BIOGRAPHICAL DIRECTORY

OF THE

AMERICAN CONGRESS

1774-1961

THE CONTINENTAL CONGRESS

SEPTEMBER 5, 1774, TO OCTOBER 21, 1788

and

THE CONGRESS OF THE UNITED STATES

FROM THE FIRST TO THE EIGHTY-SIXTH CONGRESS
MARCH 4, 1789, TO JANUARY 3, 1961, INCLUSIVE

UNITED STATES

GOVERNMENT PRINTING OFFICE

1961

THIS PUBLICATION MAY BE PURCHASED FROM THE
SUPERINTENDENT OF DOCUMENTS, U.S. GOVERNMENT PRINTING OFFICE
WASHINGTON 25, D.C., AT $11.75 PER COPY

East Front—Photo from Architect of the Capitol, by Harry L. Burnett

THE CAPITOL OF THE UNITED STATES

West Front—Photo from Architect of the Capitol, by Harry L. Burnett

THE CAPITOL OF THE UNITED STATES

HOUSE CONCURRENT RESOLUTION No. 344

EIGHTY-FIFTH CONGRESS

———

SUBMITTED BY MR. BURLESON

———

Resolved by the House of Representatives (the Senate concurring), That there shall be compiled and printed, with illustrations, as a House document, in such style and form as may be directed by the Joint Committee on Printing, a revised edition of the Biographical Directory of the American Congress up to and including the Eighty-sixth Congress (1774–1960); and that six thousand five hundred additional copies shall be printed, of which four thousand four hundred copies shall be for the use of the House of Representatives, one thousand six hundred copies for the use of the Senate, and five hundred copies for the use of the Joint Committee on Printing.

Approved by the House June 25, 1958.
Approved by the Senate July 28, 1958.

TABLE OF CONTENTS

COMPILED UNDER THE DIRECTION

OF THE

JOINT COMMITTEE ON PRINTING
CONGRESS OF THE UNITED STATES

CARL HAYDEN, Senator from Arizona, *Chairman*
OMAR BURLESON, Representative from Texas, *Vice Chairman*
MIKE MANSFIELD, Senator from Montana
JACK MILLER, Senator from Iowa
WAYNE L. HAYS, Representative from Ohio
PAUL F. SCHENCK, Representative from Ohio

JOINT COMMITTEE STAFF

John F. Haley, Staff Director

Paul C. Beach, Assistant Staff Director
Elizabeth T. Anderson, Administrative Assistant
Louis E. Shomette, Printing Technician
Tempie L. Bailey, Staff Assistant

COMPILATION STAFF

Clifford P. Reynolds, Chief Compiler and Publications Technician

Herbert V. Bibus, Editorial Assistant
Paul L. Zenor, Editorial Assistant

THE SENATE CHAMBER

THE HALL OF THE HOUSE OF REPRESENTATIVES

FOREWORD

The earliest known directory of the Federal Legislature was published in 1790 as part of an almanac for that year by John Trumbull of Norwich, Conn. "Members of Congress, Second Congress, 1792–1793," was printed in 1792 in Philadelphia. A list of the names and places of abode of the Members of the Senate and House of Representatives of the United States and their officers was published in Philadelphia in 1793. The first listing of Members of the Senate and House of Representatives published in Washington, D.C., was a 7-page pamphlet printed in 1801. A pamphlet of 12 pages published in 1803 carried the title "Alphabetical List of the Members of the Two Houses of Congress According to States, First Session of the Eighth Congress." The name of the printer was not given. A pamphlet of fifteen pages, entitled "Places of Abode of the Members of Both Houses of Congress, First Session of the Eleventh Congress," was published by R. C. Weightman in 1809. It contains the names and locations of boarding houses, arranged alphabetically, which are followed by names of Senators and Representatives residing therein. Directories containing added congressional information, compiled and printed under contract by private firms, appeared from time to time.

Though still printed by contract, the Congressional Directory for the first session of the Thirtieth Congress assumed an official air by bearing on the title-page the words "Compiled and published for the use of Congress by the Postmaster of the House of Representatives." It was issued in 1848 by J. & G. S. Gideon. Similar information was carried on titles up to and including the first session of the Thirty-eighth Congress.

The compilation and publication of the Congressional Directory under the supervision of the Joint Committee on Public Printing was first provided for at the start of the Second Session of the Thirty-eighth Congress through unanimous adoption of a joint resolution, approved February 14, 1865. After numerous sessions, during which similar foreign publications were examined, the committee decided upon a work essentially comparable to "The House of Commons," published in London since 1852.

Biographical sketches of Senators and Representatives appeared in 1867 in the first edition of the Congressional Directory for the second session of the Fortieth Congress. In the compiler's note it is called a "proof edition," and has approximately 235 biographies of Senators, Representatives, and Territorial Delegates. It is referred to as being incomplete, and in 1868 was replaced by a second edition which contained a few more sketches. The directory for the third session, printed in 1869, contains approximately 280 biographies.

Beginning with the Fortieth Congress, the names of Representatives from the various States are placed in the numerical order of the congressional districts they represented. The names of Representatives At Large appear in the order of their

[9]

seniority. By referring to the footnote references of deaths, resignations, etc., it will be easy to ascertain the particular congressional district a Member represented. The names of all Senators are given in the order of seniority, the name of the senior Senator appearing first.

The work of preparing and publishing a biographical directory to include all the preceding Congresses was first undertaken by Charles Lanman in 1859. It bears the imposing title "Dictionary of the United States Congress." There have been at least nine subsequent editions, which were intended to give up-to-date and authentic biographical data. This edition, which contains over 10,400 biographies, has been carefully compiled and revised from available biographical works and new information has been made available on earlier Members by historical associations and individuals interested in family genealogy.

This volume, compiled by Clifford P. Reynolds, Publications Technician of the Committee, is a revision of the Dictionary of the United States Congress and the General Government, published in 1859 and again revised in 1869, by Charles Lanman; the Biographical Annals of the Civil Government of the United States in 1876, by Charles Lanman and James Anglim, and the Lanman edition of 1876 as corrected by Joseph M. Morrison in 1887; the Political Register and Congressional Directory of 1878, by Ben: Perley Poore; the Biographical Congressional Directory of 1903, by O. M. Enyart; the Biographical Congressional Directory in 1911, the Biographical Directory of the American Congress of 1927, by Ansel Wold, and the 1949 edition by James L. Harrison.

Where information has been found to be in disagreement with that contained in the foregoing publications it is because later research has brought to light additional facts to disprove such records or has demonstrated the existence of errors in previous directories. Anyone discovering errors in this edition is invited to call them to the attention of the Joint Committee on Printing for reference in compiling future publications. The Committee will be especially indebted to those sufficiently interested in furnishing additional information which would add to the value of future editions.

Carl Hayden

Chairman, Joint Committee on Printing.

OFFICERS OF THE EXECUTIVE BRANCH
OF THE GOVERNMENT

EXPLANATORY NOTE

A Cabinet officer is not appointed for a fixed term and does not necessarily go out of office with the President who appointed him, and, while it is customary to tender his resignation at the time a change of administration takes place, he remains formally at the head of his department until a successor is appointed. Subordinates acting temporarily as heads of departments are not considered Cabinet officers, and in the earlier period of the Nation's history not all Cabinet officers were heads of executive departments. The names of all those exercising the duties and bearing the responsibilities of the executive departments, together with the period of service, are incorporated in the data that follows.

The dates immediately following the names of executive officers are those upon which commissions were issued, unless otherwise specifically noted. Where periods of time are indicated by dates as, for instance, March 4, 1793–March 3, 1797, both such dates are included as portions of the time period.

The Twentieth Amendment to the Constitution (effective Oct. 15, 1933) changed the terms of the President and Vice President to end at noon on the 20th day of January and the terms of Senators and Representatives to end at noon on the 3d day of January when the terms of their successors shall begin.

The National Security Act of 1947 (Pub. Law 253, 80th Cong., 1st sess.), approved July 26, 1947, created the office of Secretary of Defense and merged the War and Navy Departments into the National Military Establishment. The act was subsequently amended (Pub. Law 216, 81st Cong., 1st sess.): Section 201. (a) There is hereby established, as an executive department of the Government, the Department of Defense.

The Twenty-second Amendment to the Constitution (effective Mar. 1, 1951) limited to two the number of terms the President of the United States may serve.

The Reorganization Plan Numbered 1 of 1953 (Pub. Law 13, 83d Cong., 1st sess.), approved April 1, 1953, effective ten days later on April 11, 1953, abolished the Federal Security Agency and created the Department of Health, Education, and Welfare.

EXECUTIVE OFFICERS, 1789–1961

First Administration of GEORGE WASHINGTON

APRIL 30, 1789, TO MARCH 3, 1793

PRESIDENT OF THE UNITED STATES—George Washington, of Virginia.

VICE PRESIDENT OF THE UNITED STATES—John Adams, of Massachusetts.

SECRETARY OF STATE—John Jay, of New York, was Secretary for Foreign Affairs under the Confederation, and continued to act, at the request of Washington, until Jefferson took office. Thomas Jefferson, of Virginia, September 26, 1789; entered upon duties March 22, 1790.

SECRETARY OF THE TREASURY—Alexander Hamilton, of New York, September 11, 1789.

SECRETARY OF WAR—Henry Knox, of Massachusetts, September 12, 1789.

ATTORNEY GENERAL—Edmund Randolph, of Virginia, September 26, 1789; entered upon duties February 2, 1790.

POSTMASTER GENERAL—Samuel Osgood, of Massachusetts, September 26, 1789. Timothy Pickering, of Pennsylvania, August 12, 1791; entered upon duties August 19, 1791.

Second Administration of GEORGE WASHINGTON

MARCH 4, 1793, TO MARCH 3, 1797

PRESIDENT OF THE UNITED STATES—George Washington, of Virginia.

VICE PRESIDENT OF THE UNITED STATES—John Adams, of Massachusetts.

SECRETARY OF STATE—Thomas Jefferson, of Virginia, continued from preceding administration. Edmund Randolph, of Virginia, January 2, 1794. Timothy Pickering, of Pennsylvania (Secretary of War), ad interim, August 20, 1795. Timothy Pickering, of Pennsylvania, December 10, 1795.

SECRETARY OF THE TREASURY—Alexander Hamilton, of New York, continued from preceding administration. Oliver Wolcott, Jr., of Connecticut, February 2, 1795.

SECRETARY OF WAR—Henry Knox, of Massachusetts, continued from preceding administration. Timothy Pickering, of Pennsylvania, January 2, 1795. Timothy Pickering, of Pennsylvania (Secretary of State), ad interim, December 10, 1795, to February 5, 1796. James McHenry, of Maryland, January 27, 1796; entered upon duties February 6, 1796.

ATTORNEY GENERAL—Edmund Randolph, of Virginia, continued from preceding administration. William Bradford, of Pennsylvania, January 27, 1794; entered upon duties January 29, 1794. Charles Lee, of Virginia, December 10, 1795.

POSTMASTER GENERAL—Timothy Pickering, of Pennsylvania, continued from preceding administration. Timothy Pickering, of Pennsylvania, recommissioned June 1, 1794. Joseph Habersham, of Georgia, February 25, 1795.

Administration of JOHN ADAMS

MARCH 4, 1797, TO MARCH 3, 1801

PRESIDENT OF THE UNITED STATES—John Adams, of Massachusetts.

VICE PRESIDENT OF THE UNITED STATES—Thomas Jefferson, of Virginia.

SECRETARY OF STATE—Timothy Pickering, of Pennsylvania, continued from preceding administration; resignation requested May 10, 1800, but declining to resign, he was dismissed May 12, 1800. Charles Lee, of Virginia (Attorney General), ad interim, May 13, 1800. John Marshall, of Virginia, May 13, 1800; entered upon duties June 6, 1800. John Marshall, of Virginia (Chief Justice of the United States), ad interim, February 4, 1801, to March 3, 1801.

SECRETARY OF THE TREASURY—Oliver Wolcott, Jr., of Connecticut, continued from preceding adminstration. Samuel Dexter, of Massachusetts, January 1, 1801.

SECRETARY OF WAR—James McHenry, of Maryland, continued from preceding adminstration. Benjamin Stoddert, of Maryland (Secretary of the Navy), ad interim, June 1, 1800, to June 12, 1800. Samuel Dexter, of Massachusetts, May 13, 1800; entered upon duties June 12, 1800. Samuel Dexter, of Massachusetts (Secretary of the Treasury), ad interim, January 1, 1801.

ATTORNEY GENERAL—Charles Lee, of Virginia, continued from preceding administration.

POSTMASTER GENERAL—Joseph Habersham, of Georgia, continued from preceding administration.

SECRETARY OF THE NAVY—Benjamin Stoddert, of Maryland, May 21, 1798; entered upon duties June 18, 1798.

[13]

First Administration of THOMAS JEFFERSON

MARCH 4, 1801, TO MARCH 3, 1805

PRESIDENT OF THE UNITED STATES—THOMAS JEFFERSON, of Virginia.

VICE PRESIDENT OF THE UNITED STATES—AARON BURR, of New York.

SECRETARY OF STATE—JOHN MARSHALL, of Virginia (Chief Justice of the United States), for one day (March 4, 1801), and for a special purpose. LEVI LINCOLN, of Massachusetts (Attorney General), ad interim, March 5, 1801. JAMES MADISON, of Virginia, March 5, 1801; entered upon duties May 2, 1801.

SECRETARY OF THE TREASURY—SAMUEL DEXTER, of Massachusetts, continued from preceding administration to May 6, 1801. ALBERT GALLATIN, of Pennsylvania, May 14, 1801.

SECRETARY OF WAR—HENRY DEARBORN, of Massachusetts, March 5, 1801.

ATTORNEY GENERAL—LEVI LINCOLN, of Massachusetts, March 5, 1801, to December 31, 1804.

POSTMASTER GENERAL—JOSEPH HABERSHAM, of Georgia, continued from preceding administration. GIDEON GRANGER, of Connecticut, November 28, 1801.

SECRETARY OF THE NAVY—BENJAMIN STODDERT, of Maryland, continued from preceding administration. HENRY DEARBORN, of Massachusetts (Secretary of War), ad interim, April 1, 1801. ROBERT SMITH, of Maryland, July 15, 1801; entered upon duties July 27, 1801.

————

Second Administration of THOMAS JEFFERSON

MARCH 4, 1805, TO MARCH 3, 1809

PRESIDENT OF THE UNITED STATES—THOMAS JEFFERSON, of Virginia.

VICE PRESIDENT OF THE UNITED STATES—GEORGE CLINTON, of New York.

SECRETARY OF STATE—JAMES MADISON, of Virginia, continued from preceding administration.

SECRETARY OF THE TREASURY—ALBERT GALLATIN, of Pennsylvania, continued from preceding administration.

SECRETARY OF WAR—HENRY DEARBORN, of Massachusetts, continued from preceding administration. JOHN SMITH (chief clerk), ad interim, February 17, 1809.

ATTORNEY GENERAL—JOHN BRECKENRIDGE, of Kentucky, August 7, 1805 (died December 14, 1806). CÆSAR A. RODNEY, of Delaware, January 20, 1807.

POSTMASTER GENERAL—GIDEON GRANGER, of Connecticut, continued from preceding administration.

SECRETARY OF THE NAVY—ROBERT SMITH, of Maryland, continued from preceding administration.

————

First Administration of JAMES MADISON

MARCH 4, 1809, TO MARCH 3, 1813

PRESIDENT OF THE UNITED STATES—JAMES MADISON, of Virginia.

VICE PRESIDENT OF THE UNITED STATES—GEORGE CLINTON, of New York. (Died April 20, 1812.)

PRESIDENT PRO TEMPORE OF THE SENATE—WILLIAM H. CRAWFORD, of Georgia.

SECRETARY OF STATE—ROBERT SMITH, of Maryland, March 6, 1809. JAMES MONROE, of Virginia, April 2, 1811; entered upon duties April 6, 1811.

SECRETARY OF THE TREASURY—ALBERT GALLATIN, of Pennsylvania, continued from preceding administration.

SECRETARY OF WAR—JOHN SMITH (chief clerk), ad interim, continued from preceding administration. WILLIAM EUSTIS, of Massachusetts, March 7, 1809; entered upon duties April 8, 1809; served to December 31, 1812. JAMES MONROE, of Virginia (Secretary of State), ad interim, January 1, 1813. JOHN ARMSTRONG, of New York, January 13, 1813; entered upon duties February 5, 1813.

ATTORNEY GENERAL—CÆSAR A. RODNEY, of Delaware, continued from preceding administration; resigned December 5, 1811. WILLIAM PINKNEY, of Maryland, December 11, 1811; entered upon duties January 6, 1812.

POSTMASTER GENERAL—GIDEON GRANGER, of Connecticut, continued from preceding administration.

SECRETARY OF THE NAVY—ROBERT SMITH, of Maryland, continued from preceding administration. CHARLES W. GOLDSBOROUGH (chief clerk), ad interim, March 8, 1809. PAUL HAMILTON, of South Carolina, March 7, 1809; entered upon duties May 15, 1809; served to December 31, 1812. CHARLES W. GOLDSBOROUGH (chief clerk), ad interim, January 7, 1813, to January 18, 1813. WILLIAM JONES, of Pennsylvania, January 12, 1813; entered upon duties January 19, 1813.

Second Administration of JAMES MADISON

MARCH 4, 1813, TO MARCH 3, 1817

PRESIDENT OF THE UNITED STATES—JAMES MADISON, of Virginia.

VICE PRESIDENT OF THE UNITED STATES—ELBRIDGE GERRY, of Massachusetts.   (Died November 23, 1814.)

PRESIDENT PRO TEMPORE OF THE SENATE—JOHN GAILLARD, of South Carolina.

SECRETARY OF STATE—JAMES MONROE, of Virginia, continued from preceding administration.   JAMES MONROE, of Virginia (Secretary of War), ad interim, October 1, 1814.   JAMES MONROE, of Virginia, February 28, 1815.

SECRETARY OF THE TREASURY—ALBERT GALLATIN, of Pennsylvania, continued from preceding administration.   WILLIAM JONES, of Pennsylvania (Secretary of the Navy), performed the duties of the Secretary of the Treasury during the absence of Mr. Gallatin in Europe (April 21, 1813, to February 9, 1814).   GEORGE W. CAMPBELL, of Tennessee, February 9, 1814.   ALEXANDER J. DALLAS, of Pennsylvania, October 6, 1814; entered upon duties October 14, 1814.   WILLIAM H. CRAWFORD, of Georgia, October 22, 1816.

SECRETARY OF WAR—JOHN ARMSTRONG, of New York, continued from preceding administration.   JAMES MONROE, of Virginia (Secretary of State), ad interim, August 30, 1814.   JAMES MONROE, of Virginia, September 27, 1814; entered upon duties October 1, 1814.   JAMES MONROE, of Virginia (Secretary of State), ad interim, March 1, 1815.   ALEXANDER J. DALLAS, of Pennsylvania (Secretary of the Treasury), ad interim, March 14, 1815, to August 8, 1815.   WILLIAM H. CRAWFORD, of Georgia, August 1, 1815; entered upon duties August 8, 1815.   GEORGE GRAHAM (chief clerk), ad interim, October 22, 1816, to close of administration.

ATTORNEY GENERAL—WILLIAM PINKNEY, of Maryland, continued from preceding administration.   RICHARD RUSH, of Pennsylvania, February 10, 1814; entered upon duties the day following.

POSTMASTER GENERAL—GIDEON GRANGER, of Connecticut, continued from preceding administration.   RETURN J. MEIGS, Jr., of Ohio, March 17, 1814; entered upon duties April 11, 1814.

SECRETARY OF THE NAVY—WILLIAM JONES, of Pennsylvania, continued from preceding administration.   BENJAMIN HOMANS (chief clerk), ad interim, December 2, 1814.   BENJAMIN W. CROWNINSHIELD, of Massachusetts, December 19, 1814; entered upon duties January 16, 1815.

First Administration of JAMES MONROE

MARCH 4, 1817, TO MARCH 3, 1821

PRESIDENT OF THE UNITED STATES—JAMES MONROE, of Virginia.

VICE PRESIDENT OF THE UNITED STATES—DANIEL D. TOMPKINS, of New York.

SECRETARY OF STATE—JOHN GRAHAM (chief clerk), ad interim, March 4, 1817.   RICHARD RUSH, of Pennsylvania (Attorney General), ad interim, March 10, 1817.   JOHN QUINCY ADAMS, of Massachusetts, March 5, 1817; entered upon duties September 22, 1817.

SECRETARY OF THE TREASURY—WILLIAM H. CRAWFORD, of Georgia, continued from preceding administration.   WILLIAM H. CRAWFORD, of Georgia, recommissioned March 5, 1817.

SECRETARY OF WAR—GEORGE GRAHAM (chief clerk), ad interim, March 4, 1817.   JOHN C. CALHOUN, of South Carolina, October 8, 1817; entered upon duties December 10, 1817.

ATTORNEY GENERAL—RICHARD RUSH, of Pennsylvania, continued from preceding administration to October 30, 1817.   WILLIAM WIRT, of Virginia, November 13, 1817; entered upon duties November 15, 1817.

POSTMASTER GENERAL—RETURN J. MEIGS, Jr., of Ohio, continued from preceding administration.

SECRETARY OF THE NAVY—BENJAMIN W. CROWNINSHIELD, of Massachusetts, continued from preceding administration.   JOHN C. CALHOUN, of South Carolina (Secretary of War), ad interim, October 1, 1818.   SMITH THOMPSON, of New York, November 9, 1818; entered upon duties January 1, 1819.

Second Administration of JAMES MONROE

MARCH 4, 1821, TO MARCH 3, 1825

PRESIDENT OF THE UNITED STATES—JAMES MONROE, of Virginia.

VICE PRESIDENT OF THE UNITED STATES—DANIEL D. TOMPKINS, of New York.

SECRETARY OF STATE—JOHN QUINCY ADAMS, of Massachusetts, continued from preceding administration.

SECRETARY OF THE TREASURY—WILLIAM H. CRAWFORD, of Georgia, continued from preceding administration.

SECRETARY OF WAR—JOHN C. CALHOUN, of South Carolina, continued from preceding administration.

ATTORNEY GENERAL—WILLIAM WIRT, of Virginia, continued from preceding administration.

POSTMASTER GENERAL—RETURN J. MEIGS, Jr., of Ohio, continued from preceding administration.   JOHN McLEAN, of Ohio, commissioned June 26, 1823, to take effect July 1, 1823.

SECRETARY OF THE NAVY—SMITH THOMPSON, of New York, continued from preceding administration.   JOHN RODGERS (commodore, United States Navy, and President of the Board of Navy Commissioners), ad interim, September 1, 1823.   SAMUEL L. SOUTHARD, of New Jersey, September 16, 1823.

Administration of JOHN QUINCY ADAMS

MARCH 4, 1825, TO MARCH 3, 1829

PRESIDENT OF THE UNITED STATES—JOHN QUINCY ADAMS, of Massachusetts.

VICE PRESIDENT OF THE UNITED STATES—JOHN C. CALHOUN, of South Carolina.

SECRETARY OF STATE—DANIEL BRENT (chief clerk), ad interim, March 4, 1825. HENRY CLAY, of Kentucky, March 7, 1825.

SECRETARY OF THE TREASURY—SAMUEL L. SOUTHARD, of New Jersey (Secretary of the Navy), ad interim, March 7, 1825. RICHARD RUSH, of Pennsylvania, March 7, 1825; entered upon duties August 1, 1825.

SECRETARY OF WAR—JAMES BARBOUR, of Virginia, March 7, 1825. SAMUEL L. SOUTHARD, of New Jersey (Secretary of the Navy), ad interim, May 26, 1828. PETER B. PORTER, of New York, May 26, 1828; entered upon duties June 21, 1828.

ATTORNEY GENERAL—WILLIAM WIRT, of Virginia, continued from preceding administration.

POSTMASTER GENERAL—JOHN MCLEAN, of Ohio, continued from preceding administration.

SECRETARY OF THE NAVY—SAMUEL L. SOUTHARD, of New Jersey, continued from preceding administration.

First Administration of ANDREW JACKSON

MARCH 4, 1829, TO MARCH 3, 1833

PRESIDENT OF THE UNITED STATES—ANDREW JACKSON, of Tennessee.

VICE PRESIDENT OF THE UNITED STATES—JOHN C. CALHOUN, of South Carolina. (Resigned December 28, 1832.)

PRESIDENT PRO TEMPORE OF THE SENATE—HUGH LAWSON WHITE, of Tennessee.

SECRETARY OF STATE—JAMES A. HAMILTON, of New York, ad interim, March 4, 1829. MARTIN VAN BUREN, of New York, March 6, 1829; entered upon duties March 28, 1829. EDWARD LIVINGSTON, of Louisiana, May 24, 1831.

SECRETARY OF THE TREASURY—SAMUEL D. INGHAM, of Pennsylvania, March 6, 1829. ASBURY DICKINS (chief clerk), ad interim, June 21, 1831. LOUIS MCLANE, of Delaware, August 8, 1831.

SECRETARY OF WAR—JOHN H. EATON, of Tennessee, March 9, 1829. PHILIP G. RANDOLPH (chief clerk), ad interim, June 20, 1831. ROGER B. TANEY, of Maryland (Attorney General), ad interim, July 21, 1831. LEWIS CASS, of Ohio, August 1, 1831; entered upon duties August 8, 1831.

ATTORNEY GENERAL—JOHN M. BERRIEN, of Georgia, March 9, 1829, to June 22, 1831. ROGER B. TANEY, of Maryland, July 20, 1831.

POSTMASTER GENERAL—JOHN MCLEAN, of Ohio, continued from preceding administration. WILLIAM T. BARRY, of Kentucky, March 9, 1829; entered upon duties April 6, 1829.

SECRETARY OF THE NAVY—CHARLES HAY (chief clerk), ad interim, March 4, 1829. JOHN BRANCH, of North Carolina, March 9, 1829. JOHN BOYLE (chief clerk), ad interim, May 12, 1831. LEVI WOODBURY, of New Hampshire, May 23, 1831.

Second Administration of ANDREW JACKSON

MARCH 4, 1833, TO MARCH 3, 1837

PRESIDENT OF THE UNITED STATES—ANDREW JACKSON, of Tennessee.

VICE PRESIDENT OF THE UNITED STATES—MARTIN VAN BUREN, of New York.

SECRETARY OF STATE—EDWARD LIVINGSTON, of Louisiana, continued from preceding administration. LOUIS MCLANE, of Delaware, May 29, 1833. JOHN FORSYTH, of Georgia, June 27, 1834; entered upon duties July 1, 1834.

SECRETARY OF THE TREASURY—LOUIS MCLANE, of Delaware, continued from preceding administration. WILLIAM J. DUANE, of Pennsylvania, May 29, 1833; entered upon duties June 1, 1833. ROGER B. TANEY, of Maryland, September 23, 1833. MCCLINTOCK YOUNG (chief clerk), ad interim, June 25, 1834. LEVI WOODBURY, of New Hampshire, June 27, 1834; entered upon duties July 1, 1834.

SECRETARY OF WAR—LEWIS CASS, of Ohio, continued from preceding administration. CAREY A. HARRIS, of Tennessee (Commissioner of Indian Affairs), ad interim, October 5, 1836. BENJAMIN F. BUTLER, of New York (Attorney General), ad interim, October 26, 1836. BENJAMIN F. BUTLER, of New York, commissioned March 3, 1837, ad interim, "during the pleasure of the President, until a successor, duly appointed, shall accept such office and enter upon the duties thereof."

ATTORNEY GENERAL—ROGER B. TANEY, of Maryland, continued from preceding administration to September 23, 1833. BENJAMIN F. BUTLER, of New York, November 15, 1833; entered upon duties November 18, 1833.

POSTMASTER GENERAL—WILLIAM T. BARRY, of Kentucky, continued from preceding administration. AMOS KENDALL, of Kentucky, May 1, 1835.

SECRETARY OF THE NAVY—LEVI WOODBURY, of New Hampshire, continued from preceding administration. MAHLON DICKERSON, of New Jersey, June 30, 1834.

Administration of MARTIN VAN BUREN

MARCH 4, 1837, TO MARCH 3, 1841

PRESIDENT OF THE UNITED STATES—Martin Van Buren, of New York.

VICE PRESIDENT OF THE UNITED STATES—Richard M. Johnson, of Kentucky.

SECRETARY OF STATE—John Forsyth, of Georgia, continued from preceding administration.

SECRETARY OF THE TREASURY—Levi Woodbury, of New Hampshire, continued from preceding administration.

SECRETARY OF WAR—Benjamin F. Butler, of New York, ad interim, continued from preceding administration. Joel R. Poinsett, of South Carolina, March 7, 1837; entered upon duties March 14, 1837.

ATTORNEY GENERAL—Benjamin F. Butler, of New York, continued from preceding administration. Felix Grundy, of Tennessee, July 5, 1838, to take effect September 1, 1838. Henry D. Gilpin, of Pennsylvania, January 11, 1840.

POSTMASTER GENERAL—Amos Kendall, of Kentucky, continued from preceding administration. John M. Niles, of Connecticut, May 19, 1840, to take effect May 25, 1840; entered upon duties May 26, 1840.

SECRETARY OF THE NAVY—Mahlon Dickerson, of New Jersey, continued from preceding administration. James K. Paulding, of New York, June 25, 1838, to take effect "after the 30th instant"; entered upon duties July 1, 1838.

———

Administration of WILLIAM HENRY HARRISON

MARCH 4, 1841, TO APRIL 4, 1841

PRESIDENT OF THE UNITED STATES—William Henry Harrison, of Ohio. (Died April 4, 1841.)

VICE PRESIDENT OF THE UNITED STATES—John Tyler, of Virginia.

SECRETARY OF STATE—J. L. Martin (chief clerk), ad interim, March 4, 1841. Daniel Webster, of Massachusetts, March 5, 1841.

SECRETARY OF THE TREASURY—McClintock Young (chief clerk), ad interim, March 4, 1841. Thomas Ewing, of Ohio, March 5, 1841.

SECRETARY OF WAR—John Bell, of Tennessee, March 5, 1841.

ATTORNEY GENERAL—John J. Crittenden, of Kentucky, March 5, 1841.

POSTMASTER GENERAL—Selah R. Hobbie, of New York (First Assistant Postmaster General), ad interim, March 4, 1841. Francis Granger, of New York, March 6, 1841; entered upon duties March 8, 1841.

SECRETARY OF THE NAVY—John D. Simms (chief clerk), ad interim, March 4, 1841. George E. Badger, of North Carolina, March 5, 1841.

———

Administration of JOHN TYLER

APRIL 6, 1841, TO MARCH 3, 1845

PRESIDENT OF THE UNITED STATES—John Tyler, of Virginia.

PRESIDENT PRO TEMPORE OF THE SENATE—Samuel L. Southard, of New Jersey; Willie P. Mangum, of North Carolina.

SECRETARY OF STATE—Daniel Webster, of Massachusetts, continued from preceding administration. Hugh S. Legaré, of South Carolina (Attorney General), ad interim, May 9, 1843. William S. Derrick (chief clerk), ad interim, June 21, 1843. Abel P. Upshur, of Virginia (Secretary of the Navy), ad interim, June 24, 1843. Abel P. Upshur, of Virginia, July 24, 1843 (killed by the explosion of a gun on the U. S. S. *Princeton* February 28, 1844). John Nelson, of Maryland (Attorney General), ad interim, February 29, 1844. John C. Calhoun, of South Carolina, March 6, 1844; entered upon duties April 1, 1844.

SECRETARY OF THE TREASURY—Thomas Ewing, of Ohio, continued from preceding administration. McClintock Young (chief clerk), ad interim, September 13, 1841. Walter Forward, of Pennsylvania, September 13, 1841. McClintock Young (chief clerk), ad interim, March 1, 1843. John C. Spencer, of New York, March 3, 1843; entered upon duties March 8, 1843. McClintock Young (chief clerk), ad interim, May 2, 1844. George M. Bibb, of Kentucky, June 15, 1844; entered upon duties July 4, 1844.

SECRETARY OF WAR—John Bell, of Tennessee, continued from preceding administration. Albert M. Lea, of Maryland (chief clerk), ad interim, September 12, 1841. John C. Spencer, of New York, October 12, 1841. James M. Porter, of Pennsylvania, March 8, 1843. William Wilkins, of Pennsylvania, February 15, 1844; entered upon duties February 20, 1844.

ATTORNEY GENERAL—John J. Crittenden, of Kentucky, continued from preceding administration. Hugh S. Legaré, of South Carolina, September 13, 1841; entered upon duties September 20, 1841 (died June 20, 1843). John Nelson, of Maryland, July 1, 1843.

POSTMASTER GENERAL—Francis Granger, of New York, continued from preceding administration. Selah R. Hobbie, of New York (First Assistant Postmaster General), ad interim, September 14, 1841. Charles A. Wickliffe, of Kentucky, September 13, 1841; entered upon duties October 13, 1841.

SECRETARY OF THE NAVY—George E. Badger, of North Carolina, continued from preceding administration. John D. Simms (chief clerk), ad interim, September 11, 1841. Abel P. Upshur, of Virginia, September 13, 1841; entered upon duties October 11, 1841. David Henshaw, of Massachusetts, July 24, 1843. Thomas W. Gilmer, of Virginia, February 15, 1844; entered upon duties February 19, 1844 (killed by the explosion of a gun on the U. S. S. *Princeton* February 28, 1844). Lewis Warrington (captain, United States Navy), ad interim, February 29, 1844. John Y. Mason, of Virginia, March 14, 1844; entered upon duties March 26, 1844.

Administration of JAMES K. POLK

MARCH 4, 1845, TO MARCH 3, 1849

PRESIDENT OF THE UNITED STATES—JAMES K. POLK, of Tennessee.

VICE PRESIDENT OF THE UNITED STATES—GEORGE M. DALLAS, of Pennsylvania.

SECRETARY OF STATE—JOHN C. CALHOUN, of South Carolina, continued from preceding administration. JAMES BUCHANAN, of Pennsylvania, March 6, 1845; entered upon duties March 10, 1845.

SECRETARY OF THE TREASURY—GEORGE M. BIBB, of Kentucky, continued from preceding administration. ROBERT J. WALKER, of Mississippi, March 6, 1845; entered upon duties March 8, 1845.

SECRETARY OF WAR—WILLIAM WILKINS, of Pennsylvania, continued from preceding administration. WILLIAM L. MARCY, of New York, March 6, 1845; entered upon duties March 8, 1845.

ATTORNEY GENERAL—JOHN NELSON, of Maryland, continued from preceding administration. JOHN Y. MASON, of Virginia, March 6, 1845; entered upon duties March 11, 1845. NATHAN CLIFFORD, of Maine, October 17, 1846, to March 18, 1848, when he resigned. ISAAC TOUCEY, of Connecticut, June 21, 1848; entered upon duties June 29, 1848.

POSTMASTER GENERAL—CHARLES A. WICKLIFFE, of Kentucky, continued from preceding administration. CAVE JOHNSON, of Tennessee, March 6, 1845.

SECRETARY OF THE NAVY—JOHN Y. MASON, of Virginia, continued from preceding administration. GEORGE BANCROFT, of Massachusetts, March 10, 1845. JOHN Y. MASON, of Virginia, September 9, 1846.

Administration of ZACHARY TAYLOR

MARCH 4, 1849, TO JULY 9, 1850

PRESIDENT OF THE UNITED STATES—ZACHARY TAYLOR, of Louisiana. (Oath administered March 5, 1849. Died July 9, 1850.)

VICE PRESIDENT OF THE UNITED STATES—MILLARD FILLMORE, of New York.

SECRETARY OF STATE—JAMES BUCHANAN, of Pennsylvania, continued from preceding administration. JOHN M. CLAYTON, of Delaware, March 7, 1849.

SECRETARY OF THE TREASURY—ROBERT J. WALKER, of Mississippi, continued from preceding administration. MCCLINTOCK YOUNG (chief clerk), ad interim, March 6, 1849. WILLIAM M. MEREDITH, of Pennsylvania, March 8, 1849.

SECRETARY OF WAR—WILLIAM L. MARCY, of New York, continued from preceding administration. REVERDY JOHNSON, of Maryland (Attorney General), ad interim, March 8, 1849. GEORGE W. CRAWFORD, of Georgia, March 8, 1849; entered upon duties March 14, 1849.

ATTORNEY GENERAL—ISAAC TOUCEY, of Connecticut, continued from preceding administration. REVERDY JOHNSON, of Maryland, March 8, 1849.

POSTMASTER GENERAL—CAVE JOHNSON, of Tennessee, continued from preceding administration. SELAH R. HOBBIE, of New York (First Assistant Postmaster General), ad interim, March 6, 1849. JACOB COLLAMER, of Vermont, March 8, 1849.

SECRETARY OF THE NAVY—JOHN Y. MASON, of Virginia, continued from preceding administration. WILLIAM B. PRESTON, of Virginia, March 8, 1849.

SECRETARY OF THE INTERIOR—THOMAS EWING, of Ohio, March 8, 1849.

Administration of MILLARD FILLMORE

JULY 10, 1850, TO MARCH 3, 1853

PRESIDENT OF THE UNITED STATES—MILLARD FILLMORE, of New York.

PRESIDENT PRO TEMPORE OF THE SENATE—WILLIAM R. KING, of Alabama; DAVID R. ATCHISON, of Missouri.

SECRETARY OF STATE—JOHN M. CLAYTON, of Delaware, continued from preceding administration. DANIEL WEBSTER, of Massachusetts, July 22, 1850 (died October 24, 1852). CHARLES M. CONRAD, of Louisiana (Secretary of War), ad interim, October 25, 1852. EDWARD EVERETT, of Massachusetts, November 6, 1852.

SECRETARY OF THE TREASURY—WILLIAM M. MEREDITH, of Pennsylvania, continued from preceding administration. THOMAS CORWIN, of Ohio, July 23, 1850.

SECRETARY OF WAR—GEORGE W. CRAWFORD, of Georgia, continued from preceding administration. SAMUEL J. ANDERSON (chief clerk), ad interim, July 23, 1850. WINFIELD SCOTT (major general, U. S. Army), ad interim, July 24, 1850. CHARLES M. CONRAD, of Louisiana, August 15, 1850.

ATTORNEY GENERAL—REVERDY JOHNSON, of Maryland, continued from preceding administration, served to July 22, 1850. JOHN J. CRITTENDEN, of Kentucky, July 22, 1850; entered upon duties August 14, 1850.

POSTMASTER GENERAL—JACOB COLLAMER, of Vermont, continued from preceding administration. NATHAN K. HALL, of New York, July 23, 1850. SAMUEL D. HUBBARD, of Connecticut, August 31, 1852; entered upon duties September 14, 1852.

SECRETARY OF THE NAVY—WILLIAM B. PRESTON, of Virginia, continued from preceding administration. LEWIS WARRINGTON (captain, U. S. Navy), ad interim, July 23, 1850. WILLIAM A. GRAHAM, of North Carolina, July 22, 1850; entered upon duties August 2, 1850. JOHN P. KENNEDY, of Maryland, July 22, 1852; entered upon duties July 26, 1852.

SECRETARY OF THE INTERIOR—THOMAS EWING, of Ohio, continued from preceding administration. DANIEL C. GODDARD (chief clerk), ad interim, July 23, 1850. THOMAS M. T. MCKENNAN, of Pennsylvania, August 15, 1850. DANIEL C. GODDARD (chief clerk), ad interim, August 27, 1850. ALEXANDER H. H. STUART, of Virginia, September 12, 1850; entered upon duties September 16, 1850.

Administration of FRANKLIN PIERCE

MARCH 4, 1853, TO MARCH 3, 1857

PRESIDENT OF THE UNITED STATES—Franklin Pierce, of New Hampshire.

VICE PRESIDENT OF THE UNITED STATES—William R. King, of Alabama.   (Died April 18, 1853.)

PRESIDENT PRO TEMPORE OF THE SENATE—David R. Atchison, of Missouri; Lewis Cass, of Michigan; Jesse D. Bright, of Indiana; Charles E. Stuart, of Michigan; James M. Mason, of Virginia.

SECRETARY OF STATE—William Hunter (chief clerk), ad interim, March 4, 1853. William L. Marcy, of New York, March 7, 1853.

SECRETARY OF THE TREASURY—Thomas Corwin, of Ohio, continued from preceding administration. James Guthrie, of Kentucky, March 7, 1853.

SECRETARY OF WAR—Charles M. Conrad, of Louisiana, continued from preceding administration. Jefferson Davis, of Mississippi, March 7, 1853. Samuel Cooper (Adjutant General, U. S. Army), ad interim, March 3, 1857.

ATTORNEY GENERAL—John J. Crittenden, of Kentucky, continued from preceding administration. Caleb Cushing, of Massachusetts, March 7, 1853.

POSTMASTER GENERAL—Samuel D. Hubbard, of Connecticut, continued from preceding administration. James Campbell, of Pennsylvania, March 7, 1853.

SECRETARY OF THE NAVY—John P. Kennedy, of Maryland, continued from preceding administration. James C. Dobbin, of North Carolina, March 7, 1853.

SECRETARY OF THE INTERIOR—Alexander H. H. Stuart, of Virginia, continued from preceding administration. Robert McClelland, of Michigan, March 7, 1853.

Administration of JAMES BUCHANAN

MARCH 4, 1857, TO MARCH 3, 1861

PRESIDENT OF THE UNITED STATES—James Buchanan, of Pennsylvania.

VICE PRESIDENT OF THE UNITED STATES—John C. Breckinridge, of Kentucky.

SECRETARY OF STATE—William L. Marcy, of New York, continued from preceding administration. Lewis Cass, of Michigan, March 6, 1857. William Hunter (chief clerk), ad interim, December 15, 1860. Jeremiah S. Black, of Pennsylvania, December 17, 1860.

SECRETARY OF THE TREASURY—James Guthrie, of Kentucky, continued from preceding administration. Howell Cobb, of Georgia, March 6, 1857. Isaac Toucey, of Connecticut (Secretary of the Navy), ad interim, December 10, 1860. Philip F. Thomas, of Maryland, December 12, 1860. John A. Dix, of New York, January 11, 1861; entered upon duties January 15, 1861.

SECRETARY OF WAR—Samuel Cooper (Adjutant General, U. S. Army), ad interim, March 4, 1857. John B. Floyd, of Virginia, March 6, 1857. Joseph Holt, of Kentucky (Postmaster General), ad interim, January 1, 1861. Joseph Holt, of Kentucky, January 18, 1861.

ATTORNEY GENERAL—Caleb Cushing, of Massachusetts, continued from preceding administration. Jeremiah S. Black, of Pennsylvania, March 6, 1857; entered upon duties March 11, 1857. Edwin M. Stanton, of Pennsylvania, December 20, 1860; entered upon duties December 22, 1860.

POSTMASTER GENERAL—James Campbell, of Pennsylvania, continued from preceding administration. Aaron V. Brown, of Tennessee, March 6, 1857 (died March 8, 1859). Horatio King, of Maine (First Assistant Postmaster General), ad interim, March 9, 1859. Joseph Holt, of Kentucky, March 14, 1859. Horatio King, of Maine (First Assistant Postmaster General), ad interim, January 1, 1861. Horatio King, of Maine, February 12, 1861.

SECRETARY OF THE NAVY—James C. Dobbin, of North Carolina, continued from preceding administration. Isaac Toucey, of Connecticut, March 6, 1857.

SECRETARY OF THE INTERIOR—Robert McClelland, of Michigan, continued from preceding administration. Jacob Thompson, of Mississippi, March 6, 1857; entered upon duties March 10, 1857. Moses Kelly (chief clerk), ad interim, January 10, 1861.

First Administration of ABRAHAM LINCOLN

MARCH 4, 1861, TO MARCH 3, 1865

PRESIDENT OF THE UNITED STATES—Abraham Lincoln, of Illinois.

VICE PRESIDENT OF THE UNITED STATES—Hannibal Hamlin, of Maine.

SECRETARY OF STATE—Jeremiah S. Black, of Pennsylvania, continued from preceding administration. William H. Seward, of New York, March 5, 1861.

SECRETARY OF THE TREASURY—John A. Dix, of New York, continued from preceding administration. Salmon P. Chase, of Ohio, March 5, 1861; entered upon duties March 7, 1861. George Harrington, of the District of Columbia (Assistant Secretary), ad interim, July 1, 1864. William P. Fessenden, of Maine, July 1, 1864; entered upon duties July 5, 1864.

SECRETARY OF WAR—Joseph Holt, of Kentucky, continued from preceding administration. Simon Cameron, of Pennsylvania, March 5, 1861; entered upon duties March 11, 1861. Edwin M. Stanton, of Pennsylvania, January 15, 1862; entered upon duties January 20, 1862.

ATTORNEY GENERAL—Edwin M. Stanton, of Pennsylvania, continued from preceding administration. Edward Bates, of Missouri, March 5, 1861. James Speed, of Kentucky, December 2, 1864; entered upon duties December 5, 1864.

POSTMASTER GENERAL—Horatio King, of Maine, continued from preceding administration. Montgomery Blair, of the District of Columbia, March 5, 1861; entered upon duties March 9, 1861. William Dennison, of Ohio, September 24, 1864; entered upon duties October 1, 1864.

SECRETARY OF THE NAVY—Isaac Toucey, of Connecticut, continued from preceding administration. Gideon Welles, of Connecticut, March 5, 1861; entered upon duties March 7, 1861.

SECRETARY OF THE INTERIOR—Moses Kelly (chief clerk), ad interim, March 4, 1861. Caleb B. Smith, of Indiana, March 5, 1861. John P. Usher, of Indiana (Assistant Secretary), ad interim, January 1, 1863. John P. Usher, of Indiana, January 8, 1863.

———

Second Administration of ABRAHAM LINCOLN

MARCH 4, 1865, TO APRIL 15, 1865

PRESIDENT OF THE UNITED STATES—Abraham Lincoln, of Illinois. (Died April 15, 1865.)

VICE PRESIDENT OF THE UNITED STATES—Andrew Johnson, of Tennessee.

SECRETARY OF STATE—William H. Seward, of New York, continued from preceding administration.

SECRETARY OF THE TREASURY—George Harrington, of the District of Columbia (Assistant Secretary), ad interim, March 4, 1865. Hugh McCulloch, of Indiana, March 7, 1865; entered upon duties March 9, 1865.

SECRETARY OF WAR—Edwin M. Stanton, of Pennsylvania, continued from preceding administration.

ATTORNEY GENERAL—James Speed, of Kentucky, continued from preceding administration.

POSTMASTER GENERAL—William Dennison, of Ohio, continued from preceding administration.

SECRETARY OF THE NAVY—Gideon Welles, of Connecticut, continued from preceding administration.

SECRETARY OF THE INTERIOR—John P. Usher, of Indiana, continued from preceding administration.

———

Administration of ANDREW JOHNSON

APRIL 15, 1865, TO MARCH 3, 1869

PRESIDENT OF THE UNITED STATES—Andrew Johnson, of Tennessee.

PRESIDENT PRO TEMPORE OF THE SENATE—Lafayette S. Foster, of Connecticut; Benjamin F. Wade, of Ohio.

SECRETARY OF STATE—William H. Seward, of New York, continued from preceding administration.

SECRETARY OF THE TREASURY—Hugh McCulloch, of Indiana, continued from preceding administration.

SECRETARY OF WAR—Edwin M. Stanton, of Pennsylvania, continued from preceding administration; suspended August 12, 1867. Ulysses S. Grant (General of the Army), ad interim, August 12, 1867. Edwin M. Stanton, of Pennsylvania, reinstated January 13, 1868, to May 26, 1868. John M. Schofield, of Illinois, May 28, 1868; entered upon duties June 1, 1868.

ATTORNEY GENERAL—James Speed, of Kentucky, continued from preceding administration. J. Hubley Ashton, of Pennsylvania (Assistant Attorney General), acting, July 17, 1866. Henry Stanbery, of Ohio, July 23, 1866. Orville H. Browning, of Illinois (Secretary of the Interior), ad interim, March 13, 1868. William M. Evarts, of New York, July 15, 1868; entered upon duties July 20, 1868.

POSTMASTER GENERAL—William Dennison, of Ohio, continued from preceding administration. Alexander W. Randall, of Wisconsin (First Assistant Postmaster General), ad interim, July 17, 1866. Alexander W. Randall, of Wisconsin, July 25, 1866.

SECRETARY OF THE NAVY—Gideon Welles, of Connecticut, continued from preceding administration.

SECRETARY OF THE INTERIOR—John P. Usher, of Indiana, continued from preceding administration. James Harlan, of Iowa, May 15, 1865. Orville H. Browning, of Illinois, July 27, 1866, to take effect September 1, 1866.

First Administration of ULYSSES S. GRANT

MARCH 4, 1869, TO MARCH 3, 1873

PRESIDENT OF THE UNITED STATES—Ulysses S. Grant, of Illinois.

VICE PRESIDENT OF THE UNITED STATES—Schuyler Colfax, of Indiana.

SECRETARY OF STATE—William H. Seward, of New York, continued from preceding administration. Elihu B. Washburne, of Illinois, March 5, 1869. Hamilton Fish, of New York, March 11, 1869; entered upon duties March 17, 1869.

SECRETARY OF THE TREASURY—Hugh McCulloch, of Indiana, continued from preceding administration. John F. Hartley, of Maine (Assistant Secretary), ad interim, March 5, 1869. George S. Boutwell, of Massachusetts, March 11, 1869.

SECRETARY OF WAR—John M. Schofield, of Illinois, continued from preceding administration. John A. Rawlins, of Illinois, March 11, 1869. William T. Sherman, of Ohio, September 9, 1869; entered upon duties September 11, 1869. William W. Belknap, of Iowa, October 25, 1869; entered upon duties November 1, 1869.

ATTORNEY GENERAL—William M. Evarts, of New York, continued from preceding administration. J. Hubley Ashton, of Pennsylvania (Assistant Attorney General), acting, March 5, 1869. Ebenezer R. Hoar, of Massachusetts, March 5, 1869; entered upon duties March 11, 1869. Amos T. Akerman, of Georgia, June 23, 1870; entered upon duties July 8, 1870. George H. Williams, of Oregon, December 14, 1871, to take effect January 10, 1872.

POSTMASTER GENERAL—St. John B. L. Skinner, of New York (First Assistant Postmaster General), ad interim, March 4, 1869. John A. J. Creswell, of Maryland, March 5, 1869.

SECRETARY OF THE NAVY—William Faxon, of Connecticut (Assistant Secretary), ad interim, March 4, 1869. Adolph E. Borie, of Pennsylvania, March 5, 1869; entered upon duties March 9, 1869. George M. Robeson, of New Jersey, June 25, 1869.

SECRETARY OF THE INTERIOR—William T. Otto, of Indiana (Assistant Secretary), ad interim, March 4, 1869. Jacob D. Cox, of Ohio, March 5, 1869; entered upon duties March 9, 1869. Columbus Delano, of Ohio, November 1, 1870.

———

Second Administration of ULYSSES S. GRANT

MARCH 4, 1873, TO MARCH 3, 1877

PRESIDENT OF THE UNITED STATES—Ulysses S. Grant, of Illinois.

VICE PRESIDENT OF THE UNITED STATES—Henry Wilson, of Massachusetts. (Died November 22, 1875.)

PRESIDENT PRO TEMPORE OF THE SENATE—Thomas W. Ferry, of Michigan.

SECRETARY OF STATE—Hamilton Fish, of New York, continued from preceding administration. Hamilton Fish, of New York, recommissioned March 17, 1873.

SECRETARY OF THE TREASURY—George S. Boutwell, of Massachusetts, continued from preceding administration. William A. Richardson, of Massachusetts, March 17, 1873. Benjamin H. Bristow, of Kentucky, June 2, 1874; entered upon duties June 4, 1874. Charles F. Conant, of New Hampshire (Assistant Secretary), ad interim, June 21, 1876, to June 30, 1876. Lot M. Morrill, of Maine, June 21, 1876; entered upon duties July 7, 1876.

SECRETARY OF WAR—William W. Belknap, of Iowa, continued from preceding administration. William W. Belknap, of Iowa, recommissioned March 17, 1873. George M. Robeson, of New Jersey (Secretary of the Navy), ad interim, March 2, 1876. Alphonso Taft, of Ohio, March 8, 1876; entered upon duties March 11, 1876. James D. Cameron, of Pennsylvania, May 22, 1876; entered upon duties June 1, 1876.

ATTORNEY GENERAL—George H. Williams, of Oregon, continued from preceding administration. George H. Williams, of Oregon, recommissioned March 17, 1873. Edwards Pierrepont, of New York, April 26, 1875, to take effect May 15, 1875. Alphonso Taft, of Ohio, May 22, 1876; entered upon duties June 1, 1876.

POSTMASTER GENERAL—John A. J. Creswell, of Maryland, continued from preceding administration. John A. J. Creswell, of Maryland, recommissioned March 17, 1873. James W. Marshall, of Virginia, July 3, 1874; entered upon duties July 7, 1874. Marshall Jewell, of Connecticut, August 24, 1874; entered upon duties September 1, 1874. James N. Tyner, of Indiana, July 12, 1876.

SECRETARY OF THE NAVY—George M. Robeson, of New Jersey, continued from preceding administration. George M. Robeson, of New Jersey, recommissioned March 17, 1873.

SECRETARY OF THE INTERIOR—Columbus Delano, of Ohio, continued from preceding administration. Columbus Delano, of Ohio, recommissioned March 17, 1873. Benjamin R. Cowen, of Ohio (Assistant Secretary), ad interim, October 1, 1875. Zachariah Chandler, of Michigan, October 19, 1875.

Administration of RUTHERFORD B. HAYES

MARCH 4, 1877, TO MARCH 3, 1881

PRESIDENT OF THE UNITED STATES—RUTHERFORD B. HAYES, of Ohio.   (Oath administered March 5, 1877.)

VICE PRESIDENT OF THE UNITED STATES—WILLIAM A. WHEELER, of New York.

SECRETARY OF STATE—HAMILTON FISH, of New York, continued from preceding administration. WILLIAM M. EVARTS, of New York, March 12, 1877.

SECRETARY OF THE TREASURY—LOT M. MORRILL, of Maine, continued from preceding administration. JOHN SHERMAN, of Ohio, March 8, 1877; entered upon duties March 10, 1877.

SECRETARY OF WAR—JAMES D. CAMERON, of Pennsylvania, continued from preceding administration. GEORGE W. MCCRARY, of Iowa, March 12, 1877. ALEXANDER RAMSEY, of Minnesota, December 10, 1879; entered upon duties December 12, 1879.

ATTORNEY GENERAL—ALPHONSO TAFT, of Ohio, continued from preceding administration. CHARLES DEVENS, of Massachusetts, March 12, 1877.

POSTMASTER GENERAL—JAMES N. TYNER, of Indiana, continued from preceding administration. DAVID M. KEY, of Tennessee, March 12, 1877; resigned June 1, 1880; served to August 24, 1880. HORACE MAYNARD, of Tennessee, June 2, 1880; entered upon duties August 25, 1880.

SECRETARY OF THE NAVY—GEORGE M. ROBESON, of New Jersey, continued from preceding administration. RICHARD W. THOMPSON, of Indiana, March 12, 1877. ALEXANDER RAMSEY, of Minnesota (Secretary of War), ad interim, December 20, 1880. NATHAN GOFF, Jr., of West Virginia, January 6, 1881.

SECRETARY OF THE INTERIOR—ZACHARIAH CHANDLER, of Michigan, continued from preceding administration. CARL SCHURZ, of Missouri, March 12, 1877.

———

Administration of JAMES A. GARFIELD

MARCH 4, 1881, TO SEPTEMBER 19, 1881

PRESIDENT OF THE UNITED STATES—JAMES A. GARFIELD, of Ohio.   (Died September 19, 1881.)

VICE PRESIDENT OF THE UNITED STATES—CHESTER A. ARTHUR, of New York.

SECRETARY OF STATE—WILLIAM M. EVARTS, of New York, continued from preceding administration. JAMES G. BLAINE, of Maine, March 5, 1881; entered upon duties March 7, 1881.

SECRETARY OF THE TREASURY—HENRY F. FRENCH, of Massachusetts (Assistant Secretary), ad interim, March 4, 1881. WILLIAM WINDOM, of Minnesota, March 5, 1881; entered upon duties March 8, 1881.

SECRETARY OF WAR—ALEXANDER RAMSEY, of Minnesota, continued from preceding administration. ROBERT T. LINCOLN, of Illinois, March 5, 1881; entered upon duties March 11, 1881.

ATTORNEY GENERAL—CHARLES DEVENS, of Massachusetts, continued from preceding administration. WAYNE MACVEAGH, of Pennsylvania, March 5, 1881; entered upon duties March 7, 1881.

POSTMASTER GENERAL—HORACE MAYNARD, of Tennessee, continued from preceding administration. THOMAS L. JAMES, of New York, March 5, 1881; entered upon duties March 8, 1881.

SECRETARY OF THE NAVY—NATHAN GOFF, Jr., of West Virginia, continued from preceding administration. WILLIAM H. HUNT, of Louisiana, March 5, 1881; entered upon duties March 7, 1881.

SECRETARY OF THE INTERIOR—CARL SCHURZ, of Missouri, continued from preceding administration. SAMUEL J. KIRKWOOD, of Iowa, March 5, 1881; entered upon duties March 8, 1881.

Administration of CHESTER A. ARTHUR

SEPTEMBER 20, 1881, TO MARCH 3, 1885

PRESIDENT OF THE UNITED STATES—CHESTER A. ARTHUR, of New York.

PRESIDENT PRO TEMPORE OF THE SENATE—THOMAS F. BAYARD, of Delaware; DAVID DAVIS, of Illinois; GEORGE F. EDMUNDS, of Vermont.

SECRETARY OF STATE—JAMES G. BLAINE, of Maine, continued from preceding administration. FREDERICK T. FRELINGHUYSEN, of New Jersey, December 12, 1881; entered upon duties December 19, 1881.

SECRETARY OF THE TREASURY—WILLIAM WINDOM, of Minnesota, continued from preceding administration. CHARLES J. FOLGER, of New York, October 27, 1881; entered upon duties November 14, 1881 (died September 4, 1884). CHARLES E. COON, of New York (Assistant Secretary), ad interim, September 4, 1884. HENRY F. FRENCH, of Massachusetts (Assistant Secretary), ad interim, September 8, 1884. CHARLES E. COON, of New York (Assistant Secretary), ad interim, September 15, 1884. WALTER Q. GRESHAM, of Indiana, September 24, 1884. HENRY F. FRENCH, of Massachusetts (Assistant Secretary), ad interim, October 29, 1884. HUGH MCCULLOCH, of Indiana, October 28, 1884; entered upon duties October 31, 1884.

SECRETARY OF WAR—ROBERT T. LINCOLN, of Illinois, continued from preceding administration.

ATTORNEY GENERAL—WAYNE MACVEAGH, of Pennsylvania, continued from preceding administration. SAMUEL F. PHILLIPS, of North Carolina (Solicitor General), ad interim, November 14, 1881. BENJAMIN H. BREWSTER, of Pennsylvania, December 19, 1881; entered upon duties January 3, 1882.

POSTMASTER GENERAL—THOMAS L. JAMES, of New York, continued from preceding administration. THOMAS L. JAMES, of New York, recommissioned October 27, 1881. TIMOTHY O. HOWE, of Wisconsin, December 20, 1881; entered upon duties January 5, 1882 (died March 25, 1883). FRANK HATTON, of Iowa (First Assistant Postmaster General), ad interim, March 26, 1883. WALTER Q. GRESHAM, of Indiana, April 3, 1883; entered upon duties April 11, 1883. FRANK HATTON, of Iowa (First Assistant Postmaster General), ad interim, September 25, 1884. FRANK HATTON, of Iowa, October 14, 1884.

SECRETARY OF THE NAVY—WILLIAM H. HUNT, of Louisiana, continued from preceding administration. WILLIAM E. CHANDLER, of New Hampshire, April 12, 1882; entered upon duties April 17, 1882.

SECRETARY OF THE INTERIOR—SAMUEL J. KIRKWOOD, of Iowa, continued from preceding administration. HENRY M. TELLER, of Colorado, April 6, 1882; entered upon duties April 17, 1882.

––––––

First Administration of GROVER CLEVELAND

MARCH 4, 1885, TO MARCH 3, 1889

PRESIDENT OF THE UNITED STATES—GROVER CLEVELAND, of New York.

VICE PRESIDENT OF THE UNITED STATES—THOMAS A. HENDRICKS, of Indiana. (Died November 25, 1885.)

PRESIDENT PRO TEMPORE OF THE SENATE—JOHN SHERMAN, of Ohio; JOHN J. INGALLS, of Kansas.

SECRETARY OF STATE—FREDERICK T. FRELINGHUYSEN, of New Jersey, continued from preceding administration. THOMAS F. BAYARD, of Delaware, March 6, 1885.

SECRETARY OF THE TREASURY—HUGH MCCULLOCH, of Indiana, continued from preceding administration. DANIEL MANNING, of New York, March 6, 1885; entered upon duties March 8, 1885. CHARLES S. FAIRCHILD, of New York, April 1, 1887.

SECRETARY OF WAR—ROBERT T. LINCOLN, of Illinois, continued from preceding administration. WILLIAM C. ENDICOTT, of Massachusetts, March 6, 1885.

ATTORNEY GENERAL—BENJAMIN H. BREWSTER, of Pennsylvania, continued from preceding administration. AUGUSTUS H. GARLAND, of Arkansas, March 6, 1885; entered upon duties March 9, 1885.

POSTMASTER GENERAL—FRANK HATTON, of Iowa, continued from preceding administration. WILLIAM F. VILAS, of Wisconsin, March 6, 1885. DON M. DICKINSON, of Michigan, January 16, 1888.

SECRETARY OF THE NAVY—WILLIAM E. CHANDLER, of New Hampshire, continued from preceding administration. WILLIAM C. WHITNEY, of New York, March 6, 1885.

SECRETARY OF THE INTERIOR—MERRITT L. JOSLYN, of Illinois (Assistant Secretary), ad interim, March 4, 1885. LUCIUS Q. C. LAMAR, of Mississippi, March 6, 1885. HENRY L. MULDROW, of Mississippi (First Assistant Secretary), ad interim, January 11, 1888. WILLIAM F. VILAS, of Wisconsin, January 16, 1888.

SECRETARY OF AGRICULTURE—NORMAN J. COLMAN, of Missouri, February 13, 1889.

Administration of BENJAMIN HARRISON

MARCH 4, 1889, TO MARCH 3, 1893

PRESIDENT OF THE UNITED STATES—Benjamin Harrison, of Indiana.

VICE PRESIDENT OF THE UNITED STATES—Levi P. Morton, of New York.

SECRETARY OF STATE—Thomas F. Bayard, of Delaware, continued from preceding administration. James G. Blaine, of Maine, March 5, 1889; entered upon duties March 7, 1889. William F. Wharton, of Massachusetts (Assistant Secretary), ad interim, June 4, 1892. John W. Foster, of Indiana, June 29, 1892. William F. Wharton, of Massachusetts (Assistant Secretary), ad interim, February 23, 1893.

SECRETARY OF THE TREASURY—Charles S. Fairchild, of New York, continued from preceding administration. William Windom, of Minnesota, March 5, 1889; entered upon duties March 7, 1889 (died January 29, 1891). Allured B. Nettleton, of Minnesota (Assistant Secretary), ad interim, January 30, 1891. Charles Foster, of Ohio, February 24, 1891.

SECRETARY OF WAR—William C. Endicott, of Massachusetts, continued from preceding administration. Redfield Proctor, of Vermont, March 5, 1889. Lewis A. Grant, of Minnesota (Assistant Secretary), ad interim, December 6, 1891. Stephen B. Elkins, of West Virginia, December 22, 1891; entered upon duties December 24, 1891.

ATTORNEY GENERAL—Augustus H. Garland, of Arkansas, continued from preceding administration. William H. H. Miller, of Indiana, March 5, 1889.

POSTMASTER GENERAL—Don M. Dickinson, of Michigan, continued from preceding administration. John Wanamaker, of Pennsylvania, March 5, 1889.

SECRETARY OF THE NAVY—William C. Whitney, of New York, continued from preceding administration. Benjamin F. Tracy, of New York, March 5, 1889.

SECRETARY OF THE INTERIOR—William F. Vilas, of Wisconsin, continued from preceding administration. John W. Noble, of Missouri, March 5, 1889; entered upon duties March 7, 1889.

SECRETARY OF AGRICULTURE—Norman J. Colman, of Missouri, continued from preceding administration. Jeremiah M. Rusk, of Wisconsin, March 5, 1889; entered upon duties March 7, 1889.

Second Administration of GROVER CLEVELAND

MARCH 4, 1893, TO MARCH 3, 1897

PRESIDENT OF THE UNITED STATES—Grover Cleveland, of New York.

VICE PRESIDENT OF THE UNITED STATES—Adlai E. Stevenson, of Illinois.

SECRETARY OF STATE—William F. Wharton, of Massachusetts (Assistant Secretary), ad interim, continued from preceding administration. Walter Q. Gresham, of Illinois, March 6, 1893 (died May 28, 1895). Edwin F. Uhl, of Michigan (Assistant Secretary), ad interim, May 28, 1895. Alvey A. Adee, of the District of Columbia (Second Assistant Secretary), ad interim, May 31, 1895. Edwin F. Uhl, of Michigan (Assistant Secretary), ad interim, June 1, 1895. Richard Olney, of Massachusetts, June 8, 1895; entered upon duties June 10, 1895.

SECRETARY OF THE TREASURY—Charles Foster, of Ohio, continued from preceding administration. John G. Carlisle, of Kentucky, March 6, 1893.

SECRETARY OF WAR—Stephen B. Elkins, of West Virginia, continued from preceding administration. Daniel S. Lamont, of New York, March 6, 1893.

ATTORNEY GENERAL—William H. H. Miller, of Indiana, continued from preceding administration. Richard Olney, of Massachusetts, March 6, 1893. Judson Harmon, of Ohio, June 8, 1895; entered upon duties June 11, 1895.

POSTMASTER GENERAL—John Wanamaker, of Pennsylvania, continued from preceding administration. Wilson S. Bissell, of New York, March 6, 1893. William L. Wilson, of West Virginia, March 1, 1895; entered upon duties April 4, 1895.

SECRETARY OF THE NAVY—Benjamin F. Tracy, of New York, continued from preceding administration. Hilary A. Herbert, of Alabama, March 6, 1893.

SECRETARY OF THE INTERIOR—John W. Noble, of Missouri, continued from preceding administration. Hoke Smith, of Georgia, March 6, 1893. John M. Reynolds, of Pennsylvania (Assistant Secretary), ad interim, September 1, 1896. David R. Francis, of Missouri, September 1, 1896; entered upon duties September 4, 1896.

SECRETARY OF AGRICULTURE—Jeremiah M. Rusk, of Wisconsin, continued from preceding administration. Julius Sterling Morton, of Nebraska, March 6, 1893.

First Administration of WILLIAM McKINLEY

MARCH 4, 1897, TO MARCH 3, 1901

PRESIDENT OF THE UNITED STATES—WILLIAM MCKINLEY, of Ohio.

VICE PRESIDENT OF THE UNITED STATES—GARRET A. HOBART, of New Jersey. (Died November 21, 1899.)

PRESIDENT PRO TEMPORE OF THE SENATE—WILLIAM P. FRYE, of Maine.

SECRETARY OF STATE—RICHARD OLNEY, of Massachusetts, continued from preceding administration. JOHN SHERMAN, of Ohio, March 5, 1897. WILLIAM R. DAY, of Ohio, April 26, 1898; entered upon duties April 28, 1898. ALVEY A. ADEE (Second Assistant Secretary), ad interim, September 17, 1898. JOHN HAY, of the District of Columbia, September 20, 1898; entered upon duties September 30, 1898.

SECRETARY OF THE TREASURY—JOHN G. CARLISLE, of Kentucky, continued from preceding administration. LYMAN J. GAGE, of Illinois, March 5, 1897.

SECRETARY OF WAR—DANIEL S. LAMONT, of New York, continued from preceding administration. RUSSELL A. ALGER, of Michigan, March 5, 1897. ELIHU ROOT, of New York, August 1, 1899.

ATTORNEY GENERAL—JUDSON HARMON, of Ohio, continued from preceding administration. JOSEPH MCKENNA, of California, March 5, 1897; entered upon duties March 7, 1897. JOHN K. RICHARDS, of Ohio (Solicitor General), ad interim, January 26, 1898. JOHN W. GRIGGS, of New Jersey, January 25, 1898; entered upon duties February 1, 1898.

POSTMASTER GENERAL—WILLIAM L. WILSON, of West Virginia, continued from preceding administration. JAMES A. GARY, of Maryland, March 5, 1897. CHARLES EMORY SMITH, of Pennsylvania, April 21, 1898.

SECRETARY OF THE NAVY—HILARY A. HERBERT, of Alabama, continued from preceding administration. JOHN D. LONG, of Massachusetts, March 5, 1897.

SECRETARY OF THE INTERIOR—DAVID R. FRANCIS, of Missouri, continued from preceding administration. CORNELIUS N. BLISS, of New York, March 5, 1897. ETHAN A. HITCHCOCK, of Missouri, December 21, 1898; entered upon duties February 20, 1899.

SECRETARY OF AGRICULTURE—JULIUS STERLING MORTON, of Nebraska, continued from preceding administration. JAMES WILSON, of Iowa, March 5, 1897.

———

Second Administration of WILLIAM McKINLEY

MARCH 4, 1901, TO SEPTEMBER 14, 1901

PRESIDENT OF THE UNITED STATES—WILLIAM MCKINLEY, of Ohio. (Died September 14, 1901.)

VICE PRESIDENT OF THE UNITED STATES—THEODORE ROOSEVELT, of New York.

SECRETARY OF STATE—JOHN HAY, of the District of Columbia, continued from preceding administration. JOHN HAY, of the District of Columbia, recommissioned March 5, 1901.

SECRETARY OF THE TREASURY—LYMAN J. GAGE, of Illinois, continued from preceding administration. LYMAN J. GAGE, of Illinois, recommissioned March 5, 1901.

SECRETARY OF WAR—ELIHU ROOT, of New York, continued from preceding administration. ELIHU ROOT, of New York, recommissioned March 5, 1901.

ATTORNEY GENERAL—JOHN W. GRIGGS, of New Jersey, continued from preceding administration. JOHN W. GRIGGS, of New Jersey, recommissioned March 5, 1901. JOHN K. RICHARDS, of Ohio (Solicitor General), ad interim, April 1, 1901. PHILANDER C. KNOX, of Pennsylvania, April 5, 1901; entered upon duties April 10, 1901.

POSTMASTER GENERAL—CHARLES EMORY SMITH, of Pennsylvania, continued from preceding administration. CHARLES EMORY SMITH, of Pennsylvania, recommissioned March 5, 1901.

SECRETARY OF THE NAVY—JOHN D. LONG, of Massachusetts, continued from preceding administration. JOHN D. LONG, of Massachusetts, recommissioned March 5, 1901.

SECRETARY OF THE INTERIOR—ETHAN A. HITCHCOCK, of Missouri, continued from preceding administration. ETHAN A. HITCHCOCK, of Missouri, recommissioned March 5, 1901.

SECRETARY OF AGRICULTURE—JAMES WILSON, of Iowa, continued from preceding administration. JAMES WILSON, of Iowa, recommissioned March 5, 1901.

First Administration of THEODORE ROOSEVELT

SEPTEMBER 14, 1901, TO MARCH 3, 1905

PRESIDENT OF THE UNITED STATES—Theodore Roosevelt, of New York.

PRESIDENT PRO TEMPORE OF THE SENATE—William P. Frye, of Maine.

SECRETARY OF STATE—John Hay, of the District of Columbia, continued from preceding administration.

SECRETARY OF THE TREASURY—Lyman J. Gage, of Illinois, continued from preceding administration. Leslie M. Shaw, of Iowa, January 9, 1902; entered upon duties February 1, 1902.

SECRETARY OF WAR—Elihu Root, of New York, continued from preceding administration. William H. Taft, of Ohio, January 11, 1904, to take effect February 1, 1904.

ATTORNEY GENERAL—Philander C. Knox, of Pennsylvania, continued from preceding administration. Philander C. Knox, of Pennsylvania, recommissioned December 16, 1901. William H. Moody, of Massachusetts, July 1, 1904.

POSTMASTER GENERAL—Charles Emory Smith, of Pennsylvania, continued from preceding administration. Henry C. Payne, of Wisconsin, January 9, 1902. Robert J. Wynne, of Pennsylvania, October 10, 1904.

SECRETARY OF THE NAVY—John D. Long, of Massachusetts, continued from preceding administration. William H. Moody, of Massachusetts, April 29, 1902; entered upon duties May 1, 1902. Paul Morton, of Illinois, July 1, 1904.

SECRETARY OF THE INTERIOR—Ethan A. Hitchcock, of Missouri, continued from preceding administration.

SECRETARY OF AGRICULTURE—James Wilson, of Iowa, continued from preceding administration.

SECRETARY OF COMMERCE AND LABOR—George B. Cortelyou, of New York, February 16, 1903. Victor H. Metcalf, of California, July 1, 1904.

Second Administration of THEODORE ROOSEVELT

MARCH 4, 1905, TO MARCH 3, 1909

PRESIDENT OF THE UNITED STATES—Theodore Roosevelt, of New York.

VICE PRESIDENT OF THE UNITED STATES—Charles Warren Fairbanks, of Indiana.

SECRETARY OF STATE—John Hay, of the District of Columbia, continued from preceding administration. John Hay, of the District of Columbia, recommissioned March 6, 1905 (died July 1, 1905). Francis B. Loomis, of Ohio (Assistant Secretary), ad interim, July 1, 1905, to July 18, 1905. Elihu Root, of New York, July 7, 1905; entered upon duties July 19, 1905. Robert Bacon, of New York, January 27, 1909.

SECRETARY OF THE TREASURY—Leslie M. Shaw, of Iowa, continued from preceding administration. Leslie M. Shaw, of Iowa, recommissioned March 6, 1905. George B. Cortelyou, of New York, January 15, 1907, to take effect March 4, 1907.

SECRETARY OF WAR—William H. Taft, of Ohio, continued from preceding administration. William H. Taft, of Ohio, recommissioned March 6, 1905. Luke E. Wright, of Tennessee, June 29, 1908; entered upon duties July 1, 1908.

ATTORNEY GENERAL—William H. Moody, of Massachusetts, continued from preceding administration. William H. Moody, of Massachusetts, recommissioned March 6, 1905. Charles J. Bonaparte, of Maryland, December 12, 1906; entered upon duties December 17, 1906.

POSTMASTER GENERAL—Robert J. Wynne, of Pennsylvania, continued from preceding administration. George B. Cortelyou, of New York, March 6, 1905. George von L. Meyer, of Massachusetts, January 15, 1907, to take effect March 4, 1907.

SECRETARY OF THE NAVY—Paul Morton, of Illinois, continued from preceding administration. Paul Morton, of Illinois, recommissioned March 6, 1905. Charles J. Bonaparte, of Maryland, July 1, 1905. Victor H. Metcalf, of California, December 12, 1906; entered upon duties December 17, 1906. Truman H. Newberry, of Michigan, December 1, 1908.

SECRETARY OF THE INTERIOR—Ethan A. Hitchcock, of Missouri, continued from preceding administration. Ethan A. Hitchcock, of Missouri, recommissioned March 6, 1905. James R. Garfield, of Ohio, January 15, 1907, to take effect March 4, 1907.

SECRETARY OF AGRICULTURE—James Wilson, of Iowa, continued from preceding administration. James Wilson, of Iowa, recommissioned March 6, 1905.

SECRETARY OF COMMERCE AND LABOR—Victor H. Metcalf, of California, continued from preceding administration. Victor H. Metcalf, of California, recommissioned March 6, 1905. Oscar S. Straus, of New York, December 12, 1906; entered upon duties December 17, 1906.

Administration of WILLIAM H. TAFT

MARCH 4, 1909, TO MARCH 3, 1913

PRESIDENT OF THE UNITED STATES—WILLIAM H. TAFT, of Ohio.

VICE PRESIDENT OF THE UNITED STATES—JAMES S. SHERMAN, of New York. (Died October 30, 1912.)

PRESIDENT PRO TEMPORE OF THE SENATE—WILLIAM P. FRYE, of Maine (resigned April 27, 1911). JACOB H. GALLINGER, of New Hampshire, and AUGUSTUS O. BACON, of Georgia, alternating.

SECRETARY OF STATE—ROBERT BACON, of New York, continued from preceding administration. PHILANDER C. KNOX, of Pennsylvania, March 5, 1909.

SECRETARY OF THE TREASURY—GEORGE B. CORTELYOU, of New York, continued from preceding administration. FRANKLIN MACVEAGH, of Illinois, March 5, 1909; entered upon duties March 8, 1909.

SECRETARY OF WAR—LUKE E. WRIGHT, of Tennessee, continued from preceding administration. JACOB M. DICKINSON, of Tennessee, March 5, 1909; entered upon duties March 12, 1909. HENRY L. STIMSON, of New York, May 16, 1911; entered upon duties May 22, 1911.

ATTORNEY GENERAL—CHARLES J. BONAPARTE, of Maryland, continued from preceding administratiou. GEORGE W. WICKERSHAM, of New York, March 5, 1909.

POSTMASTER GENERAL—GEORGE VON L. MEYER, of Massachusetts, continued from preceding administration. FRANK H. HITCHCOCK, of Massachusetts, March 5, 1909.

SECRETARY OF THE NAVY—TRUMAN H. NEWBERRY, of Michigan, continued from preceding administration. GEORGE VON L. MEYER, of Massachusetts, March 5, 1909.

SECRETARY OF THE INTERIOR—JAMES R. GARFIELD, of Ohio, continued from preceding administration. RICHARD A. BALLINGER, of Washington, March 5, 1909. WALTER LOWRIE FISHER, of Illinois, March 7, 1911.

SECRETARY OF AGRICULTURE—JAMES WILSON, of Iowa, continued from preceding administration. JAMES WILSON, of Iowa, recommissioned March 5, 1909.

SECRETARY OF COMMERCE AND LABOR—OSCAR S. STRAUS, of New York, continued from preceding administration. CHARLES NAGEL, of Missouri, March 5, 1909.

First Administration of WOODROW WILSON

MARCH 4, 1913, TO MARCH 3, 1917

PRESIDENT OF THE UNITED STATES—WOODROW WILSON, of New Jersey.

VICE PRESIDENT OF THE UNITED STATES—THOMAS R. MARSHALL, of Indiana.

SECRETARY OF STATE—PHILANDER C. KNOX, of Pennsylvania, continued from preceding administration. WILLIAM JENNINGS BRYAN, of Nebraska, March 5, 1913. ROBERT LANSING, of New York (counselor), ad interim, June 9, 1915. ROBERT LANSING, of New York, June 23, 1915.

SECRETARY OF THE TREASURY—FRANKLIN MACVEAGH, of Illinois, continued from preceding administration. WILLIAM GIBBS MCADOO, of New York, March 5, 1913; entered upon duties March 6, 1913.

SECRETARY OF WAR—HENRY L. STIMSON, of New York, continued from preceding administration. LINDLEY M. GARRISON, of New Jersey, March 5, 1913. HUGH L. SCOTT (United States Army), ad interim, February 12, 1916; served from February 11 to March 8, 1916. NEWTON D. BAKER, of Ohio, March 7, 1916; entered upon duties March 9, 1916.

ATTORNEY GENERAL—GEORGE W. WICKERSHAM, of New York, continued from preceding administration. JAMES CLARK MCREYNOLDS, of Tennessee, March 5, 1913; entered upon duties March 6, 1913. THOMAS WATT GREGORY, of Texas, August 29, 1914; entered upon duties September 3, 1914.

POSTMASTER GENERAL—FRANK H. HITCHCOCK, of Massachusetts, continued from preceding administration. ALBERT SIDNEY BURLESON, of Texas, March 5, 1913.

SECRETARY OF THE NAVY—GEORGE VON L. MEYER, of Massachusetts, continued from preceding administration. JOSEPHUS DANIELS, of North Carolina, March 5, 1913.

SECRETARY OF THE INTERIOR—WALTER LOWRIE FISHER, of Illinois, continued from preceding administration. FRANKLIN KNIGHT LANE, of California, March 5, 1913.

SECRETARY OF AGRICULTURE—JAMES WILSON, of Iowa, continued from preceding administration. DAVID FRANKLIN HOUSTON, of Missouri, March 5, 1913; entered upon duties March 6, 1913.

SECRETARY OF COMMERCE—CHARLES NAGEL, of Missouri (Secretary of Commerce and Labor), continued from preceding administration. WILLIAM C. REDFIELD, of New York, March 5, 1913.

SECRETARY OF LABOR—CHARLES NAGEL, of Missouri (Secretary of Commerce and Labor), continued from preceding administration. WILLIAM BAUCHOP WILSON, of Pennsylvania, March 5, 1913.

Second Administration of WOODROW WILSON

MARCH 4, 1917, TO MARCH 3, 1921

PRESIDENT OF THE UNITED STATES—WOODROW WILSON, of New Jersey. (Oath administered March 5, 1917.)

VICE PRESIDENT OF THE UNITED STATES—THOMAS R. MARSHALL, of Indiana.

SECRETARY OF STATE—ROBERT LANSING, of New York, continued from preceding administration. FRANK L. POLK, of New York (Under Secretary), ad interim, February 14, 1920, to March 13, 1920. BAINBRIDGE COLBY, of New York, March 22, 1920; entered upon duties March 23, 1920.

SECRETARY OF THE TREASURY—WILLIAM GIBBS MCADOO, of New York, continued from preceding administration. CARTER GLASS, of Virginia, December 6, 1918; entered upon duties December 16, 1918. DAVID F. HOUSTON, of Missouri, January 31, 1920; entered upon duties February 2, 1920.

SECRETARY OF WAR—NEWTON D. BAKER, of Ohio, continued from preceding administration.

ATTORNEY GENERAL—THOMAS WATT GREGORY, of Texas, continued from preceding administration. A. MITCHELL PALMER, of Pennsylvania, March 5, 1919.

POSTMASTER GENERAL—ALBERT SIDNEY BURLESON, of Texas, continued from preceding administration. ALBERT SIDNEY BURLESON, of Texas, recommissioned January 24, 1918.

SECRETARY OF THE NAVY—JOSEPHUS DANIELS, of North Carolina, continued from preceding administration.

SECRETARY OF THE INTERIOR—FRANKLIN KNIGHT LANE, of California, continued from preceding administration. JOHN BARTON PAYNE, of Illinois, February 28, 1920; entered upon duties March 13, 1920.

SECRETARY OF AGRICULTURE—DAVID FRANKLIN HOUSTON, of Missouri, continued from preceding administration. EDWIN T. MEREDITH, of Iowa, January 31, 1920; entered upon duties February 2, 1920.

SECRETARY OF COMMERCE—WILLIAM C. REDFIELD, of New York, continued from preceding administration. JOSHUA WILLIS ALEXANDER, of Missouri, December 11, 1919; entered upon duties December 16, 1919.

SECRETARY OF LABOR—WILLIAM BAUCHOP WILSON, of Pennsylvania, continued from preceding administration.

Administration of WARREN G. HARDING

MARCH 4, 1921, TO AUGUST 2, 1923

PRESIDENT OF THE UNITED STATES—WARREN G. HARDING, of Ohio. (Died August 2, 1923.)

VICE PRESIDENT OF THE UNITED STATES—CALVIN COOLIDGE, of Massachusetts.

SECRETARY OF STATE—BAINBRIDGE COLBY, of New York, continued from preceding administration. CHARLES EVANS HUGHES, of New York, March 4, 1921; entered upon duties March 5, 1921.

SECRETARY OF THE TREASURY—DAVID F. HOUSTON, of Missouri, continued from preceding administration. ANDREW W. MELLON, of Pennsylvania, March 4, 1921; entered upon duties March 5, 1921.

SECRETARY OF WAR—NEWTON D. BAKER, of Ohio, continued from preceding administration. JOHN W. WEEKS, of Massachusetts, March 5, 1921.

ATTORNEY GENERAL—A. MITCHELL PALMER, of Pennsylvania, continued from preceding administration. HARRY M. DAUGHERTY, of Ohio, March 5, 1921.

POSTMASTER GENERAL—ALBERT SIDNEY BURLESON, of Texas, continued from preceding administration. WILL H. HAYS, of Indiana, March 5, 1921. HUBERT WORK, of Colorado, March 4, 1922. HARRY S. NEW, of Indiana, February 27, 1923; entered upon duties March 5, 1923.

SECRETARY OF THE NAVY—JOSEPHUS DANIELS, of North Carolina, continued from preceding administration. EDWIN DENBY, of Michigan, March 5, 1921.

SECRETARY OF THE INTERIOR—JOHN BARTON PAYNE, of Illinois, continued from preceding administration. ALBERT B. FALL, of New Mexico, March 5, 1921. HUBERT WORK, of Colorado, February 27, 1923; entered upon duties March 5, 1923.

SECRETARY OF AGRICULTURE—EDWIN T. MEREDITH, of Iowa, continued from preceding administration. HENRY C. WALLACE, of Iowa, March 5, 1921.

SECRETARY OF COMMERCE—JOSHUA WILLIS ALEXANDER, of Missouri, continued from preceding administration. HERBERT C. HOOVER, of California, March 5, 1921.

SECRETARY OF LABOR—WILLIAM BAUCHOP WILSON, of Pennsylvania, continued from preceding administration. JAMES J. DAVIS, of Pennsylvania, March 5, 1921.

First Administration of CALVIN COOLIDGE

AUGUST 3, 1923, TO MARCH 3, 1925

PRESIDENT OF THE UNITED STATES—Calvin Coolidge, of Massachusetts.

PRESIDENT PRO TEMPORE OF THE SENATE—Albert B. Cummins, of Iowa.

SECRETARY OF STATE—Charles Evans Hughes, of New York, continued from preceding administration.

SECRETARY OF THE TREASURY—Andrew W. Mellon, of Pennsylvania, continued from preceding administration.

SECRETARY OF WAR—John W. Weeks, of Massachusetts, continued from preceding administration.

ATTORNEY GENERAL—Harry M. Daugherty, of Ohio, continued from preceding administration. Harlan F. Stone, of New York, April 7, 1924; entered upon duties April 9, 1924.

POSTMASTER GENERAL—Harry S. New, of Indiana, continued from preceding administration.

SECRETARY OF THE NAVY—Edwin Denby, of Michigan, continued from preceding administration. Curtis D. Wilbur, of California, March 18, 1924.

SECRETARY OF THE INTERIOR—Hubert Work, of Colorado, continued from preceding administration.

SECRETARY OF AGRICULTURE—Henry C. Wallace, of Iowa, continued from preceding administration (died October 25, 1924). Howard M. Gore, of West Virginia (Assistant Secretary), ad interim, October 26, 1924, to November 22, 1924. Howard M. Gore, of West Virginia, November 21, 1924; entered upon duties November 22, 1924.

SECRETARY OF COMMERCE—Herbert C. Hoover, of California, continued from preceding administration.

SECRETARY OF LABOR—James J. Davis, of Pennsylvania, continued from preceding administration.

Second Administration of CALVIN COOLIDGE

MARCH 4, 1925, TO MARCH 3, 1929

PRESIDENT OF THE UNITED STATES—Calvin Coolidge, of Massachusetts.

VICE PRESIDENT OF THE UNITED STATES—Charles G. Dawes, of Illinois.

SECRETARY OF STATE—Charles Evans Hughes, of New York, continued from preceding administration. Frank B. Kellogg, of Minnesota, February 16, 1925; entered upon duties March 5, 1925.

SECRETARY OF THE TREASURY—Andrew W. Mellon, of Pennsylvania, continued from preceding administration.

SECRETARY OF WAR—John W. Weeks, of Massachusetts, continued from preceding administration. Dwight F. Davis, of Missouri, October 13, 1925; entered upon duties October 14, 1925.

ATTORNEY GENERAL—James M. Beck, of Pennsylvania (Solicitor General), ad interim, March 4, 1925, to March 16, 1925. John G. Sargent, of Vermont, March 17, 1925; entered upon duties March 18, 1925.

POSTMASTER GENERAL—Harry S. New, of Indiana, continued from preceding administration. Harry S. New, of Indiana, recommissioned March 5, 1925.

SECRETARY OF THE NAVY—Curtis D. Wilbur, of California, continued from preceding administration.

SECRETARY OF THE INTERIOR—Hubert Work, of Colorado, continued from preceding administration. Roy O. West, of Illinois, ad interim, July 25, 1928, to January 21, 1929. Roy O. West, January 21, 1929.

SECRETARY OF AGRICULTURE—Howard M. Gore, of West Virginia, continued from preceding administration. William M. Jardine, of Kansas, February 18, 1925; entered upon duties March 5, 1925.

SECRETARY OF COMMERCE—Herbert C. Hoover, of California, continued from preceding administration. William F. Whiting, of Massachusetts, ad interim, August 21, 1928, to December 11, 1928. William F. Whiting, December 11, 1928.

SECRETARY OF LABOR—James J. Davis, of Pennsylvania, continued from preceding administration.

Administration of HERBERT C. HOOVER

MARCH 4, 1929, TO MARCH 3, 1933

PRESIDENT OF THE UNITED STATES—HERBERT C. HOOVER, of California.

VICE PRESIDENT OF THE UNITED STATES—CHARLES CURTIS, of Kansas.

SECRETARY OF STATE—FRANK B. KELLOGG, of Minnesota, continued from preceding administration. HENRY L. STIMSON, of New York, March 4, 1929; entered upon duties March 29, 1929.

SECRETARY OF THE TREASURY—ANDREW W. MELLON, of Pennsylvania, continued from preceding administration. OGDEN L. MILLS, of New York, February 10, 1932; entered upon duties February 13, 1932.

SECRETARY OF WAR—DWIGHT F. DAVIS, of Missouri, continued from preceding administration. JAMES W. GOOD, of Illinois, March 5, 1929; entered upon duties March 6, 1929. PATRICK J. HURLEY, of Oklahoma, December 9, 1929.

ATTORNEY GENERAL—JOHN G. SARGENT, of Vermont, continued from preceding administration. JAMES DeWITT MITCHELL, of Minnesota, March 5, 1929; entered upon duties March 6, 1929.

POSTMASTER GENERAL—HARRY S. NEW, of Indiana, continued from preceding administration. WALTER F. BROWN, of Ohio, March 5, 1929; entered upon duties March 6, 1929.

SECRETARY OF THE NAVY—CURTIS D. WILBUR, of California, continued from preceding administration. CHARLES F. ADAMS, of Massachusetts, March 5, 1929.

SECRETARY OF THE INTERIOR—ROY O. WEST, of Illinois, continued from preceding administration. RAY L. WILBUR, of California, March 5, 1929.

SECRETARY OF AGRICULTURE—WILLIAM M. JARDINE, of Kansas, continued from preceding administration. ARTHUR M. HYDE, of Missouri, March 5, 1929; entered upon duties March 6, 1929.

SECRETARY OF COMMERCE—WILLIAM F. WHITING, of Massachusetts, continued from preceding administration. ROBERT P. LAMONT, of Illinois, March 5, 1929. ROY D. CHAPIN, of Michigan, ad interim, August 8, 1932, to December 14, 1932. ROY D. CHAPIN, of Michigan, December 14, 1932.

SECRETARY OF LABOR—JAMES J. DAVIS, of Pennsylvania, continued from preceding administration. WILLIAM N. DOAK, of Virginia, December 8, 1930; entered upon duties December 9, 1930.

———

First Administration of FRANKLIN DELANO ROOSEVELT

MARCH 4, 1933, TO JANUARY 20, 1937

PRESIDENT OF THE UNITED STATES—FRANKLIN DELANO ROOSEVELT, of New York.

VICE PRESIDENT OF THE UNITED STATES—JOHN N. GARNER, of Texas.

SECRETARY OF STATE—CORDELL HULL, of Tennessee, March 4, 1933.

SECRETARY OF THE TREASURY—WILLIAM H. WOODIN, of New York, March 4, 1933. HENRY MORGENTHAU, Jr., of New York (Under Secretary), ad interim, January 1, 1934, to January 8, 1934. HENRY MORGENTHAU, Jr., of New York, January 8, 1934.

SECRETARY OF WAR—GEORGE H. DERN, of Utah, March 4, 1933.

ATTORNEY GENERAL—HOMER S. CUMMINGS, of Connecticut, March 4, 1933.

POSTMASTER GENERAL—JAMES A. FARLEY, of New York, March 4, 1933.

SECRETARY OF THE NAVY—CLAUDE A. SWANSON, of Virginia, March 4, 1933.

SECRETARY OF THE INTERIOR—HAROLD L. ICKES, of Illinois, March 4, 1933.

SECRETARY OF AGRICULTURE—HENRY A. WALLACE, of Iowa, March 4, 1933.

SECRETARY OF COMMERCE—DANIEL C. ROPER, of South Carolina, March 4, 1933.

SECRETARY OF LABOR—FRANCES PERKINS, of New York, March 4, 1933.

Second Administration of FRANKLIN DELANO ROOSEVELT

JANUARY 20, 1937, TO JANUARY 20, 1941

PRESIDENT OF THE UNITED STATES—Franklin Delano Roosevelt, of New York.

VICE PRESIDENT OF THE UNITED STATES—John N. Garner, of Texas.

SECRETARY OF STATE—Cordell Hull, of Tennessee, continued from preceding administration.

SECRETARY OF THE TREASURY—Henry Morgenthau, Jr., of New York, continued from preceding administration.

SECRETARY OF WAR—George H. Dern, of Utah, continued from preceding administration (died August 27, 1936). Harry H. Woodring, of Kansas (Assistant Secretary), ad interim, September 25, 1936, to May 6, 1937. Harry H. Woodring, of Kansas, May 6, 1937. Henry L. Stimson, of New York, July 10, 1940.

ATTORNEY GENERAL—Homer S. Cummings, of Connecticut, continued from preceding administration. Frank Murphy, of Michigan, ad interim, January 2, 1939, to January 17, 1939. Frank Murphy, of Michigan, January 17, 1939. Robert H. Jackson, of New York, January 18, 1940.

POSTMASTER GENERAL—James A. Farley, of New York, continued from preceding administration. James A. Farley, of New York, recommissioned January 22, 1937. Frank C. Walker, of Pennsylvania, September 10, 1940.

SECRETARY OF THE NAVY—Claude A. Swanson, of Virginia, continued from preceding administration (died July 7, 1939). Charles Edison, of New Jersey, Acting Secretary from August 5, 1939, to December 30, 1939. Charles Edison, of New Jersey (Assistant Secretary), ad interim, December 30, 1939, to January 11, 1940. Charles Edison, of New Jersey, January 11, 1940. Frank Knox, of Illinois, July 10, 1940.

SECRETARY OF THE INTERIOR—Harold L. Ickes, of Illinois, continued from preceding administration.

SECRETARY OF AGRICULTURE—Henry A. Wallace, of Iowa, continued from preceding administration. Claude R. Wickard, of Indiana, August 27, 1940; entered upon duties September 5, 1940.

SECRETARY OF COMMERCE—Daniel C. Roper, of South Carolina, continued from preceding administration. Harry L. Hopkins, of New York, ad interim, December 24, 1938, to January 23, 1939. Harry L. Hopkins, of New York, January 23, 1939. Jesse H. Jones, of Texas, September 16, 1940; entered upon duties September 19, 1940.

SECRETARY OF LABOR—Frances Perkins, of New York, continued from preceding administration.

———

Third Administration of FRANKLIN DELANO ROOSEVELT

JANUARY 20, 1941, TO JANUARY 20, 1945

PRESIDENT OF THE UNITED STATES—Franklin Delano Roosevelt, of New York.

VICE PRESIDENT OF THE UNITED STATES—Henry A. Wallace, of Iowa.

SECRETARY OF STATE—Cordell Hull, of Tennessee, continued from preceding administration. Edward R. Stettinius, of Virginia, November 30, 1944; entered upon duties December 1, 1944.

SECRETARY OF THE TREASURY—Henry Morgenthau, Jr., of New York, continued from preceding administration.

SECRETARY OF WAR—Henry L. Stimson, of New York, continued from preceding administration.

ATTORNEY GENERAL—Robert H. Jackson, of New York, continued from preceding administration. Francis Biddle, of Pennsylvania, September 5, 1941.

POSTMASTER GENERAL—Frank C. Walker, of Pennsylvania, continued from preceding administration. Frank C. Walker, of Pennsylvania, recommissioned January 27, 1941.

SECRETARY OF THE NAVY—Frank Knox, of Illinois, continued from preceding administration (died April 28, 1944). James V. Forrestal, of New York, May 18, 1944.

SECRETARY OF THE INTERIOR—Harold L. Ickes, of Illinois, continued from preceding administration.

SECRETARY OF AGRICULTURE—Claude R. Wickard, of Indiana, continued from preceding administration.

SECRETARY OF COMMERCE—Jesse H. Jones, of Texas, continued from preceding administration.

SECRETARY OF LABOR—Frances Perkins, of New York, continued from preceding administration.

Fourth Administration of FRANKLIN DELANO ROOSEVELT

JANUARY 20, 1945, TO APRIL 12, 1945

PRESIDENT OF THE UNITED STATES—FRANKLIN DELANO ROOSEVELT, of New York. (Died April 12, 1945.)

VICE PRESIDENT OF THE UNITED STATES—HARRY S. TRUMAN, of Missouri.

SECRETARY OF STATE—EDWARD R. STETTINIUS, of Virginia, continued from preceding administration.

SECRETARY OF THE TREASURY—HENRY MORGENTHAU, Jr., of New York, continued from preceding administration.

SECRETARY OF WAR—HENRY L. STIMSON, of New York, continued from preceding administration.

ATTORNEY GENERAL—FRANCIS BIDDLE, of Pennsylvania, continued from preceding administration.

POSTMASTER GENERAL—FRANK C. WALKER, of Pennsylvania, continued from preceding administration. FRANK C. WALKER, of Pennsylvania, recommissioned February 6, 1945.

SECRETARY OF THE NAVY—JAMES V. FORRESTAL, of New York, continued from preceding administration.

SECRETARY OF THE INTERIOR—HAROLD L. ICKES, of Illinois, continued from preceding administration.

SECRETARY OF AGRICULTURE—CLAUDE R. WICKARD, of Indiana, continued from preceding administration.

SECRETARY OF COMMERCE—JESSE H. JONES, of Texas, continued from preceding administration. HENRY A. WALLACE, of Iowa, March 1, 1945; entered upon duties March 2, 1945.

SECRETARY OF LABOR—FRANCES PERKINS, of New York, continued from preceding administration.

First Administration of HARRY S. TRUMAN

APRIL 12, 1945, TO JANUARY 20, 1949

PRESIDENT OF THE UNITED STATES—HARRY S. TRUMAN, of Missouri.

PRESIDENT PRO TEMPORE OF THE SENATE—KENNETH McKELLAR, of Tennessee. ARTHUR S. VANDENBERG, of Michigan, January 4, 1947.

SECRETARY OF STATE—EDWARD R. STETTINIUS, of Virginia, continued from preceding administration. JAMES F. BYRNES, of South Carolina, July 2, 1945; entered upon duties July 3, 1945. GEORGE C. MARSHALL, of Pennsylvania, January 8, 1947; entered upon duties January 21, 1947.

SECRETARY OF THE TREASURY—HENRY MORGENTHAU, Jr., of New York, continued from preceding administration. FRED M. VINSON, of Kentucky, July 18, 1945; entered upon duties July 23, 1945. JOHN W. SNYDER, of Missouri, June 12, 1946; entered upon duties June 25, 1946.

SECRETARY OF DEFENSE—JAMES FORRESTAL, of New York, July 26, 1947; entered upon duties September 17, 1947.

SECRETARY OF WAR—HENRY L. STIMSON, of New York, continued from preceding administration. ROBERT PORTER PATTERSON, of New York, September 26, 1945; entered upon duties September 27, 1945. KENNETH C. ROYALL, of North Carolina, July 21, 1947; entered upon duties July 25, 1947, and served until September 17, 1947.

ATTORNEY GENERAL—FRANCIS BIDDLE, of Pennsylvania, continued from preceding administration. TOM C. CLARK, of Texas, June 15, 1945; entered upon duties July 1, 1945.

POSTMASTER GENERAL—FRANK C. WALKER, of Pennsylvania, continued from preceding administration. ROBERT E. HANNEGAN, of Missouri, May 8, 1945; entered upon duties July 1, 1945. JESSE M. DONALDSON, of Missouri, December 16, 1947.

SECRETARY OF THE NAVY—JAMES V. FORRESTAL, of New York, continued from preceding administration; served until September 17, 1947.

SECRETARY OF THE INTERIOR—HAROLD L. ICKES, of Illinois, continued from preceding administration. JULIUS A. KRUG, of Wisconsin, March 6, 1946; entered upon duties March 18, 1946.

SECRETARY OF AGRICULTURE—CLAUDE R. WICKARD, of Indiana, continued from preceding administration. CLINTON P. ANDERSON, of New Mexico, June 2, 1945; entered upon duties June 30, 1945. CHARLES F. BRANNAN, of Colorado, May 29, 1948; entered upon duties June 2, 1948.

SECRETARY OF COMMERCE—HENRY A. WALLACE, of Iowa, continued from preceding administration. WILLIAM AVERELL HARRIMAN, of New York, ad interim, September 28, 1946, to January 28, 1947. WILLIAM AVERELL HARRIMAN, of New York, January 28, 1947. CHARLES SAWYER, of Ohio, May 6, 1948.

SECRETARY OF LABOR—FRANCES PERKINS, of New York, continued from preceding administration. LEWIS B. SCHWELLENBACH, of Washington, June 1, 1945; entered upon duties July 1, 1945 (died June 10, 1948). MAURICE J. TOBIN, of Massachusetts, ad interim, August 13, 1948.

Second Administration of HARRY S. TRUMAN

JANUARY 20, 1949, TO JANUARY 20, 1953

PRESIDENT OF THE UNITED STATES—HARRY S. TRUMAN, of Missouri.

VICE PRESIDENT OF THE UNITED STATES—ALBEN W. BARKLEY, of Kentucky.

SECRETARY OF STATE—DEAN G. ACHESON, of Connecticut, January 19, 1949; entered upon duties January 21, 1949.

SECRETARY OF THE TREASURY—JOHN W. SNYDER, of Missouri, continued from preceding administration.

SECRETARY OF DEFENSE—JAMES FORRESTAL, of New York, continued from preceding administration. LOUIS A. JOHNSON, of West Virginia, March 23, 1949; entered upon duties March 28, 1949. GEORGE C. MARSHALL, of Pennsylvania, September 20, 1950; entered upon duties September 21, 1950. ROBERT A. LOVETT, of New York, September 14, 1951; entered upon duties September 17, 1951.

ATTORNEY GENERAL—TOM C. CLARK, of Texas, continued from preceding administration. J. HOWARD McGRATH, of Rhode Island, August 19, 1949; entered upon duties August 24, 1949. JAMES P. McGRANERY, of Pennsylvania, May 21, 1952; entered upon duties May 27, 1952.

POSTMASTER GENERAL—JESSE M. DONALDSON, of Missouri, continued from preceding administration. JESSE M. DONALDSON, of Missouri, recommissioned February 8, 1949.

SECRETARY OF THE INTERIOR—JULIUS A. KRUG, of Wisconsin, continued from preceding administration. OSCAR L. CHAPMAN, of Colorado (Under Secretary), ad interim, December 1, 1949, to January 19, 1950. OSCAR L. CHAPMAN, of Colorado, January 19, 1950.

SECRETARY OF AGRICULTURE—CHARLES F. BRANNAN, of Colorado, continued from preceding administration.

SECRETARY OF COMMERCE—CHARLES SAWYER, of Ohio, continued from preceding administration.

SECRETARY OF LABOR—MAURICE J. TOBIN, of Massachusetts, ad interim, continued from preceding administration. MAURICE J. TOBIN, of Massachusetts, February 1, 1949.

———

First Administration of DWIGHT D. EISENHOWER

JANUARY 20, 1953, TO JANUARY 20, 1957

PRESIDENT OF THE UNITED STATES—DWIGHT D. EISENHOWER, of New York.

VICE PRESIDENT OF THE UNITED STATES—RICHARD M. NIXON, of California.

SECRETARY OF STATE—JOHN FOSTER DULLES, of New York, January 21, 1953.

SECRETARY OF THE TREASURY—GEORGE M. HUMPHREY, of Ohio, January 21, 1953.

SECRETARY OF DEFENSE—CHARLES E. WILSON, of Michigan, January 26, 1953; entered upon duties January 28, 1953.

ATTORNEY GENERAL—HERBERT BROWNELL, Jr., of New York, January 21, 1953.

POSTMASTER GENERAL—ARTHUR E. SUMMERFIELD, of Michigan, January 21, 1953.

SECRETARY OF THE INTERIOR—DOUGLAS McKAY, of Oregon, January 21, 1953. FREDERICK A. SEATON, of Nebraska, June 6, 1956; entered upon duties June 8, 1956.

SECRETARY OF AGRICULTURE—EZRA TAFT BENSON, of Utah, January 21, 1953.

SECRETARY OF COMMERCE—SINCLAIR WEEKS, of Massachusetts, January 21, 1953.

SECRETARY OF LABOR—MARTIN P. DURKIN, of Maryland, January 21, 1953. JAMES P. MITCHELL, of New Jersey, ad interim, October 9, 1953, to January 19, 1954. JAMES P. MITCHELL, of New Jersey, January 19, 1954.

SECRETARY OF HEALTH, EDUCATION, AND WELFARE—OVETA CULP HOBBY, of Texas, April 10, 1953; entered upon duties April 11, 1953. MARION B. FOLSOM, of New York, July 20, 1955; entered upon duties August 1, 1955.

Second Administration of DWIGHT D. EISENHOWER

JANUARY 20, 1957, TO JANUARY 20, 1961

PRESIDENT OF THE UNITED STATES—DWIGHT D. EISENHOWER, of Pennsylvania.

VICE PRESIDENT OF THE UNITED STATES—RICHARD M. NIXON, of California.

SECRETARY OF STATE—JOHN FOSTER DULLES, of New York, continued from preceding administration. CHRISTIAN A. HERTER, of Massachusetts, April 21, 1959; entered upon duties April 22, 1959.

SECRETARY OF THE TREASURY—GEORGE M. HUMPHREY, of Ohio, continued from preceding administration. ROBERT BERNERD ANDERSON, of Connecticut, July 2, 1957; entered upon duties July 29, 1957.

SECRETARY OF DEFENSE—CHARLES E. WILSON, of Michigan, continued from preceding administration. NEIL H. MCELROY, of Ohio, August 19, 1957; entered upon duties October 9, 1957. THOMAS S. GATES, Jr., of Pennsylvania, ad interim, December 1, 1959, to January 26, 1960. THOMAS S. GATES, Jr., of Pennsylvania, January 26, 1960.

ATTORNEY GENERAL—HERBERT BROWNELL, Jr., of New York, continued from preceding administration. WILLIAM P. ROGERS, of Maryland, ad interim, November 8, 1957, to January 27, 1958. WILLIAM P. ROGERS, of Maryland, January 27, 1958.

POSTMASTER GENERAL—ARTHUR E. SUMMERFIELD, of Michigan, continued from preceding administration. ARTHUR E. SUMMERFIELD, of Michigan, recommissioned February 4, 1957.

SECRETARY OF THE INTERIOR—FREDERICK A. SEATON, of Nebraska, continued from preceding administration.

SECRETARY OF AGRICULTURE—EZRA TAFT BENSON, of Utah, continued from preceding administration.

SECRETARY OF COMMERCE—SINCLAIR WEEKS, of Massachusetts, continued from preceding administration. LEWIS L. STRAUSS, of New York, ad interim, November 13, 1958, to June 27, 1959. FREDERICK H. MUELLER, of Michigan (Under Secretary), ad interim, July 21, 1959, to August 6, 1959. FREDERICK H. MUELLER, of Michigan, August 6, 1959.

SECRETARY OF LABOR—JAMES P. MITCHELL, of New Jersey, continued from preceding administration.

SECRETARY OF HEALTH, EDUCATION, AND WELFARE—MARION B. FOLSOM, of New York, continued from preceding administration. ARTHUR S. FLEMMING, of Ohio, July 9, 1958; entered upon duties August 1, 1958.

THE CONTINENTAL CONGRESS
1774–1789

THE CONTINENTAL CONGRESS

PLACE AND TIME OF MEETING

Philadelphia, Pa	From September 5, 1774, to October 26, 1774
Philadelphia, Pa	From May 10, 1775, to December 12, 1776
Baltimore, Md	From December 20, 1776, to March 4, 1777
Philadelphia, Pa	From March 5, 1777, to September 18, 1777
Lancaster, Pa	September 27, 1777 (one day only)
York, Pa	From September 30, 1777, to June 27, 1778
Philadelphia, Pa	From July 2, 1778, to June 21, 1783
Princeton, N. J	From June 30, 1783, to November 4, 1783
Annapolis, Md	From November 26, 1783, to June 3, 1784
Trenton, N. J	From November 1, 1784, to December 24, 1784
New York City	From January 11, 1785, to November 4, 1785
New York City	From November 7, 1785, to November 3, 1786
New York City	From November 6, 1786, to October 30, 1787
New York City	From November 5, 1787, to October 21, 1788
New York City	From November 3, 1788, to March 2, 1789

PRESIDENTS OF THE CONGRESS

PEYTON RANDOLPH,[1] of Virginia	Elected September 5, 1774
HENRY MIDDLETON, of South Carolina . .	Elected October 22, 1774
PEYTON RANDOLPH,[2] of Virginia	Elected May 10, 1775
JOHN HANCOCK, of Massachusetts	Elected May 24, 1775
HENRY LAURENS, of South Carolina . . .	Elected November 1, 1777
JOHN JAY, of New York	Elected December 10, 1778
SAMUEL HUNTINGTON, of Connecticut . .	Elected September 28, 1779
THOMAS MCKEAN, of Delaware	Elected July 10, 1781
JOHN HANSON, of Maryland	Elected November 5, 1781
ELIAS BOUDINOT, of New Jersey	Elected November 4, 1782
THOMAS MIFFLIN, of Pennsylvania . . .	Elected November 3, 1783
RICHARD HENRY LEE, of Virginia	Elected November 30, 1784
JOHN HANCOCK,[3] of Massachusetts . . .	Elected November 23, 1785
NATHANIEL GORHAM, of Massachusetts .	Elected June 6, 1786
ARTHUR ST. CLAIR, of Pennsylvania . . .	Elected February 2, 1787
CYRUS GRIFFIN, of Virginia	Elected January 22, 1788

SECRETARY OF THE CONGRESS

CHARLES THOMSON, of Pennsylvania . . . Elected September 5, 1774

---

[1] Resigned October 22, 1774. [2] Died October 22, 1775. [3] Resigned May 29, 1786, never having served, owing to continued illness.

DELEGATES IN THE CONGRESS

CONNECTICUT [1]

Andrew Adams 1777–1780	Benjamin Huntington . . . 1787–1788	Jonathan Sturges 1774–1787
Andrew Adams 1781–1782	Samuel Huntington 1776–1784	John Treadwell 1785–1786
Joseph P. Cook 1784–1788	William S. Johnson 1784–1787	Joseph Trumbull 1774–1775
Silas Deane. 1774–1776	Richard Law 1778	James Wadsworth 1783–1784
Eliphalet Dyer 1774–1779	Richard Law 1783–1784	James Wadsworth 1785–1786
Eliphalet Dyer 1780–1783	Stephen M. Mitchell . . . 1781–1784	Jeremiah Wadsworth. . . . 1787–1788
Pierrepont Edwards 1787–1788	Stephen M. Mitchell . . . 1785–1786	William Williams 1776–1778
Oliver Ellsworth. 1777–1784	Stephen M. Mitchell . . . 1787–1788	William Williams 1783–1784
William Hillhouse 1783–1786	Jesse Root 1778–1783	Oliver Wolcott 1775–1778
Titus Hosmer. 1775–1776	Roger Sherman 1774–1784	Oliver Wolcott 1780–1784
Titus Hosmer. 1777–1779	Joseph Spencer 1778–1779	
Benjamin Huntington . . . 1780–1784	Jedediah Strong. 1782–1784	

DELAWARE [1]

Gunning Bedford [2] 1786–1787	Thomas McKean 1774–1776	Cæsar Rodney 1782–1784
Gunning Bedford, Jr. . . . 1783–1785	Thomas McKean 1778–1783	Thomas Rodney. 1781–1783
John Dickinson [3] 1776–1777	Nathaniel Mitchell. . . . 1786–1788	Thomas Rodney. 1785–1787
John Dickinson 1779–1780	John Patten 1785–1786	James Sykes [5] 1777–1778
Philemon Dickinson . . . 1782–1783	William Peery. 1785–1786	James Tilton 1783–1785
John Evans [3] 1776–1777	George Read 1774–1777	Nicholas Van Dyke [5] . . . 1777–1782
Dyre Kearney [4] 1787–1788	Cæsar Rodney 1774–1776	John Vining 1784–1786
Eleazer McComb 1782–1784	Cæsar Rodney 1777–1778	Samuel Wharton 1782–1783

GEORGIA [1]

Benjamin Andrew [6] 1780	John Habersham 1785	Henry Osborne [6] 1786
Abraham Baldwin 1785	Joseph Habersham [6] 1783–1784	Nathaniel Pendleton [6] 1789
Abraham Baldwin 1787–1789	Lyman Hall 1775–1778	William Pierce. 1787
Nathan Brownson 1777	Lyman Hall 1780	Samuel Stirk [6] 1781
Nathan Brownson 1783	John Houstoun 1775–1777	Edward Telfair 1778–1782
Archibald Bulloch 1775–1776	John Houstoun 1779	Edward Telfair 1784–1785
Joseph Clay [6] 1778	William Houstoun 1783–1786	Edward Telfair 1788–1789
Joseph Clay 1783	Richard Howley. 1780–1781	John Walton 1778
Samuel Elbert [7] 1784	Noble Wimberly Jones 1775	George Walton 1776–1778
William Few 1780–1788	Noble Wimberly Jones . . . 1781–1782	George Walton 1780–1781
William Gibbons 1784–1785	Lachlan McIntosh [6] 1784	George Walton 1787–1788
James Gunn [6] 1788–1789	Edward Langworthy. . . . 1777–1779	Joseph Wood 1777–1778
Button Gwinnett 1776–1777	William O'Bryen [6] 1789	John Zubly [8] 1775

---

[1] No Delegates attended from Connecticut, Delaware, and Georgia in 1788–1789, and no credentials from these States for those years are in the *Papers of the Continental Congress.*
[2] Resigned January 15, 1787.
[3] Resigned April 4, 1777.

[4] Elected to fill vacancy caused by resignation of Gunning Bedford.
[5] Elected to fill vacancies caused by resignations of John Dickinson and John Evans.
[6] Did not attend.
[7] Declined January 21, 1784.
[8] Resigned in November 1775.

MARYLAND

Robert Alexander 1775–1777
William Carmichael . . . 1778–1780
Charles Carroll ("Barris-
ter") 1776–1777
Charles Carroll of Carroll-
ton 1776–1777
Daniel Carroll 1780–1784
Jeremiah T. Chase 1783–1784
Samuel Chase 1774–1778
Samuel Chase 1784–1785
Benjamin Contee 1787–1788
James Forbes [1] 1778–1780
Uriah Forrest 1786–1787
Robert Goldsborough . . . 1774–1775
John Hall 1775

John Hall 1783–1784
John Hanson 1780–1783
William Harrison 1785–1787
William Hemsley 1782–1784
John Henry 1778–1781
John Henry 1784–1787
William Hindman 1784–1787
John E. Howard 1787–1788
Daniel Jenifer of St. Thomas . 1778–1782
Thomas Johnson 1774–1777
Thomas Sim Lee 1783–1784
Edward Lloyd 1783–1784
James McHenry 1783–1786
Luther Martin 1784–1785
William Paca 1774–1779

George Plater 1778–1781
Richard Potts 1781–1782
Nathaniel Ramsay 1785–1787
Richard Ridgely 1785–1786
John Rogers 1775–1776
David Ross 1786–1787
Benjamin Rumsey 1776–1778
Gustavus Scott 1784–1785
Joshua Seney 1787–1788
William Smith 1777–1778
Thomas Stone 1775–1779
Thomas Stone 1784–1785
Matthew Tilghman 1774–1777
Turbutt Wright 1781–1783

MASSACHUSETTS

John Adams 1774–1778
Samuel Adams 1774–1782
Thomas Cushing 1774–1776
Francis Dana 1776–1778
Francis Dana 1784
Nathan Dane 1785–1788
Elbridge Gerry 1776–1781
Elbridge Gerry 1782–1785
Nathaniel Gorham 1782–1783
Nathaniel Gorham 1785–1787

John Hancock 1775–1780
John Hancock 1785–1786
Stephen Higginson 1782–1783
Samuel Holten 1778–1780
Samuel Holten 1782–1783
Samuel Holten 1784–1785
Samuel Holten 1786–1787
Jonathan Jackson 1782
Rufus King 1784–1787
James Lovell 1776–1782

John Lowell 1782–1783
Samuel Osgood 1780–1784
Samuel A. Otis 1787–1788
Robert Treat Paine . . . 1774–1778
George Partridge 1779–1782
George Partridge 1783–1785
Theodore Sedgwick . . . 1785–1788
James Sullivan 1782
George Thacher 1787
Artemas Ward 1780–1781

NEW HAMPSHIRE

Josiah Bartlett 1775–1778
Jonathan Blanchard . . . 1783–1784
Jonathan Blanchard . . . 1787
Nathaniel Folsom 1774–1775
Nathaniel Folsom 1777–1778
Nathaniel Folsom 1779–1780
Abiel Foster 1783–1785
George Frost 1777–1779

John Taylor Gilman . . . 1782–1783
Nicholas Gilman 1786–1789
John Langdon 1775–1777
John Langdon 1786–1787
Woodbury Langdon . . . 1779–1780
Samuel Livermore 1780–1783
Samuel Livermore 1785–1786
Pierse Long 1784–1786

Nathaniel Peabody . . . 1779–1780
John Sullivan 1774–1775
John Sullivan 1780–1781
Matthew Thornton . . . 1776–1778
John Wentworth, Jr . . . 1778–1779
William Whipple 1776–1779
Phillips White 1782–1783
Paine Wingate 1787–1788

NEW JERSEY

John Beatty 1783–1785
Elias Boudinot 1777–1778
Elias Boudinot [2] 1781–1783
William Burnet [3] 1780–1781
Lambert Cadwalader . . . 1784–1787
Abraham Clark 1776–1778
Abraham Clark [4] 1779–1783
Abraham Clark 1786–1789
Silas Condict 1781–1784
John Cooper 1776
Stephen Crane 1774–1776
Jonathan Dayton [5] . . . 1787–1788
John De Hart [6] 1774–1775
John De Hart [7] 1776

Samuel Dick 1783–1785
Jonathan Elmer [8] 1776–1778
Jonathan Elmer [9] 1781–1784
Jonathan Elmer 1787–1788
John Fell 1778–1780
Frederick Frelinghuysen [10] . 1778–1779
Frederick Frelinghuysen . . 1782–1783
John Hart [11] 1776
Francis Hopkinson 1776
Josiah Hornblower 1785–1786
William C. Houston . . . 1779–1782
William C. Houston . . . 1784–1785
James Kinsey [12] 1774–1775
William Livingston 1774–1776

James Schureman 1786–1787
Nathaniel Scudder 1777–1779
Jonathan D. Sergeant [13] . . 1776
Jonathan D. Sergeant [14] . . 1776–1777
Richard Smith [15] 1774–1776
John Stevens 1783–1784
Charles Stewart 1784–1785
Richard Stockton 1776
John C. Symmes 1785–1786
John Witherspoon 1776–1779
John Witherspoon 1780–1781
John Witherspoon [16] . . . 1782

---

[1] Died March 25, 1780.
[2] Elected to fill vacancy caused by declination of William Paterson.
[3] Resigned April 1, 1781.
[4] Elected to fill vacancy caused by declination of Thomas Henderson.
[5] Elected to fill vacancy caused by declination of William Paterson.
[6] Resigned November 22, 1775.
[7] Resigned June 13, 1776.
[8] Resigned October 2, 1778.
[9] Elected to fill vacancy caused by resignation of William Burnet.
[10] Resigned May 25, 1779.
[11] Seat vacated August 30, 1776, by his election as Speaker of House of Assembly.
[12] Resigned November 22, 1775.
[13] Resigned June 22, 1776.
[14] Resigned September 6, 1777.
[15] Resigned June 12, 1776.
[16] Elected to fill vacancy caused by declination of William C. Houston.

NEW YORK

John Alsop 1774–1776	John Haring 1774–1775	Gouverneur Morris. 1777–1780
Egbert Benson 1784–1785	John Haring 1785–1788	Lewis Morris 1775–1777
Egbert Benson 1786–1788	John Jay 1774–1777	Alexander McDougall . . .1781–1782
Simon Boerum [1] 1775	John Jay 1778–1779	Alexander McDougall . . .1784–1785
George Clinton 1775–1777	John Lansing, Jr 1784–1788	Ephraim Paine 1784–1785
Charles DeWitt 1783–1785	John Laurance 1785–1786	Philip Pell 1788–1789
James Duane 1774–1784	Francis Lewis 1774–1779	Zephaniah Platt 1784–1786
William Duer 1777–1778	Ezra L'Hommedieu 1779–1783	Philip Schuyler 1775–1777
William Floyd 1774–1777	Ezra L'Hommedieu 1787–1788	Philip Schuyler 1778–1781
William Floyd 1778–1783	Philip Livingston [2] 1774–1778	John Morin Scott 1780–1783
Leonard Gansevoort 1787–1788	Robert R. Livingston. . . .1775–1777	Melancthon Smith 1785–1788
David Ghelston 1788–1789	Robert R. Livingston. . . .1779–1781	Henry Wisner 1774–1776
Alexander Hamilton 1782–1783	Walter Livingston 1784–1785	Abraham Yates 1787–1788
Alexander Hamilton 1787–1788	Isaac Low 1774–1775	Peter W. Yates 1785–1787

NORTH CAROLINA

John B. Ashe [3] 1787	Benjamin Hawkins 1786–1787	John Penn 1775–1776
Timothy Bloodworth . . .1786–1787	Joseph Hewes 1774–1777	John Penn 1777–1780
William Blount 1782–1783	Joseph Hewes [4] 1779	William Sharpe 1779–1782
William Blount 1786–1787	Whitmil Hill 1778–1781	John Sitgreaves 1784–1785
Thomas Burke 1777–1781	William Hooper 1774–1777	Richard D. Spaight 1783–1785
Robert Burton 1787–1788	Samuel Johnston 1780–1782	John Swan [6] 1787–1788
Richard Caswell 1774–1776	Allen Jones 1779–1780	James White 1786–1788
William Cumming 1784	Willie Jones 1780–1781	John Williams 1778–1779
Cornelius Harnett 1777–1780	Abner Nash 1782–1784	Hugh Williamson 1782–1785
Benjamin Hawkins 1781–1784	Abner Nash [5] 1785–1786	Hugh Williamson 1787–1788

PENNSYLVANIA

Andrew Allen 1775–1776	Edward Hand 1784–1785	Joseph Reed 1777–1778
John Armstrong 1778–1780	William Henry 1784–1786	James R. Reid 1787–1789
John Armstrong 1787–1788	Charles Humphreys 1774–1776	Samuel Rhoads 1774–1775
Samuel J. Atlee 1778–1782	Jared Ingersoll 1780–1781	Daniel Roberdeau 1777–1779
John B. Bayard 1785–1787	William Irvine 1786–1788	George Ross 1774–1777
Edward Biddle 1774–1776	David Jackson 1785–1786	Benjamin Rush 1776–1777
Edward Biddle 1778–1779	James McClene 1779–1780	Arthur St. Clair 1785–1787
William Bingham 1787–1788	Timothy Matlack 1780–1781	James Searle 1778–1780
Matthew Clarkson. 1785–1786	Samuel Meredith 1787–1788	William Shippen 1778–1780
William Clingan 1777–1779	Thomas Mifflin 1774–1776	James Smith 1776–1778
George Clymer 1776–1778	Thomas Mifflin 1782–1784	Jonathan B. Smith 1777–1778
George Clymer 1780–1783	Joseph Montgomery 1783–1784	Thomas Smith 1780–1782
Tench Coxe. 1787–1788	Cadwalader Morris 1783–1784	George Taylor 1776–1777
John Dickinson 1774–1776	Robert Morris 1776–1778	Thomas Willing 1775–1776
Thomas Fitzsimons 1782–1783	John Morton 1774–1777	James Wilson 1775–1776
Benjamin Franklin 1775–1776	Frederick A. C. Muhlenberg .1778–1780	James Wilson 1782–1783
Joseph Galloway 1774–1775	Richard Peters, Jr 1782–1783	James Wilson 1785–1787
Joseph Gardner 1784–1785	Charles Pettit 1785–1787	Henry Wynkoop 1779–1783

RHODE ISLAND

Jonathan Arnold 1782–1784	Sylvester Gardiner [8] 1788–1789	Nathan Miller 1785–1786
Peleg Arnold 1787–1789	Jonathan J. Hazard 1787–1789	Daniel Mowry, Jr 1780–1782
John Collins 1778–1783	Stephen Hopkins 1774–1780	James M. Varnum. . . .1780–1782
Ezekiel Cornell 1780–1783	David Howell 1782–1785	James M. Varnum. . . .1786–1787
William Ellery [7] 1776–1781	James Manning 1785–1786	Samuel Ward 1774–1776
William Ellery 1783–1785	Henry Marchant 1777–1780	
John Gardiner . . . , , . . .1789	Henry Marchant 1783–1784	

---

[1] Died July 11, 1775.
[2] Died June 12, 1778.
[3] Resigned November 1, 1787.
[4] Died November 10, 1779.

[5] Died December 2, 1786.
[6] Elected to fill vacancy caused by resignation of John B. Ashe.
[7] Elected to fill vacancy caused by death of Samuel Ward.
[8] Did not take his seat.

SOUTH CAROLINA

Robert Barnwell	1788–1789	Ralph Izard	1782–1783
Thomas Bee	1780–1782	John Kean	1785–1787
Richard Beresford	1783–1785	Francis Kinloch	1780–1781
John Bull	1784–1787	Henry Laurens	1777–1780
Pierce Butler	1787–1788	Thomas Lynch, Sr	1774–1776
William H. Drayton [1]	1778–1779	Thomas Lynch, Jr	1776–1777
Nicholas Eveleigh	1781–1782	John Mathews	1778–1782
Christopher Gadsden	1774–1776	Arthur Middleton	1776–1778
John L. Gervais	1782–1783	Arthur Middleton	1781–1783
Thomas Heyward, Jr	1776–1778	Henry Middleton	1774–1776
Daniel Huger	1786–1788	Isaac Motte	1780–1782
Richard Hutson	1778–1779		

John Parker	1786–1788
Charles Pinckney	1777–1778
Charles Pinckney	1784–1787
David Ramsay	1782–1784
David Ramsay	1785–1786
Jacob Read	1783–1785
Edward Rutledge	1774–1777
John Rutledge	1774–1777
John Rutledge	1782–1783
Paul Trapier	1777–1778
Thomas T. Tucker	1787–1788

VIRGINIA

Thomas Adams	1778–1780	Benjamin Harrison	1774–1778
John Banister	1778–1779	John Harvie	1777–1779
Richard Bland	1774–1775	James Henry	1780–1781
Theodorick Bland	1780–1783	Patrick Henry	1774–1776
Carter Braxton [2]	1775–1776	Thomas Jefferson	1775–1776
John Brown	1787–1788	Thomas Jefferson	1783–1785
Edward Carrington	1785–1786	Joseph Jones	1777–1778
John Dawson	1788–1789	Joseph Jones	1780–1783
William Fitzhugh	1779–1780	Arthur Lee	1781–1784
William Fleming	1779–1781	Francis Lightfoot Lee	1775–1780
William Grayson	1784–1787	Henry Lee	1785–1788
Cyrus Griffin	1778–1781	Richard Henry Lee	1774–1780
Cyrus Griffin	1787–1788	Richard Henry Lee	1784–1787
Samuel Hardy [3]	1783–1785	James Madison	1780–1783

James Madison	1786–1788
James Mercer	1779–1780
John F. Mercer	1782–1785
James Monroe	1783–1786
Thomas Nelson, Jr	1775–1777
Thomas Nelson, Jr	1779–1780
Mann Page	1777
Edmund Pendleton	1774–1775
Edmund J. Randolph	1779–1782
Peyton Randolph [4]	1774–1775
Meriwether Smith	1778–1782
George Washington	1774–1775
George Wythe	1775–1777

[1] Died September 3, 1779.
[2] Elected to fill vacancy caused by death of Peyton Randolph.
[3] Died October 17, 1785.
[4] Died October 22, 1775.

CENSUS APPORTIONMENT OF
REPRESENTATIVES

REPRESENTATIVES UNDER EACH APPORTIONMENT

States	Constitutional apportionment	1st Census 1790	2d Census 1800	3d Census 1810	4th Census 1820	5th Census 1830	6th Census 1840	7th Census 1850	8th Census 1860	9th Census 1870	10th Census 1880	11th Census 1890	12th Census 1900	13th Census 1910[1]	15th Census 1930	16th Census 1940	17th Census 1950	18th Census 1960
Alabama				[2] 1	3	5	7	7	6	8	8	9	9	10	9	9	9	8
Alaska																	[2] 1	1
Arizona														[2] 1	1	2	2	3
Arkansas						[2] 1	1	2	3	4	5	6	7	7	7	7	6	4
California							[2] 2	2	3	4	6	7	8	11	20	23	30	38
Colorado										[2] 1	1	2	3	4	4	4	4	4
Connecticut	5	7	7	7	6	6	4	4	4	4	4	4	5	5	6	6	6	6
Delaware	1	1	1	2	1	1	1	1	1	1	1	1	1	1	1	1	1	1
Florida							[2] 1	1	1	2	2	2	3	4	5	6	8	12
Georgia	3	2	4	6	7	9	8	8	7	9	10	11	11	12	10	10	10	10
Hawaii																	[2] 1	2
Idaho											[2] 1	1	1	2	2	2	2	2
Illinois				[2] 1	1	3	7	9	14	19	20	22	25	27	27	26	25	24
Indiana				[2] 1	3	7	10	11	11	13	13	13	13	13	12	11	11	11
Iowa							[2] 2	2	6	9	11	11	11	11	9	8	8	7
Kansas									1	3	7	8	8	8	7	6	6	5
Kentucky		2	6	10	12	13	10	10	9	10	11	11	11	11	9	9	8	7
Louisiana				[2] 1	3	3	4	4	5	6	6	6	7	8	8	8	8	8
Maine				[3] 7	7	8	7	6	5	5	4	4	4	4	3	3	3	2
Maryland	6	8	9	9	9	8	6	6	5	6	6	6	6	6	6	6	7	8
Massachusetts	8	14	17	[3] 13	13	12	10	11	10	11	12	13	14	16	15	14	14	12
Michigan						[2] 1	3	4	6	9	11	12	12	13	17	17	18	19
Minnesota								[2] 2	2	3	5	7	9	10	9	9	9	8
Mississippi				[2] 1	1	2	4	5	5	6	7	7	8	8	7	7	6	5
Missouri					1	2	5	7	9	13	14	15	16	16	13	13	11	10
Montana											[2] 1	1	1	2	2	2	2	2
Nebraska									[2] 1	1	3	6	6	6	5	4	4	3
Nevada									[2] 1	1	1	1	1	1	1	1	1	1
New Hampshire	3	4	5	6	6	5	4	3	3	3	2	2	2	2	2	2	2	2
New Jersey	4	5	6	6	6	6	5	5	5	7	7	8	10	12	14	14	14	15
New Mexico														[2] 1	1	2	2	2
New York	6	10	17	27	34	40	34	33	31	33	34	34	37	43	45	45	43	41
North Carolina	5	10	12	13	13	13	9	8	7	8	9	9	10	10	11	12	12	11
North Dakota											[2] 1	1	2	3	2	2	2	2
Ohio			[2] 1	6	14	19	21	21	19	20	21	21	21	22	24	23	23	24
Oklahoma													[2] 5	8	9	8	6	6
Oregon								[2] 1	1	1	1	2	2	3	3	4	4	4
Pennsylvania	8	13	18	23	26	28	24	25	24	27	28	30	32	36	34	33	30	27
Rhode Island	1	2	2	2	2	2	2	2	2	2	2	2	2	3	2	2	2	2
South Carolina	5	6	8	9	9	9	7	6	4	5	7	7	7	7	6	6	6	6
South Dakota											[2] 2	2	2	3	2	2	2	2
Tennessee		[2] 1	3	6	9	13	11	10	8	10	10	10	10	10	9	10	9	9
Texas							[2] 2	2	4	6	11	13	16	18	21	21	22	23
Utah												[2] 1	1	2	2	2	2	2
Vermont		2	4	6	5	5	4	3	3	3	2	2	2	2	1	1	1	1
Virginia	10	19	22	23	22	21	15	13	11	9	10	10	10	10	9	9	10	10
Washington											[2] 1	2	3	5	6	6	7	7
West Virginia										3	4	4	5	6	6	6	6	5
Wisconsin							[2] 2	3	6	8	9	10	11	11	10	10	10	10
Wyoming											[2] 1	1	1	1	1	1	1	1
Total	65	106	142	186	213	242	232	237	243	293	332	357	391	435	435	435	[4] 437	435

[1] No apportionment was made in 1920.

[2] The following representation was added after the several census apportionments indicated when new States were admitted and is included in the above table:

FIRST. Tennessee, 1.
SECOND. Ohio, 1.
THIRD. Alabama, 1; Illinois, 1; Indiana, 1; Louisiana, 1; Mississippi, 1.
FIFTH. Arkansas, 1; Michigan, 1.
SIXTH. California, 2; Florida, 1; Iowa, 2; Texas, 2; Wisconsin, 2.
SEVENTH. Minnesota, 2; Oregon 1.
EIGHTH. Nebraska, 1; Nevada, 1.
NINTH. Colorado, 1.
TENTH. Idaho, 1; Montana, 1; North Dakota, 1; South Dakota, 2; Washington, 1; Wyoming, 1.
ELEVENTH. Utah, 1.
TWELFTH. Oklahoma, 5.
THIRTEENTH. Arizona, 1; New Mexico, 1.
SEVENTEENTH. Alaska, 1; Hawaii, 1.

[3] Twenty Members were assigned to Massachusetts, but seven of these were credited to Maine when that area became a State.

[4] Apportionment temporarily increased by Public Laws 85-508 and 86-3 due to admission of Alaska and Hawaii as States.

THE CONGRESS OF THE UNITED STATES
1789–1961

To learn who were the colleagues of a certain Member, first refer to the biography of
the Member and ascertain the specific Congress in which he served,
then consult the personnel of that Congress

TIME AND PLACE OF MEETING

The Constitution (Art. I, sec. 4) provided that "The Congress shall assemble at least once in every year * * * on the first Monday in December, unless they shall by law appoint a different day." Pursuant to a resolution of the Continental Congress the first session of the First Congress convened March 4, 1789. Up to and including May 20, 1820, eighteen acts were passed providing for the meeting of Congress on other days in the year. Since that year Congress met regularly on the first Monday in December until January 1934. The date for convening of Congress was changed by the Twentieth Amendment to the Constitution in 1933 to the 3d day of January unless a different day shall be appointed by law. The first and second sessions of the First Congress were held in New York City; subsequently, including the first session of the Sixth Congress, Philadelphia was the meeting place; since then Congress has convened in Washington, D. C.

FIRST CONGRESS

MARCH 4, 1789, TO MARCH 3, 1791

FIRST SESSION—*March 4, 1789,[1] to September 29, 1789*

SECOND SESSION—*January 4, 1790, to August 12, 1790*

THIRD SESSION—*December 6, 1790, to March 3, 1791*

VICE PRESIDENT OF THE UNITED STATES—JOHN ADAMS, of Massachusetts

PRESIDENT PRO TEMPORE OF THE SENATE—JOHN LANGDON,[2] of New Hampshire

SECRETARY OF THE SENATE—SAMUEL A. OTIS,[3] of Massachusetts

DOORKEEPER OF THE SENATE—JAMES MATHERS,[4] of New York

SPEAKER OF THE HOUSE OF REPRESENTATIVES—FREDERICK A. C. MUHLENBERG,[5] of Pennsylvania

CLERK OF THE HOUSE—JOHN BECKLEY,[6] of Virginia

SERGEANT AT ARMS OF THE HOUSE—JOSEPH WHEATON,[7] of Rhode Island

DOORKEEPER OF THE HOUSE—GIFFORD DALLEY

CONNECTICUT

SENATORS

Oliver Ellsworth
William S. Johnson

REPRESENTATIVES

Benjamin Huntington
Roger Sherman
Jonathan Sturges
Jonathan Trumbull
Jeremiah Wadsworth

DELAWARE

SENATORS

Richard Bassett
George Read

REPRESENTATIVE

John Vining

GEORGIA

SENATORS

William Few
James Gunn

REPRESENTATIVES

Abraham Baldwin
James Jackson
George Matthews

MARYLAND

SENATORS

John Henry
Charles Carroll, *of Carrollton*

REPRESENTATIVES

Daniel Carroll
Benjamin Contee
George Gale
Joshua Seney

William Smith
Michael Jenifer Stone

MASSACHUSETTS

SENATORS

Tristram Dalton
Caleb Strong

REPRESENTATIVES

Fisher Ames
Elbridge Gerry
Benjamin Goodhue
Jonathan Grout
George Leonard
George Partridge [8]
Theodore Sedgwick
George Thacher

NEW HAMPSHIRE

SENATORS

John Langdon
Paine Wingate

---

[1] Neither a quorum of the Senate nor of the House of Representatives appeared in their respective chambers on Wednesday, March 4, 1789. But eight Senators appeared and the minority adjourned from day to day until Monday, April 6, when a quorum of the Senate was first present. Thirteen Members of the House of Representatives appeared on March 4 and a quorum was not present until April 1, when the body proceeded to the transaction of business. When both Houses were organized, on April 6, they met in joint convention, in the hall of the Senate, and proceeded to open and count the electoral vote for President and Vice-President. John Adams, the Vice President elect, appeared in the Senate Chamber and assumed the duties of the chair on Tuesday, April 21, 1789. On May 15, 1789, the Senate determined by lot the classes into which the membership should be divided agreeably to paragraph 2, section 3, of Article I of the Constitution, as follows:

Class 1, term expires March 3, 1791—Messrs. Carroll, Dalton, Ellsworth, Elmer, Maclay, Read, and Grayson.

Class 2, term expires March 3, 1793—Messrs. Bassett, Butler, Few, Lee, Strong, Paterson, and Wingate.

Class 3, term expires March 3, 1795—Messrs. Gunn, Henry, Johnson, Izard, Langdon, and Morris.

[2] Elected April 6, 1789.

[3] Elected April 8, 1789.

[4] Elected April 7, 1789.

[5] Elected April 1, 1789.

[6] Elected April 1, 1789.

[7] Elected May 12, 1789.

[8] Resigned August 14, 1790.

NEW HAMPSHIRE—Continued

REPRESENTATIVES

Abiel Foster
Nicholas Gilman
Samuel Livermore

NEW JERSEY

SENATORS

Jonathan Elmer
William Paterson [9]
Philemon Dickinson [10]

REPRESENTATIVES [11]

Elias Boudinot
Lambert Cadwalader
Thomas Sinnickson
James Schureman

NEW YORK

SENATORS

Rufus King [12]
Philip John Schuyler [13]

REPRESENTATIVES

Egbert Benson
William Floyd
John Hathorn [14]
John Laurance
Peter Silvester [15]
Jeremiah Van Rensselaer [16]

NORTH CAROLINA

SENATORS

Benjamin Hawkins [17]
Samuel Johnston [18]

REPRESENTATIVES

John Baptista Ashe [19]
Timothy Bloodworth [20]
John Sevier [21]
John Steele [22]
Hugh Williamson [23]

PENNSYLVANIA

SENATORS

William Maclay
Robert Morris

REPRESENTATIVES

George Clymer
Thomas Fitzsimons
Thomas Hartley
Daniel Hiester
Frederick A. C. Muhlenberg
John Peter G. Muhlenberg
Thomas Scott
Henry Wynkoop

RHODE ISLAND

SENATORS

Theodore Foster [24]
Joseph Stanton, Jr. [25]

REPRESENTATIVE

Benjamin Bourn [26]

SOUTH CAROLINA

SENATORS

Pierce Butler
Ralph Izard

REPRESENTATIVES

Aedanus Burke
Daniel Huger
William L. Smith [27]
Thomas Sumter
Thomas Tudor Tucker

VIRGINIA

SENATORS

William Grayson [28]
John Walker [29]
James Monroe [30]
Richard Henry Lee

REPRESENTATIVES

Theodoric Bland [31]
William B. Giles [32]
John Brown
Isaac Coles
Richard Bland Lee
James Madison
Andrew Moore
John Page
Josiah Parker
Alexander White
Samuel Griffin

---

[9] Resigned November 13, 1790, having been elected governor.
[10] Elected to fill vacancy caused by resignation of William Paterson, and took his seat December 6, 1790.
[11] The election of all four Representatives was contested, but owing to the burning of the papers and documents from the First to the Sixth Congress, by the British in 1814, it is not possible to ascertain the grounds upon which the contest was based. It is known that it related to questions of regularity and procedure, and that the decision was favorable to the sitting Members.
[12] Took his seat July 25, 1789; term to expire, as determined by lot, March 3, 1795.
[13] Took his seat July 27, 1789; term to expire, as determined by lot, March 3, 1791.
[14] Took his seat April 23, 1789.

[15] Took his seat April 22, 1789.
[16] Took his seat May 9, 1789.
[17] Took his seat January 13, 1790; term to expire, as determined by lot, March 3, 1795.
[18] Took his seat January 29, 1790; term to expire, as determined by lot, March 3, 1793.
[19] Took his seat March 24, 1790.
[20] Took his seat April 6, 1790.
[21] Took his seat June 16, 1790.
[22] Took his seat April 19, 1790.
[23] Took his seat March 19, 1790.
[24] Took his seat June 25, 1790; term to expire, as determined by lot, March 3, 1791.
[25] Took his seat June 25, 1790; term to expire, as determined by lot, March 3, 1793.
[26] Took his seat December 17, 1790.
[27] Took his seat April 13, 1789; on April 15, 1789,

David Ramsay presented a petition claiming that Smith was ineligible because at the time of his election he had not been a citizen of the United States the term of years required by the Constitution, which was referred to the Committee on Elections; the committee reported on April 18, 1789, and on May 22, 1789, the House adopted a resolution that Mr. Smith was eligible at the time he was elected.
[28] Died March 12, 1790.
[29] Appointed to fill vacancy caused by death of William Grayson, and took his seat April 26, 1790.
[30] Elected to fill vacancy caused by death of William Grayson, and took his seat December 6, 1790.
[31] Died June 1, 1790.
[32] Elected to fill vacancy caused by death of Theodoric Bland, and took his seat December 7, 1790.

SECOND CONGRESS

MARCH 4, 1791, TO MARCH 3, 1793

FIRST SESSION—*October 24, 1791, to May 8, 1792*

SECOND SESSION—*November 5, 1792, to March 2, 1793*

SPECIAL SESSION OF THE SENATE—*March 4, 1791, for one day only*

———

VICE PRESIDENT OF THE UNITED STATES—JOHN ADAMS, of Massachusetts

PRESIDENT PRO TEMPORE OF THE SENATE—RICHARD HENRY LEE,[1] of Virginia; JOHN LANGDON,[2] of New Hampshire

SECRETARY OF THE SENATE—SAMUEL A. OTIS, of Massachusetts

DOORKEEPER OF THE SENATE—JAMES MATHERS, of New York

———

SPEAKER OF THE HOUSE OF REPRESENTATIVES—JONATHAN TRUMBULL,[3] of Connecticut

CLERK OF THE HOUSE—JOHN BECKLEY,[4] of Virginia

SERGEANT AT ARMS OF THE HOUSE—JOSEPH WHEATON, of Rhode Island

DOORKEEPER OF THE HOUSE—GIFFORD DALLEY

CONNECTICUT

SENATORS

Oliver Ellsworth
William S. Johnson [5]
Roger Sherman [6]

REPRESENTATIVES

James Hillhouse
Amasa Learned
Jonathan Sturges
Jonathan Trumbull
Jeremiah Wadsworth

DELAWARE

SENATORS

Richard Bassett
George Read

REPRESENTATIVE

John Vining

GEORGIA

SENATORS

William Few
James Gunn

REPRESENTATIVES

Abraham Baldwin
Francis Willis
Anthony Wayne [7]
John Milledge [8]

KENTUCKY [9]

SENATORS

John Edwards [10]
John Brown [11]

REPRESENTATIVES

Alexander D. Orr [12]
Christopher Greenup [13]

MARYLAND

SENATORS

John Henry
Charles Carroll *of Carrollton* [14]
Richard Potts [15]

REPRESENTATIVES

Philip Key
William Pinkney [16]
John Francis Mercer [17]
William Vans Murray
Joshua Seney [18]
William Hindman [19]
Upton Sheridine
Samuel Sterett

MASSACHUSETTS

SENATORS

Caleb Strong
George Cabot

---

[1] Elected April 18, 1792.
[2] Elected November 5, 1792, and March 1, 1793.
[3] Elected October 24, 1791.
[4] Reelected October 24, 1791.
[5] Resigned March 4, 1791.
[6] Elected to fill vacancy caused by resignation of William S. Johnson, and took his seat October 24, 1791. Vacancy in this class from March 4 to June 13, 1791.
[7] Served until March 21, 1792; election contested by James Jackson, and, by separate resolutions, it was determined that neither was entitled to the seat.
[8] Elected to fill vacancy caused by declaring the seat

of Anthony Wayne vacant, and took his seat November 22, 1792.
[9] Formed from a portion of the territory of the State of Virginia; admitted as a State into the Union June 1, 1792.
[10] Took his seat November 5, 1792; term to expire, as determined by lot, March 3, 1795.
[11] Took his seat November 5, 1792; term to expire, as determined by lot, March 3, 1793.
[12] Took his seat November 8, 1792.
[13] Took his seat November 9, 1792.

[14] Resigned November 30, 1792.
[15] Elected to fill vacancy caused by resignation of Charles Carroll of Carrollton, and took his seat February 4, 1793.
[16] Resigned in November, 1791, the question of ineligibility owing to his residence being raised.
[17] Elected to fill vacancy caused by resignation of William Pinkney, and took his seat February 6, 1792.
[18] Resigned May 1, 1792.
[19] Elected to fill vacancy caused by resignation of Joshua Seney, and took his seat January 30, 1793.

MASSACHUSETTS—Continued

REPRESENTATIVES

Fisher Ames
Shearjashub Bourne
Elbridge Gerry
Benjamin Goodhue
Theodore Sedgwick
George Thacher
Artemas Ward

NEW HAMPSHIRE

SENATORS

John Langdon
Paine Wingate

REPRESENTATIVES

Nicholas Gilman
Samuel Livermore
Jeremiah Smith

NEW JERSEY

SENATORS

Philemon Dickinson
John Rutherfurd

REPRESENTATIVES

Elias Boudinot
Abraham Clark
Jonathan Dayton
Aaron Kitchell

NEW YORK

SENATORS

Rufus King
Aaron Burr

REPRESENTATIVES

Egbert Benson
James Gordon
John Laurance
Cornelius C. Schoonmaker
Peter Silvester
Thomas Tredwell [20]

NORTH CAROLINA

SENATORS

Benjamin Hawkins
Samuel Johnston

REPRESENTATIVES

John Baptista Ashe
William Barry Grove
Nathaniel Macon
John Steele
Hugh Williamson

PENNSYLVANIA

SENATORS

Robert Morris
Vacant [21]

REPRESENTATIVES

William Findley
Thomas Fitzsimons
Andrew Gregg
Thomas Hartley
Daniel Hiester
Israel Jacobs
John W. Kittera
Frederick A. C. Muhlenberg

RHODE ISLAND

SENATORS

Theodore Foster
Joseph Stanton, Jr.

REPRESENTATIVE

Benjamin Bourn

SOUTH CAROLINA

SENATORS

Pierce Butler
Ralph Izard

REPRESENTATIVES

Robert Barnwell
Daniel Huger
William L. Smith
Thomas Sumter
Thomas Tudor Tucker

VERMONT [22]

SENATORS

Moses Robinson [23]
Stephen R. Bradley [24]

REPRESENTATIVES

Nathaniel Niles [25]
Israel Smith [26]

VIRGINIA

SENATORS

Richard Henry Lee [27]
John Taylor [28]
James Monroe

REPRESENTATIVES

John Brown [29]
William B. Giles
Samuel Griffin
Richard Bland Lee
James Madison
Andrew Moore
John Page
Josiah Parker
Abraham B. Venable
Alexander White

---

[20] Elected to fill vacancy caused by death of Representative-elect James Townsend (May 24, 1790, before the commencement of the congressional term), and took his seat October 24, 1791.
[21] Credentials of Albert Gallatin were presented February 28, 1793, and ordered placed in the files; no further action taken during the Congress.
[22] Formed from a portion of the territory of the State of New York; admitted as a State into the Union March 4, 1791.
[23] Took his seat October 31, 1791; term to expire, as determined by lot, March 3, 1797.
[24] Took his seat November 4, 1791; term to expire, as determined by lot, March 3, 1795.
[25] Took his seat October 31, 1791.
[26] Took his seat October 31, 1791.
[27] Resigned October 8, 1792.
[28] Elected to fill vacancy caused by resignation of Richard Henry Lee, and took his seat December 12, 1792.
[29] Served until June 1, 1792, when the district in which he resided was admitted into the Union as the State of Kentucky; subsequently elected a Senator from the new State.

THIRD CONGRESS

MARCH 4, 1793, TO MARCH 3, 1795

FIRST SESSION—*December 2, 1793, to June 9, 1794*

SECOND SESSION—*November 3, 1794, to March 3, 1795*

SPECIAL SESSION OF THE SENATE—*March 4, 1793, for one day only*

———

VICE PRESIDENT OF THE UNITED STATES—JOHN ADAMS, of Massachusetts

PRESIDENT PRO TEMPORE OF THE SENATE—RALPH IZARD,[1] of South Carolina; HENRY TAZEWELL,[2] of Virginia

SECRETARY OF THE SENATE—SAMUEL A. OTIS, of Massachusetts

DOORKEEPER OF THE SENATE—JAMES MATHERS, of New York

———

SPEAKER OF THE HOUSE OF REPRESENTATIVES—FREDERICK A. C. MUHLENBERG,[3] of Pennsylvania

CLERK OF THE HOUSE—JOHN BECKLEY,[4] of Virginia

SERGEANT AT ARMS OF THE HOUSE—JOSEPH WHEATON, of Rhode Island

DOORKEEPER OF THE HOUSE—GIFFORD DALLEY

CONNECTICUT

SENATORS

Oliver Ellsworth
Roger Sherman [5]
Stephen M. Mitchell [6]

REPRESENTATIVES

Joshua Coit
James Hillhouse
Amasa Learned
Zephaniah Swift
Uriah Tracy
Jonathan Trumbull
Jeremiah Wadsworth

DELAWARE

SENATORS

George Read [7]
Henry Latimer [8]
John Vining

REPRESENTATIVES

John Patten [9]
Henry Latimer [10]

GEORGIA

SENATORS

James Gunn
James Jackson

REPRESENTATIVES

Abraham Baldwin
Thomas P. Carnes

KENTUCKY

SENATORS

John Edwards
John Brown

REPRESENTATIVES

Christopher Greenup
Alexander D. Orr

MARYLAND

SENATORS

John Henry
Richard Potts

REPRESENTATIVES

Gabriel Christie
George Dent
John F. Mercer [11]
Gabriel Duvall [12]
William Vans Murray
Uriah Forrest [13]
Benjamin Edwards [14]
William Hindman
Samuel Smith
Thomas Sprigg

MASSACHUSETTS

SENATORS

Caleb Strong
George Cabot

REPRESENTATIVES

Fisher Ames
Shearjashub Bourne
David Cobb
Peleg Coffin, Jr.
Henry Dearborn
Samuel Dexter

---

[1] Elected May 31, 1794. Samuel Livermore was elected February 20, 1795, but declined.
[2] Elected February 20, 1795.
[3] Elected December 2, 1793.
[4] Reelected December 2, 1793.
[5] Died July 23, 1793.
[6] Elected to fill vacancy caused by death of Roger Sherman, and took his seat December 2, 1793.
[7] Resigned September 18, 1793.
[8] Elected to fill vacancy caused by resignation of George Read, and took his seat February 28, 1795. Kensey Johns was appointed on March 19, 1794, to fill the vacancy and his credentials were presented March 24, 1794, but he was not permitted to qualify; March 28, 1794, the Senate declared he was not entitled to the seat; vacancy in this class from September 18, 1793, to February 7, 1795.
[9] Served until February 14, 1794; succeeded by Henry Latimer, who contested his election.

[10] Successfully contested the election of John Patten, and took his seat February 14, 1794; resigned February 7, 1795, having been elected Senator.
[11] Resigned April 13, 1794.
[12] Elected to fill vacancy caused by resignation of John F. Mercer, and took his seat November 11, 1794.
[13] Resigned November 8, 1794.
[14] Elected to fill vacancy caused by resignation of Uriah Forrest, and took his seat January 2, 1795.

MASSACHUSETTS—Continued

REPRESENTATIVES—continued

Dwight Foster
Benjamin Goodhue
Samuel Holten
William Lyman
Theodore Sedgwick
George Thacher
Peleg Wadsworth
Artemas Ward

NEW HAMPSHIRE

SENATORS

John Langdon
Samuel Livermore

REPRESENTATIVES

Nicholas Gilman
John S. Sherburne
Jeremiah Smith
Paine Wingate

NEW JERSEY

SENATORS

John Rutherfurd
Frederick Frelinghuysen

REPRESENTATIVES

John Beatty
Elias Boudinot
Lambert Cadwallader
Abraham Clark [15]
Aaron Kitchell [16]
Jonathan Dayton

NEW YORK

SENATORS

Rufus King
Aaron Burr

REPRESENTATIVES

Theodorus Bailey
Peter Van Gaasbeck
Ezekiel Gilbert
James Gordon
Henry Glen
Silas Talbot
Thomas Tredwell
John E. Van Alen [17]
Philip Van Cortlandt
John Watts

NORTH CAROLINA

SENATORS

Benjamin Hawkins
Alexander Martin

REPRESENTATIVES

Thomas Blount
William Johnston Dawson
James Gillespie
William Barry Grove
Matthew Locke
Nathaniel Macon
Joseph McDowell (P. G.)
Alexander Mebane
Benjamin Williams
Joseph Winston

PENNSYLVANIA

SENATORS

Robert Morris
Albert Gallatin [18]
James Ross [19]

REPRESENTATIVES

James Armstrong
William Findley
Thomas Fitzsimons
Andrew Gregg
Thomas Hartley
Daniel Hiester
William Irvine
John Wilkes Kittera
William Montgomery
Frederick A. C. Muhlenberg
John Peter G. Muhlenberg
Thomas Scott
John Smilie

RHODE ISLAND

SENATORS

Theodore Foster
William Bradford

REPRESENTATIVES

Benjamin Bourn
Francis Malbone

SOUTH CAROLINA

SENATORS

Pierce Butler
Ralph Izard

REPRESENTATIVES

Lemuel Benton
Alexander Gillon [20]
Robert Goodloe Harper [21]
John Hunter
Andrew Pickens
William L. Smith
Richard Winn

VERMONT

SENATORS

Moses Robinson
Stephen R. Bradley

REPRESENTATIVES

Nathaniel Niles
Israel Smith

VIRGINIA

SENATORS

James Monroe [22]
Stevens T. Mason [23]
John Taylor [24]
Henry Tazewell [25]

REPRESENTATIVES

Isaac Coles
Thomas Claiborne
William B. Giles
Samuel Griffin
George Hancock
Carter B. Harrison
John Heath
Richard Bland Lee
James Madison
Andrew Moore
Joseph Neville
Anthony New
John Nicholas
John Page
Josiah Parker
Francis Preston [26]
Robert Rutherford
Abraham B. Venable
Francis Walker

TERRITORY SOUTH OF THE RIVER OHIO [27]

DELEGATE

James White [28]

---

[15] Died September 15, 1794.
[16] Elected to fill vacancy caused by death of Abraham Clark, and took his seat January 29, 1795.
[17] Election unsuccessfully contested by Henry K. Van Rensselaer.
[18] Credentials presented in preceding Congress; took his seat December 2, 1793 and served until February 28, 1794, when the election was declared void, "he not having been a citizen of the United States the term of years required by the Constitution."
[19] Elected to fill vacancy caused by the Senate declaring the election of Albert Gallatin void, and took his seat April 24, 1794.
[20] Died October 6, 1794.
[21] Elected to fill vacancy caused by death of Alexander Gillon, and took his seat February 9, 1795.
[22] Resigned, effective May 27, 1794, having been appointed minister plenipotentiary to France.
[23] Elected to fill vacancy caused by the resignation of James Monroe, but did not take his seat until June 8, 1795, in the succeeding Congress.
[24] Resigned May 11, 1794.
[25] Elected to fill vacancy caused by resignation of John Taylor, and took his seat December 29, 1794.
[26] Election unsuccessfully contested by Abraham Trigg.
[27] Created a district for the purposes of temporary government by act approved May 26, 1790, from territory ceded to the United States by the State of North Carolina and granted a Delegate in Congress.
[28] Took his seat November 18, 1794.

FOURTH CONGRESS

MARCH 4, 1795, TO MARCH 3, 1797

FIRST SESSION—*December 7, 1795, to June 1, 1796*

SECOND SESSION—*December 5, 1796, to March 3, 1797*

SPECIAL SESSION OF THE SENATE—*June 8, 1795, to June 26, 1795*

VICE PRESIDENT OF THE UNITED STATES—John Adams, of Massachusetts

PRESIDENT PRO TEMPORE OF THE SENATE—Henry Tazewell,[1] of Virginia; Samuel Livermore,[2] of New Hampshire; William Bingham,[3] of Pennsylvania

SECRETARY OF THE SENATE—Samuel A. Otis, of Massachusetts

DOORKEEPER OF THE SENATE—James Mathers, of New York

SPEAKER OF THE HOUSE OF REPRESENTATIVES—Jonathan Dayton,[4] of New Jersey

CLERK OF THE HOUSE—John Beckley,[5] of Virginia

SERGEANT AT ARMS OF THE HOUSE—Joseph Wheaton, of Rhode Island

DOORKEEPER OF THE HOUSE—Thomas Claxton

CONNECTICUT

SENATORS

Oliver Ellsworth [6]
James Hillhouse [7]
Jonathan Trumbull [8]
Uriah Tracy [9]

REPRESENTATIVES

Joshua Coit
Chauncey Goodrich
Roger Griswold
James Hillhouse [10]
James Davenport [11]
Nathaniel Smith
Zephaniah Swift
Uriah Tracy [12]
Samuel Whittlesey Dana [13]

DELAWARE

SENATORS

John Vining
Henry Latimer

REPRESENTATIVE

John Patten

GEORGIA

SENATORS

James Gunn
James Jackson [14]
George Walton [15]
Josiah Tattnall [16]

REPRESENTATIVES

Abraham Baldwin
John Milledge

KENTUCKY

SENATORS

John Brown
Humphrey Marshall

REPRESENTATIVES

Christopher Greenup
Alexander D. Orr

MARYLAND

SENATORS

John Henry
Richard Potts [17]
John Eager Howard [18]

REPRESENTATIVES

Gabriel Christie
Jeremiah Crabb [19]

---

[1] Elected December 7, 1795.
[2] Elected May 6, 1796.
[3] Elected February 16, 1797.
[4] Elected December 7, 1795.
[5] Reelected December 7, 1795.
[6] Resigned March 8, 1796.
[7] Elected to fill vacancy caused by resignation of Oliver Ellsworth, and took his seat December 6, 1796.
[8] Resigned June 10, 1796.
[9] Elected to fill vacancy caused by resignation of

Jonathan Trumbull, and took his seat December 6, 1796.
[10] Resigned in the fall of 1796, having been elected Senator.
[11] Elected to fill vacancy caused by resignation of James Hillhouse, and took his seat December 5, 1796.
[12] Resigned, effective October 13, 1796, having been elected Senator.
[13] Elected to fill vacancy caused by resignation of Uriah Tracy, and took his seat January 3, 1797.

[14] Resigned in 1795.
[15] Appointed to fill vacancy caused by resignation of James Jackson, and took his seat December 18, 1795.
[16] Elected to fill vacancy caused by resignation of James Jackson, and took his seat April 12, 1796.
[17] Resigned October 24, 1796.
[18] Elected to fill vacancy caused by resignation of Richard Potts, and took his seat December 27, 1796.
[19] Resigned in 1796.

MARYLAND—Continued

REPRESENTATIVES—continued

William Craik [20]
Gabriel Duvall [21]
Richard Sprigg, Jr.[22]
George Dent
William Hindman
Samuel Smith
Thomas Sprigg
William Vans Murray

MASSACHUSETTS

SENATORS

Caleb Strong [23]
Theodore Sedgwick [24]
George Cabot [25]
Benjamin Goodhue [26]

REPRESENTATIVES

Fisher Ames
Theophilus Bradbury
Henry Dearborn
Dwight Foster
Nathaniel Freeman, Jr.
Benjamin Goodhue [27]
Samuel Sewall [28]
George Leonard
Samuel Lyman
William Lyman
John Reed
Theodore Sedgwick [29]
Thomson J. Skinner [30]
George Thacher
Joseph B. Varnum [31]
Peleg Wadsworth

NEW HAMPSHIRE

SENATORS

John Langdon
Samuel Livermore

REPRESENTATIVES

Abiel Foster
Nicholas Gilman
John S. Sherburne
Jeremiah Smith

NEW JERSEY

SENATORS

John Rutherfurd
Frederick Frelinghuysen [32]
Richard Stockton [33]

REPRESENTATIVES

Jonathan Dayton
Thomas Henderson
Aaron Kitchell
Isaac Smith
Mark Thomson

NEW YORK

SENATORS

Rufus King [34]
John Laurance [35]
Aaron Burr

REPRESENTATIVES

Theodorus Bailey
William Cooper
Ezekiel Gilbert
Henry Glen
John Hathorn
Jonathan N. Havens
Edward Livingston
John E. Van Alen
Philip Van Cortlandt
John Williams

NORTH CAROLINA

SENATORS

Alexander Martin
Timothy Bloodworth

REPRESENTATIVES

Thomas Blount
Nathan Bryan
Dempsey Burges
Jesse Franklin
James Gillespie
William Barry Grove
James Holland
Matthew Locke
Nathaniel Macon
Absalom Tatom [36]
William F. Strudwick [37]

PENNSYLVANIA

SENATORS

James Ross
William Bingham

REPRESENTATIVES

David Bard [38]
William Findley
Albert Gallatin
Andrew Gregg
Thomas Hartley
Daniel Hiester [39]
George Ege [40]
John Wilkes Kittera
Samuel Maclay
John Richards [41]
Frederick A. C. Muhlenberg
Samuel Sitgreaves
John Swanwick
Richard Thomas

RHODE ISLAND

SENATORS

Theodore Foster
William Bradford

REPRESENTATIVES

Francis Malbone
Benjamin Bourn [42]
Elisha R. Potter [43]

SOUTH CAROLINA

SENATORS

Pierce Butler [44]
John Hunter [45]
Jacob Read

REPRESENTATIVES

Lemuel Benton
Samuel Earle
Wade Hampton
Robert Goodloe Harper
William L. Smith
Richard Winn

TENNESSEE [46]

SENATORS

William Blount [47]
William Cocke [48]

---

[20] Elected to fill vacancy caused by resignation of Jeremiah Crabb, and took his seat December 5, 1796.
[21] Resigned March 28, 1796, having been elected judge of the Supreme Court of Maryland.
[22] Elected to fill vacancy caused by resignation of Gabriel Duvall, and took his seat May 5, 1796.
[23] Resigned June 1, 1796.
[24] Elected to fill vacancy caused by resignation of Caleb Strong, and took his seat December 21, 1796.
[25] Resigned June 9, 1796.
[26] Elected to fill vacancy caused by resignation of George Cabot, and took his seat December 6, 1796.
[27] Resigned in June 1796, having been elected Senator.
[28] Elected to fill vacancy caused by resignation of Benjamin Goodhue, and took his seat December 7, 1796.
[29] Resigned in June 1796, having been elected Senator.
[30] Elected to fill vacancy caused by resignation of Theodore Sedgwick, and took his seat January 27, 1797.
[31] Election contested by petition from sundry citizens of Massachusetts; Committee on Elections reported favorably for him, and added "that the attempt to deprive him of his seat was rather the act of malevolence than a desire to promote the public good." On January 25, 1797, these words were stricken out and expressions of compliment to the sitting Member were substituted, and the report was agreed to.
[32] Resigned November 12, 1796.
[33] Elected to fill vacancy caused by resignation of Frederick Frelinghuysen, and took his seat December 6, 1796.
[34] Resigned May 23, 1796, having been appointed minister to England.
[35] Elected to fill vacancy caused by resignation of Rufus King, and took his seat December 8, 1796.
[36] Resigned June 1, 1796.
[37] Elected to fill vacancy caused by resignation of Absalom Tatom, and took his seat December 13, 1796.
[38] Election of David Bard investigated on account of informality in time of making return; committee reported that Mr. Bard was entitled to the seat and the House agreed to the report.
[39] Resigned July 1, 1796.
[40] Elected to fill vacancy caused by resignation of Daniel Hiester, and took his seat December 8, 1796.
[41] Presented a memorial on December 10, 1795, claiming election, the governor having declined to issue a certificate to either candidate; the committee of election reported that James Morris had been duly elected, but having died subsequent to the election the seat had become vacant; this report was recommitted and subsequently a resolution was reported that John Richards was entitled to the seat, which was adopted by the House on January 18, 1796, and Mr. Richards took his seat the same day.
[42] Resigned in 1796, before the commencement of the Fifth Congress, to which he had been reelected.
[43] Elected to fill vacancy caused by resignation of Benjamin Bourn, and took his seat December 19, 1796.
[44] Resigned October 25, 1796.
[45] Elected to fill vacancy caused by resignation of Pierce Butler, and took his seat January 27, 1797.
[46] Admitted as a State into the Union June 1, 1796, formerly known as "Territory South of the River Ohio."
[47] Took his seat December 5, 1796; term to expire, as determined by lot, March 3, 1799.
[48] Took his seat December 5, 1796; term to expire, as determined by lot, March 3, 1797.

REPRESENTATIVE

Andrew Jackson [49]

VERMONT

SENATORS

Moses Robinson [50]
Isaac Tichenor [51]
Elijah Paine

REPRESENTATIVES

Daniel Buck
Israel Smith [52]

VIRGINIA

SENATORS

Henry Tazewell
Stevens T. Mason

REPRESENTATIVES

Richard Brent
Samuel J. Cabell
Thomas Claiborne
John Clopton [53]
Isaac Coles
William B. Giles
George Hancock
Carter B. Harrison
John Heath

George Jackson
James Madison
Andrew Moore
Anthony New
John Nicholas
John Page
Josiah Parker
Francis Preston
Robert Rutherford
Abraham B. Venable

TERRITORY SOUTH OF THE RIVER OHIO

DELEGATE

James White [54]

---

[49] Took his seat December 5, 1796.
[50] Resigned October 15, 1796.
[51] Elected to fill vacancy caused by resignation of Moses Robinson, and took his seat December 6, 1796.

[52] Election unsuccessfully contested by Matthew Lyon.
[53] Election unsuccessfully contested by Burwell Bassett.

[54] Served until June 1, 1796, when the Territory South of the River Ohio was granted statehood as the State of Tennessee.

FIFTH CONGRESS

MARCH 4, 1797, TO MARCH 3, 1799

FIRST SESSION—*May 15, 1797, to July 10, 1797*

SECOND SESSION—*November 13, 1797, to July 16, 1798*

THIRD SESSION—*December 3, 1798, to March 3, 1799*

SPECIAL SESSIONS OF THE SENATE—*March 4, 1797, for one day only; July 17, 1798, to July 19, 1798*

———

VICE PRESIDENT OF THE UNITED STATES—Thomas Jefferson, of Virginia

PRESIDENT PRO TEMPORE OF THE SENATE—William Bradford,[1] of Rhode Island; Jacob Read,[2] of South Carolina; Theodore Sedgwick,[3] of Massachusetts; John Laurance,[4] of New York; James Ross,[5] of Pennsylvania

SECRETARY OF THE SENATE—Samuel A. Otis, of Massachusetts

DOORKEEPER OF THE SENATE—James Mathers, of New York

———

SPEAKER OF THE HOUSE OF REPRESENTATIVES—Jonathan Dayton,[6] of New Jersey

CLERK OF THE HOUSE—John Beckley, of Virginia; Jonathan W. Condy,[7] of Pennsylvania

SERGEANT AT ARMS OF THE HOUSE—Joseph Wheaton, of Rhode Island

DOORKEEPER OF THE HOUSE—Thomas Claxton

CONNECTICUT

SENATORS

James Hillhouse
Uriah Tracy

REPRESENTATIVES

John Allen
Joshua Coit [8]
Jonathan Brace [9]
Samuel W. Dana
Nathaniel Smith
James Davenport [10]
William Edmond [11]
Chauncey Goodrich
Roger Griswold [12]

DELAWARE

SENATORS

John Vining [13]
Joshua Clayton [14]
William H. Wells [15]
Henry Latimer

REPRESENTATIVE

James A. Bayard

GEORGIA

SENATORS

James Gunn
Josiah Tattnall

REPRESENTATIVES

Abraham Baldwin
John Milledge

KENTUCKY

SENATORS

John Brown
Humphrey Marshall

REPRESENTATIVES

Thomas T. Davis
John Fowler

MARYLAND

SENATORS

John Henry [16]
James Lloyd [17]
John E. Howard

REPRESENTATIVES

George Baer, Jr.
William Craik
John Dennis
George Dent
William Hindman
William Matthews
Samuel Smith
Richard Sprigg, Jr.

MASSACHUSETTS

SENATORS

Benjamin Goodhue
Theodore Sedgwick

---

[1] Elected July 6, 1797.
[2] Elected November 22, 1797.
[3] Elected June 27, 1798.
[4] Elected December 6, 1798.
[5] Elected March 1, 1799.
[6] Reelected May 15, 1797; George Dent, of Maryland, was elected Speaker pro tempore for April 20, 1798, and again for May 28, 1798.
[7] Elected May 15, 1797.
[8] Died September 5, 1798.

[9] Elected to fill vacancy caused by death of Joshua Coit, and took his seat December 3, 1798.
[10] Died August 3, 1797.
[11] Elected to fill vacancy caused by death of James Davenport, and took his seat November 13, 1797.
[12] Unsuccessful motion made to expel after his personal encounter with Matthew Lyon, of Vermont, February 15, 1798.
[13] Resigned January 19, 1798.

[14] Elected to fill vacancy caused by resignation of John Vining, and took his seat February 19, 1798; died August 11, 1798.
[15] Elected to fill vacancy caused by death of Joshua Clayton, and took his seat February 4, 1799.
[16] Resigned December 10, 1797, having been elected governor.
[17] Elected to fill vacancy caused by resignation of John Henry, and took his seat January 11, 1798.

REPRESENTATIVES

Theophilus Bradbury [18]
Bailey Bartlett [19]
Stephen Bullock
Dwight Foster
Nathaniel Freeman, Jr.
Samuel Lyman
Harrison Gray Otis
Isaac Parker
John Reed
Samuel Sewall
William Shepard
Thomson J. Skinner
George Thacher
Joseph Bradley Varnum
Peleg Wadsworth

NEW HAMPSHIRE

SENATORS

John Langdon
Samuel Livermore

REPRESENTATIVES

Abiel Foster
Jonathan Freeman
William Gordon
Jeremiah Smith [20]
Peleg Sprague [21]

NEW JERSEY

SENATORS

John Rutherfurd [22]
Franklin Davenport [23]
Richard Stockton

REPRESENTATIVES

Jonathan Dayton
James H. Imlay
James Schureman [24]
Thomas Sinnickson
Mark Thompson

NEW YORK

SENATORS

John Laurance

Philip Schuyler [25]
John Sloss Hobart [26]
William North [27]
James Watson [28]

REPRESENTATIVES

David Brooks
James Cochran
Lucas C. Elmendorf
Henry Glen
Jonathan N. Havens
Hezekiah L. Hosmer
Edward Livingston
John E. Van Alen
Philip Van Cortlandt
John Williams

NORTH CAROLINA

SENATORS

Alexander Martin
Timothy Bloodworth

REPRESENTATIVES

Thomas Blount
Nathan Bryan [29]
Richard Dobbs Spaight [30]
Dempsey Burges
James Gillespie
William Barry Grove
Matthew Locke
Nathaniel Macon
Joseph McDowell
Richard Stanford
Robert Williams

PENNSYLVANIA

SENATORS

James Ross
William Bingham

REPRESENTATIVES

David Bard
Samuel Sitgreaves [31]
Robert Brown [32]
John Chapman
William Findley

Albert Gallatin
Andrew Gregg
John A. Hanna
Thomas Hartley
George Ege [33]
Joseph Hiester [34]
John Wilkes Kittera
Blair McClenachan
John Swanwick [35]
Robert Waln [36]
Richard Thomas

RHODE ISLAND

SENATORS

Theodore Foster
William Bradford [37]
Ray Greene [38]

REPRESENTATIVES

Christopher G. Champlin
Elisha R. Potter [39]
Thomas Tillinghast [40]

SOUTH CAROLINA

SENATORS

Jacob Read
John Hunter [41]
Charles Pinckney [42]

REPRESENTATIVES

Lemuel Benton
Robert Goodloe Harper
John Rutledge, Jr.
William L. Smith, [43] *Charleston district* [44]
Thomas Pinckney [45]
William Smith, *Spartan district* [44]
Thomas Sumter

TENNESSEE

SENATORS

William Blount [46]
Joseph Anderson [47]
William Cocke [48]
Andrew Jackson [49]
Daniel Smith [50]

---

[18] Resigned July 24, 1797.
[19] Elected to fill vacancy caused by resignation of Theophilus Bradbury, and took his seat November 27, 1797.
[20] Resigned July 26, 1797.
[21] Elected to fill vacancy caused by resignation of Jeremiah Smith, and took his seat December 15, 1797.
[22] Resigned November 26, 1798.
[23] Appointed to fill vacancy caused by resignation of John Rutherfurd, and took his seat December 19, 1798.
[24] Elected on February 14, 1799, to fill vacancy in Senate caused by resignation of John Rutherfurd, but did not take his seat until the following Congress, finishing out his term in the House.
[25] Resigned January 3, 1798.
[26] Elected to fill vacancy caused by resignation of Philip Schuyler, and took his seat February 2, 1798; resigned April 16, 1798, having been appointed judge of the United States district court of New York.
[27] Appointed to fill vacancy caused by resignation of John Sloss Hobart, and took his seat May 21, 1798.
[28] Elected to fill vacancy caused by resignation of John Sloss Hobart, and took his seat December 11, 1798.
[29] Died June 4, 1798.
[30] Elected to fill vacancy caused by death of Nathan Bryan, and took his seat December 10, 1798.

[31] Resigned in 1798, having been appointed commissioner to Great Britain.
[32] Elected to fill vacancy caused by resignation of Samuel Sitgreaves, and took his seat December 4, 1798.
[33] Resigned in October 1797.
[34] Elected to fill vacancy caused by resignation of George Ege, and took his seat December 1, 1797.
[35] Died August 1, 1798.
[36] Elected to fill vacancy caused by death of John Swanwick, and took his seat December 3, 1798.
[37] Resigned in October 1797.
[38] Elected to fill vacancy caused by resignation of William Bradford, and took his seat November 22, 1797.
[39] Elected to fill vacancy caused by resignation of Representative-elect Benjamin Bourn, in the preceding Congress; resigned in 1797.
[40] Elected to fill vacancy caused by resignation of Elisha R. Potter, and took his seat November 13, 1797.
[41] Resigned November 26, 1798.
[42] Elected to fill vacancy caused by resignation of John Hunter, and took his seat February 16, 1799.
[43] Resigned July 10, 1797, having been appointed minister plenipotentiary to Portugal.
[44] Many biographical errors have resulted from the fact that Smith of Charleston district and Smith of Spartan district both formerly were known as "William Smith." It was about this time that Smith

of Charleston district changed his name to "William Loughton Smith."
[45] Elected to fill vacancy caused by resignation of William L. Smith, and took his seat November 23, 1797.
[46] Expelled for "high misdemeanor" July 8, 1797.
[47] Elected to fill vacancy caused by expulsion of William Blount, and took his seat November 22, 1797, for the term ending March 3, 1799. (See foot note 50.)
[48] Appointed to fill vacancy in the term beginning March 4, 1797 (the legislature having failed to elect his successor), and took his seat May 15, 1797.
[49] Elected to fill vacancy in the term beginning March 4, 1797, and took his seat November 22, 1797; resigned in April 1798.
[50] Appointed to fill vacancy in the term beginning March 4, 1797, caused by the resignation of Andrew Jackson, and took his seat December 6, 1798; vacancy in this class from April 1798, to October 5, 1798. Joseph Anderson was elected December 12, 1798, to fill vacancy in the term beginning March 4, 1797, caused by resignation of Andrew Jackson, but did not present his credentials under this election until the Sixth Congress, continuing to serve in the other class, and on December 31, 1798, obtained leave of absence for Daniel Smith for the remainder of the session; technically, the term of Smith expired on the election of Anderson.

TENNESSEE—Continued

REPRESENTATIVE

William C. C. Claiborne [51]

VERMONT

SENATORS

Elijah Paine
Isaac Tichenor [52]
Nathaniel Chipman [53]

REPRESENTATIVES

Matthew Lyon
Lewis R. Morris

VIRGINIA

SENATORS

Henry Tazewell [54]
Stevens T. Mason

REPRESENTATIVES

Richard Brent
Samuel J. Cabell
Thomas Claiborne
Matthew Clay
John Clopton
John Dawson
William B. Giles [55]
Joseph Eggleston [56]
Thomas Evans
Carter B. Harrison
David Holmes
Walter Jones
James Machir
Daniel Morgan [57]
Anthony New
John Nicholas
Josiah Parker
Abram Trigg
John Trigg
Abraham B. Venable

---

[51] Took his seat November 23, 1797.
[52] Resigned October 17, 1797, having been elected governor.
[53] Elected to fill vacancy caused by resignation of Isaac Tichenor, and took his seat November 22, 1797.

[54] Died January 24, 1799. Letter from governor of Virginia (Senate Journal, p. 584) stating appointment would be deferred until legislature meets.
[55] Resigned October 2, 1798.

[56] Elected to fill vacancy caused by resignation of William B. Giles, and took his seat December 3, 1798.
[57] Election unsuccessfully contested by Robert Rutherford.

SIXTH CONGRESS

MARCH 4, 1799, TO MARCH 3, 1801

FIRST SESSION—*December 2, 1799, to May 14, 1800*

SECOND SESSION—*November 17, 1800, to March 3, 1801*

VICE PRESIDENT OF THE UNITED STATES—Thomas Jefferson, of Virginia

PRESIDENT PRO TEMPORE OF THE SENATE—Samuel Livermore,[1] of New Hampshire; Uriah Tracy,[2] of Connecticut; John E. Howard,[3] of Maryland; James Hillhouse,[4] of Connecticut

SECRETARY OF THE SENATE—Samuel A. Otis, of Massachusetts

DOORKEEPER OF THE SENATE—James Mathers, of New York

SPEAKER OF THE HOUSE OF REPRESENTATIVES—Theodore Sedgwick,[5] of Massachusetts

CLERK OF THE HOUSE—Jonathan W. Condy,[6] of Pennsylvania; John H. Oswald,[7] of Pennsylvania

SERGEANT AT ARMS OF THE HOUSE—Joseph Wheaton, of Rhode Island

DOORKEEPER OF THE HOUSE—Thomas Claxton

CONNECTICUT

SENATORS

James Hillhouse
Uriah Tracy

REPRESENTATIVES

Jonathan Brace [8]
John C. Smith [9]
Samuel W. Dana
John Davenport
William Edmond
Chauncey Goodrich
Elizur Goodrich
Roger Griswold

DELAWARE

SENATORS

Henry Latimer [10]
Samuel White [11]
William H. Wells

REPRESENTATIVE

James A. Bayard

GEORGIA

SENATORS

James Gunn
Abraham Baldwin

REPRESENTATIVES

James Jones [12]
Benjamin Taliaferro

KENTUCKY

SENATORS

John Brown
Humphrey Marshall

REPRESENTATIVES

Thomas T. Davis
John Fowler

MARYLAND

SENATORS

John E. Howard
James Lloyd [13]
William Hindman [14]

REPRESENTATIVES

George Baer
Gabriel Christie
William Craik
George Dent
John Dennis
Joseph H. Nicholson
Samuel Smith
John C. Thomas

MASSACHUSETTS

SENATORS

Benjamin Goodhue [15]
Jonathan Mason [16]
Samuel Dexter [17]
Dwight Foster [18]

---

[1] Elected December 2, 1799.
[2] Elected May 14, 1800.
[3] Elected November 21, 1800.
[4] Elected February 28, 1801.
[5] Elected December 2, 1799.
[6] Reelected December 2, 1799; resigned December 4, 1799.
[7] Elected December 9, 1799.
[8] Resigned in 1800.
[9] Elected to fill vacancy caused by resignation of

Jonathan Brace, and took his seat November 17, 1800.
[10] Resigned February 28, 1801.
[11] Appointed and subsequently elected to fill vacancy caused by resignation of Henry Latimer, service to date from February 28, 1801; did not take his seat until March 4, 1801, in the special session of the Senate of the Seventh Congress.
[12] Died January 13, 1801.
[13] Resigned December 1, 1800.

[14] Elected to fill vacancy caused by resignation of James Lloyd, and took his seat December 15, 1800.
[15] Resigned November 8, 1800.
[16] Elected to fill vacancy caused by resignation of Benjamin Goodhue, and took his seat December 19, 1800.
[17] Resigned May 30, 1800.
[18] Elected to fill vacancy caused by resignation of Samuel Dexter, and took his seat November 21, 1800.

MASSACHUSETTS—Continued

REPRESENTATIVES

Bailey Bartlett
Phanuel Bishop
Dwight Foster [19]
Levi Lincoln [20]
Silas Lee
Samuel Lyman [21]
Ebenezer Mattoon [22]
Harrison Gray Otis
John Reed
Theodore Sedgwick
Samuel Sewall [23]
Nathan Read [24]
William Shepard
George Thacher
Joseph B. Varnum
Peleg Wadsworth
Lemuel Williams

NEW HAMPSHIRE

SENATORS

John Langdon
Samuel Livermore

REPRESENTATIVES

Jonathan Freeman
William Gordon [25]
Samuel Tenney [26]
Abiel Foster
James Sheafe

NEW JERSEY

SENATORS

James Schureman [27]
Aaron Ogden [28]
Jonathan Dayton

REPRESENTATIVES

John Condit
Franklin Davenport
James H. Imlay
Aaron Kitchell
James Linn

NEW YORK

SENATORS

John Laurance [29]
John Armstrong [30]
James Watson [31]
Gouverneur Morris [32]

REPRESENTATIVES

Theodorus Bailey
John Bird
William Cooper
Lucas C. Elmendorf
Henry Glen
Jonathan N. Havens [33]
John Smith [34]
Edward Livingston
Jonas Platt
John Thompson
Philip Van Cortlandt

NORTH CAROLINA

SENATORS

Timothy Bloodworth
Jesse Franklin

REPRESENTATIVES

Willis Alston
Joseph Dickson
William Barry Grove
Archibald Henderson
William H. Hill
Nathaniel Macon
Richard Dobbs Spaight
Richard Stanford
David Stone
Robert Williams

PENNSYLVANIA

SENATORS

James Ross
William Bingham

REPRESENTATIVES

Robert Brown
Albert Gallatin
Andrew Gregg
John A. Hanna
Thomas Hartley [35]
John Stewart [36]
Joseph Hiester
John Wilkes Kittera
Michael Leib
John Peter G. Muhlenberg
John Smilie
Richard Thomas
Robert Waln
Henry Woods

RHODE ISLAND

SENATORS

Theodore Foster
Ray Greene

REPRESENTATIVES

John Brown
Christopher G. Champlin

SOUTH CAROLINA

SENATORS

Jacob Read
Charles Pinckney

REPRESENTATIVES

Robert Goodloe Harper
Benjamin Huger
Abraham Nott
Thomas Pinckney
John Rutledge, Jr.
Thomas Sumter

TENNESSEE

SENATORS

Joseph Anderson [37]
William Cocke

REPRESENTATIVE

William C. C. Claiborne

VERMONT

SENATORS

Elijah Paine
Nathaniel Chipman

REPRESENTATIVES

Matthew Lyon
Lewis R. Morris

VIRGINIA

SENATORS

Stevens T. Mason
Wilson C. Nicholas [38]

REPRESENTATIVES

Samuel J. Cabell
Matthew Clay
John Dawson
Joseph Eggleston
Thomas Evans
Samuel Goode

---

[19] Resigned June 6, 1800, having been elected Senator.
[20] Elected to fill vacancy caused by resignation of Dwight Foster, and took his seat February 6, 1801.
[21] Resigned November 6, 1800.
[22] Elected to fill vacancy caused by resignation of Samuel Lyman, and took his seat February 2, 1801.
[23] Resigned January 10, 1800.
[24] Elected to fill vacancy caused by resignation of Samuel Sewall, and took his seat November 25, 1800.
[25] Resigned June 12, 1800.
[26] Elected to fill vacancy caused by resignation of William Gordon, and took his seat December 8, 1800.

[27] Elected to fill vacancy caused by resignation of John Rutherfurd, in preceding Congress, and took his seat December 3, 1799; resigned February 16, 1801.
[28] Elected to fill vacancy caused by resignation of James Schureman, and took his seat March 3, 1801.
[29] Resigned in August 1800.
[30] Elected to fill vacancy caused by resignation of John Laurance, and took his seat January 8, 1801.
[31] Resigned March 19, 1800.
[32] Elected to fill vacancy caused by resignation of James Watson, and took his seat May 3, 1800.
[33] Died October 25, 1799, before Congress assembled.

[34] Elected to fill vacancy caused by death of Jonathan N. Havens, and took his seat February 27, 1800.
[35] Died December 21, 1800.
[36] Elected to fill vacancy caused by death of Thomas Hartley, and took his seat February 3, 1801.
[37] Elected December 12, 1798, to fill vacancy in the term beginning March 4, 1797, caused by resignation of Andrew Jackson, in preceding Congress, and took his seat December 2, 1799.
[38] Elected to fill vacancy caused by death of Henry Tazewell, in preceding Congress, and took his seat January 3, 1800.

Edwin Gray
David Holmes
George Jackson
Henry Lee
John Marshall [39]
Littleton W. Tazewell [40]
Anthony New

John Nicholas
Robert Page
Josiah Parker
Levin Powell
John Randolph
Abram Trigg
John Trigg

TERRITORY NORTHWEST OF THE RIVER OHIO [41]

DELEGATE

William Henry Harrison [42]
William McMillan [43]

---

[39] Resigned June 7, 1800.
[40] Elected to fill vacancy caused by resignation of John Marshall, and took his seat November 26, 1800.
[41] Created a district for the purposes of temporary government by act approved July 13, 1787, from territory ceded to the United States by the State of Virginia and granted a Delegate in Congress.
[42] Resigned in March 1800.
[43] Elected to fill vacancy caused by resignation of William Henry Harrison, and took his seat November 24, 1800.

SEVENTH CONGRESS

MARCH 4, 1801, TO MARCH 3, 1803

FIRST SESSION—*December 7, 1801, to May 3, 1802*

SECOND SESSION—*December 6, 1802, to March 3, 1803*

SPECIAL SESSION OF THE SENATE—*March 4, 1801, to March 5, 1801*

———

VICE PRESIDENT OF THE UNITED STATES—Aaron Burr, of New York

PRESIDENT PRO TEMPORE OF THE SENATE—Abraham Baldwin,[1] of Georgia; Stephen R. Bradley,[2] of Vermont

SECRETARY OF THE SENATE—Samuel A. Otis, of Massachusetts

DOORKEEPER OF THE SENATE—James Mathers, of New York

———

SPEAKER OF THE HOUSE OF REPRESENTATIVES—Nathaniel Macon,[3] of North Carolina

CLERK OF THE HOUSE—John H. Oswald, of Pennsylvania; John Beckley,[4] of Virginia

SERGEANT AT ARMS OF THE HOUSE—Joseph Wheaton, of Rhode Island

DOORKEEPER OF THE HOUSE—Thomas Claxton

CONNECTICUT

SENATORS

James Hillhouse
Uriah Tracy

REPRESENTATIVES

Samuel W. Dana
John Davenport
Roger Griswold
Calvin Goddard [5]
Elias Perkins
John C. Smith
Benjamin Tallmadge

DELAWARE

SENATORS

William H. Wells
Samuel White

REPRESENTATIVE

James A. Bayard

GEORGIA

SENATORS

Abraham Baldwin
James Jackson

REPRESENTATIVES

John Milledge [6]
Peter Early [7]
Benjamin Taliaferro [8]
David Meriwether [9]

KENTUCKY

SENATORS

John Brown
John Breckinridge

REPRESENTATIVES

Thomas T. Davis
John Fowler

MARYLAND

SENATORS

John E. Howard
William Hindman [10]
Robert Wright [11]

REPRESENTATIVES

John Archer
John Campbell
John Dennis
Daniel Hiester
Joseph H. Nicholson
Thomas Plater
Samuel Smith
Richard Sprigg, Jr. [12]
Walter Bowie [13]

MASSACHUSETTS

SENATORS

Dwight Foster [14]
Jonathan Mason

---

[1] Elected December 7, 1801; April 17, 1802.
[2] Elected December 14, 1802; February 25, 1803; March 2, 1803.
[3] Elected December 7, 1801.
[4] Elected December 7, 1801.
[5] Elected to fill vacancy caused by resignation of Representative-elect Elizur Goodrich (March 3, 1801, before the beginning of the congressional term), and took his seat December 7, 1801.

[6] Resigned in May 1802.
[7] Elected to fill vacancy caused by resignation of John Milledge, and took his seat January 10, 1803.
[8] Resigned in 1802.
[9] Elected to fill vacancy caused by resignation of Benjamin Taliaferro, and took his seat December 6, 1802.
[10] Reappointed to fill vacancy in term beginning

March 4, 1801, caused by failure of legislature to elect his successor, and took his seat March 5, 1801.
[11] Elected to fill vacancy in term beginning March 4, 1801, and took his seat December 7, 1801.
[12] Resigned February 11, 1802.
[13] Elected to fill vacancy caused by resignation of Richard Sprigg, Jr., and took his seat March 24, 1802.
[14] Resigned March 2, 1803.

REPRESENTATIVES

John Bacon
Phanuel Bishop
Manasseh Cutler
Richard Cutts
William Eustis
Silas Lee [15]
Samuel Thatcher [16]
Levi Lincoln [17]
Seth Hastings [18]
Ebenezer Mattoon
Nathan Read
William Shepard
Josiah Smith
Joseph B. Varnum
Peleg Wadsworth
Lemuel Williams

NEW HAMPSHIRE

SENATORS

Samuel Livermore [19]
Simeon Olcott [20]
James Sheafe [21]
William Plumer [22]

REPRESENTATIVES

Abiel Foster
Joseph Peirce [23]
Samuel Hunt [24]
Samuel Tenney
George B. Upham

NEW JERSEY

SENATORS

Jonathan Dayton
Aaron Ogden

REPRESENTATIVES

John Condit
Ebenezer Elmer
William Helms
James Mott
Henry Southard

NEW YORK

SENATORS

Gouverneur Morris
John Armstrong [25]
De Witt Clinton [26]

REPRESENTATIVES

John Bird [27]
John P. Van Ness [28]
Lucas C. Elmendorf
Samuel L. Mitchill
Thomas Morris
John Smith
Thomas Tillotson [29]
Theodorus Bailey [30]
David Thomas
Philip Van Cortlandt
Killian K. Van Rensselaer
Benjamin Walker

NORTH CAROLINA

SENATORS

Jesse Franklin
David Stone

REPRESENTATIVES

Willis Alston
William Barry Grove
Archibald Henderson
William H. Hill
Charles Johnson [31]
Thomas Wynns [32]
James Holland
Nathaniel Macon
Richard Stanford
John Stanly
Robert Williams

OHIO [33]

SENATORS

Vacant

REPRESENTATIVE

Vacant

PENNSYLVANIA

SENATORS

James Ross
John Peter G. Muhlenberg [34]
George Logan [35]

REPRESENTATIVES

Robert Brown
Thomas Boude
Andrew Gregg
John A. Hanna
Joseph Hiester
Joseph Hemphill
William Hoge
William Jones
Michael Leib
John Smilie
John Stewart
Isaac Van Horne
Henry Woods

RHODE ISLAND

SENATORS

Theodore Foster
Ray Greene [36]
Christopher Ellery [37]

REPRESENTATIVES

Joseph Stanton, Jr.
Thomas Tillinghast

SOUTH CAROLINA

SENATORS

Charles Pinckney [38]
Thomas Sumter [39]
John Ewing Colhoun [40]
Pierce Butler [41]

REPRESENTATIVES

William Butler
Benjamin Huger
Thomas Lowndes
Thomas Moore
John Rutledge
Thomas Sumter [42]
Richard Winn [43]

TENNESSEE

SENATORS

Joseph Anderson
William Cocke

REPRESENTATIVE

William Dickson

---

[15] Resigned August 20, 1801.
[16] Elected to fill vacancy caused by resignation of Silas Lee, and took his seat December 6, 1802.
[17] Resigned March 5, 1801, before Congress assembled having been appointed Attorney General of the United States.
[18] Elected to fill vacancy caused by resignation of Levi Lincoln, and took his seat January 11, 1802.
[19] Resigned June 12, 1801.
[20] Elected to fill vacancy caused by resignation of Samuel Livermore, and took his seat December 7, 1801.
[21] Resigned June 14, 1802.
[22] Elected to fill vacancy caused by resignation of James Sheafe, and took his seat December 14, 1802.
[23] Resigned in 1802.
[24] Elected to fill vacancy caused by resignation of Joseph Peirce, and took his seat December 6, 1802.
[25] Resigned February 5, 1802.
[26] Elected to fill vacancy caused by resignation of

John Armstrong, and took his seat February 23, 1802.
[27] Resigned July 25, 1801, before Congress assembled.
[28] Elected to fill vacancy caused by resignation of John Bird, and took his seat December 7, 1801; seat declared forfeited January 17, 1803, because he had accepted and exercised the office of major of militia, under authority of the United States, within the Territory of Columbia.
[29] Resigned August 10, 1801, before Congress assembled, having been appointed Secretary of State of New York.
[30] Elected to fill vacancy caused by resignation of Thomas Tillotson, and took his seat December 7, 1801.
[31] Died in 1802.
[32] Elected to fill vacancy caused by death of Charles Johnson, and took his seat December 7, 1802.
[33] Admitted as a State into the Union, November 29, 1802, from territory known as the "Northwest Territory," which was originally ceded to the United States by the State of Virginia.

[34] Resigned June 30, 1801; attended special session of the Senate only, March 4–5, 1801.
[35] Appointed to fill vacancy caused by resignation of John Peter G. Muhlenberg, and took his seat December 7, 1801; subsequently elected.
[36] Resigned March 5, 1801.
[37] Elected to fill vacancy caused by resignation of Ray Greene, and took his seat December 7, 1801.
[38] Resigned in 1801.
[39] Elected to fill vacancy caused by resignation of Charles Pinckney, and took his seat December 19, 1801.
[40] Died October 26, 1802.
[41] Elected on November 4, 1802, to fill vacancy caused by death of John E. Colhoun.
[42] Resigned December 15, 1801, having been elected Senator.
[43] Elected to fill vacancy caused by resignation of Thomas Sumter, and took his seat January 24, 1803.

VERMONT

SENATORS

Elijah Paine [44]
Stephen R. Bradley [45]
Nathaniel Chipman

REPRESENTATIVES

Lewis R. Morris
Israel Smith

VIRGINIA

SENATORS

Stevens T. Mason
Wilson C. Nicholas

REPRESENTATIVES

Richard Brent
Samuel J. Cabell
Thomas Claiborne
Matthew Clay
John Clopton
John Dawson
William B. Giles
Edwin Gray
David Holmes
George Jackson
Anthony New
Thomas Newton, Jr.
John Randolph
John Smith
John Stratton
John Taliaferro
Philip R. Thompson
Abram Trigg
John Trigg

MISSISSIPPI TERRITORY [46]

DELEGATE

Narsworthy Hunter [47]
Thomas M. Greene [48]

TERRITORY NORTHWEST OF THE RIVER OHIO

DELEGATE

Paul Fearing [49]

---

[44] Resigned September 1, 1801.
[45] Elected to fill vacancy caused by resignation of Elijah Paine, and took his seat December 7, 1801.
[46] Formed by act of April 7, 1798, from territory ceded to the United States by the States of Georgia and South Carolina.

[47] Died March 11, 1802.
[48] Elected to fill vacancy caused by death of Narsworthy Hunter, and took his seat December 6, 1802.

[49] Question raised as to his right to retain his seat after November 29, 1802, when the Territory was granted statehood as the State of Ohio; no other representative appearing, was permitted to retain the seat.

EIGHTH CONGRESS

MARCH 4, 1803, TO MARCH 3, 1805

FIRST SESSION—*October 17, 1803, to March 27, 1804*

SECOND SESSION—*November 5, 1804, to March 3, 1805*

———————

VICE PRESIDENT OF THE UNITED STATES—AARON BURR, of New York

PRESIDENT PRO TEMPORE OF THE SENATE—JOHN BROWN,[1] of Kentucky; JESSE FRANKLIN,[2] of North Carolina; JOSEPH ANDERSON,[3] of Tennessee

SECRETARY OF THE SENATE—SAMUEL A. OTIS, of Massachusetts

SERGEANT AT ARMS OF THE SENATE[4]—JAMES MATHERS, of New York

———————

SPEAKER OF THE HOUSE OF REPRESENTATIVES—NATHANIEL MACON,[5] of North Carolina

CLERK OF THE HOUSE—JOHN BECKLEY,[6] of Virginia

SERGEANT AT ARMS OF THE HOUSE—JOSEPH WHEATON, of Rhode Island

DOORKEEPER OF THE HOUSE—THOMAS CLAXTON

CONNECTICUT

SENATORS

James Hillhouse
Uriah Tracy

REPRESENTATIVES

Simeon Baldwin
Samuel W. Dana
John Davenport
Calvin Goddard
Roger Griswold
John C. Smith
Benjamin Tallmadge

DELAWARE

SENATORS

William H. Wells [7]
James A. Bayard [8]
Samuel White

REPRESENTATIVE

Caesar A. Rodney

GEORGIA

SENATORS

Abraham Baldwin
James Jackson

REPRESENTATIVES

Joseph Bryan
Peter Early
Samuel Hammond [9]
David Meriwether

KENTUCKY

SENATORS

John Brown
John Breckinridge

REPRESENTATIVES

George M. Bedinger
John Boyle
John Fowler
Matthew Lyon
Thomas Sandford
Matthew Walton

MARYLAND

SENATORS

Robert Wright
Samuel Smith

REPRESENTATIVES

John Archer
Walter Bowie
John Campbell
John Dennis
Nicholas R. Moore
William McCreery
Daniel Hiester [10]
Roger Nelson [11]
Joseph H. Nicholson
Thomas Plater

MASSACHUSETTS

SENATORS

Timothy Pickering [12]
John Quincy Adams

REPRESENTATIVES

Phanuel Bishop
Phineas Bruce [13]

---

[1] Elected October 17, 1803; January 23, 1804.
[2] Elected March 10, 1804.
[3] Elected January 15, 1805; February 28, 1805; March 2, 1805.
[4] Official designation of "Sergeant at Arms" was fixed March 3, 1805.
[5] Reelected October 17, 1803.

[6] Reelected October 17, 1803.
[7] Resigned November 6, 1804.
[8] Elected to fill vacancy caused by resignation of William H. Wells, and took his seat January 15, 1805.
[9] Seat declared vacant February 2, 1805, because he had accepted appointment to be civil and military governor of upper Louisiana Territory.

[10] Died March 7, 1804.
[11] Elected to fill vacancy caused by death of Daniel Hiester, and took his seat November 6, 1804.
[12] Elected to fill vacancy caused by resignation of Dwight Foster in preceding Congress, and took his seat October 17, 1803.
[13] Never qualified, owing to illness.

MASSACHUSETTS—Continued

REPRESENTATIVES—continued

Jacob Crowninshield
Manasseh Cutler
Richard Cutts
Thomas Dwight
William Eustis
Seth Hastings
Nahum Mitchell
Ebenezer Seaver
Thomson J. Skinner [14]
Simon Larned [15]
William Stedman
Samuel Taggart
Samuel Thatcher
Joseph B. Varnum
Peleg Wadsworth
Lemuel Williams

NEW HAMPSHIRE

SENATORS

Simeon Olcott
William Plumer

REPRESENTATIVES

Silas Betton
Clifton Clagett
David Hough
Samuel Hunt
Samuel Tenney

NEW JERSEY

SENATORS

Jonathan Dayton
John Condit [16]

REPRESENTATIVES

Adam Boyd
Ebenezer Elmer
William Helms
James Mott
James Sloan
Henry Southard

NEW YORK

SENATORS

De Witt Clinton [17]
John Armstrong [18]
John Smith [19]
Theodorus Bailey [20]

John Armstrong [21]
Samuel L. Mitchill [22]

REPRESENTATIVES

Isaac Bloom [23]
Daniel C. Verplanck [24]
Gaylord Griswold
Josiah Hasbrouck [25]
Henry W. Livingston
Andrew McCord
Samuel L. Mitchill [26]
George Clinton, Jr. [27]
Beriah Palmer
John Patterson
Oliver Phelps
Erastus Root
Joshua Sands
Thomas Sammons
John Smith [28]
Samuel Riker [29]
David Thomas
George Tibbitts
Philip Van Cortlandt
Killian K. Van Rensselaer

NORTH CAROLINA

SENATORS

Jesse Franklin
David Stone

REPRESENTATIVES

Nathaniel Alexander
Willis Alston
William Blackledge
James Gillespie [30]
James Holland
William Kennedy
Nathaniel Macon
Samuel D. Purviance [31]
Richard Stanford
Marmaduke Williams
Joseph Winston
Thomas Wynns

OHIO

SENATORS

John Smith [32]
Thomas Worthington [33]

REPRESENTATIVE

Jeremiah Morrow [34]

PENNSYLVANIA

SENATORS

George Logan
Samuel Maclay

REPRESENTATIVES

Isaac Anderson
David Bard
Robert Brown
Joseph Clay
Frederick Conrad
William Findley
Andrew Gregg
John A. Hanna
Joseph Hiester
William Hoge [35]
John Hoge [36]
Michael Leib
John B. C. Lucas
John Rea
Jacob Richards
John Smilie
John Stewart
Isaac Van Horne
John Whitehill

RHODE ISLAND

SENATORS

Christopher Ellery
Samuel J. Potter [37]
Benjamin Howland [38]

REPRESENTATIVES

Nehemiah Knight
Joseph Stanton, Jr.

SOUTH CAROLINA

SENATORS

Thomas Sumter
Pierce Butler [39]
John Gaillard [40]

REPRESENTATIVES

William Butler
Levi Casey
John B. Earle
Wade Hampton
Benjamin Huger
Thomas Lowndes
Thomas Moore
Richard Winn

---

[14] Resigned August 10, 1804.
[15] Elected to fill vacancy caused by resignation of Thomson J. Skinner, and took his seat November 5, 1804.
[16] Appointed to fill vacancy in term beginning March 4, 1803, to serve until the next meeting of the legislature, subsequently elected and took his seat October 17, 1803; vacancy in this class from March 4, 1803, to August 31, 1803.
[17] Resigned November 4, 1803.
[18] Appointed to fill vacancy caused by resignation of De Witt Clinton, and took his seat December 8, 1803. (See footnote 21.)
[19] Elected to fill vacancy caused by resignation of De Witt Clinton, and took his seat February 23, 1804.
[20] Resigned January 16, 1804.
[21] Elected to fill vacancy caused by resignation of Theodorus Bailey, and took his seat under the new credentials February 25, 1804; served in this class until

June 30, 1804, when he resigned, having been appointed minister to France.
[22] Elected to fill vacancy caused by resignation of John Armstrong, and took his seat November 23, 1804.
[23] Died April 26, 1803, before Congress assembled.
[24] Elected to fill vacancy caused by death of Isaac Bloom, and took his seat October 17, 1803.
[25] Elected to fill vacancy caused by resignation of Representative-elect John Cantine, before the beginning of the congressional term, and took his seat October 17, 1803.
[26] Resigned November 22, 1804, before the commencement of the Ninth Congress, to which he had been reelected, having been elected Senator.
[27] Elected to fill vacancy caused by resignation of Samuel L. Mitchill, and took his seat February 14, 1805.
[28] Resigned effective February 23, 1804, having been elected Senator.

[29] Elected to fill vacancy caused by resignation of John Smith, and took his seat November 5, 1804.
[30] Died January 10, 1805.
[31] Election unsuccessfully contested by Duncan McFarland.
[32] Took his seat October 25, 1803; term to expire, as determined by lot, March 3, 1809.
[33] Took his seat October 17, 1803; term to expire as determined by lot, March 3, 1807.
[34] Took his seat October 17, 1803.
[35] Resigned October 15, 1804.
[36] Elected to fill vacancy caused by resignation of William Hoge, and took his seat November 27, 1804.
[37] Died October 14, 1804.
[38] Elected to fill vacancy caused by death of Samuel J. Potter, and took his seat December 3, 1804.
[39] Resigned November 21, 1804.
[40] Elected to fill vacancy caused by resignation of Pierce Butler, and took his seat January 31, 1805.

TENNESSEE

SENATORS

Joseph Anderson
William Cocke

REPRESENTATIVES

George W. Campbell
William Dickson
John Rhea

VERMONT

SENATORS

Stephen R. Bradley
Israel Smith

REPRESENTATIVES

William Chamberlain
Martin Chittenden
James Elliott
Gideon Olin

VIRGINIA

SENATORS

Stevens T. Mason [41]
John Taylor [42]
Abraham B. Venable [43]
William B. Giles [44]
Andrew Moore [45]
Wilson C. Nicholas [46]
Andrew Moore [47]
William B. Giles [48]

REPRESENTATIVES

Thomas Claiborne
John Trigg [49]
Christopher Clark [50]
Matthew Clay
John Clopton
John Dawson
John W. Eppes
Peterson Goodwyn
Edwin Gray

Thomas Griffin
David Holmes
John G. Jackson
Walter Jones
Thomas Lewis [51]
Andrew Moore [52]
Alexander Wilson [53]
Anthony New
Thomas Newton, Jr.
John Randolph
Thomas M. Randolph
John Smith
James Stephenson
Philip R. Thompson
Abram Trigg
Joseph Lewis, Jr.

MISSISSIPPI TERRITORY

DELEGATE

William Lattimore

---

[41] Died May 10, 1803.
[42] Appointed to fill vacancy caused by death of Stevens T. Mason, and took his seat October 17, 1803.
[43] Elected to fill vacancy caused by death of Stevens T. Mason, and took his seat December 13, 1803; resigned June 7, 1804.
[44] Appointed to fill vacancy caused by resignation of Abraham B. Venable, and took his seat November 5, 1804; subsequently elected to fill vacancy caused by resignation of Wilson C. Nicholas. (See footnote 48.)
[45] Elected to fill vacancy caused by resignation of Abraham B. Venable, and qualified under these credentials December 17, 1804; antecedently appointed

to fill vacancy caused by resignation of Wilson C. Nicholas. (See footnote 47.)
[46] Resigned May 22, 1804.
[47] Appointed to fill vacancy caused by resignation of Wilson C. Nicholas, and took his seat November 6, 1804; subsequently elected to fill vacancy caused by resignation of Abraham B. Venable. (See footnote 45.)
[48] Elected to fill vacancy caused by resignation of Wilson C. Nicholas, and took his seat December 17, 1804; antecedently appointed to fill vacancy caused by resignation of Abraham B. Venable. (See footnote 44.)

[49] Died June 28, 1804.
[50] Elected to fill vacancy caused by death of John Trigg, and took his seat November 5, 1804.
[51] Served until March 5, 1804; succeeded by Andrew Moore, who contested his election. (Counsel were heard at bar of House in this case.)
[52] Successfully contested the election of Thomas Lewis, and took his seat March 5, 1804; resigned November 6, 1804, having been appointed Senator.
[53] Elected to fill vacancy caused by resignation of Andrew Moore, and took his seat December 4, 1804.

NINTH CONGRESS

MARCH 4, 1805, TO MARCH 3, 1807

FIRST SESSION—*December 2, 1805, to April 21, 1806*

SECOND SESSION—*December 1, 1806, to March 3, 1807*

SPECIAL SESSION OF THE SENATE—*March 4, 1805, for one day only*

————

VICE PRESIDENT OF THE UNITED STATES—George Clinton, of New York

PRESIDENT PRO TEMPORE OF THE SENATE—Samuel Smith,[1] of Maryland

SECRETARY OF THE SENATE—Samuel A. Otis, of Massachusetts

SERGEANT AT ARMS OF THE SENATE—James Mathers, of New York

————

SPEAKER OF THE HOUSE OF REPRESENTATIVES—Nathaniel Macon,[2] of North Carolina

CLERK OF THE HOUSE—John Beckley,[3] of Virginia

SERGEANT AT ARMS OF THE HOUSE—Joseph Wheaton, of Rhode Island

DOORKEEPER OF THE HOUSE—Thomas Claxton

CONNECTICUT

SENATORS

James Hillhouse
Uriah Tracy

REPRESENTATIVES

Samuel W. Dana
John Davenport
Calvin Goddard [4]
Timothy Pitkin [5]
Roger Griswold [6]
Lewis B. Sturges [7]
Jonathan O. Moseley
John Cotton Smith [8]
Theodore Dwight [9]
Benjamin Tallmadge

DELAWARE

SENATORS

Samuel White
James A. Bayard

REPRESENTATIVE

James M. Broom

GEORGIA

SENATORS

Abraham Baldwin
James Jackson [10]
John Milledge [11]

REPRESENTATIVES

Joseph Bryan [12]
Dennis Smelt [13]
Peter Early
David Meriwether
Cowles Mead [14]
Thomas Spalding [15]
William W. Bibb [16]

KENTUCKY

SENATORS

John Breckinridge [17]

John Adair [18]
Henry Clay [19]
Buckner Thruston

REPRESENTATIVES

George M. Bedinger
John Boyle
John Fowler
Matthew Lyon
Thomas Sandford
Matthew Walton

MARYLAND

SENATORS

Robert Wright [20]
Philip Reed [21]
Samuel Smith

REPRESENTATIVES

John Archer
John Campbell
Leonard Covington

---

[1] Elected December 2, 1805; March 18, 1806; and March 2, 1807.
[2] Reelected December 2, 1805.
[3] Reelected December 2, 1805.
[4] Resigned in 1805, before Congress assembled.
[5] Elected to fill vacancy caused by resignations of Calvin Goddard and Roger Griswold, and took his seat December 10, 1805.
[6] Resigned in 1805, before Congress assembled.
[7] Elected to fill vacancy caused by resignations of Calvin Goddard and Roger Griswold, and took his seat December 2, 1805.
[8] Resigned in August 1806.

[9] Elected to fill vacancy caused by resignation of John Cotton Smith, and took his seat December 1, 1806.
[10] Died March 19, 1806.
[11] Elected to fill vacancy caused by death of James Jackson, and took his seat December 11, 1806.
[12] Resigned in 1806.
[13] Elected to fill vacancy caused by resignation of Joseph Bryan, and took his seat December 26, 1806.
[14] Served until December 24, 1805; succeeded by Thomas Spalding, who contested his election.
[15] Successfully contested the election of Cowles Mead, and took his seat December 24, 1805; resigned in 1806.

[16] Elected to fill vacancy caused by resignation of Thomas Spalding, and took his seat January 26, 1807.
[17] Resigned August 7, 1805, to become Attorney General.
[18] Elected to fill vacancy caused by resignation of John Breckinridge, and took his seat December 9, 1805; resigned November 18, 1806.
[19] Elected to fill vacancy caused by resignation of John Adair, and took his seat December 29, 1806.
[20] Resigned in 1806.
[21] Elected to fill vacancy caused by resignation of Robert Wright, and took his seat December 29, 1806.

Joseph H. Nicholson [22]
Edward Lloyd [23]
Patrick Magruder
William McCreery
Nicholas R. Moore
Roger Nelson
Charles Goldsborough

MASSACHUSETTS

SENATORS

Timothy Pickering
John Quincy Adams

REPRESENTATIVES

Joseph Barker
Barnabas Bidwell
Phanuel Bishop
John Chandler
Orchard Cook
Jacob Crowninshield
Richard Cutts
William Ely
Isaiah L. Green
Seth Hastings
Jeremiah Nelson
Josiah Quincy
Ebenezer Seaver
William Stedman
Samuel Taggart
Joseph B. Varnum
Peleg Wadsworth

NEW HAMPSHIRE

SENATORS

William Plumer
Nicholas Gilman

REPRESENTATIVES

Silas Betton
Caleb Ellis
David Hough
Samuel Tenney
Thomas W. Thompson

NEW JERSEY

SENATORS

John Condit
Aaron Kitchell

REPRESENTATIVES

Ezra Darby
Ebenezer Elmer
William Helms
John Lambert
James Sloan
Henry Southard

NEW YORK

SENATORS

John Smith
Samuel L. Mitchill

REPRESENTATIVES

John Blake, Jr.
George Clinton, Jr. [24]
Silas Halsey
Henry W. Livingston
Josiah Masters
Gurdon S. Mumford [25]
John Russell
Peter Sailly
Thomas Sammons
Martin G. Schuneman
David Thomas
Uri Tracy
Philip Van Cortlandt
Killian K. Van Rensselaer
Daniel C. Verplanck
Eliphalet Wickes
Nathan Williams

NORTH CAROLINA

SENATORS

David Stone [26]
James Turner

REPRESENTATIVES

Nathaniel Alexander [27]
Evan S. Alexander [28]
Willis Alston
William Blackledge
Thomas Blount
James Holland
Thomas Kenan
Nathaniel Macon
Duncan McFarlan
Richard Stanford
Marmaduke Williams
Joseph Winston
Thomas Wynns

OHIO

SENATORS

John Smith
Thomas Worthington

REPRESENTATIVE

Jeremiah Morrow

PENNSYLVANIA

SENATORS

George Logan
Samuel Maclay

REPRESENTATIVES

Issac Anderson
David Bard
Robert Brown
Joseph Clay
Frederick Conrad
William Findley
Andrew Gregg
John Hamilton
John A. Hanna [29]
Robert Whitehill [30]
James Kelly
Michael Leib [31]
John Porter [32]
Christian Lower [33]
John B. C. Lucas [34]
Samuel Smith [35]
John Pugh
John Rea
Jacob Richards
John Smilie
John Whitehill

RHODE ISLAND

SENATORS

Benjamin Howland
James Fenner

REPRESENTATIVES

Nehemiah Knight
Joseph Stanton, Jr.

SOUTH CAROLINA

SENATORS

Thomas Sumter
John Gaillard

REPRESENTATIVES

William Butler
Levi Casey [36]
Elias Earle
Robert Marion
Thomas Moore
O'Brien Smith
David R. Williams
Richard Winn

TENNESSEE

SENATORS

Joseph Anderson
Daniel Smith

REPRESENTATIVES

George W. Campbell
William Dickson
John Rhea

---

[22] Resigned March 1, 1806.
[23] Elected to fill vacancy caused by resignation of Joseph H. Nicholson, and took his seat December 3 1806.
[24] Elected to fill vacancy caused by resignation of Representative-elect Samuel L. Mitchill in preceding Congress.
[25] Elected to fill vacancy caused by resignation of Representative-elect Daniel D. Tompkins, before the beginning of the congressional term, and took his seat December 2, 1805.
[26] Resigned about February 17, 1807.
[27] Resigned in November 1805, having been elected governor.
[28] Elected to fill vacancy caused by resignation of Nathaniel Alexander and took his seat February 24, 1806.
[29] Died July 23, 1805, before Congress assembled.
[30] Elected to fill vacancy caused by death of John A. Hanna, and took his seat December 2, 1805.
[31] Election unsuccessfully contested by John Douglas; resigned February 14, 1806.
[32] Elected to fill vacancy caused by resignation of Michael Leib, and took his seat December 8, 1806.
[33] Died December 19, 1806, never having qualified.
[34] Resigned before Congress assembled.
[35] Elected to fill vacancy caused by resignation of John B. C. Lucas, and took his seat December 2, 1805.
[36] Died February 3, 1807, before the commencement of the Tenth Congress, to which he had been reelected.

VERMONT

SENATORS

Stephen R. Bradley
Israel Smith

REPRESENTATIVES

Martin Chittenden
James Elliott
James Fisk
Gideon Olin

VIRGINIA

SENATORS

William B. Giles
Andrew Moore

REPRESENTATIVES

Burwell Bassett
John Claiborne
Christopher Clark [37]
William A. Burwell [38]
Matthew Clay
John Clopton
John Dawson
John W. Eppes
James M. Garnett
Peterson Goodwyn
Edwin Gray
David Holmes
John G. Jackson
Walter Jones
Joseph Lewis, Jr.
John Morrow
Thomas Newton, Jr.
John Randolph
Thomas M. Randolph
John Smith
Philip R. Thompson
Abram Trigg
Alexander Wilson

INDIANA TERRITORY [39]

DELEGATE

Benjamin Parke [40]

MISSISSIPPI TERRITORY

DELEGATE

William Lattimore

TERRITORY OF ORLEANS [41]

DELEGATE

Daniel Clark [42]

---

[37] Resigned July 1, 1806.
[38] Elected to fill vacancy caused by resignation of Christopher Clark, and took his seat December 1, 1806.
[39] Formed by act approved May 7, 1800, from a portion of lands of the Northwest Territory originally ceded to the United States by the State of Virginia, with seat of government at Vincennes.
[40] Took his seat December 12, 1805.
[41] Formed by act approved March 26, 1804, from a portion of lands ceded by France to the United States under the name of Louisiana by the treaty of Paris of April 30, 1803.
[42] Took his seat December 1, 1806.

TENTH CONGRESS

MARCH 4, 1807, TO MARCH 3, 1809

FIRST SESSION—*October 26, 1807, to April 25, 1808*
SECOND SESSION—*November 7, 1808, to March 3, 1809*

———

VICE PRESIDENT OF THE UNITED STATES—GEORGE CLINTON, of New York
PRESIDENT PRO TEMPORE OF THE SENATE—SAMUEL SMITH,[1] of Maryland; STEPHEN R. BRADLEY,[2] of Vermont; JOHN MILLEDGE,[3] of Georgia
SECRETARY OF THE SENATE—SAMUEL A. OTIS, of Massachusetts
SERGEANT AT ARMS OF THE SENATE—JAMES MATHERS, of New York

———

SPEAKER OF THE HOUSE OF REPRESENTATIVES—JOSEPH B. VARNUM,[4] of Massachusetts
CLERK OF THE HOUSE—JOHN BECKLEY, of Virginia; PATRICK MAGRUDER,[5] of Maryland
SERGEANT AT ARMS OF THE HOUSE—JOSEPH WHEATON, of Rhode Island; THOMAS DUNN,[6] of Maryland
DOORKEEPER OF THE HOUSE—THOMAS CLAXTON

CONNECTICUT

SENATORS

James Hillhouse, *New Haven*
Uriah Tracy,[7] *Litchfield*
Chauncey Goodrich,[8] *Hartford*

REPRESENTATIVES

Epaphroditus Champion, *East Haddam*
Samuel W. Dana, *Middlesex*
John Davenport, *Stamford*
Jonathan O. Moseley, *East Haddam*
Timothy Pitkin, *Farmington*
Lewis B. Sturges, *Fairfield*
Benjamin Tallmadge, *Litchfield*

DELAWARE

SENATORS

Samuel White, *Wilmington*
James A. Bayard, *Wilmington*

REPRESENTATIVE

James M. Broom,[9] *Wilmington*
Nicholas Van Dyke,[10] *New Castle*

GEORGIA

SENATORS

Abraham Baldwin,[11] *Augusta*

George Jones,[12] *Savannah*
William H. Crawford,[13] *Lexington*
John Milledge, *Augusta*

REPRESENTATIVES

William W. Bibb, *Petersburg*
Howell Cobb, *Louisville*
Dennis Smelt, *Savannah*
George M. Troup, *Dublin*

KENTUCKY

SENATORS

Buckner Thruston, *Lexington*
John Pope, *Springfield*

REPRESENTATIVES

John Boyle, *Lancaster*
Joseph Desha, *Mays Lick*
Benjamin Howard, *Lexington*
Richard M. Johnson, *Great Crossings*
Matthew Lyon, *Eddyville*
John Rowan, *Louisville*

MARYLAND

SENATORS

Samuel Smith, *Baltimore*
Philip Reed, *Chestertown*

REPRESENTATIVES

John Campbell, *Port Tobacco*
Charles Goldsborough, *Cambridge*
Philip B. Key,[14] *Rockville*
Edward Lloyd, *Wye Mills*
William McCreery,[15] *Reisterstown*
John Montgomery, *Bel Air*
Nicholas R. Moore, *Ruxton*
Roger Nelson, *Frederick*
Archibald Van Horne

MASSACHUSETTS

SENATORS

Timothy Pickering, *Wendham*
John Quincy Adams,[16] *Boston*
James Lloyd,[17] *Boston*

REPRESENTATIVES

Barnabas Bidwell,[18] *Stockbridge*
Ezekiel Bacon,[19] *Pittsfield*
Joseph Barker, *Middleboro*
John Chandler, *Monmouth*
Orchard Cook, *Wiscasset*
Jacob Crowninshield,[20] *Salem*
Joseph Story,[21] *Salem*
Richard Cutts, *Pepperelboro*
Josiah Dean, *Raynham*

---

[1] Elected April 16, 1808.
[2] Elected December 28, 1808.
[3] Elected January 30, 1809.
[4] Elected October 26, 1807.
[5] Elected October 26, 1807.
[6] Elected October 27, 1807.
[7] Died July 19, 1807.
[8] Elected to fill vacancy caused by death of Uriah Tracy, and took his seat November 27, 1807.
[9] Resigned before Congress assembled.
[10] Elected to fill vacancy caused by resignation of James M. Broom, and took his seat December 2, 1807.

[11] Died March 4, 1807.
[12] Appointed to fill vacancy caused by death of Abraham Baldwin, and took his seat October 26, 1807.
[13] Elected to fill vacancy caused by death of Abraham Baldwin, and took his seat December 9, 1807.
[14] Election was questioned upon the grounds that he was not a resident of the district from which elected and that he was a British pensioner; a resolution declaring him entitled to his seat was passed by a vote of 57 to 52, March 18, 1808.
[15] Election unsuccessfully contested by Joshua Barney.

[16] Resigned June 8, 1808.
[17] Elected to fill vacancy caused by resignation of John Quincy Adams, and took his seat November 7, 1808.
[18] Resigned July 13, 1807, before Congress assembled.
[19] Elected to fill vacancy caused by resignation of Barnabas Bidwell, and took his seat November 2, 1807.
[20] Died April 15, 1808.
[21] Elected to fill vacancy caused by death of Jacob Crowninshield, and took his seat December 20, 1808.

MASSACHUSETTS—Continued

REPRESENTATIVES—continued

William Ely, *Springfield*
Isaiah L. Green, *Barnstable*
Daniel Ilsley, *Falmouth*
Edward St. Loe Livermore, *Newburyport*
Josiah Quincy, *Boston*
Ebenezer Seaver, *Roxbury*
William Stedman, *Worcester*
Samuel Taggart, *Colerain*
Jabez Upham, *Brookfield*
Joseph B. Varnum, *Dracut*

NEW HAMPSHIRE

SENATORS

Nicholas Gilman, *Exeter*
Nahum Parker, *Fitzwilliam*

REPRESENTATIVES

Peter Carleton, *Landaff*
Daniel M. Durell, *Dover*
Francis Gardner, *Keene*
Jedediah K. Smith, *Amherst*
Clement Storer, *Portsmouth*

NEW JERSEY

SENATORS

John Condit, *Orange*
Aaron Kitchell, *Hanover*

REPRESENTATIVES

Ezra Darby,[22] *Scotch Plains*
Adam Boyd,[23] *Hackensack*
William Helms, *Hackettstown*
John Lambert, *Lambertville*
Thomas Newbold
James Sloan
Henry Southard, *Baskingridge*

NEW YORK

SENATORS

John Smith, *Mastic*
Samuel L. Mitchill, *New York City*

REPRESENTATIVES

John Blake, Jr., *Montgomery*
George Clinton, Jr., *New York City*
Barent Gardenier, *Kingston*
John Harris, *Aurelias*
Reuben Humphrey, *Marcellus*
William Kirkpatrick, *Salina*
Josiah Masters, *Schaghticoke*
Gurdon S. Mumford, *New York City*
Samuel Riker, *Newtown*
John Russell, *Cooperstown*
Peter Swart, *Schoharie*

David Thomas,[24] *Salem*
Nathan Wilson,[25] *Salem*
John Thompson, *Stillwater*
James I. Van Alen, *Kinderhook*
Philip Van Cortlandt, *Croton*
Killian K. Van Rensselaer, *Albany*
Daniel C. Verplanck, *Fishkill*

NORTH CAROLINA

SENATORS

James Turner, *Warrenton*
Jesse Franklin

REPRESENTATIVES

Evan S. Alexander, *Salisbury*
Willis Alston, *Greenville*
William Blackledge, *Spring Hill*
Thomas Blount, *Tarboro*
John Culpepper,[26] *Allenton*
Meshack Franklin
James Holland
Thomas Kenan, *Kenansville*
Nathaniel Macon, *Warrenton*
Lemuel Sawyer, *Elizabeth City*
Richard Stanford, *Hawfields*
Marmaduke Williams

OHIO

SENATORS

John Smith,[27] *Columbia*
Return J. Meigs, Jr,[28] *Marietta*
Edward Tiffin,[29] *Chillicothe*

REPRESENTATIVE

Jeremiah Morrow, *Montgomery*

PENNSYLVANIA

SENATORS

Samuel Maclay,[30] *Lewisburg*
Michael Leib,[31] *Philadelphia*
Andrew Gregg, *Pennvalley*

REPRESENTATIVES

David Bard, *Frankstown*
Robert Brown, *Weaversville*
Joseph Clay,[32] *Philadelphia*
Benjamin Say,[33] *Philadelphia*
William Findley, *Youngstown*
John Hiester, *Parker Ford*
William Hoge, *Washington*
Robert Jenkins, *Churchtown*
James Kelly, *Philadelphia*
William Milnor, *Philadelphia*
John Porter, *Philadelphia*
John Pugh, *Doylestown*
John Rea, *Chambersburg*

Jacob Richards, *Chester*
Matthias Richards, *Pottstown*
John Smilie, *Fayette*
Samuel Smith, *Erie*
Robert Whitehill, *Camp Hill*
Daniel Montgomery, Jr.

RHODE ISLAND

SENATORS

Benjamin Howland, *Tiverton*
James Fenner,[34] *Providence*
Elisha Mathewson,[35] *Scituate*

REPRESENTATIVES

Nehemiah Knight,[36] *Cranston*
Richard Jackson, Jr.,[37] *Providence*
Isaac Wilbour, *Little Compton*

SOUTH CAROLINA

SENATORS

Thomas Sumter, *Stateburg*
John Gaillard, *Charleston*

REPRESENTATIVES

Lemuel J. Alston, *Greenville*
William Butler, *Saluda*
Joseph Calhoun,[38] *Calhoun Mills*
Robert Marion, *Charleston*
Thomas Moore, *Prices Store*
John Taylor, *Columbia*
David R. Williams, *Society Hill*
Richard Winn, *Winnsboro*

TENNESSEE

SENATORS

Joseph Anderson
Daniel Smith, *Hendersonville*

REPRESENTATIVES

George W. Campbell, *Nashville*
John Rhea, *Sullivan*
Jesse Wharton, *Nashville*

VERMONT

SENATORS

Stephen R. Bradley, *Westminster*
Israel Smith,[39] *Rutland*
Jonathan Robinson,[40] *Bennington*

REPRESENTATIVES

Martin Chittenden, *Williston*
James Elliott, *Brattleboro*
James Fisk, *Barre*
James Witherell,[41] *Fair Haven*
Samuel Shaw,[42] *Castleton*

---

[22] Died January 28, 1808.
[23] Elected to fill vacancy caused by death of Ezra Darby, and took his seat April 1, 1808.
[24] Resigned May 1, 1808.
[25] Elected to fill vacancy caused by resignation of David Thomas, and took his seat November 7, 1808.
[26] Election contested by Duncan McFarland; the House on January 2, 1808, declared the seat vacant on account of irregularities; subsequently elected, and took his seat February 23, 1808.
[27] Tried by Senate for complicity with Aaron Burr; but resolution of expulsion negatived April 9, 1808; resigned April 25, 1808. (See Senate Election Cases, edition 1903, pp. 934–948.)

[28] Elected to fill vacancy caused by resignation of John Smith, and took his seat January 6, 1809.
[29] Resigned March 3, 1809.
[30] Resigned January 4, 1809.
[31] Elected to fill vacancy caused by resignation of Samuel Maclay, and took his seat January 19, 1809.
[32] Resigned in 1808.
[33] Elected to fill vacancy caused by resignation of Joseph Clay, and took his seat November 16, 1808.
[34] Resigned in September 1807, having been elected governor.
[35] Elected to fill vacancy caused by resignation of James Fenner, and took his seat November 20, 1807.

[36] Died June 13, 1808.
[37] Elected to fill vacancy caused by death of Nehemiah Knight, and took his seat November 11, 1808.
[38] Elected to fill vacancy caused by death of Representative-elect Levi Casey, in preceding Congress, and took his seat October 26, 1807.
[39] Resigned October 1, 1807, having been elected governor.
[40] Elected to fill vacancy caused by resignation of Israel Smith, and took his seat October 26, 1807.
[41] Resigned May 1, 1808.
[42] Elected to fill vacancy caused by resignation of James Witherell, and took his seat November 8, 1808.

VIRGINIA

SENATORS

William B. Giles, *Ladore*
Andrew Moore, *Lexington*

REPRESENTATIVES

Burwell Bassett, *Williamsburg*
William A. Burwell, *Rocky Mount*
John Claiborne,[43] *Brunswick*
Thomas Gholson, Jr.,[44] *Brunswick*
Matthew Clay, *Halifax*
John Clopton, *Tunstall*
John Dawson
John W. Eppes, *Charles City*
James M. Garnett, *Loretto*
Peterson Goodwyn, *Petersburg*
Edwin Gray
David Holmes, *Winchester*
John G. Jackson, *Clarksburg*
Walter Jones
Joseph Lewis, Jr., *Upperville*
John Love, *Alexandria*
John Morrow
Thomas Newton, Jr., *Norfolk*
Wilson C. Nicholas, *Charlottesville*
John Randolph, *Charlotte*
John Smith
Abram Trigg, *Christiansburg*
Alexander Wilson

INDIANA TERRITORY

DELEGATE

Benjamin Parke,[45] *Vincennes*
Jesse B. Thomas,[46] *Lawrenceburg*

MISSISSIPPI TERRITORY

DELEGATE

George Poindexter, *Woodville*

TERRITORY OF ORLEANS

DELEGATE

Daniel Clark, *New Orleans*

---

[43] Died October 9, 1808.
[44] Elected to fill vacancy caused by death of John Claiborne, and took his seat November 7, 1808.
[45] Resigned March 1, 1808.
[46] Elected to fill vacancy caused by resignation of Benjamin Parke, and took his seat December 1, 1808.

ELEVENTH CONGRESS

MARCH 4, 1809, TO MARCH 3, 1811

FIRST SESSION—*May 22, 1809, to June 28, 1809*

SECOND SESSION—*November 27, 1809, to May 1, 1810*

THIRD SESSION—*December 3, 1810, to March 3, 1811*

SPECIAL SESSION OF THE SENATE—*March 4, 1809, to March 7, 1809*

———

VICE PRESIDENT OF THE UNITED STATES—GEORGE CLINTON, of New York

PRESIDENT PRO TEMPORE OF THE SENATE—ANDREW GREGG,[1] of Pennsylvania; JOHN GAILLARD,[2] of South Carolina; JOHN POPE,[3] of Kentucky

SECRETARY OF THE SENATE—SAMUEL A. OTIS, of Massachusetts

SERGEANT AT ARMS OF THE SENATE—JAMES MATHERS, of New York

———

SPEAKER OF THE HOUSE OF REPRESENTATIVES—JOSEPH B. VARNUM,[4] of Massachusetts

CLERK OF THE HOUSE—PATRICK MAGRUDER,[5] of Maryland

SERGEANT AT ARMS OF THE HOUSE—THOMAS DUNN, of Maryland

DOORKEEPER OF THE HOUSE—THOMAS CLAXTON

CONNECTICUT

SENATORS

James Hillhouse,[6] *New Haven*
Samuel W. Dana,[7] *Middlesex*
Chauncey Goodrich, *Hartford*

REPRESENTATIVES

Epaphroditus Champion, *East Haddam*
Samuel W. Dana,[8] *Middlesex*
Ebenezer Huntington,[9] *Norwich*
John Davenport, *Stamford*
Jonathan O. Moseley, *East Haddam*
Timothy Pitkin, *Farmington*
Lewis B. Sturges, *Fairfield*
Benjamin Tallmadge, *Litchfield*

DELAWARE

SENATORS

Samuel White,[10] *Wilmington*
Outerbridge Horsey,[11] *Wilmington*
James A Bayard, *Wilmington*

REPRESENTATIVE

Nicholas Van Dyke, *New Castle*

GEORGIA

SENATORS

John Milledge,[12] *Augusta*
Charles Tait,[13] *Elbert*
William H. Crawford, *Lexington*

REPRESENTATIVES

William W. Bibb, *Petersburg*
Howell Cobb, *Louisville*
Dennis Smelt, *Savannah*
George M. Troup, *Dublin*

KENTUCKY

SENATORS

Buckner Thruston,[14] *Lexington*
Henry Clay,[15] *Lexington*
John Pope, *Springfield*

REPRESENTATIVES

Benjamin Howard,[16] *Lexington*
William T. Barry,[17] *Lexington*
Henry Crist, *Shepherdsville*
Joseph Desha, *Mays Lick*
Richard M. Johnson, *Great Crossings*
Matthew Lyon, *Eddyville*
Samuel McKee, *Lancaster*

MARYLAND

SENATORS

Samuel Smith,[18] *Baltimore*
Philip Reed, *Chestertown*

REPRESENTATIVES

John Brown,[19] *Centerville*
Robert Wright,[20] *Queenstown*
John Campbell, *Port Tobacco*
Charles Goldsborough, *Cambridge*
Philip B. Key, *Rockville*
Alexander McKim, *Baltimore*

---

[1] Elected June 26, 1809.
[2] Elected February 28, 1810; reelected April 17, 1810.
[3] Elected February 23, 1811.
[4] Reelected May 22, 1809.
[5] Reelected May 22, 1809.
[6] Resigned June 10, 1810.
[7] Elected to fill vacancy caused by resignation of James Hillhouse, and took his seat December 4, 1810.
[8] Resigned in May, 1810, having been elected Senator.
[9] Elected to fill vacancy caused by resignation of Samuel W. Dana, and took his seat December 3, 1810.

[10] Died November 4, 1809.
[11] Elected to fill vacancy caused by death of Samuel White, and took his seat January 29, 1810.
[12] Resigned November 14, 1809.
[13] Elected to fill vacancy caused by resignation of John Milledge, and took his seat December 28, 1809.
[14] Resigned December 18, 1809.
[15] Elected to fill vacancy caused by resignation of Buckner Thruston, and took his seat February 5, 1810.
[16] Resigned April 10, 1810, to become governor of Upper Louisiana.

[17] Elected to fill vacancy caused by resignation of Benjamin Howard, and took his seat December 13, 1810.
[18] Appointed and subsequently reelected for the term beginning March 4, 1809.
[19] Resigned in 1810, before the commencement of the Twelfth Congress, to which he had been reelected.
[20] Elected to fill vacancy caused by resignation of John Brown, and took his seat December 3, 1810.

John Montgomery, *Bel Air*
Nicholas R. Moore, *Ruxton*
Roger Nelson,[21] *Frederick*
Samuel Ringgold,[22] *Hagerstown*
Archibald Van Horne

MASSACHUSETTS

SENATORS

Timothy Pickering, *Wendham*
James Lloyd, *Boston*

REPRESENTATIVES

Ezekiel Bacon, *Pittsfield*
William Baylies,[23] *Bridgewater*
Charles Turner, Jr.,[24] *Scituate*
Orchard Cook, *Wiscasset*
Richard Cutts, *Pepperelboro*
William Ely, *Springfield*
Gideon Gardner, *Nantucket*
Barzillai Gannett, *Gardiner*
Edward St. Loe Livermore, *Newburyport*
Benjamin Pickman, Jr., *Salem*
Josiah Quincy, *Boston*
Ebenezer Seaver, *Roxbury*
William Stedman,[25] *Worcester*
Abijah Bigelow,[26] *Leominster*
Samuel Taggart, *Colerain*
Jabez Upham,[27] *Brookfield*
Joseph Allen,[28] *Worcester*
Joseph B. Varnum, *Dracut*
Laban Wheaton, *Easton*
Ezekiel Whitman, *Portland*

NEW HAMPSHIRE

SENATORS

Nicholas Gilman, *Exeter*
Nahum Parker,[29] *Fitzwilliam*
Charles Cutts,[30] *Portsmouth*

REPRESENTATIVES

Daniel Blaisdell, *Canaan*
John C. Chamberlain, *Charlestown*
William Hale, *Dover*
Nathaniel A. Haven, *Portsmouth*
James Wilson, *Peterboro*

NEW JERSEY

SENATORS

Aaron Kitchell,[31] *Hanover*
John Condit,[32] *Orange*
John Lambert, *Lambertville*

REPRESENTATIVES

Adam Boyd, *Hackensack*
James Cox,[33] *Monmouth*
John A. Scudder,[34] *Monmouth*
William Helms, *Hackettstown*
Thomas Newbold
Henry Southard, *Baskingridge*
Jacob Hufty, *Salem*

NEW YORK

SENATORS

John Smith, *Mastic*
Obadiah German, *Norwich*

REPRESENTATIVES

William Denning,[35] *New York City*
Samuel L. Mitchill,[36] *New York City*
James Emott, *Albany*
Jonathan Fisk, *Newburgh*
Barent Gardenier, *Kingston*
Thomas R. Gold, *Whitestown*
Herman Knickerbocker, *Schaghticoke*
Robert Le Roy Livingston, *Hudson*
Vincent Mathews, *Elmira*
Gurdon S. Mumford, *New York City*
John Nicholson, *Herkimer*
Peter B. Porter, *Buffalo*
Erastus Root, *Delhi*
Ebenezer Sage, *Sag Harbor*
Thomas Sammons, *Johnstown*
John Thompson, *Stillwater*
Uri Tracy, *Oxford*
Killian K. Van Rensselaer, *Albany*

NORTH CAROLINA

SENATORS

James Turner, *Warrenton*
Jesse Franklin

REPRESENTATIVES

Willis Alston, *Greenville*
James Cochran, *Roxboro*
Meshack Franklin
James Holland
Thomas Kenan, *Kenansville*
William Kennedy, *Washington*
Nathaniel Macon, *Warrenton*
Archibald McBryde, *Carthage*
Joseph Pearson, *Salisbury*
Lemuel Sawyer, *Elizabeth City*
Richard Stanford, *Hawfields*
John Stanly, *New Bern*

OHIO

SENATORS

Return J. Meigs, Jr.,[37] *Marietta*
Thomas Worthington,[38] *Chillicothe*
Stanley Griswold [39]
Alexander Campbell,[40] *Ripley*

REPRESENTATIVE

Jeremiah Morrow, *Montgomery*

PENNSYLVANIA

SENATORS

Andrew Gregg, *Pennvalley*
Michael Leib, *Philadelphia*

REPRESENTATIVES

William Anderson, *Chester*
David Bard, *Frankstown*
Robert Brown, *Weaversville*
William Crawford, *Gettysburg*
William Findley, *Youngstown*
Daniel Hiester, *West Chester*
Robert Jenkins, *Churchtown*
Aaron Lyle, *West Middletown*
William Milnor, *Philadephia*
John Porter, *Philadelphia*
John Rea, *Chambersburg*
Matthias Richards, *Pottstown*
John Ross, *Easton*
Benjamin Say,[41] *Philadelphia*
Adam Seybert,[42] *Philadelphia*
John Smilie, *Fayette*
George Smith
Samuel Smith, *Erie*
Robert Whitehill, *Camp Hill*

RHODE ISLAND

SENATORS

Elisha Mathewson, *Scituate*
Francis Malbone,[43] *Newport*
Christopher G. Champlin,[44] *Newport*

REPRESENTATIVES

Richard Jackson, Jr., *Providence*
Elisha R. Potter, *Kingston*

SOUTH CAROLINA

SENATORS

Thomas Sumter,[45] *Stateburg*
John Taylor,[46] *Columbia*
John Gaillard, *Charleston*

---

[21] Resigned May 14, 1810.
[22] Elected to fill vacancy caused by resignation of Roger Nelson, and took his seat December 7, 1810.
[23] Served until June 28, 1809; succeeded by Charles Turner, Jr., who contested his election.
[24] Successfully contested the election of William Baylies, and took his seat June 28, 1809.
[25] Resigned July 16, 1810.
[26] Elected to fill vacancy caused by resignation of William Stedman, and took his seat December 14, 1810.
[27] Resigned in 1810.
[28] Elected to fill vacancy caused by resignation of Jabez Upham, and took his seat December 13, 1810.
[29] Resigned June 1, 1810.
[30] Elected to fill vacancy caused by resignation of

Nahum Parker, and took his seat December 4, 1810.
[31] Resigned March 12, 1809.
[32] Appointed to fill vacancy caused by resignation of Aaron Kitchell, and took his seat May 24, 1809; subsequently elected.
[33] Died September 12, 1810.
[34] Elected to fill vacancy caused by death of James Cox, and took his seat December 3, 1810.
[35] Resigned before qualifying.
[36] Elected to fill vacancy caused by resignation of William Denning, and took his seat December 4, 1810.
[37] Resigned May 1, 1810.
[38] Elected to fill vacancy caused by resignation of Return J. Meigs, Jr., and took his seat January 8, 1811.

[39] Appointed to fill vacancy caused by resignation of Edward Tiffin, in preceding Congress, and took his seat June 2, 1809.
[40] Elected to fill vacancy caused by resignation of Edward Tiffin, and took his seat January 12, 1810.
[41] Resigned June, 1809.
[42] Elected to fill vacancy caused by resignation of Benjamin Say, and took his seat November 27, 1809.
[43] Died June 4, 1809.
[44] Elected to fill vacancy caused by death of Francis Malbone, and took his seat January 12, 1810.
[45] Resigned December 16, 1810.
[46] Elected on December 19, 1810, to fill vacancy caused by resignation of Thomas Sumter, and took his seat December 31, 1810.

SOUTH CAROLINA—Continued

REPRESENTATIVES

Lemuel J. Alston, *Greenville*
William Butler, *Saluda*
Joseph Calhoun, *Calhoun Mills*
Robert Marion,[47] *Charleston*
Langdon Cheves,[48] *Charleston*
Thomas Moore, *Prices Store*
John Taylor,[49] *Columbia*
Richard Winn, *Winnsboro*
Robert Witherspoon, *Mayesville*

TENNESSEE

SENATORS

Joseph Anderson [50]
Daniel Smith,[51] *Hendersonville*
Jenkin Whiteside,[52] *Knoxville*

REPRESENTATIVES

Pleasant M. Miller, *Knoxville*
John Rhea, *Sullivan*
Robert Weakley, *Nashville*

VERMONT

SENATORS

Stephen R. Bradley, *Westminster*
Jonathan Robinson, *Bennington*

REPRESENTATIVES

William Chamberlain, *Peacham*
Martin Chittenden, *Williston*
Jonathan H. Hubbard, *Windsor*
Samuel Shaw, *Castleton*

VIRGINIA

SENATORS

William B. Giles, *Ladore*
Richard Brent, *Aquia*

REPRESENTATIVES

Burwell Bassett, *Williamsburg*
James Breckinridge, *Fincastle*
William A. Burwell, *Rocky Mount*
Matthew Clay, *Halifax*
John Clopton, *Tunstall*
John G. Jackson,[53] *Clarksburg*
William McKinley [54]
John Dawson
John W. Eppes, *Charles City*
Thomas Gholson, Jr., *Brunswick*
Peterson Goodwyn, *Petersburg*
Edwin Gray
Walter Jones
Joseph Lewis, Jr., *Upperville*
John Love, *Alexandria*

Thomas Newton, Jr., *Norfolk*
Wilson C. Nicholas,[55] *Charlottesville*
David S. Garland,[56] *Clifford*
John Randolph, *Charlotte*
John Roane, *Uppowac*
Daniel Sheffey, *Wythe*
John Smith
James Stephenson, *Martinsburg*
Jacob Swoope

INDIANA TERRITORY

DELEGATE

Jonathan Jennings,[57] *Charlestown*

MISSISSIPPI TERRITORY

DELEGATE

George Poindexter, *Woodville*

TERRITORY OF ORLEANS

DELEGATE

Julien de L. Poydras, *New Orleans*

---

[47] Resigned December 4, 1810.
[48] Elected to fill vacancy caused by resignation of Robert Marion, and took his seat January 24, 1811.
[49] Resigned December 30, 1810, having been elected Senator.
[50] Appointed to fill vacancy in term commencing March 4, 1809, caused by failure of legislature to elect; subsequently elected, and took his seat May 22, 1809.
[51] Resigned March 31, 1809.
[52] Elected to fill vacancy caused by resignation of Daniel Smith, and took his seat May 26, 1809.
[53] Resigned September 28, 1810.
[54] Elected to fill vacancy caused by resignation of John G. Jackson, and took his seat December 21, 1810.
[55] Resigned November 27, 1809.
[56] Elected to fill vacancy caused by resignation of Wilson C. Nicholas, and took his seat January 17, 1810.
[57] Took his seat November 27, 1809; election unsuccessfully contested by Thomas Randolph.

TWELFTH CONGRESS

MARCH 4, 1811, TO MARCH 3, 1813

FIRST SESSION—*November 4, 1811, to July 6, 1812*
SECOND SESSION—*November 2, 1812, to March 3, 1813*

———

VICE PRESIDENT OF THE UNITED STATES—GEORGE CLINTON,[1] of New York
PRESIDENT PRO TEMPORE OF THE SENATE—WILLIAM H. CRAWFORD,[2] of Georgia
SECRETARY OF THE SENATE—SAMUEL A. OTIS, of Massachusetts
SERGEANT AT ARMS OF THE SENATE—JAMES MATHERS,[3] of New York; MOUNTJOY BAYLY,[4] of Maryland

———

SPEAKER OF THE HOUSE OF REPRESENTATIVES—HENRY CLAY,[5] of Kentucky
CLERK OF THE HOUSE—PATRICK MAGRUDER,[6] of Maryland
SERGEANT AT ARMS OF THE HOUSE—THOMAS DUNN, of Maryland
DOORKEEPER OF THE HOUSE—THOMAS CLAXTON

CONNECTICUT

SENATORS

Chauncey Goodrich, *Hartford*
Samuel W. Dana, *Middlesex*

REPRESENTATIVES

Epaphroditus Champion, *East Haddam*
John Davenport, *Stamford*
Lyman Law, *New London*
Jonathan O. Moseley, *East Haddam*
Timothy Pitkin, *Farmington*
Lewis B. Sturges, *Fairfield*
Benjamin Tallmadge, *Litchfield*

DELAWARE

SENATORS

James A. Bayard,[7] *Wilmington*
Outerbridge Horsey, *Wilmington*

REPRESENTATIVE

Henry M. Ridgely, *Dover*

GEORGIA

SENATORS

William H. Crawford, *Lexington*
Charles Tait, *Elbert*

REPRESENTATIVES

William W. Bibb, *Petersburg*
Howell Cobb,[8] *Louisville*
William Barnett,[9] *Washington*
Bolling Hall, *Milledgeville*
George M. Troup, *Dublin*

KENTUCKY

SENATORS

John Pope, *Springfield*
George M. Bibb, *Lexington*

REPRESENTATIVES

Henry Clay, *Lexington*
Joseph Desha, *Mays Lick*
Richard M. Johnson, *Great Crossings*
Samuel McKee, *Lancaster*
Anthony New, *Elkton*
Stephen Ormsby, *Louisville*

LOUISIANA [10]

SENATORS

Allan B. Magruder,[11] *Opelousas*
John N. Destréhan,[12] *Destrehan*
Thomas Posey,[13] *Attakapas*
James Brown,[14] *New Orleans*

REPRESENTATIVE

Thomas B. Robertson,[15] *New Orleans*

MARYLAND

SENATORS

Samuel Smith, *Baltimore*
Philip Reed, *Chestertown*

REPRESENTATIVES

Charles Goldsborough, *Cambridge*
Joseph Kent, *Bladensburg*
Philip B. Key, *Rockville*
Peter Little, *Baltimore*
Alexander McKim, *Baltimore*
John Montgomery,[16] *Bel Air*
Stevenson Archer,[17] *Bel Air*

---

[1] Died April 20, 1812.
[2] Elected March 24, 1812.
[3] Died September 2, 1811.
[4] Elected November 6, 1811.
[5] Elected November 4, 1811.
[6] Reelected November 4, 1811.
[7] Resigned March 3, 1813.
[8] Resigned in 1812.
[9] Elected to fill vacancy caused by resignation of Howell Cobb, and took his seat November 27, 1812.

[10] Admitted as a State into the Union April 30, 1812; formerly known as "Territory of Orleans."
[11] Took his seat November 18, 1812; term to expire, as determined by lot, March 3, 1813.
[12] Resigned October 1, 1812, never having qualified.
[13] Appointed to fill vacancy caused by resignation of John N. Destréhan, and took his seat December 7, 1812; term to expire, as determined by lot, March 3, 1817.

[14] Elected to fill vacancy caused by resignation of John N. Destréhan, and took his seat February 5, 1813.
[15] Took his seat December 23, 1812.
[16] Resigned April 29, 1811, before Congress assembled.
[17] Elected to fill vacancy caused by resignation of John Montgomery, and took his seat November 4, 1811.

MARYLAND—Continued

REPRESENTATIVES—continued

Samuel Ringgold, *Hagerstown*
Philip Stuart, *Port Tobacco*
Robert Wright,[18] *Queenstown*

MASSACHUSETTS

SENATORS

James Lloyd, *Boston*
Joseph B. Varnum,[19] *Dracut*

REPRESENTATIVES

Ezekiel Bacon, *Pittsfield*
Abijah Bigelow, *Leominster*
Elijah Brigham, *Westboro*
Richard Cutts, *Pepperelboro*
William Ely, *Springfield*
Barzillai Gannett,[20] *Gardiner*
Francis Carr,[21] *Orrington*
Isaiah L. Green, *Barnstable*
Josiah Quincy, *Boston*
William Reed, *Marblehead*
Ebenezer Seaver, *Roxbury*
Samuel Taggart, *Colerain*
Peleg Tallman, *Bath*
Charles Turner, Jr., *Scituate*
Joseph B. Varnum,[22] *Dracut*
William M. Richardson,[23] *Groton*
Laban Wheaton, *Easton*
Leonard White, *Haverhill*
William Widgery, *Portland*

NEW HAMPSHIRE

SENATORS

Nicholas Gilman, *Exeter*
Charles Cutts, *Portsmouth*

REPRESENTATIVES

Josiah Bartlett, Jr., *Stratham*
Samuel Dinsmoor, *Keene*
Obed Hall, *Bartlett*
John A. Harper, *Meredith Bridge*
George Sullivan, *Exeter*

NEW JERSEY

SENATORS

John Lambert, *Lambertville*
John Condit, *Orange*

REPRESENTATIVES

Adam Boyd, *Hackensack*
Lewis Condict, *Morristown*
Jacob Hufty, *Salem*
George C. Maxwell, *Raritan*
James Morgan, *South Amboy*
Thomas Newbold

NEW YORK

SENATORS

John Smith, *Mastic*
Obadiah German, *Norwich*

REPRESENTATIVES

Daniel Avery, *Aurora*
Harmanus Bleecker, *Albany*
Thomas B. Cooke, *Catskill*
James Emott, *Albany*
Asa Fitch, *Salem*
Thomas R. Gold, *Whitestown*
Robert Le Roy Livingston,[24] *Hudson*
Thomas P. Grosvenor,[25] *Hudson*
Arunah Metcalf, *Otsego*
Samuel L. Mitchill, *New York City*
William Paulding, Jr., *New York City*
Benjamin Pond, *Schroon*
Peter B. Porter, *Buffalo*
Ebenezer Sage, *Sag Harbor*
Thomas Sammons, *Johnstown*
Silas Stow, *Lowville*
Uri Tracy, *Oxford*
Pierre Van Cortlandt, Jr., *Peekskill*

NORTH CAROLINA

SENATORS

James Turner, *Warrenton*
Jesse Franklin

REPRESENTATIVES

Willis Alston, *Greenville*
William Blackledge, *Spring Hill*
Thomas Blount,[26] *Tarboro*
William Kennedy,[27] *Washington*
James Cochran, *Roxboro*
Meshack Franklin
William R. King, *Wilmington*
Nathaniel Macon, *Warrenton*
Archibald McBryde, *Carthage*
Joseph Pearson, *Salisbury*
Israel Pickens, *Morgantown*
Lemuel Sawyer, *Elizabeth City*
Richard Stanford, *Hawfields*

OHIO

SENATORS

Alexander Campbell, *Ripley*
Thomas Worthington, *Chillicothe*

REPRESENTATIVE

Jeremiah Morrow, *Montgomery*

PENNSYLVANIA

SENATORS

Andrew Gregg, *Pennvalley*
Michael Leib, *Philadelphia*

REPRESENTATIVES

William Anderson, *Chester*
David Bard, *Frankstown*
Robert Brown, *Weaversville*
William Crawford, *Gettysburg*
Roger Davis, *Charlestown*
William Findley, *Youngstown*
John M. Hyneman, *Reading*
Abner Lacock,[28] *Beavertown*
Joseph Lefever, *Paradise*
Aaron Lyle, *West Middletown*
James Milnor, *Philadelphia*
William Piper, *Bloodyrun*
Jonathan Roberts, *Norristown*
William Rodman, *Bristol*
Adam Seybert, *Philadelphia*
John Smilie,[29] *Fayette*
George Smith
Robert Whitehill, *Camp Hill*

RHODE ISLAND

SENATORS

Christopher G. Champlin,[30] *Newport*
William Hunter,[31] *Newport*
Jeremiah B. Howell, *Providence*

REPRESENTATIVES

Richard Jackson, Jr., *Providence*
Elisha R. Potter, *Kingston*

SOUTH CAROLINA

SENATORS

John Gaillard, *Charleston*
John Taylor, *Columbia*

REPRESENTATIVES

William Butler, *Saluda*
John C. Calhoun, *Willington*
Langdon Cheves, *Charleston*
Elias Earle, *Centerville*
William Lowndes, *Jacksonboro*
Thomas Moore, *Prices Store*
David R. Williams, *Society Hill*
Richard Winn, *Winnsboro*

TENNESSEE

SENATORS

Joseph Anderson
Jenkin Whiteside,[32] *Knoxville*
George W. Campbell,[33] *Nashville*

---

[18] Elected to fill vacancy caused by resignation of Representative-elect John Brown, in preceding Congress.
[19] Elected to fill vacancy in the term beginning March 4, 1811, caused by failure of legislature to elect, and took his seat November 4, 1811; vacancy in this class from March 4, 1811, to June 7, 1811.
[20] Resigned in 1812, never having qualified.
[21] Elected to fill vacancy caused by failure of Barzillai Gannett to qualify; took his seat June 3, 1812.
[22] Resigned June 29, 1811, before Congress assembled, having been elected Senator.

[23] Elected to fill vacancy caused by resignation of Joseph B. Varnum, and took his seat January 22, 1812.
[24] Resigned May 6, 1812.
[25] Elected to fill vacancy caused by resignation of Robert Le Roy Livingston, and took his seat January 29, 1813.
[26] Died February 7, 1812.
[27] Elected to fill vacancy caused by death of Thomas Blount, and took his seat January 30, 1813.
[28] Reelected to the Thirteenth Congress, but resigned, having been elected Senator.

[29] Died December 30, 1812, before the commencement of the Thirteenth Congress, to which he had been reelected.
[30] Resigned October 2, 1811.
[31] Elected to fill vacancy caused by resignation of Christopher G. Champlin, and took his seat November 25, 1811.
[32] Resigned October 8, 1811.
[33] Elected to fill vacancy caused by resignation of Jenkin Whiteside, and took his seat November 4, 1811.

REPRESENTATIVES

Felix Grundy, *Nashville*
John Sevier, *Knoxville*
John Rhea, *Sullivan*

VERMONT

SENATORS

Stephen R. Bradley, *Westminster*
Jonathan Robinson, *Bennington*

REPRESENTATIVES

Martin Chittenden, *Williston*
James Fisk, *Barre*
Samuel Shaw, *Castleton*
William Strong, *Hartford*

VIRGINIA

SENATORS

William B. Giles, *Lodore*
Richard Brent, *Aquia*

REPRESENTATIVES

Burwell Bassett, *Williamsburg*
James Breckinridge, *Fincastle*
William A. Burwell, *Rocky Mount*
Matthew Clay, *Halifax*
John Clopton, *Tunstall*
John Dawson
Thomas Gholson, Jr., *Brunswick*
Peterson Goodwyn, *Petersburg*
Edwin Gray
Aylett Hawes, *Woodville*
John P. Hungerford,[34] *Leedstown*
John Taliaferro,[35] *Fredericksburg*
John Baker, *Shepherdstown*
Joseph Lewis, Jr., *Upperville*
William McCoy, *Franklin*
Hugh Nelson, *Milton*
Thomas Newton, Jr., *Norfolk*
James Pleasants, *Goochland*
John Randolph, *Charlotte*
John Roane, *Uppowac*
Daniel Sheffey, *Wythe*
John Smith
Thomas Wilson, *Morgantown*

ILLINOIS TERRITORY [36]

DELEGATE

Shadrack Bond,[37] *Kaskaskia*

INDIANA TERRITORY

DELEGATE

Jonathan Jennings, *Charlestown*

MISSISSIPPI TERRITORY

DELEGATE

George Poindexter, *Woodville*

TERRITORY OF MISSOURI [38]

DELEGATE

Edward Hempstead,[39] *St. Louis*

TERRITORY OF ORLEANS [40]

DELEGATE

Vacant [41]

---

[34] Served until November 29, 1811; succeeded by John Taliaferro, who contested his election.
[35] Successfully contested the election of John P. Hungerford, and took his seat December 2, 1811.
[36] Formed by act approved February 3, 1809, from a portion of Indiana Territory and from lands originally ceded to the United States by the State of Virginia, and granted a Delegate in Congress.

[37] Took his seat December 3, 1812.
[38] Formed by the act approved June 4, 1812, from lands ceded by France to the United States by the treaty of Paris of April 30, 1803, theretofore known as the "District of Louisiana," and granted a Delegate in Congress.

[39] Took his seat January 4, 1813.
[40] Granted statehood April 30, 1812, as the State of Louisiana.
[41] Allen B. Magruder and Elegius Fromentin, agents, were accorded the privilege of the floor March 6, 1812.

THIRTEENTH CONGRESS

MARCH 4, 1813, TO MARCH 3, 1815

FIRST SESSION—*May 24, 1813, to August 2, 1813*
SECOND SESSION—*December 6, 1813, to April 18, 1814*
THIRD SESSION—*September 19, 1814, to March 3, 1815*

———

VICE PRESIDENT OF THE UNITED STATES—ELBRIDGE GERRY,[1] of Massachusetts
PRESIDENT PRO TEMPORE OF THE SENATE—JOSEPH B. VARNUM,[2] of Massachusetts; JOHN GAILLARD,[3] of South Carolina
SECRETARY OF THE SENATE—SAMUEL A. OTIS,[4] of Massachusetts; CHARLES CUTTS,[5] of New Hampshire
SERGEANT AT ARMS OF THE SENATE—MOUNTJOY BAYLY, of Maryland

———

SPEAKER OF THE HOUSE OF REPRESENTATIVES—HENRY CLAY,[6] of Kentucky; LANGDON CHEVES,[7] of South Carolina
CLERK OF THE HOUSE—PATRICK MAGRUDER,[8] of Maryland; THOMAS DOUGHERTY,[9] of Kentucky
SERGEANT AT ARMS OF THE HOUSE—THOMAS DUNN, of Maryland
DOORKEEPER OF THE HOUSE—THOMAS CLAXTON

CONNECTICUT

SENATORS

Chauncey Goodrich,[10] *Hartford*
David Daggett,[11] *New Haven*
Samuel W. Dana, *Middlesex*

REPRESENTATIVES

Epaphroditus Champion, *East Haddam*
John Davenport, *Stamford*
Lyman Law, *New London*
Jonathan O. Moseley, *East Haddam*
Timothy Pitkin, *Farmington*
Lewis B. Sturges, *Fairfield*
Benjamin Tallmadge, *Litchfield*

DELAWARE

SENATORS

Outerbridge Horsey, *Wilmington*
William H. Wells,[12] *Dagsborough*

REPRESENTATIVES

Thomas Cooper, *Georgetown*
Henry M. Ridgely, *Dover*

GEORGIA

SENATORS

William H. Crawford,[13] *Lexington*
William B. Bulloch,[14] *Savannah*
William W. Bibb,[15] *Petersburg*
Charles Tait, *Elbert*

REPRESENTATIVES

William Barnett, *Washington*
William W. Bibb,[16] *Petersburg*
Alfred Cuthbert,[17] *Eaton*
John Forsyth, *Augusta*
Bolling Hall, *Milledgeville*
Thomas Telfair, *Savannah*
George M. Troup, *Dublin*

KENTUCKY

SENATORS

George M. Bibb,[18] *Lexington*
George Walker,[19] *Nicholasville*
William T. Barry,[20] *Lexington*
Jesse Bledsoe,[21] *Lexington*
Isham Talbot,[22] *Frankfort*

REPRESENTATIVES

James Clark, *Winchester*
Henry Clay,[23] *Lexington*
Joseph H. Hawkins,[24] *Lexington*
Joseph Desha, *Mays Lick*
William P. Duval, *Bardstown*
Samuel Hopkins, *Henderson*
Richard M. Johnson, *Great Crossings*
Samuel McKee, *Lancaster*
Thomas Montgomery, *Stanford*
Stephen Ormsby,[25] *Louisville*
Solomon P. Sharp, *Russellville*

[1] Died November 23, 1814.
[2] Elected December 6, 1813.
[3] Elected April 18, 1814; November 25, 1814, upon the death of Vice President Elbridge Gerry.
[4] Died April 22, 1814.
[5] Elected October 11, 1814; Samuel Turner, Jr., the chief clerk, was appointed on September 19, 1814, to act in the interim.
[6] Reelected May 24, 1813; resigned from Congress January 19, 1814.
[7] Elected January 19, 1814, to fill vacancy caused by resignation of Henry Clay.
[8] Reelected May 24, 1813; resigned January 28, 1815, while resolution was pending to remove him from office and to elect a successor.
[9] Elected January 30, 1815.
[10] Resigned in May 1813.

[11] Elected to fill vacancy caused by resignation of Chauncey Goodrich, and took his seat May 24, 1813.
[12] Elected to fill vacancy caused by resignation of James A. Bayard, in preceding Congress, and took his seat June 10, 1813.
[13] Resigned March 23, 1813.
[14] Appointed to fill vacancy caused by resignation of William H. Crawford, and took his seat May 24, 1813.
[15] Elected to fill vacancy caused by resignation of William H. Crawford, and took his seat December 6, 1813.
[16] Resigned November 6, 1813, having been elected Senator.
[17] Elected to fill vacancy caused by resignation of William W. Bibb, and took his seat February 7, 1814.
[18] Resigned August 23, 1814.
[19] Appointed to fill vacancy caused by resignation

of George M. Bibb, and took his seat October 10, 1814.
[20] Elected to fill vacancy caused by resignation of George M. Bibb, and took his seat February 2, 1815.
[21] Resigned December 24, 1814. In response to personal inquiry, Senate passed resolution January 20, 1815, declaring seat vacant. (See Senate Election Cases, edition of 1913, p. 175.)
[22] Elected to fill vacancy caused by resignation of Jesse Bledsoe, and took his seat February 2, 1815.
[23] Resigned January 19, 1814, to accept "special and important diplomatic mission."
[24] Elected to fill vacancy caused by resignation of Henry Clay, and took his seat March 29, 1814.
[25] Elected to fill vacancy caused by death of Representative-elect John Simpson (January 22, 1813) before the beginning of the congressional term, and took his seat May 28, 1813.

LOUISIANA

SENATORS

James Brown, *New Orleans*
Eligius Fromentin, *New Orleans*

REPRESENTATIVE

Thomas B. Robertson, *New Orleans*

MARYLAND

SENATORS

Samuel Smith, *Baltimore*
Robert H. Goldsborough,[26] *Easton*

REPRESENTATIVES

Stevenson Archer, *Bel Air*
Charles Goldsborough, *Cambridge*
Alexander C. Hanson, *Rockville*
Joseph Kent, *Bladensburg*
Alexander McKim, *Baltimore*
Nicholas R. Moore, *Ruxton*
Samuel Ringgold, *Hagerstown*
Philip Stuart, *Port Tobacco*
Robert Wright, *Queenstown*

MASSACHUSETTS

SENATORS

James Lloyd,[27] *Boston*
Christopher Gore,[28] *Boston*
Jospeh B. Varnum, *Dracut*

REPRESENTATIVES

William Baylies, *Bridgewater*
Abijah Bigelow, *Leominster*
George Bradbury, *Portland*
Elijah Brigham, *Westboro*
William M. Richardson,[29] *Groton*
Samuel Dana,[30] *Groton*
Samuel Davis, *Bath*
Daniel Dewey,[31] *Williamstown*
John W. Hulbert,[32] *Pittsfield*
William Ely, *Springfield*
Levi Hubbard, *Paris*
Cyrus King, *Saco*
James Parker, *Gardiner*
Timothy Pickering, *Wendham*
John Reed, *Yarmouth*
William Reed, *Marblehead*
Nathaniel Ruggles, *Boston*
Samuel Taggart, *Colerain*
Artemas Ward, Jr., *Boston*
Laban Wheaton, *Easton*

John Wilson, *Belfast*
Abiel Wood, *Wiscasset*

NEW HAMPSHIRE

SENATORS

Nicholas Gilman,[33] *Exeter*
Thomas W. Thompson,[34] *Concord*
Charles Cutts,[35] *Portsmouth*
Jeremiah Mason,[36] *Portsmouth*

REPRESENTATIVES

Bradbury Cilley, *Nottingham*
William Hale, *Dover*
Samuel Smith, *Peterboro*
Roger Vose, *Walpole*
Daniel Webster, *Portsmouth*
Jeduthun Wilcox, *Orford*

NEW JERSEY

SENATORS

John Lambert, *Lambertville*
John Condit, *Orange*

REPRESENTATIVES

Lewis Condict, *Morristown*
William Coxe, *Burlington*
Jacob Hufty,[37] *Salem*
Thomas Bines,[38] *Pennsville*
James Schureman, *New Brunswick*
Richard Stockton, *Princeton*
Thomas Ward, *Newark*

NEW YORK

SENATORS

Obadiah German, *Norwich*
Rufus King, *New York City*

REPRESENTATIVES

Daniel Avery, *Aurora*
Egbert Benson,[39] *New York City*
William Irving,[40] *New York City*
John M. Bowers,[41] *Cooperstown*
Isaac Williams, Jr.,[42] *Cooperstown*
Alexander Boyd, *Middleburg*
Oliver C. Comstock, *Trumansburg*
Peter Denoyelles, *Haverstraw*
Jonathan Fisk, *Newburgh*
James Geddes, *Onondaga*
Thomas P. Grosvenor, *Hudson*
Abraham J. Hasbrouck, *Kingston*
Samuel M. Hopkins, *New York City*

Nathaniel W. Howell, *Canandaigua*
Moss Kent, *Leraysville*
John Lefferts, *Brooklyn*
John Lovett, *Albany*
Jacob Markell, *Manheim*
Morris S. Miller, *Utica*
Hosea Moffitt, *Nassau*
Thomas J. Oakley, *Poughkeepsie*
Jotham Post, Jr., *New York City*
Ebenezer Sage, *Sag Harbor*
Samuel Sherwood, *Delhi*
Zebulon R. Shipherd, *Granville*
William S. Smith, *Lebanon*
John W. Taylor, *Ballston Spa*
Joel Thompson, *Smyrna*
Elisha J. Winter, *Peru*

NORTH CAROLINA

SENATORS

James Turner, *Warrenton*
David Stone,[43] *Raleigh*
Francis Locke,[44] *Salisbury*

REPRESENTATIVES

Willis Alston, *Greenville*
John Culpepper, *Allenton*
Peter Forney, *Lincolnton*
Meshack Franklin
William Gaston, *New Bern*
William Kennedy, *Washington*
William R. King, *Wilmington*
Nathaniel Macon, *Warrenton*
William H. Murfree, *Murfreesburg*
Joseph Pearson, *Salisbury*
Israel Pickens, *Morgantown*
Richard Stanford, *Hawfields*
Bartlett Yancy, *Caswell*

OHIO

SENATORS

Thomas Worthington,[45] *Chillicothe*
Joseph Kerr,[46] *Chillicothe*
Jeremiah Morrow, *Montgomery*

REPRESENTATIVES

John Alexander, *Xenia*
Reasin Beall,[47] *Wooster*
David Clendenin,[48] *Youngstown*
James Caldwell, *St. Clairsville*
Duncan MacArthur,[49] *Chillicothe*
William Creighton, Jr.,[50] *Chillicothe*
James Kilbourne, *Worthington*
John McLean, *Lebanon*

---

[26] Elected for term beginning March 4, 1813, and took his seat May 27, 1813; vacancy in this class from March 4, 1813, to May 12, 1813.
[27] Resigned May 1, 1813.
[28] Appointed to fill vacancy caused by resignation of James Lloyd, and took his seat May 28, 1813; subsequently elected.
[29] Resigned April 18, 1814.
[30] Elected to fill vacancy caused by resignation of William M. Richardson, and took his seat September 22, 1814.
[31] Resigned February 24, 1814, having been appointed justice of supreme judicial court of Massachusetts.
[32] Elected to fill vacancy caused by resignation of Daniel Dewey, and took his seat September 26, 1814.
[33] Died May 2, 1814.
[34] Elected to fill vacancy caused by death of Nicholas Gilman, and took his seat September 19, 1814.

[35] Appointed to fill vacancy in term commencing March 4, 1813, there having been no election, and took his seat May 24, 1813.
[36] Elected to fill vacancy in term commencing March 4, 1813, and took his seat June 21, 1813.
[37] Died May 20, 1814.
[38] Elected to fill vacancy caused by death of Jacob Hufty, and took his seat November 2, 1814.
[39] Resigned August 2, 1813.
[40] Elected to fill vacancy caused by resignation of Egbert Benson, and took his seat January 22, 1814.
[41] Presented credentials as a Member-elect to fill vacancy caused by death of Representative-elect William Dowse (February 18, 1813, before the beginning of the congressional term), and took his seat June 21, 1813; served until December 20, 1813; succeeded by Isaac Williams, Jr., who contested his election.
[42] Successfully contested the election of John M.

Bowers, and took his seat January 24, 1814.
[43] Resigned December 24, 1814.
[44] Chosen to fill vacancy caused by resignation of David Stone, but did not qualify.
[45] Resigned December 1, 1814.
[46] Elected to fill vacancy caused by resignation of Thomas Worthington, and took his seat December 30, 1814.
[47] Elected to fill vacancy caused by death of Representative-elect John S. Edwards (February 22, 1813, before the beginning of the congressional term), and took his seat June 8, 1813; resigned June 7, 1814.
[48] Elected to fill vacancy caused by resignation of Reasin Beall, and took his seat December 22, 1814.
[49] Resigned April 5, 1813, before Congress assembled.
[50] Elected to fill vacancy caused by resignation of Duncan McArthur, and took his seat June 15, 1813.

PENNSYLVANIA

SENATORS

Michael Leib,[51] *Philadelphia*
Jonathan Roberts,[52] *Norristown*
Abner Lacock, *Beavertown*

REPRESENTATIVES

William Anderson, *Chester*
David Bard, *Frankstown*
Robert Brown, *Weaversville*
John Conard, *Germantown*
William Crawford, *Gettysburg*
Roger Davis, *Charlestown*
William Findley, *Youngstown*
Hugh Glasgow, *York*
John Gloninger,[53] *Lebanon*
Edward Crouch,[54] *Paxtang*
Isaac Griffin,[55] *New Geneva*
Jonathan Roberts,[56] *Norristown*
Samuel Henderson,[57] *Norristown*
Charles J. Ingersoll, *Philadelphia*
Samuel D. Ingham, *New Hope*
Jared Irwin, *Sunbury*
Aaron Lyle, *West Middletown*
William Piper, *Bloodyrun*
Adam Seybert, *Philadelphia*
Isaac Smith, *Jersey Shore*
Adamson Tannehill, *Pittsburgh*
John M. Hyneman,[58] *Reading*
Daniel Udree,[59] *Reading*
James Whitehill,[60] *Strasburg*
Amos Slaymaker,[61] *Lancaster*
Robert Whitehill,[62] *Camp Hill*
John Rea,[63] *Chambersburg*
Thomas Wilson,[64] *Erie*

RHODE ISLAND

SENATORS

Jeremiah B. Howell, *Providence*
William Hunter, *Newport*

REPRESENTATIVES

Richard Jackson, Jr., *Providence*
Elisha R. Potter, *Kingston*

SOUTH CAROLINA

SENATORS

John Gaillard, *Charleston*
John Taylor, *Columbia*

REPRESENTATIVES

John C. Calhoun, *Willington*
John J. Chappell, *Columbia*
Langdon Cheves, *Charleston*
Elias Earle, *Centerville*
David R. Evans, *Winnsboro*
Samuel Farrow, *Spartanburg*
Theodore Gourdin, *Pineville*
John Kershaw, *Camden*
William Lowndes, *Jacksonboro*

TENNESSEE

SENATORS

Joseph Anderson
George W. Campbell,[65] *Nashville*
Jesse Wharton,[66] *Nashville*

REPRESENTATIVES

John H. Bowen, *Gallatin*
Felix Grundy,[67] *Nashville*
Newton Cannon,[68] *Harpeth*
Thomas K. Harris,[69] *Sparta*
Parry W. Humphreys
John Rhea, *Sullivan*
John Sevier, *Knoxville*

VERMONT

SENATORS

Jonathan Robinson, *Bennington*
Dudley Chase, *Randolph*

REPRESENTATIVES

William C. Bradley, *Westminster*
Ezra Butler, *Waterbury*
James Fisk, *Barre*
Charles Rich, *Shoreham*
Richard Skinner, *Manchester*
William Strong, *Hartford*

VIRGINIA

SENATORS

William B. Giles,[70] *Lodore*
Richard Brent,[71] *Aquia*
James Barbour,[72] *Barboursville*

REPRESENTATIVES

Thomas M. Bayly,[73] *Drummondtown*
James Breckinridge, *Fincastle*
William A. Burwell, *Rocky Mount*
Hugh Caperton, *Union*
John Clopton, *Tunstall*
John Dawson [74]
Philip P. Barbour,[75] *Orange*
John W. Eppes, *Charles City*
Thomas Gholson, Jr., *Brunswick*
Peterson Goodwyn, *Petersburg*
Aylett Hawes, *Woodville*
John P. Hungerford,[76] *Leedstown*
John G. Jackson, *Clarksburg*
James Johnson, *Suffolk*
John Kerr, *Mountpleasant*
Joseph Lewis, Jr., *Upperville*
William McCoy, *Franklin*
Hugh Nelson, *Milton*
Thomas Newton, Jr., *Norfolk*
James Pleasants, *Goochland*
John Roane, *Uppowoc*
Daniel Sheffey, *Wythe*
John Smith
Francis White, *Romney*

ILLINOIS TERRITORY

DELEGATE

Shadrack Bond,[77] *Kaskaskia*
Benjamin Stephenson,[78] *Edwardsville*

INDIANA TERRITORY

DELEGATE

Jonathan Jennings, *Charlestown*

MISSISSIPPI TERRITORY

DELEGATE

William Lattimore, *Liberty*

TERRITORY OF MISSOURI

DELEGATE

Edward Hempstead,[79] *St. Louis*
Rufus Easton,[80] *St. Louis*

---

[51] Resigned February 14, 1814, to become postmaster of Philadelphia.
[52] Elected to fill vacancy caused by resignation of Michael Leib, and took his seat February 28, 1814.
[53] Resigned August 2, 1813.
[54] Elected to fill vacancy caused by resignation of John Gloninger, and took his seat December 6, 1813.
[55] Elected to fill vacancy caused by death of Representative-elect John Smilie, in preceding Congress, and took his seat May 24, 1813.
[56] Resigned February 24, 1814, having been elected Senator.
[57] Elected to fill vacancy caused by resignation of Jonathan Roberts, and took his seat November 29, 1814.
[58] Resigned August 2, 1813.
[59] Elected to fill vacancy caused by resignation of John M. Hyneman; took his seat December 6, 1813.

[60] Resigned September 1, 1814.
[61] Elected to fill vacancy caused by resignation of James Whitehill, and took his seat December 12, 1814.
[62] Died April 8, 1813.
[63] Elected to fill vacancy caused by death of Robert Whitehill, and took his seat May 28, 1813.
[64] Elected to fill vacancy caused by resignation of Representative-elect Abner Lacock, in preceding Congress, and took his seat May 28, 1813.
[65] Resigned February 11, 1814.
[66] Appointed to fill vacancy caused by resignation of George W. Campbell, and took his seat April 9, 1814.
[67] Resigned in 1814.
[68] Elected to fill vacancy caused by resignation of Felix Grundy, and took his seat October 15, 1814.
[69] Election unsuccessfully contested by William Kelly.

[70] Resigned March 3, 1815.
[71] Died December 30, 1814.
[72] Elected to fill vacancy caused by death of Richard Brent, and took his seat January 11, 1815.
[73] Election unsuccessfully contested by Burwell Bassett.
[74] Died March 31, 1814.
[75] Elected to fill vacancy caused by death of John Dawson, and took his seat September 19, 1814.
[76] Election unsuccessfully contested by John Taliaferro.
[77] Served during the first session.
[78] Presented credentials, and took his seat November 14, 1814.
[79] Served during the first and second sessions.
[80] Presented credentials and took his seat November 16, 1814.

FOURTEENTH CONGRESS

MARCH 4, 1815, TO MARCH 3, 1817

FIRST SESSION—*December 4, 1815, to April 30, 1816*
SECOND SESSION—*December 2, 1816, to March 3, 1817*

———

VICE PRESIDENT OF THE UNITED STATES [1]
PRESIDENT PRO TEMPORE OF THE SENATE—JOHN GAILLARD, of South Carolina
SECRETARY OF THE SENATE—CHARLES CUTTS, of New Hampshire
SERGEANT AT ARMS OF THE SENATE—MOUNTJOY BAYLY, of Maryland

———

SPEAKER OF THE HOUSE OF REPRESENTATIVES—HENRY CLAY,[2] of Kentucky
CLERK OF THE HOUSE—THOMAS DOUGHERTY,[3] of Kentucky
SERGEANT AT ARMS OF THE HOUSE—THOMAS DUNN, of Maryland
DOORKEEPER OF THE HOUSE—THOMAS CLAXTON

CONNECTICUT

SENATORS

Samuel W. Dana, *Middlesex*
David Daggett, *New Haven*

REPRESENTATIVES

Epaphroditus Champion, *East Haddam*
John Davenport, *Stamford*
Lyman Law, *New London*
Jonathan O. Moseley, *East Haddam*
Timothy Pitkin, *Farmington*
Lewis B. Sturges, *Fairfield*
Benjamin Tallmadge, *Litchfield*

DELAWARE

SENATORS

Outerbridge Horsey, *Wilmington*
William H. Wells, *Dagsborough*

REPRESENTATIVES

Thomas Clayton, *Dover*
Thomas Cooper, *Georgetown*

GEORGIA

SENATORS

Charles Tait, *Elbert*
William W. Bibb,[4] *Petersburg*
George M. Troup,[5] *Dublin*

REPRESENTATIVES

Alfred Cuthbert,[6] *Eatonton*
Zadock Cook,[7] *Watkinsville*
John Forsyth, *Augusta*
Bolling Hall, *Milledgeville*
Wilson Lumpkin, *Lexington*
Thomas Telfair, *Savannah*
Richard Henry Wilde, *Augusta*

INDIANA [8]

SENATORS

James Noble,[9] *Brookville*
Waller Taylor,[10] *Vincennes*

REPRESENTATIVE

William Hendricks,[11] *Madison*

KENTUCKY

SENATORS

William T. Barry,[12] *Lexington*
Martin D. Hardin,[13] *Frankfort*
Isham Talbot, *Frankfort*

REPRESENTATIVES

James Clark,[14] *Winchester*
Thomas Fletcher,[15] *Owingsville*
Henry Clay, *Lexington*
Joseph Desha, *Mays Lick*
Benjamin Hardin, *Bardstown*
Richard M. Johnson, *Great Crossings*
Alney McLean, *Greenville*
Samuel McKee, *Lancaster*
Stephen Ormsby, *Louisville*
Solomon P. Sharp, *Bowling Green*
Micah Taul, *Monticello*

LOUISIANA

SENATORS

James Brown, *New Orleans*
Eligius Fromentin, *New Orleans*

———

[1] Vice President Elbridge Gerry died in preceding Congress.
[2] Elected December 4, 1815.
[3] Reelected December 4, 1815.
[4] Resigned November 9, 1816.
[5] Elected to fill vacancy caused by resignation of William W. Bibb, and took his seat December 12, 1816.
[6] Resigned November 9, 1816.

[7] Elected to fill vacancy caused by resignation of Alfred Cuthbert, and took his seat January 23, 1817.
[8] Admitted as a State into the Union, December 11, 1816.
[9] Took his seat December 12, 1816; term to expire, as determined by lot, March 3, 1821.
[10] Took his seat December 12, 1816; term to expire, as determined by lot, March 3, 1819.

[11] Took his seat December 11, 1816.
[12] Resigned May 1, 1816.
[13] Appointed to fill vacancy caused by resignation of William T. Barry, and took his seat December 5, 1816; subsequently elected.
[14] Resigned in 1816.
[15] Elected to fill vacancy caused by resignation of James Clark, and took his seat December 2, 1816.

LOUISIANA—Continued

REPRESENTATIVE

Thomas B. Robertson, *New Orleans*

MARYLAND

SENATORS

Robert H. Goldsborough, *Easton*
Robert G. Harper,[16] *Baltimore*
Alexander C. Hanson,[17] *Rockville*

REPRESENTATIVES

Stevenson Archer, *Bel Air*
George Baer, *Frederick*
Charles Goldsborough, *Cambridge*
John C. Herbert, *Vannsville*
William Pinkney,[18] *Baltimore*
Peter Little,[19] *Baltimore*
Alexander C. Hanson,[20] *Rockville*
George Peter,[21] *Darnestown*
Nicholas R. Moore,[22] *Ruxton*
Samuel Smith,[23] *Baltimore*
Philip Stuart, *Port Tobacco*
Robert Wright, *Queenstown*

MASSACHUSETTS

SENATORS

Joseph B. Varnum, *Dracut*
Christopher Gore,[24] *Boston*
Eli P. Ashmun,[25] *Northampton*

REPRESENTATIVES

William Baylies, *Bridgewater*
George Bradbury, *Portland*
Elijah Brigham,[26] *Westboro*
Benjamin Adams,[27] *Uxbridge*
Benjamin Brown, *Waldoborough*
James Carr, *Bangor*
Samuel S. Connor, *Waterville*
John W. Hulbert, *Pittsfield*
Cyrus King, *Saco*
Elijah H. Mills, *Northampton*
Jeremiah Nelson, *Newburyport*
Albion K. Parris, *Paris*
Timothy Pickering, *Wendham*
John Reed, *Yarmouth*
Thomas Rice, *Augusta*
Nathaniel Ruggles, *Boston*
Asahel Stearns, *Charlestown*
Solomon Strong, *Westminster*
Samuel Taggart, *Colerain*

Artemas Ward, Jr., *Boston*
Laban Wheaton, *Easton*

NEW HAMPSHIRE

SENATORS

Jeremiah Mason, *Portsmouth*
Thomas W. Thompson, *Concord*

REPRESENTATIVES

Charles H. Atherton, *Amhurst*
Bradbury Cilley, *Nottingham*
William Hale, *Dover*
Roger Vose, *Walpole*
Daniel Webster, *Portsmouth*
Jeduthun Wilcox, *Orford*

NEW JERSEY

SENATORS

John Condit, *Orange*
James J. Wilson, *Trenton*

REPRESENTATIVES

Ezra Baker, *Tuckerton*
Ephraim Bateman, *Cedarsville*
Benjamin Bennet, *Middletown*
Lewis Condict, *Morristown*
Henry Southard, *Baskingridge*
Thomas Ward, *Newark*

NEW YORK

SENATORS

Rufus King, *New York City*
Nathan Sanford, *New York City*

REPRESENTATIVES

Asa Adgate,[28] *Chesterfield*
Enos T. Throop,[29] *Auburn*
Daniel Avery,[30] *Aurora*
Samuel R. Betts, *Newburgh*
James Birdsall, *Norwich*
Victory Birdseye, *Pompey*
Micah Brooks, *East Bloomfield*
Jonathan Fisk,[31] *Newburgh*
James W. Wilkin,[32] *Goshen*
Daniel Cady, *Johnston*
Oliver C. Comstock, *Trumansburg*
Henry Crocheron, *Castletown*
Thomas R. Gold, *Whitestown*
Thomas P. Grosvenor, *Hudson*
Jabez D. Hammond, *Cherry Valley*

William Irving, *New York City*
Moss Kent, *Leraysville*
John Lovett, *Albany*
Hosea Moffitt, *Nassau*
Peter B. Porter,[33] *Buffalo*
Archibald S. Clarke,[34] *Clarence*
John Adams,[35] *Catskill*
Erastus Root,[36] *Delhi*
John Savage, *Salem*
Abraham H. Schenck, *Fishkill Landing*
John W. Taylor, *Ballston Spa*
George Townsend, *Oyster Bay*
Jonathan Ward, *New Rochelle*
Peter H. Wendover, *New York City*
Westel Willoughby, Jr.,[37] *Herkimer*
John B. Yates, *Utica*

NORTH CAROLINA

SENATORS

James Turner,[38] *Warrenton*
Montfort Stokes,[39] *Wilkesboro*
Francis Locke,[40] *Salisbury*
Nathaniel Macon,[41] *Warrenton*

REPRESENTATIVES

Joseph H. Bryan, *Windsor*
James W. Clark, *Tarboro*
John Culpepper, *Allenton*
Daniel M. Forney, *Lincolnton*
William Gaston, *New Bern*
William R. King,[42] *Wilmington*
Charles Hooks,[43] *Dublin*
William C. Love, *Salisbury*
Nathaniel Macon,[44] *Warrenton*
Weldon N. Edwards,[45] *Warrenton*
William H. Murfree, *Murfreesburg*
Israel Pickens, *Morgantown*
Richard Stanford,[46] *Hawfields*
Samuel Dickens,[47] *Mount Tirzah*
Lewis Williams, *Panther Creek*
Bartlett Yancy, *Caswell*

OHIO

SENATORS

Jeremiah Morrow, *Montgomery*
Benjamin Ruggles, *St. Clairsville*

REPRESENTATIVES

John Alexander, *Xenia*
James Caldwell, *St. Clairsville*
David Clendenin, *Youngtown*

---

[16] Elected to serve "from January 29, 1816, to March 3, 1821," and took his seat February 5, 1816; resigned December 6, 1816; vacancy in this class from March 4, 1815, to January 28, 1816, caused by failure of legislature to elect.
[17] Elected to fill vacancy caused by resignation of Robert G. Harper, and took his seat January 2, 1817.
[18] Resigned April 18, 1816, having been appointed minister to Russia.
[19] Elected to fill vacancy caused by resignation of William Pinkney, and took his seat December 2, 1816.
[20] Resigned in 1816.
[21] Elected to fill vacancy caused by resignation of Alexander C. Hanson, and took his seat December 2, 1816.
[22] Resigned in 1815, before Congress assembled.
[23] Elected to fill vacancy caused by resignation of Nicholas R. Moore, and took his seat February 4, 1816.
[24] Resigned May 30, 1816.
[25] Elected to fill vacancy caused by resignation of Christopher Gore, and took his seat December 2, 1816.

[26] Died February 22, 1816.
[27] Elected to fill vacancy caused by death of Elijah Brigham, and took his seat December 2, 1816.
[28] Elected to fill vacancy caused by death of Representative-elect Benjamin Pond (October 6, 1814, before the beginning of the congressional term), and took his seat December 7, 1815.
[29] Resigned June 4, 1816.
[30] Elected to fill vacancy caused by resignation of Enos T. Throop, and took his seat December 3, 1816.
[31] Resigned in March, 1815, before Congress assembled.
[32] Elected to fill vacancy caused by resignation of Jonathan Fisk, and took his seat December 4, 1815.
[33] Resigned January 23, 1816.
[34] Elected to fill vacancy caused by resignation of Peter B. Porter, and took his seat December 2, 1816.
[35] Served until December 26, 1815; succeeded by Erastus Root, who contested his election.
[36] Successfully contested the election of John Adams, and took his seat December 26, 1815.

[37] Successfully contested the election of William S. Smith, and took his seat December 13, 1815. (Mr. Smith did not appear or claim the seat, although credentials had been presented.)
[38] Resigned November 21, 1816.
[39] Elected to fill vacancy caused by resignation of James Turner, and took his seat December 16, 1816.
[40] Resigned December 5, 1815, never having qualified.
[41] Elected to fill vacancy caused by resignation of Francis Locke, and took his seat December 13, 1815.
[42] Resigned November 4, 1816.
[43] Elected to fill vacancy caused by resignation of William R. King, and took his seat December 2, 1816.
[44] Resigned December 13, 1815, having been elected Senator.
[45] Elected to fill vacancy caused by resignation of Nathaniel Macon, and took his seat February 7, 1816.
[46] Died April 9, 1816.
[47] Elected to fill vacancy caused by death of Richard Stanford, and took his seat December 2, 1816.

William Creighton, Jr., *Chillicothe*
James Kilbourne, *Worthington*
John McLean,[48] *Lebanon*
William Henry Harrison,[49] *Cincinnati*

PENNSYLVANIA

SENATORS

Abner Lacock, *Beavertown*
Jonathan Roberts, *Norristown*

REPRESENTATIVES

David Bard,[50] *Frankstown*
Thomas Burnside,[51] *Bellefonte*
William P. Maclay,[52] *Lewistown*
William Crawford, *Gettysburg*
William Darlington, *West Chester*
William Findley, *Youngstown*
Hugh Glasgow, *York*
Isaac Griffin, *New Geneva*
John Hahn, *Pottsgrove*
Joseph Hiester, *Reading*
Joseph Hopkinson, *Philadelphia*
Samuel D. Ingham, *New Hope*
Jared Irwin, *Sunbury*
William Maclay, *Fannetsburg*
William Milnor, *Philadelphia*
William Piper, *Bloodyrun*
John Ross, *Easton*
Thomas Smith, *Darby*
Amos Ellmaker,[53] *Harrisburg*
James M. Wallace,[54] *Hummelstown*
John Whiteside, *Lancaster*
Jonathan Williams,[55] *Philadelphia*
John Sergeant,[56] *Philadelphia*
Thomas Wilson, *Erie*
William Wilson, *Williamsport*
Aaron Lyle, *West Middletown*
John Woods,[57] *Pittsburgh*

RHODE ISLAND

SENATORS

Jeremiah B. Howell, *Providence*
William Hunter, *Newport*

REPRESENTATIVES

John L. Boss, Jr., *Newport*
James B. Mason, *Providence*

SOUTH CAROLINA

SENATORS

John Gaillard, *Charleston*
John Taylor,[58] *Columbia*
William Smith,[59] *Yorkville*

REPRESENTATIVES

John J. Chappell, *Columbia*
Benjamin Huger, *Georgetown*
William Lowndes, *Jacksonboro*
William Mayrant,[60] *Stateburg*
Stephen D. Miller,[61] *Stateburg*
John C. Calhoun, *Willington*
Henry Middleton, *Charleston*
Thomas Moore, *Prices Store*
John Taylor, *Pendleton*
William Woodward, *Monticello*

TENNESSEE

SENATORS

Jesse Wharton, *Nashville*
John Williams,[62] *Knoxville*
George W. Campbell,[63] *Nashville*

REPRESENTATIVES

Newton Cannon, *Harpeth*
Bennett H. Henderson, *Hendersonville*
Samuel Powell, *Rogersville*
James B. Reynolds, *Clarksville*
John Sevier,[64] *Knoxville*
William G. Blount,[65] *Knoxville*
Isaac Thomas, *Sparta*

VERMONT

SENATORS

Dudley Chase, *Randolph*
Isaac Tichenor, *Bennington*

REPRESENTATIVES

Daniel Chipman,[66] *Middleburg*
Luther Jewett, *St. Johnsbury*
Chauncey Langdon, *Castleton*
Asa Lyon, *Grand Isle*
Charles Marsh, *Woodstock*
John Noyes, *Brattleboro*

VIRGINIA

SENATORS

James Barbour, *Barboursville*
Armistead T. Mason,[67] *Rasburg Plain*

REPRESENTATIVES

Philip P. Barbour, *Orange*
Burwell Bassett, *Williamsburg*
James Breckinridge, *Fincastle*
William A. Burwell, *Rocky Mount*
Matthew Clay,[68] *Halifax*
John Kerr,[69] *Mountpleasant*
John Clopton,[70] *Tunstall*
John Tyler,[71] *Chase City*
Peterson Goodwyn, *Petersburg*
Aylett Hawes, *Woodville*
John P. Hungerford, *Leedstown*
John G. Jackson, *Clarksburg*
James Johnson, *Suffolk*
Joseph Lewis, Jr., *Upperville*
William McCoy,[72] *Franklin*
Hugh Nelson, *Milton*
Thomas Gholson, Jr.,[73] *Brunswick*
Thomas M. Nelson,[74] *Mecklenburg*
Thomas Newton, Jr., *Norfolk*
James Pleasants, *Goochland*
John Randolph, *Charlotte*
William H. Roane, *Dunkirk*
Daniel Sheffey, *Wythe*
Ballard Smith, *Lewisburg*
Magnus Tate, *Martinsburg*
Henry St. George Tucker, *Winchester*

ILLINOIS TERRITORY

DELEGATE

Benjamin Stephenson,[75] *Edwardsville*
Nathaniel Pope,[76] *Kaskaskia*

INDIANA TERRITORY

DELEGATE

Jonathan Jennings,[77] *Charlestown*

MISSISSIPPI TERRITORY

DELEGATE

William Lattimore, *Liberty*

TERRITORY OF MISSOURI

DELEGATE

Rufus Easton,[78] *St. Louis*
John Scott,[79] *Ste. Genevieve*

---

[48] Resigned in 1816.
[49] Elected to fill vacancy caused by resignation of John McLean, and took his seat December 2, 1816.
[50] Died March 12, 1815.
[51] Elected to fill vacancy caused by death of David Bard, and took his seat December 11, 1815; resigned in April, 1816.
[52] Elected to fill vacancy caused by resignation of Thomas Burnside, and took his seat December 3, 1816.
[53] Resigned July 3, 1815, without qualifying, having been appointed judge.
[54] Elected to fill vacancy caused by resignation of Amos Ellmaker, and took his seat December 4, 1815.
[55] Died May 16, 1815, before Congress assembled.
[56] Elected to fill vacancy caused by death of Jonathan Williams, and took his seat December 6, 1815.
[57] Never qualified, owing to illness.
[58] Resigned in November, 1816.
[59] Elected to fill vacancy caused by resignation of John Taylor, and took his seat January 10, 1817.
[60] Resigned October 21, 1816.

[61] Elected to fill vacancy caused by resignation of William Mayrant, and took his seat January 2, 1817.
[62] Elected to fill vacancy in term ending March 3, 1817, caused by resignation of George W. Campbell from this class in the preceding Congress (Jesse Wharton having served by appointment from March 17, 1814, to October 10, 1815), and took his seat December 4, 1815.
[63] Elected for the term commencing March 4, 1815, and took his seat December 4, 1815; vacancy from March 4, 1815, to October 10, 1815.
[64] Died September 24, 1815, before Congress assembled.
[65] Elected to fill vacancy caused by death of John Sevier, and took his seat January 8, 1816.
[66] Resigned May 5, 1816; seat remained vacant.
[67] Elected to fill vacancy caused by resignation of William B. Giles, in preceding Congress, and took his seat January 22, 1816.
[68] Died May 27, 1815, before Congress assembled.

[69] Elected to fill vacancy caused by death of Matthew Clay, and took his seat December 5, 1815.
[70] Died September 11, 1816.
[71] Elected to fill vacancy caused by death of John Clopton, and took his seat December 17, 1816.
[72] Election unsuccessfully contested by Robert Porterfield.
[73] Died July 4, 1816.
[74] Elected to fill vacancy caused by death of Thomas Gholson, Jr., and took his seat December 4, 1816.
[75] Served during the first session.
[76] Presented credentials and took his seat December 2, 1816.
[77] Served until December 11, 1816, when Indiana Territory was granted statehood.
[78] Served during first session; unsuccessfully contested the election of John Scott in the second session.
[79] Presented credentials and took his seat December 2, 1816; Rufus Easton contested, and on January 13, 1817, the election was declared illegal and the seat vacant.

FIFTEENTH CONGRESS

MARCH 4, 1817, TO MARCH 3, 1819

FIRST SESSION—*December 1, 1817, to April 20, 1818*

SECOND SESSION—*November 16, 1818, to March 3, 1819*

SPECIAL SESSION OF THE SENATE—*March 4, 1817, to March 6, 1817*

VICE PRESIDENT OF THE UNITED STATES—DANIEL D. TOMPKINS, of New York

PRESIDENT PRO TEMPORE OF THE SENATE—JOHN GAILLARD,[1] of South Carolina; JAMES BARBOUR,[2] of Virginia

SECRETARY OF THE SENATE—CHARLES CUTTS, of New Hampshire

SERGEANT AT ARMS OF THE SENATE—MOUNTJOY BAYLY, of Maryland

SPEAKER OF THE HOUSE OF REPRESENTATIVES—HENRY CLAY,[3] of Kentucky

CLERK OF THE HOUSE—THOMAS DOUGHERTY,[4] of Kentucky

SERGEANT AT ARMS OF THE HOUSE—THOMAS DUNN, of Maryland

DOORKEEPER OF THE HOUSE—THOMAS CLAXTON

CONNECTICUT

SENATORS

Samuel W. Dana,[5] *Middlesex*
David Daggett, *New Haven*

REPRESENTATIVES

Uriel Holmes,[6] *Litchfield*
Sylvester Gilbert,[7] *Hebron*
Ebenezer Huntington, *Norwich*
Jonathan O. Moseley, *East Haddam*
Timothy Pitkin, *Farmington*
Samuel B. Sherwood, *Saugatuck*
Nathaniel Terry, *Hartford*
Thomas S. Williams, *Hartford*

DELAWARE

SENATORS

Outerbridge Horsey, *Wilmington*
Nicholas Van Dyke, *New Castle*

REPRESENTATIVES

Willard Hall, *Dover*
Louis McLane, *Wilmington*

GEORGIA

SENATORS

Charles Tait, *Elbert*
George M. Troup,[8] *Dublin*
John Forsyth,[9] *Augusta*

REPRESENTATIVES

Joel Abbot, *Washington*
Thomas W. Cobb, *Lexington*
Zadock Cook, *Watkinsville*
Joel Crawford, *Milledgeville*
John Forsyth,[10] *Augusta*
Robert R. Reid,[11] *Augusta*
William Terrell, *Sparta*

ILLINOIS [12]

SENATORS

Jesse B. Thomas,[13] *Edwardsville*
Ninian Edwards,[14] *Edwardsville*

REPRESENTATIVE

John McLean,[15] *Shawneetown*

INDIANA

SENATORS

James Noble, *Brookville*
Waller Taylor, *Vincennes*

REPRESENTATIVE

William Hendricks, *Madison*

KENTUCKY

SENATORS

Isham Talbot, *Frankfort*
John J. Crittenden,[16] *Russellville*

REPRESENTATIVES

Richard C. Anderson, Jr., *Louisville*
Henry Clay, *Lexington*
Joseph Desha, *Mays Lick*
Richard M. Johnson, *Great Crossings*
Anthony New, *Elkton*
Tunstall Quarles, *Somerset*
George Robertson, *Lancaster*
Thomas Speed, *Bardstown*
David Trimble, *Mount Sterling*
David Walker, *Russellville*

---

[1] Continuing from preceding session; elected March 6, 1817 (special session of the Senate); March 31, 1818.
[2] Elected February 15, 1819.
[3] Reelected December 1, 1817.
[4] Reelected December 1, 1817.
[5] The rule requiring Senators to stand when addressing the Chair was suspended in his favor April 9, 1818.
[6] Resigned in 1818.
[7] Elected to fill vacancy caused by resignation of

Uriel Holmes, and took his seat November 16, 1818.
[8] Resigned September 23, 1818.
[9] Elected to fill vacancy caused by resignation of George M. Troup, and took his seat November 23, 1818; resigned February 17, 1819, having been appointed minister to Spain.
[10] Resigned, effective November 23, 1818, having been elected Senator.
[11] Elected to fill vacancy caused by resignation of

John Forsyth, and took his seat February 18, 1819.
[12] Admitted as a State into the Union December 3, 1818.
[13] Took his seat December 4, 1818; term to expire, as determined by lot, March 3, 1823.
[14] Took his seat December 4, 1818; term to expire, as determined by lot, March 3, 1819.
[15] Took his seat December 4, 1818.
[16] Resigned March 3, 1819.

LOUISIANA

SENATORS

Eligius Fromentin, *New Orleans*
William C. C. Claiborne,[17] *New Orleans*
Henry Johnson,[18] *Donaldsonville*

REPRESENTATIVES

Thomas B. Robertson,[19] *New Orleans*
Thomas Butler,[20] *St. Francisville*

MARYLAND

SENATORS

Robert H. Goldsborough, *Easton*
Alexander C. Hanson, *Elkridge*

REPRESENTATIVES

Thomas Bayly, *Princess Anne*
Thomas Culbreth, *Denton*
John C. Herbert, *Vannsville*
Peter Little, *Freedom*
George Peter, *Darnestown*
Philip Reed, *Chestertown*
Samuel Ringgold, *Hagerstown*
Samuel Smith, *Baltimore*
Philip Stuart, *Port Tobacco*

MASSACHUSETTS

SENATORS

Eli P. Ashmun,[21] *Northampton*
Prentiss Mellen,[22] *Portland*
Harrison Gray Otis, *Boston*

REPRESENTATIVES

Benjamin Adams, *Uxbridge*
Samuel C. Allen, *Greenfield*
Walter Folger, Jr., *Nantucket*
Timothy Fuller, *Boston*
Joshua Gage, *Augusta*
John Holmes, *Alfred*
Jonathan Mason, *Boston*
Elijah H. Mills, *Northampton*
Marcus Morton, *Taunton*
Jeremiah Nelson, *Newburyport*
Benjamin Orr, *Brunswick*
Albion K. Parris,[23] *Paris*
Enoch Lincoln,[24] *Paris*
Thomas Rice, *Augusta*
Nathaniel Ruggles, *Boston*
Zabdiel Sampson, *Plymouth*
Henry Shaw, *Lanesboro*
Nathaniel Silsbee, *Salem*
Solomon Strong, *Westminster*
Ezekiel Whitman, *Portland*
John Wilson, *Belfast*

MISSISSIPPI [25]

SENATORS

Walter Leake,[26] *Red Bluff*
Thomas H. Williams,[27] *Washington*

REPRESENTATIVE

George Poindexter,[28] *Woodville*

NEW HAMPSHIRE

SENATORS

Jeremiah Mason,[29] *Portsmouth*
Clement Storer,[30] *Portsmouth*
David L. Morril, *Goffstown*

REPRESENTATIVES

Josiah Butler, *South Deerfield*
Clifton Clagett, *Amherst*
Salma Hale, *Keene*
Arthur Livermore, *Plymouth*
John F. Parrott, *Portsmouth*
Nathaniel Upham, *Rochester*

NEW JERSEY

SENATORS

James J. Wilson, *Trenton*
Mahlon Dickerson, *Suckasunny*

REPRESENTATIVES

Ephraim Bateman, *Cedarsville*
Benjamin Bennet, *Middletown*
Joseph Bloomfield, *Burlington*
Charles Kinsey, *Paterson*
John Linn, *Monroe*
Henry Southard, *Baskingridge*

NEW YORK

SENATORS

Rufus King, *New York City*
Nathan Sanford, *New York City*

REPRESENTATIVES

Oliver C. Comstock, *Trumansburg*
Daniel Cruger, *Bath*
John P. Cushman, *Troy*
John R. Drake, *Owego*
Benjamin Ellicott, *Batavia*
Josiah Hasbrouck, *New Paltz*
John Herkimer, *Danube*
Thomas H. Hubbard, *Hamilton*
William Irving, *New York City*
Dorrance Kirtland, *Coxsackie*
Thomas Lawyer, *Cobleskill*
David A. Ogden, *Madrid*

John Palmer, *Plattsburg*
James Porter, *Skaneateles*
John Savage, *Salem*
Philip J. Schuyler, *Rhinebeck*
Tredwell Scudder, *Islip*
John C. Spencer, *Canandaigua*
Henry R. Storrs, *Whitestown*
James Tallmadge, Jr.,[31] *Poughkeepsie*
John W. Taylor, *Ballston Spa*
Caleb Tompkins, *White Plains*
George Townsend, *Oyster Bay*
Peter H. Wendover, *New York City*
Rensselaer Westerlo, *Albany*
James W. Wilkin, *Goshen*
Isaac Williams, Jr., *Cooperstown*

NORTH CAROLINA

SENATORS

Nathaniel Macon, *Warrenton*
Montfort Stokes, *Wilkesboro*

REPRESENTATIVES

Joseph H. Bryan, *Windsor*
Weldon N. Edwards, *Warrenton*
Daniel M. Forney,[32] *Lincolnton*
William Davidson,[33] *Charlotte*
Thomas H. Hall, *Tarboro*
Alexander McMillan [34]
James Stewart,[35] *Laurinburg*
George Mumford,[36] *Salisbury*
Charles Fisher,[37] *Salisbury*
James Owen, *Elizabethtown*
Lemuel Sawyer, *Elizabeth City*
Thomas Settle, *Lenox Castle*
Jesse Slocumb, *Waynesborough*
James S. Smith, *Hillsboro*
Felix Walker, *Waynesville*
Lewis Williams, *Panther Creek*

OHIO

SENATORS

Jeremiah Morrow, *Montgomery*
Benjamin Ruggles, *St. Clairsville*

REPRESENTATIVES

Levi Barber, *Point Harmer*
Philemon Beecher, *Lancaster*
John W. Campbell, *West Union*
William Henry Harrison, *Cincinnati*
Samuel Herrick,[38] *Zanesville*
Peter Hitchcock, *Burton*

[17] Died November 23, 1817, never having qualified.
[18] Elected to fill vacancy caused by death of William C. C. Claiborne, and took his seat February 26, 1818.
[19] Resigned April 20, 1818.
[20] Elected to fill vacancy caused by resignation of Thomas B. Robertson, and took his seat November 16, 1818.
[21] Resigned May 10, 1818.
[22] Elected to fill vacancy caused by resignation of Eli P. Ashmun, and took his seat November 16, 1818.
[23] Resigned February 3, 1818.
[24] Elected to fill vacancy caused by resignation of Albion K. Parris, and took his seat November 16, 1818.
[25] Admitted as a State into the Union December 10, 1817.

[26] Took his seat December 11, 1817; term to expire, as determined by lot, March 3, 1821.
[27] Took his seat December 11, 1817; term to expire, as determined by lot, March 3, 1823.
[28] Took his seat December 15, 1817.
[29] Resigned June 16, 1817.
[30] Elected to fill vacancy caused by resignation of Jeremiah Mason, and took his seat December 1, 1817.
[31] Elected to fill vacancy caused by death of Representative-elect Henry B. Lee (February 18, 1817, before the beginning of the congressional term), and took his seat December 1, 1817.
[32] Resigned in 1818.
[33] Elected to fill vacancy caused by resignation of Daniel M. Forney, and took his seat December 2, 1818.

[34] Died before Congress assembled.
[35] Elected to fill vacancy caused by death of Alexander McMillan, and took his seat January 26, 1818.
[36] Died December 31, 1818.
[37] Elected to fill vacancy caused by death of George Mumford, and took his seat February 11, 1819.
[38] Election unsuccessfully contested by Charles Hammond. This case was one of a number in the same Congress that have been frequently referred to as determining the rights of a Representative-elect to hold a Federal office after the 4th of March—the day of the beginning of the congressional term to which they were elected. They are reported at length in Clark & Hall's publication, and also in the Digest of House Election Cases, edition of 1901, pp. 70–74.

VIRGINIA—Continued

REPRESENTATIVES—continued

James Pindall,[61] *Clarksburg*
Edward B. Jackson,[62] *Clarksburg*
James Pleasants,[63] *Goochland*
William S. Archer,[64] *Amelia*
John Randolph, *Charlotte*
Ballard Smith, *Lewisburg*
Alexander Smyth, *Wythe*
George F. Strother,[65] *Culpeper*
Thomas L. Moore,[66] *Warrenton*
George Tucker, *Lynchburg*
John Tyler, *Charles City*

Thomas Van Swearingen, *Shepherdstown*
Jared Williams, *Newton*

ALABAMA TERRITORY [67]

DELEGATE

Vacant

ARKANSAS TERRITORY [68]

DELEGATE

James W. Bates,[69] *Arkansas*

MICHIGAN TERRITORY [70]

DELEGATE

William W. Woodbridge,[71] *Detroit*
Solomon Sibley,[72] *Detroit*

TERRITORY OF MISSOURI

DELEGATE

John Scott, *Ste. Genevieve*

---

[61] Resigned July 26, 1820.
[62] Elected to fill vacancy caused by resignation of James Pindall, and took his seat November 13, 1820.
[63] Resigned December 14, 1819, having been elected Senator.
[64] Elected to fill vacancy caused by resignation of James Pleasants, and took his seat January 18, 1820.
[5] Resigned February 10, 1820.

[66] Elected to fill vacancy caused by resignation of George F. Strother, and took his seat November 13, 1820.
[67] Granted statehood December 14, 1819.
[68] Formed from a portion of lands of the Territory of Missouri and granted a Delegate in Congress by Act of March 2, 1819.
[69] Took his seat March 2, 1820.

[70] Formed by act approved January 11, 1805, from a portion of lands of Indiana Territory with Detroit as the seat of government.
[71] Took his seat March 2, 1820; resigned August 9, 1820.
[72] Elected to fill vacancy caused by resignation of William W. Woodbridge, and took his seat November 20, 1820.

SEVENTEENTH CONGRESS

MARCH 4, 1821, TO MARCH 3, 1823

FIRST SESSION—*December 3, 1821, to May 8, 1822*

SECOND SESSION—*December 2, 1822, to March 3, 1823*

———

VICE PRESIDENT OF THE UNITED STATES—Daniel D. Tompkins, of New York

PRESIDENT PRO TEMPORE OF THE SENATE—John Gaillard,[1] of South Carolina

SECRETARY OF THE SENATE—Charles Cutts, of New Hampshire

SERGEANT AT ARMS OF THE SENATE—Mountjoy Bayly, of Maryland

———

SPEAKER OF THE HOUSE OF REPRESENTATIVES—Philip P. Barbour,[2] of Virginia

CLERK OF THE HOUSE—Thomas Dougherty,[3] of Kentucky; Matthew St. Clair Clarke,[4] of Pennsylvania

SERGEANT AT ARMS OF THE HOUSE—Thomas Dunn, of Maryland

DOORKEEPER OF THE HOUSE—Benjamin Birch, of Maryland

ALABAMA

SENATORS

John W. Walker,[5] *Huntsville*
William Kelly,[6] *Huntsville*
William R. King, *Cahaba*

REPRESENTATIVE

Gabriel Moore, *Huntsville*

CONNECTICUT

SENATORS

James Lanman, *Norwich*
Elijah Boardman, *Litchfield*

REPRESENTATIVES

Noyes Barber, *Groton*
Daniel Burrows, *Hebron*
Henry W. Edwards, *New Haven*
Gideon Tomlinson, *Fairfield*
John Russ, *Hartford*
Ansel Sterling, *Sharon*
Ebenezer Stoddard, *Woodstock*

DELAWARE

SENATORS

Nicholas Van Dyke, *New Castle*
Caesar A. Rodney,[7] *Wilmington*

REPRESENTATIVES

Louis McLane, *Wilmington*
Caesar A. Rodney,[8] *Wilmington*
Daniel Rodney,[9] *Lewes*

GEORGIA

SENATORS

John Elliott, *Sunbury*
Freeman Walker,[10] *Augusta*
Nicholas Ware,[11] *Richmond*

REPRESENTATIVES

Joel Abbot, *Washington*
Alfred Cuthbert, *Eatonton*
George R. Gilmer, *Lexington*
Robert R. Reid, *Augusta*
Edward F. Tattnall, *Savannah*
Wiley Thompson, *Elberton*

ILLINOIS

SENATORS

Jesse B. Thomas, *Edwardsville*
Ninian Edwards, *Edwardsville*

REPRESENTATIVE

Daniel P. Cook, *Edwardsville*

INDIANA

SENATORS

James Noble, *Brookville*
Waller Taylor, *Vincennes*

REPRESENTATIVE

William Hendricks,[12] *Madison*
Jonathan Jennings,[13] *Charlestown*

KENTUCKY

SENATORS

Richard M. Johnson, *Great Crossings*
Isham Talbot, *Frankfort*

---

[1] Elected February 1, 1822; February 19, 1823.
[2] Elected December 4, 1821.
[3] Reelected December 4, 1821; died in 1822.
[4] Elected December 3, 1822; Samuel Burch, the principal clerk, acted as clerk in the interim.
[5] Resigned December 12, 1822.
[6] Elected to fill vacancy caused by resignation of John W. Walker, and took his seat January 21, 1823.

[7] Elected to fill vacancy in term commencing March 4, 1821, and took his seat January 24, 1822; resigned January 29, 1823, having been appointed minister to Buenos Aires; vacancy in this class from March 4, 1821, to January 23, 1822.
[8] Resigned January 24, 1822, having been elected Senator.

[9] Elected to fill vacancy caused by resignation of Caesar A. Rodney, and took his seat December 2, 1822.
[10] Resigned August 8, 1821.
[11] Elected to fill vacancy caused by resignation of Freeman Walker, and took his seat December 11, 1821.
[12] Resigned July 25, 1822.
[13] Elected to fill vacancy caused by resignation of William Hendricks, and took his seat December 2, 1822.

KENTUCKY—Continued

REPRESENTATIVES

Wingfield Bullock,[14] *Shelbyville*
James D. Breckinridge,[15] *Louisville*
Benjamin Hardin, *Bardstown*
Francis Johnson, *Bowling Green*
John T. Johnson, *Georgetown*
Thomas Metcalfe, *Carlisle*
Thomas Montgomery, *Stanford*
Anthony New, *Elkton*
George Robertson,[16] *Lancaster*
John S. Smith,[17] *Richmond*
David Trimble, *Mount Sterling*
Samuel H. Woodson, *Lexington*

LOUISIANA

SENATORS

Henry Johnson, *Donaldsonville*
James Brown, *New Orleans*

REPRESENTATIVE

Josiah S. Johnston, *Alexandria*

MAINE

SENATORS

John Chandler, *Monmouth*
John Holmes, *Alfred*

REPRESENTATIVES

Joshua Cushman, *Winslow*
Joseph Dane, *Kennebunk*
Ebenezer Herrick, *Bowdoinham*
Mark L. Hill, *Phippsburg*
Enoch Lincoln, *Paris*
Ezekiel Whitman,[18] *Portland*
Mark Harris,[19] *Portland*
William D. Williamson, *Bangor*

MARYLAND

SENATORS

Edward Lloyd, *Easton*
William Pinkney,[20] *Baltimore*
Samuel Smith,[21] *Baltimore*

REPRESENTATIVES

Thomas Bayly, *Princess Anne*
Jeremiah Cosden,[22] *Elkton*
Philip Reed,[23] *Chestertown*
Joseph Kent, *Bladensburg*
Peter Little, *Freedom*
Raphael Neale, *Leonardtown*

John Nelson, *Frederick*
Samuel Smith,[24] *Baltimore*
Isaac McKim,[25] *Baltimore*
Henry R. Warfield, *Middleburg*
Robert Wright, *Queenstown*

MASSACHUSETTS

SENATORS

Harrison Gray Otis,[26] *Boston*
James Lloyd,[27] *Boston*
Elijah H. Mills, *Northampton*

REPRESENTATIVES

Samuel C. Allen, *Greenfield*
Gideon Barstow, *Salem*
Francis Baylies, *Taunton*
Lewis Bigelow, *Petersham*
Henry W. Dwight, *Stockbridge*
William Eustis, *Boston*
Timothy Fuller, *Boston*
Benjamin Gorham, *Boston*
Aaron Hobart, *Hanover*
Samuel Lathrop, *West Springfield*
Jeremiah Nelson, *Newburyport*
John Reed, *Yarmouth*
Jonathan Russell, *Mendon*

MISSISSIPPI

SENATORS

Thomas H. Williams, *Washington*
David Holmes, *Washington*

REPRESENTATIVE

Christopher Rankin, *Natchez*

MISSOURI [28]

SENATORS

David Barton,[29] *St. Louis*
Thomas H. Benton,[30] *St. Louis*

REPRESENTATIVE

John Scott,[31] *Ste. Genevieve*

NEW HAMPSHIRE

SENATORS

David L. Morril, *Goffstown*
John F. Parrott, *Portsmouth*

REPRESENTATIVES

Josiah Butler, *South Deerfield*
Matthew Harvey, *Hopkinton*
Aaron Matson, *Stoddard*

William Plumer, Jr., *Epping*
Nathaniel Upham, *Rochester*
Thomas Whipple, Jr., *Wentworth*

NEW JERSEY

SENATORS

Mahlon Dickerson, *Succasunna*
Samuel L. Southard,[32] *Trenton*

REPRESENTATIVES

Ephraim Bateman, *Cedarville*
George Cassedy, *Hackensack*
Lewis Condict, *Morristown*
George Holcombe, *Allentown*
James Matlack, *Woodbury*
Samuel Swan, *Somerville*

NEW YORK

SENATORS

Rufus King, *New York City*
Martin Van Buren, *Albany*

REPRESENTATIVES

Selah Tuthill,[33] *Goshen*
Charles Borland, Jr.,[34] *Wardsbridge*
Churchill C. Cambreleng, *New York City*
Samuel Campbell, *Columbus*
Peter Sharpe,[35] *New York City*
Cadwallader D. Colden,[36] *New York City*
Alfred Conkling, *Canajoharie*
John D. Dickinson, *Troy*
John Gebhard, *Schoharie*
James Hawkes, *Richfield*
Thomas H. Hubbard, *Hamilton*
Joseph Kirkland, *Utica*
Elisha Litchfield, *Delphi*
Richard McCarty, *Coxsackie*
John J. Morgan, *New York City*
Walter Patterson, *Livingston*
Jeremiah H. Pierson, *Ramapo*
Nathaniel Pitcher, *Sandy Hill*
William B. Rochester, *Bath*
Charles H. Ruggles, *Kingston*
Elijah Spencer, *Benton*
Micah Sterling, *Watertown*
John W. Taylor, *Ballston Spa*
Albert H. Tracy, *Buffalo*
Solomon Van Rensselaer,[37] *Albany*
Stephen Van Rensselaer,[38] *Albany*
William W. Van Wyck, *Fishkill*
Reuben H. Walworth, *Plattsburg*
Silas Wood, *Huntington*
David Woodcock, *Ithaca*

---

[14] Died October 13, 1821, before Congress assembled.
[15] Elected to fill vacancy caused by death of Wingfield Bullock, and took his seat January 2, 1822.
[16] Resigned before Congress assembled.
[17] Elected to fill vacancy caused by resignation of George Robertson, and took his seat December 3, 1821.
[18] Resigned June 1, 1822.
[19] Elected to fill vacancy caused by resignation of Ezekiel Whitman, and took his seat December 2, 1822.
[20] Died February 25, 1822.
[21] Elected to fill vacancy caused by death of William Pinkney, and took his seat December 17, 1822.
[22] Served until March 19, 1822; succeeded by Philip Reed, who contested his election.

[23] Successfully contested the election of Jeremiah Cosden, and took his seat March 19, 1822.
[24] Resigned December 17, 1822, before the commencement of the Eighteenth Congress, to which he had been reelected, having been elected Senator
[25] Elected to fill vacancy caused by resignation of Samuel Smith, and took his seat January 8, 1823.
[26] Resigned May 30, 1822.
[27] Elected to fill vacancy caused by resignation of Harrison Gray Otis, and took his seat December 2, 1822.
[28] Admitted as a State into the Union August 10, 1821.
[29] Took his seat December 3, 1821; term to expire, as determined by lot, March 3, 1825.
[30] Took his seat December 6, 1821; term to expire, as

determined by lot, March 3, 1827.
[31] Took his seat December 3, 1821.
[32] Resigned March 3, 1823.
[33] Died September 7, 1821, before Congress assembled.
[34] Elected to fill vacancy caused by death of Selah Tuthill, and took his seat December 3, 1821.
[35] Never qualified; succeeded by Caldwallader D. Colden, who contested his election.
[36] Successfully contested the election of Peter Sharpe, and took his seat December 12, 1821.
[37] Resigned January 14, 1822.
[38] Elected to fill vacancy caused by resignation of Solomon Van Rensselaer, and took his seat March 12, 1822.

NORTH CAROLINA

SENATORS

Nathaniel Macon, *Monroe*
Montfort Stokes, *Wilkesboro*

REPRESENTATIVES

William S. Blackledge, *New Bern*
Hutchins G. Burton, *Halifax*
Henry W. Connor, *Sherrills Ford*
Josiah Crudup, *Raleigh*
Weldon N. Edwards, *Warrenton*
Thomas H. Hall, *Tarboro*
Charles Hooks, *Dublin*
John Long, *Longs Mills*
Archibald McNeill, *McNeills Store*
Romulus M. Saunders, *Milton*
Lemuel Sawyer, *Elizabeth City*
Felix Walker, *Waynesville*
Lewis Williams, *Panther Creek*

OHIO

SENATORS

Benjamin Ruggles, *St. Clairsville*
William A. Trimble,[39] *Hillsboro*
Ethan Allen Brown,[40] *Cincinnati*

REPRESENTATIVES

Levi Barber, *Point Harmer*
John W. Campbell, *West Union*
David Chambers,[41] *Zanesville*
Thomas R. Ross, *Lebanon*
John Sloane, *Wooster*
Joseph Vance,[42] *Urbana*

PENNSYLVANIA

SENATORS

Walter Lowrie, *Butler*
William Findlay,[43] *Franklinton*

REPRESENTATIVES

Henry Baldwin,[44] *Pittsburgh*
Walter Forward,[45] *Pittsburgh*
John Brown, *Lewistown*
James Buchanan, *Lancaster*
William Darlington, *West Chester*
George Denison, *Wilkes-Barre*
James Duncan,[46] *Carlisle*
John Findlay,[47] *Chambersburg*
Samuel Edwards, *Chester*

William Cox Ellis,[48] *Muncy*
Thomas Murray, Jr.,[49] *Milton*
Patrick Farrelly, *Meadville*
Samuel Gross, *Trappe*
Joseph Hemphill, *Philadelphia*
James McSherry, *Petersburg*
William Milnor,[50] *Philadelphia*
Thomas Forrest,[51] *Philadelphia*
James S. Mitchell, *Rossville*
Samuel Moore,[52] *Doylestown*
Samuel D. Ingham,[53] *New Hope*
Thomas Patterson, *West Middletown*
John Phillips, *Hummelstown*
George Plumer, *Robbstown*
Thomas J. Rogers, *Easton*
John Sergeant, *Philadelphia*
Andrew Stewart, *Uniontown*
John Tod, *Bedford*
Ludwig Worman,[54] *Pottstown*
Daniel Udree,[55] *Reading*

RHODE ISLAND

SENATORS

Nehemiah R. Knight, *Providence*
James De Wolf, *Bristol*

REPRESENTATIVES

Job Durfee, *Tiverton*
Samuel Eddy, *Providence*

SOUTH CAROLINA

SENATORS

John Gaillard, *Pendleton*
William Smith, *Pinckneyville*

REPRESENTATIVES

James Blair,[56] *Camden*
John Carter,[57] *Camden*
Joseph Gist, *Pinckneyville*
James Overstreet,[58] *King Creek*
Andrew R. Govan,[59] *Orangeburg*
William Lowndes,[60] *Jacksonboro*
James Hamilton, Jr.,[61] *Charleston*
George McDuffie, *Edgefield*
Thomas R. Mitchell, *Georgetown*
Joel R. Poinsett, *Charleston*
Starling Tucker, *Mountain Shoals*
John Wilson, *Golden Grove*

TENNESSEE

SENATORS

John Williams, *Knoxville*
John H. Eaton,[62] *Nashville*

REPRESENTATIVES

Robert Allen, *Carthage*
Henry H. Bryan,[63] *Palmyra*
Newton Cannon, *Harpeth*
John Cocke, *Rutledge*
Francis Jones, *Winchester*
John Rhea, *Sullivan*

VERMONT

SENATORS

William A. Palmer, *Danville*
Horatio Seymour, *Middlebury*

REPRESENTATIVES

Samuel C. Crafts, *Craftsbury*
Elias Keyes, *Stockbridge*
Rollin C. Mallary, *Poultney*
John Mattocks, *Peacham*
Charles Rich, *Shoreham*
Phineas White, *Putney*

VIRGINIA

SENATORS

James Barbour, *Barboursville*
James Pleasants,[64] *Goochland*
John Taylor,[65] *Port Royal*

REPRESENTATIVES

Mark Alexandria, *Lombardy Grove*
William S. Archer, *Amelia*
William L. Ball, *Nuttsville*
Philip P. Barbour, *Lucketsville*
Burwell Bassett, *Williamsburg*
John Floyd, *Newbern*
Robert S. Garnett, *Lloyds*
Edward B. Jackson, *Clarksburg*
James Jones, *Hendersonville*
Jabez Leftwich, *Liberty*
William McCoy, *Franklin*
Charles F. Mercer, *Aldie*
Thomas L. Moore, *Warrenton*
Hugh Nelson,[66] *Milton*
Thomas Newton, Jr., *Norfolk*
John Randolph, *Charlotte*
Arthur Smith, *Smithfield*

---

[39] Died December 13, 1821.
[40] Elected to fill vacancy caused by death of William A. Trimble, and took his seat January 15, 1822.
[41] Elected to fill vacancy caused by resignation of Representative-elect John C. Wright (March 3, 1821, before the beginning of the congressional term), and took his seat December 3, 1821.
[42] In previous issues of this publication this name appears as "John Vance." It is believed that this is an error arising through a printer's blunder in the first issue of the Congressional Directory for the Seventeenth Congress, caused by the typesetter carrying the name of "John" of Sloane's down to that of "Vance." The House Journal does not show that a "John Vance" was ever a Representative from Ohio, but in the same directory, under "Alphabetical List of Boarding Houses with the Members in each," the list of boarders at Miss Polk's home included "Joseph" Vance, but no "John."
[43] Elected for term beginning March 4, 1821, and

took his seat December 17, 1821; vacancy in this class from March 4, 1821, to December 9, 1821.
[44] Resigned May 8, 1822.
[45] Elected to fill vacancy caused by resignation of Henry Baldwin, and took his seat December 2, 1822.
[46] Resigned before Congress assembled.
[47] Elected to fill vacancy caused by resignation of James Duncan, and took his seat December 12, 1821.
[48] Resigned before Congress assembled.
[49] Elected to fill vacancy caused by resignation of William Cox Ellis, and took his seat December 12, 1821.
[50] Resigned May 8, 1822.
[51] Elected to fill vacancy caused by resignation of William Milnor, and took his seat December 2, 1822.
[52] Resigned May 20, 1822.
[53] Elected to fill vacancy caused by resignation of Samuel Moore, and took his seat December 2, 1822.
[54] Died October 17, 1822.
[55] Elected to fill vacancy caused by death of Ludwig Worman, and took his seat December 23, 1822.

[56] Resigned May 8, 1822.
[57] Elected to fill vacancy caused by resignation of James Blair, and took his seat December 11, 1822.
[58] Died May 24, 1822.
[59] Elected to fill vacancy caused by death of James Overstreet, and took his seat December 4, 1822.
[60] Resigned May 8, 1822.
[61] Elected to fill vacancy caused by resignation of William Lowndes, and took his seat January 6, 1823.
[62] Reelected for the term commencing March 4, 1821, and took his seat December 3, 1821; vacancy in this class from March 4, 1821, to September 26, 1821, caused by recess of legislature.
[63] Committee on Elections reported on February 17, 1823, that he had been duly elected, but appears never to have taken his seat.
[64] Resigned December 15, 1822.
[65] Elected to fill vacancy caused by resignation of James Pleasants, and took his seat December 30, 1822.
[66] Resigned January 14, 1823.

31671 O–61—7

VIRGINIA—Continued

REPRESENTATIVES—continued

William Smith, *Lewisburg*
Alexander Smyth, *Wythe*
Andrew Stevenson, *Richmond*
George Tucker, *Lynchburg*
Thomas Van Sweringen,[67] *Shepherdstown*
James Stephenson,[68] *Martinsburg*
Jared Williams, *Newton*

ARKANSAS TERRITORY

DELEGATE

James W. Bates,[69] *Arkansas*

TERRITORY OF FLORIDA [70]

DELEGATE

Joseph M. Hernandez,[71] *St. Augustine*

MICHIGAN TERRITORY

DELEGATE

Solomon Sibley, *Detroit*

TERRITORY OF MISSOURI [72]

DELEGATE

Vacant

---

[67] Died August 19, 1822.
[68] Elected to fill vacancy caused by death of Thomas Van Sweringen, and took his seat December 2, 1822.
[69] Election unsuccessfully contested by Matthew Lyon.

[70] Formed March 30, 1822, from lands ceded by Spain to the United States by treaty of Washington of February 22, 1819, and theretofore known as "East and West Florida," and granted a Delegate in Congress.

[71] Took his seat January 3, 1823.
[72] Granted statehood August 10, 1821.

EIGHTEENTH CONGRESS

MARCH 4, 1823, TO MARCH 3, 1825

FIRST SESSION—*December 1, 1823, to May 27, 1824*

SECOND SESSION—*December 6, 1824, to March 3, 1825*

———

VICE PRESIDENT OF THE UNITED STATES—DANIEL D. TOMPKINS, of New York

PRESIDENT PRO TEMPORE OF THE SENATE—JOHN GAILLARD,[1] of South Carolina

SECRETARY OF THE SENATE—CHARLES CUTTS, of New Hampshire

SERGEANT AT ARMS OF THE SENATE—MOUNTJOY BAYLY, of Maryland

———

SPEAKER OF THE HOUSE OF REPRESENTATIVES—HENRY CLAY,[2] of Kentucky

CLERK OF THE HOUSE—MATTHEW ST. CLAIR CLARKE,[3] of Pennsylvania

SERGEANT AT ARMS OF THE HOUSE—THOMAS DUNN, of Maryland; JOHN O. DUNN,[4] of District of Columbia

DOORKEEPER OF THE HOUSE—BENJAMIN BIRCH, of Maryland

ALABAMA

SENATORS

William R. King, *Cahaba*
William Kelly, *Huntsville*

REPRESENTATIVES

John McKee, *Tuscaloosa*
Gabriel Moore, *Huntsville*
George W. Owen, *Claiborne*

CONNECTICUT

SENATORS

James Lanman, *Norwich*
Elijah Boardman,[5] *Litchfield*
Henry W. Edwards,[6] *New Haven*

REPRESENTATIVES

Noyes Barber, *Groton*
Samuel A. Foote, *Cheshire*
Ansel Sterling, *Sharon*
Ebenezer Stoddard, *Woodstock*
Gideon Tomlinson, *Fairfield*
Lemuel Whitman, *Farmington*

DELAWARE

SENATORS

Nicholas Van Dyke, *New Castle*
Thomas Clayton,[7] *Dover*

REPRESENTATIVE

Louis McLane, *Wilmington*

GEORGIA

SENATORS

John Elliott, *Sunbury*
Nicholas Ware,[8] *Richmond*
Thomas W. Cobb,[9] *Greensboro*

REPRESENTATIVES

Joel Abbot, *Washington*
George Cary, *Appling*
Thomas W. Cobb,[10] *Greensboro*
Richard H. Wilde,[11] *Augusta*
Alfred Cuthbert, *Eatonton*
John Forsyth, *Augusta*
Edward F. Tattnall, *Savannah*
Wiley Thompson, *Elberton*

ILLINOIS

SENATORS

Jesse B. Thomas, *Edwardsville*
Ninian Edwards,[12] *Edwardsville*
John McLean,[13] *Shawneetown*

REPRESENTATIVE

Daniel P. Cook, *Edwardsville*

INDIANA

SENATORS

James Noble, *Brookville*
Waller Taylor, *Vincennes*

REPRESENTATIVES

Jonathan Jennings, *Charlestown*
John Test, *Brookville*
William Prince,[14] *Princeton*
Jacob Call,[15] *Princeton*

KENTUCKY

SENATORS

Richard M. Johnson, *Great Crossings*
Isham Talbot, *Frankfort*

---

[1] Elected May 21, 1824.
[2] Elected December 1, 1823.
[3] Reelected December 1, 1823.
[4] Elected December 6, 1824.
[5] Died October 8, 1823.
[6] Appointed to fill vacancy caused by death of Elijah Boardman, and took his seat December 1, 1823; subsequently elected.
[7] Elected to fill vacancy caused by resignation of

Caesar A. Rodney, in preceding Congress, and took his seat January 15, 1824. Vacancy in this class from January 29, 1823, to January 8, 1824.
[8] Died September 7, 1824.
[9] Elected to fill vacancy caused by death of Nicholas Ware, and took his seat December 6, 1824.
[10] Resigned December 6, 1824, having been elected Senator.
[11] Elected to fill vacancy caused by resignation of

Thomas W. Cobb, and took his seat February 7, 1825.
[12] Resigned March 4, 1824, having been appointed minister to Mexico.
[13] Elected to fill vacancy caused by resignation of Ninian Edwards, and took his seat December 20, 1824.
[14] Died September 4, 1824.
[15] Elected to fill vacancy caused by death of William Prince, and took his seat December 23, 1824.

KENTUCKY—Continued

REPRESENTATIVES

Richard A. Buckner, *Greensburg*
Henry Clay, *Lexington*
Robert P. Henry, *Hopkinsville*
Francis Johnson, *Bowling Green*
John T. Johnson, *Georgetown*
Robert P. Letcher, *Lancaster*
Thomas Metcalfe, *Carlisle*
Thomas P. Moore, *Harrodsburg*
Philip Thompson, *Yellow Banks*
David Trimble, *Mount Sterling*
David White, *New Castle*
Charles A. Wickliffe, *Bardstown*

LOUISIANA

SENATORS

Henry Johnson,[16] *Donaldsonville*
Dominique Bouligny,[17] *New Orleans*
James Brown,[18] *New Orleans*
Josiah S. Johnston,[19] *Alexandria*

REPRESENTATIVES

William L. Brent, *St. Martinsville*
Henry H. Gurley, *Baton Rouge*
Edward Livingston, *New Orleans*

MAINE

SENATORS

John Chandler, *Monmouth*
John Holmes, *Alfred*

REPRESENTATIVES

William Burleigh, *South Berwick*
Joshua Cushman, *Winslow*
Ebenezer Herrick, *Bowdoinham*
David Kidder, *Norridgewock*
Enoch Lincoln, *Paris*
Stephen Longfellow, *Portland*
Jeremiah O'Brien, *Machias*

MARYLAND

SENATORS

Edward Lloyd, *Easton*
Samuel Smith, *Baltimore*

REPRESENTATIVES

William Heyward, Jr., *Easton*
Joseph Kent, *Bladensburg*
John Lee, *Petersville*
Peter Little, *Freedom*
Isaac McKim,[20] *Baltimore*
George E. Mitchell, *Elkton*
Raphael Neale, *Leonardtown*
John S. Spence, *Poplartown*
Henry R. Warfield, *Middleburg*

MASSACHUSETTS

SENATORS

Elijah H. Mills, *Northampton*
James Lloyd, *Boston*

REPRESENTATIVES

Samuel C. Allen, *Greenfield*
John Bailey,[21] *Canton*
Francis Baylies, *Taunton*
Benjamin W. Crowninshield, *Salem*
Henry W. Dwight, *Stockbridge*
Timothy Fuller, *Boston*
Aaron Hobart, *Hanover*
Samuel Lathrop, *West Springfield*
John Locke, *Ashby*
Jeremiah Nelson, *Newburyport*
John Reed, *Yarmouth*
Jonas Sibley, *Worcester*
Daniel Webster, *Boston*

MISSISSIPPI

SENATORS

Thomas H. Williams, *Washington*
David Holmes, *Washington*

REPRESENTATIVE

Christopher Rankin, *Natchez*

MISSOURI

SENATORS

David Barton, *St. Louis*
Thomas H. Benton, *St. Louis*

REPRESENTATIVE

John Scott, *Ste. Genevieve*

NEW HAMPSHIRE

SENATORS

John F. Parrott, *Portsmouth*
Samuel Bell, *Chester*

REPRESENTATIVES

Ichabod Bartlett, *Portsmouth*
Matthew Harvey, *Hopkinton*
Arthur Livermore, *Plymouth*
Aaron Matson, *Stoddard*
William Plumer, Jr., *Epping*
Thomas Whipple, Jr., *Wentworth*

NEW JERSEY

SENATORS

Mahlon Dickerson, *Succasunna*
Joseph McIlvaine,[22] *Burlington*

REPRESENTATIVES

George Cassedy, *Hackensack*
Lewis Condict, *Morristown*
Daniel Garrison, *Salem*
George Holcombe, *Allentown*
James Matlack, *Woodbury*
Samuel Swan, *Somerville*

NEW YORK

SENATORS

Rufus King, *New York City*
Martin Van Buren, *Albany*

REPRESENTATIVES

John W. Cady, *Johnstown*
Churchill C. Cambreleng, *New York City*
Lot Clark, *Norwich*
Ela Collins, *Lowville*
Hector Craig, *Chester*
Rowland Day, *Simpronius*
Justin Dwinell, *Cazenovia*
Lewis Eaton, *Schoharie Bridge*
Charles A. Foote, *Delhi*
Joel Frost, *Carmel*
Moses Hayden, *York*
John Herkimer, *Danube*
James L. Hogeboom, *Castleton*
Lemuel Jenkins, *Bloomingburg*
Samuel Lawrence, *Johnsons Settlement*
Elisha Litchfield, *Delphi*
Henry C. Martindale, *Sandy Hill*
Dudley Marvin, *Canandaigua*
John J. Morgan, *New York City*
John Richards, *Johnsburg*
William B. Rochester,[23] *Bath*
William Woods,[24] *Bath*
Robert S. Rose, *Geneva*
Peter Sharpe, *New York City*
Henry R. Storrs, *Whitestown*
James Strong, *Hudson*
John W. Taylor, *Ballston Spa*
Egbert Ten Eyck, *Watertown*
Albert H. Tracy, *Buffalo*
Jacob Tyson, *Castletown*
Stephen Van Rensselaer, *Albany*
William W. Van Wyck, *Fishkill*
Isaac Williams, Jr., *Cooperstown*
Isaac Wilson,[25] *Middlebury*
Parmenio Adams,[26] *Batavia*
Silas Wood, *Huntington*

NORTH CAROLINA

SENATORS

Nathan Macon, *Monroe*
John Branch, *Enfield*

---

[16] Resigned May 27, 1824.
[17] Elected to fill vacancy caused by resignation of Henry Johnson, and took his seat December 21, 1824.
[18] Resigned December 10, 1823, having been appointed minister to France.
[19] Elected to fill vacancy caused by resignation of James Brown, and took his seat March 12, 1824.
[20] Elected to fill vacancy caused by resignation of

Representative-elect Samuel Smith, in preceding Congress.
[21] By resolution of March 18, 1824, was declared not entitled to seat; subsequently elected, and took his seat December 13, 1824.
[22] Elected to fill vacancy caused by resignation of Samuel L. Southard, in preceding Congress, and took his seat December 1, 1823.

[23] Resigned before Congress assembled.
[24] Elected to fill vacancy caused by resignation of William B. Rochester, and took his seat December 1, 1823.
[25] Served until January 7, 1824; succeeded by Parmenio Adams, who contested his election.
[26] Successfully contested the election of Isaac Wilson, and took his seat January 7, 1824.

REPRESENTATIVES

Hutchins G. Burton,[27] *Halifax*
George Outlaw,[28] *Windsor*
Henry W. Connor, *Sherrills Ford*
John Culpepper, *Lawrenceville*
Weldon N. Edwards, *Warrenton*
Alfred M. Gatlin, *Edenton*
Thomas H. Hall, *Tarboro*
Charles Hooks, *Dublin*
John Long, *Longs Mills*
Willie P. Mangum, *Red Mountain*
Romulus M. Saunders, *Milton*
Richard D. Spaight, Jr., *New Bern*
Robert B. Vance, *Nashville*
Lewis Williams, *Panther Creek*

OHIO

SENATORS

Benjamin Ruggles, *St. Clairsville*
Ethan Allen Brown, *Cincinnati*

REPRESENTATIVES

Mordecai Bartley, *Mansfield*
Philemon Beecher, *Lancaster*
John W. Campbell, *West Union*
John W. Gazlay, *Cincinnati*
Duncan McArthur, *Chillicothe*
William McLean, *Piqua*
John Patterson, *St. Clairsville*
Thomas R. Ross, *Lebanon*
John Sloane, *Wooster*
Joseph Vance, *Urbana*
Samuel F. Vinton, *Gallipolis*
Elisha Whittlesey, *Canfield*
William Wilson, *Newark*
John C. Wright, *Steubenville*

PENNSYLVANIA

SENATORS

Walter Lowrie, *Butler*
William Findlay, *Franklinton*

REPRESENTATIVES

James Allison, Jr., *Beaver*
Samuel Breck, *Philadelphia*
John Brown, *Lewistown*
James Buchanan, *Lancaster*
Samuel Edwards, *Chester*
William Cox Ellis, *Muncy*
Patrick Farrelly, *Meadville*
John Findlay, *Chambersburg*
Walter Forward, *Pittsburgh*
Robert Harris, *Harrisburg*
Joseph Hemphill, *Philadelphia*
Samuel D. Ingham, *New Hope*
George Kremer, *Lewisburg*
Samuel McKean, *Burlington*

Philip S. Markley, *Norristown*
Daniel H. Miller, *Philadelphia*
James S. Mitchell, *Rossville*
Thomas Patterson, *West Middletown*
George Plumer, *Robbstown*
Andrew Stewart, *Uniontown*
John Tod,[29] *Bedford*
Alexander Thomson,[30] *Bedford*
Daniel Udree, *Reading*
Isaac Wayne, *Warren*
Henry Wilson, *Allentown*
James Wilson, *Fairfield*
Thomas J. Rogers,[31] *Easton*
George Wolf,[32] *Easton*

RHODE ISLAND

SENATORS

Nehemiah R. Knight, *Providence*
James De Wolf, *Bristol*

REPRESENTATIVES

Job Durfee, *Tiverton*
Samuel Eddy, *Providence*

SOUTH CAROLINA

SENATORS

John Gaillard, *Pendleton*
Robert Y. Hayne, *Charleston*

REPRESENTATIVES

Robert B. Campbell, *Brownsville*
John Carter, *Camden*
Joseph Gist, *Pinckneyville*
Andrew R. Govan, *Orangeburg*
James Hamilton, Jr., *Charleston*
George McDuffie, *Edgefield*
Joel R. Poinsett, *Charleston*
Starling Tucker, *Mountain Shoals*
John Wilson, *Golden Grove*

TENNESSEE

SENATORS

John H. Eaton, *Nashville*
Andrew Jackson, *Nashville*

REPRESENTATIVES

Adam R. Alexander, *Jackson*
Robert Allen, *Carthage*
John Blair, *Jonesboro*
John Cocke, *Rutledge*
Samuel Houston, *Nashville*
Jacob C. Isacks, *Winchester*
James B. Reynolds, *Clarksville*
James T. Sandford, *Columbia*
James Standifer, *Pikeville*

VERMONT

SENATORS

William A. Palmer, *Danville*
Horatio Seymour, *Middlebury*

REPRESENTATIVES

William C. Bradley, *Westminster*
Daniel A. A. Buck, *Chelsea*
Samuel C. Crafts, *Craftsbury*
Rollin C. Mallary, *Poultney*
Charles Rich,[33] *Shoreham*
Henry Olin,[34] *Salisbury*

VIRGINIA

SENATORS

James Barbour, *Barboursville*
John Taylor,[35] *Port Royal*
Littleton W. Tazewell,[36] *Norfolk*

REPRESENTATIVES

Mark Alexander, *Lombardy Grove*
William S. Archer, *Amelia*
John S. Barbour, *Culpeper*
Philip P. Barbour, *Lucketsville*
Burwell Bassett, *Williamsburg*
John Floyd, *Newbern*
Robert S. Garnett, *Lloyds*
Joseph Johnson, *Bridgeport*
Jabez Leftwich, *Liberty*
William McCoy, *Franklin*
Charles F. Mercer, *Aldie*
Thomas Newton, Jr., *Norfolk*
John Randolph, *Charlotte*
William C. Rives, *Milton*
Arthur Smith, *Smithfield*
William Smith, *Lewisburg*
Alexander Smyth, *Wythe*
James Stephenson, *Martinsburg*
Andrew Stevenson, *Richmond*
William L. Ball,[37] *Nuttsville*
John Taliaferro,[38] *Fredericksburg*
George Tucker, *Lynchburg*
Jared Williams,[39] *Newton*

ARKANSAS TERRITORY

DELEGATE

Henry W. Conway, *Little Rock*

TERRITORY OF FLORIDA

DELEGATE

Richard K. Call, *Pensacola*

MICHIGAN TERRITORY

DELEGATE

Gabriel Richard,[40] *Detroit*

---

[27] Resigned March 23, 1824.
[28] Elected to fill vacancy caused by resignation of Hutchins G. Burton, and took his seat January 19, 1825.
[29] Resigned in 1824.
[30] Elected to fill vacancy caused by resignation of John Tod, and took his seat December 6, 1824.
[31] Resigned April 20, 1824.

[32] Elected to fill vacancy caused by resignation of Thomas J. Rogers, and took his seat December 9, 1824.
[33] Died October 15, 1824.
[34] Elected to fill vacancy caused by death of Charles Rich, and took his seat December 13, 1824.
[35] Died August 20, 1824.
[36] Elected to fill vacancy caused by death of John Taylor, and took his seat December 29, 1824.

[37] Died February 28, 1824.
[38] Elected to fill vacancy caused by death of William L. Ball, and took his seat April 8, 1824.
[39] Election unsuccessfully contested by Alfred H. Powell.
[40] Election unsuccessfully contested by John Biddle.

NINETEENTH CONGRESS

MARCH 4, 1825, TO MARCH 3, 1827

FIRST SESSION—*December 5, 1825, to May 22, 1826*

SECOND SESSION—*December 4, 1826, to March 3, 1827*

SPECIAL SESSION OF THE SENATE—*March 4, 1825, to March 9, 1825*

———

VICE PRESIDENT OF THE UNITED STATES—John C. Calhoun, of South Carolina

PRESIDENT PRO TEMPORE OF THE SENATE—John Gaillard,[1] of South Carolina; Nathaniel Macon,[2] of North Carolina

SECRETARY OF THE SENATE—Charles Cutts, of New Hampshire; Walter Lowrie,[3] of Pennsylvania

SERGEANT AT ARMS OF THE SENATE—Mountjoy Bayly, of Maryland

———

SPEAKER OF THE HOUSE OF REPRESENTATIVES—John W. Taylor,[4] of New York

CLERK OF THE HOUSE—Matthew St. Clair Clarke,[5] of Pennsylvania

SERGEANT AT ARMS OF THE HOUSE—John O. Dunn, of District of Columbia

DOORKEEPER OF THE HOUSE—Benjamin Birch, of Maryland

ALABAMA

SENATORS

William R. King, *Cahaba*
Henry H. Chambers,[6] *Madison*
Israel Pickens,[7] *Cahaba*
John McKinley,[8] *Huntsville*

REPRESENTATIVES

John McKee, *Tuscaloosa*
Gabriel Moore, *Huntsville*
George W. Owen, *Claiborne*

CONNECTICUT

SENATORS

Henry W. Edwards, *New Haven*
Calvin Willey,[9] *Tolland*

REPRESENTATIVES

John Baldwin, *Windham*
Noyes Barber, *Groton*
Ralph I. Ingersoll, *New Haven*
Orange Merwin, *New Milford*
Elisha Phelps, *Simsbury*
Gideon Tomlinson, *Fairfield*

DELAWARE

SENATORS

Nicholas Van Dyke,[10] *New Castle*
Daniel Rodney,[11] *Wilmington*
Henry M. Ridgely,[12] *Dover*
Thomas Clayton, *Dover*

REPRESENTATIVE

Louis McLane,[13] *Wilmington*

GEORGIA

SENATORS

Thomas W. Cobb, *Greensboro*
John Macpherson Berrien, *Savannah*

REPRESENTATIVES

George Cary, *Appling*
Alfred Cuthbert, *Eatonton*
John Forsyth, *Augusta*
Charles E. Haynes, *Sparta*
James Meriwether, *Athens*
Edward F. Tattnall, *Savannah*
Wiley Thompson, *Elberton*

ILLINOIS

SENATORS

Jesse B. Thomas, *Edwardsville*
Elias K. Kane, *Kaskaskia*

REPRESENTATIVE

Daniel P. Cook, *Edwardsville*

INDIANA

SENATORS

James Noble, *Brookville*
William Hendricks, *Madison*

REPRESENTATIVES

Ratliff Boon, *Boonville*
Jonathan Jennings, *Charlestown*
John Test, *Brookville*

KENTUCKY

SENATORS

Richard M. Johnson, *Great Crossings*
John Rowan, *Louisville*

---

[1] Elected March 9, 1825 (special session of the Senate).
[2] Elected May 20, 1826; January 2, 1827; and March 2, 1827.
[3] Elected December 12, 1825.
[4] Elected December 5, 1825.
[5] Reelected December 5, 1825.
[6] Died January 24, 1826.
[7] Appointed to fill vacancy caused by death of Henry Chambers, and took his seat April 10, 1826.
[8] Elected to fill vacancy caused by death of Henry Chambers, and took his seat December 21, 1826.
[9] Elected for term commencing March 4, 1825; took his seat December 5, 1825. James Lanman was appointed, but the Senate, on March 5, 1825, would not permit him to qualify; vacancy in this class from March 4, 1825, to May 4, 1825, because of recess of legislature.
[10] Died May 21, 1826.
[11] Appointed to fill vacancy caused by death of Nicholas Van Dyke, and took his seat December 4, 1826.
[12] Elected to fill vacancy caused by death of Nicholas Van Dyke, and took his seat January 23, 1827.
[13] Reelected to the Twentieth Congress, but resigned, having been elected Senator.

REPRESENTATIVES

Richard A. Buckner, *Greensburg*
Henry Clay,[14] *Lexington*
James Clark,[15] *Winchester*
Robert P. Henry,[16] *Hopkinsville*
John F. Henry,[17] *Hopkinsville*
Francis Johnson, *Bowling Green*
James Johnson,[18] *Great Crossings*
Robert McHatton,[19] *Georgetown*
Robert P. Letcher, *Lancaster*
Thomas Metcalfe, *Carlisle*
Thomas P. Moore, *Harrodsburg*
David Trimble, *Mount Sterling*
Charles A. Wickliffe, *Bardstown*
William S. Young, *Elizabethtown*
Joseph Lecompte, *New Castle*

LOUISIANA

SENATORS

Josiah S. Johnston, *Alexandria*
Dominique Bouligny, *New Orleans*

REPRESENTATIVES

William L. Brent, *St. Martinsville*
Henry H. Gurley, *Baton Rouge*
Edward Livingston, *New Orleans*

MAINE

SENATORS

John Chandler, *Monmouth*
John Holmes, *Alfred*

REPRESENTATIVES

John Anderson, *Portland*
William Burleigh, *South Berwick*
Ebenezer Herrick, *Bowdoinham*
David Kiddler, *Norridgewock*
Enoch Lincoln,[20] *Paris*
James W. Ripley,[21] *Fryeburg*
Jeremiah O'Brien, *Machias*
Peleg Sprague, *Hallowell*

MARYLAND

SENATORS

Edward Lloyd,[22] *Easton*
Ezekiel F. Chambers,[23] *Chestertown*
Samuel Smith, *Baltimore*

REPRESENTATIVES

John Barney, *Baltimore*
Clement Dorsey, *Chaptico*
Joseph Kent,[24] *Bladensburg*

John C. Weems,[25] *Waterloo*
John L. Kerr, *Easton*
Peter Little, *Freedom*
Robert N. Martin, *Princess Anne*
George E. Mitchell, *Elkton*
George Peter, *Darnestown*
Thomas C. Worthington, *Frederick*

MASSACHUSETTS

SENATORS

Elijah H. Mills, *Northampton*
James Lloyd,[26] *Boston*
Nathaniel Silsbee,[27] *Salem*

REPRESENTATIVES

Samuel C. Allen, *Greenfield*
John Bailey, *Milton*
Francis Baylies, *Taunton*
Benjamin W. Crowninshield, *Salem*
John Davis, *Worcester*
Henry W. Dwight, *Stockbridge*
Edward Everett, *Cambridge*
Aaron Hobart, *East Bridgewater*
Samuel Lathrop, *West Springfield*
John Locke, *Ashby*
John Reed, *Yarmouth*
John Varnum, *Haverhill*
Daniel Webster, *Boston*

MISSISSIPPI

SENATORS

Thomas H. Williams, *Washington*
David Holmes,[28] *Washington*
Powhatan Ellis,[29] *Winchester*
Thomas B. Reed,[30] *Natchez*

REPRESENTATIVES

Christopher Rankin,[31] *Natchez*
William Haile,[32] *Woodville*

MISSOURI

SENATORS

David Barton, *St. Louis*
Thomas H. Benton, *St. Louis*

REPRESENTATIVE

John Scott, *Ste. Genevieve*

NEW HAMPSHIRE

SENATORS

Samuel Bell, *Chester*
Levi Woodbury,[33] *Portsmouth*

REPRESENTATIVES

Ichabod Bartlett, *Portsmouth*
Titus Brown, *Francestown*
Nehemiah Eastman, *Farmington*
Jonathan Harvey, *Sutton*
Joseph Healy, *Washington*
Thomas Whipple, Jr., *Wentworth*

NEW JERSEY

SENATORS

Mahlon Dickerson, *Succasunna*
Joseph McIlvaine,[34] *Burlington*
Ephraim Bateman,[35] *Cedarville*

REPRESENTATIVES

George Cassedy, *Hackensack*
Lewis Condict, *Morristown*
Daniel Garrison, *Salem*
George Holcombe, *Allentown*
Samuel Swan, *Somerville*
Ebenezer Tucker, *Tuckerton*

NEW YORK

SENATORS

Martin Van Buren, *Albany*
Nathan Sanford,[36] *Albany*

REPRESENTATIVES

Parmenio Adams, *Batavia*
William G. Angel, *Burlington*
Henry Ashley, *Catskill*
Luther Badger, *Janesville*
Churchill C. Cambreleng, *New York City*
William Dietz, *Schoharie*
Nicoll Fosdick, *Morristown*
Daniel G. Garnsey, *Fredonia*
John Hallock, Jr., *Ridgebury*
Abraham B. Hasbrouck, *Kingston*
Moses Hayden, *York*
Michael Hoffman, *Herkimer*
Charles Humphrey, *Ithaca*
Jeromus Johnson, *New York City*
Charles Kellogg, *Kelloggsville*
William McManus, *Troy*
Henry Markell, *Palatine*
Henry C. Martindale, *Sandy Hill*
Dudley Marvin, *Canandaigua*
John Miller, *Truxton*
Timothy H. Porter, *Olean*
Robert S. Rose, *Geneva*
Henry H. Ross, *Essex*
Joshua Sands, *Brooklyn*
Henry R. Storrs, *Whitestown*
James Strong, *Hudson*

---

[14] Resigned March 6, 1825, before Congress assembled.
[15] Elected to fill vacancy caused by resignation of Henry Clay, and took his seat December 5, 1825.
[16] Died August 25, 1826.
[17] Elected to fill vacancy caused by death of Robert P. Henry, and took his seat December 11, 1826.
[18] Died August 14, 1826.
[19] Elected to fill vacancy caused by death of James Johnson, and took his seat December 7, 1826.
[20] Resigned in January, 1826, having been elected governor.
[21] Elected to fill vacancy caused by resignation of Enoch Lincoln, and took his seat December 4, 1826.

[22] Resigned in January 1826.
[23] Elected to fill vacancy caused by resignation of Edward Lloyd, and took his seat February 22, 1826.
[24] Resigned January 6, 1826, having been elected governor.
[25] Elected to fill vacancy caused by resignation of Joseph Kent, and took his seat February 7, 1826.
[26] Resigned May 23, 1826.
[27] Elected to fill vacancy caused by resignation of James Lloyd, and took his seat December 4, 1826.
[28] Resigned September 25, 1825.
[29] Appointed to fill vacancy caused by resignation of David Holmes, and took his seat December 12, 1825.

[30] Elected to fill vacancy caused by resignation of David Holmes, and took his seat March 11, 1826.
[31] Died March 14, 1826.
[32] Elected to fill vacancy caused by death of Christopher Rankin, and took his seat December 4, 1826.
[33] Elected to fill vacancy in term commencing March 4, 1825, and took his seat December 5, 1825; vacancy in this class from March 4, 1825, to June 15, 1825.
[34] Died August 19, 1826.
[35] Elected to fill vacancy caused by death of Joseph McIlvaine, and took his seat December 7, 1826.
[36] Elected to fill vacancy in term commencing March 4, 1825, and took his seat January 31, 1826; vacancy in this class from March 4, 1825, to January 14, 1826.

NEW YORK—Continued

REPRESENTATIVES—continued

John W. Taylor, *Ballston Spa*
Egbert Ten Eyck,[37] *Watertown*
Daniel Hugunin, Jr.,[38] *Oswego*
Stephen Van Rensselaer, *Albany*
Gulian C. Verplanck, *New York City*
Aaron Ward, *Mount Pleasant*
Bartow White, *Fishkill*
Elias Whitmore, *Windsor*
Silas Wood, *Huntington*

NORTH CAROLINA

SENATORS

Nathaniel Macon, *Monroe*
John Branch, *Enfield*

REPRESENTATIVES

Willis Alston, *Hyde Park*
John H. Bryan, *New Bern*
Samuel P. Carson, *Pleasant Garden*
Henry W. Connor, *Sherrills Ford*
Weldon N. Edwards, *Warrenton*
Richard Hines, *Edgecombe*
Gabriel Holmes, *Clinton*
John Long, *Longs Mills*
Archibald McNeill, *McNeills Store*
Willie P. Mangum,[39] *Red Mountain*
Daniel L. Barringer,[40] *Raleigh*
Romulus M. Saunders, *Milton*
Lemuel Sawyer, *Elizabeth City*
Lewis Williams, *Panther Creek*

OHIO

SENATORS

Benjamin Ruggles, *St. Clairsville*
William Henry Harrison, *Cincinnati*

REPRESENTATIVES

Mordecai Bartley, *Mansfield*
Philemon Beecher, *Lancaster*
John W. Campbell, *West Union*
James Findlay, *Cincinnati*
David Jennings,[41] *St. Clairsville*
Thomas Shannon,[42] *Barnesville*
William McLean, *Piqua*
John Sloane, *Wooster*
John Thomson, *Chillicothe*
Joseph Vance, *Urbana*
Samuel F. Vinton, *Gallipolis*
Elisha Whittlesey, *Canfield*

William Wilson, *Newark*
John Woods, *Hamilton*
John C. Wright, *Steubenville*

PENNSYLVANIA

SENATORS

William Findlay, *Franklinton*
William Marks, *Pittsburgh*

REPRESENTATIVES

William Addams, *Reading*
James Allison, Jr.,[43] *Beaver*
Robert Orr, Jr.,[44] *Kittanning*
James Buchanan, *Lancaster*
Samuel Edwards, *Chester*
Patrick Farrelly,[45] *Meadville*
Thomas H. Sill,[46] *Erie*
John Findlay, *Chambersburg*
Robert Harris, *Harrisburg*
Joseph Hemphill,[47] *Philadelphia*
Thomas Kittera,[48] *Philadelphia*
Samuel D. Ingham, *New Hope*
George Kremer, *Lewisburg*
Joseph Lawrence, *Washington*
Samuel McKean, *Burlington*
Philip S. Markley, *Norristown*
Daniel H. Miller, *Philadelphia*
Charles Miner, *West Chester*
James S. Mitchell, *Rossville*
John Mitchell, *Bellefonte*
George Plumer, *Robbstown*
James S. Stevenson, *Pittsburgh*
Andrew Stewart, *Uniontown*
Alexander Thomson,[49] *Bedford*
Chauncey Forward,[50] *Somerset*
Espy Van Horne, *Williamsport*
Henry Wilson,[51] *Allentown*
Jacob Krebs,[52] *Orwigsburg*
James Wilson, *Fairfield*
George Wolf, *Easton*
John Wurts, *Philadelphia*

RHODE ISLAND

SENATORS

Nehemiah R. Knight, *Providence*
James De Wolf,[53] *Bristol*
Asher Robbins,[54] *Newport*

REPRESENTATIVES

Tristam Burges, *Providence*
Dutee J. Pearce, *Newport*

SOUTH CAROLINA

SENATORS

John Gaillard,[55] *Pendleton*
William Harper,[56] *Charleston*
William Smith,[57] *Charleston*
Robert Y. Hayne, *Charleston*

REPRESENTATIVES

John Carter, *Camden*
Joel R. Poinsett,[58] *Charleston*
William Drayton,[59] *Charleston*
Joseph Gist, *Pinckneyville*
Andrew R. Govan, *Orangeburg*
James Hamilton, Jr., *Charleston*
George McDuffie, *Edgefield*
Thomas R. Mitchell, *Georgetown*
Starling Tucker, *Mountain Shoals*
John Wilson, *Golden Grove*

TENNESSEE

SENATORS

John H. Eaton, *Nashville*
Andrew Jackson,[60] *Nashville*
Hugh Lawson White,[61] *Knoxville*

REPRESENTATIVES

Adam R. Alexander, *Jackson*
Robert Allen, *Carthage*
John Blair, *Jonesboro*
John Cocke, *Rutledge*
Samuel Houston, *Nashville*
Jacob C. Isacks, *Winchester*
John H. Marable, *Yellow Creek*
James C. Mitchell, *Athens*
James K. Polk, *Columbia*

VERMONT

SENATORS

Horatio Seymour, *Middlebury*
Dudley Chase, *Randolph*

REPRESENTATIVES

William C. Bradley, *Westminster*
Rollin C. Mallary, *Poultney*
John Mattocks, *Peacham*
Ezra Meech, *Shelburn*
George E. Wales, *Hartford*

VIRGINIA

SENATORS

James Barbour,[62] *Barboursville*
John Randolph,[63] *Charlotte*
Littleton W. Tazewell, *Norfolk*

---

[37] Served until December 15, 1825; succeeded by Daniel Hugunin, Jr., who contested his election.
[38] Successfully contested the election of Egbert Ten Eyck, and took his seat December 15, 1825.
[39] Resigned March 18, 1826.
[40] Elected to fill vacancy caused by resignation of Willie P. Mangum, and took his seat December 4, 1826.
[41] Resigned May 25, 1826.
[42] Elected to fill vacancy caused by resignation of David Jennings, and took his seat December 4, 1826.
[43] Resigned before Congress assembled.
[44] Elected to fill vacancy caused by resignation of James Allison, Jr., and took his seat December 5, 1825.
[45] Died January 12, 1826.
[46] Elected to fill vacancy caused by death of Patrick Farrelly, and took his seat April 3, 1826.

[47] Resigned in 1826.
[48] Elected to fill vacancy caused by resignation of Joseph Hemphill, and took his seat December 4, 1826.
[49] Resigned May 1, 1826.
[50] Elected to fill vacancy caused by resignation of Alexander Thomson, and took his seat December 4, 1826.
[51] Died August 14, 1826.
[52] Elected to fill vacancy caused by death of Henry Wilson, and took his seat December 4, 1826.
[53] Resigned October 31, 1825.
[54] Elected to fill vacancy caused by resignation of James De Wolf, and took his seat December 5, 1825.
[55] Died February 26, 1826.
[56] Appointed to fill vacancy caused by death of John Gaillard, and took his seat March 28, 1826.

[57] Elected to fill vacancy caused by death of John Gaillard, and took his seat December 7, 1826.
[58] Resigned March 7, 1825, to become minister to Mexico.
[59] Elected to fill vacancy caused by resignation of Joel R. Poinsett, and took his seat December 5, 1825.
[60] Resigned October 14, 1825.
[61] Elected to fill vacancy caused by resignation of Andrew Jackson, and took his seat December 12, 1825.
[62] Resigned March 7, 1825.
[63] Elected to fill vacancy caused by resignation of James Barbour, and took his seat December 26, 1825; vacancy in this class from March 28, 1825, to December 8, 1825.

REPRESENTATIVES

Mark Alexander, *Lombardy Grove*
William S. Archer, *Amelia*
William Armstrong, *Romney*
John S. Barbour, *Culpeper*
Burwell Bassett, *Williamsburg*
Nathaniel H. Claiborne, *Rocky Mount*
Thomas Davenport, *Meadville*
Benjamin Estil, *Abingdon*
John Floyd, *Newbern*
Robert S. Garnett, *Lloyds*
Joseph Johnson, *Bridgeport*

William McCoy, *Franklin*
Charles F. Mercer, *Aldie*
Thomas Newton, Jr., *Norfolk*
Alfred H. Powell, *Winchester*
John Randolph,[64] *Charlotte*
George W. Crump,[65] *Cumberland*
William C. Rives, *Milton*
William Smith, *Lewisburg*
Andrew Stevenson, *Richmond*
John Taliaferro, *Fredericksburg*
Robert Taylor, *Orange*
James Trezvant, *Jerusalem*

ARKANSAS TERRITORY

DELEGATE

Henry W. Conway, *Little Rock*

TERRITORY OF FLORIDA

DELEGATE

Joseph M. White, *Pensacola*

MICHIGAN TERRITORY

DELEGATE

Austin E. Wing,[66] *Detroit*

---

[64] Resigned; effective December 26, 1825, without qualifying, having been elected Senator.

[65] Elected to fill vacancy caused by resignation of John Randolph, and took his seat February 6, 1826.

[66] Election unsuccessfully contested by John Biddle and Gabriel Richard.

TWENTIETH CONGRESS

MARCH 4, 1827, TO MARCH 3, 1829

FIRST SESSION—*December 3, 1827, to May 26, 1828*

SECOND SESSION—*December 1, 1828, to March 3, 1829*

VICE PRESIDENT OF THE UNITED STATES—JOHN C. CALHOUN, of South Carolina

PRESIDENT PRO TEMPORE OF THE SENATE—SAMUEL SMITH,[1] of Maryland

SECRETARY OF THE SENATE—WALTER LOWRIE,[2] of Pennsylvania

SERGEANT AT ARMS OF THE SENATE—MOUNTJOY BAYLY, of Maryland

SPEAKER OF THE HOUSE OF REPRESENTATIVES—ANDREW STEVENSON,[3] of Virginia

CLERK OF THE HOUSE—MATTHEW ST. CLAIR CLARKE,[4] of Pennsylvania

SERGEANT AT ARMS OF THE HOUSE—JOHN O. DUNN, of District of Columbia

DOORKEEPER OF THE HOUSE—BENJAMIN BIRCH, of Maryland

ALABAMA

SENATORS

William R. King, *Selma*
John McKinley, *Huntsville*

REPRESENTATIVES

John McKee, *Tuscaloosa*
Gabriel Moore, *Huntsville*
George W. Owen, *Claiborne*

CONNECTICUT

SENATORS

Calvin Willey, *Tolland*
Samuel A. Foote, *Cheshire*

REPRESENTATIVES

John Baldwin, *Windham*
Noyes Barber, *Groton*
Ralph I. Ingersoll, *New Haven*
Orange Merwin, *New Milford*
Elisha Phelps, *Simsbury*
David Plant, *Stratford*

DELAWARE

SENATORS

Henry M. Ridgely, *Dover*
Louis McLane, *Wilmington*

REPRESENTATIVE

Kensey Johns, Jr.,[5] *New Castle*

GEORGIA

SENATORS

Thomas W. Cobb,[6] *Greensboro*
Oliver H. Prince,[7] *Macon*
John Macpherson Berrien, *Savannah*

REPRESENTATIVES

John Floyd, *Jefferson*
John Forsyth,[8] *Augusta*
Richard H. Wilde,[9] *Augusta*
Tomlinson Fort, *Milledgeville*
Charles E. Haynes, *Sparta*
Wilson Lumpkin, *Madison*
Edward F. Tattnall,[10] *Savannah*
George R. Gilmer,[11] *Lexington*
Wiley Thompson, *Elberton*

ILLINOIS

SENATORS

Jesse B. Thomas, *Edwardsville*
Elias K. Kane, *Kaskaskia*

REPRESENTATIVE

Joseph Duncan, *Brownsville*

INDIANA

SENATORS

James Noble, *Brookville*
William Hendricks, *Madison*

REPRESENTATIVES

Thomas H. Blake, *Terre Haute*
Jonathan Jennings, *Charlestown*
Oliver H. Smith, *Connersville*

KENTUCKY

SENATORS

Richard M. Johnson, *Great Crossings*
John Rowan, *Louisville*

---

[1] Elected May 15, 1828. Nathaniel Macon, of North Carolina, was first elected on the same day, but declined to serve.
[2] Reelected December 10, 1827.
[3] Elected December 3, 1827.
[4] Reelected December 3, 1827.
[5] Elected to fill vacancy caused by resignation of Representative-elect Louis McLane, in preceding Congress, and took his seat December 3, 1827.
[6] Resigned in 1828.
[7] Elected to fill vacancy caused by resignation of Thomas W. Cobb, and took his seat December 1, 1828.
[8] Resigned; effective November 7, 1827, before Congress assembled, having been elected governor.
[9] Elected to fill vacancy caused by resignation of John Forsyth, and took his seat January 14, 1828.
[10] Resigned before Congress assembled.
[11] Elected to fill vacancy caused by resignation of Edward Tattnall, and took his seat December 3, 1827; reelected to the Twenty-first Congress but failed to signify his acceptance.

REPRESENTATIVES

Richard A. Buckner, *Greensburg*
William S. Young,[12] *Elizabethtown*
John Calhoon,[13] *Hardinsburg*
Thomas Chilton,[14] *Elizabethtown*
James Clark, *Winchester*
Henry Daniel, *Mount Sterling*
Joseph Lecompte, *New Castle*
Robert P. Letcher, *Lancaster*
Chittenden Lyon, *Eddyville*
Robert McHatton, *Georgetown*
Thomas Metcalfe,[15] *Carlisle*
John Chambers,[16] *Washington*
Thomas P. Moore, *Harrodsburg*
Charles A. Wickliffe, *Bardstown*
Joel Yancey, *Glasgow*

LOUISIANA

SENATORS

Josiah S. Johnston, *Alexandria*
Dominique Bouligny, *New Orleans*

REPRESENTATIVES

William L. Brent, *St. Martinsville*
Henry H. Gurley, *Baton Rouge*
Edward Livingston, *New Orleans*

MAINE

SENATORS

John Chandler, *Monmouth*
Albion K. Parris,[17] *Portland*
John Holmes,[18] *Alfred*

REPRESENTATIVES

John Anderson, *Portland*
Samuel Butman, *Dixmont*
William Burleigh,[19] *South Berwick*
Rufus McIntire,[20] *Parsonsfield*
Jeremiah O'Brien, *Machias*
James W. Ripley, *Fryeburg*
Peleg Sprague,[21] *Hallowell*
Joseph F. Wingate, *Bath*

MARYLAND

SENATORS

Samuel Smith, *Baltimore*
Ezekiel F. Chambers, *Chestertown*

REPRESENTATIVES

John Barney, *Baltimore*
Clement Dorsey, *Chaptico*
Levin Gale, *Elkton*
John L. Kerr, *Easton*
Peter Little, *Freedom*
Michael C. Sprigg, *Frostburg*
George C. Washington, *Rockville*
John C. Weems, *Waterloo*
Ephraim K. Wilson, *Snow Hill*

MASSACHUSETTS

SENATORS

Nathaniel Silsbee, *Salem*
Daniel Webster,[22] *Boston*

REPRESENTATIVES

Samuel C. Allen, *Greenfield*
John Baily, *Milton*
Isaac C. Bates, *Northampton*
Benjamin W. Crowninshield, *Salem*
John Davis, *Worcester*
Henry W. Dwight, *Stockbridge*
Edward Everett, *Cambridge*
James L. Hodges, *Taunton*
John Locke, *Ashby*
John Reed, *Yarmouth*
Joseph Richardson, *Hingham*
John Varnum, *Haverhill*
Daniel Webster,[23] *Boston*
Benjamin Gorham,[24] *Boston*

MISSISSIPPI

SENATORS

Thomas H. Williams, *Washington*
Powhatan Ellis, *Winchester*

REPRESENTATIVES

William Haile,[25] *Woodville*
Thomas Hinds,[26] *Greenville*

MISSOURI

SENATORS

David Barton, *St. Louis*
Thomas H. Benton, *St. Louis*

REPRESENTATIVE

Edward Bates, *St. Louis*

NEW HAMPSHIRE

SENATORS

Samuel Bell, *Chester*
Levi Woodbury, *Portsmouth*

REPRESENTATIVES

David Barker, Jr., *Rochester*
Ichabod Bartlett, *Portsmouth*
Titus Brown, *Francestown*
Jonathan Harvey, *Sutton*
Joseph Healy, *Washington*
Thomas Whipple, Jr., *Wentworth*

NEW JERSEY

SENATORS

Ephraim Bateman,[27] *Cedarville*
Mahlon Dickerson,[28] *Succasunna*
Mahlon Dickerson,[29] *Succasunna*

REPRESENTATIVES

Lewis Condict, *Morristown*
George Holcombe,[30] *Allentown*
James F. Randolph,[31] *New Brunswick*
Isaac Pierson, *Orange*
Hedge Thompson,[32] *Salem*
Thomas Sinnickson,[33] *Salem*
Samuel Swan, *Somerville*
Ebenezer Tucker, *Tuckerton*

NEW YORK

SENATORS

Martin Van Buren,[34] *Albany*
Charles E. Dudley,[35] *Albany*
Nathan Sanford, *Albany*

REPRESENTATIVES

Daniel D. Barnard, *Rochester*
George O. Belden, *Monticello*
Rudolph Bunner, *Oswego*
Churchill C. Cambreleng, *New York City*
Samuel Chase, *Cooperstown*
John C. Clark, *Bainbridge*
David E. Evans,[36] *Batavia*
Phineas L. Tracy,[37] *Batavia*
John I. De Graff, *Schenectady*
John D. Dickinson, *Troy*
Jonas Earll, Jr., *Onondaga*
Daniel G. Garnsey, *Fredonia*
Nathaniel Garrow, *Auburn*

---

[12] Died September 20, 1827, before Congress assembled.
[13] John Calhoon and Thomas Chilton were candidates to fill vacancy caused by death of William S. Young and the vote of one county being thrown out the certificate of election was given to Mr. Calhoon; by mutual agreement Calhoon resigned and both contestants then petitioned the governor for a new election.
[14] Elected to fill vacancy caused by resignation of John Calhoon, and took his seat January 11, 1828.
[15] Resigned June 1, 1828.
[16] Elected to fill vacancy caused by resignation of Thomas Metcalfe, and took his seat December 1, 1828.
[17] Resigned August 26, 1828.
[18] Elected to fill vacancy caused by resignation of Albion K. Parris, and took his seat January 26, 1829.
[19] Died July 2, 1827, before Congress assembled.
[20] Elected to fill vacancy caused by death of William Burleigh, and took his seat December 3, 1827.

[21] Reelected to the Twenty-first Congress, but resigned, having been elected Senator.
[22] Elected to fill vacancy in the term beginning March 4, 1827, caused by failure of legislature to elect, and took his seat December 17, 1827.
[23] Resigned May 30, 1827, before Congress assembled, having been elected Senator.
[24] Elected to fill vacancy caused by resignation of Daniel Webster, and took his seat December 3, 1827.
[25] Resigned September 12, 1828.
[26] Elected to fill vacancy caused by resignation of William Haile, and took his seat December 8, 1828.
[27] A remonstrance against the legality of his election was considered by a select committee of five Senators; it revealed that, as chairman of the joint convention of the general assembly of New Jersey, Mr. Bateman had voted for himself for Senator, had broken a tie vote thereby, and upon such state of facts the certificate had been issued to him; May 22, 1828, the committee

reported, that, in its opinion, he had only exercised a legal right by thus voting, and, upon its request, was discharged; resigned January 12, 1829.
[28] Elected to fill vacancy caused by resignation of Ephraim Bateman, and took his seat February 9, 1829.
[29] Resigned January 30, 1829 (see footnote 27); vacancy in this class from January 30, 1829, to March 3, 1829.
[30] Died January 14, 1828.
[31] Elected to fill vacancy caused by death of George Holcombe, and took his seat December 1, 1828.
[32] Died July 23, 1828.
[33] Elected to fill vacancy caused by death of Hedge Thompson, and took his seat December 1, 1828.
[34] Resigned December 20, 1828.
[35] Elected to fill vacancy caused by resignation of Martin Van Buren, and took his seat January 29, 1829.
[36] Resigned May 2, 1827, before Congress assembled.
[37] Elected to fill vacancy caused by resignation of David E. Evans, and took his seat December 3, 1827.

NEW YORK—Continued

REPRESENTATIVES—continued

John Hallock, Jr., *Ridgebury*
Selah R. Hobbie, *Delhi*
Michael Hoffman, *Herkimer*
Jeromus Johnson, *New York City*
Richard Keese, *Keeseville*
John Magee, *Bath*
Henry Markell, *Palatine*
Henry C. Martindale, *Sandy Hill*
Dudley Marvin, *Canandaigua*
John Maynard, *Ovid Village*
Thomas J. Oakley,[38] *Poughkeepsie*
Thomas Taber, 2d,[39] *Dover*
Henry R. Storrs, *Whitestown*
John G. Stower, *Hamilton*
James Strong, *Hudson*
John W. Taylor, *Ballston Spa*
Stephen Van Rensselaer, *Albany*
Gulian C. Verplanck, *New York City*
Aaron Ward, *Mount Pleasant*
John J. Wood, *Clarkstown*
Silas Wood, *Huntington*
David Woodcock, *Ithaca*
Silas Wright, Jr.,[40] *Canton*

NORTH CAROLINA

SENATORS

Nathaniel Macon,[41] *Warrenton*
James Iredell,[42] *Edenton*
John Branch, *Enfield*

REPRESENTATIVES

Willis Alston, *Hyde Park*
Daniel L. Barringer, *Raleigh*
John H. Bryan, *New Bern*
Samuel P. Carson, *Pleasant Garden*
Henry W. Connor, *Sherrills Ford*
John Culpepper, *Beards Store*
Thomas H. Hall, *Tarboro*
Gabriel Holmes, *Clinton*
John Long, *Longs Mills*
Lemuel Sawyer, *Elizabeth City*
Augustine H. Shepperd, *Germantown*
Daniel Turner, *Warrenton*
Lewis Williams, *Panther Creek*

OHIO

SENATORS

Benjamin Ruggles, *St. Clairsville*
William Henry Harrison,[43] *Cincinnati*
Jacob Burnet,[44] *Cincinnati*

REPRESENTATIVES

Mordecai Bartley, *Mansfield*
Philemon Beecher, *Lancaster*

William Creighton, Jr.,[45] *Chillicothe*
Francis S. Muhlenberg,[46] *Circleville*
John Davenport, *Barnesville*
James Findlay, *Cincinnati*
William McLean, *Piqua*
William Russell, *West Union*
John Sloane, *Wooster*
Joseph Vance, *Urbana*
Samuel F. Vinton, *Gallipolis*
Elisha Whittlesey, *Canfield*
William Wilson,[47] *Newark*
William Stanbery,[48] *Newark*
John Woods, *Hamilton*
John C. Wright, *Steubenville*

PENNSYLVANIA

SENATORS

Williams Marks, *Pittsburgh*
Isaac D. Barnard, *West Chester*

REPRESENTATIVES

William Addams, *Reading*
Samuel Anderson, *Providence*
Stephen Barlow, *Meadville*
James Buchanan, *Lancaster*
Richard Coulter, *Greensburg*
Chauncey Forward, *Somerset*
Joseph Fry, Jr., *Fryburg*
Innis Green, *Dauphin*
Samuel D. Ingham, *New Hope*
Adam King, *York*
George Kremer, *Lewisburg*
Joseph Lawrence, *Washington*
Samuel McKean, *Burlington*
Daniel H. Miller, *Philadelphia*
Charles Miner, *West Chester*
John Mitchell, *Bellefonte*
Robert Orr, Jr., *Kittanning*
William Ramsey, *Carlisle*
John Sergeant,[49] *Philadelphia*
John B. Sterigere, *Upper Dublin*
James S. Stevenson, *Pittsburgh*
Andrew Stewart, *Uniontown*
Joel B. Sutherland, *Philadelphia*
Espy Van Horne, *Williamsport*
James Wilson, *Fairfield*
George Wolf, *Easton*

RHODE ISLAND

SENATORS

Nehemiah R. Knight, *Providence*
Asher Robbins, *Newport*

REPRESENTATIVES

Tristam Burges, *Providence*
Dutee J. Pearce, *Newport*

SOUTH CAROLINA

SENATORS

Robert Y. Hayne, *Charleston*
William Smith, *Charleston*

REPRESENTATIVES

John Carter, *Camden*
Warren R. Davis, *Pendleton*
William Drayton, *Charleston*
James Hamilton, Jr., *Charleston*
George McDuffie, *Edgefield*
William D. Martin, *Barnwell*
Thomas R. Mitchell, *Georgetown*
William T. Nuckolls, *Spartanburg*
Starling Tucker, *Mountain Shoals*

TENNESSEE

SENATORS

John H. Eaton, *Nashville*
Hugh Lawson White, *Knoxville*

REPRESENTATIVES

John Bell, *Nashville*
John Blair, *Jonesboro*
David Crockett, *Trenton*
Robert Desha, *Gallatin*
Jacob C. Isacks, *Winchester*
Pryor Lea, *Knoxville*
John H. Marable, *Yellow Creek*
James C. Mitchell, *Athens*
James K. Polk, *Columbia*

VERMONT

SENATORS

Horatio Seymour, *Middlebury*
Dudley Chase, *Randolph*

REPRESENTATIVES

Daniel A. A. Buck, *Chelsea*
Jonathan Hunt, *Brattleboro*
Rollin C. Mallary, *Poultney*
Benjamin Swift, *St. Albans*
George E. Wales, *Hartford*

VIRGINIA

SENATORS

Littleton W. Tazewell, *Norfolk*
John Tyler, *Charles City*

REPRESENTATIVES

Mark Alexander, *Lombardy Grove*
Robert Allen, *Mount Jackson*
William S. Archer, *Elk Hill*
William Armstrong, *Romney*
John S. Barbour, *Culpeper*

---

[38] Resigned May 9, 1828.
[39] Elected to fill vacancy caused by resignation of Thomas J. Oakley, and took his seat December 1, 1828.
[40] Resigned February 16, 1829.
[41] Resigned November 14, 1828.
[42] Elected to fill vacancy caused by resignation of of Nathaniel Macon, and took his seat December 23, 1828.

[43] Resigned May 20, 1828.
[44] Elected to fill vacancy caused by resignation of William Henry Harrison, and took his seat December 29, 1828.
[45] Resigned in 1828.
[46] Elected to fill vacancy caused by resignation of William Creighton, Jr., and took his seat December 19, 1828.

[47] Died June 6, 1827, before Congress assembled.
[48] Elected to fill vacancy caused by death of William Wilson, and took his seat December 3, 1827.
[49] Election questioned by sundry citizens of Pennsylvania. On January 14, 1828, resolution was adopted declaring him entitled to his seat.

Philip P. Barbour, *Gordonsville*
Burwell Bassett, *Williamsburg*
Nathaniel H. Claiborne, *Rocky Mount*
Thomas Davenport, *Meadville*
John Floyd, *Newbern*
Isaac Leffler, *Wheeling*
Lewis Maxwell, *Weston*
Charles F. Mercer, *Aldie*
William McCoy, *Franklin*
Thomas Newton, Jr., *Norfolk*
John Randolph, *Charlotte*
William C. Rives, *Milton*

John Roane, *Rumford Academy*
Alexander Smyth, *Wythe*
Andrew Stevenson, *Richmond*
John Taliaferro, *Fredericksburg*
James Trezvant, *Jerusalem*

ARKANSAS TERRITORY

DELEGATE

Henry W. Conway, [50] *Little Rock*
Ambrose H. Sevier,[51] *Little Rock*

TERRITORY OF FLORIDA

DELEGATE

Joseph M. White, *Pensacola*

MICHIGAN TERRITORY

DELEGATE

Austin E. Wing, *Detroit*

[50] Died November 9, 1827, before Congress assembled.
[51] Elected to fill vacancy caused by death of Henry W. Conway, and took his seat February 13, 1828.

TWENTY-FIRST CONGRESS

MARCH 4, 1829, TO MARCH 3, 1831

FIRST SESSION—*December 7, 1829, to May 31, 1830*

SECOND SESSION—*December 6, 1830, to March 3, 1831*

SPECIAL SESSION OF THE SENATE—*March 4, 1829, to March 17, 1829*

VICE PRESIDENT OF THE UNITED STATES—JOHN C. CALHOUN, of South Carolina

PRESIDENT PRO TEMPORE OF THE SENATE—SAMUEL SMITH,[1] of Maryland

SECRETARY OF THE SENATE—WALTER LOWRIE,[2] of Pennsylvania

SERGEANT AT ARMS OF THE SENATE—MOUNTJOY BAYLY, of Maryland

SPEAKER OF THE HOUSE OF REPRESENTATIVES—ANDREW STEVENSON,[3] of Virginia

CLERK OF THE HOUSE—MATTHEW ST. CLAIR CLARKE,[4] of Pennsylvania

SERGEANT AT ARMS OF THE HOUSE—JOHN O. DUNN, of District of Columbia

DOORKEEPER OF THE HOUSE—BENJAMIN BIRCH, of Maryland

ALABAMA

SENATORS

William R. King, *Selma*
John McKinley, *Florence*

REPRESENTATIVES

Robert E. B. Baylor, *Tuscaloosa*
Clement C. Clay, *Huntsville*
Dixon H. Lewis, *Montgomery*

CONNECTICUT

SENATORS

Calvin Willey, *Tolland*
Samuel A. Foote, *Cheshire*

REPRESENTATIVES

Noyes Barber, *Groton*
William W. Ellsworth, *Hartford*
Jabez W. Huntington, *Litchfield*
Ralph I. Ingersoll, *New Haven*
William L. Storrs, *Middletown*
Ebenezer Young, *Killingly Center*

DELAWARE

SENATORS

Louis McLane,[5] *Wilmington*
Arnold Naudain,[6] *Wilmington*
John M. Clayton, *Dover*

REPRESENTATIVE

Kensey Johns, Jr., *New Castle*

GEORGIA

SENATORS

John Macpherson Berrien,[7] *Savannah*
John Forsyth,[8] *Augusta*
George M. Troup, *Dublin*

REPRESENTATIVES

Thomas F. Foster, *Greensboro*
Charles E. Haynes, *Sparta*
Henry G. Lamar,[9] *Macon*
Wilson Lumpkin, *Monroe*
Wiley Thompson, *Elberton*
James M. Wayne, *Savannah*
Richard H. Wilde, *Augusta*

ILLINOIS

SENATORS

Elias K. Kane, *Kaskaskia*
John McLean,[10] *Shawneetown*
David J. Baker,[11] *Shawneetown*
John M. Robinson,[12] *Carmi*

REPRESENTATIVE

Joseph Duncan, *Brownsville*

INDIANA

SENATORS

James Noble,[13] *Brookville*
William Hendricks, *Madison*

REPRESENTATIVES

Ratliff Boon, *Boonville*
Jonathan Jennings, *Charlestown*
John Test, *Lawrenceburg*

KENTUCKY

SENATORS

John Rowan, *Louisville*
George M. Bibb, *Yellow Banks*

---

[1] Elected March 13, 1829 (special session of the Senate); May 29, 1830; March 1, 1831; Littleton W. Tazewell, of Virginia, was first elected on the last-named date, but declined to serve.
[2] Reelected December 14, 1829.
[3] Reelected December 7, 1829.
[4] Reelected December 7, 1829.
[5] Resigned April 16, 1829.

[6] Elected to fill vacancy caused by resignation of Louis McLane, and took his seat January 13, 1830.
[7] Resigned March 9, 1829.
[8] Elected to fill vacancy caused by resignation of John Macpherson Berrien, and took his seat December 8, 1829.
[9] Elected to fill vacancy caused by failure of Representative-elect George R. Gilmer to signify his accept-

ance, and took his seat December 7, 1829.
[10] Died October 14, 1830.
[11] Appointed to fill vacancy caused by death of John McLean, and took his seat December 6, 1830.
[12] Elected to fill vacancy caused by death of John McLean, and took his seat January 4, 1831.
[13] Died February 26, 1831.

REPRESENTATIVES

Thomas Chilton, *Elizabethtown*
James Clark, *Winchester*
Nicholas D. Coleman, *Washington*
Henry Daniel, *Mount Sterling*
Nathan Gaither, *Columbia*
Richard M. Johnson, *Great Crossings*
John Kincaid, *Stanford*
Joseph Lecompte, *New Castle*
Robert P. Letcher, *Lancaster*
Chittenden Lyon, *Eddyville*
Charles A. Wickliffe, *Bardstown*
Joel Yancey, *Glasgow*

LOUISIANA

SENATORS

Josiah S. Johnston, *Alexandria*
Edward Livingston, *New Orleans*

REPRESENTATIVES

Henry H. Gurley, *Baton Rouge*
Walter H. Overton, *Alexandria*
Edward D. White, *Donaldsonville*

MAINE

SENATORS

John Holmes, *Alfred*
Peleg Sprague, *Hallowell*

REPRESENTATIVES

John Anderson, *Portland*
Samuel Butman, *Dixmont*
George Evans,[14] *Gardiner*
Leonard Jarvis, *Ellsworth*
Rufus McIntire, *Parsonsfield*
James W. Ripley,[15] *Fryeburg*
Cornelius Holland,[16] *Canton*
Joseph F. Wingate, *Bath*

MARYLAND

SENATORS

Samuel Smith, *Baltimore*
Ezekiel F. Chambers, *Chestertown*

REPRESENTATIVES

Elias Brown, *Freedom*
Clement Dorsey, *Chaptico*
Benjamin C. Howard, *Baltimore*
George E. Mitchell, *Elkton*
Benedict J. Semmes, *Piscataway*
Richard Spencer, *Easton*
Michael C. Sprigg, *Frostburg*
George C. Washington, *Rockville*
Ephraim K. Wilson, *Snow Hill*

MASSACHUSETTS

SENATORS

Nathaniel Silsbee, *Salem*
Daniel Webster, *Boston*

REPRESENTATIVES

John Bailey, *Milton*
Isaac C. Bates, *Northampton*
Benjamin W. Crowninshield, *Salem*
John Davis, *Worcester*
Henry W. Dwight, *Stockbridge*
Edward Everett, *Charlestown*
Benjamin Gorham, *Boston*
George Grennell, Jr., *Greenfield*
James L. Hodges, *Taunton*
Joseph G. Kendall, *Leominster*
John Reed, *Yarmouth*
Joseph Richardson, *Hingham*
John Varnum, *Haverhill*

MISSISSIPPI

SENATORS

Powhatan Ellis, *Winchester*
Thomas B. Reed,[17] *Natchez*
Robert H. Adams,[18] *Natchez*
George Poindexter,[19] *Natchez*

REPRESENTATIVE

Thomas Hinds, *Greenville*

MISSOURI

SENATORS

David Barton, *St. Louis*
Thomas H. Benton, *St. Louis*

REPRESENTATIVE

Spencer D. Pettis, *Fayette*

NEW HAMPSHIRE

SENATORS

Samuel Bell, *Chester*
Levi Woodbury, *Portsmouth*

REPRESENTATIVES

John Brodhead, *Newmarket*
Thomas Chandler, *Hillsboro*
Joseph Hammons, *Farmington*
Jonathan Harvey, *Sutton*
Henry Hubbard, *Charlestown*
John W. Weeks, *Lancaster*

NEW JERSEY

SENATORS

Mahlon Dickerson, *Succasunna*
Theodore Frelinghuysen, *Newark*

REPRESENTATIVES

Lewis Condict, *Morristown*
Richard M. Cooper, *Camden*
Thomas H. Hughes, *Cold Spring*
Isaac Pierson, *Orange*
James F. Randolph, *New Brunswick*
Samuel Swan, *Somerville*

NEW YORK

SENATORS

Nathan Sanford, *Albany*
Charles E. Dudley, *Albany*

REPRESENTATIVES

William G. Angel, *Burlington*
Benedict Arnold, *Amsterdam*
Thomas Beekman, *Peterboro*
Abraham Bockee, *Federal Store*
Peter I. Borst, *Middleburg*
Churchill C. Cambreleng, *New York City*
Timothy Childs, *Rochester*
Jonas Earll, Jr., *Onondaga*
Isaac Finch, *Jay*
George Fisher,[20] *Oswego*
Silas Wright, Jr.,[21] *Canton*
Jonah Sanford,[22] *Oswego*
Jehiel H. Halsey, *Lodi*
Joseph Hawkins, *Henderson*
Michael Hoffman, *Herkimer*
Perkins King, *Freehold*
James Lent, *Newtown*
John Magee, *Bath*
Henry C. Martindale, *Sandy Hill*
Henry B. Cowles, *Carmel*
Hector Craig,[23] *Craigville*
Samuel W. Eager,[24] *Montgomery*
Jacob Crocheron, *Smithfield*
Charles G. De Witt, *Kingston*
John D. Dickinson, *Troy*
Thomas Maxwell, *Elmira*
Robert Monell,[25] *Greene*
Ebenezer F. Norton, *Buffalo*
Gershom Powers, *Auburn*
Robert S. Rose, *Geneva*
Ambrose Spencer, *Albany*
James Strong, *Hudson*
Henry R. Storrs, *Whitestown*
John W. Taylor, *Ballston Spa*
Phineas L. Tracy, *Batavia*
Gulian C. Verplanck, *New York City*
Campbell P. White, *New York City*

---

[14] Elected to fill vacancy caused by resignation of Representative-elect Peleg Sprague, in preceding Congress, and took his seat December 7, 1829.
[15] Election unsuccessfully contested by Reuel Washburn; resigned March 12, 1830.
[16] Elected to fill vacancy caused by resignation of James W. Ripley, and took his seat December 6, 1830.
[17] Died November 26, 1829.
[18] Elected to fill vacancy caused by death of Thomas B. Reed, and took his seat Febuary 8, 1830; died July 2, 1830.
[19] Appointed to fill vacancy caused by deaths of Thomas B. Reed and Robert H. Adams, and took his seat December 6, 1830; subsequently elected.
[20] Served until February 5, 1830; election successfully contested by Silas Wright, Jr.
[21] Successfully contested the election of George Fisher, but resigned March 9, 1830, never having qualified, preferring to continue as comptroller of the State.
[22] Elected to fill vacancy caused by resignation of Silas Wright, Jr., and took his seat December 6, 1830.
[23] Resigned July 12, 1830.
[24] Elected to fill vacancy caused by resignation of Hector Craig, and took his seat December 6, 1830.
[25] Resigned February 21, 1831.

NORTH CAROLINA

SENATORS

John Branch,[26] *Enfield*
Bedford Brown,[27] *Browns Store*
James Iredell, *Edenton*

REPRESENTATIVES

Willis Alston, *Hyde Park*
Daniel L. Barringer, *Raleigh*
Samuel P. Carson, *Pleasant Garden*
Henry W. Connor, *Sherrills Ford*
Edmund Deberry, *Lawrenceville*
Thomas H. Hall, *Tarboro*
Gabriel Holmes,[28] *Clinton*
Edward B. Dudley,[29] *Wilmington*
Robert Potter, *Oxford*
Abraham Rencher, *Pittsboro*
William B. Shepard, *Elizabeth City*
Augustine H. Shepperd, *Germantown*
Jesse Speight, *Stantonsburg*
Lewis Williams, *Panther Creek*

OHIO

SENATORS

Benjamin Ruggles, *St. Clairsville*
Jacob Burnet, *Cincinnati*

REPRESENTATIVES

Mordecai Bartley, *Mansfield*
Joseph H. Crane, *Dayton*
William Creighton, Jr., *Chillicothe*
James Findlay, *Cincinnati*
John M. Goodenow,[30] *Steubenville*
Humphrey H. Leavitt,[31] *Steubenville*
William W. Irvin, *Lancaster*
William Kennon, Sr., *St. Clairsville*
William Russell, *West Union*
James Shields, *Dicks Mills*
William Stanbery, *Newark*
John Thomson, *New Lisbon*
Joseph Vance, *Urbana*
Samuel F. Vinton, *Gallipolis*
Elisha Whittlesey, *Canfield*

PENNSYLVANIA

SENATORS

William Marks, *Pittsburgh*
Isaac D. Barnard, *West Chester*

REPRESENTATIVES

James Buchanan, *Lancaster*
Richard Coulter, *Greensburg*

Thomas H. Crawford, *Chambersburg*
Joshua Evans, Jr., *Paoli*
James Ford, *Lawrenceville*
Chauncey Forward, *Somerset*
Joseph Fry, Jr., *Fryburg*
John Gilmore, *Butler*
Innis Green, *Dauphin*
Joseph Hemphill, *Philadelphia*
Samuel D. Ingham,[32] *New Hope*
Peter Ihrie, Jr.,[33] *Easton*
George Wolf,[34] *Easton*
Samuel A. Smith,[35] *Doylestown*
Thomas Irwin, *Uniontown*
Adam King, *York*
George C. Leiper, *Leiperville*
Alem Marr, *Danville*
William McCreery, *Florence*
Daniel H. Miller, *Philadelphia*
Henry A. P. Muhlenberg, *Reading*
William Ramsey, *Carlisle*
John Scott, *Alexandria*
Thomas H. Sill, *Erie*
Philander Stephens, *Montrose*
John B. Sterigere, *Norristown*
Joel B. Sutherland, *Philadelphia*
William Wilkins,[36] *Pittsburgh*
Harmar Denny,[37] *Pittsburgh*

RHODE ISLAND

SENATORS

Nehemiah R. Knight, *Providence*
Asher Robbins, *Newport*

REPRESENTATIVES

Tristam Burges, *Providence*
Dutee J. Pearce, *Newport*

SOUTH CAROLINA

SENATORS

Robert Y. Hayne, *Charleston*
William Smith, *Charleston*

REPRESENTATIVES

Robert W. Barnwell, *Beaufort*
James Blair, *Camden*
John Campbell, *Brownsville*
Warren R. Davis, *Pendleton*
William Drayton, *Charleston*
William D. Martin, *Barnwell*
George McDuffie, *Edgefield*
William T. Nuckolls, *Hancockville*
Starling Tucker, *Mountain Shoals*

TENNESSEE

SENATORS

John H. Eaton,[38] *Nashville*
Felix Grundy,[39] *Nashville*
Hugh Lawson White, *Knoxville*

REPRESENTATIVES

John Bell, *Nashville*
John Blair, *Jonesboro*
David Crockett, *Crockett*
Robert Desha, *Gallatin*
Jacob C. Isacks, *Winchester*
Cave Johnson, *Clarksville*
Pryor Lea,[40] *Knoxville*
James K. Polk, *Columbia*
James Standifer, *Mountairy*

VERMONT

SENATORS

Horatio Seymour, *Middlebury*
Dudley Chase, *Randolph*

REPRESENTATIVES

William Cahoon, *Lyndon*
Horace Everett, *Windsor*
Jonathan Hunt, *Brattleboro*
Rollin C. Mallary, *Poultney*
Benjamin Swift, *St. Albans*

VIRGINIA

SENATORS

Littleton W. Tazewell, *Norfolk*
John Tyler, *Charles City*

REPRESENTATIVES

Mark Alexander, *Lombardy Grove*
Robert Allen, *Mount Jackson*
William S. Archer, *Elk Hill*
William Armstrong, *Romney*
John S. Barbour, *Culpeper*
Philip P. Barbour,[41] *Gordonsville*
John M. Patton,[42] *Fredericksburg*
Thomas T. Bouldin, *Charlotte*
Nathaniel H. Claiborne, *Rocky Mount*
Richard Coke, Jr., *Williamsburg*
Robert Craig, *Montgomery*
Thomas Davenport, *Meadville*
Philip Doddridge, *Wellsburg*
Alexander Smyth,[43] *Wythe*
Joseph Draper,[44] *Wythe*
Thomas Newton, Jr.,[45] *Norfolk*
George Loyall,[46] *Norfolk*

---

[26] Resigned March 9, 1829, having been appointed Secretary of the Navy.
[27] Elected to fill vacancy caused by resignation of John Branch, and took his seat December 28, 1829.
[28] Died September 26, 1829, before Congress assembled.
[29] Elected to fill vacancy caused by death of Gabriel Holmes, and took his seat December 14, 1829.
[30] Resigned April 9, 1830, before Congress assembled.
[31] Elected to fill vacancy caused by resignation of John M. Goodenow, and took his seat December 6, 1830.
[32] Resigned before Congress assembled.
[33] Elected to fill in part vacancies caused by resigna-

tions of George Wolf and Samuel D. Ingham, and took his seat December 7, 1829.
[34] Resigned before Congress assembled, having been elected governor.
[35] Elected to fill in part vacancies caused by resignations of George Wolf and Samuel D. Ingham, and took his seat December 7, 1829.
[36] Resigned before Congress assembled.
[37] Elected to fill vacancy caused by resignation of William Wilkins, and took his seat December 30, 1829.
[38] Resigned March 9, 1829.
[39] Elected to fill vacancy caused by resignation of John H. Eaton, and took his seat December 7, 1829.

[40] Election unsuccessfully contested by Thomas D. Arnold.
[41] Resigned October 15, 1830.
[42] Elected to fill vacancy caused by resignation of Philip P. Barbour, and took his seat December 6, 1830.
[43] Died April 17, 1830.
[44] Elected to fill vacancy caused by death of Alexander Smyth, and took his seat December 6, 1830.
[45] Served until March 9, 1830; succeeded by George Loyall, who contested his election.
[46] Successfully contested the election of Thomas Newton, Jr., and took his seat March 9, 1830.

William C. Rives,[47] *Milton*
William F. Gordon,[48] *Lindseys Store*
Lewis Maxwell, *Weston*
William McCoy, *Franklin*
Charles F. Mercer, *Leesburg*
John Roane, *Rumford Academy*
Andrew Stevenson, *Richmond*
John Taliaferro, *Fredericksburg*
James Trezvant, *Jerusalem*

ARKANSAS TERRITORY

DELEGATE

Ambrose H. Sevier, *Little Rock*

TERRITORY OF FLORIDA

DELEGATE

Joseph M. White, *Monticello*

MICHIGAN TERRITORY

DELEGATE

John Biddle,[49] *Detroit*

---

[47] Resigned in 1829, having been appointed minister to France.

[48] Elected to fill vacancy caused by resignation of William C. Rives, and took his seat January 25, 1830.

[49] Resigned February 21, 1831.

TWENTY-SECOND CONGRESS

MARCH 4, 1831, TO MARCH 3, 1833

FIRST SESSION—*December 5, 1831, to July 16, 1832*

SECOND SESSION—*December 3, 1832, to March 2, 1833*

VICE PRESIDENT OF THE UNITED STATES—John C. Calhoun,[1] of South Carolina

PRESIDENT PRO TEMPORE OF THE SENATE—Littleton W. Tazewell,[2] of Virginia; Hugh L. White,[3] of Tennessee

SECRETARY OF THE SENATE—Walter Lowrie,[4] of Pennsylvania

SERGEANT AT ARMS OF THE SENATE—Mountjoy Bayly, of Maryland

SPEAKER OF THE HOUSE OF REPRESENTATIVES—Andrew Stevenson,[5] of Virginia

CLERK OF THE HOUSE—Matthew St. Clair Clarke,[6] of Pennsylvania

SERGEANT AT ARMS OF THE HOUSE—John O. Dunn, of District of Columbia

DOORKEEPER OF THE HOUSE—Overton Carr, of Maryland

ALABAMA

SENATORS

William R. King, *Selma*
Gabriel Moore, *Huntsville*

REPRESENTATIVES

Clement C. Clay, *Huntsville*
Dixon H. Lewis, *Montgomery*
Samuel W. Mardis, *Montevallo*

CONNECTICUT

SENATORS

Samuel A. Foote, *Cheshire*
Gideon Tomlinson, *Fairfield*

REPRESENTATIVES

Noyes Barber, *Groton*
William W. Ellsworth, *Hartford*
Jabez W. Huntington, *Litchfield*
Ralph I. Ingersoll, *New Haven*
William L. Storrs, *Middletown*
Ebenezer Young, *Killingly Center*

DELAWARE

SENATORS

John M. Clayton, *Dover*
Arnold Naudain, *Wilmington*

REPRESENTATIVE

John J. Milligan, *Wilmington*

GEORGIA

SENATORS

George M. Troup, *Dublin*
John Forsyth, *Augusta*

REPRESENTATIVES

Thomas F. Foster, *Greensboro*
Henry G. Lamar, *Macon*
Wilson Lumpkin,[7] *Monroe*
Augustin S. Clayton,[8] *Athens*
Daniel Newnan, *McDonough*
Wiley Thompson, *Elberton*
James M. Wayne, *Savannah*
Richard H. Wilde, *Augusta*

ILLINOIS

SENATORS

Elias K. Kane, *Kaskaskia*
John M. Robinson, *Carmi*

REPRESENTATIVE

Joseph Duncan, *Jacksonville*

INDIANA

SENATORS

William Hendricks, *Madison*
Robert Hanna,[9] *Brookville*
John Tipton,[10] *Logansport*

REPRESENTATIVES

Ratliff Boon, *Boonville*
John Carr, *Charlestown*
Johnathan McCarty, *Connersville*

KENTUCKY

SENATORS

George M. Bibb, *Yellow Banks*
Henry Clay,[11] *Lexington*

REPRESENTATIVES

John Adair, *Harrodsburg*
Chilton Allan, *Winchester*
Henry Daniel, *Mount Sterling*
Nathan Gaither, *Columbia*
Albert G. Hawes, *Hawesville*
Richard M. Johnson, *Great Crossings*
Joseph Lecompte, *New Castle*
Robert P. Letcher, *Lancaster*

---

[1] Resigned December 28, 1832, having been elected United States Senator.
[2] Elected July 9, 1832.
[3] Elected December 3, 1832.
[4] Reelected December 19, 1831.
[5] Reelected December 5, 1831.
[6] Reelected December 5, 1831.

[7] Resigned in 1831, before Congress assembled, having been elected governor.
[8] Elected to fill vacancy caused by resignation of Wilson Lumpkin, and took his seat January 21, 1832.
[9] Appointed to fill vacancy caused by death of James Noble, in preceding Congress, and took his seat December 5, 1831.

[10] Elected to fill vacancy caused by death of James Noble, in preceding Congress, and took his seat January 3, 1832.
[11] Elected for term beginning March 4, 1831, and took his seat December 5, 1831: vacancy in this class from March 4, 1831, to November 9, 1831.

Chittenden Lyon, *Eddyville*
Thomas A. Marshall, *Paris*
Christopher Tompkins, *Glasgow*
Charles A. Wickliffe, *Bardstown*

LOUISIANA

SENATORS

Josiah S. Johnston, *Alexandria*
Edward Livingston,[12] *New Orleans*
George A. Waggaman,[13] *New Orleans*

REPRESENTATIVES

Henry A. Bullard, *Alexandria*
Philemon Thomas, *Baton Rouge*
Edward D. White, *Donaldsonville*

MAINE

SENATORS

John Holmes, *Alfred*
Peleg Sprague, *Hallowell*

REPRESENTATIVES

John Anderson, *Portland*
James Bates, *Norridgewock*
George Evans, *Gardiner*
Cornelius Holland, *Canton*
Leonard Jarvis, *Ellsworth*
Edward Kavanagh, *Damariscotta Mills*
Rufus McIntire, *Parsonsfield*

MARYLAND

SENATORS

Samuel Smith, *Baltimore*
Ezekiel F. Chambers, *Chestertown*

REPRESENTATIVES

Benjamin C. Howard, *Baltimore*
Daniel Jenifer, *Allens Fresh*
John L. Kerr, *Easton*
George E. Mitchell,[14] *Elkton*
Charles S. Sewall,[15] *Elkton*
Benedict J. Semmes, *Piscataway*
John S. Spence, *Berlin*
Francis Thomas, *Frederick*
George C. Washington, *Rockville*
John T. H. Worthington, *Golden*

MASSACHUSETTS

SENATORS

Nathaniel Silsbee, *Salem*
Daniel Webster, *Boston*

REPRESENTATIVES

John Quincy Adams, *Quincy*
Nathan Appleton, *Boston*

Isaac C. Bates, *Northampton*
George N. Briggs, *Lanesboro*
Rufus Choate, *Salem*
John Davis, *Worcester*
Henry A. S. Dearborn, *Brookline*
Edward Everett, *Charlestown*
George Grennell, Jr., *Greenfield*
James L. Hodges, *Bristol*
Joseph G. Kendall, *Leominster*
Jeremiah Nelson, *Essex*
John Reed, *Yarmouth*

MISSISSIPPI

SENATORS

Powhatan Ellis,[16] *Winchester*
John Black,[17] *Monroe*
George Poindexter, *Wilkinson*

REPRESENTATIVE

Franklin E. Plummer, *Westville*

MISSOURI

SENATORS

Thomas H. Benton, *St. Louis*
Alexander Buckner, *Jackson*

REPRESENTATIVE

Spencer D. Pettis,[18] *Fayette*
William H. Ashley,[19] *St. Louis*

NEW HAMPSHIRE

SENATORS

Samuel Bell, *Chester*
Isaac Hill, *Concord*

REPRESENTATIVES

John Brodhead, *Newmarket*
Thomas Chandler, *Hillsboro*
Joseph Hammons, *Farmington*
Joseph M. Harper, *Canterbury*
Henry Hubbard, *Charlestown*
John W. Weeks, *Lancaster*

NEW JERSEY

SENATORS

Mahlon Dickerson, *Succasunna*
Theodore Frelinghuysen, *Newark*

REPRESENTATIVES

Lewis Condict, *Morristown*
Silas Condit, *Newark*
Richard M. Cooper, *Camden*
Thomas H. Hughes, *Cold Spring*
James F. Randolph, *New Brunswick*
Isaac Southard, *Somerville*

NEW YORK

SENATORS

Charles E. Dudley, *Albany*
William L. Marcy,[20] *Albany*
Silas Wright, Jr.,[21] *Canton*

REPRESENTATIVES

William G. Angel, *Burlington*
William Babcock, *Pen Yan*
Gamaliel H. Barstow, *Nichols*
Samuel Beardsley, *Utica*
John T. Bergen, *Brooklyn*
Joseph Bouck, *Middleburg*
John C. Brodhead, *Modena*
Churchill C. Cambreleng, *New York City*
John A. Collier, *Binghamton*
Bates Cooke, *Lewiston*
Charles Dayan, *Lowville*
John Dickson, *West Bloomfield*
Ulysses F. Doubleday, *Auburn*
Michael Hoffman, *Herkimer*
William Hogan, *Hogansburg*
Freeborn G. Jewett, *Skaneateles*
John King, *North Lebanon*
Gerrit Y. Lansing, *Albany*
James Lent,[22] *Newtown*
Edmund H. Pendleton, *Hyde Park*
Job Pierson, *Schaghticoke*
Nathaniel Pitcher, *Sandyhill*
Edward C. Reed, *Homer*
Erastus Root, *Delhi*
Nathan Soule, *Fort Plain*
John W. Taylor, *Ballston Spa*
Phineas L. Tracy, *Batavia*
Gulian C. Verplanck, *New York City*
Aaron Ward, *Mount Pleasant*
Daniel Wardwell, *Mannsville*
Grattan H. Wheeler, *Wheeler*
Campbell P. White, *New York City*
Frederick Whittlesey, *Rochester*
Samuel J. Wilkin, *Goshen*

NORTH CAROLINA

SENATORS

Bedford Brown, *Browns Store*
Willie P. Mangum, *Red Mountain*

REPRESENTATIVES

Daniel L. Barringer, *Raleigh*
Lauchlin Bethune, *Fayetteville*
John Branch,[23] *Enfield*
Samuel P. Carson, *Pleasant Garden*
Henry W. Connor, *Sherrills Ford*
Thomas H. Hall, *Tarboro*
Robert Potter,[24] *Oxford*
Micajah T. Hawkins,[25] *Warrenton*
James I. McKay, *Elizabethtown*
Abraham Rencher, *Pittsboro*

---

[12] Resigned May 24, 1831, having been appointed Secretary of State.
[13] Elected to fill vacancy caused by resignation of Edward Livingston, and took his seat January 3, 1832.
[14] Died June 28, 1832.
[15] Elected to fill vacancy caused by death of George E. Mitchell, and took his seat December 3, 1832.
[16] Resigned July 16, 1832, having been appointed judge of United States court.

[17] Appointed to fill vacancy caused by resignation of Powhatan Ellis, and took his seat December 12, 1832; subsequently elected.
[18] Died August 28, 1831, before Congress assembled.
[19] Elected to fill vacancy caused by death of Spencer D. Pettis, and took his seat December 5, 1831.
[20] Resigned January 1, 1833, having been elected governor.

[21] Elected to fill vacancy caused by resignation of William L. Marcy, and took his seat January 14, 1833.
[22] Died Febuary 22, 1833.
[23] Served as Secretary of the Navy until May 12, 1831.
[24] Resigned in November, 1831, before Congress assembled.
[25] Elected to fill vacancy caused by resignation of Robert Potter, and took his seat January 6, 1832.

NORTH CAROLINA—Continued

REPRESENTATIVES—continued

William B. Shepard, *Elizabeth City*
Augustine H. Shepperd, *Germantown*
Jesse Speight, *Stantonsburg*
Lewis Williams, *Panther Creek*

OHIO

SENATORS

Benjamin Ruggles, *St. Clairsville*
Thomas Ewing, *Lancaster*

REPRESENTATIVES

Eleutheros Cooke, *Sandusky*
Thomas Corwin, *Lebanon*
Joseph H. Crane, *Dayton*
William Creighton, Jr., *Chillicothe*
James Findlay, *Cincinnati*
William W. Irvin, *Lancaster*
William Kennon, Sr., *St. Clairsville*
Humphrey H. Leavitt, *Steubenville*
William Russell, *West Union*
William Stanbery, *Newark*
John Thomson, *New Lisbon*
Joseph Vance, *Urbana*
Samuel F. Vinton, *Gallipolis*
Elisha Whittlesey, *Canfield*

PENNSYLVANIA

SENATORS

Isaac D. Barnard,[26] *West Chester*
George M. Dallas,[27] *Philadelphia*
William Wilkins, *Pittsburgh*

REPRESENTATIVES

Robert Allison, *Huntingdon Center*
John Banks, *Mercer*
John C. Bucher, *Harrisburg*
George Burd, *Bedford*
Richard Coulter, *Greensburg*
Thomas H. Crawford, *Chambersburg*
Harmar Denny, *Pittsburgh*
Lewis Dewart, *Sunbury*
Joshua Evans, Jr., *Paoli*
James Ford, *Lawrenceville*
John Gilmore, *Butler*
William Hiester, *New Holland*
Henry Horn, *Philadelphia*
Peter Ihrie, Jr., *Easton*
Adam King, *York*
Henry King, *Allentown*
Thomas M. T. McKennan, *Washington*
Joel K. Mann, *Jenkintown*
Henry A. P. Muhlenberg, *Reading*
David Potts, Jr., *Pottstown*

William Ramsey,[28] *Carlisle*
Robert McCoy,[29] *Carlisle*
Samuel A. Smith, *Rockhill*
Philander Stephens, *Montrose*
Andrew Stewart, *Uniontown*
Joel B. Sutherland, *Philadelphia*
John G. Watmough, *Philadelphia*

RHODE ISLAND

SENATORS

Nehemiah R. Knight, *Providence*
Asher Robbins, *Newport*

REPRESENTATIVES

Tristam Burges, *Providence*
Dutee J. Pearce, *Newport*

SOUTH CAROLINA

SENATORS

Robert Y. Hayne,[30] *Charleston*
John C. Calhoun,[31] *Fort Hill*
Stephen D. Miller,[32] *Camden*

REPRESENTATIVES

Robert W. Barnwell, *Beaufort*
James Blair, *Lynchwood*
Warren R. Davis, *Pendleton*
William Drayton, *Charleston*
John M. Felder, *Orangeburg*
John K. Griffin, *Milton*
George McDuffie, *Edgefield*
Thomas R. Mitchell, *Georgetown*
William T. Nuckolls, *Hancockville*

TENNESSEE

SENATORS

Hugh Lawson White, *Knoxville*
Felix Grundy, *Nashville*

REPRESENTATIVES

Thomas D. Arnold, *Campbell Station*
John Bell, *Nashville*
John Blair, *Jonesboro*
William Fitzgerald,[33] *Dresden*
William Hall, *Green Garden*
Jacob C. Isacks, *Winchester*
Cave Johnson, *Clarksville*
James K. Polk, *Columbia*
James Standifer, *Mountairy*

VERMONT

SENATORS

Horatio Seymour, *Middlebury*
Samuel Prentiss, *Montpelier*

Heman Allen, *Burlington*
William Cahoon, *Lyndon*
Horace Everett, *Windsor*
Jonathan Hunt,[34] *Brattleboro*
Hiland Hall,[35] *Bennington*
Rollin C. Mallary,[36] *Poultney*
William Slade,[37] *Middlebury*

VIRGINIA

SENATORS

Littleton W. Tazewell,[38] *Norfolk*
William C. Rives,[39] *Milton*
John Tyler, *Gloucester*

REPRESENTATIVES

Mark Alexander, *Lombardy Grove*
Robert Allen, *Mount Jackson*
William S. Archer, *Elk Hill*
William Armstrong, *Romney*
John S. Barbour, *Culpeper*
Thomas T. Bouldin, *Charlotte*
Joseph W. Chinn, *Nuttsville*
Nathaniel H. Claiborne, *Rocky Mount*
Richard Coke, Jr., *Williamburg*
Robert Craig, *Montgomery*
Thomas Davenport, *Meadville*
Philip Doddridge,[40] *Wellsburg*
Joseph Johnson,[41] *Bridgeport*
William F. Gordon, *Lindseys Store*
Charles C. Johnston,[42] *Abingdon*
Joseph Draper,[43] *Wythe*
John Y. Mason, *Hicksford*
Lewis Maxwell, *Weston*
Charles F. Mercer, *Leesburg*
William McCoy, *Franklin*
Thomas Newton, Jr., *Norfolk*
John M. Patton, *Fredericksburg*
John J. Roane, *Rumford Academy*
Andrew Stevenson, *Richmond*

ARKANSAS TERRITORY

DELEGATE

Ambrose H. Sevier, *Little Rock*

TERRITORY OF FLORIDA

DELEGATE

Joseph M. White, *Monticello*

MICHIGAN TERRITORY

DELEGATE

Austin E. Wing, *Monroe*

---

[26] Resigned December 6, 1831.
[27] Elected to fill vacancy caused by resignation of Isaac D. Barnard, and took his seat December 21, 1831.
[28] Died September 29, 1831, before Congress assembled.
[29] Elected to fill vacancy caused by death of William Ramsey, and took his seat December 5, 1831.
[30] Resigned December 13, 1832, having been elected governor.
[31] Elected to fill vacancy caused by resignation of Robert Y. Hayne, and took his seat January 4, 1833.
[32] Resigned March 2, 1833.

[33] Election unsuccessfully contested by David Crockett.
[34] Died May 14, 1832.
[35] Elected to fill vacancy caused by death of Jonathan Hunt, and took his seat January 21, 1833.
[36] Died April 16, 1831, before Congress assembled.
[37] Elected to fill vacancy caused by death of Rollin C. Mallary, and took his seat December 5, 1831.
[38] Resigned July 16, 1832.
[39] Elected to fill vacancy caused by resignation of Littleton W. Tazewell; took his seat January 4, 1833.

[40] Died November 19, 1832.
[41] Elected to fill vacancy caused by death of Philip Doddridge, and took his seat January 21, 1833.
[42] Election unsuccessfully contested by Joseph Draper; died June 17, 1832.
[43] Unsuccessfully contested the election of Charles C. Johnston; subsequently elected to fill vacancy caused by death of Mr. Johnston, and took his seat December 12, 1832.

TWENTY-THIRD CONGRESS

MARCH 4, 1833, TO MARCH 3, 1835

FIRST SESSION—*December 2, 1833, to June 30, 1834*

SECOND SESSION—*December 1, 1834, to March 3, 1835*

———

VICE PRESIDENT OF THE UNITED STATES—MARTIN VAN BUREN, of New York

PRESIDENT PRO TEMPORE OF THE SENATE—HUGH L. WHITE, of Tennessee; GEORGE POINDEXTER,[1] of Mississippi; JOHN TYLER,[2] of Virginia

SECRETARY OF THE SENATE—WALTER LOWRIE,[3] of Pennsylvania

SERGEANT AT ARMS OF THE SENATE—MOUNTJOY BAYLY, of Maryland; JOHN SHACKFORD,[4] of New Hampshire

———

SPEAKER OF THE HOUSE OF REPRESENTATIVES—ANDREW STEVENSON,[5] of Virginia; JOHN BELL,[6] of Tennessee

CLERK OF THE HOUSE—MATTHEW ST. CLAIR CLARKE, of Pennsylvania; WALTER S. FRANKLIN,[7] of Pennsylvania

SERGEANT AT ARMS OF THE HOUSE—JOHN O. DUNN, of District of Columbia; THOMAS B. RANDOLPH,[8] of Virginia

DOORKEEPER OF THE HOUSE—OVERTON CARR, of Maryland

ALABAMA

SENATORS

William R. King, *Selma*
Gabriel Moore, *Huntsville*

REPRESENTATIVES

Clement C. Clay, *Huntsville*
Dixon H. Lewis, *Lowndesboro*
John McKinley, *Florence*
Samuel W. Mardis, *Montevallo*
John Murphy, *Claiborne*

CONNECTICUT

SENATORS

Gideon Tomlinson, *Fairfield*
Nathan Smith, *New Haven*

REPRESENTATIVES

Noyes Barber, *Groton*
William W. Ellsworth,[9] *Hartford*
Joseph Trumbull,[10] *Hartford*
Samuel A. Foote,[11] *Cheshire*
Ebenezer Jackson, Jr.,[12] *Middletown*

Jabez W. Huntington,[13] *Litchfield*
Phineas Miner,[14] *Litchfield*
Samuel Tweedy, *Danbury*
Ebenezer Young, *Killingly Center*

DELAWARE

SENATORS

John M. Clayton, *Dover*
Arnold Naudain, *Wilmington*

REPRESENTATIVE

John J. Milligan, *Wilmington*

GEORGIA

SENATORS

George M. Troup,[15] *Dublin*
John P. King,[16] *Augusta*
John Forsyth,[17] *Columbus*
Alfred Cuthbert,[18] *Monticello*

REPRESENTATIVES

Augustin S. Clayton, *Athens*
John Coffee, *Jacksonville*

Thomas F. Foster, *Greensboro*
Roger L. Gamble, *Louisville*
George R. Gilmer, *Lexington*
Seaborn Jones, *Columbus*
William Schley, *Augusta*
James M. Wayne,[19] *Savannah*
Richard H. Wilde, *Augusta*

ILLINOIS

SENATORS

Elias K. Kane, *Kaskaskia*
John M. Robinson, *Carmi*

REPRESENTATIVES

Zadoc Casey, *Mount Vernon*
Joseph Duncan,[20] *Jacksonville*
William L. May,[21] *Springfield*
Charles Slade,[22] *Carlyle*
John Reynolds,[23] *Belleville*

INDIANA

SENATORS

William Hendricks, *Madison*
John Tipton, *Logansport*

---

[1] Elected June 28, 1834.
[2] Elected March 3, 1835.
[3] Reelected December 9, 1833.
[4] Elected December 9, 1833.
[5] Reelected December 2, 1833; resigned from the House June 2, 1834; Henry Hubbard, of New Hampshire, was elected Speaker pro tempore for May 16, 1834.
[6] Elected June 2, 1834.
[7] Elected December 2, 1833.
[8] Elected December 3, 1833.
[9] Resigned July 8, 1834.
[10] Elected to fill vacancy caused by resignation of William W. Ellsworth, took his seat December 1, 1834.

[11] Resigned May 9, 1834, having been elected governor.
[12] Elected to fill vacancy caused by resignation of Samuel A. Foote, and took his seat December 1, 1834
[13] Resigned August 16, 1834, having been appointed judge of the supreme court of errors.
[14] Elected to fill vacancy caused by resignation of Jabez W. Huntington, and took his seat December 1, 1834.
[15] Resigned November 8, 1833.
[16] Elected to fill vacancy caused by resignation of George M. Troup, and took his seat December 31, 1833.

[17] Resigned June 27, 1834, having been appointed Secretary of State.
[18] Elected to fill vacancy caused by resignation of John Forsyth, and took his seat January 12, 1835.
[19] Resigned January 13, 1835.
[20] Resigned September 21, 1834, having been elected governor.
[21] Elected to fill vacancy caused by resignation of Joseph Duncan, and took his seat December 1, 1834.
[22] Died July 26, 1834.
[23] Elected to fill vacancy caused by death of Charles Slade, and took his seat December 1, 1834.

INDIANA—Continued

REPRESENTATIVES

Ratliff Boon, *Boonville*
John Carr, *Charlestown*
John Ewing, *Vincennes*
Edward A. Hannegan, *Covington*
George L. Kinnard, *Indianapolis*
Amos Lane, *Lawrenceburg*
Johnathan McCarty, *Fort Wayne*

KENTUCKY

SENATORS

George M. Bibb, *Yellow Banks*
Henry Clay, *Lexington*

REPRESENTATIVES

Chilton Allan, *Winchester*
Martin Beaty, *South Fork*
Thomas Chilton, *Elizabethtown*
Amos Davis, *Mount Sterling*
Benjamin Hardin, *Bardstown*
Albert G. Hawes, *Hawesville*
Richard M. Johnson, *Great Crossings*
Robert P. Letcher,[24] *Lancaster*
James Love, *Barbourville*
Chittenden Lyon, *Eddyville*
Thomas A. Marshall, *Paris*
Patrick H. Pope, *Louisville*
Christopher Tompkins, *Glasgow*

LOUISIANA

SENATORS

Josiah S. Johnston,[25] *Alexandria*
Alexander Porter,[26] *Attakapas*
George A. Waggaman, *New Orleans*

REPRESENTATIVES

Henry A. Bullard,[27] *Alexandria*
Rice Garland,[28] *Opelousas*
Philemon Thomas, *Baton Rouge*
Edward D. White,[29] *Donaldsonville*
Henry Johnson,[30] *Donaldsonville*

MAINE

SENATORS

Peleg Sprague,[31] *Hallowell*
John Ruggles,[32] *Thomaston*
Ether Shepley, *Saco*

REPRESENTATIVES

George Evans, *Gardiner*
Joseph Hall, *Camden*
Leonard Jarvis, *Ellsworth*
Edward Kavanagh, *Damariscotta Mills*
Moses Mason, Jr., *Bethel*
Rufus McIntire, *Parsonsfield*
Gorham Parks, *Bangor*
Francis O. J. Smith, *Portland*

MARYLAND

SENATORS

Ezekiel F. Chambers,[33] *Chestertown*
Robert H. Goldsborough,[34] *Easton*
Joseph Kent, *Bladensburg*

REPRESENTATIVES

Richard B. Carmichael, *Centerville*
Littleton P. Dennis,[35] *Princess Anne*
John N. Steele,[36] *Vienna*
James P. Heath, *Baltimore*
William Cost Johnson, *Jefferson*
Isaac McKim, *Baltimore*
John T. Stoddert, *Harris Lot*
Francis Thomas, *Frederick*
James Turner, *Wiseburg*

MASSACHUSETTS

SENATORS

Nathaniel Silsbee, *Salem*
Daniel Webster, *Boston*

REPRESENTATIVES

John Quincy Adams, *Quincy*
Isaac C. Bates, *Northampton*
William Baylies, *West Bridgewater*
George N. Briggs, *Lanesboro*
Rufus Choate,[37] *Salem*
Stephen C. Phillips,[38] *Salem*
John Davis,[39] *Worcester*
Levi Lincoln,[40] *Worcester*
Edward Everett, *Charlestown*
Benjamin Gorham, *Boston*
George Grennell, Jr., *Greenfield*
William Jackson, *Newton*
Gayton P. Osgood, *North Andover*
John Reed, *Yarmouth*

MISSISSIPPI

SENATORS

George Poindexter, *Wilkinson*
John Black,[41] *Monroe*

REPRESENTATIVES

Harry Cage, *Woodville*
Franklin E. Plummer, *Westville*

MISSOURI

SENATORS

Thomas H. Benton, *St. Louis*
Alexander Buckner,[42] *Jackson*
Lewis F. Linn,[43] *Ste. Genevieve*

REPRESENTATIVES

William H. Ashley, *St. Louis*
John Bull, *Chariton*

NEW HAMPSHIRE

SENATORS

Samuel Bell, *Chester*
Isaac Hill, *Concord*

REPRESENTATIVES

Benning M. Bean, *Moultonboro*
Robert Burns, *Hebron*
Joseph M. Harper, *Canterbury*
Henry Hubbard, *Charlestown*
Franklin Pierce, *Hillsboro*

NEW JERSEY

SENATORS

Theodore Frelinghuysen, *Newark*
Samuel L. Southard, *Trenton*

REPRESENTATIVES

Philemon Dickerson, *Paterson*
Samuel Fowler, *Hamburg*
Thomas Lee, *Port Elizabeth*
James Parker, *Perth Amboy*
Ferdinand S. Schenck, *Six Mile Run*
William N. Shinn, *Mount Holly*

NEW YORK

SENATORS

Silas Wright, Jr., *Canton*
Nathaniel P. Tallmadge, *Poughkeepsie*

REPRESENTATIVES

John Adams, *Catskill*
Samuel Beardsley, *Utica*
Abraham Bockee, *Federal Store*
Charles Bodle, *Bloomingburg*
John W. Brown, *Newburgh*
Churchill C. Cambreleng, *New York City*

---

[24] Thomas P. Moore presented credentials on December 2, 1833, but was not sworn pending a contest by Robert P. Letcher, and on June 2, 1834, the House ordered a new election, "it being impracticable for this House to determine with any certainty who is the rightful Representative of this district." Mr. Letcher was subsequently elected and took his seat December 1, 1834.
[25] Died May 19, 1833.
[26] Elected to fill vacancy caused by death of Josiah S. Johnston, and took his seat January 6, 1834.
[27] Resigned January 4, 1834, having been appointed judge of the supreme court of Louisiana.
[28] Elected to fill vacancy caused by resignation of Henry A. Bullard, and took his seat April 28, 1834.

[29] Resigned November 15, 1834, having been elected Governor.
[30] Elected to fill vacancy caused by resignation of Edward D. White, and took his seat December 1, 1834.
[31] Resigned January 1, 1835.
[32] Elected to fill vacancy caused by resignation of Peleg Sprague, and took his seat February 6, 1835.
[33] Resigned in 1834.
[34] Elected to fill vacancy caused by resignation of Ezekiel F. Chambers, and took his seat January 23, 1835.
[35] Died April 14, 1834.
[36] Elected to fill vacancy caused by death of Littleton P. Dennis, and took his seat June 9, 1834.
[37] Resigned June 30, 1834.

[38] Elected to fill vacancy caused by resignation of Rufus Choate, and took his seat December 1, 1834.
[39] Resigned January 14, 1834, having been elected governor.
[40] Elected to fill vacancy caused by resignation of John Davis, and took his seat March 5, 1834.
[41] Elected to fill vacancy in term commencing March 4, 1833, and took his seat December 23, 1833; vacancy in this class from March 4, 1833, to November 21, 1833, because of recess of legislature.
[42] Died June 6, 1833.
[43] Appointed to fill vacancy caused by death of Alexander Buckner, and took his seat December 16, 1833; subsequently elected.

Samuel Clark, *Waterloo*
John Cramer, *Waterford*
Rowland Day, *Sempronius*
John Dickson, *West Bloomfield*
Millard Fillmore, *Buffalo*
Philo C. Fuller, *Geneseo*
William K. Fuller, *Chittenango*
Ransom H. Gillet, *Ogdensburg*
Nicoll Halsey, *Trumansburg*
Gideon Hard, *Albion*
Samuel G. Hathaway, *Solon*
Abner Hazeltine, *Jamestown*
Edward Howell, *Bath*
Abel Huntington, *East Hampton*
Noadiah Johnson, *Delhi*
Gerrit Y. Lansing, *Albany*
Cornelius W. Lawrence,[44] *New York City*
John J. Morgan,[45] *New York City*
George W. Lay, *Batavia*
Charles McVean, *Canajoharie*
Abijah Mann, Jr., *Fairfield*
Henry C. Martindale, *Sandy Hill*
Henry Mitchell, *Norwich*
Sherman Page, *Unadilla*
Job Pierson, *Schaghticoke*
Dudley Selden,[46] *New York City*
Charles G. Ferris,[47] *New York City*
William Taylor, *Manlius*
Joel Turrill, *Oswego*
Aaron Vanderpoel, *Kinderhook*
Isaac B. Van Houten, *Clarkstown*
Aaron Ward, *Mount Pleasant*
Daniel Wardwell, *Mannsville*
Reuben Whallon, *Split Rock*
Campbell P. White, *New York City*
Frederick Whittlesey, *Rochester*

NORTH CAROLINA

SENATORS

Bedford Brown, *Browns Store*
Willie P. Mangum, *Red Mountain*

REPRESENTATIVES

Daniel L. Barringer, *Raleigh*
Jesse A. Bynum, *Halifax*
Henry W. Connor, *Sherrills Ford*
Edmund Deberry, *Lawrenceville*
James Graham, *Rutherfordton*
Thomas H. Hall, *Tarboro*
Micajah T. Hawkins, *Warrenton*
James I. McKay, *Elizabethtown*
Abraham Rencher, *Pittsboro*
William B. Shepard, *Elizabeth City*
Augustine H. Shepperd, *Germantown*
Jesse Speight, *Stantonsburg*
Lewis Williams, *Panther Creek*

OHIO

SENATORS

Thomas Ewing, *Lancaster*
Thomas Morris, *Bethel*

REPRESENTATIVES

William Allen,[48] *Chillicothe*
James M. Bell, *Cambridge*
John Chaney, *Courtwright*
Thomas Corwin, *Lebanon*
Joseph H. Crane, *Dayton*
Thomas L. Hamer, *Georgetown*
Benjamin Jones, *Wooster*
Humphrey H. Leavitt,[49] *Steubenville*
Daniel Kilgore,[50] *Cadiz*
Robert T. Lytle,[51] *Cincinnati*
Jeremiah McLene, *Columbus*
Robert Mitchell, *Zanesville*
William Patterson, *Mansfield*
Jonathan Sloane, *Ravenna*
David Spangler, *Coshocton*
John Thomson, *New Lisbon*
Joseph Vance, *Urbana*
Samuel F. Vinton, *Gallipolis*
Taylor Webster, *Hamilton*
Elisha Whittlesey, *Canfield*

PENNSYLVANIA

SENATORS

William Wilkins,[52] *Pittsburgh*
James Buchanan,[53] *Lancaster*
Samuel McKean, *Burlington*

REPRESENTATIVES

Joseph B. Anthony, *Williamsport*
John Banks, *Mercer*
Charles A. Barnitz, *York*
Andrew Beaumont, *Wilkes-Barre*
Horace Binney, *Philadelphia*
George Burd, *Bedford*
George Chambers, *Chambersburg*
William Clark, *Dauphin*
Richard Coulter, *Greensburg*
Edward Darlington, *Chester*
Harmar Denny, *Pittsburgh*
John Galbraith, *Franklin*
James Harper, *Philadelphia*
Samuel S. Harrison, *Kittanning*
Joseph Henderson, *Browns Mills*
William Hiester, *New Holland*
Henry King, *Allentown*
John Laporte, *Asylum*
Thomas M. T. McKennan, *Washington*
Joel K. Mann, *Jenkintown*
Jesse Miller, *Landisburg*

Henry A. P. Muhlenberg, *Reading*
David Potts, Jr., *Pottstown*
Robert Ramsey, *Hartsville*
Andrew Stewart, *Uniontown*
Joel B. Sutherland, *Philadelphia*
David D. Wagener, *Easton*
John G. Watmough, *Philadelphia*

RHODE ISLAND

SENATORS

Nehemiah R. Knight, *Providence*
Asher Robbins,[54] *Newport*

REPRESENTATIVES

Tristam Burges, *Providence*
Dutee J. Pearce, *Newport*

SOUTH CAROLINA

SENATORS

John C. Calhoun, *Fort Hill*
William C. Preston,[55] *Columbia*

REPRESENTATIVES

James Blair,[56] *Lynchwood*
Richard I. Manning,[57] *Fulton*
William K. Clowney, *Union*
Warren R. Davis,[58] *Pendleton*
John M. Felder, *Orangeburg*
William J. Grayson, *Beaufort*
John K. Griffin, *Milton*
George McDuffie,[59] *Willington*
Francis W. Pickens,[60] *Edgefield*
Henry L. Pinckney, *Charleston*
Thomas D. Singleton,[61] *Kingtree*
Robert B. Campbell,[62] *Brownsville*

TENNESSEE

SENATORS

Hugh Lawson White, *Knoxville*
Felix Grundy, *Nashville*

REPRESENTATIVES

John Bell, *Nashville*
John Blair, *Jonesboro*
Samuel Bunch, *Rutledge*
David Crockett, *Crockett*
David W. Dickinson, *Murfreesboro*
William C. Dunlap, *Bolivar*
John B. Forester, *McMinnville*
William M. Inge, *Fayetteville*
Cave Johnson, *Clarksville*
Luke Lea, *Campbells Station*
Balie Peyton, *Gallatin*
James K. Polk, *Columbia*
James Standifer, *Mountairy*

---

[44] Resigned May 14, 1834, having been elected mayor of New York City.
[45] Elected to fill vacancy caused by resignation of Cornelius W. Lawrence, and took his seat December 1, 1834.
[46] Resigned July 1, 1834.
[47] Elected to fill vacancy caused by resignation of Dudley Selden, and took his seat December 1, 1834.
[48] Election unsuccessfully contested by Duncan McArthur.
[49] Resigned July 10, 1834, having been appointed judge of the United States district court.
[50] Elected to fill vacancy caused by resignation of

Humphrey H. Leavitt, and took his seat December 1, 1834.
[51] Resigned March 10, 1834; elected to fill vacancy caused by his own resignation, and took his seat December 27, 1834.
[52] Resigned June 30, 1834, having been appointed minister to Russia.
[53] Elected to fill vacancy caused by resignation of William Wilkins, and took his seat December 15, 1834.
[54] Election unsuccessfully contested by Elisha R. Potter.
[55] Elected to fill vacancy caused by resignation of Stephen D. Miller, in preceding Congress, and took his seat December 9, 1833.

[56] Died April 1, 1834.
[57] Elected to fill vacancy caused by death of James Blair, and took his seat December 8, 1834.
[58] Died January 29, 1835, before the commencement of the Twenty-fourth Congress, to which he had been reelected.
[59] Resigned in 1834.
[60] Elected to fill vacancy caused by resignation of George McDuffie, and took his seat December 8, 1834.
[61] Died November 25, 1833, before Congress assembled.
[62] Elected to fill vacancy caused by death of Thomas D. Singleton, and took his seat February 27, 1834.

VERMONT

SENATORS

Samuel Prentiss, *Montpelier*
Benjamin Swift, *St. Albans*

REPRESENTATIVES

Heman Allen, *Burlington*
Benjamin F. Deming,[63] *Danville*
Henry F. Janes,[64] *Waterbury*
Horace Everett, *Windsor*
Hiland Hall, *Bennington*
William Slade, *Middlebury*

VIRGINIA

SENATORS

John Tyler, *Gloucester*
William C. Rives,[65] *Lindseys Store*
Benjamin W. Leigh,[66] *Richmond*

REPRESENTATIVES

John J. Allen, *Clarksburg*
William S. Archer, *Elk Hill*
James M. H. Beale, *New Market*
John Randolph,[67] *Charlotte*
Thomas T. Bouldin,[68] *Charlotte*
James W. Bouldin,[69] *Charlotte*
Joseph W. Chinn, *Nuttsville*
Nathaniel H. Claiborne, *Rocky Mount*
Thomas Davenport, *Meadville*
John H. Fulton, *Abingdon*
James H. Gholson, *Percivals*
William F. Gordon, *Lindseys Store*
George Loyall, *Norfolk*
Edward Lucas, *Charlestown*
John Y. Mason, *Hicksford*
William McComas, *Greenbrier*
Samuel McDowell Moore, *Lexington*
Charles F. Mercer, *Aldie*
John M. Patton, *Fredericksburg*

Andrew Stevenson,[70] *Richmond*
John Robertson,[71] *Richmond*
William P. Taylor, *Fredericksburg*
Edgar C. Wilson, *Morgantown*
Henry A. Wise, *Onancock*

ARKANSAS TERRITORY

DELEGATE

Ambrose H. Sevier, *Little Rock*

TERRITORY OF FLORIDA

DELEGATE

Joseph M. White, *Monticello*

MICHIGAN TERRITORY

DELEGATE

Lucius Lyon, *Bronson*

---

[63] Died July 11, 1834.
[64] Elected to fill vacancy caused by death of Benjamin F. Deming, and took his seat December 2, 1834.
[65] Resigned February 22, 1834.

[66] Elected to fill vacancy caused by resignation of William C. Rives, and took his seat March 5, 1834.
[67] Died May 24, 1833.
[68] Elected to fill vacancy caused by death of John Randolph, and took his seat December 2, 1833; died February 11, 1834, while addressing the House.

[69] Elected to fill vacancy caused by death of Thomas T. Bouldin, and took his seat March 28, 1834.
[70] Resigned June 2, 1834.
[71] Elected to fill vacancy caused by resignation of Andrew Stevenson, and took his seat December 8, 1834.

TWENTY-FOURTH CONGRESS

MARCH 4, 1835, TO MARCH 3, 1837

FIRST SESSION—*December 7, 1835, to July 4, 1836*

SECOND SESSION—*December 5, 1836, to March 3, 1837*

———

VICE PRESIDENT OF THE UNITED STATES—MARTIN VAN BUREN, of New York

PRESIDENT PRO TEMPORE OF THE SENATE—WILLIAM R. KING,[1] of Alabama

SECRETARY OF THE SENATE—WALTER LOWRIE,[2] of Pennsylvania; ASBURY DICKENS,[3] of North Carolina

SERGEANT AT ARMS OF THE SENATE—JOHN SHACKFORD, of New Hampshire

———

SPEAKER OF THE HOUSE OF REPRESENTATIVES—JAMES K. POLK,[4] of Tennessee

CLERK OF THE HOUSE—WALTER S. FRANKLIN,[5] of Pennsylvania

SERGEANT AT ARMS OF THE HOUSE—THOMAS B. RANDOLPH, of Virginia; RODERICK DORSEY,[6] of Maryland

DOORKEEPER OF THE HOUSE—OVERTON CARR, of Maryland

ALABAMA

SENATORS

William R. King, *Selma*
Gabriel Moore, *Huntsville*

REPRESENTATIVES

Reuben Chapman, *Somerville*
Joshua L. Martin, *Athens*
Joab Lawler, *Mardisville*
Dixon H. Lewis, *Lowndesboro*
Francis S. Lyon, *Demopolis*

ARKANSAS [7]

SENATORS

William S. Fulton,[8] *Little Rock*
Ambrose H. Sevier,[9] *Lake Port*

REPRESENTATIVE

Archibald Yell,[10] *Fayetteville*

CONNECTICUT

SENATORS

Gideon Tomlinson, *Fairfield*
Nathan Smith,[11] *New Haven*
John M. Niles,[12] *Hartford*

REPRESENTATIVES

Elisha Haley, *Mystic*
Andrew T. Judson,[13] *Canterbury*
Orrin Holt,[14] *Willington*
Samuel Ingham, *Saybrook*
Lancelot Phelps, *Hitchcockville*
Isaac Toucey, *Hartford*
Zalmon Wildman,[15] *Danbury*
Thomas T. Whittlesey,[16] *Danbury*

DELAWARE

SENATORS

John M. Clayton,[17] *Dover*
Thomas Clayton,[18] *New Castle*
Arnold Naudain,[19] *Wilmington*
Richard H. Bayard,[20] *Wilmington*

REPRESENTATIVE

John J. Milligan, *Wilmington*

GEORGIA

SENATORS

John P. King, *Augusta*
Alfred Cuthbert, *Monticello*

REPRESENTATIVES

George W. B. Towns,[21] *Talbotton*
Julius C. Alford,[22] *Lagrange*
William Schley,[23] *Augusta*
Jesse F. Cleveland,[24] *Decatur*
John Coffee,[25] *Jacksonville*
William C. Dawson,[26] *Greensboro*
John W. A. Sanford,[27] *Milledgeville*
Thomas Glascock,[28] *Augusta*
Seaton Grantland, *Milledgeville*
Charles E. Haynes, *Sparta*
James C. Terrell,[29] *Carnesville*
Hopkins Holsey,[30] *Hamilton*
Jabez Y. Jackson,[31] *Clarkesville*
George W. Owens, *Savannah*

[1] Elected July 1, 1836; January 28, 1837.
[2] Reelected December 15, 1835; resigned December 5, 1836.
[3] Elected December 12, 1836; Lewis H. Machen, the principal clerk, was appointed on December 5, 1836, to act in the interim.
[4] Elected December 7, 1835.
[5] Reelected December 7, 1835.
[6] Elected December 15, 1835.
[7] Admitted as a State into the Union June 15, 1836.
[8] Took his seat December 5, 1836; term to expire, as determined by lot, March 3, 1841.
[9] Took his seat December 5, 1836; term to expire, as determined by lot, March 3, 1837.
[10] Took his seat December 5, 1836.
[11] Died December 6, 1835.
[12] Appointed to fill vacancy caused by death of

Nathan Smith, and took his seat December 21, 1835; subsequently elected.
[13] Resigned July 4, 1836.
[14] Elected to fill vacancy caused by resignation of Andrew T. Judson, and took his seat December 5, 1836.
[15] Died December 10, 1835.
[16] Elected to fill vacancy caused by death of Zalmon Wildman, and took his seat April 29, 1836.
[17] Resigned December 29, 1836.
[18] Elected to fill vacancy caused by resignation of John M. Clayton, and took his seat January 19, 1837.
[19] Resigned June 16, 1836.
[20] Elected to fill vacancy caused by resignation of Arnold Naudain, and took his seat June 20, 1836.
[21] Resigned September 1, 1836.
[22] Elected to fill vacancy caused by resignation of George W. B. Towns: took his seat January 31, 1837.

[23] Resigned July 1, 1835.
[24] Elected to fill vacancy caused by resignation of William Schley, and took his seat December 7, 1835.
[25] Died September 25, 1836.
[26] Elected to fill vacancy caused by death of John Coffee, and took his seat December 26, 1836.
[27] Resigned July 25, 1835.
[28] Elected to fill vacancy caused by resignation of John W. A. Sanford, and took his seat December 7, 1835.
[29] Resigned July 8, 1835.
[30] Elected to fill vacancy caused by resignation of James C. Terrell, and took his seat December 7, 1835.
[31] Elected to fill vacancy caused by resignation of James M. Wayne in preceding Congress, and took his seat December 7, 1835.

ILLINOIS

SENATORS

Elias K. Kane,[32] *Kaskaskia*
William L. D. Ewing,[33] *Vandalia*
John M. Robinson, *Carmi*

REPRESENTATIVES

John Reynolds, *Belleville*
Zadoc Casey, *Mount Vernon*
William L. May, *Springfield*

INDIANA

SENATORS

William Hendricks, *Madison*
John Tipton, *Logansport*

REPRESENTATIVES

Ratliff Boon, *Boonville*
John W. Davis, *Carlisle*
John Carr, *Charlestown*
Amos Lane, *Lawrenceburg*
Johnathan McCarty, *Fort Wayne*
George L. Kinnard,[34] *Indianapolis*
William Herod,[35] *Columbus*
Edward A. Hannegan, *Covington*

KENTUCKY

SENATORS

Henry Clay, *Lexington*
John J. Crittenden, *Frankfort*

REPRESENTATIVES

Linn Boyd, *New Design*
Albert G. Hawes, *Hawesville*
Joseph R. Underwood, *Bowling Green*
Sherrod Williams, *Monticello*
James Harlan, *Harrodsburg*
John Calhoon, *Hardinsburg*
Benjamin Hardin, *Bardstown*
William J. Graves, *New Castle*
John White, *Richmond*
Chilton Allan, *Winchester*
Richard French, *Mount Sterling*
John Chambers, *Washington*
Richard M. Johnson, *Great Crossings*

LOUISIANA

SENATORS

Alexander Porter,[36] *Attakapas*
Alexander Mouton,[37] *Vermilionville*
Robert C. Nicholas,[38] *Donaldsonville*

REPRESENTATIVES

Henry Johnson, *Donaldsonville*
Eleazer W. Ripley, *Jackson*
Rice Garland, *Opelousas*

MAINE

SENATORS

Ether Shepley,[39] *Saco*
Judah Dana,[40] *Fryeburg*
John Ruggles, *Thomaston*

REPRESENTATIVES

Jeremiah Bailey, *Wiscasset*
George Evans, *Gardiner*
John Fairfield, *Saco*
Joseph Hall, *Camden*
Leonard Jarvis, *Ellsworth*
Moses Mason, Jr., *Bethel*
Gorham Parks, *Bangor*
Francis O. J. Smith, *Portland*

MARYLAND

SENATORS

Robert H. Goldsborough,[41] *Easton*
John S. Spence,[42] *Berlin*
Joseph Kent, *Bladensburg*

REPRESENTATIVES

John N. Steele, *Vienna*
James A. Pearce, *Chestertown*
James Turner, *Wiseburg*
Benjamin C. Howard, *Baltimore*
Isaac McKim, *Baltimore*
George C. Washington, *Rockville*
Francis Thomas, *Frederick*
Daniel Jenifer, *Harris Lot*

MASSACHUSETTS

SENATORS

Daniel Webster, *Boston*
John Davis, *Worcester*

REPRESENTATIVES

Abbott Lawrence, *Boston*
Stephen C. Phillips, *Salem*
Caleb Cushing, *Newburyport*
Samuel Hoar, *Concord*
Levi Lincoln, *Worcester*
George Grennell, Jr., *Greenfield*
George N. Briggs, *Lanesboro*
William B. Calhoun, *Springfield*
William Jackson, *Newton*
Nathaniel B. Borden, *Fall River*
John Reed, *Yarmouth*
John Quincy Adams, *Quincy*

MICHIGAN [43]

SENATORS

Lucius Lyon,[44] *Bronson*
John Norvell,[45] *Detroit*

REPRESENTATIVE

Isaac E. Crary,[46] *Marshall*

MISSISSIPPI

SENATORS

John Black, *Monroe*
Robert J. Walker, *Madisonville*

REPRESENTATIVES

John F. H. Claiborne, *Madisonville*
David Dickson,[47] *Jackson*
Samuel J. Gholson,[48] *Athens*

MISSOURI

SENATORS

Thomas H. Benton, *St. Louis*
Lewis F. Linn, *Ste. Genevieve*

REPRESENTATIVES

William H. Ashley, *St. Louis*
Albert G. Harrison, *Fulton*

NEW HAMPSHIRE

SENATORS

Isaac Hill,[49] *Concord*
John Page,[50] *Haverhill*
Henry Hubbard, *Charlestown*

REPRESENTATIVES

Benning M. Bean, *Moultonboro*
Robert Burns, *Plymouth*
Samuel Cushman, *Portsmouth*
Franklin Pierce, *Hillsboro*
Joseph Weeks, *Richmond*

NEW JERSEY

SENATORS

Samuel L. Southard, *Trenton*
Garret D. Wall, *Burlington*

REPRESENTATIVES

Philemon Dickerson,[51] *Paterson*
William Chetwood,[52] *Elizabethtown*

[32] Died December 12, 1835.
[33] Elected to fill vacancy caused by death of Elias K. Kane, and took his seat January 25, 1836.
[34] Died November 26, 1836.
[35] Elected to fill vacancy caused by death of George L. Kinnard, and took his seat January 25, 1837.
[36] Resigned January 5, 1837.
[37] Elected to fill vacancy caused by resignation of Alexander Porter, and took his seat February 2, 1837.
[38] Elected for the term beginning March 4, 1835, and took his seat March 4, 1836. Charles E. A. Gayarre was elected, but resigned on account of ill health without qualifying; vacancy in this class from March 4, 1835, to January 13, 1836.

[39] Resigned March 3, 1836.
[40] Appointed to fill vacancy caused by resignation of Ether Shepley, and took his seat December 21, 1836.
[41] Died October 5, 1836.
[42] Elected to fill vacancy caused by death of Robert H. Goldsborough, and took his seat January 11, 1837.
[43] Admitted as a State into the Union January 26, 1837.
[44] Took his seat January 26, 1837; term to expire, as determined by lot, March 3, 1839.
[45] Took his seat January 26, 1837; term to expire, as determined by lot, March 3, 1841.

[46] Took his seat January 27, 1837.
[47] Died in 1836.
[48] Elected to fill vacancy caused by death of David Dickson, and took his seat January 7, 1837.
[49] Resigned May 30, 1836, having been elected governor.
[50] Elected to fill vacancy caused by resignation of Isaac Hill, and took his seat June 13, 1836.
[51] Resigned November 3, 1836.
[52] Elected to fill vacancy caused by resignation of Philemon Dickerson and took his seat December 5, 1836.

Samuel Fowler, *Hamburg*
Thomas Lee, *Port Elizabeth*
James Parker, *Perth Amboy*
Ferdinand S. Schenck, *Six Mile Run*
William N. Shinn, *Mount Holly*

NEW YORK

SENATORS

Silas Wright, Jr., *Canton*
Nathaniel P. Tallmadge, *Poughkeepsie*

REPRESENTATIVES

Abel Huntington, *East Hampton*
Samuel Barton, *Richmond*
Churchill C. Cambreleng, *New York City*
Campbell P. White,[53] *New York City*
Gideon Lee,[54] *New York City*
John McKeon, *New York City*
Ely Moore, *New York City*
Aaron Ward, *Mount Pleasant*
Abraham Bockee, *Federal Store*
John W. Brown, *Newburgh*
Nicholas Sickles, *Kingston*
Valentine Efner, *Jefferson*
Aaron Vanderpoel, *Kinderhook*
Hiram P. Hunt, *Troy*
Gerrit Y. Lansing, *Albany*
John Cramer, *Waterford*
David A. Russell, *Salem*
Dudley Farlin, *Warrensburg*
Ranson H. Gillet, *Ogdensburg*
Matthias J. Bovee, *Amsterdam*
Abijah Mann, Jr., *Fairfield*
Samuel Beardsley,[55] *Utica*
Rutger B. Miller,[56] *Utica*
Joel Turrill, *Oswego*
Daniel Wardwell, *Mannsville*
Sherman Page, *Unadilla*
William Seymour, *Binghamton*
William Mason, *Preston*
Stephen B. Leonard, *Owego*
Joseph Reynolds, *Virgil*
William K. Fuller, *Chittenango*
William Taylor, *Manlius*
Ulysses F. Doubleday, *Auburn*
Graham H. Chapin, *Lyons*
Francis Granger, *Canandaigua*
Joshua Lee, *Penn Yan*
Timothy Childs, *Rochester*
George W. Lay, *Batavia*
Philo C. Fuller,[57] *Geneseo*
John Young,[58] *Geneseo*
Abner Hazeltine, *Jamestown*
Thomas C. Love, *Buffalo*
Gideon Hard, *Albion*

NORTH CAROLINA

SENATORS

Bedford Brown, *Browns Store*
Willie P. Mangum,[59] *Red Mountain*
Robert Strange,[60] *Fayetteville*

REPRESENTATIVES

William B. Shepard, *Elizabeth City*
Jesse A. Bynum, *Halifax*
Ebenezer Pettigrew, *Cool Spring*
Jesse Speight, *Stantonsburg*
James I. McKay, *Elizabethtown*
Micajah T. Hawkins, *Warrenton*
Edmund Deberry, *Lawrenceville*
William Montgomery, *Albrights*
Augustine H. Shepperd, *Germantown*
Abraham Rencher, *Pittsboro*
Henry W. Connor, *Sherrills Ford*
James Graham,[61] *Rutherfordton*
Lewis Williams, *Panther Creek*

OHIO

SENATORS

Thomas Ewing, *Lancaster*
Thomas Morris, *Bethel*

REPRESENTATIVES

Bellamy Storer, *Cincinnati*
Taylor Webster, *Hamilton*
Joseph H. Crane, *Dayton*
Thomas Corwin, *Lebanon*
Thomas L. Hamer, *Georgetown*
Samuel F. Vinton, *Gallipolis*
William K. Bond, *Chillicothe*
Jeremiah McLene, *Columbus*
John Chaney, *Courtwright*
Samson Mason, *Springfield*
William Kennon, Sr., *St. Clairsville*
Elias Howell, *Newark*
David Spangler, *Coshocton*
William Patterson, *Mansfield*
Jonathan Sloane, *Ravenna*
Elisha Whittlesey, *Canfield*
John Thomson, *New Lisbon*
Benjamin Jones, *Wooster*
Daniel Kilgore, *Cadiz*

PENNSYLVANIA

SENATORS

Samuel McKean, *Burlington*
James Buchanan, *Lancaster*

REPRESENTATIVES

Joel B. Sutherland, *Philadelphia*
Joseph R. Ingersoll, *Philadelphia*

James Harper, *Philadelphia*
Michael W. Ash, *Philadelphia*
Edward Darlington, *Chester*
William Hiester, *New Holland*
David Potts, Jr., *Pottstown*
Jacob Fry, Jr., *Trappe*
Mathias Morris, *Doylestown*
David D. Wagener, *Easton*
Edward B. Hubley, *Orwigsburg*
Henry A. P. Muhlenberg, *Reading*
William Clark, *Dauphin*
Henry Logan, *Dillsburg*
George Chambers, *Chambersburg*
Jesse Miller,[62] *Landisburg*
James Black,[63] *Newport*
Joseph Henderson, *Browns Mills*
Andrew Beaumont, *Wilkes-Barre*
Joseph B. Anthony, *Williamsport*
John Laporte, *Asylum*
Job Mann, *Bedford*
John Klingensmith, Jr., *Stewartsville*
Andrew Buchanan, *Waynesburg*
Thomas M. T. McKennan, *Washington*
Harmar Denny, *Pittsburgh*
Samuel S. Harrison, *Kittanning*
John Banks,[64] *Mercer*
John J. Pearson,[65] *Mercer*
John Galbraith, *Franklin*

RHODE ISLAND

SENATORS

Nehemiah R. Knight, *Providence*
Asher Robbins, *Newport*

REPRESENTATIVES

Dutee J. Pearce, *Newport*
William Sprague, *Natick*

SOUTH CAROLINA

SENATORS

John C. Calhoun, *Fort Hill*
William C. Preston, *Columbia*

REPRESENTATIVES

Robert B. Campbell, *Brownsville*
William J. Grayson, *Beaufort*
John K. Griffin, *Milton*
James H. Hammond,[66] *Silverton*
Franklin H. Elmore,[67] *Columbia*
Francis W. Pickens, *Edgefield*
Henry L. Pinckney, *Charleston*
Richard I. Manning,[68] *Fulton*
John P. Richardson,[69] *Fulton*
James Rogers, *Yorkville*
Waddy Thompson, Jr.,[70] *Greenville*

---

[53] Resigned before Congress assembled.
[54] Elected to fill vacancy caused by resignation of Campbell P. White, and took his seat December 7, 1835.
[55] Resigned March 29, 1836.
[56] Elected to fill vacancy caused by resignation of Samuel Beardsley, and took his seat December 5, 1836.
[57] Resigned September 2, 1836.
[58] Elected to fill vacancy caused by resignation of Philo C. Fuller, and took his seat December 6, 1836.
[59] Resigned November 26, 1836.

[60] Elected to fill vacancy caused by resignation of Willie P. Mangum, and took his seat December 15, 1836.
[61] Presented credentials as a Member-elect and took his seat December 7, 1835; David Newlands contested the election, and on March 29, 1836, the seat was declared vacant; subsequently elected and took his seat December 5, 1836.
[62] Resigned October 30, 1836.
[63] Elected to fill vacancy caused by resignation of Jesse Miller, and took his seat December 5, 1836.
[64] Resigned in 1836.

[65] Elected to fill vacancy caused by resignation of John Banks, and took his seat December 5, 1836.
[66] Re igned February 26, 1836.
[67] Elected to fill vacancy caused by resignation of James H. Hammond, and took his seat December 19, 1836.
[68] Died May 1, 1836.
[69] Elected to fill vacancy caused by death of Richard I. Manning, and took his seat December 19, 1836.
[70] Elected to fill vacancy caused by death of Representative-elect Warren R. Davis in preceding Congress, and took his seat December 16, 1835.

TENNESSEE

SENATORS

Hugh Lawson White, *Knoxville*
Felix Grundy, *Nashville*

REPRESENTATIVES

William B. Carter, *Elizabethton*
Samuel Bunch, *Rutledge*
Luke Lea, *Campbells Station*
James Standifer, *Mountairy*
John B. Forester, *McMinnville*
Balie Peyton, *Gallatin*
John Bell, *Nashville*
Abram P. Maury, *Franklin*
James K. Polk, *Columbia*
Ebenezer J. Shields, *Pulaski*
Cave Johnson, *Clarksville*
Adam Huntsman, *Jackson*
William C. Dunlap, *Bolivar*

VERMONT

SENATORS

Samuel Prentiss, *Montpelier*
Benjamin Swift, *St. Albans*

REPRESENTATIVES

Hiland Hall, *Bennington*
William Slade, *Middlebury*

Horace Everett, *Windsor*
Heman Allen, *Burlington*
Henry F. Janes, *Waterbury*

VIRGINIA

SENATORS

John Tyler,[71] *Gloucester*
William C. Rives,[72] *Lindseys Store*
Benjamin W. Leigh,[73] *Richmond*
Richard E. Parker,[74] *Snickersville*

REPRESENTATIVES

James M. H. Beale, *Mount Jackson*
James W. Bouldin, *Charlotte*
Nathaniel H. Claiborne, *Rocky Mount*
Walter Coles, *Robertsons Store*
Robert Craig, *Christiansburg*
George C. Dromgoole, *Gholsonville*
James Garland, *Lovingston*
George W. Hopkins, *Lebanon*
Joseph Johnson, *Bridgeport*
John W. Jones, *Petersburg*
George Loyall, *Norfolk*
Edward Lucas, *Charlestown*
William McComas, *Cabell*
John Y. Mason,[75] *Hicksford*
Charles F. Mercer, *Aldie*
William S. Morgan, *White Day*

John M. Patton, *Fredericksburg*
John Roane, *Rumford Academy*
John Robertson, *Richmond*
John Taliaferro, *Fredericksburg*
Henry A. Wise, *Accomac*

ARKANSAS TERRITORY

DELEGATE

Ambrose H. Sevier,[76] *Lake Port*

TERRITORY OF FLORIDA

DELEGATE

Joseph M. White, *Monticello*

MICHIGAN TERRITORY [77]

DELEGATE

George W. Jones,[78] *Sinsinawa Mound*

TERRITORY OF WISCONSIN [79]

DELEGATE

George W. Jones,[78] *Sinsinawa Mound*

---

[71] Resigned February 29, 1836.
[72] Elected to fill vacancy caused by resignation of John Tyler, and took his seat March 14, 1836.
[73] Resigned July 4, 1836.
[74] Elected to fill vacancy caused by resignation of Benjamin W. Leigh: took his seat December 15, 1836.

[75] Resigned January 11, 1837.
[76] Served as a Delegate until June 15, 1836, when Arkansas Territory was granted statehood; subsequently elected Senator.
[77] A portion of this Territory was granted statehood as the State of Michigan January 26, 1837.

[78] Served as a Delegate from Michigan Territory until December 5, 1836, when he became the Delegate from the new Territory of Wisconsin.
[79] Formed from a portion of Michigan Territory and granted a Delegate in Congress by Act of April 20, 1836.

TWENTY-FIFTH CONGRESS

MARCH 4, 1837, TO MARCH 3, 1839

FIRST SESSION—*September 4, 1837, to October 16, 1837*

SECOND SESSION—*December 4, 1837, to July 9, 1838*

THIRD SESSION—*December 3, 1838, to March 3, 1839*

SPECIAL SESSION OF THE SENATE—*March 4, 1837, to March 10, 1837*

———

VICE PRESIDENT OF THE UNITED STATES—RICHARD M. JOHNSON,[1] of Kentucky

PRESIDENT PRO TEMPORE OF THE SENATE—WILLIAM R. KING,[2] of Alabama

SECRETARY OF THE SENATE—ASBURY DICKENS,[3] of North Carolina

SERGEANT AT ARMS OF THE SENATE—JOHN SHACKFORD, of New Hampshire; STEPHEN HAIGHT,[4] of New York

———

SPEAKER OF THE HOUSE OF REPRESENTATIVES—JAMES K. POLK,[5] of Tennessee

CLERK OF THE HOUSE—WALTER S. FRANKLIN,[6] of Pennsylvania; HUGH A. GARLAND,[7] of Virginia

SERGEANT AT ARMS OF THE HOUSE—RODERICK DORSEY, of Maryland

DOORKEEPER OF THE HOUSE—OVERTON CARR, of Maryland

ALABAMA

SENATORS

William R. King, *Selma*
John McKinley,[8] *Florence*
Clement C. Clay,[9] *Huntsville*

REPRESENTATIVES

Reuben Chapman, *Somerville*
Joshua L. Martin, *Athens*
Joab Lawler,[10] *Mardisville*
George W. Crabb,[11] *Tuscaloosa*
Dixon H. Lewis, *Lowndesboro*
Francis S. Lyon, *Demopolis*

ARKANSAS

SENATORS

William S. Fulton, *Little Rock*
Ambrose H. Sevier, *Lake Port*

REPRESENTATIVE

Archibald Yell, *Fayetteville*

CONNECTICUT

SENATORS

John M. Niles, *Hartford*
Perry Smith, *New Milford*

REPRESENTATIVES

Isaac Toucey, *Hartford*
Samuel Ingham, *Saybrook*
Thomas T. Whittlesey, *Danbury*
Elisha Haley, *Mystic*
Lancelot Phelps, *Hitchcockville*
Orrin Holt, *Willington*

DELAWARE

SENATORS

Richard H. Bayard, *Wilmington*
Thomas Clayton, *New Castle*

REPRESENTATIVE

John J. Milligan, *Wilmington*

GEORGIA

SENATORS

Alfred Cuthbert, *Monticello*
John P. King,[12] *Augusta*
Wilson Lumpkin,[13] *Athens*

REPRESENTATIVES

Jesse F. Cleveland, *Decatur*
William C. Dawson, *Greensboro*
Thomas Glascock, *Augusta*
Seaton Grantland, *Milledgeville*
Charles E. Haynes, *Sparta*
Hopkins Holsey, *Hamilton*
Jabez Jackson, *Clarkesville*
George W. Owens, *Savannah*
George W. B. Towns, *Talbotton*

ILLINOIS

SENATORS

John M. Robinson, *Carmi*
Richard M. Young, *Quincy*

---

[1] Elected by the Senate February 8, 1837.
[2] Elected March 7, 1837 (special session of the Senate); October 13, 1837; July 2, 1838; February 25, 1839.
[3] Reelected September 11, 1837.
[4] Elected September 4, 1837.
[5] Reelected September 4, 1837.

[6] Reelected September 4, 1837; died September 20, 1838.
[7] Elected December 3, 1838; Samuel Burch, the chief clerk, acted as clerk in the interim.
[8] Resigned April 22, 1837, never having qualified.
[9] Elected to fill vacancy caused by resignation of John McKinley, and took his seat September 4, 1837.

[10] Died May 8, 1838.
[11] Elected to fill vacancy caused by death of Joab Lawler, and took his seat December 3, 1838.
[12] Resigned November 1, 1837.
[13] Elected to fill vacancy caused by resignation of John P. King, and took his seat December 13, 1837.

ILLINOIS—Continued

REPRESENTATIVES

Adam W. Snyder, *Belleville*
Zadoc Casey, *Mount Vernon*
William L. May, *Springfield*

INDIANA

SENATORS

John Tipton, *Logansport*
Oliver H. Smith, *Connersville*

REPRESENTATIVES

Ratliff Boon, *Boonville*
John Ewing, *Vincennes*
William Graham, *Vallonia*
George H. Dunn, *Lawrenceburg*
James Rariden, *Centerville*
William Herod, *Columbus*
Albert S. White, *La Fayette*

KENTUCKY

SENATORS

Henry Clay, *Lexington*
John J. Crittenden, *Frankfort*

REPRESENTATIVES

John L. Murray, *Wadesboro*
Edward Rumsey, *Greenville*
Joseph R. Underwood, *Bowling Green*
Sherrod Williams, *Monticello*
James Harlan, *Harrodsburg*
John Calhoon, *Hardinsburg*
John Pope, *Springfield*
William J. Graves, *New Castle*
John White, *Richmond*
Richard Hawes, *Winchester*
Richard H. Menifee, *Mount Sterling*
John Chambers, *Washington*
William W. Southgate, *Covington*

LOUISIANA

SENATORS

Robert C. Nicholas, *Donaldsonville*
Alexander Mouton, *Vermilionville*

REPRESENTATIVES

Henry Johnson, *Donaldsonville*
Eleazer W. Ripley,[14] *Jackson*
Rice Garland, *Opelousas*

MAINE

SENATORS

John Ruggles, *Thomaston*
Reuel Williams,[15] *Augusta*

REPRESENTATIVES

Hugh J. Anderson, *Belfast*
Timothy J. Carter,[16] *Paris*
Virgil D. Parris,[17] *Buckfield*
Jonathan Cilley,[18] *Thomaston*
Edward Robinson,[19] *Thomaston*
John Fairfield,[20] *Saco*
Joseph C. Noyes, *Eastport*
Francis O. J. Smith, *Portland*
Thomas Davee, *Blanchard*
George Evans, *Gardiner*

MARYLAND

SENATORS

Joseph Kent,[21] *Bladensburg*
William D. Merrick,[22] *Allens Fresh*
John S. Spence, *Berlin*

REPRESENTATIVES

John Dennis, *Princess Anne*
James A. Pearce, *Chestertown*
John T. H. Worthington, *Golden*
Benjamin C. Howard, *Baltimore*
Isaac McKim,[23] *Baltimore*
John P. Kennedy,[24] *Baltimore*
William Cost Johnson, *Jefferson*
Francis Thomas, *Frederick*
Daniel Jenifer, *Harris Lot*

MASSACHUSETTS

SENATORS

Daniel Webster, *Boston*
John Davis, *Worcester*

REPRESENTATIVES

Richard Fletcher, *Boston*
Stephen C. Phillips,[25] *Salem*
Leverett Saltonstall,[26] *Salem*
Caleb Cushing, *Newburyport*
William Parmenter, *East Cambridge*
Levi Lincoln, *Worcester*
George Grennell, Jr., *Greenfield*
George N. Briggs, *Lanesboro*
William B. Calhoun, *Springfield*
William S. Hastings, *Mendon*
Nathaniel B. Borden, *Fall River*
John Reed, *Yarmouth*
John Quincy Adams, *Quincy*

MICHIGAN

SENATORS

Lucius Lyon, *Bronson*
John Norvell, *Detroit*

REPRESENTATIVE

Isaac E. Crary, *Marshall*

MISSISSIPPI

SENATORS

John Black,[27] *Monroe*
James F. Trotter,[28] *Holly Springs*
Thomas H. Williams,[29] *Pontotoc*
Robert J. Walker, *Madisonville*

REPRESENTATIVES

John F. H. Claiborne,[30] *Madisonville*
Samuel J. Gholson,[30] *Athens*
Sergeant S. Prentiss,[30] *Vicksburg*
Thomas J. Word,[30] *Pontotoc*

MISSOURI

SENATORS

Thomas H. Benton, *St. Louis*
Lewis F. Linn, *Ste. Genevieve*

REPRESENTATIVES

Albert G. Harrison, *Fulton*
John Miller, *Boonville*

NEW HAMPSHIRE

SENATORS

Henry Hubbard, *Charlestown*
Franklin Pierce, *Hillsboro*

REPRESENTATIVES

Charles G. Atherton, *Nashua*
Samuel Cushman, *Portsmouth*
James Farrington, *Rochester*
Joseph Weeks, *Richmond*
Jared W. Williams, *Lancaster*

NEW JERSEY

SENATORS

Samuel L. Southard, *Trenton*
Garret D. Wall, *Burlington*

REPRESENTATIVES

John B. Aycrigg, *Hackensack*
William Halstead, *Trenton*
John P. B. Maxwell, *Belvidere*
Joseph F. Randolph, *Freehold*
Charles C. Stratton, *Swedesboro*
Thomas Jones Yorke, *Salem*

---

[14] Never qualified owing to prolonged illness.
[15] Elected to fill vacancy caused by resignation of Ether Shepley, in preceding Congress, and took his seat March 4, 1837.
[16] Died March 14, 1838.
[17] Elected to fill vacancy caused by death of Timothy J. Carter, and took his seat May 29, 1838.
[18] Killed in a duel with William J. Graves, of Kentucky, February 24, 1838.
[19] Elected to fill vacancy caused by death of Jonathan Cilley, and took his seat April 28, 1838.
[20] Resigned December 24, 1838, having been elected governor.
[21] Died November 24, 1837.
[22] Elected to fill vacancy caused by death of Joseph Kent, and took his seat January 5, 1838.

[23] Died April 1, 1838.
[24] Elected to fill vacancy caused by death of Isaac McKim, and took his seat April 30, 1838.
[25] Resigned September 28, 1838.
[26] Elected to fill vacancy caused by resignation of Stephen C. Phillips, and took his seat December 5, 1838.
[27] Resigned January 22, 1838.
[28] Elected to fill vacancy caused by resignation of John Black, and took his seat February 19, 1838; resigned July 10, 1838.
[29] Appointed to fill vacancy caused by resignation of James F. Trotter, and took his seat December 13, 1838; subsequently elected.
[30] Mississippi elected its Representatives in Novem-

ber of odd numbered years (after the beginning of the congressional term); as Congress had been called to meet in September, the governor issued writs for a special election to fill vacancies until the regular election; John F. H. Claiborne and Samuel J. Gholson presented credentials and were seated September 4, 1837, when, at their request the question of the validity of their election was referred to the Committee on Elections; on October 3, 1837, the House decided they had been elected for the full term; Sergeant S. Prentiss and Thomas J. Word presented credentials on December 27, 1837, and on February 5, 1838, the House rescinded its former decision and declared the seats vacant; Prentiss and Word were subsequently elected, and took their seats May 30, 1838.

NEW YORK

SENATORS

Silas Wright, Jr., *Canton*
Nathaniel P. Tallmadge, *Poughkeepsie*

REPRESENTATIVES

Thomas B. Jackson, *Newtown*
Abraham Vanderveer, *Brooklyn*
J. Ogden Hoffman, *New York City*
Edward Curtis, *New York City*
Churchill C. Cambreleng, *New York City*
Ely Moore, *New York City*
Gouverneur Kemble, *Cold Spring*
Obadiah Titus, *Washington*
Nathaniel Jones, *Warwick*
John C. Brodhead, *Modena*
Zadock Pratt, *Prattsville*
Robert McClellan, *Middleburg*
Henry Vail, *Troy*
Albert Gallup, *East Berne*
John I. De Graff, *Schenectady*
David A. Russell, *Salem*
John Palmer, *Plattsburg*
James B. Spencer, *Fort Covington*
John Edwards, *Ephratah*
Arphaxed Loomis, *Little Falls*
Henry A. Foster, *Rome*
Abraham P. Grant, *Oswego*
Isaac H. Bronson, *Watertown*
John H. Prentiss, *Cooperstown*
Amasa J. Parker, *Delhi*
John C. Clark, *Bainbridge*
Andrew D. W. Bruyn,[31] *Ithaca*
Cyrus Beers,[32] *Ithaca*
Hiram Gray, *Elmira*
William Taylor, *Manlius*
Bennet Bicknell, *Morrisville*
William H. Noble, *Cato*
Samuel Birdsall, *Waterloo*
Mark H. Sibley, *Canandaigua*
John T. Andrews, *North Reading*
Timothy Childs, *Rochester*
William Patterson,[33] *Warsaw*
Harvey Putnam,[34] *Attica*
Luther C. Peck, *Pike*
Richard P. Marvin, *Jamestown*
Millard Fillmore, *Buffalo*
Charles F. Mitchell, *Lockport*

NORTH CAROLINA

SENATORS

Bedford Brown, *Browns Store*
Robert Strange, *Fayetteville*

REPRESENTATIVES

Samuel T. Sawyer, *Edenton*
Jesse A. Bynum, *Halifax*

Edward Stanly, *Washington*
Charles B. Shepard, *New Bern*
James I. McKay, *Elizabethtown*
Micajah T. Hawkins, *Warrenton*
Edmund Deberry, *Lawrenceville*
William Montgomery, *Albrights*
Augustine H. Shepperd, *Bethania*
Abraham Rencher, *Pittsboro*
Henry W. Connor, *Sherrills Ford*
James Graham, *Rutherfordton*
Lewis Williams, *Panther Creek*

OHIO

SENATORS

Thomas Morris, *Bethel*
William Allen, *Chillicothe*

REPRESENTATIVES

Alexander Duncan, *Cincinnati*
Taylor Webster, *Hamilton*
Patrick G. Goode, *Sidney*
Thomas Corwin, *Lebanon*
Thomas L. Hamer, *Georgetown*
Calvary Morris, *Athens*
William K. Bond, *Chillicothe*
Joseph Ridgway, *Columbus*
John Chaney, *Courtwright*
Samson Mason, *Springfield*
James Alexander, Jr., *St. Clairsville*
Alexander Harper, *Zanesville*
Daniel P. Leadbetter, *Millersburg*
William H. Hunter, *Sandusky*
John W. Allen, *Cleveland*
Elisha Whittlesey,[35] *Canfield*
Joshua R. Giddings,[36] *Jefferson*
Andrew W. Loomis,[37] *New Lisbon*
Charles D. Coffin,[38] *New Lisbon*
Matthias Shepler, *Bethlehem*
Daniel Kilgore,[39] *Cadiz*
Henry Swearingen,[40] *Smithfield*

PENNSYLVANIA

SENATORS

Samuel McKean, *Burlington*
James Buchanan, *Lancaster*

REPRESENTATIVES

Lemuel Paynter, *Philadelphia*
John Sergeant, *Philadelphia*
George W. Toland, *Philadelphia*
Francis J. Harper,[41] *Frankford*
Charles Naylor,[42] *Philadelphia*
Edward Davies, *Churchtown*
David Potts, Jr., *Pottstown*
Edward Darlington, *Chester*
Jacob Fry, Jr., *Trappe*
Mathias Morris, *Doylestown*

David D. Wagener, *Easton*
Edward B. Hubley, *Orwigsburg*
Henry A. P. Muhlenberg,[43] *Reading*
George M. Keim,[44] *Reading*
Luther Reily, *Harrisburg*
Henry Logan, *Dillsburg*
Daniel Sheffer, *York*
Charles McClure, *Carlisle*
William W. Potter, *Bellefonte*
David Petrikin, *Danville*
Robert H. Hammond, *Milton*
Samuel W. Morris, *Wellsboro*
Charles Ogle, *Somerset*
John Klingensmith, Jr., *Stewartsville*
Andrew Buchanan, *Waynesburg*
Thomas M. T. McKennan, *Washington*
Richard Biddle, *Pittsburgh*
William Beatty, *Butler*
Thomas Henry, *Beaver*
Arnold Plumer, *Franklin*

RHODE ISLAND

SENATORS

Nehemiah R. Knight, *Providence*
Asher Robbins, *Newport*

REPRESENTATIVES

Robert B. Cranston, *Newport*
Joseph L. Tillinghast, *Providence*

SOUTH CAROLINA

SENATORS

John C. Calhoun, *Fort Hill*
William C. Preston, *Columbia*

REPRESENTATIVES

John Campbell, *Parnassus*
William K. Clowney, *Union*
Franklin H. Elmore, *Columbia*
John K. Griffin, *Milton*
Hugh S. Legare, *Charleston*
Francis W. Pickens, *Edgefield*
R. Barnwell Rhett, *Beaufort*
John P. Richardson, *Fulton*
Waddy Thompson, Jr., *Greenville*

TENNESSEE

SENATORS

Hugh Lawson White, *Knoxville*
Felix Grundy,[45] *Nashville*
Ephraim H. Foster,[46] *Nashville*

REPRESENTATIVES

William B. Carter, *Elizabethton*
Abraham McClellan, *Blountville*
Joseph L. Williams, *Knoxville*

---

[31] Died July 27, 1838.
[32] Elected to fill vacancy caused by death of Andrew D. W. Bruyn, and took his seat December 3, 1838.
[33] Died August 14, 1838.
[34] Elected to fill vacancy caused by death of William Patterson, and took his seat December 3, 1828.
[35] Resigned July 9, 1838.
[36] Elected to fill vacancy caused by resignation of Elisha Whittlesey, and took his seat December 3, 1838.
[37] Resigned October 20, 1837.

[38] Elected to fill vacancy caused by resignation of Andrew W. Loomis, and took his seat December 20, 1837.
[39] Resigned July 4, 1838.
[40] Elected to fill vacancy caused by resignation of Daniel Kilgore, and took his seat December 3, 1838.
[41] Died March 18, 1837, before Congress assembled.
[42] Elected to fill vacancy caused by death of Francis J. Harper, and took his seat September 4, 1837.

[43] Resigned February 9, 1838.
[44] Elected to fill vacancy caused by resignation of Henry A. P. Muhlenberg, and took his seat March 17, 1838.
[45] Resigned July 4, 1838.
[46] Appointed to fill vacancy caused by resignation of Felix Grundy, and took his seat December 3, 1838; subsequently elected for full term commencing March 4, 1839, but resigned March 3, 1839.

TENNESSEE—Continued

REPRESENTATIVES—continued

James Standifer,[47] *Mountairy*
William Stone,[48] *Delphi*
Hopkins L. Turney, *Winchester*
William B. Campbell, *Carthage*
John Bell, *Nashville*
Abram P. Maury, *Franklin*
James K. Polk, *Columbia*
Ebenezer J. Shields, *Pulaski*
Richard Cheatham, *Springfield*
John W. Crockett, *Paris*
Christopher H. Williams, *Lexington*

VERMONT

SENATORS

Samuel Prentiss, *Montpelier*
Benjamin Swift, *St. Albans*

REPRESENTATIVES

Hiland Hall, *Bennington*
William Slade, *Middlebury*
Horace Everett, *Windsor*

Heman Allen, *Burlington*
Isaac Fletcher, *Lyndon*

VIRGINIA

SENATORS

William C. Rives, *Lindseys Store*
Richard E. Parker,[49] *Snickersville*
William H. Roane,[50] *Richmond*

REPRESENTATIVES

Andrew Beirne, *Union*
James W. Bouldin, *Charlotte*
Walter Coles, *Robertsons Store*
Robert Craig, *Christiansburg*
George C. Dromgoole, *Gholsonville*
James Garland, *Lovingston*
George W. Hopkins, *Lebanon*
Robert M. T. Hunter, *Lloyds*
Joseph Johnson, *Bridgeport*
John W. Jones, *Petersburg*
Francis Mallory, *Hampton*
James M. Mason, *Winchester*
Charles F. Mercer, *Aldie*
William S. Morgan, *White Day*

John M. Patton,[51] *Fredericksburg*
Linn Banks,[52] *Madison*
Isaac S. Pennybacker, *Harrisonburg*
Francis E. Rives, *Littleton*
John Robertson, *Richmond*
Archibald Stuart, *Mount Airy*
John Talliaferro, *Fredericksburg*
Henry A. Wise, *Accomac*

TERRITORY OF FLORIDA

DELEGATE

Charles Downing, *St. Augustine*

TERRITORY OF IOWA [53]

DELEGATE

William W. Chapman,[54] *Burlington*

TERRITORY OF WISCONSIN

DELEGATE

George W. Jones,[55] *Sinsinawa Mound*
James D. Doty,[56] *Astor*

---

[47] Died August 20, 1837, before Congress assembled.
[48] Elected to fill vacancy caused by death of James Standifer, and took his seat October 6, 1837.
[49] Resigned March 13, 1837.
[50] Elected to fill vacancy caused by resignation of Richard E. Parker, and took his seat September 4, 1837.

[51] Resigned in 1838.
[52] Elected to fill vacancy caused by resignation of John M. Patton, and took his seat May 19, 1838.
[53] Formed from a portion of the Territory of Wisconsin and granted a Delegate in Congress by act of June 12, 1838.

[54] Took his seat December 3, 1838.
[55] Served until January 14, 1839; succeeded by James D. Doty, who contested his election.
[56] Successfully contested the election of George W. Jones, and took his seat January 14, 1839.

TWENTY-SIXTH CONGRESS

MARCH 4, 1839, TO MARCH 3, 1841

FIRST SESSION—*December 2, 1839, to July 21, 1840*

SECOND SESSION—*December 7, 1840, to March 3, 1841*

———

VICE PRESIDENT OF THE UNITED STATES—Richard M. Johnson, of Kentucky

PRESIDENT PRO TEMPORE OF THE SENATE—William R. King,[1] of Alabama

SECRETARY OF THE SENATE—Asbury Dickens,[2] of North Carolina

SERGEANT AT ARMS OF THE SENATE—Stephen Haight, of New York

———

SPEAKER OF THE HOUSE OF REPRESENTATIVES—Robert M. T. Hunter,[3] of Virginia

CLERK OF THE HOUSE—Hugh A. Garland,[4] of Virginia

SERGEANT AT ARMS OF THE HOUSE—Roderick Dorsey, of Maryland

DOORKEEPER OF THE HOUSE—Joseph Follansbee, of Massachusetts

ALABAMA

SENATORS

William R. King, *Selma*
Clement C. Clay, *Huntsville*

REPRESENTATIVES

Reuben Chapman, *Somerville*
David Hubbard, *Courtland*
George W. Crabb, *Tuscaloosa*
Dixon H. Lewis, *Lowndesboro*
James Dellet, *Claiborne*

ARKANSAS

SENATORS

William S. Fulton, *Little Rock*
Ambrose H. Sevier, *Lake Port*

REPRESENTATIVE

Edward Cross, *Washington*

CONNECTICUT

SENATORS

Perry Smith, *New Milford*
Thaddeus Betts,[5] *Norwalk*
Jabez W. Huntington,[6] *Norwich*

REPRESENTATIVES

Joseph Trumbull, *Hartford*
William L. Storrs,[7] *Middletown*
William W. Boardman,[8] *New Haven*
Thomas W. Williams, *New London*
Thomas B. Osborne, *Fairfield*
Truman Smith, *Litchfield*
John H. Brockway, *Ellington*

DELAWARE

SENATORS

Richard H. Bayard,[9] *Wilmington*
Thomas Clayton, *New Castle*

REPRESENTATIVE

Thomas Robinson, Jr., *Georgetown*

GEORGIA

SENATORS

Alfred Cuthbert, *Monticello*
Wilson Lumpkin, *Athens*

REPRESENTATIVES

Julius C. Alford, *Lagrange*
Edward J. Black, *Jacksonboro*
Walter T. Colquitt,[10] *Columbus*
Hines Holt,[11] *Columbus*
Mark A. Cooper, *Columbus*
William C. Dawson, *Greensboro*
Richard W. Habersham, *Clarkesville*
Thomas Butler King, *Waynesville*
Eugenius A. Nisbet, *Macon*
Lott Warren, *Palmyra*

ILLINOIS

SENATORS

John M. Robinson, *Carmi*
Richard M. Young, *Quincy*

REPRESENTATIVES

John Reynolds, *Cadiz*
Zadoc Casey, *Mount Vernon*
John T. Stuart, *Springfield*

INDIANA

SENATORS

Oliver H. Smith, *Indianapolis*
Albert S. White, *La Fayette*

REPRESENTATIVES

George H. Proffit, *Petersburg*
John W. Davis, *Carlisle*

---

[1] Continuing from preceding session; reelected July 3, 1840; March 3, 1841.
[2] Reelected December 9, 1839.
[3] Elected December 16, 1839.
[4] Reelected December 21, 1839.
[5] Died April 7, 1840.
[6] Elected to fill vacancy caused by death of Thaddeus Betts, and took his seat June 2, 1840.
[7] Resigned in June, 1840, to become associate judge of the court of errors.
[8] Elected to fill vacancy caused by resignation of William L. Storrs, and took his seat Decen ber 7, 1840.
[9] Resigned September 19, 1839, to become chief justice of Delaware; reelected to fill vacancy caused by his own resignation, and took his seat January 19, 1841; vacancy in this class from September 19, 1839, to January 11, 1841.
[10] Resigned July 21, 1840.
[11] Elected to fill vacancy caused by resignation of Walter T. Colquitt, and took his seat February 1, 1841.

INDIANA—Continued

REPRESENTATIVES—continued

John Carr, *Charlestown*
Thomas Smith, *Versailles*
James Rariden, *Centerville*
William W. Wick, *Indianapolis*
Tilghman A. Howard,[12] *Rockville*
Henry S. Lane,[13] *Crawfordsville*

KENTUCKY

SENATORS

Henry Clay, *Lexington*
John J. Crittenden, *Frankfort*

REPRESENTATIVES

Linn Boyd, *Cadiz*
Philip Triplett, *Owensboro*
Joseph R. Underwood, *Bowling Green*
Sherrod Williams, *Monticello*
Simeon H. Anderson,[14] *Lancaster*
John B. Thompson,[15] *Harrodsburg*
Willis Green, *Green*
John Pope, *Springfield*
William J. Graves, *New Castle*
John White, *Richmond*
Richard Hawes, *Winchester*
Landaff W. Andrews, *Flemingsburg*
Garrett Davis, *Paris*
William O. Butler, *Carrollton*

LOUISIANA

SENATORS

Robert C. Nicholas, *Donaldsonville*
Alexander Mouton, *Vermilionville*

REPRESENTATIVES

Edward D. White, *Thibodaux*
Thomas W. Chinn, *Baton Rouge*
Rice Garland,[16] *Opelousas*
John Moore,[17] *Franklin*

MAINE

SENATORS

John Ruggles, *Thomaston*
Reuel Williams, *Augusta*

REPRESENTATIVES

Hugh J. Anderson, *Belfast*
Nathan Clifford, *Newfield*
Thomas Davee, *Blanchard*
George Evans,[18] *Gardiner*

Joshua A. Lowell, *East Machias*
Virgil D. Parris, *Buckfield*
Benjamin Randall, *Bath*
Albert Smith, *Portland*

MARYLAND

SENATORS

John S. Spence,[19] *Berlin*
John L. Kerr,[20] *Easton*
William D. Merrick, *Allens Fresh*

REPRESENTATIVES

John Dennis, *Princess Anne*
Philip F. Thomas, *Easton*
John T. H. Worthington, *Shawan*
Solomon Hillen, Jr., *Baltimore*
James Carroll, *Baltimore*
William Cost Johnson, *Jefferson*
Francis Thomas, *Frederick*
Daniel Jenifer, *Milton Hill*

MASSACHUSETTS

SENATORS

Daniel Webster,[21] *Boston*
Rufus Choate,[22] *Boston*
John Davis,[23] *Worcester*
Isaac C. Bates,[24] *Northampton*

REPRESENTATIVES

Abbott Lawrence,[25] *Boston*
Robert C. Winthrop,[26] *Boston*
Leverett Saltonstall, *Salem*
Caleb Cushing, *Newburyport*
William Parmenter, *East Cambridge*
Levi Lincoln, *Worcester*
James C. Alvord,[27] *Greenfield*
Osmyn Baker,[28] *Amherst*
George N. Briggs, *Lanesboro*
William B. Calhoun, *Springfield*
William S. Hastings, *Mendon*
Henry Williams, *Taunton*
John Reed, *Yarmouth*
John Quincy Adams, *Quincy*

MICHIGAN

SENATORS

John Norvell, *Detroit*
Augustus S. Porter,[29] *Detroit*

REPRESENTATIVE

Isaac E. Crary, *Marshall*

MISSISSIPPI

SENATORS

Robert J. Walker, *Madisonville*
John Henderson, *Pass Christian*

REPRESENTATIVES

Albert G. Brown, *Gallatin*
Jacob Thompson, *Pontotoc*

MISSOURI

SENATORS

Thomas H. Benton, *St. Louis*
Lewis F. Linn, *Ste. Genevieve*

REPRESENTATIVES

Albert G. Harrison,[30] *Fulton*
John Jameson,[31] *Fulton*
John Miller, *Conners Mills*

NEW HAMPSHIRE

SENATORS

Henry Hubbard, *Charlestown*
Franklin Pierce, *Concord*

REPRESENTATIVES

Charles G. Atherton, *Nashua*
Edmund Burke, *Newport*
Ira A. Eastman, *Gilmanton*
Tristram Shaw, *Exeter*
Jared W. Williams, *Lancaster*

NEW JERSEY

SENATORS

Samuel L. Southard, *Trenton*
Garret D. Wall, *Burlington*

REPRESENTATIVES [32]

William R. Cooper, *Swedesboro*
Philemon Dickerson, *Paterson*
Joseph Kille, *Salem*
Joseph F. Randolph, *New Brunswick*
Daniel B. Ryall, *Freehold*
Peter D. Vroom, *Somerville*

NEW YORK

SENATORS

Silas Wright, Jr., *Canton*
Nathaniel P. Tallmadge, *Poughkeepsie*

---

[12] Resigned August 1, 1840.
[13] Elected to fill vacancy caused by resignation of Tilghman A. Howard, and took his seat December 7, 1840.
[14] Died August 11, 1840.
[15] Elected to fill vacancy caused by death of Simeon H. Anderson, and took his seat December 7, 1840.
[16] Resigned July 21, 1840.
[17] Elected to fill vacancy caused by resignation of Rice Garland, and took his seat December 17, 1840.
[18] Reelected to the Twenty-seventh Congress but resigned, having been elected Senator.
[19] Died October 24, 1840.
[20] Elected to fill vacancy caused by death of John S. Spence, and took his seat January 13, 1841.

[21] Resigned, effective February 22, 1841.
[22] Elected to fill vacancy caused by resignation of Daniel Webster, and took his seat March 1, 1841.
[23] Resigned January 5, 1841.
[24] Elected to fill vacancy caused by resignation of John Davis, and took his seat January 21, 1841.
[25] Resigned September 18, 1840.
[26] Elected to fill vacancy caused by resignation of Abbott Lawrence, and took his seat December 7, 1840.
[27] Died September 27, 1839, before Congress assembled.
[28] Elected to fill vacancy caused by death of James C. Alvord, and took his seat January 14, 1840.
[29] Elected to fill vacancy in term commencing March

4, 1839, caused by failure of legislature to elect, and took his seat February 7, 1840; vacancy in this class from March 4, 1839, to January 19, 1840.
[30] Died September 7, 1839.
[31] Elected to fill vacancy caused by death of Albert G. Harrison, and took his seat December 12, 1839.
[32] Messrs. Aycrigg, Maxwell, Halsted, Stratton, and Yorke contested the election of Messrs. Vroom, Dickerson, Kille, Cooper, and Ryall; the House at first declined to seat either set of candidates, but by resolution of March 10, 1840, the five last named were admitted "without prejudice to the final rights of the claimants," and, on July 17, 1840, were adjudged entitled to their seats.

REPRESENTATIVES

Thomas B. Jackson, *Newtown*
James De la Montanya, *Haverstraw*
Ogden Hoffman, *New York City*
Edward Curtis, *New York City*
Moses H. Grinnell, *New York City*
James Monroe, *New York City*
Gouverneur Kemble, *Cold Spring*
Charles Johnston, *Poughkeepsie*
Nathaniel Jones, *Warwick*
Rufus Palen, *Fallsburg*
Aaron Vanderpoel, *Kinderhook*
John Ely, *Coxsackie*
Hiram P. Hunt, *Troy*
Daniel D. Barnard, *Albany*
Anson Brown,[33] *Ballston*
Nicholas B. Doe,[34] *Waterford*
David A. Russell, *Salem*
Augustus C. Hand, *Elizabethtown*
John Fine, *Ogdensburg*
Peter J. Wagner, *Fort Plain*
Andrew W. Doig, *Lowville*
John G. Floyd, *Utica*
David P. Brewster, *Oswego*
Thomas C. Chittenden, *Adams*
John H. Prentiss, *Cooperstown*
Judson Allen, *Harpersville*
John C. Clark, *Bainbridge*
Stephen B. Leonard, *Owego*
Amasa Dana, *Ithaca*
Edward Rogers, *Madison*
Nehemiah H. Earll, *Syracuse*
Christopher Morgan, *Aurora*
Theron R. Strong, *Palmyra*
Francis Granger, *Canandaigua*
Meredith Mallory, *Hammondsport*
Thomas Kempshall, *Rochester*
Seth M. Gates, *Leroy*
Luther C. Peck, *Pike*
Richard P. Marvin, *Jamestown*
Millard Fillmore, *Buffalo*
Charles F. Mitchell, *Lockport*

NORTH CAROLINA

SENATORS

Bedford Brown,[35] *Browns Store*
Willie P. Mangum,[36] *Red Mountain*
Robert Strange,[37] *Fayetteville*
William A. Graham,[38] *Hillsboro*

REPRESENTATIVES

Kenneth Rayner, *Winton*
Jesse A. Bynum, *Halifax*
Edward Stanly, *Washington*
Charles B. Shepard, *New Bern*
James I. McKay, *Elizabethtown*

Micajah T. Hawkins, *Warrenton*
Edmund Deberry, *Lawrenceville*
William Montgomery, *Albrights*
John Hill, *Germantown*
Charles Fisher, *Salisbury*
Henry W. Connor, *Sherrills Ford*
James Graham, *Rutherfordton*
Lewis Williams, *Panther Creek*

OHIO

SENATORS

William Allen, *Chillicothe*
Benjamin Tappan, *Steubenville*

REPRESENTATIVES

Alexander Duncan, *Cincinnati*
John B. Weller, *Hamilton*
Patrick G. Goode, *Sidney*
Thomas Corwin,[39] *Lebanon*
Jeremiah Morrow,[40] *Twentymile Stand*
William Doan, *Withamsville*
Calvary Morris, *Athens*
William K. Bond, *Chillicothe*
Joseph Ridgway, *Columbus*
William Medill, *Lancaster*
Samson Mason, *Springfield*
Isaac Parrish, *Cambridge*
Jonathan Taylor, *Newark*
Daniel P. Leadbetter, *Millersburg*
George Sweeny, *Bucyrus*
John W. Allen, *Cleveland*
Joshua R. Giddings, *Jefferson*
John Hastings, *Salem*
David A. Starkweather, *Canton*
Henry Swearingen, *Smithfield*

PENNSYLVANIA

SENATORS

James Buchanan, *Lancaster*
Daniel Sturgeon,[41] *Uniontown*

REPRESENTATIVES

Lemuel Paynter, *Philadelphia*
John Sergeant, *Philadelphia*
George W. Toland, *Philadelphia*
Charles Naylor,[42] *Philadelphia*
Edward Davies, *Churchtown*
John Edwards, *Ivy Mills*
Francis James, *West Chester*
Joseph Fornance, *Norristown*
John Davis, *Davisville*
David D. Wagener, *Easton*
Peter Newhard, *Allentown*
George M. Keim, *Reading*
William Simonton, *Hummelstown*

James Gerry, *Shrewsbury*
James Cooper, *Gettysburg*
William S. Ramsey,[43] *Carlisle*
Charles McClure,[44] *Carlisle*
William W. Potter,[45] *Philadelphia*
George McCulloch,[46] *Center Line*
David Petrikin, *Danville*
Robert H. Hammond, *Milton*
Samuel W. Morris, *Wellsboro*
Charles Ogle, *Somerset*
Albert G. Marchand, *Greensburg*
Enos Hook, *Waynesburg*
Isaac Leet, *Washington*
Richard Biddle,[47] *Pittsburgh*
Henry M. Brackenridge,[48] *Tarentum*
William Beatty, *Butler*
Thomas Henry, *Beaver*
John Galbraith, *Erie*

RHODE ISLAND

SENATORS

Nehemiah R. Knight, *Providence*
Nathan F. Dixon, *Westerly*

REPRESENTATIVES

Robert B. Cranston, *Newport*
Joseph L. Tillinghast, *Providence*

SOUTH CAROLINA

SENATORS

John C. Calhoun, *Fort Hill*
William C. Preston, *Columbia*

REPRESENTATIVES

Sampson H. Butler, *Barnwell*
John Campbell, *Parnassus*
John K. Griffin, *Newberry*
Isaac E. Holmes, *Charleston*
Francis W. Pickens, *Edgefield*
R. Barnwell Rhett, *Blue House*
James Rogers, *Maybinton*
Thomas D. Sumter, *Stateburg*
Waddy Thompson, Jr., *Greenville*

TENNESSEE

SENATORS

Hugh Lawson White,[49] *Knoxville*
Alexander Anderson,[50] *Knoxville*
Felix Grundy,[51] *Nashville*
Alfred O. P. Nicholson,[52] *Columbia*

REPRESENTATIVES

William B. Carter, *Elizabethton*
Abraham McClellan, *Blountville*

---

[33] Died June 14, 1840.
[34] Elected to fill vacancy caused by death of Anson Brown, and took his seat December 7, 1840.
[35] Resigned, effective November 16, 1840.
[36] Elected to fill vacancy caused by resignation of Bedford Brown, and took his seat December 9, 1840.
[37] Resigned, effective November 16, 1840.
[38] Elected to fill vacancy caused by resignation of Robert Strange, and took his seat December 10, 1840.
[39] Resigned, effective May 30, 1840.
[40] Elected to fill vacancy caused by resignation of Thomas Corwin, and took his seat December 7, 1840.
[41] Elected January 14, 1840, to fill vacancy in the term

commencing March 4, 1839, caused by failure of the legislature to elect, and took his seat January 24, 1840.
[42] Election unsuccessfully contested by Charles J. Ingersoll.
[43] Died October 17, 1840, before the commencement of the Twenty-seventh Congress, to which he had been reelected.
[44] Elected to fill vacancy caused by death of William S. Ramsey, and took his seat December 7, 1840.
[45] Died October 28, 1839, before Congress assembled.
[46] Elected to fill vacancy caused by death of William W. Potter and took his seat December 2, 1839.
[47] Resigned in 1840.

[48] Elected to fill vacancy caused by resignation of Richard Biddle, and took his seat December 10, 1840.
[49] Resigned January 13, 1840.
[50] Elected to fill vacancy caused by resignation of Hugh L. White, and took his seat February 26, 1840.
[51] Elected to fill vacancy in the term commencing March 4, 1839, caused by resignation of Ephraim H. Foster, in preceding Congress, and took his seat January 3, 1840; vacancy in this class from March 4 to December 14, 1839; died December 19, 1840.
[52] Appointed to fill vacancy caused by death of Felix Grundy, and took his seat January 11, 1841.

TENNESSEE—Continued

REPRESENTATIVES—continued

Joseph L. Williams, *Knoxville*
Julius W. Blackwell, *Athens*
Hopkins L. Turney, *Winchester*
William B. Campbell, *Carthage*
John Bell, *Nashville*
Meredith P. Gentry, *Harpeth*
Harvey M. Watterson, *Shelbyville*
Aaron V. Brown, *Pulaski*
Cave Johnson, *Clarksville*
John W. Crockett, *Trenton*
Christopher H. Williams, *Lexington*

VERMONT

SENATORS

Samuel Prentiss, *Montpelier*
Samuel S. Phelps, *Middlebury*

REPRESENTATIVES

Hiland Hall, *Bennington*
William Slade, *Middlebury*
Horace Everett, *Windsor*

John Smith, *St. Albans*
Isaac Fletcher, *Lyndon*

VIRGINIA

SENATORS

William H. Roane, *Richmond*
William C. Rives,[53] *Lindseys Store*

REPRESENTATIVES

Linn Banks, *Madison*
Andrew Beirne, *Union*
John M. Botts, *Richmond*
Walter Coles, *Robertsons Store*
Robert Craig, *Christiansburg*
George C. Dromgoole, *Gholsonville*
James Garland, *Lovingston*
William L. Goggin, *Liberty*
John Hill, *Buckingham*
Joel Holleman,[54] *Burwell Bay*
Francis Mallory,[55] *Hampton*
George W. Hopkins, *Lebanon*
Robert M. T. Hunter, *Lloyds*
Joseph Johnson, *Bridgeport*
John W. Jones, *Petersburg*

William Lucas, *Charlestown*
Charles F. Mercer,[56] *Aldie*
William M. McCarty,[57] *Alexandria*
Francis E. Rives, *Littleton*
Green B. Samuels, *Woodstock*
Lewis Steenrod, *Wheeling*
John Taliaferro, *Fredericksburg*
Henry A. Wise, *Accomac*

TERRITORY OF FLORIDA

DELEGATE

Charles Downing, *St. Augustine*

TERRITORY OF IOWA

DELEGATE

William W. Chapman,[58] *Burlington*
Augustus C. Dodge,[59] *Burlington*

TERRITORY OF WISCONSIN

DELEGATE

James D. Doty, *Ashton*

[53] Elected to fill vacancy in term commencing March 4, 1839, caused by failure of legislature to elect, and took his seat January 30, 1841; vacancy in this class from March 4, 1839, to January 18, 1841.
[54] Resigned in 1840.
[55] Elected to fill vacancy caused by resignation of Joel Holleman, and took his seat January 7, 1841.
[56] Resigned December 26, 1839.
[57] Elected to fill vacancy caused by resignation of Charles F. Mercer, and took his seat January 25, 1840.
[58] Served until October 27, 1840, when his term expired under the provisions of the act of March 3, 1839.
[59] Elected in compliance with the act of March 3, 1839, and took his seat December 8, 1840.

TWENTY-SEVENTH CONGRESS

MARCH 4, 1841, TO MARCH 3, 1843

FIRST SESSION—*May 31, 1841, to September 13, 1841*

SECOND SESSION—*December 6, 1841, to August 31, 1842*

THIRD SESSION—*December 5, 1842, to March 3, 1843*

SPECIAL SESSION OF THE SENATE—*March 4, 1841, to March 15, 1841*

———

VICE PRESIDENT OF THE UNITED STATES—JOHN TYLER,[1] of Virginia

PRESIDENT PRO TEMPORE OF THE SENATE—WILLIAM R. KING,[2] of Alabama; SAMUEL L. SOUTHARD,[3] of New Jersey; WILLIE P. MANGUM,[4] of North Carolina

SECRETARY OF THE SENATE—ASBURY DICKENS,[5] of North Carolina

SERGEANT AT ARMS OF THE SENATE—STEPHEN HAIGHT, of New York; EDWARD DYER,[6] of Maryland

———

SPEAKER OF THE HOUSE OF REPRESENTATIVES—JOHN WHITE,[7] of Kentucky

CLERK OF THE HOUSE—HUGH A. GARLAND, of Virginia; MATTHEW ST. CLAIR CLARKE,[8] of Pennsylvania

SERGEANT AT ARMS OF THE HOUSE—RODERICK DORSEY, of Maryland; ELEAZOR M. TOWNSEND,[9] of Connecticut

DOORKEEPER OF THE HOUSE—JOSEPH FOLLANSBEE, of Massachusetts

ALABAMA

SENATORS

William R. King, *Selma*
Clement C. Clay,[10] *Huntsville*
Arthur P. Bagby,[11] *Tuscaloosa*

REPRESENTATIVES

Reuben Chapman, *Somerville*
George S. Houston, *Athens*
Dixon H. Lewis, *Lowndesboro*
William W. Payne, *Gainesville*
Benjamin G. Shields, *Demopolis*

ARKANSAS

SENATORS

William S. Fulton, *Little Rock*
Ambrose H. Sevier, *Lake Port*

REPRESENTATIVE

Edward Cross, *Washington*

CONNECTICUT

SENATORS

Perry Smith, *New Milford*
Jabez W. Huntington, *Norwich*

REPRESENTATIVES

Joseph Trumbull, *Hartford*
William W. Boardman, *New Haven*
Thomas W. Williams, *New London*
Thomas B. Osborne, *Fairfield*
Truman Smith, *Litchfield*
John H. Brockway, *Ellington*

DELAWARE

SENATORS

Richard H. Bayard, *Wilmington*
Thomas Clayton, *New Castle*

REPRESENTATIVE

George B. Rodney, *New Castle*

GEORGIA

SENATORS

Alfred Cuthbert, *Monticello*
John Macpherson Berrien, *Savannah*

REPRESENTATIVES

Julius C. Alford,[12] *Lagrange*
Edward J. Black,[13] *Jacksonboro*
William C. Dawson,[14] *Greensboro*
Walter T. Colquitt,[15] *Columbus*
Eugenius A. Nisbet,[16] *Macon*
Mark A. Cooper,[17] *Columbus*
Thomas F. Foster, *Columbus*
Roger L. Gamble, *Louisville*
Richard W. Habersham,[18] *Clarkesville*
George W. Crawford,[19] *Augusta*
Thomas Butler King, *Waynesville*
James A. Meriwether, *Edenton*
Lott Warren, *Palmyra*

---

[1] Became President upon the death of William Henry Harrison, April 4, 1841.
[2] Elected March 4, 1841 (special session of the Senate).
[3] Elected March 11, 1841 (special session of the Senate); resigned as President pro tempore May 31, 1842.
[4] Elected May 31, 1842.
[5] Reelected June 7, 1841.
[6] Elected June 7, 1841.
[7] Elected May 31, 1841.
[8] Elected May 31, 1841
[9] Elected June 8, 1841.
[10] Resigned November 15, 1841.
[11] Elected to fill vacancy caused by resignation of Clement C. Clay, and took his seat December 27, 1841.
[12] Resigned in 1841.
[13] Elected at large to fill, in part, vacancies caused by resignations of Julius C. Alford, William C. Dawson, and Eugenius A. Nisbet, and took his seat March 2, 1842.
[14] Resigned November 13, 1841.
[15] Elected at large to fill, in part, vacancies caused by resignations of Julius C. Alford, William C. Dawson and Eugenius A. Nisbet, and took his seat February 1 1842.
[16] Resigned in 1841.
[17] Elected at large to fill, in part, vacancies caused by resignations of Julius C. Alford, William C. Dawson, and Eugenius A. Nisbet, and took his seat February 1, 1842.
[18] Died December 2, 1842.
[19] Elected to fill vacancy caused by death of Richard W. Habersham, and took his seat February 1, 1843.

ILLINOIS

SENATORS

Richard M. Young, *Quincy*
Samuel McRoberts, *Danville*

REPRESENTATIVES

Zadoc Casey, *Mount Vernon*
John Reynolds, *Belleville*
John T. Stuart, *Springfield*

INDIANA

SENATORS

Oliver H. Smith, *Indianapolis*
Albert S. White, *La Fayette*

REPRESENTATIVES

George H. Proffit, *Petersburg*
Richard W. Thompson, *Bedford*
Joseph L. White, *Madison*
James H. Cravens, *Marion*
Andrew Kennedy, *Muncietown*
David Wallace, *Indianapolis*
Henry S. Lane, *Crawfordsville*

KENTUCKY

SENATORS

Henry Clay,[20] *Lexington*
John J. Crittenden,[21] *Frankfort*
James T. Morehead, *Covington*

REPRESENTATIVES

Linn Boyd, *Cadiz*
Philip Triplett, *Owensboro*
Joseph R. Underwood, *Bowling Green*
Bryan Y. Owsley, *Jamestown*
John B. Thompson, *Harrodsburg*
Willis Green, *Green*
John Pope, *Springfield*
James C. Sprigg, *Shelbyville*
John White, *Richmond*
Thomas F. Marshall, *Versailles*
Landaff W. Andrews, *Flemingsburg*
Garrett Davis, *Paris*
William O. Butler, *Carrollton*

LOUISIANA

SENATORS

Alexander Mouton,[22] *Vermilionville*
Charles M. Conrad,[23] *New Orleans*
Alexander Barrow, *Baton Rouge*

REPRESENTATIVES

Edward D. White, *Thibodaux*
John B. Dawson, *St. Francisville*
John Moore, *Franklin*

MAINE

SENATORS

Reuel Williams,[24] *Augusta*
John Fairfield,[25] *Saco*
George Evans, *Gardiner*

REPRESENTATIVES

Elisha H. Allen, *Bangor*
David Bronson,[26] *Anson*
Nathan Clifford, *Newfield*
William P. Fessenden, *Portland*
Nathaniel S. Littlefield, *Bridgeton*
Joshua A. Lowell,[27] *East Machias*
Alfred Marshall, *China*
Benjamin Randall, *Bath*

MARYLAND

SENATORS

William D. Merrick, *Allens Fresh*
John L. Kerr, *Easton*

REPRESENTATIVES

Isaac D. Jones, *Princess Anne*
James A. Pearce, *Chestertown*
James W. Williams,[28] *Churchville*
Charles S. Sewall,[29] *Elkton*
John P. Kennedy, *Baltimore*
Alexander Randall, *Annapolis*
William Cost Johnson, *Jefferson*
John T. Mason, *Hagerstown*
Augustus R. Sollers, *Prince Frederick*

MASSACHUSETTS

SENATORS

Isaac C. Bates, *Northampton*
Rufus Choate, *Boston*

REPRESENTATIVES

Robert C. Winthrop,[30] *Boston*
Nathan Appleton,[31] *Boston*
Leverett Saltonstall, *Salem*
Caleb Cushing, *Newburyport*
William Parmenter, *East Cambridge*
Levi Lincoln,[32] *Worcester*
Charles Hudson,[33] *Westminster*
Osmyn Baker, *Amherst*
George N. Briggs, *Lanesboro*
William B. Calhoun, *Springfield*
William S. Hastings,[34] *Mendon*
Nathaniel B. Borden, *Fall River*
Barker Burnell, *Nantucket*
John Quincy Adams, *Quincy*

MICHIGAN

SENATORS

Augustus S. Porter, *Detroit*
William Woodbridge, *Detroit*

REPRESENTATIVE

Jacob M. Howard, *Detroit*

MISSISSIPPI

SENATORS

Robert J. Walker, *Madisonville*
John Henderson, *Pass Christian*

REPRESENTATIVES

William M. Gwin, *Vicksburg*
Jacob Thompson, *Oxford*

MISSOURI

SENATORS

Thomas H. Benton, *St. Louis*
Lewis F. Linn, *Ste. Genevieve*

REPRESENTATIVES

John C. Edwards, *Jefferson City*
John Miller, *Conners Mills*

NEW HAMPSHIRE

SENATORS

Franklin Pierce,[35] *Concord*
Leonard Wilcox,[36] *Orford*
Levi Woodbury, *Portsmouth*

REPRESENTATIVES

Charles G. Atherton, *Nashua*
Edmund Burke, *Newport*
Ira A. Eastman, *Gilmanton*
John R. Reding, *Haverhill*
Tristram Shaw, *Exeter*

NEW JERSEY

SENATORS

Samuel L. Southard,[37] *Trenton*
William L. Dayton,[38] *Trenton*
Jacob W. Miller, *Morristown*

REPRESENTATIVES

John B. Aycrigg, *Pyramus*
William Halstead, *Trenton*
John P. B. Maxwell, *Belvidere*
Joseph F. Randolph, *New Brunswick*
Charles C. Stratton, *Swedesboro*
Thomas Jones Yorke, *Salem*

---

[20] Resigned March 31, 1842.
[21] Elected to fill vacancy caused by resignation of Henry Clay, and took his seat March 31, 1842.
[22] Resigned March 1, 1842.
[23] Elected to fill vacancy caused by resignation of Alexander Mouton, and took his seat April 14, 1842.
[24] Resigned February 15, 1843.
[25] Elected to fill vacancy caused by resignation of Reuel Williams, but did not take his seat until December 4, 1843, in the next Congress.
[26] Elected to fill vacancy caused by resignation of Representative-elect George Evans, in preceding Congress, and took his seat May 31, 1841.

[27] Election unsuccessfully protested by sundry citizens of Maine.
[28] Died December 2, 1842.
[29] Elected to fill vacancy caused by death of James W. Williams, and took his seat January 7, 1843.
[30] Resigned May 25, 1842; subsequently elected to fill vacancy caused by resignation of his own successor, Nathan Appleton, and took his seat the second time December 5, 1842.
[31] Elected to fill vacancy caused by resignation of Robert C. Winthrop, and took his seat June 9, 1842; resigned September 28, 1842.
[32] Resigned March 16, 1841, before Congress assem-

bled, having been appointed collector of the port of Boston.
[33] Elected to fill vacancy caused by resignation of Levi Lincoln, and took his seat May 3, 1841.
[34] Died June 17, 1842.
[35] Resigned February 28, 1842.
[36] Appointed to fill vacancy caused by resignation of Franklin Pierce, and took his seat March 7, 1842; subsequently elected.
[37] Died June 26, 1842.
[38] Appointed to fill vacancy caused by death of Samuel L. Southard, and took his seat July 6, 1842; subsequently elected.

NEW YORK

SENATORS

Silas Wright, Jr., *Canton*
Nathaniel P. Tallmadge, *Poughkeepsie*

REPRESENTATIVES

Charles A. Floyd, *Commack*
Joseph Egbert, *Tompkinsville*
John McKeon, *New York City*
James I. Roosevelt, *New York City*
Fernando Wood, *New York City*
Charles G. Ferris, *New York City*
Aaron Ward, *Mount Pleasant*
Richard D. Davis, *Poughkeepsie*
James G. Clinton, *Newburgh*
John Van Buren, *Kingston*
Robert McClellan, *Hudson*
Jacob Houck, Jr., *Schoharie*
Hiram P. Hunt, *Troy*
Daniel D. Barnard, *Albany*
Archibald L. Linn, *Schenectady*
Barnard Blair, *Salem*
Thomas A. Tomlinson, *Keeseville*
Henry Van B. Rensselaer, *Ogdensburg*
John Sanford, *Amsterdam*
Andrew W. Doig, *Lowville*
John G. Floyd, *Utica*
David P. Brewster, *Oswego*
Thomas C. Chittenden, *Adams*
Samuel S. Bowne, *Cooperstown*
Samuel Gordon, *Delhi*
John C. Clark, *Bainbridge*
Lewis Riggs, *Homer*
Samuel Partridge, *Elmira*
Victory Birdseye, *Pompey*
A. Lawrence Foster, *Morrisville*
Christopher Morgan, *Aurora*
John Maynard, *Seneca Falls*
Francis Granger,[39] *Canandaigua*
John Greig,[40] *Canandaigua*
William M. Oliver, *Penn Yan*
Timothy Childs, *Rochester*
Seth M. Gates, *Leroy*
John Young, *Geneseo*
Staley N. Clarke, *Ellicottsville*
Millard Fillmore, *Buffalo*
Alfred Babcock, *Gaines*

NORTH CAROLINA

SENATORS

Willie P. Mangum, *Red Mountain*
William A. Graham, *Hillsboro*

REPRESENTATIVES

Kenneth Rayner, *Winton*
John R. J. Daniel, *Halifax*
Edward Stanly, *Washington*
William H. Washington, *New Bern*
James I. McKay, *Elizabethtown*
Archibald H. Arrington, *Hilliardston*
Edmund Deberry, *Lawrenceville*
Romulus M. Saunders, *Raleigh*
Augustine H. Shepperd, *Salem*
Abraham Rencher, *Pittsboro*
Greene W. Caldwell, *Charlotte*
James Graham, *Rutherfordton*
Lewis Williams,[41] *Panther Creek*
Anderson Mitchell,[42] *Wilkesboro*

OHIO

SENATORS

William Allen, *Chillicothe*
Benjamin Tappan, *Steubenville*

REPRESENTATIVES

Nathanael G. Pendleton, *Cincinnati*
John B. Weller, *Hamilton*
Patrick G. Goode, *Sidney*
Jeremiah Morrow, *Twentymile Stand*
William Doan, *Withamsville*
Calvary Morris, *Athens*
William Russell, *Portsmouth*
Joseph Ridgway, *Columbus*
William Medill, *Lancaster*
Samson Mason, *Springfield*
Benjamin S. Cowen, *St. Clairsville*
Joshua Mathiot, *Newark*
James Mathews, *Coshocton*
George Sweeny, *Bucyrus*
Sherlock J. Andrews, *Cleveland*
Joshua R. Giddings,[43] *Jefferson*
John Hastings, *Salem*
Ezra Dean, *Wooster*
Samuel Stokely, *Steubenville*

PENNSYLVANIA

SENATORS

James Buchanan, *Lancaster*
Daniel Sturgeon, *Uniontown*

REPRESENTATIVES

Charles Brown, *Philadelphia*
John Sergeant,[44] *Philadelphia*
Joseph R. Ingersoll,[45] *Philadelphia*

George W. Toland, *Philadelphia*
Charles J. Ingersoll, *Philadelphia*
Jeremiah Brown, *Goshen*
Francis James, *West Chester*
John Edwards, *Ivy Mills*
Joseph Fornance, *Norristown*
Robert Ramsey, *Hartsville*
John Westbrook, *Dingmans Ferry*
Peter Newhard, *Allentown*
George M. Keim, *Reading*
William Simonton, *Hummelstown*
James Gerry, *Shrewsbury*
James Cooper, *Gettysburg*
Amos Gustine,[46] *Mifflintown*
James Irvin, *Milesburg*
Benjamin A. Bidlack, *Wilkes-Barre*
John Snyder, *Selinsgrove*
Davis Dimock, Jr.,[47] *Montrose*
Almon H. Read,[48] *Montrose*
Albert G. Marchand, *Greensburg*
Enos Hook,[49] *Waynesburg*
Henry W. Beeson,[50] *Uniontown*
Joseph Lawrence,[51] *Washington*
Thomas M. T. McKennan,[52] *Washington*
William W. Irwin, *Pittsburgh*
William Jack, *Brookville*
Thomas Henry, *Beaver*
Arnold Plumer, *Franklin*
Charles Ogle,[53] *Somerset*
Henry Black,[54] *Somerset*
James M. Russell,[55] *Bedford*

RHODE ISLAND

SENATORS

Nathan F. Dixon,[56] *Westerly*
William Sprague,[57] *Natick*
James F. Simmons, *Providence*

REPRESENTATIVES

Robert B. Cranston, *Newport*
Joseph L. Tillinghast, *Providence*

SOUTH CAROLINA

SENATORS

John C. Calhoun,[58] *Fort Hill*
William C. Preston,[59] *Columbia*
George McDuffie,[60] *Edgefield*

REPRESENTATIVES

Sampson H. Butler,[61] *Barnwell*
Samuel W. Trotti,[62] *Barnwell*
William Butler, *Greenville*

---

[39] Resigned March 5, 1841, having been appointed Postmaster General; subsequently elected to fill vacancy caused by resignation of his own successor, John Greig, and took his seat the second time December 7, 1841.
[40] Elected to fill vacancy caused by resignation of Francis Granger, and took his seat May 31, 1841; resigned September 25, 1841.
[41] Died February 23, 1842.
[42] Elected to fill vacancy caused by death of Lewis Williams, and took his seat April 27, 1842.
[43] Resigned March 22, 1842; subsequently elected to fill vacancy caused by his own resignation, and took his seat December 5, 1842.
[44] Resigned September 15, 1841.

[45] Elected to fill vacancy caused by resignation of John Sergeant, and took his seat December 9, 1841.
[46] Elected to fill vacancy caused by death of Representative-elect William S. Ramsey, in preceding Congress, and took his seat May 31, 1841.
[47] Died January 13, 1842.
[48] Elected to fill vacancy caused by death of Davis Dimock, Jr., and took his seat March 18, 1842.
[49] Resigned April 18, 1841.
[50] Elected to fill vacancy caused by resignation of Enos Hook, and took his seat May 31, 1841.
[51] Died April 17, 1842.
[52] Elected to fill vacancy caused by death of Joseph Lawrence, and took his seat May 30, 1842.
[53] Died May 10, 1841, before Congress assembled.

[54] Elected to fill vacancy caused by death of Charles Ogle, and took his seat June 28, 1841; died November 28, 1841.
[55] Elected to fill vacancy caused by death of Henry Black, and took his seat January 3, 1842.
[56] Died January 29, 1842.
[57] Elected to fill vacancy caused by death of Nathan F. Dixon, and took his seat February 18, 1842.
[58] Resigned March 3, 1843.
[59] Resigned November 29, 1842.
[60] Elected to fill vacancy caused by resignation of William C. Preston, and took his seat January 3, 1843.
[61] Resigned September 27, 1842.
[62] Elected to fill vacancy caused by resignation of Sampson H. Butler, and took his seat December 17, 1842.

SOUTH CAROLINA—Continued

REPRESENTATIVES—continued

Patrick C. Caldwell, *Newberry*
John Campbell, *Parnassus*
Isaac E. Holmes, *Charleston*
Francis W. Pickens, *Edgefield*
R. Barnwell Rhett, *Blue House*
James Rogers, *Maybinton*
Thomas D. Sumter, *Stateburg*

TENNESSEE

SENATORS

Alfred O. P. Nicholson,[63] *Columbia*
Vacant [64]

REPRESENTATIVES

Thomas D. Arnold, *Greeneville*
Abraham McClellan, *Blountville*
Joseph L. Williams, *Knoxville*
Thomas J. Campbell, *Athens*
Hopkins L. Turney, *Winchester*
William B. Campbell, *Carthage*
Robert L. Caruthers, *Lebanon*
Meredith P. Gentry, *Harpeth*
Harvey M. Watterson, *Shelbyville*
Aaron V. Brown, *Pulaski*
Cave Johnson, *Clarksville*
Milton Brown, *Jackson*
Christopher H. Williams, *Lexington*

VERMONT

SENATORS

Samuel Prentiss,[65] *Montpelier*
Samuel C. Crafts,[66] *Craftsbury*
Samuel S. Phelps, *Middlebury*

REPRESENTATIVES

Hiland Hall, *Bennington*
William Slade, *Middlebury*
Horace Everett, *Windsor*
Augustus Young, *Johnson*
John Mattocks, *Peacham*

VIRGINIA

SENATORS

William C. Rives, *Lindseys Store*
William S. Archer, *Elk Hill*

REPRESENTATIVES

Francis Mallory, *Hampton*
George B. Cary, *Bethlehem*
John W. Jones, *Petersburg*
William O. Goode, *Boydton*
Edmund W. Hubard, *Curdsville*
Walter Coles, *Robertsons Store*
William L. Goggin, *Otter Bridge*
Henry A. Wise, *Accomac*
Robert M. T. Hunter, *Lloyds*

John Taliaferro, *Fredericksburg*
John M. Botts, *Richmond*
Thomas W. Gilmer, *Charlottesville*
Linn Banks,[67] *Madison*
William Smith,[68] *Culpeper*
Cuthbert Powell, *Upperville*
Richard W. Barton, *Winchester*
William A. Harris, *Luray*
Alexander H. H. Stuart, *Staunton*
George W. Hopkins, *Lebanon*
George W. Summers, *Kanawha*
Samuel L. Hayes, *Stuards Creek*
Lewis Steenrod, *Wheeling*

TERRITORY OF FLORIDA

DELEGATE

David Levy (Yulee), *St. Augustine*

TERRITORY OF IOWA

DELEGATE

Augustus C. Dodge, *Burlington*

TERRITORY OF WISCONSIN

DELEGATE

Henry Dodge, *Dodgeville*

---

[63] Served until February 7, 1842; State unrepresented for the remainder of the Congress, because of failure of legislature to elect.
[64] Vacancy in this class throughout the Congress.

[65] Resigned April 11, 1842.
[66] Appointed to fill vacancy caused by resignation of Samuel Prentiss, and took his seat April 30, 1842; subsequently elected.

[67] Served until December 6, 1841; succeeded by William Smith, who contested his election.
[68] Successfully contested the election of Linn Banks, and took his seat December 6, 1841.

TWENTY-EIGHTH CONGRESS

MARCH 4, 1843, TO MARCH 3, 1845

FIRST SESSION—*December 4, 1843, to June 17, 1844*

SECOND SESSION—*December 2, 1844, to March 3, 1845*

VICE PRESIDENT OF THE UNITED STATES [1]

PRESIDENT PRO TEMPORE OF THE SENATE—WILLIE P. MANGUM, of North Carolina

SECRETARY OF THE SENATE—ASBURY DICKENS,[2] of North Carolina

SERGEANT AT ARMS OF THE SENATE—EDWARD DYER, of Maryland

SPEAKER OF THE HOUSE OF REPRESENTATIVES—JOHN W. JONES,[3] of Virginia

CLERK OF THE HOUSE—MATTHEW ST. CLAIR CLARKE, of Pennsylvania; CALEB J. MCNULTY,[4] of Ohio; BENJAMIN B. FRENCH,[5] of New Hampshire

SERGEANT AT ARMS OF THE HOUSE—ELEAZOR M. TOWNSEND, of Connecticut; NEWTON LANE,[6] of Kentucky

DOORKEEPER OF THE HOUSE—JESSE E. DOW, of Connecticut

ALABAMA

SENATORS

William R. King,[7] *Selma*
Dixon H. Lewis,[8] *Lowndesboro*
Arthur P. Bagby, *Tuscaloosa*

REPRESENTATIVES

James Dellet, *Claiborne*
James E. Belser, *Montgomery*
Dixon H. Lewis,[9] *Lowndesboro*
William L. Yancey,[10] *Wetumpka*
William W. Payne, *Cainesville*
George S. Houston, *Athens*
Reuben Chapman, *Somerville*
Felix G. McConnell, *Talladega*

ARKANSAS

SENATORS

William S. Fulton,[11] *Little Rock*
Chester Ashley,[12] *Little Rock*
Ambrose H. Sevier, *Lake Port*

REPRESENTATIVE

Edward Cross, *Washington*

CONNECTICUT

SENATORS

Jabez W. Huntington, *Norwich*
John M. Niles, *Hartford*

REPRESENTATIVES

Thomas H. Seymour, *Hartford*
John Stewart, *Middle Haddam*
George S. Catlin, *Windham*
Samuel Simons, *Bridgeport*

DELAWARE

SENATORS

Richard H. Bayard, *Wilmington*
Thomas Clayton, *New Castle*

REPRESENTATIVE

George B. Rodney, *New Castle*

GEORGIA

SENATORS

John Macpherson Berrien, *Savannah*
Walter T. Colquitt, *Columbus*

REPRESENTATIVES

Edward J. Black, *Jacksonboro*
John B. Lamar,[13] *Macon*
Absalom H. Chappell,[14] *Macon*
Howell Cobb, *Athens*
Hugh A. Haralson, *Lagrange*
William H. Stiles, *Cassville*
John H. Lumpkin, *Rome*
John Millen,[15] *Savannah*
Duncan L. Clinch,[16] *St. Marys*
Mark A. Cooper,[17] *Columbus*
Alexander H. Stephens,[18] *Crawfordville*

ILLINOIS

SENATORS

Samuel McRoberts,[19] *Danville*
James Semple,[20] *Alton*
Sidney Breese, *Carlyle*

---

[1] John Tyler became President on the death of William Henry Harrison in preceding Congress.
[2] Reelected December 11, 1843.
[3] Elected December 4, 1843; the Speaker having withdrawn, George W. Hopkins, of Virginia, was substituted to act as Speaker on February 28, 1845, and officiated as such for the remainder of the day.
[4] Elected December 6, 1843; dismissed from office January 18, 1845.
[5] Elected January 18, 1845.
[6] Elected December 7, 1843.
[7] Resigned April 15, 1844, having been appointed minister to France.
[8] Appointed to fill vacancy caused by resignation of William R. King, and took his seat May 7, 1844; subsequently elected.
[9] Resigned April 22, 1844, having been appointed Senator.
[10] Elected to fill vacancy caused by resignation of Dixon H. Lewis, and took his seat December 2, 1844.
[11] Died August 15, 1844.
[12] Elected to fill vacancy caused by death of William S. Fulton, and took his seat December 4, 1844.
[13] Resigned July 29, 1843, before Congress assembled.

[14] Elected to fill vacancy caused by resignation of John B. Lamar, and took his seat December 4, 1843.
[15] Died October 15, 1843, before Congress assembled.
[16] Elected to fill vacancy caused by death of John Millen, and took his seat February 15, 1844.
[17] Resigned June 26, 1843, before Congress assembled.
[18] Elected to fill vacancy caused by resignation of Mark A. Cooper, and took his seat December 4, 1843.
[19] Died March 27, 1843.
[20] Appointed to fill vacancy caused by death of Samuel McRoberts, and took his seat December 4, 1843; subsequently elected.

[137]

ILLINOIS—Continued

REPRESENTATIVES

Robert Smith, *Alton*
John A. McClernand, *Shawneetown*
Orlando B. Ficklin, *Charleston*
John Wentworth, *Chicago*
Stephen A. Douglas, *Quincy*
Joseph P. Hoge, *Galena*
John J. Hardin, *Jacksonville*

INDIANA

SENATORS

Albert S. White, *La Fayette*
Edward A. Hannegan, *Covington*

REPRESENTATIVES

Robert D. Owen, *New Harmony*
Thomas J. Henley, *New Washington*
Thomas Smith, *Versailles*
Caleb B. Smith, *Connersville*
William J. Brown, *Indianapolis*
John W. Davis, *Carlisle*
Joseph A. Wright, *Rockville*
John Pettit, *La Fayette*
Samuel C. Sample, *South Bend*
Andrew Kennedy, *Muncietown*

KENTUCKY

SENATORS

James T. Morehead, *Covington*
John J. Crittenden, *Frankfort*

REPRESENTATIVES

Linn Boyd, *Cadiz*
Willis Green, *Green*
Henry Grider, *Bowling Green*
George A. Caldwell, *Columbia*
James W. Stone, *Taylorsville*
John White, *Richmond*
William P. Thomasson, *Louisville*
Garrett Davis, *Paris*
Richard French, *Mount Sterling*
John W. Tibbatts, *Newport*

LOUISIANA

SENATORS

Alexander Barrow, *Baton Rouge*
Henry Johnson,[21] *New River*

REPRESENTATIVES

John Slidell, *New Orleans*
Alcée L. La Branche, *New Orleans*
John B. Dawson, *St. Francisville*
Pierre E. J. B. Bossier,[22] *Natchitoches*
Isaac E. Morse,[23] *St. Martinville*

MAINE

SENATORS

George Evans, *Gardiner*
John Fairfield, *Saco*

REPRESENTATIVES

Joshua Herrick, *Kennebunkport*
Robert P. Dunlap, *Brunswick*
Luther Severance, *Augusta*
Freeman H. Morse, *Bath*
Benjamin White,[24] *Montville*
Hannibal Hamlin, *Hampden*
Shepard Cary,[25] *Houlton*

MARYLAND

SENATORS

William D. Merrick, *Allens Fresh*
James A. Pearce, *Chestertown*

REPRESENTATIVES

John M. S. Causin, *Leonardtown*
Francis Brengle, *Frederick*
John Wethered, *Franklin*
John P. Kennedy, *Baltimore*
Jacob A. Preston, *Perryman*
Thomas A. Spence, *Snow Hill*

MASSACHUSETTS

SENATORS

Isaac C. Bates, *Northampton*
Rufus Choate, *Boston*

REPRESENTATIVES

Robert C. Winthrop, *Boston*
Daniel P. King, *South Danvers*
Amos Abbott, *Andover*
William Parmenter, *East Cambridge*
Charles Hudson, *Westminster*
Osmyn Baker, *Amherst*
Julius Rockwell, *Pittsfield*
John Quincy Adams, *Quincy*
Henry Williams, *Taunton*
Barker Burnell,[26] *Nantucket*
Joseph Grinnell,[27] *New Bedford*

MICHIGAN

SENATORS

Augustus S. Porter, *Detroit*
William Woodbridge, *Detroit*

REPRESENTATIVES

Robert McClelland, *Monroe*
James B. Hunt, *Pontiac*
Lucius Lyon, *Grand Rapids*

MISSISSIPPI

SENATORS

Robert J. Walker, *Madisonville*
John Henderson, *Pass Christian*

REPRESENTATIVES

William H. Hammett, *Princeton*
Robert W. Roberts, *Hillsboro*
Jacob Thompson, *Oxford*
Tilghman M. Tucker, *Columbus*

MISSOURI

SENATORS

Thomas H. Benton, *St. Louis*
Lewis F. Linn,[28] *Ste. Genevieve*
David R. Atchison,[29] *Platte City*

REPRESENTATIVES

Gustavus M. Bower, *Paris*
James B. Bowlin, *St. Louis*
James M. Hughes, *Liberty*
John Jameson, *Fulton*
James H. Relfe, *Caledonia*

NEW HAMPSHIRE

SENATORS

Levi Woodbury, *Portsmouth*
Charles G. Atherton, *Nashua*

REPRESENTATIVES

Edmund Burke, *Newport*
John P. Hale, *Dover*
Moses Norris, Jr., *Pittsfield*
John R. Reding, *Haverhill*

NEW JERSEY

SENATORS

Jacob W. Miller, *Morristown*
William L. Dayton, *Trenton*

REPRESENTATIVES

Lucius Q. C. Elmer, *Bridgeton*
George Sykes, *Mount Holly*
Isaac G. Farlee, *Flemington*
Littleton Kirkpatrick, *New Brunswick*
William Wright, *Newark*

NEW YORK

SENATORS

Silas Wright, Jr.,[30] *Canton*
Henry A. Foster,[31] *Rome*
John A. Dix,[32] *Albany*

---

[21] Elected for term beginning March 4, 1843, and took his seat March 4, 1844. Alexander Porter was elected for this term but his credentials were not presented, and he died January 23, 1844. Out of consideration of his prior service, 1833–1837, the Senate adopted resolutions and adjourned in respect to his memory February 2, 1844; vacancy in this class from March 4, 1843, to February 12, 1844.
[22] Died April 24, 1844.
[23] Elected to fill vacancy caused by death of Pierre E. J. B. Bossier, and took his seat December 2, 1844.
[24] Took his seat December 2, 1844.
[25] Took his seat May 10, 1844.
[26] Died June 15, 1843, before Congress assembled.
[27] Elected to fill vacancy caused by death of Barker Burnell, and took his seat December 7, 1843.
[28] Died October 3, 1843.
[29] Appointed to fill vacancy caused by death of Lewis F. Linn, and took his seat December 4, 1843; subsequently elected.
[30] Resigned November 26, 1844, having been elected governor.
[31] Appointed to fill vacancy caused by resignation of Silas Wright, Jr., and took his seat December 9, 1844.
[32] Elected to fill vacancy caused by resignation of Silas Wright, Jr., and took his seat January 27, 1845.

Nathaniel P. Tallmadge,[33] *Poughkeepsie*
Daniel S. Dickinson,[34] *Binghamton*

REPRESENTATIVES

Selah B. Strong, *Setauket*
Henry C. Murphy, *Brooklyn*
J. Phillips Phoenix, *New York City*
William B. Maclay, *New York City*
Moses G. Leonard, *New York City*
Hamilton Fish, *New York City*
Joseph H. Anderson, *White Plains*
Richard D. Davis, *Poughkeepsie*
James G. Clinton, *Newburgh*
Jeremiah Russell, *Saugerties*
Zadock Pratt, *Prattsville*
David L. Seymour, *Troy*
Daniel D. Barnard, *Albany*
Charles Rogers, *Sandy Hill*
Lemuel Stetson, *Keeseville*
Chesselden Ellis, *Waterford*
Charles S. Benton, *Mohawk*
Preston King, *Ogdensburg*
Orville Hungerford, *Watertown*
Samuel Beardsley,[35] *Utica*
Levi D. Carpenter,[36] *Waterville*
Jeremiah E. Cary, *Cherry Valley*
Smith M. Purdy, *Norwich*
Orville Robinson, *Mexico*
Horace Wheaton, *Pompey*
George Rathbun, *Auburn*
Amasa Dana, *Ithaca*
Byram Green, *Sodus*
Thomas J. Patterson, *Rochester*
Charles H. Carroll, *Groveland Center*
William S. Hubbell, *Bath*
Asher Tyler, *Ellicottsville*
William A. Moseley, *Buffalo*
Albert Smith, *Batavia*
Washington Hunt, *Lockport*

NORTH CAROLINA

SENATORS

Willie P. Mangum, *Red Mountain*
William H. Haywood, Jr., *Raleigh*

REPRESENTATIVES

Thomas L. Clingman, *Asheville*
Daniel M. Barringer, *Concord*
David S. Reid, *Reidsville*
Edmund Deberry, *Lawrenceville*
Romulus M. Saunders, *Raleigh*
James I. McKay, *Elizabethtown*
John R. J. Daniel, *Halifax*
Archibald H. Arrington, *Hilliardston*
Kenneth Rayner, *Winton*

OHIO

SENATORS

William Allen, *Chillicothe*
Benjamin Tappan, *Steubenville*

REPRESENTATIVES

Alexander Duncan, *Cincinnati*
John B. Weller, *Hamilton*
Robert C. Schenck, *Dayton*
Joseph Vance, *Urbana*
Emery D. Potter, *Toledo*
Henry St. John, *Tiffin*
Joseph J. McDowell, *Hillsboro*
John I. Vanmeter, *Piketon*
Elias Florence, *Circleville*
Heman Allen Moore,[37] *Columbus*
Alfred P. Stone,[38] *Columbus*
Jacob Brinkerhoff, *Mansfield*
Samuel F. Vinton, *Gallipolis*
Perley B. Johnson, *McConnellsville*
Alexander Harper, *Zanesville*
Joseph Morris, *Woodsfield*
James Mathews, *Coshocton*
William C. McCauslen, *Steubenville*
Ezra Dean, *Wooster*
Daniel R. Tilden, *Ravenna*
Joshua R. Giddings, *Jefferson*
Henry R. Brinkerhoff,[39] *Plymouth*
Edward S. Hamlin,[40] *Elyria*

PENNSYLVANIA

SENATORS

James Buchanan, *Lancaster*
Daniel Sturgeon, *Uniontown*

REPRESENTATIVES

Edward Joy Morris, *Philadelphia*
Joseph R. Ingersoll, *Philadelphia*
John T. Smith, *Philadelphia*
Charles J. Ingersoll, *Philadelphia*
Jacob S. Yost, *Pottstown*
Michael H. Jenks, *Newtown*
Abraham R. McIlvaine, *Brandywine*
Jeremiah Brown, *Goshen*
John Ritter, *Reading*
Richard Brodhead, *Easton*
Benjamin A. Bidlack, *Wilkes-Barre*
Almon H. Read,[41] *Montrose*
George Fuller,[42] *Montrose*
Henry Frick,[43] *Milton*
James Pollock,[44] *Milton*
Alexander Ramsey, *Harrisburg*
Henry Nes, *York*
James Black, *Newport*

James Irvin, *Milesburg*
Andrew Stewart, *Uniontown*
Henry D. Foster, *Greensburg*
John Dickey, *Beaver*
William Wilkins,[45] *Pittsburgh*
Cornelius Darragh,[46] *Pittsburgh*
Samuel Hays, *Franklin*
Charles M. Reed, *Erie*
Joseph Buffington, *Kittanning*

RHODE ISLAND

SENATORS

James F. Simmons, *Providence*
William Sprague,[47] *Natick*
John B. Francis,[48] *Providence*

REPRESENTATIVES

Henry Y. Cranston, *Newport*
Elisha R. Potter, *Kingston*

SOUTH CAROLINA

SENATORS

George McDuffie, *Edgefield*
Daniel E. Huger,[49] *Charleston*

REPRESENTATIVES

James A. Black, *Cherokee Iron Works*
Richard F. Simpson, *Pendletonville*
Joseph A. Woodward, *Winnsboro*
John Campbell, *Parnassus*
Armistead Burt, *Abbeville*
Isaac E. Holmes, *Charleston*
R. Barnwell Rhett, *Blue House*

TENNESSEE

SENATORS

Ephraim H. Foster,[50] *Nashville*
Spencer Jarnagin,[51] *Athens*

REPRESENTATIVES

Andrew Johnson, *Greeneville*
William T. Senter, *Panther Springs*
Julius W. Blackwell, *Athens*
Alvan Cullom, *Livingston*
George W. Jones, *Fayetteville*
Aaron V. Brown, *Pulaski*
David W. Dickinson, *Murfreesboro*
Joseph H. Peyton, *Gallatin*
Cave Johnson, *Clarksville*
John B. Ashe, *Brownsville*
Milton Brown, *Jackson*

---

[33] Resigned June 17, 1844, having been appointed Governor of Wisconsin Territory.
[34] Appointed to fill vacancy caused by resignation of Nathaniel P. Tallmadge, and took his seat December 9, 1844; subsequently elected.
[35] Resigned March 6, 1844.
[36] Elected to fill vacancy caused by resignation of Samuel Beardsley, and took his seat December 2, 1844.
[37] Died April 3, 1844.
[38] Elected to fill vacancy caused by death of Heman Allen Moore, and took his seat December 2, 1844.
[39] Died April 30, 1844; never qualified owing to illness.
[40] Elected to fill vacancy caused by death of Henry

R. Brinkerhoff, and took his seat December 2, 1844.
[41] Died June 3, 1844.
[42] Elected to fill vacancy caused by death of Almon H. Read, and took his seat December 2, 1844.
[43] Died March 1, 1844.
[44] Elected to fill vacancy caused by death of Henry Frick, and took his seat April 23, 1844.
[45] Resigned February 14, 1884, having been appointed Secretary of War.
[46] Elected to fill vacancy caused by resignation of William Wilkins, and took his seat March 26, 1844.
[47] Resigned January 17, 1844.
[48] Elected to fill vacancy caused by resignation of

William Sprague, and took his seat February 7, 1844.
[49] Elected to fill vacancy caused by resignation of John C. Calhoun, in preceding Congress, and took his seat December 7, 1843; resigned March 3, 1845, in order that Mr. Calhoun might return to the Senate.
[50] Elected to fill vacancy caused by death of Felix Grundy in the Twenty-sixth Congress, and took his seat December 4, 1843; vacancy in this class from October 17, 1841, to October 16, 1843, because of failure of legislature to elect.
[51] Elected October 17, 1843, to fill vacancy in term beginning March 4, 1841, caused by failure of legislature to elect, and took his seat December 4, 1843.

VERMONT

SENATORS

Samuel S. Phelps, *Middlebury*
William Upham, *Montpelier*

REPRESENTATIVES

Solomon Foot, *Rutland*
Jacob Collamer, *Woodstock*
George P. Marsh, *Burlington*
Paul Dillingham, Jr., *Waterbury*

VIRGINIA

SENATORS

William C. Rives, *Lindseys Store*
William S. Archer, *Elk Hill*

REPRESENTATIVES

Archibald Atkinson, *Smithfield*
George C. Dromgoole, *Summit*
Walter Coles, *Robertsons Store*
Edmund W. Hubard, *Curdsville*
Thomas W. Gilmer,[52] *Charlottesville*
William L. Goggin,[53] *Otter Bridge*
John W. Jones,[54] *Petersburg*
Henry A. Wise,[55] *Accomac*
Thomas H. Bayly,[56] *Accomac*
Willoughby Newton, *Hague*
Samuel Chilton, *Warrenton*
William Lucas, *Charlestown*
William Taylor, *Lexington*
Augustus A. Chapman, *Union*
George W. Hopkins, *Abingdon*
George W. Summers, *Kanawha*
Lewis Steenrod, *Wheeling*

TERRITORY OF FLORIDA [57]

DELEGATE

David Levy (Yulee), *St. Augustine*

TERRITORY OF IOWA

DELEGATE

Augustus C. Dodge, *Burlington*

TERRITORY OF WISCONSIN

DELEGATE

Henry Dodge, *Dodgeville*

---

[52] Election unsuccessfully contested by William L. Goggin; resigned February 16, 1844.
[53] Elected to fill vacancy caused by resignation of Thomas W. Gilmer, and took his seat May 10, 1844.
[54] Election unsuccessfully contested by John M. Botts.
[55] Resigned February 12, 1844.
[56] Elected to fill vacancy caused by resignation of Henry A. Wise, and took his seat May 6, 1844.
[57] Granted statehood by act of March 3, 1845.

TWENTY-NINTH CONGRESS

MARCH 4, 1845, TO MARCH 3, 1847

FIRST SESSION—*December 1, 1845, to August 10, 1846*
SECOND SESSION—*December 7, 1846, to March 3, 1847*
SPECIAL SESSION OF THE SENATE—*March 4, 1845, to March 20, 1845*

———

VICE PRESIDENT OF THE UNITED STATES—George M. Dallas, of Pennsylvania
PRESIDENT PRO TEMPORE OF THE SENATE—Ambrose H. Sevier,[1] of Arkansas; David R. Atchison,[2] of Missouri
SECRETARY OF THE SENATE—Asbury Dickens,[3] of North Carolina
SERGEANT AT ARMS OF THE SENATE—Edward Dyer,[4] of Maryland; Robert Beale,[5] of Virginia

———

SPEAKER OF THE HOUSE OF REPRESENTATIVES—John W. Davis,[6] of Indiana
CLERK OF THE HOUSE—Benjamin B. French,[7] of New Hampshire
SERGEANT AT ARMS OF THE HOUSE—Newton Lane, of Kentucky
DOORKEEPER OF THE HOUSE—Cornelius S. Whitney, of District of Columbia

ALABAMA

SENATORS

Arthur P. Bagby, *Tuscaloosa*
Dixon H. Lewis, *Lowndesboro*

REPRESENTATIVES

Reuben Chapman, *Somerville*
Edmund S. Dargan, *Mobile*
Henry W. Hilliard, *Montgomery*
George S. Houston, *Athens*
Felix G. McConnell,[8] *Talladega*
Franklin W. Bowdon,[9] *Talladega*
William W. Payne, *Gainesville*
William L. Yancey,[10] *Wetumpka*
James L. F. Cottrell,[11] *Hayneville*

ARKANSAS

SENATORS

Ambrose H. Sevier, *Lake Port*
Chester Ashley, *Little Rock*

REPRESENTATIVES

Archibald Yell,[12] *Fayetteville*
Thomas W. Newton,[13] *Little Rock*

CONNECTICUT

SENATORS

Jabez W. Huntington, *Norwich*
John M. Niles, *Hartford*

REPRESENTATIVES

James Dixon, *Hartford*
Samuel D. Hubbard, *Middletown*
John A. Rockwell, *Norwich*
Truman Smith, *Litchfield*

DELAWARE

SENATORS

Thomas Clayton, *New Castle*
John M. Clayton, *New Castle*

REPRESENTATIVE

John W. Houston, *Georgetown*

FLORIDA[14]

SENATORS

David Levy Yulee,[15] *St. Augustine*
James D. Westcott, Jr.,[16] *Tallahassee*

REPRESENTATIVE

Edward C. Cabell,[17] *Tallahassee*
William H. Brockenbrough,[18] *Tallahassee*

GEORGIA

SENATORS

John Macpherson Berrien,[19] *Savannah*
Walter T. Colquitt, *Columbus*

REPRESENTATIVES

Howell Cobb, *Athens*
Hugh A. Haralson, *Lagrange*
Seaborn Jones, *Columbus*
Thomas Butler King, *Frederica*
John H. Lumpkin, *Rome*
George W. B. Towns,[20] *Talbotton*
Alexander H. Stephens, *Crawfordville*
Robert Toombs, *Washington*

ILLINOIS

SENATORS

Sidney Breese, *Carlyle*
James Semple, *Alton*

---

[1] Served as President pro tempore one day, December 27, 1845, under designation by the Vice President.
[2] Elected August 8, 1846; January 11, 1847; March 3, 1847.
[3] Reelected December 9, 1845.
[4] Died September 8, 1845.
[5] Elected December 9, 1845.
[6] Elected December 1, 1845.
[7] Reelected December 2, 1845.
[8] Died September 10, 1846.
[9] Elected to fill vacancy caused by death of Felix G. McConnell, and took his seat December 7, 1846.
[10] Resigned September 1, 1846.
[11] Elected to fill vacancy caused by resignation of

William L. Yancey, and took his seat December 7, 1846.
[12] Resigned July 1, 1846, having been appointed colonel in the Army in Mexico.
[13] Elected to fill vacancy caused by resignation of Archibald Yell, and took his seat February 6, 1847.
[14] Admitted as a State into the Union March 3, 1845, the last day of the preceding Congress.
[15] Took his seat December 1, 1845; term to expire, as determined by lot, March 3, 1851. Presented credentials as "David Levy," but on January 12, 1846, in conformity with an act of the Florida Legislature, the Senate ordered the surname "Yulee" added to his name on the official records.
[16] Took his seat December 1, 1845; term to expire, as

determined by lot, March 3, 1849.
[17] Served until January 24, 1846; succeeded by William H. Brockenbrough, who contested his election.
[18] Successfully contested the election of Edward C. Cabell, and took his seat January 24, 1846.
[19] Resigned in May, 1845, to accept a judicial appointment in Georgia; was reelected to fill vacancy caused by his own resignation, and took his seat December 8, 1845.
[20] Elected to fill vacancy caused by resignation of Representative-elect Washington Poe on March 4, 1845, before the beginning of the congressional term, and took his seat January 27, 1846.

[141]

ILLINOIS—Continued

REPRESENTATIVES

Edward D. Baker,[21] *Springfield*
John Henry,[22] *Springfield*
Stephen A. Douglas,[23] *Quincy*
Orlando B. Ficklin, *Charleston*
Joseph P. Hoge, *Galena*
John A. McClernand, *Shawneetown*
Robert Smith, *Alton*
John Wentworth, *Chicago*

INDIANA

SENATORS

Edward A. Hannegan, *Covington*
Jesse D. Bright, *Madison*

REPRESENTATIVES

Charles W. Cathcart, *Laporte*
John W. Davis, *Carlisle*
Thomas J. Henley, *New Washington*
Andrew Kennedy, *Muncietown*
Edward W. McGaughey, *Greencastle*
Robert D. Owen, *New Harmony*
John Pettit, *La Fayette*
Caleb B. Smith, *Connersville*
Thomas Smith, *Versailles*
William W. Wick, *Indianapolis*

IOWA [24]

SENATORS

Vacant [25]

REPRESENTATIVES

S. Clinton Hastings,[26] *Bloomington*
Shepherd Leffler,[26] *Burlington*

KENTUCKY

SENATORS

James T. Morehead, *Covington*
John J. Crittenden, *Frankfort*

REPRESENTATIVES

Joshua F. Bell, *Danville*
Linn Boyd, *Cadiz*
Garrett Davis, *Paris*
Henry Grider, *Bowling Green*
John P. Martin, *Prestonburg*
John H. McHenry, *Hartford*
William P. Thomasson, *Louisville*
John W. Tibbatts, *Newport*
Andrew Trumbo, *Owingsville*
Bryan R. Young, *Elizabethtown*

LOUISIANA

SENATORS

Alexander Barrow,[27] *Baton Rouge*
Pierre Soulé,[28] *New Orleans*
Henry Johnson, *New River*

REPRESENTATIVES

John H. Harmanson, *Simmsport*
Isaac E. Morse, *St. Martinville*
John Slidell,[29] *New Orleans*
Emile La Sére,[30] *New Orleans*
Bannon G. Thibodeaux, *Thibodaux*.

MAINE

SENATORS

George Evans, *Gardiner*
John Fairfield, *Saco*

REPRESENTATIVES

Robert P. Dunlap, *Brunswick*
Hannibal Hamlin, *Hampden*
John D. McCrate, *Wiscasset*
Cullen Sawtelle, *Norridgewock*
John F. Scammon, *Saco*
Luther Severance, *Augusta*
Hezekiah Williams, *Castine*

MARYLAND

SENATORS

James A. Pearce, *Chestertown*
Reverdy Johnson, *Baltimore*

REPRESENTATIVES

John G. Chapman, *Port Tobacco*
Albert Constable, *Perryville*
William F. Giles, *Baltimore*
Thomas W. Ligon, *Ellicotts Mills*
Edward H. C. Long, *Princess Anne*
Thomas J. Perry, *Cumberland*

MASSACHUSETTS

SENATORS

Isaac C. Bates,[31] *Northampton*
John Davis,[32] *Worcester*
Daniel Webster, *Boston*

REPRESENTATIVES

Amos Abbott, *Andover*
John Quincy Adams, *Quincy*
George Ashmun, *Springfield*
Joseph Grinnell, *New Bedford*
Artemas Hale, *Bridgewater*
Charles Hudson, *Westminster*

Daniel P. King, *South Danvers*
Julius Rockwell, *Pittsfield*
Benjamin Thompson, *Charlestown*
Robert C. Winthrop, *Boston*

MICHIGAN

SENATORS

William Woodbridge, *Detroit*
Lewis Cass, *Detroit*

REPRESENTATIVES

John S. Chipman, *Centerville*
James B. Hunt, *Pontiac*
Robert McClelland, *Monroe*

MISSISSIPPI

SENATORS

Robert J. Walker,[33] *Madisonville*
Joseph W. Chalmers,[34] *Holly Springs*
Jesse Speight, *Plymouth*

REPRESENTATIVES

Stephen Adams, *Aberdeen*
Jefferson Davis,[35] *Warrenton*
Henry T. Ellett,[36] *Port Gibson*
Robert W. Roberts, *Hillsboro*
Jacob Thompson, *Oxford*

MISSOURI

SENATORS

Thomas H. Benton, *St. Louis*
David R. Atchison, *Platte City*

REPRESENTATIVES

James B. Bowlin, *St. Louis*
Sterling Price,[37] *Keytesville*
William McDaniel,[38] *Palmyra*
James H. Relfe, *Caledonia*
John S. Phelps, *Springfield*
Leonard H. Sims, *Springfield*

NEW HAMPSHIRE

SENATORS

Levi Woodbury,[39] *Portsmouth*
Benning W. Jenness,[40] *Strafford*
Joseph Cilley,[41] *Nottingham*
Charles G. Atherton, *Nashua*

REPRESENTATIVES

James H. Johnson, *Bath*
Mace Moulton, *Manchester*
Moses Norris, Jr., *Pittsfield*

---

[21] Resigned December 24, 1846, "to take effect January 15, 1847, or sooner if successor is elected"; again resigned December 30, 1846.
[22] Elected to fill vacancy caused by resignation of Edward D. Baker, and took his seat February 5, 1847.
[23] Reelected to the Thirtieth Congress, but resigned, having been elected Senator.
[24] Admitted as a State into the Union December 28, 1846.
[25] Senators were not elected to this Congress.
[26] Took his seat December 29, 1846.
[27] Died December 29, 1846.
[28] Elected to fill vacancy caused by death of Alexander Barrow, and took his seat February 3, 1847.

[29] Resigned November 10, 1845, before Congress assembled.
[30] Elected to fill vacancy caused by resignation of John Slidell, and took his seat January 29, 1846.
[31] Died March 16, 1845.
[32] Elected to fill vacancy caused by death of Isaac C. Bates, and took his seat December 1, 1845.
[33] Resigned March 5, 1845, having been appointed Secretary of the Treasury.
[34] Appointed to fill vacancy caused by resignation of Robert J. Walker, and took his seat December 1, 1845; subsequently elected.
[35] Resigned in June, 1846, to participate in the war with Mexico.

[36] Elected to fill vacancy caused by resignation of Jefferson Davis, and took his seat January 26, 1847.
[37] Resigned August 12, 1846, to command a cavalry regiment in the war with Mexico.
[38] Elected to fill vacancy caused by resignation of Sterling Price, and took his seat December 7, 1846.
[39] Resigned November 20, 1845, having been appointed to the Supreme Court of the United States.
[40] Appointed to fill vacancy caused by resignation of Levi Woodbury, and took his seat December 1, 1845.
[41] Elected to fill vacancy caused by resignation of Levi Woodbury, and took his seat June 22, 1846.

NEW JERSEY

SENATORS

Jacob W. Miller, *Morristown*
William L. Dayton, *Trenton*

REPRESENTATIVES

Joseph E. Edsall, *Hamburg*
James G. Hampton, *Bridgeton*
John Runk,[42] *Kingwood*
Samuel G. Wright,[43] *Imlaystown*
George Sykes,[44] *Mount Holly*
William Wright, *Newark*

NEW YORK

SENATORS

Daniel S. Dickinson, *Binghamton*
John A. Dix, *Albany*

REPRESENTATIVES

Joseph H. Anderson, *White Plains*
Charles S. Benton, *Mohawk*
William W. Campbell, *New York City*
Charles H. Carroll, *Groveland Center*
John F. Collin, *Hillsdale*
Erastus D. Culver, *Greenwich*
John De Mott, *Lodi*
Samuel S. Ellsworth, *Penn Yan*
Charles Goodyear, *Schoharie*
Samuel Gordon, *Delhi*
Martin Grover, *Angelica*
Richard P. Herrick,[45] *Greenbush*
Thomas C. Ripley,[46] *Schaghticoke*
Elias B. Holmes, *Brockport*
William J. Hough, *Cazenovia*
Orville Hungerford, *Watertown*
Washington Hunt, *Lockport*
Timothy Jenkins, *Oneida Castle*
Preston King, *Ogdensburg*
John W. Lawrence, *Flushing*
Abner Lewis, *Panama*
William B. Maclay, *New York City*
William S. Miller, *New York City*
William A. Moseley, *Buffalo*
Archibald C. Niven, *Monticello*
George Rathbun, *Auburn*
Joseph Russell, *Warrensburg*
Henry I. Seaman, *Richmond*
Albert Smith, *Bativia*
Stephen Strong, *Owego*
Horace Wheaton, *Pompey*
Hugh White, *Cohoes*
Bradford R. Wood, *Albany*
Thomas M. Woodruff, *New York City*
William W. Woodworth, *Hyde Park*

NORTH CAROLINA

SENATORS

Willie P. Mangum, *Red Mountain*
William H. Haywood, Jr.,[47] *Raleigh*
George E. Badger,[48] *Raleigh*

REPRESENTATIVES

Daniel M. Barringer, *Concord*
Asa Biggs, *Williamston*
Henry S. Clark, *Washington*
John R. J. Daniel, *Halifax*
James C. Dobbin, *Fayetteville*
Alfred Dockery, *Dockerys Store*
James Graham, *Rutherfordton*
James I. McKay, *Elizabethtown*
David S. Reid, *Reidsville*

OHIO

SENATORS

William Allen, *Chillicothe*
Thomas Corwin, *Lebanon*

REPRESENTATIVES

Jacob Brinkerhoff, *Mansfield*
John D. Cummins, *New Philadelphia*
Francis A. Cunningham, *Eaton*
Columbus Delano, *Mount Vernon*
James J. Faran, *Cincinnati*
George Fries, *Hanoverton*
Joshua R. Giddings, *Jefferson*
Alexander Harper, *Zanesville*
Joseph J. McDowell, *Hillsboro*
Joseph Morris, *Woodsfield*
Isaac Parrish, *Parrishs Mills*
Augustus L. Perrill, *Lithopolis*
Joseph M. Root, *Norwalk*
William Sawyer, *St. Marys*
Robert C. Schenck, *Dayton*
Henry St. John, *McCutchenville*
David A. Starkweather, *Canton*
Allen G. Thurman, *Chillicothe*
Daniel R. Tilden, *Ravenna*
Joseph Vance, *Urbana*
Samuel F. Vinton, *Gallipolis*

PENNSYLVANIA

SENATORS

James Buchanan,[49] *Lancaster*
Simon Cameron,[50] *Middletown*
Daniel Sturgeon, *Uniontown*

REPRESENTATIVES

James Black, *Newport*
John Blanchard, *Bellefonte*
Richard Brodhead, *Easton*
Joseph Buffington, *Kittanning*

John H. Campbell, *Philadelphia*
Cornelius Darragh, *Pittsburgh*
Jacob Erdman, *Coopersburg*
John H. Ewing, *Washington*
Henry D. Foster, *Greensburg*
William S. Garvin, *Mercer*
Charles J. Ingersoll, *Philadelphia*
Joseph R. Ingersoll, *Philadelphia*
Owen D. Leib, *Catawissa*
Lewis C. Levin, *Philadelphia*
Moses McClean, *Gettysburg*
Abraham R. McIlvaine, *Brandywine*
James Pollock, *Milton*
Alexander Ramsey, *Harrisburg*
John Ritter, *Reading*
Andrew Stewart, *Uniontown*
John Strohm, *New Providence*
James Thompson, *Erie*
David Wilmot, *Towanda*
Jacob S. Yost, *Pottstown*

RHODE ISLAND

SENATORS

James F. Simmons, *Providence*
Albert C. Greene, *Providence*

REPRESENTATIVES

Lemuel H. Arnold, *Wakefield*
Henry Y. Cranston, *Newport*

SOUTH CAROLINA

SENATORS

George McDuffie,[51] *Cherry Hill*
Andrew P. Butler,[52] *Edgefield*
John C. Calhoun,[53] *Pendleton*

REPRESENTATIVES

James A. Black, *Cherokee Iron Works*
Armistead Burt, *Willington*
Isaac E. Holmes, *Charleston*
R. Barnwell Rhett, *Ashepoo*
Richard F. Simpson, *Pendleton*
Alexander D. Sims, *Darlington*
Joseph A. Woodward, *Winnsboro*

TENNESSEE

SENATORS

Spencer Jarnagin, *Athens*
Hopkins L. Turney, *Winchester*

REPRESENTATIVES

Lucien B. Chase, *Clarksville*
William M. Cocke, *Rutledge*
John H. Crozier, *Knoxville*
Alvan Cullom, *Livingston*

---

[42] Election unsuccessfully contested by Isaac G. Farlee.
[43] Died July 30, 1845, before Congress assembled.
[44] Elected to fill vacancy caused by death of Samuel G. Wright, and took his seat December 1, 1845.
[45] Died June 20, 1846.
[46] Elected to fill vacancy caused by death of Richard P. Herrick, and took his seat December 7, 1846.

[47] Resigned July 25, 1846.
[48] Elected to fill vacancy caused by resignation of William H. Haywood, Jr., and took his seat December 14, 1846.
[49] Resigned March 5, 1845.
[50] Elected to fill vacancy caused by resignation of James Buchanan, and took his seat March 17, 1845.
[51] Resigned August 17, 1846.

[52] Elected to fill vacancy caused by resignation of George McDuffie, and took his seat December 21, 1846; vacancy in this class from January 17, 1846, to December 3, 1846.
[53] Elected to fill vacancy caused by resignation of Daniel E. Huger, in preceding Congress, and took his seat December 22, 1845; vacancy in this class from March 4, 1845, to November 25, 1845.

TENNESSEE—Continued

REPRESENTATIVES—continued

Joseph H. Peyton,[54] *Gallatin*
Edwin H. Ewing,[55] *Nashville*
Milton Brown, *Jackson*
Meredith P. Gentry, *Franklin*
Andrew Johnson, *Greeneville*
George W. Jones, *Fayetteville*
Barclay Martin, *Columbia*
Frederick P. Stanton, *Memphis*

TEXAS [56]

SENATORS

Sam Houston,[57] *Raven Hill*
Thomas J. Rusk,[58] *Nacogdoches*

REPRESENTATIVES

David S. Kaufman,[59] *Lowes Ferry*
Timothy Pilsbury,[60] *Brazoria*

VERMONT

SENATORS

Samuel S. Phelps, *Middlebury*
William Upham, *Montpelier*

REPRESENTATIVES

Jacob Collamer, *Woodstock*
Paul Dillingham, Jr., *Waterbury*
Solomon Foot, *Rutland*
George P. Marsh, *Burlington*

VIRGINIA

SENATORS

William S. Archer, *Elk Hill*
Isaac S. Pennybacker,[61] *New Market*
James M. Mason,[62] *Winchester*

REPRESENTATIVES

Archibald Atkinson, *Smithfield*
Thomas H. Bayly, *Accomac*
Henry Bedinger, *Charlestown*

William G. Brown, *Kingwood*
Augustus A. Chapman, *Union*
George C. Dromgoole, *Summit*
George W. Hopkins, *Abingdon*
Edmund W. Hubard, *Curdsville*
Robert M. T. Hunter, *Lloyds*
Joseph Johnson, *Bridgeport*
Shelton F. Leake, *Charlottesville*
John S. Pendleton, *Culpeper*
James A. Seddon, *Richmond*
William Taylor,[63] *Lexington*
James McDowell,[64] *Lexington*
William M. Tredway, *Danville*

TERRITORY OF IOWA

DELEGATE

Augustus C. Dodge,[65] *Burlington*

TERRITORY OF WISCONSIN

DELEGATE

Morgan L. Martin, *Green Bay*

---

[54] Died November 12, 1845, before Congress assembled.
[55] Elected to fill vacancy caused by death of Joseph H. Peyton, and took his seat January 2, 1846.
[56] Admitted as a State into the Union December 29, 1845, after compliance with certain conditions stipulated in the joint resolution approved March 1, 1845, providing for the annexation of the Republic of Texas.

[57] Took his seat March 30, 1846; term to expire, as determined by lot, March 3, 1847.
[58] Took his seat March 26, 1846; term to expire, as determined by lot, March 3, 1851.
[59] Took his seat June 1, 1846.
[60] Took his seat June 10, 1846.
[61] Died January 12, 1847.

[62] Elected to fill vacancy caused by death of Isaac S. Pennybacker, and took his seat January 25, 1847.
[63] Died January 17, 1846.
[64] Elected to fill vacancy caused by death of William Taylor, and took his seat March 6, 1846.
[65] Served until December 28, 1846, when the Territory of Iowa was granted statehood.

THIRTIETH CONGRESS

MARCH 4, 1847, TO MARCH 3, 1849

FIRST SESSION—*December 6, 1847, to August 14, 1848*

SECOND SESSION—*December 4, 1848, to March 3, 1849*

VICE PRESIDENT OF THE UNITED STATES—GEORGE M. DALLAS, of Pennsylvania

PRESIDENT PRO TEMPORE OF THE SENATE—DAVID R. ATCHISON,[1] of Missouri

SECRETARY OF THE SENATE—ASBURY DICKENS,[2] of North Carolina

SERGEANT AT ARMS OF THE SENATE—ROBERT BEALE, of Virginia

SPEAKER OF THE HOUSE OF REPRESENTATIVES—ROBERT C. WINTHROP,[3] of Massachusetts

CLERK OF THE HOUSE—BENJAMIN B. FRENCH, of New Hampshire; THOMAS J. CAMPBELL,[4] of Tennessee

SERGEANT AT ARMS OF THE HOUSE—NEWTON LANE, of Kentucky; NATHAN SARGENT,[5] of Vermont

DOORKEEPER OF THE HOUSE—ROBERT E. HORNER, of New Jersey

ALABAMA

SENATORS

Arthur P. Bagby,[6] *Tuscaloosa*
William R. King,[7] *Selma*
Dixon H. Lewis,[8] *Lowndesboro*
Benjamin Fitzpatrick,[9] *Wetumpka*

REPRESENTATIVES

John Gayle, *Mobile*
Henry W. Hilliard, *Montgomery*
Sampson W, Harris, *Wetumpka*
Samuel W. Inge, *Livingston*
George S. Houston, *Athens*
Williamson R. W. Cobb, *Bellefonte*
Franklin W. Bowdon, *Talladega*

ARKANSAS

SENATORS

Ambrose H. Sevier,[10] *Pine Bluff*
Solon Borland,[11] *Hot Springs*
Chester Ashley,[12] *Little Rock*
William K. Sebastian,[13] *Helena*

REPRESENTATIVE

Robert W. Johnson, *Little Rock*

CONNECTICUT

SENATORS

Jabez W. Huntington,[14] *Norwich*
Roger S. Baldwin,[15] *New Haven*
John M. Niles, *Hartford*

REPRESENTATIVES

James Dixon, *Hartford*
Samuel D. Hubbard, *Middletown*
John A. Rockwell, *Norwich*
Truman Smith, *Litchfield*

DELAWARE

SENATORS

John M. Clayton,[16] *New Castle*
John Wales,[17] *Wilmington*
Presley Spruance, *Smyrna*

REPRESENTATIVE

John W. Houston, *Georgetown*

FLORIDA

SENATORS

David Levy Yulee, *St. Augustine*
James D. Westcott, Jr., *Tallahassee*

REPRESENTATIVE

Edward C. Cabell, *Tallahassee*

GEORGIA

SENATORS

Walter T. Colquitt,[18] *Columbus*
Herschel V. Johnson,[19] *Milledgeville*
John Macpherson Berrien,[20] *Savannah*

REPRESENTATIVES

Thomas Butler King, *Frederica*
Alfred Iverson, *Columbus*
John W. Jones, *Griffin*
Hugh A. Haralson, *Lagrange*
John H. Lumpkin, *Rome*
Howell Cobb, *Athens*
Alexander H. Stephens, *Crawfordville*
Robert Toombs, *Washington*

---

[1] Elected February 2, 1848; June 1, 1848; June 26, 1848; July 29, 1848; December 26, 1848; and March 2, 1849.

[2] Reelected December 13, 1847.

[3] Elected December 6, 1847; Armistead Burt, of South Carolina, was elected Speaker pro tempore, and served from June 19 to 22, 1848.

[4] Elected December 7, 1847.

[5] Elected December 8, 1847.

[6] Resigned June 16, 1848.

[7] Appointed to fill vacancy caused by resignation of Arthur P. Bagby, and took his seat July 13, 1848.

[8] Died October 25, 1848.

[9] Appointed to fill vacancy caused by death of Dixon H. Lewis, and took his seat December 11, 1848.

[10] Resigned March 15, 1848.

[11] Appointed to fill vacancy caused by resignation of Ambrose H. Sevier, and took his seat April 24, 1848; subsequently elected.

[12] Died April 29, 1848.

[13] Appointed to fill vacancy caused by death of Chester Ashley, and took his seat May 31, 1848; subsequently elected.

[14] Died November 1, 1847.

[15] Appointed to fill vacancy caused by death of Jabez W. Huntington, and took his seat December 7, 1847; subsequently elected.

[16] Resigned February 23, 1849, having been appointed Secretary of State.

[17] Elected to fill vacancy caused by resignation of John M. Clayton, and took his seat February 26, 1849.

[18] Resigned in February, 1848.

[19] Appointed to fill vacancy caused by resignation of Walter T. Colquitt, and took his seat February 14, 1848.

[20] Reelected for the term beginning March 4, 1847, and took his seat December 16, 1847; vacancy in this class from March 4, 1847, to November 12, 1847.

ILLINOIS

SENATORS

Sidney Breese, *Carlyle*
Stephen A. Douglas, *Quincy*

REPRESENTATIVES

Robert Smith, *Alton*
John A. McClernand, *Shawneetown*
Orlando B. Ficklin, *Charleston*
John Wentworth, *Chicago*
William A. Richardson,[21] *Rushville*
Thomas J. Turner, *Freeport*
Abraham Lincoln, *Springfield*

INDIANA

SENATORS

Edward A. Hannegan, *Covington*
Jesse D. Bright, *Madison*

REPRESENTATIVES

Elisha Embree, *Princeton*
Thomas J. Henley, *New Washington*
John L. Robinson, *Rushville*
Caleb B. Smith, *Connersville*
William W. Wick, *Indianapolis*
George G. Dunn, *Bedford*
Richard W. Thompson, *Terre Haute*
John Pettit, *La Fayette*
Charles W. Cathcart, *Laporte*
William Rockhill, *Fort Wayne*

IOWA

SENATORS

Augustus C. Dodge,[22] *Burlington*
George W. Jones,[23] *Dubuque*

REPRESENTATIVES

William Thompson, *Mount Pleasant*
Shepherd Leffler, *Burlington*

KENTUCKY

SENATORS

John J. Crittenden,[24] *Frankfort*
Thomas Metcalfe,[25] *Forest Retreat*
Joseph R. Underwood, *Bowling Green*

REPRESENTATIVES

Linn Boyd, *Cadiz*
Beverly L. Clarke, *Franklin*
Samuel O. Peyton, *Hartford*
Aylett Buckner, *Greensburg*
John B. Thompson, *Harrodsburg*
Green Adams, *Barbourville*
W. Garnett Duncan, *Louisville*

Charles S. Morehead, *Frankfort*
Richard French, *Mount Sterling*
John P. Gaines, *Walton*

LOUISIANA

SENATORS

Henry Johnson, *New River*
Solomon W. Downs, *Monroe*

REPRESENTATIVES

Emile La Sére, *New Orleans*
Bannon G. Thibodeaux, *Thibodaux*
John H. Harmanson, *Simmsport*
Isaac E. Morse, *St. Martinville*

MAINE

SENATORS

John Fairfield,[26] *Saco*
Wyman B. S. Moor,[27] *Bangor*
Hannibal Hamlin,[28] *Hampden*
James W. Bradbury, *Augusta*

REPRESENTATIVES

David Hammons, *Lovell*
Asa W. H. Clapp, *Portland*
Hiram Belcher, *Farmington*
Franklin Clark, *Wiscasset*
Ephraim K. Smart, *Camden*
James S. Wiley, *Dover*
Hezekiah Williams, *Castine*

MARYLAND

SENATORS

James A. Pearce, *Chestertown*
Reverdy Johnson, *Baltimore*

REPRESENTATIVES

John G. Chapman, *Port Tobacco*
J. Dixon Roman, *Hagerstown*
Thomas W. Ligon, *Ellicotts Mills*
Robert M. McLane, *Baltimore*
Alexander Evans, *Elkton*
John W. Crisfield, *Princess Anne*

MASSACHUSETTS

SENATORS

Daniel Webster, *Boston*
John Davis, *Worcester*

REPRESENTATIVES

Robert C. Winthrop, *Boston*
Daniel P. King, *South Danvers*
Amos Abbott, *Andover*
John G. Palfrey, *Cambridge*

Charles Hudson, *Westminster*
George Ashmun, *Springfield*
Julius Rockwell, *Pittsfield*
John Quincy Adams,[29] *Quincy*
Horace Mann,[30] *West Newton*
Artemas Hale, *Bridgewater*
Joseph Grinnell, *New Bedford*

MICHIGAN

SENATORS

Lewis Cass,[31] *Detroit*
Thomas Fitzgerald,[32] *St. Joseph*
Alpheus Felch, *Ann Arbor*

REPRESENTATIVES

Robert McClelland, *Monroe*
Edward Bradley,[33] *Marshall*
Charles E. Stuart,[34] *Kalamazoo*
Kinsley S. Bingham, *Kensington*

MISSISSIPPI

SENATORS

Jesse Speight,[35] *Plymouth*
Jefferson Davis,[36] *Warrenton*
Henry S. Foote, *Jackson*

REPRESENTATIVES

Jacob Thompson, *Oxford*
Winfield S. Featherston, *Houston*
Patrick W. Tompkins, *Vicksburg*
Albert G. Brown, *Gallatin*

MISSOURI

SENATORS

Thomas H. Benton, *St. Louis*
David R. Atchison, *Platte City*

REPRESENTATIVES

James B. Bowlin, *St. Louis*
John Jameson, *Fulton*
James S. Green, *Canton*
Willard P. Hall, *St. Joseph*
John S. Phelps, *Springfield*

NEW HAMPSHIRE

SENATORS

Charles G. Atherton, *Nashua*
John P. Hale, *Dover*

REPRESENTATIVES

Amos Tuck, *Exeter*
Charles H. Peaslee, *Concord*
James Wilson, *Keene*
James H. Johnson, *Bath*

---

[21] Elected to fill vacancy caused by resignation of Representative-elect Stephen A. Douglas, in preceding Congress, and took his seat December 6, 1847.
[22] Took his seat December 26, 1848; term to expire, as determined by lot, March 3, 1849.
[23] Took his seat December 26, 1848; term to expire, as determined by lot, March 3, 1853.
[24] Resigned June 12, 1848.
[25] Appointed to fill vacancy caused by resignation of John J. Crittenden, and took his seat July 3, 1848; subsequently elected.

[26] Died December 24, 1847.
[27] Appointed to fill vacancy caused by death of John Fairfield, and took his seat January 17, 1848.
[28] Elected to fill vacancy caused by death of John Fairfield, and took his seat June 12, 1848.
[29] Died in the Speaker's room at the Capitol, February 23, 1848.
[30] Elected to fill vacancy caused by death of John Quincy Adams, and took his seat April 13, 1848.
[31] Resigned May 29, 1848; subsequently elected to fill vacancy caused by his own resignation, and took

his seat March 4, 1849.
[32] Appointed to fill vacancy caused by resignation of Lewis Cass, and took his seat June 20, 1848.
[33] Died August 5, 1847, before Congress assembled.
[34] Elected to fill vacancy caused by death of Edward Bradley, and took his seat December 6, 1847.
[35] Died May 1, 1847.
[36] Appointed to fill vacancy caused by death of Jesse Speight, and took his seat December 6, 1847; subsequently elected.

NEW JERSEY

SENATORS

Jacob W. Miller, *Morristown*
William L. Dayton, *Trenton*

REPRESENTATIVES

James G. Hampton, *Bridgeton*
William A. Newell, *Allentown*
Joseph E. Edsall, *Hamburg*
John Van Dyke, *New Brunswick*
Dudley S. Gregory, *Jersey City*

NEW YORK

SENATORS

Daniel S. Dickinson, *Binghamton*
John A. Dix, *Albany*

REPRESENTATIVES

Frederick W. Lord, *Greenport*
Henry C. Murphy, *Brooklyn*
Henry Nicoll, *New York City*
William B. Maclay, *New York City*
Frederick A. Tallmadge, *New York City*
David S. Jackson,[37] *New York City*
Horace Greeley,[38] *New York City*
William Nelson, *Peekskill*
Cornelius Warren, *Cold Spring*
Daniel B. St. John, *Monticello*
Eliakim Sherrill, *Shandaken*
Peter H. Silvester, *Coxsackie*
Gideon Reynolds, *Hoosick*
John I. Slingerland, *Bethlehem*
Orlando Kellogg, *Elizabethtown*
Sidney Lawrence, *Moira*
Hugh White, *Cohoes*
George Petrie, *Little Falls*
William Collins, *Lowville*
Joseph Mullin, *Watertown*
Timothy Jenkins, *Oneida Castle*
George A. Starkweather, *Cooperstown*
Ausburn Birdsall, *Binghamton*
William Duer, *Oswego*
Daniel Gott, *Pompey*
Harmon S. Conger, *Cortland*
William T. Lawrence, *Cayutaville*
John M. Holley,[39] *Lyons*
Esbon Blackmar,[40] *Newark*
Elias B. Holmes, *Brockport*
Robert L. Rose, *Allens Hill*
David Rumsey, Jr., *Bath*
Dudley Marvin, *Ripley*
Nathan K. Hall, *Buffalo*
Harvey Putnam, *Attica*
Washington Hunt, *Lockport*

NORTH CAROLINA

SENATORS

Willie P. Mangum, *Red Mountain*
George E. Badger, *Raleigh*

REPRESENTATIVES

Thomas L. Clingman, *Asheville*
Nathaniel Boyden, *Salisbury*
Daniel M. Barringer, *Concord*
Augustine H. Shepperd, *Salem*
Abraham W. Venable, *Brownsville*
John R. J. Daniel, *Halifax*
James I. McKay, *Elizabethtown*
Richard S. Donnell, *New Bern*
David Outlaw, *Windsor*

OHIO

SENATORS

William Allen, *Chillicothe*
Thomas Corwin, *Lebanon*

REPRESENTATIVES

James J. Faran, *Cincinnati*
David Fisher, *Wilmington*
Robert C. Schenck, *Dayton*
Richard S. Canby, *Bellefontaine*
William Sawyer, *St. Marys*
Rodolphus Dickinson, *Lower Sandusky*
Jonathan D. Morris,[41] *Batavia*
John L. Taylor, *Chillicothe*
Thomas O. Edwards, *Lancaster*
Daniel Duncan, *Newark*
John K. Miller, *Mount Vernon*
Samuel F. Vinton, *Gallipolis*
Thomas Ritchey, *Somerset*
Nathan Evans, *Cambridge*
William Kennon, Jr., *St. Clairsville*
John D. Cummins, *New Philadelphia*
George Fries, *Hanoverton*
Samuel Lahm, *Canton*
John Crowell, *Warren*
Joshua R. Giddings, *Jefferson*
Joseph M. Root, *Norwalk*

PENNSYLVANIA

SENATORS

Daniel Sturgeon, *Uniontown*
Simon Cameron, *Middletown*

REPRESENTATIVES

Lewis C. Levin, *Philadelphia*
Joseph R. Ingersoll, *Philadelphia*
Charles Brown, *Philadelphia*
Charles J. Ingersoll, *Philadelphia*
John Freedley, *Norristown*
John W. Hornbeck,[42] *Allentown*

Samuel A. Bridges,[43] *Allentown*
Abraham R. McIlvaine, *Brandywine*
John Strohm, *New Providence*
William Strong, *Reading*
Richard Brodhead, *Easton*
Chester P. Butler, *Wilkes-Barre*
David Wilmot, *Towanda*
James Pollock, *Milton*
George N. Eckert, *Pottsville*
Henry Nes, *York*
Jasper E. Brady, *Chambersburg*
John Blanchard, *Bellefonte*
Andrew Stewart, *Uniontown*
Job Mann, *Bedford*
John Dickey, *Beaver*
Moses Hampton, *Pittsburgh*
John W. Farrelly, *Meadville*
James Thompson, *Erie*
Alexander Irvin, *Clearfield*

RHODE ISLAND

SENATORS

Albert C. Greene, *Providence*
John H. Clarke, *Providence*

REPRESENTATIVES

Robert B. Cranston, *Newport*
Benjamin B. Thurston, *Hopkinton*

SOUTH CAROLINA

SENATORS

John C. Calhoun, *Pendleton*
Andrew P. Butler, *Edgefield*

REPRESENTATIVES

James A. Black,[44] *Cherokee Iron Works*
Daniel Wallace,[45] *Union*
Richard F. Simpson, *Pendleton*
Joseph A. Woodward, *Winnsboro*
Alexander D. Sims,[46] *Darlington*
John McQueen,[47] *Bennettsville*
Armistead Burt, *Willington*
Isaac E. Holmes, *Charleston*
R. Barnwell Rhett, *Ashepoo*

TENNESSEE

SENATORS

Hopkins L. Turney, *Winchester*
John Bell, *Nashville*

REPRESENTATIVES

Andrew Johnson, *Greeneville*
William M. Cocke, *Rutledge*
John H. Crozier, *Knoxville*
Hugh L. W. Hill, *Irving College*
George W. Jones, *Fayetteville*
James H. Thomas, *Columbia*

---

[37] Election contested by James Monroe, but the House declared, on April 19, 1848, that neither was entitled to the seat.
[38] Elected to fill vacancy declared to exist by resolutions of April 19, 1848, and took his seat December 4, 1848.
[39] Died March 8, 1848.
[40] Elected to fill vacancy caused by death of John M. Holley, and took his seat December 4, 1848.

[41] Elected to fill vacancy caused by death of Representative-elect Thomas L. Harrer (December 2, 1846, before the beginning of the congressional term, while serving in the war with Mexico), and took his seat December 6, 1847.
[42] Died January 16, 1848.
[43] Elected to fill vacancy caused by death of John W. Hornbeck, and took his seat March 6, 1848.

[44] Died April 3, 1848.
[45] Elected to fill vacancy caused by death of James A. Black, and took his seat June 12, 1848.
[46] Died November 16, 1848, before the commencement of the Thirty-first Congress, to which he had been reelected.
[47] Elected to fill vacancy caused by death of Alexander D. Sims, and took his seat February 12, 1849.

TENNESSEE—Continued

REPRESENTATIVES—continued

Meredith P. Gentry, *Franklin*
Washington Barrow, *Nashville*
Lucien B. Chase, *Clarksville*
Frederick P. Stanton, *Memphis*
William T. Haskell, *Jackson*

TEXAS

SENATORS

Sam Houston, *Raven Hill*
Thomas J. Rusk, *Nacogdoches*

REPRESENTATIVES

David S. Kaufman, *Sabine*
Timothy Pilsbury, *Brazoria*

VERMONT

SENATORS

Samuel S. Phelps, *Middlebury*
William Upham, *Montpelier*

REPRESENTATIVES

William Henry, *Bellows Falls*
Jacob Collamer, *Woodstock*
George P. Marsh, *Burlington*
Lucius B. Peck, *Montpelier*

VIRGINIA

SENATORS

James M. Mason, *Winchester*
Robert M. T. Hunter, *Lloyds*

REPRESENTATIVES

Archibald Atkinson, *Smithfield*
George C. Dromgoole,[48] *Summit*
Richard K. Meade,[49] *Petersburg*
Thomas S. Flournoy, *Halifax*
Thomas S. Bocock, *Appomattox*
William L. Goggin, *Otter Bridge*
John M. Botts, *Richmond*
Thomas H. Bayly, *Accomac*
Richard L. T. Beale, *Hague*
John S. Pendleton, *Culpeper*

Henry Bedinger, *Charlestown*
James McDowell, *Lexington*
William B. Preston, *Blacksburg*
Andrew S. Fulton, *Wytheville*
Robert A. Thompson, *Kanawha*
William G. Brown, *Kingwood*

WISCONSIN [50]

SENATORS

Henry Dodge,[51] *Dodgeville*
Isaac P. Walker,[52] *Milwaukee*

REPRESENTATIVES

Mason C. Darling,[53] *Fond du Lac*
William P. Lynde,[54] *Milwaukee*

TERRITORY OF WISCONSIN [55]

DELEGATE

John H. Tweedy,[56] *Milwaukee*
Henry H. Sibley,[57] *Mendota*

---

[48] Died April 27, 1847, before Congress assembled.
[49] Elected to fill vacancy caused by death of George C. Dromgoole, and took his seat December 6, 1847.
[50] Formed from the eastern portion of the Territory of Wisconsin by authority of act approved August 6, 1846, and admitted as a State into the Union May 29, 1848.
[51] Took his seat June 23, 1848; term to expire, as determined by lot, March 3, 1851.

[52] Took his seat June 26, 1848; term to expire, as determined by lot, March 3, 1849.
[53] Took his seat June 9, 1848.
[54] Took his seat June 5, 1848.
[55] The western portion of the Territory of Wisconsin retained its territorial organization under the same name until reorganized into the Territory of Minne-

sota by act of March 3, 1849, the eastern portion having been granted statehood as the State of Wisconsin.
[56] Served until May 29, 1848, when that portion of the Territory of Wisconsin in which he resided was admitted to statehood.
[57] Elected to fill vacancy caused by disqualification of John H. Tweedy, and took his seat January 15, 1849

THIRTY-FIRST CONGRESS

MARCH 4, 1849, TO MARCH 3, 1851

FIRST SESSION—*December 3, 1849, to September 30, 1850*

SECOND SESSION—*December 2, 1850, to March 3, 1851*

SPECIAL SESSION OF THE SENATE—*March 5, 1849, to March 23, 1849*

———

VICE PRESIDENT OF THE UNITED STATES—MILLARD FILLMORE,[1] of New York

PRESIDENT PRO TEMPORE OF THE SENATE—DAVID R. ATCHISON,[2] of Missouri; WILLIAM R. KING,[3] of Alabama

SECRETARY OF THE SENATE—ASBURY DICKINS, of North Carolina

SERGEANT AT ARMS OF THE SENATE—ROBERT BEALE, of Virginia

———

SPEAKER OF THE HOUSE OF REPRESENTATIVES—HOWELL COBB,[4] of Georgia

CLERK OF THE HOUSE—THOMAS J. CAMPBELL,[5] of Tennessee; RICHARD M. YOUNG,[6] of Illinois

SERGEANT AT ARMS OF THE HOUSE—NATHAN SARGENT, of Vermont; ADAM J. GLOSSBRENNER,[7] of Pennsylvania

DOORKEEPER OF THE HOUSE—ROBERT E. HORNER, of New Jersey

ALABAMA

SENATORS

William R. King, *Selma*
Benjamin Fitzpatrick, *Wetumpka*
Jeremiah Clemens,[8] *Huntsville*

REPRESENTATIVES

William J. Alston, *Linden*
Henry W. Hilliard, *Montgomery*
Sampson W. Harris, *Wetumpka*
Samuel W. Inge, *Livingston*
David Hubbard, *Kinlock*
Williamson R. W. Cobb, *Bellefonte*
Franklin W. Bowdon, *Talladega*

ARKANSAS

SENATORS

Solon Borland, *Hot Springs*
William K. Sebastian, *Helena*

REPRESENTATIVE

Robert W. Johnson, *Little Rock*

CALIFORNIA[9]

SENATORS

William M. Gwin,[10] *San Francisco*
John C. Fremont,[11] *San Francisco*

REPRESENTATIVES

Edward Gilbert,[12] *San Francisco*
George W. Wright,[13] *San Francisco*

CONNECTICUT

SENATORS

Roger S. Baldwin, *New Haven*
Truman Smith, *Litchfield*

REPRESENTATIVES

Loren P. Waldo, *Tolland*
Walter Booth, *Meriden*
Chauncey F. Cleveland, *Hampton*
Thomas B. Butler, *Norwalk*

DELAWARE

SENATORS

Presley Spruance, *Smyrna*
John Wales, *Wilmington*

REPRESENTATIVE

John W. Houston, *Georgetown*

FLORIDA

SENATORS

David Levy Yulee, *St. Augustine*
Jackson Morton, *Pensacola*

REPRESENTATIVE

Edward C. Cabell, *Tallahassee*

GEORGIA

SENATORS

J. Macpherson Berrien, *Savannah*
William C. Dawson, *Greensboro*

---

[1] Became President upon the death of Zachary Taylor, July 9, 1850.
[2] Elected March 5, 1849, and again March 16, 1849 (special session of the Senate). President-elect Zachary Taylor having declined to take the oath of office on March 4, 1849, because it was Sunday, the Senate was not in session on that date.
[3] Elected May 6, 1850; July 11, 1850.
[4] Elected December 22, 1849, upon the sixty-third viva voce vote and the first vote under a plurality resolution adopted that day; Robert C. Winthrop, of Massachusetts, served as Speaker pro tempore on April 19, 1850.
[5] Reelected January 11, 1850; died April 13, 1850.
[6] Elected April 17, 1850.
[7] Elected January 15, 1850.
[8] Elected to fill vacancy caused by death of Dixon H. Lewis, in preceding Congress, and took his seat December 6, 1849.
[9] Formed from a portion of the territory ceded to the United States by Mexico by the treaty of Guadalupe Hidalgo of February 2, 1848, and admitted as a State into the Union September 9, 1850.
[10] Took his seat September 10, 1850; term to expire, as determined by lot, March 3, 1855.
[11] Took his seat September 10, 1850; term to expire, as determined by lot, March 3, 1851.
[12] Took his seat September 11, 1850.
[13] Took his seat September 11, 1850.

GEORGIA—Continued

REPRESENTATIVES

Thomas Butler King,[14] *Waynesville*
Joseph W. Jackson,[15] *Savannah*
Marshall J. Wellborn, *Columbus*
Allen F. Owen, *Talbotton*
Hugh A. Haralson, *Lagrange*
Thomas C. Hackett, *Rome*
Howell Cobb, *Athens*
Alexander H. Stephens, *Crawfordville*
Robert Toombs, *Washington*

ILLINOIS

SENATORS

Stephen A. Douglas, *Chicago*
James Shields,[16] *Belleville*

REPRESENTATIVES

William H. Bissell, *Belleville*
John A. McClernand, *Shawneetown*
Timothy R. Young, *Marshall*
John Wentworth, *Chicago*
William A. Richardson, *Quincy*
Edward D. Baker, *Galena*
Thomas L. Harris, *Petersburg*

INDIANA

SENATORS

Jesse D. Bright, *Madison*
James Whitcomb, *Indianapolis*

REPRESENTATIVES

Nathaniel Albertson, *Greenville*
Cyrus L. Dunham, *Salem*
John L. Robinson, *Rushville*
George W. Julian, *Centerville*
William J. Brown, *Indianapolis*
Willis A. Gorman, *Bloomington*
Edward W. McGaughey, *Rockville*
Joseph E. McDonald, *Crawfordsville*
Graham N. Fitch, *Logansport*
Andrew J. Harlan, *Marion*

IOWA

SENATORS

Augustus C. Dodge, *Burlington*
George W. Jones, *Dubuque*

REPRESENTATIVES

William Thompson,[17] *Mount Pleasant*
Daniel F. Miller,[18] *Fort Madison*
Shepherd Leffler, *Burlington*

KENTUCKY

SENATORS

Joseph R. Underwood, *Bowling Green*
Henry Clay, *Lexington*

REPRESENTATIVES

Linn Boyd, *Cadiz*
James L. Johnson, *Owensboro*
Finis E. McLean, *Elkton*
George A. Caldwell, *Columbia*
John B. Thompson, *Harrodsburg*
Daniel Breck, *Richmond*
Humphrey Marshall, *Drennons Lick*
Charles S. Morehead, *Frankfort*
John C. Mason, *Owingsville*
Richard H. Stanton, *Maysville*

LOUISIANA

SENATORS

Solomon W. Downs, *Monroe*
Pierre Soulé, *New Orleans*

REPRESENTATIVES

Emile La Sére, *New Orleans*
Charles M. Conrad,[19] *New Orleans*
Henry A. Bullard,[20] *New Orleans*
John H. Harmanson,[21] *Simmsport*
Alexander G. Penn,[22] *Covington*
Isaac E. Morse, *St. Martinville*

MAINE

SENATORS

James W. Bradbury, *Augusta*
Hannibal Hamlin, *Hampden*

REPRESENTATIVES

Elbridge Gerry, *Waterford*
Nathaniel S. Littlefield, *Bridgeton*
John Otis, *Hallowell*
Rufus K. Goodenow, *Paris*
Cullen Sawtelle, *Norridgewock*
Charles Stetson, *Bangor*
Thomas J. D. Fuller, *Calais*

MARYLAND

SENATORS

James A. Pearce, *Chestertown*
Reverdy Johnson,[23] *Baltimore*
David Stewart,[24] *Baltimore*
Thomas G. Pratt,[25] *Annapolis*

REPRESENTATIVES

Richard J. Bowie, *Rockville*
William T. Hamilton, *Hagerstown*
Edward Hammond, *Ellicotts Mills*
Robert M. McLane, *Baltimore*
Alexander Evans, *Elkton*
John B. Kerr, *Easton*

MASSACHUSETTS

SENATORS

Daniel Webster,[26] *Boston*
Robert C. Winthrop,[27] *Boston*
Robert Rantoul, Jr.,[28] *Boston*
John Davis, *Worcester*

REPRESENTATIVES

Robert C. Winthrop,[29] *Boston*
Samuel A. Eliot,[30] *Boston*
James H. Duncan, *Haverhill*
Charles Allen, *Worcester*
George Ashmun, *Springfield*
Julius Rockwell, *Pittsfield*
Horace Mann, *West Newton*
Orin Fowler, *Fall River*
Joseph Grinnell, *New Bedford*
Daniel P. King,[31] *South Danvers*

MICHIGAN

SENATORS

Lewis Cass, *Detroit*
Alpheus Felch, *Ann Arbor*

REPRESENTATIVES

Alexander W. Buel, *Detroit*
William Sprague, *Kalamazoo*
Kinsley S. Bingham, *Kensington*

MISSISSIPPI

SENATORS

Henry S. Foote, *Jackson*
Jefferson Davis, *Palmyra*

REPRESENTATIVES

Jacob Thompson, *Oxford*
Winfield S. Featherston, *Houston*
William McWillie, *Camden*
Albert G. Brown, *Gallatin*

MISSOURI

SENATORS

Thomas H. Benton, *St. Louis*
David R. Atchison, *Platte City*

---

[14] Resigned in 1850.
[15] Elected to fill vacancy caused by resignation of Thomas Butler King, and took his seat March 4, 1850.
[16] Although seated on March 6, 1849, his election was declared void on March 15, 1849, "He not having been a citizen of the United States the term of years required as a qualification to be a Senator of the United States at the commencement of the term for which he was elected"; subsequently elected for the term beginning March 4, 1849, and took his seat December 3, 1849; vacancy in this class from March 16, 1849, to December 2, 1849.
[17] Election contested by Daniel F. Miller; served until June 29, 1850, when the House declared that

neither was entitled to the seat.
[18] Unsuccessfully contested the election of William Thompson; subsequently elected at special election, and took his seat December 20, 1850.
[19] Resigned August 17, 1850.
[20] Elected to fill vacancy caused by resignation of Charles M. Conrad, and took his seat December 5, 1850.
[21] Died October 25, 1850.
[22] Elected to fill vacancy caused by death of John H. Harmanson, and took his seat December 30, 1850.
[23] Resigned March 7, 1849.
[24] Appointed to fill vacancy caused by resignation of Reverdy Johnson, and took his seat December 8, 1849.

[25] Elected to fill vacancy caused by resignation of Reverdy Johnson, and took his seat January 14, 1850.
[26] Resigned July 22, 1850, having been appointed Secretary of State.
[27] Appointed to fill vacancy caused by resignation of Daniel Webster, and took his seat July 30, 1850.
[28] Elected to fill vacancy caused by resignation of Daniel Webster, and took his seat February 22, 1851.
[29] Resigned July 30, 1850, having been appointed Senator.
[30] Elected to fill vacancy caused by resignation of Robert C. Winthrop, and took his seat August 22, 1850.
[31] Died July 25, 1850.

REPRESENTATIVES

James B. Bowlin, *St. Louis*
William V. N. Bay, *Union*
James S. Green, *Canton*
Willard P. Hall, *St. Joseph*
John S. Phelps, *Springfield*

NEW HAMPSHIRE

SENATORS

John P. Hale, *Dover*
Moses Norris, Jr., *Manchester*

REPRESENTATIVES

Amos Tuck, *Exeter*
Charles H. Peaslee, *Concord*
James Wilson,[32] *Keene*
George W. Morrison,[33] *Manchester*
Harry Hibbard, *Bath*

NEW JERSEY

SENATORS

Jacob W. Miller, *Morristown*
William L. Dayton, *Trenton*

REPRESENTATIVES

Andrew K. Hay, *Winslow*
William A. Newell, *Allentown*
Isaac Wildrick, *Blairstown*
John Van Dyke, *New Brunswick*
James G. King, *Hoboken*

NEW YORK

SENATORS

Daniel S. Dickinson, *Binghamton*
William H. Seward, *Auburn*

REPRESENTATIVES

John A. King, *Jamaica*
David A. Bokee, *Brooklyn*
J. Phillips Phoenix, *New York City*
Walter Underhill, *New York City*
George Briggs, *New York City*
James Brooks, *New York City*
William Nelson, *Peekskill*
Ransom Halloway, *Beekman*
Thomas McKissock, *Newburgh*
Herman D. Gould, *Delhi*
Peter H. Silvester, *Coxsackie*
Gideon Reynolds, *Hoosick*
John L. Schoolcraft, *Albany*
George R. Andrews, *Ticonderoga*
John R. Thurman, *Chestertown*
Hugh White, *Cohoes*
Henry P. Alexander, *Little Falls*
Preston King, *Ogdensburg*
Charles E. Clarke, *Great Bend*

Orsamus B. Matteson, *Utica*
Hiram Walden, *Waldensville*
Henry Bennett, *New Berlin*
William Duer, *Oswego*
Daniel Gott, *Pompey*
Harmon S. Conger, *Cortland*
William T. Jackson, *Havana*
William A. Sackett, *Seneca Falls*
Abraham M. Schermerhorn, *Rochester*
Robert L. Rose, *Allens Hill*
David Rumsey, Jr., *Bath*
Elijah Risley, *Fredonia*
Elbridge G. Spaulding, *Buffalo*
Harvey Putnam, *Attica*
Lorenzo Burrows, *Albion*

NORTH CAROLINA

SENATORS

Willie P. Mangum, *Red Mountain*
George E. Badger, *Raleigh*

REPRESENTATIVES

Thomas L. Clingman, *Asheville*
Joseph P. Caldwell, *Statesville*
Edmund Deberry, *Mount Gilead*
Augustine H. Shepperd, *Salem*
Abraham W. Venable, *Brownsville*
John R. J. Daniel, *Halifax*
William S. Ashe, *Wilmington*
Edward Stanly, *Washington*
David Outlaw, *Windsor*

OHIO

SENATORS

Thomas Corwin,[34] *Lebanon*
Thomas Ewing,[35] *Lancaster*
Salmon P. Chase, *Cincinnati*

REPRESENTATIVES

David T. Disney, *Cincinnati*
Lewis D. Campbell, *Hamilton*
Robert C. Schenck, *Dayton*
Moses B. Corwin, *Urbana*
Emery D. Potter, *Toledo*
Rodolphus Dickinson,[36] *Lower Sandusky*
Amos E. Wood,[37] *Woodville*
John Bell,[38] *Fremont*
Jonathan D. Morris, *Batavia*
John L. Taylor, *Chillicothe*
Edson B. Olds, *Circleville*
Charles Sweetser, *Delaware*
John K. Miller, *Mount Vernon*
Samuel F. Vinton, *Gallipolis*
William A. Whittlesey, *Marietta*
Nathan Evans, *Cambridge*
William F. Hunter, *Woodsfield*
Moses Hoagland, *Millersburg*

Joseph Cable, *Carrollton*
David K. Cartter, *Massillon*
John Crowell, *Warren*
Joshua R. Giddings, *Jefferson*
Joseph M. Root, *Sandusky*

PENNSYLVANIA

SENATORS

Daniel Sturgeon, *Uniontown*
James Cooper, *Pottsville*

REPRESENTATIVES

Lewis C. Levin, *Philadelphia*
Joseph R. Chandler, *Philadelphia*
Henry D. Moore, *Philadelphia*
John Robbins, Jr.,[39] *Philadelphia*
John Freedley, *Norristown*
Thomas Ross, *Doylestown*
Jesse C. Dickey, *New London*
Thaddeus Stevens, *Lancaster*
William Strong, *Reading*
Milo M. Dimmick, *Stroudsburg*
David Wilmot, *Towanda*
Joseph Casey, *New Berlin*
Charles W. Pitman, *Pottsville*
Henry Nes,[40] *York*
Joel B. Danner,[41] *Gettysburg*
James X. McLanahan, *Chambersburg*
Samuel Calvin, *Hollidaysburg*
Andrew J. Ogle, *Somerset*
Job Mann, *Bedford*
Robert R. Reed, *Washington*
Moses Hampton, *Pittsburgh*
John W. Howe, *Franklin*
James Thompson, *Erie*
Alfred Gilmore, *Butler*
Chester P. Butler,[42] *Wilkes-Barre*
John Brisbin,[43] *Wilkes-Barre*

RHODE ISLAND

SENATORS

Albert C. Greene, *Providence*
John H. Clarke, *Providence*

REPRESENTATIVES

George G. King, *Newport*
Nathan F. Dixon, *Westerly*

SOUTH CAROLINA

SENATORS

John C. Calhoun,[44] *Pendleton*
Franklin H. Elmore,[45] *Columbia*
Robert W. Barnwell,[46] *Beaufort*
R. Barnwell Rhett,[47] *Charleston*
Andrew P. Butler, *Edgefield*

---

[32] Resigned September 9, 1850.
[33] Elected to fill vacancy caused by resignation of James Wilson, and took his seat December 2, 1850; election unsuccessfully contested by Jared Perkins.
[34] Resigned July 20, 1850, having been appointed Secretary of the Treasury.
[35] Appointed to fill vacancy caused by resignation of Thomas Corwin, and took his seat July 27, 1850.
[36] Died March 20, 1849.
[37] Elected to fill vacancy caused by death of

Rodolphus Dickinson, and took his seat December 3, 1849; died November 19, 1850.
[38] Elected to fill vacancy caused by death of Amos E. Wood, and took his seat January 7, 1851.
[39] Election unsuccessfully contested by John S. Littell.
[40] Died September 10, 1850.
[41] Elected to fill vacancy caused by death of Henry Nes, and took his seat December 2, 1850.
[42] Died October 5, 1850.

[43] Elected to fill vacancy caused by death of Chester P. Butler, and took his seat January 13, 1851.
[44] Died March 31, 1850.
[45] Appointed to fill vacancy caused by death of John C. Calhoun, and took his seat May 6, 1850; died May 29, 1850.
[46] Appointed to fill vacancy caused by deaths of John C. Calhoun and Franklin H. Elmore, and took his seat June 24, 1850.
[47] Elected to fill vacancy caused by death of John C. Calhoun, and took his seat January 6, 1851.

SOUTH CAROLINA—Continued

REPRESENTATIVES

Daniel Wallace, *Union*
James L. Orr, *Anderson*
Joseph A. Woodward, *Winnsboro*
John McQueen,[48] *Bennettsville*
Armistead Burt, *Willington*
Isaac E. Holmes, *Charleston*
William F. Colcock, *Grahamville*

TENNESSEE

SENATORS

Hopkins L. Turney, *Winchester*
John Bell, *Nashville*

REPRESENTATIVES

Andrew Johnson, *Greeneville*
Albert G. Watkins, *Panther Springs*
Josiah M. Anderson, *Fairview*
John H. Savage, *Smithville*
George W. Jones, *Fayetteville*
James H. Thomas, *Columbia*
Meredith P. Gentry, *Franklin*
Andrew Ewing, *Nashville*
Isham G. Harris, *Paris*
Frederick P. Stanton, *Memphis*
Christopher H. Williams, *Lexington*

TEXAS

SENATORS

Sam Houston, *Huntsville*
Thomas J. Rusk, *Nacogdoches*

REPRESENTATIVES

David S. Kaufman,[49] *Sabine*
Volney E. Howard, *San Antonio*

VERMONT

SENATORS

Samuel S. Phelps, *Middlebury*
William Upham, *Montpelier*

REPRESENTATIVES

William Henry, *Bellows Falls*
William Hebard, *Chelsea*
George P. Marsh,[50] *Burlington*
James Meacham,[51] *Middlebury*
Lucius B. Peck, *Montpelier*

VIRGINIA

SENATORS

James M. Mason, *Winchester*
Robert M. T. Hunter, *Lloyds*

REPRESENTATIVES

John S. Millson, *Norfolk*
Richard K. Meade, *Petersburg*
Thomas H. Averett, *Halifax*
Thomas S. Bocock, *Appomattox*
Paulus Powell, *Amherst*
James A. Seddon, *Richmond*
Thomas H. Bayly, *Accomac*
Alexander R. Holladay, *Mansfield*

Jeremiah Morton, *Raccoon Ford*
Richard Parker, *Berryville*
James McDowell, *Lexington*
Henry A. Edmundson, *Salem*
Fayette McMullen, *Rye Cove*
James M. H. Beale, *Point Pleasant*
Alexander Newman,[52] *Wheeling*
Thomas S. Haymond,[53] *Fairmount*

WISCONSIN

SENATORS

Henry Dodge, *Dodgeville*
Isaac P. Walker, *Milwaukee*

REPRESENTATIVES

Charles Durkee, *Kenosha*
Orsamus Cole, *Potosi*
James Duane Doty, *Menasha*

TERRITORY OF MINNESOTA [54]

DELEGATE

Henry H. Sibley,[55] *Mendota*

TERRITORY OF OREGON [56]

DELEGATE

Samuel R. Thurston,[57] *Linn City*

---

[48] Elected to fill vacancy caused by death of Representative-elect Alexander D. Sims in preceding Congress.
[49] Died January 31, 1851.
[50] Resigned in 1849, having been appointed minister to Turkey.
[51] Elected to fill vacancy caused by resignation of George P. Marsh, and took his seat December 3, 1849.

[52] Died September 8, 1949, before Congress assembled.
[53] Elected to fill vacancy caused by death of Alexander Newman and took his seat December 3, 1849.
[54] Formed March 3, 1849, from the portion of Wisconsin Territory remaining after the State of Wisconsin had been admitted to statehood (May 29, 1848), and granted a Delegate in Congress.

[55] Took his seat December 3, 1849.
[56] Formed August 14, 1848, from territory ceded to the United States by the treaty with France of April 30, 1803; the treaty with Spain of February 22, 1819, and the treaty with Great Britain of June 15, 1846, and granted a Delegate in Congress.
[57] Took his seat December 3, 1849.

THIRTY-SECOND CONGRESS

MARCH 4, 1851, TO MARCH 3, 1853

FIRST SESSION—*December 1, 1851, to August 31, 1852*

SECOND SESSION—*December 6, 1852, to March 3, 1853*

SPECIAL SESSION OF THE SENATE—*March 4, 1851, to March 13, 1851*

VICE PRESIDENT OF THE UNITED STATES [1]

PRESIDENT PRO TEMPORE OF THE SENATE—WILLIAM R. KING,[2] of Alabama; DAVID R. ATCHISON,[3] of Missouri

SECRETARY OF THE SENATE—ASBURY DICKENS, of North Carolina

SERGEANT AT ARMS OF THE SENATE—ROBERT BEALE, of Virginia

SPEAKER OF THE HOUSE OF REPRESENTATIVES—LINN BOYD,[4] of Kentucky

CLERK OF THE HOUSE—RICHARD M. YOUNG, of Illinois; JOHN W. FORNEY,[5] of Pennsylvania

SERGEANT AT ARMS OF THE HOUSE—ADAM J. GLOSSBRENNER, of Pennsylvania

DOORKEEPER OF THE HOUSE—Z. W. MCKNEW, of Maryland

ALABAMA

SENATORS

William R. King,[6] *Selma*
Benjamin Fitzpatrick,[7] *Wetumpka*
Jeremiah Clemens, *Huntsville*

REPRESENTATIVES

John Bragg, *Mobile*
James Abercrombie, *Girard*
Sampson W. Harris, *Wetumpka*
William R. Smith, *Fayette*
George S. Houston, *Athens*
Williamson R. W. Cobb, *Bellefonte*
Alexander White, *Talladega*

ARKANSAS

SENATORS

William K. Sebastian, *Helena*
Solon Borland, *Hot Springs*

REPRESENTATIVE

Robert W. Johnson, *Little Rock*

CALIFORNIA

SENATORS

William M. Gwin, *San Francisco*
John B. Weller,[8] *San Francisco*

REPRESENTATIVES

Edward C. Marshall, *Sonora*
Joseph W. McCorkle, *Marysville*

CONNECTICUT

SENATORS

Truman Smith, *Litchfield*
Isaac Toucey,[9] *Hartford*

REPRESENTATIVES

Charles Chapman, *Hartford*
Colin M. Ingersoll, *New Haven*
Chauncey F. Cleveland, *Hampton*
Origen S. Seymour, *Litchfield*

DELAWARE

SENATORS

Presley Spruance, *Smyrna*
James A. Bayard, *Wilmington*

REPRESENTATIVE

George Read Riddle, *Wilmington*

FLORIDA

SENATORS

Jackson Morton, *Pensacola*
Stephen R. Mallory,[10] *Jacksonville*

REPRESENTATIVE

Edward C. Cabell, *Tallahassee*

GEORGIA

SENATORS

John Macpherson Berrien,[11] *Savannah*
Robert M. Charlton,[12] *Savannah*
William C. Dawson, *Greensboro*

REPRESENTATIVES

Joseph W. Jackson, *Savannah*
James Johnson, *Columbus*
David J. Bailey, *Jackson*
Charles Murphey, *Decatur*
Elijah W. Chastain, *Tacoah*
Junius Hillyer, *Monroe*

---

[1] Vice President Millard Fillmore became President on the death of Zachary Taylor in preceding Congress.
[2] Resigned as President pro tempore December 20, 1852.
[3] Elected December 20, 1852.
[4] Elected December 1, 1851.
[5] Elected December 1, 1851.
[6] Resigned December 20, 1852.

[7] Appointed to fill vacancy caused by resignation of William R. King, and took his seat January 20, 1853; subsequently elected.
[8] Elected for the term beginning March 4, 1851, and took his seat March 17, 1852; vacancy in this class from March 4, 1851, to January 30, 1852.
[9] Elected for the term beginning March 4, 1851, and took his seat May 14, 1852; vacancy in this class from

March 4, 1851, to May 11, 1852, because of failure of Governor to appoint.
[10] Election unsuccessfully contested by David Levy Yulee.
[11] Resigned May 28, 1852.
[12] Appointed to fill vacancy caused by resignation of John Macpherson Berrien, and took his seat June 11, 1852.

GEORGIA—Continued

REPRESENTATIVES—continued

Alexander H. Stephens, *Crawfordville*
Robert Toombs, *Washington*

ILLINOIS

SENATORS

Stephen A. Douglas, *Chicago*
James Shields, *Belleville*

REPRESENTATIVES

William H. Bissell, *Belleville*
Willis Allen, *Marion*
Orlando B. Ficklin, *Charleston*
Richard S. Molony, *Belvidere*
William A. Richardson, *Quincy*
Thompson Campbell, *Galena*
Richard Yates, *Jacksonville*

INDIANA

SENATORS

Jesse D. Bright, *Madison*
James Whitcomb,[13] *Indianapolis*
Charles W. Cathcart,[14] *Laporte*
John Pettit,[15] *La Fayette*

REPRESENTATIVES

James Lockhart, *Evansville*
Cyrus L. Dunham, *Salem*
John L. Robinson, *Rushville*
Samuel W. Parker, *Connersville*
Thomas A. Hendricks, *Shelbyville*
Willis A. Gorman, *Bloomington*
John G. Davis, *Rockville*
Daniel Mace, *La Fayette*
Graham N. Fitch, *Logansport*
Samuel Brenton, *Fort Wayne*

IOWA

SENATORS

Augustus C. Dodge, *Burlington*
George W. Jones, *Dubuque*

REPRESENTATIVES

Bernhart Henn, *Fairfield*
Lincoln Clark, *Dubuque*

KENTUCKY

SENATORS

Joseph R. Underwood, *Bowling Green*
Henry Clay,[16] *Lexington*

David Meriwether,[17] *Louisville*
Archibald Dixon,[18] *Henderson*

REPRESENTATIVES

Linn Boyd, *Paducah*
Benjamin E. Grey, *Hopkinsville*
Presley U. Ewing, *Russellville*
William T. Ward, *Greensburg*
James W. Stone, *Elizabethtown*
Addison White, *Richmond*
Humphrey Marshall,[19] *New Castle*
William Preston,[20] *Louisville*
John C. Breckinridge, *Lexington*
John C. Mason, *Owingsville*
Richard H. Stanton, *Maysville*

LOUISIANA

SENATORS

Solomon W. Downs, *Monroe*
Pierre Soulé, *New Orleans*

REPRESENTATIVES

Louis St. Martin, *New Orleans*
J. Aristide Landry, *Donaldsonville*
Alexander G. Penn, *Covington*
John Moore, *New Iberia*

MAINE

SENATORS

James W. Bradbury, *Augusta*
Hannibal Hamlin, *Hampden*

REPRESENTATIVES

Moses Macdonald, *Biddeford*
John Appleton, *Portland*
Robert Goodenow, *Farmington*
Charles Andrews,[21] *Paris*
Isaac Reed,[22] *Waldoboro*
Ephraim K. Smart, *Camden*
Israel Washburn, Jr., *Orono*
Thomas J. D. Fuller, *Calais*

MARYLAND

SENATORS

James A. Pearce, *Chestertown*
Thomas G. Pratt, *Annapolis*

REPRESENTATIVES

Richard J. Bowie, *Rockville*
William T. Hamilton, *Hagerstown*
Edward Hammond, *Ellicotts Mills*
Thomas Yates Walsh, *Baltimore*

Alexander Evans, *Elkton*
Joseph S. Cottman, *Upper Trappe*

MASSACHUSETTS

SENATORS

John Davis, *Worcester*
Charles Sumner,[23] *Boston*

REPRESENTATIVES

William Appleton, *Boston*
Orin Fowler,[24] *Fall River*
Edward P. Little,[25] *Marshfield*
James H. Duncan, *Haverhill*
Robert Rantoul, Jr.,[26] *Beverly*
Francis B. Fay,[27] *Chelsea*
Charles Allen, *Worcester*
George T. Davis, *Greenfield*
John Z. Goodrich, *Glendale*
Horace Mann, *West Newton*
Benjamin Thompson,[28] *Charlestown*
Lorenzo Sabine,[29] *Framingham*
Zeno Scudder, *Barnstable*

MICHIGAN

SENATORS

Lewis Cass, *Detroit*
Alpheus Felch, *Ann Arbor*

REPRESENTATIVES

Ebenezer J. Penniman, *Plymouth*
Charles E. Stuart, *Kalamazoo*
James L. Conger, *Mount Clemens*

MISSISSIPPI

SENATORS

Henry S. Foote,[30] *Jackson*
Walker Brooke,[31] *Lexington*
Jefferson Davis,[32] *Palmyra*
John J. McRae,[33] *Enterprise*
Stephen Adams,[34] *Aberdeen*

REPRESENTATIVES

Benjamin D. Nabers, *Hickory Flat*
John A. Wilcox, *Aberdeen*
John D. Freeman, *Jackson*
Albert G. Brown, *Gallatin*

MISSOURI

SENATORS

David R. Atchison, *Platte City*
Henry S. Geyer, *St. Louis*

---

[13] Died October 4, 1852.
[14] Appointed to fill vacancy caused by death of James Whitcomb, and took his seat December 6, 1852.
[15] Elected to fill vacancy caused by death of James Whitcomb, and took his seat January 18, 1853.
[16] Tendered his resignation December 15, 1851, "to take effect on the first Monday of September, 1852"; died June 29, 1852.
[17] Appointed July 6, 1852, to fill vacancy caused by death of Henry Clay, and to serve "until the time the resignation of Henry Clay takes effect"; took his seat July 15, 1852, and served until the adjournment of the session, August 31, 1852.
[18] Elected December 30, 1851, to fill vacancy anticipated by the resignation of Henry Clay; credentials presented on December 6, 1852, but was not permitted

to qualify until December 20, 1852, when a resolution was adopted declaring him duly elected "to fill the vacancy occasioned by the resignation of Mr. Clay."
[19] Resigned August 4, 1852.
[20] Elected to fill vacancy caused by resignation of Humphrey Marshall, and took his seat December 6, 1852.
[21] Died April 30, 1852.
[22] Elected to fill vacancy caused by death of Charles Andrews, and took his seat June 25, 1852.
[23] Elected for term beginning March 4, 1851, and took his seat December 1, 1851; vacancy in this class from March 4, 1851, to April 23, 1851.
[24] Died September 3, 1852.
[25] Elected to fill vacancy caused by death of Orin Fowler, and took his seat December 30, 1852.

[26] Died August 7, 1852.
[27] Elected to fill vacancy caused by death of Robert Rantoul, Jr., and took his seat December 29, 1852.
[28] Died September 24, 1852.
[29] Elected to fill vacancy caused by death of Benjamin Thompson, and took his seat December 28, 1852.
[30] Resigned January 8, 1852, having been elected governor.
[31] Elected to fill vacancy caused by resignation of Henry S. Foote, and took his seat March 11, 1852.
[32] Resigned September 23, 1851.
[33] Appointed to fill vacancy caused by resignation of Jefferson Davis, and took his seat December 19, 1851.
[34] Elected to fill vacancy caused by resignation of Jefferson Davis, and took his seat March 17, 1852.

REPRESENTATIVES

John F. Darby, *St. Louis*
Gilchrist Porter, *Bowling Green*
John G. Miller, *Boonville*
Willard P. Hall, *St. Joseph*
John S. Phelps, *Springfield*

NEW HAMPSHIRE

SENATORS

John P. Hale, *Dover*
Moses Norris, Jr., *Manchester*

REPRESENTATIVES

Amos Tuck, *Exeter*
Charles H. Peaslee, *Concord*
Jared Perkins, *Winchester*
Harry Hibbard, *Bath*

NEW JERSEY

SENATORS

Jacob W. Miller, *Morristown*
Robert F. Stockton,[35] *Princeton*

REPRESENTATIVES

Nathan T. Stratton, *Mullica Hill*
Charles Skelton, *Trenton*
Isaac Wildrick, *Blairstown*
George H. Brown, *Somerville*
Rodman M. Price, *Hoboken*

NEW YORK

SENATORS

William H. Seward, *Auburn*
Hamilton Fish, *New York City*

REPRESENTATIVES

John G. Floyd, *Moriches*
Obadiah Bowne, *Richmond*
Emanuel B. Hart, *New York City*
J. H. Hobart Haws, *New York City*
George Briggs, *New York City*
James Brooks, *New York City*
Abraham P. Stephens, *Nyack*
Gilbert Dean, *Poughkeepsie*
William Murray, *Goshen*
Marius Schoonmaker, *Kingston*
Josiah Sutherland, *Hudson*
David L. Seymour, *Troy*
John L. Schoolcraft, *Albany*
John H. Boyd, *Whitehall*
Joseph Russell, *Warrensburg*
John Wells, *Johnstown*
Alexander H. Buell,[36] *Fairfield*
Preston King, *Ogdensburg*
Willard Ives, *Watertown*
Timothy Jenkins, *Oneida Castle*

William W. Snow, *Oneonta*
Henry Bennett, *New Berlin*
Leander Babcock, *Oswego*
Daniel T. Jones, *Baldwinsville*
Thomas Y. Howe, Jr., *Auburn*
Henry S. Walbridge, *Ithaca*
William A. Sackett, *Seneca Falls*
Abraham M. Schermerhorn, *Rochester*
Jerediah Horsford, *Moscow*
Reuben Robie, *Bath*
Frederick S. Martin, *Olean*
Solomon G. Haven, *Buffalo*
Augustus P. Hascall, *Le Roy*
Lorenzo Burrows, *Albion*

NORTH CAROLINA

SENATORS

Willie P. Mangum, *Red Mountain*
George E. Badger, *Raleigh*

REPRESENTATIVES

Thomas L. Clingman, *Asheville*
Joseph P. Caldwell, *Statesville*
Alfred Dockery, *Dockerys Store*
James T. Morehead, *Greensboro*
Abraham W. Venable, *Brownsville*
John R. J. Daniel, *Halifax*
William S. Ashe, *Wilmington*
Edward Stanly, *Washington*
David Outlaw, *Windsor*

OHIO

SENATORS

Salmon P. Chase, *Cincinnati*
Benjamin F. Wade,[37] *Jefferson*

REPRESENTATIVES

David T. Disney, *Cincinnati*
Lewis D. Campbell, *Hamilton*
Hiram Bell, *Greenville*
Benjamin Stanton, *Bellefontaine*
Alfred P. Edgerton, *Hicksville*
Frederick W. Green, *Tiffin*
Nelson Barrere, *Hillsboro*
John L. Taylor, *Chillicothe*
Edson B. Olds, *Circleville*
Charles Sweetser, *Delaware*
George H. Busby, *Marion*
John Welch, *Athens*
James M. Gaylord, *McConnellsville*
Alexander Harper, *Zanesville*
William F. Hunter, *Woodsfield*
John Johnson, *Coshocton*
Joseph Cable, *Carrollton*
David K. Cartter, *Massillon*
Eben Newton, *Canfield*
Joshua R. Giddings, *Jefferson*
Norton S. Townshend, *Avon*

PENNSYLVANIA

SENATORS

James Cooper, *Pottsville*
Richard Brodhead, *Easton*

REPRESENTATIVES

Thomas B. Florence, *Philadelphia*
Joseph R. Chandler, *Philadelphia*
Henry D. Moore, *Philadelphia*
John Robbins, Jr., *Kensington*
John McNair, *Norristown*
Thomas Ross, *Doylestown*
John A. Morrison, *Cochransville*
Thaddeus Stevens, *Lancaster*
J. Glancy Jones, *Reading*
Milo M. Dimmick, *Stroudsburg*
Henry M. Fuller,[38] *Wilkes-Barre*
Galusha A. Grow, *Glenwood*
James Gamble, *Jersey Shore*
Thomas M. Bibighaus, *Lebanon*
William H. Kurtz, *York*
James X. McLanahan, *Chambersburg*
Andrew Parker, *Mifflintown*
John L. Dawson, *Brownsville*
Joseph H. Kuhns, *Greensburg*
John Allison, *Beaver*
Thomas M. Howe, *Allegheny City*
John W. Howe, *Franklin*
Carlton B. Curtis, *Warren*
Alfred Gilmore, *Butler*

RHODE ISLAND

SENATORS

John H. Clarke, *Providence*
Charles T. James, *Providence*

REPRESENTATIVES

George G. King, *Newport*
Benjamin B. Thurston, *Hopkinton*

SOUTH CAROLINA

SENATORS

Andrew P. Butler, *Edgefield*
R. Barnwell Rhett,[39] *Charleston*
William F. De Saussure,[40] *Columbia*

REPRESENTATIVES

Daniel Wallace, *Jonesville*
James L. Orr, *Anderson*
Joseph A. Woodward, *Winnsboro*
John McQueen, *Bennettsville*
Armistead Burt, *Willington*
William Aiken, *Charleston*
William F. Colcock, *Grahamville*

TENNESSEE

SENATORS

John Bell, *Nashville*
James C. Jones, *Memphis*

---

[35] Resigned January 10, 1853; vacancy in this class during remainder of the Congress.
[36] Died January 29, 1853.
[37] Elected for term beginning March 4, 1851, and took his seat December 1, 1851; vacancy in this class from March 4 to 14, 1851
[38] Election unsuccessfully contested by Hendrick B. Wright.
[39] Resigned May 7, 1852.
[40] Appointed to fill vacancy caused by resignation of R. Barnwell Rhett, and took his seat May 24, 1852; subsequently elected.

TENNESSEE—Continued

REPRESENTATIVES

Andrew Johnson, *Greeneville*
Albert G. Watkins, *Panther Springs*
William M. Churchwell, *Knoxville*
John H. Savage, *Smithville*
George W. Jones, *Fayetteville*
William H. Polk, *Columbia*
Meredith P. Gentry, *Franklin*
William Cullom, *Carthage*
Isham G. Harris, *Paris*
Frederick P. Stanton, *Memphis*
Christopher H. Williams, *Lexington*

TEXAS

SENATORS

Sam Houston, *Huntsville*
Thomas J. Rusk, *Nacogdoches*

REPRESENTATIVES

Richardson Scurry, *Clarksville*
Volney E. Howard, *San Antonio*

VERMONT

SENATORS

William Upham,[41] *Montpelier*
Samuel S. Phelps,[42] *Middlebury*
Solomon Foot, *Rutland*

REPRESENTATIVES

Ahiman L. Miner, *Manchester*
William Hebard, *Chelsea*
James Meacham, *Middlebury*
Thomas Bartlett, Jr., *Lyndon*

VIRGINIA

SENATORS

James M. Mason, *Winchester*
Robert M. T. Hunter, *Lloyds*

REPRESENTATIVES

John S. Millson, *Norfolk*
Richard K. Meade, *Petersburg*
Thomas H. Averett, *Halifax*
Thomas S. Bocock, *Appomattox*
Paulus Powell, *Amherst*
John S. Caskie, *Richmond*
Thomas H. Bayly, *Accomac*
Alexander R. Holladay, *Mansfield*
James F. Strother, *Rappahannock*
Charles J. Faulkner, *Martinsburg*
John Letcher, *Lexington*
Henry A. Edmundson, *Salem*
Fayette McMullen, *Rye Cove*
James M. H. Beale, *Point Pleasant*
George W. Thompson,[43] *Wheeling*
Sherrard Clemens,[44] *Wheeling*

WISCONSIN

SENATORS

Henry Dodge, *Dodgeville*
Isaac P. Walker, *Milwaukee*

REPRESENTATIVES

Charles Durkee, *Kenosha*
Ben C. Eastman, *Platteville*
James Duane Doty, *Menasha*

TERRITORY OF MINNESOTA

DELEGATE

Henry H. Sibley, *Mendota*

TERRITORY OF NEW MEXICO [45]

DELEGATE

Richard H. Weightman,[46] *Santa Fe*

TERRITORY OF OREGON

DELEGATE

Joseph Lane, *Oregon City*

TERRITORY OF UTAH [47]

DELEGATE

John M. Bernhisel,[48] *Salt Lake City*

---

[41] Died January 14, 1853.
[42] Appointed to fill vacancy caused by death of William Upham, and took his seat January 19, 1853.
[43] Resigned July 30, 1852.
[44] Elected to fill vacancy caused by resignation of George W. Thompson, and took his seat December 6, 1852.
[45] Formed from a portion of the territory ceded to the United States by Mexico by the treaty of Guada-

lupe Hidalgo of February 2, 1848, and granted a Delegate in Congress by act of September 9, 1850. Hugh N. Smith presented credentials February 4, 1850, in the preceding Congress, but was not admitted to a seat; the committee on elections held that no territorial government existed and the matter was laid on the table.

[46] Took his seat December 1, 1851.
[47] Formed from a portion of the territory ceded to the United States by Mexico by the treaty of Guadalupe Hidalgo of February 2, 1848, and granted a Delegate in Congress by act of September 9, 1850.
[48] Took his seat December 1, 1851.

THIRTY-THIRD CONGRESS

MARCH 4, 1853, TO MARCH 3, 1855

FIRST SESSION—*December 5, 1853, to August 7, 1854*

SECOND SESSION—*December 4, 1854, to March 3, 1855*

SPECIAL SESSION OF THE SENATE—*March 4, 1853, to April 11, 1853*

VICE PRESIDENT OF THE UNITED STATES—WILLIAM R. KING,[1] of Alabama

PRESIDENT PRO TEMPORE OF THE SENATE—DAVID R. ATCHISON,[2] of Missouri; LEWIS CASS,[3] of Michigan; JESSE D. BRIGHT,[4] of Indiana

SECRETARY OF THE SENATE—ASBURY DICKENS, of North Carolina

SERGEANT AT ARMS OF THE SENATE—ROBERT BEALE, of Virginia; DUNNING R. McNAIR,[5] of Pennsylvania

SPEAKER OF THE HOUSE OF REPRESENTATIVES—LINN BOYD,[6] of Kentucky

CLERK OF THE HOUSE—JOHN W. FORNEY,[7] of Pennsylvania

SERGEANT AT ARMS OF THE HOUSE—ADAM J. GLOSSBRENNER, of Pennsylvania

DOORKEEPER OF THE HOUSE—Z. W. McKNEW, of Maryland

ALABAMA

SENATORS

Benjamin Fitzpatrick, *Wetumpka*
Clement C. Clay, Jr.,[8] *Huntsville*

REPRESENTATIVES

Philip Phillips, *Mobile*
James Abercrombie, *Girard*
Sampson W. Harris, *Wetumpka*
William R. Smith, *Fayette*
George S. Houston, *Athens*
Williamson R. W. Cobb, *Bellefonte*
James F. Dowdell, *Chambers*

ARKANSAS

SENATORS

William K. Sebastian, *Helena*
Solon Borland,[9] *Hot Springs*
Robert W. Johnson,[10] *Little Rock*

REPRESENTATIVES

Alfred B. Greenwood, *Bentonville*
Edward A. Warren, *Camden*

CALIFORNIA

SENATORS

William M. Gwin, *San Francisco*
John B. Weller, *San Francisco*

REPRESENTATIVES

Milton S. Latham, *Sacramento*
James A. McDougall, *San Francisco*

CONNECTICUT

SENATORS

Truman Smith,[11] *Litchfield*
Francis Gillette,[12] *Hartford*
Isaac Toucey, *Hartford*

REPRESENTATIVES

James T. Pratt, *Rockyhill*
Colin M. Ingersoll, *New Haven*
Nathan Belcher, *New London*
Origen S. Seymour, *Litchfield*

DELAWARE

SENATORS

James A. Bayard, *Wilmington*
John M. Clayton, *Chippewa*

REPRESENTATIVE

George Read Riddle, *Wilmington*

FLORIDA

SENATORS

Jackson Morton, *Pensacola*
Stephen R. Mallory, *Jacksonville*

REPRESENTATIVE

Augustus E. Maxwell, *Tallahassee*

GEORGIA

SENATORS

William C. Dawson, *Greensboro*
Robert Toombs, *Washington*

---

[1] Died April 18, 1853, after taking the oath of office at Habana, Cuba, a privilege accorded by special act of Congress.
[2] Elected March 4, 1853.
[3] Elected December 4, 1854, for one day only.
[4] Elected December 5, 1854.
[5] Elected March 17, 1853.

[6] Reelected December 5, 1853.
[7] Reelected December 5, 1853.
[8] Elected for term beginning March 4, 1853, and took his seat December 14, 1853; vacancy in this class from March 4, 1853, to November 28, 1853.
[9] Resigned April 3, 1853, to become minister to Nicaragua and the other Central American Republics.

[10] Appointed to fill vacancy caused by resignation of Solon Borland, and took his seat December 5, 1853; subsequently elected.
[11] Resigned, effective May 24, 1854.
[12] Elected to fill vacancy caused by resignation of Truman Smith, and took his seat May 25, 1854.

GEORGIA—Continued

REPRESENTATIVES

James L. Seward, *Thomasville*
Alfred H. Colquitt, *Newton*
David J. Bailey, *Jackson*
William B. W. Dent, *Newnan*
Elijah W. Chastain, *Tacoah*
Junius Hillyer, *Monroe*
David A. Reese, *Monticello*
Alexander H. Stephens, *Crawfordville*

ILLINOIS

SENATORS

Stephen A. Douglas, *Chicago*
James Shields, *Belleville*

REPRESENTATIVES

Elihu B. Washburne, *Galena*
John Wentworth, *Chicago*
Jesse O. Norton, *Joliet*
James Knox, *Knoxville*
William A. Richardson, *Quincy*
Richard Yates, *Jacksonville*
James C. Allen, *Palestine*
William H. Bissell, *Belleville*
Willis Allen, *Marion*

INDIANA

SENATORS

Jesse D. Bright, *Madison*
John Pettit, *La Fayette*

REPRESENTATIVES

Smith Miller, *Patoka*
William H. English, *Lexington*
Cyrus L. Dunham, *Salem*
James H. Lane, *Lawrenceburg*
Samuel W. Parker, *Connersville*
Thomas A. Hendricks, *Shelbyville*
John G. Davis, *Rockville*
Daniel Mace, *La Fayette*
Norman Eddy, *South Bend*
Ebenezer M. Chamberlain, *Goshen*
Andrew J. Harlan, *Marion*

IOWA

SENATORS

Augustus C. Dodge, *Burlington*
George W. Jones, *Dubuque*

REPRESENTATIVES

Bernhart Henn, *Fairfield*
John P. Cook, *Davenport*

KENTUCKY

SENATORS

Archibald Dixon, *Henderson*
John B. Thompson, *Harrodsburg*

REPRESENTATIVES

Linn Boyd, *Paducah*
Benjamin E. Grey, *Hopkinsville*
Presley U. Ewing,[13] *Russellville*
Francis M. Bristow,[14] *Elkton*
James S. Chrisman, *Monticello*
Clement S. Hill, *Lebanon*
John M. Elliott, *Prestonburg*
William Preston, *Louisville*
John C. Breckinridge, *Lexington*
Leander M. Cox, *Flemingsburg*
Richard H. Stanton, *Maysville*

LOUISIANA

SENATORS

Pierre Soulé,[15] *New Orleans*
John Slidell,[16] *New Orleans*
Judah P. Benjamin, *New Orleans*

REPRESENTATIVES

William Dunbar, *New Orleans*
Theodore G. Hunt, *New Orleans*
John Perkins, Jr., *Ashwood*
Roland Jones, *Shreveport*

MAINE

SENATORS

Hannibal Hamlin, *Hampden*
William Pitt Fessenden,[17] *Portland*

REPRESENTATIVES

Moses Macdonald, *Portland*
Samuel Mayall, *Gray*
E. Wilder Farley, *Newcastle*
Samuel P. Benson, *Winthrop*
Israel Washburn, Jr., *Orono*
Thomas J. D. Fuller, *Calais*

MARYLAND

SENATORS

James A. Pearce, *Chestertown*
Thomas G. Pratt, *Annapolis*

REPRESENTATIVES

John R. Franklin, *Snow Hill*
Jacob Shower, *Manchester*
Joshua Vansant, *Baltimore*
Henry May, *Baltimore*
William T. Hamilton, *Hagerstown*
Augustus R. Sollers, *Prince Frederick*

MASSACHUSETTS

SENATORS

Charles Sumner, *Boston*
Edward Everett,[18] *Boston*
Julius Rockwell,[19] *Pittsfield*
Henry Wilson,[20] *Natick*

REPRESENTATIVES

Zeno Scudder,[21] *Barnstable*
Thomas D. Eliot,[22] *New Bedford*
Samuel L. Crocker, *Taunton*
J. Wiley Edmands, *Lawrence*
Samuel H. Walley, *Roxbury*
William Appleton, *Boston*
Charles W. Upham, *Salem*
Nathaniel P. Banks, *Waltham*
Tappan Wentworth, *Lowell*
Alexander De Witt, *Oxford*
Edward Dickinson, *Amherst*
John Z. Goodrich, *Glendale*

MICHIGAN

SENATORS

Lewis Cass, *Detroit*
Charles E. Stuart, *Kalamazoo*

REPRESENTATIVES

David Stuart, *Detroit*
David A. Noble, *Monroe*
Samuel Clarke, *Kalamazoo*
Hestor L. Stevens, *Pontiac*

MISSISSIPPI

SENATORS

Stephen Adams, *Aberdeen*
Albert G. Brown,[23] *Newton*

REPRESENTATIVES

Daniel B. Wright, *Salem*
William T. S. Barry, *Greenwood*
Otho R. Singleton, *Canton*
Wiley P. Harris, *Monticello*
William Barksdale, *Columbus*

MISSOURI

SENATORS

David R. Atchison, *Platte City*
Henry S. Geyer, *St. Louis*

REPRESENTATIVES

Thomas H. Benton, *St. Louis*
Alfred W. Lamb, *Hannibal*

---

[13] Died September 27, 1854.
[14] Elected to fill vacancy caused by death of Presley U. Ewing, and took his seat December 4, 1854.
[15] Resigned April 11, 1853.
[16] Elected to fill vacancy caused by resignation of Pierre Soulé, and took his seat December 5, 1853.
[17] Elected for the term beginning March 4, 1853, and took his seat February 23, 1854; vacancy in this class from March 4, 1853, to February 10, 1854.
[18] Resigned, effective June 1, 1854.
[19] Appointed to fill vacancy caused by resignation of Edward Everett, and took his seat June 15, 1854.
[20] Elected to fill vacancy caused by resignation of Edward Everett, and took his seat February 10, 1855.
[21] Resigned March 4, 1854.
[22] Elected to fill vacancy caused by resignation of Zeno Scudder, and took his seat April 17, 1854.
[23] Elected for the term beginning March 4, 1853; took his seat January 26, 1854; vacancy in this class from March 4, 1853, to January 7, 1854.

James J. Lindley, *Monticello*
Mordecai Oliver, *Richmond*
John G. Miller, *Boonville*
John S. Phelps, *Springfield*
Samuel Caruthers, *Cape Girardeau*

NEW HAMPSHIRE

SENATORS

Moses Norris, Jr.,[24] *Manchester*
John S. Wells,[25] *Exeter*
Charles G. Atherton,[26] *Nashua*
Jared W. Williams,[27] *Lancaster*

REPRESENTATIVES

George W. Kittredge, *Newmarket*
George W. Morrison, *Manchester*
Harry Hibbard, *Bath*

NEW JERSEY

SENATORS

John R. Thomson,[28] *Princeton*
William Wright, *Newark*

REPRESENTATIVES

Nathan T. Stratton, *Mullica Hill*
Charles Skelton, *Trenton*
Samuel Lilly, *Lambertville*
George Vail, *Morristown*
Alexander C. M. Pennington, *Newark*

NEW YORK

SENATORS

William H. Seward, *Auburn*
Hamilton Fish, *New York City*

REPRESENTATIVES

James Maurice, *Maspeth*
Thomas W. Cumming, *Brooklyn*
Hiram Walbridge, *New York City*
Mike Walsh, *New York City*
William M. Tweed, *New York City*
John Wheeler, *New York City*
William A. Walker, *New York City*
Francis B. Cutting, *New York City*
Jared V. Peck, *Port Chester*
William Murray, *Goshen*
Theodore R. Westbrook, *Kingston*
Gilbert Dean,[29] *Poughkeepsie*
Isaac Teller,[30] *Mattawan*
Russell Sage, *Troy*
Rufus W. Peckham, *Albany*
Charles Hughes, *Sandy Hill*
George A. Simmons, *Keeseville*
Bishop Perkins, *Ogdensburg*
Peter Rowe, *Schenectady*

George W. Chase, *Schenevus*
Orsamus B. Matteson, *Utica*
Henry Bennett, *New Berlin*
Gerrit Smith,[31] *Petersboro*
Henry C. Goodwin,[32] *Hamilton*
Caleb Lyon, *Lyonsdale*
Daniel T. Jones, *Baldwinsville*
Edwin B. Morgan, *Aurora*
Andrew Oliver, *Penn Yan*
John J. Taylor, *Owego*
George Hastings, *Mount Morris*
Azariah Boody,[33] *Rochester*
Davis Carpenter,[34] *Brockport*
Benjamin Pringle, *Batavia*
Thomas T. Flagler, *Lockport*
Solomon G. Haven, *Buffalo*
Reuben E. Fenton, *Frewsburg*

NORTH CAROLINA

SENATORS

George E. Badger, *Raleigh*
David S. Reid,[35] *Wentworth*

REPRESENTATIVES

Henry M. Shaw, *Indian Town*
Thomas Ruffin, *Goldsboro*
William S. Ashe, *Wilmington*
Sion H. Rogers, *Raleigh*
John Kerr, Jr., *Yanceyville*
Richard C. Puryear, *Huntsville*
F. Burton Craige, *Salisbury*
Thomas L. Clingman, *Asheville*

OHIO

SENATORS

Salmon P. Chase, *Cincinnati*
Benjamin F. Wade, *Jefferson*

REPRESENTATIVES

David T. Disney, *Cincinnati*
John Scott Harrison, *Cleves*
Lewis D. Campbell, *Hamilton*
Matthias H. Nichols, *Lima*
Alfred P. Edgerton, *Hicksville*
Andrew Ellison, *Georgetown*
Aaron Harlan, *Yellow Springs*
Moses B. Corwin, *Urbana*
Frederick W. Green, *Tiffin*
John L. Taylor, *Chillicothe*
Thomas Ritchey, *Somerset*
Edson B. Olds, *Circleville*
William D. Lindsley, *Sandusky*
Harvey H. Johnson, *Ashland*
William R. Sapp, *Mount Vernon*
Edward Ball, *Zanesville*
Wilson Shannon, *St. Clairsville*

George Bliss, *Akron*
Edward Wade, *Cleveland*
Joshua R. Giddings, *Jefferson*
Andrew Stuart, *Steubenville*

PENNSYLVANIA

SENATORS

James Cooper, *Pottsville*
Richard Brodhead, *Easton*

REPRESENTATIVES

Thomas B. Florence, *Philadelphia*
Joseph R. Chandler, *Philadelphia*
John Robbins, Jr., *Kensington*
William H. Witte, *Richmond*
John McNair, *Norristown*
William Everhart, *West Chester*
Samuel A. Bridges, *Allentown*
Henry A. Muhlenberg,[36] *Berks*
J. Glancy Jones,[37] *Reading*
Isaac E. Hiester, *Lancaster*
Ner Middleswarth, *Beavertown*
Christian M. Straub, *Pottsville*
Hendrick B. Wright, *Wilkes-Barre*
Asa Packer, *Mauch Chunk*
Galusha A. Grow, *Glenwood*
James Gamble, *Jersey Shore*
Carlton B. Curtis, *Warren*
Samuel L. Russell, *Bedford*
John McCulloch, *Shavers Creek*
Augustus Drum, *Indiana*
John L. Dawson, *Brownsville*
David Ritchie, *Pittsburgh*
Thomas M. Howe, *Allegheny City*
Michael C. Trout, *Sharon*
John Dick, *Meadville*
William H. Kurtz, *York*

RHODE ISLAND

SENATORS

Charles T. James, *Providence*
Philip Allen,[38] *Providence*

REPRESENTATIVES

Thomas Davis, *Providence*
Benjamin B. Thurston, *Hopkinton*

SOUTH CAROLINA

SENATORS

Andrew P. Butler, *Edgefield*
Josiah J. Evans, *Society Hill*

REPRESENTATIVES

John McQueen, *Marlboro*
William Aiken, *Charleston*

---

[24] Died January 11, 1855.
[25] Appointed to fill vacancy caused by death of Moses Norris, Jr., and took his seat January 22, 1855.
[26] Died November 15, 1853.
[27] Appointed to fill vacancy caused by death of Charles G. Atherton, and took his seat December 12, 1853; by resolution, August 3, 1854, Senate declared representation under the appointment had expired.
[28] Elected to fill vacancy caused by resignation of Robert F. Stockton, in preceding Congress, and took his seat March 4, 1853.

[29] Resigned July 3, 1854.
[30] Elected to fill vacancy caused by resignation of Gilbert Dean, and took his seat December 4, 1854.
[31] Resigned August 7, 1854.
[32] Elected to fill vacancy caused by resignation of Gerrit Smith, and took his seat December 4, 1854.
[33] Resigned in October, 1853, before Congress assembled.
[34] Elected to fill vacancy caused by resignation of Azariah Boody, and took his seat December 5, 1853.

[35] Elected for the term beginning March 4, 1853, and took his seat December 11, 1854; vacancy in this class from March 4, 1853, to December 6, 1854.
[36] Died January 9, 1854.
[37] Elected to fill vacancy caused by death of Henry A. Muhlenberg, and took his seat February 13, 1854.
[38] Elected on May 4, 1853, for the term beginning March 4, 1853, and took his seat December 5, 1853; vacancy in this class from March 4, 1853, to July 20, 1853.

SOUTH CAROLINA—Continued

REPRESENTATIVES—continued

Laurence M. Keitt, *Orangeburg*
Preston S. Brooks, *Ninety Six*
James L. Orr, *Anderson*
William W. Boyce, *Winnsboro*

TENNESSEE

SENATORS

John Bell, *Nashville*
James C. Jones, *Memphis*

REPRESENTATIVES

Brookins Campbell,[39] *Washington College*
Nathaniel G. Taylor,[40] *Happy Valley*
William M. Churchwell, *Knoxville*
Samuel A. Smith, *Charleston*
William Cullom, *Carthage*
Charles Ready, *Murfreesboro*
George W. Jones, *Fayetteville*
Robert M. Bugg, *Lynnville*
Felix K. Zollicoffer, *Nashville*
Emerson Etheridge, *Dresden*
Frederick P. Stanton, *Memphis*

TEXAS

SENATORS

Sam Houston, *Huntsville*
Thomas J. Rusk, *Nacogdoches*

REPRESENTATIVES

George W. Smyth, *Jasper*
Peter H. Bell, *Austin*

VERMONT

SENATORS

Solomon Foot, *Rutland*
Samuel S. Phelps,[41] *Middlebury*
Lawrence Brainerd,[42] *St. Albans*

REPRESENTATIVES

James Meacham, *Middlebury*
Andrew Tracy, *Woodstock*
Alvah Sabin, *Georgia*

VIRGINIA

SENATORS

James M. Mason, *Winchester*
Robert M. T. Hunter, *Lloyds*

REPRESENTATIVES

Thomas H. Bayly, *Accomac*
John S. Millson, *Norfolk*
John S. Caskie, *Richmond*
William O. Goode, *Boydton*
Thomas S. Bocock, *Appomattox*
Paulus Powell, *Amherst*
William Smith, *Warrenton*
Charles J. Faulkner, *Martinsburg*
John Letcher, *Lexington*
Zedekiah Kidwell, *Fairmont*
John F. Snodgrass,[43] *Parkersburg*
Charles S. Lewis,[44] *Clarksburg*
Henry A. Edmundson, *Salem*
Fayette McMullen, *Rye Cove*

WISCONSIN

SENATORS

Henry Dodge, *Dodgeville*
Isaac P. Walker, *Milwaukee*

REPRESENTATIVES

Daniel Wells, Jr., *Milwaukee*
Ben C. Eastman, *Platteville*
John B. Macy, *Fond du Lac*

TERRITORY OF KANSAS [45]

DELEGATE

John W. Whitfield,[46] *Tecumseh*

TERRITORY OF MINNESOTA

DELEGATE

Henry M. Rice, *St. Paul*

TERRITORY OF NEBRASKA [47]

DELEGATE

Napoleon B. Giddings,[48] *Nebraska City*

TERRITORY OF NEW MEXICO

DELEGATE

José Manuel Gallegos,[49] *Albuquerque*

TERRITORY OF OREGON [50]

DELEGATE

Joseph Lane, *Winchester*

TERRITORY OF UTAH

DELEGATE

John M. Bernhisel, *Salt Lake City*

TERRITORY OF WASHINGTON [51]

DELEGATE

Columbia Lancaster,[52] *St. Helena*

---

[39] Died December 25, 1853, never having qualified owing to illness.
[40] Elected to fill vacancy caused by death of Brookins Campbell, December 25, 1853, who did not qualify and took his seat March 30, 1854.
[41] Appointed, in preceding Congress, to fill vacancy, caused by death of William Upham; by resolution of Senate of March 16, 1854, declared not entitled to retain his seat.
[42] Elected to fill vacancy caused by death of William Upham, in preceding Congress, and took his seat December 4, 1854; vacancy in this class from March 17, 1854, to October 13, 1854.

[43] Died June 5, 1854.
[44] Elected to fill vacancy caused by death of John F. Snodgrass, and took his seat December 4, 1854.
[45] Formed from territory ceded to the United States by France by the treaty of Paris of April 30, 1803, and by the State of Texas, in the settlement of her boundaries in 1850; erected into a Territorial government and granted a Delegate in Congress by act of May 30, 1854.
[46] Took his seat December 20, 1854.
[47] Formed from a portion of the territory ceded to the United States by France by the treaty of April 30,

1803, and granted a Delegate in Congress by act of May 30, 1854.
[48] Took his seat January 5, 1855.
[49] Election unsuccessfully contested by William Carr Lane.
[50] The Territory of Washington was formed from a portion of the Territory of Oregon by act of March 2, 1853.
[51] Formed March 2, 1853, from a portion of the Territory of Oregon, and granted a Delegate in Congress.
[52] Took his seat April 12, 1854.

THIRTY-FOURTH CONGRESS

MARCH 4, 1855, TO MARCH 3, 1857

FIRST SESSION—*December 3, 1855, to August 18, 1856*

SECOND SESSION—*August 21, 1856, to August 30, 1856*

THIRD SESSION—*December 1, 1856, to March 3, 1857*

VICE PRESIDENT OF THE UNITED STATES [1]

PRESIDENT PRO TEMPORE OF THE SENATE—JESSE D. BRIGHT,[2] of Indiana; CHARLES E. STUART,[3] of Michigan; JAMES M. MASON,[4] of Virginia

SECRETARY OF THE SENATE—ASBURY DICKENS, of North Carolina

SERGEANT AT ARMS OF THE SENATE—DUNNING R. McNAIR, of Pennsylvania

---

SPEAKER OF THE HOUSE OF REPRESENTATIVES—NATHANIEL P. BANKS,[5] of Massachusetts

CLERK OF THE HOUSE—JOHN W. FORNEY, of Pennsylvania; WILLIAM CULLOM,[6] of Tennessee

SERGEANT AT ARMS OF THE HOUSE—ADAM J. GLOSSBRENNER, of Pennsylvania

DOORKEEPER OF THE HOUSE—NATHAN DARLING, of New York

ALABAMA

SENATORS

Clement C. Clay, Jr., *Huntsville*
Benjamin Fitzpatrick,[7] *Wetumpka*

REPRESENTATIVES

Percy Walker, *Mobile*
Eli S. Shorter, *Eufaula*
James F. Dowdell, *Chambers*
William R. Smith, *Fayette*
George S. Houston, *Athens*
Williamson R. W. Cobb, *Bellefonte*
Sampson W. Harris, *Wetumpka*

ARKANSAS

SENATORS

William K. Sebastian, *Helena*
Robert W. Johnson, *Pine Bluff*

REPRESENTATIVES

Alfred B. Greenwood, *Bentonville*
Albert Rust, *El Dorado*

CALIFORNIA

SENATORS

John B. Weller, *San Francisco*
William M. Gwin,[8] *San Francisco*

REPRESENTATIVES

James W. Denver, *Weaverville*
Philemon T. Herbert, *Mariposa City*

CONNECTICUT

SENATORS

Isaac Toucey, *Hartford*
Lafayette S. Foster, *Norwich*

REPRESENTATIVES

Ezra Clark, Jr., *Hartford*
John Woodruff, *New Haven*
Sidney Dean, *Putnam*
William W. Welch, *Norfolk*

DELAWARE

SENATORS

James A. Bayard, *Wilmington*
John M. Clayton,[9] *Chippewa*
Joseph P. Comegys,[10] *Dover*
Martin W. Bates,[11] *Dover*

REPRESENTATIVE

Elisha D. Cullen, *Georgetown*

FLORIDA

SENATORS

Stephen R. Mallory, *Key West*
David Levy Yulee, *Homasassa*

REPRESENTATIVE

Augustus E. Maxwell, *Tallahassee*

GEORGIA

SENATORS

Robert Toombs, *Washington*
Alfred Iverson, *Columbus*

---

[1] Vice President William R. King died in preceding Congress.
[2] Continued from preceding Congress; again elected June 11, 1856.
[3] Served June 5, 1856; elected June 9, 1856; resigned June 11, 1856.
[4] Served January 5, 1856; elected January 6, 1857.
[5] Elected February 2, 1856, upon the one hundred and thirty-third viva voce vote and the fourth vote under a plurality resolution adopted that day.
[6] Elected February 4, 1856.
[7] Elected for term beginning March 4, 1855, and took his seat December 3, 1855; vacancy in this class from March 4, 1855, to December 2, 1855.
[8] Elected for the term beginning March 4, 1855, and took his seat February 16, 1857; vacancy in this class from March 4, 1855, to January 12, 1857.
[9] Died November 9, 1856.
[10] Appointed to fill vacancy caused by death of John M. Clayton, and took his seat December 4, 1856.
[11] Elected January 14, 1857, to fill vacancy caused by death of John M. Clayton, but did not take his seat until March 4, 1857.

GEORGIA—Continued

REPRESENTATIVES

James L. Seward, *Thomasville*
Martin J. Crawford, *Columbus*
Robert P. Trippe, *Forsyth*
Hiram Warner, *Greenville*
John H. Lumpkin, *Rome*
Howell Cobb, *Athens*
Nathaniel G. Foster, *Madison*
Alexander H. Stephens, *Crawfordville*

ILLINOIS

SENATORS

Stephen A. Douglas, *Chicago*
Lyman Trumbull, *Alton*

REPRESENTATIVES

Elihu B. Washburne, *Galena*
James H. Woodworth, *Chicago*
Jesse O. Norton, *Joliet*
James Knox, *Knoxville*
William A. Richardson,[12] *Quincy*
Jacob C. Davis,[13] *Warsaw*
Thomas L. Harris, *Petersburg*
James C. Allen,[14] *Palestine*
James L. D. Morrison,[15] *Belleville*
Samuel S. Marshall,[16] *McLeansboro*

INDIANA

SENATORS

Jesse D. Bright, *Madison*
Graham N. Fitch,[17] *Logansport*

REPRESENTATIVES

Smith Miller, *Patoka*
William H. English, *Lexington*
George G. Dunn, *Bedford*
William Cumback, *Greensburg*
David P. Holloway, *Richmond*
Lucien Barbour, *Indianapolis*
Harvey D. Scott, *Terre Haute*
Daniel Mace, *La Fayette*
Schuyler Colfax, *South Bend*
Samuel Brenton, *Fort Wayne*
John U. Pettit, *Wabash*

IOWA

SENATORS

George W. Jones, *Dubuque*
James Harlan,[18] *Mount Pleasant*

REPRESENTATIVES

Augustus Hall,[19] *Keosauqua*
James Thorington, *Davenport*

KENTUCKY

SENATORS

John B. Thompson, *Harrodsburg*
John J. Crittenden, *Frankfort*

REPRESENTATIVES

Henry C. Burnett, *Cadiz*
John P. Campbell, *Belleview*
Warner L. Underwood, *Bowling Green*
Albert G. Talbott, *Danville*
Joshua H. Jewett, *Elizabethtown*
John M. Elliott, *Prestonburg*
Humphrey Marshall, *Springport*
Alexander K. Marshall, *Nicholasville*
Leander M. Cox, *Flemingsburg*
Samuel F. Swope, *Falmouth*

LOUISIANA

SENATORS

Judah P. Benjamin, *New Orleans*
John Slidell, *New Orleans*

REPRESENTATIVES

George Eustis, Jr.,[20] *New Orleans*
Miles Taylor, *Donaldsonville*
Thomas G. Davidson, *East Feliciana*
John M. Sandidge, *Pineville*

MAINE

SENATORS

Hannibal Hamlin,[21] *Hampden*
Amos Nourse,[22] *Bath*
William Pitt Fessenden, *Portland*

REPRESENTATIVES

John M. Wood, *Portland*
John J. Perry, *Oxford*
Ebenezer Knowlton, *South Montville*
Samuel P. Benson, *Winthrop*
Israel Washburn, Jr., *Orono*
Thomas J. D. Fuller,[23] *Calais*

MARYLAND

SENATORS

James A. Pearce, *Chestertown*
Thomas G. Pratt, *Annapolis*

REPRESENTATIVES

James A. Stewart, *Cambridge*
James B. Ricaud, *Chestertown*
J. Morrison Harris, *Baltimore*
H. Winter Davis, *Baltimore*
Henry W. Hoffman, *Cumberland*
Thomas F. Bowie, *Upper Marlboro*

MASSACHUSETTS

SENATORS

Charles Sumner, *Boston*
Henry Wilson, *Natick*

REPRESENTATIVES

Robert B. Hall, *Plymouth*
James Buffinton, *Fall River*
William S. Damrell, *Dedham*
Linus B. Comins, *Roxbury*
Anson Burlingame, *Cambridge*
Timothy Davis, *Gloucester*
Nathaniel P. Banks, *Waltham*
Chauncey L. Knapp, *Lowell*
Alexander De Witt, *Oxford*
Calvin C. Chaffee, *Springfield*
Mark Trafton, *Westfield*

MICHIGAN

SENATORS

Lewis Cass, *Detroit*
Charles E. Stuart, *Kalamazoo*

REPRESENTATIVES

William A. Howard, *Detroit*
Henry Waldron, *Hillsdale*
David S. Walbridge, *Kalamazoo*
George W. Peck, *Lansing*

MISSISSIPPI

SENATORS

Stephen Adams, *Aberdeen*
Albert G. Brown, *Newton*

REPRESENTATIVES

Daniel B. Wright, *Salem*
Hendley S. Bennett, *Grenada*
William Barksdale, *Columbus*
William A. Lake, *Vicksburg*
John A. Quitman, *Natchez*

MISSOURI

SENATORS

Henry S. Geyer, *St. Louis*
James S. Green,[24] *Canton*

REPRESENTATIVES

Luther M. Kennett, *St. Louis*
Gilchrist Porter, *Hannibal*
James J. Lindley, *Monticello*
Mordecai Oliver, *Richmond*
John G. Miller,[25] *Boonville*
Thomas P. Akers,[26] *Lexington*
John S. Phelps, *Springfield*
Samuel Caruthers, *Cape Girardeau*

---

[12] Resigned August 25, 1856.
[13] Elected to fill vacancy caused by resignation of William A. Richardson, and took his seat December 4, 1856.
[14] Election contested by William B. Archer, and seat declared vacant July 18, 1856; subsequently elected, and took his seat December 1, 1856.
[15] Elected to fill vacancy caused by resignation of Representative-elect Lyman Trumbull, who was elected Senator before the beginning of the Congress, and took his seat December 1, 1856. Philip B. Fouke claimed the seat, contesting the election of Lyman Trumbull, but the House, on April 10, 1856, decided he was not entitled to it, and that the seat was vacant.
[16] Election unsuccessfully contested by L. Jay S. Turney.
[17] Elected for the term beginning March 4, 1855, and took his seat February 9, 1857; vacancy in this class from March 4, 1855, to February 3, 1857.
[18] Seat declared vacant by resolution, January 12, 1857; subsequently elected, and took his seat January 29, 1857.
[19] Election unsuccessfully contested by R. L. B. Clarke.
[20] Election unsuccessfully contested by Albert Fabre.
[21] Resigned January 7, 1857, having been elected Governor.
[22] Elected to fill vacancy caused by resignation of Hannibal Hamlin, and took his seat January 24, 1857.
[23] Election unsuccessfully contested by James A. Milliken.
[24] Elected for the term beginning March 4, 1855, and took his seat January 21, 1857; vacancy in this class from March 4, 1855, to January 11, 1857.
[25] Died May 11, 1856; never qualified owing to illness.
[26] Elected to fill vacancy caused by death of John G. Miller, and took his seat August 18, 1856.

NEW HAMPSHIRE

SENATORS

John P. Hale,[27] *Dover*
James Bell,[28] *Laconia*

REPRESENTATIVES

James Pike, *South Newmarket*
Mason W. Tappan, *Bradford*
Aaron H. Cragin, *Lebanon*

NEW JERSEY

SENATORS

John R. Thompson, *Princeton*
William Wright, *Newark*

REPRESENTATIVES

Isaiah D. Clawson, *Woodstown*
George R. Robbins, *Hamilton Square*
James Bishop, *New Brunswick*
George Vail, *Morristown*
Alexander C. M. Pennington, *Newark*

NEW YORK

SENATORS

William H. Seward, *Auburn*
Hamilton Fish, *New York*

REPRESENTATIVES

William W. Valk, *Flushing*
James S. T. Stranahan, *Brooklyn*
Guy R. Pelton, *New York City*
John Kelly, *New York City*
Thomas R. Whitney, *New York City*
John Wheeler, *New York City*
Thomas Child, Jr.,[29] *New York City*
Abram Wakeman, *New York City*
Bayard Clarke, *New York City*
Ambrose S. Murray, *Goshen*
Rufus H. King, *Catskill*
Killian Miller, *Hudson*
Russell Sage, *Troy*
Samuel Dickson, *New Scotland*
Edward Dodd, *Argyle*
George A. Simmons, *Keeseville*
Francis E. Spinner, *Mohawk*
Thomas R. Horton, *Fultonville*
Jonas A. Hughston, *Delhi*
Orsamus B. Matteson,[30] *Utica*
Henry Bennett, *New Berlin*
Andrew Z. McCarty, *Pulaski*
William A. Gilbert,[31] *Adams*
Amos P. Granger, *Syracuse*
Edwin B. Morgan, *Aurora*
Andrew Oliver, *Penn Yan*
John M. Parker, *Owego*
William H. Kelsey, *Geneseo*
John Williams, *Rochester*

Benjamin Pringle, *Batavia*
Thomas T. Flagler, *Lockport*
Solomon G. Haven, *Buffalo*
Francis S. Edwards,[32] *Fredonia*

NORTH CAROLINA

SENATORS

David S. Reid, *Pleasantville*
Asa Biggs, *Williamston*

REPRESENTATIVES

Robert T. Paine, *Edenton*
Thomas Ruffin, *Goldsboro*
Warren Winslow, *Fayetteville*
Lawrence O'B. Branch, *Raleigh*
Edwin G. Reade, *Roxboro*
Richard C. Puryear, *Huntsville*
F. Burton Craige, *Salisbury*
Thomas L. Clingman, *Asheville*

OHIO

SENATORS

Benjamin F. Wade, *Jefferson*
George E. Pugh, *Cincinnati*

REPRESENTATIVES

Timothy C. Day, *Cincinnati*
John Scott Harrison, *Cleves*
Lewis D. Campbell, *Hamilton*
Matthias H. Nichols, *Lima*
Richard Mott, *Toledo*
Jonas R. Emrie, *Hillsboro*
Aaron Harlan, *Yellow Springs*
Benjamin Stanton, *Bellefontaine*
Cooper K. Watson, *Tiffin*
Oscar F. Moore, *Portsmouth*
Valentine B. Horton, *Pomeroy*
Samuel Galloway, *Columbus*
John Sherman, *Mansfield*
Philemon Bliss, *Elyria*
William R. Sapp, *Mount Vernon*
Edward Ball, *Zanesville*
Charles J. Albright, *Cambridge*
Benjamin F. Leiter, *Canton*
Edward Wade, *Cleveland*
Joshua R. Giddings, *Jefferson*
John A. Bingham, *Cadiz*

PENNSYLVANIA

SENATORS

Richard Brodhead, *Easton*
William Bigler,[33] *Philadelphia*

REPRESENTATIVES

Thomas B. Florence, *Philadelphia*
Job R. Tyson, *Philadelphia*
William Millward, *Philadelphia*

Jacob Broom, *Philadelphia*
John Cadwalader, *Philadelphia*
John Hickman, *West Chester*
Samuel C. Bradshaw, *Quakertown*
J. Glancy Jones, *Reading*
Anthony E. Roberts, *Lancaster*
John C. Kunkel, *Harrisburg*
James H. Campbell, *Pottsville*
Henry M. Fuller, *Wilkes-Barre*
Asa Packer, *Mauch Chunk*
Galusha A. Grow, *Glenwood*
John J. Pearce, *Williamsport*
Lemuel Todd, *Carlisle*
David F. Robison, *Chambersburg*
John R. Edie, *Somerset*
John Covode, *Lockport*
Jonathan Knight, *East Bethlehem*
David Ritchie, *Pittsburgh*
Samuel A. Purviance, *Butler*
John Allison, *New Brighton*
David Barclay, *Punxsutawney*
John Dick, *Meadville*

RHODE ISLAND

SENATORS

Charles T. James, *Providence*
Philip Allen, *Providence*

REPRESENTATIVES

Nathaniel B. Durfee, *Tiverton*
Benjamin B. Thurston, *Hopkinton*

SOUTH CAROLINA

SENATORS

Andrew P. Butler, *Edgefield*
Josiah J. Evans, *Society Hill*

REPRESENTATIVES

John McQueen, *Marlboro*
William Aiken, *Charleston*
Laurence M. Keitt,[34] *Orangeburg*
Preston S. Brooks,[35] *Ninety Six*
James L. Orr, *Anderson*
William W. Boyce, *Winnsboro*

TENNESSEE

SENATORS

John Bell, *Nashville*
James C. Jones, *Memphis*

REPRESENTATIVES

Albert G. Watkins, *Panther Springs*
William H. Sneed, *Knoxville*
Samuel A. Smith, *Charleston*
John H. Savage, *Smithville*
Charles Ready, *Murfreesboro*
George W. Jones, *Fayetteville*

---

[27] Elected to fill vacancy caused by death of Charles G. Atherton, in preceding Congress, and took his seat December 4, 1855; vacancy in this class from July 16, 1854, to July 29, 1855.
[28] Elected for the term beginning March 4, 1855, and took his seat December 3, 1855; vacancy in this class

from March 4, 1855, to July 29, 1855.
[29] Never took his seat owing to prolonged illness.
[30] Resigned February 27, 1857.
[31] Resigned February 28, 1857.
[32] Resigned February 28, 1857.
[33] Elected for term beginning March 4, 1855, and took

his seat January 28, 1856; vacancy in this class from March 4, 1855, to January 13, 1856.
[34] Resigned July 16, 1856; subsequently reelected, and took his seat August 6, 1856.
[35] Resigned July 14, 1856; subsequently reelected and took his seat August 1, 1856; died January 27, 1857.

TENNESSEE—Continued

REPRESENTATIVES—continued

John V. Wright, *Purdy*
Felix K. Zollicoffer, *Nashville*
Emerson Etheridge, *Dresden*
Thomas Rivers, *Somerville*

TEXAS

SENATORS

Sam Houston, *Huntsville*
Thomas J. Rusk, *Nacogdoches*

REPRESENTATIVES

Lemuel D. Evans, *Marshall*
Peter H. Bell, *Austin*

VERMONT

SENATORS

Solomon Foot, *Rutland*
Jacob Collamer, *Woodstock*

REPRESENTATIVES

James Meacham,[36] *Middlebury*
George T. Hodges,[37] *Rutland*
Justin S. Morrill, *Strafford*
Alvah Sabin, *Georgia*

VIRGINIA

SENATORS

James M. Mason, *Winchester*
Robert M. T. Hunter, *Lloyds*

REPRESENTATIVES

Thomas H. Bayly,[38] *Accomac*
Muscoe R. H. Garnett,[39] *Lloyds*
John S. Millson, *Norfolk*
John S. Caskie, *Richmond*
William O. Goode, *Boydton*
Thomas S. Bocock, *Appomattox*
Paulus Powell, *Amherst*
William Smith, *Warrenton*
Charles J. Faulkner, *Martinsburg*
John Letcher, *Lexington*
Zedekiah Kidwell, *Fairmount*
John S. Carlile, *Clarksburg*
Henry A. Edmundson, *Salem*
Fayette, McMullen, *Rye Cove*

WISCONSIN

SENATORS

Henry Dodge, *Dodgeville*
Charles Durkee, *Kenosha*

REPRESENTATIVES

Daniel Wells, Jr., *Milwaukee*
Cadwallader C. Washburn, *Mineral Point*
Charles Billingshurst, *Juneau*

TERRITORY OF KANSAS

DELEGATE

John W. Whitfield,[40] *Tecumseh*

TERRITORY OF MINNESOTA

DELEGATE

Henry M. Rice, *St. Paul*

TERRITORY OF NEBRASKA

DELEGATE

Bird B. Chapman,[41] *Omaha City*

TERRITORY OF NEW MEXICO

DELEGATE

José Manuel Gallegos,[42] *Albuquerque*
Miguel A. Otero,[43] *Albuquerque*

TERRITORY OF OREGON

DELEGATE

Joseph Lane, *Winchester*

TERRITORY OF UTAH

DELEGATE

John M. Bernhisel, *Salt Lake City*

TERRITORY OF WASHINGTON

DELEGATE

J. Patton Anderson, *Olympia*

---

[36] Died August 23, 1856.
[37] Elected to fill vacancy caused by death of James Meacham, and took his seat December 1, 1856.
[38] Died June 23, 1856.
[39] Elected to fill vacancy caused by death of Thomas H. Bayly, and took his seat December 1, 1856.
[40] Presented credentials as a Delegate-elect to the Thirty-fourth Congress and served from March 4,

1855, until August 1, 1856, when the seat was declared vacant, the election having been unsuccessfully contested by Andrew H. Reeder; again elected to the Thirty-fourth Congress to fill vacancy caused by action of the House in declaring the seat vacant, and served from December 9, 1856, until March 3, 1857; this election also was unsuccessfully contested by Andrew H. Reeder.

[41] Election unsuccessfully contested by Hiram P. Bennett.
[42] Served until July 23, 1856; succeeded by Miguel A. Otero, who contested his election.
[43] Successfully contested the election of José Manuel Gallegos, and took his seat July 23, 1856.

THIRTY-FIFTH CONGRESS

MARCH 4, 1857, TO MARCH 3, 1859

FIRST SESSION—*December 7, 1857, to June 14, 1858*

SECOND SESSION—*December 6, 1858, to March 3, 1859*

SPECIAL SESSIONS OF THE SENATE—*March 4, 1857, to March 14, 1857; June 15, 1858, to June 16, 1858*

VICE PRESIDENT OF THE UNITED STATES—JOHN C. BRECKINRIDGE, of Kentucky

PRESIDENT PRO TEMPORE OF THE SENATE—JAMES M. MASON,[1] of Virginia; THOMAS J. RUSK,[2] of Texas; BENJAMIN FITZPATRICK,[3] of Alabama

SECRETARY OF THE SENATE—ASBURY DICKENS, of North Carolina

SERGEANT AT ARMS OF THE SENATE—DUNNING R. MCNAIR, of Pennsylvania

---

SPEAKER OF THE HOUSE OF REPRESENTATIVES—JAMES L. ORR,[4] of South Carolina

CLERK OF THE HOUSE—WILLIAM CULLOM, of Tennessee; JAMES C. ALLEN,[5] of Illinois

SERGEANT AT ARMS OF THE HOUSE—ADAM J. GLOSSBRENNER, of Pennsylvania

DOORKEEPER OF THE HOUSE—ROBERT B. HACKNEY, of Virginia

ALABAMA

SENATORS

Benjamin Fitzpatrick, *Wetumpka*
Clement C. Clay, Jr., *Huntsville*

REPRESENTATIVES

James A. Stallworth, *Evergreen*
Eli S. Shorter, *Eufaula*
James F. Dowdell, *Chambers*
Sydenham Moore, *Greensboro*
George S. Houston, *Athens*
Williamson R. W. Cobb, *Bellefonte*
Jabez L. M. Curry, *Talladega*

ARKANSAS

SENATORS

William K. Sebastian, *Helena*
Robert W. Johnson, *Pine Bluff*

REPRESENTATIVES

Alfred B. Greenwood, *Bentonville*
Edward A. Warren, *Camden*

CALIFORNIA

SENATORS

William M. Gwin, *San Francisco*
David C. Broderick, *San Francisco*

REPRESENTATIVES

Joseph C. McKibbin, *Downieville*
Charles L. Scott, *Sonora*

CONNECTICUT

SENATORS

Lafayette S. Foster, *Norwich*
James Dixon, *Hartford*

REPRESENTATIVES

Ezra Clark, Jr., *Hartford*
Samuel Arnold, *Haddam*
Sidney Dean, *Putman*
William D. Bishop, *Bridgeport*

DELAWARE

SENATORS

James A. Bayard, *Wilmington*
Martin W. Bates, *Dover*

REPRESENTATIVE

William G. Whiteley, *New Castle*

FLORIDA

SENATORS

Stephen R. Mallory, *Key West*
David Levy Yulee, *Homasassa*

REPRESENTATIVE

George S. Hawkins, *Pensacola*

GEORGIA

SENATORS

Robert Toombs, *Washington*
Alfred Iverson, *Columbus*

REPRESENTATIVES

James L. Seward, *Thomasville*
Martin J. Crawford, *Columbus*
Robert P. Trippe, *Forsyth*
Lucius J. Gartrell, *Atlanta*
Augustus R. Wright, *Rome*
James Jackson, *Athens*
Joshua Hill, *Madison*
Alexander H. Stephens, *Crawfordville*

---

[1] Elected March 4, 1857 (special session of the Senate).
[2] Elected March 14, 1857 (special session of the Senate).
[3] Elected December 7, 1857; March 29, 1858; June 14, 1858; January 25, 1859.
[4] Elected December 7, 1857.
[5] Elected December 7, 1857.

ILLINOIS

SENATORS

Stephen A. Douglas, *Chicago*
Lyman Trumbull, *Alton*

REPRESENTATIVES

Elihu B. Washburne, *Galena*
John F. Farnsworth, *Chicago*
Owen Lovejoy, *Princeton*
William Kellogg, *Canton*
Isaac N. Morris, *Quincy*
Thomas L. Harris,[6] *Petersburg*
Charles D. Hodges,[7] *Carrollton*
Aaron Shaw, *Lawrenceville*
Robert Smith, *Alton*
Samuel S. Marshall, *McLeansboro*

INDIANA

SENATORS[8]

Jesse D. Bright, *Jeffersonville*
Graham N. Fitch, *Logansport*

REPRESENTATIVES

James Lockhart,[9] *Evansville*
William E. Niblack,[10] *Vincennes*
William H. English, *Lexington*
James Hughes, *Bloomington*
James B. Foley, *Greensburg*
David Kilgore, *Yorktown*
James M. Gregg, *Danville*
John G. Davis, *Rockville*
James Wilson, *Crawfordsville*
Schuyler Colfax, *South Bend*
Samuel Brenton,[11] *Fort Wayne*
Charles Case,[12] *Fort Wayne*
John U. Pettit, *Wabash*

IOWA

SENATORS

George W. Jones, *Dubuque*
James Harlan, *Mount Pleasant*

REPRESENTATIVES

Samuel R. Curtis, *Keokuk*
Timothy Davis, *Dubuque*

KENTUCKY

SENATORS

John B. Thompson, *Harrodsburg*
John J. Crittenden, *Frankfort*

REPRESENTATIVES

Henry C. Burnett, *Cadiz*
Samuel O. Peyton, *Hartford*
Warner L. Underwood, *Bowling Green*
Albert G. Talbott, *Danville*
Joshua H. Jewett, *Elizabethtown*
John M. Elliott, *Prestonburg*
Humphrey Marshall, *Springport*
James B. Clay, *Lexington*
John C. Mason, *Owingsville*
John W. Stevenson, *Covington*

LOUISIANA

SENATORS

Judah P. Benjamin, *New Orleans*
John Slidell, *New Orleans*

REPRESENTATIVES

George Eustis, Jr., *New Orleans*
Miles Taylor, *Donaldsonville*
Thomas G. Davidson, *East Feliciana*
John M. Sandidge, *Pineville*

MAINE

SENATORS

William Pitt Fessenden, *Portland*
Hannibal Hamlin, *Hampden*

REPRESENTATIVES

John M. Wood, *Portland*
Charles J. Gilman, *Brunswick*
Nehemiah Abbott, *Belfast*
Freeman H. Morse, *Bath*
Israel Washburn, Jr., *Orono*
Stephen C. Foster, *Pembroke*

MARYLAND

SENATORS

James A. Pearce, *Chestertown*
Anthony Kennedy, *Baltimore*

REPRESENTATIVES

James A. Stewart, *Cambridge*
James B. Ricaud, *Chestertown*
J. Morrison Harris,[13] *Baltimore*
H. Winter Davis,[14] *Baltimore*
Jacob M. Kunkel, *Frederick*
Thomas F. Bowie, *Upper Marlboro*

MASSACHUSETTS

SENATORS

Charles Sumner,[15] *Boston*
Henry Wilson, *Natick*

REPRESENTATIVES

Robert B. Hall, *Plymouth*
James Buffinton, *Fall River*
William S. Damrell, *Dedham*
Linus B. Comins, *Boston*
Anson Burlingame, *Cambridge*
Timothy Davis, *Gloucester*
Nathaniel P. Banks,[16] *Waltham*
Daniel W. Gooch,[17] *Melrose*
Chauncey L. Knapp, *Lowell*
Eli Thayer, *Worcester*
Calvin C. Chaffee, *Springfield*
Henry L. Dawes, *North Adams*

MICHIGAN

SENATORS

Charles E. Stuart, *Kalamazoo*
Zachariah Chandler, *Detroit*

REPRESENTATIVES

William A. Howard, *Detroit*
Henry Waldron, *Hillsdale*
David S. Walbridge, *Kalamazoo*
De Witt C. Leach, *Lansing*

MINNESOTA [18]

SENATORS

Henry M. Rice,[19] *St. Paul*
James Shields,[20] *St. Paul*

REPRESENTATIVES [21]

James M. Cavanaugh, *Chatfield*
William W. Phelps, *Red Wing*

MISSISSIPPI

SENATORS

Albert G. Brown, *Newton*
Jefferson Davis, *Hurricane*

REPRESENTATIVES

Lucius Q. C. Lamar, *Abbeville*
Reuben Davis, *Aberdeen*
William Barksdale, *Columbus*
Otho R. Singleton, *Canton*

---

[6] Died November 24, 1858, before the commencement of the Thirty-sixth Congress, to which he had been reelected.

[7] Elected to fill vacancy caused by death of Thomas L. Harris, and took his seat January 20, 1859.

[8] A protest of certain members of the legislature was presented, in the preceding Congress, against the legality of the election of both Mr. Fitch and Mr. Bright, setting out "they were not elected by the legislature, but by a convocation of a portion of the members thereof, not authorized by State law, legislative resolution, or constitutional provision"; both the Senators were seated upon their credentials, and the credentials and protest were referred to the Committee on the Judiciary; the committee reported, May 24, 1858, that the sitting Senators were entitled to their seats, and this report was agreed to June 12, 1858. On January 24, 1859, a memorial of the State of Indiana was presented representing that it was the wish of the State that Henry S. Lane and William M. McCarty be admitted to seats as the only legally chosen Senators; February 3, 1859, the Senate Committee on the Judiciary, to which was referred the memorial, reported there was no vacancy in the Senate from the State of Indiana, and that the election of Messrs. Lane and McCarty was void; the Senate agreed to this report February 14, 1859.

[9] Died September 7, 1857, before Congress assembled.

[10] Elected to fill vacancy caused by death of James Lockhart, and took his seat December 7, 1857.

[11] Died March 29, 1857.

[12] Elected to fill vacancy caused by the death of Samuel Brenton, and took his seat December 7, 1857.

[13] Election unsuccessfully contested by William Pinkney Whyte.

[14] Election unsuccessfully contested by Henry P. Brooks.

[15] Owing to ill health was present in this Congress but one day (December 7, 1857).

[16] Resigned December 24, 1857, having been elected Governor.

[17] Elected to fill vacancy caused by resignation of Nathaniel P. Banks, and took his seat January 21, 1858.

[18] Admitted as a State into the Union May 11, 1858.

[19] Took his seat May 12, 1858; term to expire, as determined by lot, March 3, 1863.

[20] Took his seat May 12, 1858; term to expire, as determined by lot, March 3, 1859.

[21] Credentials of James M. Cavanaugh and William W. Phelps were presented on May 13, 1858, and referred to the Committee on Elections "to inquire into and report upon the right of these gentlemen to be admitted and sworn as Members of this House," and on May 22, 1858, the committee resolution "that they be admitted and sworn" was adopted; took their seats the same day.

John A. Quitman,[22] *Natchez*
John J. McRae,[23] *State Line*

MISSOURI

SENATORS

James S. Green, *Canton*
Trusten Polk, *St. Louis*

REPRESENTATIVES

Francis P. Blair, Jr., *St. Louis*
Thomas L. Anderson, *Palmyra*
John B. Clark,[24] *Fayette*
James Craig, *St. Joseph*
Samuel H. Woodson, *Independence*
John S. Phelps, *Springfield*
Samuel Caruthers, *Cape Girardeau*

NEW HAMPSHIRE

SENATORS

James Bell,[25] *Laconia*
Daniel Clark,[26] *Manchester*
John P. Hale, *Dover*

REPRESENTATIVES

James Pike, *Sanbornton Bridge*
Mason W. Tappan, *Bradford*
Aaron H. Cragin, *Lebanon*

NEW JERSEY

SENATORS

John R. Thomson, *Princeton*
William Wright, *Newark*

REPRESENTATIVES

Isaiah D. Clawson, *Woodstown*
George R. Robbins, *Hamilton Square*
Garnett B. Adrain, *New Brunswick*
John Huyler, *Hackensack*
Jacob R. Wortendyke, *Jersey City*

NEW YORK

SENATORS

William H. Seward, *Auburn*
Preston King, *Ogdensburg*

REPRESENTATIVES

John A Searing, *Hempstead Branch*
George Taylor, *Brooklyn*
Daniel E. Sickles, *New York City*
John Kelly,[27] *New York City*
Thomas J. Barr,[28] *New York City*
William B. Maclay, *New York City*
John Cochrane, *New York City*

Elijah Ward, *New York City*
Horace F. Clark, *New York City*
John B. Haskin, *Fordham*
Ambrose S. Murray, *Goshen*
William F. Russell, *Saugerties*
John Thompson, *Poughkeepsie*
Abram B. Olin, *Troy*
Erastus Corning, *Albany*
Edward Dodd, *Argyle*
George W. Palmer, *Plattsburg*
Francis E. Spinner, *Mohawk*
Clark B. Cochrane, *Schenectady*
Oliver A. Morse, *Cherry Valley*
Orsamus B. Matteson, *Utica*
Henry Bennett, *New Berlin*
Henry C. Goodwin, *Hamilton*
Charles B. Hoard, *Watertown*
Amos P. Granger, *Syracuse*
Edwin B. Morgan, *Aurora*
Emory B. Pottle, *Naples*
John M. Parker, *Owego*
William H. Kelsey, *Geneseo*
Samuel G. Andrews, *Rochester*
Judson W. Sherman, *Angelica*
Silas M. Burroughs, *Medina*
Israel T. Hatch, *Buffalo*
Reuben E. Fenton, *Frewsburg*

NORTH CAROLINA

SENATORS

David S. Reid, *Pleasantville*
Asa Biggs,[29] *Williamston*
Thomas L. Clingman,[30] *Asheville*

REPRESENTATIVES

Henry M. Shaw, *Indian Town*
Thomas Ruffin, *Goldsboro*
Warren Winslow, *Fayetteville*
Lawrence O'B. Branch, *Raleigh*
John A. Gilmer, *Greensboro*
Alfred M. Scales, *Madison*
F. Burton Craige, *Salisbury*
Thomas L. Clingman,[31] *Asheville*
Zebulon B. Vance,[32] *Asheville*

OHIO

SENATORS

Benjamin F. Wade, *Jefferson*
George E. Pugh, *Cincinnati*

REPRESENTATIVES

George H. Pendleton, *Cincinnati*
William S. Groesbeck, *Cincinnati*
Lewis D. Campbell,[33] *Hamilton*
Clement L. Vallandigham,[34] *Dayton*

Matthias H. Nichols, *Lima*
Richard Mott, *Toledo*
Joseph R. Cockerill, *West Union*
Aaron Harlan, *Yellow Springs*
Benjamin Stanton, *Bellefontaine*
Lawrence W. Hall, *Bucyrus*
Joseph Miller, *Chillicothe*
Valentine B. Horton, *Pomeroy*
Samuel S. Cox, *Columbus*
John Sherman, *Mansfield*
Philemon Bliss, *Elyria*
Joseph Burns, *Coshocton*
Cydnor B. Tompkins, *McConnellsville*
William Lawrence, *Washington*
Benjamin F. Leiter, *Canton*
Edward Wade, *Cleveland*
Joshua R. Giddings, *Jefferson*
John A. Bingham, *Cadiz*

OREGON [35]

SENATORS

Joseph Lane,[36] *Winchester*
Delazon Smith,[37] *Portland*

REPRESENTATIVE

La Fayette Grover,[38] *Salem*

PENNSYLVANIA

SENATORS

William Bigler, *Clearfield*
Simon Cameron, *Harrisburg*

REPRESENTATIVES

Thomas B. Florence, *Philadelphia*
Edward Joy Morris, *Philadelphia*
James Landy, *Philadelphia*
Henry M. Phillips, *Philadelphia*
Owen Jones, *Cabinet*
John Hickman, *West Chester*
Henry Chapman, *Doylestown*
J. Glancy Jones,[39] *Reading*
William H. Keim,[40] *Reading*
Anthony E. Roberts, *Lancaster*
John C. Kunkel, *Harrisburg*
William L. Dewart, *Sunbury*
John G. Montgomery,[41] *Danville*
Paul Leidy,[42] *Danville*
William H. Dimmick, *Honesdale*
Galusha A. Grow, *Glenwood*
Allison White, *Lock Haven*
John A. Ahl, *Newville*
Wilson Reilly, *Chambersburg*
John R. Edie, *Somerset*
John Covode, *Lockport*
William Montgomery, *Washington*

---

[22] Died July 17, 1858.
[23] Elected to fill vacancy caused by death of John A. Quitman, and took his seat December 7, 1858.
[24] Elected to fill vacancy caused by resignation of Representative-elect James S. Green (before the beginning of the congressional term), who had later been elected Senator, and took his seat December 7, 1857.
[25] Died May 26, 1857.
[26] Elected to fill vacancy caused by death of James Bell, and took his seat December 7, 1857.
[27] Resigned December 25, 1858.
[28] Elected to fill vacancy caused by resignation of John Kelly, and took his seat January 17, 1859.

[29] Resigned May 5, 1858.
[30] Appointed to fill vacancy caused by resignation of Asa Biggs, and took his seat December 6, 1858; subsequently elected.
[31] Resigned May 7, 1858, having been elected Senator.
[32] Elected to fill vacancy caused by resignation of Thomas L. Clingman, and took his seat December 7, 1858.
[33] Served until May 25, 1858; succeeded by Clement L. Vallandigham, who contested his election.
[34] Successfully contested the election of Lewis D. Campbell, and took his seat May 25, 1858.

[35] Admitted as a State into the Union February 14, 1859.
[36] Took his seat February 14, 1859; term to expire, as determined by lot, March 3, 1861.
[37] Took his seat February 14, 1859; term to expire, as determined by lot, March 3, 1859.
[38] Took his seat February 15, 1859.
[39] Resigned October 30, 1858.
[40] Elected to fill vacancy caused by resignation of J. Glancy Jones, and took his seat December 7, 1858.
[41] Died April 24, 1857, before Congress assembled.
[42] Elected to fill vacancy caused by death of John G. Montgomery, and took his seat December 7, 1857.

PENNSYLVANIA—Continued

REPRESENTATIVES—continued

David Ritchie, *Pittsburgh*
Samuel A. Purviance, *Butler*
William Stewart, *Mercer*
James L. Gillis, *Ridgway*
John Dick, *Meadville*

RHODE ISLAND

SENATORS

Philip Allen, *Providence*
James F. Simmons, *Providence*

REPRESENTATIVES

Nathaniel B. Durfee, *Tiverton*
William D. Brayton, *Warwick*

SOUTH CAROLINA

SENATORS

Andrew P. Butler,[43] *Edgefield*
James H. Hammond,[44] *Beech Island*
Josiah J. Evans,[45] *Society Hill*
Arthur P. Hayne,[46] *Charleston*
James Chestnut, Jr.,[47] *Kershaw*

REPRESENTATIVES

John McQueen, *Marlboro*
William P. Miles, *Charleston*
Laurence M. Keitt, *Orangeburg*
Milledge L. Bonham, *Edgefield*
James L. Orr, *Anderson*
William W. Boyce, *Winnsboro*

TENNESSEE

SENATORS

John Bell, *Nashville*
Andrew Johnson, *Greeneville*

REPRESENTATIVES

Albert G. Watkins, *Panther Springs*
Horace Maynard, *Knoxville*
Samuel A. Smith, *Charleston*
John H. Savage, *Smithville*
Charles Ready, *Murfreesboro*
George W. Jones, *Fayetteville*

John V. Wright, *Purdy*
Felix K. Zollicoffer, *Nashville*
John D. C. Atkins, *Paris*
William T. Avery, *Memphis*

TEXAS

SENATORS

Sam Houston, *Huntsville*
Thomas J. Rusk,[48] *Nacogdoches*
J. Pinckney Henderson,[49] *Marshville*
Matthias Ward,[50] *Jefferson*

REPRESENTATIVES

John H. Reagan, *Palestine*
Guy M. Bryan, *Brazoria*

VERMONT

SENATORS

Solomon Foot, *Rutland*
Jacob Collamer, *Woodstock*

REPRESENTATIVES

Eliakim P. Walton, *Montpelier*
Justin S. Morrill, *Strafford*
Homer E. Royce, *Berkshire*

VIRGINIA

SENATORS

James M. Mason, *Winchester*
Robert M. T. Hunter, *Lloyds*

REPRESENTATIVES

Muscoe R. H. Garnett, *Lovettsville*
John S. Millson, *Norfolk*
John S. Caskie, *Richmond*
William O. Goode, *Boydton*
Thomas S. Bocock, *Appomattox*
Paulus Powell, *Amherst*
William Smith, *Warrenton*
Charles J. Faulkner, *Martinsburg*
John Letcher, *Lexington*
Sherrard Clemens, *Wheeling*
Albert G. Jenkins, *Green Bottom*
Henry A. Edmundson, *Salem*
George W. Hopkins, *Abington*

WISCONSIN

SENATORS

Charles Durkee, *Kenosha*
James R. Doolittle, *Racine*

REPRESENTATIVES

John F. Potter, *East Troy*
Cadwallader C. Washburn, *Mineral Point*
Charles Billinghurst, *Juneau*

TERRITORY OF KANSAS

DELEGATE

Marcus J. Parrott, *Leavenworth*

TERRITORY OF MINNESOTA

DELEGATE

William W. Kingsbury,[51] *Endion*

TERRITORY OF NEBRASKA

DELEGATE

Fenner Ferguson,[52] *Belleview*

TERRITORY OF NEW MEXICO

DELEGATE

Miguel A. Otero, *Albuquerque*

TERRITORY OF OREGON

DELEGATE

Joseph Lane,[53] *Winchester*

TERRITORY OF UTAH

DELEGATE

John M. Bernhisel, *Salt Lake City*

TERRITORY OF WASHINGTON

DELEGATE

Isaac I. Stevens, *Olympia*

---

[43] Died May 25, 1857.
[44] Elected to fill vacancy caused by death of Andrew P. Butler, and took his seat January 7, 1858.
[45] Died May 6, 1858.
[46] Appointed to fill vacancy caused by death of Josiah J. Evans, and took his seat May 20, 1858.
[47] Elected to fill vacancy caused by death of Josiah J. Evans, and took his seat January 5, 1859.
[48] Died July 29, 1857.

[49] Elected to fill vacancy caused by death of Thomas J. Rusk, and took his seat March 1, 1858; died June 4, 1858.
[50] Appointed to fill vacancy caused by death of J. Pinckney Henderson, and took his seat December 6, 1858.
[51] Served until May 11, 1858, when a portion of the Territory was granted statehood; the House decided that the remainder was "without any legally organ-

ized government and not entitled to a Delegate in Congress," although William W. Kingsbury and Alpheus G. Fuller both claimed to have been elected.
[52] Election unsuccessfully contested by Bird B. Chapman.
[53] Served until February 14, 1859, when the Territory of Oregon was granted statehood; then became one of the Senators from the new State.

THIRTY-SIXTH CONGRESS

MARCH 4, 1859, TO MARCH 3, 1861

FIRST SESSION—*December 5, 1859, to June 25, 1860*

SECOND SESSION—*December 3, 1860, to March 3, 1861*

SPECIAL SESSIONS OF THE SENATE—*March 4, 1859, to March 10, 1859; June 26, 1860, to June 28, 1860*

VICE PRESIDENT OF THE UNITED STATES—JOHN C. BRECKINRIDGE, of Kentucky

PRESIDENT PRO TEMPORE OF THE SENATE—BENJAMIN FITZPATRICK,[1] of Alabama; JESSE D. BRIGHT,[2] of Indiana; SOLOMON FOOT,[3] of Vermont

SECRETARY OF THE SENATE—ASBURY DICKENS, of North Carolina

SERGEANT AT ARMS OF THE SENATE—DUNNING R. MCNAIR, of Pennsylvania

---

SPEAKER OF THE HOUSE OF REPRESENTATIVES—WILLIAM PENNINGTON,[4] of New Jersey

CLERK OF THE HOUSE—JAMES C. ALLEN, of Illinois; JOHN W. FORNEY,[5] of Pennsylvania

SERGEANT AT ARMS OF THE HOUSE—ADAM J. GLOSSBRENNER, of Pennsylvania; HENRY W. HOFFMAN,[6] of Maryland

DOORKEEPER OF THE HOUSE—GEORGE MARSTON, of New Hampshire

ALABAMA [7]

SENATORS

Benjamin Fitzpatrick,[8] *Wetumpka*
Clement C. Clay, Jr.,[8] *Huntsville*

REPRESENTATIVES

James A. Stallworth,[9] *Evergreen*
James L. Pugh,[9] *Eufaula*
David Clopton,[9] *Tuskegee*
Sydenham Moore,[9] *Greensboro*
George S. Houston,[9] *Athens*
Williamson R. W. Cobb,[10] *Bellefonte*
Jabez L. M. Curry,[9] *Talladega*

ARKANSAS

SENATORS

William K. Sebastian, *Helena*
Robert W. Johnson, *Pine Bluff*

REPRESENTATIVES

Thomas C. Hindman, *Helena*
Albert Rust, *Little Rock*

CALIFORNIA

SENATORS

William M. Gwin, *San Francisco*
David C. Broderick,[11] *San Francisco*
Henry P. Haun,[12] *Marysville*
Milton S. Latham,[13] *San Francisco*

REPRESENTATIVES

Charles L. Scott, *Sonora*
John C. Burch, *Weaverville*

CONNECTICUT

SENATORS

Lafayette S. Foster, *Norwich*
James Dixon, *Hartford*

REPRESENTATIVES

Dwight Loomis, *Rockville*
John Woodruff, *New Haven*
Alfred A. Burnham, *Windham*
Orris S. Ferry, *Norwalk*

DELAWARE

SENATORS

James A. Bayard, *Wilmington*
Willard Saulsbury, *Georgetown*

REPRESENTATIVE

Willam G. Whiteley, *New Castle*

FLORIDA [14]

SENATORS

Stephen R. Mallory,[15] *Pensacola*
David Levy Yulee,[15] *Homasassa*

---

[1] Elected March 9, 1859 (special session); December 19, 1859; February 20, 1860; June 26, 1860, in special session.
[2] Elected June 12, 1860.
[3] Elected February 16, 1861.
[4] Elected February 1, 1860, upon the forty-fourth viva voce vote.
[5] Elected February 3, 1860.
[6] Elected February 3, 1860.
[7] Seceded from the Union January 11, 1861.
[8] On January 21, 1861, David Levy Yulee, Stephen R. Mallory, Clement C. Clay, Jr., Benjamin Fitzpatrick, and Jefferson Davis announced in the Senate their intention to withdraw from the body, and they did withdraw. The Senate Journal of this date makes no record or notice of the action. On the day following the Vice President was directed to fill vacancies in the standing committees, and on January 24, 1861, the Vice President announced the appointment of members to fill places upon the standing committees, including the assignments theretofore held by the Senators named.

[9] Presented a signed communication declaring his intention, and withdrew January 21, 1861.
[10] Presented a signed communication declaring his intention, and withdrew January 30, 1861.
[11] Died September 16, 1859.
[12] Appointed to fill vacancy caused by death of David C. Broderick, and took his seat December 5, 1859.
[13] Elected to fill vacancy caused by death of David C. Broderick, and took his seat March 5, 1860.
[14] Seceded from the Union January 11, 1861.
[15] Withdrew January 21, 1861.

FLORIDA—Continued

REPRESENTATIVE

George S. Hawkins,[16] *Pensacola*

GEORGIA [17]

SENATORS

Robert Toombs,[18] *Washington*
Alfred Iverson,[19] *Columbus*

REPRESENTATIVES

Peter E. Love,[20] *Thomasville*
Martin J. Crawford,[20] *Columbus*
Thomas Hardeman, Jr.,[20] *Macon*
Lucius J. Gartrell,[20] *Atlanta*
John W. H. Underwood,[20] *Rome*
James Jackson,[20] *Athens*
Joshua Hill,[21] *Madison*
John J. Jones,[20] *Waynesboro*

ILLINOIS

SENATORS

Stephen A. Douglas, *Chicago*
Lyman Trumbull, *Alton*

REPRESENTATIVES

Elihu B. Washburne, *Galena*
John F. Farnsworth, *Chicago*
Owen Lovejoy, *Princeton*
William Kellogg, *Canton*
Isaac N. Morris, *Quincy*
John A. McClernand,[22] *Springfield*
James C. Robinson, *Marshall*
Philip B. Fouke, *Belleville*
John A. Logan, *Benton*

INDIANA

SENATORS

Jesse D. Bright, *Jeffersonville*
Graham N. Fitch, *Logansport*

REPRESENTATIVES

William E. Niblack, *Vincennes*
William H. English, *Lexington*
William McKee Dunn, *Madison*
William S. Holman, *Lawrenceburg*
David Kilgore, *Muncietown*
Albert G. Porter, *Indianapolis*
John G. Davis, *Rockville*
James Wilson, *Crawfordsville*
Schuyler Colfax, *South Bend*
Charles Case, *Fort Wayne*
John U. Pettit, *Wabash*

IOWA

SENATORS

James Harlan, *Mount Pleasant*
James W. Grimes, *Burlington*

REPRESENTATIVES

Samuel R. Curtis, *Keokuk*
William Vandever, *Dubuque*

KANSAS [23]

SENATORS

Vacant [24]

REPRESENTATIVE

Martin F. Conway,[25] *Lawrence*

KENTUCKY

SENATORS

John J. Crittenden, *Frankford*
Lazarus W. Powell, *Henderson*

REPRESENTATIVES

Henry C. Burnett, *Cadiz*
Samuel O. Peyton, *Hartford*
Francis N. Bristow, *Elkton*
William C. Anderson,[26] *Danville*
John Young Brown, *Elizabethtown*
Green Adams, *Barboursville*
Robert Mallory, *La Grange*
William E. Simms, *Paris*
Laban T. Moore, *Louisa*
John W. Stevenson, *Covington*

LOUISIANA [27]

SENATORS

Judah P. Benjamin,[28] *New Orleans*
John Slidell,[28] *New Orleans*

REPRESENTATIVES

John E. Bouligny, *New Orleans*
Miles Taylor,[29] *Donaldsonville*
Thomas G. Davidson,[30] *Baton Rouge*
John M. Landrum,[31] *Shreveport*

MAINE

SENATORS

William Pitt Fessenden, *Portland*
Hannibal Hamlin,[32] *Hampden*
Lot M. Morrill,[33] *Augusta*

REPRESENTATIVES

Daniel E. Somes, *Biddeford*
John J. Perry, *Oxford*
Ezra B. French, *Damariscotta*
Freeman H. Morse, *Bath*
Israel Washburn, Jr.,[34] *Orono*
Stephen Coburn,[35] *Skowhegan*
Stephen C. Foster, *Pembroke*

MARYLAND

SENATORS

James A. Pearce, *Chestertown*
Anthony Kennedy, *Baltimore*

REPRESENTATIVES

James A. Stewart, *Cambridge*
Edwin H. Webster, *Bel Air*
J. Morrison Harris,[36] *Baltimore*
H. Winter Davis,[37] *Baltimore*
Jacob M. Kunkel, *Frederick*
George W. Hughes, *West River*

MASSACHUSETTS

SENATORS

Charles Sumner, *Boston*
Henry Wilson, *Natick*

REPRESENTATIVES

Thomas D. Eliot, *New Bedford*
James Buffinton, *Fall River*
Charles F. Adams, *Quincy*
Alexander H. Rice, *Boston*
Anson Burlingame, *Cambridge*
John B. Alley, *Lynn*
Daniel W. Gooch, *Melrose*
Charles R. Train, *Framingham*
Eli Thayer, *Worcester*
Charles Delano, *Northampton*
Henry L. Dawes, *North Adams*

MICHIGAN

SENATORS

Zachariah Chandler, *Detroit*
Kinsley S. Bingham, *Kensington*

REPRESENTATIVES

George B. Cooper,[38] *Jackson*
William A. Howard,[39] *Detroit*
Henry Waldron, *Hillsdale*
Francis W. Kellogg, *Grand Rapids*
De Witt C. Leach, *Lansing*

---

[16] Withdrew January 21, 1861.
[17] Seceded from the Union January 28, 1861.
[18] Did not occupy his seat after February 4, 1861.
[19] Presented a signed communication declaring his intention, and withdrew January 28, 1861.
[20] Joined with his colleagues in presenting a signed communication declaring their intention, and withdrew January 23, 1861.
[21] Resigned January 23, 1861 (in written communication addressed to the Speaker).
[22] Elected to fill vacancy caused by death of Representative-elect Thomas L. Harris, in preceding Congress, and took his seat December 5, 1859.

[23] Admitted as a State into the Union January 29, 1861.
[24] Senators not elected to this Congress.
[25] Took his seat January 30, 1861.
[26] Election unsuccessfully contested by James S. Chrisman.
[27] Seceded from the Union January 26, 1861.
[28] Withdrew February 4, 1861.
[29] Bade formal adieu and withdrew February 5, 1861.
[30] Did not occupy his seat after February 5, 1861.
[31] Did not occupy his seat after February 5, 1861.
[32] Resigned effective January 17, 1861.

[33] Elected to fill vacancy caused by resignation of Hannibal Hamlin, and took his seat January 17, 1861.
[34] Resigned effective January 1, 1861.
[35] Elected to fill vacancy caused by resignation of Israel Washburn, Jr., and took his seat January 2, 1861.
[36] Election unsuccessfully contested by William P. Preston.
[37] Election unsuccessfully contested by William G. Harrison.
[38] Served until May 15, 1860; succeeded by William A. Howard, who contested his election.
[39] Successfully contested the election of George B. Cooper, and took his seat May 15, 1860.

MINNESOTA

SENATORS

Henry M. Rice, *St. Paul*
Morton S. Wilkinson, *Mankato*

REPRESENTATIVES

Cyrus Aldrich, *Minneapolis*
William Windom, *Winona*

MISSISSIPPI [40]

SENATORS

Albert G. Brown,[41] *Terry*
Jefferson Davis,[42] *Hurricane*

REPRESENTATIVES

Lucius Q. C. Lamar,[43] *Abbeville*
Reuben Davis,[41] *Aberdeen*
William Barksdale,[41] *Columbus*
Otho R. Singleton,[41] *Canton*
John J. McRae,[41] *State Line*

MISSOURI

SENATORS

James S. Green, *Canton*
Trusten Polk, *St. Louis*

REPRESENTATIVES

John R. Barret,[44] *St. Louis*
Francis P. Blair, Jr.,[45] *St. Louis*
Thomas L. Anderson, *Palmyra*
John B. Clark, *Fayette*
James Craig, *St. Joseph*
Samuel H. Woodson, *Independence*
John S. Phelps, *Springfield*
John W. Noell, *Perryville*

NEW HAMPSHIRE

SENATORS

John P. Hale, *Dover*
Daniel Clark, *Manchester*

REPRESENTATIVES

Gilman Marston, *Exeter*
Mason W. Tappan, *Bradford*
Thomas M. Edwards, *Keene*

NEW JERSEY

SENATORS

John R. Thomson, *Princeton*
John C. Ten Eyck, *Mount Holly*

REPRESENTATIVES

John T. Nixon, *Bridgeton*
John L. N. Stratton, *Mount Holly*

Garnett B. Adrain, *New Brunswick*
Jetur R. Riggs, *Paterson*
William Pennington, *Newark*

NEW YORK

SENATORS

William H. Seward, *Auburn*
Preston King, *Ogdensburg*

REPRESENTATIVES

Luther C. Carter, *Flushing*
James Humphrey, *Brooklyn*
Daniel E. Sickles,[46] *New York City*
Thomas J. Barr, *New York City*
William B. Maclay, *New York City*
John Cochrane, *New York City*
George Briggs, *New York City*
Horace F. Clark, *New York City*
John B. Haskin, *Fordham*
Charles H. Van Wyck, *Bloomingburg*
William S. Kenyon, *Kingston*
Charles L. Beale, *Kinderhook*
Abram B. Olin, *Troy*
John H. Reynolds, *Albany*
James B. McKean, *Saratoga Springs*
George W. Palmer, *Plattsburg*
Francis E. Spinner, *Mohawk*
Clark B. Cochrane, *Schenectady*
James H. Graham, *Delhi*
Roscoe Conkling, *Utica*
R. Holland Duell, *Cortland*
M. Lindley Lee, *Fulton*
Charles B. Hoard, *Watertown*
Charles B. Sedgwick, *Syracuse*
Martin Butterfield, *Palmyra*
Emory B. Pottle, *Naples*
Alfred Wells, *Ithaca*
William Irvine, *Corning*
Alfred Ely, *Rochester*
Augustus Frank, *Warsaw*
Silas M. Burroughs,[47] *Medina*
Edwin R. Reynolds,[48] *Albion*
Elbridge G. Spaulding, *Buffalo*
Reuben E. Fenton, *Frewsburg*

NORTH CAROLINA

SENATORS

Thomas L. Clingman, *Asheville*
Thomas Bragg, *Raleigh*

REPRESENTATIVES

William N. H. Smith, *Murfreesboro*
Thomas Ruffin, *Goldsboro*
Warren Winslow, *Fayetteville*
Lawrence O'B. Branch, *Raleigh*

John A. Gilmer, *Greensboro*
James M. Leach, *Lexington*
F. Burton Craige, *Salisbury*
Zebulon B. Vance, *Asheville*

OHIO

SENATORS

Benjamin F. Wade, *Jefferson*
George E. Pugh, *Cincinnati*

REPRESENTATIVES

George H. Pendleton, *Cincinnati*
John A. Gurley, *Cincinnati*
Clement L. Vallandigham, *Dayton*
William Allen, *Greenville*
James M. Ashley, *Toledo*
William Howard, *Batavia*
Thomas Corwin, *Lebanon*
Benjamin Stanton, *Bellefontaine*
John Carey, *Carey*
Carey A. Trimble, *Chillicothe*
Charles D. Martin, *Lancaster*
Samuel S. Cox, *Columbus*
John Sherman, *Mansfield*
Cyrus Spink,[49] *Wooster*
Harrison G. O. Blake,[50] *Medina*
William Helmick, *New Philadelphia*
Cydnor B. Tompkins, *McConnellsville*
Thomas C. Theaker, *Bridgeport*
Sidney Edgerton, *Tallmadge*
Edward Wade, *Cleveland*
John Hutchins, *Warren*
John A. Bingham, *Cadiz*

OREGON

SENATORS

Joseph Lane, *Winchester*
Edward D. Baker,[51] *Oregon City*

REPRESENTATIVE

Lansing Stout, *Portland*

PENNSYLVANIA

SENATORS

William Bigler, *Clearfield*
Simon Cameron, *Harrisburg*

REPRESENTATIVES

Thomas B. Florence, *Philadelphia*
Edward Joy Morris, *Philadelphia*
John P. Verree, *Philadelphia*
William Millward, *Philadelphia*
John Wood, *Conshohocken*
John Hickman, *West Chester*
Henry C. Longnecker, *Allentown*

[40] Seceded from the Union January 9, 1861.
[41] Withdrew January 12, 1861.
[42] Withdrew January 21, 1861.
[43] Retired in December, 1860.
[44] Served until June 8, 1860; succeeded by Francis P. Blair, Jr., who contested his election; subsequently elected to fill vacancy caused by resignation of Francis P. Blair, Jr., and took his seat December 3, 1860.

[45] Successfully contested the election of John R. Barret, and took his seat June 8, 1860; resigned June 25, 1860.
[46] Election unsuccessfully contested by Amor J. Williamson.
[47] Died June 3, 1860.
[48] Elected to fill vacancy caused by the death of Silas M. Burroughs, and took his seat December 5, 1860.

[49] Died May 31, 1859, before Congress assembled.
[50] Elected to fill vacancy caused by the death of Cyrus Spink, and took his seat December 5, 1859.
[51] Elected for the term beginning March 4, 1859, and took his seat December 5, 1860; vacancy in this class from March 4, 1859, to October 1, 1860.

PENNSYLVANIA—Continued

REPRESENTATIVES—continued

John Schwartz,[52] *Reading*
Jacob K. McKenty,[53] *Reading*
Thaddeus Stevens, *Lancaster*
John W. Killinger, *Lebanon*
James H. Campbell, *Pottsville*
George W. Scranton, *Scranton*
William H. Dimmick, *Honesdale*
Galusha A. Grow, *Glenwood*
James T. Hale, *Bellefonte*
Benjamin F. Junkin, *New Bloomfield*
Edward McPherson, *Gettysburg*
Samuel S. Blair, *Hollidaysburg*
John Covode, *Lockport*
William Montgomery, *Washington*
James K. Moorhead, *Pittsburgh*
Robert McKnight, *Pittsburgh*
William Stewart, *Mercer*
Chapin Hall, *Warren*
Elijah Babbitt, *Erie*

RHODE ISLAND

SENATORS

James F. Simmons, *Providence*
Henry B. Anthony, *Providence*

REPRESENTATIVES

Christopher Robinson, *Woonsocket*
William D. Brayton, *Warwick*

SOUTH CAROLINA [54]

SENATORS

James H. Hammond,[55] *Beech Island*
James Chestnut, Jr.,[56] *Camden*

REPRESENTATIVES

John McQueen,[57] *Marlboro*
W. Porcher Miles,[58] *Charleston*
Laurence M. Keitt,[59] *Orangeburg*
Milledge L. Bonham,[57] *Edgefield*
John D. Ashmore,[57] *Anderson*
William W. Boyce,[57] *Winnsboro*

TENNESSEE

SENATORS

Andrew Johnson, *Greeneville*
Alfred O. P. Nicholson,[60] *Columbia*

REPRESENTATIVES

Thomas A. R. Nelson, *Jonesboro*
Horace Maynard, *Knoxville*
Reese B. Brabson, *Chattanooga*
William B. Stokes, *Alexandria*
Robert H. Hatton, *Lebanon*
James H. Thomas, *Columbia*
John V. Wright, *Purdy*
James M. Quarles, *Clarksville*
Emerson Etheridge, *Dresden*
William T. Avery, *Memphis*

TEXAS [61]

SENATORS

Matthias Ward, *Jefferson*
Louis T. Wigfall,[62] *Marshall*
John Hemphill, *Austin*

REPRESENTATIVES

John H. Reagan, *Palestine*
Andrew J. Hamilton, *Austin*

VERMONT

SENATORS

Solomon Foot, *Rutland*
Jacob Collamer, *Woodstock*

REPRESENTATIVES

Justin S. Morrill, *Strafford*
Eliakim P. Walton, *Montpelier*
Homer E. Royce, *East Berkshire*

VIRGINIA

SENATORS

James M. Mason, *Winchester*
Robert M. T. Hunter, *Lloyds*

REPRESENTATIVES

Muscoe R. H. Garnett, *Loretto*
John S. Millson, *Norfolk*
Daniel C. DeJarnette, *Bowling Green*

William O. Goode,[63] *Boydton*
Roger A. Pryor,[64] *Petersburg*
Thomas S. Bocock, *Appomattox*
Shelton F. Leake, *Charlottesville*
William Smith, *Warrenton*
Alexander R. Boteler, *Shepherdstown*
John T. Harris, *Harrisonburg*
Sherrard Clemens, *Wheeling*
Albert G. Jenkins, *Green Bottom*
Henry A. Edmundson, *Salem*
Elbert S. Martin, *Lee*

WISCONSIN

SENATORS

Charles Durkee, *Kenosha*
James R. Doolittle, *Racine*

REPRESENTATIVES

John F. Potter, *East Troy*
Cadwallader C. Washburn, *La Crosse*
Charles H. Larrabee, *Horicon*

TERRITORY OF KANSAS

DELEGATE

Marcus J. Parrott,[65] *Leavenworth*

TERRITORY OF NEBRASKA

DELEGATE

Experience Estabrook,[66] *Omaha*
Samuel G. Daily,[67] *Peru*

TERRITORY OF NEW MEXICO

DELEGATE

Miguel A. Otero, *Albuquerque*

TERRITORY OF UTAH

DELEGATE

William H. Hooper, *Salt Lake City*

TERRITORY OF WASHINGTON

DELEGATE

Isaac I. Stevens, *Olympia*

---

[52] Died June 20, 1860.
[53] Elected to fill vacancy caused by death of John Schwartz, and took his seat December 3, 1860.
[54] Seceded from the Union December 20, 1860.
[55] Withdrew November 11, 1860.
[56] Withdrew November 10, 1860.
[57] Withdrew December 21, 1860, signed declaration of intention, of date December 21, 1860, which was read and laid on the table December 24, 1860.

[58] Did not occupy his seat after December 13, 1860.
[59] Did not occupy his seat after December 10, 1860.
[60] Withdrew March 3, 1861.
[61] Seceded from the Union February 1, 1861.
[62] Elected to fill vacancy caused by death of J. Pinckney Henderson, in preceding Congress, and took his seat January 4, 1860.
[63] Died July 3, 1859.

[64] Elected to fill vacancy caused by death of William O. Goode, and took his seat December 7, 1859.
[65] Served until January 29, 1861, when the Territory of Kansas was granted statehood.
[66] Served until May 18, 1860; succeeded by Samuel G. Daily, who contested his election.
[67] Successfully contested the election of Experience Estabrook, and took his seat May 18, 1860.

THIRTY-SEVENTH CONGRESS

MARCH 4, 1861, TO MARCH 3, 1863

FIRST SESSION—*July 4, 1861, to August 6, 1861*

SECOND SESSION—*December 2, 1861, to July 17, 1862*

THIRD SESSION—*December 1, 1862, to March 3, 1863*

SPECIAL SESSION OF THE SENATE—*March 4, 1861, to March 28, 1861*

———

VICE PRESIDENT OF THE UNITED STATES—HANNIBAL HAMLIN, of Maine

PRESIDENT PRO TEMPORE OF THE SENATE—SOLOMON FOOT,[1] of Vermont

SECRETARY OF THE SENATE—ASBURY DICKENS, of North Carolina; JOHN W. FORNEY,[2] of Pennsylvania

SERGEANT AT ARMS OF THE SENATE—DUNNING R. McNAIR, of Pennsylvania; GEORGE T. BROWN,[3] of Illinois

———

SPEAKER OF THE HOUSE OF REPRESENTATIVES—GALUSHA A. GROW,[4] of Pennsylvania

CLERK OF THE HOUSE—JOHN W. FORNEY, of Pennsylvania; EMERSON ETHERIDGE,[5] of Tennessee

SERGEANT AT ARMS OF THE HOUSE—HENRY W. HOFFMAN, of Maryland; EDWARD BALL,[6] of Ohio

DOORKEEPER OF THE HOUSE—IRA GOODNOW, of Vermont

ALABAMA

SENATORS

Clement C. Clay, Jr.,[7] *Huntsville*
Vacant

REPRESENTATIVES

Vacant

ARKANSAS [8]

SENATORS

William K. Sebastian,[9] *Helena*
Charles B. Mitchel,[9] *Little Rock*

REPRESENTATIVES

Vacant

CALIFORNIA

SENATORS

Milton S. Latham, *Sacramento*
James A. McDougall, *San Francisco*

REPRESENTATIVES [10]

Frederick F. Low,[11] *San Francisco*
Timothy G. Phelps,[12] *San Mateo*
Aaron A. Sargent,[12] *Nevada City*

CONNECTICUT

SENATORS

Lafayette S. Foster, *Norwich*
James Dixon, *Hartford*

REPRESENTATIVES

Alfred A. Burnham, *Windham*
James E. English, *New Haven*
Dwight Loomis, *Rockville*
George C. Woodruff, *Litchfield*

DELAWARE

SENATORS

James A. Bayard, *Wilmington*
Willard Saulsbury, *Georgetown*

REPRESENTATIVE

George P. Fisher, *Dover*

FLORIDA

SENATORS

Stephen R. Mallory,[13] *Pensacola*
Vacant

REPRESENTATIVE

Vacant

GEORGIA

SENATORS

Robert Toombs,[14] *Washington*
Vacant

REPRESENTATIVES

Vacant

---

[1] Elected March 23, 1861; July 18, 1861; January 15, 1862; March 31, 1862; June 19, 1862; and February 18, 1863.
[2] Elected July 15, 1861; William Hickey (chief clerk) was appointed acting secretary March 22, 1861, "to serve during the present infirmity of the secretary."
[3] Elected July 6, 1861.
[4] Elected July 4, 1861.
[5] Elected July 4, 1861.
[6] Elected July 5, 1861.

[7] Seat declared vacant by resolution of March 14, 1861.
[8] Seceded from the Union May 8, 1861.
[9] Expelled by resolution of July 11, 1861. The resolution with its preamble was revoked and annulled, so far as Mr. Sebastian was concerned, by resolution of the Senate of March 3, 1877.
[10] Elected September 4, 1861.
[11] Presented credentials and claimed a seat as a third representative from the State December 2, 1861;

declared not entitled to a seat by resolution of May 6, 1862; upon approval of the act of June 2, 1862, allowing the State of California an additional representative, appeared and took his seat June 3, 1862.
[12] Took his seat December 2, 1861.
[13] Seat declared vacant by resolution of March 14, 1861.
[14] Seat declared vacant by resolution of March 14, 1861.

ILLINOIS

SENATORS

Stephen A. Douglas,[15] *Chicago*
Orville H. Browning,[16] *Quincy*
William A. Richardson,[17] *Quincy*
Lyman Trumbull, *Alton*

REPRESENTATIVES

Isaac N. Arnold, *Chicago*
Philip B. Fouke, *Belleville*
William Kellogg, *Canton*
John A. Logan,[18] *Benton*
William J. Allen,[19] *Marion*
Owen Lovejoy, *Princeton*
John A. McClernand,[20] *Springfield*
Anthony L. Knapp,[21] *Jerseyville*
William A. Richardson,[22] *Quincy*
James C. Robinson, *Marshall*
Elihu B. Washburne, *Galena*

INDIANA

SENATORS

Jesse D. Bright,[23] *Jeffersonville*
Joseph A. Wright,[24] *Indianapolis*
David Turpie,[25] *Indianapolis*
Henry S. Lane, *Crawfordsville*

REPRESENTATIVES

Schuyler Colfax, *South Bend*
James A. Cravens, *Hardinsburg*
William McKee Dunn, *Madison*
William S. Holman, *Aurora*
George W. Julian, *Centerville*
John Law, *Evansville*
William Mitchell, *Kendallville*
Albert G. Porter, *Indianapolis*
John P. C. Shanks, *Jay Court House*
Daniel W. Voorhees, *Terre Haute*
Albert S. White, *Stockwell*

IOWA

SENATORS

James Harlan, *Mount Pleasant*
James W. Grimes, *Burlington*

REPRESENTATIVES

Samuel R. Curtis,[26] *Keokuk*
James F. Wilson,[27] *Fairfield*
William Vandever,[28] *Dubuque*

KANSAS

SENATORS

Samuel C. Pomeroy,[29] *Atchison*
James H. Lane,[30] *Lawrence*

REPRESENTATIVE

Martin F. Conway, *Lawrence*

KENTUCKY

SENATORS

Lazarus W. Powell, *Henderson*
John C. Breckinridge,[31] *Lexington*
Garrett Davis,[32] *Paris*

REPRESENTATIVES

Henry C. Burnett,[33] *Cadiz*
Samuel L. Casey,[34] *Caseyville*
John J. Crittenden, *Frankfort*
George W. Dunlap, *Lancaster*
Henry Grider, *Bowling Green*
Aaron Harding, *Greensburg*
James S. Jackson,[35] *Hopkinsville*
George H. Yeaman,[36] *Owensboro*
Robert Mallory, *La Grange*
John W. Menzies, *Covington*
William H. Wadsworth, *Maysville*
Charles A. Wickliffe, *Bardstown*

LOUISIANA

SENATORS

Judah P. Benjamin,[37] *New Orleans*
Vacant

REPRESENTATIVES

Benjamin F. Flanders,[38] *New Orleans*
Michael Hahn,[39] *New Orleans*

MAINE

SENATORS

William Pitt Fessenden, *Portland*
Lot M. Morrill, *Augusta*

REPRESENTATIVES

Samuel C. Fessenden, *Rockland*
John N. Goodwin, *South Berwick*
Anson P. Morrill, *Readfield*
Frederick A. Pike, *Calais*
John H. Rice, *Foxcroft*
Charles W. Walton,[40] *Auburn*
Thomas A. D. Fessenden,[41] *Auburn*

MARYLAND

SENATORS

James A. Pearce,[42] *Chestertown*
Thomas H. Hicks,[43] *Cambridge*
Anthony Kennedy, *Ellicotts Mills*

REPRESENTATIVES

Charles B. Calvert, *Bladensburg*
John W. Crisfield, *Princess Anne*
Cornelius L. L. Leary, *Baltimore*
Henry May, *Baltimore*
Francis Thomas, *Frankville*
Edwin H. Webster, *Bel Air*

MASSACHUSETTS

SENATORS

Charles Sumner, *Boston*
Henry Wilson, *Natick*

REPRESENTATIVES

Charles F. Adams,[44] *Quincy*
Benjamin F. Thomas,[45] *Boston*
John B. Alley, *Lynn*
William Appleton,[46] *Boston*
Samuel Hooper,[47] *Boston*
Goldsmith F. Bailey,[48] *Fitchburg*
Amasa Walker,[49] *North Brookfield*
James Buffinton, *Fall River*
Henry L. Dawes, *North Adams*
Charles Delano, *Northampton*
Thomas D. Eliot, *New Bedford*
Daniel W. Gooch, *Melrose*
Alexander H. Rice, *Boston*
Charles R. Train, *Framingham*

[15] Died June 3, 1861.
[16] Appointed to fill vacancy caused by death of Stephen A. Douglas, and took his seat July 4, 1861.
[17] Elected to fill vacancy caused by death of Stephen A. Douglas, and took his seat January 30, 1863.
[18] Resigned April 2, 1862.
[19] Elected to fill vacancy caused by resignation of John A. Logan, and took his seat June 2, 1862.
[20] Resigned October 28, 1861.
[21] Elected to fill vacancy caused by resignation of John A. McClernand, and took his seat December 12, 1861.
[22] Resigned January 29, 1863, having been elected Senator.
[23] Expelled February 5, 1862.
[24] Appointed to fill vacancy caused by expulsion of Jesse D. Bright, and took his seat March 3, 1862.
[25] Elected to fill vacancy caused by expulsion of Jesse D. Bright, and took his seat January 22, 1863.
[26] Resigned August 4, 1861.
[27] Elected to fill vacancy caused by resignation of Samuel R. Curtis, and took his seat December 2, 1861.
[28] Took his seat July 4, 1861; election contested by Le Grand Byington. By resolution of January 20,

1863, House declared contestee had not been entitled to a seat since September 24, 1861, the day he was mustered into the military service of the United States as a colonel of volunteers. Case of contestant remained undisposed of at close of the Congress.
[29] Took his seat July 4, 1861; term to expire, as determined by lot, March 3, 1867.
[30] Took his seat July 4, 1861; term to expire, as determined by lot, March 3, 1865. Election unsuccessfully contested by Frederick P. Stanton.
[31] Expelled by resolution of December 4, 1861.
[32] Elected to fill vacancy caused by expulsion of John C. Breckinridge, and took his seat December 23, 1861.
[33] Expelled by resolution of December 3, 1861.
[34] Elected to fill vacancy caused by expulsion of Henry C. Burnett, and took his seat March 10, 1862.
[35] Resigned December 13, 1861, to enter the Union Army (killed at the battle of Perryville, Ky., October 8, 1862).
[36] Elected to fill vacancy caused by death of James S. Jackson, and took his seat December 1, 1862.
[37] Seat declared vacant by resolution of March 14, 1861.

[38] Credentials presented December 19, 1862; declared entitled to his seat by resolution of February 17, 1863, and took his seat February 23, 1863.
[39] Credentials presented December 22, 1862; declared entitled to his seat by resolution of February 17, 1863, and took his seat the same day.
[40] Resigned May 26, 1862.
[41] Elected to fill vacancy caused by resignation of Charles W. Walton, and took his seat December 1, 1862.
[42] Died December 20, 1862.
[43] Appointed to fill vacancy caused by death of James A. Pearce, and took his seat January 14, 1863.
[44] Resigned May 1, 1861, having been appointed minister to England.
[45] Elected to fill vacancy caused by resignation of Charles F. Adams, and took his seat July 4, 1861.
[46] Resigned September 27, 1861.
[47] Elected to fill vacancy caused by resignation of William Appleton, and took his seat December 2, 1861.
[48] Died May 8, 1862.
[49] Elected to fill vacancy caused by death of Goldsmith F. Bailey, and took his seat December 1, 1862.

MICHIGAN

SENATORS

Zachariah Chandler, *Detroit*
Kinsley S. Bingham,[50] *Oak Grove*
Jacob M. Howard,[51] *Detroit*

REPRESENTATIVES

Fernando C. Beaman, *Adrian*
Bradley F. Granger, *Ann Arbor*
Francis W. Kellogg, *Grand Rapids*
Rowland E. Trowbridge, *Birmingham*

MINNESOTA

SENATORS

Henry M. Rice, *St. Paul*
Morton S. Wilkinson, *Mankato*

REPRESENTATIVES

Cyrus Aldrich, *Minneapolis*
William Windom, *Winona*

MISSISSIPPI

SENATORS

Albert G. Brown,[52] *Terry*
Jefferson Davis,[52] *Hurricane*

REPRESENTATIVES

Vacant

MISSOURI

SENATORS

Trusten Polk,[53] *St. Louis*
John B. Henderson,[54] *Louisiana*
Waldo Porter Johnson,[55] *Osceola*
Robert Wilson,[56] *St. Joseph*

REPRESENTATIVES

Francis P. Blair, Jr.,[57] *St. Louis*
John W. Noell, *Perryville*
Elijah H. Norton, *Platte City*
John S. Phelps, *Springfield*
John W. Reid,[58] *Jefferson City*
Thomas L. Price,[59] *Jefferson City*
James S. Rollins, *Columbia*
John B. Clark,[60] *Fayette*
William A. Hall,[61] *Huntsville*

NEW HAMPSHIRE

SENATORS

John P. Hale, *Dover*
Daniel Clark, *Manchester*

REPRESENTATIVES

Thomas M. Edwards, *Keene*
Gilman Marston, *Exeter*
Edward H. Rollins, *Concord*

NEW JERSEY

SENATORS

John R. Thomson,[62] *Princeton*
Richard S. Field,[63] *Princeton*
James W. Wall,[64] *Burlington*
John C. Ten Eyck, *Mount Holly*

REPRESENTATIVES

George T. Cobb, *Morristown*
John T. Nixon, *Bridgeton*
Nehemiah Perry, *Newark*
William G. Steele, *Somerville*
J. L. N. Stratton, *Mount Holly*

NEW YORK

SENATORS

Preston King, *Ogdensburg*
Ira Harris, *Albany*

REPRESENTATIVES

Stephen Baker, *Poughkeepsie*
Jacob P. Chamberlain, *Seneca Falls*
Ambrose W. Clark, *Watertown*
Frederick A. Conkling, *New York City*
Roscoe Conkling, *Utica*
Erastus Corning, *Albany*
Isaac C. Delaplaine, *New York City*
Alexander S. Diven, *Elmira*
R. Holland Duell, *Cortland*
Alfred Ely, *Rochester*
Reuben E. Fenton, *Frewsburg*
Richard Franchot, *Schenectady*
Augustus Frank, *Warsaw*
Edward Haight, *West Chester*
James E. Kerrigan, *New York City*
William E. Lansing, *Chittenango*
James B. McKean, *Saratoga Springs*
Moses F. Odell, *Brooklyn*
Abram B. Olin, *Troy*
Theodore M. Pomeroy, *Auburn*
Charles B. Sedgwick, *Syracuse*
Socrates N. Sherman, *Ogdensburg*
Edward H. Smith, *Smithtown*
Elbridge G. Spaulding, *Buffalo*

John B. Steele, *Kingston*
Burt Van Horn, *Newfane*
Robert B. Van Valkenburg, *Bath*
Charles H. Van Wyck, *Bloomingburg*
Chauncey Vibbard, *Schenectady*
William Wall, *Brooklyn*
Elijah Ward, *New York City*
William A. Wheeler, *Malone*
Benjamin Wood, *New York City*

NORTH CAROLINA [65]

SENATORS

Thomas L. Clingman,[66] *Asheville*
Thomas Bragg,[67] *Raleigh*

REPRESENTATIVES

Vacant

OHIO

SENATORS

Benjamin F. Wade, *Jefferson*
Salmon P. Chase,[68] *Cincinnati*
John Sherman,[69] *Mansfield*

REPRESENTATIVES

William Allen, *Greenville*
James M. Ashley, *Toledo*
John A. Bingham, *Cadiz*
Harrison G. O. Blake, *Medina*
Samuel S. Cox, *Columbus*
William P. Cutler, *Constitution*
Sidney Edgerton, *Tallmadge*
John A. Gurley, *Cincinnati*
Thomas Corwin,[70] *Lebanon*
Richard A. Harrison,[71] *London*
Valentine B. Horton, *Pomeroy*
John Hutchins, *Warren*
James R. Morris, *Woodsfield*
Warren P. Noble, *Tiffin*
Robert H. Nugen, *Newcomerstown*
George H. Pendleton, *Cincinnati*
Albert G. Riddle, *Cleveland*
Samuel Shellabarger, *Springfield*
Carey A. Trimble, *Chillicothe*
Clement L. Vallandigham, *Dayton*
Chilton A. White, *Georgetown*
John Sherman,[72] *Mansfield*
Samuel T. Worcester,[73] *Norwalk*

---

[50] Died October 5, 1861.
[51] Elected to fill vacancy caused by death of Kinsley S. Bingham, and took his seat January 17, 1862.
[52] Did not attend during this Congress; seat declared vacant by resolution of March 14, 1861.
[53] Expelled by resolution of January 10, 1862.
[54] Appointed to fill vacancy caused by expulsion of Trusten Polk, and took his seat January 29, 1862; subsequently elected.
[55] Expelled by resolution of January 10, 1862.
[56] Appointed to fill vacancy caused by expulsion of Waldo P. Johnson, and took his seat January 24, 1862.
[57] Resigned in July, 1862.
[58] Did not occupy his seat after August 3, 1861; expelled by resolution of December 2, 1861.

[59] Elected to fill vacancy caused by expulsion of John W. Reid, and took his seat January 21, 1862.
[60] Expelled by resolution of July 13, 1861, never having qualified.
[61] Elected to fill vacancy caused by expulsion of John B. Clark, and took his seat January 20, 1862.
[62] Died September 12, 1862.
[63] Appointed to fill vacancy caused by death of John R. Thomson, and took his seat December 1, 1862.
[64] Elected to fill vacancy caused by death of John R. Thomson, and took his seat January 21, 1863.
[65] Seceded from the Union May 21, 1861. Charles Henry Foster claimed the right to represent the first congressional district.
[66] Withdrew March 28, 1861; expelled by resolution

of July 11, 1861.
[67] Withdrew March 8, 1861; expelled by resolution of July 11, 1861.
[68] Resigned March 6, 1861, having been appointed Secretary of the Treasury.
[69] Elected to fill vacancy caused by resignation of Salmon P. Chase, and took his seat March 23, 1861.
[70] Resigned March 12, 1861, having been appointed minister to Mexico.
[71] Elected to fill vacancy caused by the resignation of Thomas Corwin, and took his seat July 4, 1861.
[72] Resigned March 21, 1861, having been elected Senator.
[73] Elected to fill vacancy caused by the resignation of John Sherman, and took his seat July 4, 1861.

OREGON

SENATORS

Edward D. Baker,[74] *Oregon City*
Benjamin Stark,[75] *Portland*
Benjamin F. Harding,[76] *Salem*
James W. Nesmith, *Salem*

REPRESENTATIVES

Andrew J. Thayer,[77] *Corvallis*
George K. Shiel,[78] *Salem*

PENNSYLVANIA

SENATORS

Simon Cameron,[79] *Harrisburg*
David Wilmot,[80] *Towanda*
Edgar Cowan, *Greensburg*

REPRESENTATIVES

Sydenham E. Ancona, *Reading*
Elijah Babbitt, *Erie*
Joseph Bailey, *Newport*
E. Joy Morris,[81] *Philadelphia*
Charles J. Biddle,[82] *Philadelphia*
Samuel S. Blair, *Hollidaysburg*
James H. Campbell, *Pottsville*
Thomas B. Cooper,[83] *Coopersburg*
John D. Stiles,[84] *Allentown*
John Covode, *Lockport Station*
William Morris Davis, *Milestown*
Galusha A. Grow, *Glenwood*
James T. Hale, *Bellefonte*
John Hickman, *West Chester*
Philip Johnson, *Easton*
William D. Kelley, *Philadelphia*
John W. Killinger, *Lebanon*
Jesse Lazear, *Waynesburg*
William E. Lehman,[85] *Philadelphia*
Robert McKnight, *Pittsburgh*
Edward McPherson, *Gettysburg*
James K. Moorhead, *Pittsburgh*
John Patton, *Curwinsville*
Thaddeus Stevens, *Lancaster*
John P. Verree,[86] *Philadelphia*

John W. Wallace, *New Castle*
George W. Scranton,[87] *Scranton*
Hendrick B. Wright,[88] *Wilkes-Barre*

RHODE ISLAND

SENATORS

James F. Simmons,[89] *Providence*
Samuel G. Arnold,[90] *Providence*
Henry B. Anthony, *Providence*

REPRESENTATIVES

George H. Browne, *Providence*
William P. Sheffield, *Newport*

SOUTH CAROLINA

SENATORS

James Chesnut, Jr.,[91] *Camden*
Vacant

REPRESENTATIVES

Vacant

TENNESSEE [92]

SENATORS

Andrew Johnson,[93] *Greeneville*
Alfred O. P. Nicholson,[94] *Columbia*

REPRESENTATIVES

George W. Bridges,[95] *Athens*
Andrew J. Clements,[96] *Lafayette*
Horace Maynard,[97] *Knoxville*

TEXAS

SENATORS

John Hemphill,[98] *Austin*
Louis T. Wigfall,[99] *Marshall*

REPRESENTATIVES

Vacant

VERMONT

SENATORS

Solomon Foot, *Rutland*
Jacob Collamer, *Woodstock*

REPRESENTATIVES

Portus Baxter, *Derby Line*
Justin S. Morrill, *Strafford*
Eliakim P. Walton, *Montpelier*

VIRGINIA [100]

SENATORS

James M. Mason,[101] *Winchester*
Waitman T. Willey,[102] *Morgantown*
Robert M. T. Hunter,[103] *Lloyds*
John S. Carlile,[104] *Wheeling*

REPRESENTATIVES [105]

William G. Brown, *Kingwood*
John S. Carlile,[106] *Wheeling*
Jacob B. Blair,[107] *Parkersburg*
Joseph E. Segar,[108] *Elizabeth City*
Charles H. Upton,[109] *Falls Church*
Lewis McKenzie,[110] *Alexandria*
Kellian V. Whaley, *Ceredo*

WISCONSIN

SENATORS

James R. Doolittle, *Racine*
Timothy O. Howe, *Green Gay*

REPRESENTATIVES

Luther Hanchett,[111] *Plover*
Walter D. McIndoe,[112] *Wausau*
John F. Potter, *East Troy*
A. Scott Sloan, *Beaver Dam*

TERRITORY OF COLORADO [113]

DELEGATE

Hiram P. Bennet,[114] *Denver*

[74] Died October 21, 1861.
[75] Appointed to fill vacancy caused by death of Edward D. Baker; took his seat February 27, 1862.
[76] Elected to fill vacancy caused by death of Edward D. Baker, and took his seat December 1, 1862.
[77] Served until July 30, 1861; succeeded by George K. Shiel, who contested his election.
[78] Successfully contested the election of Andrew J. Thayer, and took his seat July 30, 1861.
[79] Resigned March 4, 1861, having been appointed Secretary of War.
[80] Elected to fill vacancy caused by resignation of Simon Cameron, and took his seat March 18, 1861.
[81] Resigned June 8, 1861, having been appointed minister resident to Turkey.
[82] Elected to fill vacancy caused by resignation of E. Joy Morris, and took his seat December 2, 1861.
[83] Died April 4, 1862.
[84] Elected to fill vacancy caused by death of Thomas B. Cooper, and took his seat June 3, 1862.
[85] Election unsuccessfully contested by John M. Butler.
[86] Election unsuccessfully contested by John Kline.
[87] Died March 24, 1861.
[88] Elected to fill vacancy caused by the death of George W. Scranton, and took his seat July 4, 1861.
[89] Resigned August 15, 1862.
[90] Elected to fill vacancy caused by resignation of James F. Simmons, and took his seat December 1, 1862.

[91] Did not attend during this Congress; expelled by resolution of July 11, 1861.
[92] Seceded from the Union June 24, 1861.
[93] Resigned March 4, 1862, to become military governor of Tennessee.
[94] Did not attend during this Congress; expelled by resolution of July 11, 1861.
[95] Elected August 1, 1861; took his seat February 25, 1863.
[96] Elected August 1, 1861; presented memorial on December 3, 1861, claiming seat, and by resolution of January 13, 1862, was declared entitled to the same; took his seat same day.
[97] Elected August 1, 1861; took his seat December 2, 1861.
[98] Did not occupy his seat after March 4, 1861; expelled by resolution of July 11, 1861.
[99] Did not occupy his seat after March 23, 1861; expelled by resolution of July 11, 1861.
[100] Seceded from the Union April 17, 1861.
[101] Withdrew March 28, 1861; expelled by resolution of July 11, 1861.
[102] Elected to fill vacancy caused by withdrawal of James M. Mason, and took his seat July 13, 1861.
[103] Withdrew March 28, 1861; expelled by resolution of July 11, 1861.
[104] Elected to fill vacancy caused by withdrawal of of Robert M. T. Hunter, and took his seat July 13, 1861.
[105] J. B. McCloud and W. W. Wing both claimed election from the second district, but on February 14,

1863, the House decided that neither was entitled to the seat; Christopher L. Graffin presented credentials from the eighth district, but on March 3, 1863, was declared not entitled to seat.
[106] Resigned July 9, 1861, having been elected Senator.
[107] Elected to fill vacancy caused by resignation of John S. Carlile, and took his seat December 2, 1861.
[108] Declared not entitled to his seat under first credentials by resolution of February 11, 1862; subsequently elected and declared entitled to seat under second credentials by resolution of May 6, 1862; qualified and took his seat the same day.
[109] Presented credentials of an election held May 23, 1861, and took his seat July 4, 1861; declared not entitled to the seat February 27, 1862. S. Ferguson Beach presented memorial denying right of Upton, and claiming seat under an election held October 24, 1861, but on March 31, 1862, was declared not entitled to same.
[110] Elected to fill vacancy caused by the unseating of Charles H. Upton, and took his seat February 16, 1863.
[111] Died November 24, 1862.
[112] Elected to fill vacancy caused by death of Luther Hanchett, and took his seat January 26, 1863.
[113] Formed from portions of the territory ceded to the United States by France by the treaty of Paris of April 30, 1803, and of that ceded by Mexico by the treaty of Guadalupe Hidalgo of February 2, 1848, and granted a Delegate in Congress by act of February 28, 1861.
[114] Took his seat December 2, 1861.

TERRITORY OF DAKOTA [115]

DELEGATE

John B. S. Todd,[116] *Fort Randall*

TERRITORY OF NEBRASKA

DELEGATE

Samuel G. Daily,[117] *Peru*

TERRITORY OF NEVADA [118]

DELEGATE

John Cradlebaugh,[119] *Carson City*

TERRITORY OF NEW MEXICO

DELEGATE

John S. Watts, *Santa Fe*

TERRITORY OF UTAH

DELEGATE

John M. Bernhisel, *Salt Lake City*

TERRITORY OF WASHINGTON

DELEGATE

William H. Wallace, *Steilacoom*

---

[115] Formed from a portion of the territory ceded to the United States by France by treaty of April 30, 1803, and granted a Delegate in Congress by act of March 2, 1861.

[116] Took his seat December 9, 1861.
[117] Election unsuccessfully contested by J. Sterling Morton.
[118] Formed from a portion of the territory ceded to the

United States by Mexico by the treaty of Guadalupe Hidalgo of February 2, 1848, and granted a Delegate in Congress by act of March 2, 1861.
[119] Took his seat December 2, 1861.

THIRTY-EIGHTH CONGRESS

MARCH 4, 1863, TO MARCH 3, 1865

FIRST SESSION—*December 7, 1863, to July 4, 1864*

SECOND SESSION—*December 5, 1864, to March 3, 1865*

SPECIAL SESSION OF THE SENATE—*March 4, 1863, to March 14, 1863*

———

VICE PRESIDENT OF THE UNITED STATES—HANNIBAL HAMLIN, of Maine

PRESIDENT PRO TEMPORE OF THE SENATE—SOLOMON FOOT,[1] of Vermont; DANIEL CLARK,[2] of New Hampshire

SECRETARY OF THE SENATE—JOHN W. FORNEY, of Pennsylvania

SERGEANT AT ARMS OF THE SENATE—GEORGE T. BROWN, of Illinois

———

SPEAKER OF THE HOUSE OF REPRESENTATIVES—SCHUYLER COLFAX,[3] of Indiana

CLERK OF THE HOUSE—EMERSON ETHERIDGE, of Tennessee; EDWARD McPHERSON,[4] of Pennsylvania

SERGEANT AT ARMS OF THE HOUSE—EDWARD BALL, of Ohio; NATHANIEL G. ORDWAY,[5] of New Hampshire

DOORKEEPER OF THE HOUSE—IRA GOODNOW, of Vermont

POSTMASTER OF THE HOUSE—WILLIAM S. KING

ALABAMA

SENATORS

Vacant

REPRESENTATIVES

Vacant

ARKANSAS

SENATORS

Vacant

REPRESENTATIVES

Vacant[6]

CALIFORNIA

SENATORS

James A. McDougall, *San Francisco*
John Conness, *Sacramento*

REPRESENTATIVES

Cornelius Cole, *Santa Cruz*

William Higby, *Mokelumne Hill*
Thomas B. Shannon, *Quincy*

CONNECTICUT

SENATORS

La Fayette S. Foster, *Norwich*
James Dixon, *Hartford*

REPRESENTATIVES

Augustus Brandegee, *New London*
Henry C. Deming, *Hartford*
James E. English, *New Haven*
John H. Hubbard, *Litchfield*

DELAWARE

SENATORS

James A. Bayard,[7] *Wilmington*
George R. Riddle,[8] *Wilmington*
Willard Saulsbury, *Georgetown*

REPRESENTATIVES

William Temple,[9] *Smyrna*
Nathaniel B. Smithers,[10] *Dover*

FLORIDA

SENATORS

Vacant

REPRESENTATIVE

Vacant

GEORGIA

SENATORS

Vacant

REPRESENTATIVES

Vacant

ILLINOIS

SENATORS

Lyman Trumbull, *Alton*
William A. Richardson, *Quincy*

---

[1] Elected March 4, 1863 (special session of the Senate); December 18, 1863; February 23, 1864; March 11, 1864; and April 11, 1864.
[2] Elected April 26, 1864; February 9, 1865.
[3] Elected December 7, 1863.
[4] Elected December 8, 1863.

[5] Elected December 8, 1863.
[6] James M. Johnson, T. M. Jacks, and Anthony A. C. Rogers presented credentials as Members-elect, but their claims were not finally disposed of. By resolution of March 3, 1865, each was allowed the sum of $2,000 for "compensation, expenses, and mileage."

[7] Resigned January 29, 1864.
[8] Elected to fill vacancy caused by resignation of James A. Bayard, and took his seat February 2, 1864.
[9] Died May 28, 1863, before Congress assembled.
[10] Elected to fill vacancy caused by death of William Temple, and took his seat December 7, 1863.

REPRESENTATIVES

James C. Allen, *Palestine*
William J. Allen, *Marion*
Isaac N. Arnold, *Chicago*
John R. Eden, *Sullivan*
John F. Farnsworth, *St. Charles*
Charles M. Harris, *Oquawka*
Anthony L. Knapp, *Jerseyville*
Owen Lovejoy,[11] *Princeton*
Ebon C. Ingersoll,[12] *Peoria*
William R. Morrison, *Waterloo*
Jesse O. Norton, *Joliet*
James C. Robinson, *Marshall*
Lewis W. Ross, *Lewistown*
John T. Stuart, *Springfield*
Elihu B. Washburne, *Galena*

INDIANA

SENATORS

Henry S. Lane, *Crawfordsville*
Thomas A. Hendricks, *Indianapolis*

REPRESENTATIVES

Schuyler Colfax, *South Bend*
James A. Cravens, *Hardinsburg*
Ebenezer Dumont, *Indianapolis*
Joseph K. Edgerton, *Fort Wayne*
Henry W. Harrington, *Madison*
William S. Holman, *Aurora*
George W. Julian, *Centerville*
John Law, *Evansville*
James F. McDowell, *Marion*
Godlove S. Orth, *La Fayette*
Daniel W. Voorhees, *Terre Haute*

IOWA

SENATORS

James Harlan, *Mount Pleasant*
James W. Grimes, *Burlington*

REPRESENTATIVES

William B. Allison, *Dubuque*
Josiah B. Grinnell,[13] *Grinnell*
Asahel W. Hubbard, *Sioux City*
John A. Kasson, *Des Moines*
Hiram Price, *Davenport*
James F. Wilson, *Fairfield*

KANSAS

SENATORS

Samuel C. Pomeroy, *Atchison*
James H. Lane, *Lawrence*

REPRESENTATIVE

A. Carter Wilder, *Lawrence*

KENTUCKY

SENATORS

Lazarus W. Powell, *Henderson*
Garrett Davis, *Paris*

REPRESENTATIVES

Lucien Anderson, *Mayfield*
Brutus J. Clay, *Paris*
Henry Grider, *Bristol*
Aaron Harding, *Greensburg*
Robert Mallory, *La Grange*
William H. Randall, *London*
Green C. Smith, *Covington*
William H. Wadsworth, *Maysville*
George H. Yeaman,[14] *Owensboro*

LOUISIANA

SENATORS

Vacant

REPRESENTATIVES

Vacant [15]

MAINE

SENATORS

William Pitt Fessenden,[16] *Portland*
Nathan A. Farwell,[17] *Rockland*
Lot M. Morrill, *Augusta*

REPRESENTATIVES

James G. Blaine, *Augusta*
Sidney Perham, *Paris*
Frederick A. Pike, *Calais*
John H. Rice, *Foxcroft*
Lorenzo D. M. Sweat, *Portland*

MARYLAND

SENATORS

Thomas H. Hicks,[18] *Cambridge*
Reverdy Johnson, *Baltimore*

REPRESENTATIVES

John A. J. Creswell, *Elkton*
Henry Winter Davis, *Baltimore*
Benjamin G. Harris, *Leonardtown*
Francis Thomas, *Frankville*
Edwin H. Webster, *Bel Air*

MASSACHUSETTS

SENATORS

Charles Sumner, *Boston*
Henry Wilson, *Natick*

REPRESENTATIVES

John B. Alley, *Lynn*
Oakes Ames, *North Easton*
John D. Baldwin, *Worcester*
George S. Boutwell, *Groton*
Henry L. Dawes, *Pittsfield*
Thomas D. Eliot, *New Bedford*
Daniel W. Gooch, *Melrose*
Samuel Hooper, *Boston*
Alexander H. Rice,[19] *Boston*
William B. Washburn, *Greenfield*

MICHIGAN

SENATORS

Zachariah Chandler, *Detroit*
Jacob M. Howard, *Detroit*

REPRESENTATIVES

Augustus C. Baldwin, *Pontiac*
Fernando C. Beaman, *Adrian*
John F. Driggs, *East Saginaw*
Francis W. Kellogg, *Grand Rapids*
John W. Longyear, *Lansing*
Charles Upson, *Coldwater*

MINNESOTA

SENATORS

Morton S. Wilkinson, *Mankato*
Alexander Ramsey, *St. Paul*

REPRESENTATIVES

Ignatius Donnelly, *Nininger*
William Windom, *Winona*

MISSISSIPPI

SENATORS

Vacant

REPRESENTATIVES

Vacant

MISSOURI

SENATORS

John B. Henderson, *Louisiana*
Robert Wilson, *St. Joseph*
B. Gratz Brown,[20] *St. Louis*

REPRESENTATIVES

Francis P. Blair, Jr.,[21] *St. Louis*
Samuel Knox,[22] *St. Louis*
Henry T. Blow, *St. Louis*
Sempronius H. Boyd, *Springfield*
William A. Hall, *Huntsville*

---

[11] Died March 25, 1864.
[12] Elected to fill vacancy caused by the death of Owen Lovejoy, and took his seat May 20, 1864.
[13] Election unsuccessfully contested by Hugh M. Martin.
[14] Election unsuccessfully contested by John H. McHenry, Jr.
[15] M. F. Bonzano, A. P. Field, W. D. Mann, T. M. Welles, and Robert W. Taliaferro presented credentials as Members-elect, but their claims were not finally disposed of.
[16] Resigned July 1, 1864, to become Secretary of the Treasury.
[17] Appointed to fill vacancy caused by resignation of William Pitt Fessenden, and took his seat December 5, 1864; subsequently elected.
[18] Died February 14, 1865.
[19] Election unsuccessfully contested by John S. Sleeper.
[20] Elected, on November 13, 1863, to fill vacancy caused by expulsion of Waldo Porter Johnson, in preceding Congress, and took his seat December 14, 1863; Robert Wilson, Senator-designate in previous Congress, attended on December 7, 1863, but the following day was declared not entitled to a seat.
[21] Served until June 10, 1864; succeeded by Samuel Knox, who contested his election.
[22] Successfully contested the election of Francis P. Blair, Jr., and took his seat June 15, 1864.

MISSOURI—Continued

REPRESENTATIVES—continued

Austin A. King, *Richmond*
Benjamin F. Loan,[23] *St. Joseph*
Joseph W. McClurg,[24] *Linn Creek*
James S. Rollins, *Columbia*
John W. Noell,[25] *Perryville*
John G. Scott,[26] *Irondale*

NEVADA [27]

SENATORS

William M. Stewart,[28] *Virginia City*
James W. Nye,[29] *Carson City*

REPRESENTATIVE

Henry G. Worthington,[30] *Austin*

NEW HAMPSHIRE

SENATORS

John P. Hale, *Dover*
Daniel Clark, *Manchester*

REPRESENTATIVES

Daniel Marcy, *Portsmouth*
James W. Patterson, *Hanover*
Edward H. Rollins, *Concord*

NEW JERSEY

SENATORS

John C. Ten Eyck, *Mount Holly*
William Wright, *Newark*

REPRESENTATIVES

George Middleton, *Allentown*
Nehemiah Perry, *Newark*
Andrew J. Rogers, *Newton*
John F. Starr, *Camden*
William G. Steele, *Somerville*

NEW YORK

SENATORS

Ira Harris, *Albany*
Edwin D. Morgan, *New York City*

REPRESENTATIVES

James Brooks, *New York City*
John W. Chanler, *New York City*
Ambrose W. Clark, *Watertown*
Freeman Clarke, *Rochester*
Erastus Corning,[31] *Albany*
John V. L. Pruyn,[32] *Albany*
Thomas T. Davis, *Syracuse*
Reuben E. Fenton,[33] *Frewsburg*
Augustus Frank, *Warsaw*

John Ganson, *Buffalo*
John A. Griswold, *Troy*
Anson Herrick, *New York City*
Giles W. Hotchkiss, *Binghamton*
Calvin T. Hulburd, *Brasher Falls*
Martin Kalbfleisch, *Brooklyn*
Orlando Kellogg, *Elizabethtown*
Francis Kernan, *Utica*
De Witt C. Littlejohn, *Oswego*
James M. Marvin, *Saratoga Springs*
Samuel F. Miller, *Franklin*
Daniel Morris, *Penn Yan*
Homer A. Nelson, *Poughkeepsie*
Moses F. Odell, *Brooklyn*
Theodore M. Pomeroy, *Auburn*
William Radford, *Yonkers*
Henry G. Stebbins,[34] *New Brighton*
Dwight Townsend,[35] *Clifton*
John B. Steele, *Kingston*
Robert B. Van Valkenburg, *Bath*
Elijah Ward, *New York City*
Charles H. Winfield, *Goshen*
Benjamin Wood, *New York City*
Fernando Wood, *New York City*

NORTH CAROLINA

SENATORS

Vacant

REPRESENTATIVES

Vacant

OHIO

SENATORS

Benjamin F. Wade, *Jefferson*
John Sherman, *Mansfield*

REPRESENTATIVES

James M. Ashley, *Toledo*
George Bliss, *Wooster*
Samuel S. Cox, *Columbus*
Ephraim R. Eckley, *Carrollton*
William E. Finck, *Somerset*
James A. Garfield, *Hiram*
Wells A. Hutchins, *Portsmouth*
William Johnston, *Mansfield*
Francis C. Le Blond, *Celina*
Alexander Long, *Cincinnati*
John F. McKinney, *Piqua*
James R. Morris, *Woodsfield*
Warren P. Noble, *Tiffin*
John O'Neill, *Zanesville*
George H. Pendleton, *Cincinnati*
Robert C. Schenck, *Dayton*
Rufus P. Spalding, *Cleveland*
Chilton A. White, *Georgetown*
Joseph W. White, *Cambridge*

OREGON

SENATORS

James W. Nesmith, *Salem*
Benjamin F. Harding, *Salem*

REPRESENTATIVE

John R. McBride, *Lafayette*

PENNSYLVANIA

SENATORS

Edgar Cowan, *Greensburg*
Charles R. Buckalew, *Bloomsburg*

REPRESENTATIVES

Sydenham E. Ancona, *Reading*
Joseph Bailey, *Newport*
John M. Broomall, *Media*
Alexander H. Coffroth, *Somerset*
John L. Dawson, *Brownsville*
Charles Denison, *Wilkes-Barre*
James T. Hale, *Bellefonte*
Philip Johnson, *Easton*
William D. Kelley, *Philadelphia*
Jesse Lazear, *Waynesburg*
Archibald McAllister, *Springfield Furnace*
William H. Miller, *Harrisburg*
James K. Moorhead, *Pittsburgh*
Amos Myers, *Clarion*
Leonard Myers,[36] *Philadelphia*
Charles O'Neill, *Philadelphia*
Samuel J. Randall, *Philadelphia*
Glenni W. Schofield, *Warren*
Thaddeus Stevens, *Lancaster*
John D. Stiles, *Allentown*
Myer Strouse, *Pottsville*
M. Russell Thayer,[37] *Chestnut Hill*
Henry W. Tracy, *Standing Stone*
Thomas Williams, *Pittsburgh*

RHODE ISLAND

SENATORS

Henry B. Anthony, *Providence*
William Sprague, *Providence*

REPRESENTATIVES

Nathan F. Dixon, *Westerly*
Thomas A. Jenckes, *Providence*

SOUTH CAROLINA

SENATORS

Vacant

REPRESENTATIVES

Vacant

---

[23] Election unsuccessfully contested by John P. Bruce.
[24] Election unsuccessfully contested by Thomas L. Price.
[25] Died March 14, 1863.
[26] Elected to fill vacancy caused by the death of John W. Noell, and took his seat December 7, 1863; election unsuccessfully contested by James Lindsay.

[27] Admitted as a State into the Union October 31, 1864.
[28] Took his seat February 1, 1865; term to expire, as determined by lot, March 3, 1869.
[29] Took his seat February 1, 1865; term to expire, as determined by lot, March 3, 1867.
[30] Took his seat December 21, 1864.
[31] Resigned October 5, 1863, before Congress assembled.

[32] Elected to fill vacancy caused by the resignation of Erastus Corning, and took his seat December 7, 1863.
[33] Resigned effective December 20, 1864.
[34] Resigned October 24, 1864.
[35] Elected to fill vacancy caused by resignation of Henry G. Stebbins, and took his seat December 5, 1864.
[36] Election unsuccessfully contested by John Kline.
[37] Election unsuccessfully contested by Charles W. Carrigan.

TENNESSEE

SENATORS

Vacant

REPRESENTATIVES

Vacant

TEXAS

SENATORS

Vacant

REPRESENTATIVES

Vacant

VERMONT

SENATORS

Solomon Foot, *Rutland*
Jacob Collamer, *Woodstock*

REPRESENTATIVES

Portus Baxter, *Derby Line*
Justin S. Morrill, *Strafford*
Frederick E. Woodbridge, *Vergennes*

VIRGINIA

SENATORS

John S. Carlile, *Clarksburg*
Lemuel J. Bowden,[38] *Williamsburg*

REPRESENTATIVES

Vacant [39]

WEST VIRGINIA [40]

SENATORS

Peter G. Van Winkle,[41] *Parkersburg*
Waitman T. Willey,[42] *Morgantown*

REPRESENTATIVES

Jacob B. Blair,[43] *Parkersburg*
William G. Brown,[43] *Kingwood*
Kellian V. Whaley,[43] *Point Pleasant*

WISCONSIN

SENATORS

James R. Doolittle, *Racine*
Timothy O. Howe, *Green Bay*

REPRESENTATIVES

James S. Brown, *Milwaukee*
Amasa Cobb, *Mineral Point*
Charles A. Eldridge, *Fond du Lac*
Walter D. McIndoe, *Wausau*
Ithamar C. Sloan, *Janesville*
Ezra Wheeler, *Berlin*

TERRITORY OF ARIZONA [44]

DELEGATE

Charles D. Poston,[45] *Tubac*

TERRITORY OF COLORADO

DELEGATE

Hiram P. Bennet, *Denver*

TERRITORY OF DAKOTA

DELEGATE

William Jayne,[46] *Yankton*
John B. S. Todd,[47] *Yankton*

TERRITORY OF IDAHO [48]

DELEGATE

William H. Wallace,[49] *Lewiston*

TERRITORY OF MONTANA [50]

DELEGATE

Samuel McLean,[51] *Bannack*

TERRITORY OF NEBRASKA

DELEGATE

Samuel G. Daily, *Peru*

TERRITORY OF NEVADA

DELEGATE

Gordon N. Mott,[52] *Carson City*

TERRITORY OF NEW MEXICO

DELEGATE

Francisco Perea,[53] *Bernalillo*

TERRITORY OF UTAH

DELEGATE

John F. Kinney, *Salt Lake City*

TERRITORY OF WASHINGTON

DELEGATE

George E. Cole, *Walla Walla*

---

[38] Died January 2, 1864. On February 17, 1865, the credentials of Joseph E. Segar, to fill vacancy caused by the death of Lemuel J. Bowden, were presented but were ordered to lie on the table; no further action taken. State unrepresented in this class from this date to October 20, 1869.

[39] Joseph E. Segar, from the first district, Lucius H. Chandler, from the second district, and Bethuel M. Kitchen, from the seventh district, presented credentials. They were declared not entitled to seats, the first two by resolution of May 17, 1864; the last named by resolution of April 16, 1864. Lewis McKenzie also claimed to have been elected from the seventh district, and was declared not entitled to the seat by resolution of February 26, 1864. The first three claimants were subsequently allowed mileage and pay to the dates of the adoption of the resolutions.

[40] Formed from a portion of the State of Virginia and admitted into the Union June 19, 1863.

[41] Took his seat December 7, 1863; term to expire, as determined by lot, March 3, 1869.

[42] Took his seat December 7, 1863; term to expire, as determined by lot, March 3, 1865.

[43] Took his seat December 7, 1863.

[44] Formed from a portion of the Territory of New Mexico and granted a Delegate in Congress by act of February 24, 1863.

[45] Took his seat December 5, 1864.

[46] Served until June 17, 1864; succeeded by John B. S. Todd, who contested his election.

[47] Successfully contested the election of William Jayne, and took his seat June 17, 1864.

[48] Formed from a portion of the territory ceded to the United States by France by treaty of April 30, 1803, and granted a Delegate in Congress by act of March 3, 1863.

[49] Took his seat February 1, 1864.

[50] Formed from a portion of the territory ceded to the United States by France by treaty of April 30, 1803, and granted a Delegate in Congress by act of May 26, 1864.

[51] Took his seat January 6, 1865.

[52] Served until October 31, 1864, when the Territory of Nevada was granted statehood.

[53] Election unsuccessfully contested by José Manuel Gallegos.

THIRTY-NINTH CONGRESS

MARCH 4, 1865, TO MARCH 3, 1867

FIRST SESSION—*December 4, 1865, to July 28, 1866*

SECOND SESSION—*December 3, 1866, to March 3, 1867*

SPECIAL SESSION OF THE SENATE—*March 4, 1865, to March 11, 1865*

VICE PRESIDENT OF THE UNITED STATES—ANDREW JOHNSON,[1] of Tennessee

PRESIDENT PRO TEMPORE OF THE SENATE—LAFAYETTE S. FOSTER,[2] of Connecticut; BENJAMIN F. WADE,[3] of Ohio

SECRETARY OF THE SENATE—JOHN W. FORNEY, of Pennsylvania

SERGEANT AT ARMS OF THE SENATE—GEORGE T. BROWN, of Illinois

SPEAKER OF THE HOUSE OF REPRESENTATIVES—SCHUYLER COLFAX,[4] of Indiana

CLERK OF THE HOUSE—EDWARD MCPHERSON,[5] of Pennsylvania

SERGEANT AT ARMS OF THE HOUSE—NATHANIEL G. ORDWAY, of New Hampshire

DOORKEEPER OF THE HOUSE—IRA GOODNOW, of Vermont

POSTMASTER OF THE HOUSE—JOSIAH GIVEN

ALABAMA

SENATORS

Vacant

REPRESENTATIVES [6]

Vacant

ARKANSAS

SENATORS

Vacant

REPRESENTATIVES

Vacant

CALIFORNIA

SENATORS

James A. McDougall, *San Francisco*
John Conness, *Sacramento*

REPRESENTATIVES

Donald C. McRuer, *San Francisco*
John Bidwell, *Chico*
William Higby, *Calaveras*

CONNECTICUT

SENATORS

Lafayette S. Foster, *Norwich*
James Dixon, *Hartford*

REPRESENTATIVES

Henry C. Deming, *Hartford*
Samuel L. Warner, *Middletown*
Augustus Brandegee, *New London*
John H. Hubbard, *Litchfield*

DELAWARE

SENATORS

Willard Saulsbury, *Georgetown*
George R. Riddle, *Wilmington*

REPRESENTATIVE

John A. Nicholson, *Dover*

FLORIDA

SENATORS

Vacant [7]
Vacant [8]

REPRESENTATIVE

Vacant

GEORGIA

SENATORS

Vacant

REPRESENTATIVES

Vacant

ILLINOIS

SENATORS

Lyman Trumbull, *Chicago*
Richard Yates, *Jacksonville*

---

[1] Became President upon the death of Abraham Lincoln, April 15, 1865.
[2] Elected March 7, 1865 (special session of the Senate), "to serve in the absence of the Vice President," and did serve until March 2, 1867.
[3] Elected March 2, 1867.
[4] Reelected December 4, 1865.

[5] Reelected December 4, 1865.
[6] Credentials of Thomas J. Foster as Member-elect were presented to the House January 10, 1867, but were not acted upon.
[7] On January 19, 1866, William Marvin presented credentials as a Senator-elect for the term ending

March 3, 1867, which were ordered to lie on the table and no further action taken thereon.
[8] On June 6, 1866, Wilkinson Call presented credentials as a Senator-elect for the term ending March 3, 1869, which were ordered to lie on the table and no further action taken thereon.

REPRESENTATIVES

John Wentworth, *Chicago*
John F. Farnsworth, *St. Charles*
Elihu B. Washburne, *Galena*
Abner C. Harding, *Monmouth*
Ebon C. Ingersoll, *Peoria*
Burton C. Cook, *Ottawa*
Henry P. H. Bromwell, *Charleston*
Shelby M. Cullom, *Springfield*
Lewis W. Ross, *Lewistown*
Anthony Thornton, *Shelbyville*
Samuel S. Marshall, *McLeansboro*
Jehu Baker. *Belleville*
Andrew J. Kuykendall, *Vienna*
Samuel W. Moulton, *Shelbyville*

INDIANA

SENATORS

Henry S. Lane, *Crawfordsville*
Thomas A. Hendricks, *Indianapolis*

REPRESENTATIVES

William E. Niblack, *Vincennes*
Michael C. Kerr, *New Albany*
Ralph Hill, *Columbus*
John H. Farquhar, *Brookville*
George W. Julian, *Centerville*
Ebenezer Dumont, *Indianapolis*
Daniel W. Voorhees,[9] *Terre Haute*
Henry D. Washburn,[10] *Clinton*
Godlove S. Orth, *La Fayette*
Schuyler Colfax, *South Bend*
Joseph H. Defrees, *Goshen*
Thomas N. Stillwell, *Anderson*

IOWA

SENATORS

James Harlan,[11] *Mount Pleasant*
Samuel J. Kirkwood,[12] *Iowa City*
James W. Grimes, *Burlington*

REPRESENTATIVES

James F. Wilson, *Fairfield*
Hiram Price, *Davenport*
William B. Allison, *Dubuque*
Josiah B. Grinnell, *Grinnell*
John A. Kasson, *Des Moines*
Asahel W. Hubbard, *Sioux City*

KANSAS

SENATORS

Samuel C. Pomeroy, *Atchison*
James H. Lane,[13] *Lawrence*
Edmund G. Ross,[14] *Lawrence*

REPRESENTATIVE

Sidney Clarke, *Lawrence*

KENTUCKY

SENATORS

Garrett Davis, *Paris*
James Guthrie, *Louisville*

REPRESENTATIVES

Lawrence S. Trimble, *Paducah*
Burwell C. Ritter, *Hopkinsville*
Henry Grider,[15] *Bowling Green*
Elijah Hise,[16] *Russellville*
Aaron Harding, *Greensburg*
Lovell H. Rousseau,[17] *Louisville*
Green C. Smith,[18] *Covington*
Andrew H. Ward,[19] *Cynthiana*
George S. Shanklin, *Nicholasville*
Samuel McKee, *Mount Sterling*
William H. Randall, *London*

LOUISIANA

SENATORS

Vacant

REPRESENTATIVES

Vacant [20]

MAINE

SENATORS

Lot M. Morrill, *Augusta*
William Pitt Fessenden, *Portland*

REPRESENTATIVES

John Lynch, *Portland*
Sidney Perham, *Paris*
James G. Blaine, *Augusta*
John H. Rice, *Foxcroft*
Frederick A. Pike, *Calais*

MARYLAND

SENATORS

Reverdy Johnson, *Baltimore*
John A. J. Creswell,[21] *Elkton*

REPRESENTATIVES

Hiram McCullough, *Elkton*
Edwin H. Webster,[22] *Bel Air*
John L. Thomas, Jr.,[23] *Baltimore*
Charles E. Phelps, *Baltimore*
Francis Thomas, *Frankville*
Benjamin G. Harris, *Leonardtown*

MASSACHUSETTS

SENATORS

Charles Sumner, *Boston*
Henry Wilson, *Natick*

REPRESENTATIVES

Thomas D. Eliot, *New Bedford*
Oakes Ames, *North Easton*
Alexander H. Rice, *Boston*
Samuel Hooper, *Boston*
John B. Alley, *Lynn*
Daniel W. Gooch,[24] *Melrose*
Nathaniel P. Banks,[25] *Waltham*
George S. Boutwell, *Groton*
John D. Baldwin, *Worcester*
William B. Washburn, *Greenfield*
Henry L. Dawes, *Pittsfield*

MICHIGAN

SENATORS

Zachariah Chandler, *Detroit*
Jacob M. Howard, *Detroit*

REPRESENTATIVES

Fernando C. Beaman, *Adrian*
Charles Upson, *Coldwater*
John W. Longyear, *Lansing*
Thomas W. Ferry, *Grand Haven*
Rowland E. Trowbridge,[26] *Birmingham*
John F. Driggs, *East Saginaw*

MINNESOTA

SENATORS

Alexander Ramsey, *St. Paul*
Daniel S. Norton, *Winona*

REPRESENTATIVES

William Windom, *Winona*
Ignatius Donnelly, *Hastings*

MISSISSIPPI

SENATORS

Vacant

REPRESENTATIVES

Vacant

---

[9] Served until February 23, 1866; succeeded by Henry D. Washburn, who contested his election.
[10] Successfully contested the election of Daniel W. Voorhees, and took his seat February 23, 1866.
[11] Resigned May 15, 1865, having been appointed Secretary of the Interior.
[12] Elected to fill vacancy caused by resignation of James Harlan, and took his seat January 24, 1866.
[13] Died July 11, 1866.
[14] Appointed to fill vacancy caused by death of James H. Lane, and took his seat July 25, 1866; subsequently elected.
[15] Died September 14, 1866.

[16] Elected to fill vacancy caused by death of Henry Grider, and took his seat December 3, 1866.
[17] Resigned July 21 1866; subsequently reelected, and took his seat December 3, 1866.
[18] Resigned in 1866.
[19] Elected to fill vacancy caused by resignation of Green C. Smith, and took his seat December 3, 1866.
[20] Credentials of Jacob Barker, Robert C. Wickliffe, Louis St. Martin, John E. King, and John Ray as Members-elect were presented and referred to the Committe on Reconstruction; no further action was taken.
[21] Elected to fill vacancy caused by death of Thomas

H. Hicks, in preceding Congress, and took his seat December 4, 1865.
[22] Resigned in July, 1865, before Congress assembled, to become collector of the port of Baltimore.
[23] Elected to fill vacancy caused by resignation of Edwin H. Webster, and took his seat December 4, 1865.
[24] Resigned September 1, 1865, before Congress assembled.
[25] Elected to fill vacancy occasioned by resignation of Daniel W. Gooch, and took his seat December 4, 1865.
[26] Election unsuccessfully contested by Augustus C. Baldwin.

MISSOURI

SENATORS

John B. Henderson, *Louisiana*
B. Gratz Brown, *St. Louis*

REPRESENTATIVES

John Hogan, *St. Louis*
Henry T. Blow, *St. Louis*
Thomas E. Noell, *Perryville*
John R. Kelso,[27] *Springfield*
Joseph W. McClurg, *Linn Creek*
Robert T. Van Horn, *Kansas City*
Benjamin F. Loan, *St. Joseph*
John F. Benjamin, *Shelbyville*
George W. Anderson, *Louisiana*

NEBRASKA[28]

SENATORS

John M. Thayer,[29] *Omaha*
Thomas W. Tipton,[29] *Brownville*

REPRESENTATIVE

Turner M. Marquette,[30] *Plattsmouth*

NEVADA

SENATORS

William M. Stewart, *Virginia City*
James W. Nye, *Carson City*

REPRESENTATIVE

Delos R. Ashley, *Virginia City*

NEW HAMPSHIRE

SENATORS

Daniel Clark,[31] *Manchester*
George G. Fogg,[32] *Concord*
Aaron H. Cragin, *Lebanon*

REPRESENTATIVES

Gilman Marston, *Exeter*
Edward H. Rollins, *Concord*
James W. Patterson, *Hanover*

NEW JERSEY

SENATORS

William Wright,[33] *Newark*
Frederick T. Frelinghuysen,[34] *Newark*
John P. Stockton,[35] *Trenton*
Alexander G. Cattell,[36] *Camden*

REPRESENTATIVES

John F. Starr, *Camden*
William A. Newell, *Allentown*
Charles Sitgreaves, *Phillipsburg*
Andrew J. Rogers, *Newton*
Edwin R. V. Wright, *Hudson City*

NEW YORK

SENATORS

Ira Harris, *Albany*
Edwin D. Morgan, *New York City*

REPRESENTATIVES

Stephen Taber, *Roslyn*
Teunis G. Bergen, *New Utrecht*
James Humphrey,[37] *Brooklyn*
John W. Hunter,[38] *Brooklyn*
Morgan Jones, *New York City*
Nelson Taylor, *New York City*
Henry J. Raymond, *New York City*
John W. Chanler, *New York City*
James Brooks,[39] *New York City*
William E. Dodge,[40] *New York City*
William A. Darling, *New York City*
William Radford, *Yonkers*
Charles H. Winfield, *Goshen*
John H. Ketcham, *Dover*
Edwin N. Hubbell, *Coxsackie*
Charles Goodyear, *Schoharie*
John A. Griswold, *Troy*
Orlando Kellogg,[41] *Elizabethtown*
Robert S. Hale,[42] *Elizabethtown*
Calvin T. Hulburd, *Brasher Falls*
James M. Marvin, *Saratoga Springs*
Demas Hubbard, Jr., *Smyrna*
Addison H. Laflin, *Herkimer*
Roscoe Conkling,[43] *Utica*
Sidney T. Holmes, *Morrisville*
Thomas T. Davis, *Syracuse*
Theodore M. Pomeroy, *Auburn*
Daniel Morris, *Penn Yan*
Giles W. Hotchkiss, *Binghamton*
Hamilton Ward, *Belmont*
Roswell Hart, *Rochester*
Burt Van Horn, *Newfane*
James M. Humphrey, *Buffalo*
Henry Van Aernam, *Franklinville*

NORTH CAROLINA

SENATORS

Vacant

REPRESENTATIVES [44]

Vacant

OHIO

SENATORS

Benjamin F. Wade, *Jefferson*
John Sherman, *Mansfield*

REPRESENTATIVES

Benjamin Eggleston, *Cincinnati*
Rutherford B. Hayes, *Cincinnati*
Robert C. Schenck, *Dayton*
William Lawrence, *Bellefontaine*
Francis C. Le Blond, *Celina*
Reader W. Clarke, *Batavia*
Samuel Shellabarger, *Springfield*
James R. Hubbell, *Delaware*
Ralph P. Buckland, *Fremont*
James M. Ashley, *Toledo*
Hezekiah S. Bundy, *Reeds Mill*
William E. Finck, *Somerset*
Columbus Delano,[45] *Mount Vernon*
Martin Welker, *Wooster*
Tobias A. Plants, *Pomeroy*
John A. Bingham, *Cadiz*
Ephraim R. Eckley, *Carrolton*
Rufus P. Spalding, *Cleveland*
James A. Garfield, *Hiram*

OREGON

SENATORS

James W. Nesmith, *Salem*
George H. Williams, *Portland*

REPRESENTATIVE

James H. D. Henderson, *Eugene City*

PENNSYLVANIA

SENATORS

Edgar Cowan, *Greensburg*
Charles R. Buckalew, *Bloomsburg*

REPRESENTATIVES

Samuel J. Randall, *Philadelphia*
Charles O'Neill, *Philadelphia*
Leonard Myers, *Philadelphia*
William D. Kelley, *Philadelphia*
M. Russell Thayer, *Chestnut Hill*
Benjamin M. Boyer, *Norristown*
John M. Broomall, *Media*
Sydenham E. Ancona, *Reading*
Thaddeus Stevens, *Lancaster*
Myer Strouse, *Pottsville*
Philip Johnson,[46] *Easton*
Charles Denison, *Wilkes-Barre*
Ulysses Mercur, *Towanda*

---

[27] Election unsuccessfully contested by S. H. Boyd.
[28] Admitted as a State into the Union, March 1, 1867.
[29] Elected, but did not take his seat until March 4, 1867.
[30] Took his seat March 2, 1867.
[31] Resigned July 27, 1866.
[32] Appointed to fill vacancy caused by resignation of Daniel Clark, and took his seat December 3, 1866.
[33] Died November 1, 1866.
[34] Appointed to fill vacancy caused by death of William Wright, and took his seat December 3, 1866; subsequently elected.
[35] Presented credentials and qualified December 4,

1865; protest of members of New Jersey Legislature against his admission filed the same day; served until March 27, 1866, when the seat was declared vacant.
[36] Elected to fill vacancy caused by the Senate declaring the seat of John P. Stockton vacant, and took his seat December 3, 1866.
[37] Died June 16, 1866.
[38] Elected to fill vacancy caused by death of James Humphrey, and took his seat December 4, 1866.
[39] Served until April 7, 1866; succeeded by William E. Dodge, who contested his election.
[40] Successfully contested the election of James Brooks, and took his seat April 7, 1866.

[41] Died August 24, 1865.
[42] Elected to fill vacancy caused by death of Orlando Kellogg, and took his seat December 3, 1866.
[43] Reelected to the Fortieth Congress but resigned, effective March 4, 1867, having been elected Senator.
[44] Credentials of Alexander H. Jones and Lewis Hawes were presented and referred to the Select Committee on Reconstruction, but no further action was taken.
[45] Election unsuccessfully contested by Charles Follett.
[46] Died January 29, 1867.

George F. Miller, *Lewisburg*
Adam J. Glossbrenner, *York*
Alexander H. Coffroth,[47] *Somerset*
William H. Koontz,[48] *Somerset*
Abraham A. Barker, *Edenburg*
Stephen F. Wilson, *Wellsboro*
Glenni W. Scofield, *Warren*
Charles V. Culver, *Franklin*
John L. Dawson,[49] *Brownsville*
James K. Moorhead, *Pittsburgh*
Thomas Williams, *Pittsburgh*
George V. Lawrence, *Monongahela City*

RHODE ISLAND

SENATORS

Henry B. Anthony, *Providence*
William Sprague, *Providence*

REPRESENTATIVES

Thomas A. Jenckes, *Providence*
Nathan F. Dixon, *Westerly*

SOUTH CAROLINA

SENATORS

Vacant

REPRESENTATIVES

Vacant

TENNESSEE [50]

SENATORS

Joseph S. Fowler,[51] *Nashville*
David T. Patterson,[52] *Greeneville*

REPRESENTATIVES

Nathaniel G. Taylor,[53] *Happy Valley*
Horace Maynard,[53] *Knoxville*
William B. Stokes,[53] *Liberty*
Edmund Cooper,[54] *Shelbyville*
William B. Campbell,[55] *Lebanon*
Samuel M. Arnell,[56] *Columbia*
Isaac R. Hawkins,[55] *Huntingdon*
John W. Leftwich,[54] *Memphis*

TEXAS

SENATORS

Vacant

REPRESENTATIVES

Vacant

VERMONT

SENATORS

Solomon Foot,[57] *Rutland*
George F. Edmunds,[58] *Burlington*
Jacob Collamer,[59] *Woodstock*
Luke P. Poland,[60] *St. Johnsbury*

REPRESENTATIVES

Frederick E. Woodbridge, *Vergennes*
Justin S. Morrill, *Strafford*
Portus Baxter, *Derby Line*

VIRGINIA

SENATORS

Vacant

REPRESENTATIVES

Vacant

WEST VIRGINIA

SENATORS

Peter G. Van Winkle, *Parkersburg*
Waitman T. Willey, *Morgantown*

REPRESENTATIVES

Chester D. Hubbard, *Wheeling*
George R. Latham, *Grafton*
Kellian V. Whaley, *Point Pleasant*

WISCONSIN

SENATORS

James R. Doolittle, *Racine*
Timothy O. Howe, *Green Bay*

REPRESENTATIVES

Halbert E. Paine, *Milwaukee*
Ithamar C. Sloan, *Janesville*
Amasa Cobb, *Mineral Point*
Charles A. Eldridge, *Fond du Lac*
Philetus Sawyer, *Oshkosh*
Walter D. McIndoe, *Wausau*

TERRITORY OF ARIZONA

DELEGATE

John N. Goodwin, *Prescott*

TERRITORY OF COLORADO

DELEGATE

Allen A. Bradford, *Denver*

TERRITORY OF DAKOTA

DELEGATE

Walter A. Burleigh, *Yankton*

TERRITORY OF IDAHO

DELEGATE

Edward D. Holbrook, *Idaho City*

TERRITORY OF MONTANA

DELEGATE

Samuel McLean, *Bannack*

TERRITORY OF NEBRASKA

DELEGATE

Phineas W. Hitchcock,[61] *Omaha*

TERRITORY OF NEW MEXICO

DELEGATE

J. Francisco Chaves, *Santa Fe*

TERRITORY OF UTAH

DELEGATE

William H. Hooper, *Salt Lake City*

TERRITORY OF WASHINGTON

DELEGATE

Arthur A. Denny, *Seattle*

---

[47] Alexander H. Coffroth and William H. Koontz both claimed the election, the governor having declined to issue a certificate to either; the House, on February 19, 1866, adopted a resolution that Mr. Coffroth had the prima facie right to and should be permitted to occupy the seat without prejudice to the right to contest; took his seat the same day and served until July 18, 1866, when he was succeeded by William H. Koontz, who contested the election.
[48] Successfully contested the election of Alexander H. Coffroth, and took his seat July 18, 1866.

[49] Election unsuccessfully contested by Smith Fuller.
[50] Readmitted to representation by joint resolution of July 24, 1866.
[51] Took his seat July 25, 1866; term to expire March 3, 1871.
[52] Took his seat July 28, 1866; term to expire March 3, 1869.
[53] Took his seat July 24, 1866.
[54] Took his seat July 25, 1866.
[55] Took his seat December 3, 1866.
[56] Took his seat December 3, 1866; election unsuc-

cessfully contested by Dorsey B. Thomas.
[57] Died March 28, 1866.
[58] Appointed to fill vacancy caused by death of Solomon Foot, and took his seat April 5, 1866; subsequently elected.
[59] Died November 9, 1865.
[60] Appointed to fill vacancy caused by death of Jacob Collamer, and took his seat December 4, 1865; subsequently elected.
[61] Served until March 1, 1867, when the Territory of Nebraska was granted statehood.

FORTIETH CONGRESS

MARCH 4, 1867, TO MARCH 3, 1869

FIRST SESSION—*March 4, 1867, to March 30, 1867; July 3, 1867, to July 20, 1867;*
November 21, 1867, to December 1, 1867

SECOND SESSION—*December 2, 1867, to July 27, 1868; September 21, 1868, for one day only;*
October 16, 1868, for one day only; November 10, 1868, for one day only

THIRD SESSION—*December 7, 1868, to March 3, 1869*

SPECIAL SESSION OF THE SENATE—*April 1, 1867, to April 20, 1867*

VICE PRESIDENT OF THE UNITED STATES [1]

PRESIDENT PRO TEMPORE OF THE SENATE—BENJAMIN F. WADE, of Ohio

SECRETARY OF THE SENATE—JOHN W. FORNEY,[2] of Pennsylvania; GEORGE C. GORHAM,[3] of California

SERGEANT AT ARMS OF THE SENATE—GEORGE T. BROWN, of Illinois

SPEAKER OF THE HOUSE OF REPRESENTATIVES—SCHUYLER COLFAX,[4] of Indiana; THEODORE M. POMEROY,[5] of New York

CLERK OF THE HOUSE—EDWARD McPHERSON,[6] of Pennsylvania

SERGEANT AT ARMS OF THE HOUSE—NATHANIEL G. ORDWAY, of New Hampshire

DOORKEEPER OF THE HOUSE—CHARLES E. LIPPINCOTT, of Illinois

POSTMASTER OF THE HOUSE—WILLIAM S. KING

ALABAMA [7]

SENATORS

George E. Spencer,[8] *Decatur*
Willard Warner,[9] *Montgomery*

REPRESENTATIVES

Francis W. Kellogg,[10] *Mobile*
Charles W. Buckley,[11] *Montgomery*
Benjamin W. Norris,[11] *Elmore*
Charles W. Pierce,[11] *Demopolis*
John B. Callis,[11] *Huntsville*
Thomas Haughey,[11] *Decatur*

ARKANSAS [12]

SENATORS

Alexander McDonald,[13] *Little Rock*
Benjamin F. Rice,[14] *Little Rock*

REPRESENTATIVES

Logan H. Roots,[15] *Devall Bluff*
James Hinds,[16] *Little Rock*
James T. Elliott,[17] *Camden*
Thomas Boles,[18] *Dardanelle*

CALIFORNIA

SENATORS

John Conness, *Georgetown*
Cornelius Cole, *San Francisco*

REPRESENTATIVES [19]

Samuel B. Axtell,[20] *San Francisco*
William Higby,[20] *Calaveras*
James A. Johnson,[20] *Downieville*

CONNECTICUT

SENATORS

James Dixon, *Hartford*
Orris S. Ferry, *Norwalk*

REPRESENTATIVES

Richard D. Hubbard, *Hartford*
Julius Hotchkiss, *Middletown*
Henry H. Starkweather, *Norwich*
William H. Barnum, *Lime Rock*

DELAWARE

SENATORS

George R. Riddle,[21] *Wilmington*
James A. Bayard,[22] *Wilmington*
Willard Saulsbury, *Georgetown*

---

[1] Vice President Andrew Johnson became President in preceding Congress on the death of Abraham Lincoln.
[2] Resigned, effective June 4, 1868.
[3] Elected June 4, 1868.
[4] Reelected March 4, 1867; resigned as Speaker March 3, 1869, having been elected Vice President.
[5] Elected March 3, 1869.
[6] Reelected March 4, 1867.
[7] Readmitted to representation July 13, 1868.
[8] Took his seat July 25, 1868; term to expire March 3, 1873.

[9] Took his seat July 25, 1868; term to expire March 3, 1871.
[10] Took his seat July 22, 1868.
[11] Took his seat July 21, 1868.
[12] Readmitted to representation, by passage of bill in both Houses over the veto of President Johnson, June 22, 1868.
[13] Took his seat June 23, 1868; term to expire March 3, 1871.
[14] Took his seat June 23, 1868; term to expire March 3, 1873.

[15] Took his seat June 24, 1868.
[16] Took his seat June 24, 1868; died October 22, 1868.
[17] Elected to fill vacancy caused by death of James Hinds, and took his seat January 13, 1869.
[18] Took his seat June 24, 1868.
[19] Elected September 4, 1867.
[20] Took his seat November 21, 1867.
[21] Died March 29, 1867.
[22] Appointed to fill vacancy caused by death of George R. Riddle, and took his seat April 11, 1867; subsequently elected.

REPRESENTATIVE

At Large—John A. Nicholson, *Dover*

FLORIDA [23]

SENATORS

Thomas W. Osborn,[24] *Pensacola*
Adonijah S. Welch,[25] *Jacksonville*

REPRESENTATIVE

At Large—Charles M. Hamilton,[26]
Marianna

GEORGIA [27]

SENATORS [28]

Vacant

REPRESENTATIVES [29]

Joseph W. Clift,[30] *Savannah*
Nelson Tift,[30] *Albany*
William P. Edwards,[30] *Butler*
Samuel F. Gove,[30] *Griswoldville*
Charles H. Prince,[30] *Augusta*
Pierce M. B. Young,[30] *Cartersville*

ILLINOIS

SENATORS

Lyman Trumbull, *Chicago*
Richard Yates, *Jacksonville*

REPRESENTATIVES

Norman B. Judd, *Chicago*
John F. Farnsworth, *St. Charles*
Elihu B. Washburne, *Galena*
Abner C. Harding, *Monmouth*
Ebon C. Ingersoll, *Peoria*
Burton C. Cook, *Ottawa*
Henry P. H. Bromwell, *Charleston*
Shelby M. Cullom, *Springfield*
Lewis W. Ross, *Lewiston*
Albert G. Burr, *Winchester*
Samuel S. Marshall, *McLeansboro*

Jehu Baker, *Belleville*
Green B. Raum, *Harrisburg*
At Large—John A. Logan, *Carbondale*

INDIANA

SENATORS

Thomas A. Hendricks, *Indianapolis*
Oliver H. P. T. Morton, *Indianapolis*

REPRESENTATIVES

William E. Niblack, *Vincennes*
Michael C. Kerr, *New Albany*
Morton C. Hunter, *Bloomington*
William S. Holman, *Aurora*
George W. Julian, *Centerville*
John Coburn, *Indianapolis*
Henry D. Washburn, *Clinton*
Godlove S. Orth, *La Fayette*
Schuyler Colfax, *South Bend*
William Williams, *Warsaw*
John P. C. Shanks, *Jay Court House*

IOWA

SENATORS

James W. Grimes, *Burlington*
James Harlan, *Mount Pleasant*

REPRESENTATIVES

James F. Wilson, *Fairfield*
Hiram Price, *Davenport*
William B. Allison, *Dubuque*
William Loughridge, *Oskaloosa*
Grenville M. Dodge, *Council Bluffs*
Asahel W. Hubbard, *Sioux City*

KANSAS

SENATORS

Samuel C. Pomeroy, *Atchison*
Edmund G. Ross, *Lawrence*

REPRESENTATIVE

At Large—Sidney Clarke, *Lawrence*

KENTUCKY

SENATORS

Garrett Davis, *Paris*
James Guthrie,[31] *Louisville*
Thomas C. McCreery,[32] *Owensboro*

REPRESENTATIVES [33]

Lawrence S. Trimble,[34] *Paducah*
Elijah Hise,[35] *Russellville*
Jacob S. Golladay,[36] *Allensville*
J. Proctor Knott,[37] *Lebanon*
Asa P. Grover,[37] *Louisville*
Thomas L. Jones,[38] *Newport*
James B. Beck,[37] *Lexington*
George M. Adams,[39] *Barbourville*
Samuel McKee,[40] *Mount Sterling*

LOUISIANA [41]

SENATORS

John S. Harris,[42] *Vidalia*
William Pitt Kellogg,[43] *New Orleans*

REPRESENTATIVES

J. Hale Sypher,[44] *New Orleans*
James Mann,[45] *New Orleans*
Joseph P. Newsham,[44] *St. Francisville*
Michel Vidal,[44] *Opelousas*
W. Jasper Blackburn,[44] *Homer*

MAINE

SENATORS

Lot M. Morrill, *Augusta*
William Pitt Fessenden, *Portland*

REPRESENTATIVES

John Lynch, *Portland*
Sidney Perham, *Paris*
James G. Blaine, *Augusta*
John A. Peters, *Bangor*
Frederick A. Pike, *Calais*

---

[23] Readmitted to representation June 25, 1868.
[24] Took his seat June 30, 1868; term to expire March 3, 1873; on the same day William Marvin presented credentials dated November 28, 1866, which were read and no further action taken thereon because Mr. Osborn was seated.
[25] Took his seat July 2, 1868; term to expire March 3, 1869.
[26] Took his seat July 1, 1868.
[27] Although Georgia was not formally readmitted to representation until July 15, 1870 (in the succeeding Congress), the Representatives elected to this Congress qualified as indicated.
[28] On December 7, 1868, the credentials of Joshua Hill, elected by the legislature to fill vacancy in the term beginning March 4, 1867, were presented and referred to the Committee on the Judiciary; on January 11, 1869, the credentials of Homer V. M. Miller, elected in the same manner, for the term beginning March 4, 1865, were presented and were similarly referred; on January 25, 1869, the committee reported that the State of Georgia had not complied with the conditions of an act providing for her admission to representation, and that Mr. Hill "ought not now to be admitted"; February 17, 1869, the committee reported against admitting Mr. Miller to his seat, and

the cases remained undisposed of.
[29] John A. Wimpy and John H. Cristy both claimed election from the sixth district, but neither was seated.
[30] Took his seat July 25, 1868.
[31] Resigned February 7, 1868.
[32] Elected to fill vacancy caused by resignation of James Guthrie, and took his seat February 28, 1868.
[33] On July 3, 1867, it was proposed to seat all the Members-elect from Kentucky, but protests against the manner of holding the election and charges of disloyal acts by certain individual members of the delegation were presented and a resolution was adopted directing an investigation and referring to the Committee on Elections the credentials of Messrs Lawrence S. Trimble, John Y. Brown, J. Proctor Knott, Asa P. Grover, Thomas L. Jones, James B. Beck, and John D. Young, who were not permitted to qualify pending this investigation; Samuel E. Smith contested the election of John Y. Brown, but the House, on February 15, 1868, decided that neither was entitled to the seat, which remained vacant throughout the Congress.
[34] Election unsuccessfully contested by G. G. Symes; took his seat January 10, 1868.
[35] Died May 8, 1867, never having qualified; the election of Mr. Hise was subsequently unsuccessfully contested by George D. Blakey.

[36] Elected to fill vacancy caused by death of Elijah Hise, and took his seat December 5, 1867; George D. Blakey, claiming to have been elected from this district instead of Mr. Hise, filed a protest against the seating of Mr. Golladay, but this protest was not allowed.
[37] Charges of disloyalty were unsustained, and took his seat December 3, 1867.
[38] Charges of disloyalty were unsustained, and took his seat December 4, 1867.
[39] Took his seat July 8, 1867.
[40] Successfully contested the election of John D. Young, and took his seat June 22, 1868.
[41] Readmitted to representation July 9, 1868.
[42] Took his seat July 17, 1868; term to expire March 3, 1871.
[43] Took his seat July 17, 1868; term to expire March 3, 1873.
[44] Took his seat July 18, 1868.
[45] Took his seat July 18, 1868; died August 26, 1868; Caleb S. Hunt and J. Willis Menard claimed to have been elected to fill the vacancy, and Simon Jones claimed he was elected, instead of Mann, in the first instance. The House decided against all claimants, and the seat remained vacant for the remainder of the session.

MARYLAND

SENATORS

Reverdy Johnson,[46] *Baltimore*
William Pinkney Whyte,[47] *Baltimore*
George Vickers,[48] *Chestertown*

REPRESENTATIVES

Hiram McCullough, *Elkton*
Stevenson Archer, *Bel Air*
Charles E. Phelps, *Baltimore*
Francis Thomas, *Frankville*
Frederick Stone, *Port Tobacco*

MASSACHUSETTS

SENATORS

Charles Sumner, *Boston*
Henry Wilson, *Natick*

REPRESENTATIVES

Thomas D. Eliot, *New Bedford*
Oakes Ames, *North Easton*
Ginery Twichell, *Brookline*
Samuel Hooper, *Boston*
Benjamin F. Butler, *Lowell*
Nathaniel P. Banks, *Waltham*
George S. Boutwell, *Groton*
John D. Baldwin, *Worcester*
William B. Washburn, *Greenfield*
Henry L. Dawes, *Pittsfield*

MICHIGAN

SENATORS

Zachariah Chandler, *Detroit*
Jacob M. Howard, *Detroit*

REPRESENTATIVES

Fernando C. Beaman, *Adrian*
Charles Upson, *Coldwater*
Austin Blair, *Jackson*
Thomas W. Ferry, *Grand Haven*
Rowland E. Trowbridge, *Birmingham*
John F. Driggs, *East Saginaw*

MINNESOTA

SENATORS

Alexander Ramsey, *St. Paul*
Daniel S. Norton, *Winona*

REPRESENTATIVES

William Windom, *Winona*
Ignatius Donnelly, *Hastings*

MISSISSIPPI

SENATORS

Vacant

REPRESENTATIVES

Vacant

MISSOURI

SENATORS

John B. Henderson, *Louisiana*
Charles D. Drake, *St. Louis*

REPRESENTATIVES

William A. Pile,[49] *St. Louis*
Carman A. Newcomb, *Vineland*
Thomas E. Noell,[50] *Perryville*
James R. McCormick,[51] *Ironton*
Joseph J. Gravely, *Stockton*
Joseph W. McClurg,[52] *Linn Creek*
John H. Stover,[53] *Versailles*
Robert T. Van Horn,[54] *Kansas City*
Benjamin F. Loan, *St. Joseph*
John F. Benjamin, *Shelbyville*
George W. Anderson,[55] *Louisiana*

NEBRASKA

SENATORS

John M. Thayer,[56] *Omaha*
Thomas W. Tipton,[57] *Brownville*

REPRESENTATIVE

At Large—John Taffe, *Omaha*

NEVADA

SENATORS

William M. Stewart, *Virginia City*
James W. Nye, *Carson City*

REPRESENTATIVE

At Large—Delos R. Ashley, *Austin*

NEW HAMPSHIRE

SENATORS

Aaron H. Cragin, *Lebanon*
James W. Patterson, *Hanover*

REPRESENTATIVES

Jacob H. Ela, *Rochester*
Aaron F. Stevens, *Nashua*
Jacob Benton, *Lancaster*

NEW JERSEY

SENATORS

Alexander G. Cattell, *Camden*
Frederick T. Frelinghuysen, *Newark*

REPRESENTATIVES

William Moore, *Mays Landing*
Charles Haight, *Freehold*
Charles Sitgreaves, *Phillipsburg*
John Hill, *Boonton*
George A. Halsey, *Newark*

NEW YORK

SENATORS

Edwin D. Morgan, *New York City*
Roscoe Conkling, *Utica*

REPRESENTATIVES

Stephen Taber, *Roslyn*
Demas Barnes, *Brooklyn*
William E. Robinson, *Brooklyn*
John Fox, *New York City*
John Morrissey, *New York City*
Thomas E. Stewart, *New York City*
John W. Chanler, *New York City*
James Brooks, *New York City*
Fernando Wood, *New York City*
William H. Robertson, *Katonah*
Charles H. Van Wyck, *Middletown*
John H. Ketsham, *Dover*
Thomas Cornell, *Rondout*
John V. L. Pruyn, *Albany*
John A. Griswold, *Troy*
Orange Ferriss, *Glens Falls*
Calvin T. Hulburd, *Brasher Falls*
James M. Marvin, *Saratoga Springs*
William C. Fields, *Laurens*
Addison H. Laflin, *Herkimer*
Alexander H. Bailey,[58] *Rome*
John C. Churchill, *Oswego*
Dennis McCarthy, *Syracuse*
Theodore M. Pomeroy, *Auburn*
William H. Kelsey, *Geneseo*
William S. Lincoln, *Owego*
Hamilton Ward, *Belmont*
Lewis Selye, *Rochester*
Burt Van Horn, *Lockport*
James M. Humphrey, *Buffalo*
Henry Van Aernam, *Franklinville*

---

[46] Resigned July 10, 1868.
[47] Appointed to fill vacancy caused by resignation of Reverdy Johnson, and took his seat July 14, 1868.
[48] Elected for term beginning March 4, 1867, and took his seat March 9, 1868.   The credentials of Philip F. Thomas, Senator-elect, were presented March 18, 1867, but he was not permitted to qualify; on February 19, 1868, the Senate adopted a resolution that he was not entitled to qualify as he had "voluntarily given aid, countenance, and encouragement to persons engaged in armed hostility to the United States."

[49] Election unsuccessfully contested by John Hogan.
[50] Died October 3, 1867.
[51] Elected to fill vacancy caused by death of Thomas E. Noell, and took his seat December 17, 1867.
[52] Resigned in 1868.
[53] Elected to fill vacancy caused by resignation of Joseph W. McClurg, and took his seat December 7, 1868.
[54] Election unsuccessfully contested by James H. Birch.

[55] Election unsuccessfully contested by William F. Switzler.
[56] Took his seat March 4, 1867; term to expire, as determined by lot, March 3, 1871.
[57] Took his seat March 4, 1867; term to expire, as determined by lot, March 3, 1869.
[58] Elected to fill vacancy caused by resignation of Roscoe Conkling, in preceding Congress, and took his seat November 30, 1867.

NORTH CAROLINA [59]

SENATORS

Joseph C. Abbott,[60] *Wilmington*
John Pool,[61] *Elizabeth City*

REPRESENTATIVES

John R. French,[62] *Edenton*
David Heaton,[63] *New Bern*
Oliver H. Dockery,[64] *Richmond*
John T. Deweese,[62] *Raleigh*
Israel G. Lash,[65] *Salem*
Nathaniel Boyden,[64] *Salisbury*
Alexander H. Jones,[62] *Asheville*

OHIO

SENATORS

Benjamin F. Wade, *Jefferson*
John Sherman, *Mansfield*

REPRESENTATIVES

Benjamin Eggleston, *Cincinnati*
Rutherford B. Hayes,[66] *Cincinnati*
Samuel F. Cary,[67] *Cincinnati*
Robert C. Schenck, *Dayton*
William Lawrence, *Bellefontaine*
William Mungen, *Findlay*
Reader W. Clarke, *Batavia*
Samuel Shellabarger, *Springfield*
Cornelius S. Hamilton,[68] *Marysville*
John Beatty,[69] *Cardington*
Ralph P. Buckland, *Fremont*
James M. Ashley, *Toledo*
John T. Wilson, *Tranquility*
Philadelph Van Trump, *Lancaster*
George W. Morgan,[70] *Mount Vernon*
Columbus Delano,[71] *Mount Vernon*
Martin Welker, *Wooster*
Tobias A. Plants, *Pomeroy*
John A. Bingham, *Cadiz*
Ephraim R. Eckley, *Carrollton*
Rufus P. Spalding, *Cleveland*
James A. Garfield, *Hiram*

OREGON

SENATORS

George H. Williams, *Portland*
Henry W. Corbett, *Portland*

REPRESENTATIVE

At Large—Rufus Mallory, *Salem*

PENNSYLVANIA

SENATORS

Charles R. Buckalew, *Bloomsburg*
Simon Cameron, *Harrisburg*

REPRESENTATIVES

Samuel J. Randall, *Philadelphia*
Charles O'Neill, *Philadelphia*
Leonard Myers, *Philadelphia*
William D. Kelley, *Philadelphia*
Caleb N. Taylor, *Bristol*
Benjamin M. Boyer, *Norristown*
John M. Broomall, *Media*
J. Lawrence Getz, *Reading*
Thaddeus Stevens,[72] *Lancaster*
Oliver J. Dickey,[73] *Lancaster*
Henry L. Cake, *Tamaqua*
Daniel M. Van Auken, *Milford*
Charles Denison,[74] *Wilkes-Barre*
George W. Woodward,[75] *Wilkes-Barre*
Ulysses Mercur, *Towanda*
George F. Miller, *Lewisburg*
Adam J. Glossbrenner, *York*
William H. Koontz, *Somerset*
Daniel J. Morrell, *Johnstown*
Stephen F. Wilson, *Wellsboro*
Glenni W. Scofield, *Warren*
Darwin A. Finney,[76] *Meadville*
S. Newton Pettis,[77] *Meadville*
John Covode, *Lockport*
James K. Moorhead, *Pittsburgh*
Thomas Williams, *Allegheny*
George V. Lawrence, *Monongahela City*

RHODE ISLAND

SENATORS

Henry B. Anthony, *Providence*
William Sprague, *Providence*

REPRESENTATIVES

Thomas A. Jenckes, *Cumberland*
Nathan F. Dixon, *Westerly*

SOUTH CAROLINA [78]

SENATORS

Thomas J. Robertson,[79] *Columbia*
Frederick A. Sawyer,[80] *Charleston*

REPRESENTATIVES

B. Frank Whittemore,[81] *Darlington*
Christopher C. Bowen,[82] *Charleston*
M. Simeon Corley,[83] *Lexington*
James H. Goss,[81] *Union Court House*

TENNESSEE

SENATORS

Joseph S. Fowler, *Nashville*
David T. Patterson, *Greeneville*

REPRESENTATIVES [84]

Roderick R. Butler,[85] *Mountain City*
Horace Maynard,[86] *Knoxville*
William B. Stokes,[86] *Alexandria*
James Mullins,[86] *Shelbyville*
John Trimble,[86] *Nashville*
Samuel M. Arnell,[87] *Columbia*
Isaac R. Hawkins,[86] *Huntingdon*
David A. Nunn,[86] *Brownsville*

TEXAS

SENATORS

Vacant

REPRESENTATIVES

Vacant

VERMONT

SENATORS

George F. Edmunds, *Burlington*
Justin S. Morrill, *Strafford*

REPRESENTATIVES

Frederick E. Woodbridge, *Vergennes*
Luke P. Poland, *St. Johnsbury*
Worthington C. Smith, *St. Albans*

VIRGINIA

SENATORS

Vacant

REPRESENTATIVES

Vacant

WEST VIRGINIA

SENATORS

Peter G. Van Winkle, *Parkersburg*
Waitman T. Willey, *Morgantown*

---

[59] Readmitted to representation July 4, 1868.
[60] Took his seat July 17, 1868; term to expire March 3, 1871.
[61] Took his seat July 17, 1868; term to expire March 3, 1873.
[62] Took his seat July 6, 1868.
[63] Took his seat July 15, 1868.
[64] Took his seat July 13, 1868.
[65] Took his seat July 20, 1868.
[66] Resigned July 20, 1867.
[67] Elected to fill vacancy caused by resignation of Rutherford B. Hayes; took his seat November 21, 1867.
[68] Died December 22, 1867.
[69] Elected to fill vacancy caused by death of Cornelius S. Hamilton, and took his seat February 5, 1868.
[70] Served until June 3, 1868; succeeded by Columbus Delano, who contested his election.

[71] Successfully contested the election of George W. Morgan, and took his seat June 3, 1868.
[72] Died August 11, 1868.
[73] Elected to fill vacancy caused by death of Thaddeus Stevens, and took his seat December 7, 1868.
[74] Died June 27, 1867.
[75] Elected to fill vacancy caused by death of Charles Denison, and took his seat November 21, 1867.
[76] Died August 25, 1868.
[77] Elected to fill vacancy caused by death of Darwin A. Finney, and took his seat December 7, 1868.
[78] Readmitted to representation July 9, 1868.
[79] Took his seat July 20, 1868; term to expire March 3, 1871.
[80] Took his seat July 22, 1868; term to expire March 3, 1873.
[81] Took his seat July 18, 1868.

[82] Took his seat July 20, 1868.
[83] Took his seat July 25, 1868.
[84] The credentials of Thomas A. Hamilton, claiming to be a Member-elect from the State at large, were presented; claimant held that, inasmuch as Tennessee had voluntarily emancipated and enfranchised her slaves, she had added to her representative population a sufficient number to give her nine, instead of eight, Representatives, and he had been elected as such ninth Member. It was the first of many similar claims made by other readmitted States; the majority report was adverse to the claimant and, although the House took no formal action, he was not seated.
[85] Qualified under act of June 19, 1868, and took his seat June 26, 1868.
[86] Took his seat November 21, 1867.
[87] Took his seat November 25, 1867.

WEST VIRGINIA—Continued

REPRESENTATIVES

Chester D. Hubbard, *Wheeling*
Bethuel M. Kitchen, *Martinsburg*
Daniel Polsley, *Point Pleasant*

WISCONSIN

SENATORS

James R. Doolittle, *Racine*
Timothy O. Howe, *Green Bay*

REPRESENTATIVES

Halbert E. Paine, *Milwaukee*
Benjamin F. Hopkins, *Madison*
Amasa Cobb, *Mineral Point*
Charles A. Eldridge, *Fond du Lac*
Philetus Sawyer, *Oshkosh*
Cadwallader C. Washburn, *La Crosse*

TERRITORY OF ARIZONA

DELEGATE

Coles Bashford, *Tucson*

TERRITORY OF COLORADO

DELEGATE

George M. Chilcott,[88] *Excelsior*

TERRITORY OF DAKOTA

DELEGATE

Walter A. Burleigh, *Yankton*

TERRITORY OF IDAHO

DELEGATE

Edward D. Holbrook, *Idaho City*

TERRITORY OF MONTANA

DELEGATE

James M. Cavanaugh, *Helena*

TERRITORY OF NEW MEXICO

DELEGATE

Charles P. Clever,[89] *Santa Fe*
J. Francisco Chaves,[90] *Santa Fe*

TERRITORY OF UTAH

DELEGATE

William H. Hooper,[91] *Salt Lake City*

TERRITORY OF WASHINGTON

DELEGATE

Alvan Flanders, *Walla Walla*

---

[88] George M. Chilcott and A. C. Hunt each presented credentials on March 5, 1867, which were referred to the Committee on Elections; the committee reported that neither was entitled to the seat; Chilcott was seated March 20, 1867, and Hunt subsequently abandoned the contest.

[89] Credentials certifying his election on September 2, 1867, were presented November 21, 1867, and referred to the Committee on Elections, together with letter of secretary of New Mexico claiming fraud in election; was seated on December 19, 1867, and served until February 20, 1869; succeeded by J. Francisco Chaves, who contested his election.

[90] Successfully contested the election of Charles P. Clever, and took his seat February 20, 1869.
[91] Election unsuccessfully contested by William McGrorty.

FORTY-FIRST CONGRESS

MARCH 4, 1869, TO MARCH 3, 1871

FIRST SESSION—*March 4, 1869, to April 10, 1869*

SECOND SESSION—*December 6, 1869, to July 15, 1870*

THIRD SESSION—*December 5, 1870, to March 3, 1871*

SPECIAL SESSION OF THE SENATE—*April 12, 1869, to April 22, 1869*

———

VICE PRESIDENT OF THE UNITED STATES—SCHUYLER COLFAX, of Indiana

PRESIDENT PRO TEMPORE OF THE SENATE—HENRY B. ANTHONY,[1] of Rhode Island

SECRETARY OF THE SENATE—GEORGE C. GORHAM, of California

SERGEANT AT ARMS OF THE SENATE—GEORGE T. BROWN, of Illinois; JOHN R. FRENCH,[2] of New Hampshire

———

SPEAKER OF THE HOUSE OF REPRESENTATIVES—JAMES G. BLAINE,[3] of Maine

CLERK OF THE HOUSE—EDWARD MCPHERSON,[4] of Pennsylvania

SERGEANT AT ARMS OF THE HOUSE—NATHANIEL G. ORDWAY, of New Hampshire

DOORKEEPER OF THE HOUSE—OTIS S. BUXTON, of New York

POSTMASTER OF THE HOUSE—WILLIAM S. KING

ALABAMA

SENATORS

George E. Spencer, *Decatur*
Willard Warner, *Montgomery*

REPRESENTATIVES [5]

Alfred E. Buck, *Mobile*
Charles W. Buckley, *Montgomery*
Robert S. Heflin, *Opelika*
Charles Hays, *Eutaw*
Peter M. Dox, *Huntsville*
William C. Sherrod, *Courtland*

ARKANSAS

SENATORS

Alexander McDonald, *Little Rock*
Benjamin F. Rice, *Little Rock*

REPRESENTATIVES

Logan H. Roots, *Duvalls Bluff*
Anthony A. C. Rogers, *Pine Bluff*
Thomas Boles, *Dardanelle*

CALIFORNIA

SENATORS

Cornelius Cole, *San Francisco*
Eugene Casserly, *San Francisco*

REPRESENTATIVES

Samuel B. Axtell, *San Francisco*
Aaron A. Sargent, *Nevada City*
James A. Johnson, *Downiesville*

CONNECTICUT

SENATORS

Orris S. Ferry, *Norwalk*
William A. Buckingham, *Norwich*

REPRESENTATIVES [6]

Julius L. Strong, *Hartford*
Stephen W. Kellogg, *Waterbury*
Henry H. Starkweather, *Norwich*
William H. Barnum, *Lime Rock*

DELAWARE

SENATORS

Willard Saulsbury, *Georgetown*
Thomas F. Bayard, *Wilmington*

REPRESENTATIVE

At Large—Benjamin T. Biggs, *Summit Bridge*

FLORIDA

SENATORS

Thomas W. Osborn, *Pensacola*
Abijah Gilbert, *St. Augustine*

REPRESENTATIVE

At Large—Charles M. Hamilton, *Jacksonville*

---

[1] Elected March 23, 1869; April 9, 1869; May 28, 1870; July 1, 1870; July 14, 1870.
[2] Elected March 22, 1869.
[3] Elected March 4, 1869.
[4] Reelected March 5, 1869.
[5] Elected August 3, 1869.
[6] Elected April 5, 1869.

GEORGIA [7]

SENATORS [8]

Joshua Hill,[9] *Madison*
Homer V. M. Miller,[10] *Rome*

REPRESENTATIVES [11]

William W. Paine,[12] *Savannah*
Richard H. Whiteley,[13] *Bainbridge*
Marion Bethune,[14] *Talbotton*
Jefferson F. Long,[15] *Macon*
Stephen A. Corker,[16] *Waynesboro*
William P. Price,[14] *Dahlonega*
Pierce M. B. Young,[14] *Cartersville*

ILLINOIS

SENATORS

Lyman Trumbull, *Chicago*
Richard Yates, *Jacksonville*

REPRESENTATIVES

Norman B. Judd, *Chicago*
John F. Farnsworth, *St. Charles*
Elihu B. Washburne,[17] *Galena*
Horatio C. Burchard,[18] *Freeport*
John B. Hawley, *Rock Island*
Ebon C. Ingersoll, *Peoria*
Burton C. Cook, *Ottawa*
Jesse H. Moore, *Decatur*
Shelby M. Cullom, *Springfield*
Thompson W. McNeely, *Petersburg*
Albert G. Burr, *Carrollton*
Samuel S. Marshall, *McLeansboro*
John B. Hays, *Belleville*
John M. Crebs, *Carmi*
At Large—John A. Logan,[19] *Carbondale*

INDIANA

SENATORS

Oliver H. P. T. Morton, *Indianapolis*
Daniel D. Pratt, *Logansport*

REPRESENTATIVES

William E. Niblack, *Vincennes*
Michael C. Kerr, *New Albany*
William S. Holman, *Aurora*
George W. Julian,[20] *Centerville*
John Coburn, *Indianapolis*
Daniel W. Voorhees, *Terre Haute*
Godlove S. Orth, *La Fayette*
James N. Tyner,[21] *Peru*
John P. C. Shanks, *Jay Court House*
William Williams, *Warsaw*
Jasper Packard, *Laporte*

IOWA

SENATORS

James W. Grimes,[22] *Burlington*
James B. Howell,[23] *Keokuk*
James Harlan, *Mount Pleasant*

REPRESENTATIVES

George W. McCrary, *Keokuk*
William Smyth,[24] *Marion*
William P. Wolf,[25] *Tipton*
William B. Allison, *Dubuque*
William Loughridge, *Oskaloosa*
Frank W. Palmer, *Des Moines*
Charles Pomeroy, *Fort Dodge*

KANSAS

SENATORS

Samuel C. Pomeroy, *Atchison*
Edmund G. Ross, *Lawrence*

REPRESENTATIVE

At Large—Sidney Clarke, *Lawrence*

KENTUCKY

SENATORS

Garrett Davis, *Paris*
Thomas C. McCreery, *Owensboro*

REPRESENTATIVES

Lawrence S. Trimble, *Paducah*
William N. Sweeney, *Owensboro*
Jacob S. Golladay,[26] *Allensville*
Joseph H. Lewis,[27] *Glasgow*
J. Proctor Knott, *Lebanon*
Boyd Winchester, *Louisville*
Thomas L. Jones, *Newport*
James B. Beck, *Lexington*
George M. Adams,[28] *Barbourville*
John M. Rice,[29] *Louisa*

LOUISIANA

SENATORS

John S. Harris, *Vidalia*
William Pitt Kellogg, *New Orleans*

REPRESENTATIVES [30]

J. Hale Sypher,[31] *New Orleans*
Lionel A. Sheldon,[32] *New Orleans*
Chester B. Darrall,[33] *Brashear*
Joseph P. Newsham,[34] *St. Francisville*
Frank Morey,[35] *Monroe*

MAINE

SENATORS

William Pitt Fessenden,[36] *Portland*
Lot M. Morrill,[37] *Augusta*
Hannibal Hamlin, *Bangor*

---

[7] Formally readmitted to representation by act of July 15, 1870.

[8] The credentials of Mr. Hill and Mr. Miller, presented in the Fortieth Congress and undisposed of on the files of the Senate, were referred again to the Committee on the Judiciary March 9, 1869; they were reported back without recommendation and ordered to lie on the table March 17, 1869; they were again referred to the committee February 14, 1870. A new election was held in Georgia, and on July 15, 1870, the credentials of Richard H. Whiteley and Henry P. Farrow were presented and ordered to lie on the table, but were subsequently referred; on the same day of their presentation the act was approved readmitting Georgia to representation in Congress. The committee reported upon all the credentials January 23, 1871, resolving that Messrs. Hill and Miller were duly elected; that Mr. Hill should be permitted to take his seat, but that Mr. Miller was disqualified by reason of his service in the Confederate Army; this report was adopted February 1, 1871. A joint resolution prescribing a qualification oath for Mr. Miller was approved February 24, 1871; took his seat the same day.

[9] Took his seat under the resolution of February 1, 1871, on that day; term to expire March 3, 1873.

[10] Qualified under the terms of the joint resolution approved February 24, 1871, and took his seat on that date; term to expire March 3, 1871.

[11] Pierce M. B. Young, Nelson Tift, W. P. Edwards, J. W. Clift, Samuel F. Gove, and C. H. Prince presented credentials alleging their election as Representatives, April 20, 1868, the same election in which they were elected to the Fortieth Congress; by resolution of January 28, 1870, the House declared they were not entitled to seats. Pierce M. B. Young subsequently presented credentials under a later election and was seated.

[12] Qualified under act of July 11, 1868, and took his

seat January 23, 1871.

[13] Qualified under act of July 11, 1868, and took his seat February 9, 1871; election unsuccessfully contested by Nelson Tift.

[14] Qualified under act of July 11, 1868, and took his seat January 16, 1871.

[15] Qualified under act of July 2, 1862, and took his seat January 16, 1871.

[16] Qualified under act of July 11, 1868, and took his seat January 24, 1871; election unsuccessfully contested by Thomas P. Beard.

[17] Resigned March 6, 1869.

[18] Elected to fill vacancy caused by resignation of Elihu B. Washburne, and took his seat December 6, 1869.

[19] Reelected to the Forty-second Congress but resigned, having been elected Senator.

[20] Election unsuccessfully contested by John S. Reid.

[21] Elected to fill vacancy caused by resignation of Representative-elect Daniel D. Pratt (January 27, 1869), before the beginning of the congressional term, who had been elected Senator, and took his seat March 4, 1869.

[22] Resigned December 6, 1869.

[23] Elected to fill vacancy caused by resignation of James W. Grimes, and took his seat January 26, 1870.

[24] Died September 30, 1870.

[25] Elected to fill vacancy caused by death of William Smyth, and took his seat December 6, 1870.

[26] Resigned February 28, 1870; the Governor of Kentucky peremptorily refused to accept the resignation and requested its withdrawl; the request was complied with; on March 7, 1870, a resolution was presented in the House as a question of privilege, citing these facts and granting him the right to resume his seat; the House refused to entertain it.

[27] Elected to fill vacancy caused by resignation of Jacob S. Golladay, and took his seat May 10, 1870.

[28] Election unsuccessfully contested by Sidney M. Barnes.

[29] Seated by resolution of March 5, 1869; election unsuccessfully contested by John T. Zeigler.

[30] The Governor of Louisiana having officially declared that the election held in the State of Louisiana on November 3, 1868, "Did not elicit an honest will of the people, * * *," a resolution was adopted on March 9, 1869, directing the Committee on Elections to inquire into the validity of the elections of those presenting credentials; all seats were contested, and the Members-elect were not sworn pending the contests.

[31] Contested the election of Louis St. Martin; committee reported in favor of seating Mr. Sypher, and House adopted the report by a vote of 78 to 73, moved to reconsider by a vote of 86 to 79, then adopted a substitute resolution declaring the seat vacant by a vote of 96 to 68 (April 20, 1870); subsequently elected, and took his seat December 5, 1870.

[32] Election unsuccessfully contested by Caleb S. Hunt; took his seat April 8, 1869.

[33] Election unsuccessfully contested by Adolphe Bailey; took his seat July 6, 1870.

[34] Successfully contested the election of Michael Ryan (who had not been permitted to qualify), and took his seat May 23, 1870.

[35] Frank Morey, G. W. McCranie, and P. J. Kennedy each presented credentials claiming to be the Member-elect from the fifth congressional district; by resolution of April 28, 1870, it was declared there was no lawful election in the district. Morey presented credentials under a subsequent election, and took his seat December 6, 1870.

[36] Died September 9, 1869.

[37] Appointed to fill vacancy caused by death of William Pitt Fessenden, and took his seat December 6, 1869; subsequently elected.

MARYLAND — REPRESENTATIVES (left column continues)

REPRESENTATIVES

John Lynch, *Portland*
Samuel P. Morrill, *Farmington*
James G. Blaine, *Augusta*
John A. Peters, *Bangor*
Eugene Hale, *Ellsworth*

MARYLAND

SENATORS

George Vickers, *Chestertown*
William T. Hamilton, *Hagerstown*

REPRESENTATIVES

Samuel Hambleton, *Easton*
Stevenson Archer, *Bel Air*
Thomas Swann, *Baltimore*
Patrick Hamill, *Oakland*
Frederick Stone, *Port Tobacco*

MASSACHUSETTS

SENATORS

Charles Sumner, *Boston*
Henry Wilson, *Natick*

REPRESENTATIVES

James Buffinton, *Fall River*
Oakes Ames, *North Easton*
Ginery Twichell, *Brookline*
Samuel Hooper, *Boston*
Benjamin F. Butler, *Lowell*
Nathaniel P. Banks, *Waltham*
George S. Boutwell,[38] *Groton*
George M. Brooks,[39] *Concord*
George F. Hoar, *Worcester*
William B. Washburn, *Greenfield*
Henry L. Dawes, *Pittsfield*

MICHIGAN

SENATORS

Zachariah Chandler, *Detroit*
Jacob M. Howard, *Detroit*

REPRESENTATIVES

Fernando C. Beaman, *Adrain*
William L. Stoughton, *Sturgis*
Austin Blair, *Jackson*
Thomas W. Ferry,[40] *Grand Haven*
Omar D. Conger, *Port Huron*
Randolph Strickland, *St. Johns*

MINNESOTA

SENATORS

Alexander Ramsey, *St. Paul*
Daniel S. Norton,[41] *Winona*
William Windom,[42] *Winona*
Ozora P. Stearns,[43] *Rochester*

REPRESENTATIVES

Morton S. Wilkinson, *Mankato*
Eugene M. Wilson, *Minneapolis*

MISSISSIPPI [44]

SENATORS

Hiram R. Revels,[45] *Natchez*
Adelbert Ames,[46] *Natchez*

REPRESENTATIVES

George E. Harris,[47] *Hernando*
Joseph L. Morphis,[47] *Pontotoc*
Henry W. Barry,[48] *Columbus*
George C. McKee,[49] *Vicksburg*
Legrand W. Perce,[49] *Natchez*

MISSOURI

SENATORS

Charles D. Drake,[50] *St. Louis*
Daniel T. Jewett,[51] *St. Louis*
Francis P. Blair, Jr.,[52] *St. Louis*
Carl Schurz, *St. Louis*

REPRESENTATIVES

Erastus Wells, *St. Louis*
Gustavus A. Finkelnburg, *St. Louis*
James R. McCormick, *Ironton*
Sempronius H. Boyd, *Springfield*
Samuel S. Burdett, *Osceola*
Robert T. Van Horn,[53] *Kansas City*
Joel F. Asper, *Chillicothe*
John F. Benjamin, *Shelbyville*
David P. Dyer,[54] *Louisiana*

NEBRASKA

SENATORS

John M. Thayer, *Omaha*
Thomas W. Tipton, *Brownville*

REPRESENTATIVE

At Large—John Taffe, *Omaha*

NEVADA

SENATORS

William M. Stewart, *Virginia City*
James W. Nye, *Carson City*

REPRESENTATIVE

At Large—Thomas Fitch, *Belmont*

NEW HAMPSHIRE

SENATORS

Aaron H. Cragin, *Lebanon*
James W. Patterson, *Hanover*

REPRESENTATIVES

Jacob H. Ela, *Rochester*
Aaron F. Stevens, *Nashua*
Jacob Benton, *Lancaster*

NEW JERSEY

SENATORS

Alexander G. Cattell, *Camden*
John P. Stockton, *Trenton*

REPRESENTATIVES

William Moore, *Mays Landing*
Charles Haight, *Freehold*
John T. Bird, *Flemington*
John Hill, *Boonton*
Orestes Cleveland, *Jersey City*

NEW YORK

SENATORS

Roscoe Conkling, *Utica*
Reuben E. Fenton, *Jamestown*

REPRESENTATIVES

Henry A. Reeves, *Greenport*
John G. Schumaker, *Brooklyn*
Henry W. Slocum, *Brooklyn*
John Fox, *New York City*
John Morrissey, *New York City*
Samuel S. Cox, *New York City*
Hervey C. Calkin, *New York City*
James Brooks, *New York City*
Fernando Wood, *New York City*
Clarkson N. Potter, *New Rochelle*
George W. Greene,[55] *Goshen*
Charles H. Van Wyck,[56] *Middletown*
John H. Ketcham, *Dover*
John A. Griswold, *Catskill*
Stephen L. Mayham, *Schoharie*

---

[38] Resigned March 12, 1869, having been appointed Secretary of the Treasury.
[39] Elected to fill vacancy caused by resignation of George S. Boutwell, and took his seat December 6, 1869.
[40] Reelected to the Forty-second Congress but resigned, having been elected Senator.
[41] Died July 13, 1870.
[42] Appointed to fill vacancy caused by death of Daniel S. Norton, and took his seat December 1, 1870.
[43] Elected to fill vacancy caused by death of Daniel S. Norton, and took his seat January 23, 1871.

[44] Readmitted to representation by act of February 23, 1870.
[45] Took his seat February 25, 1870; term to expire March 3, 1871.
[46] Took his seat April 1, 1870; term to expire March 3, 1875.
[47] Qualified under act of July 11, 1868, and took his seat February 23, 1870.
[48] Took his seat April 8, 1870.
[49] Qualified under act of July 2, 1862, and took his seat February 23, 1870.
[50] Resigned December 19, 1870.

[51] Appointed to fill vacancy caused by resignation of Charles D. Drake, and took his seat December 22, 1870.
[52] Elected to fill vacancy caused by resignation of Charles D. Drake, and took his seat January 25, 1871.
[53] Election unsuccessfully contested by James Shields.
[54] Election unsuccessfully contested by William F. Switzler.
[55] Served until February 17, 1870; succeeded by Charles H. Van Wyck, who contested his election.
[56] Successfully contested the election of George W. Greene, and took his seat February 17, 1870.

NEW YORK—Continued

REPRESENTATIVES—continued

Adolphus H. Tanner, *Whitehall*
Orange Ferriss, *Glens Falls*
William A. Wheeler, *Malone*
Stephen Sanford, *Amsterdam*
Charles Knapp, *Deposit*
Addison H. Laflin, *Herkimer*
Alexander H. Bailey, *Rome*
John C. Churchill, *Oswego*
Dennis McCarthy, *Syracuse*
George W. Cowles, *Clyde*
William H. Kelsey, *Geneseo*
Giles W. Hotchkiss, *Binghamton*
Hamilton Ward, *Belmont*
Noah Davis,[57] *Albion*
Charles H. Holmes,[58] *Albion*
John Fisher, *Batavia*
David S. Bennett, *Buffalo*
Porter Sheldon, *Jamestown*

NORTH CAROLINA

SENATORS

Joseph C. Abbott, *Wilmington*
John Pool, *Elizabeth City*

REPRESENTATIVES

Clinton L. Cobb, *Elizabeth City*
David Heaton,[59] *New Bern*
Joseph Dixon,[60] *Hookerton*
Oliver H. Dockery, *Mangum*
John T. Deweese,[61] *Raleigh*
John Manning, Jr.,[62] *Pittsboro*
Israel G. Lash, *Salem*
Francis E. Shober,[63] *Salisbury*
Alexander H. Jones,[64] *Asheville*

OHIO

SENATORS

John Sherman, *Mansfield*
Allen G. Thurman, *Columbus*

REPRESENTATIVES

Peter W. Strader,[65] *Cincinnati*
Job E. Stevenson, *Cincinnati*
Robert C. Schenck,[66] *Dayton*

William Lawrence, *Bellefontaine*
William Mungen, *Findlay*
John A. Smith, *Hillsboro*
James J. Winans, *Xenia*
John Beatty, *Cardington*
Edward F. Dickinson, *Fremont*
Truman H. Hoag,[67] *Toledo*
Erasmus D. Peck,[68] *Perrysburg*
John T. Wilson, *Tranquility*
Philadelph Van Trump, *Lancaster*
George W. Morgan, *Mount Vernon*
Martin Welker, *Wooster*
Eliakim H. Moore, *Athens*
John A. Bingham, *Cadiz*
Jacob A. Ambler, *Salem*
William H. Upson, *Akron*
James A. Garfield, *Hiram*

OREGON

SENATORS

George H. Williams, *Portland*
Henry W. Corbett, *Portland*

REPRESENTATIVE

At Large—Joseph S. Smith, *Portland*

PENNSYLVANIA

SENATORS

Simon Cameron, *Harrisburg*
John Scott, *Huntingdon*

REPRESENTATIVES

Samuel J. Randall, *Philadelphia*
Charles O'Neill, *Philadelphia*
John Moffet,[69] *Philadelphia*
Leonard Myers,[70] *Philadelphia*
William D. Kelley, *Philadelphia*
John R. Reading,[71] *Somerton*
Caleb N. Taylor,[72] *Bristol*
John D. Stiles, *Allentown*
Washington Townsend, *West Chester*
J. Lawrence Getz, *Reading*
Oliver J. Dickey, *Lancaster*
Henry L. Cake, *Tamaqua*
Daniel M. Van Auken, *Milford*
George W. Woodward, *Wilkes-Barre*
Ulysses Mercur, *Towanda*
John B. Packer, *Sunbury*

Richard J. Haldeman, *Harrisburg*
John Cessna, *Bedford*
Daniel J. Morrell, *Johnstown*
William H. Armstrong, *Williamsport*
Glenni W. Scofield, *Warren*
Calvin W. Gilfillan, *Franklin*
John Covode,[73] *Lockport*
James S. Negley, *Pittsburgh*
Darwin Phelps, *Kittanning*
Joseph B. Donley, *Waynesburg*

RHODE ISLAND

SENATORS

Henry B. Anthony, *Providence*
William Sprague, *Providence*

REPRESENTATIVES

Thomas A. Jenckes, *Providence*
Nathan F. Dixon, *Westerly*

SOUTH CAROLINA

SENATORS

Thomas J. Robertson, *Columbia*
Frederick A. Sawyer, *Charleston*

REPRESENTATIVES

B. Frank Whittemore,[74] *Darlington*
Joseph H. Rainey,[75] *Georgetown*
Christopher C. Bowen, *Charleston*
Solomon L. Hoge,[76] *Columbia*
Alexander S. Wallace,[77] *Yorkville*

TENNESSEE

SENATORS

Joseph S. Fowler, *Nashville*
William G. Brownlow, *Knoxville*

REPRESENTATIVES [78]

Roderick R. Butler, *Taylorsville*
Horace Maynard, *Knoxville*
William B. Stokes, *Alexandria*
Lewis Tillman,[79] *Shelbyville*
William F. Prosser, *Nashville*
Samuel M. Arnell, *Columbia*
Isaac R. Hawkins, *Huntingdon*
William J. Smith, *Memphis*

---

[57] Resigned July 15, 1870.
[58] Elected to fill vacancy caused by resignation of Noah Davis, and took his seat December 6, 1870.
[59] Died June 25, 1870.
[60] Elected to fill vacancy caused by death of David Heaton, and took his seat December 5, 1870.
[61] Resigned February 28, 1870; on March 1, 1870, the Committee on Military Affairs reported a resolution declaring that he had made "an appointment to the United States Naval Academy in violation of law, and that such appointment was influenced by pecuniary considerations," and condemning the action; upon a roll call the resolution was agreed to by a vote of 170 to 0.
[62] Elected to fill vacancy caused by the resignation of John T. Deweese, and took his seat December 7, 1870.
[63] Election unsuccessfully contested by Nathaniel Boyden.
[64] Election unsuccessfully contested by Plato Durham.
[65] Election unsuccessfully contested by Benjamin Eggleston.
[66] Resigned January 5, 1871.
[67] Died February 5, 1870.

[68] Elected to fill vacancy caused by death of Truman H. Hoag, and took his seat April 23, 1870.
[69] Served until April 9, 1869; succeeded by Leonard Myers, who contested his election.
[70] Successfully contested the election of John Moffet, and took his seat April 9, 1869.
[71] Served until April 13, 1870; succeeded by Caleb N. Taylor, who contested his election.
[72] Successfully contested the election of John R. Reading, and took his seat April 13, 1870.
[73] Both John Covode and Henry D. Foster claimed to have been elected, while the governor refused to sign a certificate or declare either elected; the House at first refused admission to either; case was recommitted for investigation and on February 9, 1870, the House declared Mr. Covode entitled to the seat; took his seat the same day; died January 11, 1871.
[74] February 21, 1870, the Committee on Military Affairs presented a report showing he had been "influenced by improper pecuniary considerations in making appointments to the Military and Naval Academies," and a resolution for his expulsion; pending action he resigned February 24, 1870; following the

announcement, the House adopted a resolution, without a dissenting vote, declaring he had made such appointments in violation of law, that they were influenced by pecuniary considerations, that he was unworthy of a seat in the body, and condemning his conduct. June 18, 1870, credentials of his reelection were presented; on June 21, 1870, the House passed a resolution citing its previous action, declining to allow him to be sworn, and directing the return of his credentials.
[75] Elected to fill vacancy caused by B. Frank Whittemore being refused his seat; took his seat December 12, 1870.
[76] Successfully contested the election of J. P. Reed, and took his seat April 8, 1869; the House had refused to permit Mr. Reed to qualify upon the ground of disloyalty.
[77] Successfully contested the election of William D. Simpson, who was not permitted to qualify on his credentials, and took his seat May 27, 1870.
[78] John B. Rogers claimed a seat as Representative at large, but claim was not seriously considered.
[79] Election unsuccessfully contested by C. A. Sheafe.

TEXAS [80]

SENATORS

Morgan C. Hamilton,[81] *Austin*
James W. Flanagan,[82] *Wallings Ferry*

REPRESENTATIVES

George W. Whitmore,[83] *Tyler*
John C. Conner,[84] *Sherman*
William T. Clark,[83] *Galveston*
Edward Degener,[83] *San Antonio*

VERMONT

SENATORS

George F. Edmunds, *Burlington*
Justin S. Morrill, *Strafford*

REPRESENTATIVES

Charles W. Willard, *Montpelier*
Luke P. Poland, *St. Johnsbury*
Worthington C. Smith, *St. Albans*

VIRGINIA [85]

SENATORS

John W. Johnston,[86] *Abingdon*
John F. Lewis,[87] *Port Republic*

REPRESENTATIVES [88]

Richard S. Ayer,[89] *Warsaw*
James H. Platt, Jr.,[90] *Petersburg*
Charles H. Porter,[90] *Richmond*
George W. Booker,[91] *Martinsville*
Robert Ridgway,[92] *Cool Well*
Richard T. W. Duke,[93] *Charlottesville*
William Milnes, Jr.,[90] *Shenandoah Iron Works*
Lewis McKenzie,[94] *Alexandria*
James King Gibson,[95] *Abingdon*

WEST VIRGINIA

SENATORS

Waitman T. Willey, *Morgantown*
Arthur I. Boreman, *Parkersburg*

REPRESENTATIVES

Isaac H. Duval, *Wellsburg*
James C. McGrew, *Kingwood*
John S. Witcher, *Guyandotte*

WISCONSIN

SENATORS

Timothy O. Howe, *Green Bay*
Matthew H. Carpenter, *Milwaukee*

REPRESENTATIVES

Halbert E. Paine, *Milwaukee*
Benjamin F. Hopkins,[96] *Madison*
David Atwood,[97] *Madison*
Amasa Cobb, *Mineral Point*
Charles A. Eldridge, *Fond du Lac*
Philetus Sawyer, *Oshkosh*
Cadwallader C. Washburn, *La Crosse*

TERRITORY OF ARIZONA

DELEGATE

Richard C. McCormick, *Tucson*

TERRITORY OF COLORADO

DELEGATE

Allen A. Bradford, *Pueblo*

TERRITORY OF DAKOTA

DELEGATE

Solomon L. Spink, *Yankton*

TERRITORY OF IDAHO

DELEGATE

Jacob K. Shafer, *Idaho City*

TERRITORY OF MONTANA

DELEGATE

James M. Cavanaugh, *Helena*

TERRITORY OF NEW MEXICO

DELEGATE

J. Francisco Chaves, *Santa Fe*

TERRITORY OF UTAH

DELEGATE

William H. Hooper, *Salt Lake City*

TERRITORY OF WASHINGTON

DELEGATE

Selucius Garfielde, *Olympia*

TERRITORY OF WYOMING [98]

DELEGATE

Stephen F. Nuckolls,[99] *Cheyenne*

---

[80] Readmitted to representation by act of March 30, 1870.
[81] Took his seat March 31, 1870; term to expire March 3, 1871.
[82] Took his seat March 31, 1870; term to expire March 3, 1875.
[83] Qualified under act of July 2, 1862, and took his seat March 31, 1870.
[84] Qualified under act of July 2, 1862, and took his seat March 31, 1870; election unsuccessfully contested by Benjamin F. Grafton.
[85] Readmitted to representation by act of January 26, 1870.
[86] Took his seat January 28, 1870; term to expire March 3, 1871.
[87] Took his seat January 27, 1870; term to expire March 3, 1875.

[88] The Virginia constitutional convention called under reconstruction laws passed an ordinance providing for a ninth Representative at large; credentials of Joseph Segar as such Representative were presented January 25, 1870; on July 11, 1870, the House adopted a resolution, without division, declaring him not entitled to a seat.
[89] Qualified under act of July 2, 1862, and took his seat January 31, 1870.
[90] Qualified under act of July 2, 1862, and took his seat January 27, 1870.
[91] Qualified under act of July 2, 1862, and took his seat February 1, 1870; election unsuccessfully contested by George Tucker.
[92] Qualified under act of July 2, 1862, and took his seat January 27, 1870; died October 16, 1870.

[93] Elected to fill vacancy caused by death of Robert Ridgway, qualified under act of July 11, 1868, and took his seat December 5, 1870.
[94] Qualified under act of July 2, 1862, and took his seat January 31, 1870; election unsuccessfully contested by Charles Whittlesey.
[95] Qualified under act of July 11, 1868, and took his seat January 28, 1870.
[96] Died January 1, 1870.
[97] Elected to fill vacancy caused by death of Benjamin F. Hopkins, and took his seat February 23, 1870.
[98] Formed from a portion of the territory ceded to the United States by France by treaty of Paris of April 30, 1803, and granted a Delegate in Congress by act of July 25, 1868.
[99] Took his seat December 6, 1869.

FORTY-SECOND CONGRESS

MARCH 4, 1871, TO MARCH 3, 1873

FIRST SESSION—*March 4, 1871, to April 20, 1871*

SECOND SESSION—*December 4, 1871, to June 10, 1872*

THIRD SESSION—*December 2, 1872, to March 3, 1873*

SPECIAL SESSION OF THE SENATE—*May 10, 1871, to May 27, 1871*

———

VICE PRESIDENT OF THE UNITED STATES—Schuyler Colfax, of Indiana

PRESIDENT PRO TEMPORE OF THE SENATE—Henry B. Anthony,[1] of Rhode Island

SECRETARY OF THE SENATE—George C. Gorham, of California

SERGEANT AT ARMS OF THE SENATE—John R. French, of New Hampshire

———

SPEAKER OF THE HOUSE OF REPRESENTATIVES—James G. Blaine,[2] of Maine

CLERK OF THE HOUSE—Edward McPherson,[3] of Pennsylvania

SERGEANT AT ARMS OF THE HOUSE—Nathaniel G. Ordway, of New Hampshire

DOORKEEPER OF THE HOUSE—Otis S. Buxton, of New York

POSTMASTER OF THE HOUSE—William S. King

ALABAMA

SENATORS

George E. Spencer, *Decatur*
George T. Goldthwaite,[4] *Montgomery*

REPRESENTATIVES

Benjamin S. Turner, *Selma*
Charles W. Buckley, *Montgomery*
William A. Handley,[5] *Roanoke*
Charles Hays, *Eutaw*
Peter M. Dox, *Huntsville*
Joseph H. Sloss, *Tuscumbia*

ARKANSAS

SENATORS

Benjamin F. Rice, *Little Rock*
Powell Clayton, *Little Rock*

REPRESENTATIVES

James M. Hanks, *Helena*
Oliver P. Snyder, *Pine Bluff*

John Edwards,[6] *Fort Smith*
Thomas Boles,[7] *Dardanelle*

CALIFORNIA

SENATORS

Cornelius Cole, *San Francisco*
Eugene Casserly, *San Francisco*

REPRESENTATIVES [8]

Sherman O. Houghton, *San Jose*
Aaron A. Sargent, *Nevada City*
John M. Coghlan, *Suisun City*

CONNECTICUT

SENATORS

Orris S. Ferry, *Norwalk*
William A. Buckingham, *Norwich*

REPRESENTATIVES [9]

Julius L. Strong,[10] *Hartford*
Joseph R. Hawley,[11] *Hartford*
Stephen W. Kellogg, *Waterbury*
Henry H. Starkweather, *Norwich*
William H. Barnum, *Lime Rock*

DELAWARE

SENATORS

Thomas F. Bayard, *Wilmington*
Eli Saulsbury, *Dover*

REPRESENTATIVE

At Large—Benjamin T. Biggs, *Summit Bridge*

FLORIDA

SENATORS

Thomas W. Osborn, *Pensacola*
Abijah Gilbert, *St. Augustine*

---

[1] Elected March 10, 1871; April 17, 1871; May 23, 1871 (special session of the Senate); December 21, 1871; February 23, 1872; June 8, 1872; December 4, 1872; December 13, 1872; December 20, 1872; and January 24, 1873.
[2] Reelected March 4, 1871.
[3] Reelected March 4, 1871.
[4] Credentials presented February 6, 1871, in the preceding Congress; appeared to take the oath of office March 4, 1871; protest against his being seated presented the same day, and he was not permitted to qualify; on January 9, 1872, the Senate, by resolution, gave him permission to take his seat, pending further investigations; took his seat January 15, 1872; no further action.
[5] Election unsuccessfully contested by B. W. Norris.
[6] Served until February 9, 1872; succeeded by Thomas Boles, who contested his election.
[7] Successfully contested the election of John Edwards, and took his seat February 9, 1872.
[8] Elected September 5, 1871.
[9] Elected April 4, 1871.
[10] Died September 7, 1872.
[11] Elected to fill vacancy caused by death of Julius L. Strong, and took his seat December 2, 1872.

REPRESENTATIVE AT LARGE

Josiah T. Walls,[12] *Gainesville*
Silas L. Niblack,[13] *Gainesville*

GEORGIA

SENATORS

Joshua Hill, *Madison*
Thomas M. Norwood,[14] *Savannah*

REPRESENTATIVES

Archibald T. MacIntyre,[15] *Thomasville*
Richard H. Whiteley,[16] *Bainbridge*
John S. Bigby, *Newman*
Thomas J. Speer,[17] *Barnesville*
Erasmus W. Beck,[18] *Griffin*
Dudley M. DuBose,[19] *Washington*
William P. Price, *Dahlonega*
Pierce M. B. Young, *Cartersville*

ILLINOIS

SENATORS

Lyman Trumbull, *Chicago*
John A. Logan, *Carbondale*

REPRESENTATIVES

Charles B. Farwell, *Chicago*
John F. Farnsworth, *St. Charles*
Horatio C. Burchard, *Freeport*
John B. Hawley, *Rock Island*
Bradford N. Stevens, *Tiskilwa*
Burton C. Cook,[20] *Ottawa*
Henry Snapp,[21] *Joliet*
Jesse H. Moore, *Decatur*
James C. Robinson, *Springfield*
Thompson W. McNeely, *Petersburg*
Edward Y. Rice, *Hillsboro*
Samuel S. Marshall, *McLeansboro*
John B. Hay, *Belleville*
John M. Crebs, *Carmi*
At Large—John L. Beveridge,[22] *Evanston*

INDIANA

SENATORS

Oliver H. P. T. Morton, *Indianapolis*
Daniel D. Pratt, *Logansport*

REPRESENTATIVES

William E. Niblack, *Vincennes*
Michael C. Kerr, *New Albany*
William S. Holman, *Aurora*

Jeremiah M. Wilson,[23] *Connersville*
John Coburn, *Indianapolis*
Daniel W. Voorhees, *Terre Haute*
Mahlon D. Manson, *Crawfordsville*
James N. Tyner, *Peru*
John P. C. Shanks, *Jay Court House*
William Williams, *Warsaw*
Jasper Packard, *Laporte*

IOWA

SENATORS

James Harlan, *Mount Pleasant*
George G. Wright, *Des Moines*

REPRESENTATIVES

George W. McCrary, *Keokuk*
Aylett R. Cotton, *Lyons*
William G. Donnan, *Independence*
Madison M. Walden, *Centerville*
Frank W. Palmer, *Des Moines*
Jackson Orr, *Montana*

KANSAS

SENATORS[24]

Samuel C. Pomeroy, *Atchison*
Alexander Caldwell, *Leavenworth*

REPRESENTATIVE

At Large—David P. Lowe, *Fort Scott*

KENTUCKY

SENATORS

Garrett Davis,[25] *Paris*
Willis B. Machen,[26] *Eddyville*
John W. Stevenson, *Covington*

REPRESENTATIVES

Edward Crossland, *Mayfield*
Henry D. McHenry, *Hartford*
Joseph H. Lewis, *Glasgow*
William B. Read, *Hodgensville*
Boyd Winchester, *Louisville*
William E. Arthur, *Covington*
James B. Beck, *Lexington*
George M. Adams, *Barbourville*
John M. Rice, *Louisa*

LOUISIANA

SENATORS

William Pitt Kellogg,[27] *New Orleans*
J. Rodman West, *New Orleans*

REPRESENTATIVES

J. Hale Sypher, *New Orleans*
Lionel A. Sheldon, *New Orleans*
Chester B. Darrall, *Brashear*
James McCleery,[28] *Shreveport*
Aleck Boarman,[29] *Shreveport*
Frank Morey, *Monroe*

MAINE

SENATORS

Hannibal Hamlin, *Bangor*
Lot M. Morrill, *Augusta*

REPRESENTATIVES

John Lynch, *Portland*
William P. Frye, *Lewiston*
James G. Blaine, *Augusta*
John A. Peters, *Bangor*
Eugene Hale, *Ellsworth*

MARYLAND

SENATORS

George Vickers, *Chestertown*
William T. Hamilton, *Hagerstown*

REPRESENTATIVES

Samuel Hambleton, *Easton*
Stevenson Archer, *Bel Air*
Thomas Swann, *Baltimore*
John Ritchie, *Frederick*
William M. Merrick, *Ilchester*

MASSACHUSETTS

SENATORS

Charles Sumner, *Boston*
Henry Wilson,[30] *Natick*

REPRESENTATIVES

James Buffinton, *Fall River*
Oakes Ames, *North Easton*
Ginery Twichell, *Brookline*
Samuel Hooper, *Boston*
Benjamin F. Butler, *Lowell*
Nathaniel P. Banks, *Waltham*

---

[12] Served until January 29, 1873; succeeded by Silas L. Niblack, who contested his election.
[13] Successfully contested the election of Josiah T. Walls, and took his seat January 29, 1873.
[14] Took his seat December 19, 1871; Foster Blodgett presented credentials as a Senator-elect, but the Senate declared him not elected in accordance with the Constitution; vacancy in this class from March 4, 1871, to November 13, 1871.
[15] Election unsuccessfully contested by Virgil Hilyer.
[16] Election unsuccessfully contested by Nelson Tift.
[17] Died August 18, 1872.
[18] Elected to fill vacancy caused by death of Thomas J. Speer, and took his seat December 2, 1872.
[19] Election unsuccessfully contested by Isham S. Fannin.
[20] Resigned August 26, 1871.
[21] Elected to fill vacancy caused by resignation of Burton C. Cook, and took his seat December 4, 1871.

[22] Elected to fill vacancy caused by resignation of Representative-elect John A. Logan, in preceding Congress, and took his seat December 4, 1871; resigned January 4, 1873.
[23] Election unsuccessfully contested by David S. Gooding.
[24] May 11, 1872, the Committee on Privileges and Elections was authorized to investigate charges of bribery and corruption in connection with the election of both the sitting Senators; June 3, 1872, it reported that in the case of Mr. Pomeroy such charges were totally unsustained; in the case of Mr. Caldwell the report was directly to the contrary, and on February 17, 1873, it reported a resolution declaring him "not duly and legally elected"; this report was not acted upon during the Congress, but early in the succeeding Congress, during the special session of the Senate, while the report was pending and under discussion, Mr. Caldwell resigned (March 24, 1873).

[25] Died September 22, 1872.
[26] Appointed to fill vacancy caused by death of Garrett Davis, and took his seat December 2, 1872.
[27] Resigned November 1, 1872; on January 22, 1873, credentials of John Ray and William L. McMillen, each claiming to have been elected to fill the vacancy, were presented and referred; February 20, 1873, the committee reported that neither of the claimants was entitled to a seat, as no State government existed at the time in Louisiana, and recommended the passage of a bill ordering a new election; such a bill was rejected February 27, 1873; no further action was taken on the credentials and the seat remained vacant to the close of the Congress.
[28] Died November 5, 1871, never having qualified.
[29] Elected to fill vacancy caused by death of James McCleery, and took his seat December 3, 1872.
[30] Resigned March 3, 1873, having been elected Vice President.

MASSACHUSETTS—Continued

REPRESENTATIVES—continued

George M. Brooks,[31] *Concord*
Constantine C. Esty,[32] *Framingham*
George F. Hoar, *Worcester*
William B. Washburn,[33] *Greenfield*
Alvah Crocker,[34] *Fitchburg*
Henry L. Dawes, *Pittsfield*

MICHIGAN

SENATORS

Zachariah Chandler, *Detroit*
Thomas W. Ferry, *Grand Haven*

REPRESENTATIVES

Henry Waldron, *Hillsdale*
William L. Stoughton, *Sturgis*
Austin Blair, *Jackson*
Wilder D. Foster,[35] *Grand Rapids*
Omar D. Conger, *Port Huron*
Jabez G. Sutherland, *Saginaw*

MINNESOTA

SENATORS

Alexander Ramsey, *St. Paul*
William Windom, *Winona*

REPRESENTATIVES

Mark H. Dunnell, *Owatonna*
John T. Averill, *St. Paul*

MISSISSIPPI

SENATORS

Adelbert Ames, *Natchez*
James L. Alcorn,[36] *Friars Point*

REPRESENTATIVES

George E. Harris, *Hernando*
Joseph L. Morphis, *Pontotoc*
Henry W. Barry, *Columbus*
George C. McKee, *Vicksburg*
Legrand W. Perce, *Natchez*

MISSOURI

SENATORS

Carl Schurz, *St. Louis*
Francis P. Blair, Jr., *St. Louis*

REPRESENTATIVES

Erastus Wells, *St. Louis*
Gustavus A. Finkelnburg, *St. Louis*
James R. McCormick, *Arcadia*
Harrison E. Havens, *Springfield*
Samuel S. Burdett, *Osceola*
Abram Comingo, *Independence*
Isaac C. Parker, *St. Joseph*
James G. Blair, *Canton*
Andrew King, *St. Charles*

NEBRASKA

SENATORS

Thomas W. Tipton, *Brownville*
Phineas W. Hitchcock, *Omaha*

REPRESENTATIVE

At Large—John Taffe, *Omaha*

NEVADA

SENATORS

William M. Stewart, *Virginia City*
James W. Nye, *Carson City*

REPRESENTATIVE

At Large—Charles W. Kendall, *Hamilton*

NEW HAMPSHIRE

SENATORS

Aaron H. Cragin, *Lebanon*
James W. Patterson,[37] *Hanover*

REPRESENTATIVES

Ellery A. Hibbard, *Laconia*
Samuel N. Bell, *Manchester*
Hosea W. Parker, *Claremont*

NEW JERSEY

SENATORS

John P. Stockton, *Trenton*
Frederick T. Frelinghuysen, *Newark*

REPRESENTATIVES

John W. Hazelton, *Mullica Hill*
Samuel C. Forker, *Bordentown*
John T. Bird, *Flemington*
John Hill, *Boonton*
George A. Halsey, *Newark*

NEW YORK

SENATORS

Roscoe Conkling, *Utica*
Reuben E. Fenton, *Jamestown*

REPRESENTATIVES

Dwight Townsend, *Stapleton*
Thomas Kinsella, *Brooklyn*
Henry W. Slocum, *Brooklyn*
Robert B. Roosevelt, *New York City*
William R. Roberts, *New York City*
Samuel S. Cox, *New York City*
Smith Ely, Jr., *New York City*
James Brooks, *New York City*
Fernando Wood, *New York City*
Clarkson N. Potter, *New Rochelle*
Charles St. John, *Port Jervis*
John H. Ketcham, *Dover Plains*
Joseph H. Tuthill, *Ellenville*
Eli Perry, *Albany*
Joseph M. Warren, *Troy*
John Rogers, *Black Brook*
William A. Wheeler, *Malone*
John M. Carroll, *Johnstown*
Elizur H. Prindle, *Norwich*
Clinton L. Merriam, *Locust Grove*
Ellis H. Roberts, *Utica*
William E. Lansing, *Chittenango*
R. Holland Duell, *Cortland*
John E. Seeley, *Ovid*
William H. Lamport, *Canandaigua*
Milo Goodrich, *Dryden*
H. Boardman Smith, *Elmira*
Freeman Clarke, *Rochester*
Seth Wakeman, *Batavia*
William Williams, *Buffalo*
Walter L. Sessions, *Panama*

NORTH CAROLINA

SENATORS

John Pool, *Elizabeth City*
Matt W. Ransom,[38] *Weldon*

REPRESENTATIVES

Clinton L. Cobb, *Elizabeth City*
Charles R. Thomas, *New Bern*
Alfred M. Waddell, *Wilmington*
Sion H. Rogers,[39] *Raleigh*
James M. Leach, *Lexington*
Francis E. Shober, *Salisbury*
James C. Harper, *Patterson*

---

[31] Resigned May 13, 1872, to become judge of probate court.

[32] Elected to fill vacancy caused by resignation of George M. Brooks, and took his seat December 2, 1872.

[33] Resigned December 5, 1871, having been elected governor.

[34] Elected to fill vacancy caused by resignation of William B. Washburn, and took his seat February 14, 1872.

[35] Elected to fill vacancy caused by resignation of Representative-elect Thomas W. Ferry, in preceding Congress, and took his seat December 4, 1871.

[36] Elected January 18, 1870, for the term beginning March 4, 1871, but did not accept or qualify until December 4, 1871, preferring to retain the governorship.

[37] February 5, 1873, a select committee was appointed to consider matters presented in a communication from the House of Representatives and accompanying testimony, reflecting upon the conduct of certain Senators in connection with the "Credit Mobilier of America"; February 27, 1873, the committee reported, exonerating other Senators mentioned in the report, and a resolution favoring the expulsion of Mr. Patterson; as the Congress and Mr. Patterson's term expired simultaneously on March 3, 1873, no final action was reached.

[38] Joseph C. Abbott was a claimant for this seat; the Committee on Privileges and Elections reported February 28, 1872, that Zebulon B. Vance had received "a majority of the whole number of votes cast in each house," and Mr. Abbott received the next highest number of votes; the next day Mr. Vance was declared duly elected. Mr. Abbott rested his claim on what he assumed to be the legal result of the conceded ineligibility of Mr. Vance, who was barred by the provisions of the fourteenth amendment; Mr. Vance made no claim to the seat; on February 5, 1872, credentials of Mr. Ransom were presented, certifying he had been elected January 30, 1872, "to fill a vacancy existing by reason of the resignation of Zebulon B. Vance"; April 23, 1872, Senate declared, by resolution, that Mr. Abbott had not been elected, and the day following that Mr. Ransom was declared entitled to the seat; took his seat April 24, 1872; resolutions were subsequently adopted allowing mileage and salary to Mr. Abbott from March 4, 1871, to April 23, 1872, and fixing Mr. Ransom's term and pay as beginning March 4, 1871.

[39] Took his seat May 23, 1872; election unsuccessfully contested by James H. Harris.

OHIO

SENATORS

John Sherman, *Mansfield*
Allen G. Thurman, *Columbus*

REPRESENTATIVES

Aaron F. Perry,[40] *Cincinnati*
Ozro J. Dodds,[41] *Cincinnati*
Job E. Stevenson, *Cincinnati*
Lewis D. Campbell,[42] *Hamilton*
John F. McKinney, *Piqua*
Charles N. Lamison, *Lima*
John A. Smith, *Hillsboro*
Samuel Shellabarger, *Springfield*
John Beatty, *Cardington*
Charles Foster, *Fostoria*
Erasmus D. Peck, *Perrysburg*
John T. Wilson, *Tranquility*
Philadelph Van Trump, *Lancaster*
George W. Morgan, *Mount Vernon*
James Monroe, *Oberlin*
William P. Sprague, *McConnellsville*
John A. Bingham, *Cadiz*
Jacob A. Ambler, *Salem*
William H. Upson, *Akron*
James A. Garfield, *Hiram*

OREGON

SENATORS

Henry W. Corbett, *Portland*
James K. Kelly, *Portland*

REPRESENTATIVE

At Large—James H. Slater, *La Grande*

PENNSYLVANIA

SENATORS

Simon Cameron, *Harrisburg*
John Scott, *Huntingdon*

REPRESENTATIVES

Samuel J. Randall, *Philadelphia*
John V. Creely, *Philadelphia*
Leonard Myers, *Philadelphia*
William D. Kelley, *Philadelphia*
Alfred C. Harmer, *Germantown*
Ephraim L. Acker, *Norristown*
Washington Townsend, *West Chester*
J. Lawrence Getz, *Reading*
Oliver J. Dickey, *Lancaster*
John W. Killinger, *Lebanon*
John B. Storm, *Stroudsburg*
Lazarus D. Shoemaker, *Wilkes-Barre*
Ulysses Mercur,[43] *Towanda*
Frank C. Bunnell,[44] *Tunkhannock*

John B. Packer, *Sunbury*
Richard J. Haldeman, *Harrisburg*
Benjamin F. Meyers,[45] *Bedford*
R. Milton Speer, *Huntingdon*
Henry Sherwood, *Wellsboro*
Glenni W. Scofield, *Warren*
Samuel Griffith, *Mercer*
Henry D. Foster, *Greensburg*
James S. Negley, *Pittsburgh*
Ebenezer McJunkin, *Butler*
William McClelland, *Mount Jackson*

RHODE ISLAND

SENATORS

Henry B. Anthony, *Providence*
William Sprague, *Providence*

REPRESENTATIVES

Benjamin T. Eames, *Providence*
James M. Pendleton, *Westerly*

SOUTH CAROLINA

SENATORS

Thomas J. Robertson, *Columbia*
Frederick A. Sawyer, *Charleston*

REPRESENTATIVES

Joseph H. Rainey, *Georgetown*
Robert C. De Large,[46] *Charleston*
Robert B. Elliott, *Columbia*
Alexander S. Wallace,[47] *Yorkville*

TENNESSEE

SENATORS

William G. Brownlow, *Knoxville*
Henry Cooper, *Nashville*

REPRESENTATIVES [48]

Roderick R. Butler, *Taylorsville*
Horace Maynard, *Knoxville*
Abraham E. Garrett, *Carthage*
John M. Bright, *Fayetteville*
Edward I. Golladay, *Lebanon*
Washington C. Whitthorne, *Columbia*
Robert P. Caldwell, *Trenton*
William W. Vaughan, *Brownsville*

TEXAS

SENATORS

Morgan C. Hamilton,[49] *Austin*
James W. Flanagan, *Flanagans Mills*

REPRESENTATIVES [50]

William S. Herndon, *Tyler*
John C. Conner, *Sherman*
William T. Clark,[51] *Galveston*
De Witt C. Giddings,[52] *Brenham*
John Hancock, *Austin*

VERMONT

SENATORS

George F. Edmunds, *Burlington*
Justin S. Morrill, *Strafford*

REPRESENTATIVES

Charles W. Willard, *Montpelier*
Luke P. Poland, *St. Johnsbury*
Worthington C. Smith, *St. Albans*

VIRGINIA

SENATORS

John W. Johnston, *Abingdon*
John F. Lewis, *Port Republic*

REPRESENTATIVES

John Critcher, *Oak Grove*
James H. Platt, Jr., *Petersburg*
Charles H. Porter, *Richmond*
William H. H. Stowell, *Burkeville*
Richard T. W. Duke, *Charlottesville*
John T. Harris, *Harrisonburg*
Elliott M. Braxton,[53] *Fredericksburg*
William Terry, *Wytheville*

WEST VIRGINIA

SENATORS

Arthur I. Boreman, *Parkersburg*
Henry G. Davis, *Piedmont*

REPRESENTATIVES

John J. Davis, *Clarksburg*
James C. McGrew, *Kingwood*
Frank Hereford, *Union*

WISCONSIN

SENATORS

Timothy O. Howe, *Green Bay*
Matthew H. Carpenter, *Milwaukee*

REPRESENTATIVES

Alexander Mitchell, *Milwaukee*
Gerry W. Hazelton, *Columbus*
J. Allen Barber, *Lancaster*

---

[40] Resigned in 1872.
[41] Elected to fill vacancy caused by resignation of Aaron F. Perry, and took his seat December 2, 1872.
[42] Election unsuccessfully contested by R. C. Schenck.
[43] Resigned December 2, 1872.
[44] Elected to fill vacancy caused by resignation of Ulysses Mercur, and took his seat January 7, 1873.
[45] Election unsuccessfully contested by John Cessna.
[46] Election contested by Christopher C. Bowen; seat declared vacant January 24, 1873.

[47] Election unsuccessfully contested by Isaac G. McKissick.
[48] Thomas H. Reeves claimed a seat as Representative at large, but claim was not considered.
[49] Presented himself to take the oath of office March 4, 1871; a certified copy of a joint resolution of the Texas Legislature declaring his election by the preceding legislature illegal was offered and he was not permitted to qualify; March 15, 1871, credentials of Joseph J. Reynolds, claiming to be the Senator-elect, were presented; March 18, 1871, the Senate agreed to a reported

resolution declaring Mr. Hamilton duly elected; took his seat March 20, 1871.
[50] Elected October 3 to 6, 1871.
[51] Given a seat by resolution of January 10, 1872; served until May 13, 1872; succeeded by De Witt C. Giddings, who contested his election.
[52] Successfully contested the election of William T. Clark, and took his seat May 13, 1872.
[53] Election unsuccessfully contested by Lewis McKenzie.

WISCONSIN—Continued

REPRESENTATIVES—continued

Charles A. Eldredge, *Fond du Lac*
Philetus Sawyer, *Oshkosh*
Jeremiah M. Rusk, *Viroqua*

TERRITORY OF ARIZONA

DELEGATE

Richard C. McCormick, *Tucson*

TERRITORY OF COLORADO

DELEGATE

Jerome B. Chaffee, *Denver*

TERRITORY OF DAKOTA

DELEGATE

Moses K. Armstrong,[54] *Yankton*

DISTRICT OF COLUMBIA [55]

DELEGATE

Norton P. Chipman,[56] *Washington*

TERRITORY OF IDAHO

DELEGATE

Samuel A. Merritt, *Idaho City*

TERRITORY OF MONTANA

DELEGATE

William H. Clagett,[57] *Deer Lodge*

TERRITORY OF NEW MEXICO

DELEGATE

José Manuel Gallegos,[58] *Santa Fe*

TERRITORY OF UTAH

DELEGATE

William H. Hooper,[59] *Salt Lake City*

TERRITORY OF WASHINGTON

DELEGATE

Selucius Garfielde, *Olympia*

TERRITORY OF WYOMING

DELEGATE

William T. Jones, *Cheyenne*

---

[54] Election unsuccessfully contested by Walter A. Burleigh and Solomon L. Spink.

[55] Established under the seventeenth clause of the eighth section of Article I of the Constitution of the United States; formed from territory ceded to the United States by the State of Maryland, legislative act of December 23, 1788; and by the State of Virginia, legislative act of December 3, 1789; cessions accepted by Congress by act of July 16, 1790, and lines and bounds were established by proclamation of the President, George Washington, March 30, 1791. By act of July 9, 1846, Congress retroceded the county of Alexandria, incorporated in the District, to the State of Virginia; by act of February 21, 1871, a territorial form of government was provided, with the right to Delegate representation in Congress.

[56] Took his seat December 4, 1871.

[57] Elected August 7, 1871.

[58] Elected September 4, 1871.

[59] Election unsuccessfully contested by G. R. Maxwell.

FORTY-THIRD CONGRESS

MARCH 4, 1873, TO MARCH 3, 1875

FIRST SESSION—*December 1, 1873, to June 23, 1874*

SECOND SESSION—*December 7, 1874, to March 3, 1875*

SPECIAL SESSION OF THE SENATE—*March 4, 1873, to March 26, 1873*

VICE PRESIDENT OF THE UNITED STATES—Henry Wilson, of Massachusetts

PRESIDENT PRO TEMPORE OF THE SENATE—Matthew H. Carpenter,[1] of Wisconsin; Henry B. Anthony,[2] of Rhode Island

SECRETARY OF THE SENATE—George C. Gorham, of California

SERGEANT AT ARMS OF THE SENATE—John R. French, of New Hampshire

---

SPEAKER OF THE HOUSE OF REPRESENTATIVES—James G. Blaine,[3] of Maine

CLERK OF THE HOUSE—Edward McPherson,[4] of Pennsylvania

SERGEANT AT ARMS OF THE HOUSE—Nathaniel G. Ordway, of New Hampshire

DOORKEEPER OF THE HOUSE—Otis S. Buxton, of New York

POSTMASTER OF THE HOUSE—Henry Sherwood

ALABAMA

SENATORS

George E. Spencer,[5] *Decatur*
George T. Goldthwaite, *Montgomery*

REPRESENTATIVES

Frederick G. Bromberg, *Mobile*
James T. Rapier, *Montgomery*
Charles Pelham, *Talladega*
Charles Hays, *Eutaw*
John H. Caldwell, *Jacksonville*
Joseph H. Sloss, *Tuscumbia*
At Large—
    Alexander White, *Selma*
    Charles C. Sheats, *Decatur*

ARKANSAS

SENATORS

Powell Clayton, *Little Rock*
Stephen W. Dorsey, *Helena*

REPRESENTATIVES

Asa Hodges,[6] *Marion*
Oliver P. Snyder,[7] *Pine Bluff*
William W. Wilshire,[8] *Little Rock*
Thomas M. Gunther,[9] *Fayetteville*
At Large—William J. Hynes, *Little Rock*

CALIFORNIA

SENATORS

Eugene Casserly,[10] *San Francisco*
John S. Hager,[11] *San Francisco*
Aaron A. Sargent, *Nevada City*

REPRESENTATIVES

Charles Clayton, *San Francisco*
Horace F. Page, *Placerville*
John K. Luttrell, *Santa Rosa*
Sherman O. Houghton, *San Jose*

CONNECTICUT

SENATORS

Orris S. Ferry, *Norwalk*
William A. Buckingham,[12] *Norwich*
William W. Eaton,[13] *Hartford*

REPRESENTATIVES

Joseph R. Hawley, *Hartford*
Stephen W. Kellogg, *Waterbury*
Henry H. Starkweather, *Norwich*
William H. Barnum, *Lime Rock*

DELAWARE

SENATORS

Thomas F. Bayard, *Wilmington*
Eli Saulsbury, *Dover*

REPRESENTATIVE

At Large—James R. Lofland, *Milford*

---

[1] Elected March 12, 1873, and March 26, 1873 (special session of the Senate); December 11, 1873; December 23, 1874.
[2] Elected January 25, 1875, and February 15, 1875.
[3] Reelected December 1, 1873.
[4] Reelected December 1, 1873.
[5] Appeared on March 6, 1873, to take oath of office, having presented credentials in the preceding Congress; objection was made, as a memorial was on file from Francis W. Sykes, claiming the seat; on March 7, 1873, a motion to refer the credentials and memorial to the Committee on Privileges and Elections was not agreed to, and Mr. Spencer was permitted to qualify; December 8, 1873, the memorial of Mr. Sykes was re-

ferred, and April 20, 1874, the committee, upon its motion, was discharged from further consideration thereof.
[6] Credentials as Member-elect, together with notice of contest by Lucien C. Gause, were presented and referred to Committee on Elections on December 2, 1873; the House adopted resolution reported by committee that Mr. Hodges was entitled prima facie to the seat without prejudice to the right of Mr. Gause to contest; took his seat February 4, 1874; the Committee reported unfavorably on the contest.
[7] Election unsuccessfully contested by Marcus L. Bell.
[8] Credentials as Member-elect, together with notice

of contest by Thomas M. Gunter, were presented and referred to Committee on Elections on December 2, 1873; on recommendation of the committee he was seated on February 18, 1874; served until June 16, 1874, when the House decided that Mr. Gunter was entitled to the seat.
[9] Successfully contested the election of William W. Wilshire, and took his seat June 16, 1874.
[10] Resigned November 29, 1873.
[11] Elected to fill vacancy caused by resignation of Eugene Casserly, and took his seat February 9, 1874.
[12] Died February 5, 1875.
[13] Appointed to fill vacancy caused by death of William A. Buckingham.

FLORIDA

SENATORS

Abijah Gilbert, *St. Augustine*
Simon B. Conover, *Tallahassee*

REPRESENTATIVES AT LARGE

Josiah T. Walls, *Gainesville*
William J. Purman,[14] *Tallahassee*

GEORGIA

SENATORS

Thomas M. Norwood, *Savannah*
John B. Gordon, *Atlanta*

REPRESENTATIVES

Morgan Rawls,[15] *Guyton*
Andrew Sloan,[16] *Savannah*
Richard H. Whiteley, *Bainbridge*
Philip Cook, *Americus*
Henry R. Harris,[17] *Greenville*
James C. Freeman, *Griffin*
James H. Blount, *Macon*
Pierce M. B. Young, *Cartersville*
Alexander H. Stephens,[18] *Crawfordville*
Hiram P. Bell, *Cumming*

ILLINOIS

SENATORS

John A. Logan, *Chicago*
Richard J. Oglesby, *Decatur*

REPRESENTATIVES

John B. Rice,[19] *Chicago*
Bernard G. Caulfield,[20] *Chicago*
Jasper D. Ward, *Chicago*
Charles B. Farwell, *Chicago*
Stephen A. Hurlbut, *Belvidere*
Horatio C. Burchard, *Freeport*
John B. Hawley, *Rock Island*
Franklin Corwin, *Peru*
Greenbury L. Fort, *Lacon*
Granville Barrere, *Canton*
William H. Ray, *Rushville*
Robert M. Knapp, *Jerseyville*
James C. Robinson, *Springfield*
John McNulta, *Bloomington*
Joseph G. Cannon, *Tuscola*
John R. Eden, *Sullivan*
James S. Martin, *Salem*
William R. Morrison, *Waterloo*

Isaac Clements, *Carbondale*
Samuel S. Marshall, *McLeansboro*

INDIANA

SENATORS

Oliver H. P. T. Morton, *Indianapolis*
Daniel D. Pratt, *Logansport*

REPRESENTATIVES

William E. Niblack, *Vincennes*
Simeon K. Wolfe, *New Albany*
William S. Holman, *Aurora*
Jeremiah M. Wilson, *Connersville*
John Coburn, *Indianapolis*
Morton C. Hunter, *Bloomington*
Thomas J. Cason, *Lebanon*
James N. Tyner, *Peru*
John P. C. Shanks,[21] *Portland*
Henry B. Sayler, *Huntington*
Jasper Packard, *Laporte*
At Large—
    William Williams, *Warsaw*
    Godlove S. Orth, *La Fayette*

IOWA

SENATORS

George G. Wright, *Des Moines*
William B. Allison, *Dubuque*

REPRESENTATIVES

George W. McCrary, *Keokuk*
Aylett R. Cotton, *Lyons*
William G. Donnan, *Independence*
Henry O. Pratt, *Charles City*
James Wilson, *Traer*
William Loughridge, *Oskaloosa*
John A. Kasson, *Des Moines*
James W. McDill, *Afton*
Jackson Orr, *Boone*

KANSAS

SENATORS

Alexander Caldwell,[22] *Leavenworth*
Robert Crozier,[23] *Leavenworth*
James M. Harvey,[24] *Vinton*
John J. Ingalls, *Atchison*

REPRESENTATIVES

David P. Lowe, *Fort Scott*
Stephen A. Cobb, *Wyandotte*
William A. Phillips, *Salina*

KENTUCKY

SENATORS

John W. Stevenson, *Covington*
Thomas C. McCreery, *Owensboro*

REPRESENTATIVES

Edward Crossland, *Mayfield*
John Y. Brown, *Henderson*
Charles W. Milliken, *Franklin*
William B. Read, *Hodgensville*
Elisha D. Standiford, *Louisville*
William E. Arthur, *Covington*
James B. Beck, *Lexington*
Milton J. Durham, *Danville*
George M. Adams, *Barbourville*
John D. Young,[25] *Owingsville*

LOUISIANA

SENATORS

J. Rodman West, *New Orleans*
Vacant [26]

REPRESENTATIVES [27]

J. Hale Sypher,[28] *New Orleans*
Effingham Lawrence,[29] *New Orleans*
Lionel A. Sheldon,[30] *New Orleans*
Chester B. Darrall, *Brashear*
George L. Smith,[31] *Shreveport*
Frank Morey, *Monroe*
At Large—George A. Sheridan,[32] *Lake Providence*

MAINE

SENATORS

Hannibal Hamlin, *Bangor*
Lot M. Morrill, *Augusta*

REPRESENTATIVES

John H. Burleigh, *South Berwick*
William P. Frye, *Lewiston*
James G. Blaine, *Augusta*
Samuel Hersey,[33] *Bangor*
Eugene Hale, *Ellsworth*

MARYLAND

SENATORS

William T. Hamilton, *Hagerstown*
George R. Dennis, *Kingston*

---

[14] Resigned January 25, 1875.
[15] Served until March 24, 1874; succeeded by Andrew Sloan, who contested his election.
[16] Successfully contested the election of Morgan Rawls, and took his seat March 24, 1874.
[17] Election unsuccessfully contested by M. Bethune.
[18] Elected to fill vacancy caused by death of Representative-elect Ambrose R. Wright (December 21, 1872, before the beginning of the congressional term), and took his seat December 1, 1873.
[19] Died December 17, 1874.
[20] Elected to fill vacancy caused by death of John B. Rice, and took his seat February 1, 1875.
[21] Election unsuccessfully contested by John E. Neff.
[22] Resigned March 24, 1873, while a resolution was pending and under discussion declaring he "was not duly and legally elected."

[23] Appointed to fill vacancy caused by resignation of Alexander Caldwell, and took his seat December 1, 1873.
[24] Elected to fill vacancy caused by resignation of Alexander Caldwell, and took his seat February 12, 1874.
[25] Election unsuccessfully contested by John M. Burns.
[26] Pinckney B. S. Pinchback and William L. McMillen, were claimants for the seat and the contest continued throughout the Congress without settlement.
[27] A dual government existed in Louisiana at this time, and certificates of election for Representative at large and for the first, second, and fourth districts, signed by acting Governor Pinchback, were presented by Messrs. Pinchback, Lawrence, Gibson, and Davidson, respectively; credentials, signed by Governor Warmoth, were also presented by Messrs. Sheridan,

Sypher, Sheldon, and Smith, and the three last named were seated pending contests.
[28] Served until March 3, 1875; succeeded by Effingham Lawrence, who contested his election.
[29] Successfully contested the election of J. Hale Sypher, and took his seat March 3, 1875.
[30] Randall L. Gibson filed a contest, but no further action was taken.
[31] Elected to fill vacancy caused by death of Representative-elect Samuel Peters, before the beginning of the congressional term, and took his seat December 3, 1873; E. C. Davidson filed a contest under the original election, but no further action was taken.
[32] Took his seat March 3, 1875, after an unsuccessful contest by Pinckney B. S. Pinchback.
[33] Died February 3, 1875, before the commencement of the Forty-fourth Congress, to which he had been reelected.

REPRESENTATIVES

Ephraim K. Wilson, *Snow Hill*
Stevenson Archer, *Bel Air*
William J. O'Brien, *Baltimore*
Thomas Swann, *Baltimore*
William J. Albert, *Baltimore*
Lloyd Lowndes, Jr., *Cumberland*

MASSACHUSETTS

SENATORS

Charles Sumner,[34] *Boston*
William B. Washburn,[35] *Greenfield*
George S. Boutwell,[36] *Groton*

REPRESENTATIVES

James Buffinton, *Fall River*
Benjamin W. Harris, *East Bridgewater*
William Whiting,[37] *Boston*
Henry L. Pierce,[38] *Boston*
Samuel Hooper,[39] *Boston*
Daniel W. Gooch, *Melrose*
Benjamin F. Butler, *Lowell*
Ebenezer R. Hoar, *Concord*
John M. S. Williams, *Cambridge*
George F. Hoar, *Worcester*
Alvah Crocker,[40] *Fitchburg*
Charles A. Stevens,[41] *Ware*
Henry L. Dawes, *Pittsfield*

MICHIGAN

SENATORS

Zachariah Chandler, *Detroit*
Thomas W. Ferry, *Grand Haven*

REPRESENTATIVES

Moses W. Field, *Detroit*
Henry Waldron, *Hillsdale*
George Willard, *Battle Creek*
Julius C. Burrows, *Kalamazoo*
Wilder D. Foster,[42] *Grand Rapids*
William B. Williams,[43] *Allegan*
Josiah W. Begole, *Flint*
Omar D. Conger, *Port Huron*
Nathan B. Bradley, *Bay City*
Jay A. Hubbell, *Houghton*

MINNESOTA

SENATORS

Alexander Ramsey, *St. Paul*
William Windom, *Winona*

REPRESENTATIVES

Mark H. Dunnell, *Owatonna*
Horace B. Strait, *Shakopee*
John T. Averill, *St. Paul*

MISSISSIPPI

SENATORS

Adelbert Ames,[44] *Natchez*
Henry R. Pease,[45] *Jackson*
James L. Alcorn, *Friars Point*

REPRESENTATIVES

Lucius Q. C. Lamar, *Oxford*
Albert R. Howe, *Sardis*
Henry W. Barry, *Columbus*
Jason Niles, *Kosciusko*
George C. McKee, *Vicksburg*
John R. Lynch, *Natchez*

MISSOURI

SENATORS

Carl Schurz, *St. Louis*
Lewis V. Bogy, *St. Louis*

REPRESENTATIVES

Edwin O. Stanard, *St. Louis*
Erastus Wells, *St. Louis*
William H. Stone, *St. Louis*
Robert A. Hatcher, *New Madrid*
Richard P. Bland, *Lebanon*
Harrison E. Havens, *Springfield*
Thomas T. Crittenden, *Warrensburg*
Abram Comingo, *Independence*
Isaac C. Parker, *St. Joseph*
Ira B. Hyde, *Princeton*
John B. Clark, Jr., *Fayette*
John M. Glover, *La Grange*
Aylett H. Buckner, *Mexico*

NEBRASKA

SENATORS

Thomas W. Tipton, *Brownville*
Phineas W. Hitchcock, *Omaha*

REPRESENTATIVE

At Large—Lorenzo Crounse, *Fort Calhoun*

NEVADA

SENATORS

William M. Stewart, *Virginia City*
John P. Jones, *Gold Hill*

REPRESENTATIVE

At Large—Charles W. Kendall, *Hamilton*

NEW HAMPSHIRE

SENATORS

Aaron H. Cragin, *Lebanon*
Bainbridge Wadleigh, *Milford*

REPRESENTATIVES

William B. Small, *New Market*
Austin F. Pike, *Franklin*
Hosea W. Parker, *Claremont*

NEW JERSEY

SENATORS

John P. Stockton, *Trenton*
Frederick T. Frelinghuysen, *Newark*

REPRESENTATIVES

John W. Hazelton, *Mullica Hill*
Samuel A. Dobbins, *Mount Holly*
Amos Clark, Jr., *Elizabeth*
Robert Hamilton, *Newton*
William W. Phelps, *Englewood*
Marcus L. Ward, *Newark*
Isaac W. Scudder, *Jersey City*

NEW YORK

SENATORS

Roscoe Conkling, *Utica*
Reuben E. Fenton, *Jamestown*

REPRESENTATIVES

Henry J. Scudder, *New York City*
John G. Schumaker, *Brooklyn*
Stewart L. Woodford,[46] *Brooklyn*
Simeon B. Chittenden,[47] *Brooklyn*
Philip S. Crooke, *Flatbush*
William R. Roberts, *New York City*
James Brooks,[48] *New York City*
Samuel S. Cox,[49] *New York City*
Thomas J. Creamer, *New York City*
John D. Lawson, *New York City*
David B. Mellish,[50] *New York City*
Richard Schell,[51] *New York City*
Fernando Wood, *New York City*
Clarkson N. Potter, *New Rochelle*

---

[34] Died March 11, 1874.
[35] Elected to fill vacancy caused by death of Charles Sumner, and took his seat May 1, 1874.
[36] Elected to fill vacancy caused by resignation of Henry Wilson, in preceding Congress, and took his seat March 17, 1873.
[37] Died June 29, 1873, before Congress assembled.
[38] Elected to fill vacancy caused by the death of William Whiting, and took his seat December 1, 1873.
[39] Died February 13, 1875.

[40] Died December 26, 1874.
[41] Elected to fill vacancy caused by death of Alvah Crocker, and took his seat January 27, 1875.
[42] Died September 20, 1873, before Congress assembled.
[43] Elected to fill vacancy caused by death of Wilder D. Foster, and took his seat December 1, 1873.
[44] Resigned January 10, 1874, having been elected governor.
[45] Elected to fill vacancy caused by resignation of Adelbert Ames, and took his seat February 12, 1874.

[46] Resigned July 1, 1874.
[47] Elected to fill vacancy caused by resignation of Stewart L. Woodford, and took his seat December 7, 1874.
[48] Died April 30, 1873.
[49] Elected to fill vacancy caused by the death of James Brooks, and took his seat December 1, 1873.
[50] Died May 23, 1874.
[51] Elected to fill vacancy caused by death of David B. Mellish, and took his seat December 7, 1874.

NEW YORK—Continued

REPRESENTATIVES—continued

Charles St. John, *Port Jervis*
John O. Whitehouse, *Poughkeepsie*
David M. De Witt, *Kingston*
Eli Perry, *Albany*
James S. Smart, *Cambridge*
Robert S. Hale, *Elizabethtown*
William A. Wheeler, *Malone*
Henry H. Hathorn, *Saratoga Springs*
David Wilber, *Milford*
Clinton L. Merriam, *Locust Grove*
Ellis H. Roberts, *Utica*
William E. Lansing, *Chittenango*
R. Holland Duell, *Cortland*
Clinton D. MacDougall, *Auburn*
William H. Lamport, *Canandaigua*
Thomas C. Platt, *Owego*
H. Boardman Smith, *Elmira*
Freeman Clarke, *Rochester*
George G. Hoskins, *Attica*
Lyman K. Bass, *Buffalo*
Walter L. Sessions, *Panama*
At Large—Lyman Tremain, *Albany*

NORTH CAROLINA

SENATORS

Matt W. Ransom, *Weldon*
Augustus S. Merrimon, *Raleigh*

REPRESENTATIVES

Clinton L. Cobb, *Elizabeth City*
Charles R. Thomas, *New Bern*
Alfred M. Waddell, *Wilmington*
William A. Smith, *Princeton*
James M. Leach, *Lexington*
Thomas S. Ashe, *Wadesboro*
William M. Robbins, *Statesville*
Robert B. Vance, *Asheville*

OHIO

SENATORS

John Sherman, *Mansfield*
Allen G. Thurman, *Columbus*

REPRESENTATIVES

Milton Sayler, *Cincinnati*
Henry B. Banning, *Cincinnati*
John Q. Smith, *Oakland*
Lewis B. Gunckel, *Dayton*
Charles N. Lamison, *Lima*
Isaac R. Sherwood, *Bryan*
Lawrence T. Neal, *Chillicothe*
William Lawrence, *Bellefontaine*
James W. Robinson, *Marysville*
Charles Foster, *Fostoria*
Hezekiah S. Bundy, *Wellston*
Hugh J. Jewett,[52] *Columbus*
William E. Finck,[53] *Somerset*

Milton I. Southard, *Zanesville*
John Berry, *Upper Sandusky*
William P. Sprague, *McConnellsville*
Lorenzo Danford, *St. Clairsville*
Laurin D. Woodworth, *Youngstown*
James Monroe, *Oberlin*
James A. Garfield, *Hiram*
Richard C. Parsons, *Cleveland*

OREGON

SENATORS

James K. Kelly, *Portland*
John H. Mitchell, *Portland*

REPRESENTATIVE AT LARGE

Joseph G. Wilson,[54] *The Dalles*
James W. Nesmith,[55] *Rickreall*

PENNSYLVANIA

SENATORS

Simon Cameron, *Harrisburg*
John Scott, *Huntingdon*

REPRESENTATIVES

Samuel J. Randall, *Philadelphia*
Charles O'Neill, *Philadelphia*
Leonard Myers, *Philadelphia*
William D. Kelley, *Philadelphia*
Alfred C. Harmer, *Germantown*
James S. Biery, *Allentown*
Washington Townsend, *West Chester*
Hiester Clymer, *Reading*
A. Herr Smith, *Lancaster*
John W. Killinger, *Lebanon*
John B. Storm, *Stroudsburg*
Lazarus D. Shoemaker, *Wilkes-Barre*
James D. Strawbridge, *Danville*
John B. Packer, *Sunbury*
John A. Magee, *New Bloomfield*
John Cessna, *Bedford*
R. Milton Speer, *Huntingdon*
Sobieski Ross, *Coudersport*
Carlton B. Curtis, *Erie*
Hiram L. Richmond, *Meadville*
Alexander W. Taylor, *Indiana*
James S. Negley, *Pittsburgh*
Ebenezer McJunkin,[56] *Butler*
John M. Thompson,[57] *Butler*
William S. Moore, *Washington*
At Large—
  Lemuel Todd, *Carlisle*
  Glenni W. Scofield, *Warren*
  Charles Albright, *Mauch Chunk*

RHODE ISLAND

SENATORS

Henry B. Anthony, *Providence*
William Sprague, *Providence*

REPRESENTATIVES

Benjamin T. Eames, *Providence*
James M. Pendleton, *Westerly*

SOUTH CAROLINA

SENATORS

Thomas J. Robertson, *Columbia*
John J. Patterson, *Columbia*

REPRESENTATIVES

Joseph H. Rainey, *Georgetown*
Alonzo J. Ransier, *Charleston*
Robert B. Elliott,[58] *Columbia*
Lewis C. Carpenter,[59] *Columbia*
Alexander S. Wallace, *Yorkville*
At Large—Richard H. Cain, *Columbia*

TENNESSEE

SENATORS

William G. Brownlow, *Knoxville*
Henry Cooper, *Nashville*

REPRESENTATIVES

Roderick R. Butler, *Taylorsville*
Jacob M. Thornburgh, *Knoxville*
William Crutchfield, *Chattanooga*
John M. Bright, *Fayetteville*
Horace H. Harrison, *Nashville*
Washington C. Whitthorne, *Columbia*
John D. C. Atkins, *Paris*
David A. Nunn, *Brownsville*
Barbour Lewis, *Memphis*
At Large—Horace Maynard, *Knoxville*

TEXAS

SENATORS

Morgan C. Hamilton, *Austin*
James W. Flanagan, *Flanagans Mills*

REPRESENTATIVES

Asa H. Willie, *Galveston*
William S. Herndon, *Tyler*
William P. McLean, *Mount Pleasant*
De Witt C. Giddings, *Brenham*
John Hancock, *Austin*
At Large—Roger Q. Mills, *Corsicana*

VERMONT

SENATORS

George F. Edmunds, *Burlington*
Justin S. Morrill, *Strafford*

REPRESENTATIVES

Charles W. Willard, *Montpelier*
Luke P. Poland, *St. Johnsbury*
George W. Hendee, *Morrisville*

---

[52] Resigned June 23, 1874.
[53] Elected to fill vacancy caused by resignation of Hugh J. Jewett, and took his seat December 7, 1874.
[54] Died July 2, 1873, before Congress assembled.

[55] Elected to fill vacancy caused by death of Joseph G. Wilson, and took his seat December 1, 1873.
[56] Resigned January 1, 1875.
[57] Elected to fill vacancy caused by resignation of

Ebenezer McJunkin, and took his seat January 5, 1875.
[58] Resigned, effective November 1, 1874.
[59] Elected to fill vacancy caused by resignation of Robert B. Elliott, and took his seat December 7, 1874.

VIRGINIA

SENATORS

John W. Johnston, *Abingdon*
John F. Lewis, *Port Republic*

REPRESENTATIVES

James B. Sener, *Fredericksburg*
James H. Platt, Jr, *Norfolk*
J. Ambler Smith, *Richmond*
William H. H. Stowell, *Burkeville*
Alexander M. Davis,[60] *Independence*
Christopher Y. Thomas,[61] *Martinsville*
Thomas Whitehead, *Amherst*
John T. Harris, *Harrisonburg*
Eppa Hunton, *Warrenton*
Rees T. Bowen, *Maiden Spring*

WEST VIRGINIA

SENATORS

Arthur I. Boreman, *Parkersburg*
Henry G. Davis, *Piedmont*

REPRESENTATIVES

John J. Davis,[62] *Clarksburg*
John M. Hagans,[63] *Morgantown*
Frank Hereford, *Union*

WISCONSIN

SENATORS

Timothy O. Howe, *Green Bay*
Matthew H. Carpenter, *Milwaukee*

REPRESENTATIVES

Charles G. Williams, *Janesville*
Gerry W. Hazelton, *Columbus*
J. Allen Barber, *Lancaster*
Alexander Mitchell, *Milwaukee*
Charles A. Eldridge, *Fond du Lac*
Philetus Sawyer, *Oshkosh*
Jeremiah M. Rusk, *Viroqua*
Alexander S. McDill, *Plover*

TERRITORY OF ARIZONA

DELEGATE

Richard C. McCormick, *Tucson*

TERRITORY OF COLORADO

DELEGATE

Jerome B. Chaffee, *Denver*

TERRITORY OF DAKOTA

DELEGATE

Moses K. Armstrong, *Yankton*

DISTRICT OF COLUMBIA [64]

DELEGATE

Norton P. Chipman,[65] *Washington*

TERRITORY OF IDAHO

DELEGATE

John Hailey, *Boise City*

TERRITORY OF MONTANA

DELEGATE

Martin Maginnis, *Helena*

TERRITORY OF NEW MEXICO

DELEGATE

Stephen B. Elkins, *Santa Fe*

TERRITORY OF UTAH

DELEGATE

George Q. Cannon,[66] *Salt Lake City*

TERRITORY OF WASHINGTON

DELEGATE

Obadiah B. McFadden, *Olympia*

TERRITORY OF WYOMING

DELEGATE

William R. Steele, *Cheyenne*

---

[60] Served until March 5, 1874; succeeded by Christopher Y. Thomas, who contested his election.

[61] Successfully contested the election of Alexander M. Davis, and took his seat March 5, 1874.

[62] Election unsuccessfully contested by Benjamin Wilson; took his seat January 27, 1874.

[63] Election unsuccessfully contested by Benjamin F. Martin; took his seat January 27, 1874.

[64] Territorial form of government withdrawn and a government administered by a board of three commissioners, appointed by the President, by and with the advice and consent of the Senate, established by act of June 20, 1874.

[65] Served until March 3, 1875, under the provisions of the act of June 20, 1874.

[66] Election unsuccessfully contested by George R. Maxwell.

FORTY-FOURTH CONGRESS

MARCH 4, 1875, TO MARCH 3, 1877

FIRST SESSION—*December 6, 1875, to August 15, 1876*

SECOND SESSION—*December 4, 1876, to March 3, 1877*

SPECIAL SESSION OF THE SENATE—*March 5, 1875, to March 24, 1875*

VICE PRESIDENT OF THE UNITED STATES—Henry Wilson,[1] of Massachusetts

PRESIDENT PRO TEMPORE OF THE SENATE—Thomas W. Ferry,[2] of Michigan

SECRETARY OF THE SENATE—George C. Gorham, of California

SERGEANT AT ARMS OF THE SENATE—John R. French, of New Hampshire

---

SPEAKER OF THE HOUSE OF REPRESENTATIVES—Michael C. Kerr,[3] of Indiana; Samuel J. Randall,[4] of Pennsylvania

CLERK OF THE HOUSE—Edward McPherson, of Pennsylvania; George M. Adams,[5] of Kentucky

SERGEANT AT ARMS OF THE HOUSE—Nathaniel G. Ordway, of New Hampshire; John G. Thompson,[6] of Ohio

DOORKEEPER OF THE HOUSE—John H. Patterson, of New Jersey

POSTMASTER OF THE HOUSE—James M. Steuart

ALABAMA

SENATORS

George E. Spencer, *Decatur*
George T. Goldthwaite, *Montgomery*

REPRESENTATIVES

Jeremiah Haralson,[7] *Selma*
Jeremiah N. Williams, *Clayton*
Taul Bradford, *Talladega*
Charles Hays, *Haysville*
John H. Caldwell, *Jacksonville*
Goldsmith W. Hewitt, *Birmingham*
At Large—
   William H. Forney, *Jacksonville*
   Burwell B. Lewis, *Tuscaloosa*

ARKANSAS

SENATORS

Powell Clayton, *Little Rock*
Stephen W. Dorsey, *Helena*

REPRESENTATIVES

Lucien C. Gause, *Jacksonport*
William F. Slemons, *Monticello*
William W. Wilshire, *Little Rock*
Thomas M. Gunter, *Fayetteville*

CALIFORNIA

SENATORS

Aaron A. Sargent, *Nevada City*
Newton Booth, *Sacramento*

REPRESENTATIVES

William A. Piper, *San Francisco*
Horace F. Page, *Placerville*
John K. Luttrell, *Santa Rosa*
Peter D. Wigginton, *Merced*

COLORADO [8]

SENATORS

Jerome B. Chaffee,[9] *Denver*
Henry M. Teller,[10] *Central City*

REPRESENTATIVE

At Large—James B. Belford,[11] *Central City*

CONNECTICUT

SENATORS

Orris S. Ferry,[12] *Norwalk*
James E. English,[13] *New Haven*
William H. Barnum,[14] *Lime Rock*
William W. Eaton, *Hartford*

REPRESENTATIVES

George M. Landers, *New Britain*
James Phelps, *Essex*
Henry H. Starkweather,[15] *Norwich*
John Turner Wait,[16] *Norwich*
William H. Barnum,[17] *Lime Rock*
Levi Warner,[18] *Norwalk*

---

[1] Died November 22, 1875.
[2] Elected March 9, 1875, and March 19, 1875 (special session of the Senate); December 20, 1875.
[3] Elected December 6, 1875; died August 19, 1876.
[4] Elected December 4, 1876.
[5] Elected December 6, 1875.
[6] Elected December 6, 1875.
[7] Election unsuccessfully contested by Frederick G. Bromberg.
[8] Admitted as a State into the Union August 1, 1876.
[9] Took his seat December 4, 1876; term to expire, as

determined by lot, March 3, 1879.
[10] Took his seat December 4, 1876; term to expire, as determined by lot, March 3, 1877.
[11] Presented credentials as a Member-elect on December 4, 1876, which were referred to the Committee on the Judiciary, who reported favorably thereon, and the House, on January 31, 1877, decided that Colorado was a State, and that the Representative-elect should be admitted; took his seat the same day.
[12] Died November 21, 1875.
[13] Appointed to fill vacancy caused by death of Orris

S. Ferry, and took his seat December 7, 1875.
[14] Elected to fill vacancy caused by death of Orris S. Ferry, and took his seat May 22, 1876.
[15] Died January 28, 1876.
[16] Elected to fill vacancy caused by death of Henry H. Starkweather, and took his seat April 12, 1876.
[17] Resigned May 18, 1876, having been elected Senator.
[18] Elected to fill vacancy caused by resignation of William H. Barnum, and took his seat December 4, 1876.

DELAWARE

SENATORS

Thomas F. Bayard, *Wilmington*
Eli Saulsbury, *Dover*

REPRESENTATIVE

At Large—James Williams, *Kenton*

FLORIDA

SENATORS

Simon B. Conover, *Tallahassee*
Charles W. Jones, *Pensacola*

REPRESENTATIVES

William J. Purman, *Tallahassee*
Josiah T. Walls,[19] *Gainesville*
Jesse J. Finley,[20] *Jacksonville*

GEORGIA

SENATORS

Thomas M. Norwood, *Savannah*
John B. Gordon, *Atlanta*

REPRESENTATIVES

Julian Hartridge, *Savannah*
William E. Smith, *Albany*
Philip Cook, *Americus*
Henry R. Harris, *Greenville*
Milton A. Candler, *Atlanta*
James H. Blount, *Macon*
William H. Felton, *Cartersville*
Alexander H. Stephens, *Crawfordville*
Benjamin H. Hill,[21] *Atlanta*

ILLINOIS

SENATORS

John A. Logan, *Chicago*
Richard J. Oglesby, *Decatur*

REPRESENTATIVES

Bernard G. Caulfield, *Chicago*
Carter H. Harrison, *Chicago*
Charles B. Farwell,[22] *Chicago*
John V. Le Moyne,[23] *Chicago*
Stephen A. Hurlbut, *Belvidere*
Horatio C. Burchard, *Freeport*
Thomas J. Henderson, *Princeton*
Alexander Campbell, *La Salle*

Greenbury L. Fort, *Lacon*
Richard H. Whiting, *Peoria*
John C. Bagby, *Rushville*
Scott Wike, *Pittsville*
William M. Springer, *Springfield*
Adlai E. Stevenson, *Bloomington*
Joseph G. Cannon, *Tuscola*
John R. Eden, *Sullivan*
William A. J. Sparks, *Carlyle*
William R. Morrison, *Waterloo*
William Hartzell, *Chester*
William B. Anderson, *Elk Prairie*

INDIANA

SENATORS

Oliver H. P. T. Morton, *Indianapolis*
Joseph E. McDonald, *Indianapolis*

REPRESENTATIVES

Benoni S. Fuller, *Boonville*
James D. Williams,[24] *Wheatland*
Andrew Humphreys,[25] *Linton*
Michael C. Kerr,[26] *New Albany*
Nathan T. Carr,[27] *Columbus*
Jeptha D. New, *Vernon*
William S. Holman, *Aurora*
Milton S. Robinson, *Anderson*
Franklin Landers, *Indianapolis*
Morton C. Hunter, *Bloomington*
Thomas J. Cason, *Lebanon*
William S. Haymond, *Monticello*
James L. Evans, *Noblesville*
Andrew H. Hamilton, *Fort Wayne*
John H. Baker, *Goshen*

IOWA

SENATORS

George G. Wright, *Des Moines*
William B. Allison, *Dubuque*

REPRESENTATIVES

George W. McCrary, *Keokuk*
John Q. Tufts, *Wilton Junction*
Lucien L. Ainsworth, *West Union*
Henry O. Pratt, *Charles City*
James Wilson, *Traer*
Ezekiel S. Sampson, *Sigourney*
John A. Kasson, *Des Moines*
James W. McDill, *Afton*
S. Addison Oliver, *Onawa*

KANSAS

SENATORS

John J. Ingalls, *Atchison*
James M. Harvey, *Vinton*

REPRESENTATIVES

William A. Phillips, *Salina*
John R. Goodin, *Humboldt*
William R. Brown, *Hutchinson*

KENTUCKY

SENATORS

John W. Stevenson, *Covington*
Thomas C. McCreery, *Owensboro*

REPRESENTATIVES

Andrew R. Boone, *Mayfield*
John Y. Brown, *Henderson*
Charles W. Milliken, *Franklin*
J. Proctor Knott, *Lebanon*
Edward Y. Parsons,[28] *Louisville*
Henry Watterson,[29] *Louisville*
Thomas L. Jones, *Newport*
Joseph C. S. Blackburn, *Versailles*
Milton J. Durham, *Danville*
John D. White, *Manchester*
John B. Clarke, *Brooksville*

LOUISIANA

SENATORS

J. Rodman West, *New Orleans*
James B. Eustis,[30] *New Orleans*

REPRESENTATIVES

Randall L. Gibson, *New Orleans*
E. John Ellis, *New Orleans*
Chester B. Darrall,[31] *Brashear*
William M. Levy, *Natchitoches*
Frank Morey,[32] *Monroe*
William B. Spencer,[33] *Vidalia*
Charles E. Nash, *Washington*

MAINE

SENATORS

Hannibal Hamlin, *Bangor*
Lot M. Morrill,[34] *Augusta*
James G. Blaine,[35] *Augusta*

---

[19] Served until April 19, 1876; succeeded by Jesse J. Finley, who contested his election.
[20] Successfully contested the election of Josiah T. Walls, and took his seat April 19, 1876.
[21] Elected to fill vacancy caused by death of Representative-elect Garnett McMillan (January 14, 1875, before the commencement of the congressional term), and took his seat December 6, 1875; resigned, effective March 3, 1877, before the commencement of the Forty-fifth Congress, to which he had been reelected, having been elected Senator.
[22] Served until May 6, 1876; succeeded by John V. Le Moyne, who contested his election.
[23] Successfully contested the election of Charles B. Farwell, and took his seat May 6, 1876.

[24] Resigned December 1, 1876, having been elected Governor.
[25] Elected to fill vacancy caused by resignation of James D. Williams, and took his seat December 5, 1876.
[26] Died August 19, 1876.
[27] Elected to fill vacancy caused by death of Michael C. Kerr, and took his seat December 5, 1876.
[28] Died July 8, 1876.
[29] Elected to fill vacancy caused by death of Edward Y. Parsons, and took his seat August 12, 1876.
[30] Elected on January 12, 1876, for the term beginning March 4, 1873, but as his rights were not finally determined until December 10, 1877, the seat remained vacant throughout the Congress. The contest of Pinckney B. S. Pinchback and William L. McMillen

were continued from the preceding Congress, but on December 14, 1875, McMillen was permitted to withdraw his credentials, and on March 8, 1876, the Senate adopted a resolution that Pinchback "be not admitted to a seat."
[31] Election unsuccessfully contested by J. A. Preux.
[32] Served until June 8, 1876; succeeded by William B. Spencer, who contested his election.
[33] Successfully contested the election of Frank Morey, and took his seat June 8, 1876; resigned January 8, 1877.
[34] Resigned July 7, 1876, having been appointed Secretary of the Treasury.
[35] Appointed to fill vacancy caused by the resignation of Lot M. Morrill, and took his seat December 4, 1876; subsequently elected.

MAINE—Continued

REPRESENTATIVES

John H. Burleigh, *South Berwick*
William P. Frye, *Lewiston*
James G. Blaine,[36] *Augusta*
Edwin Flye,[37] *New Castle*
Harris M. Plaisted,[38] *Bangor*
Eugene Hale, *Ellsworth*

MARYLAND

SENATORS

George R. Dennis, *Kingston*
William Pinkney Whyte, *Baltimore*

REPRESENTATIVES

Philip F. Thomas, *Easton*
Charles B. Roberts, *Westminster*
William J. O'Brien, *Baltimore*
Thomas Swann, *Baltimore*
Eli J. Henkle, *Brooklyn*
William Walsh, *Cumberland*

MASSACHUSETTS

SENATORS

George S. Boutwell, *Groton*
Henry L. Dawes, *Pittsfield*

REPRESENTATIVES

James Buffinton,[39] *Fall River*
William W. Crapo,[40] *New Bedford*
Benjamin W. Harris, *East Bridgewater*
Henry L. Pierce, *Boston*
Rufus S. Frost,[41] *Chelsea*
Josiah G. Abbott,[42] *Boston*
Nathaniel P. Banks, *Waltham*
Charles P. Thompson, *Gloucester*
John K. Tarbox, *Lawrence*
William W. Warren, *Boston*
George F. Hoar, *Worcester*
Julius H. Seelye, *Amherst*
Chester W. Chapin, *Springfield*

MICHIGAN

SENATORS

Thomas W. Ferry, *Grand Haven*
Isaac P. Christiancy, *Lansing*

REPRESENTATIVES

Alpheus S. Williams, *Detroit*
Henry Waldron, *Hillsdale*
George Willard, *Battle Creek*
Allen Potter, *Kalamazoo*
William B. Williams, *Allegan*
George H. Durand, *Flint*
Omar D. Conger, *Port Huron*
Nathan B. Bradley, *Bay City*
Jay A. Hubbell, *Houghton*

MINNESOTA

SENATORS

William Windom, *Winona*
Samuel J. R. McMillan, *St. Paul*

REPRESENTATIVES

Mark H. Dunnell, *Owatonna*
Horace B. Strait,[43] *Shakopee*
William S. King, *Minneapolis*

MISSISSIPPI

SENATORS

James L. Alcorn, *Friars Point*
Blanche K. Bruce, *Floreyville*

REPRESENTATIVES

Lucius Q. C. Lamar, *Oxford*
G. Wiley Wells, *Holly Springs*
Hernando D. Money, *Winona*
Otho R. Singleton, *Canton*
Charles E. Hooker, *Jackson*
John R. Lynch, *Natchez*

MISSOURI

SENATORS

Lewis V. Bogy, *St. Louis*
Francis M. Cockrell, *Warrensburg*

REPRESENTATIVES

Edward C. Kehr, *St. Louis*
Erastus Wells, *St. Louis*
William H. Stone, *St. Louis*
Robert A. Hatcher, *New Madrid*
Richard P. Bland, *Lebanon*
Charles H. Morgan, *Lamar*
John F. Philips, *Sedalia*
Benjamin J. Franklin, *Kansas City*
David Rea, *Savannah*
Rezin A. De Bolt, *Trenton*
John B. Clark, Jr., *Fayette*
John M. Glover, *La Grange*
Aylett H. Buckner, *Mexico*

NEBRASKA

SENATORS

Phineas W. Hitchcock, *Omaha*
Algernon S. Paddock, *Beatrice*

REPRESENTATIVE

At Large—Lorenzo Crounse, *Fort Calhoun*

NEVADA

SENATORS

John P. Jones, *Gold Hill*
William Sharon, *Virginia City*

REPRESENTATIVE

At Large—William Woodburn, *Virginia City*

NEW HAMPSHIRE

SENATORS

Aaron H. Cragin, *Lebanon*
Bainbridge Wadleigh, *Milford*

REPRESENTATIVES

Frank Jones, *Portsmouth*
Samuel N. Bell, *Manchester*
Henry W. Blair, *Plymouth*

NEW JERSEY

SENATORS

Frederick T. Frelinghuysen, *Newark*
Theodore F. Randolph, *Morristown*

REPRESENTATIVES

Clement H. Sinnickson, *Salem*
Samuel A. Dobbins, *Mount Holly*
Miles Ross, *New Brunswick*
Robert Hamilton, *Newton*
Augustus W. Cutler, *Morristown*
Frederick H. Teese, *Newark*
Augustus A. Hardenbergh, *Jersey City*

NEW YORK

SENATORS

Roscoe Conkling, *Utica*
Francis Kernan, *Utica*

REPRESENTATIVES

Henry B. Metcalfe, *Westfield*
John G. Schumaker, *Brooklyn*
Simeon B. Chittenden, *Brooklyn*
Archibald M. Bliss, *Brooklyn*
Edwin R. Meade, *New York City*
Samuel S. Cox, *New York City*
Smith Ely, Jr.,[44] *New York City*
David Dudley Field,[45] *New York City*
Elijah Ward, *New York City*
Fernando Wood, *New York City*
Abram S. Hewitt, *New York City*
Benjamin A. Willis, *New York City*
N. Holmes Odell, *White Plains*
John O. Whitehouse, *Poughkeepsie*
George M. Beebe, *Monticello*
John H. Bagley, Jr., *Catskill*
Charles H. Adams, *Cohoes*

---

[36] Resigned July 10, 1876.
[37] Elected to fill vacancy caused by resignation of James G. Blaine, and took his seat December 4, 1876.
[38] Elected to fill vacancy caused by death of Representative-elect Samuel F. Hersey, in preceding Congress, and took his seat December 6, 1875.

[39] Died March 7, 1875, before Congress assembled.
[40] Elected to fill vacancy caused by death of James Buffinton, and took his seat December 6, 1875.
[41] Served until July 28, 1876; succeeded by Josiah G. Abbott, who contested his election.
[42] Successfully contested the election of Rufus S. Frost, and took his seat July 28, 1876.

[43] Election unsuccessfully contested by E. St. Julien Cox.
[44] Resigned December 11, 1876, having been elected mayor of New York City.
[45] Elected to fill vacancy caused by resignation of Smith Ely, Jr., and took his seat January 11, 1877.

Martin I. Townsend, *Troy*
Andrew Williams, *Plattsburg*
William A.. Wheeler, *Malone*
Henry H. Hathorn, *Saratoga Springs*
Samuel F. Miller, *Franklin*
George A. Bagley, *Watertown*
Scott Lord, *Utica*
William H. Baker, *Constantia*
Elias W. Leavenworth, *Syracuse*
Clinton D. MacDougall, *Auburn*
Elbridge G. Lapham, *Canandaigua*
Thomas C. Platt, *Owego*
Charles C. B. Walker, *Corning*
John M. Davy, *Rochester*
George G. Hoskins, *Attica*
Lyman K. Bass, *Buffalo*
Nelson I. Norton,[46] *Hinsdale*

NORTH CAROLINA

SENATORS

Matt W. Ransom, *Weldon*
Augustus S. Merrimon, *Raleigh*

REPRESENTATIVES

Jesse J. Yeates, *Murfreesboro*
John A. Hyman, *Warrenton*
Alfred M. Waddell, *Wilmington*
Joseph J. Davis, *Louisburg*
Alfred M. Scales, *Greensboro*
Thomas S. Ashe, *Wadesboro*
William M. Robbins, *Statesville*
Robert B. Vance, *Asheville*

OHIO

SENATORS

John Sherman, *Mansfield*
Allen G. Thurman, *Columbus*

REPRESENTATIVES

Milton Sayler, *Cincinnati*
Henry B. Banning, *Cincinnati*
John S. Savage, *Wilmington*
John A. McMahon, *Dayton*
Americus V. Rice, *Ottawa*
Frank H. Hurd, *Toledo*
Lawrence T. Neal, *Chillicothe*
William Lawrence, *Bellefontaine*
Earley F. Poppleton, *Delaware*
Charles Foster, *Fostoria*
John L. Vance, *Gallipolis*
Ansel T. Walling, *Circleville*
Milton I. Southard, *Zanesville*
Jacob P. Cowan, *Ashland*
Nelson H. Van Vorhes, *Athens*
Lorenzo Danford, *St. Clairsville*
Laurin D. Woodworth, *Youngstown*

James Monroe, *Oberlin*
James A. Garfield, *Hiram*
Henry B. Payne, *Cleveland*

OREGON

SENATORS

James K. Kelly, *Portland*
John H. Mitchell, *Portland*

REPRESENTATIVE AT LARGE

George A. La Dow,[47] *Pendleton*
La Fayette Lane,[48] *Roseburg*

PENNSYLVANIA

SENATORS

Simon Cameron, *Harrisburg*
William A. Wallace, *Clearfield*

REPRESENTATIVES

Chapman Freeman, *Philadelphia*
Charles O'Neill, *Philadelphia*
Samuel J. Randall, *Philadelphia*
William D. Kelley, *Philadelphia*
John Robbins, *Philadelphia*
Washington Townsend, *West Chester*
Alan Wood, Jr., *Conshohocken*
Hiester Clymer, *Reading*
A. Herr Smith, *Lancaster*
William Mutchler, *Easton*
Francis D. Collins, *Scranton*
Winthrop W. Ketchum,[49] *Wilkes-Barre*
William H. Stanton,[50] *Scranton*
James B. Reilly, *Pottsville*
John B. Packer, *Sunbury*
Joseph Powell, *Towanda*
Sobieski Ross, *Coudersport*
John Reilly, *Altoona*
William S. Stenger, *Chambersburg*
Levi Maish, *York*
Levi A. Mackey, *Lockhaven*
Jacob Turney, *Greensburg*
James H. Hopkins, *Pittsburgh*
Alexander G. Cochran, *Allegheny City*
John W. Wallace, *New Castle*
George A. Jenks, *Brookville*
James Sheakley, *Greenville*
Albert G. Egbert, *Franklin*

RHODE ISLAND

SENATORS

Henry B. Anthony, *Providence*
Ambrose E. Burnside, *Providence*

REPRESENTATIVES

Benjamin T. Eames, *Providence*
Latimer W. Ballou, *Woonsocket*

SOUTH CAROLINA

SENATORS

Thomas J. Robertson, *Columbia*
John J. Patterson, *Columbia*

REPRESENTATIVES

Joseph H. Rainey,[51] *Georgetown*
Edmund W. M. Mackey,[52] *Charleston*
Charles W. Buttz,[53] *Charleston*
Solomon L. Hoge, *Columbia*
Alexander S. Wallace, *Yorkville*
Robert Smalls, *Beaufort*

TENNESSEE

SENATORS

Henry Cooper, *Nashville*
Andrew Johnson,[54] *Greeneville*
David M. Key,[55] *Chattanooga*
James E. Bailey,[56] *Clarksville*

REPRESENTATIVES

William McFarland, *Morristown*
Jacob M. Thornburgh, *Knoxville*
George G. Dibrell, *Sparta*
Samuel M. Fite,[57] *Carthage*
Haywood Y. Riddle,[58] *Lebanon*
John M. Bright, *Fayetteville*
John F. House, *Clarksville*
Washington C. Whitthorne, *Columbia*
John D. C. Atkins, *Paris*
William P. Caldwell, *Gardner*
H. Casey Young, *Memphis*

TEXAS

SENATORS

Morgan C. Hamilton, *Austin*
Samuel B. Maxey, *Paris*

REPRESENTATIVES

John H. Reagan, *Palestine*
David B. Culberson, *Jefferson*
James W. Throckmorton, *McKinney*
Roger Q. Mills, *Corsicana*
John Hancock, *Austin*
Gustave Schleicher, *Cuero*

VERMONT

SENATORS

George F. Edmunds, *Burlington*
Justin S. Morrill, *Strafford*

REPRESENTATIVES

Charles H. Joyce, *Rutland*
Dudley C. Denison, *Royalton*
George W. Hendee, *Morrisville*

---

[46] Elected to fill vacancy caused by death of Representative-elect Augustus F. Allen (January 22, 1875, before the beginning of the congressional term), and took his seat December 6, 1875.
[47] Died May 1, 1875, before Congress assembled.
[48] Elected to fill vacancy caused by death of George A. La Dow, and took his seat December 6, 1875.
[49] Resigned July 19, 1876.
[50] Elected to fill vacancy caused by resignation of Winthrop W. Ketchum, and took his seat December

4, 1876.
[51] Election unsuccessfully contested by Samuel Lee.
[52] Election contested by Charles W. Buttz; seat declared vacant by resolution of July 19, 1876.
[53] Contested the election of Edmund W. M. Mackey; by resolution, July 19, 1876, House declared neither contestant nor contestee duly elected and the seat to be vacant; subsequently elected, and took his seat January 23, 1877.
[54] Died July 31, 1875.

[55] Appointed to fill vacancy caused by death of Andrew Johnson, and took his seat December 6, 1875.
[56] Elected to fill vacancy caused by death of Andrew Johnson, and took his seat January 29, 1877.
[57] Elected to fill vacancy caused by death of Representative-elect John W. Head on November 9, 1874, before the beginning of the congressional term; died October 23, 1875, before Congress assembled.
[58] Elected to fill vacancy caused by death of Samuel M. Fite, and took his seat January 5, 1876.

VIRGINIA

SENATORS

John W. Johnston, *Abingdon*
Robert E. Withers, *Wytheville*

REPRESENTATIVES

Beverly B. Douglas, *Ayletts*
John Goode, Jr.,[59] *Norfolk*
Gilbert C. Walker, *Richmond*
William H. H. Stowell, *Burkeville*
George C. Cabell, *Danville*
John R. Tucker, *Lexington*
John T. Harris, *Harrisonburg*
Eppa Hunton, *Warrenton*
William Terry, *Wytheville*

WEST VIRGINIA

SENATORS

Henry G. Davis, *Piedmont*
Allen T. Caperton,[60] *Union*
Samuel Price,[61] *Lewisburg*
Frank Hereford,[62] *Union*

REPRESENTATIVES

Benjamin Wilson, *Wilsonburg*
Charles J. Faulkner, *Martinsburg*
Frank Hereford,[63] *Union*

WISCONSIN

SENATORS

Timothy O. Howe, *Green Bay*
Angus Cameron, *La Crosse*

REPRESENTATIVES

Charles G. Williams, *Janesville*
Lucien B. Caswell, *Fort Atkinson*
Henry S. Magoon, *Darlington*
William P. Lynde, *Milwaukee*
Samuel D. Burchard, *Beaver Dam*
Alanson M. Kimball, *Pine River*
Jeremiah M. Rusk, *Viroqua*
George W. Cate, *Stevens Point*

TERRITORY OF ARIZONA

DELEGATE

Hiram S. Stevens, *Tucson*

TERRITORY OF COLORADO

DELEGATE

Thomas M. Patterson,[64] *Denver*

TERRITORY OF DAKOTA

DELEGATE

Jefferson P. Kidder, *Vermilion*

TERRITORY OF IDAHO

DELEGATE

Thomas W. Bennett,[65] *Boise City*
Stephen S. Fenn,[66] *Mount Idaho*

TERRITORY OF MONTANA

DELEGATE

Martin Maginnis, *Helena*

TERRITORY OF NEW MEXICO

DELEGATE

Stephen B. Elkins, *Santa Fe*

TERRITORY OF UTAH

DELEGATE

George Q. Cannon, *Salt Lake City*

TERRITORY OF WASHINGTON

DELEGATE

Orange Jacobs, *Seattle*

TERRITORY OF WYOMING

DELEGATE

William R. Steele, *Cheyenne*

---

[59] Election unsuccessfully contested by James H. Platt, Jr.
[60] Died July 26, 1876.
[61] Appointed to fill vacancy caused by death of Allen T. Caperton, and took his seat December 4, 1876.

[62] Elected to fill vacancy caused by death of Allen T. Caperton, and took his seat January 31, 1877.
[63] Resigned January 31, 1877, having been elected Senator.
[64] Served until August 1, 1876, when the Territory of Colorado was granted statehood by act of Congress

approved March 3, 1876.
[65] Served until June 23, 1876; succeeded by Stephen S. Fenn, who contested his election.
[66] Successfully contested the election of Thomas W. Bennett, and took his seat June 23, 1876.

FORTY-FIFTH CONGRESS

MARCH 4, 1877, TO MARCH 3, 1879

FIRST SESSION—*October 15, 1877, to December 3, 1877*

SECOND SESSION—*December 3, 1877, to June 20, 1878*

THIRD SESSION—*December 2, 1878, to March 3, 1879*

SPECIAL SESSION OF THE SENATE—*March 5, 1877, to March 17, 1877*

VICE PRESIDENT OF THE UNITED STATES—WILLIAM A. WHEELER, of New York

PRESIDENT PRO TEMPORE OF THE SENATE—THOMAS W. FERRY,[1] of Michigan

SECRETARY OF THE SENATE—GEORGE C. GORHAM, of California

SERGEANT AT ARMS OF THE SENATE—JOHN R. FRENCH, of New Hampshire

---

SPEAKER OF THE HOUSE OF REPRESENTATIVES—SAMUEL J. RANDALL,[2] of Pennsylvania

CLERK OF THE HOUSE—GEORGE M. ADAMS,[3] of Kentucky

SERGEANT AT ARMS OF THE HOUSE—JOHN G. THOMPSON, of Ohio

DOORKEEPER OF THE HOUSE—CHARLES W. FIELD, of Georgia

POSTMASTER OF THE HOUSE—JAMES M. STEUART

ALABAMA

SENATORS

George E. Spencer, *Decatur*
John T. Morgan, *Selma*

REPRESENTATIVES

James T. Jones, *Demopolis*
Hilary A. Herbert, *Montgomery*
Jeremiah N. Williams, *Clayton*
Charles M. Shelley,[4] *Selma*
Robert F. Ligon, *Tuskegee*
Goldsmith W. Hewitt, *Birmingham*
William H. Forney, *Jacksonville*
William W. Garth, *Huntsville*

ARKANSAS

SENATORS

Stephen W. Dorsey, *Helena*
Augustus H. Garland, *Little Rock*

REPRESENTATIVES

Lucien C. Gause, *Jacksonport*
William F. Slemons, *Monticello*
Jordan E. Cravens, *Clarksville*
Thomas M. Gunter, *Fayetteville*

CALIFORNIA

SENATORS

Aaron A. Sargent, *Nevada City*
Newton Booth, *Sacramento*

REPRESENTATIVES

Horace Davis, *San Francisco*
Horace F. Page, *Placerville*
John K. Luttrell, *Santa Rosa*
Romualdo Pacheco,[5] *San Luis Obispo*
Peter D. Wigginton,[6] *Merced*

COLORADO

SENATORS

Jerome B. Chaffee, *Denver*
Henry M. Teller, *Central City*

REPRESENTATIVE AT LARGE

James B. Belford,[7] *Central City*
Thomas M. Patterson,[8] *Denver*

CONNECTICUT

SENATORS

William W. Eaton, *Hartford*
William H. Barnum, *Lime Rock*

REPRESENTATIVES

George M. Landers, *New Britain*
James Phelps, *Essex*
John T. Wait, *Norwich*
Levi Warner, *Norwalk*

DELAWARE

SENATORS

Thomas F. Bayard, *Wilmington*
Eli Saulsbury, *Dover*

REPRESENTATIVE

At Large—James Williams, *Kenton*

---

[1] Elected March 5, 1877 (special session of the Senate); February 26, 1878; April 17, 1878; and March 3, 1879.
[2] Reelected October 15, 1877.
[3] Reelected October 15, 1877.

[4] Election unsuccessfully contested by Jeremiah Haralson.
[5] Served until February 7, 1878; succeeded by Peter D. Wigginton, who contested his election.
[6] Successfully contested the election of Romualdo

Pacheco, and took his seat February 7, 1878.
[7] Served until December 13, 1877; succeeded by Thomas M. Patterson, who contested his election.
[8] Successfully contested the election of James B. Belford, and took his seat December 13, 1877.

FLORIDA

SENATORS

Simon B. Conover, *Tallahassee*
Charles W. Jones, *Pensacola*

REPRESENTATIVES

Horatio Bisbee, Jr.,[9] *Jacksonville*
Jesse J. Finley,[10] *Jacksonville*
Robert H. M. Davidson, *Quincy*

GEORGIA

SENATORS

John B. Gordon, *Atlanta*
Benjamin H. Hill, *Atlanta*

REPRESENTATIVES

Julian Hartridge,[11] *Savannah*
William B. Fleming,[12] *Savannah*
William E. Smith, *Albany*
Philip Cook, *Americus*
Henry R. Harris, *Greenville*
Milton A. Candler, *Atlanta*
James H. Blount, *Macon*
William H. Felton, *Cartersville*
Alexander H. Stephens, *Crawfordville*
Hiram P. Bell,[13] *Cumming*

ILLINOIS

SENATORS

Richard J. Oglesby, *Decatur*
David Davis, *Bloomington*

REPRESENTATIVES

William Aldrich, *Chicago*
Carter H. Harrison, *Chicago*
Lorenzo Brentano, *Chicago*
William Lathrop, *Rockford*
Horatio C. Burchard, *Freeport*
Thomas J. Henderson, *Princeton*
Philip C. Hayes, *Morris*
Greenbury L. Fort, *Lacon*
Thomas A. Boyd, *Lewiston*
Benjamin F. Marsh, *Warsaw*
Robert M. Knapp, *Jerseyville*
William M. Springer, *Springfield*
Thomas F. Tipton, *Bloomington*
Joseph G. Cannon, *Danville*
John R. Eden, *Sullivan*
William A. J. Sparks, *Carlyle*

William R. Morrison, *Waterloo*
William Hartzell, *Chester*
Richard W. Townshend, *Shawneetown*

INDIANA

SENATORS

Oliver H. P. T. Morton,[14] *Indianapolis*
Daniel W. Voorhees,[15] *Terre Haute*
Joseph E. McDonald, *Indianapolis*

REPRESENTATIVES

Benoni S. Fuller, *Boonville*
Thomas R. Cobb, *Vincennes*
George A Bicknell, *New Albany*
Leonidas Sexton, *Rushville*
Thomas M. Browne, *Winchester*
Milton S. Robinson, *Anderson*
John Hanna, *Indianapolis*
Morton C. Hunter, *Bloomington*
Michael D. White, *Crawfordsville*
William H. Calkins, *Laporte*
James L. Evans, *Noblesville*
Andrew H. Hamilton, *Fort Wayne*
John H. Baker, *Goshen*

IOWA

SENATORS

William B. Allison, *Dubuque*
Samuel J. Kirkwood, *Iowa City*

REPRESENTATIVES

Joseph C. Stone, *Burlington*
Hiram Price, *Davenport*
Theodore W. Burdick, *Decorah*
Nathaniel C. Deering, *Osage*
Rush Clark, *Iowa City*
Ezekiel S. Sampson, *Sigourney*
Henry J. B. Cummings, *Winterset*
William F. Sapp, *Council Bluffs*
S. Addison Oliver, *Onawa*

KANSAS

SENATORS

John J. Ingalls, *Atchison*
Preston B. Plumb, *Emporia*

REPRESENTATIVES

William A. Phillips, *Salina*
Dudley C. Haskell, *Lawrence*
Thomas Ryan, *Topeka*

KENTUCKY

SENATORS

Thomas McCreery, *Owensboro*
James B. Beck, *Lexington*

REPRESENTATIVES

Andrew R. Boone, *Mayfield*
James A. McKenzie, *Long View*
John W. Caldwell, *Russellville*
J. Proctor Knott, *Lebanon*
Albert S. Willis, *Louisville*
John G. Carlisle, *Covington*
Joseph C. S. Blackburn, *Versailles*
Milton J. Durham, *Danville*
Thomas Turner, *Mount Sterling*
John B. Clarke, *Brooksville*

LOUISIANA

SENATORS

William Pitt Kellogg,[16] *New Orleans*
James B. Eustis,[17] *New Orleans*

REPRESENTATIVES

Randall L. Gibson, *New Orleans*
E. John Ellis, *New Orleans*
Chester B. Darrall,[18] *Brashear*
Joseph H. Acklen,[19] *Pattersonville*
Joseph B. Elam,[20] *Mansfield*
John E. Leonard,[21] *Lake Providence*
John S. Young,[22] *Homer*
Edward W. Robertson,[23] *Baton Rouge*

MAINE

SENATORS

Hannibal Hamlin, *Bangor*
James G. Blaine, *Augusta*

REPRESENTATIVES

Thomas B. Reed, *Portland*
William P. Frye, *Lewiston*
Stephen D. Lindsey, *Norridgewock*
Llewellyn Powers, *Houlton*
Eugene Hale, Ellsworth

MARYLAND

SENATORS

George R. Dennis, *Kingston*
William Pinkney Whyte, *Baltimore*

---

[9] Served until February 20, 1879; succeeded by Jesse J. Finley, who contested his election.
[10] Successfully contested the election of Horatio Bisbee, Jr., and took his seat February 20, 1879.
[11] Died January 8, 1879.
[12] Elected to fill vacancy caused by death of Julian Hartridge, and took his seat February 17, 1879.
[13] Elected to fill vacancy caused by resignation of Representative-elect Benjamin H. Hill, in preceding Congress, and took his seat October 15, 1877.
[14] Died November 1, 1877.
[15] Appointed to fill vacancy caused by death of Oliver H. P. T. Morton, and took his seat November 12, 1877; subsequently elected.
[16] This seat was claimed by Henry M. Spofford; March 5, 1877 (in the special session of the Senate), Mr. Kellogg presented himself to be sworn, but objection was made and his credentials were ordered to lie on the table; October 17, 1877, the credentials of Mr. Spofford were presented, and they, with the creden-

tials of Mr. Kellogg, were referred to the Committee on Privileges and Elections; November 26, 1877, the committee reported in favor of Mr. Kellogg; the report was adopted November 30, 1877; took his seat the same day. In the succeeding Congress the case was reopened upon petition of Mr. Spofford and a report was made in his favor, but he died August 20, 1880, before action was taken.
[17] In the preceding Congress the Committee on Privileges and Elections twice reported that Pinckney B. S. Pinchback was entitled to the seat upon credentials presented from two elections; the committee, after these decisions, was instructed to pass upon credentials of James B. Eustis and held that, inasmuch as Mr. Pinchback had a clear title, there was no vacancy; the Senate refused to adopt the report of the committee and declared Mr. Pinchback "not entitled to the seat" by a vote of 32 to 29. March 9, 1877 (in the special session of the Senate), the credentials of

Mr. Eustis were taken from the files and again referred; the committee reported December 1, 1877, holding that the Senate's action in the case of Mr. Pinchback was a final adjudication, and a resolution declaring Mr. Eustis entitled to his seat, his term of service to date from January 12, 1876; this report and resolution were adopted December 10, 1877, and Mr. Eustis appeared, qualified, and took his seat the same day.
[18] Served until February 20, 1878; succeeded by Joseph H. Acklen, who contested his election.
[19] Successfully contested the election of Chester B. Darrall, and took his seat February 20, 1878.
[20] Election unsuccessfully contested by George L. Smith.
[21] Died March 15, 1878.
[22] Elected to fill vacancy caused by death of John E. Leonard, and took his seat December 2, 1878.
[23] Election unsuccessfully contested by Charles E. Nash.

REPRESENTATIVES

Daniel M. Henry, *Cambridge*
Charles B. Roberts, *Westminster*
William Kimmel, *Baltimore*
Thomas Swann, *Baltimore*
Eli J. Henkle, *Brooklyn*
William Walsh, *Cumberland*

MASSACHUSETTS

SENATORS

Henry L. Dawes, *Pittsfield*
George F. Hoar, *Worcester*

REPRESENTATIVES

William W. Crapo, *New Bedford*
Benjamin W. Harris, *East Bridgewater*
Walbridge A. Field,[24] *Boston*
Benjamin Dean,[25] *Boston*
Leopold Morse, *Boston*
Nathaniel P. Banks, *Waltham*
George B. Loring, *Salem*
Benjamin F. Butler, *Lowell*
William Claflin, *Newton*
William W. Rice, *Worcester*
Amasa Norcross, *Fitchburg*
George D. Robinson, *Chicopee*

MICHIGAN

SENATORS

Thomas W. Ferry, *Grand Haven*
Isaac P. Christiancy,[26] *Lansing*
Zachariah Chandler,[27] *Detroit*

REPRESENTATIVES

Alpheus S. Williams,[28] *Detroit*
Edwin Willits, *Monroe*
Jonas H. McGowan, *Coldwater*
Edwin W. Keightley, *Constantine*
John W. Stone, *Grand Rapids*
Mark S. Brewer, *Pontiac*
Omar D. Conger, *Port Huron*
Charles C. Ellsworth, *Greenville*
Jay A. Hubbell, *Houghton*

MINNESOTA

SENATORS

William Windom, *Winona*
Samuel J. R. McMillan, *St. Paul*

REPRESENTATIVES

Mark H. Dunnell, *Owatonna*
Horace B. Strait, *Shakopee*
Jacob H. Stewart, *St. Paul*

MISSISSIPPI

SENATORS

Blanche K. Bruce, *Floreyville*
Lucius Q. C. Lamar, *Oxford*

REPRESENTATIVES

Henry L. Muldrow, *Starkville*
Vannoy H. Manning, *Holly Springs*
Hernando D. Money, *Winona*
Otho R. Singleton, *Canton*
Charles E. Hooker, *Jackson*
James R. Chalmers,[29] *Vicksburg*

MISSOURI

SENATORS

Lewis V. Bogy,[30] *St. Louis*
David H. Armstrong,[31] *St. Louis*
James Shields,[32] *Carrollton*
Francis M. Cockrell, *Warrensburg*

REPRESENTATIVES

Anthony Ittner, *St. Louis*
Nathan Cole, *St. Louis*
Lyne S. Metcalfe,[33] *St. Louis*
Robert A. Hatcher, *Charleston*
Richard P. Bland, *Lebanon*
Charles H. Morgan, *Lamar*
Thomas T. Crittenden, *Warrensburg*
Benjamin J. Franklin, *Kansas City*
David Rea, *Savannah*
Henry M. Pollard, *Chillicothe*
John B. Clark, Jr., *Fayette*
John M. Glover, *La Grange*
Aylett H. Buckner, *Mexico*

NEBRASKA

SENATORS

Algernon S. Paddock, *Beatrice*
Alvin Saunders, *Omaha*

REPRESENTATIVE AT LARGE

Frank Welch,[34] *Norfolk*
Thomas J. Majors,[35] *Peru*

NEVADA

SENATORS

John P. Jones, *Gold Hill*
William Sharon, *Virginia City*

REPRESENTATIVE

At Large—Thomas Wren, *Eureka*

NEW HAMPSHIRE

SENATORS

Bainbridge Wadleigh, *Milford*
Edward H. Rollins, *Concord*

REPRESENTATIVES

Frank Jones, *Portsmouth*
James F. Briggs, *Manchester*
Henry W. Blair, *Plymouth*

NEW JERSEY

SENATORS

Theodore F. Randolph, *Morristown*
John R. McPherson, *Jersey City*

REPRESENTATIVES

Clement H. Sinnickson, *Salem*
John H. Pugh, *Burlington*
Miles Ross, *New Brunswick*
Alvah A. Clark, *Somerville*
Augustus W. Cutler, *Morristown*
Thomas B. Peddie, *Newark*
Augustus A. Hardenbergh, *Jersey City*

NEW YORK

SENATORS

Roscoe Conkling, *Utica*
Francis Kernan, *Utica*

REPRESENTATIVES

James W. Covert, *Flushing*
William D. Veeder, *Brooklyn*
Simeon B. Chittenden, *Brooklyn*
Archibald M. Bliss, *Brooklyn*
Nicholas Muller, *New York City*
Samuel S. Cox, *New York City*
Anthony Eickhoff, *New York City*
Anson G. McCook, *New York City*
Fernando Wood, *New York City*
Abram S. Hewitt, *New York City*
Benjamin A. Willis, *New York City*
Clarkson N. Potter, *New Rochelle*
John H. Ketcham, *Dover Plains*
George M. Beebe, *Monticello*
Stephen L. Mayham, *Schoharie*
Terence J. Quinn,[36] *Albany*
John M. Bailey,[37] *Albany*
Martin I. Townsend, *Troy*
Andrew Williams, *Plattsburg*
Amaziah B. James, *Ogdensburg*
John H. Starin, *Fultonville*
Solomon Bundy, *Oxford*
George A. Bagley, *Watertown*
William J. Bacon, *Utica*
William H. Baker, *Constantia*
Frank Hiscock, *Syracuse*

---

[24] Served until March 28, 1878; succeeded by Benjamin Dean, who contested his election.
[25] Successfully contested the election of Walbridge A. Field, and took his seat March 28, 1878.
[26] Resigned February 10, 1879.
[27] Elected to fill vacancy caused by the resignation of Isaac P. Christiancy, and took his seat February 22, 1879.

[28] Died December 20, 1878.
[29] Election unsuccessfully contested by John R. Lynch.
[30] Died September 20, 1877.
[31] Appointed to fill vacancy caused by death of Lewis V. Bogy, and took his seat October 15, 1877.
[32] Elected to fill vacancy caused by death of Lewis V. Bogy, and took his seat January 27, 1879.

[33] Richard G. Frost filed a contest, which was referred to the Committee on Elections; the committee reported in favor of contestee; no further action taken.
[34] Died September 4, 1878.
[35] Elected to fill vacancy caused by death of Frank Welch, and took his seat December 2, 1878.
[36] Died June 18, 1878.
[37] Elected to fill vacancy caused by death of Terence J. Quinn, and took his seat December 2, 1878.

NEW YORK—Continued

REPRESENTATIVES—continued

John H. Camp, *Lyons*
Elbridge G. Lapham, *Canandaigua*
Jeremiah W. Dwight, *Dryden*
John N. Hungerford, *Corning*
E. Kirke Hart, *Albion*
Charles B. Benedict, *Attica*
Daniel N. Lockwood, *Buffalo*
George W. Patterson, *Westerfield*

NORTH CAROLINA

SENATORS

Matt W. Ransom, *Weldon*
Augustus S. Merrimon, *Raleigh*

REPRESENTATIVES

Jesse J. Yeates, *Murfreesboro*
Curtis H. Brogden, *Goldsboro*
Alfred M. Waddell, *Wilmington*
Joseph J. Davis, *Louisburg*
Alfred M. Scales, *Greensboro*
Walter L. Steele, *Rockingham*
William M. Robbins, *Statesville*
Robert B. Vance, *Asheville*

OHIO

SENATORS

John Sherman,[38] *Mansfield*
Stanley Matthews,[39] *Glendale*
Allen G. Thurman, *Columbus*

REPRESENTATIVES

Milton Sayler, *Cincinnati*
Henry B. Banning, *Cincinnati*
Mills Gardner, *Washington Court House*
John A. McMahon, *Dayton*
Americus V. Rice, *Ottawa*
Jacob D. Cox, *Toledo*
Henry L. Dickey, *Greenfield*
J. Warren Keifer, *Springfield*
John S. Jones, *Delaware*
Charles Foster, *Fostoria*
Henry S. Neal, *Ironton*
Thomas Ewing, *Lancaster*
Milton I. Southard, *Zanesville*
Ebenezer B. Finley, *Bucyrus*
Nelson H. Van Vorhes, *Athens*
Lorenzo Danford, *St. Clairsville*
William McKinley, Jr., *Canton*
James Monroe, *Oberlin*
James A. Garfield, *Mentor*
Amos Townsend, *Cleveland*

OREGON

SENATORS

John H. Mitchell, *Portland*
La Fayette Grover, *Salem*

REPRESENTATIVE

At Large—Richard Williams,[40] *Portland*

PENNSYLVANIA

SENATORS

Simon Cameron,[41] *Harrisburg*
J. Donald Cameron,[42] *Harrisburg*
William A. Wallace, *Clearfield*

REPRESENTATIVES

Chapman Freeman, *Philadelphia*
Charles O'Neill, *Philadephia*
Samuel J. Randall, *Philadelphia*
William D. Kelley, *Philadelphia*
Alfred C. Harmer, *Germantown*
William Ward, *Chester*
I. Newton Evans, *Hatboro*
Hiester Clymer, *Reading*
A. Herr Smith, *Lancaster*
Samuel A. Bridges, *Allentown*
Francis D. Collins, *Scranton*
Hendrick B. Wright, *Wilkes-Barre*
James B. Reilly, *Pottsville*
John W. Killinger, *Lebanon*
Edward Overton, Jr., *Towanda*
John I. Mitchell, *Wellsboro*
Jacob M. Campbell, *Johnstown*
William S. Stenger, *Chambersburg*
Levi Maish, *York*
Levi A. Mackey, *Lock Haven*
Jacob Turney, *Greensburg*
Russell Errett, *Pittsburgh*
Thomas M. Bayne, *Allegheny*
William S. Shallenberger, *Rochester*
Harry White, *Indiana*
John M. Thompson, *Butler*
Lewis F. Watson, *Warren*

RHODE ISLAND

SENATORS

Henry B. Anthony, *Providence*
Ambrose E. Burnside, *Providence*

REPRESENTATIVES

Benjamin T. Eames, *Providence*
Latimer W. Ballou, *Woonsocket*

SOUTH CAROLINA

SENATORS

John J. Patterson, *Charleston*
Matthew C. Butler,[43] *Edgefield*

REPRESENTATIVES

Joseph H. Rainey,[44] *Georgetown*
Richard H. Cain, *Charleston*
D. Wyatt Aiken, *Cokesbury*
John H. Evins, *Spartanburg*
Robert Smalls, *Beaufort*

TENNESSEE

SENATORS

James E. Bailey, *Clarksville*
Isham G. Harris, *Memphis*

REPRESENTATIVES

James H. Randolph, *Newport*
Jacob M. Thornburgh, *Knoxville*
George G. Dibrell, *Sparta*
Haywood Y. Riddle, *Lebanon*
John M. Bright, *Fayetteville*
John F. House, *Clarksville*
Washington C. Whitthorne, *Columbia*
John D. C. Atkins, *Paris*
William P. Caldwell, *Gardner*
H. Casey Young, *Memphis*

TEXAS

SENATORS

Samuel B. Maxey, *Paris*
Richard Coke, *Waco*

REPRESENTATIVES

John H. Reagan, *Palestine*
David B. Culberson, *Jefferson*
James W. Throckmorton, *McKinney*
Roger Q. Mills, *Corsicana*
De Witt C. Giddings, *Brenham*
Gustave Schleicher,[45] *Cuero*

VERMONT

SENATORS

George F. Edmunds, *Burlington*
Justin S. Morrill, *Strafford*

REPRESENTATIVES

Charles H. Joyce, *Rutland*
Dudley C. Denison, *Royalton*
George W. Hendee, *Morrisville*

---

[38] Resigned March 8, 1877, having been appointed Secretary of the Treasury.
[39] Elected to fill vacancy caused by resignation of John Sherman, and took his seat October 16, 1877.
[40] Election unsuccessfully contested by Samuel W. McDowell.
[41] Resigned effective March 12, 1877.
[42] Elected to fill vacancy caused by resignation of Simon Cameron, and took his seat October 15, 1877.
[43] David T. Corbin claimed this seat; his credentials, with those of Mr. Butler, were referred to the Committee on Privileges and Elections; November 26, 1877, the committee, upon its request, was discharged from further consideration of Mr. Butler's credentials; November 30, 1877, a resolution that Mr. Butler be sworn in was agreed to by a vote of 29 to 28, the Vice President voting to break a tie; appeared and qualified the same day. On February 4, 1879, the committee reported that Mr. Corbin was entitled to the seat, and a resolution that he be sworn; the Senate refused to consider this report February 25, 1879, and on February 28 following the Vice President laid before the Senate a letter from Mr. Corbin withdrawing his claim, and no further action was taken.
[44] Election unsuccessfully contested by John S. Richardson.
[45] Died January 10, 1879, before the commencement of the Forty-sixth Congress, to which he had been reelected.

VIRGINIA

SENATORS

John W. Johnston, *Abingdon*
Robert E. Withers, *Wytheville*

REPRESENTATIVES

Beverly B. Douglas,[46] *Ayletts*
Richard Lee T. Beale,[47] *Hague*
John Goode, Jr., *Norfolk*
Gilbert C. Walker, *Richmond*
Joseph Jorgensen, *Petersburg*
George C. Cabell, *Danville*
John R. Tucker, *Lexington*
John T. Harris, *Harrisonburg*
Eppa Hunton, *Warrenton*
Auburn L. Pridemore, *Jonesville*

WEST VIRGINIA

SENATORS

Henry G. Davis, *Piedmont*
Frank Hereford, *Union*

REPRESENTATIVES

Benjamin Wilson, *Wilsonburg*
Benjamin F. Martin, *Pruntytown*
John E. Kenna, *Kanawha*

WISCONSIN

SENATORS

Timothy O. Howe, *Green Bay*
Angus Cameron, *La Crosse*

REPRESENTATIVES

Charles G. Williams, *Janesville*
Lucien B. Caswell, *Fort Atkinson*
George C. Hazelton, *Boscobel*
William P. Lynde, *Milwaukee*
Edward S. Bragg, *Fond du Lac*
Gabriel Bouck, *Oshkosh*
Herman L. Humphrey, *Hudson*
Thaddeus C. Pound, *Chippewa Falls*

TERRITORY OF ARIZONA

DELEGATE

Hiram S. Stevens, *Tucson*

TERRITORY OF DAKOTA

DELEGATE

Jefferson P. Kidder, *Vermilion*

TERRITORY OF IDAHO

DELEGATE

Stephen S. Fenn, *Mount Idaho*

TERRITORY OF MONTANA

DELEGATE

Martin Maginnis, *Helena*

TERRITORY OF NEW MEXICO

DELEGATE

Trinidad Romero, *Las Vegas*

TERRITORY OF UTAH

DELEGATE

George Q. Cannon, *Salt Lake City*

TERRITORY OF WASHINGTON

DELEGATE

Orange Jacobs, *Seattle*

TERRITORY OF WYOMING

DELEGATE

William W. Corlett, *Cheyenne*

---

[46] Died December 22, 1878.
[47] Elected to fill vacancy caused by death of Beverly B. Douglas, and took his seat February 8, 1879.

FORTY-SIXTH CONGRESS

MARCH 4, 1879, TO MARCH 3, 1881

FIRST SESSION—*March 18, 1879, to July 1, 1879*

SECOND SESSION—*December 1, 1879, to June 16, 1880*

THIRD SESSION—*December 6, 1880, to March 3, 1881*

VICE PRESIDENT OF THE UNITED STATES—WILLIAM A. WHEELER, of New York

PRESIDENT PRO TEMPORE OF THE SENATE—ALLEN G. THURMAN,[1] of Ohio

SECRETARY OF THE SENATE—GEORGE C. GORHAM, of Massachusetts; JOHN C. BURCH,[2] of Tennessee

SERGEANT AT ARMS OF THE SENATE—JOHN R. FRENCH, of New Hampshire; RICHARD J. BRIGHT,[3] of Indiana

---

SPEAKER OF THE HOUSE OF REPRESENTATIVES—SAMUEL J. RANDALL,[4] of Pennsylvania

CLERK OF THE HOUSE—GEORGE M. ADAMS,[5] of Kentucky

SERGEANT AT ARMS OF THE HOUSE—JOHN G. THOMPSON, of Ohio

DOORKEEPER OF THE HOUSE—CHARLES W. FIELD, of Georgia

POSTMASTER OF THE HOUSE—A. W. C. NOWLIN

ALABAMA

SENATORS

John T. Morgan, *Selma*
George S. Houston,[6] *Athens*
Luke Pryor,[7] *Athens*
James L. Pugh,[8] *Eufaula*

REPRESENTATIVES

Thomas H. Herndon, *Mobile*
Hilary A. Herbert, *Montgomery*
William J. Samford, *Opelika*
Charles M. Shelley, *Selma*
Thomas Williams, *Wetumpka*
Burwell B. Lewis,[9] *Tuscaloosa*
Newton N. Clements,[10] *Tuscaloosa*
William H. Forney, *Jacksonville*
William M. Lowe, *Huntsville*

ARKANSAS

SENATORS

Augustus H. Garland, *Little Rock*
James D. Walker, *Fayetteville*

REPRESENTATIVES

Poindexter Dunn, *Forest City*
William F. Slemons,[11] *Monticello*
Jordan E. Cravens, *Clarksville*
Thomas M. Gunter, *Fayetteville*

CALIFORNIA

SENATORS

Newton Booth, *San Francisco*
James T. Farley, *Jackson*

REPRESENTATIVES[12]

Horace Davis, *San Francisco*
Horace F. Page, *Placerville*
Campbell P. Berry, *Wheatland*
Romualdo Pacheco, *San Luis Obispo*

COLORADO

SENATORS

Henry M. Teller, *Central City*
Nathaniel P. Hill, *Denver*

REPRESENTATIVE

At Large—James B. Belford, *Central City*

CONNECTICUT

SENATORS

William W. Eaton, *Hartford*
Orville H. Platt, *West Meriden*

REPRESENTATIVES

Joseph R. Hawley, *Hartford*
James Phelps, *Essex*
John T. Wait, *Norwich*
Frederick Miles, *Chapinville*

DELAWARE

SENATORS

Thomas F. Bayard, *Wilmington*
Eli Saulsbury, *Dover*

REPRESENTATIVE

At Large—Edward L. Martin, *Seaford*

FLORIDA

SENATORS

Charles W. Jones, *Pensacola*
Wilkinson Call, *Jacksonville*

---

[1] Elected April 15, 1879; April 7, 1880; and May 6, 1880.
[2] Elected March 24, 1879.
[3] Elected March 23, 1879.
[4] Reelected March 18, 1879.
[5] Reelected March 18, 1879.

[6] Died December 31, 1879.
[7] Appointed to fill vacancy caused by death of George S. Houston, and took his seat January 15, 1880.
[8] Elected to fill vacancy caused by death of George S. Houston, and took his seat December 6, 1880.
[9] Resigned October 1, 1880.

[10] Elected to fill vacancy caused by resignation of Burwell B. Lewis, and took his seat December 8, 1880.
[11] Election unsuccessfully contested by John M. Bradley.
[12] Elected September 3, 1879; took their seats December 1, 1879.

REPRESENTATIVES

Robert H. M. Davidson, *Quincy*
Noble A. Hull,[13] *Sanford*
Horatio Bisbee, Jr.,[14] *Jacksonville*

GEORGIA

SENATORS

Benjamin H. Hill, *Atlanta*
John B. Gordon,[15] *Atlanta*
Joseph E. Brown,[16] *Atlanta*

REPRESENTATIVES

John C. Nicholls, *Blackshear*
William E. Smith, *Albany*
Philip Cook, *Americus*
Henry Persons, *Geneva*
Nathaniel J. Hammond, *Atlanta*
James H. Blount, *Macon*
William H. Felton, *Cartersville*
Alexander H. Stephens, *Crawfordville*
Emory Speer, *Athens*

ILLINOIS

SENATORS

David Davis, *Bloomington*
John A. Logan, *Chicago*

REPRESENTATIVES

William Aldrich, *Chicago*
George R. Davis, *Chicago*
Hiram Barber, Jr., *Chicago*
John C. Sherwin, *Aurora*
Robert M. A. Hawk, *Mount Carroll*
Thomas J. Henderson, *Princeton*
Philip C. Hayes, *Morris*
Greenbury L. Fort, *Lacon*
Thomas A. Boyd, *Lewiston*
Benjamin F. Marsh, *Warsaw*
James W. Singleton, *Quincy*
William M. Springer, *Springfield*
Adlai E. Stevenson, *Bloomington*
Joseph G. Cannon, *Danville*
Albert P. Forsythe, *Isabel*
William A. J. Sparks, *Carlyle*
William R. Morrison, *Waterloo*
John R. Thomas, *Metropolis*
Richard W. Townshend, *Shawneetown*

INDIANA

SENATORS

Joseph E. McDonald, *Indianapolis*
Daniel W. Voorhees, *Terre Haute*

REPRESENTATIVES

William Heilman, *Evansville*
Thomas R. Cobb, *Vincennes*
George A. Bicknell, *New Albany*

Jeptha D. New, *Vernon*
Thomas M. Browne, *Winchester*
William R. Myers, *Anderson*
Gilbert De La Matyr, *Indianapolis*
Abraham J. Hostetler, *Bedford*
Godlove S. Orth,[17] *La Fayette*
William H. Calkins, *Laporte*
Calvin Cowgill, *Wabash*
Walpole G. Colerick, *Fort Wayne*
John H. Baker, *Goshen*

IOWA

SENATORS

William B. Allison, *Dubuque*
Samuel J. Kirkwood, *Iowa City*

REPRESENTATIVES

Moses A. McCoid, *Fairfield*
Hiram Price, *Davenport*
Thomas Updegraff, *McGregor*
Nathaniel C. Deering, *Osage*
Rush Clark,[18] *Iowa City*
William G. Thompson,[19] *Marion*
James B. Weaver, *Bloomfield*
Edward H. Gillette, *Des Moines*
William F. Sapp, *Council Bluffs*
Cyrus C. Carpenter, *Fort Dodge*

KANSAS

SENATORS

John J. Ingalls, *Atchison*
Preston B. Plumb, *Emporia*

REPRESENTATIVES

John A. Anderson, *Manhattan*
Dudley C. Haskell, *Lawrence*
Thomas Ryan, *Topeka*

KENTUCKY

SENATORS

James B. Beck, *Lexington*
John S. Williams, *Mount Sterling*

REPRESENTATIVES

Oscar Turner, *Oscar*
James A. McKenzie, *Long View*
John William Caldwell, *Russellville*
J. Proctor Knott, *Lebanon*
Albert S. Willis, *Louisville*
John G. Carlisle, *Covington*
Joseph C. S. Blackburn, *Versailles*
Philip B. Thompson, Jr., *Harrodsburg*
Thomas Turner, *Mount Sterling*
Elijah C. Phister, *Maysville*

LOUISIANA

SENATORS

William Pitt Kellogg,[20] *New Orleans*
Benjamin F. Jonas, *New Orleans*

REPRESENTATIVES

Randall L. Gibson, *New Orleans*
E. John Ellis, *New Orleans*
Joseph H. Acklen, *Franklin*
Joseph B. Elam, *Mansfield*
J. Floyd King, *Vidalia*
Edward W. Robertson, *Baton Rouge*

MAINE

SENATORS

Hannibal Hamlin, *Bangor*
James G. Blaine, *Augusta*

REPRESENTATIVES

Thomas B. Reed, *Portland*
William P. Frye, *Lewiston*
Stephen D. Lindsey, *Norridgewock*
George W. Ladd, *Bangor*
Thompson H. Murch, *Rockland*

MARYLAND

SENATORS

William Pinkney Whyte, *Baltimore*
James B. Groome, *Elkton*

REPRESENTATIVES

Daniel M. Henry, *Cambridge*
J. Fred C. Talbott, *Towsontown*
William Kimmel, *Baltimore*
Robert M. McLane, *Baltimore*
Eli J. Henkle, *Brooklyn*
Milton G. Urner, *Frederick*

MASSACHUSETTS

SENATORS

Henry L. Dawes, *Pittsfield*
George F. Hoar, *Worcester*

REPRESENTATIVES

William W. Crapo, *New Bedford*
Benjamin W. Harris, *East Bridgewater*
Walbridge A. Field, *Boston*
Leopold Morse, *Boston*
Selwyn Z. Bowman, *Somerville*
George B. Loring,[21] *Salem*
William A. Russell, *Lawrence*
William Claflin, *Newton*
William W. Rice, *Worcester*
Amasa Norcross, *Fitchburg*
George D. Robinson, *Chicopee*

---

[13] Served until January 22, 1881; succeeded by Horatio Bisbee, Jr., who contested his election.
[14] Successfully contested the election of Noble A. Hull, and took his seat January 22, 1881.
[15] Resigned in May 1880.
[16] Appointed to fill vacancy caused by resignation of John B. Gordon, and took his seat May 26, 1880; subsequently elected.

[17] Election unsuccessfully contested by James McCabe.
[18] Died April 29, 1879.
[19] Elected to fill vacancy caused by the death of Rush Clark, and took his seat December 1, 1879.
[20] The credentials of Thomas C. Manning, appointed to fill vacancy caused by the death of Henry M. Spofford (August 20, 1880), contestant for this seat in the preceding Congress, were presented December 7, 1880; inasmuch as the Senate had taken no action upon the report that was favorable to Mr. Spofford, no action was taken upon Mr. Manning's credentials beyond referring them to the committee.
[21] Election unsuccessfully contested by E. Moody Boynton.

MICHIGAN

SENATORS

Thomas W. Ferry, *Grand Haven*
Zachariah Chandler,[22] *Detroit*
Henry P. Baldwin,[23] *Detroit*

REPRESENTATIVES

John S. Newberry, *Detroit*
Edwin Willits, *Monroe*
Jonas H. McGowan, *Coldwater*
Julius C. Burrows, *Kalamazoo*
John W. Stone, *Grand Rapids*
Mark S. Brewer, *Pontiac*
Omar D. Conger,[24] *Port Huron*
Roswell G. Horr, *East Saginaw*
Jay A. Hubbell, *Houghton*

MINNESOTA

SENATORS

William Windom, *Winona*
Samuel J. R. McMillan, *St. Paul*

REPRESENTATIVES

Mark H. Dunnell, *Owatonna*
Henry Poehler, *Henderson*
William D. Washburn, *Minneapolis*

MISSISSIPPI

SENATORS

Blanche K. Bruce, *Floreyville*
Lucius Q. C. Lamar, *Oxford*

REPRESENTATIVES

Henry L. Muldrow, *Starkville*
Vannoy H. Manning, *Holly Springs*
Hernando D. Money, *Winona*
Otho R. Singleton, *Canton*
Charles E. Hooker, *Jackson*
James R. Chalmers, *Vicksburg*

MISSOURI

SENATORS

Francis M. Cockrell, *Warrensburg*
George G. Vest, *Kansas City*

REPRESENTATIVES

Martin L. Clardy, *Farmington*
Erastus Wells, *St. Louis*
Richard G. Frost, *St. Louis*
Lowndes H. Davis, *Jackson*
Richard P. Bland, *Lebanon*
James R. Waddill, *Springfield*
Alfred M. Lay,[25] *Jefferson City*

John F. Philips,[26] *Sedalia*
Samuel L. Sawyer, *Independence*
Nicholas Ford, *Rochester*
Gideon F. Rothwell, *Moberly*
John B. Clark, Jr., *Fayette*
William H. Hatch, *Hannibal*
Aylett H. Buckner, *Mexico*

NEBRASKA

SENATORS

Algernon S. Paddock, *Beatrice*
Alvin Saunders, *Omaha*

REPRESENTATIVE

At Large—Edward K. Valentine, *West Point*

NEVADA

SENATORS

John P. Jones, *Gold Hill*
William Sharon, *Virginia City*

REPRESENTATIVE

At Large—Rollin M. Daggett, *Virginia City*

NEW HAMPSHIRE

SENATORS

Edward H. Rollins, *Concord*
Charles H. Bell,[27] *Exeter*
Henry W. Blair,[28] *Plymouth*

REPRESENTATIVES

Joshua G. Hall, *Dover*
James F. Briggs, *Manchester*
Evarts W. Farr,[29] *Littleton*
Ossian Ray,[30] *Lancaster*

NEW JERSEY

SENATORS

Theodore F. Randolph, *Morristown*
John R. McPherson, *Jersey City*

REPRESENTATIVES

George M. Robeson, *Camden*
Hezekiah B. Smith, *Smithville*
Miles Ross, *New Brunswick*
Alvah A. Clark, *Somerville*
Charles H. Voorhis, *Hackensack*
John L. Blake, *Orange*
Lewis A. Brigham, *Jersey City*

NEW YORK

SENATORS

Roscoe Conkling, *Utica*
Francis Kernan, *Utica*

REPRESENTATIVES

James W. Covert, *Flushing*
Daniel O'Reilly, *Brooklyn*
Simeon B. Chittenden, *Brooklyn*
Archibald M. Bliss, *Brooklyn*
Nicholas Muller, *New York City*
Samuel S. Cox, *New York City*
Edwin Einstein, *New York City*
Anson G. McCook, *New York City*
Fernando Wood,[31] *New York City*
James O'Brien, *New York City*
Levi P. Morton, *New York City*
Waldo Hutchins,[32] *Kingsbridge*
John H. Ketcham, *Dover Plains*
John W. Ferdon, *Piermont*
William Lounsbery, *Kingston*
John M. Bailey, *Albany*
Walter A. Wood, *Hoosick Falls*
John Hammond, *Crown Point*
Amaziah B. James, *Ogdensburg*
John H. Starin, *Fultonville*
David Wilber, *Milford*
Warner Miller, *Herkimer*
Cyrus D. Prescott, *Rome*
Joseph Mason,[33] *Hamilton*
Frank Hiscock, *Syracuse*
John H. Camp, *Lyons*
Elbridge G. Lapham, *Canandaigua*
Jeremiah W. Dwight, *Dryden*
David P. Richardson, *Angelica*
John Van Voorhis, *Rochester*
Richard Crowley, *Lockport*
Ray V. Pierce,[34] *Buffalo*
Jonathan Scoville,[35] *Salisbury*
Henry Van Aernam, *Franklinville*

NORTH CAROLINA

SENATORS

Matt W. Ransom, *Weldon*
Zebulon B. Vance, *Charlotte*

REPRESENTATIVES

Joseph J. Martin,[36] *Williamston*
Jesse J. Yeates,[37] *Murfreesboro*
William H. Kitchin, *Scotland Neck*
Daniel L. Russell, *Wilmington*
Joseph J. Davis, *Louisburg*
Alfred M. Scales, *Greensborough*
Walter L. Steele, *Rockingham*
Robert F. Armfield, *Statesville*
Robert B. Vance, *Asheville*

---

[22] Died November 1, 1879.
[23] Appointed to fill vacancy caused by death of Zachariah Chandler, and took his seat December 3, 1879; subsequently elected.
[24] Resigned March 3, 1881, before the commencement of the Forty-eighth Congress to which he had been reelected, having been elected Senator.
[25] Died December 8, 1879.
[26] Elected to fill vacancy caused by the death of Alfred M. Lay, and took his seat January 26, 1880.
[27] Appointed to fill vacancy in term beginning March 4, 1879; credentials presented and referred March 18, 1879; majority of Committee on Privileges

and Elections reported resolution, April 2, 1879, declaring him not entitled to seat; by resolution, April 10, 1879, was declared entitled to seat; appeared and qualified same day.
[28] Elected to fill vacancy in term beginning March 4, 1879, and took his seat June 20, 1879.
[29] Died November 30, 1880.
[30] Elected to fill vacancy caused by death of Evarts W. Farr, and took his seat January 8, 1881.
[31] Died February 13, 1881, before the commencement of the Forty-seventh Congress, to which he had been reelected.
[32] Elected to fill vacancy caused by death of Repre-

sentative-elect Alexander Smith (November 5, 1878, before the beginning of the congressional term), and took his seat December 1, 1879.
[33] Election unsuccessfully contested by Sebastian Duffy.
[34] Resigned September 18, 1880.
[35] Elected to fill vacancy caused by resignation of Ray V. Pierce, and took his seat December 6, 1880.
[36] Served until January 29, 1881; succeeded by Jesse J. Yeates, who contested his election.
[37] Successfully contested the election of Joseph J. Martin, and took his seat January 29, 1881.

OHIO

SENATORS

Allen G. Thurman, *Columbus*
George H. Pendleton, *Cincinnati*

REPRESENTATIVES

Benjamin Butterworth, *Cincinnati*
Thomas L. Young, *Cincinnati*
John A. McMahon, *Dayton*
J. Warren Keifer, *Springfield*
Benjamin Le Fevre, *Sidney*
William D. Hill, *Defiance*
Frank H. Hurd, *Toledo*
Ebenezer B. Finley, *Bucyrus*
George L. Converse, *Columbus*
Thomas Ewing, *Lancaster*
Henry L. Dickey, *Greenfield*
Henry S. Neal, *Ironton*
Adoniram J. Warner, *Marietta*
Gibson Atherton, *Newark*
George W. Geddes, *Mansfield*
William McKinley, Jr., *Canton*
James Monroe, *Oberlin*
Jonathan T. Updegraff, *Mount Pleasant*
James A. Garfield,[38] *Mentor*
Ezra B. Taylor,[39] *Warren*
Amos Townsend, *Cleveland*

OREGON

SENATORS

La Fayette Grover, *Salem*
James H. Slater, *La Grande*

REPRESENTATIVE

At Large—John Whiteaker, *Pleasant Hill*

PENNSYLVANIA

SENATORS

William A. Wallace, *Clearfield*
J. Donald Cameron, *Harrisburg*

REPRESENTATIVES

Henry H. Bingham, *Philadelphia*
Charles O'Neill, *Philadelphia*
Samuel J. Randall, *Philadelphia*
William D. Kelley, *Philadelphia*
Alfred C. Harmer, *Germantown*
William Ward, *Chester*
William Godshalk, *New Britain*
Hiester Clymer, *Reading*
A. Herr Smith, *Lancaster*
Reuben K. Bachman, *Durham*
Robert Klotz, *Mauch Chunk*
Hendrick B. Wright, *Wilkes-Barre*
John W. Ryon, *Pottsville*
John W. Killinger, *Lebanon*
Edward Overton, Jr., *Towanda*
John I. Mitchell, *Wellsboro*
Alexander H. Coffroth, *Somerset*

Horatio G. Fisher, *Huntingdon*
Frank E. Beltzhoover, *Carlisle*
Seth H. Yocum,[40] *Bellefonte*
Morgan R. Wise, *Waynesburg*
Russell Errett, *Pittsburgh*
Thomas M. Bayne, *Allegheny*
William S. Shallenberger, *Rochester*
Harry White, *Indiana*
Samuel B. Dick, *Meadville*
James H. Osmer, *Franklin*

RHODE ISLAND

SENATORS

Henry B. Anthony, *Providence*
Ambrose E. Burnside, *Providence*

REPRESENTATIVES

Nelson W. Aldrich, *Providence*
Latimer W. Ballou, *Woonsocket*

SOUTH CAROLINA

SENATORS

Matthew C. Butler, *Edgefield*
Wade Hampton, *Columbia*

REPRESENTATIVES

John S. Richardson, *Sumter*
Michael P. O'Connor, *Charleston*
D. Wyatt Aiken, *Cokesbury*
John H. Evins, *Spartanburg*
George D. Tillman, *Edgefield*

TENNESSEE

SENATORS

James E. Bailey, *Clarksville*
Isham G. Harris, *Memphis*

REPRESENTATIVES

Robert L. Taylor, *Jonesboro*
Leonidas C. Houk, *Knoxville*
George G. Dibrell, *Sparta*
Benton McMillin, *Carthage*
John M. Bright, *Fayetteville*
John F. House, *Clarksville*
Washington C. Whitthorne, *Columbia*
John D. C. Atkins, *Paris*
Charles B. Simonton, *Covington*
H. Casey Young, *Memphis*

TEXAS

SENATORS

Samuel B. Maxey, *Paris*
Richard Coke, *Waco*

REPRESENTATIVES

John H. Reagan, *Palestine*
David B. Culberson, *Jefferson*
Olin Wellborn, *Dallas*

Roger Q. Mills, *Corsicana*
George W. Jones, *Bastrop*
Christopher C. Upson,[41] *San Antonio*

VERMONT

SENATORS

George F. Edmunds, *Burlington*
Justin S. Morrill, *Strafford*

REPRESENTATIVES

Charles H. Joyce, *Rutland*
James M. Tyler, *Brattleboro*
Bradley Barlow, *St. Albans*

VIRGINIA

SENATORS

John W. Johnston, *Abingdon*
Robert E. Withers, *Wytheville*

REPRESENTATIVES

Richard Lee T. Beale, *Hague*
John Goode, Jr., *Norfolk*
Joseph E. Johnston, *Longwood*
Joseph Jorgensen, *Petersburg*
George C. Cabell, *Danville*
John R. Tucker, *Lexington*
John T. Harris, *Harrisonburg*
Eppa Hunton, *Warrenton*
James B. Richmond, *Estillville*

WEST VIRGINIA

SENATORS

Henry G. Davis, *Piedmont*
Frank Hereford, *Union*

REPRESENTATIVES

Benjamin Wilson, *Wilsonburg*
Benjamin F. Martin, *Pruntytown*
John E. Kenna, *Kanawha*

WISCONSIN

SENATORS

Angus Cameron, *La Crosse*
Matthew H. Carpenter,[42] *Milwaukee*

REPRESENTATIVES

Charles G. Williams, *Janesville*
Lucien B. Caswell, *Fort Atkinson*
George C. Hazelton, *Boscobel*
Peter V. Deuster, *Milwaukee*
Edward S. Bragg, *Fond du Lac*
Gabriel Bouck, *Oshkosh*
Herman L. Humphrey, *Hudson*
Thaddeus C. Pound, *Chippewa Falls*

---

[38] Resigned November 8, 1880, having been elected President of the United States.
[39] Elected to fill vacancy caused by resignation of James A. Garfield, and took his seat December 13, 1880.
[40] Election unsuccessfully contested by Andrew G. Curtin.
[41] Elected to fill vacancy caused by death of Representative-elect Gustave Schleicher, in preceding Congress, and took his seat June 2, 1879.
[42] Died February 24, 1881.

TERRITORY OF ARIZONA

DELEGATE

John G. Campbell, *Prescott*

TERRITORY OF DAKOTA

DELEGATE

Granville G. Bennett, *Yankton*

TERRITORY OF IDAHO

DELEGATE

George Ainslie, *Idaho City*

TERRITORY OF MONTANA

DELEGATE

Martin Maginnis, *Helena*

TERRITORY OF NEW MEXICO

DELEGATE

Mariano S. Otero, *Peralta*

TERRITORY OF UTAH

DELEGATE

George Q. Cannon, *Salt Lake City*

TERRITORY OF WASHINGTON

DELEGATE

Thomas H. Brents, *Walla Walla*

TERRITORY OF WYOMING

DELEGATE

Stephen W. Downey, *Laramie City*

FORTY-SEVENTH CONGRESS

MARCH 4, 1881, TO MARCH 3, 1883

FIRST SESSION—*December 5, 1881, to August 8, 1882*

SECOND SESSION—*December 4, 1882, to March 3, 1883*

SPECIAL SESSIONS OF THE SENATE—*March 4, 1881, to May 20, 1881; October 10, 1881, to October 29, 1881*

———

VICE PRESIDENT OF THE UNITED STATES—CHESTER A. ARTHUR,[1] of New York

PRESIDENT PRO TEMPORE OF THE SENATE—THOMAS F. BAYARD,[2] of Delaware; DAVID DAVIS,[3] of Illinois; GEORGE F. EDMUNDS,[4] of Vermont

SECRETARY OF THE SENATE—JOHN C. BURCH,[5] of Tennessee; FRANCIS E. SHOBER[6] (Chief Clerk), of North Carolina

SERGEANT AT ARMS OF THE SENATE—RICHARD J. BRIGHT, of Indiana

———

SPEAKER OF THE HOUSE OF REPRESENTATIVES—J. WARREN KEIFER,[7] of Ohio

CLERK OF THE HOUSE—GEORGE M. ADAMS, of Kentucky; EDWARD McPHERSON,[8] of Pennsylvania

SERGEANT AT ARMS OF THE HOUSE—JOHN G. THOMPSON, of Ohio; GEORGE W. HOOKER,[9] of Vermont

DOORKEEPER OF THE HOUSE—WALTER P. BROWNLOW, of Tennessee

POSTMASTER OF THE HOUSE—HENRY SHERWOOD

ALABAMA

SENATORS

John T. Morgan, *Selma*
James L. Pugh, *Eufaula*

REPRESENTATIVES

Thomas H. Herndon, *Mobile*
Hilary A. Herbert, *Montgomery*
William C. Oates, *Abbeville*
Charles M. Shelley,[10] *Selma*
Thomas Williams, *Wetumpka*
Goldsmith W. Hewitt, *Birmingham*
William H. Forney, *Jacksonville*
Joseph Wheeler,[11] *Wheeler*
William M. Lowe,[12] *Huntsville*

ARKANSAS

SENATORS

Augustus H. Garland, *Little Rock*
James D. Walker, *Fayetteville*

REPRESENTATIVES

Poindexter Dunn, *Forest City*
James K. Jones, *Washington*
Jordan E. Cravens, *Clarksville*
Thomas M. Gunter, *Fayetteville*

CALIFORNIA

SENATORS

James T. Farley, *Jackson*
John F. Miller, *San Francisco*

REPRESENTATIVES

William S. Rosecrans, *San Francisco*
Horace F. Page, *Placerville*
Campbell P. Berry, *Wheatland*
Romualdo Pacheco, *San Luis Obispo*

COLORADO

SENATORS

Henry M. Teller,[13] *Denver*
George M. Chilcott,[14] *Denver*
Horace A. W. Tabor,[15] *Denver*
Nathaniel P. Hill, *Denver*

REPRESENTATIVE

At Large—James B. Belford, *Central City*

CONNECTICUT

SENATORS

Orville H. Platt, *West Meriden*
Joseph R. Hawley, *Hartford*

REPRESENTATIVES

John R. Buck, *Hartford*
James Phelps, *Essex*
John T. Wait, *Norwich*
Frederick Miles, *Chapinville*

[1] Became President on the death of James A. Garfield, September 19, 1881.
[2] Elected October 10, 1881 (special session of the Senate).
[3] Elected October 13, 1881 (special session of the Senate); resigned March 3, 1883.
[4] Elected March 3, 1883.
[5] Died July 28, 1881.
[6] Appointed Acting Secretary by resolution of October 24, 1881, to fill vacancy caused by death of John C. Burch; served throughout the Congress.
[7] Elected December 5, 1881.
[8] Elected December 5, 1881.
[9] Elected December 5, 1881.
[10] Election contested by James Q. Smith; report of the committee favorable to contestant, but contestant died and seat was declared vacant July 20, 1882; subsequently elected to fill vacancy thus caused, and took his seat December 4, 1882; this election was contested by John W. Jones, but was undisposed of at close of the Congress.
[11] Served until June 3, 1882; succeeded by William M. Lowe, who contested his election; subsequently elected to fill vacancy caused by the death of Mr. Lowe, and took his seat January 15, 1883.
[12] Successfully contested the election of Joseph Wheeler, and took his seat June 3, 1882; died August 12, 1882.
[13] Resigned April 17, 1882, having been appointed Secretary of the Interior.
[14] Appointed to fill vacancy caused by resignation of Henry M. Teller, and took his seat April 17, 1882.
[15] Elected to fill vacancy by caused resignation of Henry M. Teller, and took his seat February 2, 1883.

DELAWARE

SENATORS

Thomas F. Bayard, *Wilmington*
Eli Saulsbury, *Dover*

REPRESENTATIVE

At Large—Edward L. Martin, *Seaford*

FLORIDA

SENATORS

Charles W. Jones, *Pensacola*
Wilkinson Call, *Jacksonville*

REPRESENTATIVES

Robert H. M. Davidson, *Quincy*
Jesse J. Finley,[16] *Jacksonville*
Horatio Bisbee, Jr.,[17] *Jacksonville*

GEORGIA

SENATORS

Benjamin H. Hill,[18] *Atlanta*
M. Pope Barrow,[19] *Athens*
Joseph E. Brown, *Atlanta*

REPRESENTATIVES

George R. Black, *Sylvania*
Henry G. Turner, *Quitman*
Philip Cook, *Americus*
Hugh Buchanan, *Newnan*
Nathaniel J. Hammond, *Atlanta*
James H. Blount, *Macon*
Judson C. Clements, *La Fayette*
Alexander H. Stephens,[20] *Crawfordville*
Seaborn Reese,[21] *Sparta*
Emory Speer, *Athens*

ILLINOIS

SENATORS

David Davis, *Bloomington*
John A. Logan, *Chicago*

REPRESENTATIVES

William Aldrich, *Chicago*
George R. Davis, *Chicago*
Charles B. Farwell, *Chicago*
John C. Sherwin, *Aurora*
Robert M. A. Hawk,[22] *Mount Carroll*
Robert R. Hitt,[23] *Mount Morris*
Thomas J. Henderson, *Princeton*
William Cullen, *Ottawa*
Lewis E. Payson, *Pontiac*
John H. Lewis, *Knoxville*

Benjamin F. Marsh, *Warsaw*
James W. Singleton, *Quincy*
William M. Springer, *Springfield*
Dietrich C. Smith, *Pekin*
Joseph G. Cannon, *Danville*
Samuel W. Moulton, *Shelbyville*
William A. J. Sparks, *Carlyle*
William R. Morrison, *Waterloo*
John R. Thomas, *Metropolis*
Richard W. Townshend, *Shawneetown*

INDIANA

SENATORS

Daniel W. Voorhees, *Terre Haute*
Benjamin Harrison, *Indianapolis*

REPRESENTATIVES

William Heilman, *Evansville*
Thomas R. Cobb, *Vincennes*
Strother M. Stockslager, *Corydon*
William S. Holman, *Aurora*
Courtland C. Matson, *Greencastle*
Thomas M. Browne, *Winchester*
Stanton J. Peelle, *Indianapolis*
Robert B. F. Peirce, *Crawfordsville*
Godlove S. Orth,[24] *La Fayette*
Charles T. Doxey,[25] *Anderson*
Mark L. DeMotte, *Valparaiso*
George W. Steele, *Marion*
Walpole G. Colerick, *Fort Wayne*
William H. Calkins, *Laporte*

IOWA

SENATORS

William B. Allison, *Dubuque*
Samuel J. Kirkwood,[26] *Iowa City*
James W. McDill,[27] *Afton*

REPRESENTATIVES

Moses A. McCoid, *Fairfield*
Sewall S. Farwell, *Monticello*
Thomas Updegraff, *McGregor*
Nathaniel C. Deering, *Osage*
William G. Thompson, *Marion*
Marsena E. Cutts,[28] *Oskaloosa*
John C. Cook,[29] *Newton*
John A. Kasson, *Des Moines*
William P. Hepburn, *Clarinda*
Cyrus C. Carpenter, *Fort Dodge*

KANSAS

SENATORS

John J. Ingalls, *Atchison*
Preston B. Plumb, *Emporia*

REPRESENTATIVES

John A. Anderson, *Manhattan*
Dudley C. Haskell, *Lawrence*
Thomas Ryan, *Topeka*

KENTUCKY

SENATORS

James B. Beck, *Lexington*
John S. Williams, *Mount Sterling*

REPRESENTATIVES

Oscar Turner, *Oscar*
James A. McKenzie, *Long View*
John W. Caldwell, *Russellville*
J. Proctor Knott, *Lebanon*
Albert S. Willis, *Louisville*
John G. Carlisle, *Covington*
Joseph C. S. Blackburn, *Versailles*
Philip B. Thompson, Jr., *Harrodsburg*
John D. White, *Manchester*
Elijah C. Phister, *Maysville*

LOUISIANA

SENATORS

William Pitt Kellogg, *New Orleans*
Benjamin F. Jonas, *New Orleans*

REPRESENTATIVES

Randall L. Gibson, *New Orleans*
E. John Ellis, *New Orleans*
Chester B. Darrall, *Morgan City*
Newton C. Blanchard, *Shreveport*
J. Floyd King, *Vidalia*
Edward W. Robertson, *Baton Rouge*

MAINE

SENATORS

James G. Blaine,[30] *Augusta*
William P. Frye,[31] *Lewiston*
Eugene Hale, *Ellsworth*

REPRESENTATIVES

Thomas B. Reed,[32] *Portland*
William P. Frye,[33] *Lewiston*
Nelson Dingley, Jr.,[34] *Lewiston*
Stephen D. Lindsey, *Norridgewock*
George W. Ladd, *Bangor*
Thompson H. Murch, *Rockland*

MARYLAND

SENATORS

James B. Groome, *Elkton*
Arthur Pue Gorman, *Laurel*

---

[16] Served until June 1, 1882; succeeded by Horatio Bisbee, Jr., who contested his election.
[17] Successfully contested the election of Jesse J. Finley, and took his seat June 1, 1882.
[18] Died August 16, 1882.
[19] Elected to fill vacancy caused by death of Benjamin H. Hill, and took his seat December 5, 1882.
[20] Resigned November 4, 1882, having been elected governor.
[21] Elected to fill vacancy caused by resignation of Alexander H. Stephens, and took his seat December 4, 1882.
[22] Died June 29, 1882.

[23] Elected to fill vacancy caused by death of Robert M. A. Hawk, and took his seat December 4, 1882.
[24] Died December 16, 1882.
[25] Elected to fill vacancy caused by death of Godlove S. Orth, and took his seat January 17, 1883.
[26] Resigned March 7, 1881, to become Secretary of the Interior.
[27] Appointed to fill vacancy caused by resignation of Samuel J. Kirkwood, and took his seat March 14, 1881 (special session of the Senate); subsequently elected.
[28] Served until March 3, 1883; succeeded by John C. Cook, who contested his election.

[29] Successfully contested election of Marsena E. Cutts, and took his seat March 3, 1883—closing day of the Congress.
[30] Resigned March 5, 1881, having been appointed Secretary of State.
[31] Elected to fill vacancy caused by resignation of James G. Blaine, and took his seat March 18, 1881.
[32] Election unsuccessfully contested by Samuel J. Anderson.
[33] Resigned March 17, 1881, having been elected Senator.
[34] Elected to fill vacancy caused by resignation of William P. Frye, and took his seat December 5, 1881.

REPRESENTATIVES

George W. Covington, *Snow Hill*
J. Fred. C. Talbott, *Towsontown*
Fetter S. Hoblitzell, *Baltimore*
Robert M. McLane, *Baltimore*
Andrew G. Chapman, *La Plata*
Milton G. Urner, *Frederick*

MASSACHUSETTS

SENATORS

Henry L. Dawes, *Pittsfield*
George F. Hoar, *Worcester*

REPRESENTATIVES

William W. Crapo, *New Bedford*
Benjamin W. Harris, *East Bridgewater*
Ambrose A. Ranney, *Boston*
Leopold Morse, *Boston*
Selwyn Z. Bowman, *Somerville*
Eben F. Stone, *Newburyport*
William A. Russell, *Lawrence*
John W. Candler, *Brookline*
William W. Rice, *Worcester*
Amasa Norcross, *Fitchburg*
George D. Robinson, *Chicopee*

MICHIGAN

SENATORS

Thomas W. Ferry, *Grand Haven*
Omar D. Conger, *Port Huron*

REPRESENTATIVES

Henry W. Lord, *Detroit*
Edwin Willits, *Monroe*
Edward S. Lacey, *Charlotte*
Julius C. Burrows, *Kalamazoo*
George W. Webber, *Ionia*
Oliver L. Spaulding, *St. Johns*
John T. Rich,[35] *Elba*
Roswell G. Horr, *East Saginaw*
Jay A. Hubbell, *Houghton*

MINNESOTA

SENATORS

Samuel J. R. McMillan, *St. Paul*
William Windom,[36] *Winona*
Alonzo J. Edgerton,[37] *Kasson*
William Windom,[38] *Winona*

REPRESENTATIVES

Mark H. Dunnell, *Owatonna*
Horace B. Strait, *Shakopee*
William D. Washburn, *Minneapolis*

MISSISSIPPI

SENATORS

Lucius Q. C. Lamar, *Oxford*
James Z. George, *Jackson*

REPRESENTATIVES

Henry L. Muldrow, *Starkville*
Vannoy H. Manning,[39] *Holly Springs*
Hernando D. Money, *Winona*
Otho R. Singleton, *Canton*
Charles E. Hooker, *Jackson*
James R. Chalmers,[40] *Vicksburg*
John R. Lynch,[41] *Natchez*

MISSOURI

SENATORS

Francis M. Cockrell, *Warrensburg*
George G. Vest, *Kansas City*

REPRESENTATIVES

Martin L. Clardy, *Farmington*
Thomas Allen,[42] *St. Louis*
James H. McLean,[43] *St. Louis*
Richard G. Frost,[44] *St. Louis*
Gustavus Sessinghaus,[45] *St. Louis*
Lowndes H. Davis, *Jackson*
Richard P. Bland, *Lebanon*
Ira S. Hazeltine, *Springfield*
Theron M. Rice, *Booneville*
Robert T. Van Horn, *Kansas City*
Nicholas Ford, *Rochester*
Joseph H. Burrows, *Cainsville*
John B. Clark, Jr., *Fayette*
William H. Hatch, *Hannibal*
Aylett H. Buckner, *Mexico*

NEBRASKA

SENATORS

Alvin Saunders, *Omaha*
Charles H. Van Wyck, *Nebraska City*

REPRESENTATIVE [46]

At Large—Edward K. Valentine, *West Point*

NEVADA

SENATORS

John P. Jones, *Gold Hill*
James G. Fair, *Virginia City*

REPRESENTATIVE

At Large—George W. Cassidy, *Eureka*

NEW HAMPSHIRE

SENATORS

Edward H. Rollins, *Concord*
Henry W. Blair, *Plymouth*

REPRESENTATIVES

Joshua G. Hall, *Dover*
James F. Briggs, *Manchester*
Ossian Ray,[47] *Lancaster*

NEW JERSEY

SENATORS

John R. McPherson, *Jersey City*
William J. Sewell, *Camden*

REPRESENTATIVES

George M. Robeson, *Camden*
J. Hart Brewer, *Trenton*
Miles Ross, *New Brunswick*
Henry S. Harris, *Belvidere*
John Hill, *Boonton*
Phineas Jones, *Newark*
Augustus A. Hardenbergh, *Jersey City*

NEW YORK

SENATORS

Roscoe Conkling,[48] *Utica*
Elbridge G. Lapham,[49] *Canandaigua*
Thomas C. Platt,[50] *Owego*
Warner Miller,[51] *Herkimer*

REPRESENTATIVES

Perry Belmont, *Babylon*
William E. Robinson, *Brooklyn*
J. Hyatt Smith, *Brooklyn*
Archibald M. Bliss, *Brooklyn*
Benjamin Wood, *New York City*
Samuel S. Cox, *New York City*
P. Henry Dugro, *New York City*
Anson G. McCook, *New York City*
John Hardy,[52] *New York City*
Abram S. Hewitt, *New York City*
Levi P. Morton,[53] *New York City*
Roswell P. Flower,[54] *New York City*
Waldo Hutchins, *Kingsbridge*
John H. Ketcham, *Dover Plains*
Lewis Beach, *Cornwall*
Thomas Cornell, *Rondout*
Michael N. Nolan, *Albany*
Walter A. Wood, *Hoosick Falls*
John Hammond, *Crown Point*
Abraham X. Parker, *Potsdam*
George West, *Ballston Spa*

---

[35] Elected to fill vacancy caused by resignation of Representative-elect Omar D. Conger, in preceding Congress, and took his seat December 5, 1881.
[36] Resigned March 4, 1881, to become Secretary of the Treasury.
[37] Appointed to fill vacancy caused by resignation of William Windom, and took his seat March 17, 1881.
[38] Elected to fill vacancy caused by his own resignation, and took his seat December 5, 1881.
[39] Election unsuccessfully contested by George M. Buchanan.
[40] Served until April 29, 1882; succeeded by John R. Lynch, who contested his election.

[41] Successfully contested the election of James R. Chalmers, and took his seat April 29, 1882.
[42] Died April 8, 1882.
[43] Elected to fill vacancy caused by death of Thomas Allen, and took his seat December 15, 1882.
[44] Served until March 2, 1883; succeeded by Gustavus Sessinghaus, who contested his election.
[45] Successfully contested the election of Richard G. Frost, and took his seat March 2, 1883.
[46] Thomas J. Majors presented credentials as a contingent (or additional) Representative, but was not permitted to take a seat.
[47] Elected to fill vacancy caused by death of Representative-elect Evarts W. Farr, in preceding Congress.

[48] Resigned May 16, 1881.
[49] Elected to fill vacancy caused by resignation of Roscoe Conkling, and took his seat October 11, 1881.
[50] Resigned May 16, 1881.
[51] Elected to fill vacancy caused by resignation of Thomas C. Platt, and took his seat October 11, 1881.
[52] Elected to fill vacancy caused by death of Representative-elect Fernando Wood, in the preceding Congress, and took his seat December 5, 1881.
[53] Resigned, effective March 21, 1881, before Congress assembled, having been appointed minister to France.
[54] Elected to fill vacancy caused by the resignation of Levi P. Morton, and took his seat December 5, 1881.

NEW YORK—Continued

REPRESENTATIVES—continued

Ferris Jacobs, Jr., *Delhi*
Warner Miller,[55] *Herkimer*
Charles R. Skinner,[56] *Watertown*
Cyrus D. Prescott, *Rome*
Joseph Mason, *Hamilton*
Frank Hiscock, *Syracuse*
John H. Camp, *Lyons*
Elbridge G. Lapham,[57] *Canandaigua*
James W. Wadsworth,[58] *Livingstone*
Jeremiah W. Dwight, *Dryden*
David P. Richardson, *Angelica*
John Van Voorhis, *Rochester*
Richard Crowley, *Lockport*
Jonathan Scoville, *Buffalo*
Henry Van Aernam, *Franklinville*

NORTH CAROLINA

SENATORS

Matt W. Ransom, *Weldon*
Zebulon B. Vance, *Charlotte*

REPRESENTATIVES

Louis C. Latham, *Greenville*
Orlando Hubbs, *New Bern*
John W. Shackelford,[59] *Jacksonville*
William R. Cox, *Raleigh*
Alfred M. Scales, *Greensboro*
Clement Dowd, *Charlotte*
Robert F. Armfield, *Statesville*
Robert B. Vance, *Asheville*

OHIO

SENATORS

George H. Pendleton, *Cincinnati*
John Sherman,[60] *Mansfield*

REPRESENTATIVES

Benjamin Butterworth, *Cincinnati*
Thomas L. Young, *Cincinnati*
Henry L. Morey, *Hamilton*
Emanuel Shultz, *Dayton*
Benjamin Le Fevre, *Sidney*
James M. Ritchie, *Toledo*
John P. Leedom, *West Union*
J. Warren Keifer, *Springfield*
James S. Robinson, *Kenton*
John B. Rice, *Fremont*
Henry S. Neal, *Ironton*
George L. Converse, *Columbus*
Gibson Atherton, *Newark*
George W. Geddes, *Mansfield*
Rufus R. Dawes, *Marietta*

Jonathan T. Updegraff,[61] *Mount Pleasant*
Joseph D. Taylor,[62] *Cambridge*
William McKinley, Jr., *Canton*
Addison S. McClure, *Wooster*
Ezra B. Taylor, *Warren*
Amos Townsend, *Cleveland*

OREGON

SENATORS

La Fayette Grover, *Salem*
James H. Slater, *La Grande*

REPRESENTATIVE

At Large—Melvin C. George, *Portland*

PENNSYLVANIA

SENATORS

J. Donald Cameron, *Harrisburg*
John I. Mitchell, *Wellsboro*

REPRESENTATIVES

Henry H. Bingham, *Philadelphia*
Charles O'Neill, *Philadelphia*
Samuel J. Randall, *Philadelphia*
William D. Kelley, *Philadelphia*
Alfred C. Harmer, *Philadelphia*
William Ward, *Chester*
William Godshalk, *New Britain*
Daniel Ermentrout, *Reading*
A. Herr Smith, *Lancaster*
William Mutchler, *Easton*
Robert Klotz, *Mauch Chunk*
Joseph A. Scranton, *Scranton*
Charles N. Brumm, *Minersville*
Samuel F. Barr, *Harrisburg*
Cornelius C. Jadwin, *Honesdale*
Robert J. C. Walker, *Williamsport*
Jacob M. Campbell, *Johnstown*
Horatio G. Fisher, *Huntingdon*
Frank E. Beltzhoover, *Carlisle*
Andrew G. Curtin, *Bellefonte*
Morgan R. Wise, *Waynesburg*
Russell Errett, *Pittsburgh*
Thomas M. Bayne, *Allegheny*
William S. Shallenberger, *Rochester*
James Mosgrove, *Kittanning*
Samuel H. Miller, *Mercer*
Lewis F. Watson, *Warren*

RHODE ISLAND

SENATORS

Henry B. Anthony, *Providence*
Ambrose E. Burnside,[63] *Providence*
Nelson W. Aldrich,[64] *Providence*

REPRESENTATIVES

Nelson W. Aldrich,[65] *Providence*
Henry J. Spooner,[66] *Providence*
Jonathan Chace, *Providence*

SOUTH CAROLINA

SENATORS

Matthew C. Butler, *Edgefield*
Wade Hampton, *Columbia*

REPRESENTATIVES

John S. Richardson, *Sumter*
Michael P. O'Connor,[67] *Charleston*
Samuel Dibble,[68] *Orangeburg*
Edmund W. M. Mackey,[69] *Charleston*
D. Wyatt Aiken, *Cokesbury*
John H. Evins, *Spartanburg*
George D. Tillman,[70] *Edgefield*
Robert Smalls,[71] *Beaufort*

TENNESSEE

SENATORS

Isham G. Harris, *Memphis*
Howell E. Jackson, *Jackson*

REPRESENTATIVES

Augustus H. Pettibone, *Greeneville*
Leonidas C. Houk, *Knoxville*
George G. Dibrell, *Sparta*
Benton McMillin, *Carthage*
Richard Warner, *Lewisburg*
John F. House, *Clarksville*
Washington C. Whitthorne, *Columbia*
John D. C. Atkins, *Paris*
Charles B. Simonton, *Covington*
William R. Moore, *Memphis*

TEXAS

SENATORS

Samuel B. Maxey, *Paris*
Richard Coke, *Waco*

REPRESENTATIVES

John H. Reagan, *Palestine*
David B. Culberson, *Jefferson*
Olin Wellborn, *Dallas*
Roger Q. Mills, *Corsicana*
George W. Jones, *Bastrop*
Christopher C. Upson, *San Antonio*

---

[55] Resigned July 26, 1881, having been elected Senator.
[56] Elected to fill vacancy caused by resignation of Warner Miller, and took his seat December 5, 1881.
[57] Resigned July 29, 1881, having been elected Senator.
[58] Elected to fill vacancy caused by resignation of Elbridge G. Lapham, and took his seat December 5, 1881.
[59] Died January 18, 1883.
[60] Elected for the term beginning March 4, 1881. James A. Garfield was elected but declined December 23, 1880, having been elected President of the United States.

[61] Died November 30, 1882, before the commencement of the Forty-eighth Congress, to which he had been reelected.
[62] Elected to fill vacancy caused by the death of Jonathan T. Updegraff, and took his seat January 16, 1883.
[63] Died September 13, 1881.
[64] Elected to fill vacancy caused by death of Ambrose E. Burnside, and took his seat October 11, 1881.
[65] Resigned October 4, 1881, having been elected Senator.
[66] Elected to fill vacancy caused by resignation of Nelson W. Aldrich, and took his seat December 5, 1881.
[67] Died April 26, 1881, while a contest of his election

was pending, instituted by Edmund W. M. Mackey.
[68] Elected to fill vacancy caused by death of Michael P. O'Connor; took his seat December 5, 1881, and served until May 31, 1882; succeeded by Edmund W. M. Mackey, who had previously contested the election of Mr. O'Connor and continued the contest against Mr. Dibble.
[69] Successfully contested the election of Samuel Dibble, as the successor of the original contestee, Mr. O'Connor, and took his seat May 31, 1882.
[70] Served until July 19, 1882; succeeded by Robert Smalls, who contested his election.
[71] Successfully contested the election of George D. Tillman, and took his seat July 19, 1882.

VERMONT

SENATORS

George F. Edmunds, *Burlington*
Justin S. Morrill, *Strafford*

REPRESENTATIVES

Charles H. Joyce, *Rutland*
James M. Tyler, *Brattleboro*
William W. Grout, *Barton*

VIRGINIA

SENATORS

John W. Johnston, *Abingdon*
William Mahone, *Petersburg*

REPRESENTATIVES

George T. Garrison, *Accomac*
John F. Dezendorf, *Norfolk*
George D. Wise, *Richmond*
Joseph Jorgensen, *Petersburg*
George C. Cabell,[72] *Danville*
John R. Tucker, *Lexington*
John Paul, *Harrisonburg*
John S. Barbour,[73] *Alexandria*
Abram Fulkerson, *Bristol*

WEST VIRGINIA

SENATORS

Henry G. Davis, *Piedmont*
Johnson N. Camden, *Parkersburg*

REPRESENTATIVES

Benjamin Wilson, *Clarksburg*
John B. Hoge, *Martinsburg*
John E. Kenna,[74] *Kanawha*

WISCONSIN

SENATORS

Angus Cameron,[75] *La Crosse*
Philetus Sawyer, *Oshkosh*

REPRESENTATIVES

Charles G. Williams, *Janesville*
Lucien B. Caswell, *Fort Atkinson*
George C. Hazelton, *Boscobel*
Peter V. Deuster, *Milwaukee*
Edward S. Bragg, *Fond du Lac*
Richard W. Guenther, *Oshkosh*
Herman L. Humphrey, *Hudson*
Thaddeus C. Pound, *Chippewa Falls*

TERRITORY OF ARIZONA

DELEGATE

Granville H. Oury, *Florence*

TERRITORY OF DAKOTA

DELEGATE

Richard F. Pettigrew, *Sioux Falls*

TERRITORY OF IDAHO

DELEGATE

George Ainslie, *Idaho City*

TERRITORY OF MONTANA

DELEGATE

Martin Maginnis, *Helena*

TERRITORY OF NEW MEXICO

DELEGATE

Tranquilino Luna, *Los Lunas*

TERRITORY OF UTAH

DELEGATE

John T. Caine,[76] *Salt Lake City*

TERRITORY OF WASHINGTON

DELEGATE

Thomas H. Brents, *Walla Walla*

TERRITORY OF WYOMING

DELEGATE

Morton E. Post, *Cheyenne*

---

[72] Election unsuccessfully contested by John T. Stovell.
[73] Election unsuccessfully contested by S. P. Bayley.
[74] Reelected to the Forty-eighth Congress, but resigned effective March 4, 1883, having been elected Senator.
[75] Elected to fill vacancy caused by death of Matthew H. Carpenter, in preceding Congress, and took his seat March 14, 1881.
[76] Allen G. Campbell and George Q. Cannon were contestants for this seat; by resolution of April 20, 1882, it was declared that neither was entitled to qualify and seat was declared vacant; on December 4, 1882, Mr. Caine submitted a petition stating that on November 7, 1882, at the election for Delegate to the Forty-eighth Congress, he received 15,490 votes to fill the vacancy in the Forty-seventh Congress, no nomination having been made; the petition was referred to the Committee on Elections, and on January 17, 1883, a resolution was reported and adopted to the effect that he was entitled to the seat; took his seat the same day.

FORTY-EIGHTH CONGRESS

MARCH 4, 1883, TO MARCH 3, 1885

FIRST SESSION—*December 3, 1883, to July 7, 1884*

SECOND SESSION—*December 1, 1884, to March 3, 1885*

———

VICE PRESIDENT OF THE UNITED STATES [1]

PRESIDENT PRO TEMPORE OF THE SENATE—George F. Edmunds,[2] of Vermont

SECRETARY OF THE SENATE—Francis E. Shober (Chief Clerk), of North Carolina; Anson G. McCook,[3] of New York

SERGEANT AT ARMS OF THE SENATE—Richard J. Bright, of Indiana; William P. Canaday,[4] of North Carolina

———

SPEAKER OF THE HOUSE OF REPRESENTATIVES—John G. Carlisle,[5] of Kentucky

CLERK OF THE HOUSE—Edward McPherson, of Pennsylvania; John B. Clark, Jr.,[6] of Missouri

SERGEANT AT ARMS OF THE HOUSE—George W. Hooker, of Vermont; John P. Leedom,[7] of Ohio

DOORKEEPER OF THE HOUSE—James W. Wintersmith, of Texas

POSTMASTER OF THE HOUSE—Lycurgus Dalton

ALABAMA

SENATORS

John T. Morgan, *Selma*
James L. Pugh, *Eufaula*

REPRESENTATIVES

Thomas H. Herndon,[8] *Mobile*
James T. Jones,[9] *Demopolis*
Hilary A. Herbert, *Montgomery*
William C. Oates, *Abbeville*
Charles M. Shelley,[10] *Selma*
George H. Craig,[11] *Selma*
Thomas Williams, *Wetumpka*
Goldsmith W. Hewitt, *Birmingham*
William H. Forney, *Jacksonville*
Luke Pryor, *Athens*

ARKANSAS

SENATORS

Augustus H. Garland, *Little Rock*
James D. Walker, *Fayetteville*

REPRESENTATIVES

Poindexter Dunn, *Forest City*
James K. Jones,[12] *Washington*
John H. Rogers, *Fort Smith*

Samuel W. Peel, *Bentonville*
At Large—Clifton R. Breckinridge, *Pine Bluff*

CALIFORNIA

SENATORS

James T. Farley, *Jackson*
John F. Miller, *San Francisco*

REPRESENTATIVES

William S. Rosecrans, *San Francisco*
James H. Budd, *Stocken*
Barclay Henley, *Santa Rosa*
Pleasant B. Tulley, *Gilroy*
At Large—
  Charles A. Sumner, *San Francisco*
  John R. Glascock, *Oakland*

COLORADO

SENATORS

Nathaniel P. Hill, *Denver*
Thomas M. Bowen, *Del Norte*

REPRESENTATIVE

At Large—James B. Belford, *Central City*

CONNECTICUT

SENATORS

Orville H. Platt, *West Meriden*
Joseph R. Hawley, *Hartford*

REPRESENTATIVES

William W. Eaton, *Hartford*
Charles L. Mitchell, *New Haven*
John T. Wait, *Norwich*
Edward W. Seymour, *Litchfield*

DELAWARE

SENATORS

Thomas F. Bayard, *Wilmington*
Eli Saulsbury, *Dover*

REPRESENTATIVE

At Large—Charles B. Lore, *Wilmington*

FLORIDA

SENATORS

Charles W. Jones, *Pensacola*
Wilkinson Call, *Jacksonville*

---

[1] Chester A. Arthur became President on the death of James A. Garfield in preceding Congress.
[2] Reelected January 14, 1884.
[3] Elected December 18, 1883.
[4] Elected December 18, 1883.
[5] Elected December 3, 1883.
[6] Elected December 4, 1883.
[7] Elected December 4, 1883.
[8] Died March 28, 1883, before Congress assembled.
[9] Elected to fill vacancy caused by death of Thomas H. Herndon, and took his seat December 3, 1883.
[10] Served until January 9, 1885; succeeded by George

H. Craig, who contested his election.
[11] Successfully contested the election of Charles M. Shelley, and took his seat January 9, 1885.
[12] Reelected to the Forty-ninth Congress, but tendered his resignation February 19, 1885, having been elected Senator.

REPRESENTATIVES

Robert H. M. Davidson, *Quincy*
Horatio Bisbee, Jr., *Jacksonville*

GEORGIA

SENATORS

Joseph E. Brown, *Atlanta*
Alfred H. Colquitt, *Atlanta*

REPRESENTATIVES

John C. Nicholls, *Blackshear*
Henry G. Turner, *Quitman*
Charles F. Crisp, *Americus*
Hugh Buchanan, *Newnan*
Nathaniel J. Hammond, *Atlanta*
James H. Blount, *Macon*
Judson C. Clements, *La Fayette*
Seaborn Reese, *Sparta*
Allen D. Candler, *Gainesville*
At Large—Thomas Hardeman, *Macon*

ILLINOIS

SENATORS

John A. Logan, *Chicago*
Shelby M. Cullom, *Springfield*

REPRESENTATIVES

Ransom W. Dunham, *Chicago*
John F. Finerty, *Chicago*
George R. Davis, *Chicago*
George E. Adams, *Chicago*
Reuben Ellwood, *Sycamore*
Robert R. Hitt, *Mount Morris*
Thomas J. Henderson, *Princeton*
William Cullen, *Ottawa*
Lewis E. Payson, *Pontiac*
Nicholas E. Worthington, *Peoria*
William H. Neece, *Macomb*
James M. Riggs, *Winchester*
William M. Springer, *Springfield*
Jonathan H. Rowell, *Bloomington*
Joseph G. Cannon, *Danville*
Aaron Shaw, *Olney*
Samuel W. Moulton, *Shelbyville*
William R. Morrison, *Waterloo*
Richard W. Townshend, *Shawneetown*
John R. Thomas, *Metropolis*

INDIANA

SENATORS

Daniel W. Voorhees, *Terre Haute*
Benjamin Harrison, *Indianapolis*

REPRESENTATIVES

John J. Kleiner, *Evansville*
Thomas R. Cobb, *Vincennes*
Strother M. Stockslager, *Corydon*
William S. Holman, *Aurora*
Courtland C. Matson, *Greencastle*
Thomas M. Browne, *Winchester*
Stanton J. Peelle,[13] *Indianapolis*
William E. English,[14] *Indianapolis*
John E. Lamb, *Terre Haute*
Thomas B. Ward, *La Fayette*
Thomas J. Wood, *Crown Point*
George W. Steele, *Marion*
Robert Lowry, *Fort Wayne*
William H. Calkins,[15] *Laporte*
Benjamin F. Shively,[16] *South Bend*

IOWA

SENATORS

William B. Allison, *Dubuque*
James F. Wilson, *Fairfield*

REPRESENTATIVES

Moses A. McCoid, *Fairfield*
Jeremiah H. Murphy, *Davenport*
David B. Henderson, *Dubuque*
Luman H. Weller, *Nashua*
James Wilson,[17] *Traer*
Benjamin T. Frederick,[18] *Marshalltown*
Marsena E. Cutts,[19] *Oskaloosa*
John C. Cook,[20] *Newton*
John A. Kasson,[21] *Des Moines*
Hiram Y. Smith,[22] *Des Moines*
William P. Hepburn, *Clarinda*
William H. M. Pusey, *Council Bluffs*
Adoniram J. Holmes, *Boone*
Isaac S. Struble, *Le Mars*

KANSAS

SENATORS

John J. Ingalls, *Atchison*
Preston B. Plumb, *Emporia*

REPRESENTATIVES

John A. Anderson, *Manhattan*
Dudley C. Haskell,[23] *Lawrence*
Edward H. Funston,[24] *Iola*
Thomas Ryan, *Topeka*
At Large—
Edmund N. Morrill, *Hiawatha*
Lewis Hanback, *Osborne*
Samuel R. Peters,[25] *Newton*
Bishop W. Perkins, *Oswego*

KENTUCKY

SENATORS

James B. Beck, *Lexington*
John S. Williams, *Mount Sterling*

REPRESENTATIVES

Oscar Turner, *Oscar*
James F. Clay, *Henderson*
John E. Halsell, *Bowling Green*
Thomas A. Robertson, *Elizabethtown*
Albert S. Willis, *Louisville*
John G. Carlisle, *Covington*
Joseph C. S. Blackburn, *Versailles*
Philip B. Thompson, Jr., *Harrodsburg*
William W. Culbertson, *Ashland*
John D. White, *Manchester*
Frank L. Wolford, *Columbia*

LOUISIANA

SENATORS

Benjamin F. Jonas, *New Orleans*
Randall L. Gibson, *New Orleans*

REPRESENTATIVES

Carleton Hunt, *New Orleans*
E. John Ellis, *New Orleans*
William Pitt Kellogg, *New Orleans*
Newton C. Blanchard, *Shreveport*
J. Floyd King, *Vidalia*
Edward T. Lewis,[26] *Opelousas*

MAINE

SENATORS

Eugene Hale, *Ellsworth*
William P. Frye, *Lewiston*

REPRESENTATIVES AT LARGE

Thomas B. Reed, *Portland*
Nelson Dingley, Jr., *Lewiston*
Charles A. Boutelle, *Bangor*
Seth L. Milliken, *Belfast*

MARYLAND

SENATORS

James B. Groome, *Elkton*
Arthur Pue Gorman, *Laurel*

REPRESENTATIVES

George W. Covington, *Snow Hill*
J. Fred. C. Talbott, *Towsontown*
Fetter S. Hoblitzell, *Baltimore*
John V. L. Findlay, *Baltimore*
Hart B. Holton, *Powhatan*
Louis E. McComas, *Hagerstown*

---

[13] Served until May 22, 1884; succeeded by William E. English, who contested his election.
[14] Successfully contested the election of Stanton J. Peelle, and took his seat May 22, 1884.
[15] Resigned October 20, 1884.
[16] Elected to fill vacancy caused by resignation of William H. Calkins, and took his seat December 1, 1884.
[17] Served until March 3, 1885 (closing day of the Congress); succeeded by Benjamin T. Frederick, who contested his election.
[18] Successfully contested the election of James Wilson, and took his seat March 3, 1885.
[19] Died August 31, 1883, before Congress assembled.
[20] Elected to fill vacancy caused by death of Marsena E. Cutts, and took his seat December 3, 1883.
[21] Resigned July 13, 1884.
[22] Elected to fill vacancy caused by resignation of John A. Kasson, and took his seat December 2, 1884.
[23] Died December 16, 1883.
[24] Elected to fill vacancy caused by death of Dudley C. Haskell, and took his seat March 21, 1884.
[25] Election unsuccessfully contested by Samuel N. Wood.
[26] Elected to fill vacancy caused by death of Representative-elect Andrew S. Herron (November 27, 1882, before the beginning of the congressional term), and took his seat December 3, 1883.

MASSACHUSETTS

SENATORS

Henry L. Dawes, *Pittsfield*
George F. Hoar, *Worcester*

REPRESENTATIVES

Robert T. Davis, *Fall River*
John D. Long, *Hingham*
Ambrose A. Ranney, *Boston*
Patrick A. Collins, *Boston*
Leopold Morse, *Boston*
Henry B. Lovering, *Lynn*
Eben F. Stone, *Newburyport*
William A. Russell, *Lawrence*
Theodore Lyman, *Brookline*
William W. Rice, *Worcester*
William Whiting, *Holyoke*
George D. Robinson,[27] *Chicopee*
Francis W. Rockwell,[28] *Pittsfield*

MICHIGAN

SENATORS

Omar D. Conger, *Port Huron*
Thomas W. Palmer, *Detroit*

REPRESENTATIVES

William C. Maybury, *Detroit*
Nathaniel B. Eldredge, *Adrian*
Edward S. Lacey, *Charlotte*
George L. Yaple, *Mendon*
Julius Houseman, *Grand Rapids*
Edwin B. Winans, *Hamburg*
Ezra C. Carleton, *Port Huron*
Roswell G. Horr, *East Saginaw*
Byron M. Cutcheon, *Manistee*
Herschel H. Hatch, *Bay City*
Edward Breitung, *Negaunee*

MINNESOTA

SENATORS

Samuel J. R. McMillan, *St. Paul*
Dwight M. Sabin, *Stillwater*

REPRESENTATIVES

Milo White, *Chatfield*
James B. Wakefield, *Blue Earth City*
Horace B. Strait, *Shakopee*
William D. Washburn, *Minneapolis*
Knute Nelson, *Alexandria*

MISSISSIPPI

SENATORS

Lucius Q. C. Lamar, *Oxford*
James Z. George, *Jackson*

REPRESENTATIVES

Henry L. Muldrow, *Starkville*
James R. Chalmers,[29] *Sardis*
Elza Jeffords, *Mayersville*
Hernando D. Money, *Winona*
Otho R. Singleton, *Forest*
Henry S. Van Eaton, *Woodville*
Ethelbert Barksdale, *Jackson*

MISSOURI

SENATORS

Francis M. Cockrell, *Warrensburg*
George G. Vest, *Kansas City*

REPRESENTATIVES

William H. Hatch, *Hannibal*
Armstead M. Alexander, *Paris*
Alexander M. Dockery, *Gallatin*
James N. Burnes, *St. Joseph*
Alexander Graves, *Lexington*
John Cosgrove, *Boonville*
Aylett H. Buckner, *Mexico*
John J. O'Neill, *St. Louis*
James O. Broadhead, *St. Louis*
Martin L. Clardy, *Farmington*
Richard P. Bland, *Lebanon*
Charles H. Morgan, *Lamar*
Robert W. Fyan, *Marshfield*
Lowndes H. Davis, *Jackson*

NEBRASKA

SENATORS

Charles H. Van Wyck, *Nebraska City*
Charles F. Manderson, *Omaha*

REPRESENTATIVES

Archibald J. Weaver, *Falls City*
James Laird, *Hastings*
Edward K. Valentine, *West Point*

NEVADA

SENATORS

John P. Jones, *Gold Hill*
James G. Fair, *Virginia City*

REPRESENTATIVE

At Large—George W. Cassidy, *Eureka*

NEW HAMPSHIRE

SENATORS

Henry W. Blair, *Manchester*
Austin F. Pike, *Franklin*

REPRESENTATIVES

Martin A. Haynes, *Lake Village*
Ossian Ray, *Lancaster*

NEW JERSEY

SENATORS

John R. McPherson, *Jersey City*
William J. Sewell, *Camden*

REPRESENTATIVES

Thomas M. Ferrell, *Glassboro*
J. Hart Brewer, *Trenton*
John Kean, *Elizabeth*
Benjamin F. Howey, *Columbia*
William W. Phelps, *Englewood*
William H. F. Fiedler, *Newark*
William McAdoo, *Jersey City*

NEW YORK

SENATORS

Warner Miller, *Herkimer*
Elbridge G. Lapham, *Canandaigua*

REPRESENTATIVES

Perry Belmont, *Babylon*
William E. Robinson, *Brooklyn*
Darwin R. James, *Brooklyn*
Felix Campbell, *Brooklyn*
Nicholas Muller, *New York City*
Samuel S. Cox, *New York City*
William Dorsheimer, *New York City*
John J. Adams, *New York City*
John Hardy, *New York City*
Abram S. Hewitt, *New York City*
Orlando B. Potter, *New York City*
Waldo Hutchins, *Kingsbridge*
John H. Ketcham, *Dover Plains*
Lewis Beach, *Cornwall*
John H. Bagley, Jr., *Catskill*
Thomas J. Van Alstyne, *Albany*
Henry G. Burleigh, *Whitehall*
Frederick A. Johnson, *Glens Falls*
Abraham X. Parker, *Potsdam*
Edward Wemple, *Fultonville*
George W. Ray, *Chenango*
Charles R. Skinner, *Watertown*
John T. Spriggs, *Utica*
Newton W. Nutting, *Oswego*
Frank Hiscock, *Syracuse*
Sereno E. Payne, *Auburn*
James W. Wadsworth, *Geneseo*
Stephen C. Millard, *Binghamton*
John Arnot, Jr., *Elmira*
Halbert S. Greenleaf, *Rochester*
Robert S. Stevens, *Attica*
William F. Rogers, *Buffalo*
Francis B. Brewer, *Westfield*
At Large—Henry W. Slocum, *Brooklyn*

---

[27] Resigned January 7, 1884.
[28] Elected to fill vacancy caused by resignation of George D. Robinson, and took his seat January 26, 1884.
[29] Credentials of election regularly issued to Vannoy H. Manning were not filed with Clerk of the House, but were presented on December 3, 1883, and referred, with papers of contest by James R. Chalmers, to the Committee on Elections for report as to the prima facie right of one of the contestants; the committee was discharged from further consideration of the question of prima facie right on February 15, 1884, and on June 20, 1884, reported a resolution declaring Chalmers duly elected, which was adopted by the House June 25, 1884; took his seat the same day.

NORTH CAROLINA

SENATORS

Matt W. Ransom, *Weldon*
Zebulon B. Vance, *Charlotte*

REPRESENTATIVES

Walter F. Pool,[30] *Elizabeth*
Thomas G. Skinner,[31] *Hertford*
James E. O'Hara, *Enfield*
Wharton J. Green, *Fayetteville*
William R. Cox, *Raleigh*
Alfred M. Scales,[32] *Greensboro*
James W. Reid,[33] *Wentworth*
Clement Dowd, *Charlotte*
Tyre York, *Trap Hill*
Robert B. Vance, *Asheville*
At Large—Risden T. Bennett, *Wadesboro*

OHIO

SENATORS

George H. Pendleton, *Cincinnati*
John Sherman, *Mansfield*

REPRESENTATIVES

John F. Follett, *Cincinnati*
Isaac M. Jordan, *Cincinnati*
Robert M. Murray, *Piqua*
Benjamin Le Fevre, *Maplewood*
George E. Seney, *Tiffin*
William D. Hill, *Defiance*
Henry L. Morey,[34] *Hamilton*
James E. Campbell,[35] *Hamilton*
J. Warren Keifer, *Springfield*
James S. Robinson,[36] *Kenton*
Frank H. Hurd, *Toledo*
John W. McCormick, *Gallipolis*
Alphonso Hart, *Hillsboro*
George L. Converse, *Columbus*
George W. Geddes, *Mansfield*
Adoniram J. Warner, *Marietta*
Beriah Wilkins, *Urichsville*
Joseph D. Taylor,[37] *Cambridge*
William McKinley, Jr.,[38] *Canton*
Jonathan H. Wallace,[39] *New Lisbon*
Ezra B. Taylor, *Warren*
David R. Paige, *Akron*
Martin A. Foran, *Cleveland*

OREGON

SENATORS

James H. Slater, *La Grande*
Joseph N. Dolph, *Portland*

REPRESENTATIVE

At Large—Melvin C. George, *Portland*

PENNSYLVANIA

SENATORS

J. Donald Cameron, *Harrisburg*
John I. Mitchell, *Wellsboro*

REPRESENTATIVES

Henry H. Bingham, *Philadelphia*
Charles O'Neill, *Philadelphia*
Samuel J. Randall, *Philadelphia*
William D. Kelley, *Philadelphia*
Alfred C. Harmer, *Philadelphia*
James B. Everhart, *West Chester*
I. Newton Evans, *Hatboro*
Daniel Ermentrout, *Reading*
A. Herr Smith, *Lancaster*
William Mutchler, *Easton*
John B. Storm, *Stroudsburg*
Daniel W. Connolly, *Scranton*
Charles N. Brumm, *Minersville*
Samuel F. Barr, *Harrisburg*
George A. Post, *Susquehanna*
William W. Brown, *Bradford*
Jacob M. Campbell, *Johnstown*
Louis E. Atkinson, *Mifflintown*
William A. Duncan,[40] *Gettysburg*
John A. Swope,[41] *Gettysburg*
Andrew G. Curtin, *Bellefonte*
Charles E. Boyle, *Uniontown*
James H. Hopkins, *Pittsburgh*
Thomas M. Bayne, *Allegheny*
George V. Lawrence, *Monongahela*
John D. Patton, *Indiana*
Samuel H. Miller, *Mercer*
Samuel M. Brainerd, *Erie*
At Large—Mortimer F. Elliott, *Wellsboro*

RHODE ISLAND

SENATORS

Henry B. Anthony,[42] *Providence*
William P. Sheffield,[43] *Newport*
Jonathan Chace,[44] *Providence*
Nelson W. Aldrich, *Providence*

REPRESENTATIVES

Henry J. Spooner, *Providence*
Jonathan Chace,[45] *Providence*
Nathan F. Dixon,[46] *Westerly*

SOUTH CAROLINA

SENATORS

Matthew C. Butler, *Edgefield*
Wade Hampton, *Columbia*

REPRESENTATIVES

Samuel Dibble, *Orangeburg*
George D. Tillman, *Clarks Hill*
D. Wyatt Aiken, *Cokesbury*
John H. Evins,[47] *Spartanburg*
John Bratton,[48] *White Oak*
John J. Hemphill, *Chester*
George W. Dargan, *Darlington*
Edmund W. M. Mackey,[49] *Berkeley*
Robert Smalls,[50] *Beaufort*

TENNESSEE

SENATORS

Isham G. Harris, *Memphis*
Howell E. Jackson, *Nashville*

REPRESENTATIVES

Augustus H. Pettibone, *Greeneville*
Leonidas C. Houk, *Knoxville*
George G. Dibrell, *Sparta*
Benton McMillin, *Carthage*
Richard Warner, *Lewisburg*
Andrew J. Caldwell, *Nashville*
John G. Ballentine, *Pulaski*
John M. Taylor, *Lexington*
Rice A. Pierce, *Union City*
H. Casey Young, *Memphis*

TEXAS

SENATORS

Samuel B. Maxey, *Paris*
Richard Coke, *Waco*

REPRESENTATIVES

Charles Stewart, *Houston*
John H. Reagan, *Palestine*
James H. Jones, *Henderson*
David B. Culberson, *Jefferson*
James W. Throckmorton, *McKinney*
Olin Wellborn, *Dallas*
Thomas P. Ochiltree, *Galveston*
James F. Miller, *Gonzales*
Roger Q. Mills, *Corsicana*
John Hancock, *Austin*
Samuel W. T. Lanham, *Weatherford*

VERMONT

SENATORS

George F. Edmunds, *Burlington*
Justin S. Morrill, *Strafford*

REPRESENTATIVES

John W. Stewart, *Middlebury*
Luke P. Poland, *St. Johnsbury*

---

[30] Died August 25, 1883, before Congress assembled.
[31] Elected to fill vacancy caused by death of Walter F. Pool, and took his seat December 19, 1883.
[32] Resigned December 30, 1884, to become governor.
[33] Elected to fill vacancy caused by resignation of Alfred M. Scales, and took his seat January 28, 1885.
[34] Served until June 20, 1884; succeeded by James E. Campbell, who contested his election.
[35] Successfully contested the election of Henry L. Morey, and took his seat June 20, 1884.
[36] Resigned January 12, 1885.
[37] Elected to fill vacancy caused by death of Representative-elect Jonathan T. Updegraff, in preceding Congress.
[38] Served until May 27, 1884; succeeded by Jonathan H. Wallace, who contested his election.
[39] Successfully contested the election of William McKinley, Jr., and took his seat May 27, 1884.
[40] Died November 14, 1884, before the commencement of the Forty-ninth Congress, to which he had been reelected.
[41] Elected to fill vacancy caused by death of William A. Duncan, and took his seat January 5, 1885.
[42] Died September 2, 1884.
[43] Appointed to fill vacancy caused by death of Henry B. Anthony; took his seat December 2, 1884.
[44] Elected to fill vacancy caused by death of Henry B. Anthony, and took his seat January 26, 1885.
[45] Resigned January 26, 1885, having been elected Senator.
[46] Elected to fill vacancy caused by resignation of Jonathan Chace, and took his seat February 12, 1885.
[47] Died October 20, 1884.
[48] Elected to fill vacancy caused by death of John H. Evins, and took his seat December 8, 1884.
[49] Died January 27, 1884.
[50] Elected to fill vacancy caused by death of Edmund W. M. Mackey, and took his seat March 31, 1884.

VIRGINIA

SENATORS

William Mahone, *Petersburg*
Harrison H. Riddleberger, *Woodstock*

REPRESENTATIVES

Robert M. Mayo,[51] *Hague*
George T. Garrison,[52] *Accomac*
Harry Libbey, *Old Point Comfort*
George D. Wise, *Richmond*
Benjamin S. Hooper, *Farmville*
George C. Cabell, *Danville*
John R. Tucker, *Lexington*
John Paul,[53] *Harrisonburg*
Charles T. O'Ferrall,[54] *Harrisonburg*
John S. Barbour, *Alexandria*
Henry Bowen, *Tazewell*
At Large—John S. Wise, *Richmond*

WEST VIRGINIA

SENATORS

Johnson N. Camden, *Parkersburg*
John E. Kenna, *Kanawha*

REPRESENTATIVES

Nathan Goff, Jr., *Clarksburg*
William L. Wilson, *Charles Town*

Charles P. Snyder,[55] *Charleston*
Eustace Gibson, *Huntington*

WISCONSIN

SENATORS

Angus Cameron, *La Crosse*
Philetus Sawyer, *Oshkosh*

REPRESENTATIVES

John Winans, *Janesville*
Daniel H. Sumner, *Waukesha*
Burr W. Jones, *Madison*
Peter V. Deuster, *Milwaukee*
Joseph Rankin, *Manitowoc*
Richard W. Guenther, *Oshkosh*
Gilbert M. Woodward, *La Crosse*
William T. Price, *Black River Falls*
Isaac Stephenson, *Marinette*

TERRITORY OF ARIZONA

DELEGATE

Granville H. Oury, *Florence*

TERRITORY OF DAKOTA

DELEGATE

John B. Raymond, *Fargo*

TERRITORY OF IDAHO

DELEGATE

Theodore F. Singiser, *Boise City*

TERRITORY OF MONTANA

DELEGATE

Martin Maginnis,[56] *Helena*

TERRITORY OF NEW MEXICO

DELEGATE

Tranquilino Luna,[57] *Los Lunas*
Francisco A. Manzanares,[58] *Las Vegas*

TERRITORY OF UTAH

DELEGATE

John T. Caine, *Salt Lake City*

TERRITORY OF WASHINGTON

DELEGATE

Thomas H. Brents, *Walla Walla*

TERRITORY OF WYOMING

DELEGATE

Morton E. Post, *Cheyenne*

---

[51] Served until March 20, 1884; succeeded by George T. Garrison, who contested his election.
[52] Successfully contested the election of Robert M. Mayo, and took his seat March 20, 1884.
[53] Resigned September 5, 1883, before Congress assembled; succeeded by Charles T. O'Ferrall, who contested his election.
[54] Successfully contested the election of John Paul, and took his seat May 5, 1884.
[55] Elected to fill vacancy caused by resignation of Representative-elect John E. Kenna, in preceding Congress, and took his seat December 3, 1883.
[56] Election unsuccessfully contested by A. C. Botkin.
[57] Served until March 5, 1884; succeeded by Francisco A. Manzanares, who contested his election.
[58] Successfully contested the election of Tranquilino Luna, and took his seat March 5, 1884.

FORTY-NINTH CONGRESS

MARCH 4, 1885, TO MARCH 3, 1887

FIRST SESSION—*December 7, 1885, to August 5, 1886*

SECOND SESSION—*December 6, 1886, to March 3, 1887*

SPECIAL SESSION OF THE SENATE—*March 4, 1885, to April 2, 1885*

VICE PRESIDENT OF THE UNITED STATES—THOMAS A. HENDRICKS,[1] of Indiana

PRESIDENT PRO TEMPORE OF THE SENATE—JOHN SHERMAN,[2] of Ohio; JOHN J. INGALLS,[3] of Kansas

SECRETARY OF THE SENATE—ANSON G. MCCOOK, of New York

SERGEANT AT ARMS OF THE SENATE—WILLIAM P. CANADAY, of North Carolina

---

SPEAKER OF THE HOUSE OF REPRESENTATIVES—JOHN G. CARLISLE,[4] of Kentucky

CLERK OF THE HOUSE—JOHN B. CLARK, JR.,[5] of Missouri

SERGEANT AT ARMS OF THE HOUSE—JOHN P. LEEDOM, of Ohio

DOORKEEPER OF THE HOUSE—SAMUEL DONALDSON, of Tennessee

POSTMASTER OF THE HOUSE—LYCURGUS DALTON

ALABAMA

SENATORS

John T. Morgan, *Selma*
James L. Pugh, *Eufaula*

REPRESENTATIVES

James T. Jones, *Demopolis*
Hilary A. Herbert, *Montgomery*
William C. Oates, *Abbeville*
Alexander C. Davidson, *Uniontown*
Thomas W. Sadler, *Prattville*
John M. Martin, *Tuscaloosa*
William H. Forney, *Jacksonville*
Joseph Wheeler, *Wheeler*

ARKANSAS

SENATORS

Augustus H. Garland,[6] *Little Rock*
James H. Berry,[7] *Bentonville*
James K. Jones, *Washington*

REPRESENTATIVES

Poindexter Dunn, *Forest City*
Clifton R. Breckinridge, *Pine Bluff*
Thomas C. McRae,[8] *Prescott*
John H. Rogers, *Fort Smith*
Samuel W. Peel, *Bentonville*

CALIFORNIA

SENATORS

John F. Miller,[9] *San Francisco*
George Hearst,[10] *San Francisco*
Abram P. Williams,[11] *San Francisco*
Leland Stanford, *San Francisco*

REPRESENTATIVES

Barclay Henley, *Santa Rosa*
James A. Louttit, *Stockton*
Joseph McKenna, *Suisun*
William W. Morrow, *San Francisco*
Charles N. Felton, *San Francisco*
Henry H. Markham, *Pasadena*

COLORADO

SENATORS

Thomas M. Bowen, *Del Norte*
Henry M. Teller, *Central City*

REPRESENTATIVE

At Large—George G. Symes, *Denver*

CONNECTICUT

SENATORS

Orville H. Platt, *Meriden*
Joseph R. Hawley, *Hartford*

REPRESENTATIVES

John R. Buck, *Hartford*
Charles L. Mitchell, *New Haven*
John T. Wait, *Norwich*
Edward W. Seymour, *Litchfield*

---

[1] Died November 25, 1885.
[2] Elected December 7, 1885; resigned, effective February 26, 1887.
[3] Elected February 25, 1887.
[4] Reelected December 7, 1885.
[5] Reelected December 7, 1885.

[6] Resigned March 6, 1885, having been appointed Attorney General.
[7] Elected to fill vacancy caused by resignation of Augustus H. Garland, and took his seat March 25, 1885.
[8] Elected to fill vacancy caused by resignation of Representative-elect James K. Jones, in preceding

Congress, and took his seat December 7, 1885.
[9] Died March 8, 1886.
[10] Appointed to fill vacancy caused by death of John F. Miller, and took his seat April 9, 1886.
[11] Elected to fill vacancy caused by death of John F. Miller, and took his seat December 6, 1886.

DELAWARE

SENATORS

Thomas F. Bayard,[12] *Wilmington*
George Gray,[13] *New Castle*
Eli Saulsbury, *Dover*

REPRESENTATIVE

At Large—Charles B. Lore, *Wilmington*

FLORIDA

SENATORS

Charles W. Jones, *Pensacola*
Wilkinson Call, *Jacksonville*

REPRESENTATIVES

Robert H. M. Davidson, *Quincy*
Charles Dougherty, *Port Orange*

GEORGIA

SENATORS

Joseph E. Brown, *Atlanta*
Alfred H. Colquitt, *Atlanta*

REPRESENTATIVES

Thomas M. Norwood, *Savannah*
Henry G. Turner, *Quitman*
Charles F. Crisp, *Americus*
Henry R. Harris, *Greenville*
Nathaniel J. Hammond, *Atlanta*
James H. Blount, *Macon*
Judson C. Clements, *La Fayette*
Seaborn Reese, *Sparta*
Allen D. Candler, *Gainesville*
George T. Barnes, *Augusta*

ILLINOIS

SENATORS

John A. Logan,[14] *Chicago*
Charles B. Farwell,[15] *Chicago*
Shelby M. Cullom, *Springfield*

REPRESENTATIVES

Ransom W. Dunham, *Chicago*
Frank Lawler, *Chicago*
James H. Ward, *Chicago*
George E. Adams, *Chicago*
Reuben Ellwood,[16] *Sycamore*
Albert J. Hopkins,[17] *Aurora*
Robert R. Hitt, *Mount Morris*
Thomas J. Henderson, *Princeton*
Ralph Plumb, *Streator*
Lewis E. Payson, *Pontiac*
Nicholas E. Worthington, *Peoria*
William H. Neece, *Macomb*
James M. Riggs, *Winchester*
William M. Springer, *Springfield*

Jonathan H. Rowell, *Bloomington*
Joseph G. Cannon, *Danville*
Silas Z. Landes, *Mount Carmel*
John R. Eden, *Sullivan*
William R. Morrison, *Waterloo*
Richard W. Townshend, *Shawneetown*
John R. Thomas, *Metropolis*

INDIANA

SENATORS

Daniel W. Voorhees, *Terre Haute*
Benjamin Harrison, *Indianapolis*

REPRESENTATIVES

John J. Kleiner, *Evansville*
Thomas R. Cobb, *Vincennes*
Jonas G. Howard, *Jeffersonville*
William S. Holman, *Aurora*
Courtland C. Matson, *Greencastle*
Thomas M. Browne, *Winchester*
William D. Bynum, *Indianapolis*
James T. Johnston, *Rockville*
Thomas B. Ward, *La Fayette*
William D. Owen, *Logansport*
George W. Steele,[18] *Marion*
Robert Lowry, *Fort Wayne*
George Ford, *South Bend*

IOWA

SENATORS

William B. Allison, *Dubuque*
James F. Wilson, *Fairfield*

REPRESENTATIVES

Benton J. Hall, *Burlington*
Jeremiah H. Murphy, *Davenport*
David B. Henderson, *Dubuque*
William E. Fuller, *West Union*
Benjamin T. Frederick, *Marshalltown*
James B. Weaver,[19] *Bloomfield*
Edwin H. Conger, *Des Moines*
William P. Hepburn, *Clarinda*
Joseph Lyman, *Council Bluffs*
Adoniram J. Holmes, *Boone*
Isaac S. Struble, *Le Mars*

KANSAS

SENATORS

John J. Ingalls, *Atchison*
Preston B. Plumb, *Emporia*

REPRESENTATIVES

Edmund N. Morrill, *Hiawatha*
Edward H. Funston, *Iola*
Bishop W. Perkins, *Oswego*
Thomas Ryan, *Topeka*

John A. Anderson, *Manhattan*
Lewis Hanback, *Osborne*
Samuel R. Peters, *Newton*

KENTUCKY

SENATORS

James B. Beck, *Lexington*
Joseph C. S. Blackburn, *Versailles*

REPRESENTATIVES

William J. Stone, *Kuttawa*
Polk Laffoon, *Madisonville*
John E. Halsell, *Bowling Green*
Thomas A. Robertson, *Elizabethtown*
Albert S. Willis, *Louisville*
John G. Carlisle, *Covington*
William C. P. Breckinridge, *Lexington*
James B. McCreary, *Richmond*
William H. Wadsworth, *Maysville*
William P. Taulbee, *Saylersville*
Frank L. Wolford, *Columbia*

LOUISIANA

SENATORS

Randall L. Gibson, *New Orleans*
James B. Eustis, *New Orleans*

REPRESENTATIVES

Louis St. Martin, *New Orleans*
Michael Hahn,[20] *New Orleans*
Nathaniel D. Wallace,[21] *New Orleans*
Edward J. Gay, *Plaquemine*
Newton C. Blanchard, *Shreveport*
J. Floyd King, *Vidalia*
Alfred B. Irion, *Marksville*

MAINE

SENATORS

Eugene Hale, *Ellsworth*
William P. Frye, *Lewiston*

REPRESENTATIVES

Thomas B. Reed, *Portland*
Nelson Dingley, Jr., *Lewiston*
Seth L. Milliken, *Belfast*
Charles A. Boutelle, *Bangor*

MARYLAND

SENATORS

Arthur Pue Gorman, *Laurel*
Ephraim K. Wilson, *Snow Hill*

REPRESENTATIVES

Charles H. Gibson, *Easton*
Frank T. Shaw, *Westminster*
William H. Cole,[22] *Baltimore*
Harry W. Rusk,[23] *Baltimore*

---

[12] Resigned March 6, 1885, having been appointed Secretary of State.
[13] Elected to fill vacancy caused by resignation of Thomas F. Bayard, and took his seat March 19, 1885.
[14] Died December 26, 1886.
[15] Elected to fill vacancy caused by death of John A. Logan, and took his seat January 25, 1887.

[16] Died July 1, 1885, before Congress assembled.
[17] Elected to fill vacancy caused by death of Reuben Ellwood, and took his seat December 7, 1885.
[18] Election unsuccessfully contested by Meredith H. Kidd.
[19] Election unsuccessfully contested by Frank G. Campbell.

[20] Died March 15, 1886.
[21] Elected to fill vacancy caused by death of Michael Hahn, and took his seat December 9, 1886.
[22] Died July 8, 1886.
[23] Elected to fill vacancy caused by death of William H. Cole, and took his seat December 6, 1886.

John V. L. Findlay, *Baltimore*
Barnes Compton, *Laurel*
Louis E. McComas, *Hagerstown*

MASSACHUSETTS

SENATORS

Henry L. Dawes, *Pittsfield*
George F. Hoar, *Worcester*

REPRESENTATIVES

Robert T. Davis, *Fall River*
John D. Long, *Hingham*
Ambrose A. Ranney, *Boston*
Patrick A. Collins, *Boston*
Edward D. Hayden, *Woburn*
Henry B. Lovering, *Lynn*
Eben F. Stone, *Newburyport*
Charles H. Allen, *Lowell*
Frederick D. Ely, *Dedham*
William W. Rice, *Worcester*
William Whiting, *Holyoke*
Francis W. Rockwell, *Pittsfield*

MICHIGAN

SENATORS

Omar D. Conger, *Port Huron*
Thomas W. Palmer, *Detroit*

REPRESENTATIVES

William C. Maybury, *Detroit*
Nathaniel B. Eldredge, *Adrian*
James O'Donnell, *Jackson*
Julius C. Burrows, *Kalamazoo*
Charles C. Comstock, *Grand Rapids*
Edwin B. Winans, *Hamburg*
Ezra C. Carleton, *Port Huron*
Timothy E. Tarsney, *East Saginaw*
Byron M. Cutcheon, *Manistee*
Spencer O. Fisher, *West Bay City*
Seth C. Moffatt, *Traverse City*

MINNESOTA

SENATORS

Samuel J. R. McMillan, *St. Paul*
Dwight M. Sabin, *Stillwater*

REPRESENTATIVES

Milo White, *Chatfield*
James B. Wakefield, *Blue Earth City*
Horace B. Strait, *Shakopee*
John B. Gilfillan, *Minneapolis*
Knute Nelson, *Alexandria*

MISSISSIPPI

SENATORS

Lucius Q. C. Lamar,[24] *Oxford*
Edward C. Walthall,[25] *Grenada*
James Z. George, *Jackson*

REPRESENTATIVES

John M. Allen, *Tupelo*
James B. Morgan, *Hernando*
Thomas C. Catchings, *Vicksburg*
Frederick G. Barry, *West Point*
Otho R. Singleton, *Forest*
Henry S. Van Eaton, *Woodville*
Ethelbert Barksdale, *Jackson*

MISSOURI

SENATORS

Francis M. Cockrell, *Warrenburg*
George G. Vest, *Kansas City*

REPRESENTATIVES

William H. Hatch, *Hannibal*
John B. Hale, *Carrollton*
Alexander M. Dockery, *Gallatin*
James N. Burnes, *St. Joseph*
William Warner, *Kansas City*
John T. Heard, *Sedalia*
John E. Hutton, *Mexico*
John J. O'Neill, *St. Louis*
John M. Glover, *St. Louis*
Martin L. Clardy, *Farmington*
Richard P. Bland, *Lebanon*
William J. Stone, *Nevada*
William H. Wade, *Springfield*
William Dawson, *New Madrid*

NEBRASKA

SENATORS

Charles H. Van Wyck, *Nebraska City*
Charles F. Manderson, *Omaha*

REPRESENTATIVES

Archibald J. Weaver, *Falls City*
James Laird, *Hastings*
George W. E. Dorsey, *Fremont*

NEVADA

SENATORS

John P. Jones, *Gold Hill*
James G. Fair, *Virginia City*

REPRESENTATIVE

At Large—William Woodburn, *Virginia City*

NEW HAMPSHIRE

SENATORS

Austin F. Pike,[26] *Franklin*
Person C. Cheney,[27] *Manchester*
Henry W. Blair,[28] *Manchester*

REPRESENTATIVES

Martin A. Haynes, *Lake Village*
Jacob H. Gallinger, *Concord*

NEW JERSEY

SENATORS

John R. McPherson, *Jersey City*
William J. Sewell, *Camden*

REPRESENTATIVES

George Hires, *Salem*
James Buchanan, *Trenton*
Robert S. Green,[29] *Elizabeth*
James N. Pidcock, *White House Station*
William W. Phelps, *Englewood*
Herman Lehlbach, *Newark*
William McAdoo, *Jersey City*

NEW YORK

SENATORS

Warner Miller, *Herkimer*
William M. Evarts, *New York City*

REPRESENTATIVES

Perry Belmont, *Babylon*
Felix Campbell, *Brooklyn*
Darwin R. James, *Brooklyn*
Peter P. Mahoney, *Brooklyn*
Archibald M. Bliss, *Brooklyn*
Nicholas Muller, *New York City*
John J. Adams, *New York City*
Samuel S. Cox,[30] *New York City*
Timothy J. Campbell,[31] *New York City*
Joseph Pulitzer,[32] *New York City*
Samuel S. Cox,[33] *New York City*
Abram S. Hewitt,[34] *New York City*
Truman A. Merriman, *New York City*
Abraham Dowdney,[35] *New York City*
Egbert L. Viele, *New York City*
William G. Stahlnecker, *Yonkers*
Lewis Beach,[36] *Cornwall*
Henry Bacon,[37] *Goshen*
John H. Ketcham, *Dover Plains*
James G. Lindsley, *Rondout*
Henry G. Burleigh, *Whitehall*
John Swinburne, *Albany*
George West, *Ballston Spa*
Frederick A. Johnson, *Glens Falls*
Abraham X. Parker, *Potsdam*

---

[24] Resigned March 6, 1885, having been appointed Secretary of the Interior.
[25] Appointed to fill vacancy caused by resignation of Lucius Q. C. Lamar, and took his seat March 12, 1885 (special session of the Senate); subsequently elected.
[26] Died October 8, 1886.
[27] Appointed to fill vacancy caused by death of Austin F. Pike, and took his seat December 7, 1886.
[28] Appointed March 5, 1885, to fill vacancy in the term beginning March 4, 1885, to serve until the next meeting of the legislature; subsequently elected, and took his seat December 7, 1885.
[29] Resigned January 17, 1887, having been elected governor.
[30] Resigned May 20, 1885, before Congress assembled, having been appointed minister to Turkey.
[31] Elected to fill vacancy caused by resignation of Samuel S. Cox, and took his seat December 7, 1885.
[32] Resigned April 10, 1886.
[33] Elected to fill vacancy caused by resignation of Joseph Pulitzer, and took his seat December 6, 1886.
[34] Resigned December 30, 1886.
[35] Died December 10, 1886; seat vacant for remainder of the Congress.
[36] Died August 10, 1886.
[37] Elected to fill vacancy caused by death of Lewis Beach, and took his seat December 6, 1886.

NEW YORK—Continued

REPRESENTATIVES—continued

John T. Spriggs, *Utica*
John S. Pindar, *Cobleskill*
Frank Hiscock,[38] *Syracuse*
Stephen C. Millard, *Binghamton*
Sereno E. Payne, *Auburn*
John Arnot, Jr.,[39] *Elmira*
Ira Davenport, *Bath*
Charles S. Baker, *Rochester*
John G. Sawyer, *Albion*
John M. Farquhar, *Buffalo*
John B. Weber, *Buffalo*
Walter L. Sessions, *Jamestown*

NORTH CAROLINA

SENATORS

Matt W. Ransom, *Weldon*
Zebulon B. Vance, *Charlotte*

REPRESENTATIVES

Thomas G. Skinner, *Hertford*
James E. O'Hara, *Enfield*
Wharton J. Green, *Fayetteville*
William R. Cox, *Raleigh*
James W. Reid,[40] *Wentworth*
Risden T. Bennett, *Wadesboro*
John S. Henderson, *Salisbury*
William H. H. Cowles, *Wilkesboro*
Thomas D. Johnston, *Asheville*

OHIO

SENATORS

John Sherman, *Mansfield*
Henry B. Payne, *Cleveland*

REPRESENTATIVES

Benjamin Butterworth, *Cincinnati*
Charles E. Brown, *Cincinnati*
James E. Campbell, *Hamilton*
Charles M. Anderson, *Greenville*
Benjamin Le Fevre, *Maplewood*
William D. Hill, *Defiance*
George E. Seney, *Tiffin*
John Little, *Xenia*
William C. Cooper, *Mount Vernon*
Jacob Romeis,[41] *Toledo*
William W. Ellsberry, *Georgetown*
Albert C. Thompson, *Portsmouth*
Joseph H. Outhwaite, *Columbus*
Charles H. Grosvenor, *Athens*
Beriah Wilkins, *Uhrichsville*
George W. Geddes, *Mansfield*
Adoniram J. Warner, *Marietta*
Isaac H. Taylor, *Carrollton*
Ezra B. Taylor, *Warren*
William McKinley, Jr., *Canton*
Martin A. Foran, *Cleveland*

OREGON

SENATORS

Joseph N. Dolph, *Portland*
John H. Mitchell,[42] *Portland*

REPRESENTATIVE

At Large—Binger Hermann, *Roseburg*

PENNSYLVANIA

SENATORS

J. Donald Cameron, *Harrisburg*
John I. Mitchell, *Wellsboro*

REPRESENTATIVES

Henry H. Bingham, *Philadelphia*
Charles O'Neill, *Philadelphia*
Samuel J. Randall, *Philadelphia*
William D. Kelley, *Philadelphia*
Alfred C. Harmer, *Philadelphia*
James B. Everhart, *West Chester*
I. Newton Evans, *Hatboro*
Daniel Ermentrout, *Reading*
John A. Hiestand, *Lancaster*
William H. Sowden, *Allentown*
John B. Storm, *Stroudsburg*
Joseph A. Scranton, *Scranton*
Charles N. Brumm, *Minersville*
Franklin Bound, *Milton*
Frank C. Bunnell, *Tunkhannock*
William W. Brown, *Bradford*
Jacob M. Campbell, *Johnstown*
Louis E. Atkinson, *Mifflintown*
John A. Swope,[43] *Gettysburg*
Andrew G. Curtin, *Bellefonte*
Charles E. Boyle, *Uniontown*
James S. Negley, *Pittsburgh*
Thomas M. Bayne, *Allegheny*
Oscar L. Jackson, *New Castle*
Alexander C. White, *Brookville*
George W. Fleeger, *Butler*
William L. Scott, *Erie*
At Large—Edwin S. Osborne, *Wilkes-Barre*

RHODE ISLAND

SENATORS

Nelson W. Aldrich, *Providence*
Jonathan Chace, *Providence*

REPRESENTATIVES

Henry J. Spooner, *Providence*
William A. Pirce,[44] *Olneyville*
Charles H. Page,[45] *Scituate*

SOUTH CAROLINA

SENATORS

Matthew C. Butler, *Edgefield*
Wade Hampton, *Columbia*

REPRESENTATIVES

Samuel Dibble, *Orangeburg*
George D. Tillman, *Edgefield*
D. Wyatt Aiken, *Cokesbury*
William H. Perry, *Greenville*
John J. Hemphill, *Chester*
George W. Dargan, *Darlington*
Robert Smalls, *Beaufort*

TENNESSEE

SENATORS

Isham G. Harris, *Memphis*
Howell E. Jackson,[46] *Nashville*
Washington C. Whitthorne,[47] *Columbia*

REPRESENTATIVES

Augustus H. Pettibone, *Greeneville*
Leonidas C. Houk, *Knoxville*
John R. Neal, *Rhea Springs*
Benton McMillin, *Carthage*
James D. Richardson, *Murfreesboro*
Andrew J. Caldwell, *Nashville*
John G. Ballentine, *Pulaski*
John M. Taylor, *Lexington*
Presley T. Glass, *Ripley*
Zachary Taylor, *Covington*

TEXAS

SENATORS

Samuel B. Maxey, *Paris*
Richard Coke, *Waco*

REPRESENTATIVES

Charles Stewart, *Houston*
John H. Reagan,[48] *Palestine*
James H. Jones, *Henderson*
David B. Culberson, *Jefferson*
James W. Throckmorton, *McKinney*
Olin Wellborn, *Dallas*
William H. Crain, *Cuero*
James F. Miller, *Gonzales*
Roger Q. Mills, *Corsicana*
Joseph D. Sayers, *Bastrop*
Samuel W. T. Lanham, *Weatherford*

---

[38] Reelected to the Fiftieth Congress, but resigned, having been elected Senator.
[39] Died November 20, 1886; seat vacant for remainder of the Congress.
[40] Resigned December 31, 1886.
[41] Election unsuccessfully contested by Frank H. Hurd.
[42] Elected to fill vacancy in term beginning March 4, 1885, caused by failure of legislature to elect, and took his seat December 17, 1885; vacancy in this class from March 4, 1885, to November 17, 1885.
[43] Elected to fill vacancy caused by death of Representative-elect William A. Duncan, in preceding Congress, and took his seat December 7, 1885.
[44] Served until January 25, 1887, when seat was declared vacant.
[45] Elected to fill vacancy caused by declaring the seat of William A. Pirce vacant, and took his seat February 25, 1887.
[46] Resigned April 14, 1886, to become United States circuit judge, sixth circuit.
[47] Appointed to fill vacancy caused by resignation of Howell E. Jackson, and took his seat April 26, 1886; subsequently elected.
[48] Reelected to the Fiftieth Congress, but resigned, having been elected Senator.

VERMONT

SENATORS

George F. Edmunds, *Burlington*
Justin S. Morrill, *Strafford*

REPRESENTATIVES

John W Stewart, *Middlebury*
William W. Grout, *Barton*

VIRGINIA

SENATORS

William Mahone, *Petersburg*
Harrison H. Riddleberger, *Woodstock*

REPRESENTATIVES

Thomas Croxton, *Tappahannock*
Harry Libbey, *Old Point Comfort*
George D. Wise, *Richmond*
James D. Brady, *Petersburg*
George C. Cabell, *Danville*
John W. Daniel, *Lynchburg*
Charles T. O'Ferrall, *Harrisonburg*
John S. Barbour, *Alexandria*
Connally F. Trigg, *Abingdon*
John R. Tucker, *Lexington*

WEST VIRGINIA

SENATORS

Johnson N. Camden, *Parkersburg*
John E. Kenna, *Charleston*

REPRESENTATIVES

Nathan Goff, Jr., *Clarksburg*
William L. Wilson, *Charles Town*
Charles P. Snyder, *Charleston*
Eustace Gibson, *Huntington*

WISCONSIN

SENATORS

Philetus Sawyer, *Oshkosh*
John C. Spooner, *Hudson*

REPRESENTATIVES

Lucien B. Caswell, *Fort Atkinson*
Edward S. Bragg, *Fond du Lac*
Robert M. La Follette, *Madison*
Isaac W. Van Schaick, *Milwaukee*
Joseph Rankin,[49] *Manitowoc*
Thomas R. Hudd,[50] *Green Bay*
Richard W. Guenther, *Oshkosh*
Ormsby B. Thomas, *Prairie du Chien*
William T. Price,[51] *Black River Falls*
Hugh H. Price,[52] *Black River Falls*
Isaac Stephenson, *Marinette*

TERRITORY OF ARIZONA

DELEGATE

Curtis C. Bean, *Prescott*

TERRITORY OF DAKOTA

DELEGATE

Oscar S. Gifford, *Canton*

TERRITORY OF IDAHO

DELEGATE

John Hailey, *Boise City*

TERRITORY OF MONTANA

DELEGATE

Joseph K. Toole, *Helena*

TERRITORY OF NEW MEXICO

DELEGATE

Antonio Joseph, *Ojo Caliente*

TERRITORY OF UTAH

DELEGATE

John T. Caine, *Salt Lake City*

TERRITORY OF WASHINGTON

DELEGATE

Charles S. Voorhees, *Colfax*

TERRITORY OF WYOMING

DELEGATE

Joseph M. Carey, *Cheyenne*

---

[49] Died January 24, 1886.
[50] Elected to fill vacancy caused by death of Joseph Rankin, and took his seat March 8, 1886.

[51] Died December 6, 1886, before the commencement of the Fiftieth Congress, to which he had been reelected.

[52] Elected to fill vacancy caused by death of his father, William T. Price, and took his seat February 2, 1887.

FIFTIETH CONGRESS

MARCH 4, 1887, TO MARCH 3, 1889

FIRST SESSION—*December 5, 1887, to October 20, 1888*

SECOND SESSION—*December 3, 1888, to March 3, 1889*

———

VICE PRESIDENT OF THE UNITED STATES [1]

PRESIDENT PRO TEMPORE OF THE SENATE—JOHN J. INGALLS, of Kansas

SECRETARY OF THE SENATE—ANSON G. MCCOOK, of New York

SERGEANT AT ARMS OF THE SENATE—WILLIAM P. CANADAY, of North Carolina

———

SPEAKER OF THE HOUSE OF REPRESENTATIVES—JOHN G. CARLISLE,[2] of Kentucky

CLERK OF THE HOUSE—JOHN B. CLARK, Jr.,[3] of Missouri

SERGEANT AT ARMS OF THE HOUSE—JOHN P. LEEDOM, of Ohio

DOORKEEPER OF THE HOUSE—A. B. HURD, of Mississippi

POSTMASTER OF THE HOUSE—LYCURGUS DALTON

ALABAMA

SENATORS

John T. Morgan, *Selma*
James L. Pugh, *Eufaula*

REPRESENTATIVES

James T. Jones, *Demopolis*
Hilary A. Herbert, *Montgomery*
William C. Oates, *Abbeville*
Alexander C. Davidson,[4] *Uniontown*
James E. Cobb, *Tuskegee*
John H. Bankhead, *Fayette*
William H. Forney, *Jacksonville*
Joseph Wheeler, *Wheeler*

ARKANSAS

SENATORS

James K. Jones, *Washington*
James H. Berry, *Bentonville*

REPRESENTATIVES

Poindexter Dunn, *Forest City*
Clifton R. Breckinridge, *Pine Bluff*
Thomas C. McRae, *Prescott*
John H. Rogers, *Fort Smith*
Samuel W. Peel, *Bentonville*

CALIFORNIA

SENATORS

Leland Stanford, *San Francisco*
George Hearst, *San Francisco*

REPRESENTATIVES

Thomas L. Thompson, *Santa Rosa*
Marion Biggs, *Gridley*
Joseph McKenna, *Suisun*
William W. Morrow, *San Francisco*
Charles N. Felton, *San Francisco*
William Vandever,[5] *San Buenaventura*

COLORADO

SENATORS

Thomas M. Bowen, *Del Norte*
Henry M. Teller, *Central City*

REPRESENTATIVE

At Large—George G. Symes, *Denver*

CONNECTICUT

SENATORS

Orville H. Platt, *Meriden*
Joseph R. Hawley, *Hartford*

REPRESENTATIVES

Robert J. Vance, *New Britain*
Carlos French, *Seymour*
Charles A. Russell, *Killingly*
Miles T. Granger, *Canaan*

DELAWARE

SENATORS

Eli Saulsbury, *Dover*
George Gray, *New Castle*

REPRESENTATIVE

At Large—John B. Penington, *Dover*

FLORIDA

SENATORS

Wilkinson Call, *Jacksonville*
Samuel Pasco,[6] *Monticello*

REPRESENTATIVES

Robert H. M. Davidson, *Quincy*
Charles Dougherty, *Port Orange*

---

[1] Vice President Thomas A. Hendricks died in preceding Congress.
[2] Reelected December 5, 1887.
[3] Reelected December 5, 1887.
[4] Election unsuccessfully contested by John V. McDuffie.
[5] Election unsuccessfully contested by Joseph D. Lynch.

[6] Elected May 19, 1887, and took his seat December 5, 1887; Jesse J. Finley was appointed by the Governor on February 28, 1887, to fill the vacancy existing after March 4, 1887, until the next meeting of the legislature, but never qualified. Upon the request of the financial clerk of the Senate for an opinion as to his authority to pay Mr. Finley the salary due him as a Senator-designate, President pro tempore Ingalls held that it should not be done, as the appointment "was in anticipation of a vacancy, and not to fill a vacancy that existed, as contemplated by article 3 of the Constitution"; subsequently the Senate adopted a resolution to pay Mr. Finley for services rendered from March 4 to May 19, 1887.

GEORGIA

SENATORS

Joseph E. Brown, *Atlanta*
Alfred H. Colquitt, *Atlanta*

REPRESENTATIVES

Thomas M. Norwood, *Savannah*
Henry G. Turner, *Quitman*
Charles F. Crisp, *Americus*
Thomas W. Grimes, *Columbus*
John D. Stewart, *Griffin*
James H. Blount, *Macon*
Judson C. Clements, *Rome*
Henry H. Carlton, *Athens*
Allen D. Candler, *Gainesville*
George T. Barnes, *Augusta*

ILLINOIS

SENATORS

Shelby M. Cullom, *Springfield*
Charles B. Farwell, *Chicago*

REPRESENTATIVES

Ransom W. Dunham, *Chicago*
Frank Lawler, *Chicago*
William E. Mason, *Chicago*
George E. Adams, *Chicago*
Albert J. Hopkins, *Aurora*
Robert R. Hitt, *Mount Morris*
Thomas J. Henderson, *Princeton*
Ralph Plumb, *Streator*
Lewis E. Payson, *Pontiac*
Philip S. Post,[7] *Galesburg*
William H. Gest, *Rock Island*
George A. Anderson, *Quincy*
William M. Springer, *Springfield*
Jonathan H. Rowell, *Bloomington*
Joseph G. Cannon, *Danville*
Silas Z. Landes, *Mount Carmel*
Edward Lane, *Hillsboro*
Jehu Baker, *Belleville*
Richard W. Townshend, *Shawneetown*
John R. Thomas, *Metropolis*

INDIANA

SENATORS

Daniel W. Voorhees, *Terre Haute*
David Turpie, *Indianapolis*

REPRESENTATIVES

Alvin P. Hovey,[8] *Mount Vernon*
Francis B. Posey,[9] *Poseyville*
John H. O'Neall, *Washington*
Jonas G. Howard, *Jeffersonville*
William S. Holman, *Aurora*
Courtland C. Matson, *Greencastle*
Thomas M. Browne, *Winchester*
William D. Bynum, *Indianapolis*
James T. Johnston, *Rockville*

Joseph B. Cheadle, *Frankfort*
William D. Owen, *Logansport*
George W. Steele, *Marion*
James B. White,[10] *Fort Wayne*
Benjamin F. Shively, *South Bend*

IOWA

SENATORS

William B. Allison, *Dubuque*
James F. Wilson, *Fairfield*

REPRESENTATIVES

John H. Gear, *Burlington*
Walter I. Hayes, *Clinton*
David B. Henderson, *Dubuque*
William E. Fuller, *West Union*
Daniel Kerr, *Grundy Center*
James B. Weaver, *Bloomfield*
Edwin H. Conger, *Des Moines*
Albert R. Anderson, *Sidney*
Joseph Lyman, *Council Bluffs*
Adoniram J. Holmes, *Boone*
Isaac S. Struble, *Le Mars*

KANSAS

SENATORS

John J. Ingalls, *Atchison*
Preston B. Plumb, *Emporia*

REPRESENTATIVES

Edmund N. Morrill, *Hiawatha*
Edward H. Funston, *Iola*
Bishop W. Perkins, *Oswego*
Thomas Ryan, *Topeka*
John A. Anderson, *Manhattan*
Erastus J. Turner, *Hoxie*
Samuel R. Peters, *Newton*

KENTUCKY

SENATORS

James B. Beck, *Lexington*
Joseph C. S. Blackburn, *Versailles*

REPRESENTATIVES

William J. Stone, *Kuttawa*
Polk Laffoon, *Madisonville*
W. Godfrey Hunter, *Burksville*
Alexander B. Montgomery, *Elizabethtown*
Asher G. Caruth, *Louisville*
John G. Carlisle,[11] *Covington*
William C. P. Breckinridge, *Lexington*
James B. McCreary, *Richmond*
George M. Thomas, *Vanceburg*
William P. Taulbee, *Saylersville*
Hugh F. Finley, *Williamsburg*

LOUISIANA

SENATORS

Randall L. Gibson, *New Orleans*
James B. Eustis, *New Orleans*

REPRESENTATIVES

Theodore S. Wilkinson, *Plaquemines Parish*
Matthew D. Lagan, *New Orleans*
Edward J. Gay, *Plaquemine*
Newton C. Blanchard, *Shreveport*
Cherubusco Newton, *Bastrop*
Edward W. Robertson,[12] *Baton Rouge*
Samuel M. Robertson,[13] *Baton Rouge*

MAINE

SENATORS

Eugene Hale, *Ellsworth*
William P. Frye, *Lewiston*

REPRESENTATIVES

Thomas B. Reed, *Portland*
Nelson Dingley, Jr., *Lewiston*
Seth L. Milliken, *Belfast*
Charles A. Boutelle, *Bangor*

MARYLAND

SENATORS

Arthur Pue Gorman, *Laurel*
Ephraim K. Wilson, *Snow Hill*

REPRESENTATIVES

Charles H. Gibson, *Easton*
Frank T. Shaw, *Westminster*
Harry W. Rusk, *Baltimore*
Isidor Rayner, *Baltimore*
Barnes Compton, *Laurel*
Louis E. McComas, *Hagerstown*

MASSACHUSETTS

SENATORS

Henry L. Dawes, *Pittsfield*
George F. Hoar, *Worcester*

REPRESENTATIVES

Robert T. Davis, *Fall River*
John D. Long, *Hingham*
Leopold Morse, *Boston*
Patrick A. Collins, *Boston*
Edward D. Hayden, *Woburn*
Henry Cabot Lodge, *Nahant*
William Cogswell, *Salem*
Charles H. Allen, *Lowell*
Edward Burnett, *Southboro*
John E. Russell, *Leicester*
William Whiting, *Holyoke*
Francis W. Rockwell, *Pittsfield*

---

[7] Election unsuccessfully contested by Nicholas E. Worthington.
[8] Resigned January 17, 1889.
[9] Elected to fill vacancy caused by resignation of Alvin P. Hovey, and took his seat February 6, 1889.

[10] Election unsuccessfully contested by Robert Lowry.
[11] Election unsuccessfully contested by George H. Thobe.

[12] Died August 2, 1887, before Congress assembled.
[13] Elected to fill vacancy caused by death of Edward W. Robertson, and took his seat December 5, 1887.

MICHIGAN

SENATORS

Thomas W. Palmer, *Detroit*
Francis B. Stockbridge, *Kalamazoo*

REPRESENTATIVES

J. Logan Chipman, *Detroit*
Edward P. Allen, *Ypsilanti*
James O'Donnell, *Jackson*
Julius C. Burrows, *Kalamazoo*
Melbourne H. Ford, *Grand Rapids*
Mark S. Brewer, *Pontiac*
Justin R. Whiting, *St. Clair*
Timothy E. Tarsney, *East Saginaw*
Byron M. Cutcheon, *Manistee*
Spencer O. Fisher, *West Bay City*
Seth C. Moffatt,[14] *Traverse City*
Henry W. Seymour,[15] *Sault Ste. Marie*

MINNESOTA

SENATORS

Dwight M. Sabin, *Stillwater*
Cushman K. Davis, *St. Paul*

REPRESENTATIVES

Thomas Wilson, *Winona*
John Lind, *New Ulm*
John L. MacDonald, *Shakopee*
Edmund Rice, *St. Paul*
Knute Nelson, *Alexandria*

MISSISSIPPI

SENATORS

James Z. George, *Jackson*
Edward C. Walthall, *Grenada*

REPRESENTATIVES

John M. Allen, *Tupelo*
James B. Morgan, *Hernando*
Thomas C. Catchings, *Vicksburg*
Frederick G. Barry, *West Point*
Chapman L. Anderson, *Kosciusko*
Thomas R. Stockdale, *Summit*
Charles E. Hooker, *Jackson*

MISSOURI

SENATORS

Francis M. Cockrell, *Warrensburg*
George G. Vest, *Kansas City*

REPRESENTATIVES

William H. Hatch, *Hannibal*
Charles H. Mansur, *Chillicothe*
Alexander M. Dockery, *Gallatin*
James N. Burnes,[16] *St. Joseph*
Charles F. Booher,[17] *St. Joseph*

William Warner, *Kansas City*
John T. Heard, *Sedalia*
John E. Hutton, *Mexico*
John J. O'Neill, *St. Louis*
John M. Glover,[18] *St. Louis*
Martin L. Clardy, *Farmington*
Richard P. Bland, *Lebanon*
William J. Stone, *Nevada*
William H. Wade, *Springfield*
James P. Walker, *Dexter*

NEBRASKA

SENATORS

Charles F. Manderson, *Omaha*
Algernon S. Paddock, *Beatrice*

REPRESENTATIVES

John A. McShane, *Omaha*
James Laird, *Hastings*
George W. E. Dorsey, *Fremont*

NEVADA

SENATORS

John P. Jones, *Gold Hill*
William M. Stewart, *Carson City*

REPRESENTATIVE

At Large—William Woodburn, *Virginia City*

NEW HAMPSHIRE

SENATORS

Henry W. Blair, *Manchester*
Person C. Cheney, *Manchester*
William E. Chandler,[19] *Concord*

REPRESENTATIVES

Luther F. McKinney, *Manchester*
Jacob H. Gallinger, *Concord*

NEW JERSEY

SENATORS

John R. McPherson, *Jersey City*
Rufus Blodgett, *Long Branch*

REPRESENTATIVES

George Hires, *Salem*
James Buchanan, *Trenton*
John Kean, *Elizabeth*
James N. Pidcock, *White House Station*
William W. Phelps, *Englewood*
Herman Lehlbach, *Newark*
William McAdoo, *Jersey City*

NEW YORK

SENATORS

William M. Evarts, *New York City*
Frank Hiscock, *Syracuse*

REPRESENTATIVES

Perry Belmont,[20] *Babylon*
Felix Campbell, *Brooklyn*
Stephen V. White, *Brooklyn*
Peter P. Mahoney, *Brooklyn*
Archibald M. Bliss, *Brooklyn*
Amos J. Cummings, *New York City*
Lloyd S. Bryce, *New York City*
Timothy J. Campbell, *New York City*
Samuel S. Cox, *New York City*
Francis B. Spinola, *New York City*
Truman A. Merriman, *New York City*
W. Bourke Cockran, *New York City*
Ashbel P. Fitch, *New York City*
William G. Stahlnecker, *Yonkers*
Henry Bacon, *Goshen*
John H. Ketcham, *Dover Plains*
Stephen T. Hopkins, *Catskill*
Edward W. Greenman, *Troy*
Nicholas T. Kane,[21] *Albany*
Charles Tracey,[22] *Albany*
George West, *Ballston Spa*
John H. Moffitt, *Chateaugay Lake*
Abraham X. Parker, *Potsdam*
James S. Sherman, *Utica*
David Wilber, *Oneonta*
James J. Belden,[23] *Syracuse*
Milton De Lano, *Canastota*
Newton W. Nutting, *Oswego*
Thomas S. Flood, *Elmira*
Ira Davenport, *Bath*
Charles S. Baker, *Rochester*
John G. Sawyer, *Albion*
John M. Farquhar, *Buffalo*
John B. Weber, *Buffalo*
William G. Laidlaw, *Ellicottville*

NORTH CAROLINA

SENATORS

Matt W. Ransom, *Weldon*
Zebulon B. Vance, *Charlotte*

REPRESENTATIVES

Louis C. Latham, *Greenville*
Furnifold McL. Simmons, *New Bern*
Charles W. McClammy, *Scotts Hill*
John Nichols, *Raleigh*
John M. Brower, *Mount Airy*
Alfred Rowland, *Lumberton*
John S. Henderson, *Salisbury*
William H. H. Cowles, *Wilkesboro*
Thomas D. Johnston, *Asheville*

---

[14] Died December 22, 1887.
[15] Elected to fill vacancy caused by death of Seth C. Moffatt, and took his seat March 3, 1888.
[16] Died January 23, 1889, before the commencement of the Fifty-first Congress, to which he had been reelected.
[17] Elected to fill vacancy caused by death of James N. Burnes, and took his seat February 25, 1889.

[18] Election unsuccessfully contested by Nathan Frank.
[19] Elected to fill vacancy caused by death of Austin F. Pike, in preceding Congress, and took his seat December 5, 1887.
[20] Resigned December 1, 1888, having been appointed minister to Spain; seat vacant for remainder of the Congress.

[21] Died September 14, 1887, before Congress assembled.
[22] Elected to fill vacancy caused by death of Nicholas T. Kane, and took his seat December 5, 1887.
[23] Elected to fill vacancy caused by resignation of Representative-elect Frank Hiscock, in preceding Congress, and took his seat December 5, 1887.

OHIO

SENATORS

John Sherman, *Mansfield*
Henry B. Payne, *Cleveland*

REPRESENTATIVES

Benjamin Butterworth, *Cincinnati*
Charles E. Brown, *Cincinnati*
Elihu S. Williams, *Troy*
Samuel S. Yoder, *Lima*
George E. Seney, *Tiffin*
Melvin M. Boothman, *Bryan*
James E. Campbell, *Hamilton*
Robert P. Kennedy, *Bellefontaine*
William C. Cooper, *Mount Vernon*
Jacob Romeis, *Toledo*
Albert C. Thompson, *Portsmouth*
Jacob J. Pugsley, *Hillsboro*
Joseph H. Outhwaite, *Columbus*
Charles P. Wickham, *Norwalk*
Charles H. Grosvenor, *Athens*
Beriah Wilkins, *Uhrichsville*
Joseph D. Taylor, *Cambridge*
William McKinley, Jr., *Canton*
Ezra B. Taylor, *Warren*
George W. Crouse, *Akron*
Martin A. Foran, *Cleveland*

OREGON

SENATORS

Joseph N. Dolph, *Portland*
John H. Mitchell, *Portland*

REPRESENTATIVE

At Large—Binger Hermann, *Roseburg*

PENNSYLVANIA

SENATORS

J. Donald Cameron, *Harrisburg*
Matthew S. Quay, *Beaver*

REPRESENTATIVES

Henry H. Bingham, *Philadelphia*
Charles O'Neill, *Philadelphia*
Samuel J. Randall, *Philadelphia*
William D. Kelley, *Philadelphia*
Alfred C. Harmer, *Philadelphia*
Smedley Darlington, *West Chester*
Robert M. Yardley, *Doylestown*
Daniel Ermentrout, *Reading*
John A. Hiestand, *Lancaster*
William H. Sowden, *Allentown*
Charles R. Buckalew, *Bloomsburg*
John Lynch, *Wilkes-Barre*
Charles N. Brumm, *Minersville*
Franklin Bound, *Milton*
Frank C. Bunnell, *Tunkhannock*

Henry C. McCormick, *Williamsport*
Edward Scull, *Somerset*
Louis E. Atkinson, *Mifflintown*
Levi Maish, *York*
John Patton, *Curwensville*
Welty McCullogh, *Greensburg*
John Dalzell, *Pittsburgh*
Thomas M. Bayne, *Allegheny*
Oscar L. Jackson, *New Castle*
James T. Maffett, *Clarion*
Norman Hall, *Sharon*
William L. Scott, *Erie*
At Large—Edwin S. Osborne, *Wilkes-Barre*

RHODE ISLAND

SENATORS

Nelson W. Aldrich, *Providence*
Jonathan Chace, *Providence*

REPRESENTATIVES

Henry J. Spooner, *Providence*
Warren O. Arnold, *Gloucester*

SOUTH CAROLINA

SENATORS

Matthew C. Butler, *Edgefield*
Wade Hampton, *Charleston*

REPRESENTATIVES

Samuel Dibble, *Orangeburg*
George D. Tillman, *Clarks Hill*
James S. Cothran, *Abbeville*
William H. Perry, *Greenville*
John J. Hemphill, *Chester*
George W. Dargan, *Darlington*
William Elliott,[24] *Beaufort*

TENNESSEE

SENATORS

Isham G. Harris, *Memphis*
William B. Bate, *Nashville*

REPRESENTATIVES

Roderick R. Butler, *Mountain City*
Leonidas C. Houk, *Knoxville*
John R. Neal, *Rhea Springs*
Benton McMillin, *Carthage*
James D. Richardson, *Murfreesboro*
Joseph E. Washington, *Cedar Hill*
Washington C. Whitthorne, *Columbia*
Benjamin A. Enloe, *Jackson*
Presley T. Glass, *Ripley*
James Phelan, *Memphis*

TEXAS

SENATORS

Richard Coke, *Waco*
John H. Reagan, *Palestine*

REPRESENTATIVES

Charles Stewart, *Houston*
William H. Martin,[25] *Athens*
Constantine B. Kilgore, *Wills Point*
David B. Culberson, *Jefferson*
Silas Hare, *Sherman*
Jo Abbott, *Hillsboro*
William H. Crain, *Cuero*
Littleton W. Moore, *Lagrange*
Roger Q. Mills, *Corsicana*
Joseph D. Sayers, *Bastrop*
Samuel W. T. Lanham, *Weatherford*

VERMONT

SENATORS

George F. Edmunds, *Burlington*
Justin S. Morrill, *Strafford*

REPRESENTATIVES

John W. Stewart, *Middlebury*
William W. Grout, *Barton*

VIRGINIA

SENATORS

Harrison H. Riddleberger, *Woodstock*
John W. Daniel, *Lynchburg*

REPRESENTATIVES

Thomas H. B. Browne, *Accomac*
George E. Bowden, *Norfolk*
George D. Wise, *Richmond*
William E. Gaines, *Burkeville*
John R. Brown, *Martinsville*
Samuel I. Hopkins, *Lynchburg*
Charles T. O'Ferrall, *Harrisonburg*
William H. F. Lee, *Burkes Station*
Henry Bowen, *Tazewell*
Jacob Yost, *Staunton*

WEST VIRGINIA

SENATORS

John E. Kenna, *Charleston*
Charles J. Faulkner,[26] *Martinsburg*

REPRESENTATIVES

Nathan Goff, Jr., *Clarksburg*
William L. Wilson, *Charles Town*
Charles P. Snyder, *Charleston*
Charles E. Hogg, *Point Pleasant*

---

[24] Election unsuccessfully contested by Robert Smalls.
[25] Elected to fill vacancy caused by resignation of Representative-elect John H. Reagan, in preceeding Congress, and took his seat December 5, 1887.
[26] The Legislature of West Virginia had met and adjourned without electing a Senator for the term beginning March 4, 1887; on March 5, 1887, the governor appointed Daniel B. Lucas to fill such vacancy; on the same day he issued a proclamation calling the legislature in extraordinary session for eight specific purposes, the election of Senator not being named as one of them; the legislature proceeded to choose a Senator, and Charles J. Faulkner was elected; credentials of both Mr. Lucas and Mr. Faulkner were presented on December 5, 1887, and Mr. Faulkner appeared to be sworn, but objection was made and he was not permitted to qualify; December 14, 1887, the Senate adopted a report from the Committee on Privileges and Elections, to whom all papers were referred on the 12th, declaring Mr. Faulkner duly elected and entitled to the seat; appeared, qualified, and took his seat the same day.

WISCONSIN

SENATORS

Philetus Sawyer, *Oshkosh*
John C. Spooner, *Hudson*

REPRESENTATIVES

Lucien B. Caswell, *Fort Atkinson*
Richard W. Guenther, *Oshkosh*
Robert M. La Follette, *Madison*
Henry Smith, *Milwaukee*
Thomas R. Hudd, *Green Bay*
Charles B. Clark, *Neenah*
Ormsby B. Thomas, *Prairie du Chien*
Nils P. Haugen,[27] *River Falls*
Isaac Stephenson, *Marinette*

TERRITORY OF ARIZONA

DELEGATE

Marcus A. Smith, *Tombstone*

TERRITORY OF DAKOTA

DELEGATE

Oscar S. Gifford, *Canton*

TERRITORY OF IDAHO

DELEGATE

Fred T. Dubois, *Blackfoot*

TERRITORY OF MONTANA

DELEGATE

Joseph K. Toole, *Helena*

TERRITORY OF NEW MEXICO

DELEGATE

Antonio Joseph, *Ojo Caliente*

TERRITORY OF UTAH

DELEGATE

John T. Caine, *Salt Lake City*

TERRITORY OF WASHINGTON

DELEGATE

Charles S. Voorhees, *Colfax*

TERRITORY OF WYOMING

DELEGATE

Joseph M. Carey, *Cheyenne*

---

[27] Elected on January 18, 1887, to fill vacancy caused by death of Representative-elect William T. Price, in preceding Congress, but on account of illness did not take his seat until January 4, 1888.

FIFTY-FIRST CONGRESS

MARCH 4, 1889, TO MARCH 3, 1891

FIRST SESSION—*December 2, 1889, to October 1, 1890*

SECOND SESSION—*December 1, 1890, to March 2, 1891*

SPECIAL SESSION OF THE SENATE—*March 4, 1889, to April 2, 1889*

————

VICE PRESIDENT OF THE UNITED STATES—Levi P. Morton, of New York

PRESIDENT PRO TEMPORE OF THE SENATE—John J. Ingalls,[1] of Kansas; Charles F. Manderson,[2] of Nebraska

SECRETARY OF THE SENATE—Anson G. McCook, of New York

SERGEANT AT ARMS OF THE SENATE—William P. Canaday, of North Carolina; Edward K. Valentine,[3] of Nebraska

————

SPEAKER OF THE HOUSE OF REPRESENTATIVES—Thomas B. Reed,[4] of Maine

CLERK OF THE HOUSE—John B. Clark, Jr., of Missouri; Edward McPherson,[5] of Pennsylvania

SERGEANT AT ARMS OF THE HOUSE—John P. Leedom, of Ohio; Adoniram J. Holmes,[6] of Iowa

DOORKEEPER OF THE HOUSE—Charles E. Adams, of Maryland

POSTMASTER OF THE HOUSE—James L. Wheat

ALABAMA

SENATORS

John T. Morgan, *Selma*
James L. Pugh, *Eufaula*

REPRESENTATIVES

Richard H. Clarke,[7] *Mobile*
Hilary A. Herbert, *Montgomery*
William C. Oates, *Abbeville*
Louis W. Turpin,[8] *Newbern*
John V. McDuffie,[9] *Hayneville*
James E. Cobb, *Tuskegee*
John H. Bankhead, *Fayette*
William H. Forney, *Jacksonville*
Joseph Wheeler, *Wheeler*

ARKANSAS

SENATORS

James K. Jones, *Washington*
James H. Berry, *Bentonville*

REPRESENTATIVES

William H. Cate,[10] *Jonesboro*
Lewis P. Featherston,[11] *Forest City*
Clifton R. Breckinridge,[12] *Pine Bluff*
Thomas C. McRae, *Prescott*
John H. Rogers, *Fort Smith*
Samuel W. Peel, *Bentonville*

CALIFORNIA

SENATORS

Leland Stanford, *San Francisco*
George Hearst,[13] *San Francisco*

REPRESENTATIVES

John J. De Haven,[14] *Eureka*
Thomas J. Geary,[15] *Santa Rosa*
Marion Biggs, *Gridley*
Joseph McKenna, *Suisun*
William W. Morrow, *San Francisco*
Thomas J. Clunie, *San Francisco*
William Vandever, *San Buenaventura*

COLORADO

SENATORS

Henry M. Teller, *Central City*
Edward O. Wolcott, *Denver*

REPRESENTATIVE

At Large—Hosea Townsend, *Silver Cliff*

CONNECTICUT

SENATORS

Orville H. Platt, *Meriden*
Joseph R. Hawley, *Hartford*

REPRESENTATIVES

William E. Simonds, *Canton*
Washington F. Willcox, *Chester*
Charles A. Russell, *Killingly*
Frederick Miles, *Chapinville*

---

[1] Elected March 7, 1889, and April 2, 1889 (special session of the Senate); February 28, 1890, and April 3, 1890; resigned as President pro tempore, effective March 2, 1891.
[2] Elected March 2, 1891.
[3] Elected June 30, 1890.
[4] Elected December 2, 1889.
[5] Elected December 2, 1889.
[6] Elected December 2, 1889.
[7] Election unsuccessfully contested by Frank H.

Threet.
[8] Served until June 4, 1890; succeeded by John V. McDuffie, who contested his election.
[9] Successfully contested the election of Louis W. Turpin, and took his seat June 4, 1890.
[10] Served until March 5, 1890; succeeded by Lewis P. Featherston, who contested his election.
[11] Successfully contested the election of William H. Cate, and took his seat March 5, 1890.
[12] Election contested by John M. Clayton, who

died January 29, 1889 (before the beginning of the congressional term), while case was pending; served until September 5, 1890, when Clayton was declared to have been elected and the seat vacant; subsequently elected to fill vacancy caused by death of John M. Clayton, and took his seat December 1, 1890.
[13] Died February 28, 1891.
[14] Resigned October 1, 1890.
[15] Elected to fill vacancy caused by resignation of John J. De Haven, and took his seat December 9, 1890.

DELAWARE

SENATORS

George Gray, *New Castle*
Anthony Higgins, *Wilmington*

REPRESENTATIVE

At Large—John B. Penington, *Dover*

FLORIDA

SENATORS

Wilkinson Call, *Jacksonville*
Samuel Pasco, *Monticello*

REPRESENTATIVES

Robert H. M. Davidson, *Quincy*
Robert Bullock, *Ocala*

GEORGIA

SENATORS

Joseph E. Brown, *Atlanta*
Alfred H. Colquitt, *Atlanta*

REPRESENTATIVES

Rufus E. Lester, *Savannah*
Henry G. Turner, *Quitman*
Charles F. Crisp, *Americus*
Thomas W. Grimes, *Columbus*
John D. Stewart, *Griffin*
James H. Blount, *Macon*
Judson C. Clements, *Rome*
Henry H. Carlton, *Athens*
Allen D. Candler, *Gainesville*
George T. Barnes, *Augusta*

IDAHO [16]

SENATORS [17]

George L. Shoup,[18] *Salmon City*
William J. McConnell,[19] *Moscow*

REPRESENTATIVE

At Large—Willis Sweet,[20] *Moscow*

ILLINOIS

SENATORS

Shelby M. Cullom, *Springfield*
Charles B. Farwell, *Chicago*

REPRESENTATIVES

Abner Taylor, *Chicago*
Frank Lawler, *Chicago*
William E. Mason, *Chicago*
George E. Adams, *Chicago*
Albert J. Hopkins, *Aurora*

Robert R. Hitt, *Mount Morris*
Thomas J. Henderson, *Princeton*
Charles A. Hill, *Joliet*
Lewis E. Payson, *Pontiac*
Philip S. Post, *Galesburg*
William H. Gest, *Rock Island*
Scott Wike, *Pittsfield*
William M. Springer, *Springfield*
Jonathan H. Rowell, *Bloomington*
Joseph G. Cannon, *Danville*
George W. Fithian, *Newton*
Edward Lane, *Hillsboro*
William S. Forman, *Nashville*
Richard W. Townshend,[21] *Shawneetown*
James R. Williams,[22] *Carmi*
George W. Smith, *Murphysboro*

INDIANA

SENATORS

Daniel W. Voorhees, *Terre Haute*
David Turpie, *Indianapolis*

REPRESENTATIVES

William F. Parrett,[23] *Evansville*
John H. O'Neall, *Washington*
Jason B. Brown, *Seymour*
William S. Holman, *Aurora*
George W. Cooper, *Columbus*
Thomas M. Browne, *Winchester*
William D. Bynum, *Indianapolis*
Elijah V. Brookshire, *Crawfordsville*
Joseph B. Cheadle, *Frankfort*
William D. Owen, *Logansport*
Augustus N. Martin, *Bluffton*
Charles A. O. McClellan, *Auburn*
Benjamin F. Shively, *South Bend*

IOWA

SENATORS

William B. Allison, *Dubuque*
James F. Wilson, *Fairfield*

REPRESENTATIVES

John H. Gear, *Burlington*
Walter I. Hayes, *Clinton*
David B. Henderson, *Dubuque*
Joseph H. Sweney, *Osage*
Daniel Kerr, *Grundy Center*
John F. Lacey, *Oskaloosa*
Edwin H. Conger,[24] *Des Moines*
Edward R. Hays,[25] *Knoxville*
James P. Flick, *Bedford*
Joseph R. Reed, *Council Bluffs*
Jonathan P. Dolliver, *Fort Dodge*
Isaac S. Struble, *Le Mars*

KANSAS

SENATORS

John J. Ingalls, *Atchison*
Preston B. Plumb, *Emporia*

REPRESENTATIVES

Edmund N. Morrill, *Hiawatha*
Edward H. Funston, *Iola*
Bishop W. Perkins, *Oswego*
Thomas Ryan,[26] *Topeka*
Harrison Kelley,[27] *Burlington*
John A. Anderson, *Manhattan*
Erastus J. Turner, *Hoxie*
Samuel R. Peters, *Newton*

KENTUCKY

SENATORS

James B. Beck,[28] *Lexington*
John G. Carlisle,[29] *Covington*
Joseph C. S. Blackburn, *Versailles*

REPRESENTATIVES

William J. Stone, *Kuttawa*
William T. Ellis, *Owensboro*
Isaac H. Goodnight, *Franklin*
Alexander B. Montgomery, *Elizabethtown*
Asher G. Caruth, *Louisville*
John G. Carlisle,[30] *Covington*
William W. Dickerson,[31] *Williamstown*
William C. P. Breckinridge, *Lexington*
James B. McCreary, *Richmond*
Thomas H. Paynter, *Greenup*
John H. Wilson, *Barboursville*
Hugh F. Finley, *Williamsburg*

LOUISIANA

SENATORS

Randall L. Gibson, *New Orleans*
James B. Eustis, *New Orleans*

REPRESENTATIVES

Theodore S. Wilkinson, *Plaquemines Parish*
Hamilton D. Coleman, *New Orleans*
Edward J. Gay,[32] *Plaquemine*
Andrew Price,[33] *Thibodaux*
Newton C. Blanchard, *Shreveport*
Charles J. Boatner, *Monroe*
Samuel M. Robertson, *Baton Rouge*

MAINE

SENATORS

Eugene Hale, *Ellsworth*
William P. Frye, *Lewiston*

---

[16] Admitted as a State into the Union July 3, 1890.
[17] In addition to the Senators named the credentials of Fred T. Dubois, who had been elected "for the term of six years from March 4, 1891," were presented December 30, 1890, but the Senate refused to consider them prior to the beginning of the Fifty-second Congress, when they were to become effective.
[18] Took his seat December 29, 1890; term to expire, as determined by lot, March 3, 1895.
[19] Took his seat January 5, 1891; term to expire, as determined by lot, March 3, 1891.

[20] Took his seat December 1, 1890.
[21] Died March 9, 1889, before Congress assembled.
[22] Elected to fill vacancy caused by death of Richard W. Townshend, and took his seat December 2, 1889.
[23] Election unsuccessfully contested by Francis B. Posey.
[24] Resigned October 3, 1890.
[25] Elected to fill vacancy caused by resignation of Edwin H. Conger, and took his seat December 1, 1890.
[26] Resigned April 4, 1889, before Congress assembled.
[27] Elected to fill vacancy caused by resignation of

Thomas Ryan, and took his seat December 2, 1889.
[28] Died May 3, 1890.
[29] Elected to fill vacancy caused by death of James B. Beck, and took his seat May 26, 1890.
[30] Resigned May 26, 1890, having been elected Senator.
[31] Elected to fill vacancy caused by resignation of John G. Carlisle, and took his seat June 30, 1890.
[32] Died May 30, 1889, before Congress assembled.
[33] Elected to fill vacancy caused by death of Edward J. Gay, and took his seat December 2, 1889.

REPRESENTATIVES

Thomas B. Reed, *Portland*
Nelson Dingley, Jr., *Lewiston*
Seth L. Milliken, *Belfast*
Charles A. Boutelle, *Bangor*

MARYLAND

SENATORS

Arthur Pue Gorman, *Laurel*
Ephraim K. Wilson,[34] *Snow Hill*

REPRESENTATIVES

Charles H. Gibson, *Easton*
Herman Stump, *Belair*
Harry W. Rusk, *Baltimore*
Henry Stockbridge, Jr., *Baltimore*
Barnes Compton,[35] *Laurel*
Sydney E. Mudd,[36] *Bryantown*
Louis E. McComas, *Hagerstown*

MASSACHUSETTS

SENATORS

Henry L. Dawes, *Pittsfield*
George F. Hoar, *Worcester*

REPRESENTATIVES

Charles S. Randall, *New Bedford*
Elijah A. Morse, *Canton*
John F. Andrew, *Boston*
Joseph H. O'Neil, *Boston*
Nathaniel P. Banks, *Waltham*
Henry Cabot Lodge, *Nahant*
William Cogswell, *Salem*
Frederic T. Greenhalge, *Lowell*
John W. Candler, *Brookline*
Joseph H. Walker, *Worcester*
Rodney Wallace, *Fitchburg*
Francis W. Rockwell, *Pittsfield*

MICHIGAN

SENATORS

Francis B. Stockbridge, *Kalamazoo*
James McMillan, *Detroit*

REPRESENTATIVES

J. Logan Chipman, *Detroit*
Edward P. Allen, *Ypsilanti*
James O'Donnell, *Jackson*
Julius C. Burrows, *Kalamazoo*
Charles E. Belknap, *Grand Rapids*
Mark S. Brewer, *Pontiac*
Justin R. Whiting, *St. Clair*
Aaron T. Bliss, *Saginaw*

Byron M. Cutcheon, *Manistee*
Frank W. Wheeler, *West Bay City*
Samuel M. Stephenson, *Menominee*

MINNESOTA

SENATORS

Cushman K. Davis, *St. Paul*
William D. Washburn, *Minneapolis*

REPRESENTATIVES

Mark H. Dunnell, *Owatonna*
John Lind, *New Ulm*
Darwin S. Hall, *Stewart*
Samuel P. Snider, *Minneapolis*
Solomon G. Comstock, *Moorhead*

MISSISSIPPI

SENATORS

James Z. George, *Carrollton*
Edward C. Walthall, *Grenada*

REPRESENTATIVES

John M. Allen, *Tupelo*
James B. Morgan,[37] *Hernando*
Thomas C. Catchings, *Vicksburg*
Clarke Lewis, *Cliftonville*
Chapman L. Anderson, *Kosciusko*
Thomas R. Stockdale, *Summit*
Charles E. Hooker, *Jackson*

MISSOURI

SENATORS

Francis M. Cockrell, *Warrensburg*
George G. Vest, *Kansas City*

REPRESENTATIVES

William H. Hatch, *Hannibal*
Charles H. Mansur, *Chillicothe*
Alexander M. Dockery, *Gallatin*
Robert P. C. Wilson,[38] *Platte City*
John C. Tarsney, *Kansas City*
John T. Heard, *Sedalia*
Richard H. Norton, *Troy*
Frederick G. Niedringhaus, *St. Louis*
Nathan Frank, *St. Louis*
William M. Kinsey, *St. Louis*
Richard P. Bland, *Lebanon*
William J. Stone, *Nevada*
William H. Wade, *Springfield*
James P. Walker,[39] *Dexter*
Robert H. Whitelaw,[40] *Cape Girardeau*

MONTANA [41]

SENATORS [42]

Thomas C. Power,[43] *Helena*
Wilbur F. Sanders,[44] *Helena*

REPRESENTATIVE

At Large—Thomas H. Carter,[45] *Helena*

NEBRASKA

SENATORS

Charles F. Manderson, *Omaha*
Algernon S. Paddock, *Beatrice*

REPRESENTATIVES

William J. Connell, *Omaha*
James Laird,[46] *Hastings*
Gilbert L. Laws,[47] *McCook*
George W. E. Dorsey, *Fremont*

NEVADA

SENATORS

John P. Jones, *Gold Hill*
William M. Stewart, *Carson City*

REPRESENTATIVE

At Large—Horace F. Bartine, *Carson City*

NEW HAMPSHIRE

SENATORS

Henry W. Blair, *Manchester*
Gilman Marston,[48] *Exeter*
William E. Chandler,[49] *Concord*

REPRESENTATIVES

Alonzo Nute, *Farmington*
Orren C. Moore, *Nashua*

NEW JERSEY

SENATORS

John R. McPherson, *Jersey City*
Rufus Blodgett, *Long Branch*

REPRESENTATIVES

Christopher A. Bergen, *Camden*
James Buchanan, *Trenton*
Jacob A. Geissenhainer, *Freehold*
Samuel Fowler, *Newton*
Charles D. Beckwith, *Paterson*
Herman Lehlbach, *Newark*
William McAdoo, *Jersey City*

---

[34] Died February 24, 1891; had been reelected for the term beginning March 4, 1893.
[35] Served until March 20, 1890; succeeded by Sydney E. Mudd, who contested his election.
[36] Successfully contested the election of Barnes Compton, and took his seat March 20, 1890.
[37] Election unsuccessfully contested by James R. Chalmers.
[38] Elected to fill vacancy caused by death of Representative-elect James N. Burnes, in the preceding Congress, and took his seat December 2, 1889.
[39] Died July 20, 1890.

[40] Elected to fill vacancy caused by death of James P. Walker, and took his seat December 1, 1890.
[41] Admitted as a State into the Union November 8, 1889.
[42] William A. Clark and Martin Maginnis presented papers purporting to be credentials of their election January 23, 1890; the four claimants were given privileges of the floor pending the contest; by resolutions of April 16, 1890, Clark and Maginnis were declared not entitled to seats and Power and Sanders entitled thereto.

[43] Took his seat April 16, 1890; term to expire, as determined by lot, March 3, 1895.
[44] Took his seat April 16, 1890; term to expire, as determined by lot, March 3, 1893.
[45] Took his seat December 2, 1889.
[46] Died August 17, 1889, before Congress assembled.
[47] Elected to fill vacancy caused by death of James Laird, and took his seat December 2, 1889.
[48] Appointed to fill vacancy in term beginning March 4, 1889, during the recess of the legislature.
[49] Elected to fill vacancy in the term beginning March 4, 1889, and took his seat December 2, 1889.

NEW YORK

SENATORS

William M. Evarts, *New York City*
Frank Hiscock, *Syracuse*

REPRESENTATIVES

James W. Covert, *Long Island City*
Felix Campbell, *Brooklyn*
William C. Wallace, *Brooklyn*
John M. Clancy, *Brooklyn*
Thomas F. Magner, *Brooklyn*
Frank T. Fitzgerald,[50] *New York City*
Charles H. Turner,[51] *New York City*
Edward J. Dunphy, *New York City*
John H. McCarthy,[52] *New York City*
Samuel S. Cox,[53] *New York City*
Amos J. Cummings,[54] *New York City*
Francis B. Spinola, *New York City*
John Quinn, *New York City*
Roswell P. Flower, *New York City*
Ashbel P. Fitch, *New York City*
William G. Stahlnecker, *Yonkers*
Moses D. Stivers, *Middletown*
John H. Ketcham, *Dover Plains*
Charles J. Knapp, *Deposit*
John A. Quackenbush, *Stillwater*
Charles Tracey, *Albany*
John Sanford, *Amsterdam*
John H. Moffitt, *Chateaugay Lake*
Frederick Lansing, *Watertown*
James S. Sherman, *Utica*
David Wilber,[55] *Oneonta*
John S. Pindar,[56] *Cobleskill*
James J. Belden, *Syracuse*
Milton De Lano, *Canastota*
Newton W. Nutting,[57] *Oswego*
Sereno E. Payne,[58] *Auburn*
Thomas S. Flood, *Elmira*
John Raines, *Canandaigua*
Charles S. Baker, *Rochester*
John G. Sawyer, *Albion*
John M. Farquhar, *Buffalo*
John McC. Wiley, *East Aurora*
William G. Laidlaw, *Ellicottville*

NORTH CAROLINA

SENATORS

Matt W. Ransom, *Weldon*
Zebulon B. Vance, *Charlotte*

REPRESENTATIVES

Thomas G. Skinner, *Hertford*
Henry P. Cheatham, *Henderson*
Charles W. McClammy, *Scotts Hill*
Benjamin H. Bunn, *Rocky Mount*

John M. Brower, *Mount Airy*
Alfred Rowland, *Lumberton*
John S. Henderson, *Salisbury*
William H. H. Cowles, *Wilkesboro*
Hamilton G. Ewart, *Hendersonville*

NORTH DAKOTA [59]

SENATORS

Lyman R. Casey,[60] *Jamestown*
Gilbert A. Pierce,[61] *Fargo*

REPRESENTATIVE

At Large—Henry C. Hansbrough,[62] *Devils Lake*

OHIO

SENATORS

John Sherman, *Mansfield*
Henry B. Payne, *Cleveland*

REPRESENTATIVES

Benjamin Butterworth, *Cincinnati*
John A. Caldwell, *Cincinnati*
Elihu S. Williams, *Troy*
Samuel S. Yoder, *Lima*
George E. Seney, *Tiffin*
Melvin M. Boothman, *Bryan*
Henry L. Morey, *Hamilton*
Robert P. Kennedy, *Bellefontaine*
William C. Cooper, *Mount Vernon*
William E. Haynes, *Fremont*
Albert C. Thompson, *Portsmouth*
Jacob J. Pugsley, *Hillsboro*
Joseph H. Outhwaite, *Columbus*
Charles P. Wickham, *Norwalk*
Charles H. Grosvenor, *Athens*
James W. Owens, *Newark*
Joseph D. Taylor, *Cambridge*
William McKinley, Jr., *Canton*
Ezra B. Taylor, *Warren*
Martin L. Smyser, *Wooster*
Theodore E. Burton, *Cleveland*

OREGON

SENATORS

Joseph N. Dolph, *Portland*
John H. Mitchell, *Portland*

REPRESENTATIVE

At Large—Binger Hermann, *Roseburg*

PENNSYLVANIA

SENATORS

J. Donald Cameron, *Harrisburg*
Matthew S. Quay, *Beaver*

REPRESENTATIVES

Henry H. Bingham, *Philadelphia*
Charles O'Neill, *Philadelphia*
Samuel J. Randall,[63] *Philadelphia*
Richard Vaux,[64] *Philadelphia*
William D. Kelley,[65] *Philadelphia*
John E. Reyburn,[66] *Philadelphia*
Alfred C. Harmer, *Philadelphia*
Smedley Darlington, *West Chester*
Robert M. Yardley, *Doylestown*
William Mutchler, *Easton*
David B. Brunner, *Reading*
Marriott Brosius, *Lancaster*
Joseph A. Scranton, *Scranton*
Edwin S. Osborne, *Wilkes-Barre*
James B. Reilly, *Pottsville*
John W. Rife, *Middletown*
Myron B. Wright, *Susquehanna*
Henry C. McCormick, *Williamsport*
Charles R. Buckalew, *Bloomsburg*
Louis E. Atkinson, *Mifflintown*
Levi Maish, *York*
Edward Scull, *Somerset*
Samuel A. Craig, *Brookville*
John Dalzell, *Pittsburgh*
Thomas M. Bayne, *Allegheny*
Joseph W. Ray, *Waynesburg*
Charles C. Townsend, *New Brighton*
William C. Culbertson, *Girard*
Lewis F. Watson,[67] *Warren*
Charles W. Stone,[68] *Warren*
James Kerr, *Clearfield*

RHODE ISLAND

SENATORS

Nelson W. Aldrich, *Providence*
Jonathan Chace,[69] *Providence*
Nathan F. Dixon,[70] *Westerly*

REPRESENTATIVES

Henry J. Spooner, *Providence*
Warren O. Arnold, *Gloucester*

SOUTH CAROLINA

SENATORS

Matthew C. Butler, *Edgefield*
Wade Hampton, *Charleston*

---

[50] Resigned November 4, 1889, before Congress assembled.
[51] Elected to fill vacancy caused by resignation of Frank T. Fitzgerald, and took his seat December 9, 1889.
[52] Resigned January 14, 1891.
[53] Died September 10, 1889, before Congress assembled.
[54] Elected to fill vacancy caused by death of Samuel S. Cox, and took his seat December 2, 1889.
[55] Died April 1, 1890.
[56] Elected to fill vacancy caused by death of David

Wilber, and took his seat December 1, 1890.
[57] Died October 15, 1889, before Congress assembled.
[58] Elected to fill vacancy caused by death of Newton W. Nutting, and took his seat December 2, 1889.
[59] Formed from a portion of the Territory of Dakota, and admitted as a State into the Union November 2, 1889.
[60] Took his seat December 4, 1889; term to expire, as determined by lot, March 3, 1893.
[61] Took his seat December 4, 1889; term to expire, as determined by lot, March 3, 1891.
[62] Took his seat December 2, 1889.

[63] Died April 13, 1890.
[64] Elected to fill vacancy caused by death of Samuel J. Randall, and took his seat May 28, 1890.
[65] Died January 9, 1890.
[66] Elected to fill vacancy caused by death of William D. Kelley, and took his seat February 24, 1890.
[67] Died August 25, 1890.
[68] Elected to fill vacancy caused by death of Lewis F. Watson, and took his seat December 1, 1890.
[69] Resigned April 9, 1889.
[70] Elected to fill vacancy caused by resignation of Jonathan Chace, and took his seat December 2, 1889.

REPRESENTATIVES

Samuel Dibble, *Orangeburg*
George D. Tillman, *Clarks Hill*
James S. Cothran, *Abbeville*
William H. Perry, *Greenville*
John J. Hemphill, *Chester*
George W. Dargan, *Darlington*
William Elliott,[71] *Beaufort*
Thomas E. Miller,[72] *Beaufort*

SOUTH DAKOTA[73]

SENATORS

Richard F. Pettigrew,[74] *Sioux Falls*
Gideon C. Moody,[75] *Deadwood*

REPRESENTATIVES AT LARGE

Oscar S. Gifford,[76] *Canton*
John A. Pickler,[76] *Faulkton*

TENNESSEE

SENATORS

Isham G. Harris, *Memphis*
William B. Bate, *Nashville*

REPRESENTATIVES

Alfred A. Taylor, *Johnson City*
Leonidas C. Houk, *Knoxville*
H. Clay Evans, *Chattanooga*
Benton McMillin, *Carthage*
James D. Richardson, *Murfreesboro*
Joseph E. Washington, *Cedar Hill*
Washington C. Whitthorne, *Columbia*
Benjamin A. Enloe, *Jackson*
Rice A. Pierce, *Union City*
James Phelan,[77] *Memphis*

TEXAS

SENATORS

Richard Coke, *Waco*
John H. Reagan, *Palestine*

REPRESENTATIVES

Charles Stewart, *Houston*
William H. Martin, *Athens*
Constantine B. Kilgore, *Wills Point*
David B. Culberson, *Jefferson*
Silas Hare, *Sherman*
Jo Abbott, *Hillsboro*
William H. Crain, *Cuero*

Littleton W. Moore, *Lagrange*
Roger Q. Mills, *Corsicana*
Joseph D. Sayers, *Bastrop*
Samuel W. T. Lanham, *Weatherford*

VERMONT

SENATORS

George F. Edmunds, *Burlington*
Justin S. Morrill, *Strafford*

REPRESENTATIVES

John W. Stewart, *Middlebury*
William W. Grout, *Barton*

VIRGINIA

SENATORS

John W. Daniel, *Lynchburg*
John S. Barbour, *Alexandria*

REPRESENTATIVES

Thomas H. B. Browne, *Accomac*
George E. Bowden, *Norfolk*
George D. Wise,[78] *Richmond*
Edmund Waddill, Jr.,[79] *Richmond*
Edward C. Venable,[80] *Petersburg*
John M. Langston,[81] *Petersburg*
Posey G. Lester, *Floyd*
Paul C. Edmunds, *Halifax*
Charles T. O'Ferrall, *Harrisonburg*
William H. F. Lee, *Burkes Station*
John A. Buchanan,[82] *Abingdon*
Henry St. George Tucker, *Staunton*

WASHINGTON[83]

SENATORS

John B. Allen,[84] *Walla Walla*
Watson C. Squire,[85] *Seattle*

REPRESENTATIVE

At Large—John L. Wilson,[86] *Spokane Falls*

WEST VIRGINIA

SENATORS

John E. Kenna, *Charleston*
Charles J. Faulkner, *Martinsburg*

REPRESENTATIVES

John O. Pendleton,[87] *Wheeling*
George W. Atkinson,[88] *Wheeling*
William L. Wilson, *Charles Town*
John D. Alderson, *Nicholas*
J. Monroe Jackson,[89] *Parkersburg*
Charles B. Smith,[90] *Parkersburg*

WISCONSIN

SENATORS

Philetus Sawyer, *Oshkosh*
John C. Spooner, *Hudson*

REPRESENTATIVES

Lucien B. Caswell, *Fort Atkinson*
Charles Barwig, *Mayville*
Robert M. La Follette, *Madison*
Isaac W. Van Schaick, *Milwaukee*
George H. Brickner, *Sheboygan Falls*
Charles B. Clark, *Neenah*
Ormsby B. Thomas, *Prairie du Chien*
Nils P. Haugen, *River Falls*
Myron H. McCord, *Merrill*

WYOMING[91]

SENATORS

Joseph M. Carey,[92] *Cheyenne*
Francis E. Warren,[93] *Cheyenne*

REPRESENTATIVE

At Large—Clarence D. Clark,[94] *Evanston*

TERRITORY OF ARIZONA

DELEGATE

Marcus A. Smith, *Tombstone*

TERRITORY OF DAKOTA

DELEGATE

George A. Mathews,[95] *Brookings*

TERRITORY OF IDAHO

DELEGATE

Fred T. Dubois,[96] *Blackfoot*

---

[71] Served until September 23, 1890; succeeded by Thomas E. Miller, who contested his election.
[72] Successfully contested the election of William Elliott, and took his seat September 24, 1890.
[73] Formed from a portion of the Territory of Dakota, and admitted as a State into the Union November 2, 1889.
[74] Took his seat December 2, 1889; term to expire, as determined by lot, March 3, 1895.
[75] Took his seat December 2, 1889; term to expire, as determined by lot, March 3, 1891.
[76] Took his seat December 2, 1889.
[77] Died January 30, 1891.
[78] Served until April 10, 1890; succeeded by Edmond Waddill, Jr., who contested his election.
[79] Successfully contested the election of George D. Wise, and took his seat April 12, 1890.
[80] Served until September 23, 1890; succeeded by John M. Langston, who contested his election.

[81] Successfully contested the election of Edward C. Venable, and took his seat September 23, 1890. It was in connection with this case that the minority party adopted for the first time the plan of withdrawing in a body from the Hall of the House, to avoid being counted as part of a quorum.
[82] Election unsuccessfully contested by Henry Bowen.
[83] Admitted as a State into the Union November 11, 1889.
[84] Took his seat December 2, 1889; term to expire, as determined by lot, March 3, 1893.
[85] Took his seat December 2, 1889; term to expire, as determined by lot, March 3, 1891.
[86] Took his seat December 2, 1889.
[87] Served until February 26, 1890; succeeded by George W. Atkinson, who contested his election.
[88] Successfully contested the election of John O. Pendleton, and took his seat February 26, 1890.
[89] Served until February 3, 1890; succeeded by

Charles B. Smith, who contested his election. It was in connection with the final votes in this case that Speaker Reed, for the first time, made his parliamentary ruling regarding the "counting of a quorum."
[90] Successfully contested the election of J. Monroe Jackson and took his seat February 3, 1890.
[91] Admitted as a State into the Union July 10, 1890.
[92] Took his seat December 1, 1890; term to expire, as determined by lot, March 3, 1895.
[93] Took his seat December 1, 1890; term to expire, as determined by lot, March 3, 1893.
[94] Took his seat December 1, 1890.
[95] Served until November 2, 1889, when the Territory of Dakota was divided and granted statehood as the States of North and South Dakota by act of Congress approved February 22, 1889.
[96] Served until July 3, 1890, when the Territory of Idaho was granted statehood by act of Congress approved that date.

TERRITORY OF MONTANA

DELEGATE

Thomas H. Carter,[97] *Helena*

TERRITORY OF NEW MEXICO

DELEGATE

Antonio Joseph, *Ojo Caliente*

TERRITORY OF OKLAHOMA [98]

DELEGATE

David A. Harvey,[99] *Oklahoma City*

TERRITORY OF UTAH

DELEGATE

John T. Caine, *Salt Lake City*

TERRITORY OF WASHINGTON

DELEGATE

John B. Allen,[100] *Seattle*

TERRITORY OF WYOMING

DELEGATE

Joseph M. Carey,[101] *Cheyenne*

[97] Served until November 8, 1889, when the Territory of Montana was granted statehood by act of Congress approved February 22, 1889; subsequently elected the first Representative from the new State.

[98] Formed from a portion of Indian Territory and from that portion of the United States known as the "Public Land Strip," and granted a Delegate in Congress by act of May 2, 1890.

[99] Took his seat December 1, 1890.

[100] Served until November 11, 1889, when the Territory of Washington was granted statehood by act of Congress approved February 22, 1889; subsequently elected Senator from the new State.

[101] Served until July 10, 1890, when the Territory of Wyoming was granted statehood by act of Congress approved July 10, 1890; subsequently elected Senator from the new State.

FIFTY-SECOND CONGRESS

MARCH 4, 1891, TO MARCH 3, 1893

FIRST SESSION—*December 7, 1891, to August 5, 1892*

SECOND SESSION—*December 5, 1892, to March 3, 1893*

———

VICE PRESIDENT OF THE UNITED STATES—LEVI P. MORTON, of New York

PRESIDENT PRO TEMPORE OF THE SENATE—CHARLES F. MANDERSON, of Nebraska

SECRETARY OF THE SENATE—ANSON G. McCOOK, of New York

SERGEANT AT ARMS OF THE SENATE—EDWARD K. VALENTINE, of Nebraska

———

SPEAKER OF THE HOUSE OF REPRESENTATIVES—CHARLES F. CRISP,[1] of Georgia

CLERK OF THE HOUSE—EDWARD McPHERSON, of Pennsylvania; JAMES KERR,[2] of Pennsylvania

SERGEANT AT ARMS OF THE HOUSE—ADONIRAM J. HOLMES, of Iowa; SAMUEL S. YODER,[3] of Ohio

DOORKEEPER OF THE HOUSE—CHARLES H. TURNER, of New York

POSTMASTER OF THE HOUSE—J. W. HATHAWAY

ALABAMA

SENATORS

John T. Morgan, *Selma*
James L. Pugh, *Eufaula*

REPRESENTATIVES

Richard H. Clarke, *Mobile*
Hilary A. Herbert, *Montgomery*
William C. Oates, *Abbeville*
Louis W. Turpin,[4] *Newbern*
James E. Cobb, *Tuskegee*
John H. Bankhead, *Fayette*
William H. Forney, *Jacksonville*
Joseph Wheeler, *Wheeler*

ARKANSAS

SENATORS

James K. Jones, *Washington*
James H. Berry, *Bentonville*

REPRESENTATIVES

William H. Cate, *Jonesboro*
Clifton R. Breckinridge, *Pine Bluff*
Thomas C. McRae, *Prescott*
Willian L. Terry, *Little Rock*
Samuel W. Peel, *Bentonville*

CALIFORNIA

SENATORS

Leland Stanford, *San Francisco*
Charles N. Felton,[5] *San Francisco*

REPRESENTATIVES

Thomas J. Geary, *Santa Rosa*
Anthony Caminetti, *Jackson*
Joseph McKenna,[6] *Suisun*
Samuel G. Hilborn,[7] *Oakland*
John T. Cutting, *San Francisco*
Eugene F. Loud, *San Francisco*
William W. Bowers, *San Diego*

COLORADO

SENATORS

Henry M. Teller, *Central City*
Edward O. Wolcott, *Denver*

REPRESENTATIVE

At Large—Hosea Townsend, *Silver Cliff*

CONNECTICUT

SENATORS

Orville H. Platt, *Meriden*
Joseph R. Hawley, *Hartford*

REPRESENTATIVES

Lewis Sperry, *Hartford*
Washington F. Willcox, *Chester*
Charles A. Russell, *Killingly*
Robert E. De Forest, *Bridgeport*

DELAWARE

SENATORS

George Gray, *New Castle*
Anthony Higgins, *Wilmington*

REPRESENTATIVE

At Large—John W. Causey, *Milford*

FLORIDA

SENATORS

Wilkinson Call,[8] *Jacksonville*
Samuel Pasco, *Monticello*

REPRESENTATIVES

Stephen R. Mallory, *Pensacola*
Robert Bullock, *Ocala*

---

[1] Elected December 8, 1891.
[2] Elected December 8, 1891.
[3] Elected December 8, 1891.
[4] Election unsuccessfully contested by John V. McDuffie.

[5] Elected to fill vacancy caused by death of George Hearst, in preceding Congress, and took his seat December 7, 1891.
[6] Resigned March 28, 1892.

[7] Elected to fill vacancy caused by resignation of Joseph McKenna, and took his seat December 5, 1892.
[8] Election unsuccessfully contested by Robert H. M. Davidson.

GEORGIA

SENATORS

Alfred H. Colquitt, *Atlanta*
John B. Gordon, *Atlanta*

REPRESENTATIVES

Rufus E. Lester, *Savannah*
Henry G. Turner, *Quitman*
Charles F. Crisp, *Americus*
Charles L. Moses, *Turin*
Leonidas F. Livingston, *Atlanta*
James H. Blount, *Macon*
Robert W. Everett, *Fish*
Thomas G. Lawson, *Eatonton*
Thomas E. Winn, *Lawrenceville*
Thomas E. Watson, *Thomson*

IDAHO

SENATORS

George L. Shoup, *Salmon City*
Fred T. Dubois,[9] *Blackfoot*

REPRESENTATIVE

At Large—Willis Sweet, *Moscow*

ILLINOIS

SENATORS

Shelby M. Cullom, *Springfield*
John McAuley Palmer, *Springfield*

REPRESENTATIVES

Abner Taylor, *Chicago*
Lawrence E. McGann, *Chicago*
Allan C. Durborow, Jr., *Chicago*
Walter C. Newberry, *Chicago*
Albert J. Hopkins, *Aurora*
Robert R. Hitt, *Mount Morris*
Thomas J. Henderson, *Princeton*
Lewis Steward, *Plano*
Herman W. Snow, *Sheldon*
Philip S. Post, *Galesburg*
Benjamin T. Cable, *Rock Island*
Scott Wike, *Pittsfield*
William M. Springer, *Springfield*
Owen Scott, *Bloomington*
Samuel T. Busey, *Urbana*
George W. Fithian, *Newton*
Edward Lane, *Hillsboro*
William S. Forman, *Nashville*
James R. Williams, *Carmi*
George W. Smith, *Murphysboro*

INDIANA

SENATORS

Daniel W. Voorhees, *Terre Haute*
David Turpie, *Indianapolis*

REPRESENTATIVES

William F. Parrett, *Evansville*
John L. Bretz, *Jasper*
Jason B. Brown, *Seymour*
William S. Holman, *Aurora*
George W. Cooper, *Columbus*
Henry U. Johnson, *Richmond*
William D. Bynum, *Indianapolis*
Elijah V. Brookshire, *Crawfordsville*
Daniel W. Waugh, *Tipton*
David H. Patton, *Remington*
Augustus N. Martin, *Bluffton*
Charles A. O. McClellan, *Auburn*
Benjamin F. Shively, *South Bend*

IOWA

SENATORS

William B. Allison, *Dubuque*
James F. Wilson, *Fairfield*

REPRESENTATIVES

John J. Seerley, *Burlington*
Walter I. Hayes, *Clinton*
David B. Henderson, *Dubuque*
Walter H. Butler, *West Union*
John T. Hamilton, *Cedar Rapids*
Frederick E. White, *Webster*
John A. T. Hull, *Des Moines*
James P. Flick, *Bedford*
Thomas Bowman, *Council Bluffs*
Jonathan P. Dolliver, *Fort Dodge*
George D. Perkins, *Sioux City*

KANSAS

SENATORS

Preston B. Plumb,[10] *Emporia*
Bishop W. Perkins,[11] *Oswego*
William A. Peffer, *Topeka*

REPRESENTATIVES

Case Broderick, *Holton*
Edward H. Funston, *Iola*
Benjamin H. Clover, *Cambridge*
John G. Otis, *Topeka*
John Davis, *Junction City*
William Baker, *Lincoln*
Jeremiah Simpson, *Medicine Lodge*

KENTUCKY

SENATORS

Joseph C. S. Blackburn, *Versailles*
John G. Carlisle,[12] *Covington*
William Lindsay,[13] *Frankfort*

REPRESENTATIVES

William J. Stone, *Kuttawa*
William T. Ellis, *Owensboro*
Isaac H. Goodnight, *Franklin*
Alexander B. Montgomery, *Elizabethtown*
Asher G. Caruth, *Louisville*
William W. Dickerson, *Williamstown*
William C. P. Breckinridge, *Lexington*
James B. McCreary, *Richmond*
Thomas H. Paynter, *Greenup*
John W. Kendall,[14] *West Liberty*
Joseph M. Kendall,[15] *Prestonsburg*
John H. Wilson, *Barboursville*

LOUISIANA

SENATORS

Randall L. Gibson,[16] *New Orleans*
Donelson Caffery,[17] *Franklin*
Edward D. White, *New Orleans*

REPRESENTATIVES

Adolph Meyer, *New Orleans*
Matthew D. Lagan, *New Orleans*
Andrew Price, *Thibodaux*
Newton C. Blanchard, *Shreveport*
Charles J. Boatner, *Monroe*
Samuel M. Robertson, *Baton Rouge*

MAINE

SENATORS

Eugune Hale, *Ellsworth*
William P. Frye, *Lewiston*

REPRESENTATIVES

Thomas B. Reed, *Portland*
Nelson Dingley, Jr., *Lewiston*
Seth L. Milliken, *Belfast*
Charles A. Boutelle, *Bangor*

MARYLAND

SENATORS

Arthur Pue Gorman, *Laurel*
Charles H. Gibson,[18] *Easton*

REPRESENTATIVES

Henry Page,[19] *Princess Anne*
John B. Brown,[20] *Centerville*
Herman Stump, *Bel Air*
Harry W. Rusk, *Baltimore*
Isidor Rayner, *Baltimore*
Barnes Compton, *Laurel*
William M. McKaig, *Cumberland*

---

[9] Election unsuccessfully contested by William H. Clagett.
[10] Died December 20, 1891.
[11] Appointed to fill vacancy caused by death of Preston B. Plumb, and took his seat January 5, 1892.
[12] Resigned February 4, 1893.
[13] Elected to fill vacancy caused by resignation of John G. Carlisle, and took his seat February 21, 1893.

[14] Died March 7, 1892.
[15] Elected to fill vacancy caused by death of John W. Kendall, and took his seat May 5, 1892.
[16] Died December 15, 1892.
[17] Appointed to fill vacancy caused by death of Randall L. Gibson, and took his seat January 14, 1893; subsequently elected.
[18] Appointed to fill vacancy caused by death of

Ephraim K. Wilson, in preceding Congress, and took his seat December 7, 1891; subsequently elected; vacancy in this class from February 25 to November 18, 1891.
[19] Resigned September 3, 1892, having been appointed judge of first judicial district of Maryland.
[20] Elected to fill vacancy caused by resignation of Henry Page, and took his seat December 5, 1892.

MASSACHUSETTS

SENATORS

Henry L. Dawes, *Pittsfield*
George F. Hoar, *Worcester*

REPRESENTATIVES

Charles S. Randall, *New Bedford*
Elijah A. Morse, *Canton*
John F. Andrew, *Boston*
Joseph H. O'Neil, *Boston*
Sherman Hoar, *Waltham*
Henry Cabot Lodge,[21] *Nahant*
William Cogswell, *Salem*
Moses T. Stevens, *North Andover*
George F. Williams, *Dedham*
Joseph H. Walker, *Worcester*
Frederick S. Coolidge, *Ashburnham*
John C. Crosby, *Pittsfield*

MICHIGAN

SENATORS

Francis B. Stockbridge, *Kalamazoo*
James McMillan, *Detroit*

REPRESENTATIVES

J. Logan Chipman, *Detroit*
James S. Gorman, *Chelsea*
James O'Donnell, *Jackson*
Julius C. Burrows, *Kalamazoo*
Melbourne H. Ford,[22] *Grand Rapids*
Charles E. Belknap,[23] *Grand Rapids*
Byron G. Stout, *Pontiac*
Justin R. Whiting, *St. Clair*
Henry M. Youmans, *Saginaw*
Harrison H. Wheeler, *Ludington*
Thomas A. E. Weadock, *Bay City*
Samuel M. Stephenson, *Menominee*

MINNESOTA

SENATORS

Cushman K. Davis, *St. Paul*
William D. Washburn, *Minneapolis*

REPRESENTATIVES

William H. Harries, *Caledonia*
John Lind, *New Ulm*
Osee M. Hall, *Red Wing*
James N. Castle, *Stillwater*
Kittel Halvorson, *North Fork*

MISSISSIPPI

SENATORS

James Z. George, *Carrollton*
Edward C. Walthall, *Grenada*

REPRESENTATIVES

John M. Allen, *Tupelo*
John C. Kyle, *Sardis*
Thomas C. Catchings, *Vicksburg*
Clarke Lewis, *Macon*
Joseph H. Beeman, *Eley*
Thomas R. Stockdale, *Summit*
Charles E. Hooker, *Jackson*

MISSOURI

SENATORS

Francis M. Cockrell, *Warrensburg*
George G. Vest, *Kansas City*

REPRESENTATIVES

William H. Hatch, *Hannibal*
Charles H. Mansur, *Chillicothe*
Alexander M. Dockery, *Gallatin*
Robert P. C. Wilson, *Platte City*
John C. Tarsney, *Kansas City*
John T. Heard, *Sedalia*
Richard H. Norton, *Troy*
John J. O'Neill, *St. Louis*
Seth W. Cobb, *St. Louis*
Samuel Byrns, *Potosi*
Richard P. Bland, *Lebanon*
David A. De Armond, *Butler*
Robert W. Fyan, *Marshfield*
Marshall Arnold, *Benton*

MONTANA

SENATORS

Thomas C. Power, *Helena*
Wilber F. Sanders, *Helena*

REPRESENTATIVE

At Large—William W. Dixon, *Butte*

NEBRASKA

SENATORS

Charles F. Manderson, *Omaha*
Algernon S. Paddock, *Beatrice*

REPRESENTATIVES

William J. Bryan, *Lincoln*
William A. McKeighan, *Red Cloud*
Omer M. Kem, *Broken Bow*

NEVADA

SENATORS

John P. Jones, *Gold Hill*
William M. Stewart, *Carson City*

REPRESENTATIVE

At Large—Horace F. Bartine, *Carson City*

NEW HAMPSHIRE

SENATORS

William E. Chandler, *Concord*
Jacob H. Gallinger, *Concord*

REPRESENTATIVES

Luther F. McKinney, *Manchester*
Warren F. Daniell, *Franklin*

NEW JERSEY

SENATORS

John R. McPherson, *Jersey City*
Rufus Blodgett, *Long Branch*

REPRESENTATIVES

Christopher A. Bergen, *Camden*
James Buchanan, *Trenton*
Jacob A. Geissenhainer, *Freehold*
Samuel Fowler, *Newton*
Cornelius A. Cadmus, *Paterson*
Thomas D. English, *Newark*
Edward F. McDonald,[24] *Harrison*

NEW YORK

SENATORS

Frank Hiscock, *Syracuse*
David B. Hill,[25] *Elmira*

REPRESENTATIVES

James W. Covert, *Long Island City*
David A. Boody,[26] *Brooklyn*
Alfred C. Chapin,[27] *Brooklyn*
William J. Coombs, *Brooklyn*
John M. Clancy, *Brooklyn*
Thomas F. Magner, *Brooklyn*
John R. Fellows, *New York City*
Edward J. Dunphy, *New York City*
Timothy J. Campbell, *New York City*
Amos J. Cummings, *New York City*
Francis B. Spinola,[28] *New York City*
W. Bourke Cockran,[29] *New York City*
J. De Witt Warner, *New York City*
Roswell P. Flower,[30] *New York City*
Joseph J. Little,[31] *New York City*
Ashbel P. Fitch, *New York City*
William G. Stahlnecker, *Yonkers*
Henry Bacon, *Goshen*
John H. Ketcham, *Dover Plains*
Isaac N. Cox, *Ellenville*
John A. Quackenbush, *Stillwater*
Charles Tracey, *Albany*
John Sanford, *Amsterdam*
John M. Wever, *Plattsburg*
Leslie W. Russell,[32] *Ogdensburg*

---

[21] Resigned March 3, 1893, before the commencement of the Fifty-third Congress, to which he had been re-elected, having been elected Senator.
[22] Died April 20, 1891, before Congress assembled.
[23] Elected to fill vacancy caused by death of Melbourne H. Ford, and took his seat December 7, 1891.
[24] Died November 5, 1892; seat remained vacant.
[25] Elected January 21, 1891, for the term beginning March 4, 1891, and took his seat January 7, 1892; governor during interim.
[26] Resigned October 13, 1891, before Congress assembled.
[27] Elected to fill vacancy caused by resignation of David A. Boody, and took his seat December 7, 1891; resigned November 16, 1892.
[28] Died April 14, 1891, before Congress assembled.
[29] Elected to fill vacancy caused by death of Francis B. Spinola, and took his seat December 7, 1891.
[30] Resigned September 16, 1891, before Congress assembled.
[31] Elected to fill vacancy caused by resignation of Roswell P. Flower, and took his seat December 7, 1891.
[32] Resigned September 11, 1891, before Congress assembled.

NEW YORK—Continued

REPRESENTATIVES—continued

Newton M. Curtis,[33] *Ogdensburg*
Henry W. Bentley, *Boonville*
George Van Horn, *Cooperstown*
James J. Belden, *Syracuse*
George W. Ray, *Norwich*
Sereno E. Payne, *Auburn*
Hosea H. Rockwell,[34] *Elmira*
John Raines, *Canandaigua*
Halbert S. Greenleaf, *Rochester*
James W. Wadsworth, *Geneseo*
Daniel N. Lockwood, *Buffalo*
Thomas L. Bunting, *Hamburg*
Warren B. Hooker, *Fredonia*

NORTH CAROLINA

SENATORS

Matt W. Ransom, *Weldon*
Zebulon B. Vance, *Charlotte*

REPRESENTATIVES

William A. B. Branch, *Washington*
Henry P. Cheatham, *Littleton*
Benjamin F. Grady, *Wallace*
Benjamin H. Bunn, *Rocky Mount*
Archibald H. A. Williams, *Oxford*
Sydenham B. Alexander, *Charlotte*
John S. Henderson, *Salisbury*
William H. H. Cowles, *Wilkesboro*
William T. Crawford, *Waynesville*

NORTH DAKOTA

SENATORS

Lyman R. Casey, *Jamestown*
Henry C. Hansbrough, *Devils Lake*

REPRESENTATIVE

At Large—Martin N. Johnson, *Petersburg*

OHIO

SENATORS

John Sherman, *Mansfield*
Calvin S. Brice, *Lima*

REPRESENTATIVES

Bellamy Storer, *Cincinnati*
John A. Caldwell, *Cincinnati*
George W. Houk, *Dayton*
Martin K. Gantz, *Troy*
Fernando C. Layton, *Wapakoneta*
Dennis D. Donovan, *Deshler*
William E. Haynes, *Fremont*
Darius D. Hare, *Upper Sandusky*
Joseph H. Outhwaite, *Columbus*

Robert E. Doan, *Wilmington*
John M. Pattison, *Milford*
William H. Enochs, *Ironton*
Irvine Dungan, *Jackson*
James W. Owens, *Newark*
Michael D. Harter, *Mansfield*
John G. Warwick,[35] *Massillon*
Lewis P. Ohliger,[36] *Wooster*
Albert J. Pearson, *Woodsfield*
Joseph D. Taylor, *Cambridge*
Ezra B. Taylor, *Warren*
Vincent A. Taylor, *Bedford*
Tom L. Johnson, *Cleveland*

OREGON

SENATORS

Joseph N. Dolph, *Portland*
John H. Mitchell, *Portland*

REPRESENTATIVE

At Large—Binger Hermann, *Roseburg*

PENNSYLVANIA

SENATORS

J. Donald Cameron, *Harrisburg*
Matthew S. Quay, *Beaver*

REPRESENTATIVES

Henry H. Bingham, *Philadelphia*
Charles O'Neill, *Philadelphia*
William McAleer, *Philadelphia*
John E. Reyburn, *Philadelphia*
Alfred C. Harmer, *Philadelphia*
John B. Robinson, *Media*
Edwin Hallowell, *Willow Grove*
William Mutchler, *Easton*
David B. Brunner, *Reading*
Marriott Brosius, *Lancaster*
Lemuel Amerman, *Scranton*
George W. Shonk,[37] *Plymouth*
James B. Reilly, *Pottsville*
John W. Rife, *Middletown*
Myron B. Wright, *Susquehanna*
Albert C. Hopkins, *Lock Haven*
Simon P. Wolverton, *Sunbury*
Louis E. Atkinson, *Mifflintown*
Frank E. Beltzhoover, *Carlisle*
Edward Scull, *Somerset*
George F. Huff, *Greensburg*
John Dalzell, *Pittsburgh*
William A. Stone, *Allegheny*
Andrew Stewart,[38] *Uniontown*
Alexander K. Craig,[39] *Pittsburgh*
William A. Sipe,[40] *Pittsburgh*
Eugene P. Gillespie, *Greenville*
Matthew Griswold, *Erie*

Charles W. Stone, *Warren*
George F. Kribbs, *Clarion*

RHODE ISLAND

SENATORS

Nelson W. Aldrich, *Providence*
Nathan F. Dixon, *Westerly*

REPRESENTATIVES

Oscar Lapham, *Providence*
Charles H. Page, *Scituate*

SOUTH CAROLINA

SENATORS

Matthew C. Butler, *Edgefield*
John L. M. Irby, *Laurens*

REPRESENTATIVES

William H. Brawley, *Charleston*
George D. Tillman, *Clarks Hill*
George Johnstone, *Newberry*
George W. Shell, *Laurens*
John J. Hemphill, *Chester*
Eli T. Stackhouse,[41] *Little Rock*
John L. McLaurin,[42] *Bennettsville*
William Elliott, *Beaufort*

SOUTH DAKOTA

SENATORS

Richard F. Pettigrew, *Sioux Falls*
James H. Kyle, *Aberdeen*

REPRESENTATIVES AT LARGE

John R. Gamble,[43] *Yankton*
John L. Jolley,[44] *Vermilion*
John A. Pickler, *Faulkton*

TENNESSEE

SENATORS

Isham G. Harris, *Memphis*
William B. Bate, *Nashville*

REPRESENTATIVES

Alfred A. Taylor, *Johnson City*
Leonidas C. Houk,[45] *Knoxville*
John C. Houk,[46] *Knoxville*
Henry C. Snodgrass, *Sparta*
Benton McMillin, *Carthage*
James D. Richardson, *Murfreesboro*
Joseph E. Washington, *Cedar Hill*
Nicholas N. Cox, *Franklin*
Benjamin A. Enloe, *Jackson*
Rice A. Pierce, *Union City*
Josiah Patterson, *Memphis*

---

[33] Elected to fill vacancy caused by resignation of Leslie W. Russell, and took his seat December 7, 1891.
[34] Election unsuccessfully contested by Henry T. Noyes.
[35] Died August 14, 1892.
[36] Elected to fill vacancy caused by death of John G. Warwick, and took his seat December 5, 1892.
[37] Election unsuccessfully contested by John B. Reynolds.

[35] Served until February 26, 1892; succeeded by Alexander K. Craig, who contested his election.
[39] Successfully contested the election of Andrew Stewart, and took his seat February 26, 1892; died July 29, 1892.
[40] Elected to fill vacancy caused by death of Alexander K. Craig, and took his seat December 5, 1892.
[41] Died June 14, 1892.

[42] Elected to fill vacancy caused by death of Eli T. Stackhouse, and took his seat December 5, 1892.
[43] Died August 14, 1891, before Congress assembled.
[44] Elected to fill vacancy caused by death of John R. Gamble, and took his seat December 7, 1891.
[45] Died May 25, 1891, before Congress assembled.
[46] Elected to fill vacancy caused by death of Leonidas C. Houk, and took his seat December 7, 1891.

TEXAS

SENATORS

Richard Coke, *Waco*
John H. Reagan,[47] *Palestine*
Horace Chilton,[48] *Tyler*
Roger Q. Mills,[49] *Corsicana*

REPRESENTATIVES

Charles Stewart, *Houston*
John B. Long, *Rusk*
Constantine B. Kilgore, *Wills Point*
David B. Culberson, *Jefferson*
Joseph W. Bailey, *Gainesville*
Jo Abbott, *Hillsboro*
William H. Crain, *Cuero*
Littleton W. Moore, *La Grange*
Roger Q. Mills,[50] *Corsicana*
Edwin Le Roy Antony,[51] *Cameron*
Joseph D. Sayers, *Bastrop*
Samuel W. T. Lanham, *Weatherford*

VERMONT

SENATORS

George F. Edmunds,[52] *Burlington*
Redfield Proctor,[53] *Proctor*
Justin S. Morrill, *Strafford*

REPRESENTATIVES

H. Henry Powers, *Morrisville*
William W. Grout, *Barton*

VIRGINIA

SENATORS

John W. Daniel, *Lynchburg*
John S. Barbour,[54] *Alexandria*
Eppa Hunton,[55] *Warrenton*

REPRESENTATIVES

William A. Jones, *Warsaw*
John W. Lawson, *Isle of Wight*
George D. Wise, *Richmond*
James F. Epes, *Blackstone*
Posey G. Lester, *Floyd*
Paul C. Edmunds, *Halifax*
Charles T. O'Ferrall, *Harrisonburg*
William H. F. Lee,[56] *Burkes Station*
Elisha E. Meredith,[57] *Brentsville*
John A. Buchanan, *Abingdon*
Henry St. George Tucker, *Staunton*

WASHINGTON

SENATORS

John B. Allen, *Walla Walla*
Watson C. Squire, *Seattle*

REPRESENTATIVE

At Large—John L. Wilson, *Spokane*

WEST VIRGINIA

SENATORS

John E. Kenna,[58] *Charleston*
Johnson N. Camden,[59] *Parkersburg*
Charles J. Faulkner, *Martinsburg*

REPRESENTATIVES

John O. Pendleton, *Wheeling*
William L. Wilson, *Charles Town*
John D. Alderson, *Nicholas*
James Capehart, *Point Pleasant*

WISCONSIN

SENATORS

Philetus Sawyer, *Oshkosh*
William F. Vilas, *Madison*

REPRESENTATIVES

Clinton Babbitt, *Beloit*
Charles Barwig, *Mayville*
Allen R. Bushnell, *Madison*
John L. Mitchell,[60] *Milwaukee*
George H. Brickner, *Sheboygan Falls*
Lucas M. Miller, *Oshkosh*
Frank P. Coburn, *West Salem*
Nils P. Haugen, *River Falls*
Thomas Lynch, *Antigo*

WYOMING

SENATORS

Joseph M. Carey, *Cheyenne*
Francis E. Warren, *Cheyenne*

REPRESENTATIVE

At Large—Clarence D. Clark, *Evanston*

TERRITORY OF ARIZONA

DELEGATE

Marcus A. Smith, *Tombstone*

TERRITORY OF NEW MEXICO

DELEGATE

Antonio Joseph, *Ojo Caliente*

TERRITORY OF OKLAHOMA

DELEGATE

David A. Harvey, *Oklahoma City*

TERRITORY OF UTAH

DELEGATE

John T. Caine, *Salt Lake City*

---

[47] Resigned June 10, 1891.
[48] Appointed to fill vacancy caused by resignation of John H. Reagan, and took his seat December 7, 1891.
[49] Elected to fill vacancy caused by resignation of John H. Reagan, and took his seat March 30, 1892.
[50] Resigned March 28, 1892, having been elected Senator.
[51] Elected to fill vacancy caused by resignation of Roger Q. Mills, and took his seat July 28, 1892.

[52] Resigned, effective November 1, 1891.
[53] Appointed to fill vacancy caused by resignation of George F. Edmunds, and took his seat December 7, 1891; subsequently elected.
[54] Died May 14, 1892.
[55] Appointed to fill vacancy caused by death of John S. Barbour, and took his seat June 1, 1892; subsequently elected.
[56] Died October 15, 1891, before Congress assembled.

[57] Elected to fill vacancy caused by death of William H. F. Lee, and took his seat December 23, 1891.
[58] Died January 11, 1893.
[59] Elected to fill vacancy caused by death of John E. Kenna, and took his seat January 28, 1893.
[60] Resigned March 3, 1893, before the commencement of the Fifty-third Congress, to which he had been reelected, having been elected Senator.

FIFTY-THIRD CONGRESS

MARCH 4, 1893, TO MARCH 3, 1895

FIRST SESSION—*August 7, 1893, to November 3, 1893*
SECOND SESSION—*December 4, 1893, to August 28, 1894*
THIRD SESSION—*December 3, 1894, to March 3, 1895*
SPECIAL SESSION OF THE SENATE—*March 4, 1893, to April 15, 1893*

———

VICE PRESIDENT OF THE UNITED STATES—ADLAI E. STEVENSON, of Illinois
PRESIDENT PRO TEMPORE OF THE SENATE—CHARLES F. MANDERSON,[1] of Nebraska; ISHAM G. HARRIS,[2] of Tennessee; MATT W. RANSOM,[3] of North Carolina
SECRETARY OF THE SENATE—ANSON G. McCOOK, of New York; WILLIAM R. COX,[4] of North Carolina
SERGEANT AT ARMS OF THE SENATE—EDWARD K. VALENTINE, of Nebraska; RICHARD J. BRIGHT,[5] of Indiana

———

SPEAKER OF THE HOUSE OF REPRESENTATIVES—CHARLES F. CRISP,[6] of Georgia
CLERK OF THE HOUSE—JAMES KERR,[7] of Pennsylvania
SERGEANT AT ARMS OF THE HOUSE—SAMUEL S. YODER, of Ohio; HERMAN W. SNOW,[8] of Illinois
DOORKEEPER OF THE HOUSE—A. B. HURD, of Mississippi
POSTMASTER OF THE HOUSE—LYCURGUS DALTON

ALABAMA

SENATORS

John T. Morgan, *Selma*
James L. Pugh, *Eufaula*

REPRESENTATIVES

Richard H. Clarke, *Mobile*
Jesse F. Stallings, *Greenville*
William C. Oates,[9] *Abbeville*
George P. Harrison,[10] *Opelika*
Gaston A. Robbins, *Selma*
James E. Cobb,[11] *Tuskegee*
John H. Bankhead, *Fayette*
William H. Denson, *Gadsden*
Joseph Wheeler, *Wheeler*
Louis W. Turpin, *Newbern*

ARKANSAS

SENATORS

James K. Jones, *Washington*
James H. Berry, *Bentonville*

REPRESENTATIVES

Philip D. McCulloch, Jr., *Marianna*
Clifton R. Breckinridge,[12] *Pine Bluff*
John S. Little,[13] *Greenwood*
Thomas C. McRae, *Prescott*
William L. Terry, *Little Rock*
Hugh A. Dinsmore, *Fayetteville*
Robert Neill, *Batesville*

CALIFORNIA

SENATORS

Leland Stanford,[14] *San Francisco*
George C. Perkins,[15] *Oakland*
Stephen M. White, *Los Angeles*

REPRESENTATIVES

Thomas J. Geary, *Santa Rosa*
Anthony Caminetti, *Jackson*
Samuel G. Hilborn,[16] *Oakland*
Warren B. English,[17] *Oakland*
James G. Maguire, *San Francisco*
Eugene F. Loud, *San Francisco*
Marion Cannon, *Ventura*
William W. Bowers, *San Diego*

COLORADO

SENATORS

Henry M. Teller, *Central City*
Edward O. Wolcott, *Denver*

REPRESENTATIVES

Lafayette Pence, *Denver*
John C. Bell, *Montrose*

CONNECTICUT

SENATORS

Orville H. Platt, *Meriden*
Joseph R. Hawley, *Hartford*

---

[1] Resigned as President pro tempore March 22, 1893.
[2] Elected March 22, 1893 (special session of the Senate), and January 10, 1895.
[3] Elected January 7, 1895; resigned as President pro tempore January 10, 1895.
[4] Elected April 6, 1893.
[5] Elected August 8, 1893.
[6] Reelected August 7, 1893.
[7] Reelected August 7, 1893.
[8] Elected August 7, 1893.

[9] Resigned, effective November 5, 1894.
[10] Elected to fill vacancy caused by resignation of William C. Oates, and took his seat December 3, 1894.
[11] Election unsuccessfully contested by W. W. Whatley.
[12] Resigned August 14, 1894.
[13] Elected to fill vacancy caused by resignation of Clifton R. Breckinridge, and took his seat December 3, 1894.

[14] Died June 21, 1893.
[15] Appointed to fill vacancy caused by death of Leland Stanford, and took his seat August 8, 1893; subsequently elected.
[16] Served until April 4, 1894; succeeded by Warren B. English, who contested his election.
[17] Successfully contested the election of Samuel G. Hilborn, and took his seat April 4, 1894.

REPRESENTATIVES

Lewis Sperry, *Hartford*
James P. Pigott, *New Haven*
Charles A. Russell, *Killingly*
Robert E. DeForest, *Bridgeport*

DELAWARE

SENATORS

George Gray, *New Castle*
Anthony Higgins, *Wilmington*

REPRESENTATIVE

At Large—John W. Causey, *Milford*

FLORIDA

SENATORS

Wilkinson Call, *Jacksonville*
Samuel Pasco,[18] *Monticello*

REPRESENTATIVES

Stephen R. Mallory, *Pensacola*
Charles M. Cooper, *Jacksonville*

GEORGIA

SENATORS

Alfred H. Colquitt,[19] *Atlanta*
Patrick Walsh,[20] *Augusta*
John B. Gordon, *Atlanta*

REPRESENTATIVES

Rufus E. Lester, *Savannah*
Benjamin E. Russell, *Bainbridge*
Charles F. Crisp, *Americus*
Charles L. Moses, *Turin*
Leonidas F. Livingston, *Kings*
Thomas B. Cabaniss, *Forsyth*
John W. Maddox, *Rome*
Thomas G. Lawson, *Eatonton*
Farish C. Tate, *Jasper*
James C. C. Black,[21] *Augusta*
Henry G. Turner, *Quitman*

IDAHO

SENATORS

George L. Shoup, *Salmon City*
Fred T. Dubois, *Blackfoot*

REPRESENTATIVE

At Large—Willis Sweet, *Moscow*

ILLINOIS

SENATORS

Shelby M. Cullom, *Springfield*
John McAuley Palmer, *Springfield*

REPRESENTATIVES

J. Frank Aldrich, *Chicago*
Lawrence E. McGann, *Chicago*
Allan C. Durborow, Jr., *Chicago*
Julius Goldzier, *Chicago*
Albert J. Hopkins, *Aurora*
Robert R. Hitt, *Mount Morris*
Thomas J. Henderson, *Princeton*
Robert A. Childs, *Hinsdale*
Hamilton K. Wheeler, *Kankakee*
Philip S. Post,[22] *Galesburg*
Benjamin F. Marsh, *Warsaw*
John J. McDannold, *Mount Sterling*
William M. Springer, *Springfield*
Benjamin F. Funk, *Bloomington*
Joseph G. Cannon, *Danville*
George W. Fithian, *Newton*
Edward Lane, *Hillsboro*
William S. Forman, *Nashville*
James R. Williams, *Carmi*
George W. Smith, *Murphysboro*
At Large—
   John C. Black,[23] *Chicago*
   Andrew J. Hunter, *Paris*

INDIANA

SENATORS

Daniel W. Voorhees, *Terre Haute*
David Turpie, *Indianapolis*

REPRESENTATIVES

Arthur H. Taylor, *Petersburg*
John L. Bretz, *Jasper*
Jason B. Brown, *Seymour*
William S. Holman, *Aurora*
George W. Cooper, *Columbus*
Henry U. Johnson, *Richmond*
William D. Bynum, *Indianapolis*
Elijah V. Brookshire, *Crawfordsville*
Daniel W. Waugh, *Tipton*
Thomas Hammond, *Hammond*
Augustus N. Martin, *Bluffton*
William F. McNagny, *Columbia City*
Charles G. Conn, *Elkhart*

IOWA

SENATORS

William B. Allison, *Dubuque*
James F. Wilson, *Fairfield*

REPRESENTATIVES

John H. Gear, *Burlington*
Walter I. Hayes, *Clinton*
David B. Henderson, *Dubuque*
Thomas Updegraff, *McGregor*
Robert G. Cousins, *Tipton*
John F. Lacey, *Oskaloosa*
John A. T. Hull, *Des Moines*

William P. Hepburn, *Clarinda*
Alva L. Hager, *Greenfield*
Jonathan P. Dolliver, *Fort Dodge*
George D. Perkins, *Sioux City*

KANSAS

SENATORS

William A. Peffer, *Topeka*
John Martin,[24] *Topeka*

REPRESENTATIVES

Case Broderick, *Holton*
Edward H. Funston,[25] *Iola*
Horace L. Moore,[26] *Lawrence*
Thomas J. Hudson, *Fredonia*
Charles Curtis, *Topeka*
John Davis, *Junction City*
William Baker, *Lincoln*
Jeremiah Simpson, *Medicine Lodge*
At Large—William A. Harris, *Linwood*

KENTUCKY

SENATORS

Joseph C. S. Blackburn, *Versailles*
William Lindsay, *Frankfort*

REPRESENTATIVES

William J. Stone, *Kuttawa*
William T. Ellis, *Owensboro*
Isaac H. Goodnight, *Franklin*
Alexander B. Montgomery, *Elizabethtown*
Asher G. Caruth, *Louisville*
Albert S. Berry, *Newport*
William C. P. Breckinridge, *Lexington*
James B. McCreary, *Richmond*
Thomas H. Paynter,[27] *Greenup*
Marcus C. Lisle,[28] *Winchester*
William M. Beckner,[29] *Winchester*
Silas Adams, *Liberty*

LOUISIANA

SENATORS

Edward D. White,[30] *New Orleans*
Newton C. Blanchard,[31] *Shreveport*
Donelson Caffery, *Franklin*

REPRESENTATIVES

Adolph Meyer, *New Orleans*
Robert C. Davey, *New Orleans*
Andrew Price, *Thibodaux*
Newton C. Blanchard,[32] *Shreveport*
Henry W. Ogden,[33] *Benton*
Charles J. Boatner, *Monroe*
Samuel M. Robertson, *Baton Rouge*

---

[18] Reappointed to fill vacancy in the term beginning March 4, 1893, and subsequently reelected.
[19] Died March 26, 1894.
[20] Appointed to fill vacancy caused by death of Alfred H. Colquitt, and took his seat April 9, 1894; subsequently elected.
[21] Election unsuccessfully contested by Thomas E. Watson.
[22] Died January 6, 1895, before the commencement of the Fifty-fourth Congress, to which he had been reelected.
[23] Resigned January 12, 1895.

[24] Elected to fill vacancy caused by death of Preston B. Plumb in preceding Congress, and took his seat March 4, 1893; election unsuccessfully contested by Joseph W. Ady.
[25] Served until August 2, 1894; succeeded by Horace L. Moore, who contested his election.
[26] Successfully contested the election of Edward H. Funston, and took his seat August 2, 1894.
[27] Resigned, effective January 5, 1895.
[28] Died July 7, 1894.
[29] Elected to fill vacancy caused by death of Marcus C. Lisle, and took his seat December 3, 1894.

[30] Resigned, effective March 12, 1894, having been appointed Associate Justice of the United States Supreme Court.
[31] Appointed to fill vacancy caused by resignation of Edward D. White, and took his seat March 12, 1894; subsequently elected.
[32] Resigned, effective March 12, 1894, having been elected Senator.
[33] Elected to fill vacancy caused by resignation of Newton C. Blanchard, and took his seat May 12, 1894.

MAINE

SENATORS

Eugene Hale, *Ellsworth*
William P. Frye, *Lewiston*

REPRESENTATIVES

Thomas B. Reed, *Portland*
Nelson Dingley, Jr., *Lewiston*
Seth L. Milliken, *Belfast*
Charles A. Boutelle, *Bangor*

MARYLAND

SENATORS

Arthur Pue Gorman, *Laurel*
Charles H. Gibson, *Easton*

REPRESENTATIVES

Robert F. Bratton,[34] *Princess Anne*
W. Laird Henry,[35] *Cambridge*
J. Fred. C. Talbott, *Towson*
Harry W. Rusk, *Baltimore*
Isidor Rayner, *Baltimore*
Barnes Compton,[36] *Laurel*
Charles E. Coffin,[37] *Muirkirk*
William M. McKaig, *Cumberland*

MASSACHUSETTS

SENATORS

George F. Hoar, *Worcester*
Henry Cabot Lodge, *Nahant*

REPRESENTATIVES

Ashley B. Wright, *North Adams*
Frederick H. Gillett, *Springfield*
Joseph H. Walker, *Worcester*
Lewis D. Apsley, *Hudson*
Moses T. Stevens, *North Andover*
William Cogswell, *Salem*
William Everett,[38] *Quincy*
Samuel W. McCall, *Winchester*
Joseph H. O'Neil, *Boston*
Michael J. McEttrick, *Boston*
William F. Draper, *Hopedale*
Elijah A. Morse, *Canton*
Charles S. Randall, *New Bedford*

MICHIGAN

SENATORS

Francis B. Stockbridge,[39] *Kalamazoo*
John Patton, Jr.,[40] *Grand Rapids*
Julius C. Burrows,[41] *Kalamazoo*
James McMillan, *Detroit*

REPRESENTATIVES

J. Logan Chipman,[42] *Detroit*
Levi T. Griffin,[43] *Detroit*
James S. Gorman, *Chelsea*
Julius C. Burrows,[44] *Kalamazoo*
Henry F. Thomas, *Allegan*
George F. Richardson,[45] *Grand Rapids*
David D. Aitken, *Flint*
Justin R. Whiting, *St. Clair*
William S. Linton, *Saginaw*
John W. Moon, *Muskegon*
Thomas A. E. Weadock, *Bay City*
John Avery, *Greenville*
Samuel M. Stephenson, *Menominee*

MINNESOTA

SENATORS

Cushman K. Davis, *St. Paul*
William D. Washburn, *Minneapolis*

REPRESENTATIVES

James A. Tawney, *Winona*
James T. McCleary, *Mankato*
Osee M. Hall, *Red Wing*
Andrew R. Kiefer, *St. Paul*
Loren Fletcher, *Minneapolis*
Melvin R. Baldwin, *Duluth*
Haldor E. Boen, *Fergus Falls*

MISSISSIPPI

SENATORS

James Z. George, *Carrollton*
Edward C. Walthall,[46] *Grenada*
Anselm J. McLaurin,[47] *Brandon*

REPRESENTATIVES

John M. Allen, *Tupelo*
John C. Kyle, *Sardis*
Thomas C. Catchings, *Vicksburg*
Hernando D. Money, *Carrollton*
John Sharp Williams, *Yazoo City*
Thomas R. Stockdale, *Summit*
Charles E. Hooker, *Jackson*

MISSOURI

SENATORS

Francis M. Cockrell, *Warrensburg*
George G. Vest, *Kansas City*

REPRESENTATIVES

William H. Hatch, *Hannibal*
Uriel S. Hall, *Hubbard*
Alexander M. Dockery, *Gallatin*
Daniel D. Burnes, *St. Joseph*
John C. Tarsney, *Kansas City*
David A. De Armond, *Butler*
John T. Heard, *Sedalia*
Richard P. Bland, *Lebanon*
James Beauchamp Clark, *Bowling Green*
Richard Bartholdt, *St. Louis*
Charles F. Joy,[48] *St. Louis*
John J. O'Neill,[49] *St. Louis*
Seth W. Cobb, *St. Louis*
Robert W. Fyan, *Marshfield*
Marshall Arnold, *Benton*
Charles H. Morgan, *Lamar*

MONTANA

SENATORS

Thomas C. Power, *Helena*
Lee Mantle,[50] *Butte*

REPRESENTATIVE

At Large—Charles S. Hartman, *Bozeman*

NEBRASKA

SENATORS

Charles F. Manderson, *Omaha*
William V. Allen, *Madison*

REPRESENTATIVES

William J. Bryan, *Lincoln*
David H. Mercer, *Omaha*
George D. Meiklejohn, *Fullerton*
Eugene J. Hainer, *Aurora*
William A. McKeighan, *Red Cloud*
Omer M. Kem, *Broken Bow*

NEVADA

SENATORS

John P. Jones, *Gold Hill*
William M. Stewart, *Carson City*

REPRESENTATIVE

At Large—Francis G. Newlands, *Reno*

NEW HAMPSHIRE

SENATORS

William E. Chandler, *Concord*
Jacob H. Gallinger, *Concord*

REPRESENTATIVES

Henry W. Blair, *Manchester*
Henry M. Baker, *Bow*

---

[34] Died May 10, 1894.
[35] Elected to fill vacancy caused by death of Robert F. Bratton, and took his seat December 3, 1894.
[36] Resigned, effective May 15, 1894.
[37] Elected to fill vacancy caused by resignation of Barnes Compton, and took his seat December 3, 1894.
[38] Elected to fill vacancy caused by resignation of Representative-elect Henry Cabot Lodge, in preceding Congress, and took his seat August 7, 1893
[39] Died April 30, 1894.
[40] Appointed to fill vacancy caused by death of Francis B. Stockbridge, and took his seat May 10, 1894.
[41] Elected to fill vacancy caused by death of Francis B. Stockbridge, and took his seat January 23, 1895.

[42] Died August 17, 1893.
[43] Elected to fill vacancy caused by death of J. Logan Chipman, and took his seat December 4, 1893.
[44] Resigned January 23, 1895, before the commencement of the Fifty-fourth Congress, to which he had been reelected, having been elected Senator.
[45] Credentials presented December 22, 1892; credentials of Charles E. Belknap, issued by new officials, filed February 20, 1893; resolutions that Mr. Richardson be sworn adopted August 8, 1893, and he took his seat; September 9, 1893, Belknap was granted right to contest; Committee on Elections reported in favor of Richardson February 27, 1895; minority report filed for Belknap; no action by House.
[46] Resigned January 24, 1894.

[47] Elected to fill vacancy caused by resignation of Edward C. Walthall, and took his seat February 15, 1894.
[48] Served until April 3, 1894; succeeded by John J. O'Neill, who contested his election.
[49] Successfully contested the election of Charles F. Joy, and took his seat April 3, 1894.
[50] Appointed to fill vacancy in the term beginning March 4, 1893, caused by failure of legislature to elect; credentials presented March 9, 1893; on August 28, 1893, the Senate decided he was not entitled to a seat; subsequently elected and took his seat February 2, 1895; State unrepresented in this class from March 4, 1893, to January 15, 1895.

NEW JERSEY

SENATORS

John R. McPherson, *Jersey City*
James Smith, Jr., *Newark*

REPRESENTATIVES

Henry C. Loudenslager, *Paulsboro*
John J. Gardner, *Atlantic City*
Jacob A. Geissenhainer, *Freehold*
Johnston Cornish, *Washington*
Cornelius A. Cadmus, *Paterson*
Thomas D. English, *Newark*
George B. Fielder, *Jersey City*
John T. Dunn, *Elizabeth*

NEW YORK

SENATORS

David B. Hill, *Albany*
Edward Murphy, Jr., *Troy*

REPRESENTATIVES

James W. Covert, *Long Island City*
John M. Clancy, *Brooklyn*
Joseph C. Hendrix, *Brooklyn*
William J. Coombs, *Brooklyn*
John H. Graham, *Brooklyn*
Thomas F. Magner, *Brooklyn*
Franklin Bartlett, *New York City*
Edward J. Dunphy, *New York City*
Timothy J. Campbell, *New York City*
Daniel E. Sickles, *New York City*
Amos J. Cummings,[51] *New York City*
W. Bourke Cockran, *New York City*
J. De Witt Warner, *New York City*
John R. Fellows,[52] *New York City*
Lemuel E. Quigg,[53] *New York City*
Ashbel P. Fitch,[54] *New York City*
Isidor Straus,[55] *New York City*
William Ryan, *Port Chester*
Francis Marvin, *Port Jervis*
Jacob Le Fever, *New Paltz*
Charles D. Haines, *Kinderhook*
Charles Tracey, *Albany*
Simon J. Schermerhorn, *Schenectady*
Newton M. Curtis, *Ogdensburg*
John M. Wever, *Plattsburg*
Charles A. Chickering, *Copenhagen*
James S. Sherman, *Utica*
George W. Ray, *Norwich*
James J. Belden, *Syracuse*
Sereno E. Payne, *Auburn*
Charles W. Gillet, *Addison*
James W. Wadsworth, *Geneseo*
John Van Voorhis, *Rochester*
Daniel N. Lockwood, *Buffalo*
Charles Daniels, *Buffalo*
Warren B. Hooker, *Fredonia*

NORTH CAROLINA

SENATORS

Matt W. Ransom, *Weldon*
Zebulon B. Vance,[56] *Charlotte*
Thomas J. Jarvis,[57] *Greenville*
Jeter C. Pritchard,[58] *Marshall*

REPRESENTATIVES

William A. B. Branch, *Washington*
Frederick A. Woodard, *Wilson*
Benjamin F. Grady, *Wallace*
Benjamin H. Bunn, *Rocky Mount*
Thomas Settle, *Reidsville*
Sydenham B. Alexander, *Charlotte*
John S. Henderson, *Salisbury*
William H. Bower, *Lenoir*
William T. Crawford, *Waynesville*

NORTH DAKOTA

SENATORS

Henry C. Hansbrough, *Devils Lake*
William N. Roach, *Larimore*

REPRESENTATIVE

At Large—Martin N. Johnson, *Petersburg*

OHIO

SENATORS

John Sherman, *Mansfield*
Calvin S. Brice, *Lima*

REPRESENTATIVES

Bellamy Storer, *Cincinnati*
Jacob A. Caldwell,[59] *Cincinnati*
Jacob H. Bromwell,[60] *Cincinnati*
George W. Houk,[61] *Dayton*
Paul J. Sorg,[62] *Middletown*
Fernando C. Layton, *Wapakoneta*
Dennis D. Donovan, *Deshler*
George W. Hulick, *Batavia*
George W. Wilson, *London*
Luther M. Strong, *Kenton*
Byron F. Ritchie, *Toledo*
William H. Enochs,[63] *Ironton*
Hezekiah S. Bundy,[64] *Wellston*
Charles H. Grosvenor, *Athens*
Joseph H. Outhwaite, *Columbus*
Darius D. Hare, *Upper Sandusky*
Michael D. Harter, *Mansfield*
Henry C. Van Voorhis, *Zanesville*
Albert J. Pearson, *Woodsfield*
James A. D. Richards, *New Philadelphia*
George P. Ikirt, *East Liverpool*
Stephen A. Northway, *Jefferson*
William J. White, *Cleveland*
Tom L. Johnson, *Cleveland*

OREGON

SENATORS

Joseph N. Dolph, *Portland*
John H. Mitchell, *Portland*

REPRESENTATIVES

Binger Hermann, *Roseburg*
William R. Ellis, *Heppner*

PENNSYLVANIA

SENATORS

J. Donald Cameron, *Harrisburg*
Matthew S. Quay, *Beaver*

REPRESENTATIVES

Henry H. Bingham, *Philadelphia*
Charles O'Neill,[65] *Philadelphia*
Robert Adams, Jr.,[66] *Philadelphia*
William McAleer, *Philadelphia*
John E. Reyburn, *Philadelphia*
Alfred C. Harmer, *Philadelphia*
John B. Robinson, *Media*
Irving P. Wanger, *Norristown*
William Mutchler,[67] *Easton*
Howard Mutchler,[68] *Easton*
Constantine J. Erdman, *Allentown*
Marriott Brosius, *Lancaster*
Joseph A. Scranton, *Scranton*
William H. Hines, *Wilkes-Barre*
James B. Reilly, *Pottsville*
Ephraim M. Woomer, *Lebanon*
Myron B. Wright,[69] *Susquehanna*
Edwin J. Jorden,[70] *Coudersport*
Albert C. Hopkins, *Lock Haven*
Simon P. Wolverton, *Sunbury*
Thaddeus M. Mahon, *Chambersburg*
Frank E. Beltzhoover, *Carlisle*
Josiah D. Hicks, *Altoona*
Daniel B. Heiner, *Kittanning*
John Dalzell, *Pittsburgh*
William A. Stone, *Allegheny*
William A. Sipe, *Pittsburgh*
Thomas W. Phillips, *New Castle*
Joseph C. Sibley, *Franklin*
Charles W. Stone, *Warren*
George F. Kribbs, *Clarion*
At Large—
Alexander McDowell, *Sharon*
William Lilly,[71] *Mauch Chunk*
Galusha A. Grow,[72] *Glenwood*

---

[51] Resigned November 21, 1894.
[52] Resigned effective December 31, 1893.
[53] Elected to fill vacancy caused by resignation of John R. Fellows, and took his seat February 14, 1894.
[54] Resigned December 26, 1893.
[55] Elected to fill vacancy caused by resignation of Ashbel P. Fitch, and took his seat February 14, 1894.
[56] Died April 14, 1894.
[57] Appointed to fill vacancy caused by death of Zebulon B. Vance, and took his seat April 26, 1894.
[58] Elected to fill vacancy caused by death of Zebulon B. Vance, and took his seat January 24, 1895.

[59] Resigned effective May 4, 1894.
[60] Elected to fill vacancy caused by resignation of John A. Caldwell, and took his seat December 3, 1894.
[61] Died February 9, 1894.
[62] Elected to fill vacancy caused by death of George W. Houk, and took his seat May 21, 1894.
[63] Died July 13, 1893, before Congress assembled.
[64] Elected to fill vacancy caused by death of William H. Enochs, and took his seat December 4, 1893.
[65] Died November 25, 1893.
[66] Elected to fill vacancy caused by death of Charles O'Neill, and took his seat January 3, 1894.

[67] Died June 23, 1893, before Congress assembled.
[68] Elected to fill vacancy caused by death of William Mutchler, and took his seat August 7, 1893.
[69] Died November 13, 1894, before the commencement of the Fifty-fourth Congress, to which he had been reelected.
[70] Elected to fill vacancy caused by death of Myron B. Wright, and took his seat February 23, 1895.
[71] Died December 1, 1893.
[72] Elected to fill vacancy caused by death of William Lilly, and took his seat March 2, 1894.

RHODE ISLAND

SENATORS

Nelson W. Aldrich, *Providence*
Nathan F. Dixon, *Westerly*

REPRESENTATIVES

Oscar Lapham, *Providence*
Charles H. Page,[73] *Providence*

SOUTH CAROLINA

SENATORS

Matthew C. Butler, *Edgefield*
John L. M. Irby, *Laurens*

REPRESENTATIVES

William H. Brawley,[74] *Charleston*
James F. Izlar,[75] *Orangeburg*
W. Jasper Talbert, *Parksville*
Asbury C. Latimer, *Belton*
George W. Shell, *Laurens*
Thomas J. Strait, *Lancaster*
John L. McLaurin, *Bennettsville*
George W. Murray, *Sumter*

SOUTH DAKOTA

SENATORS

Richard F. Pettigrew, *Sioux Falls*
James H. Kyle, *Aberdeen*

REPRESENTATIVES AT LARGE

John A. Pickler, *Faulkton*
William V. Lucas, *Hot Springs*

TENNESSEE

SENATORS

Isham G. Harris, *Memphis*
William B. Bate, *Nashville*

REPRESENTATIVES

Alfred A. Taylor, *Johnson City*
John C. Houk, *Knoxville*
Henry C. Snodgrass, *Sparta*
Benton McMillin, *Carthage*
James D. Richardson, *Murfreesboro*
Joseph E. Washington, *Cedar Hill*
Nicholas N. Cox, *Franklin*
Benjamin A. Enloe,[76] *Jackson*
James C. McDearmon, *Trenton*
Josiah Patterson, *Memphis*

TEXAS

SENATORS

Richard Coke, *Waco*
Roger Q. Mills, *Corsicana*

REPRESENTATIVES

Joseph C. Hutcheson, *Houston*
Samuel B. Cooper, *Woodville*
Constantine, B. Kilgore, *Wills Point*
David B. Culberson, *Jefferson*
Joseph W. Bailey, *Gainesville*
Jo Abbott, *Hillsboro*
George C. Pendleton, *Belton*
Charles K. Bell, *Fort Worth*
Joseph D. Sayers, *Bastrop*
Walter Gresham, *Galveston*
William H. Crain, *Cuero*
Thomas M. Paschal, *Castroville*
Jeremiah V. Cockrell, *Anson*

VERMONT

SENATORS

Justin S. Morrill, *Strafford*
Redfield Proctor, *Proctor*

REPRESENTATIVES

H. Henry Powers, *Morrisville*
William W. Grout, *Barton*

VIRGINIA

SENATORS

John W. Daniel, *Lynchburg*
Eppa Hunton, *Warrenton*

REPRESENTATIVES

William A. Jones, *Warsaw*
D. Gardiner Tyler, *Sturgeon Point*
George D. Wise, *Richmond*
James F. Epes, *Blackstone*
Claude A. Swanson, *Chatham*
Paul C. Edmunds, *Halifax*
Charles T. O'Ferrall,[77] *Harrisonburg*
Smith S. Turner,[78] *Front Royal*
Elisha E. Meredith, *Brentsville*
James W. Marshall, *New Castle*
Henry St. George Tucker, *Staunton*

WASHINGTON

SENATORS

Watson C. Squire, *Seattle*
John L. Wilson,[79] *Spokane*

REPRESENTATIVES AT LARGE

John L. Wilson,[80] *Spokane*
William H. Doolittle, *Tacoma*

WEST VIRGINIA

SENATORS

Charles J. Faulkner, *Martinsburg*
Johnson N. Camden, *Parkersburg*

REPRESENTATIVES

John O. Pendleton, *Wheeling*
William L. Wilson, *Charles Town*
John D. Alderson, *Nicholas*
James Capehart, *Point Pleasant*

WISCONSIN

SENATORS

William F. Vilas, *Madison*
John L. Mitchell, *Milwaukee*

REPRESENTATIVES

Henry Allen Cooper, *Racine*
Charles Barwig, *Mayville*
Joseph W. Babcock, *Necedah*
Peter J. Somers,[81] *Milwaukee*
George H. Brickner, *Sheboygan Falls*
Owen A. Wells, *Fond du Lac*
George B. Shaw,[82] *Eau Claire*
Michael Griffin,[83] *Eau Claire*
Lyman E. Barnes, *Appleton*
Thomas Lynch, *Antigo*
Nils P. Haugen, *River Falls*

WYOMING

SENATORS

Joseph M. Carey, *Cheyenne*
Clarence D. Clark,[84] *Evanston*

REPRESENTATIVE

At Large—Henry A. Coffeen, *Big Horn*

TERRITORY OF ARIZONA

DELEGATE

Marcus A. Smith, *Tombstone*

TERRITORY OF NEW MEXICO

DELEGATE

Antonio Joseph, *Ojo Caliente*

TERRITORY OF OKLAHOMA

DELEGATE

Dennis T. Flynn, *Guthrie*

TERRITORY OF UTAH

DELEGATE

Joseph L. Rawlins, *Salt Lake City*

---

[73] Elected April 5, 1893, and took his seat August 7, 1893.
[74] Resigned February 12, 1894.
[75] Elected to fill vacancy caused by resignation of William H. Brawley, and took his seat April 15, 1894.
[76] Election unsuccessfully contested by P. H. Thrasher.
[77] Resigned December 28, 1893, having been elected governor.
[78] Elected to fill vacancy caused by resignation of Charles T. O'Ferrall, and took his seat February 12, 1894.
[79] Elected to fill vacancy in the term commencing March 4, 1893, and took his seat February 19, 1895.

John B. Allen was appointed to fill such vacancy, the legislature having adjourned without electing his successor; credentials presented March 20, 1893 (special session of the Senate), but he was not permitted to qualify; on August 28, 1893, the Senate decided he was not entitled to the seat. Vacancy in this class from March 4, 1893, to January 31, 1895.
[80] Resigned, effective February 18, 1895, having been elected Senator.
[81] Elected to fill vacancy caused by resignation of Representative-elect John L. Mitchell, in preceding Congress, and took his seat August 27, 1893.

[82] Died August 27, 1894.
[83] Elected to fill vacancy caused by death of George B. Shaw, and took his seat December 3, 1894.
[84] Elected to fill vacancy in the term beginning March 4, 1893, caused by failure of legislature to elect, and took his seat February 6, 1895. Asahel C. Beckwith presented credentials as a Senator-designate March 15, 1893 (special session of the Senate), but was not sworn pending investigation of his right to the seat; resigned July 11, 1893, before final action by Senate; vacancy in this class from March 4, 1893, to January 22, 1895.

FIFTY-FOURTH CONGRESS

MARCH 4, 1895, TO MARCH 3, 1897

FIRST SESSION—*December 2, 1895, to June 11, 1896*

SECOND SESSION—*December 7, 1896, to March 3, 1897*

VICE PRESIDENT OF THE UNITED STATES—Adlai E. Stevenson, of Illinois

PRESIDENT PRO TEMPORE OF THE SENATE—William P. Frye,[1] of Maine

SECRETARY OF THE SENATE—William R. Cox, of North Carolina

SERGEANT AT ARMS OF THE SENATE—Richard J. Bright, of Indiana

SPEAKER OF THE HOUSE OF REPRESENTATIVES—Thomas B. Reed,[2] of Maine

CLERK OF THE HOUSE—James Kerr, of Pennsylvania; Alexander McDowell,[3] of Pennsylvania

SERGEANT AT ARMS OF THE HOUSE—Herman W. Snow, of Illinois; Benjamin F. Russell,[4] of Missouri

DOORKEEPER OF THE HOUSE—William J. Glenn, of New York

POSTMASTER OF THE HOUSE—J. C. McElroy

ALABAMA

SENATORS

John T. Morgan, *Selma*
James L. Pugh, *Eufaula*

REPRESENTATIVES

Richard H. Clarke, *Mobile*
Jesse F. Stallings, *Greenville*
George P. Harrison,[5] *Opelika*
Gaston A. Robbins,[6] *Selma*
William F. Aldrich,[7] *Aldrich*
James E. Cobb,[8] *Tuskegee*
Albert T. Goodwyn,[9] *Robinson Springs*
John H. Bankhead, *Fayette*
Milford W. Howard, *Fort Payne*
Joseph Wheeler, *Wheeler*
Oscar W. Underwood,[10] *Birmingham*
Truman H. Aldrich,[11] *Birmingham*

ARKANSAS

SENATORS

James K. Jones, *Washington*
James H. Berry, *Bentonville*

REPRESENTATIVES

Philip D. McCulloch, Jr., *Marianna*
John S. Little, *Greenwood*
Thomas C. McRae, *Prescott*
William L. Terry, *Little Rock*
Hugh A. Dinsmore, *Fayetteville*
Robert Neill, *Batesville*

CALIFORNIA

SENATORS

Stephen M. White, *Los Angeles*
George C. Perkins, *Oakland*

REPRESENTATIVES

John A. Barham, *Santa Rosa*
Grove L. Johnson, *Sacramento*
Samuel G. Hilborn, *Oakland*
James G. Maguire, *San Francisco*
Eugene F. Loud, *San Francisco*
James McLachlan, *Pasadena*
William W. Bowers, *San Diego*

COLORADO

SENATORS

Henry M. Teller, *Central City*
Edward O. Wolcott, *Denver*

REPRESENTATIVES

John F. Shafroth, *Denver*
John C. Bell, *Montrose*

CONNECTICUT

SENATORS

Orville H. Platt, *Meriden*
Joseph R. Hawley, *Hartford*

REPRESENTATIVES

E. Stevens Henry, *Rockville*
Nehemiah D. Sperry, *New Haven*
Charles A. Russell, *Killingly*
Ebenezer J. Hill, *Norwalk*

---

[1] Elected February 7, 1896.
[2] Elected December 2, 1895.
[3] Elected December 2, 1895.
[4] Elected December 2, 1895.
[5] Election unsuccessfully contested by W. C. Robinson.

[6] Served until March 13, 1896; succeeded by William F. Aldrich, who contested his election.
[7] Successfully contested the election of Gaston A. Robbins, and took his seat March 13, 1896.
[8] Served until April 21, 1896; succeeded by Albert T. Goodwyn, who contested his election.

[9] Successfully contested the election of James E. Cobb, and took his seat April 22, 1896.
[10] Served until June 9, 1896; succeeded by Truman H. Aldrich, who contested his election.
[11] Successfully contested the election of Oscar W. Underwood, and took his seat June 9, 1896.

DELAWARE

SENATORS

George Gray, *New Castle*
Richard R. Kenney,[12] *Dover*

REPRESENTATIVE

At Large—Jonathan S. Willis, *Milford*

FLORIDA

SENATORS

Wilkinson Call, *Jacksonville*
Samuel Pasco, *Monticello*

REPRESENTATIVES

Stephen M. Sparkman, *Tampa*
Charles M. Cooper, *Jacksonville*

GEORGIA

SENATORS

John B. Gordon, *Atlanta*
Augustus O. Bacon, *Macon*

REPRESENTATIVES

Rufus E. Lester, *Savannah*
Benjamin E. Russell, *Bainbridge*
Charles F. Crisp,[13] *Americus*
Charles R. Crisp,[14] *Americus*
Charles L. Moses, *Turin*
Leonidas F. Livingston, *Kings*
Charles L. Bartlett, *Macon*
John W. Maddox,[15] *Rome*
Thomas G. Lawson, *Eatonton*
Farish C. Tate, *Jasper*
James C. C. Black,[16] *Augusta*
Henry G. Turner, *Quitman*

IDAHO

SENATORS

George L. Shoup, *Salmon City*
Fred T. Dubois, *Blackfoot*

REPRESENTATIVE

At Large—Edgar Wilson, *Boise City*

ILLINOIS

SENATORS

Shelby M. Cullom, *Springfield*
John McAuley Palmer, *Springfield*

REPRESENTATIVES

J. Frank Aldrich, *Chicago*
William Lorimer, *Chicago*
Lawrence E. McGann,[17] *Chicago*
Hugh R. Belknap,[18] *Chicago*
Charles W. Woodman, *Chicago*
George E. White, *Chicago*
Edward D. Cooke, *Chicago*
George E. Foss, *Chicago*
Albert J. Hopkins, *Aurora*
Robert R. Hitt, *Mount Morris*
George W. Prince,[19] *Galesburg*
Walter Reeves, *Streator*
Joseph G. Cannon, *Danville*
Vespasian Warner, *Clinton*
Joseph V. Graff, *Pekin*
Benjamin F. Marsh, *Warsaw*
Finis E. Downing,[20] *Virginia*
John I. Rinaker,[21] *Carlinville*
James A. Connolly, *Springfield*
Frederick Remann,[22] *Vandalia*
William F. L. Hadley,[23] *Edwardsville*
Benson Wood, *Effingham*
Orlando Burrell, *Carmi*
Everett J. Murphy, *East St. Louis*
George W. Smith, *Murphysboro*

INDIANA

SENATORS

Daniel W. Voorhees, *Terre Haute*
David Turpie, *Indianapolis*

REPRESENTATIVES

James A. Hemenway, *Boonville*
Alexander M. Hardy, *Washington*
Robert J. Tracewell, *Corydon*
James E. Watson, *Rushville*
Jesse Overstreet, *Franklin*
Henry U. Johnson, *Richmond*
Charles L. Henry, *Anderson*
George W. Faris, *Terre Haute*
J. Frank Hanly, *Williamsport*
Jethro A. Hatch, *Kentland*
George W. Steele, *Marion*
Jacob D. Leighty, *St. Joe*
Lemuel W. Royse, *Warsaw*

IOWA

SENATORS

William B. Allison, *Dubuque*
John H. Gear, *Burlington*

REPRESENTATIVES

Samuel M. Clark, *Keokuk*
George M. Curtis, *Clinton*
David B. Henderson, *Dubuque*
Thomas Updegraff, *McGregor*
Robert G. Cousins, *Tipton*
John F. Lacy, *Oskaloosa*
John A. T. Hull, *Des Moines*
William P. Hepburn, *Clarinda*
Alva L. Hager, *Greenfield*
Jonathan P. Dolliver, *Fort Dodge*
George D. Perkins, *Sioux City*

KANSAS

SENATORS

William A. Peffer, *Topeka*
Lucien Baker, *Leavenworth*

REPRESENTATIVES

Case Broderick, *Holton*
Orrin L. Miller, *Kansas City*
Snyder S. Kirkpatrick, *Fredonia*
Charles Curtis, *Topeka*
William A. Calderhead, *Marysville*
William Baker, *Lincoln*
Chester I. Long, *Medicine Lodge*
At Large—Richard W. Blue, *Pleasanton*

KENTUCKY

SENATORS

Joseph C. S. Blackburn, *Versailles*
William Lindsay, *Frankfort*

REPRESENTATIVES

John K. Hendrick, *Smithland*
John D. Clardy, *Newstead*
W. Godfrey Hunter, *Burkesville*
John W. Lewis, *Springfield*
Walter Evans, *Louisville*
Albert S. Berry, *Newport*
William C. Owens,[24] *Georgetown*
James B. McCreary, *Richmond*
Samuel J. Pugh, *Vanceburg*
Joseph M. Kendall,[25] *Prestonsburg*
Nathan T. Hopkins,[26] *Marshall*
David G. Colson, *Middlesboro*

LOUISIANA

SENATORS

Donelson Caffery, *Franklin*
Newton C. Blanchard, *Shreveport*

---

[12] A petition and papers, certifying to the election of Henry A. du Pont for the term beginning March 4, 1895, were presented December 4, 1895; numerous affidavits and papers challenging the regularity of the election were also presented; the Committee on Privileges and Elections reported favorably to Mr. du Pont, February 17, 1896, but on May 15, 1896, the Senate, by a vote of 31 to 30, decided he was not entitled to a seat; papers and legislative records were presented January 21, 1897, attesting the election of John Edwards Addicks on the day preceding, for the term beginning March 4, 1895; credentials of Richard R. Kenney, duly signed by the governor, and certifying to his election on January 19, 1897, were presented on February 5, 1897; appeared, qualified, and took his seat on the same day. The contest was continued in the succeeding Congress.

Vacancy in this class from March 4, 1895, to January 18, 1897.
[13] Died October 23, 1896.
[14] Elected to fill vacancy caused by death of his father, Charles F. Crisp, and took his seat December 19, 1896.
[15] Election unsuccessfully contested by William H. Felton.
[16] Resigned March 4, 1895, subsequently elected to fill vacancy caused by his own resignation, and took his seat December 2, 1895; election unsuccessfully contested by Thomas E. Watson.
[17] Resigned December 2, 1895; succeeded by Hugh R. Belknap, who contested his election.
[18] Successfully contested the election of Lawrence E. McGann, and took his seat December 27, 1895.

[19] Elected to fill vacancy caused by death of Representative-elect Philip S. Post, in preceding Congress, and took his seat December 2, 1895.
[20] Served until June 5, 1896; succeeded by John I. Rinaker, who contested his election.
[21] Successfully contested the election of Finis E. Downing, and took his seat June 5, 1896.
[22] Died July 14, 1895, before Congress assembled.
[23] Elected to fill vacancy caused by death of Frederick Remann, and took his seat December 2, 1895.
[24] Election unsuccessfully contested by George Denny, Jr.
[25] Served until February 18, 1897; succeeded by N. T. Hopkins, who contested his election.
[26] Successfully contested the election of Joseph M. Kendall, and took his seat February 18, 1897.

REPRESENTATIVES

Adolph Meyer, *New Orleans*
Charles F. Buck,[27] *New Orleans*
Andrew Price,[28] *Thibodaux*
Henry W. Ogden, *Benton*
Charles J. Boatner,[29] *Monroe*
Samuel M. Robertson, *Baton Rouge*

MAINE

SENATORS

Eugene Hale, *Ellsworth*
William P. Frye, *Lewiston*

REPRESENTATIVES

Thomas B. Reed, *Portland*
Nelson Dingley, Jr., *Lewiston*
Seth L. Milliken, *Belfast*
Charles A. Boutelle, *Bangor*

MARYLAND

SENATORS

Arthur Pue Gorman, *Laurel*
Charles H. Gibson, *Easton*

REPRESENTATIVES

Joshua W. Miles, *Princess Anne*
William B. Baker, *Aberdeen*
Harry W. Rusk,[30] *Baltimore*
John K. Cowen, *Baltimore*
Charles E. Coffin, *Muirkirk*
George L. Wellington, *Cumberland*

MASSACHUSETTS

SENATORS

George F. Hoar, *Worcester*
Henry Cabot Lodge, *Nahant*

REPRESENTATIVES

Ashley B. Wright, *North Adams*
Frederick H. Gillett, *Springfield*
Joseph H. Walker, *Worcester*
Lewis D. Apsley, *Hudson*
William S. Knox, *Lawrence*
William Cogswell,[31] *Salem*
William H. Moody,[32] *Haverhill*
William E. Barrett, *Melrose*
Samuel W. McCall, *Winchester*
John F. Fitzgerald, *Boston*
Harrison H. Atwood, *Boston*
William F. Draper, *Hopedale*
Elijah A. Morse, *Canton*
John Simpkins, *Yarmouth*

MICHIGAN

SENATORS

James McMillan, *Detroit*
Julius C. Burrows, *Kalamazoo*

REPRESENTATIVES

John B. Corliss, *Detroit*
George Spalding, *Monroe*
Alfred Milnes,[33] *Coldwater*
Henry F. Thomas, *Allegan*
William Alden Smith, *Grand Rapids*
David D. Aitken, *Flint*
Horace G. Snover, *Port Austin*
William S. Linton, *Saginaw*
Roswell P. Bishop, *Ludington*
Rousseau O. Crump, *West Bay City*
John Avery, *Greenville*
Samuel M. Stephenson, *Menominee*

MINNESOTA

SENATORS

Cushman K. Davis, *St. Paul*
Knute Nelson, *Alexandria*

REPRESENTATIVES

James A. Tawney, *Winona*
James T. McCleary, *Mankato*
Joel P. Heatwole, *Northfield*
Andrew R. Keifer, *St. Paul*
Loren Fletcher, *Minneapolis*
Charles A. Towne, *Duluth*
Frank M. Eddy, *Glenwood*

MISSISSIPPI

SENATORS

James Z. George, *Carrollton*
Edward C. Walthall, *Grenada*

REPRESENTATIVES

John M. Allen, *Tupelo*
John C. Kyle, *Sardis*
Thomas C. Catchings, *Vicksburg*
Hernando D. Money, *Carrollton*
John Sharp Williams, *Yazoo City*
Walter McK. Denny, *Scranton*
James G. Spencer, *Port Gibson*

MISSOURI

SENATORS

Francis M. Cockrell, *Warrensburg*
George G. Vest, *Kansas City*

REPRESENTATIVES

Charles N. Clark, *Hannibal*
Uriel S. Hall, *Hubbard*
Alexander M. Dockery, *Gallatin*
George C. Crowther, *St. Joseph*
John C. Tarsney,[34] *Kansas City*
Robert T. Van Horn,[35] *Kansas City*
David A. De Armond, *Butler*
John P. Tracey, *Springfield*
Joel D. Hubbard, *Versailles*
William M. Treloar, *Mexico*
Richard Bartholdt, *St. Louis*

Charles F. Joy, *St. Louis*
Seth W. Cobb, *St. Louis*
John H. Raney, *Piedmont*
Norman A. Mozley, *Dexter*
Charles G. Burton, *Nevada*

MONTANA

SENATORS

Lee Mantle, *Butte*
Thomas H. Carter, *Helena*

REPRESENTATIVE

At Large—Charles S. Hartman, *Bozeman*

NEBRASKA

SENATORS

William V. Allen, *Madison*
John M. Thurston, *Omaha*

REPRESENTATIVES

Jesse B. Strode, *Lincoln*
David H. Mercer, *Omaha*
George D. Meiklejohn, *Fullerton*
Eugene J. Hainer, *Aurora*
William E. Andrews, *Hastings*
Omer M. Kem, *Broken Bow*

NEVADA

SENATORS

John P. Jones, *Gold Hill*
William M. Stewart, *Carson City*

REPRESENTATIVE

At Large—Francis G. Newlands, *Reno*

NEW HAMPSHIRE

SENATORS

William E. Chandler, *Concord*
Jacob H. Gallinger, *Concord*

REPRESENTATIVES

Cyrus A. Sulloway, *Manchester*
Henry M. Baker, *Bow*

NEW JERSEY

SENATORS

James Smith, Jr., *Newark*
William J. Sewell, *Camden*

REPRESENTATIVES

Henry C. Loudenslager, *Paulsboro*
John J. Gardner, *Atlantic City*
Benjamin F. Howell, *New Brunswick*
Mahlon Pitney, *Morristown*
James F. Stewart, *Paterson*
Richard Wayne Parker, *Newark*
Thomas McEwan, Jr., *Jersey City*
Charles N. Fowler, *Elizabeth*

---

[27] Election unsuccessfully contested by H. Dudley Coleman.
[28] Election unsuccessfully contested by Taylor Beattie.
[29] Election contested by Alexis Benoit; seat declared vacant March 20, 1896; subsequently elected and took his seat December 10, 1896; this election also unsuc-

cessfully contested by Alexis Benoit.
[30] Election unsuccessfully contested by William S. Booze.
[31] Died May 22, 1895, before Congress assembled.
[32] Elected to fill vacancy caused by death of William Cogswell, and took his seat December 2, 1895.
[33] Elected to fill vacancy caused by resignation of

Representative-elect Julius C. Burrows, in preceding Congress, and took his seat December 2, 1895.
[34] Served until February 27, 1896; succeeded by Robert T. Van Horn, who contested his election.
[35] Successfully contested the election of John C. Tarsney, and took his seat February 27, 1896.

NEW YORK

SENATORS

David B. Hill, *Albany*
Edward Murphy, Jr., *Troy*

REPRESENTATIVES

Richard C. McCormick, *Jamaica*
Denis M. Hurley, *Brooklyn*
Francis H. Wilson, *Brooklyn*
Israel F. Fischer, *Brooklyn*
Charles G. Bennett, *Brooklyn*
James R. Howe, *Brooklyn*
Franklin Bartlett, *New York City*
James J. Walsh,[36] *New York City*
John M. Mitchell,[37] *New York City*
Henry Clay Miner,[38] *New York City*
Amos J. Cummings,[39] *New York City*
William Sulzer, *New York City*
George B. McClellan,[40] *New York City*
Richard C. Shannon, *New York City*
Lemuel E. Quigg, *New York City*
Philip B. Low, *New York City*
Benjamin L. Fairchild, *Pelham Heights*
Benjamin B. Odell, Jr., *Newburgh*
Jacob Le Fever, *New Paltz*
Frank S. Black,[41] *Troy*
George N. Southwick, *Albany*
David F. Wilber, *Oneonta*
Newton M. Curtis, *Ogdensburg*
Wallace T. Foote, Jr., *Port Henry*
Charles A. Chickering, *Copenhagen*
James S. Sherman, *Utica*
George W. Ray, *Norwich*
Theodore L. Poole, *Syracuse*
Sereno E. Payne, *Auburn*
Charles W. Gillet, *Addison*
James W. Wadsworth, *Geneseo*
Henry C. Brewster, *Rochester*
Rowland B. Mahany, *Buffalo*
Charles Daniels, *Buffalo*
Warren B. Hooker, *Fredonia*

NORTH CAROLINA

SENATORS

Jeter C. Pritchard, *Marshall*
Marion Butler, *Elliott*

REPRESENTATIVES

Harry Skinner, *Greenville*
Frederick A. Woodard,[42] *Wilson*
John G. Shaw,[43] *Fayetteville*
William F. Strowd, *Pittsboro*
Thomas Settle, *Reidsville*
James A. Lockhart,[44] *Wadesboro*
Charles H. Martin,[45] *Polkton*
Alonzo C. Shuford, *Newton*

Romulus Z. Linney, *Taylorsville*
Richmond Pearson, *Asheville*

NORTH DAKOTA

SENATORS

Henry C. Hansbrough, *Devils Lake*
William N. Roach, *Larimore*

REPRESENTATIVE

At Large—Martin N. Johnson, *Petersburg*

OHIO

SENATORS

John Sherman, *Mansfield*
Calvin S. Brice, *Lima*

REPRESENTATIVES

Charles P. Taft, *Cincinnati*
Jacob H. Bromwell, *Cincinnati*
Paul J. Sorg, *Middletown*
Fernando C. Layton, *Wapakoneta*
Francis B. De Witt, *Paulding*
George W. Hulick, *Batavia*
George W. Wilson, *London*
Luther M. Strong, *Kenton*
James H. Southard, *Toledo*
Lucien J. Fenton, *Winchester*
Charles H. Grosvenor, *Athens*
David K. Watson, *Columbus*
Stephen R. Harris, *Bucyrus*
Winfield S. Kerr, *Mansfield*
Henry C. Van Voorhis, *Zanesville*
Lorenzo Danford, *St. Clairsville*
Addison S. McClure, *Wooster*
Robert W. Tayler, *New Lisbon*
Stephen A. Northway, *Jefferson*
Clifton B. Beach, *Cleveland*
Theodore E. Burton, *Cleveland*

OREGON

SENATORS

John H. Mitchell, *Portland*
George W. McBride, *St. Helens*

REPRESENTATIVES

Binger Hermann, *Roseburg*
William R. Ellis, *Heppner*

PENNSYLVANIA

SENATORS

J. Donald Cameron, *Harrisburg*
Matthew S. Quay, *Beaver*

REPRESENTATIVES

Henry H. Bingham, *Philadelphia*
Robert Adams, Jr., *Philadelphia*
Frederick Halterman, *Philadelphia*
John E. Reyburn, *Philadelphia*
Alfred C. Harmer, *Philadelphia*
John B. Robinson, *Media*
Irving P. Wanger, *Norristown*
Joseph J. Hart, *Milford*
Constantine J. Erdman, *Allentown*
Marriott Brosius, *Lancaster*
Joseph A. Scranton, *Scranton*
John Leisenring, *Upper Lehigh*
Charles N. Brumm, *Minersville*
Ephraim M. Woomer, *Lebanon*
James H. Codding,[46] *Towanda*
Fred C. Leonard, *Coudersport*
Monroe H. Kulp, *Shamokin*
Thaddeus M. Mahon, *Chambersburg*
James A. Stahle, *Emigsville*
Josiah D. Hicks, *Altoona*
Daniel B. Heiner, *Kittanning*
John Dalzell, *Pittsburgh*
William A. Stone, *Allegheny*
Ernest F. Acheson, *Washington*
Thomas W. Phillips, *New Castle*
Matthew Griswold, *Erie*
Charles W. Stone, *Warren*
William C. Arnold, *Dubois*
At Large—
Galusha A. Grow, *Glenwood*
George F. Huff, *Greensburg*

RHODE ISLAND

SENATORS

Nelson W. Aldrich, *Providence*
George P. Wetmore, *Newport*

REPRESENTATIVES

Melville Bull, *Middletown*
Warren O. Arnold, *Chepatchet*

SOUTH CAROLINA

SENATORS

John L. M. Irby, *Laurens*
Benjamin R. Tillman, *Trenton*

REPRESENTATIVES

William Elliott,[47] *Beaufort*
George W. Murray,[48] *Rembert*
W. Jasper Talbert, *Parksville*
Asbury C. Latimer,[49] *Belton*
Stanyarne Wilson, *Spartanburg*
Thomas J. Strait, *Lancaster*
John L. McLaurin,[50] *Bennettsville*
J. William Stokes,[51] *Orangeburg*

---

[36] Served until June 2, 1896; succeeded by John M. Mitchell, who contested his election.
[37] Successfully contested the election of James J. Walsh, and took his seat June 2, 1896.
[38] Election unsuccessfully contested by Timothy J. Campbell.
[39] Elected to fill vacancy caused by death of Representative-elect Andrew J. Campbell (December 6, 1894, before the beginning of the congressional term), and took his seat December 2, 1895.
[40] Election unsuccessfully contested by Robert A. Chesebrough.

[41] Resigned January 7, 1897, having been elected Governor.
[42] Election unsuccessfully contested by Henry P. Cheatham.
[43] Election unsuccessfully contested by Cyrus Thompson.
[44] Served until June 5, 1896; succeeded by Charles H. Martin, who contested his election.
[45] Successfully contested election of James A. Lockhart, and took his seat June 5, 1896.
[46] Elected to fill vacancy caused by death of Representative-elect Myron B. Wright, in preceding Congress, and took his seat December 2, 1895.

[47] Served until June 4, 1896; succeeded by George W. Murray, who contested his election.
[48] Successfully contested the election of William Elliott, and took his seat June 4, 1896.
[49] Election unsuccessfully contested by Robert Moorman.
[50] Election unsuccessfully contested by Joshua E. Wilson.
[51] Election contested by James B. Johnston, but the House on June 1, 1896, declared the election invalid and seat vacant; subsequently elected and took his seat December 7, 1896.

SOUTH DAKOTA

SENATORS

Richard F. Pettigrew, *Sioux Falls*
James H. Kyle, *Aberdeen*

REPRESENTATIVES AT LARGE

John A. Pickler, *Faulkton*
Robert J. Gamble, *Yankton*

TENNESSEE

SENATORS

Isham G. Harris, *Memphis*
William B. Bate, *Nashville*

REPRESENTATIVES

William C. Anderson, *Newport*
Henry R. Gibson, *Knoxville*
Foster V. Brown, *Chattanooga*
Benton McMillin, *Carthage*
James D. Richardson, *Murfreesboro*
Joseph E. Washington, *Cedar Hill*
Nicholas N. Cox, *Franklin*
John E. McCall, *Lexington*
James C. McDearmon, *Trenton*
Josiah Patterson, *Memphis*

TEXAS

SENATORS

Roger Q. Mills, *Corsicana*
Horace Chilton, *Tyler*

REPRESENTATIVES

Joseph C. Hutcheson, *Houston*
Samuel B. Cooper, *Woodville*
Charles H. Yoakum, *Greenville*
David B. Culberson,[52] *Jefferson*
Joseph W. Bailey, *Gainesville*
Jo Abbott,[53] *Hillsboro*
George C. Pendleton, *Belton*
Charles K. Bell, *Fort Worth*
Joseph D. Sayers, *Bastrop*
Miles Crowley,[54] *Galveston*
William H. Crain,[55] *Cuero*
Rudolph Kleberg,[56] *Cuero*
George H. Noonan, *San Antonio*
Jeremiah V. Cockrell, *Anson*

UTAH [57]

SENATORS

Frank J. Cannon,[58] *Ogden*
Arthur Brown,[59] *Salt Lake City*

REPRESENTATIVE

At Large—Clarence E. Allen,[60] *Salt Lake City*

VERMONT

SENATORS

Justin S. Morrill, *Strafford*
Redfield Proctor, *Proctor*

REPRESENTATIVES

H. Henry Powers, *Morrisville*
William W. Grout, *Barton*

VIRGINIA

SENATORS

John W. Daniel, *Lynchburg*
Thomas S. Martin, *Scottsville*

REPRESENTATIVES

William A. Jones,[61] *Warsaw*
D. Gardiner Tyler, *Sturgeon Point*
Tazewell Ellett, *Richmond*
William R. McKenney,[62] *Petersburg*
Robert T. Thorp,[63] *Mecklenburg*
Claude A. Swanson,[64] *Chatham*
Peter J. Otey,[65] *Lynchburg*
Smith S. Turner, *Front Royal*
Elisha E. Meredith, *Brentsville*
James A. Walker, *Wytheville*
Henry St. George Tucker,[66] *Staunton*

WASHINGTON

SENATORS

Watson C. Squire, *Seattle*
John L. Wilson, *Spokane*

REPRESENTATIVES AT LARGE

William H. Doolittle, *Tacoma*
Samuel C. Hyde, *Spokane*

WEST VIRGINIA

SENATORS

Charles J. Faulkner, *Martinsburg*
Stephen B. Elkins, *Elkins*

REPRESENTATIVES

Blackburn B. Dovener, *Wheeling*
Alston G. Dayton, *Philippi*
James H. Huling, *Charleston*
Warren Miller, *Jackson*

WISCONSIN

SENATORS

William F. Vilas, *Madison*
John L. Mitchell, *Milwaukee*

REPRESENTATIVES

Henry Allen Cooper, *Racine*
Edward Sauerhering, *Mayville*
Joseph W. Babcock, *Necedah*
Theobold Otjen, *Milwaukee*
Samuel S. Barney, *West Bend*
Samuel A. Cook, *Neenah*
Michael Griffin, *Eau Claire*
Edward S. Minor, *Sturgeon Bay*
Alexander Stewart, *Wausau*
John J. Jenkins, *Chippewa Falls*

WYOMING

SENATORS

Clarence D. Clark, *Evanston*
Francis E. Warren, *Cheyenne*

REPRESENTATIVE

At Large—Frank W. Mondell, *Newcastle*

TERRITORY OF ARIZONA

DELEGATE

Nathan O. Murphy, *Phoenix*

TERRITORY OF NEW MEXICO

DELEGATE

Thomas B. Catron, *Santa Fe*

TERRITORY OF OKLAHOMA

DELEGATE

Dennis T. Flynn, *Guthrie*

TERRITORY OF UTAH

DELEGATE

Frank J. Cannon,[67] *Ogden*

---

[52] Election unsuccessfully contested by John H. Davis.
[53] Election unsuccessfully contested by J. C. Kearby.
[54] Election unsuccessfully contested by A. J. Rosenthal.
[55] Died February 10, 1896.
[56] Elected to fill vacancy caused by death of William H. Crain, and took his seat May 5, 1896.
[57] Admitted as a State into the Union January 4, 1896.
[58] Took his seat January 27, 1896; term to expire, as determined by lot, March 3, 1899.

[59] Took his seat January 27, 1896; term to expire, as determined by lot, March 3, 1897.
[60] Took his seat January 7, 1896.
[61] Election unsuccessfully contested by James J. McDonald.
[62] Served until May 2, 1896; succeeded by Robert T. Thorp, who contested his election.
[63] Successfully contested the election of William R. McKenney, and took his seat May 2, 1896.

[64] Election unsuccessfully contested by George W. Cornell.
[65] Election unsuccessfully contested by J. Hampton Hoge.
[66] Election unsuccessfully contested by Jacob Yost.
[67] Served until January 4, 1896, when the Territory of Utah was granted statehood; subsequently elected Senator from the new State.

FIFTY-FIFTH CONGRESS

MARCH 4, 1897, TO MARCH 3, 1899

FIRST SESSION—*March 15, 1897, to July 24, 1897*

SECOND SESSION—*December 6, 1897, to July 8, 1898*

THIRD SESSION—*December 5, 1898, to March 3, 1899*

SPECIAL SESSION OF THE SENATE—*March 4, 1897, to March 10, 1897*

———

VICE PRESIDENT OF THE UNITED STATES—GARRET A. HOBART, of New Jersey

PRESIDENT PRO TEMPORE OF THE SENATE—WILLIAM P. FRYE, of Maine

SECRETARY OF THE SENATE—WILLIAM R. COX, of North Carolina

SERGEANT AT ARMS OF THE SENATE—RICHARD J. BRIGHT, of Indiana

———

SPEAKER OF THE HOUSE OF REPRESENTATIVES—THOMAS B. REED,[1] of Maine

CLERK OF THE HOUSE—ALEXANDER McDOWELL,[2] of Pennsylvania

SERGEANT AT ARMS OF THE HOUSE—BENJAMIN F. RUSSELL, of Missouri

DOORKEEPER OF THE HOUSE—WILLIAM J. GLENN, of New York

POSTMASTER OF THE HOUSE—J. C. McELROY

ALABAMA

SENATORS

John T. Morgan, *Selma*
Edmund W. Pettus, *Selma*

REPRESENTATIVES

George W. Taylor, *Demopolis*
Jesse F. Stallings,[3] *Greenville*
Henry D. Clayton,[4] *Eufaula*
Thomas S. Plowman,[5] *Talladega*
William F. Aldrich,[6] *Aldrich*
Willis Brewer, *Hayneville*
John H. Bankhead, *Fayette*
Milford W. Howard, *Fort Payne*
Joseph Wheeler, *Wheeler*
Oscar W. Underwood,[7] *Birmingham*

ARKANSAS

SENATORS

James K. Jones, *Washington*
James H. Berry, *Bentonville*

REPRESENTATIVES

Philip D. McCulloch, Jr., *Marianna*
John S. Little, *Greenwood*
Thomas C. McRae, *Prescott*
William L. Terry, *Little Rock*
Hugh A. Dinsmore, *Fayetteville*
Stephen Brundidge, Jr., *Searcy*

CALIFORNIA

SENATORS

Stephen M. White, *Los Angeles*
George C. Perkins, *Oakland*

REPRESENTATIVES

John A. Barham, *Santa Rosa*
Marion De Vries, *Stockton*
Samuel G. Hilborn, *Oakland*
James G. Maguire, *San Francisco*
Eugene F. Loud, *San Francisco*
Charles A. Barlow, *San Luis Obispo*
Curtis H. Castle, *Merced*

COLORADO

SENATORS

Henry M. Teller, *Central City*
Edward O. Wolcott, *Denver*

REPRESENTATIVES

John F. Shafroth, *Denver*
John C. Bell, *Montrose*

CONNECTICUT

SENATORS

Orville H. Platt, *Meriden*
Joseph R. Hawley, *Hartford*

REPRESENTATIVES

E. Stevens Henry, *Rockville*
Nehemiah D. Sperry, *New Haven*
Charles A. Russell, *Killingly*
Ebenezer J. Hill, *Norwalk*

---

[1] Reelected March 15, 1897.
[2] Reelected March 15, 1897.
[3] Election unsuccessfully contested by Thomas H. Clark.

[4] Election unsuccessfully contested by George L. Comer.
[5] Served until February 9, 1898; succeeded by William F. Aldrich, who contested his election.

[6] Successfully contested the election of Thomas S. Plowman, and took his seat February 9, 1898.
[7] Election unsuccessfully contested by Grattan B. Crowe.

DELAWARE

SENATORS

George Gray, *Wilmington*
Richard R. Kenney, *Dover*

REPRESENTATIVE

At Large—Levin I. Handy,[8] *Newark*

FLORIDA

SENATORS

Samuel Pasco, *Monticello*
Stephen R. Mallory,[9] *Pensacola*

REPRESENTATIVES

Stephen M. Sparkman, *Tampa*
Robert W. Davis, *Palatka*

GEORGIA

SENATORS

Augustus O. Bacon, *Macon*
Alexander S. Clay, *Marietta*

REPRESENTATIVES

Rufus E. Lester, *Savannah*
James M. Griggs, *Dawson*
Elijah B. Lewis, *Montezuma*
William C. Adamson, *Carrollton*
Leonidas F. Livingston, *Kings*
Charles L. Bartlett, *Macon*
John W. Maddox, *Rome*
William M. Howard, *Lexington*
Farish C. Tate, *Jasper*
William H. Fleming, *Augusta*
William G. Brantley, *Brunswick*

IDAHO

SENATORS

George L. Shoup, *Boise*
Henry Heitfeld, *Lewiston*

REPRESENTATIVE

At Large—James Gunn, *Boise*

ILLINOIS

SENATORS

Shelby M. Cullom, *Springfield*
William E. Mason, *Chicago*

REPRESENTATIVES

James R. Mann, *Chicago*
William Lorimer, *Chicago*
Hugh R. Belknap, *Chicago*
Daniel W. Mills, *Chicago*

George E. White, *Chicago*
Edward D. Cooke,[10] *Chicago*
Henry S. Boutell,[11] *Chicago*
George E. Foss, *Chicago*
Albert J. Hopkins, *Aurora*
Robert R. Hitt, *Mount Morris*
George W. Prince, *Galesburg*
Walter Reeves, *Streator*
Joseph G. Cannon, *Danville*
Vespasian Warner, *Clinton*
Joseph V. Graff, *Pekin*
Benjamin F. Marsh, *Warsaw*
William H. Hinrichsen, *Jacksonville*
James A. Connolly, *Springfield*
Thomas M. Jett, *Hillsboro*
Andrew J. Hunter, *Paris*
James R. Campbell, *McLeansboro*
Jehu Baker, *Belleville*
George W. Smith, *Murphysboro*

INDIANA

SENATORS

David Turpie, *Indianapolis*
Charles W. Fairbanks, *Indianapolis*

REPRESENTATIVES

James A. Hemenway, *Boonville*
Robert W. Miers, *Bloomington*
William T. Zenor, *Corydon*
William S. Holman,[12] *Aurora*
Francis M. Griffith,[13] *Vevay*
George W. Faris, *Terre Haute*
Henry U. Johnson, *Richmond*
Jesse Overstreet, *Indianapolis*
Charles L. Henry, *Anderson*
Charles B. Landis, *Delphi*
Edgar D. Crumpacker, *Valparaiso*
George W. Steele, *Marion*
James M. Robinson, *Fort Wayne*
Lemuel W. Royse, *Warsaw*

IOWA

SENATORS

William B. Allison, *Dubuque*
John H. Gear, *Burlington*

REPRESENTATIVES

Samuel M. Clark, *Keokuk*
George M. Curtis, *Clinton*
David B. Henderson, *Dubuque*
Thomas Updegraff, *McGregor*
Robert G. Cousins, *Tipton*
John F. Lacey, *Oskaloosa*
John A. T. Hull, *Des Moines*
William P. Hepburn, *Clarinda*

Alva L. Hager, *Greenfield*
Jonathan P. Dolliver, *Fort Dodge*
George D. Perkins, *Sioux City*

KANSAS

SENATORS

Lucien Baker, *Leavenworth*
William A. Harris, *Linwood*

REPRESENTATIVES

Case Broderick, *Holton*
Mason S. Peters, *Kansas City*
Edwin R. Ridgely, *Pittsburg*
Charles Curtis, *Topeka*
William D. Vincent, *Clay Center*
Nelson B. McCormick, *Phillipsburg*
Jeremiah Simpson, *Medicine Lodge*
At Large—Jeremiah D. Botkin, *Winfield*

KENTUCKY

SENATORS

William Lindsay, *Frankfort*
William J. Deboe, *Marion*

REPRESENTATIVES

Charles K. Wheeler, *Paducah*
John D. Clardy, *Newstead*
John S. Rhea,[14] *Russellville*
David H. Smith, *Hodgensville*
Walter Evans, *Louisville*
Albert S. Berry, *Newport*
Evan E. Settle, *Owenton*
George M. Davison, *Stanford*
Samuel J. Pugh, *Vanceburg*
Thomas Y. Fitzpatrick, *Prestonburg*
David G. Colson, *Middlesboro*

LOUISIANA

SENATORS

Donelson Caffery, *Franklin*
Samuel D. McEnery, *New Orleans*

REPRESENTATIVES

Adolph Meyer,[15] *New Orleans*
Robert C. Davey, *New Orleans*
Robert F. Broussard, *New Iberia*
Henry W. Ogden, *Benton*
Samuel T. Baird, *Bastrop*
Samuel M. Robertson, *Baton Rouge*

---

[8] Election unsuccessfully contested by Jonathan S. Willis.
[9] Elected to fill vacancy in the term beginning March 4, 1897, and took his seat May 25, 1897; John A. Henderson presented credentials as a Senator-designate on March 16, 1897, which were referred to the Committee on Privileges and Elections; no further action was taken.
[10] Died June 24, 1897.
[11] Elected to fill vacancy caused by death of Edward D. Cooke, and took his seat December 6, 1897.
[12] Died April 22, 1897.

[13] Elected to fill vacancy caused by death of William S. Holman, and took his seat December 6, 1897.
[14] Election unsuccessfully contested by W. Godfrey Hunter.
[15] Election unsuccessfully contested by Joseph Gazin and Armand Romain.

MAINE

SENATORS

Eugene Hale, *Ellsworth*
William P. Frye, *Lewiston*

REPRESENTATIVES

Thomas B. Reed, *Portland*
Nelson Dingley, Jr.,[16] *Lewiston*
Seth L. Milliken,[17] *Belfast*
Edwin C. Burleigh,[18] *Augusta*
Charles A. Boutelle, *Bangor*

MARYLAND

SENATORS

Arthur Pue Gorman, *Laurel*
George L. Wellington, *Cumberland*

REPRESENTATIVES

Isaac A. Barber, *Easton*
William B. Baker, *Aberdeen*
William S. Booze, *Baltimore*
William W. McIntire, *Baltimore*
Sydney E. Mudd, *La Plata*
John McDonald, *Rockville*

MASSACHUSETTS

SENATORS

George F. Hoar, *Worcester*
Henry Cabot Lodge, *Nahant*

REPRESENTATIVES

Ashley B. Wright,[19] *North Adams*
George P. Lawrence,[20] *North Adams*
Frederick H. Gillett, *Springfield*
Joseph H. Walker, *Worcester*
George W. Weymouth, *Fitchburg*
William S. Knox, *Lawrence*
William H. Moody, *Haverhill*
William E. Barrett, *Melrose*
Samuel W. McCall, *Winchester*
John F. Fitzgerald, *Boston*
Samuel J. Barrows, *Boston*
Charles F. Sprague, *Brookline*
William C. Lovering, *Taunton*
John Simpkins,[21] *Yarmouth*
William S. Greene,[22] *Fall River*

MICHIGAN

SENATORS

James McMillan, *Detroit*
Julius C. Burrows, *Kalamazoo*

REPRESENTATIVES

John B. Corliss, *Detroit*
George Spalding, *Monroe*
Albert M. Todd, *Kalamazoo*
Edward L. Hamilton, *Niles*
William Alden Smith, *Grand Rapids*
Samuel W. Smith, *Pontiac*
Horace G. Snover, *Port Austin*
Ferdinand Brucker, *Saginaw*
Roswell P. Bishop, *Ludington*
Rousseau O. Crump, *West Bay City*
William S. Mesick, *Mancelona*
Carlos D. Shelden, *Houghton*

MINNESOTA

SENATORS

Cushman K. Davis, *St. Paul*
Knute Nelson, *Alexandria*

REPRESENTATIVES

James A. Tawney, *Winona*
James T. McCleary, *Mankato*
Joel P. Heatwole, *Northfield*
Frederick C. Stevens, *St. Paul*
Loren Fletcher, *Minneapolis*
R. Page W. Morris, *Duluth*
Frank M. Eddy, *Glenwood*

MISSISSIPPI

SENATORS

James Z. George,[23] *Carrollton*
Hernando D. Money,[24] *Carrollton*
Edward C. Walthall,[25] *Grenada*
William V. Sullivan,[26] *Oxford*

REPRESENTATIVES

John M. Allen, *Tupelo*
William V. Sullivan,[27] *Oxford*
Thomas Spight,[28] *Ripley*
Thomas C. Catchings, *Vicksburg*
Andrew F. Fox, *West Point*
John Sharp Williams, *Yazoo City*
William F. Love,[29] *Gloster*
Frank A. McLain,[30] *Gloster*
Patrick Henry, *Brandon*

MISSOURI

SENATORS

Francis M. Cockrell, *Warrensburg*
George G. Vest, *Kansas City*

REPRESENTATIVES

James T. Lloyd,[31] *Shelbyville*
Robert N. Bodine, *Paris*
Alexander M. Dockery, *Gallatin*

Charles F. Cochran, *St. Joseph*
William S. Cowherd, *Kansas City*
David A. De Armond, *Butler*
James Cooney, *Marshall*
Richard P. Bland, *Lebanon*
James Beauchamp Clark, *Bowling Green*
Richard Bartholdt, *St. Louis*
Charles F. Joy, *St. Louis*
Charles E. Pearce, *St. Louis*
Edward Robb, *Perryville*
Willard D. Vandiver, *Cape Girardeau*
Maecenas E. Benton, *Neosho*

MONTANA

SENATORS

Lee Mantle, *Butte*
Thomas H. Carter, *Helena*

REPRESENTATIVE

At Large—Charles S. Hartman, *Bozeman*

NEBRASKA

SENATORS

William V. Allen, *Madison*
John M. Thurston, *Omaha*

REPRESENTATIVES

Jesse B. Strode, *Lincoln*
David H. Mercer, *Omaha*
Samuel Maxwell, *Fremont*
William L. Stark, *Aurora*
Roderick D. Sutherland, *Nelson*
William L. Greene, *Kearney*

NEVADA

SENATORS

John P. Jones, *Gold Hill*
William M. Stewart, *Carson City*

REPRESENTATIVE

At Large—Francis G. Newlands, *Reno*

NEW HAMPSHIRE

SENATORS

William E. Chandler, *Concord*
Jacob H. Gallinger, *Concord*

REPRESENTATIVES

Cyrus A. Sulloway, *Manchester*
Frank G. Clarke, *Peterboro*

---

[16] Died January 13, 1899, before the commencement of the Fifty-sixth Congress, to which he had been reelected.
[17] Died April 18, 1897.
[18] Elected to fill vacancy caused by death of Seth L. Milliken, and took his seat July 1, 1897.
[19] Died August 14, 1897.
[20] Elected to fill vacancy caused by death of Ashley B. Wright, and took his seat December 6, 1897.
[21] Died March 27, 1898.
[22] Elected to fill vacancy caused by death of John

Simpkins, and took his seat June 15, 1898.
[23] Died August 14, 1897.
[24] Appointed to fill vacancy caused by death of James Z. George, and took his seat December 7, 1897; subsequently elected.
[25] Died April 21, 1898.
[26] Appointed to fill vacancy caused by death of Edward C. Walthall, and took his seat May 31, 1898; subsequently elected.
[27] Resigned May 31, 1898, having been appointed Senator.

[28] Elected to fill vacancy caused by resignation of William V. Sullivan, and took his seat December 5, 1898.
[29] Died October 16, 1898.
[30] Elected to fill vacancy caused by death of William F. Love, and took his seat December 12, 1898.
[31] Elected to fill vacancy caused by death of Representative-elect Richard P. Giles (November 17, 1896, before the beginning of the congressional term), and took his seat June 10, 1897.

NEW JERSEY

SENATORS

James Smith, Jr., *Newark*
William J. Sewell, *Camden*

REPRESENTATIVES

Henry C. Loudenslager, *Paulsboro*
John J. Gardner, *Atlantic City*
Benjamin F. Howell, *New Brunswick*
Mahlon Pitney,[32] *Morristown*
James F. Stewart, *Paterson*
Richard Wayne Parker, *Newark*
Thomas McEwan, Jr., *Jersey City*
Charles N. Fowler, *Elizabeth*

NEW YORK

SENATORS

Edward Murphy, Jr., *Troy*
Thomas C. Platt, *Owego*

REPRESENTATIVES

Joseph M. Belford, *Riverhead*
Denis M. Hurley,[33] *Brooklyn*
Francis H. Wilson,[34] *Brooklyn*
Edmund H. Driggs,[35] *Brooklyn*
Israel F. Fischer, *Brooklyn*
Charles G. Bennett, *Brooklyn*
James R. Howe, *Brooklyn*
John H. G. Vehslage, *New York City*
John M. Mitchell, *New York City*
Thomas J. Bradley, *New York City*
Amos J. Cummings, *New York City*
William Sulzer, *New York City*
George B. McClellan, *New York City*
Richard C. Shannon, *New York City*
Lemuel E. Quigg, *New York City*
Philip B. Low, *New York City*
William L. Ward,[36] *Port Chester*
Benjamin B. Odell, Jr., *Newburgh*
John H. Ketcham, *Dover Plains*
Aaron V. S. Cochrane, *Hudson*
George N. Southwick, *Albany*
David F. Wilber, *Oneonta*
Lucius N. Littauer, *Gloversville*
Wallace T. Foote, Jr., *Port Henry*
Charles A. Chickering, *Copenhagen*
James S. Sherman, *Utica*
George W. Ray, *Norwich*
James J. Belden, *Syracuse*
Sereno E. Payne, *Auburn*
Charles W. Gillet, *Addison*
James W. Wadsworth, *Geneseo*
Henry C. Brewster, *Rochester*
Rowland B. Mahany, *Buffalo*
De Alva S. Alexander, *Buffalo*
Warren B. Hooker,[37] *Fredonia*

NORTH CAROLINA

SENATORS

Jeter C. Pritchard, *Marshall*
Marion Butler, *Elliot*

REPRESENTATIVES

Harry Skinner, *Greenville*
George H. White, *Tarboro*
John E. Fowler, *Clinton*
William F. Strowd, *Pittsboro*
William W. Kitchin, *Roxboro*
Charles H. Martin, *Polkton*
Alonzo C. Shuford, *Newton*
Romulus Z. Linney, *Taylorsville*
Richmond Pearson, *Asheville*

NORTH DAKOTA

SENATORS

Henry C. Hansbrough, *Devils Lake*
William N. Roach, *Larimore*

REPRESENTATIVE

At Large—Martin N. Johnson, *Petersburg*

OHIO

SENATORS

John Sherman,[38] *Mansfield*
Marcus A. Hanna,[39] *Cleveland*
Joseph B. Foraker, *Cincinnati*

REPRESENTATIVES

William B. Shattuc, *Madisonville*
Jacob H. Bromwell, *Cincinnati*
John L. Brenner, *Dayton*
George A. Marshall, *Sidney*
David Meekison, *Napoleon*
Seth W. Brown, *Lebanon*
Walter L. Weaver, *Springfield*
Archibald Lybrand, *Delaware*
James H. Southard, *Toledo*
Lucien J. Fenton, *Winchester*
Charles H. Grosvenor, *Athens*
John J. Lentz, *Columbus*
James A. Norton, *Tiffin*
Winfield S. Kerr, *Mansfield*
Henry C. Van Voorhis, *Zanesville*
Lorenzo Danford, *St. Clairsville*
John A. McDowell, *Millersburg*
Robert W. Tayler, *Lisbon*
Stephen A. Northway,[40] *Jefferson*
Charles W. F. Dick,[41] *Akron*
Clifton B. Beach, *Cleveland*
Theodore E. Burton, *Cleveland*

OREGON

SENATORS

George W. McBride, *St. Helens*
Joseph Simon,[42] *Portland*

REPRESENTATIVES

Thomas H. Tongue,[43] *Hillsboro*
William R. Ellis, *Heppner*

PENNSYLVANIA

SENATORS

Matthew S. Quay, *Beaver*
Boies Penrose, *Philadelphia*

REPRESENTATIVES

Henry H. Bingham, *Philadelphia*
Robert Adams, Jr., *Philadelphia*
William McAleer,[44] *Philadelphia*
James R. Young, *Philadelphia*
Alfred C. Harmer, *Philadelphia*
Thomas S. Butler, *Westchester*
Irving P. Wanger, *Norristown*
William S. Kirkpatrick, *Easton*
Daniel Ermentrout, *Reading*
Marriott Brosius, *Lancaster*
William Connell, *Scranton*
Morgan B. Williams, *Wilkes-Barre*
Charles N. Brumm, *Minersville*
Marlin E. Olmsted, *Harrisburg*
James H. Codding, *Towanda*
Horace B. Packer, *Wellsboro*
Monroe H. Kulp, *Shamokin*
Thaddeus M. Mahon, *Chambersburg*
George J. Benner, *Gettysburg*
Josiah D. Hicks, *Altoona*
Edward E. Robbins, *Greensburg*
John Dalzell, *Pittsburgh*
William A. Stone,[45] *Allegheny*
William H. Graham,[46] *Allegheny*
Ernest F. Acheson, *Washington*
Joseph B. Showalter,[47] *Chicora*
John C. Sturtevant, *Conneautville*
Charles W. Stone, *Warren*
William C. Arnold, *Dubois*
At Large—
Galusha A. Grow, *Glenwood*
Samuel A. Davenport, *Erie*

RHODE ISLAND

SENATORS

Nelson W. Aldrich, *Providence*
George P. Wetmore, *Newport*

REPRESENTATIVES

Melville Bull, *Middletown*
Adin B. Capron, *Stillwater*

---

[32] Resigned January 10, 1899.
[33] Died February 26, 1899.
[34] Resigned September 30, 1897.
[35] Elected to fill vacancy caused by resignation of Francis H. Wilson, and took his seat December 6, 1897.
[36] Election unsuccessfully contested by Benjamin L. Fairchild.
[37] Resigned November 10, 1898, before the commencement of the Fifty-sixth Congress, to which he had been reelected.
[38] Resigned March 4, 1897, to become Secretary of State.
[39] Appointed to fill vacancy caused by resignation of John Sherman, and took his seat March 5, 1897; subsequently elected.
[40] Died September 18, 1898.
[41] Elected to fill vacancy caused by death of Stephen A. Northway, and took his seat December 5, 1898.
[42] Elected to fill vacancy in the term beginning March 4, 1897, caused by failure of legislature to elect, and took his seat December 5, 1898. Henry W. Corbett presented credentials as a Senator-designate March 15, 1897, but was not sworn; the Senate, on February 28, 1898, decided he was not entitled to the seat; vacancy in this class from March 4, 1897, to October 7, 1898.
[43] Election unsuccessfully contested by W. S. Vanderburg.
[44] Election unsuccessfully contested by Samuel E. Hudson.
[45] Resigned November 9, 1898, having been elected governor.
[46] Elected to fill vacancy caused by resignation of William A. Stone, and took his seat December 5, 1898.
[47] Elected to fill vacancy caused by death of Representative-elect James J. Davidson (January 2, 1897, before the beginning of the congressional term), and took his seat May 3, 1897.

SOUTH CAROLINA

SENATORS

Benjamin R. Tillman, *Trenton*
Joseph H. Earle,[48] *Greenville*
John L. McLaurin,[49] *Bennettsville*

REPRESENTATIVES

William Elliott, *Beaufort*
W. Jasper Talbert, *Parksville*
Asbury C. Latimer, *Belton*
Stanyarne Wilson, *Spartanburg*
Thomas J. Strait, *Lancaster*
John L. McLaurin,[50] *Bennettsville*
James Norton,[51] *Mullins*
J. William Stokes, *Orangeburg*

SOUTH DAKOTA

SENATORS

Richard F. Pettigrew, *Sioux Falls*
James H. Kyle, *Aberdeen*

REPRESENTATIVES AT LARGE

Freeman Knowles, *Deadwood*
John E. Kelley, *Flandreau*

TENNESSEE

SENATORS

Isham G. Harris,[52] *Memphis*
Thomas B. Turley,[53] *Memphis*
William B. Bate, *Nashville*

REPRESENTATIVES

Walter P. Brownlow, *Jonesboro*
Henry R. Gibson, *Knoxville*
John A. Moon, *Chattanooga*
Benton McMillin,[54] *Carthage*
James D. Richardson, *Murfreesboro*
John W. Gaines, *Nashville*
Nicholas N. Cox, *Franklin*
Thetus W. Sims, *Linden*
Rice A. Pierce, *Union City*
Edward W. Carmack,[55] *Memphis*

TEXAS

SENATORS

Roger Q. Mills, *Corsicana*
Horace Chilton, *Tyler*

REPRESENTATIVES

Thomas H. Ball, *Huntsville*
Samuel B. Cooper, *Woodville*
Reese C. De Graffenreid, *Longview*

John W. Cranford,[56] *Sulphur Springs*
Joseph W. Bailey, *Gainesville*
Robert E. Burke, *Dallas*
Robert L. Henry, *Waco*
Samuel W. T. Lanham, *Weatherford*
Joseph D. Sayers,[57] *Bastrop*
Robert B. Hawley, *Galveston*
Rudolph Kleberg, *Cuero*
James L. Slayden, *San Antonio*
John H. Stephens, *Vernon*

UTAH

SENATORS

Frank J. Cannon, *Ogden*
Joseph L. Rawlins, *Salt Lake City*

REPRESENTATIVE

At Large—William H. King, *Salt Lake City*

VERMONT

SENATORS

Justin S. Morrill,[58] *Strafford*
Jonathan Ross,[59] *St. Johnsbury*
Redfield Proctor, *Proctor*

REPRESENTATIVES

H. Henry Powers, *Morrisville*
William W. Grout, *Barton*

VIRGINIA

SENATORS

John W. Daniel, *Lynchburg*
Thomas S. Martin, *Scottsville*

REPRESENTATIVES

William A. Jones, *Warsaw*
William A. Young,[60] *Norfolk*
Richard A. Wise,[61] *Williamsburg*
John Lamb, *Richmond*
Sydney P. Epes,[62] *Blackstone*
Robert T. Thorp,[63] *Mecklenburg*
Claude A. Swanson, *Chatham*
Peter J. Otey, *Lynchburg*
James Hay, *Madison*
John F. Rixey, *Brandy*
James A. Walker, *Wytheville*
Jacob Yost, *Staunton*

WASHINGTON

SENATORS

John L. Wilson, *Spokane*
George Turner, *Spokane*

REPRESENTATIVES AT LARGE

James Hamilton Lewis, *Seattle*
William C. Jones, *Spokane*

WEST VIRGINIA

SENATORS

Charles J. Faulkner, *Martinsburg*
Stephen B. Elkins, *Elkins*

REPRESENTATIVES

Blackburn B. Dovener, *Wheeling*
Alston G. Dayton, *Philippi*
Charles P. Dorr, *Addison*
Warren Miller, *Jackson*

WISCONSIN

SENATORS

John L. Mitchell, *Milwaukee*
John C. Spooner, *Madison*

REPRESENTATIVES

Henry Allen Cooper, *Racine*
Edward Sauerhering, *Mayville*
Joseph W. Babcock, *Necedah*
Theobold Otjen, *Milwaukee*
Samuel S. Barney, *West Bend*
James H. Davidson, *Oshkosh*
Michael Griffin, *Eau Claire*
Edward S. Minor, *Sturgeon Bay*
Alexander Stewart, *Wausau*
John J. Jenkins, *Chippewa Falls*

WYOMING

SENATORS

Clarence D. Clark, *Evanston*
Francis E. Warren, *Cheyenne*

REPRESENTATIVE

At Large—John E. Osborne, *Rawlins*

TERRRITORY OF ARIZONA

DELEGATE

Marcus A. Smith, *Tucson*

TERRITORY OF NEW MEXICO

DELEGATE

Harvey B. Fergusson, *Albuquerque*

TERRITORY OF OKLAHOMA

DELEGATE

James Y. Callahan, *Kingfisher*

---

[48] Died May 20, 1897.
[49] Appointed to fill vacancy caused by death of Joseph H. Earle, and took his seat June 1, 1897; subsequently elected.
[50] Resigned May 31, 1897, having been appointed Senator.
[51] Elected to fill vacancy caused by resignation of John L. McLaurin, and took his seat December 6, 1897.
[52] Died July 8, 1897.
[53] Appointed to fill vacancy caused by death of

Isham G. Harris, and took his seat December 6, 1897; subsequently elected.
[54] Resigned January 16, 1899, having been elected governor.
[55] Election unsuccessfully contested by Josiah Patterson.
[56] Died March 2, 1899.
[57] Resigned January 16, 1899, having been elected governor.
[58] Died December 28, 1898.

[59] Appointed to fill vacancy caused by death of Justin S. Morrill, and took his seat January 16, 1899.
[60] Served until April 26, 1898; succeeded by Richard A. Wise, who contested his election.
[61] Successfully contested the election of William A. Young, and took his seat April 26, 1898.
[62] Served until March 23, 1898; succeeded by Robert T. Thorp, who contested his election.
[63] Successfully contested the election of Sydney P. Epes, and took his seat March 23, 1898.

FIFTY-SIXTH CONGRESS

MARCH 4, 1899, TO MARCH 3, 1901

FIRST SESSION—*December 4, 1899, to June 7, 1900*

SECOND SESSION—*December 3, 1900, to March 3, 1901*

———

VICE PRESIDENT OF THE UNITED STATES—GARRET A. HOBART,[1] of New Jersey

PRESIDENT PRO TEMPORE OF THE SENATE—WILLIAM P. FRYE, of Maine

SECRETARY OF THE SENATE—WILLIAM R. COX, of North Carolina; CHARLES G. BENNETT,[2] of New York

SERGEANT AT ARMS OF THE SENATE—RICHARD J. BRIGHT, of Indiana; DANIEL M. RANSDELL,[3] of Indiana

———

SPEAKER OF THE HOUSE OF REPRESENTATIVES—DAVID B. HENDERSON,[4] of Iowa

CLERK OF THE HOUSE—ALEXANDER McDOWELL,[5] of Pennsylvania

SERGEANT AT ARMS OF THE HOUSE—BENJAMIN F. RUSSELL, of Missouri; HENRY CASSON,[6] of Wisconsin

DOORKEEPER OF THE HOUSE—WILLIAM J. GLENN, of New York

POSTMASTER OF THE HOUSE—J. C. McELROY

ALABAMA

SENATORS

John T. Morgan, *Selma*
Edmund W. Pettus, *Selma*

REPRESENTATIVES

George W. Taylor, *Demopolis*
Jesse F. Stallings, *Greenville*
Henry D. Clayton, *Eufaula*
Gaston A. Robbins,[7] *Selma*
William F. Aldrich,[8] *Aldrich*
Willis Brewer, *Hayneville*
John H. Bankhead, *Fayette*
John L. Burnett, *Gadsden*
Joseph Wheeler,[9] *Wheeler*
William Richardson,[10] *Huntsville*
Oscar W. Underwood, *Birmingham*

ARKANSAS

SENATORS

James K. Jones, *Washington*
James H. Berry, *Bentonville*

REPRESENTATIVES

Philip D. McCulloch, *Marianna*
John S. Little, *Greenwood*
Thomas C. McRae, *Prescott*
William L. Terry, *Little Rock*
Hugh A. Dinsmore, *Fayetteville*
Stephen Brundidge, Jr., *Searcy*

CALIFORNIA

SENATORS

George C. Perkins, *Oakland*
Thomas R. Bard,[11] *Hueneme*

REPRESENTATIVES

John A. Barham, *Santa Rosa*
Marion De Vries,[12] *Stockton*
Samuel D. Woods,[13] *Stockton*
Victor H. Metcalf, *Oakland*
Julius Kahn, *San Francisco*
Eugene F. Loud, *San Francisco*
Russell J. Waters, *Los Angeles*
James C. Needham, *Modesto*

COLORADO

SENATORS

Henry M. Teller, *Central City*
Edward O. Wolcott, *Denver*

REPRESENTATIVES

John F. Shafroth, *Denver*
John C. Bell, *Montrose*

CONNECTICUT

SENATORS

Orville H. Platt, *Meriden*
Joseph R. Hawley, *Hartford*

REPRESENTATIVES

E. Stevens Henry, *Rockville*
Nehemiah D. Sperry, *New Haven*
Charles A. Russell, *Killingly*
Ebenezer J. Hill, *Norwalk*

---

[1] Died November 21, 1899.
[2] Elected January 29, 1900.
[3] Elected January 29, 1900.
[4] Elected December 4, 1899.
[5] Reelected December 4, 1899.
[6] Elected December 4, 1899.

[7] Served until March 8, 1900; succeeded by William F. Aldrich, who contested his election.
[8] Successfully contested the election of Gaston A. Robbins, and took his seat March 8, 1900.
[9] Resigned April 20, 1900.
[10] Elected to fill vacancy caused by resignation of Joseph Wheeler, and took his seat December 3, 1900.

[11] Elected to fill vacancy in the term beginning March 4, 1899, caused by failure of legislature to elect, and took his seat March 5, 1900; vacancy in this class from March 4, 1899, to February 6, 1900.
[12] Resigned August 20, 1900.
[13] Elected to fill vacancy caused by resignation of Marion De Vries, and took his seat December 3, 1900.

DELAWARE

SENATORS

Richard R. Kenney, *Dover*
Vacant [14]

REPRESENTATIVE AT LARGE

John H. Hoffecker,[15] *Smyrna*
Walter O. Hoffecker,[16] *Smyrna*

FLORIDA

SENATORS

Samuel Pasco,[17] *Monticello*
James P. Taliaferro,[18] *Jacksonville*
Stephen R. Mallory, *Pensacola*

REPRESENTATIVES

Stephen M. Sparkman, *Tampa*
Robert W. Davis, *Palatka*

GEORGIA

SENATORS

Augustus O. Bacon, *Macon*
Alexander S. Clay, *Marietta*

REPRESENTATIVES

Rufus E. Lester, *Savannah*
James M. Griggs, *Dawson*
Elijah B. Lewis, *Montezuma*
William C. Adamson, *Carrollton*
Leonidas F. Livingston, *Kings*
Charles L. Bartlett, *Macon*
John W. Maddox, *Rome*
William M. Howard, *Lexington*
Farish C. Tate, *Jasper*
William H. Fleming, *Augusta*
William G. Brantley, *Brunswick*

IDAHO

SENATORS

George L. Shoup, *Boise*
Henry Heitfeld, *Lewiston*

REPRESENTATIVE

At Large—Edgar Wilson, *Boise*

ILLINOIS

SENATORS

Shelby M. Cullom, *Springfield*
William E. Mason, *Chicago*

REPRESENTATIVES

James R. Mann, *Chicago*
William Lorimer, *Chicago*

George P. Foster, *Chicago*
Thomas Cusack, *Chicago*
Edward T. Noonan, *Chicago*
Henry S. Boutell, *Chicago*
George E. Foss, *Chicago*
Albert J. Hopkins, *Aurora*
Robert R. Hitt, *Mount Morris*
George W. Prince, *Galesburg*
Walter Reeves, *Streator*
Joseph G. Cannon, *Danville*
Vespasian Warner, *Clinton*
Joseph V. Graff, *Peoria*
Benjamin F. Marsh, *Warsaw*
William E. Williams, *Pittsfield*
Ben F. Caldwell, *Chatham*
Thomas M. Jett, *Hillsboro*
Joseph B. Crowley, *Robinson*
James R. Williams, *Carmi*
William A. Rodenberg, *East St. Louis*
George W. Smith, *Murphysboro*

INDIANA

SENATORS

Charles W. Fairbanks, *Indianapolis*
Albert J. Beveridge, *Indianapolis*

REPRESENTATIVES

James A. Hemenway, *Boonville*
Robert W. Miers, *Bloomington*
William T. Zenor, *Corydon*
Francis M. Griffith, *Vevay*
George W. Faris, *Terre Haute*
James E. Watson, *Rushville*
Jesse Overstreet, *Indianapolis*
George W. Cromer, *Muncie*
Charles B. Landis, *Delphi*
Edgar D. Crumpacker, *Valparaiso*
George W. Steele, *Marion*
James M. Robinson, *Fort Wayne*
Abraham L. Brick, *South Bend*

IOWA

SENATORS

William B. Allison, *Dubuque*
John H. Gear,[19] *Burlington*
Jonathan P. Dolliver,[20] *Fort Dodge*

REPRESENTATIVES

Thomas Hedge, *Burlington*
Joseph R. Lane, *Davenport*
David B. Henderson, *Dubuque*
Gilbert N. Haugen, *Northwood*
Robert G. Cousins, *Tipton*
John F. Lacey, *Oskaloosa*
John A. T. Hull, *Des Moines*
William P. Hepburn, *Clarinda*

Smith McPherson,[21] *Red Oak*
Walter I. Smith,[22] *Council Bluffs*
Jonathan P. Dolliver,[23] *Fort Dodge*
James P. Conner,[24] *Denison*
Lot Thomas, *Storm Lake*

KANSAS

SENATORS

Lucien Baker, *Leavenworth*
William A. Harris, *Linwood*

REPRESENTATIVES

Charles Curtis, *Topeka*
Justin D. Bowersock, *Lawrence*
Edwin R. Ridgely, *Pittsburg*
James M. Miller, *Council Grove*
William A. Calderhead, *Marysville*
William A. Reeder, *Logan*
Chester I. Long, *Medicine Lodge*
At Large—Willis J. Bailey, *Baileyville*

KENTUCKY

SENATORS

William Lindsay, *Frankfort*
William J. Deboe, *Marion*

REPRESENTATIVES

Charles K. Wheeler, *Paducah*
Henry D. Allen, *Morganfield*
John S. Rhea, *Russellville*
David H. Smith, *Hodgensville*
Oscar Turner,[25] *Louisville*
Albert S. Berry, *Newport*
Evan E. Settle,[26] *Owenton*
June W. Gayle,[27] *Owenton*
George G. Gilbert, *Shelbyville*
Samuel J. Pugh, *Vanceburg*
Thomas Y. Fitzpatrick, *Prestonburg*
Vincent S. Boreing,[28] *London*

LOUISIANA

SENATORS

Donelson Caffery, *Franklin*
Samuel D. McEnery, *New Orleans*

REPRESENTATIVES

Adolph Meyer, *New Orleans*
Robert C. Davey, *New Orleans*
Robert F. Broussard, *New Iberia*
Phanor Breazeale, *Natchitoches*
Samuel T. Baird,[29] *Bastrop*
Joseph E. Ransdell,[30] *Lake Providence*
Samuel M. Robertson, *Baton Rouge*

---

[14] Vacancy in this class from March 4, 1899, to March 2, 1903, because of failure of legislature to elect.
[15] Died June 16, 1900.
[16] Elected to fill vacancy caused by death of John H. Hoffecker, and took his seat December 3, 1900.
[17] Reappointed to fill vacancy in the term beginning March 4, 1899, to serve until the next meeting of the legislature.
[18] Elected to fill vacancy in the term beginning March 4, 1899, and took his seat December 4, 1899.

[19] Died July 14, 1900; had been reelected for the term beginning March 4, 1901.
[20] Appointed to fill vacancy caused by death of John H. Gear, and took his seat December 4, 1900.
[21] Resigned June 6, 1900.
[22] Elected to fill vacancy caused by resignation of Smith McPherson; took his seat December 3, 1900.
[23] Resigned August 22, 1900, having been appointed Senator.
[24] Elected to fill vacancy caused by resignation of Jonathan P. Dolliver, took his seat December 4, 1900.

[25] Election unsuccessfully contested by Walter Evans.
[26] Died November 16, 1899, before Congress assembled.
[27] Elected to fill vacancy caused by death of Evan E. Settle, and took his seat January 15, 1900.
[28] Election unsuccessfully contested by John D. White.
[29] Died April 22, 1899, before Congress assembled.
[30] Elected to fill vacancy caused by death of Samuel T. Baird, and took his seat December 4, 1899.

MAINE

SENATORS

Eugene Hale, *Ellsworth*
William P. Frye, *Lewiston*

REPRESENTATIVES

Thomas B. Reed,[31] *Portland*
Amos L. Allen,[32] *Alfred*
Charles E. Littlefield,[33] *Rockland*
Edwin C. Burleigh, *Augusta*
Charles A. Boutelle,[34] *Bangor*

MARYLAND

SENATORS

George L. Wellington, *Cumberland*
Louis E. McComas, *Williamsport*

REPRESENTATIVES

John W. Smith,[35] *Snow Hill*
Josiah L. Kerr,[36] *Cambridge*
William B. Baker, *Aberdeen*
Frank C. Wachter, *Baltimore*
James W. Denny, *Baltimore*
Sydney E. Mudd, *La Plata*
George A. Pearre, *Cumberland*

MASSACHUSETTS

SENATORS

George F. Hoar, *Worcester*
Henry Cabot Lodge, *Nahant*

REPRESENTATIVES

George P. Lawrence, *North Adams*
Frederick H. Gillett, *Springfield*
John R. Thayer, *Worcester*
George W. Weymouth, *Fitchburg*
William S. Knox, *Lawrence*
William H. Moody, *Haverhill*
Ernest W. Roberts, *Chelsea*
Samuel W. McCall, *Winchester*
John F. Fitzgerald, *Boston*
Henry F. Naphen, *Boston*
Charles F. Sprague, *Brookline*
William C. Lovering, *Taunton*
William S. Greene, *Fall River*

MICHIGAN

SENATORS

James McMillan, *Detroit*
Julius C. Burrows, *Kalamazoo*

REPRESENTATIVES

John B. Corliss, *Detroit*
Henry C. Smith, *Adrian*
Washington Gardner, *Albion*
Edward L. Hamilton, *Niles*
William Alden Smith, *Grand Rapids*
Samuel W. Smith, *Pontiac*
Edgar Weeks, *Mount Clemens*
Joseph W. Fordney, *Saginaw*
Roswell P. Bishop, *Ludington*
Rousseau O. Crump, *West Bay City*
William S. Mesick, *Mancelona*
Carlos D. Shelden, *Houghton*

MINNESOTA

SENATORS

Cushman K. Davis,[37] *St. Paul*
Charles A. Towne,[38] *Duluth*
Moses E. Clapp,[39] *St. Paul*
Knute Nelson, *Alexandria*

REPRESENTATIVES

James A. Tawney, *Winona*
James T. McCleary, *Mankato*
Joel P. Heatwole, *Northfield*
Frederick C. Stevens, *St. Paul*
Loren Fletcher, *Minneapolis*
R. Page W. Morris, *Duluth*
Frank M. Eddy, *Glenwood*

MISSISSIPPI

SENATORS

Hernando D. Money, *Carrollton*
William V. Sullivan, *Oxford*

REPRESENTATIVES

John M. Allen, *Tupelo*
Thomas Spight, *Ripley*
Thomas C. Catchings, *Vicksburg*
Andrew F. Fox, *West Point*
John Sharp Williams, *Yazoo City*
Frank McLain, *Gloster*
Patrick Henry, *Brandon*

MISSOURI

SENATORS

Francis M. Cockrell, *Warrensburg*
George G. Vest, *Sweet Springs*

REPRESENTATIVES

James T. Lloyd, *Shelbyville*
William W. Rucker, *Keytesville*
John Dougherty, *Liberty*

Charles F. Cochran, *St. Joseph*
William S. Cowherd, *Kansas City*
David A. De Armond, *Butler*
James Cooney, *Marshall*
Richard P. Bland,[40] *Lebanon*
Dorsey W. Shackleford,[41] *Jefferson City*
James Beauchamp Clark, *Bowling Green*
Richard Bartholdt, *St. Louis*
Charles F. Joy, *St. Louis*
Charles E. Pearce, *St. Louis*
Edward Robb, *Perryville*
Willard D. Vandiver, *Cape Girardeau*
Maecenas E. Benton, *Neosho*

MONTANA

SENATORS

Thomas H. Carter, *Helena*
William A. Clark,[42] *Butte*

REPRESENTATIVE

At Large—Albert J. Campbell, *Butte*

NEBRASKA

SENATORS

John M. Thurston, *Omaha*
Monroe L. Hayward,[43] *Nebraska City*
William V. Allen,[44] *Madison*

REPRESENTATIVES

Elmer J. Burkett, *Lincoln*
David H. Mercer, *Omaha*
John S. Robinson, *Madison*
William L. Stark, *Aurora*
Roderick D. Sutherland, *Nelson*
William L. Greene,[45] *Kearney*
William Neville,[46] *North Platte*

NEVADA

SENATORS

John P. Jones, *Gold Hill*
William M. Stewart, *Carson City*

REPRESENTATIVE

At Large—Francis G. Newlands, *Reno*

NEW HAMPSHIRE

SENATORS

William E. Chandler, *Concord*
Jacob H. Gallinger, *Concord*

REPRESENTATIVES

Cyrus A. Sulloway, *Manchester*
Frank G. Clarke,[47] *Peterboro*

[31] Resigned September 4, 1899, before Congress assembled.
[32] Elected to fill vacancy caused by resignation of Thomas B. Reed, and took his seat December 4, 1899.
[33] Elected to fill vacancy caused by death of Representative-elect Nelson Dingley, Jr., in preceding Congress, and took his seat December 4, 1899.
[34] Resigned March 3, 1901, before the commencement of the Fifty-seventh Congress, to which he had been reelected.
[35] Resigned January 12, 1900.
[36] Elected to fill vacancy caused by resignation of John W. Smith, and took his seat December 3, 1900.
[37] Died November 27, 1900.

[38] Appointed to fill vacancy caused by death of Cushman K. Davis, and took his seat December 10, 1900.
[39] Elected to fill vacancy caused by death of Cushman K. Davis, and took his seat January 28, 1901.
[40] Died June 15, 1899, before Congress assembled.
[41] Elected to fill vacancy caused by death of Richard P. Bland, and took his seat December 4, 1899.
[42] Protests and a memorial of certain citizens of Montana against the validity of the election were presented and referred December 4, 1899; while resolution declaring his election void was pending, tendered his resignation effective May 15, 1900; appointed by the lieutenant governor, as acting governor, to fill the vacancy caused by his own resignation, but did not

qualify. Martin Maginnis also presented credentials of appointment, signed by the governor, but was not permitted to qualify. Seat remained vacant throughout the remainder of the Congress.
[43] Elected to fill vacancy in the term beginning March 4, 1899, but died December 5, 1899, before qualifying.
[44] Appointed to fill vacancy caused by death of Monroe L. Hayward, and took his seat December 19, 1899.
[45] Died March 11, 1899, before Congress assembled.
[46] Elected to fill vacancy caused by death of William L. Greene, and took his seat December 4, 1899.
[47] Died January 9, 1901.

NEW JERSEY

SENATORS

William J. Sewell, *Camden*
John Kean, *Ursino*

REPRESENTATIVES

Henry C. Loudenslager, *Paulsboro*
John J. Gardner, *Atlantic City*
Benjamin F. Howell, *New Brunswick*
Joshua S. Salmon, *Boonton*
James F. Stewart, *Paterson*
Richard Wayne Parker, *Newark*
William D. Daly,[48] *Hoboken*
Allan L. McDermott,[49] *Jersey City*
Charles N. Fowler, *Elizabeth*

NEW YORK

SENATORS

Thomas C. Platt, *Owego*
Chauncey M. Depew, *Peekskill*

REPRESENTATIVES

Townsend Scudder, *Oyster Bay*
John J. Fitzgerald, *Brooklyn*
Edmund H. Driggs, *Brooklyn*
Bertram T. Clayton, *Brooklyn*
Frank E. Wilson, *Brooklyn*
Mitchell May, *Brooklyn*
Nicholas Muller, *New Brighton*
Daniel J. Riordan, *New York City*
Thomas J. Bradley, *New York City*
Amos J. Cummings, *New York City*
William Sulzer, *New York City*
George B. McClellan, *New York City*
Jefferson M. Levy, *New York City*
William A. Chanler, *New York City*
Jacob Ruppert, Jr., *New York City*
John Q. Underhill, *New Rochelle*
Arthur S. Tompkins, *Nyack*
John H. Ketcham, *Dover Plains*
Aaron V. S. Cochrane, *Hudson*
Martin H. Glynn, *Albany*
John K. Stewart, *Amsterdam*
Lucius N. Littauer, *Gloversville*
Louis W. Emerson, *Warrensburg*
Charles A. Chickering,[50] *Copenhagen*
Albert D. Shaw,[51] *Watertown*
James S. Sherman, *Utica*
George W. Ray, *Norwich*
Michael E. Driscoll, *Syracuse*
Sereno E. Payne, *Auburn*
Charles W. Gillet, *Addison*
James W. Wadsworth, *Geneseo*
James M. E. O'Grady, *Rochester*

William H. Ryan, *Buffalo*
De Alva S. Alexander, *Buffalo*
Edward B. Vreeland,[52] *Salamanca*

NORTH CAROLINA

SENATORS

Marion Butler, *Elliot*
Jeter C. Pritchard, *Marshall*

REPRESENTATIVES

John H. Small, *Washington*
George H. White, *Tarboro*
Charles R. Thomas, *New Bern*
John W. Atwater, *Rialto*
William W. Kitchin, *Roxboro*
John D. Bellamy, *Wilmington*
Theodore F. Kluttz, *Salisbury*
Romulus Z. Linney, *Taylorsville*
William T. Crawford,[53] *Waynesville*
Richmond Pearson,[54] *Asheville*

NORTH DAKOTA

SENATORS

Henry C. Hansbrough, *Devils Lake*
Porter J. McCumber, *Wahpeton*

REPRESENTATIVE

At Large—Burleigh F. Spalding, *Fargo*

OHIO

SENATORS

Joseph B. Foraker, *Cincinnati*
Marcus A. Hanna, *Cleveland*

REPRESENTATIVES

William B. Shattuc, *Madisonville*
Jacob H. Bromwell, *Cincinnati*
John L. Brenner, *Dayton*
Robert B. Gordon, *St. Marys*
David Meekison, *Napoleon*
Seth W. Brown, *Lebanon*
Walter L. Weaver, *Springfield*
Archibald Lybrand, *Delaware*
James H. Southard, *Toledo*
Stephen Morgan, *Oak Hill*
Charles H. Grosvenor, *Athens*
John J. Lentz, *Columbus*
James A. Norton, *Tiffin*
Winfield S. Kerr, *Mansfield*
Henry C. Van Voorhis, *Zanesville*
Lorenzo Danford,[55] *St. Clairsville*
Joseph J. Gill,[56] *Steubenville*
John A. McDowell, *Millersburg*

Robert W. Tayler, *Lisbon*
Charles W. F. Dick, *Akron*
Fremont O. Phillips, *Medina*
Theodore E. Burton, *Cleveland*

OREGON

SENATORS

George W. McBride, *St. Helens*
Joseph Simon, *Portland*

REPRESENTATIVES

Thomas H. Tongue, *Hillsboro*
Malcolm A. Moody, *The Dalles*

PENNSYLVANIA

SENATORS

Boies Penrose, *Philadelphia*
Matthew S. Quay,[57] *Beaver*

REPRESENTATIVES

Henry H. Bingham, *Philadelphia*
Robert Adams, Jr., *Philadelphia*
William McAleer, *Philadelphia*
James R. Young, *Philadelphia*
Alfred C. Harmer,[58] *Philadelphia*
Edward de V. Morrell,[59] *Torresdale*
Thomas S. Butler, *West Chester*
Irving P. Wanger, *Norristown*
Laird H. Barber, *Mauch Chunk*
Daniel Ermentrout,[60] *Reading*
Henry D. Green,[61] *Reading*
Marriott Brosius, *Lancaster*
William Connell, *Scranton*
Stanley W. Davenport, *Plymouth*
James W. Ryan, *Pottsville*
Marlin E. Olmsted, *Harrisburg*
Charles F. Wright, *Susquehanna*
Horace B. Packer, *Wellsboro*
Rufus K. Polk, *Danville*
Thaddeus M. Mahon, *Chambersburg*
Edward D. Ziegler, *York*
Joseph E. Thropp, *Everett*
Summers M. Jack, *Indiana*
John Dalzell, *Pittsburgh*
William H. Graham, *Allegheny*
Ernest F. Acheson, *Washington*
Joseph B. Showalter, *Butler*
Athelston Gaston, *Meadville*
Joseph C. Sibley, *Franklin*
James K. P. Hall, *Ridgway*
At Large—
  Galusha A. Grow, *Glenwood*
  Samuel A. Davenport, *Erie*

---

[48] Died July 31, 1900.
[49] Elected to fill vacancy caused by death of William D. Daly, and took his seat December 3, 1900.
[50] Died February 13, 1900.
[51] Elected to fill vacancy caused by death of Charles A. Chickering, and took his seat December 3, 1900; died February 10, 1901, before the commencement of the Fifty-seventh Congress, to which he had been re-elected.
[52] Elected to fill vacancy caused by resignation of Representative-elect Warren B. Hooker, in preceding Congress, and took his seat December 4, 1899.

[53] Served until May 10, 1900; succeeded by Richmond Pearson, who contested his election.
[54] Successfully contested the election of William T. Crawford, and took his seat May 10, 1900.
[55] Died June 19, 1899, before Congress assembled.
[56] Elected to fill vacancy caused by death of Lorenzo Danford, and took his seat December 4, 1899.
[57] Appointed to fill vacancy in the term beginning March 4, 1899, the legislature having met and adjourned without electing; credentials presented December 25, 1899, but not permitted to qualify; on April 24,

1900, a resolution declaring him not entitled to a seat was agreed to; subsequently elected and took his seat January 17, 1901; vacancy in this class from March 4, 1899, to January 15, 1901.
[58] Died March 6, 1900.
[59] Elected to fill vacancy caused by the death of Alfred C. Harmer, and took his seat December 3, 1900.
[60] Died September 17, 1899, before Congress assembled.
[61] Elected to fill vacancy caused by death of Daniel Ermentrout, and took his seat December 4, 1899.

RHODE ISLAND

SENATORS

Nelson W. Aldrich, *Providence*
George P. Wetmore, *Newport*

REPRESENTATIVES

Melville Bull, *Middletown*
Adin B. Capron, *Stillwater*

SOUTH CAROLINA

SENATORS

Benjamin R. Tillman, *Trenton*
John L. McLaurin, *Bennettsville*

REPRESENTATIVES

William Elliott, *Beaufort*
W. Jasper Talbert, *Parksville*
Asbury C. Latimer, *Belton*
Stanyarne Wilson, *Spartanburg*
David E. Finley, *Yorkville*
James Norton, *Mullins*
J. William Stokes, *Orangeburg*

SOUTH DAKOTA

SENATORS

Richard F. Pettigrew, *Sioux Falls*
James H. Kyle, *Aberdeen*

REPRESENTATIVES AT LARGE

Robert J. Gamble, *Yorkton*
Charles H. Burke, *Pierre*

TENNESSEE

SENATORS

William B. Bate, *Nashville*
Thomas B. Turley, *Memphis*

REPRESENTATIVES

Walter P. Brownlow, *Jonesboro*
Henry R. Gibson, *Knoxville*
John A. Moon, *Chattanooga*
Charles E. Snodgrass, *Crossville*
James D. Richardson, *Murfreesboro*
John W. Gaines, *Nashville*
Nicholas N. Cox, *Franklin*
Thetus W. Sims, *Linden*
Rice A. Pierce, *Union City*
Edward W. Carmack, *Memphis*

TEXAS

SENATORS

Horace Chilton, *Tyler*
Charles A. Culberson, *Dallas*

REPRESENTATIVES

Thomas H. Ball, *Huntsville*
Samuel B. Cooper, *Beaumont*
Reese C. De Graffenreid, *Longview*
John L. Sheppard, *Texarkana*
Joseph W. Bailey, *Gainsville*
Robert E. Burke, *Dallas*
Robert L. Henry, *Waco*
Samuel W. T. Lanham, *Weatherford*
Albert S. Burleson, *Austin*
Robert B. Hawley, *Galveston*
Rudolph Kleberg, *Cuero*
James L. Slayden, *San Antonio*
John H. Stephens, *Vernon*

UTAH

SENATORS

Joseph L. Rawlins, *Salt Lake City*
Thomas Kearns,[62] *Salt Lake City*

REPRESENTATIVE

At Large—William H. King,[63] *Salt Lake City*

VERMONT

SENATORS

Redfield Proctor, *Proctor*
Jonathan Ross, *St. Johnsbury*
William P. Dillingham,[64] *Waterbury*

REPRESENTATIVES

H. Henry Powers, *Morrisville*
William W. Grout, *Barton*

VIRGINIA

SENATORS

John W. Daniel, *Lynchburg*
Thomas S. Martin, *Scottsville*

REPRESENTATIVES

William A. Jones, *Warsaw*
William A. Young,[65] *Norfolk*
Richard A. Wise,[66] *Williamsburg*

John Lamb, *Richmond*
Sydney P. Epes,[67] *Blackstone*
Francis R. Lassiter,[68] *Petersburg*
Claude A. Swanson, *Chatham*
Peter J. Otey, *Lynchburg*
James Hay, *Madison*
John F. Rixey, *Brandy*
William F. Rhea, *Bristol*
Julian M. Quarles, *Staunton*

WASHINGTON

SENATORS

George Turner, *Spokane*
Addison G. Foster, *Tacoma*

REPRESENTATIVES AT LARGE

Wesley L. Jones, *North Yakima*
Francis W. Cushman, *Tacoma*

WEST VIRGINIA

SENATORS

Stephen B. Elkins, *Elkins*
Nathan B. Scott,[69] *Wheeling*

REPRESENTATIVES

Blackburn B. Dovener, *Wheeling*
Alston G. Dayton, *Philippi*
David E. Johnston, *Bluefield*
Romeo H. Freer, *Harrisville*

WISCONSIN

SENATORS

John C. Spooner, *Madison*
Joseph V. Quarles, *Milwaukee*

REPRESENTATIVES

Henry Allen Cooper, *Racine*
Herman B. Dahle, *Mount Horeb*
Joseph W. Babcock, *Necedah*
Theobold Otjen, *Milwaukee*
Samuel S. Barney, *West Bend*
James H. Davidson, *Oshkosh*
John J. Esch, *La Crosse*
Edward S. Minor, *Sturgeon Bay*
Alexander Stewart, *Wausau*
John J. Jenkins, *Chippewa Falls*

---

[62] Elected to fill vacancy in the term beginning March 1, 1899, caused by failure of legislature to elect, and took his seat February 4, 1901; vacancy in this class from March 4, 1899, to January 22, 1901.

[63] Brigham H. Roberts presented credentials as a Member-elect December 5, 1899, but was not sworn owing to protests against his eligibility; the House, on January 5, 1900, adopted a resolution declaring he "ought not to have or hold a seat, and the seat to which he was elected is hereby declared vacant." Mr. King was elected to fill vacancy caused by action of the House, and took his seat April 25, 1900.

[64] Elected to fill vacancy caused by death of Justin S. Morrill, in preceding Congress, and took his seat December 3, 1900.

[65] Served until March 12, 1900; succeeded by Richard A. Wise, who contested his election.

[66] Successfully contested the election of William A. Young, and took his seat March 12, 1900; died December 21, 1900.

[67] Died March 3, 1900.

[68] Elected to fill vacancy caused by death of Sydney P. Epes, and took his seat April 28, 1900.

[69] In the preceding Congress memorials were filed remonstrating against the seating of Mr. Scott; December 5, 1899, appeared, qualified, and took his seat, without objection; subsequently other memorials were filed and a resolution was introduced declaring him not entitled to a seat; the Committee on Privileges and Elections was directed to investigate the election, and reported, March 20, 1900, with a resolution declaring Mr. Scott duly elected and entitled to retain the seat; this resolution was agreed to April 27, 1900, by a vote of 52 to 3.

WYOMING

SENATORS

Clarence D. Clark, *Evanston*

Francis E. Warren, *Cheyenne*

REPRESENTATIVE

At Large—Frank W. Mondell, *Newcastle*

TERRITORY OF ARIZONA

DELEGATE

John F. Wilson, *Prescott*

TERRITORY OF HAWAII [70]

DELEGATE

Robert W. Wilcox,[71] *Honolulu*

TERRITORY OF NEW MEXICO

DELEGATE

Pedro Perea, *Bernalillo*

TERRITORY OF OKLAHOMA

DELEGATE

Dennis T. Flynn, *Guthrie*

[70] Formed from the territory of the Republic of Hawaii, annexed to the United States by act of July 7, 1898, and granted a Delegate in Congress by act of April 30, 1900.

[71] Took his seat December 15, 1900, after the investigation of charges preferred against him as to eligibility.

FIFTY-SEVENTH CONGRESS

MARCH 4, 1901, TO MARCH 3, 1903

FIRST SESSION—*December 2, 1901, to July 1, 1902*

SECOND SESSION—*December 1, 1902, to March 3, 1903*

SPECIAL SESSION OF THE SENATE—*March 4, 1901, to March 9, 1901*

———

VICE PRESIDENT OF THE UNITED STATES—THEODORE ROOSEVELT,[1] of New York

PRESIDENT PRO TEMPORE OF THE SENATE—WILLIAM P. FRYE,[2] of Maine

SECRETARY OF THE SENATE—CHARLES G. BENNETT, of New York

SERGEANT AT ARMS OF THE SENATE—DANIEL M. RANSDELL, of Indiana

———

SPEAKER OF THE HOUSE OF REPRESENTATIVES—DAVID B. HENDERSON,[3] of Iowa

CLERK OF THE HOUSE—ALEXANDER McDOWELL,[4] of Pennsylvania

SERGEANT AT ARMS OF THE HOUSE—HENRY CASSON, of Wisconsin

DOORKEEPER OF THE HOUSE—FRANK B. LYON, of New York

POSTMASTER OF THE HOUSE—J. C. McELROY

ALABAMA

SENATORS

John T. Morgan, *Selma*
Edmund W. Pettus, *Selma*

REPRESENTATIVES

George W. Taylor, *Demopolis*
Ariosto A. Wiley, *Montgomery*
Henry D. Clayton, *Eufaula*
Sydney J. Bowie, *Anniston*
Charles W. Thompson, *Tuskegee*
John H. Bankhead, *Fayette*
John L. Burnett,[5] *Gadsden*
William Richardson, *Huntsville*
Oscar W. Underwood, *Birmingham*

ARKANSAS

SENATORS

James K. Jones, *Washington*
James H. Berry, *Bentonville*

REPRESENTATIVES

Philip D. McCulloch, *Marianna*
John S. Little, *Greenwood*
Thomas C. McRae, *Prescott*
Charles C. Reid, *Morrillton*
Hugh A. Dinsmore, *Fayetteville*
Stephen Brundidge, Jr., *Searcy*

CALIFORNIA

SENATORS

George C. Perkins, *Oakland*
Thomas R. Bard, *Hueneme*

REPRESENTATIVES

Frank L. Coombs, *Napa*
Samuel D. Woods, *Stockton*
Victor H. Metcalf, *Oakland*
Julius Kahn, *San Francisco*
Eugene F. Loud, *San Francisco*
James McLachlan, *Pasadena*
James C. Needham, *Modesto*

COLORADO

SENATORS

Henry M. Teller, *Central City*
Thomas M. Patterson, *Denver*

REPRESENTATIVES

John F. Shafroth, *Denver*
John C. Bell, *Montrose*

CONNECTICUT

SENATORS

Orville H. Platt, *Meriden*
Joseph R. Hawley, *Hartford*

REPRESENTATIVES

E. Stevens Henry, *Rockville*
Nehemiah D. Sperry, *New Haven*
Charles A. Russell,[6] *Killingly*
Frank B. Brandegee,[7] *New London*
Ebenezer J. Hill, *Norwalk*

---

[1] Became President by the death of William McKinley September 14, 1901.
[2] Reelected March 7, 1901 (special session of the Senate).

[3] Elected December 2, 1901.
[4] Elected December 2, 1901.
[5] Election unsuccessfully contested by N. B. Spears.

[6] Died October 23, 1902.
[7] Elected to fill vacancy caused by death of Charles A. Russell, and took his seat December 1, 1902.

DELAWARE

SENATORS

L. Heisler Ball,[8] *Faulkland*
J. Frank Allee,[9] *Dover*

REPRESENTATIVE

At Large—L. Heisler Ball,[10] *Faulkland*

FLORIDA

SENATORS

Stephen R. Mallory, *Pensacola*
James P. Taliaferro, *Jacksonville*

REPRESENTATIVES

Stephen M. Sparkman, *Tampa*
Robert W. Davis, *Palatka*

GEORGIA

SENATORS

Augustus O. Bacon, *Macon*
Alexander S. Clay, *Marietta*

REPRESENTATIVES

Rufus E. Lester, *Savannah*
James M. Griggs, *Dawson*
Elijah B. Lewis, *Montezuma*
William C. Adamson, *Carrollton*
Leonidas F. Livingston, *Kings*
Charles L. Bartlett, *Macon*
John W. Maddox, *Rome*
William M. Howard, *Lexington*
Farish C. Tate, *Jasper*
William H. Fleming, *Augusta*
William G. Brantley, *Brunswick*

IDAHO

SENATORS

Henry Heitfeld, *Lewiston*
Fred T. Dubois, *Blackfoot*

REPRESENTATIVE

At Large—Thomas L. Glenn, *Montpelier*

ILLINOIS

SENATORS

Shelby M. Cullom, *Springfield*
William E. Mason, *Chicago*

REPRESENTATIVES

James R. Mann, *Chicago*
John J. Feely, *Chicago*
George P. Foster, *Chicago*
James McAndrews, *Chicago*
William F. Mahoney, *Chicago*

Henry S. Boutell, *Chicago*
George E. Foss, *Chicago*
Albert J. Hopkins, *Aurora*
Robert R. Hitt, *Mount Morris*
George W. Prince, *Galesburg*
Walter Reeves, *Streator*
Joseph G. Cannon, *Danville*
Vespasian Warner, *Clinton*
Joseph V. Graff, *Peoria*
J. Ross Mickey, *Macomb*
Thomas J. Selby, *Hardin*
Ben F. Caldwell, *Chatham*
Thomas M. Jett, *Hillsboro*
Joseph B. Crowley, *Robinson*
James R. Williams, *Carmi*
Frederick J. Kern, *Belleville*
George W. Smith, *Murphysboro*

INDIANA

SENATORS

Charles W. Fairbanks, *Indianapolis*
Albert J. Beveridge, *Indianapolis*

REPRESENTATIVES

James A. Hemenway, *Boonville*
Robert W. Miers, *Bloomington*
William T. Zenor, *Corydon*
Francis M. Griffith, *Vevay*
Elias S. Holliday, *Brazil*
James E. Watson, *Rushville*
Jesse Overstreet, *Indianapolis*
George W. Cromer, *Muncie*
Charles B. Landis, *Delphi*
Edgar D. Crumpacker, *Valparaiso*
George W. Steele, *Marion*
James M. Robinson, *Fort Wayne*
Abraham L. Brick, *South Bend*

IOWA

SENATORS

William B. Allison, *Dubuque*
Jonathan P. Dolliver,[11] *Fort Dodge*

REPRESENTATIVES

Thomas Hedge, *Burlington*
John N. W. Rumple,[12] *Marengo*
David B. Henderson, *Dubuque*
Gilbert N. Haugen, *Northwood*
Robert G. Cousins, *Tipton*
John F. Lacey, *Oskaloosa*
John A. T. Hull, *Des Moines*
William P. Hepburn, *Clarinda*
Walter I. Smith, *Council Bluffs*
James P. Conner, *Denison*
Lot Thomas, *Storm Lake*

KANSAS

SENATORS

William A. Harris, *Linwood*
Joseph R. Burton, *Abilene*

REPRESENTATIVES

Charles Curtis, *Topeka*
Justin D. Bowersock, *Lawrence*
Alfred M. Jackson, *Winfield*
James M. Miller, *Council Grove*
William A. Calderhead, *Marysville*
William A. Reeder, *Logan*
Chester I. Long,[13] *Medicine Lodge*
At Large—Charles F. Scott, *Iola*

KENTUCKY

SENATORS

William J. Deboe, *Marion*
Joseph C. S. Blackburn, *Versailles*

REPRESENTATIVES

Charles K. Wheeler, *Paducah*
Henry D. Allen, *Morganfield*
John S. Rhea,[14] *Russellville*
J. McKenzie Moss,[15] *Bowling Green*
David H. Smith, *Hodgensville*
Harvey S. Irwin, *Louisville*
Daniel L. Gooch, *Covington*
South Trimble, *Frankfort*
George G. Gilbert, *Shelbyville*
James N. Kehoe, *Maysville*
James B. White, *Irvine*
Vincent Boreing, *London*

LOUISIANA

SENATORS

Samuel D. McEnery, *New Orleans*
Murphy J. Foster, *Franklin*

REPRESENTATIVES

Adolph Meyer, *New Orleans*
Robert C. Davey, *New Orleans*
Robert F. Broussard, *New Iberia*
Phanor Breazeale, *Natchitoches*
Joseph E. Ransdell, *Lake Providence*
Samuel M. Robertson, *Baton Rouge*

MAINE

SENATORS

Eugene Hale, *Ellsworth*
William P. Frye, *Lewiston*

REPRESENTATIVES

Amos L. Allen, *Alfred*
Charles E. Littlefield, *Rockland*
Edwin C. Burleigh, *Augusta*
Llewellyn Powers,[16] *Houlton*

---

[8] Elected to fill vacancy in the term beginning March 4, 1899, caused by failure of legislature to elect, and took his seat March 3, 1903: vacancy in this class from March 4, 1899, to March 1, 1903.
[9] Elected to fill vacancy in the term beginning March 4, 1901, caused by failure of legislature to elect, and took his seat March 3, 1903; vacancy in this class from March 4, 1901, to March 1, 1903.

[10] Resigned March 3, 1903, having been elected Senator.
[11] Appointed to fill vacancy in the term beginning March 4, 1901, caused by death of Senator-elect John H. Gear, in preceding Congress, and took his seat March 4, 1901; subsequently elected.
[12] Died January 31, 1903.
[13] Resigned, effective March 4, 1903, before the commencement of the Fifty-eighth Congress, to which

he had been reelected, having been elected Senator.
[14] Served until March 25, 1902; succeeded by J. McKenzie Moss, who contested his election.
[15] Successfully contested the election of John S. Rhea, and took his seat March 25, 1902.
[16] Elected to fill vacancy caused by resignation of Representative-elect Charles A. Boutelle, in preceding Congress, and took his seat Deecmber 2, 1901.

MARYLAND

SENATORS

George L. Wellington, *Cumberland*
Louis E. McComas, *Williamsport*

REPRESENTATIVES

William H. Jackson, *Salisbury*
Albert A. Blakeney, *Franklinville*
Frank C. Wachter, *Baltimore*
Charles R. Schirm, *Baltimore*
Sydney E. Mudd, *La Plata*
George A. Pearre, *Cumberland*

MASSACHUSETTS

SENATORS

George F. Hoar, *Worcester*
Henry Cabot Lodge, *Nahant*

REPRESENTATIVES

George P. Lawrence, *North Adams*
Frederick H. Gillett, *Springfield*
John R. Thayer, *Worcester*
Charles Q. Tirrell, *Natick*
William S. Knox, *Lawrence*
William H. Moody,[17] *Haverhill*
Augustus P. Gardner,[18] *Hamilton*
Ernest W. Roberts, *Chelsea*
Samuel W. McCall, *Winchester*
Joseph A. Conry, *Boston*
Henry F. Naphen, *Boston*
Samuel L. Powers, *Newton*
William C. Lovering, *Taunton*
William S. Greene, *Fall River*

MICHIGAN

SENATORS

James McMillan,[19] *Detroit*
Russell A. Alger,[20] *Detroit*
Julius C. Burrows, *Kalamazoo*

REPRESENTATIVES

John B. Corliss, *Detroit*
Henry C. Smith, *Adrian*
Washington Gardner, *Albion*
Edward L. Hamilton, *Niles*
William Alden Smith, *Grand Rapids*
Samuel W. Smith, *Pontiac*
Edgar Weeks, *Mount Clemens*
Joseph W. Fordney, *Saginaw*
Roswell P. Bishop, *Ludington*
Rosseau O. Crump,[21] *West Bay City*
Henry H. Aplin,[22] *West Bay City*
Archibald B. Darragh, *St. Louis*
Carlos D. Shelden, *Houghton*

MINNESOTA

SENATORS

Knute Nelson, *Alexandria*
Moses E. Clapp, *St. Paul*

REPRESENTATIVES

James A. Tawney, *Winona*
James T. McCleary, *Mankato*
Joel P. Heatwole, *Northfield*
Frederick C. Stevens, *St. Paul*
Loren Fletcher, *Minneapolis*
R. Page W. Morris, *Duluth*
Frank M. Eddy, *Glenwood*

MISSISSIPPI

SENATORS

Hernando D. Money, *Carrollton*
Anselm J. McLaurin, *Brandon*

REPRESENTATIVES

Ezekiel S. Candler, Jr., *Corinth*
Thomas Spight, *Ripley*
Patrick Henry, *Vicksburg*
Andrew F. Fox, *West Point*
John Sharp Williams, *Yazoo City*
Frank A. McLain, *Gloster*
Charles E. Hooker, *Jackson*

MISSOURI

SENATORS

Francis M. Cockrell, *Warrensburg*
George G. Vest, *Sweet Springs*

REPRESENTATIVES

James T. Lloyd, *Shelbyville*
William W. Rucker, *Keytesville*
John Dougherty, *Liberty*
Charles F. Cochran, *St. Joseph*
William S. Cowherd, *Kansas City*
David A. De Armond, *Butler*
James Cooney, *Marshall*
Dorsey W. Shackleford, *Jefferson City*
James Beauchamp Clark, *Bowling Green*
Richard Bartholdt, *St. Louis*
Charles F. Joy, *St. Louis*
James J. Butler,[23] *St. Louis*
George C. R. Wagoner,[24] *St. Louis*
Edward Robb, *Perryville*
Willard D. Vandiver, *Cape Girardeau*
Maecenas E. Benton, *Neosho*

MONTANA

SENATORS

William A. Clark, *Butte*
Paris Gibson,[25] *Great Falls*

REPRESENTATIVE

At Large—Caldwell Edwards, *Bozeman*

NEBRASKA

SENATORS

William V. Allen, *Madison*
Charles H. Dietrich,[26] *Hastings*
Joseph H. Millard, *Omaha*

REPRESENTATIVES

Elmer J. Burkett, *Lincoln*
David H. Mercer, *Omaha*
John S. Robinson, *Madison*
William L. Stark, *Aurora*
Ashton C. Shallenberger, *Alma*
William Neville, *North Platte*

NEVADA

SENATORS

John P. Jones, *Gold Hill*
William M. Stewart, *Carson City*

REPRESENTATIVE

At Large—Francis G. Newlands, *Reno*

NEW HAMPSHIRE

SENATORS

Jacob H. Gallinger, *Concord*
Henry E. Burnham, *Manchester*

REPRESENTATIVES

Cyrus A. Sulloway, *Manchester*
Frank D. Currier, *Canaan*

NEW JERSEY

SENATORS

William J. Sewell,[27] *Camden*
John F. Dryden,[28] *Newark*
John Kean, *Ursino*

REPRESENTATIVES

Henry C. Loudenslager, *Paulsboro*
John J. Gardner, *Atlantic City*
Benjamin F. Howell, *New Brunswick*
Joshua S. Salmon,[29] *Boonton*
De Witt C. Flanagan,[30] *Morristown*
James F. Stewart, *Paterson*
Richard Wayne Parker, *Newark*
Allan L. McDermott, *Jersey City*
Charles N. Fowler, *Elizabeth*

---

[17] Resigned May 1, 1902, to become Secretary of the Navy.
[18] Elected to fill vacancy caused by resignation of William H. Moody, and took his seat December 1, 1902.
[19] Died August 10, 1902.
[20] Appointed to fill vacancy caused by death of James McMillan, and took his seat December 2, 1902; subsequently elected.
[21] Died May 1, 1901, before Congress assembled.
[22] Elected to fill vacancy caused by death of Rosseau O. Crump, and took his seat December 2, 1901.

[23] Election contested by William M. Horton; on June 28, 1902, resolution adopted declaring no valid election and seat vacant; credentials presented of a subsequent election, and took his seat December 1, 1902; served until February 26, 1903; succeeded by George C. R. Wagoner, who contested this election.
[24] Successfully contested the election of James J. Butler, and took his seat February 26, 1903.
[25] Elected to fill vacancy caused by resignation of William A. Clark, in preceding Congress, and took his seat December 2, 1901; vacancy in this class from May 16, 1900, to March 6, 1901.
[26] Elected to fill vacancy caused by death of Monroe L. Hayward, in preceding Congress, and took his seat December 2, 1901.
[27] Died December 27, 1901.
[28] Elected to fill vacancy caused by death of William J. Sewell, and took his seat February 4, 1902.
[29] Died May 6, 1902.
[30] Elected to fill vacancy caused by death of Joshua S. Salmon, and took his seat January 5, 1903.

NEW YORK

SENATORS

Thomas C. Platt, *Owego*
Chauncey M. Depew, *Peekskill*

REPRESENTATIVES

Frederic Storm, *Bayside*
John J. Fitzgerald, *Brooklyn*
Henry Bristow, *Brooklyn*
Harry A. Hanbury, *Brooklyn*
Frank E. Wilson, *Brooklyn*
George H. Lindsay, *Brooklyn*
Nicholas Muller,[31] *New York City*
Montague Lessler,[32] *New York City*
Thomas J. Creamer, *New York City*
Henry M. Goldfogle, *New York City*
Amos J. Cummings,[33] *New York City*
Edward Swann,[34] *New York City*
William Sulzer, *New York City*
George B. McClellan, *New York City*
Oliver H. P. Belmont, *New York City*
William H. Douglas, *New York City*
Jacob Ruppert, Jr., *New York City*
Cornelius A. Pugsley, *Peekskill*
Arthur S. Tompkins, *Nyack*
John H. Ketcham, *Dover Plains*
William H. Draper, *Troy*
George N. Southwick, *Albany*
John K. Stewart, *Amsterdam*
Lucius N. Littauer, *Gloversville*
Louis W. Emerson, *Warrensburg*
Charles L. Knapp,[35] *Lowville*
James S. Sherman, *Utica*
George W. Ray,[36] *Norwich*
John W. Dwight,[37] *Dryden*
Michael E. Driscoll, *Syracuse*
Sereno E. Payne, *Auburn*
Charles W. Gillet, *Addison*
James W. Wadsworth, *Geneseo*
James B. Perkins, *Rochester*
William H. Ryan, *Buffalo*
De Alva S. Alexander, *Buffalo*
Edward B. Vreeland, *Salamanca*

NORTH CAROLINA

SENATORS

Jeter C. Pritchard, *Marshall*
Furnifold McL. Simmons, *Raleigh*

REPRESENTATIVES

John H. Small, *Washington*
Claude Kitchin, *Scotland Neck*
Charles R. Thomas,[38] *New Bern*
Edward W. Pou, *Smithfield*
William W. Kitchin, *Roxboro*

John D. Bellamy, *Wilmington*
Theodore F. Kluttz, *Salisbury*
Edmond Spencer Blackburn, *Wilkesboro*
James M. Moody,[39] *Waynesville*

NORTH DAKOTA

SENATORS

Henry C. Hansbrough, *Devils Lake*
Porter J. McCumber, *Wahpeton*

REPRESENTATIVE

At Large—Thomas F. Marshall, *Oakes*

OHIO

SENATORS

Joseph B. Foraker, *Cincinnati*
Marcus A. Hanna, *Cleveland*

REPRESENTATIVES

William B. Shattuc, *Madisonville*
Jacob H. Bromwell, *Cincinnati*
Robert M. Nevin, *Dayton*
Robert B. Gordon, *St. Marys*
John S. Snook, *Paulding*
Charles Q. Hildebrant, *Wilmington*
Thomas B. Kyle, *Troy*
William R. Warnock, *Urbana*
James H. Southard, *Toledo*
Stephen Morgan, *Oak Hill*
Charles H. Grosvenor, *Athens*
Emmett Tompkins,[40] *Columbus*
James A. Norton, *Tiffin*
William W. Skiles, *Shelby*
Henry C. Van Voorhis, *Zanesville*
Joseph J. Gill, *Steubenville*
John W. Cassingham, *Coshocton*
Robert W. Tayler, *Lisbon*
Charles W. F. Dick, *Akron*
Jacob A. Beidler, *Willoughby*
Theodore E. Burton, *Cleveland*

OREGON

SENATORS

Joseph Simon, *Portland*
John H. Mitchell, *Portland*

REPRESENTATIVES

Thomas H. Tongue,[41] *Hillsboro*
Malcolm A. Moody, *The Dalles*

PENNSYLVANIA

SENATORS

Boies Penrose, *Philadelphia*
Matthew S. Quay, *Beaver*

REPRESENTATIVES

Henry H. Bingham, *Philadelphia*
Robert Adams, Jr., *Philadelphia*
Henry Burk, *Philadelphia*
James R. Young, *Philadelphia*
Edward de V. Morrell, *Torresdale*
Thomas S. Butler, *West Chester*
Irving P. Wanger, *Norristown*
Howard Mutchler, *Easton*
Henry D. Green, *Reading*
Marriott Brosius,[42] *Lancaster*
Henry B. Cassel,[43] *Marietta*
William Connell, *Scranton*
Henry W. Palmer, *Wilkes-Barre*
George R. Patterson, *Ashland*
Marlin E. Olmsted, *Harrisburg*
Charles F. Wright *Susquehanna*
Elias Deemer, *Williamsport*
Rufus K. Polk,[44] *Danville*
Alexander Billmeyer,[45] *Washingtonville*
Thaddeus M. Mahon, *Chambersburg*
Robert J. Lewis, *York*
Alvin Evans, *Ebensburg*
Summers M. Jack, *Indiana*
John Dalzell, *Pittsburgh*
William H. Graham, *Allegheny*
Ernest F. Acheson, *Washington*
Joseph B. Showalter, *Butler*
Arthur L. Bates, *Meadville*
Joseph C. Sibley, *Franklin*
James K. P. Hall,[46] *Ridgway*
At Large—
　Galusha A. Grow, *Glenwood*
　Robert H. Foerderer, *Philadelphia*

RHODE ISLAND

SENATORS

Nelson W. Aldrich, *Providence*
George P. Wetmore, *Newport*

REPRESENTATIVES

Melville Bull, *Middletown*
Adin B. Capron, *Stillwater*

SOUTH CAROLINA

SENATORS

Benjamin R. Tillman, *Trenton*
John L. McLaurin, *Bennettsville*

REPRESENTATIVES

William Elliott, *Beaufort*
William J. Talbert, *Parksville*
Asbury C. Latimer, *Belton*
Joseph T. Johnson, *Spartanburg*
David E. Finley, *Yorkville*
Robert B. Scarborough, *Conway*
J. William Stokes,[47] *Orangeburg*
Asbury F. Lever,[48] *Lexington*

---

[31] Resigned, effective December 1, 1902, before Congress assembled.
[32] Elected to fill vacancy caused by resignation of Nicholas Muller, and took his seat January 15, 1902.
[33] Died May 2, 1902.
[34] Elected to fill vacancy caused by death of Amos J. Cummings, and took his seat December 2, 1902.
[35] Elected to fill vacancy caused by death of Representative-elect Albert D. Shaw, in preceding Congress, and took his seat December 2, 1901.
[36] Resigned September 11, 1902.

[37] Elected to fill vacancy caused by resignation of George W. Ray, and took his seat December 1, 1902.
[38] Election unsuccessfully contested by John E. Fowler.
[39] Died February 5, 1903.
[40] Election unsuccessfully contested by John J. Lentz.
[41] Died January 11, 1903, before the commencement of the Fifty-eighth Congress, to which he had been reelected.

[42] Died March 16, 1901, before Congress assembled.
[43] Elected to fill vacancy caused by death of Marriott Brosius, and took his seat December 2, 1901.
[44] Died March 5, 1902.
[45] Elected to fill vacancy caused by death of Rufus K. Polk, and took his seat December 1, 1902.
[46] Resigned November 29, 1902.
[47] Died July 6, 1901, before Congress assembled.
[48] Elected to fill vacancy caused by death of J. William Stokes, and took his seat December 2, 1901.

SOUTH DAKOTA

SENATORS

James H. Kyle,[49] *Aberdeen*
Alfred B. Kittredge,[50] *Sioux Falls*
Robert J. Gamble, *Yankton*

REPRESENTATIVES AT LARGE

Charles H. Burke, *Pierre*
Eben W. Martin, *Deadwood*

TENNESSEE

SENATORS

William B. Bate, *Nashville*
Edward W. Carmack, *Memphis*

REPRESENTATIVES

Walter P. Brownlow, *Jonesboro*
Henry R. Gibson, *Knoxville*
John A. Moon, *Chattanooga*
Charles E. Snodgrass, *Crossville*
James D. Richardson, *Murfreesboro*
John W. Gaines, *Nashville*
Lemuel P. Padgett, *Columbia*
Thetus W. Sims, *Linden*
Rice A. Pierce, *Union City*
Malcolm R. Patterson, *Memphis*

TEXAS

SENATORS

Charles A. Culberson, *Dallas*
Joseph W. Bailey, *Gainsville*

REPRESENTATIVES

Thomas H. Ball, *Huntsville*
Samuel B. Cooper, *Beaumont*
Reese C. De Graffenreid,[51] *Longview*
Gordon J. Russell,[52] *Tyler*
John L. Sheppard,[53] *Texarkana*
Morris Sheppard,[54] *Texarkana*
Choice B. Randell, *Sherman*
Robert E. Burke,[55] *Dallas*
Dudley G. Wooten,[56] *Dallas*
Robert L. Henry, *Waco*
Samuel W. T. Lanham,[57] *Weatherford*
Albert S. Burleson, *Austin*
George F. Burgess, *Gonzales*
Rudolph Kleberg, *Cuero*
James L. Slayden, *San Antonio*
John H. Stephens, *Vernon*

UTAH

SENATORS

Joseph L. Rawlins, *Salt Lake City*
Thomas Kearns, *Salt Lake City*

REPRESENTATIVE

At Large—George Sutherland, *Salt Lake City*

VERMONT

SENATORS

Redfield Proctor, *Proctor*
William P. Dillingham, *Montpelier*

REPRESENTATIVES

David J. Foster, *Burlington*
Kittredge Haskins, *Brattleboro*

VIRGINIA

SENATORS

John W. Daniel, *Lynchburg*
Thomas S. Martin, *Scottsville*

REPRESENTATIVES

William A. Jones, *Warsaw*
Harry L. Maynard, *Portsmouth*
John Lamb, *Richmond*
Francis R. Lassiter, *Petersburg*
Claude A. Swanson, *Chatham*
Peter J. Otey,[58] *Lynchburg*
Carter Glass,[59] *Lynchburg*
James Hay, *Madison*
John F. Rixey, *Brandy*
William F. Rhea,[60] *Bristol*
Henry D. Flood, *Appomattox*

WASHINGTON

SENATORS

George Turner, *Spokane*
Addison G. Foster, *Tacoma*

REPRESENTATIVES AT LARGE

Wesley L. Jones, *North Yakima*
Francis W. Cushman, *Tacoma*

WEST VIRGINIA

SENATORS

Stephen B. Elkins, *Elkins*
Nathan B. Scott, *Wheeling*

REPRESENTATIVES

Blackburn B. Dovener, *Wheeling*
Alston G. Dayton, *Philippi*
Joseph Holt Gaines, *Charleston*
James A. Hughes, *Huntington*

WISCONSIN

SENATORS

John C. Spooner, *Madison*
Joseph V. Quarles, *Milwaukee*

REPRESENTATIVES

Henry Allen Cooper, *Racine*
Herman B. Dahle, *Mount Horeb*
Joseph W. Babcock, *Necedah*
Theobold Otjen, *Milwaukee*
Samuel S. Barney, *West Bend*
James H. Davidson, *Oshkosh*
John J. Esch, *La Crosse*
Edward S. Minor, *Sturgeon Bay*
Webster E. Brown, *Rhinelander*
John J. Jenkins, *Chippewa Falls*

WYOMING

SENATORS

Clarence D. Clark, *Evanston*
Francis E. Warren, *Cheyenne*

REPRESENTATIVE

At Large—Frank W. Mondell, *Newcastle*

TERRITORY OF ARIZONA

DELEGATE

Marcus A. Smith, *Tucson*

TERRITORY OF HAWAII

DELEGATE

Robert W. Wilcox, *Honolulu*

TERRITORY OF NEW MEXICO

DELEGATE

Bernard S. Rodey, *Albuquerque*

TERRITORY OF OKLAHOMA

DELEGATE

Dennis T. Flynn, *Guthrie*

PORTO RICO [61]

RESIDENT COMMISSIONER

Federico Degetau,[62] *San Juan*

---

[49] Died July 1, 1901.
[50] Appointed to fill vacancy caused by death of James H. Kyle, and took his seat December 2, 1901; subsequently elected.
[51] Died August 29, 1902.
[52] Elected to fill vacancy caused by death of Reese C. De Graffenreid, and took his seat December 2, 1902.
[53] Died October 11, 1902.
[54] Elected to fill vacancy caused by death of his father, John L. Sheppard, and took his seat December 1, 1902.
[55] Died June 5, 1901, before Congress assembled.
[56] Elected to fill vacancy caused by death of Robert E. Burke, and took his seat December 2, 1901.
[57] Resigned January 15, 1903, having been elected Governor.
[58] Died May 4, 1902.
[59] Elected to fill vacancy caused by death of Peter J. Otey, and took his seat December 1, 1902.
[60] Election unsuccessfully contested by James A. Walker.
[61] Part of the territory ceded to the United States by Spain by the treaty of Paris of December 10, 1898; granted a civil government and the right to elect a Resident Commissioner to the United States by act of April 12, 1900.
[62] Elected for a term of two years beginning March 4, 1901; granted the privilege of the floor of the House of Representatives June 28, 1902.

FIFTY-EIGHTH CONGRESS

MARCH 4, 1903, TO MARCH 3, 1905

FIRST SESSION—*November 9, 1903, to December 7, 1903*

SECOND SESSION—*December 7, 1903, to April 28, 1904*

THIRD SESSION—*December 5, 1904, to March 3, 1905*

SPECIAL SESSION OF THE SENATE—*March 5, 1903, to March 19, 1903*

VICE PRESIDENT OF THE UNITED STATES [1]

PRESIDENT PRO TEMPORE OF THE SENATE—WILLIAM P. FRYE, of Maine

SECRETARY OF THE SENATE—CHARLES G. BENNETT, of New York

SERGEANT AT ARMS OF THE SENATE—DANIEL M. RANSDELL, of Indiana

---

SPEAKER OF THE HOUSE OF REPRESENTATIVES—JOSEPH G. CANNON,[2] of Illinois

CLERK OF THE HOUSE—ALEXANDER McDOWELL,[3] of Pennsylvania

SERGEANT AT ARMS OF THE HOUSE—HENRY CASSON, of Wisconsin

DOORKEEPER OF THE HOUSE—FRANK B. LYON, of New York

POSTMASTER OF THE HOUSE—J. C. McELROY

ALABAMA

SENATORS

John T. Morgan, *Selma*
Edmund W. Pettus, *Selma*

REPRESENTATIVES

George W. Taylor, *Demopolis*
Ariosto A. Wiley, *Montgomery*
Henry D. Clayton, *Eufaula*
Sydney J. Bowie, *Anniston*
Charles W. Thompson,[4] *Tuskegee*
J. Thomas Heflin,[5] *Lafayette*
John H. Bankhead, *Fayette*
John L. Burnett, *Gadsden*
William Richardson, *Huntsville*
Oscar W. Underwood, *Birmingham*

ARKANSAS

SENATORS

James H. Berry, *Bentonville*
James P. Clarke, *Little Rock*

REPRESENTATIVES

Robert B. Macon, *Helena*
Stephen Brundidge, Jr., *Searcy*
Hugh A. Dinsmore, *Fayetteville*
John S. Little, *Greenwood*
Charles C. Reid, *Morrillton*
Joseph T. Robinson, *Lonoke*
Robert M. Wallace, *Magnolia*

CALIFORNIA

SENATORS

George C. Perkins, *Oakland*
Thomas R. Bard, *Hueneme*

REPRESENTATIVES

James N. Gillett, *Eureka*
Theodore A. Bell, *Napa*
Victor H. Metcalf,[6] *Oakland*
Joseph R. Knowland,[7] *Alameda*
Edward J. Livernash,[8] *San Francisco*
William J. Wynn, *San Francisco*
James C. Needham, *Modesto*
James McLachlan, *Pasadena*
Milton J. Daniels, *Riverside*

COLORADO

SENATORS

Henry M. Teller, *Central City*
Thomas M. Patterson, *Denver*

REPRESENTATIVES

John F. Shafroth,[9] *Denver*
Robert W. Bonynge,[10] *Denver*
Herschel M. Hogg, *Telluride*
At Large—Franklin E. Brooks, *Colorado Springs*

CONNECTICUT

SENATORS

Orville H. Platt, *Meriden*
Joseph R. Hawley, *Hartford*

REPRESENTATIVES

E. Stevens Henry, *Rockville*
Nehemiah D. Sperry, *New Haven*
Frank B. Brandegee, *New London*
Ebenezer J. Hill, *Norwalk*
At Large—George L. Lilley, *Waterbury*

---

[1] Vice President Theodore Roosevelt became President on the death of William McKinley in preceeding Congress.
[2] Elected November 9, 1903.
[3] Reelected November 9, 1903.
[4] Died March 20, 1904.
[5] Elected to fill vacancy caused by death of Charles

W. Thompson, and took his seat December 5, 1904.
[6] Resigned July 1, 1904, having been appointed Secretary of Commerce and Labor.
[7] Elected to fill vacancy caused by resignation of Victor H. Metcalf, and took his seat December 5, 1904.
[8] Election unsuccessfully contested by Julius Kahn.
[9] Election contested by Robert W. Bonynge; served

until February 15, 1904, when he declared the conviction that contestant was duly elected and entitled to seat held by him; contestant then seated by unanimous vote.
[10] Successfully contested the election of John F. Shafroth, and took his seat February 16, 1904.

[278]

DELAWARE

SENATORS

L. Heisler Ball, *Faulkland*
J. Frank Allee, *Dover*

REPRESENTATIVE

At Large—Henry A. Houston, *Millsboro*

FLORIDA

SENATORS

Stephen R. Mallory,[11] *Pensacola*
James P. Taliaferro, *Jacksonville*

REPRESENTATIVES

Stephen M. Sparkman, *Tampa*
Robert W. Davis, *Palatka*
William B. Lamar, *Monticello*

GEORGIA

SENATORS

Augustus O. Bacon, *Macon*
Alexander S. Clay, *Marietta*

REPRESENTATIVES

Rufus E. Lester, *Savannah*
James M. Griggs, *Dawson*
Elijah B. Lewis, *Montezuma*
William C. Adamson, *Carrollton*
Leonidas F. Livingston, *Covington*
Charles L. Bartlett, *Macon*
John W. Maddox, *Rome*
William M. Howard, *Lexington*
Farish C. Tate, *Jasper*
Thomas W. Hardwick, *Sandersville*
William G. Brantley, *Brunswick*

IDAHO

SENATORS

Fred T. Dubois, *Blackfoot*
Weldon B. Heyburn, *Wallace*

REPRESENTATIVE

At Large—Burton L. French, *Moscow*

ILLINOIS

SENATORS

Shelby M. Cullom, *Springfield*
Albert J. Hopkins, *Aurora*

REPRESENTATIVES

Martin Emerich, *Chicago*
James R. Mann, *Chicago*
William W. Wilson, *Chicago*
George P. Foster, *Chicago*
James McAndrews, *Chicago*
William Lorimer,[12] *Chicago*

Philip Knopf, *Chicago*
William F. Mahoney,[13] *Chicago*
Henry S. Boutell, *Chicago*
George E. Foss, *Chicago*
Howard M. Snapp, *Joliet*
Charles E. Fuller, *Belvidere*
Robert R. Hitt, *Mount Morris*
Benjamin F. Marsh, *Warsaw*
George W. Prince, *Galesburg*
Joseph V. Graff, *Peoria*
John A. Sterling, *Bloomington*
Joseph G. Cannon, *Danville*
Vespasian Warner, *Clinton*
Henry T. Rainey, *Carrollton*
Ben F. Caldwell, *Chatham*
William A. Rodenberg, *East St. Louis*
Joseph B. Crowley, *Robinson*
James R. Williams, *Carmi*
George W. Smith, *Murphysboro*

INDIANA

SENATORS

Charles W. Fairbanks,[14] *Indianapolis*
Albert J. Beveridge, *Indianapolis*

REPRESENTATIVES

James A. Hemenway,[15] *Boonville*
Robert W. Miers, *Bloomington*
William T. Zenor, *Corydon*
Francis M. Griffith, *Vevay*
Elias S. Holliday, *Brazil*
James E. Watson, *Rushville*
Jesse Overstreet, *Indianapolis*
George W. Cromer, *Muncie*
Charles B. Landis, *Delphi*
Edgar D. Crumpacker, *Valparaiso*
Frederick Landis, *Logansport*
James M. Robinson, *Fort Wayne*
Abraham L. Brick, *South Bend*

IOWA

SENATORS

William B. Allison, *Dubuque*
Jonathan P. Dolliver, *Fort Dodge*

REPRESENTATIVES

Thomas Hedge, *Burlington*
Martin J. Wade, *Iowa City*
Benjamin P. Birdsall, *Clarion*
Gilbert N. Haugen, *Northwood*
Robert G. Cousins, *Tipton*
John F. Lacey, *Oskaloosa*
John A. T. Hull, *Des Moines*
William P. Hepburn, *Clarinda*
Walter I. Smith, *Council Bluffs*
James P. Conner, *Denison*
Lot Thomas, *Storm Lake*

KANSAS

SENATORS

Joseph R. Burton, *Abilene*
Chester I. Long, *Medicine Lodge*

REPRESENTATIVES

Charles Curtis, *Topeka*
Justin D. Bowersock, *Lawrence*
Philip P. Campbell, *Pittsburg*
James M. Miller, *Council Grove*
William A. Calderhead, *Marysville*
William A. Reeder, *Logan*
Victor Murdock,[16] *Wichita*
At Large—Charles F. Scott, *Iola*

KENTUCKY

SENATORS

Joseph C. S. Blackburn, *Versailles*
James B. McCreary, *Richmond*

REPRESENTATIVES

Ollie M. James, *Marion*
Augustus O. Stanley, *Henderson*
John S. Rhea, *Russellville*
David H. Smith, *Hodgensville*
J. Swagar Sherley, *Louisville*
D. Linn Gooch, *Covington*
South Trimble, *Frankfort*
George G. Gilbert, *Shelbyville*
James N. Kehoe, *Maysville*
Frank A. Hopkins, *Prestonsburg*
Vincent Boreing,[17] *London*
W. Godfrey Hunter,[18] *Burkesville*

LOUISIANA

SENATORS

Samuel D. McEnery, *New Orleans*
Murphy J. Foster, *Franklin*

REPRESENTATIVES

Adolph Meyer, *New Orleans*
Robert C. Davey, *New Orleans*
Robert F. Broussard, *New Iberia*
Phanor Breazeale, *Natchitoches*
Joseph E. Ransdell, *Lake Providence*
Samuel M. Robertson, *Baton Rouge*
Arsène P. Pujo, *Lake Charles*

MAINE

SENATORS

Eugene Hale, *Ellsworth*
William P. Frye, *Lewiston*

REPRESENTATIVES

Amos L. Allen, *Alfred*
Charles E. Littlefield, *Rockland*
Edwin C. Burleigh, *Augusta*
Llewellyn Powers, *Houlton*

[11] Reappointed to fill vacancy in the term beginning March 4, 1903, to serve until the next meeting of the legislature; subsequently reelected.
[12] Election unsuccessfully contested by Allan C. Durborow.
[13] Died December 27, 1904.

[14] Resigned, effective March 3, 1905, having been elected Vice President of the United States.
[15] Resigned, effective March 3, 1905, before the commencement of the Fifty-ninth Congress, to which he had been reelected, having been elected Senator.
[16] Elected to fill vacancy caused by resignation of

Representative-elect Chester I. Long, in preceding Congress, and took his seat November 9, 1903.
[17] Died September 16, 1903, before Congress assembled.
[18] Elected to fill vacancy caused by death of Vincent Boreing, and took his seat December 4, 1903.

MARYLAND

SENATORS

Louis E. McComas, *Williamsport*
Arthur Pue Gorman, *Laurel*

REPRESENTATIVES

William H. Jackson, *Salisbury*
J. Fred. C. Talbott, *Towson*
Frank C. Wachter, *Baltimore*
James W. Denny, *Baltimore*
Sydney E. Mudd, *La Plata*
George A. Pearre, *Cumberland*

MASSACHUSETTS

SENATORS

George F. Hoar,[19] *Worcester*
Winthrop Murray Crane,[20] *Dalton*
Henry Cabot Lodge, *Nahant*

REPRESENTATIVES

George P. Lawrence, *North Adams*
Frederick H. Gillett, *Springfield*
John R. Thayer, *Worcester*
Charles Q. Tirrell, *Natick*
Butler Ames, *Lowell*
Augustus P. Gardner, *Hamilton*
Ernest W. Roberts, *Chelsea*
Samuel W. McCall, *Winchester*
John A. Keliher,[21] *Boston*
William S. McNary, *Boston*
John A. Sullivan, *Boston*
Samuel L. Powers, *Newton*
William S. Greene, *Fall River*
William C. Lovering, *Taunton*

MICHIGAN

SENATORS

Julius C. Burrows, *Kalamazoo*
Russell A. Alger, *Detroit*

REPRESENTATIVES

Alfred Lucking, *Detroit*
Charles E. Townsend, *Jackson*
Washington Gardner, *Albion*
Edward L. Hamilton, *Niles*
William Alden Smith, *Grand Rapids*
Samuel W. Smith, *Pontiac*
Henry McMorran, *Port Huron*
Joseph W. Fordney, *Saginaw*
Roswell P. Bishop, *Ludington*
George A. Loud, *Au Sable*
Archibald B. Darragh, *St. Louis*
H. Olin Young, *Ishpeming*

MINNESOTA

SENATORS

Knute Nelson, *Alexandria*
Moses E. Clapp, *St. Paul*

REPRESENTATIVES

James A. Tawney, *Winona*
James T. McCleary, *Mankato*
Charles R. Davis, *St. Peter*
Frederick C. Stevens, *St. Paul*
John Lind, *Minneapolis*
Clarence B. Buckman, *Little Falls*
Andrew J. Volstead, *Granite Falls*
J. Adam Bede, *Pine City*
Halvor Steenerson, *Crookston*

MISSISSIPPI

SENATORS

Hernando D. Money, *Carrollton*
Anselm J. McLaurin, *Brandon*

REPRESENTATIVES

Ezekiel S. Candler, Jr., *Corinth*
Thomas Spight, *Ripley*
Benjamin G. Humphreys, *Greenville*
Wilson S. Hill, *Winona*
Adam M. Byrd, *Philadelphia*
Eaton J. Bowers, *Bay St. Louis*
Frank A. McLain, *Gloster*
John Sharp Williams, *Yazoo City*

MISSOURI

SENATORS

Francis M. Cockrell, *Warrensburg*
William J. Stone, *Jefferson City*

REPRESENTATIVES

James T. Lloyd, *Shelbyville*
William W. Rucker, *Keytesville*
John Dougherty, *Liberty*
Charles F. Cochran, *St. Joseph*
William S. Cowherd, *Kansas City*
David A. De Armond, *Butler*
Courtney W. Hamlin, *Springfield*
Dorsey W. Shackleford, *Jefferson City*
James Beauchamp Clark, *Bowling Green*
Richard Bartholdt, *St. Louis*
John T. Hunt, *St. Louis*
James J. Butler, *St. Louis*
Edward Robb, *Perryville*
Willard D. Vandiver, *Cape Giradeau*
Maecenas E. Benton, *Neosho*
J. Robert Lamar, *Houston*

MONTANA

SENATORS

William A. Clark, *Butte*
Paris Gibson, *Great Falls*

REPRESENTATIVE

At Large—Joseph M. Dixon, *Missoula*

NEBRASKA

SENATORS

Charles H. Dietrich, *Hastings*
Joseph H. Millard, *Omaha*

REPRESENTATIVES

Elmer J. Burkett,[22] *Lincoln*
Gilbert M. Hitchcock, *Omaha*
John J. McCarthy, *Ponca*
Edmund H. Hinshaw, *Fairbury*
George W. Norris, *McCook*
Moses P. Kinkaid, *O'Neill*

NEVADA

SENATORS

William M. Stewart, *Carson City*
Francis G. Newlands, *Reno*

REPRESENTATIVE

At Large—Clarence D. Van Duzer, *Tonopah*

NEW HAMPSHIRE

SENATORS

Jacob H. Gallinger, *Concord*
Henry E. Burnham, *Manchester*

REPRESENTATIVES

Cyrus A. Sulloway, *Manchester*
Frank D. Currier, *Canaan*

NEW JERSEY

SENATORS

John Kean, *Elizabeth*
John F. Dryden, *Newark*

REPRESENTATIVES

Henry C. Loudenslager, *Paulsboro*
John J. Gardner, *Atlantic City*
Benjamin F. Howell, *New Brunswick*
William M. Lanning,[23] *Trenton*
Ira W. Wood,[24] *Trenton*
Charles N. Fowler, *Elizabeth*
William Hughes, *Paterson*
Richard Wayne Parker, *Newark*
William H. Wiley, *East Orange*
Allan Benny, *Bayonne*
Allan L. McDermott, *Jersey City*

NEW YORK

SENATORS

Thomas C. Platt, *Owego*
Chauncey M. Depew, *Peekskill*

---

[19] Died September 30, 1904.
[20] Appointed to fill vacancy caused by death of George F. Hoar, and took his seat December 6, 1904; subsequently elected.

[21] Election unsuccessfully contested by Joseph A. Conry.
[22] Resigned, effective March 4, 1905, before the commencement of the Fifty-ninth Congress, to which he had been reelected, having been elected Senator.

[23] Resigned June 6, 1904, having been appointed United States district judge for New Jersey.
[24] Elected to fill vacancy caused by resignation of William M. Lanning, and took his seat December 5, 1904.

REPRESENTATIVES

Townsend Scudder, *Glen Head*
George H. Lindsay, *Brooklyn*
Charles T. Dunwell, *Brooklyn*
Frank E. Wilson, *Brooklyn*
Edward M. Bassett, *Brooklyn*
Robert Baker, *Brooklyn*
John J. Fitzgerald, *Brooklyn*
Timothy D. Sullivan, *New York City*
Henry M. Goldfogle, *New York City*
William Sulzer, *New York City*
William R. Hearst, *New York City*
George B. McClellan,[25] *New York City*
W. Bourke Cockran,[26] *New York City*
Francis B. Harrison, *New York City*
Ira E. Rider, *New York City*
William H. Douglas, *New York City*
Jacob Ruppert, Jr., *New York City*
Francis E. Shober, *New York City*
Joseph A. Goulden, *Fordham*
Norton P. Otis,[27] *Yonkers*
Thomas W. Bradley, *Walden*
John H. Ketcham, *Dover Plains*
William H. Draper, *Troy*
George N. Southwick, *Albany*
George J. Smith, *Kingston*
Lucius N. Littauer, *Gloversville*
William H. Flack, *Malone*
James S. Sherman, *Utica*
Charles L. Knapp, *Lowville*
Michael E. Driscoll, *Syracuse*
John W. Dwight, *Dryden*
Sereno E. Payne, *Auburn*
James B. Perkins, *Rochester*
Charles W. Gillet, *Addison*
James W. Wadsworth, *Geneseo*
William H. Ryan, *Buffalo*
De Alva S. Alexander, *Buffalo*
Edward B. Vreeland, *Salamanca*

NORTH CAROLINA

SENATORS

Furnifold McL. Simmons, *Raleigh*
Lee S. Overman, *Salisbury*

REPRESENTATIVES

John H. Small, *Washington*
Claude Kitchin, *Scotland Neck*
Charles R. Thomas, *New Bern*
Edward W. Pou, *Smithfield*
William W. Kitchin, *Roxboro*
Gilbert B. Patterson, *Maxton*
Robert N. Page, *Biscoe*

Theodore F. Kluttz, *Salisbury*
Edwin Y. Webb, *Shelby*
James M. Gudger, Jr.,[28] *Asheville*

NORTH DAKOTA

SENATORS

Henry C. Hansbrough, *Devils Lake*
Porter J. McCumber, *Wahpeton*

REPRESENTATIVES AT LARGE

Thomas F. Marshall, *Oakes*
Burleigh F. Spalding, *Fargo*

OHIO

SENATORS

Joseph B. Foraker, *Cincinnati*
Marcus A. Hanna,[29] *Cleveland*
Charles W. F. Dick,[30] *Akron*

REPRESENTATIVES

Nicholas Longworth, *Cincinnati*
Herman P. Goebel, *Cincinnati*
Robert M. Nevin, *Dayton*
Harvey C. Garber, *Greenville*
John S. Snook, *Paulding*
Charles Q. Hildebrant, *Wilmington*
Thomas B. Kyle, *Troy*
William R. Warnock, *Urbana*
James H. Southard, *Toledo*
Stephen Morgan, *Oak Hill*
Charles H. Grosvenor, *Athens*
De Witt C. Badger, *Columbus*
Amos H. Jackson, *Fremont*
William W. Skiles,[31] *Shelby*
Amos R. Webber,[32] *Elyria*
Henry C. Van Voorhis, *Zanesville*
Joseph J. Gill,[33] *Steubenville*
Capell L. Weems,[34] *St. Clairsville*
John W. Cassingham, *Coshocton*
James Kennedy, *Youngstown*
Charles W. F. Dick,[35] *Akron*
William Aubrey Thomas,[36] *Niles*
Jacob A. Beidler, *Willoughby*
Theodore E. Burton, *Cleveland*

OREGON

SENATORS

John H. Mitchell, *Portland*
Charles W. Fulton, *Astoria*

REPRESENTATIVES

Binger Hermann,[37] *Roseburg*
John N. Williamson, *Prineville*

PENNSYLVANIA

SENATORS

Boies Penrose, *Philadelphia*
Matthew S. Quay,[38] *Beaver*
Philander C. Knox,[39] *Pittsburgh*

REPRESENTATIVES

Henry H. Bingham, *Philadelphia*
Robert Adams, Jr., *Philadelphia*
Henry Burk,[40] *Philadelphia*
George A. Castor,[41] *Philadelphia*
Robert H. Foerderer,[42] *Philadelphia*
Reuben O. Moon,[43] *Philadelphia*
Edward de V. Morrell, *Torresdale*
George D. McCreary, *Philadelphia*
Thomas S. Butler, *West Chester*
Irving P. Wanger, *Norristown*
Henry B. Cassel, *Marietta*
George Howell,[44] *Scranton*
William Connell,[45] *Scranton*
Henry W. Palmer, *Wilkes-Barre*
George R. Patterson, *Ashland*
Marcus C. L. Kline, *Allentown*
Charles F. Wright, *Susquehanna*
Elias Deemer, *Williamsport*
Charles H. Dickerman, *Milton*
Thaddeus M. Mahon, *Chambersburg*
Marlin E. Olmsted, *Harrisburg*
Alvin Evans, *Ebensburg*
Daniel F. Lafean, *York*
Solomon R. Dresser, *Bradford*
George F. Huff, *Greensburg*
Allen F. Cooper, *Uniontown*
Ernest F. Acheson, *Washington*
Arthur L. Bates, *Meadville*
Joseph H. Shull, *Shroudsburg*
William O. Smith, *Punxsutawney*
Joseph C. Sibley, *Franklin*
George Shiras 3d, *Allegheny*
John Dalzell, *Pittsburgh*
Henry Kirk Porter, *Pittsburgh*
James W. Brown, *Pittsburgh*

RHODE ISLAND

SENATORS

Nelson W. Aldrich, *Providence*
George P. Wetmore, *Newport*

REPRESENTATIVES

Daniel L. D. Granger, *Providence*
Adin B. Capron, *Stillwater*

---

[25] Resigned December 21, 1903, having been elected mayor of New York City.
[26] Elected to fill vacancy caused by resignation of George B. McClellan, and took his seat March 9, 1904.
[27] Died February 20, 1905.
[28] Election unsuccessfully contested by James M. Moody.
[29] Died February 15, 1904.
[30] Elected to fill vacancy caused by death of Marcus A. Hanna, and took his seat March 23, 1904.
[31] Died January 9, 1904.
[32] Elected to fill vacancy caused by death of William -W. Skiles, and took his seat December 5, 1904.

[33] Resigned October 31, 1903, before Congress assembled.
[34] Elected to fill vacancy caused by resignation of Joseph J. Gill, and took his seat November 9, 1903.
[35] Resigned March 23, 1904, having been elected Senator.
[36] Elected to fill vacancy caused by resignation of Charles W. F. Dick, and took his seat December 5, 1904.
[37] Elected to fill vacancy caused by death of Representative-elect Thomas H. Tongue, in preceding Congress, and took his seat November 9, 1903.
[38] Died May 28, 1904.

[39] Appointed to fill vacancy caused by death of Matthew S. Quay, and took his seat January 25, 1905; subsequently elected.
[40] Died December 5, 1903.
[41] Elected to fill vacancy caused by death of Henry Burk, and took his seat February 29, 1904.
[42] Died July 26, 1903, before Congress assembled.
[43] Elected to fill vacancy caused by death of Robert H. Foerderer, and took his seat November 9, 1903.
[44] Served until February 10, 1904; succeeded by William Connell, who contested his election.
[45] Successfully contested the election of George Howell, and took his seat February 10, 1904.

SOUTH CAROLINA

SENATORS

Benjamin R. Tillman, *Trenton*
Asbury C. Latimer, *Belton*

REPRESENTATIVES

George S. Legare, *Charleston*
George W. Croft,[46] *Aiken*
Theodore G. Croft,[47] *Aiken*
Wyatt Aiken, *Abbeville*
Joseph T. Johnson, *Spartanburg*
David E. Finley, *Yorkville*
Robert B. Scarborough, *Conway*
Asbury F. Lever,[48] *Lexington*

SOUTH DAKOTA

SENATORS

Robert J. Gamble, *Yankton*
Alfred B. Kittredge, *Sioux Falls*

REPRESENTATIVES AT LARGE

Charles H. Burke, *Pierre*
Eben W. Martin, *Deadwood*

TENNESSEE

SENATORS

William B. Bate, *Nashville*
Edward W. Carmack, *Memphis*

REPRESENTATIVES

Walter P. Brownlow, *Jonesboro*
Henry R. Gibson, *Knoxville*
John A. Moon, *Chattanooga*
Morgan C. Fitzpatrick, *Hartsville*
James D. Richardson, *Murfreesboro*
John W. Gaines, *Nashville*
Lemuel P. Padgett, *Columbia*
Thetus W. Sims,[49] *Linden*
Rice A. Pierce, *Union City*
Malcolm R. Patterson, *Memphis*

TEXAS

SENATORS

Charles A. Culberson, *Dallas*
Joseph W. Bailey, *Gainesville*

REPRESENTATIVES

Morris Sheppard, *Texarkana*
Samuel B. Cooper, *Beaumont*
Gordon J. Russell, *Tyler*
Choice B. Randell, *Sherman*
Jack Beall, *Waxahachie*
Scott Field, *Calvert*
Alexander W. Gregg, *Palestine*
Thomas H. Ball,[50] *Huntsville*
John M. Pinckney,[51] *Hempstead*
George F. Burgess, *Gonzales*

Albert S. Burleson, *Austin*
Robert L. Henry, *Waco*
Oscar W. Gillespie, *Fort Worth*
John H. Stephens, *Vernon*
James L. Slayden, *San Antonio*
John N. Garner, *Uvalde*
William R. Smith, *Colorado*

UTAH

SENATORS

Thomas Kearns, *Salt Lake City*
Reed Smoot, *Provo*

REPRESENTATIVE

At Large—Joseph Howell, *Logan*

VERMONT

SENATORS

Redfield Proctor, *Proctor*
William P. Dillingham, *Montpelier*

REPRESENTATIVES

David J. Foster, *Burlington*
Kittredge Haskins, *Brattleboro*

VIRGINIA

SENATORS

John W. Daniel, *Lynchburg*
Thomas S. Martin, *Scottsville*

REPRESENTATIVES

William A. Jones, *Warsaw*
Harry L. Maynard, *Portsmouth*
John Lamb, *Richmond*
Robert G. Southall, *Amelia*
Claude A. Swanson, *Chatham*
Carter Glass, *Lynchburg*
James Hay, *Madison*
John F. Rixey, *Brandy*
Campbell Slemp, *Big Stone Gap*
Henry D. Flood, *Appomattox*

WASHINGTON

SENATORS

Addison G. Foster, *Tacoma*
Levi Ankeny, *Walla Walla*

REPRESENTATIVES AT LARGE

Wesley L. Jones, *North Yakima*
Francis W. Cushman, *Tacoma*
William E. Humphrey, *Seattle*

WEST VIRGINIA

SENATORS

Stephen B. Elkins, *Elkins*
Nathan B. Scott, *Wheeling*

REPRESENTATIVES

Blackburn B. Dovener, *Wheeling*
Alston G. Dayton, *Philippi*
Joseph Holt Gaines, *Charleston*
Harry C. Woodyard, *Spencer*
James A. Hughes, *Huntington*

WISCONSIN

SENATORS

John C. Spooner, *Madison*
Joseph V. Quarles, *Milwaukee*

REPRESENTATIVES

Henry Allen Cooper, *Racine*
Henry C. Adams, *Madison*
Joseph W. Babcock, *Necedah*
Theobold Otjen, *Milwaukee*
William H. Stafford, *Milwaukee*
Charles H. Weisse, *Sheyboygan Falls*
John J. Esch, *La Crosse*
James H. Davidson, *Oshkosh*
Edward S. Minor, *Sturgeon Bay*
Webster E. Brown, *Rhinelander*
John J. Jenkins, *Chippewa Falls*

WYOMING

SENATORS

Clarence D. Clark, *Evanston*
Francis E. Warren, *Cheyenne*

REPRESENTATIVE

At Large—Frank W. Mondell, *Newcastle*

TERRITORY OF ARIZONA

DELEGATE

John F. Wilson, *Prescott*

TERRITORY OF HAWAII

DELEGATE

Jonah K. Kalanianaole, *Waikiki*

TERRITORY OF NEW MEXICO

DELEGATE

Bernard S. Rodey, *Albuquerque*

TERRITORY OF OKLAHOMA

DELEGATE

Bird S. McGuire,[52] *Pawnee*

PORTO RICO

RESIDENT COMMISSIONER[53]

Federico Degetau, *San Juan*

---

[46] Died March 10, 1904.
[47] Elected to fill vacancy caused by death of his father, George W. Croft, and took his seat December 5, 1904.
[48] Election unsuccessfully contested by Alexander D. Dantzler.

[49] Election unsuccessfully contested by F. M. Davis.
[50] Resigned effective November 16, 1903.
[51] Elected to fill vacancy caused by resignation of Thomas H. Ball, and took his seat December 7, 1903.
[52] Election unsuccessfully contested by William M. Cross.

[53] Granted same powers and privileges possessed by Delegates and made competent to serve as additional member of Committee on Insular Affairs February 2, 1904.

FIFTY-NINTH CONGRESS

MARCH 4, 1905, TO MARCH 3, 1907

FIRST SESSION—*December 4, 1905, to June 30, 1906*

SECOND SESSION—*December 3, 1906, to March 3, 1907*

SPECIAL SESSION OF THE SENATE—*March 4, 1905, to March 18, 1905*

———

VICE PRESIDENT OF THE UNITED STATES—CHARLES W. FAIRBANKS, of Indiana

PRESIDENT PRO TEMPORE OF THE SENATE—WILLIAM P. FRYE, of Maine

SECRETARY OF THE SENATE—CHARLES G. BENNETT, of New York

SERGEANT AT ARMS OF THE SENATE—DANIEL M. RANSDELL, of Indiana

———

SPEAKER OF THE HOUSE OF REPRESENTATIVES—JOSEPH G. CANNON,[1] of Illinois

CLERK OF THE HOUSE—ALEXANDER McDOWELL,[2] of Pennsylvania

SERGEANT AT ARMS OF THE HOUSE—HENRY CASSON, of Wisconsin

DOORKEEPER OF THE HOUSE—FRANK B. LYON, of New York

POSTMASTER OF THE HOUSE—J. C. McELROY

ALABAMA

SENATORS

John T. Morgan, *Selma*
Edmund W. Pettus, *Selma*

REPRESENTATIVES

George W. Taylor, *Demopolis*
Ariosto A. Wiley, *Montgomery*
Henry D. Clayton, *Eufaula*
Sydney J. Bowie, *Anniston*
J. Thomas Heflin, *Lafayette*
John H. Bankhead, *Fayette*
John L. Burnett, *Gadsden*
William Richardson, *Huntsville*
Oscar W. Underwood, *Birmingham*

ARKANSAS

SENATORS

James H. Berry, *Bentonville*
James P. Clarke, *Little Rock*

REPRESENTATIVES

Robert B. Macon, *Helena*
Stephen Brundidge, Jr., *Searcy*
John C. Floyd, *Yellville*
John S. Little,[3] *Greenwood*
Charles C. Reid, *Morrillton*
Joseph T. Robinson, *Lonoke*
Robert M. Wallace, *Magnolia*

CALIFORNIA

SENATORS

George C. Perkins, *Oakland*
Frank P. Flint, *Los Angeles*

REPRESENTATIVES

James N. Gillett,[4] *Eureka*
William F. Englebright,[5] *Nevada City*
Duncan E. McKinlay, *Santa Rosa*
Joseph R. Knowland, *Alameda*
Julius Kahn, *San Francisco*
Everis A. Hayes, *San Jose*
James C. Needham, *Modesto*
James McLachlan, *Pasadena*
Sylvester C. Smith, *Bakersfield*

COLORADO

SENATORS

Henry M. Teller, *Central City*
Thomas M. Patterson, *Denver*

REPRESENTATIVES

Robert W. Bonynge, *Denver*
Herschel M. Hogg, *Telluride*
At Large—Franklin E. Brooks, *Colorado Springs*

CONNECTICUT

SENATORS

Orville H. Platt,[6] *Meriden*
Frank B. Brandegee,[7] *New London*
Morgan G. Bulkeley, *Hartford*

REPRESENTATIVES

E. Stevens Henry, *Rockville*
Nehemiah D. Sperry, *New Haven*
Frank B. Brandegee,[8] *New London*
Edwin W. Higgins,[9] *Norwich*
Ebenezer J. Hill, *Norwalk*
At Large—George L. Lilley, *Waterbury*

---

[1] Reelected December 4, 1905.
[2] Reelected December 4, 1905.
[3] Resigned, to take effect January 14, 1907, having been elected Governor.
[4] Resigned November 4, 1906, having been elected Governor.

[5] Elected to fill vacancy caused by resignation of James N. Gillett, and took his seat January 3, 1907.
[6] Died April 21, 1905.
[7] Elected to fill vacancy caused by death of Orville H. Platt, and took his seat December 5, 1905.

[8] Resigned May 10, 1905, before Congress assembled, having been elected Senator.
[9] Elected to fill vacancy caused by resignation of Frank B. Brandegee, and took his seat December 4, 1905.

DELAWARE

SENATORS

J. Frank Allee, *Dover*
Henry A. du Pont,[10] *Winterthur*

REPRESENTATIVE

At Large—Hiram R. Burton, *Lewes*

FLORIDA

SENATORS

Stephen R. Mallory, *Pensacola*
James P. Taliaferro,[11] *Jacksonville*

REPRESENTATIVES

Stephen M. Sparkman, *Tampa*
Frank Clark, *Lake City*
William B. Lamar, *Monticello*

GEORGIA

SENATORS

Augustus O. Bacon, *Macon*
Alexander S. Clay, *Marietta*

REPRESENTATIVES

Rufus E. Lester,[12] *Savannah*
James W. Overstreet,[13] *Sylvania*
James M. Griggs, *Dawson*
Elijah B. Lewis, *Montezuma*
William C. Adamson, *Carrollton*
Leonidas F. Livingston, *Covington*
Charles L. Bartlett, *Macon*
Gordon Lee, *Chickamauga*
William M. Howard, *Lexington*
Thomas M. Bell, *Gainesville*
Thomas W. Hardwick, *Sandersville*
William G. Brantley, *Brunswick*

IDAHO

SENATORS

Fred T. Dubois, *Blackfoot*
Weldon B. Heyburn, *Wallace*

REPRESENTATIVE

At Large—Burton L. French, *Moscow*

ILLINOIS

SENATORS

Shelby M. Cullom, *Springfield*
Albert J. Hopkins, *Aurora*

REPRESENTATIVES

Martin B. Madden, *Chicago*
James R. Mann, *Chicago*
William W. Wilson, *Chicago*
Charles S. Wharton, *Chicago*
Anthony Michalek,[14] *Chicago*
William Lorimer, *Chicago*
Philip Knopf, *Chicago*
Charles McGavin, *Chicago*
Henry S. Boutell, *Chicago*
George E. Foss, *Chicago*
Howard M. Snapp, *Joliet*
Charles E. Fuller, *Belvidere*
Robert R. Hitt,[15] *Mount Morris*
Frank O. Lowden,[16] *Oregon*
Benjamin F. Marsh,[17] *Warsaw*
James McKinney,[18] *Aledo*
George W. Prince, *Galesburg*
Joseph V. Graff, *Peoria*
John A. Sterling, *Bloomington*
Joseph G. Cannon, *Danville*
William B. McKinley, *Champaign*
Henry T. Rainey, *Carrollton*
Zeno J. Rives, *Litchfield*
William A. Rodenberg, *East St. Louis*
Frank S. Dickson, *Ramsey*
Pleasant T. Chapman, *Vienna*
George W. Smith, *Murphysboro*

INDIANA

SENATORS

Albert J. Beveridge, *Indianapolis*
James A. Hemenway,[19] *Boonville*

REPRESENTATIVES

John H. Foster,[20] *Evansville*
John C. Chaney, *Sullivan*
William T. Zenor, *Corydon*
Lincoln Dixon, *North Vernon*
Elias S. Holliday, *Brazil*
James E. Watson, *Rushville*
Jesse Overstreet, *Indianapolis*
George W. Cromer, *Muncie*
Charles B. Landis, *Delphi*
Edgar D. Crumpacker, *Valparaiso*
Frederick Landis, *Logansport*
Newton W. Gilbert,[21] *Fort Wayne*
Clarence C. Gilhams,[22] *La Grange*
Abraham L. Brick, *South Bend*

IOWA

SENATORS

William B. Allison, *Dubuque*
Jonathan P. Dolliver, *Fort Dodge*

REPRESENTATIVES

Thomas Hedge, *Burlington*
Albert F. Dawson, *Preston*
Benjamin P. Birdsall, *Clarion*
Gilbert N. Haugen, *Northwood*
Robert G. Cousins, *Tipton*
John F. Lacey, *Oskaloosa*
John A. T. Hull, *Des Moines*
William P. Hepburn, *Clarinda*
Walter I. Smith, *Council Bluffs*
James P. Conner, *Denison*
Elbert H. Hubbard, *Sioux City*

KANSAS

SENATORS

Joseph R. Burton,[23] *Abilene*
Alfred W. Benson,[24] *Ottawa*
Charles Curtis,[25] *Topeka*
Chester I. Long, *Medicine Lodge*

REPRESENTATIVES

Charles Curtis,[26] *Topeka*
Justin D. Bowersock *Lawrence*
Philip P. Campbell, *Pittsburg*
James M. Miller, *Council Grove*
William A. Calderhead, *Marysville*
William A. Reeder, *Logan*
Victor Murdock, *Wichita*
At Large—Charles F. Scott, *Iola*

KENTUCKY

SENATORS

Joseph C. S. Blackburn, *Versailles*
James B. McCreary, *Richmond*

REPRESENTATIVES

Ollie M. James, *Marion*
Augustus O. Stanley, *Henderson*
James M. Richardson, *Glasgow*
David H. Smith, *Hodgensville*
J. Swagar Sherley, *Louisville*
Joseph L. Rhinock, *Covington*
South Trimble, *Frankfort*
George G. Gilbert, *Shelbyville*
Joseph B. Bennett, *Greenup*
Frank A. Hopkins, *Prestonsburg*
Don C. Edwards, *London*

LOUISIANA

SENATORS

Samuel D. McEnery, *New Orleans*
Murphy J. Foster, *Franklin*

---

[10] Elected to fill vacancy in the term beginning March 4, 1905, caused by failure of legislature to elect, and took his seat December 3, 1906; vacancy in this class from March 4, 1905, to June 12, 1906.
[11] Reappointed to fill vacancy in the term beginning March 4, 1905, to serve until the next meeting of the legislature; subsequently reelected.
[12] Died June 16, 1906.
[13] Elected to fill vacancy caused by death of Rufus E. Lester, and took his seat December 3, 1906.
[14] Protests of certain citizens of Fifth District were filed against his being seated upon grounds he was not of legal age and an alien; committee reported resolu-

tion declaring him qualified and entitled to the seat, which was agreed to March 6, 1906.
[15] Died September 19, 1906.
[16] Elected to fill vacancy caused by death of Robert R. Hitt, and took his seat December 3, 1906.
[17] Died June 2, 1905, before Congress assembled.
[18] Elected to fill vacancy caused by death of Benjamin F. Marsh, and took his seat December 4, 1905.
[19] Elected to fill vacancy caused by resignation of Charles W. Fairbanks, in preceding Congress, and took his seat March 4, 1905.
[20] Elected to fill vacancy caused by resignation of Representative-elect James A. Hemenway, in preceding Congress, and took his seat December 4, 1905.

[21] Resigned November 6, 1906, having been appointed judge in the Philippine Islands.
[22] Elected to fill vacancy caused by resignation of Newton W. Gilbert, and took his seat December 3, 1906.
[23] Resigned June 4, 1906.
[24] Appointed to fill vacancy caused by resignation of Joseph R. Burton, and took his seat June 14, 1906.
[25] Elected to fill vacancy caused by resignation of Joseph R. Burton, and took his seat January 29, 1907.
[26] Resigned January 28, 1907, before the commencement of the Sixtieth Congress, to which he had been reelected, having been elected Senator.

REPRESENTATIVES

Adolph Meyer, *New Orleans*
Robert C. Davey, *New Orleans*
Robert F. Broussard, *New Iberia*
John T. Watkins, *Minden*
Joseph E. Ransdell, *Lake Providence*
Samuel M. Robertson, *Baton Rouge*
Arsène P. Pujo, *Lake Charles*

MAINE

SENATORS

Eugene Hale, *Ellsworth*
William P. Frye, *Lewiston*

REPRESENTATIVES

Amos L. Allen, *Alfred*
Charles E. Littlefield, *Rockland*
Edwin C. Burleigh, *Augusta*
Llewellyn Powers, *Houlton*

MARYLAND

SENATORS

Arthur Pue Gorman,[27] *Laurel*
William Pinkney Whyte,[28] *Baltimore*
Isidor Rayner, *Baltimore*

REPRESENTATIVES

Thomas A. Smith, *Ridgely*
J. Fred. C. Talbott, *Towson*
Frank C. Wachter, *Baltimore*
John Gill, Jr., *Baltimore*
Sydney E. Mudd, *La Plata*
George A. Pearre, *Cumberland*

MASSACHUSETTS

SENATORS

Henry Cabot Lodge, *Nahant*
W. Murray Crane, *Dalton*

REPRESENTATIVES

George P. Lawrence, *North Adams*
Frederick H. Gillett, *Springfield*
Rockwood Hoar,[29] *Worcester*
Charles G. Washburn,[30] *Worcester*
Charles Q. Tirrell, *Natick*
Butler Ames, *Lowell*
Augustus P. Gardner, *Hamilton*
Ernest W. Roberts, *Chelsea*
Samuel W. McCall, *Winchester*
John A. Keliher, *Boston*
William S. McNary, *Boston*
John A. Sullivan, *Boston*
John W. Weeks, *Newton*
William S. Greene, *Fall River*
William C. Lovering, *Taunton*

MICHIGAN

SENATORS

Julius C. Burrows, *Kalamazoo*
Russell A. Alger,[31] *Detroit*
William Alden Smith,[32] *Grand Rapids*

REPRESENTATIVES

Edwin Denby, *Detroit*
Charles E. Townsend, *Jackson*
Washington Gardner, *Albion*
Edward L. Hamilton, *Niles*
William Alden Smith,[33] *Grand Rapids*
Samuel W. Smith, *Pontiac*
Henry McMorran, *Port Huron*
Joseph W. Fordney, *Saginaw*
Roswell P. Bishop, *Ludington*
George A. Loud, *Au Sable*
Archibald B. Darragh, *St. Louis*
H. Olin Young, *Ishpeming*

MINNESOTA

SENATORS

Knute Nelson, *Alexandria*
Moses E. Clapp, *St. Paul*

REPRESENTATIVES

James A. Tawney, *Winona*
James T. McCleary, *Mankato*
Charles R. David, *St. Peter*
Frederick C. Stevens, *St. Paul*
Loren Fletcher, *Minneapolis*
Clarence B. Buckman, *Little Falls*
Andrew J. Volstead, *Granite Falls*
J. Adam Bede, *Pine City*
Halvor Steenerson, *Crookston*

MISSISSIPPI

SENATORS

Hernando D. Money, *Carrollton*
Anselm J. McLaurin, *Brandon*

REPRESENTATIVES

Ezekiel S. Candler, Jr., *Corinth*
Thomas Spight, *Ripley*
Benjamin G. Humphreys, *Greenville*
Wilson S. Hill, *Winona*
Adam M. Byrd, *Philadelphia*
Eaton J. Bowers, *Bay St. Louis*
Frank A. McLain, *Gloster*
John Sharp Williams, *Yazoo City*

MISSOURI

SENATORS

William J. Stone, *Jefferson City*
William Warner, *Kansas City*

REPRESENTATIVES

James T. Lloyd, *Shelbyville*
William W. Rucker, *Keytesville*
Frank B. Klepper, *Kingston*
Frank B. Fulkerson, *St. Joseph*
Edgar C. Ellis, *Kansas City*
David A. De Armond, *Butler*
John Welborn, *Lexington*
Dorsey W. Shackleford, *Jefferson City*
James Beauchamp Clark, *Bowling Green*
Richard Bartholdt, *St. Louis*
John T. Hunt, *St. Louis*
Ernest E. Wood,[34] *St. Louis*
Harry M. Coudrey,[35] *St. Louis*
Marion E. Rhodes, *Potosi*
William T. Tyndall, *Sparta*
Cassius M. Shartel, *Neosho*
Arthur P. Murphy, *Rolla*

MONTANA

SENATORS

William A. Clark, *Butte*
Thomas H. Carter, *Helena*

REPRESENTATIVE

At Large—Joseph M. Dixon, *Missoula*

NEBRASKA

SENATORS

Joseph H. Millard, *Omaha*
Elmer J. Burkett, *Lincoln*

REPRESENTATIVES

Ernest M. Pollard,[36] *Nehawka*
John L. Kennedy, *Omaha*
John J. McCarthy, *Ponca*
Edmund H. Hinshaw, *Fairbury*
George W. Norris, *McCook*
Moses P. Kinkaid, *O'Neill*

NEVADA

SENATORS

Francis G. Newlands, *Reno*
George S. Nixon, *Winnemucca*

REPRESENTATIVE

At Large—Clarence D. Van Duzer, *Tonopah*

NEW HAMPSHIRE

SENATORS

Jacob H. Gallinger, *Concord*
Henry E. Burnham, *Manchester*

REPRESENTATIVES

Cyrus A. Sulloway, *Manchester*
Frank D. Currier, *Canaan*

---

[27] Died June 4, 1906.
[28] Appointed to fill vacancy caused by death of Arthur Pue Gorman, and took his seat June 11, 1906; subsequently elected.
[29] Died November 1, 1906.
[30] Elected to fill vacancy caused by death of Rockwood Hoar, and took his seat January 3, 1907.

[31] Died January 24, 1907.
[32] Elected to fill vacancy caused by death of Russell A. Alger, and took his seat February 11, 1907.
[33] Resigned effective February 9, 1907, before the commencement of the Sixtieth Congress, to which he had been reelected, having been elected Senator.

[34] Served until June 23, 1906; succeeded by Harry M. Coudrey, who contested his election.
[35] Successfully contested the election of Ernest E. Wood, and took his seat June 23, 1906.
[36] Elected to fill vacancy caused by resignation of Representative-elect Elmer J. Burkett, in preceding Congress, and took his seat December 4, 1905.

NEW JERSEY

SENATORS

John Kean, *Elizabeth*
John F. Dryden, *Newark*

REPRESENTATIVES

Henry C. Loudenslager, *Paulsboro*
John J. Gardner, *Atlantic City*
Benjamin F. Howell, *New Brunswick*
Ira W. Wood, *Trenton*
Charles N. Fowler, *Elizabeth*
Henry C. Allen, *Little Falls*
Richard Wayne Parker, *Newark*
William H. Wiley, *East Orange*
Marshall Van Winkle, *Jersey City*
Allan L. McDermott, *Jersey City*

NEW YORK

SENATORS

Thomas C. Platt, *Owego*
Chauncey M. Depew, *Peekskill*

REPRESENTATIVES

William W. Cocks, *Westbury*
George H. Lindsay, *Brooklyn*
Charles T. Dunwell, *Brooklyn*
Charles B. Law, *Brooklyn*
George E. Waldo, *Brooklyn*
William M. Calder, *Brooklyn*
John J. Fitzgerald, *Brooklyn*
Timothy D. Sullivan,[37] *New York City*
Daniel J. Riordan,[38] *New York City*
Henry M. Goldfogle, *New York City*
William Sulzer, *New York City*
William R. Hearst, *New York City*
W. Bourke Cockran, *New York City*
Herbert Parsons, *New York City*
Charles A. Towne, *New York City*
J. Van Vechten Olcott, *New York City*
Jacob Ruppert, Jr., *New York City*
William S. Bennet, *New York City*
Joseph A. Goulden, *Fordham*
John E. Andrus, *Yonkers*
Thomas W. Bradley, *Walden*
John H. Ketcham,[39] *Dover Plains*
William H. Draper, *Troy*
George N. Southwick, *Albany*
Frank J. Le Fevre, *New Paltz*
Lucius N. Littauer, *Gloversville*
William H. Flack,[40] *Malone*
James S. Sherman, *Utica*
Charles L. Knapp, *Lowville*
Michael E. Driscoll, *Syracuse*
John W. Dwight, *Dryden*
Sereno E. Payne, *Auburn*
James B. Perkins, *Rochester*
J. Sloat Fassett, *Elmira*
James W. Wadsworth, *Geneseo*

William H. Ryan, *Buffalo*
De Alva S. Alexander, *Buffalo*
Edward B. Vreeland, *Salamanca*

NORTH CAROLINA

SENATORS

Furnifold McL. Simmons, *Raleigh*
Lee S. Overman, *Salisbury*

REPRESENTATIVES

John H. Small, *Washington*
Claude Kitchin, *Scotland Neck*
Charles R. Thomas, *New Bern*
Edward W. Pou, *Smithfield*
William W. Kitchin, *Roxboro*
Gilbert B. Patterson, *Maxton*
Robert N. Page, *Biscoe*
E. Spencer Blackburn, *Wilkesboro*
Edwin Y. Webb, *Shelby*
James M. Gudger, Jr., *Asheville*

NORTH DAKOTA

SENATORS

Henry C. Hansbrough, *Devils Lake*
Porter J. McCumber, *Wahpeton*

REPRESENTATIVES AT LARGE

Thomas F. Marshall, *Oakes*
Asle J. Gronna, *Lakota*

OHIO

SENATORS

Joseph B. Foraker, *Cincinnati*
Charles W. F. Dick, *Akron*

REPRESENTATIVES

Nicholas Longworth, *Cincinnati*
Herman P. Goebel, *Cincinnati*
Robert M. Nevin, *Dayton*
Harvey C. Garber, *Greenville*
William W. Campbell, *Napoleon*
Thomas E. Scroggy, *Xenia*
J. Warren Keifer, *Springfield*
Ralph D. Cole, *Findlay*
James H. Southard, *Toledo*
Henry T. Bannon, *Portsmouth*
Charles H. Grosvenor, *Athens*
Edward L. Taylor, Jr., *Columbus*
Grant E. Mouser, *Marion*
Amos R. Webber, *Elyria*
Beman G. Dawes, *Marietta*
Capell L. Weems, *St. Clairsville*
Martin L. Smyser, *Wooster*
James Kennedy, *Youngstown*
W. Aubrey Thomas, *Niles*
Jacob A. Beidler, *Willoughby*
Theodore E. Burton, *Cleveland*

OREGON

SENATORS

John H. Mitchell,[41] *Portland*
John M. Gearin,[42] *Portland*
Frederick W. Mulkey,[43] *Portland*
Charles W. Fulton, *Astoria*

REPRESENTATIVES

Binger Hermann, *Roseburg*
John N. Williamson,[44] *Prineville*

PENNSYLVANIA

SENATORS

Boies Penrose, *Philadelphia*
Philander C. Knox, *Pittsburgh*

REPRESENTATIVES

Henry H. Bingham, *Philadelphia*
Robert Adams, Jr.,[45] *Philadelphia*
John E. Reyburn,[46] *Philadelphia*
George A. Castor,[47] *Philadelphia*
J. Hampton Moore,[48] *Philadelphia*
Reuben O. Moon, *Philadelphia*
Edward de V. Morrell, *Torresdale*
George D. McCreary, *Philadelphia*
Thomas S. Butler, *West Chester*
Irving P. Wanger, *Norristown*
Henry B. Cassel, *Marietta*
Thomas H. Dale, *Scranton*
Henry W. Palmer, *Wilkes-Barre*
George R. Patterson,[49] *Ashland*
Charles N. Brumm,[50] *Minersville*
Marcus C. L. Kline, *Allentown*
Mial E. Lilley, *Towanda*
Elias Deemer, *Williamsport*
Edmund W. Samuel, *Mount Carmel*
Thaddeus M. Mahon, *Chambersburg*
Marlin E. Olmsted, *Harrisburg*
John M. Reynolds, *Bedford*
Daniel F. Lafean, *York*
Solomon R. Dresser, *Bradford*
George F. Huff, *Greensburg*
Allen F. Cooper, *Uniontown*
Ernest F. Acheson, *Washington*
Arthur L. Bates, *Meadville*
Gustav A. Schneebeli, *Nazareth*
William O. Smith, *Punxsutawney*
Joseph C. Sibley, *Franklin*
William H. Graham, *Allegheny*
John Dalzell, *Pittsburgh*
James F. Burke, *Pittsburgh*
Andrew J. Barchfeld, *Pittsburgh*

RHODE ISLAND

SENATORS

Nelson W. Aldrich, *Providence*
George P. Wetmore, *Newport*

---

[37] Resigned July 27, 1906.
[38] Elected to fill vacancy caused by resignation of Timothy D. Sullivan, and took his seat December 3, 1906.
[39] Died November 4, 1906.
[40] Died February 2, 1907.
[41] Died December 8, 1905.

[42] Appointed to fill vacancy caused by death of John H. Mitchell, and took his seat December 21, 1905.
[43] Elected to fill vacancy caused by death of John H. Mitchell, and took his seat January 30, 1907.
[44] Never qualified.
[45] Died June 1, 1906.
[46] Elected to fill vacancy caused by death of Robert

Adams, Jr., and took his seat December 3, 1906.
[47] Died February 19, 1906.
[48] Elected to fill vacancy caused by death of George A. Castor, and took his seat December 3, 1906.
[49] Died March 21, 1906.
[50] Elected to fill vacancy caused by death of George R. Patterson, and took his seat December 3, 1906.

REPRESENTATIVES

Daniel L. D. Granger, *Providence*
Adin B. Capron, *Stillwater*

SOUTH CAROLINA

SENATORS

Benjamin R. Tillman, *Trenton*
Asbury C. Latimer, *Belton*

REPRESENTATIVES

George S. Legare,[51] *Charleston*
James O'H. Patterson,[52] *Barnwell*
Wyatt Aiken, *Abbeville*
Joseph T. Johnson, *Spartanburg*
David E. Finley, *Yorkville*
J. Edwin Ellerbe, *Marion*
Asbury F. Lever,[53] *Lexington*

SOUTH DAKOTA

SENATORS

Robert J. Gamble, *Yankton*
Alfred B. Kittredge, *Sioux Falls*

REPRESENTATIVES AT LARGE

Charles H. Burke, *Pierre*
Eben W. Martin, *Deadwood*

TENNESSEE

SENATORS

William B. Bate,[54] *Nashville*
James B. Frazier,[55] *Chattanooga*
Edward W. Carmack, *Memphis*

REPRESENTATIVES

Walter P. Brownlow, *Jonesboro*
Nathan W. Hale, *Knoxville*
John A. Moon, *Chattanooga*
Mounce G. Butler, *Gainesboro*
William C. Houston, *Woodbury*
John W. Gaines, *Nashville*
Lemuel P. Padgett, *Columbia*
Thetus W. Sims, *Linden*
Finis J. Garrett, *Dresden*
Malcolm R. Patterson,[56] *Memphis*

TEXAS

SENATORS

Charles A. Culberson, *Dallas*
Joseph W. Bailey, *Gainesville*

REPRESENTATIVES

Morris Sheppard, *Texarkana*
Moses L. Broocks,[57] *San Augustine*
Gordon J. Russell, *Tyler*

Choice B. Randell, *Sherman*
Jack Beall, *Waxahachie*
Scott Field, *Calvert*
Alexander W. Gregg, *Palestine*
John M. Pinckney,[58] *Hempstead*
John M. Moore,[59] *Richmond*
George F. Burgess, *Gonzales*
Albert S. Burleson, *Austin*
Robert L. Henry, *Waco*
Oscar W. Gillespie, *Fort Worth*
John H. Stephens, *Vernon*
James L. Slayden, *San Antonio*
John N. Garner, *Uvalde*
William R. Smith, *Colorado*

UTAH

SENATORS

Reed Smoot, *Provo*
George Sutherland, *Salt Lake City*

REPRESENTATIVE

At Large—Joseph Howell, *Logan*

VERMONT

SENATORS

Redfield Proctor, *Proctor*
William P. Dillingham, *Waterbury*

REPRESENTATIVES

David J. Foster, *Burlington*
Kittredge Haskins, *Brattleboro*

VIRGINIA

SENATORS

John W. Daniel, *Lynchburg*
Thomas S. Martin, *Charlottesville*

REPRESENTATIVES

William A. Jones, *Warsaw*
Harry L. Maynard, *Portsmouth*
John Lamb, *Richmond*
Robert G. Southall, *Amelia*
Claude A. Swanson,[60] *Chatham*
Edward W. Saunders,[61] *Rockymount*
Carter Glass, *Lynchburg*
James Hay, *Madison*
John F. Rixey,[62] *Brandy*
Campbell Slemp, *Big Stone Gap*
Henry D. Flood, *Appomattox*

WASHINGTON

SENATORS

Levi Ankeny, *Walla Walla*
Samuel H. Piles, *Seattle*

REPRESENTATIVES AT LARGE

Wesley L. Jones, *North Yakima*
Francis W. Cushman, *Tacoma*
William E. Humphrey, *Seattle*

WEST VIRGINIA

SENATORS

Stephen B. Elkins, *Elkins*
Nathan B. Scott, *Wheeling*

REPRESENTATIVES

Blackburn B. Dovener, *Wheeling*
Alston G. Dayton,[63] *Philippi*
Thomas B. Davis,[64] *Keyser*
Joseph Holt Gaines, *Charleston*
Harry C. Woodyard, *Spencer*
James A. Hughes, *Huntington*

WISCONSIN

SENATORS

John C. Spooner, *Madison*
Robert M. La Follette,[65] *Madison*

REPRESENTATIVES

Henry Allen Cooper, *Racine*
Henry C. Adams,[66] *Madison*
John M. Nelson,[67] *Madison*
Joseph W. Babcock, *Necedah*
Theobold Otjen, *Milwaukee*
William H. Stafford, *Milwaukee*
Charles H. Weisse, *Sheboygan Falls*
John J. Esch, *La Crosse*
James H. Davidson, *Oshkosh*
Edward S. Minor, *Sturgeon Bay*
Webster E. Brown, *Rhinelander*
John J. Jenkins, *Chippewa Falls*

WYOMING

SENATORS

Clarence D. Clark, *Evanston*
Francis E. Warren, *Cheyenne*

REPRESENTATIVE

At Large—Frank W. Mondell, *Newcastle*

TERRITORY OF ALASKA [68]

DELEGATE

Frank H. Waskey,[69] *Nome*

TERRITORY OF ARIZONA

DELEGATE

Marcus A. Smith, *Tucson*

TERRITORY OF HAWAII

DELEGATE

Jonah K. Kalanianaole,[70] *Waikiki*

---

[51] Election unsuccessfully contested by Aaron P. Prioleau and John A. Noland.
[52] Election unsuccessfully contested by Isaac Myers.
[53] Election unsuccessfully contested by Charles C. Jacobs.
[54] Died March 9, 1905.
[55] Elected to fill vacancy caused by death of William B. Bate, and took his seat December 4, 1905.
[56] Resigned November 5, 1906, having been elected governor.
[57] Election unsuccessfully contested by A. J. Houston.
[58] Died April 24, 1905, before Congress assembled.

[59] Elected to fill vacancy caused by death of John M. Pinckney, and took his seat December 4, 1905.
[60] Resigned to take effect January 30, 1906, having been elected governor.
[61] Elected to fill vacancy caused by resignation of Claude A. Swanson, and took his seat December 3, 1906.
[62] Died February 8, 1907, before the commencement of the Sixtieth Congress, to which he had been reelected.
[63] Resigned March 16, 1905, having been appointed United States district judge.
[64] Elected to fill vacancy caused by resignation of Alston G. Dayton, and took his seat December 4, 1905.

[65] Elected January 25, 1905, for the term beginning March 4, 1905, but did not qualify until January 4, 1906, preferring to retain the governorship.
[66] Died July 9, 1906.
[67] Elected to fill vacancy caused by death of Henry C. Adams, and took his seat December 3, 1906.
[68] Formed from territory ceded to the United States by Russia by treaty of March 30, 1867; granted a civil government without representation in Congress, by act of May 17, 1884; granted a Delegate in Congress by act of May 8, 1906.
[69] Took his seat December 3, 1906.
[70] Election unsuccessfully contested by Curtis P. Iaokea.

TERRITORY OF NEW MEXICO

DELEGATE

William H. Andrews, *Albuquerque*

TERRITORY OF OKLAHOMA

DELEGATE

Bird S. McGuire, *Pawnee*

PORTO RICO

RESIDENT COMMISSIONER

Tulio Larrinaga, *San Juan*

SIXTIETH CONGRESS

MARCH 4, 1907, TO MARCH 3, 1909

FIRST SESSION—*December 2, 1907, to May 30, 1908*

SECOND SESSION—*December 7, 1908, to March 3, 1909*

———

VICE PRESIDENT OF THE UNITED STATES—CHARLES W. FAIRBANKS, of Indiana

PRESIDENT PRO TEMPORE OF THE SENATE—WILLIAM P. FRYE,[1] of Maine

SECRETARY OF THE SENATE—CHARLES G. BENNETT, of New York

SERGEANT AT ARMS OF THE SENATE—DANIEL M. RANSDELL, of Indiana

———

SPEAKER OF THE HOUSE OF REPRESENTATIVES—JOSEPH G. CANNON,[2] of Illinois

CLERK OF THE HOUSE—ALEXANDER McDOWELL,[3] of Pennsylvania

SERGEANT AT ARMS OF THE HOUSE—HENRY CASSON, of Wisconsin

DOORKEEPER OF THE HOUSE—FRANK B. LYON, of New York

POSTMASTER OF THE HOUSE—SAMUEL LANGUM

ALABAMA

SENATORS

John T. Morgan,[4] *Selma*
John H. Bankhead,[5] *Fayette*
Edmund W. Pettus,[6] *Selma*
Joseph F. Johnston,[7] *Birmingham*

REPRESENTATIVES

George W. Taylor, *Demopolis*
Ariosto A. Wiley,[8] *Montgomery*
Oliver C. Wiley,[9] *Troy*
Henry D. Clayton, *Eufaula*
William B. Craig, *Selma*
J. Thomas Heflin, *Lafayette*
Richmond P. Hobson, *Greensboro*
John L. Burnett, *Gadsden*
William Richardson, *Huntsville*
Oscar W. Underwood, *Birmingham*

ARKANSAS

SENATORS

James P. Clarke, *Little Rock*
Jeff Davis, *Little Rock*

REPRESENTATIVES

Robert B. Macon, *Helena*
Stephen Brundidge, Jr., *Searcy*
John C. Floyd, *Yellville*
William B. Cravens, *Fort Smith*
Charles C. Reid, *Morrillton*
Joseph T. Robinson, *Lonoke*
Robert M. Wallace, *Magnolia*

CALIFORNIA

SENATORS

George C. Perkins, *Oakland*
Frank P. Flint, *Los Angeles*

REPRESENTATIVES

William F. Englebright, *Nevada City*
Duncan E. McKinlay, *Santa Rosa*
Joseph R. Knowland, *Alameda*
Julius Kahn, *San Francisco*
Everis A. Hayes, *San Jose*
James C. Needham, *Modesto*
James McLachlan, *Pasadena*
Sylvester C. Smith, *Bakersfield*

COLORADO

SENATORS

Henry M. Teller, *Central City*
Simon Guggenheim, *Denver*

REPRESENTATIVES

Robert W. Bonynge, *Denver*
Warren A. Haggott, *Idaho Springs*
At Large—George W. Cook; *Denver*

CONNECTICUT

SENATORS

Morgan G. Bulkeley, *Hartford*
Frank B. Brandegee, *New London*

REPRESENTATIVES

E. Stevens Henry, *Rockville*
Nehemiah D. Sperry, *New Haven*
Edwin W. Higgins, *Norwich*
Ebenezer J. Hill, *Norwalk*
At Large—George L. Lilley,[10] *Waterbury*

---

[1] Reelected December 5, 1907.
[2] Reelected December 2, 1907.
[3] Reelected December 2, 1907.
[4] Died June 11, 1907.
[5] Appointed to fill vacancy caused by death of John T. Morgan, subsequently elected, and took his seat January 13, 1908.
[6] Died July 27, 1907.
[7] Elected to fill vacancy caused by death of Edmund W. Pettus, and took his seat December 3, 1907.
[8] Died June 17, 1908.
[9] Elected to fill vacancy caused by death of his brother, Ariosto A. Wiley, and took his seat December 7, 1908.
[10] By resolution of January 20, 1909, seat was declared to have been vacated January 6, 1909, for the reason that incumbent had entered upon the duties of the office of Governor of Connecticut the preceding day.

DELAWARE

SENATORS

Henry A. du Pont, *Winterthur*
Harry A. Richardson, *Dover*

REPRESENTATIVE

At Large—Hiram R. Burton, *Lewes*

FLORIDA

SENATORS

Stephen R. Mallory,[11] *Pensacola*
William J. Bryan,[12] *Jacksonville*
William H. Milton,[13] *Marianna*
James P. Taliaferro, *Jacksonville*

REPRESENTATIVES

Stephen M. Sparkman, *Tampa*
Frank Clark, *Gainesville*
William B. Lamar, *Monticello*

GEORGIA

SENATORS

Augustus O. Bacon, *Macon*
Alexander S. Clay, *Marietta*

REPRESENTATIVES

Charles G. Edwards, *Savannah*
James M. Griggs, *Dawson*
Elijah B. Lewis, *Montezuma*
William C. Adamson, *Carrollton*
Leonidas F. Livingston, *Covington*
Charles L. Bartlett, *Macon*
Gordon Lee, *Chickamauga*
William M. Howard, *Lexington*
Thomas M. Bell, *Gainesville*
Thomas W. Hardwick, *Sandersville*
William G. Brantley, *Brunswick*

IDAHO

SENATORS

Weldon B. Heyburn, *Wallace*
William E. Borah, *Boise*

REPRESENTATIVE

At Large—Burton L. French, *Moscow*

ILLINOIS

SENATORS

Shelby M. Cullom, *Springfield*
Albert J. Hopkins, *Aurora*

REPRESENTATIVES

Martin B. Madden, *Chicago*
James R. Mann, *Chicago*

William W. Wilson, *Chicago*
James T. McDermott, *Chicago*
Adolph J. Sabath,[14] *Chicago*
William Lorimer, *Chicago*
Philip Knopf, *Chicago*
Charles McGavin,[15] *Chicago*
Henry S. Boutell, *Chicago*
George E. Foss, *Chicago*
Howard M. Snapp, *Joliet*
Charles E. Fuller, *Belvidere*
Frank O. Lowden, *Oregon*
James McKinney, *Aledo*
George W. Prince, *Galesburg*
Joseph V. Graff, *Peoria*
John A. Sterling, *Bloomington*
Joseph G. Cannon, *Danville*
William B. McKinley, *Champaign*
Henry T. Rainey, *Carrollton*
Benjamin F. Caldwell, *Chatham*
William A. Rodenberg, *East St. Louis*
Martin D. Foster, *Olney*
Pleasant T. Chapman, *Vienna*
George W. Smith,[16] *Murphysboro*
Napoleon B. Thistlewood,[17] *Cairo*

INDIANA

SENATORS

Albert J. Beveridge, *Indianapolis*
James A. Hemenway, *Boonville*

REPRESENTATIVES

John H. Foster, *Evansville*
John C. Chaney, *Sullivan*
William E. Cox, *Jasper*
Lincoln Dixon, *North Vernon*
Elias S. Holliday, *Brazil*
James E. Watson, *Rushville*
Jesse Overstreet, *Indianapolis*
John A. M. Adair, *Portland*
Charles B. Landis, *Delphi*
Edgar D. Crumpacker, *Valparaiso*
George W. Rauch, *Marion*
Clarence C. Gilhams, *La Grange*
Abraham L. Brick,[18] *South Bend*
Henry A. Barnhart,[19] *Rochester*

IOWA

SENATORS

William B. Allison,[20] *Dubuque*
Albert B. Cummins,[21] *Des Moines*
Jonathan P. Dolliver, *Fort Dodge*

REPRESENTATIVES

Charles A. Kennedy, *Montrose*
Albert F. Dawson, *Preston*
Benjamin P. Birdsall, *Clarion*
Gilbert N. Haugen, *Northwood*

Robert G. Cousins, *Tipton*
Daniel W. Hamilton, *Sigourney*
John A. T. Hull, *Des Moines*
William P. Hepburn, *Clarinda*
Walter I. Smith, *Council Bluffs*
James P. Conner, *Denison*
Elbert H. Hubbard, *Sioux City*

KANSAS

SENATORS

Chester I. Long, *Medicine Lodge*
Charles Curtis, *Topeka*

REPRESENTATIVES

Daniel R. Anthony, Jr.,[22] *Leavenworth*
Charles F. Scott, *Iola*
Philip P. Campbell, *Pittsburg*
James M. Miller, *Council Grove*
William A. Calderhead, *Marysville*
William A. Reeder, *Logan*
Edmond H. Madison, *Dodge City*
Victor Murdock, *Wichita*

KENTUCKY

SENATORS

James B. McCreary, *Richmond*
Thomas H. Paynter, *Greenup*

REPRESENTATIVES

Ollie M. James, *Marion*
Augustus O. Stanley, *Henderson*
Addison D. James, *Penrod*
Ben Johnson, *Bardstown*
J. Swagar Sherley, *Louisville*
Joseph L. Rhinock, *Covington*
William P. Kimball, *Lexington*
Harvey Helm, *Stanford*
Joseph B. Bennett, *Greenup*
John W. Langley, *Pikeville*
Don C. Edwards, *London*

LOUISIANA

SENATORS

Samuel D. McEnery, *New Orleans*
Murphy J. Foster, *Franklin*

REPRESENTATIVES

Adolph Meyer,[23] *New Orleans*
Albert Estopinal,[24] *Estopinal*
Robert C. Davey,[25] *New Orleans*
Robert F. Broussard, *New Iberia*
John T. Watkins, *Minden*
Joseph E. Ransdell, *Lake Providence*
George K. Favrot, *Baton Rouge*
Arsène P. Pujo, *Lake Charles*

---

[11] Died December 23, 1907.
[12] Appointed to fill vacancy caused by death of Stephen R. Mallory, and took his seat January 9, 1908; died March 22, 1908.
[13] Appointed to fill vacancy caused by deaths of Stephen R. Mallory and William J. Bryan, and took his seat April 6, 1908.
[14] Election unsuccessfully contested by Anthony Michalek.

[15] Election unsuccessfully contested by Stanley H. Kunz.
[16] Died November 30, 1907, before Congress assembled.
[17] Elected to fill vacancy caused by death of George W. Smith, and took his seat February 26, 1908.
[18] Died April 7, 1908.
[19] Elected to fill vacancy caused by death of Abraham L. Brick, and took his seat December 7, 1908.
[20] Died August 4, 1908.

[21] Elected to fill vacancy caused by death of William B. Allison, and took his seat December 8, 1908.
[22] Elected to fill vacancy caused by resignation of Representative-elect Charles Curtis, in preceding Congress, and took his seat December 2, 1907.
[23] Died March 8, 1908.
[24] Elected to fill vacancy caused by death of Adolph Meyer, and took his seat December 7, 1908.
[25] Died Dec. 26, 1908, before the commencement of the Sixty-first Congress, to which he had been reelected.

MAINE

SENATORS

Eugene Hale, *Ellsworth*
William P. Frye, *Lewiston*

REPRESENTATIVES

Amos L. Allen, *Alfred*
Charles E. Littlefield,[26] *Rockland*
John P. Swasey,[27] *Canton*
Edwin C. Burleigh, *Augusta*
Llewellyn Powers,[28] *Houlton*
Frank E. Guernsey,[29] *Dover*

MARYLAND

SENATORS

Isidor Rayner, *Baltimore*
William Pinkney Whyte,[30] *Baltimore*
John Walter Smith,[31] *Snow Hill*

REPRESENTATIVES

William H. Jackson, *Salisbury*
J. Fred. C. Talbott, *Towson*
Harry B. Wolf, *Baltimore*
John Gill, Jr., *Baltimore*
Sydney E. Mudd, *La Plata*
George A. Pearre, *Cumberland*

MASSACHUSETTS

SENATORS

Henry Cabot Lodge, *Nahant*
W. Murray Crane, *Dalton*

REPRESENTATIVES

George P. Lawrence, *North Adams*
Frederick H. Gillett, *Springfield*
Charles G. Washburn, *Worcester*
Charles Q. Tirrell, *Natick*
Butler Ames, *Lowell*
Agustus P. Gardner, *Hamilton*
Ernest W. Roberts, *Chelsea*
Samuel W. McCall, *Winchester*
John A. Keliher, *Boston*
Joseph F. O'Connell, *Boston*
Andrew J. Peters, *Boston*
John W. Weeks, *Newton*
William S. Greene, *Fall River*
William C. Lovering, *Taunton*

MICHIGAN

SENATORS

Julius C. Burrows, *Kalamazoo*
William Alden Smith, *Grand Rapids*

REPRESENTATIVES

Edwin Denby, *Detroit*
Charles E. Townsend, *Jackson*
Washington Gardner, *Albion*
Edward L. Hamilton, *Niles*

Gerrit J. Diekema,[32] *Holland*
Samuel W. Smith, *Pontiac*
Henry McMorran, *Port Huron*
Joseph W. Fordney, *Saginaw*
James C. McLaughlin, *Muskegon*
George A. Loud, *Au Sable*
Archibald B. Darragh, *St. Louis*
H. Olin Young, *Ishpeming*

MINNESOTA

SENATORS

Knute Nelson, *Alexandria*
Moses E. Clapp, *St. Paul*

REPRESENTATIVES

James A. Tawney, *Winona*
Winfield S. Hammond, *St. James*
Charles R. Davis, *St. Peter*
Frederick C. Stevens, *St. Paul*
Frank M. Nye, *Minneapolis*
Charles A. Lindbergh, *Little Falls*
Andrew G. Volstead, *Granite Falls*
J. Adam Bede, *Pine City*
Halvor Steenerson, *Crookston*

MISSISSIPPI

SENATORS

Hernando D. Money, *Mississippi City*
Anselm J. McLaurin, *Brandon*

REPRESENTATIVES

Ezekiel S. Candler, Jr., *Corinth*
Thomas Spight, *Ripley*
Benjamin G. Humphreys, *Greenville*
Wilson S. Hill, *Winona*
Adam M. Byrd, *Philadelphia*
Eaton J. Bowers, *Bay St. Louis*
Frank A. McLain, *Gloster*
John Sharp Williams, *Yazoo City*

MISSOURI

SENATORS

William J. Stone, *Jefferson City*
William Warner, *Kansas City*

REPRESENTATIVES

James T. Lloyd, *Shelbyville*
William W. Rucker, *Keytesville*
Joshua W. Alexander, *Gallatin*
Charles F. Booher, *Savannah*
Edgar C. Ellis, *Kansas City*
David A. De Armond, *Butler*
Courtney W. Hamlin, *Springfield*
Dorsey W. Shackleford, *Jefferson City*
James Beauchamp Clark, *Bowling Green*
Richard Bartholdt, *St. Louis*
Henry S. Caulfield, *St. Louis*
Harry M. Coudrey, *St. Louis*
Madison R. Smith, *Farmington*

Joseph J. Russell, *Charleston*
Thomas Hackney, *Carthage*
J. Robert Lamar, *Houston*

MONTANA

SENATORS

Thomas H. Carter, *Helena*
Joseph M. Dixon, *Missoula*

REPRESENTATIVE

At Large—Charles N. Pray, *Fort Benton*

NEBRASKA

SENATORS

Elmer J. Burkett, *Lincoln*
Norris Brown, *Kearney*

REPRESENTATIVES

Ernest M. Pollard, *Nehawka*
Gilbert M. Hitchcock, *Omaha*
John F. Boyd, *Neligh*
Edmund H. Hinshaw, *Fairbury*
George W. Norris, *McCook*
Moses P. Kinkaid, *O'Neill*

NEVADA

SENATORS

Francis G. Newlands, *Reno*
George S. Nixon, *Reno*

REPRESENTATIVE

At Large—George A. Bartlett, *Tonopah*

NEW HAMPSHIRE

SENATORS

Jacob H. Gallinger, *Concord*
Henry E. Burnham, *Manchester*

REPRESENTATIVES

Cyrus A. Sulloway, *Manchester*
Frank D. Currier, *Canaan*

NEW JERSEY

SENATORS

John Kean, *Elizabeth*
Frank O. Briggs, *Trenton*

REPRESENTATIVES

Henry C. Loudenslager, *Paulsboro*
John J. Gardner, *Atlantic City*
Benjamin F. Howell, *New Brunswick*
Ira W. Wood, *Trenton*
Charles N. Fowler, *Elizabeth*
William Hughes, *Paterson*
Richard Wayne Parker, *Newark*
Le Gage Pratt, *East Orange*
Eugene W. Leake, *Jersey City*
James A. Hamill, *Jersey City*

---

[26] Resigned effective September 30, 1908.
[27] Elected to fill vacancy caused by resignation of Charles E. Littlefield, and took his seat December 7, 1908.

[28] Died July 28, 1908.
[29] Elected to fill vacancy caused by death of Llewellyn Powers, and took his seat December 7, 1908.
[30] Died March 17, 1908.

[31] Elected to fill vacancy caused by death of William Pinkney Whyte, and took his seat March 26, 1908.
[32] Elected to fill vacancy caused by resignation of Representative-elect William Alden Smith, in preceding Congress, and took his seat December 2, 1907.

NEW YORK

SENATORS

Thomas C. Platt, *Owego*
Chauncey M. Depew, *Peekskill*

REPRESENTATIVES

William W. Cocks, *Westbury*
George H. Lindsay, *Brooklyn*
Charles T. Dunwell,[33] *Brooklyn*
Otto G. Foelker,[34] *Brooklyn*
Charles B. Law, *Brooklyn*
George E. Waldo, *Brooklyn*
William M. Calder, *Brooklyn*
John J. Fitzgerald, *Brooklyn*
Daniel J. Riordan, *New York City*
Henry M. Goldfogle, *New York City*
William Sulzer, *New York City*
Charles V. Fornes, *New York City*
W. Bourke Cockran, *New York City*
Herbert Parsons, *New York City*
William Willett, Jr., *Far Rockaway*
J. Van Vechten Olcott, *New York City*
Francis B. Harrison, *New York City*
William S. Bennet, *New York City*
Joseph A. Goulden, *Fordham*
John E. Andrus, *Yonkers*
Thomas W. Bradley, *Walden*
Samuel McMillan, *Lake Mahopac*
William H. Draper, *Troy*
George N. Southwick, *Albany*
George W. Fairchild, *Oneonta*
Cyrus Durey, *Johnstown*
George R. Malby, *Ogdensburg*
James S. Sherman, *Utica*
Charles L. Knapp, *Lowville*
Michael E. Driscoll, *Syracuse*
John W. Dwight, *Dryden*
Sereno E. Payne, *Auburn*
James B. Perkins, *Rochester*
J. Sloat Fassett, *Elmira*
Peter A. Porter, *Niagara Falls*
William H. Ryan, *Buffalo*
De Alva S. Alexander, *Buffalo*
Edward B. Vreeland, *Salamanca*

NORTH CAROLINA

SENATORS

Furnifold McL. Simmons, *Trenton*
Lee S. Overman, *Salisbury*

REPRESENTATIVES

John H. Small, *Washington*
Claude Kitchin, *Scotland Neck*
Charles R. Thomas, *New Bern*
Edward W. Pou, *Smithfield*
William W. Kitchin,[35] *Roxboro*
Hannibal L. Godwin, *Dunn*

Robert N. Page, *Biscoe*
Richard N. Hackett, *Wilkesboro*
Edwin Y. Webb, *Shelby*
William T. Crawford, *Waynesville*

NORTH DAKOTA

SENATORS

Henry C. Hansbrough, *Devils Lake*
Porter J. McCumber, *Wahpeton*

REPRESENTATIVES AT LARGE

Thomas F. Marshall, *Oakes*
Asle J. Gronna, *Lakota*

OHIO

SENATORS

Joseph B. Foraker, *Cincinnati*
Charles W. F. Dick, *Akron*

REPRESENTATIVES

Nicholas Longworth, *Cincinnati*
Herman P. Goebel, *Cincinnati*
J. Eugene Harding, *Excello*
William E. Tou Velle, *Celina*
Timothy T. Ansberry, *Defiance*
Matthew R. Denver, *Wilmington*
J. Warren Keifer, *Springfield*
Ralph D. Cole, *Findlay*
Isaac R. Sherwood, *Toledo*
Henry T. Bannon, *Portsmouth*
Albert Douglas, *Chillicothe*
Edward L. Taylor, Jr., *Columbus*
Grant E. Mouser, *Marion*
J. Ford Laning, *Norwalk*
Beman G. Dawes, *Marietta*
Capell L. Weems, *St. Clairsville*
William A. Ashbrook, *Johnstown*
James Kennedy, *Youngstown*
W. Aubrey Thomas, *Niles*
L. Paul Howland, *Cleveland*
Theodore E. Burton,[36] *Cleveland*

OKLAHOMA [37]

SENATORS

Thomas P. Gore,[38] *Lawton*
Robert L. Owen,[39] *Muskogee*

REPRESENTATIVES [40]

Bird S. McGuire, *Pawnee*
Elmer L. Fulton, *Oklahoma City*
James S. Davenport, *Vinita*
Charles D. Carter, *Ardmore*
Scott Ferris, *Lawton*

OREGON

SENATORS

Charles W. Fulton, *Astoria*
Jonathan Bourne, Jr., *Portland*

REPRESENTATIVES

Willis C. Hawley, *Salem*
William R. Ellis, *Pendleton*

PENNSYLVANIA

SENATORS

Boies Penrose, *Philadelphia*
Philander C. Knox,[41] *Pittsburgh*

REPRESENTATIVES

Henry H. Bingham, *Philadelphia*
John E. Reyburn,[42] *Philadelphia*
Joel Cook,[43] *Philadelphia*
J. Hampton Moore, *Philadelphia*
Reuben O. Moon, *Philadelphia*
William W. Foulkrod, *Philadelphia*
George D. McCreary, *Philadelphia*
Thomas S. Butler, *West Chester*
Irving P. Wanger, *Norristown*
Henry B. Cassel, *Marietta*
Thomas D. Nicholls, *Scranton*
John T. Lenahan, *Wilkes-Barre*
Charles N. Brumm,[44] *Minersville*
John H. Rothermel, *Reading*
George W. Kipp, *Towanda*
William B. Wilson, *Blossburg*
John G. McHenry, *Benton*
Benjamin K. Focht, *Lewisburg*
Marlin E. Olmsted, *Harrisburg*
John M. Reynolds, *Bedford*
Daniel F. Lafean, *York*
Charles F. Barclay, *Sinnemahoning*
George F. Huff, *Greensburg*
Allen F. Cooper, *Uniontown*
Ernest F. Acheson, *Washington*
Arthur L. Bates, *Meadville*
J. Davis Brodhead, *South Bethlehem*
Joseph G. Beale, *Leechburg*
Nelson P. Wheeler, *Endeavor*
William H. Graham, *Allegheny*
John Dalzell, *Pittsburgh*
James F. Burke, *Pittsburgh*
Andrew J. Barchfeld, *Pittsburgh*

RHODE ISLAND

SENATORS

Nelson W. Aldrich, *Providence*
George P. Wetmore,[45] *Newport*

REPRESENTATIVES

Daniel L. D. Granger,[46] *Providence*
Adin B. Capron, *Stillwater*

---

[33] Died June 12, 1908.
[34] Elected to fill vacancy caused by death of Charles T. Dunwell, and took his seat December 7, 1908.
[35] Resigned effective January 11, 1909, having been elected governor.
[36] Reelected to the Sixty-first Congress, but resigned effective March 4, 1909, having been elected Senator.
[37] Admitted as a State into the Union November 16, 1907.

[38] Took his seat December 16, 1907; term to expire, as determined by lot, March 3, 1909.
[39] Took his seat December 16, 1907; term to expire, as determined by lot, March 3, 1913.
[40] All Representatives took their seats December 2, 1907.
[41] Resigned effective March 4, 1909, having been appointed Secretary of State.
[42] Resigned March 31, 1907, before Congress assem-

bled, having been elected mayor of Philadelphia.
[43] Elected to fill vacancy caused by resignation of John E. Reyburn, and took his seat December 2, 1907.
[44] Resigned January 4, 1909.
[45] Elected to fill vacancy in term beginning March 4, 1907, caused by failure of legislature to elect, and took his seat January 27, 1908; vacancy in this class from March 4, 1907, to January 21, 1908.
[46] Died February 14, 1909.

SOUTH CAROLINA

SENATORS

Benjamin R. Tillman, *Trenton*
Asbury C. Latimer,[47] *Belton*
Frank B. Gary,[48] *Abbeville*

REPRESENTATIVES

George S. Legare,[49] *Charleston*
James O'H. Patterson,[50] *Barnwell*
Wyatt Aiken, *Abbeville*
Joseph T. Johnson, *Spartanburg*
David E. Finley, *Yorkville*
J. Edwin Ellerbe, *Marion*
Asbury F. Lever,[51] *Lexington*

SOUTH DAKOTA

SENATORS

Robert J. Gamble, *Yankton*
Alfred B. Kittredge, *Sioux Falls*

REPRESENTATIVES AT LARGE

Philo Hall, *Brookings*
William H. Parker,[52] *Deadwood*
Eben W. Martin,[53] *Deadwood*

TENNESSEE

SENATORS

James B. Frazier, *Chattanooga*
Robert L. Taylor, *Nashville*

REPRESENTATIVES

Walter P. Brownlow, *Jonesboro*
Nathan W. Hale, *Knoxville*
John A. Moon, *Chattanooga*
Cordell Hull, *Carthage*
William C. Houston, *Woodbury*
John W. Gaines, *Nashville*
Lemuel P. Padgett, *Columbia*
Thetus W. Sims, *Linden*
Finis J. Garrett, *Dresden*
George W. Gordon, *Memphis*

TEXAS

SENATORS

Charles A. Culberson, *Dallas*
Joseph W. Bailey, *Gainesville*

REPRESENTATIVES

Morris Sheppard, *Texarkana*
Samuel B. Cooper, *Beaumont*
Gordon J. Russell, *Tyler*
Choice B. Randell, *Sherman*
Jack Beall, *Waxahachie*
Rufus Hardy, *Corsicana*

Alexander W. Gregg, *Palestine*
John M. Moore, *Richmond*
George F. Burgess, *Gonzales*
Albert S. Burleson, *Austin*
Robert L. Henry, *Waco*
Oscar W. Gillespie, *Fort Worth*
John H. Stephens, *Vernon*
James L. Slayden, *San Antonio*
John N. Garner, *Uvalde*
William R. Smith, *Colorado*

UTAH

SENATORS

Reed Smoot, *Provo*
George Sutherland, *Salt Lake City*

REPRESENTATIVE

At Large—Joseph Howell, *Logan*

VERMONT

SENATORS

Redfield Proctor,[54] *Proctor*
John W. Stewart,[55] *Middlebury*
Carroll S. Page,[56] *Hyde Park*
William P. Dillingham, *Waterbury*

REPRESENTATIVES

David J. Foster, *Burlington*
Kittredge Haskins, *Brattleboro*

VIRGINIA

SENATORS

John W. Daniel, *Lynchburg*
Thomas S. Martin, *Charlottesville*

REPRESENTATIVES

William A. Jones, *Warsaw*
Harry L. Maynard, *Portsmouth*
John Lamb, *Richmond*
Francis R. Lassiter, *Petersburg*
Edward W. Saunders, *Rockymount*
Carter Glass, *Lynchburg*
James Hay, *Madison*
Charles C. Carlin,[57] *Alexandria*
Campbell Slemp,[58] *Big Stone Gap*
C. Bascom Slemp,[59] *Big Stone Gap*
Henry D. Flood, *Appomattox*

WASHINGTON

SENATORS

Levi Ankeny, *Walla Walla*
Samuel H. Piles, *Seattle*

REPRESENTATIVES AT LARGE

Wesley L. Jones, *North Yakima*
Francis W. Cushman, *Tacoma*
William E. Humphrey, *Seattle*

WEST VIRGINIA

SENATORS

Stephen B. Elkins, *Elkins*
Nathan B. Scott, *Wheeling*

REPRESENTATIVES

William P. Hubbard, *Wheeling*
George C. Sturgiss, *Morgantown*
Joseph Holt Gaines, *Charleston*
Harry C. Woodyard, *Spencer*
James A. Hughes, *Huntington*

WISCONSIN

SENATORS

John C. Spooner,[60] *Madison*
Isaac Stephenson,[61] *Marinette*
Robert M. La Follette, *Madison*

REPRESENTATIVES

Henry Allen Cooper, *Racine*
John M. Nelson, *Madison*
James W. Murphy, *Platteville*
William J. Cary, *Milwaukee*
William H. Stafford, *Milwaukee*
Charles H. Weisse, *Sheboygan Falls*
John J. Esch, *La Crosse*
James H. Davidson, *Oshkosh*
Gustav Küstermann, *Green Bay*
Elmer A. Morse, *Antigo*
John J. Jenkins, *Chippewa Falls*

WYOMING

SENATORS

Clarence D. Clark, *Evanston*
Francis E. Warren, *Cheyenne*

REPRESENTATIVE

At Large—Frank W. Mondell, *Newcastle*

TERRITORY OF ALASKA

DELEGATE

Thomas Cale, *Fairbanks*

---

[47] Died February 20, 1908.
[48] Elected to fill vacancy caused by death of Asbury C. Latimer, and took his seat March 16, 1908.
[49] Election unsuccessfully contested by Aaron P. Prioleau.
[50] Election unsuccessfully contested by Isaac Myers.
[51] Election unsuccessfully contested by Alexander D. Dantzer.

[52] Died June 26, 1908.
[53] Elected to fill vacancy caused by death of William H. Parker, and took his seat December 7, 1908.
[54] Died March 4, 1908.
[55] Appointed to fill vacancy caused by death of Redfield Proctor, and took his seat March 30, 1908.
[56] Elected to fill vacancy caused by death of Redfield Proctor, and took his seat December 7, 1908.

[57] Elected to fill vacancy caused by death of Representative-elect John F. Rixey, in preceding Congress, and took his seat December 2, 1907.
[58] Died October 13, 1907, before Congress assembled.
[59] Elected to fill vacancy caused by death of Campbell Slemp, and took his seat January 6, 1908.
[60] Resigned April 30, 1907.
[61] Elected to fill vacancy caused by resignation of John C. Spooner, and took his seat December 2, 1907.

TERRITORY OF ARIZONA

DELEGATE

Marcus A. Smith, *Tucson*

TERRITORY OF HAWAII

DELEGATE

Jonah K. Kalanianaole, *Honolulu*

TERRITORY OF NEW MEXICO

DELEGATE

William H. Andrews,[62] *Albuquerque*

TERRITORY OF OKLAHOMA [63]

DELEGATE

Vacant

PHILIPPINE ISLANDS [64]

RESIDENT COMMISSIONERS

Benito Legarda,[65] *Manila*
Pablo Ocampo,[65] *Manila*

PORTO RICO

RESIDENT COMMISSIONER

Tulio Larrinaga, *San Juan*

---

[62] Election unsuccessfully contested by Octavius A. Larrazola.
[63] Granted statehood November 16, 1907.

[64] Part of the territory ceded to the United States by Spain by the treaty of Paris of December 10, 1898; granted the right to elect two Resident Commissioners to the United States by act of July 1, 1902.

[65] Elected November 22, 1907, for a term of two years; granted the privileges of the floor of the House of Representatives, with the right of debate, February 4, 1908.

SIXTY-FIRST CONGRESS

MARCH 4, 1909, TO MARCH 3, 1911

FIRST SESSION—*March 15, 1909, to August 5, 1909*

SECOND SESSION—*December 6, 1909, to June 25, 1910*

THIRD SESSION—*December 5, 1910, to March 3, 1911*

SPECIAL SESSION OF THE SENATE—*March 4, 1909, to March 6, 1909*

———

VICE PRESIDENT OF THE UNITED STATES—JAMES S. SHERMAN, of New York

PRESIDENT PRO TEMPORE OF THE SENATE—WILLIAM P. FRYE, of Maine

SECRETARY OF THE SENATE—CHARLES G. BENNETT, of New York

SERGEANT AT ARMS OF THE SENATE—DANIEL M. RANSDELL, of Indiana

———

SPEAKER OF THE HOUSE OF REPRESENTATIVES—JOSEPH G. CANNON,[1] of Illinois

CLERK OF THE HOUSE—ALEXANDER McDOWELL,[2] of Pennsylvania

SERGEANT AT ARMS OF THE HOUSE—HENRY CASSON, of Wisconsin

DOORKEEPER OF THE HOUSE—FRANK B. LYON, of New York

POSTMASTER OF THE HOUSE—SAMUEL LANGUM

ALABAMA

SENATORS

John H. Bankhead, *Fayette*
Joseph F. Johnston, *Birmingham*

REPRESENTATIVES

George W. Taylor, *Demopolis*
S. Hubert Dent, Jr., *Montgomery*
Henry D. Clayton, *Eufaula*
William B. Craig, *Selma*
J. Thomas Heflin, *Lafayette*
Richmond P. Hobson, *Greensboro*
John L. Burnett, *Gadsden*
William Richardson, *Huntsville*
Oscar W. Underwood, *Birmingham*

ARKANSAS

SENATORS

James P. Clarke, *Little Rock*
Jeff Davis, *Little Rock*

REPRESENTATIVES

Robert B. Macon, *Helena*
William A. Oldfield, *Batesville*
John C. Floyd, *Yellville*

William B. Cravens, *Fort Smith*
Charles C. Reid, *Morrillton*
Joseph T. Robinson, *Lonoke*
Robert M. Wallace, *Magnolia*

CALIFORNIA

SENATORS

George C. Perkins, *Oakland*
Frank P. Flint, *Los Angeles*

REPRESENTATIVES

William F. Englebright, *Nevada City*
Duncan E. McKinlay, *Santa Rosa*
Joseph R. Knowland, *Alameda*
Julius Kahn, *San Francisco*
Everis A. Hayes, *San Jose*
James C. Needham, *Modesto*
James McLachlan, *Pasadena*
Sylvester C. Smith, *Bakersfield*

COLORADO

SENATORS

Simon Guggenheim, *Denver*
Charles J. Hughes, Jr.,[3] *Denver*

REPRESENTATIVES

Atterson W. Rucker, *Fort Logan*
John A. Martin, *Pueblo*
At Large—Edward T. Taylor, *Glenwood Springs*

CONNECTICUT

SENATORS

Morgan G. Bulkeley, *Hartford*
Frank B. Brandegee, *New London*

REPRESENTATIVES

E. Stevens Henry, *Rockville*
Nehemiah D. Sperry, *New Haven*
Edwin W. Higgins, *Norwich*
Ebenezer J. Hill, *Norwalk*
At Large—John Q. Tilson, *New Haven*

DELAWARE

SENATORS

Henry A. du Pont, *Winterthur*
Harry A. Richardson, *Dover*

REPRESENTATIVE

At Large—William H. Heald, *Wilmington*

---

[1] Reelected March 15, 1909. [2] Reelected March 15, 1909. [3] Died January 11, 1911.

FLORIDA

SENATORS

James P. Taliaferro, *Jacksonville*
Duncan U. Fletcher,[4] *Jacksonville*

REPRESENTATIVES

Stephen M. Sparkman, *Tampa*
Frank Clark, *Gainesville*
Dannitte H. Mays, *Monticello*

GEORGIA

SENATORS

Augustus O. Bacon, *Macon*
Alexander S. Clay,[5] *Marietta*
Joseph M. Terrell,[6] *Greenville*

REPRESENTATIVES

Charles G. Edwards, *Savannah*
James M. Griggs,[7] *Dawson*
Seaborn A. Roddenberry,[8] *Thomasville*
Dudley M. Hughes, *Danville*
William C. Adamson, *Carrollton*
Leonidas F. Livingston, *Covington*
Charles L. Bartlett, *Macon*
Gordon Lee, *Chickamauga*
William M. Howard, *Lexington*
Thomas M. Bell, *Gainesville*
Thomas W. Hardwick, *Sandersville*
William G. Brantley, *Brunswick*

IDAHO

SENATORS

Weldon B. Heyburn, *Wallace*
William E. Borah, *Boise*

REPRESENTATIVE

At Large—Thomas R. Hamer, *St. Anthony*

ILLINOIS

SENATORS

Shelby M. Cullom, *Springfield*
William Lorimer,[9] *Chicago*

REPRESENTATIVES

Martin B. Madden, *Chicago*
James R. Mann, *Chicago*
William W. Wilson. *Chicago*
James T. McDermott, *Chicago*
Adolph J. Sabath, *Chicago*
William Lorimer,[10] *Chicago*
William J. Moxley,[11] *Chicago*
Frederick Lundin, *Chicago*
Thomas Gallagher, *Chicago*

Henry S. Boutell, *Chicago*
George E. Foss, *Chicago*
Howard M. Snapp, *Joliet*
Charles E. Fuller, *Belvidere*
Frank O. Lowden, *Oregon*
James McKinney, *Aledo*
George W. Prince, *Galesburg*
Joseph V. Graff, *Peoria*
John A. Sterling, *Bloomington*
Joseph G. Cannon, *Danville*
William B. McKinley, *Champaign*
Henry T. Rainey, *Carrollton*
James M. Graham, *Springfield*
William A. Rodenberg, *East St. Louis*
Martin D. Foster, *Olney*
Pleasant T. Chapman, *Vienna*
Napoleon B. Thistlewood, *Cairo*

INDIANA

SENATORS

Albert J. Beveridge, *Indianapolis*
Benjamin F. Shively, *South Bend*

REPRESENTATIVES

John W. Boehne, *Evansville*
William A. Cullop, *Vincennes*
William E. Cox, *Jasper*
Lincoln Dixon, *North Vernon*
Ralph W. Moss, *Center Point*
William O. Barnard, *Newcastle*
Charles A. Korbly, *Indianapolis*
John A. M. Adair, *Portland*
Martin A. Morrison, *Frankfort*
Edgar D. Crumpacker, *Valparaiso*
George W. Rauch, *Marion*
Cyrus Cline, *Angola*
Henry A. Barnhart, *Rochester*

IOWA

SENATORS

Jonathan P. Dolliver,[12] *Fort Dodge*
Lafayette Young,[13] *Des Moines*
Albert B. Cummins, *Des Moines*

REPRESENTATIVES

Charles A. Kennedy, *Montrose*
Albert F. Dawson, *Preston*
Charles E. Pickett, *Waterloo*
Gilbert N. Haugen, *Northwood*
James W. Good, *Cedar Rapids*
Nathan E. Kendall, *Albia*
John A. T. Hull, *Des Moines*
William D. Jamieson,[14] *Shenandoah*
Walter I. Smith, *Council Bluffs*
Frank P. Woods, *Estherville*
Elbert H. Hubbard, *Sioux City*

KANSAS

SENATORS

Charles Curtis, *Topeka*
Joseph L. Bristow, *Salina*

REPRESENTATIVES

Daniel R. Anthony, Jr., *Leavenworth*
Charles F. Scott, *Iola*
Philip P. Campbell, *Pittsburg*
James M. Miller, *Council Grove*
William A. Calderhead, *Marysville*
William A. Reeder, *Logan*
Edmond H. Madison, *Dodge City*
Victor Murdock, *Wichita*

KENTUCKY

SENATORS

Thomas H. Paynter, *Frankfort*
William O. Bradley, *Louisville*

REPRESENTATIVES

Ollie M. James, *Marion*
Augustus O. Stanley, *Henderson*
Robert Y. Thomas, Jr., *Central City*
Ben Johnson, *Bardstown*
J. Swagar Sherley, *Louisville*
Joseph L. Rhinock, *Covington*
James C. Cantrill, *Georgetown*
Harvey Helm, *Stanford*
Joseph B. Bennett, *Greenup*
John W. Langley, *Pikeville*
Don C. Edwards, *London*

LOUISIANA

SENATORS

Samuel D. McEnery,[15] *New Orleans*
John R. Thornton,[16] *Alexandria*
Murphy J. Foster, *Franklin*

REPRESENTATIVES

Albert Estopinal,[17] *Estopinal*
Samuel L. Gilmore,[18] *New Orleans*
H. Garland Dupré,[19] *New Orleans*
Robert F. Broussard, *New Iberia*
John T. Watkins, *Minden*
Joseph E. Ransdell, *Lake Providence*
Robert C. Wickliffe, *St. Francisville*
Arsène P. Pujo, *Lake Charles*

MAINE

SENATORS

Eugene Hale, *Ellsworth*
William P. Frye, *Lewiston*

---

[4] Appointed to fill vacancy in the term beginning March 4, 1909, and took his seat March 4, 1909; subsequently elected.
[5] Died November 13, 1910.
[6] Appointed to fill vacancy caused by death of Alexander S. Clay, and took his seat December 6, 1910.
[7] Died January 5, 1910.
[8] Elected to fill vacancy caused by death of James M. Griggs, and took his seat February 28, 1910.
[9] Elected to fill vacancy in the term beginning March 4, 1909, and took his seat June 18, 1909; vacancy in this class from March 4, 1909, to May 27, 1909, because of

failure of legislature to elect; and then until June 17, 1909, because Mr. Lorimer did not resign his seat in the House until the last-named date.
[10] Resigned, effective June 17, 1909, having been elected Senator.
[11] Elected to fill vacancy caused by resignation of William Lorimer, and took his seat December 10, 1909.
[12] Died October 15, 1910.
[13] Appointed to fill vacancy caused by death of Jonathan P. Dolliver: took his seat December 6, 1910.
[14] Election unsuccessfully contested by William P. Hepburn.

[15] Died June 28, 1910.
[16] Elected to fill vacancy caused by death of Samuel D. McEnery, and took his seat December 12, 1910; vacancy from June 29, 1910, to December 6, 1910.
[17] Election unsuccessfully contested by Henry C. Warmoth.
[18] Elected to fill vacancy caused by death of Representative-elect Robert C. Davey, in preceding Congress, and took his seat April 22, 1909; died July 18, 1910.
[19] Elected to fill vacancy caused by death of Samuel L. Gilmore, and took his seat December 12, 1910.

REPRESENTATIVES

Amos L. Allen,[20] *Alfred*
John P. Swasey, *Canton*
Edwin C. Burleigh, *Augusta*
Frank E. Guernsey, *Dover*

MARYLAND

SENATORS

Isidor Rayner, *Baltimore*
John Walter Smith, *Snow Hill*

REPRESENTATIVES

J. Harry Covington, *Easton*
J. Fred. C. Talbott, *Towson*
John Kronmiller, *Baltimore*
John Gill, Jr., *Baltimore*
Sydney E. Mudd, *La Plata*
George A. Pearre, *Cumberland*

MASSACHUSETTS

SENATORS

Henry Cabot Lodge, *Nahant*
W. Murray Crane, *Dalton*

REPRESENTATIVES

George P. Lawrence, *North Adams*
Frederick H. Gillett, *Springfield*
Charles G. Washburn, *Worcester*
Charles Q. Tirrell,[21] *Natick*
John J. Mitchell,[22] *Marlboro*
Butler Ames, *Lowell*
Augustus P. Gardner, *Hamilton*
Ernest W. Roberts, *Chelsea*
Samuel W. McCall, *Winchester*
John A. Keliher, *Boston*
Joseph F. O'Connell,[23] *Boston*
Andrew J. Peters, *Boston*
John W. Weeks, *Newton*
William S. Greene, *Fall River*
William C. Lovering,[24] *Taunton*
Eugene N. Foss,[25] *Jamaica Plains*

MICHIGAN

SENATORS

Julius C. Burrows, *Kalamazoo*
William Alden Smith, *Grand Rapids*

REPRESENTATIVES

Edwin Denby, *Detroit*
Charles E. Townsend, *Jackson*
Washington Gardner, *Albion*
Edward L. Hamilton, *Niles*
Gerrit J. Diekema, *Holland*
Samuel W. Smith, *Pontiac*
Henry McMorran, *Port Huron*
Joseph W. Fordney, *Saginaw*
James C. McLaughlin, *Muskegon*
George A. Loud, *Au Sable*

Francis H. Dodds, *Mount Pleasant*
H. Olin Young, *Ishpeming*

MINNESOTA

SENATORS

Knute Nelson, *Alexandria*
Moses E. Clapp, *St. Paul*

REPRESENTATIVES

James A. Tawney, *Winona*
Winfield S. Hammond, *St. James*
Charles R. Davis, *St. Peter*
Frederick C. Stevens, *St. Paul*
Frank M. Nye, *Minneapolis*
Charles A. Lindbergh, *Little Falls*
Andrew J. Volstead, *Granite Falls*
Clarence B. Miller, *Duluth*
Halvor Steenerson, *Crookston*

MISSISSIPPI

SENATORS

Hernando D. Money, *Mississippi City*
Anselm J. McLaurin,[26] *Brandon*
James Gordon,[27] *Okolona*
Le Roy Percy,[28] *Greenville*

REPRESENTATIVES

Ezekiel S. Candler, Jr., *Corinth*
Thomas Spight, *Ripley*
Benjamin G. Humphreys, *Greenville*
Thomas U. Sisson, *Winona*
Adam M. Byrd, *Philadelphia*
Eaton J. Bowers, *Bay St. Louis*
William A. Dickson, *Centerville*
James W. Collier, *Vicksburg*

MISSOURI

SENATORS

William J. Stone, *Jefferson City*
William Warner, *Kansas City*

REPRESENTATIVES

James T. Lloyd, *Shelbyville*
William W. Rucker, *Keytesville*
Joshua W. Alexander, *Gallatin*
Charles F. Booher, *Savannah*
William P. Borland, *Kansas City*
David A. De Armond,[29] *Butler*
Clement C. Dickinson,[30] *Clinton*
Courtney W. Hamlin, *Springfield*
Dorsey W. Shackleford, *Jefferson City*
James Beauchamp Clark, *Bowling Green*
Richard Bartholdt, *St. Louis*
Patrick F. Gill, *St. Louis*
Harry M. Coudrey, *St. Louis*
Politte Elvins, *Elvins*
Charles A. Crow, *Caruthersville*
Charles H. Morgan, *Joplin*
Arthur P. Murphy, *Rolla*

MONTANA

SENATORS

Thomas H. Carter, *Helena*
Joseph M. Dixon, *Missoula*

REPRESENTATIVE

At Large—Charles N. Pray, *Fort Benton*

NEBRASKA

SENATORS

Elmer J. Burkett, *Lincoln*
Norris Brown, *Kearney*

REPRESENTATIVES

John A. Maguire, *Lincoln*
Gilbert M. Hitchcock, *Omaha*
James P. Latta, *Tekamah*
Edmund H. Hinshaw, *Fairbury*
George W. Norris, *McCook*
Moses P. Kinkaid, *O'Neill*

NEVADA

SENATORS

Francis G. Newlands, *Reno*
George S. Nixon, *Reno*

REPRESENTATIVE

At Large—George A. Bartlett, *Tonopah*

NEW HAMPSHIRE

SENATORS

Jacob H. Gallinger, *Concord*
Henry E. Burnham, *Manchester*

REPRESENTATIVES

Cyrus A. Sulloway, *Manchester*
Frank D. Currier, *Canaan*

NEW JERSEY

SENATORS

John Kean, *Elizabeth*
Frank O. Briggs, *Trenton*

REPRESENTATIVES

Henry C. Loudenslager, *Paulsboro*
John J. Gardner, *Atlantic City*
Benjamin F. Howell, *New Brunswick*
Ira W. Wood, *Trenton*
Charles N. Fowler, *Elizabeth*
William Hughes, *Paterson*
Richard Wayne Parker, *Newark*
William H. Wiley, *East Orange*
Eugene F. Kinkead, *Jersey City*
James A. Hamill, *Jersey City*

---

[20] Died February 20, 1911.
[21] Died July 31, 1910.
[22] Elected to fill vacancy caused by death of Charles Q. Tirrell, and took his seat December 5, 1910.
[23] Election unsuccessfully contested by J. Mitchell Galvin.

[24] Died February 4, 1910.
[25] Elected to fill vacancy caused by death of William C. Lovering, and took his seat April 7, 1910; resigned, effective January 4, 1911, having been elected governor.
[26] Died December 22, 1909.
[27] Appointed to fill vacancy caused by death of

Anselm J. McLaurin, and took his seat January 5, 1910.
[28] Elected to fill vacancy caused by death of Anselm J. McLaurin, and took his seat March 15, 1910.
[29] Died November 23, 1909.
[30] Elected to fill vacancy caused by death of David A. De Armond, and took his seat February 7, 1910.

NEW YORK

SENATORS

Chauncey M. Depew, *Peekskill*
Elihu Root, *New York City*

REPRESENTATIVES

William W. Cocks, *Westbury*
George H. Lindsay, *Brooklyn*
Otto G. Foelker, *Brooklyn*
Charles B. Law, *Brooklyn*
Richard Young, *Flatbush*
William M. Calder, *Brooklyn*
John J. Fitzgerald, *Brooklyn*
Daniel J. Riordan, *New York City*
Henry M. Goldfogle, *New York City*
William Sulzer, *New York City*
Charles V. Fornes, *New York City*
Michael F. Conry, *New York City*
Herbert Parsons, *New York City*
William Willett, Jr., *Long Island City*
J. Van Vechten Olcott, *New York City*
Francis B. Harrison, *New York City*
William S. Bennet, *New York City*
Joseph A. Goulden, *Fordham*
John E. Andrus, *Yonkers*
Thomas W. Bradley, *Walden*
Hamilton Fish, *Garrison*
William H. Draper, *Troy*
George N. Southwick, *Albany*
George W. Fairchild, *Oneonta*
Cyrus Durey, *Johnstown*
George R. Malby, *Ogdensburg*
Charles S. Millington, *Herkimer*
Charles L. Knapp, *Lowville*
Michael E. Driscoll, *Syracuse*
John W. Dwight, *Dryden*
Sereno E. Payne, *Auburn*
James B. Perkins,[31] *Rochester*
James S. Havens,[32] *Rochester*
J. Sloat Fassett, *Elmira*
James S. Simmons, *Niagara Falls*
Daniel A. Driscoll, *Buffalo*
De Alva S. Alexander, *Buffalo*
Edward B. Vreeland, *Salamanca*

NORTH CAROLINA

SENATORS

Furnifold McL. Simmons, *New Bern*
Lee S. Overman, *Salisbury*

REPRESENTATIVES

John H. Small, *Washington*
Claude Kitchin, *Scotland Neck*
Charles R. Thomas, *New Bern*
Edward W. Pou, *Smithfield*
John M. Morehead, *Spray*
Hannibal L. Godwin, *Dunn*

Robert N. Page, *Biscoe*
Charles H. Cowles, *Wilkesboro*
Edwin Y. Webb,[33] *Shelby*
John G. Grant, *Hendersonville*

NORTH DAKOTA

SENATORS

Porter J. McCumber, *Wahpeton*
Martin N. Johnson,[34] *Petersburg*
Fountain L. Thompson,[35] *Cando*
William E. Purcell,[36] *Wahpeton*
Asle J. Gronna,[37] *Lakota*

REPRESENTATIVES AT LARGE

Louis B. Hanna, *Fargo*
Asle J. Gronna,[38] *Lakota*

OHIO

SENATORS

Charles W. F. Dick, *Akron*
Theodore E. Burton, *Cleveland*

REPRESENTATIVES

Nicholas Longworth, *Cincinnati*
Herman P. Goebel, *Cincinnati*
James M. Cox, *Dayton*
William E. Tou Velle, *Celina*
Timothy T. Ansberry, *Defiance*
Matthew R. Denver, *Wilmington*
J. Warren Keifer, *Springfield*
Ralph D. Cole, *Findlay*
Isaac R. Sherwood, *Toledo*
Adna R. Johnson, *Ironton*
Albert Douglas, *Chillicothe*
Edward L. Taylor, Jr., *Columbus*
Carl C. Anderson, *Fostoria*
William G. Sharp, *Elyria*
James Joyce, *Cambridge*
David A. Hollingsworth, *Cadiz*
William A. Ashbrook, *Johnstown*
James Kennedy, *Youngstown*
William A. Thomas, *Niles*
L. Paul Howland, *Cleveland*
James H. Cassidy,[39] *Cleveland*

OKLAHOMA

SENATORS

Thomas P. Gore, *Lawton*
Robert L. Owen, *Muskogee*

REPRESENTATIVES

Bird S. McGuire, *Pawnee*
Dick T. Morgan, *Woodward*
Charles E. Creager, *Muskogee*
Charles D. Carter, *Ardmore*
Scott Ferris, *Lawton*

OREGON

SENATORS

Jonathan Bourne, Jr., *Portland*
George E. Chamberlain, *Portland*

REPRESENTATIVES

Willis C. Hawley, *Salem*
William R. Ellis, *Pendleton*

PENNSYLVANIA

SENATORS

Boies Penrose, *Philadelphia*
George T. Oliver,[40] *Pittsburgh*

REPRESENTATIVES

Henry H. Bingham, *Philadelphia*
Joel Cook,[41] *Philadelphia*
J. Hampton Moore, *Philadelphia*
Reuben O. Moon, *Philadelphia*
William W. Foulkrod,[42] *Philadelphia*
George D. McCreary, *Philadelphia*
Thomas S. Butler, *West Chester*
Irving P. Wanger, *Norristown*
William W. Griest, *Lancaster*
Thomas D. Nicholls, *Scranton*
Henry W. Palmer, *Wilkes-Barre*
Alfred B. Garner, *Ashland*
John H. Rothermel, *Reading*
Charles C. Pratt, *New Milford*
William B. Wilson, *Blossburg*
John G. McHenry, *Benton*
Benjamin K. Focht, *Lewisburg*
Marlin E. Olmsted, *Harrisburg*
John M. Reynolds,[43] *Bedford*
Daniel F. Lafean, *York*
Charles F. Barclay, *Sinnemahoning*
George F. Huff, *Greensburg*
Allen F. Cooper, *Uniontown*
John K. Tener,[44] *Charleroi*
Arthur L. Bates, *Meadville*
A. Mitchell Palmer, *Stroudsburg*
Jonathan N. Langham, *Indiana*
Nelson P. Wheeler, *Endeavor*
William H. Graham, *Allegheny*
John Dalzell, *Pittsburgh*
James F. Burke, *Pittsburgh*
Andrew J. Barchfeld, *Pittsburgh*

RHODE ISLAND

SENATORS

Nelson W. Aldrich, *Providence*
George P. Wetmore, *Newport*

REPRESENTATIVES

William P. Sheffield, *Newport*
Adin B. Capron, *Stillwater*

---

[31] Died March 11, 1910.
[32] Elected to fill vacancy caused by death of James B. Perkins, and took his seat April 29, 1910.
[33] Election unsuccessfully contested by John A. Smith.
[34] Died October 21, 1909.
[35] Appointed to fill vacancy caused by death of Martin N. Johnson, and took his seat December 7, 1909; resigned effective January 31, 1910.
[36] Appointed to fill vacancy caused by death of Martin N. Johnson and resignation of Fountain L.

Thompson, and took his seat February 1, 1910.
[37] Elected to fill vacancy caused by death of Martin N. Johnson, and took his seat February 2, 1911.
[38] Resigned effective February 2, 1911, having been elected Senator.
[39] Elected to fill vacancy caused by resignation of Representative-elect Theodore E. Burton, in preceding Congress, and took his seat April 26, 1909.
[40] Elected to fill vacancy caused by resignation of Philander C. Knox, in preceding Congress, and took his seat March 19, 1909.

[41] Died December 15, 1910, before the commencement of the Sixty-second Congress, to which he had been reelected.
[42] Died November 13, 1910; vacancy throughout the remainder of the Congress.
[43] Resigned January 17, 1911, having been elected Lieutenant Governor.
[44] Resigned January 16, 1911, having been elected Governor.

SOUTH CAROLINA

SENATORS

Benjamin R. Tillman, *Trenton*
Ellison D. Smith, *Florence*

REPRESENTATIVES

George S. Legare,[45] *Charleston*
James O'H. Patterson,[46] *Barnwell*
Wyatt Aiken, *Abbeville*
Joseph T. Johnson, *Spartanburg*
David E. Finley, *Yorkville*
J. Edwin Ellerbe, *Marion*
Asbury F. Lever,[47] *Lexington*

SOUTH DAKOTA

SENATORS

Robert J. Gamble, *Yankton*
Coe I. Crawford, *Huron*

REPRESENTATIVES AT LARGE

Eben W. Martin, *Deadwood*
Charles H. Burke, *Pierre*

TENNESSEE

SENATORS

James B. Frazier, *Chattanooga*
Robert L. Taylor, *Nashville*

REPRESENTATIVES

Walter P. Brownlow,[48] *Jonesboro*
Zachary D. Massey,[49] *Sevierville*
Richard W. Austin, *Knoxville*
John A. Moon, *Chattanooga*
Cordell Hull, *Carthage*
William C. Houston, *Woodbury*
Joseph W. Byrns, *Nashville*
Lemuel P. Padgett, *Columbia*
Thetus W. Sims, *Linden*
Finis J. Garrett, *Dresden*
George W. Gordon, *Memphis*

TEXAS

SENATORS

Charles A. Culberson, *Dallas*
Joseph W. Bailey, *Gainesville*

REPRESENTATIVES

Morris Sheppard, *Texarkana*
Martin Dies, *Beaumont*
Gordon J. Russell,[50] *Tyler*
Robert M. Lively,[51] *Canton*
Choice B. Randell, *Sherman*
Jack Beall, *Waxahachie*
Rufus Hardy, *Corsicana*
Alexander W. Gregg, *Palestine*

John M. Moore, *Richmond*
George F. Burgess, *Gonzales*
Albert S. Burleson, *Austin*
Robert L. Henry, *Waco*
Oscar W. Gillespie, *Fort Worth*
John H. Stephens, *Vernon*
James L. Slayden, *San Antonio*
John N. Garner, *Uvalde*
William R. Smith, *Colorado*

UTAH

SENATORS

Reed Smoot, *Provo*
George Sutherland, *Salt Lake City*

REPRESENTATIVE

At Large—Joseph Howell, *Logan*

VERMONT

SENATORS

William P. Dillingham, *Montpelier*
Carroll S. Page, *Hyde Park*

REPRESENTATIVES

David J. Foster, *Burlington*
Frank Plumley, *Northfield*

VIRGINIA

SENATORS

John W. Daniel,[52] *Lynchburg*
Claude A. Swanson,[53] *Chatham*
Thomas S. Martin, *Charlottesville*

REPRESENTATIVES

William A. Jones, *Warsaw*
Harry L. Maynard, *Portsmouth*
John Lamb, *Richmond*
Francis R. Lassiter,[54] *Petersburg*
Robert Turnbull,[55] *Lawrenceville*
Edward W. Saunders, *Rockymount*
Carter Glass, *Lynchburg*
James Hay, *Madison*
Charles C. Carlin, *Alexandria*
C. Bascom Slemp, *Big Stone Gap*
Henry D. Flood, *Appomattox*

WASHINGTON

SENATORS

Samuel H. Piles, *Seattle*
Wesley L. Jones, *North Yakima*

REPRESENTATIVES [56]

William E. Humphrey, *Seattle*
Francis W. Cushman,[57] *Tacoma*
William W. McCredie,[58] *Vancouver*
Miles Poindexter, *Spokane*

WEST VIRGINIA

SENATORS

Stephen B. Elkins,[59] *Elkins*
Davis Elkins,[60] *Morgantown*
Clarence W. Watson,[61] *Fairmont*
Nathan B. Scott, *Wheeling*

REPRESENTATIVES

William P. Hubbard, *Wheeling*
George C. Sturgiss, *Morgantown*
Joseph Holt Gaines, *Charleston*
Harry C. Woodyard, *Spencer*
James A. Hughes, *Huntington*

WISCONSIN

SENATORS

Robert M. La Follette, *Madison*
Isaac Stephenson, *Marinette*

REPRESENTATIVES

Henry Allen Cooper, *Racine*
John M. Nelson, *Madison*
Arthur W. Kopp, *Platteville*
William J. Cary, *Milwaukee*
William H. Stafford, *Milwaukee*
Charles H. Weisse, *Sheboygan Falls*
John J. Esch, *La Crosse*
James H. Davidson, *Oshkosh*
Gustav Küstermann, *Green Bay*
Elmer A. Morse, *Antigo*
Irvine L. Lenroot, *Superior*

WYOMING

SENATORS

Clarence D. Clark, *Evanston*
Francis E. Warren, *Cheyenne*

REPRESENTATIVE

At Large—Frank W. Mondell, *Newcastle*

TERRITORY OF ALASKA

DELEGATE

James Wickersham, *Fairbanks*

TERRITORY OF ARIZONA

DELEGATE

Ralph H. Cameron, *Flagstaff*

TERRITORY OF HAWAII

DELEGATE

Jonah K. Kalanianaole, *Waikiki*

---

[45] Election unsuccessfully contested by Aaron P. Prioleau.
[46] Election unsuccessfully contested by Isaac Myers.
[47] Election unsuccessfully contested by R. H. Richardson.
[48] Died July 8, 1910.
[49] Elected to fill vacancy caused by death of Walter P. Brownlow, and took his seat December 5, 1910.
[50] Resigned June 14, 1910, having been appointed a Federal judge.

[51] Elected to fill vacancy caused by resignation of Gordon J. Russell, and took his seat December 5, 1910.
[52] Died June 29, 1910; had been reelected for the term beginning March 4, 1911.
[53] Appointed to fill vacancy caused by death of John W. Daniel, and took his seat December 6, 1910.
[54] Died October 31, 1909.
[55] Elected to fill vacancy caused by death of Francis R. Lassiter, and took his seat March 16, 1910.
[56] Heretofore elected from State at large; congres-

sional districts first established in 1909.
[57] Died July 6, 1909.
[58] Elected to fill vacancy caused by death of Francis W. Cushman, and took his seat December 6, 1909.
[59] Died January 4, 1911.
[60] Appointed to fill vacancy caused by death of his father, Stephen B. Elkins, and took his seat January 9, 1911.
[61] Elected to fill vacancy caused by death of Stephen B. Elkins, and took his seat February 2, 1911.

TERRITORY OF NEW MEXICO

DELEGATE

William H. Andrews, *Albuquerque*

PHILIPPINE ISLANDS

RESIDENT COMMISSIONERS

Benito Legarda,[62] *Manila*
Pablo Ocampo,[63] *Manila*
Manuel L. Quezon,[64] *Lucena*

PORTO RICO

RESIDENT COMMISSIONER

Tulio Larrinaga, *San Juan*

---

[62] Reelected for a term of two years beginning November 23, 1909.

[63] Term expired November 22, 1909.

[64] Elected for a term of two years beginning November 23, 1909.

SIXTY-SECOND CONGRESS

MARCH 4, 1911, TO MARCH 3, 1913

FIRST SESSION—*April 4, 1911, to August 22, 1911*

SECOND SESSION—*December 4, 1911, to August 26, 1912*

THIRD SESSION—*December 2, 1912, to March 3, 1913*

VICE PRESIDENT OF THE UNITED STATES—JAMES S. SHERMAN,[1] of New York

PRESIDENT PRO TEMPORE OF THE SENATE—WILLIAM P. FRYE,[2] of Maine; CHARLES CURTIS,[3] of Kansas; AUGUSTUS O. BACON,[4] of Georgia; JACOB H. GALLINGER,[5] of New Hampshire; HENRY CABOT LODGE,[6] of Massachusetts; FRANK B. BRANDEGEE,[7] of Connecticut

SECRETARY OF THE SENATE—CHARLES G. BENNETT, of New York

SERGEANT AT ARMS OF THE SENATE—DANIEL M. RANSDELL, of Indiana; EDGAR LIVINGSTONE CORNELIUS,[8] of Maryland

---

SPEAKER OF THE HOUSE OF REPRESENTATIVES—JAMES BEAUCHAMP CLARK,[9] of Missouri

CLERK OF THE HOUSE—ALEXANDER McDOWELL, of Pennsylvania; SOUTH TRIMBLE,[10] of Kentucky

SERGEANT AT ARMS OF THE HOUSE—HENRY CASSON, of Wisconsin; ULYSSES S. JACKSON,[11] of Indiana; CHARLES F. RIDDELL,[12] of Indiana

DOORKEEPER OF THE HOUSE—JOSEPH J. SINNOTT, of Virginia

POSTMASTER OF THE HOUSE—WILLIAM M. DUNBAR

ALABAMA

SENATORS

John H. Bankhead, *Fayette*
Joseph F. Johnston, *Birmingham*

REPRESENTATIVES

George W. Taylor, *Demopolis*
S. Hubert Dent, Jr., *Montgomery*
Henry D. Clayton, *Eufaula*
Fred L. Blackmon, *Anniston*
J. Thomas Heflin, *Lafayette*
Richmond P. Hobson, *Greensboro*
John L. Burnett, *Gadsden*
William Richardson, *Huntsville*
Oscar W. Underwood, *Birmingham*

ARIZONA [13]

SENATORS

Henry F. Ashurst,[14] *Prescott*
Marcus A. Smith,[15] *Tucson*

REPRESENTATIVE

At Large—Carl Hayden,[16] *Phoenix*

ARKANSAS

SENATORS

James P. Clarke, *Little Rock*
Jeff Davis,[17] *Little Rock*
John N. Heiskell,[18] *Little Rock*
William M. Kavanaugh,[19] *Little Rock*

REPRESENTATIVES

Robert B. Macon, *Helena*
William A. Oldfield, *Batesville*
John C. Floyd, *Yellville*
William B. Cravens, *Fort Smith*
Henderson M. Jacoway, *Dardanelle*

Joseph T. Robinson,[20] *Lonoke*
Samuel M. Taylor,[21] *Pine Bluff*
William S. Goodwin, *Warren*

CALIFORNIA

SENATORS

George C. Perkins, *Oakland*
John D. Works, *Los Angeles*

REPRESENTATIVES

John E. Raker, *Alturas*
William Kent, *Kentfield*
Joseph R. Knowland, *Alameda*
Julius Kahn, *San Francisco*
Everis A. Hayes, *San Jose*
James C. Needham, *Modesto*
William D. Stephens, *Los Angeles*
Sylvester C. Smith,[22] *Bakersfield*

---

[1] Died October 30, 1912.
[2] Resigned as President pro tempore April 27, 1911.
[3] Elected to serve December 4 to 12, 1911.
[4] Elected to serve January 15 to 17, March 11 and 12, April 8, May 10, May 30 to June 3, June 13 to July 5, August 1 to 10, and August 27 to December 15, 1912; January 5 to 18 and February 2 to 15, 1913.
[5] Elected to serve February 12 to 14, April 26 and 27, May 7, July 6 to 31, August 12 to 26, 1912; December 16, 1912, to January 4, 1913; January 19 to February 1 and February 16 to March 3, 1913.
[6] Elected to serve March 25 and 26, 1912.

[7] Elected to serve May 25, 1912.
[8] Elected December 10, 1912.
[9] Elected April 4, 1911.
[10] Elected April 4, 1911.
[11] Elected April 4, 1911.
[12] Elected July 18, 1912.
[13] Admitted as a State into the Union February 14, 1912.
[14] Took his seat April 2, 1912; term to expire, as determined by lot, March 3, 1917.
[15] Took his seat April 2, 1912; term to expire, as determined by lot, March 3, 1915.

[16] Took his seat February 19, 1912.
[17] Died January 3, 1913.
[18] Appointed to fill vacancy caused by death of Jeff Davis, and took his seat January 9, 1913.
[19] Elected to fill vacancy caused by death of Jeff Davis, and took his seat January 31, 1913.
[20] Resigned effective January 14, 1913, having been elected governor.
[21] Elected to fill vacancy caused by resignation of Joseph T. Robinson, and took his seat January 27, 1913.
[22] Died January 26, 1913.

[301]

COLORADO

SENATORS

Simon Guggenheim, *Denver*
Charles S. Thomas,[23] *Denver*

REPRESENTATIVES

Atterson W. Rucker, *Fort Logan*
John A. Martin, *Pueblo*
At Large—Edward T. Taylor, *Glenwood Springs*

CONNECTICUT

SENATORS

Frank B. Brandegee, *New London*
George P. McLean, *Simsbury*

REPRESENTATIVES

E. Stevens Henry, *Rockville*
Thomas L. Reilly, *Meriden*
Edwin W. Higgins,[24] *Norwich*
Ebenezer J. Hill, *Norwalk*
At Large—John Q. Tilson, *New Haven*

DELAWARE

SENATORS

Henry A. du Pont, *Winterthur*
Harry A. Richardson, *Dover*

REPRESENTATIVE

At Large—William H. Heald, *Wilmington*

FLORIDA

SENATORS

Duncan U. Fletcher, *Jacksonville*
Nathan P. Bryan,[25] *Jacksonville*

REPRESENTATIVES

Stephen M. Sparkman, *Tampa*
Frank Clark, *Gainesville*
Dannitte H. Mays, *Monticello*

GEORGIA

SENATORS

Augustus O. Bacon, *Macon*
Joseph M. Terrell,[26] *Greenville*
Hoke Smith,[27] *Atlanta*

REPRESENTATIVES

Charles G. Edwards, *Savannah*
Seaborn A. Roddenbery, *Thomasville*

Dudley M. Hughes, *Danville*
William C. Adamson, *Carrollton*
William S. Howard, *Decatur*
Charles L. Bartlett, *Macon*
Gordon Lee, *Chickamauga*
Samuel J. Tribble, *Athens*
Thomas M. Bell, *Gainesville*
Thomas W. Hardwick, *Sandersville*
William G. Brantley, *Brunswick*

IDAHO

SENATORS

Weldon B. Heyburn,[28] *Wallace*
Kirtland I. Perky,[29] *Boise*
James H. Brady,[30] *Pocatello*
William E. Borah, *Boise*

REPRESENTATIVE

At Large—Burton L. French, *Moscow*

ILLINOIS

SENATORS

Shelby M. Cullom, *Springfield*
William Lorimer,[31] *Chicago*

REPRESENTATIVES

Martin B. Madden, *Chicago*
James R. Mann, *Chicago*
William W. Wilson,[32] *Chicago*
James T. McDermott, *Chicago*
Adolph J. Sabath, *Chicago*
Edmund J. Stack, *Chicago*
Frank Buchanan, *Chicago*
Thomas Gallagher, *Chicago*
Lynden Evans, *Chicago*
George E. Foss, *Chicago*
Ira C. Copley, *Aurora*
Charles E. Fuller, *Belvidere*
John C. McKenzie, *Elizabeth*
James McKinney, *Aledo*
George W. Prince, *Galesburg*
Claudius U. Stone, *Peoria*
John A. Sterling, *Bloomington*
Joseph G. Cannon, *Danville*
William B. McKinley, *Champaign*
Henry T. Rainey, *Carrollton*
James M. Graham, *Springfield*
William A. Rodenberg, *East St. Louis*
Martin D. Foster, *Olney*
H. Robert Fowler, *Elizabethtown*
Napoleon B. Thistlewood, *Cairo*

INDIANA

SENATORS

Benjamin F. Shively, *South Bend*
John W. Kern, *Indianapolis*

REPRESENTATIVES

John W. Boehne, *Evansville*
William A. Cullop, *Vincennes*
William E. Cox, *Jasper*
Lincoln Dixon, *North Vernon*
Ralph W. Moss, *Center Point*
Finly H. Gray, *Connersville*
Charles A. Korbly, *Indianapolis*
John A. M. Adair, *Portland*
Martin A. Morrison, *Frankfort*
Edgar D. Crumpacker, *Valparaiso*
George W. Rauch, *Marion*
Cyrus Cline, *Angola*
Henry A. Barnhardt, *Rochester*

IOWA

SENATORS

Albert B. Cummins, *Des Moines*
Lafayette Young, *Des Moines*
William S. Kenyon,[33] *Fort Dodge*

REPRESENTATIVES

Charles A. Kennedy, *Montrose*
Irvin S. Pepper, *Muscatine*
Charles E. Pickett, *Waterloo*
Gilbert N. Haugen,[34] *Northwood*
James W. Good, *Cedar Rapids*
Nathan E. Kendall, *Albia*
Solomon F. Prouty, *Des Moines*
Horace M. Towner, *Corning*
Walter I. Smith,[35] *Council Bluffs*
William R. Green,[36] *Audubon*
Frank P. Woods, *Estherville*
Elbert H. Hubbard,[37] *Sioux City*
George C. Scott,[38] *Sioux City*

KANSAS

SENATORS

Charles Curtis, *Topeka*
Joseph L. Bristow, *Salina*

REPRESENTATIVES

Daniel R. Anthony, Jr., *Leavenworth*
Alexander C. Mitchell, [39] *Lawrence*
Joseph Taggart,[40] *Kansas City*
Philip P. Campbell, *Pittsburg*
Fred S. Jackson, *Eureka*
Rollin R. Rees, *Minneapolis*
Isaac D. Young, *Beloit*

---

[23] Elected to fill vacancy caused by death of Charles J. Hughes, Jr., in preceding Congress, and took his seat January 20, 1913; vacancy in this class from January 12, 1911, to January 14, 1913, because of failure of legislature to elect.
[24] Election unsuccessfully contested by Raymond J. Jodoin.
[25] Appointed to fill vacancy in the term beginning March 4, 1911, to serve until the next meeting of the legislature, and took his seat April 4, 1911; subsequently elected.
[26] Resigned July 14, 1911.
[27] Elected July 12, 1911, to fill vacancy caused by

death of Alexander S. Clay, in preceding Congress, but did not qualify until December 4, 1911, preferring to retain the governorship.
[28] Died October 17, 1912.
[29] Appointed to fill vacancy caused by death of Weldon B. Heyburn, and took his seat December 3, 1912.
[30] Elected to fill vacancy caused by death of Weldon B. Heyburn, and took his seat February 6, 1913.
[31] Election declared invalid July 13, 1912.
[32] Election unsuccessfully contested by Fred J. Crowley.
[33] Elected to fill vacancy caused by death of Jonathan

P. Dolliver, in preceding Congress, and took his seat April 24, 1911.
[34] Election unsuccessfully contested by Daniel D. Murphy.
[35] Resigned March 15, 1911.
[36] Elected to fill vacancy caused by resignation of Walter I. Smith, and took his seat June 21, 1911.
[37] Died June 4, 1912.
[38] Elected to fill vacancy caused by death of Elbert H. Hubbard, and took his seat December 2, 1912.
[39] Died July 7, 1911.
[40] Elected to fill vacancy caused by death of Alexander C. Mitchell, and took his seat December 4, 1911.

Edmond H. Madison,[41] *Dodge City*
George A. Neeley,[42] *Hutchinson*
Victor Murdock, *Wichita*

KENTUCKY

SENATORS

Thomas H. Paynter, *Frankfort*
William O. Bradley, *Louisville*

REPRESENTATIVES

Ollie M. James, *Marion*
Augustus O. Stanley, *Henderson*
Robert Y. Thomas, Jr., *Central City*
Ben Johnson, *Bardstown*
J. Swagar Sherley, *Louisville*
Arthur B. Rouse, *Burlington*
James C. Cantrill, *Georgetown*
Harvey Helm, *Stanford*
William J. Fields, *Olive Hill*
John W. Langley, *Pikeville*
Caleb Powers, *Barbourville*

LOUISIANA

SENATORS

Murphy J. Foster, *Franklin*
John R. Thornton, *Alexandria*

REPRESENTATIVES

Albert Estopinal, *Estopinal*
H. Garland Dupré, *New Orleans*
Robert F. Broussard, *New Iberia*
John T. Watkins, *Minden*
Joseph E. Ransdell, *Lake Providence*
Robert C. Wickliffe,[43] *St. Francisville*
Lewis L. Morgan,[44] *Covington*
Arsène P. Pujo, *Lake Charles*

MAINE

SENATORS

William P. Frye,[45] *Lewiston*
Obadiah Gardner,[46] *Rockland*
Charles F. Johnson, *Waterville*

REPRESENTATIVES

Asher C. Hinds, *Portland*
Daniel J. McGillicuddy, *Lewiston*
Samuel W. Gould, *Skowhegan*
Frank E. Guernsey, *Dover*

MARYLAND

SENATORS

Isidor Rayner,[47] *Baltimore*
William P. Jackson,[48] *Salisbury*
John Walter Smith, *Snow Hill*

REPRESENTATIVES

J. Harry Covington, *Easton*
J. Fred. C. Talbott, *Towson*
George Konig, *Baltimore*
J. Charles Linthicum, *Baltimore*
Thomas Parran, *St. Leonard*
David J. Lewis, *Cumberland*

MASSACHUSETTS

SENATORS

Henry Cabot Lodge, *Nahant*
W. Murray Crane, *Dalton*

REPRESENTATIVES

George P. Lawrence, *North Adams*
Frederick H. Gillett, *Springfield*
John A. Thayer, *Worcester*
William H. Wilder, *Gardner*
Butler Ames, *Lowell*
Augustus P. Gardner, *Hamilton*
Ernest W. Roberts, *Chelsea*
Samuel W. McCall, *Winchester*
William F. Murray, *Boston*
James M. Curley, *Boston*
Andrew J. Peters, *Boston*
John W. Weeks,[49] *West Newton*
William S. Greene, *Fall River*
Robert O. Harris, *East Bridgewater*

MICHIGAN

SENATORS

William Alden Smith, *Grand Rapids*
Charles E. Townsend, *Jackson*

REPRESENTATIVES

Frank E. Doremus, *Detroit*
William W. Wedemeyer,[50] *Ann Arbor*
John M. C. Smith, *Charlotte*
Edward L. Hamilton, *Niles*
Edwin F. Sweet, *Grand Rapids*
Samuel W. Smith, *Pontiac*
Henry McMorran, *Port Huron*
Joseph W. Fordney, *Saginaw*
James C. McLaughlin, *Muskegon*
George A. Loud, *Au Sable*
Francis H. Dodds, *Mount Pleasant*
H. Olin Young, *Ishpeming*

MINNESOTA

SENATORS

Knute Nelson, *Alexandria*
Moses E. Clapp, *St. Paul*

REPRESENTATIVES

Sydney Anderson, *Lanesboro*
Winfield S. Hammond, *St. James*
Charles R. Davis, *St. Peter*
Frederick C. Stevens, *St. Paul*
Frank M. Nye, *Minneapolis*
Charles A. Lindbergh, *Little Falls*
Andrew J. Volstead, *Granite Falls*
Clarence B. Miller, *Duluth*
Halvor Steenerson, *Crookston*

MISSISSIPPI

SENATORS

Le Roy Percy, *Greenville*
John Sharp Williams, *Yazoo City*

REPRESENTATIVES

Ezekiel S. Candler, Jr., *Corinth*
Hubert D. Stephens, *New Albany*
Benjamin G. Humphreys, *Greenville*
Thomas U. Sisson, *Winona*
Samuel A. Witherspoon, *Meridian*
Pat Harrison, *Gulfport*
William A. Dickson, *Centerville*
James W. Collier, *Vicksburg*

MISSOURI

SENATORS

William J. Stone, *Jefferson City*
James A. Reed, *Kansas City*

REPRESENTATIVES

James T. Lloyd, *Shelbyville*
William W. Rucker, *Keytesville*
Joshua W. Alexander, *Gallatin*
Charles F. Booher, *Savannah*
William P. Borland, *Kansas City*
Clement C. Dickinson, *Clinton*
Courtney W. Hamlin, *Springfield*
Dorsey W. Shackleford, *Jefferson City*
James Beauchamp Clark, *Bowling Green*
Richard Bartholdt,[51] *St. Louis*
Theron E. Catlin,[52] *St. Louis*
Patrick F. Gill,[53] *St. Louis*
Leonidas C. Dyer,[54] *St. Louis*
Walter L. Hensley, *Farmington*
Joseph J. Russell, *Charleston*
James A. Daugherty, *Webb City*
Thomas L. Rubey, *Lebanon*

MONTANA

SENATORS

Joseph M. Dixon, *Missoula*
Henry L. Myers, *Hamilton*

REPRESENTATIVE

At Large—Charles N. Pray, *Fort Benton*

---

[41] Died September 18, 1911.
[42] Elected to fill vacancy caused by death of Edmond H. Madison, and took his seat January 29, 1912.
[43] Died June 11, 1912.
[44] Elected to fill vacancy caused by death of Robert C. Wickliffe, and took his seat December 2, 1912.
[45] Died August 8, 1911.
[46] Appointed to fill vacancy caused by death of William P. Frye, and took his seat December 4, 1911; subsequently elected.
[47] Died November 25, 1912.
[48] Appointed to fill vacancy caused by death of Isidor Rayner, and took his seat December 3, 1912.
[49] Reelected to the Sixty-third Congress but resigned, effective March 4, 1913, having been elected Senator.
[50] Died January 2, 1913.

[51] Election unsuccessfully contested by Charles J. Maurer.
[52] Served until August 12, 1912; succeeded by Patrick F. Gill, who contested his election.
[53] Successfully contested the election of Theron E. Catlin, and took his seat August 12, 1912.
[54] Election unsuccessfully contested by Thomas E. Kinney.

NEBRASKA

SENATORS

Norris Brown, *Kearney*
Gilbert M. Hitchcock, *Omaha*

REPRESENTATIVES

John A. Maguire, *Lincoln*
Charles O. Lobeck, *Omaha*
James P. Latta,[55] *Tekamah*
Daniel V. Stephens,[56] *Fremont*
Charles H. Sloan, *Geneva*
George W. Norris, *McCook*
Moses P. Kinkaid, *O'Neill*

NEVADA

SENATORS

Francis G. Newlands, *Reno*
George S. Nixon,[57] *Reno*
William A. Massey,[58] *Reno*
Key Pittman,[59] *Tonopah*

REPRESENTATIVE

At Large—Edwin E. Roberts, *Carson City*

NEW HAMPSHIRE

SENATORS

Jacob H. Gallinger, *Concord*
Henry E. Burnham, *Manchester*

REPRESENTATIVES

Cyrus A. Sulloway, *Manchester*
Frank D. Currier, *Canaan*

NEW JERSEY

SENATORS

Frank O. Briggs, *Trenton*
James E. Martine, *Plainfield*

REPRESENTATIVES

Henry C. Loudenslager,[60] *Paulsboro*
William J. Browning,[61] *Camden*
John J. Gardner, *Atlantic City*
Thomas J. Scully, *South Amboy*
Ira W. Wood, *Trenton*
William E. Tuttle, Jr., *Westfield*
William Hughes,[62] *Paterson*
Archibald C. Hart,[63] *Hackensack*
Edward W. Townsend, *Montclair*
Walter I. McCoy, *South Orange*
Eugene F. Kinkead, *Jersey City*
James A. Hamill, *Jersey City*

NEW MEXICO [64]

SENATORS

Thomas B. Catron,[65] *Santa Fe*
Albert B. Fall,[66] *Three Rivers*

REPRESENTATIVES AT LARGE

George Curry,[67] *Tularosa*
Harvey B. Fergusson,[68] *Albuquerque*

NEW YORK

SENATORS

Elihu Root, *New York City*
James A. O'Gorman, *New York City*

REPRESENTATIVES

Martin W. Littleton, *Port Washington*
George H. Lindsay, *Brooklyn*
James P. Maher, *Brooklyn*
Frank E. Wilson, *Brooklyn*
William C. Redfield, *Brooklyn*
William M. Calder, *Brooklyn*
John J. Fitzgerald, *Brooklyn*
Daniel J. Riordan, *New York City*
Henry M. Goldfogle, *New York City*
William Sulzer,[69] *New York City*
Charles V. Fornes, *New York City*
Michael F. Conry, *New York City*
Jefferson M. Levy, *New York City*
John J. Kindred, *Long Island City*
Thomas G. Patten, *New York City*
Francis B. Harrison, *New York City*
Henry George, Jr., *New York City*
Steven B. Ayres, *New York City*
John E. Andrus, *Yonkers*
Thomas W. Bradley, *Walden*
Richard E. Connell,[70] *Poughkeepsie*
William H. Draper, *Troy*
Henry S. De Forest, *Schenectady*
George W. Fairchild, *Oneonta*
Theron Akin, *Akin*
George R. Malby,[71] *Ogdensburg*
Edwin A. Merritt, Jr.,[72] *Potsdam*
Charles A. Talcott, *Utica*
Luther W. Mott, *Oswego*
Michael E. Driscoll, *Syracuse*
John W. Dwight, *Dryden*
Sereno E. Payne, *Auburn*
Henry G. Danforth, *Rochester*
Edwin S. Underhill, *Bath*
James S. Simmons, *Niagara Falls*
Daniel A. Driscoll, *Buffalo*
Charles B. Smith, *Buffalo*
Edward B. Vreeland, *Salamanca*

NORTH CAROLINA

SENATORS

Furnifold McL. Simmons, *New Bern*
Lee S. Overman, *Salisbury*

REPRESENTATIVES

John H. Small, *Washington*
Claude Kitchin, *Scotland Neck*
John M. Faison, *Faison*
Edward W. Pou, *Smithfield*
Charles M. Stedman, *Greensboro*
Hannibal L. Godwin, *Dunn*
Robert N. Page, *Biscoe*
Robert L. Doughton, *Laurel Springs*
Edwin Y. Webb, *Shelby*
James M. Gudger, Jr., *Asheville*

NORTH DAKOTA

SENATORS

Porter J. McCumber, *Wahpeton*
Asle J. Gronna, *Lakota*

REPRESENTATIVES AT LARGE

Louis B. Hanna,[73] *Fargo*
Henry T. Helgesen, *Milton*

OHIO

SENATORS

Theodore E. Burton, *Cleveland*
Atlee Pomerene, *Canton*

REPRESENTATIVES

Nicholas Longworth, *Cincinnati*
Alfred G. Allen, *Cincinnati*
James M. Cox,[74] *Dayton*
J. Henry Goeke, *Wapakoneta*
Timothy T. Ansberry, *Defiance*
Matthew R. Denver, *Wilmington*
James D. Post, *Washington Courthouse*
Frank B. Willis, *Ada*
Isaac R. Sherwood, *Toledo*
Robert M. Switzer, *Gallipolis*
Horatio C. Claypool, *Chillicothe*
Edward L. Taylor, Jr., *Columbus*
Carl C. Anderson,[75] *Fostoria*
William G. Sharp, *Elyria*
George White, *Marietta*
William B. Francis, *Martins Ferry*
William A. Ashbrook, *Johnstown*
John J. Whitacre, *Canton*
Ellsworth R. Bathrick, *Akron*
L. Paul Howland, *Cleveland*
Robert J. Bulkley, *Cleveland*

---

[55] Died September 11, 1911.
[56] Elected to fill vacancy caused by death of James P. Latta, and took his seat December 4, 1911.
[57] Died June 5, 1912.
[58] Appointed to fill vacancy caused by death of George S. Nixon, and took his seat July 13, 1912.
[59] Elected to fill vacancy caused by death of George S. Nixon, and took his seat February 18, 1913.
[60] Died August 12, 1911.
[61] Elected to fill vacancy caused by death of Henry C. Loudenslager, and took his seat December 4, 1911.

[62] Resigned September 27, 1912.
[63] Elected to fill vacancy caused by resignation of William Hughes, and took his seat December 2, 1912.
[64] Admitted as a State into the Union January 6, 1912.
[65] Took his seat April 2, 1912; term to expire, as determined by lot, March 3, 1917.
[66] Took his seat April 2, 1912; term to expire, as determined by lot, March 3, 1913.
[67] Took his seat January 8, 1912.
[68] Took his seat January 8, 1912.
[69] Resigned December 31, 1912, having been elected

Governor.
[70] Died October 30, 1912; vacancy throughout remainder of the Congress.
[71] Died July 5, 1912.
[72] Elected to fill vacancy caused by death of George R. Malby, and took his seat December 2, 1912.
[73] Resigned January 7, 1913, having been elected Governor.
[74] Resigned January 12, 1913, having been elected Governor.
[75] Died October 1, 1912.

OKLAHOMA

SENATORS

Thomas P. Gore, *Lawton*
Robert L. Owen, *Muskogee*

REPRESENTATIVES

Bird S. McGuire, *Pawnee*
Dick T. Morgan, *Woodward*
James S. Davenport, *Vinita*
Charles D. Carter, *Ardmore*
Scott Ferris, *Lawton*

OREGON

SENATORS

Jonathan Bourne, Jr., *Portland*
George E. Chamberlain, *Portland*

REPRESENTATIVES

Willis C. Hawley, *Salem*
Abraham W. Lafferty, *Portland*

PENNSYLVANIA

SENATORS

Boies Penrose, *Philadelphia*
George T. Oliver, *Pittsburgh*

REPRESENTATIVES

Henry H. Bingham,[76] *Philadelphia*
William S. Vare,[77] *Philadelphia*
William S. Reyburn,[78] *Philadelphia*
J. Hampton Moore, *Philadelphia*
Reuben O. Moon, *Philadelphia*
Michael Donohoe, *Philadelphia*
George D. McCreary,[79] *Philadelphia*
Thomas S. Butler,[80] *West Chester*
Robert E. Difenderfer, *Jenkintown*
William W. Griest, *Lancaster*
John R. Farr, *Scranton*
Charles C. Bowman,[81] *Pittston*
Robert E. Lee, *Pottsville*
John H. Rothermel, *Reading*
George W. Kipp,[82] *Towanda*
William D. B. Ainey,[83] *Montrose*
William B. Wilson, *Blossburg*
John G. McHenry,[84] *Benton*
Benjamin K. Focht, *Lewisburg*
Marlin E. Olmsted, *Harrisburg*
Jesse L. Hartman, *Hollidaysburg*
Daniel F. Lafean, *York*
Charles E. Patton, *Curwensville*
Curtis H. Gregg, *Greensburg*
Thomas S. Crago,[85] *Waynesburg*
Charles Matthews, *New Castle*

Arthur L. Bates, *Meadville*
A. Mitchell Palmer, *Stroudsburg*
Jonathan N. Langham, *Indiana*
Peter M. Speer, *Oil City*
Stephen G. Porter, *Pittsburgh*
John Dalzell, *Pittsburgh*
James F. Burke, *Pittsburgh*
Andrew J. Barchfeld, *Pittsburgh*

RHODE ISLAND

SENATORS

George P. Wetmore, *Newport*
Henry F. Lippitt, *Providence*

REPRESENTATIVES

George F. O'Shaunessy, *Providence*
George H. Utter,[86] *Westerly*

SOUTH CAROLINA

SENATORS

Benjamin R. Tillman, *Trenton*
Ellison D. Smith, *Florence*

REPRESENTATIVES

George S. Legare,[87] *Charleston*
James F. Byrnes, *Aiken*
Wyatt Aiken, *Abbeville*
Joseph T. Johnson, *Spartanburg*
David E. Finley, *Yorkville*
J. Edwin Ellerbe, *Marion*
Asbury F. Lever, *Lexington*

SOUTH DAKOTA

SENATORS

Robert J. Gamble, *Yankton*
Coe I. Crawford, *Huron*

REPRESENTATIVES AT LARGE

Charles H. Burke, *Pierre*
Eben W. Martin, *Deadwood*

TENNESSEE

SENATORS

Robert L. Taylor,[88] *Nashville*
Newell Sanders,[89] *Chattanooga*
William R. Webb,[90] *Bellbuckle*
Luke Lea, *Nashville*

REPRESENTATIVES

Sam R. Sells, *Johnson City*
Richard W. Austin, *Knoxville*
John A. Moon, *Chattanooga*

Cordell Hull, *Carthage*
William C. Houston, *Woodbury*
Joseph W. Byrns, *Nashville*
Lemuel P. Padgett, *Columbia*
Thetus W. Sims, *Linden*
Finis J. Garrett, *Dresden*
George W. Gordon,[91] *Memphis*
Kenneth D. McKellar,[92] *Memphis*

TEXAS

SENATORS

Charles A. Culberson, *Dallas*
Joseph W. Bailey,[93] *Gainesville*
Rienzi M. Johnston,[94] *Houston*
Morris Sheppard,[95] *Texarkana*

REPRESENTATIVES

Morris Sheppard,[96] *Texarkana*
Martin Dies, *Beaumont*
James Young, *Kaufman*
Choice B. Randell, *Sherman*
Jack Beall, *Waxahachie*
Rufus Hardy, *Corsicana*
Alexander W. Gregg, *Palestine*
John M. Moore, *Richmond*
George F. Burgess, *Gonzales*
Albert S. Burleson, *Austin*
Robert L. Henry, *Waco*
Oscar Callaway, *Comanche*
John H. Stephens, *Vernon*
James L. Slayden, *San Antonio*
John N. Garner, *Uvalde*
William R. Smith, *Colorado*

UTAH

SENATORS

Reed Smoot, *Provo*
George Sutherland, *Salt Lake City*

REPRESENTATIVE

At Large—Joseph Howell, *Logan*

VERMONT

SENATORS

William P. Dillingham, *Montpelier*
Carroll S. Page, *Hyde Park*

REPRESENTATIVES

David J. Foster,[97] *Burlington*
Frank L. Greene,[98] *St. Albans*
Frank Plumley, *Northfield*

---

[76] Died March 22, 1912.
[77] Elected to fill vacancy caused by death of Henry H. Bingham, and took his seat May 6, 1912.
[78] Elected to fill vacancy caused by death of Representative-elect Joel Cook, in preceding Congress, and took his seat June 2, 1911.
[79] Election unsuccessfully contested by Frank H. Hawkins.
[80] Election unsuccessfully contested by Eugene C. Bonniwell.
[81] Election unsuccessfully contested by George R. McLean; seat declared vacant December 12, 1912.
[82] Died July 24, 1911.
[83] Elected to fill vacancy caused by death of George W. Kipp, and took his seat December 4, 1911.
[84] Died December 27, 1912.
[85] Election unsuccessfully contested by Jesse H. Wise.
[86] Died November 3, 1912; vacancy throughout remainder of the Congress.
[87] Election unsuccessfully contested by Aaron P. Prioleau; died January 31, 1913, before the commencement of the Sixty-third Congress, to which he had been reelected.
[88] Died March 31, 1912.
[89] Appointed to fill vacancy caused by death of Robert L. Taylor, and took his seat April 11, 1912.
[90] Elected to fill vacancy caused by death of Robert L. Taylor, and took his seat February 3, 1913.
[91] Died August 9, 1911.
[92] Elected to fill vacancy caused by death of George W. Gordon, and took his seat December 4, 1911.
[93] Resigned January 3, 1913.
[94] Appointed to fill vacancy caused by resignation of Joseph W. Bailey, and took his seat January 7, 1913.
[95] Elected to fill vacancy caused by resignation of Joseph W. Bailey, and took his seat February 3, 1913.
[96] Resigned February 3, 1913, having been elected Senator.
[97] Died March 21, 1912.
[98] Elected to fill vacancy caused by death of David J. Foster, and took his seat August 14, 1912.

VIRGINIA

SENATORS

Thomas S. Martin, *Charlottesville*
Claude A. Swanson,[99] *Chatham*

REPRESENTATIVES

William A. Jones, *Warsaw*
Edward E. Holland, *Suffolk*
John Lamb, *Richmond*
Robert Turnbull, *Lawrenceville*
Edward W. Saunders, *Rockymount*
Carter Glass, *Lynchburg*
James Hay, *Madison*
Charles C. Carlin, *Alexandria*
C. Bascom Slemp, *Big Stone Gap*
Henry D. Flood, *Appomattox*

WASHINGTON

SENATORS

Wesley L. Jones, *North Yakima*
Miles Poindexter, *Spokane*

REPRESENTATIVES

William E. Humphrey, *Seattle*
Stanton Warburton, *Tacoma*
William L. La Follette, *Pullman*

WEST VIRGINIA

SENATORS

Clarence W. Watson, *Fairmont*
William E. Chilton, *Charleston*

REPRESENTATIVES

John W. Davis, *Clarksburg*
William G. Brown, Jr., *Kingwood*
Adam B. Littlepage, *Charleston*
John M. Hamilton, *Grantsville*
James A. Hughes,[100] *Huntington*

WISCONSIN

SENATORS

Robert M. La Follette, *Madison*
Isaac Stephenson, *Marinette*

REPRESENTATIVES

Henry Allen Cooper, *Racine*
John M. Nelson, *Madison*
Arthur W. Kopp, *Platteville*
William J. Cary, *Milwaukee*
Victor L. Berger, *Milwaukee*
Michael E. Burke, *Beaver Dam*
John J. Esch, *La Crosse*
James H. Davidson, *Oshkosh*
Thomas F. Konop, *Kewaunee*
Elmer A. Morse, *Antigo*
Irvine L. Lenroot, *Superior*

WYOMING

SENATORS

Clarence D. Clark, *Evanston*
Francis E. Warren, *Cheyenne*

REPRESENTATIVE

At Large—Frank W. Mondell, *Newcastle*

TERRITORY OF ALASKA

DELEGATE

James Wickersham, *Fairbanks*

TERRITORY OF ARIZONA

DELEGATE

Ralph H. Cameron,[101] *Flagstaff*

TERRITORY OF HAWAII

DELEGATE

J. Kuhio Kalanianaole, *Waikiki*

TERRITORY OF NEW MEXICO

DELEGATE

William H. Andrews,[102] *Albuquerque*

PHILIPPINE ISLANDS

RESIDENT COMMISSIONERS [103]

Benito Legarda, *Manila*
Manuel L. Quezon, *Tayabas*

PORTO RICO

RESIDENT COMMISSIONER

Luis Muñoz Rivera, *San Juan*

---

[99] Reappointed to fill vacancy in the term beginning March 4, 1911, caused by death of Senator-elect John W. Daniel in preceding Congress, to serve until the next meeting of the legislature; subsequently reelected.
[100] Election unsuccessfully contested by Rankin Wiley.

[101] Served until February 18, 1912, the Territory of Arizona having been granted statehood by act of Congress approved June 20, 1910.
[102] Served until January 7, 1912, the Territory of New Mexico having been granted statehood by act of Congress approved June 20, 1910.

[103] By act of Congress approved February 15, 1911, term of office increased to four years, beginning March 4, 1913, present Commissioners to hold office until successors are elected and qualified.

SIXTY-THIRD CONGRESS

MARCH 4, 1913, TO MARCH 3, 1915

FIRST SESSION—*April 7, 1913, to December 1, 1913*

SECOND SESSION—*December 1, 1913, to October 24, 1914*

THIRD SESSION—*December 7, 1914, to March 3, 1915*

SPECIAL SESSION OF THE SENATE—*March 4, 1913, to March 17, 1913*

VICE PRESIDENT OF THE UNITED STATES—Thomas R. Marshall, of Indiana

PRESIDENT PRO TEMPORE OF THE SENATE—James P. Clarke,[1] of Arkansas

SECRETARY OF THE SENATE—Charles G. Bennett, of New York; James M. Baker,[2] of South Carolina

SERGEANT AT ARMS OF THE SENATE—Edgar Livingstone Cornelius, of Maryland; Charles P. Higgins,[3] of Missouri

---

SPEAKER OF THE HOUSE OF REPRESENTATIVES—James Beauchamp Clark,[4] of Missouri

CLERK OF THE HOUSE—South Trimble,[5] of Kentucky

SERGEANT AT ARMS OF THE HOUSE—Charles F. Riddell, of Indiana; Robert B. Gordon,[6] of Ohio

DOORKEEPER OF THE HOUSE—Joseph J. Sinnott, of Virginia

POSTMASTER OF THE HOUSE—William M. Dunbar

ALABAMA

SENATORS

John H. Bankhead, *Jasper*
Joseph F. Johnston,[7] *Birmingham*
Frank S. White,[8] *Birmingham*

REPRESENTATIVES

George W. Taylor, *Demopolis*
S. Hubert Dent, Jr., *Montgomery*
Henry D. Clayton,[9] *Eufaula*
William O. Mulkey,[10] *Geneva*
Fred L. Blackmon, *Anniston*
J. Thomas Heflin, *Lafayette*
Richmond P. Hobson, *Greensboro*
John L. Burnett, *Gadsden*
William Richardson,[11] *Huntsville*
Christopher C. Harris,[12] *Decatur*
Oscar W. Underwood, *Birmingham*
At Large—John W. Abercrombie, *Tuscaloosa*

ARIZONA

SENATORS

Henry F. Ashurst, *Prescott*
Marcus A. Smith, *Tucson*

REPRESENTATIVE

At Large—Carl Hayden, *Phoenix*

ARKANSAS

SENATORS

James P. Clarke, *Little Rock*
Joseph T. Robinson, *Little Rock*

REPRESENTATIVES

Thaddeus H. Caraway, *Jonesboro*
William A. Oldfield, *Batesville*
John C. Floyd, *Yellville*
Otis Wingo, *De Queen*
Henderson M. Jacoway, *Dardanelle*
Samuel M. Taylor, *Pine Bluff*
William S. Goodwin, *Warren*

CALIFORNIA

SENATORS

George C. Perkins, *Oakland*
John D. Works, *Los Angeles*

REPRESENTATIVES

William Kent, *Kentfield*
John E. Raker, *Alturas*
Charles F. Curry, *Sacramento*
Julius Kahn, *San Francisco*
John I. Nolan, *San Francisco*
Joseph R. Knowland, *Alameda*
Denver S. Church, *Fresno*
Everis A. Hayes, *San Jose*
Charles W. Bell, *Pasadena*
William D. Stephens, *Los Angeles*
William Kettner, *San Diego*

COLORADO

SENATORS

Charles S. Thomas, *Denver*
John F. Shafroth, *Denver*

---

[1] Elected March 13, 1913.
[2] Elected March 13, 1913.
[3] Elected March 13, 1913.
[4] Reelected April 7, 1913.
[5] Reelected April 7, 1913.
[6] Elected April 7, 1913.
[7] Died August 8, 1913.

[8] Elected to fill vacancy caused by death of Joseph F. Johnston, and took his seat May 22, 1914. Vacancy in this class from August 8, 1913, to May 11, 1914. Henry D. Clayton was appointed by governor August 12, 1913, to fill vacancy; credentials withdrawn October 21, 1913; Frank P. Glass was appointed by governor November 17, 1913, but by Senate resolution of February 4, 1914, was declared not entitled to a seat.
[9] Resigned effective May 25, 1914.
[10] Elected to fill vacancy caused by resignation of Henry D. Clayton, and took his seat July 16, 1914.
[11] Died March 31, 1914.
[12] Elected to fill vacancy caused by death of William Richardson, and took his seat May 19, 1914.

COLORADO—Continued

REPRESENTATIVES

George J. Kindel, *Denver*
Harry H. Seldomridge, *Colorado Springs*
At Large—
Edward T. Taylor, *Glenwood Springs*
Edward Keating, *Pueblo*

CONNECTICUT

SENATORS

Frank B. Brandegee, *New London*
George P. McLean, *Simsbury*

REPRESENTATIVES

Augustine Lonergan, *Hartford*
Bryan F. Mahan, *New London*
Thomas L. Reilly, *Meriden*
Jeremiah Donovan, *South Norwalk*
William Kennedy, *Naugatuck*

DELAWARE

SENATORS

Henry A. du Pont, *Winterthur*
Willard Saulsbury, *Wilmington*

REPRESENTATIVE

At Large—Franklin Brockson, *Clayton*

FLORIDA

SENATORS

Duncan U. Fletcher, *Jacksonville*
Nathan P. Bryan, *Jacksonville*

REPRESENTATIVES

Stephen M. Sparkman, *Tampa*
Frank Clark, *Gainesville*
Emmett Wilson, *Pensacola*
At Large—Claude L'Engle, *Jacksonville*

GEORGIA

SENATORS

Augustus O. Bacon,[13] *Macon*
William S. West,[14] *Valdosta*
Thomas W. Hardwick,[15] *Sandersville*
Hoke Smith, *Atlanta*

REPRESENTATIVES

Charles G. Edwards, *Savannah*
Seaborn A. Roddenbery,[16] *Thomasville*
Frank Park,[17] *Sylvester*
Charles R. Crisp, *Americus*
William C. Adamson, *Carrollton*
William S. Howard, *Decatur*
Charles L. Bartlett, *Macon*

Gordon Lee, *Chickamauga*
Samuel J. Tribble, *Athens*
Thomas M. Bell, *Gainesville*
Thomas W. Hardwick,[18] *Sandersville*
Carl Vinson [19] *Milledgeville*
John R. Walker, *Valdosta*
Dudley M. Hughes, *Danville*

IDAHO

SENATORS

William E. Borah, *Boise*
James H. Brady, *Pocatello*

REPRESENTATIVES AT LARGE

Burton L. French, *Moscow*
Addison T. Smith, *Twin Falls*

ILLINOIS

SENATORS

James Hamilton Lewis,[20] *Chicago*
Lawrence Y. Sherman,[21] *Springfield*

REPRESENTATIVES

Martin B. Madden, *Chicago*
James R. Mann, *Chicago*
George E. Gorman, *Chicago*
James T. McDermott,[22] *Chicago*
Adolph J. Sabath, *Chicago*
James McAndrews, *Chicago*
Frank Buchanan, *Chicago*
Thomas Gallagher, *Chicago*
Fred A. Britten, *Chicago*
Charles M. Thomson, *Chicago*
Ira C. Copley, *Aurora*
William H. Hinebaugh, *Ottawa*
John C. McKenzie, *Elizabeth*
Clyde H. Tavenner, *Cordova*
Stephen A. Hoxworth, *Rapatee*
Claudius U. Stone, *Peoria*
Louis FitzHenry, *Bloomington*
Frank T. O'Hair, *Paris*
Charles M. Borchers, *Decatur*
Henry T. Rainey, *Carrollton*
James M. Graham, *Springfield*
William N. Baltz, *Millstadt*
Martin D. Foster, *Olney*
H. Robert Fowler, *Elizabethtown*
Robert P. Hill, *Marion*
At Large—
Lawrence B. Stringer, *Lincoln*
William E. Williams, *Pittsfield*

INDIANA

SENATORS

Benjamin F. Shively, *South Bend*
John W. Kern, *Indianapolis*

REPRESENTATIVES

Charles Lieb, *Rockport*
William A. Cullop, *Vincennes*
William E. Cox, *Jasper*
Lincoln Dixon, *North Vernon*
Ralph W. Moss, *Center Point*
Finly H. Gray, *Connersville*
Charles A. Korbly, *Indianapolis*
John A. M. Adair, *Portland*
Martin A. Morrison, *Frankfort*
John B. Peterson, *Crown Point*
George W. Rauch, *Marion*
Cyrus Cline, *Angola*
Henry A. Barnhart, *Rochester*

IOWA

SENATORS

Albert B. Cummins, *Des Moines*
William S. Kenyon, *Fort Dodge*

REPRESENTATIVES

Charles A. Kennedy, *Montrose*
Irvin S. Pepper,[23] *Muscatine*
Henry Vollmer,[24] *Davenport*
Maurice Connolly, *Dubuque*
Gilbert N. Haugen, *Northwood*
James W. Good, *Cedar Rapids*
Sanford Kirkpatrick, *Ottumwa*
Solomon F. Prouty, *Des Moines*
Horace M. Towner, *Corning*
William R. Green, *Audubon*
Frank P. Woods, *Estherville*
George C. Scott, *Sioux City*

KANSAS

SENATORS

Joseph L. Bristow, *Salina*
William H. Thompson, *Garden City*

REPRESENTATIVES

Daniel R. Anthony, Jr., *Leavenworth*
Joseph Taggart, *Kansas City*
Philip P. Campbell, *Pittsburg*
Dudley Doolittle, *Strong City*
Guy T. Helvering, *Marysville*
John R. Connelly, *Colby*
George A. Neeley, *Hutchinson*
Victor Murdock, *Wichita*

KENTUCKY

SENATORS

William O. Bradley,[25] *Beechmont*
Johnson N. Camden,[26] *Versailles*
Ollie M. James, *Marion*

---

[13] Reappointed to fill vacancy in the term beginning March 4, 1913, to serve until the next meeting of the legislature; subsequently reelected; died February 14, 1914.
[14] Appointed to fill vacancy caused by death of Augustus O. Bacon, and took his seat March 6, 1914.
[15] Elected to fill vacancy caused by death of Augustus O. Bacon, and took his seat December 7, 1914.
[16] Died September 25, 1913.
[17] Elected to fill vacancy caused by death of Seaborn A. Roddenbery, and took his seat November 20, 1913.

[18] Resigned effective November 2, 1914; subsequently elected Senator.
[19] Elected to fill vacancy caused by resignation of Thomas W. Hardwick; took his seat December 7, 1914.
[20] Elected to fill vacancy in the term beginning March 4, 1913, and took his seat April 17, 1913; vacancy in this class from March 4 to 25, 1913, because of recess of legislature.
[21] Elected to fill vacancy in the term ending March 3, 1915, caused by action of Senate, in preceding Congress, in declaring invalid the election of William Lor-

imer, and took his seat April 7, 1913; vacancy in this class from July 14, 1912, to March 25, 1913.
[22] Resigned July 21, 1914; vacancy throughout remainder of the Congress.
[23] Died December 22, 1913.
[24] Elected to fill vacancy caused by death of Irvin S. Pepper, and took his seat February 25, 1914.
[25] Died May 23, 1914.
[26] Appointed to fill vacancy caused by death of William O. Bradley, and took his seat June 18, 1914; subsequently elected.

REPRESENTATIVES

Alben W. Barkley, *Paducah*
Augustus O. Stanley, *Henderson*
Robert Y. Thomas, Jr., *Central City*
Ben Johnson, *Bardstown*
J. Swagar Sherley, *Louisville*
Arthur B. Rouse, *Burlington*
James C. Cantrill, *Georgetown*
Harvey Helm, *Stanford*
William J. Fields, *Olive Hill*
John W. Langley, *Pikeville*
Caleb Powers, *Barbourville*

LOUISIANA

SENATORS

John R. Thornton, *Alexandria*
Joseph E. Ransdell, *Lake Providence*

REPRESENTATIVES

Albert Estopinal, *Estopinal*
H. Garland Dupré, *New Orleans*
Robert F. Broussard, *New Iberia*
John T. Watkins, *Minden*
J. Walter Elder, *Monroe*
Lewis L. Morgan, *Covington*
Ladislas Lazaro, *Washington*
James B. Aswell, *Natchitoches*

MAINE

SENATORS

Charles F. Johnson, *Waterville*
Edwin C. Burleigh, *Augusta*

REPRESENTATIVES

Asher C. Hinds, *Portland*
Daniel J. McGillicuddy, *Lewiston*
Forrest Goodwin,[27] *Skowhegan*
John A. Peters,[28] *Ellsworth*
Frank E. Guernsey, *Dover*

MARYLAND

SENATORS

John Walter Smith, *Snow Hill*
William P. Jackson, *Salisbury*
Blair Lee,[29] *Silver Spring*

REPRESENTATIVES

J. Harry Covington,[30] *Easton*
Jesse D. Price,[31] *Salisbury*
J. Fred. C. Talbott, *Lutherville*
George Konig,[32] *Baltimore*

Charles P. Coady,[33] *Baltimore*
J. Charles Linthicum, *Baltimore*
Frank O. Smith, *Dunkirk*
David J. Lewis, *Cumberland*

MASSACHUSETTS

SENATORS

Henry Cabot Lodge, *Nahant*
John W. Weeks, *West Newton*

REPRESENTATIVES

Allen T. Treadway, *Stockbridge*
Frederick H. Gillett, *Springfield*
William H. Wilder,[34] *Gardner*
Calvin D. Paige,[35] *Southbridge*
Samuel E. Winslow, *Worcester*
John Jacob Rogers, *Lowell*
Augustus P. Gardner, *Hamilton*
Michael F. Phelan, *Lynn*
Frederick S. Deitrick, *Cambridge*
Ernest W. Roberts, *Chelsea*
William F. Murray,[36] *Boston*
Andrew J. Peters,[37] *Boston*
James M. Curley,[38] *Boston*
James A. Gallivan,[39] *Boston*
John J. Mitchell,[40] *Marlboro*
Edward Gilmore, *Brockton*
William S. Greene, *Fall River*
Thomas C. Thacher, *Yarmouth*

MICHIGAN

SENATORS

William Alden Smith, *Grand Rapids*
Charles E. Townsend, *Jackson*

REPRESENTATIVES

Frank E. Doremus, *Detroit*
Samuel W. Beakes, *Ann Arbor*
John M. C. Smith,[41] *Charlotte*
Edward L. Hamilton, *Niles*
Carl E. Mapes, *Grand Rapids*
Samuel W. Smith, *Pontiac*
Louis C. Cramton, *Lapeer*
Joseph W. Fordney, *Saginaw*
James C. McLaughlin, *Muskegon*
Roy O. Woodruff, *Bay City*
Francis O. Lindquist, *Greenville*
H. Olin Young,[42] *Ishpeming*
William J. MacDonald,[43] *Calumet*
At Large—Patrick H. Kelly, *Lansing*

MINNESOTA

SENATORS

Knute Nelson, *Alexandria*
Moses E. Clapp, *St. Paul*

REPRESENTATIVES

Sydney Anderson, *Lanesboro*
Winfield S. Hammond,[44] *St. James*
Charles R. Davis, *St. Peter*
Frederick C. Stevens, *St. Paul*
George R. Smith, *Minneapolis*
Charles A. Lindbergh, *Little Falls*
Andrew J. Volstead, *Granite Falls*
Clarence B. Miller, *Duluth*
Halvor Steenerson, *Crookston*
At Large—James Manahan, *Minneapolis*

MISSISSIPPI

SENATORS

John Sharp Williams, *Yazoo City*
James K. Vardaman, *Jackson*

REPRESENTATIVES

Ezekiel S. Candler, Jr., *Corinth*
Hubert D. Stephens, *New Albany*
Benjamin G. Humphreys, *Greenville*
Thomas U. Sisson, *Winona*
Samuel A. Witherspoon, *Meridian*
Pat Harrison, *Gulfport*
Percy E. Quin, *McComb City*
James W. Collier, *Vicksburg*

MISSOURI

SENATORS

William J. Stone, *Jefferson City*
James A. Reed, *Kansas City*

REPRESENTATIVES

James T. Lloyd, *Shelbyville*
William W. Rucker, *Keytesville*
Joshua W. Alexander, *Gallatin*
Charles F. Booher, *Savannah*
William P. Borland, *Kansas City*
Clement C. Dickinson, *Clinton*
Courtney W. Hamlin, *Springfield*
Dorsey W. Shackleford, *Jefferson City*
James Beauchamp Clark, *Bowling Green*
Richard Bartholdt, *St. Louis*
William L. Igoe, *St. Louis*
Leonidas C. Dyer,[45] *St. Louis*
Michael J. Gill,[46] *St. Louis*

---

[27] Died May 28, 1913.
[28] Elected to fill vacancy caused by death of Forrest Goodwin, and took his seat September 22, 1913.
[29] Elected on November 4, 1913, to fill vacancy caused by death of Isidor Rayner (in preceding Congress); credentials were presented on December 5, 1913, and referred to the Committee on Privileges and Elections, and pending report he did not attempt to qualify; on January 19, 1914, a resolution was reported to the effect that he had been legally elected and was entitled to the seat; on January 28, 1914, the Senate adopted the resolution and he took his seat the same day. This was the first election by popular vote held pursuant to the seventeenth amendment to the Constitution.
[30] Resigned September 30, 1914.
[31] Elected to fill vacancy caused by resignation of J. Harry Covington, and took his seat December 7, 1914.
[32] Died May 31, 1913.
[33] Elected to fill vacancy caused by death of George Konig, and took his seat November 26, 1913.
[34] Died September 11, 1913.
[35] Elected to fill vacancy caused by death of William H. Wilder, and took his seat November 29, 1913.
[36] Resigned September 28, 1914; vacancy throughout remainder of the Congress.
[37] Resigned, effective August 15, 1914, having been appointed Assistant Secretary of the Treasury; vacancy throughout remainder of the Congress.
[38] Resigned effective February 4, 1914.
[39] Elected to fill vacancy caused by resignation of James M. Curley, and took his seat April 18, 1914.
[40] Elected to fill vacancy caused by resignation of Representative-elect John W. Weeks, in preceding Congress, and took his seat April 26, 1913.
[41] Election unsuccessfully contested by Claud S. Carney.
[42] Resigned effective May 16, 1913; subsequently succeeded by William J. MacDonald, who contested his election.
[43] Successfully contested the election of H. Olin Young (who had resigned effective May 16, 1913), and took his seat August 26, 1913.
[44] Resigned January 6, 1915, having been elected Governor.
[45] Served until June 19, 1914; succeeded by Michael J. Gill, who contested his election.
[46] Successfully contested the election of Leonidas C. Dyer, and took his seat June 19, 1914.

MISSOURI—Continued

REPRESENTATIVES—continued

Walter L. Hensley, *Farmington*
Joseph J. Russell, *Charleston*
Perl D. Decker, *Joplin*
Thomas L. Rubey, *Lebanon*

MONTANA

SENATORS

Henry L. Myers, *Hamilton*
Thomas J. Walsh, *Helena*

REPRESENTATIVES AT LARGE

John M. Evans, *Missoula*
Tom Stout, *Lewistown*

NEBRASKA

SENATORS

Gilbert M. Hitchcock, *Omaha*
George W. Norris, *McCook*

REPRESENTATIVES

John A. Maguire, *Lincoln*
Charles O. Lobeck, *Omaha*
Daniel V. Stephens, *Fremont*
Charles H. Sloan, *Geneva*
Silas R. Barton, *Grand Island*
Moses P. Kinkaid, *O'Neill*

NEVADA

SENATORS

Francis G. Newlands, *Reno*
Key Pittman, *Tonopah*

REPRESENTATIVE

At Large—Edwin E. Roberts, *Carson City*

NEW HAMPSHIRE

SENATORS

Jacob H. Gallinger, *Concord*
Henry F. Hollis,[47] *Concord*

REPRESENTATIVES

Eugene E. Reed, *Manchester*
Raymond B. Stevens, *Landaff*

NEW JERSEY

SENATORS

James E. Martine, *Plainfield*
William Hughes, *Paterson*

REPRESENTATIVES

William J. Browning, *Camden*
J. Thompson Baker, *Wildwood*

Thomas J. Scully, *South Amboy*
Allan B. Walsh, *Trenton*
William E. Tuttle, Jr., *Westfield*
Lewis J. Martin,[48] *Newton*
Archibald C. Hart,[49] *Hackensack*
Robert G. Bremner,[50] *Passaic*
Dow H. Drukker,[51] *Passaic*
Eugene F. Kinkead,[52] *Jersey City*
Walter I. McCoy,[53] *East Orange*
Richard Wayne Parker,[54] *Newark*
Edward W. Townsend, *Montclair*
John J. Eagan, *Weehawken*
James A. Hamill, *Jersey City*

NEW MEXICO

SENATORS

Thomas B. Catron, *Santa Fe*
Albert B. Fall, *Three Rivers*

REPRESENTATIVE

At Large—Harvey B. Fergusson, *Albuquerque*

NEW YORK

SENATORS

Elihu Root, *New York City*
James A. O'Gorman, *New York City*

REPRESENTATIVES

Lathrop Brown, *St. James*
Denis O'Leary,[55] *Douglaston*
Frank E. Wilson, *Brooklyn*
Harry H. Dale, *Brooklyn*
James P. Maher, *Brooklyn*
William M. Calder, *Brooklyn*
John J. Fitzgerald, *Brooklyn*
Daniel J. Griffin, *Brooklyn*
James H. O'Brien, *Brooklyn*
Herman A. Metz, *Brooklyn*
Daniel J. Riordan, *New York City*
Henry M. Goldfogle, *New York City*
Timothy D. Sullivan,[56] *New York City*
George W. Loft,[57] *New York City*
Jefferson M. Levy, *New York City*
Michael F. Conry, *New York City*
Peter J. Dooling, *New York City*
John F. Carew, *New York City*
Thomas G. Patten, *New York City*
Walter M. Chandler, *New York City*
Francis B. Harrison,[58] *New York City*
Jacob A. Cantor,[59] *New York City*
Henry George, Jr., *New York City*
Henry Bruckner, *New York City*
Joseph A. Goulden, *Fordham*
Woodson R. Oglesby, *Yonkers*
Benjamin I. Taylor, *Harrison*
Edmund Platt, *Poughkeepsie*

George McClellan, *Chatham*
Peter G. Ten Eyck, *Albany*
James S. Parker, *Salem*
Samuel Wallin, *Amsterdam*
Edwin A. Merritt, Jr.,[60] *Potsdam*
Luther W. Mott, *Oswego*
Charles A. Talcott, *Utica*
George W. Fairchild, *Oneonta*
John R. Clancy, *Syracuse*
Sereno E. Payne,[61] *Auburn*
Edwin S. Underhill, *Bath*
Thomas B. Dunn, *Rochester*
Henry G. Danforth, *Rochester*
Robert H. Gittins, *Niagara Falls*
Charles B. Smith, *Buffalo*
Daniel A. Driscoll, *Buffalo*
Charles M. Hamilton, *Ripley*

NORTH CAROLINA

SENATORS

Furnifold McL. Simmons, *New Bern*
Lee S. Overman, *Salisbury*

REPRESENTATIVES

John H. Small, *Washington*
Claude Kitchin, *Scotland Neck*
John M. Faison, *Faison*
Edward W. Pou, *Smithfield*
Charles M. Stedman, *Greensboro*
Hannibal L. Godwin, *Dunn*
Robert N. Page, *Biscoe*
Robert L. Doughton, *Laurel Springs*
Edwin Y. Webb, *Shelby*
James M. Gudger, Jr., *Asheville*

NORTH DAKOTA

SENATORS

Porter J. McCumber, *Wahpeton*
Asle J. Gronna, *Lakota*

REPRESENTATIVES

Henry T. Helgesen, *Milton*
George M. Young, *Valley City*
Patrick D. Norton, *Hettinger*

OHIO

SENATORS

Theodore E. Burton, *Cleveland*
Atlee Pomerene, *Canton*

REPRESENTATIVES

Stanley E. Bowdle, *Cincinnati*
Alfred G. Allen, *Cincinnati*
Warren Gard, *Hamilton*
J. Henry Goeke, *Wapakoneta*

---

[47] Elected March 13, 1913, for the term beginning March 4, 1913, and took his seat March 15, 1913.
[48] Died May 5, 1913.
[49] Elected to fill vacancy caused by death of Lewis J. Martin, and took his seat August 12, 1913.
[50] Died February 5, 1914.
[51] Elected to fill vacancy caused by death of Robert G. Bremner, and took his seat April 22, 1914.
[52] Resigned February 4, 1915.

[53] Resigned October 3, 1914.
[54] Elected to fill vacancy caused by resignation of Walter I. McCoy, and took his seat December 7, 1914.
[55] Resigned December 31, 1914.
[56] Died August 31, 1913.
[57] Elected to fill vacancy caused by death of Timothy D. Sullivan, and took his seat November 29, 1913.
[58] Resigned, effective September 1, 1913, having been appointed Governor General of the Philippine Islands.

[59] Elected to fill vacancy caused by resignation of Francis B. Harrison, and took his seat November 29, 1913.
[60] Died December 4, 1914, before the commencement of the Sixty-fourth Congress, to which he had been reelected.
[61] Died December 10, 1914, before the commencement of the Sixty-fourth Congress, to which he had been reelected.

Timothy T. Ansberry,[62] *Defiance*
Simeon D. Fess, *Yellow Springs*
James D. Post, *Washington Courthouse*
Frank B. Willis,[63] *Ada*
Isaac R. Sherwood, *Toledo*
Robert M. Switzer, *Gallipolis*
Horatio C. Claypool, *Chillicothe*
Clement L. Brumbaugh, *Columbus*
John A. Key, *Marion*
William G. Sharp,[64] *Elyria*
George White, *Marietta*
William B. Francis, *Martins Ferry*
William A. Ashbrook, *Johnstown*
John J. Whitacre, *Canton*
Ellsworth R. Bathrick, *Akron*
William Gordon, *Cleveland*
Robert J. Bulkley, *Cleveland*
At Large—Robert Crosser, *Cleveland*

OKLAHOMA

SENATORS

Thomas P. Gore, *Lawton*
Robert L. Owen, *Muskogee*

REPRESENTATIVES

Bird S. McGuire, *Pawnee*
Dick T. Morgan, *Woodward*
James S. Davenport, *Vinita*
Charles D. Carter, *Ardmore*
Scott Ferris, *Lawton*
At Large—
    William H. Murray, *Tishomingo*
    Joseph B. Thompson, *Pauls Valley*
    Claude Weaver, *Oklahoma City*

OREGON

SENATORS

George E. Chamberlain, *Portland*
Harry Lane, *Portland*

REPRESENTATIVES

Willis C. Hawley, *Salem*
Nicholas J. Sinnott, *The Dalles*
Abraham W. Lafferty, *Portland*

PENNSYLVANIA

SENATORS

Boies Penrose, *Philadelphia*
George T. Oliver, *Pittsburgh*

REPRESENTATIVES

William S. Vare, *Philadelphia*
George S. Graham, *Philadelphia*
J. Hampton Moore, *Philadelphia*
George W. Edmonds, *Philadelphia*
Michael Donohoe, *Philadelphia*
J. Washington Logue, *Philadelphia*
Thomas S. Butler, *West Chester*
Robert E. Difenderfer, *Jenkintown*

William W. Griest, *Lancaster*
John R. Farr, *Scranton*
John J. Casey, *Wilkes-Barre*
Robert E. Lee, *Pottsville*
John H. Rothermel, *Reading*
William D. B. Ainey, *Montrose*
Edgar R. Kiess, *Williamsport*
John V. Lesher, *Sunbury*
Frank L. Dershem, *Lewisburg*
Aaron S. Kreider, *Annville*
Warren W. Bailey, *Johnstown*
Andrew R. Brodbeck, *Hanover*
Charles E. Patton, *Curwensville*
Abraham L. Keister, *Scottdale*
Wooda N. Carr, *Uniontown*
Henry W. Temple, *Washington*
Milton W. Shreve, *Erie*
A. Mitchell Palmer, *Stroudsburg*
Jonathan N. Langham, *Indiana*
Willis J. Hulings, *Oil City*
Stephen G. Porter, *Pittsburgh*
M. Clyde Kelly, *Braddock*
James F. Burke, *Pittsburgh*
Andrew J. Barchfeld, *Pittsburgh*
At Large—
    Fred E. Lewis, *Allentown*
    John M. Morin, *Pittsburgh*
    Arthur R. Rupley, *Carlisle*
    Anderson H. Walters, *Johnstown*

RHODE ISLAND

SENATORS

Henry F. Lippitt, *Providence*
LeBaron B. Colt, *Bristol*

REPRESENTATIVES

George F. O'Shaunessy, *Providence*
Peter G. Gerry, *Providence*
Ambrose Kennedy, *Woonsocket*

SOUTH CAROLINA

SENATORS

Benjamin R. Tillman, *Trenton*
Ellison D. Smith, *Florence*

REPRESENTATIVES

Richard S. Whaley,[65] *Charleston*
James F. Byrnes, *Aiken*
Wyatt Aiken, *Abbeville*
Joseph T. Johnson, *Spartanburg*
David E. Finley, *Yorkville*
J. Willard Ragsdale, *Florence*
Asbury F. Lever, *Lexington*

SOUTH DAKOTA

SENATORS

Coe I. Crawford, *Huron*
Thomas Sterling, *Vermilion*

REPRESENTATIVES

Charles H. Dillon, *Yankton*
Charles H. Burke, *Pierre*
Eben W. Martin, *Deadwood*

TENNESSEE

SENATORS

Luke Lea, *Nashville*
John K. Shields, *Knoxville*

REPRESENTATIVES

Sam R. Sells, *Johnson City*
Richard W. Austin, *Knoxville*
John A. Moon, *Chattanooga*
Cordell Hull, *Carthage*
William C. Houston, *Woodbury*
Joseph W. Byrns, *Nashville*
Lemuel P. Padgett, *Columbia*
Thetus W. Sims, *Linden*
Finis J. Garrett, *Dresden*
Kenneth D. McKellar, *Memphis*

TEXAS

SENATORS

Charles A. Culberson, *Dallas*
Morris Sheppard, *Texarkana*

REPRESENTATIVES

Horace W. Vaughan, *Texarkana*
Martin Dies, *Beaumont*
James Young, *Kaufman*
Sam Rayburn, *Bonham*
Jack Beall, *Waxahachie*
Rufus Hardy, *Corsicana*
Alexander W. Gregg, *Palestine*
Joe H. Eagle, *Houston*
George F. Burgess, *Gonzales*
Albert S. Burleson,[66] *Austin*
James P. Buchanan,[67] *Brenham*
Robert L. Henry, *Waco*
Oscar Callaway, *Comanche*
John H. Stephens, *Vernon*
James L. Slayden, *San Antonio*
John N. Garner, *Uvalde*
William R. Smith, *Colorado*
At Large—
    Daniel E. Garrett, *Houston*
    Hatton W. Sumners, *Dallas*

UTAH

SENATORS

Reed Smoot, *Provo*
George Sutherland, *Salt Lake City*

REPRESENTATIVES AT LARGE

Joseph Howell, *Logan*
Jacob Johnson, *Spring City*

---

[62] Resigned January 9, 1915.
[63] Resigned, effective January 9, 1915, having been elected Governor.
[64] Resigned, effective July 23, 1914.

[65] Elected to fill vacancy caused by death of Representative-elect George S. Legare, in preceding Congress, and took his seat May 9, 1913; election unsuccessfully contested by John P. Grace.

[66] Resigned March 6, 1913, having been appointed Postmaster General.
[67] Elected to fill vacancy caused by resignation of Albert S. Burleson, and took his seat April 17, 1913.

VERMONT

SENATORS

William P. Dillingham, *Montpelier*
Carroll S. Page, *Hyde Park*

REPRESENTATIVES

Frank L. Greene, *St. Albans*
Frank Plumley, *Northfield*

VIRGINIA

SENATORS

Thomas S. Martin, *Charlottesville*
Claude A. Swanson, *Chatham*

REPRESENTATIVES

William A. Jones, *Warsaw*
Edward E. Holland, *Suffolk*
Andrew J. Montague, *Richmond*
Walter A. Watson, *Jennings Ordinary*
Edward W. Saunders, *Rockymount*
Carter Glass, *Lynchburg*
James Hay, *Madison*
Charles C. Carlin, *Alexandria*
C. Bascom Slemp, *Big Stone Gap*
Henry D. Flood, *Appomattox*

WASHINGTON

SENATORS

Wesley L. Jones, *North Yakima*
Miles Poindexter, *Spokane*

REPRESENTATIVES

William E. Humphrey, *Seattle*
Albert Johnson, *Hoquiam*
William L. La Follette, *Pullman*
At Large—
James W. Bryan, *Seattle*
Jacob A. Falconer, *Everett*

WEST VIRGINIA

SENATORS

William E. Chilton, *Charleston*
Nathan Goff,[68] *Clarksburg*

REPRESENTATIVES

John W. Davis,[69] *Clarksburg*
Matthew M. Neely,[70] *Fairmont*
William G. Brown, Jr., *Kingwood*
Samuel B. Avis, *Charleston*
Hunter H. Moss, Jr., *Parkersburg*
James A. Hughes, *Huntington*
At Large—Howard Sutherland, *Elkins*

WISCONSIN

SENATORS

Robert M. La Follette, *Madison*
Isaac Stephenson, *Marinette*

REPRESENTATIVES

Henry Allen Cooper, *Racine*
Michael E. Burke, *Beaver Dam*
John M. Nelson, *Madison*
William J. Cary, *Milwaukee*
William H. Stafford, *Milwaukee*
Michael K. Reilly, *Fond du Lac*

John J. Esch, *La Crosse*
Edward E. Browne, *Waupaca*
Thomas F. Konop, *Kewaunee*
James A. Frear, *Hudson*
Irvine L. Lenroot, *Superior*

WYOMING

SENATORS

Clarence D. Clark, *Evanston*
Francis E. Warren, *Cheyenne*

REPRESENTATIVE

At Large—Frank W. Mondell, *Newcastle*

TERRITORY OF ALASKA

DELEGATE

James Wickersham, *Fairbanks*

TERRITORY OF HAWAII

DELEGATE

J. Kuhio Kalanianaole, *Waikiki*

PHILIPPINE ISLANDS

RESIDENT COMMISSIONERS

Manuel L. Quezon, *Tayabas*
Manuel Earnshaw, *Manila*

PORTO RICO

RESIDENT COMMISSIONER

Luis Muñoz Rivera, *San Juan*

---

[68] Elected February 21, 1913, for the term beginning March 4, 1913, but did not qualify until April 7, 1913, preferring to retain the judgeship.

[69] Resigned August 29, 1913, having been appointed Solicitor General of the United States.

[70] Elected to fill vacancy caused by resignation of John W. Davis, and took his seat November 1, 1913.

SIXTY-FOURTH CONGRESS

MARCH 4, 1915, TO MARCH 3, 1917

FIRST SESSION—*December 6, 1915, to September 8, 1916*

SECOND SESSION—*December 4, 1916, to March 3, 1917*

———

VICE PRESIDENT OF THE UNITED STATES—THOMAS R. MARSHALL, of Indiana

PRESIDENT PRO TEMPORE OF THE SENATE—JAMES P. CLARKE,[1] of Arkansas; WILLARD SAULSBURY,[2] of Delaware

SECRETARY OF THE SENATE—JAMES M. BAKER, of South Carolina

SERGEANT AT ARMS OF THE SENATE—CHARLES P. HIGGINS, of Missouri

———

SPEAKER OF THE HOUSE OF REPRESENTATIVES—JAMES BEAUCHAMP CLARK,[3] of Missouri

CLERK OF THE HOUSE—SOUTH TRIMBLE,[4] of Kentucky

SERGEANT AT ARMS OF THE HOUSE—ROBERT B. GORDON,[5] of Ohio

DOORKEEPER OF THE HOUSE—JOSEPH J. SINNOTT, of Virginia

POSTMASTER OF THE HOUSE—WILLIAM M. DUNBAR

ALABAMA

SENATORS

John H. Bankhead, *Jasper*
Oscar W. Underwood, *Birmingham*

REPRESENTATIVES

Oscar L. Gray, *Butler*
S. Hubert Dent, Jr., *Montgomery*
Henry B. Steagall, *Ozark*
Fred L. Blackmon, *Anniston*
J. Thomas Heflin, *Lafayette*
William B. Oliver, *Tuscaloosa*
John L. Burnett, *Gadsden*
Edward B. Almon, *Tuscumbia*
George Huddleston, *Birmingham*
At Large—John W. Abercrombie, *Tuscaloosa*

ARIZONA

SENATORS

Henry F. Ashurst, *Prescott*
Marcus A. Smith, *Tucson*

REPRESENTATIVE

At Large—Carl Hayden, *Phoenix*

ARKANSAS

SENATORS

James P. Clarke,[6] *Little Rock*
William F. Kirby,[7] *Little Rock*
Joseph T. Robinson, *Little Rock*

REPRESENTATIVES

Thaddeus H. Caraway, *Jonesboro*
William A. Oldfield, *Batesville*
John N. Tillman, *Fayetteville*
Otis Wingo, *De Queen*
Henderson M. Jacoway, *Dardanelle*
Samuel M. Taylor, *Pine Bluff*
William S. Goodwin, *Warren*

CALIFORNIA

SENATORS

John D. Works, *Los Angeles*
James D. Phelan, *San Francisco*

REPRESENTATIVES

William Kent, *Kentfield*
John E. Raker, *Alturas*
Charles F. Curry, *Sacramento*
Julius Kahn, *San Francisco*
John I. Nolan, *San Francisco*
John A. Elston, *Berkeley*
Denver S. Church, *Fresno*
Everis A. Hayes, *San Jose*
Charles H. Randall, *Los Angeles*
William D. Stephens,[8] *Los Angeles*
H. Stanley Benedict,[9] *Los Angeles*
William Kettner, *San Diego*

COLORADO

SENATORS

Charles S. Thomas, *Denver*
John F. Shafroth, *Denver*

REPRESENTATIVES

Benjamin C. Hilliard, *Denver*
Charles B. Timberlake, *Sterling*
Edward Keating, *Pueblo*
Edward T. Taylor, *Glenwood Springs*

CONNECTICUT

SENATORS

Frank B. Brandegee, *New London*
George P. McLean, *Simsbury*

---

[1] Reelected December 6, 1915; died October 1, 1916.
[2] Elected December 14, 1916.
[3] Reelected December 6, 1915.
[4] Reelected December 6, 1915.
[5] Reelected December 6, 1915.
[6] Died October 1, 1916.
[7] Elected to fill vacancy caused by death of James P. Clarke, and took his seat December 5, 1916.
[8] Resigned July 22, 1916.
[9] Elected to fill vacancy caused by resignation of William D. Stephens, and took his seat December 4, 1916.

CONNECTICUT—Continued

REPRESENTATIVES

P. Davis Oakey, *Hartford*
Richard P. Freeman, *New London*
John Q. Tilson, *New Haven*
Ebenezer J. Hill,[10] *Norwalk*
James P. Glynn, *Winsted*

DELAWARE

SENATORS

Henry A. du Pont, *Winterthur*
Willard Saulsbury, *Wilmington*

REPRESENTATIVE

At Large—Thomas W. Miller, *Wilmington*

FLORIDA

SENATORS

Duncan U. Fletcher, *Jacksonville*
Nathan P. Bryan, *Jacksonville*

REPRESENTATIVES

Stephen M. Sparkman, *Tampa*
Frank Clark, *Gainesville*
Emmett Wilson, *Pensacola*
William J. Sears, *Kissimmee*

GEORGIA

SENATORS

Hoke Smith, *Atlanta*
Thomas W. Hardwick, *Sandersville*

REPRESENTATIVES

Charles G. Edwards, *Savannah*
Frank Park, *Sylvester*
Charles R. Crisp, *Americus*
William C. Adamson, *Carrollton*
William S. Howard, *Kirkwood*
James W. Wise, *Fayetteville*
Gordon Lee, *Chickamauga*
Samuel J. Tribble,[11] *Athens*
Tinsley W. Rucker,[12] *Athens*
Thomas M. Bell, *Gainesville*
Carl Vinson, *Milledgeville*
John R. Walker, *Valdosta*
Dudley M. Hughes, *Danville*

IDAHO

SENATORS

William E. Borah, *Boise*
James H. Brady, *Pocatello*

REPRESENTATIVES AT LARGE

Robert M. McCracken, *Boise*
Addison T. Smith, *Twin Falls*

ILLINOIS

SENATORS

James Hamilton Lewis, *Chicago*
Lawrence Y. Sherman, *Springfield*

REPRESENTATIVES

Martin B. Madden, *Chicago*
James R. Mann, *Chicago*
William W. Wilson, *Chicago*
James T. McDermott, *Chicago*
Adolph J. Sabath, *Chicago*
James McAndrews, *Chicago*
Frank Buchanan, *Chicago*
Thomas Gallagher, *Chicago*
Fred A. Britten, *Chicago*
George E. Foss, *Chicago*
Ira C. Copley, *Aurora*
Charles E. Fuller, *Belvidere*
John C. McKenzie, *Elizabeth*
Clyde H. Tavenner, *Cordova*
Edward J. King, *Galesburg*
Claudius U. Stone, *Peoria*
John A. Sterling, *Bloomington*
Joseph G. Cannon, *Danville*
William B. McKinley, *Champaign*
Henry T. Rainey, *Carrollton*
Loren E. Wheeler, *Springfield*
William A. Rodenberg, *East St. Louis*
Martin D. Foster, *Olney*
Thomas S. Williams, *Louisville*
Edward E. Denison, *Marion*
At Large—
    Burnett M. Chiperfield, *Canton*
    William E. Williams,[13] *Pittsfield*

INDIANA

SENATORS

Benjamin F. Shively,[14] *South Bend*
Thomas Taggart,[15] *French Lick*
James E. Watson,[16] *Rushville*
John W. Kern, *Indianapolis*

REPRESENTATIVES

Charles Lieb, *Rockport*
William A. Cullop, *Vincennes*
William E. Cox, *Jasper*
Lincoln Dixon, *North Vernon*
Ralph W. Moss, *Center Point*
Finly H. Gray, *Connersville*
Merrill Moores, *Indianapolis*
John A. M. Adair, *Portland*
Martin A. Morrison, *Frankfort*
William R. Wood, *La Fayette*
George W. Rauch, *Marion*
Cyrus Cline, *Angola*
Henry A. Barnhart, *Rochester*

IOWA

SENATORS

Albert B. Cummins, *Des Moines*
William S. Kenyon, *Fort Dodge*

REPRESENTATIVES

Charles A. Kennedy, *Montrose*
Harry E. Hull, *Williamsburg*
Burton E. Sweet, *Waverly*
Gilbert N. Haugen, *Northwood*
James W. Good, *Cedar Rapids*
C. William Ramseyer, *Bloomfield*
Cassius C. Dowell, *Des Moines*
Horace M. Towner, *Corning*
William R. Green, *Council Bluffs*
Frank P. Woods, *Estherville*
Thomas J. Steele, *Sioux City*

KANSAS

SENATORS

William H. Thompson, *Garden City*
Charles Curtis, *Topeka*

REPRESENTATIVES

Daniel R. Anthony, Jr., *Leavenworth*
Joseph Taggart, *Kansas City*
Philip P. Campbell, *Pittsburg*
Dudley Doolittle, *Strong City*
Guy T. Helvering, *Marysville*
John R. Connelly, *Colby*
Jouett Shouse, *Kinsley*
William A. Ayres, *Wichita*

KENTUCKY

SENATORS

Ollie M. James, *Marion*
Joseph C. W. Beckham, *Frankfort*

REPRESENTATIVES

Alben W. Barkley, *Paducah*
David H. Kincheloe, *Madisonville*
Robert Y. Thomas, Jr., *Central City*
Ben Johnson, *Bardstown*
J. Swagar Sherley, *Louisville*
Arthur B. Rouse, *Burlington*
James C. Cantrill, *Georgetown*
Harvey Helm, *Stanford*
William J. Fields, *Olive Hill*
John W. Langley, *Pikeville*
Caleb Powers, *Barbourville*

LOUISIANA

SENATORS

Joseph E. Ransdell, *Lake Providence*
Robert F. Broussard, *New Iberia*

---

[10] Election unsuccessfully contested by Jeremiah Donovan.
[11] Died December 8, 1916, before the commencement of the Sixty-fifth Congress, to which he had been reelected.

[12] Elected to fill vacancy caused by death of Samuel J. Tribble, and took his seat January 15, 1917.
[13] Election unsuccessfully contested by J. McCan Davis.
[14] Died March 14, 1916.

[15] Appointed to fill vacancy caused by death of Benjamin F. Shively, and took his seat March 27, 1916.
[16] Elected to fill vacancy caused by death of Benjamin F. Shively, and took his seat December 5, 1916.

REPRESENTATIVES

Albert Estopinal, *Estopinal*
H. Garland Dupré, *New Orleans*
Whitmell P. Martin, *Thibodaux*
John T. Watkins, *Minden*
Riley J. Wilson, *Harrisonburg*
Lewis L. Morgan, *Covington*
Ladislas Lazaro, *Washington*
James B. Aswell, *Natchitoches*

MAINE

SENATORS

Charles F. Johnson, *Waterville*
Edwin C. Burleigh,[17] *Augusta*
Bert M. Fernald,[18] *West Poland*

REPRESENTATIVES

Asher C. Hinds, *Portland*
Daniel J. McGillicuddy, *Lewiston*
John A. Peters, *Ellsworth*
Frank E. Guernsey, *Dover*

MARYLAND

SENATORS

John Walter Smith, *Snow Hill*
Blair Lee, *Silver Spring*

REPRESENTATIVES

Jesse D. Price, *Salisbury*
J. Fred. C. Talbott, *Lutherville*
Charles P. Coady, *Baltimore*
J. Charles Linthicum, *Baltimore*
Sydney E. Mudd, *La Plata*
David J. Lewis, *Cumberland*

MASSACHUSETTS

SENATORS

Henry Cabot Lodge, *Nahant*
John W. Weeks, *West Newton*

REPRESENTATIVES

Allen T. Treadway, *Stockbridge*
Frederick H. Gillett, *Springfield*
Calvin D. Paige, *Southbridge*
Samuel E. Winslow, *Worcester*
John Jacob Rogers, *Lowell*
Augustus P. Gardner, *Hamilton*
Michael F. Phelan, *Lynn*
Frederick W. Dallinger, *Cambridge*
Ernest W. Roberts, *Chelsea*
Peter F. Tague, *Boston*
George H. Tinkham,[19] *Boston*
James A. Gallivan, *Boston*
William H. Carter, *Needham Heights*
Richard Olney, *Dedham*
William S. Greene, *Fall River*
Joseph Walsh, *New Bedford*

MICHIGAN

SENATORS

William Alden Smith, *Grand Rapids*
Charles E. Townsend, *Jackson*

REPRESENTATIVES

Frank E. Doremus, *Detroit*
Samuel W. Beakes, *Ann Arbor*
John M. C. Smith, *Charlotte*
Edward L. Hamilton, *Niles*
Carl E. Mapes, *Grand Rapids*
Patrick H. Kelley, *Lansing*
Louis C. Cramton, *Lapeer*
Joseph W. Fordney, *Saginaw*
James C. McLaughlin, *Muskegon*
George A. Loud, *Bay City*
Frank D. Scott, *Alpena*
W. Frank James, *Hancock*
Charles A. Nichols, *Detroit*

MINNESOTA

SENATORS

Knute Nelson, *Alexandria*
Moses E. Clapp, *St. Paul*

REPRESENTATIVES

Sydney Anderson, *Lanesboro*
Franklin F. Ellsworth, *Mankato*
Charles R. Davis, *St. Peter*
Carl C. Van Dyke, *St. Paul*
George R. Smith, *Minneapolis*
Charles A. Lindbergh, *Little Falls*
Andrew J. Volstead, *Granite Falls*
Clarence B. Miller, *Duluth*
Halvor Steenerson, *Crookston*
Thomas D. Schall, *Excelsior*

MISSISSIPPI

SENATORS

John Sharp Williams, *Yazoo City*
James K. Vardaman, *Jackson*

REPRESENTATIVES

Ezekiel S. Candler, Jr., *Corinth*
Hubert D. Stephens, *New Albany*
Benjamin G. Humphreys, *Greenville*
Thomas U. Sisson, *Winona*
Samuel A. Witherspoon,[20] *Meridian*
William W. Venable,[21] *Meridian*
Pat Harrison, *Gulfport*
Percy E. Quin, *McComb City*
James W. Collier, *Vicksburg*

MISSOURI

SENATORS

William J. Stone, *Jefferson City*
James A. Reed, *Kansas City*

REPRESENTATIVES

James T. Lloyd, *Shelbyville*
William W. Rucker, *Keytesville*
Joshua W. Alexander, *Gallatin*
Charles F. Booher, *Savannah*
William P. Borland, *Kansas City*
Clement C. Dickinson, *Clinton*
Courtney W. Hamlin, *Springfield*
Dorsey W. Shackleford, *Jefferson City*
James Beauchamp Clark, *Bowling Green*
Jacob E. Meeker, *St. Louis*
William L. Igoe, *St. Louis*
Leonidas C. Dyer, *St. Louis*
Walter L. Hensley, *Farmington*
Joseph J. Russell, *Charleston*
Perl D. Decker, *Joplin*
Thomas L. Rubey, *Lebanon*

MONTANA

SENATORS

Henry L. Myers, *Hamilton*
Thomas J. Walsh, *Helena*

REPRESENTATIVES AT LARGE

John M. Evans, *Missoula*
Tom Stout, *Lewistown*

NEBRASKA

SENATORS

Gilbert M. Hitchcock, *Omaha*
George W. Norris, *McCook*

REPRESENTATIVES

C. Frank Reavis, *Falls City*
Charles O. Lobeck, *Omaha*
Daniel V. Stephens, *Fremont*
Charles H. Sloan, *Geneva*
Ashton C. Shallenberger, *Alma*
Moses P. Kinkaid, *O'Neill*

NEVADA

SENATORS

Francis G. Newlands, *Reno*
Key Pittman, *Tonopah*

REPRESENTATIVE

At Large—Edwin E. Roberts, *Carson City*

NEW HAMPSHIRE

SENATORS

Jacob H. Gallinger, *Concord*
Henry F. Hollis, *Concord*

REPRESENTATIVES

Cyrus A. Sulloway, *Manchester*
Edward H. Wason, *Nashua*

---

[17] Died June 16, 1916.
[18] Elected to fill vacancy caused by death of Edwin C. Burleigh, and took his seat December 5, 1916.

[19] Election unsuccessfully contested by Francis J. Horgan.
[20] Died November 24, 1915.

[21] Elected to fill vacancy caused by death of Samuel A. Witherspoon, and took his seat January 17, 1916.

NEW JERSEY

SENATORS

James E. Martine, *Plainfield*
William Hughes, *Paterson*

REPRESENATIVES

William J. Browning, *Camden*
Isaac Bacharach, *Atlantic City*
Thomas J. Scully, *South Amboy*
Elijah C. Hutchinson, *Trenton*
John H. Capstick, *Montville*
Archibald C. Hart, *Hackensack*
Dow H. Drukker, *Passaic*
Edward W. Gray, *Newark*
Richard Wayne Parker, *Newark*
Frederick R. Lehlbach, *Newark*
John J. Eagan, *Weehawken*
James A. Hamill, *Jersey City*

NEW MEXICO

SENATORS

Thomas B. Catron, *Sante Fe*
Albert B. Fall, *Three Rivers*

REPRESENTATIVE

At Large—Benigno C. Hernandez, *Tierra Amarilla*

NEW YORK

SENATORS

James A. O'Gorman, *New York City*
James W. Wadsworth, Jr., *Groveland*

REPRESENTATIVES

Frederick C. Hicks,[22] *Port Washington*
Charles P. Caldwell, *Forest Hills*
Joseph V. Flynn, *Brooklyn*
Harry H. Dale, *Brooklyn*
James P. Maher, *Brooklyn*
Frederick W. Rowe, *Brooklyn*
John J. Fitzgerald, *Brooklyn*
Daniel J. Griffin, *Brooklyn*
Oscar W. Swift, *Brooklyn*
Reuben L. Haskell, *Brooklyn*
Daniel J. Riordan, *New York City*
Meyer London, *New York City*
George W. Loft, *New York City*
Michael F. Farley, *New York City*
Michael F. Conry,[23] *New York City*
Peter J. Dooling, *New York City*
John F. Carew, *New York City*
Thomas G. Patten, *New York City*
Walter M. Chandler, *New York City*
Isaac Siegel,[24] *New York City*
G. Murray Hulbert, *New York City*
Henry Bruckner, *New York City*
Joseph A. Goulden,[25] *Fordham*
William S. Bennet,[26] *New York City*

Woodson R. Oglesby, *Yonkers*
James W. Husted, *Peekskill*
Edmund Platt, *Poughkeepsie*
Charles B. Ward, *Debruce*
Rollin B. Sanford, *Albany*
James S. Parker, *Salem*
William B. Charles, *Amsterdam*
Bertrand H. Snell,[27] *Potsdam*
Luther W. Mott, *Oswego*
Homer P. Snyder, *Little Falls*
George W. Fairchild, *Oneonta*
Walter W. Magee, *Syracuse*
Norman J. Gould,[28] *Seneca Falls*
Harry H. Pratt, *Corning*
Thomas B. Dunn, *Rochester*
Henry G. Danforth, *Rochester*
S. Wallace Dempsey, *Lockport*
Charles B. Smith, *Buffalo*
Daniel A. Driscoll, *Buffalo*
Charles M. Hamilton, *Ripley*

NORTH CAROLINA

SENATORS

Furnifold McL. Simmons, *New Bern*
Lee S. Overman, *Salisbury*

REPRESENTATIVES

John H. Small, *Washington*
Claude Kitchin, *Scotland Neck*
George E. Hood, *Goldsboro*
Edward W. Pou, *Smithfield*
Charles M. Stedman, *Greensboro*
Hannibal L. Godwin, *Dunn*
Robert N. Page, *Biscoe*
Robert L. Doughton, *Laurel Springs*
Edwin Y. Webb, *Shelby*
James J. Britt, *Asheville*

NORTH DAKOTA

SENATORS

Porter J. McCumber, *Wahpeton*
Asle J. Gronna, *Lakota*

REPRESENTATIVES

Henry T. Helgesen, *Milton*
George M. Young, *Valley City*
Patrick D. Norton, *Hettinger*

OHIO

SENATORS

Atlee Pomerene, *Canton*
Warren G. Harding, *Marion*

REPRESENTATIVES

Nicholas Longworth, *Cincinnati*
Alfred G. Allen, *Cincinnati*
Warren Gard, *Hamilton*
J. Edward Russell, *Sidney*

Nelson E. Matthews, *Ottawa*
Charles C. Kearns, *Batavia*
Simeon D. Fess, *Yellow Springs*
John A. Key, *Marion*
Isaac R. Sherwood, *Toledo*
Robert M. Switzer, *Gallipolis*
Edwin D. Ricketts, *Logan*
Clement L. Brumbaugh, *Columbus*
Arthur W. Overmyer, *Fremont*
Seward H. Williams, *Lorain*
William C. Mooney, *Woodsfield*
Roscoe C. McCulloch, *Canton*
William A. Ashbrook, *Johnstown*
David A. Hollingsworth, *Cadiz*
John G. Cooper, *Youngstown*
William Gordon, *Cleveland*
Robert Crosser, *Cleveland*
Henry I. Emerson, *Cleveland*

OKLAHOMA

SENATORS

Thomas P. Gore, *Lawton*
Robert L. Owen, *Muskogee*

REPRESENTATIVES

James S. Davenport, *Vinita*
William W. Hastings, *Tahlequah*
Charles D. Carter, *Ardmore*
William H. Murray, *Tishomingo*
Joseph B. Thompson, *Pauls Valley*
Scott Ferris, *Lawton*
James V. McClintic, *Snyder*
Dick T. Morgan, *Woodward*

OREGON

SENATORS

George E. Chamberlain, *Portland*
Harry Lane, *Portland*

REPRESENTATIVES

Willis C. Hawley, *Salem*
Nicholas J. Sinnott, *The Dalles*
Clifton N. McArthur, *Portland*

PENNSYLVANIA

SENATORS

Boies Penrose, *Philadelphia*
George T. Oliver, *Pittsburgh*

REPRESENTATIVES

William S. Vare, *Philadelphia*
George S. Graham, *Philadelphia*
J. Hampton Moore, *Philadelphia*
George W. Edmonds, *Philadelphia*
Peter E. Costello, *Philadelphia*
George P. Darrow, *Philadelphia*
Thomas S. Butler, *West Chester*
Henry W. Watson, *Langhorne*
William W. Griest, *Lancaster*
John R. Farr, *Scranton*

---

[22] Election unsuccessfully contested by Lathrop Brown.
[23] Died March 2, 1917, before the commencement of the Sixty-fifth Congress, to which he had been reelected.

[24] Election unsuccessfully contested by Jacob A. Cantor.
[25] Died May 3, 1915.
[26] Elected to fill vacancy caused by death of Joseph A. Goulden, and took his seat December 6, 1915.

[27] Elected to fill vacancy caused by death of Representative-elect Edwin A. Merritt, Jr., in preceding Congress, and took his seat December 6, 1915.
[28] Elected to fill vacancy caused by death of Representative-elect Sereno E. Payne, in preceding Congress, and took his seat December 6, 1915.

John J. Casey, *Wilkes-Barre*
Robert D. Heaton, *Ashland*
Arthur G. Dewalt, *Allentown*
Louis T. McFadden, *Canton*
Edgar R. Kiess, *Williamsport*
John V. Lesher, *Sunbury*
Benjamin K. Focht, *Lewisburg*
Aaron S. Kreider, *Annville*
Warren W. Bailey, *Johnstown*
C. William Beales, *Gettysburg*
Charles H. Rowland, *Philipsburg*
Abraham L. Keister, *Scottdale*
Robert F. Hopwood, *Uniontown*
Henry W. Temple,[29] *Washington*
Michael Liebel, Jr., *Erie*
Henry J. Steele, *Easton*
S. Taylor North, *Punxsutawney*
Samuel H. Miller, *Mercer*
Stephen G. Porter, *Pittsburgh*
William H. Coleman, *McKeesport*
John M. Morin, *Pittsburgh*
Andrew J. Barchfeld, *Pittsburgh*
At Large—
    Thomas S. Crago, *Waynesburg*
    Mahlon M. Garland, *Pittsburgh*
    Daniel F. Lafean, *York*
    John R. K. Scott, *Philadelphia*

RHODE ISLAND

SENATORS

Henry F. Lippitt, *Providence*
LeBaron B. Colt, *Bristol*

REPRESENTATIVES

George F. O'Shaunessy, *Providence*
Walter R. Stiness, *Warwick*
Ambrose Kennedy, *Woonsocket*

SOUTH CAROLINA

SENATORS

Benjamin R. Tillman, *Trenton*
Ellison D. Smith, *Florence*

REPRESENTATIVES

Richard S. Whaley,[30] *Charleston*
James F. Byrnes, *Aiken*
Wyatt Aiken, *Abbeville*
Joseph T. Johnson,[31] *Spartanburg*
Samuel J. Nicholls,[32] *Spartanburg*
David E. Finley,[33] *Yorkville*
Paul G. McCorkle,[34] *York*
J. Willard Ragsdale, *Florence*
Asbury F. Lever, *Lexington*

SOUTH DAKOTA

SENATORS

Thomas Sterling, *Vermilion*
Edwin S. Johnson, *Yankton*

REPRESENTATIVES

Charles H. Dillon, *Yankton*
Royal C. Johnson, *Aberdeen*
Harry L. Gandy, *Rapid City*

TENNESSEE

SENATORS

Luke Lea, *Nashville*
John K. Shields, *Knoxville*

REPRESENTATIVES

Sam R. Sells, *Johnson City*
Richard W. Austin, *Knoxville*
John A. Moon, *Chattanooga*
Cordell Hull, *Carthage*
William C. Houston, *Woodbury*
Joseph W. Byrns, *Nashville*
Lemuel P. Padgett, *Columbia*
Thetus W. Sims, *Linden*
Finis J. Garrett, *Dresden*
Kenneth D. McKellar, *Memphis*

TEXAS

SENATORS

Charles A. Culberson, *Dallas*
Morris Sheppard, *Texarkana*

REPRESENTATIVES

Eugene Black, *Clarksville*
Martin Dies, *Beaumont*
James Young, *Kaufman*
Sam Rayburn, *Bonham*
Hatton W. Sumners, *Dallas*
Rufus Hardy, *Corsicana*
Alexander W. Gregg, *Palestine*
Joe H. Eagle, *Houston*
George F. Burgess, *Gonzales*
James P. Buchanan, *Brenham*
Robert L. Henry, *Waco*
Oscar Callaway, *Comanche*
John H. Stephens, *Vernon*
James L. Slayden, *San Antonio*
John N. Garner, *Uvalde*
William R. Smith, *Colorado*
At Large—
    A. Jeff. McLemore, *Houston*
    James H. Davis, *Sulphur Springs*

UTAH

SENATORS

Reed Smoot, *Provo*
George Sutherland, *Salt Lake City*

REPRESENTATIVES

Joseph Howell, *Logan*
James H. Mays, *Salt Lake City*

VERMONT

SENATORS

William P. Dillingham, *Montpelier*
Carroll S. Page, *Hyde Park*

REPRESENTATIVES

Frank L. Greene, *St. Albans*
Porter H. Dale, *Island Pond*

VIRGINIA

SENATORS

Thomas S. Martin, *Charlottesville*
Claude A. Swanson, *Chatham*

REPRESENTATIVES

William A. Jones, *Warsaw*
Edward E. Holland, *Suffolk*
Andrew J. Montague, *Richmond*
Walter A. Watson, *Jennings Ordinary*
Edward W. Saunders, *Rockymount*
Carter Glass, *Lynchburg*
James Hay,[35] *Madison*
Thomas W. Harrison,[36] *Winchester*
Charles C. Carlin, *Alexandria*
C. Bascom Slemp, *Big Stone Gap*
Henry D. Flood, *Appomattox*

WASHINGTON

SENATORS

Wesley L. Jones, *North Yakima*
Miles Poindexter, *Spokane*

REPRESENTATIVES

William E. Humphrey, *Seattle*
Lindley H. Hadley, *Bellingham*
Albert Johnson, *Hoquiam*
William L. La Follette, *Pullman*
Clarence C. Dill, *Spokane*

WEST VIRGINIA

SENATORS

William E. Chilton, *Charleston*
Nathan Goff, *Clarksburg*

REPRESENTATIVES

Matthew M. Neely, *Fairmont*
William G. Brown, Jr.,[37] *Kingwood*
George M. Bowers,[38] *Martinsburg*
Adam B. Littlepage, *Charleston*
Hunter H. Moss, Jr.,[39] *Parkersburg*
Harry C. Woodyard,[40] *Spencer*
Edward Cooper, *Bramwell*
At Large—Howard Sutherland, *Elkins*

---

[29] Elected to fill vacancy caused by death of Representative-elect William M. Brown (January 31, 1915, before the beginning of the congressional term), and took his seat December 6, 1915.
[30] Election unsuccessfully contested by Aaron P. Prioleau.
[31] Resigned April 19, 1915.

[32] Elected to fill vacancy caused by resignation of Joseph T. Johnson, and took his seat December 6, 1915.
[33] Died January 26, 1917, before the commencement of the Sixty-fifth Congress, to which he had been reelected.
[34] Elected to fill vacancy caused by death of David E. Finley, and took his seat February 24, 1917.
[35] Resigned October 1, 1916.

[36] Elected to fill vacancy caused by resignation of James Hay, and took his seat December 4, 1916.
[37] Died March 9, 1916.
[38] Elected to fill vacancy caused by death of William G. Brown, Jr., and took his seat May 18, 1916.
[39] Died July 15, 1916.
[40] Elected to fill vacancy caused by death of Hunter H. Moss, Jr., and took his seat December 4, 1916.

WISCONSIN

SENATORS

Robert M. La Follette, *Madison*
Paul O. Husting, *Mayville*

REPRESENTATIVES

Henry Allen Cooper, *Racine*
Michael E. Burke, *Beaver Dam*
John M. Nelson, *Madison*
William J. Cary,[41] *Milwaukee*
William H. Stafford, *Milwaukee*
Michael K. Reilly, *Fond du Lac*
John J. Esch, *La Crosse*
Edward E. Browne, *Waupaca*
Thomas F. Konop, *Green Bay*

James A. Frear, *Hudson*
Irvine L. Lenroot, *Superior*

WYOMING

SENATORS

Clarence D. Clark, *Evanston*
Francis E. Warren, *Cheyenne*

REPRESENTATIVE

At Large—Frank W. Mondell, *Newcastle*

TERRITORY OF ALASKA

DELEGATE

James Wickersham, *Fairbanks*

TERRITORY OF HAWAII

DELEGATE

J. Kuhio Kalanianaole, *Waikiki*

PHILIPPINE ISLANDS

RESIDENT COMMISSIONERS

Manuel L. Quezon,[42] *Tayabas*
Manuel Earnshaw, *Manila*

PORTO RICO

RESIDENT COMMISSIONER

Luis Muñoz Rivera,[43] *San Juan*

---

[41] Election unsuccessfully contested by Winfield R. Gaylord.

[42] Resigned October 15, 1916; vacancy throughout remainder of the Congress.

[43] Died November 15, 1916; vacancy until August 6, 1917.

SIXTY-FIFTH CONGRESS

MARCH 4, 1917, TO MARCH 3, 1919

FIRST SESSION—*April 2, 1917, to October 6, 1917*

SECOND SESSION—*December 3, 1917, to November 21, 1918*

THIRD SESSION—*December 2, 1918, to March 3, 1919*

SPECIAL SESSION OF THE SENATE—*March 5, 1917, to March 16, 1917*

———————

VICE PRESIDENT OF THE UNITED STATES—THOMAS R. MARSHALL, of Indiana

PRESIDENT PRO TEMPORE OF THE SENATE—WILLARD SAULSBURY, of Delaware

SECRETARY OF THE SENATE—JAMES M. BAKER, of South Carolina

SERGEANT AT ARMS OF THE SENATE—CHARLES P. HIGGINS, of Missouri

———————

SPEAKER OF THE HOUSE OF REPRESENTATIVES—JAMES BEAUCHAMP CLARK,[1] of Missouri

CLERK OF THE HOUSE—SOUTH TRIMBLE,[2] of Kentucky

SERGEANT AT ARMS OF THE HOUSE—ROBERT B. GORDON, of Ohio

DOORKEEPER OF THE HOUSE—JOSEPH J. SINNOTT, of Virginia

POSTMASTER OF THE HOUSE—WILLIAM M. DUNBAR

ALABAMA

SENATORS

John H. Bankhead, *Jasper*
Oscar W. Underwood, *Birmingham*

REPRESENTATIVES

Oscar L. Gray, *Butler*
S. Hubert Dent, Jr., *Montgomery*
Henry B. Steagall, *Ozark*
Fred L. Blackmon, *Anniston*
J. Thomas Heflin, *Lafayette*
William B. Oliver, *Tuscaloosa*
John L. Burnett, *Gadsden*
Edward B. Almon, *Tuscumbia*
George Huddleston, *Birmingham*
William B. Bankhead, *Jasper*

ARIZONA

SENATORS

Henry F. Ashurst, *Prescott*
Marcus A. Smith, *Tucson*

REPRESENTATIVE

At Large—Carl Hayden, *Phoenix*

ARKANSAS

SENATORS

Joseph T. Robinson, *Little Rock*
William F. Kirby, *Little Rock*

REPRESENTATIVES

Thaddeus H. Caraway, *Jonesboro*
William A. Oldfield, *Batesville*
John N. Tillman, *Fayetteville*
Otis Wingo, *De Queen*
Henderson M. Jacoway, *Dardanelle*
Samuel M. Taylor, *Pine Bluff*
William S. Goodwin, *Warren*

CALIFORNIA

SENATORS

James D. Phelan, *San Francisco*
Hiram W. Johnson,[3] *San Francisco*

REPRESENTATIVES

Clarence F. Lea, *Santa Rosa*
John E. Raker, *Alturas*
Charles F. Curry, *Sacramento*
Julius Kahn, *San Francisco*
John I. Nolan, *San Francisco*
John A. Elston, *Berkeley*
Denver S. Church, *Fresno*
Everis A. Hayes, *San Jose*
Charles H. Randall, *Los Angeles*
Henry Z. Osborne, *Los Angeles*
William Kettner, *San Diego*

COLORADO

SENATORS

Charles S. Thomas, *Denver*
John F. Shafroth, *Denver*

REPRESENTATIVES

Benjamin C. Hilliard, *Denver*
Charles B. Timberlake, *Sterling*
Edward Keating, *Pueblo*
Edward T. Taylor, *Glenwood Springs*

CONNECTICUT

SENATORS

Frank B. Brandegee, *New London*
George P. McLean, *Simsbury*

———————

[1] Reelected April 2, 1917.
[2] Reelected April 2, 1917.

[3] Elected November 7, 1916, for the term beginning March 4, 1917, but did not qualify until April 2, 1917, preferring to retain the governorship.

CONNECTICUT—Continued

REPRESENTATIVES

Augustine Lonergan, *Hartford*
Richard P. Freeman, *New London*
John Q. Tilson, *New Haven*
Ebenezer J. Hill,[4] *Norwalk*
Schuyler Merritt,[5] *Stamford*
James P. Glynn, *Winsted*

DELAWARE

SENATORS

Willard Saulsbury, *Wilmington*
Josiah O. Wolcott, *Dover*

REPRESENTATIVE

At Large—Albert F. Polk, *Georgetown*

FLORIDA

SENATORS

Duncan U. Fletcher, *Jacksonville*
Park Trammell, *Lakeland*

REPRESENTATIVES

Herbert J. Drane, *Lakeland*
Frank Clark, *Gainesville*
J. Walter Kehoe, *Pensacola*
William J. Sears, *Kissimmee*

GEORGIA

SENATORS

Hoke Smith, *Atlanta*
Thomas W. Hardwick, *Sandersville*

REPRESENTATIVES

James W. Overstreet, *Sylvania*
Frank Park, *Sylvester*
Charles R. Crisp, *Americus*
William C. Adamson,[6] *Carrollton*
William C. Wright,[7] *Newnan*
William S. Howard, *Kirkwood*
James W. Wise, *Fayetteville*
Gordon Lee, *Chickamauga*
Charles H. Brand,[8] *Athens*
Thomas M. Bell, *Gainesville*
Carl Vinson, *Milledgeville*
John R. Walker, *Valdosta*
William W. Larsen, *Dublin*

IDAHO

SENATORS

William E. Borah, *Boise*
James H. Brady,[9] *Pocatello*
John F. Nugent,[10] *Boise*

REPRESENTATIVES AT LARGE

Burton L. French, *Moscow*
Addison T. Smith, *Twin Falls*

ILLINOIS

SENATORS

James Hamilton Lewis, *Chicago*
Lawrence Y. Sherman, *Springfield*

REPRESENTATIVES

Martin B. Madden, *Chicago*
James R. Mann, *Chicago*
William W. Wilson, *Chicago*
Charles Martin,[11] *Chicago*
John W. Rainey,[12] *Chicago*
Adolph J. Sabath, *Chicago*
James McAndrews, *Chicago*
Niels Juul, *Chicago*
Thomas Gallagher, *Chicago*
Fred A. Britten, *Chicago*
George E. Foss, *Chicago*
Ira C. Copley, *Aurora*
Charles E. Fuller, *Belvidere*
John C. McKenzie, *Elizabeth*
William J. Graham, *Aledo*
Edward J. King, *Galesburg*
Clifford Ireland, *Peoria*
John A. Sterling,[13] *Bloomington*
Joseph G. Cannon, *Danville*
William B. McKinley, *Champaign*
Henry T. Rainey, *Carrollton*
Loren E. Wheeler, *Springfield*
William A. Rodenberg, *East St. Louis*
Martin D. Foster, *Olney*
Thomas S. Williams, *Louisville*
Edward E. Denison, *Marion*
At Large—
   Medill McCormick, *Chicago*
   William E. Mason, *Chicago*

INDIANA

SENATORS

James E. Watson, *Rushville*
Harry S. New, *Indianapolis*

REPRESENTATIVES

George K. Denton, *Evansville*
Oscar E. Bland, *Linton*
William E. Cox, *Jasper*
Lincoln Dixon, *North Vernon*
Everett Sanders, *Terre Haute*
Daniel W. Comstock,[14] *Richmond*
Richard N. Elliot,[15] *Connersville*
Merrill Moores, *Indianapolis*
Albert H. Vestal, *Anderson*
Fred S. Purnell, *Attica*

William R. Wood, *La Fayette*
Milton Kraus, *Peru*
Louis W. Fairfield, *Angola*
Henry A. Barnhart, *Rochester*

IOWA

SENATORS

Albert B. Cummins, *Des Moines*
William S. Kenyon, *Fort Dodge*

REPRESENTATIVES

Charles A. Kennedy, *Montrose*
Harry E. Hull, *Williamsburg*
Burton E. Sweet, *Waverly*
Gilbert N. Haugen, *Northwood*
James W. Good, *Cedar Rapids*
C. William Ramseyer, *Bloomfield*
Cassius C. Dowell, *Des Moines*
Horace M. Towner, *Corning*
William R. Green, *Council Bluffs*
Frank P. Woods, *Estherville*
George C. Scott,[16] *Sioux City*

KANSAS

SENATORS

William H. Thompson, *Kansas City*
Charles Curtis, *Topeka*

REPRESENTATIVES

Daniel R. Anthony, Jr., *Leavenworth*
Edward C. Little, *Kansas City*
Philip P. Campbell, *Pittsburg*
Dudley Doolittle, *Strong C'ty*
Guy T. Helvering, *Marysville*
John R. Connelly, *Colby*
Jouett Shouse, *Kinsley*
William A. Ayres, *Wichita*

KENTUCKY

SENATORS

Ollie M. James,[17] *Marion*
George B. Martin,[18] *Catlettsburg*
Joseph C. W. Beckham, *Frankfort*

REPRESENTATIVES

Alben W. Barkley, *Paducah*
David H. Kincheloe, *Madisonville*
Robert Y. Thomas, Jr., *Central City*
Ben Johnson, *Bardstown*
J. Swagar Sherley, *Louisville*
Arthur B. Rouse, *Burlington*
James C. Cantrill, *Georgetown*
Harvey Helm,[19] *Stanford*
William J. Fields, *Olive Hill*
John W. Langley, *Pikeville*
Caleb Powers, *Barbourville*

---

[4] Died September 27, 1917.
[5] Elected to fill vacancy caused by death of Ebenezer J. Hill, and took his seat December 3, 1917.
[6] Resigned December 18, 1917.
[7] Elected to fill vacancy caused by resignation of William C. Adamson, and took his seat January 24, 1918.
[8] Elected to fill vacancy caused by death of Representative-elect Samuel J. Tribble, in preceding Congress, and took his seat April 2, 1917.

[9] Died January 13, 1918.
[10] Appointed to fill vacancy caused by death of James H. Brady, and took his seat January 30, 1918; subsequently elected.
[11] Died October 28, 1917.
[12] Elected to fill vacancy caused by death of Charles Martin, and took his seat April 16, 1918.
[13] Died October 17, 1918; vacancy throughout remainder of the Congress.
[14] Died May 19, 1917.

[15] Elected to fill vacancy caused by death of Daniel W. Comstock, and took his seat July 3, 1917.
[16] Election unsuccessfully contested by Thomas J. Steele.
[17] Died August 28, 1918.
[18] Appointed to fill vacancy caused by death of Ollie M. James, and took his seat September 17, 1918.
[19] Died March 3, 1919, before the commencement of the Sixty-sixth Congress, to which he had been re-elected.

LOUISIANA

SENATORS

Joseph E. Ransdell, *Lake Providence*
Robert F. Broussard,[20] *New Iberia*
Walter Guion,[21] *Napoleonville*
Edward J. Gay,[22] *Plaquemine*

REPRESENTATIVES

Albert Estopinal, *Estopinal*
H. Garland Dupré, *New Orleans*
Whitmell P. Martin, *Thibodaux*
John T. Watkins, *Minden*
Riley J. Wilson, *Harrisonburg*
Jared Y. Sanders, *Bogalusa*
Ladislas Lazaro, *Washington*
James B. Aswell, *Natchitoches*

MAINE

SENATORS

Bert M. Fernald, *West Poland*
Frederick Hale, *Portland*

REPRESENTATIVES

Louis B. Goodall, *Sanford*
Wallace H. White, Jr., *Lewiston*
John A. Peters, *Ellsworth*
Ira G. Hersey, *Houlton*

MARYLAND

SENATORS

John Walter Smith, *Snow Hill*
Joseph I. France, *Port Deposit*

REPRESENTATIVES

Jesse D. Price, *Salisbury*
J. Fred. C. Talbott,[23] *Lutherville*
Carville D. Benson,[24] *Halethorpe*
Charles P. Coady, *Baltimore*
J. Charles Linthicum, *Baltimore*
Sydney E. Mudd, *La Plata*
Frederick N. Zihlman, *Cumberland*

MASSACHUSETTS

SENATORS

Henry Cabot Lodge, *Nahant*
John W. Weeks, *West Newton*

REPRESENTATIVES

Allen T. Treadway, *Stockbridge*
Frederick H. Gillett, *Springfield*
Calvin D. Paige, *Southbridge*
Samuel E. Winslow, *Worcester*
John Jacob Rogers, *Lowell*
Augustus P. Gardner,[25] *Hamilton*
Willfred W. Lufkin,[26] *Essex*

Michael F. Phelan, *Lynn*
Frederick W. Dallinger, *Cambridge*
Alvan T. Fuller, *Malden*
Peter F. Tague, *Boston*
George H. Tinkham, *Boston*
James A. Gallivan, *Boston*
William H. Carter, *Needham Heights*
Richard Olney, *Dedham*
William S. Greene, *Fall River*
Joseph Walsh, *New Bedford*

MICHIGAN

SENATORS

William Alden Smith, *Grand Rapids*
Charles E. Townsend, *Jackson*

REPRESENTATIVES

Frank E. Doremus, *Detroit*
Mark R. Bacon,[27] *Wyandotte*
Samuel W. Beakes,[28] *Ann Arbor*
John M. C. Smith, *Charlotte*
Edward L. Hamilton, *Niles*
Carl E. Mapes, *Grand Rapids*
Patrick H. Kelley, *Lansing*
Louis C. Cramton, *Lapeer*
Joseph W. Fordney, *Saginaw*
James C. McLaughlin, *Muskegon*
Gilbert A. Currie, *Midland*
Frank D. Scott, *Alpena*
W. Frank James, *Hancock*
Charles A. Nichols, *Detroit*

MINNESOTA

SENATORS

Knute Nelson, *Alexandria*
Frank B. Kellogg, *St. Paul*

REPRESENTATIVES

Sydney Anderson, *Lanesboro*
Franklin F. Ellsworth, *Mankato*
Charles R. Davis, *St. Peter*
Carl C. Van Dyke, *St. Paul*
Ernest Lundeen, *Minneapolis*
Harold Knutson, *St. Cloud*
Andrew J. Volstead, *Granite Falls*
Clarence B. Miller, *Duluth*
Halvor Steenerson, *Crookston*
Thomas D. Schall, *Excelsior*

MISSISSIPPI

SENATORS

John Sharp Williams, *Yazoo City*
James K. Vardaman, *Jackson*

REPRESENTATIVES

Ezekiel S. Candler, Jr., *Corinth*

Hubert D. Stephens, *New Albany*
Benjamin G. Humphreys, *Greenville*
Thomas U. Sisson, *Winona*
William W. Venable, *Meridian*
Pat Harrison, *Gulfport*
Percy E. Quin, *McComb City*
James W. Collier, *Vicksburg*

MISSOURI

SENATORS

William J. Stone,[29] *Jefferson City*
Xenophon P. Wilfley,[30] *St. Louis*
Selden P. Spencer,[31] *St. Louis*
James A. Reed, *Kansas City*

REPRESENTATIVES

Milton A. Romjue, *Macon*
William W. Rucker, *Keytesville*
Joshua W. Alexander, *Gallatin*
Charles F. Booher, *Savannah*
William P. Borland,[32] *Kansas City*
Clement C. Dickinson, *Clinton*
Courtney W. Hamlin, *Springfield*
Dorsey W. Shackleford, *Jefferson City*
James Beauchamp Clark, *Bowling Green*
Jacob E. Meeker,[33] *St. Louis*
Frederick Essen,[34] *Clayton*
William L. Igoe, *St. Louis*
Leonidas C. Dyer, *St. Louis*
Walter L. Hensley, *Farmington*
Joseph J. Russell, *Charleston*
Perl D. Decker, *Joplin*
Thomas L. Rubey, *Lebanon*

MONTANA

SENATORS

Henry L. Myers, *Hamilton*
Thomas J. Walsh, *Helena*

REPRESENTATIVES AT LARGE

John M. Evans, *Missoula*
Miss Jeannette Rankin, *Missoula*

NEBRASKA

SENATORS

Gilbert M. Hitchcock, *Omaha*
George W. Norris, *McCook*

REPRESENTATIVES

C. Frank Reavis, *Falls City*
Charles O. Lobeck, *Omaha*
Daniel V. Stephens, *Fremont*
Charles H. Sloan, *Geneva*
Ashton C. Shallenberger, *Alma*
Moses P. Kinkaid, *O'Neill*

[20] Died April 12, 1918.
[21] Appointed to fill vacancy caused by death of Robert F. Broussard, and took his seat April 24, 1918.
[22] Elected to fill vacancy caused by death of Robert F. Broussard, and took his seat December 2, 1918.
[23] Died October 5, 1918.
[24] Elected to fill vacancy caused by death of J. Fred. C. Talbott, and took his seat November 18, 1918.

[25] Resigned May 15, 1917.
[26] Elected to fill vacancy caused by resignation of Augustus P. Gardner; took his seat December 3, 1917.
[27] Served until December 13, 1917; succeeded by Samuel W. Beakes, who contested his election.
[28] Successfully contested the election of Mark R. Bacon, and took his seat December 13, 1917.
[29] Died April 14, 1918.

[30] Appointed to fill vacancy caused by death of William J. Stone, and took his seat May 7, 1918.
[31] Elected to fill vacancy caused by death of William J. Stone, and took his seat November 21, 1918.
[32] Died February 20, 1919.
[33] Died October 16, 1918.
[34] Elected to fill vacancy caused by death of Jacob E. Meeker, and took his seat November 11, 1918.

NEVADA

SENATORS

Francis G. Newlands,[35] *Reno*
Charles B. Henderson,[36] *Elko*
Key Pittman, *Tonopah*

REPRESENTATIVE

At Large—Edwin E. Roberts, *Carson City*

NEW HAMPSHIRE

SENATORS

Jacob H. Gallinger,[37] *Concord*
Irving W. Drew,[38] *Lancaster*
George H. Moses,[39] *Concord*
Henry F. Hollis, *Concord*

REPRESENTATIVES

Cyrus A. Sulloway,[40] *Manchester*
Sherman E. Burroughs,[41] *Manchester*
Edward H. Wason, *Nashua*

NEW JERSEY

SENATORS

William Hughes,[42] *Paterson*
David Baird,[43] *Camden*
Joseph S. Frelinghuysen, *Raritan*

REPRESENTATIVES

William J. Browning, *Camden*
Isaac Bacharach, *Atlantic City*
Thomas J. Scully, *South Amboy*
Elijah C. Hutchinson, *Trenton*
John H. Capstick,[44] *Montville*
William F. Birch,[45] *Dover*
John R. Ramsey, *Hackensack*
Dow H. Drukker, *Passaic*
Edward W. Gray, *Newark*
Richard Wayne Parker, *Newark*
Frederick R. Lehlbach, *Newark*
John J. Eagan, *Weehawken*
James A. Hamill, *Jersey City*

NEW MEXICO

SENATORS

Albert B. Fall, *Three Rivers*
Andrieus A. Jones, *East Las Vegas*

REPRESENTATIVE

At Large—William B. Walton, *Silver City*

NEW YORK

SENATORS

James W. Wadsworth, Jr., *Groveland*
William M. Calder, *Brooklyn*

REPRESENTATIVES

Frederick C. Hicks, *Port Washington*
Charles P. Caldwell, *Forest Hills*
Joseph V. Flynn, *Brooklyn*
Harry H. Dale,[46] *Brooklyn*
James P. Maher, *Brooklyn*
Frederick W. Rowe, *Brooklyn*
John J. Fitzgerald,[47] *Brooklyn*
John J. Delaney,[48] *Brooklyn*
Daniel J. Griffin,[49] *Brooklyn*
William E. Cleary,[50] *Brooklyn*
Oscar W. Swift, *Brooklyn*
Reuben L. Haskell, *Brooklyn*
Daniel J. Riordan, *New York City*
Meyer London, *New York City*
Christopher D. Sullivan, *New York City*
Fiorello H. LaGuardia, *New York City*
Thomas F. Smith,[51] *New York City*
Peter J. Dooling, *New York City*
John F. Carew, *New York City*
George B. Francis, *New York City*
Walter M. Chandler, *New York City*
Isaac Siegel, *New York City*
G. Murray Hulbert,[52] *New York City*
Jerome F. Donovan,[53] *New York City*
Henry Bruckner,[54] *New York City*
Anthony J. Griffin,[55] *New York City*
Daniel C. Oliver, *New York City*
Benjamin L. Fairchild, *Pelham*
James W. Husted, *Peekskill*
Edmund Platt, *Poughkeepsie*
Charles B. Ward, *Debruce*
Rollin B. Sanford, *Albany*
James S. Parker, *Salem*
George R. Lunn, *Schenectady*
Bertrand H. Snell, *Potsdam*
Luther W. Mott, *Oswego*
Homer P. Snyder, *Little Falls*
George W. Fairchild, *Oneonta*
Walter W. Magee, *Syracuse*
Norman J. Gould, *Seneca Falls*
Harry H. Pratt, *Corning*
Thomas B. Dunn,[56] *Rochester*
Archie D. Sanders, *Stafford*
S. Wallace Dempsey, *Lockport*
Charles B. Smith, *Buffalo*
William F. Waldow, *Buffalo*
Charles M. Hamilton, *Ripley*

NORTH CAROLINA

SENATORS

Furnifold McL. Simmons, *New Bern*
Lee S. Overman, *Salisbury*

REPRESENTATIVES

John H. Small, *Washington*
Claude Kitchin, *Scotland Neck*
George E. Hood, *Goldsboro*
Edward W. Pou, *Smithfield*
Charles M. Stedman, *Greensboro*
Hannibal L. Godwin, *Dunn*
Leonidas D. Robinson, *Wadesboro*
Robert L. Doughton, *Laurel Springs*
Edwin Y. Webb, *Shelby*
Zebulon Weaver,[57] *Asheville*
James J. Britt,[58] *Asheville*

NORTH DAKOTA

SENATORS

Porter J. McCumber, *Wahpeton*
Asle J. Gronna, *Lakota*

REPRESENTATIVES

Henry T. Helgesen,[59] *Milton*
John M. Baer,[60] *Fargo*
George M. Young, *Valley City*
Patrick D. Norton, *Hettinger*

OHIO

SENATORS

Atlee Pomerene, *Canton*
Warren G. Harding, *Marion*

REPRESENTATIVES

Nicholas Longworth, *Cincinnati*
Victor Heintz, *Cincinnati*
Warren Gard, *Hamilton*
Benjamin F. Welty, *Lima*
John S. Snook, *Paulding*
Charles C. Kearns, *Batavia*
Simeon D. Fess, *Yellow Springs*
John A. Key, *Marion*
Isaac R. Sherwood, *Toledo*
Robert M. Switzer, *Gallipolis*
Horatio C. Claypool, *Chillicothe*
Clement L. Brumbaugh, *Columbus*
Arthur W. Overmyer, *Fremont*
Ellsworth R. Bathrick,[61] *Akron*
Martin L. Davey,[62] *Kent*
George White, *Marietta*

---

[35] Died December 24, 1917.
[36] Appointed to fill vacancy caused by death of Francis G. Newlands, and took his seat January 24, 1918; subsequently elected.
[37] Died August 17, 1918.
[38] Appointed to fill vacancy caused by death of Jacob H. Gallinger; took his seat September 11, 1918.
[39] Elected to fill vacancy caused by death of Jacob H. Gallinger, and took his seat November 18, 1918.
[40] Died March 11, 1917.
[41] Elected to fill vacancy caused by death of Cyrus A. Sulloway, and took his seat June 7, 1917.
[42] Died January 30, 1918.
[43] Appointed to fill vacancy caused by death of William Hughes, and took his seat March 7, 1918; subsequently elected.

[44] Died March 17, 1918.
[45] Elected to fill vacancy caused by death of John H. Capstick, and took his seat November 21, 1918.
[46] Resigned January 6, 1919.
[47] Resigned December 31, 1917.
[48] Elected to fill vacancy caused by resignation of John J. Fitzgerald, and took his seat March 14, 1918.
[49] Resigned December 31, 1917.
[50] Elected to fill vacancy caused by resignation of Daniel J. Griffin, and took his seat March 14, 1918.
[51] Elected to fill vacancy caused by death of Representative-elect Michael F. Conry, in preceding Congress, and took his seat April 18, 1917.
[52] Resigned January 1, 1918.
[53] Elected to fill vacancy caused by resignation of

G. Murray Hulbert, and took his seat March 14, 1918.
[54] Resigned December 31, 1917.
[55] Elected to fill vacancy caused by resignation of Henry Bruckner, and took his seat March 14, 1918.
[56] Election unsuccessfully contested by Jacob Gerling.
[57] Served until March 1, 1919; succeeded by James J. Britt, who contested his election.
[58] Successfully contested the election of Zebulon Weaver, and took his seat March 1, 1919.
[59] Died April 10, 1917.
[60] Elected to fill vacancy caused by death of Henry T. Helgesen, and took his seat August 10, 1917.
[61] Died December 23, 1917.
[62] Elected to fill vacancy caused by death of Ellsworth R. Bathrick, and took his seat December 2, 1918.

Roscoe C. McCulloch, *Canton*
William A. Ashbrook *Johnstown*
David A. Hollinsworth, *Cadiz*
John G. Cooper, *Youngstown*
William Gordon, *Cleveland*
Robert Crosser, *Cleveland*
Henry I. Emerson, *Cleveland*

OKLAHOMA

SENATORS

Thomas P. Gore, *Lawton*
Robert L. Owen, *Muskogee*

REPRESENTATIVES

Thomas A. Chandler, *Vinita*
William W. Hastings, *Tahlequah*
Charles D. Carter, *Ardmore*
Thomas D. McKeown, *Ada*
Joseph B. Thompson, *Pauls Valley*
Scott Ferris, *Lawton*
James V. McClintic, *Snyder*
Dick T. Morgan, *Woodward*

OREGON

SENATORS

George E. Chamberlain, *Portland*
Harry Lane,[63] *Portland*
Charles L. McNary,[64] *Salem*
Frederick W. Mulkey,[65] *Portland*
Charles L. McNary,[66] *Salem*

REPRESENTATIVES

Willis C. Hawley, *Salem*
Nicholas J. Sinnott, *The Dalles*
Clifton N. McArthur, *Portland*

PENNSYLVANIA

SENATORS

Boies Penrose, *Philadelphia*
Philander C. Knox, *Pittsburgh*

REPRESENTATIVES

William S. Vare, *Philadelphia*
George S. Graham, *Philadelphia*
J. Hampton Moore, *Philadelphia*
George W. Edmonds, *Philadelphia*
Peter E. Costello, *Philadelphia*
George P. Darrow, *Philadelphia*
Thomas S. Butler, *West Chester*
Henry W. Watson, *Langhorne*
William W. Griest, *Lancaster*
John R. Farr, *Scranton*
Thomas W. Templeton, *Plymouth*
Robert D. Heaton, *Ashland*
Arthur G. Dewalt, *Allentown*
Louis T. McFadden, *Canton*

Edgar R. Kiess, *Williamsport*
John V. Lesher, *Sunbury*
Benjamin K. Focht, *Lewisburg*
Aaron S. Kreider, *Annville*
John M. Rose, *Johnstown*
Andrew R. Brodbeck, *Hanover*
Charles H. Rowland, *Philipsburg*
Edward E. Robbins,[67] *Greensburg*
Bruce F. Sterling, *Uniontown*
Henry W. Temple, *Washington*
Henry A. Clark, *Erie*
Henry J. Steele, *Easton*
Nathan L. Strong, *Brookville*
Orrin D. Bleakley,[68] *Franklin*
Earl H. Beshlin,[69] *Warren*
Stephen G. Porter, *Pittsburgh*
M. Clyde Kelly, *Braddock*
John M. Morin, *Pittsburgh*
Guy E. Campbell, *Crafton*
At Large—
  Thomas S. Crago, *Waynesburg*
  Mahlon M. Garland, *Pittsburgh*
  Joseph McLaughlin, *Philadelphia*
  John R. K. Scott,[70] *Philadelphia*

RHODE ISLAND

SENATORS

LeBaron B. Colt, *Bristol*
Peter G. Gerry, *Warwick*

REPRESENTATIVES

George F. O'Shaunessy, *Providence*
Walter R. Stiness, *Cowesett*
Ambrose Kennedy, *Woonsocket*

SOUTH CAROLINA

SENATORS

Benjamin R. Tillman,[71] *Trenton*
Christie Benet,[72] *Columbia*
William P. Pollock,[73] *Cheraw*
Ellison D. Smith, *Florence*

REPRESENTATIVES

Richard S. Whaley, *Charleston*
James F. Byrnes, *Aiken*
Fred H. Dominick, *Newberry*
Samuel J. Nicholls, *Spartanburg*
William F. Stevenson,[74] *Cheraw*
J. Willard Ragsdale, *Florence*
Asbury F. Lever, *Lexington*

SOUTH DAKOTA

SENATORS

Thomas Sterling, *Vermilion*
Edwin S. Johnson, *Yankton*

REPRESENTATIVES

Charles H. Dillon, *Yankton*
Royal C. Johnson, *Aberdeen*
Harry L. Gandy, *Rapid City*

TENNESSEE

SENATORS

John K. Shields, *Knoxville*
Kenneth D. McKellar, *Memphis*

REPRESENTATIVES

Sam R. Sells, *Johnson City*
Richard W. Austin, *Knoxville*
John A. Moon, *Chattanooga*
Cordell Hull, *Carthage*
William C. Houston, *Woodbury*
Joseph W. Byrns, *Nashville*
Lemuel P. Padgett, *Columbia*
Thetus W. Sims, *Linden*
Finis J. Garrett, *Dresden*
Hubert F. Fisher, *Memphis*

TEXAS

SENATORS

Charles A. Culberson, *Dallas*
Morris Sheppard, *Texarkana*

REPRESENTATIVES

Eugene Black, *Clarksville*
Martin Dies, *Beaumont*
James Young, *Kaufman*
Sam Rayburn, *Bonham*
Hatton W. Sumners, *Dallas*
Rufus Hardy, *Corsicana*
Alexander W. Gregg, *Palestine*
Joe H. Eagle, *Houston*
Joseph J. Mansfield, *Columbus*
James P. Buchanan, *Brenham*
Tom T. Connally, *Marlin*
James C. Wilson, *Fort Worth*
Marvin Jones, *Amarillo*
James L. Slayden, *San Antonio*
John N. Garner, *Uvalde*
Thomas L. Blanton, *Abilene*
At Large—
  A. Jeff. McLemore, *Houston*
  Daniel E. Garrett, *Houston*

UTAH

SENATORS

Reed Smoot, *Provo*
William H. King, *Salt Lake City*

REPRESENTATIVES

Milton H. Welling, *Fielding*
James H. Mays, *Salt Lake City*

---

[63] Died May 23, 1917.
[64] Appointed to fill vacancy caused by death of Harry Lane, to serve until the next general election, and took his seat June 8, 1917.
[65] Elected to fill vacancy caused by death of Harry Lane, and took his seat December 9, 1918; resigned, effective December 17, 1918.
[66] Appointed to fill vacancy caused by resignation of Frederick W. Mulkey, and took his seat December 17, 1918.
[67] Died January 25, 1919, before the commencement of the Sixty-sixth Congress, to which he had been reelected.
[68] Resigned April 3, 1917, never having qualified.
[69] Elected to fill vacancy caused by resignation of Orrin D. Bleakley, and took his seat December 3, 1917.
[70] Resigned effective January 5, 1919.
[71] Died July 3, 1918.
[72] Appointed to fill vacancy caused by death of Benjamin R. Tillman, and took his seat July 8, 1918.
[73] Elected to fill vacancy caused by death of Benjamin R. Tillman, and took his seat December 2, 1918.
[74] Elected to fill vacancy caused by death of Representative-elect David E. Finely, in preceding Congress, and took his seat April 2, 1917.

VERMONT

SENATORS

William P. Dillingham, *Montpelier*
Carroll S. Page, *Hyde Park*

REPRESENTATIVES

Frank L. Greene, *St. Albans*
Porter H. Dale, *Island Pond*

VIRGINIA

SENATORS

Thomas S. Martin, *Charlottesville*
Claude A. Swanson, *Chatham*

REPRESENTATIVES

William A. Jones,[75] *Warsaw*
Schuyler Otis Bland,[76] *Newport News*
Edward E. Holland, *Suffolk*
Andrew J. Montague, *Richmond*
Walter A. Watson, *Jennings Ordinary*
Edward W. Saunders, *Rockymount*
Carter Glass,[77] *Lynchburg*
James P. Woods,[78] *Roanoke*
Thomas W. Harrison, *Winchester*
Charles C. Carlin,[79] *Alexandria*
C. Bascom Slemp, *Big Stone Gap*
Henry D. Flood, *Appomattox*

WASHINGTON

SENATORS

Wesley L. Jones, *Seattle*
Miles Poindexter, *Spokane*

REPRESENTATIVES

John F. Miller, *Seattle*
Lindley H. Hadley, *Bellingham*
Albert Johnson, *Hoquiam*
William L. La Follette, *Pullman*
Clarence C. Dill, *Spokane*

WEST VIRGINIA

SENATORS

Nathan Goff, *Clarksburg*
Howard Sutherland,[80] *Elkins*

REPRESENTATIVES

Matthew M. Neely, *Fairmont*
George M. Bowers, *Martinsburg*
Stuart F. Reed, *Clarksburg*
Harry C. Woodyard, *Spencer*
Edward Cooper, *Bramwell*
Adam B. Littlepage, *Charleston*

WISCONSIN

SENATORS

Robert M. La Follette, *Madison*
Paul O. Husting,[81] *Mayville*
Irvine L. Lenroot,[82] *Superior*

REPRESENTATIVES

Henry Allen Cooper, *Racine*
Edward Voigt, *Sheboygan*
John M. Nelson, *Madison*
William J. Cary, *Milwaukee*
William H. Stafford, *Milwaukee*
James H. Davidson,[83] *Oshkosh*
Florian Lampert,[84] *Oshkosh*
John J. Esch, *La Crosse*

Edward E. Browne, *Waupaca*
David G. Classon, *Oconto*
James A. Frear, *Hudson*
Irvine L. Lenroot,[85] *Superior*
Adolphus P. Nelson,[86] *Grantsburg*

WYOMING

SENATORS

Francis E. Warren, *Cheyenne*
John B. Kendrick, *Sheridan*

REPRESENTATIVE

At Large—Frank W. Mondell, *Newcastle*

TERRITORY OF ALASKA

DELEGATE

Charles A. Sulzer,[87] *Sulzer*
James Wickersham,[88] *Fairbanks*

TERRITORY OF HAWAII

DELEGATE

J. Kuhio Kalanianaole, *Waikiki*

PHILIPPINE ISLANDS

RESIDENT COMMISSIONERS [89]

Jaime C. de Veyra, *Leyte*
Teodoro R. Yangco, *Zambales*

PORTO RICO

RESIDENT COMMISSIONER [90]

Felix Cordova Davila,[91] *San Juan*

---

[75] Died April 17, 1918.
[76] Elected to fill vacancy caused by death of William A. Jones, and took his seat July 3, 1918.
[77] Resigned December 16, 1918, before the commencement of the Sixty-sixth Congress, to which he had been reelected, having been appointed Secretary of the Treasury.
[78] Elected to fill vacancy caused by resignation of Carter Glass, and took his seat March 1, 1919.
[79] Resigned March 3, 1919, before the commencement of the Sixty-sixth Congress, to which he had been reelected.

[80] Election unsuccessfully contested by William E. Chilton.
[81] Died October 21, 1917.
[82] Elected to fill vacancy caused by death of Paul O. Husting, and took his seat April 18, 1918.
[83] Died August 6, 1918.
[84] Elected to fill vacancy caused by death of James H. Davidson, and took his seat December 2, 1918.
[85] Resigned April 17, 1918, having been elected Senator.
[86] Elected to fill vacancy caused by resignation of Irvine L. Lenroot, and took his seat December 2, 1918.

[87] Served until January 7, 1919; succeeded by James Wickersham, who contested his election.
[88] Successfully contested the election of Charles A. Sulzer, and took his seat January 7, 1919.
[89] By act of Congress approved August 29, 1916, term of office decreased from four to three years beginning March 4, 1917.
[90] By act of Congress approved March 2, 1917, term of office increased to four years beginning March 4, 1921.
[91] Elected July 16, 1917, to serve from August 7, 1917, to March 3, 1921.

SIXTY-SIXTH CONGRESS

MARCH 4, 1919, TO MARCH 3, 1921

FIRST SESSION—*May 19, 1919, to November 19, 1919*

SECOND SESSION—*December 1, 1919, to June 5, 1920*

THIRD SESSION—*December 6, 1920, to March 3, 1921*

———

VICE PRESIDENT OF THE UNITED STATES—THOMAS R. MARSHALL, of Indiana

PRESIDENT PRO TEMPORE OF THE SENATE—ALBERT B. CUMMINS,[1] of Iowa

SECRETARY OF THE SENATE—JAMES M. BAKER, of South Carolina; GEORGE A. SANDERSON,[2] of Illinois

SERGEANT AT ARMS OF THE SENATE—CHARLES P. HIGGINS, of Missouri; DAVID S. BARRY,[3] of Rhode Island

———

SPEAKER OF THE HOUSE OF REPRESENTATIVES—FREDERICK H. GILLETT,[4] of Massachusetts

CLERK OF THE HOUSE—SOUTH TRIMBLE, of Kentucky; WILLIAM TYLER PAGE,[5] of Maryland

SERGEANT AT ARMS OF THE HOUSE—ROBERT B. GORDON, of Ohio; JOSEPH G. ROGERS,[6] of Pennsylvania

DOORKEEPER OF THE HOUSE—BERT W. KENNEDY, of Michigan

POSTMASTER OF THE HOUSE—FRANK W. COLLIER

ALABAMA

SENATORS

John H. Bankhead,[7] *Jasper*
Braxton B. Comer,[8] *Birmingham*
J. Thomas Heflin,[9] *Lafayette*
Oscar W. Underwood, *Birmingham*

REPRESENTATIVES

John McDuffie, *Monroeville*
S. Hubert Dent, Jr., *Montgomery*
Henry B. Steagall, *Ozark*
Fred L. Blackmon,[10] *Anniston*
J. Thomas Heflin,[11] *Lafayette*
William B. Bowling,[12] *Lafayette*
William B. Oliver, *Tuscaloosa*
John L. Burnett,[13] *Gadsden*
Lilius B. Rainey,[14] *Gadsden*
Edward B. Almon, *Tuscumbia*
George Huddleston, *Birmingham*
William B. Bankhead, *Jasper*

ARIZONA

SENATORS

Henry F. Ashurst, *Prescott*
Marcus A. Smith, *Tucson*

REPRESENTATIVE

At Large—Carl Hayden, *Phoenix*

ARKANSAS

SENATORS

Joseph T. Robinson, *Little Rock*
William F. Kirby, *Little Rock*

REPRESENTATIVES

Thaddeus H. Caraway, *Jonesboro*
William A. Oldfield, *Batesville*
John N. Tillman, *Fayetteville*
Otis Wingo, *De Queen*
Henderson M. Jacoway, *Dardanelle*
Samuel M. Taylor, *Pine Bluff*
William S. Goodwin, *Warren*

CALIFORNIA

SENATORS

James D. Phelan, *San Francisco*
Hiram W. Johnson, *San Francisco*

REPRESENTATIVES

Clarence F. Lea, *Santa Rosa*
John E. Raker, *Alturas*

Charles F. Curry, *Sacramento*
Julius Kahn, *San Francisco*
John I. Nolan, *San Francisco*
John A. Elston, *Berkeley*
Henry E. Barbour, *Fresno*
Hugh S. Hersman, *Gilroy*
Charles H. Randall, *Los Angeles*
Henry Z. Osborne, *Los Angeles*
William Kettner, *San Diego*

COLORADO

SENATORS

Charles S. Thomas, *Denver*
Lawrence C. Phipps, *Denver*

REPRESENTATIVES

William N. Vaile, *Denver*
Charles B. Timberlake, *Sterling*
Guy U. Hardy, *Canon City*
Edward T. Taylor, *Glenwood Springs*

CONNECTICUT

SENATORS

Frank B. Brandegee, *New London*
George P. McLean, *Simsbury*

---

[1] Elected May 19, 1919.
[2] Elected May 19, 1919.
[3] Elected May 19, 1919.
[4] Elected May 19, 1919.
[5] Elected May 19, 1919.
[6] Elected May 19, 1919.
[7] Died March 1, 1920.

[8] Appointed to fill vacancy caused by death of John H. Bankhead, and took his seat March 15, 1920.
[9] Elected to fill vacancy caused by death of John H. Bankhead, and took his seat December 6, 1920.
[10] Died February 8, 1921.
[11] Resigned November 1, 1920, subsequently elected Senator.

[12] Elected to fill vacancy caused by resignation of J. Thomas Heflin, and took his seat December 29, 1920.
[13] Died May 13, 1919, before Congress assembled.
[14] Elected to fill vacancy caused by death of John L. Burnett, and took his seat October 13, 1919.

CONNECTICUT—Continued

REPRESENTATIVES

Augustine Lonergan, *Hartford*
Richard P. Freeman, *New London*
John Q. Tilson, *New Haven*
Schuyler Merritt, *Stamford*
James P. Glynn, *Winsted*

DELAWARE

SENATORS

Josiah O. Wolcott, *Dover*
L. Heisler Ball, *Marshallton*

REPRESENTATIVE

At Large—Caleb R. Layton, *Georgetown*

FLORIDA

SENATORS

Duncan U. Fletcher, *Jacksonville*
Park Trammell, *Lakeland*

REPRESENTATIVES

Herbert J. Drane, *Lakeland*
Frank Clark, *Gainesville*
John H. Smithwick, *Pensacola*
William J. Sears, *Kissimmee*

GEORGIA

SENATORS

Hoke Smith, *Atlanta*
William J. Harris, *Cedartown*

REPRESENTATIVES

James W. Overstreet, *Sylvania*
Frank Park, *Sylvester*
Charles R. Crisp, *Americus*
William C. Wright, *Newnan*
William D. Upshaw, *Atlanta*
James W. Wise, *Fayetteville*
Gordon Lee, *Chickamauga*
Charles H. Brand, *Athens*
Thomas M. Bell, *Gainesville*
Carl Vinson, *Milledgeville*
William C. Lankford, *Douglas*
William W. Larsen, *Dublin*

IDAHO

SENATORS

William E. Borah, *Boise*
John F. Nugent,[15] *Boise*
Frank R. Gooding,[16] *Gooding*

REPRESENTATIVES

Burton L. French, *Moscow*
Addison T. Smith, *Twin Falls*

ILLINOIS

SENATORS

Lawrence Y. Sherman, *Springfield*
Medill McCormick, *Chicago*

REPRESENTATIVES

Martin B. Madden, *Chicago*
James R. Mann, *Chicago*
William W. Wilson, *Chicago*
John W. Rainey, *Chicago*
Adolph J. Sabath, *Chicago*
James McAndrews, *Chicago*
Niels Juul, *Chicago*
Thomas Gallagher, *Chicago*
Fred A. Britten, *Chicago*
Carl R. Chindblom, *Chicago*
Ira C. Copley, *Aurora*
Charles E. Fuller, *Belvidere*
John C. McKenzie, *Elizabeth*
William J. Graham, *Aledo*
Edward J. King, *Galesburg*
Clifford Ireland, *Peoria*
Frank L. Smith, *Dwight*
Joseph G. Cannon, *Danville*
William B. McKinley, *Champaign*
Henry T. Rainey, *Carrollton*
Loren E. Wheeler, *Springfield*
William A. Rodenberg, *East St. Louis*
Edwin B. Brooks, *Newton*
Thomas S. Williams, *Louisville*
Edward E. Denison, *Marion*
At Large—
    Richard Yates, *Springfield*
    William E. Mason, *Chicago*

INDIANA

SENATORS

James E. Watson, *Rushville*
Harry S. New, *Indianapolis*

REPRESENTATIVES

Oscar R. Luhring, *Evansville*
Oscar E. Bland, *Linton*
James W. Dunbar, *New Albany*
John S. Benham, *Benham*
Everett Sanders, *Terre Haute*
Richard N. Elliott, *Connersville*
Merrill Moores, *Indianapolis*
Albert H. Vestal, *Anderson*
Fred S. Purnell, *Attica*
William R. Wood, *La Fayette*
Milton Kraus, *Peru*
Louis W. Fairfield, *Angola*
Andrew J. Hickey, *La Porte*

IOWA

SENATORS

Albert B. Cummins, *Des Moines*
William S. Kenyon, *Fort Dodge*

REPRESENTATIVES

Charles A. Kennedy, *Montrose*
Harry E. Hull, *Williamsburg*
Burton E. Sweet, *Waverly*
Gilbert N. Haugen, *Northwood*
James W. Good, *Cedar Rapids*
C. William Ramseyer, *Bloomfield*
Cassius C. Dowell, *Des Moines*
Horace M. Towner, *Corning*
William R. Green, *Council Bluffs*
Lester J. Dickinson, *Algona*
William D. Boies, *Sheldon*

KANSAS

SENATORS

Charles Curtis, *Topeka*
Arthur Capper, *Topeka*

REPRESENTATIVES

Daniel R. Anthony, Jr., *Leavenworth*
Edward C. Little, *Kansas City*
Philip P. Campbell, *Pittsburg*
Homer Hoch, *Marion*
James G. Strong, *Blue Rapids*
Hays B. White, *Mankato*
Jasper N. Tincher, *Medicine Lodge*
William A. Ayres, *Wichita*

KENTUCKY

SENATORS

Joseph C. W. Beckham, *Frankfort*
Augustus O. Stanley,[17] *Henderson*

REPRESENTATIVES

Alben W. Barkley, *Paducah*
David H. Kincheloe, *Madisonville*
Robert Y. Thomas, Jr., *Central City*
Ben Johnson, *Bardstown*
Charles F. Ogden, *Louisville*
Arthur B. Rouse, *Burlington*
James C. Cantrill, *Georgetown*
King Swope,[18] *Danville*
William J. Fields, *Olive Hill*
John W. Langley, *Pikeville*
John M. Robsion, *Barbourville*

LOUISIANA

SENATORS

Joseph E. Ransdell, *Lake Providence*
Edward J. Gay, *Plaquemine*

REPRESENTATIVES

Albert Estopinal,[19] *Estopinal*
James O'Connor,[20] *New Orleans*
H. Garland Dupré, *New Orleans*
Whitmell P. Martin, *Thibodaux*
John T. Watkins, *Minden*
Riley J. Wilson, *Harrisonburg*

[15] Resigned, effective January 14, 1921.
[16] Appointed to fill vacancy caused by resignation of John F. Nugent, and took his seat January 15, 1921.
[17] Elected November 5, 1918, for term beginning March 4, 1919, but did not qualify until May 19, 1919, preferring to retain the governorship.
[18] Elected to fill vacancy caused by death of Representative-elect Harvey Helm, in preceding Congress, and took his seat August 19, 1919.
[19] Died April 28, 1919, before Congress assembled.
[20] Elected to fill vacancy caused by death of Albert Estopinal, and took his seat June 10, 1919.

Jared Y. Sanders, *Bogalusa*
Ladislas Lazaro, *Washington*
James B. Aswell, *Natchitoches*

MAINE

SENATORS

Bert M. Fernald, *West Poland*
Frederick Hale, *Portland*

REPRESENTATIVES

Louis B. Goodall, *Sanford*
Wallace H. White, Jr., *Lewiston*
John A. Peters, *Ellsworth*
Ira G. Hersey, *Houlton*

MARYLAND

SENATORS

John Walter Smith, *Snow Hill*
Joseph I. France, *Port Deposit*

REPRESENTATIVES

William N. Andrews, *Cambridge*
Carville D. Benson, *Halethorpe*
Charles P. Coady, *Baltimore*
J. Charles Linthicum, *Baltimore*
Sydney E. Mudd, *La Plata*
Frederick N. Zihlman, *Cumberland*

MASSACHUSETTS

SENATORS

Henry Cabot Lodge, *Nahant*
David I. Walsh, *Fitchburg*

REPRESENTATIVES

Allen T. Treadway, *Stockbridge*
Frederick H. Gillett, *Springfield*
Calvin D. Paige, *Southbridge*
Samuel E. Winslow, *Worcester*
John Jacob Rogers, *Lowell*
Willfred W. Lufkin, *Essex*
Michael F. Phelan, *Lynn*
Frederick W. Dallinger, *Cambridge*
Alvan T. Fuller,[21] *Malden*
John F. Fitzgerald,[22] *Boston*
Peter F. Tague,[23] *Boston*
George H. Tinkham, *Boston*
James A. Gallivan, *Boston*
Robert Luce, *Waltham*
Richard Olney, *Dedham*
William S. Greene, *Fall River*
Joseph Walsh, *New Bedford*

MICHIGAN

SENATORS

Charles E. Townsend, *Jackson*
Truman H. Newberry, *Grosse Pointe Farms*

REPRESENTATIVES

Frank E. Doremus, *Detroit*
Earl C. Michener, *Adrian*
John M. C. Smith, *Charlotte*
Edward L. Hamilton, *Niles*
Carl E. Mapes, *Grand Rapids*
Patrick H. Kelley, *Lansing*
Louis C. Cramton, *Lapeer*
Joseph W. Fordney, *Saginaw*
James C. McLaughlin, *Muskegon*
Gilbert A. Currie, *Midland*
Frank D. Scott, *Alpena*
W. Frank James, *Hancock*
Charles A. Nichols,[24] *Detroit*
Clarence J. McLeod,[25] *Detroit*

MINNESOTA

SENATORS

Knute Nelson, *Alexandria*
Frank B. Kellogg, *St. Paul*

REPRESENTATIVES

Sydney Anderson, *Lanesboro*
Franklin F. Ellsworth, *Mankato*
Charles R. Davis, *St. Peter*
Carl C. Van Dyke,[26] *St. Paul*
Oscar E. Keller,[27] *St. Paul*
Walter H. Newton, *Minneapolis*
Harold Knutson, *St. Cloud*
Andrew J. Volstead, *Granite Falls*
William L. Carss, *Proctor*
Halvor Steenerson, *Crookston*
Thomas D. Schall, *Excelsior*

MISSISSIPPI

SENATORS

John Sharp Williams, *Yazoo City*
Pat Harrison, *Gulfport*

REPRESENTATIVES

Ezekiel S. Candler, Jr., *Corinth*
Hubert D. Stephens, *New Albany*
Benjamin G. Humphreys, *Greenville*
Thomas U. Sisson, *Winona*
William W. Venable, *Meridian*
Paul B. Johnson, *Hattiesburg*
Percy E. Quin, *McComb City*
James W. Collier, *Vicksburg*

MISSOURI

SENATORS

James A. Reed, *Kansas City*
Selden P. Spencer, *St. Louis*

REPRESENTATIVES

Milton A. Romjue, *Macon*
William W. Rucker, *Keytesville*

Joshua W. Alexander,[28] *Gallatin*
Jacob L. Milligan,[29] *Richmond*
Charles F. Booher,[30] *Savannah*
William T. Bland, *Kansas City*
Clement C. Dickinson, *Clinton*
Samuel C. Major, *Fayette*
William L. Nelson, *Columbia*
James Beauchamp Clark,[31] *Bowling Green*
Cleveland A. Newton, *St. Louis*
William L. Igoe, *St. Louis*
Leonidas C. Dyer, *St. Louis*
Marion E. Rhodes, *Potosi*
Edward D. Hays, *Cape Girardeau*
Isaac V. McPherson, *Aurora*
Thomas L. Rubey, *Lebanon*

MONTANA

SENATORS

Henry L. Myers, *Hamilton*
Thomas J. Walsh, *Helena*

REPRESENTATIVES

John M. Evans, *Missoula*
Carl W. Riddick, *Lewistown*

NEBRASKA

SENATORS

Gilbert M. Hitchcock, *Omaha*
George W. Norris, *McCook*

REPRESENTATIVES

C. Frank Reavis, *Falls City*
Albert W. Jefferis, *Omaha*
Robert E. Evans, *Dakota City*
Melvin O. McLaughlin, *York*
William E. Andrews, *Hastings*
Moses P. Kinkaid, *O'Neill*

NEVADA

SENATORS

Key Pittman, *Tonopah*
Charles B. Henderson, *Elko*

REPRESENTATIVE

At Large—Charles R. Evans, *Goldfield*

NEW HAMPSHIRE

SENATORS

George H. Moses, *Concord*
Henry K. Keyes, *Haverhill*

REPRESENTATIVES

Sherman E. Burroughs, *Manchester*
Edward H. Wason, *Nashua*

---

[21] Resigned January 5, 1921, having been elected Lieutenant Governor.
[22] Served until October 23, 1919; succeeded by Peter F. Tague, who contested his election.
[23] Successfully contested the election of John F. Fitzgerald, and took his seat October 23, 1919.
[24] Died April 25, 1920.

[25] Elected to fill vacancy caused by death of Charles A. Nichols, and took his seat December 6, 1920.
[26] Died May 20, 1919.
[27] Elected to fill vacancy caused by death of Carl C. Van Dyke, and took his seat July 28, 1919.
[28] Resigned December 15, 1919, having been appointed Secretary of Commerce.

[29] Elected to fill vacancy caused by resignation of Joshua W. Alexander, and took his seat March 20, 1920.
[30] Died January 21, 1921. Election unsuccessfully contested by Albert L. Reeves.
[31] Died March 2, 1921. Election unsuccessfully contested by James D. Salts.

NEW JERSEY

SENATORS

Joseph S. Frelinghuysen, *Raritan*
Walter E. Edge, *Atlantic City*

REPRESENTATIVES

William J. Browning,[32] *Camden*
Francis F. Patterson, Jr.,[33] *Camden*
Isaac Bacharach, *Atlantic City*
Thomas J. Scully, *South Amboy*
Elijah C. Hutchinson, *Trenton*
Ernest R. Ackerman, *Plainfield*
John R. Ramsey, *Hackensack*
Amos H. Radcliffe, *Paterson*
Cornelius A. McGlennon, *East Newark*
Daniel F. Minahan, *Orange*
Frederick R. Lehlbach, *Newark*
John J. Eagan, *Weehawken*
James A. Hamill, *Jersey City*

NEW MEXICO

SENATORS

Albert B. Fall, *Three Rivers*
Andrieus A. Jones, *East Las Vegas*

REPRESENTATIVE

At Large—Bendigno C. Hernandez, *Tierra Amarilla*

NEW YORK

SENATORS

James W. Wadsworth, Jr., *Groveland*
William M. Calder, *Brooklyn*

REPRESENTATIVES

Frederick C. Hicks, *Port Washington*
Charles P. Caldwell, *Forest Hills*
John MacCrate,[34] *Brooklyn*
Thomas H. Cullen, *Brooklyn*
John B. Johnston, *Brooklyn*
Frederick W. Rowe, *Brooklyn*
James P. Maher, *Brooklyn*
William E. Cleary, *Brooklyn*
David J. O'Connell, *Brooklyn*
Reuben L. Haskell,[35] *Brooklyn*
Lester D. Volk,[36] *Brooklyn*
Daniel J. Riordan, *New York City*
Henry M. Goldfogle, *New York City*
Christopher D. Sullivan, *New York City*
Fiorello H. LaGuardia,[37] *New York City*
Nathan D. Perlman,[38] *New York City*
Peter J. Dooling, *New York City*
Thomas F. Smith, *New York City*
Herbert C. Pell, Jr., *New York City*

John F. Carew, *New York City*
Joseph Rowan, *New York City*
Isaac Siegel, *New York City*
Jerome F. Donovan, *New York City*
Anthony J. Griffin, *New York City*
Richard F. McKiniry, *New York City*
James V. Ganly, *New York City*
James W. Husted, *Peekskill*
Edmund Platt,[39] *Poughkeepsie*
Hamilton Fish, Jr.,[40] *Garrison*
Charles B. Ward, *Debruce*
Rollin B. Sanford, *Albany*
James S. Parker, *Salem*
Frank Crowther, *Schenectady*
Bertrand H. Snell, *Potsdam*
Luther W. Mott, *Oswego*
Homer P. Snyder, *Little Falls*
William H. Hill, *Johnson City*
Walter W. Magee, *Syracuse*
Norman J. Gould, *Seneca Falls*
Alanson B. Houghton, *Corning*
Thomas B. Dunn, *Rochester*
Archie D. Sanders, *Stafford*
S. Wallace Dempsey, *Lockport*
Clarence MacGregor, *Buffalo*
James M. Mead, *Buffalo*
Daniel A. Reed, *Dunkirk*

NORTH CAROLINA

SENATORS

Furnifold McL. Simmons, *New Bern*
Lee S. Overman, *Salisbury*

REPRESENTATIVES

John H. Small, *Washington*
Claude Kitchin, *Scotland Neck*
Samuel M. Brinson, *New Bern*
Edward W. Pou, *Smithfield*
Charles M. Stedman, *Greensboro*
Hannibal L. Godwin, *Dunn*
Leonidas D. Robinson, *Wadesboro*
Robert L. Doughton, *Laurel Springs*
Edwin Y. Webb,[41] *Shelby*
Clyde R. Hoey,[42] *Shelby*
Zebulon Weaver, *Asheville*

NORTH DAKOTA

SENATORS

Porter J. McCumber, *Wahpeton*
Asle J. Gronna, *Lakota*

REPRESENTATIVES

John M. Baer, *Fargo*
George M. Young, *Valley City*
James H. Sinclair, *Kenmare*

OHIO

SENATORS

Atlee Pomerene, *Canton*
Warren G. Harding,[43] *Marion*
Frank B. Willis,[44] *Delaware*

REPRESENTATIVES

Nicholas Longworth, *Cincinnati*
Ambrose E. B. Stephens, *North Bend*
Warren Gard, *Hamilton*
Benjamin F. Welty, *Lima*
Charles J. Thomson, *Defiance*
Charles C. Kearns, *Batavia*
Simeon D. Fess, *Yellow Springs*
R. Clint. Cole, *Findlay*
Isaac R. Sherwood, *Toledo*
Israel M. Foster, *Athens*
Edwin D. Ricketts, *Logan*
Clement L. Brumbaugh, *Columbus*
James T. Begg, *Sandusky*
Martin L. Davey, *Kent*
C. Ellis Moore, *Cambridge*
Roscoe C. McCulloch, *Canton*
William A. Ashbrook, *Johnstown*
B. Frank Murphy, *Steubenville*
John G. Cooper, *Youngstown*
Charles A. Mooney, *Cleveland*
John J. Babka, *Cleveland*
Henry I. Emerson, *Cleveland*

OKLAHOMA

SENATORS

Thomas P. Gore, *Lawton*
Robert L. Owen, *Muskogee*

REPRESENTATIVES

Everette B. Howard, *Tulsa*
William W. Hastings, *Tahlequah*
Charles D. Carter, *Ardmore*
Thomas D. McKeown, *Ada*
Joseph B. Thompson,[45] *Pauls Valley*
John W. Harreld,[46] *Oklahoma City*
Scott Ferris, *Lawton*
James V. McClintic, *Snyder*
Dick T. Morgan,[47] *Woodward*
Charles Swindall,[48] *Woodward*

OREGON

SENATORS

George E. Chamberlain, *Portland*
Charles L. McNary, *Salem*

REPRESENTATIVES

Willis C. Hawley, *Salem*
Nicholas J. Sinnott, *The Dalles*
Clifton N. McArthur, *Portland*

---

[32] Died March 24, 1920.
[33] Elected to fill vacancy caused by death of William J. Browning, and took his seat December 6, 1920.
[34] Resigned December 30, 1920.
[35] Resigned December 31, 1919.
[36] Elected to fill vacancy caused by resignation of Reuben L. Haskell, and took his seat December 6, 1920.
[37] Resigned effective December 31, 1919.
[38] Elected to fill vacancy caused by resignation of

Fiorello H. LaGuardia, and took his seat December 6, 1920.
[39] Resigned June 7, 1920.
[40] Elected to fill vacancy caused by resignation of Edmund Platt, and took his seat December 6, 1920.
[41] Resigned November 10, 1919.
[42] Elected to fill vacancy caused by resignation of Edwin Y. Webb, and took his seat January 5, 1920.
[43] Resigned, effective January 13, 1921, having been

elected President of the United States.
[44] Appointed to fill vacancy caused by resignation of Warren G. Harding, and took his seat January 14, 1921.
[45] Died September 18, 1919.
[46] Elected to fill vacancy caused by death of Joseph B. Thompson, and took his seat November 17, 1919.
[47] Died July 4, 1920.
[48] Elected to fill vacancy caused by death of Dick T. Morgan, and took his seat December 6, 1920.

PENNSYLVANIA

SENATORS

Boies Penrose, *Philadelphia*
Philander C. Knox, *Pittsburgh*

REPRESENTATIVES

William S. Vare, *Philadelphia*
George S. Graham, *Philadelphia*
J. Hampton Moore,[49] *Philadelphia*
Harry C. Ransley,[50] *Philadelphia*
George W. Edmonds, *Philadelphia*
Peter E. Costello, *Philadelphia*
George P. Darrow, *Philadelphia*
Thomas S. Butler, *West Chester*
Henry W. Watson, *Langhorne*
William W. Griest, *Lancaster*
Patrick McLane,[51] *Scranton*
John R. Farr,[52] *Scranton*
John J. Casey, *Wilkes-Barre*
John Reber, *Pottsville*
Authur G. Dewalt, *Allentown*
Louis T. McFadden, *Canton*
Edgar R. Kiess, *Williamsport*
John V. Lesher, *Sunbury*
Benjamin K. Focht, *Lewisburg*
Aaron S. Kreider, *Annville*
John M. Rose, *Johnstown*
Edward S. Brooks, *York*
Evan J. Jones, *Bradford*
John H. Wilson,[53] *Butler*
Samuel A. Kendall, *Meyersdale*
Henry W. Temple, *Washington*
Milton W. Shreve, *Erie*
Henry J. Steele, *Easton*
Nathan L. Strong, *Brookville*
Willis J. Hulings, *Oil City*
Stephen G. Porter, *Pittsburgh*
M. Clyde Kelly, *Braddock*
John M. Morin, *Pittsburgh*
Guy E. Campbell, *Crafton*
At Large—
   William J. Burke, *Pittsburgh*
   Thomas S. Crago, *Waynesburg*
   Mahlon M. Garland,[54] *Pittsburgh*
   Anderson H. Walters, *Johnstown*

RHODE ISLAND

SENATORS

LeBaron B. Colt, *Bristol*
Peter G. Gerry, *Warwick*

REPRESENTATIVES

Clark Burdick, *Newport*
Walter R. Stiness, *Cowesett*
Ambrose Kennedy, *Woonsocket*

SOUTH CAROLINA

SENATORS

Ellison D. Smith, *Florence*
Nathaniel B. Dial, *Laurens*

REPRESENTATIVES

Richard S. Whaley, *Charleston*
James F. Byrnes, *Aiken*
Fred H. Dominick, *Newberry*
Samuel J. Nicholls, *Spartanburg*
William F. Stevenson, *Cheraw*
J. Willard Ragsdale,[55] *Florence*
Philip H. Stoll,[56] *Kingstree*
Asbury F. Lever,[57] *Lexington*
Edward C. Mann,[58] *St. Matthews*

SOUTH DAKOTA

SENATORS

Thomas Sterling, *Vermilion*
Edwin S. Johnson, *Yankton*

REPRESENTATIVES

Charles A. Christopherson, *Sioux Falls*
Royal C. Johnson, *Aberdeen*
Harry L. Gandy, *Rapid City*

TENNESSEE

SENATORS

John K. Shields, *Knoxville*
Kenneth D. McKellar, *Memphis*

REPRESENTATIVES

Sam R. Sells, *Johnson City*
J. Will Taylor, *La Follette*
John A. Moon, *Chattanooga*
Cordell Hull, *Carthage*
Ewin L. Davis, *Tullahoma*
Joseph W. Byrns, *Nashville*
Lemuel P. Padgett, *Columbia*
Thetus W. Sims, *Linden*
Finis J. Garrett, *Dresden*
Hubert F. Fisher, *Memphis*

TEXAS

SENATORS

Charles A. Culberson, *Dallas*
Morris Sheppard, *Texarkana*

REPRESENTATIVES

Eugene Black, *Clarksville*
John C. Box, *Jacksonville*
James Young, *Kaufman*

Sam Rayburn, *Bonham*
Hatton W. Sumners, *Dallas*
Rufus Hardy, *Corsicana*
Clay Stone Briggs, *Galveston*
Joe H. Eagle, *Houston*
Joseph J. Mansfield, *Columbus*
James P. Buchanan, *Brenham*
Tom T. Connally, *Marlin*
James C. Wilson,[59] *Fort Worth*
Fritz G. Lanham,[60] *Fort Worth*
Lucian W. Parrish, *Henrietta*
Carlos Bee, *San Antonio*
John N. Garner, *Uvalde*
Claude B. Hudspeth, *El Paso*
Thomas L. Blanton, *Abilene*
Marvin Jones, *Amarillo*

UTAH

SENATORS

Reed Smoot, *Provo*
William H. King, *Salt Lake City*

REPRESENTATIVES

Milton H. Welling, *Fielding*
James H. Mays, *Salt Lake City*

VERMONT

SENATORS

William P. Dillingham, *Montpelier*
Carroll S. Page, *Hyde Park*

REPRESENTATIVES

Frank L. Greene, *St. Albans*
Porter H. Dale, *Island Pond*

VIRGINIA

SENATORS

Thomas S. Martin,[61] *Charlottesville*
Carter Glass,[62] *Lynchburg*
Claude A. Swanson, *Chatham*

REPRESENTATIVES

Schuyler Otis Bland, *Newport News*
Edward E. Holland, *Suffolk*
Andrew J. Montague, *Richmond*
Walter A. Watson,[63] *Jennings Ordinary*
Patrick Henry Drewry,[64] *Petersburg*
Edward W. Saunders,[65] *Rockymount*
Rorer A. James,[66] *Danville*
James P. Woods,[67] *Roanoke*
Thomas W. Harrison, *Winchester*
R. Walton Moore,[68] *Fairfax*
C. Bascom Slemp, *Big Stone Gap*
Henry D. Flood, *Appomattox*

---

[49] Resigned January 4, 1920.
[50] Elected to fill vacancy caused by resignation of J. Hampton Moore, and took his seat December 6, 1920.
[51] Served until Feburary 25, 1921; succeeded by John R. Farr, who contested his election.
[52] Successfully contested the election of Patrick McLane, and took his seat February 25, 1921.
[53] Elected to fill vacancy caused by death of Representative-elect Edward E. Robbins, in preceding Congress, and took his seat May 19, 1919.
[54] Died November 19, 1920, before the commencement of the Sixty-seventh Congress, to which he had been reelected.
[55] Died July 23, 1919.

[56] Elected to fill vacancy caused by death of J. Willard Ragsdale, and took his seat October 30, 1919.
[57] Resigned August 1, 1919.
[58] Elected to fill vacancy caused by resignation of Asbury F. Lever, and took his seat October 21, 1919.
[59] Resigned March 13, 1919, before Congress assembled.
[60] Elected to fill vacancy caused by resignation of James C. Wilson, and took his seat May 19, 1919.
[61] Died November 12, 1919.
[62] Appointed November 18, 1919, to fill vacancy caused by death of Thomas S. Martin, and took his seat February 2, 1920; Secretary of the Treasury during interim; subsequently elected.

[63] Died December 24, 1919.
[64] Elected to fill vacancy caused by death of Walter A. Watson, and took his seat May 10, 1920.
[65] Resigned February 29, 1920, having been elected judge of the circuit court of appeals.
[66] Elected to fill vacancy caused by resignation of Edward W. Saunders, and took his seat December 6, 1920.
[67] Elected to fill vacancy caused by resignation of Representative-elect Carter Glass, in preceding Congress.
[68] Elected to fill vacancy caused by resignation of Representative-elect Charles C. Carlin, in preceding Congress, and took his seat June 3, 1919.

WASHINGTON

SENATORS

Wesley L. Jones, *Seattle*
Miles Poindexter, *Spokane*

REPRESENTATIVES

John F. Miller, *Seattle*
Lindley H. Hadley, *Bellingham*
Albert Johnson, *Hoquiam*
John W. Summers, *Walla Walla*
J. Stanley Webster, *Spokane*

WEST VIRGINIA

SENATORS

Howard Sutherland, *Elkins*
Davis Elkins, *Morgantown*

REPRESENTATIVES

Matthew M. Neely, *Fairmont*
George M. Bowers, *Martinsburg*
Stuart F. Reed, *Clarksburg*
Harry C. Woodyard, *Spencer*
Wells Goodykoontz, *Williamson*
Leonard S. Echols, *Charleston*

WISCONSIN

SENATORS

Robert M. La Follette, *Madison*
Irvine L. Lenroot, *Superior*

REPRESENTATIVES

Clifford E. Randall, *Kenosha*
Edward Voigt, *Sheboygan*
James G. Monahan, *Darlington*
John C. Kleczka, *Milwaukee*
Victor L. Berger,[69] *Milwaukee*
Florian Lampert, *Oshkosh*
John J. Esch, *La Crosse*
Edward E. Browne, *Waupaca*
David G. Classon, *Oconto*
James A. Frear, *Hudson*
Adolphus P. Nelson, *Grantsburg*

WYOMING

SENATORS

Francis E. Warren, *Cheyenne*
John B. Kendrick, *Sheridan*

REPRESENTATIVE

At Large—Frank W. Mondell, *Newcastle*

TERRITORY OF ALASKA

DELEGATE

Charles A. Sulzer,[70] *Sulzer*
George B. Grigsby,[71] *Juneau*
James Wickersham,[72] *Fairbanks*

TERRITORY OF HAWAII

DELEGATE

J. Kuhio Kalanianaole, *Waikiki*

PHILIPPINE ISLANDS

RESIDENT COMMISSIONERS

Jaime C. de Veyra, *Manila*
Teodoro R. Yangco,[73] *Zambales*
Isauro Gabaldon,[74] *Nueva Ecija*

PORTO RICO

RESIDENT COMMISSIONER

Felix Cordova Davila, *San Juan*

---

[69] By resolution of the House adopted November 10, 1919, Victor L. Berger was declared "not entitled to take the oath of office as a Representative, or to hold a seat therein as such"; election unsuccessfully contested by Joseph P. Carney, and seat declared vacant; Victor L. Berger again presented credentials as Representative-elect to fill vacancy occasioned by resolution of November 10, 1919, declaring Mr. Berger not eligible to hold seat; on January 10, 1920, House again declared Victor L. Berger "not entitled to a seat in the Sixty-sixth Congress and declined to permit him to take the oath or qualify as a Representative"; Henry H. Bodenstab unsuccessfully contested the election of Victor L. Berger, who had been declared ineligible, and by resolution of House adopted February 25, 1921, seat was again declared vacant.
[70] Died April 15, 1919, before Congress assembled and pending a contest for the seat.
[71] Presented credentials as a Delegate-elect to fill vacancy caused by the death of Charles A. Sulzer, and took his seat July 1, 1919; served until March 1, 1921 succeeded by James Wickersham, who contested the election of Mr. Sulzer in the first instance, and continued the contest against Mr. Grigsby.
[72] Successfully contested the election of Charles A. Sulzer and George B. Grigsby, and took his seat March 1, 1921.
[73] Term expired March 3, 1920.
[74] Elected for a term of three years beginning March 4, 1920.

SIXTY-SEVENTH CONGRESS

MARCH 4, 1921, TO MARCH 3, 1923

FIRST SESSION—*April 11, 1921, to November 23, 1921* [1]

SECOND SESSION—*December 5, 1921, to September 22, 1922* [2]

THIRD SESSION—*November 20, 1922, to December 4, 1922*

FOURTH SESSION—*December 4, 1922, to March 3, 1923*

SPECIAL SESSION OF THE SENATE—*March 4, 1921, to March 15, 1921*

———

VICE PRESIDENT OF THE UNITED STATES—CALVIN COOLIDGE, of Massachusetts

PRESIDENT PRO TEMPORE OF THE SENATE—ALBERT B. CUMMINS,[3] of Iowa

SECRETARY OF THE SENATE—GEORGE A. SANDERSON,[4] of Illinois

SERGEANT AT ARMS OF THE SENATE—DAVID S. BARRY, of Rhode Island

———

SPEAKER OF THE HOUSE OF REPRESENTATIVES—FREDERICK H. GILLETT,[5] of Massachusetts

CLERK OF THE HOUSE—WILLIAM TYLER PAGE,[6] of Maryland

SERGEANT AT ARMS OF THE HOUSE—JOSEPH G. ROGERS, of Pennsylvania

DOORKEEPER OF THE HOUSE—BERT W. KENNEDY, of Michigan

POSTMASTER OF THE HOUSE—FRANK W. COLLIER

ALABAMA

SENATORS

Oscar W. Underwood, *Birmingham*
J. Thomas Heflin, *Lafayette*

REPRESENTATIVES

John McDuffie, *Monroeville*
John R. Tyson, *Montgomery*
Henry B. Steagall, *Ozark*
Lamar Jeffers,[7] *Anniston*
William B. Bowling, *Lafayette*
William B. Oliver, *Tuscaloosa*
Lilius B. Rainey,[8] *Gadsden*
Edward B. Almon, *Tuscumbia*
George Huddleston, *Birmingham*
William B. Bankhead, *Jasper*

ARIZONA

SENATORS

Henry F. Ashurst, *Prescott*
Ralph H. Cameron, *Phoenix*

REPRESENTATIVE

At Large—Carl Hayden, *Phoenix*

ARKANSAS

SENATORS

Joseph T. Robinson, *Little Rock*
Thaddeus H. Caraway, *Jonesboro*

REPRESENTATIVES

William J. Driver, *Osceola*
William A. Oldfield, *Batesville*
John N. Tillman, *Fayetteville*
Otis Wingo, *De Queen*
Henderson M. Jacoway, *Dardanelle*
Samuel M. Taylor,[9] *Pine Bluff*
Chester W. Taylor,[10] *Pine Bluff*
Tilman B. Parks, *Hope*

CALIFORNIA

SENATORS

Hiram W. Johnson, *San Francisco*
Samuel M. Shortridge, *Menlo Park*

REPRESENTATIVES

Clarence F. Lea, *Santa Rosa*
John E. Raker, *Alturas*
Charles F. Curry, *Sacramento*
Julius Kahn, *San Francisco*
John I. Nolan,[11] *San Francisco*
Mrs. Mae E. Nolan,[12] *San Francisco*
John A. Elston,[13] *Berkeley*
James H. MacLafferty,[14] *Oakland*
Henry E. Barbour, *Fresno*
Arthur M. Free, *San Jose*
Walter F. Lineberger,[15] *Long Beach*
Henry Z. Osborne,[16] *Los Angeles*
Philip D. Swing, *El Centro*

---

[1] In recess from August 24, 1921, until September 21, 1921.
[2] The House of Representatives was in recess from June 30, 1922, until August 15, 1922.
[3] Reelected March 7, 1921.
[4] Reelected March 7, 1921.
[5] Reelected April 11, 1921.
[6] Reelected April 11, 1921.
[7] Elected to fill vacancy caused by death of Fred L. Blackmon, in preceding Congress, and took his seat June 27, 1921.

[8] Election unsuccessfully contested by Charles B. Kennamer.
[9] Died September 13, 1921.
[10] Elected to fill vacancy caused by death of his father, Samuel M. Taylor, and took his seat October 31, 1921.
[11] Died November 18, 1922, before the commencement of the Sixty-eighth Congress, to which he had been reelected.
[12] Elected to fill vacancy caused by death of her husband, John I. Nolan; took her seat February 12, 1923.

[13] Died December 15, 1921.
[14] Elected to fill vacancy caused by death of John A. Elston, and took his seat November 20, 1922.
[15] Elected to fill vacancy caused by death of Representative-elect Charles F. Van de Water (November 20, 1920, before the beginning of the congressional term), and took his seat April 11, 1921.
[16] Died February 8, 1923, before the commencement of the Sixty-eighth Congress, to which he had been reelected.

COLORADO

SENATORS

Lawrence C. Phipps, *Denver*
Samuel D. Nicholson, *Leadville*

REPRESENTATIVES

William N. Vaile, *Denver*
Charles B. Timberlake, *Sterling*
Guy U. Hardy, *Canon City*
Edward T. Taylor, *Glenwood Springs*

CONNECTICUT

SENATORS

Frank B. Brandegee, *New London*
George P. McLean, *Simsbury*

REPRESENTATIVES

E. Hart Fenn, *Wethersfield*
Richard P. Freeman, *New London*
John Q. Tilson, *New Haven*
Schuyler, Merritt, *Stamford*
James P. Glynn, *Winsted*

DELAWARE

SENATORS

Josiah O. Wolcott,[17] *Dover*
T. Coleman du Pont,[18] *Wilmington*
Thomas F. Bayard, Jr.,[19] *Wilmington*
L. Heisler Ball, *Marshallton*

REPRESENTATIVE

At Large—Caleb R. Layton, *Georgetown*

FLORIDA

SENATORS

Duncan U. Fletcher, *Jacksonville*
Park Trammell, *Lakeland*

REPRESENTATIVES

Herbert J. Drane, *Lakeland*
Frank Clark, *Gainesville*
John H. Smithwick, *Pensacola*
William J. Sears, *Kissimmee*

GEORGIA

SENATORS

William J. Harris, *Cedartown*
Thomas E. Watson,[20] *Thomson*
Mrs. Rebecca L. Felton,[21] *Cartersville*
Walter F. George,[22] *Vienna*

REPRESENTATIVES

James W. Overstreet, *Sylvania*
Frank Park, *Sylvester*
Charles R. Crisp, *Americus*
William C. Wright, *Newnan*
William D. Upshaw, *Atlanta*
James W. Wise, *Fayetteville*
Gordon Lee, *Chickamauga*
Charles H. Brand, *Athens*
Thomas M. Bell, *Gainesville*
Carl Vinson, *Milledgeville*
William C. Lankford, *Douglas*
William W. Larsen, *Dublin*

IDAHO

SENATORS

William E. Borah, *Boise*
Frank R. Gooding, *Gooding*

REPRESENTATIVES

Burton L. French, *Moscow*
Addison T. Smith, *Twin Falls*

ILLINOIS

SENATORS

Medill McCormick, *Chicago*
William B. McKinley, *Champaign*

REPRESENTATIVES

Martin B. Madden, *Chicago*
James R. Mann,[23] *Chicago*
Elliott W. Sproul, *Chicago*
John W. Rainey,[24] *Chicago*
Adolph J. Sabath,[25] *Chicago*
John J. Gorman, *Chicago*
M. Alfred Michaelson, *Chicago*
Stanley H. Kunz,[26] *Chicago*
Fred A. Britten, *Chicago*
Carl R. Chindblom, *Chicago*
Ira C. Copley, *Aurora*
Charles E. Fuller, *Belvidere*
John C. McKenzie, *Elizabeth*
William J. Graham, *Aledo*
Edward J. King, *Galesburg*
Clifford Ireland, *Peoria*
Frank H. Funk, *Bloomington*
Joseph G. Cannon, *Danville*
Allen F. Moore, *Monticello*
Guy L. Shaw,[27] *Beardstown*
Loren E. Wheeler, *Springfield*
William A. Rodenberg, *East St. Louis*
Edwin B. Brooks, *Newton*
Thomas S. Williams, *Louisville*
Edward E. Denison, *Marion*

At Large—
Richard Yates, *Springfield*
William E. Mason,[28] *Chicago*
Mrs. Winnifred S. M. Huck,[29] *Chicago*

INDIANA

SENATORS

James E. Watson, *Rushville*
Harry S. New, *Indianapolis*

REPRESENTATIVES

Oscar R. Luhring, *Evansville*
Oscar E. Bland, *Linton*
James W. Dunbar, *New Albany*
John S. Benham, *Benham*
Everett Sanders, *Terre Haute*
Richard N. Elliott, *Connersville*
Merrill Moores, *Indianapolis*
Albert H. Vestal, *Anderson*
Fred S. Purnell, *Attica*
William R. Wood, *La Fayette*
Milton Kraus, *Peru*
Louis W. Fairfield, *Angola*
Andrew J. Hickey, *La Porte*

IOWA

SENATORS

Albert B. Cummins, *Des Moines*
William S. Kenyon,[30] *Fort Dodge*
Charles A. Rawson,[31] *Des Moines*
Smith W. Brookhart,[32] *Washington*

REPRESENTATIVES

William F. Kopp, *Mount Pleasant*
Harry E. Hull, *Williamsburg*
Burton E. Sweet, *Waverly*
Gilbert N. Haugen, *Northwood*
James W. Good,[33] *Cedar Rapids*
Cyrenus Cole,[34] *Cedar Rapids*
C. William Ramseyer, *Bloomfield*
Cassius C. Dowell, *Des Moines*
Horace M. Towner, *Corning*
William R. Green, *Council Bluffs*
Lester J. Dickinson, *Algona*
William D. Boies, *Sheldon*

KANSAS

SENATORS

Charles Curtis, *Topeka*
Arthur Capper, *Topeka*

REPRESENTATIVES

Daniel R. Anthony, Jr., *Leavenworth*
Edward C. Little, *Kansas City*

[17] Resigned July 2, 1921, having been appointed State chancellor.
[18] Appointed to fill vacancy caused by resignation of Josiah O. Wolcott, and took his seat July 26, 1921.
[19] Elected to fill vacancy caused by resignation of Josiah O. Wolcott, and took his seat November 21, 1922.
[20] Died September 26, 1922.
[21] Appointed to fill vacancy caused by death of Thomas E. Watson, and took her seat November 21, 1922.
[22] Elected November 7, 1922, to fill vacancy caused by death of Thomas E. Watson, but did not present his credentials until November 22, 1922 (Mrs. Rebecca L. Felton having qualified on the day preceding), and took his seat the same day.
[23] Died November 30, 1922, before the commencement of the Sixty-eighth Congress, to which he had been reelected.
[24] Election unsuccessfully contested by John Golombiewski.
[25] Election unsuccessfully contested by Jacob Gartenstein.
[26] Election unsuccessfully contested by Dan Parillo.
[27] Election unsuccessfully contested by Henry T. Rainey.
[28] Died June 16, 1921.
[29] Elected to fill vacancy caused by death of her father, William E. Mason, and took her seat November 20, 1922.
[30] Resigned February 24, 1922.
[31] Appointed to fill vacancy caused by resignation of William S. Kenyon, and took his seat February 24, 1922.
[32] Elected to fill vacancy caused by resignation of William S. Kenyon, and took his seat December 2, 1922.
[33] Resigned June 15, 1921.
[34] Elected to fill vacancy caused by resignation of James W. Good, and took his seat July 28, 1921.

Philip P. Campbell, *Pittsburg*
Homer Hoch, *Marion*
James G. Strong, *Blue Rapids*
Hays B. White, *Mankato*
Jasper N. Tincher, *Medicine Lodge*
Richard E. Bird, *Wichita*

KENTUCKY

SENATORS

Augustus O. Stanley, *Henderson*
Richard P. Ernst, *Covington*

REPRESENTATIVES

Alben W. Barkley, *Paducah*
David H. Kincheloe, *Madisonville*
Robert Y. Thomas, Jr., *Central City*
Ben Johnson, *Bardstown*
Charles F. Ogden, *Louisville*
Arthur B. Rouse, *Burlington*
James C. Cantrill, *Georgetown*
Ralph Gilbert, *Shelbyville*
William J. Fields, *Olive Hill*
John W. Langley, *Pikeville*
John M. Robsion, *Barbourville*

LOUISIANA

SENATORS

Joseph E. Ransdell, *Lake Providence*
Edwin S. Broussard, *New Iberia*

REPRESENTATIVES

James O'Connor, *New Orleans*
H. Garland Dupré, *New Orleans*
Whitmell P. Martin, *Thibodaux*
John N. Sandlin, *Minden*
Riley J. Wilson, *Harrisonburg*
George K. Favrot, *Baton Rouge*
Ladislas Lazaro, *Washington*
James B. Aswell, *Natchitoches*

MAINE

SENATORS

Bert M. Fernald, *West Poland*
Frederick Hale, *Portland*

REPRESENTATIVES

Carroll L. Beedy, *Portland*
Wallace H. White, Jr., *Lewiston*
John A. Peters,[35] *Ellsworth*
John E. Nelson,[36] *Augusta*
Ira G. Hersey, *Houlton*

MARYLAND

SENATORS

Joseph I. France, *Port Deposit*
Ovington E. Weller, *Baltimore*

REPRESENTATIVES

T. Alan Goldsborough, *Denton*
Albert A. Blakeney, *Ten Hills*
John Philip Hill, *Baltimore*
J. Charles Linthicum, *Baltimore*
Sydney E. Mudd, *La Plata*
Frederick N. Zihlman, *Cumberland*

MASSACHUSETTS

SENATORS

Henry Cabot Lodge, *Nahant*
David I. Walsh, *Fitchburg*

REPRESENTATIVES

Allen T. Treadway, *Stockbridge*
Frederick H. Gillett, *Springfield*
Calvin D. Paige, *Southbridge*
Samuel E. Winslow, *Worcester*
John Jacob Rogers, *Lowell*
Willfred W. Lufkin,[37] *Essex*
A. Piatt Andrew, Jr.,[38] *Gloucester*
Robert S. Maloney, *Lawrence*
Frederick W. Dallinger, *Cambridge*
Charles L. Underhill, *Somerville*
Peter F. Tague, *Boston*
George H. Tinkham, *Boston*
James A. Gallivan, *Boston*
Robert Luce, *Waltham*
Louis A. Frothingham, *Easton*
William S. Greene, *Fall River*
Joseph Walsh,[39] *New Bedford*
Charles L. Gifford,[40] *Cotuit*

MICHIGAN

SENATORS

Charles E. Townsend, *Jackson*
Truman H. Newberry,[41] *Grosse Pointe Farms*
James Couzens,[42] *Detroit*

REPRESENTATIVES

George P. Codd, *Detroit*
Earl C. Michener, *Adrian*
William H. Frankhouser,[43] *Hillsdale*
John M. C. Smith,[44] *Charlotte*
John C. Ketcham, *Hastings*
Carl E. Mapes, *Grand Rapids*
Patrick H. Kelley, *Lansing*
Louis C. Cramton, *Lapeer*
Joseph W. Fordney, *Saginaw*
James C. McLaughlin, *Muskegon*
Roy O. Woodruff, *Bay City*
Frank D. Scott, *Alpena*
W. Frank James, *Hancock*
Vincent M. Brennan, *Detroit*

MINNESOTA

SENATORS

Knute Nelson, *Alexandria*
Frank B. Kellogg, *St. Paul*

REPRESENTATIVES

Sydney Anderson, *Lanesboro*
Frank Clague, *Redwood Falls*
Charles R. Davis, *St. Peter*
Oscar E. Keller, *St. Paul*
Walter H. Newton, *Minneapolis*
Harold Knutson, *St. Cloud*
Andrew J. Volstead, *Granite Falls*
Oscar J. Larson, *Duluth*
Halvor Steenerson, *Crookston*
Thomas D. Schall, *Excelsior*

MISSISSIPPI

SENATORS

John Sharp Williams, *Yazoo City*
Pat Harrison, *Gulfport*

REPRESENTATIVES

John E. Rankin, *Tupelo*
Bill G. Lowrey, *Blue Mountain*
Benjamin G. Humphreys, *Greenville*
Thomas U. Sisson, *Winona*
Ross A. Collins, *Meridian*
Paul B. Johnson, *Hattiesburg*
Percy E. Quin, *McComb City*
James W. Collier, *Vicksburg*

MISSOURI

SENATORS

James A. Reed, *Kansas City*
Selden P. Spencer, *St. Louis*

REPRESENTATIVES

Frank C. Millspaugh,[45] *Canton*
William W. Rucker, *Keytesville*
Henry F. Lawrence, *Cameron*
Charles L. Faust, *St. Joseph*
Edgar C. Ellis, *Kansas City*
William O. Atkeson, *Butler*
Roscoe C. Patterson, *Springfield*
Sidney C. Roach, *Linn Creek*
Theodore W. Hukriede, *Warrenton*
Cleveland A. Newton, *St. Louis*
Harry B. Hawes,[46] *St. Louis*
Leonidas C. Dyer, *St. Louis*
Marion E. Rhodes, *Potosi*
Edward D. Hays, *Cape Girardeau*
Isaac V. McPherson, *Aurora*
Samuel A. Shelton, *Marshfield*

---

[35] Resigned January 2, 1922.
[36] Elected to fill vacancy caused by resignation of John A. Peters, and took his seat March 27, 1922.
[37] Resigned June 30, 1921, to become collector of the port of Boston.
[38] Elected to fill vacancy caused by resignation of Willfred W. Lufkin, and took his seat October 10, 1921.
[39] Resigned August 2, 1922.

[40] Elected to fill vacancy caused by resignation of Joseph Walsh, and took his seat November 20, 1922.
[41] Election unsuccessfully contested by Henry Ford; resigned November 18, 1922.
[42] Appointed to fill vacancy caused by resignation of Truman H. Newberry, and took his seat December 7, 1922; subsequently elected.

[43] Died May 9, 1921; illness prevented his taking his seat.
[44] Elected to fill vacancy caused by death of William H. Frankhouser, and took his seat July 20, 1921.
[45] Resigned December 5, 1922; vacancy throughout remainder of the Congress.
[46] Election unsuccessfully contested by Bernard P. Bogg.

MONTANA

SENATORS

Henry L. Myers, *Hamilton*
Thomas J. Walsh, *Helena*

REPRESENTATIVES

Washington J. McCormick, *Missoula*
Carl W. Riddick, *Lewistown*

NEBRASKA

SENATORS

Gilbert M. Hitchcock, *Omaha*
George W. Norris, *McCook*

REPRESENTATIVES

C. Frank Reavis,[47] *Falls City*
Roy H. Thorpe,[48] *Lincoln*
Albert W. Jefferis, *Omaha*
Robert E. Evans, *Dakota City*
Melvin O. McLaughlin, *York*
William E. Andrews, *Hastings*
Moses P. Kinkaid,[49] *O'Neill*
Augustin R. Humphrey,[50] *Broken Bow*

NEVADA

SENATORS

Key Pittman, *Tonopah*
Tasker L. Oddie, *Reno*

REPRESENTATIVE

At Large—Samuel S. Arentz, *Simpson*

NEW HAMPSHIRE

SENATORS

George H. Moses, *Concord*
Henry W. Keyes, *Haverhill*

REPRESENTATIVES

Sherman E. Burroughs,[51] *Manchester*
Edward H. Wason, *Nashua*

NEW JERSEY

SENATORS

Joseph S. Frelinghuysen, *Raritan*
Walter E. Edge, *Atlantic City*

REPRESENTATIVES

Francis F. Patterson, Jr., *Camden*
Isaac Bacharach, *Atlantic City*
T. Frank Appleby, *Asbury Park*
Elijah C. Hutchinson, *Trenton*
Ernest R. Ackerman, *Plainfield*
Randolph Perkins, *Woodcliff Lake*
Amos H. Radcliffe, *Paterson*
Herbert W. Taylor, *Newark*

Richard Wayne Parker, *Newark*
Frederick R. Lehlbach, *Newark*
Archibald E. Olpp, *West Hoboken*
Charles F. X. O'Brien, *Jersey City*

NEW MEXICO

SENATORS

Albert B. Fall,[52] *Three Rivers*
Holm O. Bursum,[53] *Socorro*
Andrieus A. Jones, *East Las Vegas*

REPRESENTATIVE

At Large—Nestor Montoya,[54] *Albuquerque*

NEW YORK

SENATORS

James W. Wadsworth, Jr., *Groveland*
William M. Calder, *Brooklyn*

REPRESENTATIVES

Frederick C. Hicks, *Port Washington*
John J. Kindred, *Astoria*
John Kissel, *Brooklyn*
Thomas H. Cullen, *Brooklyn*
Ardolph L. Kline, *Brooklyn*
Warren I. Lee, *Brooklyn*
Michael J. Hogan, *Brooklyn*
Charles G. Bond, *Brooklyn*
Andrew N. Petersen, *Brooklyn*
Lester D. Volk, *Brooklyn*
Daniel J. Riordan, *New York City*
Meyer London, *New York City*
Christopher D. Sullivan, *New York City*
Nathan D. Perlman, *New York City*
Thomas J. Ryan, *New York City*
W. Bourke Cockran,[55] *New York City*
Ogden L. Mills, *New York City*
John F. Carew, *New York City*
Walter M. Chandler, *New York City*
Isaac Siegel, *New York City*
Martin C. Ansorge, *New York City*
Anthony J. Griffin, *New York City*
Albert B. Rossdale, *New York City*
Benjamin L. Fairchild, *Pelham*
James W. Husted, *Peekskill*
Hamilton Fish, Jr., *Garrison*
Charles B. Ward, *Debruce*
Peter G. Ten Eyck, *Albany*
James S. Parker, *Salem*
Frank Crowther, *Schenectady*
Bertrand H. Snell, *Potsdam*
Luther W. Mott, *Oswego*
Homer P. Snyder, *Little Falls*
John D. Clarke, *Fraser*
Walter W. Magee, *Syracuse*
Norman J. Gould, *Seneca Falls*
Alanson B. Houghton,[56] *Corning*

Lewis Henry,[57] *Elmira*
Thomas B. Dunn, *Rochester*
Archie D. Sanders, *Stafford*
S. Wallace Dempsey, *Lockport*
Clarence MacGregor, *Buffalo*
James M. Mead, *Buffalo*
Daniel A. Reed, *Dunkirk*

NORTH CAROLINA

SENATORS

Furnifold McL. Simmons, *New Bern*
Lee S. Overman, *Salisbury*

REPRESENTATIVES

Hallett S. Ward, *Washington*
Claude Kitchin, *Scotland Neck*
Samuel M. Brinson,[58] *New Bern*
Charles L. Abernethy,[59] *New Bern*
Edward W. Pou, *Smithfield*
Charles M. Stedman, *Greensboro*
Homer L. Lyon, *Whiteville*
William C. Hammer, *Asheboro*
Robert L. Doughton,[60] *Laurel Springs*
Alfred L. Bulwinkle, *Gastonia*
Zebulon Weaver, *Asheville*

NORTH DAKOTA

SENATORS

Porter J. McCumber, *Wahpeton*
Edwin F. Ladd, *Fargo*

REPRESENTATIVES

Olger B. Burtness, *Grand Forks*
George M. Young, *Valley City*
James H. Sinclair, *Kenmare*

OHIO

SENATORS

Atlee Pomerene, *Canton*
Frank B. Willis, *Delaware*

REPRESENTATIVES

Nicholas Longworth, *Cincinnati*
Ambrose E. B. Stephens, *North Bend*
Roy G. Fitzgerald, *Dayton*
John L. Cable, *Lima*
Charles J. Thompson, *Defiance*
Charles C. Kearns, *Batavia*
Simeon D. Fess, *Yellow Springs*
R. Clint. Cole, *Findlay*
William W. Chalmers, *Toledo*
Israel M. Foster, *Athens*
Edwin D. Ricketts, *Logan*
John C. Speaks, *Columbus*
James T. Begg, *Sandusky*
Charles L. Knight, *Akron*
C. Ellis Moore, *Cambridge*

Joseph H. Himes, *Canton*
William M. Morgan, *Newark*
B. Frank Murphy, *Steubenville*
John G. Cooper, *Youngstown*
Miner G. Norton, *Cleveland*
Harry C. Gahn, *Cleveland*
Theodore E. Burton, *Cleveland*

OKLAHOMA

SENATORS

Robert L. Owen, *Muskogee*
John W. Harreld, *Oklahoma City*

REPRESENTATIVES

Thomas A. Chandler, *Vinita*
Miss Alice M. Robertson, *Muskogee*
Charles D. Carter, *Ardmore*
Joseph C. Pringey, *Chandler*
Fletcher B. Swank, *Norman*
Lorraine M. Gensman, *Lawton*
James V. McClintic, *Snyder*
Manuel Herrick, *Perry*

OREGON

SENATORS

Charles L. McNary, *Salem*
Robert N. Stanfield, *Portland*

REPRESENTATIVES

Willis C. Hawley, *Salem*
Nicholas J. Sinnott, *The Dalles*
Clinton N. McArthur, *Portland*

PENNSYLVANIA

SENATORS

Boies Penrose,[61] *Philadelphia*
George Wharton Pepper,[62] *Philadelphia*
Philander C. Knox,[63] *Pittsburgh*
William E. Crow,[64] *Uniontown*
David A. Reed,[65] *Pittsburgh*

REPRESENTATIVES

William S. Vare,[66] *Philadelphia*
George S. Graham, *Philadelphia*
Harry C. Ransley, *Philadelphia*
George W. Edmonds, *Philadelphia*
James J. Connolly, *Philadelphia*
George P. Darrow, *Philadelphia*
Thomas S. Butler, *West Chester*
Henry W. Watson, *Langhorne*
William W. Griest, *Lancaster*
Charles R. Connell,[67] *Scranton*
Clarence D. Coughlin, *Wilkes-Barre*
John Reber, *Pottsville*
Fred B. Gernerd, *Allentown*
Louis T. McFadden, *Canton*

Edgar R. Kiess, *Williamsport*
I. Clinton Kline, *Sunbury*
Benjamin K. Focht, *Lewisburg*
Aaron S. Kreider, *Annville*
John M. Rose, *Johnstown*
Edward S. Brooks, *York*
Evan J. Jones, *Bradford*
Adam M. Wyant, *Greensburg*
Samuel A. Kendall, *Meyersdale*
Henry W. Temple, *Washington*
Milton W. Shreve, *Erie*
William H. Kirkpatrick, *Easton*
Nathan L. Strong, *Brookville*
Harris J. Bixler, *Johnsonburg*
Stephen G. Porter, *Pittsburgh*
M. Clyde Kelly, *Edgewood*
John M. Morin, *Pittsburgh*
Guy E. Campbell, *Crafton*
At Large—
  William J. Burke, *Pittsburgh*
  Thomas S. Crago,[68] *Waynesburg*
  Joseph McLaughlin, *Philadelphia*
  Anderson H. Walters, *Johnstown*

RHODE ISLAND

SENATORS

LeBaron B. Colt, *Bristol*
Peter G. Gerry, *Warwick*

REPRESENTATIVES

Clark Burdick, *Newport*
Walter R. Stiness, *Cowesett*
Ambrose Kennedy, *Woonsocket*

SOUTH CAROLINA

SENATORS

Ellison D. Smith, *Lynchburg*
Nathaniel B. Dial, *Laurens*

REPRESENTATIVES

W. Turner Logan, *Charleston*
James F. Byrnes, *Aiken*
Fred H. Dominick, *Newberry*
John J. McSwain, *Greenville*
William F. Stevenson, *Cheraw*
Philip H. Stoll, *Kingstree*
Hampton P. Fulmer, *Norway*

SOUTH DAKOTA

SENATORS

Thomas Sterling, *Vermilion*
Peter Norbeck, *Redfield*

REPRESENTATIVES

Charles A. Christopherson, *Sioux Falls*
Royal C. Johnson, *Aberdeen*
William Williamson, *Oacoma*

TENNESSEE

SENATORS

John K. Shields, *Knoxville*
Kenneth D. McKellar, *Memphis*

REPRESENTATIVES

B. Carroll Reece, *Butler*
J. Will Taylor, *La Follette*
Joseph Brown, *Chattanooga*
Wynne F. Clouse, *Cookeville*
Ewin L. Davis, *Tullahoma*
Joseph W. Byrns, *Nashville*
Lemuel P. Padgett,[69] *Columbia*
Clarence W. Turner,[70] *Waverly*
Lon A. Scott, *Savannah*
Finis J. Garrett, *Dresden*
Hubert F. Fisher, *Memphis*

TEXAS

SENATORS

Charles A. Culberson, *Dallas*
Morris Sheppard, *Texarkana*

REPRESENTATIVES

Eugene Black, *Clarksville*
John C. Box, *Jacksonville*
Morgan G. Sanders, *Canton*
Sam Rayburn, *Bonham*
Hatton W. Sumners, *Dallas*
Rufus Hardy, *Corsicana*
Clay Stone Briggs, *Galveston*
Daniel E. Garrett, *Houston*
Joseph J. Mansfield, *Columbus*
James P. Buchanan, *Brenham*
Tom T. Connally, *Marlin*
Fritz G. Lanham, *Fort Worth*
Lucian W. Parrish,[71] *Henrietta*
Guinn Williams,[72] *Decatur*
Harry M. Wurzbach, *Seguin*
John N. Garner, *Uvalde*
Claude B. Hudspeth, *El Paso*
Thomas L. Blanton, *Abilene*
Marvin Jones, *Amarillo*

UTAH

SENATORS

Reed Smoot, *Provo*
William H. King, *Salt Lake City*

REPRESENTATIVES

Don B. Colton, *Vernal*
Elmer O. Leatherwood, *Salt Lake City*

---

[61] Died December 31, 1921.
[62] Appointed to fill vacancy caused by death of Boies Penrose, and took his seat January 10, 1922; subsequently elected.
[63] Died October 12, 1921.
[64] Appointed to fill vacancy caused by death of Philander C. Knox, and took his seat October 24, 1921; died August 2, 1922.

[65] Appointed to fill vacancy caused by deaths of Philander C. Knox and William E. Crow, and took his seat August 16, 1922; subsequently elected.
[66] Resigned January 2, 1923.
[67] Died September 26, 1922; vacancy throughout remainder of the Congress.
[68] Elected to fill vacancy caused by death of Representative-elect Mahlon M. Garland, in preceding

Congress, and took his seat October 10, 1921. John P. Bracken filed a memorial claiming a seat in the Sixty-seventh Congress.
[69] Died August 2, 1922.
[70] Elected to fill vacancy caused by death of Lemuel P. Padgett, and took his seat November 20, 1922.
[71] Died March 27, 1922.
[72] Elected to fill vacancy caused by death of Lucian W. Parrish, and took his seat May 22, 1922.

VERMONT

SENATORS

William P. Dillingham, *Montpelier*
Carroll S. Page, *Hyde Park*

REPRESENTATIVES

Frank L. Greene, *St. Albans*
Porter H. Dale, *Island Pond*

VIRGINIA

SENATORS

Claude A. Swanson, *Chatham*
Carter Glass, *Lynchburg*

REPRESENTATIVES

Schuyler Otis Bland, *Newport News*
Joseph T. Deal, *Norfolk*
Andrew J. Montague, *Richmond*
Patrick Henry Drewry, *Petersburg*
Rorer A. James,[73] *Danville*
James M. Hooker,[74] *Stuart*
James P. Woods, *Roanoke*
Thomas W. Harrison,[75] *Winchester*
John Paul,[76] *Harrisonburg*
R. Walton Moore, *Fairfax*
C. Bascom Slemp, *Big Stone Gap*
Henry D. Flood,[77] *Appomattox*
Henry St. George Tucker,[78] *Lexington*

WASHINGTON

SENATORS

Wesley L. Jones, *Seattle*
Miles Poindexter, *Spokane*

REPRESENTATIVES

John F. Miller, *Seattle*
Lindley H. Hadley, *Bellingham*
Albert Johnson, *Hoquiam*
John W. Summers, *Walla Walla*
J. Stanley Webster, *Spokane*

WEST VIRGINIA

SENATORS

Howard Sutherland, *Elkins*
Davis Elkins, *Morgantown*

REPRESENTATIVES

Benjamin L. Rosenbloom, *Wheeling*
George M. Bowers, *Martinsburg*
Stuart F. Reed, *Clarksburg*
Harry C. Woodyard, *Spencer*
Wells Goodykoontz, *Williamson*
Leonard S. Echols, *Charleston*

WISCONSIN

SENATORS

Robert M. La Follette, *Madison*
Irvine L. Lenroot, *Superior*

REPRESENTATIVES

Henry Allen Cooper, *Racine*
Edward Voigt, *Sheboygan*
John M. Nelson, *Madison*
John C. Kleczka, *Milwaukee*
William H. Stafford, *Milwaukee*
Florian Lampert, *Oshkosh*
Joseph D. Beck, *Viroqua*
Edward E. Browne, *Waupaca*

David G. Classon, *Oconto*
James A. Frear, *Hudson*
Adolphus P. Nelson, *Grantsburg*

WYOMING

SENATORS

Francis E. Warren, *Cheyenne*
John B. Kendrick, *Sheridan*

REPRESENTATIVE

At Large—Frank W. Mondell,
Newcastle

TERRITORY OF ALASKA

DELEGATE

Dan A. Sutherland, *Juneau*

TERRITORY OF HAWAII

DELEGATE

J. Kuhio Kalanianaole,[79] *Waikiki*
Henry A. Baldwin,[80] *Paia*

PHILIPPINES

RESIDENT COMMISSIONERS

Jaime C. de Veyra, *Manila*
Isauro Gabaldon, *Nueva Ecija*

PORTO RICO

RESIDENT COMMISSIONER

Felix Cordova Davila, *San Juan*

---

[73] Died August 6, 1921.
[74] Elected to fill vacancy caused by death of Rorer A. James, and took his seat November 21, 1921.
[75] Served until December 15, 1922; succeeded by John Paul, who contested his election.
[76] Successfully contested the election of Thomas W. Harrison, and took his seat December 15, 1922.
[77] Died December 8, 1921.
[78] Elected to fill vacancy caused by death of Henry D. Flood, and took his seat March 25, 1922.
[79] Died January 7, 1922.
[80] Elected to fill vacancy caused by death of J. Kuhio Kalanianaole, and took his seat April 18, 1922.

SIXTY-EIGHTH CONGRESS

MARCH 4, 1923, TO MARCH 3, 1925

FIRST SESSION—*December 3, 1923, to June 7, 1924*

SECOND SESSION—*December 1, 1924, to March 3, 1925*

VICE PRESIDENT OF THE UNITED STATES—CALVIN COOLIDGE,[1] of Massachusetts

PRESIDENT PRO TEMPORE OF THE SENATE—ALBERT B. CUMMINS, of Iowa

SECRETARY OF THE SENATE—GEORGE A. SANDERSON,[2] of Illinois

SERGEANT AT ARMS OF THE SENATE—DAVID S. BARRY, of Rhode Island

---

SPEAKER OF THE HOUSE OF REPRESENTATIVES—FREDERICK H. GILLETT,[3] of Massachusetts

CLERK OF THE HOUSE—WILLIAM TYLER PAGE,[4] of Maryland

SERGEANT AT ARMS OF THE HOUSE—JOSEPH G. ROGERS, of Pennsylvania

DOORKEEPER OF THE HOUSE—BERT W. KENNEDY, of Michigan

POSTMASTER OF THE HOUSE—FRANK W. COLLIER

ALABAMA

SENATORS

Oscar W. Underwood, *Birmingham*
J. Thomas Heflin, *Lafayette*

REPRESENTATIVES

John McDuffie, *Monroeville*
John R. Tyson,[5] *Montgomery*
Lister Hill,[6] *Montgomery*
Henry B. Steagall, *Ozark*
Lamar Jeffers, *Anniston*
William B. Bowling, *Lafayette*
William B. Oliver, *Tuscaloosa*
Miles C. Allgood, *Allgood*
Edward B. Almon, *Tuscumbia*
George Huddleston, *Birmingham*
William B. Bankhead, *Jasper*

ARIZONA

SENATORS

Henry F. Ashurst, *Prescott*
Ralph H. Cameron, *Phoenix*

REPRESENTATIVE

At Large—Carl Hayden, *Phoenix*

ARKANSAS

SENATORS

Joseph T. Robinson, *Little Rock*
Thaddeus H. Caraway, *Jonesboro*

REPRESENTATIVES

William J. Driver, *Osceola*
William A. Oldfield, *Batesville*
John N. Tillman, *Fayetteville*
Otis Wingo, *De Queen*
Heartsill Ragon, *Clarksville*
Lewis E. Sawyer,[7] *Hot Springs*
James B. Reed,[8] *Lonoke*
Tilman B. Parks, *Hope*

CALIFORNIA

SENATORS

Hiram W. Johnson, *San Francisco*
Samuel M. Shortridge, *Menlo Park*

REPRESENTATIVES

Clarence F. Lea, *Santa Rosa*
John E. Raker, *Alturas*
Charles F. Curry, *Sacramento*
Julius Kahn,[9] *San Francisco*
Mrs. Mae E. Nolan,[10] *San Francisco*
James H. MacLafferty, *Oakland*
Henry E. Barbour, *Fresno*
Arthur M. Free, *San Jose*
Walter F. Lineberger, *Long Beach*
John D. Fredericks,[11] *Los Angeles*
Philip D. Swing, *El Centro*

COLORADO

SENATORS

Lawrence C. Phipps, *Denver*
Samuel D. Nicholson,[12] *Leadville*
Alva B. Adams,[13] *Pueblo*
Rice W. Means,[14] *Denver*

REPRESENTATIVES

William N. Vaile, *Denver*
Charles B. Timberlake, *Sterling*
Guy U. Hardy, *Canon City*
Edward T. Taylor, *Glenwood Springs*

CONNECTICUT

SENATORS

Frank B. Brandegee,[15] *New London*
Hiram Bingham,[16] *New Haven*
George P. McLean, *Simsbury*

---

[1] Became President upon the death of Warren G. Harding, August 3, 1923.
[2] Reelected December 17, 1923.
[3] Reelected December 3, 1923.
[4] Reelected December 3, 1923.
[5] Died March 27, 1923, before Congress assembled.
[6] Elected to fill vacancy caused by death of John R. Tyson, and took his seat December 5, 1923.
[7] Died May 5, 1923, before Congress assembled.
[8] Elected to fill vacancy caused by death of Lewis E. Sawyer, and took his seat December 5, 1923.
[9] Died December 18, 1924, before the commencement of the Sixty-ninth Congress, to which he had been reelected.
[10] Elected to fill vacancy caused by death of her husband, Representative-elect John I. Nolan, in preceding Congress.
[11] Elected to fill vacancy caused by death of Representative-elect Henry Z. Osborne, in preceding Congress, and took his seat December 5, 1923.
[12] Died March 24, 1923.
[13] Appointed to fill vacancy caused by death of Samuel D. Nicholson, and took his seat December 3, 1923.
[14] Elected to fill vacancy caused by death of Samuel D. Nicholson, and took his seat December 1, 1924.
[15] Died October 14, 1924.
[16] Elected to fill vacancy caused by death of Frank B. Brandegee, and took his seat January 9, 1925. Vacancy from October 15, 1924, to December 17, 1924.

CONNECTICUT—Continued

REPRESENTATIVES

E. Hart Fenn, *Wethersfield*
Richard P. Freeman, *New London*
John Q. Tilson, *New Haven*
Schuyler Merritt, *Stamford*
Patrick B. O'Sullivan, *Derby*

DELAWARE

SENATORS

L. Heisler Ball, *Marshallton*
Thomas F. Bayard, Jr., *Wilmington*

REPRESENTATIVE

At Large—William H. Boyce, *Dover*

FLORIDA

SENATORS

Duncan U. Fletcher, *Jacksonville*
Park Trammell, *Lakeland*

REPRESENTATIVES

Herbert J. Drane, *Lakeland*
Frank Clark, *Gainesville*
John H. Smithwick, *Pensacola*
William J. Sears, *Kissimmee*

GEORGIA

SENATORS

William J. Harris, *Cedartown*
Walter F. George, *Vienna*

REPRESENTATIVES

R. Lee Moore,[17] *Statesboro*
Frank Park, *Sylvester*
Charles R. Crisp, *Americus*
William C. Wright, *Newnan*
William D. Upshaw, *Atlanta*
James W. Wise,[18] *Fayetteville*
Gordon Lee, *Chickamauga*
Charles H. Brand, *Athens*
Thomas M. Bell, *Gainesville*
Carl Vinson, *Milledgeville*
William C. Lankford, *Douglas*
William W. Larsen, *Dublin*

IDAHO

SENATORS

William E. Borah, *Boise*
Frank R. Gooding, *Gooding*

REPRESENTATIVES

Burton L. French, *Moscow*
Addison T. Smith, *Twin Falls*

ILLINOIS

SENATORS

Medill McCormick,[19] *Chicago*
Charles S. Deneen,[20] *Chicago*
William B. McKinley, *Champaign*

REPRESENTATIVES

Martin B. Madden, *Chicago*
Morton D. Hull,[21] *Chicago*
Elliott W. Sproul, *Chicago*
John W. Rainey,[22] *Chicago*
Thomas A. Doyle,[23] *Chicago*
Adolph J. Sabath, *Chicago*
James R. Buckley,[24] *Chicago*
M. Alfred Michaelson, *Chicago*
Stanley H. Kunz, *Chicago*
Fred A. Britten, *Chicago*
Carl R. Chindblom, *Chicago*
Frank R. Reid, *Aurora*
Charles E. Fuller, *Belvidere*
John C. McKenzie, *Elizabeth*
William J. Graham,[25] *Aledo*
Edward J. King, *Galesburg*
William E. Hull, *Peoria*
Frank H. Funk, *Bloomington*
William P. Holaday, *Georgetown*
Allen F. Moore, *Monticello*
Henry T. Rainey, *Carrollton*
J. Earl Major, *Hillsboro*
Edward E. Miller, *East St. Louis*
William W. Arnold, *Robinson*
Thomas S. Williams, *Louisville*
Edward E. Denison, *Marion*
At Large—
   Richard Yates, *Springfield*
   Henry R. Rathbone, *Kenilworth*

INDIANA

SENATORS

James E. Watson, *Rushville*
Samuel M. Ralston, *Indianapolis*

REPRESENTATIVES

William E. Wilson, *Evansville*
Arthur H. Greenwood, *Washington*
Frank Gardner, *Scottsburg*
Harry C. Canfield, *Batesville*
Everett Sanders, *Terre Haute*
Richard N. Elliott, *Connersville*
Merrill Moores, *Indianapolis*
Albert H. Vestal, *Anderson*
Fred S. Purnell, *Attica*
William R. Wood, *La Fayette*
Samuel E. Cook, *Huntington*
Louis W. Fairfield, *Angola*
Andrew J. Hickey, *La Porte*

IOWA

SENATORS

Albert B. Cummins, *Des Moines*
Smith W. Brookhart, *Washington*

REPRESENTATIVES

William F. Kopp, *Mount Pleasant*
Harry E. Hull, *Williamsburg*
Thomas J. B. Robinson, *Hampton*
Gilbert N. Haugen, *Northwood*
Cyrenus Cole, *Cedar Rapids*
C. William Ramseyer, *Bloomfield*
Cassius C. Dowell, *Des Moines*
Horace M. Towner,[26] *Corning*
Hiram K. Evans,[27] *Corydon*
William R. Green, *Council Bluffs*
Lester J. Dickinson, *Algona*
William D. Boies, *Sheldon*

KANSAS

SENATORS

Charles Curtis, *Topeka*
Arthur Capper, *Topeka*

REPRESENTATIVES

Daniel R. Anthony, Jr., *Leavenworth*
Edward C. Little,[28] *Kansas City*
Ulysses S. Guyer,[29] *Kansas City*
William H. Sproul, *Sedan*
Homer Hoch, *Marion*
James G. Strong, *Blue Rapids*
Hays B. White, *Mankato*
Jasper N. Tincher, *Medicine Lodge*
William A. Ayres, *Wichita*

KENTUCKY

SENATORS

Augustus O. Stanley, *Henderson*
Richard P. Ernst, *Covington*

REPRESENTATIVES

Alben W. Barkley, *Paducah*
David H. Kincheloe, *Madisonville*
Robert Y. Thomas, Jr., *Central City*
Ben Johnson, *Bardstown*
Maurice H. Thatcher, *Louisville*
Arthur B. Rouse, *Burlington*
James C. Cantrill,[30] *Georgetown*
Joseph W. Morris,[31] *New Castle*
Ralph Gilbert, *Shelbyville*
William J. Fields,[32] *Olive Hill*
Fred M. Vinson,[33] *Louisa*
John W. Langley, *Pikeville*
John M. Robsion, *Barbourville*

---

[17] Election unsuccessfully contested by Don H. Clark.
[18] Never qualified owing to prolonged illness.
[19] Died February 25, 1925.
[20] Appointed to fill vacancy caused by death of Medill McCormick, and took his seat February 28, 1925.
[21] Elected to fill vacancy caused by death of Representative-elect James R. Mann, in preceding Congress, and took his seat December 5, 1923.

[22] Died May 4, 1923.
[23] Elected to fill vacancy caused by death of John W. Rainey, and took his seat December 5, 1923.
[24] Election unsuccessfully contested by John J. Gorman.
[25] Resigned June 7, 1924; vacancy throughout remainder of the Congress.
[26] Resigned April 1, 1923, before Congress assembled.
[27] Elected to fill vacancy caused by resignation of Horace M. Towner, and took his seat December 5, 1923.

[28] Died June 27, 1924.
[29] Elected to fill vacancy caused by death of Edward C. Little, and took his seat December 1, 1924.
[30] Died September 2, 1923, before Congress assembled.
[31] Elected to fill vacancy caused by death of James C. Cantrill, and took his seat December 5, 1923.
[32] Resigned December 11, 1923.
[33] Elected to fill vacancy caused by resignation of William J. Fields, and took his seat January 31, 1924.

LOUISIANA

SENATORS

Joseph E. Ransdell, *Lake Providence*
Edwin S. Broussard, *New Iberia*

REPRESENTATIVES

James O'Connor, *New Orleans*
H. Garland Dupré,[34] *New Orleans*
J. Zach Spearing,[35] *New Orleans*
Whitmell P. Martin, *Thibodaux*
John N. Sandlin, *Minden*
Riley J. Wilson, *Harrisonburg*
George K. Favrot, *Baton Rouge*
Ladislas Lazaro, *Washington*
James B. Aswell, *Natchitoches*

MAINE

SENATORS

Bert M. Fernald, *West Poland*
Frederick Hale, *Portland*

REPRESENTATIVES

Carroll L. Beedy, *Portland*
Wallace H. White, Jr., *Lewiston*
John E. Nelson, *Augusta*
Ira G. Hersey, *Houlton*

MARYLAND

SENATORS

Ovington E. Weller, *Baltimore*
William Cabell Bruce, *Baltimore*

REPRESENTATIVES

T. Alan Goldsborough, *Denton*
Millard E. Tydings, *Havre de Grace*
John Philip Hill, *Baltimore*
J. Charles Linthicum, *Baltimore*
Sydney E. Mudd,[36] *La Plata*
Stephen W. Gambrill,[37] *Laurel*
Frederick N. Zihlman, *Cumberland*

MASSACHUSETTS

SENATORS

Henry Cabot Lodge,[38] *Nahant*
William M. Butler,[39] *Boston*
David I. Walsh, *Fitchburg*

REPRESENTATIVES

Allen T. Treadway, *Stockbridge*
Frederick H. Gillett, *Springfield*
Calvin D. Paige, *Southbridge*
Samuel E. Winslow, *Worcester*
John Jacob Rogers, *Lowell*
A. Piatt Andrew, Jr., *Gloucester*
William P. Connery, Jr., *Lynn*
Frederick W. Dallinger, *Cambridge*
Charles L. Underhill, *Somerville*

Peter F. Tague, *Boston*
George H. Tinkham, *Boston*
James A. Gallivan, *Boston*
Robert Luce, *Waltham*
Louis A. Frothingham, *Easton*
William S. Greene,[40] *Fall River*
Robert M. Leach,[41] *Taunton*
Charles L. Gifford, *Cotuit*

MICHIGAN

SENATORS

James Couzens, *Detroit*
Woodbridge N. Ferris, *Big Rapids*

REPRESENTATIVES

Robert H. Clancy, *Detroit*
Earl C. Michener, *Adrian*
John M. C. Smith,[42] *Charlotte*
Arthur B. Williams,[43] *Battle Creek*
John C. Ketcham, *Hastings*
Carl E. Mapes, *Grand Rapids*
Grant M. Hudson, *East Lansing*
Louis C. Cramton, *Lapeer*
Bird J. Vincent, *Saginaw*
James C. McLaughlin, *Muskegon*
Roy O. Woodruff, *Bay City*
Frank D. Scott, *Alpena*
W. Frank James, *Hancock*
Clarence J. McLeod, *Detroit*

MINNESOTA

SENATORS

Knute Nelson,[44] *Alexandria*
Magnus Johnson,[45] *Kimball*
Henrik Shipstead, *Minneapolis*

REPRESENTATIVES

Sydney Anderson, *Lanesboro*
Frank Clague, *Redwood Falls*
Charles R. Davis, *St. Peter*
Oscar E. Keller, *St. Paul*
Walter H. Newton, *Minneapolis*
Harold Knutson, *St. Cloud*
O. J. Kvale, *Benson*
Oscar J. Larson, *Duluth*
Knud Wefald, *Hawley*
Thomas D. Schall, *Excelsior*

MISSISSIPPI

SENATORS

Pat Harrison, *Gulfport*
Hubert D. Stephens, *New Albany*

REPRESENTATIVES

John E. Rankin, *Tupelo*
Bill G. Lowrey, *Blue Mountain*
Benjamin G. Humphreys,[46] *Greenville*
William Y. Humphreys,[47] *Greenville*

T. Jeff. Busby, *Houston*
Ross A. Collins, *Meridian*
T. Webber Wilson, *Laurel*
Percy E. Quin, *McComb City*
James W. Collier, *Vicksburg*

MISSOURI

SENATORS

James A. Reed, *Kansas City*
Selden P. Spencer, *St. Louis*

REPRESENTATIVES

Milton A. Romjue, *Macon*
Ralph F. Lozier, *Carrollton*
Jacob L. Milligan, *Richmond*
Charles L. Faust, *St. Joseph*
Henry L. Jost, *Kansas City*
Clement C. Dickinson, *Clinton*
Samuel C. Major, *Fayette*
Sidney C. Roach, *Linn Creek*
Clarence Cannon, *Elsberry*
Cleveland A. Newton, *St. Louis*
Harry B. Hawes, *St. Louis*
Leonidas C. Dyer, *St. Louis*
J. Scott Wolff, *Festus*
James F. Fulbright, *Doniphan*
Joe J. Manlove, *Joplin*
Thomas L. Rubey, *Lebanon*

MONTANA

SENATORS

Thomas J. Walsh, *Helena*
Burton K. Wheeler, *Butte*

REPRESENTATIVES

John M. Evans, *Missoula*
Scott Leavitt, *Great Falls*

NEBRASKA

SENATORS

George W. Norris, *McCook*
Robert B. Howell, *Omaha*

REPRESENTATIVES

John H. Morehead, *Falls City*
Willis G. Sears, *Omaha*
Edgar Howard, *Columbus*
Melvin O. McLaughlin, *York*
Ashton C. Shallenberger, *Alma*
Robert G. Simmons, *Scottsbluff*

NEVADA

SENATORS

Key Pittman, *Tonopah*
Tasker L. Oddie, *Reno*

REPRESENTATIVE

At Large—Charles L. Richards, *Reno*

---

[34] Died February 21, 1924.
[35] Elected to fill vacancy caused by death of H. Garland Dupré, and took his seat May 15, 1924.
[36] Died October 11, 1924.
[37] Elected to fill vacancy caused by death of Sydney E. Mudd, and took his seat December 1, 1924.
[38] Died November 9, 1924.
[39] Appointed to fill vacancy caused by death of

Henry Cabot Lodge, and took his seat December 1, 1924.
[40] Died September 22, 1924.
[41] Elected to fill vacancy caused by death of William S. Greene, and took his seat December 1, 1924.
[42] Died March 30, 1923, before Congress assembled.
[43] Elected to fill vacancy caused by death of John M. C. Smith, and took his seat December 5, 1923.

[44] Died April 28, 1923.
[45] Elected to fill vacancy caused by death of Knute Nelson, and took his seat December 3, 1923.
[46] Died October 16, 1923, before Congress assembled.
[47] Elected to fill vacancy caused by death of his father, Benjamin G. Humphreys, and took his seat December 5, 1923.

NEW HAMPSHIRE

SENATORS

George H. Moses, *Concord*
Henry W. Keyes, *Haverhill*

REPRESENTATIVES

William N. Rogers, *Sanbornville*
Edward H. Wason, *Nashua*

NEW JERSEY

SENATORS

Walter E. Edge, *Atlantic City*
Edward I. Edwards, *Jersey City*

REPRESENTATIVES

Francis F. Patterson, Jr., *Camden*
Isaac Bacharach, *Atlantic City*
Elmer H. Geran, *Matawan*
Charles Browne, *Princeton*
Ernest R. Ackerman, *Plainfield*
Randolph Perkins, *Woodcliff Lake*
George N. Seger, *Passaic*
Frank J. McNulty, *Newark*
Daniel F. Minahan, *Orange*
Frederick R. Lehlbach, *Newark*
John J. Eagan, *Weehawken*
Charles F. X. O'Brien, *Jersey City*

NEW MEXICO

SENATORS

Andrieus A. Jones, *East Las Vegas*
Holm O. Bursum, *Socorro*

REPRESENTATIVE

At Large—John Morrow, *Raton*

NEW YORK

SENATORS

James W. Wadsworth, Jr., *Groveland*
Royal S. Copeland, *New York City*

REPRESENTATIVES

Robert L. Bacon, *Westbury*
John J. Kindred, *Astoria*
George W. Lindsay, *Brooklyn*
Thomas H. Cullen, *Brooklyn*
Loring M. Black, Jr., *Brooklyn*
Charles I. Stengle, *Brooklyn*
John F. Quayle, *Brooklyn*
William E. Cleary, *Brooklyn*
David J. O'Connell, *Brooklyn*
Emanuel Celler, *Brooklyn*
Daniel J. Riordan,[48] *New York City*
Anning S. Prall,[49] *West New Brighton*
Samuel Dickstein, *New York City*
Christopher D. Sullivan, *New York City*

Nathan D. Perlman, *New York City*
John J. Boylan, *New York City*
John J. O'Connor,[50] *New York City*
Ogden L. Mills, *New York City*
John F. Carew, *New York City*
Sol Bloom,[51] *New York City*
Fiorello H. LaGuardia,[52] *New York City*
Royal H. Weller,[53] *New York City*
Anthony J. Griffin, *New York City*
Frank Oliver, *Bronx*
James V. Ganly,[54] *Bronx*
Benjamin L. Fairchild,[55] *Pelham*
J. Mayhew Wainwright, *Rye*
Hamilton Fish, Jr., *Garrison*
Charles B. Ward, *Debruce*
Parker Corning, *Albany*
James S. Parker, *Salem*
Frank Crowther, *Schenectady*
Bertrand H. Snell, *Potsdam*
Luther W. Mott,[56] *Oswego*
Thaddeus C. Sweet,[57] *Phoenix*
Homer P. Snyder, *Little Falls*
John D. Clarke, *Fraser*
Walter W. Magee, *Syracuse*
John Taber, *Auburn*
Gale H. Stalker, *Elmira*
Meyer Jacobstein, *Rochester*
Archie D. Sanders, *Stafford*
S. Wallace Dempsey, *Lockport*
Clarence MacGregor, *Buffalo*
James M. Mead, *Buffalo*
Daniel A. Reed, *Dunkirk*

NORTH CAROLINA

SENATORS

Furnifold McL. Simmons, *New Bern*
Lee S. Overman, *Salisbury*

REPRESENTATIVES

Hallett S. Ward, *Washington*
Claude Kitchin,[58] *Scotland Neck*
John H. Kerr,[59] *Warrenton*
Charles L. Abernethy, *New Bern*
Edward W. Pou, *Smithfield*
Charles M. Stedman, *Greensboro*
Homer L. Lyon, *Whiteville*
William C. Hammer, *Asheboro*
Robert L. Doughton, *Laurel Springs*
Alfred L. Bulwinkle, *Gastonia*
Zebulon Weaver, *Asheville*

NORTH DAKOTA

SENATORS

Edwin F. Ladd, *Fargo*
Lynn J. Frazier, *Hoople*

REPRESENTATIVES

Olger B. Burtness, *Grand Forks*

George M. Young,[60] *Valley City*
Thomas Hall,[61] *Bismarck*
James H. Sinclair, *Kenmare*

OHIO

SENATORS

Frank B. Willis, *Delaware*
Simeon D. Fess, *Yellow Springs*

REPRESENTATIVES

Nicholas Longworth, *Cincinnati*
Ambrose E. B. Stephens, *North Bend*
Roy G. Fitzgerald, *Dayton*
John L. Cable, *Lima*
Charles J. Thompson, *Defiance*
Charles C. Kearns, *Batavia*
Charles Brand, *Urbana*
R. Clint. Cole, *Findlay*
Isaac R. Sherwood, *Toledo*
Israel M. Foster, *Athens*
Mell G. Underwood, *New Lexington*
John C. Speaks, *Columbus*
James T. Begg, *Sandusky*
Martin L. Davey, *Kent*
C. Ellis Moore, *Cambridge*
John McSweeney, *Wooster*
William M. Morgan, *Newark*
B. Frank Murphy, *Steubenville*
John G. Cooper, *Youngstown*
Charles A. Mooney, *Cleveland*
Robert Crosser, *Cleveland*
Theodore E. Burton, *Cleveland*

OKLAHOMA

SENATORS

Robert L. Owen, *Muskogee*
John W. Harreld, *Oklahoma City*

REPRESENTATIVES

Everette B. Howard, *Tulsa*
William W. Hastings, *Tahlequah*
Charles D. Carter, *Ardmore*
Thomas D. McKeown, *Ada*
Fletcher B. Swank, *Norman*
J. W. Elmer Thomas, *Medicine Park*
James V. McClintic, *Snyder*
Milton C. Garber, *Enid*

OREGON

SENATORS

Charles L. McNary, *Salem*
Robert N. Stanfield, *Portland*

REPRESENTATIVES

Willis C. Hawley, *Salem*
Nicholas J. Sinnott, *The Dalles*
Elton Watkins, *Portland*

PENNSYLVANIA

SENATORS

George Wharton Pepper, *Philadelphia*
David A. Reed, *Pittsburgh*

REPRESENTATIVES

William S. Vare, *Philadelphia*
George S. Graham, *Philadelphia*
Harry C. Ransley, *Philadelphia*
George W. Edmonds, *Philadelphia*
James J. Connolly, *Philadelphia*
George A. Welsh, *Philadelphia*
George P. Darrow, *Philadelphia*
Thomas S. Butler, *West Chester*
Henry W. Watson, *Langhorne*
William W. Griest, *Lancaster*
Laurence H. Watres, *Scranton*
John J. Casey, *Wilkes-Barre*
George F. Brumm, *Minersville*
William M. Croll, *Reading*
Louis T. McFadden, *Canton*
Edgar R. Kiess, *Williamsport*
Herbert W. Cummings, *Sunbury*
Edward M. Beers, *Mount Union*
Frank C. Sites, *Harrisburg*
George M. Wertz, *Johnstown*
J. Banks Kurtz, *Altoona*
Samuel F. Glatfelter, *York*
William I. Swoope, *Clearfield*
Samuel A. Kendall, *Meyersdale*
Henry W. Temple, *Washington*
Thomas W. Phillips, Jr., *Butler*
Nathan L. Strong, *Brookville*
Harris J. Bixler, *Johnsonburg*
Milton W. Shreve, *Erie*
Everett Kent, *Bangor*
Adam M. Wyant, *Greensburg*
Stephen G. Porter, *Pittsburgh*
M. Clyde Kelly, *Edgewood*
John M. Morin, *Pittsburgh*
James M. Magee, *Pittsburgh*
Guy E. Campbell, *Crafton*

RHODE ISLAND

SENATORS

LeBaron B. Colt,[62] *Bristol*
Jesse H. Metcalf,[63] *Providence*
Peter G. Gerry, *Warwick*

REPRESENTATIVES

Clark Burdick, *Newport*
Richard S. Aldrich, *Warwick*
Jeremiah E. O'Connell, *Providence*

SOUTH CAROLINA

SENATORS

Ellison D. Smith, *Lynchburg*
Nathaniel B. Dial, *Laurens*

REPRESENTATIVES

W. Turner Logan, *Charleston*
James F. Byrnes, *Aiken*
Fred H. Dominick, *Newberry*
John J. McSwain, *Greenville*
William F. Stevenson, *Cheraw*
Allard H. Gasque, *Florence*
Hampton P. Fulmer, *Norway*

SOUTH DAKOTA

SENATORS

Thomas Sterling, *Vermilion*
Peter Norbeck, *Redfield*

REPRESENTATIVES

Charles A. Christopherson, *Sioux Falls*
Royal C. Johnson, *Aberdeen*
William Williamson, *Oacoma*

TENNESSEE

SENATORS

John K. Shields, *Knoxville*
Kenneth D. McKellar, *Memphis*

REPRESENTATIVES

B. Carroll Reece, *Butler*
J. Will Taylor, *La Follette*
Sam D. McReynolds, *Chattanooga*
Cordell Hull, *Carthage*
Ewin L. Davis, *Tullahoma*
Joseph W. Byrns, *Nashville*
William C. Salmon, *Columbia*
Gordon Browning, *Huntingdon*
Finis J. Garrett, *Dresden*
Hubert F. Fisher, *Memphis*

TEXAS

SENATORS

Morris Sheppard, *Texarkana*
Earle B. Mayfield,[64] *Austin*

REPRESENTATIVES [65]

Eugene Black, *Clarksville*
John C. Box, *Jacksonville*
Morgan G. Sanders, *Canton*
Sam Rayburn, *Bonham*
Hatton W. Sumners, *Dallas*
Luther A. Johnson, *Corsicana*
Clay Stone Briggs, *Galveston*
Daniel E. Garrett, *Houston*
Joseph J. Mansfield, *Columbus*
James P. Buchanan, *Brenham*
Tom T. Connally, *Marlin*
Fritz G. Lanham, *Fort Worth*
Guinn Williams, *Decatur*
Harry M. Wurzbach, *Seguin*

John N. Garner, *Uvalde*
Claude B. Hudspeth, *El Paso*
Thomas L. Blanton, *Abilene*
Marvin Jones, *Amarillo*

UTAH

SENATORS

Reed Smoot, *Provo*
William H. King, *Salt Lake City*

REPRESENTATIVES

Don B. Colton, *Vernal*
Elmer O. Leatherwood, *Salt Lake City*

VERMONT

SENATORS

William P. Dillingham,[66] *Montpelier*
Porter H. Dale,[67] *Island Pond*
Frank L. Greene, *St. Albans*

REPRESENTATIVES

Frederick G. Fleetwood, *Morrisville*
Porter H. Dale,[68] *Island Pond*
Ernest Willard Gibson,[69] *Brattleboro*

VIRGINIA

SENATORS

Claude A. Swanson, *Chatham*
Carter Glass, *Lynchburg*

REPRESENTATIVES

Schuyler Otis Bland, *Newport News*
Joseph T. Deal, *Norfolk*
Andrew J. Montague, *Richmond*
Patrick Henry Drewry, *Petersburg*
James M. Hooker, *Stuart*
Clifton A. Woodrum, *Roanoke*
Thomas W. Harrison, *Winchester*
R. Walton Moore, *Fairfax*
George C. Peery, *Tazewell*
Henry St. George Tucker, *Lexington*

WASHINGTON

SENATORS

Wesley L. Jones, *Seattle*
Clarence C. Dill, *Spokane*

REPRESENTATIVES

John F. Miller, *Seattle*
Lindley H. Hadley, *Bellingham*
Albert Johnson, *Hoquiam*
John W. Summers, *Walla Walla*
J. Stanley Webster,[70] *Spokane*
Samuel B. Hill,[71] *Waterville*

---

[62] Died August 18, 1924.
[63] Elected to fill vacancy caused by the death of LeBaron B. Colt, and took his seat December 1, 1924.
[64] Election unsuccessfully contested by George E. B. Peddy.
[65] E. W. Cole presented credentials and claimed a seat as a Representative at large, based upon the official census of 1920, in accordance with which no reapportionment law had been enacted; House, by resolution adopted June 3, 1924, declared him not entitled to a seat.
[66] Died July 12, 1923.
[67] Elected to fill vacancy caused by death of William P. Dillingham, and took his seat December 3, 1923.
[68] Resigned August 11, 1923, before Congress assembled; subsequently elected Senator.
[69] Elected to fill vacancy caused by resignation of Porter H. Dale, and took his seat December 5, 1923.
[70] Resigned May 8, 1923, before Congress assembled.
[71] Elected to fill vacancy caused by resignation of J. Stanley Webster, and took his seat December 5, 1923.

WEST VIRGINIA

SENATORS

Davis Elkins, *Morgantown*
Matthew M. Neely, *Fairmont*

REPRESENTATIVES

Benjamin L. Rosenbloom, *Wheeling*
Robert E. L. Allen, *Morgantown*
Stuart F. Reed, *Clarksburg*
George W. Johnson, *Parkersburg*
Thomas J. Lilly, *Hinton*
J. Alfred Taylor, *Fayetteville*

WISCONSIN

SENATORS

Robert M. La Follette, *Madison*
Irvine L. Lenroot, *Superior*

REPRESENTATIVES

Henry Allen Cooper, *Racine*
Edward Voigt, *Sheboygan*
John M. Nelson, *Madison*
John C. Schafer, *Milwaukee*
Victor L. Berger, *Milwaukee*
Florian Lampert, *Oshkosh*
Joseph D. Beck, *Viroqua*
Edward E. Browne, *Waupaca*
George J. Schneider, *Appleton*
James A. Frear, *Hudson*
Hubert H. Peavey, *Washburn*

WYOMING

SENATORS

Francis E. Warren, *Cheyenne*
John B. Kendrick, *Sheridan*

REPRESENTATIVE

At Large—Charles E. Winter, *Casper*

TERRITORY OF ALASKA

DELEGATE

Dan A. Sutherland, *Fairbanks*

TERRITORY OF HAWAII

DELEGATE

William P. Jarrett, *Honolulu*

PHILIPPINE ISLANDS

RESIDENT COMMISSIONERS

Isauro Gabaldon, *Nueva Ecija*
Pedro Guevara, *Santa Cruz*

PORTO RICO

RESIDENT COMMISSIONER

Felix Cordova Davila, *San Juan*

SIXTY-NINTH CONGRESS

MARCH 4, 1925, TO MARCH 3, 1927

FIRST SESSION—*December 7, 1925, to July 3, 1926; November 10, 1926* [1]

SECOND SESSION—*December 6, 1926, to March 3, 1927*

SPECIAL SESSION OF THE SENATE—*March 4, 1925, to March 18, 1925*

VICE PRESIDENT OF THE UNITED STATES—CHARLES G. DAWES, of Illinois

PRESIDENT PRO TEMPORE OF THE SENATE—ALBERT B. CUMMINS, of Iowa; GEORGE H. MOSES,[2] of New Hampshire

SECRETARY OF THE SENATE—GEORGE A. SANDERSON,[3] of Illinois; EDWIN P. THAYER,[4] of Indiana

SERGEANT AT ARMS OF THE SENATE—DAVID S. BARRY, of Rhode Island

---

SPEAKER OF THE HOUSE OF REPRESENTATIVES—NICHOLAS LONGWORTH,[5] of Ohio

CLERK OF THE HOUSE—WILLIAM TYLER PAGE,[6] of Maryland

SERGEANT AT ARMS OF THE HOUSE—JOSEPH G. ROGERS, of Pennsylvania

DOORKEEPER OF THE HOUSE—BERT W. KENNEDY, of Michigan

POSTMASTER OF THE HOUSE—FRANK W. COLLIER

ALABAMA

SENATORS

Oscar W. Underwood, *Birmingham*
J. Thomas Heflin, *Lafayette*

REPRESENTATIVES

John McDuffie, *Monroeville*
Lister Hill, *Montgomery*
Henry B. Steagall, *Ozark*
Lamar Jeffers, *Anniston*
William B. Bowling, *Lafayette*
William B. Oliver, *Tuscaloosa*
Miles C. Allgood, *Allgood*
Edward B. Almon, *Tuscumbia*
George Huddleston, *Birmingham*
William B. Bankhead, *Jasper*

ARIZONA

SENATORS

Henry F. Ashurst, *Prescott*
Ralph H. Cameron, *Phoenix*

REPRESENTATIVE

At Large—Carl Hayden, *Phoenix*

ARKANSAS

SENATORS

Joseph T. Robinson, *Little Rock*
Thaddeus H. Caraway, *Jonesboro*

REPRESENTATIVES

William J. Driver, *Osceola*
William A. Oldfield, *Batesville*
John N. Tillman, *Fayetteville*
Otis Wingo, *De Queen*
Heartsill Ragon, *Clarksville*
James B. Reed, *Lonoke*
Tilman B. Parks, *Hope*

CALIFORNIA

SENATORS

Hiram W. Johnson, *San Francisco*
Samuel M. Shortridge, *Menlo Park*

REPRESENTATIVES

Clarence F. Lea, *Santa Rosa*
John E. Raker,[7] *Alturas*
Harry L. Englebright,[8] *Nevada City*
Charles F. Curry, *Sacramento*
Mrs. Florence P. Kahn,[9] *San Francisco*
Lawrence J. Flaherty,[10] *San Francisco*
Richard J. Welch,[11] *San Francisco*
Albert E. Carter, *Oakland*
Henry E. Barbour, *Fresno*
Arthur M. Free, *San Jose*
Walter F. Lineberger, *Long Beach*
John D. Fredericks, *Los Angeles*
Philip D. Swing, *El Centro*

COLORADO

SENATORS

Lawrence C. Phipps, *Denver*
Rice W. Means, *Denver*

REPRESENTATIVES

William N. Vaile, *Denver*
Charles B. Timberlake, *Sterling*
Guy U. Hardy, *Canon City*
Edward T. Taylor, *Glenwood Springs*

---

[1] The Senate met pursuant to adjournment for the purpose of sitting as a court of impeachment in trial of Judge George W. English; adjourned sine die the same day.
[2] Elected March 6, 1925.
[3] Reelected March 6, 1925; died April 24, 1925.
[4] Elected December 7, 1925.

[5] Elected December 7, 1925.
[6] Reelected December 7, 1925.
[7] Owing to illness, oath of office administered at his residence on January 7, 1926; died January 22, 1926.
[8] Elected to fill vacancy caused by death of John E. Raker, and took his seat December 6, 1926.

[9] Elected to fill vacancy caused by death of her husband, Representative-elect Julius Kahn, in preceding Congress, and took her seat December 7, 1925.
[10] Died June 13, 1926.
[11] Elected to fill vacancy caused by death of Lawrence J. Flaherty, and took his seat December 6, 1926.

CONNECTICUT

SENATORS

George P. McLean, *Simsbury*
Hiram Bingham, *New Haven*

REPRESENTATIVES

E. Hart Fenn, *Wethersfield*
Richard P. Freeman, *New London*
John Q. Tilson, *New Haven*
Schuyler Merritt, *Stamford*
James P. Glynn, *Winsted*

DELAWARE

SENATORS

Thomas F. Bayard, Jr., *Wilmington*
T. Coleman du Pont, *Wilmington*

REPRESENTATIVE

At Large—Robert G. Houston, *Georgetown*

FLORIDA

SENATORS

Duncan U. Fletcher, *Jacksonville*
Park Trammell, *Lakeland*

REPRESENTATIVES

Herbert J. Drane, *Lakeland*
Robert A. Green,[12] *Starke*
John H. Smithwick, *Pensacola*
William J. Sears, *Kissimmee*

GEORGIA

SENATORS

William J. Harris, *Cedartown*
Walter F. George, *Vienna*

REPRESENTATIVES

Charles G. Edwards,[13] *Savannah*
Edward E. Cox, *Camilla*
Charles R. Crisp, *Americus*
William C. Wright, *Newnan*
William D. Upshaw, *Atlanta*
Samuel Rutherford, *Forsyth*
Gordon Lee, *Chickamauga*
Charles H. Brand, *Athens*
Thomas M. Bell, *Gainesville*
Carl Vinson, *Milledgeville*
William C. Lankford, *Douglas*
William W. Larsen, *Dublin*

IDAHO

SENATORS

William E. Borah, *Boise*
Frank R. Gooding, *Gooding*

REPRESENTATIVES

Burton L. French, *Moscow*
Addison T. Smith, *Twin Falls*

ILLINOIS

SENATORS

William B. McKinley,[14] *Champaign*
Frank L. Smith,[15] *Dwight*
Charles S. Deneen, *Chicago*

REPRESENTATIVES

Martin B. Madden, *Chicago*
Morton D. Hull, *Chicago*
Elliott W. Sproul, *Chicago*
Thomas A. Doyle, *Chicago*
Adolph J. Sabath, *Chicago*
John J. Gorman, *Chicago*
M. Alfred Michaelson, *Chicago*
Stanley H. Kunz, *Chicago*
Fred A. Britten, *Chicago*
Carl R. Chindblom, *Chicago*
Frank R. Reid, *Aurora*
Charles E. Fuller,[16] *Belvidere*
William R. Johnson, *Freeport*
John C. Allen, *Monmouth*
Edward J. King, *Galesburg*
William E. Hull, *Peoria*
Frank H. Funk, *Bloomington*
William P. Holaday, *Georgetown*
Charles Adkins, *Decatur*
Henry T. Rainey, *Carrollton*
Loren E. Wheeler, *Springfield*
Edward M. Irwin, *Belleville*
William W. Arnold, *Robinson*
Thomas S. Williams, *Louisville*
Edward E. Denison, *Marion*
At Large—
　Richard Yates, *Springfield*
　Henry R. Rathbone, *Kenilworth*

INDIANA

SENATORS

James E. Watson, *Rushville*
Samuel M. Ralston,[17] *Indianapolis*
Arthur R. Robinson,[18] *Indianapolis*

REPRESENTATIVES

Harry E. Rowbottom, *Evansville*
Arthur H. Greenwood, *Washington*
Frank Gardner, *Scottsburg*
Harry C. Canfield, *Batesville*
Noble J. Johnson, *Terre Haute*
Richard N. Elliott, *Connersville*
Ralph E. Updike, *Indianapolis*
Albert H. Vestal, *Anderson*
Fred S. Purnell, *Attica*
William R. Wood, *La Fayette*
Albert R. Hall, *Marion*

David Hogg, *Fort Wayne*
Andrew J. Hickey, *La Porte*

IOWA

SENATORS

Albert B. Cummins,[19] *Des Moines*
David W. Stewart,[20] *Sioux City*
Smith W. Brookhart,[21] *Washington*
Daniel F. Steck,[22] *Ottumwa*

REPRESENTATIVES

William F. Kopp, *Mount Pleasant*
F. Dickinson Letts, *Davenport*
Thomas J. B. Robinson, *Hampton*
Gilbert N. Haugen, *Northwood*
Cyrenus Cole, *Cedar Rapids*
C. William Ramseyer, *Bloomfield*
Cassius C. Dowell, *Des Moines*
Lloyd Thurston, *Osceola*
William R. Green, *Council Bluffs*
Lester J. Dickinson, *Algona*
William D. Boies, *Sheldon*

KANSAS

SENATORS

Charles Curtis, *Topeka*
Arthur Capper, *Topeka*

REPRESENTATIVES

Daniel R. Anthony, Jr., *Leavenworth*
Chauncey B. Little, *Olathe*
William H. Sproul, *Sedan*
Homer Hoch, *Marion*
James G. Strong, *Blue Rapids*
Hays B. White, *Mankato*
Jasper N. Tincher, *Medicine Lodge*
William A. Ayres, *Wichita*

KENTUCKY

SENATORS

Richard P. Ernst, *Covington*
Frederic M. Sackett, *Louisville*

REPRESENTATIVES

Alben W. Barkley, *Paducah*
David H. Kincheloe, *Madisonville*
Robert Y. Thomas, Jr.,[23] *Central City*
John W. Moore,[24] *Morgantown*
Ben Johnson, *Bardstown*
Maurice H. Thatcher, *Louisville*
Arthur B. Rouse, *Burlington*
Virgil M. Chapman, *Paris*
Ralph Gilbert, *Shelbyville*
Fred M. Vinson, *Louisa*
John W. Langley,[25] *Pikeville*
Andrew J. Kirk,[26] *Jenkins*
John M. Robsion, *Barbourville*

[12] Election unsuccessfully contested by H. O. Brown.
[13] Election unsuccessfully contested by Don H. Clark.
[14] Died December 7, 1926.
[15] Credentials as Senator-designate to fill vacancy caused by death of William B. McKinley were presented on January 19, 1927, and were referred to the Committee on Privileges and Elections for report; meanwhile Mr. Smith was not permitted to qualify. No further action was taken.
[16] Died June 25, 1926; vacancy throughout remainder of the Congress.
[17] Died October 14, 1925.
[18] Appointed to fill vacancy caused by death of Samuel M. Ralston, and took his seat December 7, 1925; subsequently elected.
[19] Died July 30, 1926.
[20] Appointed to fill vacancy caused by death of Albert B. Cummins, and took his seat November 10, 1926; subsequently elected.
[21] Served until April 12, 1926; succeeded by Daniel F. Steck, who contested his election.
[22] Successfully contested the election of Smith W. Brookhart, and took his seat April 12, 1926.
[23] Died September 3, 1925, before Congress assembled.
[24] Elected to fill vacancy caused by death of Robert Y. Thomas, Jr., and took his seat December 7, 1925.
[25] Resigned January 11, 1926, never having qualified.
[26] Elected to fill vacancy caused by resignation of John W. Langley, and took his seat February 25, 1926.

LOUISIANA

SENATORS

Joseph E. Ransdell, *Lake Providence*
Edwin S. Broussard, *New Iberia*

REPRESENTATIVES

James O'Connor, *New Orleans*
J. Zach Spearing, *New Orleans*
Whitmell P. Martin, *Thibodaux*
John N. Sandlin, *Minden*
Riley J. Wilson, *Ruston*
Bolivar E. Kemp, *Amite*
Ladislas Lazaro, *Washington*
James B. Aswell, *Natchitoches*

MAINE

SENATORS

Bert M. Fernald,[27] *West Poland*
Arthur R. Gould,[28] *Presque Isle*
Frederick Hale, *Portland*

REPRESENTATIVES

Carroll L. Beedy, *Portland*
Wallace H. White, Jr., *Lewiston*
John E. Nelson, *Augusta*
Ira G. Hersey, *Houlton*

MARYLAND

SENATORS

Ovington E. Weller, *Baltimore*
William Cabell Bruce, *Baltimore*

REPRESENTATIVES

T. Alan Goldsborough, *Denton*
Millard E. Tydings, *Havre de Grace*
John Philip Hill, *Baltimore*
J. Charles Linthicum, *Baltimore*
Stephen W. Gambrill, *Laurel*
Frederick N. Zihlman, *Cumberland*

MASSACHUSETTS

SENATORS

William M. Butler, *Boston*
David I. Walsh,[29] *Fitchburg*
Frederick H. Gillett, *Springfield*

REPRESENTATIVES

Allen T. Treadway, *Stockbridge*
George B. Churchill,[30] *Amherst*
Henry L. Bowles,[31] *Springfield*
Frank H. Foss, *Fitchburg*
George R. Stobbs, *Worcester*
John Jacob Rogers,[32] *Lowell*
Mrs. Edith Nourse Rogers,[33] *Lowell*
A. Piatt Andrew, Jr., *Gloucester*

William P. Connery, Jr., *Lynn*
Harry I. Thayer,[34] *Wakefield*
Frederick W. Dallinger,[35] *Cambridge*
Charles L. Underhill, *Somerville*
John J. Douglass, *Boston*
George H. Tinkham, *Boston*
James A. Gallivan, *Boston*
Robert Luce, *Waltham*
Louis A. Frothingham, *Easton*
Joseph W. Martin, Jr., *North Attleboro*
Charles L. Gifford, *Cotuit*

MICHIGAN

SENATORS

James Couzens, *Detroit*
Woodbridge N. Ferris, *Big Rapids*

REPRESENTATIVES

John B. Sosnowski, *Detroit*
Earl C. Michener, *Adrian*
Arthur B. Williams,[36] *Battle Creek*
Joseph L. Hooper,[37] *Battle Creek*
John C. Ketcham, *Hastings*
Carl E. Mapes, *Grand Rapids*
Grant M. Hudson, *East Lansing*
Louis C. Cramton, *Lapeer*
Bird J. Vincent, *Saginaw*
James C. McLaughlin, *Muskegon*
Roy O. Woodruff, *Bay City*
Frank D. Scott, *Alpena*
W. Frank James, *Hancock*
Clarence J. McLeod, *Detroit*

MINNESOTA

SENATORS

Henrik Shipstead, *Minneapolis*
Thomas D. Schall, *Excelsior*

REPRESENTATIVES

Allen J. Furlow, *Rochester*
Frank Clague, *Redwood Falls*
August H. Andresen, *Red Wing*
Oscar E. Keller, *St. Paul*
Walter H. Newton, *Minneapolis*
Harold Knutson, *St. Cloud*
O. J. Kvale, *Benson*
William L. Carss, *Proctor*
Knud Wefald, *Hawley*
Godfrey G. Goodwin, *Cambridge*

MISSISSIPPI

SENATORS

Pat Harrison, *Gulfport*
Hubert D. Stephens, *New Albany*

REPRESENTATIVES

John E. Rankin, *Tupelo*
Bill G. Lowrey, *Blue Mountain*
William M. Whittington, *Greenwood*
T. Jeff. Busby, *Houston*
Ross A. Collins, *Meridian*
T. Webber Wilson, *Laurel*
Percy E. Quin, *McComb City*
James W. Collier, *Vicksburg*

MISSOURI

SENATORS

James A. Reed, *Kansas City*
Selden P. Spencer,[38] *St. Louis*
George H. Williams,[39] *St. Louis*
Harry B. Hawes,[40] *St. Louis*

REPRESENTATIVES

Milton A. Romjue, *Macon*
Ralph F. Lozier, *Carrollton*
Jacob L. Milligan, *Richmond*
Charles L. Faust, *St. Joseph*
Edgar C. Ellis, *Kansas City*
Clement C. Dickinson, *Clinton*
Samuel C. Major, *Fayette*
William L. Nelson, *Columbia*
Clarence Cannon, *Elsberry*
Cleveland A. Newton, *St. Louis*
Harry B. Hawes,[41] *St. Louis*
John J. Cochran,[42] *St. Louis*
Leonidas C. Dyer, *St. Louis*
Charles E. Kiefner, *Perryville*
Ralph E. Bailey, *Sikeston*
Joe J. Manlove, *Joplin*
Thomas L. Rubey, *Lebanon*

MONTANA

SENATORS

Thomas J. Walsh, *Helena*
Burton K. Wheeler, *Butte*

REPRESENTATIVES

John M. Evans, *Missoula*
Scott Leavitt, *Great Falls*

NEBRASKA

SENATORS

George W. Norris, *McCook*
Robert B. Howell, *Omaha*

REPRESENTATIVES

John H. Morehead, *Falls City*
Willis G. Sears, *Omaha*
Edgar Howard, *Columbus*
Melvin O. McLaughlin, *York*
Ashton C. Shallenberger, *Alma*
Robert G. Simmons, *Scottsbluff*

---

[27] Died August 23, 1926.
[28] Elected to fill vacancy caused by death of Bert M. Fernald, and took his seat December 6, 1926.
[29] Elected to fill vacancy caused by death of Henry Cabot Lodge, in preceding Congress, and took his seat December 6, 1926.
[30] Died July 1, 1925, before Congress assembled.
[31] Elected to fill vacancy caused by death of George B. Churchill, and took his seat December 7, 1925.
[32] Died March 28, 1925, before Congress assembled.

[33] Elected to fill vacancy caused by death of her husband, John Jacob Rogers, and took her seat December 7, 1925.
[34] Died March 10, 1926.
[35] Elected to fill vacancy caused by death of Harry I. Thayer, and took his seat December 6, 1926.
[36] Died May 1, 1925, before Congress assembled.
[37] Elected to fill vacancy caused by death of Arthur B. Williams, and took his seat December 7, 1925.

[38] Died May 16, 1925.
[39] Appointed to fill vacancy caused by death of Selden P. Spencer, and took his seat December 7, 1925.
[40] Elected to fill vacancy caused by death of Selden P. Spencer, and took his seat December 6, 1926.
[41] Resigned October 15, 1926, having been nominated for the Senate.
[42] Elected to fill vacancy caused by resignation of Harry B. Hawes, and took his seat December 6, 1926.

NEVADA

SENATORS

Key Pittman, *Tonopah*
Tasker L. Oddie, *Reno*

REPRESENTATIVE

At Large—Samuel S. Arentz, *Simpson*

NEW HAMPSHIRE

SENATORS

George H. Moses, *Concord*
Henry W. Keyes, *Haverhill*

REPRESENTATIVES

Fletcher Hale, *Laconia*
Edward H. Wason, *Nashua*

NEW JERSEY

SENATORS

Walter E. Edge, *Atlantic City*
Edward I. Edwards, *Jersey City*

REPRESENTATIVES

Francis F. Patterson, Jr., *Camden*
Isaac Bacharach, *Atlantic City*
Stewart H. Appleby,[43] *Asbury Park*
Charles A. Eaton, *North Plainfield*
Ernest R. Ackerman, *Plainfield*
Randolph Perkins, *Woodcliff Lake*
George N. Seger, *Passaic*
Herbert W. Taylor, *Newark*
Franklin W. Fort, *East Orange*
Frederick R. Lehlbach, *Newark*
Oscar L. Auf der Heide, *West New York*
Mrs. Mary T. Norton, *Jersey City*

NEW MEXICO

SENATORS

Andrieus A. Jones, *East Las Vegas*
Sam G. Bratton,[44] *Albuquerque*

REPRESENTATIVE

At Large—John Morrow, *Raton*

NEW YORK

SENATORS

James W. Wadsworth, Jr., *Groveland*
Royal S. Copeland, *New York City*

REPRESENTATIVES

Robert L. Bacon, *Westbury*
John J. Kindred, *Astoria*
George W. Lindsay, *Brooklyn*
Thomas H. Cullen, *Brooklyn*
Loring M. Black, Jr., *Brooklyn*
Andrew L. Somers, *Brooklyn*

John F. Quayle, *Brooklyn*
William E. Cleary, *Brooklyn*
David J. O'Connell, *Brooklyn*
Emanuel Celler, *Brooklyn*
Anning S. Prall, *West New Brighton*
Samuel Dickstein, *New York City*
Christopher D. Sullivan, *New York City*
Nathan D. Perlman,[45] *New York City*
John J. Boylan, *New York City*
John J. O'Connor, *New York City*
Ogden L. Mills, *New York City*
John F. Carew, *New York City*
Sol Bloom, *New York City*
Fiorello H. LaGuardia, *New York City*
Royal H. Weller, *New York City*
Anthony J. Griffin, *New York City*
Frank Oliver, *Bronx*
Benjamin L. Fairchild, *Pelham*
J. Mayhew Wainwright, *Rye*
Hamilton Fish, Jr., *Garrison*
Harcourt J. Pratt, *Highland*
Parker Corning, *Albany*
James S. Parker, *Salem*
Frank Crowther, *Schenectady*
Bertrand H. Snell, *Potsdam*
Thaddeus C. Sweet, *Phoenix*
Frederick M. Davenport, *Clinton*
Harold S. Tolley, *Binghamton*
Walter W. Magee, *Syracuse*
John Taber, *Auburn*
Gale H. Stalker, *Elmira*
Meyer Jacobstein, *Rochester*
Archie D. Sanders, *Stafford*
S. Wallace Dempsey, *Lockport*
Clarence MacGregor, *Buffalo*
James M. Mead, *Buffalo*
Daniel A. Reed, *Dunkirk*

NORTH CAROLINA

SENATORS

Furnifold McL. Simmons, *New Bern*
Lee S. Overman, *Salisbury*

REPRESENTATIVES

Lindsay C. Warren, *Washington*
John H. Kerr, *Warrenton*
Charles L. Abernethy, *New Bern*
Edward W. Pou, *Smithfield*
Charles M. Stedman, *Greensboro*
Homer L. Lyon, *Whiteville*
William C. Hammer, *Asheboro*
Robert L. Doughton, *Laurel Springs*
Alfred L. Bulwinkle, *Gastonia*
Zebulon Weaver, *Asheville*

NORTH DAKOTA

SENATORS

Edwin F. Ladd,[46] *Fargo*
Gerald P. Nye,[47] *Cooperstown*
Lynn J. Frazier, *Hoople*

REPRESENTATIVES

Olger B. Burtness, *Grand Forks*
Thomas Hall, *Bismarck*
James H. Sinclair, *Kenmare*

OHIO

SENATORS

Frank B. Willis, *Delaware*
Simeon D. Fess, *Yellow Springs*

REPRESENTATIVES

Nicholas Longworth, *Cincinnati*
Ambrose E. B. Stephens,[48] *North Bend*
Roy G. Fitzgerald, *Dayton*
William T. Fitzgerald, *Greenville*
Charles J. Thompson, *Defiance*
Charles C. Kearns, *Amelia*
Charles Brand, *Urbana*
Thomas Brooks Fletcher, *Marion*
William W. Chalmers, *Toledo*
Thomas A. Jenkins, *Ironton*
Mell G. Underwood, *New Lexington*
John C. Speaks, *Columbus*
James T. Begg, *Sandusky*
Martin L. Davey, *Kent*
C. Ellis Moore, *Cambridge*
John McSweeney, *Wooster*
William M. Morgan, *Newark*
B. Frank Murphy, *Steubenville*
John G. Cooper, *Youngstown*
Charles A. Mooney, *Cleveland*
Robert Crosser, *Cleveland*
Theodore E. Burton, *Cleveland*

OKLAHOMA

SENATORS

John W. Harreld, *Oklahoma City*
William B. Pine, *Okmulgee*

REPRESENTATIVES

Samuel J. Montgomery, *Bartlesville*
William W. Hastings, *Tahlequah*
Charles D. Carter, *Ardmore*
Thomas D. McKeown, *Ada*
Fletcher B. Swank, *Norman*
J. W. Elmer Thomas, *Medicine Park*
James V. McClintic, *Snyder*
Milton C. Garber, *Enid*

OREGON

SENATORS

Charles L. McNary, *Salem*
Robert N. Stanfield, *Portland*

REPRESENTATIVES

Willis C. Hawley, *Salem*
Nicholas J. Sinnott, *The Dalles*
Maurice E. Crumpacker, *Portland*

---

[43] Elected to fill vacancy caused by death of his father, Representative-elect T. Frank Appleby (December 14, 1924, before the beginning of the congressional term), and took his seat December 7, 1925.
[44] Election unsuccessfully contested by Holm O.
Bursum.
[45] Election unsuccessfully contested by William I. Sirovich.
[46] Died June 22, 1925.
[47] Appointed to fill vacancy caused by death of

Edwin F. Ladd, and took his seat January 12, 1926; subsequently elected.
[48] Died February 12, 1927, before the commencement of the Seventieth Congress, to which he had been reelected.

PENNSYLVANIA

SENATORS

George Wharton Pepper, *Philadelphia*
David A. Reed, *Pittsburgh*

REPRESENTATIVES

William S. Vare, *Philadelphia*
George S. Graham, *Philadelphia*
Harry C. Ransley, *Philadelphia*
Benjamin M. Golder, *Philadelphia*
James J. Connolly, *Philadelphia*
George A. Welsh, *Philadelphia*
George P. Darrow, *Philadelphia*
Thomas S. Butler, *West Chester*
Henry W. Watson, *Langhorne*
William W. Griest, *Lancaster*
Laurence H. Watres, *Scranton*
Edmund N. Carpenter, *Wilkes-Barre*
George F. Brumm, *Minersville*
Charles J. Esterly, *Reading*
Louis T. McFadden, *Canton*
Edgar R. Kiess, *Williamsport*
Frederick W. Magrady, *Mount Carmel*
Edward M. Beers, *Mount Union*
Joshua W. Swartz, *Harrisburg*
Anderson H. Walters,[49] *Johnstown*
J. Banks Kurtz, *Altoona*
Franklin Menges, *York*
William I. Swoope, *Clearfield*
Samuel A. Kendall, *Meyersdale*
Henry W. Temple, *Washington*
Thomas W. Phillips, Jr., *Butler*
Nathan L. Strong, *Brookville*
Harris J. Bixler, *Johnsonburg*
Milton W. Shreve, *Erie*
William R. Coyle, *Bethlehem*
Adam M. Wyant, *Greensburg*
Stephen G. Porter, *Pittsburgh*
M. Clyde Kelly, *Edgewood*
John M. Morin, *Pittsburgh*
James M. Magee, *Pittsburgh*
Guy E. Campbell, *Crafton*

RHODE ISLAND

SENATORS

Peter G. Gerry, *Warwick*
Jesse H. Metcalf, *Providence*

REPRESENTATIVES

Clark Burdick, *Newport*
Richard S. Aldrich, *Warwick*
Jeremiah E. O'Connell, *Providence*

SOUTH CAROLINA

SENATORS

Ellison D. Smith, *Lynchburg*
Coleman L. Blease, *Columbia*

REPRESENTATIVES

Thomas S. McMillan, *Charleston*
Butler B. Hare, *Saluda*

Fred H. Dominick, *Newberry*
John J. McSwain, *Greenville*
William F. Stevenson, *Cheraw*
Allard H. Gasque, *Florence*
Hampton P. Fulmer, *Orangeburg*

SOUTH DAKOTA

SENATORS

Peter Norbeck, *Redfield*
William H. McMaster, *Yankton*

REPRESENTATIVES

Charles A. Christopherson, *Sioux Falls*
Royal C. Johnson, *Aberdeen*
William Williamson, *Custer*

TENNESSEE

SENATORS

Kenneth D. McKellar, *Memphis*
Lawerence D. Tyson, *Knoxville*

REPRESENTATIVES

B. Carroll Reece, *Butler*
J. Will Taylor, *La Follette*
Sam D. McReynolds, *Chattanooga*
Cordell Hull, *Carthage*
Ewin L. Davis, *Tullahoma*
Joseph W. Byrns, *Nashville*
Edward E. Eslick, *Pulaski*
Gordon Browning, *Huntingdon*
Finis J. Garrett, *Dresden*
Hubert F. Fisher, *Memphis*

TEXAS

SENATORS

Morris Sheppard, *Texarkana*
Earle B. Mayfield, *Austin*

REPRESENTATIVES

Eugene Black, *Clarksville*
John C. Box, *Jacksonville*
Morgan G. Sanders, *Canton*
Sam Rayburn, *Bonham*
Hatton W. Sumners, *Dallas*
Luther A. Johnson, *Corsicana*
Clay Stone Briggs, *Galveston*
Daniel E. Garrett, *Houston*
Joseph J. Mansfield, *Columbus*
James P. Buchanan, *Brenham*
Tom T. Connally, *Marlin*
Fritz G. Lanham, *Fort Worth*
Guinn Williams, *Decatur*
Harry M. Wurzbach, *Seguin*
John N. Garner, *Uvalde*
Claude B. Hudspeth, *El Paso*
Thomas L. Blanton, *Abilene*
Marvin Jones, *Amarillo*

UTAH

SENATORS

Reed Smoot, *Provo*
William H. King, *Salt Lake City*

REPRESENTATIVES

Don B. Colton, *Vernal*
Elmer O. Leatherwood, *Salt Lake City*

VERMONT

SENATORS

Frank L. Greene, *St. Albans*
Porter H. Dale, *Island Pond*

REPRESENTATIVES

Elbert S. Brigham, *St. Albans*
Ernest Willard Gibson, *Brattleboro*

VIRGINIA

SENATORS

Claude A. Swanson, *Chatham*
Carter Glass, *Lynchburg*

REPRESENTATIVES

Schuyler Otis Bland, *Newport News*
Joseph T. Deal, *Norfolk*
Andrew J. Montague, *Richmond*
Patrick Henry Drewry, *Petersburg*
Joseph Whitehead, *Chatham*
Clifton A. Woodrum, *Roanoke*
Thomas W. Harrison, *Winchester*
R. Walton Moore, *Fairfax*
George C. Peery, *Tazewell*
Henry St. George Tucker, *Lexington*

WASHINGTON

SENATORS

Wesley L. Jones, *Seattle*
Clarence C. Dill, *Spokane*

REPRESENTATIVES

John F. Miller, *Seattle*
Lindley H. Hadley, *Bellingham*
Albert Johnson, *Hoquiam*
John W. Summers, *Walla Walla*
Samuel B. Hill, *Waterville*

WEST VIRGINIA

SENATORS

Matthew M. Neely, *Fairmont*
Guy D. Goff, *Clarksburg*

REPRESENTATIVES

Carl G. Bachmann, *Wheeling*
Frank L. Bowman, *Morgantown*
John M. Wolverton, *Richwood*
Harry C. Woodyard, *Spencer*
James French Strother, *Welch*
J. Alfred Taylor, *Fayetteville*

---

[49] Election unsuccessfully contested by Warren Worth Bailey.

WISCONSIN

SENATORS

Robert M. La Follette,[50] *Madison*
Robert M. La Follette, Jr.,[51] *Madison*
Irvine L. Lenroot, *Superior*

REPRESENTATIVES

Henry Allen Cooper, *Racine*
Edward Voigt, *Sheboygan*
John M. Nelson, *Madison*
John C. Schafer, *Milwaukee*
Victor L. Berger, *Milwaukee*
Florian Lampert, *Oshkosh*
Joseph D. Beck, *Viroqua*
Edward E. Browne, *Waupaca*
George J. Schneider, *Appleton*

James A. Frear, *Hudson*
Hubert H. Peavey, *Washburn*

WYOMING

SENATORS

Francis E. Warren, *Cheyenne*
John B. Kendrick, *Sheridan*

REPRESENTATIVE

At Large—Charles E. Winter, *Casper*

TERRITORY OF ALASKA

DELEGATE

Dan A. Sutherland, *Juneau*

TERRITORY OF HAWAII

DELEGATE

William P. Jarrett, *Honolulu*

PHILIPPINE ISLANDS

RESIDENT COMMISSIONERS

Isauro Gabaldon, *Nueva Ecija*
Pedro Guevara, *Santa Cruz*

PORTO RICO

RESIDENT COMMISSIONER

Felix Cordova Davila, *San Juan*

---

[50] Died June 18, 1925.
[51] Elected to fill vacancy caused by death of his father, Robert M. La Follette, and took his seat December 7, 1925.

SEVENTIETH CONGRESS

MARCH 4, 1927, TO MARCH 3, 1929

FIRST SESSION—*December 5, 1927, to May 29, 1928*
SECOND SESSION—*December 3, 1928, to March 3, 1929*

———————

VICE PRESIDENT OF THE UNITED STATES—Charles G. Dawes, of Illinois
PRESIDENT PRO TEMPORE OF THE SENATE—George H. Moses,[1] of New Hampshire
SECRETARY OF THE SENATE—Edwin P. Thayer,[2] of Indiana
SERGEANT AT ARMS OF THE SENATE—David S. Barry, of Rhode Island

———————

SPEAKER OF THE HOUSE OF REPRESENTATIVES—Nicholas Longworth,[3] of Ohio
CLERK OF THE HOUSE—William Tyler Page,[4] of Maryland
SERGEANT AT ARMS OF THE HOUSE—Joseph G. Rogers, of Pennsylvania
DOORKEEPER OF THE HOUSE—Bert W. Kennedy, of Michigan
POSTMASTER OF THE HOUSE—Frank W. Collier

ALABAMA

SENATORS

J. Thomas Heflin, *Lafayette*
Hugo L. Black, *Birmingham*

REPRESENTATIVES

John McDuffie, *Monroeville*
Lister Hill, *Montgomery*
Henry B. Steagall, *Ozark*
Lamar Jeffers, *Anniston*
William B. Bowling,[5] *Lafayette*
LaFayette L. Patterson,[6] *Alexander City*
William B. Oliver, *Tuscaloosa*
Miles C. Allgood, *Allgood*
Edward B. Almon, *Tuscumbia*
George Huddleston, *Birmingham*
William B. Bankhead, *Jasper*

ARIZONA

SENATORS

Henry F. Ashurst, *Prescott*
Carl Hayden, *Phoenix*

REPRESENTATIVE

At Large—Lewis W. Douglas, *Phoenix*

ARKANSAS

SENATORS

Joseph T. Robinson, *Little Rock*
Thaddeus H. Caraway, *Jonesboro*

REPRESENTATIVES

William J. Driver, *Osceola*
William A. Oldfield,[7] *Batesville*
Mrs. Pearl Peden Oldfield,[8] *Batesville*
John N. Tillman, *Fayetteville*
Otis Wingo, *De Queen*
Heartsill Ragon, *Clarksville*
James B. Reed, *Lonoke*
Tilman B. Parks, *Camden*

CALIFORNIA

SENATORS

Hiram W. Johnson, *San Francisco*
Samuel M. Shortridge, *Menlo Park*

REPRESENTATIVES

Clarence F. Lea, *Santa Rosa*
Harry L. Englebright, *Nevada City*
Charles F. Curry, *Sacramento*
Mrs. Florence P. Kahn, *San Francisco*

Richard J. Welch, *San Francisco*
Albert E. Carter, *Oakland*
Henry E. Barbour, *Fresno*
Arthur M. Free, *San Jose*
William E. Evans, *Glendale*
Joe Crail, *Los Angeles*
Philip D. Swing, *El Centro*

COLORADO

SENATORS

Lawrence C. Phipps, *Denver*
Charles W. Waterman, *Denver*

REPRESENTATIVES

William N. Vaile,[9] *Denver*
S. Harrison White,[10] *Denver*
Charles B. Timberlake, *Sterling*
Guy U. Hardy, *Canon City*
Edward T. Taylor, *Glenwood Springs*

CONNECTICUT

SENATORS

George P. McLean, *Simsbury*
Hiram Bingham, *New Haven*

---

[1] Reelected December 15, 1927.
[2] Reelected December 15, 1927.
[3] Reelected December 5, 1927.
[4] Reelected December 5, 1927.
[5] Resigned August 16, 1928, having been appointed a justice of the circuit court of the State of Alabama.

[6] Elected to fill vacancy caused by resignation of William B. Bowling, and took his seat December 3, 1928.
[7] Died November 19, 1928, before the commencement of the Seventy-first Congress, to which he had been reelected.

[8] Elected to fill vacancy caused by death of her husband, William A. Oldfield, and took her seat January 11, 1929.
[9] Died July 2, 1927, before Congress assembled.
[10] Elected to fill vacancy caused by death of William N. Vaile, and took his seat December 5, 1927.

CONNECTICUT—Continued

REPRESENTATIVES

E. Hart Fenn, *Wethersfield*
Richard P. Freeman, *New London*
John Q. Tilson, *New Haven*
Schuyler Merritt, *Stamford*
James P. Glynn, *Winsted*

DELAWARE

SENATORS

Thomas F. Bayard, Jr., *Wilmington*
T. Coleman du Pont,[11] *Wilmington*
Daniel O. Hastings,[12] *Wilmington*

REPRESENTATIVE

At Large—Robert G. Houston, *Georgetown*

FLORIDA

SENATORS

Duncan U. Fletcher, *Jacksonville*
Park Trammell, *Lakeland*

REPRESENTATIVES

Herbert J. Drane, *Lakeland*
Robert A. Green, *Starke*
Thomas A. Yon, *Tallahassee*
William J. Sears, *Kissimmee*

GEORGIA

SENATORS

William J. Harris, *Cedartown*
Walter F. George, *Vienna*

REPRESENTATIVES

Charles G. Edwards, *Savannah*
Edward E. Cox, *Camilla*
Charles R. Crisp, *Americus*
William C. Wright, *Newnan*
Leslie J. Steele, *Decatur*
Samuel Rutherford, *Forsyth*
Malcolm C. Tarver, *Dalton*
Charles H. Brand, *Athens*
Thomas M. Bell, *Gainesville*
Carl Vinson, *Milledgeville*
William C. Lankford, *Douglas*
William W. Larsen, *Dublin*

IDAHO

SENATORS

William E. Borah, *Boise*
Frank R. Gooding,[13] *Gooding*
John Thomas,[14] *Gooding*

REPRESENTATIVES

Burton L. French, *Moscow*
Addison T. Smith, *Twin Falls*

ILLINOIS

SENATORS

Charles S. Deneen, *Chicago*
Frank L. Smith,[15] *Dwight*
Otis F. Glenn,[16] *Murphysboro*

REPRESENTATIVES

Martin B. Madden,[17] *Chicago*
Morton D. Hull, *Chicago*
Elliott W. Sproul, *Chicago*
Thomas A. Doyle, *Chicago*
Adolph J. Sabath, *Chicago*
James T. Igoe, *Chicago*
M. Alfred Michaelson, *Chicago*
Stanley H. Kunz, *Chicago*
Fred A. Britten, *Chicago*
Carl R. Chindblom, *Chicago*
Frank R. Reid, *Aurora*
John T. Buckbee, *Rockford*
William R. Johnson, *Freeport*
John C. Allen, *Monmouth*
Edward J. King,[18] *Galesburg*
William E. Hull, *Peoria*
Homer W. Hall, *Bloomington*
William P. Holaday, *Georgetown*
Charles Adkins, *Decatur*
Henry T. Rainey, *Carrollton*
J. Earl Major, *Hillsboro*
Edward M. Irwin, *Belleville*
William W. Arnold, *Robinson*
Thomas S. Williams, *Louisville*
Edward E. Denison, *Marion*
At Large—
    Richard Yates, *Springfield*
    Henry R. Rathbone,[19] *Kenilworth*

INDIANA

SENATORS

James E. Watson, *Rushville*
Arthur R. Robinson, *Indianapolis*

REPRESENTATIVES

Harry E. Rowbottom, *Evansville*
Arthur H. Greenwood, *Washington*
Frank Gardner, *Scottsburg*
Harry C. Canfield, *Batesville*
Nobel J. Johnson, *Terre Haute*
Richard N. Elliott, *Connersville*
Ralph E. Updike, *Indianapolis*
Albert H. Vestal, *Anderson*
Fred S. Purnell, *Attica*
William R. Wood, *La Fayette*
Albert R. Hall, *Marion*
David Hogg, *Fort Wayne*
Andrew J. Hickey, *La Porte*

IOWA

SENATORS

Daniel F. Steck, *Ottumwa*
Smith W. Brookhart, *Washington*

REPRESENTATIVES

William F. Kopp, *Mount Pleasant*
F. Dickinson Letts, *Davenport*
Thomas J. B. Robinson, *Hampton*
Gilbert N. Haugen, *Northwood*
Cyrenus Cole, *Cedar Rapids*
C. William Ramseyer, *Bloomfield*
Cassius C. Dowell, *Des Moines*
Lloyd Thurston, *Osceola*
William R. Green,[20] *Council Bluffs*
Earl W. Vincent,[21] *Guthrie Center*
Lester J. Dickinson, *Algona*
William D. Boies, *Sheldon*

KANSAS

SENATORS

Charles Curtis,[22] *Topeka*
Arthur Capper, *Topeka*

REPRESENTATIVES

Daniel R. Anthony, Jr., *Leavenworth*
Ulysses S. Guyer, *Kansas City*
William H. Sproul, *Sedan*
Homer Hoch, *Marion*
James G. Strong, *Blue Rapids*
Hays B. White,[23] *Mankato*
Clifford R. Hope, *Garden City*
William A. Ayres, *Wichita*

KENTUCKY

SENATORS

Frederic M. Sackett, *Louisville*
Alben W. Barkley, *Paducah*

REPRESENTATIVES

William V. Gregory, *Mayfield*
David H. Kincheloe, *Madisonville*
John W. Moore, *Morgantown*
Henry D. Moorman, *Hardinsburg*
Maurice H. Thatcher, *Louisville*
Orie S. Ware, *Covington*
Virgil M. Chapman, *Paris*
Ralph Gilbert, *Shelbyville*
Fred M. Vinson, *Louisa*
Mrs. Katherine Langley, *Pikeville*
John M. Robsion, *Barbourville*

LOUISIANA

SENATORS

Joseph E. Ransdell, *Lake Providence*
Edwin S. Broussard, *New Iberia*

[11] Resigned December 9, 1928.
[12] Appointed to fill vacancy caused by resignation of T. Coleman du Pont, and took his seat December 13, 1928.
[13] Died June 24, 1928.
[14] Appointed to fill vacancy caused by death of Frank R. Gooding, and took his seat December 3, 1928; subsequently elected.
[15] A Senator-elect whom the Senate refused to seat and who resigned February 9, 1928.
[16] Elected to fill vacancy caused by resignation of Frank L. Smith, and took his seat December 3, 1928.
[17] Died April 27, 1928; vacancy throughout remainder of the Congress.
[18] Died February 17, 1929, before the commencement of the Seventy-first Congress, to which he had been reelected. Vacancy in the Seventieth Congress not filled.
[19] Died July 15, 1928; vacancy throughout remainder of the Congress.
[20] Resigned March 31, 1928, having been appointed a judge of the Court of Claims of the United States.
[21] Elected to fill vacancy caused by resignation of William R. Green, and took his seat December 3, 1928.
[22] Resigned effective March 3, 1929, having been elected Vice President of the United States.
[23] Election unsuccessfully contested by W. H. Clark.

REPRESENTATIVES

James O'Connor, *New Orleans*
J. Zach Spearing, *New Orleans*
Whitmell P. Martin, *Thibodaux*
John N. Sandlin, *Minden*
Riley J. Wilson, *Ruston*
Bolivar E. Kemp, *Amite*
Ladislas Lazaro,[24] *Washington*
René L. DeRouen,[25] *Ville Platte*
James B. Aswell, *Natchitoches*

MAINE

SENATORS

Frederick Hale, *Portland*
Arthur R. Gould, *Presque Isle*

REPRESENTATIVES

Carroll L. Beedy, *Portland*
Wallace H. White, Jr., *Lewiston*
John E. Nelson, *Augusta*
Ira G. Hersey, *Houlton*

MARYLAND

SENATORS

William Cabell Bruce, *Baltimore*
Millard E. Tydings, *Havre de Grace*

REPRESENTATIVES

T. Alan Goldsborough, *Denton*
William P. Cole, Jr., *Towson*
Vincent L. Palmisano, *Baltimore*
J. Charles Linthicum, *Baltimore*
Stephen W. Gambrill, *Laurel*
Frederick N. Zihlman, *Cumberland*

MASSACHUSETTS

SENATORS

Frederick H. Gillett, *Springfield*
David I. Walsh, *Fitchburg*

REPRESENTATIVES

Allen T. Treadway, *Stockbridge*
Henry L. Bowles, *Springfield*
Frank H. Foss, *Fitchburg*
George R. Stobbs, *Worcester*
Mrs. Edith Nourse Rogers, *Lowell*
A. Piatt Andrew, Jr., *Gloucester*
William P. Connery, Jr., *Lynn*
Frederick W. Dallinger, *Cambridge*
Charles L. Underhill, *Somerville*
John J. Douglass, *Boston*
George H. Tinkham, *Boston*
James A. Gallivan,[26] *Boston*
John W. McCormack,[27] *Dorchester*
Robert Luce, *Waltham*
Louis A. Frothingham,[28] *Easton*

Richard B. Wigglesworth,[29] *Milton*
Joseph W. Martin, Jr., *North Attleboro*
Charles L. Gifford, *Cotuit*

MICHIGAN

SENATORS

James Couzens, *Detroit*
Woodbridge N. Ferris,[30] *Big Rapids*
Arthur H. Vandenberg,[31] *Grand Rapids*

REPRESENTATIVES

Robert H. Clancy, *Detroit*
Earl C. Michener, *Adrian*
Joseph L. Hooper, *Battle Creek*
John C. Ketcham, *Hastings*
Carl E. Mapes, *Grand Rapids*
Grant M. Hudson, *East Lansing*
Louis C. Cramton, *Lapeer*
Bird J. Vincent, *Saginaw*
James C. McLaughlin, *Muskegon*
Roy O. Woodruff, *Bay City*
Frank P. Bohn, *Newberry*
W. Frank James, *Hancock*
Clarence J. McLeod, *Detroit*

MINNESOTA

SENATORS

Henrik Shipstead, *Minneapolis*
Thomas D. Schall, *Excelsior*

REPRESENTATIVES

Allen J. Furlow, *Rochester*
Frank Clague, *Redwood Falls*
August H. Andresen, *Red Wing*
Melvin J. Maas, *St. Paul*
Walter H. Newton, *Minneapolis*
Harold Knutson, *St. Cloud*
Ole J. Kvale, *Benson*
William L. Carss, *Proctor*
Conrad G. Selvig, *Crookston*
Godfrey G. Goodwin, *Cambridge*

MISSISSIPPI

SENATORS

Pat Harrison, *Gulfport*
Hubert D. Stephens, *New Albany*

REPRESENTATIVES

John E. Rankin, *Tupelo*
Bill G. Lowrey, *Blue Mountain*
William M. Whittington, *Greenwood*
T. Jeff. Busby, *Houston*
Ross A. Collins, *Meridian*
T. Webber Wilson, *Laurel*
Percy E. Quin, *McComb*
James W. Collier, *Vicksburg*

MISSOURI

SENATORS

James A. Reed, *Kansas City*
Harry B. Hawes, *St. Louis*

REPRESENTATIVES

Milton A. Romjue, *Macon*
Ralph F. Lozier, *Carrollton*
Jacob L. Milligan, *Richmond*
Charles L. Faust,[32] *St. Joseph*
David W. Hopkins,[33] *St. Joseph*
George H. Combs, Jr., *Kansas City*
Clement C. Dickinson, *Clinton*
Samuel C. Major, *Fayette*
William L. Nelson, *Columbia*
Clarence Cannon, *Elsberry*
Henry F. Niedringhaus, *St. Louis*
John J. Cochran, *St. Louis*
Leonidas C. Dyer, *St. Louis*
Clyde Williams, *Hillsboro*
James F. Fulbright, *Doniphan*
Joe J. Manlove, *Joplin*
Thomas L. Rubey,[34] *Lebanon*

MONTANA

SENATORS

Thomas J. Walsh, *Helena*
Burton K. Wheeler, *Butte*

REPRESENTATIVES

John M. Evans, *Missoula*
Scott Leavitt, *Great Falls*

NEBRASKA

SENATORS

George W. Norris, *McCook*
Robert B. Howell, *Omaha*

REPRESENTATIVES

John H. Morehead, *Falls City*
Willis G. Sears, *Omaha*
Edgar Howard, *Columbus*
John N. Norton, *Polk*
Ashton C. Shallenberger, *Alma*
Robert G. Simmons, *Scottsbluff*

NEVADA

SENATORS

Key Pittman, *Tonopah*
Tasker L. Oddie, *Reno*

REPRESENTATIVE

At Large—Samuel S. Arentz, *Simpson*

---

[24] Died March 30, 1927, before Congress assembled.
[25] Elected to fill vacancy caused by death of Ladislas Lazaro, and took his seat December 5, 1927.
[26] Died April 3, 1928.
[27] Elected to fill vacancy caused by death of James A. Gallivan, and took his seat December 3, 1928.
[28] Died August 23, 1928.

[29] Elected to fill vacancy caused by death of Louis A. Frothingham, and took his seat December 3, 1928.
[30] Died March 23, 1928.
[31] Appointed to fill vacancy caused by death of Woodbridge N. Ferris, and took his seat April 5, 1928; subsequently elected.
[32] Died December 17, 1928, before the commence-

ment of the Seventy-first Congress, to which he had been reelected.
[33] Elected to fill vacancy caused by death of Charles L. Faust, and took his seat February 20, 1929.
[34] Died November 2, 1928; vacancy throughout remainder of the Congress.

NEW HAMPSHIRE

SENATORS

George H. Moses, *Concord*
Henry W. Keyes, *Haverhill*

REPRESENTATIVES

Fletcher Hale, *Laconia*
Edward H. Wason, *Nashua*

NEW JERSEY

SENATORS

Walter E. Edge, *Atlantic City*
Edward I. Edwards, *Jersey City*

REPRESENTATIVES

Charles A. Wolverton, *Camden*
Isaac Bacharach, *Atlantic City*
Harold G. Hoffman, *South Amboy*
Charles A. Eaton, *North Plainfield*
Ernest R. Ackerman, *Plainfield*
Randolph Perkins, *Woodcliff Lake*
George N. Seger, *Passaic*
Paul J. Moore, *Newark*
Franklin W. Fort, *East Orange*
Frederick R. Lehlbach, *Newark*
Oscar L. Auf der Heide, *West New York*
Mrs. Mary T. Norton, *Jersey City*

NEW MEXICO

SENATORS

Andrieus A. Jones,[35] *East Las Vegas*
Bronson M. Cutting,[36] *Santa Fe*
Octaviano A. Larrazolo,[37] *Albuquerque*
Sam G. Bratton, *Albuquerque*

REPRESENTATIVE

At Large—John Morrow, *Raton*

NEW YORK

SENATORS

Royal S. Copeland, *New York City*
Robert F. Wagner, *New York City*

REPRESENTATIVES

Robert L. Bacon, *Westbury*
John J. Kindred, *Astoria*
George W. Lindsay, *Brooklyn*
Thomas H. Cullen, *Brooklyn*
Loring M. Black, Jr., *Brooklyn*
Andrew L. Somers, *Brooklyn*
John F. Quayle, *Brooklyn*
Patrick J. Carley, *Brooklyn*
David J. O'Connell, *Brooklyn*
Emanuel Celler, *Brooklyn*
Anning S. Prall, *West New Brighton*

Samuel Dickstein, *New York City*
Christopher D. Sullivan, *New York City*
William I. Sirovich, *New York City*
John J. Boylan, *New York City*
John J. O'Connor, *New York City*
William W. Cohen, *New York City*
John F. Carew, *New York City*
Sol Bloom, *New York City*
Fiorello H. LaGuardia,[38] *New York City*
Royal H. Weller,[39] *New York City*
Anthony J. Griffin, *New York City*
Frank Oliver, *Bronx*
James M. Fitzpatrick, *New York City*
J. Mayhew Wainwright, *Rye*
Hamilton Fish, Jr., *Garrison*
Harcourt J. Pratt, *Highland*
Parker Corning, *Albany*
James S. Parker, *Salem*
Frank Crowther, *Schenectady*
Bertrand H. Snell, *Potsdam*
Thaddeus C. Sweet,[40] *Phoenix*
Francis D. Culkin,[41] *Oswego*
Frederick M. Davenport, *Clinton*
John D. Clarke, *Fraser*
Walter W. Magee,[42] *Syracuse*
Clarence E. Hancock,[43] *Syracuse*
John Taber, *Auburn*
Gale H. Stalker, *Elmira*
Meyer Jacobstein, *Rochester*
Archie D. Sanders, *Stafford*
S. Wallace Dempsey, *Lockport*
Clarence MacGregor,[44] *Buffalo*
James M. Mead, *Buffalo*
Daniel A. Reed, *Dunkirk*

NORTH CAROLINA

SENATORS

Furnifold McL. Simmons, *New Bern*
Lee S. Overman, *Salisbury*

REPRESENTATIVES

Lindsay C. Warren, *Washington*
John H. Kerr, *Warrenton*
Charles L. Abernethy, *New Bern*
Edward W. Pou, *Smithfield*
Charles M. Stedman, *Greensboro*
Homer L. Lyon, *Whiteville*
William C. Hammer, *Asheboro*
Robert L. Doughton, *Laurel Springs*
Alfred L. Bulwinkle, *Gastonia*
Zebulon Weaver, *Asheville*

NORTH DAKOTA

SENATORS

Lynn J. Frazier, *Hoople*
Gerald P. Nye, *Cooperstown*

REPRESENTATIVES

Olger B. Burtness, *Grand Forks*
Thomas Hall, *Bismarck*
James H. Sinclair, *Kenmare*

OHIO

SENATORS

Frank B. Willis,[45] *Delaware*
Cyrus Locher,[46] *Cleveland*
Theodore E. Burton,[47] *Cleveland*
Simeon D. Fess, *Yellow Springs*

REPRESENTATIVES

Nicholas Longworth, *Cincinnati*
Charles Tatgenhorst, Jr.,[48] *Cleves*
Roy G. Fitzgerald, *Dayton*
William T. Fitzgerald, *Greenville*
Charles J. Thompson, *Defiance*
Charles C. Kearns, *Amelia*
Charles Brand, *Urbana*
Thomas Brooks Fletcher, *Marion*
William W. Chalmers, *Toledo*
Thomas A. Jenkins, *Ironton*
Mell G. Underwood, *New Lexington*
John C. Speaks, *Columbus*
James T. Begg, *Sandusky*
Martin L. Davey, *Kent*
C. Ellis Moore, *Cambridge*
John McSweeney, *Wooster*
William M. Morgan, *Newark*
B. Frank Murphy, *Steubenville*
John G. Cooper, *Youngstown*
Charles A. Mooney, *Cleveland*
Robert Crosser, *Cleveland*
Theodore E. Burton,[49] *Cleveland*

OKLAHOMA

SENATORS

William B. Pine, *Okmulgee*
J. W. Elmer Thomas, *Medicine Park*

REPRESENTATIVES

Everette B. Howard, *Tulsa*
William W. Hastings, *Tahlequah*
Wilburn Cartwright, *McAlester*
Thomas D. McKeown, *Ada*
Fletcher B. Swank, *Norman*
Jed Johnson, *Anadarko*
James V. McClintic, *Snyder*
Milton C. Garber, *Enid*

OREGON

SENATORS

Charles L. McNary, *Salem*
Frederick Steiwer, *Portland*

---

[35] Died December 20, 1927.
[36] Appointed to fill vacancy caused by death of Andrieus A. Jones, and took his seat January 4, 1928.
[37] Elected to fill vacancy caused by death of Andrieus A. Jones, and took his seat December 7, 1928.
[38] Election unsuccessfully contested by H. Warren Hubbard.
[39] Died March 1, 1929, before the commencement of the Seventy-first Congress, to which he had been re-elected. Vacancy in the Seventieth Congress not filled.

[40] Died May 1, 1928.
[41] Elected to fill vacancy caused by death of Thaddeus C. Sweet, and took his seat December 3, 1928.
[42] Died May 25, 1927, before Congress assembled.
[43] Elected to fill vacancy caused by death of Walter W. Magee, and took his seat December 5, 1927.
[44] Resigned December 31, 1928, having been appointed a justice to the Supreme Court of the State of New York; vacancy throughout remainder of the Congress.
[45] Died March 30, 1928.

[46] Appointed to fill vacancy caused by death of Frank B. Willis, and took his seat April 16, 1928.
[47] Elected to fill vacancy caused by death of Frank B. Willis, and took his seat December 15, 1928.
[48] Elected to fill vacancy caused by death of Representative-elect Ambrose E. B. Stephens in preceding Congress, and took his seat December 5, 1927.
[49] Resigned December 15, 1928, having been elected to the Senate; vacancy throughout remainder of the Congress.

REPRESENTATIVES

Willis C. Hawley, *Salem*
Nicholas J. Sinnott,[50] *The Dalles*
Robert R. Butler,[51] *The Dalles*
Maurice E. Crumpacker,[52] *Portland*
Franklin F. Korell,[53] *Portland*

PENNSYLVANIA

SENATORS

David A. Reed, *Pittsburgh*
William S. Vare,[54] *Philadelphia*

REPRESENTATIVES

James M. Hazlett,[55] *Philadelphia*
James M. Beck,[56] *Philadelphia*
George S. Graham, *Philadelphia*
Harry C. Ransley, *Philadelphia*
Benjamin M. Golder, *Philadelphia*
James J. Connolly, *Philadelphia*
George A. Welsh, *Philadelphia*
George P. Darrow, *Philadelphia*
Thomas S. Butler,[57] *West Chester*
James Wolfenden,[58] *Upper Darby*
Henry W. Watson, *Langhorne*
William W. Griest, *Lancaster*
Laurence H. Watres, *Scranton*
John J. Casey, *Wilkes-Barre*
Cyrus M. Palmer, *Pottsville*
Robert G. Bushong, *Sinking Spring*
Louis T. McFadden, *Canton*
Edgar R. Kiess, *Williamsport*
Frederick W. Magrady, *Mount Carmel*
Edward M. Beers, *Mount Union*
Isaac H. Doutrich, *Harrisburg*
J. Russell Leech, *Ebensburg*
J. Banks Kurtz, *Altoona*
Franklin Menges, *York*
J. Mitchell Chase, *Clearfield*
Samuel A. Kendall, *Meyersdale*
Henry W. Temple, *Washington*
J. Howard Swick, *Beaver Falls*
Nathan L. Strong, *Brookville*
Thomas C. Cochran, *Mercer*
Milton W. Shreve, *Erie*
Everett Kent, *Bangor*
Adam M. Wyant, *Greensburg*
Stephen G. Porter, *Pittsburgh*
M. Clyde Kelly, *Edgewood*
John M. Morin, *Pittsburgh*
Harry A. Estep, *Pittsburgh*
Guy E. Campbell, *Crafton*

RHODE ISLAND

SENATORS

Peter G. Gerry, *Warwick*
Jesse H. Metcalf, *Providence*

REPRESENTATIVES

Clark Burdick, *Newport*

Richard S. Aldrich, *Warwick*
Louis Monast, *Pawtucket*

SOUTH CAROLINA

SENATORS

Ellison D. Smith, *Lynchburg*
Coleman L. Blease, *Columbia*

REPRESENTATIVES

Thomas S. McMillan, *Charleston*
Butler B. Hare, *Saluda*
Fred H. Dominick, *Newberry*
John J. McSwain, *Greenville*
William F. Stevenson, *Cheraw*
Allard H. Gasque, *Florence*
Hampton P. Fulmer, *Orangeburg*

SOUTH DAKOTA

SENATORS

Peter Norbeck, *Redfield*
William H. McMaster, *Yankton*

REPRESENTATIVES

Charles A. Chistopherson, *Sioux Falls*
Royal C. Johnson, *Aberdeen*
William Williamson, *Rapid City*

TENNESSEE

SENATORS

Kenneth D. McKellar, *Memphis*
Lawrence D. Tyson, *Knoxville*

REPRESENTATIVES

B. Carroll Reece, *Butler*
J. Will Taylor, *La Follette*
Sam D. McReynolds, *Chattanooga*
Cordell Hull, *Carthage*
Ewin L. Davis, *Tullahoma*
Joseph W. Byrns, *Nashville*
Edward E. Eslick, *Pulaski*
Gordon Browning, *Huntingdon*
Finis J. Garrett, *Dresden*
Hubert F. Fisher, *Memphis*

TEXAS

SENATORS

Morris Sheppard, *Texarkana*
Earle B. Mayfield, *Austin*

REPRESENTATIVES

Eugene Black, *Clarksville*
John C. Box, *Jacksonville*
Morgan G. Sanders, *Canton*
Sam Rayburn, *Bonham*
Hatton W. Sumners, *Dallas*
Luther A. Johnson, *Corsicana*
Clay Stone Briggs, *Galveston*
Daniel E. Garrett, *Houston*

Joseph J. Mansfield, *Columbus*
James P. Buchanan, *Brenham*
Tom T. Connally, *Marlin*
Fritz G. Lanham, *Fort Worth*
Guinn Williams, *Decatur*
Harry M. Wurzbach, *Seguin*
John N. Garner, *Uvalde*
Claude B. Hudspeth, *El Paso*
Thomas L. Blanton, *Abilene*
Marvin Jones, *Amarillo*

UTAH

SENATORS

Reed Smoot, *Provo*
William H. King, *Salt Lake City*

REPRESENTATIVES

Don B. Colton, *Vernal*
Elmer O. Leatherwood, *Salt Lake City*

VERMONT

SENATORS

Frank L. Greene, *St. Albans*
Porter H. Dale, *Island Pond*

REPRESENTATIVES

Elbert S. Brigham, *St. Albans*
Ernest Willard Gibson, *Brattleboro*

VIRGINIA

SENATORS

Claude A. Swanson, *Chatham*
Carter Glass, *Lynchburg*

REPRESENTATIVES

Schuyler Otis Bland, *Newport News*
Joseph T. Deal, *Norfolk*
Andrew J. Montague, *Richmond*
Patrick Henry Drewry, *Petersburg*
Joseph Whitehead, *Chatham*
Clifton A. Woodrum, *Roanoke*
Thomas W. Harrison, *Winchester*
R. Walton Moore, *Fairfax*
George C. Peery, *Tazewell*
Henry St. George Tucker, *Lexington*

WASHINGTON

SENATORS

Wesley L. Jones, *Seattle*
Clarence C. Dill, *Spokane*

REPRESENTATIVES

John F. Miller, *Seattle*
Lindley H. Hadley, *Bellingham*
Albert Johnson, *Hoquiam*
John W. Summers, *Walla Walla*
Samuel B. Hill, *Waterville*

---

[50] Resigned May 31, 1928, having been appointed a judge of the Court of Claims of the United States.
[51] Elected to fill vacancy caused by resignation of Nicholas J. Sinnott, and took his seat December 3, 1928.
[52] Died July 24, 1927, before Congress assembled.
[53] Elected to fill vacancy caused by death of Maurice

E. Crumpacker, and took his seat December 5, 1927.
[54] Credentials as Senator-elect were presented and referred to the Committee on Privileges and Elections for report; meanwhile Mr. Vare was not permitted to qualify. No action taken during the session.
[55] Resigned October 20, 1927, before Congress assembled.

[56] Elected to fill vacancy caused by resignation of James M. Hazlett, and took his seat December 5, 1927. Election unsuccessfully contested by House Resolution No. 9.
[57] Died May 26, 1928.
[58] Elected to fill vacancy caused by death of Thomas S. Butler, and took his seat December 3, 1928.

WEST VIRGINIA

SENATORS

Matthew M. Neely, *Fairmont*
Guy D. Goff, *Clarksburg*

REPRESENTATIVES

Carl G. Bachmann, *Wheeling*
Frank L. Bowman, *Morgantown*
William S. O'Brien, *Buckhannon*
James A. Hughes, *Huntington*
James French Strother, *Welch*
Edward T. England,[59] *Charleston*

WISCONSIN

SENATORS

Robert M. La Follette, Jr., *Madison*
John J. Blaine, *Boscobel*

REPRESENTATIVES

Henry Allen Cooper, *Racine*
Charles A. Kading, *Watertown*
John M. Nelson, *Madison*
John C. Schafer, *Milwaukee*
Victor L. Berger, *Milwaukee*
Florian Lampert, *Oshkosh*
Joseph D. Beck, *Viroqua*
Edward E. Browne, *Waupaca*
George J. Schneider, *Appleton*
James A. Frear, *Hudson*
Hubert H. Peavey, *Washburn*

WYOMING

SENATORS

Francis E. Warren, *Cheyenne*
John B. Kendrick, *Sheridan*

REPRESENTATIVE

At Large—Charles E. Winter, *Casper*

TERRITORY OF ALASKA

DELEGATE

Dan A. Sutherland, *Juneau*

TERRITORY OF HAWAII

DELEGATE

Victor S. K. Houston, *Honolulu*

PHILIPPINE ISLANDS

RESIDENT COMMISSIONERS

Isauro Gabaldon,[60] *Nueva Ecija*
Pedro Guevara, *Santa Cruz*

PORTO RICO

RESIDENT COMMISSIONER

Felix Cordova Davila, *San Juan*

---

[59] Election unsuccessfully contested by J. Alfred Taylor.
[60] Resigned July 16, 1928, having been nominated for election to the Philippine House of Representatives; vacancy throughout the remainder of the Congress.

SEVENTY-FIRST CONGRESS

MARCH 4, 1929, TO MARCH 3, 1931

FIRST SESSION—*April 15, 1929, to November 22, 1929*

SECOND SESSION—*December 2, 1929, to July 3, 1930*

THIRD SESSION—*December 1, 1930, to March 3, 1931*

SPECIAL SESSIONS OF THE SENATE—*March 4, 1929, to March 5, 1929; July 7, 1930, to July 21, 1930*

VICE PRESIDENT OF THE UNITED STATES—Charles Curtis, of Kansas

PRESIDENT PRO TEMPORE OF THE SENATE—George H. Moses, of New Hampshire

SECRETARY OF THE SENATE—Edwin P. Thayer, of Indiana

SERGEANT AT ARMS OF THE SENATE—David S. Barry, of Rhode Island

---

SPEAKER OF THE HOUSE OF REPRESENTATIVES—Nicholas Longworth,[1] of Ohio

CLERK OF THE HOUSE—William Tyler Page,[2] of Maryland

SERGEANT AT ARMS OF THE HOUSE—Joseph G. Rogers, of Pennsylvania

DOORKEEPER OF THE HOUSE—Bert W. Kennedy, of Michigan

POSTMASTER OF THE HOUSE—Frank W. Collier

ALABAMA

SENATORS

J. Thomas Heflin, *Lafayette*
Hugo L. Black, *Birmingham*

REPRESENTATIVES

John McDuffie, *Monroeville*
Lister Hill, *Montgomery*
Henry B. Steagall, *Ozark*
Lamar Jeffers, *Anniston*
LaFayette L. Patterson, *Alexander City*
William B. Oliver, *Tuscaloosa*
Miles C. Allgood, *Allgood*
Edward B. Almon, *Tuscumbia*
George Huddleston, *Birmingham*
William B. Bankhead, *Jasper*

ARIZONA

SENATORS

Henry F. Ashurst, *Prescott*
Carl Hayden, *Phoenix*

REPRESENTATIVE

At Large—Lewis W. Douglas, *Phoenix*

ARKANSAS

SENATORS

Joseph T. Robinson, *Little Rock*
Thaddeus H. Caraway, *Jonesboro*

REPRESENTATIVES

William J. Driver, *Osceola*
Mrs. Pearl Peden Oldfield,[3] *Batesville*
Claude A. Fuller, *Eureka Springs*
Otis Wingo,[4] *De Queen*
Mrs. Effiegene (Locke) Wingo,[5] *De Queen*
Heartsill Ragon, *Clarksville*
David D. Glover, *Malvern*
Tilman B. Parks, *Camden*

CALIFORNIA

SENATORS

Hiram W. Johnson, *San Francisco*
Samuel M. Shortridge, *Menlo Park*

REPRESENTATIVES

Clarence F. Lea, *Santa Rosa*
Harry L. Englebright, *Nevada City*
Charles F. Curry,[6] *Sacramento*

Mrs. Florence P. Kahn, *San Francisco*
Richard J. Welch, *San Francisco*
Albert E. Carter, *Oakland*
Henry E. Barbour, *Fresno*
Arthur M. Free, *San Jose*
William E. Evans, *Glendale*
Joe Crail, *Los Angeles*
Philip D. Swing, *El Centro*

COLORADO

SENATORS

Lawrence C. Phipps, *Denver*
Charles W. Waterman, *Denver*

REPRESENTATIVES

William R. Eaton, *Denver*
Charles B. Timberlake, *Sterling*
Guy U. Hardy, *Canon City*
Edward T. Taylor, *Glenwood Springs*

CONNECTICUT

SENATORS

Hiram Bingham, *New Haven*
Frederic C. Walcott, *Norfolk*

---

[1] Reelected April 15, 1929.
[2] Reelected April 15, 1929.
[3] Elected to fill vacancy caused by death of her hus- band, Representative-elect William A. Oldfield, in preceding Congress.
[4] Died October 21, 1930.

[5] Elected to fill vacancy caused by death of her hus- band, Otis Wingo, and took her seat December 1, 1930.
[6] Died October 10, 1930; vacancy throughout remain- der of the Congress.

CONNECTICUT—Continued

REPRESENTATIVES

E. Hart Fenn, *Wethersfield*
Richard P. Freeman, *New London*
John Q. Tilson, *New Haven*
Schuyler Merritt, *Stamford*
James P. Glynn,[7] *Winsted*
Edward W. Goss,[8] *Waterbury*

DELAWARE

SENATORS

Daniel O. Hastings, *Wilmington*
John G. Townsend, Jr., *Selbyville*

REPRESENTATIVE

At Large—Robert G. Houston, *Georgetown*

FLORIDA

SENATORS

Duncan U. Fletcher, *Jacksonville*
Park Trammell, *Lakeland*

REPRESENTATIVES

Herbert J. Drane, *Lakeland*
Robert A. Green, *Starke*
Thomas A. Yon, *Tallahassee*
Mrs. Ruth Bryan Owen,[9] *Miami*

GEORGIA

SENATORS

William J. Harris, *Cedartown*
Walter F. George, *Vienna*

REPRESENTATIVES

Charles G. Edwards, *Savannah*
Edward E. Cox, *Camilla*
Charles R. Crisp, *Americus*
William C. Wright, *Newnan*
Leslie J. Steele,[10] *Decatur*
Robert Ramspeck,[11] *Decatur*
Samuel Rutherford, *Forsyth*
Malcolm C. Tarver, *Dalton*
Charles H. Brand, *Athens*
Thomas M. Bell, *Gainesville*
Carl Vinson, *Milledgeville*
William C. Lankford, *Douglas*
William W. Larsen, *Dublin*

IDAHO

SENATORS

William E. Borah, *Boise*
John Thomas, *Gooding*

REPRESENTATIVES

Burton L. French, *Moscow*
Addison T. Smith, *Twin Falls*

ILLINOIS

SENATORS

Charles S. Deneen, *Chicago*
Otis F. Glenn, *Murphysboro*

REPRESENTATIVES

Oscar De Priest, *Chicago*
Morton D. Hull, *Chicago*
Elliott W. Sproul, *Chicago*
Thomas A. Doyle, *Chicago*
Adolph J. Sabath, *Chicago*
James T. Igoe, *Chicago*
M. Alfred Michaelson, *Chicago*
Stanley H. Kunz, *Chicago*
Fred A. Britten, *Chicago*
Carl R. Chindblom, *Chicago*
Frank R. Reid, *Aurora*
John T. Buckbee, *Rockford*
William R. Johnson, *Freeport*
John C. Allen, *Monmouth*
Burnett M. Chiperfield,[12] *Canton*
William E. Hull, *Peoria*
Homer W. Hall, *Bloomington*
William P. Holaday, *Georgetown*
Charles Adkins, *Decatur*
Henry T. Rainey, *Carrollton*
Frank M. Ramey, *Hillsboro*
Edward M. Irwin, *Belleville*
William W. Arnold, *Robinson*
Thomas S. Williams,[13] *Louisville*
Claude V. Parsons,[14] *Golconda*
Edward E. Denison, *Marion*
At Large—
　Richard Yates, *Springfield*
　Mrs. Ruth Hanna McCormick, *Byron*

INDIANA

SENATORS

James E. Watson, *Rushville*
Arthur R. Robinson, *Indianapolis*

REPRESENTATIVES

Harry E. Rowbottom, *Evansville*
Arthur H. Greenwood, *Washington*
James W. Dunbar, *New Albany*
Harry C. Canfield, *Batesville*
Noble J. Johnson, *Terre Haute*
Richard N. Elliott, *Connersville*
Louis Ludlow,[15] *Indianapolis*
Albert H. Vestal, *Anderson*
Fred S. Purnell, *Attica*
William R. Wood, *La Fayette*

Albert R. Hall, *Marion*
David Hogg, *Fort Wayne*
Andrew J. Hickey, *La Porte*

IOWA

SENATORS

Daniel F. Steck, *Ottumwa*
Smith W. Brookhart, *Washington*

REPRESENTATIVES

William F. Kopp, *Mount Pleasant*
F. Dickinson Letts, *Davenport*
Thomas J. B. Robinson, *Hampton*
Gilbert N. Haugen, *Northwood*
Cyrenus Cole, *Cedar Rapids*
C. William Ramseyer, *Bloomfield*
Cassius C. Dowell, *Des Moines*
Lloyd Thurston, *Osceola*
Charles E. Swanson, *Council Bluffs*
Lester J. Dickinson, *Algona*
Ed H. Campbell, *Battle Creek*

KANSAS

SENATORS

Arthur Capper, *Topeka*
Henry J. Allen,[16] *Wichita*
George McGill,[17] *Wichita*

REPRESENTATIVES

William P. Lambertson, *Fairview*
Ulysses S. Guyer, *Kansas City*
William H. Sproul, *Sedan*
Homer Hoch, *Marion*
James G. Strong, *Blue Rapids*
Charles I. Sparks, *Goodland*
Clifford R. Hope, *Garden City*
William A. Ayres, *Wichita*

KENTUCKY

SENATORS

Frederic M. Sackett,[18] *Louisville*
John M. Robsion,[19] *Barbourville*
Ben M. Williamson,[20] *Ashland*
Alben W. Barkley, *Paducah*

REPRESENTATIVES

William V. Gregory, *Mayfield*
David H. Kincheloe,[21] *Madisonville*
John L. Dorsey, Jr.,[22] *Henderson*
Charles W. Roark,[23] *Greenville*
John W. Moore,[24] *Morgantown*
John D. Craddock, *Munfordville*
Maurice H. Thatcher, *Louisville*
J. Lincoln Newhall, *Covington*
Robert E. Lee Blackburn, *Lexington*
Lewis L. Walker, *Lancaster*

---

[7] Died March 6, 1930.
[8] Elected to fill vacancy caused by death of James P. Glynn, and took his seat December 1, 1930.
[9] Election unsuccessfully contested by William C. Lawson.
[10] Died July 24, 1929.
[11] Elected to fill vacancy caused by death of Leslie J. Steele, and took his seat November 11, 1929.
[12] Elected to fill vacancy caused by death of Representative-elect Edward J. King, in preceding Congress, and took his seat December 1, 1930.
[13] Resigned November 11, 1929, having been appointed a judge for the Court of Claims of the United States.

[14] Elected to fill vacancy caused by the resignation of Thomas S. Williams, and took his seat December 1, 1930.
[15] Election unsuccessfully contested by Ralph E. Updike.
[16] Appointed to fill vacancy caused by resignation of Charles Curtis, in preceding Congress, and took his seat April 15, 1929.
[17] Elected to fill vacancy caused by resignation of Charles Curtis, in preceding Congress, and took his seat December 1, 1930.
[18] Resigned January 9, 1930, having been appointed ambassador to Germany.

[19] Appointed to fill vacancy caused by resignation of Frederic M. Sackett, and took his seat January 11, 1930.
[20] Elected to fill vacancy caused by resignation of Frederic M. Sackett, and took his seat December 1, 1930.
[21] Resigned October 5, 1930, having been appointed a judge for the United States Customs Court.
[22] Elected to fill vacancy caused by resignation of David H. Kincheloe, and took his seat December 1, 1930.
[23] Died April 5, 1929, before Congress assembled.
[24] Elected to fill vacancy caused by death of Charles W. Roark, and took his seat June 19, 1929.

Elva R. Kendall, *Carlisle*
Mrs. Katherine Langley, *Pikeville*
John M. Robsion,[25] *Barbourville*
Charles Finley,[26] *Williamsburg*

LOUISIANA

SENATORS

Joseph E. Ransdell, *Lake Providence*
Edwin S. Broussard, *New Iberia*

REPRESENTATIVES

James O'Connor, *New Orleans*
J. Zach Spearing, *New Orleans*
Whitmell P. Martin,[27] *Thibodaux*
Numa F. Montet,[28] *Thibodaux*
John N. Sandlin, *Minden*
Riley J. Wilson, *Ruston*
Bolivar E. Kemp, *Amite*
René L. DeRouen, *Ville Platte*
James B. Aswell, *Natchitoches*

MAINE

SENATORS

Frederick Hale, *Portland*
Arthur R. Gould, *Presque Isle*

REPRESENTATIVES

Carroll L. Beedy, *Portland*
Wallace H. White, Jr., *Lewiston*
John E. Nelson, *Augusta*
Donald F. Snow, *Bangor*

MARYLAND

SENATORS

Millard E. Tydings, *Havre de Grace*
Phillips Lee Goldsborough, *Baltimore*

REPRESENTATIVES

T. Alan Goldsborough, *Denton*
Linwood L. Clark, *Baltimore*
Vincent L. Palmisano,[29] *Baltimore*
J. Charles Linthicum, *Baltimore*
Stephen W. Gambrill, *Laurel*
Frederick N. Zihlman, *Cumberland*

MASSACHUSETTS

SENATORS

Frederick H. Gillett, *Springfield*
David I. Walsh, *Fitchburg*

REPRESENTATIVES

Allen T. Tredway, *Stockbridge*
William Kirk Kaynor,[30] *Springfield*
William J. Granfield,[31] *Longmeadow*
Frank H. Foss, *Fitchburg*

George R. Stobbs, *Worcester*
Mrs. Edith Nourse Rogers, *Lowell*
A. Piatt Andrew, Jr., *Gloucester*
William P. Connery, Jr., *Lynn*
Frederick W. Dallinger, *Cambridge*
Charles L. Underhill, *Somerville*
John J. Douglass, *Boston*
George H. Tinkham, *Boston*
John W. McCormack, *Dorchester*
Robert Luce, *Waltham*
Richard B. Wigglesworth, *Milton*
Joseph W. Martin, Jr., *North Attleboro*
Charles L. Gifford, *Cotuit*

MICHIGAN

SENATORS

James Couzens, *Detroit*
Arthur H. Vandenberg, *Grand Rapids*

REPRESENTATIVES

Robert H. Clancy, *Detroit*
Earl C. Michener, *Adrian*
Joseph L. Hooper, *Battle Creek*
John C. Ketcham, *Hastings*
Carl E. Mapes, *Grand Rapids*
Grant M. Hudson, *East Lansing*
Louis C. Cramton, *Lapeer*
Bird J. Vincent, *Saginaw*
James C. McLaughlin, *Muskegon*
Roy O. Woodruff, *Bay City*
Frank P. Bohn, *Newberry*
W. Frank James, *Hancock*
Clarence J. McLeod, *Detroit*

MINNESOTA

SENATORS

Henrik Shipstead, *Minneapolis*
Thomas D. Schall, *Excelsior*

REPRESENTATIVES

Victor Christgau, *Austin*
Frank Clague, *Redwood Falls*
August H. Andresen, *Red Wing*
Melvin J. Maas, *St. Paul*
Walter H. Newton,[32] *Minneapolis*
William I. Nolan,[33] *Minneapolis*
Harold Knutson, *St. Cloud*
Ole J. Kvale,[34] *Benson*
Paul J. Kvale,[35] *Benson*
William A. Pittenger, *Duluth*
Conrad G. Selvig, *Crookston*
Godfrey G. Goodwin, *Cambridge*

MISSISSIPPI

SENATORS

Pat Harrison, *Gulfport*
Hubert D. Stephens, *New Albany*

REPRESENTATIVES

John E. Rankin, *Tupelo*
Wall Doxey, *Holly Springs*
William M. Whittington, *Greenwood*
T. Jeff. Busby, *Houston*
Ross A. Collins, *Meridian*
Robert S. Hall, *Hattiesburg*
Percy E. Quin, *McComb*
James W. Collier, *Vicksburg*

MISSOURI

SENATORS

Harry B. Hawes, *St. Louis*
Roscoe C. Patterson, *Kansas City*

REPRESENTATIVES

Milton A. Romjue, *Macon*
Ralph F. Lozier, *Carrollton*
Jacob L. Milligan,[36] *Richmond*
David W. Hopkins,[37] *St. Joseph*
Edgar C. Ellis, *Kansas City*
Thomas J. Halsey, *Holden*
John W. Palmer, *Sedalia*
William L. Nelson, *Columbia*
Clarence Cannon, *Elsberry*
Henry F. Niedringhaus, *St. Louis*
John J. Cochran, *St. Louis*
Leonidas C. Dyer, *St. Louis*
Charles E. Kiefner, *Perryville*
Dewey Short, *Galena*
Joe J. Manlove, *Joplin*
Rowland L. Johnston, *Rolla*

MONTANA

SENATORS

Thomas J. Walsh, *Helena*
Burton K. Wheeler, *Butte*

REPRESENTATIVES

John M. Evans, *Missoula*
Scott Leavitt, *Great Falls*

NEBRASKA

SENATORS

George W. Norris, *McCook*
Robert B. Howell, *Omaha*

REPRESENTATIVES

John H. Morehead, *Falls City*
Willis G. Sears, *Omaha*
Edgar Howard, *Columbus*
Charles H. Sloan, *Geneva*
Fred G. Johnson, *Hastings*
Robert G. Simmons, *Scottsbluff*

---

[25] Resigned January 10, 1930, having been appointed a Senator.
[26] Elected to fill vacancy caused by resignation of John M. Robsion, and took his seat March 1, 1930.
[27] Died April 6, 1929, before Congress assembled.
[28] Elected to fill vacancy caused by death of Whitmell P. Martin, and took his seat October 14, 1929.
[29] Election unsuccessfully contested by John P. Hill.

[30] Died December 20, 1929.
[31] Elected to fill vacancy caused by death of William Kirk Kaynor, and took his seat February 17, 1930.
[32] Resigned June 30, 1929, having been appointed Secretary to the President.
[33] Elected to fill vacancy caused by resignation of Walter H. Newton, and took his seat October 14, 1929.
[34] Died September 11, 1929.

[35] Elected to fill vacancy caused by death of his father, Ole J. Kvale, and took his seat November 11, 1929.
[36] Election unsuccessfully contested by Henry F. Lawrence.
[37] Elected to fill vacancy caused by death of Representative-elect Charles L. Faust, in preceding Congress.

NEVADA

SENATORS

Key Pittman, *Tonopah*
Tasker L. Oddie, *Reno*

REPRESENTATIVE

At Large—Samuel S. Arentz, *Simpson*

NEW HAMPSHIRE

SENATORS

George H. Moses, *Concord*
Henry W. Keyes, *Haverhill*

REPRESENTATIVES

Fletcher Hale, *Laconia*
Edward H. Wason, *Nashua*

NEW JERSEY

SENATORS

Walter E. Edge,[38] *Atlantic City*
David Baird, Jr.,[39] *Camden*
Dwight W. Morrow,[40] *Englewood*
Hamilton F. Kean, *Elizabeth*

REPRESENTATIVES

Charles A. Wolverton, *Camden*
Isaac Bacharach, *Atlantic City*
Harold G. Hoffman, *South Amboy*
Charles A. Eaton, *North Plainfield*
Ernest R. Ackerman, *Plainfield*
Randolph Perkins, *Woodcliff Lake*
George N. Seger, *Passaic*
Fred A. Hartley, Jr., *Kearny*
Franklin W. Fort, *East Orange*
Frederick R. Lehlbach, *Newark*
Oscar L. Auf der Heide, *West New York*
Mrs. Mary T. Norton, *Jersey City*

NEW MEXICO

SENATORS

Sam G. Bratton, *Albuquerque*
Bronson M. Cutting, *Santa Fe*

REPRESENTATIVE

At Large—Albert Gallatin Simms, *Albuquerque*

NEW YORK

SENATORS

Royal S. Copeland, *New York City*
Robert F. Wagner, *New York City*

REPRESENTATIVES

Robert L. Bacon, *Westbury*
William F. Brunner, *Rockaway Park*
George W. Lindsay, *Brooklyn*
Thomas H. Cullen, *Brooklyn*
Loring M. Black, Jr., *Brooklyn*
Andrew L. Somers, *Brooklyn*
John F. Quayle,[41] *Brooklyn*
Patrick J. Carley, *Brooklyn*
David J. O'Connell,[42] *Brooklyn*
Emanuel Celler, *Brooklyn*
Anning S. Prall, *West New Brighton*
Samuel Dickstein, *New York City*
Christopher D. Sullivan, *New York City*
William I. Sirovich, *New York City*
John J. Boylan, *New York City*
John J. O'Connor, *New York City*
Mrs. Ruth S. B. Pratt, *New York City*
John F. Carew,[43] *New York City*
Martin J. Kennedy,[44] *New York City*
Sol Bloom, *New York City*
Fiorello H. LaGuardia, *New York City*
Joseph A. Gavagan,[45] *New York City*
Anthony J. Griffin, *New York City*
Frank Oliver, *Bronx*
James M. Fitzpatrick, *New York City*
J. Mayhew Wainwright, *Rye*
Hamilton Fish, Jr., *Garrison*
Harcourt J. Pratt, *Highland*
Parker Corning, *Albany*
James S. Parker, *Salem*
Frank Crowther, *Schenectady*
Bertrand H. Snell, *Potsdam*
Francis D. Culkin, *Oswego*
Frederick M. Davenport, *Clinton*
John D. Clarke, *Fraser*
Clarence E. Hancock, *Syracuse*
John Taber, *Auburn*
Gale H. Stalker, *Elmira*
James L. Whitley, *Rochester*
Archie D. Sanders, *Stafford*
S. Wallace Dempsey, *Lockport*
Edmund F. Cooke, *Alden*
James M. Mead, *Buffalo*
Daniel A. Reed, *Dunkirk*

NORTH CAROLINA

SENATORS

Furnifold McL. Simmons, *New Bern*
Lee S. Overman,[46] *Salisbury*
Cameron Morrison,[47] *Charlotte*

REPRESENTATIVES

Lindsay C. Warren, *Washington*
John H. Kerr, *Warrenton*
Charles L. Abernethy, *New Bern*

Edward W. Pou, *Smithfield*
Charles M. Stedman,[48] *Greensboro*
Franklin W. Hancock, Jr.,[49] *Oxford*
J. Bayard Clark, *Fayetteville*
William C. Hammer,[50] *Asheboro*
Hinton James,[51] *Laurinburg*
Robert L. Doughton, *Laurel Springs*
Charles A. Jonas, *Lincolnton*
George M. Pritchard, *Asheville*

NORTH DAKOTA

SENATORS

Lynn J. Frazier, *Hoople*
Gerald P. Nye, *Cooperstown*

REPRESENTATIVES

Olger B. Burtness, *Grand Forks*
Thomas Hall, *Bismarck*
James H. Sinclair, *Kenmare*

OHIO

SENATORS

Simeon D. Fess, *Yellow Springs*
Theodore E. Burton,[52] *Cleveland*
Roscoe C. McCulloch,[53] *Canton*
Robert J. Bulkley,[54] *Cleveland*

REPRESENTATIVES

Nicholas Longworth, *Cincinnati*
William E. Hess, *Cincinnati*
Roy G. Fitzgerald, *Dayton*
John L. Cable, *Lima*
Charles J. Thompson, *Defiance*
Charles C. Kearns, *Amelia*
Charles Brand, *Urbana*
Grant E. Mouser, Jr., *Marion*
William W. Chalmers, *Toledo*
Thomas A. Jenkins, *Ironton*
Mell G. Underwood, *New Lexington*
John C. Speaks, *Columbus*
Joseph E. Baird, *Bowling Green*
Francis Seiberling, *Akron*
C. Ellis Moore, *Cambridge*
Charles B. McClintock, *Canton*
William M. Morgan, *Newark*
B. Frank Murphy, *Steubenville*
John G. Cooper, *Youngstown*
Charles A. Mooney, *Cleveland*
Robert Crosser, *Cleveland*
Chester C. Bolton, *Cleveland*

OKLAHOMA

SENATORS

William B. Pine, *Okmulgee*
J. W. Elmer Thomas, *Medicine Park*

[38] Resigned November 21, 1929, having been appointed ambassador to France.
[39] Appointed to fill vacancy caused by resignation of Walter E. Edge, and took his seat December 9, 1929.
[40] Elected to fill vacancy caused by resignation of Walter E. Edge, and took his seat December 3, 1930.
[41] Died November 27, 1930, before the commencement of the Seventy-second Congress, to which he had been reelected. Vacancy in the Seventy-first Congress not filled.
[42] Died December 29, 1930, before the commencement of the Seventy-second Congress, to which he had been reelected. Vacancy in the Seventy-first Congress

not filled.
[43] Resigned December 28, 1929, having been appointed a justice of the Supreme Court of the State of New York.
[44] Elected to fill vacancy caused by resignation of John F. Carew, and took his seat April 16, 1930.
[45] Elected to fill vacancy caused by death of Representative-elect Royal H. Weller, in preceding Congress, and took his seat November 21, 1929.
[46] Died December 12, 1930.
[47] Appointed to fill vacancy caused by death of Lee S. Overman, and took his seat December 17, 1930.
[48] Died September 23, 1930.

[49] Elected to fill vacancy caused by death of Charles M. Stedman, and took his seat December 1, 1930.
[50] Died September 26, 1930.
[51] Elected to fill vacancy caused by death of William C. Hammer, and took his seat December 1, 1930.
[52] Died October 28, 1929.
[53] Appointed to fill vacancy caused by death of Theodore E. Burton, and took his seat November 12, 1929.
[54] Elected to fill vacancy caused by death of Theodore E. Burton, and took his seat December 1, 1930.

REPRESENTATIVES

Charles O'Connor, *Tulsa*
William W. Hastings, *Tahlequah*
Wilburn Cartwright, *McAlester*
Thomas D. McKeown, *Ada*
Ulysses S. Stone, *Norman*
Jed Johnson, *Anadarko*
James V. McClintic, *Snyder*
Milton C. Garber, *Enid*

OREGON

SENATORS

Charles L. McNary, *Salem*
Frederick Steiwer, *Portland*

REPRESENTATIVES

Willis C. Hawley, *Salem*
Robert R. Butler, *The Dalles*
Franklin F. Korell, *Portland*

PENNSYLVANIA

SENATORS

David A. Reed, *Pittsburgh*
William S. Vare,[55] *Philadelphia*
Joseph R. Grundy,[56] *Bristol*
James J. Davis,[57] *Pittsburgh*

REPRESENTATIVES

James M. Beck, *Philadelphia*
George S. Graham, *Philadelphia*
Harry C. Ransley, *Philadelphia*
Benjamin M. Golder, *Philadelphia*
James J. Connolly, *Philadelphia*
George A. Welsh, *Philadelphia*
George P. Darrow, *Philadelphia*
James Wolfenden, *Upper Darby*
Henry W. Watson, *Langhorne*
William W. Griest,[58] *Lancaster*
J. Roland Kinzer,[59] *Lancaster*
Laurence H. Watres, *Scranton*
John J. Casey,[60] *Wilkes-Barre*
C. Murray Turpin,[61] *Kingston*
George F. Brumm, *Minersville*
Charles J. Esterly, *Sally Ann Furnace*
Louis T. McFadden, *Canton*
Edgar R. Kiess,[62] *Williamsport*
Robert F. Rich,[63] *Woolrich*
Frederick W. Magrady, *Mount Carmel*
Edward M. Beers, *Mount Union*
Isaac H. Doutrich, *Harrisburg*
J. Russell Leech, *Ebensburg*
J. Banks Kurtz, *Altoona*
Franklin Menges, *York*
J. Mitchell Chase, *Clearfield*
Samuel A. Kendall, *Meyersdale*

Henry W. Temple, *Washington*
J. Howard Swick, *Beaver Falls*
Nathan L. Strong, *Brookville*
Thomas C. Cochran, *Mercer*
Milton W. Shreve, *Erie*
William R. Coyle, *Bethlehem*
Adam M. Wyant, *Greensburg*
Stephen G. Porter,[64] *Pittsburgh*
Edmund F. Erk,[65] *Pittsburgh*
M. Clyde Kelly, *Edgewood*
Patrick J. Sullivan, *Pittsburgh*
Harry A. Estep, *Pittsburgh*
Guy E. Campbell, *Crafton*

RHODE ISLAND

SENATORS

Jesse H. Metcalf, *Providence*
Felix Hébert, *West Warwick*

REPRESENTATIVES

Clark Burdick, *Newport*
Richard S. Aldrich, *Warwick*
Jeremiah E. O'Connell,[66] *Providence*
Francis B. Condon,[67] *Central Falls*

SOUTH CAROLINA

SENATORS

Ellison D. Smith, *Lynchburg*
Coleman L. Blease, *Columbia*

REPRESENTATIVES

Thomas S. McMillan, *Charleston*
Butler B. Hare, *Saluda*
Fred H. Dominick, *Newberry*
John J. McSwain, *Greenville*
William F. Stevenson, *Cheraw*
Allard H. Gasque, *Florence*
Hampton P. Fulmer, *Orangeburg*

SOUTH DAKOTA

SENATORS

Peter Norbeck, *Redfield*
William H. McMaster, *Yankton*

REPRESENTATIVES

Charles A. Christopherson, *Sioux Falls*
Royal C. Johnson, *Aberdeen*
William Williamson, *Rapid City*

TENNESSEE

SENATORS

Kenneth D. McKellar, *Memphis*
Lawrence D. Tyson,[68] *Knoxville*
William E. Brock,[69] *Chattanooga*

REPRESENTATIVES

B. Carroll Reece, *Butler*
J. Will Taylor, *La Follette*
Sam D. McReynolds, *Chattanooga*
Cordell Hull, *Carthage*
Ewin L. Davis, *Tullahoma*
Joseph W. Byrns, *Nashville*
Edward E. Eslick, *Pulaski*
Gordon Browning, *Huntingdon*
Jere Cooper, *Dyersburg*
Hubert F. Fisher, *Memphis*

TEXAS

SENATORS

Morris Sheppard, *Texarkana*
Tom T. Connally, *Marlin*

REPRESENTATIVES

Wright Patman, *Texarkana*
John C. Box, *Jacksonville*
Morgan G. Sanders, *Canton*
Sam Rayburn, *Bonham*
Hatton W. Sumners, *Dallas*
Luther A. Johnson, *Corsicana*
Clay Stone Briggs, *Galveston*
Daniel E. Garrett, *Houston*
Joseph J. Mansfield, *Columbus*
James P. Buchanan, *Brenham*
Oliver H. Cross, *Waco*
Fritz G. Lanham, *Fort Worth*
Guinn Williams, *Decatur*
Augustus McCloskey,[70] *San Antonio*
Harry M. Wurzbach,[71] *Seguin*
John N. Garner, *Uvalde*
Claude B. Hudspeth, *El Paso*
Robert Q. Lee,[72] *Cisco*
Thomas L. Blanton,[73] *Abilene*
Marvin Jones, *Amarillo*

UTAH

SENATORS

Reed Smoot, *Provo*
William H. King, *Salt Lake City*

REPRESENTATIVES

Don B. Colton, *Vernal*
Elmer O. Leatherwood,[74] *Salt Lake City*
Frederick C. Loofbourow,[75] *Salt Lake City*

[55] Credentials as Senator-elect were presented, in preceding Congress, and referred to the Committee on Privileges and Elections for report; meanwhile Mr. Vare was not permitted to qualify, and by Senate Resolution No. 111, of December 6, 1929, was declared not entitled to a seat.
[56] Appointed to fill vacancy caused by refusal of the Senate to seat William S. Vare, and took his seat December 12, 1929.
[57] Elected to fill vacancy caused by refusal of the Senate to seat William S. Vare, and took his seat December 2, 1930.
[58] Died December 5, 1929.
[59] Elected to fill vacancy caused by death of William

W. Griest, and took his seat February 4, 1930.
[60] Died May 5, 1929.
[61] Elected to fill vacancy caused by death of John J. Casey, and took his seat June 11, 1929.
[62] Died July 20, 1930.
[63] Elected to fill vacancy caused by death of Edgar R. Kiess, and took his seat December 1, 1930.
[64] Died June 27, 1930.
[65] Elected to fill vacancy caused by death of Stephen G. Porter, and took his seat December 1, 1930.
[66] Resigned May 9, 1930, having been appointed an associate justice of the Superior Court of Rhode Island.
[67] Elected to fill vacancy caused by resignation of Jeremiah E. O'Connell: took his seat December 1, 1930.

[68] Died August 24, 1929.
[69] Appointed to fill vacancy caused by death of Lawrence D. Tyson, and took his seat September 9, 1929; subsequently elected.
[70] Served until February 10, 1930; succeeded by Harry M. Wurzbach, who contested his election.
[71] Successfully contested the election of Augustus McCloskey, and took his seat February 10, 1930.
[72] Died April 18, 1930.
[73] Elected to fill vacancy caused by death of Robert Q. Lee, and took his seat June 2, 1930.
[74] Died December 24, 1929.
[75] Elected to fill vacancy caused by death of Elmer O. Leatherwood, and took his seat December 1, 1930.

VERMONT

SENATORS

Frank L. Greene,[76] *St. Albans*
Frank C. Partridge,[77] *Proctor*
Porter H. Dale, *Island Pond*

REPRESENTATIVES

Elbert S. Brigham, *St. Albans*
Ernest Willard Gibson, *Brattleboro*

VIRGINIA

SENATORS

Claude A. Swanson, *Chatham*
Carter Glass, *Lynchburg*

REPRESENTATIVES

Schuyler Otis Bland, *Newport News*
Menalcus Lankford, *Norfolk*
Andrew J. Montague, *Richmond*
Patrick Henry Drewry, *Petersburg*
Joseph Whitehead, *Chatham*
Clifton A. Woodrum, *Roanoke*
Jacob A. Garber, *Harrisonburg*
R. Walton Moore, *Fairfax*
Joseph C. Shaffer, *Wytheville*
Henry St. George Tucker, *Lexington*

WASHINGTON

SENATORS

Wesley L. Jones, *Seattle*
Clarence C. Dill, *Spokane*

REPRESENTATIVES

John F. Miller, *Seattle*
Lindley H. Hadley, *Bellingham*
Albert Johnson, *Hoquiam*
John W. Summers, *Walla Walla*
Samuel B. Hill, *Waterville*

WEST VIRGINIA

SENATORS

Guy D. Goff, *Clarksburg*
Henry D. Hatfield, *Huntington*

REPRESENTATIVES

Carl G. Bachmann, *Wheeling*
Frank L. Bowman, *Morgantown*
John M. Wolverton, *Richwood*
James A. Hughes,[78] *Huntington*
Robert L. Hogg,[79] *Point Pleasant*
Hugh Ike Shott, *Bluefield*
Joe L. Smith, *Beckley*

WISCONSIN

SENATORS

Robert M. La Follette, Jr., *Madison*
John J. Blaine, *Boscobel*

REPRESENTATIVES

Henry Allen Cooper,[80] *Racine*
Charles A. Kading, *Watertown*
John M. Nelson, *Madison*
John C. Schafer, *Milwaukee*
William H. Stafford, *Milwaukee*
Florian Lampert,[81] *Oshkosh*
Michael K. Reilly,[82] *Fond du Lac*

Merlin Hull, *Black River Falls*
Edward E. Browne, *Waupaca*
George J. Schneider, *Appleton*
James A. Frear, *Hudson*
Hubert H. Peavey, *Washburn*

WYOMING

SENATORS

Francis E. Warren,[83] *Cheyenne*
Patrick J. Sullivan,[84] *Casper*
Robert D. Carey,[85] *Careyhurst*
John B. Kendrick, *Sheridan*

REPRESENTATIVE

At Large—Vincent M. Carter, *Kemmerer*

TERRITORY OF ALASKA

DELEGATE

Dan A. Sutherland, *Juneau*

TERRITORY OF HAWAII

DELEGATE

Victor S. K. Houston, *Honolulu*

PHILIPPINE ISLANDS

RESIDENT COMMISSIONERS

Pedro Guevara, *Santa Cruz*
Camilo Osias, *Balaoan*

PORTO RICO

RESIDENT COMMISSIONER

Felix Cordova Davila, *San Juan*

---

[76] Died December 17, 1930.
[77] Appointed to fill vacancy caused by death of Frank L. Greene, and took his seat January 5, 1931.
[78] Died March 2, 1930.
[79] Elected to fill vacancy caused by death of James A. Hughes, and took his seat December 1, 1930.

[80] Died March 1, 1931, before the commencement of the Seventy-second Congress, to which he had been reelected. Vacancy in the Seventy-first Congress not filled.
[81] Died July 18, 1930.
[82] Elected to fill vacancy caused by death of Florian

Lampert, and took his seat December 1, 1930.
[83] Died November 24, 1929.
[84] Appointed to fill vacancy caused by death of Francis E. Warren, and took his seat December 9, 1929.
[85] Elected to fill vacancy caused by death of Francis E. Warren, and took his seat December 1, 1930.

SEVENTY-SECOND CONGRESS

MARCH 4, 1931, TO MARCH 3, 1933

FIRST SESSION—*December 7, 1931, to July 16, 1932*

SECOND SESSION—*December 5, 1932, to March 3, 1933*

VICE PRESIDENT OF THE UNITED STATES—CHARLES CURTIS, of Kansas

PRESIDENT PRO TEMPORE OF THE SENATE—GEORGE H. MOSES, of New Hampshire

SECRETARY OF THE SENATE—EDWIN P. THAYER, of Indiana

SERGEANT AT ARMS OF THE SENATE—DAVID S. BARRY, of Rhode Island

---

SPEAKER OF THE HOUSE OF REPRESENTATIVES—JOHN N. GARNER,[1] of Texas

CLERK OF THE HOUSE—SOUTH TRIMBLE,[2] of Kentucky

SERGEANT AT ARMS OF THE HOUSE—JOSEPH G. ROGERS, of Pennsylvania; KENNETH ROMNEY,[3] of Montana

DOORKEEPER OF THE HOUSE—JOSEPH J. SINNOTT, of Virginia

POSTMASTER OF THE HOUSE—FINIS E. SCOTT

ALABAMA

SENATORS

Hugo L. Black, *Birmingham*
John H. Bankhead 2d, *Jasper*

REPRESENTATIVES

John McDuffie, *Monroeville*
Lister Hill, *Montgomery*
Henry B. Steagall, *Ozark*
Lamar Jeffers, *Anniston*
LaFayette L. Patterson, *Gadsden*
William B. Oliver, *Tuscaloosa*
Miles C. Allgood, *Gadsden*
Edward B. Almon, *Tuscumbia*
George Huddleston, *Birmingham*
William B. Bankhead, *Jasper*

ARIZONA

SENATORS

Henry F. Ashurst, *Prescott*
Carl Hayden, *Phoenix*

REPRESENTATIVE

At Large—Lewis W. Douglas,[4] *Phoenix*

ARKANSAS

SENATORS

Joseph T. Robinson, *Little Rock*
Thaddeus H. Caraway,[5] *Jonesboro*
Mrs. Hattie W. Caraway,[6] *Jonesboro*

REPRESENTATIVES

William J. Driver, *Osceola*
John E. Miller, *Searcy*
Claude A. Fuller, *Eureka Springs*
Mrs. Effiegene (Locke) Wingo, *De Queen*
Heartsill Ragon, *Clarksville*
David D. Glover, *Malvern*
Tilman B. Parks, *Camden*

CALIFORNIA

SENATORS

Hiram W. Johnson, *San Francisco*
Samuel M. Shortridge, *Menlo Park*

REPRESENTATIVES

Clarence F. Lea, *Santa Rosa*
Harry L. Englebright, *Nevada City*
Charles F. Curry, Jr., *Sacramento*
Mrs. Florence P. Kahn, *San Francisco*
Richard J. Welch, *San Francisco*

Albert E. Carter, *Oakland*
Henry E. Barbour, *Fresno*
Arthur M. Free, *San Jose*
William E. Evans, *Glendale*
Joe Crail, *Los Angeles*
Philip D. Swing, *El Centro*

COLORADO

SENATORS

Charles W. Waterman,[7] *Denver*
Walter Walker,[8] *Grand Junction*
Karl C. Schuyler,[9] *Denver*
Edward P. Costigan, *Denver*

REPRESENTATIVES

William R. Eaton, *Denver*
Charles B. Timberlake, *Sterling*
Guy U. Hardy, *Canon City*
Edward T. Taylor, *Glenwood Springs*

CONNECTICUT

SENATORS

Hiram Bingham, *New Haven*
Frederic C. Walcott, *Norfolk*

---

[1] Elected December 7, 1931.
[2] Elected December 7, 1931.
[3] Elected December 7, 1931.
[4] Resigned, effective March 4, 1933, before the commencement of the Seventy-third Congress, to which he had been reelected, having been appointed Director of the Bureau of the Budget.
[5] Died November 6, 1931.
[6] Appointed to fill vacancy caused by death of Thaddeus H. Caraway, and took her seat December 8, 1931; subsequently elected.
[7] Died August 27, 1932.
[8] Appointed to fill vacancy caused by death of Charles W. Waterman, and took his seat December 5, 1932.
[9] Elected to fill vacancy caused by death of Charles W. Waterman, and took his seat December 7, 1932.

CONNECTICUT—Continued

REPRESENTATIVES

Augustine Lonergan, *Hartford*
Richard P. Freeman, *New London*
John Q. Tilson,[10] *New Haven*
William L. Tierney, *Greenwich*
Edward W. Goss, *Waterbury*

DELAWARE

SENATORS

Daniel O. Hastings, *Wilmington*
John G. Townsend, Jr., *Selbyville*

REPRESENTATIVE

At Large—Robert G. Houston, *George-town*

FLORIDA

SENATORS

Duncan U. Fletcher, *Jacksonville*
Park Trammell, *Lakeland*

REPRESENTATIVES

Herbert J. Drane, *Lakeland*
Robert A. Green, *Starke*
Thomas A. Yon, *Tallahassee*
Mrs. Ruth Bryan Owen, *Miami*

GEORGIA

SENATORS

William J. Harris,[11] *Cedartown*
John S. Cohen,[12] *Atlanta*
Richard B. Russell,[13] *Winder*
Walter F. George, *Vienna*

REPRESENTATIVES

Charles G. Edwards,[14] *Savannah*
Homer C. Parker,[15] *Statesboro*
Edward E. Cox, *Camilla*
Charles R. Crisp,[16] *Americus*
Bryant T. Castellow,[17] *Cuthbert*
William C. Wright, *Newnan*
Robert Ramspeck, *Atlanta*
Samuel Rutherford,[18] *Forsyth*
W. Carlton Mobley,[19] *Forsyth*
Malcolm C. Tarver, *Dalton*
Charles H. Brand, *Athens*
John S. Wood, *Canton*
Carl Vinson, *Milledgeville*
William C. Lankford, *Douglas*
William W. Larsen, *Dublin*

IDAHO

SENATORS

William E. Borah, *Boise*
John Thomas, *Gooding*

REPRESENTATIVES

Burton L. French, *Moscow*
Addison T. Smith, *Twin Falls*

ILLINOIS

SENATORS

Otis F. Glenn, *Murphysboro*
J. Hamilton Lewis, *Chicago*

REPRESENTATIVES

Oscar De Priest, *Chicago*
Morton D. Hull, *Chicago*
Edward A. Kelly, *Chicago*
Harry P. Beam, *Chicago*
Adolph J. Sabath, *Chicago*
James T. Igoe, *Chicago*
Leonard W. Schuetz, *Chicago*
Peter C. Granata,[20] *Chicago*
Stanley H. Kunz,[21] *Chicago*
Fred A Britten, *Chicago*
Carl R. Chindblom, *Evanston*
Frank R. Reid, *Aurora*
John T. Buckbee, *Rockford*
William R. Johnson, *Freeport*
John C. Allen, *Monmouth*
Burnett M. Chiperfield, *Canton*
William E. Hull, *Peoria*
Homer W. Hall, *Bloomington*
William P. Holaday, *Georgetown*
Charles Adkins, *Decatur*
Henry T. Rainey, *Carrollton*
J. Earl Major, *Hillsboro*
Charles A. Karch,[22] *East St. Louis*
William W. Arnold, *Robinson*
Claude V. Parsons, *Golconda*
Kent E. Keller, *Ava*
At Large—
   Richard Yates, *Springfield*
   William H. Dieterich, *Beardstown*

INDIANA

SENATORS

James E. Watson, *Rushville*
Arthur R. Robinson, *Indianapolis*

REPRESENTATIVES

John W. Boehne, Jr., *Evansville*
Arthur H. Greenwood, *Washington*
Eugene B. Crowe, *Bedford*
Harry C. Canfield, *Batesville*
Courtland C. Gillen, *Greencastle*
William H. Larrabee, *New Palestine*
Louis Ludlow, *Indianapolis*

Albert H. Vestal,[23] *Anderson*
Fred S. Purnell, *Attica*
William R. Wood, *La Fayette*
Glenn Griswold, *Peru*
David Hogg, *Fort Wayne*
Samuel B. Pettengill, *South Bend*

IOWA

SENATORS

Smith W. Brookhart, *Washington*
Lester J. Dickinson, *Algona*

REPRESENTATIVES

William F. Kopp, *Mount Pleasant*
Bernhard M. Jacobsen, *Clinton*
Thomas J. B. Robinson, *Hampton*
Gilbert N. Haugen, *Northwood*
Cyrenus Cole, *Cedar Rapids*
C. William Ramseyer, *Bloomfield*
Cassius C. Dowell, *Des Moines*
Lloyd Thurston, *Osceola*
Charles E. Swanson, *Council Bluffs*
Fred C. Gilchrist, *Laurens*
Ed H. Campbell, *Battle Creek*

KANSAS

SENATORS

Arthur Capper, *Topeka*
George McGill, *Wichita*

REPRESENTATIVES

William P. Lambertson, *Fairview*
Ulysses S. Guyer, *Kansas City*
Harold McGugin, *Coffeyville*
Homer Hoch, *Marion*
James G. Strong, *Blue Rapids*
Charles I. Sparks, *Goodland*
Clifford R. Hope, *Garden City*
William A. Ayres, *Wichita*

KENTUCKY

SENATORS

Alben W. Barkley, *Paducah*
Marvel M. Logan, *Bowling Green*

REPRESENTATIVES

William V. Gregory, *Mayfield*
Glover H. Cary, *Owensboro*
John W. Moore, *Morgantown*
Cap R. Carden, *Munfordville*
Maurice H. Thatcher, *Louisville*
Brent Spence, *Fort Thomas*
Virgil M. Chapman, *Paris*
Ralph Gilbert, *Shelbyville*
Fred M. Vinson, *Ashland*
Andrew J. May, *Prestonsburg*
Charles Finley, *Williamsburg*

---

[10] Resigned December 3, 1932; vacancy throughout remainder of the Congress.
[11] Died April 18, 1932.
[12] Appointed to fill vacancy caused by death of William J. Harris, and took his seat April 27, 1932.
[13] Elected to fill vacancy caused by death of William J. Harris, and took his seat January 12, 1933.
[14] Died July 13, 1931.

[15] Elected to fill vacancy caused by death of Charles G. Edwards, and took his seat December 7, 1931.
[16] Resigned October 7, 1932, having been appointed a member of the United States Tariff Commission.
[17] Elected to fill vacancy caused by resignation of Charles R. Crisp, and took his seat December 5, 1932.
[18] Died February 4, 1932.
[19] Elected to fill vacancy caused by death of Samuel Rutherford, and took his seat March 7, 1932.

[20] Served until April 5, 1932; succeeded by Stanley H. Kunz, who contested his election.
[21] Successfully contested the election of Peter C. Granata, and took his seat April 5, 1932.
[22] Died November 6, 1932; vacancy throughout remainder of the Congress.
[23] Died April 1, 1932; vacancy throughout remainder of the Congress.

LOUISIANA

SENATORS

Edwin S. Broussard, *New Iberia*
Huey P. Long,[24] *New Orleans*

REPRESENTATIVES

Joachim O. Fernandez, *New Orleans*
Paul H. Maloney, *New Orleans*
Numa F. Montet, *Thibodaux*
John N. Sandlin, *Minden*
Riley J. Wilson, *Ruston*
Bolivar E. Kemp, *Amite*
René L. DeRouen, *Ville Platte*
James B. Aswell,[25] *Natchitoches*
John H. Overton,[26] *Alexandria*

MAINE

SENATORS

Frederick Hale, *Portland*
Wallace H. White, Jr., *Auburn*

REPRESENTATIVES

Carroll L. Beedy, *Portland*
Donald B. Partridge, *Norway*
John E. Nelson, *Augusta*
Donald F. Snow, *Bangor*

MARYLAND

SENATORS

Millard E. Tydings, *Havre de Grace*
Phillips Lee Goldsborough, *Baltimore*

REPRESENTATIVES

T. Alan Goldsborough, *Denton*
William P. Cole, Jr., *Towson*
Vincent L. Palmisano, *Baltimore*
J. Charles Linthicum,[27] *Baltimore*
Ambrose J. Kennedy,[28] *Baltimore*
Stephen W. Gambrill, *Laurel*
David J. Lewis, *Cumberland*

MASSACHUSETTS

SENATORS

David I. Walsh, *Fitchburg*
Marcus A. Coolidge, *Fitchburg*

REPRESENTATIVES

Allen T. Treadway, *Stockbridge*
William J. Granfield, *Springfield*
Frank H. Foss, *Fitchburg*
Pehr G. Holmes, *Worcester*
Mrs. Edith Nourse Rogers, *Lowell*
A. Piatt Andrew, Jr., *Gloucester*
William P. Connery, Jr., *Lynn*
Frederick W. Dallinger,[29] *Cambridge*

Charles L. Underhill, *Somerville*
John J. Douglass, *Boston*
George H. Tinkham, *Boston*
John W. McCormack, *Dorchester*
Robert Luce, *Waltham*
Richard B. Wigglesworth, *Milton*
Joseph W. Martin, Jr., *North Attleboro*
Charles L. Gifford, *Cotuit*

MICHIGAN

SENATORS

James Couzens, *Detroit*
Arthur H. Vandenberg, *Grand Rapids*

REPRESENTATIVES

Robert H. Clancy, *Detroit*
Earl C. Michener, *Adrian*
Joseph L. Hooper, *Battle Creek*
John C. Ketcham, *Hastings*
Carl E. Mapes, *Grand Rapids*
Seymour H. Person, *Lansing*
Jesse P. Wolcott, *Port Huron*
Bird J. Vincent,[30] *Saginaw*
Michael J. Hart,[31] *Saginaw*
James C. McLaughlin,[32] *Muskegon*
Roy O. Woodruff, *Bay City*
Frank P. Bohn, *Newberry*
W. Frank James, *Hancock*
Clarence J. McLeod, *Detroit*

MINNESOTA

SENATORS

Henrik Shipstead, *Minneapolis*
Thomas D. Schall, *Excelsior*

REPRESENTATIVES

Victor Christgau, *Austin*
Frank Clague, *Redwood Falls*
August H. Andresen, *Red Wing*
Melvin J. Maas, *St. Paul*
William I. Nolan, *Minneapolis*
Harold Knutson, *St. Cloud*
Paul J. Kvale, *Benson*
William A. Pittenger, *Duluth*
Conrad G. Selvig, *Crookston*
Godfrey G. Goodwin,[33] *Cambridge*

MISSISSIPPI

SENATORS

Pat Harrison, *Gulfport*
Hubert D. Stephens, *New Albany*

REPRESENTATIVES

John E. Rankin, *Tupelo*
Wall Doxey, *Holly Springs*

William M. Whittington, *Greenwood*
T. Jeff. Busby, *Houston*
Ross A. Collins, *Meridian*
Robert S. Hall, *Hattiesburg*
Percy E. Quin,[34] *McComb*
Lawrence Russell Ellzey,[35] *Wesson*
James W. Collier, *Vicksburg*

MISSOURI

SENATORS

Harry B. Hawes,[36] *St. Louis*
Joel Bennett Clark,[37] *St. Louis*
Roscoe C. Patterson, *Kansas City*

REPRESENTATIVES

Milton A. Romjue, *Macon*
Ralph F. Lozier, *Carrollton*
Jacob L. Milligan, *Richmond*
David W. Hopkins, *St. Joseph*
Joseph B. Shannon, *Kansas City*
Clement C. Dickinson, *Clinton*
Samuel C. Major,[38] *Fayette*
Robert D. Johnson,[39] *Marshall*
William L. Nelson, *Columbia*
Clarence Cannon, *Elsberry*
Henry F. Niedringhaus, *St. Louis*
John J. Cochran, *St. Louis*
Leonidas C. Dyer, *St. Louis*
Clyde Williams, *Hillsboro*
James F. Fulbright, *Doniphan*
Joe J. Manlove, *Joplin*
William E. Barton, *Houston*

MONTANA

SENATORS

Thomas J. Walsh,[40] *Helena*
Burton K. Wheeler, *Butte*

REPRESENTATIVES

John M. Evans, *Missoula*
Scott Leavitt, *Great Falls*

NEBRASKA

SENATORS

George W. Norris, *McCook*
Robert B. Howell, *Omaha*

REPRESENTATIVES

John H. Morehead, *Falls City*
H. Malcolm Baldrige, *Omaha*
Edgar Howard, *Columbus*
John N. Norton, *Polk*
Ashton C. Shallenberger, *Alma*
Robert G. Simmons, *Scottsbluff*

---

[24] Elected November 4, 1930, for the term beginning March 4, 1931, but did not qualify until January 25, 1932, preferring to retain the governorship.
[25] Died March 16, 1931.
[26] Elected to fill vacancy caused by death of James B. Aswell, and took his seat December 7, 1931.
[27] Died October 5, 1932.
[28] Elected to fill vacancy caused by death of J. Charles Linthicum, and took his seat December 5, 1932.
[29] Resigned October 1, 1932, having been appointed a judge of the United States Customs Court; vacancy

throughout remainder of the Congress.
[30] Died July 18, 1931.
[31] Elected to fill vacancy caused by death of Bird J. Vincent, and took his seat December 7, 1931.
[32] Died November 29, 1932; vacancy throughout remainder of the Congress.
[33] Died February 16, 1933; vacancy throughout remainder of the Congress.
[34] Died February 4, 1932.
[35] Elected to fill vacancy caused by death of Percy E. Quin, and took his seat March 30, 1932.

[36] Resigned February 3, 1933.
[37] Appointed to fill vacancy caused by resignation of Harry B. Hawes, and took his seat February 3, 1933; was previously elected for the term commencing March 4, 1933.
[38] Died July 28, 1931.
[39] Elected to fill vacancy caused by death of Samuel C. Major, and took his seat December 7, 1931.
[40] Died March 2, 1933; vacancy throughout remainder of the Congress.

NEVADA

SENATORS

Key Pittman, *Tonopah*
Tasker L. Oddie, *Reno*

REPRESENTATIVE

At Large—Samuel S. Arentz, *Simpson*

NEW HAMPSHIRE

SENATORS

George H. Moses, *Concord*
Henry W. Keyes, *Haverhill*

REPRESENTATIVES

Fletcher Hale,[41] *Laconia*
William N. Rogers,[42] *Sanbornville*
Edward H. Wason, *Nashua*

NEW JERSEY

SENATORS

Hamilton F. Kean, *Elizabeth*
Dwight W. Morrow,[43] *Englewood*
W. Warren Barbour,[44] *Locust*

REPRESENTATIVES

Charles A. Wolverton, *Camden*
Isaac Bacharach, *Atlantic City*
William H. Sutphin, *Matawan*
Charles A. Eaton, *North Plainfield*
Ernest R. Ackerman,[45] *Plainfield*
Percy H. Stewart,[46] *Plainfield*
Randolph Perkins, *Woodcliff Lake*
George N. Seger, *Passaic*
Fred A. Hartley, Jr., *Kearny*
Peter A. Cavicchia, *Newark*
Frederick R. Lehlbach, *Newark*
Oscar L. Auf der Heide, *West New York*
Mrs. Mary T. Norton, *Jersey City*

NEW MEXICO

SENATORS

Sam G. Bratton, *Albuquerque*
Bronson M. Cutting, *Santa Fe*

REPRESENTATIVE

At Large—Dennis Chavez, *Albuquerque*

NEW YORK

SENATORS

Royal S. Copeland, *New York City*
Robert F. Wagner, *New York City*

REPRESENTATIVES

Robert L. Bacon, *Westbury*
William F. Brunner, *Rockaway Park*
George W. Lindsay, *Brooklyn*
Thomas H. Cullen, *Brooklyn*
Loring M. Black, Jr., *Brooklyn*
Andrew L. Somers, *Brooklyn*
Matthew V. O'Malley,[47] *Brooklyn*
John J. Delaney,[48] *Brooklyn*
Patrick J. Carley, *Brooklyn*
Stephen A. Rudd,[49] *Brooklyn*
Emanuel Celler, *Brooklyn*
Anning S. Prall, *West New Brighton*
Samuel Dickstein, *New York City*
Christopher D. Sullivan, *New York City*
William I. Sirovich, *New York City*
John J. Boylan, *New York City*
John J. O'Connor, *New York City*
Mrs. Ruth S. B. Pratt, *New York City*
Martin J. Kennedy, *New York City*
Sol Bloom, *New York City*
Fiorello H. LaGuardia, *New York City*
Joseph A. Gavagan, *New York City*
Anthony J. Griffin, *New York City*
Frank Oliver, *Bronx*
James M. Fitzpatrick, *New York City*
Charles D. Millard, *Tarrytown*
Hamilton Fish, Jr., *Garrison*
Harcourt J. Pratt, *Highland*
Parker Corning, *Albany*
James S. Parker, *Salem*
Frank Crowther, *Schenectady*
Bertrand H. Snell, *Potsdam*
Francis D. Culkin, *Oswego*
Frederick M. Davenport, *Clinton*
John D. Clarke, *Fraser*
Clarence E. Hancock, *Syracuse*
John Taber, *Auburn*
Gale H. Stalker, *Elmira*
James L. Whitley, *Rochester*
Archie D. Sanders, *Stafford*
Walter G. Andrews, *Buffalo*
Edmund F. Cooke, *Alden*
James M. Mead, *Buffalo*
Daniel A. Reed, *Dunkirk*

NORTH CAROLINA

SENATORS

Cameron Morrison,[50] *Charlotte*
Robert R. Reynolds,[51] *Asheville*
Josiah W. Bailey, *Raleigh*

REPRESENTATIVES

Lindsay C. Warren, *Washington*
John H. Kerr, *Warrenton*
Charles L. Abernethy, *New Bern*
Edward W. Pou, *Smithfield*

Franklin W. Hancock, Jr., *Oxford*
J. Bayard Clark, *Fayetteville*
J. Walter Lambeth, *Thomasville*
Robert L. Doughton, *Laurel Springs*
Alfred L. Bulwinkle, *Gastonia*
Zebulon Weaver, *Asheville*

NORTH DAKOTA

SENATORS

Lynn J. Frazier, *Hoople*
Gerald P. Nye, *Cooperstown*

REPRESENTATIVES

Olger B. Burtness, *Grand Forks*
Thomas Hall, *Bismarck*
James H. Sinclair, *Kenmare*

OHIO

SENATORS

Simeon D. Fess, *Yellow Springs*
Robert J. Bulkley, *Cleveland*

REPRESENTATIVES

Nicholas Longworth,[52] *Cincinnati*
John B. Hollister,[53] *Cincinnati*
William E. Hess, *Cincinnati*
Byron B. Harlan, *Dayton*
John L. Cable, *Lima*
Frank C. Kniffin, *Napoleon*
James G. Polk, *Highland*
Charles Brand, *Urbana*
Grant E. Mouser, Jr., *Marion*
Wilbur M. White, *Toledo*
Thomas A. Jenkins, *Ironton*
Mell G. Underwood, *New Lexington*
Authur P. Lamneck, *Columbus*
William L. Fiesinger, *Sandusky*
Francis Seiberling, *Akron*
C. Ellis Moore, *Cambridge*
Charles B. McClintock, *Canton*
Charles West, *Granville*
B. Frank Murphy, *Steubenville*
John G. Cooper, *Youngstown*
Charles A. Mooney,[54] *Cleveland*
Martin L. Sweeney,[55] *Cleveland*
Robert Crosser, *Cleveland*
Chester C. Bolton, *Cleveland*

OKLAHOMA

SENATORS

J. W. Elmer Thomas, *Medicine Park*
Thomas P. Gore, *Oklahoma City*

---

[41] Died October 22, 1931.
[42] Elected to fill vacancy caused by death of Fletcher Hale, and took his seat January 20, 1932.
[43] Died October 5, 1931.
[44] Appointed to fill vacancy caused by death of Dwight W. Morrow, and took his seat December 8, 1931; subsequently elected.
[45] Died October 18, 1931.
[46] Elected to fill vacancy caused by death of Ernest R. Ackerman, and took his seat December 7, 1931.

[47] Elected February 17, 1931, to fill vacancy caused by death of Representative-elect John F. Quayle, in preceding Congress; died May 26, 1931, before Congress assembled, and was therefore not sworn in.
[48] Elected to fill vacancy caused by deaths of Representatives-elect John F. Quayle and Matthew V. O'Malley, and took his seat December 7, 1931.
[49] Elected to fill vacancy caused by death of Representative-elect David J. O'Connell, in preceding Congress, and took his seat December 7, 1931.

[50] Appointed to fill vacancy caused by death of Lee S. Overman in preceding Congress.
[51] Elected to fill vacancy caused by death of Lee S. Overman, in preceding Congress, and took his seat December 5, 1932.
[52] Died April 9, 1931.
[53] Elected to fill vacancy caused by death of Nicholas Longworth, and took his seat December 7, 1931.
[54] Died May 29, 1931.
[55] Elected to fill vacancy caused by death of Charles A. Mooney, and took his seat December 7, 1931.

OREGON

REPRESENTATIVES

Wesley E. Disney, *Tulsa*
William W. Hastings, *Tahlequah*
Wilburn Cartwright, *McAlester*
Thomas D. McKeown, *Ada*
Fletcher B. Swank, *Norman*
Jed Johnson, *Anadarko*
James V. McClintic, *Snyder*
Milton C. Garber, *Enid*

OREGON

SENATORS

Charles L. McNary, *Salem*
Frederick Steiwer, *Portland*

REPRESENTATIVES

Willis C. Hawley, *Salem*
Robert R. Butler,[56] *The Dalles*
Charles H. Martin, *Portland*

PENNSYLVANIA

SENATORS

David A. Reed, *Pittsburgh*
James J. Davis, *Pittsburgh*

REPRESENTATIVES

James M. Beck, *Philadelphia*
George S. Graham,[57] *Philadelphia*
Edward L. Stokes,[58] *Philadelphia*
Harry C. Ransley, *Philadelphia*
Benjamin M. Golder, *Philadelphia*
James J. Connolly, *Philadelphia*
George A. Welsh,[59] *Philadelphia*
Robert L. Davis,[60] *Philadelphia*
George P. Darrow, *Philadelphia*
James Wolfenden, *Upper Darby*
Henry W. Watson, *Langhorne*
J. Roland Kinzer, *Lancaster*
Patrick J. Boland, *Scranton*
C. Murray Turpin, *Kingston*
George F. Brumm, *Minersville*
Norton L. Lichtenwalner, *Allentown*
Louis T. McFadden, *Canton*
Robert F. Rich, *Woolrich*
Frederick W. Magrady, *Mount Carmel*
Edward M. Beers,[61] *Mount Union*
Joseph F. Biddle,[62] *Huntingdon*
Isaac H. Doutrich, *Harrisburg*
J. Russell Leech,[63] *Ebensburg*
Howard W. Stull,[64] *Johnstown*
J. Banks Kurtz, *Altoona*
Harry L. Haines, *Red Lion*
J. Mitchell Chase, *Clearfield*
Samuel A. Kendall,[65] *Meyersdale*
Henry W. Temple, *Washington*

J. Howard Swick, *Beaver Falls*
Nathan L. Strong, *Brookville*
Thomas C. Cochran, *Mercer*
Milton W. Shreve, *Erie*
William R. Coyle, *Bethlehem*
Adam M. Wyant, *Greensburg*
Edmund F. Erk, *Pittsburgh*
M. Clyde Kelly, *Edgewood*
Patrick J. Sullivan, *Pittsburgh*
Harry A. Estep, *Pittsburgh*
Guy E. Campbell, *Crafton*

RHODE ISLAND

SENATORS

Jesse H. Metcalf, *Providence*
Felix Hébert, *West Warwick*

REPRESENTATIVES

Clark Burdick, *Newport*
Richard S. Aldrich, *Warwick*
Francis B. Condon, *Central Falls*

SOUTH CAROLINA

SENATORS

Ellison D. Smith, *Lynchburg*
James F. Byrnes, *Spartanburg*

REPRESENTATIVES

Thomas S. McMillan, *Charleston*
Butler B. Hare, *Saluda*
Fred H. Dominick, *Newberry*
John J. McSwain, *Greenville*
William F. Stevenson, *Cheraw*
Allard H. Gasque, *Florence*
Hampton P. Fulmer, *Orangeburg*

SOUTH DAKOTA

SENATORS

Peter Norbeck, *Redfield*
William J. Bulow, *Beresford*

REPRESENTATIVES

Charles A. Christopherson, *Sioux Falls*
Royal C. Johnson, *Aberdeen*
William Williamson, *Rapid City*

TENNESSEE

SENATORS

Kenneth D. McKellar, *Memphis*
Cordell Hull,[66] *Carthage*

REPRESENTATIVES

Oscar B. Lovette, *Greeneville*
J. Will Taylor, *La Follette*
Sam D. McReynolds, *Chattanooga*
John R. Mitchell, *Cookeville*
Ewin L. Davis, *Tullahoma*
Joseph W. Byrns, *Nashville*
Edward E. Eslick,[67] *Pulaski*
Mrs. Willa M. B. Eslick,[68] *Pulaski*
Gordon Browning, *Huntingdon*
Jere Cooper, *Dyersburg*
Edward H. Crump, *Memphis*

TEXAS

SENATORS

Morris Sheppard, *Texarkana*
Tom T. Connally, *Marlin*

REPRESENTATIVES

Wright Patman, *Texarkana*
Martin Dies, Jr., *Orange*
Morgan G. Sanders, *Canton*
Sam Rayburn, *Bonham*
Hatton W. Sumners, *Dallas*
Luther A. Johnson, *Corsicana*
Clay Stone Briggs, *Galveston*
Daniel E. Garrett,[69] *Houston*
Joe H. Eagle,[70] *Houston*
Joseph J. Mansfield, *Columbus*
James P. Buchanan, *Brenham*
Oliver H. Cross, *Waco*
Fritz G. Lanham, *Fort Worth*
Guinn Williams, *Decatur*
Harry M. Wurzbach,[71] *Seguin*
Richard M. Kleberg,[72] *Corpus Christi*
John N. Garner,[73] *Uvalde*
R. Ewing Thomason, *El Paso*
Thomas L. Blanton, *Abilene*
Marvin Jones, *Amarillo*

UTAH

SENATORS

Reed Smoot, *Provo*
William H. King, *Salt Lake City*

REPRESENTATIVES

Don B. Colton, *Vernal*
Frederick C. Loofbourow, *Salt Lake City*

VERMONT

SENATORS

Porter H. Dale, *Island Pond*
Frank C. Partridge,[74] *Proctor*
Warren R. Austin,[75] *Burlington*

[56] Died January 7, 1933; vacancy throughout remainder of the Congress.
[57] Died July 4, 1931.
[58] Elected to fill vacancy caused by death of George S. Graham, and took his seat December 7, 1931.
[59] Resigned May 31, 1932, having been appointed judge of the United States district court, eastern district of Pennsylvania.
[60] Elected to fill vacancy caused by resignation of George A. Welsh, and took his seat December 5, 1932.
[61] Died April 21, 1932.
[62] Elected to fill vacancy caused by death of Edward M. Beers, and took his seat December 5, 1932.
[63] Resigned January 29, 1932, having been appointed

a member of the United States Board of Tax Appeals.
[64] Elected to fill vacancy caused by resignation of J. Russell Leech, and took his seat May 6, 1932.
[65] Died January 8, 1933; vacancy throughout remainder of the Congress.
[66] Resigned, effective March 3, 1933, having been appointed Secretary of State.
[67] Died June 14, 1932.
[68] Elected to fill vacancy caused by death of her husband, Edward E. Eslick, and took her seat December 5, 1932.
[69] Died December 13, 1932, before the commencement of the Seventy-third Congress, to which he had been reelected.

[70] Elected to fill vacancy caused by death of Daniel E. Garrett, and took his seat February 7, 1933.
[71] Died November 6, 1931.
[72] Elected to fill vacancy caused by death of Harry M. Wurzbach, and took his seat December 7, 1931.
[73] Resigned, effective March 3, 1933, before the commencement of the Seventy-third Congress, to which he had been reelected, having been elected Vice President of the United States.
[74] Appointed to fill vacancy caused by death of Frank L. Greene in preceding Congress.
[75] Elected March 31, 1931, to fill vacancy caused by death of Frank L. Greene, in preceding Congress. His term commenced April 1, 1931.

VERMONT—Continued

REPRESENTATIVES

John E. Weeks, *Middlebury*
Ernest Willard Gibson, *Brattleboro*

VIRGINIA

SENATORS

Claude A. Swanson,[76] *Chatham*
Carter Glass, *Lynchburg*

REPRESENTATIVES

Schuyler Otis Bland, *Newport News*
Menalcus Lankford, *Norfolk*
Andrew J. Montague, *Richmond*
Patrick Henry Drewry, *Petersburg*
Thomas G. Burch, *Martinsville*
Clifton A. Woodrum, *Roanoke*
John W. Fishburne, *Charlottesville*
Howard W. Smith, *Alexandria*
John W. Flannagan, Jr., *Bristol*
Henry St. George Tucker,[77] *Lexington*
Joel W. Flood,[78] *Appomattox*

WASHINGTON

SENATORS

Wesley L. Jones,[79] *Seattle*
Elijah S. Grammer,[80] *Seattle*
Clarence C. Dill, *Spokane*

REPRESENTATIVES

Ralph A. Horr, *Seattle*
Lindley H. Hadley, *Bellingham*

Albert Johnson, *Hoquiam*
John W. Summers, *Walla Walla*
Samuel B. Hill, *Waterville*

WEST VIRGINIA

SENATORS

Henry D. Hatfield, *Huntington*
Matthew M. Neely, *Fairmont*

REPRESENTATIVES

Carl G. Bachmann, *Wheeling*
Frank L. Bowman, *Morgantown*
Lynn S. Hornor, *Clarksburg*
Robert L. Hogg, *Point Pleasant*
Hugh Ike Shott, *Bluefield*
Joe L. Smith, *Beckley*

WISCONSIN

SENATORS

Robert M. La Follette, Jr., *Madison*
John J. Blaine, *Boscobel*

REPRESENTATIVES

Thomas R. Amlie,[81] *Elkhorn*
Charles A. Kading, *Watertown*
John M. Nelson, *Madison*
John C. Schafer, *Milwaukee*
William H. Stafford, *Milwaukee*
Michael K. Reilly, *Fond du Lac*
Gardner R. Withrow, *La Crosse*
Gerald J. Boileau, *Wausau*
George J. Schneider, *Appleton*

James A. Frear, *Hudson*
Hubert H. Peavey, *Washburn*

WYOMING

SENATORS

John B. Kendrick, *Sheridan*
Robert D. Carey, *Careyhurst*

REPRESENTATIVE

At Large—Vincent M. Carter, *Kemmerer*

TERRITORY OF ALASKA

DELEGATE

James Wickersham, *Juneau*

TERRITORY OF HAWAII

DELEGATE

Victor S. K. Houston, *Honolulu*

PHILIPPINE ISLANDS

RESIDENT COMMISSIONERS

Pedro Guevara, *Santa Cruz*
Camilo Osias, *Balaoan*

PUERTO RICO [82]

RESIDENT COMMISSIONERS

Felix Cordova Davila,[83] *San Juan*
José L. Pesquera,[84] *Bayamon*

---

[76] Resigned, effective March 3, 1933, having been appointed Secretary of the Navy.
[77] Died July 23, 1932.
[78] Elected to fill vacancy caused by death of Henry St. George Tucker, and took his seat December 5, 1932.
[79] Died November 19, 1932.

[80] Appointed to fill vacancy caused by death of Wesley L. Jones, and took his seat December 5, 1932.
[81] Elected to fill vacancy caused by death of Representative-elect Henry Allen Cooper, in preceding Congress, and took his seat December 7, 1931.
[82] The spelling of this name was changed from Porto

Rico to Puerto Rico by an act of Congress (47 Stat. 158), approved May 17, 1932.
[83] Resigned April 11, 1932.
[84] Appointed to fill vacancy caused by resignation of Felix Cordova Davila, and took his seat April 28, 1932.

SEVENTY-THIRD CONGRESS

MARCH 4, 1933, TO JANUARY 3,[1] 1935

FIRST SESSION—*March 9, 1933, to June 15, 1933*

SECOND SESSION—*January 3,[1] 1934, to June 18, 1934*

SPECIAL SESSION OF THE SENATE—*March 4, 1933, to March 6, 1933*

————

VICE PRESIDENT OF THE UNITED STATES—JOHN N. GARNER, of Texas

PRESIDENT PRO TEMPORE OF THE SENATE—KEY PITTMAN,[2] of Nevada

SECRETARY OF THE SENATE—EDWIN A. HALSEY,[3] of Virginia

SERGEANT AT ARMS OF THE SENATE—CHESLEY W. JURNEY,[4] of Texas

————

SPEAKER OF THE HOUSE OF REPRESENTATIVES—HENRY T. RAINEY,[5] of Illinois

CLERK OF THE HOUSE—SOUTH TRIMBLE,[6] of Kentucky

SERGEANT AT ARMS OF THE HOUSE—KENNETH ROMNEY, of Montana

DOORKEEPER OF THE HOUSE—JOSEPH J. SINNOTT, of Virginia

POSTMASTER OF THE HOUSE—FINIS E. SCOTT

ALABAMA

SENATORS

Hugo L. Black, *Birmingham*
John H. Bankhead 2d, *Jasper*

REPRESENTATIVES

John McDuffie, *Monroeville*
Lister Hill, *Montgomery*
Henry B. Steagall, *Ozark*
Lamar Jeffers, *Anniston*
Miles C. Allgood, *Gadsden*
William B. Oliver, *Tuscaloosa*
William B. Bankhead, *Jasper*
Edward B. Almon,[7] *Tuscumbia*
Archibald H. Carmichael,[8] *Tuscumbia*
George Huddleston, *Birmingham*

ARIZONA

SENATORS

Henry F. Ashurst, *Prescott*
Carl Hayden, *Phoenix*

REPRESENTATIVE

At Large—Mrs. Isabella S. Greenway,[9] *Ajo*

ARKANSAS

SENATORS

Joseph T. Robinson, *Little Rock*
Mrs. Hattie W. Caraway, *Jonesboro*

REPRESENTATIVES

William J. Driver, *Osceola*
John E. Miller, *Searcy*
Claude A. Fuller, *Eureka Springs*
William B. Cravens, *Fort Smith*
Heartsill Ragon,[10] *Clarksville*
David D. Terry,[11] *Little Rock*
David D. Glover, *Malvern*
Tilman B. Parks, *Camden*

CALIFORNIA

SENATORS

Hiram W. Johnson, *San Francisco*
William Gibbs McAdoo, *Los Angeles*

REPRESENTATIVES

Clarence F. Lea, *Santa Rosa*
Harry L. Englebright, *Nevada City*

Frank H. Buck, *Vacaville*
Mrs. Florence P. Kahn, *San Francisco*
Richard J. Welch, *San Francisco*
Albert E. Carter, *Oakland*
Ralph R. Eltse, *Berkeley*
John J. McGrath, *San Mateo*
Denver S. Church, *Fresno*
Henry E. Stubbs, *Santa Maria*
William E. Evans, *Glendale*
John H. Hoeppel, *Arcadia*
Charles Kramer, *Los Angeles*
Thomas F. Ford, *Los Angeles*
William I. Traeger, *Los Angeles*
John F. Dockweiler, *Los Angeles*
Charles J. Colden, *San Pedro*
John H. Burke, *Long Beach*
Samuel L. Collins, *Fullerton*
George Burnham,[12] *San Diego*

COLORADO

SENATORS

Edward P. Costigan, *Denver*
Alva B. Adams, *Pueblo*

————

[1] Pursuant to the twentieth amendment to the Constitution, the regular sessions of Congress will hereafter begin on January 3 of each year.
[2] Elected March 9, 1933.
[3] Unanimously elected March 9, 1933.
[4] Elected March 9, 1933.
[5] Elected March 9, 1933; died August 19, 1934.

[6] Reelected March 9, 1933.
[7] Died June 22, 1933.
[8] Elected to fill vacancy caused by death of Edward B. Almon, and took his seat January 3, 1934.
[9] Elected to fill vacancy caused by resignation of Representative-elect Lewis W. Douglas, in preceding Congress, and took her seat January 3, 1934.

[10] Resigned June 16, 1933, having been appointed a judge of the United States district court, western district of Arkansas.
[11] Elected to fill vacancy caused by resignation of Heartsill Ragon, and took his seat January 3, 1934.
[12] Election unsuccessfully contested by Claude Chandler.

COLORADO—Continued

REPRESENTATIVES

Lawrence Lewis, *Denver*
Fred Cummings, *Fort Collins*
John A. Martin, *Pueblo*
Edward T. Taylor, *Glenwood Springs*

CONNECTICUT

SENATORS

Frederic C. Walcott, *Norfolk*
Augustine Lonergan, *Hartford*

REPRESENTATIVES

Herman P. Kopplemann, *Hartford*
William L. Higgins,[13] *South Coventry*
Francis T. Maloney, *Meriden*
Schuyler Merritt, *Stamford*
Edward W. Goss,[14] *Waterbury*
At Large—Charles M. Bakewell, *New Haven*

DELAWARE

SENATORS

Daniel O. Hastings, *Wilmington*
John G. Townsend, Jr., *Selbyville*

REPRESENTATIVE

At Large—Wilbur L. Adams, *Wilmington*

FLORIDA

SENATORS

Duncan U. Fletcher, *Jacksonville*
Park Trammell, *Lakeland*

REPRESENTATIVES

J. Hardin Peterson, *Lakeland*
Robert A. Green, *Starke*
Millard F. Caldwell, *Milton*
J. Mark Wilcox, *West Palm Beach*
At Large—William J. Sears, *Jacksonville*

GEORGIA

SENATORS

Walter F. George, *Vienna*
Richard B. Russell, *Winder*

REPRESENTATIVES

Homer C. Parker, *Statesboro*
Edward E. Cox, *Camilla*
Bryant T. Castellow, *Cuthbert*
Emmett M. Owen, *Griffin*
Robert Ramspeck, *Decatur*
Carl Vinson, *Milledgeville*
Malcolm C. Tarver, *Dalton*

Braswell D. Deen, *Alma*
John S. Wood, *Canton*
Charles H. Brand,[15] *Athens*
Paul Brown,[16] *Elberton*

IDAHO

SENATORS

William E. Borah, *Boise*
James P. Pope, *Boise*

REPRESENTATIVES

Compton I. White, *Clark Fork*
Thomas C. Coffin,[17] *Pocatello*

ILLINOIS

SENATORS

J. Hamilton Lewis, *Chicago*
William H. Dieterich, *Beardstown*

REPRESENTATIVES

Oscar De Priest, *Chicago*
Patrick H. Moynihan, *Chicago*
Edward A. Kelly, *Chicago*
Harry P. Beam, *Chicago*
Adolph J. Sabath, *Chicago*
Thomas J. O'Brien, *Chicago*
Leonard W. Schuetz, *Chicago*
Leo Kocialkowski, *Chicago*
Fred A. Britten,[18] *Chicago*
James Simpson, Jr.,[19] *Wadsworth*
Frank R. Reid, *Aurora*
John T. Buckbee, *Rockford*
Leo E. Allen, *Galena*
Chester C. Thompson, *Rock Island*
J. Leroy Adair, *Quincy*
Everett M. Dirksen, *Pekin*
James Frank Gillespie, *Bloomington*
James A. Meeks, *Danville*
Donald C. Dobbins, *Champaign*
Henry T. Rainey,[20] *Carrollton*
J. Earl Major,[21] *Hillsboro*
Edwin M. Schaefer, *Belleville*
William W. Arnold, *Robinson*
Claude V. Parsons, *Golconda*
Kent E. Keller, *Ava*
At Large—
    Martin A. Brennan, *Bloomington*
    Walter Nesbit, *Belleville*

INDIANA

SENATORS

Arthur R. Robinson, *Indianapolis*
Frederick Van Nuys, *Indianapolis*

REPRESENTATIVES

William T. Schulte, *Hammond*
George R. Durgan, *La Fayette*

Samuel B. Pettengill, *South Bend*
James I. Farley, *Auburn*
Glenn Griswold, *Peru*
Mrs. Virginia E. Jenckes, *Terre Haute*
Arthur H. Greenwood, *Washington*
John W. Boehne, Jr., *Evansville*
Eugene B. Crowe, *Bedford*
Finly H. Gray, *Connersville*
William H. Larrabee, *New Palestine*
Louis Ludlow, *Indianapolis*

IOWA

SENATORS

Lester J. Dickinson, *Algona*
Richard Louis Murphy, *Dubuque*

REPRESENTATIVES

Edward C. Eicher, *Washington*
Bernhard M. Jacobsen, *Clinton*
Albert C. Willford, *Waterloo*
Fred Biermann, *Decorah*
Lloyd Thurston,[22] *Osceola*
Cassius C. Dowell, *Des Moines*
Otha D. Wearin, *Hastings*
Fred C. Gilchrist, *Laurens*
Guy M. Gillette, *Cherokee*

KANSAS

SENATORS

Arthur Capper, *Topeka*
George McGill, *Wichita*

REPRESENTATIVES

William P. Lambertson, *Fairview*
Ulysses S. Guyer, *Kansas City*
Harold McGugin, *Coffeyville*
William Randolph Carpenter, *Marion*
William A. Ayres,[23] *Wichita*
Miss Kathryn E. O'Loughlin,[24] *Hays*
Clifford R. Hope, *Garden City*

KENTUCKY

SENATORS

Alben W. Barkley, *Paducah*
Marvel M. Logan, *Bowling Green*

REPRESENTATIVES AT LARGE

Fred M. Vinson, *Ashland*
John Y. Brown, *Lexington*
Andrew J. May, *Prestonsburg*
Brent Spence, *Fort Thomas*
Virgil M. Chapman, *Paris*
Glover H. Cary, *Owensboro*
William V. Gregory, *Mayfield*
Cap R. Carden, *Munfordville*
Finley Hamilton, *London*

---

[13] Election unsuccessfully contested by William C. Fox.
[14] Election unsuccessfully contested by Martin E. Gormley.
[15] Died May 17, 1933.
[16] Elected to fill vacancy caused by death of Charles H. Brand, and took his seat January 3, 1934.
[17] Died June 8, 1934; vacancy throughout remainder of the Congress.

[18] Election unsuccessfully contested by James McAndrews.
[19] Election unsuccessfully contested by Charles H. Weber.
[20] Died August 19, 1934; vacancy throughout remainder of the Congress.
[21] Resigned October 6, 1933, having been appointed a judge of the United States district court, southern

district of Illinois; vacancy throughout remainder of the Congress.
[22] Election unsuccessfully contested by Lloyd Ellis.
[23] Resigned August 22, 1934, having been appointed a member of the Federal Trade Commission; vacancy throughout remainder of the Congress.
[24] After election was married and name changed to Kathryn O'Loughlin McCarthy.

LOUISIANA

SENATORS

Huey P. Long, *New Orleans*
John H. Overton, *Alexandria*

REPRESENTATIVES

Joachim O. Fernandez, *New Orleans*
Paul H. Maloney, *New Orleans*
Numa F. Montet, *Thibodaux*
John N. Sandlin, *Minden*
Riley J. Wilson, *Ruston*
Bolivar E. Kemp,[25] *Amite*
Jared Y. Sanders, Jr.,[26] *Baton Rouge*
René L. DeRouen, *Ville Platte*
Cleveland Dear, *Alexandria*

MAINE

SENATORS

Frederick Hale, *Portland*
Wallace H. White, Jr., *Auburn*

REPRESENTATIVES

Carroll L. Beedy, *Portland*
Edward C. Moran, Jr., *Rockland*
John G. Utterback,[27] *Bangor*

MARYLAND

SENATORS

Millard E. Tydings, *Havre de Grace*
Phillips Lee Goldsborough, *Baltimore*

REPRESENTATIVES

T. Alan Goldsborough, *Denton*
William P. Cole, Jr., *Towson*
Vincent L. Palmisano, *Baltimore*
Ambrose J. Kennedy, *Baltimore*
Stephen W. Gambrill, *Laurel*
David J. Lewis, *Cumberland*

MASSACHUSETTS

SENATORS

David I. Walsh, *Fitchburg*
Marcus A. Coolidge, *Fitchburg*

REPRESENTATIVES

Allen T. Treadway, *Stockbridge*
William J. Granfield, *Springfield*
Frank H. Foss, *Fitchburg*
Pehr G. Holmes, *Worcester*
Mrs. Edith Nourse Rogers, *Lowell*
A. Piatt Andrew, Jr., *Gloucester*
William P. Connery, Jr., *Lynn*
Arthur D. Healey, *Somerville*
Robert Luce, *Waltham*
George H. Tinkham, *Boston*

John J. Douglass, *Boston*
John W. McCormack, *Dorchester*
Richard B. Wigglesworth, *Milton*
Joseph W. Martin, Jr., *North Attleboro*
Charles L. Gifford, *Cotuit*

MICHIGAN

SENATORS

James Couzens, *Detroit*
Arthur H. Vandenberg, *Grand Rapids*

REPRESENTATIVES

George G. Sadowski, *Detroit*
John C. Lehr, *Monroe*
Joseph L. Hooper,[28] *Battle Creek*
George E. Foulkes, *Hartford*
Carl E. Mapes, *Grand Rapids*
Claude E. Cady, *Lansing*
Jesse P. Wolcott, *Port Huron*
Michael J. Hart, *Saginaw*
Harry W. Musselwhite, *Manistee*
Roy O. Woodruff, *Bay City*
Prentiss M. Brown, *St. Ignace*
W. Frank James, *Hancock*
Clarence J. McLeod, *Detroit*
Carl M. Weideman, *Detroit*
John D. Dingell,[29] *Detroit*
John Lesinski, *Dearborn*
George A. Dondero, *Royal Oak*

MINNESOTA

SENATORS

Henrik Shipstead, *Miltona*
Thomas D. Schall, *Excelsior*

REPRESENTATIVES AT LARGE

Magnus John, *Kimball*
Paul J. Kvale, *Benson*
Henry Arens, *Jordan*
Ernest Lundeen, *Minneapolis*
Theodore Christianson, *Minneapolis*
Einar Hoidale, *Minneapolis*
Ray P. Chase, *Anoka*
Francis H. Shoemaker, *Red Wing*
Harold Knutson, *St. Cloud*

MISSISSIPPI

SENATORS

Pat Harrison, *Gulfport*
Hubert D. Stephens, *New Albany*

REPRESENTATIVES

John E. Rankin, *Tupelo*
Wall Doxey, *Holly Springs*
William M. Whittington, *Greenwood*
T. Jeff. Busby, *Houston*

Ross A. Collins, *Meridian*
William M. Colmer, *Pascagoula*
Lawrence Russell Ellzey,[30] *Wesson*

MISSOURI

SENATORS

Roscoe C. Patterson, *Kansas City*
Joel Bennett Clark, *St. Louis*

REPRESENTATIVES AT LARGE

John J. Cochran, *St. Louis*
James R. Claiborne, *St. Louis*
Joseph B. Shannon, *Kansas City*
Clyde Williams, *Hillsboro*
Clarence Cannon, *Elsberry*
Frank H. Lee, *Joplin*
James E. Ruffin, *Springfield*
Ralph F. Lozier, *Carrollton*
Jacob L. Milligan, *Richmond*
Reuben T. Wood, *Springfield*
Milton A. Romjue, *Macon*
Richard M. Duncan, *St. Joseph*
Clement C. Dickinson, *Clinton*

MONTANA

SENATORS

Burton K. Wheeler, *Butte*
John E. Erickson,[31] *Kalispell*
James E. Murray,[32] *Butte*

REPRESENTATIVES

Joseph P. Monaghan, *Butte*
Roy E. Ayers, *Lewistown*

NEBRASKA

SENATORS

George W. Norris, *McCook*
Robert B. Howell,[33] *Omaha*
William H. Thompson,[34] *Grand Island*
Richard C. Hunter,[35] *Omaha*

REPRESENTATIVES

John H. Morehead, *Falls City*
Edward R. Burke, *Omaha*
Edgar Howard, *Columbus*
Ashton C. Shallenberger, *Alma*
Terry M. Carpenter, *Scottsbluff*

NEVADA

SENATORS

Key Pittman, *Tonopah*
Patrick A. McCarran, *Reno*

REPRESENTATIVE

At Large—James G. Scrugham, *Reno*

---

[25] Died June 19, 1933.
[26] Contested the election of Mrs. Bolivar E. Kemp, who had presented credentials as a Member-elect to fill the vacancy caused by the death of her husband, Bolivar E. Kemp, but who was not permitted to qualify, the seat being declared vacant; subsequently elected to fill this vacancy, and took his seat May 21, 1934.
[27] Election unsuccessfully contested by Ralph O. Brewster.

[28] Died February 22, 1934; vacancy throughout remainder of the Congress.
[29] Election unsuccessfully contested by Charles Bowles.
[30] Election unsuccessfully contested by L. G. Reese.
[31] Appointed to fill vacancy caused by death of Thomas J. Walsh, in preceding Congress, and took his seat March 20, 1933.
[32] Elected November 6, 1934, to fill vacancy caused

by death of Thomas J. Walsh, and took his seat January 3, 1935.
[33] Died March 11, 1933.
[34] Appointed to fill vacancy caused by death of Robert B. Howell, and took his seat May 26, 1933.
[35] Elected to fill vacancy caused by death of Robert B. Howell, and served from November 7, 1934, to January 3, 1935.

NEW HAMPSHIRE

SENATORS

Henry W. Keyes, *Haverhill*
Fred H. Brown, *Somersworth*

REPRESENTATIVES

William N. Rogers, *Sanbornville*
Charles W. Tobey, *Temple*

NEW JERSEY

SENATORS

Hamilton F. Kean, *Elizabeth*
W. Warren Barbour, *Locust*

REPRESENTATIVES

Charles A. Wolverton, *Camden*
Isaac Bacharach, *Atlantic City*
William H. Sutphin, *Matawan*
D. Lane Powers, *Trenton*
Charles A. Eaton, *North Plainfield*
Donald H. McLean, *Elizabeth*
Randolph Perkins, *Woodcliff Lake*
George N. Seger, *Passaic*
Edward A. Kenney, *Cliffside Park*
Fred A. Hartley, Jr., *Kearny*
Peter A. Cavicchia, *Newark*
Frederick R. Lehlbach, *Newark*
Mrs. Mary T. Norton, *Jersey City*
Oscar L. Auf der Heide, *West New York*

NEW MEXICO

SENATORS

Sam G. Bratton,[36] *Albuquerque*
Carl A. Hatch,[37] *Clovis*
Bronson M. Cutting, *Santa Fe*

REPRESENTATIVE

At Large—Dennis Chavez, *Albuquerque*

NEW YORK

SENATORS

Royal S. Copeland, *New York City*
Robert F. Wagner, *New York City*

REPRESENTATIVES

Robert L. Bacon, *Old Westbury*
William F. Brunner, *Rockaway Park*
George W. Lindsay, *Brooklyn*
Thomas H. Cullen, *Brooklyn*
Loring M. Black, Jr., *Brooklyn*
Andrew L. Somers, *Brooklyn*
John J. Delaney, *Brooklyn*
Patrick J. Carley, *Brooklyn*
Stephen A. Rudd, *Brooklyn*
Emanuel Celler, *Brooklyn*
Anning S. Prall, *West New Brighton*
Samuel Dickstein, *New York City*

Christopher D. Sullivan, *New York City*
William I. Sirovich, *New York City*
John J. Boylan, *New York City*
John J. O'Connor, *New York City*
Theodore A. Peyser, *New York City*
Martin J. Kennedy, *New York City*
Sol Bloom, *New York City*
James J. Lanzetta, *New York City*
Joseph A. Gavagan, *New York City*
Anthony J. Griffin, *New York City*
Frank Oliver,[38] *Bronx*
James M. Fitzpatrick, *New York City*
Charles D. Millard, *Tarrytown*
Hamilton Fish, Jr., *Garrison*
Philip A. Goodwin, *Coxsackie*
Parker Corning, *Albany*
James S. Parker,[39] *Salem*
William D. Thomas,[40] *Hoosick Falls*
Frank Crowther, *Schenectady*
Bertrand H. Snell, *Potsdam*
Francis D. Culkin, *Oswego*
Fred J. Sisson, *Whitesboro*
John D. Clarke,[41] *Fraser*
Mrs. Marian W. Clarke,[42] *Fraser*
Clarence E. Hancock, *Syracuse*
John Taber, *Auburn*
Gale H. Stalker, *Elmira*
James L. Whitley, *Rochester*
James W. Wadsworth, Jr., *Geneseo*
Walter G. Andrews, *Buffalo*
Alfred F. Beiter, *Williamsville*
James M. Mead, *Buffalo*
Daniel A. Reed, *Dunkirk*
At Large—
　Elmer E. Studley, *Flushing*
　John Fitzgibbons, *Oswego*

NORTH CAROLINA

SENATORS

Josiah W. Bailey, *Raleigh*
Robert R. Reynolds, *Asheville*

REPRESENTATIVES

Lindsay C. Warren, *Washington*
John H. Kerr, *Warrenton*
Charles L. Abernethy, *New Bern*
Edward W. Pou,[43] *Smithfield*
Harold D. Cooley,[44] *Nashville*
Franklin W. Hancock, Jr., *Oxford*
William B. Umstead, *Durham*
J. Bayard Clark, *Fayetteville*
J. Walter Lambeth, *Thomasville*
Robert L. Doughton, *Laurel Springs*
Alfred L. Bulwinkle, *Gastonia*
Zebulon Weaver, *Asheville*

NORTH DAKOTA

SENATORS

Lynn J. Frazier, *Hoople*
Gerald P. Nye, *Cooperstown*

REPRESENTATIVES AT LARGE

James H. Sinclair, *Kenmare*
William Lemke, *Fargo*

OHIO

SENATORS

Simeon D. Fess, *Yellow Springs*
Robert J. Bulkley, *Cleveland*

REPRESENTATIVES

John B. Hollister, *Cincinnati*
William E. Hess, *Cincinnati*
Byron B. Harlan, *Dayton*
Frank L. Kloeb, *Celina*
Frank C. Kniffin, *Napoleon*
James G. Polk, *Highland*
Leroy T. Marshall, *Xenia*
Thomas Brooks Fletcher, *Marion*
Warren J. Duffey, *Toledo*
Thomas A. Jenkins, *Ironton*
Mell G. Underwood, *New Lexington*
Arthur P. Lamneck, *Columbus*
William L. Fiesinger, *Sandusky*
Dow W. Harter, *Akron*
Robert T. Secrest, *Senecaville*
William R. Thom, *Canton*
Charles West, *Granville*
Lawrence E. Imhoff, *St. Clairsville*
John G. Cooper, *Youngstown*
Martin L. Sweeney, *Cleveland*
Robert Crosser, *Cleveland*
Chester C. Bolton, *Cleveland*
At Large—
　Charles V. Truax, *Bucyrus*
　Stephen M. Young, *Cleveland*

OKLAHOMA

SENATORS

J. W. Elmer Thomas, *Medicine Park*
Thomas P. Gore, *Oklahoma City*

REPRESENTATIVES

Wesley E. Disney, *Tulsa*
William W. Hastings, *Tahlequah*
Wilburn Cartwright, *McAlester*
Thomas D. McKeown, *Ada*
Fletcher B. Swank, *Norman*
Jed Johnson, *Anadarko*
James V. McClintic, *Snyder*
Ernest W. Marland, *Ponca City*
At Large—Will Rogers, *Oklahoma City*

OREGON

SENATORS

Charles L. McNary, *Salem*
Frederick Steiwer, *Portland*

---

[36] Resigned June 24, 1933, having been appointed a judge of the Circuit Court of Appeals of the United States.
[37] Appointed to fill vacancy caused by resignation of Sam G. Bratton, and took his seat January 3, 1934; subsequently elected.
[38] Resigned June 18, 1934, having been appointed a

magistrate in the city of New York; vacancy throughout remainder of the Congress.
[39] Died December 19, 1933.
[40] Elected to fill vacancy caused by death of James S. Parker, and took his seat February 5, 1934.
[41] Died November 5, 1933.
[42] Elected to fill vacancy caused by death of her hus-

band, John D. Clarke, and took her seat January 3, 1934.
[43] Died April 1, 1934.
[44] Elected to fill vacancy caused by death of Edward W. Pou, and served from July 7, 1934, to January 3, 1935.

REPRESENTATIVES

James W. Mott, *Salem*
Walter M. Pierce, *La Grande*
Charles H. Martin, *Portland*

PENNSYLVANIA

SENATORS

David A. Reed, *Pittsburgh*
James J. Davis, *Pittsburgh*

REPRESENTATIVES

Harry C. Ransley, *Philadelphia*
James M. Beck,[45] *Philadelphia*
Alfred M. Waldron, *Philadelphia*
George W. Edmonds, *Philadelphia*
James J. Connolly, *Philadelphia*
Edward L. Stokes, *Philadelphia*
George P. Darrow, *Philadelphia*
James Wolfenden, *Upper Darby*
Henry W. Watson,[46] *Langhorne*
Oliver W. Frey,[47] *Allentown*
J. Roland Kinzer, *Lancaster*
Patrick J. Boland, *Scranton*
C. Murray Turpin,[48] *Kingston*
George F. Brumm,[49] *Minersville*
William E. Richardson, *Reading*
Louis T. McFadden, *Canton*
Robert F. Rich, *Woolrich*
J. William Ditter, *Ambler*
Benjamin K. Focht, *Lewisburg*
Isaac H. Doutrich, *Harrisburg*
Thomas C. Cochran, *Mercer*
Francis E. Walter, *Easton*
Harry L. Haines, *Red Lion*
J. Banks Kurtz, *Altoona*
J. Buell Snyder, *Perryopolis*
Charles I. Faddis, *Waynesburg*
J. Howard Swick, *Beaver Falls*
Nathan L. Strong, *Brookville*
William M. Berlin, *Greensburg*
Charles N. Crosby, *Meadville*
J. Twing Brooks, *Sewickley*
M. Clyde Kelly, *Edgewood*
Michael J. Muldowney, *Pittsburgh*
Henry Ellenbogen,[50] *Pittsburgh*
Matthew A. Dunn, *Pittsburgh*

RHODE ISLAND

SENATORS

Jesse H. Metcalf, *Providence*
Felix Hébert, *West Warwick*

REPRESENTATIVES

Francis B. Condon, *Central Falls*
John M. O'Connell, *Westerly*

SOUTH CAROLINA

SENATORS

Ellison D. Smith, *Lynchburg*
James F. Byrnes, *Spartanburg*

REPRESENTATIVES

Thomas S. McMillan, *Charleston*
Hampton P. Fulmer, *Orangeburg*
John C. Taylor, *Anderson*
John J. McSwain, *Greenville*
James P. Richards, *Lancaster*
Allard H. Gasque, *Florence*

SOUTH DAKOTA

SENATORS

Peter Norbeck, *Redfield*
William J. Bulow, *Beresford*

REPRESENTATIVES

Fred H. Hildebrandt, *Watertown*
Theodore B. Werner, *Rapid City*

TENNESSEE

SENATORS

Kenneth D. McKellar, *Memphis*
Nathan L. Bachman,[51] *Chattanooga*

REPRESENTATIVES

B. Carroll Reece,[52] *Johnson City*
J. Will Taylor, *La Follette*
Sam D. McReynolds, *Chattanooga*
John R. Mitchell, *Cookeville*
Joseph W. Byrns, *Nashville*
Clarence W. Turner, *Waverly*
Gordon Browning, *Huntingdon*
Jere Cooper, *Dyersburg*
Edward H. Crump, *Memphis*

TEXAS

SENATORS

Morris Sheppard, *Texarkana*
Tom T. Connally, *Marlin*

REPRESENTATIVES

Wright Patman, *Texarkana*
Martin Dies, Jr., *Orange*
Morgan G. Sanders, *Canton*
Sam Rayburn, *Bonham*

Hatton W. Sumners, *Dallas*
Luther A. Johnson, *Corsicana*
Clay Stone Briggs,[53] *Galveston*
Clark W. Thompson,[54] *Galveston*
Joe H. Eagle,[55] *Houston*
Joseph J. Mansfield, *Columbus*
James P. Buchanan, *Brenham*
Oliver H. Cross, *Waco*
Fritz G. Lanham, *Fort Worth*
William D. McFarlane, *Graham*
Richard M. Kleberg, *Corpus Christi*
Milton H. West,[56] *Brownsville*
R. Ewing Thomason, *El Paso*
Thomas L. Blanton, *Abilene*
Marvin Jones, *Amarillo*
At Large—
    George B. Terrell, *Alto*
    Sterling P. Strong, *Dallas*
    Joseph W. Bailey, Jr., *Dallas*

UTAH

SENATORS

William H. King, *Salt Lake City*
Elbert D. Thomas, *Salt Lake City*

REPRESENTATIVES

Abe Murdock, *Beaver*
J. W. Robinson, *Provo*

VERMONT

SENATORS

Porter H. Dale,[57] *Island Pond*
Ernest Willard Gibson,[58] *Brattleboro*
Warren R. Austin, *Burlington*

REPRESENTATIVE AT LARGE

Ernest Willard Gibson,[59] *Brattleboro*
Charles A. Plumley,[60] *Northfield*

VIRGINIA

SENATORS

Carter Glass, *Lynchburg*
Harry Flood Byrd,[61] *Berryville*

REPRESENTATIVES AT LARGE

Clifton A. Woodrum, *Roanoke*
Andrew J. Montague, *Richmond*
Schuyler Otis Bland, *Newport News*
Thomas G. Burch, *Martinsville*
A. Willis Robertson, *Lexington*
Howard W. Smith, *Alexandria*
Patrick Henry Drewry, *Petersburg*
Colgate W. Darden, Jr., *Norfolk*
John W. Flannagan, Jr., *Bristol*

---

[45] Election unsuccessfully contested by John J. Shanahan; resigned September 30, 1934; vacancy throughout remainder of the Congress.
[46] Died August 27, 1933.
[47] Elected to fill vacancy caused by death of Henry W. Watson, and took his seat January 3, 1934.
[48] Election unsuccessfully contested by John J. Casey.
[49] Died May 29, 1934; vacancy throughout remainder of the Congress.
[50] Election unsuccessfully contested by Harry E. Estep.

[51] Appointed to fill vacancy caused by resignation of Cordell Hull, and took his seat March 4, 1933; subsequently elected.
[52] Election unsuccessfully contested by O. B. Lovette.
[53] Died April 29, 1933.
[54] Elected to fill vacancy caused by death of Clay Stone Briggs, and took his seat January 3, 1934.
[55] Elected to fill vacancy caused by death of Representative-elect Daniel E. Garrett, in preceding Congress.
[56] Elected to fill vacancy caused by resignation of

Representative-elect John N. Garner, in preceding Congress, and took his seat May 2, 1933.
[57] Died October 6, 1933.
[58] Appointed to fill vacancy caused by death of Porter H. Dale, and took his seat February 1, 1934; subsequently elected.
[59] Resigned October 19, 1933, having been appointed Senator.
[60] Elected to fill vacancy caused by resignation of Ernest W. Gibson, and took his seat January 18, 1934.
[61] Appointed to fill vacancy caused by resignation of Claude A. Swanson, and took his seat March 4, 1933; subsequently elected.

WASHINGTON

SENATORS

Clarence C. Dill, *Spokane*
Homer T. Bone, *Tacoma*

REPRESENTATIVES

Marion A. Zioncheck, *Seattle*
Monrad C. Wallgren, *Everett*
Martin F. Smith, *Hoquiam*
Knute Hill, *Prosser*
Samuel B. Hill, *Waterville*
Wesley Lloyd, *Tacoma*

WEST VIRGINIA

SENATORS

Henry D. Hatfield, *Huntington*
Matthew M. Neely, *Fairmont*

REPRESENTATIVES

Robert L. Ramsay, *Follansbee*
Jennings Randolph, *Elkins*
Lynn S. Hornor,[62] *Clarksburg*
Andrew Edmiston,[63] *Weston*
George W. Johnson, *Parkersburg*

John Kee, *Bluefield*
Joe L. Smith *Beckley*

WISCONSIN

SENATORS

Robert M. La Follette, Jr., *Madison*
F. Ryan Duffy, *Fond du Lac*

REPRESENTATIVES

George W. Blanchard, *Edgerton*
Charles W. Henney, *Portage*
Gardner R. Withrow, *La Crosse*
Raymond J. Cannon, *Milwaukee*
Thomas O'Malley, *Milwaukee*
Michael K. Reilly, *Fond du Lac*
Gerald J. Boileau, *Wausau*
James F. Hughes, *De Pere*
James A. Frear, *Hudson*
Hubert H. Peavey, *Washburn*

WYOMING

SENATORS

John B. Kendrick,[64] *Sheridan*
Joseph C. O'Mahoney,[65] *Cheyenne*
Robert D. Carey, *Careyhurst*

REPRESENTATIVE

At Large—Vincent M. Carter, *Kemmerer*

TERRITORY OF ALASKA

DELEGATE

Anthony J. Dimond, *Valdez*

TERRITORY OF HAWAII

DELEGATE

Lincoln L. McCandless, *Honolulu*

PHILIPPINE ISLANDS

RESIDENT COMMISSIONERS

Pedro Guevara, *Santa Cruz*
Camilo Osias, *Balaoan*

PUERTO RICO

RESIDENT COMMISSIONER

Santiago Iglesias, *San Juan*

---

[62] Died September 23, 1933.
[63] Elected to fill vacancy caused by death of Lynn S. Hornor, and took his seat January 3, 1934.
[64] Died November 3, 1933.

[65] Appointed to fill vacancy caused by death of John B. Kendrick, and took his seat January 3, 1934; subsequently elected.

SEVENTY-FOURTH CONGRESS

JANUARY 3, 1935, TO JANUARY 3, 1937

FIRST SESSION—*January 3, 1935, to August 26, 1935*

SECOND SESSION—*January 3, 1936, to June 20, 1936*

VICE PRESIDENT OF THE UNITED STATES—John N. Garner, of Texas

PRESIDENT PRO TEMPORE OF THE SENATE—Key Pittman,[1] of Nevada

SECRETARY OF THE SENATE—Edwin A. Halsey, of Virginia

SERGEANT AT ARMS OF THE SENATE—Chesley W. Jurney, of Texas

SPEAKER OF THE HOUSE OF REPRESENTATIVES—Joseph W. Byrns,[2] of Tennessee; William B. Bankhead,[3] of Alabama

CLERK OF THE HOUSE—South Trimble,[4] of Kentucky

SERGEANT AT ARMS OF THE HOUSE—Kenneth Romney, of Montana

DOORKEEPER OF THE HOUSE—Joseph J. Sinnott, of Virginia

POSTMASTER OF THE HOUSE—Finis E. Scott

ALABAMA

SENATORS

Hugo L. Black, *Birmingham*
John H. Bankhead 2d, *Jasper*

REPRESENTATIVES

John McDuffie,[5] *Monroeville*
Frank W. Boykin,[6] *Mobile*
Lister Hill, *Montgomery*
Henry B. Steagall, *Ozark*
Sam Hobbs, *Selma*
Joe Starnes, *Guntersville*
William B. Oliver, *Tuscaloosa*
William B. Bankhead, *Jasper*
Archibald H. Carmichael, *Tuscumbia*
George Huddleston, *Birmingham*

ARIZONA

SENATORS

Henry F. Ashurst, *Prescott*
Carl Hayden, *Phoenix*

REPRESENTATIVE

At Large—Mrs. Isabella S. Greenway, *Ajo*

ARKANSAS

SENATORS

Joseph T. Robinson, *Little Rock*
Mrs. Hattie W. Caraway, *Jonesboro*

REPRESENTATIVES

William J. Driver, *Osceola*
John E. Miller, *Searcy*
Claude A. Fuller, *Eureka Springs*
William B. Cravens, *Fort Smith*
David D. Terry, *Little Rock*
John L. McClellan, *Malvern*
Tilman B. Parks, *Camden*

CALIFORNIA

SENATORS

Hiram W. Johnson, *San Francisco*
William Gibbs McAdoo, *Los Angeles*

REPRESENTATIVES

Clarence F. Lea, *Santa Rosa*
Harry L. Englebright, *Nevada City*
Frank H. Buck, *Vacaville*
Mrs. Florence P. Kahn, *San Francisco*
Richard J. Welch, *San Francisco*
Albert E. Carter, *Oakland*
John H. Tolan, *Oakland*
John J. McGrath, *San Mateo*

Bertrand W. Gearhart, *Fresno*
Henry E. Stubbs, *Santa Maria*
John S. McGroarty, *Tujunga*
John H. Hoeppel, *Arcadia*
Charles Kramer, *Los Angeles*
Thomas F. Ford, *Los Angeles*
John M. Costello, *Hollywood*
John F. Dockweiler, *Los Angeles*
Charles J. Colden, *San Pedro*
Byron N. Scott, *Long Beach*
Samuel L. Collins, *Fullerton*
George Burnham, *San Diego*

COLORADO

SENATORS

Edward P. Costigan, *Denver*
Alva B. Adams, *Pueblo*

REPRESENTATIVES

Lawrence Lewis, *Denver*
Fred Cummings, *Fort Collins*
John A. Martin, *Pueblo*
Edward T. Taylor, *Glenwood Springs*

CONNECTICUT

SENATORS

Augustine Lonergan, *Hartford*
Francis T. Maloney, *Meriden*

---

[1] Reelected January 7, 1935.
[2] Elected January 3, 1935; died June 4, 1936.
[3] Elected June 4, 1936.

[4] Reelected January 3, 1935.
[5] Resigned March 2, 1935, having been appointed a judge in the United States District Court.

[6] Elected to fill vacancy caused by resignation of John McDuffie, and took his seat August 12, 1935.

CONNECTICUT—Continued

REPRESENTATIVES

Herman P. Kopplemann, *Hartford*
William L. Higgins, *South Coventry*
James A. Shanley, *New Haven*
Schuyler Merritt, *Stamford*
J. Joseph Smith, *Waterbury*
At Large—William M. Citron, *Middletown*

DELAWARE

SENATORS

Daniel O. Hastings, *Wilmington*
John G. Townsend, Jr., *Selbyville*

REPRESENTATIVE

At Large—John G. Stewart, *Wilmington*

FLORIDA

SENATORS

Duncan U. Fletcher,[7] *Jacksonville*
William L. Hill,[8] *Gainesville*
Claude Pepper,[9] *Tallahassee*
Park Trammell,[10] *Lakeland*
Scott M. Loftin,[11] *Jacksonville*
Charles O. Andrews,[12] *Orlando*

REPRESENTATIVES

J. Hardin Peterson, *Lakeland*
Robert A. Green, *Starke*
Millard F. Caldwell, *Milton*
J. Mark Wilcox, *West Palm Beach*
At Large—William J. Sears, *Jacksonville*

GEORGIA

SENATORS

Walter F. George, *Vienna*
Richard B. Russell, *Winder*

REPRESENTATIVES

Hugh Peterson, *Ailey*
Edward E. Cox, *Camilla*
Bryant T. Castellow, *Cuthbert*
Emmett M. Owen, *Griffin*
Robert Ramspeck, *Atlanta*
Carl Vinson, *Milledgeville*
Malcolm C. Tarver, *Dalton*
Braswell D. Deen, *Alma*
B. Frank Whelchel, *Gainesville*
Paul Brown, *Elberton*

IDAHO

SENATORS

William E. Borah, *Boise*
James P. Pope, *Boise*

REPRESENTATIVES

Compton I. White, *Clark Fork*
D. Worth Clark, *Pocatello*

ILLINOIS

SENATORS

J. Hamilton Lewis, *Chicago*
William H. Dieterich, *Beardstown*

REPRESENTATIVES

Arthur W. Mitchell, *Chicago*
Raymond S. McKeough, *Chicago*
Edward A. Kelly, *Chicago*
Harry P. Beam, *Chicago*
Adolph J. Sabath, *Chicago*
Thomas J. O'Brien, *Chicago*
Leonard W. Schuetz, *Chicago*
Leo Kocialkowski, *Chicago*
James McAndrews, *Chicago*
Ralph E. Church, *Evanston*
Chauncey W. Reed, *West Chicago*
John T. Buckbee,[13] *Rockford*
Leo E. Allen, *Galena*
Chester C. Thompson, *Rock Island*
J. Leroy Adair, *Quincy*
Everett M. Dirksen, *Pekin*
Leslie C. Arends, *Melvin*
James A. Meeks, *Danville*
Donald C. Dobbins, *Champaign*
Scott W. Lucas, *Havana*
Harry H. Mason, *Pawnee*
Edwin M. Schaefer, *Belleville*
William W. Arnold,[14] *Robinson*
Claude V. Parsons, *Golconda*
Kent E. Keller, *Ava*
At Large—
    Martin A. Brennan, *Bloomington*
    Michael L. Igoe,[15] *Chicago*

INDIANA

SENATORS

Frederick Van Nuys, *Indianapolis*
Sherman Minton, *New Albany*

REPRESENTATIVES

William T. Schulte, *Hammond*
Charles A. Halleck,[16] *Rensselaer*
Samuel B. Pettengill, *South Bend*
James I. Farley, *Auburn*
Glenn Griswold, *Peru*
Mrs. Virginia E. Jenckes, *Terre Haute*
Arthur H. Greenwood, *Washington*
John W. Boehne, Jr., *Evansville*
Eugene B. Crowe, *Bedford*

Finly H. Gray, *Connersville*
William H. Larrabee, *New Palestine*
Louis Ludlow, *Indianapolis*

IOWA

SENATORS

Lester J. Dickinson, *Algona*
Richard Louis Murphy,[17] *Dubuque*
Guy M. Gillette,[18] *Cherokee*

REPRESENTATIVES

Edward C. Eicher, *Washington*
Bernhard M. Jacobsen,[19] *Clinton*
John W. Gwynne, *Waterloo*
Fred Biermann, *Decorah*
Lloyd Thurston, *Osceola*
Hubert Utterback, *Des Moines*
Otha D. Wearin, *Hastings*
Fred C. Gilchrist, *Laurens*
Guy M. Gillette,[20] *Cherokee*

KANSAS

SENATORS

Arthur Capper, *Topeka*
George McGill, *Wichita*

REPRESENTATIVES

William P. Lambertson, *Fairview*
Ulysses S. Guyer, *Kansas City*
Edward W. Patterson, *Pittsburg*
William Randolph Carpenter, *Marion*
John M. Houston, *Newton*
Frank Carlson, *Concordia*
Clifford R. Hope, *Garden City*

KENTUCKY

SENATORS

Alben W. Barkley, *Paducah*
Marvel M. Logan, *Bowling Green*

REPRESENTATIVES

William V. Gregory,[21] *Mayfield*
Glover H. Cary,[22] *Owensboro*
Emmet O'Neal, *Louisville*
Cap R. Carden,[23] *Munfordville*
Edward W. Creal,[24] *Hodgenville*
Brent Spence, *Fort Thomas*
Virgil M. Chapman, *Paris*
Andrew J. May, *Prestonsburg*
Fred M. Vinson, *Ashland*
John M. Robsion, *Barbourville*

---

[7] Died June 17, 1936.
[8] Appointed to fill vacancy caused by death of Duncan U. Fletcher, and served from July 1, 1936, to November 3, 1936, but was unable to be sworn in as Congress was not in session.
[9] Elected to fill vacancy caused by death of Duncan U. Fletcher, and took his seat January 5, 1937.
[10] Died May 8, 1936.
[11] Appointed to fill vacancy caused by death of Park Trammell, and took his seat May 27, 1936.
[12] Elected to fill vacancy caused by death of Park Trammell, and took his seat January 5, 1937.
[13] Died April 23, 1936; vacancy throughout remainder of the Congress.
[14] Resigned September 16, 1935, having been

appointed a member of the United States Board of Tax Appeals; vacancy throughout remainder of the Congress.
[15] Resigned June 2, 1935, having been appointed a United States attorney, northern district of Illinois; vacancy throughout remainder of the Congress.
[16] Elected to fill vacancy caused by death of Representative-elect Frederick Landis (November 15, 1934, before the beginning of the congressional term), and took his seat February 5, 1935.
[17] Died July 16, 1936; vacancy in this class from July 17, 1936, to November 3, 1936.
[18] Elected November 3, 1936, to fill vacancy caused by death of Richard Louis Murphy, and took his seat January 5, 1937.

[19] Died June 30, 1936; vacancy throughout remainder of the Congress.
[20] Resigned November 3, 1936; subsequently elected Senator; vacancy throughout the remainder of the Congress.
[21] Died October 10, 1936; vacancy throughout remainder of the Congress.
[22] Died December 5, 1936, before the commencement of the Seventy-fifth Congress, to which he had been reelected; vacancy throughout remainder of the Congress.
[23] Died June 13, 1935.
[24] Elected to fill vacancy caused by death of Cap R. Carden, and took his seat January 3, 1936.

LOUISIANA

SENATORS

Huey P. Long,[25] *New Orleans*
Mrs. Rose McConnell Long,[26] *New Orleans*
John H. Overton, *Alexandria*

REPRESENTATIVES

Joachim O. Fernandez, *New Orleans*
Paul H. Maloney, *New Orleans*
Numa F. Montet, *Thibodaux*
John N, Sandlin, *Minden*
Riley J. Wilson, *Ruston*
Jared Y. Sanders, Jr., *Baton Rouge*
René L. DeRouen, *Ville Platte*
Cleveland Dear, *Alexandria*

MAINE

SENATORS

Frederick Hale, *Portland*
Wallace H. White, Jr., *Auburn*

REPRESENTATIVES

Simon M. Hamlin, *South Portland*
Edward C. Moran, Jr., *Rockland*
Ralph O. Brewster, *Dexter*

MARYLAND

SENATORS

Millard E. Tydings, *Havre de Grace*
George L. Radcliffe, *Baltimore*

REPRESENTATIVES

T. Alan Goldsborough, *Denton*
William P. Cole, Jr., *Towson*
Vincent L. Palmisano, *Baltimore*
Ambrose J. Kennedy, *Baltimore*
Stephen W. Gambrill, *Laurel*
David J. Lewis, *Cumberland*

MASSACHUSETTS

SENATORS

David I. Walsh, *Fitchburg*
Marcus A. Coolidge, *Fitchburg*

REPRESENTATIVES

Allen T. Treadway, *Stockbridge*
William J. Granfield, *Springfield*
Joseph E. Casey, *Clinton*
Pehr G. Holmes, *Worcester*
Mrs. Edith Nourse Rogers, *Lowell*
A. Piatt Andrew, Jr.,[27] *Gloucester*
William P. Connery, Jr., *Lynn*
Arthur D. Healey, *Somerville*
Richard M. Russell, *Cambridge*
George H. Tinkham, *Boston*

John P. Higgins, *Boston*
John W. McCormack, *Dorchester*
Richard B. Wigglesworth, *Milton*
Joseph W. Martin, Jr., *North Attleboro*
Charles L. Gifford, *Cotuit*

MICHIGAN

SENATORS

James Couzens,[28] *Detroit*
Prentiss M. Brown,[29] *St. Ignace*
Arthur H. Vandenberg, *Grand Rapids*

REPRESENTATIVES

George G. Sadowski, *Detroit*
Earl C. Michener, *Adrian*
Henry M. Kimball,[30] *Kalamazoo*
Verner W. Main,[31] *Battle Creek*
Clare E. Hoffman, *Allegan*
Carl E. Mapes, *Grand Rapids*
William W. Blackney, *Flint*
Jesse P. Wolcott, *Port Huron*
Fred L. Crawford, *Saginaw*
Albert J. Engel, *Lake City*
Roy O. Woodruff, *Bay City*
Prentiss M. Brown,[32] *St. Ignace*
Frank E. Hook, *Ironwood*
Clarence J. McLeod, *Detroit*
Louis C. Rabaut, *Detroit*
John D. Dingell, *Detroit*
John Lesinski, *Dearborn*
George A. Dondero, *Royal Oak*

MINNESOTA

SENATORS

Henrik Shipstead, *Minneapolis*
Thomas D. Schall,[33] *Excelsior*
Elmer A. Benson,[34] *Appleton*
Guy V. Howard,[35] *Minneapolis*

REPRESENTATIVES

August H. Andresen, *Red Wing*
Elmer J. Ryan, *South St. Paul*
Ernest Lundeen, *Minneapolis*
Melvin J. Maas, *St. Paul*
Theodore Christianson, *Minneapolis*
Harold Knutson, *St. Cloud*
Paul J. Kvale, *Benson*
William A. Pittenger, *Duluth*
Richard T. Buckler, *Crookston*

MISSISSIPPI

SENATORS

Pat Harrison, *Gulfport*
Theodore G. Bilbo, *Poplarville*

REPRESENTATIVES

John E. Rankin, *Tupelo*

Wall Doxey, *Holly Springs*
William M. Whittington, *Greenwood*
Aaron Lane Ford, *Ackerman*
Aubert C. Dunn, *Meridian*
William M. Colmer, *Pascagoula*
Dan R. McGehee, *Meadville*

MISSOURI

SENATORS

Joel Bennett Clark, *St. Louis*
Harry S. Truman, *Independence*

REPRESENTATIVES

Milton A. Romjue, *Macon*
William L. Nelson, *Columbia*
Richard M. Duncan, *St. Joseph*
C. Jasper Bell, *Kansas City*
Joseph B. Shannon, *Kansas City*
Reuben T. Wood, *Springfield*
Dewey Short, *Galena*
Clyde Williams, *Hillsboro*
Clarence Cannon, *Elsberry*
Orville Zimmerman, *Kennett*
Thomas C. Hennings, Jr., *St. Louis*
James R. Claiborne, *St. Louis*
John J. Cochran, *St. Louis*

MONTANA

SENATORS

Burton K. Wheeler, *Butte*
James E. Murray, *Butte*

REPRESENTATIVES

Joseph P. Monaghan, *Butte*
Roy E. Ayers, *Lewistown*

NEBRASKA

SENATORS

George W. Norris, *McCook*
Edward R. Burke, *Omaha*

REPRESENTATIVES

Henry C. Luckey, *Lincoln*
Charles F. McLaughlin, *Omaha*
Karl Stefan, *Norfolk*
Charles G. Binderup, *Minden*
Harry B. Coffee, *Chadron*

NEVADA

SENATORS

Key Pittman, *Tonopah*
Patrick A. McCarran, *Reno*

REPRESENTATIVE

At Large—James G. Scrugham, *Reno*

---

[25] Died September 10, 1935; vacancy in this class from September 11, 1935, to January 30, 1936.
[26] Appointed to fill vacancy caused by death of her husband, Huey P. Long, and took her seat February 10, 1936; subsequently elected.
[27] Died June 3, 1936; vacancy throughout remainder of the Congress.
[28] Died October 22, 1936; vacancy in this class from October 23, 1936, to November 18, 1936.

[29] Appointed to fill vacancy caused by death of James Couzens, and served from November 19, 1936; was previously elected for term commencing January 3, 1937.
[30] Died October 19, 1935.
[31] Elected to fill vacancy caused by death of Henry M. Kimball, and took his seat January 3, 1936.
[32] Resigned November 18, 1936, having been appointed a Senator; vacancy throughout remainder of the Congress.

[33] Died December 22, 1935.
[34] Appointed to fill vacancy caused by death of Thomas D. Schall, and took his seat January 3, 1936.
[35] Elected to fill vacancy caused by death of Thomas D. Schall, and served from November 4, 1936, to January 3, 1937, but was unable to be sworn in as Congress was not in session.

NEW HAMPSHIRE

SENATORS

Henry W. Keyes, *Haverhill*
Fred H. Brown, *Somersworth*

REPRESENTATIVES

William N. Rogers, *Sanbornville*
Charles W. Tobey, *Temple*

NEW JERSEY

SENATORS

W. Warren Barbour, *Locust*
A. Harry Moore, *Jersey City*

REPRESENTATIVES

Charles A. Wolverton, *Camden*
Isaac Bacharach, *Atlantic City*
William H. Sutphin, *Matawan*
D. Lane Powers, *Trenton*
Charles A. Eaton, *North Plainfield*
Donald H. McLean, *Elizabeth*
Randolph Perkins,[36] *Woodcliff Lake*
George N. Seger, *Passaic*
Edward A. Kenney, *Cliffside Park*
Fred A. Hartley, Jr., *Kearny*
Peter A. Cavicchia, *Newark*
Frederick R. Lehlbach, *Newark*
Mrs. Mary T. Norton, *Jersey City*
Edward J. Hart, *Jersey City*

NEW MEXICO

SENATORS

Bronson M. Cutting,[37] *Santa Fe*
Dennis Chavez,[38] *Albuquerque*
Carl A. Hatch, *Clovis*

REPRESENTATIVE

At Large—John J. Dempsey, *Santa Fe*

NEW YORK

SENATORS

Royal S. Copeland, *New York City*
Robert F. Wagner, *New York City*

REPRESENTATIVES

Robert L. Bacon, *Old Westbury*
William F. Brunner,[39] *Rockaway Park*
William B. Barry,[40] *Hollis*
Joseph L. Pfeifer, *Brooklyn*
Thomas H. Cullen, *Brooklyn*
Marcellus H. Evans, *Brooklyn*
Andrew L. Somers, *Brooklyn*
John J. Delaney, *Brooklyn*
Richard J. Tonry, *Brooklyn*

Stephen A. Rudd,[41] *Brooklyn*
Emanuel Celler, *Brooklyn*
James A. O'Leary, *West New Brighton*
Samuel Dickstein, *New York City*
Christopher D. Sullivan, *New York City*
William I. Sirovich, *New York City*
John J. Boylan, *New York City*
John J. O'Connor, *New York City*
Theodore A. Peyser, *New York City*
Martin J. Kennedy, *New York City*
Sol Bloom, *New York City*
Vito Marcantonio,[42] *New York City*
Joseph A. Gavagan, *New York City*
Anthony J. Griffin,[43] *New York City*
Edward W. Curley,[44] *New York City*
Charles A. Buckley, *New York City*
James M. Fitzpatrick, *New York City*
Charles D. Millard, *Tarrytown*
Hamilton Fish, Jr., *Garrison*
Philip A. Goodwin, *Coxsackie*
Parker Corning, *Albany*
William D. Thomas,[45] *Hoosick Falls*
Frank Crowther, *Schenectady*
Bertrand H. Snell, *Potsdam*
Francis D. Culkin, *Oswego*
Fred J. Sisson, *Whitesboro*
Bert Lord, *Afton*
Clarence E. Hancock, *Syracuse*
John Taber, *Auburn*
W. Sterling Cole, *Bath*
James P. B. Duffy, *Rochester*
James W. Wadsworth, Jr., *Geneseo*
Walter G. Andrews, *Buffalo*
Alfred F. Beiter, *Williamsville*
James M. Mead, *Buffalo*
Daniel A. Reed, *Dunkirk*
At Large—
    Matthew J. Merritt, *Flushing*
    Mrs. Caroline O'Day, *Rye*

NORTH CAROLINA

SENATORS

Josiah W. Bailey, *Raleigh*
Robert R. Reynolds, *Asheville*

REPRESENTATIVES

Lindsay C. Warren, *Washington*
John H. Kerr, *Warrenton*
Graham A. Barden, *New Bern*
Harold D. Cooley, *Nashville*
Franklin W. Hancock, Jr., *Oxford*
William B. Umstead, *Durham*
J. Bayard Clark, *Fayetteville*
J. Walter Lambeth, *Thomasville*
Robert L. Doughton, *Laurel Springs*
Alfred L. Bulwinkle, *Gastonia*
Zebulon Weaver, *Asheville*

NORTH DAKOTA

SENATORS

Lynn J. Frazier, *Hoople*
Gerald P. Nye, *Cooperstown*

REPRESENTATIVES AT LARGE

Usher L. Burdick, *Bismarck*
William Lemke, *Fargo*

OHIO

SENATORS

Robert J. Bulkley, *Cleveland*
A. Victor Donahey, *Huntsville, R.F.D.*

REPRESENTATIVES

John B. Hollister, *Cincinnati*
William E. Hess, *Cincinnati*
Byron B. Harlan, *Dayton*
Frank L. Kloeb, *Celina*
Frank C. Kniffin, *Napoleon*
James G. Polk, *Highland*
Leroy T. Marshall, *Xenia*
Thomas Brooks Fletcher, *Marion*
Warren J. Duffey,[46] *Toledo*
Thomas A. Jenkins, *Ironton*
Mell G. Underwood,[47] *New Lexington*
Peter F. Hammond,[48] *Lancaster*
Arthur P. Lamneck, *Columbus*
William L. Fiesinger, *Sandusky*
Dow W. Harter, *Akron*
Robert T. Secrest, *Caldwell*
William R. Thom, *Canton*
William A. Ashbrook, *Johnstown*
Lawrence E. Imhoff, *St. Clairsville*
John G. Cooper,[49] *Youngstown*
Martin L. Sweeney, *Cleveland*
Robert Crosser, *Cleveland*
Chester C. Bolton, *Cleveland*
At Large—
    Charles V. Truax,[50] *Bucyrus*
    Daniel S. Earhart,[51] *Columbus*
    Stephen M. Young, *Cleveland*

OKLAHOMA

SENATORS

J. W. Elmer Thomas, *Medicine Park*
Thomas P. Gore, *Oklahoma City*

REPRESENTATIVES

Wesley E. Disney, *Tulsa*
Jack Nichols, *Eufaula*
Wilburn Cartwright, *McAlester*
P. L. Gassaway, *Coalgate*
Josh Lee, *Norman*

---

[36] Died May 25, 1936; vacancy throughout remainder of the Congress.
[37] Died May 6, 1935.
[38] Appointed to fill vacancy caused by death of Bronson M. Cutting, and took his seat May 20, 1935; subsequently elected.
[39] Resigned September 27, 1935, having been nominated and elected sheriff of Queens County, N. Y.
[40] Elected to fill vacancy caused by resignation of William F. Brunner, and took his seat January 3, 1936.
[41] Died March 31, 1936; vacancy throughout remainder of the Congress.

[42] Election unsuccessfully contested by James J. Lanzetta.
[43] Died January 13, 1935.
[44] Elected to fill vacancy caused by death of Anthony J. Griffin, and took his seat January 3, 1936.
[45] Died May 17, 1936; vacancy throughout remainder of the Congress.
[46] Died July 7, 1936; vacancy throughout remainder of the Congress.
[47] Resigned effective April 10, 1936, having been appointed a judge of the United States District Court for the Southern District of Ohio on February 12, 1936.

[48] Elected to fill vacancy caused by resignation of Mell G. Underwood, and served from November 3, 1936, to January 3, 1937, but was unable to be sworn in as Congress was not in session.
[49] Election unsuccessfully contested by Locke Miller.
[50] Died August 9, 1935.
[51] Elected to fill vacancy caused by death of Charles V. Truax, and served from November 3, 1936, to January 3, 1937, but was unable to be sworn in as Congress was not in session.

Jed Johnson, *Anadarko*
Sam C. Massingale, *Cordell*
Phil Ferguson, *Woodward*
At Large—Will Rogers, *Oklahoma City*

OREGON

SENATORS

Charles L. McNary, *Salem*
Frederick Steiwer, *Portland*

REPRESENTATIVES

James W. Mott, *Salem*
Walter M. Pierce, *La Grande*
William A. Ekwall, *Portland*

PENNSYLVANIA

SENATORS

James J. Davis, *Pittsburgh*
Joseph F. Guffey, *Pittsburgh*

REPRESENTATIVES

Harry C. Ransley, *Philadelphia*
William H. Wilson, *Philadelphia*
Clare G. Fenerty, *Philadelphia*
J. Burrwood Daly, *Philadelphia*
Frank J. G. Dorsey, *Philadelphia*
Michael J. Stack, *Philadelphia*
George P. Darrow, *Philadelphia*
James Wolfenden, *Upper Darby*
Oliver W. Frey, *Allentown*
J. Roland Kinzer, *Lancaster*
Patrick J. Boland, *Scranton*
C. Murray Turpin, *Kingston*
James H. Gildea, *Coaldale*
William E. Richardson, *Reading*
C. Elmer Dietrich, *Tunkhannock*
Robert F. Rich, *Woolrich*
J. William Ditter, *Ambler*
Benjamin K. Focht, *Lewisburg*
Isaac H. Doutrich, *Harrisburg*
D. J. Driscoll, *St. Marys*
Francis E. Walter, *Easton*
Harry L. Haines, *Red Lion*
Don Gingery, *Clearfield*
J. Buell Snyder, *Perryopolis*
Charles I. Faddis, *Waynesburg*
Charles R. Eckert, *Beaver*
Joseph Gray, *Spangler*
William M. Berlin, *Greensburg*
Charles N. Crosby, *Meadville*
J. Twing Brooks, *Sewickley*
James L. Quinn, *Braddock*
Theodore L. Moritz, *Pittsburgh*
Henry Ellenbogen, *Pittsburgh*
Matthew A. Dunn, *Pittsburgh*

RHODE ISLAND

SENATORS

Jesse H. Metcalf, *Providence*
Peter G. Gerry, *Warwick*

REPRESENTATIVES

Francis B. Condon,[52] *Central Falls*
Charles F. Risk,[53] *Saylesville*
John M. O'Connell, *Westerly*

SOUTH CAROLINA

SENATORS

Ellison D. Smith, *Lynchburg*
James F. Byrnes, *Spartanburg*

REPRESENTATIVES

Thomas S. McMillan, *Charleston*
Hampton P. Fulmer, *Orangeburg*
John C. Taylor, *Anderson*
John J. McSwain,[54] *Greenville*
G. Heyward Mahon, Jr.,[55] *Greenville*
James P. Richards, *Lancaster*
Allard H. Gasque, *Florence*

SOUTH DAKOTA

SENATORS

Peter Norbeck,[56] *Redfield*
Herbert E. Hitchcock,[57] *Mitchell*
William J. Bulow, *Beresford*

REPRESENTATIVES

Fred H. Hildebrandt, *Watertown*
Theodore B. Werner, *Rapid City*

TENNESSEE

SENATORS

Kenneth D. McKellar, *Memphis*
Nathan L. Bachman, *Chattanooga*

REPRESENTATIVES

B. Carroll Reece, *Johnson City*
J. Will Taylor, *La Follette*
Sam D. McReynolds, *Chattanooga*
John R. Mitchell, *Cookeville*
Joseph W. Byrns,[58] *Nashville*
Clarence W. Turner, *Waverly*
Herron Pearson, *Jackson*
Jere Cooper, *Dyersburg*
Walter Chandler, *Memphis*

TEXAS

SENATORS

Morris Sheppard, *Texarkana*
Tom T. Connally, *Marlin*

REPRESENTATIVES

Wright Patman, *Texarkana*
Martin Dies, Jr., *Orange*
Morgan G. Sanders, *Canton*
Sam Rayburn, *Bonham*
Hatton W. Sumners, *Dallas*
Luther A. Johnson, *Corsicana*
Nat Patton, *Crockett*
Joe H. Eagle, *Houston*
Joseph J. Mansfield, *Columbus*
James P. Buchanan, *Brenham*
Oliver H. Cross, *Waco*
Fritz G. Lanham, *Fort Worth*
William D. McFarlane, *Graham*
Richard M. Kleberg, *Corpus Christi*
Milton H. West, *Brownsville*
R. Ewing Thomason, *El Paso*
Thomas L. Blanton, *Abilene*
Marvin Jones, *Amarillo*
George H. Mahon, *Colorado*
Maury Maverick, *San Antonio*
Charles L. South, *Coleman*

UTAH

SENATORS

William H. King, *Salt Lake City*
Elbert D. Thomas, *Salt Lake City*

REPRESENTATIVES

Abe Murdock, *Beaver*
J. W. Robinson, *Provo*

VERMONT

SENATORS

Warren R. Austin, *Burlington*
Ernest Willard Gibson, *Brattleboro*

REPRESENTATIVE

At Large—Charles A. Plumley, *Northfield*

VIRGINIA

SENATORS

Carter Glass, *Lynchburg*
Harry Flood Byrd, *Berryville*

REPRESENTATIVES

Schuyler Otis Bland, *Newport News*
Colgate W. Darden, Jr., *Norfolk*
Andrew J. Montague, *Richmond*
Patrick Henry Drewry, *Petersburg*
Thomas C. Burch, *Martinsville*
Clifton A. Woodrum, *Roanoke*
A. Willis Robertson, *Lexington*
Howard W. Smith, *Alexandria*
John W. Flannagan, Jr., *Bristol*

---

[52] Resigned January 10, 1935, having been appointed an associate justice of the Supreme Court of the State of Rhode Island.
[53] Elected to fill vacancy caused by the resignation of Francis B. Condon, and took his seat August 19, 1935.

[54] Died August 6, 1936.
[55] Elected to fill vacancy caused by death of John J. McSwain, and served from November 3, 1936, to January 3, 1937, but was unable to be sworn in as Congress was not in session.

[56] Died December 20, 1936.
[57] Appointed to fill vacancy caused by death of Peter Norbeck, and took his seat January 5, 1937.
[58] Died June 4, 1936; vacancy throughout remainder of the Congress.

WASHINGTON

SENATORS

Homer T. Bone, *Tacoma*
Lewis B. Schwellenbach, *Neppel*

REPRESENTATIVES

Marion A. Zioncheck,[59] *Seattle*
Monrad C. Wallgren, *Everett*
Martin F. Smith, *Hoquiam*
Knute Hill, *Prosser*
Samuel B. Hill,[60] *Waterville*
Wesley Lloyd,[61] *Tacoma*

WEST VIRGINIA

SENATORS

Matthew M. Neely, *Fairmont*
Rush D. Holt,[62] *Weston*

REPRESENTATIVES

Robert L. Ramsay, *Follansbee*
Jennings Randolph, *Elkins*
Andrew Edmiston, *Weston*
George W. Johnson, *Parkersburg*
John Kee, *Bluefield*
Joe L. Smith, *Beckley*

WISCONSIN

SENATORS

Robert M. La Follette, Jr., *Madison*
F. Ryan Duffy, *Fond du Lac*

REPRESENTATIVES

Thomas R. Amlie, *Elkhorn*
Harry Sauthoff, *Madison*
Gardner R. Withrow, *La Crosse*
Raymond J. Cannon, *Milwaukee*
Thomas O'Malley, *Milwaukee*
Michael K. Reilly, *Fond du Lac*
Gerald J. Boileau, *Wausau*
George J. Schneider, *Appleton*
Merlin Hull, *Black River Falls*
Bernard J. Gehrmann, *Mellon, R.F.D.*

WYOMING

SENATORS

Robert D. Carey, *Careyhurst*
Joseph C. O'Mahoney, *Cheyenne*

REPRESENTATIVE

At Large—Paul R. Greever, *Cody*

TERRITORY OF ALASKA

DELEGATE

Anthony J. Dimond, *Valdez*

TERRITORY OF HAWAII

DELEGATE

Samuel W. King,[63] *Honolulu*

PHILIPPINE ISLANDS [64]

RESIDENT COMMISSIONERS

Pedro Guevara,[64] *Santa Cruz*
Francisco A. Delgado,[64] *Bulacan*
Quintin Paredes,[65] *Bangued, Abra*

PUERTO RICO

RESIDENT COMMISSIONER

Santiago Iglesias, *San Juan*

---

[59] Died August 7, 1936; vacancy throughout remainder of the Congress.

[60] Resigned effective June 25, 1936, having been appointed a member of the United States Board of Tax Appeals on May 21, 1936; vacancy throughout remainder of the Congress.

[61] Died January 10, 1936; vacancy throughout remainder of the Congress.

[62] Elected for the term commencing January 3, 1935, but not having attained the age required by the Constitution, did not take his seat until June 21, 1935.

[63] Election unsuccessfully contested by Lincoln L. McCandless.

[64] The terms of office of the Resident Commissioners of the Philippine Islands expired when the new government of the Commonwealth of the Philippine Islands was inaugurated; both served until February 14, 1936, when a selected successor qualified. (See 48 Stat. 456.) This law also reduced from 2 to 1 the number of Resident Commissioners.

[65] Appointed December 21, 1935, to fill the vacancy caused by the expiration of the terms of Pedro Guevara and Francisco A. Delgado, due to the new form of government, and took his seat February 14, 1936.

SEVENTY-FIFTH CONGRESS

JANUARY 3,[1] 1937, TO JANUARY 3, 1939

FIRST SESSION—*January 5,[1] 1937, to August 21, 1937*

SECOND SESSION—*November 15, 1937, to December 21, 1937*

THIRD SESSION—*January 3, 1938, to June 16, 1938*

VICE PRESIDENT OF THE UNITED STATES—John N. Garner, of Texas
PRESIDENT PRO TEMPORE OF THE SENATE—Key Pittman, of Nevada
SECRETARY OF THE SENATE—Edwin A. Halsey, of Virginia
SERGEANT AT ARMS OF THE SENATE—Chesley W. Jurney, of Texas

SPEAKER OF THE HOUSE OF REPRESENTATIVES—William B. Bankhead,[2] of Alabama
CLERK OF THE HOUSE—South Trimble,[3] of Kentucky
SERGEANT AT ARMS OF THE HOUSE—Kenneth Romney, of Montana
DOORKEEPER OF THE HOUSE—Joseph J. Sinnott, of Virginia
POSTMASTER OF THE HOUSE—Finis E. Scott

ALABAMA

SENATORS

Hugo L. Black,[4] *Birmingham*
Mrs. Dixie Bibb Graves,[5] *Montgomery*
Lister Hill,[6] *Montgomery*
John H. Bankhead 2d, *Jasper*

REPRESENTATIVES

Frank W. Boykin, *Mobile*
Lister Hill,[7] *Montgomery*
George M. Grant,[8] *Troy*
Henry B. Steagall, *Ozark*
Sam Hobbs, *Selma*
Joe Starnes, *Guntersville*
Pete Jarman, *Livingston*
William B. Bankhead, *Jasper*
John J. Sparkman, *Huntsville*
Luther Patrick, *Birmingham*

ARIZONA

SENATORS

Henry F. Ashurst, *Prescott*
Carl Hayden, *Phoenix*

REPRESENTATIVE

At Large—John R. Murdock, *Tempe*

ARKANSAS

SENATORS

Joseph T. Robinson,[9] *Little Rock*
John E. Miller,[10] *Searcy*
Mrs. Hattie W. Caraway, *Jonesboro*

REPRESENTATIVES

William J. Driver, *Osceola*
John E. Miller,[11] *Searcy*
Claude A. Fuller, *Eureka Springs*
William B. Cravens, *Fort Smith*
David D. Terry, *Little Rock*
John L. McClellan, *Malvern*
Wade H. Kitchens, *Magnolia*

CALIFORNIA

SENATORS

Hiram W. Johnson, *San Francisco*
William Gibbs McAdoo,[12] *Los Angeles*
Thomas M. Storke,[13] *Santa Barbara*

REPRESENTATIVES

Clarence F. Lea, *Santa Rosa*
Harry L. Englebright, *Nevada City*
Frank H. Buck, *Vacaville*
Franck R. Havenner, *San Francisco*
Richard J. Welch, *San Francisco*
Albert E. Carter, *Oakland*
John H. Tolan, *Oakland*
John J. McGrath, *San Mateo*
Bertrand W. Gearhart, *Fresno*
Henry E. Stubbs,[14] *Santa Maria*
Alfred J. Elliott,[15] *Tulare*
John S. McGroarty, *Tujunga*
H. Jerry Voorhis, *San Dimas*
Charles Kramer, *Los Angeles*
Thomas F. Ford, *Los Angeles*
John M. Costello, *Hollywood*
John F. Dockweiler, *Los Angeles*
Charles J. Colden,[16] *San Pedro*
Byron N. Scott, *Long Beach*
Harry R. Sheppard, *Yucaipa*
Edouard V. M. Izac, *San Diego*

---

[1] By joint resolution (Pub. Law No. 120, 74th Cong.) the date of assembling the first session of the Seventy-fifth Congress was fixed for January 5, 1937.
[2] Reelected January 5, 1937.
[3] Reelected January 5, 1937.
[4] Resigned August 19, 1937, having been appointed an Associate Justice of the Supreme Court of the United States.
[5] Appointed to fill vacancy caused by resignation of Hugo L. Black, and took her seat August 20, 1937; resigned January 10, 1938.
[6] Appointed to fill vacancy caused by resignations of Hugo L. Black and Mrs. Dixie Bibb Graves, and took

his seat January 11, 1938; subsequently elected.
[7] Resigned January 11, 1938, having been appointed Senator.
[8] Elected to fill vacancy caused by resignation of Lister Hill, and served from June 14, 1938, to January 3, 1939, but was not sworn in as Congress adjourned shortly after his election.
[9] Died July 14, 1937.
[10] Elected to fill vacancy caused by death of Joseph T. Robinson, and took his seat November 15, 1937; vacancy in this class from July 15, 1937, to November 14, 1937.
[11] Resigned November 14, 1937, having been elected

Senator; vacancy throughout remainder of the Congress.
[12] Resigned November 8, 1938.
[13] Appointed to fill vacancy caused by resignation of William Gibbs McAdoo, and served from November 9, 1938, to January 3, 1939, but was unable to be sworn in as Congress was not in session.
[14] Died February 28, 1937.
[15] Elected to fill vacancy caused by death of Henry E. Stubbs, and took his seat June 7, 1937.
[16] Died April 15, 1938; vacancy throughout remainder of the Congress.

COLORADO

SENATORS

Alva B. Adams, *Pueblo*
Edwin C. Johnson, *Denver*

REPRESENTATIVES

Lawrence Lewis, *Denver*
Fred Cummings, *Fort Collins*
John A. Martin, *Pueblo*
Edward T. Taylor, *Glenwood Springs*

CONNECTICUT

SENATORS

Augustine Lonergan, *Hartford*
Francis T. Maloney, *Meriden*

REPRESENTATIVES

Herman P. Kopplemann, *Hartford*
William J. Fitzgerald, *Norwich*
James A. Shanley, *New Haven*
Alfred N. Phillips, Jr., *Stamford*
J. Joseph Smith, *Waterbury*
At Large—William M. Citron, *Middletown*

DELAWARE

SENATORS

John G. Townsend, Jr., *Selbyville*
James H. Hughes, *Dover*

REPRESENTATIVE

At Large—William F. Allen, *Seaford*

FLORIDA

SENATORS

Charles O. Andrews, *Orlando*
Claude Pepper, *Tallahasse*

REPRESENTATIVES

J. Hardin Peterson, *Lakeland*
Robert A. Green, *Starke*
Millard F. Caldwell, *Milton*
J. Mark Wilcox, *West Palm Beach*
Joe Hendricks, *De Land*

GEORGIA

SENATORS

Walter F. George, *Vienna*
Richard B. Russell, *Winder*

REPRESENTATIVES

Hugh Peterson, *Ailey*
Edward E. Cox, *Camilla*
Stephen Pace, *Americus*
Emmett M. Owen, *Griffin*
Robert Ramspeck, *Atlanta*

Carl Vinson, *Milledgeville*
Malcolm C. Tarver, *Dalton*
Braswell D. Deen, *Alma*
B. Frank Whelchel, *Gainesville*
Paul Brown, *Elberton*

IDAHO

SENATORS

William E. Borah, *Boise*
James P. Pope, *Boise*

REPRESENTATIVES

Compton I. White, *Clark Fork*
D. Worth Clark, *Pocatello*

ILLINOIS

SENATORS

J. Hamilton Lewis, *Chicago*
William H. Dieterich, *Beardstown*

REPRESENTATIVES

Arthur W. Mitchell, *Chicago*
Raymond S. McKeough, *Chicago*
Edward A. Kelly, *Chicago*
Harry P. Beam, *Chicago*
Adolph J. Sabath, *Chicago*
Thomas J. O'Brien, *Chicago*
Leonard W. Schuetz, *Chicago*
Leo Kocialkowski, *Chicago*
James McAndrews, *Chicago*
Ralph E. Church, *Evanston*
Chauncey W. Reed, *West Chicago*
Noah M. Mason, *Oglesby*
Leo E. Allen, *Galena*
Chester C. Thompson, *Rock Island*
Lewis L. Boyer, *Quincy*
Everett M. Dirksen, *Pekin*
Leslie C. Arends, *Melvin*
James A. Meeks, *Danville*
Hugh M. Rigney, *Arthur*
Scott W. Lucas, *Havana*
Frank W. Fries, *Carlinville*
Edwin M. Schaefer, *Belleville*
Laurence F. Arnold, *Newton*
Claude V. Parsons, *Golconda*
Kent E. Keller, *Ava*
At Large—
  Edwin V. Champion, *Peoria*
  Lewis M. Long, *Sandwich*

INDIANA

SENATORS

Frederick Van Nuys, *Indianapolis*
Sherman Minton, *New Albany*

REPRESENTATIVES

William T. Schulte, *Hammond*
Charles A. Halleck, *Rensselaer*

Samuel B. Pettengill, *South Bend*
James I. Farley, *Auburn*
Glenn Griswold, *Peru*
Mrs. Virginia E. Jenckes, *Terre Haute*
Arthur H. Greenwood, *Washington*
John W. Boehne, Jr., *Evansville*
Eugene B. Crowe, *Bedford*
Finly H. Gray, *Connersville*
William H. Larrabee, *New Palestine*
Louis Ludlow, *Indianapolis*

IOWA

SENATORS

Guy M. Gillette, *Cherokee*
Clyde L. Herring, *Des Moines*

REPRESENTATIVES

Edward C. Eicher,[17] *Washington*
William S. Jacobsen, *Clinton*
John W. Gwynne, *Waterloo*
Fred Biermann, *Decorah*
Lloyd Thurston, *Osceola*
Cassius C. Dowell, *Des Moines*
Otha D. Wearin, *Hastings*
Fred C. Gilchrist, *Laurens*
Vincent F. Harrington, *Sioux City*

KANSAS

SENATORS

Arthur Capper, *Topeka*
George McGill, *Wichita*

REPRESENTATIVES

William P. Lambertson, *Fairview*
Ulysses S. Guyer, *Kansas City*
Edward W. Patterson, *Pittsburg*
Edward H. Rees, *Emporia*
John M. Houston, *Newton*
Frank Carlson, *Concordia*
Clifford R. Hope, *Garden City*

KENTUCKY

SENATORS

Alben W. Barkley, *Paducah*
Marvel M. Logan, *Bowling Green*

REPRESENTATIVES

Noble J. Gregory, *Mayfield*
Beverly M. Vincent,[18] *Brownsville*
Emmet O'Neal, *Louisville*
Edward W. Creal, *Hodgenville*
Brent Spence, *Fort Thomas*
Virgil M. Chapman, *Paris*
Andrew J. May, *Prestonsburg*
Fred M. Vinson,[19] *Ashland*
Joe B. Bates,[20] *Greenup*
John M. Robsion, *Barbourville*

---

[17] Resigned December 2, 1938, having been appointed a commissioner of the Securities and Exchange Commission; vacancy throughout remainder of the Congress.

[18] Elected to fill vacancy caused by death of Representative-elect Glover H. Cary, in preceding Congress, and took his seat March 11, 1937.
[19] Resigned May 12, 1938, having been appointed an

associate justice of the United States Court of Appeals for the District of Columbia.
[20] Elected to fill vacancy caused by resignation of Fred M. Vinson, and took his seat June 9, 1938.

LOUISIANA

SENATORS

John H. Overton, *Alexandria*
Allen J. Ellender, *Houma*

REPRESENTATIVES

Joachim O. Fernandez, *New Orleans*
Paul H. Maloney, *New Orleans*
Robert L. Mouton, *Lafayette*
Overton Brooks, *Shreveport*
Newt V. Mills, *Mer Rouge*
John K. Griffith, *Slidell*
René L. DeRouen, *Ville Platte*
A. Leonard Allen, *Winnfield*

MAINE

SENATORS

Frederick Hale, *Portland*
Wallace H. White, Jr., *Auburn*

REPRESENTATIVES

James C. Oliver, *South Portland*
Clyde H. Smith, *Skowhegan*
Ralph O. Brewster, *Dexter*

MARYLAND

SENATORS

Millard E. Tydings, *Havre de Grace*
George L. Radcliffe, *Baltimore*

REPRESENTATIVES

T. Alan Goldsborough, *Denton*
William P. Cole, Jr., *Towson*
Vincent L. Palmisano, *Baltimore*
Ambrose J. Kennedy, *Baltimore*
Stephen W. Gambrill,[21] *Laurel*
David J. Lewis, *Cumberland*

MASSACHUSETTS

SENATORS

David I. Walsh, *Fitchburg*
Henry Cabot Lodge, Jr., *Beverly*

REPRESENTATIVES

Allen T. Treadway, *Stockbridge*
Charles R. Clason, *Springfield*
Joseph E. Casey, *Clinton*
Pehr G. Holmes, *Worcester*
Mrs. Edith Nourse Rogers, *Lowell*
George J. Bates, *Salem*
William P. Connery, Jr.,[22] *Lynn*
Lawrence J. Connery,[23] *Lynn*
Arthur D. Healey, *Somerville*
Robert Luce, *Waltham*
George H. Tinkham, *Boston*
John P. Higgins,[24] *Boston*
Thomas A. Flaherty,[25] *Boston*

John W. McCormack, *Dorchester*
Richard B. Wigglesworth, *Milton*
Joseph W. Martin, Jr., *North Attleboro*
Charles L. Gifford, *Cotuit*

MICHIGAN

SENATORS

Arthur H. Vandenberg, *Grand Rapids*
Prentiss M. Brown, *St. Ignace*

REPRESENTATIVES

George G. Sadowski, *Detroit*
Earl C. Michener, *Adrian*
Paul W. Shafer, *Battle Creek*
Clare E. Hoffman, *Allegan*
Carl E. Mapes, *Grand Rapids*
Andrew J. Transue, *Flint*
Jesse P. Wolcott, *Port Huron*
Fred L. Crawford, *Saginaw*
Albert J. Engel, *Lake City*
Roy O. Woodruff, *Bay City*
John Luecke, *Escanaba*
Frank E. Hook, *Ironwood*
George D. O'Brien, *Detroit*
Louis C. Rabaut, *Detroit*
John D. Dingell, *Detroit*
John Lesinski, *Dearborn*
George A. Dondero, *Royal Oak*

MINNESOTA

SENATORS

Henrik Shipstead, *Minneapolis*
Ernest Lundeen, *Minneapolis*

REPRESENTATIVES

August H. Andresen, *Red Wing*
Elmer J. Ryan, *South St. Paul*
Henry G. Teigan, *Minneapolis*
Melvin J. Maas, *St. Paul*
Dewey W. Johnson, *Minneapolis*
Harold Knutson, *St. Cloud*
Paul J. Kvale, *Benson*
John T. Bernard, *Eveleth*
Richard T. Buckler, *Crookston*

MISSISSIPPI

SENATORS

Pat Harrison, *Gulfport*
Theodore G. Bilbo, *Poplarville*

REPRESENTATIVES

John E. Rankin, *Tupelo*
Wall Doxey, *Holly Springs*
William M. Whittington, *Greenwood*
Aaron Lane Ford, *Ackerman*
Ross A. Collins, *Meridian*
William M. Colmer, *Pascagoula*
Dan R. McGehee, *Meadville*

MISSOURI

SENATORS

Joel Bennett Clark, *St. Louis*
Harry S. Truman, *Independence*

REPRESENTATIVES

Milton A. Romjue, *Macon*
William L. Nelson, *Columbia*
Richard M. Duncan, *St. Joseph*
C. Jasper Bell, *Kansas City*
Joseph B. Shannon, *Kansas City*
Reuben T. Wood, *Springfield*
Dewey Short, *Galena*
Clyde Williams, *Hillsboro*
Clarence Cannon, *Elsberry*
Orville Zimmerman, *Kennett*
Thomas C. Hennings, Jr., *St. Louis*
C. Arthur Anderson, *St. Louis*
John J. Cochran, *St. Louis*

MONTANA

SENATORS

Burton K. Wheeler, *Butte*
James E. Murray, *Butte*

REPRESENTATIVES

Jerry J. O'Connell, *Butte*
James F. O'Connor, *Livingston*

NEBRASKA

SENATORS

George W. Norris, *McCook*
Edward R. Burke, *Omaha*

REPRESENTATIVES

Henry C. Luckey, *Lincoln*
Charles F. McLaughlin, *Omaha*
Karl Stefan, *Norfolk*
Charles G. Binderup, *Minden*
Harry B. Coffee, *Chadron*

NEVADA

SENATORS

Key Pittman, *Tonopah*
Patrick A. McCarran, *Reno*

REPRESENTATIVE

At Large—James G. Scrugham, *Reno*

NEW HAMPSHIRE

SENATORS

Fred H. Brown, *Somersworth*
H. Styles Bridges, *East Concord*

REPRESENTATIVES

Arthur B. Jenks,[26] *Manchester*
Alphonse Roy,[27] *Manchester*
Charles W. Tobey, *Temple*

---

[21] Died December 19, 1938, before the commencement of the Seventy-sixth Congress, to which he had been reelected; vacancy throughout remainder of the Congress.
[22] Died June 15, 1937.

[23] Elected to fill vacancy caused by death of his brother, William P. Connery, Jr., and took his seat November 15, 1937.
[24] Resigned September 30, 1937, having been appointed chief justice of the Superior Court of Massachusetts.

[25] Elected to fill vacancy caused by resignation of John P. Higgins, and took his seat January 3, 1938.
[26] Served until June 9, 1938; succeeded by Alphonse Roy, who contested his election.
[27] Successfully contested the election of Arthur B. Jenks, and took his seat June 9, 1938.

NEW JERSEY

SENATORS

A. Harry Moore,[28] *Jersey City*
John Milton,[29] *Jersey City*
W. Warren Barbour,[30] *Locust*
William H. Smathers,[31] *Atlantic City*

REPRESENTATIVES

Charles A. Wolverton, *Camden*
Elmer H. Wene, *Vineland*
William H. Sutphin, *Matawan*
D. Lane Powers, *Trenton*
Charles A. Eaton, *North Plainfield*
Donald H. McLean, *Elizabeth*
J. Parnell Thomas, *Allendale*
George N. Seger, *Passaic*
Edward A. Kenney,[32] *Cliffside Park*
Fred A. Hartley, Jr., *Kearny*
Edward L. O'Neill, *Newark*
Frank W. Towey, Jr., *Caldwell*
Mrs. Mary T. Norton, *Jersey City*
Edward J. Hart, *Jersey City*

NEW MEXICO

SENATORS

Carl A. Hatch, *Clovis*
Dennis Chavez, *Albuquerque*

REPRESENTATIVE

At Large—John J. Dempsey, *Santa Fe*

NEW YORK

SENATORS

Royal S. Copeland,[33] *New York City*
James M. Mead,[34] *Buffalo*
Robert F. Wagner, *New York City*

REPRESENTATIVES

Robert L. Bacon,[35] *Old Westbury*
William B. Barry, *Hollis*
Joseph L. Pfeifer, *Brooklyn*
Thomas H. Cullen, *Brooklyn*
Marcellus H. Evans, *Brooklyn*
Andrew L. Somers, *Brooklyn*
John J. Delaney, *Brooklyn*
Donald L. O'Toole, *Brooklyn*
Eugene J. Keogh, *Brooklyn*
Emanuel Celler, *Brooklyn*
James A. O'Leary, *West New Brighton*
Samuel Dickstein, *New York City*
Christopher D. Sullivan, *New York City*
William I. Sirovich, *New York City*
John J. Boylan,[36] *New York City*
John J. O'Connor, *New York City*
Theodore A. Peyser,[37] *New York City*

Bruce Barton,[38] *New York City*
Martin J. Kennedy, *New York City*
Sol Bloom, *New York City*
James J. Lanzetta, *New York City*
Joseph A. Gavagan, *New York City*
Edward W. Curley, *New York City*
Charles A. Buckley, *New York City*
James M. Fitzpatrick, *New York City*
Charles D. Millard,[39] *Tarrytown*
Ralph A. Gamble,[40] *Larchmont*
Hamilton Fish, Jr., *Garrison*
Philip A. Goodwin,[41] *Coxsackie*
Lewis K. Rockefeller,[42] *Chatham*
William T. Byrne, *Loudonville*
E. Harold Cluett, *Troy*
Frank Crowther, *Schenectady*
Bertrand H. Snell, *Potsdam*
Francis D. Culkin, *Oswego*
Fred J. Douglas, *Utica*
Bert Lord, *Afton*
Clarence E. Hancock, *Syracuse*
John Taber, *Auburn*
W. Sterling Cole, *Bath*
George B. Kelly, *Rochester*
James W. Wadsworth, Jr., *Geneseo*
Walter G. Andrews, *Buffalo*
Alfred F. Beiter, *Williamsville*
James M. Mead,[43] *Buffalo*
Daniel A. Reed, *Dunkirk*
At Large—
Matthew J. Merritt, *Flushing*
Mrs. Caroline O'Day, *Rye*

NORTH CAROLINA

SENATORS

Josiah W. Bailey, *Raleigh*
Robert R. Reynolds, *Asheville*

REPRESENTATIVES

Lindsay C. Warren, *Washington*
John H. Kerr, *Warrenton*
Graham A. Barden, *New Bern*
Harold D. Cooley, *Nashville*
Franklin W. Hancock, Jr., *Oxford*
William B. Umstead, *Durham*
J. Bayard Clark, *Fayetteville*
J. Walter Lambeth, *Thomasville*
Robert L. Doughton, *Laurel Springs*
Alfred L. Bulwinkle, *Gastonia*
Zebulon Weaver, *Asheville*

NORTH DAKOTA

SENATORS

Lynn J. Frazier, *Hoople*
Gerald P. Nye, *Cooperstown*

REPRESENTATIVES AT LARGE

Usher L. Burdick, *Bismarck*
William Lemke, *Fargo*

OHIO

SENATORS

Robert J. Bulkley, *Cleveland*
A. Victor Donahey, *Huntsville, R.F.D.*

REPRESENTATIVES

Joseph A. Dixon, *Cincinnati*
Herbert S. Bigelow, *Cincinnati*
Byron B. Harlan, *Dayton*
Frank L. Kloeb,[44] *Celina*
Walter H. Albaugh,[45] *Troy*
Frank C. Kniffin, *Napoleon*
James G. Polk, *Highland*
Arthur W. Aleshire, *Springfield*
Thomas Brooks Fletcher, *Marion*
John F. Hunter, *Toledo*
Thomas A. Jenkins, *Ironton*
Harold K. Claypool, *Chillicothe*
Arthur P. Lamneck, *Columbus*
Dudley A. White, *Norwalk*
Dow W. Harter, *Akron*
Robert T. Secrest, *Caldwell*
William R. Thom, *Canton*
William A. Ashbrook, *Johnstown*
Lawrence E. Imhoff, *St. Clairsville*
Michael J. Kirwan, *Youngstown*
Martin L. Sweeney, *Cleveland*
Robert Crosser, *Cleveland*
Anthony A. Fleger, *Parma*
At Large—
John McSweeney, *Wooster*
Harold G. Mosier, *Cleveland*

OKLAHOMA

SENATORS

J. W. Elmer Thomas, *Medicine Park*
Josh Lee, *Norman*

REPRESENTATIVES

Wesley E. Disney, *Tulsa*
Jack Nichols, *Eufaula*
Wilburn Cartwright, *McAlester*
Lyle H. Boren, *Seminole*
Robert P. Hill,[46] *Oklahoma City*
Gomer Smith,[47] *Oklahoma City*
Jed Johnson, *Anadarko*
Sam C. Massingale, *Cordell*
Phil Ferguson, *Woodward*
At Large—Will Rogers, *Oklahoma City*

---

[28] Resigned January 18, 1938, having been elected Governor of New Jersey.
[29] Appointed to fill vacancy caused by resignation of A. Harry Moore, and took his seat January 24, 1938.
[30] Elected November 8, 1938, to fill vacancy caused by resignation of A. Harry Moore, and took his seat January 3, 1939.
[31] Elected November 3, 1936, for the term beginning January 3, 1937, but did not qualify until April 15, 1937, serving as a State senator until that time.
[32] Died January 27, 1938; vacancy throughout remainder of the Congress.
[33] Died June 17, 1938.
[34] Elected November 8, 1938, to fill vacancy caused by death of Royal S. Copeland, and took his seat Jan-

uary 3, 1939; vacancy in this class from June 18, 1938, to December 2, 1938.
[35] Died September 12, 1938; vacancy throughout remainder of the Congress.
[36] Died October 5, 1938; vacancy throughout remainder of the Congress.
[37] Died August 8, 1937.
[38] Elected to fill vacancy caused by death of Theodore A. Peyser, and took his seat November 15, 1937.
[39] Resigned September 29, 1937, having been elected surrogate of Westchester County, N. Y.
[40] Elected to fill vacancy caused by resignation of Charles D. Millard, and took his seat November 15, 1937.
[41] Died June 6, 1937.

[42] Elected to fill vacancy caused by death of Philip A. Goodwin, and took his seat November 15, 1937.
[43] Resigned December 2, 1938, having been elected Senator; vacancy throughout remainder of the Congress.
[44] Resigned August 19, 1937, having been appointed a judge of the United States district court, northern district of Ohio.
[45] Elected to fill vacancy caused by resignation of Frank L. Kloeb, and served from November 8, 1938, to January 3, 1939, but was unable to be sworn in as Congress was not in session.
[46] Died October 29, 1937.
[47] Elected to fill vacancy caused by death of Robert P. Hill, and took his seat January 3, 1938.

OREGON

SENATORS

Charles L. McNary, *Salem*
Frederick Steiwer,[48] *Portland*
Alfred Evan Reames,[49] *Medford*
Alexander G. Berry,[50] *Portland*

REPRESENTATIVES

James W. Mott, *Salem*
Walter M. Pierce, *La Grande*
Mrs. Nan W. Honeyman, *Portland*

PENNSYLVANIA

SENATORS

James J. Davis, *Pittsburgh*
Joseph F. Guffey, *Pittsburgh*

REPRESENTATIVES

Leon Sacks, *Philadelphia*
James P. McGranery, *Philadelphia*
Michael J. Bradley, *Phildelphia*
J. Burrwood Daly, *Philadelphia*
Frank J. G. Dorsey, *Philadelphia*
Michael J. Stack, *Philadelphia*
Ira W. Drew, *Philadelphia*
James Wolfenden, *Upper Darby*
Oliver W. Frey, *Allentown*
J. Roland Kinzer, *Lancaster*
Patrick J. Boland, *Scranton*
J. Harold Flannery, *Pittston*
James H. Gildea, *Coaldale*
Guy L. Moser, *Douglassville*
Albert G. Rutherford, *Honesdale*
Robert F. Rich, *Woolrich*
J. William Ditter, *Ambler*
Benjamin K. Focht,[51] *Lewisburg*
Richard M. Simpson,[52] *Huntingdon*
Guy J. Swope, *Harrisburg*
Benjamin Jarrett, *Farrell*
Francis E. Walter, *Easton*
Harry L. Haines, *Red Lion*
Don Gingery, *Clearfield*
J. Buell Snyder, *Perryopolis*
Charles I. Faddis, *Waynesburg*
Charles R. Eckert, *Beaver*
Joseph Gray, *Spangler*
Robert G. Allen, *Greensburg*
Charles N. Crosby, *Meadville*
Peter J. DeMuth, *Pittsburgh*
James L. Quinn, *Braddock*
Herman P. Eberharter, *Pittsburgh*
Henry Ellenbogen,[53] *Pittsburgh*
Matthew A. Dunn, *Pittsburgh*

RHODE ISLAND

SENATORS

Peter G. Gerry, *Warwick*
Theodore F. Green, *Providence*

REPRESENTATIVES

Aime J. Forand, *Central Falls*
John M. O'Connell, *Westerly*

SOUTH CAROLINA

SENATORS

Ellison D. Smith, *Lynchburg*
James F. Byrnes, *Spartanburg*

REPRESENTATIVES

Thomas S. McMillan, *Charleston*
Hampton P. Fulmer, *Orangeburg*
John C. Taylor, *Anderson*
G. Heyward Mahon, Jr., *Greenville*
James P. Richards, *Lancaster*
Allard H. Gasque,[54] *Florence*
Mrs. Elizabeth H. Gasque,[55] *Florence*

SOUTH DAKOTA

SENATORS

William J. Bulow, *Beresford*
Herbert E. Hitchcock,[56] *Mitchell*
Miss Gladys Pyle,[57] *Huron*

REPRESENTATIVES

Fred H. Hildebrandt, *Watertown*
Francis H. Case, *Custer*

TENNESSEE

SENATORS

Kenneth D. McKellar, *Memphis*
Nathan L. Bachman,[58] *Chattanooga*
George L. Berry,[59] *Pressmen's Home*
A. Tom Stewart,[60] *Winchester*

REPRESENTATIVES

B. Carroll Reece, *Johnson City*
J. Will Taylor, *La Follette*
Sam D. McReynolds, *Chattanooga*
John R. Mitchell, *Cookeville*
Richard M. Atkinson, *Nashville*
Clarence W. Turner, *Waverly*
Herron C. Pearson, *Jackson*
Jere Cooper, *Dyersburg*
Walter Chandler, *Memphis*

TEXAS

SENATORS

Morris Sheppard, *Texarkana*
Tom T. Connally, *Marlin*

REPRESENTATIVES

Wright Patman, *Texarkana*
Martin Dies, Jr., *Orange*
Morgan G. Sanders, *Canton*
Sam Rayburn, *Bonham*
Hatton W. Sumners, *Dallas*
Luther A. Johnson, *Corsicana*
Nat Patton, *Crockett*
Albert Thomas, *Houston*
Joseph J. Mansfield, *Columbus*
James P. Buchanan,[61] *Brenham*
Lyndon B. Johnson,[62] *Johnson City*
William R. Poage, *Waco*
Fritz G. Lanham, *Fort Worth*
William D. McFarlane, *Graham*
Richard M. Kleberg, *Corpus Christi*
Milton H. West, *Brownsville*
R. Ewing Thomason, *El Paso*
Clyde L. Garrett, *Eastland*
Marvin Jones, *Amarillo*
George H. Mahon, *Colorado*
Maury Maverick, *San Antonio*
Charles L. South, *Coleman*

UTAH

SENATORS

William H. King, *Salt Lake City*
Elbert D. Thomas, *Salt Lake City*

REPRESENTATIVES

Abe Murdock, *Beaver*
J. W. Robinson, *Provo*

VERMONT

SENATORS

Warren R. Austin, *Burlington*
Ernest Willard Gibson, *Brattleboro*

REPRESENTATIVE

At Large—Charles A. Plumley, *Northfield*

VIRGINIA

SENATORS

Carter Glass, *Lynchburg*
Harry Flood Byrd, *Berryville*

---

[48] Resigned January 31, 1938.
[49] Appointed to fill vacancy caused by resignation of Frederick Steiwer, and took his seat February 11, 1938.
[50] Elected to fill vacancy caused by resignation of Frederick Steiwer, and served from November 9, 1938, to January 3, 1939, but was unable to be sworn in as Congress was not in session.
[51] Died March 27, 1937.
[52] Elected to fill vacancy caused by death of Benjamin K. Focht, and took his seat May 24, 1937.
[53] Resigned January 3, 1938, having been elected judge of the common pleas court of Allegheny County, Pa.; vacancy throughout remainder of the Congress.
[54] Died June 17, 1938.
[55] Elected to fill vacancy caused by death of her husband, Allard H. Gasque, and served from September 13, 1938, to January 3, 1939, but was unable to be sworn in as Congress was not in session.
[56] Appointed to fill vacancy caused by death of Peter Norbeck in preceding Congress.
[57] Elected to fill vacancy caused by death of Peter Norbeck, in preceding Congress, and served from November 9, 1938, to January 3, 1939, but was unable to be sworn in as Congress was not in session.
[58] Died April 23, 1937.
[59] Appointed to fill vacancy caused by death of Nathan L. Bachman, and took his seat May 10, 1937.
[60] Elected November 8, 1938, to fill vacancy caused by death of Nathan L. Bachman, and took his seat January 16, 1939.
[61] Died February 22, 1937.
[62] Elected to fill vacancy caused by death of James B Buchanan, and took his seat May 13, 1937.

VIRGINIA—Continued

REPRESENTATIVES

Schuyler Otis Bland, *Newport News*
Norman R. Hamilton, *Portsmouth*
Andrew J. Montague,[63] *Richmond*
Dave E. Satterfield, Jr.,[64] *Richmond*
Patrick Henry Drewry, *Petersburg*
Thomas G. Burch, *Martinsville*
Clifton A. Woodrum, *Roanoke*
A. Willis Robertson, *Lexington*
Howard W. Smith, *Alexandria*
John W. Flannagan, Jr., *Bristol*

WASHINGTON

SENATORS

Homer T. Bone, *Tacoma*
Lewis B. Schwellenbach, *Neppel*

REPRESENTATIVES

Warren G. Magnuson, *Seattle*
Monrad C. Wallgren, *Everett*
Martin F. Smith, *Hoquiam*
Knute Hill, *Prosser*
Charles H. Leavy, *Spokane*
John M. Coffee, *Tacoma*

WEST VIRGINIA

SENATORS

Matthew M. Neely, *Fairmont*
Rush D. Holt, *Weston*

REPRESENTATIVES

Robert L. Ramsay, *Follansbee*
Jennings Randolph, *Elkins*
Andrew Edmiston, *Weston*
George W. Johnson, *Parkersburg*
John Kee, *Bluefield*
Joe L. Smith, *Beckley*

WISCONSIN

SENATORS

Robert M. La Follette, Jr., *Madison*
F. Ryan Duffy, *Fond du Lac*

REPRESENTATIVES

Thomas R. Amlie, *Elkhorn*
Harry Sauthoff, *Madison*
Gardner R. Withrow, *La Crosse*
Raymond J. Cannon, *Milwaukee*
Thomas O'Malley, *Milwaukee*
Michael K. Reilly, *Fond du Lac*
Gerald J. Boileau, *Wausau*
George J. Schneider, *Appleton*
Merlin Hull, *Black River Falls*
Bernard J. Gehrmann, *Mellon, R.F.D.*

WYOMING

SENATORS

Joseph C. O'Mahoney, *Cheyenne*
H. H. Schwartz, *Casper*

REPRESENTATIVE

At Large—Paul R. Greever, *Cody*

TERRITORY OF ALASKA

DELEGATE

Anthony J. Dimond, *Valdez*

TERRITORY OF HAWAII

DELEGATE

Samuel W. King, *Honolulu*

COMMONWEALTH OF THE PHILIPPINES

RESIDENT COMMISSIONER

Quintin Paredes,[65] *Bangued Abra*
Joaquin M. Elizalde,[66] *Manila*

PUERTO RICO

RESIDENT COMMISSIONER

Santiago Iglesias, *San Juan*

---

[63] Died January 24, 1937.
[64] Elected to fill vacancy caused by death of Andrew J. Montague, and took his seat November 15, 1937.
[65] Resigned September 29, 1938.

[66] Appointed September 29, 1938, to fill vacancy caused by resignation of Quintin Paredes, and took his seat January 3, 1939, upon the convening of the Seventy-sixth Congress.

SEVENTY-SIXTH CONGRESS

JANUARY 3, 1939, TO JANUARY 3, 1941

FIRST SESSION—*January 3, 1939, to August 5, 1939*

SECOND SESSION—*September 21, 1939, to November 3, 1939*

THIRD SESSION—*January 3, 1940, to January 3, 1941*

———

VICE PRESIDENT OF THE UNITED STATES—JOHN N. GARNER, of Texas

PRESIDENT PRO TEMPORE OF THE SENATE—KEY PITTMAN,[1] of Nevada; WILLIAM H. KING,[2] of Utah

SECRETARY OF THE SENATE—EDWIN A. HALSEY, of Virginia

SERGEANT AT ARMS OF THE SENATE—CHESLEY W. JURNEY, of Texas

———

SPEAKER OF THE HOUSE OF REPRESENTATIVES—WILLIAM B. BANKHEAD,[3] of Alabama; SAM RAYBURN,[4] of Texas

CLERK OF THE HOUSE—SOUTH TRIMBLE,[5] of Kentucky

SERGEANT AT ARMS OF THE HOUSE—KENNETH ROMNEY, of Montana

DOORKEEPER OF THE HOUSE—JOSEPH J. SINNOTT, of Virginia

POSTMASTER OF THE HOUSE—FINIS E. SCOTT

ALABAMA

SENATORS

John H. Bankhead 2d, *Jasper*
Lister Hill, *Montgomery*

REPRESENTATIVES

Frank W. Boykin, *Mobile*
George M. Grant, *Troy*
Henry B. Steagall, *Ozark*
Sam Hobbs, *Selma*
Joe Starnes, *Guntersville*
Pete Jarman, *Livingston*
William B. Bankhead,[6] *Jasper*
Zadoc L. Weatherford,[7] *Red Bay*
John J. Sparkman, *Huntsville*
Luther Patrick, *Birmingham*

ARIZONA

SENATORS

Henry F. Ashurst, *Prescott*
Carl Hayden, *Phoenix*

REPRESENTATIVE

At Large—John R. Murdock, *Tempe*

ARKANSAS

SENATORS

Mrs. Hattie W. Caraway, *Jonesboro*
John E. Miller, *Searcy*

REPRESENTATIVES

Ezekiel C. Gathings, *West Memphis*
Wilbur D. Mills, *Kensett*
Clyde T. Ellis, *Bentonville*
William B. Cravens,[8] *Fort Smith*
Fadjo Cravens,[9] *Fort Smith*
David D. Terry, *Little Rock*
William F. Norrell, *Monticello*
Wade H. Kitchens, *Magnolia*

CALIFORNIA

SENATORS

Hiram W. Johnson, *San Francisco*
Sheridan Downey, *Atherton*

REPRESENTATIVES

Clarence F. Lea, *Santa Rosa*
Harry L. Englebright, *Nevada City*
Frank H. Buck, *Vacaville*
Franck R. Havenner, *San Francisco*
Richard J. Welch, *San Francisco*
Albert E. Carter, *Oakland*
John H. Tolan, *Oakland*
John Z. Anderson, *San Juan Bautista*
Bertrand W. Gearhart, *Fresno*
Alfred J. Elliott, *Tulare*
Carl Hinshaw, *Pasadena*
H. Jerry Voorhis, *San Dimas*
Charles Kramer, *Los Angeles*
Thomas F. Ford, *Los Angeles*
John M. Costello, *Hollywood*
Leland M. Ford, *Santa Monica*
Lee E. Geyer, *Gardena*
Thomas M. Eaton,[10] *Long Beach*
Harry R. Sheppard, *Yucaipa*
Edouard V. M. Izac, *San Diego*

COLORADO

SENATORS

Alva B. Adams, *Pueblo*
Edwin C. Johnson, *Denver*

REPRESENTATIVES

Lawrence Lewis, *Denver*
Fred Cummings, *Fort Collins*
John A. Martin,[11] *Pueblo*
William E. Burney,[12] *Pueblo*
Edward T. Taylor, *Glenwood Springs*

---

[1] Died November 10, 1940.
[2] Elected November 19, 1940.
[3] Reelected January 3, 1939; died September 15, 1940.
[4] Elected September 16, 1940.
[5] Reelected January 3, 1939.
[6] Died September 15, 1940.

[7] Elected to fill vacancy caused by death of William B. Bankhead, and took his seat November 11, 1940.
[8] Died January 13, 1939.
[9] Elected to fill vacancy caused by death of his father, William B. Cravens, and took his seat September 21, 1939.

[10] Died September 16, 1939; vacancy throughout remainder of the Congress; election unsuccessfully contested by Byron N. Scott.
[11] Died December 23, 1939.
[12] Elected to fill vacancy caused by death of John A. Martin, and took his seat November 28, 1940.

CONNECTICUT

SENATORS

Francis T. Maloney, *Meriden*
John A. Danaher, *Hartford*

REPRESENTATIVES

William J. Miller, *Wethersfield*
Thomas R. Ball, *Old Lyme*
James A. Shanley, *New Haven*
Albert E. Austin, *Old Greenwich*
J. Joseph Smith, *Waterbury*
At Large—Boleslaus J. Monkiewicz, *New Britain*

DELAWARE

SENATORS

John G. Townsend, Jr., *Selbyville*
James H. Hughes, *Dover*

REPRESENTATIVE

At Large—George S. Williams, *Millsboro*

FLORIDA

SENATORS

Charles O. Andrews, *Orlando*
Claude Pepper, *Tallahassee*

REPRESENTATIVES

J. Hardin Peterson, *Lakeland*
Robert A. Green, *Starke*
Millard F. Caldwell, *Milton*
Arthur P. Cannon, *Miami*
Joe Hendricks, *De Land*

GEORGIA

SENATORS

Walter F. George, *Vienna*
Richard B. Russell, *Winder*

REPRESENTATIVES

Hugh Peterson, *Ailey*
Edward E. Cox, *Camilla*
Stephen Pace, *Americus*
Emmett M. Owen,[13] *Griffin*
A. Sidney Camp,[14] *Newnan*
Robert Ramspeck, *Atlanta*
Carl Vinson, *Milledgeville*
Malcolm C. Tarver, *Dalton*
W. Benjamin Gibbs,[15] *Jesup*
Mrs. Florence R. Gibbs,[16] *Jesup*
B. Frank Whelchel, *Gainesville*
Paul Brown, *Elberton*

IDAHO

SENATORS

William E. Borah,[17] *Boise*
John Thomas,[18] *Gooding*
D. Worth Clark, *Pocatello*

REPRESENTATIVES

Compton I. White, *Clark Fork*
Henry C. Dworshak, *Burley*

ILLINOIS

SENATORS

J. Hamilton Lewis,[19] *Chicago*
James M. Slattery,[20] *Chicago*
C. Wayland Brooks,[21] *Chicago*
Scott W. Lucas, *Havana*

REPRESENTATIVES

Arthur W. Mitchell, *Chicago*
Raymond S. McKeough, *Chicago*
Edward A. Kelly, *Chicago*
Harry P. Beam, *Chicago*
Adolph J. Sabath, *Chicago*
Anton F. Maciejewski, *Cicero*
Leonard W. Schuetz, *Chicago*
Leo Kocialkowski, *Chicago*
James McAndrews, *Chicago*
Ralph E. Church, *Evanston*
Chauncey W. Reed, *West Chicago*
Noah M. Mason, *Oglesby*
Leo E. Allen, *Galena*
Anton J. Johnson, *Macomb*
Robert B. Chiperfield, *Canton*
Everett M. Dirksen, *Pekin*
Leslie C. Arends, *Melvin*
Miss Jessie Sumner, *Milford*
William H. Wheat, *Rantoul*
James M. Barnes, *Jacksonville*
Frank W. Fries, *Carlinville*
Edwin M. Schaefer, *Belleville*
Laurence F. Arnold, *Newton*
Claude V. Parsons, *Golconda*
Kent E. Keller, *Ava*
At Large—
John C. Martin, *Salem*
Thomas V. Smith, *Chicago*

INDIANA

SENATORS

Frederick Van Nuys, *Indianapolis*
Sherman Minton, *New Albany*

REPRESENTATIVES

William T. Schulte, *Hammond*
Charles A. Halleck, *Rensselaer*
Robert A. Grant, *South Bend*
George W. Gillie, *Fort Wayne*

Forest A. Harness, *Kokomo*
Noble J. Johnson, *Terre Haute*
Gerald W. Landis, *Linton*
John W. Boehne, Jr., *Evansville*
Eugene B. Crowe, *Bedford*
Raymond S. Springer, *Connersville*
William H. Larrabee, *New Palestine*
Louis Ludlow, *Indianapolis*

IOWA

SENATORS

Guy M. Gillette, *Cherokee*
Clyde L. Herring, *Des Moines*

REPRESENTATIVES

Thomas E. Martin, *Iowa City*
William S. Jacobsen, *Clinton*
John W. Gwynne, *Waterloo*
Henry O. Talle, *Decorah*
Karl M. LeCompte, *Corydon*
Cassius C. Dowell,[22] *Des Moines*
Robert K. Goodwin,[23] *Redfield*
Ben F. Jensen, *Exira*
Fred C. Gilchrist, *Laurens*
Vincent F. Harrington,[24] *Sioux City*

KANSAS

SENATORS

Arthur Capper, *Topeka*
Clyde M. Reed, *Parsons*

REPRESENTATIVES

William P. Lambertson, *Fairview*
Ulysses S. Guyer, *Kansas City*
Thomas D. Winter, *Girard*
Edward H. Rees, *Emporia*
John M. Houston, *Newton*
Frank Carlson, *Concordia*
Clifford R. Hope, *Garden City*

KENTUCKY

SENATORS

Alben W. Barkley, *Paducah*
Marvel M. Logan,[25] *Bowling Green*
Albert B. Chandler,[26] *Versailles*

REPRESENTATIVES

Noble J. Gregory, *Mayfield*
Beverly M. Vincent, *Brownsville*
Emmet O'Neal, *Louisville*
Edward W. Creal, *Hodgenville*
Brent Spence, *Fort Thomas*
Virgil M. Chapman, *Paris*
Andrew J. May, *Prestonsburg*
Joe B. Bates, *Greenup*
John M. Robsion, *Barbourville*

[13] Died June 21, 1939.
[14] Elected to fill vacancy caused by death of Emmett M. Owen, and took his seat August 5, 1939.
[15] Died August 7, 1940.
[16] Elected to fill vacancy caused by death of her husband, W. Benjamin Gibbs, and took her seat October 3, 1940
[17] Died January 19, 1940.
[18] Appointed to fill vacancy caused by death of

William E. Borah, and took his seat February 6, 1940; subsequently elected.
[19] Died April 9, 1939.
[20] Appointed to fill vacancy caused by death of J. Hamilton Lewis, and took his seat April 24, 1939.
[21] Elected November 5, 1940, to fill vacancy caused by death of J. Hamilton Lewis, and took his seat November 22, 1940
[22] Died February 4, 1940.

[23] Elected to fill vacancy caused by death of Cassius C. Dowell, and took his seat March 12, 1940.
[24] Election unsuccessfully contested by Albert F. Swanson.
[25] Died October 3, 1939.
[26] Appointed to fill vacancy caused by death of Marvel M. Logan, and took his seat October 10, 1939; subsequently elected.

LOUISIANA

SENATORS

John H. Overton, *Alexandria*
Allen J. Ellender, *Houma*

REPRESENTATIVES

Joachim O. Fernandez, *New Orleans*
Paul H. Maloney,[27] *New Orleans*
Robert L. Mouton, *Lafayette*
Overton Brooks, *Shreveport*
Newt V. Mills, *Monroe*
John K. Griffith, *Slidell*
René L. DeRouen, *Ville Platte*
A. Leonard Allen, *Winnfield*

MAINE

SENATORS

Frederick Hale, *Portland*
Wallace H. White, Jr., *Auburn*

REPRESENTATIVES

James C. Oliver, *South Portland*
Clyde H. Smith,[28] *Skowhegan*
Mrs. Margaret Chase Smith,[29] *Skowhegan*
Ralph O. Brewster, *Dexter*

MARYLAND

SENATORS

Millard E. Tydings, *Havre de Grace*
George L. Radcliffe, *Baltimore*

REPRESENTATIVES

T. Alan Goldsborough,[30] *Denton*
David J. Ward,[31] *Salisbury*
William P. Cole, Jr., *Towson*
Thomas D'Alesandro, Jr., *Baltimore*
Ambrose J. Kennedy, *Baltimore*
Lansdale G. Sasscer,[32] *Upper Marlboro*
William D. Byron, *Williamsport*

MASSACHUSETTS

SENATORS

David I. Walsh, *Fitchburg*
Henry Cabot Lodge, Jr., *Beverly*

REPRESENTATIVES

Allen T. Treadway, *Stockbridge*
Charles R. Clason, *Springfield*
Joseph E. Casey, *Clinton*
Pehr G. Holmes, *Worcester*
Mrs. Edith Nourse Rogers, *Lowell*
George J. Bates, *Salem*
Lawrence J. Connery, *Lynn*
Arthur D. Healey, *Somerville*
Robert Luce, *Waltham*

George H. Tinkham, *Boston*
Thomas A. Flaherty, *Boston*
John W. McCormack, *Dorchester*
Richard B. Wigglesworth, *Milton*
Joseph W. Martin, Jr., *North Attleboro*
Charles L. Gifford, *Cotuit*

MICHIGAN

SENATORS

Arthur H. Vandenberg, *Grand Rapids*
Prentiss M. Brown, *St. Ignace*

REPRESENTATIVES

Rudolph G. Tenerowicz, *Detroit*
Earl C. Michener, *Adrian*
Paul W. Shafer, *Battle Creek*
Clare E. Hoffman, *Allegan*
Carl E. Mapes,[33] *Grand Rapids*
Bartel J. Jonkman,[34] *Grand Rapids*
William W. Blackney, *Flint*
Jesse P. Wolcott, *Port Huron*
Fred L. Crawford, *Saginaw*
Albert J. Engel, *Muskegon*
Roy O. Woodruff, *Bay City*
Frederick V. Bradley, *Rogers City*
Frank E. Hook, *Ironwood*
Clarence J. McLeod, *Detroit*
Louis C. Rabaut, *Detroit*
John D. Dingell, *Detroit*
John Lesinski, *Dearborn*
George A. Dondero, *Royal Oak*

MINNESOTA

SENATORS

Henrik Shipstead, *Minneapolis*
Ernest Lundeen,[35] *Wayzata, R.F.D.*
Joseph H. Ball,[36] *St. Paul*

REPRESENTATIVES

August H. Andresen, *Red Wing*
Elmer J. Ryan, *South St. Paul*
John G. Alexander, *Minneapolis*
Melvin J. Maas, *St. Paul*
Oscar Youngdahl, *Minneapolis*
Harold Knutson, *St. Cloud*
H. Carl Andersen, *Tyler*
William A. Pittenger, *Duluth*
Richard T. Buckler, *Crookston*

MISSISSIPPI

SENATORS

Pat Harrison, *Gulfport*
Theodore G. Bilbo, *Poplarville*

REPRESENTATIVES

John E. Rankin, *Tupelo*
Wall Doxey, *Holly Springs*

William M. Whittington, *Greenwood*
Aaron Lane Ford, *Ackerman*
Ross A. Collins, *Meridian*
William M. Colmer, *Pascagoula*
Dan R. McGehee, *Meadville*

MISSOURI

SENATORS

Joel Bennett Clark, *St. Louis*
Harry S. Truman, *Independence*

REPRESENTATIVES

Milton A. Romjue, *Macon*
William L. Nelson, *Columbia*
Richard M. Duncan, *St. Joseph*
C. Jasper Bell, *Kansas City*
Joseph B. Shannon, *Kansas City*
Reuben T. Wood, *Springfield*
Dewey Short, *Galena*
Clyde Williams, *Hillsboro*
Clarence Cannon, *Elsberry*
Orville Zimmerman, *Kennett*
Thomas C. Hennings, Jr.,[37] *St. Louis*
C. Arthur Anderson, *St. Louis*
John J. Cochran, *St. Louis*

MONTANA

SENATORS

Burton K. Wheeler, *Butte*
James E. Murray, *Butte*

REPRESENTATIVES

Jacob Thorkelson, *Butte*
James F. O'Connor, *Livingston*

NEBRASKA

SENATORS

George W. Norris, *McCook*
Edward R. Burke, *Omaha*

REPRESENTATIVES

George H. Heinke,[38] *Nebraska City*
John Hyde Sweet,[39] *Nebraska City*
Charles F. McLaughlin, *Omaha*
Karl Stefan, *Norfolk*
Carl T. Curtis, *Minden*
Harry B. Coffee, *Chadron*

NEVADA

SENATORS

Key Pittman,[40] *Tonopah*
Berkeley L. Bunker,[41] *Las Vegas*
Patrick A. McCarran, *Reno*

REPRESENTATIVE

At Large—James G. Scrugham, *Reno*

---

[27] Resigned December 15, 1940; vacancy throughout remainder of the Congress.
[28] Died April 8, 1940.
[29] Elected to fill vacancy caused by death of her husband, Clyde H. Smith, and took her seat June 10, 1940.
[30] Resigned April 5, 1939, having been appointed an associate justice of the District Court of the United States for the District of Columbia.
[31] Elected to fill vacancy caused by resignation of

T. Alan Goldsborough, and took his seat June 13, 1939.
[32] Elected to fill vacancy caused by death of Representative-elect Stephen W. Gambrill in preceding Congress, and took his seat February 16, 1939.
[33] Died December 12, 1939.
[34] Elected to fill vacancy caused by death of Carl E. Mapes, and took his seat February 29, 1940.
[35] Died August 31, 1940.
[36] Appointed to fill vacancy caused by death of Ernest Lundeen, and took his seat October 17, 1940.

[37] Resigned December 31, 1940, to become circuit attorney for the city of St. Louis; vacancy throughout remainder of the Congress.
[38] Died January 2, 1940.
[39] Elected to fill vacancy caused by death of George H. Heinke, and took his seat April 17, 1940.
[40] Died November 10, 1940.
[41] Appointed to fill vacancy caused by death of Key Pittman, and took his seat December 12, 1940.

NEW HAMPSHIRE

SENATORS

H. Styles Bridges, *East Concord*
Charles W. Tobey, *Temple*

REPRESENTATIVES

Arthur B. Jenks, *Manchester*
Foster Stearns, *Hancock*

NEW JERSEY

SENATORS

William H. Smathers, *Atlantic City*
W. Warren Barbour, *Locust*

REPRESENTATIVES

Charles A. Wolverton, *Camden*
Walter S. Jeffries, *Atlantic City*
William H. Sutphin, *Matawan*
D. Lane Powers, *Trenton*
Charles A. Eaton, *North Plainfield*
Donald H. McLean, *Elizabeth*
J. Parnell Thomas, *Allendale*
George N. Seger,[42] *Passaic*
Frank C. Osmers, Jr., *Haworth*
Fred A. Hartley, Jr., *Kearny*
Albert L. Vreeland, *East Orange*
Robert W. Kean, *Livingston*
Mrs. Mary T. Norton, *Jersey City*
Edward J. Hart, *Jersey City*

NEW MEXICO

SENATORS

Carl A. Hatch, *Clovis*
Dennis Chavez, *Albuquerque*

REPRESENTATIVE

At Large—John J. Dempsey, *Santa Fe*

NEW YORK

SENATORS

Robert F. Wagner, *New York City*
James M. Mead, *Buffalo*

REPRESENTATIVES

Leonard W. Hall, *Oyster Bay*
William B. Barry, *St. Albans*
Joseph L. Pfeifer, *Brooklyn*
Thomas H. Cullen, *Brooklyn*
Marcellus H. Evans, *Brooklyn*
Andrew L. Somers, *Brooklyn*
John J. Delaney, *Brooklyn*
Donald L. O'Toole, *Brooklyn*
Eugene J. Keogh, *Brooklyn*
Emanuel Celler, *Brooklyn*
James A. O'Leary, *West New Brighton*

Samuel Dickstein, *New York City*
Christopher D. Sullivan, *New York City*
William I. Sirovich,[43] *New York City*
M. Michael Edelstein,[44] *New York City*
Michael J. Kennedy, *New York City*
James H. Fay, *New York City*
Bruce Barton, *New York City*
Martin J. Kennedy, *New York City*
Sol Bloom, *New York City*
Vito Marcantonio, *New York City*
Joseph A. Gavagan, *New York City*
Edward W. Curley,[45] *New York City*
Walter A. Lynch,[46] *New York City*
Charles A. Buckley, *New York City*
James M. Fitzpatrick, *New York City*
Ralph A. Gamble, *Larchmont*
Hamilton Fish, Jr., *Garrison*
Lewis K. Rockefeller, *Chatham*
William T. Byrne, *Loudonville*
E. Harold Cluett, *Troy*
Frank Crowther, *Schenectady*
Wallace E. Pierce,[47] *Plattsburgh*
Clarence E. Kilburn,[48] *Malone*
Francis D. Culkin, *Oswego*
Fred J. Douglas, *Utica*
Bert Lord,[49] *Afton*
Edwin Arthur Hall,[50] *Binghamton*
Clarence E. Hancock, *Syracuse*
John Taber, *Auburn*
W. Sterling Cole, *Bath*
Joseph J. O'Brien, *East Rochester*
James W. Wadsworth, Jr., *Geneseo*
Walter G. Andrews, *Buffalo*
J. Francis Harter, *Eggertsville*
Pius L. Schwert, *Buffalo*
Daniel A. Reed, *Dunkirk*
At Large—
 Matthew J. Merritt, *Flushing*
 Mrs. Caroline O'Day, *Rye*

NORTH CAROLINA

SENATORS

Josiah W. Bailey, *Raleigh*
Robert R. Reynolds, *Asheville*

REPRESENTATIVES

Lindsay C. Warren,[51] *Washington*
Herbert C. Bonner,[52] *Washington*
John H. Kerr, *Warrenton*
Graham A. Barden, *New Bern*
Harold D. Cooley, *Nashville*
Alonzo D. Folger, *Mount Airy*
Carl T. Durham, *Chapel Hill*
J. Bayard Clark, *Fayetteville*
William O. Burgin, *Lexington*
Robert L. Doughton, *Laurel Springs*
Alfred L. Bulwinkle, *Gastonia*
Zebulon Weaver, *Asheville*

NORTH DAKOTA

SENATORS

Lynn J. Frazier, *Hoople*
Gerald P. Nye, *Cooperstown*

REPRESENTATIVES AT LARGE

Usher L. Burdick, *Williston*
William Lemke, *Fargo*

OHIO

SENATORS

A. Victor Donahey, *Huntsville, R.F.D.*
Robert A. Taft, *Cincinnati*

REPRESENTATIVES

Charles H. Elston, *Newtown, R.F.D.*
William E. Hess, *Cincinnati*
Harry N. Routzohn, *Dayton*
Robert F. Jones, *Lima*
Cliff Clevenger, *Bryan*
James G. Polk,[53] *Highland*
Clarence J. Brown, *Blanchester*
Frederick C. Smith, *Marion*
John F. Hunter, *Toledo*
Thomas A. Jenkins, *Ironton*
Harold K. Claypool, *Chillicothe*
John M. Vorys, *Columbus*
Dudley A. White, *Norwalk*
Dow W. Harter, *Akron*
Robert T. Secrest, *Caldwell*
James Seccombe, *Canton*
William A. Ashbrook,[54] *Johnstown*
J. Harry McGregor,[55] *West Lafayette*
Earl R. Lewis, *St. Clairsville*
Michael J. Kirwan, *Youngstown*
Martin L. Sweeney, *Cleveland*
Robert Crosser, *Cleveland*
Chester C. Bolton,[56] *Lyndhurst*
Mrs. Frances P. Bolton,[57] *Lyndhurst*
At Large—
 George H. Bender, *Cleveland Heights*
 Lycurgus L. Marshall, *Euclid*

OKLAHOMA

SENATORS

J. W. Elmer Thomas, *Medicine Park*
Josh Lee, *Norman*

REPRESENTATIVES

Wesley E. Disney, *Tulsa*
Jack Nichols, *Eufaula*
Wilburn Cartwright, *McAlester*
Lyle H. Boren, *Seminole*
A. S. Mike Monroney, *Oklahoma City*
Jed Johnson, *Anadarko*
Sam C. Massingale, *Cordell*
Phil Ferguson, *Woodward*
At Large—Will Rogers, *Oklahoma City*

---

[42] Died August 26, 1940; vacancy throughout remainder of the Congress.
[43] Died December 17, 1939.
[44] Elected to fill vacancy caused by death of William I. Sirovich, and took his seat February 14, 1940.
[45] Died January 6, 1940.
[46] Elected to fill vacancy caused by death of Edward W. Curley, and took his seat March 4, 1940.
[47] Died January 3, 1940.

[48] Elected to fill vacancy caused by death of Wallace E. Pierce, and took his seat February 21, 1940.
[49] Died May 24, 1939.
[50] Elected to fill vacancy caused by death of Bert Lord, and took his seat January 3, 1940.
[51] Resigned October 31, 1940, having been appointed Comptroller General of the United States.
[52] Elected to fill vacancy caused by resignation of Lindsay C. Warren; took his seat November 11, 1940.

[53] Election unsuccessfully contested by Emory F. Smith.
[54] Died January 1, 1940.
[55] Elected to vacancy caused by death of William A. Ashbrook, and took his seat March 5, 1940.
[56] Died October 29, 1939.
[57] Elected to fill vacancy caused by death of her husband, Chester C. Bolton, and took her seat March 5, 1940.

OREGON

SENATORS

Charles L. McNary, *Salem*
Rufus C. Holman, *Portland*

REPRESENTATIVES

James W. Mott, *Salem*
Walter M. Pierce, *La Grande*
Homer D. Angell, *Portland*

PENNSYLVANIA

SENATORS

James J. Davis, *Pittsburgh*
Joseph F. Guffey, *Pittsburgh*

REPRESENTATIVES

Leon Sacks, *Philadelphia*
James P. McGranery, *Philadelphia*
Michael J. Bradley, *Philadelphia*
J. Burrwood Daly,[58] *Philadelphia*
John Edward Sheridan,[59] *Philadelphia*
Fred C. Gartner, *Philadelphia*
Francis J. Myers, *Philadelphia*
George P. Darrow, *Philadelphia*
James Wolfenden, *Upper Darby*
Charles L. Gerlach, *Allentown*
J. Roland Kinzer, *Lancaster*
Patrick J. Boland, *Scranton*
J. Harold Flannery, *Pittston*
Ivor D. Fenton, *Mahanoy City*
Guy L. Moser, *Douglassville*
Albert G. Rutherford, *Honesdale*
Robert F. Rich, *Woolrich*
J. William Ditter, *Ambler*
Richard M. Simpson, *Huntingdon*
John C. Kunkel, *Harrisburg*
Benjamin Jarrett, *Farrell*
Francis E. Walter, *Easton*
Chester H. Gross, *Manchester*
James E. Van Zandt, *Altoona*
J. Buell Snyder, *Perryopolis*
Charles I. Faddis, *Waynesburg*
Louis E. Graham, *Beaver*
Harve Tibbott, *Ebensburg*
Robert G. Allen, *Greensburg*
Robert L. Rodgers, *Erie*
Robert J. Corbett, *Bellevue*
John McDowell, *Wilkinsburg*
Herman P. Eberharter, *Pittsburgh*
Joseph A. McArdle, *Pittsburgh*
Matthew A. Dunn, *Pittsburgh*

RHODE ISLAND

SENATORS

Peter G. Gerry, *Warwick*
Theodore F. Green, *Providence*

REPRESENTATIVES

Charles F. Risk, *Saylesville*
Harry Sandager, *Cranston*

SOUTH CAROLINA

SENATORS

Ellison D. Smith, *Lynchburg*
James F. Byrnes, *Spartanburg*

REPRESENTATIVES

Thomas S. McMillan,[60] *Charleston*
Mrs. Clara G. McMillan,[61] *Charleston*
Hampton P. Fulmer, *Orangeburg*
Butler B. Hare, *Saluda*
Joseph R. Bryson, *Greenville*
James P. Richards, *Lancaster*
John L. McMillan, *Florence*

SOUTH DAKOTA

SENATORS

William J. Bulow, *Beresford*
J. Chandler Gurney, *Yankton*

REPRESENTATIVES

Karl E. Mundt, *Madison*
Francis H. Case, *Custer*

TENNESSEE

SENATORS

Kenneth D. McKellar, *Memphis*
A. Tom Stewart,[62] *Winchester*

REPRESENTATIVES

B. Carroll Reece, *Johnson City*
J. Will Taylor,[63] *La Follette*
John Jennings, Jr.,[64] *Knoxville*
Sam D. McReynolds,[65] *Chattanooga*
Estes Kefauver,[66] *Chattanooga*
Albert A. Gore, *Carthage*
Joseph W. Byrns, Jr., *Nashville*
Clarence W. Turner,[67] *Waverly*
Wirt Courtney,[68] *Franklin*
Herron Pearson, *Jackson*
Jere Cooper, *Dyersburg*
Walter Chandler,[69] *Memphis*
Clifford Davis,[70] *Memphis*

TEXAS

SENATORS

Morris Sheppard, *Texarkana*
Tom T. Connally, *Marlin*

REPRESENTATIVES

Wright Patman, *Texarkana*
Martin Dies, Jr., *Orange*

Lindley Beckworth, *Gilmer*
Sam Rayburn, *Bonham*
Hatton W. Sumners, *Dallas*
Luther A. Johnson, *Corsicana*
Nat Patton, *Crockett*
Albert Thomas, *Houston*
Joseph J. Mansfield, *Columbus*
Lyndon B. Johnson, *Johnson City*
William R. Poage, *Waco*
Fritz G. Lanham, *Fort Worth*
Ed Gossett, *Wichita Falls*
Richard M. Kleberg, *Corpus Christi*
Milton H. West, *Brownsville*
R. Ewing Thomason, *El Paso*
Clyde L. Garrett, *Eastland*
Marvin Jones,[71] *Amarillo*
George H. Mahon, *Colorado City*
Paul J. Kilday, *San Antonio*
Charles L. South, *Coleman*

UTAH

SENATORS

William H. King, *Salt Lake City*
Elbert D. Thomas, *Salt Lake City*

REPRESENTATIVES

Abe Murdock, *Beaver*
J. W. Robinson, *Provo*

VERMONT

SENATORS

Warren R. Austin, *Burlington*
Ernest Willard Gibson,[72] *Brattleboro*
Ernest William Gibson,[73] *Brattleboro*

REPRESENTATIVE

At Large—Charles A. Plumley, *Northfield*

VIRGINIA

SENATORS

Carter Glass, *Lynchburg*
Harry Flood Byrd, *Berryville*

REPRESENTATIVES

Schuyler Otis Bland, *Newport News*
Colgate W. Darden, Jr., *Norfolk*
Dave E. Satterfield, Jr., *Richmond*
Patrick Henry Drewry, *Petersburg*
Thomas G. Burch, *Martinsville*
Clifton A. Woodrum, *Roanoke*
A. Willis Robertson, *Lexington*
Howard W. Smith, *Alexandria*
John W. Flannagan, Jr., *Bristol*

---

[58] Died March 12, 1939.
[59] Elected to fill the vacancy caused by the death of J. Burrwood Daly, and took his seat January 3, 1940.
[60] Died September 29, 1939.
[61] Elected to fill vacancy caused by death of her husband, Thomas S. McMillan, and took her seat January 3, 1940.
[62] Elected November 8, 1938, to fill vacancy caused by death of Nathan L. Bachman in preceding Congress, but did not qualify until January 16, 1939;

vacancy from November 9, 1938, to January 15, 1939. Election unsuccessfully contested by John R. Neal.
[63] Died November 14, 1939.
[64] Elected to fill vacancy caused by death of J. Will Taylor, and took his seat January 8, 1940.
[65] Died July 11, 1939.
[66] Elected to fill vacancy caused by death of Sam D. McReynolds, and took his seat September 21, 1939.
[67] Died March 23, 1939.
[68] Elected to fill vacancy caused by death of Clarence W. Turner, and took his seat May 24, 1939.

[69] Resigned January 2, 1940, to serve as mayor of Memphis, Tenn.
[70] Elected to fill vacancy caused by resignation of Walter Chandler, and took his seat February 21, 1940.
[71] Resigned November 20, 1940, having been appointed judge of the United States Court of Claims; vacancy throughout remainder of the Congress.
[72] Died June 20, 1940.
[73] Appointed to fill vacancy caused by death of his father, Ernest Willard Gibson, and took his seat July 3, 1940.

WASHINGTON

SENATORS

Homer T. Bone, *Tacoma*
Lewis B. Schwellenbach,[74] *Neppel*
Monrad C. Wallgren,[75] *Everett*

REPRESENTATIVES

Warren G. Magnuson, *Seattle*
Monrad C. Wallgren,[76] *Everett*
Martin F. Smith, *Hoquiam*
Knute Hill, *Prosser*
Charles H. Leavy, *Veradale*
John M. Coffee, *Tacoma*

WEST VIRGINIA

SENATORS

Matthew M. Neely, *Fairmont*
Rush D. Holt, *Weston*

REPRESENTATIVES

Andrew C. Schiffler, *Wheeling*
Jennings Randolph, *Elkins*
Andrew Edmiston, *Weston*
George W. Johnson, *Parkersburg*

John Kee, *Bluefield*
Joe L. Smith, *Beckley*

WISCONSIN

SENATORS

Robert M. La Follette, Jr., *Madison*
Alexander Wiley, *Chippewa Falls*

REPRESENTATIVES

Stephen Bolles, *Janesville*
Charles Hawks, Jr., *Horicon*
Harry W. Griswold,[77] *West Salem*
John C. Schafer, *Milwaukee*
Lewis D. Thill, *Milwaukee*
Frank B. Keefe, *Oshkosh*
Reid F. Murray, *Waupaca*
Joshua L. Johns, *Appleton*
Merlin Hull, *Black River Falls*
Bernard J. Gehrmann, *Mellon, R.F.D.*

WYOMING

SENATORS

Joseph C. O'Mahoney, *Cheyenne*
H. H. Schwartz, *Casper*

REPRESENTATIVE

At Large—Frank O. Horton, *Saddlestring*

TERRITORY OF ALASKA

DELEGATE

Anthony J. Dimond, *Valdez*

TERRITORY OF HAWAII

DELEGATE

Samuel W. King, *Honolulu*

COMMONWEALTH OF THE PHILIPPINES

RESIDENT COMMISSIONER

Joaquin M. Elizalde, *Manila*

PUERTO RICO

RESIDENT COMMISSIONER

Santiago Iglesias,[78] *San Juan*
Bolívar Pagán,[79] *San Juan*

---

[74] Resigned December 16, 1940, having been appointed United States district judge for the Eastern District of Washington.
[75] Appointed to fill vacancy caused by resignation of Lewis B. Schwellenbach, and took his seat December 19, 1940.

[76] Resigned December 19, 1940, having been appointed United States Senator; vacancy throughout remainder of the Congress.
[77] Died July 4, 1939; vacancy throughout remainder of the Congress.

[78] Died December 5, 1939.
[79] Appointed December 26, 1939, to fill vacancy caused by death of Santiago Iglesias, and took his seat January 3, 1940.

SEVENTY-SEVENTH CONGRESS

JANUARY 3, 1941, TO JANUARY 3, 1943

FIRST SESSION—*January 3, 1941, to January 2, 1942*

SECOND SESSION—*January 5,*[1] *1942, to December 16, 1942*

———

VICE PRESIDENT[2] OF THE UNITED STATES—JOHN N. GARNER,[3] of Texas; HENRY A. WALLACE,[4] of Iowa

PRESIDENT PRO TEMPORE OF THE SENATE—PAT HARRISON,[5] of Mississippi; CARTER GLASS,[6] of Virginia

SECRETARY OF THE SENATE—EDWIN A. HALSEY, of Virginia

SERGEANT AT ARMS OF THE SENATE—CHESLEY W. JURNEY, of Texas

———

SPEAKER OF THE HOUSE OF REPRESENTATIVES—SAM RAYBURN,[7] of Texas

CLERK OF THE HOUSE—SOUTH TRIMBLE,[8] of Kentucky

SERGEANT AT ARMS OF THE HOUSE—KENNETH ROMNEY, of Montana

DOORKEEPER OF THE HOUSE—JOSEPH J. SINNOTT, of Virginia

POSTMASTER OF THE HOUSE—FINIS E. SCOTT

ALABAMA

SENATORS

John H. Bankhead 2d, *Jasper*
Lister Hill, *Mongomery*

REPRESENTATIVES

Frank W. Boykin, *Mobile*
George M. Grant, *Troy*
Henry B. Steagall, *Ozark*
Sam Hobbs, *Selma*
Joe Starnes, *Guntersville*
Pete Jarman, *Livingston*
Walter W. Bankhead,[9] *Jasper*
Carter Manasco,[10] *Jasper*
John J. Sparkman, *Huntsville*
Luther Patrick, *Birmingham*

ARIZONA

SENATORS

Carl Hayden, *Phoenix*
Ernest W. McFarland, *Florence*

REPRESENTATIVE

At Large—John R. Murdock, *Tempe*

ARKANSAS

SENATORS

Mrs. Hattie W. Caraway, *Jonesboro*
John E. Miller,[11] *Searcy*
George Lloyd Spencer,[12] *Hope*

REPRESENTATIVES

Ezekiel C. Gathings, *West Memphis*
Wilbur D. Mills, *Kensett*
Clyde T. Ellis, *Bentonville*
Fadjo Cravens, *Fort Smith*
David D. Terry, *Little Rock*
William F. Norrell, *Monticello*
Oren Harris, *El Dorado*

CALIFORNIA

SENATORS

Hiram W. Johnson, *San Francisco*
Sheridan Downey, *Atherton*

REPRESENTATIVES

Clarence F. Lea, *Santa Rosa*
Harry L. Englebright, *Nevada City*
Frank H. Buck,[13] *Vacaville*
Thomas Rolph, *San Francisco*
Richard J. Welch, *San Francisco*
Albert E. Carter, *Oakland*
John H. Tolan, *Oakland*
John Z. Anderson, *San Juan Bautista*
Bertrand W. Gearhart, *Fresno*
Alfred J. Elliott, *Tulare*
Carl Hinshaw, *Pasadena*
H. Jerry Voorhis, *San Dimas*
Charles Kramer, *Los Angeles*
Thomas F. Ford, *Los Angeles*
John M. Costello, *Hollywood*
Leland M. Ford, *Santa Monica*
Lee E. Geyer,[14] *Gardena*
Cecil R. King,[15] *Los Angeles*
Ward Johnson, *Long Beach*
Harry R. Sheppard, *Yucaipa*
Edouard V. M. Izac, *San Diego*

COLORADO

SENATORS

Alva B. Adams,[16] *Pueblo*
Eugene D. Millikin,[17] *Denver*
Edwin C. Johnson, *Denver*

REPRESENTATIVES

Lawrence Lewis, *Denver*
William S. Hill, *Fort Collins*
J. Edgar Chenoweth, *Trinidad*
Edward T. Taylor,[18] *Glenwood Springs*
Robert F. Rockwell,[19] *Paonia*

CONNECTICUT

SENATORS

Francis T. Maloney, *Meriden*
John A. Danaher, *Hartford*

REPRESENTATIVES

Herman P. Kopplemann, *Hartford*
William J. Fitzgerald, *Norwich*
James A. Shanley, *New Haven*
Le Roy D. Downs, *South Norwalk*
J. Joseph Smith,[20] *Prospect*
Joseph E. Talbot,[21] *Naugatuck*
At Large—Lucien J. Maciora, *New Britain*

DELAWARE

SENATORS

James H. Hughes, *Dover*
James M. Tunnell, *Georgetown*

REPRESENTATIVE

At Large—Philip A. Traynor, *Wilmington*

FLORIDA

SENATORS

Charles O. Andrews, *Orlando*
Claude Pepper, *Tallahassee*

REPRESENTATIVES

J. Hardin Peterson, *Lakeland*
Robert A. Green, *Starke*
Robert L. F. Sikes, *Crestview*
Arthur P. Cannon, *Miami*
Joe Hendricks, *De Land*

GEORGIA

SENATORS

Walter F. George, *Vienna*
Richard B. Russell, *Winder*

REPRESENTATIVES

Hugh Peterson, *Ailey*
Edward E. Cox, *Camilla*
Stephen Pace, *Americus*

A. Sidney Camp, *Newnan*
Robert Ramspeck, *Atlanta*
Carl Vinson, *Milledgeville*
Malcolm C. Tarver, *Dalton*
John S. Gibson, *Douglas*
B. Frank Whelchel, *Gainesville*
Paul Brown, *Elberton*

IDAHO

SENATORS

D. Worth Clark, *Pocatello*
John Thomas, *Gooding*

REPRESENTATIVES

Compton I. White, *Clark Fork*
Henry C. Dworshak, *Burley*

ILLINOIS

SENATORS

Scott W. Lucas, *Havana*
C. Wayland Brooks, *Chicago*

REPRESENTATIVES

Arthur W. Mitchell, *Chicago*
Raymond S. McKeough, *Chicago*
Edward A. Kelly, *Chicago*
Harry P. Beam,[22] *Chicago*
Adolph J. Sabath, *Chicago*
Anton F. Maciejewski,[23] *Cicero*
Leonard W. Schuetz, *Chicago*
Leo Kocialkowski, *Chicago*
Charles S. Dewey, *Chicago*
George A. Paddock, *Evanston*
Chauncey W. Reed, *West Chicago*
Noah M. Mason, *Oglesby*
Leo E. Allen, *Galena*
Anton J. Johnson, *Macomb*
Robert B. Chiperfield, *Canton*
Everett M. Dirksen, *Pekin*
Leslie C. Arends, *Melvin*
Miss Jessie Sumner, *Milford*
William H. Wheat, *Rantoul*
James M. Barnes, *Jacksonville*
Evan Howell, *Springfield*
Edwin M. Schaefer, *Belleville*
Laurence F. Arnold, *Newton*
James V. Heidinger, *Fairfield*
Cecil W. (Runt) Bishop, *Carterville*
At Large—
Stephen A. Day, *Evanston*
William G. Stratton, *Morris*

INDIANA

SENATORS

Frederick Van Nuys, *Indianapolis*
Raymond E. Willis, *Angola*

REPRESENTATIVES

William T. Schulte, *Hammond*
Charles A. Halleck, *Rensselaer*

Robert A. Grant, *South Bend*
George W. Gillie, *Fort Wayne*
Forest A. Harness, *Kokomo*
Noble J. Johnson, *Terre Haute*
Gerald W. Landis, *Linton*
John W. Boehne, Jr., *Evansville*
Earl Wilson, *Huron*
Raymond S. Springer, *Connersville*
William H. Larrabee, *New Palestine*
Louis Ludlow, *Indianapolis*

IOWA

SENATORS

Guy M. Gillette, *Cherokee*
Clyde L. Herring, *Des Moines*

REPRESENTATIVES

Thomas E. Martin, *Iowa City*
William S. Jacobsen, *Clinton*
John W. Gwynne, *Waterloo*
Henry O. Talle, *Decorah*
Karl M. LeCompte, *Corydon*
Paul Cunningham, *Des Moines*
Ben F. Jensen, *Exira*
Fred C. Gilchrist, *Laurens*
Vincent F. Harrington,[24] *Sioux City*
Harry E. Narey,[25] *Spirit Lake*

KANSAS

SENATORS

Arthur Capper, *Topeka*
Clyde M. Reed, *Parsons*

REPRESENTATIVES

William P. Lambertson, *Fairview*
Ulysses S. Guyer, *Kansas City*
Thomas D. Winter, *Girard*
Edward H. Rees, *Emporia*
John M. Houston, *Wichita, R.F.D.*
Frank Carlson, *Concordia*
Clifford R. Hope, *Garden City*

KENTUCKY

SENATORS

Alben W. Barkley, *Paducah*
Albert B. Chandler, *Versailles*

REPRESENTATIVES

Noble J. Gregory, *Mayfield*
Beverly M. Vincent, *Brownsville*
Emmet O'Neal, *Louisville*
Edward W. Creal, *Hodgenville*
Brent Spence, *Fort Thomas*
Virgil M. Chapman, *Paris*
Andrew J. May, *Prestonsburg*
Joe B. Bates, *Greenup*
John M. Robsion, *Barbourville*

---

[16] Died December 1, 1941.
[17] Appointed to fill vacancy caused by death of Alva B. Adams, and took his seat January 5, 1942; subsequently elected.
[18] Died September 3, 1941.
[19] Elected to fill vacancy caused by death of Edward

T. Taylor, and took his seat January 5, 1941.
[20] Resigned November 4, 1942.
[21] Elected to fill vacancy caused by resignation of J. Joseph Smith, and took his seat February 5, 1942.
[22] Resigned December 6, 1942; vacancy throughout remainder of the Congress.

[23] Resigned December 8, 1942; vacancy throughout remainder of the Congress.
[24] Resigned September 5, 1942.
[25] Elected to fill vacancy caused by resignation of Vincent F. Harrington, and took his seat November 16, 1942.

LOUISIANA

SENATORS

John H. Overton, *Alexandria*
Allen J. Ellender, *Houma*

REPRESENTATIVES

F. Edward Hébert, *New Orleans*
T. Hale Boggs, *New Orleans*
James Domengeaux, *Lafayette*
Overton Brooks, *Shreveport*
Newt V. Mills, *Monroe*
Jared Y. Sanders, Jr., *Baton Rouge*
Vance Plauché, *Lake Charles*
A. Leonard Allen, *Winnfield*

MAINE

SENATORS

Wallace H. White, Jr., *Auburn*
Ralph O. Brewster, *Dexter*

REPRESENTATIVES

James C. Oliver, *South Portland*
Mrs. Margaret Chase Smith, *Skowhegan*
Frank Fellows, *Bangor*

MARYLAND

SENATORS

Millard E. Tydings, *Havre de Grace*
George L. Radcliffe, *Baltimore*

REPRESENTATIVES

David J. Ward, *Salisbury*
William P. Cole, Jr.,[26] *Towson*
Thomas D'Alesandro, Jr., *Baltimore*
John A. Meyer, *Baltimore*
Lansdale G. Sasscer, *Upper Marlboro*
William D. Byron,[27] *Williamsport*
Mrs. Katharine E. Byron,[28] *Williamsport*

MASSACHUSETTS

SENATORS

David I. Walsh, *Fitchburg*
Henry Cabot Lodge, Jr., *Beverly*

REPRESENTATIVES

Allen T. Treadway, *Stockbridge*
Charles R. Clason, *Springfield*
Joseph E. Casey, *Clinton*
Pehr G. Holmes, *Worcester*
Mrs. Edith Nourse Rogers, *Lowell*
George J. Bates, *Salem*
Lawrence J. Connery,[29] *Lynn*
Thomas J. Lane,[30] *Lawrence*

Arthur D. Healey,[31] *Somerville*
Thomas H. Eliot, *Cambridge*
George H. Tinkham, *Boston*
Thomas A. Flaherty, *Boston*
John W. McCormack, *Boston*
Richard B. Wigglesworth, *Milton*
Joseph W. Martin, Jr., *North Attleboro*
Charles L. Gifford, *Cotuit*

MICHIGAN

SENATORS

Arthur H. Vandenberg, *Grand Rapids*
Prentiss M. Brown, *St. Ignace*

REPRESENTATIVES

Rudolph G. Tenerowicz, *Detroit*
Earl C. Michner, *Adrian*
Paul W. Shafer, *Battle Creek*
Clare E. Hoffman, *Allegan*
Bartel J. Jonkman, *Grand Rapids*
William W. Blackney, *Flint*
Jesse P. Wolcott, *Port Huron*
Fred L. Crawford, *Saginaw*
Albert J. Engel, *Muskegon*
Roy O. Woodruff, *Bay City*
Frederick V. Bradley, *Rogers City*
Frank E. Hook, *Ironwood*
George D. O'Brien, *Detroit*
Louis C. Rabaut, *Detroit*
John D. Dingell, *Detroit*
John Lensinki, *Dearborn*
George A. Dondero, *Royal Oak*

MINNESOTA

SENATORS

Henrik Shipstead, *Minneapolis*
Joseph H. Ball,[32] *St. Paul*
Arthur E. Nelson,[33] *St. Paul*

REPRESENTATIVES

August H. Andresen, *Red Wing*
Joseph P. O'Hara, *Glencoe*
Richard P. Gale, *Mound*
Melvin J. Maas, *St. Paul*
Oscar Youngdahl, *Minneapolis*
Harold Knutson, *St. Cloud*
H. Carl Andersen, *Tyler*
William A. Pittenger, *Duluth*
Richard T. Buckler, *Crookston*

MISSISSIPPI

SENATORS

Pat Harrison,[34] *Gulfport*
James O. Eastland,[35] *Ruleville*

Wall Doxey,[36] *Holly Springs*
Theodore G. Bilbo, *Poplarville*

REPRESENTATIVES

John E. Rankin, *Tupelo*
Wall Doxey,[37] *Holly Springs*
Jamie L. Whitten,[38] *Charleston*
William M. Whittington, *Greenwood*
Aaron Lane Ford, *Ackerman*
Ross A. Collins, *Meridian*
William M. Colmer, *Pascagoula*
Dan R. McGehee, *Meadville*

MISSOURI

SENATORS

Joel Bennett Clark, *St. Louis*
Harry S. Truman, *Independence*

REPRESENTATIVES

Milton A. Romjue, *Macon*
William L. Nelson, *Columbia*
Richard M. Duncan, *St. Joseph*
C. Jasper Bell, *Blue Springs*
Joseph B. Shannon, *Kansas City*
Philip A. Bennett,[39] *Springfield*
Dewey Short, *Galena*
Clyde Williams, *Hillsboro*
Clarence Cannon, *Elsberry*
Orville Zimmerman, *Kennett*
John B. Sullivan, *St. Louis*
Walter C. Ploeser, *St. Louis*
John J. Cochran, *St. Louis*

MONTANA

SENATORS

Burton K. Wheeler, *Butte*
James E. Murray, *Butte*

REPRESENTATIVES

Miss Jeannette Rankin, *Missoula*
James F. O'Connor, *Livingston*

NEBRASKA

SENATORS

George W. Norris, *McCook*
Hugh A. Butler, *Omaha*

REPRESENTATIVES

Oren S. Copeland, *Lincoln*
Charles F. McLaughlin, *Omaha*
Karl Stefan, *Norfolk*
Carl T. Curtis, *Minden*
Harry B. Coffee, *Chadron*

---

[26] Resigned October 26, 1942; vacancy throughout remainder of the Congress.
[27] Died February 27, 1941.
[28] Elected to fill vacancy caused by death of her husband, William D. Byron, and took her seat June 11, 1941.
[29] Died October 19, 1941.
[30] Elected to fill vacancy caused by death of Lawrence J. Connery, and took his seat January 12, 1942.

[31] Resigned August 3, 1942; vacancy throughout remainder of the Congress.
[32] Appointed in preceding Congress to fill vacancy caused by death of Ernest Lundeen.
[33] Elected to fill vacancy caused by death of Ernest Lundeen, in preceding Congress, and took his seat November 18, 1942.
[34] Died June 22, 1941.
[35] Appointed to fill vacancy caused by death of Pat Harrison, and took his seat June 30, 1941.

[36] Elected to fill vacancy caused by death of Pat Harrison, and took his seat September 29, 1941.
[37] Resigned September 29, 1941, having been elected Senator.
[38] Elected to fill vacancy caused by resignation of Wall Doxey, and took his seat November 14, 1941.
[39] Died December 7, 1942, before the commencement of the Seventy-eighth Congress, to which he had been reelected; vacancy throughout remainder of the Congress.

NEVADA

SENATORS

Patrick A. McCarran, *Reno*
Berkeley L. Bunker,[40] *Las Vegas*
James G. Scrugham,[41] *Reno*

REPRESENTATIVE

At Large—James G. Scrugham,[42] *Reno*

NEW HAMPSHIRE

SENATORS

H. Styles Bridges, *Concord*
Charles W. Tobey, *Temple*

REPRESENTATIVES

Arthur B. Jenks, *Manchester*
Foster Stearns, *Hancock*

NEW JERSEY

SENATORS

William H. Smathers, *Atantic City*
W. Warren Barbour, *Locust*

REPRESENTATIVES

Charles A. Wolverton, *Camden*
Elmer H. Wene, *Vineland*
William H. Sutphin, *Matawan*
D. Lane Powers, *Trenton*
Charles A. Eaton, *North Plainfield*
Donald H. McLean, *Elizabeth*
J. Parnell Thomas, *Allendale*
Gordon Canfield, *Paterson*
Frank C. Osmers, Jr., *Haworth*
Fred A. Hartley, Jr., *Kearny*
Albert L. Vreeland, *East Orange*
Robert W. Kean, *Livington*
Mrs. Mary T. Norton, *Jersey City*
Edward J. Hart, *Jersey City*

NEW MEXICO

SENATORS

Carl A. Hatch, *Clovis*
Dennis Chavez, *Albuquerque*

REPRESENTATIVE

At Large—Clinton P. Anderson, *Albuquerque*

NEW YORK

SENATORS

Robert F. Wagner, *New York City*
James M. Mead, *Buffalo*

REPRESENTATIVES

Leonard W. Hall, *Oyster Bay*
William B. Barry, *St. Albans*
Joseph L. Pfeifer, *Brooklyn*
Thomas H. Cullen, *Brooklyn*
James J. Heffernan, *Brooklyn*
Andrew L. Somers, *Brookyln*
John J. Delaney, *Brooklyn*
Donald L. O'Toole, *Brooklyn*
Eugene J. Keogh, *Brooklyn*
Emanuel Celler, *Brooklyn*
James A. O'Leary, *West New Brighton*
Samuel Dickstein, *New York City*
Louis J. Capozzoli, *New York City*
M. Michael Edelstein,[43] *New York City*
Arthur G. Klein,[44] *New York City*
Michael J. Kennedy, *New York City*
William T. Pheiffer, *New York City*
Kenneth F. Simpson,[45] *New York City*
Joseph Clark Baldwin,[46] *New York City*
Martin J. Kennedy, *New York City*
Sol Bloom, *New York City*
Vito Marcantonio, *New York City*
Joseph A. Gavagan, *New York City*
Walter A. Lynch, *New York City*
Charles A. Buckley, *New York City*
James M. Fitzpatrick, *New York City*
Ralph A. Gamble, *Larchmont*
Hamilton Fish, Jr., *Garrison*
Lewis K. Rockefeller, *Chatham*
William T. Byrne, *Loudonville*
E. Harold Cluett, *Troy*
Frank Crowther, *Schenectady*
Clarence E. Kilburn, *Malone*
Francis D. Culkin, *Oswego*
Fred J. Douglas, *Utica*
Edwin Arthur Hall, *Binghamton*
Clarence E. Hancock, *Syracuse*
John Taber, *Auburn*
W. Sterling Cole, *Bath*
Joseph J. O'Brien, *East Rochester*
James W. Wadsworth, Jr., *Geneseo*
Walter G. Andrews, *Buffalo*
Alfred F. Beiter, *Williamsville*
Pius L. Schwert,[47] *Buffalo*
John C. Butler,[48] *Buffalo*
Daniel A. Reed, *Dunkirk*
At Large—
 Matthew J. Merritt, *Flushing*
 Mrs. Caroline O'Day, *Rye*

NORTH CAROLINA

SENATORS

Josiah W. Bailey, *Raleigh*
Robert R. Reynolds, *Asheville*

REPRESENTATIVES

Herbert C. Bonner, *Washington*
John H. Kerr, *Warrenton*

Graham A. Barden, *New Bern*
Harold D. Cooley, *Nashville*
Alonzo D. Folger,[49] *Mount Airy*
John H. Folger,[50] *Mount Airy*
Carl T. Durham, *Chapel Hill*
J. Bayard Clark, *Fayetteville*
William O. Burgin, *Lexington*
Robert L. Doughton, *Laurel Springs*
Alfred L. Bulwinkle, *Gastonia*
Zebulon Weaver, *Asheville*

NORTH DAKOTA

SENATORS

Gerald P. Nye, *Cooperstown*
William Langer, *Bismarck*

REPRESENTATIVES AT LARGE

Usher L. Burdick, *Williston*
Charles R. Robertson, *Bismarck*

OHIO

SENATORS

Robert A. Taft, *Cincinnati*
Harold H. Burton, *Cleveland*

REPRESENTATIVES

Charles H. Elston, *Newtown, R.F.D.*
William E. Hess, *Cincinnati*
Greg J. Holbrock, *Hamilton*
Robert F. Jones, *Lima*
Cliff Clevenger, *Bryan*
Jacob E. Davis, *Waverly*
Clarence J. Brown, *Blanchester*
Frederick C. Smith, *Marion*
John F. Hunter, *Toledo*
Thomas A. Jenkins, *Ironton*
Harold K. Claypool, *Chillicothe*
John M. Vorys, *Columbus*
Albert D. Baumhart, Jr.,[51] *Vermilion*
Dow W. Harter, *Akron*
Robert T. Secrest,[52] *Caldwell*
William R. Thom, *Canton*
J. Harry McGregor, *West Lafayette*
Lawrence E. Imhoff, *St. Clairsville*
Michael J. Kirwan, *Youngstown*
Martin L. Sweeney, *Cleveland*
Robert Crosser, *Cleveland*
Mrs. Frances P. Bolton, *Lyndhurst*
At Large—
 George H. Bender, *Cleveland Heights*
 Stephen M. Young, *Cleveland*

OKLAHOMA

SENATORS

J. W. Elmer Thomas, *Medicine Park*
Josh Lee, *Norman*

---

[40] Appointed in preceding Congress to fill vacancy caused by death of Key Pittman.
[41] Elected to fill vacancy caused by death of Key Pittman in preceding Congress, and took his seat December 7, 1942.
[42] Resigned December 7, 1942, having been elected Senator; vacancy throughout remainder of the Congress.
[43] Died June 4, 1941.

[44] Elected to fill vacancy caused by death of M. Michael Edelstein, and took his seat August 7, 1941.
[45] Died January 25, 1941.
[46] Elected to fill vacancy caused by death of Kenneth F. Simpson, and took his seat March 19, 1941.
[47] Died March 11, 1941.
[48] Elected to fill vacancy caused by death of Pius L. Schwert, and his seat May 5, 1941.

[49] Died April 30, 1941.
[50] Elected to fill vacancy caused by death of his brother, Alonzo D. Folger, and took his seat June 20, 1941.
[51] Resigned September 2, 1942; vacancy throughout remainder of the Congress.
[52] Resigned August 3, 1942; vacancy throughout remainder of the Congress.

REPRESENTATIVES

Wesley E. Disney, *Tulsa*
Jack Nichols, *Eufaula*
Wilburn Cartwright, *McAlester*
Lyle H. Boren, *Seminole*
A. S. Mike Monroney, *Oklahoma City*
Jed Johnson, *Anadarko*
Sam C. Massingale,[53] *Cordell*
Victor Wickersham,[54] *Mangum*
Ross Rizley, *Guymon*
At Large—Will Rogers, *Oklahoma City*

OREGON

SENATORS

Charles L. McNary, *Salem*
Rufus C. Holman, *Portland*

REPRESENTATIVES

James W. Mott, *Salem*
Walter M. Pierce, *La Grande*
Homer D. Angell, *Portland*

PENNSYLVANIA

SENATORS

James J. Davis, *Pittsburgh*
Joseph F. Guffey, *Pittsburgh*

REPRESENTATIVES

Leon Sacks, *Philadelphia*
James P. McGranery, *Philadelphia*
Michael J. Bradley, *Philadelphia*
John Edward Sheridan, *Philadelphia*
Francis R. Smith, *Philadelphia*
Francis J. Myers, *Philadelphia*
Hugh D. Scott, Jr., *Philadelphia*
James Wolfenden, *Upper Darby*
Charles L. Gerlach, *Allentown*
J. Roland Kinzer, *Lancaster*
Patrick J. Boland,[55] *Scranton*
Mrs. Veronica G. Boland,[56] *Scranton*
J. Harold Flannery,[57] *Pittston*
Thomas Byron Miller,[58] *Plymouth*
Ivor D. Fenton, *Mahanoy City*
Guy L. Moser, *Douglassville*
Albert G. Rutherford,[59] *Honesdale*
Wilson D. Gillette,[60] *Towanda*
Robert F. Rich, *Woolrich*
J. William Ditter, *Ambler*
Richard M. Simpson, *Huntingdon*
John C. Kunkel, *Harrisburg*
Benjamin Jarrett, *Farrell*
Francis E. Walter, *Easton*
Harry L. Haines, *Red Lion*
James E. Van Zandt, *Altoona*
J. Buell Snyder, *Perryopolis*

Charles I. Faddis,[61] *Waynesburg*
Louis E. Graham, *Beaver*
Harve Tibbott, *Ebensburg*
Augustine B. Kelley, *Greensburg*
Robert L. Rodgers, *Erie*
Thomas E. Scanlon, *Pittsburgh*
Samuel A. Weiss, *Glassport*
Herman P. Eberharter, *Pittsburgh*
Joseph A. McArdle,[62] *Pittsburgh*
Elmer J. Holland,[63] *Pittsburgh*
James A. Wright, *Carnegie*

RHODE ISLAND

SENATORS

Peter G. Gerry, *Warwick*
Theodore F. Green, *Providence*

REPRESENTATIVES

Aime J. Forand, *Cumberland*
John E. Fogarty, *Harmony*

SOUTH CAROLINA

SENATORS

Ellison D. Smith, *Lynchburg*
James F. Byrnes,[64] *Spartanburg*
Alva M. Lumpkin,[65] *Columbia*
Roger C. Peace,[66] *Greenville*
Burnet R. Maybank,[67] *Charleston*

REPRESENTATIVES

L. Mendel Rivers, *North Charleston*
Hampton P. Fulmer, *Orangeburg*
Butler B. Hare, *Saluda*
Joseph R. Bryson, *Greenville*
James P. Richards, *Lancaster*
John L. McMillan, *Florence*

SOUTH DAKOTA

SENATORS

William J. Bulow, *Beresford*
J. Chandler Gurney, *Yankton*

REPRESENTATIVES

Karl E. Mundt, *Madison*
Francis H. Case, *Custer*

TENNESSEE

SENATORS

Kenneth D. McKellar, *Memphis*
A. Tom Stewart, *Winchester*

REPRESENTATIVES

B. Carroll Reece, *Johnson City*
John Jennings, Jr., *Knoxville*

Estes Kefauver, *Chattanooga*
Albert A. Gore, *Carthage*
J. Percy Priest, *Nashville*
Wirt Courtney, *Franklin*
Herron Pearson, *Jackson*
Jere Cooper, *Dyersburg*
Clifford Davis, *Memphis*

TEXAS

SENATORS

Morris Sheppard,[68] *Texarkana*
Andrew Jackson Houston,[69] *La Porte*
W. Lee O'Daniel,[70] *Fort Worth*
Tom T. Connally, *Marlin*

REPRESENTATIVES

Wright Patman, *Texarkana*
Martin Dies, Jr., *Orange*
Lindley Beckworth, *Gilmer*
Sam Rayburn, *Bonham*
Hatton W. Sumners, *Dallas*
Luther A. Johnson, *Corsicana*
Nat Patton, *Crockett*
Albert Thomas, *Houston*
Joseph J. Mansfield, *Columbus*
Lyndon B. Johnson, *Johnson City*
William R. Poage, *Waco*
Fritz G. Lanham, *Fort Worth*
Ed Gossett, *Wichita Falls*
Richard M. Kleberg, *Corpus Christi*
Milton H. West, *Brownsville*
R. Ewing Thomason, *El Paso*
Sam M. Russell, *Stephenville*
Eugene Worley, *Shamrock*
George H. Mahon, *Colorado City*
Paul J. Kilday, *San Antonio*
Charles L. South, *Coleman*

UTAH

SENATORS

Elbert D. Thomas, *Salt Lake City*
Abe Murdock, *Beaver*

REPRESENTATIVES

Walter K. Granger, *Cedar City*
J. W. Robinson, *Provo*

VERMONT

SENATORS

Warren R. Austin, *Burlington*
George D. Aiken,[71] *Putney*

REPRESENTATIVE

At Large—Charles A. Plumley, *Northfield*

---

[53] Died January 17, 1941.
[54] Elected to fill vacancy caused by death by Sam C. Massingale, and took his seat April 14, 1941.
[55] Died May 18, 1942.
[56] Elected to fill vacancy caused by death of her husband, Patrick J. Boland, and took her seat November 19, 1942.
[57] Resigned January 3, 1942.
[58] Elected to fill vacancy caused by resignation of J. Harold Flannery, and took his seat June 15, 1942.
[59] Died August 10, 1941.
[60] Elected to fill vacancy caused by death of Albert G. Rutherford, and took his seat December 4, 1941.

[61] Resigned December 4, 1942; vacancy throughout remainder of the Congress.
[62] Resigned January 5, 1942.
[63] Elected to fill vacancy caused by resignation of Joseph A. McArdle, and took his seat June 15, 1942.
[64] Resigned July 8, 1941, having been appointed Associate Justice of the United States Supreme Court.
[65] Appointed to fill vacancy caused by resignation of James F. Byrnes, and took his seat July 22, 1941; died August 1, 1941, while serving as an appointee.
[66] Appointed to fill vacancy caused by resignation of James F. Byrnes and death of Alva M. Lumpkin, and took his seat August 6, 1941.

[67] Elected to fill vacancy caused by resignation of James F. Byrnes, and took his seat November 5, 1941.
[68] Died April 9, 1941.
[69] Appointed to fill vacancy caused by death of Morris Sheppard, and took his seat June 2, 1941; died June 26, 1941, while serving as an appointee.
[70] Elected June 28, 1941, to fill vacancy caused by deaths of Morris Sheppard and Andrew Jackson Houston, but did not qualify until August 4, 1941; vacancy from June 27 to August 3, 1941.
[71] Elected November 5, 1940, to fill vacancy caused by death of Ernest Willard Gibson in preceding Congress, but did not qualify until January 10, 1941; vacancy from January 3 to 9, 1941.

VIRGINIA

SENATORS

Carter Glass, *Lynchburg*
Harry Flood Byrd, *Berryville*

REPRESENTATIVES

Schuyler Otis Bland, *Newport News*
Colgate W. Darden, Jr.,[72] *Norfolk*
Winder R. Harris,[73] *Norfolk*
Dave E. Satterfield, Jr., *Richmond*
Patrick Henry Drewry, *Petersburg*
Thomas G. Burch, *Martinsville*
Clifton A. Woodrum, *Roanoke*
A. Willis Robertson, *Lexington*
Howard W. Smith, *Alexandria*
John W. Flannagan, Jr., *Bristol*

WASHINGTON

SENATORS

Homer T. Bone, *Tacoma*
Monrad C. Wallgren, *Everett*

REPRESENTATIVES

Warren G. Magnuson, *Seattle*
Henry M. Jackson, *Everett*
Martin F. Smith, *Hoquiam*
Knute Hill, *Prosser*
Charles H. Leavy,[74] *Spokane*
John M. Coffee, *Tacoma*

WEST VIRGINIA

SENATORS

Matthew M. Neely,[75] *Fairmont*
Joseph Rosier,[76] *Fairmont*
Hugh Ike Shott,[77] *Bluefield*
Harley M. Kilgore, *Beckley*

REPRESENTATIVES

Robert L. Ramsay, *Follansbee*
Jennings Randolph, *Elkins*
Andrew Edmiston, *Weston*
George W. Johnson, *Parkersburg*
John Kee, *Bluefield*
Joe L. Smith, *Beckley*

WISCONSIN

SENATORS

Robert M. La Follette, Jr., *Madison*
Alexander Wiley, *Chippewa Falls*

REPRESENTATIVES

Stephen Bolles,[78] *Janesville*
Lawrence H. Smith,[79] *Racine*
Harry Sauthoff, *Madison*
William H. Stevenson, *La Crosse*
Thaddeus F. B. Wasielewski, *Milwaukee*
Lewis D. Thill, *Milwaukee*
Frank B. Keefe, *Oshkosh*
Reid F. Murray, *Ogdensburg*
Joshua L. Johns, *Appleton*

Merlin Hull, *Black River Falls*
Bernard J. Gehrmann, *Mellon, R.F.D.*

WYOMING

SENATORS

Joseph C. O'Mahoney, *Cheyenne*
H. H. Schwartz, *Casper*

REPRESENTATIVE

At Large—John J. McIntyre, *Douglas*

TERRITORY OF ALASKA

DELEGATE

Anthony J. Dimond, *Valdez*

TERRITORY OF HAWAII

DELEGATE

Samuel W. King, *Honolulu*

COMMONWEALTH OF THE PHILIPPINES

RESIDENT COMMISSIONER

Joaquin M. Elizalde, *Manila*

PUERTO RICO

RESIDENT COMMISSIONER

Bolívar Pagán, *San Juan*

---

[72] Resigned March 1, 1941.
[73] Elected to fill vacancy caused by resignation of Colgate W. Darden, Jr., and took his seat April 15, 1941.
[74] Resigned August 1, 1942; vacancy throughout remainder of the Congress.
[75] Resigned January 12, 1941.

[76] The outgoing Governor of West Virginia having appointed Clarence E. Martin and the incoming Governor Joseph Rosier to fill the vacancy caused by the resignation of Matthew M. Neely, the Senate decided on May 13, 1941 (S. Res. 106), that Joseph Rosier was entitled to a seat as a Senator from West Virginia, and he took his seat May 14, 1941.

[77] Elected to fill vacancy caused by resignation of Matthew M. Neely and took his seat November 18, 1942.
[78] Died July 8, 1941.
[79] Elected to fill vacancy caused by death of Stephen Bolles, and took his seat September 16, 1941.

SEVENTY-EIGHTH CONGRESS

JANUARY 3, 1943, TO JANUARY 3, 1945

FIRST SESSION—*January 6,[1] 1943, to December 21, 1943*

SECOND SESSION—*January 10,[2] 1944, to December 19, 1944*

VICE PRESIDENT OF THE UNITED STATES—HENRY A. WALLACE, of Iowa

PRESIDENT PRO TEMPORE OF THE SENATE—CARTER GLASS, of Virginia

SECRETARY OF THE SENATE—EDWIN A. HALSEY, of Virginia

SERGEANT AT ARMS OF THE SENATE—CHESLEY W. JURNEY, of Texas; WALL DOXY,[3] of Mississippi

---

SPEAKER OF THE HOUSE OF REPRESENTATIVES—SAM RAYBURN,[4] of Texas

CLERK OF THE HOUSE—SOUTH TRIMBLE,[5] of Kentucky

SERGEANT AT ARMS OF THE HOUSE—KENNETH ROMNEY, of Montana

DOORKEEPER OF THE HOUSE—JOSEPH J. SINNOTT, of Virginia

POSTMASTER OF THE HOUSE—FINIS E. SCOTT

ALABAMA

SENATORS

John H. Bankhead 2d, *Jasper*
Lister Hill, *Montgomery*

REPRESENTATIVES

Frank W. Boykin, *Mobile*
George M. Grant, *Troy*
Henry B. Steagall,[6] *Ozark*
George W. Andrews,[7] *Union Springs*
Sam Hobbs, *Selma*
Joe Starnes, *Guntersville*
Pete Jarman, *Livingston*
Carter Manasco, *Jasper*
John J. Sparkman, *Huntsville*
John P. Newsome, *Birmingham*

ARIZONA

SENATORS

Carl Hayden, *Phoenix*
Ernest W. McFarland, *Florence*

REPRESENTATIVES AT LARGE

Richard F. Harless, *Phoenix*
John R. Murdock, *Tempe*

ARKANSAS

SENATORS

Mrs. Hattie W. Caraway, *Jonesboro*
John L. McClellan, *Camden*

REPRESENTATIVES

Ezekiel C. Gathings, *West Memphis*
Wilbur D. Mills, *Kensett*
J. William Fulbright, *Fayetteville*
Fadjo Cravens, *Fort Smith*
Brooks Hays, *Little Rock*
William F. Norrell, *Monticello*
Oren Harris, *El Dorado*

CALIFORNIA

SENATORS

Hiram W. Johnson, *San Francisco*
Sheridan Downey, *Claremont*

REPRESENTATIVES

Clarence F. Lea, *Santa Rosa*
Harry L. Englebright,[8] *Nevada City*
Clair Engle,[9] *Red Bluff*
Leroy Johnson, *Stockton*
Thomas Rolph, *San Francisco*
Richard J. Welch, *San Francisco*
Albert E. Carter, *Oakland*
John H. Tolan, *Oakland*

John Z. Anderson, *San Juan Bautista*
Bertrand W. Gearhart, *Fresno*
Alfred J. Elliott, *Tulare*
George E. Outland, *Santa Barbara*
H. Jerry Voorhis, *San Dimas*
Norris Poulson, *Los Angeles*
Thomas F. Ford, *Los Angeles*
John M. Costello, *Hollywood*
Will Rogers, Jr.,[10] *Culver City*
Cecil R. King, *Los Angeles*
Ward Johnson, *Long Beach*
Chet Holifield, *Montebello*
Carl Hinshaw, *Pasadena*
Harry R. Sheppard, *Yucaipa*
John Phillips, *Banning*
Edouard V. M. Izac, *San Diego*

COLORADO

SENATORS

Edwin C. Johnson, *Craig*
Eugene D. Millikin, *Denver*

REPRESENTATIVES

Lawrence Lewis,[11] *Denver*
Dean M. Gillespie,[12] *Denver*
William S. Hill, *Fort Collins*
J. Edgar Chenoweth, *Trindad*
Robert F. Rockwell, *Paonia*

---

[1] By joint resolution (Pub. Law 819, 77th Cong., 2d sess.) the date of assembling the first session of the Seventy-eighth Congress was fixed for January 6, 1943.
[2] By joint resolution (Pub. Law 210, 78th Cong., 1st sess.) the date of assembling the second session of the Seventy-eighth Congress was fixed for January 10, 1944.
[3] Elected February 1, 1943.

[4] Reelected January 6, 1943.
[5] Reelected January 6, 1943.
[6] Died November 22, 1943.
[7] Elected to fill vacancy caused by death of Henry B. Steagall, and took his seat March 20, 1944.
[8] Died May 13, 1943.
[9] Elected to fill vacancy caused by death of Harry L.

Englebright, and took his seat September 23, 1943.
[10] Resigned May 23, 1944; vacancy throughout remainder of the Congress.
[11] Died December 9, 1943.
[12] Elected to fill vacancy caused by death of Lawrence Lewis, and took his seat March 30, 1944

CONNECTICUT

SENATORS

Francis T. Maloney, *Meriden*
John A. Danaher, *Portland*

REPRESENTATIVES

William J. Miller, *Wethersfield*
John D. McWilliams, *Norwich*
Ranulf Compton, *Madison*
Mrs. Clare Boothe Luce, *Greenwich*
Joseph E. Talbot, *Naugatuck*
At Large—Boleslaus J. Monkiewicz, *New Britain*

DELAWARE

SENATORS

James M. Tunnell, *Georgetown*
C. Douglass Buck, *Wilmington*

REPRESENTATIVE

At Large—Earle D. Willey, *Dover*

FLORIDA

SENATORS

Charles O. Andrews, *Orlando*
Claude Pepper, *Tallahassee*

REPRESENTATIVES

J. Hardin Peterson, *Lakeland*
Emory H. Price, *Jacksonville*
Robert L. F. Sikes,[13] *Crestview*
Arthur P. Cannon, *Miami*
Joe Hendricks, *De Land*
At Large—Robert A. Green,[14] *Starke*

GEORGIA

SENATORS

Walter F. George, *Vienna*
Richard B. Russell, *Winder*

REPRESENTATIVES

Hugh Peterson,[15] *Ailey*
Edward E. Cox, *Camilla*
Stephen Pace, *Americus*
A. Sidney Camp, *Newnan*
Robert Ramspeck, *Atlanta*
Carl Vinson, *Milledgeville*
Malcolm C. Tarver, *Dalton*
John S. Gibson, *Douglas*
B. Frank Whelchel, *Gainesville*
Paul Brown, *Elberton*

IDAHO

SENATORS

D. Worth Clark, *Pocatello*
John Thomas, *Gooding*

REPRESENTATIVES

Compton I. White, *Clark Fork*
Henry C. Dworshak, *Burley*

ILLINOIS

SENATORS

Scott W. Lucas, *Havana*
C. Wayland Brooks, *Chicago*

REPRESENTATIVES

William L. Dawson, *Chicago*
William A. Rowan, *Chicago*
Fred E. Busbey, *Chicago*
Martin Gorski, *Chicago*
Adolph J. Sabath, *Chicago*
Thomas J. O'Brien, *Chicago*
Leonard W. Schuetz,[16] [17] *Chicago*
Thomas S. Gordon, *Chicago*
Charles S. Dewey, *Chicago*
Ralph E. Church, *Evanston*
Chauncey W. Reed, *West Chicago*
Noah M. Mason, *Oglesby*
Leo E. Allen, *Galena*
Anton J. Johnson, *Macomb*
Robert B. Chiperfield, *Canton*
Everett M. Dirksen, *Pekin*
Leslie C. Arends, *Melvin*
Miss Jessie Sumner, *Milford*
William H. Wheat,[18] *Rantoul*
Rolla C. McMillen,[19] *Decatur*
Sidney E. Simpson, *Carrollton*
Evan Howell, *Springfield*
Calvin D. Johnson, *Belleville*
Charles W. Vursell, *Salem*
James V. Heidinger, *Fairfield*
Cecil W. (Runt) Bishop, *Carterville*
At Large—Stephen A. Day, *Evanston*

INDIANA

SENATORS

Frederick Van Nuys,[20] *Indianapolis*
Samuel D. Jackson,[21] *Fort Wayne*
William E. Jenner,[22] *Bedford*
Raymond E. Willis, *Angola*

REPRESENTATIVES

Ray J. Madden, *Gary*
Charles A. Halleck, *Rensselaer*
Robert A. Grant, *South Bend*

George W. Gillie, *Fort Wayne*
Forest A. Harness, *Kokomo*
Noble J. Johnson, *Terre Haute*
Gerald W. Landis, *Linton*
Charles M. La Follette, *Evansville*
Earl Wilson, *Bedford*
Raymond S. Springer, *Connersville*
Louis Ludlow, *Indianapolis*

IOWA

SENATORS

Guy M. Gillette, *Cherokee*
George A. Wilson, *Des Moines*

REPRESENTATIVES

Thomas E. Martin, *Iowa City*
Henry O. Talle, *Decorah*
John W. Gwynne, *Waterloo*
Karl M. LeCompte, *Corydon*
Paul Cunningham, *Des Moines*
Fred C. Gilchrist, *Laurens*
Ben F. Jensen, *Exira*
Charles B. Hoeven, *Alton*

KANSAS

SENATORS

Arthur Capper, *Topeka*
Clyde M. Reed, *Parsons*

REPRESENTATIVES

William P. Lambertson, *Fairview*
Ulysses S. Guyer,[23] *Kansas City*
Errett P. Scrivner,[24] *Kansas City*
Thomas D. Winter, *Girard*
Edward H. Rees, *Emporia*
Clifford R. Hope, *Garden City*
Frank Carlson, *Concordia*

KENTUCKY

SENATORS

Alben W. Barkley, *Paducah*
Albert B. Chandler, *Versailles*

REPRESENTATIVES

Noble J. Gregory, *Mayfield*
Beverly M. Vincent, *Brownsville*
Emmet O'Neal, *Louisville*
Edward W. Creal,[25] *Hodgenville*
Chester O. Carrier,[26] *Leitchfield*
Brent Spence, *Fort Thomas*
Virgil M. Chapman, *Paris*
Andrew J. May, *Prestonsburg*
Joe B. Bates, *Greenup*
John M. Robsion, *Barbourville*

---

[13] Resigned October 19, 1944; vacancy throughout remainder of the Congress.
[14] Resigned November 25, 1944; vacancy throughout remainder of the Congress.
[15] Election unsuccessfully contested by Edward T. McEvoy.
[16] Election unsuccessfully contested by James C. Moreland.

[17] Died February 13, 1944; vacancy throughout remainder of the Congress.
[18] Died January 16, 1944.
[19] Elected to fill vacancy caused by death of William H. Wheat, and took his seat August 1, 1944.
[20] Died January 25, 1944.
[21] Appointed to fill vacancy caused by death of Frederick Van Nuys; took his seat January 31, 1944.

[22] Elected to fill vacancy caused by death of Frederick Van Nuys, and took his seat November 14, 1944.
[23] Died June 5, 1943.
[24] Elected to fill vacancy caused by death of Ulysses S. Guyer, and took his seat September 28, 1943.
[25] Died October 13, 1943.
[26] Elected to fill vacancy caused by death of Edward W. Creal, and took his seat December 10, 1943.

LOUISIANA

SENATORS

John H. Overton, *Alexandria*
Allen J. Ellender, *Houma*

REPRESENTATIVES

F. Edward Hébert, *New Orleans*
Paul H. Maloney, *New Orleans*
James Domengeaux,[27] *Lafayette*
Overton Brooks, *Shreveport*
Charles E. McKenzie, *Monroe*
James H. Morrison, *Hammond*
Henry D. Larcade, Jr., *Opelousas*
A. Leonard Allen, *Winnfield*

MAINE

SENATORS

Wallace H. White, Jr., *Auburn*
Ralph O. Brewster, *Dexter*

REPRESENTATIVES

Robert Hale, *Portland*
Mrs. Margaret Chase Smith, *Skowhegan*
Frank Fellows, *Bangor*

MARYLAND

SENATORS

Millard E. Tydings, *Havre de Grace*
George L. Radcliffe, *Baltimore*

REPRESENTATIVES

David J. Ward, *Salisbury*
H. Streett Baldwin, *Towson*
Thomas D'Alesandro, Jr., *Baltimore*
Daniel Ellison, *Baltimore*
Lansdale G. Sasscer, *Upper Marlboro*
J. Glenn Beall, *Frostburg*

MASSACHUSETTS

SENATORS

David I. Walsh, *Clinton*
Henry Cabot Lodge, Jr.,[28] *Beverly*
Sinclair Weeks,[29] *West Newton*

REPRESENTATIVES

Allen T. Treadway, *Stockbridge*
Charles R. Clason, *Springfield*
Philip J. Philbin, *Clinton*
Pehr G. Holmes, *Worcester*
Mrs. Edith Nourse Rogers, *Lowell*
George J. Bates, *Salem*
Thomas J. Lane, *Lawrence*
Angier L. Goodwin, *Melrose*
Charles L. Gifford, *Cotuit*
Christian A. Herter, *Boston*
James M. Curley, *Boston*
John W. McCormack, *Boston*

Richard B. Wigglesworth, *Milton*
Joseph W. Martin, Jr., *North Attleboro*

MICHIGAN

SENATORS

Arthur H. Vandenberg, *Grand Rapids*
Homer Ferguson, *Detroit*

REPRESENTATIVES

George G. Sadowski, *Detroit*
Earl C. Michener, *Adrian*
Paul W. Shafer, *Battle Creek*
Clare E. Hoffman, *Allegan*
Bartel J. Jonkman, *Grand Rapids*
William W. Blackney, *Flint*
Jesse P. Wolcott, *Port Huron*
Fred L. Crawford, *Saginaw*
Albert J. Engel, *Muskegon*
Roy O. Woodruff, *Bay City*
Frederick V. Bradley, *Rogers City*
John B. Bennett, *Ontonagon*
George D. O'Brien, *Detroit*
Louis C. Rabaut, *Detroit*
John D. Dingell, *Detroit*
John Lesinski, *Dearborn*
George A. Dondero, *Royal Oak*

MINNESOTA

SENATORS

Henrik Shipstead, *Carlos, R.F.D.*
Joseph H. Ball, *St. Paul*

REPRESENTATIVES

August H. Andresen, *Red Wing*
Joseph P. O'Hara, *Glencoe*
Richard P. Gale, *Mound*
Melvin J. Maas, *St. Paul*
Walter H. Judd, *Minneapolis*
Harold Knutson, *St. Cloud*
H. Carl Andersen, *Tyler*
William A. Pittenger, *Duluth*
Harold C. Hagen, *Crookston*

MISSISSIPPI

SENATORS

Theodore G. Bilbo, *Poplarville*
James O. Eastland, *Ruleville*

REPRESENTATIVES

John E. Rankin, *Tupelo*
Jamie L. Whitten, *Charleston*
William M. Whittington, *Greenwood*
Thomas G. Abernethy, *Okolona*
W. Arthur Winstead, *Philadelphia*
William M. Colmer, *Pascagoula*
Dan R. McGehee, *Meadville*

MISSOURI

SENATORS

Joel Bennett Clark, *St. Louis*
Harry S. Truman, *Independence*

REPRESENTATIVES

Samuel W. Arnold, *Kirksville*
Max Schwabe, *Columbia*
William C. Cole, *St. Joseph*
C. Jasper Bell, *Blue Springs*
Roger C. Slaughter, *Kansas City*
Marion T. Bennett,[30] *Springfield*
Dewey Short, *Galena*
William P. Elmer, *Salem*
Clarence Cannon, *Elsberry*
Orville Zimmerman, *Kennett*
Louis E. Miller,[31] *St. Louis*
Walter C. Ploeser, *St. Louis*
John J. Cochran, *St. Louis*

MONTANA

SENATORS

Burton K. Wheeler, *Butte*
James E. Murray, *Butte*

REPRESENTATIVES

Mike Mansfield, *Missoula*
James F. O'Connor, *Livingston*

NEBRASKA

SENATORS

Hugh A. Butler, *Omaha*
Kenneth S. Wherry, *Pawnee City*

REPRESENTATIVES

Carl T. Curtis, *Minden*
Howard H. Buffett, *Omaha*
Karl Stefan, *Norfolk*
Arthur L. Miller, *Kimball*

NEVADA

SENATORS

Patrick A. McCarran, *Reno*
James G. Scrugham, *Reno*

REPRESENTATIVE

At Large—Maurice J. Sullivan, *Reno*

NEW HAMPSHIRE

SENATORS

H. Styles Bridges, *Concord*
Charles W. Tobey, *Temple*

REPRESENTATIVES

Chester E. Merrow, *Center Ossipee*
Foster Stearns, *Hancock*

---

[27] Resigned April 15, 1944; subsequently reelected, and took his seat November 20, 1944.
[28] Resigned February 3, 1944.
[29] Appointed to fill vacancy caused by resignation of Henry Cabot Lodge, Jr., and took his seat February 15, 1944.
[30] Elected to fill vacancy caused by death of his father, Philip A. Bennett, in preceding Congress and took his seat January 21, 1943.
[31] Election unsuccessfully contested by John B. Sullivan.

NEW JERSEY

SENATORS

W. Warren Barbour,[32] *Locust*
Arthur Walsh,[33] *South Orange*
H. Alexander Smith,[34] *Princeton*
Albert W. Hawkes, *Montclair*

REPRESENTATIVES

Charles A. Wolverton, *Camden*
Elmer H. Wene, *Vineland*
James C. Auchincloss, *Rumson*
D. Lane Powers, *Trenton*
Charles A. Eaton, *North Plainfield*
Donald H. McLean, *Elizabeth*
J. Parnell Thomas, *Allendale*
Gordon Canfield, *Paterson*
Harry L. Towe, *Rutherford*
Fred A. Hartley, Jr., *Kearney*
Frank L. Sundstrom, *East Orange*
Robert W. Kean, *Livingston*
Mrs. Mary T. Norton, *Jersey City*
Edward J. Hart, *Jersey City*

NEW MEXICO

SENATORS

Carl A. Hatch, *Clovis*
Dennis Chavez, *Albuquerque*

REPRESENTATIVES AT LARGE

Clinton P. Anderson, *Albuquerque*
Antonio M. Fernandez, *Santa Fe*

NEW YORK

SENATORS

Robert F. Wagner, *New York City*
James M. Mead, *Buffalo*

REPRESENTATIVES

Leonard W. Hall, *Oyster Bay*
William B. Barry, *St. Albans*
Joseph L. Pfeifer, *Brooklyn*
Thomas H. Cullen,[35] *Brooklyn*
John J. Rooney,[36] *Brooklyn*
James J. Heffernan, *Brooklyn*
Andrew L. Somers, *Brooklyn*
John. J. Delaney, *Brooklyn*
Donald L. O'Toole, *Brooklyn*
Eugene J. Keogh, *Brooklyn*
Emanuel Celler, *Brooklyn*
James A. O'Leary,[37] *West New Brighton*
Ellsworth B. Buck,[38] *Staten Island*
Samuel Dickstein, *New York City*
Louis J. Capozzoli, *New York City*
Arthur G. Klein, *New York City*
Thomas F. Burchill, *New York City*
James H. Fay, *New York City*
Joseph Clark Baldwin, *New York City*

Martin J. Kennedy, *New York City*
Sol Bloom, *New York City*
Vito Marcantonio, *New York City*
Joseph A. Gavagan,[39] *New York City*
James H. Torrens,[40] *New York City*
Walter A. Lynch, *New York City*
Charles A. Buckley, *New York City*
James M. Fitzpatrick, *New York City*
Ralph A. Gamble, *Larchmont*
Hamilton Fish, Jr., *Garrison*
Jay LeFevre, *New Paltz*
William T. Byrne, *Loudonville*
Dean P. Taylor, *Troy*
Bernard W. Kearney, *Gloversville*
Clarence E. Kilburn, *Malone*
Francis D. Culkin,[41] *Oswego*
Hadwen C. Fuller,[42] *Parish*
Fred J. Douglas, *Utica*
Edwin Arthur Hall, *Binghamton*
Clarence E. Hancock, *Syracuse*
John Taber, *Auburn*
W. Sterling Cole, *Bath*
Joseph J. O'Brien, *East Rochester*
James W. Wadsworth, Jr., *Geneseo*
Walter G. Andrews, *Buffalo*
Joseph Mruk, *Buffalo*
John C. Butler, *Buffalo*
Daniel A. Reed, *Dunkirk*
At Large—
    Matthew J. Merritt, *Flushing*
    Miss Winifred C. Stanley, *Buffalo*

NORTH CAROLINA

SENATORS

Josiah W. Bailey, *Raleigh*
Robert R. Reynolds, *Asheville*

REPRESENTATIVES

Herbert C. Bonner, *Washington*
John H. Kerr, *Warrenton*
Graham A. Barden, *New Bern*
Harold D. Cooley, *Nashville*
John H. Folger, *Mount Airy*
Carl T. Durham, *Chapel Hill*
J. Bayard Clark, *Fayetteville*
William O. Burgin, *Lexington*
Robert L. Doughton, *Laurel Springs*
Cameron Morrison, *Charlotte*
Alfred L. Bulwinkle, *Gastonia*
Zebulon Weaver, *Asheville*

NORTH DAKOTA

SENATORS

Gerald P. Nye, *Cooperstown*
William Langer, *Bismarck*

REPRESENTATIVES AT LARGE

Usher L. Burdick, *Williston*
William Lemke, *Fargo*

OHIO

SENATORS

Robert A. Taft, *Cincinnati*
Harold H. Burton, *Cleveland*

REPRESENTATIVES

Charles H. Elston, *Cincinnati*
William E. Hess, *Cincinnati*
Harry P. Jeffrey, *Dayton*
Robert F. Jones, *Lima*
Cliff Clevenger, *Bryan*
Edward O. McCowen, *Wheelersburg*
Clarence J. Brown, *Blanchester*
Frederick C. Smith, *Marion*
Homer A. Ramey, *Toledo*
Thomas A. Jenkins, *Ironton*
Walter E. Brehm, *Logan*
John M. Vorys, *Columbus*
Alvin F. Weichel, *Sandusky*
Ed Rowe, *Akron*
Percy W. Griffiths, *Marietta*
Henderson H. Carson, *Canton*
J. Harry McGregor, *West Lafayette*
Earl R. Lewis, *St. Clairsville*
Michael J. Kirwan, *Youngstown*
Michael A. Feighan, *Cleveland*
Robert Crosser, *Cleveland*
Mrs. Frances P. Bolton, *Lyndhurst*
At Large—George H. Bender, *Cleveland Heights*

OKLAHOMA

SENATORS

J. W. Elmer Thomas, *Medicine Park*
Edward H. Moore, *Tulsa*

REPRESENTATIVES

Wesley E. Disney, *Tulsa*
Jack Nichols,[43][44] *Eufaula*
William C. Stigler,[45] *Stigler*
Paul Stewart, *Antlers*
Lyle H. Boren, *Seminole*
A. S. Mike Monroney, *Oklahoma City*
Jed Johnson, *Anadarko*
Victor Wickersham, *Mangum*
Ross Rizley, *Guymon*

OREGON

SENATORS

Charles L. McNary,[46] *Salem*
Guy Cordon,[47] *Roseburg*
Rufus C. Holman, *Portland*

REPRESENTATIVES

James W. Mott, *Salem*
Lowell Stockman, *Pendleton*

---

[32] Died November 22, 1943.
[33] Appointed to fill vacancy caused by death of W. Warren Barbour, and took his seat December 2, 1943.
[34] Elected to fill vacancy caused by death of W. Warren Barbour, and took his seat December 7, 1944.
[35] Died March 1, 1944.
[36] Elected to fill vacancy caused by death of Thomas H. Cullen, and took his seat June 15, 1944.
[37] Died March 16, 1944.

[38] Elected to fill vacancy caused by death of James A. O'Leary, and took his seat June 14, 1944.
[39] Resigned December 30, 1943, having been elected a justice of the New York Supreme Court.
[40] Elected to fill vacancy caused by resignation of Joseph A. Gavagan, and took his seat March 9, 1944.
[41] Died August 4, 1943.
[42] Elected to fill vacancy caused by death of Francis D. Culkin, and took his seat November 10, 1943.

[43] Election unsuccessfully contested by E. O. Clark.
[44] Resigned July 3, 1943.
[45] Elected to fill vacancy caused by resignation of Jack Nichols, and took his seat April 12, 1944.
[46] Died February 25, 1944.
[47] Appointed to fill vacancy caused by death of Charles L. McNary, and took his seat March 13, 1944; subsequently elected.

Homer D. Angell, *Portland*
Harris Ellsworth, *Roseburg*

PENNSYLVANIA

SENATORS

James J. Davis, *Pittsburgh*
Joseph F. Guffey, *Pittsburgh*

REPRESENTATIVES

James Gallagher, *Philadelphia*
James P. McGranery,[48] *Philadelphia*
Joseph M. Pratt,[49] *Philadelphia*
Michael J. Bradley, *Philadelphia*
John Edward Sheridan, *Philadelphia*
C. Frederick Pracht, *Philadelphia*
Francis J. Myers, *Philadelphia*
Hugh D. Scott, Jr., *Philadelphia*
James Wolfenden, *Upper Darby*
Charles L. Gerlach, *Allentown*
J. Roland Kinzer, *Lancaster*
John W. Murphy, *Dunmore*
Thomas Byron Miller, *Plymouth*
Ivor D. Fenton, *Mahanoy City*
Daniel K. Hoch, *Reading*
Wilson D. Gillette, *Towanda*
Thomas E. Scanlon, *Pittsburgh*
J. William Ditter,[50] *Ambler*
Samuel K. McConnell, Jr.,[51] *Penn Wynne*
Richard M. Simpson, *Huntingdon*
John C. Kunkel, *Harrisburg*
Leon H. Gavin, *Oil City*
Francis E. Walter, *Easton*
Chester H. Gross, *Manchester*
James E. Van Zandt,[52] *Altoona*
D. Emmert Brumbaugh,[53] *Claysburg*
J. Buell Snyder, *Perryopolis*
Grant Furlong, *Donora*
Louis E. Graham, *Beaver*
Harve Tibbott, *Ebensburg*
Augustine B. Kelley, *Greensburg*
Robert L. Rodgers, *Erie*
Samuel A. Weiss, *Glassport*
Herman P. Eberharter, *Pittsburgh*
James A. Wright, *Carnegie*
At Large—William I. Troutman,[54]
  Shamokin

RHODE ISLAND

SENATORS

Peter G. Gerry, *Warwick*
Theodore F. Green, *Providence*

REPRESENTATIVES

Aime J. Forand, *Cumberland*
John E. Fogarty,[55] *Harmony*

SOUTH CAROLINA

SENATORS

Ellison D. Smith,[56] *Lynchburg*
Wilton E. Hall,[57] *Anderson*
Burnet R. Maybank, *Charleston*

REPRESENTATIVES

L. Mendel Rivers, *North Charleston*
Hampton P. Fulmer,[58] *Orangeburg*
Mrs. Willa E. Fulmer,[59] *Orangeburg*
Butler B. Hare, *Saluda*
Joseph R. Bryson, *Greenville*
James P. Richards, *Lancaster*
John L. McMillan, *Florence*

SOUTH DAKOTA

SENATORS

J. Chandler Gurney, *Yankton*
Harlan J. Bushfield, *Miller*

REPRESENTATIVES

Karl E. Mundt, *Madison*
Francis H. Case, *Custer*

TENNESSEE

SENATORS

Kenneth D. McKellar, *Memphis*
A. Tom Stewart, *Winchester*

REPRESENTATIVES

B. Carroll Reece, *Johnson City*
John Jennings, Jr., *Knoxville*
Estes Kefauver, *Chattanooga*
Albert A. Gore,[60] *Carthage*
Jim Nance McCord, *Lewisburg*
J. Percy Priest, *Nashville*
Wirt Courtney, *Franklin*
Thomas J. Murray, *Jackson*
Jere Cooper, *Dyersburg*
Clifford Davis, *Memphis*

TEXAS

SENATORS

Tom T. Connally, *Marlin*
W. Lee O'Daniel, *Fort Worth*

REPRESENTATIVES

Wright Patman, *Texarkana*
Martin Dies, Jr., *Orange*
Lindley Beckworth, *Gilmer*
Sam Rayburn, *Bonham*
Hatton W. Sumners, *Dallas*
Luther A. Johnson, *Corsicana*
Nat Patton, *Crockett*
Albert Thomas, *Houston*

Joseph J. Mansfield, *Columbus*
Lyndon B. Johnson, *Johnson City*
William R. Poage, *Waco*
Fritz G. Lanham, *Fort Worth*
Ed Gossett, *Wichita Falls*
Richard M. Kleberg, *Corpus Christi*
Milton H. West, *Brownsville*
R. Ewing Thomason, *El Paso*
Sam M. Russell, *Stephenville*
Eugene Worley, *Shamrock*
George H. Mahon, *Colorado City*
Paul J. Kilday, *San Antonio*
O. Clark Fisher, *San Angelo*

UTAH

SENATORS

Elbert D. Thomas, *Salt Lake City*
Abe Murdock, *Beaver*

REPRESENTATIVES

Walter K. Granger, *Cedar City*
J. W. Robinson, *Provo*

VERMONT

SENATORS

Warren R. Austin, *Burlington*
George D. Aiken, *Putney*

REPRESENTATIVE

At Large—Charles A. Plumley, *Northfield*

VIRGINIA

SENATORS

Carter Glass, *Lynchburg*
Harry Flood Byrd, *Berryville*

REPRESENTATIVES

Schuyler Otis Bland, *Newport News*
Winder R. Harris,[61] *Norfolk*
Ralph H. Daughton,[62] *Norfolk*
Dave E. Satterfield, Jr., *Richmond*
Patrick Henry Drewry, *Petersburg*
Thomas G. Burch, *Martinsville*
Clifton A. Woodrum, *Roanoke*
A. Willis Robertson, *Lexington*
Howard W. Smith, *Alexandria*
John W. Flannagan, Jr., *Bristol*

WASHINGTON

SENATORS

Homer T. Bone,[63] *Tacoma*
Warren G. Magnuson,[64] *Seattle*
Monrad C. Wallgren, *Everett*

---

[48] Resigned November 17, 1943.
[49] Elected to fill vacancy caused by resignation of James P. McGranery, and took his seat February 8, 1944.
[50] Died November 21, 1943.
[51] Elected to fill vacancy caused by death of J. William Ditter, and took his seat February 8, 1944.
[52] Resigned September 24, 1943.
[53] Elected to fill vacancy caused by resignation of James E. Van Zandt, took his seat November 23, 1943.

[54] Resigned January 2, 1945.
[55] Resigned December 7, 1944; vacancy throughout remainder of the Congress.
[56] Died November 17, 1944.
[57] Appointed to fill vacancy caused by death of Ellison D. Smith, and took his seat November 27, 1944.
[58] Died October 19, 1944.
[59] Elected to fill vacancy caused by death of Hampton P. Fulmer, and took her seat November 16, 1944.

[60] Resigned December 4, 1944; vacancy throughout remainder of the Congress.
[61] Resigned September 15, 1944.
[62] Elected to fill vacancy caused by resignation of Winder R. Harris, and took his seat November 14, 1944.
[63] Resigned November 13, 1944.
[64] Appointed to fill vacancy caused by resignation of Homer T. Bone, and took his seat December 14, 1944.

WASHINGTON—Continued

REPRESENTATIVES

Warren G. Magnuson,[65] *Seattle*
Henry M. Jackson, *Everett*
Fred Norman, *Raymond*
Hal Holmes, *Ellensburg*
Walter F. Horan, *Wenatchee*
John M. Coffee, *Tacoma*

WEST VIRGINIA

SENATORS

Harley M. Kilgore, *Beckley*
Chapman Revercomb, *Charleston*

REPRESENTATIVES

Andrew C. Schiffler, *Wheeling*
Jennings Randolph, *Elkins*
Edward G. Rohrbough, *Glenville*
Hubert S. Ellis, *Huntington*
John Kee, *Bluefield*
Joe L. Smith, *Beckley*

WISCONSIN

SENATORS

Robert M. La Follette, Jr., *Madison*
Alexander Wiley, *Chippewa Falls*

REPRESENTATIVES

Lawrence H. Smith, *Racine*
Harry Sauthoff, *Madison*
William H. Stevenson, *La Crosse*
Thaddeus F. B. Wasielewski,[66] *Milwaukee*
Howard J. McMurray,[67] *Milwaukee*
Frank B. Keefe, *Oshkosh*
Reid F. Murray, *Ogdensburg*
LaVern R. Dilweg, *Green Bay*
Merlin Hull, *Black River Falls*
Alvin E. O'Konski, *Mercer*

WYOMING

SENATORS

Joseph C. O'Mahoney, *Cheyenne*
Edward V. Robertson, *Cody*

REPRESENTATIVE

At Large—Frank A. Barrett, *Lusk*

TERRITORY OF ALASKA

DELEGATE

Anthony J. Dimond, *Valdez*

TERRITORY OF HAWAII

DELEGATE

Joseph R. Farrington, *Honolulu*

COMMONWEALTH OF THE PHILIPPINES

RESIDENT COMMISSIONER

Joaquin M. Elizalde,[68] *Manila*
Carlos P. Romulo,[69] *Manila*

PUERTO RICO

RESIDENT COMMISSIONER

Bolívar Pagán, *San Juan*

---

[65] Resigned December 13, 1944; vacancy throughout remainder of the Congress.
[66] Election unsuccessfully contested by John C. Schafer.
[67] Election unsuccessfully contested by Lewis D. Thill.
[68] Resigned August 9, 1944.
[69] Appointed to fill vacancy caused by resignation of Joaquin M. Elizalde, and took his seat August 21, 1944.

SEVENTY-NINTH CONGRESS

JANUARY 3, 1945, TO JANUARY 3, 1947

FIRST SESSION—*January 3, 1945, to December 21, 1945*

SECOND SESSION—*January 14,[1] 1946, to August 2, 1946*

———

VICE PRESIDENT OF THE UNITED STATES—Henry A. Wallace,[2] of Iowa; Harry S. Truman,[3][4] of Missouri

PRESIDENT PRO TEMPORE OF THE SENATE—Kenneth McKellar,[5] of Tennessee

SECRETARY OF THE SENATE—Edwin A. Halsey,[6] of Virginia; Leslie L. Biffle,[7] of Arkansas

SERGEANT AT ARMS OF THE SENATE—Wall Doxey, of Mississippi

———

SPEAKER OF THE HOUSE OF REPRESENTATIVES—Sam Rayburn,[8] of Texas

CLERK OF THE HOUSE—South Trimble,[9] of Kentucky; Harry Newlin Megill[10]

SERGEANT AT ARMS OF THE HOUSE—Kenneth Romney, of Montana

DOORKEEPER OF THE HOUSE—Ralph R. Roberts, of Indiana

POSTMASTER OF THE HOUSE—Finis E. Scott

ALABAMA

SENATORS

John H. Bankhead 2d,[11] *Jasper*
George R. Swift,[12] *Atmore*
John J. Sparkman,[13] *Huntsville*
Lister Hill, *Montgomery*

REPRESENTATIVES

Frank W. Boykin, *Mobile*
George M. Grant, *Troy*
George W. Andrews, *Union Springs*
Sam Hobbs, *Selma*
Albert Rains, *Gadsden*
Pete Jarman, *Livingston*
Carter Manasco, *Jasper*
John J. Sparkman,[14] *Huntsville*
Luther Patrick, *Birmingham*

ARIZONA

SENATORS

Carl Hayden, *Phoenix*
Ernest W. McFarland, *Florence*

REPRESENTATIVES AT LARGE

Richard F. Harless, *Phoenix*
John R. Murdock, *Tempe*

ARKANSAS

SENATORS

John L. McClellan, *Camden*
J. William Fulbright, *Fayetteville*

REPRESENTATIVES

Ezekiel C. Gathings, *West Memphis*
Wilbur D. Mills, *Kensett*
James W. Trimble, *Berryville*
Fadjo Cravens, *Fort Smith*
Brooks Hays, *Little Rock*
William F. Norrell, *Monticello*
Oren Harris, *El Dorado*

CALIFORNIA

SENATORS

Hiram W. Johnson,[15] *San Francisco*
William F. Knowland,[16] *Piedmont*
Sheridan Downey, *Laguna Beach*

REPRESENTATIVES

Clarence F. Lea, *Santa Rosa*
Clair Engle, *Red Bluff*
Leroy Johnson, *Stockton*
Franck R. Havenner, *San Francisco*
Richard J. Welch, *San Francisco*
George P. Miller, *Alameda*

John H. Tolan, *Oakland*
John Z. Anderson, *San Juan Bautista*
Bertrand W. Gearhart, *Fresno*
Alfred J. Elliott, *Tulare*
George E. Outland, *Santa Barbara*
H. Jerry Voorhis, *San Dimas*
Ned R. Healy, *Los Angeles*
Mrs. Helen Gahagan Douglas, *Los Angeles*
Gordon L. McDonough, *Los Angeles*
Ellis E. Patterson, *Los Angeles*
Cecil R. King, *Los Angeles*
Clyde G. Doyle, *Long Beach*
Chet Holifield, *Montebello*
Carl Hinshaw, *Pasadena*
Harry R. Sheppard, *Yucaipa*
John Phillips, *Banning*
Edouard V. M. Izac, *San Diego*

COLORADO

SENATORS

Edwin C. Johnson, *Craig*
Eugene D. Millikin, *Denver*

REPRESENTATIVES

Dean M. Gillespie, *Denver*
William S. Hill, *Fort Collins*
J. Edgar Chenoweth, *Trinidad*
Robert F. Rockwell, *Paonia*

---

[1] By joint resolution (Pub. Law 289, 79th Cong., 1st sess.) the date of assembling the second session of the Seventy-ninth Congress was fixed for January 14, 1946.
[2] Term expired at noon on January 20, 1945.
[3] Term began at noon on January 20, 1945.
[4] Became President upon the the death of Franklin D. Roosevelt, April 12, 1945.
[5] Elected January 6, 1945.
[6] Died January 29, 1945.

[7] Elected February 8, 1945.
[8] Reelected January 3, 1945.
[9] Reelected January 3, 1945; died November 23, 1946.
[10] Harry Newlin Megill, Assistant to the Clerk, acted as Clerk during the interim.
[11] Died June 12, 1946.
[12] Appointed to fill vacancy caused by death of John H. Bankhead 2d, and took his seat June 20, 1946.

[13] Elected November 5, 1946, to fill vacancy caused by death of John H. Bankhead 2d, but was unable to be sworn in as Congress was not in session.
[14] Resigned November 5, 1946, having been elected Senator.
[15] Died August 6, 1945.
[16] Appointed to fill vacancy caused by death of Hiram W. Johnson, and took his seat September 5, 1945.

CONNECTICUT

SENATORS

Francis T. Maloney,[17] *Meriden*
Thomas C. Hart,[18] *Sharon*
Raymond E. Baldwin,[19] *Stratford*
Brien McMahon, *Norwalk*

REPRESENTATIVES

Herman P. Kopplemann, *Hartford*
Mrs. Chase Going Woodhouse, *New London*
James P. Geelan, *New Haven*
Mrs. Clare Boothe Luce, *Greenwich*
Joseph E. Talbot, *Naugatuck*
At Large—Joseph F. Ryter, *Hartford*

DELAWARE

SENATORS

James M. Tunnell, *Georgetown*
C. Douglass Buck, *Wilmington*

REPRESENTATIVE

At Large—Philip A. Traynor, *Wilmington*

FLORIDA

SENATORS

Charles O. Andrews,[20] *Orlando*
Spessard L. Holland,[21] *Bartow*
Claude Pepper, *Tallahassee*

REPRESENTATIVES

J. Hardin Peterson, *Lakeland*
Emory H. Price, *Jacksonville*
Robert L. F. Sikes, *Crestview*
Arthur P. Cannon, *Miami*
Joe Hendricks, *De Land*
Dwight L. Rogers, *Fort Lauderdale*

GEORGIA

SENATORS

Walter F. George, *Vienna*
Richard B. Russell, *Winder*

REPRESENTATIVES

Hugh Peterson, *Ailey*
Edward E. Cox, *Camilla*
Stephen Pace, *Americus*
A. Sidney Camp, *Newnan*
Robert Ramspeck,[22] *Atlanta*
Mrs. Helen Douglas Mankin,[23] *Atlanta*
Carl Vinson, *Milledgeville*
Malcolm C. Tarver, *Dalton*
John S. Gibson, *Douglas*
John S. Wood, *Canton*
Paul Brown, *Elberton*

IDAHO

SENATORS

John Thomas,[24] *Gooding*
Charles C. Gossett,[25] *Nampa*
Henry C. Dworshak,[26] *Burley*
Glen H. Taylor, *Pocatello*

REPRESENTATIVES

Compton I. White, *Clark Fork*
Henry C. Dworshak,[27] *Burley*

ILLINOIS

SENATORS

Scott W. Lucas, *Havana*
C. Wayland Brooks, *Chicago*

REPRESENTATIVES

William L. Dawson, *Chicago*
William A. Rowan, *Chicago*
Edward A. Kelly, *Chicago*
Martin Gorski, *Chicago*
Adolph J. Sabath, *Chicago*
Thomas J. O'Brien, *Chicago*
William W. Link, *Chicago*
Thomas S. Gordon, *Chicago*
Alexander J. Resa, *Chicago*
Ralph E. Church, *Evanston*
Chauncey W. Reed, *West Chicago*
Noah M. Mason, *Oglesby*
Leo E. Allen, *Galena*
Anton J. Johnson, *Macomb*
Robert B. Chiperfield, *Canton*
Everett M. Dirksen, *Pekin*
Leslie C. Arends, *Melvin*
Miss Jessie Sumner, *Milford*
Rolla C. McMillen, *Decatur*
Sidney E. Simpson, *Carrollton*
Evan Howell, *Springfield*
Charles Melvin Price, *East St. Louis*
Charles W. Vursell, *Salem*
James V. Heidinger,[28] *Fairfield*
Roy Clippinger,[29] *Carmi*
Cecil W. (Runt) Bishop, *Carterville*
At Large—Mrs. Emily Taft Douglas, *Chicago*

INDIANA

SENATORS

Raymond E. Willis, *Angola*
Homer E. Capehart, *Washington*

REPRESENTATIVES

Ray J. Madden, *Gary*
Charles A. Halleck, *Rensselaer*
Robert A. Grant, *South Bend*
George W. Gillie, *Fort Wayne*

Forest A. Harness, *Kokomo*
Noble J. Johnson, *Terre Haute*
Gerald W. Landis, *Linton*
Charles M. La Follette, *Evansville*
Earl Wilson, *Huron*
Raymond S. Springer, *Connersville*
Louis Ludlow, *Indianapolis*

IOWA

SENATORS

George A. Wilson, *Des Moines*
Bourke B. Hickenlooper, *Cedar Rapids*

REPRESENTATIVES

Thomas E. Martin, *Iowa City*
Henry O. Talle, *Decorah*
John W. Gwynne, *Waterloo*
Karl M. LeCompte, *Corydon*
Paul Cunningham, *Des Moines*
James I. Dolliver, *Fort Dodge*
Ben F. Jensen, *Exira*
Charles B. Hoeven, *Alton*

KANSAS

SENATORS

Arthur Capper, *Topeka*
Clyde M. Reed, *Parsons*

REPRESENTATIVES

Albert M. Cole, *Holton*
Errett P. Scrivner, *Kansas City*
Thomas D. Winter, *Girard*
Edward H. Rees, *Emporia*
Clifford R. Hope, *Garden City*
Frank Carlson, *Concordia*

KENTUCKY

SENATORS

Alben W. Barkley, *Paducah*
Albert B. Chandler,[30] *Versailles*
William A. Stanfill,[31] *Hazard*
John Sherman Cooper,[32] *Somerset*

REPRESENTATIVES

Noble J. Gregory, *Mayfield*
Earle C. Clements, *Morganfield*
Emmet O'Neal, *Louisville*
Frank L. Chelf, *Lebanon*
Brent Spence, *Fort Thomas*
Virgil M. Chapman, *Paris*
Andrew J. May, *Prestonsburg*
Joe B. Bates, *Greenup*
John M. Robsion, *Barbourville*

[17] Died January 16, 1945.
[18] Appointed to fill vacancy caused by death of Francis T. Maloney; took his seat February 15, 1945.
[19] Elected November 5, 1946, to fill vacancy caused by death of Francis T. Maloney, but was unable to be sworn in as Congress was not in session.
[20] Died September 18, 1946.
[21] Appointed September 25, 1946, to fill vacancy caused by death of Charles O. Andrews, but was unable to be sworn in as Congress was not in session.
[22] Resigned December 31, 1945.

[23] Elected to fill vacancy caused by resignation of Robert Ramspeck, and took her seat February 25, 1946.
[24] Died November 10, 1945.
[25] Appointed to fill vacancy caused by death of John Thomas, and took his seat November 29, 1945.
[26] Elected November 5, 1946, to fill vacancy caused by death of John Thomas, but was unable to be sworn in as Congress was not in session.
[27] Resigned November 5, 1946, having been elected Senator; vacancy throughout remainder of the Congress.

[28] Died March 22, 1945.
[29] Elected to fill vacancy caused by death of James V. Heidinger, and took his seat November 26, 1945.
[30] Resigned November 1, 1945.
[31] Appointed to fill vacancy caused by resignation of Albert B. Chandler, and took his seat November 23, 1945.
[32] Elected November 5, 1946, to fill vacancy caused by resignation of Albert B. Chandler, but was unable to be sworn in as Congress was not in session.

LOUISIANA

SENATORS

John H. Overton, *Alexandria*
Allen J. Ellender, *Houma*

REPRESENTATIVES

F. Edward Hébert, *New Orleans*
Paul H. Maloney, *New Orleans*
James Domengeaux, *Lafayette*
Overton Brooks, *Shreveport*
Charles E. McKenzie, *Monroe*
James H. Morrison, *Hammond*
Henry D. Larcade, Jr., *Opelousas*
A. Leonard Allen, *Winnfield*

MAINE

SENATORS

Wallace H. White, Jr., *Auburn*
Ralph O. Brewster, *Dexter*

REPRESENTATIVES

Robert Hale, *Portland*
Mrs. Margaret Chase Smith, *Skowhegan*
Frank Fellows, *Bangor*

MARYLAND

SENATORS

Millard E. Tydings, *Havre de Grace*
George L. Radcliffe, *Baltimore*

REPRESENTATIVES

Dudley G. Roe, *Sudlersville*
H. Streett Baldwin, *Hydes*
Thomas D'Alesandro, Jr., *Baltimore*
George H. Fallon, *Baltimore*
Lansdale G. Sasscer, *Upper Marlboro*
J. Glenn Beall, *Frostburg*

MASSACHUSETTS

SENATORS

David I. Walsh, *Clinton*
Leverett Saltonstall,[33] *Chestnut Hill*

REPRESENTATIVES

John W. Heselton, *Deerfield*
Charles R. Clason, *Springfield*
Philip J. Philbin, *Clinton*
Pehr G. Holmes, *Worcester*
Mrs. Edith Nourse Rogers, *Lowell*
George J. Bates, *Salem*
Thomas J. Lane, *Lawrence*
Angier L. Goodwin, *Melrose*
Charles L. Gifford, *Cotuit*
Christian A. Herter, *Boston*
James M. Curley, *Boston*
John W. McCormack, *Boston*
Richard B. Wigglesworth, *Milton*
Joseph W. Martin, Jr., *North Attleboro*

MICHIGAN

SENATORS

Arthur H. Vandenberg, *Grand Rapids*
Homer Ferguson, *Detroit*

REPRESENTATIVES

George G. Sadowski, *Detroit*
Earl C. Michener, *Adrian*
Paul W. Shafer, *Battle Creek*
Clare E. Hoffman, *Allegan*
Bartel J. Jonkman, *Grand Rapids*
William W. Blackney, *Flint*
Jesse P. Wolcott, *Port Huron*
Fred L. Crawford, *Saginaw*
Albert J. Engel, *Muskegon*
Roy O. Woodruff, *Bay City*
Frederick V. Bradley, *Rogers City*
Frank E. Hook, *Ironwood*
George D. O'Brien, *Detroit*
Louis C. Rabaut, *Detroit*
John D. Dingell, *Detroit*
John Lesinski, *Dearborn*
George A. Dondero,[34] *Royal Oak*

MINNESOTA

SENATORS

Henrik Shipstead, *Carlos, R.F.D.*
Joseph H. Ball, *St. Paul*

REPRESENTATIVES

August H. Andresen, *Red Wing*
Joseph P. O'Hara, *Glencoe*
William J. Gallagher,[35] *Minneapolis*
Frank T. Starkey, *St. Paul*
Walter H. Judd, *Minneapolis*
Harold Knutson, *St. Cloud*
H. Carl Andersen, *Tyler*
William A. Pittenger, *Duluth*
Harold C. Hagen, *Crookston*

MISSISSIPPI

SENATORS

Theodore G. Bilbo, *Poplarville*
James O. Eastland, *Ruleville*

REPRESENTATIVES

John E. Rankin, *Tupelo*
Jamie L. Whitten, *Charleston*
William M. Whittington, *Greenwood*
Thomas G. Abernethy, *Okolona*
W. Arthur Winstead, *Philadelphia*
William M. Colmer, *Pascagoula*
Dan R. McGehee, *Meadville*

MISSOURI

SENATORS

Harry S. Truman,[36] *Independence*
Frank P. Briggs,[37] *Macon*
Forrest C. Donnell, *Webster Groves*

REPRESENTATIVES

Samuel W. Arnold, *Kirksville*
Max Schwabe, *Columbia*
William C. Cole, *St. Joseph*
C. Jasper Bell, *Blue Springs*
Roger C. Slaughter, *Kansas City*
Marion T. Bennett, *Springfield*
Dewey Short, *Galena*
Albert S. J. Carnahan, *Ellsinore*
Clarence Cannon, *Elsberry*
Orville Zimmerman, *Kennett*
John B. Sullivan, *St. Louis*
Walter C. Ploeser, *Clayton*
John J. Cochran, *St. Louis*

MONTANA

SENATORS

Burton K. Wheeler, *Butte*
James E. Murray, *Butte*

REPRESENTATIVES

Mike Mansfield, *Missoula*
James F. O'Connor,[38] *Livingston*
Wesley A. D'Ewart,[39] *Wilsall*

NEBRASKA

SENATORS

Hugh A. Butler, *Omaha*
Kenneth S. Wherry, *Pawnee City*

REPRESENTATIVES

Carl T. Curtis, *Minden*
Howard H. Buffett, *Omaha*
Karl Stefan, *Norfolk*
Arthur L. Miller, *Kimball*

NEVADA

SENATORS

Patrick A. McCarran, *Reno*
James G. Scrugham,[40] *Reno*
Edward P. Carville,[41] *Reno*

REPRESENTATIVE

At Large—Berkeley L. Bunker, *Las Vegas*

NEW HAMPSHIRE

SENATORS

H. Styles Bridges, *Concord*
Charles W. Tobey, *Temple*

REPRESENTATIVES

Chester E. Merrow, *Center Ossipee*
Sherman Adams, *Lincoln*

---

[33] Elected November 7, 1944, to fill vacancy caused by resignation of Henry Cabot Lodge, Jr., in preceding Congress, and took his seat January 10, 1945.
[34] Election unsuccessfully contested by John W. L. Hicks.

[35] Died August 13, 1946; vacancy throughout remainder of the Congress.
[36] Resigned January 17, 1945, having been elected Vice President of the United States.
[37] Appointed to fill vacancy caused by resignation of Harry S. Truman, and took his seat January 22, 1945.

[38] Died January 15, 1945.
[39] Elected to fill vacancy caused by death of James F. O'Connor, and took his seat June 25, 1945.
[40] Died June 23, 1945.
[41] Appointed to fill vacancy caused by death of James G. Scrugham, and took his seat July 26, 1945.

NEW JERSEY

SENATORS

Albert W. Hawkes, *Montclair*
H. Alexander Smith, *Princeton*

REPRESENTATIVES

Charles A. Wolverton, *Camden*
T. Millet Hand, *Cape May City*
James C. Auchincloss, *Rumson*
D. Lane Powers,[42] *Trenton*
Frank A. Mathews, Jr.,[43] *Riverton*
Charles A. Eaton, *North Plainfield*
Clifford P. Case, *Rahway*
J. Parnell Thomas, *Allendale*
Gordon Canfield *Paterson*
Harry L. Towe, *Rutherford*
Fred A. Hartley, Jr., *Kearney*
Frank L. Sundstrom, *East Orange*
Robert W. Kean, *Livingston*
Mrs. Mary T. Norton, *Jersey City*
Edward J. Hart, *Jersey City*

NEW MEXICO

SENATORS

Carl A. Hatch, *Clovis*
Dennis Chavez, *Albuquerque*

REPRESENTATIVES AT LARGE

Clinton P. Anderson,[44] *Albuquerque*
Antonio M. Fernandez, *Santa Fe*

NEW YORK

SENATORS

Robert F. Wagner, *New York City*
James M. Mead, *Buffalo*

REPRESENTATIVES

Edgar A. Sharp, *Patchogue*
Leonard W. Hall, *Oyster Bay*
Henry J. Latham, *Queens Village*
William B. Barry,[45] *St. Albans*
James A. Roe, *Flushing*
James J. Delaney, *Long Island City*
John J. Delaney, *Brooklyn*
Joseph L. Pfeifer, *Brooklyn*
Eugene J. Keogh, *Brooklyn*
Andrew L. Somers, *Brooklyn*
James J. Heffernan, *Brooklyn*
John J. Rooney, *Brooklyn*
Donald L. O'Toole, *Brooklyn*
Leo F. Rayfiel, *Brooklyn*
Emanuel Celler, *Brooklyn*
Ellsworth B. Buck, *Staten Island*
Joseph Clark Baldwin, *New York City*
Vito Marcantonio, *New York City*

Samuel Dickstein,[46] *New York City*
Arthur G. Klein,[47] *New York City*
Sol Bloom, *New York City*
James H. Torrens, *New York City*
Adam C. Powell, Jr., *New York City*
Walter A. Lynch, *New York City*
Benjamin J. Rabin, *New York City*
Charles A. Buckley, *New York City*
Peter A. Quinn, *New York City*
Ralph W. Gwinn, *Bronxville*
Ralph A. Gamble, *Larchmont*
Augustus W. Bennet, *Newburgh*
Jay LeFevre, *New Paltz*
Bernard W. Kearney, *Gloversville*
William T. Byrne, *Loudonville*
Dean P. Taylor, *Troy*
Clarence E. Kilburn, *Malone*
Hadwin C. Fuller, *Parish*
Clarence E. Hancock, *Syracuse*
Edwin Arthur Hall, *Binghamton*
John Taber, *Auburn*
W. Sterling Cole, *Bath*
George F. Rogers, *Rochester*
James W. Wadsworth, Jr., *Geneseo*
Walter G. Andrews, *Buffalo*
Edward J. Elsaesser, *Buffalo*
John C. Butler, *Buffalo*
Daniel A. Reed, *Dunkirk*

NORTH CAROLINA

SENATORS

Josiah W. Bailey,[48] *Raleigh*
William B. Umstead,[49] *Durham*
Clyde R. Hoey, *Shelby*

REPRESENTATIVES

Herbert C. Bonner, *Washington*
John H. Kerr, *Warrenton*
Graham A. Barden, *New Bern*
Harold D. Cooley, *Nashville*
John H. Folger, *Mount Airy*
Carl T. Durham, *Chapel Hill*
J. Bayard Clark, *Fayetteville*
William O. Burgin,[50] *Lexington*
Miss Eliza Jane Pratt,[51] *Lexington*
Robert L. Doughton, *Laurel Springs*
Joe W. Ervin,[52] *Charlotte*
Sam J. Ervin, Jr.,[53] *Morganton*
Alfred L. Bulwinkle, *Gastonia*
Zebulon Weaver, *Asheville*

NORTH DAKOTA

SENATORS

William Langer, *Bismarck*
John Moses,[54] *Hazen*
Milton R. Young,[55] *Berlin*

REPRESENTATIVES AT LARGE

William Lemke, *Fargo*
Charles R. Robertson, *Bismarck*

OHIO

SENATORS

Robert A. Taft, *Cincinnati*
Harold H. Burton,[56] *Cleveland*
James W. Huffman,[57] *Columbus*
Kingsley A. Taft,[58] *Shaker Heights*

REPRESENTATIVES

Charles H. Elston, *Cincinnati*
William E. Hess, *Cincinnati*
Edward J. Gardner, *Hamilton*
Robert F. Jones, *Lima*
Cliff Clevenger, *Bryan*
Edward O. McCowen, *Wheelersburg*
Clarence J. Brown, *Blanchester*
Frederick C. Smith, *Marion*
Homer A. Ramey, *Toledo*
Thomas A. Jenkins, *Ironton*
Walter E. Brehm, *Logan*
John M. Vorys, *Columbus*
Alvin F. Weichel, *Sandusky*
Walter B. Huber, *Akron*
Percy W. Griffiths, *Marietta*
William R. Thom, *Canton*
J. Harry McGregor, *West Lafayette*
Earl R. Lewis, *St. Clairsville*
Michael J. Kirwan, *Youngstown*
Michael A. Feighan, *Cleveland*
Robert Crosser, *Cleveland*
Mrs. Frances P. Bolton, *Lyndhurst*
At Large—George H. Bender, *Cleveland Heights*

OKLAHOMA

SENATORS

J. W. Elmer Thomas, *Medicine Park*
Edward H. Moore, *Tulsa*

REPRESENTATIVES

George B. Schwabe, *Tulsa*
William G. Stigler, *Stigler*
Paul Stewart, *Antlers*
Lyle H. Boren, *Seminole*
A. S. Mike Monroney, *Oklahoma City*
Jed Johnson, *Anadarko*
Victor Wickersham, *Mangum*
Ross Rizley, *Guymon*

OREGON

SENATORS

Guy Cordon, *Roseburg*
Wayne L. Morse, *Eugene*

---

[42] Resigned August 30, 1945.
[43] Elected to fill vacancy caused by resignation of D. Lane Powers, and took his seat November 27, 1945.
[44] Resigned June 30, 1945; vacancy throughout remainder of the Congress.
[45] Died October 20, 1946; vacancy throughout remainder of the Congress.
[46] Resigned December 30, 1945.
[47] Elected to fill vacancy caused by resignation of Samuel Dickstein, and took his seat March 4, 1946.
[48] Died December 15, 1946.

[49] Appointed December 18, 1946, to fill vacancy caused by death of Josiah W. Bailey, but was unable to be sworn in as Congress was not in session.
[50] Died April 11, 1946.
[51] Elected to fill vacancy caused by death of William O. Burgin, and took her seat June 3, 1946.
[52] Died December 25, 1945.
[53] Elected to fill vacancy caused by death of Joe W. Ervin, and took his seat February 4, 1946.
[54] Died March 3, 1945.
[55] Appointed to fill vacancy caused by death of John

Moses, and took his seat March 19, 1945; subsequently elected.
[56] Resigned September 30, 1945, having been appointed Associate Justice of the Supreme Court of the United States.
[57] Appointed to fill vacancy caused by resignation of Harold H. Burton, and took his seat October 9, 1945.
[58] Elected to fill vacancy caused by resignation of Harold H. Burton and served from November 6, 1946, to January 3, 1947, but was unable to be sworn in as Congress was not in session.

REPRESENTATIVES

James W. Mott,[59] *Salem*
A. Walter Norblad, Jr.,[60] *Astoria*
Lowell Stockman, *Pendleton*
Homer D. Angell, *Portland*
Harris Ellsworth, *Roseburg*

PENNSYLVANIA

SENATORS

Joseph F. Guffey, *Pittsburgh*
Francis J. Myers, *Philadelphia*

REPRESENTATIVES

William A. Barrett, *Philadelphia*
William T. Granahan, *Philadelphia*
Michael J. Bradley, *Philadelphia*
John Edward Sheridan, *Philadelphia*
William J. Green, Jr., *Philadelphia*
Herbert J. McGlinchey, *Philadelphia*
James Wolfenden, *Upper Darby*
Charles L. Gerlach, *Allentown*
J. Roland Kinzer, *Lancaster*
John W. Murphy,[61] *Dunmore*
James P. Scoblick,[62] *Archbald*
Daniel J. Flood, *Wilkes-Barre*
Ivor D. Fenton, *Mahanoy City*
Daniel K. Hoch, *Reading*
Wilson D. Gillette, *Towanda*
Robert F. Rich, *Woolrich*
Samuel K. McConnell, Jr., *Penn Wynne*
Richard M. Simpson, *Huntingdon*
John C. Kunkel, *Harrisburg*
Leon H. Gavin, *Oil City*
Francis E. Walter, *Easton*
Chester H. Gross, *Manchester*
D. Emmert Brumbaugh, *Claysburg*
J. Buell Snyder,[63] *Perryopolis*
Carl H. Hoffman,[64] *Somerset*
Thomas E. Morgan, *Fredericktown*
Louis E. Graham, *Beaver*
Harve Tibbott, *Ebensburg*
Augustine B. Kelley, *Greensburg*
Robert L. Rodgers, *Erie*
Howard E. Campbell, *Pittsburgh*
Robert J. Corbett, *Bellevue*
James G. Fulton, *Dormont*
Herman P. Eberharter, *Pittsburgh*
Samuel A. Weiss,[65] *Glassport*
Frank Buchanan,[66] *McKeesport*

RHODE ISLAND

SENATORS

Peter G. Gerry, *Providence*
Theodore F. Green, *Providence*

REPRESENTATIVES

Aime J. Forand, *Cumberland*
John E. Fogarty, *Harmony*

SOUTH CAROLINA

SENATORS

Burnet R. Maybank, *Charleston*
Olin D. Johnston, *Spartanburg*

REPRESENTATIVES

L. Mendel Rivers, *North Charleston*
John J. Riley, *Sumter*
Butler B. Hare, *Saluda*
Joseph R. Bryson, *Greenville*
James P. Richards, *Lancaster*
John L. McMillan, *Florence*

SOUTH DAKOTA

SENATORS

J. Chandler Gurney, *Yankton*
Harlan J. Bushfield, *Miller*

REPRESENTATIVES

Karl E. Mundt, *Madison*
Francis H. Case, *Custer*

TENNESSEE

SENATORS

Kenneth D. McKellar, *Memphis*
A. Tom Stewart, *Winchester*

REPRESENTATIVES

B. Carroll Reece, *Johnson City*
John Jennings, Jr., *Knoxville*
Estes Kefauver, *Chattanooga*
Albert A. Gore, *Carthage*
Harold H. Earthman, *Murfreesboro*
J. Percy Priest, *Nashville*
Wirt Courtney, *Franklin*
Thomas J. Murray, *Jackson*
Jere Cooper, *Dyersburg*
Clifford Davis, *Memphis*

TEXAS

SENATORS

Tom T. Connally, *Marlin*
W. Lee O'Daniel, *Fort Worth*

REPRESENTATIVES

Wright Patman, *Texarkana*
Jesse M. Combs, *Beaumont*
Lindley Beckworth, *Gladewater*

Sam Rayburn, *Bonham*
Hatton W. Sumners, *Dallas*
Luther A. Johnson,[67] *Corsicana*
Olin E. Teague,[68] *College Station*
Tom Pickett, *Palestine*
Albert Thomas, *Houston*
Joseph J. Mansfield, *Columbus*
Lyndon B. Johnson, *Johnson City*
William R. Poage, *Waco*
Fritz G. Lanham, *Fort Worth*
Ed Gossett, *Wichita Falls*
John E. Lyle, Jr., *Corpus Christi*
Milton H. West, *Brownsville*
R. Ewing Thomason, *El Paso*
Sam M. Russell, *Stephenville*
Eugene Worley, *Shamrock*
George H. Mahon, *Colorado City*
Paul J. Kilday, *San Antonio*
O. Clark Fisher, *San Angelo*

UTAH

SENATORS

Elbert D. Thomas, *Salt Lake City*
Abe Murdock, *Beaver*

REPRESENTATIVES

Walter K. Granger, *Cedar City*
J. W. Robinson, *Provo*

VERMONT

SENATORS

Warren R. Austin,[69] *Burlington*
Ralph E. Flanders,[70] *Springfield*
George D. Aiken, *Putney*

REPRESENTATIVE

At Large—Charles A. Plumley, *Northfield*

VIRGINIA

SENATORS

Carter Glass,[71] *Lynchburg*
Thomas G. Burch,[72] *Martinsville*
A. Willis Robertson,[73] *Lexington*
Harry Flood Byrd, *Berryville*

REPRESENTATIVES

Schuyler Otis Bland, *Newport News*
Ralph H. Daughton, *Norfolk*
Dave E. Satterfield, Jr.,[74] *Richmond*
J. Vaughan Gary,[75] *Richmond*
Patrick Henry Drewry, *Petersburg*
Thomas G. Burch,[76] *Martinsville*
Thomas B. Stanley,[77] *Stanleytown*

---

[59] Died November 12, 1945.
[60] Elected to fill vacancy caused by death of James W. Mott, and took his seat January 29, 1946.
[61] Resigned July 17, 1946.
[62] Elected on November 5, 1946, to fill vacancy caused by resignation of John W. Murphy, but was unable to be sworn in as Congress was not in session.
[63] Died February 24, 1946.
[64] Elected to fill vacancy caused by death of J. Buell Snyder, and took his seat June 11, 1946.
[65] Resigned January 7, 1946.
[66] Elected to fill vacancy caused by resignation of

Samuel A. Weiss, and took his seat June 19, 1946.
[67] Resigned July 17, 1946.
[68] Elected August 24, 1946, to fill vacancy caused by resignation of Luther A. Johnson, but was unable to be sworn in as Congress was not in session.
[69] Resigned August 2, 1946.
[70] Appointed November 1, 1946, to fill vacancy caused by resignation of Warren R. Austin, but was unable to be sworn in as Congress was not in session.
[71] Died May 28, 1946.
[72] Appointed to fill vacancy caused by death of Carter Glass, and took his seat May 31, 1946.

[73] Elected November 5, 1946, to fill vacancy caused by death of Carter Glass, but was unable to be sworn in as Congress was not in session.
[74] Resigned February 15, 1945.
[75] Elected to fill vacancy caused by resignation of Dave E. Satterfield, Jr., and took his seat March 16, 1945.
[76] Resigned May 31, 1946, having been appointed Senator.
[77] Elected November 5, 1946, to fill vacancy caused by resignation of Thomas B. Burch, but was unable to be sworn in as Congress was not in session.

VIRGINIA—Continued

REPRESENTATIVES—continued

Clifton A. Woodrum,[78] *Roanoke*
J. Lindsay Almond, Jr.,[79] *Roanoke*
A. Willis Robertson,[80] *Lexington*
Burr P. Harrison,[81] *Winchester*
Howard W. Smith, *Alexandria*
John W. Flannagan, Jr., *Bristol*

WASHINGTON

SENATORS

Warren G. Magnuson, *Seattle*
Monrad C. Wallgren,[82] *Everett*
Hugh B. Mitchell,[83] *Everett*
Harry P. Cain,[84] *Tacoma*

REPRESENTATIVES

Hugh De Lacy, *Seattle*
Henry M. Jackson, *Everett*
Charles R. Savage, *Shelton*
Hal Holmes, *Ellensburg*
Walter F. Horan, *Wenatchee*
John M. Coffee, *Tacoma*

WEST VIRGINIA

SENATORS

Harley M. Kilgore, *Beckley*
Chapman Revercomb, *Charleston*

REPRESENTATIVES

Matthew M. Neely, *Fairmont*
Jennings Randolph, *Elkins*
Cleveland M. Bailey, *Clarksburg*
Hubert S. Ellis, *Huntington*
John Kee, *Bluefield*
Erland H. Hedrick, *Beckley*

WISCONSIN

SENATORS

Robert M. La Follette, Jr., *Madison*
Alexander Wiley, *Chippewa Falls*

REPRESENTATIVES

Lawrence H. Smith, *Racine*
Robert K. Henry,[85] *Jefferson*
William H. Stevenson, *La Crosse*
Thaddeus F. B. Wasielewski, *Milwaukee*
Andrew J. Biemiller, *Milwaukee*
Frank B. Keefe, *Oshkosh*
Reid F. Murray, *Ogdensburg*
John W. Byrnes, *Green Bay*
Merlin Hull, *Black River Falls*
Alvin E. O'Konski, *Mercer*

WYOMING

SENATORS

Joseph C. O'Mahoney, *Cheyenne*
Edward V. Robertson, *Cody*

REPRESENTATIVE

At Large—Frank A. Barrett, *Lusk*

TERRITORY OF ALASKA

DELEGATE

Edward L. Bartlett, *Juneau*

TERRITORY OF HAWAII

DELEGATE

Joseph R. Farrington, *Honolulu*

COMMONWEALTH OF THE PHILIPPINES

RESIDENT COMMISSIONER

Carlos P. Romulo,[86] *Manila*

PUERTO RICO

RESIDENT COMMISSIONER

Jesús T. Piñero,[87] *Canovanas*
A. Fernós-Isern,[88] *San Juan*

---

[78] Resigned December 31, 1945.
[79] Elected to fill vacancy caused by resignation of Clifton A. Woodrum, and took his seat February 4, 1946.
[80] Resigned November 5, 1946, having been elected Senator.
[81] Elected November 5, 1946, to fill vacancy caused by resignation of A. Willis Robertson, but was unable to be sworn in as Congress was not in session.

[82] Resigned January 9, 1945.
[83] Appointed to fill vacancy caused by resignation of Monrad C. Wallgren, and took his seat January 18, 1945; resigned December 25, 1946.
[84] Appointed December 26, 1946, to fill vacancy caused by resignation of Monrad C. Wallgren and Hugh B. Mitchell, but was unable to be sworn in as Congress was not in session.

[85] Died November 20, 1946; vacancy throughout remainder of the Congress.
[86] Office of Resident Commissioner terminated on July 4, 1946 (Public Law 127, 73d Cong.).
[87] Resigned September 2, 1946.
[88] Appointed September 11, 1946, to fill vacancy caused by resignation of Jesús T. Piñero, but was unable to be sworn in as Congress was not in session.

EIGHTIETH CONGRESS

JANUARY 3, 1947, TO JANUARY 3, 1949

FIRST SESSION—*January 3, 1947, to December 19, 1947*

SECOND SESSION—*January 6,*[1] *1948, to December 31, 1948*

VICE PRESIDENT OF THE UNITED STATES [2]

PRESIDENT PRO TEMPORE OF THE SENATE—ARTHUR H. VANDENBERG,[3] of Michigan

SECRETARY OF THE SENATE—CARL A. LOEFFLER,[4] of Pennsylvania

SERGEANT AT ARMS OF THE SENATE—EDWARD F. McGINNIS,[5] of Illinois

---

SPEAKER OF THE HOUSE OF REPRESENTATIVES—JOSEPH W. MARTIN, Jr.,[6] of Massachusetts

CLERK OF THE HOUSE—JOHN ANDREWS,[7] of Massachusetts

SERGEANT AT ARMS OF THE HOUSE—WILLIAM F. RUSSELL, of Pennsylvania

DOORKEEPER OF THE HOUSE—M. L. MELETIO, of Missouri

POSTMASTER OF THE HOUSE—FRANK COLLIER

ALABAMA

SENATORS

Lister Hill, *Montgomery*
John J. Sparkman, *Huntsville*

REPRESENTATIVES

Frank W. Boykin, *Mobile*
George M. Grant, *Troy*
George W. Andrews, *Union Springs*
Sam Hobbs, *Selma*
Albert Rains, *Gadsden*
Pete Jarman, *Livingston*
Carter Manasco, *Jasper*
Robert E. Jones, Jr.,[8] *Scottsboro*
Laurie C. Battle, *Birmingham*

ARIZONA

SENATORS

Carl Hayden, *Phoenix*
Ernest W. McFarland, *Florence*

REPRESENTATIVES AT LARGE

Richard F. Harless, *Phoenix*
John R. Murdock, *Tempe*

ARKANSAS

SENATORS

John L. McClellan, *Camden*
J. William Fulbright, *Fayetteville*

REPRESENTATIVES

Ezekiel C. Gathings, *West Memphis*
Wilbur D. Mills, *Kensett*
James W. Trimble, *Berryville*
Fadjo Cravens, *Fort Smith*
Brooks Hays, *Little Rock*
William F. Norrell, *Monticello*
Oren Harris, *El Dorado*

CALIFORNIA

SENATORS

Sheridan Downey, *San Francisco*
William F. Knowland, *Piedmont*

REPRESENTATIVES

Clarence F. Lea, *Santa Rosa*
Clair Engle, *Red Bluff*
Leroy Johnson, *Stockton*
Franck R. Havenner, *San Francisco*
Richard J. Welch, *San Francisco*
George P. Miller, *Alameda*
John J. Allen, Jr., *Oakland*

John Z. Anderson, *San Juan Bautista*
Bertrand W. Gearhart, *Fresno*
Alfred J. Elliott, *Tulare*
Ernest K. Bramblett, *Pacific Grove*
Richard M. Nixon, *Whittier*
Norris Poulson, *Los Angeles*
Mrs. Helen Gahagan Douglas, *Los Angeles*
Gordon L. McDonough, *Los Angeles*
Donald L. Jackson, *Santa Monica*
Cecil R. King, *Los Angeles*
Willis W. Bradley, *Long Beach*
Chet Holifield, *Montebello*
Carl Hinshaw, *Pasadena*
Harry R. Sheppard, *Yucaipa*
John Phillips, *Banning*
Charles K. Fletcher, *San Diego*

COLORADO

SENATORS

Edwin C. Johnson, *Craig*
Eugene D. Millikin, *Denver*

REPRESENTATIVES

John A. Carroll, *Denver*
William S. Hill, *Fort Collins*
J. Edgar Chenoweth, *Trinidad*
Robert F. Rockwell, *Paonia*

---

[1] By joint resolution (Pub. Law 358, 80th Cong., 1st sess.), the date of assembling the second session of the Eightieth Congress was fixed for January 6, 1948.
[2] Harry S. Truman became President on the death of Franklin D. Roosevelt in the preceding Congress.

[3] Elected January 4, 1947.
[4] Elected January 4, 1947.
[5] Elected January 4, 1947.
[6] Elected January 3, 1947.
[7] Elected January 3, 1947.

[8] Elected to fill vacancy caused by resignation of Representative-elect John J. Sparkman, in preceding Congress, and took his seat February 5, 1947.

CONNECTICUT

SENATORS

Brien McMahon, *Norwalk*
Raymond E. Baldwin, *Stratford*

REPRESENTATIVES

William J. Miller, *Wethersfield*
Horace Seely-Brown, Jr., *Pomfret Center*
Ellsworth B. Foote, *North Branford*
John Davis Lodge, *Westport*
James T. Patterson, *Naugatuck*
At Large—Antoni N. Sadlak, *Rockville*

DELAWARE

SENATORS

C. Douglass Buck, *Wilmington*
John J. Williams, *Millsboro*

REPRESENTATIVE

At Large—J. Caleb Boggs, *Wilmington*

FLORIDA

SENATORS

Claude D. Pepper, *Tallahassee*
Spessard L. Holland, *Bartow*

REPRESENTATIVES

J. Hardin Peterson, *Lakeland*
Emory H. Price, *Jacksonville*
Robert L. F. Sikes, *Crestview*
George A. Smathers, *Miami*
Joe Hendricks, *De Land*
Dwight L. Rogers, *Fort Lauderdale*

GEORGIA

SENATORS

Walter F. George, *Vienna*
Richard B. Russell, *Winder*

REPRESENTATIVES

Prince H. Preston, Jr., *Statesboro*
Edward E. Cox, *Camilla*
Stephen Pace, *Americus*
A. Sidney Camp, *Newnan*
James C. Davis,[9] *Stone Mountain*
Carl Vinson, *Milledgeville*
Henderson L. Lanham, *Rome*
William M. Wheeler, *Alma*
John S. Wood, *Canton*
Paul Brown, *Elberton*

IDAHO

SENATORS

Glen H. Taylor, *Pocatello*
Henry C. Dworshak, *Burley*

REPRESENTATIVES

Abe McGregor Goff, *Moscow*
John C. Sanborn, *Hagerman*

ILLINOIS

SENATORS

Scott W. Lucas, *Havana*
C. Wayland Brooks, *Chicago*

REPRESENTATIVES

William L. Dawson, *Chicago*
Richard B. Vail, *Chicago*
Fred E. Busbey, *Chicago*
Martin Gorski, *Chicago*
Adolph J. Sabath, *Chicago*
Thomas J. O'Brien, *Chicago*
Thomas L. Owens,[10] *Chicago*
Thomas S. Gordon, *Chicago*
Robert J. Twyman, *Chicago*
Ralph E. Church, *Evanston*
Chauncey W. Reed, *West Chicago*
Noah M. Mason, *Oglesby*
Leo E. Allen, *Galena*
Anton J. Johnson, *Macomb*
Robert B. Chiperfield, *Canton*
Everett M. Dirksen, *Pekin*
Leslie C. Arends, *Melvin*
Edward H. Jenison, *Paris*
Rolla C. McMillen, *Decatur*
Sidney E. Simpson, *Carrollton*
Evan Howell,[11] *Springfield*
Charles Melvin Price, *East St. Louis*
Charles W. Vursell, *Salem*
Roy Clippinger, *Carmi*
Cecil W. (Runt) Bishop, *Carterville*
At Large—William G. Stratton, *Morris*

INDIANA

SENATORS

Homer E. Capehart, *Washington*
William E. Jenner, *Bedford*

REPRESENTATIVES

Ray J. Madden, *Gary*
Charles A. Halleck, *Rensselaer*
Robert A. Grant, *South Bend*
George W. Gillie, *Fort Wayne*
Forest A. Harness, *Kokomo*
Noble J. Johnson,[12] *Terre Haute*
Gerald W. Landis, *Linton*
Edward A. Mitchell, *Evansville*
Earl Wilson, *Bedford*
Raymond S. Springer,[13] *Connersville*
Ralph Harvey,[14] *New Castle*
Louis Ludlow, *Indianapolis*

IOWA

SENATORS

George A. Wilson, *Des Moines*
Bourke B. Hickenlooper, *Cedar Rapids*

REPRESENTATIVES

Thomas E. Martin, *Iowa City*
Henry O. Talle, *Decorah*
John W. Gwynne, *Waterloo*
Karl M. LeCompte, *Corydon*
Paul Cunningham, *Des Moines*
James I. Dolliver, *Fort Dodge*
Ben F. Jensen, *Exira*
Charles B. Hoeven, *Alton*

KANSAS

SENATORS

Arthur Capper, *Topeka*
Clyde M. Reed, *Parsons*

REPRESENTATIVES

Albert M. Cole, *Holton*
Errett P. Scrivner, *Kansas City*
Herbert A. Meyer, *Independence*
Edward H. Rees, *Emporia*
Clifford R. Hope, *Garden City*
Wint Smith, *Mankato*

KENTUCKY

SENATORS

Alben W. Barkley, *Paducah*
John Sherman Cooper, *Somerset*

REPRESENTATIVES

Noble J. Gregory, *Mayfield*
Earle C. Clements,[15] *Morganfield*
John A. Whitaker,[16] *Russellville*
Thruston Ballard Morton, *Glenview*
Frank L. Chelf, *Lebanon*
Brent Spence, *Fort Thomas*
Virgil M. Chapman, *Paris*
W. Howes Meade, *Paintsville*
Joe B. Bates, *Greenup*
John M. Robsion,[17] *Barbourville*
William Lewis,[18] *London*

LOUISIANA

SENATORS

John H. Overton,[19] *Alexandria*
William C. Feazel,[20] *West Monroe*
Russell B. Long,[21] *Baton Rouge*
Allen J. Ellender, *Houma*

REPRESENTATIVES

F. Edward Hébert, *New Orleans*
T. Hale Boggs, *New Orleans*

---

[9] Election unsuccessfully contested by Mrs. Helen Douglas Mankin and Wyman C. Lowe.
[10] Died June 7, 1948.
[11] Resigned October 5, 1947.
[12] Resigned July 1, 1948.
[13] Died August 28, 1947.
[14] Elected to fill vacancy caused by death of Raymond S. Springer, and took his seat November 17, 1947.
[15] Resigned January 6, 1948.
[16] Elected to fill vacancy caused by resignation of Earle C. Clements, and took his seat April 26, 1948.
[17] Died February 17, 1948.
[18] Elected to fill vacancy caused by death of John M. Robsion, and took his seat May 3, 1948.
[19] Died May 14, 1948.
[20] Appointed to fill vacancy caused by death of John H. Overton, and took his seat May 24, 1948.
[21] Elected to fill vacancy caused by death of John H. Overton, and took his seat December 31, 1948.

James Domengeaux, *Lafayette*
Overton Brooks, *Shreveport*
Otto E. Passman, *Monroe*
James H. Morrison, *Hammond*
Henry D. Larcade, Jr., *Opelousas*
A. Leonard Allen, *Winnfield*

MAINE

SENATORS

Wallace H. White, Jr., *Auburn*
Ralph O. Brewster, *Dexter*

REPRESENTATIVES

Robert Hale, *Portland*
Mrs. Margaret Chase Smith, *Skowhegan*
Frank Fellows, *Bangor*

MARYLAND

SENATORS

Millard E. Tydings, *Havre de Grace*
Herbert R. O'Conor,[22] *Baltimore*

REPRESENTATIVES

Edward T. Miller, *Easton*
Hugh A. Meade, *Baltimore*
Thomas D'Alesandro, Jr.,[23] *Baltimore*
Edward A. Garmatz,[24] *Baltimore*
George H. Fallon, *Baltimore*
Lansdale G. Sasscer, *Upper Marlboro*
J. Glenn Beall, *Frostburg*

MASSACHUSETTS

SENATORS

Leverett Saltonstall, *Dover*
Henry Cabot Lodge, Jr., *Beverly*

REPRESENTATIVES

John W. Heselton, *Deerfield*
Charles R. Clason, *Springfield*
Philip J. Philbin, *Clinton*
Harold D. Donohue, *Worcester*
Mrs. Edith Nourse Rogers, *Lowell*
George J. Bates, *Salem*
Thomas J. Lane, *Lawrence*
Angier L. Goodwin, *Melrose*
Charles L. Gifford,[25] *Cotuit*
Donald W. Nicholson,[26] *Wareham*
Christian A. Herter, *Boston*
John F. Kennedy, *Boston*
John W. McCormack, *Dorchester*
Richard B. Wigglesworth, *Milton*
Joseph W. Martin, Jr., *North Attleboro*

MICHIGAN

SENATORS

Arthur H. Vandenberg, *Grand Rapids*
Homer Ferguson, *Detroit*

REPRESENTATIVES

George G. Sadowski, *Detroit*
Earl C. Michener, *Adrian*
Paul W. Shafer, *Battle Creek*
Clare E. Hoffman, *Allegan*
Bartel J. Jonkman, *Grand Rapids*
William W. Blackney, *Flint*
Jesse P. Wolcott, *Port Huron*
Fred L. Crawford, *Saginaw*
Albert J. Engel, *Muskegon*
Roy O. Woodruff, *Bay City*
Frederick V. Bradley,[27] *Rogers City*
Charles E. Potter,[28] *Cheboygan*
John B. Bennett, *Ontonagon*
Howard A. Coffin, *Detroit*
Harold F. Youngblood, *Detroit*
John D. Dingell, *Detroit*
John Lesinski, *Dearborn*
George A. Dondero, *Royal Oak*

MINNESOTA

SENATORS

Joseph H. Ball, *Stillwater*
Edward J. Thye, *Northfield*

REPRESENTATIVES

August H. Andresen, *Red Wing*
Joseph P. O'Hara, *Glencoe*
George E. MacKinnon, *Minneapolis*
Edward J. Devitt, *St. Paul*
Walter H. Judd, *Minneapolis*
Harold Knutson, *Manhattan Beach*
H. Carl Andersen, *Tyler*
John A. Blatnik, *Chisholm*
Harold C. Hagen, *Crookston*

MISSISSIPPI

SENATORS

Theodore G. Bilbo,[29] *Poplarville*
John C. Stennis,[30] *De Kalb*
James O. Eastland, *Doddsville*

REPRESENTATIVES

John E. Rankin, *Tupelo*
Jamie L. Whitten, *Charleston*
William M. Whittington, *Greenwood*
Thomas G. Abernethy, *Okolona*
W. Arthur Winstead, *Philadelphia*
William M. Colmer, *Pascagoula*
John Bell Williams, *Raymond*

MISSOURI

SENATORS

Forrest C. Donnell, *Webster Groves*
James P. Kem, *Kansas City*

REPRESENTATIVES

Samuel W. Arnold, *Kirksville*
Max Schwabe, *Columbia*
William C. Cole, *St. Joseph*
C. Jasper Bell, *Blue Springs*
Albert L. Reeves, Jr., *Kansas City*
Marion T. Bennett, *Springfield*
Dewey Short, *Galena*
Parke M. Banta, *Arcadia*
Clarence Cannon, *Elsberry*
Orville Zimmerman,[31] *Kennett*
Paul C. Jones,[32] *Kennett*
Claude I. Bakewell, *St. Louis*
Walter C. Ploeser, *Chesterfield*
Frank M. Karsten, *St. Louis*

MONTANA

SENATORS

James E. Murray, *Butte*
Zales N. Ecton, *Manhattan*

REPRESENTATIVES

Mike Mansfield, *Missoula*
Wesley A. D'Ewart, *Wilsall*

NEBRASKA

SENATORS

Hugh A. Butler, *Omaha*
Kenneth S. Wherry, *Pawnee City*

REPRESENTATIVES

Carl T. Curtis, *Minden*
Howard H. Buffett, *Omaha*
Karl Stefan, *Norfolk*
Arthur L. Miller, *Kimball*

NEVADA

SENATORS

Patrick A. McCarran, *Reno*
George W. Malone, *Reno*

REPRESENTATIVE

At Large—Charles H. Russell, *Ely*

NEW HAMPSHIRE

SENATORS

H. Styles Bridges, *Concord*
Charles W. Tobey, *Temple*

REPRESENTATIVES

Chester E. Merrow, *Center Ossipee*
Norris Cotton, *Lebanon*

---

[22] Election unsuccessfully contested by David J. Markey.
[23] Resigned May 16, 1947.
[24] Elected to fill vacancy caused by resignation of Thomas D'Alesandro, Jr., and took his seat July 24, 1947.

[25] Died August 23, 1947.
[26] Elected to fill vacancy caused by death of Charles L. Gifford, and took his seat November 28, 1947.
[27] Died May 24, 1947.
[28] Elected to fill vacancy caused by death of Frederick V. Bradley, and took his seat November 17, 1947.

[29] Died August 21, 1947.
[30] Elected to fill vacancy caused by death of Theodore G. Bilbo, and took his seat November 17, 1947.
[31] Died April 7, 1948.
[32] Elected to fill vacancy caused by death of Orville Zimmerman, and took his seat December 31, 1948.

NEW JERSEY

SENATORS

Albert W. Hawkes, *Montclair*
H. Alexander Smith, *Princeton*

REPRESENTATIVES

Charles A. Wolverton, *Merchantville*
T. Millet Hand, *Cape May City*
James C. Auchincloss, *Rumson*
Frank A. Mathews, Jr., *Riverton*
Charles A. Eaton, *Plainfield*
Clifford P. Case, *Rahway*
J. Parnell Thomas, *Allendale*
Gordon Canfield, *Paterson*
Harry L. Towe, *Rutherford*
Fred A. Hartley, Jr., *Pittstown*
Frank L. Sundstrom, *East Orange*
Robert W. Kean, *Livingston*
Mrs. Mary T. Norton, *Jersey City*
Edward J. Hart, *Jersey City*

NEW MEXICO

SENATORS

Carl A. Hatch, *Clovis*
Dennis Chavez, *Albuquerque*

REPRESENTATIVES AT LARGE

Antonio M. Fernandez, *Santa Fe*
Mrs. Georgia L. Lusk, *Santa Fe*

NEW YORK

SENATORS

Robert F. Wagner, *New York City*
Irving M. Ives, *Norwich*

REPRESENTATIVES

W. Kingsland Macy, *Islip*
Leonard W. Hall, *Oyster Bay*
Henry J. Latham, *Queens Village*
Gregory McMahon, *Ozone Park*
Robert Tripp Ross, *Jackson Heights*
Robert J. Nodar, Jr., *Maspeth*
John J. Delaney,[33] *Brooklyn*
Joseph L. Pfeifer, *Brooklyn*
Eugene J. Keogh, *Brooklyn*
Andrew L. Somers, *Brooklyn*
James J. Heffernan, *Brooklyn*
John J. Rooney, *Brooklyn*
Donald L. O'Toole, *Brooklyn*
Leo F. Rayfiel,[34] *Brooklyn*
Abraham J. Multer,[35] *Brooklyn*
Emanuel Celler, *Brooklyn*
Ellsworth B. Buck, *Staten Island*
Frederic R. Coudert, Jr., *New York City*
Vito Marcantonio, *New York City*
Arthur G. Klein, *New York City*
Sol Bloom, *New York City*
Jacob K. Javits, *New York City*

Adam C. Powell, Jr., *New York City*
Walter A. Lynch, *New York City*
Benjamin J. Rabin,[36] *New York City*
Leo Isacson,[37] *New York City*
Charles A. Buckley, *New York City*
David M. Potts, *New York City*
Ralph W. Gwinn, *Bronxville*
Ralph A. Gamble, *Larchmont*
Mrs. Katharine St. George, *Tuxedo Park*
Jay LeFevre, *New Paltz*
Bernard W. Kearney, *Gloversville*
William T. Byrne, *Loudonville*
Dean P. Taylor, *Troy*
Clarence E. Kilburn, *Malone*
Hadwen C. Fuller, *Parish*
R. Walter Riehlman, *Tully*
Edwin Arthur Hall, *Binghamton*
John Taber, *Auburn*
W. Sterling Cole, *Bath*
Kenneth B. Keating, *Rochester*
James W. Wadsworth, Jr., *Geneseo*
Walter G. Andrews, *Buffalo*
Edward J. Elsaesser, *Buffalo*
John C. Butler, *Buffalo*
Daniel A. Reed, *Dunkirk*

NORTH CAROLINA

SENATORS

Clyde R. Hoey, *Shelby*
William B. Umstead,[38] *Durham*
J. Melville Broughton,[39] *Raleigh*

REPRESENTATIVES

Herbert C. Bonner, *Washington*
John H. Kerr, *Warrenton*
Graham A. Barden, *New Bern*
Harold D. Cooley, *Nashville*
John H. Folger, *Mount Airy*
Carl T. Durham, *Chapel Hill*
J. Bayard Clark, *Fayetteville*
Charles B. Deane, *Rockingham*
Robert L. Doughton, *Sparta*
Hamilton C. Jones, *Charlotte*
Alfred L. Bulwinkle, *Gastonia*
Monroe M. Redden, *Hendersonville*

NORTH DAKOTA

SENATORS

William Langer, *Wheatland*
Milton R. Young, *Berlin*

REPRESENTATIVES AT LARGE

William Lemke, *Fargo*
Charles R. Robertson, *Bismarck*

OHIO

SENATORS

Robert A. Taft, *Cincinnati*
John W. Bricker, *Columbus*

REPRESENTATIVES

Charles H. Elston, *Cincinnati*
William E. Hess, *Cincinnati*
Raymond H. Burke, *Hamilton*
Robert F. Jones,[40] *Lima*
William M. McCulloch,[41] *Piqua*
Cliff Clevenger, *Bryan*
Edward O. McCowen, *Wheelersburg*
Clarence J. Brown, *Blanchester*
Frederick C. Smith, *Marion*
Homer A. Ramey, *Toledo*
Thomas A. Jenkins, *Ironton*
Walter E. Brehm, *Logan*
John M. Vorys, *Columbus*
Alvin F. Weichel, *Sandusky*
Walter B. Huber, *Akron*
Percy W. Griffiths, *Marietta*
Henderson H. Carson, *Canton*
J. Harry McGregor, *West Lafayette*
Earl R. Lewis, *St. Clairsville*
Michael J. Kirwan, *Youngstown*
Michael A. Feighan, *Cleveland*
Robert Crosser, *Cleveland*
Mrs. Frances P. Bolton, *Lyndhurst*
At Large—George H. Bender, *Cleveland Heights*

OKLAHOMA

SENATORS

J. W. Elmer Thomas, *Medicine Park*
Edward H. Moore, *Tulsa*

REPRESENTATIVES

George B. Schwabe, *Tulsa*
William G. Stigler, *Stigler*
Carl Albert, *McAlester*
Glen D. Johnson, *Okemah*
A. S. Mike Monroney, *Oklahoma City*
Toby Morris, *Lawton*
Preston E. Peden, *Altus*
Ross Rizley, *Guymon*

OREGON

SENATORS

Guy Cordon, *Roseburg*
Wayne L. Morse, *Eugene*

REPRESENTATIVES

A. Walter Norblad, Jr., *Astoria*
Lowell Stockman, *Pendleton*
Homer D. Angell, *Portland*
Harris Ellsworth, *Roseburg*

PENNSYLVANIA

SENATORS

Francis J. Myers, *Philadelphia*
Edward Martin, *Washington*

---

[33] Died November 18, 1948.
[34] Resigned September 13, 1947.
[35] Elected to fill vacancy caused by resignation of Leo F. Rayfiel, and took his seat November 17, 1947.
[36] Resigned December 31, 1947.

[37] Elected to fill vacancy caused by resignation of Benjamin J. Rabin, and took his seat March 1, 1948.
[38] Appointed to fill vacancy caused by death of Josiah W. Bailey, in preceding Congress.
[39] Elected to fill vacancy caused by death of Josiah

W. Bailey, in preceding Congress, and took his seat December 31, 1948.
[40] Resigned September 2, 1947.
[41] Elected to fill vacancy caused by resignation of Robert F. Jones, and took his seat November 17, 1947.

REPRESENTATIVES

James Gallagher, *Philadelphia*
Robert N. McGarvey, *Philadelphia*
Hardie Scott, *Philadelphia*
Franklin J. Maloney, *Philadelphia*
George W. Sarbacher, Jr., *Philadelphia*
Hugh D. Scott, Jr., *Philadelphia*
E. Wallace Chadwick, *Rose Valley*
Charles L. Gerlach,[42] *Allentown*
Franklin H. Lichtenwalter,[43] *Center Valley*
Paul B. Dague, *Downingtown*
James P. Scoblick, *Archbald*
Mitchell Jenkins, *Trucksville*
Ivor D. Fenton, *Mahanoy City*
Frederick A. Muhlenberg, *Wernersville*
Wilson D. Gillette, *Towanda*
Robert F. Rich, *Woolrich*
Samuel K. McConnell, Jr., *Wynnewood*
Richard M. Simpson, *Huntingdon*
John C. Kunkel, *Harrisburg*
Leon H. Gavin, *Oil City*
Francis E. Walter, *Easton*
Chester H. Gross, *York*
James E. Van Zandt, *Altoona*
William J. Crow, *Uniontown*
Thomas E. Morgan, *Fredericktown*
Louis E. Graham, *Beaver*
Harve Tibbott, *Ebensburg*
Augustine B. Kelley, *Greensburg*
Carroll D. Kearns, *Farrell*
John R. McDowell, *Wilkinsburg*
Robert J. Corbett, *Bellevue*
James G. Fulton, *Dormont*
Herman P. Eberharter, *Pittsburgh*
Frank Buchanan, *McKeesport*

RHODE ISLAND

SENATORS

Theodore F. Green, *Providence*
J. Howard McGrath, *Providence*

REPRESENTATIVES

Aime J. Forand, *Valley Falls*
John E. Fogarty, *Harmony*

SOUTH CAROLINA

SENATORS

Burnet R. Maybank, *Charleston*
Olin D. Johnston, *Spartanburg*

REPRESENTATIVES

L. Mendel Rivers, *North Charleston*
John J. Riley, *Sumter*
W. J. Bryan Dorn, *Greenwood*
Joseph R. Bryson, *Greenville*
James P. Richards, *Lancaster*
John L. McMillan, *Florence*

SOUTH DAKOTA

SENATORS

J. Chandler Gurney, *Yankton*
Harlan J. Bushfield,[44] *Miller*
Mrs. Vera C. Bushfield,[45] *Miller*
Karl E. Mundt,[46] *Madison*

REPRESENTATIVES

Karl E. Mundt,[47] *Madison*
Francis H. Case, *Custer*

TENNESSEE

SENATORS

Kenneth D. McKellar, *Memphis*
A. Tom Stewart, *Winchester*

REPRESENTATIVES

Dayton E. Phillips, *Elizabethton*
John Jennings, Jr., *Knoxville*
Estes Kefauver, *Chattanooga*
Albert A. Gore, *Carthage*
Joseph L. Evins, *Smithville*
J. Percy Priest, *Nashville*
Wirt Courtney, *Franklin*
Thomas J. Murray, *Jackson*
Jere Cooper, *Dyersburg*
Clifford Davis, *Memphis*

TEXAS

SENATORS

Tom T. Connally, *Marlin*
W. Lee O'Daniel, *Fort Worth*

REPRESENTATIVES

Wright Patman, *Texarkana*
Jesse M. Combs, *Beaumont*
Lindley Beckworth, *Gladewater*
Sam Rayburn, *Bonham*
J. Frank Wilson, *Dallas*
Olin E. Teague, *College Station*
Tom Pickett, *Palestine*
Albert Thomas, *Houston*
Joseph J. Mansfield,[48] *Columbus*
Clark W. Thompson,[49] *Galveston*
Lyndon B. Johnson, *Johnson City*
William R. Poage, *Waco*
Wingate H. Lucas, *Grapevine*
Ed Gossett, *Wichita Falls*
John E. Lyle, Jr., *Corpus Christi*
Milton H. West,[50] *Brownsville*
Lloyd M. Bentsen, Jr.,[51] *McAllen*
R. Ewing Thomason,[52] *El Paso*
Kenneth M. Regan,[53] *Midland*
Omar T. Burleson, *Anson*

Eugene Worley, *Shamrock*
George H. Mahon, *Colorado City*
Paul J. Kilday, *San Antonio*
O. Clark Fisher, *San Angelo*

UTAH

SENATORS

Elbert D. Thomas, *Salt Lake City*
Arthur V. Watkins, *Orem*

REPRESENTATIVES

Walter K. Granger,[54] *Cedar City*
William A. Dawson, *Layton*

VERMONT

SENATORS

George D. Aiken, *Putney*
Ralph E. Flanders, *Springfield*

REPRESENTATIVE

At Large—Charles A. Plumley, *Northfield*

VIRGINIA

SENATORS

Harry Flood Byrd, *Berryville*
A. Willis Robertson, *Lexington*

REPRESENTATIVES

Schuyler Otis Bland, *Newport News*
Porter Hardy, Jr., *Churchland*
J. Vaughan Gary, *Richmond*
Patrick Henry Drewry,[55] *Petersburg*
Watkins M. Abbitt,[56] *Appomattox*
Thomas B. Stanley, *Stanleytown*
J. Lindsay Almond, Jr.,[57] *Roanoke*
Clarence G. Burton,[58] *Lynchburg*
Burr P. Harrison, *Winchester*
Howard W. Smith, *Alexandria*
John W. Flannagan, Jr., *Bristol*

WASHINGTON

SENATORS

Warren G. Magnuson, *Seattle*
Harry P. Cain, *Tacoma*

REPRESENTATIVES

Homer R. Jones, *Bremerton*
Henry M. Jackson, *Everett*
Fred B. Norman,[59] *Raymond*
Russell V. Mack,[60] *Hoquiam*
Hal Holmes, *Ellensburg*
Walter F. Horan, *Wenatchee*
Thor C. Tollefson, *Tacoma*

---

[42] Died May 5, 1947.
[43] Elected to fill vacancy caused by death of Charles L. Gerlach, and took his seat November 17, 1947.
[44] Died September 27, 1948.
[45] Appointed to fill vacancy caused by death of Harlan J. Bushfield, but did not take her seat as Congress was not in session; resigned December 27, 1948.
[46] Elected to fill vacancy caused by death of Harlan J. Bushfield, and took his seat December 31, 1948.
[47] Resigned December 30, 1948.
[48] Died July 12, 1947.

[49] Elected to fill vacancy caused by death of Joseph J. Mansfield, and took his seat November 17, 1947.
[50] Died October 28, 1948.
[51] Elected to fill vacancy caused by death of Milton H. West, and took his seat December 31, 1948.
[52] Resigned July 31, 1947.
[53] Elected to fill vacancy caused by resignation of R. Ewing Thomason, and took his seat November 17, 1947.
[54] Election unsuccessfully contested by David J. Wilson.

[55] Died December 21, 1947.
[56] Elected to fill vacancy caused by death of Patrick H. Drewry, and took his seat February 26, 1948.
[57] Resigned April 17, 1948.
[58] Elected to fill vacancy caused by resignation of J. Lindsay Almond, Jr., and took his seat December 31, 1948.
[59] Died April 18, 1947.
[60] Elected to fill vacancy caused by death of Fred B. Norman, and took his seat June 25, 1947.

WEST VIRGINIA

SENATORS

Harley M. Kilgore, *Beckley*
Chapman Revercomb, *Charleston*

REPRESENTATIVES

Francis J. Love, *Wheeling*
Melvin C. Snyder, *Kingwood*
Edward G. Rohrbough, *Glenville*
Hubert S. Ellis, *Huntington*
John Kee, *Bluefield*
Erland H. Hedrick, *Beckley*

WISCONSIN

SENATORS

Alexander Wiley, *Chippewa Falls*
Joseph R. McCarthy, *Appleton*

REPRESENTATIVES

Lawrence H. Smith, *Racine*
Glenn R. Davis,[61] *Waukesha*
William H. Stevenson, *La Crosse*
John C. Brophy, *Milwaukee*
Charles J. Kersten, *Milwaukee*
Frank B. Keefe, *Oshkosh*
Reid F. Murray, *Ogdensburg*
John W. Byrnes, *Green Bay*
Merlin Hull, *Black River Falls*
Alvin E. O'Konski, *Mercer*

WYOMING

SENATORS

Joseph C. O'Mahoney, *Cheyenne*
Edward V. Robertson, *Cody*

REPRESENTATIVE

At Large—Frank A. Barrett, *Lusk*

TERRITORY OF ALASKA

DELEGATE

Edward L. Bartlett, *Juneau*

TERRITORY OF HAWAII

DELEGATE

Joseph R. Farrington, *Honolulu*

PUERTO RICO

RESIDENT COMMISSIONER

A. Fernós-Isern, *San Juan*

[61] Elected to fill vacancy caused by death of Representative-elect Robert K. Henry, in preceding Congress, and took his seat May 5, 1947.

EIGHTY-FIRST CONGRESS

JANUARY 3, 1949, TO JANUARY 3, 1951

FIRST SESSION—*January 3, 1949, to October 19, 1949*

SECOND SESSION—*January 3, 1950, to January 2, 1951*

———

VICE PRESIDENT OF THE UNITED STATES—ALBEN W. BARKLEY,[1] of Kentucky

PRESIDENT PRO TEMPORE OF THE SENATE—KENNETH D. McKELLAR,[2] of Tennessee

SECRETARY OF THE SENATE—LESLIE L. BIFFLE,[2] of Arkansas

SERGEANT AT ARMS OF THE SENATE—JOSEPH C. DUKE,[2] of Arizona

———

SPEAKER OF THE HOUSE OF REPRESENTATIVES—SAM RAYBURN,[2] of Texas

CLERK OF THE HOUSE—RALPH R. ROBERTS,[2] of Indiana

SERGEANT AT ARMS OF THE HOUSE—JOSEPH H. CALLAHAN,[2] of Kentucky

DOORKEEPER OF THE HOUSE—WILLIAM M. MILLER,[2] of Mississippi

POSTMASTER OF THE HOUSE—FINIS E. SCOTT,[2] of Tennessee

ALABAMA

SENATORS

Lister Hill, *Montgomery*

John J. Sparkman, *Huntsville*

REPRESENTATIVES

Frank W. Boykin, *Mobile*

George M. Grant, *Troy*

George W. Andrews, *Union Springs*

Sam Hobbs, *Selma*

Albert Rains, *Gadsden*

Edward deGraffenried, *Tuscaloosa*

Carl A. Elliott, *Jasper*

Robert E. Jones, Jr., *Scottsboro*

Laurie C. Battle, *Birmingham*

ARIZONA

SENATORS

Carl Hayden, *Phoenix*

Ernest W. McFarland, *Florence*

REPRESENTATIVES

John R. Murdock, *Tempe*

Harold A. Patten, *Tucson*

ARKANSAS

SENATORS

John L. McClellan, *Camden*

J. William Fulbright, *Fayetteville*

REPRESENTATIVES

Ezekiel C. Gathings, *West Memphis*

Wilbur D. Mills, *Kensett*

James W. Trimble, *Berryville*

Boyd Tackett, *Nashville*

Brooks Hays, *Little Rock*

William F. Norrell, *Monticello*

Oren Harris, *El Dorado*

CALIFORNIA

SENATORS

Sheridan Downey,[3] *San Francisco*

Richard M. Nixon,[4] *Whittier*

William F. Knowland, *Piedmont*

REPRESENTATIVES

Hubert B. Scudder, *Sebastopol*

Clair Engle, *Red Bluff*

Leroy Johnson, *Stockton*

Franck R. Havenner, *San Francisco*

Richard J. Welch,[5] *San Francisco*

John F. Shelley,[6] *San Francisco*

George P. Miller, *Alameda*

John J. Allen, Jr., *Oakland*

John Z. Anderson, *San Juan Bautista*

Cecil F. White, *Fresno*

Thomas H. Werdel, *Bakersfield*

Ernest K. Bramblett, *Pacific Grove*

Richard M. Nixon,[7] *Whittier*

Norris Poulson, *Los Angeles*

Mrs. Helen Gahagan Douglas, *Los Angeles*

Gordon L. McDonough, *Los Angeles*

Donald L. Jackson, *Santa Monica*

Cecil R. King, *Los Angeles*

Clyde G. Doyle, *Long Beach*

Chet Holifield, *Montebello*

Carl Hinshaw, *Pasadena*

Harry R. Sheppard, *Yucaipa*

John Phillips, *Banning*

Clinton D. McKinnon, *San Diego*

COLORADO

SENATORS

Edwin C. Johnson, *Craig*

Eugene D. Millikin, *Denver*

REPRESENTATIVES

John A. Carroll, *Denver*

William S. Hill, *Fort Collins*

John H. Marsalis, *Pueblo*

Wayne N. Aspinall, *Palisade*

---

[1] Elected Vice President and took the oath of office January 20, 1949.

[2] Elected January 3, 1949.

[3] Resigned November 30, 1950

[4] Appointed to fill vacancy caused by resignation of Sheridan Downey, and took his seat December 4, 1950.

[5] Died September 10, 1949.

[6] Elected to fill vacancy caused by death of Richard J. Welch, and took his seat January 3, 1950.

[7] Resigned November 30, 1950; vacancy throughout remainder of the Congress.

CONNECTICUT

SENATORS

Brien McMahon, *Norwalk*
Raymond E. Baldwin,[8] *Stratford*
William Benton,[9] *Southport*

REPRESENTATIVES

Abraham A. Ribicoff, *Hartford*
Mrs. Chase Going Woodhouse, *Sprague*
John A. McGuire, *Wallingford*
John Davis Lodge, *Westport*
James T. Patterson, *Naugatuck*
At Large—Antoni N. Sadlak, *Rockville*

DELAWARE

SENATORS

John J. Williams, *Millsboro*
J. Allen Frear, Jr., *Dover*

REPRESENTATIVE

At Large—J. Caleb Boggs, *Wilmington*

FLORIDA

SENATORS

Claude D. Pepper, *Tallahassee*
Spessard L. Holland, *Bartow*

REPRESENTATIVES

J. Hardin Peterson, *Lakeland*
Charles E. Bennett, *Jacksonville*
Robert L. F. Sikes, *Crestview*
George A. Smathers, *Miami*
Albert S. Herlong, Jr., *Leesburg*
Dwight L. Rogers, *Fort Lauderdale*

GEORGIA

SENATORS

Walter F. George, *Vienna*
Richard B. Russell, *Winder*

REPRESENTATIVES

Prince H. Preston, Jr., *Statesboro*
Edward E. Cox, *Camilla*
Stephen Pace, *Americus*
A. Sidney Camp, *Newnan*
James C. Davis, *Stone Mountain*
Carl Vinson, *Milledgeville*
Henderson L. Lanham, *Rome*
William M. Wheeler, *Alma*
John S. Wood, *Canton*
Paul Brown, *Elberton*

IDAHO

SENATORS

Glen H. Taylor, *Pocatello*
Bert H. Miller,[10] *Boise*
Henry C. Dworshak,[11] *Burley*

REPRESENTATIVES

Compton I. White, *Clark Fork*
John C. Sanborn, *Hagerman*

ILLINOIS

SENATORS

Scott W. Lucas, *Havana*
Paul H. Douglas, *Chicago*

REPRESENTATIVES

William L. Dawson, *Chicago*
Barratt O'Hara, *Chicago*
Neil J. Linehan, *Chicago*
James V. Buckley, *Lansing*
Martin Gorski,[12] *Chicago*
Thomas J. O'Brien, *Chicago*
Adolph J. Sabath, *Chicago*
Thomas S. Gordon, *Chicago*
Sidney R. Yates, *Chicago*
Richard W. Hoffman, *Berwyn*
Chester A. Chesney, *Chicago*
Edgar A. Jonas, *Chicago*
Ralph E. Church,[13] *Evanston*
Chauncey W. Reed, *West Chicago*
Noah M. Mason, *Oglesby*
Leo E. Allen, *Galena*
Leslie C. Arends, *Melvin*
Harold H. Velde, *Pekin*
Robert B. Chiperfield, *Canton*
Sidney E. Simpson, *Carrollton*
Peter F. Mack, Jr., *Carlinville*
Rolla C. McMillen, *Decatur*
Edward H. Jenison, *Paris*
Charles W. Vursell, *Salem*
Charles Melvin Price, *East St. Louis*
Cecil W. (Runt) Bishop, *Carterville*

INDIANA

SENATORS

Homer E. Capehart, *Washington*
William E. Jenner, *Bedford*

REPRESENTATIVES

Ray J. Madden, *Gary*
Charles A. Halleck, *Rensselaer*
Thurman C. Crook, *South Bend*
Edward H. Kruse, Jr., *Fort Wayne*
John R. Walsh, *Anderson*
Mrs. Cecil M. Harden, *Covington*
James E. Noland, *Bloomington*
Winfield K. Denton, *Evansville*
Earl Wilson, *Bedford*
Ralph Harvey, *New Castle*
Andrew Jacobs, Sr., *Indianapolis*

IOWA

SENATORS

Bourke B. Hickenlooper, *Cedar Rapids*
Guy M. Gillette, *Cherokee*

REPRESENTATIVES

Thomas E. Martin, *Iowa City*
Henry O. Talle, *Decorah*
Harold R. Gross, *Waterloo*
Karl M. LeCompte, *Corydon*
Paul Cunningham,[14] *Des Moines*
James I. Dolliver, *Fort Dodge*
Ben F. Jensen, *Exira*
Charles B. Hoeven, *Alton*

KANSAS

SENATORS

Clyde M. Reed,[15] *Parsons*
Harry Darby,[16] *Kansas City*
Frank Carlson,[17] *Concordia*
Andrew F. Schoeppel, *Wichita*

REPRESENTATIVES

Albert M. Cole, *Holton*
Errett P. Scrivner, *Kansas City*
Herbert A. Meyer,[18] *Independence*
Myron V. George,[19] *Altamont*
Edward H. Rees, *Emporia*
Clifford R. Hope, *Garden City*
Wint Smith, *Mankato*

KENTUCKY

SENATORS

Alben W. Barkley,[20] *Paducah*
Garrett L. Withers,[21] *Dixon*
Earle C. Clements,[22] *Morganfield*
Virgil M. Chapman, *Paris*

REPRESENTATIVES

Noble J. Gregory, *Mayfield*
John A. Whitaker, *Russellville*
Thruston Ballard Morton, *Glenview*
Frank L. Chelf, *Lebanon*
Brent Spence, *Fort Thomas*
Thomas R. Underwood, *Lexington*
Carl D. Perkins, *Hindman*
Joe B. Bates, *Greenup*
James S. Golden, *Pineville*

[8] Resigned December 16, 1949.
[9] Appointed to fill vacancy caused by resignation of Raymond E. Baldwin, and took his seat January 3, 1950; subsequently elected.
[10] Died October 8, 1949.
[11] Appointed to fill vacancy caused by death of Bert H. Miller, and took his seat October 15, 1949; subsequently elected.
[12] Died December 4, 1949; vacancy throughout remainder of the Congress.
[13] Died March 21, 1950; vacancy throughout remainder of the Congress.
[14] Election unsuccessfully contested by Vincent L. Browner.
[15] Died November 8, 1949.
[16] Appointed to fill vacancy caused by death of Clyde M. Reed, and took his seat January, 3, 1950.
[17] Elected to fill vacancy caused by death of Clyde M. Reed, and took his seat November 29, 1950.
[18] Died October 2, 1950.
[19] Elected to fill vacancy caused by death of Herbert A. Meyer, and took his seat November 27, 1950.
[20] Resigned January 19, 1949, having been elected Vice President of the United States.
[21] Appointed to fill vacancy caused by resignation of Alben W. Barkley, and took his seat January 20, 1949.
[22] Elected to fill vacancy caused by resignation of Alben W. Barkley, and took his seat November 27, 1950.

LOUISIANA

SENATORS

Allen J. Ellender, Sr., *Houma*
Russell B. Long, *Baton Rouge*

REPRESENTATIVES

F. Edward Hébert, *New Orleans*
T. Hale Boggs, *New Orleans*
Edwin E. Willis, *St. Martinville*
Overton Brooks, *Shreveport*
Otto E. Passman, *Monroe*
James H. Morrison, *Hammond*
Henry D. Larcade, Jr., *Opelousas*
A. Leonard Allen, *Winnfield*

MAINE

SENATORS

Ralph O. Brewster, *Dexter*
Mrs. Margaret Chase Smith, *Skowhegan*

REPRESENTATIVES

Robert Hale, *Portland*
Charles P. Nelson, *Augusta*
Frank Fellows, *Bangor*

MARYLAND

SENATORS

Millard E. Tydings, *Havre de Grace*
Herbert R. O'Conor, *Baltimore*

REPRESENTATIVES

Edward T. Miller, *Easton*
William P. Bolton, *Towson*
Edward A. Garmatz, *Baltimore*
George H. Fallon, *Baltimore*
Lansdale G. Sasscer, *Upper Marlboro*
J. Glenn Beall, *Frostburg*

MASSACHUSETTS

SENATORS

Leverett Saltonstall, *Dover*
Henry Cabot Lodge, Jr., *Beverly*

REPRESENTATIVES

John W. Heselton, *Deerfield*
Foster Furcolo, *Longmeadow*
Philip J. Philbin, *Clinton*
Harold D. Donohue, *Worcester*
Mrs. Edith Nourse Rogers, *Lowell*
George J. Bates,[23] *Salem*
William H. Bates,[24] *Salem*
Thomas J. Lane, *Lawrence*
Angier L. Goodwin, *Melrose*
Donald W. Nicholson, *Wareham*
Christian A. Herter, *Boston*
John F. Kennedy, *Boston*
John W. McCormack, *Dorchester*
Richard B. Wigglesworth, *Milton*
Joseph W. Martin, Jr., *North Attleboro*

MICHIGAN

SENATORS

Arthur H. Vandenberg, *Grand Rapids*
Homer Ferguson, *Detroit*

REPRESENTATIVES

George G. Sadowski, *Detroit*
Earl C. Michener, *Adrian*
Paul W. Shafer, *Battle Creek*
Clare E. Hoffman, *Allegan*
Gerald R. Ford, Jr., *Grand Rapids*
William W. Blackney,[25] *Flint*
Jesse P. Wolcott, *Port Huron*
Fred L. Crawford, *Saginaw*
Albert J. Engel, *Muskegon*
Roy O. Woodruff, *Bay City*
Charles E. Potter, *Cheboygan*
John B. Bennett, *Ontonagon*
George D. O'Brien, *Detroit*
Louis C. Rabaut, *Grosse Pointe Park*
John D. Dingell, *Detroit*
John Lesinski,[26] *Dearborn*
George A. Dondero, *Royal Oak*

MINNESOTA

SENATORS

Edward J. Thye, *Northfield*
Hubert H. Humphrey, *Minneapolis*

REPRESENTATIVES

August H. Andresen, *Red Wing*
Joseph P. O'Hara, *Glencoe*
Roy W. Wier, *Minneapolis*
Eugene J. McCarthy, *St. Paul*
Walter H. Judd, *Minneapolis*
Fred Marshall, *Grove City*
H. Carl Andersen, *Tyler*
John A. Blatnik, *Chisholm*
Harold C. Hagen, *Crookston*

MISSISSIPPI

SENATORS

James O. Eastland, *Doddsville*
John C. Stennis, *De Kalb*

REPRESENTATIVES

John E. Rankin, *Tupelo*
Jamie L. Whitten, *Charleston*
William M. Whittington, *Greenwood*
Thomas G. Abernethy, *Okolona*
W. Arthur Winstead, *Philadelphia*
William M. Colmer, *Pascagoula*
John Bell Williams, *Raymond*

MISSOURI

SENATORS

Forrest C. Donnell, *Webster Groves*
James P. Kem, *Kansas City*

REPRESENTATIVES

Clare Magee, *Unionville*
Morgan M. Moulder, *Camdenton*
Philip J. Welch, *St. Joseph*
Theodore Leonard Irving, *Independence*
Richard W. Bolling, *Kansas City*
George H. Christopher, *Amoret*
Dewey Short, *Galena*
Albert S. J. Carnahan, *Ellsinore*
Clarence Cannon, *Elsberry*
Paul C. Jones, *Kennett*
John B. Sullivan, *St. Louis*
Raymond W. Karst, *St. Louis*
Frank M. Karsten, *St. Louis*

MONTANA

SENATORS

James E. Murray, *Butte*
Zales N. Ecton, *Manhattan*

REPRESENTATIVES

Mike Mansfield, *Missoula*
Wesley A. D'Ewart, *Wilsall*

NEBRASKA

SENATORS

Hugh A. Butler, *Omaha*
Kenneth S. Wherry, *Pawnee City*

REPRESENTATIVES

Carl T. Curtis, *Minden*
Eugene D. O'Sullivan, *Omaha*
Karl Stefan, *Norfolk*
Arthur L. Miller, *Kimball*

NEVADA

SENATORS

Patrick A. McCarran, *Reno*
George W. Malone, *Reno*

REPRESENTATIVE

At Large—Walter S. Baring, *Reno*

NEW HAMPSHIRE

SENATORS

H. Styles Bridges, *Concord*
Charles W. Tobey, *Temple*

REPRESENTATIVES

Chester E. Merrow, *Center Ossipee*
Norris Cotton, *Lebanon*

NEW JERSEY

SENATORS

H. Alexander Smith, *Princeton*
Robert C. Hendrickson, *Woodbury*

---

[23] Died November 1, 1949.
[24] Elected to fill vacancy caused by death of his father, George J. Bates; took his seat February 28, 1950.

[25] Election unsuccessfully contested by George D. Stevens.

[26] Died May 27, 1950; vacancy throughout remainder of the Congress.

NEW JERSEY—Continued

REPRESENTATIVES

Charles A. Wolverton, *Merchantville*
T. Millet Hand, *Cape May City*
James C. Auchincloss, *Rumson*
Charles R. Howell, *Pennington*
Charles A. Eaton, *Plainfield*
Clifford P. Case, *Rahway*
J. Parnell Thomas,[27] *Allendale*
William B. Widnall,[28] *Saddle River*
Gordon Canfield, *Paterson*
Harry L. Towe, *Rutherford*
Peter W. Rodino, Jr., *Newark*
Hugh J. Addonizio, *Newark*
Robert W. Kean, *Livingston*
Mrs. Mary T. Norton, *Jersey City*
Edward J. Hart, *Jersey City*

NEW MEXICO

SENATORS

Dennis Chavez, *Albuquerque*
Clinton P. Anderson, *Albuquerque*

REPRESENTATIVES AT LARGE

Antonio M. Fernandez, *Santa Fe*
John E. Miles, *Santa Fe*

NEW YORK

SENATORS

Robert F. Wagner,[29] *New York City*
John Foster Dulles,[30] *New York City*
Herbert H. Lehman,[31] *New York City*
Irving M. Ives, *Norwich*

REPRESENTATIVES

W. Kingsland Macy, *Islip*
Leonard W. Hall, *Oyster Bay*
Henry J. Latham, *Queens Village*
L. Gary Clemente, *Ozone Park*
T. Vincent Quinn, *Jackson Heights*
James J. Delaney, *Long Island City*
Louis B. Heller,[32] *Brooklyn*
Joseph L. Pfeifer, *Brooklyn*
Eugene J. Keogh, *Brooklyn*
Andrew L. Somers,[33] *Brooklyn*
Mrs. Edna F. Kelly,[34] *Brooklyn*
James J. Heffernan, *Brooklyn*
John J. Rooney, *Brooklyn*
Donald L. O'Toole, *Brooklyn*
Abraham J. Multer, *Brooklyn*
Emanuel Celler, *Brooklyn*
James J. Murphy, *Staten Island*
Frederic R. Coudert, Jr., *New York City*
Vito Marcantonio, *New York City*
Arthur G. Klein, *New York City*

Sol Bloom,[35] *New York City*
Franklin D. Roosevelt, Jr.,[36] *New York City*
Jacob K. Javits, *New York City*
Adam C. Powell, Jr., *New York City*
Walter A. Lynch, *New York City*
Isidore Dollinger, *New York City*
Charles A. Buckley, *New York City*
Christopher C. McGrath, *New York City*
Ralph W. Gwinn, *Bronxville*
Ralph A. Gamble, *Larchmont*
Mrs. Katharine St. George, *Tuxedo Park*
Jay LeFevre, *New Paltz*
Bernard W. Kearney, *Gloversville*
William T. Byrne, *Loudonville*
Dean P. Taylor, *Troy*
Clarence E. Kilburn, *Malone*
John C. Davies,[37] *Utica*
R. Walter Riehlman, *Tully*
Edwin Arthur Hall, *Binghamton*
John Taber, *Auburn*
W. Sterling Cole, *Bath*
Kenneth B. Keating, *Rochester*
James W. Wadsworth, Jr., *Geneseo*
William L. Pfeiffer, *Kenmore*
Anthony F. Tauriello, *Buffalo*
Chester C. Gorski, *Buffalo*
Daniel A. Reed, *Dunkirk*

NORTH CAROLINA

SENATORS

Clyde R. Hoey, *Shelby*
J. Melville Broughton,[38] *Raleigh*
Frank P. Graham,[39] *Chapel Hill*
Willis Smith,[40] *Raleigh*

REPRESENTATIVES

Herbert C. Bonner, *Washington*
John H. Kerr, *Warrenton*
Graham A. Barden, *New Bern*
Harold D. Cooley, *Nashville*
Richard Thurmond Chatham, *Winston-Salem*
Carl T. Durham, *Chapel Hill*
F. Ertel Carlyle, *Lumberton*
Charles B. Deane, *Rockingham*
Robert L. Doughton, *Sparta*
Hamilton C. Jones, *Charlotte*
Alfred L. Bulwinkle,[41] *Gastonia*
Woodrow W. Jones,[42] *Rutherfordton*
Monroe M. Redden, *Hendersonville*

NORTH DAKOTA

SENATORS

William Langer, *Wheatland*
Milton R. Young, *La Moure*

REPRESENTATIVES AT LARGE

William Lemke,[43] *Fargo*
Usher L. Burdick, *Williston*

OHIO

SENATORS

Robert A. Taft, *Cincinnati*
John W. Bricker, *Columbus*

REPRESENTATIVES

Charles H. Elston, *Cincinnati*
Earl T. Wagner, *Cincinnati*
Edward F. Breen, *Dayton*
William M. McCulloch, *Piqua*
Cliff Clevenger, *Bryan*
James G. Polk, *Highland*
Clarence J. Brown, *Blanchester*
Frederick C. Smith, *Marion*
Thomas H. Burke, *Toledo*
Thomas A. Jenkins, *Ironton*
Walter E. Brehm, *Millersport*
John M. Vorys, *Columbus*
Alvin F. Weichel, *Sandusky*
Walter B. Huber, *Akron*
Robert T. Secrest, *Senecaville*
John McSweeney, *Wooster*
J. Harry McGregor, *West Lafayette*
Wayne L. Hays, *Flushing*
Michael J. Kirwan, *Youngstown*
Michael A. Feighan,[44] *Cleveland*
Robert Crosser, *Cleveland*
Mrs. Frances P. Bolton, *Lyndhurst*
At Large—Stephen M. Young, *Cleveland*

OKLAHOMA

SENATORS

J. W. Elmer Thomas, *Medicine Park*
Robert S. Kerr, *Oklahoma City*

REPRESENTATIVES

William Franklin (Dixie) Gilmer, *Tulsa*
William G. Stigler, *Stigler*
Carl Albert, *McAlester*
Thomas J. Steed, *Shawnee*
A. S. Mike Monroney, *Oklahoma City*
Toby Morris, *Lawton*
Victor E. Wickersham, *Mangum*
George H. Wilson, *Enid*

OREGON

SENATORS

Guy Cordon, *Roseburg*
Wayne L. Morse, *Eugene*

---

[27] Resigned January 2, 1950.
[28] Elected to fill vacancy caused by resignation of J. Parnell Thomas, and took his seat February 14, 1950.
[29] Resigned June 28, 1949.
[30] Appointed to fill vacancy caused by resignation of Robert F. Wagner, and took his seat July 8, 1949.
[31] Elected to fill vacancy caused by resignation of Robert F. Wagner, and took his seat January 3, 1950.
[32] Elected to fill vacancy caused by death of Representative-elect John J. Delaney in preceding Congress, and took his seat February 28, 1949.

[33] Died April 6, 1949.
[34] Elected to fill vacancy caused by death of Andrew L. Somers, and took her seat January 3, 1950.
[35] Died March 7, 1949.
[36] Elected to fill vacancy caused by death of Sol Bloom, and took his seat June 14, 1949.
[37] Election unsuccessfully contested by Hadwen C. Fuller.
[38] Died March 6, 1949.
[39] Appointed to fill vacancy caused by death of J.

Melville Broughton, and took his seat March 29, 1949.
[40] Elected to fill vacancy caused by death of J. Melville Broughton, and took his seat November 27, 1950.
[41] Died August 31, 1950.
[42] Elected to fill vacancy caused by death of Alfred L. Bulwinkle, and took his seat November 30, 1950.
[43] Died May 30, 1950; vacancy throughout remainder of the Congress.
[44] Election unsuccessfully contested by James F. Thierry.

REPRESENTATIVES

A. Walter Norblad, Jr., *Astoria*
Lowell Stockman, *Pendleton*
Homer D. Angell, *Portland*
Harris Ellsworth, *Roseburg*

PENNSYLVANIA

SENATORS

Francis J. Myers, *Philadelphia*
Edward Martin, *Washington*

REPRESENTATIVES

William A. Barrett, *Philadelphia*
William T. Granahan, *Philadelphia*
Hardie Scott, *Philadelphia*
Earl Chudoff, *Philadelphia*
William J. Green, Jr., *Philadelphia*
Hugh D. Scott, Jr., *Philadelphia*
Benjamin F. James, *Rosemont*
Franklin H. Lichtenwalter, *Center Valley*
Paul B. Dague, *Downingtown*
Harry P. O'Neill, *Dunmore*
Daniel J. Flood, *Wilkes-Barre*
Ivor D. Fenton, *Mahanoy City*
George M. Rhodes, *Reading*
Wilson D. Gillette, *Towanda*
Robert F. Rich, *Woolrich*
Samuel K. McConnell, Jr., *Wynnewood*
Richard M. Simpson, *Huntingdon*
John C. Kunkel, *Harrisburg*
Leon H. Gavin, *Oil City*
Francis E. Walter, *Easton*
James F. Lind, *York*
James E. Van Zandt, *Altoona*
Anthony Cavalcante, *Uniontown*
Thomas E. Morgan, *Fredericktown*
Louis E. Graham, *Beaver*
Robert L. Coffey, Jr.,[45] *Johnstown*
John P. Saylor,[46] *Johnstown*
Augustine B. Kelley, *Greensburg*
Carroll D. Kearns, *Farrell*
Harry J. Davenport, *Pittsburgh*
Robert J. Corbett, *Pittsburgh*
James G. Fulton, *Pittsburgh*
Herman P. Eberharter, *Pittsburgh*
Frank Buchanan, *McKeesport*

RHODE ISLAND

SENATORS

Theodore F. Green, *Providence*
J. Howard McGrath,[47] *Providence*
Edward L. Leahy,[48] *Bristol*
John O. Pastore,[49] *Providence*

REPRESENTATIVES

Aime J. Forand, *Valley Falls*
John E. Fogarty, *Harmony*

SOUTH CAROLINA

SENATORS

Burnet R. Maybank, *Charleston*
Olin D. Johnston, *Spartanburg*

REPRESENTATIVES

L. Mendel Rivers, *Charleston*
Hugo S. Sims, Jr., *Orangeburg*
James B. Hare, *Saluda*
Joseph R. Bryson, *Greenville*
James P. Richards, *Lancaster*
John L. McMillan, *Florence*

SOUTH DAKOTA

SENATORS

J. Chandler Gurney, *Yankton*
Karl E. Mundt, *Madison*

REPRESENTATIVES

Harold O. Lovre, *Watertown*
Francis H. Case, *Custer*

TENNESSEE

SENATORS

Kenneth D. McKellar, *Memphis*
Estes Kefauver, *Chattanooga*

REPRESENTATIVES

Dayton E. Phillips, *Elizabethton*
John Jennings, Jr., *Knoxville*
James B. Frazier, Jr., *Chattanooga*
Albert A. Gore, *Carthage*
Joseph L. Evins, *Smithville*
J. Percy Priest, *Nashville*
James P. Sutton, *Lawrenceburg*
Thomas J. Murray, *Jackson*
Jere Cooper, *Dyersburg*
Clifford Davis, *Memphis*

TEXAS

SENATORS

Tom T. Connally, *Marlin*
Lyndon B. Johnson, *Johnson City*

REPRESENTATIVES

Wright Patman, *Texarkana*
Jesse M. Combs, *Beaumont*
Lindley Beckworth, *Gladewater*
Sam Rayburn, *Bonham*
J. Frank Wilson, *Dallas*
Olin E. Teague, *College Station*
Tom Pickett, *Palestine*
Albert Thomas, *Houston*
Clark W. Thompson, *Galveston*
W. Homer Thornberry, *Austin*
William R. Poage, *Waco*
Wingate H. Lucas, *Grapevine*

Ed Gossett, *Wichita Falls*
John E. Lyle, Jr., *Corpus Christi*
Lloyd M. Bentsen, Jr., *McAllen*
Kenneth M. Regan, *Midland*
Omar T. Burleson, *Anson*
Eugene Worley,[50] *Shamrock*
Ben H. Guill,[51] *Pampa*
George H. Mahon, *Colorado City*
Paul J. Kilday, *San Antonio*
O. Clark Fisher, *San Angelo*

UTAH

SENATORS

Elbert D. Thomas, *Salt Lake City*
Arthur V. Watkins, *Orem*

REPRESENTATIVES

Walter K. Granger, *Cedar City*
Mrs. Reva Z. B. Bosone, *Salt Lake City*

VERMONT

SENATORS

George D. Aiken, *Putney*
Ralph E. Flanders, *Springfield*

REPRESENTATIVE

At Large—Charles A. Plumley, *Northfield*

VIRGINIA

SENATORS

Harry Flood Byrd, *Berryville*
A. Willis Robertson, *Lexington*

REPRESENTATIVES

Schuyler Otis Bland,[52] *Newport News*
Edward J. Robeson, Jr.,[53] *Newport News*
Porter Hardy, Jr., *Churchland*
J. Vaughan Gary, *Richmond*
Watkins M. Abbitt, *Appomattox*
Thomas B. Stanley, *Stanleytown*
Clarence G. Burton, *Lynchburg*
Burr P. Harrison, *Winchester*
Howard W. Smith, *Alexandria*
Thomas B. Fugate, *Ewing*

WASHINGTON

SENATORS

Warren G. Magnuson, *Seattle*
Harry P. Cain, *Tacoma*

REPRESENTATIVES

Hugh B. Mitchell, *Seattle*
Henry M. Jackson, *Everett*
Russell V. Mack, *Hoquiam*
Hal Holmes, *Ellensburg*
Walter F. Horan, *Wenatchee*
Thor C. Tollefson, *Tacoma*

---

[45] Died April 20, 1949.
[46] Elected to fill vacancy caused by death of Robert L. Coffey, Jr., and took his seat September 28, 1949.
[47] Resigned August 23, 1949.
[48] Appointed to fill vacancy caused by resignation of J. Howard McGrath; took his seat August 24, 1949.
[49] Elected to fill vacancy caused by resignation of J. Howard McGrath, and took his seat December 19, 1950.
[50] Resigned April 3, 1950.
[51] Elected to fill vacancy caused by resignation of Eugene Worley, and took his seat May 15, 1950.
[52] Died February 16, 1950.
[53] Elected to fill vacancy caused by death of Schuyler Otis Bland, and took his seat May 11, 1950.

WEST VIRGINIA

SENATORS

Harley M. Kilgore, *Beckley*
Matthew M. Neely, *Fairmont*

REPRESENTATIVES

Robert L. Ramsay, *Follansbee*
Harley O. Staggers, *Keyser*
Cleveland M. Bailey, *Clarksburg*
Maurice G. Burnside, *Huntington*
John Kee, *Bluefield*
Erland H. Hedrick, *Beckley*

WISCONSIN

SENATORS

Alexander Wiley, *Chippewa Falls*
Joseph R. McCarthy, *Appleton*

REPRESENTATIVES

Lawrence H. Smith, *Racine*
Glenn R. Davis, *Waukesha*
Gardner R. Withrow, *La Crosse*
Clement J. Zablocki, *Milwaukee*
Andrew J. Biemiller, *Milwaukee*
Frank B. Keefe, *Oshkosh*
Reid F. Murray, *Ogdensburg*
John W. Byrnes, *Green Bay*
Merlin Hull, *Black River Falls*
Alvin E. O'Konski, *Mercer*

WYOMING

SENATORS

Joseph C. O'Mahoney, *Cheyenne*
Lester C. Hunt, *Lander*

REPRESENTATIVE

At Large—Frank A. Barrett,[54] *Lusk*

TERRITORY OF ALASKA

DELEGATE

Edward L. Bartlett, *Juneau*

TERRITORY OF HAWAII

DELEGATE

Joseph R. Farrington, *Honolulu*

PUERTO RICO

RESIDENT COMMISSIONER

A. Fernós-Isern, *Santurce*

---

[54] Resigned December 31, 1950; vacancy throughout remainder of the Congress.

EIGHTY-SECOND CONGRESS

JANUARY 3, 1951, TO JANUARY 3, 1953

FIRST SESSION—*January 3, 1951, to October 20, 1951*

SECOND SESSION—*January 8,[1] 1952, to July 7, 1952*

VICE PRESIDENT OF THE UNITED STATES—ALBEN W. BARKLEY, of Kentucky

PRESIDENT PRO TEMPORE OF THE SENATE—KENNETH D. MCKELLAR, of Tennessee

SECRETARY OF THE SENATE—LESLIE L. BIFFLE, of Arkansas

SERGEANT AT ARMS OF THE SENATE—JOSEPH C. DUKE,[2] of Arizona

SPEAKER OF THE HOUSE OF REPRESENTATIVES—SAM RAYBURN,[2] of Texas

CLERK OF THE HOUSE—RALPH R. ROBERTS,[2] of Indiana

SERGEANT AT ARMS OF THE HOUSE—JOSEPH H. CALLAHAN,[2] of Kentucky

DOORKEEPER OF THE HOUSE—WILLIAM M. MILLER,[2] of Mississippi

POSTMASTER OF THE HOUSE—FINIS E. SCOTT,[2] of Tennessee

ALABAMA

SENATORS

Lister Hill, *Montgomery*
John J. Sparkman, *Huntsville*

REPRESENTATIVES

Frank W. Boykin, *Mobile*
George M. Grant, *Troy*
George W. Andrews, *Union Springs*
Kenneth A. Roberts, *Piedmont*
Albert Rains, *Gadsden*
Edward deGraffenried, *Tuscaloosa*
Carl A. Elliott, *Jasper*
Robert E. Jones, Jr., *Scottsboro*
Laurie C. Battle, *Birmingham*

ARIZONA

SENATORS

Carl Hayden, *Phoenix*
Ernest W. McFarland, *Florence*

REPRESENTATIVES

John R. Murdock, *Tempe*
Harold A. Patten, *Tucson*

ARKANSAS

SENATORS

John L. McClellan, *Camden*
J. William Fulbright, *Fayetteville*

REPRESENTATIVES

Ezekiel C. Gathings, *West Memphis*
Wilbur D. Mills, *Kensett*
James W. Trimble, *Berryville*
Boyd Tackett, *Nashville*
Brooks Hays, *Little Rock*
William F. Norrell, *Monticello*
Oren Harris, *El Dorado*

CALIFORNIA

SENATORS

William F. Knowland, *Piedmont*
Richard M. Nixon,[3] *Whittier*
Thomas H. Kuchel,[4] *Anaheim*

REPRESENTATIVES

Hubert B. Scudder, *Sebastopol*
Clair Engle, *Red Bluff*
Leroy Johnson, *Stockton*
Franck R. Havenner, *San Francisco*
John F. Shelley, *San Francisco*
George P. Miller, *Alameda*

John J. Allen, Jr., *Oakland*
John Z. Anderson, *San Juan Bautista*
Allan O. Hunter, *Fresno*
Thomas H. Werdel, *Bakersfield*
Ernest K. Bramblett, *Pacific Grove*
Patrick J. Hillings, *Arcadia*
Norris Poulson, *Los Angeles*
Samuel W. Yorty, *Los Angeles*
Gordon L. McDonough, *Los Angeles*
Donald L. Jackson, *Pacific Palisades*
Cecil R. King, *Los Angeles*
Clyde G. Doyle, *Long Beach*
Chet Holifield, *Montebella*
Carl Hinshaw, *Pasadena*
Harry R. Sheppard, *Yucaipa*
John Phillips, *Banning*
Clinton D. McKinnon, *San Diego*

COLORADO

SENATORS

Edwin C. Johnson, *Craig*
Eugene D. Millikin, *Denver*

REPRESENTATIVES

Byron G. Rogers, *Denver*
William S. Hill, *Fort Collins*
J. Edgar Chenoweth, *Trinidad*
Wayne N. Aspinall, *Palisade*

---

[1] By joint resolution (Pub. Law 244, 82d Cong., 1st sess.), the date of assembling the second session of the Eighty-second Congress was fixed for January 8, 1952.

[2] Reelected January 3, 1951.
[3] Resigned January 1, 1953.

[4] Appointed to fill vacancy caused by resignation of Richard M. Nixon, and took his seat January 3, 1953.

CONNECTICUT

SENATORS

Brien McMahon,[5] *Norwalk*
William A. Purtell,[6] *West Hartford*
Prescott S. Bush,[7] *Greenwich*
William Benton, *Southport*

REPRESENTATIVES

Abraham A. Ribicoff, *Hartford*
Horace Seely-Brown, Jr., *Pomfret Center*
John A. McGuire, *Wallingford*
Albert P. Morano, *Greenwich*
James T. Patterson, *Naugatuck*
At Large—Antoni N. Sadlak, *Rockville*

DELAWARE

SENATORS

John J. Williams, *Millsboro*
J. Allen Frear, Jr., *Dover*

REPRESENTATIVE

At Large—J. Caleb Boggs, *Wilmington*

FLORIDA

SENATORS

Spessard L. Holland, *Bartow*
George A. Smathers, *Miami*

REPRESENTATIVES

Chester B. McMullen, *Clearwater*
Charles E. Bennett, *Jacksonville*
Robert L. F. Sikes, *Crestview*
William C. Lantaff, *Miami Springs*
Albert S. Herlong, Jr., *Leesburg*
Dwight L. Rogers, *Fort Lauderdale*

GEORGIA

SENATORS

Walter F. George, *Vienna*
Richard B. Russell, *Winder*

REPRESENTATIVES

Prince H. Preston, Jr., *Statesboro*
Edward E. Cox,[8] *Camilla*
Elijah L. Forrester, *Leesburg*
A. Sidney Camp, *Newnan*
James C. Davis, *Stone Mountain*
Carl Vinson, *Milledgeville*
Henderson L. Lanham, *Rome*
William M. Wheeler, *Alma*
John S. Wood, *Canton*
Paul Brown, *Elberton*

IDAHO

SENATORS

Henry C. Dworshak, *Burley*
Herman Welker, *Payette*

REPRESENTATIVES

John T. Wood, *Coeur d'Alene*
Hamer H. Budge, *Boise*

ILLINOIS

SENATORS

Paul H. Douglas, *Chicago*
Everett M. Dirksen, *Pekin*

REPRESENTATIVES

William L. Dawson, *Chicago*
Richard B. Vail, *Chicago*
Fred E. Busbey, *Chicago*
William E. McVey, *Harvey*
John C. Kluczynski, *Chicago*
Thomas J. O'Brien, *Chicago*
Adolph J. Sabath,[9] *Chicago*
Thomas S. Gordon, *Chicago*
Sidney R. Yates, *Chicago*
Richard W. Hoffman, *Berwyn*
Timothy P. Sheehan, *Chicago*
Edgar A. Jonas, *Chicago*
Mrs. Marguerite Stitt Church, *Evanston*
Chauncey W. Reed, *West Chicago*
Noah M. Mason, *Oglesby*
Leo E. Allen, *Galena*
Leslie C. Arends, *Melvin*
Harold H. Velde, *Pekin*
Robert B. Chiperfield, *Canton*
Sidney E. Simpson, *Carrollton*
Peter F. Mack, Jr., *Carlinville*
William L. Springer, *Champaign*
Edward H. Jenison, *Paris*
Charles W. Vursell, *Salem*
Charles Melvin Price, *East St. Louis*
Cecil W. (Runt) Bishop, *Carterville*

INDIANA

SENATORS

Homer E. Capehart, *Washington*
William E. Jenner, *Bedford*

REPRESENTATIVES

Ray J. Madden, *Gary*
Charles A. Halleck, *Rensselaer*
Shepard J. Crumpacker, Jr., *South Bend*
E. Ross Adair, *Fort Wayne*
John V. Beamer, *Wabash*
Mrs. Cecil M. Harden, *Covington*
William G. Bray, *Martinsville*
Winfield K. Denton, *Evansville*

Earl Wilson, *Bedford*
Ralph Harvey, *Mount Summit*
Charles B. Brownson, *Indianapolis*

IOWA

SENATORS

Bourke B. Hickenlooper, *Cedar Rapids*
Guy M. Gillette, *Cherokee*

REPRESENTATIVES

Thomas E. Martin, *Iowa City*
Henry O. Talle, *Decorah*
Harold R. Gross, *Waterloo*
Karl M. LeCompte, *Corydon*
Paul Cunningham, *Des Moines*
James I. Dolliver, *Fort Dodge*
Ben F. Jensen, *Exira*
Charles B. Hoeven, *Alton*

KANSAS

SENATORS

Andrew F. Schoeppel, *Wichita*
Frank Carlson, *Concordia*

REPRESENTATIVES

Albert M. Cole, *Holton*
Errett P. Scrivner, *Kansas City*
Myron V. George, *Altamont*
Edward H. Rees, *Emporia*
Clifford R. Hope, *Garden City*
Wint Smith, *Mankato*

KENTUCKY

SENATORS

Virgil M. Chapman,[10] *Paris*
Thomas R. Underwood,[11] *Lexington*
John Sherman Cooper,[12] *Somerset*
Earle C. Clements, *Morganfield*

REPRESENTATIVES

Noble J. Gregory, *Mayfield*
John A. Whitaker,[13] *Russellville*
Garrett L. Withers,[14] *Dixon*
Thruston Ballard Morton, *Glenview*
Frank L. Chelf, *Lebanon*
Brent Spence, *Fort Thomas*
Thomas R. Underwood,[15] *Lexington*
John C. Watts,[16] *Nicholasville*
Carl D. Perkins, *Hindman*
Joe B. Bates, *Greenup*
James S. Golden, *Pineville*

LOUISIANA

SENATORS

Allen J. Ellender, Sr., *Houma*
Russell B. Long, *Baton Rouge*

---

[5] Died July 28, 1952.
[6] Appointed August 29, 1952, to fill vacancy caused by death of Brien McMahon, but was unable to be sworn in as Congress was not in session.
[7] Elected to fill vacancy caused by death of Brien McMahon, and took his seat January 3, 1953.
[8] Died December 24, 1952, before the commencement of the Eighty-third Congress, to which he had been re-elected. Vacancy in the Eighty-second Congress not filled.

[9] Died November 6, 1952, before the commencement of the Eighty-third Congress, to which he had been re-elected. Vacancy in the Eighty-second Congress not filled.
[10] Died March 8, 1951.
[11] Appointed to fill vacancy caused by death of Virgil M. Chapman, and took his seat March 19, 1951.
[12] Elected November 4, 1952, to fill vacancy caused by death of Virgil M. Chapman, and took his seat January 3, 1953.

[13] Died December 15, 1951.
[14] Elected August 2, 1952, to fill vacancy caused by death of John A. Whitaker, but was unable to be sworn in as Congress was not in session.
[15] Resigned March 17, 1951.
[16] Elected April 14, 1951, to fill vacancy caused by resignation of Thomas R. Underwood, and took his seat April 23, 1951.

REPRESENTATIVES

F. Edward Hébert, *New Orleans*
T. Hale Boggs, *New Orleans*
Edwin E. Willis, *St. Martinville*
Overton Brooks, *Shreveport*
Otto E. Passman, *Monroe*
James H. Morrison, *Hammond*
Henry D. Larcade, Jr., *Opelousas*
A. Leonard Allen, *Winnfield*

MAINE

SENATORS

Ralph O. Brewster,[17] *Dexter*
Mrs. Margaret Chase Smith, *Skowhegan*

REPRESENTATIVES

Robert Hale, *Portland*
Charles P. Nelson, *Augusta*
Frank Fellows,[18] *Bangor*
Clifford G. McIntire,[19] *Perham*

MARYLAND

SENATORS

Herbert R. O'Conor, *Baltimore*
John Marshall Butler, *Baltimore*

REPRESENTATIVES

Edward T. Miller, *Easton*
James P. S. Devereux, *Stevenson*
Edward A. Garmatz, *Baltimore*
George H. Fallon, *Baltimore*
Lansdale G. Sasscer, *Upper Marlboro*
J. Glenn Beall, *Frostburg*

MASSACHUSETTS

SENATORS

Leverett Saltonstall, *Dover*
Henry Cabot Lodge, Jr., *Beverly*

REPRESENTATIVES

John W. Heselton, *Deerfield*
Foster Furcolo,[20] *Longmeadow*
Philip J. Philbin, *Clinton*
Harold D. Donohue, *Worcester*
Mrs. Edith Nourse Rogers, *Lowell*
William H. Bates, *Salem*
Thomas J. Lane, *Lawrence*
Angier L. Goodwin, *Melrose*
Donald W. Nicholson, *Wareham*
Christian A. Herter, *Boston*
John F. Kennedy, *Boston*
John W. McCormack, *Dorchester*
Richard B. Wigglesworth, *Milton*
Joseph W. Martin, Jr., *North Attleboro*

MICHIGAN

SENATORS

Arthur H. Vandenberg,[21] *Grand Rapids*
Arthur Edson Blair Moody,[22] *Detroit*
Charles E. Potter,[23] *Cheboygan*
Homer Ferguson, *Detroit*

REPRESENTATIVES

Thaddeus M. Machrowicz, *Hamtramck*
George Meader, *Ann Arbor*
Paul W. Shafer, *Battle Creek*
Clare E. Hoffman, *Allegan*
Gerald R. Ford, Jr., *Grand Rapids*
William W. Blackney, *Flint*
Jesse P. Wolcott, *Port Huron*
Fred L. Crawford, *Saginaw*
Miss Ruth Thompson, *Whitehall*
Roy O. Woodruff, *Bay City*
Charles E. Potter,[24] *Cheboygan*
John B. Bennett, *Ontonagon*
George D. O'Brien, *Detroit*
Louis C. Rabaut, *Grosse Pointe Park*
John D. Dingell, *Detroit*
John Lesinski, Jr., *Dearborn*
George A. Dondero, *Royal Oak*

MINNESOTA

SENATORS

Edward J. Thye, *Northfield*
Hubert H. Humphrey, *Minneapolis*

REPRESENTATIVES

August H. Andresen, *Red Wing*
Joseph P. O'Hara, *Glencoe*
Roy W. Wier, *Minneapolis*
Eugene J. McCarthy, *St. Paul*
Walter H. Judd, *Minneapolis*
Fred Marshall, *Grove City*
H. Carl Andersen, *Tyler*
John A. Blatnik, *Chisholm*
Harold C. Hagen, *Crookston*

MISSISSIPPI

SENATORS

James O. Eastland, *Doddsville*
John C. Stennis, *De Kalb*

REPRESENTATIVES

John E. Rankin, *Tupelo*
Jamie L. Whitten, *Charleston*
Frank E. Smith, *Greenwood*
Thomas G. Abernethy, *Okolona*
W. Arthur Winstead, *Philadelphia*
William M. Colmer, *Pascagoula*
John Bell Williams, *Raymond*

MISSOURI

SENATORS

James P. Kem, *Kansas City*
Thomas C. Hennings, Jr., *St. Louis*

REPRESENTATIVES

Clare Magee, *Unionville*
Morgan M. Moulder, *Camdenton*
Philip J. Welch, *St. Joseph*
Theodore Leonard Irving, *Independence*
Richard W. Bolling, *Kansas City*
Orland K. Armstrong, *Springfield*
Dewey Short, *Galena*
Albert S. J. Carnahan, *Ellsinore*
Clarence Cannon, *Elsberry*
Paul C. Jones, *Kennett*
John B. Sullivan,[25] *St. Louis*
Claude I. Bakewell,[26] *St. Louis*
Thomas B. Curtis, *Webster Groves*
Frank M. Karsten, *St. Louis*

MONTANA

SENATORS

James E. Murray, *Butte*
Zales N. Ecton, *Manhattan*

REPRESENTATIVES

Mike Mansfield, *Missoula*
Wesley A. D'Ewart, *Wilsall*

NEBRASKA

SENATORS

Hugh A. Butler, *Omaha*
Kenneth S. Wherry,[27] *Pawnee City*
Frederick A. Seaton,[28] *Hastings*
Dwight P. Griswold,[29] *Scotts Bluff*

REPRESENTATIVES

Carl T. Curtis, *Minden*
Howard H. Buffett, *Omaha*
Karl Stefan,[30] *Norfolk*
Robert D. Harrison,[31] *Norfolk*
Arthur L. Miller, *Kimball*

NEVADA

SENATORS

Patrick A. McCarran, *Reno*
George W. Malone, *Reno*

REPRESENTATIVE

At Large—Walter S. Baring, *Reno*

---

[17] Resigned December 31, 1952.
[18] Died August 27, 1951.
[19] Elected October 22, 1951, to fill vacancy caused by death of Frank Fellows; took his seat January 8, 1952.
[20] Resigned September 30, 1952; vacancy throughout remainder of the Congress.
[21] Died April 18, 1951.
[22] Appointed to fill vacancy caused by death of Arthur H. Vandenberg, and took his seat April 25, 1951.

[23] Elected November 4, 1952, to fill vacancy caused by death of Arthur H. Vandenberg; also elected to full term, and took his seat January 3, 1953.
[24] Resigned November 4, 1952; vacancy throughout remainder of the Congress.
[25] Died January 29, 1951.
[26] Elected March 9, 1951, to fill vacancy caused by death of John B. Sullivan, and took his seat March 19, 1951.
[27] Died November 29, 1951.

[28] Appointed to fill vacancy caused by death of Kenneth S. Wherry, and took his seat January 8, 1952.
[29] Elected November 4, 1952, to fill vacancy caused by death of Kenneth S. Wherry, and took his seat January 3, 1953.
[30] Died October 2, 1951.
[31] Elected December 4, 1951, to fill vacancy caused by death of Karl Stefan, and took his seat January 8, 1952.

NEW HAMPSHIRE

SENATORS

H. Styles Bridges, *Concord*
Charles W. Tobey, *Temple*

REPRESENTATIVES

Chester E. Merrow, *Center Ossipee*
Norris Cotton, *Lebanon*

NEW JERSEY

SENATORS

H. Alexander Smith, *Princeton*
Robert C. Hendrickson, *Woodbury*

REPRESENTATIVES

Charles A. Wolverton, *Merchantville*
T. Millet Hand, *Cape May City*
James C. Auchincloss, *Rumson*
Charles R. Howell, *Pennington*
Charles A. Eaton, *Watchung*
Clifford P. Case, *Rahway*
William B. Widnall, *Saddle River*
Gordon Canfield, *Paterson*
Harry L. Towe,[32] *Tenafly*
Frank C. Osmers, Jr.,[33] *Haworth*
Peter W. Rodino, Jr., *Newark*
Hugh J. Addonizio, *Newark*
Robert W. Kean, *Livingston*
Alfred D. Sieminski, *Jersey City*
Edward J. Hart, *Jersey City*

NEW MEXICO

SENATORS

Dennis Chavez, *Albuquerque*
Clinton P. Anderson, *Albuquerque*

REPRESENTATIVES AT LARGE

Antonio M. Fernandez, *Santa Fe*
John J. Dempsey, *Santa Fe*

NEW YORK

SENATORS

Irving M. Ives, *Norwich*
Herbert H. Lehman, *New York City*

REPRESENTATIVES

Ernest Greenwood, *Bay Shore*
Leonard W. Hall,[34] *Oyster Bay*
Henry J. Latham, *Queens Village*
L. Gary Clemente, *Ozone Park*
T. Vincent Quinn,[35] *Jackson Heights*
Robert Tripp Ross,[36] *Jackson Heights*
James J. Delaney, *Long Island City*
Louis B. Heller, *Brooklyn*
Victor L. Anfuso, *Brooklyn*

Eugene J. Keogh, *Brooklyn*
Mrs. Edna F. Kelly, *Brooklyn*
James J. Heffernan, *Brooklyn*
John J. Rooney, *Brooklyn*
Donald L. O'Toole, *Brooklyn*
Abraham J. Multer, *New York City*
Emanuel Celler, *Brooklyn*
James J. Murphy, *Staten Island*
Frederic R. Coudert, Jr., *New York City*
James G. Donovan, *New York City*
Arthur G. Klein, *New York City*
Franklin D. Roosevelt, Jr., *New York City*
Jacob K. Javits, *New York City*
Adam C. Powell, Jr., *New York City*
Sidney A. Fine, *New York City*
Isidore Dollinger, *New York City*
Charles A. Buckley, *New York City*
Christopher C. McGrath, *New York City*
Ralph W. Gwinn, *Bronxville*
Ralph A. Gamble, *Larchmont*
Mrs. Katharine St. George, *Tuxedo Park*
J. Ernest Wharton, *Richmondville*
Bernard W. Kearney, *Gloversville*
William T. Byrne,[37] *Loudonville*
Leo W. O'Brien,[38] *Albany*
Dean P. Taylor, *Troy*
Clarence E. Kilburn, *Malone*
William R. Willams, *Cassville*
R. Walter Riehlman, *Tully*
Edwin Arthur Hall, *Binghamton*
John Taber, *Auburn*
W. Sterling Cole, *Bath*
Kenneth B. Keating, *Rochester*
Harold C. Ostertag, *Attica*
William E. Miller, *Lockport*
Edmund P. Radwan, *Buffalo*
John C. Butler, *Buffalo*
Daniel A. Reed, *Dunkirk*

NORTH CAROLINA

SENATORS

Clyde R. Hoey, *Shelby*
Willis Smith, *Raleigh*

REPRESENTATIVES

Herbert C. Bonner, *Washington*
John H. Kerr, *Warrenton*
Graham A. Barden, *New Bern*
Harold D. Cooley, *Nashville*
Richard Thurmond Chatham, *Winston-Salem*
Carl T. Durham, *Chapel Hill*
F. Ertel Carlyle, *Lumberton*
Charles B. Deane, *Rockingham*
Robert L. Doughton, *Laurel Springs*
Hamilton C. Jones, *Charlotte*
Woodrow W. Jones, *Rutherfordton*
Monroe M. Redden, *Hendersonville*

NORTH DAKOTA

SENATORS

William Langer, *Wheatland*
Milton R. Young, *La Moure*

REPRESENTATIVES AT LARGE

Usher L. Burdick, *Williston*
Fred G. Aandahl, *Litchville*

OHIO

SENATORS

Robert A. Taft, *Cincinnati*
John W. Bricker, *Columbus*

REPRESENTATIVES

Charles H. Elston, *Cincinnati*
William E. Hess, *Cincinnati*
Edward F. Breen,[39] *Dayton*
Paul F. Schenck,[40] *Dayton*
William M. McCulloch, *Piqua*
Cliff Clevenger, *Bryan*
James G. Polk, *Highland*
Clarence J. Brown, *Blanchester*
Jackson E. Betts, *Findlay*
Henry Frazier Reams, *Toledo*
Thomas A. Jenkins, *Ironton*
Walter E. Brehm, *Millersport*
John M. Vorys, *Columbus*
Alvin F. Weichel, *Sandusky*
William H. Ayres, *Akron*
Robert T. Secrest, *Senacaville*
Frank T. Bow, *Canton*
J. Harry McGregor, *West Lafayette*
Wayne L. Hays, *Flushing*
Michael J. Kirwan, *Youngstown*
Michael A. Feighan, *Cleveland*
Robert Crosser, *Cleveland*
Mrs. Frances P. Bolton, *Lyndhurst*
At Large—George H. Bender, *Chagrin Falls*

OKLAHOMA

SENATORS

Robert S. Kerr, *Oklahoma City*
A. S. Mike Monroney, *Oklahoma City*

REPRESENTATIVES

George B. Schwabe,[41] *Tulsa*
William G. Stigler,[42] *Stigler*
Carl Albert, *McAlester*
Thomas J. Steed, *Shawnee*
John Jarman, *Oklahoma City*
Toby Morris, *Lawton*
Victor E. Wickersham, *Mangum*
Page H. Belcher, *Enid*

---

[32] Resigned September 7, 1951.
[33] Elected November 6, 1951, to fill vacancy caused by resignation of Harry L. Towe, and took his seat January 8, 1952.
[34] Resigned December 31, 1952; vacancy throughout remainder of the Congress.
[35] Resigned December 30, 1951.

[36] Elected February 19, 1952, to fill vacancy caused by resignation of T. Vincent Quinn, and took his seat February 26, 1952.
[37] Died January 27, 1952.
[38] Elected April 1, 1952, to fill vacancy caused by death of William T. Byrne, and took his seat April 9, 1952.

[39] Resigned October 1, 1951.
[40] Elected November 6, 1951, to fill vacancy caused by resignation of Edward F. Breen, and took his seat January 8, 1952.
[41] Died April 2, 1952; vacancy throughout remainder of the Congress.
[42] Died August 21, 1952; vacancy throughout remainder of the Congress.

OREGON

SENATORS

Guy Cordon, *Roseberg*
Wayne L. Morse, *Eugene*

REPRESENTATIVES

A. Walter Norblad, Jr., *Astoria*
Lowell Stockman, *Pendleton*
Homer D. Angell, *Portland*
Harris Ellsworth, *Roseberg*

PENNSYLVANIA

SENATORS

Edward Martin, *Washington*
James H. Duff, *Carnegie*

REPRESENTATIVES

William A. Barrett, *Philadelphia*
William T. Granahan, *Philadelphia*
Hardie Scott, *Philadelphia*
Earl Chudoff, *Philadelphia*
William J. Green, Jr., *Philadelphia*
Hugh D. Scott, Jr., *Philadelphia*
Benjamin F. James, *Rosemont*
Albert C. Vaughn,[43] *Fullerton*
Karl C. King,[44] *Morrisville*
Paul B. Dague, *Downingtown*
Harry P. O'Neill, *Dunmore*
Daniel J. Flood, *Wilkes-Barre*
Ivor D. Fenton, *Mahanoy City*
George M. Rhodes, *Reading*
Wilson D. Gillette,[45] *Towanda*
Joseph L. Carrigg,[46] *Susquehanna*
Alvin R. Bush, *Muncy*
Samuel K. McConnell, Jr., *Wynnewood*
Richard M. Simpson, *Huntingdon*
Walter M. Mumma, *Harrisburg*
Leon H. Gavin, *Oil City*
Francis E. Walter, *Easton*
James F. Lind, *York*
James E. Van Zandt, *Altoona*
Edward L. Sittler, Jr., *Uniontown*
Thomas E. Morgan, *Fredericktown*
Louis E. Graham, *Beaver*
John P. Saylor, *Johnstown*
Augustine B. Kelley, *Greensburg*
Carroll D. Kearns, *Farrell*
Harmar D. Denny, Jr., *Pittsburgh*
Robert J. Corbett, *Pittsburgh*
James G. Fulton, *Pittsburgh*
Herman P. Eberharter, *Pittsburgh*
Frank Buchanan,[47] *McKeesport*
Mrs. Vera D. Buchanan,[48] *McKeesport*

RHODE ISLAND

SENATORS

Theodore F. Green, *Providence*
John O. Pastore, *Providence*

REPRESENTATIVES

Aime J. Forand, *Cumberland*
John E. Fogarty, *Harmony*

SOUTH CAROLINA

SENATORS

Burnet R. Maybank, *Charleston*
Olin D. Johnston, *Spartanburg*

REPRESENTATIVES

L. Mendel Rivers, *Charleston*
John J. Riley, *Sumter*
W. J. Bryan Dorn, *Greenwood*
Joseph R. Bryson, *Greenville*
James P. Richards, *Lancaster*
John L. McMillan, *Florence*

SOUTH DAKOTA

SENATORS

Karl E. Mundt, *Madison*
Francis H. Case, *Custer*

REPRESENTATIVES

Harold O. Lovre, *Watertown*
Ellis Y. Berry, *McLaughlin*

TENNESSEE

SENATORS

Kenneth D. McKellar, *Memphis*
Estes Kefauver, *Chattanooga*

REPRESENTATIVES

B. Carroll Reece, *Johnson City*
Howard H. Baker, *Huntsville*
James B. Frazier, Jr., *Chattanooga*
Albert A. Gore, *Carthage*
Joseph L. Evins, *Smithville*
J. Percy Priest, *Nashville*
James P. Sutton, *Lawrenceburg*
Thomas J. Murray, *Jackson*
Jere Cooper, *Dyersburg*
Clifford Davis, *Memphis*

TEXAS

SENATORS

Tom T. Connally, *Marlin*
Lyndon B. Johnson, *Johnson City*

REPRESENTATIVES

Wright Patman, *Texarkana*
Jesse M. Combs, *Beaumont*
Lindley Beckworth, *Gladewater*
Sam Rayburn, *Bonham*
J. Frank Wilson, *Dallas*
Olin E. Teague, *College Station*
Tom Pickett,[49] *Palestine*
John V. Dowdy,[50] *Athens*
Albert Thomas, *Houston*
Clark W. Thompson, *Galveston*

W. Homer Thornberry, *Austin*
William R. Poage, *Waco*
Wingate H. Lucas, *Grapevine*
Ed Gossett,[51] *Wichita Falls*
Frank N. Ikard,[52] *Wichita Falls*
John E. Lyle, Jr., *Corpus Christi*
Lloyd M. Bentsen, Jr., *McAllen*
Kenneth M. Regan, *Midland*
Omar T. Burleson, *Anson*
Walter E. Rogers, *Pampa*
George H. Mahon, *Lubbock*
Paul J. Kilday, *San Antonio*
O. Clark Fisher, *San Angelo*

UTAH

SENATORS

Arthur V. Watkins, *Orem*
Wallace F. Bennett, *Salt Lake City*

REPRESENTATIVES

Walter K. Granger, *Cedar City*
Mrs. Reva Z. B. Bosone, *Salt Lake City*

VERMONT

SENATORS

George D. Aiken, *Putney*
Ralph E. Flanders, *Springfield*

REPRESENTATIVE

At Large—Winston L. Prouty, *Newport*

VIRGINIA

SENATORS

Harry Flood Byrd, *Berryville*
A. Willis Robertson, *Lexington*

REPRESENTATIVES

Edward J. Robeson, Jr., *Newport News*
Porter Hardy, Jr., *Churchland*
J. Vaughan Gary, *Richmond*
Watkins M. Abbitt, *Appomattox*
Thomas B. Stanley, *Stanleytown*
Clarence G. Burton, *Lynchburg*
Burr P. Harrison, *Winchester*
Howard W. Smith, *Alexandria*
Thomas B. Fugate, *Ewing*

WASHINGTON

SENATORS

Warren G. Magnuson, *Seattle*
Harry P. Cain, *Tacoma*

REPRESENTATIVES

Hugh B. Mitchell, *Seattle*
Henry M. Jackson, *Everett*
Russell V. Mack, *Hoquiam*
Hal Holmes, *Ellensburg*
Walter F. Horan, *Wenatchee*
Thor C. Tollefson, *Tacoma*

---

[43] Died September 1, 1951.
[44] Elected November 6, 1951, to fill vacancy caused by death of Albert C. Vaughn, and took his seat January 8, 1952.
[45] Died August 7, 1951.
[46] Elected November 6, 1951, to fill vacancy caused by death of Wilson D. Gillette, and took his seat January 8, 1952.
[47] Died April 27, 1951.
[48] Elected July 24, 1951, to fill vacancy caused by death of Frank Buchanan, and took her seat August 1, 1951.
[49] Resigned June 30, 1952.
[50] Elected September 23, 1952, to fill vacancy caused by resignation of Tom Pickett, but was unable to be sworn in as Congress was not in session.
[51] Resigned July 31, 1951.
[52] Elected September 8, 1951, to fill vacancy caused by resignation of Ed Gossett, and took his seat September 17, 1951.

WEST VIRGINIA

SENATORS

Harley M. Kilgore, *Beckley*
Matthew M. Neely, *Fairmont*

REPRESENTATIVES

Robert L. Ramsay, *Follansbee*
Harley O. Staggers, *Keyser*
Cleveland M. Bailey, *Clarksburg*
Maurice G. Burnside, *Huntington*
John Kee,[53] *Bluefield*
Mrs. Maude Elizabeth Kee,[54] *Bluefield*
Erland H. Hedrick, *Beckley*

WISCONSIN

SENATORS

Alexander Wiley, *Chippewa Falls*
Joseph R. McCarthy, *Appleton*

REPRESENTATIVES

Lawrence H. Smith, *Racine*
Glenn R. Davis, *Waukesha*
Gardner R. Withrow, *La Crosse*
Clement J. Zablocki, *Milwaukee*
Charles J. Kersten, *Milwaukee*
William K. Van Pelt, *Fond du Lac*
Reid F. Murray,[55] *Ogdensburg*
John W. Byrnes, *Green Bay*
Merlin Hull, *Black River Falls*
Alvin E. O'Konski, *Mercer*

WYOMING

SENATORS

Joseph C. O'Mahoney, *Cheyenne*
Lester C. Hunt, *Lander*

REPRESENTATIVE

At Large—William H. Harrison, *Sheridan*

TERRITORY OF ALASKA

DELEGATE

Edward L. Bartlett, *Juneau*

TERRITORY OF HAWAII

DELEGATE

Joseph R. Farrington, *Honolulu*

COMMONWEALTH OF PUERTO RICO [56]

RESIDENT COMMISSIONER

A. Fernós-Isern, *Santurce*

---

[53] Died May 8, 1951.
[54] Elected July 17, 1951, to fill vacancy caused by death of her husband, John Kee, and took her seat July 26, 1951.

[55] Died April 29, 1952; vacancy throughout remainder of the Congress.

[56] Became a Commonwealth by enactment of Public Law 447, 82d Congress (66 Stat. 327), effective July 25, 1952.

EIGHTY-THIRD CONGRESS

JANUARY 3, 1953, TO JANUARY 3, 1955

FIRST SESSION—*January 3, 1953, to August 3, 1953*

SECOND SESSION—*January 6,[1] 1954, to December 2,[2] 1954*

VICE PRESIDENT OF THE UNITED STATES—ALBEN W. BARKLEY,[3] of Kentucky; RICHARD M. NIXON,[4] of California

PRESIDENT PRO TEMPORE OF THE SENATE—STYLES BRIDGES,[5] of New Hampshire

SECRETARY OF THE SENATE—J. MARK TRICE,[5] of Maryland

SERGEANT AT ARMS OF THE SENATE—FOREST A. HARNESS,[5] of Indiana

---

SPEAKER OF THE HOUSE OF REPRESENTATIVES—JOSEPH W. MARTIN, Jr.,[5] of Massachusetts

CLERK OF THE HOUSE—LYLE O. SNADER,[5] of Illinois

SERGEANT AT ARMS OF THE HOUSE—WILLIAM F. RUSSELL,[6] of Pennsylvania; LYLE O. SNADER,[7] of Illinois; WILLIAM R. BONSELL,[8] of Pennsylvania

DOORKEEPER OF THE HOUSE—TOM KENNAMER,[5] of Missouri

POSTMASTER OF THE HOUSE—BEECHER HESS,[5] of Ohio

ALABAMA

SENATORS

Lister Hill, *Montgomery*
John J. Sparkman, *Huntsville*

REPRESENTATIVES

Frank W. Boykin, *Mobile*
George M. Grant, *Troy*
George W. Andrews, *Union Springs*
Kenneth A. Roberts, *Piedmont*
Albert Rains, *Gadsden*
Armistead I. Selden, Jr., *Greensboro*
Carl A. Elliott, *Jasper*
Robert E. Jones, Jr., *Scottsboro*
Laurie C. Battle, *Birmingham*

ARIZONA

SENATORS

Carl Hayden, *Phoenix*
Barry M. Goldwater, *Phoenix*

REPRESENTATIVES

John J. Rhodes, *Mesa*
Harold A. Patten, *Tucson*

ARKANSAS

SENATORS

John L. McClellan, *Camden*
J. William Fulbright, *Fayetteville*

REPRESENTATIVES

Ezekiel C. Gathings, *West Memphis*
Wilbur D. Mills, *Kensett*
James W. Trimble, *Berryville*
Oren Harris, *El Dorado*
Brooks Hays, *Little Rock*
William F. Norrell, *Monticello*

CALIFORNIA

SENATORS

William F. Knowland, *Piedmont*
Thomas H. Kuchel, *Anaheim*

REPRESENTATIVES

Hubert B. Scudder, *Sebastopol*
Clair Engle, *Red Bluff*
John E. Moss, Jr., *Sacramento*
William S. Mailliard, *San Francisco*

John F. Shelley, *San Francisco*
Robert L. Condon, *Walnut Creek*
John J. Allen, Jr., *Oakland*
George P. Miller, *Alameda*
J. Arthur Younger, *San Mateo*
Charles S. Gubser, *Gilroy*
Leroy Johnson, *Stockton*
Allan O. Hunter, *Fresno*
Ernest K. Bramblett, *Pacific Grove*
Harlan F. Hagen, *Hanford*
Gordon L. McDonough, *Los Angeles*
Donald L. Jackson, *Pacific Palisades*
Cecil R. King, *Los Angeles*
Craig Hosmer, *Long Beach*
Chet Holifield, *Montebello*
Carl Hinshaw, *Pasadena*
Edgar W. Hiestand, *Altadena*
Joseph F. Holt, *Van Nuys*
Clyde G. Doyle, *South Gate*
Norris Poulson,[9] *Los Angeles*
Glenard P. Lipscomb,[10] *Los Angeles*
Patrick J. Hillings, *Arcadia*
Samuel W. Yorty, *Los Angeles*
Harry R. Sheppard, *Yucaipa*
James B. Utt, *Santa Ana*
John Phillips, *Banning*
Robert C. Wilson, *Chula Vista*

---

[1] By joint resolution (Pub. Law 199, 83d Cong., 1st sess.) the date of assembling the second session of the Eighty-third Congress was fixed for January 6, 1954.
[2] The House adjourned sine die August 20, 1954, and the Senate adjourned sine die December 2, 1954.
[3] Term expired at noon January 20, 1953.

[4] Term began at noon January 20, 1953.
[5] Elected January 3, 1953.
[6] Elected January 3, 1953; died July 7, 1953.
[7] Served from July 8, 1953, to September 15, 1953, to fill vacancy.

[8] Appointed September 15, 1953.
[9] Resigned June 11, 1953.
[10] Elected to fill vacancy caused by resignation of Norris Paulson, and took his seat January 6, 1954.

COLORADO

SENATORS

Edwin C. Johnson, *Craig*
Eugene D. Millikin, *Denver*

REPRESENTATIVES

Byron G. Rogers, *Denver*
William S. Hill, *Fort Collins*
J. Edgar Chenoweth, *Trinidad*
Wayne N. Aspinall, *Palisade*

CONNECTICUT

SENATORS

Prescott S. Bush, *Greenwich*
William A. Purtell, *West Hartford*

REPRESENTATIVES

Thomas J. Dodd, *West Hartford*
Horace Seely-Brown, Jr., *Pomfret Center*
Albert W. Cretella, *North Haven*
Albert P. Morano, *Greenwich*
James T. Patterson, *Watertown*
At Large—Antoni N. Sadlak, *Rockville*

DELAWARE

SENATORS

John J. Williams, *Millsboro*
J. Allen Frear, Jr., *Dover*

REPRESENTATIVE

At Large—Herbert B. Warburton, *Wilmington*

FLORIDA

SENATORS

Spessard L. Holland, *Bartow*
George A. Smathers, *Miami*

REPRESENTATIVES

Courtney W. Campbell, *Clearwater*
Charles E. Bennett, *Jacksonville*
Robert L. F. Sikes, *Crestview*
William C. Lantaff, *Miami Springs*
Albert S. Herlong, Jr., *Leesburg*
Dwight L. Rogers,[11] *Fort Lauderdale*
James A. Haley, *Sarasota*
Donald R. Matthews, *Gainesville*

GEORGIA

SENATORS

Walter F. George, *Vienna*
Richard B. Russell, *Winder*

REPRESENTATIVES

Prince H. Preston, Jr., *Statesboro*
John L. Pilcher,[12] *Meigs*
Elijah L. Forrester, *Leesburg*

A. Sidney Camp,[13] *Newnan*
John James Flynt, Jr.,[14] *Griffin*
James C. Davis, *Stone Mountain*
Carl Vinson, *Milledgeville*
Henderson L. Lanham, *Rome*
William M. Wheeler, *Alma*
Phillip M. Landrum, *Jasper*
Paul Brown, *Elberton*

IDAHO

SENATORS

Henry C. Dworshak, *Burley*
Herman Welker, *Payette*

REPRESENTATIVES

Mrs. Gracie B. Pfost, *Nampa*
Hamer H. Budge, *Boise*

ILLINOIS

SENATORS

Paul H. Douglas, *Chicago*
Everett M. Dirksen, *Pekin*

REPRESENTATIVES

William L. Dawson, *Chicago*
Barratt O'Hara, *Chicago*
Fred E. Busbey, *Chicago*
William E. McVey, *Harvey*
John C. Kluczynski, *Chicago*
Thomas J. O'Brien, *Chicago*
James B. Bowler,[15] *Chicago*
Thomas S. Gordon, *Chicago*
Sidney R. Yates, *Chicago*
Richard W. Hoffman, *Riverside*
Timothy P. Sheehan, *Chicago*
Edgar A. Jonas, *Chicago*
Mrs. Marguerite Stitt Church, *Evanston*
Chauncey W. Reed, *West Chicago*
Noah M. Mason, *Oglesby*
Leo E. Allen, *Galena*
Leslie C. Arends, *Melvin*
Harold H. Velde, *Pekin*
Robert B. Chiperfield, *Canton*
Sidney E. Simpson, *Carrollton*
Peter F. Mack, Jr., *Carlinville*
William L. Springer, *Champaign*
Charles W. Vursell, *Salem*
Charles Melvin Price, *East St. Louis*
Cecil W. (Runt) Bishop, *Carterville*

INDIANA

SENATORS

Homer E. Capehart, *Washington*
William E. Jenner, *Bedford*

REPRESENTATIVES

Ray J. Madden, *Gary*
Charles A. Halleck, *Rensselaer*
Shepard J. Crumpacker, Jr., *South Bend*

E. Ross Adair, *Fort Wayne*
John V. Beamer, *Wabash*
Mrs. Cecil M. Harden, *Covington*
William G. Bray, *Martinsville*
D. Bailey Merrill, *Evansville*
Earl Wilson, *Bedford*
Ralph Harvey, *Mount Summit*
Charles B. Brownson, *Indianapolis*

IOWA

SENATORS

Bourke B. Hickenlooper, *Cedar Rapids*
Guy M. Gillette, *Cherokee*

REPRESENTATIVES

Thomas E. Martin, *Iowa City*
Henry O. Talle, *Decorah*
Harold R. Gross, *Waterloo*
Karl M. LeCompte, *Corydon*
Paul Cunningham, *Des Moines*
James I. Dolliver, *Fort Dodge*
Ben F. Jensen, *Exira*
Charles B. Hoeven, *Alton*

KANSAS

SENATORS

Andrew F. Schoeppel, *Wichita*
Frank Carlson, *Concordia*

REPRESENTATIVES

Howard S. Miller, *Hiawatha*
Errett P. Scrivner, *Kansas City*
Myron V. George, *Altamont*
Edward H. Rees, *Emporia*
Clifford R. Hope, *Garden City*
Wint Smith, *Mankato*

KENTUCKY

SENATORS

Earle C. Clements, *Morganfield*
John Sherman Cooper, *Somerset*

REPRESENTATIVES

Noble J. Gregory, *Mayfield*
Garrett L. Withers,[16] *Dixon*
William H. Natcher,[17] *Bowling Green*
John M. Robsion, Jr., *Louisville*
Frank L. Chelf, *Lebanon*
Brent Spence, *Fort Thomas*
John C. Watts, *Nicholasville*
Carl D. Perkins, *Hindman*
James S. Golden, *Pineville*

LOUISIANA

SENATORS

Allen J. Ellender, Sr., *Houma*
Russell B. Long, *Baton Rouge*

---

[11] Died December 1, 1954, before the commencement of the Eighty-fourth Congress to which he had been reelected. Vacancy in the Eighty-third Congress not filled.
[12] Elected to fill vacancy caused by death of Representative-elect Edward E. Cox, in preceding Congress,

and took his seat February 9, 1953.
[13] Died July 24, 1954.
[14] Elected November 2, 1954, to fill vacancy caused by death of A. Sidney Camp, but was unable to be sworn in as Congress was not in session.
[15] Elected to fill vacancy caused by death of Repre-

sentative-elect Adolph J. Sabath, in preceding Congress, and took his seat July 13, 1953.
[16] Died April 30, 1953.
[17] Elected to fill vacancy caused by death of Garrett L. Withers, and took his seat January 6, 1954.

REPRESENTATIVES

F. Edward Hébert, *New Orleans*
T. Hale Boggs, *New Orleans*
Edwin E. Willis, *St. Martinville*
Overton Brooks, *Shreveport*
Otto E. Passman, *Monroe*
James H. Morrison, *Hammond*
T. Ashton Thompson, *Ville Platte*
George S. Long, *Pineville*

MAINE

SENATORS

Mrs. Margaret Chase Smith, *Skowhegan*
Frederick G. Payne, *Waldoboro*

REPRESENTATIVES

Robert Hale, *Portland*
Charles P. Nelson, *Augusta*
Clifford G. McIntire, *Perham*

MARYLAND

SENATORS

John Marshall Butler, *Baltimore*
J. Glenn Beall, *Frostburg*

REPRESENTATIVES

Edward T. Miller, *Easton*
James P. S. Devereux, *Stevenson*
Edward A. Garmatz, *Baltimore*
George H. Fallon, *Baltimore*
Frank Small, Jr., *Clinton*
DeWitt S. Hyde, *Bethesda*
Samuel N. Friedel, *Baltimore*

MASSACHUSETTS

SENATORS

Leverett Saltonstall, *Dover*
John F. Kennedy, *Boston*

REPRESENTATIVES

John W. Heselton, *Deerfield*
Edward P. Boland, *Springfield*
Philip J. Philbin, *Clinton*
Harold D. Donohue, *Worcester*
Mrs. Edith Nourse Rogers, *Lowell*
William H. Bates, *Salem*
Thomas J. Lane, *Lawrence*
Angier L. Goodwin, *Melrose*
Donald W. Nicholson, *Wareham*
Laurence Curtis, *Boston*
Thomas P. O'Neill, Jr., *Cambridge*
John W. McCormack, *Dorchester*
Richard B. Wigglesworth, *Milton*
Joseph W. Martin, Jr., *North Attleboro*

MICHIGAN

SENATORS

Homer Ferguson, *Detroit*
Charles E. Potter, *Cheboygan*

REPRESENTATIVES

Thaddeus M. Machrowicz, *Hamtramck*
George Meader, *Ann Arbor*
Paul W. Shafer,[18] *Battle Creek*
Clare E. Hoffman, *Allegan*
Gerald R. Ford, Jr., *Grand Rapids*
Kit Clardy, *East Lansing*
Jesse P. Wolcott, *Port Huron*
Alvin M. Bentley, *Owosso*
Miss Ruth Thompson, *Whitehall*
Elford A. Cederberg, *Bay City*
Victor A. Knox, *Sault Ste. Marie*
John B. Bennett, *Ontonagon*
George D. O'Brien, *Detroit*
Louis C. Rabaut, *Grosse Pointe Park*
John D. Dingell, *Detroit*
John Lesinski, Jr., *Dearborn*
Charles G. Oakman, *Detroit*
George A. Dondero, *Royal Oak*

MINNESOTA

SENATORS

Edward J. Thye, *Northfield*
Hubert H. Humphrey, *Minneapolis*

REPRESENTATIVES

August H. Andresen, *Red Wing*
Joseph P. O'Hara, *Glencoe*
Roy W. Wier, *Minneapolis*
Eugene J. McCarthy, *St. Paul*
Walter H. Judd, *Minneapolis*
Fred Marshall, *Grove City*
H. Carl Andersen, *Tyler*
John A. Blatnik, *Chisholm*
Harold C. Hagen, *Crookston*

MISSISSIPPI

SENATORS

James O. Eastland, *Doddsville*
John C. Stennis, *De Kalb*

REPRESENTATIVES

Thomas G. Abernethy, *Okolona*
Jamie L. Whitten, *Charleston*
Frank E. Smith, *Greenwood*
John Bell Williams, *Raymond*
W. Arthur Winstead, *Philadelphia*
William M. Colmer, *Pascagoula*

MISSOURI

SENATORS

Thomas C. Hennings, Jr., *St. Louis*
Stuart Symington, *Creve Coeur*

REPRESENTATIVES

Frank M. Karsten, *St. Louis*
Thomas B. Curtis, *Webster Groves*
Mrs. Leonor Kretzer Sullivan, *St. Louis*
Jeffrey P. Hillelson, *Independence*
Richard W. Bolling, *Kansas City*
William C. Cole, *St. Joseph*
Dewey Short, *Galena*
Albert S. J. Carnahan, *Ellsinore*
Clarence Cannon, *Elsberry*
Paul C. Jones, *Kennett*
Morgan M. Moulder, *Camdenton*

MONTANA

SENATORS

James E. Murray, *Butte*
Mike Mansfield, *Missoula*

REPRESENTATIVES

Lee Metcalf, *Helena*
Wesley A. D'Ewart, *Wilsall*

NEBRASKA

SENATORS

Hugh A. Butler,[19] *Omaha*
Sam W. Reynolds,[20] *Omaha*
Roman L. Hruska,[21] *Omaha*
Dwight P. Griswold,[22] *Scottsbluff*
Mrs. Eva K. Bowring,[23] *Merriman*
Mrs. Hazel H. Abel,[24] *Lincoln*
Carl T. Curtis,[25] *Minden*

REPRESENTATIVES

Carl T. Curtis,[26] *Minden*
Roman L. Hruska,[27] *Omaha*
Robert D. Harrison, *Norfolk*
Arthur L. Miller, *Kimball*

NEVADA

SENATORS

Patrick A. McCarran,[28] *Reno*
Ernest S. Brown,[29] *Reno*
Alan H. Bible,[30] *Reno*
George W. Malone, *Reno*

REPRESENTATIVE

At Large—Clifton Young, *Reno*

---

[18] Died August 17, 1954; vacancy throughout remainder of the Congress.
[19] Died July 1, 1954.
[20] Appointed to fill vacancy caused by death of Hugh A. Butler, and took his seat July 7, 1954.
[21] Elected November 2, 1954, to fill vacancy caused by death of Hugh A. Butler, and took his seat November 8, 1954.
[22] Died April 12, 1954.

[23] Appointed to fill vacancy caused by death of Dwight P. Griswold, and took her seat April 26, 1954.
[24] Elected November 2, 1954, to fill vacancy caused by death of Dwight P. Griswold, and took her seat November 8, 1954; resigned December 31, 1954.
[25] Appointed January 1, 1954, to fill vacancy caused by resignation of Hazel H. Abel, but was unable to be sworn in as Congress was not in session.
[26] Resigned December 31, 1954; vacancy throughout remainder of the Congress.

[27] Resigned November 8, 1954; vacancy throughout remainder of the Congress.
[28] Died September 28, 1954.
[29] Appointed to fill vacancy caused by death of Patrick A. McCarran, and took his seat November 8, 1954.
[30] Elected November 2, 1954, to fill vacancy caused by death of Patrick A. McCarran, and took his seat December 2, 1954.

NEW HAMPSHIRE

SENATORS

H. Styles Bridges, *Concord*
Charles W. Tobey,[31] *Temple*
Robert W. Upton,[32] *Concord*
Norris Cotton,[33] *Lebanon*

REPRESENTATIVES

Chester E. Merrow, *Center Ossipee*
Norris Cotton,[34] *Lebanon*

NEW JERSEY

SENATORS

H. Alexander Smith, *Princeton*
Robert C. Hendrickson, *Woodbury*

REPRESENTATIVES

Charles A. Wolverton, *Merchantville*
T. Millet Hand, *Cape May City*
James C. Auchincloss, *Rumson*
Charles R. Howell, *Pennington*
Peter H. B. Frelinghuysen, Jr., *Morristown*
Clifford P. Case,[35] *Rahway*
Harrison A. Williams, Jr.,[36] *Plainfield*
William B. Widnall, *Saddle River*
Gordon Canfield, *Paterson*
Frank C. Osmers, Jr., *Haworth*
Peter W. Rodino, Jr., *Newark*
Hugh J. Addonizio, *Newark*
Robert W. Kean, *Livingston*
Alfred D. Sieminski, *Jersey City*
Edward J. Hart, *Jersey City*

NEW MEXICO

SENATORS

Dennis Chavez, *Albuquerque*
Clinton P. Anderson, *Albuquerque*

REPRESENTATIVES AT LARGE

Antonio M. Fernandez, *Santa Fe*
John J. Dempsey, *Santa Fe*

NEW YORK

SENATORS

Irving M. Ives, *Norwich*
Herbert H. Lehman, *New York City*

REPRESENTATIVES

Stuyvesant Wainwright 2d, *Wainscott*
Steven B. Derounian, *Roslyn*
Frank J. Becker, *Lynbrook*
Henry J. Latham, *Queens Village*
Albert H. Bosch, *Richmond Hill*

Lester Holtzman, *Rego Park*
James J. Delaney, *Long Island City*
Louis B. Heller,[37] *Brooklyn*
Eugene J. Keogh, *Brooklyn*
Mrs. Edna F. Kelly, *Brooklyn*
Emanuel Celler, *Brooklyn*
Francis E. Dorn, *Brooklyn*
Abraham J. Multer, *Brooklyn*
John J. Rooney, *Brooklyn*
John H. Ray, *Staten Island*
Adam C. Powell, Jr., *New York City*
Frederic R. Coudert, Jr., *New York City*
James G. Donovan, *New York City*
Arthur G. Klein, *New York City*
Franklin D. Roosevelt, Jr., *New York City*
Jacob K. Javits,[38] *New York City*
Sidney A. Fine, *New York City*
Isidore Dollinger, *New York City*
Charles A. Buckley, *New York City*
Paul A. Fino, *New York City*
Ralph A. Gamble, *Larchmont*
Ralph W. Gwinn, *Bronxville*
Mrs. Katharine St. George, *Tuxedo Park*
J. Ernest Wharton, *Richmondville*
Leo W. O'Brien, *Albany*
Dean P. Taylor, *Troy*
Bernard W. Kearney, *Gloversville*
Clarence E. Kilburn, *Malone*
William R. Williams, *Cassville*
R. Walter Riehlman, *Tully*
John Taber, *Auburn*
W. Sterling Cole, *Bath*
Kenneth B. Keating, *Rochester*
Harold C. Ostertag, *Attica*
William E. Miller, *Lockport*
Edmund P. Radwan, *Buffalo*
John R. Pillion, *Lackawanna*
Daniel A. Reed, *Dunkirk*

NORTH CAROLINA

SENATORS

Clyde R. Hoey,[39] *Shelby*
Samuel J. Ervin, Jr.,[40] *Morganton*
Willis Smith,[41] *Raleigh*
Alton A. Lennon,[42] *Wilmington*
W. Kerr Scott,[43] *Haw River*

REPRESENTATIVES

Herbert C. Bonner, *Washington*
Lawrence H. Fountain, *Tarboro*
Graham A. Barden, *New Bern*
Harold D. Cooley, *Nashville*
Richard Thurmond Chatham, *Elkin*
Carl T. Durham, *Chapel Hill*
F. Ertel Carlyle, *Lumberton*

Charles B. Deane, *Rockingham*
Hugh Q. Alexander, *Kannapolis*
Charles Raper Jonas, *Lincolnton*
Woodrow W. Jones, *Rutherfordton*
George A. Shuford, *Asheville*

NORTH DAKOTA

SENATORS

William Langer, *Wheatland*
Milton R. Young, *La Moure*

REPRESENTATIVES AT LARGE

Usher L. Burdick, *Williston*
Otto Krueger, *Fessenden*

OHIO

SENATORS

Robert A. Taft,[44] *Cincinnati*
Thomas A. Burke,[45] *Cleveland*
George H. Bender,[46] *Chagrin Falls*
John W. Bricker, *Columbus*

REPRESENTATIVES

Gordon H. Scherer, *Cincinnati*
William E. Hess, *Cincinnati*
Paul F. Schenck, *Dayton*
William M. McCulloch, *Piqua*
Cliff Clevenger, *Bryan*
James G. Polk, *Highland*
Clarence J. Brown, *Blanchester*
Jackson E. Betts, *Findlay*
Henry Frazier Reams, *Toledo*
Thomas A. Jenkins, *Ironton*
Oliver P. Bolton, *Mentor*
John M. Vorys, *Columbus*
Alvin F. Weichel, *Sandusky*
William H. Ayers, *Akron*
Robert T. Secrest,[47] *Senecaville*
Frank T. Bow, *Canton*
J. Harry McGregor, *West Lafayette*
Wayne L. Hayes, *Flushing*
Michael J. Kirwan, *Youngstown*
Michael A. Feighan, *Cleveland*
Robert Crosser, *Cleveland*
Mrs. Frances P. Bolton, *Lyndhurst*
George H. Bender,[48] *Chagrin Falls*

OKLAHOMA

SENATORS

Robert S. Kerr, *Oklahoma City*
A. S. Mike Monroney, *Oklahoma City*

REPRESENTATIVES

Page H. Belcher, *Enid*
Edmond Edmondson, *Muskogee*

---

[31] Died July 24, 1953.
[32] Appointed to fill vacancy caused by death of Charles W. Tobey, and took his seat January 6, 1954.
[33] Elected November 2, 1954, to fill vacancy caused by death of Charles W. Tobey, and took his seat November 8, 1954.
[34] Resigned November 7, 1954; vacancy throughout remainder of the Congress.
[35] Resigned August 16, 1953.
[36] Elected to fill vacancy caused by resignation of Clifford P. Case, and took his seat January 6, 1954.

[37] Resigned July 21, 1954; vacancy throughout remainder of the Congress.
[38] Resigned December 31, 1954; vacancy throughout remainder of the Congress.
[39] Died May 12, 1954.
[40] Appointed to fill vacancy caused by death of Clyde R. Hoey, and took his seat June 11, 1954; subsequently elected.
[41] Died June 26, 1953.
[42] Appointed to fill vacancy caused by death of Willis Smith, and took his seat July 15, 1953.

[43] Elected to fill vacancy caused by death of Willis Smith, and took his seat November 29, 1954.
[44] Died July 31, 1953.
[45] Appointed to fill vacancy caused by death of Robert A. Taft, and took his seat January 6, 1954.
[46] Elected November 2, 1954, to fill vacancy caused by death of Robert A. Taft, but was unable to be sworn in as Congress was not in session.
[47] Resigned September 26, 1954; vacancy throughout remainder of the Congress.
[48] Resigned December 15, 1954; vacancy throughout remainder of the Congress.

Carl Albert, *McAlester*
Thomas J. Steed, *Shawnee*
John Jarman, *Oklahoma City*
Victor E. Wickersham, *Mangum*

OREGON

SENATORS

Guy Cordon, *Roseburg*
Wayne L. Morse, *Eugene*

REPRESENTATIVES

A. Walter Norblad, *Stayton*
Samuel H. Coon, *Baker*
Homer D. Angell, *Portland*
Harris Ellsworth, *Roseburg*

PENNSYLVANIA

SENATORS

Edward Martin, *Washington*
James H. Duff, *Carnegie*

REPRESENTATIVES

William A. Barrett, *Philadelphia*
William T. Granahan, *Philadelphia*
James A. Byrne, *Philadelphia*
Earl Chudoff, *Philadelphia*
William J. Green, Jr., *Philadelphia*
Hugh D. Scott, Jr., *Philadelphia*
Benjamin F. James, *Rosemont*
Karl C. King, *Morrisville*
Paul B. Dague, *Downingtown*
Joseph L. Carrigg, *Susquehanna*
Edward J. Bonin, *Hazleton*
Ivor D. Fenton, *Mahanoy City*
Samuel K. McConnell, Jr., *Wynnewood*
George M. Rhodes, *Reading*
Francis E. Walter, *Easton*
Walter M. Mumma, *Harrisburg*
Alvin R. Bush, *Muncy*
Richard M. Simpson, *Huntingdon*
S. Walter Stauffer, *York*
James E. Van Zandt, *Altoona*
Augustine B. Kelly, *Greensburg*
John P. Saylor, *Johnstown*
Leon H. Gavin, *Oil City*
Carroll D. Kearns, *Farrell*
Louis E. Graham, *Beaver*
Thomas E. Morgan, *Fredericktown*
James G. Fulton, *Pittsburgh*
Herman P. Eberharter, *Pittsburgh*
Robert J. Corbett, *Pittsburgh*
Mrs. Vera D. Buchanan, *McKeesport*

RHODE ISLAND

SENATORS

Theodore F. Green, *Providence*
John O. Pastore, *Providence*

REPRESENTATIVES

Aime J. Forand, *Cumberland*
John E. Fogarty, *Harmony*

SOUTH CAROLINA

SENATORS

Burnet R. Maybank,[49] *Charleston*
Charles E. Daniel,[50] *Greenville*
James Strom Thurmond,[51] *Aiken*
Olin D. Johnston, *Spartanburg*

REPRESENTATIVES

L. Mendel Rivers, *Charleston*
John J. Riley, *Sumter*
W. J. Bryan Dorn, *Greenwood*
Joseph R. Bryson,[52] *Greenville*
Robert T. Ashmore,[53] *Greenville*
James P. Richards, *Lancaster*
John L. McMillan, *Florence*

SOUTH DAKOTA

SENATORS

Karl E. Mundt, *Madison*
Francis H. Case, *Custer*

REPRESENTATIVES

Harold O. Lovre, *Watertown*
Ellis Y. Berry, *McLaughlin*

TENNESSEE

SENATORS

Estes Kefauver, *Chattanooga*
Albert A. Gore, *Carthage*

REPRESENTATIVES

B. Carroll Reece, *Johnson City*
Howard H. Baker, *Huntsville*
James B. Frazier, Jr., *Chattanooga*
Joseph L. Evins, *Smithville*
J. Percy Priest, *Nashville*
James P. Sutton, *Lawrenceburg*
Thomas J. Murray, *Jackson*
Jere Cooper, *Dyersburg*
Clifford Davis, *Memphis*

TEXAS

SENATORS

Lyndon B. Johnson, *Johnson City*
Marion Price Daniel, *Liberty*

REPRESENTATIVES

Wright Patman, *Texarkana*
Jack B. Brooks, *Beaumont*
Brady P. Gentry, *Tyler*
Sam Rayburn, *Bonham*
J. Frank Wilson, *Dallas*
Olin E. Teague, *College Station*

John V. Dowdy, *Athens*
Albert Thomas, *Houston*
Clark W. Thompson, *Galveston*
W. Homer Thornberry, *Austin*
William R. Poage, *Waco*
Wingate H. Lucas, *Grapevine*
Frank N. Ikard, *Wichita Falls*
John E. Lyle, Jr., *Corpus Christi*
Lloyd M. Bentsen, Jr., *McAllen*
Kenneth M. Regan, *Midland*
Omar T. Burleson, *Anson*
Walter E. Rogers, *Pampa*
George H. Mahon, *Lubbock*
Paul J. Kilday, *San Antonio*
O. Clark Fisher, *San Angelo*
At Large—Martin Dies, Jr., *Lufkin*

UTAH

SENATORS

Arthur V. Watkins, *Orem*
Wallace F. Bennett, *Salt Lake City*

REPRESENTATIVES

Douglas R. Stringfellow, *Ogden*
William A. Dawson, *Salt Lake City*

VERMONT

SENATORS

George D. Aiken, *Putney*
Ralph E. Flanders, *Springfield*

REPRESENTATIVE

At Large—Winston L. Prouty, *Newport*

VIRGINIA

SENATORS

Harry Flood Byrd, *Berryville*
A. Willis Robertson, *Lexington*

REPRESENTATIVES

Edward J. Robeson, Jr., *Warwick*
Porter Hardy, Jr., *Churchland*
J. Vaughan Gary, *Richmond*
Watkins M. Abbitt, *Appomattox*
Thomas B. Stanley,[54] *Stanleytown*
William M. Tuck,[55] *South Boston*
Richard H. Poff, *Radford*
Burr P. Harrison, *Winchester*
Howard W. Smith, *Broad Run*
William C. Wampler, *Bristol*
Joel T. Broyhill, *Arlington*

WASHINGTON

SENATORS

Warren G. Magnuson, *Seattle*
Henry M. Jackson, *Everett*

---

[49] Died September 1, 1954.
[50] Appointed to fill vacancy caused by death of Burnet R. Maybank, and took his seat November 8, 1954; resigned December 23, 1954.
[51] Appointed December 24, 1954, to fill vacancy caused by the death of Burnet R. Maybank, but was unable to be sworn in as Congress was not in session.
[52] Died March 10, 1953.
[53] Elected to fill vacancy caused by death of Joseph R. Bryson, and took his seat June 15, 1953.
[54] Resigned February 3, 1953.
[55] Elected to fill vacancy caused by resignation of Thomas B. Stanley, and took his seat April 21, 1953.

WASHINGTON—Continued

REPRESENTATIVES

Thomas M. Pelly, *Seattle*
Alfred John Westland, *Everett*
Russell V. Mack, *Hoquiam*
Hal Holmes, *Ellensburg*
Walter F. Horan, *Wenatchee*
Thor C. Tollefson, *Tacoma*
At Large—Don Magnuson, *Seattle*

WEST VIRGINIA

SENATORS

Harley M. Kilgore, *Beckley*
Matthew M. Neely, *Fairmont*

REPRESENTATIVES

Robert H. Mollohan, *Fairmont*
Harley O. Staggers, *Keyser*
Cleveland M. Bailey, *Clarksburg*
William E. Neal, *Huntington*
Mrs. Maude Elizabeth Kee, *Bluefield*
Robert C. Byrd, *Beckley*

WISCONSIN

SENATORS

Alexander Wiley, *Chippewa Falls*
Joseph R. McCarthy, *Appleton*

REPRESENTATIVES

Lawrence H. Smith, *Racine*
Glenn R. Davis, *Waukesha*
Gardner R. Withrow, *La Crosse*
Clement J. Zablocki, *Milwaukee*
Charles J. Kersten, *Milwaukee*
William K. Van Pelt, *Fond du Lac*
Melvin R. Laird, *Marshfield*
John W. Byrnes, *Green Bay*
Merlin Hull,[56] *Black River Falls*
Lester R. Johnson,[57] *Black River Falls*
Alvin E. O'Konski, *Mercer*

WYOMING

SENATORS

Lester C. Hunt,[58] *Lander*
Edward D. Crippa,[59] *Rock Springs*

Joseph C. O'Mahoney,[60] *Cheyenne*
Frank A. Barrett, *Lusk*

REPRESENTATIVE

At Large—William H. Harrison, *Sheridan*

TERRITORY OF ALASKA

DELEGATE

Edward L. Bartlett, *Juneau*

TERRITORY OF HAWAII

DELEGATE

Joseph R. Farrington,[61] *Honolulu*
Mrs. Mary Elizabeth Pruett Farrington,[62] *Honolulu*

COMMONWEALTH OF PUERTO RICO

RESIDENT COMMISSIONER

A. Fernós-Isern, *Santurce*

---

[56] Died May 17, 1953.
[57] Elected to fill vacancy caused by death of Merlin Hull, and took his seat January 6, 1954.
[58] Died June 19, 1954.

[59] Appointed to fill vacancy caused by death of Lester C. Hunt, and took his seat June 28, 1954.
[60] Elected to fill vacancy caused by death of Lester C. Hunt, and took his seat November 29, 1954.

[61] Died June 19, 1954.
[62] Elected to fill vacancy caused by death of her husband, Joseph R. Farrington, and took her seat August 4, 1954.

EIGHTY-FOURTH CONGRESS

JANUARY 3, 1955, TO JANUARY 3, 1957

FIRST SESSION—*January 5,*[1] *1955, to August 2, 1955*
SECOND SESSION—*January 3, 1956, to July 27, 1956*

———

VICE PRESIDENT OF THE UNITED STATES—RICHARD M. NIXON, of California
PRESIDENT PRO TEMPORE OF THE SENATE—WALTER F. GEORGE,[2] of Georgia
SECRETARY OF THE SENATE—FELTON McLELLAN JOHNSTON,[2] of Mississippi
SERGEANT AT ARMS OF THE SENATE—JOSEPH C. DUKE,[2] of Arizona

———

SPEAKER OF THE HOUSE OF REPRESENTATIVES—SAM RAYBURN,[2] of Texas
CLERK OF THE HOUSE—RALPH R. ROBERTS,[2] of Indiana
SERGEANT AT ARMS OF THE HOUSE—ZEAKE W. JOHNSON, JR.,[2] of Tennessee
DOORKEEPER OF THE HOUSE—WILLIAM M. MILLER,[2] of Mississippi
POSTMASTER OF THE HOUSE—H. H. MORRIS,[2] of Kentucky

ALABAMA

SENATORS

Lister Hill, *Montgomery*
John J. Sparkman, *Huntsville*

REPRESENTATIVES

Frank W. Boykin, *Mobile*
George M. Grant, *Troy*
George W. Andrews, *Union Springs*
Kenneth A. Roberts, *Anniston*
Albert Rains, *Gadsden*
Armistead I. Selden, Jr., *Greensboro*
Carl A. Elliott, *Jasper*
Robert E. Jones, Jr., *Scottsboro*
George Huddleston, Jr., *Birmingham*

ARIZONA

SENATORS

Carl Hayden, *Phoenix*
Barry M. Goldwater, *Phoenix*

REPRESENTATIVES

John J. Rhodes, *Mesa*
Stewart L. Udall, *Tucson*

ARKANSAS

SENATORS

John L. McClellan, *Camden*
J. William Fulbright, *Fayetteville*

REPRESENTATIVES

Ezekiel C. Gathings, *West Memphis*
Wilbur D. Mills, *Kensett*
James W. Trimble, *Berryville*
Oren Harris, *El Dorado*
Brooks Hays, *Little Rock*
William F. Norrell, *Monticello*

CALIFORNIA

SENATORS

William F. Knowland, *Piedmont*
Thomas H. Kuchel, *Anaheim*

REPRESENTATIVES

Hubert B. Scudder, *Sebastopol*
Clair Engle, *Red Bluff*
John E. Moss, Jr., *Sacramento*
William S. Mailliard, *San Francisco*
John F. Shelley, *San Francisco*
John F. Baldwin, Jr., *Martinez*
John J. Allen, Jr., *Oakland*
George P. Miller, *Alameda*

J. Arthur Younger, *San Mateo*
Charles S. Gubser, *Gilroy*
Leroy Johnson, *Stockton*
Bernice F. Sisk, *Fresno*
Charles M. Teague, *Ojai*
Harlan F. Hagen, *Hanford*
Gordon L. McDonough, *Los Angeles*
Donald L. Jackson, *Pacific Palisades*
Cecil R. King, *Los Angeles*
Craig Hosmer, *Long Beach*
Chet Holifield, *Montebello*
Carl Hinshaw,[3] *Pasadena*
Edgar W. Hiestand, *Altadena*
Joseph F. Holt, *Van Nuys*
Clyde G. Doyle, *South Gate*
Glenard P. Lipscomb, *Los Angeles*
Patrick J. Hillings, *Arcadia*
James Roosevelt, *Los Angeles*
Harry R. Sheppard, *Yucaipa*
James B. Utt, *Santa Ana*
John Phillips, *Banning*
Robert C. Wilson, *Chula Vista*

COLORADO

SENATORS

Eugene D. Millikin, *Denver*
Gordon L. Allott, *Lamar*

---

[1] By joint resolution (Pub. Law 700, 83d Cong., 2d sess.) the date of assemblying the first session of the Eighty-fourth Congress was fixed for January 5, 1955.
[2] Elected January 5, 1955.
[3] Died August 5, 1956; vacancy throughout remainder of the Congress.

31671 O–61—28

COLORADO—Continued

REPRESENTATIVES

Byron G. Rogers, *Denver*
William S. Hill, *Fort Collins*
J. Edgar Chenoweth, *Trinidad*
Wayne N. Aspinall, *Palisade*

CONNECTICUT

SENATORS

Prescott S. Bush, *Greenwich*
William A. Purtell, *West Hartford*

REPRESENTATIVES

Thomas J. Dodd, *West Hartford*
Horace Seely-Brown, Jr., *Pomfret Center*
Albert W. Cretella, *North Haven*
Albert P. Morano, *Greenwich*
James T. Patterson, *Watertown*
At Large—Antoni N. Sadlak, *Rockville*

DELAWARE

SENATORS

John J. Williams, *Millsboro*
J. Allen Frear, Jr., *Dover*

REPRESENTATIVE

At Large—Harris B. McDowell, Jr., *Middletown*

FLORIDA

SENATORS

Spessard L. Holland, *Bartow*
George A. Smathers, *Miami*

REPRESENTATIVES

William C. Cramer, *St. Petersburg*
Charles E. Bennett, *Jacksonville*
Robert L. F. Sikes, *Crestview*
Dante B. Fascell, *Miami*
Albert S. Herlong, Jr., *Leesburg*
Paul G. Rogers,[4] *West Palm Beach*
James A. Haley, *Sarasota*
Donald R. Matthews, *Gainesville*

GEORGIA

SENATORS

Walter F. George, *Vienna*
Richard B. Russell, *Winder*

REPRESENTATIVES

Prince H. Preston, Jr., *Statesboro*
John L. Pilcher, *Meigs*
Elijah L. Forrester, *Leesburg*
John James Flynt, Jr., *Griffin*
James C. Davis, *Stone Mountain*
Carl Vinson, *Milledgeville*
Henderson L. Lanham, *Rome*

Mrs. Iris F. Blitch, *Homerville*
Phillip M. Landrum, *Jasper*
Paul Brown, *Elberton*

IDAHO

SENATORS

Henry C. Dworshak, *Burley*
Herman Welker, *Payette*

REPRESENTATIVES

Mrs. Gracie B. Pfost, *Nampa*
Hamer H. Budge, *Boise*

ILLINOIS

SENATORS

Paul H. Douglas, *Chicago*
Everett M. Dirksen, *Pekin*

REPRESENTATIVES

William L. Dawson, *Chicago*
Barratt O'Hara, *Chicago*
James C. Murray, *Chicago*
William E. McVey, *Harvey*
John C. Kluczynski, *Chicago*
Thomas J. O'Brien, *Chicago*
James B. Bowler, *Chicago*
Thomas S. Gordon, *Chicago*
Sidney R. Yates, *Chicago*
Richard W. Hoffman, *Riverside*
Timothy P. Sheehan, *Chicago*
Charles A. Boyle, *Chicago*
Mrs. Marguerite Stitt Church, *Evanston*
Chauncey W. Reed,[5] *West Chicago*
Noah M. Mason, *Oglesby*
Leo E. Allen, *Galena*
Leslie C. Arends, *Melvin*
Harold H. Velde, *Pekin*
Robert B. Chiperfield, *Canton*
Sidney E. Simpson, *Carrollton*
Peter F. Mack, Jr., *Carlinville*
William L. Springer, *Champaign*
Charles W. Vursell, *Salem*
Charles Melvin Price, *East St. Louis*
Kenneth J. Gray, *West Frankfort*

INDIANA

SENATORS

Homer E. Capehart, *Washington*
William E. Jenner, *Bedford*

REPRESENTATIVES

Ray J. Madden, *Gary*
Charles A. Halleck, *Rensselaer*
Shepard J. Crumpacker, Jr., *South Bend*
E. Ross Adair, *Fort Wayne*
John V. Beamer, *Wabash*
Mrs. Cecil M. Harden, *Covington*
William G. Bray, *Martinsville*
Winfield K. Denton, *Evansville*

Earl Wilson, *Bedford*
Ralph Harvey, *Mount Summit*
Charles B. Brownson, *Indianapolis*

IOWA

SENATORS

Bourke B. Hickenlooper, *Cedar Rapids*
Thomas E. Martin, *Iowa City*

REPRESENTATIVES

Frederick D. Schwengel, *Davenport*
Henry O. Talle, *Decorah*
Harold R. Gross, *Waterloo*
Karl M. LeCompte, *Corydon*
Paul Cunningham, *Des Moines*
James I. Dolliver, *Fort Dodge*
Ben F. Jensen, *Exira*
Charles B. Hoeven, *Alton*

KANSAS

SENATORS

Andrew F. Schoeppel, *Wichita*
Frank Carlson, *Concordia*

REPRESENTATIVES

William H. Avery, *Wakefield*
Errett P. Scrivner, *Kansas City*
Myron V. George, *Altamont*
Edward H. Rees, *Emporia*
Clifford R. Hope, *Garden City*
Wint Smith, *Mankato*

KENTUCKY

SENATORS

Earle C. Clements, *Morganfield*
Alben W. Barkley,[6] *Paducah*
Robert Humphreys,[7] *Frankfort*
John Sherman Cooper,[8] *Somerset*

REPRESENTATIVES

Noble J. Gregory, *Mayfield*
William H. Natcher, *Bowling Green*
John M. Robsion, Jr., *Louisville*
Frank L. Chelf, *Lebanon*
Brent Spence, *Fort Thomas*
John C. Watts, *Nicholasville*
Carl D. Perkins, *Hindman*
Eugene Siler, *Williamsburg*

LOUISIANA

SENATORS

Allen J. Ellender, Sr., *Houma*
Russell B. Long, *Baton Rouge*

REPRESENTATIVES

F. Edward Hébert, *New Orleans*
T. Hale Boggs, *New Orleans*
Edwin E. Willis, *St. Martinville*
Overton Brooks, *Shreveport*

---

[4] Elected to fill vacancy caused by death of his father, Representative-elect Dwight L. Rogers, in the preceding Congress, and took his seat January 13, 1955.

[5] Died February 9, 1956; vacancy throughout remainder of the Congress.
[6] Died April 30, 1956.
[7] Appointed to fill vacancy caused by death of Alben W. Barkley, and took his seat June 25, 1956.
[8] Elected to fill vacancy caused by death of Alben W. Barkley, and took his seat January 3, 1957.

Otto E. Passman, *Monroe*
James H. Morrison, *Hammond*
T. Ashton Thompson, *Ville Platte*
George S. Long, *Pineville*

MAINE

SENATORS

Mrs. Margaret Chase Smith, *Skowhegan*
Frederick G. Payne, *Waldoboro*

REPRESENTATIVES

Robert Hale, *Portland*
Charles P. Nelson, *Waterville*
Clifford G. McIntire, *Perham*

MARYLAND

SENATORS

John Marshall Butler, *Baltimore*
J. Glenn Beall, *Frostburg*

REPRESENTATIVES

Edward T. Miller, *Easton*
James P. S. Devereux, *Stevenson*
Edward A. Garmatz, *Baltimore*
George H. Fallon, *Baltimore*
Richard E. Lankford, *Annapolis*
DeWitt S. Hyde, *Bethesda*
Samuel N. Friedel, *Baltimore*

MASSACHUSETTS

SENATORS

Leverett Saltonstall, *Dover*
John F. Kennedy, *Boston*

REPRESENTATIVES

John W. Heselton, *Deerfield*
Edward P. Boland, *Springfield*
Philip J. Philbin, *Clinton*
Harold D. Donohue, *Worcester*
Mrs. Edith Nourse Rogers, *Lowell*
William H. Bates, *Salem*
Thomas J. Lane, *Lawrence*
Torbert H. Macdonald, *Malden*
Donald W. Nicholson, *Wareham*
Laurence Curtis, *Boston*
Thomas P. O'Neill, Jr., *Cambridge*
John W. McCormack, *Dorchester*
Richard B. Wigglesworth, *Milton*
Joseph W. Martin, Jr., *North Attleboro*

MICHIGAN

SENATORS

Charles E. Potter, *Cheboygan*
Patrick V. McNamara, *Detroit*

REPRESENTATIVES

Thaddeus M. Machrowicz, *Hamtramck*
George Meader, *Ann Arbor*
August E. Johansen, *Battle Creek*

Clare E. Hoffman, *Allegan*
Gerald R. Ford, Jr., *Grand Rapids*
Don Hayworth, *East Lansing*
Jesse P. Wolcott, *Port Huron*
Alvin M. Bentley, *Owosso*
Miss Ruth Thompson, *Whitehall*
Elford A. Cederberg, *Bay City*
Victor A. Knox, *Sault Ste. Marie*
John B. Bennett, *Ontonagon*
Charles C. Diggs, Jr., *Detroit*
Louis C. Rabaut, *Grosse Pointe Park*
John D. Dingell,[9] *Detroit*
John D. Dingell, Jr.,[10] *Detroit*
John Lesinski, Jr., *Dearborn*
Mrs. Martha W. Griffiths, *Detroit*
George A. Dondero, *Royal Oak*

MINNESOTA

SENATORS

Edward J. Thye, *Northfield*
Hubert H. Humphrey, *Minneapolis*

REPRESENTATIVES

August H. Andresen, *Red Wing*
Joseph P. O'Hara, *Glencoe*
Roy W. Wier, *Minneapolis*
Eugene J. McCarthy, *St. Paul*
Walter H. Judd, *Minneapolis*
Fred Marshall, *Grove City*
H. Carl Andersen, *Tyler*
John A. Blatnik, *Chisholm*
Mrs. Coya G. Knutson, *Oklee*

MISSISSIPPI

SENATORS

James O. Eastland, *Doddsville*
John C. Stennis, *De Kalb*

REPRESENTATIVES

Thomas G. Abernethy, *Okolona*
Jamie L. Whitten, *Charleston*
Frank E. Smith, *Greenwood*
John Bell Williams, *Raymond*
W. Arthur Winstead, *Philadelphia*
William M. Colmer, *Pascagoula*

MISSOURI

SENATORS

Thomas C. Hennings, Jr., *St. Louis*
Stuart Symington, *Creve Coeur*

REPRESENTATIVES

Frank M. Karsten, *St. Louis*
Thomas B. Curtis, *Webster Groves*
Mrs. Leonor Kretzer Sullivan, *St. Louis*
George H. Christopher, *Butler*
Richard W. Bolling, *Kansas City*
William R. Hull, Jr., *Weston*
Dewey Short, *Galena*
Albert S. J. Carnahan, *Ellsinore*

Clarence Cannon, *Elsberry*
Paul C. Jones, *Kennett*
Morgan M. Moulder, *Camdenton*

MONTANA

SENATORS

James E. Murray, *Butte*
Mike Mansfield, *Missoula*

REPRESENTATIVES

Lee Metcalf, *Helena*
Orvin B. Fjare, *Big Timber*

NEBRASKA

SENATORS

Roman L. Hruska, *Omaha*
Carl T. Curtis, *Minden*

REPRESENTATIVES

Phillip H. Weaver, *Falls City*
Jackson B. Chase, *Omaha*
Robert D. Harrison, *Norfolk*
Arthur L. Miller, *Kimball*

NEVADA

SENATORS

George W. Malone, *Reno*
Alan H. Bible, *Reno*

REPRESENTATIVE

At Large—Clifton Young, *Reno*

NEW HAMPSHIRE

SENATORS

H. Styles Bridges, *Concord*
Norris Cotton, *Lebanon*

REPRESENTATIVES

Chester E. Merrow, *Center Ossipee*
Perkins Bass, *Peterborough*

NEW JERSEY

SENATORS

H. Alexander Smith, *Princeton*
Clifford P. Case, *Rahway*

REPRESENTATIVES

Charles A. Wolverton, *Merchantville*
T. Millet Hand,[11] *Cape May City*
James C. Auchincloss, *Rumson*
Frank Thompson, Jr., *Trenton*
Peter H. B. Frelinghuysen, Jr., *Morristown*
Harrison A. Williams, Jr., *Westfield*
William B. Widnall, *Saddle River*
Gordon Canfield, *Paterson*
Frank C. Osmers, Jr., *Tenafly*
Peter W. Rodino, Jr., *Newark*

[9] Died September 19, 1955.
[10] Elected to fill vacancy caused by death of his father, John D. Dingell; took his seat January 3, 1956.

[11] Died December 26, 1956, before the commencement of the Eighty-fifth Congress to which he had been reelected. Vacancy in the Eighty-fourth Congress not filled.

NEW JERSEY—Continued

REPRESENTATIVES—continued

Hugh J. Addonizio, *Newark*
Robert W. Kean, *Livingston*
Alfred D. Sieminski, *Jersey City*
T. James Tumulty, *Jersey City*

NEW MEXICO

SENATORS

Dennis Chavez, *Albuquerque*
Clinton P. Anderson, *Albuquerque*

REPRESENTATIVES AT LARGE

Antonio M. Fernandez,[12] *Santa Fe*
John J. Dempsey, *Santa Fe*

NEW YORK

SENATORS

Irving M. Ives, *Norwich*
Herbert H. Lehman, *New York City*

REPRESENTATIVES

Stuyvesant Wainwright, *Wainscott*
Steven B. Derounian, *Roslyn*
Frank J. Becker, *Lynbrook*
Henry J. Latham, *Queens Village*
Albert H. Bosch, *Richmond Hill*
Lester Holtzman, *Rego Park*
James J. Delaney, *Long Island City*
Victor L. Anfuso, *Brooklyn*
Eugene J. Keogh, *Brooklyn*
Mrs. Edna F. Kelly, *Brooklyn*
Emanuel Celler, *Brooklyn*
Francis E. Dorn, *Brooklyn*
Abraham J. Multer, *Brooklyn*
John J. Rooney, *Brooklyn*
John H. Ray, *Staten Island*
Adam C. Powell, Jr., *New York City*
Frederic R. Coudert, Jr., *New York City*
James G. Donovan, *New York York City*
Arthur G. Klein,[13] *New York City*
Irwin D. Davidson,[13] *New York City*
Herbert Zelenko, *New York City*
Sidney A. Fine,[14] *New York City*
James C. Healey,[15] *New York City*
Isidore Dollinger, *New York City*
Charles A. Buckley, *New York City*
Paul A. Fino, *New York City*
Ralph A. Gamble, *Larchmont*
Ralph W. Gwinn, *Bronxville*
Mrs. Katharine St. George, *Tuxedo Park*
J. Ernest Wharton, *Richmondville*
Leo W. O'Brien, *Albany*
Dean P. Taylor, *Troy*
Bernard W. Kearney, *Gloversville*
Clarence E. Kilburn, *Malone*
William R. Williams, *Cassville*
R. Walter Riehlman, *Tully*
John Taber, *Auburn*

W. Sterling Cole, *Bath*
Kenneth B. Keating, *Rochester*
Harold C. Ostertag, *Attica*
William E. Miller, *Lockport*
Edmund P. Radwan, *Buffalo*
John R. Pillion, *Lackawanna*
Daniel A. Reed, *Dunkirk*

NORTH CAROLINA

SENATORS

Samuel J. Ervin, Jr., *Morganton*
W. Kerr Scott, *Haw River*

REPRESENTATIVES

Herbert C. Bonner, *Washington*
Lawrence H. Fountain, *Tarboro*
Graham A. Barden, *New Bern*
Harold D. Cooley, *Nashville*
Richard Thurmond Chatham, *Winston-Salem*
Carl T. Durham, *Chapel Hill*
F. Ertel Carlyle, *Lumberton*
Charles B. Deane, *Rockingham*
Hugh Q. Alexander, *Kannapolis*
Charles Raper Jonas, *Lincolnton*
Woodrow W. Jones, *Rutherfordton*
George A. Shuford, *Asheville*

NORTH DAKOTA

SENATORS

William Langer, *Wheatland*
Milton R. Young, *La Moure*

REPRESENTATIVES AT LARGE

Usher L. Burdick, *Williston*
Otto Krueger, *Fessenden*

OHIO

SENATORS

John W. Bricker, *Columbus*
George H. Bender, *Chagrin Falls*

REPRESENTATIVES

Gordon H. Scherer, *Cincinnati*
William E. Hess, *Cincinnati*
Paul F. Schenck, *Dayton*
William M. McCulloch, *Piqua*
Cliff Clevenger, *Bryan*
James G. Polk, *Highland*
Clarence J. Brown, *Blanchester*
Jackson E. Betts, *Findlay*
Thomas L. Ashley, *Toledo*
Thomas A. Jenkins, *Ironton*
Oliver P. Bolton, *Mentor*
John M. Vorys, *Columbus*
Albert D. Baumhart, Jr., *Vermilion*
William H. Ayres, *Akron*
John E. Henderson, *Cambridge*
Frank T. Bow, *Canton*

J. Harry McGregor, *West Lafayette*
Wayne L. Hays, *Flushing*
Michael J. Kirwan, *Youngstown*
Michael A. Feighan, *Cleveland*
Charles A. Vanik, *Cleveland*
Mrs. Frances P. Bolton, *Lyndhurst*
William E. Minshall, *Rocky River*

OKLAHOMA

SENATORS

Robert S. Kerr, *Oklahoma City*
A. S. Mike Monroney, *Oklahoma City*

REPRESENTATIVES

Page H. Belcher, *Enid*
Edmond Edmondson, *Muskogee*
Carl Albert, *McAlester*
Thomas J. Steed, *Shawnee*
John Jarman, *Oklahoma City*
Victor E. Wickersham, *Mangum*

OREGON

SENATORS

Wayne L. Morse, *Eugene*
Richard L. Neuberger, *Portland*

REPRESENTATIVES

A. Walter Norblad, *Stayton*
Samuel H. Coon, *Baker*
Mrs. Edith S. Green, *Portland*
Harris Ellsworth, *Roseburg*

PENNSYLVANIA

SENATORS

Edward Martin, *Washington*
James H. Duff, *Carnegie*

REPRESENTATIVES

William A. Barrett, *Philadelphia*
William T. Granahan,[16] *Philadelphia*
Mrs. Kathryn E. Granahan,[17] *Philadelphia*
James A. Byrne, *Philadelphia*
Earl Chudoff, *Philadelphia*
William J. Green, Jr., *Philadelphia*
Hugh D. Scott, Jr., *Philadelphia*
Benjamin F. James, *Rosemont*
Karl C. King, *Morrisville*
Paul B. Dague, *Downingtown*
Joseph L. Carrigg, *Susquehanna*
Daniel J. Flood, *Wilkes-Barre*
Ivor D. Fenton, *Mahanoy City*
Samuel K. McConnell, Jr., *Wynnewood*
George M. Rhodes, *Reading*
Francis E. Walter, *Easton*
Walter M. Mumma, *Harrisburg*
Alvin R. Bush, *Muncy*
Richard M. Simpson, *Huntingdon*
James M. Quigley, *Highland Park*

---

[12] Died November 7, 1956, before the commencement of the Eighty-fifth Congress to which he had been re-elected. Vacancy in the Eighty-fourth Congress not filled.

[13] Resigned December 31, 1956; vacancy throughout remainder of the Congress.
[14] Resigned January 2, 1956.
[15] Elected to fill vacancy caused by resignation of Sidney A. Fine, and took his seat February 20, 1956.

[16] Died May 25, 1956.
[17] Elected November 6, 1956, to fill vacancy caused by death of her husband, William T. Granahan, but was unable to be sworn in as Congress was not in session.

James E. Van Zandt, *Altoona*
Augustine B. Kelley, *Greensburg*
John P. Saylor, *Johnstown*
Leon H. Gavin, *Oil City*
Carroll D. Kearns, *Farrell*
Frank M. Clark, *Bessemer*
Thomas E. Morgan, *Fredericktown*
James G. Fulton, *Pittsburgh*
Herman P. Eberharter, *Pittsburgh*
Robert J. Corbett, *Pittsburgh*
Mrs. Vera D. Buchanan,[18] *McKeesport*
Elmer J. Holland,[19] *Pittsburgh*

RHODE ISLAND

SENATORS

Theodore F. Green, *Providence*
John O. Pastore, *Providence*

REPRESENTATIVES

Aime J. Forand, *Cumberland*
John E. Fogarty, *Harmony*

SOUTH CAROLINA

SENATORS

Olin D. Johnston, *Spartanburg*
James Strom Thurmond,[20] *Aiken*
Thomas A. Wofford,[21] *Greenville*
James Strom Thurmond,[22] *Aiken*

REPRESENTATIVES

L. Mendel Rivers, *Charleston*
John J. Riley, *Sumter*
W. J. Bryan Dorn, *Greenwood*
Robert T. Ashmore, *Greenville*
James P. Richards, *Lancaster*
John L. McMillan, *Florence*

SOUTH DAKOTA

SENATORS

Karl E. Mundt, *Madison*
Francis H. Case, *Custer*

REPRESENTATIVES

Harold O. Lovre, *Watertown*
Ellis Y. Berry, *McLaughlin*

TENNESSEE

SENATORS

Estes Kefauver, *Chattanooga*
Albert A. Gore, *Carthage*

REPRESENTATIVES

B. Carroll Reece, *Johnson City*
Howard H. Baker, *Huntsville*
James B. Frazier, Jr., *Chattanooga*
Joseph L. Evins, *Smithville*

J. Percy Priest,[23] *Nashville*
Ross Bass, *Pulaski*
Thomas J. Murray, *Jackson*
Jere Cooper, *Dyersburg*
Clifford Davis, *Memphis*

TEXAS

SENATORS

Lyndon B. Johnson, *Johnson City*
Marion Price Daniel, *Liberty*

REPRESENTATIVES

Wright Patman, *Texarkana*
Jack B. Brooks, *Beaumont*
Brady P. Gentry, *Tyler*
Sam Rayburn, *Bonham*
Bruce R. Alger, *Dallas*
Olin E. Teague, *College Station*
John V. Dowdy, *Athens*
Albert Thomas, *Houston*
Clark W. Thompson, *Galveston*
W. Homer Thornberry, *Austin*
William R. Poage, *Waco*
James C. Wright, Jr., *Weatherford*
Frank N. Ikard, *Wichita Falls*
John J. Bell, *Cuero*
Joe M. Kilgore, *McAllen*
J. T. Rutherford, *Odessa*
Omar T. Burleson, *Anson*
Walter E. Rogers, *Pampa*
George H. Mahon, *Lubbock*
Paul J. Kilday, *San Antonio*
O. Clark Fisher, *San Angelo*
At Large—Martin Dies, Jr., *Lufkin*

UTAH

SENATORS

Arthur V. Watkins, *Orem*
Wallace F. Bennett, *Salt Lake City*

REPRESENTATIVES

Henry Aldous Dixon, *Ogden*
William A. Dawson, *Salt Lake City*

VERMONT

SENATORS

George D. Aiken, *Putney*
Ralph E. Flanders, *Springfield*

REPRESENTATIVE

At Large—Winston L. Prouty, *Newport*

VIRGINIA

SENATORS

Harry Flood Byrd, *Berryville*
A. Willis Robertson, *Lexington*

REPRESENTATIVES

Edward J. Robeson, Jr., *Warwick*
Porter Hardy, Jr., *Churchland*
J. Vaughan Gary, *Richmond*
Watkins M. Abbitt, *Appomattox*
William M. Tuck, *South Boston*
Richard H. Poff, *Radford*
Burr P. Harrison, *Winchester*
Howard W. Smith, *Broad Run*
William Pat Jennings, *Marion*
Joel T. Broyhill, *Arlington*

WASHINGTON

SENATORS

Warren G. Magnuson, *Seattle*
Henry M. Jackson, *Everett*

REPRESENTATIVES

Thomas M. Pelly, *Seattle*
Alfred John Westland, *Everett*
Russell V. Mack, *Hoquiam*
Hal Holmes, *Ellensburg*
Walter F. Horan, *Wenatchee*
Thor C. Tollefson, *Tacoma*
At Large—Donald H. Magnuson, *Seattle*

WEST VIRGINIA

SENATORS

Harley M. Kilgore,[24] *Beckley*
William R. Laird 3d,[25] *Fayetteville*
Chapman Revercomb,[26] *Charleston*
Matthew M. Neely, *Fairmont*

REPRESENTATIVES

Robert H. Mollohan, *Fairmont*
Harley O. Staggers, *Keyser*
Cleveland M. Bailey, *Clarksburg*
Maurice G. Burnside, *Huntington*
Mrs. Maude Elizabeth Kee, *Bluefield*
Robert C. Byrd, *Beckley*

WISCONSIN

SENATORS

Alexander Wiley, *Chippewa Falls*
Joseph R. McCarthy, *Appleton*

REPRESENTATIVES

Lawrence H. Smith, *Racine*
Glenn R. Davis, *Waukesha*
Gardner R. Withrow, *La Crosse*
Clement J. Zablocki, *Milwaukee*
Henry S. Reuss, *Milwaukee*
William K. Van Pelt, *Fond du Lac*
Melvin R. Laird, *Marshfield*
John W. Byrnes, *Green Bay*
Lester R. Johnson, *Black River Falls*
Alvin E. O'Konski, *Mercer*

---

[18] Died November 26, 1955.
[19] Elected to fill vacancy caused by death of Vera D. Buchanan, and took his seat February 8, 1956.
[20] Resigned April 4, 1956.
[21] Appointed to fill vacancy caused by resignation of James Strom Thurmond, and took his seat April 9, 1956.
[22] Elected to fill vacancy caused by his own resignation, and took his seat January 3, 1957.
[23] Died October 12, 1956; vacancy throughout remainder of the Congress.
[24] Died February 28, 1956.
[25] Appointed to fill vacancy caused by death of Harley M. Kilgore, and took his seat March 15, 1956.
[26] Elected to fill vacancy caused by death of Harley M. Kilgore, and took his seat January 3, 1957.

WYOMING

SENATORS

Frank A. Barrett, *Lusk*
Joseph C. O'Mahoney, *Cheyenne*

REPRESENTATIVE

At Large—E. Keith Thomson, *Cheyenne*

TERRITORY OF ALASKA

DELEGATE

Edward L. Bartlett, *Juneau*

TERRITORY OF HAWAII

DELEGATE

Mrs. Mary Elizabeth Pruett Farrington, *Honolulu*

COMMONWEALTH OF PUERTO RICO

RESIDENT COMMISSIONER

A. Fernós-Isern, *Santurce*

EIGHTY-FIFTH CONGRESS

JANUARY 3, 1957, TO JANUARY 3, 1959

FIRST SESSION—*January 3, 1957, to August 30, 1957*
SECOND SESSION—*January 7,[1] 1958, to August 24, 1958*

VICE PRESIDENT OF THE UNITED STATES—RICHARD M. NIXON, of California
PRESIDENT PRO TEMPORE OF THE SENATE—CARL HAYDEN,[2] of Arizona
SECRETARY OF THE SENATE—FELTON McLELLAN JOHNSTON,[3] of Mississippi
SERGEANT AT ARMS OF THE SENATE—JOSEPH C. DUKE,[3] of Arizona

SPEAKER OF THE HOUSE OF REPRESENTATIVES—SAM RAYBURN,[3] of Texas
CLERK OF THE HOUSE—RALPH R. ROBERTS,[3] of Indiana
SERGEANT AT ARMS OF THE HOUSE—ZEAKE W. JOHNSON, JR.,[3] of Tennessee
DOORKEEPER OF THE HOUSE—WILLIAM M. MILLER,[3] of Mississippi
POSTMASTER OF THE HOUSE—H. H. MORRIS,[3] of Kentucky

ALABAMA

SENATORS

Lister Hill, *Montgomery*
John J. Sparkman, *Huntsville*

REPRESENTATIVES

Frank W. Boykin, *Mobile*
George M. Grant, *Troy*
George W. Andrews, *Union Springs*
Kenneth A. Roberts, *Anniston*
Albert Rains, *Gadsden*
Armistead I. Selden, Jr., *Greensboro*
Carl A. Elliott, *Jasper*
Robert E. Jones, Jr., *Scottsboro*
George Huddleston, Jr., *Birmingham*

ARIZONA

SENATORS

Carl Hayden, *Phoenix*
Barry M. Goldwater, *Phoenix*

REPRESENTATIVES

John J. Rhodes, *Mesa*
Stewart L. Udall, *Tucson*

ARKANSAS

SENATORS

John L. McClellan, *Camden*
J. William Fulbright, *Fayetteville*

REPRESENTATIVES

Ezekiel C. Gathings, *West Memphis*
Wilbur D. Mills, *Kensett*
James W. Trimble, *Berryville*
Oren Harris, *El Dorado*
Brooks Hays, *Little Rock*
William F. Norrell, *Monticello*

CALIFORNIA

SENATORS

William F. Knowland, *Piedmont*
Thomas H. Kuchel, *Anaheim*

REPRESENTATIVES

Hubert B. Scudder, *Sebastopol*
Clair Engle, *Red Bluff*
John E. Moss, Jr., *Sacramento*
William S. Mailliard, *San Francisco*
John F. Shelley, *San Francisco*
John F. Baldwin, Jr., *Martinez*
John J. Allen, Jr., *Oakland*
George P. Miller, *Alameda*
J. Arthur Younger, *San Mateo*
Charles S. Gubser, *Gilroy*
John J. McFall, *Manteca*
Bernice F. Sisk, *Fresno*
Charles M. Teague, *Ojai*
Harlan F. Hagen, *Hanford*
Gordon L. McDonough, *Los Angeles*
Donald L. Jackson, *Pacific Palisades*
Cecil R. King, *Los Angeles*
Craig Hosmer, *Long Beach*
Chet Holifield, *Montebello*
H. Allen Smith, *Glendale*
Edgar W. Hiestand, *Altadena*
Joseph F. Holt, *Van Nuys*
Clyde G. Doyle, *South Gate*
Glenard P. Lipscomb, *Los Angeles*
Patrick J. Hillings, *Arcadia*
James Roosevelt, *Los Angeles*
Harry R. Sheppard, *Yucaipa*
James B. Utt, *Santa Ana*
Dalip S. Saund, *Westmorland*
Robert C. Wilson, *Chula Vista*

COLORADO

SENATORS

Gordon L. Allott, *Lamar*
John A. Carroll, *Denver*

REPRESENTATIVES

Byron G. Rogers, *Denver*
William S. Hill, *Fort Collins*
J. Edgar Chenoweth, *Trinidad*
Wayne N. Aspinall, *Palisade*

---

[1] By joint resolution (Pub. Law 85-290, 85th Cong., 1st sess.) the date of assembling the second session of the Eighty-fifth Congress was fixed for January 7, 1958.
[2] Elected January 3, 1957.
[3] Reelected January 3, 1957.

CONNECTICUT

SENATORS

Prescott S. Bush, *Greenwich*
William A. Purtell, *West Hartford*

REPRESENTATIVES

Edwin H. May, Jr., *Wethersfield*
Horace Seely-Brown, Jr., *Pomfret Center*
Albert W. Cretella, *North Haven*
Albert P. Morano, *Greenwich*
James T. Patterson, *Watertown*
At Large—Antoni N. Sadlak, *Rockville*

DELAWARE

SENATORS

John J. Williams, *Millsboro*
J. Allen Frear, Jr., *Dover*

REPRESENTATIVE

At Large—Harry G. Haskell, Jr., *Wilmington*

FLORIDA

SENATORS

Spessard L. Holland, *Bartow*
George A. Smathers, *Miami*

REPRESENTATIVES

William C. Cramer, *St. Petersburg*
Charles E. Bennett, *Jacksonville*
Robert L. F. Sikes, *Crestview*
Dante B. Fascell, *Miami*
Albert S. Herlong, Jr., *Leesburg*
Paul G. Rogers, *West Palm Beach*
James A. Haley, *Sarasota*
Donald R. Matthews, *Gainesville*

GEORGIA

SENATORS

Richard B. Russell, *Winder*
Herman E. Talmadge, *Lovejoy*

REPRESENTATIVES

Prince H. Preston, Jr., *Statesboro*
John L. Pilcher, *Meigs*
Elijah L. Forrester, *Leesburg*
John James Flynt, Jr., *Griffin*
James C. Davis, *Stone Mountain*
Carl Vinson, *Milledgeville*
Henderson L. Lanham,[4] *Rome*
Harlan Erwin Mitchell,[5] *Dalton*
Mrs. Iris F. Blitch, *Homerville*
Phillip M. Landrum, *Jasper*
Paul Brown, *Elberton*

IDAHO

SENATORS

Henry C. Dworshak, *Burley*
Frank Church, *Boise*

REPRESENTATIVES

Mrs. Gracie B. Pfost, *Nampa*
Hamer H. Budge, *Boise*

ILLINOIS

SENATORS

Paul H. Douglas, *Chicago*
Everett M. Dirksen, *Pekin*

REPRESENTATIVES

William L. Dawson, *Chicago*
Barratt O'Hara, *Chicago*
Emmet F. Byrne, *Chicago*
William E. McVey,[6] *Harvey*
John C. Kluczynski, *Chicago*
Thomas J. O'Brien, *Chicago*
James B. Bowler,[7] *Chicago*
Roland V. Libonati,[8] *Chicago*
Thomas S. Gordon, *Chicago*
Sidney R. Yates, *Chicago*
Harold R. Collier, *Berwyn*
Timothy P. Sheehan, *Chicago*
Charles A. Boyle, *Chicago*
Mrs. Marguerite Stitt Church, *Evanston*
Russell W. Keeney,[9] *Wheaton*
Noah M. Mason, *Oglesby*
Leo E. Allen, *Galena*
Leslie C. Arends, *Melvin*
Robert H. Michel, *Peoria*
Robert B. Chiperfield, *Canton*
Sidney E. Simpson,[10] *Carrollton*
Peter F. Mack, Jr., *Carlinville*
William L. Springer, *Champaign*
Charles W. Vursell, *Salem*
Charles Melvin Price, *East St. Louis*
Kenneth J. Gray, *West Frankfort*

INDIANA

SENATORS

Homer E. Capehart, *Washington*
William E. Jenner, *Bedford*

REPRESENTATIVES

Ray J. Madden, *Gary*
Charles A. Halleck, *Rensselaer*
F. Jay Nimtz, *South Bend*
E. Ross Adair, *Fort Wayne*
John V. Beamer, *Wabash*
Mrs. Cecil M. Harden, *Covington*
William G. Bray, *Martinsville*
Winfield K. Denton, *Evansville*
Earl Wilson, *Bedford*
Ralph Harvey, *New Castle*
Charles B. Brownson, *Indianapolis*

IOWA

SENATORS

Bourke B. Hickenlooper, *Cedar Rapids*
Thomas E. Martin, *Iowa City*

REPRESENTATIVES

Frederick D. Schwengel, *Davenport*
Henry O. Talle, *Decorah*
Harold R. Gross, *Waterloo*
Karl M. LeCompte,[11] *Corydon*
Paul Cunningham, *Des Moines*
Merwin Coad, *Boone*
Ben F. Jensen, *Exira*
Charles B. Hoeven, *Alton*

KANSAS

SENATORS

Andrew F. Schoeppel, *Wichita*
Frank Carlson, *Concordia*

REPRESENTATIVES

William H. Avery, *Wakefield*
Errett P. Scrivner, *Kansas City*
Myron V. George, *Altamont*
Edward H. Rees, *Emporia*
J. Floyd Breeding, *Rolla*
Wint Smith, *Mankato*

KENTUCKY

SENATORS

John Sherman Cooper, *Somerset*
Thruston B. Morton, *Glenview*

REPRESENTATIVES

Nobel J. Gregory, *Mayfield*
William H. Natcher, *Bowling Green*
John M. Robsion, Jr., *Louisville*
Frank L. Chelf, *Lebanon*
Brent Spence, *Fort Thomas*
John C. Watts, *Nicholasville*
Carl D. Perkins, *Hindman*
Eugene Siler, *Williamsburg*

LOUISIANA

SENATORS

Allen J. Ellender, *Houma*
Russell B. Long, *Baton Rouge*

REPRESENTATIVES

F. Edward Hébert, *New Orleans*
T. Hale Boggs, *New Orleans*
Edwin E. Willis, *St. Martinville*
Overton Brooks, *Shreveport*
Otto E. Passman, *Monroe*
James H. Morrison, *Hammond*
T. Ashton Thompson, *Ville Platte*
George S. Long,[12] *Pineville*

---

[4] Died November 10, 1957.
[5] Elected to fill vacancy caused by death of Henderson L. Lanham, and took his seat January 13, 1958.
[6] Died August 10, 1958; vacancy throughout remainder of the Congress.

[7] Died July 18, 1957.
[8] Elected to fill vacancy caused by death of James B. Bowler, and took his seat January 7, 1958.
[9] Died January 11, 1958; vacancy throughout remainder of the Congress.

[10] Died October 26, 1958; vacancy throughout remainder of the Congress.
[11] Election unsuccessfully contested by Steven V. Carter.
[12] Died March 22, 1958; vacancy throughout remainder of the Congress.

MAINE

SENATORS

Mrs. Margaret Chase Smith, *Skowhegan*
Frederick G. Payne, *Waldoboro*

REPRESENTATIVES

Robert Hale,[13] *Portland*
Frank M. Coffin, *Lewiston*
Clifford G. McIntire, *Perham*

MARYLAND

SENATORS

John Marshall Butler, *Baltimore*
J. Glenn Beall, *Frostburg*

REPRESENTATIVES

Edward T. Miller, *Easton*
James P. S. Devereux, *Stevenson*
Edward A. Garmatz, *Baltimore*
George H. Fallon, *Baltimore*
Richard E. Lankford, *Annapolis*
DeWitt S. Hyde, *Bethesda*
Samuel N. Friedel, *Baltimore*

MASSACHUSETTS

SENATORS

Leverett Saltonstall, *Dover*
John F. Kennedy, *Boston*

REPRESENTATIVES

John W. Heselton, *Deerfield*
Edward P. Boland, *Springfield*
Philip J. Philbin, *Clinton*
Harold D. Donohue, *Worcester*
Mrs. Edith Nourse Rogers, *Lowell*
William H. Bates, *Salem*
Thomas J. Lane, *Lawrence*
Torbert H. Macdonald, *Malden*
Donald W. Nicholson, *Wareham*
Laurence Curtis, *Boston*
Thomas P. O'Neill, Jr., *Cambridge*
John W. McCormack, *Dorchester*
Richard B. Wigglesworth,[14] *Milton*
Joseph W. Martin, Jr., *North Attleboro*

MICHIGAN

SENATORS

Charles E. Potter, *Cheboygan*
Patrick V. McNamara, *Detroit*

REPRESENTATIVES

Thaddeus M. Machrowicz, *Hamtramck*
George Meader, *Ann Arbor*
August E. Johansen, *Battle Creek*
Clare E. Hoffman, *Allegan*
Gerald R. Ford, Jr., *Grand Rapids*
Charles E. Chamberlain, *East Lansing*
Robert J. McIntosh, *Port Huron*

Alvin M. Bentley, *Owosso*
Robert P. Griffin, *Traverse City*
Elford A. Cederberg, *Bay City*
Victor A. Knox, *Sault Ste. Marie*
John B. Bennett, *Ontonagon*
Charles C. Diggs, Jr., *Detroit*
Louis C. Rabaut, *Grosse Pointe Park*
John D. Dingell, Jr., *Detroit*
John Lesinski, Jr., *Dearborn*
Mrs. Martha W. Griffiths, *Detroit*
William S. Broomfield, *Royal Oak*

MINNESOTA

SENATORS

Edward J. Thye, *Northfield*
Hubert H. Humphrey, *Minneapolis*

REPRESENTATIVES

August H. Andresen,[15] *Red Wing*
Albert H. Quie,[16] *Dennison*
Joseph P. O'Hara, *Glencoe*
Roy W. Wier, *Minneapolis*
Eugene J. McCarthy, *St. Paul*
Walter H. Judd, *Minneapolis*
Fred Marshall, *Grove City*
H. Carl Andersen, *Tyler*
John A. Blatnik, *Chisholm*
Mrs. Coya G. Knutson, *Oklee*

MISSISSIPPI

SENATORS

James O. Eastland, *Doddsville*
John C. Stennis, *De Kalb*

REPRESENTATIVES

Thomas G. Abernethy, *Okolona*
Jamie L. Whitten, *Charleston*
Frank E. Smith, *Greenwood*
John Bell Williams, *Raymond*
W. Arthur Winstead, *Philadelphia*
William M. Colmer, *Pascagoula*

MISSOURI

SENATORS

Thomas C. Hennings, Jr., *St. Louis*
Stuart Symington, *Creve Coeur*

REPRESENTATIVES

Frank M. Karsten, *St. Louis*
Thomas B. Curtis, *Webster Groves*
Mrs. Leonor Kretzer Sullivan, *St. Louis*
George H. Christopher, *Butler*
Richard W. Bolling, *Kansas City*
William R. Hull, Jr., *Weston*
Charles H. Brown, *Springfield*
Albert S. J. Carnahan, *Ellsinore*
Clarence Cannon, *Elsberry*
Paul C. Jones, *Kennett*
Morgan M. Moulder, *Camdenton*

MONTANA

SENATORS

James E. Murray, *Butte*
Mike Mansfield, *Missoula*

REPRESENTATIVES

Lee Metcalf, *Helena*
LeRoy H. Anderson, *Conrad*

NEBRASKA

SENATORS

Roman L. Hruska, *Omaha*
Carl T. Curtis, *Minden*

REPRESENTATIVES

Phillip H. Weaver, *Falls City*
Glenn C. Cunningham, *Omaha*
Robert D. Harrison, *Norfolk*
Arthur L. Miller, *Kimball*

NEVADA

SENATORS

George W. Malone, *Reno*
Alan H. Bible, *Reno*

REPRESENTATIVE

At Large—Walter S. Baring, *Reno*

NEW HAMPSHIRE

SENATORS

H. Styles Bridges, *Concord*
Norris Cotton, *Lebanon*

REPRESENTATIVES

Chester E. Merrow, *Center Ossipee*
Perkins Bass, *Peterborough*

NEW JERSEY

SENATORS

H. Alexander Smith, *Princeton*
Clifford P. Case, *Rahway*

REPRESENTATIVES

Charles A. Wolverton, *Merchantville*
Milton W. Glenn,[17] *Margate City*
James C. Auchincloss, *Rumson*
Frank Thompson, Jr., *Trenton*
Peter H. B. Frelinghuysen, Jr., *Morristown*
Mrs. Florence P. Dwyer, *Elizabeth*
William B. Widnall, *Saddle River*
Gordon Canfield, *Paterson*
Frank C. Osmers, Jr., *Tenafly*
Peter W. Rodino, Jr., *Newark*
Hugh J. Addonizio, *Newark*
Robert W. Kean, *Livingston*
Alfred D. Sieminski, *Jersey City*
Vincent J. Dellay, *West New York*

---

[13] Election unsuccessfully contested by James C. Oliver.
[14] Resigned November 13, 1958; vacancy throughout remainder of the Congress.

[15] Died January 14, 1958.
[16] Elected to fill vacancy caused by death of August H. Andresen, and took his seat March 6, 1958.

[17] Elected to fill vacancy caused by death of Representative-elect T. Millet Hand, in the preceding Congress, and took his seat January 7, 1958.

NEW MEXICO

SENATORS

Dennis Chavez, *Albuquerque*
Clinton P. Anderson, *Albuquerque*

REPRESENTATIVES AT LARGE

John J. Dempsey,[18] *Santa Fe*
Joseph M. Montoya,[19] *Santa Fe*

NEW YORK

SENATORS

Irving M. Ives, *Norwich*
Jacob K. Javits, *New York City*

REPRESENTATIVES

Stuyvesant Wainwright, *Wainscott*
Steven B. Derounian, *Roslyn*
Frank J. Becker, *Lynbrook*
Henry J. Latham,[20] *Queens Village*
Albert H. Bosch, *Woodhaven*
Lester Holtzman, *Rego Park*
James J. Delaney, *Long Island City*
Victor L. Anfuso, *Brooklyn*
Eugene J. Keogh, *Brooklyn*
Mrs. Edna F. Kelly, *Brooklyn*
Emanuel Celler, *Brooklyn*
Francis E. Dorn, *Brooklyn*
Abraham J. Multer, *Brooklyn*
John J. Rooney, *Brooklyn*
John H. Ray, *Staten Island*
Adam C. Powell, Jr., *New York City*
Frederic R. Coudert, Jr., *New York City*
Alfred E. Santangelo, *New York City*
Leonard Farbstein, *New York City*
Ludwig Teller, *New York City*
Herbert Zelenko, *New York City*
James C. Healey, *New York City*
Isidore Dollinger, *New York City*
Charles A. Buckley, *New York City*
Paul A. Fino, *New York City*
Edwin B. Dooley, *Mamaroneck*
Ralph W. Gwinn, *Bronxville*
Mrs. Katharine St. George, *Tuxedo Park*
J. Ernest Wharton, *Richmondville*
Leo W. O'Brien, *Albany*
Dean P. Taylor, *Troy*
Bernard W. Kearney, *Lake Pleasant*
Clarence E. Kilburn, *Malone*
William R. Williams, *Cassville*
R. Walter Riehlman, *Tully*
John Taber, *Auburn*
W. Sterling Cole,[21] *Bath*
Howard W. Robison,[22] *Owego*
Kenneth B. Keating, *Rochester*
Harold C. Ostertag, *Attica*
William E. Miller, *Lockport*
Edmund P. Radwan, *Buffalo*

John R. Pillion, *Hamburg*
Daniel A. Reed, *Dunkirk*

NORTH CAROLINA

SENATORS

Samuel J. Ervin, Jr., *Morganton*
W. Kerr Scott,[23] *Haw River*
B. Everett Jordan,[24] *Saxapahaw*

REPRESENTATIVES

Herbert C. Bonner, *Washington*
Lawrence H. Fountain, *Tarboro*
Graham A. Barden, *New Bern*
Harold D. Cooley, *Nashville*
Ralph J. Scott, *Danbury*
Carl T. Durham, *Chapel Hill*
Alton A. Lennon, *Wilmington*
A. Paul Kitchin, *Wadesboro*
Hugh Q. Alexander, *Kannapolis*
Charles Raper Jonas, *Lincolnton*
Basil L. Whitener, *Gastonia*
George A. Shuford, *Asheville*

NORTH DAKOTA

SENATORS

William Langer, *Wheatland*
Milton R. Young, *La Moure*

REPRESENTATIVES AT LARGE

Usher L. Burdick, *Williston*
Otto Krueger, *Fessenden*

OHIO

SENATORS

John W. Bricker, *Columbus*
Frank J. Lausche, *Cleveland*

REPRESENTATIVES

Gordon H. Scherer, *Cincinnati*
William E. Hess, *Cincinnati*
Paul F. Schenck, *Dayton*
William M. McCulloch, *Piqua*
Cliff Clevenger, *Bryan*
James G. Polk, *Highland*
Clarence J. Brown, *Blanchester*
Jackson E. Betts, *Findlay*
Thomas L. Ashley, *Waterville*
Thomas A. Jenkins, *Ironton*
David S. Dennison, *Warren*
John M. Vorys, *Columbus*
Albert D. Baumhart, Jr., *Vermilion*
William H. Ayres, *Akron*
John E. Henderson, *Cambridge*
Frank T. Bow, *Canton*
J. Harry McGregor,[25] *West Lafayette*
Wayne L. Hayes, *Flushing*

Michael J. Kirwan, *Youngstown*
Michael A. Feighan, *Cleveland*
Charles A. Vanik, *Cleveland*
Mrs. Frances P. Bolton, *Lyndhurst*
William E. Minshall, *Rocky River*

OKLAHOMA

SENATORS

Robert S. Kerr, *Oklahoma City*
A. S. Mike Monroney, *Oklahoma City*

REPRESENTATIVES

Page H. Belcher, *Enid*
Edmond Edmondson, *Muskogee*
Carl Albert, *McAlester*
Thomas J. Steed, *Shawnee*
John Jarman, *Oklahoma City*
Toby Morris, *Lawton*

OREGON

SENATORS

Wayne L. Morse, *Eugene*
Richard L. Neuberger, *Portland*

REPRESENTATIVES

A. Walter Norblad, *Stayton*
Albert C. Ullman, *Baker*
Mrs. Edith S. Green, *Portland*
Charles O. Porter, *Eugene*

PENNSYLVANIA

SENATORS

Edward Martin, *Washington*
Joseph S. Clark, *Philadelphia*

REPRESENTATIVES

William A. Barrett, *Philadelphia*
Mrs. Kathryn E. Granahan, *Philadelphia*
James A. Byrne, *Philadelphia*
Earl Chudoff,[26] *Philadelphia*
Robert N. C. Nix,[27] *Philadelphia*
William J. Green, Jr., *Philadelphia*
Hugh D. Scott, Jr., *Philadelphia*
Benjamin F. James, *Rosemont*
Willard S. Curtin, *Morrisville*
Paul B. Dague, *Downingtown*
Joseph L. Carrigg, *Susquehanna*
Daniel J. Flood, *Wilkes-Barre*
Ivor D. Fenton, *Mahanoy City*
Samuel K. McConnell, Jr.,[28] *Wynnewood*
John A. Lafore, Jr.,[29] *Haverford*
George M. Rhodes, *Reading*
Francis E. Walter, *Easton*
Walter M. Mumma, *Harrisburg*
Alvin R. Bush, *Muncy*
Richard M. Simpson, *Huntingdon*

---

[18] Died March 11, 1958; vacancy throughout remainder of the Congress.
[19] Elected to fill vacancy caused by death of Representative-elect Antonio M. Fernandez, in the preceding Congress, and took his seat April 29, 1957.
[20] Resigned December 31, 1958; vacancy throughout remainder of the Congress.
[21] Resigned December 1, 1957.

[22] Elected to fill vacancy caused by resignation of Sterling Cole, and took his seat January 20, 1958.
[23] Died April 16, 1958.
[24] Appointed to fill vacancy caused by death of W. Kerr Scott, and took his seat May 5, 1958; subsequently elected.
[25] Died October 7, 1958; vacancy throughout remainder of the Congress.

[26] Resigned January 5, 1958.
[27] Elected to fill vacancy caused by resignation of Earl Chudoff, and took his seat June 4, 1958.
[28] Resigned September 1, 1957.
[29] Elected to fill vacancy caused by resignation of Samuel K. McConnell, Jr., and took his seat **January 7, 1958.**

S. Walter Stauffer, *York*
James E. Van Zandt, *Altoona*
Augustine B. Kelley,[30] *Greensburg*
John H. Dent,[31] *Jeannette*
John P. Saylor, *Johnstown*
Leon H. Gavin, *Oil City*
Carroll D. Kearns, *Farrell*
Frank M. Clark, *Bessemer*
Thomas E. Morgan, *Fredericktown*
James G. Fulton, *Dormont*
Herman P. Eberharter,[32] *Pittsburgh*
Robert J. Corbett, *Ben Avon Heights*
Elmer J. Holland, *Pittsburgh*

RHODE ISLAND

SENATORS

Theodore F. Green, *Providence*
John O. Pastore, *Providence*

REPRESENTATIVES

Aime J. Forand, *Cumberland*
John E. Fogarty, *Harmony*

SOUTH CAROLINA

SENATORS

Olin D. Johnston, *Spartanburg*
James Strom Thurmond, *Aiken*

REPRESENTATIVES

L. Mendel Rivers, *Charleston*
John J. Riley, *Sumter*
W. J. Bryan Dorn, *Greenwood*
Robert T. Ashmore, *Greenville*
Robert W. Hemphill, *Chester*
John L. McMillan, *Florence*

SOUTH DAKOTA

SENATORS

Karl E. Mundt, *Madison*
Francis H. Case, *Custer*

REPRESENTATIVES

George S. McGovern, *Mitchell*
Ellis Y. Berry, *McLaughlin*

TENNESSEE

SENATORS

Estes Kefauver, *Chattanooga*
Albert A. Gore, *Carthage*

REPRESENTATIVES

B. Carroll Reece, *Johnson City*
Howard H. Baker, *Huntsville*
James B. Frazier, Jr., *Chattanooga*

Joseph L. Evins, *Smithville*
J. Carlton Loser, *Nashville*
Ross Bass, *Pulaski*
Thomas J. Murray, *Jackson*
Jere Cooper,[33] *Dyersburg*
Robert A. Everett,[34] *Union City*
Clifford Davis, *Memphis*

TEXAS

SENATORS

Lyndon B. Johnson, *Johnson City*
Marion Price Daniel,[35] *Liberty*
William A. Blakley,[36] *Dallas*
Ralph W. Yarborough,[37] *Austin*

REPRESENTATIVES

Wright Patman, *Texarkana*
Jack B. Brooks, *Beaumont*
Lindley G. Beckworth, *Gladewater*
Sam Rayburn, *Bonham*
Bruce R. Alger, *Dallas*
Olin E. Teague, *College Station*
John V. Dowdy, *Athens*
Albert Thomas, *Houston*
Clark W. Thompson, *Galveston*
W. Homer Thornberry, *Austin*
William R. Poage, *Waco*
James C. Wright, Jr., *Fort Worth*
Frank N. Ikard, *Wichita Falls*
John A. Young, *Corpus Christi*
Joe M. Kilgore, *McAllen*
J. T. Rutherford, *Odessa*
Omar T. Burleson, *Anson*
Walter E. Rogers, *Pampa*
George H. Mahon, *Lubbock*
Paul J. Kilday, *San Antonio*
O. Clark Fisher, *San Angelo*
At Large—Martin Dies, Jr., *Lufkin*

UTAH

SENATORS

Arthur V. Watkins, *Orem*
Wallace F. Bennett, *Salt Lake City*

REPRESENTATIVES

Henry Aldous Dixon, *Ogden*
William A. Dawson, *Salt Lake City*

VERMONT

SENATORS

George D. Aiken, *Putney*
Ralph E. Flanders, *Springfield*

REPRESENTATIVE

At Large—Winston L. Prouty, *Newport*

VIRGINIA

SENATORS

Harry Flood Byrd, *Berryville*
A. Willis Robertson, *Lexington*

REPRESENTATIVES

Edward J. Robeson, Jr., *Warwick*
Porter Hardy, Jr., *Churchland*
J. Vaughan Gary, *Richmond*
Watkins M. Abbitt, *Appomattox*
William M. Tuck, *South Boston*
Richard H. Poff, *Radford*
Burr P. Harrison, *Winchester*
Howard W. Smith, *Broad Run*
William Pat Jennings, *Marion*
Joel T. Broyhill, *Arlington*

WASHINGTON

SENATORS

Warren G. Magnuson, *Seattle*
Henry M. Jackson, *Everett*

REPRESENTATIVES

Thomas M. Pelly, *Port Blakely*
Alfred John Westland, *Everett*
Russell V. Mack, *Hoquiam*
Hal Holmes, *Ellensburg*
Walter F. Horan, *Wenatchee*
Thor C. Tollefson, *Tacoma*
At Large—Donald H. Magnuson, *Seattle*

WEST VIRGINIA

SENATORS

Matthew M. Neely,[38] *Fairmont*
John D. Hoblitzell, Jr.,[39] *Ravenswood*
Jennings Randolph,[40] *Elkins*
Chapman Revercomb, *Charleston*

REPRESENTATIVES

Arch A. Moore, Jr., *Glendale*
Harley O. Staggers, *Keyser*
Cleveland M. Bailey, *Clarksburg*
William E. Neal, *Huntington*
Mrs. Maude Elizabeth Kee, *Bluefield*
Robert C. Byrd, *Beckley*

WISCONSIN

SENATORS

Alexander Wiley, *Chippewa Falls*
Joseph R. McCarthy,[41] *Appleton*
William Proxmire,[42] *Madison*

---

[30] Died November 20, 1957.
[31] Elected to fill vacancy caused by death of Augustine B. Kelley, and took his seat January 27, 1958.
[32] Died September 9, 1958; vacancy throughout remainder of the Congress.
[33] Died December 18, 1957.
[34] Elected to fill vacancy caused by death of Jere Cooper, and took his seat February 10, 1958.

[35] Resigned January 14, 1957.
[36] Appointed to fill vacancy caused by resignation of Marion Price Daniel, and took his seat January 17, 1957.
[37] Elected to fill vacancy caused by resignation of Marion Price Daniel, and took his seat April 29, 1957.
[38] Died January 18, 1958.

[39] Appointed to fill vacancy caused by death of Matthew M. Neely, and took his seat January 27, 1958.
[40] Elected to fill vacancy caused by death of Matthew M. Neely, and took his seat January 7, 1959.
[41] Died May 2, 1957.
[42] Elected to fill vacancy caused by death of Joseph R. McCarthy, and took his seat August 29, 1957.

WISCONSIN—Continued

REPRESENTATIVES

Lawrence H. Smith,[43] *Racine*
Donald E. Tewes, *Waukesha*
Gardner R. Withrow, *La Crosse*
Clement J. Zablocki, *Milwaukee*
Henry S. Reuss, *Milwaukee*
William K. Van Pelt, *Fond du Lac*
Melvin R. Laird, *Marshfield*
John W. Byrnes, *Green Bay*
Lester R. Johnson, *Black River Falls*
Alvin E. O'Konski, *Mercer*

WYOMING

SENATORS

Frank A. Barrett, *Lusk*
Joseph C. O'Mahoney, *Cheyenne*

REPRESENTATIVE

At Large—E. Keith Thomson, *Cheyenne*

TERRITORY OF ALASKA

DELEGATE

Edward L. Bartlett, *Juneau*

TERRITORY OF HAWAII

DELEGATE

John A. Burns, *Honolulu*

COMMONWEALTH OF PUERTO RICO

RESIDENT COMMISSIONER

A. Fernós-Isern, *Santurce*

[43] Died January 22, 1958; vacancy throughout remainder of the Congress.

EIGHTY-SIXTH CONGRESS

JANUARY 3, 1959, TO JANUARY 3, 1961

FIRST SESSION—*January 7, 1959,*[1] *to September 15, 1959*

SECOND SESSION—*January 6, 1960,*[2] *to September 1, 1960*

VICE PRESIDENT OF THE UNITED STATES—Richard M. Nixon, of California

PRESIDENT PRO TEMPORE OF THE SENATE—Carl Hayden, of Arizona

SECRETARY OF THE SENATE—Felton McLellan Johnston, of Mississippi

SERGEANT AT ARMS OF THE SENATE—Joseph C. Duke, of Arizona

SPEAKER OF THE HOUSE OF REPRESENTATIVES—Sam Rayburn,[3] of Texas

CLERK OF THE HOUSE—Ralph R. Roberts,[3] of Indiana

SERGEANT AT ARMS OF THE HOUSE—Zeake W. Johnson, Jr.,[3] of Tennessee

DOORKEEPER OF THE HOUSE—William M. Miller,[3] of Mississippi

POSTMASTER OF THE HOUSE—H. H. Morris,[3] of Kentucky

ALABAMA

SENATORS

Lister Hill, *Montgomery*
John J. Sparkman, *Huntsville*

REPRESENTATIVES

Frank W. Boykin, *Mobile*
George M. Grant, *Troy*
George W. Andrews, *Union Springs*
Kenneth A. Roberts, *Anniston*
Albert Rains, *Gadsden*
Armistead I. Selden, Jr., *Greensboro*
Carl A. Elliott, *Jasper*
Robert E. Jones, Jr., *Scottsboro*
George Huddleston, Jr., *Birmingham*

ALASKA [4]

SENATORS

Edward L. Bartlett,[5] *Juneau*
Ernest Gruening,[6] *Juneau*

REPRESENTATIVE

At Large—Ralph J. Rivers,[7] *Fairbanks*

ARIZONA

SENATORS

Carl Hayden, *Phoenix*
Barry M. Goldwater, *Phoenix*

REPRESENTATIVES

John J. Rhodes, *Mesa*
Stewart L. Udall, *Tucson*

ARKANSAS

SENATORS

John L. McClellan, *Camden*
J. William Fulbright, *Fayetteville*

REPRESENTATIVES

Ezekiel C. Gathings, *West Memphis*
Wilbur D. Mills, *Kensett*
James W. Trimble, *Berryville*
Oren Harris, *El Dorado*
T. Dale Alford,[8] *Little Rock*
William F. Norrell, *Monticello*

CALIFORNIA

SENATORS

Thomas H. Kuchel, *Anaheim*
Clair Engle, *Red Bluff*

REPRESENTATIVES

Clement W. Miller, *Corte Madera*
Harold T. Johnson, *Roseville*
John E. Moss, Jr., *Sacramento*
William S. Mailliard, *San Francisco*
John F. Shelley, *San Francisco*
John F. Baldwin, *Martinez*
Jeffery Cohelan, *Berkeley*
George P. Miller, *Alameda*
J. Arthur Younger, *San Mateo*
Charles S. Gubser, *Gilroy*
John J. McFall, *Manteca*
Bernice F. Sisk, *Fresno*
Charles M. Teague, *Ojai*
Harlan F. Hagen, *Hanford*
Gordon L. McDonough, *Los Angeles*
Donald L. Jackson, *Pacific Palisades*
Cecil R. King, *Los Angeles*
Craig Hosmer, *Long Beach*
Chet Holifield, *Montebello*
H. Allen Smith, *Glendale*
Edgar W. Hiestand, *Burbank*
Joseph F. Holt, *Van Nuys*
Clyde G. Doyle, *South Gate*
Glenard P. Lipscomb, *Los Angeles*
George A. Kasem, *West Covina*
James Roosevelt, *Los Angeles*
Harry R. Sheppard, *Yucaipa*

---

[1] By joint resolution (Pub. Law 85-819, 85th Cong., 2d sess.) the date of assembling the first session of the Eighty-sixth Congress was fixed for January 7, 1959.
[2] By joint resolution (Pub. Law 86-305, 86th Cong., 1st sess.) the date of assembling the second session of the Eighty-sixth Congress was fixed for January 6, 1960.
[3] Reelected January 7, 1959.
[4] Admitted as a State into the Union January 3, 1959.
[5] Took his seat January 7, 1959; term to expire, as determined by lot, January 3, 1961.
[6] Took his seat January 7, 1959; term to expire, as determined by lot, January 3, 1963.
[7] Took his seat January 7, 1959.
[8] Election investigated by order of the House (H. Res. 1). H. Res. 380 declared T. Dale Alford was entitled to his seat.

CALIFORNIA—Continued

REPRESENTATIVES—continued

James B. Utt, *Santa Ana*
Dalip S. Saund, *Westmorland*
Robert C. Wilson, *Chula Vista*

COLORADO

SENATORS

Gordon L. Allott, *Lamar*
John A. Carroll, *Denver*

REPRESENTATIVES

Byron G. Rogers, *Denver*
Byron L. Johnson, *Denver*
J. Edgar Chenoweth, *Trinidad*
Wayne N. Aspinall, *Palisade*

CONNECTICUT

SENATORS

Prescott S. Bush, *Greenwich*
Thomas J. Dodd, *West Hartford*

REPRESENTATIVES

Emilio Q. Daddario, *Hartford*
Chester Bowles, *Essex*
Robert N. Giaimo, *North Haven*
Donald J. Irwin, *Norwalk*
John S. Monagan, *Waterbury*
At Large—Frank Kowalski, *Meriden*

DELAWARE

SENATORS

John J. Williams, *Millsboro*
J. Allen Frear, Jr., *Dover*

REPRESENTATIVE

At Large—Harris B. McDowell, Jr., *Middletown*

FLORIDA

SENATORS

Spessard L. Holland, *Bartow*
George A. Smathers, *Miami*

REPRESENTATIVES

William C. Cramer, *St. Petersburg*
Charles E. Bennett, *Jacksonville*
Robert L. F. Sikes, *Crestview*
Dante B. Fascell, *Miami*
Albert S. Herlong, Jr., *Leesburg*
Paul G. Rogers, *West Palm Beach*
James A. Haley, *Sarasota*
Donald R. Matthews, *Gainesville*

GEORGIA

SENATORS

Richard B. Russell, *Winder*
Herman E. Talmadge, *Lovejoy*

REPRESENTATIVES

Prince H. Preston, Jr., *Statesboro*
John L. Pilcher, *Meigs*
Elijah L. Forrester, *Leesburg*
John James Flynt, Jr., *Griffin*
James C. Davis, *Stone Mountain*
Carl Vinson, *Milledgeville*
Harlan Erwin Mitchell, *Dalton*
Mrs. Iris F. Blitch, *Homerville*
Phillip M. Landrum, *Jasper*
Paul Brown, *Elberton*

HAWAII [9]

SENATORS

Hiram L. Fong,[10] *Honolulu*
Oren E. Long,[11] *Honolulu*

REPRESENTATIVE

At Large—Daniel K. Inouye,[12] *Honolulu*

IDAHO

SENATORS

Henry C. Dworshak, *Burley*
Frank Church, *Boise*

REPRESENTATIVES

Mrs. Gracie B. Pfost, *Nampa*
Hamer H. Budge, *Boise*

ILLINOIS

SENATORS

Paul H. Douglas, *Chicago*
Everett M. Dirksen, *Pekin*

REPRESENTATIVES

William L. Dawson, *Chicago*
Barratt O'Hara, *Chicago*
William T. Murphy, *Chicago*
Edward J. Derwinski, *Chicago*
John C. Kluczynski, *Chicago*
Thomas J. O'Brien, *Chicago*
Roland V. Libonati, *Chicago*
Daniel D. Rostenkowski, *Chicago*
Sidney R. Yates, *Chicago*
Harold R. Collier, *Berwyn*
Roman C. Pucinski, *Chicago*
Charles A. Boyle,[13] *Chicago*
Mrs. Marguerite Stitt Church, *Evanston*
Elmer J. Hoffman, *Wheaton*
Noah M. Mason, *Oglesby*
Leo E. Allen, *Galena*

Leslie C. Arends, *Melvin*
Robert H. Michel, *Peoria*
Robert B. Chiperfield, *Canton*
Mrs. Edna Oakes Simpson, *Carrollton*
Peter F. Mack, Jr., *Carlinville*
William L. Springer, *Champaign*
George E. Shipley, *Olney*
Charles Melvin Price, *East St. Louis*
Kenneth J. Gray, *West Frankfort*

INDIANA

SENATORS

Homer E. Capehart, *Washington*
Vance Hartke, *Evansville*

REPRESENTATIVES

Ray J. Madden, *Gary*
Charles A. Halleck, *Rensselaer*
John Brademas, *South Bend*
E. Ross Adair, *Fort Wayne*
J. Edward Roush, *Huntington*
Fred Wampler, *Terre Haute*
William G. Bray, *Martinsville*
Winfield K. Denton, *Evansville*
Earl Hogan, *Hope*
Randall S. Harmon, *Muncie*
Joseph W. Barr, *Indianapolis*

IOWA

SENATORS

Bourke B. Hickenlooper, *Cedar Rapids*
Thomas E. Martin, *Iowa City*

REPRESENTATIVES

Frederick D. Schwengel, *Davenport*
Leonard G. Wolf, *Elkader*
Harold R. Gross, *Waterloo*
Steven V. Carter,[14] *Leon*
John H. Kyl,[15] *Bloomfield*
Neal Smith, *Altoona*
Merwin Coad, *Boone*
Ben F. Jensen, *Exira*
Charles B. Hoeven, *Alton*

KANSAS

SENATORS

Andrew F. Schoeppel, *Wichita*
Frank Carlson, *Concordia*

REPRESENTATIVES

William H. Avery, *Wakefield*
Newell A. George, *Kansas City*
Denver D. Hargis, *Coffeyville*
Edward H. Rees, *Emporia*
J. Floyd Breeding, *Rolla*
Wint Smith,[16] *Mankato*

---

[9] Admitted as a State into the Union August 21, 1959.
[10] Took his seat August 24, 1959; term to expire, as determined by lot, January 3, 1965.
[11] Took his seat August 24, 1959; term to expire, as determined by lot, January 3, 1963.

[12] Took his seat August 24, 1959.
[13] Died November 4, 1959; vacancy throughout remainder of the Congress.
[14] Died November 4, 1959.

[15] Elected to fill vacancy caused by death of Steven V. Carter, and took his seat January 6, 1960.
[16] Election unsuccessfully contested by Elmo J. Mahoney.

KENTUCKY

SENATORS

John Sherman Cooper, *Somerset*
Thruston B. Morton, *Glenview*

REPRESENTATIVES

Frank A. Stubblefield, *Murray*
William H. Natcher, *Bowling Green*
Frank W. Burke, *Louisville*
Frank L. Chelf, *Lebanon*
Brent Spence, *Fort Thomas*
John C. Watts, *Nicholasville*
Carl D. Perkins, *Hindman*
Eugene Siler, *Williamsburg*

LOUISIANA

SENATORS

Allen J. Ellender, *Houma*
Russell B. Long, *Baton Rouge*

REPRESENTATIVES

F. Edward Hébert, *New Orleans*
T. Hale Boggs, *New Orleans*
Edwin E. Willis, *St. Martinville*
Overton Brooks, *Shreveport*
Otto E. Passman, *Monroe*
James H. Morrison, *Hammond*
T. Ashton Thompson, *Ville Platte*
Harold B. McSween, *Alexandria*

MAINE

SENATORS

Mrs. Margaret Chase Smith, *Skowhegan*
Edmund S. Muskie, *Waterville*

REPRESENTATIVES

James C. Oliver, *South Portland*
Frank M. Coffin, *Lewiston*
Clifford G. McIntire, *Perham*

MARYLAND

SENATORS

John Marshall Butler, *Baltimore*
J. Glenn Beall, *Frostburg*

REPRESENTATIVES

Thomas F. Johnson, *Berlin*
Daniel B. Brewster, *Glyndon*
Edward A. Garmatz, *Baltimore*
George H. Fallon, *Baltimore*
Richard E. Lankford, *Annapolis*
John R. Foley, *Kensington*
Samuel N. Friedel, *Baltimore*

MASSACHUSETTS

SENATORS

Leverett Saltonstall, *Dover*
John F. Kennedy,[17] *Boston*
Benjamin A. Smith II,[18] *Gloucester*

REPRESENTATIVES

Silvio O. Conte, *Pittsfield*
Edward P. Boland, *Springfield*
Philip J. Philbin, *Clinton*
Harold D. Donohue, *Worcester*
Mrs. Edith Nourse Rogers,[19] *Lowell*
William H. Bates, *Salem*
Thomas J. Lane, *Lawrence*
Torbert H. Macdonald, *Malden*
Hastings Keith, *West Bridgewater*
Laurence Curtis, *Boston*
Thomas P. O'Neill, Jr., *Cambridge*
John W. McCormack, *Dorchester*
James A. Burke, *Milton*
Joseph W. Martin, Jr., *North Attleboro*

MICHIGAN

SENATORS

Patrick V. McNamara, *Detroit*
Philip A. Hart, *Mackinac Island*

REPRESENTATIVES

Thaddeus M. Machrowicz, *Hamtramck*
George Meader, *Ann Arbor*
August E. Johansen, *Battle Creek*
Clare E. Hoffman, *Allegan*
Gerald R. Ford, Jr., *Grand Rapids*
Charles E. Chamberlain, *East Lansing*
James G. O'Hara, *Utica*
Alvin M. Bentley, *Owosso*
Robert P. Griffin, *Traverse City*
Elford A. Cederberg, *Bay City*
Victor A. Knox, *Sault Ste. Marie*
John B. Bennett, *Ontonagon*
Charles C. Diggs, Jr., *Detroit*
Louis C. Rabaut, *Grosse Pointe Park*
John D. Dingell, Jr., *Detroit*
John Lesinski, Jr., *Dearborn*
Mrs. Martha W. Griffiths, *Detroit*
William S. Broomfield, *Royal Oak*

MINNESOTA

SENATORS

Hubert H. Humphrey, *Waverly*
Eugene J. McCarthy, *St. Paul*

REPRESENTATIVES

Albert H. Quie, *Dennison*
Ancher Nelsen, *Hutchinson*
Roy W. Wier, *Minneapolis*
Joseph E. Karth, *St. Paul*
Walter H. Judd, *Minneapolis*

Fred Marshall, *Grove City*
H. Carl Andersen, *Tyler*
John A. Blatnik, *Chisholm*
Odin Langen, *Kennedy*

MISSISSIPPI

SENATORS

James O. Eastland, *Doddsville*
John C. Stennis, *De Kalb*

REPRESENTATIVES

Thomas G. Abernethy, *Okolona*
Jamie L. Whitten, *Charleston*
Frank E. Smith, *Greenwood*
John Bell Williams, *Raymond*
W. Arthur Winstead, *Philadelphia*
William M. Colmer, *Pascagoula*

MISSOURI

SENATORS

Thomas C. Hennings, Jr.,[20] *St. Louis*
Edward V. Long,[21] *Bowling Green*
Stuart Symington, *Richmond Heights*

REPRESENTATIVES

Frank M. Karsten, *St. Louis*
Thomas B. Curtis, *Webster Groves*
Mrs. Leonor Kretzer Sullivan, *St. Louis*
George H. Christopher,[22] *Butler*
William J. Randall,[23] *Independence*
Richard W. Bolling, *Kansas City*
William R. Hull, Jr., *Weston*
Charles H. Brown, *Springfield*
Albert S. J. Carnahan, *Ellsinore*
Clarence Cannon, *Elsberry*
Paul C. Jones, *Kennett*
Morgan M. Moulder, *Camdenton*

MONTANA

SENATORS

James E. Murray, *Butte*
Mike Mansfield, *Missoula*

REPRESENTATIVES

Lee Metcalf, *Helena*
LeRoy H. Anderson, *Conrad*

NEBRASKA

SENATORS

Roman L. Hruska, *Omaha*
Carl T. Curtis, *Minden*

REPRESENTATIVES

Phillip H. Weaver, *Falls City*
Glenn C. Cunningham, *Omaha*
Lawrence Brock, *Wakefield*
Donald F. McGinley, *Ogallala*

---

[17] Resigned December 22, 1960.
[18] Appointed to fill vacancy caused by resignation of John F. Kennedy but was unable to be sworn in as Congress was not in session.

[19] Died September 10, 1960; vacancy throughout remainder of the Congress.
[20] Died September 13, 1960.
[21] Appointed September 23, 1960, to fill vacancy

caused by death of Thomas C. Hennings, Jr.; subsequently elected.
[22] Died January 23, 1959.
[23] Elected to fill vacancy caused by death of George H. Christopher, and took his seat March 9, 1959.

NEVADA

SENATORS

Alan H. Bible, *Reno*
Howard W. Cannon, *Las Vegas*

REPRESENTATIVE

At Large—Walter S. Baring, *Reno*

NEW HAMPSHIRE

SENATORS

H. Styles Bridges, *Concord*
Norris Cotton, *Lebanon*

REPRESENTATIVES

Chester E. Merrow, *Center Ossipee*
Perkins Bass, *Peterborough*

NEW JERSEY

SENATORS

Clifford P. Case, *Rahway*
Harrison A. Williams, Jr., *Westfield*

REPRESENTATIVES

William T. Cahill, *Collingswood*
Milton W. Glenn, *Margate City*
James C. Auchincloss, *Rumson*
Frank Thompson, Jr., *Trenton*
Peter H. B. Frelinghuysen, Jr., *Morristown*
Mrs. Florence P. Dwyer, *Elizabeth*
William B. Widnall, *Saddle River*
Gordon Canfield, *Paterson*
Frank C. Osmers, Jr., *Tenafly*
Peter W. Rodino, Jr., *Newark*
Hugh J. Addonizio, *Newark*
George M. Wallhauser, *Maplewood*
Cornelius E. Gallagher, *Bayonne*
Dominick V. Daniels, *Jersey City*

NEW MEXICO

SENATORS

Dennis Chavez, *Albuquerque*
Clinton P. Anderson, *Albuquerque*

REPRESENTATIVES AT LARGE

Joseph M. Montoya, *Santa Fe*
Thomas G. Morris, *Tucumcari*

NEW YORK

SENATORS

Jacob K. Javits, *New York City*
Kenneth B. Keating, *Rochester*

REPRESENTATIVES

Stuyvesant Wainwright, *Wainscott*
Steven B. Derounian, *Roslyn*

Frank J. Becker, *Lynbrook*
Seymour Halpern, *Forest Hills*
Albert H. Bosch,[24] *Woodhaven*
Lester Holtzman, *Rego Park*
James J. Delaney, *Long Island City*
Victor L. Anfuso, *Brooklyn*
Eugene J. Keogh, *Brooklyn*
Mrs. Edna F. Kelly, *Brooklyn*
Emanuel Celler, *Brooklyn*
Francis E. Dorn, *Brooklyn*
Abraham J. Multer, *Brooklyn*
John J. Rooney, *Brooklyn*
John H. Ray, *Staten Island*
Adam C. Powell, Jr., *New York City*
John V. Lindsay, *New York City*
Alfred E. Santangelo, *New York City*
Leonard Farbstein, *New York City*
Ludwig Teller, *New York City*
Herbert Zelenko, *New York City*
James C. Healey, *New York City*
Isidore Dollinger,[25] *New York City*
Jacob H. Gilbert,[26] *New York City*
Charles A. Buckley, *New York City*
Paul A. Fino, *New York City*
Edwin B. Dooley, *Mamaroneck*
Robert R. Barry, *Yonkers*
Mrs. Katharine St. George, *Tuxedo Park*
J. Ernest Wharton, *Richmondville*
Leo W. O'Brien, *Albany*
Dean P. Taylor, *Troy*
Samuel S. Stratton, *Schenectady*
Clarence E. Kilburn, *Malone*
Alexander Pirnie, *Utica*
R. Walter Riehlman, *Tully*
John Taber, *Auburn*
Howard W. Robison, *Owego*
Mrs. Jessica McC. Weis, *Rochester*
Harold C. Ostertag, *Attica*
William E. Miller, *Olcott*
Thaddeus J. Dulski, *Buffalo*
John R. Pillion, *Hamburg*
Daniel A. Reed,[27] *Dunkirk*
Charles E. Goodell,[28] *Jamestown*

NORTH CAROLINA

SENATORS

Samuel J. Ervin, Jr., *Morganton*
B. Everett Jordan, *Saxapahaw*

REPRESENTATIVES

Herbert C. Bonner, *Washington*
Lawrence H. Fountain, *Tarboro*
Graham A. Barden, *New Bern*
Harold D. Cooley, *Nashville*
Ralph J. Scott, *Danbury*
Carl T. Durham, *Chapel Hill*
Alton A. Lennon, *Wilmington*
A. Paul Kitchin, *Wadesboro*
Hugh Q. Alexander, *Kannapolis*

Charles Raper Jonas, *Lincolnton*
Basil L. Whitener, *Gastonia*
David M. Hall,[29] *Sylva*
Roy A. Taylor,[30] *Black Mountain*

NORTH DAKOTA

SENATORS

William Langer,[31] *Wheatland*
C. Norman Brunsdale,[32] *Mayville*
Quentin N. Burdick,[33] *Fargo*
Milton R. Young, *La Moure*

REPRESENTATIVES AT LARGE

Quentin N. Burdick,[34] *Fargo*
Don L. Short, *Medora*

OHIO

SENATORS

Frank J. Lausche, *Cleveland*
Stephen M. Young, *Cleveland*

REPRESENTATIVES

Gordon H. Scherer, *Cincinnati*
William E. Hess, *Cincinnati*
Paul F. Schenck, *Dayton*
William M. McCulloch, *Piqua*
Delbert L. Latta, *Bowling Green*
James G. Polk,[35] *Highland*
Ward M. Miller,[36] *Portsmouth*
Clarence J. Brown, *Blanchester*
Jackson E. Betts, *Findlay*
Thomas L. Ashley, *Waterville*
Walter H. Moeller, *Lancaster*
Robert E. Cook, *Ravenna*
Samuel L. Devine, *Columbus*
Albert D. Baumhart, Jr., *Vermilion*
William H. Ayres, *Akron*
John E. Henderson, *Cambridge*
Frank T. Bow, *Canton*
Robert W. Levering, *Fredericktown*
Wayne L. Hays, *Flushing*
Michael J. Kirwan, *Youngstown*
Michael A. Feighan, *Cleveland*
Charles A. Vanik, *Cleveland*
Mrs. Frances P. Bolton, *Lyndhurst*
William E. Minshall, *Rocky River*

OKLAHOMA

SENATORS

Robert S. Kerr, *Oklahoma City*
A. S. Mike Monroney, *Oklahoma City*

REPRESENTATIVES

Page H. Belcher, *Enid*
Edmond Edmondson, *Muskogee*

---

[24] Resigned December 31, 1960; vacancy throughout remainder of the Congress.
[25] Resigned December 31, 1959.
[26] Elected to fill vacancy caused by resignation of Isidore Dollinger, and took his seat March 11, 1960.
[27] Died February 19, 1959.
[28] Elected to fill vacancy caused by death of Daniel A. Reed, and took his seat June 2, 1959.

[29] Died January 29, 1960.
[30] Elected to fill vacancy caused by death of David M. Hall, and took his seat July 2, 1960.
[31] Died November 8, 1959.
[32] Appointed to fill vacancy caused by death of William Langer, and took his seat January 6, 1960.
[33] Elected to fill vacancy caused by death of William Langer, and took his seat August 8, 1960.

[34] Resigned August 8, 1960, having been elected Senator; vacancy throughout remainder of the Congress.
[35] Died April 28, 1959.
[36] Elected November 8, 1960, to fill vacancy caused by death of James G. Polk but was unable to be sworn in as Congress was not in session.

Carl Albert, *McAlester*
Thomas J. Steed, *Shawnee*
John Jarman, *Oklahoma City*
Toby Morris, *Lawton*

OREGON

SENATORS

Wayne L. Morse, *Eugene*
Richard L. Neuberger,[37] *Portland*
Hall S. Lusk,[38] *Portland*
Maurine B. Neuberger,[39] *Portland*

REPRESENTATIVES

A. Walter Norblad, *Stayton*
Albert C. Ullman, *Baker*
Mrs. Edith S. Green, *Portland*
Charles O. Porter, *Eugene*

PENNSYLVANIA

SENATORS

Joseph S. Clark, *Philadelphia*
Hugh D. Scott, Jr., *Philadelphia*

REPRESENTATIVES

William A. Barrett, *Philadelphia*
Mrs. Kathryn E. Granahan, *Philadelphia*
James A. Byrne, *Philadelphia*
Robert N. C. Nix, *Philadelphia*
William J. Green, Jr., *Philadelphia*
Herman Toll, *Philadelphia*
William H. Milliken, Jr., *Sharon Hill*
Willard S. Curtin, *Morrisville*
Paul B. Dague, *Downingtown*
Stanley A. Prokop, *Lake Ariel*
Daniel J. Flood, *Wilkes-Barre*
Ivor D. Fenton, *Mahanoy City*
John A. Lafore, Jr., *Haverford*
George M. Rhodes, *Reading*
Francis E. Walter, *Easton*
Walter M. Mumma, *Harrisburg*
Alvin R. Bush,[40] *Muncy*
Herman T. Schneebeli,[41] *Williamsport*
Richard M. Simpson,[42] *Huntingdon*
Douglas H. Elliott,[43] [44] *Chambersburg*
J. Irving Whalley,[45] *Windber*
James M. Quigley, *Camp Hill*
James E. Van Zandt, *Altoona*
John H. Dent, *Jeannette*
John P. Saylor, *Johnstown*
Leon H. Gavin, *Oil City*
Carroll D. Kearns, *Farrell*
Frank M. Clark, *Bessemer*
Thomas E. Morgan, *Fredericktown*
James G. Fulton, *Dormont*
William S. Moorhead, *Pittsburgh*
Robert J. Corbett, *Pittsburgh*
Elmer J. Holland, *Pittsburgh*

RHODE ISLAND

SENATORS

Theodore F. Green, *Providence*
John O. Pastore, *Cranston*

REPRESENTATIVES

Aime J. Forand, *Cumberland*
John E. Fogarty, *Harmony*

SOUTH CAROLINA

SENATORS

Olin D. Johnston, *Spartanburg*
James Strom Thurmond, *Aiken*

REPRESENTATIVES

L. Mendel Rivers, *Charleston*
John J. Riley, *Sumter*
W. J. Bryan Dorn, *Greenwood*
Robert T. Ashmore, *Greenville*
Robert W. Hemphill, *Chester*
John L. McMillan, *Florence*

SOUTH DAKOTA

SENATORS

Karl E. Mundt, *Madison*
Francis H. Case, *Custer*

REPRESENTATIVES

George S. McGovern, *Mitchell*
Ellis Y. Berry, *McLaughlin*

TENNESSEE

SENATORS

Estes Kefauver, *Chattanooga*
Albert A. Gore, *Carthage*

REPRESENTATIVES

B. Carroll Reece, *Johnson City*
Howard H. Baker, *Huntsville*
James B. Frazier, Jr., *Chattanooga*
Joseph L. Evins, *Smithville*
J. Carlton Loser, *Nashville*
Ross Bass, *Pulaski*
Thomas J. Murray, *Jackson*
Robert A. Everett, *Union City*
Clifford Davis, *Memphis*

TEXAS

SENATORS

Lyndon B. Johnson, *Johnson City*
Ralph W. Yarborough, *Austin*

REPRESENTATIVES

Wright Patman, *Texarkana*
Jack B. Brooks, *Beaumont*

Lindley G. Beckworth, *Gladewater*
Sam Rayburn, *Bonham*
Bruce R. Alger, *Dallas*
Olin E. Teague, *College Station*
John V. Dowdy, *Athens*
Albert Thomas, *Houston*
Clark W. Thompson, *Galveston*
W. Homer Thornberry, *Austin*
William R. Poage, *Waco*
James C. Wright, Jr., *Fort Worth*
Frank N. Ikard, *Wichita Falls*
John A. Young, *Corpus Christi*
Joe M. Kilgore, *McAllen*
J. T. Rutherford, *Odessa*
Omar T. Burleson, *Anson*
Walter E. Rogers, *Pampa*
George H. Mahon, *Lubbock*
Paul J. Kilday, *San Antonio*
O. Clark Fisher, *San Angelo*
Robert R. Casey, *Houston*

UTAH

SENATORS

Wallace F. Bennett, *Salt Lake City*
Frank E. Moss, *Salt Lake City*

REPRESENTATIVES

Henry Aldous Dixon, *Ogden*
David S. King, *Salt Lake City*

VERMONT

SENATORS

George D. Aiken, *Putney*
Winston L. Prouty, *Newport*

REPRESENTATIVE

At Large—William H. Meyer, *West Rupert*

VIRGINIA

SENATORS

Harry Flood Byrd, *Berryville*
A. Willis Robertson, *Lexington*

REPRESENTATIVES

Thomas N. Downing, *Newport News*
Porter Hardy, Jr., *Churchland*
J. Vaughan Gary, *Richmond*
Watkins M. Abbitt, *Appomattox*
William M. Tuck, *South Boston*
Richard H. Poff, *Radford*
Burr P. Harrison, *Winchester*
Howard W. Smith, *Broad Run*
William Pat Jennings, *Marion*
Joel T. Broyhill, *Arlington*

---

[37] Died March 9, 1960.
[38] Appointed to fill vacancy caused by death of Richard L. Neuberger, and took his seat March 23, 1960.
[39] Elected November 8, 1960, to fill vacancy caused by death of her husband, Richard L. Neuberger, for the term ending January 3, 1961, but was unable to be sworn in as Congress was not in session.
[40] Died November 5, 1959.
[41] Elected to fill vacancy caused by death of Alvin R. Bush, and took his seat May 5, 1960.
[42] Died January 7, 1960.

[43] Elected to fill vacancy caused by death of Richard M. Simpson, and took his seat May 5, 1960.
[44] Died June 19, 1960.
[45] Elected November 8, 1960, to fill vacancy caused by death of Douglas H. Elliott, but was unable to be sworn in as Congress was not in session.

WASHINGTON

SENATORS

Warren G. Magnuson, *Seattle*
Henry M. Jackson, *Everett*

REPRESENTATIVES

Thomas M. Pelly, *Port Blakely*
Alfred John Westland, *Everett*
Russell V. Mack,[46] *Hoquiam*
Mrs. Julia Butler Hansen,[47] *Cathlamet*
Mrs. Catherine D. May, *Yakima*
Walter F. Horan, *Wenatchee*
Thor C. Tollefson, *Tacoma*
Donald H. Magnuson, *Seattle*

WEST VIRGINIA

SENATORS

Jennings Randolph, *Elkins*
Robert C. Byrd, *Sophia*

REPRESENTATIVES

Arch A. Moore, Jr., *Glendale*
Harley O. Staggers, *Keyser*
Cleveland M. Bailey, *Clarksburg*
Kenneth Hechler, *Huntington*
Mrs. Maude Elizabeth Kee, *Bluefield*
John M. Slack, Jr., *Charleston*

WISCONSIN

SENATORS

Alexander Wiley, *Chippewa Falls*
William Proxmire, *Madison*

REPRESENTATIVES

Gerald T. Flynn, *Racine*
Robert W. Kastenmeier, *Watertown*
Gardner R. Withrow, *La Crosse*
Clement J. Zablocki, *Milwaukee*
Henry S. Reuss, *Milwaukee*

William K. Van Pelt, *Fond du Lac*
Melvin R. Laird, *Marshfield*
John W. Byrnes, *Green Bay*
Lester R. Johnson, *Black River Falls*
Alvin E. O'Konski, *Mercer*

WYOMING

SENATORS

Joseph C. O'Mahoney, *Cheyenne*
Gale W. McGee, *Laramie*

REPRESENTATIVE

At Large—E. Keith Thomson,[48] *Cheyenne*

COMMONWEALTH OF PUERTO RICO

RESIDENT COMMISSIONER

A. Fernós-Isern, *Santurce*

---

[46] Died March 28, 1960.
[47] Elected November 8, 1960, to fill vacancy caused by death of Russell V. Mack, but was unable to be sworn in as Congress was not in session.

[48] Died December 9, 1960; vacancy throughout remainder of the Congress.

MEMBERS OF THE EIGHTY-SEVENTH CONGRESS
SERVING THEIR FIRST TERM

SENATORS

J. J. Hickey, Democrat, *Cheyenne, Wyo.*
Jack R. Miller, Republican, *Sioux City, Iowa*
Claiborne Pell, Democrat, *Newport, R.I.*
John G. Tower, Republican, *Wichita Falls, Tex.*

REPRESENTATIVES

Joseph P. Addabbo, Democrat, 5th District, *Ozone Park, N.Y.*
John B. Anderson, Republican, 16th District, *Rockford, Ill.*
John M. Ashbrook, Republican, 17th District, *Johnstown, Ohio*
James F. Battin, Republican, 2d District, *Billings, Mont.*
Ralph F. Beermann, Republican, 3d District, *Dakota City, Nebr.*
Alphonzo Bell, Republican, 16th District, *Santa Monica, Calif.*
James E. Bromwell, Republican, 2d District, *Cedar Rapids, Iowa*
Donald C. Bruce, Republican, 11th District, *Indianapolis, Ind.*
Hugh L. Carey, Democrat, 12th District, *Brooklyn, N.Y.*
Donald D. Clancy, Republican, 2d District, *Cincinnati, Ohio*
James C. Corman, Democrat, 22d District, *Van Nuys, Calif.*
John W. Davis, Democrat, 7th District, *Summerville, Ga.*
Robert J. Dole, Republican, 6th District, *Russell, Kans.*
Peter H. Dominick, Republican, 2d District, *Englewood, Colo.*
Edwin R. Durno, Republican, 4th District, *Medford, Oreg.*
Robert F. Ellsworth, Republican, 2d District, *Lawrence, Kans.*
Paul Findley, Republican, 20th District, *Pittsfield, Ill.*
Edward R. Finnegan, Democrat, 12th District, *Chicago, Ill.*
Peter A. Garland, Republican, 1st District, *Saco, Maine*
Henry B. Gonzalez, Democrat, 20th District, *San Antonio, Tex.*
George A. Goodling, Republican, 19th District, *Loganville, Pa.*
G. Elliott Hagan, Democrat, 1st District, *Sylvania, Ga.*
Durward G. Hall, Republican, 7th District, *Springfield, Mo.*
Ralph R. Harding, Democrat, 2d District, *Blackfoot, Idaho*
William H. Harsha, Jr., Republican, 6th District, *Portsmouth, Ohio*
James Harvey, Republican, 8th District, *Saginaw, Mich.*
David N. Henderson, Democrat, 3d District, *Wallace, N.C.*
Richard H. Ichord, Democrat, 8th District, *Houston, Mo.*

Charles S. Joelson, Democrat, 8th District, *Paterson, N.J.*
Carleton J. King, Republican, 31st District, *Saratoga Springs, N.Y.*
Horace R. Kornegay, Democrat, 6th District, *Greensboro, N.C.*
Clark MacGregor, Republican, 3d District, *Plymouth, Minn.*
David T. Martin, Republican, 4th District, *Kearney, Nebr.*
Charles McC. Mathias, Jr., Republican, 6th District, *Frederick, Md.*
Walter L. McVey, Republican, 3d District, *Independence, Kans.*
Tom V. Moorehead, Republican, 15th District, *Zanesville, Ohio*
F. Bradford Morse, Republican, 5th District, *Lowell, Mass.*
Charles A. Mosher, Republican, 13th District, *Oberlin, Ohio*
Lucien N. Nedzi, Democrat, 1st District, *Detroit, Mich.*
Mrs. Catherine D. Norrell, Democrat, 6th District, *Monticello, Ark.*
Hjalmar C. Nygaard, Republican, At Large, *Enderlin, N. Dak.*
Arnold Olsen, Democrat, 1st District, *Helena, Mont.*
M. Blaine Peterson, Democrat, 1st District, *Ogden, Utah*
Otis G. Pike, Democrat, 1st District, *Riverhead, N.Y.*
Mrs. Louise G. Reece, Republican, 1st District, *Johnson City, Tenn.*
Ben Reifel, Republican, 1st District, *Aberdeen, S. Dak.*
Richard L. Roudebush, Republican, 6th District, *Noblesville, Ind.*
John H. Rousselot, Republican, 25th District, *San Gabriel, Calif.*
William Fitts Ryan, Democrat, 20th District, *New York City, N.Y.*
Fernand J. St Germain, Democrat, 1st District, *Woonsocket, R.I.*
Henry C. Schadeberg, Republican, 1st District, *Burlington, Wis.*
Richard S. Schweiker, Republican, 13th District, *Lansdale, Pa.*
William W. Scranton, Republican, 10th District, *Dalton, Pa.*
Garner E. Shriver, Republican, 4th District, *Wichita, Kans.*
Abner W. Sibal, Republican, 4th District, *Norwalk, Conn.*
Robert T. Stafford, Republican, At Large, *Rutland, Vt.*
Robert G. Stephens, Jr., Democrat, 10th District, *Athens, Ga.*
Vernon W. Thomson, Republican, 3d District, *Richland Center, Wis.*
Stanley R. Tupper, Republican, 2d District, *Boothbay Harbor, Maine*
Morris K. Udall, Democrat, 2d District, *Tucson, Ariz.*

BIOGRAPHIES

BIOGRAPHIES

AANDAHL, Fred George, a Representative from North Dakota; born in Litchville, Barnes County, N. Dak., April 9, 1897; attended a one-room country school and Litchville High School; was graduated from the University of North Dakota at Grand Forks in 1921; engaged in agricultural pursuits since 1921; superintendent of schools in Litchville, N. Dak., 1922–1927; member of the North Dakota Senate in the 1931, 1939, and 1941 sessions; Governor of North Dakota 1945–1950; elected as a Republican to the Eighty-second Congress (January 3, 1951–January 3, 1953); was not a candidate for renomination in 1952, but was unsuccessful for the Republican senatorial nomination; appointed Assistant Secretary of the Department of the Interior, Washington, D. C., and served from February 10, 1953, until January 20, 1961; is a resident of Litchville, N. Dak.

ABBITT, Watkins Moorman, a Representative from Virginia; born in Appomattox, Appomattox County, Va., May 21, 1908; attended the public schools; was graduated from Appomattox Agricultural High School in 1925 and from the law department of the University of Richmond in 1931; was admitted to the bar in 1931 and commenced practice in Appomattox, Va.; Commonwealth attorney of Appomattox County 1932–1948; member of the Virginia Constitutional Convention of 1945; director of Farmers National Bank; delegate to Democratic State Conventions in 1932, 1936, 1940, 1944, 1948, and 1952; member of Democratic State executive committee since 1937; elected as a Democrat to the Eightieth Congress to fill the vacancy caused by the death of Patrick H. Drewry; reelected to the Eighty-first and to the five succeeding Congresses and served from February 17, 1948, to January 3, 1961. *Reelected to the Eighty-seventh Congress.*

ABBOTT, Amos, a Representative from Massachusetts; born in Andover, Mass., September 10, 1786; attended the district school and Bradford Academy; engaged in mercantile pursuits; highway surveyor in 1812, 1814, and 1816; clerk of the market in 1819 and 1820–22; town clerk in 1822, 1826, and 1828; town treasurer 1824–1829; member of the school committee 1828–1829 and again in 1830; one of the founders of the Boston & Portland (now the Boston & Maine) Railroad in 1833, serving as director 1833–1841; member of the State house of representatives in 1835, 1836, 1837, and again in 1843; served in the State senate 1840–1842; elected as a Whig to the Twenty-eighth, Twenty-ninth, and Thirtieth Congresses (March 4, 1843–March 3, 1849); was not a candidate for reelection in 1848; resumed his former mercantile pursuits; died in Andover, Mass., November 2, 1868; interment in South Parish Cemetery.

ABBOTT, Jo (Joseph), a Representative from Texas; born near Decatur, Morgan County, Ala., January 15, 1840; attended the public schools; moved with his parents to Freestone County, Tex., in 1853; during the Civil War served in the Confederate Army as first lieutenant in the Twelfth Regiment, Texas Cavalry; studied law; was admitted to the bar in 1866 and commenced practice in Springfield, Limestone County, Tex.; subsequently moved to Hillsboro and continued the practice of law; member of the State house of representatives in 1870 and 1871;

appointed district judge of the twenty-eighth judicial district by Governor Roberts in February 1879; subsequently elected in November 1880 for a term of four years; elected as a Democrat to the Fiftieth and to the four succeeding Congresses (March 4, 1887–March 3, 1897); was not a candidate for renomination in 1896; resumed the practice of law in Hillsboro, Hill County, Tex., and died there February 11, 1908; interment in Old Cemetery.

ABBOTT, Joel, a Representative from Georgia; born in Fairfield, Conn., March 17, 1776; pursued an academic course; studied medicine under his father in Fairfield, Conn.; moved to Washington, Ga., in 1794 and practiced medicine; held several local offices; member of the State house of representatives in 1809 and twice reelected; elected as a Democrat to the Fifteenth and to the three succeeding Congresses (March 4, 1817–March 3, 1825); resumed the practice of medicine; delegate to the convention which met in Philadelphia, Pa., in 1820 to prepare the first National Pharmacopoeia; died in Washington, Wilkes County, Ga., November 19, 1826; interment in Rest Haven Cemetery.

ABBOTT, Joseph Carter, a Senator from North Carolina; born in Concord, N. H., July 15, 1825; was graduated from Phillips Academy, Andover, Mass., in 1846; studied law; was admitted to the bar in 1852; editor and proprietor of the Manchester American 1852–1857; appointed adjutant general of New Hampshire in July 1855 and served until his resignation in 1861; editor of the Boston Atlas in 1859; member of the commission to adjust the boundary line between New Hampshire and Canada; served in the Union Army during the Civil War; was commissioned lieutenant colonel of the Seventh Regiment, New Hampshire Volunteer Infantry, December 13, 1861, and colonel November 17, 1863; brevetted brigadier general of Volunteers January 15, 1865, "for gallant and meritorious services in the capture of Fort Fisher, N. C.," where he commanded a brigade; honorably mustered out July 17, 1865; moved to Wilmington, N. C., and was for a time commandant of the city; delegate to the State constitutional convention in 1868; upon the readmission of the State of North Carolina to representation was elected as a Republican to the United States Senate and served from July 14, 1868, to March 3, 1871; collector of the port of Wilmington under President Grant; inspector of posts along the eastern line of the southern coast under President Hayes; established the town of Abbottsburg, in Bladen County, N. C.; engaged in the manufacture of lumber; employed as a special agent in the United States Treasury Department; editor of the Wilmington Post; died in Wilmington, New Hanover County, N. C., October 8, 1881; interment in Valley Cemetery, Manchester, N. H.

ABBOTT, Josiah Gardner, a Representative from Massachusetts; born in Chelmsford, Middlesex County, Mass., November 1, 1814; attended the common schools and Chelmsford Academy; was graduated from Harvard University in 1832; taught school; studied law; was admitted to the bar in 1835 and commenced practice in Lowell, Mass., in 1837; member of the State house of representatives in 1836; served in the State senate in 1841 and 1842; member of the staff of Governor Morton in 1843; master in chancery 1850–1855; member of the State constitutional convention in 1853; appointed justice of the superior court of Suffolk County in 1855 and served until 1858, when he resigned; resumed the practice of law; one of the overseers of Harvard College 1859–1865; several times was the unsuccessful Democratic candidate for United States Senator; declined an appointment to the supreme court bench in 1860; moved to Boston in 1861 and continued the practice of law; declined the Democratic nomination for attorney general in 1861; successfully contested as a Democrat the election of Rufus S. Frost to the Forty-fourth Congress and served from July 28, 1876, to March 3, 1877; was not a candidate for renomination in 1876; appointed a member of the Electoral Commission created by the act of Congress approved January 29, 1877, to decide the contests in various States in the presidential election of 1876; resumed the practice of law; also interested in manufacturing and various other enterprises; died in Wellesley Hills, near Boston, Mass., June 2, 1891; interment in St. Mary's Cemetery, Newton Lower Falls, Mass.

ABBOTT, Nehemiah, a Representative from Maine; born in Sidney, Maine, March 29, 1804; studied law at the Litchfield (Conn.) Law School; was admitted to the bar in 1836 and commenced practice at Calais, Maine; moved to Columbus, Miss., in 1839 and continued the practice of law; returned to Maine in 1840 and settled in Belfast, Waldo County, where he resumed the practice of law; member of the State house of representatives in 1842, 1843, and 1845; elected as a Republican to the Thirty-fifth Congress (March 4, 1857–March 3, 1859); engaged in the practice of his profession until his death; mayor of Belfast in 1865 and 1866; died in Belfast, Maine, July 26, 1877; interment in Grove Cemetery.

ABEL, Hazel Hempel, a Senator from Nebraska; born in Plattsmouth, Cass County, Nebr., July 10, 1888; attended the public schools of Omaha, Nebr., was graduated from the University of Nebraska at Lincoln in 1908; high school teacher of mathematics and principal of high schools in Papillion, Ashland, and Crete, Nebr., 1908–1916; president of Abel Construction Co. 1937–1952; chairman of the board of directors of Abel Investment Co., Lincoln, Nebr., in 1952 and 1953; delegate to State Republican Conventions 1939–1948 and 1952–1956; vice chairman of State Republican Central Committee in 1954; elected as a Republican to the United States Senate to fill the vacancy in the term ending January 3, 1955, caused by the deaths of Kenneth S. Wherry and Dwight Griswold, and served from November 8, 1954, until her resignation December 31, 1954; delegate to White House Conference on Education in 1955; chairman of Nebraska delegation to the Republican National Convention in 1956; member of the Theodore Roosevelt Centennial Commission 1955–1959; chairman, board of trustees, Doane College; member, board of trustees of Nebraska Wesleyan College; is a resident of Lincoln, Nebr.

ABERCROMBIE, James, a Representative from Alabama; born in Hancock County, Ga., in 1795; attended the common schools; moved to Alabama about 1812 and settled in Monroe (now Dallas) County, and later, in 1819, in Montgomery County; during the War of 1812 served as a corporal in Maj. F. Freeman's Squadron of Georgia Cavalry; studied law; member of the State house of representatives 1820–1822 and in 1824; captain in the Alabama Militia and in command of the cavalry at the reception for General Lafayette in 1825; served in the State senate 1825–1833; moved to Russell County in 1834; again a member of the State house of representatives in 1838 and 1839; again served in the State senate 1847–1850; elected as a Union Whig to the Thirty-second and Thirty-third Congresses (March 4, 1851–March 3, 1855); was not a candidate for renomination in 1854;

moved to Florida in 1856 and became engaged as a Government brick contractor; died in Pensacola, Fla., July 2, 1861; interment in Linwood Cemetery, Columbus, Ga.

ABERCROMBIE, John William, a Representative from Alabama; born near Kellys Creek Post Office, St. Clair County, Ala., May 17, 1866; attended the rural schools; was graduated from Oxford (Ala.) College in 1886 and from the law department of the University of Alabama at Tuscaloosa in 1888; was admitted to the bar in 1888 and practiced in Cleburne County, Ala., in 1889 and 1890; high-school principal, city school superintendent, and college president 1888–1898; member of the State senate 1896–1898; State superintendent of education 1898–1902; president of the University of Alabama 1902–1911; member of the Alabama Textbook Commission 1903–1908; chairman of the Rhodes Scholarship Commission of Alabama 1903–1911; president of the Southern Educational Association in 1906 and 1907; organizer and president of the Alabama Association of Colleges 1908–1912; elected as a Democrat to the Sixty-third and Sixty-fourth Congresses (March 4, 1913–March 3, 1917); served as Solicitor and Acting Secretary in the United States Department of Labor 1918–1920; appointed and subsequently elected State superintendent of education for the term 1920–1927; member of the Alabama State Board of Education; died in Montgomery, Ala., July 2, 1940; interment in Greenwood Cemetery.

ABERNETHY, Charles Laban, a Representative from North Carolina; born in Rutherford College, Burke County, N. C., March 18, 1872; attended the public schools, Mount Olive (N. C.) High School, and Rutherford College; moved to Beaufort, Carteret County, N. C., in 1893; founded the Beaufort Herald in 1893; studied law at the University of North Carolina at Chapel Hill; was admitted to the bar in 1895 and commenced practice in Beaufort, N. C.; solicitor of the third (later the fifth) judicial circuit for twelve years; member of the State Democratic executive committee 1898–1900; presidential elector on the Democratic ticket of Bryan and Stevenson in 1900 and of Parker and Davis in 1904; moved to New Bern, N. C., in 1913 and continued the practice of law; elected as a Democrat to the Sixty-seventh Congress to fill the vacancy caused by the death of Samuel M. Brinson; reelected to the Sixty-eighth and to the five succeeding Congresses and served from November 7, 1922, to January 3, 1935; unsuccessful candidate for renomination in 1934; resumed the practice of law until his retirement in 1938; died in New Bern, N. C., February 23, 1955; interment in Cedar Grove Cemetery.

ABERNETHY, Thomas Gerstle, a Representative from Mississippi; born in Eupora, Webster County, Miss., May 16, 1903; attended the public schools, the University of Alabama at Tuscaloosa, the University of Mississippi at Oxford, and was graduated from the law department of Cumberland University, Lebanon, Tenn., in 1924; was admitted to the bar in 1924 and commenced practice in Eupora, Miss., in 1925; mayor of Eupora 1927–1929; moved to Okolona, Miss., in 1929 and continued the practice of law; district attorney of the third judicial district of Mississippi 1935–1942; elected as a Democrat to the Seventy-eighth and to the eight succeeding Congresses (January 3, 1943–January 3, 1961). *Reelected to the Eighty-seventh Congress.*

ACHESON, Ernest Francis, a Representative from Pennsylvania; born in Washington, Washington County, Pa., September 19, 1855; attended the public schools; was graduated from Washington and Jefferson College, Washington, Pa., in 1875; studied law; was admitted to the bar in 1877 and practiced until 1879; purchased the Washington Weekly Observer, of which he was editor; delegate to the Republican National Conventions in

1884 and 1896; established a daily edition of the Observer in 1889; elected president of the Pennsylvania Editorial Association in January 1893 and in June of the same year was chosen recording secretary of the National Editorial Association; trustee of Washington and Jefferson College 1894–1917; elected as a Republican to the Fifty-fourth and to the six succeeding Congresses (March 4, 1895–March 3, 1909); unsuccessful candidate for renomination in 1908; resumed editorial work; discontinued active business pursuits in 1912 and lived in retirement until his death in Washington, Pa., May 16, 1917; interment in Washington Cemetery.

ACKER, Ephraim Leister, a Representative from Pennsylvania; born in Marlboro Township, Montgomery County, Pa., January 11, 1827; attended the common schools and the academy at Sumneytown; was graduated from Marshall College, Mercersburg, Pa., September 8, 1847; taught school for two years; was graduated in medicine from the University of Pennsylvania at Philadelphia in March 1852; editor and publisher of the Norristown Register 1853–1877; superintendent of the schools of Montgomery County from June 1854 to June 1860; appointed postmaster of Norristown, Pa., in March 1860 by President Buchanan and after serving eleven months was removed by President Lincoln; served as inspector of Montgomery County Prison for three years; elected as a Democrat to the Forty-second Congress (March 4, 1871–March 3, 1873); unsuccessful candidate for reelection in 1872 to the Forty-third Congress; resumed the publication of his newspaper until 1877, when he began the study of law; was admitted to the bar and practiced until his death in Norristown, Pa., May 12, 1903; interment in Norris City Cemetery, Norriton Township, Montgomery County, Pa.

ACKERMAN, Ernest Robinson, a Representative from New Jersey; born in New York City, N. Y., June 17, 1863; moved with his parents to Plainfield, N. J., very shortly thereafter; educated at public and private schools and was graduated from the Plainfield High School in 1880; engaged in cement manufacturing; member of the common council of Plainfield, N. J., in 1891 and 1892; presidential elector on the Republican ticket of McKinley and Hobart in 1896; secretary of the New Jersey presidential electors in 1897; member of the State senate 1905–1911, serving as president in 1911; delegate to the Republican National Conventions at Chicago in 1908 and in 1916; member of the board of trustees of Rutgers College, New Brunswick, N. J., 1916–1920; Federal food administrator for Union County during the First World War; member of the State board of education 1918–1920; member of the New Jersey Geological Survey and associate of the American Society of Civil Engineers; elected as a Republican to the Sixty-sixth and to the six succeeding Congresses and served from March 4, 1919, until his death in Plainfield, N. J., October 18, 1931; interment in the family plot, Hillside Cemetery.

ACKLEN, Joseph Hayes, a Representative from Louisiana; born in Nashville, Tenn., May 20, 1850; educated by private tutors; attended Burlington Military College, near Burlington, N. J., in 1864 and 1865, and was graduated from two foreign universities (École de Neuilly, Paris, and Swiss University, Vevay); returned to the United States and was graduated from the Lebanon Law School, Lebanon, Tenn., in 1871; commenced the practice of law in Nashville and later practiced in Memphis, Tenn.; abandoned the practice of law and moved to Louisiana to superintend his sugar plantations near Pattersonville (now Patterson), St. May Parish; colonel in the Louisiana Militia in 1876; successfully contested as a Democrat the election of Chester B. Darrall to the Forty-fifth Congress; reelected to the Forty-sixth Congress and served from February 20, 1878, to March 3, 1881; was not a candidate for renomination in 1880; resumed the prac-

tice of law at Franklin, La.; declined to accept the position of judge of the Federal district court of Louisiana tendered by President Hayes in 1880; unsuccessful candidate for election in 1882 to the Forty-eighth Congress; returned to Nashville, Tenn., in 1885 and continued the practice of law; chairman of the Davidson County Democratic executive committee 1886–1894; member of the Nashville City Council 1900–1904; president of the State bar association in 1901 and 1902; general insurance counsel of Tennessee 1903–1907; State warden of the department of game, fish, and forestry 1903–1913; general counsel of the National Association of Game and Fish Commissioners of the United States 1905–1912, when elected president; middle Tennessee counsel of the St. Louis & San Francisco Railroad 1907–1911; chief game warden of the United States in 1913 and 1914; author of numerous articles on ornithology, fish culture, forestry, and field sports; chairman of the State central committee on the constitutional convention 1923–1927; died in Nashville, Tenn., September 28, 1938; interment in Mount Olivet Cemetery.

ADAIR, Edwin Ross, a Representative from Indiana; born in Albion, Noble County, Ind., December 14, 1907; attended grade and high schools in Albion, Ind.; was graduated from Hillsdale (Mich.) College in 1928 and from George Washington University Law School, Washington, D. C., in 1933; was admitted to the Indiana bar in 1933 and commenced the practice of law in Fort Wayne, Ind.; probate commissioner of Allen County, Ind., 1940–1950; during World War II was called to active duty as a second lieutenant in the Quartermaster Corps Reserve in September 1941 and served until October 1945; awarded battle stars for the Normandy, Northern France, Ardennes, Rhine, and Central European campaigns; elected as a Republican to the Eighty-second and to the four succeeding Congresses (January 3, 1951–January 3, 1961). *Reelected to the Eighty-seventh Congress.*

ADAIR, Jackson Leroy, a Representative from Illinois; born in Clayton, Adams County, Ill., February 23, 1887; attended public and high schools, and Illinois College at Jacksonville; was graduated from the law department of the University of Michigan at Ann Arbor in 1911; was admitted to the bar the same year and commenced practice in Muskogee, Okla.; moved to Quincy, Ill., in 1913 and continued the practice of law; also engaged in agricultural pursuits and in the manufacture of medicine for livestock; city attorney 1914–1916; prosecuting attorney of Adams County 1916–1920 and 1924–1928; member of the State senate 1928–1932; elected as a Democrat to the Seventy-third and Seventy-fourth Congresses (March 4, 1933–January 3, 1937); was not a candidate for renomination in 1936; appointed United States district judge for the southern district of Illinois in 1937 by President Franklin D. Roosevelt and served until his death in Quincy, Ill., January 19, 1956; interment in South Side Cemetery, Clayton, Ill.

ADAIR, John, a Senator and a Representative from Kentucky; born in Chester District, Chester County, S. C., January 9, 1757; attended the public schools and high school at Charlotte, N. C.; served in the Revolutionary War; member of the South Carolina convention that ratified the Constitution of the United States; moved to Kentucky in 1788; major of volunteers in an expedition against the Indians under General Wilkinson in 1791 and 1792; was a lieutenant colonel under General Scott in 1793; member of the Kentucky constitutional convention in 1792; member of the State house of representatives 1793–1795, 1798, and 1800–1803, serving as speaker in 1802 and 1803; register of the United States land office in 1805; elected as a Democrat to the United States Senate to fill the vacancy caused by the resignation of John Breckinridge and served from November 8, 1805, until November 18, 1806, when he resigned, having been an unsuccessful candidate for reelection; aide to Governor Shelby in the Battle of the Thames in 1813; commander of the Kentucky rifle brigade which served under General Jackson in 1814 and 1815; again a member of the State house of representatives in 1817; appointed adjutant general with the brevet rank of brigadier general; Governor of Kentucky 1820–1824; elected as a Democrat to the Twenty-second Congress (March 4, 1831–March 3, 1833); was not a candidate for renomination in 1832; died at White Hall, Mercer County, Ky., May 19, 1840; interment in the State Cemetery, Frankfort, Ky., where a monument to his memory was erected by the State.

ADAIR, John Alfred McDowell, a Representative from Indiana; born near Portland, Jay County, Ind., December 22, 1864; attended the public schools and Portland High School; engaged in mercantile pursuits; clerk of the city of Portland 1888–1890; clerk of Jay County 1890–1895; studied law; was admitted to the bar in 1895 and commenced practice in Portland, Ind.; member of the State house of representatives in 1902 and 1903; engaged in banking, being elected president of the First National Bank of Portland in 1904; elected as a Democrat to the Sixtieth and to the four succeeding Congresses (March 4, 1907–March 3, 1917); did not seek renomination in 1916, having become a gubernatorial candidate; unsuccessful Democratic nominee for Governor of Indiana in 1916; resumed the banking business in Portland, Ind.; moved to Washington, D. C., in 1924 and served as vice president of Southern Dairies (Inc.) until 1931; chairman of the board of the Finance Service Co., in Baltimore, Md., 1933-1935; vice president of the Atlas Tack Corporation, Fairhaven, Mass., 1935–1937; director of the Artloom Corporation, Philadelphia, Pa., in 1937; died in Portland, Ind., October 5, 1938; interment in Green Park Cemetery.

ADAMS, Alva Blanchard, a Senator from Colorado; born in Del Norte, Rio Grande County, Colo., October 29, 1875; attended the common schools; was graduated from Phillips Academy, Andover, Mass., in 1893, from Yale University in 1896, and from Columbia Law School at New York City, in 1899; was admitted to the bar in 1899 and commenced practice in Pueblo, Colo.; county attorney of Pueblo County 1909–1911; member of the charter convention of Pueblo in 1911; regent of the State University of Colorado 1911 and 1912; city attorney of Pueblo 1911–1915; delegate to the Democratic National Convention at St. Louis in 1916; delegate to every Democratic State convention from 1899 to 1926; during the First World War served as major in the Judge Advocate General's Department in 1918 and 1919; appointed as a Democrat to the United States Senate to fill the vacancy caused by the death of Samuel D. Nicholson and served from May 17, 1923, to November 30, 1924, when a successor was elected and qualified; unsuccessful candidate for election in 1924 to fill the vacancy; resumed the practice of law; elected to the United States Senate in 1932; reelected in 1938 and served from March 4, 1933, until his death in Washington, D. C., on December 1, 1941; interment in Roselawn Cemetery, Pueblo, Colo.

ADAMS, Andrew, a Delegate from Connecticut; born in Stratford, Conn., January 7, 1736; pursued preparatory studies; was graduated from Yale College in 1760; studied law, and was admitted to the Fairfield County bar; prosecuting attorney of Litchfield County in 1772; moved in 1774 to Litchfield, which thereafter remained his home; member of the Connecticut Council of Safety for two years; served in the Revolutionary War with the rank of colonel; member of the State house of representatives 1776–1781, serving as speaker in 1779 and 1780; Member of the Continental Congress 1777–1782; signer of the Articles of Confederation in 1778; member of the executive

council in 1789; appointed chief justice of the Connecticut Supreme Court in 1793 and served in this position until his death in Litchfield, Conn., November 26, 1797; interment in East Cemetery.

ADAMS, Benjamin, a Representative from Massachusetts; born in Mendon, Mass., December 16, 1764; attended the public schools, and was graduated from Brown University in 1788; studied law; was admitted to the bar and commenced practice in Uxbridge; member of the State house of representatives 1809–1814; served in the State senate in 1814, 1815, and 1822–1825; elected as a Federalist to the Fourteenth Congress to fill the vacancy caused by the death of Elijah Brigham; reelected to the Fifteenth and Sixteenth Congresses and served from December 2, 1816, to March 3, 1821; unsuccessful candidate for reelection in 1820 to the Seventeenth Congress and for election in 1822 to the Eighteenth Congress; resumed the practice of his profession; died in Uxbridge, Worcester County, Mass., March 28, 1837; interment in Prospect Hill Cemetery.

ADAMS, Charles Francis (son of John Quincy Adams and grandson of John Adams), a Representative from Massachusetts; born in Boston, Mass., August 18, 1807; spent several years with his parents in St. Petersburg, Russia; attended the Boston Latin School, and was graduated from Harvard University in 1825; studied law; was admitted to the bar on January 6, 1829, and commenced practice in Boston; member of the State house of representatives in 1831; served in the State senate 1835–1840; founded the Boston Whig in 1846; unsuccessful candidate of the Free-Soil Party for Vice President of the United States on the ticket with Martin Van Buren in 1848; elected as a Republican to the Thirty-sixth and Thirty-seventh Congresses and served from March 4, 1859, to May 1, 1861, when he resigned to accept a diplomatic position; appointed by President Lincoln as Minister to England and served from March 20, 1861, to May 13, 1868; declined the presidency of Harvard University but became one of its overseers in 1869; died in Boston, Mass., November 21, 1886; interment in Mount Wollaston Cemetery, Quincy, Norfolk County, Mass.

ADAMS, Charles Henry, a Representative from New York; born in Coxsackie, Greene County, N. Y., April 10, 1824; attended the public schools; studied law; was admitted to the bar about 1845 and commenced practice in New York City; moved to Cohoes, Albany County, N. Y., in 1850; appointed with rank of colonel to Governor Hunt's staff in 1851; member of the State assembly in 1858; engaged in the manufacture of knit underwear, and in banking; retired from active business in 1870; served as first mayor of Cohoes 1870–1872; delegate to the Republican National Convention at Philadelphia in 1872; served in the State senate in 1872 and 1873; United States commissioner from New York to the Vienna Exposition in 1873; elected as a Republican to the Forty-fourth Congress (March 4, 1875–March 3, 1877); unsuccessful candidate for renomination in 1876; resumed banking in Cohoes, N. Y., until 1892, when he retired from active business pursuits and moved to New York City, where he died December 15, 1902; interment in Woodlawn Cemetery.

ADAMS, George Everett, a Representative from Illinois; born in Keene, Cheshire County, N. H., June 18, 1840; moved with his parents to Chicago, Ill., in 1853; attended Phillips Exeter Academy, Exeter, N. H.; was graduated from Harvard University in 1860; during the Civil War enlisted in the First Regiment, Illinois Volunteer Artillery; attended the Harvard Law School, Cambridge, Mass; was admitted to the bar in 1865 and commenced practice in Chicago, Ill.; member of the State senate from 1880 until March 3, 1883, when he resigned to enter Congress; elected as a Republican to the Forty-eighth and to the three succeeding Congresses (March 4, 1883–March 3, 1891); was an unsuccessful candidate for reelection in 1890 to the Fifty-second Congress; resumed the practice of his profession in Chicago, Ill., until his death at his summer home in Peterborough, Hillsborough County, N. H., October 5, 1917; interment in Pine Hill Cemetery.

ADAMS, George Madison (nephew of Green Adams), a Representative from Kentucky; born in Barbourville, Knox County, Ky., December 20, 1837; received private instruction from his father and attended Centre College, Danville, Ky.; studied law; clerk of the circuit court of Knox County, Ky., 1859–1861; during the Civil War raised a company of volunteers and was captain of Company H, Seventh Regiment, Kentucky Volunteer Infantry, from 1861 to 1863; in 1864 was commissioned paymaster with the rank of major; elected as a Democrat to the Fortieth and to the three succeeding Congresses (March 4, 1867–March 3, 1875); unsuccessful candidate for reelection in 1874 to the Fourty-fourth Congress; elected Clerk of the National House of Representatives December 6, 1875, during the Forty-fourth Congress, and served until the commencement of the Forty-seventh Congress, December 5, 1881; appointed register of the Kentucky land office by Gov. J. Proctor Knott and served from 1884 to 1887; appointed secretary of state for Kentucky by Gov. Simon B. Buckner and served from 1887 to 1891; appointed State railroad commissioner in 1891; appointed United States pension agent at Louisville by President Cleveland and served from 1894 to 1898; after retirement resided at Winchester, Clark County, Ky., until his death April 6, 1920; interment in Lexington Cemetery, Lexington, Ky.

ADAMS, Green (uncle of George Madison Adams), a Representative from Kentucky; born in Barbourville, Knox County, Ky., August 20, 1812; pursued preparatory studies; studied law; was admitted to the bar and practiced; member of the State house of representatives in 1839; presidential elector on the Whig ticket of Clay and Frelinghuysen in 1844; elected as a Whig to the Thirtieth Congress (March 4, 1847–March 3, 1849); was not a candidate for renomination in 1848; judge of the circuit court of Kentucky 1851–1856; elected as the candidate of the American Party to the Thirty-sixth Congress (March 4, 1859–March 3, 1861); was not a candidate for renomination in 1860; Sixth Auditor of the Treasury Department from April 17, 1861, to October 26, 1864; resumed the practice of law in Philadelphia; Chief Clerk of the National House of Representatives during the Forty-fourth, Forty-fifth, and Forty-sixth Congresses 1875–1881; discontinued active pursuits; lived in retirement until his death in Philadelphia, Pa., January 18, 1884; interment in West Laurel Hill Cemetery.

ADAMS, Henry Cullen, a Representative from Wisconsin; born in Verona, Oneida County, N. Y., November 28, 1850; moved to Wisconsin in 1851 with his parents, who settled in Fort Atkinson, Jefferson County; attended the public schools, Albion Academy, and the University of Wisconsin at Madison; engaged in agricultural pursuits; member of the Wisconsin Assembly 1883–1885; State superintendent of public property 1884–1890; engaged in work with the Wisconsin farmers' institutes 1887–1889; president of the Wisconsin Dairy Association and secretary of the State Horticultural Society; State dairy and food commissioner 1895–1902; elected as a Republican to the Fifty-eighth and Fifty-ninth Congresses and served from March 4, 1903, until his death in Chicago, Ill., July 9, 1906; interment in Forest Hill Cemetery, Madison, Wis.

ADAMS, John (father of John Quincy Adams and grandfather of Charles Francis Adams), a Delegate from Massachusetts and a Vice President and a President of the United States; born in Braintree, Mass., October 30, 1735; was graduated from Harvard College in 1755; studied law; was admitted to the bar in 1758 and commenced practice in Suffolk County; joined the Sons of Liberty and appeared before Governor Hutchinson, with Otis and Gridley, to argue against the Stamp Act; was elected to represent Boston, to which city he had moved, in the general court in 1768; Member of the First Continental Congress 1774–1778; signed the Declaration of Independence and proposed George Washington, of Virginia, for General of the American Army; became head of the War Department, but resigned and was appointed commissioner, superseding Deane, with Franklin and Arthur Lee, to the Court of France; later made Minister Plenipotentiary to Holland to negotiate a loan in 1782; obtained the loan and negotiated a treaty of amity and commerce; was the first Minister to England, serving from 1785 until 1788; elected in 1788 as the first Vice President of the United States on the Federalist ticket with George Washington as President; reelected in 1792 and served from April 30, 1789, to March 3, 1797; elected President of the United States as a member of the Federalist Party and served from March 4, 1797, to March 3, 1801; his last act in office was to appoint John Marshall as Chief Justice of the United States; at the age of eighty-five served as a delegate to the constitutional convention of Massachusetts; died in Quincy, Mass., July 4, 1826; interment under the old First Congregational Church.

ADAMS, John, a Representative from New York; born in Oak Hill, town of Durham, Greene County, N. Y., August 26, 1778; attended the common schools; taught school in Durham; studied law; was admitted to the bar in 1805 and commenced practice in Durham; appointed surrogate of Greene County by Governor Tompkins in 1810; member of the State assembly in 1812 and 1813; presented credentials as a Democratic Member-elect to the Fourteenth Congress and served from March 4 to December 26, 1815, when he was succeeded by Erastus Root, who contested his election; elected as a Jackson Democrat to the Twenty-third Congress (March 4, 1833–March 3, 1835); was not a candidate for renomination in 1834; moved to Catskill, Greene County, N. Y., and continued the practice of law until his death; elected a director of the Catskill-Canajoharie Railroad in 1835; died in Catskill, N. Y., September 25, 1854; interment in Thomson Street Cemetery.

ADAMS, John Joseph, a Representative from New York; born in Douglas Town, Province of New Brunswick, Dominion of Canada, September 16, 1848; attended the local school; came to the United States and settled in New York City in 1864; engaged as a clerk with a dry-goods firm until 1874; was graduated from Columbia Law School in 1876; was admitted to the bar the same year and commenced practice in New York City; elected as an Independent Democrat to the Forty-eighth and Forty-ninth Congresses (March 4, 1883–March 3, 1887); was not a candidate for renomination in 1886; resumed the practice of law in New York City and died there February 16, 1919; interment in Greenwood Cemetery, Brooklyn, N. Y.

ADAMS, John Quincy (son of John Adams and father of Charles Francis Adams), a Senator and a Representative from Massachusetts and a President of the United States; born in Braintree, Mass., July 11, 1767; acquired his early education in Europe; attended the University of Leyden; was graduated from Harvard University in 1788; studied law; was admitted to the bar and commenced practice in Boston, Mass.; elected to the State senate in 1802; unsuccessful candidate for election in 1802 to the Eighth Congress; elected as a Federalist to the United

States Senate and served from March 4, 1803, until June 8, 1808, when he resigned; Minister to Russia 1809–1814; member of the commission which ne otiated the Treaty of Ghent in 1815; Minister to England 1815–1817 and assisted in concluding the convention of commerce with Great Britain; Secretary of State in the Cabinet of President Monroe 1817–1825; in 1825 the election of the President of the United States fell, according to the Constitution of the United States, upon the House of Representatives, as neither of the candidates had secured a majority of the electors chosen by the States, and Mr. Adams, who stood second to Andrew Jackson in the electoral vote, was chosen and served from March 4, 1825, to March 3, 1829; elected as a Whig to the Twenty-second and to the eight succeeding Congresses and served from March 4, 1831, until his death; unsuccessful candidate for Governor of Massachusetts in 1834; died in the National Capitol at Washington, D. C., February 23, 1848; interment in the family burial ground at Quincy, Mass.

ADAMS, Parmenio, a Representative from New York; born in Hartford, Conn., September 9, 1776; attended the common schools; moved in 1806 to "Phelps Corners," then in the township of Batavia, Genesee County (now Attica, Wyoming County), N. Y.; held commissions in the New York State Militia from 1806 to 1816 as lieutenant of light Infantry, captain of Grenadiers, second and first major, and division inspector of Infantry; served in the War of 1812 as major and commandant of New York Volunteers for some months on the Niagara frontier and was recommended for a majority in the United States Army by Gov. Daniel D. Tompkins, of New York; twice appointed sheriff of Genesee County, serving from March 16, 1815, to March 1, 1816, and from March 16, 1818, to February 22, 1821; engaged in agricultural pursuits and also was a construction contractor on the Erie Canal; successfully contested, as an Adams supporter, the election of Isaac Wilson to the Eighteenth Congress; reelected to the Nineteenth Congress and served from January 7, 1824, to March 3, 1827; died in Alexander, Genesee County, N. Y., February 19, 1832.

ADAMS, Robert, Jr., a Representative from Pennsylvania; born in Philadelphia, Pa., February 26, 1849; attended Doctor Fairies Physical Institute, Philadelphia, Pa., and was graduated from the University of Pennsylvania at Philadelphia in 1869; studied law; was admitted to the bar April 27, 1872, and practiced; member of the United States Geological Survey during the explorations of Yellowstone Park 1871–1875; member of the State militia 1881–1895; served in the State senate 1883–1886; was graduated from the Wharton School of Economy and Finance of the University of Pennsylvania in 1884; appointed United States Minister to Brazil on April 1, 1889, and served until June 1, 1890, when he resigned; elected as a Republican to the Fifty-third Congress to fill the vacancy caused by the death of Charles O'Neill; reelected to the Fifty-fourth and to the five succeeding Congresses and served from December 19, 1893, until his death in Washington, D. C., June 1, 1906; interment in Laurel Hill Cemetery, Philadelphia, Pa.

ADAMS, Robert Huntington, a Senator from Mississippi; born in Rockbridge County, Va., in 1792; apprenticed to the cooper's trade; was graduated from Washington College (now Washington and Lee University) at Lexington in 1806; studied law; was admitted to the bar and commenced practice in Knoxville, Tenn.; moved to Natchez, Miss., in 1819; member of the State house of representatives in 1828; elected as a Jackson Democrat to the United States Senate to fill the vacancy caused by the death of Thomas B. Reed and served from January 6, 1830, until his death in Natchez, Miss., July 2, 1830; interment in Natchez City Cemetery.

ADAMS, Samuel (uncle of Joseph Allen and grandfather of Charles Allen), a Delegate from Massachusetts; born in Boston, Mass., September 27, 1722; was graduated from Harvard College in 1740; engaged in the brewing business; appointed tax collector of Boston; drafted the instructions given by the town of Boston to its newly chosen representatives with reference to Lord Grenville's proposed Stamp Act in May 1764; member of the general court of Massachusetts 1765–1774; Member of the Continental Congress from 1774 to 1782, when he resigned; a signer of the Declaration of Independence; member of the Massachusetts constitutional convention in 1779; president of the State senate in 1781; member of the State constitutional convention in 1788; unsuccessful candidate for election in 1788 to the First Congress; Lieutenant Governor 1789–1794; Governor 1794–1797; died in Boston, Mass., October 2, 1803; interment in Granary Burial Ground.

ADAMS, Sherman, a Representative from New Hampshire; born in East Dover, Windham County, Vt., January 8, 1899; as an infant moved with his parents to Providence, R. I.; attended the public schools of Providence; served in the United States Marine Corps during the First World War; was graduated from Dartmouth College, Hanover, N. H., in 1920; engaged in the lumber business in Healdville, Vt., in 1921 and 1922 and in the paper and lumber business in Lincoln, N. H., 1923–1944; also engaged in banking; member of the New Hampshire House of Representatives 1941–1944, serving as speaker in 1943 and 1944; chairman of the Grafton County Republican Committee 1942–1944; delegate to the Republican National Conventions in 1944 and 1952; elected as a Republican to the Seventy-ninth Congress (January 3, 1945–January 3, 1947); was not a candidate for renomination in 1946, but was an unsuccessful Republican candidate for the gubernatorial nomination; engaged as a representative of the American Pulpwood Industry in New York City 1946–1948; Governor of New Hampshire January 1, 1949–January 1, 1953; appointed The Assistant to President Eisenhower January 21, 1953, and served until his resignation September 22, 1958; engaged in writing and lecturing; is a resident of Lincoln, N. H.

ADAMS, Silas, a Representative from Kentucky; born in Pulaski County, Ky., February 9, 1839; moved to Casey County with his parents in 1841; attended the public schools, Kentucky University at Harrodsburg, and Transylvania University at Lexington; entered the Union Army during the Civil War as a first lieutenant, First Regiment, Kentucky Volunteer Cavalry; promoted to captain, lieutenant colonel, and colonel of the regiment; was mustered out December 31, 1864; entered Lexington Law School in 1867; was admitted to the bar and practiced; served two terms as county attorney; member of the State house of representatives 1889–1892; unsuccessful Republican candidate for the United States Senate in 1892; elected as a Republican to the Fifty-third Congress (March 4, 1893–March 3, 1895); unsuccessful independent candidate for reelection in 1894 to the Fifty-fourth Congress; resumed the practice of law; died in Liberty, Casey County, Ky., May 5, 1896; interment in Brown Cemetery, Humphrey, Ky.

ADAMS, Stephen, a Representative and a Senator from Mississippi; born in the Pendleton District, S. C., October 17, 1807; moved with his parents to Franklin County, Tenn., in 1812; attended the public schools; studied law; was admitted to the bar in 1829; member of the State senate in 1833–1834; moved to Aberdeen, Miss., in 1834 and commenced the practice of law; circuit court judge 1837–1845; elected as a Democrat to the Twenty-ninth Congress (March 4, 1845–March 3, 1847); again became judge of the circuit court in 1848; member of the State house of representatives in 1850; delegate to the State constitutional convention in 1851; elected as a Union Democrat to the United States Senate on February 19, 1852, to fill the vacancy caused by the resignation of Jefferson Davis and served from March 17, 1852, to March 3, 1857; moved to Memphis, Tenn., and resumed the practice of his profession; died in Memphis, Tenn., May 11, 1857; interment in Elmwood Cemetery.

ADAMS, Thomas, a Delegate from Virginia; born in New Kent County, Va., in 1730; attended the common schools; clerk of Henrico County; journeyed to England in 1762 and attended to his extensive business interests there until 1774; returned before the Revolutionary War; member of the Virginia House of Burgesses and signed the Articles of Association May 27, 1774; chairman of the New Kent County Committee of Safety in 1774; Member of the Continental Congress 1778–1780; a signer of the Articles of Confederation; moved to Augusta County, Va., in 1780; member of the State senate 1783–1786; died on his estate, "Cowpasture," in Augusta County, Va., in August 1788.

ADAMS, Wilbur Louis, a Representative from Delaware; born in Georgetown, Sussex County, Del., October 23, 1884; attended the public schools, Delaware College, Newark, Del., and Dickinson College, Carlisle, Pa.; was graduated from the law department of the University of Pennsylvania at Philadelphia in 1907; was admitted to the bar the same year and commenced practice in Wilmington, Del.; unsuccessful candidate for election as attorney general in 1924; elected as a Democrat to the Seventy-third Congress (March 4, 1933–January 3, 1935); was not a candidate for renomination in 1934, but was an unsuccessful candidate for election to the United States Senate; moved to Georgetown, Del., in 1934 and continued the practice of law; acting postmaster of Georgetown, Del., from May 6, 1937, until his death; died while confined in a hospital in Lewes, Del., on December 4, 1937; interment in Union Cemetery, Georgetown, Del.

ADAMSON, William Charles, a Representative from Georgia; born in Bowdon, Carroll County, Ga., August 13, 1854; attended the common schools; was graduated from Bowdon College in 1874; studied law; was admitted to the bar in 1876 and commenced practice in Carrollton, Carroll County, Ga.; judge of the city court of Carrollton 1885–1889; attorney for the city of Carrollton for a number of years; delegate to the Democratic National Convention at Chicago in 1892; presidential elector on the Democratic ticket of Cleveland and Stevenson in 1892; elected as a Democrat to the Fifty-fifth and to the ten succeeding Congresses and served from March 4, 1897, until December 18, 1917, when he resigned; appointed on December 17, 1917, a member of the Board of United States General Appraisers (now the United States Customs Court) and served until January 20, 1928, when he resigned; resumed the practice of law in Carrollton, Ga.; died while on a visit in New York City, January 3, 1929; interment in City Cemetery, Carrollton, Ga.

ADDAMS, William, a Representative from Pennsylvania; born in Lancaster County, Pa., April 11, 1777; moved to Berks County, near Reading, and served as auditor in 1813 and 1814; commissioner of Berks County 1814–1817; member of the State house of representatives 1822–1824; elected as a Democrat to the Nineteenth and Twentieth Congresses (March 4, 1825–March 3, 1829); unsuccessful candidate for renomination in 1828; member of the committee for the Deaf and Dumb Institution for the States of New York and Ohio; elected associate judge of Berks County and served from 1839 to 1842; captain of the Reading City Troop; largely interested in agricultural pursuits; died in Spring Township, Berks County, Pa., May 30, 1858; interment in St. John's Church Cemetery, Sinking Springs, Pa.

ADDONIZIO, Hugh Joseph, a Representative from New Jersey; born in Newark, Essex County, N. J., January 31, 1914; attended the public schools; graduated from West Side High School, Newark, N. J., in 1933, St. Benedict's Prep School, Newark, N. J., in 1935, and Fordham University, New York, N. Y., in 1939; employed with A & C Clothing Co., of Newark, N. J., in 1939 and became vice president 1946; during World War II entered the United States Army as a private on January 13, 1941; attended Officers Candidate School, Fort Benning, Ga., and commissioned a second lieutenant of Infantry; served thirty-seven months overseas with the Sixtieth Infantry, Ninth Division, participating in eight major campaigns (Algiers, French Morocco, Tunisia, Sicily, Normandy, Northern France Battle of the Bulge, and Rhineland) from the invasion of North Africa to the end of the war in Germany; discharged as a captain in February 1946; awarded European-African Middle Eastern Theater campaign ribbon with bronze arrowhead and eight campaign stars, Bronze Star Medal, Combat Infantryman's Badge, World War II Victory Medal, American Defense Service Medal, and American Theater Campaign Ribbon; elected as a Democrat to the Eighty-first and to the five succeeding Congresses (January 3, 1949–January 3, 1961). *Reelected to the Eighty-seventh Congress.*

ADGATE, Asa, a Representative from New York; born in Canaan, N. Y., November 17, 1767; in 1793 moved to what became known as Adgates Falls, on the Ausable River, then in the township of Peru, Clinton County, N. Y., (now Ausable Chasm, Chesterfield Township, Essex County, N. Y.), where he engaged in the manufacture of iron and agricultural pursuits; upon the organization of the town of Peru in 1793 was elected town clerk and reelected in 1794; supervisor in 1795; assessor in 1796 and 1797; commissioner of schools in 1798; member of the State general assembly from Clinton County in 1798; lieutenant of Infantry, Clinton County, New York Militia, in 1798 and 1799; named by Gov. John Jay, of New York, March 9, 1799, in the first commission of the peace for Essex County, as one of the judges of the court of common pleas and served for several years; elected as a Democrat to the Fourteenth Congress to fill the vacancy caused by the death of Benjamin Pond and served from June 7, 1815, to March 3, 1817; was not a candidate for renomination in 1816; resumed his former occupations; again a member of the State general assembly from Essex County, in 1823; retired to private life; died at Ausable Chasm, Chesterfield Township, Essex County, N. Y., February 15, 1832; interment in Ausable Chasm Cemetery, Ausable Township, Clinton County, N. Y.

ADKINS, Charles, a Representative from Illinois; born on a farm in Pickaway County, Ohio, near Mount Sterling, February 7, 1863; attended the common schools; taught school for several years; moved to Illinois in 1885 and settled on a farm in Piatt County near Bement; engaged in agricultural pursuits; president of the Piatt County (Ill.) Farmers' Institute; member of the board of education of Bement, Ill., 1900–1920; member of the board of supervisors of Piatt County 1902–1906; member of the State house of representatives 1907–1913, serving as speaker 1911–1913; president of the Illinois Livestock Breeders' Association in 1914 and 1915; appointed State director of agriculture during the administration of Gov. Frank M. Lowden and served from 1916 to 1920; moved to Decatur, Macon County, Ill., in 1918; elected as a Republican to the Sixty-ninth and to the three succeeding Congresses (March 4, 1925–March 3, 1933); unsuccessful candidate for reelection in 1932 to the Seventy-third Congress; retired from active pursuits and resided in Decatur, Ill., until his death there on March 31, 1941; interment in Bement Cemetery, Bement, Ill.

ADRAIN, Garnett Bowditch, a Representative from New Jersey; born in New York City December 15, 1815; moved with his parents to New Brunswick, N. J.; attended the public schools; was graduated from Rutgers College, New Brunswick, in 1833; studied law in the office of his brother; was licensed as an attorney in 1836 and as a counselor in 1839; commenced the practice of law in New Brunswick, N. J.; elected as a Democrat to the Thirty-fifth and Thirty-sixth Congresses (March 4, 1857–March 3, 1861); retired from active political life and resumed the practice of his profession; died in New Brunswick, Middlesex County, N. J., August 17, 1878; interment in Van Liew Cemetery.

AHL, John Alexander, a Representative from Pennsylvania; born in Strasburg, Franklin County, Pa., August 16, 1813; moved with his parents to Newville, Cumberland County, Pa., in 1825; attended the public schools; taught school for several terms; studied medicine and was graduated from the University of Maryland, Baltimore, Md., in 1832; practiced his profession at Centerville, Pa., until 1856; moved to Newville, Pa., in 1856 and engaged in the real-estate business; also operated a paper mill; delegate to the Democratic National Convention at Cincinnati in 1856; elected as a Democrat to the Thirty-fifth Congress (March 4, 1857–March 3, 1859); declined to be a candidate for renomination in 1858; resumed the manufacture of paper and operated an iron furnace at Antietam, Md.; served as surgeon in the State militia; projector and major builder of the Harrisburg & Potomac Railroad; died in Newville, Pa., April 25, 1882; interment in Big Spring Presbyterian Cemetery.

AIKEN, David Wyatt (father of Wyatt Aiken and cousin of William Aiken), a Representative from South Carolina; born in Winnsboro, Fairfield County, S. C., March 17, 1828; received his early education under private tutors; attended Mount Zion Institute, Winnsboro, and was graduated from South Carolina University, at Columbia, in 1849; taught school two years; engaged in agricultural pursuits in 1852; during the Civil War served in the Confederate Army as a private; appointed adjutant and later elected colonel of the Seventh Regiment of Volunteers; relieved from service by reason of wounds received on September 17, 1862, at Antietam; member of the State house of representatives 1864–1868; delegate to the Democratic National Convention at St. Louis in 1876; elected as a Democrat to the Forty-fifth and to the four succeeding Congresses (March 4, 1877–March 3, 1887); was not a candidate for renomination in 1886, being an invalid throughout his last term; died in Cokesbury, S. C., April 6, 1887; interment in Magnolia Cemetery, Greenwood, S. C.

AIKEN, George David, a Senator from Vermont; born in Dummerston, Windham County, Vt., August 20, 1892; moved to Putney, Vt., with his parents in 1893; attended the public schools of Putney and was graduated from the Brattleboro (Vt.) High School in 1909; engaged in fruit farming in 1912; also conducted an extensive nursery business, and in 1926 engaged in the commercial cultivation of wildflowers; served as school director of Putney 1920–1937; member of the State house of representatives 1931–1934 and served as speaker in 1933 and 1934; Lieutenant Governor of Vermont 1935–1937 and Governor 1937–1941; elected as a Republican to the United States Senate on November 5, 1940, to fill the vacancy in the term ending January 3, 1945, caused by the death of Ernest W. Gibson, but did not assume office until January 10, 1941; reelected in 1944, 1950, and again in 1956 for the term ending January 3, 1963.

AIKEN, William (cousin of David Wyatt Aiken), a Representative from South Carolina; born in Charleston, S. C., August 4, 1806; attended private schools; was graduated from the College of South Carolina (now the University of South Carolina) at Columbia in 1825; engaged in agricultural pursuits; member of the State house of representatives 1838–1842; served in the State senate 1842–1844; Governor of South Carolina 1844–1846; elected as a Democrat to the Thirty-second, Thirty-third, and Thirty-fourth Congresses (March 4, 1851–March 3, 1857); was an unsuccessful candidate for Speaker of the House of Representatives after 133 ballots in the Thirty-fourth Congress; was not a candidate for renomination in 1856; presented credentials as a Member-elect to the Thirty-ninth Congress February 12, 1867, but was not permitted to qualify; resumed his former pursuits near Charleston, S. C.; died at Flat Rock, Henderson County, N. C., September 7, 1887; interment in Magnolia Cemetery, Charleston, S. C.

AIKEN, Wyatt (son of David Wyatt Aiken), a Representative from South Carolina; born near Macon, Ga., December 14, 1863; reared in Cokesbury, Abbeville (now Greenwood) County, S. C.; attended the public schools of Cokesbury and of Washington, D. C.; official court reporter for the second South Carolina judicial circuit and, later, for the eighth circuit; volunteered as a private in Company A, First South Carolina Regiment of Infantry, during the war with Spain; later appointed battalion adjutant by Governor Ellerbe, and acted as regimental quartermaster during the greater portion of his service; was mustered out in Columbia, S. C., November 10, 1898; delegate to several State conventions; elected as a Democrat to the Fifty-eighth and to the six succeeding Congresses (March 4, 1903–March 3, 1917); unsuccessful candidate for renomination in 1916 and again in 1918; discontinued active pursuits and lived in retirement until his death in Abbeville, S. C., February 6, 1923; interment in Melrose Cemetery.

AINEY, William David Blakeslee, a Representative from Pennsylvania; born in New Milford, Pa., April 8, 1864; attended the public schools, the State Normal School at Mansfield, and Lehigh University, Bethlehem, Pa., in 1887; studied law; was admitted to the bar in 1887 and commenced practice in Montrose, Pa.; district attorney for Susquehanna County 1890–1896; organized Company G of the Pennsylvania National Guard and served as captain 1889–1894; elected as a Republican to the Sixty-second Congress to fill the vacancy caused by the death of George W. Kipp; reelected to the Sixty-third Congress and served from November 7, 1911, to March 3, 1915; was not a candidate for reelection in 1914 to the Sixty-fourth Congress; delegate to the International Parliamentary Union for International Peace held at Geneva, Switzerland, in 1912, and at The Hague in 1913; secretary and president of the Japanese-American group of interparliamentarians and delegate in 1914 to Tokyo, Japan, and to Stockholm, Sweden; resumed the practice of law in Montrose, Pa.; appointed a member of the Public Service Commission of Pennsylvania May 20, 1915, and on August 20, 1915, was elected chairman; reappointed for a ten-year term as member and chairman on July 1, 1917, and again on July 1, 1927; appointed chairman of the Pennsylvania Fuel Commission in August 1922; president of the National Association of Railroad and Utilities Commissioners in 1924; died in Harrisburg, Pa., September 4, 1932; interment in Montrose Cemetery, Montrose, Pa.

AINSLIE, George, a Delegate from the Territory of Idaho; born near Boonville, Cooper County, Mo., October 30, 1838; attended the common schools, and St. Louis (Mo.) University in 1856 and 1857; was graduated from the Jesuit College at St. Louis; studied law; was admitted to the bar in 1860 and commenced practice in Boonville, Mo.; moved to Colorado the same year, and in 1862 moved to that portion of the Territory of Washington that later became the Territory of Idaho; engaged in mining and also practiced law; member of the Territorial house of representatives in 1865 and 1866; edited the Idaho World from 1869 to 1873; district attorney of the second district in 1874 and 1876; elected as a Democrat to the Forty-sixth and Forty-seventh Congresses (March 4, 1879–March 3, 1883); unsuccessful candidate for reelection in 1882 to the Forty-eighth Congress; built the first electric street railway in Boise City, Idaho; settled in Oakland, Calif., and retired from active business pursuits; died in Oakland, Calif., May 19, 1913; the remains were cremated and the ashes deposited in the columbarium, Odd Fellows Cemetery, San Francisco, Calif.

AINSWORTH, Lucien Lester, a Representative from Iowa; born in New Woodstock, Madison County, N. Y., June 21, 1831; attended the public schools, and the Oneida Conference Seminary, Cazenovia, N. Y.; studied law; was admitted to the bar in Madison County, N. Y., in 1854; moved to Belvidere, Ill., and commenced practice the same year; moved to Iowa in 1855 and continued the practice of law, in West Union; member of the State senate 1860–1862; during the Civil War entered the Union Army in 1862 as captain of Company C, Sixth Regiment, Iowa Volunteer Cavalry, and served three years against the Indians in the Northwest; after leaving the Army returned to West Union and resumed the practice of law; member of the State house of representatives 1871–1873; elected as an anti-Monopolist to the Forty-fourth Congress (March 4, 1875–March 3, 1877); declined to accept a renomination in 1876; resumed the practice of law in West Union, Fayette County, Iowa, and died there April 19, 1902; interment in West Union Cemetery.

AITKEN, David Demerest, a Representative from Michigan; born on a farm in Flint Township, Genesee County, Mich., September 5, 1853; attended the district schools and the local high school in Flint; taught in a district school of Genesee County in 1871 and 1872; moved to New Jersey in 1872 and was employed as a bookkeeper; studied law in New York City; was admitted to the bar in 1878 and commenced practice in Flint, Mich.; city clerk 1883–1886; city attorney 1886–1890; elected as a Republican to the Fifty-third and Fifty-fourth Congresses (March 4, 1893–March 3, 1897); was not a candidate for renomination, being an unsuccessful candidate for Governor of Michigan in 1896; resumed the practice of law; also engaged in banking and subsequently became interested in the manufacture of automobiles; served as mayor of Flint in 1905 and 1906; died in Flint, Mich., May 26, 1930; interment in Glenwood Cemetery.

AKERS, Thomas Peter, a Representative from Missouri; born in Knox County, Ohio, October 4, 1828; attended school in Cleveland, Ohio; was graduated from an Ohio college; studied law; was admitted to the bar; taught school for a time in Kentucky; moved to Lexington, Mo., in 1853; professor of mathematics and moral philosophy in Masonic College, Lexington, Mo., in 1855 and 1856; pastor of the local Methodist Church; elected by the American Party to the Thirty-fourth Congress to fill the vacancy caused by the death of John G. Miller and served from August 18, 1856, to March 3, 1857; moved to New York City in 1861 and became vice president of the gold board; owing to ill health moved to Utah, and shortly thereafter returned to Lexington, Lafayette County, Mo., where he died on April 3, 1877; interment in Machpelah Cemetery.

AKIN, Theron, a Representative from New York; born in Johnstown, Fulton County, N. Y., May 23, 1855; attended the common schools of Amsterdam, N. Y., and also was privately tutored at home; engaged in agricultural pursuits; studied dentistry, was graduated from the New York Dental College, and practiced for twelve years in Amsterdam, N. Y.; moved to Akin

(subsequently changed to Fort Johnson), N. Y., and became extensively engaged in agricultural pursuits in Montgomery County; served as president of the village of Fort Johnson, N. Y.; elected as a Progressive Republican to the Sixty-second Congress (March 4, 1911–March 3, 1913); unsuccessful candidate for renomination on the Progressive ticket in 1912; resumed agricultural pursuits; unsuccessful candidate for election to the Sixty-fourth Congress on the Progressive ticket in 1914; mayor of Amsterdam, Montgomery County, N. Y., 1920–1923; resumed his former pursuits; unsuccessful candidate for the Republican and Democratic mayoralty nomination in 1927; retired from active pursuits; died in Amsterdam, N. Y., March 26, 1933; interment in Pine Grove Cemetery, Tribes Hill, Montgomery County, N. Y.

ALBAUGH, Walter Hugh, a Representative from Ohio; born in Phoneton, Miami County, Ohio, January 2, 1890; attended the public and high schools of his native city; was graduated from the law department of Ohio State University at Columbus in 1914; was admitted to the bar the same year and commenced practice in Troy, Ohio; during the First World War served in the United States Infantry as a private unassigned, from May 28, 1918, to December 13, 1918; member of the State house of representatives 1921–1925; also engaged as a civil engineer, surveying fuel lands in Ohio and West Virginia 1910–1911; elected as a Republican to the Seventy-fifth Congress to fill the vacancy caused by the resignation of Frank L. Kloeb and served from November 8, 1938, until January 3, 1939; was not a candidate for nomination in 1938 to the full term; resumed the practice of law in Troy, Ohio, and died there January 21, 1942; interment in Memorial Park Cemetery, Dayton, Ohio.

ALBERT, Carl, a Representative from Oklahoma; born in North McAlester, Pittsburg County, Okla., May 10, 1908; attended Flowery Mound Rural School; was graduated from McAlester High School in 1927, from the University of Oklahoma at Norman in 1931, and (having been awarded a Rhodes Scholarship) from Oxford University in England in 1934; studied law; was admitted to the bar in 1935 and commenced practice in McAlester, Okla.; during World War II enlisted in the United States Army on June 16, 1941, as a private; served in the Pacific Theater and was discharged a lieutenant colonel on February 17, 1946; awarded the Bronze Star; resumed the practice of law; elected as a Democrat to the Eightieth and to the six succeeding Congresses (January 3, 1947–January 3, 1961). *Reelected to the Eighty-seventh Congress.*

ALBERT, William Julian, a Representative from Maryland; born in Baltimore, Md., August 4, 1816; was graduated from Mount St. Mary's College, near Emmittsburg, Md., in 1833; engaged in the hardware business until 1855 and, later, in banking; president of the electoral college of Maryland in 1864 and voted for Abraham Lincoln for President of the United States; was a prominent Union leader in Maryland and took an important part in preventing the secession of the State; Federal finances being greatly depleted in 1860 to the extent that there was danger that the December interest on Government bonds might not be paid, he offered to place his entire fortune at the service of the depository in Baltimore, should it be required; one of the founders and directors of the First National Bank of Maryland; director of several insurance companies, savings banks, and manufacturing companies; unsuccessful candidate for election in 1866 to the Fortieth Congress and in 1868 to the Forty-first Congress; elected as a Republican to the Forty-third Congress (March 4, 1873–March 3, 1875); resumed his former business pursuits; died in Baltimore, Md., March 29, 1879; interment in Greenmount Cemetery.

ALBERTSON, Nathaniel, a Representative from Indiana; born in Fairfax, Fairfax County, Va., June 10, 1800; moved to Salem, Washington County, Ind., and engaged in agricultural pursuits; member of the State house of representatives 1838–1840; moved to Floyd County in 1835 and settled in Greenville, near New Albany, and resumed agricultural pursuits; elected as a Democrat to the Thirty-first Congress (March 4, 1849–March 3, 1851); unsuccessful candidate for reelection in 1850 to the Thirty-second Congress; resumed agricultural pursuits in Floyd County; moved to Keokuk, Iowa, in 1853 and engaged in mercantile pursuits; moved to Boonville, Mo., in 1856 and continued mercantile pursuits; settled in Central City, Gilpin County, Colo., in 1860 and engaged in the hotel business; also became interested in mining; died in Central City, Colo., December 16, 1863; interment in Central City Graveyard.

ALBRIGHT, Charles, a Representative from Pennsylvania; born in Bucks County, Pa., December 13, 1830; attended Dickinson College, Carlisle, Pa.; studied law; was admitted to the bar in 1852 and commenced practice in Mauch Chunk, Pa.; moved to the Territory of Kansas in 1854 and participated in its early development; returned to Pennsylvania and resumed the practice of law in Mauch Chunk in 1856; delegate to the Republican National Convention at Chicago in 1860; during the Civil War served in the Union Army and was promoted to major of the One Hundred and Thirty-second Regiment, Pennsylvania Volunteer Infantry, on August 21, 1862; lieutenant colonel September 18, 1862; colonel January 24, 1863; honorably mustered out May 24, 1865; recommissioned colonel of the Thirty-fourth Pennsylvania Militia July 3, 1863, and honorably mustered out August 10, 1863; recommissioned colonel of the Two Hundred and Second Regiment, Pennsylvania Volunteer Infantry, September 4, 1864; breveted brigadier general of Volunteers March 7, 1865; honorably mustered out August 3, 1865; resumed the practice of law in Mauch Chunk, Pa.; delegate to the Republican National Convention at Philadelphia in 1872; elected as a Republican to the Forty-third Congress (March 4, 1873–March 3, 1875); resumed the practice of law and also engaged in manufacturing in Mauch Chunk, Pa., until his death there September 28, 1880; interment in Mauch Chunk Cemetery.

ALBRIGHT, Charles Jefferson, a Representative from Ohio; born in Carlisle, Cumberland County, Pa., May 9, 1816; moved with his parents in 1824 to Allegheny County, Pa.; received a limited schooling; was employed in a harness shop and, later, as a clerk in a rural store; apprenticed as a printer; moved to Guernsey County, Ohio, in 1832 and settled on a farm near Cambridge; owner and publisher of the Guernsey Times 1840–1845 and 1848–1855; served as secretary of the Guernsey County Board of School Examiners 1841–1844; elected as a Republican to the Thirty-fourth Congress (March 4, 1855–March 3, 1857); unsuccessful candidate for reelection in 1856 to the Thirty-fifth Congress; served as vice president at the Republican State convention in 1855; delegate to the first and second Republican National Conventions, at Philadelphia in 1856 and at Chicago in 1860; during the Civil War served as chairman of the Guernsey County Military Committee; internal-revenue collector for the sixteenth Ohio district, by appointment of President Lincoln, 1862–1869; delegate to the third State constitutional convention in 1873; member of the State board of charities in 1875; president of the board of school examiners of the Cambridge Union School 1881–1883; died in Cambridge, Ohio, October 21, 1883; interment in South Cemetery.

ALCORN, James Lusk, a Senator from Mississippi; born near Golconda, Ill., November 4, 1816; attended the public schools of Livingston County, Ky., and was graduated from Cumberland College, Kentucky; deputy sheriff of Livingston County 1839–1844; member of the Kentucky House of Representatives in 1843; studied law; was admitted to the bar in 1844 and commenced practice in Delta, Panola County, Miss.; member of the Mississippi House of Representatives 1846, 1856, and 1857; served in the State senate 1848–1854; delegate to the State constitutional conventions in 1851 and 1861; presidential elector on the Whig ticket of Scott and Graham in 1852; unsuccessful candidate for election in 1856 to the Thirty-fifth Congress; declined the nomination for Governor in 1857; founder of the Mississippi levee system and was made president of the levee board of the Mississippi-Yazoo Delta in 1858; served in the Confederate Army during the Civil War; presented credential as a United States Senator-elect in 1865 but was not permitted to take his seat; again a member of the State constitutional convention in 1868; elected Governor of Mississippi in 1869 and served from March 1870 until his resignation on November 30, 1871, having previously been elected Senator; elected as a Republican to the United States Senate on January 18, 1870, for the term beginning March 4, 1871, but did not assume these duties until later, preferring to continue as Governor; served as Senator from December 1, 1871, to March 3, 1877; unsuccessful candidate for Governor in 1873; resumed the practice of law in Friar Point; member of the State constitutional convention in 1890; died at his plantation home, "Eagles Nest," in Coahoma County, Miss., December 19, 1894; interment in the family cemetery on his estate.

ALDERSON, John Duffy, a Representative from West Virginia; born at Nicholas Court House (now Summersville), W. Va., November 29, 1854; attended the common schools; sergeant at arms of the State senate 1871–1873; doorkeeper in 1872 and 1873; studied law; was admitted to the bar in 1876 and commenced practice at Nicholas Court House; appointed prosecuting attorney for the counties of Nicholas and Webster in 1876; elected prosecuting attorney for these counties, reelected in 1880 and 1884, and served until January 1, 1889; clerk of the State senate 1883–1887; elected as a Democrat to the Fifty-first, Fifty-second, and Fifty-third Congresses (March 4, 1889–March 3, 1895); unsuccessful candidate for reelection in 1894 to the Fifty-fourth Congress; resumed the practice of law in Nicholas, W. Va.; delegate to the Democratic National Conventions in 1900 and 1908; delegate to many State conventions; died in Richwood, Nicholas County, W. Va., December 5, 1910; interment in a private burial ground at Summersville, W. Va.

ALDRICH, Cyrus, a Representative from Minnesota; born in Smithfield, R. I., June 18, 1808; attended the common schools; followed the occupations of sailor, boatman, farmer, contractor on public works, and mail contractor; moved to Illinois and settled in Alton in 1837; member of the State house of representatives 1845–1847; register of deeds of Jo Daviess County 1847–1849; receiver of the United States land office at Dixon, Ill., 1849–1853; moved to Minneapolis, Minn., in 1855 and engaged in the lumber business; member of the State constitutional convention in 1857; elected as a Republican to the Thirty-sixth and Thirty-seventh Congresses (March 4, 1859–March 3, 1863); was not a candidate for renomination in 1862; unsuccessful candidate for election in 1863 to the United States Senate; member of the State house of representatives in 1865; elected chairman of the board of supervisors of the town of Minneapolis in 1865; appointed by President Lincoln in 1863 one of the commissioners to examine claims for indemnity of those who had suffered from the Sioux War of 1862; postmaster of Minneapolis, Minn., from September 11, 1867, until April 15, 1871, when a successor was appointed; died in Minneapolis, Minn., October 5, 1871; interment in Lakewood Cemetery.

ALDRICH, James Franklin (son of William Aldrich), a Representative from Illinois; born at Two Rivers, Manitowoc County, Wis., April 6, 1853; moved with his parents to Chicago, Ill., in April 1861; attended the public schools and Chicago University; was graduated from Rensselaer Polytechnic Institute, Troy, N. Y., in 1877; engaged in the manufacture of linseed oil and later engaged in the gas business; member of the Cook County Board of Commissioners 1886–1888, serving as president in 1887; member of the county board of education in 1887; commissioner of public works of Chicago from May 1, 1891, to January 1, 1893; elected as a Republican to the Fifty-third and Fifty-fourth Congresses (March 4, 1893–March 3, 1897); was not a candidate for renomination in 1896; appointed consul general at Habana, Cuba, in 1897, but did not reach his post to serve owing to the sinking of the battleship *Maine* and to the war with Spain which followed; receiver of national banks, and railroad appraiser, from 1898 until 1923; died in Chicago, Ill., March 8, 1933; interment in Rosehill Cemetery.

ALDRICH, Nelson Wilmarth (father of Richard Steere Aldrich and cousin of William Aldrich), a Representative and a Senator from Rhode Island; born in Foster, R. I., November 6, 1841; attended the public schools of East Killingly, Conn., and the Academy of East Greenwich, R. I.; entered the wholesale grocery business in Providence; during the Civil War enlisted as a private in Company D, First Regiment, Rhode Island National Guard, in 1862; member of the city council 1869–1874, serving as president in 1872 and 1873; member of the State house of representatives in 1875 and 1876, being elected speaker in 1876; delegate to the Republican National Convention at Cincinnati in 1876; elected as a Republican to the Forty-sixth and Forty-seventh Congresses and served from March 4, 1879, until October 4, 1881, when he resigned to become Senator; elected to the United States Senate to fill the vacancy caused by the death of Ambrose E. Burnside; reelected 1886, 1892, 1898, and 1904 and served from October 5, 1881, to March 3, 1911; was not a candidate for reelection in 1911; chairman of the National Monetary Commission 1908–1912; did not engage in active business pursuits but lived in retirement in Providence, R. I.; died in New York City, April 16, 1915; interment in Swan Point Cemetery, Providence, R. I.

ALDRICH, Richard Steere (son of Nelson Wilmarth Aldrich), a Representative from Rhode Island; born in Washington, D. C., February 29, 1884; attended the public schools in Providence, R. I.; was graduated from Hope Street High School at Providence in 1902, from Yale University in 1906, and from the law department of Harvard University in 1909; was admitted to the bar in 1911 and commenced the practice of law in New York City the same year; returned to Providence, R. I., in 1913 and continued the practice of his profession; member of the Rhode Island House of Representatives 1914–1916; served in the State senate 1916–1918; elected as a Republican to the Sixty-eighth and to the four succeeding Congresses (March 4, 1923–March 3, 1933); was not a candidate for renomination in 1932; resumed legal pursuits in Providence, R. I., until his death there on December 25, 1941; interment in Swan Point Cemetery.

ALDRICH, Truman Heminway (brother of William Farrington Aldrich), a Representative from Alabama; born in Palmyra, Wayne County, N. Y., October 17, 1848; attended the public schools, the military academy at West Chester, Pa., and was graduated from the Rensselaer Polytechnic Institute, Troy, N. Y., in 1869; engaged in engineering in New York and New Jersey; moved to Selma, Ala., in 1871; engaged in banking and in the mining of coal, becoming vice president and general manager of the Tennessee Coal, Iron & Railroad Co. in 1892; founder of the Cahaba Coal Mining Co.; member of the American Institute of Mining Engineers; successfully contested as a Republican the election of Oscar W. Underwood to the Fifty-fourth Congress and served from June 9, 1896, to March 3, 1897; was not a candidate for renomination in 1896; served as postmaster at Birmingham, Ala., by appointment of President Taft, from September 1, 1911, to December 15, 1915; delegate to the Republican National Convention at Chicago in 1904 which nominated Theodore Roosevelt for President; served as a dollar-per-year man on the War Industries Board during the First World War; after the war was engaged as a mining engineer and geologist; died in Birmingham, Ala., April 28, 1932; interment in Elmwood Cemetery.

ALDRICH, William (father of James Franklin Aldrich and cousin of Nelson Wilmarth Aldrich), a Representative from Illinois; born in Greenfield Center, Saratoga County, N. Y., January 19, 1820; attended the common schools and the local academy; taught school until twenty-six years of age; moved to Jackson, Mich., in 1846 and engaged in mercantile pursuits; moved to Wisconsin and settled in Two Rivers, Manitowoc County, in 1851; continued mercantile pursuits and also engaged in the manufacture of lumber, woodenware, and furniture; superintendent of schools 1855 and 1856; chairman of the county board of supervisors 1857 and 1858; member of the State house of representatives in 1859; moved to Chicago, Ill., in 1861 and engaged in the wholesale grocery business; member of the Chicago City Council in 1876, serving as chairman; elected as a Republican to the Forty-fifth, Forty-sixth, and Forty-seventh Congresses (March 4, 1877–March 3, 1883); unsuccessful candidate for renomination in 1882; resumed his former business pursuits in Chicago and was also interested in the milling business at Fond du Lac, Wis., where he died, while on a business trip, December 3, 1885; interment in Rosehill Cemetery, Chicago, Ill.

ALDRICH, William Farrington (brother of Truman Heminway Aldrich), a Representative from Alabama; born in Palmyra, Wayne County, N. Y., March 11, 1853; attended the public schools of his native city; moved with his father to New York City in 1865; attended several schools, and was graduated from Warren's Military Academy in Poughkeepsie, N. Y., in 1873; moved to Alabama in 1874; engaged in mining and manufacturing; built up the town that bears his name; successfully contested as a Republican the election of Gaston A. Robbins to the Fifty-fourth Congress and served from March 13, 1896, to March 3, 1897; successfully contested the election of Thomas S. Plowman to the Fifty-fifth Congress and served from February 9, 1898, to March 3, 1899; again successfully contested the election of Gaston A. Robbins to the Fifty-sixth Congress and served from March 8, 1900, to March 3, 1901; declined to be a candidate for renomination in 1900; editor, owner, and publisher of the Birmingham (Ala.) Times; delegate to the Republican National Convention at Chicago in 1904; engaged in the development of mineral lands until his death in Birmingham, Ala., October 30, 1925; the remains were cremated and the ashes placed in an urn and deposited in the family vault in Rock Creek Cemetery, Washington, D. C.

ALESHIRE, Arthur William, a Representative from Ohio; born near Luray, Page County, Va., February 15, 1900; attended the rural schools; moved to Clark County, Ohio, in 1912 with his parents, who settled on a farm near Springfield; employed by a railway express company in 1921 and 1922; engaged in dairy farming near Springfield, Ohio, in 1922 and 1923; due to an accident in 1923 lost the use of his legs and in a wheelchair operated a filling station and grocery store until elected to Congress; elected as a Democrat to the Seventy-fifth Congress (January 3, 1937–January 3, 1939); unsuccessful candidate for reelection in

1938 to the Seventy-sixth Congress; resumed his former business pursuits near Springfield, Ohio; died in Springfield, Ohio, March 11, 1940; interment in Ferncliff Cemetery.

ALEXANDER, Adam Rankin, a Representative from Tennessee; born in Rockbridge County, Va.; became a surveyor by profession; moved to Tennessee in 1801 and located in Blount County; moved to what is now Madison County, Tenn., about 1806 and established the town of Alexandria, named for him; member of the State senate in 1817; register of the land office for the tenth surveyors' district; member of the first county court of Madison County in 1821; elected as a Federalist to the Eighteenth and Nineteenth Congresses (March 4, 1823–March 3, 1827); unsuccessful candidate for reelection in 1828 to the Twentieth Congress; moved to Shelby County, Tenn., and represented that county at the State abolitionist convention in 1834; member of the State house of representatives in 1841 and 1843; died in Jackson, Madison County, Tenn.

ALEXANDER, Armstead Milton, a Representative from Missouri; born near Winchester, Clark County, Ky., May 26, 1834; moved to Monroe County, Mo., with his parents, who settled near Paris; attended the common schools; worked at the blacksmith trade in 1848; engaged in gold mining in California in 1849; was graduated from Bethany College, Bethany, Va. (now West Virginia), in 1853; moved to Paris, Mo., and became engaged in business; served in the Confederate Army during the Civil War; studied law; was admitted to the bar in 1870 and commenced practice at Paris, Mo., but did not sign the record there until 1881; prosecuting attorney of Monroe County 1872–1876; delegate to the State constitutional convention in 1875; elected as a Democrat to the Forty-eighth Congress (March 4, 1883–March 3, 1885); unsuccessful candidate for renomination in 1884; resumed the practice of law in his adopted city; died in Paris, Mo., November 7, 1892; interment in Walnut Grove Cemetery.

ALEXANDER, De Alva Stanwood, a Representative from New York; born in Richmond, Sagadahoc County, Maine, July 17, 1846; attended the common schools; moved with his mother to Ohio in 1859; at the age of fifteen enlisted in the Union Army as a private in the One Hundred and Twenty-eighth Regiment, Ohio Volunteer Infantry, and served from 1862 until the close of the Civil War, when he entered the Edward Little Institute, Auburn, Maine, to prepare for college; was graduated from Bowdoin College, Brunswick, Maine, in 1870 and served many years as a member and president of its board of overseers; moved to Fort Wayne, Ind., in 1870; one of the editors and proprietors of the Daily Gazette 1871–1874; delegate to the Republican National Convention at Philadelphia in 1872; moved to Indianapolis, Ind., in 1874 and became a staff correspondent of the Cincinnati Gazette; secretary of the Indiana Republican State committee 1874–1878; studied law; was admitted to the bar in 1877 and commenced practice in Indianapolis, Ind.; appointed Fifth Auditor of the Treasury Department in 1881 and served until 1885; commander of the Department of the Potomac, Grand Army of the Republic, for one term; moved to Buffalo, N. Y., in 1885; appointed United States attorney for the northern district of New York in May 1889 and served until his resignation in December 1893; elected as a Republican to the Fifty-fifth and to the six succeeding Congresses (March 4, 1897–March 3, 1911); unsuccessful candidate for reelection in 1910 to the Sixty-second Congress; resumed the practice of law; died in Buffalo, N. Y., January 30, 1925; interment in Forest Lawn Cemetery.

ALEXANDER, Evan Shelby (cousin of Nathaniel Alexander), a Representative from North Carolina; born in Mecklenburg County, N. C., about 1767; attended the common schools; was graduated from Princeton College in 1787; studied law; was admitted to the bar and commenced practice in Salisbury, Rowan County, N. C.; member of the State house of commons 1796–1803; trustee of the University of North Carolina at Chapel Hill 1799–1809; elected to the Ninth Congress to fill the vacancy caused by the resignation of Nathaniel Alexander; reelected to the Tenth Congress and served from February 24, 1806, to March 3, 1809; died October 28, 1809.

ALEXANDER, Henry Porteous, a Representative from New York; born in Little Falls, Herkimer County, N. Y., September 13, 1801; attended the public schools; engaged in mercantile pursuits in Little Falls; also engaged in banking; president of the village of Little Falls in 1834 and 1835; became president of the Herkimer County Bank at Little Falls in 1839 and served until his death; unsuccessful candidate for election in 1846 to the Thirtieth Congress; elected as a Whig to the Thirty-first Congress (March 4, 1849–March 3, 1851); unsuccessful candidate for reelection in 1850 to the Thirty-second Congress; resumed his former business pursuits; died in Little Falls, N. Y., February 22, 1867; interment in Church Street Cemetery.

ALEXANDER, Hugh Quincy, a Representative from North Carolina; born on a farm near Glendon, Moore County, N. C., August 7, 1911; attended the public schools; graduated from Duke University, Durham, N. C., in 1932, and from the University of North Carolina, Chapel Hill, N. C., in 1937; studied law; was admitted to the bar in 1937 and began practice in Kannapolis, N. C.; during World War II served in the United States Navy 1942–1946 and had thirty-four months overseas duty; member of North Carolina House of Representatives in 1947 and 1949; solicitor, Cabarrus County Recorders Court, 1950–1952; elected as a Democrat to the Eighty-third and to the three succeeding Congresses (January 3, 1953–January 3, 1961). *Reelected to the Eighty-seventh Congress.*

ALEXANDER, James, Jr., a Representative from Ohio; born near Delta, York County, Pa., October 17, 1789; moved to the Northwest Territory in 1799 with his father, who settled in what is now known as St. Clairsville, Belmont County, Ohio; engaged in agricultural pursuits, in river transportation on the Ohio and Mississippi Rivers, and, later, in mercantile pursuits in St. Clairsville; member of the State house of representatives in 1830 and again in 1833 and 1834; served as associate judge of the court of common pleas in 1831; elected as a Democrat to the Twenty-fifth Congress (March 4, 1837–March 3, 1839); unsuccessful candidate for reelection in 1838 to the Twenty-sixth Congress; returned to St. Clairsville, Ohio, and resumed his former business pursuits; purchased a large tract of property in Wheeling, Va. (now West Virginia), in 1843 and moved to that city and established his permanent residence, living in retirement until his death; was an extensive owner of farming land in the State of Illinois; died, while visiting his son, in McNabb, Putnam County, Ill., September 5, 1846; interment in Scotch Ridge Cemetery, eight miles north of St. Clairsville, Ohio.

ALEXANDER, John, a Representative from Ohio; born at Crowsville, in the Spartanburg District, S. C., April 16, 1777; attended the public schools; moved to Butler County, Ohio, and thence to Miamisburg, Montgomery County, in 1803; studied law; was admitted to the bar and commenced practice in 1804; moved to Xenia, Greene County, Ohio, in 1805 and continued his profession there, also practicing in Columbus, Chillicothe, and before the Supreme Court of the United States at Washington, D. C.; appointed prosecuting attorney in 1808 and held that office until 1833, except during the time he was a Member of Congress; elected as a Democrat to the Thirteenth and Fourteenth Congresses (March 4, 1813–March 3, 1817); unsuccessful candidate for reelection in 1816 to the Fifteenth Congress; resumed the practice of law at Xenia; member of the State senate in 1822 and 1823; served in the State house of representatives two terms; retired from the practice of his profession in 1834; died at Xenia, Ohio, June 28, 1848; interment in Woodlawn Cemetery.

ALEXANDER, John Grant, a Representative from Minnesota; born in Texas Valley, Cortland County, N. Y., July 16, 1893; attended the public schools; was graduated from the law department of Cornell University, Ithaca, N. Y., in 1916; was admitted to the New York bar the same year; moved to Redwood Falls, Minn., in 1916; was admitted to the Minnesota bar in 1917 and commenced practice in Lynd, Minn.; engaged in the banking business 1917–1923; during the First World War served as a private in the Three Hundred and Eighty-sixth Ambulance Company in 1918; engaged in the insurance business and in real-estate management in Minneapolis, Minn., in 1924; member of the Minnesota National Guard 1927–1937; elected as a Republican to the Seventy-sixth Congress (January 3, 1939–January 3, 1941); unsuccessful candidate for renomination in 1940; resumed the real-estate and insurance business; unsuccessful candidate for the Republican nomination for Governor in 1942; is a resident of Minneapolis, Minn.

ALEXANDER, Joshua Willis, a Representative from Missouri; born in Cincinnati, Ohio, January 22, 1852; moved to Missouri with his mother, who settled in Canton, Daviess County, in 1863; attended public, private, and high schools, and was graduated from Christian University (now Culver-Stockton College), Canton, Mo., in 1872; moved to Gallatin, Mo., in 1873; studied law; was admitted to the bar in 1875 and commenced practice in Gallatin; public administrator of Daviess County 1877–1881; served as secretary and then as president of the board of education of Gallatin, Mo., 1882–1901; member of the State house of representatives 1883–1887, serving as speaker in 1887; mayor of Gallatin in 1891 and 1892; member of the board of managers of State Hospital No. 2, 1893–1896; judge of the seventh judicial circuit of Missouri 1901–1907; elected as a Democrat to the Sixtieth and to the six succeeding Congresses and served from March 4, 1907, until December 15, 1919, when he resigned to accept a Cabinet portfolio; served as chairman of the commissioners of the United States to the International Conference on Safety of Life at Sea, which met in London on November 12, 1913, and continued until January 20, 1914; appointed Secretary of Commerce in the Cabinet of President Wilson and served from December 16, 1919, until March 4, 1921; returned to Gallatin, Mo., in 1921 and resumed the practice of law; delegate at large to the State constitutional convention in 1922; died in Gallatin, Mo., February 27, 1936; interment in Brown Cemetery.

ALEXANDER, Mark, a Representative from Virginia; born on a plantation near Boydton, Mecklenburg County, Va., February 7, 1792; attended the public schools; was graduated from the University of North Carolina at Chapel Hill, in 1811; studied law; was admitted to the bar and commenced the practice of law in Boydton, Va.; member of the State house of delegates 1817–1819; elected as a State Rights Democrat to the Sixteenth and to the six succeeding Congresses (March 4, 1819–March 3, 1833); declined to be a candidate for renomination in 1832; delegate to the State constitutional convention in 1829; retired from political life and engaged in the management of his large estate; died in Scotland Neck, Halifax County, N. C., October 7, 1883; interment in the cemetery of the old Episcopal Church.

ALEXANDER, Nathaniel (cousin of Evan Shelby Alexander) a Representative from North Carolina; born near Concord, Mecklenburg County, N. C., March 5, 1756; attended the common schools; was graduated from Princeton College in 1776; studied medicine and surgery; served in the Revolutionary War as a surgeon 1778–1782; after independence was established, practiced his profession at the High Hills of Santee in South Carolina; subsequently returned to Charlotte, N. C., and continued practice; member of the State house of commons in 1797; served in the State senate in 1801 and 1802; elected to the Eighth and Ninth Congresses and served from March 4, 1803, until November 1805, when he resigned to become Governor; Governor of North Carolina 1805–1807; died in Salisbury, Rowan County, N. C., March 7, 1808; interment in Old Cemetery, Charlotte, N. C.

ALEXANDER, Robert, a Delegate from Maryland; born on the family estate in Cecil County (now part of the city of Elkton), Md.; studied law; was admitted to the bar and practiced; member of the provincial convention of Maryland 1774, 1775, and 1776; secretary of the Baltimore committee of observation and member of the council of safety in 1775; commissioned a first lieutenant in the Baltimore militia June 6, 1776; elected as a Member of the Continental Congress December 9, 1775, and reelected July 4, 1776, but soon after the promulgation of the Declaration of Independence he fled from Maryland to the British Fleet, joined the Associated Loyalists of America, and in 1782 sailed for London, England, where he remained; in 1780 he was adjudged guilty of high treason and his property was confiscated; died in London, England.

ALEXANDER, Sydenham Benoni (cousin of Adlai Ewing Stevenson and John Sharp Williams), a Representative from North Carolina; born at "Rosedale," near Charlotte, Mecklenburg County, N. C., December 8, 1840; attended preparatory schools at Rocky River and Wadesboro, N. C.; was graduated from the University of North Carolina at Chapel Hill in 1860; during the Civil War enlisted in the Confederate Army in 1861 as a private in the First Regiment, North Carolina Volunteer Infantry; elected captain of Company K, Forty-second North Carolina Regiment, in June 1862; detached from his company in 1864 and served as inspector general on the staff of Maj. Gen. Robert F. Hoke; member of the State senate in 1879, 1883, 1885, 1887, and 1901; was instrumental in the establishment of the North Carolina Agricultural and Mechanical College and served as a member of its board of trustees; president of the North Carolina Railroad; elected as a Democrat to the Fifty-second and Fifty-third Congresses (March 4, 1891–March 3, 1895); was not a candidate for renomination in 1894; retired to his estate, "Enderly Plantation," in Mecklenburg County, N. C., and engaged in agricultural pursuits; moved to Charlotte, N. C., in 1906 and died there June 14, 1921; interment in Elmwood Cemetery.

ALFORD, Julius Caesar, a Representative from Georgia; born in Greensboro, Ga., May 10, 1799; attended the common schools; studied law; was admitted to the bar and commenced practice in Lagrange, Ga.; also engaged in planting; member of the State house of representatives; commanded a company in the Creek War of 1836; elected as a State Rights Whig to the Twenty-fourth Congress to fill the vacancy caused by the resignation of George W. B. Towns and served from January 2 to March 3, 1837; unsuccessful candidate for reelection in 1836 to the Twenty-fifth Congress; elected as a Harrison Whig to the Twenty-sixth and Twenty-seventh Congresses and served from March 4, 1839, to October 1, 1841, when he resigned; moved to Tuskegee, Ala., and subsequently settled near Montgomery, Ala.; delegate to the Union convention at Montgomery in 1852; resumed the practice of law; unsuccessful candidate for election in 1855 to the Thirty-fourth Congress; member of the secession convention in 1861; died on his plantation near Montgomery, Ala., January 1, 1863; interment in the family cemetery on his estate near Montgomery.

ALFORD, Thomas Dale, a Representative from Arkansas; born in Pike County, near Murfreesboro, Ark., January 28, 1916; attended the public schools of Rector, Ark., Arkansas State College at Jonesboro, State Teachers College at Conway, and graduated from the University of Arkansas School of Medicine at Little Rock; postgraduate training at the University of Illinois in Chicago; during World War II served in the United States Army Medical Corps with service at the Army and Navy General Hospital, Hot Springs, Ark. 1941–1943; and in the European Theater 1943–1945; private practice of medicine at Atlanta, Ga., 1946–1948, at which time was on the clinical staff of Emory University College of Medicine; in 1948 returned to Little Rock, Ark., and continued the practice of medicine; member of active teaching faculty, University of Arkansas School of Medicine, 1948–1958; member of Little Rock Board of Education 1955–1958 and Little Rock University Board of Trustees 1955–1958; elected as a Democrat, a write-in candidate, to the Eighty-sixth Congress (January 3, 1959–January 3, 1961). *Reelected to the Eighty-seventh Congress.*

ALGER, Bruce Reynolds, a Representative from Texas; born in Dallas, Tex., June 12, 1918; moved to Webster Groves, Mo., with his parents in 1924, and attended the public schools; graduated from Princeton University, Princeton, N. J., in 1940; field representative with RCA Victor Manufacturing Co., 1940 and 1941; enlisted as an aviation cadet in the Army Air Corps in September 1941, served as a B–29 commander in the Pacific Area, and discharged in November 1945; returned to Dallas, Tex., and engaged in the real-estate and construction business; elected as a Republican to the Eighty-fourth, Eighty-fifth, and Eighty-sixth Congresses (January 3, 1955–January 3, 1961). *Reelected to the Eighty-seventh Congress.*

ALGER, Russell Alexander, a Senator from Michigan; born in Lafayette Township, Medina County, Ohio, February 27, 1836; at the age of eleven years his parents died; for seven years he worked on a farm; attended Richfield Academy, Summit County, Ohio, in winters, and subsequently taught country school; studied law in Akron, Ohio; was admitted to the bar in March 1859; moved to Grand Rapids, Mich., and engaged in the lumber business; moved to Detroit; during the Civil War enlisted in the Army in August 1861 as a private; commissioned captain of Company C, Second Regiment, Michigan Volunteer Cavalry, September 2, 1861; major of the regiment April 2, 1862; lieutenant colonel, Sixth Regiment, Michigan Volunteer Cavalry, October 30, 1862; colonel, Fifth Regiment, Michigan Volunteer Cavalry, June 11, 1863; brevetted brigadier general, United States Volunteers, "for gallant and meritorious services, to rank from the Battle of Trevillon Station," June 11, 1864; brevetted major general, United States Volunteers, June 11, 1865, "for gallant and meritorious services during the war," having participated in sixty-six battles and skirmishes; after the close of the war he resumed the lumber business; was elected commander in chief of the Grand Army of the Republic in 1889; delegate to the Republican National Convention at Chicago in 1884; elected Governor of Michigan the same year; declined a renomination in 1886; presidential elector at large on the Republican ticket of Harrison and Morton in 1888; was appointed Secretary of War in the Cabinet of President McKinley on March 5, 1897, and resigned August 1, 1899; appointed and subsequently

elected as a Republican to the United States Senate to fill the vacancy caused by the death of James McMillan and served from September 27, 1902, until his death in Washington, D. C., January 24, 1907; interment in Elmwood Cemetery, Detroit, Mich.

ALLAN, Chilton, a Representative from Kentucky; born in Albemarle County, Va., April 6, 1786; moved with his mother to Winchester, Clark County, Ky., in 1797; attended the common schools, and also received private instructions; served an apprenticeship of three years as a wheelwright, studying law in his leisure time; was admitted to the bar in 1808 and commenced practice in Winchester; member of the State house of representatives in 1811, 1815, 1822, and 1830; member of the State senate 1823–1827; elected as a Clay Democrat to the Twenty-second, Twenty-third, and Twenty-fourth Congresses (March 4, 1831–March 3, 1837); was not a candidate for renomination in 1836; appointed president of the State board of internal improvements in 1837 and served until 1839, when he resigned; resumed the practice of law; again a member of the State house of representatives, in 1842; died in Winchester, Ky., September 3, 1858; interment in Winchester Cemetery.

ALLEE, James Frank, a Senator from Delaware; born in Dover, Del., December 2, 1857; attended the common schools; learned the trade of jeweler and watchmaker from his father, whom he succeeded in business; chairman of the Republican State committee 1886–1896; member of the State senate from January 3, 1899, to March 2, 1903, when he resigned to become a United States Senator; delegate to the Republican National Conventions in 1900 and 1904; elected as a Republican to the United States Senate on March 2, 1903, to fill the vacancy in the term commencing March 3, 1901, caused by the failure of the legislature to elect, and served from March 3, 1903, to March 3, 1907; was not a candidate for reelection in 1907; resumed his former business pursuits; discontinued the jewelry business in 1908 and became engaged in the fruit- and vegetable-canning industry; delegate to the National Progressive Convention at Chicago in 1912; retired from active pursuits and devoted his time to the management of his business interests; died in Dover, Del., October 12, 1938; interment in Christ Church Cemetery.

ALLEN, Alfred Gaither, a Representative from Ohio; born on a farm near Wilmington, Clinton County, Ohio, July 23, 1867; attended the public schools; was graduated from Wilmington High School in 1886 and from the law school of the University of Cincinnati, Ohio, in 1890; was admitted to the bar in 1890 and commenced practice in Cincinnati, Ohio; United States commissioner 1896–1900; delegate to the Democratic State conventions at Columbus in 1901 and 1908; member of the city council 1906–1908; member of the board of the sinking-fund trustees of Cincinnati 1908–1910; elected as a Democrat to the Sixty-second, Sixty-third, and Sixty-fourth Congresses (March 4, 1911–March 3, 1917); declined to be a candidate for renomination in 1916; resumed the practice of his profession in Cincinnati; delegate to the Democratic National Convention at San Francisco in 1920; served as president of the Cincinnati Bar Association in 1925 and 1926; died in Cincinnati, Ohio, December 9, 1932; interment in Sugar Grove Cemetery, Wilmington, Ohio.

ALLEN, Amos Lawrence, a Representative from Maine; born in Waterboro, York County, Maine, March 17, 1837; attended the common schools, Whitestown Seminary, Whitestown, N. Y., and was graduated from Bowdoin College, Brunswick, Maine, in 1860; studied law at Columbian Law School, Washington, D. C.; was admitted to the bar of York County in 1866 but never practiced; served as a clerk in the United States Treasury Department for about three years; elected clerk of the courts for

York County, Maine, in 1870, reelected three times, and served until January 1, 1883; member of the State house of representatives in 1886 and 1887; private secretary to Speaker Thomas B. Reed in three Congresses; delegate at large to the Republican National Convention at St. Louis in 1896, which nominated McKinley and Hobart; elected as a Republican to the Fifty-sixth Congress to fill the vacancy caused by the resignation of Thomas B. Reed; reelected to the Fifty-seventh and to the four succeeding Congresses and served from November 6, 1899, until his death in Washington, D. C., February 20, 1911; interment in Evergreen Cemetery, Alfred, Maine.

ALLEN, Andrew, a Delegate from Pennsylvania; born in Philadelphia, Pa., in June 1740; was graduated from the University of Pennsylvania at Philadelphia in 1759; completed law studies at the Temple in London, England; was admitted to the bar in 1765 and commenced practice in Philadelphia; member of the provisional assembly and of the provisional council 1765–1775; appointed attorney general in 1766; member of the common council of Philadelphia in 1768; member of the committee of safety in 1775 and 1776; Member of the Continental Congress in 1775 and 1776, but disapproved of independence and withdrew in June 1776; when the Royalist Army entered New York he went within the British lines, took the oath of allegiance to the King, renouncing those he had taken as a Member of the Continental Congress, and went to London, England; was attainted of treason and his estates confiscated; compensated by the British Government with a pension of £400 per annum; died in London, England, March 7, 1825.

ALLEN, Asa Leonard, a Representative from Louisiana; born on a farm near Winnfield, Winn Parish, La., January 5, 1891; attended the rural schools; was graduated from Louisiana State University at Baton Rouge in 1914; taught in the rural schools of Louisiana; principal of the Georgetown (La.) High School in 1914 and 1915 and of the Verda (La.) High School 1915–1917; superintendent of Winn Parish schools 1917–1922; studied law; was admitted to the bar in 1922 and commenced practice in Winnfield, La.; served as city attorney of Winnfield for several years; elected as a Democrat to the Seventy-fifth and to the seven succeeding Congresses (January 3, 1937–January 3, 1953); was not a candidate for renomination in 1952; retired; is a resident of Winnfield, La.

ALLEN, Charles (grandson of Samuel Adams), a Representative from Massachusetts; born in Worcester, Mass., August 9, 1797; attended the Leicester Academy 1809–1811 and Yale College in 1811 and 1812; studied law; was admitted to the bar in 1818 and commenced practice in New Braintree; moved to Worcester in 1824 and continued the practice of law; member of the State house of representatives 1830, 1833, 1835, and 1840; served in the State senate 1836 and 1837; member of the Northeastern Boundary Commission in 1842; judge of the court of common pleas 1842–1845; delegate to the Whig National Convention at Philadelphia in 1848; elected by the Free-Soil Party to the Thirty-first and Thirty-second Congresses (March 4, 1849–March 3, 1853); was not a candidate for renomination in 1852; resumed the practice of law; member of the State constitutional convention in 1853; chief justice of the Suffolk County Superior Court 1859–1867; delegate to the peace convention held at Washington, D. C., in 1861, in an effort to devise means to prevent the impending war; died in Worcester, Mass., August 6, 1869; interment in the Rural Cemetery.

ALLEN, Charles Herbert, a Representative from Massachusetts; born in Lowell, Mass., April 15, 1848; attended public and private schools; was graduated from Amherst College,

Mass., in 1869; engaged in the manufacture of wooden boxes and in the lumber business with his father; held various local offices; member of the Massachusetts House of Representatives in 1881 and 1882; served in the Massachusetts Senate in 1883; colonel and aide-de-camp on the staff of Governor Robinson in 1884; elected as a Republican to the Forty-ninth and Fiftieth Congresses (March 4, 1885–March 3, 1889); declined to be a candidate for renomination in 1888; unsuccessful candidate for Governor of Massachusetts in 1890; served as Massachusetts Prison Commissioner in 1897 and 1898; Assistant Secretary of the Navy 1898–1900; served as first civil Governor of Puerto Rico 1900–1902; returned to Lowell, Mass., in 1902 and became financially interested in banking and other enterprises, serving as vice president of the Morton Trust Co. and of the Guaranty Trust Co. of New York and as president of the American Sugar Refining Co.; died in Lowell, Mass., April 20, 1934; interment in Lowell Cemetery.

ALLEN, Clarence Emir, a Representative from Utah; born in Girard Township, Erie County, Pa., September 8, 1852; attended the district school and Girard (Pa.) Academy; was graduated from Western Reserve College, then at Hudson, Ohio, in 1877; moved to Salt Lake City, Utah, in August 1881 and was an instructor in Salt Lake Academy until 1886, when he resigned to engage in mining pursuits; member of the Territorial house of representatives in 1888, 1890, and again in 1894; elected county clerk of Salt Lake County in August 1890 and served until January 1, 1893; studied law; was admitted to the bar in 1893 and commenced practice in Salt Lake City; unsuccessful Liberal candidate for election in 1892 as a Delegate to the Fifty-third Congress; delegate to the Republican National Convention at Minneapolis in 1892, which nominated Benjamin Harrison and Whitelaw Reid, and at St. Louis in 1896, which nominated William McKinley and Garret A. Hobart; upon the admission of Utah as a State into the Union was elected as a Republican to the Fifty-fourth Congress and served from January 4, 1896, to March 3, 1897; declined to be a candidate for renomination in 1896; resumed his former mining pursuits until 1922, when he retired from active business and resided in Columbus, Ohio, until 1931; died in Escondido, Calif., July 9, 1932; the remains were cremated and the ashes interred in Mount Olivet Cemetery, Salt Lake City, Utah.

ALLEN, Edward Payson, a Representative from Michigan; born in Sharon, Washtenaw County, Mich., October 28, 1839; attended the district and select schools; was graduated from the State normal school in 1864; enlisted and helped to raise a company for the Twenty-ninth Regiment, Michigan Volunteer Infantry; commissioned first lieutenant in September 1864 and later, captain; mustered out with his regiment in September 1865; was graduated from the law school of Michigan University at Ann Arbor in March 1867; was admitted to the bar; commenced practice in Ypsilanti, Washtenaw County; assistant assessor of internal revenue in 1869; prosecuting attorney of Washtenaw County in 1872; alderman of Ypsilanti 1872–1874; elected to the Michigan House of Representatives in 1876 and again in 1878, at which time he was elected speaker pro tempore; mayor of Ypsilanti in 1880; appointed United States Indian agent for Michigan in August 1882 and served until December 1885; elected as a Republican to the Fiftieth and Fifty-first Congresses (March 4, 1887–March 3, 1891); unsuccessful candidate for reelection in 1890 to the Fifty-second Congress; resumed the practice of law; member of the State board of agriculture 1897–1903; again mayor of Ypsilanti in 1899 and 1900; member of the State soldiers' home board 1903–1909; died in Ypsilanti, Mich., November 25, 1909; interment in Highland Cemetery.

ALLEN, Elisha Hunt (son of Samuel Clesson Allen), a Representative from Maine; born in New Salem, Mass., January 28, 1804; attended New Salem Academy, and was graduated from Williams College, Williamstown, Mass., in 1823; studied law; was admitted to the bar in 1825 and commenced practice in Brattleboro, Vt.; moved to Bangor, Maine, and continued the practice of law; member of the Maine House of Representatives 1836–1841, serving as speaker from 1838 to 1841; elected as a Whig to the Twenty-seventh Congress (March 4, 1841–March 3, 1843); unsuccessful candidate for reelection in 1842 to the Twenty-eighth Congress; again elected to the Maine House of Representatives, in 1846; moved to Boston, Mass., in 1847 and resumed the practice of his profession; elected to the Massachusetts House of Representatives in 1849; appointed consul to Honolulu in 1850; was prominently connected with the government of the Hawaiian Islands as chief justice and regent, and as envoy to the United States in 1856 and 1864; served as minister from the Kingdom of Hawaii to the United States from 1869 until his sudden death January 1, 1883, while attending a diplomatic reception given by President Chester A. Arthur in the White House at Washington, D.C.; interment in Mount Auburn Cemetery, Boston, Mass.

ALLEN, Heman (of Milton), a Representative from Vermont; born in Ashfield (now Deerfield), Mass., June 14, 1777; attended an academy in Chesterfield, N. H., for two years; moved to Grand Isle, Vt.; studied law; was admitted to the bar in 1803 and commenced practice in Milton, Vt.; member of the State house of representatives 1810–1814, 1816, 1817, 1822, and 1824–1826; moved to Burlington, Chittenden County, Vt., in 1828 and continued the practice of his profession; elected as a Whig to the Twenty-second and to the three succeeding Congresses (March 4, 1831–March 3, 1839); unsuccessful candidate for reelection in 1838 to the Twenty-sixth Congress; resumed the practice of law; died in Burlington, Vt., on December 11, 1844; interment in Elmwood Avenue Cemetery.

ALLEN, Heman (of Colchester), a Representative from Vermont; born in Poultney, Vt., February 23, 1779; attended the common schools; was graduated from Dartmouth College, Hanover, N. H., in 1795; studied law; was admitted to the bar in 1801 and commenced practice in Colchester, Vt.; sheriff of Chittenden County in 1808 and 1809; chief justice of the county court 1811–1814; member of the State house of representatives 1812–1817; elected as a Democrat to the Fifteenth Congress and served from March 4, 1817, to April 20, 1818, when he resigned to become marshal; appointed United States marshal for the district of Vermont on December 14, 1818, and reappointed on December 24, 1822; United States Minister Plenipotentiary to Chile from January 27, 1823, to July 31, 1827; president of the Burlington branch of the United States Bank from 1830 until the expiration of its charter in 1836; resumed the practice of his profession in Highgate, Franklin County, Vt., where he died April 7, 1852; interment in Allen Cemetery, Burlington, Vt.

ALLEN, Henry Crosby, a Representative from New Jersey; born in Paterson, N. J., May 13, 1872; attended private and public schools of his native city; was graduated from St. Paul's School, Garden City, Long Island, in 1889, from Yale University in 1893, and from the New York Law School in 1895; was admitted to the bar in 1895 and commenced practice in Paterson, N. J.; elected as a Republican to the Fifty-ninth Congress (March 4, 1905–March 3, 1907); was not a candidate for renomination in 1906; resumed the practice of law in Paterson, N. J.; postmaster of Paterson 1926–1935; died in Mystic, Conn., March 7, 1942, while visiting his daughter; interment in Cedar Lawn Cemetery, Paterson, N. J.

ALLEN, Henry Dixon, a Representative from Kentucky; born near Henderson, Henderson County, Ky., June 24, 1854; moved with his parents to Morganfield, Union County, in 1855; attended the common schools and Morganfield Collegiate Institute; taught school in Union County 1869–1875; studied medicine and was graduated from the Missouri Medical College, St. Louis, Mo., in 1877; practiced medicine in Union County from 1877 to 1878; abandoned medicine and studied law; was admitted to the bar in 1878 and commenced practice in Morganfield, Ky.; county school commissioner 1879–1881; prosecuting attorney of Union County 1882–1891; elected as a Democrat to the Fifty-sixth and Fifty-seventh Congresses (March 4, 1899–March 3, 1903); was not a candidate for renomination in 1902; resumed the practice of law; also engaged in banking and agricultural pursuits; died in Morganfield, Ky., March 9, 1924; interment in Masonic Cemetery.

ALLEN, Henry Justin, a Senator from Kansas; born in Pittsfield, Warren County, Pa., September 11, 1868; moved to Kansas in 1870 with his parents, who settled on a farm near Clifton, Clay County; attended the public schools, Washburn College, Topeka, Kans., and was graduated from Baker University, Baldwin, Kans., in 1890; located in Ottawa, Kans., and became a newspaper reporter and editorial writer; during the Spanish-American War served as a war correspondent in Cuba with Shafter's Corps; member of the press galleries of the United States Congress 1914–1916; proprietor of several Kansas newspapers; served with the American Red Cross in France as head of the home communication service during the First World War; Governor of Kansas 1919–1923; special commissioner of the Near East Relief to Armenia, Turkey, Greece, and Southern Russia in 1923 and 1924; director of publicity for the Republican National Committee in the campaign of 1928; appointed as a Republican to the United States Senate to fill the vacancy caused by the resignation of Charles Curtis and served from April 1, 1929, to November 30, 1930, when a duly elected successor qualified; unsuccessful candidate for election to fill the vacancy; engaged in special writing and in newspaper publishing; editor of the Topeka State Journal and chairman of the board of directors of the Wichita Beacon; died in Wichita, Kans., January 17, 1950, interment in Maple Grove Cemetery.

ALLEN, James Cameron, a Representative from Illinois; born in Shelby County, Ky., January 29, 1822; attended the public schools; moved to Indiana in 1830; studied law; was admitted to the bar in 1843 and commenced practice in Sullivan, Ind.; prosecuting attorney for the seventh judicial district of Indiana 1846–1848; moved to Palestine, Ill., in 1848 and continued the practice of law; member of the State house of representatives in 1850 and 1851; elected as a Democrat to the Thirty-third Congress (March 4, 1853–March 3, 1855); presented credentials as a Member-elect to the Thirty-fourth Congress and served from March 4, 1855, to July 18, 1856, when the House decided he was not entitled to the seat; subsequently elected to fill the vacancy thus caused and served from November 4, 1856, to March 3, 1857; was not a candidate for renomination in 1856; Clerk of the National House of Representatives in the Thirty-fifth Congress 1857–1859; unsuccessful candidate for Governor in 1860; elected circuit court judge in April 1861 and served until he resigned in 1863; elected to the Thirty-eighth Congress (March 4, 1863–March 3, 1865); unsuccessful candidate for reelection in 1864 to the Thirty-ninth Congress; resumed the practice of law; reelected circuit court judge in 1873 and upon the establishment of the appellate court was appointed its judge, occupying both positions and serving from 1873 to 1879; moved to Olney, Richland County, Ill., in 1876 and practiced law; retired from the practice of his profession in 1907; died in Olney, Ill., January 30, 1912; interment in Olney Cemetery.

ALLEN, John (father of John William Allen), a Representative from Connecticut; born in Great Barrington, Mass., June 12, 1763; attended the common schools; studied law at the Litchfield Law School; was admitted to the bar in 1786 and commenced practice in Litchfield, Conn.; member of the State house of representatives 1793–1796, serving as clerk in 1796; elected as a Federalist to the Fifth Congress (March 4, 1797–March 3, 1799); declined to be a candidate for renomination in 1798; member of the State council and of the supreme court of errors 1800–1806; continued the practice of law in Litchfield, Conn., until his death on July 31, 1812; interment in East Cemetery.

ALLEN, John Beard, a Delegate from the Territory of Washington and a Senator from Washington; born in Crawfordsville, Montgomery County, Ind., May 18, 1845; attended the public schools and Wabash College, Crawfordsville, Ind.; during the Civil War served as a private in the One Hundred and Thirty-eighth Regiment, Indiana Volunteer Infantry; moved to Rochester, Minn., in 1865 and engaged in business as a grain dealer; graduated from the law department of Michigan University at Ann Arbor, and was admitted to the bar in 1869; moved to Washington Territory in March 1870 and commenced the practice of law in Olympia; appointed United States attorney for the Territory of Washington in April 1875 by President Grant and served in that capacity until July 1885; reporter for the supreme court of the Territory 1878–1885; moved to Walla Walla in 1881; elected as a Republican Delegate to the Fifty-first Congress and served from March 4 until November 11, 1889, when, the Territory being admitted as a State, he was elected to the United States Senate and served from November 20, 1889, to March 3, 1893; presented credentials as a Senator-designate in 1893 but was not permitted to qualify; moved to Seattle and resumed the practice of law; died in Seattle, Wash., January 28, 1903; interment in Lakeview Cemetery.

ALLEN, John Clayton, a Representative from Illinois; born in Hinesburg, Chittenden County, Vt., February 14, 1860; attended the common schools and Beeman Academy, New Haven, Vt.; moved to Lincoln, Nebr., in 1881, and to McCook, Redwillow County, Nebr., in 1886 and engaged in mercantile pursuits at both places; member of the McCook City Council 1887–1889; mayor of McCook, Nebr., in 1890; secretary of state of Nebraska 1891–1895; moved to Monmouth, Warren County, Ill., in 1896 and became president of the John C. Allen Co. department store and of the People's National Bank of Monmouth; member of the State normal school board 1917–1927; elected as a Republican to the Sixty-ninth and to the three succeeding Congresses (March 4, 1925–March 3, 1933); unsuccessful candidate for reelection in 1932 to the Seventy-third Congress and for election in 1934 to the Seventy-fourth Congress; resumed his former business pursuits in Monmouth, Ill., until his death there on January 12, 1939; interment in Vermont Cemetery, Vermont, Ill.

ALLEN, John James (brother of Robert Allen), a Representative from Virginia; born in Woodstock, Shenandoah County, Va., September 25, 1797; attended Dickinson College, Carlisle, Pa., in 1811 and 1812, and Washington College (now Washington and Lee University), Lexington, Va., in 1814 and 1815; studied law; was admitted to the bar in 1819 and commenced practice at Campbell Courthouse; moved to Clarksburg, Harrison County, Va., and continued practice; member of the State senate 1828–1831; Commonwealth attorney for Harrison, Lewis, and Preston Counties in 1834, serving while a Member of Congress; elected as a Whig to the Twenty-third Congress (March 4, 1833–March 3, 1835); unsuccessful candidate for reelection in 1834 to the Twenty-fourth Congress; judge of the seventeenth circuit court of Virginia 1836–1840; judge of the State supreme court of appeals 1840–1865, serving as presiding justice 1852–1865; president of the executive council in 1861; author of the "Botetourt resolutions" of 1861; retired to private life and engaged in the management of his large estate; died at Beaverdam, near Fincastle, Botetourt County, Va., September 18, 1871; interment in the family burying ground in Lauderdale Cemetery, near his estate in Botetourt County, Va.

ALLEN, John Joseph, Jr., a Representative from California; born in Oakland, Alameda County, Calif., November 27, 1899; attended the public schools; while a student in college enlisted during the First World War in the United States Navy and served as an apprentice seaman; was graduated from the University of California at Berkeley in 1920 and from its law department in 1922; was admitted to the bar in 1922 and commenced practice in Oakland, Calif.; member of the Oakland Board of Education 1923–1943, serving several terms as president; president of the California State School Trustees Association 1936–1938; member of the County Republican Central Committee 1936–1944; during World War II served as a lieutenant commander in the United States Navy 1942–1945, with twenty months in the South Pacific area; vice chairman of the State commission on school districts in 1946 and 1947; elected as a Republican to the Eightieth and to the five succeeding Congresses (January 3, 1947–January 3, 1959); unsuccessful for reelection in 1958 to the Eighty-sixth Congress; appointed Under Secretary of Commerce for Transportation January 5, 1959, serving until January 20, 1961; resumed the practice of law; resides in Oakland, Calif.

ALLEN, John Mills, a Representative from Mississippi; born in Tishomingo County, Miss., July 8, 1846; attended the common schools; during the Civil War enlisted as a private in the Confederate Army and served throughout the war; attended the law school of Cumberland University, Lebanon, Tenn., and was graduated from the law department of the University of Mississippi in 1870; was admitted to the bar the same year and commenced practice in Tupelo, Lee County, Miss.; district attorney for the first judicial district of Mississippi 1875–1879; elected as a Democrat to the Forty-ninth and to the seven succeeding Congresses (March 4, 1885–March 3, 1901); declined to be a candidate for reelection in 1900 to the Fifty-seventh Congress; appointed in March 1901 a United States commissioner to the St. Louis Exposition of 1904; resumed the practice of law in Tupelo, Miss., and died there October 30, 1917; interment in Glenwood Cemetery.

ALLEN, John William (son of John Allen), a Representative from Ohio; born in Litchfield, Conn., in August 1802; attended preparatory schools; moved to Chenango County, N. Y., in 1818, where he received a classical education and studied law; moved to Cleveland, Ohio, in 1825 and continued the study of law; was admitted to the bar in 1826 and commenced practice in Cleveland; president of the village 1831–1835; member of the board of directors of the Commercial Bank of Lake Erie upon its reorganization in 1832; one of the incorporators of the Cleveland & Newburg Railroad Co. in 1834 and an organizer of the Ohio Railroad Co. in 1836; served in the State senate in 1836 and 1837; elected as a Whig to the Twenty-fifth and Twenty-sixth Congresses (March 4, 1837–March 3, 1841); was not a candidate for reelection; elected mayor of Cleveland in 1841; elected president of the Cleveland, Columbus & Cincinnati Railroad in 1845; delegate to the first convention on river and harbor improvement, held in Chicago in 1847; appointed postmaster of Cleveland by President Grant on April 4, 1870, reappointed April 4, 1874, and served until his resignation January 11, 1875; one of the first bank commissioners of Ohio; died in Cleveland, Ohio, October 5, 1887; interment in Erie Street Cemetery.

ALLEN, Joseph (nephew of Samuel Adams), a Representative from Massachusetts; born in Boston, Mass., September 2, 1749; was graduated from Harvard College in 1774; engaged in business in Leicester, Mass.; moved to Worcester in 1776; member of the State constitutional convention of 1788; Federalist presidential elector in 1797 and voted for John Adams; appointed clerk of the courts and held that office until 1810, when he resigned to serve in Congress; elected to the Eleventh Congress to fill the vacancy caused by the resignation of Jabez Upham and served from October 8, 1810, to March 3, 1811; declined to be a candidate for reelection in 1810; State councilor from 1815 to 1818; died in Worcester, Mass., September 2, 1827; interment in Mechanic Street Burying Ground.

ALLEN, Judson, a Representative from New York; born in Plymouth, Conn., April 3, 1797; attended the public schools; engaged in the lumber business; moved to Harpursville (formerly Harpersville), Broome County, N. Y.; appointed postmaster of Harpursville March 19, 1830, and served until November 20, 1839; judge of the Broome County Court for eight years; member of the State assembly in 1836 and 1837; elected as a Democrat to the Twenty-sixth Congress (March 4, 1839–March 3, 1841); was not a candidate for renomination in 1840; moved to St. Louis, Mo., and engaged in the produce, lumber, marble, and grocery business until his death in St. Louis, August 6, 1880; interment in Bellefontaine Cemetery.

ALLEN, Leo Elwood, a Representative from Illinois; born in Elizabeth, Jo Daviess County, Ill., October 5, 1898; attended the public schools; during the First World War served as a sergeant in the One Hundred and Twenty-third Field Artillery 1917–1919; was graduated from the University of Michigan at Ann Arbor in 1923; taught school at Galena, Ill., in 1922 and 1923; clerk of the circuit court of Jo Daviess County 1924–1932; studied law; was admitted to the bar in 1930 and commenced practice in Galena, Ill.; elected as a Republican to the Seventy-third and to the thirteen succeeding Congresses (March 4, 1933–January 3, 1961); was not a candidate for renomination in 1960; is a resident of Galena, Ill.

ALLEN, Nathaniel (father-in-law of Robert Lawson Rose), a Representative from New York; born in East Bloomfield, N. Y., in 1780; attended the common schools; worked as a blacksmith at Canandaigua, Ontario County, N. Y.; started a blacksmith shop at Richmond, near Allens Hill, in 1796; served as an officer in the militia; appointed postmaster of Honeoye Falls, N. Y., July 1, 1811; was commissioner and paymaster on the Niagara frontier in 1812; member of the State assembly in 1812; sheriff of Ontario County, N. Y., 1815–1819; elected to the Sixteenth Congress (March 4, 1819–March 3, 1821); was not a candidate for renomination in 1820; supervisor of the town of Richmond 1824–1826; engaged in the prosecution of claims for money due in connection with the construction of the Louisville & Portland Canal; died in the Gault House at Louisville, Ky., while on a business trip to that city, December 22, 1832; interment in the churchyard of the Episcopal Church, Allens Hill, Ontario County, N. Y.

ALLEN, Philip, a Senator from Rhode Island; born in Providence, R. I., September 1, 1785; received his early education from private tutors; attended Taunton Academy and Robert Rogers School at Newport; was graduated from Rhode Island College (now Brown University) in 1803; engaged in mercantile pursuits and foreign commerce; when shipping was suspended during the War of 1812 he engaged in the manufacture of cotton goods in Smithfield, R. I.; member of the State house of representatives 1819–1821; appointed pension agent and president

of the Rhode Island branch of the United States Bank in 1827; continued the manufacture of cotton goods and began the printing of calicos at Providence, R. I., in 1831; elected Governor of Rhode Island in 1851 as a Tariff Democrat; reelected in 1852 and 1853 and served until July 20, 1853, when he resigned to become Senator; elected on May 4, 1853, to the United States Senate for the term beginning March 4, 1853, and served from July 20, 1853, to March 3, 1859; was not a candidate for reelection in 1859 and retired from active political and business pursuits; died in Providence, R. I., December 16, 1865; interment in the North Burial Ground.

ALLEN, Robert, a Representative from Tennessee; born in Augusta County, Va., June 19, 1778; attended the rural schools and William and Mary College, Williamsburg, Va.; studied law and practiced; moved to Carthage, Tenn., in 1804 and engaged in the mercantile business; clerk of Smith County many years; during the War of 1812 served as colonel and commanded a regiment of Tennessee Volunteers under Gen. Andrew Jackson; elected as a Democrat to the Sixteenth and to the three succeeding Congresses (March 4, 1819–March 3, 1827); declined to be a candidate for renomination in 1826; engaged in agricultural and mercantile pursuits in Carthage, Tenn.; delegate to the State convention in 1834; died in Carthage, Tenn., August 19, 1844; interment in Greenwood Cemetery, Lebanon, Tenn.

ALLEN, Robert (brother of John James Allen), a Representative from Virginia; born in the village of Woodstock, Shenandoah County, Va., July 30, 1794; attended the rural schools, and Dickinson College at Carlisle 1811–1812; was graduated from Washington College (now Washington and Lee University), Lexington, Va., in 1815; engaged in agricultural pursuits in Shenandoah County; studied law; was admitted to the bar and commenced practice in Woodstock; prosecuting attorney of Shenandoah County; member of the State senate in 1821–1826; elected as a Democrat to the Twentieth, Twenty-first, and Twenty-second Congresses (March 4, 1827–March 3, 1833); moved to Bedford County and continued agricultural pursuits; died in Mount Prospect, Va., December 30, 1859; interment in Longwood Cemetery, Liberty (now Bedford City), Va.

ALLEN, Robert Edward Lee, a Representative from West Virginia; born in Lima, Tyler County, W. Va., November 28, 1865; attended the country schools, Fairmont Normal School, and Peabody College, Nashville, Tenn.; was graduated from the literary department of the University of West Virginia at Morgantown in 1894 and from its law department in 1895; was admitted to the bar in 1895 and commenced practice at Morgantown, Monongalia County, W. Va.; member of the city council from 1895 to 1917; deputy collector of internal revenue for the district of West Virginia 1917–1921; judge of the city court 1921–1923; elected as a Democrat to the Sixty-eighth Congress (March 4, 1923–March 3, 1925); was an unsuccessful candidate for reelection in 1924 to the Sixty-ninth Congress and for election in 1926 to the Seventieth Congress; resumed the practice of law in Morgantown, W. Va., until his retirement in 1927; moved to Preston County, W. Va., and operated a summer resort at Brookside 1929–1939; resided in Aurora, W. Va., until his death in Mountain Lake Park, Md., January 28, 1951; interment in Kingwood Cemetery, Kingwood, W. Va.

ALLEN, Robert Gray, a Representative from Pennsylvania; born in Winchester, Middlesex County, Mass., August 24, 1902; moved to Minneapolis, Minn., in 1906 and attended public and private schools; was graduated from Phillips Academy at Andover, Mass., in 1922 and later attended Harvard University at Cambridge, Mass.; moved to Greensburg, Pa., in 1929 and engaged in the valve and fittings manufacturing business as salesman and sales manager until 1937; district administrator of the Works Progress Administration in 1935 and 1936; elected as a Democrat to the Seventy-fifth and Seventy-sixth Congresses (January 3, 1937–January 3, 1941); was not a candidate for renomination in 1940; president of the Duff-Norton Manufacturing Co., Pittsburgh, Pa., 1940–1943; commissioned a major in the Ordnance Branch, United States Army, in July 1942, promoted to lieutenant colonel in February 1943, and served until his discharge in January 1945; sales manager for the Baldwin Locomotive Works from March 1945 to June 1946; vice president of Fisher Plastics Corporation, Boston, Mass., from June 1946 to June 1947; vice president of Great Lakes Carbon Corporation and general manager of its electrode division at Niagara Falls, N. Y., and Morganton, N. C., 1947–1954, president, Pesco Products, division of Borg-Warner Corporation, Bedford, Ohio, 1954–1957; vice president of Bucyrus-Erie Co., South Milwaukee, Wis., in 1957 and 1958 and president since 1958; chairman of the board and president of Bucyrus-Erie Co. of Canada, Ltd., Guelph, Ontario, and chairman of the board of Ruston-Bucyrus, Ltd., Lincoln, England; director of the First Wisconsin National Bank of Milwaukee; is a resident of Milwaukee, Wis.

ALLEN, Samuel Clesson (father of Elisha Hunt Allen), a Representative from Massachusetts; born in Bernardston, Mass., January 5, 1772; attended the public schools of New Salem, and was graduated from Dartmouth College, Hanover, N. H., in 1794; studied theology; was ordained as a minister, became pastor of the Congregational Church in Northfield in 1795, and served until 1798; studied law; was admitted to the bar in 1800 and practiced in New Salem; member of the State house of representatives 1806–1810; served in the State senate 1812–1815; elected to the Fifteenth and to the five succeeding Congresses (March 4, 1817–March 3, 1829); member of the Governor's executive council of Massachusetts 1829–1830; again elected to the State senate in 1831; retired from politics and was not a candidate for renomination in 1828; engaged as a lecturer at Amherst College; member of the board of trustees of Amherst College and of the University of Vermont; died in Northfield, Mass., February 8, 1842; interment in the Village Cemetery, Bernardston, Franklin County, Mass.

ALLEN, Thomas, a Representative from Missouri; born in Pittsfield, Mass., August 29, 1813; attended Pittsfield Academy and Berkshire Gymnasium; was graduated from Union College in 1832; studied law in New York City; was admitted to the bar in 1835 and commenced practice in New York City in 1832; moved to Washington, D. C., and established the Madisonian in 1837; printer to the House of Representatives 1837–1839; printer to the United States Senate 1839–1842; moved to St. Louis, Mo., in 1842; member of the State senate 1850–1854; was a contractor upon internal improvements and projected and built more than 1,000 miles of railway; in 1852 took the first steam locomotive across the Mississippi River; president of the St. Louis, Iron Mountain & Southern Railway, but subsequently sold all his railway interests and retired from active pursuits; elected as a Democrat to the Forty-seventh Congress and served from March 4, 1881, until his death in Washington, D. C., April 8, 1882; interment in Pittsfield Cemetery, Pittsfield, Mass.

ALLEN, William, a Representative and a Senator from Ohio; born in Edenton, Chowan County, N. C., December 27, 1803; moved with his sister to Lynchburg, Va., and attended private schools; moved to Chillicothe, Ohio, in 1819; attended Chillicothe Academy; studied law; was admitted to the bar in 1827 and commenced practice in Chillicothe; elected as a Democrat to the

Twenty-third Congress (March 4, 1833–March 3, 1835); unsuccessful candidate for reelection in 1834 to the Twenty-fourth Congress; elected to the United States Senate in January 1837; reelected in 1843 and served from March 4, 1837, to March 3, 1849; was not a candidate for reelection; retired to his estate, "Fruit Hill," near Chillicothe, Ross County, Ohio, and engaged in farming and stock raising; Governor of Ohio 1874–1876; unsuccessful candidate for reelection in 1875; resumed agricultural pursuits; died at "Fruit Hill," July 11, 1879; interment in Grand View Cemetery, Chillicothe, Ohio.

ALLEN, William, a Representative from Ohio; born near Hamilton, Butler County, Ohio, August 13, 1827; attended the public schools; taught school; studied law; was admitted to the bar in 1849 and commenced practice in Greenville, Ohio, in 1850; prosecuting attorney of Darke County 1850–1854; elected as a Democrat to the Thirty-sixth and Thirty-seventh Congresses (March 4, 1859–March 3, 1863); declined to be a candidate for renomination in 1862; resumed the practice of law; affiliated with the Republican Party at the close of the Civil War; appointed judge of the court of common pleas of the second judicial district in 1865; declined the Republican nomination for election to the Forty-sixth Congress in 1878 because of failing health; interested in banking until his death in Greenville, Darke County, Ohio, July 6, 1881; interment in Greenville Cemetery.

ALLEN, William Franklin, a Representative from Delaware; born in Bridgeville, Sussex County, Del., January 19, 1883; attended the public schools at Bridgeville, and Laurel, Del.; moved to Seaford, Del., and was employed as an agent and train dispatcher by a railroad company 1902–1922; served as school commissioner at Seaford, Del., 1920–1924; delegate to the Democratic National Convention at San Francisco, Calif., in 1920; member of the State senate 1925–1929, serving as president pro tempore in 1927; engaged in the manufacture of fruit packages and in the packing and shipping of farm products in 1926; also engaged in the brokerage of oil and petroleum in 1926; elected as a Democrat to the Seventy-fifth Congress (January 3, 1937–January 3, 1939); unsuccessful candidate for reelection in 1938 to the Seventy-sixth Congress; resumed the oil and gasoline distribution business; died in a hospital at Lewes, Del., June 14, 1946; interment in Odd Fellows Cemetery, Seaford, Del.

ALLEN, William Joshua (son of Willis Allen), a Representative from Illinois; born in Wilson County, Tenn., June 9, 1829; moved with his father to Franklin (now Williamson) County, Ill., about 1830, and in 1839 settled in Marion; attended the common schools; studied law; was admitted to the bar in 1849 and commenced practice in Metropolis; enrolling and engrossing clerk of the State house of representatives in 1849 and 1851; moved to Marion, Ill., in 1853 and continued the practice of his profession; appointed prosecuting attorney for the twenty-sixth judicial circuit of Illinois in 1854; member of the State senate in 1855; elected judge of the circuit court of the twenty-sixth judicial circuit on June 24, 1859, and served until 1861; elected as a Democrat to the Thirty-seventh Congress to fill the vacancy caused by the resignation of John A. Logan; reelected to the Thirty-eighth Congress and served from June 2, 1862, to March 3, 1865; was not a candidate for reelection in 1864; member of the State constitutional conventions in 1862 and 1870; delegate to all Democratic National Conventions from 1864 to 1888; moved to Springfield, Ill., in 1886; appointed United States district judge for the southern district of Illinois on April 18, 1887, and served until his death January 26, 1901, while visiting in Hot Springs, Ark.; interment in Oak Ridge Cemetery, Springfield, Ill.

ALLEN, William Vincent, a Senator from Nebraska; born in Midway, Madison County, Ohio, January 28, 1847; moved to Iowa with his parents in 1857; attended the common schools, and Upper Iowa University at Fayette; served as a private in Company G, Thirty-second Iowa Volunteer Infantry, during the Civil War, the last five months being on the staff of Gen. J. I. Gilbert; studied law at West Union, Iowa; was admitted to the bar in 1869 and practiced in the State of Iowa until 1884, when he moved to Madison, Madison County, Nebr.; served as judge of the district court of the ninth judicial district of Nebraska from 1891 to 1893; permanent chairman of the Populist State conventions in 1892, 1894, and 1896; elected as a Populist to the United States Senate and served from March 4, 1893, to March 3, 1899; unsuccessful candidate for reelection in 1899; appointed and subsequently elected judge of the district court of the ninth judicial district of Nebraska and served from March 9, 1899, until December 1899, when he resigned; appointed to the United States Senate to fill the vacancy caused by the death of Monroe L. Hayward and served from December 13, 1899, until March 28, 1901, when a successor was elected; was not an active candidate for election to this vacancy; delegate to the Populist National Convention at St. Louis in 1896, serving as presiding officer; resumed the practice of law in Madison, Nebr.; again elected judge of the district court of the ninth judicial district of Nebraska in 1917 and served in this capacity until his death; died in Los Angeles, Calif., January 12, 1924; interment in Crown Hill Cemetery, Madison, Nebr.

ALLEN, Willis (father of William Joshua Allen), a Representative from Illinois; born near Roanoke, Va., December 15, 1806; attended the common schools; taught school; moved to Tennessee and settled in Wilson County; moved to Franklin (now Williamson) County, Ill., in 1830 and engaged in agricultural pursuits; studied law; was admitted to the bar and commenced practice in Marion; sheriff of Franklin County 1834–1838; member of the State house of representatives 1838–1840; prosecuting attorney of the first judicial circuit in 1841; presidential elector on the Democratic ticket of Polk and Dallas in 1844; member of the State senate 1844–1847; member of the State constitutional convention in 1847 and 1848; elected as a Democrat to the Thirty-second and Thirty-third Congresses (March 4, 1851–March 3, 1855); voluntarily retired from public life and resumed the practice of his profession; elected judge of the twenty-sixth circuit court of Illinois March 2, 1859, and served until his death while holding court in Harrisburg, Saline County, Ill., April 15, 1859; interment in Marion Cemetery, Marion, Ill.

ALLEY, John Bassett, a Representative from Massachusetts; born in Lynn, Essex County, Mass., January 7, 1817; attended the common schools; at the age of fourteen was apprenticed as a shoemaker, but was released at nineteen; moved to Cincinnati, Ohio, in 1836; freighted merchandise up and down the Mississippi River; moved to Lynn, Mass., in 1838 and entered the shoe manufacturing business; established a hide and leather house in Boston in 1847; member of the first board of aldermen of Lynn in 1850; member of the Governor's council 1847–1851; served in the State senate in 1852; member of the constitutional convention of 1853; elected as a Republican to the Thirty-sixth and to the three succeeding Congresses (March 4, 1859–March 3, 1867); was not a candidate for renomination in 1866; became connected with the Union Pacific Railroad; abandoned active business pursuits in 1886 and took an extensive European trip; lived in retirement until his death in West Newton, Mass., January 19, 1896; interment in Pine Grove Cemetery, Lynn, Mass.

ALLGOOD, Miles Clayton, a Representative from Alabama; born in Chepultepec (now Allgood), Blount County, Ala., Feb-

ruary 22, 1878; attended the common schools of his native county and was graduated from the State Normal College at Florence, Ala., in 1898; taught school in Blount County; tax assessor of Blount County, Ala., 1900–1909; member of the State Democratic executive committee 1908–1910; Blount County agricultural demonstration agent 1910–1913; State auditor of Alabama 1914–1918; State commissioner of agriculture and industries 1918–1922; elected as a delegate at large from Alabama to the Democratic National Convention at San Francisco in 1920; elected as a Democrat to the Sixty-eighth Congress and to the five succeeding Congresses (March 4, 1923–January 3, 1935); unsuccessful candidate for renomination in 1934; served as a member of the Farm Security Administration from September 4, 1935, until he retired on December 1, 1943; made an unsuccessful campaign for State treasurer in 1954; is a resident of Mentone, Ala.

ALLISON, James, Jr. (father of John Allison), a Representative from Pennsylvania; born near Elkton, Cecil County, Md., October 4, 1772; moved with his parents to Washington County, Pa., in 1774; at seventeen years of age he enrolled in the school of David Johnson, of Beaver, Pa., who taught the first Latin grammar class established west of the Allegheny Mountains; saw service in the Indian warfare at Yellow Creek, Bedford County, Pa.; studied law; was admitted to the bar in 1796 and commenced practice in Washington, Pa.; returned to Beaver in 1803 and continued the practice of law until 1822, when he was elected to Congress; prosecuting attorney of Beaver County 1803–1809; elected as a Whig to the Eighteenth and Nineteenth Congresses and served from March 4, 1823, until his resignation in 1825 before the assembling of the Nineteenth Congress; resumed the practice of law until 1848, after which he discontinued active pursuits and lived in retirement until his death in Beaver, Beaver County, Pa., June 17, 1854; interment in Old Cemetery.

ALLISON, John (son of James Allison, Jr.), a Representative from Pennsylvania; born in Beaver, Pa., August 5, 1812; attended the common schools; studied law; was admitted to the bar but did not practice extensively; engaged in the manufacture of hats; also operated a tannery; member of the State house of representatives in 1846, 1847, and 1849; elected as a Whig to the Thirty-second Congress (March 4, 1851–March 3, 1853); unsuccessful candidate for reelection in 1852 to the Thirty-third Congress; elected to the Thirty-fourth Congress (March 4, 1855–March 3, 1857); declined to be a candidate for renomination in 1856; delegate to the Republican National Convention at Philadelphia in 1856 and nominated Abraham Lincoln as a candidate for Vice President of the United States; also a delegate to the Republican National Convention at Chicago in 1860; appointed Register of the Treasury April 3, 1869, and served until his death in Washington, D. C., on March 23, 1878; interment in Beaver Cemetery, Beaver, Pa.

ALLISON, Robert, a Representative from Pennsylvania; born near Greencastle, Franklin County, Pa., March 10, 1777; attended local and private schools; moved to Huntingdon, Pa., in 1795; employed as a clerk in his brother's office; studied law; was admitted to the bar in April 1798 and commenced the practice of law in Huntingdon; served as a captain in the Huntingdon Volunteers during the War of 1812; at the close of the war returned to Huntingdon and resumed the practice of law; burgess of Huntingdon, Pa., in 1815, 1817, 1819, 1821–1824, and again in 1826; unsuccessful candidate for election in 1824 to the Nineteenth Congress, in 1826 to the Twentieth Congress, and in 1828 to the Twenty-first Congress; elected as a Whig to the Twenty-second Congress (March 4, 1831–March 3, 1833); was not a candidate for renomination in 1832 to the Twenty-third Congress;

continued the practice of his profession in Huntingdon, Huntingdon County, Pa., until his death there on December 2, 1840; interment in River View Cemetery.

ALLISON, William Boyd, a Representative and a Senator from Iowa; born in Perry, Wayne County, Ohio, March 2, 1829; attended country schools, the academy in Wooster, Ohio, and Allegheny College, Meadville, Pa.; was graduated from Western Reserve College, Hudson (now in Cleveland), Ohio, in 1849; studied law; was admitted to the bar in 1852 and commenced practice in Ashland, Ohio; unsuccessful candidate for district attorney in 1856; settled in Dubuque, Iowa, in 1857 and resumed the practice of law; delegate to the Republican National Convention at Chicago in 1860 that nominated Abraham Lincoln for President; appointed a special aide with title of lieutenant colonel of Volunteers by Gov. S. J. Kirkwood in 1861 and rendered marked service in fitting the troops of Iowa for participation in the Civil War; elected as a Republican to the Thirty-eighth and to the three succeeding Congresses (March 4, 1863–March 3, 1871); declined to be a candidate for renomination in 1870, but was an unsuccessful candidate for the United States Senate; resumed the practice of law in Dubuque; elected to the United States Senate in 1872; reelected in 1878, 1884, 1890, 1896, and again in 1902, and served from March 4, 1873, until his death; had been nominated in a State preferential primary as a candidate for reelection to the Senate; his service as a Senator covered a period of thirty-five years and five months; died in Dubuque, Dubuque County, Iowa, August 4, 1908; interment in Linwood Cemetery.

ALLOTT, Gordon Llewellyn, a Senator from Colorado; born in Pueblo, Colo., January 2, 1907; attended the public and high schools of Pueblo, Colo.; was graduated from the University of Colorado at Boulder in 1927 and from its law school in 1929; was admitted to the bar in 1929 and commenced the practice of law in Pueblo, Colo.; moved to Lamar, Colo., in 1930 and continued practicing law; county attorney of Prowers County, Colo., in 1934 and 1941–1946; director, First Federal Savings & Loan Association of Lamar, Colo., 1934–1960; city attorney, Lamar, Colo., 1937–1941; during World War II served as a major in the United States Air Force from August 10, 1942, to March 1, 1946, with nineteen months of service in the South Pacific Theater; participated in seven campaigns and won seven battle stars; district attorney, fifteenth judicial district, 1946–1949; member of legislative council 1952–1955; vice chairman State Board of Paroles 1951–1955; Lieutenant Governor of Colorado January 1951 to January 1955; delegate to the Republican National Conventions in 1948, 1952, and 1956; elected as a Republican to the United States Senate for the term commencing January 3, 1955, and ending January 3, 1961. *Reelected in 1960 for the term ending January 3, 1967.*

ALMON, Edward Berton, a Representative from Alabama; born near Moulton, Lawrence County, Ala., April 18, 1860; attended the rural schools; was graduated from the State Normal College, Florence, Ala., and from the law department of the University of Alabama, at Tuscaloosa, in 1883; was admitted to the bar in 1885 and commenced practice in Tuscumbia, Colbert County, Ala.; served in the State senate 1892–1894; presidential elector on the Democratic ticket of Bryan and Sewall in 1896; judge of the circuit court of the eleventh judicial circuit of Alabama 1898–1906; member of the State house of representatives 1910–1915, serving as speaker in 1911; elected as a Democrat to the Sixty-fourth and to the nine succeeding Congresses and served from March 4, 1915, until his death in Washington, D. C., June 22, 1933; interment in Oakwood Cemetery, Tuscumbia, Ala.

ALMOND, James Lindsay, Jr., a Representative from Virginia; born in Charlottesville, Albemarle County, Va., June 15, 1898; attended the graded schools in Locust Grove, Va., and was graduated from the law department of the University of Virginia at Charlottesville in 1923; was admitted to the bar the same year and commenced practice in Roanoke, Va.; during the First World War served as a private in the Students Army Training Corps at the University of Virginia in 1917 and 1918; taught school at Locust Grove, Va., in 1919; principal of Zoar High School in 1921 and 1922; served as assistant Commonwealth's attorney of Virginia 1930–1933; judge of the Hustings Court of Roanoke City, Va., 1933–1945; elected as a Democrat to the Seventy-ninth Congress to fill the vacancy caused by the resignation of Clifton A. Woodrum; reelected to the Eightieth Congress and served from January 22, 1946, until his resignation on April 17, 1948, having been elected attorney general of Virginia, in which capacity he served until August 28, 1957, when he resigned; elected Governor of Virginia in 1957 for the term ending January 1962; is a resident of Roanoke, Va.

ALSOP, John, a Delegate from New York; born in New Windsor, Orange County, N. Y., in 1724; completed preparatory studies; moved to New York City and engaged in mercantile pursuits and importing; represented New York City in the colonial legislature; one of the incorporators of the New York Hospital, serving as its governor 1770–1784; Member of the Continental Congress from September 14 to October 26, 1774, and from May 10, 1775, to the latter part of that year; member of a committee of one hundred appointed in 1775 by the citizens of the city to take charge of the government until a convention could be assembled; served as the eighth president of the New York Chamber of Commerce in 1784 and 1785; died in Newtown, Long Island, N. Y., November 22, 1794; interment in Trinity Church Cemetery, New York City.

ALSTON, Lemuel James, a Representative from South Carolina; born in the eastern part of Granville (now Warren) County, N. C., in 1760; moved to South Carolina after the Revolutionary War and settled near Greens Mill, which soon became the town of Greenville; studied law; was admitted to the bar and commenced practice in Greenville; elected to the Tenth and Eleventh Congresses (March 4, 1807–March 3, 1811); moved in 1816 to Clarke County, Ala., and settled near Grove Hill, where he presided over the orphans' court and the county court from November 1816 until May 1821; died at "Alston Place," Clarke County, Ala., in 1836.

ALSTON, William Jeffreys, a Representative from Alabama; born in Milledgeville, Ga., December 31, 1800; attended a private school in South Carolina; moved to Alabama and settled in Marengo County; taught school for several years; studied law; was admitted to the bar and commenced practice in Linden, Marengo County, in 1821; judge of the Marengo County Court for several years; member of the State house of representatives in 1837; served in the State senate 1839–1842; elected as a Whig to the Thirty-first Congress (March 4, 1849–March 3, 1851); was not a candidate for renomination in 1850; resumed the practice of his profession; again became a member of the State house of representatives, in 1855; engaged in agricultural pursuits; died in Magnolia, Marengo County, Ala., June 10, 1876; interment in Magnolia Cemetery.

ALSTON, Willis (nephew of Nathaniel Macon), a Representative from North Carolina; born near Littleton, Halifax County, N. C., in 1769; completed preparatory studies and attended Princeton College; engaged in agricultural pursuits; member of the State house of commons 1790–1792; served in the State senate 1794–1796; elected as a War Democrat to the Sixth and to the seven succeeding Congresses (March 4, 1799–March 3, 1815); during the war with Great Britain in 1812 was a member of the Ways and Means Committee of Congress; again a member of the State house of commons 1820–1824; elected to the Nineteenth, Twentieth, and Twenty-first Congresses (March 4, 1825–March 3, 1831); resumed agricultural pursuits; died in Halifax, N. C., April 10, 1837; interment in a private burying ground on his plantation home, "Butterwood," near Littleton, Halifax County, N. C.

ALVORD, James Church, a Representative from Massachusetts; born in Greenwich, Mass., April 14, 1808; completed preparatory studies and was graduated from Dartmouth College, Hanover, N. H., in 1827; studied law; was admitted to the bar in 1830 and commenced the practice of his profession in Greenfield, Mass.; member of the State house of representatives in 1837; served in the State senate in 1838; elected as a Whig to to the Twenty-sixth Congress and served from March 4, 1839, until his death, before the Congress assembled, in Greenfield, Franklin County, Mass., on September 27, 1839; interment in Federal Street Cemetery.

AMBLER, Jacob A., a Representative from Ohio; born in Pittsburgh, Pa., February 18, 1829; attended the local schools of Allegheny City and also received private instruction; moved to Salem, Ohio, and studied law in his brother's law office; was admitted to the bar on March 27, 1851, and commenced practice in Salem, Columbiana County, Ohio; elected to the State house of representatives in 1857 and served two terms; appointed judge of the ninth judicial district in 1859 and served until 1867; elected as a Republican to the Forty-first and Forty-second Congresses (March 4, 1869–March 3, 1873); declined to be a candidate for renomination in 1872; resumed the practice of law and also became interested in various business enterprises in Salem, Ohio; served as vice president of a bank and of a steel and wire nail mill corporation and also as president of a publishing company; delegate to the Republican National Conventions in 1876, 1880, 1884, 1888, 1892, and 1896; appointed a member of the United States Tariff Commission by President Arthur in 1882; retired from the general practice of law in 1898 but continued active business pursuits until his death in Canton, Stark County, Ohio, September 22, 1906; interment in Hope Cemetery, Salem, Ohio.

AMERMAN, Lemuel, a Representative from Pennsylvania; born near Danville, Montour County, Pa., October 29, 1846; attended the common schools and Danville Academy; was graduated from Bucknell University, Lewisburg, Pa., in 1869; taught school three years; studied law; was admitted to the bar in 1873 and commenced practice in Philadelphia, Pa.; moved to Scranton, Pa., in 1876 and continued the practice of law; also engaged in banking; solicitor for Lackawana County 1879 and 1880; member of the State house of representatives 1881–1884; elected city comptroller of Scranton in 1885 and 1886; reporter of the decisions of the supreme court of Pennsylvania in 1886 and 1887; elected as a Democrat to the Fifty-second Congress (March 4, 1891–March 3, 1893); unsuccessful candidate for reelection in 1892 to the Fifty-third Congress; continued the practice of his profession in Scranton, Pa., until his death in Blossburg, Tioga County, Pa., October 7, 1897; interment in Forest Hill Cemetery, Scranton, Pa.

AMES, Adelbert (father of Butler Ames), a Senator from Mississippi; born in Rockland, Knox County, Maine, October 31, 1835; attended the common schools; was graduated from the United States Military Academy at West Point in 1861; during the Civil War served with the Union Army from 1861 to 1865 as lieutenant, colonel, and brigadier general; received the brevet of major in the United States Army and the Congressional Medal of Honor for gallantry at the Battle of Bull Run; brevetted colonel in the United States Army for meritorious service at Gettysburg July 1, 1863; captain in the Fifth Artillery of the Regular Army 1864–1866; lieutenant colonel of the Twenty-fourth United States Infantry from 1866 until 1870, when he resigned; appointed Provisional Governor of Mississippi on March 15, 1868; appointed to the command of the fourth military district (Department of Mississippi) March 17, 1869; upon the readmission of the State of Mississippi to representation was elected as a Republican to the United States Senate and served from February 23, 1870, until January 10, 1874, when he resigned, having been elected Governor in 1873; Governor of Mississippi from January 4, 1874, until March 29, 1876, when he resigned; moved to New York City and later to Lowell, Mass.; engaged in the flour business, with mills in Minnesota; also interested in various manufacturing industries in Lowell; was appointed brigadier general of Volunteers in the war with Spain June 20, 1898, and served until January 3, 1899; discontinued active business pursuits and lived in retirement in Lowell, Mass.; died at his winter home in Ormond, Fla., April 12, 1933; interment in Hildreth Cemetery, Lowell, Mass.

AMES, Butler (son of Adelbert Ames and grandson of Benjamin Franklin Butler), a Representative from Massachusetts; born in Lowell, Mass., August 22, 1871; attended the public schools and Phillips Exeter Academy, Exeter, N. H.; was graduated from the United States Military Academy at West Point in 1894; resigned from the United States Army after appointment as second lieutenant to the Eleventh Regiment, United States Infantry; took a postgraduate course at Massachusetts Institute of Technology and was graduated in 1896 as a mechanical and electrical engineer; engaged in the manufacture of bunting and also of ignition and generating apparatus; served as a member of the common council of Lowell in 1896; enlisted during the Spanish-American War and was commissioned lieutenant and adjutant of the Sixth Regiment, Massachusetts Volunteer Infantry; while at Camp Alger, near Washington, D. C., was appointed acting engineer officer of the Second Army Corps under General Graham, in addition to his duties as adjutant; went from Charlestown to Cuba and Puerto Rico under General Miles; was at the landing at Guanica and in the skirmish at Yauco Road in July 1898; was promoted to lieutenant colonel in August of the same year; served as civil administrator of the Arecibo district of Puerto Rico until November 1898; member of the Massachusetts House of Representatives 1897–1899; elected as a Republican to the Fifty-eighth and to the four succeeding Congresses (March 4, 1903–March 3, 1913); was not a candidate for renomination in 1912; retired from political activities and resumed manufacturing pursuits; former president of United States Cartridge Co., and treasurer of Heinze Electrical Co., of Lowell; at time of death was treasurer and a director of Wamesit Power Co., of Lowell, Mass.; director of Union Land and Grazing Co., Colorado Springs, Colo., and vice president and a director of Ames Textile Corp., Lowell, Mass.; died in Tewksbury, Mass., November 6, 1954; interment in Hildreth Family Cemetery, Lowell, Mass.

AMES, Fisher, a Representative from Massachusetts; born in Dedham, Mass., April 9, 1758; attended the town school of his native city and also received private instruction; was graduated from Harvard College in 1774; while teaching school, studied law; was admitted to the bar and commenced practice in Dedham in 1781; served in the State house of representatives in 1788; member of the Massachusetts convention called for the ratification of the Federal Constitution in 1788; elected as a Federalist to the First and to the three succeeding Congresses (March 4, 1789–March 3, 1797); was not a candidate for renomination in 1796; resumed the practice of law in Dedham; member of the Governor's council in 1799 and 1800; chosen president of Harvard University in 1804, but declined to accept because of failing health; died in Dedham, Mass., July 4, 1808; interment in Old First Parish Cemetery.

AMES, Oakes, a Representative from Massachusetts; born in Easton, Mass., January 10, 1804; attended the public schools and Dighton (Mass.) Academy; engaged in the manufacture of shovels in North Easton; member of the executive council of Massachusetts in 1860; elected as a Republican to the Thirty-eighth and to the four succeeding Congresses (March 4, 1863–March 3, 1873); was not a candidate for renomination in 1872; instrumental in accomplishing the construction of the first transcontinental railroad; received the censure of Congress for "seeking to procure congressional attention to the affairs of a corporation in which he was interested," which was in connection with the Crédit Mobilier; in 1883 the legislature of Massachusetts passed resolutions of gratitude for his work and faith in his integrity and petitioned the United States Congress to extend him a like acknowledgment; died in North Easton, Mass., May 8, 1873; interment in Unity Cemetery.

AMLIE, Thomas Ryum, a Representative from Wisconsin; born on a farm near Binford, Griggs County, N. Dak., April 17, 1897; attended the public schools, Cooperstown (N. Dak.) High School, the University of North Dakota at Grand Forks, and the University of Minnesota at Minneapolis; was graduated from the law department of the University of Wisconsin at Madison in 1923; was admitted to the Wisconsin bar the same year and commenced the practice of law in Beloit, Wis.; moved to Elkhorn, Wis., in 1927 and continued the practice of law; served as president of the Walworth County Bar Association in 1931 and 1932; elected as a Republican (Progressive) to the Seventy-second Congress to fill the vacancy caused by the death of Henry Allen Cooper and served from October 13, 1931, to March 3, 1933; was an unsuccessful candidate for renomination in 1932 to the Seventy-third Congress; elected as a Progressive to the Seventy-fourth and Seventy-fifth Congresses (January 3, 1935–January 3, 1939); was not a candidate for renomination in 1938, but was an unsuccessful Progressive candidate for nomination for United States Senator; nominated by President Franklin D. Roosevelt in 1939 to be a member of the Interstate Commerce Commission but subsequently requested that his name be withdrawn; resumed the practice of law in Madison, Wis., where he now resides.

ANCONA, Sydenham Elnathan, a Representative from Pennsylvania; born near Lititz, Lancaster County, Pa., November 20, 1824; moved to Berks County, Pa., in 1826 with his parents, who settled near Sculls Hill; attended public and private schools; taught school; moved in 1856 to Reading, Pa., where he entered the employ of the Reading Railroad Co.; member of the board of education; elected as a Democrat to the Thirty-seventh, Thirty-eighth, and Thirty-ninth Congresses (March 4, 1861–March 3, 1867); unsuccessful candidate for renomination in 1866; became engaged in the trust, fire-insurance, and relief-association businesses in Reading, Pa.; delegate to the Democratic National Convention at Cincinnati in 1880 that nominated Hancock and English; during a visit to the Capitol at Washington, D. C., in 1912 was tendered a reception on the floor of the House of Representatives, it being stated at the time that he was the last surviving Member of the Thirty-seventh Congress which assembled at the extraordinary session called by Abraham Lincoln on July 4,

1861; engaged in banking and in the insurance business until his death in Reading, Pa., on June 20, 1913; interment in Charles Evans Cemetery.

ANDERSEN, Herman Carl, a Representative from Minnesota; born in Newcastle, Kings County, Wash., January 27, 1897; moved with his parents to a farm near Tyler, Lincoln County, Minn., in 1901; attended the rural schools; engaged in cattle raising and agricultural pursuits 1919–1925 and as a civil engineer 1925–1930; resumed agricultural pursuits near Tyler, Minn., 1930–1938; member of the State house of representatives in 1935; elected as a Republican to the Seventy-sixth and to the ten succeeding Congresses (January 3, 1939–January 3, 1961). *Reelected to the Eighty-seventh Congress.*

ANDERSON, Albert Raney, a Representative from Iowa; born in Adams County, Ohio, November 8, 1837; moved with his parents to Galesburg, Ill.; attended the common schools and Knox College, Galesburg, Ill.; moved to Taylor County, Iowa, in 1857; studied law; was admitted to the bar in 1860 and commenced practice in Clarinda, Iowa; appointed postmaster of Clarinda by President Lincoln in 1861; resigned to enlist in the Union Army during the Civil War as a private in Company K, Fourth Regiment, Iowa Volunteer Infantry; promoted to first lieutenant after the Battle of Pea Ridge; while before Vicksburg was promoted to captain; when serving as adjutant general of his brigade in the Atlanta campaign was commissioned major of his regiment; wounded at Jonesboro August 31, 1864, and again at Bentonville, N. C., March 19, 1865; commissioned lieutenant colonel in 1865; mustered out in August 1865 and returned to Clarinda, Iowa; moved to Sidney, Iowa, in 1866; resumed the practice of law; assessor of internal revenue 1868–1871; delegate to the Republican National Convention at Philadelphia in 1872; district attorney 1876–1880; State railroad commissioner in 1881; unsuccessful candidate for election in 1882 to the Forty-eighth Congress; elected as an Independent Republican to the Fiftieth Congress (March 4, 1887–March 3, 1889); unsuccessful candidate for reelection in 1888 to the Fifty-first Congress; moved to Hot Springs, S. Dak., in 1892 and continued the practice of his profession; served as mayor of Hot Springs, Fall River County, S. Dak., in 1895 and 1896; elected State attorney of Fall River County November 8, 1898; died at Hot Springs, S. Dak., November 17, 1898; interment in Sidney Cemetery, Sidney, Iowa.

ANDERSON, Alexander Outlaw (son of Joseph Anderson), a Senator from Tennessee; born at "Soldiers' Rest," Jefferson County, Tenn., November 10, 1794; attended preparatory schools; was graduated from Washington College at Greeneville, Tenn.; enlisted in the War of 1812 at the age of eighteen under Gen. Andrew Jackson and fought in the Battle of New Orleans; studied law in Washington, D. C., and in 1814 was admitted to the bar in Dandridge, Tenn., where he began the practice of his profession; later moved to Knoxville; superintendent of the United States land office in Alabama in 1836; Government agent for removing the Indians from Alabama and Florida in 1838; elected as a Democrat to the United States Senate to fill the vacancy caused by the resignation of Hugh L. White and served from February 26, 1840, to March 3, 1841; was not a candidate for reelection; leader of an overland company which went to California in 1849; member of the State senate in 1850 and 1851; supreme court judge of California 1851–1853; returned to Tennessee in 1853; later practiced law in Washington, D. C., before the Court of Claims and before the Supreme Court of the United States; during the Civil War moved to Alabama and practiced law in Mobile and Camden; died in Knoxville, Tenn., May 23, 1869; interment in the Old Gray Cemetery.

ANDERSON, Carl Carey, a Representative from Ohio; born in Bluffton, Allen County, Ohio, December 2, 1877; moved to Sandusky County in 1881 with his parents, who settled in Fremont; attended the common schools; became employed as a traveling salesman; moved to Fostoria, Seneca County, and engaged in the manufacture of underwear; elected mayor of Fostoria, Ohio, in 1905 and again in 1907, on each occasion for a term of two years; president of the city hospital board and director in a number of manufacturing enterprises; elected as a Democrat to the Sixty-first and Sixty-second Congresses and served from March 4, 1909, until his death in an automobile accident near Fostoria, Ohio, October 1, 1912; interment in Oakwood Cemetery, Fremont, Ohio.

ANDERSON, Chapman Levy, a Representative from Mississippi; born near Macon, Noxubee County, Miss., March 15, 1845; attended the common schools in Jackson, Miss., and the University of Mississippi at Oxford; during the Civil War enlisted in the Confederate Army on March 5, 1862, as a private in the Thirty-ninth Regiment, Mississippi Volunteer Infantry; was promoted through the successive grades of noncommissioned officer until July 1864, when he was transferred to Bradford's cavalry corps of scouts with the rank of second lieutenant, in which capacity he served until the close of the war; studied law; was admitted to the bar in 1868 and commenced practice in Kosciusko, Miss.; mayor of Kosciusko, Miss., in 1875; member of the State house of representatives in 1879 and 1880; elected as a Democrat to the Fiftieth and Fifty-first Congresses (March 4, 1887–March 3, 1891); unsuccessful candidate for renomination in 1890; United States district attorney for the northern district of Mississippi in 1896 and 1897; engaged in the practice of law in Kosciusko, Miss., until his death, April 27, 1924; interment in Kosciusko Cemetery.

ANDERSON, Charles Arthur, a Representative from Missouri; born in St. Louis, Mo., September 26, 1899; attended the public schools; was graduated from St. Charles Military Academy in 1916 and from the law school of St. Louis University in 1924; during the First World War served in the One Hundred and Twenty-eighth Field Artillery, Thirty-fifth Division, from April 1, 1917, to July 2, 1919, with nineteen months' service overseas; was admitted to the bar in 1924 and commenced practice in St. Louis, Mo.; prosecuting attorney of St. Louis County 1933–1937; nominated for the St. Louis outstanding-citizen award in 1935 and 1936; elected as a Democrat to the Seventy-fifth and Seventy-sixth Congresses (January 3, 1937–January 3, 1941); unsuccessful candidate for reelection in 1940 to the Seventy-seventh Congress; chairman of the Democratic State convention at St. Louis in 1940; resumed the practice of law in St. Louis, Mo., where he now resides.

ANDERSON, Charles Marley, a Representative from Ohio; born near Mifflintown, Juniata County, Pa., January 5, 1845; moved to Ohio in 1855 with his parents, who settled in Darke County; attended the common schools; was graduated from the Lebanon Normal School, Lebanon, Ohio, in 1868; enlisted in the Union Army during the Civil War and served from March 15, 1861, in Company B, Seventy-first Regiment, Ohio Volunteer Infantry, until discharged on November 30, 1865; studied law; was admitted to the bar in 1868 and commenced practice in Greenville, Ohio; manager of the Central Branch of the National Soldiers' Home, Dayton, Ohio, for twenty years; elected as a Democrat to the Forty-ninth Congress (March 4, 1885–March 3, 1887); was an unsuccessful candidate for renomination in 1886; resumed the practice of law; Ohio State commissioner to the World's Fair at Chicago in 1892 and 1893; died in Greenville, Ohio, December 28, 1908; interment in Greenville Cemetery.

ANDERSON, Clinton Presba, a Representative and a Senator from New Mexico; born in Centerville, Turner County, S. Dak., October 23, 1895; attended the public schools, Dakota Wesleyan University, Mitchell, S. Dak., and the University of Michigan at Ann Arbor; moved to Albuquerque, N. Mex., in 1917; newspaper reporter and editor at Albuquerque 1918–1922; engaged in the general insurance business at Albuquerque 1922–1946; also interested in dairy farming; served as treasurer of State of New Mexico in 1933 and 1934; administrator of the New Mexico Relief Administration in 1935; field representative of the Federal Emergency Relief Administration in 1935 and 1936; chairman and executive director of the Unemployment Compensation Commission of New Mexico 1936–1938; managing director of the United States Coronado Exposition Commission in 1939 and 1940; elected as a Democrat to the Seventy-seventh, Seventy-eighth, and Seventy-ninth Congresses and served from January 3, 1941, until his resignation on June 30, 1945, having been appointed Secretary of Agriculture; served as Secretary of Agriculture from June 30, 1945, until his resignation May 10, 1948; elected as a Democrat to the United States Senate in 1948, and again in 1954, and served from January 3, 1949, to January 3, 1961. *Reelected in 1960 for the term ending January 3, 1967.*

ANDERSON, George Alburtus, a Representative from Illinois; born in Botetourt County, Va., March 11, 1853; moved to Illinois in 1855 with his parents, who settled in Hancock County; attended the common schools; was graduated from Carthage (Ill.) College in 1876; studied law in Lincoln, Nebr., and Sedalia, Mo.; was admitted to the bar in 1878 and commenced practice in Quincy, Ill., in 1880; unsuccessful candidate for city attorney of Quincy in 1883; elected city attorney in 1884 and again in 1885; elected as a Democrat to the Fiftieth Congress (March 4, 1887–March 3, 1889); declined to be a candidate for renomination in 1888; engaged in the practice of law until his death in Quincy, Ill., January 31, 1896; interment in Woodlawn Cemetery.

ANDERSON, George Washington, a Representative from Missouri; born in Jefferson County, Tenn., May 22, 1832; attended the public schools; was graduated from Franklin College, Tennessee; moved to St. Louis, Mo., in 1853; studied law; was admitted to the bar in Louisiana, Pike County, Mo., in 1854 and began the practice of law; member of the State house of representatives in 1859 and 1860; presidential elector on the Republican ticket of Lincoln and Hamlin in 1860; served in the State senate in 1862; during the Civil War was captain of Company A, Pike County (Missouri), Home Guards from June 12 to July 17, 1861, when he was elected colonel of the regiment, and served until the organization was disbanded on September 3, 1861; colonel of the Forty-ninth Regiment, Enrolled Missouri Militia, from August 13, 1862, to January 25, 1863, and from September 29 to December 1, 1864; elected as a Radical Republican to the Thirty-ninth and Fortieth Congresses (March 4, 1865–March 3, 1869); declined to be a candidate for renomination in 1868; resumed the practice of law; died while on a visit to his brother at Rhea Springs, Tenn., February 26, 1902; interment in Leuty Cemetery, near Rhea Springs.

ANDERSON, Hugh Johnston, a Representative from Maine; born in Wiscasset, Maine, May 10, 1801; attended the local schools; moved to Belfast, Maine, in 1815 and was employed as a clerk in the mercantile establishment of his uncle; clerk of the Waldo County courts 1824–1836; studied law; elected as a Democrat to the Twenty-fifth and Twenty-sixth Congresses (March 4, 1837–March 3, 1841); Governor of Maine 1844–1847; was a candidate for United States Senator in 1847 but subsequently withdrew; presidential elector on the Democratic ticket of Cass and Butler in 1848; moved to Washington, D. C., and served as commissioner of customs in the United States Treasury Department 1853–1858; appointed head of the commission to reorganize and adjust the affairs of the United States Mint at San Francisco, Calif., in 1857; Sixth Auditor of the Treasury 1866–1869; retired from public life in 1880 and settled in Portland, Oreg., where he died May 31, 1881; interment in Grove Cemetery, Belfast, Maine.

ANDERSON, Isaac, a Representative from Pennsylvania; born at "Anderson Place," in Charlestown Township, near Valley Forge, Chester County, Pa., November 23, 1760; as a mere youth was the carrier of dispatches between the headquarters of the Revolutionary Army under General Washington at Valley Forge and the Congress then in session at York; served three terms of service in the Revolutionary War before attaining the age of eighteen and ultimately became an ensign in the Fifth Battalion of Chester County Militia; commissioned on May 24, 1779, as first lieutenant, Fifth Battalion, Sixth Company; justice of the peace in Charlestown Township for several years; member of the Pennsylvania House of Representatives in 1801; elected as a Jefferson Democrat to the Eighth and Ninth Congresses (March 4, 1803–March 3, 1807); was not a candidate for renomination in 1806; engaged in agricultural pursuits and sawmilling; presidential elector on the Democratic ticket of James Monroe and Daniel T. Tompkins in 1816; died at "Anderson Place," Charlestown Township, Pa., October 27, 1838; interment in the family burying ground near Valley Forge, Schuylkill Township, Chester County, Pa.

ANDERSON, James Patton, a Delegate from the Territory of Washington; born near Winchester, Franklin County, Tenn., February 16, 1822; was graduated from Jefferson College, Canonsburg, Pa., in 1842; moved to Kentucky; studied law at Montrose Law School, Frankfort, Ky.; was admitted to the bar and practiced in Hernando, Miss., from 1842 to 1846; raised a company of volunteers for the Mexican War; elected lieutenant colonel of the Second Battalion, Mississippi Rifles, and served in that capacity until the close of the war; member of the State house of representatives in 1850; appointed United States marshal for the Territory of Washington in 1853 and settled in Olympia; elected as a Democrat to the Thirty-fourth Congress (March 4, 1855–March 3, 1857); was not a candidate for renomination in 1856; appointed Governor of the Territory of Washington by President Buchanan in 1857, but declined the office; moved to his plantation, "Casabianca," near Monticello, Fla., the same year; served in the Provisional Congress of the Confederate States; during the Civil War entered the Confederate Army as colonel of the First Regiment, Florida Infantry; appointed brigadier general February 10, 1862; promoted to major general February 17, 1864, and assigned to the command of the district of Florida; after the close of the war settled in Memphis, Tenn., and conducted a publication devoted to agriculture; collector of delinquent State taxes for Shelby County; died in Memphis, Tenn., September 20, 1872; interment in Elmwood Cemetery.

ANDERSON, John, a Representative from Maine; born in Windham, Maine, July 30, 1792; attended the common schools; was graduated from Bowdoin College, Brunswick, Maine, in 1813; studied law; was admitted to the bar in 1816 and commenced practice in Portland, Maine; member of the State senate in 1823; elected as a Jefferson Democrat to the Nineteenth and to the three succeeding Congresses (March 4, 1825–March 3, 1833); was not a candidate for renomination in 1832; mayor of Portland 1833–1836 and again in 1842; United States attorney for the district of Maine 1833–1836; collector of customs for the port of Portland 1837–1841 and 1843–1848; resumed the practice

of law; died in Portland, Maine, August 21, 1853; interment in Town Cemetery (then a part of the farm of his ancestors) on River Road, Windham, Maine.

ANDERSON, John Alexander, a Representative from Kansas; born near Pigeon Creek, Washington County, Pa., June 26, 1834; attended public and private schools; was graduated from Miami University, Oxford, Ohio, in 1853; ordained a Presbyterian minister in 1857 and began preaching in Stockton, Calif.; elected trustee of the State insane asylum in 1860; appointed chaplain of the Third Regiment, California Volunteer Infantry, in 1862; accompanied General Connor's expedition to Salt Lake City in July 1862; mustered into the Federal service March 1863; resigned June 1863; California correspondent and agent of the United States Sanitary Commission 1863–1867; moved to Junction City, Kans., in 1868, where he erected the First Presbyterian Church, of which he was pastor for five years; regent of the University of Kansas in 1872 and 1873; president of the Kansas State Agricultural College 1873–1879; elected as a Republican to the Forty-sixth and to the three succeeding Congresses (March 4, 1879–March 3, 1887); unsuccessful candidate for renomination in 1886; became an Independent candidate and was elected to the Fiftieth Congress and reelected as a Republican to the Fifty-first Congress (March 4, 1887–March 3, 1891); unsuccessful candidate for renomination in 1890; appointed United States consul general to Cairo, Egypt, March 4, 1891, and remained there until shortly before his death in a hospital in Liverpool, England, May 18, 1892, en route to his home; interment in Highland Cemetery, Junction City, Kans.

ANDERSON, John Zuinglius, a Representative from California; born in Oakland, Alameda County, Calif., March 22, 1904; moved with his parents to Santa Cruz, Calif., the same year, and to San Jose, Calif., in 1913; attended the public schools; was graduated from San Jose High School in 1923; moved to San Juan Bautista, San Benito County, Calif., in 1925 and engaged in agricultural pursuits and fruit growing; elected as a Republican to the Seventy-sixth and to the six succeeding Congresses (January 3, 1939–January 3, 1953); was not a candidate for renomination in 1952; member of board of directors of Bank of America; president of California Canning Pear Association and Pacific States Canning Pear Association; with Department of Agriculture in 1954 and 1955; administrative assistant to President Eisenhower from December 15, 1956, to January 20, 1961; member of staff of Veterans Affairs Committee, House of Representatives; resides in Arlington, Va.

ANDERSON, Joseph (father of Alexander Outlaw Anderson), a Senator from Tennessee; born near Philadelphia, Pa., November 5, 1757; studied law; served throughout the Revolutionary War and attained the rank of brevet major; was admitted to the bar and practiced in Delaware for several years; appointed United States judge of the Territory South of the River Ohio in 1791; member of the first constitutional convention of Tennessee; elected in 1797 to the United States Senate to fill the vacancy in the term ending March 3, 1799, caused by the expulsion of William Blount; again elected December 12, 1798, to fill the vacancy in the term ending March 3, 1803, caused by the resignation of Andrew Jackson; reelected in 1803; appointed and subsequently reelected in 1809 for the ensuing term and served continuously from September 26, 1797, to March 3, 1815; President pro tempore of the Senate January 13, February 28, and March 2, 1805; during the Madison administration was appointed First Comptroller of the Treasury and served from March 4, 1815, to July 1, 1836; lived in retirement until his death in Washington, D. C., on April 17, 1837; interment in the Congressional Cemetery.

ANDERSON, Joseph Halstead, a Representative from New York; born in the town of Harrison, near White Plains, Westchester County, N. Y., August 25, 1800; attended the common schools; engaged in agricultural pursuits; member of the State assembly in 1833 and 1834; sheriff of Westchester County 1835–1838; elected as a Democrat to the Twenty-eighth and Twenty-ninth Congresses (March 4, 1843–March 3, 1847); was not a candidate for renomination in 1846; resumed farming pursuits; died in White Plains, N. Y., June 23, 1870; interment in a private burying ground at "Anderson Hill," near White Plains, N. Y.

ANDERSON, Josiah McNair, a Representative from Tennessee; born near Pikeville, Bledsoe County, Tenn., November 29, 1807; attended the common schools; studied law; was admitted to the bar and commenced practice in Jasper, Tenn.; member of the State house of representatives 1833–1837, serving as speaker; member of the State senate 1843–1845, serving as presiding officer; elected as a Whig to the Thirty-first Congress (March 4, 1849–March 3, 1851); unsuccessful candidate for reelection in 1850 to the Thirty-second Congress; delegate from Tennessee to the peace convention of 1861, held in Washington, D. C., in an effort to devise means to prevent the impending war; colonel in the Tennessee State Militia 1861; was killed at Looneys Creek, near the present town of Whitwell, Marion County, Tenn., November 8, 1861, just after having made a secession speech; interment on a farm seven miles southeast of Dunlap, Sequatchie County, Tenn.

ANDERSON, LeRoy Hagen, a Representative from Montana; born in Ellendale, Dickey County, N. Dak., February 2, 1906; moved with his parents to Conrad, Mont., in 1909; was graduated from Montana State College at Bozeman in 1927; postgraduate work in mathematics and physical chemistry in 1938 at California Institute of Technology in Pasadena; wheat and cattle rancher; during World War II served as commander of armored task force in the European Theater of Operations in combat from Normandy to the Elbe River; separated from the service as a lieutenant colonel in 1945; awarded Silver Star Medal and Croix de Guerre Medal with Palm; major general in Army Reserve, commanding the 96th Infantry Division Reserve 1948–1960; member of the State house of representatives in 1947 and 1948 and the State senate 1949–1956, serving as Democratic floor leader 1954–1956; unsuccessful candidate for election in 1954 to the Eighty-fourth Congress; elected as a Democrat to the Eighty-fifth and Eighty-sixth Congresses (January 3, 1957–January 3, 1961); was not a candidate for renomination in 1960 but was unsuccessful for the Democratic nomination for United States Senator; is a resident of Conrad, Mont.

ANDERSON, Lucian, a Representative from Kentucky; born near Mayfield, Graves County, Ky., June 23, 1824; attended the public schools; studied law; was admitted to the bar in 1845 and commenced practice in Mayfield; presidential elector on the Whig ticket of Scott and Graham in 1852; member of the State house of representatives 1855–1857; elected as a Unionist to the Thirty-eighth Congress (March 4, 1863–March 3, 1865); declined to be a candidate for renomination in 1864; delegate to the Republican National Convention at Baltimore in 1864; resumed the practice of his profession; died in Mayfield, Ky., October 18, 1898; interment in the Anderson family cemetery.

ANDERSON, Richard Clough, Jr., a Representative from Kentucky; born at "Soldiers' Retreat," near Louisville, Ky., August 4, 1788; attended private schools; was graduated from William and Mary College, Williamsburg, Va., in 1804; studied law; was admitted to the bar and commenced practice in Louis-

ville; member of the State house of representatives in 1815; elected to the Fifteenth and Sixteenth Congresses (March 4, 1817–March 3, 1821); declined to be a candidate for reelection in 1820; again a member of the State house of representatives, in 1821 and 1822, serving as speaker the latter year; appointed the first United States Minister to the Republic of Colombia January 27, 1823; took his leave June 7, 1823, having been commissioned Envoy Extraordinary and Minister Plenipotentiary to the Panama Congress of Nations, but died, en route to his post, in Turbaco, near Cartagena, Colombia, July 24, 1826; interment at "Soldiers' Retreat," near Louisville, Ky.

ANDERSON, Samuel, a Representative from Pennsylvania; born in Middletown, Dauphin County, Pa., in 1773; completed preparatory studies; studied medicine; was admitted to practice in 1796; entered the United States Navy as assistant surgeon in 1799; promoted to the rank of surgeon in 1800; resigned his commission and in 1801 settled in Chester, Pa., where he practiced his profession; during the War of 1812; raised a body of volunteers known as the Mifflin Guards; commissioned captain on September 10, 1814; served in the Pennsylvania Militia and was promoted to the rank of lieutenant colonel in the One Hundredth Regiment, Second Brigade, Third Division, on August 3, 1821; member of the State house of representatives 1815–1818 and 1823–1825; sheriff of Delaware County 1819–1823; again entered the naval service in 1823 as special physician to Admiral David Porter, who was then in command of the West Indian Squadron, but was soon forced to resign because of ill health; elected to the Twentieth Congress (March 4, 1827–March 3, 1829); again a member of the State house of representatives 1829–1835 and served as speaker in 1833; appointed inspector of customs in 1841; elected justice of the peace in 1846 and served until his death in Chester, Chester County, Pa., January 17, 1850; interment in Middletown Presbyterian Cemetery, near Media, Delaware County, Pa.

ANDERSON, Simeon H. (father of William Clayton Anderson), a Representative from Kentucky; born near Lancaster, Garrard County, Ky., March 2, 1802; pursued preparatory studies; studied law; was admitted to the bar in 1823 and commenced practice in Lancaster, Ky.; member of the State house of representatives 1828, 1829, 1832, and 1836–1838; elected as a Whig to the Twenty-sixth Congress and served from March 4, 1839, until his death near Lancaster, Garrard County, Ky., August 11, 1840; interment in the Anderson family cemetery.

ANDERSON, Sydney, a Representative from Minnesota; born in Zumbrota, Goodhue County, Minn., September 18, 1881; attended the common schools; was graduated from high school in 1899; attended Highland Park College, Des Moines, Iowa, and the University of Minnesota at Minneapolis; studied law; was admitted to the bar in 1903 and commenced practice in Minneapolis, Minn.; moved to Kansas City, Mo., and thence to Lanesboro, Minn., and continued the practice of law from 1904 to 1911; served as a private in Company D, Fourteenth Regiment, Minnesota Volunteer Infantry, during the Spanish-American War; elected as a Republican to the Sixty-second and to the six succeeding Congresses (March 4, 1911–March 3, 1925); declined to be a candidate for reelection in 1924 to the Sixty-ninth Congress; chairman of the Congressional Joint Commission of Agricultural Inquiry in 1921 and 1922; chairman of the National Wheat Conference held in Chicago, Ill., on June 19 and 20, 1923; president of the Wheat Council of the United States at Chicago in 1923 and 1924; vice chairman of the research council of the National Transportation Institute at Washington, D. C., in 1923 and 1924; president of the Millers' National Federation, Chicago, Ill., and Washington, D. C., 1924–1929; vice president, secretary, and, later, member of the board of directors of General Mills, Inc., Minneapolis, Minn., 1930–1948; president of the Transportation Association of America, Chicago, Ill., 1943–1948; died in Minneapolis, Minn., October 8, 1948, interment in Lakewood Cemetery.

ANDERSON, Thomas Lilbourne, a Representative from Missouri; born near Bowling Green, Green County, Ky., December 8, 1808; attended the rural schools; studied law; was admitted to the bar in 1828 and commenced practice in Franklin, Simpson County, Ky.; moved in 1830 to Palmyra, Marion County, Mo., where he continued the practice of law; member of the State house of representatives 1840–1844; presidential elector on the Whig ticket in 1844, 1848, 1852, and 1856; member of the State constitutional convention in 1845; elected by the American Party to the Thirty-fifth Congress and as an Independent Democrat to the Thirty-sixth Congress (March 4, 1857–March 3, 1861); was not a candidate for renomination in 1860; resumed the practice of law in Marion County, Mo.; died in Palmyra, Mo., March 6, 1885; interment in the City Cemetery.

ANDERSON, William, a Representative from Pennsylvania; born in Virginia in 1762; attended the common schools; during the Revolutionary War joined the Continental Army at the age of fifteen and served until the end of the war; was a major on the staff of General Lafayette and distinguished himself at Germantown and Yorktown; engaged in the hotel business as landlord of the Columbia House, Chester, Pa., in 1796; county auditor in 1804; county director of the poor in 1805; elected as a Jeffersonian Democrat to the Eleventh, Twelfth, and Thirteenth Congresses (March 4, 1809–March 3, 1815); elected to the Fifteenth Congress (March 4, 1817–March 3, 1819); appointed an associate judge of the county court on January 5, 1826; resigned in 1828 to become an inspector of customs in Philadelphia and served until his death in Chester, Pa., December 16, 1829; interment in Old St. Paul's Cemetery.

ANDERSON, William Black, a Representative from Illinois; born in Mount Vernon, Ill., April 2, 1830; attended the common schools; was graduated from McKendree College, Lebanon, Ill., in 1850; surveyor of Jefferson County in 1851; studied law; was admitted to the bar but never practiced; engaged in agricultural pursuits; member of the State house of representatives in 1856 and 1858; during the Civil War entered the Union Army as a private in the Sixtieth Regiment, Illinois Volunteer Infantry; commissioned lieutenant colonel of the regiment February 17, 1862, and colonel, April 4, 1863; brevetted brigadier general of Volunteers March 13, 1865, "for gallant and meritorious services during the war"; resigned December 26, 1864; member of the constitutional convention of Illinois in 1869; served in the State senate in 1871; elected as an Independent Democrat to the Forty-fourth Congress (March 4, 1875–March 3, 1877); was not a candidate for renomination in 1876; collector of internal revenue for the southern district of Illinois 1885–1889; United States pension agent in Chicago from November 9, 1893, to January 17, 1898; died in Chicago, Ill., August 28, 1901; interment in Oakwood Cemetery, Mount Vernon, Ill.

ANDERSON, William Clayton (son of Simeon H. Anderson and nephew of Albert Gallatin Talbott), a Representative from Kentucky; born in Lancaster, Garrard County, Ky., December 26, 1826; attended private schools and was graduated from Centre College, Danville, Ky., in 1845; studied law; was admitted to the bar and commenced practice in Lancaster; moved to Danville, Boyle County, in 1847 and continued the practice of law; member of the State house of representatives 1851–1853; presidential elector on the American Party ticket of Fillmore and

Donaldson in 1856; unsuccessful candidate for election in 1856 to the Thirty-fifth Congress; elected by the American Party to the Thirty-sixth Congress (March 4, 1859–March 3, 1861); was not a candidate for renomination in 1860; elected as a Unionist to the State house of representatives in 1861; died, during the session of the legislature, at Frankfort, Ky., December 23, 1861; interment in Bell View Cemetery, Danville, Ky.

ANDERSON, William Coleman, a Representative from Tennessee; born at Tusculum, near Greeneville, Greene County, Tenn., July 10, 1853; attended a rural school; was graduated from Tusculum College, Greeneville, Tenn., in 1876; moved to Newport, Tenn., in 1876; while studying law was assistant clerk of Cocke County 1877–1878; was admitted to the bar in 1878 and commenced practice in Newport; member of the State house of representatives 1881–1883; was a principal examiner in the General Land Office at Washington, D. C., 1889–1892; promoted to chief of the contest division February 1, 1892, but resigned August 7, 1892; chief of the General Land Office from November 23, 1892, until April 11, 1893; returned to Newport, Cocke County, in 1893 and resumed the practice of law; elected as a Republican to the Fifty-fourth Congress (March 4, 1895–March 3, 1897); unsuccessful candidate for renomination in 1896; founder and editor of Plain Talk, a weekly newspaper published in Newport; member of the city council at the time of his death in Newport, Tenn., September 8, 1902; interment in Union Cemetery.

ANDRESEN, August Herman, a Representative from Minnesota; born in Newark, Kendall County, Ill., October 11, 1890; attended the public schools; moved with his parents to Grand Forks, N. Dak., in 1900, to Eagle Grove, Iowa, in 1902, and to Red Wing, Goodhue County, Minn., in 1905, attending the local schools in each place; was graduated from Red Wing (Minn.) Seminary, and from St. Olaf College, Northfield, Minn., in 1912; special investigator for the Minnesota Department of Weights and Measures 1912–1915; was graduated from the St. Paul (Minn.) College of Law; was admitted to the bar in 1914 and commenced practice in Red Wing in 1915; member of the Minnesota Home Guards in 1918 and 1919; president of the Goodhue County Red Cross, the Goodhue County Soldiers' Memorial Association, and the Red Wing Chamber of Commerce; interested in financial and business enterprises and also engaged in agricultural pursuits; elected as a Republican to the Sixty-ninth and to the three succeeding Congresses (March 4, 1925–March 3, 1933); unsuccessful candidate for reelection in 1932 to the Seventy-third Congress; elected to the Seventy-fourth and to the eleven succeeding Congresses, and served from January 3, 1935, until his death in the naval hospital, Bethesda, Md., January 14, 1958; interment in Oakwood Cemetery, Red Wing, Minn.

ANDREW, Abram Piatt, Jr., a Representative from Massachusetts; born in La Porte, La Porte County, Ind., February 12, 1873; attended the public schools and the Lawrenceville (N. J.) School; was graduated from Princeton College in 1893; member of the Harvard Graduate School of Arts and Sciences 1893–1898; pursued postgraduate studies in the Universities of Halle, Berlin, and Paris; moved to Gloucester, Mass., and was instructor and assistant professor of economics at Harvard University 1900–1909; expert assistant and editor of publications of the National Monetary Commission 1908–1911; director of the Mint 1909 and 1910; Assistant Secretary of the Treasury 1910–1912; served in France continuously for four and a half years during the First World War, first with the French Army and later with the United States Army; commissioned major, United States National Army, in September 1917 and promoted to lieutenant colonel in September 1918; awarded the Croix de Guerre and the Legion of Honor Medal by the Republic of France in 1917 and the Distinguished-Service Medal by the United States Government in 1918; elected as a Republican to the Sixty-seventh Congress to fill the vacancy caused by the resignation of Willfred W. Lufkin; reelected to the Sixty-eighth and to the six succeeding Congresses and served from September 27, 1921, until his death; delegate to the Republican National Conventions in 1924 and 1928; member of the board of trustees of Princeton University 1932–1936; died in Gloucester, Mass., June 3, 1936; remains were cremated and the ashes scattered from an airplane flying over his estate at Eastern Point, Gloucester, Mass.

ANDREW, Benjamin, a Delegate from Georgia; born in Dorchester, S. C., in 1730; moved to Georgia in 1754 and became a planter in St. John's Parish; president of State Executive Council in 1777; elected as a Delegate to the Continental Congress in 1780; associate justice for the County of Liberty for several terms; died in Liberty County, Georgia, about 1799.

ANDREW, John Forrester, a Representative from Massachusetts; born in Hingham, Plymouth County, Mass., November 26, 1850; attended private schools in Hingham and the Phillips School and Brooks School in Boston; was graduated from Harvard University in 1872 and from Harvard Law School in 1875; was admitted to the Suffolk bar in 1875 and commenced practice in Boston; member of the State house of representatives 1880–1882; served in the State senate in 1884 and 1885; commissioner of parks for Boston 1885–1890 and again in 1894; unsuccessful Democratic candidate for Governor in 1886; elected as a Democrat to the Fifty-first and Fifty-second Congresses (March 4, 1889–March 3, 1893); unsuccessful candidate for reelection in 1892 to the Fifty-third Congress; resumed the practice of his profession; died in Boston, Mass., May 30, 1895; interment in Mount Auburn Cemetery, Cambridge, Mass.

ANDREWS, Charles, a Representative from Maine; born in Paris, Oxford County, Maine, Feburary 11, 1814; attended the district school; was graduated from Hebron (Maine) Academy; studied law; was admitted to the bar in 1837 and commenced practice in Turner, Androscoggin County, Maine; returned to Paris, Maine; member of the State house of representatives 1839–1843, serving as speaker in 1842; became clerk of the courts for Oxford County, Maine, on January 1, 1845, and served three years; delegate to the Democratic National Convention at Baltimore in 1848; elected as a Democrat to the Thirty-second Congress and served from March 4, 1851, until his death in Paris, Maine, April 30, 1852; interment in Hillside Cemetery.

ANDREWS, Charles Oscar, a Senator from Florida; born in Ponce de Leon, Holmes County, Fla., March 7, 1877; attended the public schools and the South Florida Military Institute at Bartow, Fla.; was graduated from the Florida State Normal School at Gainesville, Fla., in 1901 and the University of Florida at Gainesville in 1907; during the Spanish-American War served as a captain in Company M in the Florida National Guard; captain in the Florida National Guard 1903–1905; secretary of the Florida State senate 1905–1907 and 1909–1911; studied law; was admitted to the bar in 1907 and commenced practice in De Funiak Springs, Fla.; judge of the criminal court of record of Walton County, Fla., in 1910 and 1911; assistant attorney general of Florida 1912–1919; circuit judge of the seventeenth judicial circuit 1919–1925; general counsel of the Florida Real Estate Commission 1925–1928; member of the State house of representatives in 1927; attorney for Orlando, Fla., 1926–1929; State supreme court commissioner 1929–1932; elected as a Democrat to the United States Senate to fill the vacancy caused by the death of Park Trammell; reelected in 1940 and served from November 4, 1936, until his death; was not a candidate for renomination in 1946; died in Washington, D. C., on September 18, 1946: interment in Greenwood Cemetery, Orlando, Fla.

ANDREWS, George Rex, a Representative from New York; born in Ticonderoga, Essex County, N. Y., September 21, 1808; attended the common schools and was graduated from the Albany Law School; was admitted to the bar in 1836 and commenced the practice of law in Ticonderoga; elected as a Whig to the Thirty-first Congress (March 4, 1849–March 3, 1851); moved to Oshkosh, Wis., in 1852 and engaged in the timber and lumber business; died in Oshkosh, Wis., December 5, 1873; interment in Riverside Cemetery.

ANDREWS, George William, a Representative from Alabama; born in Clayton, Barbour County, Ala., December 12, 1906; attended the public schools; was graduated from the University of Alabama at Tuscaloosa in 1928; was admitted to the bar in 1928 and commenced practice in Union Springs, Ala.; circuit solicitor for the third judicial circuit of Alabama 1931–1943; during World War II served as a lieutenant (jg) in the United States Naval Reserve from January 1943 until his election to Congress, at which time he was serving at Pearl Harbor, Hawaii; elected as a Democrat to the Seventy-eighth Congress to fill the vacancy caused by the death of Henry B. Steagall; reelected to the Seventy-ninth and to the seven succeeding Congresses and served from March 14, 1944 to January 3, 1961. *Reelected to the Eighty-seventh Congress.*

ANDREWS, John Tuttle, a Representative from New York; born near Schoharie Creek, Greene County, N. Y., May 29, 1803; moved with his parents in 1813 to Reading, near Dundee, Yates County; attended the district school and also was privately tutored; taught school for several years; engaged in mercantile pursuits in Irelandville and Watkins; justice of the peace and sheriff of Steuben County in 1836 and 1837; elected as a Democrat to the Twenty-fifth Congress (March 4, 1837–March 3, 1839); was not a candidate for renomination in 1838; after his term in Congress retired from active business and settled in Dundee, N. Y.; again engaged in mercantile pursuits, from 1866 until 1877, when he again retired from business pursuits to care for his personal estate; died in Dundee, N. Y., June 11, 1894; interment in Hillside Cemetery, Dundee, N. Y.

ANDREWS, Landaff Watson, a Representative from Kentucky; born in Flemingsburg, Fleming County, Ky., February 12, 1803; attended the public schools; was graduated from the law department of Transylvania University, Lexington, Ky., in 1826; was admitted to the bar the same year and commenced practice in Flemingsburg; prosecuting attorney of Fleming County 1829–1839; member of the State house of representatives 1834–1838; elected as a Whig to the Twenty-sixth and Twenty-seventh Congresses (March 4, 1839–March 3, 1843); unsuccessful candidate for reelection in 1842 to the Twenty-eighth Congress; presidential elector on the Whig ticket of Clay and Frelinghuysen in 1845; served in the State senate as an independent candidate in 1857; again elected a member of the State house of representatives, in 1861, and served until 1862, when he resigned; judge of the circuit court 1862–1868; resumed the practice of law in Flemingsburg, Ky., where he died December 23, 1887; interment in Fleming County Cemetery.

ANDREWS, Samuel George, a Representative from New York; born in Derby, Conn., October 16, 1796; attended the public schools, and a classical academy in Chester, Conn.; moved to New York in 1815 with his parents, who settled in Rochester;

became engaged in the mercantile business; clerk of the State assembly in 1831 and 1832; clerk of Monroe County 1834–1837; member of the board of aldermen in 1838; secretary of the State senate in 1840 and 1841; clerk of the court of errors for two years; appointed postmaster of Rochester on January 8, 1842, and served until July 18, 1845, when his successor was appointed; mayor of Rochester in 1846 and again in 1850; elected as a Republican to the Thirty-fifth Congress (March 4, 1857–March 3, 1859); engaged in the milling business; died in Rochester, N. Y., June 11, 1863; interment in Mount Hope Cemetery.

ANDREWS, Sherlock James, a Representative from Ohio; born in Wallingford, New Haven County, Conn., November 17, 1801; attended Cheshire Academy, Connecticut; was graduated from Union College, Schenectady, N. Y., in 1821; studied law at the New Haven (Conn.) Law School; was admitted to the bar and commenced practice in Cleveland, Cuyahoga County, Ohio, in 1825; prosecuting attorney of Cuyahoga County, Ohio, in 1830; elected as a Whig to the Twenty-seventh Congress (March 4, 1841–March 3, 1843); declined to be a candidate for renomination in 1842; resumed the practice of law in Cleveland; judge of the superior court of Cleveland 1848–1850; delegate to the second and third State constitutional conventions in 1849 and 1873; member of the village council of Cleveland, Ohio; was the first president of the Cleveland Bar Association in 1873; president of the board of library managers in Cleveland; died in Cleveland, Ohio, February 11, 1880; interment in Lakeview Cemetery.

ANDREWS, Walter Gresham, a Representative from New York; born in Evanston, Cook County, Ill., July 16, 1889; moved with his parents to Buffalo, N. Y., in 1902; attended the public schools of Buffalo, N. Y.; was graduated from the Lawrenceville (N. J.) Academy in 1908 and from the law department of Princeton University, Princeton, N. J., in 1913; coach of the Princeton University football team in 1913 and 1915; served on the Mexican border as a private, Troop I, First New York Cavalry, in 1916; commissioned second lieutenant, Machine Gun Group, First New York Cavalry, in 1917; machine-gun instructor, Twenty-seventh New York National Guard Division, Camp Wadsworth, Spartanburg, S. C.; first lieutenant and captain, One Hundred and Fifth Machine Gun Battalion, Twenty-seventh Division, in 1918; served in France with the One Hundred and Seventh United States Infantry, Twenty-seventh Division; wounded in action; promoted to major; awarded the Distinguished Service Cross; superintendent and central sales manager, Pratt & Lambert, Inc., Buffalo, N. Y., 1914–1925; supervisor of the fifteenth federal census for the seventh district of New York in 1929 and 1930; director of the Buffalo General Hospital; elected as a Republican to the Seventy-second and to the eight succeeding Congresses (March 4, 1931–January 3, 1949); was not a candidate for renomination in 1948; died at Daytona Beach, Fla., March 5, 1949; interment in Old Fort Niagara Cemetery, Youngstown, N. Y.

ANDREWS, William Ezekiel, a Representative from Nebraska; born near Oskaloosa, Mahaska County, Iowa, December 17, 1854; became an orphan in early youth; worked as a farm hand, and attended the country schools in the winter; was graduated from Simpson College, Indianola, Iowa, in 1874, and from Parsons College, Fairfield, Iowa, in 1875; was elected superintendent of schools of Ringgold County in 1879; delegate to the Republican State convention in 1880; member of the faculty of Hastings (Nebr.) College from January 1, 1885, to January 1, 1893; elected vice president of Hastings College in 1889 and president of the Nebraska State Teachers' Association in 1890;

served as private secretary to the Governor of Nebraska in 1893 and 1894; was an unsuccessful candidate for election in 1892 to the Fifty-third Congress; elected as a Republican to the Fifty-fourth Congress (March 4, 1895–March 3, 1897); was an unsuccessful candidate for reelection in 1896 to the Fifty-fifth Congress; auditor for the Treasury Department, Washington, D. C., 1897–1915; elected to the Sixty-sixth and Sixty-seventh Congresses (March 4, 1919–March 3, 1923); was an unsuccessful candidate for reelection in 1922 to the Sixty-eighth Congress; established his residence in Washington, D. C., in 1923, when he retired from active business pursuits and political life; died in Washington, D. C., January 19, 1942; interment in Parkview Cemetery, Hastings, Nebr.

ANDREWS, William Henry, a Delegate from the Territory of New Mexico; born in Youngsville, Warren County, Pa., January 14, 1846; attended the public schools; engaged in mercantile pursuits at Cincinnati, Ohio, and at Meadville and Titusville, Pa., 1880–1890; was also a builder of railroads; president of the Santa Fe Central Railway Co.; chairman of the Republican State committee of Pennsylvania 1889–1891; member of the State house of representatives 1889–1893; served in the State senate in 1895; moved to the Territory of New Mexico in 1900 and engaged in the mining business in Sierra County; was a member of the Territorial council in 1903 and 1904; elected as a Republican to the Fifty-ninth, Sixtieth, Sixty-first, and Sixty-second Congresses and served from March 4, 1905, to January 7, 1912, when, pursuant to law, his term expired, the Territory of New Mexico having been admitted as a State into the Union and the Representative-elect having qualified; became engaged in the development of oil in the southern part of New Mexico in 1912; died in Carlsbad, Eddy County, N. Mex., January 16, 1919; interment in Woodlawn Cemetery, Titusville, Crawford County, Pa.

ANDREWS, William Noble, a Representative from Maryland; born in Hurlock, Dorchester County, Md., November 13, 1876; attended the public schools of the county and Dixon College; was graduated from Wesley Collegiate Institute, Dover, Del., in 1898 and from the law department of the University of Maryland at Baltimore in 1903; was admitted to the bar in 1903 and commenced the practice of law in Cambridge, Md.; served as State attorney for Dorchester County from 1904 to 1911; member of the State house of delegates in 1914; served in the State senate from 1918 until 1919, when he resigned to enter Congress; elected as a Republican to the Sixty-sixth Congress (March 4, 1919–March 3, 1921); unsuccessful candidate for reelection in 1920 to the Sixty-seventh Congress; resumed the practice of law in Cambridge, Md., until his death there on December 27, 1937; interment in Washington Cemetery, Hurlock, Md.

ANDRUS, John Emory, a Representative from New York; born in Pleasantville, Westchester County, N. Y., February 16, 1841; attended the local schools, and Charlotteville Seminary in Schoharie County, N. Y.; was graduated from Wesleyan University, Middletown, Conn., in 1862; taught school in New Jersey for four years; engaged in the manufacture of medicine in Yonkers, N. Y.; president of the New York Pharmaceutical Association, and of the Palisade Manufacturing Co. of Yonkers, Westchester County; trustee of Wesleyan University; mayor of Yonkers in 1903; elected as a Republican to the Fifty-ninth and to the three succeeding Congresses (March 4, 1905–March 3, 1913); was not a candidate for renomination in 1912; resumed his former business pursuits in Yonkers, N. Y., until his death there on December 26, 1934; interment in Kensico Cemetery, Valhalla, N. Y.

ANFUSO, Victor L'Episcopo, a Representative from New York; born in Gagliano Castelferrato, Sicily, Italy, March 10, 1905; immigrated to the United States in 1914 and settled in Brooklyn, N. Y.; attended elementary and Commercial High School in Brooklyn, N. Y.; preparatory courses at Columbia University in 1926 and 1927; was graduated from St. Lawrence University Law School (now Brooklyn Law School) in 1927; was admitted to the bar in 1928 and commenced the practice of law in New York City; during World War II served with the Office of Strategic Services in the Mediterranean Theater 1943–1945; special assistant to the Commissioner of Immigration 1944–1946; elected as a Democrat to the Eighty-second Congress (January 3, 1951–January 3, 1953); did not seek renomination in 1952; appointed city magistrate of Brooklyn, N. Y., in February 1954 and resigned in July 1954 to run for Congress; elected to the Eighty-fourth, Eighty-fifth, and Eighty-sixth Congresses (January 3, 1955–January 3, 1961). *Reelected to the Eighty-seventh Congress.*

ANGEL, William G., a Representative from New York; born in New Shoreham, Block Island, R. I., July 17, 1790; moved with his parents to Litchfield, Otsego County, N. Y., in 1792; attended the common schools; began the study of medicine in 1807; studied law; was admitted to the bar and commenced practice in Burlington, N. Y., in 1817; elected as a John Quincy Adams Democrat to the Nineteenth Congress (March 4, 1825–March 3, 1827); elected as a Jackson Democrat to the Twenty-first and Twenty-second Congresses (March 4, 1829–March 3, 1833); resumed the practice of law in Hammondsport, Steuben County, N. Y.; member of the State constitutional convention of 1846; was elected judge of Allegany County in 1847; died in Angelica, Allegany County, N. Y., on August 13, 1858; interment in Until the Day Dawn Cemetery.

ANGELL, Homer Daniel, a Representative from Oregon; born on a farm near The Dalles, Wasco County, Oreg., January 12, 1875; attended the public schools; was graduated from the University of Oregon at Eugene in 1900 and from the law school of Columbia University, New York, N. Y., in 1903; was admitted to the New York and Oregon bars the same year and commenced practice in Portland, Oreg.; member of the State house of representatives in 1929, 1931, and 1935; served in the State senate in 1937 and 1938, resigning to become a candidate for Congress; elected as a Republican to the Seventy-sixth and to the seven succeeding Congresses (January 3, 1939–January 3, 1955); unsuccessful candidate for renomination in 1954; retired; is a resident of Portland, Oreg.

ANKENY, Levi, a Senator from Washington; born near St. Joseph, Buchanan County, Mo., August 1, 1844; crossed the plains to Oregon in 1850 with his parents, who settled in Portland; attended the rural schools and Kingsley Academy, Portland, Oreg.; engaged in mercantile pursuits in Lewiston, Orofino, and Florence, Idaho; interested in the cattle business; first mayor of Lewiston, the Government having deeded to him, as trustee, the public land on which that city is located; moved to Walla Walla, Wash., and engaged in banking; organized the First National Bank of Walla Walla in 1878; president of seven banks in Washington and Oregon; member of the Walla Walla Common Council; delegate to the Republican National Convention at Philadelphia in 1900; member of the Republican National Committee 1904–1908; appointed a member of the Pan American Exposition Commission and became its chairman; elected as a Republican to the United States Senate and served from March 4, 1903, to March 3, 1909; unsuccessful candidate for renomination in a State primary in 1908; engaged in banking in Walla Walla, Wash., until his death on March 29, 1921; interment in Masonic Cemetery.

ANSBERRY, Timothy Thomas, a Representative from Ohio; born in Defiance, Defiance County, Ohio, December 24, 1871; attended the public schools; was graduated from the University of Notre Dame, South Bend, Ind., in June 1893; was admitted to the bar and commenced practice in Defiance, Ohio; justice of the peace 1893–1895; prosecuting attorney of Defiance County 1895–1903; was an unsuccessful candidate for election in 1904 to the Fifty-ninth Congress; elected as a Democrat to the Sixtieth and to the three succeeding Congresses and served from March 4, 1907, until January 9, 1915, when he resigned to accept a judicial position; appointed associate judge of the Ohio Court of Appeals, in which capacity he served until his resignation in 1916; presidential elector on the Democratic ticket of Woodrow Wilson and Thomas R. Marshall in 1916; delegate to the Democratic National Conventions at San Francisco in 1920 and at New York in 1924; moved to Washington, D. C., in 1916 and engaged in the practice of law until his death; died in New York City, N. Y., July 5, 1943; interment in Mount Olivet Cemetery, Washington, D. C.

ANSORGE, Martin Charles, a Representative from New York; born in Corning, Steuben County, N. Y., January 1, 1882; attended the public schools and the College of the City of New York; was graduated from Columbia College in 1903 and from the Columbia Law School in 1906; was admitted to the bar in 1906 and commenced practice in New York City; chairman of the Triborough Bridge Committee 1918–1921; delegate to all of the Republican State conventions from 1910 to 1925; unsuccessful Republican candidate for election to Congress in 1912, 1914, and 1916; declined the Republican nomination for Congress in 1918; during the First World War enlisted in the Motor Transport Corps; elected as a Republican to the Sixty-seventh Congress (March 4, 1921–March 3, 1923); unsuccessfully contested the election in 1922 of Royal H. Weller to the Sixty-eighth Congress; unsuccessful candidate for judge of the court of general sessions of New York City in 1924; unsuccessful candidate for justice of the supreme court of New York in 1927 and in 1928; resumed the practice of law in New York City; director of United Air Lines 1934–1961; engaged in general practice of law and is a resident of New York City, N. Y.

ANTHONY, Daniel Read, Jr., a Representative from Kansas; born in Leavenworth, Kans., August 22, 1870; attended the public schools, the Michigan Military Academy at Orchard Lake, and the University of Michigan at Ann Arbor; studied law; was admitted to the bar but did not practice extensively; engaged in newspaper work; appointed postmaster of Leavenworth, Kans., on June 22, 1898, and served until June 30, 1902, when a successor was appointed; mayor of Leavenworth 1903–1905; became manager and editor of the Leavenworth Daily Times in 1904; elected as a Republican to the Sixtieth Congress to fill the vacancy caused by the resignation of Charles Curtis; reelected to the Sixty-first and to the nine succeeding Congresses and served from May 23, 1907, to March 3, 1929; was not a candidate for renomination in 1928; resumed his former business pursuits; died in Leavenworth, Kans., August 4, 1931; interment in Mount Muncie Cemetery.

ANTHONY, Henry Bowen, a Senator from Rhode Island; born in Coventry, R. I., April 1, 1815; attended a private school in Providence, R. I., and was graduated from Brown University in 1833; editor of the Providence Journal in 1838, and afterwards became one of its proprietors; elected Governor of Rhode Island in 1849 and reelected in 1850; declined to be a candidate for renomination; resumed editorial pursuits; elected as a Republican to the United States Senate in 1858, reelected in 1864, 1870, 1876, and again in 1882, and served from March 4, 1859, until his death; was elected president pro tempore of the Senate March 23, 1869, April 8, 1869, May 28, 1870, July 1, and July 14, 1870, and repeatedly in 1871; also elected to that position in 1884, but because of ill health declined to serve; died in Providence, R. I., September 2, 1884; interment in Swan Point Cemetery.

ANTHONY, Joseph Biles, a Representative from Pennsylvania; born in Philadelphia, Pa., June 19, 1795; attended the public schools; studied law; was admitted to the bar and practiced; member of the State senate 1830–1833; elected as a Democrat to the Twenty-third and Twenty-fourth Congresses (March 4, 1833–March 3, 1837); appointed judge of the "Nichelson court"; engaged in the sale of titles to large tracts of lands in Pennsylvania; was elected president judge of the eighth district in 1844 and served until his death in Williamsport, Lycoming County, Pa., January 10, 1851; interment in Williamsport Cemetery.

ANTONY, Edwin Le Roy, a Representative from Texas; born in Waynesboro, Burke County, Ga., January 5, 1852; moved with his parents to Texas in 1859 and settled in Brazoria County; moved to Milam County in 1867; attended the common schools, and was graduated from the University of Georgia at Athens in 1873; studied law; was admitted to the bar in 1874 and commenced practice in Cameron, Tex.; prosecuting attorney of Milam County 1876, being also ex officio district attorney for his county; was appointed special judge during the illness of the regular district judge in 1886; member of the board of aldermen of Cameron 1890–1892; elected as a Democrat to the Fifty-second Congress to fill the vacancy caused by the resignation of Roger Q. Mills, and served from June 14, 1892, to March 3, 1893; unsuccessful candidate for renomination in 1892; resumed the practice of law in Cameron, Tex.; died in Dallas, Tex., January 16, 1913; interment in Oakland Cemetery.

APLIN, Henry Harrison, a Representative from Michigan; born in Thetford Township, Genesee County, Mich., April 15, 1841; moved with his parents to Flint, Mich., in 1848; attended the public and high schools; at the outbreak of the Civil War enlisted July 3, 1861, in Company C, Sixteenth Regiment, Michigan Volunteer Infantry; served until July 16, 1865, with the rank of second lieutenant; returned to Michigan and engaged in mercantile pursuits at Wenona (now West Bay City); postmaster of West Bay City from November 1869 to June 1886; served as township clerk and township treasurer, each for three years; delegate to the Republican National Convention at Chicago in 1884; elected auditor general of the State in 1886 and 1888; interested in the construction of the electric railways of West Bay City and served as general manager until 1891; member of the Michigan House of Representatives in 1894 and 1895; was again appointed postmaster of West Bay City and served from October 1, 1898, to June 1902; elected as a Republican to the Fifty-seventh Congress to fill the vacancy caused by the death of Rousseau O. Crump and served from October 20, 1901, to March 3, 1903; unsuccessful candidate for renomination in 1902; engaged in agricultural pursuits and was also interested in the manufacture of ice; died in West Bay City, Mich., July 23, 1910; interment in Elm Lawn Cemetery, Bay City, Mich.

APPLEBY, Stewart Hoffman (son of Theodore Frank Appleby), a Representative from New Jersey; born in Asbury Park, Monmouth County, N. J., May 17, 1890; attended the public schools of Asbury Park, and Mercersburg Academy; was graduated from Rutgers University, New Brunswick, N. J., in 1913;

engaged in the real estate and insurance business; organized and served as vice president of the First National Bank of Avon-by-the-Sea, N. J.; during the First World War enlisted in the United States Marine Corps on May 17, 1917, and served until May 17, 1921, being awarded the Good-conduct Medal; commissioned a captain in the United States Marine Corps Reserve on November 24, 1925; elected as a Republican to the Sixty-ninth Congress to fill the vacancy caused by the death of his father, Representative-elect T. Frank Appleby, and served from November 3, 1925, to March 3, 1927; was not a candidate for renomination in 1926; during World War II served in the United States Coast Guard, being discharged in September 1945 as a coxswain; retired, and resides in Hallandale, Fla.

APPLEBY, Theodore Frank (father of Stewart Hoffman Appleby), a Representative from New Jersey; born in Old Bridge, Middlesex County, N. J., October 10, 1864; moved with his parents to Asbury Park, N. J., in 1875; attended the public schools and Pennington (N. J.) Seminary; was graduated from Fort Edwards Collegiate Institute, Glens Falls, N. Y., in 1885; engaged in the real estate and insurance business; member of the Asbury Park Board of Education 1887–1897; member of the State board of education 1894–1902; delegate to the Republican National Convention at St. Louis in 1896; member of the city council 1899–1906; mayor of Asbury Park 1908–1912; member of the Monmouth County Board of Taxation 1917–1920; elected as a Republican to the Sixty-seventh Congress (March 4, 1921–March 3, 1923); unsuccessful candidate for reelection in 1922 to the Sixty-eighth Congress; had been elected to the Sixty-ninth Congress, but died before the commencement of the congressional term in a hospital at Baltimore, Md., December 15, 1924; interment in Chestnut Hill Cemetery, Old Bridge, N. J.

APPLETON, John, a Representative from Maine; born in Beverly, Mass., February 11, 1815; was graduated from Bowdoin College, Brunswick, Maine, in 1834; studied law at the Cambridge Law School; was admitted to the Cumberland bar in 1837 and commenced practice in Portland, Maine; engaged in editorial work on the Eastern Argus and became editor in 1838; register of probate for Cumberland County, Maine, 1840 and 1842–1844; chief clerk of the Navy Department 1845–1848 and of the Department of State from January 26 to April 25, 1848; Minister to Bolivia from March 30, 1848, to May 4, 1849; elected as a Democrat to the Thirty-second Congress (March 4, 1851–March 3, 1853); resumed the practice of law; secretary of the legation in London from February 19 to November 16, 1855; Assistant Secretary of State from April 4, 1857, to June 8, 1860; Minister to Russia from June 1860 to June 7, 1861, when he resigned; died in Portland, Maine, August 22, 1864; interment in Evergreen Cemetery.

APPLETON, Nathan (cousin of William Appleton), a Representative from Massachusetts; born in New Ipswich, N. H., October 6, 1779; attended the common schools, the local academy in New Ipswich, N. H., and Dartmouth College, Hanover, N. H.; clerked in his brother's importing house in Boston; one of the founders of the cotton-mill industry of Waltham, Mass.; also one of the founders of the city of Lowell in 1821; served in the Massachusetts House of Representatives in 1815, 1816, 1821, 1823, 1824, and 1827; elected as a High-tariff Whig to the Twenty-second Congress (March 4, 1831–March 3, 1833); was not a candidate for renomination in 1832 to the Twenty-third Congress; elected to the Twenty-seventh Congress to fill the vacancy caused by the resignation of Robert C. Winthrop and served from June 9 to September 28, 1842, when he resigned; engaged in mercantile pursuits; died in Boston, Mass., July 14, 1861; interment in Mount Auburn Cemetery, Cambridge, Mass.

APPLETON, William (cousin of Nathan Appleton), a Representative from Massachusetts; born in Brookfield, Mass., November 16, 1786; attended schools in New Ipswich, N. H., Francestown, N. H., and Tyngsboro, Mass.; worked in a country store at Temple, Hillsboro County, N. H., when fifteen years of age; moved to Boston in 1807; engaged in mercantile pursuits; president of the Boston Branch of the United States Bank 1832–1836; elected as a Whig to the Thirty-second and Thirty-third Congresses (March 4, 1851–March 3, 1855); unsuccessful candidate for reelection in 1854 to the Thirty-fourth Congress and for election in 1856 to the Thirty-fifth Congress; elected to the Thirty-seventh Congress and served from March 4, 1861, to September 27, 1861, when he resigned because of failing health; died at Longwood (Brookline), Mass., February 15, 1862; interment in Mount Auburn Cemetery, Cambridge, Mass.

APSLEY, Lewis Dewart, a Representative from Massachusetts; born in Northumberland, Pa., September 29, 1852; moved with his parents to Lock Haven, Clinton County, Pa., in 1861; attended public and private schools; moved to Philadelphia and engaged in business; early identified himself with the rubber-goods trade; moved to Massachusetts in 1877 and became a manufacturer of rubber clothing in Hudson in 1885; president of the Apsley Rubber Co., succeeded by the Firestone Apsley Rubber Co.; president of the Hudson Board of Trade and a director of the Hudson National Bank; elected as a Republican to the Fifty-third and Fifty-fourth Congresses (March 4, 1893–March 3, 1897); declined to be a candidate for renomination in 1896; resumed his former business pursuits in Hudson, Mass.; served two terms as vice chairman of the Republican National Congressional Committee; died in Colon, Panama, April 11, 1925; interment in Forestvale Cemetery, Hudson, Mass.

ARCHER, John (father of Stevenson Archer), a Representative from Maryland; born near Churchville, Harford (then Baltimore) County, Md., May 5, 1741; attended the West Nottingham Academy in Cecil County and was graduated from Princeton College in 1760; studied theology, but owing to a throat affection abandoned the same and began the study of medicine; was graduated as a physician from the College of Philadelphia in 1768, receiving the first medical diploma issued on the American Continent; commenced the practice of his profession in Harford County in 1769; member of the Revolutionary committee 1774–1776; raised a military company during the Revolution; member of the first State constitutional convention of 1776; served in the State house of delegates 1777–1779; during the Revolutionary War was aide-de-camp to Gen. Anthony Wayne at Stony Point; June 1, 1779, was made a captain and subsequently a major in the Continental Army; on June 26, 1779, was the bearer of General Wayne's letter announcing the victory at Stony Point; presidential elector in 1797 and 1801; elected as a Democrat to the Seventh, Eighth, and Ninth Congresses (March 4, 1801–March 3, 1807); founded with his son, Dr. Thomas Archer, the medical and chirurgical faculty of Maryland in 1799; died at his country home, "Medical Hall," near Churchville, Harford County, Md., September 28, 1810; interment in the Presbyterian Cemetery, Churchville, Md.

ARCHER, Stevenson (son of John Archer), a Representative from Maryland; born at "Medical Hall," near Churchville, Harford County, Md., October 11, 1786; attended Nottingham Academy, Maryland, and was graduated from Princeton College in 1805; studied law; was admitted to the bar of Harford County in 1808 and commenced practice the same year; member of the State house of delegates 1809–1810; elected as a Democrat to the Twelfth Congress to fill the vacancy caused by the resignation of John Montgomery; reelected to the Thirteenth and Fourteenth Congresses and served from October 26, 1811, to March 3, 1817; paymaster to the Fortieth Maryland Militia during the War of 1812; appointed on March 5, 1817, by President Madison as United States judge for the Territory of Mississippi, with powers of Governor, holding court at St. Stephens; resigned within a year and returned to Maryland and practiced law; elected to the Sixteenth Congress (March 4, 1819–March 3, 1821); appointed chief judge of the judicial circuit court of Baltimore and Harford Counties and Baltimore city in 1823; in 1844 was appointed by Governor Pratt as chief justice of the Maryland Court of Appeals and served until his death at "Medical Hall," near Churchville, Harford County, Md., June 26, 1848; interment in the Presbyterian Cemetery, Churchville, Md.

ARCHER, Stevenson (son of the preceding and grandson of John Archer), a Representative from Maryland; born at "Medical Hall," near Churchville, Harford County, Md., February 28, 1827; attended Bel Air Academy, and was graduated from Princeton College in 1848; studied law; was admitted to the bar in 1850 and commenced practice the same year; member of the State house of delegates in 1854; elected as a Democrat to the Fortieth and to the three succeeding Congresses (March 4, 1867–March 3, 1875); unsuccessful candidate for renomination in 1874; engaged in the practice of his chosen profession in Bel Air, Md., until his death on August 2, 1898; interment in the Presbyterian Cemetery, Churchville, Md.

ARCHER, William Segar (nephew of Joseph Eggleston), a Representative and a Senator from Virginia; born at "The Lodge," a plantation about nine miles north of Amelia Court House, Amelia County, Va., March 5, 1789; received private instruction; was graduated from William and Mary College, Williamsburg, Va., in 1806; studied law; was admitted to the bar in 1810 and practiced in Amelia and Powhatan Counties; member of the State house of delegates in 1812; reelected annually until 1819, with the exception of a single year; elected to the Sixteenth Congress to fill the vacancy caused by the resignation of James Pleasants; reelected to the Seventeenth and to the six succeeding Congresses and served from January 3, 1820, to March 3, 1835; unsuccessful candidate for reelection in 1834 to the Twenty-fourth Congress; elected as a Whig to the United States Senate and served from March 4, 1841, to March 3, 1847; unsuccessful candidate for reelection in 1846; resumed the practice of law; died at "The Lodge," in Amelia County, Va., March 28, 1855; interment in a private cemetery at "The Lodge."

ARENDS, Leslie Cornelius, a Representative from Illinois; born in Melvin, Ford County, Ill., September 27, 1895; attended public and high schools and Oberlin (Ohio) College; during the First World War served in the United States Navy in 1918 and 1919; engaged in agricultural pursuits and banking; in 1935 became member of the Ford County (Ill.) Farm Bureau and in 1938 a member of the board of trustees of the Illinois Wesleyan University at Bloomington; elected as a Republican to the Seventy-fourth and to the twelve succeeding Congresses (January 3, 1935–January 3, 1961); Republican whip since 1943. *Reelected to the Eighty-seventh Congress.*

ARENS, Henry, a Representative from Minnesota; born in Westphalia, Germany, November 21, 1873; attended the public schools and an agricultural school in Germany; immigrated to the United States in 1889 and settled near Jordan, Scott County, Minn.; engaged in agricultural pursuits in 1903; member of the board of aldermen of Jordan, Minn., 1905–1913; served on the board of education 1913–1919; member of the State house of representatives 1919–1923; served in the State senate 1923–1929; Lieutenant Governor of Minnesota 1929–1931; elected as a

Farmer-Laborite to the Seventy-third Congress (March 4, 1933–January 3, 1935); unsuccessful candidate for reelection in 1934 to the Seventy-fourth Congress and for election in 1936 to the Seventy-fifth Congress; resumed agricultural pursuits; unsuccessful candidate in 1942 for the Farmer-Labor nomination for United States Senator; retired from business pursuits in 1944 and resides in Jordan, Minn.

ARENTZ, Samuel Shaw (Ulysses), a Representative from Nevada; born in Chicago, Ill., January 8, 1879; attended the public and high schools; was graduated from the Chicago Manual Training School in 1897 and from the South Dakota School of Mines at Rapid City in 1904; member of the South Dakota National Guard at Rapid City 1901–1904; moved to Ludering, Lyon County, Nev., in 1907, and to Salt Lake City, Utah, in 1912, and was engaged as surveyor, assessor, miner, and timberman in Bear Gulch and Butte, Mont., Bingham Canyon and Stockton, Utah, and the Lake Superior copper country; mining engineer and superintendent of mines in Idaho, Utah, Arizona, and Nevada; chief engineer of railway companies in Nevada; consulting engineer of the United States Bureau of Mines; member of sundry engineering and mining associations; captain of Engineers, United States Army, during the First World War; moved to a ranch in Lyon County, Nev., near Simpson, in 1917; also engaged in mining and irrigation projects; elected as a Republican to the Sixty-seventh Congress (March 4, 1921–March 3, 1923); was not a candidate for renomination, having become a candidate for Senator; unsuccessful candidate in the 1922 primary election for the Republican nomination for United States Senator; elected to the Sixty-ninth and to the three succeeding Congresses (March 4, 1925–March 3, 1933); unsuccessful candidate for reelection in 1932 to the Seventy-third Congress; delegate to the Republican National Conventions in 1928 and 1932; again engaged as a rancher near Simpson; also resumed mining activities in Nevada and Utah; died in Reno, Nev., where he had gone to receive medical treatment, on June 17, 1934; interment in Mountain View Cemetery, Reno, Nev.

ARMFIELD, Robert Franklin, a Representative from North Carolina; born near Greensboro, Guilford County, N. C., July 9, 1829; attended the common schools and was graduated from Trinity College, Durham, N. C.; studied law; was admitted to the bar in 1845 and began practice in Yadkinville, N. C.; enlisted in the Confederate Army in 1861; served as lieutenant and later as lieutenant colonel of the Thirty-eighth Regiment of North Carolina State troops during the Civil War; moved to Statesville, N. C., and continued the practice of law; State solicitor for the sixth district in 1862 while on furlough from the Army; member of the State senate in 1874 and 1875, serving as president in 1874; Lieutenant Governor of North Carolina in 1875 and 1876; elected as a Democrat to the Forty-sixth and Forty-seventh Congresses (March 4, 1879–March 3, 1883); was not a candidate for renomination in 1882; resumed the practice of law; appointed and subsequently elected judge of the superior court and served from 1889 until January 1, 1895, when he retired; died in Statesville, Iredell County, N. C., November 9, 1898; interment in Oakwood Cemetery.

ARMSTRONG, David Hartley, a Senator from Missouri; born in Nova Scotia, Canada, October 21, 1812; attended Maine Wesleyan Seminary; taught school in New Bedford, Mass., 1833–1837; moved to St. Louis, Mo., in 1837, and thence to Lebanon, Ill., where he taught in McKendree College; returned to Missouri and was principal of the public school at Benton 1838–1847; comptroller of St. Louis 1847–1850; postmaster of St. Louis 1854–1858; member of the board of police commissioners 1873–1876; served as a member of the board of freeholders which framed the present city charter of St. Louis in 1876; was appointed as a Democrat to the United States Senate to fill the vacancy caused by the death of Lewis V. Bogy and served from September 29, 1877, to January 26, 1879, when a successor was elected and qualified; was not a candidate for election in 1879; died in St. Louis, Mo., March 18, 1893; interment in Bellefontaine Cemetery.

ARMSTRONG, James (brother of John Armstrong), a Representative from Pennsylvania; born in Carlisle, Cumberland County, Pa., August 29, 1748; attended the Philadelphia Academy and the College of New Jersey (now Princeton University); studied medicine in Dr. John Morgan's School in Philadelphia and was graduated from the University of Pennsylvania at Philadelphia in 1769; commenced the practice of medicine in Winchester, Frederick County, Va.; was a medical officer during the Revolutionary War; pursued medical studies in London, England, for three years; returned to Carlisle, Pa., in 1788; moved to Mifflin County, Pa., and practiced medicine there for twelve years; was appointed an associate judge, and on September 13, 1791, repelled a riot at the courthouse by the use of firearms; elected as a Federalist to the Third Congress (March 4, 1793–March 3, 1795); was not a candidate for renomination in 1794; returned to Carlisle in 1796 and continued the practice of his profession; appointed as an associate judge of the Cumberland County Court and served from September 12, 1808, until his death in Carlisle, Pa., May 6, 1828; interment in the Old Carlisle Cemetery.

ARMSTRONG, John (father of James Armstrong and John Armstrong), a Delegate from Pennsylvania; born in Brookbor, County Fermanagh, Ireland, October 13, 1717; attended school in Ireland, and became a civil engineer; immigrated to the United States and settled in Carlisle, Cumberland County, Pa.; was presented a medal by the city of Philadelphia for destroying the Kittanning Indian towns, September 8, 1756; rendered distinguished service in the Continental Army, was commissioned a brigadier general in 1776, and served until April 4, 1777; appointed a major general of the Pennsylvania State Militia and served throughout the Revolutionary War, with the exception of the term of his congressional service; Member of the Continental Congress 1778–1780 and again in 1787 and 1788; died in Carlisle, Pa., March 9, 1795; interment in Old Carlisle Cemetery.

ARMSTRONG, John (son of the preceding and brother of James Armstrong), a Senator from New York; born in Carlisle, Cumberland County, Pa., November 25, 1755; attended Princeton College but left college to enter the Revolutionary Army; served on the staffs of Generals Mercer and Gates; secretary of state of Pennsylvania 1783–1787; adjutant general for several years; moved to Dutchess County, N. Y., in 1789 and settled near Lexington Manor; elected to the United States Senate to fill the vacancy in the term ending March 3, 1801, caused by the resignation of John Laurance; reelected in 1801 and served from November 6, 1800, to February 5, 1802, when he resigned; was appointed to fill the vacancy in the term ending March 3, 1807, caused by the resignation of his successor, De Witt Clinton; subsequently elected to fill the vacancy in the term ending March 3, 1809, caused by the resignation of Theodorus Bailey, and served from November 10, 1803, until June 30, 1804, when he again resigned, to enter the diplomatic service; Minister to France from June 30, 1804, to September 14, 1810; also acted as Minister to Spain in 1806; during the War of 1812 was commissioned brigadier general on July 6, 1812; appointed Secretary of War in the Cabinet of President Madison during his two administrations and served from January 13, 1813, until September 27,

1814, when he resigned; engaged in literary pursuits; died in Red Hook, Dutchess County, N. Y., April 1, 1843; interment in Rhinebeck Cemetery, Rhinebeck, N. Y.

ARMSTRONG, Moses Kimball, a Delegate from the Territory of Dakota; born in Milan, Erie County, Ohio, September 19, 1832; attended Huron Institute and Western Reserve College, Cleveland, Ohio; moved to the Territory of Minnesota in 1856; elected surveyor of Mower County, and assigned to survey the United States lands in 1858; moved to Yankton, then a small Indian village, in Dakota Territory, when Minnesota Territory was admitted as a State; was a member of the first Territorial house of representatives in 1861; reelected in 1862 and 1863, serving as speaker in 1863; edited the Dakota Union in 1864; appointed clerk of the supreme court in 1865; elected to the Territorial council in 1866 and in 1867 was chosen president; acted as secretary of the Indian peace commission in 1867; established the great meridian and standard lines for United States surveys in southern Dakota and in the northern Red River Valley; again elected to the Territorial council, in 1869; elected as a Democrat to the Forty-second and Forty-third Congresses (March 4, 1871–March 3, 1875); unsuccessful candidate for reelection in 1874 to the Forty-fourth Congress; moved to St. James, Watonwan County, Minn., and engaged in banking and in the real-estate business; died in Albert Lea, Minn., on January 11, 1906; interment in Lakewood Cemetery, Minneapolis, Minn.

ARMSTRONG, Orland Kay, a Representative from Missouri; born in Willow Springs, Howell County, Mo., October 2, 1893; was graduated from Drury College, Springfield, Mo., in 1916, Cumberland University Law School, Lebanon, Tenn., in 1922, and from the University of Missouri School of Journalism at Columbia in 1925; was admitted to the bar in 1922, but did not practice; teacher of English and public speaking at Southwest Baptist College, Bolivar, Mo., in 1916 and 1917; during the First World War served from private to lieutenant in the United States Army Air Corps 1917–1919; Y. M. C. A. welfare representative in France in 1919 and 1920; established department of journalism at University of Florida at Gainesville in 1925 and served as director 1925–1928; author, magazine writer, and newspaper correspondent; secretary of Missouri Century of Progress Commission 1930–1932; member of the State house of representatives 1932–1936 and 1942–44; became a member of editorial staff of Reader's Digest in 1944; member of the staff of the United States Senate Committee on Post Office and Civil Service in 1947 and 1948; elected as a Republican to the Eighty-second Congress (January 3, 1951–January 3, 1953); was not a candidate for renomination in 1952; is a resident of Springfield, Mo.

ARMSTRONG, William, a Representative from Virginia; born in Lisburn, County Antrim, Ireland, December 23, 1782; immigrated to the United States in 1792 with his parents, who settled in Virginia; studied law in Winchester; United States tax collector in 1818 and 1819; member of the State house of delegates in 1822 and 1823; presidential elector on the Democratic ticket of Monroe and Tompkins in 1820, and of Crawford and Macon in 1824; elected to the Nineteenth and to the three succeeding Congresses (March 4, 1825–March 3, 1833); engaged in the tavern business in Romney, W. Va., until 1862; died in Keyser, W. Va., May 10, 1865; interment in Indian Mound Cemetery, Romney, W. Va.

ARMSTRONG, William Hepburn, a Representative from Pennsylvania; born in Williamsport, Lycoming County, Pa., September 7, 1824; attended the common schools, and was graduated from Princeton College in 1847; studied law; was admitted to the bar and commenced practice in Williamsport, Pa.; served in the State house of representatives in 1860 and 1861; declined a commission as president judge of the twenty-sixth judicial circuit of Pennsylvania in 1862; elected as a Republican to the Forty-first Congress (March 4, 1869–March 3, 1871); unsuccessful candidate for reelection in 1870 to the Forty-second Congress; declined the office of commissioner of Indian affairs tendered by President Grant; commissioner of railroads 1882–1885; resumed the practice of law in Washington, D. C., and Philadelphia, Pa., until 1898, when he retired from active business pursuits; moved to Wilmington, Del., where he died on May 14, 1919; interment in Wilmington and Brandywine Cemetery.

ARNELL, Samuel Mayes, a Representative from Tennessee; born at Zion Settlement, near Columbia, Maury County, Tenn., May 3, 1833; attended Amherst College, Amherst, Mass.; studied law; was admitted to the bar and commenced practice in Columbia; member of the constitutional convention of Tennessee in 1865; served in the State house of representatives in 1865 and 1866; upon the readmission of the State of Tennessee to representation was elected as a Republican to the Thirty-ninth Congress; reelected to the Fortieth and Forty-first Congresses and served from July 24, 1866, to March 3, 1871; was not a candidate for renomination in 1870; resumed the practice of law in Washington, D. C.; returned to Columbia, Tenn.; postmaster of Columbia 1879–1884; superintendent of schools 1884–1886; devoted his later years to literature; died in Johnson City, Washington County, Tenn., July 20, 1903; interment in Monte Vista Cemetery.

ARNOLD, Benedict (brother-in-law of Matthias J. Bovee), a Representative from New York; born in Amsterdam, Montgomery County, N. Y., October 5, 1780; attended the common schools; engaged in mercantile pursuits and also was an extensive landowner and philanthropist; supervisor of Amsterdam 1813–1816; member of the State assembly in 1816 and 1817; elected to the Twenty-first Congress (March 4, 1829–March 3, 1831); was not a candidate for reelection in 1830; president of the board of trustees of the village of Amsterdam in 1832; did not resume active business pursuits, but lived in retirement until his death in Amsterdam, N. Y., March 3, 1849; interment in Green Hill Cemetery.

ARNOLD, Isaac Newton, a Representative from Illinois; born in Hartwick, Otsego County, N. Y., November 30, 1815; attended the district and select schools and Hartwick Seminary; taught school in Otsego County 1832–1835; studied law; was admitted to the bar in 1835 and commenced practice in Cooperstown, Otsego County, N. Y.; moved to Chicago, Cook County, Ill., in 1836 and continued the practice of law; was elected as city clerk of Chicago in 1837, but had served only a short time when he resigned to devote his entire efforts to his law practice; delegate to the Democratic State convention in 1842; member of the State house of representatives in 1842 and 1843; presidential elector on the Democratic ticket of Polk and Dallas in 1844; delegate to the Free-Soil National Convention at Buffalo in 1848; again a member of the State house of representatives in 1855 and was an unsuccessful candidate for speaker; unsuccessful candidate for the Republican nomination to Congress in 1858; elected as a Republican to the Thirty-seventh and Thirty-eighth Congresses (March 4, 1861–March 3, 1865); declined to be a candidate for renomination in 1864; during the Civil War acted as aide to Colonel Hunter at the Battle of Bull Run; served as Sixth Auditor of the United States Treasury, Washington, D. C., from April 29, 1865, to

September 29, 1866, when he resigned; resumed the practice of law and also engaged in literary pursuits; died in Chicago, Ill., April 24, 1884; interment in Graceland Cemetery.

ARNOLD, Jonathan (father of Lemuel Hastings Arnold and great-great-grandfather of Theodore Francis Green), a Delegate from Rhode Island; born in Providence, R. I., December 3, 1741; studied medicine and practiced; member of the general assembly of Rhode Island from Providence in 1776; served in the Revolutionary Army as surgeon; director of the Army hospital in Providence; Member of the Continental Congress 1782–1784; moved to St. Johnsbury, Vt., in 1787 and engaged in agricultural pursuits; appointed a member of the Governor's council; was appointed judge of Orange County and served until his death in St. Johnsbury, Caledonia County, Vt., February 1, 1793; interment in Mount Pleasant Cemetery.

ARNOLD, Laurence Fletcher, a Representative from Illinois; born in Newton, Jasper County, Ill., June 8, 1891; attended the public and high schools of his native city and the University of Chicago, Chicago, Ill.; studied law; engaged in banking and in the wholesale hay and grain business at Newton, Ill., in 1916; served in the State house of representatives 1923–1927 and 1933–1937; delegate to the Democratic National Convention at New York in 1924; elected as a Democrat to the Seventy-fifth, Seventy-sixth, and Seventy-seventh Congresses (January 3, 1937–January 3, 1943); unsuccessful candidate for reelection in 1942 to the Seventy-eighth Congress and for election in 1950 to the Eighty-second Congress; resumed former business interests; president, Peoples State Bank; is a resident of Newton, Ill.

ARNOLD, Lemuel Hastings (son of Jonathan Arnold and great-great-uncle of Theodore Francis Green), a Representative from Rhode Island; born in St. Johnsbury, Vt., January 29, 1792; was graduated from Dartmouth College, Hanover, N. H., in 1811; studied law; was admitted to the bar in 1814 and commenced practice in Providence, R. I.; engaged in manufacturing and mercantile pursuits in 1821; member of the State house of representatives 1826–1831; Governor of Rhode Island in 1831 and 1832; member of the executive council during the Dorr Rebellion in 1842 and 1843; unsuccessful candidate for United States Senator in 1845; elected as a Liberation Whig to the Twenty-ninth Congress (March 4, 1845–March 3, 1847); was not a candidate for renomination in 1846; moved to South Kingston in 1847 and continued the practice of law until his death on June 27, 1852; interment in Swan Point Cemetery, Providence, R. I.

ARNOLD, Marshall, a Representative from Missouri; born at Cook Settlement, near Farmington, St. Francois County, Mo., October 21, 1845; attended the common schools; professor at Arcadia College in 1870 and 1871; deputy clerk of the circuit, county, and probate courts of St. Francois County, Mo.; studied law; was admitted to the bar in 1872 and commenced practice in Commerce, Scott County, Mo.; prosecuting attorney of Scott County 1873–1876; member of the State house of representatives 1877–1879; presidential elector on the Democratic ticket of Hancock and English in 1880; elected as a Democrat to the Fifty-second and Fifty-third Congresses (March 4, 1891–March 3, 1895); unsuccessful candidate for reelection in 1894 to the Fifty-fourth Congress; resumed the practice of law in Benton, Scott County, Mo., and died there June 12, 1913; interment in Benton Cemetery.

ARNOLD, Peleg, a Delegate from Rhode Island; born in Smithfield, R. I., June 10, 1751; attended the common schools, and Brown University, Providence, R. I.; studied law; was admitted to the bar and practiced; elected deputy to the general assembly of Rhode Island, serving from October 1777 to October 1778 and from May 1782 to May 1783; colonel of the Second Regiment of Providence County Militia in 1780; Member of the Continental Congress 1787–1789; keeper of the "Peleg Arnold Tavern," at Smithfield, R. I.; Assistant Governor of Rhode Island in 1790; incorporator of the Providence Society for the Abolition of Slavery in 1790; unsuccessful Anti-Federalist candidate for election to the Fourth Congress in 1794 and also an unsuccessful Republican candidate for election to the same Congress to fill the vacancy caused by the resignation of Benjamin Bourne in 1796; chief justice of the supreme court of Rhode Island from June 1795 to June 1809 and again from May 1810 to May 1812; president of the Smithfield Union Bank in 1803; president of Smithfield Academy in 1810; again served as deputy to the general assembly of Rhode Island from October 1817 to May 1819; died in Smithfield, R. I., February 13, 1820; interment in Union Cemetery, opposite the Friends Meeting House, in Union Village, near Woonsocket, R. I.

ARNOLD, Samuel, a Representative from Connecticut; born in Haddam, Conn., June 1, 1806; attended the local academy at Plainfield, Conn., and Westfield Academy, Massachusetts; devoted most of his life to agricultural pursuits; acquired a controlling interest in a stone quarry and became owner of a line of schooners operating between New York and Philadelphia; was, also, for a number of years, president of the Bank of East Haddam; member of the State house of representatives in 1839, 1842, 1844, and again in 1851; elected as a Democrat to the Thirty-fifth Congress (March 4, 1857–March 3, 1859); declined to be a candidate for renomination in 1858; resumed agricultural pursuits and quarrying; died in Haddam, Middlesex County, Conn., May 5, 1869; interment in a mausoleum on his estate near Haddam.

ARNOLD, Samuel Greene (granduncle of Theodore Francis Green), a Senator from Rhode Island; born in Providence, R. I., April 12, 1821; received his early education under private tutors; was graduated from Brown University, Providence, R. I., in 1841 and from the law department of Harvard University in 1845; was admitted to the bar in 1845; spent three years in travel and study in Europe and South America; commenced practice in Providence, R. I., in 1848; also engaged in historical research; trustee of Brown University 1848–1880; elected Lieutenant Governor of Rhode Island in 1852 and in the absence of Governor Sprague was Acting Governor; member of the peace commission held at Washington, D. C., in 1861 in an effort to devise means to prevent the impending war; again elected Lieutenant Governor, in 1861 and 1862; during the Civil War organized a company of Light Artillery which went to Washington, D. C., and was mustered into the Union Army; elected as a Republican to the United States Senate to fill the vacancy caused by the resignation of James F. Simmons and served from December 1, 1862, to March 3, 1863; again engaged in historical research; president of the Rhode Island Historical Society 1868–1880; died in Providence, R. I., February 14, 1880; interment in Swan Point Cemetery.

ARNOLD, Samuel Washington, a Representative from Missouri; born on a farm near Downing, Schuyler County, Mo., September 21, 1879; attended the Coffey, Mo., rural schools and was graduated from Kirksville (Mo.) State Teachers College in 1902; taught school in the Coffey, Mo., school district in 1896; superintendent of the public schools in Middletown, Mo., in 1901 and 1902 and in Atlanta, Mo., in 1903; employed in the St. Louis, Mo., internal revenue office in 1904; engaged in the retail lumber business at Atlanta, Mo., 1905–1908; moved to Kirksville, Mo., in 1908 and organized the Arnold Lumber Co.; elected as a Republican to the Seventy-eighth, Seventy-ninth, and Eightieth Congresses (January 3, 1943–January 3, 1949); unsuccessful candidate for reelection in 1948 to the Eighty-first Congress, for election in 1950 to the Eighty-second Congress, and in 1952 to the Eighty-third Congress; retired from political and business activities in 1952; is a resident of Kirksville, Mo.

ARNOLD, Thomas Dickens, a Representative from Tennessee; born in Spotsylvania County, Va., May 3, 1798; moved with his parents to Knox County, Tenn., in 1808; was tutored privately; at the age of fourteen enlisted as a drummer boy in the War of 1812; taught school in Knox and Grainger Counties; studied law; was admitted to the bar in 1820 and commenced practice in Knoxville, Tenn.; elected as a Whig to the Twenty-second Congress (March 4, 1831–March 3, 1833); an attempt was made by Morgan A. Heard to assassinate him in April 1833 as he descended the west steps of the Capitol; was made brigadier general of the Tennessee Militia in 1836; moved to Greeneville, Tenn.; presidential elector on the Whig ticket of Harrison and Tyler in 1840; elected to the Twenty-seventh Congress (March 4, 1841–March 3, 1843); resumed the practice of law in Greeneville; died while attending court in Jonesboro, Washington County, Tenn., May 26, 1870; interment in Oak Grove Cemetery, Greeneville, Tenn.

ARNOLD, Warren Otis, a Representative from Rhode Island; born in Coventry, Kent County, R. I., June 3, 1839; attended the common schools; engaged in mercantile pursuits at Coventry from 1857 to 1864; was a manufacturer of cotton goods in Chepachet and Westerly, R. I., until 1866, when he began the manufacture of woolen goods; elected as a Republican to the Fiftieth and Fifty-first Congresses (March 4, 1887–March 3, 1891); was a candidate for reelection in 1890 to the Fifty-second Congress, but as neither candidate received a majority the general assembly ordered a new election, in which he declined to be a participant; elected to the Fifty-fourth Congress (March 4, 1895–March 3, 1897); declined to be a candidate for renomination in 1896; continued his former manufacturing pursuits until his death in Westerly, Washington County, R. I., April 1, 1910; interment in Acotes Hill Cemetery, Chepachet, R. I.

ARNOLD, William Carlile, a Representative from Pennsylvania; born in Luthersburg, Clearfield County, Pa., July 15, 1851; attended the public schools and Phillips Academy, Andover, Mass.; studied law; was admitted to the bar in Clearfield County, Pa., June 18, 1875, and practiced in Curwensville and Du Bois, Clearfield County, Pa.; elected as a Republican to the Fifty-fourth and Fifty-fifth Congresses (March 4, 1895–March 3, 1899); unsuccessful candidate for reelection in 1898 to the Fifty-sixth Congress; resumed the practice of law in Clearfield County, Pa.; died in Muskegon, Mich., while on a business trip to that city, March 20, 1906; interment in Oak Hill Cemetery, Curwensville, Pa.

ARNOLD, William Wright, a Representative from Illinois; born in Oblong, Crawford County, Ill., October 14, 1877; attended the country schools of his native county and Austin College, Effingham, Ill.; was graduated from the law department of the University of Illinois at Urbana in 1901; was admitted to the bar the same year and commenced the practice of law in Robinson, Crawford County, Ill.; was continuously engaged in the practice of his chosen profession until elected to Congress; elected as a Democrat to the Sixty-eighth and to the six succeeding Congresses and served from March 4, 1923, until his resignation, effective September 16, 1935, having been appointed July 29, 1935, a member of the United States Board of Tax Appeals (now

the Tax Court of the United States); reappointed in 1944 and served until his retirement June 30, 1950; owned and operated two large farms; director of the Second National Bank, Farmers and Producers Bank, and the First National Bank of Robinson; died in Robinson, Ill., November 23, 1957; interment in New Cemetery.

ARNOT, John, Jr., a Representative from New York; born in Elmira, Chemung County, N. Y., March 11, 1831; educated at private schools in his native city; entered Yale College, but left before graduation to enter business; upon the death of his father became engaged in banking in Elmira; president of the village 1859–1864; president of the board of trustees of the village of Elmira in 1859, 1860, and 1864; during the Civil War served as Army paymaster with the rank of major in Elmira; when the village of Elmira was chartered as a city was elected mayor in 1864, 1870, and 1874; declined the proffered nomination as Democratic candidate for Congress in 1882, but accepted nomination at a subsequent convention; elected as a Democrat to the Forty-eighth and Forty-ninth Congresses and served from March 4, 1883, until his death in Elmira, N. Y., November 20, 1886; interment in Woodlawn Cemetery.

ARRINGTON, Archibald Hunter (uncle of Archibald Hunter Arrington Williams), a Representative from North Carolina; born near Nashville, Nash County, N. C., November 13, 1809; attended the local academy at Hilliardston and Louisburg (N. C.) College; studied law; was a large landowner, extensively engaged in planting; elected as a Democrat to the Twenty-seventh and Twenty-eighth Congresses (March 4, 1841–March 3, 1845); unsuccessful candidate for reelection in 1844 to the Twenty-ninth Congress; was a supporter of the Confederacy and a member of the secession convention in 1861; member of the First Confederate Congress in 1861; unsuccessful candidate for reelection in 1863 to the Second Confederate Congress; delegate to the Union National Convention at Philadelphia in 1866; chairman of the court of common pleas and quarter sessions for Nash County in 1866 and 1867; county commissioner in 1868; engaged in the management of his estate; died at his country home near Nashville, Nash County, N. C., July 20, 1872; interment in the family graveyard on his plantation.

ARTHUR, Chester Alan, a Vice President and a President of the United States; born in Fairfield, Franklin County, Vt., October 5, 1830; attended the public schools, and was graduated from Union College, Schenectady, N. Y., in 1848; became principal of an academy in North Pownal, Vt., in 1851; studied law; was admitted to the bar in 1854 and commenced practice in New York City; delegate to the Republican State convention at Saratoga in 1856; took an active part in the reorganization of the State militia and was made judge advocate of the Second Brigade in 1857; appointed engineer in chief on the staff of Governor Morgan, with the rank of brigadier general, in 1860; became acting quartermaster general of the State in April 1861; commissioned inspector general February 10, 1862, and served until appointed quartermaster general with the rank of brigadier general July 10, 1862, and served until December 31, 1862; resumed the practice of law in New York City; counsel for the city department of assessment and taxes; appointed by President Grant as collector of the port of New York in 1871; reappointed in 1875 and served from November 24, 1871, until July 11, 1878; resumed the practice of law in New York City; delegate to the Republican National Convention at Chicago in 1880; elected Vice President of the United States on the Republican ticket with James A. Garfield as President for the term beginning March 4, 1881; upon the death of President Garfield became President of the United States on September 20, 1881, and served until March 3, 1885; returned to New York City where he died November 18, 1886; interment in the Rural Cemetery Albany, N. Y.

ARTHUR, William Evans, a Representative from Kentucky; born in Cincinnati, Ohio, March 3, 1825; moved with his parents to Covington, Ky., where he received instruction from private tutors and also in private schools; studied law; was admitted to the bar in 1850 and commenced practice in Covington; Commonwealth attorney for the ninth judicial district of Kentucky 1856–1862; presidential elector on the Democratic ticket of Breckinridge and Lane in 1860; appointed judge of the ninth judicial circuit in 1866 and served until 1868, when he resigned; elected as a Democrat to the Forty-second and Forty-third Congresses (March 4, 1871–March 3, 1875); was not a candidate for renomination in 1874; resumed the practice of law in Covington; became judge of the twelfth judicial circuit of Kentucky in 1886 and served until 1893, when he resigned; engaged in the practice of law until his death in Covington, Ky., May 18, 1897; interment in Linden Grove Cemetery.

ASH, Michael Woolston, a Representative from Pennsylvania; born in Philadelphia, Pa., March 5, 1789; studied law; was admitted to the bar June 21, 1811, and commenced practice in Philadelphia; served as a first lieutenant and lieutenant colonel in the First Regular Pennsylvania Volunteers during the War of 1812; at the close of the war he went into partnership with James Buchanan, who subsequently was a President of the United States, and continued the practice of his profession in Philadelphia; elected to the Twenty-fourth Congress (March 4, 1835–March 3, 1837); was not a candidate for reelection in 1836 to the Twenty-fifth Congress; again engaged in the practice of his profession until his death in Philadelphia, Pa., December 14, 1858; interment in Christ Church Burial Ground, located at Fifth and Arch Streets.

ASHBROOK, William Albert, a Representative from Ohio; born near Johnstown, Licking County, Ohio, July 1, 1867; attended the public schools, and Bartlett's Business College, Lansing, Mich.; in 1885 engaged in the newspaper publishing business in Johnstown, Ohio; also engaged in banking; served as postmaster of Johnstown from 1893 to 1897, when his successor was appointed; secretary of the National Editorial Association 1902–1906; member of the State house of representatives in 1904 and 1905; elected as a Democrat to the Sixtieth and to the six succeeding Congresses (March 4, 1907–March 3, 1921); unsuccessful candidate for reelection in 1920 to the Sixty-seventh Congress; resumed the newspaper publishing business and banking in Johnstown, Ohio; elected to the Seventy-fourth, Seventy-fifth, and Seventy-sixth Congresses and served from January 3, 1935, until his death in Johnstown, Ohio, January 1, 1940; interment in Green Hill Cemetery.

ASHE, John Baptista (uncle of John Baptista Ashe of Tennessee, Thomas Samuel Ashe, and William Shepperd Ashe), a Delegate and a Representative from North Carolina; born in Rocky Point, N. C., in 1748; was privately tutored at home; engaged in agricultural pursuits; served throughout the Revolutionary War and attained the rank of colonel in command of North Carolina troops at Valley Forge and at the Battle of Eutaw, S. C.; member of the State house of commons 1784–1786, serving as speaker of the house in 1786; Member of the Continental Congress in 1787 and served until November 1, 1787, when he resigned; served as chairman of the committee of the whole in the State convention of 1789 that ratified the Constitution of the United States; member of the State senate in 1789; elected as a Federalist to the First and Second Congresses

(March 4, 1789–March 3, 1793); resumed agricultural pursuits; again served in the State senate in 1795; elected Governor of North Carolina in 1802, but died in Halifax, N. C., November 27, 1802, before being inaugurated; interment in the Churchyard Cemetery, Halifax, N. C.

ASHE, John Baptista (brother of William Shepperd Ashe, nephew of the preceding, and cousin of Thomas Samuel Ashe), a Representative from Tennessee; born in Rocky Point, Pender County, N. C., in 1810; attended Fayetteville Academy and was graduated from Trinity College, Hartford, Conn., in 1830; studied law; was admitted to the bar in 1832; moved to Tennessee and commenced practice in Brownsville; elected as a Whig to the Twenty-eighth Congress (March 4, 1843–March 3, 1845); moved to Galveston County, Tex., and settled near Galveston; continued the practice of his chosen profession until his death in Galveston, Tex., December 29, 1857; interment in a cemetery near Galveston.

ASHE, Thomas Samuel (nephew of John Baptista Ashe of North Carolina and cousin of John Baptista Ashe of Tennessee and of William Shepperd Ashe), a Representative from North Carolina; born in Hawfields, near Graham, Alamance County (then a part of Orange County), N. C., July 21, 1812; attended Bingham's Academy, Hillsboro, N. C., and was graduated from the University of North Carolina at Chapel Hill in 1832; studied law; was admitted to the bar in 1834 and commenced practice in Wadesboro, Anson County, in 1835; member of the State house of commons in 1842; solicitor of the fifth judicial district of North Carolina 1847–1851; elected to the State senate in 1854; Member of the Confederate House of Representatives 1861–1864; elected to the Confederate Senate in 1864, but did not serve due to the termination of the Civil War; served as State councilor in 1866; unsuccessful candidate for Governor of North Carolina in 1868; elected as a Conservative to the Forty-third Congress and as a Democrat to the Forty-fourth Congress (March 4, 1873–March 3, 1877); declined to be a candidate for renomination in 1876; resumed the practice of law at Wadesboro; elected associate justice of the State supreme court in 1878; reelected in 1886 for a term of eight years and served until his death in Wadesboro, Anson County, N. C., on February 4, 1887; interment in East View Cemetery.

ASHE, William Shepperd (brother of John Baptista Ashe of Tennessee and nephew of John Baptista Ashe of North Carolina), a Representative from North Carolina; born in Rocky Point, N. C., August 12, 1813; attended school at Fayetteville, N. C., and pursued classical studies in Trinity College, Hartford, Conn.; engaged in the cultivation of rice; studied law; was admitted to the North Carolina bar in 1836 and commenced the practice of law in New Hanover County, N. C., the same year; presidential elector of the Democratic ticket of James K. Polk and George M. Dallas in 1844; member of the North Carolina Senate 1846–1848; elected as a Democrat to the Thirty-first, Thirth-second, and Thirty-third Congresses (March 4, 1849–March 3, 1855); was not a candidate for renomination in 1854; served as president of the Wilmington & Weldon Railroad Company from 1854 until his death; again a member of the North Carolina Senate 1859–1861; delegate to the Democratic National Convention at Charleston in 1860; member of the North Carolina Constitutional Convention in 1861; during the Civil War served as a major in the Confederate Army, in charge of all transportation from the South to Virginia; killed in a railroad accident near Wilmington, N. C., September 14, 1862; interment in the family burying ground at "The Neck," near Ashton, Pender County, N. C.

ASHLEY, Chester, a Senator from Arkansas; born in Westfield, Mass., June 1, 1790; moved with his parents to Hudson, N. Y., during infancy; attended the common schools and was graduated from Williams College, Williamstown, Mass., and the Litchfield (Conn.) Law School; was admitted to the bar in 1817 and commenced the practice of law in Hudson, N. Y.; moved to Edwardsville, Ill., in 1818, to St. Louis, Mo., in 1819, and to Little Rock, Ark., in 1820, where he permanently established himself in the practice of law; elected as a Democrat to the United States Senate in 1844 to fill the vacancy caused by the death of William S. Fulton; reelected in 1846 and served from November 8, 1844, until his death in Washington, D. C., April 29, 1848; interment in the Congressional Cemetery.

ASHLEY, Delos Rodeyn, a Representative from Nevada; born at The Post, Ark., February 19, 1828; received an academic education; studied law; was admitted to the bar in 1849 and practiced; moved to California in 1849 and continued the practice of law in Monterey in 1850; district attorney 1851–1853; member of the State house of representatives in 1854 and 1855; served in the State senate in 1856 and 1857; State treasurer of California in 1862 and 1863; moved to Virginia City, Storey County, Nev., in 1864 and continued the practice of law; elected as a Republican to the Thirty-ninth and Fortieth Congresses (March 4, 1865–March 3, 1869); was not a candidate for renomination in 1868; moved to Pioche, Lincoln County, Nev., in 1871 and resumed the practice of law; due to failing health moved to San Francisco, Calif., in 1872, and lived in retirement until his death there July 18, 1873; interment in Calvary Cemetery.

ASHLEY, Henry, a Representative from New York; born in Winchester, Cheshire County, N. H., February 19, 1778; attended the common schools; clerk of Winchester village in 1811; justice of the peace in 1817; engaged in the manufacture of leather in Catskill, Greene County, N. Y.; chairman of the tanners' association in 1825; elected to the Nineteenth Congress (March 4, 1825–March 3, 1827); was not a candidate for reelection in 1826; resumed his former business pursuits; president of the board of trustees of the village of Catskill in 1828; trustee of the apprentices' library in 1828; died in Catskill, N. Y., January 14, 1829; interment in Thomson Street Cemetery.

ASHLEY, James Mitchell (great-grandfather of Thomas William Ludlow Ashley), a Representative from Ohio; born near Pittsburgh, Pa., November 14, 1824; instructed himself in elementary subjects while employed as a clerk on boats operating on the Ohio and Mississippi Rivers; editor of the Dispatch, and afterwards of the Democrat, in Portsmouth, Ohio; studied law; was admitted to the bar in 1849 but never practiced; moved to Toledo, Ohio, and engaged in the wholesale drug business; elected as a Republican to the Thirty-sixth and to the four succeeding Congresses (March 4, 1859–March 3, 1869); unsuccessful Republican candidate for reelection in 1868 to the Forty-first Congress; delegate to the Philadelphia Loyalists' Convention in 1866; Governor of the Territory of Montana in 1869 and 1870; constructed the Toledo, Ann Arbor & Northern Railroad, and served as president from 1877 to 1893; died in Alma, Gratiot County, Mich., September 16, 1896; interment in Woodlawn Cemetery, Toledo, Ohio.

ASHLEY, Thomas William Ludlow (great-grandson of James M. Ashley), a Representative from Ohio; born in Toledo, Lucas County, Ohio, January 11, 1923; attended the Monroe and Glenwood elementary schools, and Kent School, Kent, Conn., 1939–1942; during World War II served in the United States Army as a corporal with service in the Pacific Theater of Operations 1943–1945; was graduated from Yale University, New Haven, Conn., in 1948; associated with Toledo Publicity and Efficiency Commission in 1948; studied law in evening classes at the University of Toledo Law School; graduated from Ohio State University Law School at Columbus in 1951; was admitted to the bar in 1951 and commenced the practice of law in Whitehouse and Toledo, Ohio; in 1952 joined the staff of Radio Free Europe, serving in Europe as codirector of the press section and later as assistant director of special projets, resigning March 1, 1954; elected as a Democrat to the Eighty-fourth, Eighty-fifth, and Eighty-sixth Congresses (January 3, 1955–January 3, 1961). *Reelected to the Eighty-seventh Congress.*

ASHLEY, William Henry, a Representative from Missouri; born in Powhatan County, Va., in 1778; attended the common schools; moved to St. Genevieve, Mo. (then Upper Louisiana), in 1803; engaged in the manufacture of saltpeter; became a merchant and later a surveyor; moved to St. Louis, Mo., in 1808; brigadier general of militia during the War of 1812; traded with the Indians and dealt in furs; founded an organization which in 1830 became the Rocky Mountain Fur Co., and conducted trading and exploring expeditions to the headwaters of the Missouri River; elected as the first Lieutenant Governor of Missouri and served from 1820 to 1824; was an unsuccessful candidate for Governor in 1831; elected as a Whig to the Twenty-second Congress to fill the vacancy caused by the death of Spencer D. Pettis; reelected to the Twenty-third and Twenty-fourth Congresses and served from October 31, 1831, to March 3, 1837; did not seek renomination in 1836, again having become a gubernatorial aspirant; unsuccessful candidate for Governor of Missouri in 1836; died near Boonville, Mo., March 26, 1838; interment in an Indian mound overlooking the Missouri River, near his home, on the Lamine River, in Cooper County, Mo.

ASHMORE, John Durant, a Representative from South Carolina; born in Greenville District, S. C., August 18, 1819; attended the common schools; studied law; was admitted to the bar but never practiced; engaged in agricultural pursuits; member of the State house of representatives 1848–1852; comptroller general of the State 1853–1857; elected as a Democrat to the Thirty-sixth Congress and served from March 4, 1859, until his retirement on December 21, 1860; during the Civil War was elected colonel of the Fourth South Carolina Regiment, but resigned before the regiment was called into service; engaged in mercantile pursuits in Greenville, S. C.; died in Sardis, Miss., December 5, 1871; interment in Black Jack Cemetery, near Sardis, in Panola County.

ASHMORE, Robert Thomas, a Representative from South Carolina; born on a farm near Greenville, S. C., February 22, 1904; attended the public schools of Greenville; was graduated from Furman University Law School, Greenville, S. C., in 1927; while a student, engaged in agricultural work, retail sales, and as a substitute rural mail carrier; was admitted to the bar in January 1928 and engaged in the practice of law in Greenville, S. C.; solicitor of Greenville County Court 1930–1934; solicitor of the thirteenth judicial circuit of South Carolina 1936–1953; during World War II, while on official leave from duties as solicitor, volunteered for service in the United States Army in December 1942, serving in this country and overseas for three years and five months, until discharged from active duty in May 1946, as a lieutenant colonel in the United States Army Reserve; promoted to colonel in 1955; elected as a Democrat to the Eighty-third Congress to fill the vacancy caused by the death of Joseph R. Bryson; reelected to the Eighty-fourth, Eighty-fifth, and Eighty-sixth Congresses, and served from June 2, 1953, to January 3, 1961. *Reelected to the Eighty-seventh Congress.*

ASHMUN, Eli Porter (father of George Ashmun), a Senator from Massachusetts; born in Blandford, Hampden County, Mass., June 24, 1770; attended the village school; member of the State house of representatives in 1803 and 1804; was graduated from Middlebury College, Middlebury, Vt., in 1807; studied law; was admitted to the bar the same year and commenced practice in Blandford; moved with his mother to Northampton, Mass., in 1807 and continued the practice of law; member of the State house of representatives for several years; served in the State senate 1808–1810 and in 1813; member of the Governor's council in 1816; elected to the United States Senate to fill the vacancy caused by the resignation of Christopher Gore and served from June 12, 1816, to May 10, 1818, when he resigned; died in Northampton, Mass., May 10, 1819; interment in Bridge Street Cemetery.

ASHMUN, George (son of Eli Porter Ashmun), a Representative from Massachusetts; born in Blandford, Hampden County, Mass., December 25, 1804; moved to Northampton with his parents in 1807; attended the local schools; was graduated from Yale College in 1823; studied law; was admitted to the bar and commenced practice in Springfield in 1828; member of the State house of representatives in 1833, 1835, 1836, 1838, and 1841, serving as speaker in 1841; member of the State senate in 1838 and 1839; elected as a Whig to the Twenty-ninth, Thirtieth, and Thirty-first Congresses (March 4, 1845–March 3, 1851); was not a candidate for renomination in 1850; resumed the practice of law in Springfield; chairman of the Republican National Convention at Chicago that nominated Abraham Lincoln as a candidate for President in 1860; director of the Union Pacific Railroad Co.; delegate to the Union National Convention at Philadelphia in 1866; died in Springfield, Hampden County, Mass., July 16, 1870; interment in Springfield Cemetery.

ASHURST, Henry Fountain, a Senator from Arizona; born in Winnemucca, Humboldt County, Nev., September 13, 1874; moved to Arizona in 1875 with his parents, who settled near the present town of Flagstaff, Coconino County; attended the public schools of Flagstaff and was graduated from the Stockton (Calif.) Business College in 1896; studied law and political economy at the University of Michigan at Ann Arbor; was admitted to the bar in 1897 and commenced practice in Williams, Ariz.; member of the Territorial house of representatives in 1897 and 1899, serving as speaker in 1899; served in the Territorial senate in 1903; district attorney of Coconino County 1905–1908; moved to Prescott, Ariz., in 1909 and continued the practice of law; upon the admission of Arizona as a State into the Union was elected as a Democrat to the United States Senate by the unanimous vote of the first State legislative assembly on March 27, 1912, was reelected in 1916, 1922, 1928, and again in 1934, and served from March 27, 1912, to January 3, 1941; unsuccessful candidate for renomination in 1940; appointed a member of the Board of Immigration Appeals in the Department of Justice on April 8, 1941, and served until February 28, 1943, when he retired; resides in Washington, D. C.

ASPER, Joel Funk, a Representative from Missouri; born in Adams County, Pa., April 20, 1822; moved to Ohio with his parents, who settled in Trumbull County in 1827; attended the public schools and the local college in Warren, Ohio; studied law; was admitted to the bar in 1844 and commenced practice in Warren, Ohio; justice of the peace in 1846; prosecuting attorney of Geauga County in 1847; delegate to the Buffalo Free-Soil Convention in 1848; editor of the Western Reserve Chronicle in 1849; moved to Iowa in 1850 and published the Chardon Democrat; raised a company for the Civil War in 1861 and served as its captain; was wounded in the Battle of Win-

chester; promoted to the rank of lieutenant colonel in 1862; mustered out of the service in 1863 because of wounds received in action; moved to Chillicothe, Livingston County, Mo., in 1864 and resumed the practice of law; founded the Spectator in 1866; delegate to the Republican National Convention at Chicago in 1868; elected as a Radical Republican to the Forty-first Congress (March 4, 1869–March 3, 1871); was not a candidate for renomination in 1870; practiced law until his death; died in Chillicothe, Mo., October 1, 1872; interment in Edgewood Cemetery.

ASPINALL, Wayne Norviel, a Representative from Colorado; born in Middleburg, Logan County, Ohio, April 3, 1896; moved with his parents to Palisade, Mesa County, Colo., in 1904; attended the public schools; studied at the University of Denver until the First World War, then enlisted in the Air Service of the Signal Corps and served as a corporal and staff sergeant until discharged as a flying cadet; returned to the University of Denver and graduated in 1919; taught school in Palisade, Colo., 1919–1921; president of the Mount Lincoln School District School Board 1920–1922; graduated from the Denver Law School in 1925; was admitted to the bar the same year and commenced practice in Palisade, Colo.; also engaged in peach-orchard industry; again taught school 1925–1933; member of Palisade Board of Trustees 1926–1934; district counsel of the Home Owners Loan Corporation in western Colorado in 1933 and 1934; member of the State house of representatives 1931–1934 and in 1937 and 1938, serving as Democratic caucus chairman in 1931, Democratic whip in 1933, and as speaker in 1937 and 1938; served in the State senate 1939–1948 and was Democratic whip in 1939, majority floor leader in 1941, and minority floor leader 1943–1947; during World War II was commissioned a captain in Military Government in 1943, serving overseas as a legal expert with the American and English forces; participated in the Normandy drive with the English Second Army; was discharged on December 14, 1944; delegate to the Democratic State Conventions 1922–1960 and to the Democratic National Conventions in 1948 and 1960; elected as a Democrat to the Eighty-first and to the five succeeding Congresses (January 3, 1949–January 3, 1961). *Reelected to the Eighty-seventh Congress.*

ASWELL, James Benjamin, a Representative from Louisiana; born near Vernon, Jackson Parish, La., December 23, 1869; attended the public schools; was graduated from Peabody Normal College, Nashville, Tenn., in 1892 and from the University of Nashville in 1893; taught in country schools and high schools, and later attended Chicago University; State institution conductor 1897–1900; president of the Louisiana Polytechnic Institute 1900–1904; State superintendent of public education 1904–1908, and while serving in that capacity reorganized the public-school system of Louisiana; was elected chancellor of the University of Mississippi at University in 1907 but declined to accept; president of the Louisiana State Normal College at Natchitoches 1908–1911; elected as a Democrat to the Sixty-third and to the nine succeeding Congresses and served from March 4, 1913, until his death in Washington, D. C., March 16, 1931; interment in Rock Creek Cemetery.

ATCHISON, David Rice, a Senator from Missouri; born in Frogtown, Ky., August 11, 1807; attended Transylvania University, Lexington, Ky.; studied law; was admitted to the bar and commenced practice in Liberty, Clay County, Mo., in 1829; also engaged in agricultural pursuits; member of the State house of representatives in 1834, and again in 1838; appointed judge of the Platte County circuit court in 1841; appointed and subsequently elected in 1843 as a Whig to the United States Senate to fill the vacancy caused by the death of Lewis F. Linn; elected President pro tempore of the Senate

August 8, 1846, January 11 and March 3, 1847, February 2, June 1, June 26, July 29, and December 26, 1848, and March 1 and 2, 1849; term of office as Senator expired on March 3, 1849; reelected in 1849 for the term commencing March 4, 1849, but this day falling on Sunday he did not qualify until Monday, March 5, 1849, and was thereupon elected president pro tempore of the Senate for the purpose of administering the oath of office to the Senators-elect; again elected President pro tempore of the Senate on March 16, 1849, May 2 and 6 and July 10, 1850, December 20, 1852, and again on March 4, 1853, and served throughout the session; served as United States Senator from October 14, 1843, to March 3, 1855; resumed the practice of law; died at his home near Gower, Clinton County, Mo., January 26, 1886; interment in Greenlawn Cemetery, Plattsburg, Mo.

ATHERTON, Charles Gordon (son of Charles Humphrey Atherton), a Representative and a Senator from New Hampshire; born in Amherst, Hillsborough County, N. H., July 4, 1804; was graduated from Harvard University in 1822; studied law in the office of his father; was admitted to the bar in 1825 and commenced practice in Dunstable (now Nashua), N. H.; member of the State house of representatives 1830 and 1833–1835, serving as speaker 1833–1835; elected as a Democrat to the Twenty-fifth, Twenty-sixth, and Twenty-seventh Congresses (March 4, 1837– March 3, 1843); did not seek reelection in 1842, having become a candidate for Senator; elected to the United States Senate in 1843 and served from March 4, 1843, to March 3, 1849; resumed the practice of law in Nashua; again elected to the United States Senate in 1852 for the term beginning March 4, 1853, but never qualified, having suffered a stroke of paralysis while attending court; died in Manchester, N. H., November 15, 1853; interment in Nashua Cemetery, Nashua, N. H.

ATHERTON, Charles Humphrey (father of Charles Gordon Atherton), a Representative from New Hampshire; born in Amherst, Hillsborough County, N. H., August 14, 1773; attended the common schools and was graduated from Harvard University in 1794; studied law; was admitted to the bar in 1797 and commenced practice in Amherst; register of probate 1798–1807; elected as a Federalist to the Fourteenth Congress (March 4, 1815–March 3, 1817); declined to be a candidate for renomination in 1816; member of the State house of representatives 1823–1839; resumed the practice of law; died in Amherst, N. H., January 8, 1853; interment in the Old Cemetery.

ATHERTON, Gibson, a Representative from Ohio; born near Newark, Licking County, Ohio, January 19, 1831; attended Denison University, Granville, Ohio, and was graduated from Miami University, Oxford, Ohio, in 1853; principal of the local academy at Osceola, Mo., in 1853 and 1854; studied law; was admitted to the bar in 1855 and commenced practice in Newark, Ohio; president of the board of education of Newark for fifteen years; elected prosecuting attorney of Licking County in 1857 and reelected in 1859 and 1861; mayor of Newark 1860–1864; unsuccessful Democratic candidate for the State senate in 1863 and for judge of the court of common pleas in 1866; member of the city council of Newark for two years; delegate to the Democratic National Convention at St. Louis in 1876; elected as a Democrat to the Forty-sixth and Forty-seventh Congresses (March 4, 1879–March 3, 1883); did not seek renomination, having become an aspirant for the bench; unsuccessful candidate for election as judge of the supreme court of Ohio in 1882; appointed to that position by Governor Hoadly the same year and served until the election of his successor six months later; resumed the practice of law; died in Newark, Ohio, November 10, 1887; interment in Cedar Hill Cemetery.

ATKESON, William Oscar, a Representative from Missouri; born on a farm near Buffalo, Putnam County, Va. (now West Virginia), August 24, 1854; attended the public schools and the University of Kentucky at Lexington; taught school in Mason County, W. Va., in 1874 and at New Haven, W. Va., in 1875; was graduated from Fairmont (W. Va.) Normal School in 1875; moved to Point Pleasant, W. Va., in 1876 and edited and published the West Virginia Monitor; studied law; was admitted to the bar in 1877 and commenced practice in Council Grove, Kans.; moved to Rich Hill, Bates County, Mo., in 1882 and to Butler, Bates County, Mo., in 1889, and continued to practice law; prosecuting attorney of Bates County, Mo., 1891–1893; unsuccessful candidate for circuit judge of the twenty-ninth judicial circuit in 1892; owner and editor of the Butler Free Press 1894–1902; unsuccessful candidate for election in 1906 to the Sixtieth Congress and in 1908 to the Sixty-first Congress; served as deputy State hotel inspector in 1910 and 1911 and as deputy State labor commissioner 1911–1913; owner and editor of the Bates County Record 1915–1918; elected as a Republican to the Sixty-seventh Congress (March 4, 1921–March 3, 1923); unsuccessful candidate for reelection in 1922 to the Sixty-eighth Congress; served as State warehouse commissioner in Kansas City, Mo., from July 1, 1923, until February 5, 1925, when he resigned; resumed the practice of law and also engaged in literary pursuits; died in Butler, Mo., October 16, 1931; interment in Oak Hill Cemetery.

ATKINS, John DeWitt Clinton, a Representative from Tennessee; born near Manly's Chapel, Henry County, Tenn., June 4, 1825; attended a private school in Paris, Tenn., and was graduated from the East Tennessee University at Knoxville in 1846; studied law; was admitted to the bar but did not practice; engaged in agricultural pursuits; member of the State house of representatives 1849–1851; served in the State senate 1855–1857; presidential elector on the Democratic ticket of Buchanan and Breckinridge in 1856; elected as a Democrat to the Thirty-fifth Congress (March 4, 1857–March 3, 1859); unsuccessful candidate for reelection in 1858 to the Thirty-sixth Congress; during the Civil War served as lieutenant colonel of the Fifth Tennessee Regiment in the Confederate Army in 1861; elected to the Confederate Provisional Congress in August and November 1861 and in November 1863; elected as a Democrat to the Forty-third and to the four succeeding Congresses (March 4, 1873–March 3, 1883); was not a candidate for renomination in 1882; engaged in agricultural pursuits near Paris, Henry County, Tenn.; presidential elector on the Democratic ticket of Cleveland and Hendricks in 1884; appointed United States Commissioner of Indian Affairs by President Cleveland on March 21, 1885, and served until June 13, 1888, when he resigned; was an unsuccessful candidate for the Democratic nomination for United States Senator in 1888; again engaged in agricultural pursuits; retired from active pursuits in 1898 and moved to Paris, Tenn., where he lived in retirement until his death on June 2, 1908; interment in the City Cemetery.

ATKINSON, Archibald, a Representative from Virginia; born in Isle of Wight County, Va., September 15, 1792; received a liberal education; attended the law department of William and Mary College, Williamsburg, Va.; served during the War of 1812; was admitted to the bar and commenced practice in Smithfield, Isle of Wight County, Va.; member of the State house of delegates 1815–1817 and 1828–1831; served in the State senate 1839–1843; elected as a Democrat to the Twenty-eighth, Twenty-ninth, and Thirtieth Congresses (March 4, 1843–March 3, 1849); was not a candidate for renomination in 1848 to the Thirty-first Congress; served as prosecuting attorney for Isle of Wight

County; died in Smithfield, Va., on January 7, 1872; interment in the graveyard of Old St. Luke's Church, four miles southeast of Smithfield, Va.

ATKINSON, George Wesley, a Representative from West Virginia; born near Charleston, Kanawha County, Va. (now West Virginia), June 29, 1845; attended the public schools of Charleston and was graduated from the Ohio Wesleyan University at Delaware in 1870; collector of tolls on the Kanawha River Board 1869–1871; postmaster of Charleston 1871–1877; was graduated from Mount Union College, Alliance, Ohio, and Howard University Law School, Washington, D. C.; was admitted to the bar in 1875 and commenced practice in Charleston; later attended lectures on law at Columbia University; moved to Wheeling, Ohio County, W. Va., in 1877; editor of the Wheeling Standard in 1877 and 1878; internal-revenue agent of the Treasury Department 1879–1881; United States marshal for the district of West Virginia 1881–1885; successfully contested as a Republican the election of John O. Pendleton to the Fifty-first Congress and served from February 26, 1890, to March 3, 1891; declined to be a candidate for reelection in 1890; resumed the practice of law in Wheeling, W. Va.; editor of the West Virginia Journal 1891–1896; Governor of West Virginia 1897–1901; served as United States district attorney for the southern district of West Virginia from July 1, 1901, to April 18, 1905; appointed associate judge of the Court of Claims at Washington, D. C., on April 15, 1905, and served until April 16, 1916, when he retired; died in Charleston, W. Va., April 4, 1925; interment in Spring Hill Cemetery.

ATKINSON, Louis Evans, a Representative from Pennsylvania; born in Delaware Township, Juniata County, Pa., April 16, 1841; attended the common schools and Airy View and Milnwood Academies; studied medicine and was graduated from the medical department of the College of the City of New York March 4, 1861; during the Civil War entered the medical department of the United States Army on September 5, 1861; served as assistant surgeon in the First Pennsylvania Reserve Cavalry and as surgeon of the One Hundred and Eighty-eighth Pennsylvania Volunteer Infantry, until mustered out in December 1865; was disabled while in the Army and, being unable to practice medicine, studied law; was admitted to the bar in September 1870 and commenced practice in Mifflintown, Pa.; elected as a Republican to the Forty-eighth and to the four succeeding Congresses (March 4, 1883–March 3, 1893); became a candidate for renomination in 1892, but ultimately withdrew; resumed the practice of law in Mifflintown, Pa.; appointed president judge of the forty-first Pennsylvania district and served one year; died in Mifflintown, Juniata County, Pa., February 5, 1910; interment in Presbyterian Cemetery.

ATKINSON, Richard Merrill, a Representative from Tennessee; born in Nashville, Davidson County, Tenn., February 6, 1894; attended the public schools; was graduated from Wallace University School, Nashville, Tenn., in 1912, from Vanderbilt University, Nashville, Tenn., in 1916, and from the law department of Cumberland University, Lebanon, Tenn., in 1917; was admitted to the bar in 1917 and commenced the practice of law in Nashville, Tenn., in 1920; during the First World War served from June 30, 1917, until honorably discharged on August 29, 1919, as a member of the Forty-seventh Company, United States Marines, Second Division, serving in France with the American Expeditionary Forces; attorney general of the tenth judicial circuit of Tennessee from September 1, 1926, to September 1, 1934; State commissioner of Smoky Mountain National Park 1931–1933; elected as a Democrat to the Seventy-fifth Congress (January 3,

1937–January 3, 1939); unsuccessful candidate for renomination in 1938; engaged in the practice of law in Nashville, Tenn., until his death there on April 29, 1947; interment in Spring Hill Cemetery.

ATLEE, Samuel John, a Delegate from Pennsylvania; born in Trenton, N. J., in 1739, during the temporary residence of his parents at that place; moved with his mother to Lancaster, Pa., in 1745; educated by a private tutor and subsequently commenced the study of law, but abandoned it to enter the Army; during the French and Indian War at the age of sixteen was placed in command of a company of the provincial service from Lancaster County, Pa.; commissioned ensign in Col. William Clapham's Augusta regiment on April 23, 1756, and promoted to lieutenant December 7, 1757; served in the Forbes campaign and participated in a battle near Fort Duquesne, September 15, 1758; was commissioned captain May 13, 1759; appointed colonel of the Pennsylvania Musketry Battalion on March 21, 1776; during the Revolutionary War was captured by the British on August 27, 1776, at the Battle of Long Island and held as a prisoner until October 1, 1778, when he was exchanged; Member of the Continental Congress 1778–1782; served in the general assembly in 1782, 1785, and 1786; elected supreme executive councilor for Lancaster County in 1783; appointed a member of the board of commissioners to treat with the Indians in 1784 for the unpurchased lands in Pennsylvania; one of the charter members of the Society of the Cincinnati; died in Philadelphia, Pa., November 25, 1786, while attending a session of the assembly; interment in Christ Churchyard.

ATWATER, John Wilbur, a Representative from North Carolina; born near Rialto now (Fearington), Chatham County, N. C., December 27, 1840; attended the common schools and the old William Closs Academy; engaged in agricultural pursuits; during the Civil War enlisted in the Confederate Army and served in Company D, First Regiment, North Carolina Volunteer Infantry, and was with the army of Gen. Robert E. Lee until the surrender at Appomattox; joined the Farmers' Alliance in 1887; first president of Chatham County Alliance; elected to the State senate in 1890 as an Alliance Democrat, and also in 1892 and 1896 as a Populist; elected as a Populist to the Fifty-sixth Congress (March 4, 1899–March 3, 1901); was an unsuccessful candidate for reelection in 1900 to the Fifty-seventh Congress; resumed agricultural pursuits; died in Fearington, N. C., on July 4, 1910; interment in Mount Pleasant Church Cemetery, near Pittsboro, N. C.

ATWOOD, David, a Representative from Wisconsin; born in Bedford, N. H., December 15, 1815; attended the public schools; moved to Hamilton, N. Y., in 1832; apprenticed as a printer and subsequently became publisher of the Hamilton Palladium; moved to Freeport, Ill., in 1845 and engaged in agricultural pursuits; moved to Madison, Wis., in 1847 and for forty-two years was editor and publisher of the State Journal, Madison, Wis.; was commissioned major general in the Wisconsin Militia in 1858; member of the State assembly in 1861; United States assessor for four years; mayor of Madison in 1868 and 1869; elected as a Republican to the Forty-first Congress to fill the vacancy caused by the death of Benjamin F. Hopkins and served from February 23, 1870, until March 3, 1871; declined to be a candidate for renomination in 1870; resumed his former newspaper activities; United States Centennial Exposition commissioner, representing the State of Wisconsin, 1872–1876; delegate to the Republican National Convention at Philadelphia in 1872 and at Cincinnati in 1876; died in Madison, Wis., December 11, 1889; interment in Forest Hill Cemetery.

ATWOOD, Harrison Henry, a Representative from Massachusetts; born at the home of his grandmother in North Londonderry, Vt., August 26, 1863; attended the public schools of Boston, Mass.; studied architecture and engaged in that profession in Boston, Mass.; member of the Massachusetts House of Representatives 1887–1889; city architect of Boston in 1889 and 1890; member of the Republican State committee 1887–1889; member and secretary of the Boston Republican city committee 1888–1894; delegate to the Republican National Conventions in 1888 and 1892; elected as a Republican to the Fifty-fourth Congress (March 4, 1895–March 3, 1897); unsuccessful candidate for renomination in 1896 to the Fifty-fifth Congress; resumed his former profession in Boston; again a member of the Massachusetts House of Representatives in 1915, 1917, 1918, 1923, 1924, 1927, and 1928; was an unsuccessful candidate for election in 1918 to the Sixty-sixth Congress; resumed his profession as an architect in Boston, Mass.; moved to Wellesley Hills, Mass., in April 1938; died in Boston, Mass., October 22, 1954; interment in Forest Hills Cemetery.

AUCHINCLOSS, James Coats, a Representative from New Jersey; born in New York City, N. Y., January 19, 1885; attended Cutler School, New York City, and Groton School, Groton, Mass.; was graduated from Yale University, New Haven, Conn., in 1908; engaged in financial and stock brokerage business in New York City 1908–1940; served in the Seventh Regiment, New York National Guard, 1909–1913; during the First World War served as captain, Military Intelligence; deputy police commissioner of New York City; founder, treasurer, president, and chairman of the board of the New York Better Business Bureau; member of the borough council, Rumson, N. J., 1930–1937; mayor of Rumson, N. J., 1938–1943; elected as a Republican to the Seventy-eighth and to the eight succeeding Congresses (January 3, 1943–January 3, 1961). *Reelected to the Eighty-seventh Congress.*

AUF DER HEIDE, Oscar Louis, a Representative from New Jersey; born in New York City, N. Y., December 8, 1874; attended the public schools; moved with his parents to West New York, Hudson County, N. J., in 1887; engaged in the real-estate business; member of the town council 1899–1902; member and president of the board of education in 1903 and 1904; member of the State house of assembly 1908–1911; served on the board of assessors of West New York in 1912 and 1913; mayor of West New York 1914–1917; elected a member and subsequently a director of the Board of Chosen Freeholders of Hudson County and served from 1915 to 1924; director of the First National Bank of West New York, Hamilton National Bank of Weehawken, and Liberty National Bank of Guttenberg; elected as a Democrat to the Sixty-ninth and to the four succeeding Congresses (March 4, 1925–January 3, 1935); was not a candidate for renomination in 1934 to the Seventy-fourth Congress; resumed the real estate and insurance business; died in West New York, N. J., March 29, 1945; interment in Hoboken Cemetery, North Bergen, N. J.

AUSTIN, Albert Elmer (stepfather of Clare Boothe Luce), a Representative from Connecticut; born in Medway, Norfolk County, Mass., November 15, 1877; attended the public schools and was graduated from Amherst (Mass.) College in 1899 and from Jefferson Medical College, Philadelphia, Pa., in 1905; member of the faculty of Attleboro (Mass.) High School 1899–1900; practicing physician in Old Greenwich, Conn., 1907–1939; health officer of Greenwich, Conn., 1917–1937; engaged in banking in Old Greenwich, Conn., 1926–1942; during the First World War served as regimental surgeon in the Two Hundred and Fourteenth Engineers, Fourteenth (Wolverine) Division,

1918–1919; member of the State house of representatives 1917–1919 and 1921–1923; elected as a Republican to the Seventy-sixth Congress (January 3, 1939–January 3, 1941); unsuccessful candidate for reelection in 1940 to the Seventy-seventh Congress; continued his former professional pursuits until his death in Greenwich, Conn., January 26, 1942; interment in Ferncliff Cemetery, Hartsdale, Westchester County, N. Y.

AUSTIN, Archibald, a Representative from Virginia; born near Buckingham, Buckingham County, Va., August 11, 1772; studied law; was admitted to the bar and commenced practice in Buckingham County; member of the State house of delegates in 1815 and 1816; elected as a Democrat to the Fifteenth Congress (March 4, 1817–March 3, 1819); was not a candidate for renomination in 1818; resumed the practice of his profession; presidential elector on the Democratic ticket of Jackson and Van Buren in 1832; again a member of the State house of delegates 1835–1837; presidential elector on the Democratic ticket of Van Buren and Johnson in 1836; died near Buckingham Court House, Buckingham County, Va., October 16, 1837; interment in the family cemetery on his estate.

AUSTIN, Richard Wilson, a Representative from Tennessee; born in Decatur, Morgan County, Ala., August 26, 1857; attended the common schools, Loudon High School, and the University of Tennessee at Knoxville in 1873; studied law; was admitted to the bar in 1878 and commenced practice in Knoxville, Tenn.; clerk in the Post Office Department at Washington, D. C., 1879–1881; Assistant Doorkeeper of the National House of Representatives in the Forty-seventh Congress 1881–1883; special agent of the War Department 1883–1885; engaged in newspaper work in Knoxville, Tenn., in 1885; returned to Decatur, Ala., and continued the practice of law; private secretary to Congressman Leonidas C. Houk from Tennessee in 1888; served as city attorney of Decatur, Ala.; unsuccessful Republican candidate for election 1890 to the Fifty-second Congress; delegate to the Republican National Convention at Minneapolis in 1892; returned to Knoxville, Tenn., in 1893 and edited the Knoxville Republican; United States marshal for the eastern district of Tennessee 1897–1906; appointed United States consul at Glasgow, Scotland, and served from July 1906 to November 1907, when he resigned; elected as a Republican to the Sixty-first and to the four succeeding Congresses (March 4, 1909–March 3, 1919); unsuccessful candidate for renomination in 1918; became ill prior to the expiration of his term in Congress, and after prolonged sickness died in Washington, D. C., April 20, 1919; interment in the Old Gray Cemetery, Knoxville, Tenn.

AUSTIN, Warren Robinson, a Senator from Vermont; born in Highgate Center, Franklin County, Vt., November 12, 1877; attended the public schools; was graduated from Brigham Academy, Bakersfield, Vt., in 1895 and from the University of Vermont, at Burlington, in 1899; studied law; was admitted to the bar in 1902 and commenced practice at St. Albans, Vt.; served as State's attorney of Franklin County, Vt., 1904–1906; United States commissioner 1907–1915; chairman of the Republican State Convention in 1908; mayor of St. Albans in 1909; delegate to the Congress of the Mint in 1912; trustee of the University of Vermont 1914–1941; special counsel for Vermont in the boundary-line dispute between Vermont and New Hampshire in 1925–1937; member of the United States Court for China in 1917; delegate to the Republican National Conventions in 1928, 1940, and 1944; elected as a Republican to the United States Senate on March 31, 1931, to fill the vacancy caused by the death of Frank L. Greene; reelected in 1934 and 1940 and served from April 1, 1931, until his resignation on August 2,

1946, to become United States representative on the Security Council of the United Nations, serving until his retirement January 25, 1953; is a resident of Burlington, Vt.

AVERETT, Thomas Hamlet, a Representative from Virginia; born near Halifax, Halifax County, Va., July 10, 1800; attended the common schools; served as a drummer boy in the War of 1812; studied medicine; was graduated from Jefferson Medical College, Philadelphia, Pa., and practiced in Halifax and the adjacent counties; served in the State senate in 1848 and 1849; unsuccessful candidate for election in 1846 to the Thirtieth Congress; elected as a Democrat to the Thirty-first and Thirty-second Congresses (March 4, 1849–March 3, 1853); unsuccessful candidate for renomination in 1852; resumed the practice of medicine in Halifax County; died near Halifax Court House, Va., June 30, 1855; interment in the family burial ground near Halifax Court House, Va.

AVERILL, John Thomas, a Representative from Minnesota; born in Alna, Lincoln County, Maine, March 1, 1825; attended the common schools; moved with his parents to Montville, Maine, in 1838; was graduated from the Maine Wesleyan Seminary at Readfield in 1846; taught school for a short time, and subsequently engaged in lumbering for one year; moved to Winthrop, Maine, and engaged in mercantile pursuits for three years; moved to northern Pennsylvania in 1852 and again engaged in lumbering until 1857, when he journeyed westward and settled in Lake City, Minn.; engaged in mercantile pursuits and the grain business; member of the State senate 1858–1860; served in the Union Army during the Civil War; commissioned lieutenant colonel of the Sixth Regiment, Minnesota Volunteer Infantry, August 22, 1862; promoted to colonel on November 22, 1864; honorably mustered out on September 28, 1865; brevetted brigadier general of Volunteers on October 18, 1865, "for meritorious services in the recruitment of the Army of the United States"; moved to St. Paul, Minn., in 1866 and engaged in the wholesale paper and stationery business; member of the Republican National Committee 1868–1880; elected as a Republican to the Forty-second and Forty-third Congresses (March 4, 1871–March 3, 1875); was not a candidate for renomination in 1874; resumed his business activities in St. Paul, Minn., where he died on October 3, 1889; interment in Oakland Cemetery.

AVERY, Daniel, a Representative from New York; born in Groton, Conn., September 18, 1766; attended the common schools; appointed ensign in the Sixth Company, Eighth Regiment of the Connecticut Militia, and served as lieutenant and captain until May 1794; moved to Aurora, N. Y., in 1795 and subsequently became the owner of a large tract of land which was farmed by tenants; elected as a Democrat to the Twelfth and Thirteenth Congresses (March 4, 1811–March 3, 1815); elected to the Fourteenth Congress to fill the vacancy caused by the resignation of Enos T. Throop and served from September 30, 1816, to March 3, 1817; resumed the management of his estate; connected with the land office at Albany, N. Y., for twenty years; died in Aurora, Cayuga County, N. Y., January 30, 1842; interment in Oak Glen Cemetery.

AVERY, John, a Representative from Michigan; born in Watertown, Jefferson County, N. Y., February 29, 1824; moved with his parents to Michigan in 1836; attended the common schools; entered Grass Lake Academy, Jackson, Mich., where he studied medicine for two years; was graduated from the Cleveland Medical College in 1850 and commenced the practice of medicine in Ionia, Mich.; moved to Otsego, Mich., in 1852 and continued the practice of his profession; during the Civil War was assistant surgeon and surgeon of the Twenty-first

Regiment, Michigan Volunteer Infantry; served in the Army of the Cumberland in Kentucky and Tennessee and was with Sherman on his march to the sea; settled in Greenville, Mich., in 1868 and again engaged in the practice of medicine; member of the State house of representatives in 1869 and 1870; appointed a member of the State board of health in 1880 and reappointed in 1886; elected as a Republican to the Fifty-third and Fifty-fourth Congresses (March 4, 1893–March 3, 1897); was not a candidate for renomination in 1896; engaged in the practice of medicine in Greenville, Mich., where he died January 21, 1914; interment in Forest Home Cemetery.

AVERY, William Henry, a Representative from Kansas; born in Wakefield, Clay County, Kans., August 11, 1911; attended the public schools; was graduated from the University of Kansas at Lawrence in 1934, majoring in political science; engaged in business as a farmer and stockman near Wakefield, Kans., since 1935; director of the Wakefield Rural High School Board of Education since 1946; served in the Kansas State House of Representatives from 1951 until elected to Congress; member of Legislative Council of Kansas 1953–1955; elected as a Republican to the Eighty-fourth, Eighty-fifth, and Eighty-sixth Congresses (January 3, 1955–January 3, 1961). *Reelected to the Eighty-seventh Congress.*

AVERY, William Tecumsah, a Representative from Tennessee; born in Hardeman County, Tenn., November 11, 1819; attended the common schools and was graduated from old Jackson College near Columbia, Maury County, Tenn.; studied law; was admitted to the bar; moved to Memphis, Tenn., in 1840 and engaged in the practice of law; member of the State house of representatives in 1843; elected as a Democrat to the Thirty-fifth and Thirty-sixth Congresses (March 4, 1857–March 3, 1861); was not a candidate for renomination in 1860; during the Civil War served as lieutenant colonel in the Confederate Army; clerk of the criminal court of Shelby County 1870–1874; resumed the practice of law in Memphis, Tenn.; accidentally drowned in Ten Mile Bayou, Crittenden County, Ark., opposite Memphis, Tenn., May 22, 1880; interment in Elmwood Cemetery, Memphis, Tenn.

AVIS, Samuel Brashear, a Representative from West Virginia; born in Harrisonburg, Rockingham County, Va., February 19, 1872; attended the public schools and Staunton (Va.) Military Academy; was graduated from the law department of Washington and Lee University, Lexington, Va.; was admitted to the bar in 1893 and commenced practice in Charleston, W. Va.; commissioned senior captain of Company A, Second West Virginia Volunteer Infantry, during the Spanish-American War in 1898; served until 1899, when he was honorably discharged; prosecuting attorney of Kanawha County, W. Va., from January 1, 1900, to December 31, 1912; assistant United States attorney for the southern district of West Virginia from August 22 to November 15, 1904; elected as a Republican to the Sixty-third Congress (March 4, 1913–March 3, 1915); unsuccessful candidate for reelection in 1914 to the Sixty-fourth Congress; resumed the practice of law; was killed by lightning in Charleston, W. Va., June 8, 1924; interment in Spring Hill Cemetery, Spring Hill, W. Va.

AXTELL, Samuel Beach, a Representative from California; born near Columbus, Franklin County, Ohio, October 14, 1819; attended the local schools and Oberlin College; was graduated from Western Reserve College, Hudson, Ohio; studied law; was admitted to the bar in 1843 and commenced practice in Mount Clemens, Mich.; went to California in 1851 and engaged in mining in Amador County; prosecuting attorney of Amador

County 1854–1860; moved to San Francisco in 1860 and practiced law; elected as a Democrat to the Fortieth and Forty-first Congresses (March 4, 1867–March 3, 1871); was not a candidate for renomination in 1870; affiliated with the Republican Party during the administration of President Grant; appointed Governor of Utah Territory in 1874 and subsequently, in 1875, transferred to the office of Governor of the Territory of New Mexico; chief justice of the supreme court of the Territory of New Mexico from August 1882 until his resignation, tendered May 1, 1885, to take effect May 25 of the same year; engaged in the practice of law in Santa Fe, N. Mex.; at the time of his death was counsel of the Southern Pacific Railroad Co. and chairman of the Republican Territorial committee; died while on a visit to Morristown, Morris County, N. J., August 6, 1891; interment in First Presbyterian Church Cemetery.

AYCRIGG, John Bancker, a Representative from New Jersey; born in New York City July 9, 1798; studied medicine; was graduated from the College of Physicians and Surgeons (now the medical department of Columbia University), New York City, in 1818 and was admitted to practice in New York; moved to New Jersey and located at Paramus; elected as a Whig to the Twenty-fifth Congress (March 4, 1837–March 3, 1839); presented credentials as a Member-elect to the Twenty-sixth Congress but was not permitted to qualify; elected to the Twenty-seventh Congress (March 4, 1841–March 3, 1843); was not a candidate for renomination in 1842 to the Twenty-eighth Congress; resumed the practice of medicine in Paramus; moved to Passaic, N. J., and died there November 8, 1856; interment in Paramus Church Cemetery, Ridgewood, N. J.

AYER, Richard Small, a Representative from Virginia; born in Montville, Waldo County, Maine, October 9, 1829; attended the common schools; was engaged for a number of years in agricultural and mercantile pursuits; during the Civil War enlisted in 1861 in the Union Army as a private in Company A, Fourth Regiment, Maine Volunteer Infantry; subsequently promoted to first lieutenant and was mustered out as a captain on March 22, 1863, for disability; settled in Virginia in 1865 and located near Warsaw; delegate to the Virginia constitutional convention in 1867; upon the readmission of the State of Virginia to representation was elected as a Republican to the Forty-first Congress and served from January 31, 1870, until March 3, 1871; was not a candidate for renomination in 1870; engaged in agricultural pursuits; returned to Montville, Maine; member of the State house of representatives in 1888; died in Liberty, Waldo County, Maine, December 14, 1896; interment in Mount Repose Cemetery, Montville, Maine.

AYERS, Roy Elmer, a Representative from Montana; born on a ranch near Lewistown, Fergus County, Mont., November 9, 1882; attended the rural schools and Lewistown High School; was graduated from the law department of Valparaiso (Ind.) University in 1903; was admitted to the bar the same year and commenced practice in Lewistown, Mont.; also became engaged in ranching and the raising of livestock; served as attorney of Fergus County, Mont., 1905–1909; member of the Montana Board of Education 1908–1912; judge of the tenth judicial district of Montana 1913–1921 and justice of the State supreme court from January 1922 until his resignation on November 22, 1922, when he resumed the private practice of law in Lewistown, Mont.; during the First World War served as chairman of the Fergus County Exemption Board; delegate to the Democratic National Conventions in 1920 and 1940 and to every State Democratic Convention 1906–1940; elected as a Democrat to the Seventy-third and Seventy-fourth Congresses (March 4, 1933–January 3, 1937); was not a candidate for renomination, having become a gubernatorial candidate for the Democratic nomination; elected Governor of Montana and served from January 4, 1937, until January 6, 1941; resumed his ranching activities; died in Lewistown, Mont., May 23, 1955; interment in Lewistown City Cemetery.

AYRES, Steven Beckwith, a Representative from New York; born in Fort Dodge, Iowa, October 27, 1861; moved with his parents to Elmira, N. Y., in 1866; attended the grammar school; moved to Penn Yan, N. Y., in 1873; attended the Penn Yan Academy and was graduated from Syracuse (N. Y.) University, in 1882; engaged in the publishing business at Penn Yan and was editor of the Yates County Chronicle; delegate to the Republican State convention in 1884; moved to New York City in 1893 and engaged in the advertising business; declined the Democratic nomination as candidate for the New York State Assembly in 1910; elected as an Independent Democrat to the Sixty-second Congress (March 4, 1911–March 3, 1913); unsuccessful candidate for reelection as an Independent Democrat in 1912 to the Sixty-third Congress; author of several books and many historical articles; lecturer in the New York University Summer School in 1914; engaged in the cultivation of oranges at Clearwater, Fla., in winter and in the real-estate business at Woodstock, N. Y., during the summer; died in New York City, N. Y., June 1, 1929; interment in the Clearwater Cemetery, Clearwater, Fla.

AYRES, William Augustus, a Representative from Kansas; born in Elizabethtown, Hardin County, Ill., April 19, 1867; moved with his parents to Sedgwick County, Kans., in 1881; attended the common schools and Garfield University (now Friends University), Wichita, Kans.; was admitted to the bar in 1893 and commenced practice in Wichita, Kans.; clerk of the Court of Appeals of Kansas 1897–1901; prosecuting attorney of Sedgwick County 1906–1910; elected as a Democrat to the Sixty-fourth, Sixty-fifth, and Sixty-sixth Congresses (March 4, 1915–March 3, 1921); unsuccessful candidate for reelection in 1920 to the Sixty-seventh Congress; elected to the Sixty-eighth and to the five succeeding Congresses and served from March 4, 1923, until his resignation effective August 22, 1934, having been appointed a member of the Federal Trade Commission on June 30, 1934, in which capacity he served until his death in Washington, D. C., February 17, 1952; interment in Old Mission Cemetery, Wichita, Kans.

AYRES, William Hanes, a Representative from Ohio; born in Eagle Rock, Botetourt County, Va., February 5, 1916; moved with his parents to West Virginia and later to Lorain County, Ohio; attended the Weller Township High School; was graduated from Western Reserve University, Cleveland, Ohio, in 1936; salesman for heating equipment in Akron, Ohio, 1936–1944; during World War II served as a private in the United States Army until discharged December 17, 1945; president of the Ayres Heating & Insulation Co., Akron, Ohio, since 1946; elected as a Republican to the Eighty-second and to the four succeeding Congresses (January 3, 1951–January 3, 1961). *Reelected to the Eighty-seventh Congress.*

B

BABBITT, Clinton, a Representative from Wisconsin; born in Westmoreland, Cheshire County, N. H., November 16, 1831; attended the common schools and was graduated from Keene (N. H.) Academy; moved to Wisconsin in 1853 and settled near Beloit, Rock County; engaged in agricultural pursuits; elected alderman and was a member of the first city council of Beloit; unsuccessful Democratic candidate for election in 1880 to the

Forty-seventh Congress; appointed postmaster of Beloit by President Cleveland on August 2, 1886, and served until August 17, 1889, when a successor was appointed; appointed secretary of the State agricultural society of Wisconsin in 1885 and served until 1899; elected as a Democrat to the Fifty-second Congress (March 4, 1891–March 3, 1893); unsuccessful candidate for reelection in 1892 to the Fifty-third Congress; retired from public life and active business pursuits and resided in Beloit, Wis., until his death there on March 11, 1907; interment in the Protestant Cemetery.

BABBITT, Elijah, a Representative from Pennsylvania; born in Providence, R. I., July 29, 1795; moved with his parents to New York State in 1805; received an academic education; moved to Milton, Northumberland County, Pa., in 1816; studied law; was admitted to the bar in March 1824 and commenced practice in Milton; moved to Erie, Pa., in 1826 and continued the practice of law; served as attorney for the borough and subsequently for the city of Erie; prosecuting attorney for Erie County in 1833; deputy attorney general for the State in 1834 and 1835; member of the State house of representatives in 1836 and 1837; served in the State senate 1843–1846; elected as a Unionist to the Thirty-sixth Congress and as a Republican to the Thirty-seventh Congress (March 4, 1859–March 3, 1863); was not a candidate for reelection in 1862 to the Twenty-eighth Congress; resumed the practice of his profession; died in Erie, Pa., January 9, 1887; interment in Erie Cemetery.

BABCOCK, Alfred, a Representative from New York; born in Hamilton, Madison County, N. Y., April 15, 1805; attended the local schools and Gaines (N. Y.) Academy; studied medicine; moved to Gaines, Orleans County, N. Y., where he practiced his profession; elected a member of the board of trustees of the village of Gaines at its first election on May 28, 1839; elected as a Whig to the Twenty-seventh Congress (March 4, 1841–March 3, 1843); resumed the practice of medicine in Gaines, N. Y.; moved to Illinois in 1850 and settled in Galesburg, Knox County, where he continued the practice of his profession until his death on May 16, 1871; interment in Hope Cemetery.

BABCOCK, Joseph Weeks (grandson of Joseph Weeks), a Representative from Wisconsin; born in Swanton, Franklin County, Vt., March 6, 1850; moved to Linn County, Iowa, with his parents, who settled near Mount Vernon in 1855; attended the common schools of Mount Vernon and Cedar Falls; moved to Necedah, Juneau County, Wis., in 1872 and engaged in the lumber business; member of the Wisconsin State Assembly 1889–1893; chairman of the Republican National Congressional Committee in 1894 and 1902; delegate at large to the Republican National Convention at Chicago in 1904; elected as a Republican to the Fifty-third and to the six succeeding Congresses (March 4, 1893–March 3, 1907); declined to be a candidate for renomination in 1906; retired from public life and active business pursuits and resided in Washington, D. C., until his death there on April 27, 1909; remains were cremated and the ashes deposited in the monument on the family plot in Rock Creek Cemetery.

BABCOCK, Leander, a Representative from New York; born in Paris, Oneida County, N. Y., March 1, 1811; was graduated from Union College, Schenectady, N. Y., in 1830; studied law; was admitted to the bar in 1834; moved to Oswego, N. Y., and commenced the practice of law; district attorney for Oswego County 1841–1843; mayor of Oswego in 1850 and 1851; elected as a Democrat to the Thirty-second Congress (March 4, 1851–March 3, 1853); president of the board of education in 1853 and 1855; died in Richfield Springs, N. Y., August 18, 1864; interment in Riverside Cemetery, Oswego, N. Y.

BABCOCK, William, a Representative from New York; born in Hinsdale, Westmoreland County, N. H., in 1785; moved to Penn Yan, N. Y., in 1813 and engaged in mercantile pursuits; upon the formation of Yates County was appointed by the Governor as the first county treasurer; elected to the Twenty-second Congress (March 4, 1831–March 3, 1833); resumed mercantile pursuits and also was engaged as a hotel keeper; died in Penn Yan, Yates County, N. Y., October 20, 1838; interment in City Hill Cemetery in Torrey Township, near Penn Yan.

BABKA, John Joseph, a Representative from Ohio; born in Cleveland, Ohio, March 16, 1884; attended the public schools; was graduated from the Cleveland Law School in 1908; was admitted to the bar the same year and commenced practice in Cleveland, Ohio; special counsel to the attorney general of Ohio in 1911 and 1912; assistant prosecuting attorney of Cuyahoga County 1912–1919; elected as a Democrat to the Sixty-sixth Congress (March 4, 1919–March 3, 1921); unsuccessful candidate for reelection in 1920 to the Sixty-seventh Congress; resumed the practice of law; delegate to the Democratic National Conventions in 1920 and 1932; appointed deputy superintendent of building and loans to assist in liquidating the City Savings & Loan Co. in 1935, and at the time of his death was acting as liquidating attorney for the division of savings and loan associations of the department of commerce of Ohio; died at Cleveland, Ohio, March 22, 1937; interment in Calvary Cemetery.

BACHARACH, Isaac, a Representative from New Jersey; born in Philadelphia, Pa., January 5, 1870; moved to New Jersey in 1881 with his parents, who settled in Atlantic City; attended the public schools; entered the real-estate business and also became interested in the lumber business and in banking; member of the council of Atlantic City, N. J., 1905–1910; member of the State house of assembly in 1911; delegate to the Republican National Convention at Chicago in 1920; elected as a Republican to the Sixty-fourth and to the ten succeeding Congresses (March 4, 1915–January 3, 1937); unsuccessful candidate for reelection in 1936 to the Seventy-fifth Congress; engaged in the real-estate and insurance business in Atlantic City, N. J., until his death there on September 5, 1956; interment in Mount Sinai Cemetery, Philadelphia, Pa.

BACHMAN, Nathan Lynn, a Senator from Tennessee; born in Chattanooga, Tenn., August 2, 1878; attended the public schools, Baylor Preparatory School for Boys, Chattanooga, Tenn., Southwestern Presbyterian University, Clarksville, Tenn., Central University, Danville, Ky., Washington and Lee University, Lexington, Va., and the University of Chattanooga Law School, Chattanooga, Tenn.; was graduated from the law department of the University of Virginia at Charlottesville in 1903, admitted to the bar in 1903, and commenced practice in Chattanooga, Tenn., in the same year; city attorney of Chattanooga 1906–1908; served as judge of the circuit court of Hamilton County, Tenn., 1912–1918; served as associate justice of the Supreme Court of Tennessee from 1918 until his resignation in 1924, to seek the nomination for United States Senator; unsuccessful candidate for nomination for United States Senator in 1924; resumed the practice of law the same year; appointed and subsequently elected as a Democrat to the United States Senate to fill the vacancy caused by the resignation of Cordell Hull; reelected in 1936 and served from February 28, 1933, until his death in Washington, D. C., April 23, 1937; interment in Forest Hills Cemetery, Chattanooga, Tenn.

BACHMAN, Reuben Knecht, a Representative from Pennsylvania; born in Williams Township, Northampton County, Pa., August 6, 1834; attended the common schools; taught school for several years; entered the mercantile and milling business in Durham, Bucks County, Pa.; elected as a Democrat to the Forty-sixth Congress (March 4, 1879–March 3, 1881); was not a candidate for renomination in 1880; delegate to the Democratic National Convention at Chicago in 1884; engaged in the lumber business and the manufacture of builders' millwork at Riegelsville, Pa., and Phillipsburg, N. J.; died in Easton Pa., September 19, 1911; interment in Durham Cemetery, near Durham, Bucks County, Pa.

BACHMANN, Carl George, a Representative from West Virginia; born in Wheeling, Ohio County, W. Va., May 14, 1890; attended the public schools; was graduated from Linsly Institute, Wheeling, W. Va., in 1908; attended Washington and Jefferson College, Washington, Pa., for two years; was graduated from the department of arts and science of West Virginia University at Morgantown in 1913 and from its law department in 1915; was admitted to the bar in 1915 and commenced practice in Wheeling; appointed assistant prosecuting attorney of Ohio County in January 1917; was subsequently elected prosecuting attorney in January 1921 and served until January 1925; delegate to the Republican State conventions 1920–1944; alternate delegate to the Republican National Convention in 1932 and delegate in 1936, 1944, 1948, and 1952; elected as a Republican to the Sixty-ninth and to the three succeeding Congresses (March 4, 1925–March 3, 1933); unsuccessful candidate for reelection in 1932 to the Seventy-third Congress and for election in 1934 to the Seventy-fourth Congress; resumed the practice of law in Wheeling, W. Va.; served on the city council of Wheeling, W. Va., 1939–1941; member of the West Virginia State liquor control commission 1941–1944; elected mayor of Wheeling in 1947 for the term ending June 30, 1951; engaged in banking and the practice of law; is a resident of Wheeling, W. Va.

BACON, Augustus Octavius (cousin of William S. Howard), a Senator from Georgia; born in Bryan County, Ga., October 20, 1839; attended the common schools in Liberty and Troup Counties; was graduated from the literary department of the University of Georgia at Athens in 1859 and from its law department in 1860; was admitted to the bar in 1860 and commenced practice in Atlanta, Ga.; entered the Confederate Army at the beginning of the Civil War and served during the campaigns of 1861 and 1862 as adjutant of the Ninth Georgia Regiment in the Army of Northern Virginia; subsequently commissioned captain in the Provisional Army of the Confederacy and assigned to general staff duty; at the close of the war resumed the practice of law in Macon, Ga.; presidential elector on the Democratic ticket of Seymour and Blair in 1868; member of the State house of representatives 1871–1886, serving as speaker pro tempore for two terms and as speaker eight years; president of the Democratic State convention in 1880; delegate to the Democratic National Convention at Chicago in 1884; elected as a Democrat to the United States Senate in 1894; reelected in 1900; appointed and subsequently reelected in 1907, and again in 1913, and served from March 4, 1895, until his death in Washington, D. C., February 14, 1914; funeral services were held in the Chamber of the United States Senate; interment in Rose Hill Cemetery, Macon, Ga.

BACON, Ezekiel (son of John Bacon and father of William Johnson Bacon), a Representative from Massachusetts; born in Boston, Mass., September 1, 1776; received a liberal schooling and was graduated from Yale College in 1794; attended the Litchfield Law School and afterwards studied with Nathan Dane in Beverly; was admitted to the bar in 1800 and commenced practice in Stockbridge, Mass.; member of the State house of representatives in 1805 and 1806; elected as a Democrat

to the Tenth Congress to fill the vacancy caused by the resignation of Barnabas Bidwell; reelected to the Eleventh and Twelfth Congresses and served from September 16, 1807, to March 3, 1813; chief justice of the court of common pleas for the western district of Massachusetts 1811–1814; First Comptroller of the United States Treasury from February 11, 1814, to February 28, 1815, when he resigned; moved to Utica, Oneida County, N. Y., in 1816; appointed associate justice of the court of common pleas in 1818; member of the State assembly in 1819; delegate to the State constitutional convention in 1821; unsuccessful candidate for election in 1824 to the Nineteenth Congress; at time of his death he was the oldest surviving Member of Congress and the last representative of the administration of President Madison; died in Utica, N. Y., October 18, 1870; interment in Forest Hill Cemetery.

BACON, Henry, a Representative from New York; born in Brooklyn, N. Y., March 14, 1846; attended the Mount Pleasant Academy in Sing Sing, the Episcopal Academy in Cheshire, Conn., and was graduated from Union College in 1865; studied law; was admitted to the bar in 1866 and commenced practice in Goshen, N. Y.; elected as a Democrat to the Forty-ninth Congress to fill the vacancy caused by the death of Lewis Beach; reelected to the Fiftieth Congress and served from December 6, 1886, until March 3, 1889; unsuccessful candidate for reelection in 1888 to the Fifty-first Congress; elected to the Fifty-second Congress (March 4, 1891–March 3, 1893); unsuccessful candidate for renomination in 1892; resumed the practice of law in Goshen; delegate to the Democratic National Convention at Chicago in 1892; corporation counsel of Goshen 1909–1915; died in Goshen, N. Y., on March 25, 1915; interment in Slate Hill Cemetery.

BACON, John (father of Ezekiel Bacon and grandfather of William Johnson Bacon), a Representative from Massachusetts; born in Canterbury, Conn., April 5, 1738; was graduated from Princeton College in 1765; studied theology; had charge of the Old South Church, Boston, from September 25, 1771, until dismissed February 8, 1775, owing to differences of opinion; located in Stockbridge; studied law; was admitted to the bar and practiced; served on the committee of correspondence, inspection, and safety in 1777; member of the State constitutional convention in 1779 and 1780; member of the State house of representatives 1780, 1783, 1784, 1786, 1789–1791, and in 1793; member of the State senate 1781, 1782, 1794–1796, 1798, and 1803–1806, serving as president in 1806; elected to the Seventh Congress (March 4, 1801–March 3, 1803); presidential elector on the Democratic ticket of Jefferson and Clinton in 1804; presiding judge of the court of common pleas; chief justice of the State supreme court in 1809; died in Stockbridge, Berkshire County, Mass., October 25, 1820; interment in Stockbridge Cemetery.

BACON, Mark Reeves, a Representative from Michigan; born in Phillipstown, White County, Ill., February 29, 1852; attended the public schools of his native city; taught school at Bolivar (Mo.) Academy in 1871; studied law; was admitted to the bar on July 4, 1876, and commenced practice in Fairfield, Wayne County, Ill.; city attorney of Fairfield, Ill.; delegate to several State conventions; moved to Orlando, Fla., in 1882 and to Jacksonville, Fla., in 1886 and engaged in the abstract business; moved to Wyandotte, Wayne County, Mich., in 1895 and became associated with the Michigan Alkali Co., manufacturers of soda ash and allied materials; presented credentials as a Republican Member-elect to the Sixty-fifth Congress and served from March 4 until December 13, 1917, when he was succeeded by Samuel W. Beakes, who contested his election; was not a candidate for renomination in 1918; retired from public life and active business pursuits in 1918 and resided in Wyandotte, Mich., until 1927, when he spent the winters at his Pasadena, Calif., home and the summers at his Wyandotte home; died at his winter home in Pasadena, Calif., August 20, 1941; interment in San Gabriel Cemetery, San Gabriel, Calif.

BACON, Robert Low, a Representative from New York; born in Jamaica Plains, Boston, Mass., July 23, 1884; attended the public schools; was graduated from Harvard University in 1907 and from its law school in 1910; was an employee of the United States Treasury Department in 1910 and 1911; moved to Old Westbury, N. Y., in 1911 and engaged in the banking business in New York City 1911–1922; delegate to several State conventions; delegate to the Republican National Convention at Chicago in 1920; attended the business men's training camp at Plattsburg in 1915; served on the Texas border with the New York National Guard in 1916; during the First World War served with the United States military forces from April 24, 1917, to January 2, 1919, attaining the rank of major; awarded the Distinguished Service Medal; commissioned in the United States Officers' Reserve Corps with the rank of lieutenant colonel in 1919; promoted to colonel in January 1923 and served until his death; elected as a Republican to the Sixty-eighth and to the seven succeeding Congresses and served from March 4, 1923, until his death at Lake Success, Long Island, N. Y., en route from a visit to New York City, September 12, 1938; interment in Arlington National Cemetery, Fort Myer, Va.

BACON, William Johnson (son of Ezekiel Bacon and grandson of John Bacon), a Representative from New York; born in Williamstown, Mass., February 18, 1803; moved with his parents to Utica, N. Y., in 1815; was graduated from Hamilton College, Clinton, N. Y., in 1822; studied law and was graduated from the Litchfield Law School in 1824; was admitted to the bar the same year and commenced practice in Utica, Oneida County, N. Y.; appointed city attorney in 1837; member of the State assembly in 1850; elected trustee of Hamilton College in 1851; elected judge of the State supreme court of the fifth district in 1854 and served until 1870; president of the Utica Cemetery Association in 1874; elected as a Republican to the Forty-fifth Congress (March 4, 1877–March 3, 1879); was not a candidate for renomination in 1878; resumed the practice of law; died in Utica, N. Y., July 3, 1889; interment in Forest Hill Cemetery.

BADGER, De Witt Clinton, a Representative from Ohio; born near London, Madison County, Ohio, August 7, 1858; attended the country schools in Madison County and Mount Union College, Alliance, Ohio; taught school from 1875 to 1880; studied law; was admitted to the bar in 1881 and commenced practice in London, Ohio; prosecuting attorney of Madison County 1882–1885; moved to Columbus, Ohio, and was elected judge of the court of common pleas in 1893; reelected in 1897 and served until 1903, when he resigned, having been elected to Congress; elected as a Democrat to the Fifty-eighth Congress (March 4, 1903–March 3, 1905); declined to be a candidate for renomination in 1904; resumed the practice of law in Columbus, Ohio; mayor of Columbus 1906–1908; died in Columbus, Ohio, May 20, 1926; interment in Green Lawn Cemetery.

BADGER, George Edmund, a Senator from North Carolina; born in New Bern, N. C., April 17, 1795; instructed by private teachers and attended preparatory school at New Bern; attended Yale College 1810 and 1811; studied law; was admitted to the bar in 1814 and commenced practice in New Bern; member of the house of commons of North Carolina in 1816; elected judge of the superior court in 1820 and served until 1825, when he resigned; moved to Raleigh, N. C.; appointed Secretary of the Navy in the Cabinet of President William H. Harrison March 5, 1841; reappointed by President John Tyler and served until September 11, 1841, when he resigned to resume the practice of his profession; elected as a Whig to the United States Senate in 1846 to fill the vacancy caused by the resignation of William H. Haywood; reelected in 1849 and served from November 25, 1846, to March 3, 1855; was not a candidate for reelection; was nominated by President Fillmore as an Associate Justice of the Supreme Court in 1853, but was not confirmed by the Senate; upon his retirement from the Senate March 3, 1855, that body, in executive session, unanimously adopted a resolution expressing regret at his retirement—an unusual action; returned to Raleigh and resumed the practice of law; member of the State convention in 1861; died in Raleigh, N. C., May 11, 1866; interment in Oakwood Cemetery.

BADGER, Luther, a Representative from New York; born in Partridgefield (now Peru), Mass., April 10, 1785; moved with his father to New York in 1786; attended Hamilton College in 1807; studied law; was admitted to the bar in 1812 and commenced practice in Jamesville, Onondaga County, N. Y.; judge advocate of the Twenty-seventh Brigade, New York Militia, 1819–1827; elected to the Nineteenth Congress (March 4, 1825–March 3, 1827); resumed the practice of his profession; moved to Broome County in 1832; examiner in chancery 1833–1847; appointed commissioner of United States loans in 1840, and served until 1843; elected district attorney of Broome County and served from July 5, 1847, until his resignation in November 1849; resumed the practice of law in Jordan, Onondaga County, N. Y., where he died in 1869; interment in Jordan Cemetery.

BAER, George, Jr., a Representative from Maryland; born in Frederick, Md., in 1763; attended the common schools; engaged in mercantile pursuits; member of the State house of delegates in 1794; elected as a Federalist to the Fifth and Sixth Congresses (March 4, 1797–March 3, 1801); again a member of the State house of delegates, in 1808 and 1809; judge of the orphans' court of Frederick County in 1813; elected to the Fourteenth Congress (March 4, 1815–March 3, 1817); resumed his former mercantile pursuits; mayor of Frederick in 1820; died in Frederick, Frederick County, Md., April 3, 1834; interment in Mount Olivet Cemetery.

BAER, John Miller, a Representative from North Dakota; born at Blackcreek, Outagamie County, Wis., March 29, 1886; attended the public schools; was graduated from Lawrence University, Appleton, Wis., in 1909; moved to Beach, Golden Valley County, N. Dak., in 1909; engaged as a civil engineer and in agricultural pursuits 1909–1915; also furnished cartoons and articles to newspapers 1909–1917; postmaster of Beach, N. Dak., 1909–1915; elected as a Nonpartisan League candidate to the Sixty-fifth Congress to fill the vacancy caused by the death of Henry T. Helgesen; reelected as a Republican to the Sixty-sixth Congress and served from July 10, 1917, to March 3, 1921; unsuccessful candidate for reelection in 1920 to the Sixty-seventh Congress; resumed activities as a cartoonist and journalist; is a resident of Chevy Chase, Md.

BAGBY, Arthur Pendleton, a Senator from Alabama; born in Louise County, Va., in 1794; studied law; was admitted to the bar in 1819 and commenced practice in Claiborne, Ala.; member of the State house of representatives in 1821, 1822, 1824, and 1834–1836, serving as speaker in 1822 and 1836; served in the State senate in 1825; Governor of Alabama 1837–1841; elected as a Democrat to the United States Senate to fill the vacancy caused by the resignation of Clement C. Clay and served from November 24, 1841, until June 16, 1848, when he resigned to accept a position in the diplomatic corps; United States Minister to Russia from June 17, 1848, until May 14, 1849; member of the commission to codify the State laws of Alabama in 1852; moved to Mobile, Ala., in 1856, where he died September 21, 1858; interment in Magnolia Cemetery, Mobile, Ala.

BAGBY, John Courts, a Representative from Illinois; born in Glasgow, Ky., January 24, 1819; attended the public schools; was graduated as a civil engineer from Bacon College, Harrodsburg, Ky., in June 1840; studied law; was admitted to the bar in March 1845 and commenced practice in Rushville, Schuyler County, Ill., in April 1846; elected as a Democrat to the Forty-fourth Congress (March 4, 1875–March 3, 1877); was not a candidate for renomination in 1876; resumed the practice of his profession in Rushville, Ill.; judge of Schuyler County 1882–1885; judge of the sixth judicial circuit court of Illinois 1885–1891; resumed the practice of law; died in Rushville, Ill., April 4, 1896; interment in Rushville Cemetery.

BAGLEY, George Augustus, a Representative from New York; born in Watertown, Jefferson County, N. Y., July 22, 1826; received an academic training; studied law; was admitted to the New York bar in 1847 and commenced practice in Watertown, N. Y.; retired from the practice of his profession in 1853 to engage in the manufacture of iron; president of the village of Watertown in 1866; supervisor of the town 1865–1868; elected as a Republican to the Forty-fourth and Forty-fifth Congresses (March 4, 1875–March 3, 1879); resumed the manufacture of iron; died in Watertown, N. Y., May 12, 1915; interment in Brookside Cemetery.

BAGLEY, John Holroyd, Jr., a Representative from New York; born in Hudson, Columbia County, N. Y., November 26, 1832; attended the common schools; went to California in 1851 and engaged in mining and other pursuits; returned to New York and engaged in steamboating on the Hudson River; settled in Catskill and engaged in mercantile pursuits and the manufacture of leather; supervisor of the town of Catskill 1860–1864; elected as a Democrat to the Forty-fourth Congress (March 4, 1875–March 3, 1877); was not a candidate for renomination in 1876; resumed his former mercantile pursuits; elected to the Forty-eighth Congress (March 4, 1883–March 3, 1885); was not a candidate for renomination in 1884; engaged in banking and the insurance business and also served as vice president of the Catskill Mountain Railway Co.; trustee of the village of Catskill, Greene County, N. Y.; member of the State assembly in 1888; unsuccessful candidate for election in 1896 to the Fifty-fifth Congress; died in Catskill, N. Y., October 23, 1902; interment in the Village Cemetery.

BAILEY, Alexander Hamilton, a Representative from New York; born in Minisink, N. Y., August 14, 1817; was graduated from Princeton College in 1837; studied law; was admitted to the bar and commenced practice; examiner in chancery of Greene County 1840–1842; justice of the peace of the town of Catskill for four years; member of the State assembly in 1849; judge of Greene County 1851–1855; moved to Rome, Oneida County, N. Y., in 1856 and continued the practice of law; served in the State senate 1861–1864; elected as a Republican to the Fortieth Congress to fill the vacancy caused by the resignation of Roscoe Conkling; reelected to the Forty-first Congress and served from November 30, 1867, to March 3, 1871; was not a candidate for renomination in 1870; elected judge of the Oneida County Court in 1871 and served until his death in Rome, Oneida County, N. Y., April 20, 1874; interment in Rome Cemetery.

BAILEY, Cleveland Monroe, a Representative from West Virginia; born on a farm near St. Marys, Pleasants County, W.

Va., July 15, 1886; attended the public schools, and West Liberty State College, West Liberty, W. Va.; was graduated from Geneva College, Beaver Falls, Pa., in 1908; high school principal at Clarksburg, W. Va., in 1917 and 1918; district supervisor of schools 1919–1922; councilman of Clarksburg, W. Va., 1921–1923; Associated Press editor in Clarksburg, W. Va., 1923–1933; assistant State auditor from March 4, 1933, to May 15, 1941; State budget director 1941–1944; delegate to the Democratic National Convention at Chicago in 1932; elected as a Democrat to the Seventy-ninth Congress (January 3, 1945–January 3, 1947); unsuccessful candidate for reelection in 1946 to the Eightieth Congress; State tax statistician in 1947 and 1948; elected to the Eighty-first and to the five succeeding Congresses (January 3, 1949–January 3, 1961). *Reelected to the Eighty-seventh Congress.*

BAILEY, David Jackson, a Representative from Georgia; born in Lexington, Ga., March 11, 1812; educated by a private tutor; moved to Jackson, Butts County, in 1829; studied law; was admitted to the bar in 1831 and practiced; elected to the State legislature before he was twenty-one, but was not permitted to take his seat because he was not of legal age; served as captain of a company through the Seminole and Creek Wars; served in the State house of representatives in 1835 and 1847; member of the State senate in 1838, 1849, and 1850; delegate to the Democratic county conventions in 1839 and 1850; secretary of the State senate 1839–1841; elected as a State Rights Democrat to the Thirty-second and Thirty-third Congresses (March 4, 1851–March 3, 1855); unsuccessful candidate for reelection in 1854 to the Thirty-fourth Congress; again a member of the State senate, in 1855 and 1856, and served as president; resumed the practice of law in Jackson, Ga.; member of the secession convention in 1861; entered the Confederate Army during the Civil War and became colonel of the Thirtieth Regiment, Georgia Infantry; moved to Griffin, Spalding County, Ga., in 1861, where he died June 14, 1897; interment in Oak Hill Cemetery.

BAILEY, Goldsmith Fox, a Representative from Massachusetts; born in Westmoreland, Cheshire County, N. H., July 17, 1823; attended the public schools of Fitchburg, Mass.; editor and publisher of the Bellows Falls (Vt.) Gazette in 1844; studied law; was admitted to the bar in 1848 and commenced practice in Fitchburg, Mass.; served on the school committee 1849–1854; appointed postmaster of Fitchburg on May 3, 1851 and served until May 4, 1853, when his successor was appointed; member of the State house of representatives in 1857; served in the State senate 1858–1860; elected as a Republican to the Thirty-seventh Congress and served from March 4, 1861, until his death in Fitchburg, Worcester County, Mass., May 8, 1862; interment in Laurel Hill Cemetery.

BAILEY, James Edmund, a Senator from Tennessee; born in Montgomery County, Tenn., August 15, 1822; attended the Clarksville Academy and the University of Nashville; studied law; was admitted to the Tennessee bar in 1843 and commenced practice in Clarksville, Montgomery County; elected as a Whig to the Tennessee House of Representatives in 1853; during the Civil War served in the Confederate Army as colonel of the Forty-ninth Tennessee Regiment; was appointed a member of the court of arbitration by the Governor of Tennessee in 1874; elected as a Democrat to the United States Senate to fill the vacancy caused by the death of Andrew Johnson and served from January 19, 1877, to March 3, 1881; was an unsuccessful candidate for reelection in 1880; resumed the practice of law; died in Clarksville, Tenn., December 29, 1885; interment in Greenwood Cemetery.

BAILEY, Jeremiah, a Representative from Maine; born in Little Compton, R. I., May 1, 1773; attended the common schools and was graduated from Brown University, Providence, R. I., in 1794; studied law; was admitted to the bar and commenced practice in Wiscasset, Maine (until 1820 a district of Massachusetts), in 1798; presidential elector on the Federalist ticket of Pinckney and King in 1808; member of the general court 1811–1814; judge of probate 1816–1834; elected as a Whig to the Twenty-fourth Congress (March 4, 1835–March 3, 1837); unsuccessful candidate for reelection in 1836 to the Twenty-fifth Congress; collector of customs of Wiscasset 1849–1853; died in Wiscasset, Lincoln County, Maine, July 6, 1853; interment in Evergreen Cemetery.

BAILEY, John, a Representative from Massachusetts; born in 1786 in that part of Stoughton, Norfolk County, Mass., which in 1797 was set apart and named Canton; was graduated from Brown University, Providence, R. I., in 1807; tutor and librarian at Providence, R. I., 1807–1814; member of the Massachusetts State House of Representatives 1814–1817; clerk in the Department of State in Washington, D. C., 1817–1823; presented credentials as a Member-elect to the Eighteenth Congress, but the election was contested on the ground that he was not a resident of the district he purported to represent, and by resolution of March 18, 1824, the House declared he was not entitled to the seat; returned to Canton, Mass., and was subsequently elected to fill the vacancy thus caused in this Congress; reelected to the Nineteenth, Twentieth, and Twenty-first Congresses and served from December 13, 1824, to March 3, 1831; was not a candidate for renomination in 1830; member of the State senate in 1831 and 1834; unsuccessful Anti-Masonic candidate for Governor in 1834; died in Dorchester, Mass., June 26, 1835; interment in Oak Grove Cemetery.

BAILEY, John Mosher, a Representative from New York; born in Bethlehem, N. Y., August 24, 1838; attended the public schools, and Hudson River Institute at Claverack, N. Y.; was graduated from Union College, Schenectady, N. Y., in 1861; during the Civil War entered the Union Army as a first lieutenant and adjutant of the One Hundred and Seventy-seventh Regiment, New York Volunteer Infantry, and served in the Department of the Gulf in 1862; graduated from the Albany Law School in 1864; was admitted to the bar the same year and commenced practice in Albany, N. Y.; assistant district attorney of Albany County 1865–1867; collector of internal revenue 1871–1874; district attorney of Albany County 1874–1877; elected as a Republican to the Forty-fifth Congress to fill the vacancy caused by the death of Terence J. Quinn; reelected to the Forty-sixth Congress and served from November 5, 1878, to March 3, 1881; was not a candidate for renomination in 1880; United States consul to Hamburg, Germany, by appointment of President Garfield 1881–1885; delegate to the Republican National Convention at Chicago in 1888; appointed by President Harrison as surveyor of customs at Albany, N. Y., 1889–1894; resumed the practice of law; died in Albany, N. Y., February 21, 1916; interment in Elmwood Cemetery, Bethlehem, N. Y.

BAILEY, Joseph, a Representative from Pennsylvania; born in Pennsbury Township, Chester County, Pa., March 18, 1810; attended the common schools; learned the trade of a hatter, which he carried on in Parkersville; served in the State house of representatives in 1840; member of the State senate in 1843; moved to Perry County in 1845; again a member of the State senate 1851–1853; State treasurer of Pennsylvania in 1854; studied law; was admitted to the bar in 1860; elected as a Democrat to the Thirty-seventh and Thirty-eighth Congresses (March 4, 1861–March 3, 1865); member of the State constitutional

convention in 1872; died at Bailey Station, Perry County, Pa., on August 26, 1885; interment in Bloomfield Cemetery, New Bloomfield, Pa.

BAILEY, Joseph Weldon, a Representative and a Senator from Texas; born near Crystal Springs, Copiah County, Miss., October 6, 1862; attended the common schools; studied law; was admitted to the bar in 1883 and commenced practice in Hazlehurst, Miss.; presidential elector on the Democratic ticket of Cleveland and Hendricks in 1884; moved to Gainesville, Tex., in 1885 and continued the practice of law; presidential elector on the Democratic ticket of Cleveland and Thurman in 1888; elected as a Democrat to the Fifty-second and to the four succeeding Congresses (March 4, 1891–March 3, 1901); was not a candidate for renomination in 1900; upon the organization of the Fifty-fifth Congress was the Democratic nominee for Speaker of the House of Representatives; elected to the United States Senate in 1901, reelected in 1907, and served from March 4, 1901, until January 3, 1913, when he resigned; resumed the practice of law in Washington, D. C.; subsequently, on March 3, 1921, moved to Dallas, Tex., and engaged in the practice of his profession; was an unsuccessful candidate for Governor of Texas in 1920; died in a courtroom in Sherman, Tex., on April 13, 1929, while defending a client; interment in Gainesville Cemetery, Gainesville, Tex.

BAILEY, Joseph Weldon, Jr. (son of the preceding), a Representative from Texas; born in Gainesville, Cooke County, Tex., December 15, 1892; attended the public schools in Gainesville, Tex., and Washington, D. C.; was graduated from Princeton University, Princeton, N. J., in 1915 and from the University of Virginia at Charlottesville in 1919; during the First World War served as a first lieutenant in the Three Hundred and Fourteenth Regiment of Field Artillery from August 15, 1917, to March 24, 1919; studied law; was admitted to the bar in 1920 and commenced practice in Fort Worth, Tex.; moved to Dallas, Tex., the same year and continued the practice of his profession; delegate to the Democratic State conventions from 1922 to 1934; elected as a Democrat to the Seventy-third Congress (March 4, 1933–January 3, 1935); was not a candidate for renomination in 1934, but was an unsuccessful candidate for the Democratic nomination for United States Senator; resumed the practice of law in Dallas, Tex.; during World War II served as a captain in the Marine Corps from May 13, 1942, until his death in an Army hospital at Gainesville, Tex., July 17, 1943; interment in Gainesville Cemetery.

BAILEY, Josiah William, a Senator from North Carolina; born in Warrenton, Warren County, N. C., September 14, 1873; moved with his parents to Raleigh, N. C., in 1877; attended the public schools and Raleigh (N. C.) Male Academy; was graduated from Wake Forest (N. C.) College in 1893; editor of the Biblical Recorder 1893–1907; member of the State board of agriculture 1896–1900; studied law; was admitted to the bar in 1908 and commenced practice in Raleigh, N. C.; presidential elector in 1908 on the ticket of Bryan and Kern; United States collector of internal revenue for North Carolina 1913–1921; member of the North Carolina Constitutional Commission in 1915; trustee of the University of North Carolina 1930; elected as a Democrat to the United States Senate in 1930; reelected in 1936 and again in 1942 and served from March 4, 1931, until his death in Raleigh, N. C., on December 15, 1946; interment in Oakwood Cemetery.

BAILEY, Ralph Emerson, a Representative from Missouri; born in Cainsville, Harrison County, Mo., July 14, 1878; moved to Illinois with his parents, who settled in Benton,

Franklin County, in 1880; attended the graded and high schools at Benton; moved to Bloomfield, Stoddard County, Mo., in 1897; was graduated from the Southeast Missouri Teachers' College at Cape Girardeau in 1901; afterwards took a special course in the University of Missouri at Columbia; studied law; was admitted to the bar in 1907 and commenced practice in Bloomfield, Mo.; moved to Sikeston, Scott County, Mo., in 1910 and continued the practice of law; city attorney 1912–1914 and again 1918–1922; served as a member of the board of regents of the Southeast Missouri Teachers' College; elected as a Republican to the Sixty-ninth Congress (March 4, 1925–March 3, 1927); was not a candidate for renomination in 1926 to the Seventieth Congress; resumed the practice of law in Sikeston, Mo.; died in Cape Girardeau, Mo., April 8, 1948; interment in the City Cemetery, Sikeston, Mo.

BAILEY, Theodorus, a Representative and a Senator from New York; born near Fishkill, Dutchess County, N. Y., October 12, 1758; attended the rural schools; studied law; was admitted to the bar in 1778 and commenced practice in Poughkeepsie, N. Y.; served as adjutant in Colonel Freer's regiment, New York Militia, and later in Col. Morris Graham's regiment during the Revolutionary War; served in the State militia as a major in 1786, as lieutenant colonel in 1797, and as brigadier general from 1801 until his resignation in 1805; elected as a Democrat to the Third and Fourth Congresses (March 4, 1793–March 3, 1797; elected to the Sixth Congress (March 4, 1799–March 3, 1801); elected to the Seventh Congress to fill the vacancy caused by the resignation of Thomas Tillotson and served from October 6, 1801, to March 3, 1803; served in the State assembly in 1802; elected to the United States Senate and served from March 4, 1803, to January 16, 1804, when he resigned to accept the position of postmaster of the city of New York, which position he held until his death there on September 6, 1828; interment in the Dutch Burying Ground; reinterment in the Rural Cemetery, Poughkeepsie, N. Y., January 8, 1864.

BAILEY, Warren Worth, a Representative from Pennsylvania; born in New Winchester, Hendricks County, Ind., January 8, 1855; moved to Illinois with his parents, who settled in Edgar County in 1863; attended the country schools; became a telegrapher, at which he worked until 1875, when he joined the Kansas (Ill.) News and learned the printing trade; engaged in the publishing business with his brother at Carlisle, Ind., in 1877; subsequently they purchased the Vincennes News, which they published until 1887; delegate to the Democratic State convention in 1884; moved to Chicago in 1887 and became a member of the staff of the Daily News and later of the Evening Mail; moved to Johnstown, Pa., in 1893 and published the Daily Democrat, devoted to the single-tax principle; unsuccessful Democratic candidate for election in 1906 to the Sixtieth Congress; delegate at large to the Democratic National Convention at Baltimore in 1912; elected as a Democrat to the Sixty-third and Sixth-fourth Congresses (March 4, 1913–March 3, 1917); unsuccessful candidate for reelection in 1916 to the Sixth-fifth Congress and for election in 1920, 1922, and 1926 to the Sixty-seventh, Sixty-eighth, and Seventieth Congresses, respectively; unsuccessfully contested the election of Anderson H. Walters to the Sixty-ninth Congress; resumed journalism in Johnstown, Cambria County, Pa., where he died November 9, 1928; interment in Grandview Cemetery.

BAILEY, Willis Joshua, a Representative from Kansas; born near Mount Carroll, Carroll County, Ill., October 12, 1854; attended the common schools, Mount Carroll High School, and the University of Illinois at Urbana; moved to Nemaha County,

Kans., in 1879; engaged in agricultural pursuits, stock raising, and banking; founded the town of Baileyville, Kans.; member of the Kansas House of Representatives 1888–1890; president of the Republican State League in 1893; member of the Kansas State Board of Agriculture 1895–1899; elected as a Republican to the Fifty-sixth Congress (March 4, 1899–March 3, 1901); was not a candidate for renomination in 1900 to the Fifty-seventh Congress; Governor of Kansas 1903–1905; moved to Atchison, Kans., in 1907 and engaged in the banking business; elected a director of the Federal Reserve Bank of Kansas City, Mo., in 1914, governor in 1922, and served until his death; was a resident of Mission Hills, Johnson County, Kans. (a suburb of Kansas City, Mo.), where he died May 19, 1932; interment in Mount Vernon Cemetery, Atchison, Kans.

BAIRD, David, a Senator from New Jersey; born in Londonderry, County Derry, Ireland, April 7, 1839; attended the common schools; immigrated to the United States in 1856 and entered the lumber business in Port Deposit, Md.; moved in 1860 to Camden, N. J., where he continued in the lumber business and also engaged in banking; member of the board of chosen freeholders of Camden County 1876–1880; sheriff of Camden County 1887–1889 and 1895–1897; member of the State board of assessors in 1895 and 1901–1909; presidential elector on the Republican ticket of McKinley and Roosevelt in 1900; unsuccessful candidate for election to the United States Senate in 1910; delegate to all the Republican National Conventions held between 1892 and 1916; appointed and subsequently elected as a Republican to the United States Senate to fill the vacancy caused by the death of William Hughes and served from February 23, 1918, to March 3, 1919; was not a candidate for renomination in 1918; resumed his former business pursuits in Camden, N. J., where he died February 25, 1927; interment in Harleigh Cemetery.

BAIRD, David, Jr. (son of the preceding), a Senator from New Jersey; born in Camden, N. J., October 10, 1881; attended the Raymond Academy at Camden and Penn Charter School at Philadelphia, Pa.; was graduated from Lawrenceville (N. J.) School in 1899 and from Princeton University, Princeton, N. J., in 1903; engaged as a lumber merchant in Camden, N. J., in 1903; also interested in banking; member of the State senate in 1929 and 1930; delegate to the Republican State conventions 1927–1934; appointed as a Republican to the United States Senate to fill the vacancy caused by the resignation of Walter E. Edge and served from November 30, 1929, to December 2, 1930, when a duly elected successor qualified; was not a candidate for election to the vacancy in 1930; unsuccessful candidate for Governor of New Jersey in 1931; resumed former business pursuits; moved to a farm at Ashland, Delaware Township, near Haddonfield, N. J., in 1936; in 1938 was appointed by the Governor to the Delaware River Joint Commission (now the Delaware River Port Authority) to fill an unexpired term; retired from political activities in 1938 to devote time to insurance brokerage business and was elected president of the Smith-Austermuhl Co.; died in Camden, N. J., February 28, 1955; interment in Harleigh Cemetery.

BAIRD, Joseph Edward, a Representative from Ohio; born at Perrysburg, Wood County, Ohio, November 12, 1865; attended the public schools; was graduated from the Perrysburg High School in 1885 and from the law department of the University of Michigan at Ann Arbor in 1893; was admitted to the bar in 1893 but did not practice; moved to Bowling Green, Ohio, in 1894 and served as county clerk of Wood County 1894–1900; engaged as a dealer in oil and farm lands from 1900 to 1921; served as mayor of Bowling Green 1902–1905, and as postmaster

1910–1914; secretary of the Ohio Public Utilities Commission 1921–1923; served as assistant secretary of state 1923–1929; elected as a Republican to the Seventy-first Congress (March 4, 1929–March 3, 1931); unsuccessful candidate for reelection in 1930 to the Seventy-second Congress; retired from active business pursuits and political activities; died in Bowling Green, Ohio, June 14, 1942; interment in Oak Grove Cemetery.

BAIRD, Samuel Thomas, a Representative from Louisiana; born in Oak Ridge, Morehouse Parish, La., May 5, 1861; educated under private tutors and attended the Vincennes (Ind.) University; studied law; was admitted to the bar in 1882 and commenced practice in Bastrop, Morehouse Parish, La.; district attorney of the sixth judicial district 1884–1888; district judge of the sixth judicial district 1888–1892; resumed the practice of law in Bastrop; member of the State senate in 1896; delegate to the Democratic National Convention at Chicago in 1896; elected as a Democrat to the Fifty-fifth and Fifty-sixth Congresses and served from March 4, 1897, until his death in Washington, D. C., April 22, 1899; interment in Christ Church Cemetery, Bastrop, La.

BAKER, Caleb, a Representative from New York; born in Providence, R. I., in 1762; moved to New York in 1790 and resided in the towns of Chemung, Ashland, and Newtown, Tioga County, from 1790 to 1836, and in Southport, Chemung County, from 1836 until his death; studied law; was admitted to the bar and practiced; assessor of the town of Chemung in 1791; taught school on the site of the present Baptist Graveyard at Wellsburg, Chemung County, in 1803 and 1804; appointed surrogate of Tioga County on April 7, 1806, April 13, 1825, and again in 1829; appointed judge of common pleas in 1810; member of the State assembly in 1814, 1815, and again in 1829; justice of the peace of the town of Chemung in 1816; elected to the Sixteenth Congress (March 4, 1819–March 3, 1821); when Chemung County was formed in 1836 he served as foreman of its first grand jury the same year; died in Southport (now a part of Elmira), Chemung County, N. Y., June 26, 1849; interment in Fitzsimmons Cemetery, lower Maple Avenue.

BAKER, Charles Simeon, a Representative from New York; born in Churchville, Monroe County, N. Y., February 18, 1839; attended the common schools, Cary Collegiate Institute of Oakfield, and the New York Seminary at Lima; taught school; studied law; was admitted to the bar in December 1860 and commenced practice in Rochester, N. Y.; served in the Union Army during the Civil War as first lieutenant, Company E, Twenty-seventh Regiment, New York Volunteer Infantry; disabled in the first Battle of Bull Run and honorably discharged; member of the New York State Assembly 1879–1882; served in the State senate in 1884 and 1885; elected as a Republican to the Forty-ninth, Fiftieth, and Fifty-first Congresses (March 4, 1885–March 3, 1891); resumed the practice of law in Rochester, N. Y.; died in Washington, D. C., April 21, 1902; interment in Mount Hope Cemetery, Rochester, N. Y.

BAKER, David Jewett, a Senator from Illinois; born in East Haddam, Conn., September 7, 1792; moved with his parents to Ontario County, N. Y.; attended the common schools and was graduated from Hamilton College, Clinton, N. Y., in 1816; studied law; was admitted to the Illinois bar in 1819 and commenced the practice of law in Kaskaskia, Ill.; probate judge of Randolph County from August 1827 until December 6, 1830, when he resigned to become Senator; appointed as a Democrat to the United States Senate to fill the vacancy caused by the death of John McLean and served from November 12,

1830, to December 11, 1830, when a successor was elected and qualified; was not a candidate for election in 1830 to fill the vacancy; appointed United States district attorney for the district of Illinois in 1833 and served until 1841; resumed the practice of his profession; died in Alton, Madison County, Ill., August 6, 1869; interment in City Cemetery.

BAKER, Edward Dickinson, a Representative from Illinois and a Senator from Oregon; born in London, England, February 24, 1811; immigrated to the United States in 1815 with his parents, who settled in Philadelphia, Pa.; moved to Carrollton, Ill., in 1825; studied law; was admitted to the bar in 1830 and commenced practice in Springfield; member of the State house of representatives in 1837; served in the State senate 1840–1844; elected as a Whig to the Twenty-ninth Congress and served from March 4, 1845, until he tendered his resignation in writing on December 24, 1846, to take effect on January 15, 1847; orally resigned from the House of Representatives on December 30, 1846; commissioned colonel of the Fourth Regiment, Illinois Volunteer Infantry, on July 4, 1846; participated in the siege of Vera Cruz and commanded a brigade at Cerro Gordo; honorably mustered out May 29, 1847; after the war moved to Galena, Ill.; elected as a Republican to the Thirty-first Congress (March 4, 1849–March 3, 1851); was not a candidate for renomination in 1850; moved to San Francisco, Calif., in 1851 and resumed the practice of law; moved to Oregon in 1860; elected as a Republican to the United States Senate to fill the vacancy in the term beginning March 4, 1859, and served from October 2, 1860, until his death; raised a regiment in New York City and Philadelphia during the Civil War; commissioned brigadier general of Volunteers May 17, 1861, but declined; colonel of the Seventy-first Regiment, Pennsylvania Volunteer Infantry, June 22, 1861; appointed major general of Volunteers September 21, 1861; killed in the Battle of Balls Bluff, Va., October 21, 1861; interment in San Francisco National Cemetery, Presidio of San Francisco, Fort Mason, Calif.

BAKER, Ezra, a Representative from New Jersey; born in Tuckerton, N. J.; moved with his parents to the Province of East Jersey about 1765; educated for the medical profession and commenced practice; moved to Absecon, N. J., in 1799; served as collector of customs at the port of Great Egg Harbor, N. J., from February 18, 1813, to March 1, 1815; elected to the Fourteenth Congress (March 4, 1815–March 3, 1817); moved westward to the "Wabash country" with his sons in 1818 and engaged in the culture of castor beans for the New Orleans market; died in the "Wabash country."

BAKER, Henry Moore, a Representative from New Hampshire; born in Bow, near Concord, N. H., January 11, 1841; attended the common schools, Pembroke, Tilton, and Hopkinton Academies, New Hampshire; was graduated from the New Hampshire Conference Seminary in 1859, Dartmouth College, Hanover, N. H., in 1863, and the law school of Columbian (now George Washington) University, Washington, D. C., in 1866; was admitted to the bar in 1866; clerk in the War and Treasury Departments 1864–1874; commenced the practice of law in Washington, D. C., in 1874; judge advocate general of the National Guard of New Hampshire in 1886 and 1887 with rank of brigadier general; member of the State senate in 1891 and 1892; elected as a Republican to the Fifty-third and Fifty-fourth Congresses (March 3, 1893–March 3, 1897); was not a candidate for renomination in 1896; resumed the practice of his profession in Washington, D. C., but retained his legal residence in Bow, N. H.; member of the New Hampshire House of Representatives 1905–1909; died in Washington, D. C., May 30, 1912; interment in Alexander Cemetery, Bow, N. H.

BAKER, Howard Henry, a Representative from Tennessee; born in Somerset, Pulaski County, Ky., January 12, 1902; moved with his parents to Huntsville, Scott County, Tenn.; attended the public schools of Scott and Knox Counties, Tenn.; was graduated from the University of Tennessee at Knoxville in 1922 and from its law school in 1924; was admitted to the Tennessee bar in 1923 and commenced the practice of law in Huntsville, Tenn.; served in the Tennessee House of Representatives in 1929 and 1930; member of Scott County Board of Education in 1931 and 1932; attorney general of the nineteenth judicial circuit of Tennessee 1934–1948; vice president and general counsel of the Oneida & Western Railroad Co., in 1945; member of the board of directors, First National Bank of Oneida, Tenn.; unsuccessful Republican candidate for Governor in 1938 and for United States Senator in 1940; delegate to the Republican National Conventions in 1940, 1948, 1952, and 1956; elected as a Republican to the Eighty-second and to the four succeeding Congresses (January 3, 1951–January 3, 1961). *Reelected to the Eighty-seventh Congress.*

BAKER, Jacob Thompson, a Representative from New Jersey; born near Cowan, Union County, Pa., April 13, 1847; attended the public schools and Bucknell University, Lewisburg, Pa.; studied law; was admitted to the bar in 1870 and commenced practice in Lewisburg, Pa.; chairman of the Democratic State convention in 1905; moved to New Jersey and was one of the founders of Wildwood and the borough of Wildwood Crest; first mayor of the consolidated city of Wildwood in 1911 and 1912; delegate to the Democratic National Convention at Baltimore in 1912; elected as a Democrat to the Sixty-third Congress (March 4, 1913–March 3, 1915); unsuccessful candidate for reelection in 1914 to the Sixty-fourth Congress; resumed real-estate activities in Wildwood, N. J.; died in Philadelphia, Pa., December 7, 1919; interment in Cold Spring Cemetery, Cold Spring, Cape May County, N. J.

BAKER, Jehu, a Representative from Illinois; born near Lexington, Fayette County, Ky., November 4, 1822; moved with his father to Lebanon, Ill., in 1829; attended the common schools and McKendree College at Lebanon; studied law; was admitted to the bar in 1846 and commenced practice at Belleville, St. Clair County, Ill.; master in chancery of St. Clair County 1861–1865; elected as a Republican to the Thirty-ninth and Fortieth Congresses (March 4, 1865–March 3, 1869); served as United States Minister to Venezuela 1878–1881 and 1882–1885, being Minister Resident and consul general for a time during the latter portion of his service; elected as a Republican to the Fiftieth Congress (March 4, 1887–March 3, 1889); unsuccessful candidate for reelection in 1888 to the Fifty-first Congress; continued the practice of law; elected as a Fusionist to the Fifty-fifth Congress (March 4, 1897–March 3, 1899); declined to be a candidate for renomination in 1898 to the Fifty-sixth Congress; resumed the practice of law; died in Belleville, Ill., on March 1, 1903; interment in Walnut Hill Cemetery.

BAKER, John, a Representative from Virginia; born in Frederick County, Md.; attended Washington College (now Washington and Lee University), Lexington, Va., for three years; studied law; was admitted to the bar and began practice in Berkeley County, Va. (now Jefferson County, W. Va.); member of the State house of delegates 1798–1799; one of the lawyers who defended Aaron Burr when he was tried for treason; elected as a Federalist to the Twelfth Congress (March 4, 1811–March 3, 1813); resumed the practice of law; Commonwealth attorney for Jefferson County; died in Shepherdstown, Jefferson County, Va. (now West Virginia), August 18, 1823; interment in the Old Episcopal Church Cemetery.

BAKER, John Harris, a Representative from Indiana; born in Parma Township, Monroe County, N. Y., February 28, 1832; moved with his parents to the present county of Fulton, Ohio; attended the public schools; taught school; attended the Wesleyan University in Delaware, Ohio, two years; studied law in Adrian, Mich.; was admitted to the bar in 1857 and commenced practice in Goshen, Ind.; member of the State senate in 1862, but, being a notary public at the time, was unseated because the State constitution forbid the simultaneous holding of two lucrative offices; elected as a Republican to the Forty-fourth, Forty-fifth, and Forty-sixth Congresses (March 4, 1875–March 3, 1881); declined to be a candidate for renomination in 1880; resumed the practice of law in Goshen, Ind.; delegate to the Republican National Convention at Chicago in 1888 that nominated Harrison and Morton; appointed judge of the United States District Court for Indiana by President Harrison in 1892 and served until his retirement in 1904; resided in Goshen, Elkhart County, Ind., until his death on October 21, 1915; interment in Oak Ridge Cemetery.

BAKER, Lucien, a Senator from Kansas; born near Cleveland, Fulton County, Ohio, June 8, 1846; moved with his parents to Morenci, Mich.; attended the public schools and was graduated from Adrian College, Michigan, and from the law department of the University of Michigan at Ann Arbor; was admitted to the bar in 1868 and commenced practice in Leavenworth, Kans., in 1869; city attorney of Leavenworth 1872–1874; member of the State senate 1893–1895; elected as a Republican to the United States Senate and served from March 4, 1895, to March 3, 1901; unsuccessful candidate for renomination; resumed the practice of law in Leavenworth, Leavenworth County, Kans., where he died on June 21, 1907; interment in Mount Muncie Cemetery.

BAKER, Osmyn, a Representative from Massachusetts; born in Amherst, Mass., May 18, 1800; attended Amherst Academy; was graduated from Yale College in 1822; studied law; was admitted to the bar and commenced practice in Amherst in 1825; member of the State house of representatives 1833, 1834, 1836, and 1837; county commissioner of Hampshire County 1834–1837; elected as a Whig to the Twenty-sixth Congress to fill the vacancy caused by the death of James C. Alvord; reelected to the Twenty-seventh and Twenty-eighth Congresses and served from January 14, 1840, to March 3, 1845; was not a candidate for renomination in 1844; resumed the practice of law at Northampton in 1845; first president of Smith Charities 1860–1870; died in Northampton, Mass., February 9, 1875; interment in Bridge Street Cemetery.

BAKER, Robert, a Representative from New York; born at Bury St. Edmunds, England, in April 1862; attended the common schools; immigrated to the United States in 1882 and settled in Albany, N. Y.; moved to Brooklyn, N. Y., in 1889; unsuccessful candidate for election to the State assembly in 1894; auditor of New York City in 1902; elected as a Democrat to the Fifty-eighth Congress (March 4, 1903–March 3, 1905); unsuccessful candidate for reelection in 1904 to the Fifty-ninth Congress and for election in 1906 to the Sixtieth Congress; became secretary of the New York City Department of Docks and Ferries in 1906; engaged in stone paving and in the general real-estate business in Brooklyn, N. Y., until his death there on June 15, 1943; interment in Evergreen Cemetery.

BAKER, Stephen, a Representative from New York; born in New York City, August 12, 1819; attended the common schools; engaged as importer and jobber in woolen goods; moved to Poughkeepsie, Dutchess County, N. Y., in 1850; elected as a

Republican to the Thirty-seventh Congress (March 4, 1861–March 3, 1863); abandoned active business pursuits and lived in retirement until his death, while en route to California for his health, on a train near Ogden, Utah, June 9, 1875; interment in the Rural Cemetery, Poughkeepsie, N. Y.

BAKER, William, a Representative from Kansas; born near Centerville, Washington County, Pa., April 29, 1831; attended the public schools and was graduated from the Waynesboro College in 1856; taught school; moved to Iowa in 1859 and became principal of the public schools in Council Bluffs; studied law and was admitted to the bar in 1860 but never practiced; returned to Bealsville, Washington County, Pa., in 1865; engaged in mercantile pursuits 1865–1878; moved to Lincoln County, Kans., in 1878; engaged in agricultural pursuits and stock raising; elected as a candidate of the People's Party to the Fifty-second, Fifty-third, and Fifty-fourth Congresses (March 4, 1891–March 3, 1897); was not a candidate for renomination in 1896; resumed agricultural pursuits; died in Lincoln, Kans., February 11, 1910; interment in Lincoln Center Cemetery.

BAKER, William Benjamin, a Representative from Maryland; born near Aberdeen, Harford County, Md., July 22, 1840; attended the common schools and was privately tutored; engaged in agricultural pursuits until 1872, when he became interested in the canning industry, and later in banking; delegate to several State and congressional conventions; member of the State house of delegates in 1881; served in the State senate in 1893; elected as a Republican to the Fifty-fourth, Fifty-fifth, and Fifty-sixth Congresses (March 4, 1895–March 3, 1901); was not a candidate for renomination in 1900; resumed the canning business; died in Aberdeen, Md., May 17, 1911; interment in Baker's Cemetery.

BAKER, William Henry, a Representative from New York; born in Lenox Township, Madison County, N. Y., January 17, 1827; moved with his parents to Oswego County in 1829; attended the common schools and Red Creek and Mexico Academies; studied law; was admitted to the bar in Syracuse, N. Y., in November 1851 and commenced practice in Cleveland, N. Y.; moved to Constantia, N. Y., in 1853; served as district attorney for Oswego County from January 1863 to January 1870; elected as a Republican to the Forty-fourth and Forty-fifth Congresses (March 4, 1875–March 3, 1879); declined to be a candidate for renomination in 1878; delegate to the State constitutional convention in 1884; engaged in agricultural pursuits; died in Constantia, Oswego County, N. Y., November 25, 1911; interment in Trinity Church Cemetery.

BAKEWELL, Charles Montague, a Representative from Connecticut; born in Pittsburgh, Pa., April 24, 1867; attended the public schools and the preparatory department of Western University of Pennsylvania (now the University of Pittsburgh); was graduated from the University of California at Berkeley in 1889 and from Harvard University, Cambridge, Mass., in 1894; attended the Universities of Berlin, Strassburg, and Paris 1894–1896; instructor in philosophy at Harvard University in 1896 and 1897 and at the University of California in 1897 and 1898; associate professor at Bryn Mawr College 1898–1900; associate professor and professor at the University of California 1900–1905; professor of philosophy at Yale University 1905–1933; president of the American Philosophical Association in 1910; during the First World War served as inspector and historian, with rank of major and deputy commissioner, under the Italian Commission of the American Red Cross in Italy, and received the Order of the Crown of Italy, and the Silver Medal of Honor from the Italian Red Cross served in the State senate

1920–1924; served as chairman of the commission to revise and codify the educational laws of the State of Connecticut 1921–1923; member and chairman of the Connecticut State Board of Healing Arts 1925–1949; also engaged as an author and editor; elected as a Republican to the Seventy-third Congress (March 4, 1933–January 3, 1935); unsuccessful candidate for reelection in 1934 to the Seventy-fourth Congress; Sheldon Clark professor emeritus of philosophy, Yale University, at time of death; died in New Haven, Conn., September 19, 1957; interment in Grove Street Cemetery.

BAKEWELL, Claude Ignatius, a Representative from Missouri; born in St. Louis, Mo., August 9, 1912; attended the St. Louis University High School; was graduated from Georgetown University, Washington, D. C., in 1932 and from St. Louis University School of Law in 1935; was admitted to the bar in 1935 and commenced practice in St. Louis; member of the board of aldermen of St. Louis 1941–1945; during World War II served in the United States Navy as lieutenant (jg) with service in the South Pacific and at the Philadelphia Navy Base from October 1944 to April 1946; elected as a Republican to the Eightieth Congress (January 3, 1947–January 3, 1949); unsuccessful candidate for reelection in 1948 to the Eighty-first Congress; elected to the Eighty-second Congress to fill the vacancy caused by the death of John B. Sullivan, and served from March 9, 1951, to January 3, 1953; unsuccessful candidate for reelection in 1952 to the Eighty-third Congress; resumed the practice of law; is a resident of St. Louis, Mo.

BALDRIGE, Howard Malcolm, a Representative from Nebraska; born in Omaha, Nebr., June 23, 1894; attended the public schools and was graduated from the Omaha High School; attended Phillips Academy, Andover, Mass., and was graduated from Yale University in 1918; during the First World War served as captain of Battery F, Three Hundred and Thirty-eighth Field Artillery; was graduated from the Nebraska Law School, at Lincoln, in 1921; was admitted to the bar the same year and commenced practice in Omaha, Nebr.; served in the State house of representatives in 1923; delegate to the Republican National Conventions in 1924 and 1928; elected as a Republican to the Seventy-second Congress (March 4, 1931–March 3, 1933); unsuccessful candidate for reelection in 1932 to the Seventy-third Congress; resumed the practice of law; during World War II entered the Army on June 10, 1942, as a major in the Air Corps and was discharged as a colonel on October 25, 1945; resumed the practice of law with offices in New York, N. Y., and Washington, D. C.; is a resident of Omaha, Nebr.

BALDWIN, Abraham, a Delegate, a Representative, and a Senator from Georgia; born in North Guilford, Conn., November 2, 1754; moved with his father to New Haven, Conn., in 1769; attended private schools; was graduated from Yale College in 1772; subsequently studied theology at the college and was licensed to preach September 26, 1775; appointed in 1775 as a tutor in that institution and served until 1779, when he resigned to enter the Army; chaplain in the Second Connecticut Brigade, Revolutionary Army, from 1777 until 1783, when the troops disbanded; studied law during his service in the Army; was admitted to the bar in 1783 and practiced at Fairfield; moved to Augusta, Ga., in 1784 and continued the practice of law; member of the State house of representatives in 1785; originator of the plan for, and author of, the charter of the University of Georgia and was its president for a number of years; Member of the Continental Congress in 1785 and 1787–1789; member of the United States Constitutional Convention in 1787; elected as a Federalist to the First and to the four succeeding Congresses (March 4, 1789–March 3, 1799); elected to the United States Senate in 1799;

reelected in 1805 and served from March 4, 1799, until his death; elected President pro tempore of the Senate December 7, 1801, and April 17, 1802; died in Washington, D. C., March 4, 1807; interment in Rock Creek Cemetery.

BALDWIN, Augustus Carpenter, a Representative from Michigan; born in Salina (now Syracuse), Onondaga County, N. Y., December 24, 1817; attended the public schools; moved to Oakland County, Mich., in 1837 and taught school; studied law; was admitted to the bar in 1842 and commenced practice in Milford, Oakland County; member of the State house of representatives 1844–1846, serving as speaker pro tempore in 1846; moved to Pontiac, Mich., in March 1849; prosecuting attorney for Oakland County 1853 and 1854; delegate to the Democratic National Conventions at Charleston and Baltimore in 1860; elected as a Union Democrat to the Thirty-eighth Congress (March 4, 1863– March 3, 1865); unsuccessfully contested the election of Rowland E. Trowbridge to the Thirty-ninth Congress; delegate to the peace convention at Philadelphia in 1866; member of the Pontiac School Board 1868–1886; mayor of Pontiac in 1874; judge of the sixth judicial circuit court of Michigan from 1875 until April 15, 1880, when he resigned and resumed the practice of law; member of the board of trustees of the Eastern Michigan Asylum; died in Pontiac, Oakland County, Mich., January 21, 1903; interment in Oak Hill Cemetery.

BALDWIN, Harry Streett, a Representative from Maryland; born in Baldwin, Baltimore County, Md., August 21, 1894; attended the public and high schools, and the University of Maryland at College Park, Md.; owner and operator of a large truck farm; served in the State house of delegates in 1931; member of the board of county commissioners 1934–1942, serving as president 1938–1942; elected as a Democrat to the Seventy-eighth and Seventy-ninth Congresses (January 3, 1943–January 3, 1947); was not a candidate for renomination in 1946 to the Eightieth Congress; unsuccessful Democratic candidate for the gubernatorial nomination in 1946; resumed agricultural pursuits; again elected to the board of county commissioners in 1950 and was serving as chairman at time of death; died in Union Memorial Hospital, Baltimore, Md., October 19, 1952; interment in Chestnut Grove Cemetery, Jacksonville, Md.

BALDWIN, Henry, a Representative from Pennsylvania; born in New Haven, Conn., January 14, 1780; was graduated from Hopkins Grammar School in 1793 and from Yale College in 1797; studied law; was admitted to the Philadelphia bar in 1798 and commenced practice in Pittsburgh, Pa., in 1801; moved to Meadville, Crawford County, Pa.; elected as a Federalist to the Fifteenth, Sixteenth, and Seventeenth Congresses and served from March 4, 1817, until his resignation on May 8, 1822; engaged in the manufacture of iron at Bear Creek, Butler County, Pa.; resumed the practice of law in Pittsburgh, Pa., appointed an Associate Justice of the United States Supreme Court on January 6, 1830, and served until his death in Philadelphia, Pa., April 21, 1844; interment in Greendale Cemetery, Meadville, Pa.

BALDWIN, Henry Alexander, a Delegate from the Territory of Hawaii; born in Paliuli, Maui County, Hawaii, January 12, 1871; attended Haiku School in Haiku, and Punahou School in Honolulu; was graduated from Phillips Academy in Andover, Mass., in 1889 and from Massachusetts Institute of Technology, Boston, Mass., in 1894; engaged in sugar planting; member of the Territorial senate 1913–1921; served as a lieutenant colonel and later as colonel in the Third Regiment of the Hawaii National Guard 1915–1917; elected as a Republican to the Sixty-seventh Congress to fill the vacancy caused by the death of J. Kuhio Kalanianaole and served from March 25, 1922, to March 3, 1923;

declined to be a candidate for renomination in 1922; resumed his former business pursuits and was also interested in banking; served in the Hawaii House of Representatives in 1933; member of the Hawaii Senate 1934–1937, serving as president during the 1937 session; died at Paia, Maui County, Hawaii, October 8, 1946; interment in Makawao Cemetery, Makawao, Hawaii.

BALDWIN, Henry Porter, a Senator from Michigan; born in Coventry, R. I., February 22, 1814; attended the common schools; moved to Detroit, Mich., and established a mercantile house in 1838; member of the convention which organized the Republican Party in Jackson, Mich., in 1854; director of the Michigan State Bank and president of the Second National Bank of Detroit from its organization in 1863 until 1887; member of the State senate in 1861 and 1862; Governor of Michigan 1869–1873; delegate to the Republican National Convention at Cincinnati in 1876; appointed and subsequently elected as a Republican to the United States Senate to fill the vacancy caused by the death of Zachariah Chandler and served from November 17, 1879, to March 3, 1881; was not a candidate for reelection; resumed his former business pursuits; president of the Detroit National Bank 1883– 1887; died in Detroit, Mich., December 31, 1892; interment in Elmwood Cemetery.

BALDWIN, John, a Representative from Connecticut; born in Mansfield, Conn., April 5, 1772; attended the common schools; was graduated from Brown University, Providence, R. I., in 1797; studied law; was admitted to the bar in 1800 and commenced practice in Windham, Conn.; probate judge of Windham County 1818–1824; elected to the Nineteenth and Twentieth Congresses (March 4, 1825–March 3, 1829); affiliated with the Whig Party after its formation; resumed the practice of law; died in Windham, Windham County, Conn., March 27, 1850; interment in Windham Cemetery.

BALDWIN, John Denison, a Representative from Massachusetts; born in North Stonington, Conn., September 28, 1809; moved with his parents to Chenango County, N. Y., in 1816; returned to North Stonington in 1823; attended schools in Chenango County, N. Y., and in North Stonington, Conn.; studied law for a time but discontinued the study for theology; was graduated from the Yale Divinity School in 1834; was licensed to preach and assumed Congregational pastorates in West Woodstock, Conn., 1834–1837, in North Branford 1838– 1845, and in North Killingly 1846–1849; member of the State house of representatives 1847–1852; engaged in newspaper work in Hartford, Conn., 1849–1852, in Boston, Mass., 1852–1859, and was connected with the Worcester Spy from 1859 until his death; delegate to the Republican National Convention at Chicago in 1860, and it was at his suggestion that Hannibal Hamlin was nominated on the Republican ticket with Abraham Lincoln; elected as a Republican to the Thirty-eighth, Thirty-ninth, and Fortieth Congresses (March 4, 1863–March 3, 1869); was not a candidate for reelection in 1868; resumed his newspaper interests; died in Worcester, Mass., July 8, 1883; interment in the Rural Cemetery.

BALDWIN, John Finley, Jr., a Representative from California; born in Oakland, Alameda County, Calif., June 28, 1915; graduated from San Ramon Valley Union High School in Danville, Calif., and from the University of California at Berkeley in 1935, majoring in accounting and finance; assistant manager of South-Western Publishing Co., of San Francisco, 1936–1941; enlisted as a private in the United States Army in April 1941; served as director of training, Army Finance School, in 1943 and 1944; Chief of Foreign Fiscal Affairs Branch, Office of Fiscal Director, War Department, in 1945, and executive officer,

Office of Fiscal Director, Mediterranean Theater, in 1946; discharged as a lieutenant colonel in October 1946; decorated by Italian Government for work in the devaluation of the lira currency in 1946; graduated from the University of California Boalt Hall School of Law in Berkeley in 1949; was admitted to the bar in 1950 and commenced the practice of law in Martinez, Calif.; elected as a Republican to the Eighty-fourth, Eighty-fifth, and Eighty-sixth Congresses (January 3, 1955–January 3, 1961). *Reelected to the Eighty-seventh Congress.*

BALDWIN, Joseph Clark, a Representative from New York; born in New York City, N. Y., January 11, 1897; attended private schools; was graduated from St. Paul's School, Concord, N. H., in 1916 and from Harvard University, Cambridge, Mass., in 1920; enlisted in the Navy in 1917 and was transferred to the Army in 1918, serving overseas as a private in the Machine Gun Company of the Three Hundred and Fifth Infantry; received a commission and commanded the First Platoon, Machine Gun Company, Thirty-ninth Infantry; officer of the French Legion of Honor; political reporter for the New York Tribune and later associate editor for the North Westchester Times 1922–1930; established a public relations firm in 1930; served as a member of the board of aldermen of New York City 1929–1934; member of the State senate 1934–1936; delegate to the New York State constitutional convention in 1938; member of the New York City Council 1937–1941; elected as a Republican to the Seventy-seventh Congress to fill the vacancy caused by the death of Kenneth F. Simpson; reelected to the Seventy-eighth and Seventy-ninth Congresses and served from March 11, 1941, to January 3, 1947; unsuccessful candidate for renomination in 1946 to the Eightieth Congress; became a representative for United Dye and Chemical Corp., and William Recht Co., Inc.; died in New York City, N. Y., October 27, 1957; interment in Woodlawn Cemetery.

BALDWIN, Melvin Riley, a Representative from Minnesota; born near Chester, Windsor County, Vt., April 12, 1838; moved with his parents to Oshkosh, Winnebago County, Wis., in 1847; attended the common schools; entered Lawrence University, Appleton, Wis., in 1855; studied law but adopted civil engineering as a profession; engaged on the Chicago & North Western Railway until April 19, 1861, when he enlisted, during the Civil War, as a private in Company E, Second Regiment, Wisconsin Volunteer Infantry; commissioned captain of his company; was captured at Gettysburg and confined in Libby Prison, Richmond, Va., at Macon, Ga., and at Charleston and Columbia, S. C., being prisoner for eighteen months; after the war engaged in operative railway work in Kansas; general superintendent for four years; moved to Duluth, St. Louis County, Minn., in 1885; elected as a Democrat to the Fifty-third Congress (March 4, 1893–March 3, 1895); unsuccessful candidate for reelection in 1894 to the Fifty-fourth Congress; chairman of the Chippewa Indian Commission 1894–1897; went to Alaska in November 1897; died in Seattle, Wash., April 15, 1901; interment in Forest Hill Cemetery, Duluth, Minn.

BALDWIN, Raymond Earl, a Senator from Connecticut; born in Rye, Westchester County, N. Y., August 31, 1893; moved to Middletown, Conn., in 1901 and attended the public schools; was graduated from the Middletown High School in 1912 and from Wesleyan University, Middletown, Conn., in 1916; entered Yale University, New Haven, Conn., in 1916 but, when war was declared, enlisted as a seaman in the United States Navy; was assigned to Officers' Training School, commissioned an ensign at Annapolis, Md., in February 1918 and assigned to a destroyer, the U. S. S. *Talbot,* serving in trans-Atlantic escort duty and antisubmarine warfare off the Irish Coast, in the English Chan-

nel, and in the Bay of Biscay; was promoted to lieutenant (jg) in September 1918 and following Armistice served in the Mediterranean and Adriatic Seas; resigned from the Navy in August 1919 and returned to Yale University Law School, graduating in 1921; was admitted to the bar in 1921 and practiced in New Haven, Conn., until July 1, 1924, when he became associated with a law firm in Bridgeport, Conn.; prosecutor of Stratford Town Court 1927–1930; judge of Stratford Town Court 1931–1933; member of the State house of representatives 1931–1933, serving as chairman of the judiciary committee and majority leader in 1933; resumed the private practice of law 1933–1938; also interested in the insurance business; town chairman of Stratford, Conn., 1935–1937; delegate to all Republican State conventions since 1938 and to all Republican National Conventions since 1940; Governor of Connecticut in 1939 and 1940; unsuccessful candidate for reelection as Governor in 1940; again elected Governor, in 1942 and 1944, and served from January 6, 1943, until his resignation on December 25, 1946, having been elected United States Senator; elected as a Republican to the United States Senate on November 5, 1946, to fill the vacancy in the term ending January 3, 1947, caused by the death of Francis T. Maloney, but did not assume his duties until December 27, 1946, and at the same time was elected for the term commencing January 3, 1947, and served until his resignation on December 16, 1949; took the oath of office December 17, 1949, as an associate justice of the Connecticut Supreme Court of Errors; is a resident of Glastonbury, Conn.

BALDWIN, Roger Sherman (son of Simeon Baldwin), a Senator from Connecticut; born in New Haven, Conn., January 4, 1793; attended the common schools and the Hopkins Grammar School; was graduated from Yale College in 1811; studied law in his father's office and in 1812 entered the Litchfield Law School; was admitted to the bar in 1814 and commenced practice in New Haven, Conn.; member of the State senate in 1837 and 1838; served in the State house of representatives in 1840 and 1841; Governor of Connecticut 1844–1846; appointed and subsequently elected as a Whig to the United States Senate to fill the vacancy caused by the death of Jabez W. Huntington and served from November 11, 1847, to March 3, 1851; presidential elector on the Republican ticket of Lincoln and Hamlin in 1860; member of the peace convention held in Washington, D. C., in 1861 in an effort to devise means to prevent the impending war; died in New Haven, Conn., February 19, 1863; interment in the Grove Street Cemetery.

BALDWIN, Simeon (father of Roger Sherman Baldwin), a Representative from Connecticut; born in Norwich, Conn., December 14, 1761; completed preparatory studies; was graduated from Yale College, New Haven, Conn., in 1781; was preceptor of the academy at Albany in 1782; tutor at Yale College from October 1783 until his resignation in September 1786; studied law; was admitted to the bar in 1786 and commenced practice in New Haven, Conn., the same year; elected city clerk in 1789 and served until June 1800; in 1790 was appointed clerk of the District and Circuit Courts of the United States for the District of Connecticut and served until November 1803, when he resigned, having been elected to Congress; elected as a Federalist to the Eighth Congress (March 4, 1803–March 3, 1805); declined to be a candidate for reelection in 1804; again appointed to his former clerkship, but was removed by Judge Edwards in 1806; associate judge of the superior court and of the supreme court of errors 1806–1817; president of the board of commissioners that located the Farmington Canal 1822–1830, when he resigned; mayor of New Haven in 1826; died in New Haven, Conn., May 26, 1851; interment in the Grove Street Cemetery.

BALL, Edward, a Representative from Ohio; born in Fairfax County, near Falls Church, Va., November 6, 1811; attended the village school; moved to Ohio and located near Zanesville; engaged in agricultural pursuits; deputy sheriff of Muskingum County in 1837 and 1838 and sheriff 1839–1843; member of the State house of representatives 1845–1849; became editor of the Zanesville Courier in 1849; elected as a Whig to the Thirty-third and Thirty-fourth Congresses (March 4, 1853–March 3, 1857); was not a candidate for renomination in 1856; studied law; was admitted to the bar in 1860 and commenced practice in Zanesville; delegate to the Republican National Convention at Chicago in 1860; presidential elector on the Republican ticket of Lincoln and Hamlin in 1860; Sergeant at Arms of the National House of Representatives in the Thirty-seventh Congress 1861–1863; resumed the practice of law; again a member of the State house of representatives 1868–1870; accidentally killed by a railroad train near Zanesville, Ohio, on November 22, 1872; interment in Greenwood Cemetery.

BALL, Joseph Hurst, a Senator from Minnesota; born in Crookston, Polk County, Minn., November 3, 1905; attended the public schools; student at Antioch College, Yellow Springs, Ohio, 1922–1924, Eau Claire (Wis.) Normal School in 1925, and the University of Minnesota at Minneapolis in 1926 and 1927; newspaper reporter in Minneapolis, Minn., in 1927 and 1928; free-lance and fiction writer in 1928 and 1929; general assignment reporter and rewrite man on a St. Paul newspaper 1929–1934; State political writer 1934–1940; appointed as a Republican to the United States Senate to fill the vacancy caused by the death of Ernest Lundeen for the term ending January 3, 1943, and served from October 14, 1940, to November 17, 1942, when a duly elected successor qualified; elected in 1942 for the term commencing January 3, 1943, and ending January 3, 1949; unsuccessful candidate for reelection in 1948; resumed journalistic activities; vice president of the Association of American Ship Owners 1949–1953; vice president of the States Marine Lines 1953–; resides in New York City, N. Y.

BALL, Lewis Heisler, a Representative and a Senator from Delaware; born near Stanton, New Castle County, Del., September 21, 1861; attended the common schools and Rugby Academy at Wilmington; was graduated from Delaware College, Newark, Del., in 1882 and from the medical department of the University of Pennsylvania at Philadelphia in 1885; commenced the practice of medicine at Brandywine Springs, Del., in 1887; State treasurer of Delaware 1899–1901; elected as a Republican to the Fifty-seventh Congress and served from March 4, 1901, to March 3, 1903, when he resigned to become Senator; unsuccessful candidate for reelection in 1902 to the Fifty-eighth Congress; elected to the United States Senate on March 2, 1903, to fill the vacancy in the term commencing March 4, 1899; caused by the failure of the legislature to elect, and served from March 3, 1903, to March 3, 1905; resumed the practice of medicine at Brandywine Springs, Del.; again elected to the United States Senate and served from March 4, 1919, to March 3, 1925; unsuccessful candidate for renomination in 1924; appointed a member of the Rent Commission of Washington, D. C., in 1925 and served during its entire existence; resumed the practice of medicine; died in Faulkland, Del., October 18, 1932; interment in St. James Cemetery, Stanton, Del.

BALL, Thomas Henry, a Representative from Texas; born in Huntsville, Walker County, Tex., January 14, 1859; attended private schools; was graduated from Austin College, Sherman, Tex., in 1876; studied law at the University of Virginia at Charlottesville; was admitted to the bar in 1886 and commenced practice in Huntsville, Tex.; mayor of Huntsville 1887–1893; chairman of the Democratic executive committee of Walker County 1884–1896; delegate to all State conventions from 1886 to 1924, with three exceptions; delegate to the Democratic National Conventions in 1892, 1924, and 1928; elected as a Democrat to the Fifty-fifth and to the three succeeding Congresses and served from March 4, 1897, to November 16, 1903, when he resigned; resumed the practice of his profession; unsuccessful candidate for the Democratic gubernatorial nomination in 1914; general counsel for the State council of defense during the First World War; general counsel for the port commission of the Houston Harbor and Ship Channel from May 1922 to August 1931, when he retired; died in Houston, Tex., May 7, 1944; interment in Forest Park Cemetery.

BALL, Thomas Raymond, a Representative from Connecticut; born in New York City, N. Y., February 12, 1896; attended the public schools, Anglo-Saxon School, Paris, France, Heathcote School, Harrison, N. Y., and the Art Students League, New York, N. Y.; engaged as a designer in 1916; during the First World War served in the Depot Battalion, Seventh New York Infantry, in 1917, and overseas with the Camouflage Section, Fortieth United States Engineers, 1918–1919; after the war located in Old Lyme, Conn., and engaged in architectural pursuits; member of the board of education 1926–1938, and also served as selectman of Old Lyme, Conn.; served in the State house of representatives 1927–1937; elected as a Republican to the Seventy-sixth Congress (January 3, 1939–January 3, 1941); unsuccessful candidate for reelection in 1940 to the Seventy-seventh Congress; resumed his former pursuits at Old Lyme, Conn.; died in Old Lyme, Conn., June 16, 1943; interment in Duck River Cemetery.

BALL, William Lee, a Representative from Virginia; born in Lancaster County, Va., January 2, 1781; received a liberal schooling; served as paymaster in the War of 1812 and was assigned to the Ninety-second Virginia Regiment; elected as a Democrat to the Fifteenth, and to the three succeeding Congresses and served from March 4, 1817, until his death in Washington, D. C., February 28, 1824; interment in the Congressional Cemetery.

BALLENTINE, John Goff, a Representative from Tennessee; born in Pulaski, Giles County, Tenn., May 20, 1825; was graduated from Wurtemberg Academy in 1841, from the University of Nashville in 1845, and from the law department of Harvard University in 1848; was a member of the faculty of Livingston Law School in New York; commenced the practice of law in Pulaski; moved to Mississippi about 1854; continued the practice of law and engaged in agricultural pursuits; settled in Memphis, Tenn., in 1860; served as a colonel in the Confederate Army during the Civil War; returned to Pulaski, Tenn.; elected as a Democrat to the Forty-eighth and Forty-ninth Congresses (March 4, 1883–March 3, 1887); declined to be a candidate for renomination in 1886; retired from active pursuits; died in Pulaski, Tenn., on November 23, 1915; interment in the New Pulaski Cemetery.

BALLOU, Latimer Whipple, a Representative from Rhode Island; born in Cumberland, R. I., March 1, 1812; attended the public schools and the local academies in his native town; moved to Cambridge, Mass., in 1828 and learned the art of printing at the University Press; was instrumental in establishing the Cambridge Press in 1835 and continued in the printing business until 1842, when he moved to Woonsocket, R. I.; engaged in banking in 1850; was active in the organization of the Republican Party in 1856; presidential elector on the Republican ticket of Lincoln and Hamlin in 1860; delegate to the Republican National Convention at Philadelphia in 1872; elected as a Republican to the Forty-fourth, Forty-fifth and Forty-sixth Congresses (March 4, 1875–March 3, 1881); declined to be a candidate for renomination in 1880; engaged in his former business pursuits until his death in Woonsocket, Providence County, R. I., May 9, 1900; interment in Oak Hill Cemetery.

BALTZ, William Nicolas, a Representative from Illinois; born in Millstadt, St. Clair County, Ill., February 5, 1860; attended the public schools; engaged in agricultural pursuits, milling, and banking; member of the Millstadt Board of Education and served as president 1892–1917; member of the St. Clair County Board of Supervisors 1897–1913, serving as presiding officer from 1908 to 1911; member of the Democratic county central committee 1905–1913; elected as a Democrat to the Sixty-third Congress (March 4, 1913–March 3, 1915); unsuccessful candidate for reelection in 1914 to the Sixty-fourth Congress; mayor of Millstadt six years; resumed agricultural and industrial pursuits at Millstadt, Ill., until his death there August 22, 1943; interment in Mount Evergreen Cemetery.

BANISTER, John, a Delegate from Virginia; born at "Hatcher's Run," near Petersburg, Dinwiddie County, Va., December 26, 1734; attended a private school at Wakefield, England, and was graduated in law from the Temple in London; returned to Virginia and commenced the practice of law in Petersburg; also engaged as a planter; became an active organizer in anti-Revolutionary movements; member of the Virginia Assembly in 1765, 1766–1774, and 1775; distinguished member of the conventions of 1775 and 1776; served in the State house of delegates in 1776, 1777, and 1781–1783; Member of the Continental Congress from March 16, 1778, to September 24, 1779; one of the framers and signers of the Articles of Confederation; during the Revolutionary War served as major and lieutenant colonel of the Virginia Militia; died on his estate, "Hatcher's Run," near Petersburg, Dinwiddie County, Va., on September 30, 1788; interment in the family burying ground on his estate.

BANKHEAD, John Hollis (father of John Hollis Bankhead 2d and William Brockman Bankhead, and grandfather of Walter Will Bankhead), a Representative and a Senator from Alabama; born in Moscow, Marion (now Lamar) County, Ala., September 13, 1842; attended the common schools; engaged as a planter; served in the Confederate Army during the Civil War as Captain of Company K, Sixteenth Regiment, Alabama Infantry; member of the State house of representatives 1865–1867 and again in 1880 and 1881; served in the State senate in 1876 and 1877; warden of the State penitentiary at Wetumpka 1881–1885; moved to Fayette, Ala., in 1885 and resumed planting; in 1912 moved to Jasper, Ala.; elected as a Democrat to the Fiftieth and to the nine succeeding Congresses (March 4, 1887–March 3, 1907); unsuccessful candidate for renomination in 1906; appointed a member of the Inland Waterways Commission in 1907; appointed and subsequently elected to the United States Senate in 1907 to fill the vacancy caused by the death of John T. Morgan; reelected in 1912 and 1918 and served from June 18, 1907, until his death in Washington, D. C., March 1, 1920; interment in Oak Hill Cemetery, Jasper, Ala.

BANKHEAD, John Hollis 2d (son of the preceding, brother of William Brockman Bankhead, and father of Walter Will Bankhead), a Senator from Alabama; born on a farm near Old Moscow, Lamar County, Ala., July 8, 1872; attended the public schools; was graduated from the University of Alabama at Tuscaloosa in 1891 and from the law department of Georgetown University, Washington, D. C., in 1893; was admitted to the bar in 1893 and commenced practice in Jasper, Ala.; served in the Alabama

National Guard with rank of major 1901–1903; member of the State house of representatives 1904–1905; president of the Bankhead Coal Co. 1911–1925; trustee of the University of Alabama 1917–1919 and 1931–1946; elected as a Democrat to the United States Senate in 1930; reelected in 1936 and again in 1942 and served from March 4, 1931, until his death in the United States Naval Hospital, Bethesda, Md., on June 12, 1946; interment in Oak Hill Cemetery, Jasper, Ala.

BANKHEAD, Walter Will (son of John Hollis Bankhead 2d, grandson of John Hollis Bankhead, and nephew of William Brockman Bankhead), a Representative from Alabama; born in Jasper, Walker County, Ala., July 21, 1897; attended the public schools; was graduated from Marion (Ala.) Military Institute in 1916, from the University of Alabama at Tuscaloosa in 1919, and from the law department of the same university in 1920; was admitted to the bar in 1920 and commenced practice in Jasper, Ala.; delegate to the Democratic National Convention at Chicago in 1940; elected as a Democrat to the Seventy-seventh Congress and served from January 3, 1941, until February 1, 1941, when he resigned; resumed the practice of law; chairman of the board of Bankhead Mining Co., Inc., and Bankhead Development Co., Inc.; president of Mammoth Packing Co. and Bankhead Broadcasting Co., Inc.; vice chairman, board of directors, First National Bank of Jasper; is a resident of Jasper, Ala.

BANKHEAD, William Brockman (son of John Hollis Bankhead, brother of John Hollis Bankhead 2d, and uncle of Walter Will Bankhead), a Representative from Alabama; born in Moscow, Lamar County, Ala., April 12, 1874; attended the country schools; was graduated from the University of Alabama at Tuscaloosa in 1893 and from the Georgetown University Law School at Washington, D. C., in 1895; was admitted to the bar the same year and commenced practice in Huntsville, Ala.; member of the State house of representatives in 1900 and 1901; city attorney of Huntsville 1898–1902; moved to Jasper, Walker County, Ala., in 1905 and continued the practice of law; solicitor of the fourteenth judicial circuit of Alabama 1910–1914; elected as a Democrat to the Sixty-fifth and to the eleven succeeding Congresses and served from March 4, 1917, until his death; elected Democratic majority leader of the House of Representatives in the Seventy-fourth Congress; elected Speaker during the Seventy-fourth Congress and served until his death; delegate to the Democratic National Convention at Chicago in 1940; died in Washington, D. C., September 15, 1940; funeral services were held in the Hall of the House of Representatives; interment in Oak Hill Cemetery, Jasper, Ala.

BANKS, John, a Representative from Pennsylvania; born near Lewisburg, Juniata County, Pa., October 17, 1793; received a liberal education; studied law; was admitted to the bar and commenced practice in Juniata County in 1819; moved to Mercer County and continued the practice of law; elected as a Whig to the Twenty-second, Twenty-third, and Twenty-fourth Congresses and served from March 4, 1831, until his resignation in 1836; judge of the Berks judicial district from 1836 until he resigned to accept a State position; State treasurer of Pennsylvania in 1847; resumed the practice of law in Reading, Pa., where he died April 3, 1864; interment in Charles Evans Cemetery.

BANKS, Linn, a Representative from Virginia; born in Madison (then Culpeper) County, Va., January 23, 1784; studied law; was admitted to the bar in Madison County April 10, 1809; member of the Virginia House of Delegates 1812–1838, for twenty successive years serving as speaker; elected as a Democrat to the Twenty-fifth Congress to fill the vacancy caused by the resignation of John M. Patton; reelected to the Twenty-sixth

Congress and served from April 28, 1838, to March 3, 1841; presented credentials as a Member-elect to the Twenty-seventh Congress and served from March 4, 1841, until December 6, 1841, when he was succeeded by William Smith, who contested the election; was not a candidate for renomination in 1842; resumed the practice of law; served as a colonel in the Virginia Militia; was drowned while attempting to ford the Conway River near Wolftown, Madison County, Va., January 13, 1842; interment in the family burying ground on his estate, Vale Evergreen, near Graves Mill, Madison County, Va.

BANKS, Nathaniel Prentice, a Representative from Massachusetts; born in Waltham, Mass., January 30, 1816; attended the common schools; a machinist by trade; editor of a weekly paper in Waltham, Mass.; clerk in the customhouse in Boston, Mass.; studied law; was admitted to the Suffolk County bar and commenced practice in Boston; member of the State house of representatives 1849–1852, for two years serving as speaker; member of the State constitutional convention of 1853; elected as a Coalition Democrat to the Thirty-third Congress and as the candidate of the American Party to the Thirty-fourth Congress, of which he was chosen Speaker; elected as a Republican to the Thirty-fifth Congress and served from March 4, 1853, until he resigned December 24, 1857, to become Governor; Governor of Massachusetts from January 1858, until January 1861; moved to Chicago, Ill.; vice president of the Illinois Central Railroad; entered the Union Army as a major general of Volunteers May 16, 1861; received the thanks of Congress January 18, 1864, "for the skill, courage, and endurance which compelled the surrender of Port Hudson, and thus removed the last obstruction to the free navigation of the Mississippi River"; honorably mustered out August 24, 1865; returned to Massachusetts; elected as a Union Republican to the Thirty-ninth Congress to fill the vacancy caused by the resignation of Daniel W. Gooch; reelected as a Republican to the Fortieth, Forty-first, and Forty-second Congresses and served from December 4, 1865, to March 3, 1873; unsuccessful Liberal and Democratic candidate for reelection in 1872 to the Forty-third Congress; member of the State senate in 1874; elected as a Liberal Republican to the Forty-fourth and Forty-fifth Congresses (March 4, 1875–March 3, 1879); unsuccessful candidate for renomination in 1878 to the Forty-sixth Congress; appointed United States marshal on March 11, 1879, and served until April 23, 1888; elected as a Republican to the Fifty-first Congress (March 4, 1889–March 3, 1891); unsuccessful candidate for renomination in 1890 to the Fifty-second Congress; died in Waltham, Middlesex County, Mass., September 1, 1894; interment in Grove Hill Cemetery.

BANNING, Henry Blackstone, a Representative from Ohio; born in Bannings Mills, Ohio, November 10, 1836; attended the Clinton district school, Mount Vernon Academy, and Kenyon College, Gambier, Ohio; studied law; was admitted to the bar in 1857 and commenced practice in Mount Vernon, Ohio; during the Civil War enlisted April 1861 in the Union Army as a private; commissioned captain of the Fourth Regiment, Ohio Volunteer Infantry, June 5, 1861; colonel of the Eighty-seventh Regiment, Ohio Volunteer Infantry, June 25, 1862; honorably mustered out October 4, 1862; commissioned lieutenant colonel of the One Hundred and Twenty-fifth Regiment, Ohio Volunteer Infantry, January 1, 1863; transferred to the One Hundred and Twenty-first Regiment, Ohio Volunteer Infantry, April 5, 1863; colonel November 10, 1863; brevetted brigadier general and major general of Volunteers March 13, 1865, "for gallant and meritorious services during the Civil War"; resigned January 1, 1865; member of the State house of representatives in 1866 and 1867; moved to Cincinnati, Ohio, in 1869 and resumed the practice of law; elected as a Democrat to the Forty-third, Forty-fourth, and Forty-fifth

Congresses (March 4, 1873–March 3, 1879); unsuccessful candidate for renomination in 1878 to the Forty-sixth Congress, and for election in 1880 to the Forty-seventh Congress; resumed the practice of law; died in Cincinnati, Ohio, December 10, 1881; interment in Spring Grove Cemetery.

BANNON, Henry Towne, a Representative from Ohio; born near Portsmouth, Scioto County, Ohio, June 5, 1867; attended the public schools of Portsmouth, Ohio State University at Columbus in 1885 and 1886, and was graduated from the University of Michigan at Ann Arbor in 1889; studied law; was admitted to the Ohio bar in 1891 and practiced in Portsmouth, Ohio; prosecuting attorney of Scioto County 1897–1902; elected as a Republican to the Fifty-ninth and Sixtieth Congresses (March 4, 1905–March 3, 1909); was not a candidate for renomination in 1908; resumed the practice of law; delegate to the Republican National Conventions in 1924, 1928, 1932, 1936, and 1940; served as a director of the First National Bank, National Bank of Portsmouth, Oak Hill Savings Bank, and the Selby Shoe Co.; also engaged in literary pursuits; died in Portsmouth, Ohio, September 6, 1950; interment in Greenlawn Cemetery.

BANTA, Parke Monroe, a Representative from Missouri; born in Berryman, Crawford County, Mo., November 21, 1891; attended the public schools, and William Jewell College at Liberty, Mo.; was graduated from Northwestern University Law School at Evanston-Chicago, Ill., in 1914; was admitted to the bar in 1913 and practiced at Potosi, Mo., 1914–1925 and at Ironton, Mo., 1925–1941; prosecuting attorney of Washington County, Mo., in 1917 and 1918; during the First World War served in the United States Army as a private and through the ranks to first lieutenant from April 1918 to August 1919; member of the board of trustees of Arcadia, Mo., in 1928 and 1929; member of Ironton-Arcadia School Board in 1932 and 1933; administrator of the Missouri State Social Security Commission 1941–1945; delegate to the Republican State Conventions in 1916, 1920, 1922, 1924, and 1926; elected as a Republican to the Eightieth Congress (January 3, 1947–January 3, 1949); unsuccessful candidate for reelection in 1948 to the Eighty-first Congress and for election in 1950 to the Eighty-second Congress; resumed the practice of law in Ironton, Mo.; general counsel for Department of Health, Education, and Welfare, Washington, D. C., from April 11, 1953, until January 20, 1961; is a resident of Potosi, Mo.

BARBER, Hiram, Jr., a Representative from Illinois; born in Queensbury, Warren County, N. Y., March 24, 1835; moved to Horicon, Dodge County, Wis., in 1846; attended the University of Wisconsin at Madison; studied law in Albany, N. Y.; was admitted to the bar in 1856 and commenced practice at Juneau, Wis.; prosecuting attorney of Jefferson County, Wis., in 1861 and 1862; assistant attorney general of Wisconsin in 1865 and 1866; moved to Chicago, Ill., and resumed the practice of law in 1866; elected as a Republican to the Forty-sixth Congress (March 4, 1879–March 3, 1881); unsuccessful candidate for renomination in 1880; receiver of the land office at Mitchell, S. Dak., 1881–1888; returned to Chicago and continued the practice of law; served as master in chancery of the Cook County Superior Court from 1891 to 1914; retired from public life and active business pursuits; died at Lake Geneva, Wis., August 5, 1924; interment in Juneau Cemetery, Juneau, Wis.

BARBER, Isaac Ambrose, a Representative from Maryland; born near Salem, Salem County, N. J., January 26, 1852; attended the common schools, and studied medicine in Hahnemann Medical College, Philadelphia, Pa., from which he was graduated in 1872; commenced practice in Woodstown, N. J.; moved to Easton, Talbot County, Md., in 1873 and continued the practice of medicine for fifteen years; engaged in the milling business; member of the State house of delegates in 1895; president of the Farmers & Merchants' National Bank of Easton; elected as a Republican to the Fifty-fifth Congress (March 4, 1897–March 3, 1899); resumed the milling business and also engaged in agricultural pursuits; chairman of the Republican State central committee 1900–1904; died in Easton, Md., March 1, 1909; interment in Spring Hill Cemetery.

BARBER, Joel Allen, a Representative from Wisconsin; born in Georgia (near St. Albans), Franklin County, Vt., January 17, 1809; attended the common schools, Georgia Academy, and the University of Vermont, Burlington, Vt.; studied law; was admitted to the bar in 1834 in Prince Georges County, Md., where he was teaching school, and commenced practice in Fairfield, Vt.; moved to Wisconsin in 1837 and settled in Lancaster, Grant County, and continued the practice of his profession; county clerk for four years and district attorney three terms; member of the first constitutional convention of Wisconsin in 1846; elected to the State assembly in 1852, 1853, 1863, and 1864, serving as speaker in 1864; member of the State senate in 1856 and 1857; founded Lancaster Academy; elected as a Republican to the Forty-second and Forty-third Congresses (March 4, 1871–March 3, 1875); was not a candidate for renomination in 1874; resumed the practice of law; died in Lancaster, Wis., June 17, 1881; interment in Hillside Cemetery.

BARBER, Laird Howard, a Representative from Pennsylvania; born on a farm near Mifflinburg, Union County, Pa., October 25, 1848; prepared for college in the Mifflinburg Academy, and was graduated from Lafayette College, Easton, Pa., in 1871; taught school at Mount Carmel and was principal of the Mauch Chunk Public Schools from 1875 to 1880; studied law; was admitted to the bar in Carbon County June 20, 1881, and commenced practice at Mauch Chunk; elected in 1890 a director of the Mauch Chunk School Board and served as president and treasurer; also served as secretary of the town council; unsuccessful candidate for election in 1896 to the Fifty-fifth Congress; elected as a Democrat to the Fifty-sixth Congress (March 4, 1899–March 3, 1901); was not a candidate for renomination in 1900 to the Fifth-seventh Congress; resumed the practice of law in Mauch Chunk; elected president judge of the fifty-sixth judicial district of Pennsylvania in 1913; reelected in 1923 and served from January 5, 1914, until his death in Mauch Chunk, Carbon County, Pa., February 16, 1928; interment in Evergreen Cemetery, East Mauch Chunk, Pa.

BARBER, Levi, a Representative from Ohio; born in Simsbury, Hartford County, Conn., October 16, 1777; moved to Ohio; was a surveyor in the employ of the Federal Government; member of the State house of representatives in 1806; was commissioned receiver of the United States land office in Marietta, Ohio, on April 1, 1807; aide to Governor Meigs during the War of 1812; elected to the Fifteenth Congress (March 4, 1817–March 3, 1819); unsuccessful candidate for reelection in 1818 to the Sixteenth Congress; elected to the Seventeenth Congress (March 4, 1821–March 3, 1823); unsuccessful candidate for reelection in 1822 to the Eighteenth Congress; clerk of the court of common pleas and the court of Washington County; justice of the peace; president of the Bank of Marietta; died in Harmar (now a part of Marietta), Ohio, April 23, 1833; interment in Harmar Cemetery.

BARBER, Noyes (uncle of Edwin Barbour Morgan and Christopher Morgan), a Representative from Connecticut; born in Groton, New London County, Conn., April 28, 1781; attended the common schools; engaged in mercantile pursuits;

major of the Eighth Connecticut Regiment in the War of 1812; detailed to defend the coast towns during the blockade by the British Fleet; member of the State house of representatives in 1818; elected as a Democrat to the Seventeenth and to the six succeeding Congresses (March 4, 1821–March 3, 1835); unsuccessful candidate for reelection in 1834 to the Twenty-fourth Congress; resumed mercantile pursuits; member of all Whig State conventions from 1836; died in Groton, Conn., January 3, 1844; interment in Starr Cemetery.

BARBOUR, Henry Ellsworth, a Representative from California; born in Ogdensburg, St. Lawrence County, N. Y., March 8, 1877; attended the public schools of his native city, the local Free Academy at Ogdensburg, Union College at Schenectady, N. Y., and the law department of George Washington University, Washington, D. C.; was admitted to the New York bar in 1901; moved to Fresno, Fresno County, Calif., in 1902 and engaged in the practice of law; member of the Fresno County Bar Association; elected as a Republican to the Sixty-sixth and to the six succeeding Congresses (March 4, 1919–March 3, 1933); unsuccessful candidate for reelection in 1932 to the Seventy-third Congress; resumed the practice of his profession in Fresno, Calif., where he died on March 21, 1945; interment in Belmont Memorial Cemetery.

BARBOUR, James (brother of Philip Pendleton Barbour and cousin of John Strode Barbour), a Senator from Virginia; born at "Frascati," near Gordonsville, Orange County, Va., June 10, 1775; attended the common schools; deputy sheriff of Orange County; studied law; was admitted to the bar in 1794 at Orange Court House; member of the Virginia House of Delegates 1796–1812, serving as speaker from 1809 to 1812; Governor of Virginia 1812–1814; elected as an Anti-Democrat and State Rights candidate to the United States Senate in 1814 for the term commencing March 4, 1815; subsequently elected to fill the vacancy in the term ending March 3, 1815, caused by the death of Richard Brent; reelected in 1821 and served from January 2, 1815, to March 7, 1825, when he resigned to accept a Cabinet portfolio; elected President pro tempore of the Senate on February 15, 1819; appointed Secretary of War by President John Quincy Adams and served from March 7, 1825, to May 26, 1828, when he resigned to accept a diplomatic position; United States Minister to England from May 26, 1828, to September 23, 1829; chairman of the Whig National Convention in 1839 that nominated Harrison and Tyler; founder of the Orange County Humane Society, established for the advancement of education; died in Barboursville, Orange County, Va., June 7, 1842; interment in the family cemetery.

BARBOUR, John Strode (cousin of James Barbour and Philip Pendleton Barbour), a Representative from Virginia; born at "Fleetwood," near Brandy Station, Culpeper County, Va., August 8, 1790; attended private schools; was graduated from William and Mary College, Williamsburg, Va., in 1808; studied law; was admitted to the bar in 1811 and commenced practice in Culpeper, Va.; served in the War of 1812 as aide-de-camp to General Madison; member of the State house of delegates 1813–1816, 1820–1823, 1833, and 1834; elected as a State Rights Democrat to the Eighteenth and to the four succeeding Congresses (March 4, 1823–March 3, 1833); was not a candidate for renomination in 1832; member of the Virginia constitutional conventions in 1829 and 1830; chairman of the Democratic National Convention at Baltimore that nominated Franklin Pierce as a candidate for President in 1852; resumed the practice of law; died on his estate, "Fleetwood," near Culpeper, Culpeper County, Va., on January 12, 1855; interment in the family burying ground on his estate.

BARBOUR, John Strode (son of the preceding), a Representative and a Senator from Virginia; born at "Catalpa," near Culpeper, Culpeper County, Va., December 29, 1820; attended the common schools and was graduated from the law department of the University of Virginia at Charlottesville; was admitted to the bar in 1841 and commenced practice in Culpeper; member of the State house of delegates 1847–1851; elected president of the Orange & Alexandria Railroad Co. (now a part of the main line of the Southern Railway in Virginia) in 1852 and served until his resignation in 1881; elected as a Democrat to the Forty-seventh, Forty-eighth, and Forty-ninth Congresses (March 4, 1881–March 3, 1887); declined to be a candidate for renomination in 1886; chairman of the Democratic State committee in 1883 and conducted the series of campaigns which resulted in the defeat of the Mahone coalition movement in Virginia, resigning in 1890; delegate at large to the Democratic National Conventions in 1884 and 1888; member of the Democratic National Committee 1884–1892; elected as a Democrat to the United States Senate and served from March 4, 1889, until his death in Washington, D. C., May 14, 1892; interment in the burial ground of his wife's family at "Poplar Hill," Prince Georges County, Md.

BARBOUR, Lucien, a Representative from Indiana; born in Canton, Hartford County, Conn., March 4, 1811; was graduated from Amherst (Mass.) College in 1837; moved to Indiana the same year and settled in Madison, Jefferson County; studied law; was admitted to the bar and commenced practice in Indianapolis, Ind., in 1839; acted a number of times as arbitrator between the State of Indiana and private corporations; appointed United States district attorney for the district of Indiana by President Polk; member of the commission to codify the laws of Indiana in 1852; elected by a combination of the Free Soil, Temperance, and Know Nothing Parties to the Thirty-fourth Congress (March 4, 1855–March 3, 1857); was not a candidate for renomination in 1856; affiliated with the Republican Party in 1860; practiced law in Indianapolis, Ind., until his death in that city on July 19, 1880; interment in Crown Hill Cemetery.

BARBOUR, Philip Pendleton (brother of James Barbour and cousin of John Strode Barbour), a Representative from Virginia; born at "Frascati," near Gordonsville, Orange County, Va., May 25, 1783; attended common and private schools; was graduated from William and Mary College, Williamsburg, Va., in 1799; studied law; was admitted to the bar in 1800 and commenced practice in Bardstown, Ky.; returned to Virginia in 1801 and practiced law in Gordonsville, Orange County; member of the State house of delegates 1812–1814; elected as a Democrat to the Thirteenth Congress to fill the vacancy caused by the death of John Dawson; reelected to the Fourteenth and to the four succeeding Congresses and served from September 19, 1814, to March 3, 1825; was not a candidate for renomination in 1824; served as Speaker of the House of Representatives in the Seventeenth Congress; offered the professorship of law in the University of Virginia in 1825, but declined; appointed a judge of the general court of Virginia and served for two years, resigning in 1827; elected to the Twentieth and Twenty-first Congresses and served from March 4, 1827, until his resignation on October 15, 1830; president of the Virginia constitutional convention in 1829; appointed by President Jackson, June 1, 1830, judge of the United States Circuit Court for the Eastern District of Virginia, declining the chancellorship and the post of attorney general; refused nominations for judge of the court of appeals, for Governor, and for United States Senator; appointed Associate Justice of the United States Supreme Court and served from March 15, 1836, until his death in Washington, D. C., February 25, 1841; interment in Congressional Cemetery.

BARBOUR, William Warren, a Senator from New Jersey; born in Monmouth Beach, Monmouth County, N. J., July 31, 1888; attended the public schools and was graduated from the Browning School, New York City, N. Y., in 1906; also attended Princeton University, Princeton, N. J.; amateur heavyweight boxing champion of the United States and Canada in 1910 and 1911; member of the New York National Guard for ten years, serving on the Mexican border in 1916 as a first lieutenant and advancing to the rank of captain; member of the Rumson (N. J.) Borough Council in 1922; served as mayor of Rumson, N. J., 1923–1928; moved to Locust, Monmouth County, N. J., in 1930; engaged in the thread-manufacturing business and other industrial enterprises; appointed and subsequently elected as a Republican to the United States Senate to fill the vacancy caused by the death of Dwight W. Morrow and served from December 1, 1931, to January 3, 1937; unsuccessful candidate for reelection in 1936; resumed his former pursuits; member of the New Jersey Unemployment Compensation Commission in 1937; again elected to the United States Senate to fill the vacancy caused by the resignation of A. Harry Moore, reelected in 1940, and served from November 9, 1938, until his death in Washington, D. C., on November 22, 1943; interment in Cedar Lawn Cemetery, Paterson, N. J.

BARCHFELD, Andrew Jackson, a Representative from Pennsylvania; born in Pittsburgh, Pa., May 18, 1863; attended the public schools and the Pittsburgh Central High School; was graduated from Jefferson Medical College, Philadelphia, Pa., in 1884; commenced the practice of medicine in Pittsburgh, and was for many years president of the South Side Hospital; member of the American Medical Association and the Allegheny County Medical Society; member of the common council of Pittsburgh 1886 and 1887; delegate to the Republican State conventions of 1886, 1894, and 1901; for many years a member of the Republican State committee; unsuccessful candidate for election in 1902 to the Fifty-eighth Congress; elected as a Republican to the Fifty-ninth and to the five succeeding Congresses (March 4, 1905–March 3, 1917); unsuccessful candidate for reelection in 1916 to the Sixty-fifth Congress; delegate to the peace congress at Brussels in 1905; member of the commission to the Philippine Islands in 1910 and of the Panama Canal Commission in 1912; continued to reside in Washington, D. C., after leaving Congress and was killed in the Knickerbocker Theater disaster in that city on January 28, 1922; interment in South Side Cemetery, Pittsburgh, Pa.

BARCLAY, Charles Frederick, a Representative from Pennsylvania; born in Owego, Tioga County, N. Y., May 9, 1844; moved with his parents to Pennsylvania in 1845; attended Painted Post (N. Y.) High School and Coudersport (Pa.) Academy; taught school for several years; during the Civil War enlisted as a private in Company K, One Hundred and Forty-ninth Regiment, Pennsylvania Volunteer Infantry, in 1862 and served until 1865, when he was mustered out with the rank of captain; attended Belfast Seminary, New York, and subsequently studied law at the University of Michigan at Ann Arbor, but never practiced; with an elder brother was engaged extensively in the lumber business in Sinnamahoning, Pa.; presidential elector on the Republican ticket of Benjamin Harrison and Whitelaw Reid in 1892; delegate to the Republican National Convention at Philadelphia in 1900; elected as a Republican to the Sixtieth and Sixty-first Congresses (March 4, 1907–March 3, 1911); was not a candidate for renomination in 1910 to the Sixty-second Congress; engaged in business in Washington, D. C., until his death March 9, 1914; interment in Wyside Cemetery, Sinnamahoning, Cameron County, Pa.

BARCLAY, David, a Representative from Pennsylvania; born in Punxsutawney, Jefferson County, Pa., in 1823; attended Washington (now Washington and Jefferson) College, Washington, Pa.; studied law in Pittsburgh; was admitted to the bar and practiced in Punxsutawney, Brookville, and Kittanning, Pa.; one of the editors and publishers of the Pittsburgh Union and Legal Journal 1850–1855; while a resident of Brookville was elected as a Democrat to the Thirty-fourth Congress (March 4, 1855–March 3, 1857); resumed the practice of law; died in Freeport, Armstrong County, Pa., September 10, 1889; interment in Freeport Cemetery.

BARD, David, a Representative from Pennsylvania; born at "Carroll's Delight," Adams County, Pa., in 1744; was graduated from Princeton College, New Jersey, in 1773; studied theology and was licensed to preach by the Donegal Presbytery in 1777; was ordained to the Presbyterian ministry at Lower Conotheague in 1779; missionary in Virginia and west of the Allegheny Mountains; pastor at Bedford, Pa., 1786–1789, and later at Frankstown (now Hollidaysburg), Blair County, Pa.; elected to the Fourth and Fifth Congresses (March 4, 1795–March 3, 1799); elected to the Eighth and to the six succeeding Congresses and served from March 4, 1803, until his death in Alexandria, Huntingdon County, Pa., March 12, 1815; interment in Sinking Valley Cemetery, near Arch Spring, Blair County, Pa.

BARD, Thomas Robert, a Senator from California; born in Chambersburg, Franklin County, Pa., December 8, 1841; attended the common schools, and was graduated from the Chambersburg Academy in 1858; studied law, but before completing his studies secured a position with the Pennsylvania Railroad Co., later becoming assistant to the superintendent of the Cumberland Valley Railroad and had charge of the movement of trains carrying military supplies; was engaged in the grain business at Hagerstown, Md.; during the early part of the Civil War served as a volunteer Union scout during the invasions of Maryland and Pennsylvania by the Confederates; moved to Ventura County, Calif., in 1864; member of the board of supervisors of Santa Barbara County 1868–1873; laid out the town of Hueneme; one of the commissioners appointed to organize Ventura County in 1871; delegate to the Republican National Convention at Chicago in 1884; director of the State board of agriculture in 1886 and 1887; in 1892 he was the only presidential elector chosen on the Republican ticket of Harrison and Reid, the other electors being Democrats; elected as a Republican to the United States Senate to fill the vacancy in the term beginning March 4, 1899, and served from February 7, 1900, to March 3, 1905; was an unsuccessful candidate for reelection in 1904; died at his home, "Berylwood," in Hueneme, Ventura County, Calif., March 5, 1915; interment in the family cemetery on his estate.

BARDEN, Graham Arthur, a Representative from North Carolina; born in Turkey Township, Sampson County, N. C., September 25, 1896; moved to Burgaw, Pender County, N. C., in 1908; attended the public schools; during the First World War served as a seaman in the United States Navy in 1918 and 1919; was graduated from the law department of the University of North Carolina at Chapel Hill in 1920; was admitted to the bar the same year and commenced practice in New Bern, N. C.; teacher in the New Bern (N. C.) High School in 1920; judge of the county court of Craven County, N. C., 1920–1924; member of the State house of representatives in 1933; elected as a Democrat to the Seventy-fourth and to the twelve succeeding Congresses (January 3, 1935–January 3, 1961); was not a candidate for renomination in 1960; is a resident of New Bern, N. C.

BARHAM, John All, a Representative from California; born on a farm in Cass County, Mo., July 17, 1843; moved to California in 1849 with his parents, who settled in Woodland; attended the common schools and Hesperian College in Woodland, Calif.; taught in the public schools 1864–1876; studied law; was admitted to the bar in 1865 and commenced practice in Watsonville, San Francisco, and Santa Rosa; elected as a Republican to the Fifty-fourth, Fifty-fifth, and Fifty-sixth Congresses (March 4, 1895–March 3, 1901); was not a candidate for renomination in 1900; engaged in the practice of law until his death in Santa Rosa, Sonoma County, Calif., January 22, 1926; interment in Rural Cemetery.

BARING, Walter Stephan, a Representative from Nevada; born in Goldfield, Esmeralda County, Nev., September 9, 1911; graduated from Reno High School in 1929 and from the University of Nevada at Reno in 1934; holder of high-school teacher's certificate; elected chairman of the Democratic Central Committee of Washoe County, Nev., in 1936; elected assemblyman from Washoe County to the State assembly in 1936, reelected in 1942, and served until his resignation to enlist in the United States Navy; served in the Navy from September 26, 1942, until May 31, 1945; engaged in the furniture business at Reno, Nev., 1945–1948; member of the Reno City Council in 1947; elected as a Democrat to the Eighty-first and Eighty-second Congresses (January 3, 1949–January 3, 1953); unsuccessful candidate for reelection in 1952 to the Eighty-third Congress; delegate to the Democratic National Conventions in 1952 and 1956; engaged in the insurance business; unsuccessful candidate for election in 1954 to the Eighty-fourth Congress; elected to the Eighty-fifth and Eighty-sixth Congresses (January 3, 1957–January 3, 1961). *Reelected to the Eighty-seventh Congress.*

BARKER, Abraham Andrews, a Representative from Pennsylvania; born in Lovell, Oxford County, Maine, March 30, 1816; attended the common schools; engaged in agricultural pursuits and also in the shook business; moved to Carrolltown, Pa., in 1854 and to Ebensburg, Cambria County, Pa., where he continued the shook business; also engaged in the mercantile business in 1858 and later in the lumber business; delegate to the Republican National Convention at Chicago in 1860; served in Company E, Fourth Regiment, Pennsylvania Emergency Troops, during the Civil War; elected as a Union Republican to the Thirty-ninth Congress (March 4, 1865–March 3, 1867); unsuccessful candidate for renomination in 1866 and for election as a Republican in 1872 to the Forty-third Congress; reengaged in the lumber and shook business until 1880, when he retired from active pursuits; died in Altoona, Pa., while on a visit for medical treatment, March 18, 1898; interment in Lloyd Cemetery, Ebensburg, Pa.

BARKER, David, Jr., a Representative from New Hampshire; born in Stratham, N. H., January 8, 1797; attended Phillips Exeter Academy, Exeter, N. H., and was graduated from Harvard University in 1815; studied law; was admitted to the bar in 1819 and commenced practice in Rochester, N. H.; member of the State house of representatives in 1823, 1825, and 1826; elected to the Twentieth Congress (March 4, 1827–March 3, 1829); resumed the practice of law; was an original member of the New Hampshire Historical Society; died in Rochester, N. H., April 1, 1834; interment in the Old Rochester Cemetery.

BARKER, Joseph, a Representative from Massachusetts; born in Branford, Conn., October 19, 1751; attended the common schools in Branford, Harvard College for two years, and was graduated from Yale College in 1771; studied theology; licensed to preach January 3, 1775, ordained to the ministry December

5, 1781, and was installed as pastor of the First Congregational Church of Middleboro, Plymouth County, Mass.; elected as a Democrat to the Ninth and Tenth Congresses (March 4, 1805–March 3, 1809); was not a candidate for renomination in 1808; member of the State house of representatives in 1812 and 1813; continued in the ministry at Middleboro, Mass., until his death, July 5, 1815; interment in Green Cemetery.

BARKLEY, Alben William, a Representative and a Senator from Kentucky and a Vice President of the United States; born near Lowes, Graves County, Ky., November 24, 1877; attended the public schools and was graduated from Marvin College, Clinton, Ky., in 1897; afterwards attended Emory College, Oxford, Ga., and the University of Virginia Law School, Charlottesville, Va.; was admitted to the bar in 1901 and commenced practice in Paducah, McCracken County, Ky.; prosecuting attorney for McCracken County, Ky., 1905–1909; judge of McCracken County Court 1909–1913; chairman of the Democratic State Conventions in 1919 and 1924; delegate to all Democratic National Conventions from 1920 to 1940, inclusive, serving as temporary chairman in 1932 and 1936 and as permanent chairman in 1940; elected as a Democrat to the Sixty-third and to the six succeeding Congresses (March 4, 1913–March 3, 1927); did not seek renomination in 1926, having become a candidate for United States Senator; elected to the United States Senate in 1926; reelected in 1932, 1938, and again in 1944, and served from March 4, 1927, until his resignation on January 19, 1949; served as Democratic majority leader of the Senate 1937–1947 and as Democratic minority leader of the Senate in 1947 and 1948; elected Vice President of the United States on the Democratic ticket with President Harry S. Truman in 1948, and was inaugurated January 20, 1949, for the term ending January 20, 1953; again elected to the United States Senate and served from January 3, 1955, until his death in Lexington, Va., April 30, 1956; interment in Mount Kenton Cemetery, on Lone Oak Road, near Paducah, Ky.

BARKSDALE, Ethelbert (brother of William Barksdale), a Representative from Mississippi; born in Smyrna, Rutherford County, Tenn., January 4, 1824; moved to Jackson, Hinds County, Miss.; adopted journalism as a profession; edited the official journal of the State 1854–1861 and 1876–1883; member of the Confederate Congress 1861–1865; delegate to the Democratic National Conventions in 1860, 1868, 1872, and 1880; presidential elector on the Democratic ticket of Tilden and Hendricks in 1876 and president of the State electoral college; chairman of the Democratic State executive committee 1877–1879; elected as a Democrat to the Forty-eighth and Forty-ninth Congresses (March 4, 1883–March 3, 1887); unsuccessful candidate for renomination in 1886; engaged in agricultural pursuits in Yazoo County; died in Yazoo City, Miss., February 17, 1893; interment in Greenwood Cemetery, Jackson, Miss.

BARKSDALE, William (brother of Ethelbert Barksdale), a Representative from Mississippi; born in Rutherford County, Tenn., August 21, 1821; attended the University of Nashville; studied law; was admitted to the bar in 1839 and commenced practice in Columbus, Lowndes County, Miss.; served in the Mexican War as quartermaster of the Mississippi Volunteers; delegate to the Democratic National Convention at Baltimore in 1852; elected as a State Rights Democrat to the Thirty-third and to the three succeeding Congresses and served from March 4, 1853, until January 12, 1861, when he withdrew; accompanied Representative Preston S. Brooks, of South Carolina, to the Senate Chamber when the latter made an attack upon Senator Charles Sumner, of Massachusetts, and made himself somewhat conspicuous in preventing the interference of others present;

entered the Confederate Army during the Civil War as colonel of the Thirteenth Regiment of Mississippi Volunteers; promoted to the rank of brigadier general on August 12, 1862; commanded a Mississippi brigade in Longstreet's corps; killed in the Battle of Gettysburg, Pa., July 2, 1863; interment in Greenwood Cemetery, Jackson, Miss.

BARLOW, Bradley, a Representative from Vermont; born in Fairfield, Franklin County, Vt., May 12, 1814; attended the common schools; engaged in mercantile pursuits in Philadelphia until 1858, when he moved to St. Albans, Vt.; delegate to the State constitutional conventions in 1843, 1850, and 1857, acting as assistant secretary in 1843; member of the State house of representatives in 1845, 1850–1852, 1864, and 1865; engaged in banking and in the railroad business 1860–1883 chairman of the school committee in St. Albans; president of the village corporation and treasurer of Franklin County 1860–1867; served in the State senate 1866–1868; elected as a National Republican to the Forty-sixth Congress (March 4, 1879–March 3, 1881); was not a candidate for renomination in 1880; died in Denver, Colo., on November 6, 1889; interment in Greenwood Cemetery, St. Albans, Vt.

BARLOW, Charles Averill, a Representative from California; born in Cleveland, Ohio, March 17, 1858; attended the common schools; engaged in agricultural and commercial pursuits; moved to Ventura, Calif., in 1875 and to San Luis Obispo County in 1889, engaging in wheat farming; member of the State assembly in 1892 and 1893; chairman of the People's Party State convention in 1896; elected as a Populist and Democrat to the Fifty-fifth Congress (March 4, 1897–March 3, 1899); was not a candidate for renomination; moved to Kern County in 1901 and engaged in mining, fruit growing, and the production of oil; delegate to the Democratic National Conventions in 1912 and 1920; died in Bakersfield, Calif., on October 3, 1927; interment in Union Cemetery.

BARLOW, Stephen, a Representative from Pennsylvania; born in Redding, Fairfield County, Conn., June 13, 1779; attended the common schools and Yale College; moved to Meadville, Pa., in 1816; studied law; was admitted to the bar and commenced practice in Meadville, Crawford County, Pa.; elected as a Democrat to the Twentieth Congress (March 4, 1827–March 3, 1829); unsuccessful candidate for reelection in 1828 to the Twenty-first Congress; resumed the practice of his profession; served in the State house of representatives 1829–1831; appointed as an associate judge of Crawford County in January 1831 and served until his death in Meadville, Pa., August 24, 1845; interment in Greendale Cemetery.

BARNARD, Daniel Dewey, a Representative from New York; born in Sheffield, Berkshire County, Mass., July 16, 1797; attended the common schools and was graduated from Williams College, Williamstown, Mass., in 1818; studied law; was admitted to the bar in 1821 and began practice in Rochester, N. Y.; prosecuting attorney of Monroe County in 1826; elected to the Twentieth Congress (March 4, 1827–March 3, 1829); unsuccessful candidate for reelection in 1828 to the Twenty-first Congress; traveled in Europe in 1831; moved to Albany, N. Y., in 1832 and continued the practice of law; member of the State assembly in 1838; elected as a Whig to the Twenty-sixth, Twenty-seventh, and Twenty-eighth Congresses (March 4, 1839–March 3, 1845); was not a candidate for reelection in 1844; appointed Minister to Prussia and served from September 3, 1850, to September 21, 1853; retired from active business pursuits in 1853 and engaged in literary pursuits; died in Albany, N. Y., April 24, 1861; interment in Albany Rural Cemetery.

BARNARD, Isaac Dutton, a Senator from Pennsylvania; born in Aston Township, Delaware County, Pa., July 18, 1791; moved with his parents to a farm near Chester, Pa.; attended the public schools; moved to Philadelphia, where he remained until 1811, when he returned to Chester; while studying law was appointed captain and major in the Fourteenth Regiment, United States Infantry, May 12, 1812, and served during the War of 1812; resumed his legal studies; was admitted to the bar in 1816 and commenced practice in West Chester, Chester County, Pa.; deputy attorney general for Chester County 1817–1821; member of the State senate 1820–1826; secretary of State in 1826; elected as a Federalist to the United States Senate and served from March 4, 1827, until December 6, 1831, when he resigned; died in West Chester, Pa., February 28, 1834; interment in Oakland's Cemetery, near West Chester, Pa.

BARNARD, William Oscar, a Representative from Indiana; born near Liberty, Union County, Ind., October 25, 1852; moved with his parents to Dublin, Wayne County, Ind., in 1854, to Fayette County in 1856, and to Henry County in 1866; attended the common schools, and Spiceland Academy, Spiceland, Ind.; taught school for five years in Henry and Wayne Counties; studied law; was admitted to the bar in 1876 and commenced practice in Newcastle, Ind.; prosecuting attorney of the eighteenth and fifty-third judicial circuits 1887–1893; judge of the fifty-third judicial circuit court of Indiana 1896–1902; resumed the practice of law in Newcastle; elected as a Republican to the Sixty-first Congress (March 4, 1909–March 3, 1911); unsuccessful candidate for reelection in 1910 to the Sixty-second Congress; resumed the practice of law in Newcastle, Ind., until his death there on April 8, 1939; interment in Southmound Cemetery.

BARNES, Demas, a Representative from New York; born in Gorham Township, Ontario County, N. Y., April 4, 1827; attended the public schools; engaged in mercantile pursuits; moved to New York City in 1849 and engaged in the drug business; crossed the continent in a wagon and studied the mineral resources of Colorado, Nevada, and California; returned to New York City and wrote articles and published works concerning his experiences; elected as a Democrat to the Fortieth Congress (March 4, 1867–March 3, 1869); was not a candidate for renomination in 1868; established and edited the Brooklyn Argus in 1873 and was also engaged in the real-estate business; member of the board of education; one of the original trustees of the Brooklyn Bridge when it was a private enterprise; died in New York City May 1, 1888; interment in Greenwood Cemetery.

BARNES, George Thomas, a Representative from Georgia; born in a suburb (now called Summerville) of Augusta, Richmond County, Ga., August 14, 1833; attended private schools, Richmond Academy, and Franklin College; was graduated from the University of Georgia at Athens in 1853; studied law; was admitted to the bar in 1855 and commenced practice in Augusta; during the Civil War served in the Confederate Army in the Washington Light Artillery Company of Augusta, Ga., as second lieutenant and major brevet; member of the State house of representatives 1860–1865; member of the Democratic National Committee 1876–1884; elected as a Democrat to the Forty-ninth, Fiftieth, and Fifty-first Congresses (March 4, 1885–March 3, 1891); unsuccessful candidate for reelection in 1890 to the Fifty-second Congress; resumed the practice of law; died in Augusta, Ga., October 24, 1901; interment in the City Cemetery.

BARNES, James Martin, a Representative from Illinois; born in Jacksonville, Morgan County, Ill., January 9, 1899; attended the public schools; during the First World War served overseas as a private in the United States Marine Corps in 1918 and 1919; was graduated from Illinois College at Jacksonville in 1921 and from the law department of Harvard University, Cambridge, Mass., in 1924; was admitted to the bar in 1924 and commenced the practice of law in Jacksonville, Ill.; served as county judge of Morgan County, Ill., 1926–1934; resumed the practice of law 1934–1939; elected as a Democrat to the Seventy-sixth and Seventy-seventh Congresses (January 3, 1939–January 3, 1943); unsuccessful candidate for reelection in 1942 to the Seventy-eighth Congress; appointed administrative assistant to President Franklin D. Roosevelt on March 1, 1943, and served until July 15, 1945; resumed the practice of law in Washington, D. C., where he died June 8, 1958; interment in Arlington National Cemetery, Fort Myer, Va.

BARNES, Lyman Eddy, a Representative from Wisconsin; born in Weyauwega, Waupaca County, Wis., June 30, 1855; attended the public schools and the law department of Columbia College, New York City; was admitted to the bar in 1876 and commenced practice in Appleton, Outagamie County, Wis., the same year; moved to Rockledge, Brevard County, Fla., in 1882, where he remained about five years and continued the practice of law; returned to Appleton, Wis., and was elected district attorney of Outagamie County; elected as a Democrat to the Fifty-third Congress (March 4, 1893–March 3, 1895); unsuccessful candidate for reelection in 1894 to the Fifty-fourth Congress; resumed the practice of his profession; died in Appleton, Wis., on January 16, 1904; interment in Riverside Cemetery.

BARNETT, William, a Representative from Georgia; born in Amherst County, Va., March 4, 1761; moved to Georgia with his father, who settled in Columbia County; at the outbreak of the Revolutionary War returned to Virginia with his brother and joined a military company from Amherst County under the leadership of the Marquis de Lafayette and was present at the surrender of Cornwallis at Yorktown; returned to Georgia at the close of the war and settled on Broad River, Elbert County; sheriff of Elbert County for several years; member of the State senate and served as president of that body; elected as a State Rights Democrat to the Twelfth Congress to fill the vacancy caused by the resignation of Howell Cobb; reelected to the Thirteenth Congress and served from October 5, 1812, to March 3, 1815; appointed commissioner to establish the boundaries of the Creek Indian Reservation in 1815; moved to Montgomery County, Ala., and engaged in planting; died in Montgomery County, Ala., April 1832; interment in the Gilmer-Christian-Barnett cemetery, near Mathews Station, Montgomery County, Ala.

BARNEY, John, a Representative from Maryland; born in Baltimore, Md., January 18, 1785; appointed a captain and assistant district quartermaster general in the United States Army August 15, 1814, and served until June 15, 1815, when he was honorably discharged; unsuccessful candidate for election in 1822 to the Eighteenth Congress; elected as a Federalist to the Nineteenth and Twentieth Congresses (March 4, 1825–March 3, 1829); unsuccessful candidate for reelection in 1828 to the Twenty-first Congress; engaged in literary pursuits until his death in Washington, D. C., January 26, 1857; interment in Greenmount Cemetery, Baltimore, Md.

BARNEY, Samuel Stebbins, a Representative from Wisconsin; born in Hartford, Washington County, Wis., January 31, 1846; attended the public schools and Lombard University, Galesburg, Ill.; taught in the high school at Hartford for four years; studied law in West Bend, Wis.; was admitted to the bar in 1873 and commenced practice in West Bend; superintendent of schools of Washington County 1876–1880; delegate to the Republican National Convention at Chicago in 1884; unsuccessful candidate for election in 1884 to the Forty-ninth Congress; elected as a Republican to the Fifty-fourth and to the three succeeding Congresses (March 4, 1895–March 3, 1903); was not a candidate for renomination in 1902; appointed associate justice of the court of claims, Washington, D. C., in 1904 and served until 1919; died in Milwaukee, Wis., December 31, 1919; interment in Union Cemetery, West Bend, Washington County, Wis.

BARNHART, Henry A., a Representative from Indiana; born near Twelve Mile, Cass County, Ind., September 11, 1858; attended the common schools, Amboy Academy, and Wabash Normal Training School; taught school; moved to Liberty Township, Fulton County, in 1881 and engaged in agricultural pursuits until 1884; moved to Rochester, Ind., in 1885 and served as surveyor of Fulton County 1885–1887; owner and editor of the Rochester Sentinel 1886–1924; president and manager of the Rochester Telephone Co. 1895–1934; president of the Indiana Telephone Association; president of the National Telephone Association; director of the United States Bank & Trust Co.; appointed a director of the Indiana State Prison in 1893 and a trustee of the State hospital for the insane in 1903; elected as a Democrat to the Sixtieth Congress to fill the vacancy caused by the death of Abram L. Brick; reelected to the Sixty-first and to the four succeeding Congresses and served from November 3, 1908, to March 3, 1919; unsuccessful candidate for reelection in 1918 to the Sixty-sixth Congress; resumed his activities in the newspaper publishing business and in the telephone business; also engaged as a lecturer and in agricultural pursuits; died in Rochester, Ind., March 26, 1934; interment in the Mausoleum.

BARNITZ, Charles Augustus, a Representative from Pennsylvania; born in York, York County, Pa., September 11, 1780; attended York County Academy, York, Pa.; studied law; was admitted to the bar in 1811 and commenced practice in York; member of the State senate 1815–1819; from 1820 until his death served as agent of the heirs of William Penn for their interests in Springettsbury Manor, the center of which is now the city of York; elected as a Whig to the Twenty-third Congress (March 4, 1833–March 3, 1835); was not a candidate for reelection in 1834 to the Twenty-fourth Congress; resumed the practice of law at York, Pa.; also engaged in banking and served as president of the York Bank; member of the State constitutional convention in 1838; delegate to the Whig National Conventions at Harrisburg in 1840 and at Baltimore in 1844; died in York, Pa., January 8, 1850; interment in the First Presbyterian Churchyard.

BARNUM, William Henry, a Representative and a Senator from Connecticut; born in Boston Corner, Columbia County, N. Y., September 17, 1818; attended the common schools; apprenticed to the trade of iron founder and subsequently admitted to partnership by his father, who was engaged in the iron business at Lime Rock, Conn.; member of the State house of representatives in 1851 and 1852; elected as a Democrat to the Fortieth and to the four succeeding Congresses and served from March 4, 1867, until May 18, 1876, when he resigned to become Senator; elected to the United States Senate to fill the vacancy caused by the death of Orris S. Ferry and served from May 18, 1876, to March 3, 1879; delegate to the Democratic National Conventions in 1868, 1872, 1876, 1880, 1884, and 1888; chairman of the Democratic National Committee from 1876 to

1889; resumed his former manufacturing pursuits; died at Lime Rock, Litchfield County, Conn., April 30, 1889; interment in the Lime Rock Cemetery.

BARNWELL, Robert (father of Robert Woodward Barnwell), a Delegate and a Representative from South Carolina; born in Beaufort, S. C., December 21, 1761; educated in the common schools and by private teachers; volunteered for service in the Revolutionary War when sixteen years of age; received seventeen wounds in the battle on Johns Island, S. C.; finally recovered and served as lieutenant with his company at the siege of Charleston in 1780; at the fall of that city was sent aboard the prison ship *Pack Horse*, but was released in the general exchange of prisoners in June 1781; was for many years president of the board of trustees of Beaufort College; Member of the Continental Congress in 1788 and 1789; member of the convention of South Carolina for the adoption of the Federal Constitution in 1788; elected as a Federalist to the Second Congress (March 4, 1791–March 3, 1793); declined to be a candidate for renomination in 1792 to the Third Congress; member of the South Carolina House of Representatives 1795–1797, serving as speaker in 1795; member of the South Carolina Senate in 1805 and 1806, serving as president in 1805; died in Beaufort, Beaufort County, S. C., October 24, 1814; interment in St. Helena's Churchyard.

BARNWELL, Robert Woodward (son of Robert Barnwell), a Representative and a Senator from South Carolina; born in Beaufort, Beaufort County, S. C., August 10, 1801; attended private schools in Beaufort and Charleston, S. C., and was graduated from Harvard University in 1821; studied law; was admitted to the bar and commenced practice in Beaufort, S. C., in 1824; member of the State house of representatives 1826–1828; elected as a Democrat to the Twenty-first and Twenty-second Congresses (March 4, 1829–March 3, 1833); was not a candidate for renomination in 1832; president of South Carolina College (now the University of South Carolina) at Columbia from 1835 to 1841, when he resigned; appointed to the United States Senate to fill the vacancy caused by the death of Franklin H. Elmore and served from June 4 to December 8, 1850, when a successor was elected and qualified; was not a candidate for election; member of the Nashville convention in 1850; commissioner to the Federal Government from South Carolina regarding the secession of that State in December 1860; delegate to the convention of the seceding States in Montgomery, Ala., his being the deciding vote in the South Carolina delegation which carried the State for Jefferson Davis and made him President of the Southern Confederacy; member of the Confederate States Senate 1861–1865; chairman of the faculty of the University of South Carolina from 1866 until 1872, when he conducted a private school; died in Columbia, Richland County, S. C., November 24, 1882; interment in St. Helena's Churchyard, Beaufort, S. C.

BARR, Joseph Walker, a Representative from Indiana; born in Bicknell, Knox County, Ind., January 17, 1918; graduated from DePauw University in 1939 and from Harvard University in 1941; during World War II served in the United States Navy 1942–1945 with subchaser duty in the Mediterranean and Atlantic; rode assault wave in invasion of Sicily, Salerno, Anzio, and South France; received Bronze Star for sinking submarine off Anzio Beach; engaged in the operation of grain elevators, theaters, real-estate, and publishing business; member of the Juvenile Court Advisory Board and Central Indiana Boy Scouts of America Board; elected as a Democrat to the Eighty-sixth Congress (January 3, 1959–January 3, 1961); unsuccessful candidate for reelection in 1960 to the Eighty-seventh Congress; appointed assistant to the Secretary of the Treasury in 1961; resides in Potomac, Md.

BARR, Samuel Fleming, a Representative from Pennsylvania; born near Coleraine, County Antrim, Ireland, June 15, 1829; immigrated to the United States in 1831 with his parents, who settled in Harrisburg, Pa.; attended the common schools; freight agent of the Pittsburgh, Fort Wayne & Chicago Railroad in 1855 and 1856; early in the Civil War was employed upon Government railways in and about Washington, D. C.; editor of the Harrisburg (Pa.) Telegraph 1873–1878; elected as a Republican to the Forty-seventh and Forty-eighth Congresses (March 4, 1881–March 3, 1885); declined to be a candidate for renomination in 1884; discontinued active business pursuits and lived in retirement until his death, residing in San Diego, Calif., in the winter and in Seal Harbor, Maine, during the summer season; died in San Diego, Calif., May 29, 1919; interment in Odd Fellows Cemetery.

BARR, Thomas Jefferson, a Representative from New York; born in New York City in 1812; attended the public schools; moved to Scotch Plains, N. J., in 1835 and conducted a roadhouse; returned to New York City in 1842; assistant alderman of the sixth ward in 1849 and 1850 and alderman in 1852 and 1853; served in the State senate in 1854 and 1855; elected on January 6, 1859, as a Democrat to the Thirty-fifth Congress to fill the vacancy caused by the resignation of John Kelly; reelected to the Thirty-sixth Congress as an Independent Democrat and served from January 17, 1859, to March 3, 1861; was not a candidate for renomination in 1860; appointed a police commissioner of New York City in 1870 and served until 1873, when the police board was abolished; was subsequently employed in the customhouse; died in New York City March 27, 1881; interment in Calvary Cemetery, Long Island, N. Y.

BARRERE, Granville (nephew of Nelson Barrere), a Representative from Illinois; born in New Market, near Hillsboro, Highland County, Ohio, July 11, 1829; attended the common schools, Augusta College, Augusta, Ky., and was graduated from Marietta College, Marietta, Ohio; studied law; was admitted to the bar in Chillicothe, Ross County, Ohio, in 1853 and commenced practice in Marion, Crittenden County, Ark.; moved to Bloomington, McLean County, Ill., in 1855, and then to Canton, Fulton County, Ill., the same year, and continued the practice of his profession; member of the city board of education; member of the board of supervisors of Canton; elected as a Republican to the Forty-third Congress (March 4, 1873–March 3, 1875); unsuccessful candidate for renomination in 1874; resumed the practice of law; died in Canton, Fulton County, Ill., January 13, 1889; interment in Greenwood Cemetery.

BARRERE, Nelson (uncle of Granville Barrere), a Representative from Ohio; born in New Market, near Hillsboro, Highland County, Ohio, April 1, 1808; attended the common schools, and Hillsboro High School in 1827; was graduated from Augusta (Ky.) College in 1830; studied law; was admitted to the bar in 1833 and commenced practice in Hillsboro; moved to West Union, Adams County, Ohio, in 1834 and continued the practice of law; in 1846 returned to Hillsboro, where he resided until his death; member of the State house of representatives in 1837 and 1838; elected as a Whig to the Thirty-second Congress (March 4, 1851–March 3, 1853); unsuccessful candidate for reelection in 1852 to the Thirty-third Congress; resumed the practice of law; died in Hillsboro, Highland County, Ohio, August 20, 1883; interment in Presbyterian Cemetery, New Market, Ohio.

BARRET, John Richard, a Representative from Missouri; born in Greensburg, Green County, Ky., August 21, 1825; attended the common schools and Centre College, Danville, Ky.; moved to St. Louis, Mo., in 1839; was graduated from the St. Louis University in 1843; studied law and practiced; elected to the State house of representatives in 1852 and served four terms; became identified with the St. Louis Agricultural Society and organized its exhibitions; presented credentials as a Democratic Member-elect to the Thirty-sixth Congress and served from March 4, 1859, to June 8, 1860, when he was succeeded by Francis P. Blair, Jr., who contested his election; subsequently elected to the same Congress to fill the vacancy caused by the resignation of Francis P. Blair, Jr., and served from December 3, 1860, to March 3, 1861; unsuccessful for reelection in 1860 to the Thirty-seventh Congress; moved to New York City and engaged in numerous occupations; died in New York City on November 2, 1903; interment in Cave Hill Cemetery, Louisville Ky.

BARRETT, Frank A., a Representative and a Senator from Wyoming; born in Omaha, Douglas County, Nebr., November 10, 1892; attended the public schools; was graduated from Creighton University, Omaha, Nebr., in 1913 and from its law department in 1916; during the First World War served as a sergeant in the Balloon Corps, United States Army, 1917–1919; was admitted to the bar in 1919 and commenced practice in Lusk, Wyo.; also engaged in livestock ranching in 1924; county attorney of Niobrara County, Wyo., 1923–1932; member of the State senate 1933–1935; member of the board of trustees of the University of Wyoming since 1939; elected as a Republican to the Seventy-eighth and to the three succeeding Congresses and served from January 3, 1943, until his resignation on December 31, 1950, having been elected Governor of Wyoming; served as Governor from January 1951 until his resignation January 2, 1953, having been elected a Senator; elected to the United States Senate for the term commencing January 3, 1953, and ending January 3, 1959; unsuccessful candidate for reelection in 1958; general counsel, Department of Agriculture, Washington, D. C., and member of board of directors of Commodity Credit Corporation from May 11, 1959, to March 15, 1960, when he resigned; unsuccessful for the Republican nomination for United States Senator in 1960; is a resident of Lusk, Wyo.

BARRETT, William A., a Representative from Pennsylvania; born August 14, 1896; was graduated from Brown Preparatory School in Philadelphia, Pa., and from St. Joseph's College, Philadelphia, Pa.; engaged in the real-estate business; member of the Board of Mercantile Appraisers, Philadelphia, Pa., for four years; served as district director of the War Bond and War Chest campaigns; member of the Democratic city committee; elected as a Democrat to the Seventy-ninth Congress (January 3, 1945–January 3, 1947); unsuccessful candidate for reelection in 1946 to the Eightieth Congress; elected to the Eighty-first and to the five succeeding Congresses (January 3, 1949–January 3, 1961). *Reelected to the Eighty-seventh Congress.*

BARRETT, William Emerson, a Representative from Massachusetts; born in Melrose, Middlesex County, Mass., December 29, 1858; attended the public schools; was graduated from Dartmouth College, Hanover, N. H., in 1880; assistant editor of the St. Albans Daily Messenger; joined the staff of the Boston Daily Advertiser in 1882; Washington correspondent of the Boston Advertiser 1882–1886; recalled to Boston to become editor in chief and in 1888 became chief proprietor and manager of the Boston Daily Advertiser and the Boston Evening Record; member of the State house of representatives 1887–1892 and served as speaker the last five years; elected as a Republican to the Fifty-fourth and Fifty-fifth Congresses (March 4, 1895–March 3, 1899); declined to be a candidate for renomination in 1898; returned to Boston and resumed active management of his newspaper interests; president of the Union Trust Co. of Boston; died in Newton, Mass., February 12, 1906; interment in Newton Cemetery.

BARRINGER, Daniel Laurens (uncle of Daniel Moreau Barringer), a Representative from North Carolina; born at "Poplar Grove," Cabarrus County, N. C., October 1, 1788; studied law; was admitted to the bar and commenced practice in Raleigh, Wake County, N. C.; member of the State house of commons in 1813, 1814, and 1819–1822; elected as a Democrat to the Nineteenth Congress to fill the vacancy caused by the resignation of Willie P. Mangum; reelected to the Twentieth and to the three succeeding Congresses and served from December 4, 1826, to March 3, 1835; unsuccessful candidate for reelection in 1834 to the Twenty-fourth Congress; moved to Bedford County, Tenn., about 1830 and settled in Shelbyville, where he continued the practice of law; member and speaker of the State house of representatives 1843–1845; presidential elector on the Whig ticket of Clay and Frelinghuysen in 1844; died in Shelbyville, Bedford County, Tenn., October 16, 1852; interment in Willow Mount Cemetery.

BARRINGER, Daniel Moreau (nephew of Daniel Laurens Barringer), a Representative from North Carolina; born at "Poplar Grove," near Concord, Cabarrus County, N. C., July 30, 1806; was graduated from the University of North Carolina at Chapel Hill in 1826; studied law in Hillsboro; was admitted to the bar and commenced practice in Concord, N. C., in 1829; member of the State house of commons 1829–1834, 1840, and 1842; member of the State constitutional convention in 1835; elected as a Whig to the Twenty-eighth, Twenty-ninth, and Thirtieth Congresses (March 4, 1843–March 3, 1849); declined a renomination; appointed by President Taylor and reappointed by President Fillmore Minister to Spain and served from June 18, 1849, until September 4, 1853; again elected to the State house of commons in 1854; delegate to the peace convention held in Washington, D. C., in 1861 in an effort to devise means to prevent the impending war; delegate to the Union National Convention at Philadelphia in August 1866; chairman of the Democratic State committee in 1872; died at White Sulphur Springs, Greenbrier County, Va., September 1, 1873; interment in Greenmount Cemetery, Baltimore, Md.

BARROW, Alexander, a Senator from Louisiana; born near Nashville, Tenn., March 27, 1801; attended the United States Military Academy, West Point, N. Y., 1816–1818; studied law; was admitted to the bar in 1822 and commenced practice in Nashville, Tenn.; moved soon afterwards to Louisiana and settled in Feliciana Parish and continued the practice of law; abandoned the practice of law and became a planter; member of the State house of representatives for several terms; elected in 1840 as a Whig to the United States Senate and served from March 4, 1841, until his death at Barnum's Hotel, while on a visit in Baltimore, Md., December 29, 1846; interment in a private cemetery at Afton Villa plantation, near Bayou Sara, La.

BARROW, Middleton Pope (grandson of Wilson Lumpkin), a Senator from Georgia; born near Antioch (now Stephens), Oglethorpe County, Ga., August 1, 1839; attended a private academy; was graduated from the law department of the University of Georgia at Athens in 1860; was admitted to the bar in 1860 and commenced practice in Athens, Clarke County, Ga.; during the Civil War entered the Confederate service in 1861 as aide-de-camp to Maj. Gen. Howell Cobb and served throughout the war;

resumed the practice of law in Athens; member of the State constitutional convention in 1877; served in the State house of representatives in 1880 and 1881; elected as a Democrat to the United States Senate in 1882 to fill the vacancy caused by the death of Benjamin H. Hill and served from November 15, 1882, to March 3, 1883; was not a candidate for reelection; again resumed the practice of law in Athens, Ga.; moved to Savannah, Ga., in 1893; judge of the eastern judicial circuit of Georgia from January 6, 1902, until his death in Savannah, Ga., December 23, 1903; interment in a private cemetery on the family plantation in Oglethorpe County, Ga.

BARROW, Washington, a Representative from Tennessee; born in Davidson County, Tenn., October 5, 1807; received a classical education; studied law; was admitted to the bar in 1827 and commenced practice in Nashville; Minister to Portugal from August 16, 1841, to February 24, 1844; editor of the Nashville Republican Banner 1845–1847; elected as a Whig to the Thirtieth Congress (March 4, 1847–March 3, 1849); was not a candidate for renomination in 1848; president of the Nashville Gas Co. in 1848; member of the State senate in 1860 and 1861; prominently identified with the Confederacy during the Civil War and was arrested by order of Gov. Andrew Jackson March 28, 1862, and imprisoned in Nashville; released the following week by order of President Lincoln; resumed newspaper interests; died in St. Louis, Mo., October 19, 1866; interment in the vault of Dr. John Shelby on a private estate in East Nashville, Tenn.

BARROWS, Samuel June, a Representative from Massachusetts; born in New York City May 26, 1845; after attending primary school was graduated from the Harvard Divinity School in the fall of 1871; while at Harvard University was the Boston correspondent of the New York Tribune; went with the Yellowstone Expedition of 1873, under the command of General Stanley, and with the Black Hills Expedition in 1874, commanded by General Custer; in 1873 took part in the Battles of Tongue River and the Big Horn; pastor of the first parish, Dorchester (Boston), Mass., from 1876–1881, when he resigned to become editor of the Christian Register, which position he held for 16 years; American representative to the International Prison Congress of 1895, 1900, and 1905, at which he was elected to serve as president of the 1910 congress; elected as a Republican to the Fifty-fifth Congress (March 4, 1897–March 3, 1899); unsuccessful candidate for reelection in 1898 to the Fifty-sixth Congress; secretary of the New York Prison Association 1899–1909; died in New York City April 21, 1909; remains were cremated and the ashes placed in a private burying ground near Georgeville, Quebec, Canada.

BARRY, Alexander Grant, a Senator from Oregon; born in Astoria, Clatsop County, Oreg., August 23, 1892; attended the public schools of Astoria and Portland, Oreg., the University of Washington at Seattle, the University of Oregon Law School, and Northwest College of Law at Portland, Oreg.; was admitted to the bar July 18, 1917, and commenced practice in Portland, Oreg.; during the First World War was commissioned a second lieutenant and served in the Field Artillery, Thirty-first Separate Artillery Brigade, and later with the Fifty-fifth and Forty-sixth Coast Artillery Corps, from November 27, 1917, to February 21, 1919, with overseas service; member of the Oregon Relief Committee in 1932, the Oregon Relief Commission in 1933, and the Oregon Liquor Control Commission 1933–1935; chairman of School District No. 1 Civil Service Board in 1937 and 1938; elected as a Republican to the United States Senate to fill the vacancy caused by the resignation of Frederick Steiwer and served from November 9, 1938, to January 3, 1939; was not a candidate for election to the full term; resumed the practice of law; member of the State house of representatives 1945–1950; died in Portland, Oreg., December 28, 1952; interment in Willamette National Cemetery.

BARRY, Frederick George, a Representative from Mississippi; born in Woodbury, Cannon County, Tenn., January 12, 1845; received a limited education; served as a private in Company E, Eighth Confederate Cavalry, Col. William B. Wade's regiment, during the Civil War; studied law; was admitted to the bar and commenced practice in Aberdeen, Monroe County, Miss.; moved to West Point, Miss., in 1873 and continued the practice of law; member of the State senate 1875–1879; presidential elector at large on the Democratic ticket of Hancock and English in 1880; elected as a Democrat to the Forty-ninth and Fiftieth Congresses (March 4, 1885–March 3, 1889); was not a candidate for renomination in 1888; resumed the practice of law in West Point, Clay County, Miss., where he died May 7, 1909; interment in Odd Fellows Rest Cemetery, Aberdeen, Miss.

BARRY, Henry W., a Representative from Mississippi; born in Schoharie County, N. Y., in April 1840; self-educated; principal of Locust Grove Academy in Kentucky; during the Civil War enlisted in the Union Army; organized a regiment of colored troops in Kentucky; commissioned first lieutenant of the Tenth Regiment, Kentucky Volunteer Infantry, November 21, 1861; colonel of the Eighth United States Colored Artillery April 28, 1864; brevetted brigadier general of Volunteers March 13, 1865, "for faithful and meritorious services during the war"; mustered out May 11, 1866; was graduated from the law department of Columbian College (now George Washington University), Washington, D. C., in 1867; was admitted to the bar the same year and commenced practice in Columbus, Lowndes County, Miss.; delegate to the State constitutional convention in 1867; member of the State senate in 1868; upon the readmission of the State of Mississippi to representation was elected as a Republican to the Forty-first, Forty-second, and Forty-third Congresses and served from February 23, 1870, to March 3, 1875; died in Washington, D. C., June 7, 1875; interment in Oak Hill Cemetery.

BARRY, Robert Raymond, a Representative from New York; born in Omaha, Nebr., May 15, 1915; received early education in the public schools of Evanston, Ill.; attended Hamilton College, Clinton, N. Y., 1933–1936, and the Tuck School of Business Administration at Dartmouth College in 1937; studied law and finance at New York University Graduate School in 1938; engaged in investment banking with Kidder, Peabody & Co., in 1937 and 1938 and commercial banking with Manufacturers Trust Co., in 1938 and 1939; executive of Bendix Aviation Corp., 1940–1943 and Yale & Towne Manufacturing Co., 1945–1950; also engaged in farming, mining, and real-estate development; served on the political staffs of Gov. Thomas E. Dewey and of President Dwight D. Eisenhower; chairman of the United Nations Committee to Build World House at the United Nations; during World War II served in the office of the Under Secretary of the Navy; maintains a ranch home at Palm Springs, Calif., and has mining operations at Portola, Calif.; United States delegate to the 1959 NATO Parliamentarians Conference; elected as a Republican to the Eighty-sixth Congress (January 3, 1959–January 3, 1961). *Reelected to the Eighty-seventh Congress.*

BARRY, William Bernard, a Representative from New York; born in County Mayo, Ireland, July 21, 1902; immigrated to the United States in 1907 with his parents, who settled in Queens County, N. Y.; attended the public schools; was graduated from New York University at New York City in 1925 and from its law school in 1929; was admitted to the bar in 1929 and commenced practice in New York City, N. Y.; assistant district attorney of Queens County, N. Y., in 1932 and 1933; special United States attorney for the Department of Justice 1933–1935; member of the Democratic executive committee of Queens County 1930–1935; elected as a Democrat to the Seventy-fourth Congress to fill the vacancy caused by the resignation of William F. Brunner; reelected to the Seventy-fifth and to the four succeeding Congresses and served from November 5, 1935, until his death; had been renominated to the Eightieth Congress; died in New York, N. Y., on October 20, 1946; interment in Mount St. Mary's Cemetery, Flushing, N. Y.

BARRY, William Taylor, a Representative and a Senator from Kentucky; born near Lunenburg, Lunenburg County, Va., February 15, 1784; moved to Kentucky in 1796 with his parents, who settled in Fayette County; attended the common schools, Pisgah Academy and Kentucky Academy in Woodford County, Ky., Transylvania University at Lexington, Ky., and was graduated from William and Mary College at Williamsburg, Va., in 1803; studied law; was admitted to the bar in 1805 and commenced practice at Lexington, Ky.; appointed Commonwealth attorney; member of the State house of representatives in 1807; elected as a Democrat to the Eleventh Congress to fill the vacancy caused by the resignation of Benjamin Howard and served from August 8, 1810, to March 3, 1811; secretary and aide-de-camp to Governor Shelby in the War of 1812, being present at the Battle of the Thames October 5, 1813; again a member of the State house of representatives in 1814 and was chosen speaker; elected as a Democrat to the United States Senate to fill the vacancy caused by the resignation of George M. Bibb and served from December 16, 1814, until his resignation effective May 1, 1816, having been appointed to a judicial position; appointed judge of the circuit court for the eleventh district of Kentucky 1816–1817; member of the State senate 1817–1821; elected Lieutenant Governor of Kentucky in 1820; professor of law and politics in Transylvania University in 1822; appointed secretary of state of Kentucky in 1824; appointed chief justice of the State court of appeals January 10, 1825; unsuccessful Democratic candidate for election as Governor of Kentucky in 1828; appointed Postmaster General by President Jackson March 9, 1829, and served until April 10, 1835, when he resigned; appointed Envoy Extraordinary and Minister Plenipotentiary to Spain May 1, 1835; died in Liverpool, England, August 30, 1835, while en route to Madrid, Spain; interment in England; reinterment in the State Cemetery at Frankfort, Ky., November 8, 1854.

BARRY, William Taylor Sullivan, a Representative from Mississippi; born in Columbus, Lowndes County, Miss., December 10, 1821; was graduated from Yale College in 1841; studied law; was admitted to the bar in 1844 and commenced practice in Columbus; also engaged in planting; member of the State house of representatives 1849–1851; elected as a Democrat to the Thirty-third Congress (March 4, 1853–March 3, 1855); president of the State secession convention in 1861; again a member of the State house of representatives and served as speaker in 1855; member of the Provisional Confederate Congress; during the Civil War entered the Confederate Army and raised the Thirty-fifth Regiment of Mississippi Infantry, at times acting as brigade commander; captured at Mobile April 12, 1865; resumed the practice of law in Columbus, Miss., where he died January 29, 1868; interment in Odd Fellows Cemetery.

BARSTOW, Gamaliel Henry, a Representative from New York; born in Sharon, Litchfield County, Conn., July 20, 1784; moved to Tioga County, N. Y., in 1812; worked on his father's farm and taught school; studied medicine in Barrington, Mass., and practiced; member of the State assembly 1815–1819; appointed first judge of the Tioga County Court in 1818 and served until 1823; served in the State senate 1819–1822; again a member of the State assembly 1823–1826; State treasurer 1825–1828 and again in 1838; supervisor of Nichols, N. Y., in 1830; elected as a National-Republican to the Twenty-second Congress (March 4, 1831–March 3, 1833); continued the practice of medicine and engaged in agricultural pursuits in Nichols, N.Y., until his death there March 30, 1865; interment in Ashbury Cemetery, near Nichols, N. Y.

BARSTOW, Gideon, a Representative from Massachusetts; born in Mattapoisett, Plymouth County, Mass., September 7, 1783; attended the common schools and Brown University, Providence, R. I., 1799–1801; studied medicine; was admitted to practice and settled in Salem, Essex County, Mass.; member of the State constitutional convention in 1820; elected as a Democrat to the Seventeenth Congress (March 4, 1821–March 3, 1823); was not a candidate for renomination in 1822; member of the State house of representatives in 1823, 1829, 1833, and 1837; served in the State senate in 1827 and 1834; presidential elector on the Whig ticket of Clay and Sergeant in 1832; because of ill health moved to St. Augustine, St. Johns County, Fla., and engaged in mercantile pursuits; died in St. Augustine, Fla., March 26, 1852; interment in Huguenot Cemetery.

BARTHOLDT, Richard, a Representative from Missouri; born in Schleiz, Germany, November 2, 1855; attended the public schools and Schleiz College (Gymnasium); immigrated to the United States in April 1872 and settled in Brooklyn, N. Y.; learned the printing trade and became a newspaper writer and publisher; moved to Missouri and settled in St. Louis in 1877; was connected with several papers as reporter, legislative correspondent, and editor, and at the time of his election to Congress was editor in chief of the St. Louis Tribune; member of the St. Louis Board of Education from 1888 to 1892, serving as president from 1890 to 1892; elected as a Republican to the Fifty-third and to the ten succeeding Congresses (March 4, 1893–March 3, 1915); was not a candidate for renomination in 1914; engaged in literary pursuits; served as chairman of the Republican State convention at St. Joseph, Mo., in 1896; in 1911, while a Member of Congress, was appointed by President Taft as a special envoy to the German Emperor to present to him and to the German people a statue of Baron Steuben as a gift from Congress and the American people; elected president of the Interparliamentary Union at the conference held in St. Louis in 1903, and for many years was president of the arbitration group in Congress, which he founded in 1903; died in St. Louis, Mo., March 19, 1932; his body was cremated and the ashes interred in Concordia Cemetery.

BARTINE, Horace Franklin, a Representative from Nevada; born in New York City March 21, 1848; moved with his parents to New Jersey in 1858; attended the common schools until fifteen years of age, when he enlisted as a private in the Eighth Regiment, New Jersey Volunteer Infantry, in July 1863 and served during the last two years of the Civil War; was severely wounded at the Battle of the Wilderness; participated in many of the engagements of the Army of the Potomac and was present at the surrender of the Confederate forces at Appomattox Court House; returned to New Jersey and engaged in agricultural pursuits; moved to Carson City, Nev., in 1869; from 1869 to 1876 engaged in the manufacture of copper sulphate for milling purposes; studied law; was admitted to the bar in 1880 and practiced in the courts of Nevada; served as district attorney of Ormsby County 1880–1882; elected as a Republican to the Fifty-first and Fifty-second Congresses (March 4, 1889–March

3, 1893); was not a candidate for renomination in 1892; editor of the National Bimetallist, published in Chicago, Ill., and Washington, D. C.; returned to Carson City, Nev., in 1902; appointed State tax examiner in 1904; appointed railroad commissioner in March 1907 and served as chief commissioner and chairman of the commission until his death in Winnemucca, Humboldt County, Nev., August 27, 1918; interment in Lone Mountain Cemetery, Carson City, Ormsby County, Nev.

BARTLETT, Bailey, a Representative from Massachusetts; born in Haverhill, Essex County, Mass., January 29, 1750; attended the common schools; engaged in mercantile pursuits until 1789; member of the State house of representatives 1781–1784 and in 1788; member of the convention which adopted the Constitution of the United States in 1788; served in the State senate in 1789; appointed high sheriff of Essex County by Gov. John Hancock and served from July 1, 1789, until December 5, 1811; elected as a Federalist to the Fifth Congress to fill the vacancy caused by the resignation of Theophilus Bradbury; reelected to the Sixth Congress and served from November 27, 1797, to March 3, 1801; was not a candidate for renomination in 1800; served as treasurer of Essex County in 1812; again appointed high sheriff of Essex County on June 20, 1812, and served until his death; delegate to the State constitutional convention in 1820; died in Haverhill, Mass., September 9, 1830; interment in Pentucket Cemetery.

BARTLETT, Charles Lafayette, a Representative from Georgia; born in Monticello, Jasper County, Ga., January 31, 1853; attended private schools in Monticello and was graduated from the University of Georgia at Athens in 1870; studied law at the University of Virginia at Charlottesville, and was graduated from the law department of the University of Georgia in 1872; was admitted to the bar the same year and commenced practice in Monticello in August 1872; moved to Macon, Ga., in 1875 and continued the practice of law; appointed solicitor general for the Macon Judicial Court on January 31, 1877, and served in that capacity until January 31, 1881; member of the State house of representatives 1882–1885; city attorney of Macon 1887–1892; served in the State senate in 1888 and 1889; appointed judge of the superior court of the Macon circuit in October 1892, and elected to the same office January 1, 1893, serving until May 1, 1894, when he resigned; elected as a Democrat to the Fifty-fourth and to the nine succeeding Congresses (March 4, 1895–March 3, 1915); was not a candidate for renomination in 1914; delegate to the Democratic National Convention at St. Louis in 1916; resumed the practice of law in Macon, Ga., also engaged in banking; died in Macon, Ga., April 21, 1938; interment in Rose Hill Cemetery.

BARTLETT, Edward Lewis (Bob), a Delegate from the Territory of Alaska and a Senator from Alaska; born in Seattle, King County, Wash., April 20, 1904; attended Fairbanks (Alaska) High School, University of Washington 1922–1924, and University of Alaska in 1924 and 1925; reporter Fairbanks (Alaska) Daily News-Miner 1925–1933; secretary to Delegate Anthony J. Dimond of Alaska in 1933 and 1934; gold miner in Alaska 1936–1939; chairman of the Unemployment Compensation Commission of Alaska 1937–1939; appointed secretary of Alaska by President Franklin D. Roosevelt on January 30, 1939, and served until his resignation on February 6, 1944, to become a candidate for Delegate to Congress; president of the Alaska Tuberculosis Association 1940–1944; member of the Alaska War Council 1942–1944; elected as a Democrat, a Delegate to the Seventy-ninth and to the six succeeding Congresses (January 3, 1945–January 3, 1959); was not a candidate for renomination in 1958 having become a candidate for the United States Senate;

elected as a Democrat to the United States Senate on November 25, 1958, and upon the admission of Alaska as a State into the Union on January 3, 1959, in the classification of Senators from that State, drew the two-year term beginning on that day and ending January 3, 1961. *Reelected in 1960 for the term ending January 3, 1967.*

BARTLETT, Franklin, a Representative from New York; born in Worcester County, Mass., September 10, 1847; was graduated from the Brooklyn Polytechnic Institute in 1865 and from Harvard University in 1869; attended Columbia College Law School in 1869; was admitted to the bar in 1870; attended Exeter College, Oxford University, England, in 1870 and 1871; concluded the course at Columbia College Law School in 1873; served as a member of the constitutional commission of the State of New York in 1890; delegate to the Democratic National Convention at Chicago in 1892; elected as a Democrat to the Fifty-third and Fifty-fourth Congresses (March 4, 1893–March 3, 1897); unsuccessful candidate for reelection in 1896 to the Fifty-fifth Congress; colonel of Volunteers in the war with Spain in 1898; died in New York City on April 23, 1909; interment in Greenwood Cemetery, Brooklyn, N. Y.

BARTLETT, George Arthur, a Representative from Nevada; born in San Francisco, Calif., November 30, 1869; moved with his parents to Eureka, Eureka County, Nev.; attended the common schools; was graduated from the law department of Georgetown University, Washington, D. C., in 1894; was admitted to the bar the same year and commenced the practice of law in the courts of Nevada; district attorney of Eureka County, Nev., in 1889 and 1890; elected as a Democrat to the Sixtieth and Sixty-first Congresses (March 4, 1907–March 3, 1911); voluntarily retired from public life and was not a candidate for renomination in 1910; resumed the practice of law in Reno, Nev.; appointed United States assistant district attorney for the district of Nevada on March 3, 1915, and served until March 30, 1918, when he resigned; appointed judge of the second judicial district court of Nevada on April 1, 1918, in which capacity he served, with the exception of about two years, until January 1931, when he resumed the private practice of law; author of several books; died in Reno, Nev., June 1, 1951; interment in Mountain View Cemetery.

BARTLETT, Ichabod, a Representative from New Hampshire; born in Salisbury, N. H., July 24, 1786; received a classical education and was graduated from Dartmouth College, Hanover, N. H., in 1808; studied law; was admitted to the bar in 1811 and commenced practice in Durham, Strafford County, N. H.; moved to Portsmouth in 1816 and continued the practice of law; clerk of the State senate in 1817 and 1818; State solicitor for Rockingham County 1819–1821; member of the State house of representatives 1819–1821; served as speaker in 1821; elected as an Anti-Democrat to the Eighteenth, Nineteenth, and Twentieth Congresses (March 4, 1823–March 3, 1829); declined the appointment as chief justice of the court of common pleas in 1825; again a member of the State house of representatives 1830, 1838, 1851, and 1852; unsuccessful candidate for Governor in 1832; member of the State constitutional convention in 1850; died in Portsmouth, N. H., October 19, 1853; interment in Harmony Grove Cemetery.

BARTLETT, Josiah, a Delegate from New Hampshire; born in Amesbury, Mass., November 21, 1729; attended the public schools; studied medicine, and commenced practice in Kingston, N. H., in 1750; was medical agent to Gen. John Stark at Bennington; member of the colonial legislature of New Hampshire 1765–1775; Member of the Continental Congress in 1775 and 1776; signer of the Articles of Confederation and second signer of the Declaration of Independence; again elected to the Continental Congress, in 1778, but resigned the same year and became chief justice of the court of common pleas; became justice of the superior court in 1784 and chief justice in 1788; member of the convention which framed the Federal Constitution in 1788; in 1789 was elected to the United States Senate from New Hampshire, but declined, and at the same time resigned as chief justice; Governor of the State of New Hampshire 1790–1794; member of the constitutional convention of 1792 which changed the title from president to that of Governor; presidential elector in 1792; retired in 1794; died in Kingston, N. H., May 19, 1795; interment in the First Cemetery, in rear of the Universalist Church.

BARTLETT, Josiah, Jr. (son of the preceding), a Representative from New Hampshire; born in Kingston, N. H., August 29, 1768; attended the common schools and was graduated from Exeter Academy, Exeter, N. H.; studied medicine and commenced practice in Stratham, Rockingham County, N. H.; member of the State senate in 1809 and 1810; elected to the Twelfth Congress (March 4, 1811–March 3, 1813); resumed the practice of medicine; treasurer of Rockingham County; again elected to the State senate, in 1824, and served as president; presidential elector in 1824 and supported John Quincy Adams; resumed the practice of medicine; died in Stratham, N. H., April 16, 1838; interment in the Old Congregational Cemetery.

BARTLETT, Thomas, Jr., a Representative from Vermont; born in Sutton, Caledonia County, Vt., June 18, 1808; attended the common schools; studied law; was admitted to the bar in 1833 and commenced practice in Groton, Vt.; moved to Lyndon, Vt., in 1836 and continued the practice of law; State's attorney for Caledonia County 1839–1842; member of the State senate in 1841 and 1842; served in the State house of representatives in 1849, 1850, 1854, and 1855; delegate to the State constitutional conventions in 1850 and 1857; elected as a Democrat to the Thirty-second Congress (March 4, 1851–March 3, 1853); unsuccessful candidate for reelection in 1852 to the Thirty-third Congress; resumed the practice of law; died in Lyndon, Vt., September 12, 1876; interment in Lyndon Town Cemetery, Lyndon Center, Vt.

BARTLEY, Mordecai, a Representative from Ohio; born in Fayette County, Pa., December 16, 1783; attended school in Virginia; moved to Ohio in 1809 and settled in Jefferson County; served in the War of 1812 as captain and was promoted to adjutant; settled on a farm in Richland County in 1814 and engaged in agricultural pursuits; member of the State senate in 1817 and 1818; elected register of the land office of Virginia military district school lands in 1818 and served until his resignation in 1823, having been elected to Congress; elected to the Eighteenth and to the three succeeding Congresses (March 4, 1823–March 3, 1831); declined to be a candidate for renomination in 1830; resumed agricultural pursuits; moved to Mansfield in 1834 and engaged in mercantile pursuits; Governor of Ohio 1844–1846; declined reelection, retired from public life, and again engaged in agricultural pursuits; died in Mansfield, Richland County, Ohio, October 10, 1870; interment in Mansfield Cemetery.

BARTON, Bruce, a Representative from New York; born in Robbins, Scott County, Tenn., August 5, 1886; educated in the public schools of Ohio, Massachusetts, and Illinois; graduated from Amherst (Mass.) College in 1907; moved to Chicago, Ill., in 1900 and engaged in literary and editorial pursuits; moved to New York, N. Y., in 1912 and continued literary work; also engaged in the magazine and advertising business; elected as a Republican to the Seventy-fifth Congress to fill the vacancy caused by the death of Theodore A. Peyser; reelected to the

Seventy-sixth Congress and served from November 2, 1937, to January 3, 1941; was not a candidate for renomination in 1940, having become a candidate for United States Senator; unsuccessful candidate for election in 1940 to the United States Senate; delegate to the Republican State convention in 1938 and to the Republican National Convention at Philadelphia in 1940; engaged in the advertising business and resides in New York City, N. Y.

BARTON, David, a Senator from Missouri; born in Greene County, N. C. (now Tennessee), December 14, 1783; moved to the Territory of Missouri in 1809; elected attorney general in 1813; first circuit judge of Howard County in 1815 and presiding judge in 1816; member of the Territorial house of representatives in 1818 and served as speaker; member and president of the convention which formed the State constitution in 1820; upon the admission of Missouri as a State into the Union was elected to the United States Senate; reelected in 1825, and served from August 10, 1821, to March 3, 1831; unsuccessful candidate for reelection; member of the State senate in 1834; became circuit judge in 1835, with residence in Boonville, Cooper County, Mo., and served until his death in Boonville on September 28, 1837; interment in Walnut Grove Cemetery, Boonville, Mo.

BARTON, Richard Walker, a Representative from Virginia; born at "Shady Oak," near Winchester, Frederick County, Va., in 1800; pursued academic studies; studied law; was admitted to the bar and commenced practice in Winchester, Va.; member of the State assembly in 1823, 1824, 1832, 1835, and 1839; elected as a Whig to the Twenty-seventh Congress (March 4, 1841–March 3, 1843); unsuccessful candidate for reelection in 1842 to the Twenty-eighth Congress; resumed the practice of his profession in Winchester, Va.; died on his estate, "Springdale," near Winchester, Frederick County, Va., March 15, 1859; interment in the family burying ground at "Springdale."

BARTON, Samuel, a Representative from New York; born in New Dorp, Richmond County, N. Y., July 27, 1785; attended the common schools; agent for Commodore Vanderbilt's steamship lines; served in the State militia as a major in 1818 and as a colonel in 1833; member of the State assembly in 1821 and 1822; served on the Andrew Jackson reception committee in 1833; elected as a Jacksonian Democrat to the Twenty-fourth Congress (March 4, 1835–March 3, 1837); was not a candidate for renomination in 1836; resumed his former pursuits in the steamship business; director of the Tompkinsville Lyceum in 1842; died in New Dorp, Richmond County, N. Y., January 29, 1858; interment in Moravian Cemetery.

BARTON, Silas Reynolds, a Representative from Nebraska; born in New London, Henry County, Iowa, May 21, 1872; moved to Hamilton County, Nebr., in 1873 with his parents; was graduated from the Aurora High School and attended the Peru (Nebr.) State Normal School; engaged in agricultural pursuits and taught school; deputy treasurer of Hamilton County 1898–1901; grand recorder of the Ancient Order of United Workmen of Nebraska 1901–1908; president for two terms of the Grand Recorders' Association of the United States; State auditor 1909–1913; during his two terms as auditor and insurance commissioner was a member of the National Executive Committee of Insurance Commissioners; elected as a Republican to the Sixty-third Congress (March 4, 1913–March 3, 1915); was a candidate for election to the Sixty-fifth Congress, but died before election day in Grand Island, Hall County, Nebr., November 7, 1916; interment in Aurora Cemetery, Aurora, Hamilton County, Nebr.

BARTON, William Edward (cousin of Courtney Walker Hamlin), a Representative from Missouri; born in Pickens District (now County), S. C., April 11, 1868; in 1869 moved to Missouri with his parents, who settled in Crawford County, near Bourbon; attended the public schools and the Steelville Normal and Business Institute, Steelville, Mo.; employed as a farm hand, miner, and in a railroad office; taught school near Bourbon, Mo., 1889–1892; graduated from the law department of the Missouri University at Columbia in 1894; was admitted to the bar the same year and commenced practice in Houston, Mo.; delegate to the State judicial conventions in 1896 and 1906; during the Spanish-American War served as a sergeant in Company M, Second Regiment, Missouri Volunteer Infantry; prosecuting attorney of Texas County in 1901 and 1902; judge of the nineteenth judicial circuit 1923–1928; elected as a Democrat to the Seventy-second Congress (March 4, 1931–March 3, 1933); unsuccessful candidate for renomination in 1932 to the Seventy-third Congress; again elected judge of the nineteenth judicial circuit of Missouri and served from 1934 to 1946; resumed the private practice of law; died in Houston, Mo., July 29, 1955; interment in Houston Cemetery.

BARWIG, Charles, a Representative from Wisconsin; born in Hesse-Darmstadt, Germany, March 19, 1837; immigrated to the United States in 1845 with his parents, who settled in Milwaukee, Wis.; attended the public schools and was graduated from the Spencerian Business College at Milwaukee in 1857; moved to Mayville in 1865 and engaged in the wholesale liquor business; mayor of Mayville 1886–1888; elected as a Democrat to the Fifty-first, Fifty-second, and Fifty-third Congresses (March 4, 1889–March 3, 1895); unsuccessful candidate for reelection in 1894 to the Fifty-fourth Congress; engaged in the real-estate business; died in Mayville, Wis., on February 15, 1912; interment in Graceland Cemetery.

BASHFORD, Coles, a Delegate from the Territory of Arizona; born near Cold Spring, Putnam County, N. Y., January 24, 1816; attended the Wesleyan Seminary (now Genesee College), Lima, N. Y.; studied law; was admitted to the bar in 1842; district attorney for Wayne County 1847–1850; resigned in 1850 and moved to Oshkosh, Wis.; member of the Wisconsin Senate in 1853 and 1855; first Republican Governor of Wisconsin 1855–1858; declined renomination; moved to Arizona in 1863; first attorney general of Arizona 1864–1866; presiding officer of first Territorial Council in 1865; elected as an Independent to the Fortieth Congress (March 4, 1867–March 3, 1869); secretary of state of Arizona 1869–1876; resigned and moved to Prescott, Ariz., in 1876, where he engaged in business; died in Prescott, Ariz., April 25, 1878; interment in Mountain View Cemetery, Oakland, Calif.

BASS, Lyman Kidder, a Representative from New York; born in the town of Alden, Erie County, N. Y., November 13, 1836; attended the common schools and was graduated from Union College, Schenectady, N. Y., in 1856; studied law; was admitted to the bar in 1858 and commenced practice in Buffalo, N. Y.; district attorney for Erie County 1865–1872; renominated in 1871, but declined to accept; unsuccessful Republican candidate for election in 1870 to the Forty-second Congress; elected as a Republican to the Forty-third and Forty-fourth Congresses (March 4, 1873–March 3, 1877); because of ill health declined to be a candidate for renomination in 1876; moved to Colorado Springs, Colo., in 1877 and continued the practice of law; served as general counsel for the Denver & Rio Grande Railroad Co. from 1878 to 1884; died in New York City, while on a visit, May 11, 1889; interment in Forest Lawn Cemetery, Buffalo, N. Y.

BASS, Perkins, a Representative from New Hampshire; born in East Walpole, Norfolk County, Mass., October 6, 1912; graduated from Dartmouth College, Hanover, N. H., in 1934 and from Harvard Law School, Cambridge, Mass., in 1938; was admitted to the New Hampshire bar in 1938 and commenced the practice of law in Manchester, N. H.; law clerk to Judge Woodbury of First Circuit Court of Appeals in 1941 and 1942; during World War II entered military service April 9, 1942, and served as air combat intelligence officer with General Chennault's Fourteenth Air Force in China from 1943 until discharged with rank of major in 1945; awarded the Bronze Star Medal and from the Nationalist Government of China received the Yun-Ma Medal for distinguished and meritorious service; resumed practice of law in Manchester and Peterborough, N. H.; member of the New Hampshire House of Representatives 1939, 1941, 1947, and 1951; served in the State senate 1949–1951 as president; trustee of the New Hampshire Savings Bank of Concord; director and member of the executive committee of Bird & Son, Inc., East Walpole, Mass.; president of the Monadnock Community Hospital, Peterborough, N. H., 1952–1954; elected as a Republican to the Eighty-fourth, Eighty-fifth, and Eighty-sixth Congresses (January 3, 1955–January 3, 1961). *Reelected to the Eighty-seventh Congress.*

BASS, Ross, a Representative from Tennessee; born on a farm in Giles County, near Pulaski, Tenn., March 17, 1918; attended the public schools in Middle, Tenn.; was graduated from Martin College, Pulaski, Tenn., in 1941, majoring in political science, law, and economics; during World War II enlisted as a private in the Infantry of the United States Army in 1942; commissioned a captain and transferred to the Air Force; received his wings and flew combat missions with the Eighth Air Force in Europe until discharged in 1946; awarded the Air Medal and Oak Leaf Cluster; owner and operator of a soft-drink bottling plant, Pulaski, Tenn., 1946–1948; operated a florist and nursery business in 1946 and 1947; postmaster of Pulaski, Tenn., from August 16, 1947, to February 1, 1954; delegate to the Democratic National Convention in 1960; elected as a Democrat to the Eighty-fourth, Eighty-fifth, and Eighty-sixth Congresses (January 3, 1955–January 3, 1961). *Reelected to the Eighty-seventh Congress.*

BASSETT, Burwell, a Representative from Virginia; born in New Kent County, Va., March 18, 1764; attended William and Mary College, Williamsburg, Va.; member of the State house of delegates 1787–1789; served in the State senate 1793–1805; unsuccessfully contested the election of John Clopton to the Fourth Congress; elected as a Democrat to the Ninth and to the three succeeding Congresses (March 4, 1805–March 3, 1813); unsuccessful candidate for reelection in 1812 to the Thirteenth Congress; elected to the Fourteenth and Fifteenth Congresses (March 4, 1815–March 3, 1819); again a member of the State house of delegates 1819–1821; elected to the Seventeenth and to the three succeeding Congresses (March 4, 1821–March 3, 1829); unsuccessful candidate for reelection in 1828 to the Twenty-first Congress; died in New Kent County, Va., February 26, 1841.

BASSETT, Edward Murray, a Representative from New York; born in Brooklyn, N. Y., February 7, 1863; attended the public schools in Brooklyn and Watertown, N. Y., and Hamilton College, Clinton, N. Y., in 1881 and 1882; was graduated from Amherst (Mass.) College in 1884 and from Columbia Law School, New York City, in 1886; was admitted to the New York State bar in 1886 and commenced practice in Buffalo, N. Y.; moved to New York City in 1892 and continued the practice of law; member of the Brooklyn School Board 1899–1903; elected as a Democrat to the Fifty-eighth Congress (March 4, 1903–March 3, 1905); declined to be a candidate for renomination in 1904; resumed the practice of law; member of the New York Public Service Commission 1907–1911; chairman of the Heights of Buildings Commission 1913–1915; chairman of the Zoning Commission in 1916 and 1917; appointed by Secretary Hoover in 1922 as a member of the Department of Commerce, Advisory Committee on Zoning; writer on bankruptcy, eminent domain, and police power; died in Brooklyn, N. Y., October 27, 1948; interment in Ashfield Plains Cemetery, Ashfield, Mass.

BASSETT, Richard (grandfather of Richard Henry Bayard and James Asheton Bayard, Jr.), a Senator from Delaware; born on his father's plantation in Kent County, Md., April 2, 1745; pursued preparatory studies; studied law; was admitted to the bar and practiced in Delaware; captain of a Delaware troop in the Colonial Army; member of the State constitutional conventions in 1776 and 1792; member of the State senate in 1782; served in the State house of representatives in 1786; delegate to the convention which framed the Constitution of the United States in 1787; member of the Delaware convention which ratified the Federal Constitution in 1787; elected to the United States Senate and served from March 4, 1789, to March 3, 1793; is credited with being the first man to cast his vote to locate the Capital of the United States on the Potomac River; chief justice of the court of common pleas from September 6, 1793, to January 8, 1799; presidential elector on the Adams ticket in 1797; Governor of Delaware from January 9, 1799, to March 3, 1801; appointed United States circuit judge by President Adams on March 3, 1801; died on his estate, "Bohemia Manor," in Cecil County, Md., August 15, 1815; interment in Wilmington and Brandywine Cemetery, Wilmington, Del.

BATE, William Brimage, a Senator from Tennessee; born near Castalian Springs, Sumner County, Tenn., October 7, 1826; completed an academic course of study; served as a private in Louisiana and Tennessee regiments throughout the Mexican War; member of the State house of representatives 1849–1851; was graduated from the law department of Lebanon University, Lebanon, Tenn., in 1852; was admitted to the bar and commenced practice in Gallatin, Tenn.; elected attorney general for the Nashville district in 1854; presidential elector on the Breckinridge and Lane ticket in 1860; during the Civil War served as private, captain, colonel, brigadier general, and major general in the Confederate Army, surrendering with the Army of the Tennessee in 1865; after the close of the war returned to Tennessee and resumed the practice of law at Gallatin; delegate to the Democratic National Convention at New York City in 1868; served on the Democratic national executive committee for Tennessee twelve years; presidential elector at large on the Democratic ticket of Tilden and Hendricks in 1876; elected Governor of Tennessee in 1882 and reelected in 1884; elected as a Democrat to the United States Senate in 1887; reelected in 1893, 1899, and again in 1905, and served from March 4, 1887, until his death in Washington, D. C., March 9, 1905; funeral services were held in the Chamber of the United States Senate; interment in Mount Olivet Cemetery, Nashville, Tenn.

BATEMAN, Ephraim, a Representative and a Senator from New Jersey; born in Cedarville, N. J., July 9, 1780; attended the local schools and Nathaniel Ogden's Latin school; apprenticed as a tailor in 1796; taught in the local school 1799–1801; studied medicine with Dr. Jonathan Elmer in 1801, at the University of Pennsylvania at Philadelphia in 1802 and 1803, and practiced in Cedarville; member of the State house of assembly in 1808,

1809, 1811, and 1813, serving as speaker in 1813; elected as a Democrat to the Fourteenth and to the three succeeding Congresses (March 4, 1815–March 3, 1823); member of the State council in 1826 and served as president, casting the deciding vote which elected him, instead of Theodore Frelinghuysen, United States Senator; elected to the United States Senate to fill the vacancy caused by the death of Joseph McIlvaine and served from November 10, 1826, to January 12, 1829, when he resigned because of failing health; died in Cedarville, Cumberland County, N. J., January 28, 1829; interment in Old Stone Church Cemetery, Fairfield Township, N. J., between Cedarville and Fairton.

BATES, Arthur Laban (nephew of John Milton Thayer), a Representative from Pennsylvania; born in Meadville, Crawford County, Pa., June 6, 1859; studied under tutors and was graduated from Allegheny College, Meadville, Pa., in 1880; studied law; was admitted to the bar in 1882; attended Oxford University, London, England, in 1882 and 1883; commenced the practice of law in Meadville, Pa., in 1884; also engaged in the newspaper publishing business in 1899; city solicitor of Meadville 1889–1896; elected as a Republican to the Fifty-seventh and to the five succeeding Congresses (March 4, 1901–March 3, 1913); declined to be a candidate for renomination in 1912; delegate to the International Peace Conference at Brussels in 1905 and at Rome in 1911; delegate to the Republican State convention at Harrisburg in 1908; resumed the practice of law and the publishing business in Meadville; also engaged in banking; trustee of Allegheny College; director of the Pennsylvania College of Music and of the Meadville City Hospital; president of the Meadville Free Library; presidential elector on the Republican ticket of Hughes and Fairbanks in 1916; delegate to the Republican National Convention at Cleveland in 1924; died in Meadville, Pa., August 26, 1934; interment in Greendale Cemetery.

BATES, Edward (brother of James Woodson Bates), a Representative from Missouri; born in Belmont, Goochland County, Va., September 4, 1793; attended Charlotte Hall Academy, Maryland; acted as sergeant in a volunteer brigade during the War of 1812; moved to St. Louis, Mo., in 1814; studied law; was admitted to the bar in 1817 and practiced; circuit prosecuting attorney in 1818; member of the State constitutional convention in 1820; State's attorney in 1820; member of the State house of representatives in 1822; United States district attorney 1821–1826; elected as an Adams Anti-Democrat to the Twentieth Congress (March 4, 1827–March 3, 1829); unsuccessful candidate for reelection in 1828 to the Twenty-first Congress; resumed the practice of law; member of the State senate in 1830; again a member of the State house of representatives in 1834; declined the appointment as Secretary of War in 1850 in the Cabinet of President Fillmore; judge of the St. Louis land court 1853–1856; presided at the Whig National Convention at Baltimore in 1856; appointed by President Lincoln as Attorney General of the United States and served from March 5, 1861, to September 1864; died in St. Louis, Mo., March 25, 1869; interment in Bellefontaine Cemetery.

BATES, George Joseph (father of William Henry Bates), a Representative from Massachusetts; born in Salem, Essex County, Mass., February 25, 1891; attended the public schools; member of the State house of representatives 1918–1924; served as mayor of Salem, Mass., 1924–1937; elected as a Republican to the Seventy-fifth and to the six succeeding Congresses and served from January 3, 1937, until his death in an airplane accident at the Washington (D. C.) National Airport on November 1, 1949; interment in St. Mary's Cemetery, Salem, Mass.

BATES, Isaac Chapman, a Representative and a Senator from Massachusetts; born in Granville, Mass., January 23, 1779; tutored privately; was graduated from Yale College in 1802; was admitted to the bar and commenced the practice of law in Northampton, Hampshire County, Mass., in 1808; member of the State house of representatives in 1808 and 1809; elected as an anti-Jackson man to the Twentieth and to the three succeeding Congresses (March 4, 1827–March 3, 1835); declined to be a candidate for renomination in 1834; presidential elector on the Whig tickets of Daniel Webster and Francis Granger in 1836 and of William Henry Harrison and John Tyler in 1840; elected as a Whig to the United States Senate to fill the vacancy in the term ending March 3, 1841, caused by the resignation of John Davis and on the same day elected for the term commencing March 4, 1841, and served from January 13, 1841, until his death in Washington, D. C., March 16, 1845; interment in Bridge Street Cemetery, Northampton, Mass.

BATES, James, a Representative from Maine; born in Greene, Lincoln (now Kennebec) County, Maine, September 24, 1789; attended the common schools; studied medicine at Harvard Medical University, Boston, Mass.; served as a surgeon during the War of 1812 and was present at the surrender of Fort Erie; was in charge of the general military hospital near Buffalo, N. Y., until his resignation in May 1815; practiced medicine in Hallowell, Maine, 1815–1819; moved to Norridgewock in 1819 and continued practice; elected as a Democrat to the Twenty-second Congress (March 4, 1831–March 3, 1833); superintendent of the State hospital for the insane 1845–1851; resumed the practice of medicine in Gardiner and Fairfield, Maine; moved to Yarmouth, Cumberland County, Maine, in 1858 and engaged in practice until his death there February 25, 1882; interment in what is now known as the Old Oak Cemetery, Norridgewock, Somerset County, Maine.

BATES, James Woodson (brother of Edward Bates), a Delegate from the Territory of Arkansas; born in Goochland County, Va., August 25, 1788; attended Yale College and was graduated from Princeton College in 1807; studied law; was admitted to the bar and commenced practice in Virginia; moved to St. Louis, Mo., in 1816, and thence to the Post of Arkansas in 1819; elected as first Delegate from Arkansas to the Sixteenth and Seventeenth Congresses and served from December 21, 1819, to March 3, 1823; unsuccessful candidate for reelection in 1822 to the Eighteenth Congress; resumed the practice of law in Batesville, Ark.; judge of the fourth judicial circuit of Arkansas Territory 1824–1828; judge of the superior court of Arkansas 1828–1832; delegate to the State constitutional convention in 1835; judge of the probate court of Crawford County in 1836; register of the land office in Clarksville 1841–1845; died in Van Buren, Crawford County, Ark., December 26, 1846; interment in the family burying ground at Moores Rock, Crawford (now Sebastian) County, Ark.

BATES, Joseph Bengal, a Representative from Kentucky; born in Republican, Ky., October 29, 1893; attended the public schools and the Mountain Training School at Hindman, Ky.; was graduated from Eastern Kentucky State Teachers College at Richmond in 1916; studied law; taught in the rural schools of Knott County, Ky., 1912–1915; high school superintendent at Raceland, Ky., 1917–1919; county clerk of Greenup County, Ky., 1922–1938; elected as a Democrat to the Seventy-fifth Congress to fill the vacancy caused by the resignation of Fred M. Vinson; reelected to the Seventy-sixth and to the six succeeding Congresses and served from June 4, 1938, to January 3, 1953; unsuccessful candidate for renomination in 1952, and was unsuccessful for the Democratic nomination in 1956 for the United States Senate; engaged in the practice of law; is a resident of Greenup, Ky.

BATES, Martin Waltham, a Senator from Delaware; born in Salisbury, Conn., February 24, 1787; attended the common schools; moved to Delaware and taught school for several years; studied medicine, and later studied law; was admitted to the bar October 5, 1822, and commenced practice in Dover, Kent County, Del.; member of the State house of representatives in 1826; delegate to the State constitutional convention in 1852; elected as a Democrat to the United States Senate to fill the vacancy caused by the death of John M. Clayton and served from January 14, 1857, to March 3, 1859; unsuccessful candidate for reelection in 1858; resumed the practice of law until his death in Dover, Del., January 1, 1869; interment in the Old Methodist Cemetery.

BATES, William Henry (son of George Joseph Bates), a Representative from Massachusetts; born in Salem, Essex County, Mass., April 26, 1917; attended the public schools; was graduated from Worchester Academy in 1936, from Brown University, Providence, R. I., in 1940, and from Harvard Graduate School of Business Administration, Boston, Mass., in 1947; during World War II enlisted in the United States Navy in July 1940 and served until February 24, 1950, resigning his commission as lieutenant commander after being elected to Congress; elected as a Republican to the Eighty-first Congress to fill the vacancy caused by the death of his father, George J. Bates; reelected to the Eighty-second and to the four succeeding Congresses and served from February 14, 1950, to January 3, 1961. *Reelected to the Eighty-seventh Congress.*

BATHRICK, Elsworth Raymond, a Representative from Ohio; born near Pontiac, Oakland County, Mich., January 6, 1863; attended the country schools and was graduated from the Pontiac High School; moved to New York City in 1890 and engaged in the importation of edible oils; moved to Akron, Ohio, in 1900 and engaged in the real-estate business; elected as a Democrat to the Sixty-second and Sixty-third Congresses (March 4, 1911–March 3, 1915); unsuccessful candidate for reelection in 1914 to the Sixty-fourth Congress; resumed his former business pursuits; elected to the Sixty-fifth Congress and served from March 4, 1917, until his death in Akron, Summit County, Ohio, December 23, 1917; interment in Glendale Cemetery.

BATTLE, Laurie Calvin, a Representative from Alabama; born in Wilsonville, Shelby County, Ala., May 10, 1912; attended the elementary school at Inglenook, Jefferson County, Ala.; moved to Tuscumbia in 1926; was graduated from Deshler High School in 1930 and from Birmingham-Southern College at Birmingham in 1934; student Vanderbilt University and Scarritt College, Nashville, Tenn., in 1934 and 1935; graduated from Ohio State University at Columbus in 1939; engaged as a driver-salesman and assistant personnel and claims director for a dairy company, Cleveland, Ohio, in 1937 and 1938; laborer and district clerk for the Southern Natural Gas Co., Birmingham, Ala., in 1940 and 1941; sociology teacher at Ohio State University in 1940; during World War II served in the United States Army as a private and through the ranks to major, with service in the Asiatic-Pacific Theater from February 19, 1942, until discharged on March 6, 1946; awarded the Bronze Star Medal, Philippine Liberation Medal, Victory Medal, Asiatic-Pacific Theater Medal with eight battle stars; student at University of Alabama in 1946; elected as a Democrat to the Eightieth and to the three succeeding Congresses (January 3, 1947–January 3, 1955); was not a candidate for renomination in 1954, but was an unsuccessful

candidate for the Democratic nomination for the United States Senate; engaged in the insurance business in Birmingham, Ala.; public relations representative in Washington, D. C.; resides in Temple Hills, Md.

BAUMHART, Albert David, Jr., a Representative from Ohio; born in Vermilion, Erie County, Ohio, June 15, 1908; attended the public schools and was graduated from the Ohio University at Athens in 1931; publishing house representative at Vermilion, Ohio, 1932–1939; member of the State senate 1937–1940; elected as a Republican to the Seventy-seventh Congress and served from January 3, 1941, until his resignation on September 2, 1942, to accept a commission in the United States Navy, in which he served until discharged as a lieutenant commander on January 17, 1946; member of the public relations staff of Owens-Corning Fiberglas Corp., Toledo, Ohio, 1946–1953; director, Republican National Committee in 1953 and 1954; elected as a Republican to the Eighty-fourth, Eighty-fifth, and Eighty-sixth Congresses (January 3, 1955–January 3, 1961); was not a candidate for renomination in 1960; is a resident of Vermilion, Ohio.

BAXTER, Portus, a Representative from Vermont; born in Brownington, Orleans County, Vt., December 4, 1806; attended the common schools, Norwich Military Academy, and the University of Vermont at Burlington; moved to Derby Line, Orleans County, Vt., in 1828; presidential elector on the Whig ticket of Scott and Graham in 1852 and on the Republican ticket of Frémont and Dayton in 1856; elected as a Republican to the Thirty-seventh, Thirty-eighth, and Thirty-ninth Congresses (March 4, 1861–March 3, 1867); declined to be a candidate for renomination in 1866; died in Washington, D. C., March 4, 1868; interment in Strafford Cemetery, Strafford, Orange County, Vt.

BAY, William Van Ness, a Representative from Missouri; born in Hudson, N. Y., November 23, 1818; attended the public schools; studied law; was admitted to the bar; moved to Union, Franklin County, Mo., in 1836 and commenced the practice of law; member of the State house of representatives 1844–1848; elected as a Democrat to the Thirty-first Congress (March 4, 1849–March 3, 1851); resumed the practice of law; appointed judge of the State supreme court in 1862; elected to this position in 1863 and served until removed by Governor Fletcher in 1865; moved to St. Louis, Mo., and again resumed the practice of law; retired in 1886 and moved to Eureka, Mo., where he died February 10, 1894; interment in Oak Hill Cemetery, Kirkwood, St. Louis County, Mo.

BAYARD, James Asheton, Sr. (father of Richard Henry Bayard and James Asheton Bayard, Jr., grandfather of Thomas Francis Bayard, Sr., and great-grandfather of Thomas Francis Bayard, Jr.), a Representative and a Senator from Delaware; born in Philadelphia, Pa., July 28, 1767; was graduated from Princeton College in 1784; studied law under Gen. Joseph Reed; was admitted to the bar in 1787 and commenced practice in Wilmington, Del.; declined the appointment as Minister to France tendered by President John Adams in 1801; elected as a Federalist to the Fifth, Sixth, and Seventh Congresses (March 4, 1797–March 3, 1803); unsuccessful candidate for reelection in 1802 to the Eighth Congress; one of the managers appointed by the House of Representatives in 1798 to conduct the impeachment proceedings against William Blount, a Senator from Tennessee; elected to the United States Senate to fill the vacancy caused by the resignation of William Hill Wells; reelected in 1805 and 1811 and served from November 13, 1804, to March 3, 1813, when he resigned; appointed a member of the commission to negotiate peace with Great Britain; went to Europe in

May 1813 and aided in negotiating the treaty of Ghent, signed December 24, 1814; declined the appointment as Minister to Russia tendered by President Madison in 1815; died in Wilmington, Del., August 6, 1815; interment at Bohemia Manor, Cecil County, Md.; reinterment about 1842 in Wilmington and Brandywine Cemetery, Wilmington, Del.

BAYARD, James Asheton, Jr. (son of James Asheton Bayard, Sr., grandson of Richard Bassett, father of Thomas Francis Bayard, Sr., and grandfather of Thomas Francis Bayard, Jr.), a Senator from Delaware; born in Wilmington, Del., November 15, 1799; pursued classical studies; studied law; was admitted to the bar and commenced practice in Wilmington; United States district attorney for Delaware 1838–1843; elected as a Democrat to the United States Senate in 1851; reelected in 1857 and 1863 and served from March 4, 1851, to January 29, 1864, when he resigned; resumed the practice of law in Wilmington; appointed in 1867 to the United States Senate to fill the vacancy caused by the death of George Read Riddle; was subsequently elected, and served from April 5, 1867, to March 3, 1869; was not a candidate for reelection; delegate to the Democratic National Convention at New York City in 1868; again resumed the practice of law; died in Wilmington, Del., June 13, 1880; interment in the Old Swedes Burial Ground.

BAYARD, John Bubenheim (uncle of James Asheton Bayard, Sr.), a Delegate from Pennsylvania; born at Bohemia Manor, Cecil County, Md., August 11, 1738; moved to Pennsylvania in 1756 and settled in Philadelphia, where he became one of the leading merchants; member of the general assembly 1776–1779 and in 1784, serving several terms as speaker; member of the council of safety in 1776 and 1777; during the Revolutionary War was colonel of the Second Regiment of Philadelphia Volunteers and served in the Battles of Brandywine, Germantown, and Princeton; Member of the Continental Congress 1785–1787; moved to New Brunswick, N. J., in 1788; city mayor in 1790 and, later, judge of the court of common pleas; died in New Brunswick, N. J., January 7, 1807; interment in the First Presbyterian Churchyard.

BAYARD, Richard Henry (son of James Asheton Bayard, Sr., and grandson of Richard Bassett), a Senator from Delaware; born in Wilmington, Del., September 23, 1796; was graduated from Princeton College in 1814; studied law; was admitted to the bar in New Castle, Del., in 1818 and commenced practice in Wilmington; first mayor of Wilmington in 1832; elected as a Whig to the United States Senate to fill the vacancy caused by the resignation of Arnold Naudain and served from June 17, 1836, to September 19, 1839, when he resigned to become chief justice of Delaware; served as chief justice until January 12, 1841, when he resigned, having been again elected to the United States Senate to fill the vacancy caused by his own resignation, and served from January 12, 1841, to March 3, 1845; was not a candidate for reelection in 1845; Chargé d'Affaires to Belgium from December 10, 1850, to September 12, 1853; died in Philadelphia, Pa., March 4, 1868; interment in the Wilmington and Brandywine Cemetery, Wilmington, Del.

BAYARD, Thomas Francis, Sr. (son of James Asheton Bayard, Jr., and father of Thomas Francis Bayard, Jr.), a Senator from Delaware; born in Wilmington, Del., October 29, 1828; attended Doctor Hawkes' school in Flushing; studied law; was admitted to the bar in 1851 and commenced practice in Wilmington, Del.; appointed United States district attorney for Delaware in 1853, but resigned in 1854; moved to Philadelphia and practiced law in copartnership with William Shippen, Jr.; returned to Wilmington in 1858; at the expiration of his father's term in 1869 was elected as a Democrat to the United States Senate; reelected in 1875 and 1881 and served from March 4, 1869, to March 6, 1885, when he resigned to become Secretary of State; elected President pro tempore of the Senate October 10, 1881; was appointed a member of the Electoral Commission created by the act of Congress approved on January 29, 1877, to decide the contests in various States in the presidential election of 1876; served as Secretary of State in the Cabinet of President Grover Cleveland from March 6, 1885, to March 5, 1889; Ambassador to Great Britain 1893–1897; died at the home of his daughter in Dedham, Mass., on September 28, 1898; interment in Old Swedes Cemetery, Wilmington, Del.

BAYARD, Thomas Francis, Jr. (son of the preceding), a Senator from Delaware; born in Wilmington, Del., June 4, 1868; attended the common schools of his native city and St. Paul's School, Concord, N. H., from 1880 to 1886; was graduated from Yale University in 1890; was a student at the Yale Law School in 1890 and 1891; from 1891 to 1893 continued the study of law; was admitted to the Delaware bar in 1893 and commenced practice in Wilmington; moved to New York City, N. Y., and was appointed an assistant corporation counsel in 1897; practiced law in New York until September 1901, when he returned to Wilmington, Del., and resumed the practice of his profession; served as chairman of the Democratic State committee from 1906 to 1916; solicitor of the city of Wilmington 1917–1919; elected on November 7, 1922, as a Democrat to the United States Senate to fill the vacancy caused by the resignation of Josiah O. Wolcott and on the same day was also elected for the full term commencing March 4, 1923, and served from November 8, 1922, to March 3, 1929; unsuccessful candidate for reelection in 1928; resumed the practice of law in Wilmington, Del.; unsuccessful Democratic candidate for election to the United States Senate in 1930; died in Wilmington, Del., July 12, 1942; interment in Old Swedes Cemetery.

BAYLIES, Francis (brother of William Baylies), a Representative from Massachusetts; born in Taunton, Mass., October 16, 1784; studied law; was admitted to the bar in 1810 and commenced practice in Taunton, Mass.; register of probate for Bristol County 1812–1820; unsuccessful candidate for election in 1818 to the Sixteenth Congress; elected to the Seventeenth, Eighteenth, and Nineteenth Congresses (March 4, 1821–March 3, 1827); unsuccessful candidate in 1827 for reelection to the Twentieth Congress; member of the State house of representatives 1827–1832; commissioned Chargé d'Affaires to Argentina January 3, 1832; again elected to the State house of representatives in 1835; engaged in literary pursuits; died in Taunton, Bristol County, Mass., October 28, 1852; interment in the Old Plain Cemetery.

BAYLIES, William (brother of Francis Baylies), a Representative from Massachusetts; born in Dighton, Mass., September 15, 1776; was graduated from Brown University, Providence, R. I., in 1795; studied law; was admitted to the bar and commenced practice in Bridgewater (west parish) in 1799; member of the State house of representatives in 1808, 1809, 1812, and 1813; served in the State senate in 1825 and 1826; presented credentials as a War Democrat to the Eleventh Congress and served from March 4, 1809, until June 28, 1809, when he was succeeded by Charles Turner, Jr., who contested the election; elected to the Thirteenth and Fourteenth Congresses (March 4, 1813–March 3, 1817); again a member of the State house of representatives in 1820 and 1821; again served in the State senate in 1830 and 1831; elected to the Twenty-third Congress (March 4, 1833–March 3, 1835); unsuccessful candidate for reelection in 1834 to the Twenty-fourth Congress; resumed the practice of his profession; died in Taunton, Bristol County, Mass., on September 27, 1865; interment in the Old Cemetery, Dighton, Mass.

BAYLOR, Robert Emmett Bledsoe (nephew of Jesse Bledsoe), a Representative from Alabama; born in Lincoln County, Ky., May 10, 1793; served in the War of 1812; studied law; was admitted to the bar and practiced; member of the Kentucky House of Representatives in 1819, but resigned and moved to Alabama in 1820, continuing the practice of law; studied theology, was licensed to preach, and was ordained to the Baptist ministry; member of the Alabama House of Representatives in 1824; elected as a Democrat to the Twenty-first Congress (March 4, 1829–March 3, 1831); unsuccessful candidate for election in 1830 to the Twenty-third Congress; commanded an Alabama regiment during the Creek War; moved to Texas in 1839; elected judge of the district and supreme courts of the Republic; member of the convention that framed the State constitution of Texas in 1845; district judge for twenty-five years; one of the founders of Baylor University at Independence, Tex. (now located at Waco, Tex.), and Baylor Female College at Belton, Tex.; professor of law in Baylor University; died at Gay Hill, Washington County, Tex., on January 6, 1874; interment in the Baylor University grounds; later the remains were removed to the campus of Baylor Female College at Belton, Tex.

BAYLY, Thomas, a Representative from Maryland; born at "Wellington," near Quantico, Somerset (now Wicomico) County, Md., September 13, 1775; attended private schools and was graduated from Princeton College in 1797; studied law; was admitted to the bar and practiced in Somerset and Worcester Counties, Md.; member of the State house of delegates 1804–1814; elected as a Democrat to the Fifteenth, Sixteenth, and Seventeenth Congresses (March 4, 1817–March 3, 1823); resumed the practice of law; died at his home, "Wellington," near Quantico, Md., in 1829; interment in the family cemetery on the grounds of his estate.

BAYLY, Thomas Henry (son of Thomas Monteagle Bayly), a Representative from Virginia; born at "Mount Custis," the family estate, near Drummondtown, Accomac County, Va., December 11, 1810; attended the common schools; was graduated from the University of Virginia at Charlottesville in 1829; studied law; was admitted to the bar in 1830 and commenced practice in Accomac County; also engaged in agricultural pursuits; elected to the Virginia House of Delegates in 1835 and served until his resignation in 1840; appointed brigadier general of the Twenty-first Brigade, Virginia Militia, in 1837 and served until 1842; elected judge of the superior court of law and chancery in 1842 and served until 1844, having been elected to Congress; elected as a State Rights Democrat to the Twenty-eighth Congress to fill the vacancy caused by the resignation of Henry A. Wise; reelected to the Twenty-ninth and to the five succeeding Congresses and served from May 6, 1844, until his death on his estate, "Mount Custis," near Drummondtown, Accomac County, Va., June 23, 1856; interment in the family burying ground on his estate.

BAYLY, Thomas Monteagle (father of Thomas Henry Bayly), a Representative from Virginia; born at Hills Farm, near Drummondtown, Accomac County, Va., on March 26, 1775; attended Washington Academy, Maryland, and was graduated from Princeton College in 1794; studied law; was admitted to the bar about 1796 and commenced practice in Accomac County; also engaged in planting; member of the State house of delegates 1798–1801; member of the State senate 1801–1809; served during the War of 1812 as colonel of militia; elected as a Democrat to

the Thirteenth Congress (March 4, 1813–March 3, 1815); was not a candidate for renomination in 1814; resumed agricultural pursuits and the practice of law; again a member of the State house of delegates 1819, 1820, and 1828–1831; delegate to the State constitutional convention in 1829 and 1830; died on his plantation, "Mount Custis," near Accomac, Accomac County, Va., January 7, 1834; interment in the family cemetery on his estate, "Mount Custis."

BAYNE, Thomas McKee, a Representative from Pennsylvania; born in Bellevue, Allegheny County, Pa., June 14, 1836; attended the public schools and Westminster College, New Wilmington, Pa.; studied law; during the Civil War entered the Union Army in July 1862 as colonel of the One Hundred and Thirty-sixth Regiment, Pennsylvania Volunteer Infantry; took part in the Battles of Fredericksburg and Chancellorsville; resumed the study of law in 1865; was admitted to the bar of Allegheny County in April 1866; elected district attorney for Allegheny County in October 1870 and held the office until January 1, 1874; unsuccessful candidate for election in 1874 to the Forty-fourth Congress; elected as a Republican to the Forty-fifth and to the six succeeding Congresses (March 4, 1877–March 3, 1891); was renominated as a candidate for reelection to the Fifty-second Congress, but declined to accept the nomination, retiring from public life and active business pursuits; died in Washington, D. C., on June 16, 1894; interment in Uniondale Cemetery, Pittsburgh, Pa.

BEACH, Clifton Bailey, a Representative from Ohio; born in Sharon, Medina County, Ohio, September 16, 1845; moved to Cleveland with his parents in 1857; attended the common schools and was graduated from Western Reserve College, Hudson, Ohio, in 1871; studied law; was admitted to the bar in 1872 and commenced practice in Cleveland; served as deputy collector of customs at Cleveland; retired from the practice of law in 1884 and engaged in the manufacture of wire nails, staples, and rods; elected as a Republican to the Fifty-fourth and Fifty-fifth Congresses (March 4, 1895–March 3, 1899); was not a candidate for renomination in 1898; resumed his former manufacturing pursuits in Cleveland; died at Rocky River, Cuyahoga County, Ohio, November 15, 1902; interment in Lake View Cemetery, Cleveland, Ohio.

BEACH, Lewis, a Representative from New York; born in New York City March 30, 1835; was graduated from the Yale Law School in 1856; was admitted to the bar the same year and commenced practice in New York; took up residence in Orange County, N. Y., in 1861; member and treasurer of the Democratic State central committee 1877–1879; elected as a Democrat to the Forty-seventh, Forty-eighth, and Forty-ninth Congresses and served from March 4, 1881, until his death at his home, "Knoll View," Cornwall, Orange County, N. Y., August 10, 1886; interment in Greenwood Cemetery, Brooklyn, N. Y.

BEAKES, Samuel Willard, a Representative from Michigan; born in Burlingham, Sullivan County, N. Y., January 11, 1861; attended Wallkill Academy, Middletown, N. Y.; was graduated from the law department of the University of Michigan at Ann Arbor in 1883; was admitted to the bar the same year and commenced practice in Westerville, Ohio; editor and proprietor of the Westerville Review in 1884, of the Adrian (Mich.) Daily Record 1884–1886, and of the Ann Arbor (Mich.) Argus 1886–1905; mayor of Ann Arbor 1888–1890; postmaster of Ann Arbor under President Cleveland 1894–1898; city treasurer 1891–1893 and 1903–1905; city assessor 1906–1913; delegate to numerous Democratic State conventions and to the Democratic National Convention at St. Louis in 1916; elected as a Democrat to the

Sixty-third and Sixty-fourth Congresses (March 4, 1913–March 3, 1917); successfully contested the election of Mark R. Bacon to the Sixty-fifth Congress and served from December 13, 1917, to March 3, 1919; unsuccessful candidate for reelection in 1918 to the Sixty-sixth Congress; after his service in Congress located in Washington, D. C.; assistant chief of the industrial cooperation service of the United States Department of Commerce from April to July 1919; staff member of the United States Veterans' Bureau from 1919 until his death in Washington, D. C., February 9, 1927; interment in Forest Hill Cemetery, Ann Arbor, Mich.

BEALE, Charles Lewis, a Representative from New York; born in Canaan, Columbia County, N. Y., March 5, 1824; was graduated from Union College, Schenectady, N. Y., in 1844; studied law; was admitted to the bar in 1849 and commenced practice in Canaan, N. Y.; moved to Kinderhook, N. Y., in 1852 and continued the practice of law; elected as a Republican to the Thirty-sixth Congress (March 4, 1859–March 3, 1861); unsuccessful candidate for reelection in 1860 to the Thirty-seventh Congress; presidential elector on the Republican ticket of Lincoln and Johnson in 1864; delegate to the Union National Convention at Philadelphia in 1866; resumed the practice of law; died in Hudson, N. Y., on January 29, 1900; interment in Kinderhook Cemetery, Kinderhook, N. Y.

BEALE, James Madison Hite, a Representative from Virginia; born in Mount Airy, Shenandoah County, Va., February 7, 1786; pursued preparatory studies; engaged in agricultural pursuits; elected as a Democrat to the Twenty-third and Twenty-fourth Congresses (March 4, 1833–March 3, 1837); resumed agricultural pursuits; elected to the Thirty-first and Thirty-second Congresses (March 4, 1849–March 3, 1853); declined to be a candidate for renomination in 1852; resumed agricultural pursuits; died in Putnam County, W. Va., August 2, 1866; interment in Beale Cemetery, near Gallipolis Ferry, Mason County, W. Va.

BEALE, Joseph Grant, a Representative from Pennsylvania; born in Allegheny County, near Freeport, Armstrong County, Pa., March 26, 1839; attended the common schools; was graduated from Caton Academy, Turtle Creek, Pa., and from Iron City Commercial College, Pittsburgh, Pa.; during the Civil War enlisted in the Friend Rifles for three months, and later served as captain of Company C, Ninth Regiment, Pennsylvania Reserves, for three years; was taken prisoner and confined in Libby Prison, Richmond, Va., until released on parole; studied law; served as major in the Pennsylvania State Militia; discontinuing the study of law, he engaged in the coal business in the suburbs of Pittsburgh; moved to Leechburg, Armstrong County, in the spring of 1868 and actively engaged in the iron and steel business; president of the Leechburg Banking Co.; elected as a Republican to the Sixtieth Congress (March 4, 1907–March 3, 1909); unsuccessful candidate for renomination in 1908 to the Sixty-first Congress; resumed his former business pursuits; died in Leechburg, Pa., May 21, 1915; interment in Evergreen Cemetery.

BEALE, Richard Lee Turberville, a Representative from Virginia; born in Hickory Hill, Westmoreland County, Va., May 22, 1819; attended private schools in Westmoreland County, Northumberland Academy and Rappahannock Academy, Virginia, and Dickinson College, Carlisle, Pa.; studied law; was graduated from the University of Virginia at Charlottesville in 1837; was admitted to the bar in 1839 and commenced practice at Hague, Westmoreland County, Va.; elected as a Democrat to the Thirtieth Congress (March 4, 1847–March 3, 1849); declined to be a candidate for renomination in 1848; member of the convention to form a constitution for Virginia

in 1851; member of the State senate 1858–1860; during the Civil War rose through a series of promotions from lieutenant to brigadier general in the Confederate Army; elected to the Forty-fifth Congress to fill the vacancy caused by the death of Beverly B. Douglas; reelected to the Forty-sixth Congress and served from January 23, 1879, to March 3, 1881; resumed the practice of law; died near Hague, Westmoreland County, April 21, 1893; interment in Hickory Hill Cemetery.

BEALES, Cyrus William, a Representative from Pennsylvania; born on a farm near York Spring, Adams County, Pa., December 16, 1877; attended the common schools; at the age of thirteen, upon the death of his father, took over the operation of his father's farm; was graduated from the pharmaceutical department of the Ohio Northern University at Ada in 1899; settled at York Springs and was employed as a pharmacist; moved to Gettysburg, Pa., in 1903 upon his appointment as mercantile appraiser of Adams County; clerk to the county commissioners in 1904 and 1905; engaged in the drug, banking, manufacturing, and printing businesses; postmaster of Gettysburg from April 1, 1910, to May 8, 1914; elected as a Republican to the Sixty-fourth Congress (March 4, 1915–March 3, 1917); was not a candidate for renomination in 1916; member of the State senate 1917–1921; engaged in the drug business in Gettysburg, and died there November 14, 1927; interment in the family plot in Evergreen Cemetery.

BEALL, James Andrew (Jack), a Representative from Texas; born on a farm near Midlothian, Ellis County, Tex., October 25, 1866; attended the country schools; taught school in 1884 and 1885; was graduated from the law department of the University of Texas at Austin in 1890; was admitted to the bar the same year and commenced practice in Waxahachie, Ellis County, Tex.; member of the State house of representatives 1892–1895; served in the State senate 1895–1899; elected as a Democrat to the Fifty-eighth and to the five succeeding Congresses (March 4, 1903–March 3, 1915); was not a candidate for renomination in 1914; moved to Dallas, Tex., in 1914 and resumed the practice of law; also engaged in banking; served as president of the Texas Electric Railway Co. from 1921 until his death in Dallas, Tex., on February 12, 1929; interment in Oakland Cemetery.

BEALL, James Glenn, a Representative and a Senator from Maryland; born in Frostburg, Allegany County, Md., June 5, 1894; attended the public schools and Gettysburg (Pa.) College; during the First World War served in the Ordnance Corps, United States Army, in 1918 and 1919, being discharged as a sergeant; engaged in the insurance and real-estate business; member of the Allegany County Road Commission 1923–1930; served in the State senate 1930–1934; member and chairman of the Maryland State Road Commission in 1938 and 1939; elected as a Republican to the Seventy-eighth and to the four succeeding Congresses (January 3, 1943–January 3, 1953); was not a candidate for renomination in 1952; elected to the United States Senate in 1952 for the term commencing January 3, 1953, and reelected in 1958 for the term ending January 3, 1965.

BEALL, Reasin, a Representative from Ohio; born in Montgomery County, Md., December 3, 1769; received a limited schooling; served as an officer under General Harmer in 1790; appointed ensign in the United States Army March 7, 1792, and battalion quartermaster in 1793, and served under General Wayne in the campaign against the Indians; moved to New Lisbon, Ohio, in 1803; was commissioned brigadier general of Volunteers in 1812; moved to Wooster, Ohio, in 1815; elected as a Whig to the Thirteenth Congress to fill the vacancy caused by the death of John S. Edwards and served from April 20, 1813, until his resignation on June 7, 1814; served as register of the land offices at Canton and Wooster, Ohio, from 1814 to 1824; presided over the Whig mass convention held at Columbus, Ohio, February 22, 1840; presidential elector on the Whig ticket of Harrison and Tyler in 1840; died in Wooster, Wayne County, Ohio, February 20, 1843; interment in Wooster Cemetery.

BEAM, Harry Peter, a Representative from Illinois; born in Peoria, Ill., November 23, 1892; moved with his parents to Chicago, Ill., in 1899; attended St. Mary's School, Marshalltown, Iowa, and Holy Family School, Chicago, Ill.; was graduated from St. Ignatius College, Chicago, Ill., in 1912 and from the law department of Loyola University, Chicago, Ill., in 1916; was admitted to the bar the same year and commenced practice in Chicago, Ill.; during the First World War served as a seaman, first class, in the United States Navy from May 1918 to December 1918; assistant corporation counsel of Chicago 1923–1927; elected as a Democrat to the Seventy-second and to the five succeeding Congresses and served from March 4, 1931, until his resignation on December 6, 1942; elected as a judge of the municipal court of Chicago in 1942, reelected in 1948, and again in 1954 for the term ending in 1960; engaged in legal practice; is a resident of Chicago, Ill.

BEAMAN, Fernando Cortez, a Representative from Michigan; born in Chester, Vt., June 28, 1814; moved with his parents to a farm in Franklin County, N. Y., in 1819; attended the district schools and Malone Academy, Malone, N. Y.; taught school; moved to Rochester, N. Y., in 1836; studied law; moved to Manchester, Mich., in 1838; was admitted to the bar and commenced practice in 1839; moved to Tecumseh in 1841 and practiced law there and in Clinton; moved to Adrian in 1843, having been appointed prosecuting attorney for Lenawee County, and served until 1850; city attorney of Adrian; member of the convention that organized the Republican Party "under the oaks" at Jackson, Mich., in 1854; delegate to the first Republican National Convention, at Philadelphia in 1856; presidential elector on the Republican ticket of Frémont and Dayton in 1856; mayor of Adrian in 1856; judge of the probate court of Lenawee County 1856–1860; elected as a Republican to the Thirty-seventh and to the four succeeding Congresses (March 4, 1861–March 3, 1871); declined to be a candidate for renomination in 1870; returned to Adrian and resumed the practice of law; appointed judge of probate of Lenawee County in 1871, elected to the same position in 1872, and reelected in 1876; appointed United States Senator to fill the vacancy caused by the death of Zachariah Chandler in 1879, but declined the appointment owing to ill health; declined appointments to the State supreme court and as United States Commissioner of Indian Affairs; died in Adrian, Lenawee County, Mich., September 27, 1882; interment in Oakwood Cemetery.

BEAMER, John Valentine, a Representative from Indiana; born on a farm in Wabash County, Ind., November 17, 1896; attended the public schools of Roann, Ind.; was graduated from Wabash College, Crawfordsville, Ind., in 1918; during the First World War served in the Field Artillery; employed with Service Motor Truck Co., Wabash, Ind., 1919–1921; representative for the Century Co., school textbook publisher, New York and Chicago, 1921–1928; vice president and general manager, Wabash (Ind.) Baking Powder & Chemical Co., 1928–1941; vice president and sales manager, Union Rock Wool Corp., Wabash, Ind., 1935–1942; owner and operator of a farm near Wabash, Ind.; served in the State house of representatives in 1949 and 1950; member of the Wabash Carnegie Library Board 1934–1949, Wabash City School Board 1937–1949, and board of trustees of Estelle Peabody Memorial Home; elected as a Republican to the Eighty-second and to the three succeeding Congresses (January 3, 1951–January 3, 1959); unsuccessful candidate for reelection in 1958 to the Eighty-sixth Congress; member of the National Selective Service Appeal Board from March 1960 until his resignation September 1, 1961; is a resident of Wabash, Ind.

BEAN, Benning Moulton, a Representative from New Hampshire; born in Moultonboro, Carroll County, N. H., on January 9, 1782; attended the public schools of Moultonboro and received private tutoring; engaged in teaching and in agricultural pursuits; selectman of Moultonboro 1811–1829 and 1832–1838; justice of the peace in 1816; trustee of Sandwich Academy in 1824; member of the State house of representatives 1815–1823; served in the State senate 1824–1826; again a member of the State house of representatives in 1827; member of the Governor's council in 1829; again served in the State senate, in 1831 and 1832, being president the latter year; elected as a Democrat to the Twenty-third and Twenty-fourth Congresses (March 4, 1833–March 3, 1837); declined to be a candidate for renomination in 1836; resumed teaching and agricultural pursuits in Moultonboro, Carroll County, N. H., where he died February 6, 1866; interment in Bean Cemetery.

BEAN, Curtis Coe, a Delegate from the Territory of Arizona; born in Tamworth, Carroll County, N. H., January 4, 1828; upon the death of his father moved with his mother to Gilmanton, Belknap County, N. H., in 1837; attended Gilmanton Academy, Phillips Exeter Academy, Exeter, N. H., and Union College, Schenectady, N. Y.; moved to New York City in the early fifties and was employed in the United States customhouse; also engaged in the brokerage business; studied law; was admitted to the bar but did not practice extensively; moved to Tennessee in 1864 and settled in Columbia and later in Nashville; member of the State house of representatives in 1867 and 1868; moved to Arizona Territory and settled in Prescott in June 1868; engaged in mining; unsuccessful candidate for election in 1876 to the Forty-fifth Congress; member of the Territorial senate in 1879; elected as a Republican to the Forty-ninth Congress (March 4, 1885–March 3, 1887); unsuccessful candidate for reelection in 1886 to the Fiftieth Congress; returned to Arizona and resumed mining operations; moved to New York City in 1889 but maintained his citizenship and business interests in Arizona; died in New York City on February 1, 1904; interment in Greenwood Cemetery, Brooklyn, N. Y.

BEARDSLEY, Samuel, a Representative from New York; born in Hoosick, Rensselaer County, N. Y., February 6, 1790; pursued academic studies; taught school; studied law in Rome, N. Y.; served as a lieutenant in the War of 1812 and took part in the defense of Sackets Harbor in 1813; was admitted to the bar in 1815 and commenced practice in Watertown; judge advocate in the State militia; returned to Rome in 1816 and continued the practice of law; prosecuting attorney in 1821; member of the State senate in 1823; moved to Utica, Oneida County, in 1823; United States attorney for the northern district of New York 1823–1830; elected as a Democrat to the Twenty-second, Twenty-third, and Twenty-fourth Congresses and served from March 4, 1831, to March 29, 1836, when he resigned; appointed circuit judge in 1836; attorney general of the State of New York 1836–1838; was elected to the Twenty-eighth Congress and served from March 4, 1843, to February 29, 1844, when he resigned to accept a judicial appointment; served as associate judge of the New York Supreme Court from 1844 to 1847, and was appointed chief justice in the latter year; declined another term of service and resumed the practice of law; died in Utica, N. Y., May 6, 1860; interment in Forest Hill Cemetery.

BEATTY, John, a Delegate and a Representative from New Jersey; born in Neshaminy, Bucks County, Pa., December 10, 1749; was graduated from the College of New Jersey (now Princeton University) in 1769; studied medicine in Philadelphia and practiced in Bucks County; entered the Revolutionary Army in 1775 and had attained the rank of major when he was made prisoner at the surrender of Fort Washington; after his exchange was appointed commissary general of prisoners with the rank of colonel May 28, 1778; resigned March 31, 1780, and resumed the practice of medicine in Princeton, N. J.; member of the State council 1781–1783; Member of the Continental Congress from January 13, 1784, to June 3, 1784, and from November 11, 1784, to November 7, 1785; appointed by President Lee as one of the special committee to receive and take leave of General Lafayette in the name of the Continental Congress while it was in session at Trenton on December 11, 1784; member of the State convention that adopted the Federal Constitution in 1787; member of the State general assembly in 1789 and 1790, serving as speaker; elected to the Third Congress (March 4, 1793–March 3, 1795); brigadier general of the Somerset Militia 1793–1796; secretary of state of New Jersey 1795–1805; served as trustee of the College of New Jersey from 1787 until 1802; president of the Trenton Banking Co. from 1815 to 1826; died in Trenton, N. J., May 30, 1826; interment in First Presbyterian Church Cemetery.

BEATTY, John, a Representative from Ohio; born near Sandusky, Erie County, Ohio, December 16, 1828; attended the common schools; entered the banking business in 1852, and subsequently, with his brother, conducted a bank in Cardington, Morrow County, Ohio; presidential elector on the Republican ticket of Lincoln and Hamlin in 1860; at the beginning of the Civil War volunteered as a private in the Third Regiment, Ohio Volunteer Infantry; was appointed lieutenant colonel in 1861; promoted to colonel in 1862 and took a prominent part in the campaigns in the Southwest; commanded a regiment at Perryville and a brigade at Stone River; commissioned brigadier general in 1863 and commanded a brigade at Tullahoma, Chickamauga, and Marion Ridge; elected as a Republican to the Fortieth Congress to fill the vacancy caused by the death of Cornelius S. Hamilton; reelected to the Forty-first and Forty-second Congresses and served from February 5, 1868, to March 3, 1873; moved to Columbus, Ohio, in 1873 and organized the Citizens Savings Bank, serving as its president until 1903, when he retired from active business pursuits; unsuccessful candidate for the Republican nomination as Governor in 1882; presidential elector on the Republican ticket of Blaine and Logan in 1884; member of the State board of charities in 1886 and 1887; president of the Ohio Chickamauga National Military Park Commission 1891–1895; died in Columbus, Ohio, December 21, 1914; interment in Oakland Cemetery, Sandusky, Ohio.

BEATTY, William, a Representative from Pennsylvania; born in Stewartstown, County Tyrone, Ireland, in 1787; immigrated to the United States in 1807 and settled in Butler, Butler County, Pa.; was a sergeant in Captain Thompson's company in the War of 1812; sheriff of Butler County 1823–1826; elected as a Van Buren Democrat to the Twenty-fifth and Twenty-sixth Congresses (March 4, 1837–March 3, 1841); member of the State house of representatives 1840–1842; appointed deputy sheriff of Butler County; died in Butler, Pa., April 12, 1851; interment in the Old Butler Cemetery.

BEATY, Martin, a Representative from Kentucky; born in Abingdon, Va.; operated an iron furnace; moved to Wayne County, Ky., in 1817 and engaged in drilling wells for brine and in the manufacture of salt at Saltville, Ky.; member of the State

senate 1824–1828 and in 1832; presidential elector on the Whig tickets of Clay and Sergeant in 1832 and Harrison and Granger in 1836; was an unsuccessful candidate for election in 1828 to the Twenty-first Congress and in 1830 to the Twenty-second Congress; elected as a Whig to the Twenty-third Congress (March 4, 1833–March 3, 1835); unsuccessful candidate for reelection in 1834 to the Twenty-fourth Congress; member of the State house of representatives in 1848; moved to a farm near Belmont, Tex., in 1856 and engaged in agricultural pursuits and cattle raising; died in Southfork, Owsley County, Ky.; interment in Belmont Cemetery.

BEAUMONT, Andrew, a Representative from Pennsylvania; born in Lebanon, New London County, Conn., January 24, 1790; moved to Pennsylvania in 1808; studied law but never practiced; collector of revenue in 1814; prothonotary and clerk of the courts of Luzerne County, Pa., 1816–1819; member of the State house of representatives in 1821, 1822, and 1826; postmaster of Wilkes-Barre 1826–1832; elected as a Democrat to the Twenty-third and Twenty-fourth Congresses (March 4, 1833–March 3, 1837); was not a candidate for renomination; commissioner of public buildings in Washington, D. C., from November 5, 1846, to March 3, 1847; again a member of the State house of representatives, in 1849; died in Wilkes-Barre, Pa., September 30, 1853; interment in Hollenback Cemetery.

BECK, Erasmus Williams, a Representative from Georgia; born in McDonough, Henry County, Ga., October 21, 1833; attended the local schools of his native county, a private school, and Mercer University, Macon, Ga., for two years; in 1855, on account of ill health, returned to McDonough and began the study of law; moved to Griffin, Ga., in 1856 and continued his law studies; was admitted to the bar in 1856 and commenced practice in Griffin, Ga.; served for a short period in the Confederate Army during the Civil War, but was invalided home on account of ill health; during the war was solicitor general of the Flint circuit; elected as a Democrat to the Forty-second Congress to fill the vacancy caused by the death of Thomas J. Speer and served from December 2, 1872, to March 3, 1873; was not a candidate for renomination in 1872; resumed the practice of his profession at Griffin, Ga.; judge of the city court of Griffin from 1890 until his death in that city on July 22, 1898; interment in Oak Hill Cemetery.

BECK, James Burnie, a Representative and a Senator from Kentucky; born in Dumfriesshire, Scotland, February 13, 1822; received an academic education; immigrated to the United States in 1838 and settled in Wyoming County, N. Y.; moved to Lexington, Ky., in 1843 and was graduated from Transylvania University, Lexington, Ky., in 1846; was admitted to the bar and commenced the practice of law in Lexington; delegate to the Democratic National Conventions at Charleston and Baltimore in 1860; elected as a Democrat to the Fortieth and to the three succeeding Congresses (March 4, 1867–March 3, 1875); appointed in May 1876 a member of the commission to define the boundary line between Maryland and Virginia; elected to the United States Senate in 1876; reelected in 1882, again in 1888, and served from March 4, 1877, until his death in Washington, D. C., on May 3, 1890; interment in Lexington Cemetery, Lexington, Ky.

BECK, James Montgomery, a Representative from Pennsylvania; born in Philadelphia, Pa., July 9, 1861; attended the public schools and was graduated from Moravian College, Bethlehem, Pa., in 1880; employed as clerk for a railway company in 1880 and studied law at night; was admitted to the bar in 1884 and commenced practice in Philadelphia; admitted to the bar of

New York City in 1903, and to the bar of England in 1922; served as assistant United States attorney for the eastern district of Pennsylvania 1888–1892 and as United States attorney 1896–1900; appointed by President William McKinley as assistant to the Attorney General of the United States in 1900 and served until his resignation in 1903; continued the practice of law in Philadelphia, New York City, and Washington from 1903 to 1921; during the First World War he championed the cause of the Allies and was elected a bencher of Gray's Inn in 1914, being the first foreigner in 600 years to receive that distinction; also received decorations from France and Belgium; author of several books and articles on the war and on the Constitution of the United States; appointed by President Warren G. Harding as Solicitor General of the United States in 1921 and served until his resignation in 1925; resumed the practice of law; elected as a Republican to the Seventieth Congress to fill the vacancy caused by the resignation of James M. Hazlett; reelected to the Seventy-first, Seventy-second, and Seventy-third Congresses and served from November 8, 1927, until his resignation on September 30, 1934; resumed the practice of law and was also engaged as an author; died in Washington, D. C., April 12, 1936; interment in Rock Creek Cemetery.

BECK, Joseph David, a Representative from Wisconsin; born near Bloomingdale, Vernon County, Wis., March 14, 1866; attended the common schools; taught in the public schools of the State for twelve years; was graduated from the State Normal School, Stevens Point, Wis., in 1897 and from the University of Wisconsin at Madison in 1903; clerk of the State bureau of statistics of Wisconsin in 1901; deputy commissioner of statistics in 1902; delegate to the Republican State convention at Madison in 1902; chief of the department of labor statistics 1903–1913; president of the International Association of Labor Bureau Officials 1911–1913; chairman of the Industrial Commission of Wisconsin 1913–1917; engaged in agricultural pursuits and in stock raising near Viroqua, Vernon County, in 1917; elected as a Republican to the Sixty-seventh and to the three succeeding Congresses (March 4, 1921–March 3, 1929); was not a candidate for renomination, but was an unsuccessful candidate for the Republican nomination for Governor of Wisconsin in 1928; resumed agricultural pursuits; appointed a member of the State department of agriculture and markets in 1931 and served until his death in Madison, Wis., November 8, 1936; interment in Viroqua Cemetery, Viroqua, Wis.

BECKER, Frank John, a Representative from New York; born in Brooklyn, N. Y., August 27, 1899; moved with his parents to Lynbrook, Nassau County, L. I., in November 1905; attended the public schools of Lynbrook and Brown's Business College, Jamaica, L. I.; during the First World War enlisted in the United States Army July 22, 1918, and served overseas in France and England; was discharged from the service on September 22, 1919; engaged in the insurance business in Lynbrook, N. Y.; member of the State assembly of New York 1945–1953; Republican committeeman since 1931; director, Lynbrook Federal Savings & Loan Association since 1945; delegate to the Republican National Convention in 1956; elected as a Republican to the Eighty-third and to the three succeeding Congresses (January 3, 1953–January 3, 1961). *Reelected to the Eighty-seventh Congress.*

BECKHAM, John Crepps Wickliffe (grandson of Charles Anderson Wickliffe and cousin of Robert Charles Wickliffe), a Senator from Kentucky; born in Wickland, near Bardstown, Nelson County, Ky., August 5, 1869; attended the Roseland Academy at Bardstown and Central University, Richmond, Ky.; served as a page in the State house of representatives in 1881 and 1882; principal of the Bardstown High School 1888–1891; studied law;

was admitted to the bar in 1889 and commenced practice in Bardstown in 1893; member of the State house of representatives 1894–1898, serving as speaker in 1898; Lieutenant Governor of Kentucky in 1899, becoming Governor upon the death of Governor Goebel, February 3, 1900; subsequently elected for the unexpired term ending December 8, 1903, and reelected for the term 1903–1907; delegate to the Democratic National Conventions in 1904, 1908, 1912, 1916, and 1920; elected as a Democrat to the United States Senate and served from March 4, 1915, to March 3, 1921; unsuccessful candidate for reelection in 1920; resumed the practice of law in Louisville, Ky.; unsuccessful candidate for Governor of Kentucky in 1927; unsuccessful candidate for nomination to the United States Senate in 1936; died in Louisville, Ky., January 9, 1940; interment in Frankfort Cemetery, Frankfort, Ky.

BECKNER, William Morgan, a Representative from Kentucky; born in Moorefield, Nichols County, Ky., June 19, 1841; attended the public schools, Rand and Richeson Seminary, Maysville, Ky., and Centre College, Danville, Ky.; worked on a farm and was subsequently a clerk in a country store at Bethel, Bath County, Ky.; became a private tutor and taught school for two years in Orangeburg and Maysville; studied law; was admitted to the bar in 1864 and commenced practice in Winchester, Ky.; city judge in 1865; served as prosecuting attorney in 1866 and 1867; was elected judge of Clark County in 1870; established the Clark County Democrat in 1867, which he owned and edited for a number of years; appointed State prison commissioner in 1880; served as State railroad commissioner from 1882 until 1884, when he resigned; president of the interstate educational conventions held in Louisville in 1883 and 1885; member of the State constitutional convention in 1890; member of the State house of representatives in 1893; chairman of the Democratic State convention in 1893; elected as a Democrat to the Fifty-third Congress to fill the vacancy caused by the death of Marcus C. Lisle and served from December 3, 1894, to March 3, 1895; unsuccessful candidate for renomination in 1894; resumed the practice of law; died in Winchester, Ky., March 14, 1910; interment in Winchester Cemetery.

BECKWITH, Charles Dyer, a Representative from New Jersey; born near Coveville, Saratoga County, N. Y., October 22, 1838; attended private schools in Troy, N. Y., Philadelphia, Pa., Worcester, Mass., and a military institution in New Haven, Conn.; moved to Paterson, Passaic County, N. J., in 1860 and engaged in the manufacture of iron; member of the board of aldermen in 1882; mayor of Paterson, N. J., 1885–1889; elected as a Republican to the Fifty-first Congress (March 4, 1889–March 3, 1891); unsuccessful candidate for reelection in 1890 to the Fifty-second Congress; resumed manufacturing pursuits; returned to the State of New York and settled on a farm in the town of Chatham, Columbia County, in 1897 and engaged in the management of his farm until his death near Chatham Center, Columbia County, N. Y., on March 27, 1921; interment in Chatham Center Rural Cemetery.

BECKWORTH, Lindley Gary, a Representative from Texas; born on a farm in the South Bouie community near Mabank, Kaufman County, Tex., June 30, 1913; attended the rural schools, East Texas State Teachers College, Commerce, Tex., Sam Houston State Teachers College, Huntsville, Tex., and Southern Methodist University, Dallas, Tex.; taught school in Upshur County, Tex., for three years; attended the law department of Baylor University, Waco, Tex., and the University of Texas at Austin; was admitted to the bar in 1937 and commenced practice in Gilmer, Tex.; member of the State house of representatives 1936–1938; elected as a Democrat to the Seventy-sixth and to the six succeeding Congresses (January 3, 1939–January 3, 1953); was not a candidate for renomination in 1952, but was unsuccessful for the Democratic nomination for United States Senator; resumed the practice of law in Longview, Tex.; elected to the Eighty-fifth and Eighty-sixth Congresses (January 3, 1957–January 3, 1961). *Reelected to the Eighty-seventh Congress.*

BEDE, James Adam, a Representative from Minnesota; born on a farm in North Eaton Township, Lorain County, Ohio, January 13, 1856; attended the public schools of Ohio, Oberlin (Ohio) College, and Tabor (Iowa) College; read law while learning the printing trade; taught school in Iowa, Ohio, and Arkansas; editor and publisher of several newspapers and periodicals; served as a representative for several western newspapers in Washington, D. C., 1888–1891; engaged in newspaper work at Pine City, Pine County, Minn.; served as United States marshal for the district of Minnesota in 1894 during the great railway strike; elected as a Republican to the Fifty-eighth, Fifty-ninth, and Sixtieth Congresses (March 4, 1903–March 3, 1909); unsuccessful candidate for renomination in 1908 to the Sixty-first Congress; returned to Pine City; engaged as a publisher and lecturer; moved to Duluth, Minn., in 1927 and engaged in his former pursuits; also was interested in the St. Lawrence inland waterway project; died in Duluth, Minn., April 11, 1942; interment in Birchwood Cemetery, Pine City, Minn.

BEDFORD, Gunning (cousin of Gunning Bedford, Jr.), a Delegate from Delaware; born in Philadelphia, Pa., April 7, 1742; became a major in the Continental Army in 1775; lieutenant colonel in Haslet's Regiment in 1776, being wounded in the battle of White Plains; subsequently appointed muster-master-general in 1776; was admitted to the bar in 1779; member of the Delaware General Assembly from New Castle County 1784–1786; elected a Member of the Continental Congress for the term 1786–1787 but declined to serve and resigned January 15, 1787; member of the Delaware convention in 1787 which ratified the Federal Constitution; presidential elector in 1788; elected as Governor of Delaware in 1796 and served until his death in New Castle, Del., September 30, 1797; interment in Immanuel Churchyard.

BEDFORD, Gunning, Jr. (cousin of Gunning Bedford), a Delegate from Delaware; born in Philadelphia, Pa., in 1747; was graduated from Princeton College in 1771; studied law in Philadelphia; was admitted to the Delaware bar in 1779 and commenced practice in Dover, Del.; moved to Wilmington, Del.; Member of the Continental Congress 1783–1785; appointed attorney general of the State on April 26, 1784, and served until September 26, 1789; appointed a commissioner to the convention held at Annapolis, Md., in September 1786 but did not attend; member of the Federal constitutional convention at Philadelphia in 1787 and signed the Constitution; delegate to the State convention that ratified the Federal Constitution in 1787; member of the State senate in 1788; presidential elector in 1789, when George Washington was the unanimous choice for President, and again in 1793; appointed United States judge for the district of Delaware September 26, 1789, which position he held until his death in Wilmington, Del., March 30, 1812; interment in First Presbyterian Churchyard; reinterment at the Masonic Home, on the Lancaster Turnpike, in Christiana Hundred, Del.

BEDINGER, George Michael (uncle of Henry Bedinger), a Representative from Kentucky; born in Hanover, York County, Pa., December 10, 1756; attended an English school and obtained the best education possible at that time; immigrated to Virginia about 1762 and to Kentucky in 1779 and settled at Boones-

borough; adjutant in the expedition against Chillicothe in May 1779; major in the Battle of Blue Licks, August 19, 1782; major in Drake's Regiment in 1791; major commanding the Winchester Battalion of Sharpshooters in the St. Clair expedition in 1791; major commanding the Third Sublegion of the United States Infantry from April 11, 1792, to February 28, 1793; member of the State house of representatives of the first legislature of Kentucky in 1792, representing Bourbon and Nicholas Counties; served in the State senate in 1800 and 1801; elected to the Eighth and Ninth Congresses (March 4, 1803–March 3, 1807); engaged in agricultural pursuits; died at Blue Licks Springs, Ky., December 7, 1843; interment in the family cemetery on his farm (later owned by E. R. Sampson) near Lower Blue Licks Springs, Ky.

BEDINGER, Henry (nephew of George Michael Bedinger), a Representative from Virginia; born near Shepherdstown, Jefferson County, Va. (now West Virginia), February 3, 1812; attended the common schools; studied law; was admitted to the bar in 1832 and commenced practice in Shepherdstown; moved to Charlestown, Va., and continued the practice of law; elected as a Democrat to the Twenty-ninth and Thirtieth Congresses (March 4, 1845–March 3, 1849); was an unsuccessful candidate for reelection in 1848 to the Thirty-first Congress; resumed the practice of law; appointed Chargé d'Affaires to Denmark on May 24, 1853, and Minister Resident June 29, 1854, in which capacity he served until August 10, 1858, when he resigned; died in Shepherdstown, W. Va., November 26, 1858; interment in Elmwood Cemetery.

BEE, Carlos (great-grandson of Thomas Bee), a Representative from Texas; born in Saltillo, Mexico, July 8, 1867, where his parents had moved after the collapse of the Confederacy; returned with his parents to San Antonio, Tex., in 1874; attended the public schools and the Agricultural and Mechanical College; studied law while working as a railway mail clerk; was admitted to the bar in 1893 and commenced practice in San Antonio, Tex.; United States commissioner for the western district of Texas in 1893; district attorney of the thirty-seventh judicial district 1898–1905; chairman of the Democratic State convention in 1904; delegate to the Democratic National Convention at St. Louis, Mo., in 1904 and at Denver, Colo., in 1908; served as a member of the city school board of San Antonio 1906–1908; president of the county school board of Bexar County, Tex., 1912–1914; member of the State senate 1915–1919; elected as a Democrat to the Sixty-sixth Congress (March 4, 1919–March 3, 1921); unsuccessful candidate for reelection in 1920 to the Sixty-seventh Congress; engaged in the practice of law in San Antonio, Tex., until his death there on April 20, 1932; interment in the Confederate Cemetery.

BEE, Thomas (great-grandfather of Carlos Bee), a Delegate from South Carolina; born in Charleston, S. C., in 1725; educated in Charleston, and later at Oxford University, England; studied law; was admitted to the bar at Charleston, S. C., January 27, 1761, and practiced there; also engaged in planting; member of Commons House, Province of South Carolina, for St. Pauls 1762–1764, for St. Peters 1765, and for St. Andrews 1772–1776; justice of the peace in 1775; Delegate to the First and Second Provincial Congresses 1775 and 1776; member of the State house of representatives 1776–1779 and 1782, serving as speaker 1777–1779; took an active part in the Revolution and was a member of the council of safety 1775 and 1776; law judge 1776–1778; member of the State legislative council 1776–1778; Lieutenant Governor of South Carolina in 1779 and 1780; Member of the Continental Congress 1780–1782; appointed judge of the United States Court for the District of South Carolina by President Washington June 14, 1790; published reports of the district court of South Carolina in 1810; died in Pendleton, S. C., February 18, 1812; interment in Woodstock Cemetery, Goose Creek, S. C.

BEEBE, George Monroe, a Representative from New York; born in New Vernon, Orange County, N. Y., October 28, 1836; attended the common schools, and Walkill Academy, Middletown, N. Y.; studied law and was graduated from the Albany Law University in 1857; was admitted to the bar the same year and commenced practice in Monticello, Sullivan County, N. Y.; moved to Peoria, Ill., in 1857 and became editor of the Central Illinois Democrat; moved to Troy, Doniphan County, Territory of Kansas, in 1858 and continued the practice of law; member of the Territorial council in 1858 and 1859; appointed by President Buchanan as secretary of the Territory in 1859; Acting Governor in 1860 and 1861; moved to St. Joseph, Mo., in 1861 and to Virginia City, Nev., in 1863, continuing the practice of his profession; unsuccessful candidate for associate judge of the State supreme court in 1865; declined the appointment as collector of internal revenue tendered in 1865 by President Johnson; returned to Monticello, N. Y., and became editor of the Republican Watchman in 1866; unsuccessful candidate for the State senate in 1871; member of the State assembly in 1872 and 1873; delegate to the Democratic State conventions of New York in 1873 and 1874, serving as chairman; commissioned by Governor Dix as chief of artillery with the rank of colonel in the Fifth Division, National Guard of New York, in 1873; resigned in 1874 to enter Congress; elected as a Democrat to the Forty-fourth and Forty-fifth Congresses (March 4, 1875–March 3, 1879); unsuccessful candidate for reelection in 1878 to the Forty-sixth Congress; resumed his former newspaper pursuits; delegate to the Democratic National Conventions in 1876, 1880, and 1892; member of the State court of claims from 1883 until 1900; resided at Monticello until 1892 when he moved to Ellenville, N. Y.; retired from active business pursuits in 1900; died in Ellenville, Ulster County, N. Y., on March 1, 1927; interment in Woodlawn Cemetery, Newburgh, N. Y.

BEECHER, Philemon, a Representative from Ohio; born in Kent, Litchfield County, Conn., in 1775; received a classical education; studied law; was admitted to the bar and practiced; moved to Lancaster, Ohio, in 1801 and continued the practice of law; member of the State house of representatives in 1803 and 1805–1807, serving as speaker in 1807; unsuccessful candidate in 1807 for election to the United States Senate, and also as judge of the Ohio Supreme Court; major general in the State militia; elected as a Federalist to the Fifteenth and Sixteenth Congresses (March 4, 1817–March 3, 1821); unsuccessful candidate for reelection in 1820 to the Seventeenth Congress; elected to the Eighteenth, Nineteenth, and Twentieth Congresses (March 4, 1823–March 3, 1829); unsuccessful candidate for reelection in 1828 to the Twenty-first Congress; engaged in the practice of law in Lancaster, Fairfield County, Ohio, until his death there November 30, 1839; interment in Elmwood Cemetery.

BEEDY, Carroll Lynwood, a Representative from Maine; born in Phillips, Franklin County, Maine, August 3, 1880; attended the public schools of Lewiston, Androscoggin County, Maine; was graduated from Bates College, Lewiston, Maine, in 1903 and from the law department of Yale University, New Haven, Conn., in 1906; was admitted to the bar in 1907 and commenced practice in Portland, Maine; prosecuting attorney of Cumberland County 1917–1921; elected as a Republican to the Sixty-seventh and to the six succeeding Congresses (March 4, 1921–

January 3, 1935); unsuccessful candidate for reelection in 1934 to the Seventy-fourth Congress; engaged in the practice of law in Washington, D. C., until his death there August 30, 1947; interment in Evergreen Cemetery, Portland, Maine.

BEEKMAN, Thomas, a Representative from New York; born in Wayne County, N. Y.; town clerk of Smithfield, N. Y., in 1824; elected to the Twenty-first Congress (March 4, 1829–March 3, 1831); died in Peterboro, N. Y.

BEEMAN, Joseph Henry, a Representative from Mississippi; born near Gatesville, Gates County, N. C., November 17, 1833; moved with his parents to Morgan County, Ala., in 1847 and to Mississippi in 1849; received an academic education; taught school for several years; engaged in mercantile pursuits; served as a lieutenant in the Confederate Army during the Civil War; member of the State house of representatives 1883–1891; connected with the Farmers' Alliance and served as chairman of its executive committee; delegate to several State conventions; elected as a Democrat to the Fifty-second Congress (March 4, 1891–March 3, 1893); engaged in agricultural pursuits until his death near Lena, Scott County, Miss., July 31, 1909; interment in Beeman Cemetery, Lena, Miss.

BEERS, Cyrus, a Representative from New York; born in Newtown, Conn., June 21, 1786; moved with his parents to New York City; obtained a limited education in the public schools; engaged in mercantile pursuits and also in the lumber business; moved to Ithaca, N. Y., in 1821 and engaged in the mercantile business; delegate to the Democratic State convention at Herkimer in 1830; appointed commissioner of deeds at Ithaca in 1837; elected as a Democrat to the Twenty-fifth Congress to fill the vacancy caused by the death of Andrew D. W. Bruyn and served from December 3, 1838, to March 3, 1839; was not a candidate for renomination in 1838; delegate to the New York and Erie Railroad Convention at Ithaca in 1839; resumed his former business pursuits in Ithaca, Tompkins County, N. Y., where he died June 5, 1850; interment in the City Cemetery.

BEERS, Edward McMath, a Representative from Pennsylvania; born in Nossville, Huntingdon County, Pa., May 27, 1877; attended the public schools; moved with his parents to Mount Union, Pa., in 1889; was graduated from Mount Union High School in 1895; upon the death of his father, succeeded him in the hotel business in 1895; also interested in agricultural pursuits; delegate to the Republican State convention at Harrisburg in 1898; mayor of Mount Union 1910–1914; member of the board of directors of the First National Bank of Mount Union and of the Grange Trust Co. of Huntingdon, Pa.; associate judge of Huntingdon County 1914–1923; elected as a Republican to the Sixty-eighth and to the four succeeding Congresses and served from March 4, 1923, until his death in Washington, D. C., on April 21, 1932; interment in the Odd Fellows' Cemetery, Mount Union, Pa.

BEESON, Henry White, a Representative from Pennsylvania; born in Uniontown, Fayette County, Pa., September 14, 1791; attended the public schools; engaged in agricultural pursuits; colonel in the Fayette County Militia; elected as a Democrat to the Twenty-seventh Congress to fill the vacancy caused by the resignation of Enos Hook and served from May 31, 1841, to March 3, 1843; unsuccessful candidate for reelection in 1842 to the Twenty-eighth Congress; resumed agricultural pursuits; died in North Union Township, near Uniontown, Pa., October 28, 1863; interment in Oak Hill Cemetery.

BEGG, James Thomas, a Representative from Ohio; born on a farm near Lima, Allen County, Ohio, February 16, 1877; attended the public and high schools of Columbus Grove, and Lima (Ohio) College; was graduated from the Wooster (Ohio) University in 1903; taught school; superintendent of public schools at Columbus Grove 1905–1910, at Ironton, Ohio, 1910–1913, and at Sandusky, Ohio, 1913–1917; employed as a campaign director and lectured throughout the United States for the American City Bureau of New York in chamber-of-commerce work 1917–1919; elected as a Republican to the Sixty-sixth and to the four succeeding Congresses (March 4, 1919–March 3, 1929); was not a candidate for renomination in 1928 to the Seventy-first Congress; engaged in the banking business; unsuccessful candidate for election in 1942 to the Seventy-eighth Congress; business consultant and dairy farmer; moved to Oklahoma City, Okla., in 1959, where he now resides.

BEGOLE, Josiah Williams, a Representative from Michigan; born in Groveland, Livingston County, N. Y., January 20, 1815; attended the public schools in Mount Morris and Temple Hill Academy, Geneseo, N. Y.; moved to Flint, Genesee County, Mich., in August 1836; taught school in 1837 and 1838; engaged in agricultural pursuits from 1839 to 1856; school inspector; justice of the peace and township treasurer; county treasurer 1856–1864; engaged in the lumber business in 1863; member of the State senate in 1870 and 1871; member of the city council for three years; delegate to the Republican National Convention at Philadelphia in 1872 and a member of the delegation which informed Grant and Wilson of their nomination; elected as a Republican to the Forty-third Congress (March 4, 1873–March 3, 1875); was an unsuccessful candidate for reelection in 1874 to the Forty-fourth Congress; resumed the lumber business and later engaged in the manufacture of wagons; also engaged in banking; Governor of Michigan 1883–1885; resumed his former business activities; died in Flint, Mich., June 5, 1896; interment in Glenwood Cemetery.

BEIDLER, Jacob Atlee, a Representative from Ohio; born in Tredyffrin Township, near Valley Forge, Chester County, Pa., November 2, 1852; attended the country schools, and Locke's Seminary, Norristown, Pa.; moved to Ohio and settled in Willoughby, Lake County, in 1873; engaged in business as a coal dealer and later as an operator; elected a member of the city council of Willoughby in 1881; moved to his farm, "Belle Vernon," near Willoughby, in 1881 and engaged in raising dairy cattle; president of the Belle Vernon-Mapes Dairy Co.; vice president of the Cleveland, Painesville & Eastern Railroad Co.; elected as a Republican to the Fifty-seventh, Fifty-eighth, and Fifty-ninth Congresses (March 4, 1901–March 3, 1907); owing to ill health declined to be a candidate for renomination in 1906 to the Sixtieth Congress; resumed his former business activities; president of the Rhodes & Beidler Coal Co.; member of the State board of agriculture; died at "Belle Vernon," near Willoughby, Lake County, Ohio, September 13, 1912; interment in Lake View Cemetery, Cleveland, Ohio.

BEIRNE, Andrew, a Representative from Virginia; born in Dangan, County Roscommon, Ireland, in 1771; received a classical education and was graduated from Trinity University, Dublin, Ireland; immigrated to the United States in 1793 and settled in Union, Monroe County, Va.; engaged in mercantile and agricultural pursuits; member of the State house of delegates in 1807 and 1808; during the War of 1812 served as captain of a rifle company and as colonel of the Monroe County Militia; delegate to the Virginia constitutional convention in 1829 and 1830; member of the State senate 1831–1836; presidential elector on the Democratic ticket of Van Buren and Johnson in 1836; elected as a Van Buren Democrat to the Twenty-fifth and Twenty-sixth Congresses (March 4, 1837–March 3, 1841); was not a candidate for reelection in 1840 to the Twenty-seventh Congress; resumed his former business activities; died while on a visit in Gainesville, Sumter County, Ala., March 16, 1845; interment in the family burying ground at Union, Monroe County, Va. (now West Virginia).

BEITER, Alfred Florian, a Representative from New York; born in Clarence, Erie County, N. Y., July 7, 1893; attended the elementary schools, Williamsville (N. Y.) High School, and Niagara University, Niagara Falls, N. Y.; moved to Williamsville, N. Y., and engaged in the general merchandising business from 1915 to 1929; supervisor of the town of Amherst, N. Y., 1930–1934; elected as a Democrat to the Seventy-third, Seventy-fourth, and Seventy-fifth Congresses (March 4, 1933–January 3, 1939); unsuccessful candidate for reelection in 1938 to the Seventy-sixth Congress; assistant to the Secretary of the Interior in 1939 and 1940; elected to the Seventy-seventh Congress (January 3, 1941–January 3, 1943); unsuccessful candidate for reelection in 1942 to the Seventy-eighth Congress; owned and operated a hatchery and feed business in Buffalo, N. Y., 1944–1948; president of the National Customs Service Association 1949–1961; Deputy Commissioner of Customs, Treasury Department, Washington, D. C., 1961–; is a resident of Chevy Chase, Md.

BELCHER, Hiram, a Representative from Maine; born in Hallowell, Maine, February 23, 1790; attended the rural schools and the local academy at Hallowell 1805–1807; studied law; was admitted to the bar and commenced practice in Farmington, Kennebec County, Maine, in 1812; elected town clerk of Farmington and served from 1814 to 1819; member of the State house of representatives in 1822, 1829, and 1832; served in the State senate in 1838 and 1839; elected as a Whig to the Thirtieth Congress (March 4, 1847–March 3, 1849); was not a candidate for reelection in 1848 to the Thirty-first Congress; engaged in the practice of his profession until his death in Farmington, Maine, May 6, 1857; interment in Center Meeting House Cemetery.

BELCHER, Nathan, a Representative from Connecticut; born in Preston (now a part of Griswold), Conn., June 23, 1813; completed academic studies; was graduated from Amherst (Mass.) College in 1832; studied law at the Cambridge Law School; was admitted to the bar in 1836 and commenced practice in Clinton, Conn.; moved in 1841 to New London, where he engaged in manufacturing tools, hardware, and kitchen utensils; member of the State house of representatives 1846 and 1847; served in the State senate in 1850; presidential elector on the Democratic ticket of Pierce and King in 1852; elected as a Democrat to the Thirty-third Congress (March 4, 1853–March 3, 1855); was not a candidate for renomination in 1854; resumed his former manufacturing pursuits; also engaged in banking; died in New London, New London County, Conn., June 2, 1891; interment in Cedar Grove Cemetery.

BELCHER, Page Henry, a Representative from Oklahoma; born in Jefferson, Grant County, Okla., April 21, 1899, on the claim his father took in the opening of the Cherokee Strip; attended high school at Jefferson and Medford, Okla.; student at Friends University, Wichita, Kans., and the University of Oklahoma at Norman; veteran of the First World War; court clerk of Garfield County, Okla., 1934–1938; studied law, was admitted to the bar in 1936 and commenced the practice of law in Enid, Okla.; municipal judge, Enid, Okla., in 1938; secretary to Congressman Ross Rizley in 1941; member of Enid Board of Education;

elected as a Republican to the Eighty-second and to the four succeeding Congresses (January 3, 1951–January 3, 1961). *Reelected to the Eighty-seventh Congress.*

BELDEN, George Ogilvie, a Representative from New York; born in Norwalk, Conn., March 28, 1797; attended the public schools; studied law with Charles Baker, of Bloomingburg, N. Y.; was admitted to the bar and practiced in Monticello, Sullivan County, N. Y.; elected as a Democrat to the Twentieth Congress (March 4, 1827–March 3, 1829); resumed the practice of law; served as general of the Twenty-third Brigade of Infantry of the State of New York in 1831; died in Monticello, Sullivan County, N. Y., October 9, 1833; interment in the Old Cemetery on St. John Street.

BELDEN, James Jerome, a Representative from New York; born in Fabius, Onondaga County, N. Y., September 30, 1825; attended the common schools; engaged in the banking business at Syracuse, N. Y., in 1880; also interested in the construction of railroads and public works; served as mayor of Syracuse, N. Y., in 1877 and 1878; elected as a Republican to the Fiftieth Congress to fill the vacancy caused by the resignation of Frank Hiscock; reelected to the Fifty-first, Fifty-second, and Fifty-third Congresses and served from November 8, 1887, to March 3, 1895; was not a candidate for renomination in 1894; elected to the Fifty-fifth Congress (March 4, 1897–March 3, 1899); was not a candidate for renomination in 1898; died in Syracuse, Onondaga County, N. Y., January 1, 1904; interment in Oakwood Cemetery.

BELFORD, James Burns, a Representative from Colorado; born in Lewistown, Mifflin County, Pa., September 28, 1837; attended the common schools and Dickinson College, Carlisle, Pa.; studied law; was admitted to the bar in 1859; moved to California, Moniteau County, Mo., and commenced practice; moved to La Porte, La Porte County, Ind., in 1860; member of the State house of representatives in 1867; presidential elector on the Republican ticket of Lincoln and Johnson in 1864; appointed an associate justice of the supreme court of Colorado in 1870 and moved to Central City; moved to Denver in 1883; upon the admission of Colorado as a State into the Union was elected as a Republican to the Forty-fourth Congress and served from October 3, 1876, until March 3, 1877; presented credentials as a Member-elect to the Forty-fifth Congress and served from March 4, 1877, until December 13, 1877, when he was succeeded by Thomas M. Patterson, who contested his election; elected to the Forty-sixth, Forty-seventh, and Forty-eighth Congresses (March 4, 1879–March 3, 1885); unsuccessful candidate for renomination in 1884; engaged in the practice of law in Denver, Colo., until his death there January 10, 1910; interment in Riverside Cemetery.

BELFORD, Joseph McCrum, a Representative from New York; born in Mifflintown, Juniata County, Pa., August 5, 1852; attended Dickinson Seminary, Williamsport, Pa., and was graduated from Dickinson College, Carlisle, Pa., in 1871; moved to Long Island, N. Y., in 1884 and engaged in teaching at the Franklinville and Riverhead Academies; studied law; was admitted to the bar in 1889 and commenced the practice of law in Riverhead, Long Island, N. Y.; served as secretary and chairman of the Suffolk County Republican committee; clerk of the surrogate court; elected as a Republican to the Fifty-fifth Congress (March 4, 1897–March 3, 1899); was not a candidate for renomination in 1898 to the Fifty-sixth Congress; delegate to the Republican National Convention at Philadelphia in 1900 that nominated William McKinley and Theodore Roosevelt;

resumed the practice of his chosen profession in Riverhead, Suffolk County, Long Island, N. Y.; also engaged in the banking business; served as surrogate of Suffolk County from 1904 to 1910; died suddenly in Grand Central Station, New York City, May 3, 1917; interment in Riverhead Cemetery, Riverhead, Long Island, N. Y.

BELKNAP, Charles Eugene, a Representative from Michigan; born in Massena, St. Lawrence County, N. Y., October 17, 1846; moved with his parents to Grand Rapids, Mich., in 1855; attended the common schools; left school August 14, 1862, and enlisted in the Twenty-first Regiment, Michigan Volunteer Infantry; received a captain's commission January 8, 1864; brevet major August 1864; brevet lieutenant colonel June 1865; served until June 1865 with the Army of the Cumberland; engaged in the manufacture of wagons and sleighs in 1871; member of the board of education of Grand Rapids 1871–1878; served on the board of aldermen 1880–1882; elected mayor of Grand Rapids in 1884; trustee of the State institution for the deaf 1885–1891; president of the State hospital board 1905–1915; elected as a Republican to the Fifty-first Congress (March 4, 1889–March 3, 1891); was not a candidate for renomination in 1890, but was subsequently nominated and elected to the Fifty-second Congress to fill the vacancy caused by the death of Melbourne H. Ford and served from November 3, 1891, to March 3, 1893; unsuccessfully contested the election of George F. Richardson to the Fifty-third Congress; resumed the manufacture of wagons and sleighs; served on staff duty at Fort Oglethorpe during the Spanish-American War; appointed by Gov. John T. Rich as president of the Michigan Commission of the Chickamauga and Chattanooga National Military Park in 1898; during the First World War was appointed a member of the local selective draft board of the city of Grand Rapids; retired from active business pursuits; engaged in literary pursuits; died in Grand Rapids, Mich., January 16, 1929; interment in the Greenwood Cemetery.

BELKNAP, Hugh Reid, a Representative from Illinois; born in Keokuk, Lee County, Iowa, September 1, 1860; attended the public schools, Adams Academy, Quincy, Mass., and Phillips Academy, Andover, Mass.; at the age of eighteen entered the service of the Baltimore & Ohio Railroad Co. in a minor capacity; remained with this company for twelve years, filling various positions in practical railroading in the operating department, and retired as chief clerk to the general manager in 1892 to become superintendent of the South Side Rapid Transit Railroad of Chicago; successfully contested as a Republican the election of Lawrence E. McGann to the Fifty-fourth Congress; reelected to the Fifty-fifth Congress and served from December 27, 1895, to March 3, 1899; unsuccessful candidate for reelection in 1898 to the Fifty-sixth Congress; resided in Chicago, Ill., until 1901; appointed a paymaster in the United States Army with the rank of major and served from February 2, 1901, until his death in Calamba, Laguna, P. I., November 12, 1901; interment in Arlington National Cemetery, Fort Myer, Va.

BELL, Charles Henry (nephew of Samuel Bell and cousin of James Bell), a Senator from New Hampshire; born in Chester, Rockingham County, N. H., November 18, 1823; was graduated from Dartmouth College, Hanover, N. H., in 1844; studied law; was admitted to the bar and practiced in Chester, Great Falls, and Exeter; was county solicitor for ten years; member of the State house of representatives 1858–1860, serving as speaker in 1860; member of the State senate in 1863 and 1864, serving as president in 1894; appointed as a Republican to the United States Senate to fill the vacancy in the term beginning March 4, 1879, and served from March 13, 1879, to June 18, 1879, when a successor was elected; was not a candidate for election to the Senate in 1879; resumed the practice of law at Exeter and also engaged in literary pursuits; Governor of New Hampshire from June 1881 to June 1883; president of the State constitutional convention in 1889; president of the New Hampshire Historical Society 1868–1887; died in Exeter, Rockingham County, N. H., November 11, 1893; interment in Exeter Cemetery.

BELL, Charles Jasper, a Representative from Missouri; born in Lake City, Hinsdale County, Colo., January 16, 1885; attended the country schools in Jackson County, Mo., Lees Summit (Mo.) High School, and the University of Missouri at Columbia; was graduated from Kansas City (Mo.) School of Law in 1913; was admitted to the bar the same year and commenced practice in Kansas City, Mo.; member of the city council of Kansas City 1926–1930; member of the committee to draft the administrative code which comprises the general law of Kansas City, Mo.; judge of the circuit court of Jackson County, Mo., from 1931 until his resignation in 1934; elected as a Democrat to the Seventy-fourth and to the six succeeding Congresses (January 3, 1935–January 3, 1949); member of the Filipino Rehabilitation Commission in 1945 and 1946; awarded the Distinguished Service Star by the Philippine Republic; was not a candidate for renomination in 1948; continued the practice of law until his retirement and is a resident of Kansas City, Mo.

BELL, Charles Keith (nephew of Reese Bowen Brabson), a Representative from Texas; born in Chattanooga, Tenn., April 18, 1853; attended the public schools and Sewanee (Tenn.) College; moved to Texas in 1871; studied law; was admitted to the bar in 1874 and commenced practice in Hamilton, Tex.; prosecuting attorney of Hamilton County in 1876; district attorney 1880–1882; delegate to the Democratic National Convention at Chicago in 1884; member of the State senate 1884–1888; judge of the twenty-ninth judicial district of Texas 1888–1890; elected as a Democrat to the Fifty-third and Fifty-fourth Congresses (March 4, 1893–March 3, 1897); was not a candidate for renomination in 1896; resumed the practice of law in Fort Worth, Tex.; attorney general of Texas 1901–1904; again resumed the practice of law in Fort Worth, where he died April 21, 1913; interment in East Oakwood Cemetery.

BELL, Charles Webster, a Representative from California; born in Albany, N. Y., June 11, 1857; attended the public schools; moved to California in 1877 and settled in Pasadena, Los Angeles County; engaged in fruit growing and the real-estate business; county clerk of Los Angeles County 1899–1903; member of the State senate 1907–1912; elected as a Progressive Republican to the Sixty-third Congress (March 4, 1913–March 3, 1915); unsuccessful candidate for reelection in 1914 to the Sixty-fourth Congress; resumed his former business pursuits in Pasadena, Calif.; served as secretary of the Pasadena Mercantile Finance Corporation; died in Pasadena, Calif., April 19, 1927; interment in Mountain View Cemetery.

BELL, Hiram, a Representative from Ohio; born in Salem, Vt., April 22, 1808; attended the public schools of his native city; moved with his parents to Hamilton, Ohio, in 1826; studied law; was admitted to the bar in 1829 and commenced practice in Greenville, Darke County, Ohio; auditor of Darke County in 1829 and 1834; member of the State house of representatives in 1836, 1837, and 1840; elected as a Whig to the Thirty-second Congress (March 4, 1851–March 3, 1853); was not a candidate for renomination in 1852; engaged in the practice of his profession until his death in Greenville, Ohio, December 21, 1855; interment in the Greenville Cemetery.

BELL, Hiram Parks, a Representative from Georgia; born near Jefferson, Jackson County, Ga., January 19, 1827; attended the public schools at Cumming, Forsyth County, Ga.; taught school for two years, during which time he studied law; was admitted to the bar in 1849 and commenced practice in Cumming; member of the secession convention in 1861 and opposed the secession ordinance; commissioner from Georgia to solicit the cooperation of Tennessee in the formation of a southern confederacy; member of the State senate in 1861, but resigned to enter the Confederate Army; during the Civil War was commissioned captain and later promoted to lieutenant colonel and colonel of the Forty-third Georgia Regiment; member of the Second Confederate Congress in 1864 and 1865; presidential elector on the Democratic ticket of Seymour and Blair in 1868; member of the Democratic State executive committee 1868–1871; elected as a Democrat to the Forty-third Congress (March 4, 1873–March 3, 1875); delegate to the Democratic National Convention at St. Louis in 1876; was chosen a member of the Democratic National Committee from the State at large; elected to the Forty-fifth Congress to fill the vacancy caused by the resignation of Benjamin H. Hill and served from March 13, 1877, to March 3, 1879; unsuccessful candidate for renomination in 1878; member of the State house of representatives in 1898 and 1899; served in the State senate in 1900 and 1901; died in Atlanta, Ga., August 17, 1907; interment in Cumming Cemetery, Cumming, Ga.

BELL, James (son of Samuel Bell, uncle of Samuel Newell Bell, and cousin of Charles Henry Bell), a Senator from New Hampshire; born in Francistown, Hillsboro County, N. H., November 13, 1804; attended Phillips Academy, Andover, Mass., and was graduated from Bowdoin College, Brunswick, Maine, in 1822; studied law at Litchfield Law School, Litchfield, Conn.; was admitted to the bar in 1825 and commenced practice in Gilmanton, N. H.; moved to Exeter in 1831 and to Gilford in 1846; member of the New Hampshire House of Representatives in 1846 and 1850; delegate to the State constitutional convention in 1850; was an unsuccessful candidate for Governor of New Hampshire in 1854 and 1855; elected as a Whig to the United States Senate for the term beginning March 4, 1855, and served from July 30, 1855, until his death in Laconia, Belknap County, N. H., May 26, 1857; interment in Exeter Cemetery, Exeter, N. H.

BELL, James Martin, a Representative from Ohio; born in Huntingdon County, Pa., October 16, 1796; attended the public schools; studied law in Steubenville, Ohio; was admitted to the bar in 1817 and commenced practice in Cambridge, Guernsey County, Ohio; served as major general of the Fifteenth Division, Ohio Militia; prosecuting attorney of Guernsey County 1818–1832; member of the State house of representatives 1826–1831, serving as speaker in 1830 and 1831; master commissioner in 1827; justice of the peace in 1830; county school examiner in 1830; elected as a Democrat to the Twenty-third Congress (March 4, 1833–March 3, 1835); unsuccessful candidate for reelection in 1834 to the Twenty-fourth Congress; resumed the practice of law; served as mayor of Cambridge from 1838 to 1840; died in Cambridge, Ohio, on April 4, 1849; interment in Founders' Burial Ground.

BELL, John, a Representative from Ohio; born in Pennsboro, Lycoming County, Pa., June 19, 1796; received a limited education; moved to Ohio in 1810 with his parents, who settled in Greene County, near Xenia; moved to Lower Sandusky in 1823; city mayor in 1830; probate judge of Sandusky County several terms; commissioned major general of State militia in 1834; commanded Ohio forces in the Toledo war in 1835; served as postmaster of Lower Sandusky from November 14, 1838, to May 3, 1841; member of the State house of representatives in 1844 and 1845; mayor of Fremont, Ohio, in 1845 and 1846; elected as a Whig to the Thirty-first Congress to fill the vacancy caused by the death of Amos E. Wood and served from January 7 to March 3, 1851; probate judge 1852–1855 and 1858–1863; died in Fremont, Sandusky County, Ohio, May 4, 1869; interment in Oakwood Cemetery.

BELL, John, a Representative and a Senator from Tennessee; born near Nashville, Tenn., February 15, 1797; was graduated from the University of Nashville in 1814; studied law; was admitted to the bar in 1816 and commenced practice in Franklin, Tenn.; served in the State senate in 1817; declined to be a candidate for reelection and moved to Nashville; elected as a Democrat to the Twentieth and as a Whig to the Twenty-first and to the five succeeding Congresses (March 4, 1827–March 3, 1841); Speaker of the National House of Representatives during the second session of the Twenty-third Congress in 1834; appointed by President Harrison as Secretary of War March 5, 1841, and served until September 12, 1841, when he resigned; member of the State house of representatives in 1847; elected as a Whig to the United States Senate in 1847; reelected in 1853, and served from November 22, 1847, to March 3, 1859; unsuccessful candidate for President of the United States on the Constitutional Union ticket with Edward Everett for Vice President in 1860; interested in ironworks at Cumberland Furnace and Chattanooga, Tenn.; died at his home on the banks of the Cumberland River, near Cumberland Furnace, September 10, 1869; interment in Mount Olivet Cemetery, near Nashville, Tenn.

BELL, John Calhoun, a Representative from Colorado; born near Sewanee, Franklin County, Tenn., December 11, 1851; attended public and private schools in Franklin County; studied law in Winchester, Tenn., and was admitted to the bar in 1874; moved to Colorado in 1874 and commenced practice in Del Norte, moving to Saguache, Colo., the same year; county attorney of Saguache County, Colo., from 1874 to May 1876; moved to Lake City, Colo., in 1876; elected county clerk of Hinsdale County in 1878; mayor of Lake City in 1885; moved to Montrose, Montrose County, Colo., in 1886 and continued the practice of law; served as judge of the seventh judicial district of Colorado from 1889 until his resignation in 1892, having been elected to Congress; elected as a Democrat to the Fifty-third and to the four succeeding Congresses (March 4, 1893–March 3, 1903); unsuccessful candidate for reelection in 1902 to the Fifty-eighth Congress; member of the United States Industrial Commission in 1900 and 1901; resumed the practice of law in Montrose, Colo.; judge of the Court of Appeals of Colorado 1913–1915; again resumed the practice of law; member of the State board of agriculture 1931–1933; died in Montrose, Colo., August 12, 1933; interment in the Cedar Cemetery.

BELL, John Junior, a Representative from Texas; born in Cuero, De Witt County, Tex., May 15, 1910; attended the public schools; was graduated from the University of Texas at Austin in 1932 and from its law school in 1936; was admitted to the bar in 1936 and commenced the practice of law in Cuero, Tex.; served in the State house of representatives 1937–1947; president of a company operating compresses in Victoria, Shiner, Cuero, and Taft, Tex.; during World War II served as a private in the United States Army from May 1944 to March 1945; member of the State senate 1947–1954; delegate to the Democratic National Conventions in 1948 and 1952; elected as a Democrat to the Eighty-fourth Congress (January 3, 1955–January 3, 1957); unsuccessful candidate for renomination in 1956; lawyer, rancher, and farmer; is a resident of Cuero, Tex.

BELL, Joshua Fry, a Representative from Kentucky; born in Danville, Boyle County, Ky., November 26, 1811; attended the public schools; was graduated from Centre College, Danville, Ky., in 1828; studied law in Lexington, Ky.; traveled in Europe for several years before admission to the bar; commenced practice in Danville, Boyle County, Ky.; elected as a Whig to the Twenty-ninth Congress (March 4, 1845–March 3, 1847); declined to be a candidate for renomination in 1846; secretary of state of Kentucky in 1849; presidential elector on the Whig ticket of Scott and Graham in 1852; chosen by the legislature as one of six commissioners to the peace convention of 1861 held in Washington, D. C., in an effort to devise means to prevent the impending war; delegate to the Border State convention in 1861; nominated in 1863 by the Union Democrats for Governor of Kentucky, but declined to accept the nomination; member of the State house of representatives 1862–1867; died in Danville, Ky., August 17, 1870; interment in Bellevue Cemetery.

BELL, Peter Hansbrough, a Representative from Texas; born in Spotsylvania County, Va., March 11, 1810; attended the public schools; moved to Texas in 1836 during the war for Texan independence; participated in the Battle of San Jacinto April 21, 1836; assistant adjutant general of the Texan forces in 1837 and inspector general in 1839; served in the Mexican War as captain of the Texas Volunteer Rangers in 1845 and 1846 and as lieutenant colonel of mounted volunteers; colonel of a Texan volunteer regiment in 1848 and 1849; Governor of Texas 1849–1853; elected as a Democrat to the Thirty-third and Thirty-fourth Congresses (March 4, 1853–March 3, 1857); was not a candidate for renomination in 1856; moved to North Carolina in 1857 and settled in Halifax County; died in Littleton, Halifax County, N. C., March 8, 1898; interment in City Cemetery.

BELL, Samuel (father of James Bell, grandfather of Samuel Newell Bell, and uncle of Charles Henry Bell), a Senator from New Hampshire; born in Londonderry, N. H., February 9, 1770; attended the common schools and was graduated from Dartmouth College, Hanover, N. H., in 1793; studied law; was admitted to the bar in 1796 and commenced practice in Francestown, N. H.; moved to Amherst in 1810 and to Chester in 1812 and continued the practice of law; member of the State house of representatives 1804–1807, serving as speaker 1805–1807; served in the State senate and was president of that body 1807–1809; State councilor in 1809 and 1810; judge of the State supreme court 1816–1819; Governor of New Hampshire 1819–1823; elected to the United States Senate in 1823; reelected in 1829, and served from March 4, 1823, to March 3, 1835; was not a candidate for reelection; affiliated with the Whig Party upon its formation in 1834; resumed the practice of law; died in Chester, Rockingham County, N. H., on December 23, 1850; interment in the Village Cemetery.

BELL, Samuel Newell (grandson of Samuel Bell and nephew of James Bell), a Representative from New Hampshire; born in Chester, Rockingham County, N. H., March 25, 1829; attended school in Francestown, N. H., and Phillips Academy, Andover, Mass.; was graduated from Dartmouth College, Hanover, N. H., in 1847; studied law; was admitted to the bar in 1849 and commenced practice in Meredith, Belknap County, N. H.; elected as a Democrat to the Forty-second Congress (March 4, 1871–March 3, 1873); unsuccessful candidate for reelection in 1872 to the Forty-third Congress; elected to the Forty-fourth Congress (March 4, 1875–March 3, 1877); was not a candidate for reelection in 1876; resumed the practice of law in Meredith; also interested in large real-estate holdings; served as president of several railroads and vice president of the New Hampshire Fire Insurance Co.; appointed chief justice of the superior court of New Hampshire, but declined to accept; retired from public life; died while on a visit in North Woodstock, N. H., February 8, 1889; interment in the Valley Cemetery, Manchester, N. H.

BELL, Theodore Arlington, a Representative from California; born in Vallejo, Solano County, Calif., July 25, 1872; moved with his parents to St. Helena, Napa County, in 1876; attended the common schools; studied law; was admitted to the bar in 1893 and commenced practice at Napa, Calif.; district attorney of Napa County 1895-1903; elected as a Democrat to the Fifty-eighth Congress (March 4, 1903-March 3, 1905); unsuccessful candidate for reelection in 1904 to the Fifty-ninth Congress; moved to San Francisco in 1906 and continued the practice of his profession; unsuccessful candidate for Governor of California in 1906 and 1910; delegate to the Democratic National Convention at Denver in 1908, serving as temporary chairman; also a delegate to the convention at Baltimore in 1912; became affiliated with the Republican Party in 1921; was accidentally killed near San Rafael, Marin County, Calif., September 4, 1922; interment in Odd Fellows Cemetery, St. Helena, Calif.

BELL, Thomas Montgomery, a Representative from Georgia; born in Nacoochee Valley, near Cleveland, White County, Ga., March 17, 1861; attended the common schools, a private school in Cleveland, Ga., and Moore's Business University at Atlanta; taught in the public schools of Cleveland in 1878 and 1879; in the following year became employed as a traveling salesman and was connected with many wholesale business houses at Atlanta, Ga., and Baltimore, Md.; moved to Gainesville, Ga., in 1885 and continued his former pursuits; elected clerk of the superior court of Hall County in 1898; reelected in 1900 and again in 1902 and served until 1904; elected as a Democrat to the Fifty-ninth and to the twelve succeeding Congresses (March 4, 1905-March 3, 1931); unsuccessful candidate for renomination in 1930; employed as a representative of a marble company; died in Gainesville, Ga., March 18, 1941; interment in Alta Vista Cemetery.

BELLAMY, John Dillard, a Representative from North Carolina; born in Wilmington, N. C., March 24, 1854; attended the common schools and Cape Fear Military Academy; was graduated from Davidson College, Davidson, N. C., in 1873 and from the University of Virginia at Charlottesville in 1875; was admitted to the bar in 1875 and commenced the practice of law in Wilmington, N. C.; city attorney of Wilmington 1892-1894; member of the State senate 1900-1902; delegate at large to the Democratic National Conventions in 1892, 1908, and 1920; elected as a Democrat to the Fifty-sixth and Fifty-seventh Congresses (March 4, 1899-March 3, 1903); unsuccessful candidate for renomination in 1902 to the Fifty-eighth Congress; resumed the practice of law in Wilmington, N. C.; also engaged as an author; during the First World War served as a member of the draft board; district counsel for the Seaboard Air Line Railway Co., the Southern Bell Telephone Co., and the Western Union Telegraph Co.; also connected with the street railway company and cotton mills in Wilmington, N. C.; served as president of the New Hanover County Bar Association and in 1926 and 1927 as president of the North Carolina State Bar Association; appointed by Governor McLean as a commissioner from North Carolina to the celebration of the one hundred and fiftieth anniversary of the birth of George Washington, held in Washington, D. C., in 1932; died in Wilmington, N. C., September 25, 1942; interment in Oakdale Cemetery.

BELLINGER, Joseph, a Representative from South Carolina; born at Bellinger Plantation in Saint Bartholomew Parish, Ashepoo, Colleton County, S. C., in 1773; planter and owner of "Aeolian Lawn" plantation; member of the State house of representatives 1802-1810 and of the State senate from Barnwell District 1810-1813; presidential elector on the Democratic ticket of Madison and Clinton in 1808; elected to the Fifteenth Congress (March 4, 1817-March 3, 1819); was not a candidate for reelection to the Sixteenth Congress; died at Charleston, S. C., January 10, 1830; interment in the Bellinger private burial ground, Poco Sabo Plantation, Ashepoo, S. C.

BELMONT, Oliver Hazard Perry (brother of Perry Belmont), a Representative from New York; born in New York City November 12, 1858; attended St. Paul's School, Concord, N. H., and was graduated from the United States Naval Academy, Annapolis, Md., June 10, 1880; was commissioned as a midshipman and served until June 1, 1881, when he resigned; at one time a member of the banking firm of August Belmont & Co., New York City; became publisher of the Verdict, a weekly paper; delegate to the Democratic National Convention at Kansas City in 1900; elected as a Democrat to the Fifty-seventh Congress (March 4, 1901-March 3, 1903); was not a candidate for renomination in 1902; died in Hempstead, N. Y., on June 10, 1908; interment in Woodlawn Cemetery, New York City.

BELMONT, Perry (brother of Oliver Hazard Perry Belmont), a Representative from New York; born in New York City December 28, 1851; attended Everest Military Academy, Hamden, Conn., and was graduated from Harvard University in 1872; studied civil law at the University of Berlin; was graduated from the Columbia Law School, New York City, in 1876; was admitted to the bar the same year and commenced practice in New York City; elected as a Democrat to the Forty-seventh and to the three succeeding Congresses and served from March 4, 1881, to December 1, 1888, when he resigned to accept a diplomatic position; declined to be a candidate for renomination to Congress in 1888; United States Minister to Spain in 1888 and 1889; delegate to the Democratic National Conventions in 1892, 1896, 1904, and 1912; during the Spanish-American War served as major and inspector general of the First Division, Second Army Corps, United States Volunteers; in 1905 successfully initiated and organized the movement for the Federal and State campaign-publicity legislation, which was enacted into law in 1911, and was elected president of the National Association for Campaign Publicity Law; during the First World War was commissioned a captain in the remount service; resumed the practice of law in New York City in 1920; author of a number of books pertaining to national and political affairs; went abroad in 1932 for three years, residing mostly at Paris, France; returned, and made Newport, R. I., his permanent residence; died at Newport, R. I., May 25, 1947; interment in Island Cemetery.

BELSER, James Edwin, a Representative from Alabama; born in Charleston, S. C., December 22, 1805; attended the public schools; in 1820 moved with his parents to Sumter District, S. C., where he continued his schooling under a private tutor; moved to Alabama in 1825 and settled in Montgomery; studied law; was admitted to the bar and commenced practice in Montgomery; elected clerk of the county court; member of the State house of representatives in 1828; edited the Planters Gazette for several years; appointed solicitor of Montgomery County in 1828 and later elected to that position; appointed by Governor Fitzpatrick in 1842 as a commissioner of the State to procure a settlement of the claims against the Federal Government for money advanced in the Indian War of 1836; elected as a Democrat to the Twenty-eighth Congress (March 4, 1843-March 3, 1845); declined to be a candidate for renomination in 1844; resumed the practice of law in Montgomery; affiliated with the

Whig Party in 1848; again elected a member of the State house of representatives in 1853 and reelected in 1857; died in Montgomery, Ala., January 16, 1859; interment in Oakwood Cemetery.

BELTZHOOVER, Frank Eckels, a Representative from Pennsylvania; born in Silver Spring Township, Cumberland County, Pa., November 6, 1841; attended Big Spring Academy, Newville; was graduated from Pennsylvania College at Gettysburg in 1862; studied law; was admitted to the bar in 1864 and commenced practice in Carlisle, Pa.; chairman of the Democratic committee of Cumberland County 1868 and 1873; district attorney 1874–1877; delegate to the Democratic National Convention at St. Louis in 1876; elected as a Democrat to the Forty-sixth and Forty-seventh Congresses (March 4, 1879–March 3, 1883); was not a candidate for renomination in 1882; elected to the Fifty-second and Fifty-third Congresses (March 4, 1891–March 3, 1895); was not a candidate for renomination in 1894; resumed the practice of law in Carlisle, Cumberland County, Pa.; discontinued the practice of his profession in 1910 and moved to Los Angeles, Calif., where he lived in retirement until his death on June 2, 1923; interment in Ashland Cemetery, Carlisle, Pa.

BENDER, George Harrison, a Representative and a Senator from Ohio; born in Cleveland, Ohio, September 29, 1896; attended the public schools; engaged in the insurance business in 1930; in 1934 founded and became editor and publisher of the National Republican magazine; served in the State senate 1920–1930; chairman of the Republican central committee of Cuyahoga County 1936–1954; unsuccessful candidate for election to the United States House of Representatives in 1930, 1932, 1934, and 1936; elected as a Republican to the Seventy-sixth and to the four succeeding Congresses (January 3, 1939–January 3, 1949); unsuccessful candidate for reelection in 1948 to the Eighty-first Congress; elected to the Eighty-second and Eighty-third Congresses and served from January 3, 1951, until his resignation effective December 15, 1954; elected to the United States Senate to fill the vacancy in the term ending January 3, 1957, caused by the death of Robert A. Taft, and served from December 16, 1954, to January 3, 1957; unsuccessful candidate for reelection in 1956; special assistant to Secretary of the Interior, Washington, D. C., from June 10, 1957, to May 16, 1958; died in Chagrin Falls, Ohio, June 18, 1961; interment in Knollwood Cemetery, Mayfield Heights, Cleveland, Ohio.

BENEDICT, Charles Brewster, a Representative from New York; born in Attica Township, Wyoming County, N. Y., February 7, 1828; attended the public schools and Oberlin College, Oberlin, Ohio; taught school and also engaged in agricultural pursuits; studied law; was admitted to the bar in 1856 and commenced practice in Attica, N. Y.; justice of the peace 1854–1860; engaged in banking in 1859; member of the board of supervisors of Wyoming County 1869–1871 and 1873–1875, serving a part of the time as chairman; member of the Democratic State committee in 1875; presidential elector on the Democratic ticket of Tilden and Hendricks in 1876; elected as a Democrat to the Forty-fifth Congress (March 4, 1877–March 3, 1879); was not a candidate for renomination in 1878; resumed banking in Attica, N. Y.; one of the organizers of the First National Bank at Moorhead, Minn., and also operated farming lands extensively in that vicinity; died in Attica, N. Y., October 3, 1901; interment in Forest Hill Cemetery.

BENEDICT, Henry Stanley, a Representative from California; born in Boonville, Cooper County, Mo., February 20, 1878; moved with his parents to Los Angeles, Calif., in 1888; attended

the grammer schools and high school; attended the University of Southern California College of Law, Los Angeles, Calif.; was admitted to the bar in 1910 and commenced practice in Los Angeles, Calif.; member of the State house of representatives 1910–1914; served in the State senate 1914–1916; elected as a Republican to the Sixty-fourth Congress to fill the vacancy caused by the resignation of William D. Stephens and served from November 7, 1916, to March 3, 1917; was nominated by the Progressive Party for the Sixty-fifth Congress, but withdrew in behalf of the Republican nominee; continued the practice of law and also engaged in banking; member of the State department of finance of California (State board of control) from 1919 to 1921; served as a member of the California State Railroad Commission from 1921 to 1923; resumed the practice of law in Los Angeles, Calif., until his death; died while on a visit in London, England, July 10, 1930; interment in Forest Lawn Memorial Park, Glendale, Calif.

BENET, Christie, a Senator from South Carolina; born in Abbeville, Abbeville County, S. C., December 26, 1879; attended the common schools, the College of Charleston, the University of South Carolina at Columbia, and the University of Virginia at Charlottesville; studied law; was admitted to the bar and commenced practice in Columbia, Richland County, S. C., in 1903; solicitor of the fifth judicial circuit in 1908; attorney for the city of Columbia 1910–1912; three times secretary of the Democratic State committee; during the First World War served as vice president and member of the executive committee of the State Council of Defense of South Carolina in 1917 and 1918; appointed as a Democrat to the United States Senate to fill the vacancy caused by the death of Benjamin R. Tillman and served from July 6 to November 5, 1918, when a successor was elected; unsuccessful candidate for election in 1918 to the Senate to fill the vacancy; resumed the practice of law; member and later chairman of the board of regents of South Carolina State Hospital 1915–1946; life trustee of Clemson Agricultural College; during World War II served as chairman of the War Finance Committee for South Carolina and was serving as chairman of the Alien Enemy Hearing Board for the eastern district of South Carolina at time of death; died in Columbia, S. C., March 30, 1951; interment in Elmwood Cemetery.

BENHAM, John Samuel, a Representative from Indiana; born on a farm near Benham, Ripley County, Ind., October 24, 1863; attended the public schools, a business college in Delaware, Ohio, and a normal school in Brookville, Ind.; taught school in the winter and attended college in the summer, being engaged as a teacher in various places in Indiana from 1882 to 1907; was graduated from Indiana State Normal School at Terre Haute, Ind., in 1893 and from Indiana University at Bloomington, Ind., in 1903; specialized in history at the University of Chicago for several terms; superintendent of schools for Ripley County for fourteen years; returned to Benham, Ind., in 1907 and engaged in the timber, milling, and contracting business; also followed agricultural pursuits; served as chairman of the Republican county committee in 1916; delegate to the Republican National Convention at Chicago in 1916 that nominated Hughes and Fairbanks; elected as a Republican to the Sixty-sixth and Sixty-seventh Congresses (March 4, 1919–March 3, 1923); unsuccessful candidate for reelection in 1922 to the Sixty-eighth Congress; moved to Batesville, Ripley County, Ind., in 1923 and engaged as a building contractor; again superintendent of schools for Ripley County, Ind., 1924–1929; retired from active business pursuits in 1931 and resided in Batesville, Ind., until his death there on December 11, 1935; interment in Benham Church Cemetery, near Benham, Ind.

BENJAMIN, John Forbes, a Representative from Missouri; born in Cicero, Onondaga County, N. Y., January 23, 1817; attended the public schools; moved to Texas in 1845 and to Missouri in 1848; studied law; was admitted to the bar and commenced practice in Shelbyville, Shelby County, Mo., in 1848; member of the State house of representatives 1850–1852; presidential elector on the Democratic ticket of Buchanan and Breckinridge in 1856; entered the Union Army as a private in 1861 and was subsequently promoted to the ranks of captain, major, lieutenant colonel, and brigadier general; provost marshal of the Eighth District of Missouri in 1863 and 1864; delegate to the Republican National Convention at Baltimore in 1864; elected as a Radical Republican to the Thirty-ninth, Fortieth, and Forty-first Congresses (March 4, 1865–March 3, 1871); was not a candidate for renomination in 1870; resumed the practice of law in Shelbyville; unsuccessful candidate for election in 1872 to the Forty-third Congress; moved to Washington, D. C., in 1874 and engaged in banking; died in Washington, D. C., March 8, 1877; interment in a private cemetery at Shelbina, Shelby County, Mo.

BENJAMIN, Judah Philip, a Senator from Louisiana; born on the island of St. Croix, Danish West Indies (now Virgin Islands), August 6, 1811; immigrated to Savannah, Ga., in 1816 with his parents, who later settled in Wilmington, N. C.; attended the common schools and Yale College; moved to New Orleans, La., in 1831 and taught school; studied law; was admitted to the bar in 1832 and commenced practice in New Orleans; member of the State constitutional convention in 1845; presidential elector on the Whig ticket of Taylor and Fillmore in 1848; elected as a Whig to the United States Senate in 1853; reelected as a Democrat in 1859 and served from March 4, 1853, to February 4, 1861, when he withdrew; appointed Attorney General in the Cabinet under the provisional government of the Confederate States February 21, 1861; appointed Acting Secretary of War of the Confederate States in August 1861 and served until November 10, 1861, when he was appointed Secretary of War; served in this capacity until February 7, 1862, when he resigned to accept the appointment as Secretary of State in the Cabinet of President Jefferson Davis, in which capacity he served until the end of the war; moved to Great Britain in 1865; studied English law at Lincoln's Inn, London, was admitted to the bar in that city in 1866, and practiced; engaged in newspaper and magazine work; became one of the most prominent barristers in England and received the appointment of Queen's counsel in 1872; retired in 1883 from active practice and public life; moved to Paris, France, and died there May 8, 1884; interment in Père la Chaise Cemetery.

BENNER, George Jacob, a Representative from Pennsylvania; born in Gettysburg, Adams County, Pa., April 13, 1859; attended the public schools and was graduated from Pennsylvania College at Gettysburg in 1878; taught school for several years; studied law; was admitted to the Adams County bar in 1881 and commenced practice in Gettysburg; delegate to the Democratic State convention in 1886; elected as a Democrat to the Fifty-fifth Congress (March 4, 1897–March 3, 1899); was not a candidate for renomination in 1898 to the Fifty-sixth Congress; resumed the practice of law in Gettysburg, Pa.; unsuccessful candidate for election as president judge of the thirty-first judicial district in 1925; died in Gettysburg, Pa., December 30, 1930; interment in Evergreen Cemetery.

BENNET, Augustus Witschief (son of William Stiles Bennet), a Representative from New York; born in New York, N. Y., October 7, 1897; attended the public schools of New York City, N. Y., and Washington, D. C., and was graduated from Amherst (Mass.) College in 1918; during the First World War served in the United States Naval Reserve Flying Corps with the rating of chief quartermaster from June 8, 1918, to January 19, 1919; was graduated from the Columbia University Law School at New York, N. Y., in 1921; was admitted to the bar the same year and commenced practice in Newburgh, N. Y.; United States referee in bankruptcy 1923–1944; elected as a Republican to the Seventy-ninth Congress (January 3, 1945–January 3, 1947); unsuccessful candidate for renomination in 1946; resumed the practice of law and is a resident of Newburgh, N. Y.

BENNET, Benjamin, a Representative from New Jersey; born in Bucks County, Pa., October 31, 1764; attended the common schools; studied theology; was ordained as a minister in Middletown, Monmouth County, N. J., in 1793 and served as pastor of a Baptist church in that city; also engaged in agricultural pursuits; elected to the Fourteenth and Fifteenth Congresses (March 4, 1815–March 3, 1819); resumed agricultural pursuits; died on his farm near Middletown, N. J., October 8, 1840; interment in the Baptist Cemetery, Holmdel, N. J.

BENNET, Hiram Pitt, a Delegate from the Territory of Colorado; born in Carthage, Franklin County, Maine, September 2, 1826; moved to Ohio with his parents, who settled in Richland County in 1831; attended public and private schools and the Ohio Wesleyan University at Delaware; taught school in northwestern Missouri in 1850; studied law; was admitted to the bar in 1851 and practiced in western Iowa and later at Glenwood, Iowa; judge of the circuit court of Iowa in 1852; moved to Nebraska Territory in 1854, settled in Nebraska City, and continued the practice of law; unsuccessfully contested in 1855 as a Republican the election of Bird B. Chapman to the Thirty-fourth Congress; member of the Territorial council in 1856; member of the Territorial house of representatives in 1858 and served as speaker; moved to Denver, Colo., in 1859 and continued the practice of law; upon the admission of the Territory to representation was elected as a Conservative Republican a Delegate to the Thirty-seventh Congress; reelected to the Thirty-eighth Congress and served from August 19, 1861, to March 3, 1865; was not a candidate for renomination in 1864; secretary of state of Colorado in 1867; appointed postmaster of Denver, Colo., on March 26, 1869, and served until May 27, 1874, when a successor was appointed; member of the first State senate in 1876; appointed "State agent" in 1888, and served until 1895 in recovering lands belonging to the State of Colorado which had been wrongfully disposed of; retired from active duties and the practice of his profession in 1899 and resided in Denver, Colo., until his death, November 11, 1914; interment in Riverside Cemetery.

BENNET, William Stiles (father of Augustus Witschief Bennet), a Representative from New York; born in Port Jervis, Orange County, N. Y., November 9, 1870; attended the common schools; was graduated from Port Jervis Academy in 1889 and from Albany Law School in 1892; was admitted to the bar in 1892 and commenced practice the same year; official reporter of the Orange County Board of Supervisors in 1892 and 1893; member of the State assembly in 1901 and 1902; justice of the municipal court of New York City in 1903; member of the United States Immigration Commission 1907–1910; delegate to the Republican National Conventions in 1908 and 1916; elected as a Republican to the Fifty-ninth, Sixtieth, and Sixty-first Congresses (March 4, 1905–March 3, 1911); unsuccessful candidate for reelection in 1910 to the Sixty-second Congress; resumed the practice of law in New York City; elected to the Sixty-fourth Congress to fill the vacancy caused by the death of Joseph A. Goulden and served from November 2, 1915, to March 3, 1917; unsuccessful candidate for reelection in 1916 to the Sixty-fifth Congress; resumed the practice of law in New York City; official parliamentarian of the Republican National Convention at Chicago in 1916; moved to Chicago in 1920 and continued the practice of law; American delegate to the Seventeenth International Congress Against Alcoholism held at Copenhagen in 1923; general counsel and vice president of the Edward Hines associated lumber, coal, and railroad organizations 1920–1932; returned to New York City in 1933 and resumed the practice of law; unsuccessful candidate for election in 1936 to the Seventy-fifth Congress; received a majority of the Republican primary votes cast in Oregon for nomination as Vice President of the United States in 1936; served as a delegate to the State constitutional convention in 1938; unsuccessful candidate at a special election in 1944 to fill a vacancy in the Seventy-eighth Congress; is a resident of Westchester County, N. Y.

BENNETT, Charles Edward, a Representative from Florida; born in Canton, St. Lawrence County, N. Y., December 2, 1910; moved with his parents to Tampa, Fla., in 1913 and to Jacksonville, Fla., in 1932; attended the Tampa schools and was graduated from the University of Florida at Gainesville in 1934; was admitted to the bar the same year and commenced the practice of law in Jacksonville, Fla.; member of the State house of representatives in 1941; during World War II enlisted in the United States Army on March 13, 1942, and discharged as a captain of Infantry on January 13, 1947; served overseas in New Guinea and the Philippines, including guerrilla fighting on Luzon; awarded the Silver Star, Bronze Star, and Combat Infantry Badge; elected as a Democrat to the Eighty-first and to the five succeeding Congresses (January 3, 1949–January 3, 1961). *Reelected to the Eighty-seventh Congress.*

BENNETT, Charles Goodwin, a Representative from New York; born in Brooklyn, N. Y., December 11, 1863; attended the public schools; was graduated from the Brooklyn High School and from the New York Law School in 1882; was admitted to the bar in 1882 and commenced practice in Brooklyn, N. Y.; unsuccessful candidate for election 1892 to the Fifty-third Congress; elected as a Republican to the Fifty-fourth and Fifty-fifth Congresses (March 4, 1895–March 3, 1899); unsuccessful candidate for reelection in 1898 to the Fifty-sixth Congress; Secretary of the United States Senate from January 29, 1900, to March 3, 1913, when a successor was elected; returned to Brooklyn, N. Y., discontinued active business pursuits, and lived in retirement until his death on May 25, 1914; interment in Evergreen Cemetery.

BENNETT, David Smith, a Representative from New York; born on a farm near Camillus, Onondaga County, N. Y., May 3, 1811; attended the common schools and the local academy in Onondaga; engaged in agricultural pursuits; moved to Syracuse and engaged in the produce business, afterwards extending his business to New York City; moved to Buffalo in 1853 and built and operated several grain elevators; also purchased the original Dart grain elevator; elected a member of the State senate in 1865; elected as a Republican to the Forty-first Congress (March 4, 1869–March 3, 1871); declined to be a candidate for renomination in 1870; resumed his former business pursuits in Buffalo, N. Y., where he died November 6, 1894; interment in Oakwood Cemetery, Syracuse, N. Y.

BENNETT, Granville Gaylord, a Delegate from the Territory of Dakota; born near Bloomingburg, Fayette County, Ohio, October 9, 1833; moved to Illinois in 1849 with his parents, who settled in Fulton County, and to Washington, Iowa, in 1855; attended Howe's Academy, Mount Pleasant, Iowa, and Wash-

ington College, Iowa; studied law; was admitted to the bar in 1859 and commenced practice in Washington, Iowa; during the Civil War served in the Union Army as a commissioned officer from July 1861 to August 1865 and was assigned to the Seventh and Nineteenth Regiments of Iowa Volunteer Infantry; returned to Washington, Iowa; member of the State house of representatives 1865–1867; served in the State senate 1867–1871; appointed associate justice of the supreme court of the Territory of Dakota on February 24, 1875, and served until August 23, 1878, when he resigned, having been nominated for Congress; elected as a Republican to the Forty-sixth Congress (March 4, 1879–March 3, 1881); was not a candidate for reelection in 1880 to the Forty-seventh Congress; resumed the practice of law in Deadwood, S. Dak.; elected judge of the probate court of Lawrence County and served three terms; died at Hot Springs, Fall River County, S. Dak., June 28, 1910; interment in Mount Moriah Cemetery, Deadwood, S. Dak.

BENNETT, Hendley Stone, a Representative from Mississippi; born near Franklin, Williamson County, Tenn., April 7, 1807; attended the public schools in West Point, Miss.; studied law; was admitted to the bar in 1830 and commenced practice in Columbus, Miss.; judge of the circuit court 1846–1854; elected as a Democrat to the Thirty-fourth Congress (March 4, 1855–March 3, 1857); unsuccessful candidate for renomination in 1856; resumed the practice of law in Columbus; moved to Paris, Tex., in 1859 and continued the practice of law; served as a captain in Company G, Thirty-second Regiment, Texas Cavalry, Confederate States Army, from August 5, 1861, to August 31, 1862; resumed the practice of law; in 1886 returned to Tennessee and settled in Franklin, Williamson County, and continued the practice of his profession; died in Franklin, Tenn., December 15, 1891; interment in Mount Hope Cemetery.

BENNETT, Henry, a Representative from New York; born in New Lisbon, Otsego County, N. Y., September 29, 1808; attended the public schools; studied law; was admitted to the bar in 1832 and commenced practice in New Berlin, Chenango County, N. Y.; served as clerk of the town of New Berlin in 1846; elected as a Whig to the Thirty-first Congress and as a Republican to the Thirty-second and to the three succeeding Congresses (March 4, 1849–March 3, 1859); unsuccessful candidate for renomination in 1858 to the Thirty-sixth Congress; resumed the practice of law in New Berlin, N. Y., until his death there on May 10, 1868; interment in St. Andrews' Cemetery.

BENNETT, John Bonifas, a Representative from Michigan; born in Garden, Delta County, Mich., January 10, 1904; attended the public schools; was graduated from Watersmeet (Mich.) High School, from Marquette University Law School, Milwaukee, Wis., in 1925, and took a postgraduate course at Chicago (Ill.) University Law School; was admitted to the Wisconsin bar in 1925 and to the Michigan bar in 1926; practiced law in Ontonagon, Mich., 1926–1942; prosecuting attorney of Ontonagon County 1929–1934; deputy commissioner of the State department of labor and industry 1935–1937; elected as a Republican to the Seventy-eighth Congress (January 3, 1943–January 3, 1945); unsuccessful candidate for reelection in 1944 to the Seventy-ninth Congress; resumed the practice of law; elected in 1946 to the Eightieth and to the six succeeding Congresses (January 3, 1947–January 3, 1961). *Reelected to the Eighty-seventh Congress.*

BENNETT, Joseph Bentley, a Representative from Kentucky; born in Greenup County, Ky., April 21, 1859; attended the common schools and Greenup Academy, Greenup, Ky.; taught in the public schools; studied law; was admitted to the bar in 1878 and commenced practice in 1880; entered the mercantile business in 1885; judge of Greenup County 1894–1897; reelected in 1897 and served until 1901; member of the Republican State central committee in 1900 and 1904; elected as a Republican to the Fifty-ninth, Sixtieth, and Sixty-first Congresses (March 4, 1905–March 3, 1911); unsuccessful candidate for reelection in 1910 to the Sixty-second Congress; continued the practice of his profession until his death in Greenup, Greenup County, Ky., November 7, 1923; interment in Riverview Cemetery.

BENNETT, Marion Tinsley (son of Philip A. Bennett), a Representative from Missouri; born in Buffalo, Dallas County, Mo., June 6, 1914; attended the public schools of Buffalo, Jefferson City, and Springfield, Mo.; was graduated from Southwest Missouri State Teachers College at Springfield in 1935 and from Washington University School of Law, St. Louis, Mo., in 1938; was admitted to the bar in 1938 and commenced practice in Springfield, Mo.; served as secretary to his father, Congressman Philip A. Bennett, 1941–1943; volunteered for combat duty in World War II but was rejected; captain in United States Air Force Reserve; member of the Greene County (Mo.) Republican central committee 1938–1942; elected as a Republican to the Seventy-eighth Congress to fill the vacancy caused by the death of his father; reelected to the Seventy-ninth and Eightieth Congresses and served from January 12, 1943, to January 3, 1949; was an unsuccessful candidate for reelection in 1948 to the Eighty-first Congress; commissioner of the United States Court of Claims, Washington, D. C., since January 4, 1949; is a resident of Springfield, Mo.

BENNETT, Philip Allen (father of Marion T. Bennett), a Representative from Missouri; born on a farm near Buffalo, Dallas County, Mo., March 5, 1881; attended the public schools and Buffalo (Mo.) High School; was graduated from Springfield (Mo.) Normal and Business College in 1902; taught school at Independence, Mo., in 1899 and at Boyd, Mo., in 1900; purchased the Buffalo (Mo.) Reflex, which he edited and published 1904–1921; chairman of the Dallas County (Mo.) Republican committee for eight years; delegate to the Republican National Convention at Chicago in 1912; served in the State senate 1921–1925; moved to Springfield, Mo., in 1922 and engaged in the real estate and loan business; Federal land bank appraiser 1923–1925; Lieutenant Governor of Missouri 1925–1929; unsuccessful candidate for the Republican nomination for Governor in 1928; engaged in the insurance and loan business; unsuccessful candidate for election in 1938 to the Seventy-sixth Congress; elected as a Republican to the Seventy-seventh Congress and served from January 3, 1941, until his death before the close of the Seventy-seventh Congress; had been reelected to the Seventy-eighth Congress; died in Washington, D. C., December 7, 1942; interment in Hazelwood Cemetery, Springfield, Mo.

BENNETT, Risden Tyler, a Representative from North Carolina; born in Wadesboro, Anson County, N. C., June 18, 1840; attended the common schools and Anson Institute; was graduated from Cumberland University and from Lebanon Law School, Tennessee, in 1859; during the Civil War enlisted in the Confederate Army as a private on April 30, 1861, and left the service as colonel of the Fourteenth North Carolina Troops, having been wounded on three occasions; solicitor of Anson County in 1866 and 1867; member of the State house of representatives 1872–1874; delegate to the State constitutional convention in 1875; judge of the superior court from 1880 until his resignation in 1882; elected as a Democrat to the Forty-eighth and Forty-ninth Congresses (March 4, 1883–March 3, 1887); engaged in the practice of law in Wadesboro, N. C., and died there July 21, 1913; interment in the family cemetery near Wadesboro, N. C.

BENNETT, Thomas Warren, a Delegate from the Territory of Idaho; born in Union County, Ind., February 16, 1831; attended the common schools and was graduated from the law department of the Indiana Asbury (now De Pauw) University in July 1854; was admitted to the bar in 1855 and commenced practice in Liberty, Union County, Ind.; elected a member of the State senate in 1858 and resigned in 1861, upon the outbreak of the Civil War, to enter the Union Army; was commissioned a captain in the Fifteenth Regiment, Indiana Volunteer Infantry, in April 1861; became major of the Thirty-sixth Regiment in September 1861; colonel of the Sixty-ninth Regiment in August 1862 and was appointed brigadier general in March 1865; returned to Richmond, Ind.; again elected a member of the State senate, in October 1864, and served until March 1867; mayor of the city of Richmond, Ind., in 1869 and 1870; in September 1871 was appointed Governor of the Territory of Idaho by President Grant and served until December 4, 1875, when he resigned, having been elected to Congress; presented credentials as an Independent Member-elect to the Forty-fourth Congress and served from March 4, 1875, to June 23, 1876, when he was succeeded by Stephen S. Fenn, who contested his election; was not a candidate for renomination in 1876; resumed the practice of law in Richmond, Ind.; again served as city mayor 1877–1883 and 1885–1887; died in Richmond, Wayne County, Ind., February 2, 1893; interment in Earlham Cemetery.

BENNETT, Wallace Foster, a Senator from Utah; born in Salt Lake City, Utah, November 13, 1898; attended the public schools and the University of Utah; in 1918 during the First World War served as a second lieutenant of Infantry; returned to the University of Utah and graduated in 1919; principal, San Luis State Academy, Manassa, Colo., in 1919 and 1920; office clerk with Bennett Glass & Paint Co. (now Bennett's) in 1920, serving as chairman of the board since 1950; president, Bennett Motor Co., 1939–1950 and chairman of board of directors since 1950; director, Utah Oil Refining Co. and Utah Home Fire Insurance Co.; vice president, National Paint, Varnish & Lacquer Association in 1935 and 1936; president, National Association of Manufacturers in 1949; elected as a Republican to the United States Senate in 1950 for the term commencing January 3, 1951; reelected in 1956 for the term ending January 3, 1963.

BENNY, Allan, a Representative from New Jersey; born in Brooklyn, N. Y., July 12, 1867; attended the public schools of Bayonne, Hudson County, N. J.; studied law; was admitted to the bar in 1889 and commenced practice in Bayonne; member of the city council 1892–1894; member of the State house of assembly 1898–1900; prosecuting attorney of Bayonne from 1900 to 1903, when he resigned, having been elected to Congress; elected as a Democrat to the Fifty-eighth Congress (March 4, 1903–March 3, 1905); unsuccessful candidate for reelection in 1904 to the Fifty-ninth Congress; resumed the practice of his chosen profession; and was assistant librarian of the law library in the courthouse at Jersey City until his death; died in Bayonne, N. J., November 6, 1942; interment in Moravian Cemetery, Staten Island, N. Y.

BENSON, Alfred Washburn, a Senator from Kansas; born in Poland, Chautauqua County, N. Y., July 15, 1843; moved to Jamestown, N. Y., in 1860; attended Jamestown and Randolph Academies; during the Civil War enlisted in 1862 as a private soldier in the One Hundred and Fifty-fourth Regiment, New York Volunteer Infantry, and at the close of the war held a commission as major; studied law; was admitted to the bar in Buffalo, N. Y., in 1866 and commenced practice in Sherman, N. Y.; moved to Ottawa, Franklin County, Kans., in 1869; held various local offices; member of the State senate 1881–1885;

judge of the fourth judicial district of Kansas 1885–1897; appointed as a Republican to the United States Senate to fill the vacancy caused by the resignation of Joseph R. Burton and served from June 11, 1906, to January 23, 1907, when a successor was elected; unsuccessful candidate for election in 1907 to the United States Senate to fill this vacancy; appointed and subsequently elected associate justice of the supreme court of Kansas and served from August 1, 1907, until January 11, 1915, when he resigned; retired from political life and the practice of his profession; died in Topeka, Kans., January 1, 1916; interment in Highland Cemetery, Ottawa, Kans.

BENSON, Carville Dickinson, a Representative from Maryland; born near Halethorpe, Baltimore County, Md., August 24, 1872; attended the public schools of Baltimore, preparatory schools, and Lehigh University, Bethlehem, Pa., in 1890; was graduated from the law department of Baltimore University in 1893; was admitted to the bar the same year and commenced practice in Baltimore; member of the State house of representatives 1904–1910 and again in 1918, serving as speaker in 1906; member of the State senate 1912–1914; elected as a Democrat to the Sixty-fifth Congress to fill the vacancy caused by the death of Joshua F. C. Talbott; reelected to the Sixty-sixth Congress and served from November 5, 1918, to March 3, 1921; unsuccessful candidate for reelection in 1920 to the Sixty-seventh Congress; resumed the practice of law in Baltimore, Md., and resided in Halethorpe, Md.; appointed State insurance commissioner of Maryland in 1924 and served until his death in a hospital in Baltimore, Md., February 8, 1929; interment in Cedar Hill Cemetery, Brooklyn Station, Baltimore, Md.

BENSON, Egbert, a Delegate and a Representative from New York; born in New York City June 21, 1746; was graduated from Kings (now Columbia) College in 1765; studied law; was admitted to the bar and commenced practice in New York City; deputy to the provincial convention in 1775; member of the council of safety in 1777 and 1778; in 1777 was appointed the first attorney general of New York and served until 1789; member of the State assembly 1777–1781 and again in 1788; in 1783 was appointed one of the three commissioners to direct the embarkation of the Tory refugees for the loyal British provinces; associate judge of the supreme court of New York 1784–1801; Member of the Continental Congress 1784–1788; member of the State constitutional convention in 1788, which ratified the Federal Constitution; elected to the First and Second Congresses (March 4, 1789–March 3, 1793); regent of the New York University 1789–1802; appointed judge of the United States Circuit Court, second circuit, February 20, 1801; served as the first president of the New York Historical Society from 1804 to 1816; elected to the Thirteenth Congress and served from March 4, 1813, to August 2, 1813, when he resigned; died in Jamaica, Long Island, N. Y., August 24, 1833; interment in Prospect Cemetery.

BENSON, Elmer Austin, a Senator from Minnesota; born in Appleton, Swift County, Minn., September 22, 1895; attended the public and high schools; was graduated from the St. Paul (Minn.) College of Law in 1918; during the First World War served as a private in the United States Army from April 16, 1918, to January 28, 1919, with overseas service; employed as assistant cashier in a bank in 1922 and 1923; was admitted to the bar in 1919 but did not practice; engaged in the retail clothing business 1919–1933; cashier of a bank 1923–1933; State commissioner of securities in 1933 and State commissioner of banks 1933–1935; appointed as a Farmer-Laborite to the United States Senate to fill the vacancy caused by the death of Thomas D. Schall and served from December 27, 1935, until November 3, 1936, when a successor was elected; was not a candidate for elec-

tion to fill the vacancy, but was elected Governor of Minnesota in 1936 and served from January 4, 1937, to January 1, 1939; unsuccessful candidate in 1938 for reelection as Governor; unsuccessful candidate for election to the United States Senate in 1940 and 1942; presently engaged in agricultural pursuits and is a resident of Appleton, Minn.

BENSON, Samuel Page, a Representative from Maine; born in Winthrop, Maine, November 28, 1804; received instruction from private teachers and attended the Monmouth (Maine) Academy; was graduated from Bowdoin College, Brunswick, Maine, in 1825; studied law; was admitted to the Kennebec County bar in 1828 and commenced practice in Unity, Maine; returned to Winthrop and practiced law until 1850; railroad builder; secretary of the Androscoggin & Kennebec (now Maine Central) Railroad; member of the State house of representatives in 1833 and 1834; served in the State senate in 1836 and 1837; secretary of state 1838–1841; overseer of Bowdoin College 1838–1876 and president of the board for sixteen years; chairman of the board of selectmen 1844–1848; elected as a Whig to the Thirty-third Congress and as a Republican to the Thirty-fourth Congress (March 4, 1853–March 3, 1857); resumed the practice of law; died in Yarmouth, Cumberland County, Maine, August 12, 1876; interment in Maple Cemetery, Winthrop, Maine.

BENTLEY, Alvin Morell, a Representative from Michigan; born in Portland, Maine, August 30, 1918; graduated from Southern Pines (N. C.) High School in 1934, Asheville (N. C.) Prep School in 1936, and the University of Michigan in 1940; attended Turner's Diplomatic School, Washington, D. C., to qualify for diplomatic service; served as vice consul and secretary with the United States Diplomatic Corps in Mexico in May 1942, then going to Colombia, Hungary, and Italy; returned to Washington, D. C., March 15, 1950, for work in the State Department; resigned from the diplomatic service in 1950; returned to Owosso, Mich., and began a crusade against communism; delegate to Republican State Conventions in 1950, 1951, and 1952; vice president, Lake Huron Broadcasting Co., Saginaw, Mich., since 1952; director of Mitchell-Bentley Corp.; elected as a Republican to the Eighty-third and to the three succeeding Congresses (January 3, 1953–January 3, 1961); was not a candidate for renomination in 1960, but was unsuccessful for election to the United States Senate; delegate to First German-American Conference at Bad Godesburg, Germany, in October 1959 and to the Eighth Pan-American Highway Congress at Bogotá, Colombia, in May 1960; is a resident of Owosso, Mich.

BENTLEY, Henry Wilbur, a Representative from New York; born in DeRuyter, Madison County, N. Y., September 30, 1838; moved with his parents to Morrisville, N. Y.; attended Union School, Yates Polytechnic Institute at Chittenango, and Judd's private school at Berkshire; taught school for several years; studied law; was admitted to the bar in 1861 and commenced practice in Boonville, N. Y.; chairman of the Oneida County Building Commission; president of Boonville in 1874, 1889–1891, and 1899; elected as a Democrat to the Fifty-second Congress (March 4, 1891–March 3, 1893); unsuccessful candidate for reelection in 1892 to the Fifty-third Congress; continued the practice of law in Boonville, Oneida County, N. Y., until his death there on January 27, 1907; interment in Boonville Cemetery.

BENTON, Charles Swan, a Representative from New York; born in Fryeburg, Oxford County, Maine, July 12, 1810; pursued preparatory studies; moved to Herkimer County, N. Y., in 1824 to live with an elder brother; attended Lowville Academy, Lowville, N. Y.; learned the tanner's trade; editor of the Mohawk Courier and the Little Falls Gazette 1830–1832; studied law; was admitted to the bar in 1835 and commenced practice at Little Falls, N. Y.; surrogate of Herkimer County in 1837; judge advocate of the State militia; elected as a Democrat to the Twenty-eighth and Twenty-ninth Congresses (March 4, 1843–March 3, 1847); was not a candidate for renomination in 1846; clerk of the court of appeals 1847–1849; moved to Milwaukee, Wis., in 1855 and subsequently became editor of the Milwaukee News; appointed by President Franklin Pierce in 1856 as register of the United States land office at La Crosse, Wis., and served until 1861; was an unsuccessful candidate for election in 1862 to the Thirty-eighth Congress; engaged in agricultural pursuits near West Salem, Wis., and later, in 1865, at Galesburg, Ill.; returned to La Crosse, Wis., in 1869; judge of La Crosse County 1874–1881; died in La Crosse, Wis., May 4, 1882; interment in Oak Grove Cemetery.

BENTON, Jacob, a Representative from New Hampshire; born in Waterford, Caledonia County, Vt., August 19, 1814; attended the common schools, Lyndon (Vt.) Academy, and Randolph (Vt.) Academy, and was graduated from Burr and Burton Seminary at Manchester in 1839; taught school for several years; moved to Lancaster, Coos County, N. H., in 1842; studied law; was admitted to the bar in 1843 and commenced practice in Lancaster; member of the State house of representatives 1854–1856; delegate to the Republican National Convention at Chicago in 1860; brigadier general, commanding State Volunteers; elected as a Republican to the Fortieth and Forty-first Congresses (March 4, 1867–March 3, 1871); declined to be a candidate for renomination in 1870; resumed the practice of law; died in Lancaster, Coos County, N. H., September 29, 1892; interment in the Summer Street Cemetery.

BENTON, Lemuel (great-grandfather of George William Dargan), a Representative from South Carolina; born in Granville County, N. C., in 1754; as a young man moved to that section of Cheraw District which is now Darlington County, S. C., engaged as a planter and subsequently became an extensive landowner; elected major of the Cheraw Regiment in 1777 and served throughout the Revolutionary War, being promoted to the rank of colonel in 1781; resigned his commission in 1794; member of the State house of representatives 1781–1784 and 1787; county court justice of Darlington County in 1785 and 1791; escheator of Cheraw District (composed of what is now Chesterfield, Darlington, and Marlboro Counties) in 1787; delegate to the State convention at Charleston that ratified the Federal Constitution in 1788; sheriff of Cheraw District in 1789 and 1791; delegate to the State constitutional convention at Columbia in 1790; elected as a Democrat to the Third, Fourth, and Fifth Congresses (March 4, 1793–March 3, 1799); unsuccessful candidate for reelection in 1798 to the Sixth Congress; resumed agricultural pursuits; died in Darlington, Darlington County, S. C., May 18, 1818; interment on his estate, "Stony Hill," near Darlington, S. C.

BENTON, Maecenas Eason, a Representative from Missouri; born near Dyersburg, Obion County, Tenn., January 29, 1848; attended two west Tennessee academies and St. Louis University; was graduated from the law department of Cumberland University, Lebanon, Tenn., in 1870; served in the Confederate Army during the Civil War; was admitted to the bar and commenced practice in Neosho, Newton County, Mo.; was many times a delegate to Democratic State conventions, serving as president in 1890, 1896, and 1898; prosecuting attorney of Newton County 1878–1884; United States attorney from March 1885 to July 1889; delegate to the Democratic National Convention at Chicago in 1896; elected as a Democrat to the Fifty-fifth, Fifty-sixth, Fifty-seventh, and Fifty-eighth Congresses (March 4, 1897–March 3, 1905); unsuccessful candidate

for reelection in 1904 to the Fifty-ninth Congress; resumed the practice of law in Neosho, Mo.; member of the State constitutional conventions in 1922 and 1924; died in Springfield, Greene County, Mo., April 27, 1924; interment in the Odd Fellows Cemetery, Neosho, Mo.

BENTON, Thomas Hart, a Senator and a Representative from Missouri; born at Harts Mill, near Hillsboro, N. C., March 14, 1782; attended Chapel Hill College (now the University of North Carolina) and the law department of William and Mary College, Williamsburg, Va.; was admitted to the bar at Nashville, Tenn., in 1806 and commenced practice in Franklin, Williamson County, Tenn.; member of the State senate 1809–1811; served as aide-de-camp to General Jackson; colonel of a regiment of Tennessee volunteers from December 1812 to April 1813; lieutenant colonel of the Thirty-ninth United States Infantry 1813–1815; moved to St. Louis, Mo., where he edited the Missouri Inquirer and continued the practice of law; upon the admission of Missouri as a State into the Union was elected as a Democrat to the United States Senate; reelected in 1827, 1833, 1839, and 1845 and served from August 10, 1821, to March 3, 1851, the first Senator to serve thirty consecutive years; author of the resolution to expunge from the Senate Journal the resolution of censure on Andrew Jackson; unsuccessful candidate for reelection to the Senate in 1850; elected as a Missouri Compromise Democrat to the Thirty-third Congress (March 4, 1853–March 3, 1855); unsuccessful candidate for reelection in 1854 to the Thirty-fourth Congress and for Governor of Missouri in 1856; engaged in literary pursuits in Washington, D. C., until his death there on April 10, 1858; interment in Bellefontaine Cemetery, St. Louis, Mo.

BENTON, William, a Senator from Connecticut; born in Minneapolis, Hennepin County, Minn., April 1, 1900; attended Shattuck Military Academy, Faribault, Minn., and Carleton College, Northfield, Minn., in 1917 and 1918; was graduated from Yale University, New Haven, Conn., in 1921; worked for advertising agencies in New York and Chicago until 1929 and then founded the firm of Benton & Bowles, New York advertising agency, serving as president until 1935 and chairman of the board until 1936; in 1932 established residence in Norwalk, Conn.; part-time vice president of the University of Chicago 1937–1945; Assistant Secretary of State, Washington, D. C., August 31, 1945, to September 30, 1947; member of United States delegation Inter-American Conference on War and Peace, Mexico City, in 1945; United States delegate to Constitutional Convention, United Nations Educational, Scientific and Cultural Organization, London, 1945; chairman of United States delegation to first general conference of UNESCO, at Paris in 1946; the second general conference at Mexico City in 1947; and the United States delegation to United Nations Conference on Freedom of Information, Geneva, Switzerland, in 1948; member advisory committee to Coordinator of Inter-American Affairs 1940–1945; vice chairman, United States Commission, Inter-American Development Commission 1942–1945; founding vice chairman, Committee for Economic Development 1942–1945, and trustee 1947–1960; chairman of board and publisher of Encyclopaedia Britannica 1943–1945 and 1947–1960; trustee of Shattuck Military Academy 1938–1945, University of Chicago 1947–1960, Carleton College 1948–1960, University of Connecticut 1957–1960, and University of Bridgeport 1958–1960; appointed and subsequently elected as a Democrat to the United States Senate to fill the vacancy caused by the resignation of Raymond E. Baldwin, and served from December 17, 1949, to January 3, 1953; unsuccessful candidate for election for the full term in 1952; delegate to the Democratic National Conventions in 1952 and 1956; resides in Southport, Conn.

BENTSEN, Lloyd Millard, Jr., a Representative from Texas; born in Mission, Hidalgo County, Tex., February 11, 1921; attended the public schools; was graduated from the law school of the University of Texas at Austin in 1942 and was admitted to the bar the same year; during World War II enlisted as a private in the United States Army in April 1942 and served until discharged as a major in July 1945; commenced the practice of law in McAllen, Tex., in 1945; elected county judge of Hidalgo County, Tex., in 1946 and served until March 1948; elected as a Democrat on November 2, 1948, to the Eighty-first Congress, and, at a special election on December 4, 1948, to fill the vacancy in the Eightieth Congress caused by the death of Milton H. West; reelected to the Eighty-second and Eighty-third Congresses and served from December 4, 1948, to January 3, 1955; was not a candidate for renomination in 1954; founded Consolidated American Life Insurance Co., and in 1958 merged with Lincoln Liberty Life Insurance Co., with headquarters in Houston, Tex., where he now resides.

BERESFORD, Richard, a Delegate from South Carolina; born near Charleston, St. Thomas and St. Denis Parish, Berkeley County, S. C., in 1755; educated in South Carolina and in England; studied law at the Middle Temple in London; was admitted to the bar in 1773 and practiced in Charleston, S. C.; engaged in planting, with extensive estates in Berkeley and Colleton Counties, S. C., and in England; took an active part in the Revolution, serving under General Huger in the Georgia campaign in 1778; was captured at the fall of Charleston in 1780 and imprisoned at St. Augustine until 1781, when he was exchanged; member of the State house of representatives in 1781; elected by the State general assembly a member of the privy council in 1782; elected Lieutenant Governor in January 1783, but resigned shortly afterwards, having been elected to Congress; Member of the Continental Congress from May 30, 1783, to June 3, 1784; resumed planting; later engaged in literary pursuits; published the Vigil in Charleston in 1798; died in Charleston, S. C., February 6, 1803.

BERGEN, Christopher Augustus, a Representative from New Jersey; born in Bridge Point, Somerset County, N. J., August 2, 1841; attended Harlingen School and Edge Hill Classical School and was graduated from the academic department of Princeton College in 1863; studied law; was licensed by the supreme court of New Jersey in 1866 as an attorney and commenced practice in Camden, N. J.; licensed as a counselor in 1869; elected as a Republican to the Fifty-first and Fifty-second Congresses (March 4, 1889–March 3, 1893); unsuccessful candidate for renomination in 1892; resumed the practice of law; in 1903 moved to Haverford, Montgomery County, Pa., where he died on February 18, 1905; interment in Evergreen Cemetery, Camden, N. J.

BERGEN, John Teunis (second cousin of Teunis Garret Bergen), a Representative from New York; born in Gowanus, Brooklyn, N. Y., in 1786; completed preparatory studies; appointed a lieutenant in the New York State Militia in 1812 and promoted to captain in 1815; served in the War of 1812; sheriff of Kings County, N. Y., 1821–1825 and again from 1828 until 1831, when he resigned; purchased the Long Island Patriot in 1829, the name of which was subsequently changed to the Brooklyn Advocate, and which ultimately became the Brooklyn Daily Eagle; elected as a Democrat to the Twenty-second Congress (March 4, 1831–March 3, 1833); was not a candidate for renomination in 1832; engaged in agricultural pursuits near Bay Ridge, New Utrecht, N. Y.; moved to Brooklyn, N. Y., and engaged in the grocery business; in 1837, with his sons, conducted a planing mill in New York City; moved to Genesee County and engaged in agricultural pursuits; died in Batavia, Genesee County, N. Y., on March 9, 1855; interment in Batavia Cemetery.

BERGEN, Teunis Garret (second cousin of John Teunis Bergen), a Representative from New York; born in Brooklyn, N. Y., October 6, 1806; attended the common schools and Erasmus Hall Academy, Flatbush, N.·Y.; engaged in agricultural pursuits and surveying; supervisor of New Utrecht, Kings County, N. Y., 1836–1859; member of the State constitutional conventions in 1846, 1867, and 1868; delegate to the Democratic National Conventions at Baltimore and Charleston in 1860; elected as a Democrat to the Thirty-ninth Congress (March 4, 1865–March 3, 1867); was not a candidate for renomination in 1866; resumed agricultural pursuits and surveying near New Utrecht; also engaged in literary and historical work; served as ensign, captain, adjutant, lieutenant colonel, and colonel of the Two Hundred and Forty-first Regiment, New York State Militia, known as Kings County Troop; died in Brooklyn, N. Y., April 24, 1881; interment in Greenwood Cemetery.

BERGER, Victor Luitpold, a Representative from Wisconsin; born in Nieder Rebbach, Austria-Hungary, February 28, 1860; attended the Gymnasia at Leutschau and the universities at Budapest and Vienna; immigrated to the United States in 1878 with his parents, who settled near Bridgeport, Conn.; moved to Milwaukee, Wis., in 1880; taught school 1880–1890; editor of the Milwaukee Daily Vorwaerts 1892–1898; editor of the Wahrheit, the Social Democratic Herald, and the Milwaukee Leader, being publisher of the last named at the time of his death; delegate to the People's Party Convention at St. Louis in 1896; one of the organizers of the Social Democracy in 1897 and of the Social Democratic Party in 1898, known since 1900 as the Socialist Party; unsuccessful candidate of the Socialist Party for election in 1904 to the Fifty-ninth Congress; elected a member of the charter convention of Milwaukee in 1907, and alderman at large in 1910; elected as a Socialist to the Sixty-second Congress (March 4, 1911–March 3, 1913); presented credentials as a Member-elect to the Sixty-sixth Congress, but the House by a resolution adopted on November 10, 1919, declared him not entitled to take the oath of office as a Representative or to hold a seat as such; having been opposed to the entrance of the United States in the First World War and having written articles expressing his opinion on that question, he was indicted in various places in the Federal courts, tried at Chicago, found guilty, and sentenced by Judge Kenesaw M. Landis in February 1919 to serve twenty years in the Federal penitentiary; this judgment was reversed by the United States Supreme Court in 1921, whereupon the Government withdrew all cases against him in 1922; his election to the Sixty-sixth Congress was unsuccessfully contested by Joseph P. Carney and the seat was declared vacant; presented credentials as a Member-elect to fill the vacancy caused by the action of the House and on January 10, 1920, the House again decided that he was not entitled to a seat in the Sixty-sixth Congress and declined to permit him to take the oath or qualify as a Representative; Henry H. Bodenstab unsuccessfully contested this election, and on February 25, 1921, the House again declared the seat vacant; elected as a Socialist to the Sixty-eighth, Sixty-ninth, and Seventieth Congresses (March 4, 1923–March 3, 1929); unsuccessful candidate for reelection in 1928 to the Seventy-first Congress; resumed his editorial work; died in Milwaukee, Wis., August 7, 1929; interment in Forest Home Cemetery.

BERLIN, William Markle, a Representative from Pennsylvania; born on a farm near Delmont, Westmoreland County, Pa., March 29, 1880; attended the public schools; was graduated from Laird Institute at Murrysville, Pa., in 1896; moved to Greensburg, Pa., in 1916 and engaged as an automobile distributor, in the wholesale oil and gas business, and in coal mining; chairman of the Democratic County Committee in 1916; elected as a Democrat to the Seventy-third and Seventy-fourth Congresses (March 4, 1933–January 3, 1937); unsuccessful candidate for renomination in 1936; clerk of the court of Westmoreland County, Pa., 1937–1941; resumed the mining of coal in Pennsylvania and West Virginia in 1941; assistant librarian, United States House of Representatives, since February 1, 1957; is a resident of Greensburg, Pa.

BERNARD, John Toussaint, a Representative from Minnesota; born in Bastia, Island of Corsica, France, March 6, 1893; in 1907 immigrated to the United States with his parents, who settled in Eveleth, St. Louis County, Minn.; attended public schools in France and in Eveleth, Minn.; employed as an iron-ore miner 1910–1917 and as city fireman 1920–1936; served in the United States Army during the First World War as a corporal in the One Hundred and Twenty-fifth Field Artillery, and also as a civilian employee in the Army and Navy Intelligence 1917–1919, serving overseas fifteen months; delegate to the State Farmer-Labor Party Conventions in 1936, 1938, and 1940; elected as a Farmer-Laborite to the Seventy-fifth Congress (January 3, 1937–January 3, 1939); unsuccessful candidate for reelection in 1938 to the Seventy-sixth Congress and for election in 1940 to the Seventy-seventh Congress; engaged as a labor organizer in Chicago, Ill., where he now resides.

BERNHISEL, John Milton, a Delegate from the Territory of Utah; born at Sandy Hill, Tyrone Township, near Harrisburg, Cumberland County, Pa., July 23, 1799; attended the common schools; was graduated from the medical department of the University of Pennsylvania at Philadelphia; commenced the practice of medicine in New York City; moved to Nauvoo, Hancock County, Ill., in 1843, and thence to the Territory of Utah: settled in Salt Lake City in 1848 and continued the practice of medicine; elected as a Whig to the Thirty-second and to the three succeeding Congresses (March 4, 1851–March 3, 1859); was not a candidate for renomination in 1858; resumed the practice of medicine; elected to the Thirty-seventh Congress (March 4, 1861–March 3, 1863); was not a candidate for renomination in 1862; resumed the practice of his profession; served as regent of the University of Utah; died in Salt Lake City September 28, 1881; interment in Salt Lake City Cemetery.

BERRIEN, John Macpherson, a Senator from Georgia; born at Rocky Hill, near Princeton, N. J., August 23, 1781; moved with his parents to Savannah, Ga., in 1782; was graduated from Princeton College in 1796; studied law in Savannah; was admitted to the bar and began practice in Louisville, then the capital of Georgia, in 1799; returned to Savannah; elected solicitor of the eastern judicial circuit of Georgia in 1809; judge of the same circuit from 1810 until January 30, 1821, when he resigned; captain of the Georgia Hussars, a Savannah volunteer company, in the War of 1812; member of the State senate in 1822 and 1823; elected as a Democrat to the United States Senate and served from March 4, 1825, until March 9, 1829; resigned to accept the position of Attorney General in the Cabinet of President Jackson and served from March 9, 1829, until June 22, 1831, when he resigned; resumed the practice of law; again elected, as a Whig, to the United States Senate and served from March 4, 1841, until May 1845, when he again resigned to accept an appointment to the supreme court of Georgia; delegate to the Whig National Convention at Baltimore in 1844; again elected to the United States Senate to fill the vacancy caused by his second

resignation and served from November 14, 1845, to March 3, 1847; subsequently elected to succeed himself for the term commencing March 4, 1847, and served from November 13, 1847, until May 28, 1852, when he resigned for a third time; president of the American Party convention at Milledgeville in 1855; died in Savannah, Ga, January 1, 1856; interment in Laurel Grove Cemetery.

BERRY, Albert Seaton, a Representative from Kentucky; born in Fairfield (now Dayton), Campbell County, Ky., May 13, 1836; attended the public schools; was graduated from Miami University, Oxford, Ohio, in 1855 and from the Cincinnati Law School in 1858; was admitted to the bar and practiced; prosecuting attorney of Newport, Ky., in 1859; served in the Confederate Army throughout the Civil War; mayor of Newport in 1870 and served five terms; member of the State senate in 1878 and 1884; elected as a Democrat to the Fifty-third and to the three succeeding Congresses (March 4, 1893–March 3, 1901); unsuccessful candidate for renomination in 1900; resumed the practice of law; appointed and subsequently elected judge of the seventeenth judicial district of Kentucky and served from 1905 until his death in Newport, Campbell County, Ky., January 6, 1908; interment in Evergreen Cemetery.

BERRY, Campbell Polson (cousin of James Henderson Berry), a Representative from California; born in Jackson County, Ala., November 7, 1834; moved to Arkansas in 1841 with his parents, who settled in Berryville; attended the grammar school; moved to California in 1857 and settled near Yuba City; was graduated from the Pacific Methodist College, Vacaville, Solano County, Calif., in 1865; served as supervisor of Sutter County 1866–1869; engaged in agricultural pursuits and for a short time, in 1872, was also in the mercantile business; member of the State assembly in 1869, 1871, 1873, 1875, 1877, and 1878, serving as speaker in 1877 and 1878; elected as a Democrat to the Forty-sixth and Forty-seventh Congresses (March 4, 1879–March 3, 1883); declined to be a candidate for renomination in 1882; subtreasurer of the United States at San Francisco, Calif., 1894–1898; died in Wheatland, Yuba County, Calif., on January 8, 1901; interment in Fairview Cemetery, Sutter County, Calif.

BERRY, Ellis Yarnal, a Representative from South Dakota; born in Larchwood, Lyon County, Iowa, October 6, 1902; attended Philip (S. Dak.) High School; student in Morningside College, Sioux City, Iowa, 1920–1922; was graduated from the law school of the University of South Dakota at Vermillion in 1927; was admitted to the bar the same year and commenced the practice of law in Kennebec, Lyman County, S. Dak., and at McLaughlin, Corson County, in 1929; served as State's attorney, mayor of McLaughlin, and judge, Probate Court, Corson County, 1931–1939; publisher of the McLaughlin Messenger since 1938; delegate to State Republican Conventions in 1934, 1936, and 1938; editor of the State Bar Association Journal 1938–1950; member of the State senate in 1939 and 1941 legislative sessions, and legislative assistant to the Governor during the 1943 session; member of the Missouri River States Committee 1940–1943; member of the State Board of Regents of Education 1946–1950; elected as a Republican to the Eighty-second and to the four succeeding Congresses (January 3, 1951–January 3, 1961). *Reelected to the Eighty-seventh Congress.*

BERRY, George Leonard, a Senator from Tennessee; born in Lee Valley, Hawkins County, Tenn., September 12, 1882; attended the common schools, but went to work at an early age to learn the pressman's trade and was employed as a pressman from 1891 to 1907 in various cities; served in the American

Expeditionary Forces during the First World War, with rank of major, in the Railroad Transportation Engineers from November 10, 1918 until April 17, 1919; received the Victory Medal and the French Legion of Honor; president of the International Pressmen and Assistants' Union of North America 1907–1948; also engaged in agricultural pursuits and banking; delegate to many national and international labor conventions in the United States and abroad; appointed as a Democrat to the United States Senate to fill the vacancy caused by the death of Nathan L. Bachman and served from May 6, 1937, to November 8, 1938, when a successor was elected; unsuccessful candidate for nomination in 1938 to fill the vacancy; resumed the presidency of the International Pressmen and Assistants' Union of North America, and also his agricultural pursuits at Pressmen's Home, Tenn., until his death on December 4, 1948; interment in Pressmen's Home Cemetery.

BERRY, James Henderson (cousin of Campbell Polson Berry), a Senator from Arkansas; born in Jackson County, Ala., May 15, 1841; moved to Arkansas with his parents, who settled in Carroll County in 1848; attended a private school in Berryville, Ark.; entered the Confederate Army in 1861 as a second lieutenant, Sixteenth Regiment, Arkansas Infantry; lost a leg in the Battle of Corinth, Miss., in 1862; studied law; was admitted to the bar in 1866 and commenced practice in Berryville, Carroll County, Ark.; elected to the State house of representatives in 1866; reelected in 1872, and served as speaker at the extraordinary session of 1874; moved to Bentonville, Ark., in 1869 and continued the practice of law; chairman of the Democratic State convention in 1876; judge of the circuit court 1878–1882; elected Governor of Arkansas in 1882; elected as a Democrat to the United States Senate in 1885 to fill the vacancy caused by the resignation of Augustus H. Garland; reelected in 1889, 1895, and 1901, and served from March 20, 1885, to March 3, 1907; unsuccessful candidate for reelection in 1906; returned to Bentonville, Ark.; member of the commission for marking the graves of the Confederate dead 1910–1912; died in Bentonville, Benton County, Ark., January 30, 1913; interment in the Knights of Pythias Cemetery.

BERRY, John, a Representative from Ohio; born near Carey, in that portion of Crawford County which is now Wyandot County, Ohio, April 26, 1833; attended the public schools, and Ohio Wesleyan University at Delaware; was graduated from the law department of Cincinnati College, Ohio, in 1857; was admitted to the bar in April 1857 and commenced practice in Upper Sandusky; elected prosecuting attorney of Wyandot County in 1862; reelected in 1864; mayor of Upper Sandusky, Ohio, in 1864; elected as a Democrat to the Forty-third Congress (March 4, 1873–March 3, 1875); declined to be a candidate for renomination in 1874; resumed the practice of law in Upper Sandusky, Ohio, where he died May 18, 1879; interment in Oak Hill Cemetery, near Upper Sandusky, Ohio.

BESHLIN, Earl Hanley, a Representative from Pennsylvania; born in Conewango Township, Warren County, Pa., April 28, 1870; was raised on a farm; attended the public schools and was graduated from Warren High School; studied law; was admitted to the bar of Warren County in 1893 and commenced practice in Warren, Warren County, Pa.; elected burgess of Warren County in 1906 for a term of three years; served as borough solicitor from 1914 to 1918; elected as a Democrat and Prohibitionist to the Sixty-fifth Congress to fill the vacancy caused by the resignation of Orrin D. Bleakley and served from November 8, 1917, to March 3, 1919; unsuccessful candidate for reelection in 1918 to the Sixty-sixth Congress; resumed the practice of law at Warren, Pa., where he now resides.

BETHUNE, Lauchlin, a Representative from North Carolina; born near Fayetteville, Cumberland County, N. C., April 15, 1785; attended private schools and Lumberton (N. C.) Male Academy; engaged in agricultural pursuits; member of the State senate in 1817, 1818, 1822–1825, and 1827; elected as a Jacksonian Democrat to the Twenty-second Congress (March 4, 1831–March 3, 1833); unsuccessful candidate for reelection to the Twenty-third, Twenty-fourth, and Twenty-fifth Congresses; returned to his plantation near Fayetteville, N. C., and continued agricultural pursuits until his death on October 10, 1874; interment in the Presbyterian Cemetery, Aberdeen, Moore County, N. C.

BETHUNE, Marion, a Representative from Georgia; born near Greensboro, Greene County, Ga., April 8, 1816; attended private schools and De Hagan's Academy; moved with his widowed mother to Talbotton, Talbot County, Ga., in 1829; engaged in mercantile pursuits; studied law; was admitted to the bar in 1842 and commenced practice at Talbotton; probate judge of Talbot County from 1852 to 1868, when he voluntarily retired; member of the constitutional convention of Georgia at the time of the repeal of the ordinance of secession; member of the State house of representatives 1867–1871; elected as a Republican to the Forty-first Congress to fill the vacancy caused by the House declaring that William P. Edwards was not entitled to the seat and served from December 22, 1870, to March 3, 1871; unsuccessful candidate for reelection in 1870 to the Forty-second Congress; resumed the practice of law; unsuccessful candidate for election in 1872 to the Forty-third Congress; United States census supervisor in 1890; died in Talbotton, Ga., February 20, 1895; interment in Oakhill Cemetery.

BETTON, Silas, a Representative from New Hampshire; born in Londonderry, N. H., August 26, 1768; studied under a private tutor, and was graduated from Dartmouth College, Hanover, N. H., in 1787; studied law; was admitted to the bar and commenced practice in Salem, Rockingham County, N. H., in 1790; member of the State house of representatives 1797–1799; member of the State senate 1801–1803; elected to the Eighth and Ninth Congresses (March 4, 1803–March 3, 1807); resumed the practice of law; again a member of the State house of representatives in 1810 and 1811; served as high sheriff of Rockingham County 1813–1818; died in Salem, N. H., January 22, 1822; interment in Old Parish Cemetery, Center Village, Salem, N. H.

BETTS, Jackson Edward, a Representative from Ohio; born in Findlay, Hancock County, Ohio, May 26, 1904; attended the public schools of Findlay, Ohio; graduated from Kenyon College, Gambier, Ohio, in 1926, and from Yale Law School, New Haven, Conn., in 1929; was admitted to the bar in 1930, and commenced the practice of law in Findlay, Ohio; prosecuting attorney of Hancock County, Ohio, 1933–1937; member of the State house of representatives 1937–1947, serving as speaker in 1945 and 1946; elected as a Republican to the Eighty-second and to the four succeeding Congresses (January 3, 1951–January 3, 1961). *Reelected to the Eighty-seventh Congress.*

BETTS, Samuel Rossiter, a Representative from New York; born in Richmond, Berkshire County, Mass., June 8, 1787; was graduated from Williams College, Williamstown, Mass., in 1806; studied law in Hudson, N. Y.; was admitted to the bar in 1807 and commenced practice in Monticello, Sullivan County, N. Y.; served as judge advocate of Volunteers in the War of 1812; elected as a Democrat to the Fourteenth Congress (March 4, 1815–March 3, 1817); was not a candidate for renomination in 1816; moved to Newburgh, Orange County, N. Y., where he continued the practice of law; appointed circuit judge under the new State constitution in 1823; appointed and subsequently elected judge of the United States District Court for the Southern District of New York and served from 1826 until 1867, when he resigned; died in New Haven, Conn., November 2, 1868; interment in Woodlawn Cemetery, New York City.

BETTS, Thaddeus, a Senator from Connecticut; born in Norwalk, Conn., February 4, 1789; completed preparatory studies; was graduated from Yale College, New Haven, Conn., in 1807; studied law; was admitted to the bar in 1810 and commenced practice in Norwalk; member of the State house of representatives in 1815 and 1830; served in the State senate in 1831; elected Lieutenant Governor of Connecticut in 1832 and 1836; elected as a Whig to the United States Senate and served from March 4, 1839, until his death in Washington, D. C., April 7, 1840; interment in Union Cemetery, Norwalk, Conn.

BEVERIDGE, Albert Jeremiah, a Senator from Indiana; born near Sugar Tree Ridge, Concord Township, Highland County, Ohio, October 6, 1862; attended the common schools; was graduated from Indiana Asbury (now De Pauw) University, Greencastle, Ind., in 1885; studied law; was admitted to the bar in 1887 and commenced practice in Indianapolis, Ind.; elected as a Republican to the United States Senate on January 17, 1899, reelected in 1905, and served from March 4, 1899, until March 3, 1911; unsuccessful candidate for reelection in 1910; returned to Indianapolis and engaged in literary pursuits; unsuccessful Progressive candidate for Governor of Indiana in 1912; chairman of the National Progressive Convention at Chicago in 1912; unsuccessful candidate as a Progressive in 1914 and as a Republican in 1922 for election to the United States Senate; died in Indianapolis, Ind., April 27, 1927; interment in Crown Hill Cemetery.

BEVERIDGE, John Lourie, a Representative from Illinois; born in Greenwich, Washington County, N. Y., July 6, 1824; attended the public schools; moved with his parents to De Kalb, Ill., in 1842; attended the Rock River Seminary, Mount Morris, Ill.; moved to Tennessee in 1845 and taught school until 1851; studied law; was admitted to the bar and practiced; returned to Illinois in 1851 and settled in Sycamore and continued the practice of law; moved to Evanston in 1854 and practiced law in Chicago; during the Civil War served in the Union Army; appointed major of the Eighth Illinois Cavalry September 18, 1861; colonel of the Seventeenth Illinois Cavalry January 28, 1864; brevetted brigadier general and mustered out February 7, 1866; elected sheriff of Cook County, Ill., in 1866; member of the State senate in 1871; resigned, having been elected as a Republican to the Forty-second Congress to fill the vacancy caused by the resignation of John A. Logan and served from November 7, 1871, until January 4, 1873, when he resigned; elected Lieutenant Governor of Illinois in 1872 and upon the resignation of Gov. R. J. Oglesby in 1873 became Governor and served from January 23, 1873, to January 1877; United States subtreasurer at Chicago 1877–1881; moved to California in 1895 and resided in Hollywood, Los Angeles County, until his death on May 3, 1910; interment in Rose Hill Cemetery, Chicago, Ill.

BIBB, George Motier, a Senator from Kentucky; born in Prince Edward County, Va., October 30, 1776; pursued preparatory studies; was graduated from Hampden-Sidney (Va.) College and from William and Mary College, Williamsburg, Va., in 1792; studied law; was admitted to the bar and practiced for a short time in Virginia; moved to Lexington, Ky., in 1798; elected from Fayette County a member of the State house of representatives to fill the vacancy caused by the resignation of Henry Clay,

November 26, 1806, served a few days, and then resigned; reelected from Logan County in 1810 and from Franklin County in 1817; appointed judge of the Kentucky Court of Appeals January 30, 1808; chief justice of that court May 30, 1809, and served until March 1810, when he resigned; elected to the United States Senate and served from March 4, 1811, to August 23, 1814, when he resigned; resumed the practice of law in Lexington; moved to Frankfort in 1816; was again appointed chief justice of the court of appeals January 5, 1827, and served until December 23, 1828, when he again resigned; again elected to the United States Senate and served from March 4, 1829, to March 3, 1835; chancellor of the Louisville chancery court from its establishment in 1835 to 1844; appointed Secretary of the Treasury in the Cabinet of President Tyler and served from July 4, 1844, to March 3, 1845; resumed the practice of law in Washington, D. C., and was an assistant in the office of the Attorney General; died in Georgetown, D. C., April 14, 1859; interment in the State Cemetery, Frankfort, Ky.

BIBB, William Wyatt, a Representative and a Senator from Georgia; born in Prince Edward County, Va., October 1, 1780; pursued an academic course; attended William and Mary College at Williamsburg and was graduated from the medical department of the University of Pennsylvania at Philadelphia in 1801; moved to Petersburg, Elbert County, Ga., and began the practice of medicine; member of the State house of representatives 1803–1805; resumed the practice of medicine; elected as a Democrat to the Ninth Congress to fill the vacancy caused by the resignation of Thomas Spalding; reelected to the Tenth and to the three succeeding Congresses and served from January 26, 1807, until his resignation November 6, 1813, having been elected Senator; elected to the United States Senate to fill the vacancy caused by the resignation of William H. Crawford and served from November 6, 1813, to November 9, 1816, when he resigned; moved to Alabama Territory and was appointed the first Territorial Governor; elected as the first Governor under the State Constitution and served from March 1817 until his death near Coosada Station, Elmore County, Ala., July 9, 1820; interment in the family cemetery, Coosada Station, Ala.

BIBIGHAUS, Thomas Marshal, a Representative from Pennsylvania; born in Philadelphia, Pa., March 17, 1817; attended the common schools; studied law; was admitted to the bar in 1839 and commenced practice in Lebanon, Pa.; elected as a Whig to the Thirty-second Congress (March 4, 1851–March 3, 1853); was not a candidate for renomination in 1852 to the Thirty-third Congress owing to ill health; resumed the practice of law in Lebanon, Lebanon County, Pa., and died there June 18, 1853; interment in Mount Lebanon Cemetery.

BIBLE, Alan Harvey, a Senator from Nevada; born in Lovelock, Pershing County, Nev., November 20, 1909; graduated from the University of Nevada at Reno in 1930 and from Georgetown University Law School, Washington, D. C., in 1934; was admitted to the Nevada bar in 1935 and commenced the practice of law in Reno, Nev.; district attorney of Storey County 1935–1938; appointed deputy attorney general of Nevada in 1938 and elected attorney general in 1942; reelected in 1946 and served until 1950; private practice of law since January 1951; elected as a Democrat to the United States Senate to fill the vacancy caused by the death of Patrick A. McCarran and served from December 2, 1954, to January 3, 1957; reelected in 1956 for the term ending January 3, 1963.

BICKNELL, Bennet, a Representative from New York; born in Mansfield, Conn., November 14, 1781; attended the public schools; moved to Morrisville, N. Y., in 1808; served in the **War**

of 1812; member of the State assembly in 1812; served in the State senate 1814–1818; clerk of Madison County, N. Y., 1821–1825; editor of the Madison Observer; elected as a Democrat to the Twenty-fifth Congress (March 4, 1837–March 3, 1839); unsuccessful candidate for reelection in 1838 to the Twenty-sixth Congress; died in Morrisville, Madison County, N. Y., September 15, 1841; interment in Morrisville Rural Cemetery.

BICKNELL, George Augustus, a Representative from Indiana; born in Philadelphia, Pa., February 6, 1815; was graduated from the University of Pennsylvania at Philadelphia in 1831; attended Yale Law School one year; completed the study of law; was admitted to the bar in 1836 and commenced practice in New York City; moved to Lexington, Scott County, Ind., in 1846; elected prosecuting attorney of Scott County in 1848; circuit prosecutor in 1850; moved to New Albany in 1851; judge of the second judicial circuit of Indiana 1852–1876; professor of law at the University of Indiana 1861–1870; elected as a Democrat to the Forty-fifth and Forty-sixth Congresses (March 4, 1877–March 3, 1881); unsuccessful candidate for renomination in 1880; appointed commissioner of appeals in the supreme court of Indiana in 1881, which office he held until the completion of its work in 1885; resumed the practice of law; elected judge of the circuit court of Indiana in 1889 and held that office until his death, April 11, 1891, in New Albany, Floyd County, Ind.; interment in Fairview Cemetery.

BIDDLE, Charles John (nephew of Richard Biddle), a Representative from Pennsylvania; born in Philadelphia, Pa., April 30, 1819; was graduated from Princeton College in 1837; studied law; was admitted to the bar and commenced practice in Philadelphia in 1840; served in the Mexican War and was brevetted major for meritorious services; resumed the practice of law in Philadelphia; during the Civil War entered the Union Army in 1861 as colonel of a regiment of the Pennsylvania Reserve Corps; elected as a Democrat to the Thirty-seventh Congress to fill the vacancy caused by the resignation of E. Joy Morris and served from July 2, 1861, to March 3, 1863; unsuccessful candidate for reelection in 1862 to the Thirty-eighth Congress; chairman of the Democratic State central committee in 1863; one of the proprietors and editor in chief of the Philadelphia Age until his death in Philadelphia September 28, 1873; interment in Old St. Peter's Church Cemetery.

BIDDLE, Edward (uncle of Richard Biddle), a Delegate from Pennsylvania; born in Philadelphia, Pa., in 1738; entered the provincial army as an ensign in 1754, promoted to lieutenant and captain, and served until 1763, when he resigned; studied law; was admitted to the bar and commenced practice in Reading, Pa.; member of the State assembly 1767–1775, serving as speaker in 1774; member of the provincial convention held at Philadelphia in 1775; again a member of the State assembly in 1778; Member of the Continental Congress 1774–1776, 1778, and 1779; died at Chatsworth, near Baltimore, Md., September 5, 1779; interment in St. Paul's Churchyard, Baltimore, Md.

BIDDLE, John, a Delegate from the Territory of Michigan; born in Philadelphia, Pa., March 2, 1792; attended the common schools and Princeton College; enlisted in the War of 1812; appointed a second lieutenant in the Third Artillery July 6, 1812, first lieutenant March 13, 1813, and captain in the Forty-second Infantry October 1, 1813; assistant inspector general with the rank of major June 19, 1817, until June 1, 1821; attached to the staff of General Scott on the Niagara frontier; paymaster and Indian agent at Green Bay, Wis., 1821 and 1822; register of the land office at Detroit, Territory of Michigan, 1823–1837; commissioner for determining the ancient land claims at Detroit,

Mackinaw, Sault Ste. Marie, Green Bay, and Prairie du Chien; mayor of Detroit in 1827 and 1828; elected as a Whig a Delegate from the Territory of Michigan to the Twenty-first Congress and served from March 4, 1829, until February 21, 1831, when he resigned; president of the convention that framed the State constitution for Michigan in 1835; president of the Michigan Central Railroad Co. in 1835; unsuccessful candidate for election in 1835 to the United States Senate; unsuccessful candidate for Governor of Michigan; member of the State house of representatives in 1841 and served as speaker; retired from public life and active pursuits and resided on his farm near Wyandotte, Mich.; later spent much time on his estate near St. Louis, Gratiot County, Mich.; went to White Sulphur Springs, Va., for the summer, and died there August 25, 1859; interment in Elmwood Cemetery, Detroit, Mich.

BIDDLE, Joseph Franklin, a Representative from Pennsylvania; born near Bedford, Bedford County, Pa., September 14, 1871; educated in the public schools; was graduated from Millersville State Teachers' College at Millersville, Pa., in 1894 and from the law department of Dickinson College, Carlisle, Pa., in 1897; was admitted to the bar in 1897 and commenced practice in Bedford, Pa.; moved to Everett, Pa., in 1903 and engaged in the practice of law and in newspaper publishing; moved to Huntingdon, Pa., in 1918 and engaged in the printing and publishing business and in banking; member of the Pennsylvania Publishers' Association 1924–1936; director of the National Editorial Association 1926–1936; member of the Republican State Committee 1932–1936; elected as a Republican to the Seventy-second Congress to fill the vacancy caused by the death of Edward M. Beers and served from November 8, 1932, to March 3, 1933; was not a candidate for election to the Seventy-third Congress in 1932; resumed the printing and newspaper publishing business in Huntingdon, Pa., where he died on December 3, 1936; interment in Trinity Churchyard, Friends' Cove, near Bedford, Pa.

BIDDLE, Richard (nephew of Edward Biddle and uncle of Charles John Biddle), a Representative from Pennsylvania; born in Philadelphia, Pa., March 25, 1796; pursued classical studies; was graduated from the University of Pennsylvania at Philadelphia in 1811; served as a volunteer in the Washington Guards during the War of 1812; studied law; was admitted to the bar in Philadelphia in 1817 and commenced practice in Pittsburgh the same year; went to England in 1827, remained there three years, and published valuable works upon American discovery and travel; elected as a Whig to the Twenty-fifth and Twenty-sixth Congresses and served from March 4, 1837, until his resignation in 1840; resumed the practice of law in Pittsburgh, Pa., where he died on July 6, 1847; interment in Allegheny Cemetery.

BIDLACK, Benjamin Alden, a Representative from Pennsylvania; born in Paris, Oneida County, N. Y., September 8, 1804; moved to Wilkes-Barre, Pa.; attended the public schools; was graduated from the Wilkes-Barre Academy; studied law; was admitted to the bar in 1825 and commenced practice in Wilkes-Barre; elected district attorney of Luzerne County in 1825; moved to Milford, Pike County, Pa., in 1830; county treasurer in 1834; returned to Wilkes-Barre; elected a member of the State house of representatives in 1835 and 1836; editor of the Republican Farmer and the Democratic Journal, Wilkes-Barre; elected as a Democrat to the Twenty-seventh and Twenty-eighth Congresses (March 4, 1841–March 3, 1845); appointed Chargé d'Affaires to Colombia May 14, 1845; successfully negotiated a "treaty of peace, amity, and navigation" with Colombia and secured for the United States the right to build a canal or railroad across the Isthmus of Panama; died in Bogota, Colombia, February 6, 1849; interment in the English Cemetery.

BIDWELL, Barnabas, a Representative from Massachusetts; born in Tyringham (now Monterey), Mass., August 23, 1763; was graduated from Yale College in 1785; studied law at Brown University, Providence, R. I.; was admitted to the bar in 1805 and commenced practice in Stockbridge, Mass.; served in the State senate 1801–1804; member of the State house of representatives 1805–1807; elected to the Ninth and Tenth Congresses and served from March 4, 1805, until his resignation on July 13, 1807; attorney general of Massachusetts from June 15, 1807, to August 30, 1810; moved to Canada about 1815 and settled near Kingston; became interested in political affairs and engaged in the practice of law; died in Kingston, Ontario, Canada, July 27, 1833; interment in Cataraqui Cemetery, Cataraqui, Ontario.

BIDWELL, John, a Representative from California; born in Chautauqua County, N. Y., August 5, 1819; moved with his parents to Erie, Pa., in 1829 and to Ashtabula County, Ohio, in 1831; attended the country schools and Kingsville Academy, Ashtabula, Ohio; taught school in Ohio; spent two years in Missouri and taught school; crossed the Rockies and Sierras with the first overland expedition, arriving in the Sacramento Valley, California, on November 4, 1841; secured employment on the ranch of John A. Sutter; later engaged in mining; served in the War with Mexico, attaining the rank of major; member of the State constitutional convention; member of the State senate in 1849; supervisor in California of the United States census in 1850 and in 1860; delegate to the Democratic National Convention at Charleston in 1860; during the Civil War was appointed brigadier general of the California Militia in 1863; delegate to the Republican National Convention at Baltimore in 1864 that nominated Lincoln and Johnson; elected as a Unionist to the Thirty-ninth Congress (March 4, 1865–March 3, 1867); was not a candidate for renomination in 1866; engaged extensively in agricultural pursuits; unsuccessful candidate for Governor of California in 1875 on the Anti-Monopoly ticket; presided over the Prohibition State convention in 1888 and was the unsuccessful candidate of that party for Governor of California in 1890 and for President of the United States in 1892; died in Chico, Butte County, Calif., April 4, 1900; interment in Chico Cemetery.

BIEMILLER, Andrew John, a Representative from Wisconsin; born in Sandusky, Erie County, Ohio, July 23, 1906; attended the public schools; was graduated from Cornell University, Ithaca, N. Y., in 1926, and also took graduate work at the University of Pennsylvania at Philadelphia; taught history at Syracuse (N. Y.) University 1926–1928 and at the University of Pennsylvania at Philadelphia 1929–1931; moved to Milwaukee, Wis., in 1932; organizer from the Wisconsin State Federation of Labor (A. F. of L.); member of the State assembly 1937–1941, serving as party floor leader 1939–1941; assistant to the vice chairman for labor production, War Production Board, Washington, D. C., 1941–1944; elected as a Democrat to the Seventy-ninth Congress (January 3, 1945–January 3, 1947); unsuccessful candidate for reelection in 1946 to the Eightieth Congress; engaged as a public relations counselor; elected to the Eighty-first Congress (January 3, 1949–January 3, 1951); unsuccessful candidate for reelection in 1950 to the Eighty-second Congress; resumed activities as a public relations counselor in Washington, D. C.; resides in Bethesda, Md.

BIERMANN, Frederick Elliott, a Representative from Iowa; born in Rochester, Olmstead County, Minn., March 20, 1884; moved to Decorah, Iowa, in 1888; attended the public and high schools of Decorah, Iowa, and the University of Minnesota at Minneapolis; was graduated from Columbia University, New York, N. Y., in 1905 and later attended Valder's Business College, Decorah, Iowa, and Harvard Law School; homesteaded in North Dakota in 1906 and 1907; editor and publisher of the Decorah (Iowa) Journal 1908–1931; volunteered for service in the United States Army during the First World War; was commissioned a second lieutenant August 15, 1917, and a first lieutenant on December 31, 1917, in the Eighty-eighth Division; served from April 1917 until June 1919, being overseas ten months; postmaster of Decorah, Iowa, 1913–1923; served as park commissioner of Decorah since 1922; chairman of the Winneshiek County, Iowa, Democratic central committee about twenty-five years and member of the Democratic State central committee for eight years; delegate to the Democratic National Conventions in 1928, 1940, and 1956; delegate to the Interparliamentary Union Conference at Paris, France, in 1937; elected as a Democrat to the Seventy-third, Seventy-fourth, and Seventy-fifth Congresses (March 4, 1933–January 3, 1939); unsuccessful candidate for reelection in 1938 to the Seventy-sixth Congress; appointed United States Marshal for northern Iowa in October 1940, in which capacity he served until 1953; is a resident of Decorah, Iowa.

BIERY, James Soloman, a Representative from Pennsylvania; born on a farm near Emlenton, Venango County, Pa., March 2, 1839; attended the district schools, a select school of the county, and Emlenton (Pa.) Academy; taught school for three years in the oil regions of Pennsylvania; moved to Allentown, Lehigh County, Pa., in 1861 and continued teaching for eight years; studied theology for two years; subsequently studied law; was admitted to the bar in 1868 and commenced practice in Allentown; member of the State house of representatives in 1869; elected as a Republican to the Forty-third Congress (March 4, 1873–March 3, 1875); was not a candidate for renomination in 1874; resumed the practice of law at Allentown and also engaged in literary pursuits; died in Allentown, Pa., December 3, 1904; interment in Fairview Cemetery.

BIGBY, John Summerfield, a Representative from Georgia; born near Newnan, Coweta County, Ga., February 13, 1832; attended the common schools; was graduated from Emory College, Oxford, Ga., in 1853; studied law; was admitted to the bar in 1856 and commenced practice in Newnan, Coweta County, Ga.; member of the State constitutional convention of 1867–68; solicitor general of the Tallapoosa circuit from August 1867 to September 22, 1868; judge of the superior court of the same circuit from September 22, 1868, to March 3, 1871; elected as a Republican to the Forty-second Congress (March 4, 1871–March 3, 1873); unsuccessful candidate for reelection in 1872 to the Forty-third Congress; resumed the practice of law in Atlanta, Ga.; delegate to the Republican National Convention at Cincinnati in 1876; became president of the Atlanta & West Point Railroad in 1876; died in Atlanta, Ga., March 28, 1898; interment in West View Cemetery.

BIGELOW, Abijah, a Representative from Massachusetts; born in Westminster, Mass., on December 5, 1775; attended Leicester (Mass.) Academy and an academy at New Ipswich, N. H.; was graduated from Dartmouth College, Hanover, N. H., in 1795; studied law in Groton, Mass.; was admitted to the bar in 1798 and commenced practice in Leominster, Mass., in the same year; town clerk of Leominster 1803–1809; member of the State house of representatives 1807–1809; justice of the peace 1809–1860 and justice of the quorum 1812–1860; elected as a Federalist to the Eleventh Congress to fill the vacancy caused by the resignation of William Stedman; reelected to the Twelfth and Thirteenth Congresses and served from October 8, 1810, to March 3, 1815; moved to Worcester in 1817; clerk of the courts of Worcester County 1817–1833; resumed the practice of law; served as trustee of Leicester Academy in 1819 and 1820 and as treasurer 1820–1853; appointed a master in chancery in 1838; died in Worcester, Worcester County, Mass., April 5, 1860; interment in the Rural Cemetery.

BIGELOW, Herbert Seely, a Representative from Ohio; born in Elkhart, Elkhart County, Ind., January 4, 1870; attended the public schools, and Oberlin College, Oberlin, Ohio; was graduated from Western Reserve University, Cleveland, Ohio, in 1894; moved to Cincinnati, Ohio, and studied in Lane Theological Seminary; ordained as a Congregational minister in 1895 and became pastor of the Vine Street Congregational Church in Cincinnati, Ohio; delegate to the fourth constitutional convention of Ohio in 1912, serving as president; member of the State house of representatives in 1913 and 1914; served in the Cincinnati City Council from January 1, 1936, to January 1, 1937; elected as a Democrat to the Seventy-fifth Congress (January 3, 1937–January 3, 1939); unsuccessful candidate for reelection in 1938 to the Seventy-sixth Congress; member of the city council in 1940 and 1941; resumed his duties as pastor of the Vine Street Congregational Church (Peoples Church), Cincinnati, Ohio, where he died November 11, 1951; remains were cremated and the ashes scattered over his farm near Forestville, Hamilton County, Ohio.

BIGELOW, Lewis, a Representative from Massachusetts; born in Petersham, Worcester County, Mass., August 18, 1785; was graduated from Williams College, Williamstown, Mass., in 1803; studied law; was admitted to the bar and commenced practice in Petersham; member of the State senate 1819–1821; editor of the first seventeen volumes of Massachusetts Reports and of a digest of six volumes of Pickering's Reports; elected to the Seventeenth Congress (March 4, 1821–March 3, 1823); moved to Peoria, Ill., in 1831 and continued the practice of law; interested in the real-estate business and in the operation of ferry boats; served as justice of the peace; appointed clerk of the circuit court of Peoria County, November 26, 1835, and served until his death in Peoria, Ill., October 2, 1838; interment presumed to be in the Old Centre Cemetery, Petersham, Mass.

BIGGS, Asa, a Representative and a Senator from North Carolina; born in Williamston, Martin County, N. C., February 4, 1811; attended the common schools; pursued classical studies; studied law; was admitted to the bar in 1831 and commenced practice in Williamston, N. C.; member of the State constitutional convention in 1835; member of the State house of commons in 1840 and 1842; served in the State senate in 1844 and 1854; elected as a Democrat to the Twenty-ninth Congress (March 4, 1845–March 3, 1847); unsuccessful candidate for reelection in 1846 to the Thirtieth Congress; one of a commission to codify the State laws of North Carolina in 1851; elected to the United States Senate and served from March 4, 1855, until May 5, 1858, when he resigned, having been appointed United States judge of the district of North Carolina by President Buchanan; served as judge of the district court until 1861; member of the secession convention of North Carolina in 1861; Confederate States judge 1861–1865; resumed the practice of law in Tarboro, Edgecombe County, N. C., in 1865; moved to Norfolk, Va., in 1869 and continued the practice of law until his death in that city March 6, 1878; interment in Elmwood Cemetery.

BIGGS, Benjamin Thomas, a Representative from Delaware; born near Summit Bridge, New Castle County, Del., October 1, 1821; attended the public schools and Pennington Seminary in New Jersey; taught school for a short time and later attended the Wesleyan University, Middletown, Conn.; engaged in agricultural pursuits; member of the State constitutional convention in 1853; became interested in railroad operations and was a director of the Kent & Queen Annes Railroad; unsuccessful Democratic candidate for election in 1860 to the Thirty-seventh Congress; elected as a Democrat to the Forty-first and Forty-second Congresses (March 4, 1869–March 3, 1873); was not a candidate for renomination in 1872; delegate to the Democratic National Convention at Baltimore in 1872; elected Governor of Delaware and served from January 1887 to January 1891; died in Middletown, New Castle County, Del., December 25, 1893; interment in Bethel Cemetery, near Chesapeake City, Cecil County, Md.

BIGGS, Marion, a Representative from California; born near Curryville, Pike County, Mo., May 2, 1823; attended the common schools; moved to California in 1850; returned to Missouri; was elected sheriff of Monroe County, Mo., in 1852 and reelected in 1854; returned to California in 1864; was a cattle buyer and was also engaged in agricultural pursuits; elected to the State assembly from Sacramento County in 1867 and from Butte County in 1869; elected to the State constitutional convention from the State at large in 1878; alternate presidential elector on the Democratic ticket of Samuel J. Tilden and Thomas A. Hendricks in 1876 and an elector on the Democratic ticket of Grover Cleveland and Thomas A. Hendricks in 1884; elected as a Democrat to the Fiftieth and Fifty-first Congresses (March 4, 1887–March 3, 1891); was not a candidate for renomination in 1890 to the Fifty-second Congress; commissioner to attend the centennial celebration of the inauguration of George Washington as President of the United States, in 1888; resided in Gridley, Butte County, Calif., and lived in retirement until his death there on August 2, 1910; interment in Helvetia Cemetery, Sacramento, Calif.

BIGLER, William, a Senator from Pennsylvania; born in Shiremanstown, Cumberland County, Pa., on January 1, 1814; attended the public schools; in 1829 was apprenticed to the printing trade; moved to Clearfield, Clearfield County, Pa., in 1833 and established the Clearfield Democrat; engaged in the lumber business in 1836; member of the State senate 1841–1847, twice serving as speaker; elected Governor in 1851; elected as a Democrat to the United States Senate to fill the vacancy in the term commencing March 4, 1855, caused by failure of the legislature to elect and served from January 14, 1856, to March 3, 1861; unsuccessful candidate for reelection; delegate to the Democratic National Convention at Chicago in 1864, to the Union National Convention at Philadelphia in 1866, and to the Democratic National Convention at New York in 1868; member of the constitutional convention of Pennsylvania; member of the board of finance of the Centennial Exposition in 1876; president of the Philadelphia & Erie Railroad; died in Clearfield, Pa., August 9, 1880; interment in Hillcrest Cemetery.

BILBO, Theodore Gilmore, a Senator from Mississippi; born on a farm near Poplarville, Pearl River County, Miss., October 13, 1877; attended the public schools, Peabody College, Nashville, Tenn., the law department of Vanderbilt University, Nashville, Tenn., and the University of Michigan at Ann Arbor; teacher in district and high schools of Mississippi for five years; was admitted to the bar in 1908 and commenced practice in Poplarville, Miss.; member of the State senate 1908–1912; served as

Lieutenant Governor 1912–1916 and as Governor 1916–1920 and 1928–1932; elected as a Democrat to the United States Senate in 1934, 1940 and again in 1946, but did not take the oath of office at the beginning of the Eightieth Congress, and served from January 3, 1935, until his death August 21, 1947, in a hospital at New Orleans, La., where he had gone for treatment; interment in Juniper Grove Cemetery, near Poplarville, Miss.

BILLINGHURST, Charles, a Representative from Wisconsin; born in Brighton, Franklin County, N. Y., July 27, 1818; attended the common schools; studied law; was admitted to the bar in 1847 and commenced practice in Rochester, N. Y.; moved to Wisconsin the same year and settled in Juneau, Dodge County; continued the practice of his profession; elected as a member of the first State Legislature of Wisconsin in 1848; was elected a presidential elector on the Democratic ticket of Pierce and King in 1852; elected as a Republican to the Thirty-fourth and Thirty-fifth Congresses (March 4, 1855–March 3, 1859); unsuccessful candidate for reelection in 1858 to the Thirty-sixth Congress; resumed the practice of law in Juneau, Wis., where he died August 18, 1865; interment in Juneau Cemetery.

BILLMEYER, Alexander, a Representative from Pennsylvania; born in Liberty Township, Montour County, Pa., January 7, 1841; attended the common schools; engaged in agricultural pursuits; interested in the manufacture of lumber; director of a national bank in Washingtonville, Montour County, Pa.; elected as a Democrat to the Fifty-seventh Congress to fill the vacancy caused by the death of Rufus K. Polk and served from November 4, 1902, to March 3, 1903; was not a candidate for renomination in 1902; resumed agricultural pursuits in Montour County, Pa.; died near Washingtonville, Pa., May 24, 1924; interment in Odd Fellows Cemetery, Danville, Pa.

BINDERUP, Charles Gustav, a Representative from Nebraska; born in Horsens, Denmark, March 5, 1873; when six months old immigrated to the United States with his parents, who settled on a farm near Hastings, Adams County, Nebr.; attended the county schools and Grand Island (Nebr.) Business College; engaged in agricultural pursuits near Hastings and Minden, Nebr., and also in the mercantile and creamery business at Minden, Nebr.; elected as a Democrat to the Seventy-fourth and Seventy-fifth Congresses (January 3, 1935–January 3, 1939); was an unsuccessful candidate for reelection in 1938 to the Seventy-sixth Congress and for election as an Independent in 1940 to the Seventy-seventh Congress; organized and was active in the Constitutional Money League of America in Minden, Nebr., until his death; died in Minden, Nebr., August 19, 1950; interment in Minden Cemetery.

BINES, Thomas, a Representative from New Jersey; born in Trenton, N. J.; attended the common schools; appointed coroner for Salem County on October 16, 1802; elected sheriff of Salem County in 1808 and served until 1810; elected as a Democrat to the Thirteenth Congress to fill the vacancy caused by the death of Jacob Hufty and served from November 2, 1814, to March 3, 1815; was not a candidate for renomination in 1814 to the Fourteenth Congress; elected justice of the peace of Lower Penns Neck Township in 1822 and served in this capacity until 1826; died in Lower Penns Neck Township, Salem County, April 9, 1826.

BINGHAM, Henry Harrison, a Representative from Pennsylvania; born in Philadelphia, Pa., December 4, 1841; was graduated from Jefferson College, Canonsburg, Pa., in 1862 and from the law department of Washington and Jefferson College, Washington, Pa.; during the Civil War entered the

Union Army as a first lieutenant in the One Hundred and Fortieth Regiment, Pennsylvania Volunteer Infantry, August 22, 1862; commissioned captain September 9, 1862; major and judge advocate September 20, 1864; brevetted major of Volunteers August 1, 1864, "for good conduct and conspicuous gallantry, especially at the Wilderness, Spotsylvania, and Gettysburg"; brevetted lieutenant colonel of Volunteers April 9, 1865, "for highly meritorious services during the recent campaign terminating with the surrender of the insurgent army under Gen. Robert E. Lee"; colonel and brigadier general of Volunteers April 9, 1865, "for conspicuous gallantry and meritorious service during the war"; honorably mustered out of service July 2, 1866; awarded a Congressional Medal of Honor August 26, 1893, "for distinguished gallantry in the Battle of the Wilderness, Virginia, May 6, 1864, where he rallied and led into action a portion of the troops which had given way under the fierce assaults of the enemy"; appointed postmaster of Philadelphia in March 1867 and served until December 1872, when he resigned to accept the clerkship of the courts of oyer and terminer and quarter sessions of the peace in Philadelphia, having been elected by the people; reelected clerk of courts in 1875; delegate at large to the Republican National Convention at Philadelphia in 1872; also a delegate from the first congressional district to the Republican National Conventions in 1876, 1884, 1888, 1892, 1896, and 1900; elected as a Republican to the Forty-sixth and to the sixteen succeeding Congresses and served from March 4, 1879, until his death, his service covering a period of thirty-three years and nineteen days; died in Philadelphia, Pa., March 22, 1912; interment in Laurel Hill Cemetery.

BINGHAM, Hiram, a Senator from Connecticut; born in Honolulu, Hawaii, November 19, 1875; educated at Punahou School and Oahu College, Hawaii, 1882–1892, Phillips Academy, Andover, Mass., 1892–1894, Yale University 1894–1898, University of California at Berkeley 1899–1900, and Harvard University 1900–1905; taught history at Harvard University 1902–1905, history and politics at Princeton University in 1905 and 1906, and history of South America at Yale University 1907–1917; in 1906 and 1907 explored Bolivar's route across Venezuela and Colombia, and, in 1908 and 1909, the Spanish trade route from Buenos Aires to Lima; United States Government delegate to the First Pan American Scientific Congress at Santiago, Chile, in 1908; directed the Yale Peruvian expedition in 1911; made further Peruvian explorations under the auspices of Yale University and the National Geographic Society 1912–1915; captain of Headquarters Company, Tenth Field Artillery, Connecticut National Guard, in 1916; became an aviator in the spring of 1917; organized the United States Schools of Military Aeronautics in May 1917; commissioned major, Aviation Section, Signal Corps, June 6, 1917; promoted to lieutenant colonel October 25, 1917; commanded the flying school at Issoudun, France, from August to December 1918; alternate at large to the Republican National Conventions in 1916 and 1920 and delegate at large in 1924, 1928, 1932, and 1936; presidential elector on the Republican ticket of Hughes and Fairbanks in 1916; Lieutenant Governor of Connecticut 1922–1924; elected Governor of Connecticut on November 4, 1924; elected as a Republican to the United States Senate on December 16, 1924, to fill the vacancy caused by the death of Frank B. Brandegee in the term ending March 3, 1927; reelected in 1926 and served from December 17, 1924, to March 3, 1933; appointed a member of the President's Aircraft Board by President Coolidge on September 12, 1925, and served until its final report in December 1925; unsuccessful candidate for reelection to the United States Senate in 1932; engaged in banking and literary work in Washington, D. C.; during World War II lectured at naval training schools in 1942 and 1943; chairman of the Civil Service Commission's Loyalty Review

Board from January 8, 1951, to September 24, 1953; died in Washington, D. C., June 6, 1956; interment in Arlington National Cemetery, Fort Myer, Va.

BINGHAM, John Armor, a representative from Ohio; born in Mercer, Mercer County, Pa., January 21, 1815; pursued academic studies; apprentice in a printing office for two years; attended Franklin College, Ohio; studied law; was admitted to the bar in 1840 and commenced practice in New Philadelphia, Tuscarawas County, Ohio; district attorney for Tuscarawas County, Ohio, 1846–1849; elected as a Republican to the Thirty-fourth and to the three succeeding Congresses (March 4, 1855–March 3, 1863); unsuccessful candidate for reelection in 1862 to the Thirty-eighth Congress; appointed by President Lincoln as judge advocate of the Union Army with the rank of major in 1864; later appointed solicitor of the court of claims; special judge advocate in the trial of the conspirators against the life of President Lincoln; elected to the Thirty-ninth and to the three succeeding Congresses (March 4, 1865–March 3, 1873); unsuccessful candidate for renomination in 1872; one of the managers appointed by the House of Representatives in 1862 to conduct the impeachment proceedings against West H. Humphreys, United States judge for the several districts of Tennessee, and in 1868 in the proceedings against Andrew Johnson, President of the United States; appointed Minister to Japan and served from May 31, 1873, until July 2, 1885; died in Cadiz, Harrison County, Ohio, March 19, 1900; interment in Cadiz Cemetery.

BINGHAM, Kinsley Scott, a Representative and a Senator from Michigan; born in Camillus, Onondaga County, N. Y., December 16, 1808; attended the common schools and pursued an academic course; studied law in Syracuse, N. Y.; moved to Green Oak, Mich., in 1833; admitted to the bar and practiced; engaged in agricultural pursuits; held a number of local offices, including those of justice of the peace, postmaster, and first judge of probate of Livingston County; member of the first house of representatives of Michigan in 1837, the year of the State's admission to the Union, and was reelected four times; speaker of the State house of representatives three terms; elected as a Democrat to the Thirtieth and Thirty-first Congresses (March 4, 1847–March 3, 1851); was not a candidate for renomination in 1850 to the Thirty-second Congress; resumed agricultural pursuits; elected Governor in 1854, heading the first ticket ever designated as "Republican," and was reelected in 1856; was instrumental in the establishment of the Michigan Agricultural College and other educational institutions; elected as a Republican to the United States Senate and served from March 4, 1859, until his death in Green Oak, Livingston County, Mich., October 5, 1861; interment in Old Village Cemetery, Brighton, Livingston County, Mich.

BINGHAM, William, a Delegate and a Senator from Pennsylvania; born in Philadelphia, Pa., March 8, 1752; was graduated from Philadelphia College in 1768; agent of the Continental Congress at Martinique, and afterwards consul at St. Pierre, in the West Indies, the two services covering the period 1777–1780; Member of the Continental Congress in 1787 and 1788; member of the State house of representatives in 1790 and 1791, serving as speaker in 1791; served in, and was president of, the State senate in 1794 and 1795; elected to the United States Senate and served from March 4, 1795, to March 3, 1801; elected President pro tempore of the Senate February 16, 1797; was not a candidate for reelection; withdrew from public life and engaged in the management of his extensive estates; moved in 1801 to Bath, England, and resided with his daughter until his death in that city on February 7, 1804; interment in Paris Church, Bath, England.

BINNEY, Horace, a Representative from Pennsylvania; born in Philadelphia, Pa., January 4, 1780; attended a classical school in Bordentown, N. J., three years; was graduated from Harvard University in 1797; studied law; was admitted to the bar and commenced practice in Philadelphia in 1800; member of the State house of representatives in 1806 and 1807; between 1807 and 1814 prepared and published six volumes of reported decisions of the supreme court of Pennsylvania; director of the United States Bank; elected as a Whig to the Twenty-third Congress (March 4, 1833–March 3, 1835); was not a candidate for renomination in 1834; except for his appearance before the supreme court in 1844 as counsel for Philadelphia in the Girard will case, he retired from his practice in the courts and confined himself to giving written opinions; died in Philadelphia, Pa., August 12, 1875; interment in St. James the Less Cemetery, Falls of the Schuylkill (now a part of Philadelphia), Pa.

BIRCH, William Fred, a Representative from New Jersey; born in Newark, N. J., August 30, 1870; moved with his parents to Phillipsburg, N. J., in 1872 and to Dover, Morris County, N. J., in 1874; attended the public schools and was graduated from the New Jersey State Model School at Trenton and from Coleman's Business College at Newark in 1887; engaged in the manufacture of boilers and smokestacks at Dover; member of the Dover Common Council for several years; city recorder 1904–1909; member of the State house of assembly 1910–1912; elected as a Republican to the Sixty-fifth Congress to fill the vacancy caused by the death of John H. Capstick and served from November 5, 1918, to March 3, 1919; was not a candidate for renomination in 1918; resumed his former manufacturing pursuits; also engaged in the fire-insurance and automobile businesses and was interested in banking; trustee of the Dover General Hospital; retired from business activities in 1941; died in a hospital at Glen Ridge, N. J., January 25, 1946; interment in Orchard Street Cemetery, Dover, N. J.

BIRD, John, a Representative from New York; born in Litchfield, Conn., November 22, 1768; pursued classical studies; was graduated from Yale College in 1786; studied law; was admitted to the bar and commenced practice in Litchfield, Conn.; moved to Troy, N. Y., in 1793 and engaged in the practice of law; member of the State assembly 1796–1798; elected as a Democrat to the Sixth and Seventh Congresses and served from March 4, 1799, to July 25, 1801, when he resigned; again resumed the practice of his profession; died in Troy, N. Y., on February 2, 1806; interment in Mount Ida Cemetery.

BIRD, John Taylor, a Representative from New Jersey; born in Bloomsbury, Hunterdon County, N. J., August 16, 1829; attended the public schools, and a classical academy at Hackettstown, N. J.; studied law; was admitted to the bar in 1855 and commenced practice in Bloomsbury, N. J.; moved to Clinton in 1858; prosecutor of the pleas for Hunterdon County 1862–1867; moved to Flemington in 1865; elected as a Democrat to the Forty-first and Forty-second Congresses (March 4, 1869–March 3, 1873); was not a candidate for renomination in 1872; resumed the practice of law in Flemington, N. J.; member of the New Jersey constitutional convention in 1876; moved to Trenton, N. J., in 1882; vice chancellor of New Jersey 1882–1896; master in chancery 1900–1909; died in Trenton, N. J., May 6, 1911; interment in Riverview Cemetery.

BIRD, Richard Ely, a Representative from Kansas; born in Cincinnati, Ohio, November 4, 1878; moved with his parents to Wichita, Sedgwick County, Kans., in 1887; attended the public schools and was graduated from Wichita High School in 1898; studied law; was admitted to the bar in 1901 and commenced practice in Wichita; judge of the district court of the eighteenth judicial district of Kansas 1916–1921; elected as a Republican to the Sixty-seventh Congress (March 4, 1921–March 3, 1923); unsuccessful candidate for reelection in 1922 to the Sixty-eighth Congress; resumed the practice of law; United States referee in bankruptcy, Wichita, Kans., 1925–1927; retired from public life in 1937 and moved to Long Beach, Calif., where he died January 10, 1955, interment in Maplegrove Cemetery, Wichita, Kans.

BIRDSALL, Ausburn, a Representative from New York; born in Otego, Otsego County, N. Y.; moved to Binghamton, Broome County, N. Y.; studied law; was admitted to the bar and practiced; district attorney of Broome County; elected as a Democrat to the Thirtieth Congress (March 4, 1847–March 3, 1849); appointed United States naval storekeeper in New York City; returned to Binghamton, N. Y., and resumed the practice of law until 1890, when he retired and moved to New York City, where he resided until his death July 10, 1903; interment in Woodlawn Cemetery, New York City.

BIRDSALL, Benjamin Pixley, a Representative from Iowa; born in Weyauwega, Waupaca County, Wis., October 26, 1858; attended the common schools of Iowa and Iowa State University, Iowa City; studied law; was admitted to the bar in 1878 and practiced; served as district judge of the eleventh judicial district of Iowa from January 1893 to October 1900; elected as a Republican to the Fifty-eighth, Fifty-ninth, and Sixtieth Congresses (March 4, 1903–March 3, 1909); resumed the practice of law in Clarion, Wright County, Iowa, where he died May 26, 1917; interment in Evergreen Cemetery.

BIRDSALL, James, a Representative from New York; born in that State in 1783; studied law; was admitted to the bar in 1806 and was the first lawyer to settle in Norwich, Chenango County, N. Y.; surrogate of Chenango County, N. Y., in 1811; elected as a Democrat to the Fourteenth Congress (March 4, 1815–March 3, 1817); member of the State assembly in 1827; one of the incorporators of the Bank of Chenango; moved to Fenton, Genesee County, Mich., in 1839 and later to Flint, Mich., where he died July 20, 1856; interment in Glenwood Cemetery.

BIRDSALL, Samuel, a Representative from New York; born in Hillsdale, Columbia County, N. Y., May 14, 1791; attended the common schools; studied law in the office of Martin Van Buren; was admitted to the bar in 1812 and commenced practice in Cooperstown, N. Y.; master in chancery in 1815; moved to Waterloo, N. Y., in 1817; division judge advocate with rank of colonel in 1819; counselor in the supreme court and solicitor in chancery in 1823; surrogate of Seneca County 1827–1837; bank commissioner in 1832; elected as a Democrat to the Twenty-fifth Congress (March 4, 1837–March 3, 1839); was not a candidate for renomination in 1838; admitted to practice before the United States Supreme Court in 1838; district attorney of Seneca County in 1846; postmaster of Waterloo, Seneca County, N. Y., 1853–1863; died in Waterloo, N. Y., February 8, 1872; interment in Maple Grove Cemetery.

BIRDSEYE, Victory, a Representative from New York; born in Cornwall, Conn., December 25, 1782; attended the public schools, and was graduated from Williams College, Williamstown, Mass., in 1804; studied law; was admitted to the bar in 1807 and commenced practice in Pompey Hill, Onondaga County, N. Y.; elected to the Fourteenth Congress (March 4, 1815–March 3, 1817); was not a candidate for renomination in 1816; postmaster of Pompey Hill 1817–1838; district attorney of Onon-

daga County 1818–1833; master of chancery of Onondaga County 1818–1822; delegate to the State constitutional convention in 1821; served in the State senate in 1827; member of the State assembly 1823 and 1838–1840; unsuccessful candidate for election in 1838 to the Twenty-sixth Congress; elected as a Whig to the Twenty-seventh Congress (March 4, 1841–March 3, 1843); was not a candidate for renomination in 1842; resumed the practice of law; died in Pompey, Onondaga County, N. Y., September 16, 1853; interment in Pompey Hill Cemetery.

BISBEE, Horatio, Jr., a Representative from Florida; born in Canton, Oxford County, Maine, May 1, 1839; attended the public schools, and was graduated from Tufts College, Medford, Mass., in 1863; during the Civil War served as a private for three months in the Fifth Regiment, Massachusetts Volunteer Infantry; mustered out the middle of July 1861; appointed captain in the Ninth Regiment, Maine Volunteer Infantry, in September 1861; promoted to the rank of lieutenant colonel and afterwards to the rank of colonel; honorably mustered out of the service with the latter rank in March 1863; moved to Illinois in 1863; studied law; was admitted to the bar in Chicago in 1864 and commenced practice in Jacksonville, Fla., in 1865; United States attorney for the northern district of Florida 1869–1873 and for a short period filled the office of attorney general of the State; presented credentials as a Republican Member-elect to the Forty-fifth Congress and served from March 4, 1877, to February 20, 1879, when he was succeeded by Jesse J. Finley, who contested the election; successfully contested the election of Noble A. Hull to the Forty-sixth Congress and served from January 22, 1881, to March 3, 1881; successfully contested the election of Jesse J. Finley to the Forty-seventh Congress and served from June 1, 1882, to March 3, 1883; reelected to the Forty-eighth Congress (March 4, 1883–March 3, 1885); unsuccessful candidate for reelection in 1884 to the Forty-ninth Congress; resumed the practice of his profession; died in Dixfield, Oxford County, Maine, March 27, 1916; interment in Greenwood Cemetery.

BISHOP, Cecil William (Runt), a Representative from Illinois; born on a farm near West Vienna, Johnson County, Ill., June 29, 1890; attended the public schools, and Union Academy, Anna, Ill.; learned the tailoring trade; worked as coal miner, telephone linesman, professional football and baseball player and manager; city clerk of Carterville, Ill., 1915–1918; engaged in the cleaning-tailoring business 1910–1922; postmaster at Carterville, Ill., 1923–1933; elected as a Republican to the Seventy-seventh and to the six succeeding Congresses (January 3, 1941–January 3, 1955); unsuccessful candidate for reelection in 1954 to the Eighty-fourth Congress; congressional liaison assistant, Post Office Department, Washington, D. C., 1955–1957; superintendent of Division of Industrial Planning and Development, State of Illinois, in 1957 and 1958; Department of Labor conciliator for State of Illinois 1958–1960; retired; is a resident of Carterville, Ill.

BISHOP, James, a Representative from New Jersey; born in New Brunswick, N. J., May 11, 1816; attended Spaulding School and Rutgers College Preparatory School, New Brunswick, N. J.; engaged in mercantile pursuits in New Brunswick; member of the State house of assembly in 1849 and 1850; elected as a Whig to the Thirty-fourth Congress (March 4, 1855–March 3, 1857); unsuccessful candidate for reelection in 1856 to the Thirty-fifth Congress; prominent in the rubber trade in New York City; chief of the bureau of labor statistics of New Jersey 1878–1893 and a resident of Trenton; died at Kemble Hall, near Morristown, Morris County, N. J., May 10, 1895; interment in Elmwood Cemetery, New Brunswick, Middlesex County, N. J.

BISHOP, Phanuel, a Representative from Massachusetts; born in Rehoboth, Mass., September 3, 1739; attended the common schools; was an innkeeper; served in the State senate 1787–1791; member of the State house of representatives in 1792, 1793, 1797, and 1798; elected to the Sixth, Seventh, Eighth, and Ninth Congresses (March 4, 1799–March 3, 1807); died in Rehoboth, Mass., January 6, 1812; interment in Old Cemetery, Rumford, East Providence, R. I.

BISHOP, Roswell Peter, a Representative from Michigan; born in Sidney, Delaware County, N. Y., January 6, 1843; attended Unadilla Academy, Cooperstown Seminary, and Walton Academy, New York; taught school several years; during the Civil War enlisted as a private in Company C, Forty-third Regiment, New York Volunteer Infantry, in 1861 and was discharged in December 1862 because of a wound which necessitated the amputation of his right arm; entered the University of Michigan, Ann Arbor, in September 1868 where he remained until December 1872; studied law; was admitted to the bar in Ann Arbor in May 1875 and commenced practice in Ludington, Mason County, Mich.; elected prosecuting attorney of Mason County in 1876, 1878, and 1884; member of the State house of representatives in 1882 and 1892; elected as a Republican to the Fifty-fourth and to the five succeeding Congresses (March 4, 1895–March 3, 1907); unsuccessful candidate for renomination in 1906; resumed the practice of law in Ludington, Mich.; served as a member of the Michigan constitutional convention in 1907; was appointed a member of the Spanish Treaty Claims Commission in December 1907 and served until the work of the commission was completed; moved to Hollister, Calif., in 1910 and engaged in fruit growing; died at Pacific Grove, Monterey County, Calif., March 4, 1920; interment in the El Carmelo Cemetery.

BISHOP, William Darius, a Representative from Connecticut; born in Bloomfield, Essex County, N. J., September 14, 1827; pursued preparatory studies; was graduated from Yale College in 1849; studied law; was admitted to the bar but did not practice, instead carrying on his father's railroad enterprises which involved the construction of the Naugatuck and the New York and New Haven Railroads in Connecticut and the railroad between Saratoga Springs and Whitehall in New York; founder of the Eastern Railroad Association and its president until the time of his death; elected as a Democrat to the Thirty-fifth Congress (March 4, 1857–March 3, 1859); unsuccessful candidate for relection in 1858 to the Thirty-sixth Congress; commissioner of patents from May 23, 1859, to January 1860; vice president and president of the New York, New Haven & Hartford Railroad Co.; member of the State house of representatives in 1866 and 1871; served in the State senate in 1877 and 1878; died in Bridgeport, Conn., February 4, 1904; interment in Mountain Grove Cemetery.

BISSELL, William Harrison, a Representative from Illinois; born in Hartwick, Otsego County, N. Y., on April 25, 1811; attended the public schools, and was graduated from the Philadelphia Medical College in 1835; moved to Monroe County, Ill., in 1837; taught school and practiced medicine until 1840; member of the State house of representatives 1840–1842; studied law; was admitted to the bar and commenced practice in Belleville, St. Clair County, Ill.; prosecuting attorney of St. Clair County in 1844; served in the Mexican War as colonel of the Second Regiment, Illinois Volunteer Infantry; elected as a Democrat to the Thirty-first, Thirty-second, and Thirty-third Congresses (March 4, 1849–March 3, 1855); was not a candidate for renomination in 1854; elected Governor of Illinois in 1856

and served from January 12, 1857, until his death; died in Springfield, Sangamon County, Ill., March 18, 1860; interment in Oak Ridge Cemetery.

BIXLER, Harris Jacob, a Representative from Pennsylvania; born in New Buffalo, Perry County, Pa., September 16, 1870; attended the public schools and Lock Haven State Normal School; taught school in the country districts in Perry and Clinton Counties 1878–1892; attended Potts Business College, Williamsport, Pa.; moved to Johnsonburg, Elk County, Pa., in 1892 and worked as a shipping clerk; later was engaged in banking and manufacturing; director of the Johnsonburg National Bank; served as president of the city council 1900–1904 and as president of the board of education 1904–1910; mayor of Johnsonburg 1908–1912; sheriff of Elk County, Pa., 1916–1920; chairman of the Republican county committee 1916–1925; chairman of the draft board, Elk County, during the First World War; treasurer of Elk County 1920–1922; elected as a Republican to the Sixty-seventh, Sixty-eighth, and Sixty-ninth Congresses (March 4, 1921–March 3, 1927); unsuccessful candidate for renomination in 1926; engaged in business as a freight contractor and also interested in agricultural pursuits; died in Johnsonburg, Pa., on March 29, 1941; interment in Duncannon Cemetery, Duncannon, Pa.

BLACK, Edward Junius (father of George Robison Black), a Representative from Georgia; born in Beaufort, S. C., October 30, 1806; attended the common schools and was graduated from Richmond Academy, Augusta, Ga.; studied law; was admitted to the bar in 1827 and commenced practice in Augusta, Ga.; member of the State house of representatives 1829–1831; moved to Screven County, Ga., in 1832; elected as a State Rights Whig to the Twenty-sixth Congress (March 4, 1839–March 3, 1841); unsuccessful Democratic candidate for reelection in 1840 to the Twenty-seventh Congress; subsequently elected as a Democrat to the Twenty-seventh Congress to fill in part the vacancies caused by the resignations of Julius C. Alford, William C. Dawson, and Eugenius A. Nisbet; reelected to the Twenty-eighth Congress and served from January 3, 1842, to March 3, 1845; unsuccessful candidate for reelection in 1844 to the Twenty-ninth Congress; resumed the practice of law; died in Millettville, Barnwell District, S. C., September 1, 1846; interment in the family burying ground near Millettville, Allendale County, S. C.

BLACK, Eugene, a Representative from Texas; born near Blossom, Lamar County, Tex., July 2, 1879; attended the public schools of Blossom; taught school in Lamar County 1898–1900; employed in the post office at Blossom; was graduated from the law department of Cumberland University, Lebanon, Tenn., in 1905; was admitted to the bar the same year and commenced practice in Clarksville, Red River County, Tex.; was also engaged in the wholesale grocery business; elected as a Democrat to the Sixty-fourth and to the six succeeding Congresses (March 4, 1915–March 3, 1929); unsuccessful candidate for renomination in 1928; appointed by President Hoover to the United States Board of Tax Appeals (now the Tax Court of the United States) in November 1929 to fill an unexpired term; reappointed in 1932 and again in 1944 by President Franklin D. Roosevelt for a term of twelve years and served until his retirement November 30, 1953; recalled December 1, 1953, to perform further judicial service with Tax Court of the United States; is a resident of Washington, D. C.

BLACK, Frank Swett, a Representative from New York; born near Limington, York County, Maine, March 8, 1853;

attended the district schools, and was graduated from Lebanon Academy, West Lebanon, Maine, in 1871; taught school for several years; was graduated from Dartmouth College, Hanover, N. H., in 1875; editor of the Johnstown (N. Y.) Journal; moved to Troy, N. Y., and engaged in newspaper work; studied law; was admitted to the bar in 1879 and commenced practice in Troy; elected as a Republican to the Fifty-fourth Congress and served from March 4, 1895, to January 7, 1897, when he resigned to become Governor; Governor of New York 1897–1899; resumed the practice of law in New York City; died in Troy, N. Y., March 22, 1913; the remains were cremated and placed in a sepulcher on his farm near Freedom, Carroll County, N. H.

BLACK, George Robison (son of Edward Junius Black), a Representative from Georgia; born on his father's plantation near Jacksonboro, Screven County, Ga., March 24, 1835; attended the common schools, the University of Georgia at Athens, and the University of South Carolina at Columbia; studied law; was admitted to the bar in 1857 and commenced practice in Savannah, Ga.; during the Civil War entered the Confederate service as first lieutenant of the Phoenix Riflemen and afterwards was promoted to lieutenant colonel of the Sixty-third Georgia Regiment; delegate to the State constitutional convention in 1865; delegate to the Democratic National Convention at Baltimore in 1872; member of the State senate 1874–1877; vice president of the Georgia State Agricultural Society; elected as a Democrat to the Forty-seventh Congress (March 4, 1881–March 3, 1883); was an unsuccessful candidate for renomination in 1882 to the Forty-eighth Congress; died in Sylvania, Screven County, Ga., November 3, 1886; interment in Sylvania Cemetery.

BLACK, Henry, a Representative from Pennsylvania; born near the borough of Somerset, Somerset County, Pa., February 25, 1783; attended the common schools; engaged in agricultural pursuits; member of the State house of representatives 1816–1818; justice of the peace; associate judge of Somerset County, Pa., 1820–1840; elected as a Whig to the Twenty-seventh Congress to fill the vacancy caused by the death of Charles Ogle and served from June 28, 1841, until his death in Somerset, Pa., on November 28, 1841; interment in the family cemetery, Stony Creek Township, Somerset County, Pa.

BLACK, Hugo Lafayette, a Senator from Alabama; born near Ashland, Clay County, Ala., February 27, 1886; attended the public schools and Ashland College, Ashland, Ala.; was graduated from the law department of the University of Alabama at Tuscaloosa in 1906; was admitted to the Alabama bar the same year and commenced the practice of law in Ashland, Ala.; moved to Birmingham, Ala., in 1907 and continued the practice of law; during the First World War served as a captain of the Eighty-first Field Artillery and as company regimental adjutant in the Nineteenth Artillery Brigade from November 27, 1917, to December 5, 1918; served as a police court judge in Birmingham, Ala., for one and one-half years; prosecuting attorney of Jefferson County, Ala., for two years and seven months; was a delegate to the Democratic National Convention at Philadelphia in 1936; elected as a Democrat to the United States Senate in 1926; reelected in 1932, and served from March 4, 1927, until his resignation on August 19, 1937, having been appointed by President Franklin D. Roosevelt as an Associate Justice of the United States Supreme Court; was confirmed by the Senate on August 17, 1937, and took his seat as an Associate Justice on October 4, 1937, in which capacity he is now serving; is a legal resident of Birmingham, Ala.

BLACK, James, a Representative from Pennsylvania; born in Newport, Perry County, Pa., March 6, 1793; attended the common schools; engaged in mercantile pursuits; member of the State house of representatives in 1830 and 1831; elected as a Democrat to the Twenty-fourth Congress to fill the vacancy caused by the resignation of Jesse Miller and served from December 5, 1836, to March 3, 1837; associate judge of Perry County in 1842 and 1843; elected to the Twenty-eighth and Twenty-ninth Congresses (March 4, 1843–March 3, 1847); State collector of tolls on the Juniata Canal; died in New Bloomfield, Perry County, Pa., on June 21, 1872; interment in New Bloomfield Cemetery.

BLACK, James Augustus, a Representative from South Carolina; born on his father's plantation in Ninety Six District, near Abbeville, S. C., in 1793; attended the common schools on his father's plantation; during the War of 1812 was appointed a second lieutenant in the Eighth Infantry March 12, 1812; promoted to first lieutenant December 2, 1813, and was honorably discharged June 15, 1815; engaged in the mining of iron ore on what is now the present site of Cherokee Falls, S. C.; moved to Georgia and settled in Savannah; engaged in cotton dealing; served as tax collector of Chatham County, Ga.; returned to South Carolina and settled in Columbia; cashier of the State (branch) bank; elected as a Calhoun Democrat to the Twenty-eighth, Twenty-ninth, and Thirtieth Congresses and served from March 4, 1843, until his death in Washington, D. C., on April 3, 1848; interment in the graveyard of the First Presbyterian Church, Columbia, S. C.

BLACK, James Conquest Cross, a Representative from Georgia; born in Stamping Ground, Scott County, Ky., May 9, 1842; attended the common schools and the high school at Newcastle, Ky., and was graduated from Georgetown College, Kentucky, in 1862; during the Civil War enlisted as a private in Company A, Ninth Kentucky Cavalry, in the Confederate Army; moved to Augusta, Ga., in 1865; studied law; was admitted to the bar in 1866 and commenced practice in Augusta, Ga.; member of the State house of representatives 1873–1877; served as president of the Augusta Orphan Asylum 1879–1886; presidential elector on the Democratic ticket of Hancock and English in 1880; member of the city council; served as city attorney; elected as a Democrat to the Fifty-third and Fifty-fourth Congresses and served from March 4, 1893, to March 4, 1895, when he resigned; subsequently elected to fill the vacancy caused by his own resignation and served from October 2, 1895, to March 3, 1897; was not a candidate for renomination in 1896; resumed the practice of law in Augusta, Ga., until his death there on October 1, 1928; interment in Magnolia Cemetery.

BLACK, John, a Senator from Mississippi; born in Massachusetts; engaged in teaching for a few years; studied law; commenced practice in Louisiana; moved to Mississippi; elected judge of the fourth circuit and supreme court in 1826 and served until 1832; appointed to the United States Senate to fill the vacancy caused by the resignation of Powhatan Ellis and served from November 12, 1832, to March 3, 1833; elected to the United States Senate to fill the vacancy in the term commencing March 4, 1833, caused by the recess of the legislature, and served from November 22, 1833, to January 22, 1838, when he resigned; affiliated with the Whig Party after its formation; resumed the practice of law in Winchester, Va., and died there August 29, 1854; interment in Mount Hebron Cemetery.

BLACK, John Charles, a Representative from Illinois; born in Lexington, Holmes County, Miss., January 27, 1839; moved to Danville, Vermilion County, Ill., in 1847; attended the common schools and Wabash College, Crawfordsville, Ind., but was not graduated until after the close of the Civil War; during the Civil War served in the Union Army from April 14, 1861, to August 15, 1865; entered as a private, and was successively sergeant major, major, lieutenant colonel, and colonel; brevetted brigadier general for gallant service in the storming of Fort Blakeley on April 9, 1865; received the Congressional Medal for conspicuous bravery in action; studied law in Chicago, Ill.; was admitted to the bar in 1867 and commenced practice in Danville, Ill.; appointed United States Commissioner of Pensions by President Cleveland and served from March 17, 1885, to March 27, 1889, during which time he inaugurated many reforms which reduced the expenses of the bureau and at the same time saved not less than a million dollars in pension attorney's fees; elected as a Democrat to the Fifty-third Congress and served from March 4, 1893, to January 12, 1895, when he resigned; United States attorney for the northern district of Illinois 1895–1899; department commander of the Loyal Legion of Illinois 1895–1897; department commander of the Illinois department, Grand Army of the Republic, in 1898; commander in chief of the Grand Army of the Republic in 1903 and 1904; member of the United States Civil Service Commission 1904–1913 and served as its president; resigned and returned to Chicago, Ill., where he died August 17, 1915; interment in Spring Hill Cemetery, Danville, Ill.

BLACK, Loring Milton, Jr., a Representative from New York; born in New York City, N. Y., May 17, 1886; attended the public schools and was graduated from Fordham University, New York City, in 1907; studied law at Columbia University, New York City; was admitted to the bar in 1909 and commenced practice in New York City; member of the State senate in 1911 and 1912; resumed the practice of his profession in New York City; again a member of the State senate in 1919 and 1920; elected as a Democrat to the Sixty-eighth and to the five succeeding Congresses (March 4, 1923–January 3, 1935); was not a candidate for renomination in 1934; resumed the practice of law in New York City and Washington, D. C.; died in Washington, D. C., May 21, 1956; interment in Fort Lincoln Cemetery.

BLACKBURN, Edmond Spencer, a Representative from North Carolina; born near Boone, Watauga County, N. C., September 22, 1868; attended the common schools and academies of his native State; studied law; was admitted to the bar in 1890 and commenced practice in Jefferson, Ashe County, N. C.; reading clerk of the State senate in 1894 and 1895; member of the State house of representatives in 1896 and 1897, serving as speaker pro tempore the latter year; assistant United States attorney in 1898; elected as a Republican to the Fifty-seventh Congress (March 4, 1901–March 3, 1903); unsuccessful candidate for reelection in 1902 to the Fifty-eighth Congress; elected to the Fifty-ninth Congress (March 4, 1905–March 3, 1907); was not a candidate for renomination in 1906; resumed the practice of law in Greensboro, N. C.; died in Elizabethton, Carter County, Tenn., March 10, 1912; interment in Old Hopewell Cemetery, near Boone, N. C.

BLACKBURN, Joseph Clay Stiles, a Representative and a Senator from Kentucky; born near Spring Station, Woodford County, Ky., October 1, 1838; attended Sayres Institute, Frankfort, Ky., and was graduated from Centre College, Danville, Ky., in 1857; studied law in Lexington, Ky.; was admitted to the bar in 1858 and practiced in Chicago, Ill., until 1860, when he returned to Woodford County, Ky.; entered the Confederate Army as a private in 1861 and was promoted to the rank of lieutenant colonel before the close of the Civil War; settled in Arkansas in 1865, where he was engaged as lawyer and planter in Desha County until 1868, when he returned to Ken-

tucky and opened law offices in Versailles; member of the State house of representatives 1871–1875; elected as a Democrat to the Forty-fourth and to the four succeeding Congresses (March 4, 1875–March 3, 1885); elected to the United States Senate in 1885; reelected in 1890, and served from March 4, 1885, to March 3, 1897; unsuccessful candidate for reelection in 1897 due to Democratic Party dissension; delegate to the Democratic National Conventions in 1896, 1900, and 1904; again elected to the United States Senate and served from March 4, 1901, to March 3, 1907; unsuccessful candidate for reelection in 1907; appointed Governor of the Canal Zone, Isthmus of Panama, by President Theodore Roosevelt on April 1, 1907; resigned in November 1909 and returned to his estate in Woodford County, Ky.; died in Washington, D. C., September 12, 1918; interment in the State Cemetery, Frankfort, Ky.

BLACKBURN, Robert E. Lee, a Representative from Kentucky; born on a farm near Furnace, Estill County, Ky., April 9, 1870; as an infant moved with his parents to Stanton, Powell County, Ky.; attended the county schools, and Elliott Academy at Kirksville, Madison County, Ky.; traveling salesman for an oil company 1891–1900; during the Spanish-American War served as a second lieutenant in Company C, Fourth Infantry, United States Volunteers; engaged in general merchandising at Stanton, Ky., and in agricultural pursuits 1900–1907; member of the State house of representatives in 1904 and 1905; served as clerk of the court of Powell County 1906 to 1910; was engaged in the insurance and stock brokerage business 1910–1919; moved to Lexington, Ky., in 1919 and continued the insurance and brokerage business; also engaged in the oil-development business; appointed a member of the State board of agriculture in 1926 and served until 1928; elected as a Republican to the Seventy-first Congress (March 4, 1929–March 3, 1931); unsuccessful candidate for reelection in 1930 to the Seventy-second Congress and for election in 1932 to the Seventy-third Congress; resumed his former activities in the oil business and resided in Lexington, Ky., until his death there on September 20, 1935; interment in Stanton Cemetery, Stanton, Ky.

BLACKBURN, William Jasper, a Representative from Louisiana; born on the Fourche de Mau, Randolph County, Ark., on July 24, 1820; received his early education from his mother; moved to Batesville in 1839 and learned the printer's trade; moved to Little Rock in 1845, to Fort Smith in 1846, and to Minden, La., in 1849, where he established the Minden Herald; moved to Homer, La., and established the Homer Iliad in 1859; member of the State constitutional convention in 1867; county judge of Claiborne Parish, La., for four years; upon the readmission of the State of Louisiana to representation was elected as a Republican to the Fortieth Congress and served from July 18, 1868, to March 3, 1869; was not a candidate for renomination in 1868; member of the State senate 1874–1878; returned to Little Rock, Ark., in 1880; published the Arkansas Republican from 1881 to 1884 and the Free South from 1885 to 1892; died in Little Rock, Ark., November 10, 1899; interment in Mount Holly Cemetery.

BLACKLEDGE, William (father of William Salter Blackledge), a Representative from North Carolina; born in Craven County, N. C.; member of the State house of commons 1797–1799 and again in 1809; elected as a Democrat to the Eighth, Ninth, and Tenth Congresses (March 4, 1803–March 3, 1809); unsuccessful candidate for reelection in 1808 to the Eleventh Congress; one of the managers appointed by the House of Representatives in 1804 to conduct the impeachment proceedings against John Pickering, judge of the United States District Court for New Hampshire; elected to the Twelfth Congress

(March 4, 1811–March 3, 1813); unsuccessful candidate for reelection in 1812 to the Thirteenth Congress; died at Spring Hill, Craven County, N. C., October 19, 1828.

BLACKLEDGE, William Salter (son of William Blackledge), a Representative from North Carolina; born in Pitt County, N. C., in 1793; moved to Craven County, N. C., and settled in New Bern; graduated from the University of North Carolina at Chapel Hill in 1813; member of the State house of commons in 1820; elected as a Democrat to the Sixteenth Congress to fill the vacancy caused by the death of Jesse Slocumb; reelected to the Seventeenth Congress and served from February 7, 1821, until March 3, 1823; died in New Bern, Craven County, N. C., March 21, 1857; interment in New Bern Cemetery.

BLACKMAR, Esbon, a Representative from New York; born in Freehold, Greene County, N. Y., June 19, 1805; attended the district schools and was graduated from the high school; engaged in the general merchandise business; member of the State senate in 1838 and 1841; elected as a Whig to the Thirtieth Congress to fill the vacancy caused by the death of John M. Holley and served from December 4, 1848, to March 3, 1849; resumed his former business activities; died in Newark, Wayne County, N. Y., on November 19, 1857; interment in Willow Avenue Cemetery.

BLACKMON, Fred Leonard, a Representative from Alabama; born at Lime Branch, Polk County, Ga., September 15, 1873; moved with his parents to Calhoun County, Ala., in 1883; attended the public schools in Dearmanville and Choccolocco, the State normal college at Jacksonville, Ala., Douglasville (Ga.) College, and Mountain City Business College, Chattanooga, Tenn.; was graduated from the law department of the University of Alabama at Tuscaloosa in 1894; was admitted to the bar in the same year and commenced practice in Anniston, Calhoun County, Ala.; city attorney for Anniston 1898–1902; member of the State senate 1900–1910; chairman of the congressional committee for the fourth Alabama district from 1906 until 1910, when he resigned; elected as a Democrat to the Sixty-second and to the four succeeding Congresses and served from March 4, 1911, until his death; had also been reelected to the Sixty-seventh Congress; died in Bartow, Polk County, Fla., on February 8, 1921; interment in the Hillside Cemetery, Anniston, Ala.

BLACKNEY, William Wallace, a Representative from Michigan; born in Clio, Genesee County, Mich., August 28, 1876; attended the public schools, Olivet College, Olivet, Mich., and Ferris School, Big Rapids, Mich.; moved to Flint, Mich., in 1904; served as county clerk of Genesee County 1905–1912; was graduated from the law department of the University of Michigan at Ann Arbor in 1912; was admitted to the bar the same year and commenced practice in Flint, Mich.; served as assistant prosecuting attorney of Genesee County 1913–1917; member of the Flint School Board 1924–1934; member of the Republican State central committee 1925–1930; instructor in the General Motors Co. technical night school for sixteen years; elected as a Republican to the Seventy-fourth Congress (January 3, 1935–January 3, 1937); unsuccessful candidate for reelection in 1936 to the Seventy-fifth Congress; elected to the Seventy-sixth and to the six succeeding Congresses (January 3, 1939–January 3, 1953); was not a candidate for renomination in 1952; retired; is a resident of Flint, Mich.

BLACKWELL, Julius W., a Representative from Tennessee; born in Virginia; attended the public schools; moved to Tennessee and settled in Athens, McMinn County; elected as a

Van Buren Democrat to the Twenty-sixth Congress (March 4, 1839–March 3, 1841); unsuccessful candidate for reelection in 1840 to the Twenty-seventh Congress; elected to the Twenty-eighth Congress (March 4, 1843–March 3, 1845); unsuccessful candidate for reelection in 1844 to the Twenty-ninth Congress.

BLAINE, James Gillespie, a Representative and a Senator from Maine; born in West Brownsville, Washington County, Pa., January 31, 1830; was graduated from Washington College, Washington, Pa., in 1847; was for a time teacher in the Western Military Institute, Blue Lick Springs, Ky.; returned to Pennsylvania; studied law; taught advanced subjects in the Pennsylvania Institution for the Blind at Philadelphia 1852–1854; moved in 1854 to Maine, where he edited the Portland Advertiser and the Kennebec Journal; member of the State house of representatives 1859–1862, serving the last two years as speaker; elected as a Republican to the Thirty-eighth and to the six succeeding Congresses and served from March 4, 1863, to July 10, 1876, when he resigned; served in the Forty-first, Forty-second, and Forty-third Congresses as Speaker; was a leading candidate for the nomination for President on the Republican ticket in 1876 and 1880; appointed and subsequently elected to the United States Senate to fill the vacancy caused by the resignation of Lot M. Morrill; reelected and served from July 10, 1876, to March 5, 1881, when he resigned to become Secretary of State in the Cabinet of President Garfield; Secretary of State of the United States from March 5 to December 12, 1881; unsuccessful Republican candidate for President of the United States in 1884; Secretary of State in the Cabinet of President Benjamin Harrison and served from March 7, 1889, to June 4, 1892, when he resigned; aided in organizing and was the first president of the Pan American Congress; died in Washington, D. C., January 27, 1893; interment in Oak Hill Cemetery; reinterment at the request of the State of Maine in the Blaine Memorial Park, Augusta, Maine, in June 1920.

BLAINE, John James, a Senator from Wisconsin; born on a farm in Wingville Township, Grant County, Wis., May 4, 1875; attended the common schools; was graduated from Montford (Wis.) High School, and from the law department of Valparaiso (Ind.) University in 1896; was admitted to the bar in 1896 and commenced practice in Montford; moved to Boscobel in 1897 and continued the practice of law; mayor of Boscobel 1901–1904 and 1906–1907; member of the Grant County Board of Supervisors 1901–1904; served in the State senate 1909–1913; unsuccessful candidate for Governor in 1914; delegate to the Republican National Conventions in 1916, 1920, and 1924; attorney general of the State of Wisconsin 1919–1921; Governor of Wisconsin 1921–1927; elected as a Republican to the United States Senate for the term beginning March 4, 1927, and ending March 3, 1933; unsuccessful candidate for renomination in 1932; resumed the practice of law at Boscobel; appointed a director of the Reconstruction Finance Corporation in 1933 and served until his death in Boscobel, Wis., April 18, 1934; interment in Hillside Cemetery.

BLAIR, Austin, a Representative from Michigan; born in Caroline, Tompkins County, N. Y., February 8, 1818; attended the common schools, Cazenovia Seminary, and Hamilton College, Clinton, N. Y.; was graduated from Union College, Schenectady, N. Y., in 1837; studied law in Oswego; was admitted to the bar in Tioga County, N. Y., in 1841; moved to Michigan and settled in Eaton Rapids, where he commenced the practice of his profession in 1842; county clerk of Eaton County; moved to Jackson, Mich., in 1844; elected to the State house of representatives in 1845; delegate to the Free-Soil National Convention at Buffalo, N. Y., in 1848; elected prosecuting attorney of

Jackson County in 1852; elected to the State senate in 1854; was present at the organization of the Republican Party in Jackson, Mich., on July 6, 1854, and was a member of the platform committee; delegate to the Republican National Convention at Chicago in 1860; Governor of Michigan from January 1, 1861, to January 1, 1865; elected as a Republican to the Fortieth, Forty-first, and Forty-second Congresses (March 4, 1867–March 3, 1873); was not a candidate for renomination in 1872, having become the Liberal Republican candidate for Governor, but was unsuccessful; resumed the practice of law in Jackson, Jackson County, Mich., and died there August 6, 1894; interment in Mount Evergreen Cemetery.

BLAIR, Bernard, a Representative from New York; born in Williamstown, Mass., May 24, 1801; attended the public schools and pursued preparatory studies; was graduated from Williams College, Williamstown, Mass., in 1825; moved to Salem, Washington County, N. Y., in 1825; studied law; was admitted to the bar in 1828 and commenced practice in Salem, subsequently being admitted as counselor and solicitor in chancery; elected as a Whig to the Twenty-seventh Congress (March 4, 1841–March 3, 1843); discontinued the practice of his profession and engaged in business pursuits; died in Salem, Washington County, N. Y., May 7, 1880; interment in Evergreen Cemetery.

BLAIR, Francis Preston, Jr., a Representative and a Senator from Missouri; born in Lexington, Ky., on February 19, 1821; when nine years of age moved with his father to Washington, D. C.; attended a private school in that city and the University of North Carolina at Chapel Hill; was graduated from Princeton College in 1841; studied law at Transylvania University, Lexington, Ky.; was admitted to the bar in 1842 and commenced practice in St. Louis in 1843; enlisted as a private in the regiment of Colonel Doniphan during the Mexican War, and served as attorney general of the Territory after General Kearny took New Mexico; resumed the practice of law in St. Louis; member of the State house of representatives 1852–1856; elected as a Free-Soiler to the Thirty-fifth Congress (March 4, 1857–March 3, 1859); successfully contested the election of John R. Barret to the Thirty-sixth Congress and served from June 8 to June 25, 1860, when he resigned; unsuccessful candidate for reelection to the Thirty-sixth Congress to fill the vacancy caused by his own resignation; delegate to the Republican National Convention at Chicago in 1860; elected to the Thirty-seventh Congress and served from March 4, 1861, until his resignation in July 1862 to become a colonel in the Union Army; served on the staff of Gen. William T. Sherman; presented credentials as a Member-elect to the Thirty-eighth Congress and served from March 4, 1863, to June 10, 1864, when he was succeeded by Samuel Knox, who contested the election; unsuccessful Democratic candidate for Vice President of the United States in 1868; again a member of the State house of representatives in 1870; elected as a Democrat to the United States Senate to fill the vacancy caused by the resignation of Charles D. Drake and served from January 20, 1871, to March 3, 1873; was not a candidate for reelection owing to ill health; State insurance commissioner in 1874; died in St. Louis, Mo., July 8, 1875; interment in Bellefontaine Cemetery; the people of Missouri erected a statue to his memory in Forest Park, St. Louis, and the State legislature presented to the United States Government the statue of him which stands in Statuary Hall of the Capitol, Washington, D. C.

BLAIR, Henry William, a Representative and a Senator from New Hampshire; born in Campton, Grafton County, N. H., December 6, 1834; attended the common schools and Tilton Academy; studied law; was admitted to the bar in 1859 and commenced practice in Plymouth, N. H.; appointed prosecuting attorney for Grafton County in 1860; during the Civil War served in the Union Army as lieutenant colonel of the Fifteenth Regiment, New Hampshire Volunteer Infantry; member of the State house of representatives in 1866; served in the State senate in 1867 and 1868; elected as a Republican to the Forty-fourth and Forty-fifth Congresses (March 4, 1875–March 3, 1879); was not a candidate for renomination in 1878; elected to the United States Senate on June 17, 1879, and took his seat June 20, 1879, for the vacancy in the term ending March 3, 1885; appointed on March 5, 1885, and elected on June 17, 1885, to fill the vacancy in the term beginning March 4, 1885, and served until March 3, 1891; unsuccessful candidate for renomination in the caucus in 1891; declined an appointment as judge of the district court for the district of New Hampshire tendered by President Harrison in 1891; was appointed Envoy Extraordinary and Minister Plenipotentiary to China March 6, 1891; he was objected to by the Chinese Government as being persona non grata, although our Government protested against the insufficiency of the objections; subsequently he tendered his resignation which was accepted October 6, 1891; elected to the Fifty-third Congress (March 4, 1893–March 3, 1895); was not a candidate for reelection in 1894; engaged in the practice of law in Washington, D. C., until his death on March 14, 1920; interment in Campton Cemetery, Campton, N. H.

BLAIR, Jacob Beeson, a Representative from Virginia and from West Virginia; born in Parkersburg, Wood County, Va. (now West Virginia), April 11, 1821; attended the public schools; studied law; was admitted to the bar in 1844 and commenced practice at Harrisville, Ritchie County, Va. (now West Virginia); prosecuting attorney of Ritchie County for several years; returned to Parkersburg in 1856; elected as a Unionist from Virginia to the Thirty-seventh Congress to fill the vacancy caused by the resignation of John S. Carlile and served from December 2, 1861, to March 3, 1863; upon the admission of West Virginia as a State into the Union was elected to the Thirty-eighth Congress and served from December 7, 1863, to March 3, 1865; United States Minister to Costa Rica 1868–1873; served as an associate justice of the supreme court of Wyoming 1876–1888; moved to Utah in 1888; probate judge for Salt Lake County, Utah, 1892–1895; surveyor general of Utah from 1897 until his death in Salt Lake City on February 12, 1901; interment in Mount Olivet Cemetery.

BLAIR, James, a Representative from South Carolina; born in the Waxhaw settlement, Lancaster County, S. C., about 1790; engaged in planting; sheriff of Lancaster District; elected as a Democrat to the Seventeenth Congress and served from March 4, 1821, to May 8, 1822, when he resigned; elected as a Union Democrat to the Twenty-first Congress; reelected as a Democrat to the Twenty-second and Twenty-third Congresses and served from March 4, 1829, until his death in Washington, D. C., April 1, 1834; interment in Congressional Cemetery.

BLAIR, James Gorrall, a Representative from Missouri; born near Blairville, Ky., January 1, 1825; was self-educated, having attended the public schools only three months; moved to Monticello, Lewis County, Mo., in 1840 and engaged in agricultural pursuits; elected circuit clerk in 1848 and served until 1854; studied law; was admitted to the bar and commenced practice in Canton, Mo., in 1854; delegate to the Republican State convention in 1870; elected as a Liberal Republican to the Forty-second Congress (March 4, 1871–March 3, 1873); was not a candidate for renomination in 1872; resumed the practice of law and also engaged in agricultural pursuits; died in Monticello, Lewis County, Mo., March 1, 1904; interment in Forest Grove Cemetery, Canton, Mo.

BLAIR, John, a Representative from Tennessee; born at Blairs Mill, near Jonesborough (now Jonesboro), Washington County, Tenn., September 13, 1790; attended Martain Academy, and was graduated from Washington (Tenn.) College in 1809; studied law; was admitted to the bar in 1813 and practiced; member of the State house of representatives 1815–1817; served in the State senate 1817–1821; elected as a Democrat to the Eighteenth and to the five succeeding Congresses (March 4, 1823–March 3, 1835); unsuccessful candidate for reelection in 1834 to the Twenty-fourth Congress; retired to private life; again a member of the State house of representatives, in 1849 and 1850; resumed the practice of law; died in Jonesboro, Tenn., July 9, 1863; interment in the Old Cemetery.

BLAIR, Samuel Steel, a Representative from Pennsylvania; born in Indiana, Indiana County, Pa., December 5, 1821; attended the public schools, and was graduated from Jefferson College, Canonsburg, Pa., in 1838; studied law; was admitted to the bar in 1845 and commenced practice in Hollidaysburg, Blair County, Pa., in 1846; delegate to several State conventions; delegate to the Republican National Convention at Philadelphia in 1856; elected as a Republican to the Thirty-sixth and Thirty-seventh Congresses (March 4, 1859–March 3, 1863); unsuccessful candidate for reelection in 1862 to the Thirty-eighth Congress; resumed the practice of law; unsuccessful candidate for election in 1874 to the Forty-fourth Congress; died in Hollidaysburg, Pa., December 8, 1890; interment in the Presbyterian Cemetery.

BLAISDELL, Daniel, a Representative from New Hampshire; born in Amesbury, Mass., January 22, 1762; attended the public schools; served in the Revolutionary War from August 1776 to August 1777; moved to Canaan, N. H., in 1780; taught school and also acquired some legal knowledge; engaged in agricultural pursuits; held several local offices; member of the State house of representatives in 1793, 1795, and 1799; served as a member of the executive council 1803–1808; moderator of Canaan in 1808, 1809, 1812, 1822, 1824, 1826, and 1830; elected as a Federalist to the Eleventh Congress (March 4, 1809–March 3, 1811); served in the War of 1812; again a member of the State house of representatives, in 1812, 1813, 1824, and 1825; served as selectman of Canaan in 1813, 1815, and 1818; resumed agricultural pursuits; member of the State senate in 1814 and 1815; chief justice of the court of sessions in 1822; died in Canaan, Grafton County, N. H., January 10, 1833; interment in Wells Cemetery.

BLAKE, Harrison Gray Otis, a Representative from Ohio; born in Newfane, Windham County, Vt., March 17, 1818; moved to Salem, N. Y., and in 1830 to Guilford, Medina County, Ohio; attended the public schools; studied medicine at Seville for one year; moved to Medina in 1836 and engaged in mercantile pursuits; also studied law; was admitted to the bar and commenced practice in Medina; member of the State house of representatives in 1846 and 1847; member of the State senate in 1848 and 1849, serving as its president; elected as a Republican to the Thirty-sixth Congress to fill the vacancy caused by the death of Cyrus Spink; reelected to the Thirty-seventh Congress and served from October 11, 1859, to March 3, 1863; was not a candidate for renomination in 1862 to the Thirty-eighth Congress; during the Civil War entered the Union Army in 1864 as colonel of the One Hundred and Sixty-sixth Regiment; declined the appointment of Governor of Idaho Territory; resumed the practice of law; also interested in banking and mercantile pursuits; delegate to the Loyalist Convention at Philadelphia in 1866; died in Medina, Medina County, Ohio, April 16, 1876; interment in Spring Grove Cemetery.

BLAKE, John, Jr., a Representative from New York; born in Ulster County, N. Y., December 5, 1762; attended the public schools; during the Revolutionary War served in the New York State Militia; appointed deputy sheriff of Ulster County in 1793; member of the State assembly 1798–1800; sheriff of Orange County 1803–1805; elected to the Ninth and Tenth Congresses (March 4, 1805–March 3, 1809); again a member of the State assembly in 1812 and 1813; judge of the court of common pleas for Orange County 1815–1818; again served in the State assembly in 1819; supervisor of the town of Montgomery fifteen terms; died in Montgomery, Orange County, N. Y., January 13, 1826; interment in the Berea Churchyard, near Newburgh, N. Y.

BLAKE, John Lauris, a Representative from New Jersey; born in Boston, Mass., March 25, 1831; received a classical education; moved to Orange, N. J., in 1846; studied law; was admitted to the bar in 1852 and commenced practice in Orange, N. J.; member of the State house of assembly in 1857; delegate to the Republican National Convention at Cincinnati in 1876; elected as a Republican to the Forty-sixth Congress (March 4, 1879–March 3, 1881); declined to be a candidate for renomination in 1880; resumed the practice of his profession in Orange; became president of the Citizens' Gas Light Co. of Newark, N. J., in 1893; died in West Orange, Essex County, N. J., October 10, 1899; interment in Rosedale Cemetery, Orange, N. J.

BLAKE, Thomas Holdsworth, a Representative from Indiana; born in Calvert County, Md., June 14, 1792; attended the public schools; studied law in Washington, D. C.; member of the militia of the District of Columbia which took part in the Battle of Bladensburg in 1814; moved to Kentucky and thence to Indiana; was admitted to the bar and commenced practice in Terre Haute, Ind.; prosecuting attorney and judge of the circuit court; abandoned the practice of law to engage in business; member of the State house of representatives; elected as an Adams Republican to the Twentieth Congress (March 4, 1827–March 3, 1829); was an unsuccessful candidate for reelection in 1828 to the Twenty-first Congress; declined to be a candidate for the Twenty-second Congress; was appointed Commissioner of the General Land Office by President Tyler on May 19, 1842, and served until April 1845; chosen president of the Erie & Wabash Canal Co.; visited England as financial agent of the State of Indiana and, while returning, died in Cincinnati, Ohio, November 28, 1849; interment in Woodlawn Cemetery, Terre Haute, Ind.

BLAKENEY, Albert Alexander, a Representative from Maryland; born in Riderwood, Baltimore County, Md., September 28, 1850; attended private schools; learned the business of cotton manufacturing and established the large cotton-duck mills located in Franklinville, Md.; commissioner of Baltimore County 1895–1899; elected as a Republican to the Fifty-seventh Congress (March 4, 1901–March 3, 1903); declined to be a candidate for renomination in 1902; resumed his former business activities in Franklinville, Baltimore County, Md.; elected to the Sixty-seventh Congress (March 4, 1921–March 3, 1923); unsuccessful candidate for reelection in 1922 to the Sixty-eighth Congress; died in Baltimore, Md., October 15, 1924; interment in the Baltimore Cemetery.

BLAKLEY, William A., a Senator from Texas; born in Miami Station, Saline County, Mo., November 17, 1898; moved with his parents to Arapaho, Custer County, Okla., and graduated from Arapaho High School; during the First World War served in the United States Army; attorney and certified public accountant in Dallas, Tex., since 1924; has interests in oil fields, ranching, and real estate; appointed as a Democrat by Gov. Allan Shivers to the United States Senate to fill the vacancy caused by the resignation of Price Daniel and served from January 15, 1957, to April 28, 1957; declined to be a candidate for election to the vacancy; unsuccessful candidate for the Democratic nomination for a full term to the United States Senate in 1958; appointed to the United States Senate to fill the vacancy caused by the resignation of Lyndon B. Johnson and served from January 3, 1961, to June 14, 1961; was unsuccessful for election to fill the vacancy; resumed former business interests; is a resident of Dallas, Tex.

BLANCHARD, George Washington, a Representative from Wisconsin; born in Colby, Marathon County, Wis., January 26, 1884; attended the graded and high schools; was graduated from the University of Wisconsin at Madison in 1906 and from its law department in 1910; was admitted to the bar in 1910 and commenced practice in Edgerton, Rock County, Wis.; city attorney of Edgerton from 1912 until his resignation in 1932, having been elected to Congress; member of the State assembly 1925–1927; served in the State senate 1927–1933; elected as a Republican to the Seventy-third Congress (March 3, 1933–January 3, 1935); was a candidate for renomination, but withdrew after being nominated; resumed the practice of law in Edgerton, Wis., where he now resides.

BLANCHARD, John, a Representative from Pennsylvania; born in Peacham Township, Caledonia County, Vt., September 30, 1787; attended the common schools; taught school; was graduated from Dartmouth College, Hanover, N. H., in 1812; moved to Pennsylvania and settled in York, York County, in 1812, where he again taught school; studied law; was admitted to the bar March 31, 1815, and commenced practice in Lewistown, Mifflin County, Pa.; moved to Bellefonte the same year and continued the practice of law; elected as a Whig to the Twenty-ninth and Thirtieth Congresses (March 4, 1845–March 3, 1849); was not a candidate for renomination in 1848; died in Columbia, Lancaster County, Pa., en route from Washington, D. C., to his home, March 9, 1849; interment in Union Cemetery, Bellefonte, Centre County, Pa.

BLANCHARD, Jonathan, a Delegate from New Hampshire; born in Dunstable, N. H., September 18, 1738; attended the public schools; chosen a member of the council of twelve in 1775; delegate to the Fifth Provincial Congress in 1775; served in the first house of representatives of the State in 1776; appointed State attorney general in 1777; member of the committee of safety in 1777 and 1778; one of the commissioners from New Hampshire to the convention at New Haven, Conn., in 1778 to regulate prices; Member of the Continental Congress in 1783, 1784, and 1787; first judge of probate under the State constitution of 1784; brigadier general of militia 1784–1788; died in Dunstable, N. H., July 16, 1788; interment in the Old South Burying Ground at Dunstable, now merged into the town of Nashua, N. H.

BLANCHARD, Newton Crain, a Representative and a Senator from Louisiana; born in Rapides Parish, La., January 29, 1849; completed academic studies; studied law in Alexandria, La., in 1868 and was graduated from the law department of the University of Louisiana in 1870; was admitted to the bar and commenced practice in Shreveport, La., in 1871; elected chairman of the Democratic committee of Caddo Parish in 1876; delegate to the State constitutional convention in 1879; appointed major on the staffs of Governors Wiltz and McEnery; trustee for Louisiana of the University of the South at Sewanee, Tenn.; elected as a Democrat to the Forty-seventh and to the six succeeding Con-

gresses and served from March 4, 1881, until his resignation, effective March 12, 1894; appointed and subsequently elected to the United States Senate to fill the vacancy caused by the resignation of Edward D. White and served from March 12, 1894, to March 3, 1897; was not a candidate for reelection; delegate to the Democratic National Conventions in 1896 and 1912; elected associate justice of the supreme court of Louisiana and served from 1897 to 1903, when he resigned; elected Governor of Louisiana and served from 1904 to 1908; resumed the practice of law in Shreveport, La.; member of the State constitutional convention in 1913 and served as president; died in Shreveport, La., June 22, 1922; interment in Greenwood Cemetery.

BLAND, Oscar Edward, a Representative from Indiana; born near Bloomfield, Green County, Ind., November 21, 1877; attended the public schools, Valparaiso University, Valparaiso, Ind., and the University of Indiana at Bloomington; taught school for three years; studied law; was admitted to the bar in 1901 and commenced practice in Linton, Ind.; member of the State senate 1907–1909; unsuccessful Republican candidate for election to Congress in 1910, 1912, and 1914; elected as a Republican to the Sixty-fifth, Sixty-sixth, and Sixty-seventh Congresses (March 4, 1917–March 3, 1923); unsuccessful candidate for reelection in 1922 to the Sixty-eighth Congress; appointed by President Warren G. Harding as associate judge of the United States Court of Customs Appeals (now the United States Court of Customs and Patent Appeals) on March 4, 1923, and served until his resignation on December 1, 1949; resumed the private practice of law in Washington, D. C., where he died August 3, 1951; interment in Fort Lincoln Cemetery.

BLAND, Richard (uncle of Theodorick Bland), a Delegate from Virginia; born in Orange County, Va., May 6, 1710; completed preparatory studies; was graduated from William and Mary College, Williamsburg, Va., and the University of Edinburgh; member of the Virginia House of Burgesses 1745–1775; was known as "The Virginia Antiquary"; member of the Virginia Committee of Correspondence in 1773; took a leading part in the Revolutionary War; Member of the Continental Congress in 1774 and 1775; again chosen, but declined to serve; member of the Revolutionary conventions of 1775 and 1776; died in Williamsburg, Va., October 26, 1776; interment in a private cemetery on the Jordan Point plantation, on the James River.

BLAND, Richard Parks, a Representative from Missouri; born near Hartford, Ohio County, Ky., August 19, 1835; received an academic education; moved to Missouri in 1855, thence to California, and later to that portion of Utah which is now the State of Nevada; taught school for several years; studied law; was admitted to the bar and commenced practice in Virginia City; also interested in mining; treasurer of Carson County from 1860 until the organization of the State government of Nevada; returned to Missouri in 1865 and continued the practice of law in Rolla; moved to Lebanon, Laclede County, in August 1869; elected as a Democrat to the Forty-third and to the ten succeeding Congresses (March 4, 1873–March 3, 1895); unsuccessful candidate for reelection in 1894 to the Fifty-fourth Congress; elected to the Fifty-fifth and Fifty-sixth Congresses and served from March 4, 1897, until his death; in 1896 was a prominent candidate for the Democratic nomination for President, receiving two hundred and ninety votes; died in Lebanon, Mo., June 15, 1899; interment in Lebanon Cemetery.

BLAND, Schuyler Otis, a Representative from Virginia; born near Gloucester, Gloucester County, Va., May 4, 1872; attended private schools, Gloucester (Va.) Academy, and William and Mary College, Williamsburg, Va.; taught school in Accomac and

Northampton Counties for several years; studied law; was admitted to the bar in 1900 and commenced practice in Newport News, Va.; served at different periods as president of the Newport News Chamber of Commerce; vice president of the Virginia State Bar Association and president of the Newport News Bar Association; elected as a Democrat to the Sixty-fifth Congress to fill the vacancy caused by the death of William A. Jones; reelected to the Sixty-sixth and to the fifteen succeeding Congresses and served from July 2, 1918, until his death at the naval hospital, Bethesda, Md., February 16, 1950; interment in Greenlawn Cemetery, Newport News, Va.

BLAND, Theodorick (nephew of Richard Bland), a Delegate and a Representative from Virginia; born at Cawsons, on the Appomattox River, near Petersburg, Prince George County, Va., March 21, 1742; was sent to England to be educated; studied medicine in Edinburgh and was admitted to practice; returned to his home in 1759 and engaged in extensive practice; took an active part in the Revolutionary War; entered the Continental Army as captain of the First Troop of Virginia Cavalry; Member of the Continental Congress 1780–1783; appointed by Governor Henry as lieutenant of Prince George County Militia in 1785; member of the Virginia convention of 1788 on the adoption of the Federal Constitution and was one of the minority which opposed its ratification; elected to the First Congress and served from March 4, 1789, until his death in New York City June 1, 1790; interment in Trinity Churchyard; reinterred in the Congressional Cemetery, Washington, D. C., August 31, 1828.

BLAND, William Thomas (grandson of John George Jackson and cousin of James Monroe Jackson), a Representative from Missouri; born in Weston, Lewis County, Va. (now West Virginia), January 21, 1861; was graduated from the University of West Virginia at Morgantown in 1883 and from the law department of that university in 1884; took a special course in law at the University of Virginia at Charlottesville in 1885; was admitted to the bar and commenced practice in Weston, W. Va.; moved to Atchison, Kans., in 1887; prosecuting attorney of Atchison County, Kans., 1890–1892; declined a reelection; mayor of Atchison in 1894; elected judge of the second Kansas district in 1896; reelected in 1900, and served until 1901, when he resigned; engaged in the wholesale drug business in 1901; moved to Kansas City, Mo., in 1904 and continued in business as a wholesale druggist; retired from the drug business in 1917 and engaged in banking; elected president of the Manufacturers and Merchants' Association in 1907 and president of the Kansas City Chamber of Commerce in 1909; chairman of the Kansas City River and Harbor Improvement Commission 1909–1918; director of the National Rivers and Harbors Congress; vice president of the Mississippi Valley Waterway Association; elected to the Kansas City Board of Education in 1912 for a six-year term and served as vice president and president; chairman of the first Liberty loan campaign and also chairman of the Missouri and Kansas Red Cross drives during the First World War; elected as a Democrat to the Sixty-sixth Congress (March 4, 1919–March 3, 1921); unsuccessful candidate for reelection in 1920 to the Sixty-seventh Congress; moved to Florida and settled in Orlando in 1921; engaged in banking; served as a member of the Orlando Utilities Commission for three years; died in Orlando, Orange County, Fla., January 15, 1928; interment in Greenwood Cemetery.

BLANTON, Thomas Lindsay, a Representative from Texas; born in Houston, Harris County, Tex., October 25, 1872; educated in the public schools; was graduated from the law department of the University of Texas at Austin in 1897, with three years in the academic department; was admitted to the bar in 1897 and commenced practice in Cleburne, Tex.; moved to Albany, Tex., and continued the practice of law until 1908, when he was elected judge of the forty-second judicial district of Texas; reelected in 1912 and served in that capacity from 1908 until elected to Congress; elected as a Democrat to the Sixty-fifth and to the five succeeding Congresses (March 4, 1917–March 3, 1929); was not a candidate for renomination in 1928, but was an unsuccessful candidate for nomination to the United States Senate; subsequently elected on May 20, 1930, to the Seventy-first Congress to fill the vacancy caused by the death of Robert Q. Lee; reelected to the Seventy-second, Seventy-third, and Seventy-fourth Congresses and served from May 20, 1930, to January 3, 1937; unsuccessful candidate for renomination in 1936; engaged in the practice of law in Washington, D. C., in 1937 and 1938; returned to Albany, Tex., in 1938, and continued practicing law; also engaged in the raising of Hereford cattle; died in Albany, Tex., August 11, 1957; interment in Albany Cemetery.

BLATNIK, John Anton, a Representative from Minnesota; born in Chisholm, St. Louis County, Minn., August 17, 1911; attended the public schools and was graduated from Chisholm High School in June 1929; taught a one-room rural school in St. Louis County in 1930 and 1931; was graduated from State Teachers College, Winona, Minn., in June 1935; also attended the University of Chicago during summer of 1938 and the University of Minnesota at Minneapolis in 1941 and 1942; engaged in CCC work in Superior National Forest in Minnesota from September 1935 to September 1937; taught chemistry in high school at Chisholm, Minn., from September 1937 to June 1939; assistant county superintendent of schools of St. Louis County, Minn., from June 1939 to September 1941; member of the State senate 1941–1946; during World War II served with the United States Army Air Forces and the Office of Strategic Services from August 1942 until his discharge as a captain on January 1946 with eighteen months' service overseas; awarded the Bronze Star Medal with Oak Leaf Cluster and the Air Medal; elected as a Democrat to the Eightieth and to the six succeeding Congresses (January 3, 1947–January 3, 1961). *Reelected to the Eighty-seventh Congress.*

BLEAKLEY, Orrin Dubbs, a Representative from Pennsylvania; born in Franklin, Venango County, Pa., May 15, 1854; attended the common schools, the local academy of his native city, and the University of Bonn, Bonn, Prussia; engaged in banking with his father until 1876; interested in the production of oil from 1876 to 1883; organized the Franklin Trust Company in the latter year, and became its president; delegate at large to the Republican National Convention at Chicago in 1904; served as chairman of the Venango County Republican committee; elected as a Republican to the Sixty-fifth Congress and served from March 4 to April 3, 1917, when he resigned without having qualified; resumed banking in Franklin, Pa.; died in Robinson, Ill., December 3, 1927; interment in Franklin Cemetery, Franklin, Pa.

BLEASE, Coleman Livingston, a Senator from South Carolina; born near Newberry, Newberry County, S. C., October 8, 1868; attended the common schools, and was graduated from the law department of Georgetown University, Washington, D. C., in 1889; was admitted to the bar the same year and commenced practice in Newberry, S. C.; member of the State house of representatives 1890–1894, 1899, and 1900, serving as speaker pro tempore 1892–1894; mayor of Helena, S. C., in 1897; presidential elector on the Democratic ticket of Bryan and Sewell in 1896 and of Bryan and Stevenson in 1900; delegate to several State conventions, being president of the Democratic State convention in 1926; member of the Democratic State executive committee for eighteen years; city attorney of Newberry in 1901 and 1902; member of the State senate 1905–1909, serving as president pro tempore in 1906 and 1907; mayor of Newberry in 1910; Governor of South Carolina 1911–1915; elected as a Democrat to the United States Senate and served from March 4, 1925, to March 3, 1931; unsuccessful candidate for renomination in 1930; unsuccessful candidate for the Democratic gubernatorial nominations in 1934 and 1938; elected a member of the State unemployment compensation commission for a four-year term beginning in 1941; died in Columbia, S. C., January 19, 1942; interment in Rosemont Cemetery, Newberry, S. C.

BLEDSOE, Jesse (uncle of Robert Emmett Bledsoe Baylor), a Senator from Kentucky; born in Culpeper County, Va., April 6, 1776; when quite young moved with an elder brother to Kentucky; attended Transylvania Seminary and Transylvania University, Lexington, Ky.; studied law in Lexington; was admitted to the bar about 1800 and practiced; appointed secretary of state under Gov. Charles Scott in 1808; member of the State house of representatives in 1812; elected to the United States Senate and served from March 4, 1813, until his resignation on December 24, 1814; member of the State senate 1817–1820; presidential elector on the Democratic ticket in 1820; judge of the Lexington circuit in 1822; settled in Lexington and was professor of law in Transylvania University; minister in the Disciples Church; moved to Mississippi in 1833 and to Texas in 1835; was engaged in collecting historical material at the time of his death; died near Nacogdoches, Nacogdoches County, Tex., June 25, 1836.

BLEECKER, Harmanus, a Representative from New York; born in Albany, N. Y., October 9, 1779; studied law; was admitted to the bar in 1801 and commenced practice in Albany; elected as a Federalist to the Twelfth Congress (March 4, 1811–March 3, 1813); was not a candidate for renomination in 1812; resumed the practice of law in Albany, N. Y.; member of the State assembly in 1814 and 1815; regent of the University of the State of New York 1822–1834; Chargé d'Affaires to the Netherlands May 12, 1837, to June 28, 1842; retired from public life and business pursuits; died in Albany, N. Y., July 19, 1849; interment in the Rural Cemetery.

BLISS, Aaron Thomas, a Representative from Michigan; born in Peterboro, Madison County, N. Y., May 22, 1837; attended the common schools; employed as a clerk in a store in Morrisville, N. Y., in 1853 and 1854; attended a select school in Munnsville, N. Y., in 1854; moved to Bouckville, N. Y., in 1855 and engaged in mercantile pursuits; during the Civil War enlisted as a private in the Tenth Regiment, New York Volunteer Cavalry, October 1, 1861; served three years, being confined six months of this time in the prisons of Andersonville, Charleston, Macon, and Columbia; made his escape from Columbia, and after eighteen nights of travel through enemy territory reached the Union lines; rose while in the service from private to captain; moved to Saginaw, Mich., in December 1865 and engaged in the manufacture of lumber; member of the State senate in 1882; appointed aide-de-camp on the staff of Governor Alger in 1885; held the same position on the staff of the commander in chief of the Grand Army of the Republic in 1888; elected as a Republican to the Fifty-first Congress (March 4, 1889–March 3, 1891); unsuccessful candidate for reelection in 1890 to the Fifty-second Congress; resumed the lumber business and also engaged in banking; department commander of the Grand Army of the Republic in Michigan in 1897; Governor of Michigan 1900–1904; died in Milwaukee, Wis., September 16, 1906, while on a visit for medical treatment; interment in Forest Lawn Cemetery, Saginaw, Mich.

BLISS, Archibald Meserole, a Representative from New York; born in Brooklyn, N. Y., January 25, 1838; attended the common schools; alderman of Brooklyn, N. Y., 1864–1867, serving as president of the board of aldermen in 1866; unsuccessful Republican candidate for mayor of Brooklyn in 1867; delegate to the Republican National Convention at Baltimore in 1864 and at Chicago in 1868, to the Liberal National Convention at Cincinnati in 1872, and to the Democratic National Conventions in 1876, 1880, 1884, and 1888; member of the board of water commissioners of Brooklyn in 1871 and 1872; president and vice president of the Bushwick Railroad Co. 1868–1878; director of the New York & Long Island Bridge Co.; elected as a Democrat to the Forty-fourth and to the three succeeding Congresses (March 4, 1875–March 3, 1883); was not a candidate for renomination in 1882 to the Forty-eighth Congress; elected to the Forty-ninth and Fiftieth Congresses (March 4, 1885–March 3, 1889); was not a candidate for renomination in 1888 to the Fifty-first Congress; engaged in the real-estate business in Washington, D. C., until his death there on March 19, 1923; interment in Cypress Hills Cemetery, Brooklyn, N. Y.

BLISS, George, a Representative from Ohio; born in Jericho. Vt., January 1, 1813; attended Granville College; studied law; was admitted to the bar in 1841 and commenced practice in Akron, Ohio; appointed presiding judge of the eighth judicial district in 1850 and served until the office was discontinued, owing to a change in the constitution; elected as a Democrat to the Thirty-third Congress (March 4, 1853–March 3, 1855); was a candidate for renomination in 1855 but subsequently withdrew; moved to Wooster, Ohio, and continued the practice of law; elected to the Thirty-eighth Congress (March 4, 1863–March 3, 1865); unsuccessful candidate for reelection in 1864 to the Thirty-ninth Congress; delegate to the Union National Convention at Philadelphia in 1866; died in Wooster, Ohio, October 24, 1868; interment in Oak Hill Cemetery.

BLISS, Philemon, a Representative from Ohio; born in Canton, Conn., July 28, 1813; attended Fairfield Academy and Hamilton College; studied law; was admitted to the bar in 1840 and commenced practice at Cuyahoga Falls, Ohio; later practiced in Elyria, Ohio; presiding judge of the fourteenth judicial circuit of Ohio 1848–1851; elected as a Republican to the Thirty-fourth and Thirty-fifth Congresses (March 4, 1855–March 3, 1859); was not a candidate for renomination in 1858; appointed chief justice of the supreme court of the Territory of Dakota by President Lincoln in 1861; subsequently moved to St. Joseph, Mo.; associate justice of the supreme court of Missouri 1868–1872; dean of the law division of the State University of Missouri at Columbia 1872–1889; died in St. Paul, Minn., August 25, 1889; interment in the Columbia Cemetery, Columbia, Mo.

BLITCH, Iris Faircloth, a Representative from Georgia; born in Toombs County, near Vidalia, Ga., April 25, 1912; attended the public schools of Vidalia, Douglas, Fitzgerald, and Homerville, Ga., and Hagerstown, Md.; student at the University of Georgia at Athens in 1929 and attended South Georgia College at Douglas in 1949; associated with husband in drug business, naval stores operations, and farming in Homerville, Ga.; unsuccessful candidate for election to the State house of representatives in 1940; elected to the State senate in 1946; elected to the State house of representatives in 1948 and defeated for reelection in 1950; again elected to the State senate in 1952 and served until December 31, 1954; Democratic national committeewoman for Georgia 1948–1956; elected as a Democrat to the Eighty-fourth, Eighty-fifth, and Eighty-sixth Congresses (January 3, 1955–January 3, 1961). *Reelected to the Eighty-seventh Congress.*

BLODGETT, Rufus, a Senator from New Jersey; born in Dorchester, N. H., October 9, 1834; attended the common schools and Wentworth (N. H.) Academy; learned the machinist's trade; moved to New Jersey in 1866 and settled in Long Branch; builder of railroad equipment; president of the Long Branch City Bank; member of the State assembly in 1878 and 1879; delegate to the Democratic National Conventions in 1880 and 1896; superintendent of the New York & Long Branch Railroad 1884–1910; elected as a Democrat to the United States Senate and served from March 4, 1887, to March 3, 1893; was not a candidate for reelection; mayor of Long Branch 1893–1898; engaged in the railroad business and in banking; died in Long Branch, Monmouth County, N. J., October 3, 1910; interment in Village Cemetery, Wentworth, Grafton County, N. H.

BLOODWORTH, Timothy, a Delegate, a Representative, and a Senator from North Carolina; born in New Hanover County, N. C., in 1736; educated at his own expense; was a master of many trades but subsequently became a teacher; in June 1776 was employed in making muskets and bayonets for the Continental Army; member of the State house of commons in 1778 and 1779; treasurer of Wilmington District in 1781 and 1782; appointed commissioner of confiscated property in 1783; Member of the Continental Congress from 1786 to August 13, 1787, when he resigned; served in the State senate in 1788 and 1789; elected to the First Congress and served from April 6, 1790, to March 3, 1791; member of the State house of representatives in 1793 and 1794; elected to the United States Senate and served from March 4, 1795, to March 3, 1801; collector of customs at Wilmington; died in Wilmington, N. C., August 24, 1814.

BLOOM, Isaac, a Representative from New York, born in Jamaica, Queens County, N. Y., about 1716; moved to Dutchess County about 1740; captain of minutemen of Charlotte precinct, Dutchess County, in 1775; was engaged in mercantile pursuits in 1784; member of the State assembly 1788–1792; delegate to the State convention in 1801; served in the State senate 1800–1802; elected to the Eighth Congress and served from March 4, 1803, until his death in Clinton, Dutchess County, N. Y., April 26, 1803; interment probably in Jamaica.

BLOOM, Sol, a Representative from New York; born in Pekin, Tazewell County, Ill., March 9, 1870; moved with his parents to San Francisco, Calif., in 1873; attended the public schools; engaged in the newspaper, theatrical, and music-publishing businesses; superintendent of construction of the Midway Plaisance at the World's Columbian Exposition at Chicago in 1893; moved to New York City in 1903 and engaged in the real estate and construction business; captain in the New York Naval Reserve in 1917; director of the United States George Washington Bicentennial Commission; director general of the United States Constitution Sesquicentennial Commission; chairman of the Committee on Celebration of the One Hundred and Fiftieth Anniversary of the United States Supreme Court; director and United States Commissioner, New York World's Fair, in 1939; elected as a Democrat to the Sixty-eighth Congress on January 30, 1923, to fill the vacancy caused by the death of Representative-elect Samuel Marx; reelected to the Sixty-ninth and to the twelve succeeding Congresses and served from March 4, 1923, until his death in Washington, D. C., March 7, 1949; interment in Mount Eden Cemetery, Westchester Hills, N. Y.

BLOOMFIELD, Joseph, a Representative from New Jersey; born in Woodbridge, Middlesex County, N. J., October 5, 1753; educated at Rev. Enoch Green's school in Deerfield, N. J.; studied law; was admitted to the bar in 1775 and commenced practice in Bridgeton, N. J.; entered the Revolutionary Army as captain of the Third New Jersey Regiment on February 9, 1776; attained the rank of major; resumed the practice of law in Burlington, N. J.; registrar of the admiralty court 1779–1783; State attorney general from 1783 to 1792, when he resigned; presidential elector on the Washington and Adams ticket in 1792; trustee of Princeton College from 1793 until his resignation in 1801; Governor of New Jersey 1801–1812; commissioned brigadier general on March 13, 1812. and served until June 15, 1815; elected as a Democrat to the Fifteenth and Sixteenth Congresses (March 4, 1817–March 3, 1821); unsuccessful candidate for reelection to the Seventeenth Congress; died in Burlington, Burlington County, N. J., October 3, 1823; interment in St. Mary's Episcopal Churchyard.

BLOUNT, James Henderson, a Representative from Georgia; born near Clinton, Jones County, Ga., September 12, 1837; attended private schools in Clinton, Ga., and Tuscaloosa, Ala.; was graduated from the University of Georgia at Athens in 1858; studied law; was admitted to the bar in 1859 and commenced practice in Clinton, Jones County, Ga.; moved to Macon, Ga., in 1872 and continued the practice of law; during the Civil War served in the Confererate Army as a private in the Second Georgia Battalion, Floyd Rifles, for two years, and was later lieutenant colonel for two years; delegate to the State constitutional convention in 1865; elected as a Democrat to the Forty-third and to the nine succeeding Congresses (March 4, 1873–March 3, 1893); was not a candidate for renomination in 1892; appointed by President Cleveland commissioner to the Hawaiian Islands on March 20, 1893; retired from that position in 1893 and devoted his time to his plantation interests; died in Macon, Ga., March 8, 1903; interment in Rose Hill Cemetery.

BLOUNT, Thomas (brother of William Blount and uncle of William Grainger Blount), a Representative from North Carolina; born at "Blount Hall," Craven (now Pitt) County, N. C., May 10, 1759; educated at home; at the age of sixteen years entered the Continental Army; was captured and sent to England as a prisoner of war; after the Revolutionary War engaged in the mercantile business in Tarboro, Edgecombe County, N. C.; member of the State house of commons in 1788; elected as a Democrat to the Third, Fourth, and Fifth Congresses (March 4, 1793–March 3, 1799); unsuccessful candidate for reelection in 1802 to the Eighth Congress; elected to the Ninth and Tenth Congresses (March 4, 1805–March 3, 1809); unsuccessful candidate for election in 1808 to the Eleventh Congress; elected to the Twelfth Congress and served from March 4, 1811, until his death in Washington, D. C., February 7, 1812; interment in the Congressional Cemetery.

BLOUNT, William (father of William Grainger Blount and brother of Thomas Blount), a Delegate from North Carolina and a Senator from Tennessee; born near Windsor, Bertie County, N. C., March 26, 1749; pursued preparatory studies in New Bern, N. C.; paymaster of the Continental troops, North Carolina Line, in 1777; served in the State house of commons 1780–1784; Member of the Continental Congress in 1782, 1783, 1786, and 1787; delegate to the convention that framed the Federal Constitution in 1787; member of the State senate 1788–1790; appointed Governor of the Territory South of the River Ohio by President Washington in 1790; Superintendent of Indian Affairs 1790–1796; chairman of the convention which framed the first State constitution of Tennessee, February 6, 1796; upon the admission of Tennessee as a State into the Union was elected to the United States Senate and served from August 2, 1796, until he was found guilty "of a high misdemeanor, entirely inconsistent with his public trust and duty as a Senator," and was expelled July 8, 1797; was active in a plan to incite the Creeks and Cherokees to aid the British in conquering the Spanish territory of West Florida; impeachment proceedings were instituted but dismissed; during the trial was elected to the State senate of Tennessee and chosen its president at the opening of the session, December 3, 1797; died in Knoxville, Tenn., March 21, 1800; interment in the First Presbyterian Church Cemetery.

BLOUNT, William Grainger (son of William Blount and nephew of Thomas Blount), a Representative from Tennessee; born near New Bern, Craven County, N. C., in 1784; attended the New Bern Academy; moved with his parents to Knoxville, Tenn., in 1792; studied law; was admitted to the bar in 1805 and commenced practice in Knoxville, Tenn.; also engaged in agricultural pursuits; member of State house of representatives in 1811; secretary of state of Tennessee 1811–1815; elected as a Democrat to the Fourteenth Congress to fill the vacancy caused by the death of John Sevier; reelected to the Fifteenth Congress and served from December 8, 1815, to March 3, 1819; declined to be a candidate for renomination; resumed the practice of his profession in Knoxville; moved to Paris, Henry County, Tenn., in 1826 and continued the practice of law until his death on May 21, 1827; interment in the City Cemetery.

BLOW, Henry Taylor, a Representative from Missouri; born in Southampton County, Va., July 15, 1817; moved to St. Louis, Mo., in 1830; attended St. Louis University in 1830 and 1831; engaged in the paint and oil business and later became especially interested in lead mines; member of the State senate 1854–1858; served as Minister Resident at Venezuela from June 8, 1861, to February 22, 1862; elected as a Republican to the Thirty-eighth and Thirty-ninth Congresses (March 4, 1863–March 3, 1867); was not a candidate for renomination in 1866; resumed his former business pursuits; Minister to Brazil from May 1, 1869, to February 11, 1871; was a member of the Board of Commissioners of the District of Columbia in 1874 and 1875; died in Saratoga, Saratoga County, N. Y., September 11, 1875; interment in Bellefontaine Cemetery, St. Louis, Mo.

BLUE, Richard Whiting, a Representative from Kansas; born near Parkersburg, Wood County, Va. (now West Virginia), September 8, 1841; worked on a farm in the summertime and studied in the select schools of that locality during the winter season; attended Monongalia Academy, Morgantown, Va., in 1859 and Washington (Pa.) College until his enlistment, on June 29, 1863, as a private in Company A, Third Regiment, West Virginia Volunteer Infantry, during the Civil War; became second and then first lieutenant of the company; wounded in the Battle of Rocky Gap, West Virginia, August 26, 1863; prisoner of war in Libby Prison, Richmond, Va., and in Danville, Va., from October to December 1864; honorably discharged May 22, 1866, at Leavenworth, Kans., when he returned to Grafton, W. Va.; taught school; studied law; was admitted to the bar in Virginia, and commenced practice in Linn County, Kans., in 1871; probate judge of Linn County 1872–1876; county attorney 1876–1880; member of the State senate 1880–1888; elected as a Republican to the Fifty-fourth Congress (March 4, 1895–March 3, 1897); unsuccessful candidate for reelection in 1896 to the Fifty-fifth Congress; engaged in the practice of law until his death in Bartlesville, Washington County, Okla., January 28, 1907; interment in Pleasanton Cemetery, Pleasanton, Linn County, Kans.

BOARDMAN, Elijah (father of William Whiting Boardman), a Senator from Connecticut; born in New Milford, Conn., March 7, 1760; educated under private tutors; served in the Revolutionary War in Col. Charles Webb's regiment; employed as clerk in a mercantile establishment; engaged in mercantile pursuits 1781–1812; served in the State house of representatives 1803–1805 and again in 1816; member of the upper house, as it was then called, in 1817 and 1818; when the new State constitution was adopted served in the State senate 1819–1821; elected as a Democrat to the United States Senate and served from March 4, 1821, until his death while on a visit to Boardman, Ohio, October 8, 1823; interment in the Center Cemetery, New Milford, Conn.

BOARDMAN, William Whiting (son of Elijah Boardman), a Representative from Connecticut; born in New Milford, Conn., October 10, 1794; attended Bacon Academy, Colchester, Conn.; was graduated from Yale College in 1812; studied law in Cambridge and Litchfield Law Schools and commenced the practice of his profession in New Haven in 1819; clerk of the State senate in 1820; judge of probate; member of the State house of representatives 1836–1839, serving as speaker in 1836 and 1839; elected as a Whig to the Twenty-sixth Congress to fill the vacancy caused by the resignation of William L. Storrs; reelected to the Twenty-seventh Congress and served from December 7, 1840, to March 3, 1843; was not a candidate for renomination in 1842 to the Twenty-eighth Congress; member of the State house of representatives in 1845, 1849, and 1851, serving as speaker in 1845; resumed the practice of law; died in New Haven, Conn., August 27, 1871; interment in Grove Street Cemetery.

BOARMAN, Alexander (Aleck), a Representative from Louisiana; born in Yazoo City, Yazoo County, Miss., December 10, 1839; lost his parents in infancy and was raised by relatives in Shreveport, Caddo Parish, La.; attended the common schools of Shreveport, La., and Kentucky Military Institute at Frankfort; was graduated from the University of Kentucky at Lexington in 1860; at the outbreak of the Civil War enlisted in the Confederate Army and served as lieutenant of the Caddo Rifles; was subsequently promoted to the rank of captain and served throughout the war; studied law; was admitted to the bar in 1866 and commenced practice in Shreveport, La.; mayor of Shreveport from May 7, 1866, to August 8, 1867; city attorney of Shreveport 1868–1872; unsuccessful candidate for election as secretary of state in 1872; elected as a Liberal to the Forty-second Congress to fill the vacancy caused by the death of Representative-elect James McCleery and served from December 3, 1872, to March 3, 1873; unsuccessful candidate for renomination in 1872; resumed the practice of law in Shreveport, La.; judge of the tenth judicial district court, Caddo Parish, La., 1877–1880; appointed United States judge for the western district of Louisiana by President Garfield on May 18, 1881, and served until his death, while on a visit, at Loon Lake, Franklin County, N. Y., August 30, 1916; interment in Oakland Cemetery, Shreveport, La.

BOATNER, Charles Jahleal, a Representative from Louisiana; born in Columbia, Caldwell Parish, La., January 23, 1849; completed preparatory studies; studied law; was admitted to the bar in 1870 and practiced; member of the State senate from 1876 until May 1878; elected as a Democrat to the Fifty-first, Fifty-second, and Fifty-third Congresses (March 4, 1889–March 3, 1895); presented credentials as a Member-elect to the Fifty-fourth Congress but on March 20, 1896, the House declared the seat vacant, the election having been contested by Alexis Benoit; elected to fill the vacancy caused by the House declaring the seat vacant and served from June 10, 1896, to March 3, 1897; declined to be a candidate for reelection in 1896; moved to New Orleans and resumed the practice of law; died in New Orleans, La., on March 21, 1903; interment in Monroe Cemetery, Monroe, La.

BOCKEE, Abraham, a Representative from New York; born in Shekomeko, Dutchess County, N. Y., February 3, 1784; attended the public schools; was graduated from Union College, Schenectady, N. Y., May 4, 1803; studied law in Poughkeepsie; was admitted to the bar in 1806 and practiced in Poughkeepsie until 1815, when he returned to Shekomeko; engaged in agricultural pursuits; member of the State assembly in 1820; elected as a Jackson Democrat to the Twenty-first Congress (March 4, 1829–March 3, 1831); elected to the Twenty-third and Twenty-fourth Congresses (March 4, 1833–March 3, 1837); served in the State senate 1840–1844; elected judge of the court of errors in 1843; first judge of the Dutchess County Court in 1846; died in Shekomeko, N. Y., June 1, 1865; interment on his estate near Shekomeko.

BOCOCK, Thomas Stanhope, a Representative from Virginia; born at Buckingham Court House, Buckingham (now Appomattox) County, Va., May 18, 1815; educated by private tutors; was graduated from Hampden-Sidney College, Virginia, in 1838; studied law; was admitted to the bar in 1840 and commenced practice at Buckingham Court House; member of the State house of delegates 1842–1844; served as prosecuting attorney of Appomattox County in 1845 and 1846; elected as a Democrat to the Thirtieth and to the six succeeding Congresses (March 4, 1847- March 3, 1861); elected a Representative to the Confederate Congress in 1861, being chosen speaker of that body February 18, 1862; again served as a member of the State house of delegates in 1869, 1870, 1877, and 1878; was a delegate to the Democratic National Conventions in 1868, 1876, and 1880; died in Appomattox County, Va., on August 5, 1891; interment in Old Bocock Cemetery (private burying ground), near Wildway, Va.

BODEN, Andrew, a Representative from Pennsylvania; born in Carlisle, Cumberland County, Pa.; attended the public schools; studied law; was admitted to the bar and practiced; also engaged in the real-estate business; elected to the Fifteenth and Sixteenth Congresses (March 4, 1817–March 3, 1821); resumed the practice of law; died in Carlisle, Pa., December 20, 1835.

BODINE, Robert Nall, a Representative from Missouri; born near Paris, Monroe County, Mo., December 17, 1837; attended Paris Academy and was graduated from the University of Missouri at Columbia in 1859; principal of the Paris public schools; studied law; was admitted to the bar and began practice in Paris, Mo.; prosecuting attorney of Monroe County; delegate to the State convention in 1890; member of the State house of representatives 1895–1897; elected as a Democrat to the Fifty-fifth Congress (March 4, 1897–March 3, 1899); unsuccessful candidate for renomination in 1898; resumed the practice of law in Paris, Mo., and died there March 16, 1914; interment in Walnut Grove Cemetery.

BODLE, Charles, a Representative from New York; born near Poughkeepsie, Dutchess County, N. Y., in 1787; was a wagon maker by trade; justice of the peace; held several political offices in Bloomingburg, Sullivan County; elected to the Twenty-third Congress (March 4, 1833–March 3, 1835); died in New York City October 31, 1835; interment in Bloomingburg Cemetery, Bloomingburg, N. Y.

BOEHNE, John William, a Representative from Indiana; born in Scott Township, Vanderburgh County, Ind., October 28, 1856; attended the district schools, the German parochial school of the Lutheran Church, and Evansville Business College; moved to Evansville, Ind., in 1872, becoming an accountant; engaged in the manufacture of stoves and ranges and was interested in other manufacturing enterprises; elected councilman at large in 1897 and reelected in 1899; unsuccessful Democratic candidate for mayor of Evansville in 1901; mayor 1905–1908; delegate to the Democratic National Convention at Denver in 1908; elected as a Democrat to the Sixty-first and Sixty-second Congresses (March 4, 1909–March 3, 1913); was not a candidate for renomination in 1912; director of the Federal Reserve Bank at St. Louis, Mo.; retired from active business pursuits; died in Evansville, Ind., December 27, 1946; interment in the Lutheran Cemetery.

BOEHNE, John William, Jr. (son of the preceding), a Representative from Indiana; born in Evansville, Vanderburgh County, Ind., March 2, 1895; attended the public and parochial schools; was graduated from the University of Wisconsin at Madison in 1918; during the First World War served as a private and sergeant in the Detached Service, Ordnance, United States Army, from January 9, 1918, to April 8, 1919; secretary and treasurer of the Indiana Stove Works at Evansville, Ind., 1920–1931; elected as a Democrat to the Seventy-second and to the five succeeding Congresses (March 4, 1931–January 3, 1943); unsuccessful candidate for reelection in 1942 to the Seventy-eighth Congress; corporation tax counselor in Washington, D. C.; resides in Kensington, Md.

BOEN, Haldor Erickson, a Representative from Minnesota; born in Sondre Aurdal, Valders, Norway, January 2, 1851; immigrated to the United States in 1868 and settled in Mower County, Minn.; attended the St. Cloud Normal School in 1869 and 1870; located near Fergus Falls, Ottertail County, January 1, 1871; employed in the auditor's office in 1872, computing the first taxes levied in Ottertail County; taught in the common schools of that county 1874–1879; justice of the peace 1875–1900; elected county commissioner in 1880; register of deeds 1888–1892; elected as a candidate of the People's Party to the Fifty-third Congress (March 4, 1893–March 3, 1895); unsuccessful candidate for reelection in 1894 to the Fifty-fourth Congress; editor of the Fergus Falls Globe; resumed agricultural pursuits in Ottertail County, Minn.; died in Aurdal Township, Ottertail County, Minn., July 23, 1912; interment in Aurdal Cemetery, near Fergus Falls, Minn.

BOERUM, Simon, a Delegate from New York; born in New Lots (now Brooklyn), Long Island, N. Y., February 29, 1724; attended the Dutch school at Flatbush, N. Y., from which he was graduated; engaged in agricultural pursuits and milling; appointed county clerk of Kings County by Governor Clinton in 1750; also became clerk of the board of supervisors and held both positions until his death; member of the colonial assembly 1761–1775; deputy to the provincial convention in April 1775; Member of the Continental Congress in 1775; died in Brooklyn, N. Y., July 11, 1775; interment in Glenwood Cemetery.

BOGGS, James Caleb, a Representative and a Senator from Delaware; born in Cheswold, Kent County, Del., May 15, 1909; attended the rural schools; was graduated from the University of Delaware at Newark in 1931 and from Georgetown University Law School, Washington, D. C., in 1937; was admitted to the bar in 1938 and commenced practice in Dover, Del.; during World War II served as an officer in the United States Army from February 10, 1941, until discharged as a colonel January 3, 1946; deputy judge of the family court of New Castle County, Del., in 1946; elected as a Republican to the Eightieth, Eighty-first, and Eighty-second Congresses (January 3, 1947–January 3, 1953); was not a candidate for renomination in 1952 to the Eighty-third Congress; elected Governor of Delaware in 1952 for the term beginning January 1953 and reelected in 1956 for the term ending January 17, 1961, but resigned December 30, 1960. *Elected to the United States Senate for the term beginning January 3, 1961, and ending January 3, 1967.*

BOGGS, Thomas Hale, a Representative from Louisiana; born in Long Beach, Harrison County, Miss., February 15, 1914; attended the public and parochial schools of Jefferson Parish, La.; was graduated from Tulane University, New Orleans, La., in 1935 and from the law department of the same university in 1937; was admitted to the bar in 1937 and commenced practice in New Orleans, La.; elected as a Democrat to the Seventy-seventh Congress (January 3, 1941–January 3, 1943); unsuccessful candidate for renomination in 1942; resumed the practice of law in New Orleans, La.; enlisted in the United States Naval Reserve in November 1943; was commissioned an ensign and attached to the Potomac River Naval Command and the United States Maritime Service until separated in January 1946; again elected as a Democrat to the Eightieth and to the six succeeding Congresses (January 3, 1947–January 3, 1961). *Reelected to the Eighty-seventh Congress.*

BOGY, Lewis Vital, a Senator from Missouri; born in Ste. Genevieve, Mo., April 9, 1813; attended the public schools; employed as clerk in a mercantile establishment; studied law in Illinois; was graduated from a law school in Lexington, Ky., in 1835 and commenced practice in St. Louis; served in the Black Hawk War; member of the board of aldermen of St. Louis in 1838; member of the State house of representatives in 1840, 1841, 1854, and 1855; Commissioner of Indian Affairs in 1867 and 1868; president of the city council of St. Louis in 1872; one of the projectors of the St. Louis & Iron Mountain Railway, acting as president for two years; elected as a Democrat to the United States Senate and served from March 4, 1873, until his death in St. Louis, Mo., September 20, 1877; interment in Calvary Cemetery.

BOHN, Frank Probasco, a Representative from Michigan; born in Charlottesville, Hancock County, Ind., July 14, 1866; attended the common and high schools and the Danville (Ind.) Normal College; was graduated from the Medical College of Indiana, Indianapolis, Ind., in 1890; moved to Seney, Mich., in in 1890 and engaged in the practice of medicine; moved to Newberry, Luce County, Mich., in 1898 and practiced his profession until 1923; also engaged in banking in 1905; served as village president of Newberry 1904 to 1919; member of the Newberry School Board 1908–1914; member of the State senate 1923–1926; elected as a Republican to the Seventieth, Seventy-first, and Seventy-second Congresses (March 4, 1927–March 3, 1933); unsuccessful candidate for reelection in 1932 to the Seventy-third Congress; resumed banking activities in Newberry, Mich.; member of the Michigan State Hospital Commission 1935-1937; died in Newberry, Mich., June 1, 1944; interment in Forest Home Cemetery.

BOIES, William Dayton, a Representative from Iowa; born on a farm in Boone County, Ill., January 3, 1857; moved with his parents to Buchanan County, Iowa, in 1873 and settled near Quasqueton; attended country schools and the public schools of Belvidere, Ill.; was graduated in law from the State University of Iowa at Iowa City in 1880; was admitted to the bar in 1881 and commenced practice in Sanborn, O'Brien County, Iowa; moved to Sheldon, Iowa, in 1887 and continued the practice of law; unsuccessful candidate for election as judge of the district court in 1890; member of the school board of the independent school district of Sheldon 1900–1912; appointed judge of the district court of the fourth judicial district of Iowa January 1, 1913; on a division of this district became judge of the twenty-first judicial district of the State and in 1914 was elected for a

term of four years, which position he resigned on March 31, 1918 to become a candidate for the Republican nomination for Congress; elected as a Republican to the Sixty-sixth and to the four succeeding Congresses (March 4, 1919–March 3, 1929); one of the managers appointed by the House of Representatives in 1926 to conduct the impeachment proceedings against George W. English, judge of the United States District Court for the Eastern District of Illinois; was not a candidate for renomination in 1928; retired from active business and political pursuits; died in Sheldon, Iowa, May 31, 1932; interment in Eastlawn Cemetery.

BOILEAU, Gerald John, a Representative from Wisconsin; born in Woodruff, Oneida County, Wis., January 15, 1900; moved to Minocqua, Oneida County, Wis., in 1909; attended the public and high schools; during the First World War enlisted in the United States Army on February 25, 1918, as a private in the Eleventh Field Artillery, Battery D, and was honorably discharged as a corporal on July 16, 1919, having served twelve months overseas; was graduated from the law department of Marquette University, Milwaukee, Wis., in 1923; was admitted to the bar the same year and commenced practice in Wausau, Marathon County, Wis.; served as district attorney of Marathon County, Wis., 1926–1931; delegate to the Republican National Convention at Kansas City, Mo., in 1928; elected as a Republican to the Seventy-second and Seventy-third Congresses and as a Progressive to the Seventy-fourth and Seventy-fifth Congresses (March 4, 1931–January 3, 1939); unsuccessful candidate for reelection in 1938 to the Seventy-sixth Congress and for election in 1940 to the Seventy-seventh Congress; resumed the practice of law; elected circuit judge of the sixteenth judicial circuit of Wisconsin in 1942; reelected in 1945, 1951, and again in 1957 for a six-year term; is a resident of Wausau, Wis.

BOKEE, David Alexander, a Representative from New York; born in New York City, October 6, 1805; attended the public schools; engaged in mercantile pursuits; studied law; was admitted to the bar and practiced; president of the Brooklyn Board of Aldermen 1840–1843 and 1845–1848; member of the State senate 1846–1849; trustee of the New York Life Insurance Co. 1848–1860; elected as a Whig to the Thirty-first Congress (March 4, 1849–March 3, 1851); appointed by President Fillmore as naval officer of customs of the port of New York and served from 1851 to 1853; engaged as a shipping merchant; died in Washington, D. C., March 15, 1860; interment in Greenwood Cemetery, Brooklyn, N. Y.

BOLAND, Edward Patrick, a Representative from Massachusetts; born in Springfield, Hampden County, Mass., October 1, 1911; educated in classical high school, Bay Path Institute, and Boston College Law School; member of the State house of representatives 1935–1940; register of deeds for Hampden County 1941–1952; during World War II enlisted in May 1942 as a private in the United States Army and served through the ranks until his discharge as a captain in 1946, serving eleven months overseas in the Philippines; elected as a Democrat to the Eighty-third and to the three succeeding Congresses (January 3, 1953–January 3, 1961). *Reelected to the Eighty-seventh Congress.*

BOLAND, Patrick Joseph (husband of Veronica G. Boland), a Representative from Pennsylvania; born in Scranton, Lackawanna County, Pa., January 6, 1880; attended the parochial schools and St. Thomas College, Scranton, Pa.; began work as a carpenter; member of the firm of Boland Brothers, general building contractors; also associated with a sewer and paving contract company; member of the city council of Scranton, Pa., 1905–1906; served on the school board of Scranton 1907–1909; county commissioner of Lackawanna County, Pa., 1915–

1919; elected as a Democrat to the Seventy-second and to the five succeeding Congresses and served from March 4, 1931, until his death in Scranton, Pa., May 18, 1942; interment in Cathedral Cemetery.

BOLAND, Veronica Grace (widow of Patrick J. Boland), a Representative from Pennsylvania; born in Scranton, Lackawanna County, Pa., March 18, 1899; attended the public schools and Scranton Technical High School; elected as a Democrat to the Seventy-seventh Congress to fill the vacancy caused by the death of her husband, Patrick J. Boland, and served from November 19, 1942, to January 3, 1943; was not a candidate for reelection to the Seventy-eighth Congress; is a resident of Scranton, Pa.

BOLES, Thomas, a Representative from Arkansas; born near Clarksville, Johnson County, Ark., July 16, 1837; attended the common schools; taught school for several years; sheriff of Yell County in 1858; deputy clerk of the circuit court of Yell County in 1859 and 1860; studied law; was admitted to the bar in 1860 and commenced practice in Danville, Ark.; during the Civil War served as captain of Company E, Third Regiment, Arkansas Volunteer Cavalry; judge of the fourth judicial circuit from 1865 to April 20, 1868, when he resigned; upon the readmission of Arkansas to representation was elected as a Republican to the Fortieth Congress; reelected to the Forty-first Congress and served from June 22, 1868, until March 3, 1871; successfully contested the election of John Edwards to the Forty-second Congress and served from February 9, 1872, until March 3, 1873; was not a candidate for renomination in 1872; resumed the practice of law at Dardanelle, Yell County, Ark.; served many years as school director and alderman; appointed receiver of the land office at Dardanelle by President Hayes in February 1878; United States marshal for the western district of Arkansas 1881–1889; delegate to every Republican State convention from the organization of the party until his death; clerk of the United States Circuit Court for the Eighth Judicial Circuit from September 1897 until his death in Fort Smith, Sebastian County, Ark., March 13, 1905; interment in Brealey Cemetery, Dardanelle, Ark.

BOLLES, Stephen, a Representative from Wisconsin; born in Springboro, Crawford County, Pa., June 25, 1866; attended the public schools; was graduated from the State Normal School of Pennsylvania at Slippery Rock, Pa., in 1888 and from the law department of Milton College, Milton, Wis.; served as reporter, correspondent, managing editor, and publisher of many newspapers in Ohio, Pennsylvania, and New York 1893–1901; chairman of the congressional committee of the Eleventh Ohio District and secretary of the Republican city committee of Toledo in 1894; chairman of the congressional committee of the Twenty-sixth Pennsylvania District and secretary of the Pennsylvania Republican League of Clubs in 1896; superintendent of the press department of the Pan American Exposition at Buffalo, N. Y., in 1901; secretary of the McKinley National Memorial Association, Cleveland, Ohio, in 1901 and 1902; managing editor of the Buffalo (N. Y.) Enquirer in 1902 and 1903; superintendent of graphic arts of the St. Louis Exposition 1903–1905, during which time he was also director and editor of the exposition catalogue for which France decorated him Officier d'Academie; director of publicity of the Jamestown Exposition in 1907; engaged as a special writer and also in private business, including the brokerage business, in Atlanta, Ga., 1907–1919; moved to Janesville, Wis., in 1920 and again engaged as a newspaper editor until elected to Congress; delegate to the Republican National Convention at Kansas City in 1928; president of the Wisconsin State Chamber of Commerce in 1931 and president of

the Wisconsin Associated Press Association in 1933 and 1934; elected as a Republican to the Seventy-sixth and Seventy-seventh Congresses and served from January 3, 1939, until his death in Washington, D. C., July 8, 1941; interment in Oak Hill Cemetery, Janesville, Wis.

BOLLING, Richard Walker, a Representative from Missouri; born in New York City, N. Y., May 17, 1916; attended grade schools and Phillips-Exeter Academy, Exeter, N. H.; at the age of fifteen, upon his father's death, returned to his home in Huntsville, Ala.; was graduated from the University of the South, Sewanee, Tenn., in 1937; graduate work at University of the South in 1937 and 1938, and at Vanderbilt University, Nashville, Tenn., in 1940 and 1941; taught at Sewanee Military Academy in 1938 and 1939; served as assistant to the head of the Department of Education, Florence State Teachers College, in Alabama, in 1940; educational administrator by profession; during World War II entered the United States Army as a private in April 1941, and served until discharged as a lieutenant colonel in July 1946, with four years' overseas service in Australia, New Guinea, Philippines, and in Japan as assistant chief of staff to General MacArthur; awarded the Legion of Merit and Bronze Star Medal; veterans' adviser at the University of Kansas City in 1946 and 1947; midwest director of Americans for Democratic Action from May 1947 until July 1947; elected as a Democrat to the Eighty-first and to the five succeeding Congresses (January 3, 1949–January 3, 1961). *Reelected to the Eighty-seventh Congress.*

BOLTON, Chester Castle (husband of Frances P. Bolton), a Representative from Ohio; born in Cleveland, Ohio, September 5, 1882; attended the public schools; was graduated from the University School, Cleveland, Ohio, in 1901 and from Harvard University, Cambridge, Mass., in 1905; employed in the steel industry in Cleveland 1905–1917; member of the Ohio National Guard 1905–1915; during the First World War was commissioned a captain in the Reserve Corps and ordered into active service in March 1917; detailed first to the War Industries Board, then served as aide to the Assistant Secretary of War; transferred to the General Staff in 1917 and ordered to the War College for a course of instruction in officers' field training in 1918; promoted to the rank of lieutenant colonel and detailed to the One Hundred and First Division as Assistant Chief of Staff; discharged in December 1918; after the war returned to Cleveland, Ohio, and served as a director of several large business corporations and as trustee of various civic and educational institutions; also engaged in raising and breeding cattle; member of the Lyndhurst Village Council 1918–1921; served in the State senate 1923–1928, serving as president pro tempore in 1927 and 1928; delegate to the Republican National Convention at Kansas City in 1928; elected as a Republican to the Seventy-first and to the three succeeding Congresses (March 4, 1929–January 3, 1937); unsuccessful candidate for reelection in 1936 to the Seventy-fifth Congress; served as chairman of the Republican Congressional Campaign Committee in 1934 and 1936; resumed his former business pursuits; elected to the Seventy-sixth Congress and served from January 3, 1939, until his death in Cleveland, Ohio, October 29, 1939; interment in Lake View Cemetery.

BOLTON, Frances Payne (widow of Chester C. Bolton, granddaughter of Henry B. Payne, and mother of Oliver P. Bolton), a Representative from Ohio; born in Cleveland, Ohio, March 29, 1885; attended the public schools; engaged in public health nursing, nursing education and other social service, educational, and philanthropic work; trustee of Lakeside Hospitals, East End Community Center, and School of Nursing at Western Reserve University, Cleveland, Ohio; vice regent for Ohio of the Mount

Vernon Ladies' Association, which has charge of George Washington's former home; member of the Republican State Central Committee 1937–1940; elected as a Republican to the Seventy-sixth Congress to fill the vacancy caused by the death of her husband, Chester C. Bolton; reelected to the Seventy-seventh and to the nine succeeding Congresses and served from February 27, 1940, to January 3, 1961. *Reelected to the Eighty-seventh Congress.*

BOLTON, Oliver Payne (son of Chester Castle Bolton and Frances Payne Bolton and great-grandson of Henry B. Payne), a Representative from Ohio; born in Cleveland, Ohio, February 22, 1917; graduated from Milton (Mass.) Academy in 1935, Harvard College in 1939, and Western Reserve University Law School in 1947; was admitted to the bar in 1947 and began practice in Cleveland, Ohio; member of the One Hundred and Seventh Cavalry, Ohio National Guard, 1939–1941; during World War II spent five years in the service 1941–1946, one of which was in the Pacific Theater on the staff of C–2 section of Fifth Amphibious Corps; chairman of Ohio Young Republicans in 1948 and 1949; Young Republicans national committeeman from Ohio in 1950 and 1951; publisher of Lake County News Herald, Willoughby, Ohio, and the Daily Reporter, Dover, Ohio; elected as a Republican to the Eighty-third and Eighty-fourth Congresses (January 3, 1953–January 3, 1957); was not a candidate for renomination in 1956; director of commerce, State of Ohio, from February 4 to August 2, 1957; is a resident of Mentor, Ohio.

BOLTON, William P., a Representative from Maryland; born near Whiteford, Harford County, Md., July 2, 1885; attended the public schools and St. Francis Parochial School in Baltimore County, Md.; was graduated from the Baltimore University Law School in 1909; was admitted to the bar in 1909 and commenced the practice of law in Towson, Md.; served as trial magistrate 1941–1946; member of the State senate 1946–1948; elected as a Democrat to the Eighty-first Congress (January 3, 1949–January 3, 1951); was an unsuccessful candidate for reelection in 1950 to the Eighty-second Congress; resumed the practice of law in Towson, Md.; Baltimore County Civil Defense director since 1951; resides in Towson, Md.

BOND, Charles Grosvenor (nephew of Charles Henry Grosvenor), a Representative from New York; born in Columbus, Franklin County, Ohio, May 29, 1877; attended the public schools; was graduated from the law department of Ohio State University at Columbus in 1899; was admitted to the bar the same year and commenced the practice of law in Columbus, Ohio; moved to New York City in 1903 and continued the practice of his profession; elected as a Republican to the Sixty-seventh Congress (March 4, 1921–March 3, 1923); unsuccessful candidate for reelection in 1922 to the Sixty-eighth Congress; resumed the practice of law; also interested in banking; unsuccessful Republican candidate for president of the borough of Brooklyn in 1926; delegate to the Republican National Convention at Cleveland in 1936; commissioner of the New York City Alcoholic Beverage Control Board since 1914; is a resident of Brooklyn, N. Y.

BOND, Shadrack, a Delegate from Illinois Territory; born in Frederick, Md., November 24, 1773; received a common-school education; moved to Kaskaskia, Ill. (then Indiana Territory), in 1794 and engaged in agricultural pursuits; member of the legislative council of Indiana Territory 1805–1808; when Illinois Territory was formed was elected on October 10, 1812, as a Democrat to Congress for a term of two years (Twelfth and Thirteenth Congresses); served as receiver of public moneys in the general land office at Kaskaskia, Ill., 1814–1818; upon the admission of Illinois as a State into the Union was elected its first Governor and served from 1818 to 1822; appointed register of the land office for the district of Kaskaskia on January 28, 1823, and served until his death in Kaskaskia, Randolph County, Ill., April 12, 1832; interment in Evergreen Cemetery, Chester, Randolph County, Ill.

BOND, William Key, a Representative from Ohio; born in St. Marys County, Md., October 2, 1792; attended the schools at Litchfield, Conn., where he also studied law at the Litchfield Law School; moved to Chillicothe, Ohio, in 1812; was admitted to the bar in 1813 and commenced practice in Chillicothe; elected as a Whig to the Twenty-fourth, Twenty-fifth, and Twenty-sixth Congresses (March 4, 1835–March 3, 1841); declined to be a candidate for renomination in 1840; moved to Cincinnati in 1841 and continued the practice of his profession; appointed surveyor of the port of Cincinnati by President Fillmore May 2, 1849, and served until September 28, 1853; became interested in the development of railroads in the West; died in Cincinnati, Ohio, February 17, 1864; interment in Spring Grove Cemetery.

BONE, Homer Truett, a Senator from Washington; born in Franklin, Johnson County, Ind., January 25, 1883; attended the public schools; employed in the postal service and as a clerk in the accounting and credit department of a chain furniture company; was graduated from the Tacoma (Wash.) Law School in 1911; was admitted to the bar the same year and commenced practice in Tacoma, Wash.; special deputy prosecuting attorney of Pierce County, Wash., in 1912; corporation counsel of the port of Tacoma, Wash., 1918–1932; member of the State house of representatives in 1923 and 1924; unsuccessful candidate for the Republican nomination in 1928 to the Seventy-first Congress; elected as a Democrat to the United States Senate in 1932; reelected in 1938 and served from March 4, 1933, until his resignation on November 13, 1944; appointed a judge of the United States Circuit Court of Appeals for the Ninth Judicial Circuit, took the oath of office on November 16, 1944, and served until his retirement on January 1, 1956; is a resident of Tacoma, Wash.

BONHAM, Milledge Luke, a Representative from South Carolina; born near Red Bank (now Saluda), Edgefield District, S. C., December 25, 1813; attended private schools in Edgefield District and at Abbeville, S. C.; was graduated from South Carolina College (now the University of South Carolina) at Columbia in 1834; studied law; was admitted to the bar and commenced practice in Edgefield in 1837; served as major and adjutant general of the South Carolina Brigade in the Seminole War in Florida in 1836; during the Mexican War was lieutenant colonel and colonel of the Twelfth Regiment, United States Infantry; major general of the South Carolina Militia; member of the State house of representatives 1840–1844; solicitor of the southern circuit of South Carolina 1848–1857; elected as a State Rights Democrat to the Thirty-fifth and Thirty-sixth Congresses and served from March 4, 1857, until his retirement on December 21, 1860; appointed major general and commander of the Army of South Carolina by Gov. F. W. Pickens in February 1861; appointed brigadier general in the Confederate Army April 19, 1861; commanded in the center of General Beauregard's army in the first Battle of Manassas; resigned his commission January 27, 1862, to enter the Confederate Congress; elected Governor of South Carolina in December 1862 and served until December 1864; appointed brigadier general of Cavalry in the Confederate Army in February 1865; again a member of the State house of representatives 1865–1867; delegate to the Democratic National Convention at New York City in 1868; member of the South Carolina taxpayers' convention in 1871 and 1874; delegate to the Democratic State convention in 1876; resumed the practice of law in Edgefield, engaged in planting, and also conducted an insurance business in Edgefield, S. C., and Atlanta, Ga., 1865–1878; appointed State railroad commissioner in 1878 and served until his death at White Sulphur Springs, N. C., August 27, 1890; interment in Elmwood Cemetery, Columbia, S. C.

BONIN, Edward John, a Representative from Pennsylvania; born in Hazleton, Luzerne County, Pa., December 23, 1904; attended the parochial and public schools of Hazleton; served in the United States Navy 1922–1926; graduated from Wyoming Seminary, Kingston, Pa., in 1929, Dickinson College, Carlisle, Pa., in 1933, and Temple University, Philadelphia, Pa., in 1937; studied law; was admitted to the bar in February 1938 and began practice in Hazleton, Pa.; during World War II served in the United States Army 1942–1944; resumed law practice; assistant district attorney of Luzerne County 1949–1952; mayor of Hazleton, Pa., 1951–1953; elected as a Republican to the Eighty-third Congress (January 3, 1953–January 3, 1955); was an unsuccessful candidate for reelection in 1954 to the Eighty-fourth Congress; assistant to Philadelphia regional director, Post Office Department, from February 1955 to May 1961; is a resident of Hazleton, Pa.

BONNER, Herbert Covington, a Representative from North Carolina; born in Washington, Beaufort County, N. C., May 16, 1891; attended a private school; was graduated from Graham School, Warrenton, N. C.; engaged as a salesman and in agricultural pursuits; during the First World War served as sergeant in Company I, Three Hundred and Twenty-second Infantry, with overseas service in the Eighty-first Division; secretary to Congressman Lindsay C. Warren 1924–1940; elected as a Democrat on November 5, 1940, to the Seventy-sixth Congress to fill the vacancy caused by the resignation of Lindsay C. Warren and on the same day was elected to the Seventy-seventh Congress; reelected to the Seventy-eighth and to the eight succeeding Congresses and served from November 5, 1940, to January 3, 1961. *Reelected to the Eighty-seventh Congress.*

BONYNGE, Robert William, a Representative from Colorado; born in New York City September 8, 1863; attended the public schools; was graduated from the College of the City of New York in 1882 and from the law department of Columbia College, New York City, in 1885; was admitted to the bar in 1885 and commenced practice in New York City; moved to Denver, Colo., in 1888 and continued the practice of law; member of the State house of representatives in 1893 and 1894; unsuccessful candidate for election in 1900 to the Fifty-seventh Congress; contested the election to the Fifty-eighth Congress of John F. Shafroth, who in an address before the House of Representatives conceded his defeat and withdrew from the contest; reelected as a Republican to the Fifty-ninth and Sixtieth Congresses and served from February 16, 1904, until March 3, 1909; unsuccessful candidate for reelection in 1908 to the Sixty-first Congress; member of the National Monetary Commission 1908–1912; resumed the practice of law in Denver, Colo.; moved to New York City in November 1912 and continued the practice of law; chief counsel of the New York State Industrial Commission 1916–1918; appointed United States agent before the Mixed Claims Commission (United States and Germany) in 1923 and before the Tripartite Claims Commission (United States, Austria, and Hungary) in 1927; died in New York City, N. Y., September 22, 1939; interment in Woodlawn Cemetery.

BOODY, Azariah, a Representative from New York; born in Stanstead County, Province of Quebec, Canada, April 21, 1815; moved to Massachusetts with his parents, who settled in Lowell; attended the common schools; moved to Rochester, N. Y., in 1850 and engaged in agricultural pursuits; donated a portion of his farm to the University of Rochester for a campus in 1853; trustee of the University of Rochester 1853–1865; elected as a Whig to the Thirty-third Congress and served from March 4 until his resignation in October 1853, before the convening of Congress; moved to New York City, N. Y., in 1855 and engaged in the construction of railroads, canals, and bridges; served as president of the Wabash Railroad Co.; retired from active business pursuits in 1875, retaining his residence in New York City, where he died on November 18, 1885; interment in Mount Hope Cemetery, Rochester, N. Y.

BOODY, David Augustus, a Representative from New York; born in Jackson, Waldo County, Maine, August 13, 1837; attended the common schools and Phillips Academy, Andover, Mass.; studied law; was admitted to the bar in 1860 at Belfast, Maine, and commenced practice in Camden, Maine; moved to Brooklyn, N. Y., in 1862 and engaged in the banking and brokerage business; unsuccessful candidate for election in 1882 to the Forty-eighth Congress; delegate to the Democratic National Conventions at Chicago in 1884 and 1892; president of Berkeley Institute, Brooklyn, N. Y., 1886–1922; delegate to the New York State Democratic convention in 1890; elected as a Democrat to the Fifty-second Congress and served from March 4 to October 13, 1891, when he resigned, having become a candidate for mayor; mayor of Brooklyn in 1892 and 1893; resumed his former banking and brokerage business; served as president of the board of trustees of the Brooklyn Public Library from 1897 until his death; donated $50,000 in November 1927 to establish the David A. Boody Foundation of the Brooklyn Public Library; presidential elector on the Democratic ticket of Wilson and Marshall in 1912; was a member of the New York Stock Exchange but retired in 1926, and resided in Brooklyn, N. Y., until his death there on January 20, 1930; interment in Greenwood Cemetery.

BOOHER, Charles Ferris, a Representative from Missouri; born on a farm near East Groveland, Livingston County, N. Y., January 31, 1848; attended the common schools and the Geneseo Academy, Geneseo, N. Y.; taught school and studied law; was admitted to the bar in 1871 and commenced practice in Rochester, Mo.; moved to Savannah, Mo., in 1875, having been appointed prosecuting attorney of Andrew County, in which capacity he served until 1877, and again from 1883 to 1885; resumed the practice of law in Savannah, Mo., and also, in 1888, engaged in the loan and real-estate business; presidential elector on the Democratic ticket of Hancock and English in 1880; mayor of Savannah, Mo., 1886–1890; elected as a Democrat to the Fiftieth Congress to fill the vacancy caused by the death of James N. Burnes and served from February 19 to March 3, 1889; was not a candidate for election for the full term; elected to the Sixtieth and to the six succeeding Congresses and served from March 4, 1907, until his death; was not a candidate for renomination in 1920; died in Savannah, Andrew County, Mo., January 21, 1921; interment in City Cemetery.

BOOKER, George William, a Representative from Virginia; born near Stuart, Patrick County, Va.; December 5, 1821; attended the public schools; taught school; studied law; was admitted to the bar in 1846 and commenced practice in Patrick County; elected a justice of the peace in Henry County; member and presiding justice of the county court from August 1856 to February 1868; member of the State house of delegates in 1865 and 1873; nominated by the Republican Party and elected attorney general in 1868, but resigned in 1869; upon the readmission of the State of Virginia to representation was elected as a Conservative to the Forty-first Congress and served from

January 26, 1870, to March 3, 1871; resumed the practice of law in Martinsville, Henry County, Va., where he died June 4, 1883; interment in the family cemetery.

BOON, Ratliff, a Representative from Indiana; born in Franklin County, N. C., January 18, 1781; moved with his parents to Warren County, Ky.; attended the public schools; moved to Danville, Ky., and learned the gunsmith's trade; moved to what is now Boon Township, Warrick County, Ind., in 1809; on the organization of Warrick County was appointed its first treasurer in 1813; member of the State house of representatives in 1816 and 1817; served in the State senate in 1818; elected Lieutenant Governor of Indiana in 1819; upon the resignation of Jonathan Jennings became Governor and served from September 12 to December 5, 1822; reelected Lieutenant Governor in August 1822 and served until January 30, 1824, when he resigned to become a candidate for Congress; elected as a Jacksonian Democrat to the Nineteenth Congress (March 4, 1825–March 3, 1827); unsuccessful candidate for reelection in 1826 to the Twentieth Congress; elected to the Twenty-first and to the four succeeding Congresses (March 4, 1829–March 3, 1839); unsuccessful candidate for election to the United States Senate in 1836; moved to Pike County, Mo., in 1839; died in Louisiana, Mo., on November 20, 1844; interment in Riverview Cemetery.

BOONE, Andrew Rechmond, a Representative from Kentucky; born in Davidson County, Tenn., April 4, 1831; moved with his parents to Mayfield, Graves County, Ky., in 1833; attended the public schools; studied law; was admitted to the bar in 1852 and practiced in Mayfield; elected judge of the Graves County Court in 1854; reelected in 1858 and served until 1861, when he resigned; member of the State house of representatives in 1861; circuit judge for the first judicial district of Kentucky 1868–1874; elected as a Democrat to the Forty-fourth and Forty-fifth Congresses (March 4, 1875–March 3, 1879); was not a candidate for reelection in 1878; chairman of the State railroad commission 1882–1886; died in Mayfield, Ky., January 26, 1886; interment in Mayfield Cemetery.

BOOTH, Newton, a Senator from California; born in Salem, Washington County, Ind., December 25, 1825; attended the common schools, and was graduated from Asbury (later De Pauw) University, Greencastle, Ind., in 1846; studied law in Terre Haute, Ind.; was admitted to the bar in 1850; moved the same year to California, where he temporarily engaged in the wholesale grocery business at Sacramento; returned to Terre Haute in 1857 and engaged in the practice of law until 1860, when he returned to Sacramento, Calif., and again engaged in mercantile pursuits; member of the State senate in 1863; elected Governor of California in 1871 and served until March 1874, when he resigned, having been elected Senator; elected as an Anti-Monopolist to the United States Senate and served from March 4, 1875, to March 3, 1881; was not a candidate for renomination in 1880; engaged in the wholesale mercantile business in Sacramento, Calif., where he died July 14, 1892; interment in the City Cemetery.

BOOTH, Walter, a Representative from Connecticut; born in Woodbridge, Conn., December 8, 1791; attended the common schools; settled in Meriden and engaged in manufacturing; colonel of the Tenth Regiment, Second Battalion of Militia, 1825–1827, brigadier general in 1827 and 1828, and major general of the First Division 1831–1834; judge of the county court in 1834; member of the State house of representatives in 1838; elected as a Free-Soiler to the Thirty-first Congress (March 4, 1849–March 3, 1851); unsuccessful candidate for reelection in

1850 to the Thirty-second Congress; resumed his former manufacturing pursuits; died in Meriden, New Haven County, Conn., April 30, 1870; interment in East Cemetery.

BOOTHMAN, Melvin Morella, a Representative from Ohio; born near Bryan, Williams County, Ohio, October 16, 1846; attended the public schools; engaged in agricultural pursuits; enlisted in Company H, Thirty-eighth Regiment, Ohio Volunteer Infantry, January 4, 1864, "for three years, or during the Civil War"; served through the Atlanta campaign; was graduated from the law department of Michigan University at Ann Arbor in 1871; was admitted to the bar and commenced practice in Bryan, Ohio; elected treasurer of Williams County in 1871 and reelected in 1873; elected as a Republican to the Fiftieth and Fifty-first Congresses (March 4, 1887–March 3, 1891); was not a candidate for renomination in 1890; resumed the practice of law in Bryan, Ohio, and died there March 5, 1904; interment in Fountain City Cemetery.

BOOZE, William Samuel, a Representative from Maryland; born in Baltimore, Md., January 9, 1862; attended the public schools; was graduated from Baltimore City College in 1879 and afterwards attended the University of Maryland School of Medicine; was graduated in medicine from the College of Physicians and Surgeons, New York City, in 1882 and practiced his profession in Baltimore until 1896, when he was elected to Congress; unsuccessfully contested the election of Harry Welles Rusk to the Fifty-fourth Congress; elected as a Republican to the Fifty-fifth Congress (March 4, 1897–March 3, 1899); was not a candidate for renomination in 1898; engaged in banking and in the brokerage business in Baltimore, Md., until 1915, when he again engaged in the practice of medicine; delegate to the Republican National Conventions at Chicago in 1904 and 1908; died in Wilmington, Del., December 6, 1933, while en route to his home from a trip to South America; interment in Loudoun Park Cemetery, Baltimore, Md.

BORAH, William Edgar, a Senator from Idaho; born on a farm near Fairfield, Wayne County, Ill., June 29, 1865; attended the common schools of Wayne County and Southern Illinois Academy at Enfield; was graduated from the University of Kansas at Lawrence in 1889; studied law; was admitted to the bar in September 1890 and commenced practice in Lyons, Kans.; moved to Boise, Idaho, in 1891 and devoted his time exclusively to the practice of his profession; unsuccessful candidate on the Silver Republican ticket for election in 1896 to the Fifty-fifth Congress; unsuccessful candidate for nomination as United States Senator in 1903; member of the Republican National Committee 1908–1912; delegate to the Republican National Convention at Chicago in 1912 that nominated Taft and Sherman; elected as a Republican to the United States Senate in 1907; reelected in 1913, 1918, 1924, 1930, and again in 1936, and served from March 4, 1907, until his death; unsuccessful candidate for the Republican presidential nomination in 1936; died in Washington, D. C., January 19, 1940; funeral services were held in the Chamber of the United States Senate; interment in Morris Hill Cemetery, Boise, Idaho.

BORCHERS, Charles Martin, a Representative from Illinois; born in Lockville, Fairfield County, Ohio, November 18, 1869; moved to Illinois with his parents, who settled in Macon County in 1875; attended the common schools; taught school in Macon County for seven years; studied law; was admitted to the bar in 1897 and commenced practice in Decatur, Macon County, Ill.; mayor of Decatur 1909–1911; elected as a Democrat to the Sixty-third Congress (March 4, 1913–March 3, 1915); unsuccessful candidate for reelection in 1914 to the Sixty-fourth

Congress; resumed the practice of law; again served as mayor of Decatur 1919–1923; unsuccessful Democratic candidate for Governor in 1924; died in Decatur, Ill., December 2, 1946; interment in Frantz Cemetery, Macon County, Ill.

BORDEN, Nathaniel Briggs, a Representative from Massachusetts; born in Fall River, Mass., April 15, 1801; attended the district school and Plainfield (Conn.) Academy; organized the Pocasset Manufacturing Co. in Fall River, Mass.; member of the State house of representatives in 1831 and 1834; elected as a Van Buren Democrat to the Twenty-fourth and Twenty-fifth Congresses (March 4, 1835–March 3, 1839); unsuccessful Whig candidate for reelection to the Twenty-sixth Congress in 1838; elected as a Whig to the Twenty-seventh Congress (March 4, 1841–March 3, 1843); member of the State senate from 1845 to 1848; served in the State house of representatives in 1851; elected mayor of Fall River in 1856 and reelected in 1857; again a member of the State house of representatives in 1864; engaged in banking and served as president of the Fall River Savings Bank and of the Fall River Union Bank; was president also of the Fall River Railroad Co.; died in Fall River, Bristol County, Mass., April 10, 1865; interment in Oak Grove Cemetery.

BOREING, Vincent, a Representative from Kentucky; born near Jonesboro, Washington County, Tenn., November 24, 1839; moved with his father to Laurel County, Ky., in 1847; attended Laurel Seminary, London, Ky., and Tusculum College, Greenville, Tenn.; enlisted as a private in the Union Army during the Civil War in Company A, Twenty-fourth Regiment, Kentucky Volunteer Infantry, November 1, 1861; for meritorious conduct was commissioned first lieutenant; was severely wounded in the battle at Reseca, Ga., May 14, 1863; county superintendent of public schools 1868–1872; established the Mountain Echo at London, Ky., in 1875, the first Republican newspaper published in southeastern Kentucky; county judge in 1886; president of the Cumberland Valley Land Co. in 1887; president of the First National Bank of London in 1888; department commander of the Grand Army of the Republic in Kentucky in 1889; elected as a Republican to the Fifty-sixth, Fifty-seventh, and Fifty-eighth Congresses and served from March 4, 1899, until his death in London, Laurel County, Ky., September 16, 1903; interment in Pine Grove Cemetery.

BOREMAN, Arthur Inghram, a Senator from West Virginia; born in Waynesburg, Pa., July 24, 1823; moved to Virginia with his parents, who settled in Middlebourne, Tyler County, in 1827, and in Moundsville, Marshall County, in 1840; attended the public schools; studied law; was admitted to the bar in May 1843 and commenced practice in Parkersburg the same year; member of the Virginia House of Delegates 1855–1860; also served in the house of delegates at the extra session of the legislature in 1861, taking an active part against the secession movement; presided over the convention of supporters of the Union of the northwestern counties of Virginia held at Wheeling, June 19, 1861, to form the new State of West Virginia; elected judge of the circuit court, nineteenth circuit of Virginia, in October 1861 and held the office until 1863; unanimously elected the first Governor of West Virginia in 1863; twice reelected, and served from June 20, 1863, until February 26, 1869, when he resigned to accept the nomination as United States Senator; elected as a Republican to the United States Senate and served from March 4, 1869, to March 3, 1875; was not a candidate for reelection in 1874; resumed the practice of his profession in Parkersburg, W. Va.; elected judge of the circuit court for the fifth judicial circuit of West Virginia in 1888 and served until his death in Parkersburg, Wood County, W. Va., April 19, 1896; interment in the Odd Fellows Cemetery.

BOREN, Lyle H., a Representative from Oklahoma; born near Waxahachie, Ellis County, Tex., May 11, 1909; moved to Lawton, Okla., in 1917; attended the public schools; was graduated from the East Central College at Ada, Okla., in 1930 and from Oklahoma Agricultural and Mechanical College at Stillwater; teacher in the schools at Wolf, Okla., 1930–1935; served as a deputy procurement officer of the United States Treasury Department; engaged in agricultural pursuits and also was interested in the mercantile business; author; lieutenant commander in the United States Naval Reserve; elected as a Democrat to the Seventy-fifth and to the four succeeding Congresses (January 3, 1937–January 3, 1947); unsuccessful candidate for renomination in 1946; resumed former mercantile business and agricultural pursuits; president of a petroleum corporation; representative of the Association of Western Railways in Washington, D. C., where he resides.

BORLAND, Charles, Jr., a Representative from New York; born in Minisink, Orange County, N. Y., June 29, 1786; pursued preparatory studies; was graduated from Union College, Schenectady, N. Y., in 1811; studied law; was admitted to the bar and practiced; president of the board of trustees of Montgomery for ten years; member of the State assembly in 1820 and 1821; elected to the Seventeenth Congress to fill the vacancy caused by the death of Selah Tuthill and served from November 8, 1821, to March 3, 1823; district attorney of Orange County 1835–1841; again a member of the State assembly, in 1836; died in Wardsbridge, N. Y., February 23, 1852; interment in Riverside Cemetery, Montgomery, N. Y.

BORLAND, Solon, a Senator from Arkansas; born near Suffolk, Nansemond County, Va., September 21, 1808; attended preparatory schools in North Carolina; studied medicine and afterwards practiced; located in Little Rock, Ark.; served throughout the Mexican War as major of Yell's Arkansas Volunteer Cavalry and as volunteer aide to Major General Worth; was appointed and subsequently elected as a Democrat to the United States Senate to fill the vacancy caused by the resignation of Ambrose H. Sevier and served from March 30, 1848, to April 3, 1853, when he resigned; served as United States Minister to Nicaragua and to the other Central American Republics from April 18, 1853, to June 30, 1854; declined an appointment as Governor of the Territory of New Mexico; returned to Arkansas and resumed the practice of medicine in Little Rock until 1861; during the Civil War raised a brigade of troops for the Confederate Army and took possession of Fort Smith on April 24, 1861; subsequently raised the Third Regiment, Arkansas Confederate Cavalry, and became its colonel; later was appointed a brigadier general in the Confederate service; died near Houston, Tex., on January 1, 1864; interment in City Cemetery, Houston, Tex.

BORLAND, William Patterson, a Representative from Missouri; born in Leavenworth, Kans., October 14, 1867; attended the public schools; was graduated from the law department of the University of Michigan at Ann Arbor in 1892; was admitted to the bar and commenced the practice of law in Kansas City, Mo., the same year; assisted in the organization of the Kansas City School of Law and served as dean 1895–1909; member of the board of freeholders directed to draft a charter for Kansas City in 1898; also engaged as an author on law subjects; elected as a Democrat to the Sixty-first and to the four succeeding Congresses and served from March 4, 1909, until his death; unsuccessful candidate for renomination in 1918 to the Sixty-sixth Congress; died near Coblenz, Germany, while on a Masonic mission abroad, on February 20, 1919; interment in Elmwood Cemetery, Kansas City, Mo.

BORST, Peter I., a Representative from New York; born in Middleburg, Schoharie County, N. Y., April 24, 1797; attended the common schools; served as an officer of State troops and on the staff of Gov. William C. Bouck; held various local positions; elected as a Jackson Democrat to the Twenty-first Congress (March 4, 1829–March 3, 1831); served as a member of the committee appointed by the county board of supervisors to oversee the building of the first county almshouse in 1838; died in Middleburg, N. Y., November 14, 1848; interment in the family burying ground on his estate, "The Hook," in Schoharie County.

BOSCH, Albert Henry, a Representative from New York; born in New York City, N. Y., October 30, 1908; attended the public schools and was graduated from the School of Law, St. Johns College, in 1933; was admitted to the bar in 1938 and commenced the practice of law in New York City; also admitted to practice before the Treasury Department and the Supreme Court of the United States; trustee of Hamburg Savings Bank, Ridgewood, N. Y.; elected as a Republican to the Eighty-third and to the three succeeding Congresses and served from January 3, 1953, until his resignation December 31, 1960, having been elected judge of County Court of Queens for a 14-year term; is a resident of Woodhaven, N. Y.

BOSONE, Reva Zilpha Beck, a Representative from Utah; born in American Fork, Utah County, Utah; attended the public schools; graduated from Westminster Junior College in 1917 and from the University of California at Berkeley in 1919; taught in American Fork (Utah) Senior High School in 1920 and 1921, Delta (Utah) High School in 1921 and 1922, and Ogden (Utah) High School 1922–1927; graduated from the University of Utah College of Law at Salt Lake City in 1930 and was admitted to the bar the same year; practiced law in Helper, Carbon County, Utah, 1931–1933 and Salt Lake City, Utah, 1933–1936; member of the State house of representatives 1933–1935, serving as floor leader in 1935; elected Salt Lake City judge in 1936 and served until elected to Congress; during World War II was chairman of Women's Army Corps Civilian Advisory Committee of the Ninth Service Command; official observer at United Nations Conference at San Francisco in 1945; first director of Utah State Board for Education on Alcoholism in 1947 and 1948; elected as a Democrat to the Eighty-first and Eighty-second Congresses (January 3, 1949–January 3, 1953); unsuccessful candidate for reelection in 1952 to the Eighty-third Congress and for election in 1954 to the Eighty-fourth Congress; delegate to Democratic National Conventions in 1952 and 1956; resumed the practice of law in Salt Lake City, Utah, 1953–1957; legal counsel to Safety and Compensation Subcommittee of House Committee on Education and Labor 1957–1960; judicial officer, Post Office Department in 1961; resides in Washington, D. C.

BOSS, John Linscom, Jr., a Representative from Rhode Island; born in Charleston, S. C., September 7, 1780; completed preparatory studies; studied law; was admitted to the bar and commenced practice in Newport, R. I.; held many important local offices; member of the State house of representatives from 1806 to 1815; elected to the Fourteenth and Fifteenth Congresses (March 4, 1815–March 3, 1819); died in Newport, R. I., August 1, 1819; interment in the Common Burial Ground.

BOSSIER, Pierre Evariste John Baptiste, a Representative from Louisiana; born in Natchitoches, La., March 22, 1797, of a Creole family which was among the first to settle in the French colony; received a classical education; engaged as a sugar and cotton planter; member of the State senate 1833–1843; elected as a Calhoun Democrat to the Twenty-eighth Congress

and served from March 4, 1843, until his death in Washington, D. C., on April 24, 1844; interment in the Congressional Cemetery, Washington, D. C.; reinterment in the Catholic Cemetery, Natchitoches, La.

BOTELER, Alexander Robinson, a Representative from Virginia; born in Shepherdstown, Jefferson County, Va. (now West Virginia), May 16, 1815; was graduated from Princeton College in 1835; engaged in agriculture and literary pursuits; elected as the candidate of the American Party to the Thirty-sixth Congress (March 4, 1859–March 3, 1861); during the Civil War entered the Confederate Army and was a member of Stonewall Jackson's staff; chosen by the State convention a Representative from Virginia to the Confederate Provisional Congress November 19, 1861; elected from Virginia to the Confederate Congress, serving from February 1862 to February 1864; appointed a member of the Centennial Commission in 1876; appointed a member of the Tariff Commission by President Arthur and subsequently made pardon clerk in the Department of Justice by Attorney General Brewster; died in Shepherdstown, Jefferson County, W. Va., May 8, 1892; interment in Elmwood Cemetery.

BOTKIN, Jeremiah Dunham, a Representative from Kansas; born near Atlanta, Logan County, Ill., April 24, 1849; attended the country schools; spent one year at De Pauw University, Greencastle, Ind., pursued theological studies, and entered the Methodist ministry in 1870; unsuccessful Prohibition candidate for Governor of Kansas in 1888; unsuccessful candidate for election in 1894 to the Fifty-fourth Congress; chaplain of the Kansas Senate in 1897; elected as a Fusionist to the Fifty-fifth Congress (March 4, 1897–March 3, 1899); unsuccessful candidate for reelection in 1898 to the Fifty-sixth Congress; resumed ministerial duties; unsuccessful candidate for Governor in 1908; warden of the State penitentiary, Lansing, Kans., 1913–1915; again resumed his ministerial duties; became a Chautauqua lecturer in 1921; died in Liberal, Seward County, Kans., December 29, 1921; interment in Winfield Cemetery, Winfield, Cowley County, Kans.

BOTTS, John Minor, a Representative from Virginia; born in Dumfries, Va., September 16, 1802; attended the common schools in Richmond, Va.; studied law; was admitted to the bar in 1830 and commenced practice in Richmond, Va.; moved to Henrico County and engaged in agricultural pursuits; member of the State house of delegates 1833–1839; elected as a Henry Clay Whig to the Twenty-sixth and Twenty-seventh Congresses (March 4, 1839–March 3, 1843); unsuccessful candidate for reelection in 1842 to the Twenty-eighth Congress; elected to the Thirtieth Congress (March 4, 1847–March 3, 1849); unsuccessful candidate for reelection in 1848 and 1850 to the Thirty-first and Thirty-second Congresses, respectively; resumed the practice of law in Richmond, Va., in 1852; delegate to the Southern Loyalists' Convention in 1866; died in Richmond, Va., January 8, 1869; interment in Shockoe Hill Cemetery.

BOUCK, Gabriel (nephew of Joseph Bouck), a Representative from Wisconsin; born in Fultonham, Schoharie County, N. Y., December 16, 1828; was graduated from Union College, Schenectady, N. Y., in 1847; studied law; moved to Oshkosh, Winnebago County, Wis., in 1848; was admitted to the bar the same year and commenced practice in Oshkosh; attorney general of the State in 1858 and 1859; member of the State assembly in 1860 and 1874, serving the last year as speaker; during the Civil War served in the Union Army as captain of Company E, Second Regiment, Wisconsin Volunteer Infantry, from July 11, 1861, to April 21, 1862, and as colonel of the Eighteenth Regiment,

Wisconsin Volunteer Infantry, from April 22, 1862, to January 4, 1864; delegate to the Democratic National Conventions in 1868 and 1872; unsuccessful Democratic candidate for election in 1874 to the Forty-fourth Congress; elected as a Democrat to the Forty-fifth and Forty-sixth Congresses (March 4, 1877–March 3, 1881); unsuccessful candidate for reelection in 1880 to the Forty-seventh Congress; resumed the practice of law in Oshkosh, Wis., and died there on February 21, 1904; interment in the Riverside Cemetery.

BOUCK, Joseph (uncle of Gabriel Bouck), a Representative from New York; born on Bouck's Island, near Fultonham, Schoharie County, N. Y., July 22, 1788; attended the rural schools of his native county; engaged in agricultural pursuits for many years in Schoharie County until his change of residence to Middleburgh; served as inspector of turnpike roads in Schoharie County in 1828; elected as a Democrat to the Twenty-second Congress (March 4, 1831–March 3, 1833); resided in Middleburgh, N. Y., until his death on March 30, 1858; interment in his son's plot in Middleburgh Cemetery.

BOUDE, Thomas, a Representative from Pennsylvania; born in Lancaster, Pa., May 17, 1752; attended private schools; during the Revolutionary War served as a lieutenant under Gen. Anthony Wayne with the Second, Fourth, and Fifth Pennsylvania Battalions from January 5, 1776, to November 3, 1783, and was promoted to captain and brevet major; engaged in business as a lumber dealer in Columbia, Pa.; member and one of the organizers of the Society of the Cincinnati; member of the State house of representatives 1794–1796; elected as a Federalist to the Seventh Congress (March 4, 1801–March 3, 1803); unsuccessful candidate for reelection in 1802 to the Eighth Congress; resumed his former business as a lumber dealer; died in Columbia, Lancaster County, Pa., October 24, 1822; interment in that part of Mount Bethel Cemetery known as the "Brick Graveyard."

BOUDINOT, Elias, a Delegate and a Representative from New Jersey; born in Philadelphia, Pa., May 2, 1740; received a classical education; studied law; was admitted to the bar in 1760 and commenced practice in Elizabethtown, N. J.; member of the board of trustees of Princeton College 1772–1821; member of the committee of safety in 1775; commissary general of prisoners in the Revolutionary Army 1776–1779; Member of the Continental Congress in 1777, 1778, and 1781–1783, serving as President in 1782 and 1783, and signing the treaty of peace with England; resumed the practice of law; elected to the First, Second, and Third Congresses (March 4, 1789–March 3, 1795); was not a candidate for renomination in 1794 to the Fourth Congress; Director of the Mint from October 1795 to July 1805, when he resigned; elected first president of the American Bible Society, in 1816; died in Burlington, Burlington County, N. J., October 24, 1821; interment in St. Mary's Protestant Episcopal Church Cemetery.

BOULDIN, James Wood (brother of Thomas Tyler Bouldin), a Representative from Virginia; born in Charlotte County, Va., in 1792; attended the common schools; studied law; was admitted to the bar April 12, 1813, and commenced practice at Charlotte Court House, Va.; elected as a Jacksonian Democrat to the Twenty-third Congress to fill the vacancy caused by the death of Thomas T. Bouldin; reelected to the Twenty-fourth and Twenty-fifth Congresses and served from March 15, 1834, to March 3, 1839; resumed the practice of law and also engaged in agricultural pursuits; died at his country home, "Forest Hill," Charlotte County, Va., March 30, 1854; interment in the private burial ground on his estate.

BOULDIN, Thomas Tyler (brother of James Wood Bouldin), a Representative from Virginia; born near Charlotte Court House, Charlotte County, Va., in 1781; attended the country schools; studied law; was admitted to the bar December 6, 1802, and commenced practice at Charlotte Court House, Va.; appointed judge of the circuit court; elected as a Democrat to the Twenty-first and Twenty-second Congresses (March 4, 1829–March 3, 1833); unsuccessful candidate for reelection to the Twenty-third Congress; subsequently elected to the Twenty-third Congress to fill the vacancy caused by the death of John Randolph and served from August 26, 1833, until his death in Washington, D. C., February 11, 1834, while addressing the House of Representatives; interment in a private cemetery on his farm, "Golden Hills," near Drakes Branch, Charlotte County, Va.

BOULIGNY, Charles Joseph Dominique (uncle of John Edward Bouligny), a Senator from Louisiana; born in New Orleans, La., August 22, 1773; was educated by private tutors; served as ensign in his father's Spanish Regiment; commissioner of the municipal council in 1800; assumed American citizenship when the United States acquired Louisiana through the Louisiana Purchase in 1803; studied law; was admitted to the bar and practiced in New Orleans; served in the house of representatives of Louisiana Territory in 1806; resigned from the legislature in 1807 and was appointed justice of the peace in New Orleans; served on the committee on public defense during the British invasion in 1814 and 1815; elected to the United States Senate to fill the vacancy caused by the resignation of Henry Johnson and served from November 19, 1824, to March 3, 1829; died in New Orleans, La., on March 6, 1833; interment in St. Louis Cemetery No. 1.

BOULIGNY, John Edward (nephew of Charles Joseph Dominique Bouligny), a Representative from Louisiana; born in New Orleans, La., February 5, 1824; attended the public schools; studied law; was admitted to the bar and commenced practice in New Orleans; held several local offices; elected as the candidate of the American Party to the Thirty-sixth Congress (March 4, 1859–March 3, 1861); was strongly opposed to secession and was the only Louisiana Member to retain his seat after the State seceded on January 26, 1861; retired to private life and remained in the North during the Civil War; died in Washington, D. C., February 20, 1864; interment in the Congressional Cemetery.

BOUND, Franklin, a Representative from Pennsylvania; born in Milton, Northumberland County, Pa., April 9, 1829; attended the common schools and old Milton Academy; studied law at Easton, Pa.; was admitted to the bar in 1853 and commenced practice in Milton; member of the State senate 1860–1863; delegate to the Republican National Convention at Chicago in 1868; served as a private in one of the emergency regiments called for the defense of the State; was mustered into the United States service and discharged with his regiment; elected as a Republican to the Forty-ninth and Fiftieth Congresses (March 4, 1885–March 3, 1889); was not a candidate for renomination in 1888; resumed the practice of law; died in Milton, Pa., on August 8, 1910; interment in Milton Cemetery.

BOURN, Benjamin, a Representative from Rhode Island; born in Bristol, R. I., September 9, 1755; was graduated from Harvard College in 1775; studied law; was admitted to the bar and commenced practice in Providence; held several public offices; quartermaster of the Second Rhode Island Regiment in 1776; member of the general assembly in 1789 and 1790; member of the committee which presented a petition from Rhode Island to the Continental Congress; upon the ratification of the Constitution by the State of Rhode Island was elected as a Federalist to the First and to the four succeeding Congresses and served from August 31, 1790, until his resignation in 1796, before the close of the Fourth Congress; appointed judge of the United States District Court for the District of Rhode Island in 1801 and, later, judge of the United States Circuit Court for the Eastern Circuit; died in Bristol, R. I., September 17, 1808; interment in Juniper Hill Cemetery.

BOURNE, Jonathan, Jr., a Senator from Oregon; born in New Bedford, Bristol County, Mass., February 23, 1855; attended private schools and Harvard University; settled in Portland, Oreg., May 16, 1878; studied law; was admitted to the bar in 1881 and practiced in Portland; became especially interested in mining, farming, and commercial enterprises; president of a number of Oregon corporations and of the Bourne cotton mills in Fall River, Mass.; member of the Oregon House of Representatives in 1885, 1886, and 1897; delegate to the Republican National Conventions in 1888 and 1892; member of the Republican National Committee 1888–1892; elected as a Republican to the United States Senate and served from March 4, 1907, to March 3, 1913; unsuccessful candidate in the State preferential primary for the Republican renomination of United States Senator in 1912; president of the National Republican Progressive League; resumed his former pursuits in Oregon and Massachusetts; also operated a citrus plantation in Alabama, and engaged in newspaper work in Washington, D. C., until his death there September 1, 1940; interment in Cedar Hill Cemetery.

BOURNE, Shearjashub, a Representative from Massachusetts; born in Barnstable, Mass., June 14, 1746; was graduated from Harvard College in 1764; studied law; was admitted to the bar and commenced practice in Boston; member of the State house of representatives 1782–1785 and 1788–1790; member of the convention in 1788 which ratified the Constitution; elected to the Second and Third Congresses (March 4, 1791–March 3, 1795); served as justice of the court of common pleas of Suffolk County from 1799 until his death in Boston, Mass., March 11, 1806.

BOUTELL, Henry Sherman, a Representative from Illinois; born in Boston, Mass., March 14, 1856; moved to Chicago, Ill., in 1863; pursued academic studies; was graduated from Northwestern University, Evanston, Ill., in 1874 and from Harvard University in 1876; studied law; was admitted to the bar in 1879 and commenced practice in Chicago, Ill.; member of the State house of representatives in 1884 and 1885 and was one of the "103" who elected General Logan to the United States Senate; elected as a Republican to the Fifty-fifth Congress to fill the vacancy caused by the death of Edward D. Cooke; reelected to the Fifty-sixth and to the five succeeding Congresses and served from November 23, 1897, to March 3, 1911; unsuccessful candidate for reelection in 1910 to the Sixty-second Congress; trustee of Northwestern University 1899–1911; delegate to the Republican National Convention at Chicago in 1908; appointed Envoy Extraordinary and Minister Plenipotentiary to Portugal March 2, 1911, and to Switzerland April 24, 1911, and served until 1913, when he resigned; professor of constitutional law at Georgetown University, Washington, D. C., 1914–1923; died while on a trip to Europe in San Remo, Italy, March 11, 1926; interment in Pine Grove Cemetery, Westboro, Worcester County, Mass.

BOUTELLE, Charles Addison, a Representative from Maine; born in Damariscotta, Lincoln County, Maine, February 9, 1839; attended the public schools at Brunswick and the Yarmouth Academy; adopted the profession of shipmaster; in the spring of 1862 volunteered and was appointed acting master in the United States Navy; served in the North and South Atlantic and West Gulf Squadrons; took part in the blockade of Charleston and Wilmington, the Pocotaligo expedition, the capture of St. Johns Bluff, and the occupation of Jacksonville, Fla.; while an officer of the United States steamer *Sassacus* was promoted to lieutenant "for gallant conduct in the engagement with the Confederate ironclad *Albermarle*," May 5, 1864; afterward in command of the U. S. S. *Nyanza*; participated in the capture of Mobile and in receiving surrender of the Confederate Fleet; afterwards assigned to command of naval forces in Mississippi Sound; honorably discharged January 14, 1866; engaged in business in New York; became managing editor of the Bangor (Maine) Whig and Courier in 1870 and purchased controlling ownership in 1874; delegate to the Republican National Convention at Cincinnati in 1876; elected as a Republican to the Forty-eighth and to the nine succeeding Congresses and served from March 4, 1883, until his resignation, March 3, 1901, before the commencement of the Fifty-seventh Congress, to which he had been reelected; by joint resolution of Congress on January 16, 1901, was placed on the retired list of the Navy, with the rank of captain; died in Waverley, Middlesex County, Mass., May 21, 1901; interment in Mount Hope Cemetery, Bangor, Maine.

BOUTWELL, George Sewel, a Representative and a Senator from Massachusetts; born in Brookline, Mass., January 28, 1818; attended the public schools; taught school in Shirley, Mass.; engaged in mercantile pursuits in Groton, Mass., in 1841; appointed postmaster of Groton in 1841; studied law; was admitted to the bar but did not enter into active practice for many years; member of the State house of representatives 1842–1844 and 1847–1850; unsuccessful Democratic candidate for election to the Twenty-ninth, Thirtieth, and Thirty-first Congresses; unsuccessful Democratic candidate for Governor of Massachusetts in 1849 and 1850; State bank commissioner 1849–1851; Governor of Massachusetts in 1851 and 1852; member of the State constitutional convention in 1853; secretary of the State board of education from October 1855 until January 1861; member of the board of overseers of Harvard University from 1850 until 1860; member of the peace convention of 1861 held in Washington, D. C., in an effort to devise means to prevent the impending war; served on the military commission under the War Department in 1862; first Commissioner of Internal Revenue in 1862 and 1863; elected as a Republican to the Thirty-eighth and to the three succeeding Congresses and served from March 4, 1863, to March 12, 1869, when he resigned; one of the managers appointed by the House of Representatives in 1868 to conduct the impeachment proceedings against Andrew Johnson, President of the United States; appointed Secretary of the Treasury by President Grant and served from March 12, 1869, to March 17, 1873, when he resigned; elected to the United States Senate to fill the vacancy caused by the resignation of Henry Wilson and served from March 17, 1873, until March 3, 1877; appointed by President Hayes as commissioner to codify and edit the Statutes at Large in March 1877; United States counsel before the French and American Claims Commission in 1880; declined appointment as Secretary of the Treasury in 1884; practiced law in Washington, D. C.; counsel for Haiti in 1885, for Hawaii in 1886, and for Chile in 1893 and 1894; president of the Anti-Imperialist League 1898–1905; died in Groton, Middlesex County, Mass., February 27, 1905; interment in Groton Cemetery.

BOVEE, Matthias Jacob, a Representative from New York; born in Amsterdam, Montgomery County, N. Y., July 24, 1793; attended the rural school until the death of his father in 1807; taught school in winter and worked the family farm in summer; engaged in mercantile pursuits in 1815; chairman of the town of Amsterdam; member of the county board of supervisors; elected a member of the State assembly in 1826; trustee of the village of Amsterdam in 1831; elected as a Jacksonian Democrat to the Twenty-fourth Congress (March 4, 1835–March 3, 1837); returned to Amsterdam and resumed mercantile pursuits; moved to Milwaukee, Wis., in June 1843 and two months later settled near Eagle, Waukesha County, and engaged in agricultural pursuits; justice of the peace for 10 years; died in Eagle, Wis., September 12, 1872; interment in Oak Ridge Cemetery.

BOW, Frank Townsend, a Representative from Ohio; born in Canton, Stark County, Ohio, February 20, 1901; attended the public schools in Canton and Plain Township, Stark County, Ohio, the University School, Cleveland, Ohio, and Culver Military Academy, Culver, Ind.; attended the law school of Ohio Northern University at Ada in 1921; postgraduate work at Columbia University, New York City, N. Y.; was admitted to the bar in 1923 and commenced the practice of law in Canton, Ohio; assistant attorney general of Ohio 1929–1932; during World War II became news editor of radio station WHBC, Canton, Ohio, and in 1945 was selected to serve as a war correspondent with Ohio's Thirty-seventh Division in the Philippines; general counsel to Subcommittee on Expenditures and to the Select Committee To Investigate the Federal Communications Commission during the Eightieth Congress; served as legislative assistant to Senator Andrew F. Schoeppel in the Eighty-first Congress; elected as a Republican to the Eighty-second and to the four succeeding Congresses (January 3, 1951–January 3, 1961). *Reelected to the Eighty-seventh Congress.*

BOWDEN, George Edwin (nephew of Lemuel Jackson Bowden), a Representative from Virginia; born in Williamsburg, James City County, Va., July 6, 1852; attended a private school; studied law; was admitted to the bar but never practiced; engaged in banking; collector of customs for the port of Norfolk from September 1879 until May 1885; elected as a Republican to the Fiftieth and Fifty-first Congresses (March 4, 1887–March 3, 1891); unsuccessful candidate for reelection in 1890 to the Fifty-second Congress; again collector of customs for the port of Norfolk; clerk of the United States Court for the Eastern District of Virginia from March 10, 1899, until his death in Norfolk, Va., January 22, 1908; interment in Elmwood Cemetery.

BOWDEN, Lemuel Jackson (uncle of George Edwin Bowden), a Senator from Virginia; born in Williamsburg, James City County, Va., January 16, 1815; was graduated from William and Mary College, Williamsburg, Va.; studied law; was admitted to the bar in 1838 and commenced practice in Williamsburg; member of the State house of delegates 1841–1846; delegate to the Virginia constitutional conventions in 1849 and 1851; presidential elector on the Constitutional Union ticket of Bell and Everett in 1860; elected as a Republican to the United States Senate and served from March 4, 1863, until his death in Washington, D. C., on January 2, 1864; interment in Congressional Cemetery.

BOWDLE, Stanley Eyre, a Representative from Ohio; born in Clifton, Hamilton County, Ohio, September 4, 1868; attended the public schools until fifteen years of age; served an apprenticeship of three years in the machine shops of Cramp's shipyard, Philadelphia, Pa.; studied law, and was graduated from the Cincinnati Law School in 1889; was admitted to the bar the same year and commenced practice in Cincinnati; because of ill health, moved to Colorado and later to Mexico, where he

resided from 1897 to 1900; returned to Cincinnati and resumed his profession; member of the State constitutional convention in 1912; elected as a Democrat to the Sixty-third Congress (March 4, 1913–March 3, 1915); unsuccessful candidate for reelection in 1914 and 1916 to the Sixty-fourth and Sixty-fifth Congresses, respectively; mayor of Clifton, Ohio; engaged in the practice of law in Cincinnati, Ohio, until his death there April 6, 1919; interment in Spring Grove Cemetery.

BOWDON, Franklin Welsh (uncle of Sydney Johnston Bowie), a Representative from Alabama; born in Chester District, S. C., February 17, 1817; attended the common schools and was graduated from the University of Alabama at Tuscaloosa in 1836; studied law; was admitted to the bar and commenced practice in Talladega, Ala.; member of the State house of representatives in 1844 and 1845; elected as a Democrat to the Twenty-ninth Congress to fill the vacancy caused by the death of Felix G. McConnell; reelected to the Thirtieth and Thirty-first Congresses and served from December 7, 1846, to March 3, 1851; was not a candidate for renomination in 1850; moved to Henderson, Rusk County, Tex., in 1852, where he resumed the practice of his profession; presidential elector on the Democratic ticket of Buchanan and Breckinridge in 1856; died in Henderson, Tex., June 8, 1857; interment in the City Cemetery.

BOWEN, Christopher Columbus, a Representative from South Carolina; born in Providence, R. I., January 5, 1832; attended the public schools; moved to Georgia in 1850; engaged in agricultural pursuits; studied law; was admitted to the bar in 1862 and commenced practice in Charleston, S. C.; during the Civil War enlisted in the Confederate Army and served throughout the war as a captain in the Coast Guard; resumed the practice of law in Charleston, S. C.; member of the Republican State convention at Charleston in May 1867; first chairman of the Republican State central committee; delegate to the State constitutional convention in November 1867; upon the readmission of South Carolina to representation was elected as a Republican to the Fortieth and Forty-first Congresses and served from July 20, 1868, to March 3, 1871; unsuccessful candidate for reelection in 1870 to the Forty-second Congress; elected sheriff of Charleston in November 1872; died in New York City, June 23, 1880; interment in St. Laurence Cemetery, Charleston, S. C.

BOWEN, Henry (son of Rees Tate Bowen, nephew of John Warfield Johnston, and cousin of William Bowen Campbell), a Representative from Virginia; born at "Maiden Springs," near Tazewell, Tazewell County, Va., December 26, 1841; attended the public schools and Emory and Henry College, Emory, Va.; engaged in agricultural pursuits and grazing; during the Civil War entered the Confederate Army in 1861 as a captain of Cavalry in Payne's brigade, Lee's division, Army of Northern Virginia, and served until December 21, 1864, when he was captured by Sheridan's cavalry at Lacy Springs, Va.; released June 19, 1865; returned to his native county and resumed farming and grazing; member of the State house of delegates 1869–1873; elected as a Readjuster to the Forty-eighth Congress (March 4, 1883–March 3, 1885); unsuccessful candidate for renomination in 1884; elected as a Republican to the Fiftieth Congress (March 4, 1887–March 3, 1889); unsuccessful candidate for reelection in 1888 to the Fifty-first Congress; delegate to the Republican National Convention at Minneapolis in 1892; resumed agricultural interests and stock raising in Tazewell County, Va.; died at his home, "Maiden Springs," in Tazewell County, April 29, 1915; interment in Jeffersonville Cemetery, Tazewell, Va.

BOWEN, John Henry, a Representative from Tennessee; born in Washington County, Va., in September 1780; attended the schools of Lexington, Ky.; studied law; was admitted to the bar and commenced practice in Gallatin, Tenn.; elected as a Democrat to the Thirteenth Congress (March 4, 1813–March 3, 1815); engaged in the practice of law in Gallatin, Cherokee County, Tenn., until his death there September 25, 1822.

BOWEN, Rees Tate (father of Henry Bowen), a Representative from Virginia; born at "Maiden Springs," near Tazewell, Tazewell County, Va., January 10, 1809; attended Abingdon Academy, Virginia; engaged in agricultural pursuits; appointed brigadier general of the State militia; member of the State house of delegates 1863 and 1864; magistrate of Tazewell County for several years prior to the war and presiding justice of the county court a portion of that time; elected as a Conservative to the Forty-third Congress (March 4, 1873–March 3, 1875); was not a candidate for renomination in 1874; resumed agricultural pursuits; died at his home, "Maiden Springs," in Tazewell County, Va., August 29, 1879; interment in the family burying ground on his estate, "Maiden Springs."

BOWEN, Thomas Mead, a Senator from Colorado; born near the present site of Burlington, Iowa, October 26, 1835; attended the public schools and the academy at Mount Pleasant, Iowa; studied law; was admitted to the bar in 1853 and practiced; moved to Wayne County, Iowa, in 1856 and to Kansas in 1858; during the Civil War served in the Union Army from June 1861 until July 1865, first as a captain in the First Regiment, Nebraska Volunteer Infantry, after which he raised and commanded, as colonel, the Thirteenth Regiment, Kansas Infantry; brigadier general by brevet and in command of a brigade the last two years of the war; located in Arkansas after the war; delegate to the Republican National Convention at Baltimore in 1864; member and president of the constitutional convention of Arkansas which convened under the reconstruction acts of Congress in 1866; justice of the supreme court of Arkansas 1867–1871; appointed Governor of Idaho Territory by President Grant in 1871; resigned and returned to Arkansas; moved to Colorado in January 1875 and resumed the practice of law; upon the organization of the State government was elected judge of the fourth judicial district in 1876 and served until 1880; member of the State house of representatives in 1882; resigned, having been elected as a Republican to the United States Senate, and served from March 4, 1883, to March 3, 1889; engaged in mining in Colorado, with residence in Pueblo, Colo., where he died December 30, 1906; interment in Roselawn Cemetery.

BOWER, Gustavus Miller, a Representative from Missouri; born near Culpeper, Culpeper County, Va., December 12, 1790; attended the public schools; studied medicine in Philadelphia, Pa.; moved to Kentucky prior to 1812 and resided near Nicholasville; enlisted during the War of 1812 as a surgeon-dresser; was one of the few survivors of the massacre at Frenchtown, near Detroit, January 23, 1813; moved to Monroe County, Mo., in 1833, settled near Paris, and engaged in the practice of medicine and also in agricultural pursuits; elected as a Democrat to the Twenty-eighth Congress (March 4, 1843–March 3, 1845); resumed the practice of medicine; died near Paris, Monroe County, Mo., November 17, 1864; interment in the family burying ground north of Paris, Mo.

BOWER, William Horton, a Representative from North Carolina; born near Wilkesboro, Wilkes County, N. C., June 6, 1850; attended the Finley High School at Lenoir, N. C.; studied law; was admitted to the bar in 1870 and commenced practice in Lenoir; moved to California in 1876 and taught school there four years; returned to Lenoir, N. C., in 1881; member of the State house of representatives in 1882; served in the State senate in 1884; solicitor of the tenth judicial district of North Carolina in 1885 and 1886; unsuccessful candidate for Congress in 1890; elected as a Democrat to the Fifty-third Congress (March 4, 1893–March 3, 1895); unsuccessful candidate for reelection in 1894 to the Fifty-fourth Congress; resumed the practice of law in Lenoir, Caldwell County, N. C., and died there May 11, 1910; interment in Elkville Cemetery, Caldwell County, N. C.

BOWERS, Eaton Jackson, a Representative from Mississippi; born in Canton, Madison County, Miss., June 17, 1865; attended the public schools, and Mississippi Military Institute at Pass Christian; studied law; was admitted to the bar in 1883 at the age of seventeen and practiced in Canton until August 1884, when he moved to Bay St. Louis; engaged in the practice of law and in newspaper work; editor and proprietor of the Gulf Coast Progress at Bay St. Louis; member of the Democratic State executive committee 1886–1900; presidential elector on the Democratic ticket of Cleveland and Thurman in 1888 and of Cleveland and Stevenson in 1892; retired from the newspaper business in 1890; member of the State senate in 1896; served in the State house of representatives in 1900; delegate to the Democratic National Conventions in 1900 and 1916; elected as a Democrat to the Fifty-eighth and to the three succeeding Congresses (March 4, 1903–March 3, 1911); was not a candidate for renomination in 1910 to the Sixty-second Congress; resumed the practice of law in Bay St. Louis, Hancock County, Miss.; moved to New Orleans, La., and continued the practice of law until his death there October 26, 1939; interment in Cedar Rest Cemetery, Bay St. Louis, Miss.

BOWERS, George Meade, a Representative from West Virginia; born in Gerrardstown, Berkeley County, W. Va., September 13, 1863; educated by private tutors and attended high school; engaged in banking; member of the State house of delegates 1883–1887; supervisor of the United States census for West Virginia in 1890; delegate to the Republican National Convention at Minneapolis in 1892; member and treasurer of the board of World's Fair commissioners for West Virginia in 1893; Commissioner of Fisheries from 1898 to 1913, when he resigned; elected as a Republican to the Sixty-fourth Congress to fill the vacancy caused by the death of William G. Brown, Jr.; reelected to the Sixty-fifth, Sixty-sixth, and Sixty-seventh Congresses and served from May 9, 1916, to March 3, 1923; unsuccessful candidate for reelection in 1922 to the Sixty-eighth Congress; president of the People's Trust Co.; died in Martinsburg, W. Va., December 7, 1925; interment in the Presbyterian Cemetery, Gerrardstown, W. Va.

BOWERS, John Myer, a Representative from New York; born in Boston, Mass., September 25, 1772; attended the common schools and was graduated from Columbia College, New York City; studied law; was admitted to the bar in 1802 and commenced practice in Cooperstown, N. Y.; moved to his country home, "Lakelands," near Cooperstown, in 1805; presented credentials as a Member-elect to the Thirteenth Congress to fill the vacancy caused by the death of Representative-elect William Dowse and served from May 26, 1813, to December 20, 1813, when he was succeeded by Isaac William, Jr., who contested the election; resumed the practice of law in Cooperstown, Otsego County, N. Y., where he died February 24, 1846; interment in Lakewood Cemetery.

BOWERS, William Wallace, a Representative from California; born in Whitestown, Oneida County, N. Y., October 20, 1834; attended the common schools; moved to Wisconsin in 1854; enlisted as a private in Company I, First Wisconsin Cavalry, February 22, 1862; discharged from the service as second sergeant February 22, 1865; moved to San Diego, Calif., in 1869; engaged in ranching; member of the State assembly in 1873 and 1874; appointed collector of customs of the port of San Diego, Calif., September 25, 1874, and served until his resignation on February 3, 1879; owned and operated a hotel in San Diego 1884–1891; member of the State senate 1887–1889; elected as a Republican to the Fifty-second, Fifty-third, and Fifty-fourth Congresses (March 4, 1891–March 3, 1897); unsuccessful candidate for reelection in 1896 to the Fifty-fifth Congress; again appointed collector of customs of the port of San Diego, Calif., on March 15, 1902, and served until March 4, 1906; resided in San Diego, Calif., in retirement until his death there on May 2, 1917; interment in the Masonic Cemetery.

BOWERSOCK, Justin De Witt, a Representative from Kansas; born near Columbiana, Columbiana County, Ohio, September 19, 1842; moved to Iowa City, Iowa, in 1860 and engaged in mercantile pursuits and grain shipping; moved to Lawrence, Kans., in 1877 and engaged in banking and in the manufacture of flour, paper, and barbed wire, and was closely connected with nearly all the business enterprises of Lawrence; mayor of Lawrence 1881–1885; elected to the Kansas House of Representatives in 1887; member of the State senate in 1895; elected as a Republican to the Fifty-sixth and to the three succeeding Congresses (March 4, 1899–March 3, 1907); was not a candidate for renomination in 1906; interested in banking and the manufacture of flour, ice, paperboard, and shipping containers in Lawrence, Douglas County, Kans., until his death there on October 27, 1922; interment in Oak Hill Cemetery.

BOWIE, Richard Johns, a Representative from Maryland; born in Georgetown, D. C., June 23, 1807; attended the public schools and Brookville Academy; studied law and was graduated from the Georgetown Law School in 1826; commenced practice in Washington, D. C., in 1826; admitted to practice before the Supreme Court in 1829; moved to Rockville, Md., and engaged in agricultural pursuits and also practiced law; member of the State house of delegates 1835–1837; served in the State senate 1837–1841; delegate to the Whig National Convention at Harrisburg, Pa., in 1840; presidential elector on the Whig ticket of Harrison and Tyler in 1840; State's attorney for Montgomery County 1844–1849; elected as a Whig to the Thirty-first and Thirty-second Congresses (March 4, 1849–March 3, 1853); unsuccessful Whig candidate for Governor in 1853; resumed the practice of his profession in Rockville; chief judge of the court of appeals of Maryland 1861–1867; chief judge of the sixth judicial circuit, and as such also an associate judge of the court of appeals of Maryland, from November 7, 1871, until his death near Rockville, Montgomery County, Md., March 12, 1888; interment in Rockville Cemetery.

BOWIE, Sydney Johnston (nephew of Franklin Welsh Bowdon), a Representative from Alabama; born in Talladega, Talladega County, Ala., July 26, 1865; attended private schools, and was graduated from the law department of the University of Alabama at Tuscaloosa in 1885; was admitted to the bar June 1, 1885, and commenced practice in Talladega, Ala.; city clerk of Talladega in 1885 and 1886; member of the board of aldermen in 1891; member of the Democratic State executive committee 1894–1899; moved to Anniston, Ala., in 1899; chairman of the Democratic executive committee having in charge the ratification of the new constitution in Calhoun County in 1901; elected as a Democrat to the Fifty-seventh, Fifty-eighth, and Fifty-ninth Congresses (March 4, 1901–March 3, 1907); declined to be a candidate for renomination in 1906; moved to Birmingham and

continued the practice of law until 1919, when he engaged in business there as an automobile dealer; member of the Southern Education Board in 1908 and 1909; member of the Birmingham Board of Education 1915–1919; chairman of the State educational commission in 1920; delegate at large from Alabama to the Democratic National Convention at San Francisco in 1920 and chairman of the delegation; president of the Alabama Tuberculosis Commission 1920–1922; general chairman of the Birmingham Semicentennial Committee in 1921; delegate to the Democratic State convention in 1922; member of the State harbor commission in 1922 and 1923; State chairman of the Woodrow Wilson Memorial Committee in 1923 and 1924; died in Birmingham, Ala., May 7, 1928; interment in Elmwood Cemetery.

BOWIE, Thomas Fielder (grandnephew of Walter Bowie and brother-in-law of Reverdy Johnson), a Representative from Maryland; born in Queen Anne, Prince Georges County, Md., April 7, 1808; attended Charlotte Hall Academy in St. Marys County, Md., and Princeton College, Princeton, N. J.; was graduated from Union College, Schenectady, N. Y., in 1827; studied law; was admitted to the bar in 1829 and commenced practice in Upper Marlboro, Md.; deputy attorney general for Prince Georges County 1833–1842; member of the State house of delegates 1842–1846; unsuccessful candidate for Governor in 1843; unsuccessful candidate for election in 1850 to the Thirty-second Congress; member of the State constitutional convention in 1851; member of the judicial committee assisting in framing the State's new constitution; presidential elector on the Whig ticket of Scott and Graham in 1852; elected as a Democrat to the Thirty-fourth and Thirty-fifth Congresses (March 4, 1855–March 3, 1859); was an unsuccessful candidate for renomination in 1858 to the Thirty-sixth Congress; resumed the practice of his profession; died in Upper Marlboro, Md., October 30, 1869; interment in the Waring family burying ground at Mount Pleasant, near Upper Marlboro, Md.

BOWIE, Walter (granduncle of Thomas Fielder Bowie), a Representative from Maryland; born in Mattaponi, near Nottingham, Prince Georges County, Md., in 1748; attended Rev. John Eversfield's School, near Nottingham, the common schools in Annapolis, and Craddock's School, near Baltimore, Md.; engaged in agricultural pursuits, was a large landowner, and also was interested in shipping; member of the State constitutional convention in 1776; captain and, later, major of a Prince Georges County company during the Revolution; member of the State house of delegates 1780–1800; served in the State senate 1800–1802; elected as a Democrat to the Seventh Congress to fill the vacancy caused by the resignation of Richard Sprigg, Jr.; reelected to the Eighth Congress and served from March 24, 1802, to March 3, 1805; declined to be a candidate for renomination in 1804 to the Ninth Congress; died near Collington, Prince Georges County, Md., November 9, 1810; interment in the family burying ground on his estate.

BOWLER, James Bernard, a Representative from Illinois; born in Chicago, Ill., February 5, 1875; attended the parochial and public schools; professional bicycle rider and racer; member of the Chicago City Council 1906–1923; served as commissioner of compensation for the city of Chicago 1923–1927; public vehicle license commissioner for the city of Chicago in 1934; again served as a member in the city council 1928–1953, serving as president pro tempore for eight years; engaged in the insurance business; elected as a Democrat to the Eighty-third Congress to fill the vacancy caused by the death of Adolph J. Sabath; reelected to the Eighty-fourth and Eighty-fifth Congresses and served from July 7, 1953, until his death in Chicago, Ill., July 18, 1957; interment in All Saints Cemetery, Des Plaines, Ill.

BOWLES, Chester Bliss, a Representative from Connecticut; born in Springfield, Hampden County, Mass., April 5, 1901; graduated from Choate School, Wallingford, Conn., in 1919 and from Yale University in 1924; businessman in Springfield, Mass. and New York City, N. Y., 1924–1929; cofounder Benton & Bowles, Inc., an advertising agency, New York, N. Y., in 1929 and was chairman of the board 1936–1941; Connecticut State rationing administrator in 1942, State director in 1942 and 1943, and general manager July–October 1943; price administrator, Office of Price Administration, 1943–1946; member, War Production Board and Petroleum Board for War 1943–1946; chairman, Economic Stabilization Board, 1946; delegate to the United Nations Economic, Scientific and Cultural Organization Conference at Paris in 1946; Governor of Connecticut 1949–1951; Ambassador to India and Nepal 1951–1953; author and lecturer; trustee of Rockefeller Foundation, Woodrow Wilson Foundation, and Franklin D. Roosevelt Foundation; delegate to the Democratic National Conventions in 1940, 1948, and 1956; chairman of the platform committee, Democratic National Convention, in 1960; elected as a Democrat to the Eighty-sixth Congress (January 3, 1959–January 3, 1961); was not a candidate for renomination in 1960; Under Secretary of State since January 20, 1961; is a resident of Essex, Conn.

BOWLES, Henry Leland, a Representative from Massachusetts; born in Athens, Windham County, Vt., January 6, 1866; attended the district schools at Kendricks Corner and Vermont Academy at Saxtons River, Vt.; at the age of eighteen moved to Osage, Iowa, and engaged in agricultural pursuits; later moved to California, where for four years he worked as lumberjack, rancher, and farmer; returned east and settled in Massachusetts, working in Waltham, Salem, and Lynn at various businesses; trustee of the Vermont Academy; moved to Springfield, Mass., in 1898 and became engaged in the operation of a chain of restaurants; member of the Governor's council in 1913, 1918, and 1919; during the First World War was a member of the local selective draft board of Springfield, Mass., in 1917 and 1918; delegate to the Republican National Convention at Chicago in 1920 and at Cleveland in 1924; elected as a Republican to the Sixty-ninth Congress to fill the vacancy caused by the death of George B. Churchill; reelected to the Seventieth Congress and served from September 29, 1925, to March 3, 1929; was not a candidate for renomination in 1928; resumed his former business pursuits; died in Springfield, Mass., May 17, 1932; the remains were cremated and the ashes interred in Springfield Cemetery.

BOWLIN, James Butler, a Representative from Missouri; born near Fredericksburg, Spotsylvania County, Va., January 16, 1804; apprenticed to a trade, but abandoned it to teach school; received a classical education; moved to Lewisburg, Greenbrier County, Va., in 1825; studied law; was admitted to the bar in 1826 and commenced practice in Greenbrier County; moved to St. Louis, Mo., in 1833 and continued the practice of law; established the Farmers and Mechanics' Advocate; chief clerk of the State house of representatives in 1836; member of the State house of representatives in 1836 and 1837; appointed district attorney for St. Louis in 1837; unsuccessful candidate for the State house of representatives in 1838; elected judge of the criminal court in 1839 and served until his resignation in 1842; elected as a Democrat to the Twenty-eighth and to the three succeeding Congresses (March 4, 1843–March 3, 1851); unsuccessful candidate for reelection in 1850 to the Thirty-second Congress; appointed Minister Resident to New Granada by President Pierce December 13, 1854; appointed commissioner to Paraguay by President Buchanan September 9, 1858, and served until February 10, 1859; resumed the practice of law; died in St. Louis, Mo., July 19, 1874; interment in Bellefontaine Cemetery.

BOWLING, William Bismarck, a Representative from Alabama; born near Iron City, Calhoun County, Ala., September 24, 1870; attended the common schools, and was graduated from the State normal school, Jacksonville, Ala., in 1892; taught in the public schools of Montgomery, Ala., 1893–1895 and of Columbus, Ga., 1896–1899; moved to Lafayette, Chambers County, Ala.; studied law; was admitted to the bar in 1900 and commenced practice in Lafayette; solicitor of the fifth judicial circuit of Alabama 1905–1920; member of the board of trustees of Alabama Polytechnic Institute at Auburn; elected as a Democrat to the Sixty-sixth Congress to fill the vacancy caused by the resignation of J. Thomas Heflin; reelected to the Sixty-seventh and to the three succeeding Congresses and served from December 14, 1920, until his resignation effective August 16, 1928, having been appointed judge for the fifth judicial circuit of Alabama, in which capacity he served until his death; died in Lafayette, Ala., on December 27, 1946; interment in Lafayette Cemetery.

BOWMAN, Charles Calvin, a Representative from Pennsylvania; born in Troy, Rensselaer County, N. Y., November 14, 1852; attended the public schools and Lansingburg Academy, Troy, N. Y.; learned the woodworking trade; was graduated in civil engineering from Union College, Schenectady, N. Y., in 1875; engaged in civil engineering work for the State of Massachusetts at Danvers in 1875; organized the western shipping department of the Pennsylvania Coal Co., Pittston, Pa., in 1876, which he managed until 1883; served as general manager of the Florence Coal Co. in 1883 and 1884, later operating as an independent miner and shipper of anthracite coal; trustee of the Pittston Hospital Association; secretary of the soldiers' relief association; mayor of the city of Pittston in 1886; also served as a member of the city council for sixteen terms; treasurer of the Pittston State Armory Board and president of the New England Society of Northeastern Pennsylvania; delegate to the Independent Republican State convention in 1890 and to the Republican State convention in 1898; presented credentials as a Republican Member-elect to the Sixty-second Congress and served from March 4, 1911, to December 12, 1912, when the seat was declared vacant; unsuccessful candidate for election in 1912 to the Sixty-third Congress; resumed the coal business, serving as vice president of the Roden Coal Co., director of the Raub Coal Co., and secretary-treasurer of the Franklin Coal Co.; died in Pittston, Pa., July 3, 1941; interment in Pittston Cemetery.

BOWMAN, Frank Llewellyn, a Representative from West Virginia; born in Masontown, Fayette County, Pa., January 21, 1879; attended the public schools; moved with his parents to Morgantown, W. Va.; was graduated from the University of West Virginia at Morgantown in 1902; teller in a bank at Morgantown from 1902 until 1904, when he resigned to take up the study of law; was admitted to the bar in 1905 and commenced practice in Morgantown, W. Va.; was also interested in coal mining; appointed postmaster of Morgantown May 25, 1911, and served until April 14, 1915, when a successor was appointed; city mayor in 1916 and 1917; declined renomination for mayor; elected as a Republican to the Sixty-ninth and to the three succeeding Congresses (March 4, 1925–March 3, 1933); unsuccessful candidate for reelection in 1932 to the Seventy-third Congress; organized a coal company in Washington, D. C., and served as president until appointed a member of the Board of Veterans Appeals of the Veterans' Administration in 1935 and served until his death in Washington, D. C., on September 15, 1936; interment in Oak Grove Cemetery, Morgantown, W. Va.

BOWMAN, Selwyn Zadock, a Representative from Massachusetts; born in Charlestown, Middlesex County, Mass., May 11, 1840; attended the Charlestown public schools; moved to

Somerville, Mass., with his parents in 1855; was graduated from Harvard University in 1860 and from its law school in 1863; was admitted to the bar in 1863 and commenced practice in Boston, Mass., and continued his residence in Somerville, Mass.; member of the State house of representatives in 1870, 1871, and again in 1875; city solicitor of Somerville, Mass., in 1872 and 1873; served in the State senate in 1876 and 1877; elected as a Republican to the Forty-sixth and Forty-seventh Congresses (March 4, 1879–March 3, 1883); unsuccessful candidate for reelection in 1882 to the Forty-eighth Congress; returned to Somerville, Mass., and resumed the practice of law in Boston, Mass.; again served as city solicitor of Somerville, Mass., 1888–1897; moved to Cohasset, Mass., in 1914, and continued the practice of law in Boston, Mass.; died while on a visit for medical treatment in Framingham, Mass., September 30, 1928; interment in Mount Auburn Cemetery, Cambridge, Mass.

BOWMAN, Thomas, a Representative from Iowa; born in Wiscasset, Lincoln County, Maine, May 25, 1848; moved to Council Bluffs, Iowa, in 1868; engaged in mercantile pursuits; elected treasurer of Pottawattamie County in 1875, and reelected in 1877 and 1879; mayor of Council Bluffs in 1882; appointed postmaster in 1885 and served until 1889, when he resigned; purchased controlling ownership of the Council Bluffs Globe in 1883; elected as a Democrat to the Fifty-second Congress (March 4, 1891–March 3, 1893); was not a candidate for renomination in 1892; again postmaster of Council Bluffs 1904–1908; engaged in railroad contracting; died in Council Bluffs, Iowa, December 1, 1917; interment in Pine Grove Cemetery, Dresden Mills, Maine.

BOWNE, Obadiah, a Representative from New York; born near Richmond, Richmond County, Staten Island, N. Y., May 19, 1822; attended private schools, and was a student at Princeton College 1838–1840; held several local offices; elected as a Whig to the Thirty-second Congress (March 4, 1851–March 3, 1853); declined to be a candidate for renomination in 1852; quarantine commissioner 1857–1859; presidential elector on the Republican ticket of Lincoln and Johnson in 1864; died in Richmond Village, Staten Island, N. Y., April 27, 1874; interment in St. Andrew's Cemetery.

BOWNE, Samuel Smith, a Representative from New York; born in New Rochelle, Westchester County, N. Y., April 11, 1800; moved to Otsego County with his parents, who settled near Morris, N. Y.; attended the common schools; engaged in agricultural pursuits; moved to Laurens, Otsego County, in 1825; studied law; was admitted to the bar in 1832 and commenced practice in Laurens; moved to Cooperstown, N. Y.; member of the State assembly in 1834; elected as a Van Buren Democrat to the Twenty-seventh Congress (March 4, 1841–March 3, 1843); was not a candidate for renomination in 1842; moved to Rochester, N. Y., in 1846 and continued the practice of his profession; judge of Otsego County 1851–1855; resumed the practice of law; died on his farm near Morris, Otsego County, N. J., July 9, 1865; interment in Friends Burying Ground.

BOWRING, Eva Kelly, a Senator from Nebraska; born in Nevada, Vernon County, Mo., January 9, 1892; engaged in ranching as owner and operator of Bar-99 Ranch, near Merriman, Nebr.; former chairman of the Nebraska Stockgrowers Association Brand Committee and an active member of the Northwest Nebraska Hereford Breeders Association; vice chairman of the Nebraska Republican Central Committee 1946–1954; vice chairman of the twenty-one State Midwest Vice Chairman's Association in 1954 and director of the Women's Division of the Republican Party in Nebraska 1946–1954; appointed as a Republican to

the United States Senate April 16, 1954, to fill the vacancy caused by the death of Dwight Palmer Griswold, and served until November 7, 1954; was not a candidate for election to fill the vacancy; member of the National Advisory Council, National Institutes of Health, 1954–1958 and 1960–1961; appointed a member of the Board of Parole, Department of Justice, in September 1956 and reappointed in September 1958 for a six-year term ending September 30, 1964; is a legal resident of Merriman, Nebr.

BOX, John Calvin, a Representative from Texas; born near Crockett, Houston County, Tex., March 28, 1871; attended the country schools, and Alexander Collegiate Institute (later Lon Morris College), Kilgore, Tex.; studied law; was admitted to the bar in 1893 and commenced practice in Lufkin, Tex.; moved to Jacksonville, Cherokee County, Tex., in 1897 and continued the practice of his profession; also a licensed Methodist minister; judge of the Cherokee County Court 1898–1901; mayor of Jacksonville 1902–1905; member of the Democratic State committee 1908–1910; member of the board of education and served as chairman 1913–1918; elected as a Democrat to the Sixty-sixth and to the five succeeding Congresses (March 4, 1919–March 3, 1931); unsuccessful candidate for renomination in 1930; reengaged in the practice of law in Jacksonville, Tex., until his death there May 17, 1941; interment in the City Cemetery.

BOYCE, William Henry, a Representative from Delaware; born at Peppers Mills, near Laurel, Sussex County, Del., November 28, 1855; attended the public schools and Laurel Academy; was principal of the public schools at Laurel 1875–1880 and at Oxford, Md., in 1880 and 1881; recorder of deeds for Sussex County at Georgetown 1881–1886; studied law; was admitted to the bar in 1887 and practiced in Georgetown, Del., until 1897; president of the board of education 1883–1886; captain of Company G, Delaware National Guard, 1887–1890; president of the town commissioners 1895–1897; chairman of the Sussex County Democratic committee 1893–1897; delegate to the Democratic National Conventions in 1896 and 1924; appointed secretary of state of Delaware January 19, 1897, and served until June 17, 1897, when he resigned; associate judge of the Delaware Supreme Court 1897–1921 and ex officio judicial reporter 1909–1921; retired June 15, 1921; elected as a Democrat to the Sixty-eighth Congress (March 4, 1923–March 3, 1925); renominated by acclamation but was unsuccessful for reelection in 1924 to the Sixty-ninth Congress; president of the Elizabeth W. Murphy School for Indigent Children of Kent and Sussex Counties and also president of the Delaware Citizens' Association; resumed the practice of law until retirement from active practice in 1936; died in Dover, Del., February 6, 1942; interment in Christ Church Cemetery.

BOYCE, William Waters, a Representative from South Carolina; born in Charleston, S. C., October 24, 1818; attended South Carolina College (now the University of South Carolina) at Columbia and the University of Virginia at Charlottesville; studied law; was admitted to the bar in 1839 and practiced in Winnsboro, S. C.; member of the State house of representatives; elected as a State Rights Democrat to the Thirty-third and to the three succeeding Congresses and served from March 4, 1853, until his retirement on December 21, 1860; appointed a delegate for South Carolina to the Confederate Provisional Congress January 4, 1861; elected as a member of the First and Second Confederate Congresses 1862–1864; moved to Washington, D. C., in 1866 and practiced law until his retirement a few years before his death; died at his country home, "Ashland," in Fairfax County, Va., February 3, 1890; interment in the Episcopal Cemetery, Winnsboro, Fairfield County, S. C.

BOYD, Adam, a Representative from New Jersey; born in Mendham, N. J., March 21, 1746; moved to Bergen County about 1770 and to Hackensack a few years later; member of the board of freeholders and justices in 1773, 1784, 1791, 1794, and 1798; sheriff of Bergen County 1778–1781 and again in 1789; member of the State house of assembly in 1782, 1783, 1787, 1794, and 1795; judge of the court of common pleas of Bergen County 1803–1805; elected as a Democrat to the Eighth Congress (March 4, 1803–March 3, 1805); elected to the Tenth Congress to fill the vacancy caused by the death of Ezra Darby; reelected to the Eleventh and Twelfth Congresses and served from March 8, 1808, to March 3, 1813; again judge of the court of common pleas 1813–1833; died in Hackensack, Bergen County, N. J., August 15, 1835; interment in the First Reformed Church Cemetery.

BOYD, Alexander, a Representative from New York; born in Albany, N. Y., September 14, 1764; moved to Middleburg, Schoharie County, N. Y., and engaged in agricultural pursuits; elected as a Whig to the Thirteenth Congress (March 4, 1813–March 3, 1815); died in the town of Esperence, Schoharie County, N. Y., April 8, 1857; interment in Schoharie Cemetery, Schoharie, N. Y.

BOYD, John Frank, a Representative from Nebraska; born in Connellsville, Fayette County, Pa., August 8, 1853; moved with his parents to Henry County, Ill., in 1857; attended the public schools and Abingdon (Ill.) College; studied law; was admitted to the bar in 1878 and commenced practice in Galva, Ill.; moved to Nebraska in 1883 and settled in Oakdale, Antelope County; prosecuting attorney of Antelope County, Nebr., 1888–1894; judge of the Ninth Judicial District Court of Nebraska 1900–1907; moved to Neligh, Antelope County, Nebr., in 1901; elected as a Republican to the Sixtieth Congress (March 4, 1907–March 3, 1909); unsuccessful candidate for reelection in 1908 to the Sixty-first Congress; resumed the practice of law in Neligh, Nebr., until 1929, when he retired and moved to Los Angeles, Calif.; died in Los Angeles, Calif., May 28, 1945; interment in Forest Lawn Cemetery.

BOYD, John Huggins, a Representative from New York; born in Salem, N. Y., July 31, 1799; attended the common schools, and was graduated from Washington Academy, Salem, N. Y., in 1818; studied law; was admitted to the bar in 1823 and commenced practice in Salem, N. Y., but shortly afterward moved to Whitehall, N. Y.; elected justice of the peace in 1828 and served for many years; member of the State assembly in 1840; supervisor of Whitehall in 1845, 1848, and 1849; elected as a Whig to the Thirty-second Congress (March 4, 1851–March 3, 1853); special surrogate of Washington County 1857–1859; elected president of the village; resumed the practice of law; died in Whitehall, Washington County, N. Y., on July 2, 1868; interment in Evergreen Cemetery, Salem, N. Y.

BOYD, Linn, a Representative from Kentucky; born in Nashville, Tenn., November 22, 1800; pursued preparatory studies; moved with his parents to New Design, Trigg County, Ky.; engaged in agricultural pursuits in Calloway County; member of the State house of representatives 1827–1832; returned to Trigg County in 1834; elected as a Democrat to the Twenty-fourth Congress (March 4, 1835–March 3, 1837); unsuccessful candidate for reelection in 1836 to the Twenty-fifth Congress; elected to the Twenty-sixth and to the seven succeeding Congresses (March 4, 1839–March 3, 1855); served as Speaker of the House of Representatives in the Thirty-second and Thirty-third Congresses; moved to Paducah, Paducah County, Ky., in 1852; elected Lieutenant Governor of Kentucky in 1859, but when the senate convened was too ill to preside over its deliberations; died in Paducah, Ky., December 17, 1859; interment in Oak Grove Cemetery.

BOYD, Sempronius Hamilton, a Representative from Missouri; born near Nashville, Williamson County, Tenn., May 28, 1828; moved to Missouri in 1840 with his parents, who settled on a farm near Springfield, Greene County; educated by private tutors; moved to California in 1849, where he prospected for gold and taught school; returned to Missouri in 1854; clerk of the court of Greene County 1854–1856; studied law; was admitted to the bar in 1856 and commenced practice in Springfield, Mo.; mayor of Springfield in 1856; during the Civil War raised the Twenty-fourth Missouri Infantry and served as colonel until his election to Congress; elected as an Emancipationist to the Thirty-eighth Congress (March 4, 1863–March 3, 1865); appointed judge of the court of the fourteenth judicial district in 1865; member of the Republican National Committee 1864–1868; delegate to the Republican National Convention at Baltimore in 1864; interested in building and operating the Southwest Pacific Railroad 1867–1874; elected as a Republican to the Forty-first Congress (March 4, 1869–March 3, 1871); operated a wagon factory 1874–1876; resumed the practice of law; appointed Minister Resident and consul general to Siam by President Harrison on October 1, 1890, and served until October 26, 1892; died in Springfield, Greene County, Mo., June 22, 1894; interment in the Hazelwood Cemetery.

BOYD, Thomas Alexander, a Representative from Illinois; born near Bedford, Adams County, Pa., June 25, 1830; attended the public schools; was graduated from Marshall College, Mercersburg, Pa., in 1848; studied law in Chambersburg, Pa.; was admitted to the bar and commenced practice in Bedford, Pa.; moved to Lewistown, Ill., in 1856 and engaged in the practice of law until 1861; during the Civil War enlisted in the Seventeenth Regiment, Illinois Infantry, in 1861 and obtained the commission of captain; member of the State senate in 1866 and was reelected in 1870; elected as a Republican to the Forty-fifth and Forty-sixth Congresses (March 4, 1877–March 3, 1881); was not a candidate for renomination in 1880; resumed the practice of law; died in Lewistown, Fulton County, Ill., May 28, 1897; interment in Oak Hill Cemetery.

BOYDEN, Nathaniel, a Representative from North Carolina; born in Conway, Mass., August 16, 1796; attended the common schools; served in the War of 1812; was graduated from Union College, Schenectady, N. Y., in 1821; moved to Stokes County, N. C., in 1822; taught school for several years; studied law; was admitted to the bar and practiced; member of the State house of commons in 1838 and 1840; moved to Salisbury, N. C., in 1842 and continued the practice of law; served in the State senate in 1844; elected as a Whig to the Thirtieth Congress (March 4, 1847–March 3, 1849); was not a candidate for renomination in 1848; resumed the practice of law; member of the State constitutional convention of 1865; upon the readmission of North Carolina to representation was elected as a Republican to the Fortieth Congress and served from July 13, 1868, to March 3, 1869; unsuccessfully contested the election of Francis E. Shober to the Forty-first Congress; resumed the practice of law until elected associate justice of the supreme court of North Carolina in 1872 and served until his death in Salisbury, N. C., November 20, 1873; interment in the Lutheran Cemetery.

BOYER, Benjamin Markley, a Representative from Pennsylvania; born in Pottstown, Montgomery County, Pa., January 22, 1823; attended the common schools, and was graduated from the University of Pennsylvania at Philadelphia in 1841;

studied law; was admitted to the bar in 1844 and practiced; deputy attorney general of Montgomery County, Pa., 1848–1850; elected as a Democrat to the Thirty-ninth and Fortieth Congresses (March 4, 1865–March 3, 1869); was not a candidate for renomination in 1868; appointed judge of Montgomery County Court in 1882 and served until his death in Norristown, Pa., August 16, 1887; interment in West Laurel Hill Cemetery, Philadelphia, Pa.

BOYER, Lewis Leonard, a Representative from Illinois; born on a farm near Richfield, Richfield Township, Adams County, Ill., May 19, 1886; attended the rural schools; taught school at Douglas, Franklin, Pin Oak, and Liberty, Ill., 1904–1915, and, while teaching, studied civil engineering; moved to Quincy, Ill., in 1915 and engaged in engineering as county superintendent of highways of Adams County, Ill., from March 1915 until December 1936; elected as a Democrat to the Seventy-fifth Congress (January 3, 1937–January 3, 1939); unsuccessful candidate for reelection in 1938 to the Seventy-sixth Congress; unsuccessful candidate for the State senate in 1940 and 1942; retired from public life because of a heart ailment; died in Quincy, Ill., March 12, 1944; interment in Zander Cemetery, Liberty, Ill.

BOYKIN, Frank William, a Representative from Alabama; born in Bladon Springs, Choctaw County, Ala., February 21, 1885; attended the public schools; moved to Fairford, Ala., in 1890 and was employed as a clerk in a store and later as store manager; moved to Malcolm, Ala., in 1905 and engaged in the manufacture of railroad cross ties; moved to Mobile, Ala., in 1915 and was occupied with real estate, farming, livestock, timber, lumber, and naval stores in southern Alabama; during the First World War served as an official in shipbuilding companies; elected as a Democrat to the Seventy-fourth Congress to fill the vacancy caused by the resignation of John McDuffie; reelected to the Seventy-fifth and to the eleven succeeding Congresses and served from July 30, 1935, to January 3, 1961. *Reelected to the Eighty-seventh Congress.*

BOYLAN, John Joseph, a Representative from New York; born in New York City September 20, 1878; attended the public schools, Cathedral School, De La Salle Institute, and Manhattan College, all in New York City; employed as a postal clerk and afterward engaged in the real-estate business; member of the State assembly 1909–1913; served in the State senate 1913–1922; during the First World War served as a member of the draft board of New York City; elected as a Democrat to the Sixty-eighth and to the seven succeeding Congresses and served from March 4, 1923, until his death; was not a candidate for renomination in 1938 to the Seventy-sixth Congress; died in New York City, N. Y., October 5, 1938; interment in Calvary Cemetery, Long Island City, N. Y.

BOYLE, Charles Augustus, a Representative from Illinois; born in Spring Lake, Ottawa County, Mich., August 13, 1907; after leaving the farm of his parents he graduated from Chicago, Ill., Mount Carmel High School in 1925; worked way through college as a conductor, checker, investigator, driver, and inspector for the Chicago Motor Coach Co.; was graduated from Loyola University, Chicago, Ill., in 1930 and from Loyola Law School in 1933; was admitted to the Illinois bar in 1934 and commenced the practice of law in Chicago, Ill.; zone attorney for the Federal Housing Administration in 1937 and 1938; elected as a Democrat to the Eighty-fourth, Eighty-fifth, and Eighty-sixth Congresses and served from January 3, 1955, until his death in an automobile accident in Chicago, Ill., November 4, 1959; interment in All Saints Cemetery, Des Plaines, Ill.

BOYLE, Charles Edmund, a Representative from Pennsylvania; born in Uniontown, Fayette County, Pa., February 4, 1836; attended the common schools, and Waynesburg College, Waynesburg, Greene County, Pa.; studied law; was admitted to the bar in December 1861 and practiced; elected district attorney for Fayette County in 1862; member of the State house of representatives in 1865 and 1866; president of the Democratic State convention in 1867 and 1871; delegate to the Democratic National Convention in 1876 and 1880; elected as a Democrat to the Forty-eighth and Forty-ninth Congresses (March 4, 1883–March 3, 1887); was not a candidate for renomination in 1886; appointed judge of the Territory of Washington in September 1888 and served until his death in Seattle, Wash., December 15, 1888; interment in Oak Grove Cemetery, Uniontown, Pa.

BOYLE, John, a Representative from Kentucky; born at "Castle Woods," Botetourt County, Va., October 28, 1774; moved with his father to Whitleys Station, Ky., in 1779; educated by private tutors and in private schools; studied law; was admitted to the bar in 1797 and commenced practice in Lancaster, Ky.; member of the State house of representatives in 1800; elected as a Democrat to the Eighth, Ninth, and Tenth Congresses (March 4, 1803–March 3, 1809); one of the managers appointed by the House of Representatives, in January 1804, to conduct the impeachment proceedings against John Pickering, judge of the United States District Court for New Hampshire, and, in December of the same year, against Samuel Chase, Associate Justice of the Supreme Court of the United States; appointed Governor of Illinois Territory in 1809, but declined; judge of the Court of Appeals of Kentucky from April 1809 to April 1810, serving as chief justice from April 1810 to November 8, 1826, when he resigned; United States judge for the district of Kentucky from November 9, 1826, until his death near Danville, Boyle County, Ky., February 28, 1834; interment in Bellevue Cemetery.

BRABSON, Reese Bowen (uncle of Charles Keith Bell), a Representative from Tennessee; born at Brabsons Ferry, near Knoxville, Tenn., September 16, 1817; attended the Dandridge Academy, Dandridge, Tenn.; was graduated from Maryville College, Maryville, Tenn., in 1840; studied law; was admitted to the bar in 1848 and commenced practice in Chattanooga, Tenn.; also engaged in agricultural pursuits; member of the State house of representatives in 1851 and 1852; elected as a Democrat to the Thirty-sixth Congress (March 4, 1859–March 3, 1861); was not a candidate for renomination in 1860; engaged in the practice of his profession until his death in Chattanooga, Tenn., August 16, 1863; interment in the Citizens Cemetery.

BRACE, Jonathan, a Representative from Connecticut; born in Harwinton, Conn., November 12, 1754; pursued preparatory studies; was graduated from Yale College in 1779; studied law; was admitted to the bar in Bennington, Vt., in 1779 and commenced practice in Pawlet, Vt.; moved to Manchester, Vt., in 1782 and continued the practice of law; member of the council of censors to revise the constitution; prosecuting attorney for Bennington County 1784–1785; moved to Glastonbury, Conn., in January 1786 but was not admitted to the Connecticut bar until 1790; member of the general assembly 1788 and 1791–1794 and was chosen assistant in the council in May 1798; moved to Hartford, Conn., in 1794; judge of the city court from 1797 until 1815, with the exception of two years; elected as a Federalist to the Fifth Congress to fill the vacancy caused by the death of Joshua Coit; reelected to the Sixth Congress and served from December 3, 1798, until his resignation in 1800; assistant in the council of the State 1802–1818; appointed prosecuting attorney for Hartford County in December 1807 and served until May 1809, when he resigned; appointed judge of the county court and of probate in May 1809; continued as judge of the county court until 1821 and as judge of probate until 1824; mayor of Hartford 1815–1824; member of the State senate in 1819 and 1820; died in Hartford, Conn., August 26, 1837; interment in the Old North Cemetery.

BRACKENRIDGE, Henry Marie, a Representative from Pennsylvania; born in Pittsburgh, Pa., May 11, 1786; instructed by his father and private tutors; attended a French academy at St. Genevieve, La.; studied law; was admitted to the bar in 1806 and practiced in Somerset, Pa., until 1810; appointed deputy attorney general of the Territory of Orleans (Louisiana) in 1811; district judge of Louisiana in 1812; appointed secretary of a mission to South America in 1817; judge for the western district of Florida 1821–1832; returned to Pennsylvania in 1832 and became owner of a large tract of land upon which he founded the town of Tarentum, Pa.; elected as a Whig to the Twenty-sixth Congress to fill the vacancy caused by the resignation of Richard Biddle and served from October 13, 1840, to March 3, 1841; unsuccessful candidate for renomination in 1840; member of the commission under the treaty with Mexico in 1841; engaged in literary pursuits until his death in Pittsburgh, Pa., January 18, 1871; interment in Prospect Cemetery, Brackenridge, Pa.

BRADBURY, George, a Representative from Massachusetts; born in Falmouth, Mass., October 10, 1770; was graduated from Harvard University in 1789; studied law; was admitted to the bar and commenced practice in Portland, Maine (until 1820 a district of Massachusetts); member of the Massachusetts House of Representatives 1806–1810, 1811, and 1812; elected as a Federalist to the Thirteenth and Fourteenth Congresses (March 4, 1813–March 3, 1817); unsuccessful candidate for renomination in 1816; resumed the practice of law; associate clerk of the Portland Court 1817–1820; member of the State senate in 1820; charter member of the Maine Historical Society; died in Portland, Maine, November 7, 1823; interment in Eastern Cemetery.

BRADBURY, James Ware, a Senator from Maine; born in Parsonsfield, Maine, June 10, 1802; attended the common schools and Gorham Academy; was graduated from Bowdoin College, Brunswick, Maine, in 1825; principal of Hallowell Academy and founder of the first normal school in New England, at Effingham, N. H., in 1829; studied law; was admitted to the bar and commenced practice in Augusta, Maine, in 1830; prosecuting attorney 1834–1838; presidential elector on the Democratic ticket of Polk and Dallas in 1844; elected as a Democrat to the United States Senate and served from March 4, 1847, until March 3, 1853; declined to be a candidate for renomination; one of the trustees of Bowdoin College in 1861; president of the Maine Historical Society 1867–1887; practiced law in Augusta, Maine, until after he had passed his ninety-first birthday; died in Augusta, Maine, January 7, 1901; interment in Forest Grove Cemetery.

BRADBURY, Theophilus, a Representative from Massachusetts; born in Newbury, Mass., November 13, 1739; was graduated from Harvard College in 1757; taught school and studied law in Portland, Maine; was admitted to the bar and commenced practice in Portland in 1761; moved to Newburyport, Mass., in 1764 and continued the practice of law; member of the State senate 1791–1794; elected as a Federalist to the Fourth and Fifth Congresses and served from March 4, 1795, until July 24, 1797, when he resigned; appointed judge of the supreme court of Massachusetts in 1797, which position he held until his death; member of the electoral college in 1800; died in Newburyport, Mass., September 6, 1803; interment in Newburyport Cemetery.

BRADEMAS, John, a Representative from Indiana; born in Mishawaka, Saint Joseph County, Ind., March 2, 1927; graduate of Central High School, South Bend, Ind.; during World War II served in the United States Navy in 1945 and 1946; graduated from Harvard University in 1949 and from Oxford University (Rhodes Scholar for Indiana) in 1954; legislative assistant to United States Senator Pat McNamara of Michigan in 1955; administrative assistant to Representative Thomas L. Ashley of Ohio in 1955; executive assistant to Adlai E. Stevenson in 1955 and 1956; assistant professor of political science, Saint Mary's College, Notre Dame, Ind., in 1957 and 1958; member of congressional delegation to First Inter-American Conference, Lima, Peru, in 1959; unsuccessful Democratic candidate for election to the Eighty-fourth Congress in 1954 and to the Eighty-fifth Congress in 1956; elected as a Democrat to the Eighty-sixth Congress (January 3, 1959–January 3, 1961). *Reelected to the Eighty-seventh Congress.*

BRADFORD, Allen Alexander, a Delegate from the Territory of Colorado; born in Friendship, Maine, July 23, 1815; moved to Missouri in 1841; studied law; was admitted to the bar and practiced; clerk of the circuit court of Atchison County, Mo., 1845–1851; moved to Iowa and was judge of the sixth judicial district 1852–1855; moved to the Territory of Nebraska; served as a member of the Territorial house of representatives in 1856, 1857, and 1858; moved to the Territory of Colorado in 1860; appointed judge of the supreme court of the Territory by President Abraham Lincoln on June 6, 1862; elected as a Republican to the Thirty-ninth Congress (March 4, 1865–March 3, 1867); resumed the practice of law; elected to the Forty-first Congress (March 4, 1869–March 3, 1871); engaged in the practice of law in Pueblo, Colo., until his death there March 12, 1888; interment in the City Cemetery.

BRADFORD, Taul, a Representative from Alabama; born in Talladega, Talladega County, Ala., January 20, 1835; attended the local school; was graduated from the University of Alabama at Tuscaloosa in 1854; studied law; was admitted to the bar in 1855 and commenced practice in Talladega, Ala.; during the Civil War served in the Confederate Army as major of the Tenth Regiment, Alabama Infantry, and subsequently became lieutenant colonel of the Thirtieth Regiment, Alabama Infantry; member of the State house of representatives in 1871 and 1872; elected as a Democrat to the Forty-fourth Congress (March 4, 1875–March 3, 1877); was not a candidate for renomination in 1876; continued the practice of law in Talladega, Ala., until his death on October 28, 1883; interment in Oak Hill Cemetery, Talladega, Ala.

BRADFORD, William, a Senator from Rhode Island; born in Plympton, Plymouth County, Mass., November 4, 1729; studied medicine in Hingham, Mass., and afterwards practiced in Warren, R. I.; moved to Bristol, R. I.; abandoned the profession of medicine and studied law; was admitted to the Rhode Island bar in 1767 and commenced practice in Bristol; member of the Rhode Island House of Representatives in 1764 and 1765, serving as speaker; member of the Rhode Island Committee of Correspondence in 1773; Deputy Governor of Rhode Island from November 1775 to May 1778; elected as a Delegate to the Continental Congress but did not serve; member of the Rhode Island House of Representatives, serving as speaker for one year; elected to the United States Senate and served from March 4, 1793, until October 1797, when he resigned; elected president pro tempore of the Senate July 6, 1797; retired to his home in Bristol, R. I., and died there on July 6, 1808; interment in East Burial Ground.

BRADLEY, Edward, a Representative from Michigan; born in East Bloomfield, Ontario County, N. Y., in April 1808; attended the common schools and the local academy in Canandaigua; associate judge of the common pleas court of Ontario County, N. Y., in 1836; moved to Detroit, Mich., in 1839; studied law; was admitted to the bar in 1841 and commenced practice in Marshall, Calhoun County, Mich.; prosecuting attorney of Calhoun County in 1842; member of the State senate in 1842 and 1843; elected as a Democrat to the Thirtieth Congress and served from March 4, 1847, until his death on August 5, 1847, in New York City while en route to Washington, D. C., before the assembling of Congress; interment in the Congressional Cemetery, Washington, D. C.

BRADLEY, Frederick Van Ness, a Representative from Michigan; born in Chicago, Ill., April 12, 1898; moved to Rogers City, Mich., in 1910; attended the public schools, Roger City (Mich.) High School, and Montclair (N. J.) Academy; served in the Student Army Training Corps at Plattsburg, N. Y., in 1918; was graduated from Cornell University, Ithaca, N. Y., in 1921; salesman with the Michigan Limestone and Chemical Co., Buffalo, N. Y., 1921–1923, and purchasing agent 1928–1938; also purchasing agent, Bradley Transportation Co., Rogers City, Mich., 1924–1938; elected as a Republican to the Seventy-sixth and to the four succeeding Congresses and served from January 3, 1939, until his death May 24, 1947, at New London, Conn., while there as a member of the Board of Visitors to the Coast Guard Academy; interment in Rogers City Memorial Park, Rogers City, Mich.

BRADLEY, Michael Joseph, a Representative from Pennsylvania; born in Philadelphia, Pa., May 24, 1897; attended the parochial and public high schools; engaged as a telegrapher 1914–1917; during the First World War served overseas as a chief radio electrician in the United States Navy 1917–1919; engaged in the security and brokerage business in Philadelphia, Pa., 1923–1935; deputy insurance commissioner of Pennsylvania 1935–1937; unsuccessful candidate for election in 1934 to the Seventy-fourth Congress; elected as a Democrat to the Seventy-fifth and to the four succeeding Congresses (January 3, 1937–January 3, 1947); was not a candidate for renomination in 1946; chairman of the Democratic county executive committee of Philadelphia from January 1946 to January 1948; collector of customs for district No. 11 from April 1948 to June 1953; deputy managing director, city of Philadelphia, June 1953 to April 1955; member and secretary of Independence National Park Advisory Commission since 1949; member of Pennsylvania Navigation Commission for the Delaware River since 1954; member of Board of Revision of Taxes, city of Philadelphia, since April 1955; is a resident of Philadelphia, Pa.

BRADLEY, Nathan Ball, a Representative from Michigan; born in Lee, Berkshire County, Mass., May 28, 1831; moved with his parents to Lorain County, Ohio, in 1835; attended the common schools; moved to Wisconsin in 1849; employed in a sawmill in the pine region; returned to Ohio in 1850 and built and operated a sawmill until 1852, when he moved to Lexington, Mich., and engaged in the manufacture of lumber; moved to St. Charles, in the Saginaw Valley, in 1855 and engaged in the lumber industry; purchased a mill in Bay City, Mich., which he operated from 1858 to 1864; engaged in the salt industry in Bay City; justice of the peace three terms, a supervisor one term, an alderman three terms, and the first mayor of Bay City after it obtained its charter in 1865; member of the State senate 1866–1868; engaged in banking in 1867; vice president of the First National Bank of Bay City; elected as a Republican to the Forty-third and Forty-fourth Congresses (March 4, 1873–March 3, 1877); was not a

candidate for renomination in 1876 to the Forty-fifth Congress; again engaged in the lumber business in Bay City and also was instrumental in establishing the first beet-sugar factory in the State; died in Bay City, Bay County, Mich., November 8, 1906; interment in Elm Lawn Cemetery.

BRADLEY, Stephen Row (father of William Czar Bradley), a Senator from Vermont; born in Wallingford, Conn., February 20, 1754; was graduated from Yale College in 1775; studied law; was admitted to the bar in 1779 and commenced practice in Westminster, Vt.; captain of a volunteer company during the Revolutionary War and served as aide-de-camp to General Wooster; State's attorney for Cumberland County in 1780; register of probate for Westminster in 1782; appointed judge of Windham County in 1783; member of the State house of representatives in 1785, serving as speaker; appointed associate judge of the superior court of Vermont in 1788; member of the city council of Westminster in 1798; upon the admission of Vermont as a State into the Union was elected as a Democrat to the United States Senate and served from October 17, 1791, to March 3, 1795; unsuccessful candidate for reelection in 1795; again elected to the United States Senate, in 1801, to fill the vacancy caused by the resignation of Elijah Paine; reelected in 1807, and served from October 15, 1801, to March 3, 1813; elected President pro tempore of the Senate December 14, 1802, February 25, 1803, March 2, 1803, and December 28, 1808; voluntarily retired from public life and returned to Westminster; moved to Walpole, N. H., in 1818 and died there December 9, 1830; interment in the Old Cemetery, Westminster, Vt.

BRADLEY, Thomas Joseph, a Representative from New York; born in New York City January 2, 1870; attended the public schools; was graduated from the College of the City of New York in 1887; taught in the public schools of New York City from 1887 until 1891; was graduated from the law department of the University of New York, New York City, in 1889; was admitted to the bar in 1891 and commenced practice in New York City; deputy assistant district attorney of the county of New York 1892–1895; resumed the practice of law; elected as a Democrat to the Fifty-fifth and Fifty-sixth Congresses (March 4, 1897–March 3, 1901); was not a candidate for renomination in 1900; continued the practice of law until his death in New York City April 1, 1901; interment in Calvary Cemetery.

BRADLEY, Thomas Wilson, a Representative from New York; born in Yorkshire, England, April 6, 1844; immigrated to the United States in 1846 with his parents, who settled in Walden, N. Y.; attended school until nine years of age; during the Civil War entered the Union Army as a private; promoted to captain in the One Hundred and Twenty-fourth Regiment, New York Volunteer Infantry; was aide-de-camp to Major General Mott, Third Division, Second Army Corps; awarded the Congressional Medal of Honor "for gallantry at Chancellorsville"; was brevetted major of United States Volunteers "for meritorious services during the campaign terminating at Appomattox"; member of the State house of assembly in 1876; delegate to the Republican National Conventions in 1892, 1896, and 1900; elected as a Republican to the Fifty-eighth and to the three succeeding Congresses (March 4, 1903–March 3, 1913); was not a candidate for renomination in 1912; engaged in banking; president and treasurer of the New York Knife Co.; died in Walden, Orange County, N. Y., May 30, 1920; interment in Wallkill Valley Cemetery.

BRADLEY, William Czar (son of Stephen Row Bradley), a Representative from Vermont; born in Westminster, Vt., March 23, 1782; received his early education in the schools of Cheshire,

Conn., and Charlestown, N. H., and for a short time attended Yale College, New Haven, Conn.; studied law; was admitted to the bar in 1802 and commenced practice in Westminster; prosecuting attorney for Windham County 1804–1811; member of the State house of representatives in 1806, 1807, and 1819; member of the Governor's council in 1812; elected as a War Democrat to the Thirteenth Congress (March 4, 1813–March 3, 1815); agent of the United States under the treaty of Ghent to fix the boundary line between Maine and Canada 1815–1820; elected as a Democrat to the Eighteenth and Nineteenth Congresses (March 4, 1823–March 3, 1827); resumed the practice of law; unsuccessful Democratic candidate for Governor in 1830, 1834, and 1838; again a member of the State house of representatives in 1850; presidential elector on the Republican ticket of Frémont and Dayton in 1856; member of the State constitutional convention in 1857; retired from the practice of his profession in 1858; died in Westminster, Windham County, Vt., March 3, 1867; interment in the Old Cemetery.

BRADLEY, William O'Connell, a Senator from Kentucky; born near Lancaster, Garrard County, Ky., March 18, 1847; educated by private tutors and at a private school in Somerset, Ky.; during the Civil War entered the Union Army at the age of fifteen, but because of his youth served only a short time; served as a page in the State house of representatives in 1861; studied law and when only eighteen years of age was licensed to practice by a special act of the legislature in 1865; prosecuting attorney of Garrard County in 1870; presidential elector on the Liberal Republican ticket of Greeley and Brown in 1872; delegate at large to the Republican National Conventions in 1880, 1884, 1888, 1892, 1896, 1900, and 1904; member of the Republican National Committee from 1890 until 1896, when he resigned; appointed Minister to Korea (Chosen) in 1889 but declined; was the first Republican Governor elected in the State of Kentucky and served from 1895 to 1899; elected as a Republican to the United States Senate and served from March 4, 1909, until his death in Washington, D. C., May 23, 1914; interment in State Cemetery, Frankfort, Ky.

BRADLEY, Willis Winter, a Representative from California; born in Ransomville, Niagara County, N. Y., June 28, 1884; moved with his parents to Milnor, N. Dak., in July 1884 and to Forman, N. Dak., in 1891; attended the public schools, and Hamlin University, St. Paul, Minn.; deputy registrant of deeds of Sargent County, N. Dak., in 1902 and 1903; was graduated from the United States Naval Academy in 1906; reported for duty on the U. S. S. *Virginia* attached to the Atlantic Fleet; during the First World War served as gunnery officer aboard the U. S. S. *Pittsburgh* and as chief of the Explosives Section, Bureau of Ordnance, Navy Department; awarded the Congressional Medal of Honor; Governor of Guam 1929–1931; in command of the U. S. S. *Bridge* 1931–1933; captain of the Pearl Harbor Navy Yard 1933–1935; in command of the U. S. S. *Portland* 1935–1937; commander of Destroyer Squadron 31 and of Caribbean Patrol in 1939 and 1940; attached to the Board of Inspection and Survey, Pacific Coast Section, 1940–1946; in 1946, after forty-three years of service, retired from the United States Navy because of physical incapacity incurred in line of duty; took up residence in Long Beach, Calif., in 1931; elected as a Republican to the Eightieth Congress (January 3, 1947–January 3, 1949); was an unsuccessful candidate for reelection in 1948 to the Eighty-first Congress; assistant to the president of the Pacific Coast Steamship Co., 1949–1952; member of the State assembly from 1952 until his death; appointed by the Governor to the State Fair Exposition Board; died in Santa Barbara, Calif., August 27, 1954; interment in Fort Rosecrans National Cemetery, San Diego, Calif.

BRADSHAW, Samuel Carey, a Representative from Pennsylvania; born in Plumstead, Bucks County, Pa., June 10, 1809; attended the public schools; was graduated from Pennsylvania Medical College in 1833 and practiced in Quakertown, Bucks County, Pa.; elected as a Whig to the Thirty-fourth Congress (March 4, 1855–March 3, 1857); unsuccessful candidate for reelection in 1856 to the Thirty-fifth Congress; died in Quakertown, Pa., June 9, 1872; interment in Friends Burial Ground.

BRADY, James Dennis, a Representative from Virginia, born in Portsmouth, Va., April 3, 1843; moved to New York City when twelve years of age; attended the public schools; engaged in mercantile pursuits; during the Civil War enlisted as a private in the Thirty-seventh New York Volunteers and was successively promoted to the grades of lieutenant and adjutant, captain, major, and lieutenant colonel of the Sixty-third New York Volunteers, holding the latter rank when mustered out of service in July 1865; returned to Portsmouth, Va., after the war and was elected clerk of the corporation court of Portsmouth, which position he held until June 1877; appointed collector of internal revenue for the second district of Virginia and served from June 1877 until his death, with the exception of eight years (1885–1889 and 1893–1897) under the two Cleveland administrations; delegate to the Republican National Conventions in 1880, 1888, and 1896; elected as a Republican to the Forty-ninth Congress (March 4, 1885–March 3, 1887); was not a candidate for renomination in 1886; member of the Republican National Committee 1888–1892; studied law; was admitted to the bar in 1892 and commenced practice in Washington, D. C.; died in Petersburg, Dinwiddie County, Va., November 30, 1900; interment in St. Joseph's Cemetery.

BRADY, James Henry, a Senator from Idaho; born in Indiana County, Pa., June 12, 1862; moved with his parents to Johnson County, Kans., in 1865; attended the public schools and Leavenworth Normal College; taught school; edited a newspaper in Enterprise, Kans.; engaged in the real-estate business at Abilene, Kans.; moved to Chicago, Ill., in 1890 and engaged in the sale of Texas lands; moved to Idaho in 1895 and became interested in the development of water power and in irrigation projects; delegate to the Republican National Conventions in 1900 and 1908; chairman of the Republican State central committee 1904–1908; president of the Trans-Mississippi Commercial Congress; vice president of the National Irrigation Congress 1904–1906; Governor of Idaho 1909–1911; elected as a Republican to the United States Senate on January 24, 1913, to fill the vacancy caused by the death of Weldon B. Heyburn; reelected in 1914, and served from February 6, 1913, until his death in Washington, D. C., January 13, 1918; remains were cremated and the ashes deposited in the James H. Brady Memorial Chapel in Mountain View Cemetery, Pocatello, Bannock County, Idaho.

BRADY, Jasper Ewing, a Representative from Pennsylvania; born in Sunbury, Northumberland County, Pa., March 4, 1797; attended the common schools; learned the hatter's trade; taught school in Franklin County, Pa.; studied law; was admitted to the bar in 1827 and commenced practice in Chambersburg, Franklin County, Pa.; served as treasurer of Franklin County for three years; member of the State house of representatives in 1844 and 1845; elected as a Whig to the Thirtieth Congress (March 4, 1847–March 3, 1849); unsuccessful candidate for reelection in 1848 to the Thirty-first Congress; moved to Pittsburgh, Pa., in September 1849 and resumed the practice of law; clerk in the office of the paymaster general in the War Department, Washington, D. C., 1861–1869; retired from active business pursuits in 1869 and resided in Washington, D. C., until his death in that city on January 26, 1871; interment in City Cemetery, Sunbury, Northumberland County, Pa.; reinterment in Rock Creek Cemetery, Washington, D. C., in 1893.

BRAGG, Edward Stuyvesant, a Representative from Wisconsin; born in Unadilla, Otsego County, N. Y., February 20, 1827; attended the district schools, the local academy, and Geneva (later Hobart) College at Geneva, N. Y.; studied law; was admitted to the bar in 1848 and commenced practice in Unadilla; moved to Fond du Lac, Wis., in 1850 and continued the practice of law; elected district attorney in 1853; delegate to the Democratic National Convention at Charleston in 1860; during the Civil War entered the Union Army as a captain in the Sixth Regiment, Wisconsin Volunteer Infantry, July 16, 1861; major September 17, 1861; lieutenant colonel June 21, 1862; colonel March 24, 1863; brigadier general of Volunteers June 25, 1864; mustered out of the service October 9, 1865; appointed postmaster of Fond du Lac by President Johnson in 1866; member of the State senate in 1868 and 1869; delegate to the Democratic National Convention in 1872, 1880, and 1896; unsuccessful candidate for election to the United States Senate in 1874; elected as a Democrat to the Forty-fifth, Forty-sixth, and Forty-seventh Congresses (March 4, 1877–March 3, 1883); was not a candidate for renomination in 1882; again elected to the Forty-ninth Congress (March 4, 1885–March 3, 1887); was not a candidate for renomination in 1886; resumed the practice of law in Fond du Lac, Wis.; appointed Envoy Extraordinary and Minister Plenipotentiary to Mexico January 16, 1888, and served from March 5, 1888, to May 27, 1889; appointed consul general at Habana, Cuba, May 19, 1902, and assumed charge June 30, 1902; appointed consul general at Hong Kong, China, September 15, 1902, and assumed his duties March 1, 1903; resigned, effective May 1, 1906; retired from public life and the practice of his profession; died in Fond du Lac, Wis., June 20, 1912; interment in the Rienzi Cemetery.

BRAGG, John, a Representative from Alabama; born near Warrenton, Warren County, N. C., January 14, 1806; attended the local academy at Warrenton, and was graduated from the University of North Carolina at Chapel Hill in 1824; studied law; was admitted to the bar in 1830 and commenced practice in Warrenton; member of the State house of commons of North Carolina 1830–1834; moved to Mobile, Ala., in 1836 and continued the practice of law; was appointed judge of the tenth judicial circuit in 1842; member of the State house of representatives; elected as a State Rights Democrat to the Thirty-second Congress (March 4, 1851–March 3, 1853); declined to be a candidate for reelection in 1852; resumed the practice of his profession; delegate from Mobile to the State constitutional convention in 1861; died in Mobile, Ala., August 10, 1878; interment in Magnolia Cemetery

BRAGG, Thomas, a Senator from North Carolina; born in Warrenton, Warren County, N. C., November 10, 1810; attended the Warrenton Academy; was graduated from Captain Partridge's Military Academy, Middletown, Conn.; studied law; was admitted to the bar in 1833 and commenced practice in Jackson, Northampton County, N. C.; member of the State house of commons in 1842 and 1843; presidential elector on the Democratic ticket of Pierce and King in 1852; prosecuting attorney for Northampton County; delegate to the Democratic National Conventions in 1844, 1848, and 1852; Governor of North Carolina 1855–1859; elected as a Democrat to the United States Senate and served from March 4, 1859, until March 6, 1861, when he withdrew; appointed Attorney General of the

Confederate States November 21, 1861, and served two years; resumed the practice of law; died in Raleigh, N. C., January 21, 1872; interment in Oakwood Cemetery.

BRAINERD, Lawrence, a Senator from Vermont; born in East Hartford, Conn., March 16, 1794; when nine years of age went to Troy, N. Y., to reside with an uncle and in 1808 moved with him to St. Albans, Vt.; completed preparatory studies; taught school; employed as a clerk in a mercantile establishment until 1816; engaged in mercantile, banking, navigation, and railroad enterprises; affiliated with the Whig Party until 1840, when he became a member of the Liberty Party; unsuccessful candidate for Governor; elected as a member of the Free-Soil Party to the United States Senate to fill the vacancy caused by the death of William Upham and served from October 14, 1854, to March 3, 1855; was not a candidate for reelection; subsequently received the unanimous nomination for Governor, but declined the honor; resumed business activities; chairman of the delegation at Chicago in 1860 that nominated Abraham Lincoln for President; died in St. Albans, Franklin County, Vt., May 9, 1870; interment in Greenwood Cemetery.

BRAINERD, Samuel Myron, a Representative from Pennsylvania; born in Albion, Erie County, Pa., November 13, 1842; attended the public schools, Edinboro Normal School, and Ann Arbor (Mich.) Law School; studied law; was admitted to the bar in 1869 and commenced practice in North East, Erie County, Pa.; district attorney of Erie County 1872–1875; moved to Erie, Pa., in 1874 and continued the practice of law; chairman of the Republican county committee in 1880; elected as a Republican to the Forty-eighth Congress (March 4, 1883–March 3, 1885); unsuccessful candidate for renomination in 1884; resumed the practice of law in Erie, Pa., and died there November 21, 1898; interment in the City Cemetery.

BRAMBLETT, Ernest King, a Representative from California; born in Fresno, Calif., April 25, 1901; attended the public schools; was graduated from Stanford University in 1925; took graduate work at Stanford, Fresno State, San Jose State, and the University of Southern California; engaged in the insurance and automobile business 1925–1928, and in educational work 1928–1946; mayor of Pacific Grove 1939–1947; coordinator of Monterey County schools 1943–1946; member of the Republican Central Committee 1944–1946; elected as a Republican to the Eightieth and to the three succeeding Congresses (January 3, 1947–January 3, 1955); was not a candidate for renomination in 1954; engaged as a consultant in southern California; is a resident of Woodland Hills, Calif.

BRANCH, John (uncle of Lawrence O'Bryan Branch), a Senator and a Representative from North Carolina; born in Halifax, Halifax County, N. C., November 4, 1782; appointed commissioner for valuation of lands and dwellings and enumeration of slaves, third district of North Carolina, in 1799; was graduated from the University of North Carolina at Chapel Hill in 1801; studied law; was admitted to the bar and commenced practice in Halifax, Halifax County, N. C.; member of the State senate 1811–1817 and again in 1822, serving as speaker 1815–1817; Governor of North Carolina 1817–1820; appointed Federal judge for the western district of Florida by President Monroe on April 17, 1822; elected as a Democrat to the United States Senate in 1822; reelected in 1829, and served from March 4, 1823, to March 9, 1829, when he resigned; appointed Secretary of the Navy by President Jackson and served from March 9, 1829, until his resignation, effective May 12, 1831, having been elected to Congress; elected as a Democrat to the Twenty-second Congress and served from May 12, 1831, to March 3, 1833; was not a candidate for renomination in 1832; member of the State constitutional convention in 1835; appointed Governor of Florida by President Tyler and served from June 21, 1844, until the election of a Governor under the State constitution in 1845; died in Enfield, Halifax County, N. C., January 3, 1863; interment in the family burial ground.

BRANCH, Lawrence O'Bryan (nephew of John Branch), a Representative from North Carolina; born in Enfield, Halifax County, N. C., November 28, 1820; pursued a preparatory course under a private teacher in Washington, D. C., and at the Bingham Military Academy in North Carolina; attended the University of North Carolina at Chapel Hill for a short time and was graduated from Princeton College in 1838; studied law at Nashville, Tenn., and owned and edited a newspaper there; moved to Tallahassee, Fla., in 1840; was admitted to the bar in Florida in 1840 by a special act of the legislature and commenced practice in Tallahassee; fought in the Seminole War in 1841; moved to Raleigh, N. C., in 1852 and continued the practice of law; president of the Raleigh & Gaston Railroad Co.; presidential elector on the Democratic ticket of Pierce and King in 1852; elected as a Democrat to the Thirty-fourth, Thirty-fifth, and Thirty-sixth Congresses (March 4, 1855–March 3, 1861); was not a candidate for renomination in 1860; appointed Secretary of the Treasury by President Buchanan December 2, 1860, but declined; entered the Confederate Army in May 1861 and was appointed brigadier general the same year; was in command when New Bern was captured by General Burnside; senior brigadier general in A. P. Hill's division, Stonewall Jackson's corps; killed in the Battle of Antietam, Sharpsburg, Md., while in command of the Fourth Brigade, North Carolina Troops, September 17, 1862; interment in Old City Cemetery, Raleigh, N. C.

BRANCH, William Augustus Blount (son of Lawrence O'Bryan Branch), a Representative from North Carolina; born in Tallahassee, Fla., February 26, 1847; moved with his father to Raleigh, N. C., in 1852; attended Lovejoy's Academy, Raleigh, N. C., Bingham Military Academy near Mebane, N. C., the University of North Carolina at Chapel Hill, and Virginia Military Institute at Lexington; joined the Confederate Army and served as a courier on the staff of Gen. R. F. Hoke; surrendered with Gen. Joseph E. Johnston's army in 1865; studied law but never practiced; in 1867 took charge of his landed estate near Washington, Beaufort County, N. C., and engaged in agricultural pursuits; elected as a Democrat to the Fifty-second and Fifty-third Congresses (March 4, 1891–March 3, 1895); unsuccessful candidate for reelection in 1894 to the Fifty-fourth Congress; again engaged in agricultural pursuits on his estate near Washington, Beaufort County, N. C.; member of the State house of representatives in 1896; died in Washington, N. C., November 18, 1910; interment in Oakdale Cemetery.

BRAND, Charles, a Representative from Ohio; born in Urbana, Champaign County, Ohio, November 1, 1871; attended the graded schools of his native city and Ohio Wesleyan University, Delaware, Ohio; engaged in agricultural pursuits, manufacturing, and banking at Urbana; member of the Urbana City Council in 1911 and 1912 and was its president; member of the State senate in 1921 and 1922; served as a member of the advisory committee of the War Finance Corporation in 1921; elected as a Republican to the Sixty-eighth and to the four succeeding Congresses (March 4, 1923–March 3, 1933); was not a candidate for renomination in 1932; resumed former business pursuits until his retirement; is a resident of Melbourne Beach, Fla.

BRAND, Charles Hillyer, a Representative from Georgia; born in Loganville, Walton County, Ga., April 20, 1861; attended the common schools, and was graduated from the University of Georgia at Athens in 1881; was admitted to the bar in 1882 and commenced practice in Lawrenceville, Gwinnett County, Ga.; member of the State senate in 1894 and 1895 and served as president pro tempore; served as president and director of the Brand Banking Co., Lawrenceville, Ga., and director of the Georgia National Bank and of the American State Bank, Athens, Ga.; solicitor general for the western judicial circuit of Georgia 1896–1904; judge of the superior court 1906–1917; elected as a Democrat to the Sixty-fifth Congress to fill the vacancy caused by the death of Representative-elect Samuel J. Tribble; reelected to the Sixty-sixth and to the seven succeeding Congresses and served from March 4, 1917, until his death in Athens, Ga., on May 17, 1933; interment in Shadow Lawn Cemetery, Lawrenceville, Ga.

BRANDEGEE, Augustus (father of Frank Bosworth Brandegee), a Representative from Connecticut; born in New London, Conn., July 15, 1828; pursued preparatory studies; was graduated from Yale College in 1849 and from the Yale Law School in 1851; was admitted to the bar in 1851 and commenced practice in New London; member of the State house of representatives 1854, 1858, 1859, and 1861, and served as speaker the last term; presidential elector on the Republican ticket of Lincoln and Hamlin in 1860; elected as a Republican to the Thirty-eighth and Thirty-ninth Congresses (March 4, 1863–March 3, 1867); was not a candidate for reelection in 1866; delegate to the Republican National Convention at Baltimore in 1864, the Loyalist Convention at Philadelphia in 1866, and the Republican National Conventions at Chicago in 1880 and 1884; resumed the practice of law; corporation counsel of New London in 1897 and 1898; died in New London, Conn., November 10, 1904; interment in Cedar Grove Cemetery.

BRANDEGEE, Frank Bosworth (son of Augustus Brandegee), a Representative and a Senator from Connecticut; born in New London, Conn., July 8, 1864; attended the common schools, and was graduated from Yale College in 1885; studied law; was admitted to the bar in 1888 and practiced in New London; member of the State house of representatives in 1888; corporation counsel of New London from October 1889 to October 1893 and from October 1894 until October 1897, when he resigned; delegate to the Republican National Conventions in 1888, 1892, 1900, and 1904; again a member of the State house of representatives in 1899, and served as speaker; again elected corporation counsel of New London in October 1901 and served until October 1902, when he resigned to become a Member of Congress; chairman of the Republican State convention in 1904; elected as a Republican to the Fifty-seventh Congress to fill the vacancy caused by the death of Charles A. Russell; reelected to the Fifty-eighth and Fifty-ninth Congresses and served from November 5, 1902, until May 10, 1905, when he resigned, having been elected a United States Senator to fill the vacancy caused by the death of Orville H. Platt; reelected in 1908, 1914, and 1920, and served from May 10, 1905, until his death in Washington, D. C., October 14, 1924; interment in Cedar Grove Cemetery, New London, Conn.

BRANTLEY, William Gordon, a Representative from Georgia; born in Blackshear, Pierce County, Ga., September 18, 1860; attended the public schools, and the University of Georgia at Athens; studied law; was admitted to the bar in 1881 and commenced practice in Blackshear, Pierce County, Ga.; member of the State house of representatives in 1884 and 1885; served in the State senate in 1886 and 1887; solicitor general (prosecuting attorney) of the Brunswick Circuit Court of Georgia 1888–1896; moved to Brunswick in 1889 and continued the practice of law; elected as a Democrat to the Fifty-fifth and to the seven succeeding Congress (March 4, 1897–March 3, 1913); was not a candidate for renomination in 1912; delegate to the Democratic National Convention at Baltimore in 1912; moved from Brunswick, Ga., to Washington, D. C., in 1913 and resumed the practice of law; died in Washington, D. C., September 11, 1934; interment in Blackshear Cemetery, Blackshear, Ga.

BRATTON, John, a Representative from South Carolina; born in Winnsboro, Fairfield County, S. C., March 7, 1831; attended the Academy of Mount Zion Institute in Winnsboro; was graduated from South Carolina College at Columbia in 1850 and from South Carolina Medical College at Charleston in 1853; engaged in the practice of medicine in Winnsboro from 1853 to 1861; also engaged as a planter; volunteered in the Confederate Army as a private and served throughout the Civil War, attaining the rank of brigadier general; member of the State constitutional convention in 1865; served in the State senate in 1866; chairman of the South Carolina delegation in the Democratic National Convention at St. Louis in 1876; delegate to the Democratic National Convention at Cincinnati in 1880; elected comptroller general of South Carolina by the legislature, to fill a vacancy, in 1881; elected to the Forty-eighth Congress to fill the vacancy caused by the death of John H. Evins and served from December 8, 1884, to March 3, 1885; was not a candidate for renomination in 1884; retired from active politics and again engaged in planting at "Farmington," near Winnsboro; died in Winnsboro, S. C., January 12, 1898; interment in the Episcopal Cemetery.

BRATTON, Robert Franklin, a Representative from Maryland; born in Barren Creek Springs, Somerset (now Wicomico) County, Md., May 13, 1845; was graduated from Washington College, Chestertown, Md., in 1864; deputy register of wills for Somerset County; admitted to the bar in 1867; member of the State convention of 1865 which sent delegates to a peace convention held in Philadelphia in the following year; member of several State and congressional conventions; member of the State house of representatives in 1869; served in the State senate in 1873, 1879, 1887, and 1890; elected president of the senate in 1890; engaged in the practice of law in Princess Anne, Somerset County, Md.; elected as a Democrat to the Fifty-third Congress and served from March 4, 1893, until his death in Princess Anne, Md., May 10, 1894; interment in St. Andrew's Cemetery.

BRATTON, Sam Gilbert, a Senator from New Mexico; born in Kosse, Limestone County, Tex., August 19, 1888; attended the public schools; studied law; was admitted to the bar in 1909 and commenced practice in Farwell, Parmer County, Tex.; moved to Clovis, N. Mex., in 1915 and continued the practice of law; judge of the district court for the fifth judicial district of New Mexico from January 1, 1919, to January 1, 1921, when, this district being divided, he became judge of the ninth judicial district and served from January 1, 1921, to January 1, 1923; associate justice of the supreme court of New Mexico from January 1, 1923, to September 16, 1924, when he resigned to accept the nomination for Senator, which had been tendered him by the Democratic convention; elected as a Democrat to the United States Senate in 1924; reelected in 1930 and served from March 4, 1925, until his resignation, effective June 24, 1933, having been appointed circuit judge of the United States Circuit Court of Appeals for the Tenth Judicial Circuit; retired from active service on the Court of Appeals, effective March 1, 1961; is a resident of Albuquerque, N. Mex.

BRAWLEY, William Huggins (cousin of John James Hemphill and great-uncle of Robert Witherspoon Hemphill), a Representative from South Carolina; born in Chester, Chester County, S. C., May 13, 1841; attended the common schools, and was graduated from South Carolina College at Columbia in 1860; during the Civil War enlisted as a private in Company F, Sixth Regiment, South Carolina Infantry, Confederate States Army, April 11, 1861; lost an arm in the Battle of Seven Pines and was retired from service; traveled and studied in Europe in 1864 and 1865; studied law; was admitted to the bar in 1866 and commenced practice at Chester, S. C.; elected solicitor of the sixth judicial circuit of South Carolina in 1868 and served until his resignation in 1874; moved to Charleston and continued the practice of his profession; member of the State house of representatives 1882–1890; elected as a Democrat to the Fifty-second and Fifty-third Congresses and served from March 4, 1891, until February 12, 1894, when he resigned to accept a position on the bench; appointed January 18, 1894, United States district judge of the district of South Carolina and served from February 12, 1894, until his resignation June 14, 1911; withdrew from public life and active business pursuits and lived in retirement until his death in Charleston, S. C., November 15, 1916; interment in Magnolia Cemetery.

BRAXTON, Carter (great-grandfather of Elliott Muse Braxton), a Delegate from Virginia; born at "Newington," on the Mattaponi River, near King and Queen Court House, Va., September 16, 1736; was graduated from William and Mary College, Williamsburg, Va., in 1755; spent three years in England and attended the University of Cambridge; member of the Virginia House of Burgesses 1761–1771 and in 1775; elected a Member of the Continental Congress to fill the vacancy caused by the death of Peyton Randolph and served from August 15, 1775, until August 11, 1776, when Virginia reduced her representation from seven to five; one of the signers of the Declaration of Independence; reelected to the Continental Congress at the first session of the general assembly of Virginia under the new constitution and served from 1777 to 1783, and again in 1785; member of the Virginia Council of State 1786–1791 and from 1794 until his death in Richmond, Va., October 10, 1797; interment on his estate, "Chericoke," King William County, Va.

BRAXTON, Elliott Muse (great-grandson of Carter Braxton), a Representative from Virginia; born in Matthews, Matthews County, Va., October 8, 1823; attended the common schools; studied law; was admitted to the bar in 1849 and commenced practice in Richmond, Va.; subsequently moved to Richmond County; member of the State senate 1851–1855; moved to Fredericksburg, Spotsylvania County, in 1860 and continued the practice of law; during the Civil War raised a company for the Confederate Army and was elected its captain; subsequently commissioned a major and served on the staff of Gen. John R. Cooke; elected a member of the common council of Fredericksburg in 1866; elected as a Democrat to the Forty-second Congress (March 4, 1871–March 3, 1873); unsuccessful candidate for reelection in 1872 to the Forty-third Congress; resumed the practice of law in Fredericksburg, Va., where he died on October 2, 1891; interment in Confederate Cemetery.

BRAY, William Gilmer, a Representative from Indiana; born on a farm near Mooresville, Morgan County, Ind., June 17, 1903; attended the public schools of Mooresville, Ind.; was graduated from Indiana University Law School at Bloomington in 1927 and was admitted to the bar the same year; prosecuting attorney of the fifteenth judicial district of Indiana, Martinsville, Ind., 1926–1930; commenced the private practice of law in Martinsville, Ind., in 1930; during World War II was called from the

Army Reserve June 21, 1941, with the rank of captain and served with a tank company throughout the Pacific campaign, receiving the Silver Star; after the war was transferred to Military Government and served nine months in Korea as deputy property custodian; released from active duty in November 1946 with the rank of colonel; returned to private law practice in Martinsville, Ind.; elected as a Republican to the Eighty-second and to the four succeeding Congresses (January 3, 1951–January 3, 1961). *Reelected to the Eighty-seventh Congress.*

BRAYTON, William Daniel, a Representative from Rhode Island; born in Warwick, Kent County, R. I., November 6, 1815; attended Kent Academy in East Greenwich and Kingston Academy; spent two years in Brown University, Providence, R. I.; engaged in mercantile pursuits; major of the Fourth Regiment of Rhode Island Militia in the Dorr Rebellion; town clerk of Warwick in 1844; member of the town council; member of the State house of representatives in 1841 and 1851; served in the State senate in 1848 and 1853; presidential elector on the Republican ticket of Frémont and Dayton in 1856; elected as a Republican to the Thirty-fifth and Thirty-sixth Congresses (March 4, 1857–March 3, 1861); unsuccessful candidate for reelection in 1860 to the Thirty-seventh Congress; appointed collector of internal revenue for the second district of Rhode Island in 1862 and served until 1871, when he resigned; delegate to the Republican National Convention at Philadelphia in 1872; for a number of years in charge of the money-order division of the Providence post office; died in Providence, R. I., June 30, 1887; interment in Brayton Cemetery, Apponaug, R. I.

BREAZEALE, Phanor, a Representative from Louisiana; born in Natchitoches Parish, La., December 29, 1858; attended private schools; moved to Natchitoches, La., in 1877; clerked in a mercantile establishment for two years; studied law; clerk in the supreme court of the State; was graduated from the law department of Tulane University, New Orleans, La., in 1881; was admitted to the bar the same year and commenced practice in Natchitoches; also engaged in newspaper work 1882–1884; president of the school board of Natchitoches Parish 1888–1891; district attorney for the tenth judicial district 1892–1900; member of the State constitutional convention in 1898; elected as a Democrat to the Fifty-sixth, Fifty-seventh, and Fifty-eighth Congresses (March 4, 1899–March 3, 1905); unsuccessful candidate for renomination in 1904; resumed the practice of law in Natchitoches, La.; appointed in October 1908 member of a commission to codify the criminal laws of Louisiana and to prepare a code of criminal procedure; member of the Democratic State central committee since 1908 and a member of the executive committee; delegate to the Democratic National Convention at Denver in 1908 and at St. Louis in 1916; member of the constitutional convention to frame a constitution for the State of Louisiana at Baton Rouge in 1921; presidential elector on the Democratic ticket of Davis and Bryan in 1924; died in Natchitoches, La., April 29, 1934; interment in the Catholic Cemetery.

BRECK, Daniel (brother of Samuel Breck), a Representative from Kentucky; born in Topsfield, Essex County, Mass., February 12, 1788; attended the local school; taught school; was graduated from Dartmouth College, Hanover, N. H., in 1812; studied law; was admitted to the bar in 1814 and commenced practice in Richmond, Ky., in October of the same year; judge of the Richmond County Court; member of the State house of representatives 1824–1827 and again in 1834; presidential elector on the Whig ticket of Harrison and Tyler in 1841; president of the Richmond branch of the State Bank of Kentucky 1835–1843; appointed associate judge of the supreme court of Kentucky April 7, 1843, and served until 1849; elected as a Whig to the

Thirty-first Congress (March 4, 1849–March 3, 1851); returned to Richmond, Ky., and again served as president to the Richmond branch of the State bank; died in Richmond, Madison County, Ky., February 4, 1871; interment in Richmond Cemetery.

BRECK, Samuel (brother of Daniel Breck), a Representative from Pennsylvania; born in Boston, Mass., July 17, 1771; attended the Royal Military School of Loreze, France; moved to Pennsylvania and settled in Philadelphia in 1792, where he engaged in business as a merchant; served as corporal during the Whisky Rebellion; member of the State house of representatives 1817–1820; served in the State senate 1832–1834; elected as a Federalist to the Eighteenth Congress (March 4, 1823–March 3, 1825); withdrew from active business pursuits and lived in retirement until his death in Philadelphia, Pa., August 31, 1862; interment in St. Peter's Churchyard.

BRECKINRIDGE, Clifton Rodes (son of John Cabell Breckinridge and great-grandson of John Breckinridge), a Representative from Arkansas; born near Lexington, Ky., November 22, 1846; attended the rural schools; served in the Confederate Army and was a midshipman in the Navy; after the Civil War he attended Washington College (now Washington and Lee University), Lexington, Va., for three years; settled near Pine Bluff, Ark., in 1870 and engaged in cotton planting and in the commission business for 13 years; elected as a Democrat to the Forty-eighth, Forty-ninth, and Fiftieth Congresses (March 4, 1883–March 3, 1889); presented credentials as a Member-elect to the Fifty-first Congress and served from March 4, 1889, until September 5, 1890, when John M. Clayton was declared to have been duly elected, but, owing to the death of Mr. Clayton while the contest was pending, the seat was declared vacant; subsequently elected to the Fifty-first Congress to fill the vacancy thus caused; reelected to the Fifty-second and Fifty-third Congresses and served from November 4, 1890, to August 14, 1894, when he resigned to accept a consular position; unsuccessful candidate for renomination for Congress in 1894; appointed Minister to Russia by President Cleveland July 20, 1894, and served until December 13, 1897, when he returned to Pine Bluff, Ark.; from June 1900 to July 1905 was a member of the Dawes Commission which was engaged in distributing the estates of the Five Civilized Tribes of Indians in the then Indian Territory; engaged in banking at Fort Smith, Ark., serving as president of the Arkansas Valley Trust Co.; member of the State constitutional convention in 1917; was a resident of Fort Smith, Ark., until 1925, when he moved to Wendover, Leslie County, Ky., where he died on December 3, 1932; interment in Old Lexington Cemetery, Lexington, Ky.

BRECKINRIDGE, James (brother of John Breckinridge), a Representative from Virginia; born near Fincastle, Botetourt County, Va., March 7, 1763; studied under private tutors; during the Revolutionary War served in Colonel Preston's rifle regiment under General Greene; attended Washington College (now Washington and Lee University), Lexington, Va., and was graduated from William and Mary College, Williamsburg, Va., in 1785; studied law; was admitted to the bar and practiced in Fincastle; member of the State house of delegates 1789–1802, 1806–1808, 1820, 1821, 1823, and 1824; took a special interest in the construction of the Chesapeake & Ohio Canal; was an associate of Thomas Jefferson in the establishment of the University of Virginia, Charlottesville, Va.; served as brigadier general in the War of 1812; elected as a Federalist to the Eleventh and to the three succeeding Congresses (March 4, 1809–March 3, 1817); resumed the practice of law; died at his country home, "Grove Hill," Botetourt County, Va., May 13, 1833; interment in the family burial plot on his estate near Fincastle, Va.

BRECKINRIDGE, James Douglas, a Representative from Kentucky; born in Woodville, near Louisville, Jefferson County, Ky.; attended Washington College (now Washington and Lee University), Lexington, Va., 1800–1803; studied law; was admitted to the bar and commenced practice in Louisville, Ky. member of the State house of representatives 1809–1811; appointed judge by Gov. Robert Desha in April 1826, but declined to serve; elected to the Seventeenth Congress to fill the vacancy caused by the death of Wingfield Bullock and served from November 21, 1821, to March 3, 1823; unsuccessful candidate for reelection in 1822 to the Eighteenth Congress; resumed the practice of law; died in Louisville, Ky., May 6, 1849; interment in St. John's Cemetery; reinterment in St. Louis Catholic Cemetery at Louisville in 1867.

BRECKINRIDGE, John (brother of James Breckinridge, grandfather of John Cabell Breckinridge and William Campbell Preston Breckinridge, and great-grandfather of Clifton Rodes Breckinridge), a Senator from Kentucky; born near Staunton, Augusta County, Va., December 2, 1760; educated at Augusta Academy, near Staunton (now Washington and Lee University), Lexington, Va., and at William and Mary College, Williamsburg, Va.; elected a member of the house of burgesses in 1780 when nineteen years of age, but being under age was not allowed to take his seat until elected the third time; served as subaltern in the Virginia Militia in the latter part of the Revolutionary War; studied law; was admitted to the bar in 1785 and commenced practice in Charlottesville, Va.; elected as a Democrat a Representative to the Third Congress, but resigned in 1792 before the commencement of the congressional term; moved to Kentucky in 1793 and resumed the practice of law in Lexington; unsuccessful candidate for election to the United States Senate in 1794; appointed attorney general of Kentucky in 1795 and served until November 30, 1797, when he resigned; member of the State house of representatives 1798–1800 serving as speaker in 1799 and 1800; member of the State constitutional convention in 1799; elected as a Democrat to the United States Senate and served from March 4, 1801, until August 7, 1805, when he resigned to accept the position of Attorney General of the United States in the Cabinet of President Jefferson; served in this capacity until his death at "Cabell's Dale," near Lexington, Ky., December 14, 1806; interment in Lexington Cemetery, Lexington, Ky.

BRECKINRIDGE, John Cabell (grandson of John Breckinridge, father of Clifton Rodes Breckinridge, and cousin of Henry Donnel Foster), a Representative and a Senator from Kentucky and a Vice President of the United States; born at "Cabell's Dale," near Lexington, Ky., January 21, 1821; attended Pisgah Academy, Woodford County, Ky.; was graduated from Centre College, Danville, Ky., in 1839; later attended Princeton College; studied law in the Transylvania Institute, Lexington, Ky.; was admitted to the bar in 1840; moved to Burlington, Iowa, but soon returned and began practice in Lexington, Ky.; major of the Third Kentucky Volunteers during the Mexican War in 1847 and 1848; member of the State house of representatives in 1849; elected as a Democrat to the Thirty-second and Thirty-third Congresses (March 4, 1851–March 3, 1855); was not a candidate for renomination in 1854; was tendered the mission to Spain by President Pierce, but declined; elected Vice President of the United States in 1856 on the Democratic ticket, with James Buchanan as President, being the youngest Vice President who had ever held that office; defeated as a candidate for President in 1860 by Abraham Lincoln; elected to the United States Senate and served from March 4, 1861, until expelled by resolution of December 4, 1861; entered the Confederate Army during the Civil War as brigadier

general and soon became a major general; Secretary of War in the Cabinet of the Confederate States from January until April 1865; resided in Europe for a year or more; returned to Lexington, Ky., and resumed the practice of law; vice president of the Elizabethtown, Lexington & Big Sandy Railroad Co.; died in Lexington, Ky., May 17, 1875; interment in Lexington Cemetery.

BRECKINRIDGE, William Campbell Preston (grandson of John Breckinridge and uncle of Levin Irving Handy), a Representative from Kentucky; born in Baltimore, Md., August 28, 1837; attended the common schools, Jefferson College, Chambersburg, Pa., and Pisgah Academy, Woodford County, Ky.; was graduated from Centre College, Danville, Ky., in 1855 and from the law department of the University of Louisville in 1857; was admitted to the bar in 1857 and commenced practice in Lexington, Ky.; during the Civil War entered the Confederate Army in 1861 as captain and was subsequently promoted to the rank of colonel in the Ninth Kentucky Cavalry; was in command of the Kentucky cavalry designated to act as bodyguard for President Jefferson Davis and the members of his Cabinet at the close of the Civil War; returned to Lexington, Ky., and was attorney for Fayette County; edited the Lexington (Ky.) Observer and Reporter 1866–1868; professor of equity and jurisprudence in the University of Kentucky at Lexington; delegate to the Democratic National Conventions in 1876 and 1888; elected as a Democrat to the Forty-ninth and to the four succeeding Congresses (March 4, 1885–March 3, 1895); unsuccessful candidate for election in 1896 to the Fifty-fifth Congress; resumed the practice of law and also edited the Lexington Herald; died in Lexington, Ky., November 18, 1904; interment in Lexington Cemetery.

BREEDING, James Floyd, a Representative from Kansas; born near Robinson, Brown County, Kans., September 28, 1901; educated in grade schools, Moonlight, Dickinson County, Kans., and Berryton High School in Shawnee County, Kans.; attended Kansas State College at Manhattan in 1921 and 1922; moved to Rolla, Kans., in 1928; farmer-stockman near Rolla, Morton County, since 1928; member of State house of representatives 1947–1949, serving as minority leader in 1949 session; Democratic nominee for Lieutenant Governor of Kansas in 1950; president of Western Kansas Development Association in 1951; delegate to the Democratic National Convention in 1960; elected as a Democrat to the Eighty-fifth and Eighty-sixth Congresses (January 3, 1957–January 3, 1961). *Reelected to the Eighty-seventh Congress.*

BREEN, Edward F., a Representative from Ohio; born in Dayton, Montgomery County, Ohio, June 10, 1908; attended Corpus Christi Grammar School; graduated from the University of Dayton and attended the Ohio State University; engaged in the hotel business in Dayton; during World War II served as a major in the United States Air Force in North Africa and Italy until released from active service as a lieutenant colonel in the Infantry Reserve; mayor of Dayton, Ohio, from November 1945 until his resignation in April 1948 to seek nomination to Congress; elected as a Democrat to the Eighty-first and Eighty-second Congresses and served from January 3, 1949, until his resignation October 1, 1951, due to ill health; member of Montgomery County Board of Commissioners 1955–1960; engaged in the real-estate and insurance business; is a resident of Dayton, Ohio.

BREESE, Sidney, a Senator from Illinois; born in Whitesboro, N. Y., July 15, 1800; attended Hamilton College, Clinton, N. Y., and was graduated from Union College, Schenectady,

N. Y., in 1818; moved to Illinois; studied law; was admitted to the bar in 1820 and commenced practice in Kaskaskia; appointed postmaster of Kaskaskia in 1821; prosecuting attorney of the third judicial circuit 1822–1826; United States district attorney for Illinois 1827–1829; compiled and published the first volume of Illinois Supreme Court Reports in 1831; was the first reporter of the proceedings of the State supreme court in 1831; held several commissions in the militia and served as a lieutenant colonel of Volunteers in the Black Hawk War in 1832; circuit judge of the second district 1835–1841; judge of the State supreme court in 1841 and 1842; elected as a Democrat to the United States Senate and served from March 4, 1843, to March 3, 1849; unsuccessful candidate for renomination in 1849; member of the State house of representatives in 1851 and 1852, serving as speaker in the former year; judge of the circuit court of Illinois 1855–1857; judge of the supreme court of Illinois from 1857 until his death; served as chief justice 1867–1870, 1873, and 1874; died in Pinkneyville, Perry County, Ill., June 28, 1878; interment in Carlyle Cemetery, Carlyle, Ill.

BREHM, Walter Ellsworth, a Representative from Ohio; born in Somerset, Perry County, Ohio, May 25, 1892; attended the public schools, Boston (Mass.) University, and Ohio Wesleyan University at Delaware, Ohio; was graduated from the Ohio State University Dental School at Columbus in 1917; worked in steel mills, rubber factories, and oil fields after graduation from high school, preparing himself financially for college; member of Company D, Seventh Regiment, Ohio Infantry, 1908–1913; engaged in the practice of dentistry in Logan, Ohio, 1921–1942; treasurer of the executive committee of Logan City Council 1936–1938; served in the State house of representatives 1938–1942; elected as a Republican to the Seventy-eighth and to the four succeeding Congresses (January 3, 1943–January 3, 1953); was not a candidate for renomination in 1952; retired and resides at Summerland Beach, Millersport, Ohio.

BREITUNG, Edward, a Representative from Michigan; born in the city of Schalkau, Duchy of Saxe-Meiningen, Germany, November 10, 1831; attended the College of Mining, Meiningen, Germany, in 1849; after the revolution in Germany immigrated to the United States and settled in Kalamazoo County, Mich.; moved to Detroit in 1851 and became a clerk in a mercantile house; moved to Marquette, Mich., and engaged in mercantile pursuits until 1859, when he went to Negaunee, Marquette County; sold out his mercantile business to engage exclusively in iron-mining operations in 1864; explored the iron range in Marquette and Menominee Counties, locating several profitable mines, 1864–1867; later became interested in gold and silver mining in Colorado; member of the State house of representatives in 1873 and 1874; member of the State senate in 1877 and 1878; served as mayor of Negaunee, Mich., in 1879, 1880, and 1882; elected as a Republican to the Forty-eighth Congress (March 4, 1883–March 3, 1885); declined to be a candidate for renomination in 1884; died in Negaunee, Marquette County, Mich., March 3, 1887; interment in Park Cemetery, Marquette, Mich.

BREMNER, Robert Gunn, a Representative from New Jersey; born in Keiss, Caithness, Scotland, December 17, 1874; immigrated with his parents to Canada; attended the public schools; moved to the United States, and was employed as a carpenter and electrician in New York City in 1894 and 1895; became a newspaper reporter in Paterson, N. J., in 1895; served as a private in Company C, Second Regiment, New Jersey Volunteer Infantry, during the Spanish-American War; resumed newspaper work in Paterson; editor and publisher of the Daily Herald, Passaic, N. J., 1902–1914; elected as a Democrat to the Sixty-third Congress and served from March 4, 1913, until his death in a hospital in Baltimore, Md., February 5, 1914; interment in Laurel Grove Cemetery, Totowa Borough, N. J.

BRENGLE, Francis, a Representative from Maryland; born in Frederick, Md., November 26, 1807; completed academic studies; studied law; was admitted to the bar and practiced in Frederick, Md.; member of the State house of delegates 1832, 1834, and 1836; elected as a Whig to the Twenty-eighth Congress (March 4, 1843–March 3, 1845); died in Frederick, Frederick County, Md., December 10, 1846; interment in Mount Olivet Cemetery.

BRENNAN, Martin Adlai, a Representative from Illinois; born in Bloomington, McLean County, Ill., September 21, 1879; attended parochial schools; employed as a reporter for the Bloomington Bulletin; was graduated from the Wesleyan College of Law, Bloomington, Ill., in 1902; was admitted to the bar the same year and commenced practice in Bloomington, Ill.; served as presiding judge of the Illinois Court of Claims 1913–1917; served as census supervisor for McLean County, Ill., in 1920; member of the State house of representatives 1921–1923; delegate to the Democratic National Convention at New York City in 1924; elected as a Democrat to the Seventy-third and Seventy-fourth Congresses (March 4, 1933–January 3, 1937); was not a candidate for renomination in 1936; resumed the practice of law in Bloomington, Ill., until his death there on July 4, 1941; interment in St. Mary's Cemetery.

BRENNAN, Vincent Morrison, a Representative from Michigan; born in Mount Clemens, Macomb County, Mich., April 22, 1890; moved with his parents to Detroit in 1895; was graduated from SS. Peter and Paul's Parochial School, from Detroit College in 1909, from the law department of Harvard University in 1912, and from the University of Detroit in 1914; was admitted to the bar in 1912 and commenced practice in Detroit; legal adviser to the Michigan State Labor Department in 1912 and 1913; assistant corporation counsel for the city of Detroit 1915–1920; member of the State senate in 1919 and 1920; drafted the automobile traffic ordinance of Detroit, used as a model for many other cities; elected as a Republican to the Sixty-seventh Congress (March 4, 1921–March 3, 1923); was not a candidate for reelection in 1922; elected judge of the circuit court of Wayne County, Mich., for the term commencing in January 1924; reelected for six successive terms and served until his resignation December 31, 1954; practiced law; died in Detroit, Mich., February 4, 1959; interment in Holy Sepulchre Cemetery, Birmingham, Mich.

BRENNER, John Lewis, a Representative from Ohio; born in Wayne Township, Montgomery County, Ohio, February 2, 1832; attended the common schools and Springfield (Ohio) Academy; engaged in agricultural pursuits until 1862, interested in the nursery business until 1872, and then engaged in the production of tobacco; moved to Dayton, Ohio, in 1866; member of the board of police commissioners 1885–1887; elected as a Democrat to the Fifty-fifth and Fifty-sixth Congresses (March 4, 1897–March 3, 1901); unsuccessful candidate for renomination in 1900; resumed his former occupation as a dealer in leaf tobacco; died in Dayton, Montgomery County, Ohio, November 1, 1906; interment in Woodland Cemetery.

BRENT, Richard (uncle of William Leigh Brent and nephew of Daniel Carroll), a Representative and a Senator from Virginia; born at "Richland," on the Potomac River, at Aquia Creek, Stafford County, Va., in 1757; studied law; was admitted to the bar and practiced; member of the Virginia House of Delegates from Stafford County in 1788 and from Prince William County in 1793, 1794, 1800, and 1801; elected to the Fourth and Fifth Congresses (March 4, 1795–March 3, 1799); elected to the Seventh Congress (March 4, 1801–March 3, 1803); served in the State senate 1808–1810; elected to the United States Senate and served from March 4, 1809, until his death in Washington, D. C., on December 30, 1814; interment in the family burial ground at "Richland," on the Potomac River, at Aquia Creek.

BRENT, William Leigh (nephew of Richard Brent), a Representative from Louisiana; born at Port Tobacco, Charles County, Md., February 20, 1784; studied law and was admitted to the bar; moved to Louisiana about 1809 and commenced practice; appointed by President Madison as deputy attorney general for the western district of the Territory of Orleans; elected to the Eighteenth, Nineteenth, and Twentieth Congresses (March 4, 1823–March 3, 1829); affiliated with the Whig Party upon its formation; resumed the practice of law in Louisiana, and in Washington, D. C.; died in St. Martinsville, La., July 7, 1848; interment in St. Martin's Catholic Cemetery.

BRENTANO, Lorenzo, a Representative from Illinois; born in Manneheim, Grand Duchy of Baden, Germany, November 4, 1813; studied jurisprudence in the Universities of Heidelberg and Freiburg and was graduated; practiced before the supreme court of Baden; elected to the Chamber of Deputies and in 1848 to the Frankfort Parliament; president of the provisional republic established by the revolutionists in 1849; sentenced to imprisonment for life after the failure of the revolution, but sought refuge in the United States; settled in Kalamazoo County, Mich., and engaged in agricultural pursuits; moved to Chicago in 1859; was admitted to the bar in 1859 and commenced practice in Chicago, Ill.; became editor in chief and principal proprietor of the Illinois Staats-Zeitung; member of the State house of representatives in 1862; member of the Chicago Board of Education 1862–1868; delegate to the Republican National Convention at Baltimore in 1864; presidential elector on the Republican ticket of Grant and Colfax in 1868; appointed United States consul at Dresden in 1872 and served until April 1876; elected as a Republican to the Forty-fifth Congress (March 4, 1877–March 3, 1879); unsuccessful candidate for renomination in 1878; engaged in literary pursuits; died in Chicago, Ill., September 18, 1891; interment in Graceland Cemetery.

BRENTON, Samuel, a Representative from Indiana; born in Gallatin County, Ky., November 22, 1810; attended the public schools; was ordained to the Methodist ministry in 1830 and served as a minister; located at Danville, Ind., in 1834 because of ill health, and studied law; member of the State house of representatives 1838–1841; in 1841, upon the restoration of his health, returned to the ministry and served at Crawfordsville, Perryville, Lafayette, and finally at Fort Wayne, where he suffered a paralytic stroke in 1848 and was compelled to abandon his ministerial duties; appointed register of the land office at Fort Wayne, Ind., on May 2, 1849, and served until July 31, 1851, when he resigned; elected as a Whig to the Thirty-second Congress (March 4, 1851–March 3, 1853); unsuccessful candidate for reelection in 1852 to the Thirty-third Congress; elected as a Republican to the Thirty-fourth and Thirty-fifth Congresses and served from March 4, 1855, until his death in Fort Wayne, Ind., March 29, 1857; interment in Lindenwood Cemetery.

BRENTS, Thomas Hurley, a Delegate from the Territory of Washington; born near Florence, Pike County, Ill., December 24, 1840; attended the common schools, Portland (Oreg.) Academy, Baptist Seminary, Oregon City, Oreg., and McMinnville (Oreg.) College; justice of the peace in 1862; engaged in the general mercantile business at Canyon City, Oreg., 1863–1866; postmaster of Canyon City in 1863 and 1864; clerk of Grant County, Oreg., 1864–1866; delegate to the Union-Republican convention of Oregon in 1866; member of the State house of representatives in 1866; studied law; was admitted to the bar in 1866 and commenced practice in San Francisco, Calif., in 1867; moved to Walla Walla, Wash., in 1870; city attorney of Walla Walla in 1871 and 1872; presided over the Republican Territorial convention at Vancouver in 1874; elected as a Republican to the Forty-sixth, Forty-seventh, and Forty-eighth Congresses (March 4, 1879–March 3, 1885); unsuccessful candidate for renomination in 1884; resumed the practice of law; judge of the superior court of Walla Walla 1896–1913; died in Walla Walla, Wash., October 23, 1916; interment in Blue Mountain Cemetery.

BRETZ, John Lewis, a Representative from Indiana; born near Huntingburg, Dubois County, Ind., September 21, 1852; attended the country schools and Huntingburg High School; taught school 1876–1880; studied law, and was graduated from the Cincinnati Law School in 1880; was admitted to the bar and commenced practice in Jasper, Ind.; prosecuting attorney of the eleventh judicial circuit 1884–1890; elected as a Democrat to the Fifty-second and Fifty-third Congresses (March 4, 1891–March 3, 1895); unsuccessful candidate for reelection in 1894 to the Fifty-fourth Congress; judge of the circuit court of Pike and Dubois Counties from 1895 until his death; delegate to the Democratic National Convention at Kansas City in 1900; died in Jasper, Dubois County, Ind., December 25, 1920; interment in Fairmount Cemetery, Huntingburg, Ind.

BREVARD, Joseph, a Representative from South Carolina; born in Iredell, Iredell County, N. C., July 19, 1766; entered the Continental Army when still a boy; was commissioned lieutenant in the North Carolina Line in 1782 and served throughout the Revolutionary War; moved to Camden, S. C.; sheriff of Camden District 1789–1791; commissioner in equity October 14, 1791; studied law; was admitted to the bar in 1792 and commenced practice in Camden, S. C.; engaged in the compilation of the law reports which bear his name 1793–1815; elected judge of the State supreme court December 17, 1801, and served until December 1815, when he resigned; resumed the practice of law in Camden; elected as a Whig to the Sixteenth Congress (March 4, 1819–March 3, 1821); was not a candidate for renomination in 1820; unsuccessful candidate for Congress at a special election held in 1821; died in Camden, Kershaw County, S. C., October 11, 1821; interment in the Quaker Cemetery.

BREWER, Francis Beattie, a Representative from New York; born in Keene, Cheshire County, N. H., October 8, 1820; attended the Barnet (Vt.) public schools, Newbury (Vt.) Seminary, and Kimball Union Academy at Meriden, N. H.; was graduated from Dartmouth College, Hanover, N. H., in 1843 and from the medical department of the same institution in 1846; practiced medicine in Barnet, Vt., Plymouth, Mass., and Titusville, Pa., from 1849 to 1861; pioneer oil operator and lumberman in Titusville, Pa.; moved to Westfield, N. Y., in 1861 and engaged in banking, manufacturing, and agricultural pursuits; State military agent with rank of major during the Civil War; member of the board of supervisors of Chautauqua County, N. Y., 1868–1879; delegate to the Republican National Convention at Philadelphia in 1872; member of the State assembly in 1873 and 1874; Government director of the Union Pacific Railroad four years under Presidents Grant and Hayes; appointed manager of the State insane asylum, Buffalo, N. Y., in 1881; elected as a Republican to the Forty-eighth

Congress (March 4, 1883–March 3, 1885); was not a candidate for reelection in 1884; resumed the practice of medicine; died in Westfield, Chautauqua County, N. Y., July 29, 1892; interment in Allegheny Cemetery, Pittsburgh, Pa.

BREWER, John Hart, a Representative from New Jersey; born in Hunterdon County, N. J., March 29, 1844; attended the Lawrenceville schools and Trenton Academy; was graduated from the Delaware Literary Institution, Franklin, Delaware County, N. Y., in 1862; moved to Trenton, N. J., in 1865 and engaged in the manufacture of pottery; member of the State house of assembly in 1876; president of the National Potters' Association in 1879; elected as a Republican to the Forty-seventh and Forty-eighth Congresses (March 4, 1881–March 3, 1885); resumed the manufacture of pottery until 1895, when he engaged in the insurance business; appointed assistant appraiser of merchandise at the port of New York City by President McKinley and served until his death in Trenton, N. J., December 21, 1900; interment in Riverview Cemetery.

BREWER, Mark Spencer, a Representative from Michigan; born in Addison Township, Oakland County, Mich., October 22, 1837; attended the rural schools and Romeo and Oxford Academies; studied law; was admitted to the bar in 1864 and commenced practice in Pontiac, Mich.; city attorney of Pontiac in 1866 and 1867; circuit court commissioner for Oakland County 1866–1869; member of the State senate 1872–1874; elected as a Republican to the Forty-fifth and Forty-sixth Congresses (March 4, 1877–March 3, 1881); appointed consul general to Berlin on June 30, 1881, by President Garfield and served from August 29, 1881, until June 7, 1885; elected to the Fiftieth and Fifty-first Congresses (March 4, 1887–March 3, 1891); declined to be a candidate for renomination in 1890; resumed the practice of law in Pontiac, Mich.; delegate to the Republican National Convention at St. Louis in 1896; appointed a member of the United States Civil Service Commission by President William McKinley January 18, 1898, and served until his death in Washington, D. C., March 18, 1901; interment in Oak Hill Cemetery, Pontiac, Mich.

BREWER, Willis, a Representative from Alabama; born near Livingston, Sumter County, Ala., March 15, 1844; attended the common schools; entered the military service of the Confederate Army at the age of eighteen years; journalist, author, and planter; studied law; was admitted to the bar in 1870 and commenced practice at Haynesville, Ala.; treasurer of Lowndes County in 1871; State auditor 1876–1880; member of the State house of representatives 1880–1882; served in the State senate 1882–1890; again a member of the State house of representatives 1890–1894; presidential elector on the Democratic ticket of Cleveland and Stevenson in 1892; again served in the State senate 1894–1897; elected as a Democrat to the Fifty-fifth and Fifty-sixth Congresses (March 4, 1897–March 3, 1901); unsuccessful candidate for renomination in 1900; resumed the practice of law and continued his work as an author until his death in Montgomery, Ala., on October 30, 1912; interment in the family mausoleum on Cedars plantation, near Montgomery, Ala.

BREWSTER, Daniel Baugh, a Representative from Maryland; born in Baltimore County, Md., November 23, 1923; educated at Gilman School, Baltimore, Md., St. Paul's School, Concord, N. H., Princeton University, and Johns Hopkins University; during World War II enlisted as a private in the United States Marine Corps in 1942; commissioned as a second lieutenant in 1943 and served two years in the South Pacific as troop commander in Raider Battalion; landed in assault waves on Guam and Okinawa invasions; wounded in three different engagements;

awarded the Purple Heart Medal, a Gold Star in lieu of second Purple Heart, and Bronze Star; separated from active service in 1946; major in the United States Marine Corps Reserve; graduated from the University of Maryland Law School in 1949; was admitted to the bar in 1949 and commenced practice of law in Towson, Md.; elected to the Maryland House of Delegates in 1950; reelected in 1954 and served until 1958; member of Veterans Advisory Commission in 1947, Commission To Study Maryland Unemployment Compensation Law in 1951, and Burke Commission To Study Judiciary of Maryland in 1952; Baltimore County representative on Port of Baltimore Commission in 1954 and 1955; vice chairman of Commission to Review State Roads Commission program in 1957; owns and operates a grain and cattle farm in Baltimore County, near Glyndon, Md.; elected as a Democrat to the Eighty-sixth Congress (January 3, 1959–January 3, 1961). *Reelected to the Eighty-seventh Congress.*

BREWSTER, David P., a Representative from New York; born in Cairo, Greene County, N. Y., June 15, 1801; attended the common schools, and was graduated from Union College, Schenectady, N. Y., in 1823; moved to New York City; studied law; was admitted to the bar in 1825 and commenced practice in Oswego, N. Y.; trustee of the village of Oswego in 1828, 1836, and 1845; prosecuting attorney of Oswego County 1829–1833; treasurer of the village of Oswego 1832–1834, and served as its president in 1837; judge of the court of common pleas 1833–1841; elected as a Democrat to the Twenty-sixth and Twenty-seventh Congresses (March 4, 1839–March 3, 1843); appointed postmaster of Oswego, N. Y., on July 21, 1845, and served until January 10, 1849, when his successor was appointed; resumed the practice of law; also engaged in agricultural pursuits; member of the excise board commission and served as president 1870–1873; died in Oswego, Oswego County, N. Y., February 20, 1876; interment in Riverside Cemetery.

BREWSTER, Henry Colvin, a Representative from New York; born in Rochester, N. Y., September 7, 1845; attended the public schools; became a clerk in the Traders' National Bank in 1863; employed as cashier 1868–1894, president 1907–1917, and chairman of the board 1917–1923; vice president of the New York State League of Republican Clubs and president of the Monroe County League; president of the Rochester Chamber of Commerce in 1893 and 1902; one of the organizers of the New York State Bankers' Association, serving as vice president in 1894 and president in 1899; elected as a Republican to the Fifty-fourth and Fifty-fifth Congresses (March 4, 1895–March 3, 1899); was not a candidate for renomination in 1898; vice president of the National League of Republican Clubs in 1897; resumed banking and other business activities; governor of the Mayflower Society; delegate to the Republican National Convention at Philadelphia in 1900; retired from active business pursuits in 1923; died January 29, 1928, in Canandaigua, N. Y., while on a visit; interment in Mount Hope Cemetery, Rochester, N. Y.

BREWSTER, Ralph Owen, a Representative and a Senator from Maine; born in Dexter, Penobscot County, Maine, February 22, 1888; attended the public schools; was graduated from Bowdoin College, Brunswick, Maine, in 1909, and from the law department of Harvard University, Cambridge, Mass., in 1913; principal of Castine High School in 1910; was admitted to the bar in 1913 and commenced practice in Portland, Maine; member of the Portland school committee 1915–1923; served in the State house of representatives in 1917 and 1918, but resigned to enter military service; served successively as private, second lieutenant, captain, and regimental adjutant, Third Infantry, Maine National Guard; entered Central Officers' Training School, Camp

Zachary Taylor, Louisville, Ky., in 1918; again served in the State house of representatives 1921–1923; member of the State senate 1923–1925; Governor of Maine 1925–1929; unsuccessful candidate for election to the Seventy-third Congress in 1932; elected as a Republican to the Seventy-fourth, Seventy-fifth, and Seventy-sixth Congresses (January 3, 1935–January 3, 1941); did not seek renomination in 1940, having become a candidate for United States Senator; elected to the United States Senate in 1940; reelected in 1946 and served from January 3, 1941, until his resignation December 31, 1952; unsuccessful candidate for renomination in 1952; retired from political activities and resides in Dexter, Maine.

BRICE, Calvin Stewart, a Senator from Ohio; born in Denmark, Ashtabula County, Ohio, September 17, 1845; attended Miami University, Oxford, Ohio; during the Civil War enlisted in Captain Dodd's university company in April 1861 and served in West Virginia; was graduated from Miami University in June 1863; recruited a company, reentered the Civil War as captain of Company E, One Hundred and Eightieth Regiment, Ohio Volunteer Infantry, and served until July 1865, attaining the rank of lieutenant colonel; studied law at the University of Michigan at Ann Arbor; was admitted to the Cincinnati bar in 1866 and commenced practice in Lima, Allen County, Ohio; presidential elector on the Democratic ticket of Tilden and Hendricks in 1876 and of Cleveland and Hendricks in 1884; delegate to the Democratic National Convention at St. Louis in 1888; member of the Democratic National Committee, serving as chairman in 1889; elected as a Democrat to the United States Senate and served from March 4, 1891, to March 3, 1897; was not a candidate for reelection; died in New York City December 15, 1898; interment in Woodlawn Cemetery, Lima, Ohio.

BRICK, Abraham Lincoln, a Representative from Indiana; born on his father's farm, near South Bend, St. Joseph County, Ind., May 27, 1860; attended the common schools and was graduated from the South Bend High School; later attended Cornell and Yale Colleges, and was graduated from the law department of the University of Michigan at Ann Arbor in 1883; was admitted to the bar the same year and commenced practice in South Bend, St. Joseph County, Ind.; prosecuting attorney for the counties of St. Joseph and La Porte in 1886; delegate to the Republican National Convention at St. Louis in 1896; elected as a Republican to the Fifty-sixth and to the four succeeding Congresses and served from March 4, 1899, until his death; died in Indianapolis, Ind., April 7, 1908; interment in Riverview Cemetery, South Bend, Ind.

BRICKER, John William, a Senator from Ohio; born on a farm near Mount Sterling, Madison County, Ohio, September 6, 1893; attended the country schools and Mount Sterling High School; was graduated from Ohio State University at Columbus in 1916 and from its law department in 1920; was admitted to the bar in 1917 and commenced practice in Columbus, Ohio, in 1920; during the First World War served as first lieutenant and chaplain in the United States Army in 1917 and 1918; solicitor for Grandview Heights, Ohio, 1920–1928; assistant attorney general of Ohio 1923–1927; member of the Public Utilities Commission of Ohio 1929–1932; attorney general of Ohio 1933–1937; Governor of Ohio 1939–1945; Republican candidate for Vice President in 1944; delegate to the Republican National Conventions in 1940 and 1948; trustee of Denison University, Defiance College, Franklin University, and Ohio State University; elected as a Republican to the United States Senate in 1946, reelected in 1952 and served from January 3, 1947, to January 3, 1959; unsuccessful candidate for reelection in 1958; resumed the practice of law in Columbus, Ohio.

BRICKNER, George H., a Representative from Wisconsin; born in Anspach, Bavaria, Germany, January 21, 1834; immigrated to the United States in 1840 with his parents, who settled in Seneca County, Ohio; attended the public schools; engaged in mercantile pursuits in Tiffin, Ohio, 1850–1855; moved to Cascade, Wis., in 1855 and again engaged in mercantile pursuits; operated a flour mill until 1868, when he engaged in the manufacture of woolens at Sheboygan Falls, Wis.; established a glass factory in Tiffin, Ohio, in 1889; elected as a Democrat to the Fifty-first, Fifty-second, and Fifty-third Congresses (March 4, 1889–March 3, 1895); was not a candidate for reelection in 1894 to the Fifty-fourth Congress; withdrew from public life and active business pursuits and lived in retirement in Sheboygan Falls, Sheboygan County, Wis., until his death on August 12, 1904; interment in St. Mary's Cemetery.

BRIDGES, George Washington, a Representative from Tennessee; born in Charleston, Bradley County, Tenn., October 9, 1825; attended East Tennessee University at Knoxville; studied law; was admitted to the bar in 1848 and commenced practice in Athens, McMinn County, Tenn.; also engaged in agricultural pursuits; attorney general of Tennessee 1849–1860; elected as a Unionist to the Thirty-seventh Congress, but was arrested by Confederate troops while en route to Washington, D. C., taken back to Tennessee, and held as a prisoner for more than a year; finally made his escape and went to Washington, D. C., and assumed his duties; qualified and took his seat in the House of Representatives on February 25, 1863, and served until March 3, 1863; during the Civil War enlisted in the Union Army as a captain on August 25, 1863; mustered in as a lieutenant colonel in the Tenth Tennessee Volunteer Cavalry February 23, 1864, and was discharged December 29, 1864; elected circuit judge of the fourth judical district of Tennessee in 1866 and served about one year; died in Athens, Tenn., March 16, 1873; interment in Cedar Grove Cemetery.

BRIDGES, Henry Styles, a Senator from New Hampshire; born in West Pembroke, Washington County, Maine, September 9, 1898; attended the public schools; was graduated from the University of Maine at Orono in 1918; instructor at Sanderson Academy, Ashfield, Mass., in 1918 and 1919; member of the extension staff of the University of New Hampshire at Durham in 1921 and 1922; secretary of the New Hampshire Farm Bureau Federation in 1922 and 1923; editor of the Granite Monthly Magazine 1924–1926; director and secretary of the New Hampshire Investment Co. 1924–1929; also interested in the banking and publishing businesses; lieutenant in the Reserve Corps, United States Army, 1925–1937; member of the New Hampshire Public Service Commission 1930–1934; Governor of New Hampshire 1934–1936; delegate to the Republican National Conventions in 1936 and 1940; elected as a Republican to the United States Senate in 1936, 1942, 1948, and again in 1954, and served from January 3, 1937, to January 3, 1961. *Reelected in 1960 for the term ending January 3, 1967.*

BRIDGES, Samuel Augustus, a Representative from Pennsylvania; born in Colchester, Conn., January 27, 1802; pursued an academic course, and was graduated from Williams College, Williamstown, Mass., in 1826; studied law; was admitted to the bar in 1829 and commenced practice in Doylestown, Pa.; moved to Allentown, Lehigh County, Pa., in 1830, where he continued the practice of law; town clerk 1837–1842; deputy attorney general of the State for Lehigh County 1837–1844; delegate to the Democratic State convention in 1841; elected as a Democrat to the Thirtieth Congress to fill the vacancy caused by the death of John W. Hornbeck and served from March 6, 1848, to March 3, 1849; was not a candidate for renomination in 1848; elected to the Thirty-third Congress (March 4, 1853–March 3, 1855); unsuccessful candidate for reelection in 1854 to the Thirty-fourth Congress; resumed the practice of law; elected to the Forty-fifth Congress (March 4, 1877–March 3, 1879); was not a candidate for renomination in 1878; continued the practice of law in Allentown, Pa., where he died January 14, 1884; interment in Union Cemetery.

BRIGGS, Clay Stone, a Representative from Texas; born in Galveston, Tex., January 8, 1876; attended private and public schools, the University of Texas at Austin, and Harvard University, Cambridge, Mass.; was graduated from the law department of Yale University, New Haven, Conn., in 1899; was admitted to the bar the same year and commenced the practice of law in Galveston, Tex.; member of the State house of representatives 1906–1908; served as judge of the tenth judicial district of Texas from June 15, 1909, until February 1, 1919, when he resigned, having been elected to Congress; elected as a Democrat to the Sixty-sixth and to the seven succeeding Congresses and served from March 4, 1919, until his death in Washington, D. C., April 29, 1933; interment in Oakwood Cemetery, Syracuse, N. Y.

BRIGGS, Frank Obadiah (son of James Frankland Briggs), a Senator from New Jersey; born in Concord, N. H., August 12, 1851; attended the public schools, Francestown (N. H.) Academy, and Phillips Exeter Academy, Exeter, N. H.; was graduated from the United States Military Academy at West Point in 1872; served in the Second Regiment, United States Infantry, as second lieutenant until 1877, when he resigned from the Army; moved to Trenton, N. J., in 1877 and engaged in the manufacture of wire and of wire products; member of the Trenton School Board 1884–1892; mayor of Trenton 1899–1902; member of the State board of education in 1901 and 1902; State treasurer 1902–1907; chairman of the Republican State committee 1904–1911; elected as a Republican to the United States Senate and served from March 4, 1907, to March 3, 1913; unsuccessful candidate for reelection; delegate to the Republican National Convention at Chicago in 1908; resumed his former business pursuits in Trenton, N. J., where he died May 8, 1913; interment in Riverview Cemetery.

BRIGGS, Frank Parks, a Senator from Missouri; born in Armstrong, Howard County, Mo., February 25, 1894; attended the Armstrong and Fayette schools and Central College at Fayette, Mo., 1911–1914; was graduated from the University of Missouri at Columbia in 1915; engaged in the newspaper business in 1915 and in the publishing business at Macon, Mo., in 1925; served as mayor of Macon, Mo., 1930–1932; member of the State senate 1933–1944; appointed as a Democrat to the United States Senate to fill the vacancy caused by the resignation of Harry S. Truman and served from January 18, 1945, to January 3, 1947; unsuccessful candidate for election to the United States Senate in 1946; resumed the newspaper publishing business; chairman, Missouri State Conservation Commission in 1955 and 1956; appointed Assistant Secretary of the Interior for Fish and Wildlife in 1961; is a resident of Macon, Mo.

BRIGGS, George, a Representative from New York; born near Broadalbin, Fulton County, N. Y., May 6, 1805; moved to Vermont, in 1812 with his parents, who settled in Bennington; attended the public schools; engaged in business as a dealer in hardware; member of the Vermont House of Representatives in 1837; returned to New York, settled in New York City in 1838, and continued in the hardware business; elected as a Whig to the Thirty-first and Thirty-second Congresses (March 4, 1849–March 3, 1853); declined to be a candidate for renomination in 1852; elected as the candidate of the American Party to the Thirty-sixth Congress (March 4, 1859–March 3, 1861); declined

to be a candidate for renomination in 1860; retired from public life and active business pursuits; delegate to the Union National Convention at Philadelphia in 1866; died at his summer home, "Woodlawn," at Saratoga Springs, N. Y., June 1, 1869; interment in Greenwood Cemetery, New York City.

BRIGGS, George Nixon, a Representative from Massachusetts; born in Adams, Mass., April 12, 1796; when seven years of age moved with his parents to Manchester, Vt., and, two years later, to White Creek, N. Y.; attended the public schools; moved to Lanesboro, Mass., in 1814; apprenticed to the hatter's trade; studied law; was admitted to the bar in 1818 and commenced practice in Lanesboro; register of deeds for Berkshire County 1824–1831; elected town clerk in 1824; appointed chairman of the board of commissioners of highways in 1826; elected as a Whig to the Twenty-second and to the five succeeding Congresses (March 4, 1831–March 3, 1843); was not a candidate for renomination in 1842; moved to Pittsfield in 1843; Governor of Massachusetts 1844–1851; resumed the practice of law in Pittsfield; member of the State constitutional convention in 1853; judge of the court of common pleas 1853–1858; appointed in 1861 as a member of a commission to adjust differences between the United States and New Granada; accidentally killed in Pittsfield, Berkshire County, Mass., on September 11, 1861; interment in the Pittsfield Cemetery.

BRIGGS, James Frankland (father of Frank Obadiah Briggs), a Representative from New Hampshire; born in Bury, Lancashire, England, October 23, 1827; immigrated to the United States in 1829 with his parents, who settled in Holderness (now Ashland), N. H.; attended the common schools and Newbury Academy; studied law; was admitted to the bar in 1851 and practiced in Hillsboro, N. H., until 1871; moved to Manchester, N. H.; member of the State house of representatives 1856–1858 and in 1874; during the Civil War served as major of the Eleventh Regiment, New Hampshire Volunteer Infantry; served in the State senate in 1876; elected as a Republican to the Forty-fifth, Forty-sixth, and Forty-seventh Congresses (March 4, 1877–March 3, 1883); was not a candidate for renomination in 1882; resumed the practice of law; again a member of the State house of representatives in 1883, 1891, and 1897, serving as speaker in 1897; delegate to the State constitutional convention in 1889; died in Manchester, N. H., January 21, 1905; interment in Green Grove Cemetery, Ashland, Grafton County, N. H.

BRIGHAM, Elbert Sidney, a Representative from Vermont; born in St. Albans, Franklin County, Vt., October 19, 1877; attended the graded schools; was graduated from St. Albans High School in 1898 and from Middlebury (Vt.) College in 1903; engaged in agricultural pursuits; auditor for the town of St. Albans in 1911 and 1912; State commissioner of agriculture 1913–1924; member of the New England Regional Milk Commission in 1917 and 1918; member of the National Agricultural Advisory Committee and of the United States Food Administration, Washington, D. C., in 1918, during the First World War; trustee of Middlebury College 1922–1960; director, National Life Insurance Co., in 1925; elected as a Republican to the Sixty-ninth, Seventieth, and Seventy-first Congresses (March 4, 1925–March 3, 1931); was not a candidate for renomination in 1930; president, National Life Insurance Co., Montpelier, Vt., 1937–1948; president, Franklin County Savings Bank & Trust Co., St. Albans, Vt., 1944–1957 and chairman of the board 1957–; is a resident of St. Albans, Vt.

BRIGHAM, Elijah, a Representative from Massachusetts; born in Westboro (now Northboro), Mass., July 7, 1751; was graduated from Dartmouth College, Hanover, N. H., in 1778;

studied law, but did not practice; engaged in mercantile pursuits at Westboro; member of the State house of representatives 1791–1793; justice of the court of common pleas 1795–1811; served in the State senate in 1796, 1798, 1801–1805, and 1807–1810; State councilor in 1799, 1800, and 1806; elected as a Federalist to the Twelfth, Thirteenth, and Fourteenth Congresses and served from March 4, 1811, until his death in Washington, D. C., February 22, 1816; interment in the Congressional Cemetery.

BRIGHAM, Lewis Alexander, a Representative from New Jersey; born at New York Mills, Oneida County, N. Y., January 2, 1831; attended the district schools and Whitestown Seminary, Whitesboro, N. Y.; was graduated from Hamilton College, Clinton, N. Y., in 1849; studied law; was admitted to the bar in 1855 and commenced practice in New York City; superintendent of public schools, Bergen, N. J., 1866–1870; member of the board of police commissioners of Jersey City 1874–1876; member of the State house of assembly in 1877; elected as a Republican to the Forty-sixth Congress (March 4, 1879–March 3, 1881); unsuccessful candidate for reelection in 1880 to the Forty-eighth Congress; resumed the practice of law in New York City; died in Jersey City, N. J., February 19, 1885; interment in Old Bergen Church Cemetery.

BRIGHT, Jesse David, a Senator from Indiana; born in Norwich, Chenango County, N. Y., December 18, 1812; moved with his parents to Madison, Ind., in 1820; attended the public schools; studied law; was admitted to the bar in 1831 and commenced practice in Madison, Jefferson County, Ind.; elected judge of the probate court of Jefferson County in 1834; United States marshal for the district of Indiana from January 9, 1840, until December 6, 1841, when he became a member of the State senate, in which he served until 1843; Lieutenant Governor of Indiana 1843–1845; elected as a Democrat to the United States Senate in 1845; reelected in 1850 and 1856, and served from March 4, 1845, to February 5, 1862, when he was expelled for having (in a letter to him) recognized Jefferson Davis as "President of the Confederate States"; was elected President pro tempore of the Senate December 5, 1854, June 11, 1856, and June 12, 1860; unsuccessful candidate for election in 1863 to the United States Senate to fill the vacancy caused by his expulsion; moved to Carrollton, Ky., in 1863 and then to Covington, Ky.; member of the State house of representatives in 1866; president of the Raymond City Coal Co., in 1871; moved to Baltimore in 1874, still retaining his connection with the coal company; died in Baltimore, Md., May 20, 1875; interment in Greenmount Cemetery.

BRIGHT, John Morgan, a Representative from Tennessee; born in Fayetteville, Lincoln County, Tenn., January 20, 1817; attended the schools of Fayetteville and Bingham's School, Hillsboro, N. C.; was graduated from Nashville (Tenn.) University in September 1839 and from the law department of Transylvania University, Lexington, Ky., in March 1841; was admitted to the bar in 1841 and commenced practice in Fayetteville, Tenn.; member of the State house of representatives in 1847 and 1848; served as general on the staff of Gov. Isham G. Harris 1861–1865; elected as a Democrat to the Forty-second and to the four succeeding Congresses (March 4, 1871–March 3, 1881); unsuccessful candidate for reelection in 1880 to the Forty-seventh Congress; resumed the practice of law; died in Fayetteville, Tenn., October 3, 1911; interment in the Presbyterian Churchyard.

BRINKERHOFF, Henry Roelif (cousin of Jacob Brinkerhoff), a Representative from Ohio; born in Adams County, Pa., September 23, 1787; moved with his parents to Cayuga County,

N. Y., in 1793; attended the country schools, supplementing his education later by reading and study; commanded a company of militia in the War of 1812, distinguishing himself in the Battle of Queenstown Heights; engaged in agricultural pursuits; member of the State assembly in 1828 and 1829; senior major general of the New York State Militia in 1824; commanded the military escort which accompanied General Lafayette in his progress through the State; moved to Huron County, Ohio, in 1837; elected as a Democrat to the Twenty-eighth Congress and served from March 4, 1843, until his death in Huron County, Ohio, April 30, 1844; interment in the Pioneer Cemetery, Plymouth, Richland County, Ohio.

BRINKERHOFF, Jacob (cousin of Henry Roelif Brinkerhoff), a Representative from Ohio; born in Niles, Cayuga County, N. Y., August 31, 1810; attended the public schools and Plattsburg Academy, Steuben County, N. Y.; studied law; was admitted to the bar in 1837 and commenced practice in Mansfield, Richland County, Ohio; moved to Plymouth, Ohio; prosecuting attorney of Richland County, Ohio, 1839–1843; elected as a Democrat to the Twenty-eighth and Twenty-ninth Congresses (March 4, 1843–March 3, 1847); resumed the practice of law in Mansfield, Ohio; affiliated with the Republican Party on its formation in 1856; delegate to numerous Republican National Conventions; justice of the supreme court of Ohio 1856–1871; died in Mansfield, Ohio, July 19, 1880; interment in Mansfield Cemetery.

BRINSON, Samuel Mitchell, a Representative from North Carolina; born in New Bern, Craven County, N. C., March 20, 1870; attended private and public schools, and was graduated from Wake Forest College, North Carolina, in 1891; taught school in New Bern one year; was graduated from the law department of the University of North Carolina at Chapel Hill in 1895; was admitted to the North Carolina bar in 1896 and commenced the practice of law in New Bern, N. C.; served as county superintendent of public instruction in Craven County 1902–1919; president of the Atlantic & North Carolina Railroad Company in 1918; elected as a Democrat to the Sixty-sixth and Sixty-seventh Congresses and served from March 4, 1919, until his death in New Bern, N. C., April 13, 1922, interment in Cedar Grove Cemetery.

BRISBIN, John, a Representative from Pennsylvania; born in Sherburne, Chenango County, N. Y., July 13, 1818; taught school; studied law; was admitted to the bar and commenced practice in Tunkhannock, Wyoming County, Pa., about 1843; elected as a Whig to the Thirty-first Congress to fill the vacancy caused by the death of Chester Butler and served from January 13 to March 3, 1851; president of the Delaware, Lackawanna & Western Railway Co. 1863–1867 and member of the board of managers and general counsel from 1867 until his death in Newark, N. J., February 3, 1880; interment in Evergreen Cemetery, Elizabeth, N. J.

BRISTOW, Francis Marion, a Representative from Kentucky; born in Clark County, Ky., August 11, 1804; pursued preparatory studies; studied law; was admitted to the bar and commenced practice in Elkton; member of the State house of representatives 1831–1833; served in the State senate in 1846; delegate to the State constitutional convention in 1849; elected as a Whig to the Thirty-third Congress to fill the vacancy caused by the death of Presley Underwood Ewing and served from December 4, 1854, to March 3, 1855; elected to the Thirty-sixth Congress (March 4, 1859–March 3, 1861); was not a candidate for reelection in 1860; resumed the practice of law; member of the peace convention of 1861 held in Washington,

D. C., in an effort to devise means to prevent the impending war; died in Elkton, Todd County, Ky., June 10, 1864; interment in the family burying ground.

BRISTOW, Henry, a Representative from New York; born in St. Michael, Azores Islands, June 5, 1840; immigrated to the United States with his parents, who settled in Brooklyn, N. Y.; attended public and private schools; engaged in mercantile pursuits until 1896; during the Civil War served as a private in Company B, Seventh Regiment, New York State Militia, from April 26, 1861, to June 3, 1861; appointed city magistrate in 1896; member of the board of education of Brooklyn 1880–1889; elected as a Republican to the Fifty-seventh Congress (March 4, 1901–March 3, 1903); unsuccessful candidate for reelection in 1902 to the Fifty-eighth Congress; appointed public administrator of Brooklyn, N. Y., in 1904 and served until his death in that city October 11, 1906; interment in Greenwood Cemetery.

BRISTOW, Joseph Little, a Senator from Kansas; born near Hazelgreen, Wolf County, Ky., July 22, 1861; moved with his father to Fredonia, Kans., in 1873; attended the country schools, and was graduated from Baker University, Baldwin, Kans., in 1886; clerk of the district court of Douglas County 1886–1890; in 1890 bought the Salina (Kans.) Daily Republican, which he edited for five years; elected secretary of the Republican State committee in 1894; private secretary to Gov. E. N. Morrill 1895–1897; purchased the Ottawa (Kans.) Herald, which he owned for more than ten years; again elected secretary of the Republican State committee, in 1898; Fourth Assistant Postmaster General 1897–1905; under the direction of the President made an investigation of the Cuban postal frauds in 1900; purchased the Salina Daily Republican-Journal in 1903; appointed a special commissioner of the Panama Railroad in 1905; elected as a Republican to the United States Senate and served from March 4, 1909, to March 3, 1915; was an unsuccessful candidate for reelection in 1914; temporarily engaged in agricultural pursuits with his son near Fairfax, Va.; chairman of the Kansas Utilities Commission 1915–1918; reengaged in agricultural pursuits on his estate, Ossian Hall, near Fairfax, Va., from 1918 until his death there July 14, 1944; interment in Gypsum Hill Cemetery, Salina, Kans.

BRITT, James Jefferson, a Representative from North Carolina; born in Unico County, near Johnson City, Tenn., March 4, 1861; attended the common schools and studied under private tutors; principal of Burnsville (N. C.) Academy 1886–1893; superintendent of the public schools of Mitchell County 1894–1896; headmaster of Bowman Academy, Bakersville, N. C., 1895–1896; deputy collector of internal revenue at Asheville, N. C., 1896–1899; studied law at the University of North Carolina at Chapel Hill; was admitted to the bar in 1900 and commenced practice in Asheville, N. C.; delegate to the Republican National Convention at St. Louis in 1904; presidential elector on the Republican ticket of Roosevelt and Fairbanks in 1904; unsuccessful candidate for election in 1906 to the Sixtieth Congress; special assistant United States attorney in 1906 and 1907; member of the State senate 1909–1911; special counsel to the Post Office Department from July 1, 1909, to December 1, 1910; special assistant to the Attorney General from July 13, 1910, to December 1, 1910; appointed Third Assistant Postmaster General by President Taft on December 1, 1910, and served until March 17, 1913; elected as a Republican to the Sixty-fourth Congress (March 4, 1915–March 3, 1917); successfully contested the election of Zebulon Weaver to the Sixty-fifth Congress and served from March 1, to March 3, 1919; unsuccessful candidate in 1918 for reelection to the Sixty-sixth Congress; resumed the practice of law in Asheville, N. C.; served as chief counsel for the Bureau of Prohibition, Treasury Department, 1922–1932; was an unsuccessful candidate for chief justice of the supreme court of North Carolina in 1926; resumed the practice of law in 1933; died in Asheville, N. C., on December 26, 1939; interment in Riverside Cemetery.

BRITTEN, Frederick Albert, a Representative from Illinois; born in Chicago, Cook County, Ill., November 18, 1871; attended the public schools, and Healds Business College at San Francisco, Calif.; engaged in general building construction work in Chicago in 1893; member of the Chicago City Council 1908–1912; member of the city civil service committee in 1909, serving as chairman; member of the executive committee of the American group of the Interparliamentary Union 1923–1934; became a member of the Republican National Congressional Committee in 1926; delegate to the Republican National Convention at Cleveland in 1936; elected as a Republican to the Sixty-third and to the ten succeeding Congresses (March 4, 1913–January 3, 1935); unsuccessful candidate for relection in 1934 to the Seventy-fourth Congress; corporation executive in Chicago and New York; retired from public life and resided in Washington, D. C., until his death at the naval hospital in Bethesda, Md., on May 4, 1946; interment in Abbey Mausoleum (adjoining Arlington National Cemetery), Arlington, Va.

BROADHEAD, James Overton, a Representative from Missouri; born in Charlottesville, Va., May 29, 1819; attended the high school in Albemarle County and the University of Virginia at Charlottesville; moved to Missouri in 1837; studied law; was admitted to the bar in 1842 and commenced practice in Bowling Green, Pike County, Mo.; delegate to the State constitutional conventions in 1845, 1861, 1863, and 1875; member of the State house of representatives in 1846 and 1847; served in the State senate 1850–1853; moved to St. Louis in 1859 and continued the practice of law; appointed United States attorney for the eastern district of Missouri in 1861; commissioned by President Lincoln as lieutenant colonel of Volunteers and appointed provost marshal general of Missouri in 1863; delegate to the Democratic National Conventions in 1868 and 1872; appointed by President Grant as special United States attorney to assist in the prosecution of the so-called "whisky ring" at St. Louis in 1876; president of the American Bar Association in 1878; elected as a Democrat to the Forty-eighth Congress (March 4, 1883–March 3, 1885); was not a candidate for renomination in 1884; appointed a special commissioner on French spoliation claims by President Cleveland in 1885; Minister to Switzerland 1893–1897; died in St. Louis, Mo., August 7, 1898; interment in Bellefontaine Cemetery.

BROCK, Lawrence, a Representative from Nebraska; born in Platte County, near Columbus, Nebr., August 16, 1906; graduated from Leigh High School and from the University of Nebraska College of Pharmacy at Lincoln, Nebr., in 1929; engaged as a pharmacist in Madison, Nebr.; cattle feeder and farmer; former president of Nebraska Livestock Feeders Association, Cornbelt Livestock Feeders Association, and Northeast Nebraska Rural Electric Association; past vice president Nebraska Rural Electric Association; former member Nebraska Highway Advisory Commission; member of executive committee of Better Nebraska Association; delegate to the Democratic National Convention in 1956; elected as a Democrat to the Eighty-sixth Congress (January 3, 1959–January 3, 1961); was an unsuccessful candidate for reelection in 1960 to the Eighty-seventh Congress; appointed assistant administrator, Farmers Home Administration, Washington, D. C., in February 1961; resides in Alexandria, Va.

BROCK, William Emerson, a Senator from Tennessee; born near Mocksville, Davie County, N. C., March 14, 1872; attended the public schools; engaged in agricultural pursuits until 1894; moved to Winston-Salem, N. C., in 1894 and was employed as a clerk in a general store until 1896; tobacco salesman 1896–1901; moved to Chattanooga, Tenn., in 1909 and became engaged in the manufacture of candy; also was interested in banking and various other business enterprises and was director in a life and accident insurance company; during the First World War served as chairman of the Liberty loan drives and as member of the executive committees of other drives; served as trustee of the University of Chattanooga, Emory and Henry College, and Martha Washington College for Girls; appointed and subsequently elected as a Democrat to the United States Senate to fill the vacancy caused by the death of Lawrence D. Tyson and served from September 2, 1929, to March 3, 1931; was not a candidate for election to the full term; resumed the candy manufacturing business until his death in Chattanooga, Tenn., August 5, 1950; interment in Forest Hills Cemetery.

BROCKENBROUGH, William Henry, a Representative from Florida; born in Virginia February 23, 1812; studied law; was admitted to the bar and settled in Tallahassee, Fla.; member of the State house of representatives in 1837; served in the State senate 1840–1844, being its president in 1842; United States district attorney 1841–1843; upon the admission of Florida as a State into the Union successfully contested as a Democrat the election of Edward C. Cabell to the Twenty-ninth Congress and served from January 24, 1846, to March 3, 1847; died in Tallahassee, Fla., January 28, 1850; interment in the Episcopal Cemetery.

BROCKSON, Franklin, a Representative from Delaware; born in Blackbird Hundred, Newcastle County, Del., August 6, 1865; attended the public schools; was graduated from the Wilmington Conference Academy at Dover, Del., in 1890; engaged in mercantile pursuits; teacher and principal in the public schools at Port Penn and Marshallton, Del.; was graduated from the law department of Washington and Lee University, Lexington, Va., in 1896; was admitted to the bar September 21, 1896, and commenced practice in Wilmington, Del.; unsuccessful candidate in 1896 for election as delegate to the State constitutional convention; member of the State house of representatives 1908–1910; elected as a Democrat to the Sixty-third Congress (March 4, 1913–March 3, 1915); represented Delaware at the rededication of Congress Hall in Philadelphia, Pa., on October 25, 1913; unsuccessful candidate for reelection in 1914 to the Sixty-fourth Congress; resumed the practice of law in Clayton, and Wilmington, Del.; died in Clayton, Del., March 16, 1942; interment in Odd Fellows Cemetery, Smyrna, Del.

BROCKWAY, John Hall, a Representative from Connecticut; born in Ellington, Tolland County, Conn., January 31, 1801; pursued preparatory studies and was graduated from Yale College, New Haven, Conn., in 1820; taught school; studied law; was admitted to the bar in 1823 and commenced practice in Ellington; member of the State house of representatives 1832–1838; served in the State senate in 1834; elected as a Whig to the Twenty-sixth and Twenty-seventh Congresses (March 4, 1839–March 3, 1843); prosecuting attorney for Tolland County from 1849 to 1867, when he resigned; died in Ellington, Conn., July 29, 1870; interment in Ellington Center Cemetery.

BRODBECK, Andrew R., a Representative from Pennsylvania; born in Jefferson (now Codorus), York County, Pa., April 11, 1860; attended the public schools; engaged in agricul-

tural pursuits; taught in the public schools of York County 1878–1880; moved to Hanover, Pa., in 1880 and engaged in the farm implement and fertilizer business until 1896; sheriff of York County, Pa., 1896–1899; delegate to several State conventions; served on the State central committee; alternate delegate to the Democratic National Convention at Kansas City in 1900; member of the board of directors of various business enterprises; served on the board of directors of Hood College, Frederick, Md., and of Ursinus College, Collegeville, Pa., over twenty-five years; unsuccessful candidate for election in 1910 to the Sixty-second Congress; elected as a Democrat to the Sixty-third Congress (March 4, 1913–March 3, 1915); unsuccessful candidate for reelection in 1914 to the Sixty-fourth Congress; elected to the Sixty-fifth Congress (March 4, 1917–March 3, 1919); unsuccessful candidate for reelection in 1918 to the Sixty-sixth Congress; delegate at large to the Democratic National Convention at San Francisco in 1920; retired from active business pursuits in 1920; died in Hanover, Pa., February 27, 1937; interment in Mount Olivet Cemetery.

BRODERICK, Case (cousin of David Colbreth Broderick and Andrew Kennedy), a Representative from Kansas; born near Marion, Grant County, Ind., September 23, 1839; attended the common schools; moved to Holton, Jackson County, Kans., in 1858 and engaged in agricultural pursuits; during the Civil War enlisted as a private in the Second Kansas Battery in 1862 and was mustered out at Leavenworth in August 1865; studied law; was admitted to the bar in 1870 and commenced practice in Holton, Kans.; mayor of Holton in 1874 and 1875; prosecuting attorney of Jackson County 1876–1880; member of the State senate 1880–1884; appointed by President Arthur as an associate justice of the supreme court of the Territory of Idaho in March 1884 and took up his residence in Boise City, Ada County, Idaho; served until the fall of 1888, when he returned to Holton, Kans., and resumed the practice of law; elected as a Republican to the Fifty-second and to the three succeeding Congresses (March 4, 1891–March 3, 1899); unsuccessful candidate for renomination in 1898; again engaged in the practice of law in Holton, Kans.; presidential elector on the Republican ticket of Taft and Sherman in 1908; retired from the practice of law and devoted his time to farming and livestock interests; died in Holton, Kans., April 1, 1920; interment in Holton Cemetery.

BRODERICK, David Colbreth (cousin of Andrew Kennedy), a Senator from California; born in Washington, D. C., February 4, 1820, his father having emigrated from Ireland to work as a stonecutter on the Capitol; moved with his parents to New York, in 1823; attended the common schools; apprenticed to a stonecutter in early youth; unsuccessful candidate for election in 1846 to the Thirtieth Congress; moved to California in 1849 and engaged in smelting and assaying gold; delegate to the constitutional convention of California in 1849; member of the State senate in 1850 and 1851, serving as president of that body in the latter year; elected as a Democrat to the United States Senate and served from March 4, 1857, until mortally wounded in a duel with David S. Terry, chief justice of the supreme court of California; died near San Francisco, Calif., September 16, 1859; interment under a monument erected by the people of the State in Lone Mountain Cemetery, San Francisco.

BRODHEAD, John, a Representative from New Hampshire; born in Lower Smithfield, Pa., October 5, 1770; attended the common schools and Stroudsburg (Pa.) Academy; studied theology; was ordained a minister and active in ministerial service for forty-four years; moved in 1796 to New England where he became supervisor of Methodist societies in the Connecticut Valley; settled in Canaan, N. H., in 1801; moved to Newfields Village, Newmarket, N. H., in 1809; member of the State senate 1817–1827; officiated as chaplain of the State house of representatives in 1825; elected as a Democrat to the Twenty-first and Twenty-second Congresses (March 4, 1829–March 3, 1833); declined to be a candidate for renomination in 1832 and resumed his ministerial duties; died in Newfields, Rockingham County, N. H., April 7, 1838; interment in Locust Cemetery.

BRODHEAD, John Curtis, a Representative from New York; born in Modena, Ulster County, N. Y., October 27, 1780; attended the district schools; engaged in mercantile and agricultural pursuits; sheriff of Ulster County 1825–1828; elected as a Democrat to the Twenty-second Congress (March 4, 1831–March 3, 1833); elected to the Twenty-fifth Congress (March 4, 1837–March 3, 1839); declined to be a candidate for renomination in 1838; resumed mercantile and agricultural pursuits; died in Modena, Ulster County, N. Y., January 2, 1859; interment in Modena Rural Cemetery.

BRODHEAD, Joseph Davis (son of Richard Brodhead), a Representative from Pennsylvania; born in Easton, Northampton County, Pa., January 12, 1859; attended the public schools; studied law; was admitted to the bar in 1881 and commenced practice in Stroudsburg, Monroe County, Pa.; elected district attorney of Northampton County in 1889; delegate to the Democratic National Conventions in 1892 and 1904; elected to the Sixtieth Congress (March 4, 1907–March 3, 1909); unsuccessful candidate for renomination in 1908; resumed the practice of law in South Bethlehem, Northampton County, Pa.; appointed judge of the courts of record of Northampton County in 1914; died in Washington, D. C., April 23, 1920; interment in Easton Cemetery, Easton, Pa.

BRODHEAD, Richard (father of Joseph Davis Brodhead), a Representative and a Senator from Pennsylvania; born in Lehman Township, Pike County, Pa., January 5, 1811; moved to Easton in 1830; studied law; was admitted to the bar in 1836 and commenced practice in Easton; member of the State house of representatives 1837–1839; appointed treasurer of Northampton County in 1841; elected as a Democrat to the Twenty-eighth, Twenty-ninth, and Thirtieth Congresses (March 4, 1843–March 3, 1849); was not a candidate for renomination in 1848; elected to the United States Senate and served from March 4, 1851, to March 3, 1857; died in Easton, Pa., September 16, 1863; interment in Easton Cemetery.

BROGDEN, Curtis Hooks, a Representative from North Carolina; born in Goldsboro, Wayne County, N. C., November 6, 1816; pursued academic studies; member of the State house of representatives 1840–1850; comptroller of the State 1857–1867; presidential elector on the Republican ticket of Grant and Colfax in 1868; appointed collector of internal revenue in 1869; member of the State senate 1868–1872; Lieutenant Governor of North Carolina in 1872 and Governor upon the death of Governor Caldwell, July 14, 1874; elected as a Republican to the Forty-fifth Congress (March 4, 1877–March 3, 1879); again a member of the State house of representatives 1886–1888; represented North Carolina at the centennial celebration in Philadelphia, Pa., in 1876; died in Goldsboro, N. C., January 5, 1901; interment in Willowdale Cemetery.

BROMBERG, Frederick George, a Representative from Alabama; born in New York City June 19, 1837; moved with his parents to Mobile, Ala., in February 1838; attended the public schools; was graduated from Harvard University in 1858; studied chemistry at Harvard University 1861–1863; tutor of mathematics at Harvard University 1863–1865; appointed treasurer of the city of Mobile in July 1867 by Maj. Gen. John Pope, who commanded the department, and served until January 19, 1869; member of the State senate 1868–1872; appointed postmaster of Mobile in July 1869 but was removed in June 1871; chairman of the Alabama delegation to the Liberal Republican Convention at Cincinnati in 1872; elected by the Liberal Republicans and Democrats to the Forty-third Congress (March 4, 1873–March 3, 1875); unsuccessfully contested the election of Jeremiah Haralson to the Forty-fourth Congress; studied law; was admitted to the bar in 1877 and commenced practice in Mobile, Ala.; Alabama commissioner of the World's Columbian Exposition at Chicago in 1893; president of the State bar association in 1906; died in Mobile, Ala., on September 4, 1930; interment in Magnolia Cemetery.

BROMWELL, Henry Pelham Holmes, a Representative from Illinois; born in Baltimore, Md., August 26, 1823; moved with his parents to Cincinnati, Ohio, in 1824, and thence to Cumberland, Ill., in 1836; attended private schools in Ohio and Illinois, and Marshall Academy, Marshall, Ill.; becoming an instructor in that academy in 1844; studied law; was admitted to the bar in 1853 and commenced practice in Vandalia, Ill.; edited his father's newspaper for several years; judge of Fayette County 1853–1857; took an active part in the founding and building of the Republican Party; moved to Charleston, Coles County, Ill., in 1857; presidential elector on the Republican ticket of Lincoln and Hamlin in 1860; delegate to the State constitutional convention in 1870; elected as a Republican to the Thirty-ninth and Fortieth Congresses (March 4, 1865–March 3, 1869); unsuccessful candidate for renomination in 1868; moved to Denver, Colo., in 1870 and continued the practice of law; president of the Denver School Board 1871–1874; member of the Territorial council in 1874; delegate to the constitutional convention of Colorado in 1875; declined the office as judge of Arapahoe County in 1878 and the appointment as chief justice of Utah Territory in 1879; appointed by the Governor in 1879 to compile the general statutes of Colorado; died in Denver, Colo., January 7, 1903; interment in Riverside Cemetery.

BROMWELL, Jacob Henry, a Representative from Ohio; born in Cincinnati, Ohio, May 11, 1848; resided during his boyhood in Newport, Ky.; attended the public schools of Cincinnati and was graduated from Hughes High School in 1864; taught in the public schools of southern Indiana and of Cincinnati for twenty-three years; was graduated from Cincinnati Law College in 1870; was admitted to the bar of Hamilton County in 1888 and commenced practice in Cincinnati, Ohio; mayor of Wyoming, Hamilton County, Ohio, 1880–1886; assistant county solicitor of Hamilton County 1888–1892; elected as a Republican to the Fifty-third Congress to fill the vacancy caused by the resignation of John A. Caldwell; reelected to the Fifty-fourth and to the three succeeding Congresses and served from December 3, 1894, to March 3, 1903; was not a candidate for renomination in 1902; resumed the practice of law in Cincinnati, Ohio; judge of the court of common pleas of Hamilton County 1907–1913; declined to be a candidate for renomination; again engaged in the practice of law; died in Wyoming, Ohio, June 4, 1924; interment in Spring Grove Cemetery, Cincinnati, Ohio.

BRONSON, David, a Representative from Maine; born in Suffield, Conn., February 8, 1800; was graduated from Dartmouth College, Hanover, N. H., in 1819; studied law; was admitted to the bar in 1823 and commenced practice in North Anson, Maine; member of the State house of representatives in 1832 and 1834; justice of the peace; elected as a Whig to the

Twenty-seventh Congress to fill the vacancy caused by the resignation of George Evans and served from May 31, 1841, to March 3, 1843; moved to Augusta, Maine, in 1843 and resumed the practice of law; member of the State senate in 1846; moved to Bath, Maine, in 1850; served as collector of customs in Bath, Maine, 1850–1853; judge of probate for Sagadahoc County 1854–1857; unsuccessful candidate for election in 1856 to the Thirty-fifth Congress; died in St. Michaels, Talbot County, Md., November 20, 1863; interment in the Episcopal Cemetery of St. Michael's Parish.

BRONSON, Isaac Hopkins, a Representative from New York; born in Rutland, N. Y., October 16, 1802; attended the public schools; studied law; was admitted to the bar in 1822 and commenced practice in Watertown, Jefferson County, N. Y.; elected as a Democrat to the Twenty-fifth Congress (March 4, 1837–March 3, 1839); unsuccessful candidate for reelection in 1838 to the Twenty-sixth Congress; appointed judge of the fifth judicial district of New York April 18, 1838; moved to St. Augustine, Fla., and a number of years later moved to Palatka, Putnam County, Fla.; appointed United States judge for the eastern district of Florida March 14, 1840; upon the admission of Florida as a State into the Union in 1845 was unanimously chosen as judge for the eastern circuit; appointed United States judge for the district of Florida August 8, 1846; when the State was divided he retained the judgeship of the northern district and served until his death in Palatka, Fla., on August 13, 1855; interment in the Episcopal Church Cemetery.

BROOCKS, Moses Lycurgus, a Representative from Texas; born near San Augustine, San Augustine County, Tex., November 1, 1864; attended the common schools; was graduated from the law department of the University of Texas at Austin in 1891 and commenced practice at San Augustine; member of the State house of representatives in 1892; moved to Beaumont, Jefferson County, Tex.; elected district attorney of the first judicial district of Texas in 1896 and served one term; elected as a Democrat to the Fifty-ninth Congress (March 4, 1905–March 3, 1907); resumed the practice of law in San Augustine, Tex., and died there May 27, 1908; interment in Old Broocks Cemetery, about four miles east of San Augustine, Tex.

BROOKE, Walker, a Senator from Mississippi; born at Page Brooke, near Winchester, Clarke County, Va., December 25, 1813; attended the public schools in Richmond, Va., and Georgetown, D. C.; was graduated from the University of Virginia at Charlottesville in 1835; studied law; was admitted to the bar in 1838 and commenced practice in Lexington, Miss.; member of the State house of representatives in 1848; served in the State senate in 1850 and 1852; elected as a Whig to the United States Senate to fill the vacancy caused by the resignation of Henry S. Foote and served from February 18, 1852, to March 3, 1853; was not a candidate for reelection; resumed the practice of law; moved to Vicksburg, Miss., in 1857 and continued the practice of law; delegate to the State constitutional convention in 1861; became affiliated with the Democratic Party in 1861; elected a member of the Provisional Confederate Congress from Mississippi in 1861 and served one year; appointed a member of the permanent military court of the Confederate States; died in Vicksburg, Miss., February 18, 1869; interment in Vicksburg Cemetery.

BROOKHART, Smith Wildman, a Senator from Iowa; born in a farm cabin near Arbela, Scotland County, Mo., February 2, 1869; attended the country schools; was graduated from the high school at Bloomfield, Iowa, in 1886 and from the Southern Iowa Normal and Scientific Institute at Bloomfield in 1889; taught school for five years at Keosauqua; studied law; was admitted to the bar in 1892 and commenced practice in Washington, Iowa; served in the Iowa National Guard 1894–1917; attorney of Washington County 1895–1901; during the Spanish-American War served as second lieutenant in Company D, Fiftieth Regiment, Iowa Volunteer Infantry; resumed the practice of law and also engaged in agricultural pursuits; chairman of the Republican State Convention in 1912; major during the Mexican border troubles in 1916; major and lieutenant colonel during the First World War and served as chief instructor in marksmanship at Camp Perry and Camp Benning schools; elected as a Progressive Republican to the United States Senate to fill the vacancy caused by the resignation of William S. Kenyon and served from November 7, 1922, to March 3, 1925; presented credentials as a Senator-elect for the term commencing March 4, 1925, and served until April 12, 1926, when he was succeeded by Daniel F. Steck, who contested his election; again elected in 1926 and served from March 4, 1927, to March 3, 1933; unsuccessful candidate for renomination in 1932 and for election as an independent candidate; appointed foreign-trade advisor in the Agricultural Adjustment Administration May 25, 1933, and served until January 15, 1935; unsuccessful candidate for the Republican senatorial nomination in 1936; practiced law in Washington, D. C., until 1943, when he retired from active business and political life; died in a veterans' hospital in Whipple, Ariz., November 15, 1944; interment in Elm Grove Cemetery, Washington, Iowa.

BROOKS, Charles Wayland, a Senator from Illinois; born in West Bureau, Ill., March 8, 1897; attended the public schools, the high school at Wheaton, Ill., the University of Illinois at Urbana, and Northwestern University, Chicago, Ill.; during the First World War served as a first lieutenant in the Sixth Regiment, Second Division, United States Marines, 1917–1919; wounded seven times; decorated with the United States Distinguished Service Cross, the American Navy Cross, the Purple Heart, and the Croix de Guerre of France; was graduated from the law department of Northwestern University, Chicago, Ill., in 1926; was admitted to the bar the same year and commenced practice in Chicago, Ill.; instructor of law at Northwestern University in 1926 and 1927; served as assistant State's attorney 1926–1932; unsuccessful Republican candidate for Governor in 1936; delegate to the Republican National Conventions in 1936, 1940, 1944, and 1948; elected as a Republican to the United States Senate to fill the vacancy caused by the death of James Hamilton Lewis, reelected in 1942, and served from November 22, 1940, to January 3, 1949; unsuccessful candidate for reelection in 1948; resumed the practice of law in Chicago, Ill.; owned a farm on the Fox River in La Salle County, Ill.; in 1952 became Republican National Committeeman for Illinois; died in Chicago, Ill., January 14, 1957; interment in Pleasant View Cemetery, Kewanee, Ill.

BROOKS, David, a Representative from New York; born in Philadelphia, Pa., in 1756; attended the public schools; during the Revolutionary War entered the Continental Army as a lieutenant in the Pennsylvania Battalion of the Flying Camp in 1776; was captured at Fort Washington November 16, 1776, and exchanged in January 1780; appointed assistant clothier general; studied law; was admitted to the bar and practiced; after the war settled in New York County, N. Y.; member of the State assembly 1787 and 1788; moved to Dutchess County, N. Y.; member of the State assembly 1794–1796 and 1810; judge of Dutchess County 1795–1807; elected to the Fifth Congress (March 4, 1797–March 3, 1799); unsuccessful candidate for reelection in 1798 to the Sixth Congress and in 1800 to the Seventh Congress; appointed commissioner to negotiate a treaty with the

Seneca Indians; clerk of Dutchess County June 5, 1807, to January 25, 1809, and from February 9, 1810, to February 14, 1811; and again from February 23, 1813, to February 13, 1815; appointed an officer in the United States Customs Service; an original member of the Society of the Cincinnati; died in Poughkeepsie, Dutchess County, N. Y., August 30, 1838; interment probably in Old the Rural Cemetery.

BROOKS, Edward Schroeder, a Representative from Pennsylvania; born in York, Pa.; June 14, 1867; attended the public schools, York County Academy, York, Pa., and York (Pa.) Collegiate Institute; engaged as a banker, manufacturer of steel forgings, and as a contractor; member of the city council 1897–1902; treasurer of York County 1903–1905; member of the Republican State committee in 1917 and 1918; elected as a Republican to the Sixty-sixth and Sixty-seventh Congresses (March 4, 1919–March 3, 1923); was not a candidate for renomination in 1922; acting postmaster of York, Pa., from September 30, 1925, until February 23, 1926, and postmaster 1926–1931; engaged in the clothing business from 1937 until his retirement; died in York, Pa., July 12, 1957; interment in Prospect Hill Cemetery.

BROOKS, Edwin Bruce (cousin of Edmund Howard Hinshaw), a Representative from Illinois; born in Newton, Jasper County, Ill., September 20, 1868; attended the public schools, and was graduated from Valparaiso (Ind.) University in 1892; superintendent of schools at Newman 1894–1897, at Newton 1897–1903, at Greenville 1903–1905, and at Paris 1905–1912; engaged in banking at Newton, Ill., 1912–1914; county superintendent of schools of Jasper County 1914–1918; elected as a Republican to the Sixty-sixth and Sixty-seventh Congresses (March 4, 1919–March 3, 1923); unsuccessful candidate for reelection in 1922 to the Sixty-eighth Congress; superintendent of charities for the State of Illinois in 1924–1930; assistant attorney general 1930–1932; died in Newton, Ill., September 18, 1933; interment in River Side Cemetery.

BROOKS, Franklin Eli, a Representative from Colorado; born in Sturbridge, Worcester County, Mass., November 19, 1860; attended the public schools; was graduated from Southbridge High School in 1879 and from Brown University, Providence, R. I., in 1883; taught school for several years; attended the law school of Boston University in 1887 and 1888; was admitted to the bar in 1888 and commenced practice in Boston, Mass.; moved to Colorado Springs, El Paso County, Colo., in 1891, where he continued the practice of law; delegate to the Republican State conventions in 1900 and 1907, serving as chairman the latter year; elected as a Republican to the Fifty-eighth and Fifty-ninth Congresses (March 4, 1903–March 3, 1907); was not a candidate for renomination in 1906 to the Sixtieth Congress; resumed the practice of law in Colorado Springs, Colo., but devoted himself principally to land development, being president of the Costilla Estates Development Company; appointed a member of the State board of agriculture and trustee of the State agricultural college, Fort Collins, Colo., in 1907; trustee of Brown University; died February 7, 1916, in St. Augustine, Fla., where he had gone in search of health; interment in Evergreen Cemetery, Colorado Springs, Colo.

BROOKS, George Merrick, a Representative from Massachusetts; born in Concord, Mass., July 26, 1824; attended an academy in Concord and a boarding school at Waltham; was graduated from Harvard University in 1844; studied law; was admitted to the bar in 1847 and commenced practice in Concord; member of the State house of representatives in 1858; served in the State senate in 1859; member of the joint committee of the senate and house chosen in 1859 to revise the statutes of Massachusetts; elected as a Republican to the Forty-first Congress to fill the vacancy caused by the resignation of George S. Boutwell; reelected to the Forty-second Congress and served from November 2, 1869, to May 13, 1872, when he resigned, having been appointed to a judicial position; judge of probate for Middlesex County and served until his death in Concord, Mass., September 22, 1893; interment in Sleepy Hollow Cemetery.

BROOKS, Jack Bascom, a Representative from Texas; born in Crowley, Acadia Parish, La., December 18, 1922; moved with his family to Beaumont, Tex., in 1927; attended public schools and Lamar Junior College, Beaumont, Tex., 1939–1941; graduated from the University of Texas at Austin in 1943; enlisted as a private in the United States Marine Corps November 7, 1942, serving overseas twenty-three and one-half months on Guadalcanal, Guam, Okinawa, and in North China, and discharged as a first lieutenant April 23, 1946; lieutenant colonel in the United States Marine Corps Reserve; member of State house of representatives 1946–1950; graduated from the law school of the University of Texas in 1949; was admitted to the bar the same year and commenced the practice of law in Beaumont, Tex.; owns and operates a farm; elected as a Democrat to the Eighty-third and to the three succeeding Congresses (January 3, 1953–January 3, 1961). *Reelected to the Eighty-seventh Congress.*

BROOKS, James, a Representative from New York; born in Portland, Maine, November 10, 1810; attended the public schools; employed in Lewiston, Maine, as clerk in a drug store at eleven years of age; attended the academy at Monmouth, Maine; taught school at sixteen years of age in Lewiston; was graduated from Waterville (Maine) College in 1831; studied law and also edited the Portland Advertiser, and in 1832 was its Washington correspondent; member of the State house of representatives in 1835; unsuccessful candidate for election in 1836 to the Twenty-fifth Congress; moved to New York City in 1836 and established the New York Daily Express, of which he was editor in chief the remainder of his life; served in the State assembly in 1847; elected as a Whig to the Thirty-first and Thirty-second Congresses (March 4, 1849–March 3, 1853); unsuccessful candidate for reelection in 1852 to the Thirty-third Congress; resumed his editorial pursuits; affiliated with the Democratic Party; elected as a Democrat to the Thirty-eighth Congress (March 4, 1863–March 3, 1865); presented credentials as a Member-elect to the Thirty-ninth Congress and served from March 4, 1865, to April 7, 1866, when he was succeeded by William E. Dodge, who contested the election; elected to the Fortieth and to the three succeeding Congresses and served from March 4, 1867, until his death; member of the State constitutional convention in 1867; appointed a Government director of the Union Pacific Railroad in October 1867; died in Washington, D. C., April 30, 1873; interment in Greenwood Cemetery, Brooklyn, N. Y.

BROOKS, Joshua Twing, a Representative from Pennsylvania; born in Edgeworth (now Sewickley), Allegheny County, Pa., February 27, 1884; attended the public schools and was graduated from the Sheffield Scientific School of Yale University, New Haven, Conn., in 1908; engaged in the steel industry; during the First World War served in the Quartermaster Division in Washington, D. C., purchasing steel products for the Army; returned to Sewickley, Pa., and continued in the steel industry; later established his own business, being a distributor of railway supplies and steel products; elected as a Democrat to the Seventy-third and Seventy-fourth Congresses (March 4, 1933–January 3, 1937); unsuccessful candidate for renomination in 1936; member of the State Liquor Board at Harrisburg, Pa., 1937–1939;

assistant director of aviation for Allegheny County, Pa., 1940–; manager of Allegheny County Airport 1949–; is a resident of Sewickley, Pa.

BROOKS, Micah, a Representative from New York; born in Brooksvale, near Cheshire, Conn., May 14, 1775; received his early education from his father; a pioneer and one of the earliest surveyors of western New York; justice of the peace in 1806; member of the State assembly in 1808 and 1809; colonel on the frontier and at Fort Erie 1812–1814; major general of the New York State Infantry 1828–1830; elected to the Fourteenth Congress (March 4, 1815–March 3, 1817); engaged in agricultural pursuits; delegate from Ontario County to the State constitutional convention in 1821; presidential elector on the Adams ticket in 1824; died in Fillmore, Allegany County, N. Y., on July 7, 1857; interment in Nunda Cemetery, Nunda, Livingston County, N. Y.

BROOKS, Overton (nephew of John Holmes Overton), a Representative from Louisiana; born near Baton Rouge, East Baton Rouge Parish, La., December 21, 1897; attended the public schools; during the First World War served overseas as an enlisted man in the Sixth Field Artillery, First Division, Regular Army, in 1918 and 1919; was graduated from the law department of Louisiana State University at Baton Rouge in 1923; was admitted to the bar the same year and commenced practice in Shreveport, La.; served as United States Commissioner 1925–1935; elected as a Democrat to the Seventy-fifth and to the twelve succeeding Congresses and served from January 3, 1937, until his death in the naval hospital at Bethesda, Md., September 16, 1961; interment in Forest Hills Cemetery, Shreveport, La.

BROOKS, Preston Smith, a Representative from South Carolina; born in Edgefield District, S. C., August 5, 1819; attended the common schools and was graduated from South Carolina College (now the University of South Carolina) at Columbia in 1839; studied law; was admitted to the bar in 1845 and commenced practice in Edgefield, S. C.; member of the State house of representatives in 1844; served in the Mexican War as captain in the Palmetto Regiment of South Carolina Volunteers; elected as a State Rights Democrat to the Thirty-third and Thirty-fourth Congresses and served from March 4, 1853, until July 15, 1856, when he resigned even though the attempt to expel him for his assault upon Charles Sumner on May 22, 1856, had failed through lack of the necessary two-thirds vote; reelected to the Thirty-fourth Congress to fill the vacancy caused by his own resignation and served from August 1, 1856, until his death in Washington, D. C., January 27, 1857; interment in Willow Brook Cemetery, Edgefield, S. C.

BROOKSHIRE, Elijah Voorhees, a Representative from Indiana; born near Ladoga, Montgomery County, Ind., August 15, 1856; attended the common schools, and was graduated from Central Indiana Normal College at Ladoga in August 1878; taught in the common schools of Montgomery County, Ind., 1879–1882; also engaged in agricultural pursuits; studied law; was admitted to the bar in 1883 and commenced practice in Crawfordsville the same year; elected as a Democrat to the Fifty-first, Fifty-second, and Fifty-third Congresses (March 4, 1889–March 3, 1895); unsuccessful candidate for reelection in 1894 to the Fifty-fourth Congress; resumed the practice of law in Washington, D. C., and was admitted to practice before the United States Supreme Court in 1894; moved to Los Angeles, Calif., in 1925, and to Seattle, Wash., in 1935, having retired from active law practice in 1925; died in Seattle, Wash., April 14, 1936; interment in Harshbarger Cemetery, near Ladoga, Montgomery County, Ind.

BROOM, Jacob (son of James Madison Broom), a Representative from Pennsylvania; born in Baltimore, Md., July 25, 1808; received a classical education; moved to Philadelphia, Pa., with his parents in 1819; studied law; was admitted to the bar in 1832 and commenced practice in Philadelphia, Pa.; appointed deputy auditor of the State in 1840; clerk of the Philadelphia orphans' court 1848–1852; nominated by the Native American Party in 1852 for President of the United States; elected as an American Whig to the Thirty-fourth Congress (March 4, 1855–March 3, 1857); unsuccessful candidate for renomination in 1856 and for election to the Thirty-sixth Congress in 1858; died in Washington, D. C., November 28, 1864; interment in Congressional Cemetery.

BROOM, James Madison (father of Jacob Broom), a Representative from Delaware; born near Wilmington, Del., in 1776; was graduated from Princeton College in 1794; studied law; was admitted to the bar in 1801 and practiced in New Castle and Wilmington, Del., and Baltimore, Md.; elected as a Federalist to the Ninth and Tenth Congresses and served from March 4, 1805, until his resignation in 1807, before the assembling of the Tenth Congress; moved to Philadelphia, Pa., in 1819 and resumed the practice of law; member of the Pennsylvania House of Representatives in 1824; died in Philadelphia, Pa., January 15, 1850; interment in St. Mary's Churchyard, Hamilton Village (now a part of Philadelphia), Pa.

BROOMALL, John Martin, a Representative from Pennsylvania; born in Upper Chichester Township, Delaware County, Pa., January 19, 1816; attended private schools; taught school for several years; studied law; was admitted to the bar in 1840 and commenced practice in Chester, Pa.; member of the State house of representatives in 1851 and 1852; served on the State revenue board in 1854; unsuccessful candidate for election in 1854 to the Thirty-fourth Congress and in 1858 to the Thirty-sixth Congress; delegate to the Republican National Convention at Chicago in 1860; presidential elector on the Republican ticket of Lincoln and Hamlin in 1860 and of Grant and Wilson in 1872; moved to Media in 1860 and continued the practice of law; during the Civil War served in the Union Army as captain of Company C, Twenty-ninth Regiment, Pennsylvania Emergency Men, from June 18 to August 1, 1863; elected as a Republican to the Thirty-eighth, Thirty-ninth, and Fortieth Congresses (March 4, 1863–March 3, 1869); was not a candidate for renomination in 1868; resumed the practice of law; delegate to the State constitutional convention in 1874; appointed judge of the courts of Delaware County in March 1874 and served until January 1875, being an unsuccessful candidate for election to succeed himself; again resumed the practice of law in Media, Delaware County, Pa.; died in Philadelphia, Pa., June 3, 1894; interment in Media Cemetery, Media, Pa.

BROOMFIELD, William S., a Representative from Michigan; born in Royal Oak, Oakland County, Mich., April 28, 1922; graduated from high school in 1940; attended Michigan State College at East Lansing; during World War II served in the United States Army Air Corps; engaged in the real-estate and property-management business; president of the Broomfield-Bishop-Ruge Co., insurance underwriters, in Berkley, Mich.; member of the State house of representatives 1949–1954, serving as speaker pro tempore in 1953; served in the State senate in 1955 and 1956; elected as a Republican to the Eighty-fifth and Eighty-sixth Congresses (January 3, 1957–January 3, 1961). *Reelected to the Eighty-seventh Congress.*

BROPHY, John Charles, a Representative from Wisconsin; born in Eagle, Waukesha County, Wis., October 8, 1901; attended the public and parochial schools of Milwaukee, Wis.;

was graduated from St. Patricks and Marquette Academy; enlisted in the United States Navy during the First World War and served as a seaman from August 1919 until honorably discharged in May 1921; worked as a mechanic 1922–1938; alderman of the city of Milwaukee from April 1939 to December 1946; elected as a Republican to the Eightieth Congress (January 3, 1947–January 3, 1949); unsuccessful candidate for reelection in 1948 to the Eighty-first Congress and for election in 1950 to the Eighty-second Congress; employed as a salesman and is a resident of Milwaukee, Wis.

BROSIUS, Marriott, a Representative from Pennsylvania; born in Colerain Township, Lancaster County, Pa., March 7, 1843; attended the common schools and Thomas Baker's Academy in Colerain Township; during the Civil War enlisted as a private in Company K, Ninety-seventh Regiment, Pennsylvania Volunteers, in October 1861, for three years, and reenlisted May 20, 1864; honorably discharged December 28, 1864, and on February 28, 1865, was commissioned a second lieutenant for bravery on the field of battle; after the war attended the State normal school at Millersville and the law department of the University of Michigan at Ann Arbor; was admitted to the bar in 1868 and commenced practice in Lancaster, Lancaster County, Pa.; elected as a Republican to the Fifty-first and to the six succeeding Congresses and served from March 4, 1889, until his death in Lancaster, Pa.. March 16, 1901; interment in Greenwood Cemetery.

BROUGHTON, Joseph Melville, a Senator from North Carolina; born in Raleigh, Wake County, N. C., November 17, 1888; attended the public schools; was graduated from Hugh Morson Academy in 1906 and Wake Forest (N. C.) College in 1910; taught school in Bunn, N. C., 1910–1912; reporter on a newspaper in Winston-Salem, N. C., in 1912; attended Harvard University Law School, Cambridge, Mass., in 1912 and 1913; was admitted to the bar in 1914 and commenced practice in Raleigh, N. C., the same year; also engaged in agricultural pursuits; member of the State senate 1927–1929; Governor of North Carolina 1941–1945; served as a member of the board of trustees of Wake Forest College and of the University of North Carolina; elected as a Democrat to the United States Senate on November 2, 1948, to fill the vacancy in the term ending January 3, 1949, caused by the death of Josiah W. Bailey and at the same time was elected for the full term commencing January 3, 1949, and served from December 31, 1948, until his death in Washington, D. C., March 6, 1949; interment in Montlawn Memorial Park, Raleigh, N. C.

BROUSSARD, Edwin Sidney (brother of Robert Foligny Broussard), a Senator from Louisiana; born near Loreauville, in Iberia Parish, La., December 4, 1874; attended the public schools and was graduated from the Louisiana State University and Agricultural and Mechanical College at Baton Rouge in 1896; taught in the public schools of Iberia and St. Martin Parishes 1896–1898; at the outbreak of the Spanish-American War volunteered for service; joined the Second United States Volunteer Infantry, and was elected captain of Company I; participated in the Santiago campaign and served in Cuba from June 23, 1898, until June 22, 1899; accompanied the Taft Commission to the Philippine Islands in 1899 and served as an assistant secretary; returned to the United States in 1900; was graduated from the law department of Tulane University, New Orleans, La., in 1901, and was president of his class; was admitted to the bar the same year, and commenced practice in New Iberia, La.; prosecuting attorney for the nineteenth district of Louisiana 1903–1908; unsuccessful candidate for Lieutenant Governor in 1916; elected as a Democrat to the United States Senate in 1920; reelected in 1926 and served from March 4, 1921, to March 3, 1933; un-

successful candidate for renomination in 1932; resumed the practice of law in New Iberia, La., where he died on November 19, 1934; interment in St. Peters Cemetery.

BROUSSARD, Robert Foligny (brother of Edwin Sidney Broussard), a Representative and a Senator from Louisiana; born on the Mary Louise plantation, near New Iberia, Iberia Parish, La., August 17, 1864; attended public and private schools; attended Georgetown University, Washington, D. C., 1879–1882; appointed night inspector of customs in New Orleans July 1, 1885, and served until July 7, 1888, when he was appointed assistant weigher and statistician, serving in this capacity until January 12, 1889; studied law at Tulane University, New Orleans, La., and was graduated in 1889; was admitted to the bar the same year and commenced practice in New Iberia; elected prosecuting attorney of the nineteenth judicial district in 1892 and served until 1897, when he resigned to enter Congress; elected as a Democrat to the Fifty-fifth and to the eight succeeding Congresses (March 4, 1897–March 3, 1915); did not seek renomination in 1914, having become a candidate for Senator; elected in 1914 to the United States Senate and served from March 4, 1915, until his death in New Iberia, La., April 12, 1918; interment in the Catholic Cemetery.

BROWER, John Morehead, a Representative from North Carolina; born in Greensboro, Guilford County, N. C., July 19, 1845; moved to Surry County, N. C., with his parents, who settled in Mount Airy in 1845; educated by private tutors and attended the Mount Airy Male Academy; engaged in agricultural pursuits, the raising and processing of tobacco, and mercantile pursuits; delegate to all Republican State conventions from 1872 to 1896; member of the State senate 1876–1878; elected as a Republican to the Fiftieth and Fifty-first Congresses (March 4, 1887–March 3, 1891); unsuccessful candidate for reelection in 1890 to the Fifty-second Congress; member of the State house of representatives 1896–1898; resumed his former agricultural and business pursuits; moved to Oklahoma and settled in Boswell, Choctaw County, in 1907 and engaged in the manufacture of lumber, agricultural pursuits, and stock raising; died in a hospital in Paris, Lamar County, Tex., where he had gone for medical treatment, August 5, 1913; interment in Oakdale Cemetery, Mount Airy, N. C.

BROWN, Aaron Venable, a Representative from Tennessee; born in Brunswick County, Va., August 15, 1795; attended Westrayville Academy, North Carolina, and was graduated from the University of North Carolina at Chapel Hill in 1814; moved to Nashville, Tenn., in 1815; studied law; was admitted to the bar in 1817 and commenced practice in Nashville; moved to Giles County in 1818 and continued the practice of law; became the partner of James K. Polk, who subsequently was a President of the United States; served in the State senate 1821–1825; member of the State house of representatives 1831–1833; elected as a Democrat to the Twenty-sixth, Twenty-seventh, and Twenty-eighth Congresses (March 4, 1839–March 3, 1845); was not a candidate for reelection in 1844; Governor of Tennessee 1845–1847; unsuccessful candidate for reelection; delegate to the Democratic National Convention at Baltimore in 1852; appointed Postmaster General in the Cabinet of President James Buchanan on March 6, 1857, and served until his death in Washington, D. C., on March 8, 1859; interment in Mount Olivet Cemetery, Nashville, Tenn.

BROWN, Albert Gallatin, a Representative and a Senator from Mississippi; born in Chester District, S. C., May 31, 1813; moved with his parents to Copiah County, Miss., in 1823; attended Mississippi College, Clinton, Miss., and Jefferson College, Washington, Miss.; studied law; was admitted to the bar in 1833 and commenced practice in Gallatin, Miss.; member of the State house of representatives 1835–1839; elected as a Democrat to the Twenty-sixth Congress (March 4, 1839–March 3, 1841); declined to be a candidate for renomination in 1840; judge of the circuit superior court in 1842 and 1843; Governor of Mississippi 1844–1848; elected to the Thirtieth, Thirty-first, and Thirty-second Congresses (March 4, 1847–March 3, 1853); was not a candidate for reelection in 1852; elected to the United States Senate in 1854 to fill the vacancy in the term beginning March 4, 1853; reelected in 1859 and served from January 7, 1854, until January 12, 1861, when he withdrew; during the Civil War entered the Confederate Army as a captain, Company H, Eighteenth Mississippi Infantry; elected a member of the Confederate Senate in 1862 and served in the First and Second Confederate Congresses; engaged in agricultural pursuits; died near Terry, Hinds County, Miss., June 12, 1880; interment in Greenwood Cemetery, Jackson, Miss.

BROWN, Anson, a Representative from New York; born in Charlton, Saratoga County, N. Y., in 1800; attended the public schools, and was graduated from Union College, Schenectady, N. Y., in 1819; studied law; was admitted to the bar and commenced practice in Ballston Spa; one of the first directors of the Ballston Spa State Bank (later the Ballston Spa National Bank), which was organized in 1830; elected as a Whig to the Twenty-sixth Congress and served from March 4, 1839, until his death in Ballston Spa, N. Y., June 14, 1840; interment in the cemetery of the Ballston Spa Cemetery Association.

BROWN, Arthur, a Senator from Utah; born near Kalamazoo, Kalamazoo County, Mich., March 8, 1843; attended the common schools, and was graduated from Antioch College, Yellow Springs, Ohio, in 1862; took a postgraduate course at the University of Michigan at Ann Arbor; was graduated from the law department of the University of Michigan in 1864; was admitted to the bar and commenced practice in Kalamazoo; moved to Salt Lake City, Utah, in 1879; upon the admission of Utah as a State into the Union was elected as a Republican to the United States Senate and served from January 22, 1896, until March 3, 1897; was not a candidate for renomination; resumed the practice of law in Salt Lake City; delegate to the Republican National Convention at St. Louis in 1896 and at Philadelphia in 1900; assassinated in Washington, D. C., while on a business trip, December 12, 1906; interment in Mount Olivet Cemetery, Salt Lake City, Utah.

BROWN, Bedford, a Senator from North Carolina; born in Caswell County, N. C., near Greensboro, June 6, 1795; was graduated from the University of North Carolina at Chapel Hill in 1813; studied law; was admitted to the bar in 1815 but did not practice; engaged as a planter; elected to the House of Commons of North Carolina in 1815, 1816, 1817, and 1823; member of the State senate in 1828 and 1829; elected as a Democrat to the United States Senate to fill the vacancy caused by the resignation of John Branch; reelected in 1835 and served from December 9, 1829, until November 16, 1840, when he resigned, because he would not obey the instructions of the general assembly of North Carolina; again elected to the State senate in 1842; unsuccessful candidate for election to the United States Senate in 1842; moved to Missouri in 1843; subsequently moved to Virginia and built a place known as Waverly; returned to North Carolina and engaged in agricultural pursuits; again a member of the State senate in 1858 and 1860; delegate to the reconstruction convention in 1865; again elected to the State senate in 1868, but was not permitted to take his seat; delegate to the Democratic National Convention at New York City in 1868; died at "Rose Hill," Caswell County, N. C., near Greensboro, December 6, 1870; interment in the family cemetery at "Rose Hill."

BROWN, Benjamin (nephew of John Brown), a Representative from Massachusetts; born in Swansea, Mass., September 23, 1756; pursued academic studies; studied medicine and commenced practice in Waldoboro, Maine (until 1820 a district of Massachusetts); surgeon in 1778 on the American frigate *Boston*, commanded by Commodore Tucker, which conveyed John Adams as American commissioner to France; with Commander Tucker, was captured in 1781 on the American warship *Thorne* at the mouth of the St. Lawrence River and imprisoned on Prince Edward Island; escaped in an open boat and reached Boston, Mass.; member of the Massachusetts House of Representatives in 1809, 1811, 1812, and again in 1819; elected to the Fourteenth Congress (March 4, 1815–March 3, 1817); resumed the practice of medicine; died in Waldoboro, Lincoln County, Maine, September 17, 1831; interment in Waldoboro Cemetery.

BROWN, Benjamin Gratz (grandson of John Brown of Virginia and Kentucky), a Senator from Missouri; born in Lexington, Ky., May 28, 1826; completed preparatory studies; was graduated from Transylvania University, Lexington, Ky., in 1845 and from Yale College in 1847; studied law in Louisville, Ky.; was admitted to the bar in 1849 and commenced practice in St. Louis, Mo.; member of the State house of representatives 1852–1858; one of the founders of the Missouri Democrat and its chief editor in 1854; unsuccessful candidate for election in 1857 as Governor of Missouri; took an active part in preventing the secession of Missouri in 1861; during the Civil War enlisted in the Union Army; raised a regiment and commanded it; led a brigade against Price and Van Dorn; elected as a Democrat to the United States Senate to fill the vacancy caused by the expulsion of Waldo P. Johnson and served from November 13, 1863, to March 3, 1867; Governor of Missouri in 1871; unsuccessful Democratic candidate for Vice President of the United States on the ticket with Horace Greeley in 1872; resumed the practice of law; died in Kirkwood, near St. Louis, Mo., December 13, 1885; interment in Oak Hill Cemetery, Kirkwood, Mo.

BROWN, Charles, a Representative from Pennsylvania; born in Philadelphia, Pa., September 23, 1797; attended the public schools; also received private instruction; in early boyhood moved with his father to Cumberland County, N. J., and resided near Bridgeton; officer in the State militia 1817–1819; town clerk of Dover Township 1819; taught school at Dividing Creek in 1820 and 1821; returned to Philadelphia in 1823 and engaged in the cordwood business; appointed a director of the Philadelphia public schools in 1828; member of the Philadelphia City Council in 1830 and 1831; served in the State house of representatives 1830–1833; delegate to the convention to revise the constitution of Pennsylvania 1834–1838; served in the State senate 1838–1841; elected as a Democrat to the Twenty-seventh Congress (March 4, 1841–March 3, 1843); was not a candidate for reelection in 1842; president of the State convention to nominate candidates for the board of canal commissioners in 1843; member of the board of commissioners, Northern Liberties Township, in 1843; elected to the Thirtieth Congress (March 4, 1847–March 3, 1849); was not a candidate for reelection in 1848; member of the board of inspectors of the Eastern State Penitentiary 1851–1853; collector of customs at the port of Philadelphia 1853–1857; member of the board of guardians of the poor of Philadelphia in 1860; moved to Dover, Del., in 1861 and engaged in agricultural pursuits; town commissioner of Dover in 1864 and 1865; delegate to the Union

National Convention at Philadelphia in 1866; president of the board of trustees of the Dover public schools 1871–1878; died at Dover, Del., September 4, 1883; interment in Laurel Hill Cemetery, Philadelphia, Pa.

BROWN, Charles Elwood, a Representative from Ohio; born in Cincinnati, Ohio, July 4, 1834; attended the common schools and Greenfield Academy, and was graduated from Miami University, Oxford, Ohio, in 1854; went south and, while serving as tutor at Baton Rouge, La., studied law; was admitted to the bar in 1859 and commenced practice in Chillicothe, Ohio; prosecuting attorney of Ross County in 1859 and 1860; during the Civil War enlisted as a private in Company B, Sixty-third Regiment, Ohio Volunteers, September 2, 1861, and was commissioned captain October 23, 1861; promoted to major March 10, 1863, for meritorious conduct; lieutenant colonel May 17, 1865; colonel June 6, 1865, and brevetted brigadier general March 13, 1865, for "gallant and meritorious services" during the war; mustered out July 8, 1865; resumed the practice of law in Chillicothe, Ross County, Ohio; postmaster of Chillicothe 1866–1872; commissioned pension agent at Cincinnati in 1872, which position he held until President Hayes's administration; elected as a Republican to the Forty-ninth and Fiftieth Congresses (March 4, 1885–March 3, 1889); was not a candidate for renomination in 1888; resumed the practice of law; member of the State senate in 1900 and 1901; died at College Hill, Hamilton County, Ohio, on May 22, 1904; interment in Spring Grove Cemetery, Cincinnati, Ohio.

BROWN, Charles Harrison, a Representative from Missouri; born in Coweta, Wagoner County, Okla., October 22, 1920; attended the public schools in Humansville and Republic, Mo., and high school in Springfield, Mo.; attended Drury College, Springfield, Mo., in 1937, 1938, and 1940, and George Washington University, Washington, D. C., in 1939; program director for radio station KWTO in Springfield, Mo., in 1937 and 1938; radio publicity director for Missouri Conservation Commission in 1940; account executive for Gardner Advertising Co., St. Louis, Mo., 1943–1945; founder and president of Brown Radio-TV Productions, Inc., Springfield, Mo.; partner, Brown Brothers Advertising Agency, Nashville, St. Louis, and Springfield; elected as a Democrat to the Eighty-fifth and Eighty-sixth Congresses (January 3, 1957–January 3, 1961); unsuccessful candidate for reelection in 1960 to the Eighty-seventh Congress; public relations consultant in Washington, D. C., where he now resides.

BROWN, Clarence J., a Representative from Ohio; born in Blanchester, Clinton County, Ohio, July 14, 1893; attended the Blanchester public schools and the law school of Washington and Lee University, Lexington, Va., 1913–1915; State statistician in 1915 and 1916; engaged in newspaper work at Blanchester, Ohio, in 1917 and was publisher of several country newspapers; president of the Brown Publishing Co., Blanchester, Ohio; also engaged in agricultural pursuits as owner and operator of several large farms; Lieutenant Governor of Ohio 1919–1923; secretary of state of Ohio 1927–1933; Republican nominee for Governor in 1934; delegate to the Republican National Conventions in 1936, 1940, 1944, and 1948; member of the Republican National Committee since 1944; elected as a Republican to the Seventy-sixth and to the ten succeeding Congresses (January 3, 1939–January 3, 1961). *Reelected to the Eighty-seventh Congress.*

BROWN, Elias, a Representative from Maryland; born near Baltimore, Md., on May 9, 1793; attended the common schools; presidential elector on the Democratic ticket of Mon-

roe and Tompkins in 1820 and on the Whig ticket of Adams and Rush in 1828; elected as a Whig to the Twenty-first Congress (March 4, 1829–March 3, 1831); member of the State house of representatives in 1834 and 1835; member of the State senate 1836–1838; presidential elector on the Whig ticket of Harrison and Tyler in 1836; delegate to the State constitutional convention in 1836; died near Baltimore, Md., July 7, 1857; interment in a private cemetery near Eldersburg, Carroll County, Md.

BROWN, Ernest S., a Senator from Nevada; born in Alturas, Modoc County, Calif., September 25, 1903; moved with family to Reno, Nev., in 1906; attended the public schools; graduated from the University of Nevada at Reno in 1926; studied law; was admitted to the bar in 1927 and commenced the practice of law in Reno, Nev.; member of the State assembly from Washoe County in 1933; district attorney of Washoe County 1935–1941, resigning in December 1941 to enter active service in the United States Army as a second lieutenant; commissioned a colonel and discharged in December 1945; returned to Reno and resumed the practice of law; member of active Army Reserve since 1926; appointed as a Republican to the United States Senate October 1, 1954, to fill the vacancy caused by the death of Pat McCarran, and served until December 1, 1954; was unsuccessful for election to the vacancy; is a resident of Reno, Nev.

BROWN, Ethan Allen, a Senator from Ohio; born in Darien, Conn., July 4, 1776; pursued academic studies; studied law under Alexander Hamilton; was admitted to the bar in 1802; moved to Cincinnati in 1804, where he began the practice of law; associate judge of the supreme court of Ohio 1810–1818; Governor of Ohio 1818–1822; resigned on being elected as a Democrat to the United States Senate to fill the vacancy caused by the death of William A. Trimble and served from January 3, 1822, to March 3, 1825; unsuccessful candidate for reelection in 1825; canal commissioner of Ohio 1825–1830; appointed Chargé d'Affaires to Brazil May 26, 1830, and served until April 11, 1834; commissioner of the General Land Office in Washington from July 24, 1835, to October 31, 1836; moved to Rising Sun, Ohio County, Ind., November 1, 1836; member of the Indiana House of Representatives in 1842; died in Indianapolis, Ind., February 24, 1852, while attending the Democratic State convention as a delegate; interment in the City Cemetery, Rising Sun, Ind.

BROWN, Foster Vincent (father of Joseph Edgar Brown), a Representative from Tennessee; born near Sparta, White County, Tenn., December 24, 1852; attended the common schools; was graduated from Burritt College, Spencer, Van Buren County, Tenn., in 1871 and from the law department of Cumberland University, Lebanon, Tenn., in 1873; was admitted to the bar and commenced practice in Jasper, Tenn., in 1874; delegate to the Republican National Conventions in 1884, 1896, 1900, and 1916; attorney general of the fourth judicial district 1886–1894; moved to Chattanooga, Tenn., in May 1890 and continued the practice of law; elected as a Republican to the Fifty-fourth Congress (March 4, 1895–March 3, 1897); declined to be a candidate for renomination in 1896; resumed the practice of law; appointed attorney general of Puerto Rico on May 10, 1910, and served until April 20, 1912, when he resigned; resumed the practice of law in Chattanooga, Tenn., until his death there on March 26, 1937; interment in Forest Hills Cemetery.

BROWN, Fred Herbert, a Senator from New Hampshire; born in Ossippee, Carroll County, N. H., April 12, 1879; attended the public schools and Dow Academy, Franconia, N. H., Dartmouth College, Hanover, N. H., and Boston (Mass.) University School of Law; was admitted to the bar in 1907 and commenced practice in Somersworth, N. H.; city solicitor 1910–1914; delegate to the State constitutional convention in 1912; presidential elector on the Democratic ticket of Wilson and Marshall in 1912; mayor of Somersworth, N. H., 1914–1922; United States attorney for the district of New Hampshire 1914–1922; Governor of New Hampshire in 1923 and 1924; member of the New Hampshire Public Service Commission 1925–1933; elected as a Democrat to the United States Senate and served from March 4, 1933, to January 3, 1939; unsuccessful candidate for reelection in 1938; appointed Comptroller General of the United States by President Franklin D. Roosevelt in April 1939 and served until his resignation on June 19, 1940; served as a member of the United States Tariff Commission from August 1940 to June 16, 1941; retired from public and political activities; died in Somersworth, N. H., February 3, 1955; interment in Ossipee Cemetery, Ossipee, N. H.

BROWN, George Houston, a Representative from New Jersey; born in Lawrenceville, N. J., February 12, 1810; attended the common schools and Lawrenceville Academy and was graduated from Princeton College in 1828; teacher in Lawrenceville Academy 1828–1830; studied law in the law department of Yale College for one year and also in a law office in Somerville, N. J.; was admitted to the bar in 1835 and commenced practice in Somerville, N. J.; member of the State council 1842–1845; delegate to the State constitutional convention in 1844; elected as a Whig to the Thirty-second Congress (March 4, 1851–March 3, 1853); was not a candidate for renomination in 1852; resumed the practice of law; associate justice of the supreme court of New Jersey from 1861 until his death in Somerville, Somerset County, N. J., August 1, 1865; interment in the Old Cemetery.

BROWN, James (brother of John Brown of Virginia and Kentucky), a Senator from Louisiana; born near Staunton, Va., September 11, 1776; attended Washington College (now Washington and Lee University), Lexington, Va., and William and Mary College, Williamsburg, Va.; studied law; was admitted to the bar and commenced practice in Frankfort, Ky.; commanded a company of sharpshooters in an expedition against the Indians in 1789; secretary to Governor Shelby in 1792; soon after the cession of the Territory of Louisiana moved to New Orleans and served as secretary of the Territory; United States district attorney; elected to the United States Senate on December 1, 1812, to fill the vacancy caused by the resignation of John N. Destréhan, and served from February 5, 1813, to March 3, 1817; unsuccessful candidate for reelection; again elected to the United States Senate in 1819 and served from March 4, 1819, until December 10, 1823, when he resigned; appointed United States Minister to France and served from December 10, 1823, to June 28, 1829; returned to the United States and settled in Philadelphia, Pa., where he died April 7, 1835.

BROWN, James Sproat, a Representative from Wisconsin; born in Hampden, Penobscot County, Maine, February 1, 1824; attended the public schools; moved to Cincinnati, Ohio, in 1840; studied law; was admitted to the bar in 1843 and commenced practice in Milwaukee, Wis., in 1844; elected prosecuting attorney for Milwaukee County in 1846; attorney general of Wisconsin in 1848 and 1849; mayor of Milwaukee in 1861; elected as a Democrat to the Thirty-eighth Congress (March 4, 1863–March 3, 1865); unsuccessful candidate for reelection in 1864 to the Thirty-ninth Congress; in 1865 went to Europe to recuperate his health; returned to the United States in 1873; resumed the practice of law in Milwaukee, Wis.; died on April 15, 1878, in Chicago, Ill., where he had gone for medical treatment; interment in Forest Home Cemetery, Milwaukee, Wis.

BROWN, James W. (son-in-law of Thomas Marshall Howe); a Representative from Pennsylvania; born in Pittsburgh, Pa., July 14, 1844; attended the common schools of Allegheny County and also private schools; became interested in the iron and steel industry and served as vice president of the Crucible Steel Co.; also engaged in banking and was trustee of the Dollar Savings Bank; elected as a Republican to the Fifty-eighth Congress (March 4, 1903–March 3, 1905); declined to be a candidate for renomination in 1904; resumed his former business pursuits and served as president of the Colonial Steel Co.; died at Point Mouille, Mich., on October 23, 1909; interment in Allegheny Cemetery, Pittsburgh, Pa.

BROWN, Jason Brevoort, a Representative from Indiana; born in Dillsboro, Dearborn County, Ind., February 26, 1839; attended the common schools and Wilmington Academy, Dearborn County, Ind.; studied law; was admitted to the bar in 1860 and commenced practice in Brownstown, Ind.; member of the State house of representatives 1862–1866; presidential elector on the Democratic ticket of Seymour and Blair in 1868; member of the State senate in 1870; secretary of the Territory of Wyoming 1873–1875; moved to Seymour, Ind., in 1875; again a member of the State senate 1880–1883; elected as a Democrat to the Fifty-first, Fifty-second, and Fifty-third Congresses (March 4, 1889–March 3, 1895); unsuccessful candidate for renomination in 1894; resumed the practice of law in Seymour, Jackson County, Ind., and died there March 10, 1898; interment in Riverview Cemetery.

BROWN, Jeremiah, a Representative from Pennsylvania; born in Little Britain (now Fulton) Township, Lancaster County, Pa., April 14, 1785; learned the trade of miller; engaged in milling and agricultural pursuits; member of the State house of representatives in 1826; delegate to the convention to revise the constitution of the State in 1836; elected as a Whig to the Twenty-seventh and Twenty-eighth Congresses (March 4, 1841–March 3, 1845); was not a candidate for renomination in 1844 to the Twenty-ninth Congress; first associate judge for Lancaster and served from 1851 to 1856; died in Goshen (then a post office), Fulton Township, Lancaster County, Pa., March 2, 1858; interment in the cemetery adjoining Penn Hill Quaker Meeting House, Little Britain (later Fulton) Township, Pa.

BROWN, John (uncle of Benjamin Brown and grandfather of John Brown Francis), a Representative from Rhode Island; born in Providence, R. I., January 27, 1736; engaged in mercantile pursuits; one of the party which destroyed the British sloop of war *Gaspee* in Narragansett Bay June 17, 1772; sent in irons to Boston for trial, but released through the efforts of his brother Moses; laid the cornerstone of the first building of the College of Rhode Island (now Brown University) May 14, 1770; trustee of Brown University, Providence, R. I., 1774–1803; treasurer 1775–1796; member of the State house of representatives 1782–1784; chosen as a Delegate to the Continental Congress in 1784, but did not serve; elected as a Federalist to the Sixth Congress (March 4, 1799–March 3, 1801); resumed his former business pursuits; died in Providence, R. I., September 20, 1803; interment in the North Burial Ground.

BROWN, John, a Representative from Maryland; member of the State house of delegates in 1807 and 1808; elected as a Democrat to the Eleventh and Twelfth Congresses and served from March 4, 1809, until his resignation in 1810, before the close of the Eleventh Congress, to accept an appointment as clerk of the court of Queen Annes County, Md., which office he held until his death in Centerville, Queen Annes County, December 13, 1815; interment in Chesterfield Cemetery.

BROWN, John (brother of James Brown and grandfather of Benjamin Gratz Brown), a Delegate and a Representative from Virginia and a Senator from Kentucky; born in Staunton, Va., September 12, 1757; attended Washington College (now Washington and Lee University), Lexington, Va., and Princeton College; enlisted in the Revolutionary Army and served until the close of the war; completed his studies at William and Mary College, Williamsburg, Va.; taught school for several years; studied law; was admitted to the bar in 1782 and commenced practice in Frankfort, Ky.; member of the Virginia Senate from the district of Kentucky 1784–1788; Delegate from the Kentucky district of Virginia to the Continental Congress in 1787 and 1788; elected from Virginia to the First and Second Congresses and served from March 4, 1789, to June 1, 1792, when that portion of Virginia which is now Kentucky was admitted as a State into the Union; elected on June 18, 1792, to the United States Senate from Kentucky for the term ending March 3, 1793; reelected on December 11, 1792, and again in 1799 and served from June 18, 1792, to March 3, 1805; elected President pro tempore of the Senate on October 17, 1803, and January 23, 1804; member of the local board of war for the district of Kentucky in 1791; resumed the practice of law; died in Frankfort, Ky., August 29, 1837, being the last survivor of the Continental Congress; interment in Frankfort Cemetery.

BROWN, John, a Representative from Pennsylvania; born in Kishacoquillas Valley, near Lewistown, Mifflin County, Pa., August 12, 1772; attended the common schools; moved to Lewistown, Mifflin County, Pa., in 1800; engaged in the gristmill and sawmill business at Lewiston; member of the State house of representatives 1809–1813; elected to the Seventeenth and Eighteenth Congresses (March 4, 1821–March 3, 1825); resumed his former business pursuits; moved to Limestone, Buncombe County, N. C., in 1827 and engaged in agricultural pursuits and in the real-estate business; died in a section of Buncombe County, N. C., then called Limestone, near Skyland, on October 12, 1845; interment in Riverside Cemetery, Asheville, N. C.

BROWN, John Brewer, a Representative from Maryland; born in Philadelphia, Pa., May 13, 1836; attended Centerville (Maryland) Academy and Dickinson College, Carlisle, Pa.; studied law; was admitted to the bar in 1857 and practiced in Centerville, Queen Annes County; member of the State house of delegates in 1870; served in the State senate 1888–1892; elected as a Democrat to the Fifty-second Congress to fill the vacancy caused by the resignation of Henry Page and served from November 8, 1892, to March 3, 1893; declined to be a candidate for renomination in 1892; resumed the practice of law; died in Centerville, Queen Annes County, Md., May 16, 1898; interment in Chesterfield Cemetery.

BROWN, John Robert, a Representative from Virginia; born near Snow Creek, Franklin County, Va., January 14, 1842; attended private schools in Franklin and Henry Counties; during the Civil War entered the Confederate Army in 1861 as a private in Company D, Twenty-fourth Regiment, Virginia Volunteers; formed a partnership with his father in the tobacco business at Shady Grove in 1870; moved to Martinsville, Henry County, in 1882 and continued in the tobacco business; also engaged in banking; mayor of Martinsville 1884–1888; elected as an Independent Republican to the Fiftieth Congress (March 4, 1887–March 3, 1889); unsuccessfully contested the election of Claude A. Swanson to the Fifty-fifth Congress; again engaged in the tobacco business; retired from active business pursuits; died in Martinsville, Va., August 4, 1927; interment in Oakwood Cemetery.

BROWN, John W., a Representative from New York; born in Dundee, Scotland, October 11, 1796; immigrated to the United States in 1802 with his father, who settled in Newburgh, N. Y.; attended the public schools; studied law; was admitted to the New York bar in 1818 and commenced the practice of law in Newburgh, N. Y.; elected justice of the peace in 1820; elected as a Democrat to the Twenty-third and Twenty-fourth Congresses (March 4, 1833–March 3, 1837); resumed the practice of law; elected judge of the supreme court for the second judicial district of New York in 1849; reelected in 1857, and served until 1865; resumed the practice of law; died in Newburgh, Orange County, N. Y., September 6, 1875; interment in Cedar Hill Cemetery.

BROWN, John Young (nephew of Bryan Rust Young and William Singleton Young), a Representative from Kentucky; born in Claysville, Hardin County, Ky., June 28, 1835; was graduated from Centre College, Danville, Ky., in 1855; studied law; was admitted to the bar in 1857 and commenced practice in Elizabethtown, Ky.; elected as a Democrat to the Thirty-sixth Congress (March 4, 1859–March 3, 1861), but because he had not attained the age required by the Constitution of the United States he did not take his seat until the second session; member of the Douglas National Committee in 1860; elected to the Fortieth Congress, but his seat was declared vacant because of alleged disloyalty; elected to the Forty-third and Forty-fourth Congresses (March 4, 1873–March 3, 1877); voluntarily retired from politics and resumed the practice of law in Louisville; Governor of Kentucky 1891–1895; returned to Louisville, where he practiced law until his death in Henderson, Henderson County, Ky., January 11, 1904; interment in Fernwood Cemetery.

BROWN, John Young, a Representative from Kentucky; born on a farm near Geigers Lake, Union County, Ky., February 1, 1900; attended the county schools and the high school at Sturgis, Ky.; was graduated from Centre College, Danville, Ky., in 1921, and from the law department of the University of Kentucky at Lexington in 1926; was admitted to the bar the same year and commenced practice in Lexington, Ky.; also engaged in agricultural pursuits; city representative of Lexington, Ky., in 1930; county representative of Fayette County, Ky., in 1932 and again in 1946; member of the State house of representatives 1930 to 1932, serving as speaker in 1932; elected as a Democrat to the Seventy-third Congress (March 4, 1933–January 3, 1935); unsuccessful candidate for renomination in 1934; resumed the practice of law; unsuccessful Democratic candidate for election to the United States Senate in 1946; member State legislature in 1953 and 1954; defeated for the Democratic nomination in 1960 for United States Senator; is a resident of Lexington, Ky.

BROWN, Joseph Edgar (son of Foster Vincent Brown), a Representative from Tennessee; born in Jasper, Marion County, Tenn., February 11, 1880; attended Baylor's Preparatory School, Chattanooga, Tenn., and was graduated from Cumberland University, Lebanon, Tenn., in 1902; studied law; was admitted to the Tennessee bar in 1904 and commenced practice in Jasper, Tenn.; moved to Chattanooga, Tenn., in 1907 and continued the practice of law; elected as a Republican to the Sixty-seventh Congress (March 4, 1921–March 3, 1923); was not a candidate for renomination in 1922; served as chairman of the Republican State executive committee 1922–1924; resumed the practice of law in Chattanooga, Tenn.; delegate to the Republican National Convention at Cleveland in 1924; died in Chattanooga, Tenn., June 13, 1939; interment in Forest Hills Cemetery.

BROWN, Joseph Emerson, a Senator from Georgia; born in the Pickens District of South Carolina April 15, 1821; moved to Georgia; attended Calhoun Academy in South Carolina; taught school; studied law; was admitted to the bar in 1845 and later was graduated from the Yale Law School; returned to Georgia and commenced practice in 1846; member of the State senate in 1849; presidential elector on the Democratic ticket of Pierce and King in 1852; judge of the superior court of the Blue Ridge circuit in 1855; elected Governor of Georgia in 1855; reelected in 1859, 1861, and 1863 and served until June 25, 1865, when he resigned; appointed by Governor Bullock as chief justice of the supreme court of Georgia, which position he held until December 1870, when he resigned and accepted the presidency of the Western & Atlantic Railroad Co.; appointed and subsequently elected as a Democrat to the United States Senate to fill the vacancy caused by the resignation of John B. Gordon; reelected in 1885 and served from May 26, 1880, until March 3, 1891; died in Atlanta, Ga., November 30, 1894; interment in Oakland Cemetery.

BROWN, Lathrop, a Representative from New York; born in New York City February 26, 1883; was graduated from Groton School, Massachusetts, in 1900 and from Harvard University in 1903; engaged in the real-estate business; served in Squadron A, National Guard of New York, for five years; elected as a Democrat to the Sixty-third Congress (March 4, 1913–March 3, 1915); unsuccessfully contested the election of Frederick C. Hicks to the Sixty-fourth Congress; special assistant to the Secretary of the Interior from March 1917 to October 1918; served as a private in the Tank Corps during the First World War; joint secretary of President Wilson's Industrial Conference in 1919; delegate to the Democratic National Conventions in 1920, 1924, and 1936; studied monetary theory at the Graduate School of Harvard University 1928–1932; moved to California in 1946 and settled on a cattle ranch; elected to the sheriff's posse of Monterey County in 1947, member of committee to supervise Graduate School of Public Administration of Harvard University in 1954 and 1955; is a resident of Big Sur, Calif.

BROWN, Milton, a Representative from Tennessee; born in Lebanon, Ohio, February 28, 1804; moved to Nashville, Tenn.; studied law; was admitted to the bar and commenced practice in Paris, Tenn.; later moved to Jackson, Tenn.; became judge of the chancery court of west Tennessee in 1835 and held this position until elected as a Whig to the Twenty-seventh, Twenty-eighth, and Twenty-ninth Congresses (March 4, 1841–March 3, 1847); resumed the practice of law; one of the founders of Southwestern University (later Union University) and of Lambuth College, both in Jackson, Madison County, Tenn.; president of the Mississippi Central & Tennessee Railroad Co. 1854–1856; president of the Mobile & Ohio Railroad Co. 1856–1871; died in Jackson, Tenn., on May 15, 1883; interment in Riverside Cemetery.

BROWN, Norris, a Senator from Nebraska; born in Maquoketa, Jackson County, Iowa, May 2, 1863; attended the common schools; was graduated from the law department of the University of Iowa at Iowa City in 1883; was admitted to the bar in 1884 and commenced practice in Perry, Dallas County, Iowa; moved to Kearney, Buffalo County, Nebr., in 1888 and continued the practice of law; prosecuting attorney of Buffalo County 1892–1896; deputy attorney general of Nebraska 1900–1904; attorney general of Nebraska 1904–1906; elected as a Republican to the United States Senate and served from March 4, 1907, to March 3, 1913; unsuccessful candidate for renomination as Senator in 1912; delegate at large to the Republican National Convention at Chicago in 1908; practiced law in Omaha, Nebr., 1913–1942;

retired and moved to Seattle, Wash., where he died January 5, 1960; interment in Forest Lawn Cemetery, Omaha, Nebr.

BROWN, Paul, a Representative from Georgia; born near Hartwell, Hart County, Ga., March 31, 1880; attended the public schools; was graduated in 1901 from the Lumpkin Law School, University of Georgia, at Athens; was admitted to the bar the same year and practiced law in Lexington, Ga., until 1920; also engaged in agricultural pursuits; mayor of Lexington, Ga., 1908–1914; member of the State house of representatives in 1907 and 1908; moved to Elberton, Ga., in 1920; county attorney of Elbert County 1928–1933; delegate to the Democratic National Convention in 1932; elected as a Democrat to the Seventy-third Congress to fill the vacancy caused by the death of Charles H. Brand; reelected to the Seventy-fourth and to the twelve succeeding Congresses and served from July 5, 1933, to January 3, 1961; was not a candidate for renomination in 1960; died in Elberton, Ga., September 24, 1961; interment in Elmhurst Cemetery.

BROWN, Prentiss Marsh, a Representative and a Senator from Michigan; born in St. Ignace, Mackinac County, Mich., June 18, 1889; attended the public schools, and the University of Illinois at Urbana; was graduated from Albion (Mich.) College in 1911; secretary to the dean of the University of Illinois 1912–1914; studied law; was admitted to the bar in 1914 and commenced practice in St. Ignace, Mich.; prosecuting attorney of Mackinac County 1914–1926; city attorney of St. Ignace 1916–1928; unsuccessful candidate for election in 1924 to the Sixty-ninth Congress and for election in 1928 as justice of the Michigan Supreme Court; chairman of the Democratic State conventions in 1924, 1932, 1934, 1936, 1938, and 1940; member of the State board of law examiners 1930–1942; elected as a Democrat to the Seventy-third and Seventy-fourth Congresses and served from March 4, 1933, until his resignation, effective November 18, 1936; elected on November 3, 1936, to the United States Senate for the term beginning January 3, 1937; subsequently appointed to the United States Senate to fill the vacancy caused by the death of James Couzens for the term ending January 3, 1937, and served from November 19, 1936, to January 3, 1943; unsuccessful candidate for reelection in 1942; served as Administrator in the Office of Price Administration from January 19, 1943, until his resignation on October 21, 1943; resumed the practice of law, with offices in Washington, D. C., and Detroit, Mich.; chairman of the board of the Detroit Edison Co., 1934–1954; chairman of the Mackinac Bridge Authority; incorporator of the Atomic Reactor Development Co., Detroit, Mich.; is a resident of St. Ignace, Mich.

BROWN, Robert, a Representative from Pennsylvania; born in Weaversville, East Allen Township, Northampton County, Pa., December 25, 1744; attended the common schools and was apprenticed to the blacksmith trade; at the beginning of the Revolutionary War was commissioned first lieutenant in the Pennsylvania "Flying Camp" on September 10, 1776; captured at the surrender of Fort Washington November 16, 1776; worked at the blacksmith trade while a prisoner; later put aboard the prison ship *Judith* and subsequently imprisoned in the old city hall, New York City; paroled on board ship December 10, 1777; member of the State senate 1783–1787; elected as a Democrat to the Fifth Congress to fill the vacancy caused by the resignation of Samuel Sitgreaves; reelected to the Sixth and to the seven succeeding Congresses and served from December 4, 1798, to March 3, 1815; was not a candidate for renomination in 1814; retired from public life and lived on his farm; died near Weaversville, Northampton County, Pa., February 26, 1823; interment in East Allen Presbyterian Churchyard.

BROWN, Seth W., a Representative from Ohio; born near Waynesville, Warren County, Ohio, January 4, 1841; attended the public schools; during the Civil War served in Company H, Seventy-ninth Regiment, Ohio Volunteer Infantry; engaged in the newspaper business; studied law; was admitted to the bar in 1873 and commenced practice in Waynesville, Ohio; prosecuting attorney for Warren County 1880–1883; resumed the practice of law in Lebanon, Ohio; member of the State house of representatives 1883–1887; presidential elector on the Republican ticket of Harrison and Morton in 1888; elected as a Republican to the Fifty-fifth and Fifty-sixth Congresses (March 4, 1897–March 3, 1901); unsuccessful candidate for renomination in 1900; resumed the practice of law in Lebanon and Cincinnati, Ohio; writer on political and governmental subjects; died in Lebanon, Warren County, Ohio, February 24, 1923; interment in Miami Cemetery, Waynesville, Ohio.

BROWN, Titus, a Representative from New Hampshire; born in Alstead, Cheshire County, N. H., February 11, 1786; was graduated from Middlebury (Vt.) College in 1811; studied law; was admitted to the bar and commenced practice in Reading, Vt., in 1814; moved to Francestown, N. H., in 1817 and continued the practice of law; member of the State house of representatives 1820–1825; solicitor of Hillsborough County 1823–1825 and 1829–1834; elected to the Nineteenth and Twentieth Congresses (March 4, 1825–March 3, 1829); was not a candidate for reelection in 1828; member of the State senate and served as its president in 1842; chairman of the boards of bank and railroad commissioners at the time of his death; died in Francestown, Hillsborough County, N. H., January 29, 1849; interment in Mill Village Cemetery.

BROWN, Webster Everett, a Representative from Wisconsin; born near Peterboro village, Madison County, N. Y., July 16, 1851; moved with his parents to Wisconsin in 1857; resided for a time in Newport, Columbia County, and then in Hull and Stockton, Portage County; attended the common schools; completed a preparatory course at Lawrence University, Appleton, Wis., and later, in 1870, a business course at the Spencerian Business College, Milwaukee, Wis.; was graduated from the University of Wisconsin at Madison in 1874; engaged in the logging and lumber business at Stevens Point, Wis., in 1875; moved to Rhinelander, Oneida County, Wis., in 1882 and continued in the logging and lumber business; also engaged in manufacture of paper; mayor of Rhinelander in 1894 and 1895; elected as a Republican to the Fifty-seventh, Fifty-eighth, and Fifty-ninth Congresses (March 4, 1901–March 3, 1907); was not a candidate for renomination in 1906; resumed his former business and manufacturing pursuits in Rhinelander, Wis.; died in Chicago, Ill., while on a visit for medical treatment, December 14, 1929; interment in Forest Home Cemetery, Rhinelander, Wis.

BROWN, William, a Representative from Kentucky; born in Frederick County, Va., April 19, 1779; attended the common schools; moved with his father to Bourbon County, Ky., in 1784 and to Cynthiana, Harrison County, Ky., about 1795; studied law; was admitted to the bar and practiced; served as a colonel in the War of 1812; member of the State house of representatives; elected to the Sixteenth Congress (March 4, 1819–March 3, 1821); moved to Jacksonville, Morgan County, Ill., in 1832, where he died October 6, 1833.

BROWN, William Gay, a Representative from Virginia and from West Virginia; born in Kingwood, Preston County, Va. (now West Virginia), September 25, 1800; attended the public schools; studied law; was admitted to the bar in 1823 and commenced practice in Kingwood, Va.; member of the State house of delegates in 1832 and 1840–1843; elected as a Democrat from Virginia to the Twenty-ninth and Thirtieth Congresses (March 4, 1845–March 3, 1849); delegate to the State constitutional conventions in 1850 and 1861; delegate to the Democratic National Conventions at Charleston and Baltimore in 1860; elected as a Unionist to the Thirty-seventh Congress (March 4, 1861–March 3, 1863); upon the admission of West Virginia as a State into the Union was elected to the Thirty-eighth Congress and served from December 7, 1863, to March 3, 1865; died in Kingwood, W. Va., April 19, 1884; interment in Maplewood Cemetery.

BROWN, William Gay, Jr. (son of the preceding), a Representative from West Virginia; born in Kingwood, Preston County, Va. (now West Virginia), April 7, 1856; attended the common schools; was graduated from the University of West Virginia at Morgantown in 1877; studied law; was admitted to the bar in 1877 and commenced practice in Preston County, W. Va.; also engaged in banking; presidential elector on the Democratic ticket of Bryan and Kern in 1908; elected as a Democrat to the Sixty-second, Sixty-third, and Sixty-fourth Congresses and served from March 4, 1911, until his death in Washington, D. C., March 9, 1916; interment in Kingwood Cemetery, Kingwood, W. Va.

BROWN, William John, a Representative from Indiana; born near Washington, Mason County, Ky., August 15, 1805; moved to Clermont County, Ohio, in 1808 with his parents, who settled near New Richmond; attended the common schools and Franklin Academy in Clermont County; moved to Rushville, Rush County, Ind., in 1821; studied law; was admitted to the bar in 1826 and commenced practice in Rushville; member of the State house of representatives 1829–1832; prosecuting attorney 1831–1835; secretary of state of Indiana 1836–1840; moved to Indianapolis, Ind., in 1837; again a member of the State house of representatives 1841–1843; elected as a Democrat to the Twenty-eighth Congress (March 4, 1843–March 3, 1845); appointed Second Assistant Postmaster General by President Polk and served from 1845 until 1849; elected to the Thirty-first Congress (March 4, 1849–March 3, 1851); unsuccessful candidate for renomination in 1850; chief editor of the Indianapolis Sentinel 1850–1855; many times chairman of the Democratic State central committee of Indiana; appointed by President Pierce as special agent of the Post Office Department for Indiana and Illinois, which position he held from 1853 until his death near Indianapolis, Ind., March 18, 1857; interment in Crown Hill Cemetery.

BROWN, William Ripley, a Representative from Kansas; born in Buffalo, N. Y., July 16, 1840; was prepared for college in Phillips Exeter Academy, Exeter, N. H., and was graduated from Union College, Schenectady, N. Y., in 1862; went immediately to Kansas and settled in Emporia; studied law; was admitted to the bar in 1864 and commenced practice in Emporia, Lyon County, Kans.; judge of the ninth judicial district of Kansas 1867–1877; elected as a Republican to the Forty-fourth Congress (March 4, 1875–March 3, 1877); unsuccessful candidate for renomination in 1876; resumed the practice of law in Hutchinson, Kans.; register of the United States land office in Larned, Kans., 1883–1885; moved to El Reno, Okla., in 1892; probate judge of Canadian County 1894–1898; died in Kansas City, Mo., March 3, 1916; interment in Lawrence Cemetery, Lawrence, Douglas County, Kans.

BROWN, William Wallace, a Representative from Pennsylvania; born in Summer Hill, Cayuga County, N. Y., April 22, 1836; moved with his parents to Elk County, Pa., in 1838; attended the common schools and Smethport Academy; was graduated from Alfred University, Allegany County, N. Y., in 1861; during the Civil War enlisted in the Twenty-third New York Volunteers in 1861; transferred to the First Pennsylvania Rifles

December 18, 1861; appointed recorder of deeds of McKean County in 1864 and its superintendent of schools in 1866; studied law; was admitted to the bar in 1866 and practiced; elected district attorney of McKean County the same year; moved in 1869 to Corry, Erie County, Pa., where he served three years as city attorney and two years in the city council; member of the State house of representatives 1872–1876; appointed aide-de-camp to Governor Hartranft in 1876 and was associated with the National Guard of Pennsylvania; moved to Bradford, Pa., in 1878 and continued the practice of law; trustee of Alfred (N. Y.) University from 1879 until his death; elected as a Republican to the Forty-eighth and Forty-ninth Congresses (March 4, 1883–March 3, 1887); unsuccessful candidate for renomination in 1886; resumed the practice of law; city solicitor of Bradford 1892–1897; auditor for the War Department 1897–1899; auditor for the Navy Department 1899–1907; appointed by President Theodore Roosevelt in 1907, and served until 1910, as Assistant Attorney General, in charge of defense of Spanish treaty claims; resumed the practice of law in Bradford, McKean County, Pa., where he died November 4, 1926; interment in Alfred Cemetery, Alfred, Allegany County, N. Y.

BROWNE, Charles, a Representative from New Jersey; born in Philadelphia, Pa., September 28, 1875; attended private schools in Philadelphia; was graduated from Princeton University, Princeton, N. J., in 1896; studied medicine, and was graduated from the University of Pennsylvania at Philadelphia in 1900; attended the University of Berlin in 1902 and 1903; overseer of the poor, Princeton, N. J., 1912–1914; mayor of Princeton 1914–1923; during the First World War served as first lieutenant and captain in the Medical Corps from March 1917 to April 1919; resumed the practice of his profession in Princeton, N. J.; elected as a Democrat to the Sixty-eighth Congress (March 4, 1923–March 3, 1925); unsuccessful candidate for reelection in 1924 to the Sixty-ninth Congress; member of the Board of Public Utility Commissioners of New Jersey 1925–1931; served in the New Jersey House of Assembly 1937–1939, and again in 1941 and 1942; adviser in the department of politics at Princeton University; died in Princeton, N. J., August 17, 1947; remains were cremated and the ashes interred in the grounds of his home in Princeton, N. J.

BROWNE, Edward Everts, a Representative from Wisconsin; born in Waupaca, Waupaca County, Wis., February 16, 1868; attended the public schools and Waupaca High School; was graduated from the University of Wisconsin at Madison in 1890 and from the law department of the same university in 1892; was admitted to the bar in 1892 and commenced practice in Waupaca, Wis.; district attorney of Waupaca County 1898–1905; delegate to the Republican State conventions in 1902, 1904, and 1906; member of the board of regents of the University of Wisconsin in 1905 and 1906; member of the State senate 1907–1912; elected as a Republican to the Sixty-third and to the eight succeeding Congresses (March 4, 1913–March 3, 1931); unsuccessful candidate for renomination in 1930; resumed the practice of law in Waupaca, Wis.; member of the State conservation commission 1936–1941; died in a hospital at Evanston, Ill., November 23, 1945; interment in Lakeside Cemetery, Waupaca, Wis.

BROWNE, George Huntington, a Representative from Rhode Island; born in Gloucester, R. I., January 6, 1811; attended the public schools and was graduated from Brown University in 1840; studied law; was admitted to the bar in 1843 and commenced practice in Providence, R. I.; elected a representative to the so-called "Charter" General Assembly of Rhode Island in 1842; at the same time was elected a representative to what was termed the "Suffrage" legislature and attended the latter; member of the general assembly under the constitution 1849–1852;

appointed United States district attorney in 1852 and served until 1861 when he resigned; delegate to the Charleston and Baltimore Democratic National Conventions in 1860; delegate to the peace convention held in Washington, D. C., in 1861 in an effort to devise means to prevent the impending war; elected as a Democrat to the Thirty-seventh Congress (March 4, 1861–March 3, 1863); unsuccessful candidate for reelection in 1862 to the Thirty-eighth Congress; declined the appointment as Governor of the Territory of Arizona in 1861; entered the Union Army as colonel of the Twelfth Regiment, Rhode Island Volunteer Infantry, October 13, 1862, and served throughout the Civil War; member of the State senate in 1872 and 1873; elected chief justice of the supreme court of Rhode Island in May 1874 but declined the office; died in Providence, R. I., September 26, 1885; interment in Swan Point Cemetery.

BROWNE, Thomas Henry Bayly, a Representative from Virginia; born at Accomac Court House, Accomac County, Va., February 8. 1844; instructed by private tutors; attended Hanover and Bloomfield Academies in Virginia; during the Civil War enlisted as a private in Company F, Thirty-ninth Regiment, Virginia Volunteer Infantry, Confederate Army; afterwards served as a private in Chew's battery of the Stuart Horse Artillery; was surrendered with the Army of Northern Virginia in April 1865; was graduated from the law department of the University of Virginia at Charlottesville in 1867; admitted to the bar in 1868 and commenced practice in Accomac, Va.; elected prosecuting attorney for Accomac County in 1873; presidential elector on the Republican ticket of Blaine and Logan in 1884; elected as a Republican to the Fiftieth and Fifty-first Congresses (March 4, 1887–March 3, 1891); unsuccessful candidate for reelection in 1890 to the Fifty-second Congress; resumed the practice of law; died in Accomac, Va., August 27, 1892; interment in Mount Curtis Cemetery.

BROWNE, Thomas McLelland, a Representative from Indiana; born in New Paris, Preble County, Ohio, April 19, 1829; moved to Indiana in January 1844; attended the common schools; moved to Winchester, Ind., in 1848; studied law; was admitted to the bar in 1849 and commenced practice in Winchester; elected prosecuting attorney for the thirteenth judicial circuit in 1855; reelected in 1857 and 1859; secretary of the State senate in 1861; member of the State senate in 1863; assisted in organizing the Seventh Regiment, Indiana Volunteer Cavalry of the Union Army, and went to the field with that regiment as captain of Company B, August 28, 1863; commissioned lieutenant colonel October 1, 1863; promoted to colonel October 10, 1865, and subsequently commissioned by President Lincoln as brigadier general by brevet March 13, 1865, "for gallant and meritorious services during the war"; mustered out February 18, 1866; appointed United States attorney for the district of Indiana in April 1869 and served until his resignation August 1, 1872; unsuccessful candidate for Governor in 1872; delegate to the Republican National Convention at Cincinnati in 1876; elected as a Republican to the Forty-fifth and to the six succeeding Congresses (March 4, 1877–March 3, 1891); was not a candidate for renomination in 1890; died in Winchester, Randolph County, Ind., July 17, 1891; interment in Fountain Park Cemetery.

BROWNING, Gordon, a Representative from Tennessee; born near Atwood, Carroll County, Tenn., November 22, 1889; attended the public schools; was graduated from the high school at Milan, Tenn., in 1908, from Valparaiso University, Valparaiso, Ind., in 1913, and from Cumberland University Law School in 1915; was admitted to the bar and commenced practice in Huntingdon, Tenn., in 1915; during the First World War enlisted in the National Guard in June 1917, and on July 25,

1917, was commissioned a second lieutenant of the First Tennessee Field Artillery, afterwards the One Hundred and Fourteenth Field Artillery, Thirtieth Division; promoted to first lieutenant November 23, 1917, and to captain May 10, 1918, and commanded a battery during all its engagements in France; was discharged from the service in 1919 and resumed the practice of law in Huntingdon, Tenn.; unsuccessful candidate for election in 1920 to the Sixty-seventh Congress; elected as a Democrat to the Sixty-eighth and to the five succeeding Congresses (March 4, 1923–January 3, 1935); was not a candidate for renomination in 1934, but was an unsuccessful candidate for the Democratic nomination for United States Senator; one of the managers appointed by the House of Representatives in 1933 to conduct the impeachment proceedings against Harold Louderback, judge of the United States District Court for the Northern District of California; again resumed the practice of law; Governor of Tennessee 1937–1939; chancellor of the Eighth Tennessee Chancery Division 1942–1949; during World War II was appointed a captain in the United States Army on February 17, 1943; attended the School of Military Government at Charlottesville, Va.; advanced through the ranks to lieutenant colonel; acted as deputy head of the Belgium-Luxembourg missions until January 1946; with the military government in Germany for one year, serving as civil-affairs adviser on the supreme commander's staff, in policy enforcement in Bavaria, and as director of the Bremen enclave; again Governor of Tennessee from January 1949 to January 1953; engaged in the practice of law and in the operation of a dairy farm; is a resident of Huntingdon, Tenn.

BROWNING, Orville Hickman, a Senator from Illinois; born in Cynthiana, Harrison County, Ky., February 10, 1806; attended Augusta College; studied law; was admitted to the bar in 1831; moved to Quincy, Ill., in 1831 and practiced; served in the Illinois Volunteers through the Black Hawk War in 1832; member of the State senate 1836–1843; unsuccessful candidate for election as a Whig in 1850 to the Thirty-second Congress and in 1852 to the Thirty-third Congress; delegate to the anti-Nebraska convention held at Bloomington, Ill., on May 29, 1856, which laid the foundations of the Republican Party; delegate to the Republican National Convention at Chicago in 1860; appointed as a Republican to the United States Senate to fill the vacancy caused by the death of Stephen A. Douglas and served from June 26, 1861, to January 12, 1863, when a successor was elected; was not a candidate for election in 1863; member of the Union executive committee in 1866; appointed by President Johnson as Secretary of the Interior July 27, 1866, to take effect September 1, 1866, and served until March 3, 1869, also discharging for a time the duties of Attorney General; delegate to the State constitutional convention in 1869; resumed the practice of law; died in Quincy, Adams County, Ill., August 10, 1881; interment in Woodland Cemetery.

BROWNING, William John, a Representative from New Jersey; born in Camden, N. J., April 11, 1850; attended the Friends' School; at an early age engaged in the wholesale dry-goods business in Camden; member of the Camden Board of Education and of the city council; appointed postmaster of Camden on June 18, 1889, and served until June 1, 1894, when his successor was appointed; Chief Clerk of the House of Representatives of the United States 1895–1911; elected as a Republican to the Sixty-second Congress to fill the vacancy caused by the death of Henry C. Loudenslager; reelected to the Sixty-third and to the three succeeding Congresses and served from November 7, 1911, until his death in the Capitol Building, Washington, D. C., March 24, 1920; interment in Harleigh Cemetery, Camden, N. J.

BROWNLOW, Walter Preston (nephew of William Gannaway Brownlow), a Representative from Tennessee; born in Abingdon, Washington County, Va., March 27, 1851; attended the common schools; employed as a telegraph messenger boy when only ten years of age; became an apprentice in the tinning business at the age of fourteen and later became a locomotive engineer; entered upon newspaper work as a reporter for the Knoxville Whig and Chronicle in 1876; in the same year purchased the Herald and Tribune in Jonesboro, Tenn.; delegate to the Republican National Conventions in 1880, 1884, 1896, 1900, and 1904; appointed postmaster at Jonesboro in March 1881; resigned in the following December to accept the position of Doorkeeper of the National House of Representatives in the Forty-seventh Congress and served in that capacity from 1881 to 1883; member of the Republican National Committee in 1884, 1896, and 1900; elected as a Republican to the Fifty-fifth and to the six succeeding Congresses and served from March 4, 1897, until his death; elected as a member of the Board of Managers for the National Soldiers' Home for Disabled Volunteer Soldiers and served from 1902 to 1910; died at the National Soldiers' Home, Johnson City, Washington County, Tenn., July 8, 1910; interment in the Soldiers' Home Cemetery.

BROWNLOW, William Gannaway (uncle of Walter Preston Brownlow), a Senator from Tennessee; born near Wytheville, Wythe County, Va., August 29, 1805; attended the common schools; entered the Methodist ministry in 1826; moved to Elizabethton, Tenn., in 1828 and continued his ministerial duties; published and edited a newspaper called the Whig at Elizabethton in 1838; moved the paper to Jonesboro, Tenn., in 1839 and to Knoxville, Tenn., in 1849 and from his caustic and trenchant editorials became widely known as "the fighting parson"; unsuccessful candidate for election in 1842 to the Twenty-eighth Congress; appointed by President Fillmore in 1850 a member of the Tennessee River Commission for the Improvement of Navigation; delegate to the constitutional convention which reorganized the State government of Tennessee in 1864; elected Governor in 1865 and again in 1867; elected as a Republican to the United States Senate and served from March 4, 1869, to March 3, 1875; was not a candidate for reelection; returned to Knoxville, Tenn., and lived in retirement until his death there on April 29, 1877; interment in the Old Grey Cemetery.

BROWNSON, Charles Bruce, a Representative from Indiana; born in Jackson, Mich., February 5, 1914; moved with his parents to Flint, Mich., in 1916; attended the public schools and Flint Central High School; was graduated from the University of Michigan at Ann Arbor in 1935; entered Thomasson Act training as second lieutenant, Infantry Reserve, Fort Sheridan, Ill., August 1, 1935; moved to Indianapolis, Ind., in October 1936 and established the Central Wallpaper & Paint Corp.; during World War II entered on active duty as first lieutenant, Infantry Reserve, Chanute Field, Ill., February 10, 1941; served as Assistant Chief of Staff, G–1, Eighty-third Infantry Division, Camp Atterbury, Ind., in 1943; graduated from Adjutants General School in 1942 and Command and General Staff, Fort Leavenworth, Kans., in 1943; executive officer to Assistant Chief of Staff, G–1, First Army, during invasion planning in England and combat in Europe until V–E Day; transferred with First Army Planning Headquarters to Canlubang, Philippine Islands, August 5, 1945; released from active duty February 27, 1946, as lieutenant colonel, Army Reserve, and promoted to colonel in 1960; awarded five battle stars and invasion arrowhead on European Theater Ribbon, Legion of Merit, Bronze Star, and French Medaille de Reconnaissance; chairman Marion County Juvenile Court Advisory Council in 1948 and 1949; elected as a Republican to the Eighty-second and to the three succeeding Congresses (January 3, 1951–January 3, 1959); unsuccessful candidate for reelection in 1958 to the Eighty-sixth Congress; assistant administrator for public affairs and congressional liaison, Housing and Home Finance Agency, Washington, D. C., from August 12, 1959, to January 20, 1961; editor and publisher of Congressional Staff Directory; engaged in public relations in Washington, D. C., where he resides.

BROWNSON, Nathan, a Delegate from Georgia; born in Woodbury, Conn., May 14, 1742; was graduated from Yale College in 1761; studied medicine and practiced in Woodbury; moved to Liberty County, Ga., about 1764; member of the Provincial Congress in 1775; surgeon in the Revolutionary Army; Member of the Continental Congress in 1777 and 1783; member of the State house of representatives in 1781 and served as speaker; chosen by that body as Governor of Georgia in 1782; again elected to the State house of representatives in 1788 and served as speaker; delegate to the State convention to ratify the Federal Constitution in 1788 and to the State constitutional convention in 1789; member of the State senate 1789–1791 and served as president of that body; died on his plantation near Riceboro, Liberty County, Ga., November 6, 1796; interment in the Old Midway Burial Ground.

BROYHILL, Joel Thomas, a Representative from Virginia; born in Hopewell, Prince George County, Va., November 4, 1919; attended the public schools, Fork Union Military Academy, Fork Union, Va., and George Washington University, Washington, D. C., 1939–1941; engaged in the building business in the firm of M. T. Broyhill & Sons since 1945; during World War II entered the United States Army in February 1942 as an enlisted man; served in European Theater as captain in One Hundred and Sixth Infantry Division and was taken prisoner in Battle of the Bulge; after six months in German prison camps escaped and rejoined advancing American forces; after four years of service was released from active duty November 1, 1945, as a captain of Infantry; elected as a Republican to the Eighty-third and to the three succeeding Congresses (January 3, 1953–January 3, 1961). *Reelected to the Eighty-seventh Congress.*

BRUCE, Blanche Kelso, a Senator from Mississippi; born near Farmville, Prince Edward County, Va., March 1, 1841; was of the Negro race and raised as a slave; was tutored by his master's son; left his master at the beginning of the Civil War; taught school for a time in Hannibal, Mo., and later attended Oberlin College, Ohio; after the war became a planter in Mississippi; member of the Mississippi Levee Board; sheriff and tax collector of Bolivar County 1872–1875; elected as a Republican to the United States Senate and served from March 4, 1875, to March 3, 1881; delegate to several Republican National Conventions; appointed Register of the Treasury by President Garfield May 19, 1881; recorder of deeds for the District of Columbia 1891–1893; again Register of the Treasury from 1897 until his death in Washington, D. C., on March 17, 1898; interment in Woodlawn Cemetery.

BRUCE, Phineas, a Representative from Massachusetts; born in Mendon, Mass., June 7, 1762; received a classical education and was graduated from Yale College in 1786; studied law; was admitted to the bar in 1790 and commenced practice in Machias, Maine (then a district of Massachusetts); member of the Massachusetts House of Representatives 1791–1798 and in 1800; elected to the Eighth Congress commencing March 4, 1803, but was prevented by illness from qualifying; died in Uxbridge, Mass., October 4, 1809; interment in the Old Burying Ground; reinterment in Prospect Hill Cemetery.

BRUCE, William Cabell, a Senator from Maryland; born in Staunton Hill, Charlotte County, Va., March 12, 1860; received an academic education at Norwood High School and College, Nelson County, Va.; attended the University of Virginia at Charlottesville in 1879 and 1880; was graduated from the University of Maryland Law School at Baltimore in 1882; was admitted to the Maryland bar the same year and commenced practice in Baltimore, Md.; member of the State senate 1894–1896, serving as president of that body in 1896; head of the city law department of Baltimore from 1903 until 1908; member of the Baltimore Charter Commission in 1910; general counsel to the Public Service Commission of Maryland from 1910 to 1922, when he resigned; unsuccessful candidate for the Democratic nomination for United States Senator in 1916; author of many books; elected as a Democrat to the United States Senate and served from March 4, 1923, to March 3, 1929; unsuccessful candidate for reelection in 1928; resumed the practice of law in Baltimore until 1937, when he retired; died in Ruxton, Baltimore County, Md., May 9, 1946; interment in St. Thomas' Episcopal Church Cemetery, Garrison, Md.

BRUCKER, Ferdinand, a Representative from Michigan; born in Bridgeport, Saginaw County, Mich., January 8, 1858; attended the common schools; member of the State militia 1878–1881; was graduated from the law department of the University of Michigan at Ann Arbor in 1881; was admitted to the bar the same year and commenced practice in Saginaw, Mich.; alderman of East Saginaw 1882–1884; judge of the probate court of Saginaw County 1888–1896; delegate to the Democratic National Convention at Chicago in 1896; elected as a Democrat to the Fifty-fifth Congress (March 4, 1897–March 3, 1899); was an unsuccessful candidate for reelection in 1898 to the Fifty-sixth Congress; resumed the practice of law; died in Saginaw, Mich., on March 3, 1904; interment in Bridgeport Cemetery, Bridgeport, Mich.

BRUCKNER, Henry, a Representative from New York; born in New York City, June 17, 1871; attended the common and high schools in New York; became engaged in the manufacture of mineral waters in 1892; member of the State assembly in 1901; commissioner of public works for the Borough of the Bronx, New York City, 1902–1905; elected as a Democrat to the Sixty-third, Sixty-fourth, and Sixty-fifth Congresses and served from March 4, 1913, until December 31, 1917, when he resigned; resumed his former business pursuits in New York City; also interested in banking; president of the Borough of the Bronx 1918–1933; died in New York City on April 14, 1942; interment in Woodlawn Cemetery.

BRUMBAUGH, Clement Laird, a Representative from Ohio; born on a farm near Pikeville, Darke County, Ohio, February 28, 1863; attended the district schools and the Greenville (Ohio) High School; taught school, worked on a farm, and tutored; was graduated from National Normal University, Lebanon, Ohio, in 1887; founded and conducted the Van Buren Academy 1887–1891; attended Ohio Wesleyan University, Delaware, Ohio, 1891–1893; was graduated from Harvard University in 1894; taught school in Washington, D. C., 1894–1896; superintendent of schools in Greenville, Ohio, 1896–1900; studied law; was admitted to the bar in 1900 and commenced practice in Columbus, Ohio; member of the State house of representatives 1900–1904, serving as minority leader; elected as a Democrat to the Sixty-third and to the three succeeding Congresses (March 4, 1913–March 3, 1921); was not a candidate for renomination in 1920; lived in retirement in Columbus, Ohio, until his death there on September 28, 1921; interment in Greenville Cemetery, Greenville, Ohio.

BRUMBAUGH, David Emmert, a Representative from Pennsylvania; born in Martinsburg, Blair County, Pa., October 8, 1894; attended the public schools of North Woodbury Township, Pa., and the summer normal school at Martinsburg, Pa.; student of the International Correspondence School of Scranton, Pa., majoring in the commercial course; in 1914 became interested in banking at Claysburg, Pa.; during the First World War was a private in the Thirty-third Division, Fifty-eighth Brigade Headquarters, serving overseas in 1918 and 1919; in 1921 became interested in the lumber business and later established an insurance agency; trustee of the Pennsylvania Industrial School, Huntingdon, Pa., 1939–1943; in 1934 became chairman of the Blair County Chapter, American Red Cross; member of the Blair County War Fund Committee 1940–1945; chairman of Blair County Selective Service Board No. 1, Hollidaysburg, Pa., 1940–1943; elected as a Republican to the Seventy-eighth Congress to fill the vacancy caused by the resignation of James E. Van Zandt; reelected to the Seventy-ninth Congress and served from November 2, 1943, to January 3, 1947; was not a candidate for renomination in 1946; secretary of banking of the Commonwealth of Pennsylvania, Harrisburg, Pa., 1947–1951; resumed banking interests as president of the First National Bank of Claysburg; is a resident of Claysburg, Pa.

BRUMM, Charles Napoleon (father of George Franklin Brumm), a Representative from Pennsylvania; born in Pottsville, Schuylkill County, Pa., June 9, 1838; attended the common schools and Pennsylvania College, Gettysburg, Pa.; studied law for two years; under the first call of President Lincoln for three-months' men enlisted as a private and was elected first lieutenant of Company I, Fifth Regiment, Pennsylvania Volunteer Infantry; reenlisted September 15, 1861, for three years and was elected first lieutenant of Company K, Seventy-sixth Regiment, Pennsylvania Volunteer Infantry, November 18, 1861; detailed on the staff of General Barton as assistant quartermaster and aide-de-camp, which position he held under Generals Barton and Pennypacker until the expiration of his term of service in 1871; resumed the study of law; was admitted to the bar in 1871 and commenced practice in Pottsville, Schuylkill County; unsuccessful candidate for election in 1878 to the Forty-sixth Congress; elected as a Republican Greenbacker to the Forty-seventh and to the three succeeding Congresses (March 4, 1881–March 3, 1889); unsuccessful candidate for reelection in 1888 to the Fifty-first Congress; delegate to the Republican National Convention at Chicago in 1884; declined to accept the appointment of First Assistant Postmaster General tendered by President Harrison; elected to the Fifty-fourth and Fifty-fifth Congresses (March 4, 1895–March 3, 1899); unsuccessful candidate for renomination in 1898; declined to accept appointment as Minister to Belgium tendered by President McKinley; elected to the Fifty-ninth Congress to fill the vacancy caused by the death of George R. Patterson; reelected to the Sixtieth Congress and served from November 6, 1906, to January 4, 1909, when he resigned, having been elected judge of the court of common pleas of Schuylkill County, in which capacity he served until his death at Minersville, Pa., January 11, 1917; interment in Charles Baber Cemetery, Pottsville, Pa.

BRUMM, George Franklin (son of Charles Napoleon Brumm), a Representative from Pennsylvania; born in Minersville, Schuylkill County, Pa., January 24, 1880; attended the common schools of Minersville, Washington, and Pottsville; was graduated from the University of Pennsylvania at Philadelphia in 1901 and from its law school in 1907; was admitted to the bar of Pennsylvania in 1908 and commenced practice in Pottsville, Pa.; served in 1916 as a private and corporal in Company C, Pennsylvania Engineers, on the Mexican border; appointed by Governor Brumbaugh in 1918 as election commissioner for Texas to take the vote of

servicemen at cantonments; during the First World War was attorney for the conscription board; in 1918 and 1920 was unsuccessful Republican candidate for the nomination to Congress; elected as a Republican to the Sixty-eighth and Sixty-ninth Congresses (March 4, 1923–March 3, 1927); unsuccessful candidate for renomination in 1926; resumed the practice of law in Minersville, Pa.; elected to the Seventy-first, Seventy-second, and Seventy-third Congresses and served from March 4, 1929, until his death in the Methodist Hospital, Philadelphia, Pa., May 29, 1934; interment in Charles Baber Cemetery, Pottsville, Pa.

BRUNDIDGE, Stephen, Jr., a Representative from Arkansas; born in Searcy, White County, Ark., January 1, 1857; educated by private tutors and in the public schools in his native city; studied law; was admitted to the bar in 1879 and commenced practice in Newport, Ark.; returned to Searcy, Ark., in 1880 and continued the practice of law; elected prosecuting attorney of the first judicial district of Arkansas in 1886; reelected in 1888 and served until 1890; resumed the practice of law; member of the Democratic State central committee 1890–1892; elected as a Democrat to the Fifty-fifth and to the five succeeding Congresses (March 4, 1897–March 3, 1909); was not a candidate for renomination in 1908, but was an unsuccessful candidate for Governor that year; resumed the practice of law in Searcy, Ark.; unsuccessful candidate for election to the United States Senate in 1918; died in Searcy, Ark., January 14, 1938; interment in Oak Grove Cemetery.

BRUNNER, David B., a Representative from Pennsylvania; born in Amity, Berks (now Washington) County, Pa., March 7, 1835; attended the common schools; learned the carpenter's trade; taught school from 1853 to 1856, during which time he studied the classics; was graduated from Dickinson College, Carlisle, Pa., in 1860; principal of Reading Classical Academy, Reading, Pa., 1860–1869; established the Reading Business College in 1880; elected as a Democrat to the Fifty-first and Fifty-second Congresses (March 4, 1889–March 3, 1893); was not a candidate for renomination in 1892; retired from public life and engaged in teaching in the Reading Business College; died in Reading Pa., on November 29, 1903; interment in Amityville Cemetery, Berks County, Pa.

BRUNNER, William Frank, a Representative from New York; born in Woodhaven, Queens County, N. Y., September 15, 1887; attended the public schools, the high school at Far Rockaway, N. Y., and Packard Commercial School at New York City, N. Y.; moved to Rockaway Park, Queens County, N. Y., in 1901; engaged in the general insurance and real-estate business; during the First World War served in the United States Navy as a yeoman first class 1917–1919; member of the State assembly 1922–1928; elected as a Democrat to the Seventy-first and to the three succeeding Congresses and served from March 4, 1929, until his resignation on September 27, 1935, having been elected sheriff of Queens County, N. Y.; served as sheriff from 1935 until his resignation in 1936; president of the board of aldermen of New York City 1936–1938; resumed the insurance and real-estate business; commissioner of borough works, Queens County, N. Y., from July 1 to December 31, 1941; unsuccessful candidate for the Democratic nomination in 1942 and for election on the American Labor ticket to the Seventy-eighth Congress; president of Rockaway Beach Hospital; insurance and real-estate broker; is a resident of Rockaway Park, N. Y.

BRUNSDALE, Clarence Norman, a Senator from North Dakota; born in Sherbrooke, Traill County, N. Dak., July 9, 1891; resided on a farm near Hatton, N. Dak., until 1899, when family moved to Portland, N. Dak.; attended private and public schools, and a course in business; graduated from Luther College, Decorah, Iowa, in 1913; taught business school at Portland, N. Dak., in 1913 and 1914; managed Brunsdale Farms, a family partnership, near Mayville, N. Dak., 1914–1939; director and vice president of Goose River Bank, Mayville, N. Dak., 1924–1951; member of North Dakota State Senate 1927–1935 and 1940–1951, serving as president pro tempore in 1943 and majority floor leader 1945–1947; Governor of North Dakota 1951–1957; North Dakota Republican national committeeman 1948–1952; delegate to the Republican National Conventions in 1940, 1948, and 1956; appointed as a Republican to the United States Senate to fill the vacancy caused by the death of William Langer, and served from November 19, 1959, to August 7, 1960; was not a candidate for election to the vacancy; is a resident of Mayville, N. Dak.

BRUSH, Henry, a Representative from Ohio; born in Dutchess County, N. Y., in June 1778; completed preparatory studies; studied law; was admitted to the bar in 1803 and commenced practice in Chillicothe, Ohio; member of the State house of representatives in 1810; served in the State senate in 1814; moved to London, Ohio; elected to the Sixteenth Congress (March 4, 1819–March 3, 1821); unsuccessful candidate for reelection in 1820 to the Seventeenth Congress; judge of the supreme court of Ohio in 1828; retired to his farm near London, Madison County, Ohio, where he died January 19, 1855; interment in Oak Hill Cemetery.

BRUYN, Andrew DeWitt, a Representative from New York; born in Warwarsing, Ulster County, N. Y., November 18, 1790; attended Kingston Academy, Kingston, N. Y., and was graduated from Princeton College in 1810; studied law; was admitted to the bar in 1814 and commenced practice in Ithaca, Tompkins County, N. Y.; justice of the peace in 1817; first surrogate of Tompkins County 1817–1821; member of the State assembly in 1818; appointed trustee of Ithaca in 1821; president of the village in 1822; unsuccessful candidate for election to the State senate in 1825; county supervisor in 1825; treasurer of the village 1826–1828; judge of the court of common pleas 1826–1836; served as a director of the Ithaca & Owego Railroad in 1828; also interested in banking; presidential elector on the Democratic ticket of Jackson and Calhoun in 1828; elected as a Democrat to the Twenty-fifth Congress and served from March 4, 1837, until his death in Ithaca, Tompkins County, N. Y., on July 27, 1838; interment in Ithaca City Cemetery.

BRYAN, Guy Morrison, a Representative from Texas; born in Herculaneum, Jefferson County, Mo., January 12, 1821; moved to the Mexican State of Texas in 1831 with his parents, who settled near San Felipe; attended private schools; joined the Texas Army at San Jacinto in 1836 and fought for the cause of the Republic; was graduated from Kenyon College, Gambier, Ohio, in 1842; studied law, but never practiced; engaged in planting; served as a private in the Brazoria company, under the command of Captain Ballowe, during the Mexican War with the Texas Volunteers on the eastern bank of the Rio Grande; member of the State house of representatives 1847–1853; served in the State senate 1853–1857; delegate to the Democratic National Convention at Cincinnati in 1856; chairman of the Texas delegation in the Democratic National Convention at Baltimore in 1860; elected as a Democrat to the Thirty-fifth Congress (March 4, 1857–March 3, 1859); was not a candidate for renomination in 1858; during the Civil War served as volunteer aide-de-camp on the staff of General Herbert and afterwards as assistant adjutant general, with the rank of major, of the trans-Mississippi Department; established a cotton bureau in Houston, Tex., in order to escape the blockade along the Gulf; moved to Galveston, Tex., in 1872; again a member of the State house of representatives in 1873, 1879, and 1887–1891, and served as speaker in 1873; moved to Quintana, Tex., in 1890 and to Austin, Travis County, Tex., in 1898; elected president of the Texas Veterans Association in 1892 and served until his death in Austin, Tex., June 4, 1901; interment in the State Cemetery.

BRYAN, Henry H., a Representative from Tennessee; born in Martin County, N. C.; attended grammar and high schools; moved to Tennessee and held several local offices; elected to the Sixteenth Congress (March 4, 1819–March 3, 1821); had been reelected to the Seventeenth Congress but did not qualify; died in Montgomery County, Tenn., May 7, 1835.

BRYAN, James Wesley, a Representative from Washington; born in Lake Charles, Calcasieu Parish, La., March 11, 1874; attended the public schools and Lake Charles College at Lake Charles, La.; was graduated from Baylor University, Waco, Tex., in 1895 and from Yale University in 1897; studied law; was admitted to the bar in 1898 and commenced practice at Lake Charles, La.; moved to Bremerton, Wash., in 1905 and continued the practice of law; city attorney in 1907, 1908, and again in 1911; member of the State senate 1908–1912; elected as a Progressive Republican to the Sixty-third Congress (March 4, 1913–March 3, 1915); was an unsuccessful candidate for renomination in 1914 to the Sixty-fourth Congress; affiliated with the Republican Party in 1904; owned and published the Navy Yard American from 1915 to 1917; resumed the practice of law; prosecuting attorney of Kitsap County 1926–1930; president of the Bremerton Port Commission 1933–1936; practiced law in Bremerton, Wash., until his death there on August 26, 1956; interment in Forest Lawn Cemetery.

BRYAN, John Heritage, a Representative from North Carolina; born in New Bern, N. C., November 4, 1798; studied under private teachers and attended New Bern Academy; was graduated from the University of North Carolina in 1815; studied law; was admitted to the bar in 1819 and commenced practice in New Bern, N. C.; member of the State senate in 1823 and 1824; trustee of the University of North Carolina at Chapel Hill 1823–1868; elected as a Whig to the Nineteenth and Twentieth Congresses (March 4, 1825–March 3, 1829); was not a candidate for renomination in 1828; resumed the practice of law in New Bern; moved to Raleigh in 1839 and continued the practice of law; died in Raleigh, N. C., May 19, 1870; interment in Oakwood Cemetery.

BRYAN, Joseph, a Representative from Georgia; born in Savannah, Ga., August 18, 1773; was educated by private tutors and attended Oxford University in England; traveled in France during the Revolutionary War; engaged in agricultural pursuits on Wilmington Island, Ga.; elected as a Democrat to the Eighth and Ninth Congresses and served from March 4, 1803, until his resignation in 1806; engaged in planting; died on his estate, "Nonchalance," Wilmington Island, near Savannah, Ga., on September 12, 1812; interment in the family burial ground on his estate.

BRYAN, Joseph Hunter, a Representative from North Carolina; born in Windsor, Bertie County, N. C.; member of the State house of commons 1804, 1805, and 1807–1809; trustee of the University of North Carolina at Chapel Hill, 1809–1817, and was sent to Tennessee on behalf of the university to secure from the general assembly of Tennessee its claims to escheated lands; elected to the Fourteenth and Fifteenth Congresses (March 4, 1815–March 3, 1819).

BRYAN, Nathan, a Representative from North Carolina; born in Craven (now Jones) County, N. C., in 1748; member of the house of commons of North Carolina in 1787 and 1791–1794; elected to the Fourth and Fifth Congresses and served from March 4, 1795, until his death in Philadelphia, Pa., June 4, 1798; interment in the Baptist burial ground on Second Street between Christ Church burial ground and Arch Street; reinterred at an unknown location when the burial ground was used as a building site.

BRYAN, Nathan Philemon (brother of William James Bryan), a Senator from Florida; born near Fort Mason, Orange (now Lake) County, Fla., April 23, 1872; attended the common schools; was graduated from Emory College, Oxford, Ga., (now Emory University, Atlanta, Ga.) in 1893 and from the law department of Washington and Lee University, Lexington, Va., in 1895; was admitted to the bar in 1895 and commenced practice in Jacksonville, Fla.; chairman of the board of control of the Florida State institutions of higher education 1905–1909; appointed on February 22, 1911 (the legislature having failed to elect) and subsequently elected as a Democrat to the United States Senate and served from March 4, 1911, to March 3, 1917; unsuccessful candidate for renomination in 1916; resumed the practice of law; declined the appointment as Governor General of the Philippine Islands by President Wilson in 1917; served as trustee of Emory University; appointed judge of the United States Circuit Court of Appeals of the Fifth Judicial Circuit in April 1920 and served until his death in Jacksonville, Fla., on August 8, 1935; interment in Evergreen Cemetery.

BRYAN, William James (brother of Nathan Philemon Bryan), a Senator from Florida; born near Fort Mason, Orange (now Lake) County, Fla., October 10, 1876; attended the public schools; was graduated from Emory College, Oxford, Ga., in 1896 and from the law department of Washington and Lee University, Lexington, Va., in 1899; was admitted to the bar in 1899 and commenced practice in Jacksonville, Fla.; solicitor of the Duval County Criminal Court of Record 1902–1907; delegate to the Democratic National Convention at St. Louis in 1904; appointed to the United States Senate to fill the vacancy caused by the death of Stephen R. Mallory and served from December 26, 1907, until his death in Washington, D. C., March 22, 1908; interment in Evergreen Cemetery, Jacksonville, Fla.

BRYAN, William Jennings (father of Ruth Bryan Owen), a Representative from Nebraska; born in Salem, Marion County, Ill., March 19, 1860; attended the public schools and Whipple Academy, Jacksonville, Ill.; was graduated from Illinois College, Jacksonville, Ill., in 1881; studied law at Union College in Chicago; was graduated in 1883 and commenced practice at Jacksonville, Ill., in 1883; moved to Lincoln, Nebr., in 1887 and continued the practice of law; delegate to the Democratic State convention in 1888; elected as a Democrat to the Fifty-second and Fifty-third Congresses (March 4, 1891–March 3, 1895); declined to be a candidate for reelection in 1894; unsuccessful candidate for election to the United States Senate in 1894; delegate to the Democratic National Conventions in 1896, 1904, 1912, 1920, and 1924; unsuccessful Democratic candidate for President of the United States in 1896, 1900, and again in 1908; was indorsed by the Populist and Silver Republican Parties in the first and second campaigns; during the Spanish-American War raised the Third Regiment, Nebraska Volunteer Infantry, in May 1898 and was commissioned colonel; established a newspaper, "The Commoner," at Lincoln, Nebr., in 1901; made a tour of the world in 1905 and 1906; engaged in editorial writing and delivering Chautauqua lectures; Secretary of State in the Cabinet of President Wilson and served from March 4, 1913, until June 9,

1915, when he resigned; resumed his former pursuits of lecturing and writing; established his home in Miami, Fla., in 1921; died while attending court in Dayton, Tenn., July 26, 1925; interment in Arlington National Cemetery, Fort Myer, Va.

BRYCE, Lloyd Stephens, a Representative from New York; born in Flushing, Queens County, N. Y., September 20, 1850; attended the public schools and Georgetown University, Washington, D. C.; was graduated from Oxford College, England, in 1869; studied law at Columbia Law School, New York City; paymaster general for the State of New York in 1886 and 1887; elected as a Democrat to the Fiftieth Congress (March 4, 1887–March 3, 1889); unsuccessful candidate for reelection in 1888 to the Fifty-first Congress; editor of the North American Review 1889–1896; appointed Envoy Extraordinary and Minister Plenipotentiary to the Netherlands August 12, 1911, and served to September 10, 1913; died in Flushing, N. Y., April 2, 1917; interment in Greenwood Cemetery, Brooklyn, N. Y.

BRYSON, Joseph Raleigh, a Representative from South Carolina; born in Brevard, Transylvania County, N. C., January 18, 1893; moved, with his parents, to Greenville, Greenville County, S. C., in 1900; attended the public schools; was graduated from Furman University, Greenville, S. C., in 1917 and from the law department of the University of South Carolina at Columbia in 1920; during the First World War enlisted on September 28, 1915, as a private in Company A, First Infantry, South Carolina National Guard, and served until discharged on August 9, 1916; reenlisted on August 3, 1917, in the Medical Reserve Corps, being discharged as a second lieutenant of Infantry on December 12, 1918; was admitted to the bar in 1920 and commenced practice in Greenville, S. C.; member of the State house of representatives 1921–1924; served in the State senate 1929–1932; elected as a Democrat to the Seventy-sixth and to the seven succeeding Congresses, and served from January 3, 1939, until his death in the naval hospital at Bethesda, Md., March 10, 1953; interment in Woodlawn Memorial Park, Greenville, S. C.

BUCHANAN, Andrew, a Representative from Pennsylvania; born in Chester County, Pa., April 8, 1780; was graduated from Dickinson College, Carlisle, Pa.; studied law; was admitted to the bar in 1798 and commenced practice in York, Pa.; located in Waynesburg, Greene County, Pa., in 1803; member of the State house of representatives; served in the State senate; elected as a Democrat to the Twenty-fourth and Twenty-fifth Congresses (March 4, 1835–March 3, 1839); resumed the practice of his profession until his death in Waynesburg, Pa., on December 2, 1848; interment in Greene Mount Cemetery.

BUCHANAN, Frank, a Representative from Illinois; born on a farm near Madison, Jefferson County, Ind., June 14, 1862; attended the rural schools of the county; engaged in agricultural pursuits at home and subsequently became a bridge builder and structural-iron worker in Chicago; served as business agent for the Bridge and Structural Iron Worker's Union and was elected president of the International Structural Iron Worker's Union in 1901; unsuccessful candidate for election in 1906 to the Sixtieth Congress and again in 1908 to the Sixty-first Congress; elected as a Democrat to the Sixty-second, Sixty-third, and Sixty-fourth Congresses (March 4, 1911–March 3, 1917); unsuccessful candidate for reelection in 1916 to the Sixty-fifth Congress; resumed his former business pursuits as a structural-iron worker; died in Chicago, Ill., April 18, 1930; interment in Irving Park Boulevard Cemetery.

BUCHANAN, Frank (husband of Vera Daerr Buchanan), a Representative from Pennsylvania; born in McKeesport, Allegheny County, Pa., December 1, 1902; attended the public schools and was graduated from the University of Pittsburgh in 1925; teacher in high schools of Homestead and McKeesport, Pa., 1924–1928 and 1931–1942; automobile dealer 1928–1931; economic consultant 1928–1946; served as mayor of McKeesport, Pa., 1942–1946; elected as a Democrat to the Seventy-ninth Congress to fill the vacancy caused by the resignation of Samuel A. Weiss; reelected to the Eightieth, Eighty-first, and Eighty-second Congresses and served from May 21, 1946, until his death in the naval hospital at Bethesda, Md., April 27, 1951; interment in Mount Vernon Cemetery, Elizabeth Township (near McKeesport), Pa.

BUCHANAN, Hugh, a Representative from Georgia; born in Argyleshire, Scotland, September 15, 1823; immigrated to the United States and settled in Vermont; attended the public schools of that State; studied law; was admitted to the bar in 1845 and commenced practice in Newnan, Coweta County, Ga., in 1846; member of the State senate in 1855 and 1857; delegate to the Democratic National Conventions in 1856 and 1868; presidential elector on the Democratic ticket of Breckinridge and Lane in 1860; during the Civil War enlisted in the Confederate Army in June 1861 and served until 1865; elected to the Thirty-ninth Congress, but his credentials were not presented to the House as the State had not been readmitted to representation; appointed judge of the superior court of the Coweta circuit in August 1872 and served until September 1880; delegate to the State constitutional convention of 1877; elected as a Democrat to the Forty-seventh and Forty-eighth Congresses (March 4, 1881–March 3, 1885); because of ill health was not a candidate for renomination in 1884; died in Newnan, Ga., June 11, 1890; interment in Oak Hill Cemetery.

BUCHANAN, James, a Representative and a Senator from Pennsylvania and a President of the United States; born at Cove Gap, near Mercersburg, Franklin County, Pa., April 23, 1791; moved to Mercersburg, Pa., with his parents in 1799; was privately tutored and then attended the village academy; was graduated from Dickinson College, Carlisle, Pa., in 1809; moved to Lancaster, Pa., the same year; studied law; was admitted to the bar in 1812 and practiced in Lancaster; although a Federalist, was one of the first volunteers in the War of 1812 and served under Judge Shippen in the defense of Baltimore; member of the State house of representatives in 1814 and 1815; unsuccessful candidate for election in 1818 to the Sixteenth Congress; elected to the Seventeenth and to the four succeeding Congresses (March 4, 1821–March 3, 1831); was not a candidate for renomination in 1830; one of the managers appointed by the House of Representatives in 1830 to conduct the impeachment proceedings against James H. Peck, judge of the United States District Court for the District of Missouri; Minister to Russia from June 1832 to August 1834; elected as a Democrat to the United States Senate to fill the vacancy caused by the resignation of William Wilkins; reelected in 1837 and 1843 and served from December 6, 1834, until he resigned on March 5, 1845, to accept a Cabinet portfolio; Secretary of State in the Cabinet of President Polk from March 6, 1845, to March 7, 1849; Minister to Great Britain 1853–1856; elected President of the United States in 1856 as the candidate of the Democratic Party and served from March 4, 1857, to March 3, 1861; retired to his home in Wheatland, near Lancaster, Pa., where he died June 1, 1868; interment in Woodward Hill Cemetery, Lancaster, Pa.

BUCHANAN, James, a Representative from New Jersey; born in Ringoes, Hunterdon County, N. J., June 17, 1839; attended the public schools and Clinton Academy; studied law at Albany University; was admitted to the bar in 1864 and commenced practice in Trenton, N. J.; reading clerk of the New Jersey House of Assembly in 1866; member of the Trenton Board of Education in 1868 and 1869; presiding judge of Mercer County 1872–1877; delegate to the Republican National Convention at Philadelphia in 1872; appointed a member of the board of trustees of Peddie Institute, Hightstown, N. J., in 1875; member of the Common Council of Trenton 1883–1885; elected as a Republican to the Forty-ninth and to the three succeeding Congresses (March 4, 1885–March 3, 1893); declined to be a candidate for renomination in 1892; resumed the practice of law in Trenton; elected city solicitor of Trenton May 7, 1900, and served until his death; trustee of Bucknell College, Lewisburg, Pa.; died in Trenton, N. J., on October 30, 1900; interment in Mountain View Cemetery, Cherryville, Hunterdon County, N. J.

BUCHANAN, James Paul (cousin of Edward William Pou), a Representative from Texas; born in Midway, Orangeburg County, S. C., April 30, 1867; moved to Texas in 1867 with his parents, who settled near Chapel Hill, Washington County; attended the district school; was graduated from the law department of the University of Texas at Austin in 1889; was admitted to the bar and commenced practice in Brenham, Washington County, Tex.; justice of the peace of Washington County 1889–1892; prosecuting attorney 1892–1899; district attorney for the twenty-first judicial district of Texas 1899–1906; served as a member of the State house of representatives 1906–1913; elected as a Democrat to the Sixty-third Congress to fill the vacancy caused by the resignation of Albert Sidney Burleson; reelected to the Sixth-fourth and to the eleven succeeding Congresses and served from April 5, 1913, until his death in Washington, D. C., February 22, 1937; interment in Prairie Lea Cemetery, Brenham, Tex.

BUCHANAN, John Alexander, a Representative from Virginia; born near Groseclose, Smyth County, Va., October 7, 1843; attended the "old field" school and the local academies at Chatham Hill and Marion, Va.; during the Civil War served as a private in Company D, Virginia Infantry, Stonewall Brigade, of the Confederate Army; was captured at the Battle of Gettysburg July 3, 1863, and remained a prisoner until February 1865; attended Emory and Henry College, Emory, Va., 1865–1870 and was graduated in June 1870; studied law at the University of Virginia at Charlottesville in 1870 and 1871; was admitted to the bar in 1872 and commenced practice in Abingdon, Va.; member of the State house of delegates 1885–1887; elected as a Democrat to the Fifty-first and Fifty-second Congresses (March 4, 1889–March 3, 1893); declined to be a candidate for renomination in 1892 to the Fifty-third Congress; engaged in the practice of law in Abingdon, Va., 1893 and 1894; elected associate judge of the court of appeals of Virginia January 1, 1895, and served until January 1915; retired from political activities and engaged in agricultural pursuits; died near Emory, Washington County, Va., on September 2, 1921; interment in the Old Glade Spring Presbyterian Cemetery, Glade Spring, Va.

BUCHANAN, Vera Daerr (wife of Frank Buchanan), a Representative from Pennsylvania; born in Wilson (later a part of Clairton), Allegheny County, Pa., July 20, 1902; moved to Duquesne, Pa., and attended the public and parochial schools; elected as a Democrat to the Eighty-second Congress to fill the vacancy caused by the death of her husband, Frank Buchanan; reelected to the Eighty-third and Eighty-fourth Congresses and served from July 24, 1951, until her death in McKeesport, Pa.,

November 26, 1955; interment in Mount Vernon Cemetery, in Elizabeth Township (near McKeesport), Pa.

BUCHER, John Conrad, a Representative from Pennsylvania; born in Harrisburg, Pa., December 28, 1792; attended the public schools; studied law; was admitted to the bar and commenced practice in Harrisburg; clerk of the land department of Pennsylvania in 1813; member of the borough council of Harrisburg; member of the board of school directors; elected to the Twenty-second Congress (March 4, 1831–March 3, 1833); trustee of Harrisburg Academy, Franklin College, Lancaster, Pa., and Marshall College, Mercersburg, Pa.; by appointment of Governor Porter was an associate judge of Dauphin County from 1839 until his death in Harrisburg, Pa., October 15, 1851; interment in the City Cemetery.

BUCK, Alfred Eliab, a Representative from Alabama; born in Foxcroft, Piscataquis County, Maine, February 7, 1832; was graduated from Waterville (Maine) College in 1859; during the Civil War entered the Union Army as captain of Company C, Thirteenth Regiment, Maine Volunteer Infantry; appointed lieutenant colonel of the Ninety-first United States Colored Troops in August 1863; transferred to the Fifty-first United States Colored Troops in October 1864; brevetted colonel of Volunteers for gallant conduct; mustered out of the service at Baton Rouge, La., in June 1866; delegate to the constitutional convention of Alabama in 1867; clerk of the circuit court of Mobile County in 1867 and 1868; presidential elector on the Republican ticket of Ulysses S. Grant and Schuyler Colfax in 1868; elected as a Republican to the Forty-first Congress (March 4, 1869–March 3, 1871); appointed president of the city council of Mobile in 1873; served as clerk of the United States circuit and district courts in Atlanta, Ga., 1874–1889; United States marshal for the northern district of Georgia 1889–1893; appointed Minister to Japan by President William McKinley in April 1897 and served until his death in Tokyo, Japan, on December 4, 1902; interment in Arlington National Cemetery, Fort Myer, Va.

BUCK, Charles Francis, a Representative from Louisiana; born in Durrheim, Grand Duchy of Baden, Germany, November 5, 1841; immigrated to the United States in 1852 with his parents, who settled in New Orleans, La.; was graduated from the high school of New Orleans in 1861; attended Louisiana State Seminary and Military Academy at Alexandria; studied law; was admitted to the bar in 1867 and commenced practice in New Orleans, La.; member of the school board of New Orleans for many years; city attorney of New Orleans 1880–1884; elected as a Democrat to the Fifty-fourth Congress (March 4, 1895–March 3, 1897); declined to be a candidate for reelection in 1896; resumed the practice of law; unsuccessful candidate for mayor of New Orleans in 1896 and again in 1904; member of the supreme court board of examiners for admission to the bar 1898–1900; died in New Orleans, La., January 19, 1918; interment in the Metairie Cemetery.

BUCK, Clayton Douglass (great-grandnephew of John M. Clayton), a Senator from Delaware; born at "Buena Vista," the family estate, in New Castle County, Del., March 21, 1890; was graduated from Friends School, Wilmington, Del., and for two years attended the University of Pennsylvania Engineering School at Philadelphia; engaged in road-building and engineering work in Delaware; chief engineer of the Delaware State Highway Department 1922–1929; Governor of Delaware 1929–1937; engaged in the banking business since 1931; member of the Republican National Committee 1930–1937; elected as a Republican to the United States Senate in 1942 and served from January 3, 1943, to January 3, 1949; unsuccessful candidate for reelection in 1948; resumed the banking business; tax commissioner of Delaware 1953–1957; resides in Buena Vista, New Castle County, Del.

BUCK, Daniel (father of Daniel Azro Ashley Buck), a Representative from Vermont; born in Hebron, Conn., November 9, 1753; studied law; was admitted to the bar in 1783 and practiced in Thetford, Vt.; prosecuting attorney of Orange County 1783–1785; clerk of the court in 1783 and 1784; moved to Norwich, Vt., in 1785; delegate to the State constitutional convention in 1791; member of the State house of representatives in 1793 and 1794 and served as speaker; elected as a Federalist to the Fourth Congress (March 4, 1795–March 3, 1797); unsuccessful candidate for renomination in 1796; attorney general of Vermont in 1802 and 1803; moved to Chelsea, Vt., about 1805; again a member of the State house of representatives in 1806 and 1807; resumed the practice of law in Chelsea, Vt., where he died August 16, 1816; interment in the Old Cemetery.

BUCK, Daniel Azro Ashley (son of Daniel Buck), a Representative from Vermont; born in Norwich, Vt., April 19, 1789; moved with his parents to Chelsea; was graduated from Middlebury College in 1807 and from the United States Military Academy at West Point in 1808; commissioned a lieutenant in the Engineer Corps of the United States Army in the latter year; resigned in 1811 and studied law; appointed a second lieutenant in the Third Artillery in 1811; raised a volunteer company of rangers in 1813 and served until 1815; appointed a captain of the Thirty-first Infantry in 1813; was honorably discharged June 15, 1815, at the close of the War of 1812; was admitted to the bar in 1814 and commenced the practice of law in Chelsea, Vt.; member of the State house of representatives 1816–1826, 1828–1830, and 1833–1835 and served as speaker of the house 1820–1822, 1825, 1826, and 1829; State attorney for Orange County 1819–1822 and 1830–1834; presidential elector on the Democratic ticket of Monroe and Tompkins in 1820; elected as a Democrat to the Eighteenth Congress (March 4, 1823–March 3, 1825); elected to the Twentieth Congress (March 4, 1827–March 3, 1829); unsuccessful candidate for renomination in 1828; was a clerk in the War Department 1835–1839; clerk in the Treasury Department in 1840; died in Washington, D. C., December 24, 1841; interment in the Congressional Cemetery.

BUCK, Ellsworth Brewer, a Representative from New York; born in Chicago, Cook County, Ill., July 3, 1892; attended the public schools in Chicago, Ill., and Morgan Park (Ill.) Academy; was graduated from Dartmouth College, Hanover, N. H., in 1914; engaged in the chewing-gum industry 1914–1917; enlisted in the United States Naval Reserve on July 5, 1917; attended Naval Aviation Ground School, Massachusetts Institute of Technology; commissioned an ensign and assigned as instructor in meteorology from April 1918 to August 1918 and as custodian of meteorological instruments at the United States Naval Observatory, Washington, D. C., from August to December 1918; moved to Staten Island, N. Y., in 1919 and became associated with L. A. Dreyfus Co., serving as chairman of the board 1932–1957; chairman of the Chewing Gum Code Authority, under N. R. A., in 1934 and 1935; member of the board of education of New York City 1935–1944, serving as vice president 1938–1942 and as president 1942–1944; former trustee of Staten Island Hospital, Staten Island Academy, Staten Island Savings Bank, and of the American Museum of Natural History; trustee and treasurer, Staten Island Zoological Society; vice president and director, Thunder Mountain Ranch Co.; elected as a Republican to the Seventy-eighth Congress to fill the vacancy caused by the death of James A. O'Leary; reelected to the Seventy-ninth and

Eightieth Congresses and served from June 6, 1944, to January 3, 1949; was not a candidate for renomination in 1948; delegate to the Republican National Convention in 1952; director, Office of Trade Investment and Monetary Affairs, Foreign Operations Administration, in 1954; public advisor, United States delegation to United Nations Economic and Social Council, Geneva, Switzerland, in 1955; is a resident of Staten Island, N. Y.

BUCK, Frank Henry, a Representative from California; born on a ranch near Vacaville, Solano County, Calif., September 23, 1887; attended the public schools; was graduated from the University of California at Berkeley in 1908 and from the law department of Harvard University, Cambridge, Mass., in 1911; was admitted to the bar the same year and commenced practice in San Francisco, Calif.; fruit grower and farmer at Vacaville, Calif.; also engaged in the lumber business and in oil refining; delegate to the Democratic National Conventions in 1928, 1936, and 1940; elected as a Democrat to the Seventy-third and to the four succeeding Congresses and served from March 4, 1933, until his death in Washington, D. C., September 17, 1942; interment in Vacaville-Elmira Cemetery, Vacaville, Calif.

BUCK, John Ransom, a Representative from Connecticut; born in Glastonbury, Hartford County, Conn., December 6, 1835; attended the common schools, Wilbraham (Mass.) Academy, and Wesleyan University, Middletown, Conn.; taught school; studied law; was admitted to the bar in 1862 and practiced in Hartford; assistant clerk of the State house of representatives in 1864 and clerk in 1865; clerk of the senate in 1866; president of the Hartford Court of Common Council in 1868; city attorney 1871–1873; treasurer of Hartford County 1873–1881; member of the State senate in 1880 and 1881; secretary of the State bar association 1875–1881; elected as a Republican to the Forty-seventh Congress (March 4, 1881–March 3, 1883); unsuccessful candidate for reelection in 1882 to the Forty-eighth Congress; elected to the Forty-ninth Congress (March 4, 1885–March 3, 1887); unsuccessful candidate for reelection in 1886 to the Fiftieth Congress; resumed the practice of law in Hartford, Conn., where he died February 6, 1917; interment in Cedar Hill Cemetery.

BUCKALEW, Charles Rollin, a Senator and a Representative from Pennsylvania; born in Fishing Creek Township, Columbia County, Pa., December 28, 1821; was graduated from Harford Academy, Susquehanna County, Pa.; studied law; was admitted to the bar in 1843 and commenced practice in Bloomsburg, Pa., in 1844; prosecuting attorney for Columbia County 1845–1847; served in the State senate 1850–1853; commissioner to exchange ratifications of a treaty with Paraguay in 1854; presidential elector on the Democratic ticket of Buchanan and Breckinridge in 1856; chairman of the Democratic State committee in 1857; again a member of the State senate, in 1857 and 1858; appointed one of the commissioners to revise the penal code of the State in 1857; appointed Minister Resident to the Republic of Ecuador in 1858 and served three years; elected as a Democrat to the United States Senate and served from March 4, 1863, to March 3, 1869; again served in the State senate in 1869; unsuccessful candidate for Governor in 1872; delegate to the constitutional convention of 1873; elected as a Democrat to the Fiftieth and Fifty-first Congresses (March 4, 1887–March 3, 1891); resumed the practice of his profession in Bloomsburg, Columbia County, Pa., where he died on May 19, 1899; interment in Rosemont Cemetery.

BUCKBEE, John Theodore, a Representative from Illinois; born on a farm near Rockford, Winnebago County, Ill., August 1, 1871; attended the public schools of Rockford; studied agriculture and horticulture in Austria, France, Holland, Denmark, Sweden, Belgium, Italy, and Great Britain; established and engaged in a seed business in Rockford, Ill.; elected as a Republican to the Seventieth Congress; reelected to the Seventy-first and to the three succeeding Congresses and served from March 4, 1927, until his death; was not a candidate for renomination in 1936; died in Rockford, Ill., April 23, 1936; interment in Greenwood Cemetery.

BUCKINGHAM, William Alfred, a Senator from Connecticut; born in Lebanon, Conn., May 28, 1804; attended the common schools and Bacon Academy, Colchester, Conn.; engaged in mercantile pursuits and in manufacturing; mayor of Norwich in 1849, 1850, 1856, and 1857; presidential elector on the Republican ticket of Frémont and Dayton in 1856; Governor of Connecticut 1858–1866; resumed his former business pursuits; elected as a Republican to the United States Senate and served from March 4, 1869, until his death in Norwich, Conn., February 5, 1875; his statue as the "War Governor of Connecticut" adorns the battle flag vestibule of the statehouse in Hartford, Conn.; interment in Yantic Cemetery, Norwich, Conn.

BUCKLAND, Ralph Pomeroy, a Representative from Ohio; born in Leyden, Mass., January 20, 1812; moved with his parents to Ravenna, Ohio, the same year; attended the country schools, Tallmadge (Ohio) Academy, and Kenyon College, Gambier, Ohio; studied law; was admitted to the bar in 1837 and commenced practice in Fremont, Ohio; mayor of Fremont 1843–1845; delegate to the Whig National Convention in 1848; member of the State senate 1855–1859; during the Civil War entered the Union Army as colonel of the Seventy-second Regiment, Ohio Volunteer Infantry, January 10, 1862; commissioned brigadier general of Volunteers November 29, 1862; brevetted major general March 13, 1865, for faithful and meritorious services; resigned from the Army January 6, 1865; elected as a Republican to the Thirty-ninth and Fortieth Congresses (March 4, 1865–March 3, 1869); was not a candidate for renomination in 1868 to the Forty-first Congress; resumed the practice of law; delegate to the Philadelphia Loyalists' Convention in 1866 and to the Pittsburgh Soldiers' Convention; delegate to the Republican National Convention at Cincinnati in 1876; Government director of the Union Pacific Railroad 1877–1880; died in Fremont, Sandusky County, Ohio, May 27, 1892; interment in Oakwood Cemetery.

BUCKLER, Richard Thompson, a Representative from Minnesota; born on a farm near Oakland, Coles County, Ill., October 27, 1865; attended the public schools; engaged in agricultural pursuits in Cole County, Ill.; moved to Andover Township, Polk County, Minn., in 1904 and continued agricultural pursuits; active in Farm Bureau and Farmers' Union organizations; held numerous township and local school-district offices; served in the State senate 1915–1919, 1923–1927, and 1931–1933; elected on the Farmer-Labor ticket to the Seventy-fourth and to the three succeeding Congresses (January 3, 1935–January 3, 1943); was not a candidate for renomination in 1942; resumed agricultural pursuits; died in Crookston, Minn., January 23, 1950; interment in Oakdale Cemetery.

BUCKLEY, Charles Anthony, a Representative from New York; born in New York City, N. Y., June 23, 1890; attended the public schools; contractor and builder in New York City since 1914; member of the board of aldermen of New York City 1918–1923; State tax appraiser 1923–1929; chamberlain of New York City 1929–1933; elected as a Democrat to the Seventy-fourth and to the 12 succeeding Congresses (January 3, 1935–January 3, 1961). *Reelected to the Eighty-seventh Congress.*

BUCKLEY, Charles Waldron, a Representative from Alabama; born in Unadilla, Otsego County, N. Y., February 18, 1835; attended the public schools in that town and also in Freeport, Ill., where his parents moved in 1846; was graduated from Beloit College, Wisconsin, in 1860 and from the Union Theological Seminary in New York City in 1863; entered the Union Army February 9, 1864, and served as chaplain of the Forty-seventh Regiment, United States Colored Volunteer Infantry, and of the Eighth Regiment, Louisiana Colored Infantry, until January 5, 1866, when he was mustered out; Alabama superintendent of education for the bureau of refugees and freedmen in 1866 and 1867 and resided in Montgomery; delegate to the convention which framed the constitution of Alabama in 1867; engaged in agricultural pursuits, banking, the fire-insurance business, and mining; upon the readmission of the State of Alabama to representation was elected as a Republican to the Fortieth Congress; reelected to the Forty-first and Forty-second Congresses and served from July 21, 1868, to March 3, 1873; was not a candidate for renomination in 1872; probate judge of Montgomery County 1874–1878; resumed banking and also engaged in the fire-insurance business; postmaster of Montgomery 1881–1885, 1890–1893, and 1897–1906; delegate to the Republican National Convention in St. Louis in 1896; died in Montgomery, Ala., on December 4, 1906; interment in Woodlawn Cemetery, New York City.

BUCKLEY, James Richard, a Representative from Illinois; born in Chicago, Ill., November 18, 1870; attended the public and parochial schools and Christian Brothers' Commercial Academy; engaged in mercantile pursuits; permit clerk of the department of public works 1893–1897; deputy city gas inspector 1897–1910; unsuccessful Democratic candidate for clerk of the supreme court of Cook County, Ill., in 1908; member of the Chicago Board of Aldermen 1910–1912; delegate to the Democratic National Convention in 1908, 1912, 1916; chief deputy criminal court clerk 1912–1918; manager of the State personal property tax collection department 1918–1923; elected as a Democrat to the Sixty-eighth Congress (March 4, 1923–March 3, 1925); unsuccessful candidate for reelection in 1924 to the Sixty-ninth Congress; vice president of the Universal Granite Quarries; was serving as chief drain inspector at the time of his death in Chicago, Ill., on June 22, 1945; interment in Calvary Cemetery, Evanston, Ill.

BUCKLEY, James Vincent, a Representative from Illinois; born on a farm in Saginaw County, Mich., May 15, 1894; attended the public schools of Saginaw County, Mich.; moved to Chicago, Ill., at an early age and worked in the automobile industry; engaged in the real-estate and building business in the Calumet region of Cook County, Ill., and Lake County, Ind.; during World War II was active in war-plant production service and was elected president of Local Union 714, United Automobile Workers; elected as a Democrat to the Eighty-first Congress (January 3, 1949–January 3, 1951); unsuccessful candidate for reelection in 1950 to the Eighty-second Congress; engaged in the real-estate and building business at Calumet City, Ill., from 1951 until his death; died in Hammond, Ind., July 30, 1954; interment in Calvary Cemetery, Gary, Ind.

BUCKMAN, Clarence Bennett, a Representative from Minnesota; born in Doylestown, Bucks County, Pa., April 1, 1851; attended the public and normal schools; moved to Minnesota in 1872 and settled in what is now known as Buckman; engaged in agricultural pursuits and in the lumber business; appointed justice of the peace in 1873; member of the State house of representatives 1881–1883; served in the State senate 1887–1891 and 1899–1903; elected as a Republican to the Fifty-

eighth and Fifty-ninth Congresses (March 4, 1903–March 3, 1907); unsuccessful candidate for renomination in 1906; deputy United States marshal 1912–1917; resumed the lumber business in Little Falls, Morrison County, Minn.; died in a local hospital in Battle Creek, Mich., March 1, 1917; interment in Oakland Cemetery, Little Falls, Minn.

BUCKNER, Alexander, a Senator from Missouri; born in Jefferson County, Ky., in 1785; studied law; moved to Charleston, Clark County, Ind., in 1812; moved to Missouri in 1818 and settled near Jackson, Cape Girardeau County; practiced law and also engaged in agricultural pursuits; appointed by the Territorial Governor as circuit attorney for the Cape Girardeau district; president of the State constitutional convention in 1820; member of the State senate 1822–1826; elected to the United States Senate and served from March 4, 1831, until his death in Cape Girardeau County, Mo., June 6, 1833; interment on his farm in Cape Girardeau County; reinterment in City Cemetery, Cape Girardeau, Mo., in 1897.

BUCKNER, Aylette (son of Richard Aylett Buckner), a Representative from Kentucky; born in Greensburg, Green County, Ky., July 21, 1806; attended the New Athens Seminary; studied law; was admitted to the bar and commenced practice in Greensburg; member of the State house of representatives in 1842 and 1843; elected as a Whig to the Thirtieth Congress (March 4, 1847–March 3, 1849); unsuccessful candidate in 1848 for reelection to the Thirty-first Congress; moved to St. Louis, Mo., and continued the practice of his profession; returned to Lexington, Ky., in 1864, where he died July 3, 1869; interment in Lexington Cemetery.

BUCKNER, Aylett Hawes (nephew of Aylett Hawes and cousin of Richard Hawes and Albert Gallatin Hawes), a Representative from Missouri; born in Fredericksburg, Va., December 14, 1816; attended Georgetown College, Washington, D. C., and the University of Virginia at Charlottesville; engaged in teaching for several years; moved to Palmyra, Mo., in 1837; served as deputy sheriff; studied law; was admitted to the bar in 1838 and commenced practice in Bowling Green, Mo.; became editor of the Salt River Journal; elected clerk of the Pike County Court in 1841; moved to St. Louis, Mo., in 1850 and continued the practice of law; attorney for the Bank of the State of Missouri in 1852; appointed commissioner of public works in 1854 and served until 1855; returned to Pike County and settled on a farm near Bowling Green; elected judge of the third judicial circuit in 1857; delegate to the convention held in Washington, D. C., in 1861 in an effort to devise means to prevent the impending war; moved to St. Charles, Mo., in 1862 and became interested in the manufacture of tobacco in St. Louis; also engaged in mercantile pursuits; moved to Mexico, Audrain County; member of the Democratic central committee in 1868; delegate to the Democratic National Convention at Baltimore in 1872; elected as a Democrat to the Forty-third and to the five succeeding Congresses (March 4, 1873–March 3, 1885); declined to be a candidate for reelection in 1884 and retired from public life; died in Mexico, Mo., February 5, 1894; interment in Elmwood Cemetery.

BUCKNER, Richard Aylett (father of Aylette Buckner), a Representative from Kentucky; born in Fauquier County, Va., July 16, 1763; received a liberal education; moved to Green County, Ky., in 1803; studied law; was admitted to the bar; taught school; moved to Greensburg in 1811 and practiced law; county attorney and Commonwealth's attorney of Green County; member of the State house of representatives in 1813 and 1815; elected as an Anti-Democrat to the Eighteenth, Nineteenth, and Twentieth Congresses (March 4, 1823–March 3, 1829); unsuccessful candidate for reelection in 1828 to the Twenty-first Congress; appointed associate judge of the court of appeals December 31, 1831, but resigned shortly afterwards; unsuccessful Whig candidate for Governor of Kentucky in 1832; again a member of the State house of representatives 1837–1839; presidential elector on the Harrison tickets in 1836 and 1840; circuit judge in 1845; judge of the Court of Appeals of Kentucky; died in Greensburg, Ky., December 8, 1847; interment in the family graveyard at the ancestral home, "Buckner's Hill."

BUDD, James Herbert, a Representative from California; born in Janesville, Rock County, Wis., May 18, 1851; moved to California in 1859 with his parents, who settled in Stockton; attended the public schools in Stockton and Brayton College, Oakland, in 1869; was graduated from the University of California at Berkeley in 1873; served as lieutenant colonel on the Governor's staff in 1873 and 1874; deputy district attorney in 1873 and 1874; studied law; was admitted to the bar in 1874 and commenced practice in Stockton; served as first lieutenant in the California National Guard and was promoted to major of the line; elected as a Democrat to the Forty-eighth Congress (March 4, 1883–March 3, 1885); declined to be a candidate for reelection in 1884; appointed police and fire commissioner of Stockton in 1889; trustee of the Stockton City Library for six years; member of the board for drafting the city charter in 1889; Governor of California 1894–1898; resumed the practice of law in San Francisco; died in Stockton, Calif., July 30, 1908; interment in Rural Cemetery.

BUDGE, Hamer Harold, a Representative from Idaho; born in Pocatello, Bannock County, Idaho, November 21, 1910; attended the public schools of Boise, Idaho, and the College of Idaho at Caldwell 1928–1930; graduated from Stanford University, Palo Alto, Calif., in 1933, and from the law school of the University of Idaho at Moscow in 1936; was admitted to the bar in 1936 and commenced the practice of law in Boise, Idaho; member of the State house of representatives in 1939 and 1941, serving as assistant Republican floor leader; during World War II served in the United States Navy from 1942 until discharged in 1945 as a lieutenant commander, United States Naval Reserve; again a member of the State house of representatives in 1949, serving as Republican floor leader; elected as a Republican to the Eighty-second and to the four succeeding Congresses (January 3, 1951–January 3, 1961); unsuccessful candidate for reelection in 1960 to the Eighty-seventh Congress; appointed a judge of the third judicial district of Idaho in June 1961; is a resident of Boise, Idaho.

BUEL, Alexander Woodruff, a Representative from Michigan; born in Castleton, Vt., December 13, 1813; attended the public schools in Poultney, Vt., and was graduated from Middlebury College, Vermont, in 1830; taught school and studied law; moved to Detroit, Mich., in 1834; was admitted to the bar in 1835 and commenced practice in Detroit, Mich.; city attorney in 1837; member of the State house of representatives in 1838 and 1848, serving as speaker the latter year; prosecuting attorney for Wayne County 1843–1846; elected as a Democrat to the Thirty-first Congress (March 4, 1849–March 3, 1851); unsuccessful candidate for reelection in 1850 to the Thirty-second Congress; resumed the practice of law; again a member of the State house of representatives, in 1859 and 1860; appointed postmaster of Detroit on September 28, 1860, and served until March 18, 1861; died in Detroit, Mich., April 19, 1868; interment in Elmwood Cemetery.

BUELL, Alexander Hamilton, a Representative from New York; born in Fairfield, Herkimer County, N. Y., July 14, 1801; attended the district schools and Fairfield Academy; engaged in

mercantile pursuits in Fairfield, N. Y., and maintained general stores in other cities; served as a member of the State assembly in 1845; elected as a Democrat to the Thirty-second Congress and served from March 4, 1851, until his death in Washington, D. C., on January 29, 1853; interment in the Episcopal Cemetery, Fairfield, N. Y.

BUFFETT, Howard Homan, a Representative from Nebraska; born in Omaha, Douglas County, Nebr., August 13, 1903; attended the public schools, and was graduated from the University of Nebraska at Lincoln in 1925; engaged in the investment business in 1926; member of the Omaha Board of Education 1939–1942; elected as a Republican to the Seventy-eighth, Seventy-ninth, and Eightieth Congresses (January 3, 1943–January 3, 1949); unsuccessful candidate for reelection in 1948 to the Eighty-first Congress; elected to the Eighty-second Congress (January 3, 1951–January 3, 1953); was not a candidate for renomination in 1952; resumed former business pursuits; is a resident of Omaha, Nebr.

BUFFINGTON, Joseph, a Representative from Pennsylvania; born in West Chester, Pa., November 27, 1803; attended the common schools and Western University, Pittsburgh, Pa.; moved to Butler County, Pa., and edited a weekly newspaper; studied law; was admitted to the bar in 1826 and commenced practice in Butler; moved to Kittanning, Pa., in 1827 and continued the practice of law; elected as a Whig to the Twenty-eighth and Twenty-ninth Congresses (March 4, 1843–March 3, 1847); was not a candidate for renomination in 1846; appointed president judge of the eighteenth district in 1849 and served until 1851; declined the appointment as chief justice of the Territory of Utah tendered by President Fillmore in 1852; judge of the tenth district of Pennsylvania from 1855 until his retirement in 1871; died in Kittanning, Armstrong County, Pa., February 3, 1872; interment in Kittanning Cemetery.

BUFFIN(G)TON, James, a Representative from Massachusetts; born in Fall River, Mass., March 16, 1817; attended the common schools, and Friends College, Providence, R. I.; studied medicine but never practiced; engaged in mercantile pursuits in Fall River; mayor of Fall River in 1854 and 1855; elected as a Republican to the Thirty-fourth and to the three succeeding Congresses (March 4, 1855–March 3, 1863); was not a candidate for renomination in 1862; during the Civil War was mustered into the service April 24, 1861, and was discharged June 15, 1861; special agent of the United States Treasury and internal-revenue collector for the district of Massachusetts 1867–1869; elected to the Forty-first and to the three succeeding Congresses and served from March 4, 1869, until his death in Fall River, Mass., March 7, 1875; interment in Oak Grove Cemetery.

BUFFUM, Joseph, Jr., a Representative from New Hampshire; born in Fitchburg, Mass., September 23, 1784; attended the public schools and the local academy; was graduated from Dartmouth College, Hanover, N. H., in 1806; studied law and practiced in Westmoreland and Keene, N. H.; elected as a Democrat to the Sixteenth Congress (March 4, 1819–March 3, 1821); appointed judge of the court of common pleas on January 21, 1825; engaged in agricultural pursuits; died in Westmoreland, Cheshire County, N. H., February 24, 1874; interment in South Village Cemetery.

BUGG, Robert Malone, a Representative from Tennessee; born in Boydton, Mecklenburg County, Va., January 20, 1805; attended the public schools; moved to Tennessee and settled in Williamson County in 1825, where he taught school for several years; moved to Giles County and engaged in agricultural pursuits; justice of the peace in 1840; member of the State house of representatives in 1851 and 1852; elected as a Whig to the Thirty-third Congress (March 4, 1853–March 3, 1855); declined to be a candidate for renomination in 1854; resumed agricultural pursuits; served in the State senate in 1871 and 1872; died in Lynnville, Giles County, Tenn., February 18, 1887; interment in McLaurine Cemetery, near Lynnville, Tenn.

BULKELEY, Morgan Gardner (cousin of Edwin Dennison Morgan), a Senator from Connecticut; born in East Haddam, Middlesex County, Conn., December 26, 1837; attended the district schools; moved with his parents to Hartford, Conn., in 1846; engaged in mercantile pursuits in Brooklyn, N. Y., 1852–1872; member of the Republican general committee of Kings County; during the Civil War enlisted in the Thirteenth Regiment, New York National Guard, and served at Baltimore and at Suffolk, Va., under the command of Brig. Gen. Max Weber; returned to Hartford, Conn., in 1872; engaged in the life insurance business and served as president of the Ætna Life Insurance Co. from 1879 until his death; served in the city council in 1874; member of the board of aldermen in 1875 and 1876; first president of the National League of Professional Base Ball Clubs in 1876; mayor of Hartford 1880–1888; Governor of Connecticut 1889–1893; delegate to the Republican National Conventions in 1888 and 1896; elected commander of the Department of Connecticut, Grand Army of the Republic, in 1903; elected as a Republican to the United States Senate and served from March 4, 1905, to March 3, 1911; unsuccessful candidate for reelection; resumed his former business pursuits; died in Hartford, Conn., on November 6, 1922; interment in Cedar Hill Cemetery.

BULKLEY, Robert Johns, a Representative and a Senator from Ohio; born in Cleveland, Cuyahoga County, Ohio, October 8, 1880; attended the University School, Cleveland, Ohio, and was graduated from Harvard University, Cambridge, Mass., in 1902; studied law at Harvard Law School; was admitted to the bar in 1906 and commenced practice in Cleveland, Ohio; elected as a Democrat to the Sixty-second and Sixty-third Congresses (March 4, 1911–March 3, 1915); delegate to the Democratic State Convention in 1912; delegate to the Democratic National Conventions in 1912, 1916, 1932, 1936, 1940, 1944, 1948, 1952, and 1960; during the First World War served as chief of the legal section of the War Industries Board in 1917 and 1918; resumed the practice of law; elected to the United States Senate on November 4, 1930, to fill the vacancy caused by the death of Theodore E. Burton; reelected in 1932 for the term beginning March 4, 1933, and served from December 1, 1930, to January 3, 1939; unsuccessful candidate for reelection in 1938; resumed the practice of law; during World War II served as a member of the board of appeals in visa cases; is a resident of Cleveland, Ohio.

BULL, John, a Delegate from South Carolina; born in Prince William's Parish, South Carolina, about 1740; justice of the peace of Greenville County; member of the Provincial house of commons in 1772; deputy secretary of the Province in 1772; delegate to the First and Second Provincial Congresses in 1775 and 1776; member of the first general assembly in 1776; served in the State house of representatives 1778–1781 and in 1784; Member of the Continental Congress 1784–1787; served in the State senate in 1798; died in South Carolina in 1802; interment in Prince William's Parish Churchyard, Beaufort County, S. C.

BULL, John, a Representative from Missouri; born in Virginia in 1803; studied medicine in Baltimore, Md.; moved to Howard County, Mo., and settled near Glasgow; engaged in the practice of medicine; studied theology; was ordained to the ministry and became a Methodist minister in that locality; unsuccessful candi-

date for Governor of Missouri; presidential elector on the Democratic ticket of Jackson and Calhoun in 1828; elected as a Whig to the Twenty-third Congress (March 4, 1833–March 3, 1835); resumed his ministerial duties and also the practice of medicine; died near Rothville, Chariton County, Mo., in February 1863; interment in Hutcheson Cemetery, a family burial ground, near Rothville, Mo.

BULL, Melville, a Representative from Rhode Island; born in Newport, R. I., September 29, 1854; attended Phillips Exeter Academy, Exeter, N. H., and was graduated from Harvard University in 1877; engaged in agricultural pursuits near Newport; member of the State house of representatives 1883–1885; served in the State senate 1885–1892; member of the Republican State central committee; delegate to the Republican National Convention at Chicago in 1888; Lieutenant Governor of Rhode Island 1892–1894; elected as a Republican to the Fifty-fourth and to the three succeeding Congresses (March 4, 1895–March 3, 1903); unsuccessful candidate for reelection in 1902 to the Fifty-eighth Congress; owing to ill health, discontinued active business pursuits and lived in retirement until his death in Middletown, Newport County, R. I., July 5, 1909; interment in Island Cemetery, Newport, R. I.

BULLARD, Henry Adams, a Representative from Louisiana; born in Pepperell, Mass., September 9, 1788; was graduated from Harvard University in 1807; studied law in Boston and Philadelphia; was admitted to the bar about 1812; accompanied Gen. José Álvarez Toledo as military secretary on his revolutionary expedition into Texas in 1813, which was repulsed by the Spanish troops under General Arredondo at the Battle of Medina, near San Antonio, Tex., August 18, 1813; moved to Natchitoches, La., and commenced the practice of law; appointed district judge in 1822, but resigned after a few years' service, returning to the bench later for another period of service; elected as a Whig to the Twenty-second and Twenty-third Congresses and served from March 4, 1831, until January 4, 1834, when he resigned, having been appointed judge; judge of the supreme court of Louisiana from 1834 to 1846; acted as secretary of state of Louisiana in 1839; resumed the practice of law in New Orleans, La.; appointed professor of civil law in the Law School of Louisiana in 1847; served as a member of the State house of representatives in 1850; elected to the Thirty-first Congress to fill the vacancy caused by the resignation of Charles M. Conrad and served from December 5, 1850, to March 3, 1851; died in New Orleans, La., on April 17, 1851; interment in Girod Street Cemetery.

BULLOCH, Archibald (father of William Bellinger Bulloch and great-great-grandfather of Theodore Roosevelt), a Delegate from Georgia; born in Charleston, S. C., about 1730; completed preparatory studies; studied law, was admitted to the bar and practiced; commissioned lieutenant in a South Carolina regiment in 1757; moved to Savannah, Ga., about 1762; appointed a member of the committee to correspond with Franklin for redress of grievances in 1768 and of the committee to sympathize with the citizens of Boston; elected speaker of the Georgia Royal Assembly in 1772; president of the Georgia Provincial Congress in 1775 and 1776; Member of the Continental Congress in 1775 and 1776, and on November 9, 1775, signed the secret pact or declaration, and was the first man in Georgia to read the Declaration of Independence; led a company to clear Tybee Island of the enemy; elected by the Provincial Congress president and commander in chief of Georgia and served from June 20, 1776, to February 5, 1777, when the State government was adopted; signed the first constitution of Georgia; died in Savannah, Ga., February 22, 1777; interment in Colonial Cemetery.

BULLOCH, William Bellinger (son of Archibald Bulloch), a Senator from Georgia; born in Savannah, Ga., in 1777; studied law; was admitted to the bar and commenced practice in Savannah in 1797; appointed United States district attorney in 1804; mayor of Savannah in 1812 and alderman in 1814; during the War of 1812 served in the Savannah Heavy Artillery; solicitor general of the State; second vice president of the Georgia Historical Society in 1829; collector of customs in 1849 and 1850; member of the State house of representatives; served in the State senate; appointed as a Democrat to the United States Senate to fill the vacancy caused by the resignation of William H. Crawford and served from April 8, 1813, until November 6, 1813, when a successor was elected and qualified; one of the founders of the State Bank of Georgia and served as its president 1816–1843; died in Savannah, Ga., May 6, 1852; interment in Laurel Grove Cemetery.

BULLOCK, Robert, a Representative from Florida; born in Greenville, Pitt County, N. C., December 8, 1828; attended the common schools; moved to Florida in 1844 and settled at Fort King, then a United States Government post, near the present city of Ocala; taught in the first school in Sumter County; clerk of the circuit court of Marion County from November 13, 1849, to November 11, 1855; commissioned by the Governor in 1856 a captain to raise a mounted company of volunteers for the suppression of Indian hostilities; the company was mustered into the service of the United States and served eighteen months, until the cessation of hostilities; during the Civil War entered the Confederate Army as captain in the Seventh Regiment Florida Volunteers, in 1862 and served until the close of the war; promoted to lieutenant colonel in 1863 and to brigadier general in 1865; studied law; was admitted to the bar in 1866 and began practice in Marion County; judge of probate court 1866–1868; presidential elector on the Democratic ticket of Tilden and Hendricks in 1876; member of the State house of representatives in 1879; again clerk of the circuit court of Marion County from February 11, 1881, to February 9, 1889; elected as a Democrat to the Fifty-first and Fifty-second Congresses (March 4, 1889–March 3, 1893); was not a candidate for renomination in 1892; engaged in agricultural pursuits; elected judge of Marion County in 1903 and served until his death in Ocala, Marion County, Fla., July 27, 1905; interment in Evergreen Cemetery.

BULLOCK, Stephen, a Representative from Massachusetts; born in Rehoboth, Mass., October 10, 1735; attended the common schools; taught school; during the Revolutionary War was captain of the Sixth Company in Col. Thomas Carpenter's Regiment, and was in the Battle of Rhode Island in 1778; delegate to the first State constitutional convention in 1780; member of the State house of representatives in 1783, 1785, 1786, 1795, and 1796; elected as a Federalist to the Fifth Congress (March 4, 1797–March 3, 1799); judge of the court of common pleas for Bristol County; member of the Governor's council 1803–1805; died in Rehoboth, Bristol County, Mass., February 2, 1816; interment in Burial Place Hill.

BULLOCK, Wingfield, a Representative from Kentucky; born in Spotsylvania, Va.; studied law; moved to Kentucky; member of the State senate from Shelby County 1812–1814; elected to the Seventeenth Congress and served from March 4, 1821, until his death in Shelbyville, Shelby County, Ky., October 13, 1821; interment in an old burying ground near Shelbyville.

BULOW, William John, a Senator from South Dakota; born on a farm near Moscow, Clermont County, Ohio, January 13, 1869; attended the public schools in Moscow, Ohio, and was graduated from the law department of the University of Michigan at Ann Arbor in 1893; was admitted to the bar the same year and commenced practice in Beresford, Union County, S. Dak., in 1894; member of the State senate in 1899; served as city attorney of Beresford, S. Dak., 1902–1912 and 1913–1927; mayor of Beresford in 1912 and 1913; county judge of Union County, S. Dak., in 1918; Governor of South Dakota 1927–1931; delegate to the Democratic National Convention at Houston, Tex., in 1928, and to a number of Democratic State conventions; elected as a Democrat to the United States Senate in 1930; reelected in 1936 and served from March 4, 1931, to January 3, 1943; unsuccessful candidate for renomination in 1942; retired and resided in Washington, D. C., until his death there on February 26, 1960; interment in St. John's Catholic Cemetery, Beresford, S. Dak.

BULWINKLE, Alfred Lee, a Representative from North Carolina; born in Charleston, Charleston County, S. C., April 21, 1883; moved with his parents to Dallas, N. C., in 1891; attended the common schools; studied law at the University of North Carolina at Chapel Hill; was admitted to the bar in 1904 and commenced practice in Dallas, Gaston County, N. C.; delegate to practically all the Democratic State conventions since 1904; prosecuting attorney for the municipal court of Gastonia 1913–1916; captain in Company B, First Infantry, North Carolina National Guard, 1909–1917; served on the Mexican border in 1916 and 1917; during the First World War served as a major in command of the Second Battalion, One Hundred and Thirteenth Field Artillery, Fifty-fifth Brigade, Thirtieth Division, American Expeditionary Forces; elected as a Democrat to the Sixty-seventh and to the three succeeding Congresses (March 4, 1921–March 3, 1929); unsuccessful candidate for reelection in 1928 to the Seventy-first Congress; elected to the Seventy-second and to the nine succeeding Congresses and served from March 4, 1931, until his death; delegate to the International Aviation Conference at Chicago, Ill., in 1944; United States adviser, International Civil Aviation Organization at Montreal, Canada, and Geneva, Switzerland, in 1947; died in Gastonia, N. C., August 31, 1950; interment in Oakwood Cemetery.

BUNCH, Samuel, a Representative from Tennessee; born in Grainger County, Tenn., December 4, 1786; attended the public schools; engaged in agricultural pursuits; served in the Creek War as captain of a company of mounted riflemen under General Jackson and participated in the attack on Hillibeetown November 18, 1813; sheriff of Grainger County for several years; elected as a Whig to the Twenty-third and Twenty-fourth Congresses (March 4, 1833–March 3, 1837); resumed agricultural pursuits; died on his farm near Rutledge, Grainger County, Tenn., September 5, 1849; interment in a private cemetery on his farm (later known as the Walter Manly farm), near Rutledge.

BUNDY, Hezekiah Sanford, a Representative from Ohio; born in Marietta, Ohio, August 15, 1817; moved with his parents to Athens County in 1819; attended the public schools; engaged in agricultural pursuits; studied law; was admitted to the bar in 1850 and practiced until 1860, when he became engaged in the iron business; member of the State house of representatives in 1848 and 1850; served in the State senate in 1855; presidential elector on the Republican ticket of Lincoln and Hamlin in 1860; unsuccessful candidate for election in 1862 to the Thirty-eighth Congress; elected as a Republican to the Thirty-ninth Congress (March 5, 1865–March 3, 1867); declined to be a candidate for renomination in 1866; elected to the Forty-third Congress (March 4, 1873–March 3, 1875); unsuccessful candidate for reelection in 1874 to the Forty-fourth Congress; moved to Wellston, Jackson County, in 1887 and resumed the practice of law; elected to the Fifty-third Congress to fill the vacancy caused by the death of William H. Enochs and served from December 4, 1893, to March 3, 1895; died in Wellston, Jackson County, Ohio, December 12, 1895; interment in the City Cemetery.

BUNDY, Solomon, a Representative from New York; born in Oxford, Chenango County, N. Y., May 22, 1823; attended the common schools and Oxford (N. Y.) Academy; taught school for several years; engaged in mercantile pursuits; studied law; was admitted to the bar in 1859 and commenced practice in Oxford; while studying law served as justice of the peace and clerk of the Board of Supervisors of Chenango County; district attorney of Chenango County 1862–1865; elected as a Republican to the Forty-fifth Congress (March 4, 1877–March 3, 1879); was not a candidate for renomination in 1878; resumed the practice of law; died in Oxford, N. Y., January 13, 1889; interment in Riverview Cemetery.

BUNKER, Berkeley Lloyd, a Senator and a Representative from Nevada; born in what was then St. Thomas, Clark County, Nev., August 12, 1906; attended the public schools, and was graduated from the high school at Las Vegas, Nev., in 1926; became engaged in the tire and oil business in Las Vegas, Nev., in 1934; member of the State assembly 1936–1941, serving as speaker in 1939; appointed as a Democrat to the United States Senate to fill the vacancy caused by the death of Key Pittman for the term ending January 3, 1941, and also for the term ending January 3, 1947, and served from November 27, 1940, until December 6, 1942, when a duly elected successor qualified; unsuccessful candidate for nomination in 1942 for the vacancy; engaged in the life-insurance business in Las Vegas, Nev.; elected as a Democrat to the Seventy-ninth Congress (January 3, 1945–January 3, 1947); was not a candidate for renomination in 1946; unsuccessful Democratic candidate for election to the United States Senate in 1946; investment broker and vice president of a mortuary establishment; is a resident of Las Vegas, Nev.

BUNN, Benjamin Hickman, a Representative from North Carolina; born on a farm in Nash County, near Rocky Mount, N. C., October 19, 1844; attended the local schools; during the Civil War enlisted in the Confederate Army as a second lieutenant in Company A, Forty-seventh North Carolina Regiment; promoted successively and became captain of the Fourth Company of Sharpshooters, MacRae's brigade, Army of Northern Virginia, 1861–1865; studied law; was admitted to the bar in 1866 and commenced practice in Rocky Mount, N. C.; elected mayor of Rocky Mount in 1867; delegate to the State constitutional convention in 1875 and to the Democratic National Convention at Cincinnati in 1880; member of the State house of representatives 1883–1885; presidential elector on the Democratic ticket of Cleveland and Hendricks in 1884; elected as a Democrat to the Fifty-first, Fifty-second, and Fifty-third Congresses (March 4, 1889–March 3, 1895); was not a candidate for renomination in 1894; postmaster of Rocky Mount, N. C., from April 23, 1895, until the appointment of his successor on July 27, 1897; resumed the practice of law; died in Nash County, near Rocky Mount, N. C., August 25, 1907; interment in Pineview Cemetery, Rocky Mount, Edgecombe County, N. C.

BUNNELL, Frank Charles, a Representative from Pennsylvania; born in Washington Township, Luzerne County, Pa., March 19, 1842; attended the district rural school and Wyoming Seminary, Kingston, Pa., until the beginning of the Civil War, when he enlisted as a private in Company B, Fifty-second Regiment, Pennsylvania Volunteers, in September 1861; promoted and served as quartermaster sergeant of his regiment during the peninsular campaign under General McClellan;

discharged from the service April 2, 1863, on a surgeon's certificate of disability; engaged in mercantile pursuits 1864–1869; moved to Tunkhannock and engaged in agricultural pursuits and in banking; unsuccessful candidate for nomination in 1872 to the Forty-third Congress; subsequently elected to the Forty-second Congress to fill the vacancy caused by the resignation of Ulysses Mercur and served from December 24, 1872, to March 3, 1873; president of the Wyoming County Agricultural Society for over twenty years; elected burgess and borough treasurer of Tunkhannock, Wyoming County, in 1884; elected as a Republican to the Forty-ninth and Fiftieth Congresses (March 4, 1885–March 3, 1889); was not a candidate for renomination in 1888; retired from active business pursuits and political life; died in Philadelphia, Pa., September 11, 1911; interment in Gravel Hill Cemetery, Tunkhannock, Pa.

BUNNER, Rudolph, a Representative from New York; born in Savannah, Wayne County, N. Y., August 17, 1779; was graduated from Columbia College, at New York City, in 1798; studied law; was admitted to the bar and practiced in Newburgh, Orange County, N. Y., from 1819 until 1822; moved to Oswego, Oswego County, N. Y., in October 1822; engaged in manufacturing and served as a director in the Oswego Cloth & Carpet Manufacturing Co.; also was an extensive landowner; member of the first board of directors of the Oswego Canal Co.; elected as an Adams Democrat to the Twentieth Congress (March 4, 1827–March 3, 1829); died in Oswego, N. Y., July 16, 1837; interment in Riverside Cemetery.

BUNTING, Thomas Lathrop, a Representative from New York; born in Eden, Erie County, N. Y., April 24, 1844; was educated in the common schools and the Griffith Institute, Springville, N. Y.; taught school in winters and attended the academy in summer months; illness having interrupted his preparation for college, he moved to Hamburg, N. Y., in 1868 and entered a store in the position of clerk and after one year established a general mercantile store; later engaged in the canning business; elected as a Democrat to the Fifty-second Congress (March 4, 1891–March 3, 1893); declined to be a candidate for renomination in 1892; resumed the canning business and also became interested in farming, dairying, and stock raising; died in Buffalo, N. Y., December 27, 1898; interment in Forest Lawn Cemetery at Hamburg, Erie County, N. Y.

BURCH, John Chilton, a Representative from California; born in Boone County, Mo., February 1, 1826; attended the Bonne Femme Academy and Kemper College; studied law in Jefferson City; was admitted to the bar and practiced; deputy clerk of Cole County; assistant adjutant general of Missouri; moved to California in 1850 and worked in the mines until 1851; elected clerk of the newly organized Trinity County; appointed district attorney in 1853; member of the State assembly in 1856; served in the State senate 1857–1859; elected as a Democrat to the Thirty-sixth Congress (March 4, 1859–March 3, 1861); resumed the practice of law in San Francisco; appointed a code commissioner and served four years; declined to be a candidate for judge of the supreme court of California; died in San Francisco, Calif., August 31, 1885; interment in the City Cemetery, Sacramento, Calif.

BURCH, Thomas Granville, a Representative and a Senator from Virginia; born on a farm near Dyer's Store, in Henry County, Va., July 3, 1869; attended the public schools; engaged in agricultural pursuits and in the tobacco manufacturing business; moved to Martinsville, Va., in 1886 and engaged in the banking business; also interested in the insurance and real-estate business; member of the State board of agriculture 1910–1913;

mayor of Martinsville, Va., 1912–1914; served on the board of visitors of the State normal school, Radford, Va., 1913–1915 and of the Virginia School for the Deaf and the Blind 1922–1931; United States marshal for the western district of Virginia 1914–1921; member of the commission in 1927 to simplify and reorganize the State government; served with the State transportation and public utility advisory commission in 1929; member of the State board of education in 1930 and 1931; delegate to the Democratic National Conventions in 1908, 1912, 1924, 1932, 1936, and 1940; elected as a Democrat to the Seventy-second Congress and to the seven succeeding Congresses and served from March 4, 1931, to May 31, 1946, when he resigned, having been appointed to the United States Senate to fill the vacancy caused by the death of Carter Glass and served until November 5, 1946, when a duly elected successor qualified; was not a candidate for election to the vacancy in 1946; chairman of Governor's Commission on Reorganization of the State Government in 1947; member of the board of visitors, Virginia Military Institute, Lexington, Va.; president of a real-estate and insurance brokerage firm, and a member of the board of directors of Bassett Furniture Industries, Inc.; died in Martinsville, Va., March 20, 1951; interment in Oakwood Cemetery.

BURCHARD, Horatio Chapin, a Representative from Illinois; born in Marshall, Oneida County, N. Y., September 22, 1825; attended the public schools and private preparatory schools; was graduated from Hamilton College, Clinton, N. Y., in 1850; studied law; was admitted to the bar in 1854 and commenced practice in Freeport, Ill.; member of the State house of representatives 1863–1866; elected as a Republican to the Forty-first Congress to fill the vacancy caused by the resignation of Elihu B. Washburne; reelected to the Forty-second and to the three succeeding Congresses and served from December 6, 1869, to March 3, 1879; unsuccessful candidate for renomination in 1878; director of the United States Mints 1879–1885; resumed the practice of law in Freeport, Ill.; member of the commission to revise the State revenue laws in 1885 and 1886; was placed in charge of the jury of awards of the mining department of the World's Columbian Exposition at Chicago in 1893; died in Freeport, Ill., May 14, 1908; interment in Oakland Cemetery.

BURCHARD, Samuel Dickinson, a Representative from Wisconsin; born in Leyden, N. Y., July 17, 1836; moved with his father to Beaver Dam, Wis., in 1845; attended Madison (now Colgate) University, Hamilton, N. Y.; engaged in the wool manufacturing business in Beaver Dam; during the Civil War entered the Union Army as a lieutenant in the Missouri Militia; appointed assistant quartermaster of United States Volunteers with the rank of captain; was stationed at New York, where he had charge of the purchase of forage for the forces on the Atlantic coast; was mustered out with the rank of major; member of the Wisconsin Senate 1872–1874; elected as a Democrat to the Forty-fourth Congress (March 4, 1875–March 3, 1877); engaged in agricultural pursuits; died in Greenwood, Wise County, Tex., September 1, 1901; interment in Greenwood Cemetery.

BURCHILL, Thomas Francis, a Representative from New York; born in New York City, N. Y., August 3, 1882; attended St. Francis Xavier High School in New York City and Niagara University, Niagara Falls, N. Y.; auctioneer, appraiser, and also interested in the insurance business in New York City since 1900; member of the State assembly 1919–1924; served in the State senate 1924–1938; appointed a member of the New York World's Fair Commission in 1938; elected as a Democrat to the Seventy-eighth Congress (January 3, 1943–January 3, 1945); was not a candidate for renomination in 1944; resumed his former business pursuits and is a resident of New York City.

BURD, George, a Representative from Pennsylvania; born in 1793; studied law; was admitted to the bar in 1810 at Carlisle, Cumberland County, Pa., and practiced; elected to the Twenty-second and Twenty-third Congresses (March 4, 1831–March 3, 1835); moved to Mercer County in 1843; died in Bedford, Bedford County, Pa., on January 13, 1844; interment in Bedford Cemetery.

BURDETT, Samuel Swinfin, a Representative from Missouri; born at Sutton-in-the-Elms, Leicestershire, England, February 21, 1836; when twelve years of age immigrated to the United States; worked on a farm in Lorain County, Ohio, and attended the common schools; studied law at Oberlin College, Ohio, was admitted to the bar in 1858 and commenced practice in Dewitt, Iowa; during the Civil War entered the Union Army as a private in the First Regiment, Iowa Volunteer Cavalry, in May 1861; promoted to the rank of lieutenant, later becoming captain, and served until August 1864; assistant provost marshal general from March 1 until August 1, 1864; presidential elector on the Republican ticket of Lincoln and Johnson in 1864; moved to Osceola, St. Clair County, Mo., in December 1865; attorney for the seventh circuit in 1868 and 1869; delegate to the Republican National Convention at Chicago in 1868; elected as a Republican to the Forty-first and Forty-second Congresses (March 4, 1869–March 3, 1873); unsuccessful candidate in 1872 for reelection to the Forty-third Congress; resumed the practice of law in Osceola, Mo.; appointed Commissioner of the General Land Office in 1874; engaged in the practice of law in Washington, D. C., residing at Glencarlyn, Va., during his last years; commander in chief of the Grand Army of the Republic in 1885 and 1886; died at Sutton-in-the-Elms, Leicestershire, England, September 24, 1914; interment in Arlington National Cemetery, Fort Myer, Va.

BURDICK, Clark, a Representative from Rhode Island; born in Newport, R. I., January 13, 1868; attended the public schools and Rogers High School in Newport; was a student at the Harvard Law School 1893–1895; was admitted to the bar in 1894 and commenced practice in Newport; also interested in banking and served as president of the Newport Trust Co.; member of the First Division, Rhode Island Naval Militia, in 1896 and 1897; member of the city school board 1899–1901; city solicitor of Newport in 1901, 1902, and again in 1907 and 1908; member of the State house of representatives 1906–1908; delegate to the Republican National Convention at Chicago in 1912 and to numerous Republican State conventions; member of the Newport Representative Council 1906–1916, serving as chairman; served in the State senate in 1915 and 1916; awarded the third class order of the Sacred Treasury of Japan for services rendered the representatives of the Emperor of Japan in 1917; mayor of Newport in 1917 and 1918; elected as a Republican to the Sixty-sixth and to the six succeeding Congresses (March 4, 1919–March 3, 1933); unsuccessful candidate for reelection in 1932 to the Seventy-third Congress; reengaged in the practice of law and also in his banking interests in Newport, R. I., until his death on August 27, 1948; interment in St. Mary's Episcopal Cemetery, Portsmouth, R. I.

BURDICK, Quentin Northrop (son of Usher L. Burdick and brother-in-law of Robert W. Levering), a Representative and a Senator from North Dakota; born in Munich, Cavalier County, N. Dak., June 19, 1908; attended the public schools; graduated from the University of Minnesota in 1931 and from the law department of the same university in 1932; was admitted to the bar the same year and commenced the practice of law in Fargo, N. Dak.; delegate to the Democratic National Convention in 1956; elected as a Democrat to the Eighty-sixth Congress and served from January 3, 1959, until his resignation August 8, 1960; elected to the United States Senate June 28, 1960, to fill the vacancy caused by the death of William Langer and took his seat August 8, 1960, for the term ending January 3, 1965.

BURDICK, Theodore Weld, a Representative from Iowa; born in Evansburg, Crawford County, Pa., October 7, 1836; attended the common schools; moved with his parents to Decorah, Iowa, in 1853 and engaged in banking; deputy treasurer and recorder of Winneshiek County 1854–1857; treasurer and recorder from 1858 to 1862, when he resigned to recruit a company for the Union Army during the Civil War; was commissioned as captain and assigned to the Sixth Regiment, Iowa Volunteer Cavalry, in which he served for three years in the Department of the Northwest; after the regiment was mustered out in 1865 he returned to Decorah and became cashier of the First National Bank; elected as a Republican to the Forty-fifth Congress (March 4, 1877–March 3, 1879); declined to be a candidate for renomination in 1878; resumed banking at Decorah, Iowa, and Sault Ste. Marie, Mich.; member of the State senate in 1886 and 1887; declined to be a candidate for renomination; died in Decorah, Winneshiek County, Iowa, July 16, 1898; interment in Phelps Cemetery.

BURDICK, Usher Lloyd (father of Quentin N. Burdick and father-in-law of Robert W. Levering), a Representative from North Dakota; born in Owatonna, Steele County, Minn., February 21, 1879; moved with his parents to Dakota Territory in 1882; raised among the Sioux Indians; was graduated from the State normal school at Mayville, N. Dak., in 1900; deputy superintendent of schools of Benson County, N. Dak., 1900–1902; was graduated from the law department of the University of Minnesota at Minneapolis in 1904, teaching school in a business college while attending the university; was admitted to the bar in 1904 and commenced practice in Munich, N. Dak.; member of the State house of representatives 1907–1911, serving as speaker in 1909; moved to Williston, N. Dak., in 1910 and continued the practice of law; Lieutenant Governor 1911–1913; State's attorney of Williams County 1913–1915; assistant United States district attorney for North Dakota 1929–1932; unsuccessful candidate for the Republican nomination to the Seventy-third Congress in 1932; also engaged in livestock breeding and farming; author; elected as a Republican to the Seventy-fourth and to the four succeeding Congresses (January 3, 1935–January 3, 1945); was not a candidate for renomination in 1944, but was an unsuccessful candidate for the Republican nomination for United States Senator; unsuccessful Independent candidate for election in 1944 to the Seventy-ninth Congress; elected to the Eighty-first and to the four succeeding Congresses (January 3, 1949–January 3, 1959); was not a candidate for renomination in 1958; died in Washington, D. C., August 19, 1960; interment on his ranch at Williston, N. Dak.

BURGES, Dempsey, a Representative from North Carolina; born in Shiloh, Camden County, N. C., in 1751; member of the Provincial Congress in 1775 and 1776; took an active part in the Revolutionary War, serving first as major of the Pasquotank Minutemen and later as lieutenant colonel of Gregory's Continental Regiment; elected to the Fourth and Fifth Congresses (March 4, 1795–March 3, 1799); died in Camden County, N. C., January 13, 1800; interment in Shiloh Baptist Churchyard.

BURGES, Tristam (great-great-uncle of Theodore Francis Green), a Representative from Rhode Island; born in Rochester, Mass., February 26, 1770; attended the common schools; studied medicine at a school in Wrentham; upon the death of his father he abandoned the study of medicine; was graduated from Rhode Island College (now Brown University), Providence, R. I., in 1796; studied law; was admitted to the bar in 1799 and commenced practice in Providence, R. I.; member of the State house of representatives in 1811 and was prominent as a member of the Federal Party; appointed chief justice of the supreme court of Rhode Island in May 1815; unsuccessful candidate for election to the same in 1816; professor of oratory in Brown University; elected to the Nineteenth and to the four succeeding Congresses (March 4, 1825–March 3, 1835); unsuccessful candidate for reelection; unsuccessful Whig candidate for Governor in 1836; resumed the practice of law; died on his estate, "Watchemoket Farm" (now a part of East Providence, R. I.), October 13, 1853; interment in North Burial Ground, Providence, R. I.

BURGESS, George Farmer, a Representative from Texas; born in Wharton, Wharton County, Tex., September 21, 1861; attended the common schools; moved with his mother to Fayette County in 1880 and engaged in agricultural pursuits near Flatonia; was later employed as a clerk in a country store; studied law; was admitted to the bar in 1882 and commenced practice in La Grange, Tex.; moved to Gonzales in 1884; prosecuting attorney of Gonzales County from 1886 to 1889, when he resigned; presidential elector on the Democratic ticket of Cleveland and Stevenson in 1892; elected as a Democrat to the Fifty-seventh and to the seven succeeding Congresses (March 4, 1901–March 3, 1917); unsuccessful candidate for the Democratic nomination of United States Senator in 1916; resumed the practice of law at Gonzales, Tex., where he died December 31, 1919; interment in the Masonic Cemetery.

BURGIN, William Olin, a Representative from North Carolina; born on a farm near Marion, McDowell County, N. C., July 28, 1877; moved with his parents to Rutherfordton, N. C., where he attended the public schools and Rutherfordton Military Institute; also attended the Law School of the University of North Carolina at Chapel Hill; engaged as a clerk in a general store in Rutherfordton in 1893 and later as a traveling salesman and merchant; moved to Thomasville and engaged in the mercantile business; was admitted to the bar; mayor of Thomasville, N. C., 1906–1910; moved to Lexington, N. C., and continued the practice of law; president and attorney of the Industrial Bank of Lexington; director in a number of business enterprises in Lexington; served in the State house of representatives in 1931; member of the State senate in 1933; elected as a Democrat to the Seventy-sixth and to the three succeeding Congresses and served from January 3, 1939, until his death in Washington, D. C., on April 11, 1946; interment in Lexington Cemetery, Lexington, N. C.

BURK, Henry, a Representative from Pennsylvania; born in Wurttemberg, Germany, September 26, 1850; immigrated to the United States in 1854 with his parents, who settled in Philadelphia, Pa.; attended the public schools about three years; became a repairer of shoemaking machinery and subsequently engaged in supplying this machinery to the trade; engaged in the manufacture of leather and in 1887 invented the alum and sumac process, which revolutionized the industry; president of the Manufacturers' National Association in 1895; elected as a Republican to the Fifty-seventh and Fifty-eighth Congresses and served from March 4, 1901, until his death in Philadelphia, Pa., December 5, 1903; interment in Holy Sepulchre Cemetery.

BURKE, Aedanus, a Representative from South Carolina; born in Galway, Ireland, June 16, 1743; attended the theological college at St. Omer, France; visited the West Indies; immigrated to the American Colonies and settled in Charles Town (now Charleston), S. C.; served in the militia forces of South Carolina during the Revolutionary War; appointed a judge of the State circuit court in 1778 and served until the enemy overran the State; member of the South Carolina House of Representatives 1779–1782; again served in the Revolutionary Army 1780–1782; when the courts were reestablished resumed his seat on the bench, and in 1785 was appointed one of three commissioners to prepare a digest of the State laws; member of the convention in 1788 called to consider ratification of the Constitution of the United States, which he opposed; elected to the First Congress (March 4, 1789–March 3, 1791); declined to be a candidate for reelection in 1790 to the Second Congress, the legislature having passed a law prohibiting a State judge from leaving the State; elected a chancellor of the courts of equity in 1799 and served until his death in Charleston, S. C., March 30, 1802; interment in O'Brien Smith's lot in the cemetery of the Chapel of Ease (later commonly called the "Burnt Church") of St. Bartholomew's Parish, near Jacksonboro, Colleton County, S. C.

BURKE, Charles Henry, a Representative from South Dakota; born on a farm near Batavia, Genesee County, N. Y., April 1, 1861; attended the public schools of Batavia, N. Y.; moved to the Territory of Dakota in 1882 and settled on a homestead in Beadle County; moved to Hughes County in 1883; studied law; was admitted to the bar in 1886; engaged in the real-estate investment business in Pierre, S. Dak.; member of the State house of representatives in 1895 and 1897; elected as a Republican to the Fifty-sixth and to the three succeeding Congresses (March 4, 1899–March 3, 1907); unsuccessful candidate for renomination in 1906 to the Sixtieth Congress; elected to the Sixty-first, Sixty-second, and Sixty-third Congresses (March 4, 1909–March 3, 1915); did not seek renomination in 1914 having received the Republican nomination for United States Senator, but was unsuccessful for election; resumed the investment business; engaged in war-relief work during the First World War; appointed Commissioner of Indian Affairs, Washington, D. C., on April 1, 1921, and served until his resignation on June 30, 1929; engaged in the real-estate and loan business in Pierre S. Dak., and also worked in the interest of Indians in Washington, D. C.; died in Washington, D. C., April 7, 1944; interment in Riverside Cemetery, Pierre, S. Dak.

BURKE, Edmund, a Representative from New Hampshire; born in Westminster, Vt., January 23, 1809; attended the public schools; studied law; was admitted to the bar in 1826 and commenced practice in Colebrook, N. H.; moved to Claremont, N. H., in 1833 and assumed editorial management of the New Hampshire Argus; moved to Newport in 1834 and united the Argus with the Spectator of that place, continuing as editor for several years; commissioned as adjutant in the State militia in 1837 and as brigade inspector in 1838; elected as a Democrat to the Twenty-sixth, Twenty-seventh, and Twenty-eighth Congresses (March 4, 1839–March 3, 1845); was not a candidate for renomination in 1844; appointed Commissioner of Patents by President Polk and served from May 5, 1846, to September 3, 1850; resumed the practice of law in Newport, N. H.; delegate to the Democratic National Conventions at Baltimore in 1844 and 1852; delegate to the Democratic State convention in 1867, and served as presiding officer; member of the State board of agriculture in 1871; died in Newport, Sullivan County, N. H., January 25, 1882; interment in Maple Grove Cemetery.

BURKE, Edward Raymond, a Representative and a Senator from Nebraska; born at Running Water, Bon Homme County, S. Dak., November 28, 1880; moved with his parents to Sparta, Monroe County, Wis., in 1880; educated in the public schools of Sparta, Wis.; moved to Beloit, Rock County, in 1902; was graduated from Beloit (Wis.) College in 1906; taught school in Chad-

ron, Nebr., 1906–1908; was graduated from the law department of Harvard University, Cambridge, Mass., in 1911; was admitted to the bar the same year and commenced practice in Omaha, Nebr.; during the First World War enlisted on November 17, 1917, was commissioned a second lieutenant in the Air Service and served until March 11, 1919; president of the board of education of Omaha 1927–1930; delegate to the Democratic State conventions in 1928, 1930, and 1932; elected as a Democrat to the Seventy-third Congress (March 4, 1933–January 3, 1935); did not seek renomination in 1934, having become a candidate for United States Senator; elected to the United States Senate in 1934 and served from January 3, 1935, to January 3, 1941; unsuccessful candidate for renomination in 1940; resumed the practice of law in Omaha, Nebr.; moved to Washington, D. C., in 1942 and served as president of Southern Coal Producers Association until 1947; Washington representative and general counsel for Hawaiian Statehood Commission until 1950; is a resident of Kensington, Md.

BURKE, Frank Welsh, a Representative from Kentucky; born in Louisville, Jefferson County, Ky., June 1, 1920; educated in parochial schools of Louisville and St. Xavier High School; attended the University of Southern California; graduated from Xavier University, Cincinnati, Ohio, in 1942 and from the University of Louisville in 1948; was admitted to the bar in 1948 and commenced the practice of law in Louisville, Ky.; served in the United States Army 1942–1946; assistant city attorney of Louisville in 1950 and 1951; director of public safety of Louisville in 1952; executive assistant to the mayor of Louisville in 1952 and 1953; member of the Kentucky House of Representatives in 1957 and 1958; elected as a Democrat to the Eighty-sixth Congress (January 3, 1959–January 3, 1961). *Reelected to the Eighty-seventh Congress.*

BURKE, James Anthony, a Representative from Massachusetts; born in Boston, Mass., March 30, 1910; educated in the Boston public schools and Lincoln Preparatory School; graduated from Suffolk University; registrar of vital statistics for the city of Boston; during World War II was special agent in the Counter-Intelligence, attached to the Seventy-seventh Infantry Division in the South Pacific; awarded four battle stars; member of the Massachusetts General Court for ten years; member of the Massachusetts House of Representatives for four years, serving as assistant majority leader; vice chairman of the Massachusetts Democratic State Committee for four years; elected as a Democrat to the Eighty-sixth Congress (January 3, 1959–January 3, 1961). *Reelected to the Eighty-seventh Congress.*

BURKE, James Francis, a Representative from Pennsylvania; born in Petroleum Center, Venango County, Pa., October 21, 1867; attended the public schools, and was graduated from the law department of the University of Michigan at Ann Arbor in 1892; was admitted to the bar the same year and commenced practice in Pittsburgh, Pa.; secretary of the Republican National Committee in 1892, resigning during the same year to devote his entire time to his duties as president of the American Republican College League; appointed by President Harrison to codify the navigation laws of the United States; officer of, or a delegate to, the Republican National Conventions from 1892 to 1924, with the exception of the year 1912; appointed a delegate to the Parliamentary Peace Conference at Brussels in 1905; elected as a Republican to the Fifty-ninth and to the four succeeding Congresses (March 4, 1905–March 3, 1915); was not a candidate for renomination in 1914; United States Government director of War Savings during the First World War; resumed the practice of law; elected general counsel of the Republican National Committee in December 1927 and served until his death; parliamentarian of the Republican National Convention at Kansas City, Mo., in 1928; died in Washington, D. C., August 8, 1932; interment in Calvary Cemetery, Pittsburgh, Pa.

BURKE, John Harley, a Representative from California; born in Excelsior, Richland County, Wis., June 2, 1894; moved to Milaca, Minn., with his parents in 1897, to San Pedro, Calif., in 1900, and to Long Beach, Calif., in 1909; attended the public schools, and was graduated from Long Beach Polytechnic High School in 1913; attended the University of Santa Clara at Santa Clara and the law department of the University of Southern California at Los Angeles; was admitted to the bar in 1917 and commenced practice in Long Beach, Calif.; during the First World War served as a private, first class, in the Twelfth Training Battery, Field Artillery, Camp Taylor, Ky.; in 1921 engaged in the oil business as an independent producer; elected as a Democrat to the Seventy-third Congress (March 4, 1933– January 3, 1935); was not a candidate for renomination in 1934; engaged in the real-estate business in Long Beach, Calif., until his death there May 14, 1951; interment in Calvary Cemetery, Los Angeles, Calif.

BURKE, Michael Edmund, a Representative from Wisconsin; born at Beaver Dam, Dodge County, Wis., October 15, 1863; attended the public schools and was graduated from the Wayland Academy at Beaver Dam in 1884; studied law at the University of Wisconsin at Madison in 1886 and 1887; was admitted to the bar in 1888 and commenced practice at Beaver Dam; town clerk 1887–1889; member of the State assembly 1891–1893; served in the State senate 1895–1899; city attorney of Beaver Dam 1893–1908; delegate to the Democratic National Convention at St. Louis in 1904; elected mayor of Beaver Dam and served from 1908 to 1910; elected as a Democrat to the Sixty-second, Sixty-third, and Sixty-fourth Congresses (March 4, 1911–March 3, 1917); unsuccessful candidate for reelection in 1916; died at Beaver Dam, Wis., December 12, 1918; interment in St. Patrick's Cemetery.

BURKE, Raymond Hugh, a Representative from Ohio; born in Nicholsville, Clermont County, Ohio, November 4, 1881; attended Jackson School; worked on a farm and in the village while studying to teach in rural schools; taught at Pendleton School near Point Pleasant in 1899 and 1900; student at Oberlin Academy and College 1900–1905; was graduated from the University of Chicago, Chicago, Ill., in 1906; taught in Miami University at Oxford, Ohio, 1906–1915; personnel and employment manager 1918–1923; secretary-treasurer of an automobile agency 1923–1926; special representative for an insurance company at Hamilton, Ohio, 1926–1954; mayor of Hamilton 1928–1940 and councilman 1928–1942; member of the State senate 1942–1946; elected as a Republican to the Eightieth Congress (January 3, 1947–January 3, 1949); unsuccessful candidate for reelection in 1948 to the Eighty-first Congress; lecturer in the finance department of Miami University in 1949 and 1950; died in Hamilton, Ohio, August 18, 1954; interment in Greenwood Cemetery.

BURKE, Robert Emmet, a Representative from Texas; born near Dadeville, Tallapoosa County, Ala., August 1, 1847; attended the public schools of his native city; volunteered as a private in Company D, Tenth Georgia Cavalry, Confederate Army, at the age of sixteen and served throughout the Civil War; moved to Jefferson, Tex., in 1866; studied law; was admitted to the bar in November 1870 and commenced practice in Dallas, Tex., in 1871; judge of Dallas County 1878– 1888; judge of the fourteenth judicial district of Texas 1888– 1896; elected as a Democrat to the Fifty-fifth, Fifty-sixth, and

Fifty-seventh Congresses and served from March 4, 1897, until his death in Dallas, Tex., June 5, 1901; interment in Greenwood Cemetery.

BURKE, Thomas, a Delegate from North Carolina; born in Galway, Ireland, about 1747; studied medicine; immigrated to America in 1764, settled in Accomac County, Va., and practiced; studied law; was admitted to the bar and commenced practice in Norfolk, Va.; moved to Hillsboro, N. C., in 1771; delegate to the State convention at New Bern and Hillsboro in 1775 and at Halifax in 1776; member of the State house of commons in 1777; Member of the Continental Congress from December 1776 to June 26, 1781, when he became the third Governor of North Carolina under its State constitution; kidnaped by the Tories September 13, 1781, and carried to Charleston, S. C., where he was held as a hostage; succeeded in escaping and made an exchange; resumed his duties as Governor February 1, 1782, and served until April 22, 1782; died at "Tyaquin," near Hillsboro, Orange County, N. C., December 2, 1783; interment in Mars Hill Churchyard, near Hillsboro, N. C.

BURKE, Thomas A., a Senator from Ohio; born in Cleveland, Cuyahoga County, Ohio, October 30, 1898; attended St. Agnes Parochial School; was graduated from Loyola High School, Cleveland, Ohio, in 1916, Holy Cross College, Worcester, Mass., in 1920, and Western Reserve University Law School, Cleveland, Ohio, in 1923; during the First World War served in the United States Army; was admitted to the bar in 1923 and commenced practice in Cleveland, Ohio; assistant prosecutor of Cuyahoga County 1930–1936; special counsel to the Ohio attorney general in 1937; director of law for the city of Cleveland 1942–1945; mayor of the city of Cleveland 1945–1953; president of the National Conference of Mayors in 1953; delegate to the Democratic National Conventions in 1952, 1956, and 1960; appointed as a Democrat to the United States Senate October 12, 1953, to fill the vacancy caused by the death of Robert A. Taft and served from November 10, 1953, to December 2, 1954; unsuccessful candidate for election in 1954 to the vacancy; engaged in the practice of law; is a resident of Cleveland, Ohio.

BURKE, Thomas Henry, a Representative from Ohio; born in Toledo, Lucas County, Ohio, May 6, 1904; attended St. Patrick's grade school and St. John's College in Toledo, Ohio; served in the United States Navy as pharmacist's mate 1923–1927 and in the Naval Fleet Reserve 1927–1939; worked for Dana Corp., Toledo, Ohio, 1928–1937; official of United Automobile Workers Union 1938–1948; member of the Ohio State House of Representatives in 1941 and 1942; member of Toledo city council 1944–1948; vice mayor of Toledo in 1948; elected as a Democrat to the Eighty-first Congress (January 3, 1949–January 3, 1951); unsuccessful candidate for reelection in 1950 to the Eighty-second Congress; labor and manpower adviser in the National Production Authority in 1951; unsuccessful candidate for election in 1952 to the Eighty-third Congress; moved to Alexandria, Va.; legislative representative, United Automobile Workers' Union; died in Arlington, Va., September 12, 1959; interment in Arlington National Cemetery, Fort Myer, Va.

BURKE, William Joseph, a Representative from Pennsylvania; born near London, England, September 25, 1862; immigrated to the United States in 1866 with his parents, who settled in Reynoldsville, Jefferson County, Pa., attended the public schools employed in the coal mines at the age of twelve; entered the railroad service in 1878 as a brakeman and was later promoted to passenger conductor with residence in Pittsburgh, Pa.; was a member of the Allegheny Common Council for four years, and from 1906 to 1910 was a member of the greater city council of Pittsburgh; became extensively interested in the production of oil near Callery, Butler County, in 1904; identified with organized labor as chairman of the general committee of adjustment, Order of Railroad Conductors, of the Baltimore & Ohio Railroad system; elected a member of the State senate in 1914 and served until January 1, 1918, when he resigned to become a member of the Pittsburgh City Council, serving until January 1919, when he resigned, having been elected to Congress; elected as a Republican to the Sixty-sixth and Sixty-seventh Congresses (March 4, 1919–March 3, 1923); did not seek renomination, but became a candidate for the Republican nomination as United States Senator; unsuccessful candidate for election as United States Senator in 1922; resumed activities with organized labor and served as chairman of the general committee of the Brotherhood of Railroad Conductors; also engaged in agricultural pursuits and in the production of oil; died at his summer home in Callery Junction, Butler County, near Pittsburgh, Pa., November 7, 1925; interment in Calvary Cemetery, Pittsburgh, Pa.

BURKETT, Elmer Jacob, a Representative and a Senator from Nebraska; born on a farm near Glenwood, Mills County, Iowa, December 1, 1867; attended the public schools; was graduated from Tabor (Iowa) College in 1890 and from the law department of the University of Nebraska at Lincoln in 1893; principal of the Leigh, Nebr., public schools 1890–1892; was admitted to the bar in 1893 and commenced practice in Lincoln, Nebr.; trustee of Tabor College 1895–1905; member of the State house of representatives 1896–1898; elected as a Republican to the Fifty-sixth, Fifty-seventh, and Fifty-eighth Congresses (March 4, 1899–March 3, 1905); had been reelected to the Fifty-ninth Congress, but resigned, effective March 4, 1905, to become Senator; elected to the United States Senate and served from March 4, 1905, to March 3, 1911; unsuccessful candidate for renomination in 1910; delegate to the Republican National Conventions in 1908 and 1912; resumed the practice of law in Lincoln, Nebr.; declined the candidacy for Governor of Nebraska in 1912; was an unsuccessful candidate for the Vice Presidential nomination in 1912; died in Lincoln, Nebr., May 23, 1935; interment in the Wyuka Cemetery.

BURLEIGH, Edwin Chick, a Representative and a Senator from Maine; born in Linneus, Aroostook County, Maine, November 27, 1843; attended the common schools and was graduated from the Houlton (Maine) Academy; taught school; clerk in the adjutant general's office; engaged in surveying; clerk in the State land office at Bangor 1870–1876; moved to Augusta in 1876; State land agent 1876–1878; assistant clerk in the State house of representatives in 1878; clerk in the office of the State treasurer 1880–1884; State treasurer 1884–1888; became principal owner of the Kennebec Journal in 1887; Governor of Maine 1889–1892; delegate to the Republican National Convention at St. Louis in 1896; elected as a Republican to the Fifty-fifth Congress to fill the vacancy caused by the death of Seth L. Milliken; reelected to the Fifty-sixth and to the five succeeding Congresses and served from June 21, 1897, to March 3, 1911; unsuccessful candidate for reelection in 1910; resumed newspaper publishing in Augusta, Maine, and the management of timberlands; elected to the United States Senate and served from March 4, 1913, until his death in Augusta, Maine, June 16, 1916; interment in Forest Grove Cemetery.

BURLEIGH, Henry Gordon, a Representative from New York; born in Canaan, Grafton County, N. H., June 2, 1832; attended the common schools; moved to New York in 1846 with his parents, who settled in Ticonderoga, Essex County;

engaged in the mining of iron ore and in the lumber, coal, and transportation business; supervisor of the town of Ticonderoga in 1864 and 1865; moved to Whitehall, Washington County, N. Y., in 1867; member of the State assembly in 1876; delegate to the Republican National Conventions in 1880, 1884, 1888, 1892, and 1896; elected as a Republican to the Forty-eighth and Forty-ninth Congresses (March 4, 1883–March 3, 1887); unsuccessful candidate for reelection in 1886 to the Fiftieth Congress; died in Whitehall, N. Y., August 10, 1900; interment in Mount Hope Cemetery, Ticonderoga, N. Y.

BURLEIGH, John Holmes (son of William Burleigh), a Representative from Maine; born in South Berwick, York County, Maine, October 9, 1822; attended the local academy; became a sailor when sixteen years of age and commanded a ship on foreign voyages from 1846 until 1853 when he engaged in woolen manufacturing at South Berwick, Maine; also engaged in banking; member of the State house of representatives in 1862, 1864, 1866, and again in 1872; delegate to the Republican National Convention at Baltimore in 1864; elected as a Republican to the Forty-third and Forty-fourth Congresses (March 4, 1873–March 3, 1877); was an unsuccessful candidate for renomination in 1876; resumed his former manufacturing pursuits; died in South Berwick, Maine, December 5, 1877; interment in the Portland Street Cemetery.

BURLEIGH, Walter Atwood, a Delegate from the Territory of Dakota; born in Waterville, Maine, October 25, 1820; attended the public schools; served as a private in the Aroostook War in 1839; studied medicine in Burlington, Vt., and New York City, and commenced practice in Richmond, Maine; moved to Kittanning, Pa., in 1852; continued the practice of medicine and studied law; declined a foreign mission tendered by President Lincoln in 1861; Indian agent at Greenwood, Dak., 1861–1865; elected as a Republican to the Thirty-ninth and Fortieth Congresses (March 4, 1865–March 3, 1869); unsuccessful candidate for reelection in 1868 to the Forty-first Congress; member of the Dakota Territorial Council in 1877; engaged as a contractor and in agricultural pursuits; moved to Miles City, Mont., in 1879 and practiced law; member of the special session of the Montana Territorial Council in 1887; delegate to the State convention that framed the constitution of Montana in 1889; member of the first State house of representatives; prosecuting attorney of Custer County in 1889 and 1890; returned to South Dakota in 1893; served in the State senate in 1893; resumed the practice of law; died in Yankton, Yankton County, S Dak., March 7, 1896; interment in Yankton Cemetery.

BURLEIGH, William (father of John Holmes Burleigh), a Representative from Maine; born in Northwood, Rockingham County, N. H., October 24, 1785; moved with his parents to Gilmanton, N. H., in 1788; attended the common schools and taught for several years; studied law; was admitted to the bar in 1815 and commenced practice in South Berwick, Maine; elected as an Adams Democrat to the Eighteenth, Nineteenth, and Twentieth Congresses and served from March 4, 1823, until his death in South Berwick, York County, Maine, July 2, 1827; interment in Portland Street Cemetery.

BURLESON, Albert Sidney, a Representative from Texas; born in San Marcos, Hays County, Tex., June 7, 1863; attended the public schools and Coronal Institute, San Marcos, Tex., and the Agricultural and Mechanical College, College Station, Tex.; was graduated from Baylor University, Waco, Tex., in 1881 and from the law department of the University of Texas at Austin in 1884; was admitted to the bar in 1884 and commenced practice in Austin, Travis County, Tex., in 1885; assistant city attorney of Austin 1885–1890; served as district attorney of the twenty-sixth judicial district 1891–1898; elected as a Democrat to the Fifty-sixth and to the seven succeeding Congresses and served from March 4, 1899, until March 6, 1913, when he resigned to accept a Cabinet portfolio; appointed Postmaster General in the Cabinet of President Wilson and served from March 7, 1913, to March 4, 1921, when he retired from public life; chairman of the United States Telegraph and Telephone Administration in 1918; chairman of the United States Commission to the International Wire Communication Conference in 1920; returned to Austin, Tex., and engaged in banking; also interested in agricultural pursuits and the raising of livestock; died in Austin, Tex., November 24, 1937; interment in Oakwood Cemetery.

BURLESON, Omar Truman, a Representative from Texas; born in Anson, Jones County, Tex., March 19, 1906; attended the public schools, Abilene Christian College, and Hardin-Simmons University at Abilene, Tex.; was graduated from Cumberland University, Lebanon, Tenn., in 1929; was admitted to the bar the same year and commenced practice in Gorman, Tex.; county attorney of Jones County, Tex., 1931–1934; judge of Jones County, Tex., 1934–1940; special agent of the Federal Bureau of Investigation in 1940 and 1941; secretary to Congressman Sam Russell of Texas in 1941 and 1942; general counsel for the Housing Authority, District of Columbia, in 1942; during World War II served in the United States Navy from December 1942 to April 1946, with service in the South Pacific Theater; member of the board of trustees of Abilene Christian College since 1939; elected as a Democrat to the Eightieth and to the six succeeding Congresses (January 3, 1947–January 3, 1961). *Reelected to the Eighty-seventh Congress.*

BURLINGAME, Anson, a Representative from Massachusetts; born in New Berlin, N. Y., November 14, 1820; moved with his parents to Seneca County, Ohio, in 1823, and to Detroit, Mich., in 1833; attended private schools and the Detroit branch of the University of Michigan; was graduated from the law department of Harvard University in 1846; was admitted to the bar and commenced practice in Boston; served in the State senate in 1852; member of the Massachusetts constitutional convention in 1853; elected as a candidate of the American Party to the Thirty-fourth and Thirty-fifth Congresses (March 4, 1855–March 3, 1859); reelected as a Republican to the Thirty-sixth Congress (March 4, 1859–March 3, 1861); unsuccessful candidate for reelection in 1860 to the Thirty-seventh Congress; appointed Minister to Austria March 22, 1861, but was not accepted by the Austrian Government because of certain opinions he was known to entertain regarding Hungary and Sardinia; Minister to China from June 14, 1861, to November 21, 1867; appointed December 1, 1867, by the Chinese Government its ambassador to negotiate treaties with foreign powers; died in St. Petersburg, Russia, February 23, 1870; interment in Mount Auburn Cemetery, Cambridge, Mass.

BURNELL, Barker, a Representative from Massachusetts; born in Nantucket, Mass., January 30, 1798; member of the State house of representatives in 1819; member of the Massachusetts constitutional convention in 1820; served in the State senate in 1824 and 1825; delegate to the Whig National Convention at Harrisburg, Pa., in 1840; elected as a Whig to the Twenty-seventh and Twenty-eighth Congresses and served from March 4, 1841, until his death in Washington, D. C., June 15, 1843; interment in Congressional Cemetery; reinterment in Prospect Hill Cemetery, Nantucket, Mass., in 1844.

BURNES, Daniel Dee, a Representative from Missouri; born in Ringgold, Platte County, Mo., January 4, 1851; received his early schooling at Weston, Mo.; was graduated from St. Louis University, St. Louis, Mo., in 1873 and from the law department of Harvard University in 1874; went to Germany and studied at Heidelberg University; returned to the United States and settled in St. Joseph, Mo., where he engaged in the practice of law; elected as a Democrat to the Fifty-third Congress (March 4, 1893–March 3, 1895); declined to be a candidate for reelection in 1894; resumed the practice of law; died on his estate, "Ayr Lawn," at St. Joseph, Buchanan County, Mo., November 2, 1899; interment in Mount Mora Cemetery.

BURNES, James Nelson, a Representative from Missouri; born in Marion County, Ind., August 22, 1827; moved with his parents to Platte County, Mo., in 1837; attended the common schools; was graduated from the Harvard Law School in 1853; was admitted to the bar and commenced practice in Missouri; attorney of the district of Missouri in 1856; presidential elector on the Democratic ticket of Buchanan and Breckinridge in 1856; judge of the court of common pleas 1868–1872; engaged in banking and the construction of railroads; served as president of the Missouri Valley Railroad Co.; principal owner and president of the St. Joseph Waterworks Co.; elected as a Democrat to the Forty-eighth, Forty-ninth, and Fiftieth Congresses and served from March 4, 1883, until his death; had been reelected to the Fifty-first Congress, but died before the commencement of the congressional term in Washington, D. C., on January 23, 1889; interment in Mount Mora Cemetery, St. Joseph, Buchanan County, Mo.

BURNET, Jacob (son of William Burnet), a Senator from Ohio; born in Newark, N. J., February 22, 1770; pursued preparatory studies; was graduated from Princeton College in 1791; studied law; was admitted to the bar in 1796 and commenced practice in Cincinnati, Ohio; one of three judges appointed to hold court in Cincinnati, Vincennes, and Detroit; member of the Territorial councils of Ohio 1799–1802; member of the State house of representatives in 1812 and 1813; appointed judge of the Ohio Supreme Court in 1821 and served until his resignation in December 1828; elected as a Federalist to the United States Senate to fill the vacancy caused by the resignation of William H. Harrison and served from December 10, 1828, to March 3, 1831; was not a candidate for renomination in 1831; member of the commission appointed in 1831 by the States of Virginia and Kentucky to settle their controversy over the statute of limitation passed by Kentucky; resumed the practice of law; president of the Cincinnati College and the Medical College of Ohio; president of the Cincinnati branch of the United States Bank; died in Cincinnati, Ohio, on May 10, 1853; interment in Spring Grove Cemetery.

BURNET, William (father of Jacob Burnet), a Delegate from New Jersey; born in Newark, N. J., December 2, 1730; was graduated from Princeton College in 1749; studied medicine in New York and commenced practice in Newark; chairman of the committee of public safety in Newark in 1775; superintendent of a military hospital in Newark in 1775; surgeon general of the eastern district of the United States 1776–1783; returned to Newark and engaged in agricultural pursuits; appointed presiding judge of the court of common pleas by the State legislature in 1776; Member of the Continental Congress from December 11, 1780, to April 1, 1781, when he resigned; first judge of Essex County in 1781; president of the State medical society in 1787; died in Newark, N. J., October 7, 1791; interment in the First Presbyterian Churchyard.

BURNETT, Edward, a Representative from Massachusetts; born in Boston, Mass., March 16, 1849; attended St. Paul's School; was graduated from St. Mark's School, Southboro, Mass., in 1867 and from Harvard University in 1871; engaged in agricultural pursuits near Southboro, Mass.; elected as a Democrat to the Fiftieth Congress (March 4, 1887–March 3, 1889); unsuccessful candidate for reelection in 1888 to the Fifty-first Congress; general manager of Flosham Farms, Madison, N. J., 1892–1900; became engaged as a farm architect in New York City from 1900 to 1925, when he retired from active pursuits; died in Milton, Mass., November 5, 1925; interment in St. Mark's Churchyard, Southboro, Worcester County, Mass.

BURNETT, Henry Cornelius, a Representative from Kentucky; born in Essex County, Va., October 5, 1825; moved with his parents to Kentucky in early childhood; attended the common schools and an academy at Hopkinsville; studied law; was admitted to the bar in 1847 and commenced practice in Cadiz, Ky.; clerk of the Trigg County circuit court 1851–1853; elected as a Democrat to the Thirty-fourth and to the three succeeding Congresses and served from March 4, 1855, to December 3, 1861, when he was expelled; colonel of the Eighth Regiment, Kentucky Infantry, in the Confederate Army during the Civil War; president of the Kentucky Southern Conference in Russellville October 29, 1861, and of the sovereignty convention in Russellville, November 18, which passed an ordinance of secession and organized a State government; representative from Kentucky to the Provisional Confederate Congress and served from November 18, 1861, to February 17, 1862; elected as a Senator from Kentucky to the First and Second Confederate Congresses and served from February 19, 1862, to February 18, 1865; resumed the practice of law; died in Hopkinsville, Christian County, Ky., October 1, 1866; interment in East End Cemetery, Cadiz, Trigg County, Ky.

BURNETT, John Lawson, a Representative from Alabama; born in Cedar Bluff, Cherokee County, Ala., January 20, 1854; attended the common schools of the county, Wesleyan Institute, Cave Spring, Ga., and the local high school at Gaylesville, Ala.; studied law and was graduated from Vanderbilt University, Nashville, Tenn.; was admitted to the bar in Cherokee County, Ala., in 1876 and commenced practice in Gadsden; served in the State house of representatives in 1884; member of the State senate in 1886; elected as a Democrat to the Fifty-sixth and to the ten succeeding Congresses and served from March 4, 1899, until his death; member of the United States Immigration Commission 1907–1910; died in Gadsden, Etowah County, Ala., May 13, 1919; interment in Forest Cemetery.

BURNEY, William Evans, a Representative from Colorado; born in Hubbard, Hill County, Tex., September 11, 1893; attended the public schools in Texas and the University of New Mexico at Albuquerque; during the First World War served in the United States Navy as a torpedoman with service on the destroyer U. S. S. *McKee;* moved to Pueblo, Colo., in 1924 and engaged in the life insurance business until 1942; member of the Pueblo Board of Education 1937–1943; member of the United States Army Reserve Corps 1924–1942, serving in all grades up to major; elected as a Democrat to the Seventy-sixth Congress to fill the vacancy caused by the death of John A. Martin and served from November 5, 1940, to January 3, 1941; was not a candidate for election to the full term in the Seventy-seventh Congress; was called to active duty in the Army as a major in January 1942 and was promoted to the rank of lieutenant colonel in October 1942; commanding officer of the Three Hundred and Seventy-third, Three Hundred and Eighty-fifth, and Five Hundred and Third Port Battalions at various times; participated in the New Guinea campaign; organized and commanded basic military and technical training units at Camp Stoneman, Pittsburg, Calif.; served as commanding officer of troops aboard the U. S. S. *Republic* and the U. S. S. *Admiral Benson;* returned to the United States from India and took command of Camp Ross in May 1945; requested inactive duty on point system in December 1945 with the rank of colonel; resumed the life insurance business until his retirement; is a resident of Denver, Colo.

BURNHAM, Alfred Avery, a Representative from Connecticut; born in Windham, Windham County, Conn., on March 8, 1819; completed a preparatory course and attended college one year; studied law; was admitted to the bar in 1843 and commenced practice in Windham; member of the State house of representatives in 1844, 1845, 1850, and 1858, serving as speaker in 1858; clerk of the State senate in 1847; Lieutenant Governor in 1857; elected as a Republican to the Thirty-sixth and Thirty-seventh Congresses (March 4, 1859–March 3, 1863); was not a candidate for renomination in 1862; again a member of the State house of representatives in 1870 and served as speaker; died in Windham, Conn., April 11, 1879; interment in Windham Cemetery, Windham Center, Conn.

BURNHAM, George, a Representative from California; born in London, England, December 28, 1868; attended the public schools; immigrated in 1881 to the United States with his parents, who settled in Spring Valley, Minn.; employed as a clerk 1884–1886; moved to Jackson, Minn., in 1887 and engaged in the retail shoe business until 1901, when he moved to Spokane, Wash., and engaged in the real-estate business and in ranching; moved to San Diego, Calif., in 1903 and continued in the real-estate business until 1917 when he took up banking; one of the organizers of the Panama-California Exposition in 1909, serving as vice president from 1909 to 1916; member of the Honorary Commercial Commission to China in 1910; member of the San Diego Library Commission 1926–1932 and of the San Diego Scientific Library 1926–1932; elected as a Republican to the Seventy-third and Seventy-fourth Congresses (March 4, 1933–January 3, 1937); was not a candidate for renomination in 1936; vice president of the California-Pacific International Exposition 1935–1936; retired from active pursuits and resided in San Diego, Calif., until his death there on June 28, 1939; interment in Greenwood Cathedral Mausoleum, Greenwood Memorial Park.

BURNHAM, Henry Eben, a Senator from New Hampshire; born in Dunbarton, Merrimack County, N. H., November 8, 1844; attended the public schools; prepared for college at Kimball Union Academy and was graduated from Dartmouth College, Hanover, N. H., in 1865; studied law; was admitted to the bar in 1868 and commenced practice in Manchester; president of the Mechanics Savings Bank and a member of the board of directors of the Amoskeag National Bank and the New Hampshire Fire Insurance Co., Manchester; member of the State house of representatives in 1873 and 1874; treasurer of Hillsboro County 1875–1877; judge of probate for Hillsboro County 1876–1879; member of the constitutional convention of 1889; chairman of the Republican State convention in 1888; served as ballot-law commissioner 1892–1900; elected as a Republican to the United States Senate in 1901; reelected in 1907 and served from March 4, 1901, to March 3, 1913; was not a candidate for reelection; resumed the practice of law; died in Manchester, N. H., February 8, 1917; interment in Pine Grove Cemetery.

BURNS, John Anthony, a Delegate from the Territory of Hawaii; born in Fort Assinneboine, Mont., March 30, 1909; resident of Hawaii since May 30, 1913; attended school in

Honolulu and Kansas; graduated from St. Louis High School in Honolulu; attended the University of Hawaii in 1930 and 1931; police officer, city and county of Honolulu, 1934–1945; chairman, Traffic Safety Commission, city and county of Honolulu, 1950–1954; president of Burns & Co., Ltd., real-estate broker; Honolulu Civil Defense Administrator 1951–1955; delegate to the Democratic National Conventions in 1952 and 1956; chairman of Honolulu County Democratic Committee 1948–1952; chairman of Territorial Democratic Central Committee 1952–1956; elected as a Democrat a Delegate to the Eighty-fifth and Eighty-sixth Congresses and served from January 3, 1957, to August 21, 1959, when Hawaii became a State in the Union; unsuccessful candidate for election as Governor of the State of Hawaii in 1959; real-estate broker; resides in Kailua, city and county of Honolulu, Hawaii.

BURNS, Joseph, a Representative from Ohio; born in Waynesboro, Augusta County, Va., March 11, 1800; moved to Ohio with his parents, who settled in New Philadelphia in 1815, and near Coshocton, Coshocton County, in 1816; attended the rural schools; engaged in agricultural pursuits; auditor of Coshocton County 1821–1838; member of the State house of representatives 1838–1840; county clerk 1843–1851; served as a major general in the State militia; elected as a Democrat to the Thirty-fifth Congress (March 4, 1857–March 3, 1859); unsuccessful candidate for reelection in 1858 to the Thirty-sixth Congress; engaged in the drug business in Coshocton, Ohio; probate judge of Coshocton County; died in Coshocton, Ohio, May 12, 1875; interment in Oak Ridge Cemetery.

BURNS, Robert, a Representative from New Hampshire; born in Hudson, Hillsboro County, N. H., December 12, 1792; moved with his parents in childhood to Rumney, Grafton County; studied medicine in Warren; taught school; attended Dartmouth Medical School in 1815; returned to Warren and commenced the practice of medicine; moved to Hebron, Grafton County, in 1818 and continued the practice of his profession until 1835; fellow of the New Hampshire Medical Society in 1824; member of the State senate in 1831; elected as a Democrat to the Twenty-third and Twenty-fourth Congresses (March 4, 1833–March 3, 1837); continued the practice of medicine in Plymouth, N. H., until his death June 26, 1866; interment in the churchyard of Trinity Church, Holderness, Grafton County, N. H.

BURNSIDE, Ambrose Everett, a Senator from Rhode Island; born in Liberty, Ind., May 23, 1824; attended a seminary at Liberty and Beach Grove Academy; was graduated from the United States Military Academy at West Point in 1847; served in the Mexican and Indian wars; resigned in 1852 to manufacture a breech-loading rifle of his own invention; moved to Illinois, and was appointed treasurer of the Illinois Central Railroad in 1858; during the Civil War entered the Union Army May 2, 1861, as colonel of the First Regiment, Rhode Island Volunteer Infantry; commanded a brigade at the first Battle of Bull Run; honorably mustered out August 2, 1861; commissioned brigadier general of Volunteers August 6, 1861; major general March 18, 1862; commanded successively the expedition to North Carolina in 1862, the left wing of the Union Army at Antietam, the Army of the Potomac, and the Ninth Army Corps; received the thanks of Congress for himself and the officers and men who fought under his command for "gallantry, good conduct, and soldierlike endurance" by resolution of January 28, 1864; resigned April 15, 1865; Governor of Rhode Island 1866–1868; visited Europe in 1870 and was admitted within the German and French lines in and around Paris; acted as a medium of communication between the hostile nations in the interests of conciliation; elected as a

Republican to the United States Senate in 1874; reelected in 1880 and served from March 4, 1875, until his death in Bristol, R. I., September 13, 1881; interment in Swan Point Cemetery, Providence, R. I.

BURNSIDE, Maurice Gwinn, a Representative from West Virginia; born near Columbia, Richland County, S. C., August 23, 1902; attended the public schools of South Carolina; student at The Citadel, Charleston, S. C., 1920–1922; studied law at Furman University, Greenville, S. C., graduating in 1926; graduated from the University of Texas at Austin in 1928; studied and traveled in Europe and Asia 1928–1931; instructor in Greenville (S. C.) High School in 1931 and 1932; purchaser of rare documents for Duke University Library, Durham, N. C., 1933–1935; instructor in Alabama Polytechnic Institute at Auburn in 1936 and 1937; professor of political science at Marshall College, Huntington, W. Va., 1937–1948; member of Parole and Probation Examination Board of West Virginia 1939–1941; chairman of Workers Education for West Virginia 1943–1945; regional coordinator of Inter-American Affairs for West Virginia, eastern and southern Ohio, and eastern Kentucky; elected as a Democrat to the Eighty-first and Eighty-second Congresses (January 3, 1949–January 3, 1953); unsuccessful candidate for reelection in 1952 to the Eighty-third Congress; with the National Security Agency, Washington, D. C., from February 20 to March 27, 1953; elected to the Eighty-fourth Congress (January 3, 1955–January 3, 1957); unsuccessful candidate for election in 1956 to the Eighty-fifth Congress; president of Tri-State Tobacco Warehouse, Inc., since 1957; legislative representative in Washington, D. C., for National Education Association since 1959; delegate to the Democratic National Convention in 1960; resides in Alexandria, Va.

BURNSIDE, Thomas, a Representative from Pennsylvania; born near Newton Stewart, County Tyrone, Ireland, July 28, 1782; immigrated to the United States with his father's family, who settled in Norristown, Montgomery County, Pa., in 1793; studied law; was admitted to the bar in 1804 and commenced practice in Bellefonte; appointed deputy attorney general January 12, 1809; served in the State senate in 1811 and 1812; elected to the Fourteenth Congress to fill the vacancy caused by the death of David Bard and served from October 10, 1815, to April 1816, when he resigned; appointed president judge of the Luzerne district courts in 1815, and resigned in 1819; again a member of the State senate and its presiding officer in 1823; president judge of the fourth judicial district 1826–1841 and later presided in the same capacity over the seventh judicial district; appointed an associate justice of the supreme court of Pennsylvania in 1845, which office he held until his death in Germantown, Pa., March 25, 1851; interment in Union Cemetery, Bellefonte, Centre County, Pa.

BURR, Aaron (cousin of Theodore Dwight), a Senator from New York and a Vice President of the United States; born in Newark, N. J., February 6, 1756; was graduated from Princeton College in 1772; studied theology in Litchfield, Conn., in 1773; but soon abandoned it for the law; during the Revolutionary War entered the Continental Army in 1775; distinguished himself at Quebec, Monmouth, and New Haven, and resigned March 10, 1779, owing to ill health; studied law; was admitted to the bar April 17, 1782, and practiced in Albany, N. Y.; moved to New York City in 1783; member of the State assembly 1784, 1785, 1798, and 1799; attorney general of New York in 1789 and 1790; commissioner on Revolutionary claims in 1791; elected as a Democrat to the United States Senate and served from March 4, 1791, to March 3, 1797; unsuccessful candidate for reelection; president of the State constitutional convention in 1801; at the presidential election of 1801 Burr and Jefferson each had seventy-three votes, and the House of Representatives on the thirty-sixth ballot elected Jefferson President and Burr Vice President; unsuccessful candidate for Governor in 1804; challenged and mortally wounded Alexander Hamilton in a duel fought at Weehawken, N. J., July 11, 1804, the result of charges made by Hamilton in the gubernatorial election; the coroner's jury returned a verdict of murder, and he escaped to South Carolina; returned to Washington and completed his term of service as Vice President; arrested and tried for treason in August 1807 for attempting to form a republic in the Southwest of which he was to be the head, but was acquitted; went abroad in 1808; returned to New York City in 1812 and resumed the practice of law; died in Port Richmond, Staten Island, N. Y., September 14, 1836; interment in the President's lot, Princeton Cemetery, Princeton, N. J.

BURR, Albert George, a Representative from Illinois; born near Batavia, Genesee County, N. Y., November 8, 1829; moved to Illinois with his mother, who settled near Springfield, Sangamon County, in 1830; completed preparatory studies; taught school for several years at Vandalia, Ill.; moved to Winchester, Scott County, in 1850 and engaged in mercantile pursuits; studied law; was admitted to the bar in 1856 and commenced practice in Winchester; member of the State house of representatives 1861–1864; moved to Carrollton, Greene County, in 1868 and continued the practice of law; member of the State constitutional convention in 1870; elected as a Democrat to the Fortieth and Forty-first Congresses (March 4, 1867–March 3, 1871); was not a candidate for renomination in 1870; resumed the practice of law in Carrollton, Ill.; elected circuit judge of the seventh judicial circuit in 1877 and served until his death; died in Carrollton, Ill., June 10, 1882; interment in the Carrollton Cemetery.

BURRELL, Orlando, a Representative from Illinois; born in Newton, Bradford County, Pa., July 26, 1826; moved with his parents to White County, Ill., in 1834; attended the common schools; engaged in agricultural pursuits; during the Civil War raised a company of Cavalry in June 1861, was elected its captain, and was attached to the First Regiment, Illinois Volunteer Cavalry; judge of White County 1873–1881; sheriff of White County 1892–1894; delegate to the Republican National Convention at Minneapolis in 1892; elected as a Republican to the Fifty-fourth Congress (March 4, 1895–March 3, 1897); unsuccessful candidate for reelection in 1896 to the Fifty-fifth Congress; retired from public life and resumed his agricultural pursuits; died in Carmi, White County, Ill., June 7, 1922; interment in Maple Ridge Cemetery.

BURRILL, James, Jr. (great-grandfather of Theodore Francis Green), a Senator from Rhode Island; born in Providence, R. I., April 25, 1772; was graduated from Brown University at Providence in 1788; studied law; was admitted to the bar in 1791 and commenced practice in Providence; attorney general of Rhode Island 1797–1814; member of the State house of representatives 1813–1816 and served as speaker 1814–1816; chief justice of the State supreme court in 1816; elected to the United States Senate and served from March 4, 1817, until his death in Washington, D. C., December 25, 1820; interment in Congressional Cemetery.

BURROUGHS, Sherman Everett, a Representative from New Hampshire; born in Dunbarton, Merrimack County, N. H., February 6, 1870; attended the public schools, and was graduated from Dartmouth College, Hanover, N. H., in 1894; private

secretary to Henry M. Baker, Member of Congress from the second New Hampshire district 1894–1897; was graduated from the law school of Columbian College (now George Washington University), Washington, D. C., in 1896; was admitted to the bar in 1896 and commenced practice in Manchester, N. H., in 1897; member of the State house of representatives in 1901 and 1902; member of the State board of charities and corrections 1901–1907; member of the State board of equalization in 1909 and 1910; elected as a Republican to the Sixty-fifth Congress on May 29, 1917, to fill the vacancy caused by the death of Cyrus A. Sulloway; reelected to the Sixty-sixth and Sixty-seventh Congresses and served from June 7, 1917, until his death; declined to be a candidate for reelection in 1922 to the Sixty-eighth Congress; died in Washington, D. C., January 27, 1923; interment in Valley Cemetery, Manchester, N. H.

BURROUGHS, Silas Mainville, a Representative from New York; born in Ovid, N. Y., July 16, 1810; completed a preparatory course; village clerk of Medina, Orleans County, N. Y., in 1835; village trustee in 1836 and 1839–1843; studied law; was admitted to the bar in Orleans County in 1840 and commenced practice in Medina; again trustee of Medina 1845–1847; village attorney 1845–1847; served as brigadier general in the New York State Militia 1848–1858; member of the State assembly in 1837, 1850, 1851, and 1853; elected as a Republican to the Thirty-fifth and Thirty-sixth Congresses and served from March 4, 1857, until his death in Medina, N. Y., June 3, 1860; interment in Boxwood Cemetery.

BURROWS, Daniel (uncle of Lorenzo Burrows), a Representative from Connecticut; born at Fort Hill, Groton, Conn., October 26, 1766; pursued preparatory studies; engaged in the manufacture of carriages and wagons at New London, Conn.; studied theology; was ordained as a minister of the Methodist Church; member of the State house of representatives 1816–1820 and in 1826; delegate to the State constitutional convention in 1818; one of the commissioners to establish the boundary line between the States of Connecticut and Massachusetts; elected as a Democrat to the Seventeenth Congress (March 4, 1821–March 3, 1823); was not a candidate for renomination in 1822; resident of Middletown, Conn., 1823–1854; surveyor and inspector of customs for the port of Middletown 1823–1847; died in Mystic, New London County, Conn., January 23, 1858; interment in Elm Grove Cemetery.

BURROWS, Joseph Henry, a Representative from Missouri; born in Manchester, England, May 15, 1840; immigrated to the United States with his parents, who settled in Quincy, Ill.; attended the common schools at Quincy, Ill., and Keokuk, Iowa; engaged in mercantile pursuits and later in agricultural pursuits; moved to Cainsville, Harrison County, Mo., in 1862; was ordained as a minister in Cainsville in 1867; member of the State house of representatives 1870–1874 and 1878–1880; elected as a Greenbacker to the Forty-seventh Congress (March 4, 1881–March 3, 1883); unsuccessful candidate for reelection in 1882 to the Forty-eighth Congress; resumed ministerial duties and also engaged in agricultural pursuits; died in Cainsville, Mo., April 28, 1914; interment in Oak Lawn Cemetery, near Cainsville.

BURROWS, Julius Caesar, a Representative and a Senator from Michigan; born in North East, Erie County, Pa., January 9, 1837; moved with his parents while a youth to Ashtabula County, Ohio; attended district school, Kingsville Academy, and Grand River Institute, Austinburg, Ohio; studied law; was admitted to the bar at Jefferson, Ohio, in 1859; moved to Richland, Kalamazoo County, Mich., in 1860, and was principal of the Richland Seminary one year; commenced the practice of law in Kalamazoo in 1861; raised a company for the Seventeenth Regiment, Michigan Volunteer Infantry, in 1862; served as its captain until the fall of 1863, and participated in the engagements at South Mountain, Antietam, Fredericksburg, Vicksburg, Jackson, and Knoxville; elected circuit court commissioner in 1864; prosecuting attorney for Kalamazoo County 1866–1870; declined appointment as supervisor of internal revenue for Michigan and Wisconsin in 1868; elected as a Republican to the Forty-third Congress (March 4, 1873–March 3, 1875); unsuccessful candidate for reelection in 1874 to the Forty-fourth Congress; elected to the Forty-sixth and Forty-seventh Congresses (March 4, 1879–March 3, 1883); unsuccessful candidate for reelection in 1882 to the Forty-eighth Congress; delegate at large to the Republican National Convention at Chicago in 1884; tendered appointment as Solicitor of the Treasury by President Arthur in 1884, which he declined; elected to the Forty-ninth and to the five succeeding Congresses and served from March 4, 1885, until his resignation on January 23, 1895, before the close of the Fifty-third Congress, having been elected Senator; was twice appointed Speaker pro tempore in the Fifty-first Congress; elected to the United States Senate to fill the vacancy caused by the death of Francis B. Stockbridge; reelected in 1899 and 1905 and served from January 24, 1895, to March 3, 1911; unsuccessful candidate for renomination; was delegate at large and temporary chairman of the Republican National Convention at Chicago in 1908; member of the National Monetary Commission and its vice chairman during its existence from May 30, 1908, to March 31, 1912; retired from active business pursuits and political life; died in Kalamazoo, Mich., November 16, 1915; interment in Mountain Home Cemetery.

BURROWS, Lorenzo (nephew of Daniel Burrows), a Representative from New York; born in Groton, Conn., March 15, 1805; attended the academies at Plainfield, Conn., and Westerly, R. I.; moved to New York and settled in Albion, Orleans County, in 1824; employed as a clerk until 1826, when he engaged in mercantile pursuits; assisted in establishing the Bank of Albion in 1839, and served as cashier; treasurer of Orleans County in 1840; assignee in bankruptcy for Orleans County in 1841; presidential elector on the Whig ticket of Clay and Frelinghuysen in 1844; supervisor of the town of Barre in 1845; elected as a Whig to the Thirty-first and Thirty-second Congresses (March 4, 1849–March 3, 1853); comptroller of the State of New York 1855–1857; director and president of the Niagara Falls International Bridge Co.; chosen a regent of the University of New York in 1858 and appointed one of the commissioners of Mount Albion Cemetery in 1862, serving in both of these capacities at the time of his death in Albion, Orleans County, N. Y., March 6, 1885; interment in Mount Albion Cemetery.

BURSUM, Holm Olaf, a Senator from New Mexico; born at Fort Dodge, Webster County, Iowa, February 10, 1867; attended the public schools; moved to New Mexico in 1881; settled near Socorro, Socorro County, and engaged in stock raising; member of the Territorial senate in 1899 and 1900; delegate to the Republican National Conventions in 1904, 1908, and 1912; chairman of the Territorial central committee in 1905 and 1911; member of the State constitutional convention in 1910; member of the Republican National Committee 1920–1924; appointed, and subsequently elected, as a Republican to the United States Senate to fill the vacancy caused by the resignation of Albert B. Fall and served from March 11, 1921, to March 3, 1925; unsuccessful candidate for reelection in 1924; engaged in the newspaper business at Washington, D. C., and subsequently returned to Socorro, N. Mex., and resumed his former business interests until his death in Colorado Springs, Colo., August 7, 1953; interment in Socorro Protestant Cemetery, Socorro, N. Mex.

BURT, Armistead, a Representative from South Carolina; born at Clouds Creek, near Edgefield, Edgefield District, S. C., November 13, 1802; moved with his parents to Pendleton, S. C.; completed preparatory studies; studied law; was admitted to the bar in 1823 and practiced in Pendleton; moved to Abbeville, S. C., in 1828 and continued the practice of law; also engaged in agricultural pursuits; elected as a Democrat to the Twenty-eighth and to the four succeeding Congresses (March 4, 1843–March 3, 1853); was not a candidate for renomination in 1852; served as Speaker pro tempore of the House of Representatives during the absence of Speaker Winthrop in 1848; resumed the practice of law in Abbeville; delegate to the Democratic National Convention at New York City in 1868; died in Abbeville, Abbeville County, S. C., October 30, 1883; interment in Episcopal Cemetery.

BURTNESS, Olger Burton, a Representative from North Dakota; born on a farm near Mekinock, Grand Forks County, N. Dak., March 14, 1884; attended the country school; was graduated from the academic department of the University of North Dakota at Grand Forks in 1906 and from its law department in 1907; was admitted to the bar the same year and commenced practice in Grand Forks; prosecuting attorney of Grand Forks County 1911–1916; delegate to the Republican National Conventions in 1916, 1936, and 1948; member of the State house of representatives in 1919 and 1920; elected as a Republican to the Sixty-seventh and to the five succeeding Congresses (March 4, 1921–March 3, 1933); unsuccessful candidate for renomination in 1932; resumed the practice of law; city attorney of Grand Forks, N. Dak., in 1936 and 1937; judge of the first judicial district of North Dakota from November 1950 until his death; died in Grand Forks, N. Dak., January 20, 1960; interment in Memorial Park Cemetery.

BURTON, Charles Germman, a Representative from Missouri; born in Cleveland, Ohio, April 4, 1846; moved to Warren, Ohio, and attended the public schools; during the Civil War enlisted as a private September 7, 1861, in Company C, Nineteenth Regiment, Ohio Volunteer Infantry, and served with the regiment until discharged October 29, 1862; corporal in Company A, One Hundred and Seventy-first Regiment, Ohio National Guard, during the "one hundred days'" campaign of 1864; studied law; was admitted to the bar in Warren, Ohio, in 1867; moved to Virgil City, Mo., in 1868, to Erie, Kans., in 1869, and Nevada, Vernon County, Mo., in 1871, where he practiced law; circuit attorney and judge of the twenty-fifth circuit; delegate to the Republican National Convention at Chicago in 1884; elected as a Republican to the Fifty-fourth Congress (March 4, 1895–March 3, 1897); unsuccessful candidate for reelection in 1896 to the Fifty-fifth Congress; resumed the practice of law; delegate at large to the Republican National Convention at Chicago in 1904; collector of internal revenue at Kansas City, Mo., 1907–1915; commander in chief of the Grand Army of the Republic in 1908; died in Kansas City, Mo., February 25, 1926; interment in Deepwood Cemetery, Nevada, Mo.

BURTON, Clarence Godber, a Representative from Virginia; born in Providence, R. I., December 14, 1886; moved with his parents to Lynchburg, Campbell County, Va., at an early age; attended the public schools; was graduated from Piedmont Business College, Lynchburg, Va.; engaged in the hosiery manufacturing industry, becoming treasurer of a firm in 1907 and president in 1921; also engaged in cattle raising and banking; president of Memorial Hospital; chairman of Lynchburg Local Draft Board No. 2 1940–1943; chairman of Virginia Appeal Board No. 5 1943–1946; member of the Lynchburg School Board 1938–1943, serving as vice chairman; member of the Lynchburg City Council

1942–1948, serving as mayor 1946–1948; elected as a Democrat to the Eightieth Congress on November 2, 1948, to fill the vacancy caused by the resignation of J. Lindsay Almond, Jr., and at the same time was elected to the Eighty-first Congress; reelected to the Eighty-second Congress and served from November 2, 1948, to January 3, 1953; unsuccessful candidate for reelection in 1952 to the Eighty-third Congress; president of Lynchburg Hosiery Mills, Inc., Commercial Trust & Savings Bank, and Lynchburg Federal Savings & Loan Association; is a resident of Lynchburg, Va.

BURTON, Harold Hitz, a Senator from Ohio; born in Jamaica Plain, Mass., June 22, 1888; attended the public schools; was graduated from Bowdoin College, Brunswick, Maine, in 1909 and from the law department of Harvard University, Cambridge, Mass., in 1912; was admitted to the bar in 1912 and commenced practice in Cleveland, Ohio; assistant attorney for a power company in Salt Lake City, Utah, 1914–1916 and attorney for a power company in Boise, Idaho, in 1916 and 1917; during the First World War served overseas as lieutenant, and later as captain, in the Three Hundred and Sixty-first Infantry, Ninety-first Division, in 1917 and 1918; received the citation and the Order of the Purple Heart of the United States and the Croix de Guerre of Belgium; resumed the practice of law in Cleveland, Ohio, in 1919; instructor in Western Reserve University, Cleveland, Ohio, 1923–1925; member of the board of education of East Cleveland in 1928 and 1929; served in the State house of representatives in 1929; director of law of Cleveland 1929–1932; mayor of Cleveland 1935–1940; elected as a Republican to the United States Senate in 1940 and served from January 3, 1941, until his resignation on September 30, 1945, to become associate justice of the Supreme Court of the United States, in which capacity he served until his retirement October 13, 1958; is a legal resident of Cleveland, Ohio.

BURTON, Hiram Rodney, a Representative from Delaware; born in Lewes, Sussex County, Del., November 13, 1841; attended the public schools and St. Peter's Academy at Lewes; taught for two years in the schools of Sussex County; engaged in the dry goods business in Washington, D. C., 1862–1865; was graduated from the medical department of the University of Pennsylvania at Philadelphia in 1868 and practiced in Frankford, Del., from 1868 until 1872, when he moved to Lewes, Del.; deputy collector of customs for the port of Lewes 1877–1888; acting assistant surgeon in the United States Marine Hospital Service 1890–1893, stationed at Lewes; unsuccessful candidate for the State senate in 1898; delegate to the Republican National Conventions in 1896, 1900, and 1908; elected as a Republican to the Fifty-ninth and Sixtieth Congresses (March 4, 1905–March 3, 1909); unsuccessful candidate for renomination in 1908 to the Sixty-first Congress; resumed the practice of medicine in Lewes, Del.; director of Lewes National Bank; died in Lewes, Del., June 17, 1927; interment in St. Paul's Episcopal Churchyard, Georgetown, Sussex County, Del.

BURTON, Hutchins Gordon (nephew of Robert Burton), a Representative from North Carolina; born in Virginia in 1782; when three years of age his father died and he was sent to Granville County, where he was reared by his uncle, Col. Robert Burton; moved to Mecklenburg County, N. C., in 1803; studied law; was admitted to the bar in 1806 and practiced; member of the State house of commons in 1809; elected attorney general of North Carolina in 1810 and served until his resignation in November 1816; moved to Halifax, N. C., in 1816, and again elected a member of the State house of commons in 1817; elected as an Anti-Democrat to the Sixteenth, Seventeenth, and Eighteenth Congresses and served from December 6, 1819, until

March 23, 1824, when he resigned, having been elected Governor; Governor of North Carolina 1824–1827; resumed the practice of law in Halifax; was the host of General Lafayette when the latter visited Raleigh during his tour of the United States in 1825; died while on a visit to relatives in Iredell County, N. C., April 21, 1836; interment in Unity Churchyard, Beattys Ford, Lincoln County, N. C.

BURTON, Joseph Ralph, a Senator from Kansas; born near Mitchell, Lawrence County, Ind., November 16, 1850; attended the common schools, Franklin (Ind.) College, and De Pauw University at Greencastle; studied law; was admitted to the bar in 1875 and commenced practice in Princeton, Ind.; moved to Abilene, Dickinson County, Kans., in 1878; member of the State house of representatives 1882–1886; appointed a member of the World's Fair Columbian Commission at Chicago in 1893, representing the State of Kansas; elected as a Republican to the United States Senate and served from March 4, 1901, until June 4, 1906, when he resigned; returned to Abilene, Kans., and engaged in the newspaper business; died in Los Angeles, Calif., February 27, 1923; the remains were cremated and the ashes deposited in the columbarium of the Los Angeles Crematory Association.

BURTON, Robert (uncle of Hutchins Gordon Burton), a Delegate from North Carolina; born near Chase City, Mecklenburg County, Va., October 20, 1747; attended private schools; moved to Granville County, N. C., in 1775; engaged as a planter; served in the Revolutionary Army and as quartermaster general attained the rank of colonel; member of the Governor's council in 1783 and 1784; Member of the Continental Congress in 1787 and 1788; member of the commission to establish the boundary line between the States of North Carolina, South Carolina, and Georgia in 1801; died in Granville (now Vance) County, N. C., May 31, 1825; interment on his estate, "Montpelier," at Williamsboro (now Henderson), Vance County, N. C.

BURTON, Theodore Elijah, a Representative and a Senator from Ohio; born in Jefferson, Ashtabula County, Ohio, December 20, 1851; attended the public schools, Grand River Institute, Austinburg, Ohio, and Iowa College, Grinnell, Iowa; was graduated from Oberlin (Ohio) College in 1872; studied law; was admitted to the bar in 1875 and commenced practice in Cleveland, Ohio; elected as a Republican to the Fifty-first Congress (March 4, 1889–March 3, 1891); unsuccessful candidate for reelection in 1890 to the Fifty-second Congress; declined to be a candidate for the Republican nomination to Congress in 1892; elected to the Fifty-fourth and to the seven succeeding Congresses and served from March 4, 1895, until his resignation, effective March 3, 1909, before the beginning of the Sixty-first Congress, having been elected United States Senator; chosen a member of the American group of the Interparliamentary Union in 1904; delegate to the Republican National Conventions in 1904, 1908, 1912, and 1924; by appointment of President Theodore Roosevelt, served as chairman of the Inland Waterways Commission in 1907 and 1908 and of the National Waterways Commission 1908–1912; member of the National Monetary Commission 1908–1912; elected to the United States Senate and served from March 4, 1909, to March 3, 1915; was not a candidate for renomination in 1914; traveled abroad and subsequently became interested in banking in New York City; unanimously supported by the Ohio delegation for the Republican Presidential nomination in 1916; elected to the Sixty-seventh and to the three succeeding Congresses and served from March 4, 1921, until his resignation on December 15, 1928; did not seek renomination, having become a candidate for Senator; appointed by President Harding as a member of the World War Debt Funding Commission in 1922; chairman of the United States delegation to the conference for the control of international traffic in arms at Geneva, Switzerland, in 1925; elected to the United States Senate to fill the vacancy caused by the death of Frank B. Willis and served from December 15, 1928, until his death in Washington, D. C., October 28, 1929; funeral services were held in the Chamber of the United States Senate; interment in Lake View Cemetery, Cleveland, Ohio.

BURWELL, William Armisted, a Representative from Virginia; born near Boydton, Mecklenburg County, Va., on March 15, 1780; was graduated from William and Mary College, Williamsburg, Va.; moved to Franklin County in 1802; elected a member of the State house of delegates; private secretary to President Jefferson; elected as a Democrat to the Ninth Congress to fill the vacancy caused by the resignation of Christopher Clark; reelected to the Tenth and to the six succeeding Congresses and served from December 1, 1806, until his death in Washington, D. C., February 16, 1821; interment in Congressional Cemetery.

BUSBEY, Fred Ernst, a Representative from Illinois; born in Tuscola, Douglas County, Ill., February 8, 1895; attended the public schools, Armour Institute of Technology, Chicago, Ill., and Northwestern University, Evanston, Ill.; during the First World War enlisted September 24, 1917, in the United States Regular Army and served overseas as a sergeant until after the Armistice, when he was made a battalion sergeant major in the One Hundred and Twenty-fourth Field Artillery, Thirty-third Division, being discharged June 8, 1919; participated in the St. Mihiel, Argonne, and Meuse-Argonne offensives; in 1930 engaged in the investment brokerage business in Chicago, Ill.; elected as a Republican to the Seventy-eighth Congress (January 3, 1943–January 3, 1945); unsuccessful candidate for reelection in 1944 to the Seventy-ninth Congress; elected in 1946 to the Eightieth Congress (January 3, 1947–January 3, 1949); unsuccessful candidate for reelection in 1948 to the Eighty-first Congress; elected to the Eighty-second and Eighty-third Congresses (January 3, 1951–January 3, 1955); unsuccessful candidate for reelection in 1954 to the Eighty-fourth Congress; resumed the investment brokerage business until his retirement in 1958; resides in Cocoa Beach, Fla.

BUSBY, George Henry, a Representative from Ohio; born in Davistown, Pa., June 10, 1794; attended the public schools; moved to Ohio in 1810 with his father, who settled in Royalton, Fairfield County; engaged in the general mercantile business; major of militia in the War of 1812; moved to Marion County in 1823 and helped organize the town of Marion, where he continued mercantile pursuits; clerk of the Marion County courts and clerk of the supreme court 1824–1828; recorder of deeds 1831–1835; elected as a Democrat to the Thirty-second Congress (March 4, 1851–March 3, 1853); was not a candidate for renomination in 1852; resumed mercantile pursuits; member of the State senate 1853–1855; probate judge of Marion County from 1866 until his death in Marion, Ohio, August 22, 1869; interment in Marion Cemetery.

BUSBY, Thomas Jefferson, a Representative from Mississippi; born near Short, Tishomingo County, Miss., July 26, 1884; attended the common schools of his native city, Oakland College, Yale, Miss., and Iuka Normal College at Iuka, Miss., taught in the public schools of Tishomingo, Alcorn, and Chickasaw Counties, Miss., 1903–1908; was graduated from the George Robertson Christian College, Henderson, Tenn., in 1905 and from the law department of the University of Mississippi at Oxford in 1909; was admitted to the bar in 1909 and commenced practice of law

at Houston, Miss.; prosecuting attorney of Chickasaw County 1912–1920; elected as a Democrat to the Sixty-eighth and to the five succeeding Congresses (March 4, 1923–January 3, 1935); unsuccessful candidate for renomination in 1934; resumed the practice of law in Houston, Miss., where he resides.

BUSEY, Samuel Thompson, a Representative from Illinois; born in Greencastle, Putnam County, Ind., November 16, 1835; moved with his parents to Urbana, Ill.; attended the public schools; studied law; attended commercial college and law lectures in 1859 and 1860; during the Civil War served as first sergeant and then first lieutenant of the Urbana Zouaves in 1861 and 1862; town collector in 1862; second lieutenant in the recruiting service in June 1862 and helped to organize the Seventy-sixth Regiment, Illinois Volunteer Infantry; captain of Company B of that regiment June 22, 1862; lieutenant colonel August 22, 1862; colonel January 7, 1863; brevetted brigadier general of Volunteers April 9, 1865, "for gallant conduct in leading his regiment in the assault on Fort Blakeley, Ala."; mustered out of the service July 22, 1865, in Chicago, Ill.; engaged in banking from 1867 to 1888; mayor of Urbana 1880–1889; elected as a Democrat to the Fifty-second Congress (March 4, 1891–March 3, 1893); unsuccessful candidate for reelection in 1892 to the Fifty-third Congress; again engaged in banking; died in Urbana, Ill., August 12, 1909; interment in Woodlawn Cemetery.

BUSH, Alvin Ray, a Representative from Pennsylvania; born on a farm in Boggs Township, Clearfield County, Pa., June 4, 1893; attended the public schools; at the age of thirteen started work as a laborer in Pennsylvania coal mines and later was an apprentice in a machine shop; during the First World War served overseas as a corporal with the Five Hundred and Forty-first Motor Truck Company; established an automobile repair business in Philipsburg, Pa.; purchased a bus line serving Philipsburg and neighboring communities, later becoming president and general manager of the Williamsport Transportation Co.; operated a dairy farm in Lycoming County, Pa.; director of Lowry Electric Co. and Muncy Valley Hospital; elected as a Republican to the Eighty-second and to the four succeeding Congresses and served from January 3, 1951, until his death in Williamsport, Pa., November 5, 1959; interment in Twin Hills Cemetery, near Montoursville, Pa.

BUSH, Prescott Sheldon, a Senator from Connecticut; born in Columbus, Franklin County, Ohio, May 15, 1895; attended the Periglas School of Columbus, Ohio, and St. George's School, Newport, R. I., 1908–1913; graduated from Yale University in 1917; enlisted in Connecticut National Guard in 1916 and served as captain of Field Artillery in American Expeditionary Forces 1917–1919; after war service engaged in hardware business as a warehouse clerk in St. Louis, Mo., and later went to New York City to enter the banking field; moved to Greenwich, Conn., in 1924; engaged in investment banking business in New York City since 1926 and as partner in the firm of Brown Bros., Harriman & Co. since 1930; moderator, Greenwich Representative Town Meeting 1935–1952; chairman, National Campaign United Service Organizations in 1942, National War Fund Campaign in 1943 and 1944, Connecticut Republican Finance Committee 1947–1950; trustee, Yale University and Episcopal Church Foundation of the United States; Republican nominee for the United States Senate in 1950; delegate at large to the Republican National Convention in 1952; elected as a Republican to the United States Senate to fill the vacancy caused by the death of Brien McMahon and served from November 4, 1952, to January 3, 1957; reelected in 1956 for the term ending January 3, 1963.

BUSHFIELD, Harlan John (husband of Vera C. Bushfield), a Senator from South Dakota; born in Atlantic, Cass County, Iowa, August 6, 1882; moved with his parents to South Dakota in 1883; attended the public schools in Miller, S. Dak., and Dakota Wesleyan University, Mitchell, S. Dak., 1899–1901; was graduated from the Minnesota University Law School at Minneapolis in 1904; was admitted to the bar the same year and commenced practice in Miller, S. Dak.; Governor of South Dakota 1939–1942; elected as a Republican to the United States Senate in 1942 and served from January 3, 1943, until his death in Miller, S. Dak., September 27, 1948; interment in the G. A. R. Cemetery.

BUSHFIELD, Vera Cahalan (widow of Harlan J. Bushfield), a Senator from South Dakota; born in Miller, Hand County, S. Dak., August 9, 1889; attended the public schools; was graduated from Miller High School in 1908 and from Stout Institute, Menominee, Wis., in 1912; also attended Dakota Wesleyan University and the University of Minnesota; appointed as a Republican to the United States Senate to fill the vacancy caused by the death of her husband, Harlan J. Bushfield, and served from October 6, 1948, until her resignation on December 26, 1948; is a resident of Miller, S. Dak.

BUSHNELL, Allen Ralph, a Representative from Wisconsin; born in Hartford, Trumbull County, Ohio, July 18, 1833; attended the public schools and the academies of Oberlin and Hiram, Ohio; moved to Wisconsin in 1854 and settled in Platteville; studied law; was admitted to the bar in 1857 and commenced practice in Platteville; elected district attorney of Grant County in 1860; resigned to enter the Union Army, during the Civil War, in August 1861; served as first lieutenant and afterwards as captain of Company C, Seventh Regiment, Wisconsin Volunteer Infantry; member of the Iron Brigade; moved to Lancaster in 1864; district attorney of Grant County in 1864; member of the State assembly in 1872; elected first mayor of Lancaster, Wis., in 1875; United States district attorney for the western district of Wisconsin 1886–1890; moved to Madison, Wis., in 1891; elected as a Democrat to the Fifty-second Congress (March 4, 1891–March 3, 1893); was not a candidate for renomination in 1892; resumed the practice of law in Madison, Wis., and died there March 29, 1909; interment in Hillside Cemetery, Lancaster, Wis.

BUSHONG, Robert Grey (grandson of Anthony Ellmaker Roberts), a Representative from Pennsylvania; born in Reading, Berks County, Pa., June 10, 1883; attended Phillips Academy, Andover, Mass.; was graduated from Yale University, New Haven, Conn., in 1903 and from the law school of Columbia University, New York, N. Y., in 1906; was admitted to the bar in 1906 and commenced practice in Reading, Pa.; member of the Pennsylvania House of Representatives in 1908 and 1909; president judge of the orphans' court of Berks County in 1914 and 1915; delegate to the Republican National Conventions in 1916 and 1924; elected as a Republican to the Seventieth Congress (March 4, 1927–March 3, 1929); was not a candidate for renomination in 1928; resumed the practice of law in Reading, Pa., and resided in Sinking Springs, Pa.; died in Reading, Pa., April 6, 1951; interment in Charles Evans Cemetery.

BUTLER, Andrew Pickens (son of William Butler), a Senator from South Carolina; born in Edgefield, S. C., November 19, 1796; attended Doctor Waddell's Academy at Willington, Abbeville County, S. C., and was graduated from South Carolina College (now the University of South Carolina) at Columbia in 1817; studied law; was admitted to the bar in 1818 and practiced in Columbia, Edgefield, Lexington, Barnwell, and Newberry; member of the State house of representatives; served in the State senate 1824–1833; appointed an aide on the staff of Governor Manning in December 1824, and as such attended General Lafayette on his visit to the State in March 1825; appointed judge of the session court in 1833; judge of the State court of common pleas 1835–1846; appointed and subsequently elected as a State Rights Democrat to the United States Senate to fill the vacancy caused by the resignation of George McDuffie; reelected in 1848 and again in 1854 and served from December 4, 1846, until his death near Edgefield, S. C., May 25, 1857; interment in Big Creek Butler Churchyard, Edgefield, S. C.

BUTLER, Benjamin Franklin (grandfather of Butler Ames), a Representative from Massachusetts; born in Deerfield, N. H., November 5, 1818; moved with his mother to Lowell, Mass., in 1828; attended high school and Exeter Academy, and was graduated from Waterville College (now Colby University), Waterville, Maine, in 1838; studied law; was admitted to the bar in 1840 and commenced practice in Lowell, Mass.; member of the State house of representatives in 1853; served in the State senate in 1859; delegate to the Democratic National Conventions at Charleston and Baltimore in 1860; entered the Union Army April 17, 1861, as a brigadier general; promoted to major general May 16, 1861, and assigned to the command of Fort Monroe and the Department of Eastern Virginia; resigned November 30, 1865; elected as a Republican to the Fortieth and to the three succeeding Congresses (March 4, 1867–March 3, 1875); one of the managers appointed by the House of Representatives in 1868 to conduct the impeachment proceedings against Andrew Johnson, President of the United States; unsuccessful candidate for the Republican nomination for Governor in 1871 and 1872 and for reelection to the Forty-fourth Congress in 1874; elected to the Forty-fifth Congress (March 4, 1877–March 3, 1879); declined to be a candidate for renomination; unsuccessful candidate for Governor as an independent in 1878 and as a Democrat in 1879; elected Governor in 1882 by the combined efforts of the Greenback and Democratic Parties; unsuccessful candidate for President of the United States on the Greenback and Anti-Monopolist ticket in 1884; died while attending court in Washington, D. C., January 11, 1893; interment in Hildreth Cemetery, Lowell, Mass.

BUTLER, Chester Pierce, a Representative from Pennsylvania; born in Wilkes-Barre, Luzerne County, Pa., March 21, 1798; attended Wilkes-Barre Academy and was graduated from Princeton College in 1817; trustee of Wilkes-Barre Academy 1818–1838 and served as secretary; studied law at Litchfield Law School; was admitted to the bar in 1820 and commenced practice in Wilkes-Barre; register and recorder of Luzerne County 1821–1824; member of the State house of representatives in 1832, 1838, 1839, and again in 1843; elected as a Whig to the Thirtieth and Thirty-first Congresses and served from March 4, 1847, until his death in Philadelphia, Pa., October 5, 1850; interment in Hollenbeck Cemetery, Wilkes-Barre, Pa.

BUTLER, Ezra, a Representative from Vermont; born in Lancaster, Worcester County, Mass., September 24, 1763; moved with his parents to West Windsor, Vt., in 1770; engaged in agricultural pursuits in Claremont, N. H.; served in the Revolutionary War for a short time; moved to Waterbury, Vt., in 1785; studied law; was admitted to the bar and commenced practice in Waterbury, Vt., in 1786; town clerk in 1790; one of the first three town selectmen; member of the State house of representatives 1794–1797, 1799–1804, 1807, and 1808; served in the executive council for fifteen years; first judge of the Chittenden County Court 1803–1806; chief justice 1806–1811; when Jefferson County (which has since become

Washington County) was formed in 1812 he was elected chief justice and held the position continuously, with the exception of his congressional service, until 1825; elected as a Democrat to the Thirteenth Congress (March 4, 1813–March 3, 1815); member of the State constitutional convention in 1822; Governor of Vermont 1826–1828; died in Waterbury, Washington County, Vt., July 12, 1838; interment in Waterbury Cemetery.

BUTLER, Hugh Alfred, a Senator from Nebraska; born on a farm near Missouri Valley, Harrison County, Iowa, February 28, 1878; attended the public schools and was graduated from Doane College at Crete, Nebr., in 1900; construction engineer with the Chicago, Burlington & Quincy Railroad 1900–1908; member of the city board of Curtis, Nebr., 1908–1913; engaged in the flour-milling and grain business at Curtis, Crete, and Omaha, Nebr., 1908–1940; member of the board of education of Omaha, Nebr., 1919–1946; Republican National committeeman for Nebraska 1936–1940; elected as a Republican to the United States Senate in 1940; reelected in 1946 and again in 1952 and served from January 3, 1941, until his death in the naval hospital at Bethesda, Md., July 1, 1954; interment in Forest Lawn Cemetery, Omaha, Nebr.

BUTLER, James Joseph, a Representative from Missouri; born in St. Louis, Mo., August 29, 1862; attended the public schools; served an apprenticeship as a blacksmith, and worked at that trade for several years; was graduated from St. Louis (Mo.) University in 1881; studied law at Washington University, St. Louis, Mo.; was admitted to the bar in 1884 and commenced practice in St. Louis, Mo.; served as city attorney of St. Louis 1886–1894; presented credentials as a Democratic Member-elect to the Fifty-seventh Congress and served from March 4, 1901, until June 28, 1902, when the seat was declared vacant; subsequently presented credentials as a Member-elect to fill the vacancy thus caused and served from November 4, 1902, until February 26, 1903, when he was succeeded by George C. R. Wagoner, who contested his election; elected to the Fifty-eighth Congress (March 4, 1903–March 3, 1905); delegate to the Democratic National Convention at St. Louis in 1904 and at Denver in 1908; resumed the practice of law in St. Louis, Mo., and died there May 31, 1917; interment in Calvary Cemetery.

BUTLER, John Cornelius, a Representative from New York; born in Buffalo, Erie County, N. Y., July 2, 1887; attended the public schools and Old Central High School, Buffalo, N. Y.; from boyhood was employed in waterfront industries in Buffalo; held many offices in longshoremen's, grain elevator employees', and electrical workers' unions; superintendent of Marine "A" and "B" Grain Elevators 1925–1941; elected as a Republican to the Seventy-seventh Congress to fill the vacancy caused by the death of Pius L. Schwert; reelected to the Seventy-eighth, Seventy-ninth, and Eightieth Congresses and served from April 22, 1941, to January 3, 1949; unsuccessful candidate for reelection in 1948 to the Eighty-first Congress; sales manager of Fire Equipment Sales Co., and estimator for Beacon Electrical Engineering and Construction Co., Buffalo, N. Y.; elected to the Eighty-second Congress (January 3, 1951–January 3, 1953); unsuccessful candidate for renomination in 1952; died in Buffalo, N. Y., August 13, 1953; interment in Forest Lawn Cemetery.

BUTLER, John Marshall, a Senator from Maryland; born in Baltimore, Md., July 21, 1897; attended the public schools; during the First World War enlisted in the United States Army and served as a private in the One Hundred and Tenth Field Artillery, Twenty-ninth Division, 1917–1919, with 12 months'

overseas service; student Johns Hopkins University 1919–1921, and graduated from the University of Maryland Law School in 1926; was admitted to the bar in 1926 and commenced the practice of law in Baltimore, Md.; member of City Service Commission of Baltimore from April 1947 to June 1949; delegate to the Republican National Conventions in 1952 and 1956; elected as a Republican in 1950 to the United States Senate for the term commencing January 3, 1951; reelected in 1956 for the term ending January 3, 1963.

BUTLER, Josiah, a Representative from New Hampshire; born in Pelham, N. H., December 4, 1779; attended the Londonderry and Atkinson Academies and was instructed by private tutors; was graduated from Harvard University in 1803; taught school in Virginia for three years; studied law; was admitted to the bar of Virginia in 1807; returned to Pelham, N. H., and commenced practice in 1807; moved to Deerfield in 1809; sheriff of Rockingham County 1810–1813; clerk of the court of common pleas; unsuccessful candidate for election in 1812 to the Thirteenth Congress; member of the State house of representatives in 1815 and 1816; elected as a Democrat to the Fifteenth, Sixteenth, and Seventeenth Congresses (March 4, 1817–March 3, 1823); associate justice of the State court of common pleas 1825–1835; died in Deerfield, Rockingham County, N. H., October 27, 1854; interment in Granite Cemetery, South Deerfield, N. H.

BUTLER, Marion, a Senator from North Carolina; born near Clinton, Sampson County, N. C., May 20, 1863; attended Salem High School and was graduated from the University of North Carolina at Chapel Hill in 1885; taught school for three years; moved to Clinton, N. C., in 1888 and became editor and publisher of the Clinton Caucasian; moved to Raleigh in 1894, but continued the publication of the paper; elected as a Democrat to the State senate in 1890; chairman of the Populist State committee during the campaign of 1892; president of the State Farmers' Alliance in 1892 and 1893; president of the National Farmers' Alliance and Industrial Union in 1894 and 1895; chairman of the People's Party State committee in 1894; trustee and member of the executive committee of the University of North Carolina 1891–1899; studied law; was admitted to the bar in 1899 and commenced practice in Raleigh, N. C.; elected as a Populist to the United States Senate and served from March 4, 1895, to March 3, 1901; unsuccessful candidate for reelection in 1901; chairman of the Populist National Executive Committee 1896–1904; affiliated with the Republican Party since 1904; delegate to the Republican National Conventions in 1912, 1916, 1920, 1924, 1928, and 1932; largely interested in agriculture and assisted in organizing the Cotton and Tobacco Cooperative Marketing Association of the South in 1923 and 1924; resumed the practice of law in Washington, D. C.; died June 3, 1938, in Takoma Park, Md., where he had been confined in a hospital; interment in Clinton Cemetery, Clinton, N. C.

BUTLER, Matthew Calbraith (son of William Butler), a Senator from South Carolina; born near Greenville, Greenville County, S. C., March 8, 1836; attended the local academy in Edgefield, S. C., and South Carolina College at Columbia; studied law; was admitted to the bar in 1857 and commenced practice in Edgefield; elected to the State house of representatives in 1860; entered the Confederate Army as captain of Cavalry in the Hampton Legion in June 1861 and served throughout the Civil War, attaining the rank of major general; again elected to the State house of representatives in 1866; unsuccessful candidate for Lieutenant Governor of South Carolina in 1870; elected as a Democrat to the United States Senate in 1876; reelected in 1882 and again in 1888 and served from March 4, 1877, until March 3,

1895; unsuccessful candidate for reelection; resumed the practice of law in Washington, D. C.; during the Spanish-American War was appointed major general of United States Volunteers, and was one of the commissioners appointed to supervise the evacuation of Cuba by the Spanish forces in 1898; returned to Edgefield, S. C., and resumed the practice of his profession; died in Columbia, S. C., April 14, 1909; interment in Willow Brook Cemetery, Edgefield, S. C.

BUTLER, Mounce Gore, a Representative from Tennessee; born in Gainesboro, Jackson County, Tenn., May 11, 1849; attended the common schools, Old Philomath Academy, and the law department of Cumberland University, Lebanon, Tenn.; was admitted to the bar in 1871 and commenced the practice of law in Gainesboro; delegate to all Democratic State conventions from 1872 to 1916; attorney general for the fifth judicial circuit of Tennessee 1894–1902; elected as a Democrat to the Fifty-ninth Congress (March 4, 1905–March 3, 1907); unsuccessful candidate for renomination in 1906; resumed the practice of his profession in Gainesboro, Jackson County, Tenn., and died there February 13, 1917; interment in Gainesboro Cemetery.

BUTLER, Pierce, a Delegate and a Senator from South Carolina; born in Ireland, July 11, 1744; pursued preparatory studies; came to America as an officer in the British Army and was stationed in Boston; resigned prior to the Revolutionary War and settled in Charles Town (now Charleston), S. C.; member of the Continental Congress in 1787 and 1788; member of the convention which framed the Federal Constitution in 1787; elected as a Democrat to the United States Senate January 22, 1789, for the term ending March 3, 1793; reelected December 5, 1792, and served from March 4, 1789, to October 25, 1796, when he resigned; again elected to the United States Senate to fill the vacancy caused by the death of John Ewing Colhoun and served from November 4, 1802, until his resignation November 21, 1804; died in Philadelphia, Pa., February 15, 1822; interment in Christ Churchyard, Philadelphia, Pa.

BUTLER, Robert Reyburn (grandson of Roderick Random Butler), a Representative from Oregon; born in Butler, Johnson County, Tenn., September 24, 1881; attended the public schools and Holly Springs College; was graduated from the law department of Cumberland University, Lebanon, Tenn., in 1903; was admitted to the bar and commenced practice in Mountain City, Tenn.; moved to Condon, Oreg., in 1906 and resumed the practice of law; mayor of Condon, Oreg.; presidential elector on the Republican ticket of Taft and Sherman in 1908 and of Hughes and Fairbanks in 1916; appointed circuit judge for the eleventh judicial district of Oregon and served from February 1909 until his retirement in January 1911; moved to The Dalles in 1911 and resumed the practice of law; member of the State senate 1913–1917 and 1925–1929; elected on November 6, 1928, as a Republican to the Seventieth Congress to fill the vacancy caused by the resignation of Nicholas J. Sinnott and on the same day was elected to the Seventy-first Congress; reelected to the Seventy-second Congress and served until his death; unsuccessful candidate for reelection in 1932 to the Seventy-third Congress; died in Washington, D. C., January 7, 1933; interment in the Odd Fellows Cemetery, The Dalles, Oreg.

BUTLER, Roderick Random (grandfather of Robert Reyburn Butler), a Representative from Tennessee; born in Wytheville, Va., April 9, 1827; bound as an apprentice and learned the tailor's trade; moved to Taylorsville (now Mountain City), Tenn.; attended night school; studied law; was admitted to the bar in 1853 and commenced practice in Taylorsville, Tenn.; appointed postmaster of Taylorsville by President Fillmore; major of the

First Battalion of Tennessee Militia; member of the State senate 1859–1863; during the Civil War served in the Union Army as lieutenant colonel of the Thirteenth Regiment, Tennessee Volunteer Cavalry, from November 5, 1863, until April 25, 1864, when he was honorably discharged; delegate to the Republican National Convention at Baltimore in 1864; delegate to the State constitutional convention in 1865; county judge and judge of the first judicial circuit of Tennessee in 1865; chairman of the first State Republican executive committee of Tennessee; delegate to the Baltimore Border State Convention; elected as a Republican to the Fortieth and to the three succeeding Congresses (March 4, 1867–March 3, 1875); unsuccessful candidate for reelection in 1874 to the Forty-fourth Congress; president of the Republican State conventions in 1869 and 1882; delegate to the Republican National Convention at Philadelphia in 1872 and at Cincinnati in 1876; member of the State house of representatives 1879–1885; elected to the Fiftieth Congress (March 4, 1887–March 3, 1889); was not a candidate for renomination in 1888; resumed the practice of law; again a member of the State senate 1893–1901; died in Mountain City, Johnson County, Tenn., August 18, 1902; interment in Mountain View Cemetery.

BUTLER, Sampson Hale, a Representative from South Carolina; born near Ninety Six, Edgefield District, S. C., January 3, 1803; attended the country schools and South Carolina College (now the University of South Carolina) at Columbia; studied law; was admitted to the bar in 1825 and commenced practice in Edgefield, S. C.; moved to Barnwell, S. C., and continued the practice of law; sheriff of Barnwell County 1832–1839; member of the State house of representatives 1836–1839; elected as a Democrat to the Twenty-sixth and Twenty-seventh Congresses and served from March 4, 1839, until September 27, 1842, when he resigned; resumed the practice of law; moved to Florida; died in Tallahassee, Fla., March 16, 1848; interment in a cemetery in that city.

BUTLER, Thomas, a Representative from Louisiana; born near Carlisle, Cumberland County, Pa., April 14, 1785; attended the common schools and received a college education in Pittsburgh, Pa.; studied law; was admitted to the bar in 1806 and commenced practice at Pittsburgh, Pa.; moved to Mississippi Territory about 1807; admitted to the bar there in 1808; captain of a Cavalry troop in the Mississippi Territory Militia in 1810; purchased land in the parish of Feliciana, Orleans Territory, and settled there in 1811; appointed parish judge December 14, 1812; appointed judge of the third district by Governor Claiborne of Louisiana March 4, 1813; elected to the Fifteenth Congress to fill the vacancy caused by the resignation of Thomas B. Robertson; reelected to the Sixteenth Congress and served from November 16, 1818, to March 3, 1821; unsuccessful candidate for renomination in 1820; appointed special judge of the third judicial district in 1822 and again in 1840; member of the Whig Party and afterwards affiliated with the American Party; owing to ill health declined to be a candidate for Congress in 1844; owner of sugar and cotton plantations; president of the board of trustees of the Louisiana College, Jackson, La.; member of the Pennsylvania Society of the Cincinnati; died in St. Louis, Mo., August 7, 1847; interment on his plantation, "The Cottage," near St. Francisville, West Feliciana Parish, La.

BUTLER, Thomas Belden, a Representative from Connecticut; born in Wethersfield, Conn., August 22, 1806; attended the common schools; was graduated from the medical department of Yale University in 1828 and commenced practice in Norwalk, Conn.; member of the State house of representatives 832–1846; studied law; was admitted to the bar in 1837 and commenced practice in Norwalk; served in the State senate in 1847 and 1848; elected as a Whig to the Thirty-first Congress (March 4, 1849–March 3, 1851); unsuccessful candidate for reelection in 1850 to the Thirty-second Congress; judge of the superior court in 1855; appointed associate justice of the State supreme court in 1861 and became chief justice of the same court in 1870; died in Norwalk, Conn., June 8, 1873; interment in Norwalk Cemetery.

BUTLER, Thomas Stalker, a Representative from Pennsylvania; born in Uwchland Township, Chester County, Pa., November 4, 1855; attended the common schools, West Chester State Normal School, and Wyer's Academy, West Chester, Pa.; studied law; was admitted to the bar in 1877 and commenced practice in West Chester, Pa.; served as trustee of the West Chester State Normal School 1885–1889 and again in 1927 and 1928; appointed judge of the fifteenth judicial district of Pennsylvania in 1888; unsuccessful candidate for reelection in 1889; delegate to the Republican National Convention at Minneapolis in 1892; elected as a Republican to the Fifty-fifth and to the fifteen succeeding Congresses and served from March 4, 1897, until his death in Washington, D. C., May 26, 1928; interment in Oaklands Cemetery, West Chester, Pa.

BUTLER, Walter Halben, a Representative from Iowa; born in Springboro, Crawford County, Pa., February 13, 1852; moved to Minnesota in 1868 with his parents, who settled in Mankato, Blue Earth County; attended public and private schools, and was graduated from the University of Wisconsin at Madison in 1875; studied law; was admitted to the bar in 1875 and commenced practice in Princeton, Green Lake County, Wis.; moved to Iowa in 1876 and taught school at La Porte City until 1878 and at Manchester until 1880; moved to West Union, Iowa, in 1883 and became owner and publisher of the Fayette County Union; served as superintendent of the tenth division, railway mail service, at St. Paul, Minn., 1885–1889; returned to West Union, Iowa, and resumed his former newspaper pursuits; elected as a Democrat to the Fifty-second Congress (March 4, 1891–March 3, 1893); was an unsuccessful candidate for reelection in 1892 to the Fifty-third Congress; moved to Des Moines, Iowa, in 1897 and to Kansas City, Mo., in 1907; engaged in the real estate and loan business and, later, in banking; died in Kansas City, Mo., April 24, 1931; interment in Forest Hill Cemetery.

BUTLER, William (father of Andrew Pickens Butler), a Representative from South Carolina; born in Prince William County, Va., December 17, 1759; attended grammar schools; moved to South Carolina; served in the Snow campaign under General Richardson in 1775 and in Gen. Andrew Williamson's expedition against the Cherokee Indians in 1776; lieutenant in Pulaski's legion, under Gen. Benjamin Lincoln, in 1779; served under Gen. Andrew Pickens at the siege of Augusta in 1780, as captain under General Henderson in 1781, and as captain of Mounted Rangers under General Pickens in 1782; member of the State convention which adopted the Federal Constitution; member of the State house of representatives in 1787 and 1788; sheriff of the Ninety-sixth District in 1794; elected major general of the upper division of State militia in 1796; elected as an Anti-Federalist to the Seventh and to the five succeeding Congresses (March 4, 1801–March 3, 1813); was not a candidate for reelection; major general commanding the troops raised for the defense of South Carolina during the War of 1812; retired to his plantation on the Saluda River, near Mount Willing, Edgefield County, S. C., and died there September 15, 1821; interment in the family burial ground at Butler Methodist Church, near Saluda, Edgefield (now Saluda) County, S. C.

BUTLER, William (son of the preceding, brother of Andrew Pickens Butler, and father of Matthew Calbraith Butler), a Representative from South Carolina; born in the Edgefield District, S. C., near the present town of Saluda, February 1, 1790; attended the common schools, and was graduated from South Carolina College at Columbia in 1810; studied medicine and was licensed to practice; served as a surgeon in the Battle of New Orleans during the War of 1812; continued his service in the Navy until June 6, 1820, when he resigned; elected as a Whig to the Twenty-seventh Congress (March 4, 1841–March 3, 1843); agent of the Cherokee Indians from May 29, 1849, until his death in Fort Gibson, Indian Territory (now Oklahoma), September 25, 1850; interment near Van Buren, Ark.

BUTLER, William Morgan, a Senator from Massachusetts; born in New Bedford, Mass., January 29, 1861; attended the public schools; studied law; was admitted to the bar in 1883; was graduated from the law department of Boston University in 1884; practiced his profession in New Bedford until 1895; member of the State house of representatives in 1890 and 1891; served in the State senate 1892–1895, being president of that body in 1894 and 1895; moved to Boston, Mass., in 1895 and continued the practice of law until 1912, when he engaged in the manufacture of cotton goods; member of the commission to revise the statutes of Massachusetts 1896–1900; chairman of the Republican National Committee in 1924; appointed as a Republican to the United States Senate to fill the vacancy caused by the death of Henry Cabot Lodge and served from November 13, 1924, to December 6, 1926, when a successor was elected; unsuccessful candidate for election to fill the vacancy; engaged extensively in manufacturing, with office and residence in Boston, until his death there on March 29, 1937; interment in Forest Hills Cemetery.

BUTLER, William Orlando, a Representative from Kentucky; born in Jessamine County, Ky., April 19, 1791; moved with his parents to Maysville, Ky.; pursued preparatory studies; was graduated from Transylvania University, Lexington, Ky., in 1812; studied law at Lexington; during the War of 1812 served as captain, and was brevetted major for distinguished service in the Battle of New Orleans; aide to General Jackson in 1816 and 1817; was admitted to the bar in 1817 and commenced practice at Carrollton, Ky.; member of the State house of representatives in 1817 and 1818; elected as a Democrat to the Twenty-sixth and Twenty-seventh Congresses (March 4, 1839–March 3, 1843); was not a candidate for reelection; during the war with Mexico was commissioned major general of Volunteers June 29, 1846; received the thanks of Congress and a sword for gallantry in the storming of Monterey, Mexico; unsuccessful Democratic candidate for Vice President in 1848; declined appointment as Governor of Nebraska Territory in 1855; delegate to the peace convention held in Washington, D. C., in 1861 in an effort to devise means to prevent the impending war; died in Carrollton, Ky., August 6, 1880; interment in a private burying ground at the foot of Butlers Hill, near Carrollton, Ky.

BUTMAN, Samuel, a Representative from Maine; born in Worcester, Worcester County, Mass., in 1788; moved to Maine in 1804, and settled in Dixmont, Penobscot County; engaged in agricultural pursuits; served as a captain in the War of 1812; member of the State constitutional convention in 1820; member of the house of representatives of Maine in 1822, 1826, and 1827; elected to the Twentieth and Twenty-first Congresses (March 4, 1827–March 3, 1831); county commissioner of Penobscot County in 1846; served in the State senate and was its president in 1853; died in Plymouth, Maine, October 9, 1864.

BUTTERFIELD, Martin, a Representative from New York; born in Westmoreland, N. H., December 8, 1790; attended the common schools; moved to Palmyra, Wayne County, N. Y., in 1828 and engaged in the hardware business and also in the manufacture of rope and cordage; presidential elector on the Whig ticket of Taylor and Fillmore in 1848; elected as a Republican to the Thirty-sixth Congress (March 4, 1859–March 3, 1861); declined to be a candidate for renomination in 1860; resumed his former business pursuits; died in Palmyra, N. Y., August 6, 1866; interment in the Village Cemetery.

BUTTERWORTH, Benjamin, a Representative from Ohio; born near Maineville, Warren County, Ohio, October 22, 1837; attended the common schools of Warren County, the academy in Maineville, Ohio, and Ohio University in Athens; studied law; was admitted to the bar in 1861 and commenced practice in Cincinnati, Ohio; appointed assistant United States district attorney in 1868; member of the State senate in 1874 and 1875; elected as a Republican to the Forty-sixth and Forty-seventh Congresses (March 4, 1879–March 3, 1883); unsuccessful candidate for reelection in 1882 to the Forty-eighth Congress; delegate to the Republican National Convention at Chicago in 1880; Regent of the Smithsonian Institution; appointed a commissioner of the Northern Pacific Railroad by President Arthur in 1883; special Government counsel to prosecute the South Carolina election cases in 1883; elected to the Forty-ninth, Fiftieth, and Fifty-first Congresses (March 4, 1885–March 3, 1891); was not a candidate for renomination in 1890; resumed the practice of his profession in Washington, D. C.; served as Commissioner of Patents from 1896 until his death; died, while on a visit to regain his health, in Thomasville, Ga., January 16, 1898; interment in Rock Creek Cemetery, Washington, D. C.

BUTTZ, Charles Wilson, a Representative from South Carolina; born in Stroudsburg, Monroe County, Pa., November 16, 1837; moved with his parents to Buttzville, N. J., in 1839; completed academic studies; studied law in Belvidere, N. J.; during the Civil War entered the Union Army in 1861 as second lieutenant in the Eleventh Pennsylvania Cavalry; was promoted to first lieutenant in 1862; received two brevet ranks from the President, one as captain "for gallant and meritorious services in capturing from the enemy a full rocket battery," and the other as major "for gallant and meritorious services in front of Suffolk, Va.," both dating May 1865; was wounded in 1863; resigned on account of impaired health in October 1863; was admitted to the bar in 1863 and commenced the practice of law in Norfolk, Va.; delegate to the Republican National Convention at Baltimore in 1864; appointed director of the Exchange Bank of Virginia in 1864; Commonwealth attorney for King William County in 1866; moved to Charleston, S. C., in 1870; solicitor of the first judicial circuit 1872–1880; contested as a Republican the election of Edmund W. M. Mackey to the Forty-fourth Congress, but the House decided that neither was entitled to the seat; subsequently elected to fill the vacancy caused by the decision of the House and served from November 7, 1876, to March 3, 1877; was not a candidate for renomination in 1876; moved to Fargo, N. Dak., in 1878; procured the official organization of Ransom County in 1882, and established his residence in what is now known as Buttzville, N. Dak.; State's attorney 1884–1886; member of the State house of representatives 1903–1909; died in Lisbon, Ransom County, N. Dak., July 20, 1913; interment in Oakwood Cemetery.

BYNUM, Jesse Atherton, a Representative from North Carolina; born in Halifax County, N. C., May 23, 1797; attended Princeton College in 1818 and 1819; studied law; was admitted to the bar and commenced practice in Halifax, N. C.; member of the House of Commons of North Carolina in 1823, 1824, and 1827–1830; elected as a Democrat to the Twenty-third and to the three succeeding Congresses (March 4, 1833–March 3, 1841); moved to Alexandria, Rapides Parish, La., where he engaged in agricultural pursuits; died in Alexandria, La., September 23, 1868; interment in Rapides Cemetery, Pineville, La.

BYNUM, William Dallas, a Representative from Indiana; born near Newberry, Greene County, Ind., June 26, 1846; attended the country schools, and was graduated from the University of Indiana at Bloomington in 1869; studied law; was admitted to the bar in 1872 and commenced practice in Washington, Ind.; served as the first city clerk; city attorney of Washington, Ind., 1871–1875; mayor of Washington, Ind., 1875–1879; presidential elector on the Democratic ticket of Tilden and Hendricks in 1876; moved from Daviess County to Indianapolis in 1880; member of the State house of representatives 1881–1885, and served as speaker in 1885; elected as a Democrat to the Forty-ninth and to the four succeeding Congresses (March 4, 1885–March 3, 1895); unsuccessful candidate for reelection in 1894 to the Fifty-fourth Congress; served for some time as whip of the Democratic minority; was active in the organization of the National (Gold-Standard) Democratic Party in 1896, and was chairman of its national committee 1896–1898; settled in Washington, D. C.; appointed by President McKinley in 1900 a member of the commission to codify the United States criminal laws and served until 1906; member of the board of trustees of the Indiana State School for the Blind 1917–1927; retired from the practice of law; died in Indianapolis, Ind., October 21, 1927; interment in Oak Grove Cemetery, Washington, Ind.

BYRD, Adam Monroe, a Representative from Mississippi; born in Sumter County, Ala., July 6, 1859; moved to Neshoba County, Miss.; attended the common schools and Cooper Institute in Daleville; was graduated from the law department of Cumberland University, Lebanon, Tenn., in 1884; was admitted to the bar in 1885 and commenced practice in Philadelphia, Neshoba County, Miss.; superintendent of education for Neshoba County 1887–1889; member of the State senate 1889–1896; served in the State house of representatives in 1896 and 1897, when he resigned; prosecuting attorney for the tenth judicial district in 1897; judge of the sixth chancery district from 1897 until his resignation in 1903; elected as a Democrat to the Fifty-eighth and to the three succeeding Congresses (March 4, 1903–March 3, 1911); unsuccessful candidate for renomination in 1910; resumed the practice of law in Philadelphia, Miss.; died at Hot Springs, Ark., June 21, 1912; interment in Town Cemetery, Philadelphia, Miss.

BYRD, Harry Flood (nephew of Henry De La Warr Flood and Joel West Flood), a Senator from Virginia; born in Martinsburg, Berkeley County, W. Va., June 10, 1887; moved with his parents to Winchester, Va., in 1887; attended the public schools and Shenandoah Valley Academy at Winchester, Va.; entered the newspaper publishing business in 1903 and became publisher of the Winchester (Va.) Star; also engaged extensively in agricultural pursuits near Berryville, Va., in 1906, specializing in growing and storing apples and peaches; president of the Valley Turnpike Co. 1908–1918; member of the State senate 1915–1925; State fuel commissioner in 1918; was elected chairman of the Democratic State committee in 1922; served as Governor of Virginia 1926–1930; Democratic National committeeman 1928–1940; was appointed and subsequently elected as a Democrat to the United States Senate to fill the vacancy caused by the resignation of Claude A. Swanson and served from March 4, 1933, to March 4, 1935; reelected in 1934, 1940, 1946, 1952, and again in 1958 for the term ending January 3, 1965.

BYRD, Robert Carlyle, a Representative and a Senator from West Virginia; born in North Wilkesboro, Wilkes County, N. C., January 15, 1918; attended the public schools; student at Beckley College, Concord College, Morris Harvey College in 1950 and 1951, Marshall College in 1951 and 1952, all in West Virginia, George Washington University and American University Law School, Washington, D. C.; member of the West Virginia House of Delegates 1947–1950; member of the West Virginia Senate in 1951 and 1952, resigning when elected to Congress; elected as a Democrat to the Eighty-third, Eighty-fourth, and Eighty-fifth Congresses (January 3, 1953–January 3, 1959); was not a candidate for renomination to the House of Representatives in 1958; elected as a Democrat to the United States Senate for the term commencing January 3, 1959, and ending January 3, 1965.

BYRNE, Emmet Francis, a Representative from Illinois; born in Chicago, Cook County, Ill., December 6, 1896; educated in the public and parochial schools of Chicago and graduated from St. Ignatius Academy; attended Loyola University in 1916; veteran of the First World War; graduated from De Paul University Law School, Chicago, Ill., in 1920; was admitted to the bar in 1919 and commenced the practice of law in Chicago, Ill.; assistant corporation counsel for city of Chicago from June 1921 to June 1923; assistant State's attorney for Cook County, Ill., from June 1, 1923, to December 1, 1928; unsuccessful candidate for election as judge of the Municipal Court of Chicago in 1934 and again in 1936; chairman of Draft Board No. 86, Selective Service, during World War II; hearing officer for Illinois Commerce Commission in 1947 and 1948 and again in 1955 and 1956; elected as a Republican to the Eighty-fifth Congress (January 3, 1957–January 3, 1959); unsuccessful candidate for reelection in 1958 to the Eighty-sixth Congress; resumed law practice; is a resident of Chicago, Ill.

BYRNE, James Aloysius, a Representative from Pennsylvania; born in Philadelphia, Pa., June 22, 1906; attended the parochial school, St. Joseph's Preparatory School, public high school, and St. Joseph's College in Philadelphia; engaged in business as a mortician 1937–1950; county registrar, Bureau of Vital Statistics, 1934–1939; chief deputy United States marshal 1940–1943, and United States marshal for eastern district of Pennsylvania 1943–1945; senior disbursing officer of Pennsylvania State Treasury 1945–1950; delegate to the Democratic National Convention in Philadelphia in 1936; member State house of representatives in 1951 and 1952; elected as a Democrat to the Eighty-third and to the three succeeding Congresses (January 3, 1953–January 3, 1961). *Reelected to the Eighty-seventh Congress.*

BYRNE, William Thomas, a Representative from New York; born in the town of Florida, Montgomery County, N. Y., March 6, 1876; attended the public schools; was graduated from Albany (N. Y.) Law School (branch of Union College) in 1904; was admitted to the bar the same year and commenced practice in Albany, N. Y.; member of the State senate 1923–1936; elected as a Democrat to the Seventy-fifth and to the seven succeeding Congresses and served from January 3, 1937, until his death in a hospital in Troy, N. Y., January 27, 1952; interment in St. John's Cemetery, West Albany, Town of Colonie, N. Y.

BYRNES, James Francis, a Representative and a Senator from South Carolina; born in Charleston, S. C., May 2, 1879; attended the public schools; official court reporter for the second circuit of South Carolina 1900–1908; editor of the Journal and Review, Aiken, S. C., 1903–1907; studied law; was admitted to the bar in 1903 and commenced practice in Aiken, S. C.; solicitor for the second circuit of South Carolina 1908–1910; elected as a Democrat to the Sixty-second and to the six succeeding Congresses (March 4, 1911–March 3, 1925); was not a candidate for renomination in 1924, but was an unsuccessful candidate for United States Senator; delegate at large to the Democratic National Conventions in 1920, 1932, 1936, and 1940; resumed the practice of law in Spartanburg, S. C.; elected to the United States Senate on November 4, 1930; reelected in 1936 and served from March 4, 1931, until his resignation on July 8, 1941, having been appointed to the Supreme Court; served as an Associate Justice of the United States Supreme Court until his resignation on October 3, 1942, to head the wartime Office of Economic Stabilization, in which office he served until May 27, 1943, when he became director of the Office of War Mobilization and served until his resignation on April 2, 1945; was sworn in as Secretary of State on July 3, 1945, and served until his resignation January 21, 1947; resumed the practice of law in Washington, D. C.; elected Governor of South Carolina in 1950 and served from January 16, 1951, until January 19, 1955; is a resident of Columbia, S. C.

BYRNES, John William, a Representative from Wisconsin; born in Green Bay, Brown County, Wis., June 12, 1913; attended the public and parochial schools; was graduated from the University of Wisconsin at Madison in 1936 and from the law school of the same university in 1938; was admitted to the bar in 1938 and commenced practice in Green Bay, Wis.; served as a special deputy commissioner of banking for the State of Wisconsin from 1938 until his resignation in 1940 to assume his duties as State senator; member of the State senate 1940–1944, serving as majority floor leader in 1943; elected as a Republican to the Seventy-ninth and to the seven succeeding Congresses (January 3, 1945–January 3, 1961). *Reelected to the Eighty-seventh Congress.*

BYRNS, Joseph Wellington, a Representative from Tennessee; born near Cedar Hill, Robertson County, Tenn., July 20, 1869; attended the common schools; was graduated from Nashville High School in 1887 and from the law department of Vanderbilt University, Nashville, Tenn., in 1890; was admitted to the bar in 1890 and commenced the practice of law in Nashville, Tenn.; member of the State house of representatives in 1895, 1897, and again in 1899, serving as speaker during the latter term; member of the State senate in 1901; unsuccessful candidate for district attorney general of Davidson County in 1902; presidential elector on the Democratic ticket of Parker and Davis in 1904; elected as a Democrat to the Sixty-first and to the thirteen succeeding Congresses and served from March 4, 1909, until his death; was a nominee for reelection to the Seventy-fifth Congress at the time of his death; chairman of the Democratic National Congressional Campaign Committee 1928–1930; served as Democratic majority leader during the Seventy-third Congress and as Speaker of the House of Representatives during the Seventy-fourth Congress; died in Washington, D. C., on June 4, 1936; funeral services were held in the Hall of the House of Representatives; interment in Mount Olivet Cemetery, Nashville, Tenn.

BYRNS, Joseph Wellington, Jr. (son of the preceding), a Representative from Tennessee; born in Nashville, Tenn., August 15, 1903; attended the public schools; was graduated from Emerson Institute at Washington, D. C., in 1922 and from the law department of Vanderbilt University at Nashville, Tenn., in 1928; was admitted to the bar in 1928 and commenced practice in Nashville, Tenn.; member of the Air Corps Reserve 1930–1938, with the rank of captain; elected as a Democrat to the Seventy-sixth Congress (January 3, 1939–January 3, 1941); unsuccessful candidate for reelection in 1940 to the Seventy-seventh Congress; resumed the practice of law; served in the

United States Army from June 23, 1942, to August 17, 1945, with two and one-half years overseas in the European Theater of Operations; retired; is a resident of Carson City, Nev.

BYRNS, Samuel, a Representative from Missouri; born on a farm in Jefferson County, Mo., March 4, 1848; received a good English education; studied law; was admitted to the bar in 1872 and commenced practice in Hillsboro, Mo.; collector of revenue for Jefferson County in 1872; presidential elector on the Democratic ticket of Tilden and Hendricks in 1876 and of Cleveland and Thurman in 1888; member of the State house of representatives in 1876 and 1877; served in the State senate in 1878; member of the Democratic State central committee 1886–1888; elected as a Democrat to the Fifty-second Congress (March 4, 1891–March 3, 1893); was an unsuccessful candidate for renomination in 1892 to the Fifty-third Congress; resumed the practice of his chosen profession in De Soto, Jefferson County, Mo., where he died on July 9, 1914; interment in Hillsboro Cemetery, Hillsboro, Mo.

BYRON, Katharine Edgar (widow of William D. Byron), a Representative from Maryland; born in Detroit, Mich., October 25, 1903; attended the public schools, Westover School, Middlebury, Conn., and Holton Arms School, Washington, D. C.; moved to Williamsport, Md., in 1922; president of the parent-teachers' association of Williamsport in 1935; chairman of Red Cross flood disaster committee of Williamsport in 1936; town commissioner of Williamsport 1938–1940; elected as a Democrat to the Seventy-seventh Congress to fill the vacancy caused by the death of her husband, William D. Byron, and served from May 27, 1941, to January 3, 1943; did not seek renomination in 1942; retired and resides in Washington, D. C.

BYRON, William Devereux (husband of Katharine E. Byron), a Representative from Maryland; born in Danville, Pittsylvania County, Va., May 15, 1895; moved to Williamsport, Washington County, Md. with his parents in 1899; attended the public schools, Phillips Exeter Academy, Exeter, N. H., and Pratt Institute, Brooklyn, N. Y.; during the First World War enlisted as a private in the Aviation Corps; commissioned a first lieutenant, and was assigned as an instructor in flying and in aerial gunnery; engaged in the leather-manufacturing business in 1919; served as mayor of Williamsport 1926–1930; member of the State senate 1930–1934; member of the Maryland Roads Commission in 1934 and 1935; elected as a Democrat to the Seventy-sixth and Seventy-seventh Congresses and served from January 3, 1939, until his death in an airplane crash at Jonesboro, near Atlanta, Ga., February 27, 1941; interment in Riverview Cemetery, Williamsport, Md.

C

CABANISS, Thomas Banks (cousin of Thomas Chipman McRae), a Representative from Georgia; born in Forsyth, Monroe County, Ga., August 31, 1835; attended private schools and Penfield College; was graduated from the University of Georgia at Athens in 1853; studied law; was admitted to the bar in 1861; entered the Confederate Army April 1, 1861, and served throughout the Civil War; returned to Forsyth, Ga., and commenced the practice of law; member of the State house of representatives 1865–1867; appointed assistant secretary of the State senate in 1870 and secretary in 1873; resigned to become solicitor general of the Flint circuit, which office he held until 1877; served in the State senate 1878–1880 and 1884–1886; elected as a Democrat to the Fifty-third Congress (March 4, 1893–March 3, 1895); unsuccessful candidate for renomination in 1894; appointed a member of the Dawes Commission

to adjust affairs in the Indian Territory; mayor of Forsyth, Ga., in 1910; judge of the city court in 1913 and 1914; died in Forsyth, Ga., August 14, 1915; interment in Oakland Cemetery.

CABELL, Edward Carrington, a Representative from Florida; born in Richmond, Va., February 5, 1816; attended Washington College (now Washington and Lee University), Lexington, Va., in 1832 and 1833 and Reynolds' Classical Academy in 1833 and 1834; was graduated from the University of Virginia at Charlottesville in 1836; moved to Florida in 1837 and engaged in agricultural pursuits near Tallahassee; delegate to the Territorial convention to form a State constitution in 1838; returned to Virginia; studied law; was admitted to the bar in 1840; returned to Tallahassee, Fla.; upon the admission of Florida as a State into the Union presented credentials as a Member-elect to the Twenty-ninth Congress and served from October 6, 1845, to January 24, 1846, when he was succeeded by William H. Brockenbrough, who contested the election; elected as a Whig to the Thirtieth, Thirty-first, and Thirty-second Congresses (March 4, 1847–March 3, 1853); unsuccessful candidate in 1852 for reelection to the Thirty-third Congress; resumed the practice of law in Tallahassee; moved to St. Louis, Mo., in 1859; during the Civil War served in the Confederate Army with rank of lieutenant colonel; engaged in the practice of law in New York City 1868–1872, and subsequently in St. Louis, Mo.; member of the State senate of Missouri 1878–1882; died in St. Louis, Mo., February 28, 1896; interment in Bellefontaine Cemetery.

CABELL, George Craighead, a Representative from Virginia; born in Danville, Pittsylvania County, Va., January 25, 1836; attended the Danville Academy, and the law school of the University of Virginia at Charlottesville in 1857; was admitted to the bar and commenced practice in Danville in 1858; edited the Republican and later the Democratic Appeal in Danville; elected Commonwealth attorney for Danville in September 1858, and served until April 23, 1861, when he volunteered as a private in the Confederate Army; commissioned major in June 1861 and was assigned to the Eighteenth Regiment, Virginia Infantry; promoted to the rank of colonel and served until the close of the Civil War; resumed the practice of his profession; elected as a Democrat to the Forty-fourth and to the five succeeding Congresses (March 4, 1875–March 3, 1887); unsuccessful candidate for reelection in 1886 to the Fiftieth Congress; resumed the practice of law in Danville, Va.; died in Baltimore, Md., June 23, 1906; interment in Green Hill Cemetery, Danville, Va.

CABELL, Samuel Jordan, a Representative from Virginia; born in Albemarle (now Nelson) County, Va., December 15, 1756; attended William and Mary College, Williamsburg, Va.; left school to enter the Revolutionary Army; appointed captain of Amherst County Volunteers in 1776; assigned to the Sixth Virginia Regiment; promoted to the rank of major for gallantry at Saratoga in 1777; served in Washington's army in 1778 and 1779 and attained the rank of lieutenant colonel; was taken prisoner by the British May 12, 1780, at the capture of Charleston; after the war returned to Virginia and engaged in planting; member of the State house of delegates 1785–1792; elected as a Democrat to the Fourth and to the three succeeding Congresses (March 4, 1795–March 3, 1803); was not a candidate for reelection in 1802; died on his estate "Soldiers' Joy," near New Market (now Norwood), Nelson County, Va., August 4, 1818; interment in the family burying ground on his farm near Norwood, Va.

CABLE, Benjamin Taylor, a Representative from Illinois; born in Georgetown, Scott County, Ky., August 11, 1853; moved with his parents to Rock Island, Ill., in September 1856; attended the public schools, the Rock Island High School, and Racine College, Racine, Wis.; was graduated from the University of Michigan at Ann Arbor in 1876; engaged in agricultural pursuits and also became interested in various manufacturing enterprises; chairman of the western branch of the Democratic National Committee in 1892; chairman of the Democratic executive committee in 1902; delegate to the Democratic National Convention at St. Louis in 1904; elected as a Democrat to the Fifty-second Congress (March 4, 1891–March 3, 1893); declined to be a candidate for renomination in 1892 and retired from public life; engaged in agricultural pursuits as joint owner of a ranch near San Antonio, Tex., during a part of the year; died in Rock Island, Ill., on December 13, 1923; interment in Chippiannock Cemetery.

CABLE, John Levi (great-grandson of Joseph Cable), a Representative from Ohio; born in Lima, Allen County, Ohio, April 15, 1884; attended the public schools; was graduated from Kenyon College, Gambier, Ohio, in 1906 and from the law department of George Washington University, Washington, D. C., in 1909; was admitted to the bar in 1909 and commenced practice in Lima, Ohio; prosecuting attorney of Allen County 1917–1921; elected as a Republican to the Sixty-seventh and Sixty-eighth Congresses (March 4, 1921–March 3, 1925); was not a candidate for renomination in 1924; resumed the practice of law; again elected to the Seventy-first and Seventy-second Congresses (March 4, 1929–March 3, 1933); unsuccessful candidate for reelection in 1932 to the Seventy-third Congress; resumed the practice of law; special assistant to attorney general of Ohio 1933–1937; Republican presidential elector in 1936; special counsel to the Reconstruction Finance Corporation in the liquidation of the Lima First American Bank & Trust Co.; appointed Government appeal agent of Selective Service Board No. 2, Lima, Ohio, in 1948; is a resident of Lima, Ohio.

CABLE, Joseph (great-grandfather of John Levi Cable), a Representative from Ohio; born in Jefferson County, then in the Territory Northwest of the River Ohio (now in the State of Ohio), April 17, 1801; attended the public schools; studied law; was admitted to the bar and commenced practice in Jefferson County; established and published the Jeffersonian and Democrat at Steubenville, Ohio, in 1831 and later the Ohio Patriot at New Lisbon, Ohio; elected as a Democrat to the Thirty-first and Thirty-second Congresses (March 4, 1849–March 3, 1853); was not a candidate for renomination in 1852; moved to Sandusky, Ohio, in 1853 and published the Daily Sandusky Minor; in 1857 established the American and later the Bulletin at Van Wert, Ohio; moved to Wauseon, Ohio, and established the Wauseon Republican; subsequently moved to Paulding, where he published the Political Review; died in Paulding, Ohio, May 1, 1880; interment in Live Oak Cemetery.

CABOT, George (great-grandfather of Henry Cabot Lodge), a Senator from Massachusetts; born in Salem, Mass., December 16, 1751; received a classical education and attended Harvard College; member of the State provincial congress in 1775; delegate to the State constitutional convention in 1777 and to the convention which ratified the Constitution of the United States in 1787; elected as a Federalist to the United States Senate and served from March 4, 1791, to June 9, 1796, when he resigned; appointed the first Secretary of the Navy in the Cabinet of President Adams May 3, 1798, but declined; member of the executive council of Massachusetts in 1808; delegate to the Hartford convention of 1814 and served as its presiding officer; died in Boston, Mass., April 18, 1823; interment in the Granary Burial Ground, Boston, Mass.; reinterment in Mount Auburn Cemetery, Cambridge, Mass.

CADMUS, Cornelius Andrew, a Representative from New Jersey; born at Dundee Lake, Bergen County, N. J., October 7, 1844; attended the public schools; engaged in the feed and grain business in Paterson, N. J.; member of the State house of assembly in 1884 and 1885; sheriff of Passaic County 1887–1890; elected as a Democrat to the Fifty-second and Fifty-third Congresses (March 4, 1891–March 3, 1895); was not a candidate for renomination in 1894; member of the board of inspectors of the State prison; resumed his former business pursuits; died in Paterson, N. J., January 20, 1902; interment in Cedar Lawn Cemetery, near Paterson, N. J.

CADWALADER, John, a Representative from Pennsylvania; born in Philadelphia, Pa., April 1, 1805; was graduated from the University of Pennsylvania at Philadelphia in 1821; studied law; was admitted to the bar in 1825 and commenced practice in Philadelphia; solicitor for the Bank of the United States in 1830; captain of a military company during the riots of 1844 in Philadelphia; elected as a Democrat to the Thirty-fourth Congress (March 4, 1855–March 3, 1857); declined to be a candidate for renomination in 1856; resumed the practice of law in Philadelphia; appointed judge of the United States District Court for the Eastern District of Pennsylvania in 1858 and served until his death in Philadelphia, Pa., January 26, 1879; interment in Christ Churchyard.

CADWALADER, Lambert, a Delegate and a Representative from New Jersey; born near Trenton, N. J., in 1742; attended Dr. Allison's Academy, and the Universtity of Pennsylvania at Philadelphia in 1760; member of the common council of Philadelphia at the beginning of the Revolution; signed the nonimportation agreement; delegate to the provincial convention in Pennsylvania in 1775 and to the State constitutional convention in 1776; entered the Revolutionary Army and commanded a regiment of "The Greens"; lieutenant colonel of the Third Pennsylvania Battalion in 1776; colonel of the Fourth Pennsylvania Line; after being taken a prisoner at Fort Washington on the Hudson resigned from the Army; Member of the Continental Congress 1784–1787; elected to the First Congress (March 4, 1789–March 3, 1791); elected to the Third Congress (March 4, 1793–March 3, 1795); died on his estate, "Greenwood," near Trenton, N. J., September 13, 1823; interment in the Friends Burying Ground, Trenton, N. J.

CADY, Claude Ernest, a Representative from Michigan; born in Lansing, Ingham County, Mich., May 28, 1878; attended the common schools and the high school of his native city; engaged in the wholesale and retail grocery business from 1899 to 1913; was active in the amusement business, being owner of three theaters in Lansing, and also had financial interests in other Michigan cities 1914–1925; in the wholesale candy and fountain supplies business from 1925 to 1932; served as a member of the board of aldermen 1910–1917; member of the Lansing Police and Fire Commission 1918–1928; elected as a Democrat to the Seventy-third Congress (March 4, 1933–January 3, 1935); unsuccessful candidate for reelection in 1934 to the Seventy-fourth Congress; served as postmaster at Lansing, Mich., 1935–1943; retired from political and business life; died in Lansing, Mich., November 30, 1953; interment in Mount Hope Cemetery.

CADY, Daniel (uncle of John Watts Cady), a Representative from New York; born in Canaan, Columbia County, N. Y., April 29, 1773; attended the public schools; studied law in Albany, N. Y.; was admitted to the bar in 1795 and commenced practice in Florida, N. Y.; moved to Johnstown (then in Montgomery County), N. Y., and continued the practice of law; member of the State assembly 1808–1813; village trustee in 1808 and supervisor in 1809 and 1810; district attorney of the fifth district in 1813; elected as a Federalist to the Fourteenth Congress (March 4, 1815–March 3, 1817); was not a candidate for renomination in 1816; resumed the practice of law; served as justice of the State supreme court, fourth district, from June 7, 1847, to January 1, 1855, when he resigned; served as judge of the court of appeals in 1853; presidential elector on the Republican ticket of Frémont and Dayton in 1856 and served as president of the State electoral college; died in Johnstown, N. Y., October 31, 1859; interment in Johnstown Cemetery.

CADY, John Watts (nephew of Daniel Cady), a Representative from New York; born in Florida, Montgomery County, N. Y., June 28, 1790; attended school at the Old Stone Manse at Fort Hunter, and was graduated from Union College, Schenectady, N. Y., in 1808; studied law; was admitted to the bar and commenced practice in Johnstown (then in Montgomery County), N. Y.; town clerk of Johnstown 1814, 1816, and 1817; county supervisor 1818–1822 and 1826–1829; member of the State assembly in 1822; elected as a Whig to the Eighteenth Congress (March 4, 1823–March 3, 1825); was not a candidate for renomination in 1824; resumed the practice of law at Johnstown, N. Y.; district attorney of Fulton County 1840–1846; justice of the peace of Johnstown in 1853; died in Johnstown, N. Y., January 5, 1854; interment in Johnstown Cemetery.

CAFFERY, Donelson, a Senator from Louisiana; born near Franklin, St. Mary Parish, La., September 10, 1835; attended private schools in Franklin, St. Mary's College, Baltimore, Md., and Louisiana University at New Orleans; studied law, but abandoned the same to enter the Confederate Army; during the Civil War served as a lieutenant in the Thirteenth Louisiana Regiment and subsequently on the staff of Gen. W. W. Walker; served as clerk of court in 1866; was admitted to the bar in 1867 and commenced the practice of law in Franklin, La.; also engaged in sugar planting; delegate to the State constitutional convention in 1879; member of the State senate in 1892 and 1893; appointed and subsequently elected in 1894 as a Democrat to the United States Senate to fill the vacancy caused by the death of Randall Lee Gibson and served from December 31, 1892, to March 3, 1901; was not a candidate for reelection in 1900; resumed the practice of law; died in New Orleans, La., on December 30, 1906; interment in Franklin Cemetery, Franklin, La.

CAGE, Harry, a Representative from Mississippi; born at Cages Bend of the Cumberland River, Sumner County, Tenn.; moved to Wilkinson County, Miss., in early youth; studied law; was admitted to the bar and commenced practice in Woodville, Miss.; judge of the supreme court of Mississippi 1829–1832; elected to the Twenty-third Congress (March 4, 1833–March 3, 1835); retired from the practice of law and settled on Woodlawn plantation in the parish of Terrebonne, near the town of Houme, in Louisiana; died while on a visit to New Orleans, La., in 1859; interment in the cemetery of the Stewart family in Wilkinson County, Miss.

CAHILL, William Thomas, a Representative from New Jersey; born in Philadelphia, Pa., June 25, 1912; moved with his parents to New Jersey in 1919; graduated from Camden (N. J.) Catholic High School in 1929, St. Joseph's College in 1933, and Rutgers Law School in 1937; special agent of the Federal Bureau of Investigation in 1937 and 1938; was admitted to the bar in 1939 and commenced the practice of law in Camden, N. J.; city prosecutor of Camden, N. J., in 1944 and 1945; first assistant prosecutor of Camden County 1948–1951; special deputy attorney general of the State of New Jersey in 1951; member of the New Jersey General Assembly 1951–1953; elected as a Republican to the Eighty-sixth Congress (January 3, 1959–January 3, 1961). *Reelected to the Eighty-seventh Congress.*

CAHOON, William, a Representative from Vermont; born in Providence, R. I., January 12, 1774; attended the common schools; moved with his parents to Lyndon, Vt., in 1791 and engaged in milling and agricultural pursuits; member of the State house of representatives 1802–1810; succeeded his father as town clerk in 1808; Democratic presidential elector in 1808 and voted for Madison and Langdon; was the messenger to deliver the electoral vote of Vermont; county judge 1811–1819; appointed major general in the militia in 1808 and served during the War of 1812; delegate to the State constitutional conventions in 1814 and 1828; member of the executive council 1815–1820; Lieutenant Governor of Vermont in 1820 and 1821; elected on the Anti-Masonic ticket to the Twenty-first and Twenty-second Congresses (March 4, 1829–March 3, 1833); unsuccessful candidate in 1832 for reelection to the Twenty-third Congress; died in Lyndon, Vt., May 30, 1833; interment in Lyndon Town Cemetery, Lyndon Center, Vt.

CAIN, Harry Pulliam, a Senator from Washington; born in Nashville, Davidson County, Tenn., January 10, 1906; moved with his parents to Tacoma, Pierce County, Wash., in 1911; attended the public schools and Hill Military Academy at Portland, Oreg.; was graduated from the University of the South, Sewanee, Tenn.; graduate study in England and Germany; engaged in newspaper work in Portland, Oreg., in 1924 and 1925 and in the banking business at Tacoma, Wash., 1929–1939; elected mayor of Tacoma, Wash., in 1940, and again in 1942 for a four-year term; took leave of absence in May 1943 to enter the United States Army as a major; served overseas and was honorably discharged as a colonel on December 31, 1945; promoted on Ardennes battlefield to colonel; awarded five battle stars, Bronze Star with two clusters, Purple Heart, Legion of Merit, and Belgian and French Croix de Guerre with Palm; reassumed his duties as mayor of Tacoma until June 15, 1946; elected as a Republican to the United States Senate on November 5, 1946, for the term commencing January 3, 1947, and ending January 3, 1953; subsequently appointed on December 26, 1946, to fill the vacancy in the term ending January 3, 1947, caused by the resignation of Hugh B. Mitchell, who had been appointed to fill the unexpired term of Mon C. Wallgren, and served from December 26, 1946, to January 3, 1953; unsuccessful candidate for reelection in 1952; member of the Subversive Activities Control Board, Washington, D. C., from April 1953 to September 1956; moved to Florida in 1957 to become associated with the First Federal Savings & Loan Association of Miami as a vice president; resides on Bay Harbor Island, Miami Beach, Fla.

CAIN, Richard Harvey, a Representative from South Carolina; born in Greenbrier County, Va., April 12, 1825; was of the Negro race; moved with his father to Gallipolis, Ohio, in 1831 and attended school; entered the ministry, and was a pastor in Brooklyn, N. Y., from 1861 to 1865; moved to South Carolina in 1865 and settled in Charleston; delegate to the constitutional convention of South Carolina in 1868; member of the State senate 1868–1872; manager of a newspaper in Charleston in 1868; elected as a Republican to the Forty-third Congress (March 4, 1873–March 3, 1875); was not a candidate for renomination in 1874; elected to the Forty-fifth Congress (March 4, 1877–March 3, 1879); was not a candidate for renomination in 1878; appointed a bishop of the African Methodist Episcopal Church in 1880 and served until his death in Washington, D. C., January 18, 1887; interment in Graceland Cemetery.

CAINE, John Thomas, a Delegate from the Territory of Utah; born in the parish of Kirk Patrick, Isle of Man, January 8, 1829; attended the common schools in Douglas, Isle of Man; immigrated to the United States in 1846 and lived in New York City until 1848, when he went to St. Louis; settled in the Territory of Utah in 1852 and taught school; served as secretary of the Territorial council during the sessions of 1856, 1857, 1859, and 1860; one of the founders of the Salt Lake Herald in 1870; managing editor and president of the company; delegate to the constitutional conventions in 1872 and 1882; member of the Territorial council in 1874, 1876, 1880, and 1882; recorder of Salt Lake City in 1876, 1878, 1880, and 1882; elected as a Democrat to the Forty-seventh Congress to fill the vacancy caused by the action of the House declaring the Delegate-elect ineligible; reelected as a Democrat to the Forty-eighth, Forty-ninth, and Fiftieth Congresses and on the People's Party ticket to the Fifty-first and Fifty-second Congresses and served from November 7, 1882, to March 3, 1893; was not a candidate for renomination in 1892; was an unsuccessful Democratic candidate for Governor of Utah in 1895; member of the State senate in 1896; resumed the management of the Salt Lake Herald; died in Salt Lake City, Utah, September 20, 1911; interment in Salt Lake City Cemetery.

CAKE, Henry Lutz, a Representative from Pennsylvania; born near Northumberland, Northumberland County, Pa., on October 6, 1827; attended the common and private schools; learned the art of printing, and published the Pottsville (Pa.) Mining Record until the Civil War; entered the Union Army April 17, 1861, as a second lieutenant, and was elected colonel of the Twenty-fifth Regiment, Pennsylvania Volunteer Infantry, in Washington, D. C., May 1, 1861; reorganized the regiment after three months' service; commanded the Ninety-sixth Regiment, Pennsylvania Volunteer Infantry, from September 23, 1861, to March 12, 1863, when he resigned and settled in Tamaqua, Schuylkill County, Pa.; engaged in the mining and shipping of anthracite coal; elected as a Republican to the Fortieth and Forty-first Congresses (March 4, 1867–March 3, 1871); unsuccessful candidate for renomination in 1870; resumed the mining and shipping of coal; died in Northumberland, Pa., August 26, 1899; interment in Riverview Cemetery.

CALDER, William Musgrave, a Representative and a Senator from New York; born in Brooklyn, N. Y., March 3, 1869; attended the public schools of Brooklyn; apprenticed to the carpenter's trade, and studied at the evening school of Cooper Institute, New York City; engaged in building construction in 1893; building commissioner of the Borough of Brooklyn in 1902 and 1903; delegate to many Republican State conventions and to the Republican National Conventions in 1908, 1912, 1916, 1920, 1924, 1928, 1932, 1936, and 1940; elected as a Republican to the Fifty-ninth and to the four succeeding Congresses (March 4, 1905–March 3, 1915); was not a candidate for reelection in 1914; elected to the United States Senate and served from March 4, 1917, to March 3, 1923; unsuccessful candidate for reelection in 1922; again engaged in building construction and was also a director in many Brooklyn financial institutions; died in Brooklyn, N. Y., March 3, 1945; interment in Greenwood Cemetery.

CALDERHEAD, William Alexander, a Representative from Kansas; born on a farm near New Lexington, Perry County, Ohio, September 26, 1844; received private schooling and also attended the common schools and Franklin College, New Athens, Ohio; during the Civil War enlisted in August 1862 as a private in Company H, One Hundred and Twenty-sixth Regiment, Ohio Volunteer Infantry; was transferred to Company

D, Ninth Veteran Reserves, for disability incurred in service and discharged June 27, 1865; moved to Harvey County, Kans., in 1868 and engaged in agricultural pursuits near Newton; moved to Newton, Kans., in 1872 and taught school and studied law; was admitted to the bar in 1875; moved to Atchison, Kans., and continued to study law; also engaged in teaching; settled in Marysville, Marshall County, Kans., in 1879 and commenced the practice of law; served as prosecuting attorney of Marshall County 1889–1891; elected as a Republican to the Fifty-fourth Congress (March 4, 1895–March 3, 1897); unsuccessful candidate for reelection in 1896 to the Fifty-fifth Congress; elected to the Fifty-sixth and to the five succeeding Congresses (March 4, 1899–March 3, 1911); unsuccessful candidate for renomination in 1910; resumed the practice of law in Marysville, Kans., until 1920, when he retired from active business pursuits and moved to Enid, Okla., where he died on December 18, 1928; interment in Marysville Cemetery, Marysville, Kans.

CALDWELL, Alexander, a Senator from Kansas; born at Drakes Ferry, Huntingdon County, Pa., March 1, 1830; attended the public schools; enlisted in 1847 as a private in the Mexican War; moved to Columbia, Pa., in 1848; employed in a bank and subsequently went into business for himself; moved to Leavenworth, Kans., in 1861 and engaged in the transportation of military supplies to the various posts on the plains; became largely interested in the building of railroads, especially the Missouri River and Kansas Central Railroad in 1865; elected as a Republican to the United States Senate and served from March 4, 1871, to March 24, 1873, when he resigned; engaged in the manufacture of wagons and carriages, with general offices at Leavenworth, Kans., 1877–1897; president of the First National Bank of Leavenworth from 1897 until 1915; died in Kansas City, Mo., May 19, 1917; interment in Mount Muncie Cemetery, Leavenworth, Kans.

CALDWELL, Andrew Jackson, a Representative from Tennessee; born in Montevallo, Shelby County, Ala., July 22, 1837; moved to Tennessee in 1844 with his parents, who settled near Nashville; attended the common schools; was graduated from Franklin College, Tennessee, in 1854; taught school in Nashville 1854–1857; moved to Trenton in 1857 and studied law; during the Civil War served in the Confederate Army as a private and regimental quartermaster in the First Regiment, Tennessee Cavalry; resumed his law studies; was admitted to the Tennessee bar in 1867 and commenced the practice of law in Nashville, Tenn.; attorney general for the district of Davidson and Rutherford Counties, Tenn., 1870–1878; served as a member of the State house of representatives in 1880 and 1882; elected as a Democrat to the Forty-eighth and Forty-ninth Congresses (March 4, 1883–March 3, 1887); resumed the practice of law; died in Nashville, Tenn., November 22, 1906; interment in Mount Olivet Cemetery.

CALDWELL, Ben Franklin, a Representative from Illinois; born near Carrollton, Greene County, Ill., August 2, 1848; moved to Illinois in April 1853 with his parents, who settled near Chatham, Ill.; attended the public schools; engaged in agricultural pursuits; member of the Board of Supervisors of Sangamon County in 1877 and 1878; member of the State house of representatives 1882–1886; served in the State senate 1890–1894; upon his election to Congress in 1898 he resigned the presidency of the Farmers' National Bank of Springfield, which office he had held since 1885; president of the Caldwell State Bank of Chatham; elected as a Democrat to the Fifty-sixth, Fifty-seventh, and Fifty-eighth Congresses (March 4, 1899–March 3, 1905); unsuccessful candidate for reelection in 1904 to the Fifty-ninth Congress; elected to the Sixtieth Congress (March 4, 1907–

March 3, 1909); was not a candidate for renomination in 1908; again engaged in banking in Chatham, Ill.; died in Springfield, Ill., on December 29, 1924; interment in Oak Ridge Cemetery.

CALDWELL, Charles Pope, a Representative from New York; born near Bastrop, Bastrop County, Tex., June 18, 1875; attended the public schools; was graduated from the law department of the University of Texas at Austin in 1898 and the law department of Yale University in 1899; was admitted to the bar in Austin, Tex., in 1898, and later in New York City, where he commenced practice in 1900; appointed by Governor Dix a delegate to the Atlantic Deeper Water Ways Convention in 1910; delegate to the Democratic National Convention at Baltimore in 1912; elected as a Democrat to the Sixty-fourth, Sixty-fifth, and Sixty-sixth Congresses (March 4, 1915–March 3, 1921); declined to be a candidate for renomination in 1920; resumed the practice of law in New York City; appointed associate justice of the court of special sessions of New York City January 1, 1926, and served until December 1935; resumed the practice of law in Long Island, N. Y.; died in Sunnyside, Queens County, N. Y., July 31, 1940; remains were cremated and the ashes scattered over his ancestral estate in Bastrop County, Tex.

CALDWELL, George Alfred, a Representative from Kentucky; born in Columbia, Adair County, Ky., October 18, 1814; attended the common schools; studied law; was admitted to the bar in 1837 and commenced practice in Adair County; member of the State house of representatives in 1839 and 1840; elected as a Democrat to the Twenty-eighth Congress (March 4, 1843–March 3, 1845); commissioned major and quartermaster of Volunteers in the war with Mexico June 26, 1846; major of Infantry March 3, 1847, and major of voltigeurs April 9, 1847; brevetted lieutenant colonel September 13, 1847, "for gallant and meritorious services in the Battle of Chapultepec, Mexico"; honorably mustered out August 25, 1848; elected to the Thirty-first Congress (March 4, 1849–March 3, 1851); resumed the practice of law in Louisville; delegate to the Union National Convention at Philadelphia in 1866; died in Louisville, Ky., September 17, 1866; interment in Cave Hill Cemetery.

CALDWELL, Greene Washington, a Representative from North Carolina; born in Belmont, Gaston County, N. C., April 13, 1806; pursued academic studies; was graduated from the medical department of the University of Pennsylvania at Philadelphia in 1831 and practiced; assistant surgeon in the United States Army from July 13 to October 19, 1832; studied law; was admitted to the bar and practiced in Charlotte, N. C.; member of the State house of commons 1836–1841; elected as a Democrat to the Twenty-seventh Congress (March 4, 1841–March 3, 1843); was not a candidate for renomination in 1842; appointed superintendent of the United States Mint at Charlotte in 1844; participated in the war with Mexico as captain of Infantry; commissioned captain of the Third Dragoons April 9, 1847, and was mustered out July 20, 1848; member of the State senate in 1849; unsuccessful candidate for election in 1850 to the Thirty-second Congress; resumed the practice of medicine; died in Charlotte, N. C., July 10, 1864; interment in the Old Cemetery.

CALDWELL, James, a Representative from Ohio; born in Baltimore, Md., November 30, 1770; moved with his father to Virginia (now West Virginia) in 1772 and settled on what is now the site of the city of Wheeling; received a liberal schooling; moved to St. Clairsville, Ohio, in 1799; engaged in mercantile pursuits and later in banking; delegate to the convention which framed the first constitution of Ohio; clerk of the court of Belmont County, Ohio, 1806–1810; captain in an Ohio regiment in

the War of 1812; member of the State senate 1809–1812; elected as a Democrat to the Thirteenth and Fourteenth Congresses (March 4, 1813–March 3, 1817); Democratic presidential elector on the Monroe and Tompkins ticket in 1820 and on the Clay and Sanford ticket in 1824; resumed banking and mercantile business in St. Clairsville, Ohio; died in Wheeling, Va. (now West Virginia), in May 1838; interment in Episcopal Cemetery, St. Clairsville, Belmont County, Ohio.

CALDWELL, John Alexander, a Representative from Ohio; born in Fairhaven, Preble County, Ohio, April 21, 1852; educated in the common schools of his native county and also by private teachers; taught school for several years; was graduated from the Cincinnati Law College in 1876; was admitted to the bar the same year; again engaged in teaching; commenced the practice of law in Cincinnati, Ohio, in 1878; prosecuting attorney of the Cincinnati police court 1881–1885; elected judge of the city police court in 1887; elected president of the Ohio League of Republican Clubs in 1887; elected as a Republican to the Fifty-first, Fifty-second, and Fifty-third Congresses and served from March 4, 1889, until May 4, 1894, when he resigned; mayor of Cincinnati 1894–1897; Lieutenant Governor of Ohio 1899–1901; elected judge of the court of common pleas in 1902, and served until his death in Cincinnati, Ohio, May 24, 1927; interment in Spring Grove Cemetery.

CALDWELL, John Henry, a Representative from Alabama; born in Huntsville, Ala., April 4, 1826; attended the common schools of Huntsville and Bacon College, Harrodsburg, Ky.; taught school in Limestone County, Ala., four years; moved to Jacksonville, Ala., in 1848; was principal of the Jacksonville Female Academy 1848–1852 and of the Jacksonville Male Academy 1853–1857; edited the Jacksonville Republican in 1851 and 1852 and assumed the editorship of the Sunny South in 1855; member of the State house of representatives in 1857 and 1858; studied law; was admitted to the bar in 1859 and commenced practice in Jacksonville, Ala.; during the Civil War enlisted in the Confederate Army and organized Company A of the Tenth Alabama Regiment, from St. Clair and Calhoun Counties, and served throughout the war; promoted to major and then to lieutenant colonel; served in the Army of Virginia; elected solicitor for the tenth judicial circuit in 1863 but was deposed by the Provisional Governor in 1865; reelected the same year, and in 1867 was removed from office for refusing to obey military orders; elected as a Democrat to the Forty-third and Forty-fourth Congresses (March 4, 1873–March 3, 1877); was not a candidate for renomination in 1876; resumed the practice of law; died in Jacksonville, Ala., September 4, 1902; interment in Jacksonville Cemetery.

CALDWELL, John William, a Representative from Kentucky; born in Russellville, Logan County, Ky., January 15, 1837; attended the common schools and Bethel College; moved with his uncle to Texas in 1850, where he worked on a farm; engaged as a clerk and as a surveyor; returned to Kentucky and studied law in the Louisville University; was admitted to the bar in 1858 and commenced practice in Russellville, Ky.; during the Civil War volunteered as a private in the Confederate Army in 1861 and was immediately elected captain of the "Logan Grays"; promoted to major, lieutenant colonel, and colonel of the Ninth Regiment, Kentucky Infantry; resumed the practice of law in Russellville in 1865; elected judge of the Logan County Court in 1866 and reelected in 1870; elected as a Democrat to the Forty-fifth, Forty-sixth, and Forty-seventh Congresses (March 4, 1877–March 3, 1883); declined to be a candidate for reelection; president of the Logan County Bank; died in Russellville, Ky., July 4, 1903; interment in Maple Grove Cemetery.

CALDWELL, Joseph Pearson, a Representative from North Carolina; born near Olin, Iredell County, N. C., March 5, 1808; attended Bethany Academy, near Statesville, N. C.; studied law; was admitted to the bar and commenced practice in Statesville, N. C.; served in the State senate in 1833 and 1834; member of the State house of commons 1838–1844; elected as a Whig to the Thirty-first and Thirty-second Congresses (March 4, 1849–March 3, 1853); was not a candidate for renomination in 1852; died in Statesville, N. C., June 30, 1853; interment in Old Statesville Cemetery.

CALDWELL, Millard Fillmore, a Representative from Florida; born in Knoxville, Knox County, Tenn., February 6, 1897; attended the public schools, Carson-Newman College, Jefferson City, Tenn., the University of Mississippi at Oxford, and the University of Virginia at Charlottesville; during the First World War enlisted in the United States Army on April 3, 1918, was commissioned a second lieutenant in the Field Artillery, and was discharged January 11, 1919; studied law; was admitted to the bar in 1922 and commenced practice in Milton, Fla., in 1925; served as prosecuting attorney and county attorney of Santa Rosa County, Fla., 1926–1932; member of the State house of representatives 1929–1932; elected as a Democrat to the Seventy-third and to the three succeeding Congresses (March 4, 1933–January 3, 1941); was not a candidate for renomination in 1940; resumed the practice of law; Governor of Florida from January 2, 1945, to January 4, 1949; chairman of the National Governors' Conference in 1946 and 1947; chairman of the Regional Board of Control for Southern Regional Education 1948–1950; Administrator, Federal Civil Defense Administration 1950–1952; engaged in farming, banking, and practice of law; is a resident of Tallahassee, Fla.

CALDWELL, Patrick Calhoun, a Representative from South Carolina; born near Newberry, S. C., March 10, 1801; was graduated from South Carolina College (now the University of South Carolina) at Columbia in 1820; studied law; was admitted to the bar in 1822 and commenced practice in South Carolina; member of the State house of representatives 1836–1838; elected as a State Rights Democrat to the Twenty-seventh Congress (March 4, 1841–March 3, 1843); served in the State senate in 1848; died in South Carolina November 22, 1855.

CALDWELL, Robert Porter, a Representative from Tennessee; born in Adair County, Ky., December 16, 1821; moved with his parents to Henry County, Tenn.; a few years later moved to Obion County; attended the public schools at Troy and Lebanon; studied law at Troy; was admitted to the bar and commenced practice in Trenton in 1845; member of the State house of representatives in 1847 and 1848; served in the State senate in 1855 and 1856; elected attorney general for the sixteenth judicial circuit of Tennessee in 1858; during the Civil War was a major in the Twelfth Regiment, Tennessee Infantry, of the Confederate Army; elected as a Democrat to the Forty-second Congress (March 4, 1871–March 3, 1873); unsuccessful candidate for renomination in 1872 to the Forty-third Congress; resumed the practice of law in Trenton, Tenn.; died in Trenton March 12, 1885; interment in Oakland Cemetery.

CALDWELL, William Parker, a Representative from Tennessee; born in Christmasville, Carroll County, Tenn., November 8, 1832; attended school at McLemoresville, Tenn., and at Princeton, Ky.; studied law at Cumberland University, Lebanon, Tenn.; was admitted to the bar in 1853 and practiced in Dresden and Union City, Tenn.; member of the State house of representatives 1857–1859; presidential elector on the Democratic ticket of Douglas and Johnson in 1860; delegate to the Democratic

National Convention at New York City in 1868; elected as a Democrat to the Forty-fourth and Forty-fifth Congresses (March 4, 1875–March 3, 1879); resumed the practice of law in Gardner, Tenn.; member of the State senate 1891–1893; died in Gardner, Weakley County, Tenn., June 7, 1903; interment in the Caldwell Cemetery.

CALE, Thomas, a Delegate from the Territory of Alaska; born in Underhill, Chittenden County, Vt., September 17, 1848; attended the district schools and Bell Academy, Underhill Flats, Vt.; moved to Fort Edward, Washington County, N. Y., in 1866; taught school near Underhill Center, Vt., in 1867 and 1868; moved to Fond du Lac, Wis., in 1869; taught school in several districts in Fond du Lac County and then engaged in agricultural pursuits near Eden, Wis.; town clerk of Eden, Wis., 1881–1884; member of the board of commissioners of Fond du Lac County 1884–1886; returned to Fond du Lac, Wis., and served as undersheriff of Fond du Lac County 1886–1888; county sheriff 1888–1890; engaged as a salesman of farm machinery; moved to Fairbanks, Alaska, in 1898 and engaged in mining; elected as an Independent to the Sixtieth Congress (March 4, 1907–March 3, 1909); was not a candidate for renomination in 1908; engaged in farming near McLaughlin, S. Dak., 1910–1915 and near Stevens Point, Wis., 1915–1920; retired from active pursuits in 1920 and resided in Fond du Lac, Wis., until his death in that city on February 3, 1941; interment in Calvary Cemetery.

CALHOON, John, a Representative from Kentucky; born in Henry County, Ky., in 1797; studied law; was admitted to the bar and practiced; member of the State house of representatives in 1820, 1821, 1829, and 1830; unsuccessful candidate for election to the Twentieth Congress; received the credentials of an election to the Twentieth Congress, held November 5–7, 1827, to fill the vacancy caused by the death of William S. Young, but, in order to avoid a contest, resigned and, together with his opponent, Thomas Chilton, petitioned the Governor for a new election; was again unsuccessful; elected as a Whig to the Twenty-fourth and Twenty-fifth Congresses (March 4, 1835–March 3, 1839); moved to St. Louis, Mo., in 1839; resumed the practice of law; returned to Kentucky; appointed judge of the fourteenth judicial district in January 1842.

CALHOUN, John Caldwell (cousin of John Ewing Colhoun and Joseph Calhoun), a Representative and a Senator from South Carolina and a Vice President of the United States; born near Calhoun Mills, Abbeville District (now Mount Carmel, McCormick County), S. C., March 18, 1782; attended the common schools and Willington Academy; was graduated from Yale College in 1804 and from Litchfield (Conn.) Law School in 1806; was admitted to the bar in 1807 and commenced practice in Abbeville, S. C.; also engaged in agricultural pursuits; member of the State house of representatives in 1808 and 1809; elected as a War Democrat to the Twelfth and to the three succeeding Congresses and served from March 4, 1811, to November 3, 1817, when he resigned; appointed Secretary of War and served from December 10, 1817, to March 3, 1825; elected Vice President of the United States in 1824; reelected in 1828 on the Jackson ticket and served from March 4, 1825, to December 28, 1832, when he resigned, having been elected to the United States Senate on December 12, 1832, to fill the vacancy caused by the resignation of Robert Y. Hayne; reelected in 1834 and 1840 and served from December 29, 1832, until his resignation, effective March 3, 1843; appointed Secretary of State March 6, 1844, entered upon his duties April 1, 1844, and served until March 6, 1845; declined the offer of the English mission tendered by Presidents Polk and Adams; again elected to the United

States Senate to fill the vacancy caused by the resignation of Daniel E. Huger; reelected in 1846 and served from November 26, 1845, until his death in Washington, D. C., March 31, 1850; interment in St. Philip's Churchyard, Charleston, S. C.

CALHOUN, Joseph (cousin of John Caldwell Calhoun and John Ewing Colhoun), a Representative from South Carolina; born in Staunton, Augusta County, Va., October 22, 1750; moved with his father to South Carolina in 1756 and settled in Granville District, on Little River, near the present town of Abbeville; received a limited education; engaged in agricultural pursuits; served as a member of the South Carolina House of Representatives in 1804 and 1805; colonel of State militia; elected as a Democrat to the Tenth Congress to fill the vacancy caused by the death of Levi Casey; reelected to the Eleventh Congress and served from June 2, 1807, to March 3, 1811; declined to be a candidate for reelection in 1810 to the Twelfth Congress; resumed agricultural pursuits and engaged in milling; died in Calhoun Mills, Abbeville District (now Mount Carmel, McCormick County), April 14, 1817; interment in the family burying ground near his home.

CALHOUN, William Barron, a Representative from Massachusetts; born in Boston, Mass., December 29, 1796; was graduated from Yale College in 1814; studied law; was admitted to the bar and commenced practice in Springfield; member of the State house of representatives 1825–1834, serving as speaker 1828–1834; elected as a Whig to the Twenty-fourth and to the three succeeding Congresses (March 4, 1835–March 3, 1843); was not a candidate for renomination in 1842; member of the State senate in 1846 and 1847, serving as its president; secretary of State of Massachusetts 1848–1851; State bank commissioner 1853–1855; presidential elector on the Whig ticket of Clay and Frelinghuysen in 1844; mayor of Springfield in 1859; again a member of the State house of representatives in 1861 and 1862; died in Springfield, Mass., November 8, 1865; interment in Springfield Cemetery.

CALKIN, Hervey Chittenden, a Representative from New York; born in Malden, Ulster County, N. Y., March 23, 1828; attended the public schools; moved to New York City in 1847; employed in the Morgan Iron Works for five years; in 1852 commenced business as a dealer in metals and identified with the shipping interests of the country; school officer in his ward; elected as a Democrat to the Forty-first Congress (March 4, 1869–March 3, 1871); resumed his former business pursuits in New York City until 1904, when he retired; died in the Borough of the Bronx, New York City, April 20, 1913; interment in Woodlawn Cemetery.

CALKINS, William Henry, a Representative from Indiana; born in Pike County, Ohio, February 18, 1842; studied law; was admitted to the bar and practiced; during the Civil War served in the Union Army from May 1861 to December 1865, except three months in 1863, attached to the Fourteenth Iowa Infantry and the Twelfth Indiana Cavalry; took up his residence in La Porte, Ind.; State's attorney for the ninth Indiana judicial circuit 1866–1870; member of the State house of representatives in 1871; elected as a Republican to the Forty-fifth and to the three succeeding Congresses and served from March 4, 1877, to October 20, 1884, when he resigned; moved to Tacoma, Wash., and resumed the practice of law; appointed United States associate justice of the Territory of Washington in April 1889 and served until November 11, 1889, when the Territory was admitted as a State into the Union; died in Tacoma, Wash., on January 29, 1894; interment in Tacoma Cemetery.

CALL, Jacob, a Representative from Indiana; born in Kentucky; was graduated from an academy in Kentucky; studied law; was admitted to the bar and practiced in Vincennes and Princeton, Ind.; judge of the Knox County Circuit Court in 1817, 1818, and 1822–1824; elected to the Eighteenth Congress to fill the vacancy caused by the death of William Prince and served from December 23, 1824, to March 3, 1825; died in Frankfort, Ky., April 20, 1826.

CALL, Richard Keith (uncle of Wilkinson Call), a Delegate from the Territory of Florida; born near Petersburg, Va., October 24, 1792; attended the common schools and Mount Pleasant Academy; in 1814 entered the United States Army as first lieutenant in the Forty-fourth Infantry; special aide to Major General Jackson in the Battle of New Orleans; promoted to captain in July 1818 and resigned May 1, 1822; settled in the Territory of Florida; studied law; was admitted to the bar and practiced in Pensacola; member of the Territorial council in 1822; brigadier general of the West Florida Militia in 1823; elected as a Democrat to the Eighteenth Congress (March 4, 1823–March 3, 1825); receiver of the land office of the Territory of Florida; Governor of the Territory 1835–1840 and 1841–1844; unsuccessful candidate of the Whig Party for Governor of the new State in 1845; devoted the remaining years of his life in a gallant defense of the Union as opposed to the growing sentiment for secession; died in Tallahassee, Fla., September 14, 1862; interment in a private cemetery on his estate.

CALL, Wilkinson (nephew of Richard Keith Call and cousin of James David Walker), a Senator from Florida; born in Russellville, Logan County, Ky., January 9, 1834; attended the common schools; moved to Jacksonville, Fla.; studied law; was admitted to the bar and practiced; served as adjutant general in the Confederate Army during the Civil War; elected to the United States Senate on December 29, 1865, but was not permitted to take the seat; Democratic presidential elector on the Greeley and Brown ticket in 1872 and on the Tilden and Hendricks ticket in 1876; member of the Democratic National Executive Committee; delegate to the Democratic National Convention at St. Louis in 1876; practiced law in Jacksonville; elected as a Democrat to the United States Senate in 1879; reelected in 1885 and 1891 and served from March 4, 1879, to March 3, 1897; retired, and resided in Washington, D. C., until his death on August 24, 1910; interment in Oak Hill Cemetery.

CALLAHAN, James Yancy, a Delegate from the Territory of Oklahoma; born on a farm near Salem, Dent County, Mo., December 19, 1852; attended the common schools; entered the ministry in 1880; engaged in agricultural pursuits, saw-milling, and mining; moved to Stanton County, Kans., in 1885; elected register of deeds in 1886; reelected in 1888 and served until December 1889, when he resigned; returned to Dent County, Mo.; moved to Oklahoma in 1892 and settled near Kingfisher, Kingfisher County, and engaged in agricultural pursuits; elected on the Free Silver ticket to the Fifty-fifth Congress (March 4, 1897–March 3, 1899); was not a candidate for renomination in 1898; published the Jacksonian at Enid, Garfield County, Okla., until January 1, 1913; retired from active business pursuits and resided in Enid, Okla., until his death there on May 3, 1935; interment in Enid Cemetery.

CALLAWAY, Oscar, a Representative from Texas; born in Harmony Hill (Nip-and-Tuck), Rusk County, Tex., October 2, 1872; moved with his parents to Comanche County in 1876; attended the public schools, and was graduated from the Comanche High School in 1894; taught school 1894–1897; attended the University of Texas at Austin 1897–1899, and was graduated from the law department of that university in 1900; was admitted to the bar the same year and commenced practice in Comanche, Tex.; prosecuting attorney of Comanche County 1900–1902; delegate to Democratic State conventions in 1896, 1898, 1900–1916, and 1920–1926; elected as a Democrat to the Sixty-second, Sixty-third, and Sixty-fourth Congresses (March 4, 1911–March 3, 1917); unsuccessful candidate for renomination in 1916; returned to his ranch near Comanche, Tex., where he engaged in agricultural pursuits and stock raising, and also in the practice of law in Comanche; died in Comanche, Tex., January 31, 1947; interment in Oakwood Cemetery.

CALLIS, John Benton, a Representative from Alabama; born in Fayetteville, Cumberland County, N. C., January 3, 1828; moved to Tennessee in 1834 with his parents, who settled in Carroll County, and thence, in 1840, to Lancaster, Grant County, Wis.; attended the common schools; studied medicine for three years, but then abandoned its further study; went to Minnesota in 1849 and was one of the contractors who built Fort Gaines (now Fort Ripley); crossed the Plains to California in 1851 and engaged in mining and the mercantile business; went to Central America in 1853; returned to Lancaster, Wis., in the fall of that year and again engaged in mercantile pursuits; during the Civil War entered the Union Army as a lieutenant, and was promoted to captain in the Seventh Regiment, Wisconsin Volunteer Infantry (later forming a part of the Iron Brigade), August 30, 1861; major January 5, 1863; appointed by President Lincoln military superintendent of the War Department at Washington, D. C., in 1864; promoted to lieutenant colonel February 11, 1865; brevetted colonel and brigadier general of Volunteers March 13, 1865, "for efficient and meritorious services"; appointed captain in the Forty-fifth Regiment, United States Infantry, and brevetted major March 7, 1867, "for gallant and meritorious services in the Battle of Gettysburg, Pa."; settled in Huntsville, Ala., in 1865; resigned his commission in the Army on February 4, 1868; upon the readmission of the State of Alabama to representation was elected as a Republican to the Fortieth Congress and served from July 21, 1868, to March 3, 1869; was not a candidate for renomination in 1868; returned to Lancaster, Wis., and engaged in the real-estate business; member of the State assembly in 1874; retired from active pursuits; died in Lancaster, Wis., on September 24, 1898; interment in Hillside Cemetery.

CALVERT, Charles Benedict, a Representative from Maryland; born in Riverdale, Prince Georges County, Md., August 24, 1808; completed preparatory studies at Bladensburg Academy, Maryland; was graduated from the University of Virginia at Charlottesville in 1827; engaged in agricultural pursuits and stock breeding; member of the State house of delegates in 1839, 1843, and 1844; president of the Prince Georges County Agricultural Society and the Maryland State Agricultural Society; vice president of the United States Agricultural Society; founded the first agricultural research college in America (later the Maryland Agricultural College at College Park), chartered in 1856; one of the early advocates for the establishment of the United States Department of Agriculture; elected as a Union Whig to the Thirty-seventh Congress (March 4, 1861–March 3, 1863); was not a candidate for renomination in 1862; resumed agricultural pursuits; died in Riverdale, Prince Georges County, Md., May 12, 1864; interment in Calvert Cemetery.

CALVIN, Samuel, a Representative from Pennsylvania; born in Washingtonville, Pa., July 30, 1811; attended the common schools and Milton Academy; taught in Huntingdon Academy; studied law; was admitted to the bar in 1836 and commenced practice in Hollidaysburg, Pa.; elected as a Whig to the Thirty-first Congress (March 4, 1849–March 3, 1851); declined to be a candidate for renomination in 1850; resumed the practice of law; director of the Hollidaysburg School Board for thirty years; member of the State revenue board; member of the State constitutional convention in 1873; died in Hollidaysburg, Blair County, Pa., on March 12, 1890; interment in Presbyterian Cemetery.

CAMBRELENG, Churchill Caldom, a Representative from New York; born in Washington, Beaufort County, N. C., October 24, 1786; attended school in New Bern, N. C.; moved to New York City in 1802, where he became a clerk and subsequently engaged in the mercantile business; elected as a Democrat to the Seventeenth and to the eight succeeding Congresses (March 4, 1821–March 3, 1839); unsuccessful candidate for reelection in 1838 to the Twenty-sixth Congress; appointed United States Minister to Russia by President Van Buren and served from May 20, 1840, to July 13, 1841; member of the State constitutional convention in 1846; retired from active business pursuits; died at his residence near Huntington, Suffolk County, N. Y., April 30, 1862; interment in Greenwood Cemetery, Brooklyn, N. Y.

CAMDEN, Johnson Newlon, a Senator from West Virginia; born in Collins Settlement, Lewis County, Va. (now West Virginia), March 6, 1828; attended school in Sutton, Va. (now West Virginia); appointed as a cadet to the United States Military Academy at West Point in 1846 and served until 1848, when he resigned; studied law; was admitted to the bar and commenced practice in Sutton in 1851; appointed the same year prosecuting attorney for Braxton County; elected prosecuting attorney for Nicholas County in 1852; in 1858 engaged in the development of petroleum and in manufacturing in Parkersburg, Va. (now West Virginia); president of the First National Bank of Parkersburg at its organization in 1862; nominee of the Democratic Party for Governor of the State in 1868 and again in 1872; delegate to the Democratic National Convention at New York City in 1868, at Baltimore in 1872, and at St. Louis in 1876; elected as a Democrat to the United States Senate and served from March 4, 1881, to March 3, 1887; resumed the practice of law at Parkersburg; again elected to the United States Senate to fill the vacancy caused by the death of John E. Kenna, and served from January 25, 1893, to March 3, 1895; continued former business pursuits; died in Baltimore, Md., April 25, 1908; interment in Odd Fellows Cemetery, Parkersburg, W. Va.

CAMDEN, Johnson Newlon, Jr. (son of the preceding), a Senator from Kentucky; born in Parkersburg, Wood County, W. Va., January 5, 1865; attended Episcopal High School, Alexandria, Va., Phillips Academy, Andover, Mass., Virginia Military Institute, Lexington, Va., Columbia Law School, New York City, and the summer law school of the University of Virginia at Charlottesville; was admitted to the bar in 1888 but never practiced; moved to Spring Hill Farm, near Versailles, Woodford County, Ky., in 1890; engaged in agricultural pursuits and in the breeding and raising of fine cattle and thoroughbred horses; also interested in the opening and development of the coal fields of eastern Kentucky; served on both the executive and financial committees of the Democratic State Committee in 1911; appointed and subsequently elected as a Democrat to the United States Senate to fill the vacancy caused by the death of William O. Bradley and served from June 16, 1914, to March 3, 1915; declined to be a candidate for renomination in 1914; resumed agricultural pursuits on a farm near Paris, Ky., until his death on August 16, 1942; interment in Frankfort Cemetery, Frankfort, Ky.

CAMERON, Angus, a Senator from Wisconsin; born in Caledonia, Livingston County, N. Y., July 4, 1826; attended the public schools and the Genesee Wesleyan Seminary, Lima, N. Y.; taught school; studied law in Buffalo, N. Y.; was graduated from the National Law School, Ballston Spa, N. Y., in 1853; was admitted to the bar the same year and commenced practice in Buffalo, N. Y.; engaged in banking for a year; moved to La Crosse, Wis., in 1857 and resumed the practice of law; served in the State senate in 1863, 1864, 1871, and 1872; member of the State assembly in 1866 and 1867, and served as speaker in 1867; delegate to the Republican National Convention at Baltimore in 1864; regent of the University of Wisconsin 1866–1875; elected as a Republican to the United States Senate on February 3, 1875, and served from March 4, 1875, until March 3, 1881; was not a candidate for reelection in 1881; elected March 10, 1881, to fill the vacancy caused by the death of Matthew H. Carpenter and took his seat March 14, 1881, and served until March 3, 1885; was not a candidate for reelection; resumed the practice of law in La Crosse, Wis., and died there March 30, 1897; interment in Oak Grove Cemetery.

CAMERON, James Donald (son of Simon Cameron), a Senator from Pennsylvania; born in Middletown, Dauphin County, Pa., May 14, 1833; was graduated from Princeton College in 1853; entered the Middletown Bank as clerk and subsequently became its cashier; president of the Northern Central Railway Co. of Pennsylvania 1866–1874; appointed Secretary of War in the Cabinet of President Grant and served from May 22, 1876, to March 12, 1877; delegate to the Republican National Conventions in 1868, 1876, and 1880; chairman of the Republican National Committee in 1880; elected as a Republican to the United States Senate to fill the vacancy caused by the resignation of his father, Simon Cameron, March 5, 1877; reelected in 1879, 1885, and 1890, and served from March 20, 1877, to March 3, 1897; was not a candidate for reelection; engaged in several business enterprises in Harrisburg, Pa.; died at his country home, "Donegal," in Lancaster County, Pa., August 30, 1918; interment in the Harrisburg Cemetery, Harrisburg, Pa.

CAMERON, Ralph Henry, a Delegate and a Senator from Arizona; born in Southport, Lincoln County, Maine, October 21, 1863; attended the common schools; emigrated to the West and became interested in mining and stock raising; locator and builder of the Bright Angel trail into the Grand Canyon of the Colorado in Arizona; moved to the Territory of Arizona in 1883; sheriff of Coconino County in 1891 and 1894–1898; delegate to the Republican National Convention at St. Louis in 1896; member of the board of supervisors of Coconino County 1905–1907 and served as chairman; elected as a Republican a Delegate to the Sixty-first and Sixty-second Congresses and served from March 4, 1909, to February 18, 1912, when, pursuant to law, his term expired, Arizona having been admitted as a State into the Union and the Representative-elect having qualified; resumed mining pursuits at Phoenix, Ariz.; elected to the United States Senate in 1920 and served from March 4, 1921, to March 3, 1927; unsuccessful candidate for reelection in 1926 and for election in 1928; engaged in mica mining in North Carolina and Georgia and in gold mining in California; resided in Los Angeles, Calif., and Yuma, Ariz., until his death in Washington, D. C., while on a business trip, February 12, 1953; interment in the American Legion Cemetery, Grand Canyon, Ariz.

CAMERON, Simon (father of James Donald Cameron), a Senator from Pennsylvania; born in Maytown, Lancaster County, Pa., March 8, 1799; apprenticed as a printer at the age of ten years; successfully conducted and edited the Doylestown (Pa.) Democrat; purchased the Harrisburg Republican and rechristened it the Intelligencer in 1821; cashier of a bank, president of two railroad companies, and adjutant general of Pennsylvania; elected to the United States Senate to fill the vacancy caused by the resignation of James Buchanan, and acted with the Democratic Party; served from March 13, 1845, to March 3, 1849; left the Democratic Party in 1854 and assisted in the formation of the People's Party; elected as a Republican to the United States Senate and served from March 4, 1857, to March 4, 1861, when he resigned, having been appointed Secretary of War; had strong support as a presidential candidate in 1860, but failed to secure the nomination for Vice President on the ticket with Abraham Lincoln; Secretary of War in the Cabinet of President Lincoln from March 11, 1861, until January 11, 1862, when he resigned and organized the Union forces for service in the field; was immediately appointed United States Minister to Russia; resigned this portfolio on November 8, 1862; delegate to the Republican National Convention at Baltimore in 1864 and to the Loyalists' Convention at Philadelphia in 1866; was again elected to the United States Senate in 1867; reelected in 1873, and served from March 4, 1867, until his resignation, effective March 12, 1877; retired from active business pursuits and traveled extensively in Europe and the West Indies; died near Maytown, Lancaster County, Pa., June 26, 1889; interment in Harrisburg Cemetery, Harrisburg, Pa.

CAMINETTI, Anthony, a Representative from California; born in Jackson, Amador County, Calif., July 30, 1854; attended the public schools of his native county, the grammar schools in San Francisco, and the University of California at Berkeley; studied law; was admitted to the bar in 1877 and commenced practice in Jackson, Calif.; district attorney of Amador County 1878–1882; Democratic alternate elector for the second congressional district in 1880; served in the State assembly in 1883–1885; member of the State senate 1885–1887; Democratic presidential elector on the Cleveland and Thurman ticket in 1888 and on the Wilson and Marshall ticket in 1912; the first native citizen of the State of California elected to Congress; elected as a Democrat to the Fifty-second and Fifty-third Congresses (March 4, 1891–March 3, 1895); unsuccessful candidate in 1894 for reelection to the Fifty-fourth Congress; delegate to the Democratic National Convention at Chicago in 1896; again a member of the State assembly 1896–1900; in April 1897 was appointed code commissioner and served until July 31, 1899; member of the State senate 1907–1913; served as United States commissioner of immigration from 1913 to 1921; when war was declared with Germany in 1917 was appointed a member of the War Industries Board and after the war was sent to Europe to investigate conditions there; engaged in the practice of his profession in Jackson, Amador County, Calif., until his death, November 17, 1923; interment in the Protestant Cemetery.

CAMP, Albert Sidney, a Representative from Georgia; born on a farm near Moreland, Coweta County, Ga., July 26, 1892; attended the public schools, and was graduated from the law department of the University of Georgia at Athens in 1915; was admitted to the bar the same year and commenced practice at Newnan, Ga.; during the First World War served overseas as a member of Headquarters Detachment of the Eighty-second Division 1917–1919; delegate to the Democratic National Convention in New York City in 1924; member of the State house of representatives 1923–1928; assistant United States attorney for the northern district of Georgia 1934–1939; elected as a Democrat to the Seventy-sixth Congress to fill the vacancy caused by the death of Emmett M. Owen; reelected to the Seventy-seventh and to the six succeeding Congresses and served from August 1, 1939, until his death in the naval hospital at Bethesda, Md., July 24, 1954; interment in Oak Hill Cemetery, Newnan, Ga.

CAMP, John Henry, a Representative from New York; born in Ithaca, Tompkins County, N. Y., April 4, 1840; attended the common schools, and was graduated from the Albany Law School in 1860; was admitted to the bar the same year and commenced practice in Lyons, N. Y.; clerk of the surrogate court in 1863; prosecuting attorney of Wayne County 1867–1870; presidential elector on the Republican ticket of Grant and Wilson in 1872, and elected secretary of the Electoral College; elected as a Republican to the Forty-fifth, Forty-sixth, and Forty-seventh Congresses (March 4, 1877–March 3, 1883); resumed the practice of law in Lyons, Wayne County, N. Y., where he died October 12, 1892; interment in Grove Cemetery, Trumansburg, N. Y.

CAMPBELL, Albert James, a Representative from Montana; born in Pontiac, Oakland County, Mich., December 12, 1857; attended the common schools and the Michigan Agricultural College at Lansing; taught school for several years; studied law; was admitted to the bar in 1881 and commenced practice in Oxford, Mich.; moved to Clarke, Mich., in 1882, and resumed the practice of law; prosecuting attorney of Lake County, Mich., from 1886 to 1888 when he resigned; moved to Butte, Mont., on November 16, 1889, and continued the practice of his profession; member of the State house of representatives in 1897; elected as a Democrat to the Fifty-sixth Congress (March 4, 1899–March 3, 1901); declined to be a candidate for renomination in 1900; resumed the practice of law in Butte, Mont.; died in New York City, N. Y., August 9, 1907; interment in Mount Moriah Cemetery, Butte, Mont.

CAMPBELL, Alexander, a Senator from Ohio; born in Frederick County, Va., in 1779; moved with his parents to east Tennessee and later to Kentucky, settling near Lexington; moved with his mother to Woodford County, Ky.; educated at Pisgah Academy, Woodford County, Ky.; studied medicine at Transylvania University and commenced practice in Cynthiana, Ky., in 1801; member of the State house of representatives from Harrison County in 1803; moved to that part of Adams County in 1804, later set off to Brown County, Ohio, where he continued the practice of medicine; also engaged in mercantile pursuits; member of the State house of representatives from Adams County in 1807; reelected in 1808 and 1809, and served as speaker in 1808 and 1809; unsuccessful candidate for United States Senator in 1808; elected to the United States Senate to fill the vacancy caused by the resignation of Edward Tiffin and served from December 11, 1809, to March 3, 1813; resumed the practice of medicine; moved to Staunton (now Ripley), Ohio, in 1815; was the first physician in that town; declined a professorship in the Ohio Medical College in Cincinnati; member of the State house of representatives from Clermont County in 1819, and served as speaker pro tempore; presidential elector on the Democratic ticket of Monroe and Tompkins in 1820 and on the Whig ticket of Harrison and Granger in 1836; member of the State senate 1822–1824; unsuccessful candidate for Governor in 1826; again a member of the State house of representatives in 1832 and 1833; served as vice president of the first general antislavery society of Ohio in 1835; mayor of Ripley 1838–1840; died in Ripley, Brown County, Ohio, November 5, 1857; interment in Maplewood Cemetery.

CAMPBELL, Alexander, a Representative from Illinois; born on a farm near Concord, Franklin County, Pa., October 4, 1814; attended the public schools; became a clerk in an iron works and was subsequently promoted to superintendent, continuing in the business of managing iron works in Pennsylvania, Kentucky, and Missouri until 1850, when he moved to La Salle, Ill., and became interested in the coal fields; mayor of La Salle in 1852 and 1853; member of the State house of representatives in 1858 and 1859; delegate to the State constitutional convention in 1862; elected as an Independent to the Forty-fourth Congress (March 4, 1875–March 3, 1877); unsuccessful candidate for reelection in 1876 to the Forty-fifth Congress; was called the "Father of the Greenback Party"; retired from public life; died in La Salle, Ill., August 8, 1898; interment in Oakwood Cemetery.

CAMPBELL, Brookins, a Representative from Tennessee; born in Washington County, Tenn., in 1808; attended the rural schools and was graduated from Washington College (now Washington and Lee University) at Lexington; studied law; was admitted to the bar and practiced; member of the State house of representatives 1835–1839, 1841–1846, and 1851–1853, and served as speaker in 1845; during the Mexican War was appointed by President Polk in 1846 an assistant quartermaster to the Army with the rank of major; elected as a Democrat to the Thirty-third Congress and served from March 4, 1853, until his death in Washington, D. C., December 25, 1853, without having qualified; interment in Providence Presbyterian Churchyard, Greene County, Tenn.

CAMPBELL, Courtney Warren, a Representative from Florida; born in Chillicothe, Livingston County, Mo., April 29, 1895; educated in Westminster College, Fulton, Mo., and the University of Missouri at Columbia, Mo.; during the First World War served as a second lieutenant in the United States Army; studied law; was admitted to the bar in Missouri and Florida in 1924 and practiced in Tampa, Fla., 1924–1928; farmer, citrus grower, banker, and land developer; became vice president and general manager of Food Machinery & Chemical Corp., Lakeland, Fla., in 1927; assistant attorney general State of Florida; member Florida State Road Board 1942–1947; founder of Florida State Roadside Parks in 1944 and builder of Courtney Campbell Parkway between Clearwater and Tampa in 1947; chairman Pinellas County Park Board in 1948 and 1949; member Florida War Labor Relations Board 1941–1946; elected as a Democrat to the Eighty-third Congress (January 3, 1953–January 3, 1955); unsuccessful for reelection in 1954 to the Eighty-fourth Congress; resumed business interests; is a resident of Clearwater, Fla.

CAMPBELL, Ed Hoyt, a Representative from Iowa; born in Battle Creek, Ida County, Iowa, March 6, 1882; attended the public schools of his native city, and was graduated from the law department of the State University of Iowa at Iowa City in 1906; was admitted to the bar the same year and commenced practice in Battle Creek; mayor of Battle Creek 1908–1911; member of the State house of representatives 1911–1913; during the First World War served as a private in Company Six, First Officers Training School, Fort Snelling, Minn.; member of the State senate 1920–1928, serving as president pro tempore 1924–1926; elected as a Republican to the Seventy-first and Seventy-second Congresses (March 4, 1929–March 3, 1933); unsuccessful candidate for reelection in 1932 to the Seventy-third Congress; resumed the practice of law and is a resident of Battle Creek, Iowa.

CAMPBELL, Felix, a Representative from New York; born in Brooklyn, N. Y., February 28, 1829; attended the common schools; became a manufacturer of iron pipe and a consulting engineer; president of the board of supervisors in 1858; appointed by Governor Tilden a member of the board of commissioners from New York to the Centennial Exhibition at Philadelphia in 1876; elected as a Democrat to the Forty-eighth and to the three succeeding Congresses (March 4, 1883–March 3, 1891); declined to be a candidate for renomination in 1890; died in Brooklyn, N. Y., November 8, 1902; interment in Holy Cross Cemetery.

CAMPBELL, George Washington, a Representative and a Senator from Tennessee; born in the parish of Tongue, Sutherlandshire, Scotland, February 9, 1769; immigrated with his parents to North Carolina in 1772; taught school; was graduated from Princeton College in 1794; studied law while teaching; was admitted to the bar in North Carolina and commenced practice in Knoxville, Tenn.; elected as a Democrat to the Eighth, Ninth, and Tenth Congresses (March 4, 1803–March 3, 1809); one of the managers appointed by the House of Representatives in January 1804 to conduct the impeachment proceedings against John Pickering, judge of the United States District Court for New Hampshire, and in December of the same year against Samuel Chase, Associate Justice of the Supreme Court of the United States; judge of the State supreme court of errors and appeals 1809–1811; elected to the United States Senate to fill the vacancy caused by the resignation of Jenkin Whiteside and served from October 8, 1811, to February 11, 1814, when he resigned; appointed Secretary of the Treasury in the Cabinet of President Madison and served from February 9, 1814, to October 6, 1814, when he resigned because of ill health; again elected to the United States Senate and served from October 10, 1815, until his resignation, effective April 20, 1818; Minister to Russia 1818–1821; member of the French Spoliation Claims Commission in 1831; died in Nashville, Tenn., February 17, 1848; interment in the City Cemetery.

CAMPBELL, Guy Edgar, a Representative from Pennsylvania; born in Fetterman, Taylor County, W. Va., October 9, 1871; attended the grammar and high schools; moved to Pennsylvania with his parents, who located in Pittsburgh in 1889, and subsequently, in 1893, to Crafton Borough, Allegheny County; attended Iron City Business College at Pittsburgh; was employed as a clerk in the offices of the Baltimore & Ohio Railroad at Pittsburgh, Pa., until June 1896, when he resigned; was engaged in the general insurance business in Pittsburgh until 1903; was interested in the production of oil and gas in Pennsylvania and West Virginia; elected as a Democrat to the Sixty-fifth, Sixty-sixth, and Sixty-seventh Congresses (March 4, 1917–March 3, 1923), and as a Republican to the Sixty-eighth and to the four succeeding Congresses (March 4, 1923–March 3, 1933); unsuccessful candidate for reelection in 1932 to the Seventy-third Congress; engaged in an advisory capacity in Washington, D. C.; died at Willoughby, Ohio, February 17, 1940; interment in Mount Union Cemetery, Robinson Township, Allegheny County, Pa.

CAMPBELL, Howard Edmond, a Representative from Pennsylvania; born in Pittsburgh, Allegheny County, Pa., January 4, 1890; attended the public schools and the University of Pittsburgh, Pittsburgh, Pa.; engaged in the real-estate and insurance business in Pittsburgh, Pa., in 1922; president of the Pittsburgh Real Estate Board in 1943 and 1944; elected as a Republican to the Seventy-ninth Congress (January 3, 1945–January 3, 1947); was not a candidate for renomination in 1946; resumed the real-estate and insurance business; president of East Liberty Chamber of Commerce in 1954 and 1955; is a resident of Pittsburgh, Pa.

CAMPBELL, Jacob Miller, a Representative from Pennsylvania; born at "White Horse," near Somerset, Allegheny Township, Somerset County, Pa., November 20, 1821; moved with his parents to Allegheny City, Pa., in 1826; attended the public schools; learned the art of printing in the office of the Somerset Whig; later was connected with a magazine-publishing company in Pittsburgh and with leading newspapers in New Orleans, La.; engaged in steamboating on the lower Mississippi River 1814–1847 and in gold mining in California in 1851; aided in the building of the Cambria Iron Works in Johnstown, Pa., in 1853, and was employed by that company until 1861, when he resigned;

delegate to the first Republican National Convention at Philadelphia in 1856; served in the Union Army as first lieutenant and quartermaster of Company G, Third Regiment, Pennsylvania Volunteer Infantry; recruited the Fifty-fourth Regiment of Infantry and was commissioned its colonel February 27, 1862; brevetted brigadier general March 13, 1865, "for gallant and meritorious conduct at the Battle of Piedmont, Virginia"; honorably discharged September 3, 1864; returned to Johnstown, Pa.; surveyor general (later secretary of internal affairs) of Pennsylvania 1865–1871; declined a renomination; engaged in mechanical and other industrial pursuits; elected as a Republican to the Forty-fifth Congress (March 4, 1877–March 3, 1879); unsuccessful candidate for reelection in 1878 to the Forty-sixth Congress; elected to the Forty-seventh, Forty-eighth, and Forty-ninth Congresses (March 4, 1881–March 3, 1887); unsuccessful candidate for renomination in 1886; financially interested in banking and in the manufacture of steel; chairman of the Republican State convention in 1887; died in Johnstown, Cambria County, Pa., September 27, 1888; interment in Grand View Cemetery.

CAMPBELL, James Edwin (nephew of Lewis Davis Campbell), a Representative from Ohio; born in Middletown, Butler County, Ohio, July 7, 1843; attended the public schools and Miami University, Oxford, Ohio; during the Civil War entered the Union Army as a member of the Mississippi Squadron, November 29, 1863, and served as master's mate on the gunboats *Elk* and *Naiad* until honorably discharged September 24, 1864; studied law; was admitted to the bar in 1865; deputy collector of internal revenue, third district; commenced the practice of law in Hamilton, Ohio, in 1867; prosecuting attorney of Butler County 1876–1880; successfully contested as a Democrat the election of Henry L. Morey to the Forty-eighth Congress; reelected to the Forty-ninth and Fiftieth Congresses and served from June 20, 1884, to March 3, 1889; was not a candidate for renomination in 1888; Governor of Ohio in 1889; unsuccessful candidate for Governor in 1891, and again in 1895; delegate to the Democratic National Conventions in 1892, 1920, and 1924; served on the commission to codify the State laws 1908–1911; resumed the practice of law in Columbus, Ohio, and died there on December 18, 1924; interment in Green Lawn Cemetery.

CAMPBELL, James Hepburn, a Representative from Pennsylvania; born in Williamsport, Lycoming County, Pa., February 8, 1820; attended the common schools, and was graduated from the law department of Dickinson College, Carlisle, Pa., in 1841; was admitted to the bar the same year and commenced practice in Pottsville, Pa.; delegate to the Whig National Convention at Baltimore in 1844; elected as a Whig to the Thirty-fourth Congress (March 4, 1855–March 3, 1857); unsuccessful candidate for reelection in 1856 to the Thirty-fifth Congress; elected to the Thirty-sixth and Thirty-seventh Congresses (March 4, 1859–March 3, 1863); was not a candidate for renomination in 1862; during the Civil War served as major of the Twenty-fifth Regiment of Pennsylvania Infantry; appointed Minister to Sweden by President Lincoln in May 1864 and served until March 29, 1867; declined the diplomatic mission to Colombia in 1867; located in Philadelphia, Pa., in 1867 and continued the practice of law; retired from active practice and engaged in agricultural pursuits; died on his estate "Aeola," near Wayne, Delaware County, Pa., April 12, 1895; interment in Woodlands Cemetery, Philadelphia, Pa.

CAMPBELL, James Romulus, a Representative from Illinois; born near McLeansboro, Hamilton County, Ill., May 4, 1853; attended the public schools and the University of Notre

Dame, Notre Dame, Ind.; studied law; was admitted to the bar in 1877 and commenced practice in McLeansboro, Ill.; owned and edited the McLeansboro Times 1870–1898; member of the State house of representatives 1884–1888; served in the State senate 1888–1896; elected as a Democrat to the Fifty-fifth Congress (March 4, 1897–March 3, 1899); served in the war with Spain in the Ninth Regiment, Illinois Volunteer Infantry; commissioned colonel June 28, 1898; after the muster out of that regiment was appointed lieutenant colonel of the Thirtieth Regiment, United States Volunteers, on July 5, 1899, and assigned to service in the Philippine Islands; commissioned brigadier general of Volunteers January 3, 1901, and was honorably discharged March 25, 1901; engaged in milling and banking in McLeansboro, Ill., and died there August 12, 1924; interment in Odd Fellows Cemetery.

CAMPBELL, John, a Representative from Maryland; born near Port Tobacco, Charles County, Md., September 11, 1765; studied law; was admitted to the bar and practiced; held several local offices; member of the State senate for three years; elected as a Federalist to the Seventh and to the four succeeding Congresses (March 4, 1801–March 3, 1811); judge of the orphans' court of Charles County; died at "Charleston" farm, Charles County, Md., June 23, 1828; interment in the private burying ground on the estate of Daniel Jenifer.

CAMPBELL, John (brother of Robert Blair Campbell), a Representative from South Carolina; born near Brownsville, Marlboro County, S. C.; was graduated from South Carolina College (now the University of South Carolina) at Columbia in 1819; studied law; was admitted to the bar and commenced practice in Brownsville, S. C.; moved to Parnassus, Marlboro District, and continued the practice of law; elected as a State Rights Whig to the Twenty-first Congress (March 4, 1829–March 3, 1831); elected as a State Rights Democrat to the Twenty-fifth and to the three succeeding Congresses (March 4, 1837–March 3, 1845); died in Parnassus (now Blenheim), Marlboro County, S. C., on May 19, 1845; interment in a private cemetery near Blenheim, S. C.

CAMPBELL, John Goulder, a Delegate from the Territory of Arizona; born in Glasgow, Scotland, June 25, 1827; immigrated to the United States in 1841 and settled in the State of New York; attended the public and high schools; moved to California in 1849 and engaged in numerous occupations; moved to Prescott, Ariz., in 1863 and engaged in mercantile pursuits and stock raising; member of the Territorial house of representatives 1868–1874; county supervisor of Yavapai County; elected as a Democrat to the Forty-sixth Congress (March 4, 1879–March 3, 1881); resumed his former business pursuits; also engaged in the hotel business and in stock raising; retired in 1901; died in Prescott, Ariz., December 22, 1903; interment in Mountain View Cemetery.

CAMPBELL, John Hull, a Representative from Pennsylvania; born in York, York County, Pa., October 10, 1800; studied law; was admitted to the bar in Philadelphia, Pa., in 1823 and commenced practice in that city; member of the State house of representatives in 1831; elected as a Whig to the Twenty-ninth Congress (March 4, 1845–March 3, 1847); declined to be a candidate for renomination in 1846; resumed the practice of law; died in Philadelphia, Pa., on January 19, 1868; interment in Monument Cemetery.

CAMPBELL, John Pierce, Jr., a Representative from Kentucky; born near Hopkinsville, Christian County, Ky., December 8, 1820; pursued an academic course; studied law; was admitted to the bar in 1841 and commenced practice in Lexington, Mo.; member of the Missouri House of Representatives 1848–1852; returned to Hopkinsville, Ky., and engaged in agricultural pursuits; elected by the American Party to the Thirty-fourth Congress (March 4, 1855–March 3, 1857); declined to be a candidate for reelection; president of the Henderson & Nashville Railroad in 1870; organized the Mastodon Coal & Iron Co., which was succeeded by the St. Bernard Coal Co.; devoted the latter years of his life to his large landed estates; died in Hopkinsville, Ky., October 29, 1888; interment in Riverside Cemetery.

CAMPBELL, John Wilson, a Representative from Ohio; born near Miller's Iron Works, Augusta County, Va., February 23, 1782; attended the common schools; taught school; studied law; was admitted to the bar in 1808 and commenced practice in West Union, Ohio; justice of the peace of Tiffin Township, Adams County, 1809–1815; prosecuting attorney of Adams County in 1809; member of the State house of representatives in 1810, 1813, and 1815; elected as a Democrat to the Fifteenth and to the four succeeding Congresses (March 4, 1817–March 3, 1827); declined to be a candidate for renomination in 1826; judge of the United States Court for the District of Ohio from 1829 until his death in Delaware, Delaware County, Ohio, September 24, 1833; interment in the Old North Cemetery, Columbus, Ohio.

CAMPBELL, Lewis Davis (uncle of James Edwin Campbell), a Representative from Ohio; born in Franklin, Warren County, Ohio, August 9, 1811; attended the public schools; apprenticed to learn the art of printing 1828–1831; published a Clay Whig newspaper in Hamilton, Ohio, 1831–1835; studied law; was admitted to the bar in 1835 and practiced in Hamilton until 1850; engaged in agricultural pursuits; unsuccessful candidate for election in 1840, 1842, and 1844 to the Twenty-seventh, Twenty-eighth, and Twenty-ninth Congresses; elected as a Whig to the Thirty-first and to the three succeeding Congresses (March 4, 1849–March 3, 1857); presented credentials as a Member-elect to the Thirty-fifth Congress and served from March 4, 1857, to May 25, 1858, when he was succeeded by Clement L. Vallandigham, who successfully contested the election; was an unsuccessful candidate for reelection in 1858 to the Thirty-sixth Congress; served in the Union Army during the Civil War as colonel of the Sixty-ninth Regiment, Ohio Volunteer Infantry, in 1861 and 1862; resigned on account of poor health; appointed by President Andrew Johnson as Envoy Extraordinary and Minister Plenipotentiary to Mexico on May 4, 1866, and served until June 16, 1867, when he resigned; elected to the State senate in 1869 and resigned in 1870; elected as a Democrat to the Forty-second Congress (March 4, 1871–March 3, 1873); was not a candidate for relection in 1872 to the Forty-third Congress; delegate to the third State constitutional convention in 1873; resumed agricultural pursuits; died in Hamilton, Butler County, Ohio, on November 26, 1882; interment in Greenwood Cemetery.

CAMPBELL, Philip Pitt, a Representative from Kansas; born in Cape Breton, Nova Scotia, Canada, April 25, 1862; moved with his parents to Neosho County, Kans., in 1867; attended the common schools, and was graduated from Baker University, Baldwin, Kans., in 1888; studied law; was admitted to the bar in 1889 and commenced practice in Pittsburg, Kans.; elected as a Republican to the Fifty-eighth and to the nine succeeding Congresses (March 4, 1903–March 3, 1923); unsuccessful candidate for reelection in 1922 to the Sixty-eighth Congress; parliamentarian of the Republican National Convention at Cleveland in 1924; resumed the practice of law in Washington, D. C., with residence in Arlington, Va.; died in Emergency Hospital, Washington, D. C., May 26, 1941; interment in Abbey Mausoleum (near Arlington National Cemetery), Arlington, Va.

CAMPBELL, Robert Blair (brother of John Campbell of South Carolina), a Representative from South Carolina; born in Marlboro County, S. C.; educated by a private tutor; attended school in Fayetteville, N. C., and was graduated from South Carolina College (now the University of South Carolina) at Columbia in 1809; engaged in agricultural pursuits; commissioned captain in South Carolina Militia in 1814; unsuccessful candidate in 1820 for election to the Seventeenth Congress; served in the State senate 1821–1823; elected to the Eighteenth Congress (March 4, 1823–March 3, 1825); unsuccessful candidate for reelection in 1824 to the Nineteenth Congress and for election in 1826 to the Twentieth Congress and in 1830 to the Twenty-second Congress; elected to the State senate in 1830; elected as a Nullifier to the Twenty-third Congress to fill the vacancy caused by the death of Thomas B. Singleton; reelected as a Whig to the Twenty-fourth Congress and served from February 27, 1834, to March 3, 1837; in 1833 during the nullification movement was commissioned general of South Carolina troops; moved to Lowndes County, Ala., about 1840; member of the State house of representatives in 1840; appointed on September 28, 1842, consul at Habana, Cuba, and served until July 22, 1850; moved to San Antonio, Tex.; was appointed on March 16, 1853, a commissioner for the United States to aid in settlement of the disputed boundary line between Texas and Mexico; appointed consul at London, England, and served from August 3, 1854, to March 1861, when he was recalled; moved to Ealing, London, England, where he died July 12, 1862; interment in the crypt of Kensington Church.

CAMPBELL, Samuel, a Representative from New York; born in Mansfield, Conn., July 11, 1773; attended the common schools; moved to Columbus, N. Y., and engaged in agricultural pursuits; supervisor of the town of Columbus in 1807, 1808, 1821, and 1840; member of the State assembly in 1808, 1809, 1812, and 1820; served on the staff of Maj. Gen. Nathaniel King as division quartermaster in the War of 1812; associate judge of Chenango County Court in 1814; justice of the peace in Columbus for twenty-five years; sheriff of Chenango County 1815–1819; elected to the Seventeenth Congress (March 4, 1821–March 3, 1823); affiliated with the Whig Party after its formation; resumed agricultural pursuits; died in Columbus, near Sherburne, Chenango County, N. Y., June 2, 1853; interment in Lambs Corners Cemetery.

CAMPBELL, Thomas Jefferson, a Representative from Tennessee; born in Rhea County, Tenn., in 1786; attended the public schools; assistant inspector general to Major General Cole's division of the East Tennessee Militia from September 25, 1813, to March 12, 1814; clerk of the State house of representatives 1817–1819, 1821, and 1825–1831, and a member of that body 1833–1837; presidential elector on the Whig ticket of Harrison and Tyler in 1840; elected as a Whig to the Twenty-seventh Congress (March 4, 1841–March 3, 1843); unsuccessful candidate for reelection in 1842 to the Twenty-eighth Congress; Clerk of the National House of Representatives in the Thirtieth and Thirty-first Congresses and served from December 7, 1847, until his death in Washington, D. C., April 13, 1850; interment at Calhoun, McMinn County, Tenn.

CAMPBELL, Thompson, a Representative from Illinois; born in Ireland in 1811; immigrated to the United States with his parents, who settled in Chester County, Pa.; attended the public schools; studied law; was admitted to the bar in Pittsburgh, Pa.; moved to Galena, Ill., and engaged in mining; secretary of state of Illinois from 1843 until he resigned in 1846; delegate to the State constitutional convention in 1847; elected as a Democrat to the Thirty-second Congress (March 4, 1851–March 3, 1853); unsuccessful candidate for reelection in 1852 to the Thirty-third Congress; delegate to the Democratic National Convention at Baltimore in 1852; appointed United States land commissioner for California by President Pierce in 1853 and served until he resigned in 1855; returned to Illinois; delegate to the Democratic National Convention at Charleston in 1860; was nominated elector at large on the Breckinridge and Lane ticket in 1860; returned to California and served in the California House of Representatives as a member of the Union Party in 1863 and 1864; delegate to the Republican National Convention at Baltimore in 1864; died in San Francisco, Calif., December 6, 1868; interment in Laurel Hill Cemetery.

CAMPBELL, Timothy John, a Representative from New York; born in County Cavan, Ireland, January 8, 1840; immigrated with his parents to the United States in 1845; attended the public schools of New York City; learned the printer's trade; studied law; was admitted to the bar in 1869 and commenced practice in New York City; member of the State assembly 1868–1873, 1875, and 1883; justice of the fifth district civil court in New York City 1875–1883; served in the State senate in 1884 and 1885; elected as a Democrat to the Forty-ninth Congress to fill the vacancy caused by the resignation of Samuel S. Cox; reelected to the Fiftieth Congress and served from November 3, 1885, to March 3, 1889; unsuccessful candidate for reelection in 1888 to the Fifty-first Congress; elected to the Fifty-second and Fifty-third Congresses (March 4, 1891–March 3, 1895); unsuccessful candidate in 1894 for reelection to the Fifty-fourth Congress; resumed the practice of his profession in New York City; died in New York City, N. Y., on April 7, 1904; interment in Calvary Cemetery, Long Island City, N. Y.

CAMPBELL, William Bowen (cousin of Henry Bowen), a Representative from Tennessee; born near Hendersonville, Sumner County, Tenn., February 1, 1807; attended private schools; studied law in Abingdon and Winchester, Va.; was admitted to the bar in 1829 and commenced practice in Carthage, Smith County, Tenn.; also engaged in agricultural pursuits and banking; elected district attorney in 1831; member of the State house of representatives in 1835 and 1836; captain of a company in Trousdale's regiment of Tennessee Mounted Volunteers in the Florida War; mustered out January 14, 1837; elected as a Whig to the Twenty-fifth, Twenty-sixth, and Twenty-seventh Congresses (March 4, 1837–March 3, 1843); declined to be a candidate for reelection to the Twenty-eighth Congress; elected colonel of the First Tennessee Volunteers in the Mexican War June 3, 1846, and was mustered out May 25, 1847; unanimously elected judge of the fourth circuit of Tennessee after his return from Mexico and served from 1847 to 1851; served as Governor of Tennessee from 1851 to 1853; declined renomination; elected judge of the circuit court in 1857; during the Civil War was appointed by President Lincoln brigadier general of Volunteers June 30, 1862; resigned January 26, 1863, on account of ill health; upon the readmission of the State of Tennessee to representation was elected as a Democrat to the Thirty-ninth Congress and served from July 24, 1866, to March 3, 1867; resumed banking and agricultural pursuits; died near Lebanon, Wilson County, Tenn., August 19, 1867; interment in Cedar Grove Cemetery.

CAMPBELL, William W., a Representative from New York; born in Cherry Valley; N. Y., June 10, 1806; attended the common schools; was graduated from Union College, Schenectady, N. Y., in 1827; studied law; was admitted to the bar in 1831 and commenced practice in New York City; was appointed master in chancery in 1841; commissioner in bankruptcy; elected by the American Party to the Twenty-ninth Congress (March 4, 1845–March 3, 1847); was not a candidate for renomination in 1846; justice of the superior court of New York City 1849–1855; returned to Cherry Valley in December 1855; judge of the supreme court for the sixth district of New York 1857–1865; retired from public life; author and engaged in historical work; died in Cherry Valley, Otsego County, N. Y., September 7, 1881; interment in Cherry Valley Cemetery.

CAMPBELL, William Wildman, a Representative from Ohio; born in Rochester, Windsor County, Vt., April 2, 1853; attended the public schools, Goddard Seminary, Barre, Vt., and Tufts College, Medford, Mass.; studied law; was admitted to the bar in 1878 and commenced practice at Napoleon, Henry County, Ohio; served as prosecuting attorney for Henry County, Ohio, 1893–1896; elected as a Republican to the Fifty-ninth Congress (March 4, 1905–March 3, 1907); unsuccessful candidate for reelection in 1906 to the Sixtieth Congress and for election in 1908 to the Sixty-first Congress; resumed the practice of law in Napoleon, Ohio; member of the State constitutional convention of 1911 and 1912; died in Napoleon, Ohio, August 13, 1927; interment in Forest Hill Cemetery.

CANBY, Richard Sprigg, a Representative from Ohio; born in Lebanon, Ohio, September 30, 1808; completed preparatory studies; attended Miami University, Oxford, Ohio, 1826–1828; engaged in mercantile pursuits and while thus employed studied law; was admitted to the bar about 1840 and commenced practice in Bellefontaine, Ohio; member of the State house of representatives in 1845 and 1846; elected as a Whig to the Thirtieth Congress (March 4, 1847–March 3, 1849); engaged in agricultural pursuits; upon its formation in 1856 affiliated with the Republican Party; moved to Olney, Richland County, Ill., in 1863, where he resumed the practice of law; elected judge of the second judicial circuit court of Illinois in 1867 and served for several years; again resumed the practice of his profession in Olney; discontinued active business pursuits in 1882, and lived in retirement until his death; died in Olney, Ill., July 27, 1895; interment in Haven Hill Cemetery.

CANDLER, Allen Daniel (cousin of Ezekiel Samuel Candler, Jr., and Milton Anthony Candler), a Representative from Georgia; born in Homer, Banks County, Ga., November 4, 1834; attended country schools, and was graduated from Mercer University, Macon, Ga., in 1859; studied law; during the Civil War entered the Confederate Army as a private in Company H, Thirty-fourth Regiment of Georgia Infantry on May 12, 1862; was elected first lieutenant May 17, 1862; promoted to captain October 26, 1862; appointed lieutenant colonel May 16, 1864; promoted to colonel December 27, 1864; engaged in agricultural pursuits; member of the State house of representatives 1873–1877; served in the State senate in 1878 and 1879; engaged in manufacturing and was president of a railroad; elected as a Democrat to the Forty-eighth and to the three succeeding Congresses (March 4, 1883–March 3, 1891); was not a candidate for reelection in 1890; secretary of state of Georgia from May 28, 1894, until March 1, 1898, when he resigned; served as Governor of Georgia from 1898 to 1902; compiler of the records of the State of Georgia from 1903 until his death in Atlanta, Ga., October 26, 1910; interment in Alta Vista Cemetery, Gainesville, Ga.

CANDLER, Ezekiel Samuel, Jr. (nephew of Milton A. Candler and cousin of Allen Daniel Candler), a Representative

from Mississippi; born in Belleville, Hamilton County, Fla., January 18, 1862; moved with his parents to Tishomingo County, Miss., in 1870; attended the common schools and Iuka (Miss.) Male Academy; was graduated from the law department of the University of Mississippi at Oxford in 1881; was admitted to the bar the same year and commenced practice in Iuka, Miss.; chairman of the Democratic executive committee of Tishomingo County in 1884; moved to Corinth in 1887 and continued the practice of law; presidential elector on the Democratic ticket of Cleveland and Thurman in 1888; member of the Democratic executive committee of Alcorn County for several years; elected as a Democrat to the Fifty-seventh and to the nine succeeding Congresses (March 4, 1901–March 3, 1921); unsuccessful candidate for renomination in 1920; resumed the practice of his profession; mayor of Corinth, Miss., 1933–1937; died in Corinth, Miss., December 18, 1944; interment in Henry Cemetery.

CANDLER, John Wilson, a Representative from Massachusetts; born in Boston, Mass., February 10, 1828; attended the Marblehead Academy and Dummer Academy, Byfield, Mass.; entered a countingroom in Boston in 1845; merchant, engaged in shipping and commerce with the East and West Indies and South America; served as a member of the Massachusetts House of Representatives in 1866; chairman of the commissioners of prisons of Massachusetts; president of the Boston Board of Trade and of the Commercial Club of Boston; elected as a Republican to the Forty-seventh Congress (March 4, 1881–March 3, 1883); unsuccessful candidate for reelection 1882 to the Forty-eighth Congress; again elected to the Fifty-first Congress (March 4, 1889–March 3, 1891); unsuccessful candidate for reelection in 1890 to the Fifty-second Congress; engaged in mercantile pursuits; retired from active business pursuits and political life in 1893; died at the home of his son-in-law in Providence, R. I., March 16, 1903; interment in Mount Auburn Cemetery.

CANDLER, Milton Anthony (uncle of Ezekiel Samuel Candler, Jr., and cousin of Allen Daniel Candler), a Representative from Georgia; born near Campbellton, Campbell County, Ga., January 11, 1837; attended private schools; was graduated from the University of Georgia at Athens in 1854; studied law; was admitted to the bar in 1856 and commenced practice in Cassville, Bartow County, Ga.; moved to Decatur in 1857; member of the State house of representatives 1861–1863; delegate to the State constitutional convention in 1865; served in the State senate 1868–1872; delegate to the Democratic National Convention at Baltimore in 1872 and at St. Louis in 1876; elected as a Democrat to the Forty-fourth and Forty-fifth Congresses (March 4, 1875–March 3, 1879); was a candidate for renomination in 1878 to the Forty-sixth Congress, but withdrew because of the adoption of a free-silver plank by the district convention; resumed the practice of law; died in Decatur, De Kalb County, Ga., August 8, 1909; interment in Decatur Cemetery.

CANFIELD, Gordon, a Representative from New Jersey; born in Salamanca, Cattaraugus County, N. Y., April 15, 1898; attended the public schools of Binghamton, N. Y.; during the First World War served as a private in the Signal Corps, United States Army, in 1917 and 1918; reporter in Passaic, N. J., 1919–1923; studied law at New Jersey Law School in Newark and was graduated from National University, Washington, D. C., in 1926; was admitted to the District of Columbia bar in 1927; served as secretary to Representative George N. Seger 1923–1940; elected as a Republican to the Seventy-seventh and to the nine succeeding Congresses (January 3, 1941–January

3, 1961); in World War II served during the Congressional recess in 1944 as an ordinary seaman, North Atlantic tanker duty, United States Merchant Marine; was not a candidate for renomination in 1960; is a resident of Paterson, N. J.

CANFIELD, Harry Clifford, a Representative from Indiana; born near Moores Hill, Dearborn County, Ind., November 22, 1875; attended the public schools, Moores Hill College, Central Normal College, Danville, Ind., and Vorhies Business College, Indianapolis, Ind.; taught school in Dearborn County 1896–1898; moved to Batesville, Ripley County, in 1899 and engaged in the manufacture of furniture; also interested in the jobbing of furniture, and in farming and banking; elected as a Democrat to the Sixty-eighth and to the four succeeding Congresses (March 4, 1923–March 3, 1933); unsuccessful candidate for renomination in 1932; resumed the furniture manufacturing business in Batesville, Ind.; died in Batesville, Ind., February 9, 1945; interment in the First Methodist Episcopal Cemetery.

CANNON, Arthur Patrick, a Representative from Florida; born in Powder Springs, Cobb County, Ga., May 22, 1904; moved to Laurens County, S. C.; attended the public schools, Wofford College, Spartanburg, S. C., and John B. Stetson University, De Land, Fla.; was graduated from the law college of the University of Miami, Miami, Fla., in 1931; was admitted to the bar the same year and commenced practice in Miami; elected as a Democrat to the Seventy-sixth and to the three succeeding Congresses (January 3, 1939–January 3, 1947); unsuccessful candidate for renomination in 1946; resumed the practice of law; elected circuit judge of Dade County, Fla., in 1952, reelected in 1954, and again in 1960 for a six-year term; is a resident of Miami, Fla.

CANNON, Clarence, a Representative from Missouri; born in Elsberry, Lincoln County, Mo., April 11, 1879; was graduated from La Grange Junior College, Hannibal, Mo., in 1901, from William Jewell College, Liberty, Mo., in 1903, and from the law department of the University of Missouri at Columbia in 1908; was admitted to the bar in 1908 and commenced practice in Troy, Mo.; parliamentarian of the House of Representatives in the Sixty-fourth, Sixty-fifth, and Sixty-sixth Congresses; parliamentarian of the Democratic National Conventions 1920–1960; author of "A Synopsis of the Procedure of the House (1918)," "Procedure in the House of Representatives (1920)," and "Cannon's Procedure (1928)," subsequent editions of the latter (1935 and 1949) being published by resolutions of the House; editor and compiler of "Precedents of the House of Representatives" by act of Congress; regent of the Smithsonian Institution; elected as a Democrat to the Sixty-eighth and to the eighteen succeeding Congresses (March 3, 1923–January 3, 1961). *Reelected to the Eighty-seventh Congress.*

CANNON, Frank Jenne (son of George Quayle Cannon), a Delegate from the Territory of Utah and a Senator from Utah; born in Salt Lake City, Utah, January 25, 1859; attended the public schools, and was graduated from the University of Utah at Salt Lake City in 1878; engaged as a newspaper writer; moved to San Francisco, Calif., in 1880 and was engaged as a newspaper reporter; moved to Ogden, Utah, in 1882, and served as deputy county clerk and recorder; elected county recorder in 1884; became editor of the Ogden Herald in 1887 and established the Ogden Standard in 1888; unsuccessful candidate for election in 1892 to the Fifty-third Congress; interested in the building of the Ogden Canyon electric power plant in 1893; delegate to the Republican National Convention at Minneapolis in 1892 and at St. Louis in 1896; elected as a Republican to the Fifty-fourth Congress and served from March 4, 1895, to January 4, 1896,

when the Territory was admitted as a State into the Union; was then elected to the United States Senate and served from January 22, 1896, to March 3, 1899; unsuccessful candidate for reelection in 1898; affiliated with the Democratic Party in 1900 and served as State chairman 1902–1904; again became interested in newspaper publishing and established the Daily Utah State Journal at Ogden in 1903; moved to Denver, Colo., in 1909 and engaged in newspaper work and mining; died in Denver, Colo., July 25, 1933; interment in Ogden City Cemetery, Ogden, Utah.

CANNON, George Quayle (father of Frank Jenne Cannon), a Delegate from the Territory of Utah; born in Liverpool, England, January 11, 1827; attended the common schools; immigrated to the United States in 1842 with his parents, who settled in Nauvoo, Ill.; moved to Great Salt Lake (then Mexican territory), Utah, in 1847; went to California in 1849 and a year later to the Hawaiian Islands as a missionary; returned to Salt Lake City, Utah, in 1854; learned the art of printing; editor of the Western Standard in 1856 and 1857 and of the Deseret News 1867–1874 and 1877–1879; member of the Territorial council 1865, 1866, and 1869–1872; member of the board of regents of the Deseret University (now the University of Utah) and later chancellor; elected by the constitutional convention in 1872 a delegate to present the constitution and memorial to Congress for admission of the Territory as a State into the Union; elected as a Republican to the Forty-third and to the three succeeding Congresses (March 4, 1873–March 3, 1881); contested the election of Allen G. Campbell to the Forty-seventh Congress, but the House, on April 20, 1882, decided that neither was entitled to the seat; returned to Salt Lake City; director of the Union Pacific Railroad and a member of the board of directors of many important financial and industrial enterprises at the time of his death; died in Monterey, Monterey County, Calif., April 12, 1901; interment in Salt Lake City Cemetery, Salt Lake City, Utah.

CANNON, Howard Walter, a Senator from Nevada; born in St. George, Washington County, Utah, January 26, 1912; graduated from Dixie High School, St. George, Utah, in 1929, Dixie Junior College in 1931, Arizona State Teachers College in 1933, and University of Arizona Law School in 1937; was admitted to the bar in Arizona in 1937, Utah in 1938, and Nevada in 1946; reference attorney, Utah State Senate in 1939; elected county attorney of Washington County, Utah, in 1940; member of the Utah National Guard and in March 1941 entered on active duty as a first lieutenant with the One Hundred and Fifteenth Combat Engineers; in 1942 transferred to Air Force and served twenty months overseas; was shot down over Holland and evaded capture for forty-two days before reaching Allied lines; separated from the service in July 1946 with rank of lieutenant colonel; colonel in the Active Air Force Reserves; awarded the Distinguished Flying Cross, Air Medal with two Oak Leaf Clusters, Purple Heart, European Theater Ribbon with seven Battle Stars, American Defense Citation, Presidential Unit Citation, and French Croix de Guerre with Silver Star; elected city attorney of Las Vagas, Nev., in June 1949 and served for four consecutive terms; Nevada State chairman of the National Institute of Municipal Law Officers for seven years; charter member of the Southern Nevada Industrial Foundation, Inc.; elected as a Democrat to the United States Senate for the term commencing January 3, 1959, and ending January 3, 1965.

CANNON, Joseph Gurney, a Representative from Illinois; born in Guilford, Guilford County, N. C., May 7, 1836; moved with his parents to Bloomingdale, Ind., in 1840; completed preparatory studies; studied law at the Cincinnati Law School;

was admitted to the bar in 1858 and commenced practice in Terre Haute, Ind., in 1858; moved to Tuscola, Ill., in 1859; State's attorney for the twenty-seventh judicial district of Illinois from March 1861 to December 1868; elected as a Republican to the Forty-third and to the eight succeeding Congresses (March 4, 1873–March 3, 1891); moved to Danville, Ill., in 1878; unsuccessful candidate for reelection in 1890 to the Fifty-second Congress; elected to the Fifty-third and to the nine succeeding Congresses (March 4, 1893–March 3, 1913); served as Speaker of the House of Representatives in the Fifty-eighth, Fifty-ninth, Sixtieth, and Sixty-first Congresses; received fifty-eight votes for the presidential nomination at the Republican National Convention at Chicago in 1908; unsuccessful candidate for reelection in 1912 to the Sixty-third Congress; again elected to the Sixty-fourth and to the three succeeding Congresses (March 4, 1915–March 3, 1923); declined renomination for Congress at the end of the Sixty-seventh Congress; retired from public life; died in Danville, Vermilion County, Ill., November 12, 1926; interment in Spring Hill Cemetery.

CANNON, Marion, a Representative from California; born near Morgantown, Va. (now West Virginia), October 30, 1834; attended the district school; learned the blacksmith trade; moved to California in 1852 and engaged in mining in Nevada County for twenty-one years; elected county recorder of Nevada County in 1869 and served two years; moved to Ventura County, Calif., and settled near Ventura in 1874; engaged in agricultural pursuits; elected first State president of the Farmers' Alliance November 20, 1890, and reelected October 22, 1891; organized the People's Party of California October 20, 1891; chosen a representative to the supreme council in Indianapolis November 1891; selected by that body to represent California in the industrial conference at St. Louis February 22, 1892; served as chairman of the California delegation to the People's Party National Convention at Omaha in 1892; elected as the candidate of the People's and Democratic Parties to the Fifty-third Congress (March 4, 1893–March 3, 1895); was not a candidate for renomination in 1894; resumed agricultural pursuits near Ventura, Ventura County, Calif., until his death at "Ranch Home," near Ventura, August 27, 1920; interment in Ivy Lawn Cemetery, Ventura, Calif.

CANNON, Newton, a Representative from Tennessee; born in Guilford County, N. C., May 22, 1781; attended the common schools; moved to Tennessee at an early period and settled near Nashville, Williamson County; engaged in agricultural pursuits; member of the State house of representatives in 1811 and 1812; enlisted in the War of 1812 and became colonel of a regiment of Tennessee Mounted Rifles; elected as a Democrat to the Thirteenth Congress to fill the vacancy caused by the resignation of Felix Grundy; reelected to the Fourteenth Congress and served from September 16, 1814, to March 3, 1817; appointed by President Monroe a commissioner to negotiate a treaty with the Chickasaw Indians in 1819; elected to the Sixteenth and Seventeenth Congresses (March 4, 1819–March 3, 1823); resumed agricultural pursuits; Governor of Tennessee 1835–1839; died in Nashville, September 16, 1841; interment in a cemetery on his estate near Allisona, Williamson County, Tenn.

CANNON, Raymond Joseph, a Representative from Wisconsin; born in Ironwood, Gogebic County, Mich., August 26, 1894; his parents having died when he was six months old, he spent his early life in a home for dependent children; attended the public and high schools; taught school at Minocqua, Wis., in 1910 and 1911; professional baseball player 1908–1922; attended the law department of Marquette University, Milwaukee, Wis., for two years; was admitted to the bar in 1914 and commenced practice

in Milwaukee, Wis.; unsuccessful candidate for election as associate justice of the Wisconsin Supreme Court in 1930; elected as a Democrat to the Seventy-third, Seventy-fourth, and Seventy-fifth Congresses (March 4, 1933–January 3, 1939); was an unsuccessful candidate for renomination as a Democrat and for reelection in 1938 as an Independent to the Seventy-sixth Congress; resumed the practice of law; unsuccessful candidate for the Democratic gubernatorial nomination in 1940 and 1942 and for the Democratic nomination for Congress in 1944; died in Milwaukee, Wis., November 25, 1951; interment in Holy Cross Cemetery.

CANTOR, Jacob Aaron, a Representative from New York; born in New York City December 6, 1854; attended the graded and high schools; reporter on the New York World for several years; was graduated from the law department of the College of the City of New York in 1875; was admitted to the bar and commenced practice in New York City; served in the State assembly 1885–1887; member of the State senate 1887–1898 and served as president in 1893 and 1894; elected president of the Borough of Manhattan in 1901; declined to be a candidate for renomination; elected as a Democrat to the Sixty-third Congress to fill the vacancy caused by the resignation of Francis Burton Harrison and served from November 4, 1913, to March 3, 1915; unsuccessfully contested the election of Isaac Siegel to the Sixty-fourth Congress; resumed the practice of law in New York City; president of the Tax Commission Board of New York City at the time of his death there on July 2, 1921; interment in Mount Hope Cemetery, Mount Hope, Westchester County, N. Y.

CANTRILL, James Campbell, a Representative from Kentucky; born in Georgetown, Scott County, Ky., July 9, 1870; attended the common schools, Georgetown (Ky.) College, and the University of Virginia at Charlottesville; engaged in agricultural pursuits until his death; chairman of the Scott County Democratic committee in 1895; elected a member of the State house of representatives in 1897, and again in 1899; served in the State senate 1901–1905; was nominated for Congress in 1904, but declined; delegate to the Democratic National Convention at St. Louis in 1904; elected president of the American Society of Equity for Kentucky, an organization of farmers, in 1908; elected as a Democrat to the Sixty-first and to the seven succeeding Congresses and served from March 4, 1909, until his death during his campaign as the Democratic nominee for Governor of Kentucky; died in Louisville, Ky., September 2, 1923; interment in Georgetown Cemetery, Georgetown, Ky.

CAPEHART, Homer Earl, a Senator from Indiana; born in Algiers, Pike County, Ind., June 6, 1897; attended the public schools; was graduated from the high school at Polo, Ill., in 1916; interested in agricultural pursuits since 1916; during the First World War enlisted as a private in the United States Army; promoted to sergeant and served in the Twelfth Infantry 1917–1919; engaged in the radio, phonograph, and television manufacturing business; elected as a Republican to the United States Senate in 1944 for the term commencing January 3, 1945; reelected in 1950 and again in 1956 for the term ending January 3, 1963.

CAPEHART, James, a Representative from West Virginia; born in Point Pleasant, Mason County, Va. (now West Virginia), March 7, 1847; attended the public schools and Marietta College, Ohio; studied at Duff's Commercial College, Pittsburgh, Pa.; clerk and bookkeeper in his father's store; engaged in agricultural pursuits and stock breeding 1867–1903; president of Mason County Court in 1871, 1872, and again 1880–1885; delegate to the Democratic National Convention at St. Louis in 1888; elected as a Democrat to the Fifty-second and Fifty-third Congresses

(March 4, 1891–March 3, 1895); was not a candidate for reelection in 1894; president of the Point Pleasant National Bank in 1901; after 1903 he became interested in fruit growing in Brevard County, Fla.; resided in Cocoa, Fla., until his death on April 28, 1921; interment in Lone Oak Cemetery, Point Pleasant, W. Va.

CAPERTON, Allen Taylor (son of Hugh Caperton), a Senator from West Virginia; born near Union, Monroe County, Va. (now West Virginia), November 21, 1810; attended the public schools of Virginia and Huntsville, Ala., and the University of Virginia at Charlottesville; was graduated from Yale College in 1832; studied law in Staunton, Va.; was admitted to the bar and practiced; Whig member of the Virginia House of Delegates in 1841 and 1842; served in the State senate 1844–1848; delegate to the Whig National Convention at Philadelphia in 1848; delegate to the State constitutional conventions in 1850 and 1861; again a member of the State house of delegates 1857–1861; elected by the Legislature of Virginia a member of the Confederate States Senate and served until 1865; elected as a Democrat to the United States Senate from West Virginia and served from March 4, 1875, until his death in Washington, D. C., July 26, 1876; interment in Green Hill Cemetery, Union, W. Va.

CAPERTON, Hugh (father of Allen Taylor Caperton), a Representative from Virginia; born in Greenbrier County, Va. (now West Virginia), April 17, 1781; was a planter and also engaged in mercantile pursuits; moved to Monroe County; sheriff of Monroe County in 1805; member of the State house of delegates 1810–1818 and again 1826–1830; elected as a Federalist to the Thirteenth Congress (March 4, 1813–March 3, 1815); resumed agricultural and mercantile pursuits; died on his estate, "Elmwood," in Monroe County, near Union, Va. (now West Virginia), February 9, 1847; interment in Green Hill Cemetery, Union, W. Va.

CAPOZZOLI, Louis Joseph, a Representative from New York; born in Cosenza, Italy, March 6, 1901; immigrated to the United States in 1906; attended the public schools in New York City; was graduated from the law department of Fordham University, New York, N. Y., in 1922; was admitted to the bar in 1923 and commenced practice in New York, N. Y.; assistant district attorney of New York County 1930–1937; member of the State assembly in 1939 and 1940; elected as a Democrat to the Seventy-seventh and Seventy-eighth Congresses (January 3, 1941–January 3, 1945); was not a candidate for renomination in 1944; resumed the practice of law; elected a justice of the New York City Court in 1946 and served from 1947 to 1950; elected to the Court of General Sessions, County of New York, in 1950, and served until January 1957; appointed and served as a judge of the New York Supreme Court from January 21, 1957, to December 31, 1957; elected to the New York Supreme Court for a fourteen-year term ending December 31, 1971; resides in New York City.

CAPPER, Arthur, a Senator from Kansas; born in Garnett, Anderson County, Kans., July 14, 1865; attended the common and high schools; learned the art of printing and subsequently became a newspaper reporter; owner and publisher of the Topeka Daily Capital, Capper's Weekly, Capper's Farmer, the Household Magazine, and other publications; owner of two radio stations; delegate to the Republican National Convention at Chicago in 1908; president of the board of regents, Kansas Agricultural College, 1910–1913; unsuccessful candidate for Governor of Kansas in 1912; Governor of Kansas 1915–1919; elected as a Republican to the United States Senate in 1918 for the term commencing March 4, 1919; reelected in 1924, 1930, 1936, and

again in 1942 for the term ending January 3, 1949; was not a candidate for renomination in 1948; returned to Topeka, Kans., and continued publishing business; died in Topeka, Kans., December 19, 1951; interment in Topeka Cemetery.

CAPRON, Adin Ballou, a Representative from Rhode Island; born in Mendon, Worcester County, Mass., January 9, 1841; attended the Woonsocket High School and Westbrook Seminary, near Portland, Maine; settled in Stillwater, Providence County, R. I., and engaged in milling and dealing in grain; enlisted as a sergeant in the Second Regiment, Rhode Island Volunteer Infantry, in May 1861; promoted to the rank of sergeant major July 11, 1861; commissioned lieutenant in September 1861 and ordered on detached service in the Signal Corps in December 1861; served in the Signal Corps until the close of the Civil War, having been commissioned first lieutenant on March 3, 1863, and subsequently promoted to the rank of captain and major by brevet; member of the State house of representatives 1887–1892 and served as speaker in 1891 and 1892; unsuccessful candidate for election in 1892 to the Fifty-third Congress; elected as a Republican to the Fifty-fifth and to the six succeeding Congresses (March 4, 1897–March 3, 1911); was not a candidate for renomination in 1910; resumed his former business activities in Stillwater, Providence County, R. I., where he died March 17, 1911; interment in Swan Point Cemetery, Providence, R. I.

CAPSTICK, John Henry, a Representative from New Jersey; born in Lawrence, Mass., September 2, 1856; attended the public schools of Lawrence; moved with his parents to Providence, R. I., in 1868; attended a business college; member of the Rhode Island Militia in 1870 and 1871; moved to Montville, N. J., in 1883, and engaged in the manufacture of textile fabrics the same year; member of the State sewerage commission 1905–1908; president of the State board of health 1908–1914; elected as a Republican to the Sixty-fourth and Sixty-fifth Congresses and served from March 4, 1915, until his death in Montville, Morris County, N. J., March 17, 1918; interment in Greenwood Cemetery, Boonton, N. J.

CARAWAY, Hattie Wyatt (wife of Thaddeus Horatius Caraway), a Senator from Arkansas; born in Bakerville, Humphreys County, Tenn., February 1, 1878; attended the public schools and was graduated from Dickson (Tenn.) Normal College in 1896; married and thereafter located in Jonesboro, Ark.; appointed as a Democrat on November 13, 1931, and elected on January 12, 1932, to the United States Senate to fill the vacancy in the term ending March 3, 1933, caused by the death of her husband, Thaddeus H. Caraway; reelected in 1932, and again in 1938 for the term ending January 3, 1945; unsuccessful candidate for renomination in 1944; member of the United States Employees' Compensation Commission (now Bureau of Employees' Compensation) in 1945 and 1946; member of the Employees' Compensation Appeals Board from July 16, 1946, until her death in Falls Church, Va., December 21, 1950; interment in West Lawn Cemetery, Jonesboro, Ark.

CARAWAY, Thaddeus Horatius (husband of Hattie Watt Caraway), a Representative and a Senator from Arkansas; born on a farm near Springhill, Stoddard County, Mo., October 17, 1871; attended the common schools; moved to Arkansas in 1883 with his parents, who settled in Clay County; was graduated from Dickson (Tenn.) College in 1896; taught in country schools 1896–1899; studied law in a law office; was admitted to the bar in 1900 and commenced practice in Osceola, Ark.; moved to Lake City, Craighead County, Ark., in 1900 and to Jonesboro, Ark., in 1901 and continued the practice of law; prosecuting attorney for the second judicial circuit of Arkansas 1908–1912; elected as a Democrat to the Sixty-third and to the three succeeding Congresses (March 4, 1913–March 3, 1921); did not seek renomination, having become a candidate for Senator; elected to the United States Senate in 1920 and took his seat March 4, 1921; reelected in 1926 and served until his death in Little Rock, Ark., November 6, 1931; interment in West Lawn Cemetery, Jonesboro, Ark.

CARDEN, Cap Robert, a Representative from Kentucky; born on a farm near Munfordville, Hart County, Ky., December 17, 1866; attended the rural schools and Bowling Green (Ky.) Business and Normal School; studied law; was admitted to the bar in 1895 and commenced practice in Munfordville, Hart County, Ky.; also engaged in agricultural pursuits and in banking; sheriff of Hart County 1887–1890; was elected county attorney of Hart County in 1890 and served from 1891 to 1894; served as master commissioner of the circuit court of Hart County 1900–1915; elected as a Democrat to the Seventy-second, Seventy-third, and Seventy-fourth Congresses and served from March 4, 1931, until his death in the Kentucky Baptist Hospital, at Louisville, Ky., on June 13, 1935; interment in Munfordville Cemetery, Munfordville, Ky.

CAREW, John Francis (nephew of Thomas Francis Magner), a Representative from New York; born in Williamsburg, Brooklyn, N. Y., April 16, 1873; attended the public schools of Brooklyn and New York City and the College of the City of New York; was graduated from Columbia College in 1893 and from Columbia University Law School in New York City in 1896; was admitted to the bar in 1897 and commenced practice in New York City; member of the State assembly in 1904; delegate to all Democratic State conventions from 1912 to 1924; delegate to the Democratic National Conventions in 1912 and 1924; elected as a Democrat to the Sixty-third and to the eight succeeding Congresses and served from March 4, 1913, until his resignation on December 28, 1929, having been appointed a justice of the New York State Supreme Court; was subsequently elected to the same office in November 1930 for a fourteen-year term, but retired December 31, 1943, due to age limitation; served as official referee of the New York Supreme Court; died in Rockville Centre, N. Y., April 10, 1951; interment in Calvary Cemetery, New York City, Queens County, N. Y.

CAREY, John, a Representative from Ohio; born in Monongalia County, Va. (now West Virginia), April 5, 1792; moved with his parents to the Northwest Territory in 1798; at the age of twelve carried the United States mail on horseback between Chillicothe and Portsmouth, Ohio; served under General Hull in the War of 1812; associate judge 1825–1832; appointed Indian agent at the Wyandotte Reservation in 1829; member of the Ohio House of Representatives in 1828, 1836, 1843; promoter and first president of the Mad River Railroad, from Sandusky to Dayton, about 1845; established the town of Carey, Wyandot County, Ohio; elected as a Republican to the Thirty-sixth Congress (March 4, 1859–March 3, 1861); died in Carey, Ohio, March 17, 1875; interment in the family burial ground on the home farm; reinterment in 1919 in Spring Grove Cemetery, Carey, Ohio.

CAREY, Joseph Maull (father of Robert Davis Carey), a Delegate from the Territory of Wyoming and a Senator from Wyoming; born in Milton, Sussex County, Del., January 19, 1845; attended the common schools, Fort Edward Collegiate Institute, and Union College, New York; was graduated from the law department of the University of Pennsylvania at Philadelphia in 1864; was admitted to the bar in 1867 and commenced practice in Philadelphia; named United States attorney for the Territory of Wyoming upon its organization in 1869 and served until his resignation in 1871; associate justice of the supreme court of the Territory of Wyoming 1871–1876; retired from the bench and engaged in the cattle and ranching business; member of the United States Centennial Commission 1872–1876; member of the Republican National Committee 1876–1897; mayor of Cheyenne 1881–1885; elected as a Republican to the Forty-ninth, Fiftieth, and Fifty-first Congresses and served from March 4, 1885, until July 10, 1890, when the Territory became a State; was then elected to the United States Senate and served from November 15, 1890, until March 3, 1895; unsuccessful candidate in 1895 for reelection; resumed the practice of law in Cheyenne, Wyo.; Governor of Wyoming 1911–1915; one of the organizers of the Progressive Party in 1912; vice president of the Federal Land Bank; member of the board of trustees of the University of Wyoming at Laramie; died in Cheyenne, Wyo., February 5, 1924; interment in Lakeview Cemetery.

CAREY, Robert Davis (son of Joseph Maull Carey), a Senator from Wyoming; born in Cheyenne, Laramie County, Wyo., August 12, 1878; attended the public schools, and Hill School at Pottstown, Pa.; was graduated from Yale University at New Haven, Conn., in 1900; moved to Careyhurst, Converse County, Wyo., in 1900; engaged in the raising of livestock and in agricultural pursuits; also interested in banking and various other activities; chairman of the Converse County Republican central committee in 1908 and 1909; president of the Wyoming State Fair Commission in 1909 and 1910; member of the Progressive National Committee for Wyoming 1912–1916; served as chairman of the Wyoming State Highway Commission in 1917 and 1918; president of the Wyoming Stock Growers' Association 1917–1921; member of the State council of national defense in 1917 and 1918; Governor of Wyoming 1919–1923; delegate to the Republican National Convention at Cleveland in 1924; appointed by President Coolidge in 1924 as chairman of the agricultural conference to investigate and report on the agricultural situation in the United States; elected as a Republican to the United States Senate on November 4, 1930, to fill the vacancy caused by the death of Francis E. Warren and on the same day was also elected for the term commencing March 4, 1931, and served from December 1, 1930, to January 3, 1937; unsuccessful candidate for reelection in 1936; resumed agricultural pursuits and ranching; died in Cheyenne, Wyo., January 17, 1937; interment in Lakeview Cemetery.

CARLETON, Ezra Child, a Representative from Michigan; born in St. Clair, St. Clair County, Mich., September 6, 1838; attended the common schools, and was graduated from the Port Huron High School in 1859; engaged in business as a hardware merchant in Port Huron, St. Clair County; mayor of Port Huron, Mich., in 1881 and 1882; elected as a Democrat to the Forty-eighth and Forty-ninth Congresses (March 4, 1883–March 3, 1887); engaged in his former mercantile pursuits in Port Huron, Mich., until his death there July 24, 1911; interment in Lakeside Cemetery.

CARLETON, Peter, a Representative from New Hampshire; born in Haverhill, Mass., September 19, 1755; attended the public schools; engaged in agricultural pursuits; served in a Massachusetts regiment during the Revolutionary War; moved to Landaff, N. H., about 1789; member of the State constitutional convention in 1790; member of the State house of representatives in 1803 and 1804; served in the State senate in 1806 and 1807; elected as a Democrat to the Tenth Congress (March 4, 1807–March 3, 1809); died in Landaff, Grafton County, N. H., on April 29, 1828; interment in the City Cemetery.

CARLEY, Patrick J., a Representative from New York; born in County Roscommon, Ireland, February 2, 1866; immigrated to the United States with his parents at an early age; attended the public schools; was naturalized on October 28, 1892; engaged in the building and construction business; also interested in banking; director of the Bay Ridge Memorial Hospital; elected as a Democrat to the Seventieth and to the three succeeding Congresses (March 4, 1927–January 3, 1935); was not a candidate for renomination in 1934; resumed the building and construction business until his retirement; died in Brooklyn, N. Y., February 25, 1936; interment in Calvary Cemetery, Queens County, N. Y.

CARLILE, John Snyder, a Representative and a Senator from Virginia; born in Winchester, Va., on December 16, 1817; educated by his mother; clerked in a store at the age of 14 and when 17 commenced business for himself; also studied law; was admitted to the bar in 1840 and commenced practice in Beverly, Va. (now West Virginia) in 1842; moved to Philippi and later to Clarksburg and continued the practice of law; member of the State senate 1847–1851; delegate to the State constitutional convention in 1850; elected as the candidate of the American Party to the Thirty-fourth Congress (March 4, 1855–March 3, 1857); delegate to the State secession convention in February 1861; elected to the Thirty-seventh Congress and served from March 4, 1861, until July 9, 1861, when he resigned to become Senator; elected as a Unionist to the United States Senate to fill the vacancy caused by the retirement of Robert M. T. Hunter and served from July 9, 1861, to March 3, 1865; member of the convention that submitted the new State ordinance in August 1861; died in Clarksburg, Harrison County, W. Va., October 24, 1878; interment in Odd Fellows Cemetery.

CARLIN, Charles Creighton, a Representative from Virginia; born in Alexandria, Va., April 8, 1866; attended the public schools and Alexandria Academy; was graduated from National University Law School, Washington, D. C.; was admitted to the bar in 1891 and commenced practice in Alexandria, Va.; postmaster at Alexandria, Va., 1893–1897; served as delegate to Democratic National Conventions for forty years; presidential elector on the Democratic ticket of Parker and Davis in 1904; elected as a Democrat to the Sixtieth Congress to fill the vacancy caused by the death of John F. Rixey; reelected to the Sixty-first and to the five succeeding Congresses and served from November 5, 1907, to March 3, 1919, when he resigned before the commencement of the Sixty-sixth Congress, to which he had been reelected; resumed the practice of law in Alexandria, Va., and Washington, D. C.; also engaged in the newspaper publishing business at Alexandria, Va.; moved to Washington, D. C., in 1936 and continued the practice of law; died in Washington, D. C., October 14, 1938; interment in Ivy Hill Cemetery, Alexandria, Va.

CARLISLE, John Griffin, a Representative and a Senator from Kentucky; born in Campbell (now Kenton) County, Ky., September 5, 1835; attended the common schools; taught school in Covington and elsewhere for five years; studied law; was admitted to the bar in March 1858 and commenced practice in Covington, Ky.; member of the State house of representatives 1859–1861; nominated for presidential elector on the Democratic ticket in 1864, but declined to run; member of the State senate in 1866; reelected in August 1869 and resigned in 1871; delegate at large to the Democratic National Convention at New York City in 1868; Lieutenant Governor of Kentucky, serving from August 1871 to September 1875; was editor of the Louisville Daily Ledger in 1872; alternate presidential elector at large in 1876; elected as a Democrat to the Forty-fifth and to the six succeeding Congresses and served from March 4, 1877, to May

26, 1890, when he resigned, having been elected Senator; served as Speaker of the House of Representatives in the Forty-eighth, Forty-ninth, and Fiftieth Congresses; elected to the United States Senate to fill the vacancy caused by the death of James B. Beck and took his seat May 26, 1890, and served until February 4, 1893, when he resigned to accept a Cabinet portfolio; Secretary of the Treasury 1893–1897; moved to New York City and resumed the practice of law; died in New York City July 31, 1910; interment in Linden Grove Cemetery, Covington, Ky.

CARLSON, Frank, a Representative and a Senator from Kansas; born in Concordia, Cloud County, Kans., January 23, 1893; attended the public schools, Concordia (Kans.) Normal and Business College, and Kansas State College at Manhattan; during the First World War served as a private in the United States Army from October 21, 1918, to March 31, 1919; engaged in agricultural pursuits and stock raising; member of the State house of representatives 1929–1933; chairman of the Republican State committee 1932–1934; elected as a Republican to the Seventy-fourth and to the five succeeding Congresses (January 3, 1935–January 3, 1947); was not a candidate for renomination in 1946; elected Governor of Kansas in 1946 and again in 1948 and served from January 1947 until his resignation on November 28, 1950, having been elected a Senator; chairman of the Interstate Oil Compact Commission in 1949; chairman of the National Governors' Conference in Colorado Springs in 1949; vice chairman of President's National Safety Conference in 1950; elected as a Republican to the United States Senate in 1950 to fill the vacancy caused by the death of Clyde M. Reed for the term ending January 3, 1951, and also for the full term commencing January 3, 1951, and served from November 29, 1950, to January 3, 1957; reelected in 1956 for the term ending January 3, 1963.

CARLTON, Henry Hull, a Representative from Georgia; born in Athens, Ga., May 14, 1835; attended the public schools and the University of Georgia at Athens for two years; was graduated in medicine and surgery from Jefferson Medical College, Philadelphia, Pa., in 1857, and practiced until 1872; during the Civil War served four years in the Confederate Army under Gen. Robert E. Lee, holding the ranks of lieutenant, captain, and major of artillery; member of the State house of representatives 1873–1877, serving as speaker pro tempore in 1877; editor and proprietor of the Athens Banner (Banner Watchman) until 1880; studied law; was admitted to the bar in 1881 and commenced practice in Athens, Ga.; city attorney of Athens in 1881 and 1882; member and president of the State senate in 1884 and 1885; elected as a Democrat to the Fiftieth and Fifty-first Congresses (March 4, 1887–March 3, 1891); again a member of the State house of representatives in 1899; declined reelection; volunteered for service in the Spanish-American War and was made inspector general with the rank of major; engaged in the insurance business; died in Athens, Ga., October 26, 1905; interment in Oconee Cemetery.

CARLYLE, Frank Ertel, a Representative from North Carolina; born in Lumberton, Robeson County, N. C., April 7, 1897; educated in the schools of Robeson County, N. C., and Wilson Memorial Academy, Nyack, N. Y.; graduated from the University of North Carolina at Chapel Hill; during the First World War served in the United States Navy; licensed to practice law on January 31, 1921, and commenced practice in Lumberton, N. C.; elected solicitor of the ninth judicial district of North Carolina in 1938, 1942, and 1946, and served until elected to Congress; elected as a Democrat to the Eighty-first and to the three succeeding Congresses (January 3, 1949–January 3, 1957); unsuccessful for renomination in 1956; died in Lumberton, N. C., October 2, 1960; interment in Meadowbrook Cemetery.

CARMACK, Edward Ward, a Representative and a Senator from Tennessee; born near Castalian Springs, Sumner County, Tenn., November 5, 1858; attended Webb's School, Culleoka, Tenn.; studied law; was admitted to the bar in 1879 and practiced in Columbia, Tenn.; city attorney of Columbia in 1881; elected to the State house of representatives in 1884; joined the staff of the Nashville Democrat in 1888; editor in chief of the Nashville American when the papers were merged; editor of the Memphis Commercial in 1892; delegate to the Democratic National Conventions in 1896, 1900, and 1904; elected as a Democrat to the Fifty-fifth and Fifty-sixth Congresses (March 4, 1897–March 3, 1901); elected to the United States Senate and served from March 4, 1901, to March 3, 1907; unsuccessful candidate in 1906 for reelection; resumed the practice of law; unsuccessful candidate for nomination as Governor in 1908; was assassinated in Nashville, Tenn., November 9, 1908; interment in Rose Hill Cemetery, Columbia, Tenn.; an act of the State legislature of 1909 provided that a statue be erected to his memory on the capitol grounds in Nashville.

CARMICHAEL, Archibald Hill, a Representative from Alabama; born near Sylvan Grove in Dale County, Ala., June 17, 1864; attended the public schools; was graduated from the law department of the University of Alabama at Tuscaloosa in 1886; was admitted to the bar the same year and commenced practice in Tuscumbia, Ala.; served as solicitor of the eighth judicial district of Alabama 1890–1894; delegate to the State constitutional convention in 1901; member of the State house of representatives 1907–1911 and 1915–1919, serving as speaker in 1907 and 1911; delegate at large to the Democratic National Conventions in 1916, 1928, and 1932; served in the State senate 1919–1923; member of the State Board of Education 1919–1947 and of the Tuscumbia Board of Education 1920–1947; trustee of the University of Alabama 1924–1947; elected as a Democrat to the Seventy-third Congress to fill the vacancy caused by the death of Edward B. Almon; reelected to the Seventy-fourth Congress and served from November 14, 1933, to January 3, 1937; was not a candidate for renomination in 1936; resumed the practice of law and was also interested in banking until his death in Tuscumbia, Ala., on July 15, 1947; interment in Oakwood Cemetery.

CARMICHAEL, Richard Bennett (grandnephew of William Carmichael), a Representative from Maryland; born in Centerville, Queen Annes County, Md., December 25, 1807; attended the academy at Centerville, and Dickinson College, Carlisle, Pa.; was graduated from Princeton College in 1828; studied law; was admitted to the bar in 1830 and commenced practice in Centerville, Queen Annes County, Md.; member of the State house of delegates in 1831 and 1841–1866; elected as a Jackson Democrat to the Twenty-third Congress (March 4, 1833–March 3, 1835); resumed the practice of law; delegate to the Democratic National Conventions in 1856, 1864, 1868, and 1876; judge of the circuit court 1858–1864; presiding judge of the county court of Queen Annes County in 1861; member and president of the State constitutional convention in 1867; died at "Wye," near Carmichael, Queen Annes County, Md., October 21, 1884; interment in the family burying ground at "Wye."

CARMICHAEL, William (granduncle of Richard Bennett Carmichael), a Delegate from Maryland; born at "Round Top," in Queen Annes County, Md., near Chestertown, Md.; studied law; was admitted to the bar and practiced in Centerville, Md.; was in London, England, at the beginning of the Revolution; assistant to Silas Deane, secret agent of Congress, at Paris, France, in 1776; went to Berlin, Prussia, in American interests in 1776; named secretary to the American commissioners in France in 1777, but did not serve, returning to the United States in May 1778; Member of the Continental Congress 1778–1780; went to Spain in September 1779 and served as secretary of the legation; appointed Chargé d'Affaires at Madrid, Spain, April 20, 1782, and served until May 1794; died in Madrid, Spain, February 9, 1795; interment in a lot adjoining the Roman Catholic Cemetery.

CARNAHAN, Albert Sidney Johnson, a Representative from Missouri; born on a farm near Ellsinore, Carter County, Mo., January 9, 1897; attended the local country schools and high schools at Ellsinore and Cape Girardeau, Mo.; was graduated from State Teachers College at Cape Girardeau in 1926 and from the University of Missouri at Columbia in 1934; taught school, served as high school principal for one year, and held school administrative positions in Carter, Reynolds, and Shannon Counties 1920–1944; during the First World War served overseas in the United States Navy as a yeoman third class with a naval aviation unit in 1918 and 1919; elected as a Democrat to the Seventy-ninth Congress (January 3, 1945–January 3, 1947); unsuccessful candidate for reelection in 1946 to the Eightieth Congress; superintendent of schools at Ellsinore, Mo.; elected to the Eighty-first and to the five succeeding Congresses (January 3, 1949–January 3, 1961); unsuccessful candidate for renomination in 1960; confirmed as Ambassador to Sierra Leone May 11, 1961; is a resident of Ellsinore, Mo.

CARNES, Thomas Petters, a Representative from Georgia; born in Maryland in 1762; completed preparatory studies; studied law; was admitted to the bar and practiced in Milledgeville, Ga.; member of the State house of representatives 1786, 1787, 1789, and 1797; solicitor general for the western circuit of Georgia; attorney general of Georgia from December 22, 1789, until December 8, 1792, when he resigned; elected to the Third Congress (March 4, 1793–March 3, 1795); resumed the practice of law; judge of the western circuit court of Georgia from January 27, 1798, until May 20, 1803, when he resigned, and from December 1809 to November 1810; member of the State constitutional convention in 1798; appointed one of the commissioners to settle the boundary disputes between the States of Georgia and North Carolina in 1806; again a member of the State house of representatives in 1807 and 1808; died on his farm in Franklin (now Hart) County, Ga., May 5, 1822; interment in the garden on his estate.

CARPENTER, Cyrus Clay, a Representative from Iowa; born near Harford, Susquehanna County, Pa., November 24, 1829; attended the common schools, and was graduated from Harford Academy in 1853; moved to Iowa in 1854 and engaged in teaching and afterwards in land surveying; studied law but never practiced; county surveyor of Webster County in 1856; member of the State house of representatives 1858–1860; during the Civil War was appointed captain of Volunteers March 24, 1862; lieutenant colonel from September 26, 1864, to July 14, 1865; brevetted colonel of Volunteers "for efficient and meritorious services" July 12, 1865; mustered out July 14, 1865; register of the State land office 1866–1868; Governor of Iowa 1872–1876; Second Comptroller of the Treasury from January 1876 to September 1877; appointed railroad commissioner of Iowa March 26, 1878; elected as a Republican to the Forty-sixth and Forty-seventh Congresses (March 4, 1879–March 3, 1883); was not a candidate for renomination in 1882 to the Forty-eighth Congress; again served in the State house of representatives 1884–1886; postmaster of Fort Dodge 1889–1893; engaged in the management of his farm and in the real-estate business; died in Fort Dodge, Iowa, May 29, 1898; interment in Oakland Cemetery.

CARPENTER, Davis, a Representative from New York; born in Walpole, Cheshire County, N. H., December 25, 1799; studied medicine; was graduated from Middlebury (Vt.) College in 1824; studied law; was admitted to the bar and commenced practice in Brockport, N. Y.; elected as a Whig to the Thirty-third Congress to fill the vacancy caused by the resignation of Azariah Boody and served from November 8, 1853, to March 3, 1855; unsuccessful candidate for reelection in 1854 to the Thirty-fourth Congress; engaged in the practice of medicine in Brockport, Monroe County, N. Y., and died there October 22, 1878; interment in High Street Cemetery.

CARPENTER, Edmund Nelson, a Representative from Pennsylvania; born in Wilkes-Barre, Pa., June 27, 1865; attended the public schools in Wilkes-Barre and the Wyoming Seminary, Kingston, Pa.; interested in mining and the manufacture of sheet-metal products; enlisted as a private in 1893 and attained the rank of major in the Pennsylvania National Guard; during the Spanish-American War served as first lieutenant and quartermaster in the Ninth Regiment, Pennsylvania Volunteer Infantry, from April 27, 1898, to October 29, 1898; chairman of the Wyoming Valley Chapter of the American Red Cross during the First World War; unsuccessful candidate for election in 1918 to the Sixty-sixth Congress; elected as a Republican to the Sixty-ninth Congress (March 4, 1925–March 3, 1927); unsuccessful candidate for reelection in 1926 to the Seventieth Congress; resumed his manufacturing interests; died in Fairmount Farms, Inc., a hospital in (Roxborough) Philadelphia, Pa., November 4, 1952; interment in Hollenback Cemetery, Wilkes-Barre, Pa.

CARPENTER, Levi D., a Representative from New York; born in Waterville, Oneida County, N. Y., August 21, 1802; attended the public schools; studied law; was admitted to the bar and commenced practice in Waterville, N. Y.; supervisor of the town of Sangerfield in 1835; elected as a Democrat to the Twenty-eighth Congress to fill the vacancy caused by the resignation of Samuel Beardsley and served from November 5, 1844, to March 3, 1845; was not a candidate for reelection in 1844 to the Twenty-ninth Congress; resumed the practice of law in Waterville, N. Y., and died there October 27, 1856; interment in the City Cemetery.

CARPENTER, Lewis Cass, a Representative from South Carolina; born in Putnam, Conn., February 20, 1836; attended the public schools; moved to New Jersey, where he taught school; appointed State inspector of public schools in New Jersey in 1863; at an early age began writing for the press, and was connected with the New York papers for several years; went to Washington, D. C., in 1864 and was employed in the Treasury Department; studied law at Columbian (now George Washington) University; was admitted to the bar and practiced; Washington newspaper correspondent; moved to Charleston, S. C., in 1867 and became editor of the Charleston Courier; assisted in establishing the Charleston Republican in 1868; secretary to United States Senator William H. Buckingham, of Connecticut, 1868–1873; elected as a Republican to the Forty-third Congress to fill the vacancy caused by the resignation of Robert B. Elliott and served from November 3, 1874, to March 3, 1875; unsuccessful candidate for election to the Forty-fifth Congress; moved to Denver, Colo., in 1878, and thence, in 1879, to Leadville, where he edited a newspaper; appointed supervisor of the census for Colorado in 1880; appointed United States post-office inspector in 1881 and resigned in 1883; engaged in the insurance business 1883–1890; resumed the practice of law; died in Denver, Colo., March 6, 1908; interment in Fairmount Cemetery.

CARPENTER, Matthew Hale, a Senator from Wisconsin; born in Moretown, Washington County, Vt., December 22, 1824; attended the common schools; entered the United States Military Academy at West Point in 1843 and remained two years; studied law in the office of Rufus Choate; was admitted to the bar in 1847 and practiced in Boston, Mass.; moved to Beloit, Wis., in 1848; district attorney of Rock County 1850–1854; moved to Milwaukee in 1858; until the commencement of the Civil War belonged to the Douglas wing of the Democratic Party; represented the Government in the celebrated McCardle case, and brought to trial the validity of the reconstruction act of March 7, 1867, for the government of the States then in rebellion, and won the case in the Supreme Court; elected as a Republican to the United States Senate and served from March 4, 1869, to March 3, 1875; elected President pro tempore of the Senate March 12, 1873, March 26, 1873, December 11, 1873, and December 22, 1874; unsuccessful candidate for reelection in 1875; resumed the practice of law in Washington and in Milwaukee; again elected as a Republican to the United States Senate and served from March 4, 1879, until his death in Washington, D. C., February 24, 1881; interment in Forest Home Cemetery, Milwaukee, Wis.

CARPENTER, Terry McGovern, a Representative from Nebraska; born in Cedar Rapids, Linn County, Iowa, March 28, 1900; attended the public schools of Cedar Rapids; moved to Scottsbluff, Nebr., in 1916 and was employed in various positions with a railroad company; was engaged in the wholesale candy and tobacco business in 1922 and 1923; moved to Long Beach, Calif., in 1923 and was employed as manager of the municipal gas and water department; returned to Scottsbluff, Nebr., in 1927 and engaged in the garage business until 1930, when he became owner of a gasoline filling station; also in the retail coal business; unsuccessful candidate for mayor in 1931; elected as a Democrat to the Seventy-third Congress (March 4, 1933–January 3, 1935); was not a candidate for renomination in 1934; unsuccessful for the Democratic gubernatorial nomination in 1934, for election to the United States Senate in 1936 and 1948 and again for the gubernatorial nomination in 1950; changed political affiliation in 1952; unsuccessful for the Republican nomination in 1954 to the United States Senate; delegate to the Republican National Convention in 1956; elected to the State legislature in 1954, 1956, and 1958; defeated for the Republican gubernatorial nomination in 1960; engaged in operating Terry Carpenter, Inc., in Terrytown, Nebr.; resides in Scottsbluff, Nebr.

CARPENTER, William Randolph, a Representative from Kansas; born in Marion, Marion County, Kans., April 24, 1894; attended public and high schools; was graduated from the law department of the University of Michigan at Ann Arbor in 1917; was admitted to the bar the same year and commenced practice in Marion, Kans.; also interested in agricultural pursuits; organized Company M, Third Regiment Infantry, Kansas National Guard, serving as second lieutenant; during the First World War was transferred to Company M, One Hundred and Thirty-ninth Infantry, Thirty-fifth Division, was promoted to first lieutenant during the Argonne offensive, and served from August 5, 1917, until his discharge on May 8, 1919; member of the Marion Board of Education 1925–1933; served in the State house of representatives 1929–1933; elected as a Democrat to the Seventy-third and Seventy-fourth Congresses (March 4, 1933–January 3, 1937); was not a candidate for renomination in 1936; resumed the practice of law; appointed acting United States attorney for the district of Kansas on February 21, 1945, and as United States attorney for the same district on April 7, 1945, and served until his resignation in 1948 to become a candidate for Governor; unsuccessful

Democratic candidate for Governor in 1948; member of the United States Motor Carrier Claims Commission 1950–1952; member of board of directors of Sherwood Manufacturing Co., Independence, Mo.; vice president of Columbian Title & Trust Company, Topeka, Kans., at the time of his death; died in Topeka, Kans., July 26, 1956; interment in Highland Cemetery, Marion, Kans.

CARR, Francis (father of James Carr), a Representative from Massachusetts; born in Newbury, Mass., December 6, 1751; attended the common schools; engaged in the mercantile business; member of the State house of representatives from Haverhill 1791–1795 and 1801–1803, and from Orrington, Maine (then Massachusetts), 1806–1808; served in the State senate 1809–1811; elected as a Democrat to the Twelfth Congress to fill the vacancy caused by the resignation of Barzillai Gannett and served from April 6, 1812, to March 3, 1813; unsuccessful candidate for reelection in 1812 to the Thirteenth Congress; resumed mercantile pursuits; died in Bangor, Maine, October 6, 1821; interment in Mount Hope Cemetery.

CARR, James (son of Francis Carr), a Representative from Massachusetts; born in Bangor, Maine (then a part of Massachusetts), September 9, 1777; attended Exeter and Byfield Academies; clerk on U. S. S. *Crescent;* appointed as secretary to the United States consul at Algiers and served two years; engaged in mercantile pursuits in Orrington, Maine (then Massachusetts); member of the State house of representatives 1806–1811; elected to the Fourteenth Congress (March 4, 1815–March 3, 1817); was drowned in the Ohio River August 24, 1818; memorial headstone placed in Mount Hope Cemetery, Bangor, Maine.

CARR, John, a Representative from Indiana; born in Uniontown, Perry County, Ind., April 9, 1793; moved with his parents to Clark County, Ind., in 1806; attended the public schools; fought in the Battle of Tippecanoe; appointed lieutenant in a company of United States Rangers, authorized by an act of Congress for defense of western frontiers, in 1812; brigadier general and major general of the Indiana Militia until his death; county clerk 1824–1830; presidential elector on the Democratic ticket of Jackson and Calhoun in 1824; elected as a Democrat to the Twenty-second, Twenty-third, and Twenty-fourth Congresses (March 4, 1831–March 3, 1837); unsuccessful candidate in 1836 for reelection to the Twenty-fifth Congress; elected to the Twenty-sixth Congress (March 4, 1839–March 3, 1841); died in Charlestown, Clark County, Ind., January 20, 1845; interment in the Old Cemetery.

CARR, Nathan Tracy, a Representative from Indiana; born in Corning, Steuben County, N. Y., December 25, 1833; attended the common schools, and was graduated from Starkey Academy in 1851; moved to Midland County, Mich.; studied law; was admitted to the Midland County bar in 1858 and commenced practice at Vassar, Mich.; member of the State house of representatives 1858–1860; recorder of Midland County in 1861 and 1862; during the Civil War served as a lieutenant in the Second Regiment, Michigan Volunteer Infantry, in 1862; moved to Columbus, Ind., in 1867; prosecuting attorney for Bartholomew, Shelby, Jackson, and Brown Counties in 1870; elected as a Democrat to the Forty-fourth Congress to fill the vacancy caused by the death of Michael C. Kerr and served from December 5, 1876, to March 3, 1877; unsuccessful candidate for renomination in 1876; resumed the practice of law in Columbus, Bartholomew County, Ind.; appointed judge of the ninth judicial circuit court of Indiana in 1878; died in Columbus, Ind., May 28, 1885; interment in the City Cemetery.

CARR, Wooda Nicholas, a Representative from Pennsylvania; born in Allegheny City (now a part of Pittsburgh), Pa., February 6, 1871; attended the public schools and Madison College; was graduated from Monongahela College, Pennsylvania, in 1891; editor of the Uniontown (Pa.) News and the Uniontown Democrat in 1892; studied law; was admitted to the Pennsylvania bar in 1895 and commenced practice in Uniontown; delegate to the Democratic State conventions in 1898, 1899, 1900, and 1904; served as chairman of the Democratic committee of Fayette County in 1901, 1902, and 1920; elected as a Democrat to the Sixty-third Congress (March 4, 1913–March 3, 1915); was an unsuccessful candidate for reelection in 1914 to the Sixty-fourth Congress; resumed the practice of law; president of the Fayette County Bar Association in 1924; was appointed postmaster of Uniontown, Pa., on August 2, 1934, and served until his retirement in 1947; died in Uniontown, Pa., on June 28, 1953; interment in Oak Grove Cemetery.

CARRIER, Chester Otto, a Representative from Kentucky; born on a farm near Brownsville, Edmonson County, Ky., May 5, 1897; attended the public schools of Grayson County, Ky., the University of West Virginia at Morgantown, and was graduated from the law department of the University of Louisville at Louisville, Ky., in 1924; engaged in ranching in Wyoming for one year; took up railroading in Pennsylvania in 1920; was admitted to the bar in 1923 and commenced practice in Leitchfield, Grayson County, Ky.; county attorney of Grayson County, Ky., 1925–1943; elected as a Republican to the Seventy-eighth Congress to fill the vacancy caused by the death of Edward W. Creal and served from November 30, 1943, to January 3, 1945; unsuccessful candidate for reelection in 1944 to the Seventy-ninth Congress; resumed the practice of his profession and is a resident of Leitchfield, Ky.

CARRIGG, Joseph Leonard, a Representative from Pennsylvania; born in Susquehanna, Pa., February 23, 1901; attended Laurel Hill Academy, Susquehanna, Pa., was graduated from Niagara University, Niagara Falls, N. Y., in 1922, Albany Law School, Albany, N. Y., in 1924, and Dickinson Law School, Carlisle, Pa., in 1925; was admitted to the bar in 1926 and commenced the practice of law in Susquehanna, Pa.; district attorney of Susquehanna County, Pa., 1936–1948; burgess of borough of Susquehanna 1948–1951; elected as a Republican to the Eighty-second Congress to fill the vacancy caused by the death of Wilson D. Gillette; reelected to the Eighty-third, Eighty-fourth, and Eighty-fifth Congresses and served from November 6, 1951, to January 3, 1959; unsuccessful candidate for reelection in 1958 to the Eighty-sixth Congress; director of practice, Internal Revenue Service, Washington, D. C., 1959–1960; secretary to Representative Scranton of Pennsylvania in 1961; is a resident of Susquehanna, Pa.

CARRINGTON, Edward, a Delegate from Virginia; born in Goochland County, Va., February 11, 1748; member of the county committee in 1775 and 1776; served in the Revolutionary Army; commissioned lieutenant colonel of Artillery November 30, 1776; served as quartermaster general on the staff of General Greene; commanded the Artillery at the Battle of Hobkirks Hill, April 24, 1781, and at Yorktown; Member of the Continental Congress in 1785 and 1786; appointed by President Washington marshal of Virginia in 1789; foreman of the jury during the trial of Aaron Burr for treason in 1807; died in Richmond, Va., October 28, 1810; interment in St. John's Cemetery.

CARROLL, Charles ("Barrister") (cousin of Charles Carroll of Carrollton and Daniel Carroll), a Delegate from Maryland; born in Annapolis, Md., March 22, 1723; received his education at the

English House, West Lisbon, Portugal, at Eaton in London, at the University of Cambridge, and studied law in the Middle Temple, Garden Court, England; returned to Annapolis, Md., in 1746 and commenced the practice of law; elected to the Maryland Lower House of Assembly in 1755 to fill the vacancy caused by the death of his father, Dr. Charles Carroll; served on many important committees in the conventions of Maryland and framed many important State documents and public papers, among them the "Declaration of Rights" adopted by the convention of Maryland on November 3, 1776; became a member of the Council of Safety in August 1775; elected a Delegate to the Continental Congress on November 10, 1776, to succeed his cousin, Charles Carroll of Carrollton, serving until February 15, 1777; was elected in 1777 to the first State senate, having previously declined the position of chief judge of the general court of Maryland; was reelected in 1781 and held that office until his death at his residence, Mount Clare, near Baltimore, Md., March 23, 1783.

CARROLL, Charles (of Carrollton) (cousin of Charles Carroll, "Barrister," and Daniel Carroll), a Delegate and a Senator from Maryland; born in Annapolis, Md., September 19, 1737; attended the Jesuits' College of Bohemia at Hermans Manor, Md., and the College of St. Omer in France; studied civil law at the College of Louis le Grand in Rheims, and common law in London; returned to Annapolis, Md., in 1765; delegate to the revolutionary convention of Maryland in 1775; Continental commissioner to Canada in 1776; member of the Board of War 1776–1777; elected as a Delegate to the Continental Congress on July 4, 1776, and served until November 15, 1776; again elected on February 15, 1777, and served until 1778, when he resigned; again elected to the Continental Congress in 1780, but declined to serve; member of the State senate of Maryland 1777 to 1800; was a signer of the Declaration of Independence; elected as a Federalist to the United States Senate; reelected in 1791 and served from March 4, 1789, to November 30, 1792, when, preferring to remain a State senator, he resigned because of a law passed by the Maryland Legislature disqualifying the members of the State senate who held seats in Congress; retired to private life in 1801; set the stone marking the beginning of the Baltimore & Ohio Railroad Company on July 4, 1828; died in Baltimore, Md., November 14, 1832; at the time of his death was the last surviving signer of the Declaration of Independence; interment in the chapel of Doughoregan Manor, near Ellicott City, Howard County, Md.

CARROLL, Charles Hobart (great-grandson of Daniel Carroll), a Representative from New York; born in Bellevue, Georgetown Heights, D. C., May 4, 1794; was graduated from St. Mary's College, Baltimore, Md., in 1812; moved to Livingston County, N. Y.; studied law but never practiced; engaged in agricultural pursuits; land agent; supervisor of Groveland, Livingston County, in 1817, 1818, 1822, 1839, 1840, and 1848; county judge 1823–1829; served in the State senate in 1827 and 1828; member of the State assembly in 1836; elected as a Clay Whig to the Twenty-eighth and Twenty-ninth Congresses (March 4, 1843–March 3, 1847); was not a candidate for renomination in 1846; managed his large landed estate near Groveland, N. Y.; presidential elector on the American Party ticket of Fillmore and Donelson in 1856; died in Groveland, N. Y., June 8, 1865; interment in Williamsburgh Cemetery.

CARROLL, Daniel (uncle of Richard Brent, cousin of Charles Carroll of Carrollton and Charles Carroll, "Barrister," and great-grandfather of Charles Hobart Carroll), a Delegate and a Representative from Maryland; born in Upper Marlboro, Prince Georges County, Md., July 22, 1730; educated at the Jesuit

School at Bohemia Manor, Md., and at St. Omer's College, France; returned to Maryland in 1748; Member of the Continental Congress 1780–1784, signing the Articles of Confederation on March 1, 1781; appointed a delegate on May 26, 1787, to the convention that framed the Federal Constitution; member of the first State senate of Maryland and up to the time of his death was a member of the senate of Maryland, or the executive council of Maryland; elected as a Federalist to the First Congress (March 4, 1789–March 3, 1791); took an active part in fixing the seat of government for the United States; appointed by President Washington on January 22, 1791, as one of the Commissioners to locate the District of Columbia and the Federal City and served until July 25, 1795, when he resigned; engaged in agricultural pursuits, his farm being the site of the present city of Washington; died at Rock Creek (Forest Glen), near Washington, D. C., May 7, 1796; interment in St. John's Catholic Cemetery, Forest Glen, Md.

CARROLL, James, a Representative from Maryland; born in Baltimore, Md., December 2, 1791; was graduated from old St. Mary's College at Baltimore in 1808; studied law but did not practice; settled on a farm on West River; returned to Baltimore, Md., in 1831; judge of the orphans' court; trustee of the poor; served as a director of the Baltimore & Ohio Railroad Company and the Chesapeake & Ohio Canal Company; elected as a Democrat to the Twenty-sixth Congress (March 4, 1839–March 3, 1841); was not a candidate for renomination in 1840 to the Twenty-seventh Congress; unsuccessful candidate for Governor of Maryland in 1844; retired from political life; died in Baltimore, Md., January 16, 1873; interment in St. Paul's Burying Ground.

CARROLL, John Albert, a Representative and a Senator from Colorado; born in Denver, Colo., July 30, 1901; attended the public schools; was graduated from Westminster Law School, Denver, Colo., in 1929; was admitted to the bar the same year and commenced practice in Denver, Colo.; assistant United States district attorney in 1933 and 1934; district attorney of Denver 1937–1941; regional attorney for the Office of Price Administration (Rocky Mountain Area) in 1942 and 1943; during the First World War served as an enlisted man in the United States Army at Corregidor, Philippine Islands, from January 11, 1918, to August 26, 1919, and in World War II as a commissioned officer in the United States Army with service in Africa, Italy, Corsica, and France, from May 17, 1943, to July 15, 1945; resumed the practice of law; elected as a Democrat to the Eightieth and Eighty-first Congresses (January 3, 1947–January 3, 1951); was not a candidate for renomination in 1950 but was an unsuccessful candidate for election to the United States Senate in 1950 and again in 1954; special assistant to President Truman in 1951 and 1952; elected to the United States Senate in 1956 for the term commencing January 3, 1957, and ending January 3, 1963.

CARROLL, John Michael, a Representative from New York; born in Springfield, Otsego County, N. Y., April 27, 1823; attended the public schools; was graduated from Fairfield Seminary, Fairfield, N. Y., and from Union College, Schenectady, N. Y., in 1846; studied law; was admitted to the bar in 1848 and commenced practice in Broadalbin, Fulton County, N. Y.; prosecuting attorney of Fulton County 1859–1862; moved to Johnstown, N. Y., in 1862 and continued the practice of law; elected as a Democrat to the Forty-second Congress (March 4, 1871–March 3, 1873); declined to be a candidate for renomination in 1872; engaged in the practice of law in Johnstown, Fulton County, N. Y., until his death there on May 8, 1901; interment in Johnstown Cemetery.

CARSON, Henderson Haverfield, a Representative from Ohio; born on a farm near Cadiz, Harrison County, Ohio, October 25, 1893; attended the public and high schools; was graduated from the Cleveland (Ohio) Law School, and from Baldwin Wallace College at Berea, Ohio, in 1919; became affiliated with the legal department of the Pennsylvania Railroad Co. in 1915; during the First World War enlisted in the Field Artillery in 1918; was transferred to Base Hospital, One Hundred and Nineteenth Unit, Camp Zachary Taylor, Ky., and served there until honorably discharged in 1919 as a corporal; was admitted to the bar in 1919 and commenced practice in Canton, Ohio, in 1922, still retaining his railroad connection, specializing in insurance law; member of the faculty of McKinley Law School 1926–1942; elected as a Republican to the Seventy-eighth Congress (January 3, 1943–January 3, 1945); unsuccessful candidate for reelection in 1944 to the Seventy-ninth Congress; elected to the Eightieth Congress (January 3, 1947–January 3, 1949); was an unsuccessful candidate for reelection in 1948 to the Eighty-first Congress; resumed the practice of law in Canton, Ohio, and Washington, D. C.; is a resident of Canton, Ohio.

CARSON, Samuel Price, a Representative from North Carolina; born in Pleasant Gardens, N. C., January 22, 1798; studied under private tutors in Pleasant Gardens; engaged in agricultural pursuits; member of the State senate 1822–1824; elected as a Democrat to the Nineteenth and to the three succeeding Congresses (March 4, 1825–March 3, 1833); unsuccessful candidate in 1833 for reelection to the Twenty-third Congress because of the sentiment against the nullification doctrine of Calhoun which he supported; again elected to the State senate in 1834; delegate to the State constitutional convention in 1835; moved to Texas in 1836; member of the Texas convention that adopted the constitution of that Republic in 1836; appointed Secretary of State for the Republic of Texas in September 1836 and served until 1838; sent as a commissioner to Washington, D. C., to intercede for the recognition of the independence of Texas in 1836; died at Hot Springs, Ark., November 2, 1838; interment in the Government Cemetery, Hot Springs, Ark.

CARSS, William Leighton, a Representative from Minnesota; born in Pella, Marion County, Iowa, February 15, 1865; moved with his parents to Des Moines, Iowa, in 1867; attended the public schools; studied civil and mechanical engineering and followed that profession for a number of years; moved to St. Louis County, Minn., in 1893 and settled in Proctor; engaged as a locomotive engineer; elected as an Independent to the Sixty-sixth Congress (March 4, 1919–March 3, 1921); unsuccessful candidate for reelection as a Democrat in 1920 to the Sixty-seventh Congress and for election in 1922 to the Sixty-eighth Congress; elected on the Farmer-Labor ticket to the Sixty-ninth and Seventieth Congresses (March 4, 1925–March 3, 1929); unsuccessful candidate for reelection in 1928 to the Seventy-first Congress and for election in 1930 to the Seventy-second Congress; moved to Duluth, Minn., in 1929; resumed his position as locomotive engineer at Proctor, Minn.; died in Duluth, Minn., May 31, 1931; interment in Oneota Cemetery.

CARTER, Albert Edward, a Representative from California; born near Visalia, Tulare County, Calif., July 5, 1881; attended the public schools; was graduated from San Jose State Normal School in 1903; taught school six years; was graduated from the law department of the University of California at Berkeley in 1913; was admitted to the bar the same year and commenced practice in Oakland, Calif.; representative of the United States War Department Commission on Training Camps 1917–1919; attorney for the California State Board of Pharmacy in 1920

and 1921; commissioner of public works of Oakland 1921–1925 and in 1923 initiated the plan for a comprehensive development of the harbor on the east side of San Francisco Bay; president of the Pacific Coast Association of Port Authorities; elected as a Republican to the Sixty-ninth and to the nine succeeding Congresses (March 4, 1925–January 3, 1945); unsuccessful candidate for reelection in 1944 to the Seventy-ninth Congress; resumed the practice of law in California and Washington, D. C., and is a resident of Oakland, Calif.

CARTER, Charles David, a Representative from Oklahoma; born near Boggy Depot, Choctaw Nation, Indian Territory (now Oklahoma), August 16, 1868; moved with his father to Mill Creek, a stage stand on the western frontier of the Chickasaw Nation, in April 1876; attended the Indian day schools and Chickasaw Manual Training Academy at Tishomingo; employed on a ranch from 1887 to 1889 and in a mercantile establishment in Ardmore, Okla., from 1889 to 1892; auditor of public accounts of the Chickasaw Nation 1892–1894; member of the Chickasaw Council in 1895; superintendent of schools of the Chickasaw Nation in 1897; appointed mining trustee of Indian Territory by President McKinley in November 1900 and served four years; secretary of the first Democratic executive committee of the proposed State of Oklahoma from June to December 1906; upon the admission of Oklahoma as a State into the Union was elected as a Democrat to the Sixtieth and to the nine succeeding Congresses and served from November 16, 1907, to March 3, 1927; unsuccessful candidate for renomination in 1926; appointed a member of the State highway commission on March 5, 1927, and served until April 1, 1929; died in Ardmore, Okla., April 9, 1929; interment in Rose Hill Cemetery.

CARTER, John, a Representative from South Carolina; born on the Black River, near Camden, Sumter District, S. C., September 10, 1792; was graduated from South Carolina College (now the University of South Carolina) at Columbia in 1811; studied law; was admitted to the bar in 1814 and commenced practice in Camden, S. C.; served as commissioner in equity 1814–1820; elected to the Seventeenth Congress to fill the vacancy caused by the resignation of James Blair; reelected to the Eighteenth, Nineteenth, and Twentieth Congresses and served from December 11, 1822, to March 3, 1829; resumed the practice of law in Camden, S. C.; moved to Georgetown, D. C., in 1836, and died there June 20, 1850.

CARTER, Luther Cullen, a Representative from New York; born in Bethel, Maine, February 25, 1805; moved to New York City and engaged in mercantile pursuits; member of the Board of Education of New York City in 1853; retired from business and moved to Long Island City, where he engaged in agricultural pursuits; elected as a Union Republican to the Thirty-sixth Congress (March 4, 1859–March 3, 1861); unsuccessful candidate for reelection in 1860 to the Thirty-seventh Congress; died in New York City January 3, 1875; interment in Greenwood Cemetery, Brooklyn, N. Y.

CARTER, Steven V., a Representative from Iowa; born in Carterville, Utah, October 8, 1915; at the age of 14 years moved with his parents to Lamoni, Decatur County, Iowa, and attended the public schools; graduated from Graceland College, Lamoni, Iowa, in 1934, University of Iowa in 1937, and State University of Iowa College of Law in 1939; was admitted to the bar in 1939 and commenced the practice of law in Leon, Iowa; county attorney, Decatur County, 1940–1944; during World War II served as a supply officer in the United States Navy 1943–1946, with service in the South Pacific Theater; city attorney, Leon, Iowa, 1946–1948; member of the executive board of the Southern Iowa

Area Council of Boy Scouts of America; unsuccessful Democratic candidate for election to the Eighty-fifth Congress in 1956, and later unsuccessfully contested the election; elected as a Democrat to the Eighty-sixth Congress and served from January 3, 1959, until his death in the naval hospital at Bethesda, Md., November 4, 1959; interment in Leon Cemetery, Leon, Iowa.

CARTER, Thomas Henry, a Delegate, a Representative, and a Senator from Montana; born near Portsmouth, Scioto County, Ohio, October 30, 1854; while a child his parents moved to Pana, Ill.; attended the common schools in Illinois; engaged in farming, school teaching, and railroading; at the same time studied law and was admitted to the bar; in 1882 moved from Burlington, Iowa, to Helena, Mont.; elected as a Republican a Delegate to the Fifty-first Congress and served from March 4, 1889, to November 7, 1889, when the Territory was admitted as a State into the Union; elected as its first Representative and served from November 8, 1889, to March 3, 1891; unsuccessful candidate in 1890 for reelection to the Fifty-second Congress; Commissioner of the General Land Office from March 1891 to July 1892, when he was elected chairman of the Republican National Committee; delegate to the Republican National Conventions in 1896, 1900, and 1904; elected as a Republican to the United States Senate and served from March 4, 1895, until March 3, 1901; caucus nominee for reelection by his party, which was in the minority; appointed by President McKinley a member of the board of commissioners of the Louisiana Purchase Exposition and served as its president; again elected to the United States Senate and served from March 4, 1905, to March 3, 1911; again the caucus nominee for reelection by his party, which was in the minority; chairman of the United States section of the International Joint Commission created to prevent disputes regarding the use of boundary waters between the United States and Canada from March 11, 1911, until his death in Washington, D. C., September 17, 1911; interment in Mount Olivet Cemetery.

CARTER, Timothy Jarvis, a Representative from Maine; born in Bethel, in the Maine district of Massachusetts, August 18, 1800; attended the town schools of Bethel; studied law at Northampton, Mass., was admitted to the bar in 1826 and commenced practice in Rumford, Oxford County, Maine; moved to Paris, Oxford County, Maine, in 1827 and continued the practice of law; secretary of the State senate of Maine in 1833; county attorney 1833–1837; elected as a Democrat to the Twenty-fifth Congress and served from September 4, 1837, until his death in Washington, D. C., March 14, 1838; interment in the Congressional Cemetery.

CARTER, Vincent Michael, a Representative from Wyoming; born in St. Clair, Schuylkill County, Pa., November 6, 1891; moved with his parents to Pottsville, Pa., in 1893; attended the public and high schools, the United States Naval Academy Preparatory School, Annapolis, Md., and Fordham University, New York City, N. Y.; was graduated from the law department of Catholic University, Washington, D. C., in 1915; was admitted to the bar in 1919 and commenced practice in Casper, Wyo., the same year; moved to Kemmerer, Wyo., in 1929 and continued the practice of law; during the First World War served in the Marine Corps as a lieutenant in the Eighth Regiment, Third Brigade; captain in the State militia 1919–1921; deputy attorney general of Wyoming 1919–1923; State auditor 1923–1929; elected as a Republican to the Seventy-first, Seventy-second, and Seventy-third Congresses (March 4, 1929–January 3, 1935); was not a candidate for renomination in 1934, but was an unsuccessful candidate for election to the United States

Senate; resumed the practice of law in Cheyenne, Wyo.; delegate to the Republican National Conventions in 1936 and 1940; is a resident of Cheyenne, Wyo.

CARTER, William Blount, a Representative from Tennessee; born in Elizabethton, Carter County, Tenn., October 22, 1792; attended the public schools; during the War of 1812 served as a colonel; member of the State house of representatives; served in the State senate; delegate to the State constitutional convention in 1834 and served as its presiding officer; elected as a Whig to the Twenty-fourth, Twenty-fifth, and Twenty-sixth Congresses (March 4, 1835–March 3, 1841); died in Elizabethton, Tenn., April 17, 1848; interment in Carter Cemetery.

CARTER, William Henry, a Representative from Massachusetts; born at Needham Heights, Norfolk County, Mass., June 15, 1864; attended the Avery graded schools and Needham High School; was graduated from Comers Commercial College, Boston, Mass.; served as a mechanic, foreman, superintendent, and general superintendent in the knit-underwear manufacturing plant of the William Carter Co.; member of the State house of representatives in 1906; member of the Republican State committee in 1907 and 1908; elected as a Republican to the Sixty-fourth and Sixty-fifth Congresses (March 4, 1915–March 3, 1919); was not a candidate for reelection in 1918; interested in real-estate development; was elected president of the William Carter Co. in 1918 and continued manufacturing activities until his death; died in Needham, Mass., April 23, 1955; interment in Needham Cemetery.

CARTTER, David Kellogg, a Representative from Ohio; born in Jefferson County, N. Y., in June 22, 1812; pursued preparatory studies; studied law in Rochester, N. Y.; was admitted to the bar in 1832 and commenced practice in Rochester, N. Y.; four years later moved to Akron, Ohio, and then to Massillon, Ohio, and continued the practice of law; elected as a Democrat to the Thirty-first and Thirty-second Congresses (March 4, 1849–March 3, 1853); moved to Cleveland, Ohio, in 1856 and continued law practice; delegate to the Republican National Convention at Chicago in 1860; appointed United States Minister to Bolivia by President Lincoln, and served from March 27, 1861, to March 10, 1862; appointed chief justice of the Supreme Court of the District of Columbia in 1863, and served until his death in Washington, D. C., on April 16, 1887; interment in Lakeview Cemetery, Cleveland, Ohio.

CARTWRIGHT, Wilburn, a Representative from Oklahoma; born on a farm near Georgetown, Meigs County, Tenn., January 12, 1892; moved with his parents to the Choctaw Nation, Indian Territory, in 1903; attended the public schools at Wapanucka and Ada, Okla., and State Teachers College at Durant, Okla.; taught in the rural, village, and city schools of Coal, Atoka, Bryan, and Pittsburg Counties, Okla., 1914–1926; member of the State house of representatives 1914–1918; studied law; was admitted to the bar in 1917 and commenced practice in McAlester Okla.; during the First World War served as a private in the Student Army Training Corps in 1917 and 1918; member of the State senate 1918–1922; was graduated from the law department of the University of Oklahoma at Norman in 1920; took postgraduate work at the University of Chicago, Chicago, Ill.; vocational adviser for disabled veterans at McAlester, Okla., in 1921 and 1922; unsuccessful candidate for the Democratic nomination for Congress in 1922 and 1924; superintendent of schools at Krebs, Okla., 1922–1926; elected as a Democrat to the Seventieth and to the seven succeeding Congresses (March 4, 1927–January 3, 1943); unsuccessful candidate for renomination in 1942; during World War II served as a major in the United States Army, Allied Military Government, with service in Africa and Europe from 1943 until injured; returned to the United States as an instructor at Fort Custer, Mich., in 1945; employed with the Veterans' Administration at Muskogee, Okla., in 1945 and 1946; elected secretary of state of Oklahoma for four-year term in 1946; elected State auditor for four-year term in 1950; elected State corporat on commissioner for six-year term in 1954 and reelected in 1960; is a resident of Oklahoma City, Okla.

CARUTH, Asher Graham, a Representative from Kentucky; born in Scottsville, Allen County, Ky., on February 7, 1844; attended the public schools; was graduated from the high school of Louisville in June 1864 and from the law department of the University of Louisville, Kentucky, in March 1866; was admitted to the bar and commenced practice in Hopkinsville, Christian County, Ky.; established the Kentucky Weekly New Era; moved to Louisville in 1871 and continued the practice of law; attorney of the board of trustees of the public schools of Louisville from 1873 to 1880; presidential elector on the Democratic ticket of Tilden and Hendricks in 1876; elected Commonwealth attorney for the ninth judicial district of Kentucky in 1880 for six years and reelected in August 1886; resigned the office in March 1887; elected as a Democrat to the Fiftieth and to the three succeeding Congresses (March 4, 1887–March 3, 1895); unsuccessful candidate for renomination in 1894; resumed the practice of law in Louisville, Ky.; judge of the criminal division of the Jefferson County Circuit Court in 1902; commissioner of the St. Louis Exposition in 1904; died in Louisville, Ky., November 25, 1907; interment in Cave Hill Cemetery.

CARUTHERS, Robert Looney, a Representative from Tennessee; born in Smith County, Tenn., July 31, 1800; engaged in mercantile pursuits 1817–1819; attended Woodward's Academy, near Columbia, Tenn., and Greenville College in 1820 and 1821; studied law; was admitted to the bar in 1823; clerk of the State house of representatives in 1824; clerk of the chancery court of Smith County and editor of the Tennessee Republican; moved to Lebanon, Wilson County, Tenn., in 1826; State's attorney 1827–1832; member of the State house of representatives in 1835; was the founder of Cumberland University, Lebanon, Tenn., in 1842 and of its law department in 1847; presidential elector on the Whig ticket of Clay and Frelinghuysen in 1844; elected as a Whig to the Twenty-seventh Congress (March 4, 1841–March 3, 1843); appointed judge of the supreme court of Tennessee in 1852 to fill a vacancy and elected to the position in 1854, which he held until the beginning of the Civil War; member of the peace convention of 1861 held in Washington, D. C., in an effort to devise means to prevent the impending war; elected Governor in 1862, but because of the occupation of the State by Federal forces never assumed the duties of the office; at the close of the Civil War became professor of law in Cumberland University and served in that capacity until his death in Lebanon, Tenn., October 2, 1882; interment in Cedar Grove Cemetery.

CARUTHERS, Samuel, a Representative from Missouri; born in Madison County, Mo., October 13, 1820; was graduated from Cumberland University, Lebanon, Tenn.; studied law; was admitted to the bar and commenced practice in Fredericktown, Madison County, Mo.; moved to Cape Girardeau, Mo., in 1844; held several local offices; elected as a Whig to the Thirty-third and Thirty-fourth Congresses (March 4, 1853–March 3, 1857); reelected as a Democrat to the Thirty-fifth Congress (March 4, 1857–March 3, 1859); died in Cape Girardeau, Cape Girardeau County, Mo., July 20, 1860.

CARVILLE, Edward Peter, a Senator from Nevada; born in Mound Valley, Nev., May 14, 1885; attended the public and high schools in Elko County, Nev.; was graduated from the University of Notre Dame, South Bend, Ind., in 1909; was admitted to the bar in 1909 and commenced practice in Elko, Nev.; district attorney of Elko County, Nev., 1912–1918; district judge of Elko County 1928–1934; United States attorney for Nevada 1934–1938; elected Governor of Nevada in 1938; reelected in 1942 and served until his resignation; appointed July 24, 1945, as a Democrat to the United States Senate to fill the vacancy caused by the death of James G. Scrugham and served from July 25, 1945, until January 3, 1947; unsuccessful candidate for the Democratic nomination for United States Senator in 1946; resumed the practice of law in Reno, Nev., until his death there June 27, 1956; interment in Nevada Memorial Park Mausoleum, Reno, Nev.

CARY, George, a Representative from Georgia; born near Allens Fresh, Charles County, Md., August 7, 1789; received a classical education; studied law; was admitted to the bar and commenced practice in Frederick, Md.; also engaged in agricultural pursuits; moved to Appling, Ga.; member of the State house of representatives 1819–1821; elected to the Eighteenth and Nineteenth Congresses (March 4, 1823–March 3, 1827); engaged in the newspaper business and edited the Hickory Nut; again a member of the State house of representatives in 1834; died in Thomaston, Upson County, Ga., September 10, 1843; interment in the Methodist Churchyard.

CARY, George Booth, a Representative from Virginia; born at "Bonny Doon," near Courtland, Southampton County, Va., in 1811; received a liberal education; engaged in planting; elected as a Democrat to the Twenty-seventh Congress (March 4, 1841–March 3, 1843); resumed agricultural pursuits; died in Bethlehem, Va., March 5, 1850; interment in the family cemetery on his estate, "Bonny Doon," near Courtland, Southampton County, Va.

CARY, Glover H., a Representative from Kentucky; born in Calhoun, McLean County, Ky., May 1, 1885; attended public and private schools, and Centre College, Danville, Ky.; employed as deputy clerk, bank cashier, and newspaper editor; studied law; was admitted to the bar in June 1909 and commenced practice in Calhoun, Ky.; member of the State house of representatives 1914–1917; prosecuting attorney of McLean County 1918–1922; served as Commonwealth's attorney for the sixth judicial district from 1922 until his resignation on February 28, 1931, having been elected to Congress; moved to Owensboro, Ky., in 1926; elected as a Democrat to the Seventy-second, Seventy-third, and Seventy-fourth Congresses and served from March 4, 1931, until his death; had been reelected to the Seventy-fifth Congress; delegate to the Democratic National Convention at Chicago in 1932; died in Cincinnati, Ohio, while on a visit for medical treatment, on December 5, 1936; interment in Calhoun Cemetery, Calhoun, Ky.

CARY, Jeremiah Eaton, a Representative from New York; born in Coventry, R. I., April 30, 1803; attended the public schools; moved to Cherry Valley, N. Y., in 1820; studied law; was admitted to the bar in 1829 and commenced practice in New York City; elected as a Democrat to the Twenty-eighth Congress (March 4, 1843–March 3, 1845); resumed the practice of law in New York City; moved to Plainfield, N. J., in 1860, where he continued the practice of law; died in June 1888 while on a visit at Rockville Center, Long Island, N. Y.; interment in Grace Episcopal Church Cemetery, Plainfield, N. J.

CARY, Samuel Fenton, a Representative from Ohio; born in Cincinnati, Ohio, February 18, 1814; attended the public schools of College Hill, a suburb of Cincinnati; was graduated from Miami University, Oxford, Ohio, in 1835 and from the Cincinnati Law School in 1837; was admitted to the bar in the latter year and commenced practice in Cincinnati; elected judge of the State supreme court but declined; continued the practice of his profession until 1845, when he devoted himself to temperance and other reforms; delegate to the Republican National Convention at Baltimore in 1864; served as paymaster general for the State of Ohio under Governors Bartley and Bebb; collector of internal revenue for the first district of Ohio in 1865; elected as a Republican to the Fortieth Congress to fill the vacancy caused by the resignation of Rutherford B. Hayes and served from November 21, 1867, to March 3, 1869; was an unsuccessful candidate for reelection in 1868 to the Forty-first Congress; unsuccessful candidate for Lieutenant Governor of Ohio in 1875; was nominated in 1876 by the Greenback National Convention at Indianapolis as a candidate for Vice President of the United States; writer and lecturer for twenty years; died at the Cary homestead in College Hill, Cincinnati, Ohio, September 29, 1900; interment in Spring Grove Cemetery.

CARY, Shepard, a Representative from Maine; born in New Salem, Mass., July 3, 1805; attended the common schools; moved with his parents to Houlton, Maine, in 1822; engaged in extensive lumber operations and also in agricultural and mercantile pursuits; member of the State house of representatives in 1832, 1833, 1839–1842, 1848, 1849, and 1862; presidential elector on the Democratic ticket of Van Buren and Johnson in 1836; served in the State senate in 1843 and 1850–1853; elected as a Democrat to the Twenty-eighth Congress; took his seat May 10, 1844, and served until March 3, 1845; candidate of the Liberty Party for Governor in 1854; died in Houlton, Aroostook County, Maine, August 9, 1866; interment in Evergreen Cemetery.

CARY, William Joseph, a Representative from Wisconsin; born in Milwaukee, Wis., March 22, 1865; educated in the public schools and St. John's Academy; was left an orphan at the age of eleven, when he became a messenger boy; studied telegraphy and was employed as a telegraph operator 1883–1895; engaged in the brokerage business 1895–1905; elected a member of the board of aldermen of Milwaukee in 1900 and was reelected in 1902 for the term ending in 1904; served as sheriff of Milwaukee County 1904–1906; elected as a Republican to the Sixtieth and to the five succeeding Congresses (March 4, 1907–March 3, 1919); unsuccessful candidate for renomination in 1918 to the Sixty-sixth Congress; served as county clerk of Milwaukee County 1921–1933; died in Milwaukee, Wis., January 2, 1934; interment in Calvary Cemetery.

CASE, Charles, a Representative from Indiana; born in Austinburg, Ohio, December 21, 1817; studied law; was admitted to the bar and commenced practice in Fort Wayne, Ind.; elected as a Democrat to the Thirty-fifth Congress to fill the vacancy caused by the death of Samuel Brenton; reelected to the Thirty-sixth Congress and served from December 7, 1857, to March 3, 1861; unsuccessful candidate for reelection in 1860 to the Thirty-seventh Congress; during the Civil War served as first lieutenant and adjutant of the Forty-fourth Regiment, Indiana Volunteer Infantry; subsequently became a major in the Third Regiment, Indiana Volunteer Cavalry, and served from November 26, 1861, to August 15, 1862; resumed the practice of his profession in Washington, D. C.; died in Brighton, Washington County, Iowa, June 30, 1883; interment in the Congressional Cemetery, Washington, D. C.

CASE, Clifford Philip, a Representative and a Senator from New Jersey; born in Franklin Park, Somerset County, N. J., April 16, 1904; attended the public schools of Poughkeepsie, N. Y.; was graduated from Rutgers University, New Brunswick, N. J., in 1925 and from Columbia University Law School, New York, N. Y., in 1928; was admitted to the bar in 1928 and commenced practice in New York City, N. Y.; member of the Rahway (N. J.) Common Council 1938–1942; served in the New Jersey House of Assembly in 1943 and 1944; trustee of Rutgers University; elected as a Republican to the Seventy-ninth and to the four succeeding Congresses, and served from January 3, 1945, until his resignation August 16, 1953; president of The Fund for the Republic, created and financed by The Ford Foundation from August 1953 to March 1954; elected as a Republican to the United States Senate for the term commencing January 3, 1955, and ending January 3, 1961. *Reelected in 1960 for the term ending January 3, 1967.*

CASE, Francis Higbee, a Representative and a Senator from South Dakota; born in Everly, Clay County, Iowa, December 9, 1896; moved with his parents to Sturgis, S. Dak., in 1909; attended the public schools; was graduated from Hot Springs (S. Dak.) High School in 1914, from Dakota Wesleyan University, Mitchell, S. Dak., in 1918, and from Northwestern University, Evanston, Ill., in 1920; during the First World War served as a private in the United States Marine Corps in 1918; lieutenant in the United States Army Reserves 1924–1931; captain in the United States Marine Corps Reserves since 1937; assistant editor, Epworth Herald, Chicago, Ill., 1920–1922; telegraph editor and editorial writer on the Rapid City (S. Dak.) Daily Journal 1922–1925; editor and publisher of the Hot Springs (S. Dak.) Star 1925–1931; editor and publisher of the Custer (S. Dak.) Chronicle since 1931; member of the State regents of education 1931–1933; unsuccessful candidate for election in 1934 to the Seventy-fourth Congress; elected as a Republican to the Seventy-fifth and to the six succeeding Congresses (January 3, 1937–January 3, 1951); was not a candidate for renomination in 1950, having become a candidate for United States Senator; elected to the United States Senate in 1950 for the term commencing January 3, 1951; reelected in 1956 for the term ending January 3, 1963.

CASE, Walter, a Representative from New York; born in Pleasant Valley, Dutchess County, N. Y., in 1776; educated by private tutors; attended Newburgh Academy, and was graduated from Union College, Schenectady, N. Y., in 1799; studied law; was admitted to the bar in 1802 and commenced practice in Newburgh; elected to the Sixteenth Congress (March 4, 1819–March 3, 1821); affiliated with the Whig Party after its formation; resumed the practice of law; moved to New York City in 1844 and continued the practice of law until 1848, when he retired; died in Fishkill, Dutchess County, N. Y., October 7, 1859; interment in Fishkill Rural Cemetery.

CASEY, John Joseph, a Representative from Pennsylvania; born in Wilkes-Barre Township, Luzerne County, Pa., May 26, 1875; attended the public schools and St. Mary's parochial school; member of the State house of representatives 1907–1909; elected as a Democrat to the Sixty-third and Sixty-fourth Congresses (March 4, 1913–March 3, 1917); unsuccessful candidate for reelection in 1916 to the Sixty-fifth Congress; appointed a member of the advisory council to the Secretary of Labor in 1918; appointed labor adviser and executive of the labor adjustment division, Emergency Fleet Corporation, United States Shipping Board, during the First World War; elected to the Sixty-sixth Congress (March 4, 1919–March 3, 1921); unsuccessful candidate for reelection in 1920 to the Sixty-seventh Congress; elected to the Sixty-eighth Congress (March 4, 1923–March 3, 1925);

unsuccessful candidate for reelection in 1924 to the Sixty-ninth Congress; business agent for the Plumbers and Steam Fitters' Union; elected to the Seventieth and Seventy-first Congresses and served from March 4, 1927, until his death at Balboa, Canal Zone, May 5, 1929; interment in St. Mary's Cemetery, Hanover Township, Luzerne County, Pa.

CASEY, Joseph, a Representative from Pennsylvania; born at Ringgold Manor, Washington County, Md., December 17, 1814; studied law in Carlisle, Pa.; was admitted to the bar in 1838 and commenced practice in Bloomfield, Perry County, Pa.; moved to New Berlin, Pa., and resumed the practice of law; elected as a Whig to the Thirty-first Congress (March 4, 1849–March 3, 1851); declined to be a candidate for renomination in 1850; again engaged in the practice of his profession; in 1856 was appointed reporter of the decisions of the supreme court of Pennsylvania, which position he held until 1861; was appointed in 1861 by President Lincoln one of the judges of the court of claims; upon the reorganization of that court in 1863 was appointed chief justice and was the first person to serve in that capacity, holding the position until December 1870, when he resigned; engaged in the practice of law in Washington, D. C., until his death, February 10, 1879; interment in Oak Hill Cemetery.

CASEY, Joseph Edward, a Representative from Massachusetts; born in Clinton, Worcester County, Mass., December 27, 1898; attended the public schools; during the First World War served as a private in the United States Army at Camp Lee, Va., in 1918; was graduated from the law department of Boston University, Boston, Mass., in 1920; was admitted to the bar in 1920 and commenced practice in Clinton, Mass.; delegate to the Democratic National Conventions in 1924, 1932, 1936, 1940, and 1944; elected as a Democrat to the Seventy-fourth and to the three succeeding Congresses (January 3, 1935–January 3, 1943); was not a candidate for renomination in 1942 to the Seventy-eighth Congress, but was an unsuccessful candidate for election to the United States Senate; resumed the practice of law in Boston, Mass., and in Washington, D. C., where he now resides.

CASEY, Levi, a Representative from South Carolina; born in that State about 1752; served in the Continental Army during the Revolutionary War; elected brigadier general of militia; justice of Newberry County Court in 1785; member of the State senate in 1781 and 1782 and 1800–1802; member of the State house of representatives 1786–1788; elected to the Eighth and Ninth Congresses and served from March 4, 1803, until his death, before the close of the Ninth Congress; had been reelected to the Tenth Congress; died in Washington, D. C., February 3, 1807; interment in the Congressional Cemetery.

CASEY, Lyman Rufus, a Senator from North Dakota; born in York, Livingston County, N. Y., May 6, 1837; moved with his parents to Ypsilanti, Mich., in 1853; received a classical education; engaged in the hardware business for many years; moved to Carrington, Foster County, Territory of Dakota, in 1882; engaged in agricultural pursuits and owned one of the largest ranches of that period, containing about 100,000 acres; chairman of the North Dakota Committee on Irrigation; commissioner of Foster County in 1887; upon the admission of North Dakota as a State into the Union was elected as a Republican to the United States Senate and served from November 25, 1889, to March 3, 1893; moved to New York City; unsuccessful candidate for renomination in 1892; returned to Washington, D. C., and died there January 26, 1914; interment in Greenmount Cemetery, Baltimore, Md.

CASEY, Robert Randolph (Bob), a Representative from Texas; born in Joplin, Jasper County, Mo., July 27, 1915; moved with his parents to Houston, Tex., in 1930 and graduated from San Jacinto High School; student at the University of Houston, also the South Texas School of Law 1934–1940; was admitted to the Texas bar in 1940 and commenced the practice of law in Alvin, Tex.; served as city attorney of Alvin, Tex., in 1942 and 1943; member of the school board; in 1943 returned to Houston, Tex., as an assistant district attorney in Harris County in charge of the civil department; in 1948 was elected to the State house of representatives and served in the regular and special sessions of the fifty-first legislature; elected county judge of Harris County in 1950, 1952, and again in 1954 for a four-year term; member of board of regents of the South Texas College of Law, board of directors of the Speech and Hearing Center, and director of the South Texas Law Journal, Inc.; elected as a Democrat to the Eighty-sixth Congress (January 3, 1959–January 3, 1961). *Reelected to the Eighty-seventh Congress.*

CASEY, Samuel Lewis, a Representative from Kentucky; born near Caseyville, Union County, Ky., February 12, 1821; attended the country schools; engaged in mercantile pursuits; member of the State house of representatives 1860–1862; elected as a Republican to the Thirty-seventh Congress to fill the vacancy caused by the expulsion of Henry C. Burnett and served from March 10, 1862, to March 3, 1863; retired from active business pursuits; died in St. Joseph, Mo., August 25, 1902; the remains were cremated in St. Louis, Mo., and the ashes interred in Caseyville Cemetery, Caseyville, Ky.

CASEY, Zadoc, a Representative from Illinois; born in Greene County, Ga., March 7, 1796; attended the common schools; moved to Illinois in 1819 and settled near the present site of Mount Vernon, Jefferson County; member of the State house of representatives 1822–1826; served in the State senate 1826–1830; elected Lieutenant Governor of Illinois in 1830; volunteer in the Black Hawk War in 1832; elected as a Jackson Democrat to the Twenty-third and to the four succeeding Congresses (March 4, 1833–March 3, 1843); unsuccessful candidate for reelection in 1842 to the Twenty-eighth Congress; delegate to the State constitutional conventions in 1848 and 1860; again a member of the State house of representatives 1848–1852, and served as speaker in 1852; again served in the State senate 1860–1862; retired to his farm, "Elm Hill," near Mount Vernon, Ill.; died in Caseyville, St. Clair County, Ill., which was named after him, September 4, 1862; interment in old Union Cemetery, near Mount Vernon, Ill.

CASKIE, John Samuels, a Representative from Virginia; born in Richmond, Va., November 8, 1821; was graduated from the University of Virginia at Charlottesville in 1842; studied law; was admitted to the bar about 1842 and practiced in Richmond; prosecuting attorney of the city of Richmond 1842–1846; judge of the Richmond and Henrico circuits 1846–1849; elected as a Democrat to the Thirty-second and to the three succeeding Congresses (March 4, 1851–March 3, 1859); unsuccessful candidate for renomination in 1858; resumed the practice of law; died in Richmond, Va., December 16, 1869; interment in Hollywood Cemetery.

CASON, Thomas Jefferson, a Representative from Indiana; born near Brownsville, Union County, Ind., September 13, 1828; moved to Boone County with his parents, who settled on a farm near Thorntown in 1832; attended the common schools; taught school in Boone County for several years; studied law in Crawfordsville; was admitted to the bar in 1850 and commenced practice in Lebanon, Ind.; member of the State house of representatives 1861–1864; member of the State senate 1864–1867; appointed by Governor Baker common pleas judge of Boone County in April 1867 and was subsequently elected to the same office in October 1867 for a term of four years; declined reelection and resumed the practice of law; elected as a Republican to the Forty-third and Forty-fourth Congresses (March 4, 1873–March 3, 1877); unsuccessful candidate for renomination in 1876; resumed the practice of law in Lebanon, Ind.; retired in 1897 and moved to Washington, D. C., where he died July 10, 1901; interment in Oak Hill Cemetery, Lebanon, Boone County, Ind.

CASS, Lewis, a Senator from Michigan; born in Exeter, N. H., October 9, 1782; attended Exeter Academy; moved with his parents to Wilmington, Del., in 1799 and taught school there; set out on foot for the Northwest Territory in 1801 and settled on a farm near Zanesville, Ohio; studied law under Governor Meigs in Marietta, Ohio, and was admitted to the bar in 1802; member of the State house of representatives in 1806; United States marshal for the district of Ohio from 1807 until 1812, when he resigned to enlist in the Army; colonel of the Twenty-seventh Regiment, United States Infantry, February 20, 1813; promoted to rank of brigadier general March 20, 1813; contributed much to General Harrison's decisive victory over the British under Proctor and the Indians under Tecumseh, his name being associated with that of Perry, who fought with him side by side; resigned May 1, 1814; military and civil Governor of Michigan Territory 1813–1831; settled in Detroit; appointed Secretary of War by President Jackson and served in his Cabinet from August 1, 1831, to October 5, 1836, when he resigned, having been appointed to a diplomatic post; Envoy Extraordinary and Minister Plenipotentiary to France from October 24, 1836, to November 12, 1842; elected as a Democrat to the United States Senate and served from March 4, 1845, until May 29, 1848, when he resigned, having been nominated for President of the United States; unsuccessful candidate for President on the Democratic ticket in 1848; again elected to the United States Senate on January 20, 1849, to fill the vacancy caused by his own resignation; was reelected, and served from March 4, 1849, to March 3, 1857; appointed Secretary of State in the Cabinet of President Buchanan and served from March 6, 1857, until December 14, 1860, when he resigned; returned to Detroit, Mich., and engaged in literary pursuits; died in Detroit, Mich., June 17, 1866; interment in Elmwood Cemetery.

CASSEDY, George, a Representative from New Jersey; born in Hackensack, Bergen County, N. J., September 16, 1783; attended the common schools; studied law; was admitted to the bar in 1809 and commenced practice in Hackensack, N. J.; postmaster of Hackensack from June 10, 1805, to January 1, 1806; elected as a Democrat to the Seventeenth, Eighteenth, and Nineteenth Congresses (March 4, 1821–March 3, 1827); died in Hackensack, Bergen County, N. J., December 31, 1842; interment in the cemetery of the First Reformed Church.

CASSEL, Henry Burd, a Representative from Pennsylvania; born in Marietta, Lancaster County, Pa., October 19, 1855; attended the public schools of Marietta and Columbia Classical Institute; engaged in the wholesale and retail lumber business; member of the Republican county committee in 1881; chairman of the county committee in 1893; delegate to the Republican National Convention at St. Louis in 1896; member of the State house of representatives in 1898 and 1900; elected as a Republican to the Fifty-seventh Congress to fill the vacancy caused by the death of Marriott Brosius; reelected to the Fifty-eighth, Fifty-ninth, and Sixtieth Congresses and served from November

5, 1901, to March 3, 1909; engaged in business as a manufacturer and contractor; died in Marietta, Pa., April 28, 1926; interment in Marietta Cemetery.

CASSERLY, Eugene, a Senator from California; born in Mullingar, County Westmeath, Ireland, November 13, 1820; immigrated to the United States in 1822 with his parents, who settled in New York; prepared for college by his father, who was a student of the classics; was graduated from Georgetown College, Washington, D. C.; studied law; was admitted to the bar in 1844 and commenced practice in New York City; editor of the Freeman's Journal and contributor to newspapers in other cities; corporation counsel of New York City in 1846 and 1847; moved to San Francisco, Calif., in 1850 and published the Public Balance, the True Balance, and the Standard; elected State printer May 1, 1851; retired from journalism and resumed the practice of law; elected as a Democrat to the United States Senate and served from March 4, 1869, until November 29, 1873, when he resigned; again engaged in the practice of law in San Francisco, Calif.; member of the constitutional convention of California in 1878 and 1879; died in San Francisco June 14, 1883; interment in Calvary Cemetery.

CASSIDY, George Williams, a Representative from Nevada; born near Paris, Bourbon County, Ky., April 25, 1836; attended the public schools and was educated by private tutors; studied law but never practiced; moved to Eureka, Nev., in 1870; engaged in newspaper work; member of the State senate 1872–1879 and served as president during the session of 1879; elected as a Democrat to the Forty-seventh and Forty-eighth Congresses (March 4, 1881–March 3, 1885); unsuccessful candidate for reelection in 1884 to the Forty-ninth Congress; appointed national bank examiner for Nevada, Utah, California, and Colorado by President Cleveland and served from 1886 to 1890; unsuccessful candidate for election in 1888 to the Fifty-first Congress and in 1890 to the Fifty-second Congress; delegate to the Democratic National Convention at Chicago in 1892; nominated as a candidate for election to the Fifty-third Congress but died before the election; died in Reno, Nev., June 24, 1892; interment in Hillside Cemetery.

CASSIDY, James Henry, a Representative from Ohio; born in Cleveland, Ohio, October 28, 1869; attended the public schools; studied law at the Cleveland Law School; was admitted to the bar in 1899 and commenced practice in Cleveland, Ohio; served as clerk of the Committee on Rivers and Harbors, House of Representatives, from December 1901 until January 11, 1909, when he resigned; elected as a Republican to the Sixty-first Congress to fill the vacancy caused by the resignation of Theodore E. Burton, and served from April 20, 1909, to March 3, 1911; was an unsuccessful candidate for reelection in 1910 to the Sixty-second Congress; resumed the practice of his profession in Cleveland, Ohio; appointed as receiver of the Cleveland & Pittsburgh Coal Co.; moved to New York in 1915 and engaged in the brokerage business; president of an express company; died in Forest Hills Gardens, N. Y., August 23, 1926; interment in Maple Grove Cemetery, Kew Gardens, Long Island, N. Y.

CASSINGHAM, John Wilson, a Representative from Ohio; born in Coshocton, Coshocton County, Ohio, June 22, 1840; attended the public schools; deputy county treasurer 1857–1868; engaged in the mercantile business from 1868 to 1875 and in the mining of coal in 1875; later also engaged in the manufacture of paper and in banking; county auditor 1880–1887; trustee of the public library of Coshocton; member of the board of education; president of the Coshocton Board of Trade; delegate to the

Democratic National Convention at Chicago in 1896; elected as a Democrat to the Fifty-seventh and Fifty-eighth Congresses (March 4, 1901–March 3, 1905); declined to be a candidate for reelection in 1904 to the Fifty-ninth Congress; reengaged in his former business interests in Coschoton, Ohio, until 1915, when he retired from active pursuits; died in Coshocton, Ohio, March 14, 1930; interment in South Lawn Cemetery.

CASTELLOW, Bryant Thomas, a Representative from Georgia; born on a farm near Georgetown, Quitman County, Ga., July 29, 1876; attended the local school, high schools at Eufaula, Ala., and Coleman, Ga., and Mercer University, Macon, Ga.; was graduated from the law department of the University of Georgia, at Athens in 1897; was admitted to the bar in 1897 and commenced practice in Fort Gaines, Ga., in 1898; superintendent of the public schools in Coleman, Ga., in 1897 and 1898; captain of Company D, Fourth Infantry, Georgia State Troops, 1899–1902; solicitor of Clay County Court in 1900 and 1901; judge of Clay County Court 1901–1905; moved to Cuthbert, Randolph County, Ga., in 1906 and served as referee in bankruptcy for the western division of the northern district of Georgia 1906–1912; solicitor general of the Pataula judicial circuit from January 1, 1913, until his resignation on October 7, 1932, having been nominated for Congress; elected on November 8, 1932, as a Democrat to the Seventy-second Congress to fill the vacancy caused by the resignation of Charles R. Crisp and on the same day was elected to the Seventy-third Congress; reelected to the Seventy-fourth Congress and served from November 8, 1932, to January 3, 1937; was not a candidate for renomination in 1936; retired from public life and the practice of law in order to devote more time to travel and to the study of world conditions; is a resident of Cuthbert, Ga.

CASTLE, Curtis Harvey, a Representative from California; born near Galesburg, Knox County, Ill., October 4, 1848; attended the public schools and Knox College, Galesburg, Ill.; was graduated from Northwestern University, Evanston, Ill., in 1872; served as principal of the Washington, Tex., public schools 1872–1876; was graduated from the College of Physicians and Surgeons, Keokuk, Iowa, in 1878; practiced his profession for a brief period in Fulton County, Ill., and in Wayland, Henry County, Iowa, until 1882; moved to Point Arena, Calif., in 1882 and to Merced, Merced County, Calif., in 1888, and continued the practice of medicine; served from 1894 to 1896 as a member of the American Academy of Medicine, as chairman of the Populist executive committee of Merced County, and as a member of the State executive committee; elected as the candidate of the Populist and Democratic Parties to the Fifty-fifth Congress (March 4, 1897–March 3, 1899); unsuccessful candidate for reelection in 1898 to the Fifty-sixth Congress; resumed the practice of medicine in Merced, Calif.; retired from active practice from 1915 until the start of the First World War, when he resumed practice until the close of the war; again retired, and moved to Santa Barbara, Calif., where he lived in retirement until his death on July 12, 1928; remains were cremated and the ashes deposited in the mausoleum of the Santa Barbara Cemetery and Crematory.

CASTLE, James Nathan, a Representative from Minnesota; born in Shefford, Province of Quebec, Canada, May 23, 1836; attended the public schools; studied law; moved to Afton, Washington County, Minn., in 1862 and taught school; completed his law studies; was admitted to the bar and practiced; moved to Stillwater, Washington County, Minn., in 1865 and continued the practice of law; elected county attorney in 1866 to fill the unexpired term of his deceased brother; city attorney in 1868; elected to the State senate in 1868 and 1878,

and again in 1882; elected as a Democrat to the Fifty-second Congress (March 4, 1891–March 3, 1893); unsuccessful candidate for reelection in 1892 to the Fifty-third Congress; engaged in the practice of law until his death in Stillwater, Minn., January 2, 1903; interment in Fairview Cemetery.

CASTOR, George Albert, a Representative from Pennsylvania; born in Holmesburg (a part of the city of Philadelphia), Pa., August 6, 1855; attended the public schools; entered a cloth house early in life and subsequently became a merchant tailor with large establishments in New York City, Boston, and Philadelphia; retired from active business pursuits in 1875; unsuccessful candidate for the Republican nomination of Congressman at Large in 1892; member of the Republican city committee for fifteen years; elected as a Republican to the Fifty-eighth Congress to fill the vacancy caused by the death of Henry Burk; reelected to the Fifty-ninth Congress and served from February 16, 1904, until his death in Philadelphia, Pa., February 19, 1906; interment in Emanuel Protestant Episcopal Cemetery, Holmesburg, Pa.

CASWELL, Lucien Bonaparte, a Representative from Wisconsin; born in Swanton, Franklin County, Vt., November 27, 1827; moved to Wisconsin in 1837 with his parents, who settled near Lake Koshkonong, in Rock County; attended the common schools, Milton Academy, and Beloit College; studied law; was admitted to the bar in 1851 and commenced practice in Fort Atkinson, Wis.; district attorney of Jefferson County in 1855 and 1856; served on the local school board for nearly sixty-five years; organized the First National Bank of Fort Atkinson in 1863, serving as president at the time of his death; member of the State assembly in 1863, 1872, and 1874; during the Civil War served as commissioner of the second district board of enrollment from September 1863 to May 5, 1865; organized the Northwestern Manufacturing Co. in 1866 and continued in its activities during his lifetime; delegate to the Republican National Convention at Chicago in 1868; elected as a Republican to the Forty-fourth and to the three succeeding Congresses (March 4, 1875–March 3, 1883); unsuccessful candidate for renomination in 1882; organized the Citizens' State Bank in 1885, serving as its president for many years; elected to the Forty-ninth, Fiftieth, and Fifty-first Congresses (March 4, 1885–March 3, 1891); unsuccessful candidate for renomination in 1890; resumed the practice of law in Fort Atkinson, Jefferson County, Wis.; died in Fort Atkinson, Wis., April 26, 1919; interment in Evergreen Cemetery.

CASWELL, Richard, a Delegate from North Carolina; born in Harford (now Baltimore) County, Md., August 3, 1729; moved to North Carolina in 1746; appointed deputy surveyor of the colony in 1750; clerk of the court of Orange County 1752–1754; studied law; was admitted to the bar in 1754 and commenced practice in Hillsboro, N. C.; member of the colonial house of delegates 1754–1771, and served as speaker the last two years; commanded the right wing of Governor Tryon's army at the Battle of Alamance in 1771; served in the Revolutionary Army; Member of the Continental Congress 1774–1776; commanded the patriots at the Battle of Moores Creek Bridge, North Carolina, February 23, 1776; appointed brigadier general of the New Bern District by the Provincial Congress in 1776; delegate to the State constitutional convention and its president in 1776; Governor of North Carolina 1776–1780, serving without pay from 1776 to 1778; commanded the North Carolina troops at the Battle of Camden in 1780; comptroller general in 1782; member of the State senate 1782–1784 and served as speaker; again elected Governor in 1785 and served until 1788; appointed delegate from North Carolina to the convention that framed the Federal Constitution in 1787, but did not attend; member of the State convention at Fayetteville, N. C., that adopted the Federal Constitution in 1789; member and speaker of the State house of commons in 1789 and served until his death in Fayetteville, N. C., November 10, 1789; interment in the family cemetery on his estate near Kinston, Lenoir County, N. C.

CATCHINGS, Thomas Clendinen, a Representative from Mississippi; born near Brownsville, Hinds County, Miss., January 11, 1847; was tutored at home; attended the University of Mississippi at Oxford in 1859 and Oakland College in 1861; during the Civil War entered the Confederate Army in 1861 and served as a private in Company A, Eighteenth Mississippi Infantry, and subsequently in Company C, Eleventh (Perrin's) Mississippi Cavalry; studied law; was admitted to the bar in 1866 and commenced practice in Vicksburg; elected to the State senate in 1875 but resigned in 1877, having been nominated as a candidate for attorney general; elected attorney general of Mississippi in 1877; reelected in 1881 and served until February 16, 1885, when he resigned, having been elected to Congress; elected as a Democrat to the Forty-ninth and to the seven succeeding Congresses (March 4, 1885–March 3, 1901); resumed the practice of law; also served as division counsel for the Southern Railway Co.; member of the Mississippi Code Commission by appointment of Governor Vardaman; died in Vicksburg, Miss., December 24, 1927; interment in the City Cemetery.

CATE, George Washington, a Representative from Wisconsin; born in Montpelier, Washington County, Vt., September 17, 1825; attended the common schools; studied law and was admitted to the bar at Montpelier in 1845; moved to Wisconsin the same year and commenced the practice of law in Plover, Portage County; member of the State assembly in 1852 and 1853; moved to Stevens Point; elected judge of the circuit court in April 1854 and served in that capacity until March 4, 1875, when he resigned, having been elected to Congress; elected as an Independent Reformer to the Forty-fourth Congress (March 4, 1875–March 3, 1877); unsuccessful candidate for reelection in 1876 to the Forty-fifth Congress; resumed the practice of law in Stevens Point, Portage County, Wis., and died there March 7, 1905; interment in Forest Cemetery.

CATE, William Henderson, a Representative from Arkansas; born near Murfreesboro, Rutherford County, Tenn., November 11, 1839; attended the common schools, and an academy at Abingdon, Va.; was graduated from the University of Tennessee at Knoxville in 1857; taught school in the South and West; served in the Confederate Army during the Civil War and was promoted to captain; moved to Jonesboro, Craighead County, Ark., in 1865; studied law; was admitted to the Arkansas bar in 1866 and commenced practice in Jonesboro; member of the Arkansas House of Representatives 1871–1873 and during the extra session of 1874; elected prosecuting attorney in 1878; was appointed and subsequently elected judge of the second judicial circuit of Arkansas in 1884; organized the Bank of Jonesboro in 1887; presented credentials as a Democratic Member-elect to the Fifty-first Congress and served from March 4, 1889, to March 5, 1890, when he was succeeded by Lewis P. Featherstone, who contested the election; elected to the Fifty-second Congress (March 4, 1891–March 3, 1893); declined to be a candidate for renomination in 1892 to the Fifty-third Congress; resumed the practice of law in Jonesboro, Ark.; died while on a visit in Toledo, Ohio, August 23, 1899; interment in the City Cemetery, Jonesboro, Ark.

CATHCART, Charles William, a Representative and a Senator from Indiana; born July 24, 1809, in Funchal, Island of Madeira, where his father was the United States consul; came to the United States with his parents in 1815; sailed with his parents to Cadiz, Spain, in 1817; attended private schools; returned to the United States in 1819; became a sailor before the mast; moved to Washington, D. C., in 1830, and was a clerk in the General Land Office; went with the ammunition team to Fort Dearborn (now Chicago), Ill., in 1832; joined a military company under the command of Captain Finch; justice of the peace at New Durham Township, Ind., in 1833; engaged in agricultural pursuits near La Porte, Ind., in 1837; United States land surveyor; member of the State senate 1837–1840; presidential elector on the Democratic ticket of Polk and Dallas in 1844; elected as a Democrat to the Twenty-ninth and Thirtieth Congresses (March 4, 1845–March 3, 1849); appointed to the United States Senate to fill the vacancy caused by the death of James Whitcomb and served from December 6, 1852, to March 3, 1853; unsuccessful candidate for election in 1860 to the Thirty-seventh Congress; engaged in agricultural pursuits; died on his farm near La Porte, La Porte County, Ind., August 22, 1888; interment in Pine Lake Cemetery.

CATLIN, George Smith, a Representative from Connecticut; born in Harwinton, Conn., August 24, 1808; attended the common schools, Amherst (Mass.) College, and the Litchfield (Conn.) Law School; was admitted to the bar in 1828 and practiced in Windham, Conn., 1829–1851; member of the State house of representatives in 1831 and again in 1846; secretary to the Governor 1831–1833: prosecuting attorney for Windham County in 1842 and 1843; elected as a Democrat to the Twenty-eighth Congress (March 4, 1843–March 3, 1845); unsuccessful Democratic candidate for Governor of Connecticut in 1848; served in the State senate in 1850; judge of the Windham County Court in 1850 and 1851; died in Windham, Conn., December 26, 1851; interment in Windham Cemetery.

CATLIN, Theron Ephron, a Representative from Missouri; born in St. Louis, Mo., May 16, 1878; attended private schools; was graduated from Harvard University in 1899 and from the law department of the same institution in 1902; was admitted to the bar in 1903 and commenced practice in St. Louis, Mo.; member of the State house of representatives 1907–1909; presented credentials as a Republican Member-elect to the Sixty-second Congress and served from March 4, 1911, to August 12, 1912, when he was succeeded by Patrick F. Gill, who contested the election; unsuccessful for election in 1912 to the Sixty-third Congress; resumed the practice of law; member of the board of directors of St. Louis Union Trust Co.; died in St. Louis, Mo., March 19, 1960; interment in Bellefontaine Cemetery.

CATRON, Thomas Benton, a Delegate and a Senator from New Mexico; born near Lexington, Lafayette County, Mo., October 6, 1840; attended the common schools, and was graduated from the University of Missouri at Columbia in 1860; served four years in the Confederate Army during the Civil War; moved to New Mexico in 1866; studied law; was admitted to the bar in 1867 and commenced practice in Las Cruces, N. Mex.; district attorney of the third district 1866–1868; in 1869 was appointed attorney general of the Territory; resigned to take the position of United States attorney, to which he had been appointed by President Grant; member of the Territorial council in 1884, 1888, 1890, 1899, 1905, and 1909; unsuccessful candidate for election in 1892 to the Fifty-third Congress; elected as a Republican a Delegate to the Fifty-fourth Congress (March 4, 1895–March 3, 1897); unsuccessful candidate for reelection in

1896 to the Fifty-fifth Congress; resumed the practice of law in Santa Fe, N. Mex.; upon the admission of New Mexico as a State into the Union was elected to the United States Senate and served from March 27, 1912, to March 3, 1917; was not an active candidate for renomination in 1916; discontinued active pursuits and lived in retirement until his death in Santa Fe, N. Mex., May 15, 1921; interment in Fairview Cemetery.

CATTELL, Alexander Gilmore, a Senator from New Jersey; born in Salem, N. J., February 12, 1816; received an academic education; engaged in mercantile pursuits in his native town until 1846; member of the New Jersey General Assembly in 1840, and served as clerk of that body 1842–1844; member of the State constitutional convention in 1844; moved to Philadelphia in 1846 and engaged in business and banking; member of the Philadelphia City Council 1848–1853; organized the Corn Exchange Bank and was president 1858–1871; moved to Merchantville, N. J., in 1863; elected as a Republican to the United States Senate to succeed John P. Stockton, whose seat was declared vacant, and served from September 19, 1866, to March 3, 1871; was not a candidate for reelection; appointed by President Grant a member of the first United States Civil Service Commission and served two years, resigning to accept the position of United States financial agent in London, serving in 1873 and 1874; member of New Jersey Board of Tax Assessors 1884–1891, and was president 1889–1891; appointed member of the State board of education in 1891 for a term of three years; died in Jamestown, Chautauqua County, N. Y., April 8, 1894; interment in Colestown Cemetery, near Merchantville, Camden County, N. J.

CAULFIELD, Bernard Gregory, a Representative from Illinois; born in Alexandria, Va., October 18, 1828; received a classical education; was graduated from Georgetown College, Washington, D. C., in 1848 and from the law department of the University of Pennsylvania at Philadelphia in 1850; was admitted to the bar in 1850 and commenced the practice of law in Lexington, Ky.; moved to Chicago, Ill., in 1853 and continued the practice of his profession; elected as a Democrat to the Forty-third Congress to fill the vacancy caused by the death of John B. Rice; reelected to the Forty-fourth Congress and served from February 1, 1875, to March 3, 1877; was not a candidate for renomination 1876; resumed the practice of law; moved to Dakota Territory in 1878 and settled in Deadwood; continued the practice of law and became a large landowner; died in Deadwood, Territory of Dakota (now S. Dak.), December 19, 1887; interment in Calvary Cemetery, St. Louis, Mo.

CAULFIELD, Henry Stewart, a Representative from Missouri; born in St. Louis, Mo., December 9, 1873; attended the St. Louis public schools and St. Charles (Mo.) College; was graduated from the law department of Washington University, St. Louis, Mo., in 1895; was admitted to the bar the same year and commenced practice in St. Louis; unsuccessful candidate for election in 1904 to the Fifty-ninth Congress; elected as a Republican to the Sixtieth Congress (March 4, 1907–March 3, 1909); was not a candidate for renomination in 1908; excise commissioner of St. Louis in 1909 and 1910; judge of the St. Louis Court of Appeals 1910–1912; member of the St. Louis Public Library Board 1918–1921; city counselor in 1921 and 1922; chairman of the board of freeholders to merge the city of St. Louis and St. Louis County, serving from June 5, 1925, to June 3, 1926; Governor of Missouri, January 14, 1929, to January 9, 1933; member of the St. Louis Board of Election Commissioners from February 10, 1937, to May 27, 1938; unsuccessful Republican nominee for United States Senator in 1938; director of public welfare of St. Louis from June 2, 1941, to April 21, 1949; resumed the practice of law; member of the State Reorganization Commission of Missouri; is a resident of St. Louis, Mo.

CAUSEY, John Williams, a Representative from Delaware; born in Milford, Kent County, Del., September 19, 1841; attended a private school and Albany Academy, New York, and was graduated from the Pennsylvania Agricultural College; engaged in agricultural pursuits; member of the State senate 1875–1877; delegate to the Democratic National Convention at Chicago in 1884; appointed internal-revenue collector for Delaware by President Cleveland in 1885 and served until 1887; elected as a Democrat to the Fifty-second and Fifty-third Congresses (March 4, 1891–March 3, 1895); was not a candidate for renomination in 1894; resumed agricultural pursuits; president of an insurance company; died in Milford, Del., October 1, 1908; interment in Odd Fellows Cemetery.

CAUSIN, John M. S., a Representative from Maryland; born in St. Marys County, Md., in 1811; studied law; was admitted to the bar in Prince Georges County about 1836; returned to St. Marys County and commenced the practice of law in Leonardtown, Md.; member of the State house of representatives in 1837 and again 1843; elected as a Whig to the Twenty-eighth Congress (March 4, 1843–March 3, 1845); moved to Annapolis, Md., delegate to the State constitutional convention; presidential elector on the Whig ticket of Taylor and Fillmore in 1848; moved to Chicago, Ill., in 1858 and resumed the practice of law; died in Cairo, Alexander County, Ill., January 30, 1861, while en route to his home after a visit with relatives in Little Rock, Ark.; interment in the City Cemetery (now Lincoln Park), Chicago, Ill.

CAVALCANTE, Anthony, a Representative from Pennsylvania; born in Vanderbilt, Fayette County, Pa., February 6, 1897; graduated from German Township High School; during the First World War served overseas with Company D, One Hundred and Tenth Infantry, Twenty-eighth Division, from May 3, 1918, to May 6, 1919; awarded the Purple Heart Medal; student at Bucknell University, Lewisburg, Pa., in 1920 and 1921 and Pennsylvania State College in 1921; graduated from the law school of Dickinson College, Carlisle, Pa., in 1924; was admitted to the bar the same year and commenced the practice of law in Uniontown, Pa.; member of the State senate 1935–1943; chief counsel for United Mine Workers of America, District Four of German Township School District, German Township Road Supervisors, and South Union Township Road Supervisors; elected as a Democrat to the Eighty-first Congress (January 3, 1949–January 3, 1951); unsuccessful for reelection in 1950; engaged in the practice of law; resides in Uniontown, Pa.

CAVANAUGH, James Michael, a Representative from Minnesota and a Delegate from the Territory of Montana; born in Springfield, Mass., July 4, 1823; received an academic education; engaged in newspaper work; studied law; was admitted to the bar in 1854 and began practice in Davenport, Iowa; moved to Chatfield, Fillmore County, Minn., in 1854 and continued the practice of law; upon the admission of Minnesota as a State into the Union was elected as a Democrat to the Thirty-fifth Congress and served from May 11, 1858, to March 3, 1859; unsuccessful candidate for reelection in 1858 to the Thirty-sixth Congress; moved to Colorado in 1861 and resumed the practice of law; also engaged in mining; member of the State constitutional convention in 1865; moved to Montana in 1866; elected as a Democrat a Delegate to the Fortieth and Forty-first Congresses (March 4, 1867–March 3, 1871);

unsuccessful candidate for renomination in 1870; engaged in the practice of law in New York City; returned to Colorado in 1879 and settled in Leadville, where he died October 30, 1879; interment in Greenwood Cemetery, New York City.

CAVICCHIA, Peter Angelo, a Representative from New Jersey; born in Roccamandolf, Province of Campobasso, Italy, May 22, 1879; immigrated to the United States in 1888 with his parents, who settled in Newark, N. J.; attended the public schools; was graduated from the American International (formerly French-American) College, Springfield, Mass., in 1906 and from the law department of the New York University, New York City, in 1908; was admitted to the bar in 1909 and commenced practice in Newark, N. J.; also served as director and counsel for several building and loan associations; appointed supervisor of inheritance tax of Essex County in 1917; member of the Newark Board of Education 1917–1931, serving as president 1924–1926; professor of law and trustee of Mercer Beasley School of Law (now part of Rutgers University), Newark, N. J., 1925–1931; elected as a Republican to the Seventy-second, Seventy-third, and Seventy-fourth Congresses (March 4, 1931–January 3, 1937); unsuccessful candidate for reelection in 1936 to the Seventy-fifth Congress; resumed the practice of law and again served as supervisor of inheritance tax for Essex County, N. J., 1937–1956; chairman of Central Planning Board of Newark, N. J., 1946–1957; is a resident of Newark, N. J.

CEDERBERG, Elford Alfred, a Representative from Michigan; born in Bay City, Bay County, Mich., March 6, 1918; attended the public schools and Bay City Junior College 1935–1937; entered the United States Army in April 1941, commissioned a second lieutenant in July 1942, a captain in 1943, and assigned to the Eighty-third Infantry; went overseas and participated in the Normandy invasion and fought in France and Germany; received five battle stars and the Bronze Star Medal; discharged as a captain in the Reserves in December 1945; manager of Nelson Manufacturing Co. of Bay City, Mich., 1946–1952; mayor of Bay City 1949–1953; elected as a Republican to the Eighty-third and to the three succeeding Congresses (January 3, 1953–January 3, 1961). *Reelected to the Eighty-seventh Congress.*

CELLER, Emanuel, a Representative from New York; born in Brooklyn, N. Y., May 6, 1888; attended the public schools; was graduated from the Boys' High School of Brooklyn in 1906, from Columbia College, New York City, in 1910, and from Columbia University Law School, New York City, in 1912; was admitted to the bar in 1912 and commenced practice in New York City; Government appeal agent on the draft board during the First World War; delegate to the Democratic State conventions in 1922 and 1924; elected as a Democrat to the Sixty-eighth and to the eighteen succeeding Congresses (March 4, 1923–January 3, 1961). *Reelected to the Eighty-seventh Congress.*

CESSNA, John, a Representative from Pennsylvania; born near Bedford County, Pa., June 29, 1821; attended the common schools and Hall's Military Academy, Bedford, Pa.; was graduated from Marshall College, Mercersburg, Pa., in 1842; taught school; studied law; was admitted to the bar in 1845 and commenced practice in Bedford; member of the State house of representatives in 1850, 1851, 1862, and 1863, and served as speaker of the house in 1850 and 1863; delegate to the Democratic National Convention at Cincinnati in 1856 and at Charleston and Baltimore in 1860; affiliated with the Republican Party in 1863; chairman of the Republican State convention in 1865; elected chairman of the Republican State central committee in 1865; delegate to the Republican National Conventions in 1868, 1876, and 1880; elected as a Republican to

the Forty-first Congress (March 4, 1869–March 3, 1871); unsuccessful candidate for reelection 1870 to the Forty-second Congress; elected to the Forty-third Congress (March 4, 1873–March 3, 1875); was not a candidate for renomination in 1874; again a member of the State house of representatives in 1892; resumed the practice of law in Bedford, Pa., where he died December 13, 1893; interment in Bedford Cemetery.

CHACE, Jonathan, a Representative and a Senator from Rhode Island; born at Fall River, Mass., July 22, 1829; attended the public schools and Friends' School at Providence, R. I.; moved to Central Falls, R. I.; engaged in cotton manufacturing; member of the State senate in 1876 and 1877; elected as a Republican to the Forty-seventh and Forty-eighth Congresses and served from March 4, 1881, to January 26, 1885, when he resigned; elected to the United States Senate to fill the vacancy caused by the death of Henry B. Anthony; reelected, and served from January 20, 1885, to April 9, 1889, when he resigned; president of the Phenix National Bank of Providence, R. I., and interested in several manufacturing enterprises; died in Providence, R. I., June 30, 1917; interment in the North Burial Ground.

CHADWICK, E. Wallace, a Representative from Pennsylvania; born in Vincennes, Knox County, Ind., January 17, 1884; moved with his parents to Chester, Delaware County, Pa., in 1890; attended the public schools; was graduated from Chester High School, from the University of Pennsylvania in 1906, and from the law school of the same university in 1910; was admitted to the bar in 1910 and commenced practice in Chester, Pa.; also interested in the banking business; president judge of the Delaware County Orphans' Court in 1945; elected as a Republican to the Eightieth Congress (January 3, 1947–January 3, 1949); unsuccessful candidate for renomination in 1948; resumed the practice of law in Chester, Pa.; in 1954 was named chief counsel of special Senate committee to study censure charges against Senator Joseph R. McCarthy; public member, Tenth Foreign Service Selection Board, State Department, 1956; is a resident of Rose Valley, Delaware County, Pa.

CHAFFEE, Calvin Clifford, a Representative from Massachusetts; born at Saratoga Springs, N. Y., on August 28, 1811; attended the common schools; studied medicine, and was graduated from the medical school of Middlebury College, Middlebury, Vt., in 1835; settled in Springfield, Mass., where he began the practice of his profession; elected on the American Party ticket to the Thirty-fourth and Thirty-fifth Congresses (March 4, 1855–March 3, 1859); was not a candidate for renomination in 1858; librarian of the National House of Representatives 1859–1861; settled in Washington, D. C., and engaged in the practice of medicine until 1876, when he moved to Springfield, Mass.; president of the Union Relief Association 1880–1893; president of Hampden County Children's Aid Association; died in Springfield, Hampden County, Mass., on August 8, 1896; interment in Springfield Cemetery.

CHAFFEE, Jerome Bunty, a Delegate from the Territory of Colorado and a Senator from Colorado; born in Niagara County, N. Y., April 17, 1825; attended the public schools of Lockport, N. Y.; moved to Adrian, Mich., in 1844, where he taught school and clerked in a store; moved in 1852 to St. Joseph, Mo., and later to Elmwood, Kans., where he engaged in banking and the real-estate business; moved to the Territory of Colorado in 1860 and engaged in mining and stamp-mill operations at Lake Gulch, Gilpin County; member of the Territorial house of representatives 1861–1863, and served in 1863 as speaker of the house; one of the founders of the city of Denver; president of the First National Bank of Denver from

1865 until 1880; elected as a Republican a Delegate to the Forty-second and Forty-third Congresses (March 4, 1871–March 3, 1875); upon the admission of Colorado as a State into the Union was elected as a Republican to the United States Senate and served from November 15, 1876, to March 3, 1879; was not a candidate for reelection; chairman of the Republican State executive committee in 1884; died in Salem Center, Westchester County, N. Y., March 9, 1886; interment in Adrian Cemetery, Adrian, Lenawee County, Mich.

CHALMERS, James Ronald (son of Joseph Williams Chalmers), a Representative from Mississippi; born near Lynchburg, Halifax County, Va., January 12, 1831; moved with his parents in 1835 to Jackson, Tenn., and in 1839 to Holly Springs, Miss.; attended St. Thomas Hall, Holly Springs, Miss., and was graduated from South Carolina College (now the University of South Carolina) at Columbia in 1851; studied law; was admitted to the bar in 1853 and commenced practice at Holly Springs; delegate to the Democratic National Convention at Baltimore in 1852; district attorney for the seventh judicial district of Mississippi in 1858; member of the secession convention of Mississippi in 1861; during the Civil War entered the Confederate Army as a captain in March 1861; elected colonel of the Ninth Mississippi Regiment in April 1861; promoted to the rank of brigadier general in February 1862; transferred to the Cavalry service in 1863; in command of the first division of Forrest's cavalry corps; surrendered in May 1865; member of the State senate in 1876 and 1877; elected as a Democrat to the Forty-fifth and Forty-sixth Congresses (March 4, 1877–March 3, 1881); presented credentials as a Member-elect to the Forty-seventh Congress and served from March 4, 1881, to April 29, 1882, when he was succeeded by John R. Lynch, who contested the election; elected as an Independent to the Forty-eighth Congress and, after a contest with Van H. Manning as to the legality of his election, took his seat June 25, 1884, and served until March 3, 1885; unsuccessful candidate for reelection in 1884 to the Forty-ninth Congress; resumed the practice of law in Memphis, Tenn., where he died April 9, 1898; interment in Elmwood Cemetery.

CHALMERS, Joseph Williams (father of James Ronald Chalmers), a Senator from Mississippi; born in Halifax County, Va., December 20, 1806; studied law in the University of Virginia at Charlottesville, and in Richmond; was admitted to the bar and practiced; moved to Jackson, Tenn., in 1835 and to Holly Springs, Miss., in 1839, engaging in the practice of his profession in both places; vice chancellor of the northern Mississippi district in 1842 and 1843; appointed and subsequently elected as a Democrat to the United States Senate to fill the vacancy caused by the resignation of Robert J. Walker and served from November 3, 1845, to March 3, 1847; presidential elector on the Democratic ticket of Cass and Butler in 1848; engaged in the practice of law in Holly Springs, Marshall County, Miss., until his death in that city June 16, 1853; interment in Hill Crest Cemetery.

CHALMERS, William Wallace, a Representative from Ohio; born in Strathroy, Ontario, Canada, November 1, 1861; moved with his parents to Kent County, near Grand Rapids, Mich., in 1865; attended the public schools, Grand Rapids (Mich.) High School, and Michigan State Normal School; was graduated from the University of Michigan at Ann Harbor in 1887, from Eureka (Ill.) College in 1889, and from Heidelberg University, Tiffin, Ohio, in 1904; teacher and principal of schools until 1890; superintendent of schools in Grand Rapids, Mich., 1890–1898 and in Toledo, Ohio, 1898–1905; president of Toledo University in 1904; engaged at different periods in farming, lumbering and,

in the real-estate and insurance business at Toledo, Ohio; elected as a Republican to the Sixty-seventh Congress (March 4, 1921–March 3, 1923); unsuccessful candidate for reelection in 1922 to the Sixty-eighth Congress; elected to the Sixty-ninth, Seventieth, and Seventy-first Congresses (March 4, 1925–March 3, 1931); unsuccessful candidate for renomination in 1930; retired from active business pursuits and political life; died in Indianapolis, Ind., on October 1, 1944; interment in Crown Hill Cemetery.

CHAMBERLAIN, Charles Ernest, a Representative from Michigan; born on a farm in Locke Township, Ingham County, Mich., July 22, 1917; attended Lansing, Mich., public schools and graduated from the University of Virginia at Charlottesville in 1941 and from the law school of the same university in 1949; admitted to Virginia and Michigan bars in 1949 and commenced practice of law in Lansing, Mich., in 1950; during World War II served as an apprentice seaman in the United States Coast Guard from February 1942 to February 1946 and attained the rank of lieutenant commander; Internal Revenue agent, Treasury Department, in 1946 and 1947; assistant prosecutor Ingham County in 1950; city attorney of East Lansing and legal counsel to Michigan Senate Judiciary Committee in 1953 and 1954; prosecuting attorney of Ingham County in 1955 and 1956; elected as a Republican to the Eighty-fifth and Eighty-sixth Congresses (January 3, 1957–January 3, 1961). *Reelected to the Eighty-seventh Congress.*

CHAMBERLAIN, Ebenezer Mattoon, a Representative from Indiana; born in Orrington, Maine, August 20, 1805; attended the public schools; employed in his father's shipyard; studied law; moved to Connersville, Ind., where he completed his studies; was admitted to the bar in 1832 and commenced practice in Elkhart County in 1833; member of the State house of representatives 1835–1837; served in the State senate 1839–1842; elected prosecuting attorney of the ninth judicial circuit in 1842; elected president judge of the ninth judicial district in 1843, reelected in 1851 and served until he resigned, having been elected to Congress; delegate to the Democratic National Convention at Baltimore in 1844; elected as a Democrat to the Thirty-third Congress (March 4, 1853–March 3, 1855); engaged in the practice of law in Goshen, Elkhart County, Ind., until his death there March 14, 1861; interment in Oak Ridge Cemetery.

CHAMBERLAIN, George Earle, a Senator from Oregon; born on a plantation near Natchez, Adams County, Miss., January 1, 1854; attended private and public schools in Natchez; clerk in a general merchandise store in Natchez 1870–1872; was graduated from the literary and law departments of Washington and Lee University, Lexington, Va., in June 1876; moved to Oregon in December 1876; taught school in Linn County; deputy clerk of Linn County from 1877 to 1879, when he resigned; was admitted to the bar in 1879 and commenced the practice of law in Albany, Linn County, Oreg.; member of the State house of representatives 1880–1882; district attorney for the third judicial district 1884–1886; appointed and subsequently elected attorney general of Oregon, and served from 1891 to 1894, with residence in Portland; continued the practice of law in Portland; district attorney for the fourth judicial district 1900–1902; elected Governor of Oregon in 1902 and reelected in 1906; resigned as Governor after serving two years of his second term, having been elected Senator; elected in 1908 as a Democrat to the United States Senate; reelected in 1914 and served from March 4, 1909, to March 3, 1921; was chairman of the Senate Committee on Military Affairs during the entire period of the First World War; unsuccessful candidate for reelection to the Senate in 1920; member of the United States Shipping Board from June 13, 1921, to June 30, 1923, when he resigned; engaged in the practice of law in Washington, D. C., and died there on July 9, 1928; interment in Arlington National Cemetery, Fort Myer, Va.

CHAMBERLAIN, Jacob Payson, a Representative from New York; born in Dudley, Mass., August 1, 1802; moved with his parents to Seneca Falls, N. Y., in 1807; attended the public schools; operated flour mills, malt houses, and woolen mills; organized the first savings bank of the village; supervisor of Seneca Falls; member of the board of education; member of the State assembly 1859–1861; elected as a Republican to the Thirty-seventh Congress (March 4, 1861–March 3, 1863); was not a candidate for renomination; resumed the flour-milling business; died at Seneca Falls, Seneca County, N. Y., October 5, 1878; interment in Restvale Cemetery.

CHAMBERLAIN, John Curtis, a Representative from New Hampshire; born in Worcester, Mass., June 5, 1772; was graduated from Harvard College in 1793; studied law; was admitted to the bar in 1796 and commenced practice in Alstead, Cheshire County, N. H.; member of the State house of representatives 1802–1804; moved to Charlestown, N. H., in 1804; elected as a Federalist to the Eleventh Congress (March 4, 1809–March 3, 1811); resumed the practice of law; again a member of the State house of representatives in 1818; moved to Honeoye Falls, Monroe County, N. Y., in 1826, and thence to Utica, N. Y., where he died December 8, 1834.

CHAMBERLAIN, William, a Representative from Vermont; born in Hopkinton, Mass., April 27, 1755; attended the common schools; moved with his father to Loudon, N. H., in 1774; served as a sergeant during the Revolutionary War; engaged in land surveying and farming; moved to Peacham, Vt., in 1780; clerk of the proprietors of the town the same year; town clerk 1785–1797; town representative twelve years; member of the State house of representatives 1785, 1787–1796, 1805, and 1808; justice of the peace 1786–1796; delegate to the State constitutional convention in 1791; brigadier general of State militia in 1794; major general in 1799; assistant judge of Orange County in 1795 and chief judge of Caledonia County 1796–1803; secretary of the board of trustees of the Caledonia County Grammar School 1795–1812, and president 1813–1828; State councilor 1796–1803; Federalist presidential elector in 1800; elected as a Federalist to the Eighth Congress (March 4, 1803–March 3, 1805); reelected to the Eleventh Congress (March 4, 1809–March 3, 1811); Lieutenant Governor of Vermont 1813–1815; delegate to the State constitutional convention in 1814; died in Peacham, Caledonia County, Vt., September 27, 1828; interment in Peacham Cemetery.

CHAMBERS, David, a Representative from Ohio; born in Allentown, Pa., November 25, 1780; tutored by his father; was a confidential express rider for President Washington during the Whisky Insurrection in 1794; learned the art of printing; moved to Zanesville, Ohio, in 1810, where he established a newspaper and was elected State printer; volunteer aide-de-camp to General Cass in the War of 1812; served as recorder and mayor of Zanesville; member of the State house of representatives in 1814, 1828, 1836–1838, 1841, and 1842; clerk of the Ohio State Senate in 1817; clerk of the court of common pleas of Muskingum County 1817–1821; unsuccessful candidate for election in 1820 to the Seventeenth Congress; subsequently elected to the Seventeenth Congress to fill the vacancy caused by the resignation of Representative-elect John C. Wright and served from October 9, 1821, to March 3, 1823; was not a candidate for renomination; affiliated with the Whig Party after its formation; member of the State

senate in 1843 and 1844; president of the senate in 1844; delegate to the State constitutional convention of 1850; engaged in agricultural pursuits until 1856; died in Zanesville, Muskingum County, Ohio, August 8, 1864; interment in Greenwood Cemetery.

CHAMBERS, Ezekiel Forman, a Senator from Maryland; born in Chestertown, Kent County, Md., February 28, 1788; was graduated from Washington College at Chestertown in 1805; studied law; was admitted to the bar in 1808 and commenced practice in Chestertown, Md.; served in the War of 1812, attaining the rank of brigadier general; member of the State senate in 1822; elected as a Whig to the United States Senate to fill the vacancy caused by the resignation of Edward Lloyd; reelected in 1831 and served from January 24, 1826, until his resignation on December 20, 1834; presiding judge of the second judicial circuit of Maryland and judge of the court of appeals 1834–1851; was offered the position of Secretary of the Navy by President Fillmore in 1852, but declined; unsuccessful Democratic candidate for Governor in 1864; died in Chestertown, Md., January 30, 1867; interment in Chester Cemetery.

CHAMBERS, George, a Representative from Pennsylvania; born in Chambersburg, Pa., February 24, 1786; received a classical education and attended the Chambersburg Academy; was graduated from Princeton College in 1804; studied law; was admitted to the bar in 1807 and commenced practice in Chambersburg; elected as a Whig to the Twenty-third and Twenty-fourth Congresses (March 4, 1833–March 3, 1837); resumed the practice of law; member of the State constitutional convention in 1837; appointed a justice of the Pennsylvania Supreme Court April 12, 1851, which position he held until it was vacated by constitutional provision; died in Chambersburg, Franklin County, Pa., March 25, 1866; interment in Falling Spring Presbyterian Churchyard.

CHAMBERS, Henry H., a Senator from Alabama; born near Kenbridge, Lunenburg County, Va., October 1, 1790; was graduated from William and Mary College, Williamsburg, Va., in 1808 and from the medical department of the University of Pennsylvania at Philadelphia in 1811; moved to Madison, Ala., in 1812 and engaged in the practice of medicine; served in the earlier Indian wars as a surgeon on the staff of Gen. Andrew Jackson; returned to Alabama and settled in Huntsville; member of the State constitutional convention in 1819; member of the State house of representatives in 1820; unsuccessful candidate for Governor in 1821 and 1823; Democratic presidential elector on the Jackson ticket in 1824; elected as a Democrat to the United States Senate and served from March 4, 1825, until his death near Kenbridge, Lunenburg County, Va., February 24, 1826, while en route to Washington, D. C., to attend the opening session of the Twenty-seventh Congress; interment in the family burial ground near Kenbridge, Va.

CHAMBERS, John, a Representative from Kentucky; born at Bromley Bridge, Somerset County, N. J., October 6, 1780; attended the public schools and the Transylvania Seminary. Lexington, Ky.; moved with his father to Washington, Mason County, Ky., in 1794; studied law; was admitted to the bar in 1800 and commenced practice in Washington, Ky.; served as aide-de-camp to General Harrison in the War of 1812 and was at the Battle of the Thames; member of the State house of representatives in 1812, 1815, 1830, and 1831; appointed judge of the court of appeals in 1825; resigned in 1827; elected as a Whig to the Twentieth Congress to fill the vacancy caused by the resignation of Thomas Metcalfe and served from December 1, 1828, to March 3, 1829; elected to the Twenty-fourth and Twenty-fifth Congresses (March 4, 1835–March 3, 1839); Governor of the

Territory of Iowa 1841–1845; commissioner to negotiate a treaty with the Sioux Indians in 1849; died near Paris, Bourbon County, Ky., September 21, 1852; interment in the family burial ground at Washington, Mason County, Ky.

CHAMPION, Edwin Van Meter, a Representative from Illinois; born in Mansfield, Piatt County, Ill., September 18, 1890; attended the public schools; was graduated from the law department of the University of Illinois at Urbana in 1912; was admitted to the bar the same year and commenced practice in Peoria, Ill.; during the First World War entered the Officers' Training Camp at Fort Sheridan, Ill., on May 15, 1917; commissioned second lieutenant and assigned to service overseas with the Three Hundred and Forty-first Infantry, Company C, Eighty-sixth Division; discharged with rank of captain on February 6, 1919; served as assistant State's attorney of Peoria County, Ill., in 1919 and 1920 and as State's attorney 1932–1936; president of the Illinois State's Attorneys' Association in 1935; elected as a Democrat to the Seventy-fifth Congress (January 3, 1937–January 3, 1939); was not a candidate for renomination in 1938; resumed the practice of law in Peoria, Ill., where he now resides.

CHAMPION, Epaphroditus, a Representative from Connecticut; born in Westchester parish, Colchester, Conn., April 6, 1756; educated by private tutors and in the common schools; served during the Revolutionary War in the commissary and purchasing departments of the American Army; moved to East Haddam, Conn., in 1782; served as captain in the Twenty-fourth Regiment of State militia 1784–1792, as major 1793 and 1794, as lieutenant colonel 1795–1798, and as brigadier general of the Seventh Brigade 1800–1803; merchant, shipowner, exporter, and importer; member of the State assembly 1791–1806; elected as a Federalist to the Tenth and to the four succeeding Congresses (March 4, 1807–March 3, 1817); resumed his former business activities, but soon retired to private life; died in East Haddam, Conn., December 22, 1834; interment in Riverview Cemetery.

CHAMPLIN, Christopher Grant, a Representative and a Senator from Rhode Island; born in Newport, R. I., April 12, 1768; completed preparatory studies; was graduated from Harvard College in 1786 and continued his studies at the College of St. Omer in France; elected to the Fifth and Sixth Congresses (March 4, 1797–March 3, 1801); engaged in mercantile pursuits; elected to the United States Senate to fill the vacancy caused by the death of Francis Malbone and served from June 26, 1809, to October 2, 1811, when he resigned; president of the Rhode Island Bank until a short time before his death in Newport, Newport County, R. I., March 18, 1840; interment in Common Burial Ground.

CHANDLER, Albert Benjamin, a Senator from Kentucky; born in Corydon, Henderson County, Ky., July 14, 1898; attended the public schools, and Harvard University, Cambridge, Mass.; served as a private in the United States Army in 1918 and 1919; was graduated from Transylvania College, Lexington, Ky., in 1921 and from the law department of the University of Kentucky at Lexington in 1924; was admitted to the bar in 1925 and commenced practice in Versailles, Ky.; served in the State senate 1930–1931; master commissioner of the Woodford circuit in 1928; receiver of the Inter-Southern Life Insurance Co. in 1932; Lieutenant Governor 1931–1935; captain in the Judge Advocate General's Reserve in 1934 and 1935; elected Governor of Kentucky in 1935 and served until his resignation October 9, 1939; appointed as a Democrat and subsequently elected to the United States Senate to fill the vacancy caused by the death of

Marvel Mills Logan; reelected in 1942 and served from October 10, 1939, until his resignation on November 1, 1945, to become commissioner of organized baseball, in which capacity he served until 1950; engaged in the practice of law, raising of tobacco, and the publication of a weekly newspaper; again Governor of Kentucky, December 1955 to December 1959; is a resident of Versailles, Ky.

CHANDLER, John (brother of Thomas Chandler and uncle of Zachariah Chandler), a Representative from Massachusetts and a Senator from Maine; born in Epping, N. H., February 1, 1762; self-educated; served in the Revolutionary War; moved to the Maine district of Massachusetts and settled on a farm near Monmouth; member of the Massachusetts Senate 1803–1805; elected to the Ninth and Tenth Congresses (March 4, 1805–March 3, 1809); was not a candidate for renomination in 1808; appointed sheriff of Kennebec County the same year; during the War of 1812 was a major general of Maine Militia and was commissioned brigadier general July 8, 1812; honorably discharged June 15, 1815; member of the Massachusetts General Court in 1819; first president of the Maine Senate; member of the Maine constitutional convention 1819–1820; upon the admission of Maine as a State into the Union was elected as a Democrat to the United States Senate; reelected in 1823 and served from June 14, 1820, to March 3, 1829; was not a candidate for renomination; collector of customs at Portland 1829–1837; died in Augusta, Kennebec County, Maine, September 25, 1841; interment in Mount Pleasant Cemetery.

CHANDLER, Joseph Ripley, a Representative from Pennsylvania; born in Kingston, Mass., August 22, 1792; attended the common schools; engaged in commercial work in Boston; moved to Philadelphia, Pa., in 1815; founded a young ladies' seminary; editor of the United States Gazette 1822–1847, member of the Philadelphia City Council 1832–1848; member of the State constitutional convention in 1837; elected as a Whig to the Thirty-first, Thirty-second, and Thirty-third Congresses (March 4, 1849–March 3, 1855); unsuccessful candidate for reelection in 1854 to the Thirty-fourth Congress; appointed by President Buchanan as Minister to the Two Sicilies and served from June 15, 1858, to November 15, 1860; president of the board of directors of Girard College; interested in prison reform and was a delegate to the International Prison Congress held at London in 1872; died in Philadelphia, Pa., July 10, 1880; interment in New Cathedral Cemetery.

CHANDLER, Thomas (brother of John Chandler and uncle of Zachariah Chandler), a Representative from New Hampshire; born in Bedford, N. H., August 10, 1772; attended the public schools; justice of the peace in 1808; captain of militia in 1815; member of the State house of representatives in 1818 and again in 1827; elected as a Democrat to the Twenty-first and Twenty-second Congresses (March 4, 1829–March 3, 1833); innkeeper and also engaged in agricultural pursuits; died in Bedford, N. H., January 28, 1866; interment in Bedford Cemetery.

CHANDLER, Thomas Alberter, a Representative from Oklahoma; born near Eucha, Delaware County, Indian Territory (now Oklahoma), July 26, 1871; attended the public schools, Worcester Academy, Vinita, Indian Territory, in 1888, and, later, Drury College, Springfield, Mo.; appointed a Cherokee revenue collector in 1891; Cherokee town-site commissioner 1895–1898; United States deputy clerk of the court for the northern district of Indian Territory 1900–1907; studied law; was admitted to the bar in 1907 and commenced practice in Vinita, Indian Territory; delegate to the Republican National Convention at Chicago in 1908; member of the first Board of Public Affairs for the State of Oklahoma in 1909 and 1910; resumed the practice of law; also engaged in the production of oil, in agricultural pursuits, and in the real-estate business; elected as a Republican to the Sixty-fifth Congress (March 4, 1917–March 3, 1919); unsuccessful candidate for reelection 1918 to the Sixty-sixth Congress; elected to the Sixty-seventh Congress (March 4, 1921–March 3, 1923); unsuccessful candidate for reelection in 1922 to the Sixty-eighth Congress; resumed the practice of law; died in Vinita, Okla., June 22, 1953; interment in Fairview Cemetery.

CHANDLER, Walter (Clift), a Representative from Tennessee; born in Jackson, Madison County, Tenn., October 5, 1887; attended the public schools and was graduated from the law department of the University of Tennessee at Knoxville in 1909; admitted to the bar the same year and commenced practice in Memphis, Tenn.; assistant district attorney general in 1916; member of the State house of representatives in 1917; served in the State senate 1921–1923; city attorney of Memphis 1928–1934; during the First World War served as a captain in the One Hundred and Fourteenth Field Artillery, Thirtieth Division, American Expeditionary Forces, from July 25, 1917, to April 19, 1919; delegate to the Democratic National Conventions in 1940 and 1944; elected as a Democrat to the Seventy-fourth, Seventy-fifth, and Seventy-sixth Congresses and served from January 3, 1935, until his resignation on January 2, 1940, having been elected mayor of Memphis; reelected mayor in 1943 and served until September 1, 1946; resumed the practice of law; temporary president, Tennessee Constitutional Convention, in 1953; Mayor of Memphis in 1955 for unexpired term; is a resident of Memphis, Tenn.

CHANDLER, Walter Marion, a Representative from New York; born near Yazoo City, Yazoo County, Miss., December 8, 1867; attended the public schools, the University of Virginia at Charlottesville, and the University of Mississippi at Oxford; taught school; was graduated from the University of Michigan at Ann Arbor in 1897; studied history and jurisprudence at the Universities of Berlin and Heidelberg, Germany; was admitted to the bar in 1897 and commenced the practice of law in Dallas, Tex.; moved to New York City in 1900 and continued the practice of law; also engaged in writing and lecturing; elected as a Progressive to the Sixty-third, Sixty-fourth, and Sixty-fifth Congresses (March 4, 1913–March 3, 1919); unsuccessful candidate for reelection in 1918 to the Sixty-sixth Congress; elected as a Republican to the Sixty-seventh Congress (March 4, 1921–March 3, 1923); unsuccessful candidate for reelection in 1922 to the Sixty-eighth Congress and also unsuccessfully contested the election of Sol Bloom to fill a vacancy in the Sixty-eighth Congress; unsuccessful candidate for election in 1924 to the Sixty-ninth Congress; member of the faculty and lecturer at the American Expeditionary Forces University at Beaune, France, during the First World War; resumed the practice of law in New York City, N. Y.; also traveled extensively and engaged in lecturing and writing; died in New York City, N. Y., on March 16, 1935; interment in the West Evergreen Cemetery, Jacksonville, Fla.

CHANDLER, William Eaton, a Senator from New Hampshire; born in Concord, N. H., December 28, 1835; attended the common schools and the academies in Thetford, Vt., and Pembroke, N. H.; was graduated from Harvard Law School in 1854; was admitted to the bar in 1855 and commenced practice in Concord, N. H.; appointed reporter of the decisions of the supreme court of New Hampshire in 1859; member of the State house of representatives 1862–1864 and served as speaker during the last two years; appointed by President Lincoln solicitor and judge advocate general of the Navy Department

March 9, 1865; appointed First Assistant Secretary of the Treasury on June 17, 1865, and served until November 30, 1867, when he resigned; member of the State constitutional convention in 1876; again a member of the State house of representatives in 1881; appointed by President Arthur as Secretary of the Navy on April 12, 1882, and served until March 7, 1885; elected as a Republican to the United States Senate to fill the vacancy caused by the death of Austin F. Pike and served from June 14, 1887, to March 3, 1889; subsequently elected for the term beginning March 4, 1889; reelected in 1895 and served from June 18, 1889, to March 3, 1901; unsuccessful candidate for renomination; appointed by President McKinley as president of the Spanish Claims Treaty Commission in 1901; resigned in 1908 and resumed the practice of law in Concord, N. H., and Washington, D. C.; died in Concord, N. H., November 20, 1917; interment in Blossom Hill Cemetery.

CHANDLER, Zachariah (nephew of John Chandler and Thomas Chandler, and grandfather of Frederick Hale); a Senator from Michigan; born in Bedford, N. H., December 10, 1813; attended the common schools; taught school; moved to Detroit, Mich., in December 1833 and engaged in mercantile pursuits; mayor of Detroit in 1851; unsuccessful Whig candidate for Governor in 1852; was prominent in the organization of the Republican Party in 1854; elected as a Republican to the United States Senate in 1857; reelected in 1863 and again in 1869 and served from March 4, 1857, to March 3, 1875; unsuccessful candidate for reelection in 1874; appointed Secretary of the Interior in the Cabinet of President Grant and served from October 19, 1875, to March 3, 1877; chairman of the Republican National Executive Committee in 1868 and 1876; again elected in 1879 to the United States Senate to fill the vacancy caused by the resignation of Isaac P. Christiancy and served from February 22, 1879, until his death while on a speaking tour in Chicago, Ill., on November 1, 1879; interment in Elmwood Cemetery, Detroit, Mich.

CHANEY, John, a Representative from Ohio; born in Washington County, Md., January 12, 1790; moved with his parents to Pennsylvania; received a limited schooling; moved to Ohio in 1810 and settled in Bloom Township, Fairfield County; engaged in agricultural pursuits; justice of the peace in 1821, 1824, and 1827; trustee of Bloom Township for twenty-three years; major, colonel, and paymaster in the Ohio State Militia; member of the State house of representatives 1828–1830; elected associate judge of Fairfield County in 1831; Democratic presidential elector on the Jackson ticket in 1832; elected as a Jackson Democrat to the Twenty-third, Twenty-fourth, and Twenty-fifth Congresses (March 4, 1833–March 3, 1839); returned to Ohio and settled in Canal Winchester, Franklin County; again a member of the State house of representatives in 1842 and served as speaker; member of the village council; served in the State senate in 1844 and 1845; again a member of the State house of representatives in 1855; served as a delegate to the Maryland Constitutional Convention in 1851; died at Canal Winchester, Ohio, April 10, 1881; interment in Union Grove Cemetery.

CHANEY, John Crawford, a Representative from Indiana; born near New Lisbon, Columbiana County, Ohio, February 1, 1853; in 1854 moved to Lafayette Township, Allen County, Ind., with his parents, who settled on a farm near Fort Wayne; attended the common schools; was graduated from Ascension Seminary, Farmersburg, Sullivan County, Ind., in 1874 and later from the Terre Haute Commercial College; taught school and served as superintendent of schools for five years; was graduated from the law school of Cincinnati University in June

1882; was admitted to the bar in 1883 and commenced practice in Sullivan, Sullivan County, Ind.; member of the State central committee from the second district in 1884 and 1885; presidential elector on the Harrison and Morton ticket in 1888; appointed by President Harrison as assistant to the Attorney General in the Department of Justice in July 1889, which position he filled until August 1893, when he resigned and resumed the practice of law; elected as a Republican to the Fifty-ninth and Sixtieth Congresses (March 4, 1905–March 3, 1909); unsuccessful candidate for reelection in 1908 to the Sixty-first Congress; continued the practice of law in Sullivan, Sullivan County, Ind.; trustee of Hanover College, Hanover, Ind.; president of the Sullivan County Historical Society; died in Sullivan, Ind., April 26, 1940; interment in Center Ridge Cemetery.

CHANLER, John Winthrop (father of William Astor Chanler), a Representative from New York; born in New York City September 14, 1826; received his early education from private tutors, and was graduated from Columbia College, New York City, in 1847; attended the University of Heidelberg, Germany; studied law; was admitted to the bar and practiced; member of the State assembly in 1858 and 1859; was nominated as a candidate for State senator in 1860 but declined; unsuccessful candidate for election in 1860 to the Thirty-seventh Congress; elected as a Democrat to the Thirty-eighth, Thirty-ninth, and Fortieth Congresses (March 4, 1863–March 3, 1869); died near Rhinebeck, Dutchess County, N. Y., October 19, 1877; interment in Trinity Cemetery, Red Hook, N. Y.

CHANLER, William Astor (son of John Winthrop Chanler), a Representative from New York; born in Newport, R. I., June 11, 1867; attended St. John's School, Ossining, N. Y., Phillips Academy, Exeter, N. H., and Harvard University for two years; Fellow of the Royal Geographic Society of London; explored the territory in the vicinity of Mount Kilimanjaro in 1891; delegate to the State republican convention at Saratoga in 1896; member of the State assembly in 1897; during the Spanish-American War was appointed captain and assistant adjutant general of Volunteers on May 10, 1898; served as acting ordnance officer, Cavalry Division, Fifth Army Corps, from May 23 to August 23, 1898; participated in the Battle of Santiago; elected as a Democrat to the Fifty-sixth Congress (March 4, 1899–March 3, 1901); was not a candidate for renomination in 1900; traveler, author, and explorer; retired from active life and moved to Europe in 1920; died in Menton, A. M., France, March 4, 1934; interment in Trinity Church Cemetery, New York City, N. Y.

CHAPIN, Alfred Clark, a Representative from New York; born in South Hadley, Hampshire County, Mass., March 8, 1848; resided in Springfield, Mass., in Keene, N. H., and in Rutland, Vt.; attended the public and private schools; was graduated from Williams College, Williamstown, Mass., in 1869 and from Harvard Law School in 1871; was admitted to the bar in 1872 and commenced practice in New York City with residence in Brooklyn, N. Y.; member of the State assembly in 1882 and 1883, serving as speaker in the latter year; State comptroller 1884–1887; mayor of Brooklyn 1888–1891; elected as a Democrat to the Fifty-second Congress to fill the vacancy caused by the resignation of David A. Boody and served from November 3, 1891, to November 16, 1892, when he resigned; served as railroad commissioner of New York State 1892–1897; continued the practice of law and was also financially interested in various enterprises; retired from active business pursuits in 1923; died while on a visit in Montreal, Canada, October 2, 1936; interment in Woodlawn Cemetery, New York City, Borough of the Bronx, N. Y.

CHAPIN, Chester Williams, a Representative from Massachusetts; born in Ludlow, Mass., December 16, 1798; attended the common schools and Westfield Academy, Westfield, Mass.; engaged in mercantile pursuits; mail contractor, running post coaches and steamboats; member of the constitutional convention of Massachusetts in 1853; president and director of the Western Railroad Corporation 1854–1867; president of the Boston & Albany Railroad Co. 1868–1878, and one of the directors 1868–1880; elected as a Democrat to the Forty-fourth Congress (March 4, 1875–March 3, 1877); unsuccessful candidate for reelection in 1876 to the Forty-fifth Congress; died in Springfield, Hampden County, Mass., on June 10, 1883; interment in Springfield Cemetery.

CHAPIN, Graham Hurd, a Representative from New York; born in Salisbury, Conn., February 10, 1799; moved to Lyons, Wayne County, N. Y., in 1817; was graduated from Yale College in 1819; studied law; was admitted to the bar in 1823 and practiced in Lyons; surrogate of Wayne County 1826–1833; district attorney of Wayne County in 1829 and 1830; moved to Rochester, N. Y., in 1833 and continued the practice of law; elected as a Democrat to the Twenty-fourth Congress (March 4, 1835–March 3, 1837); died in Mount Morris, Livingston County, N. Y., September 8, 1843.

CHAPMAN, Andrew Grant (son of John Grant Chapman), a Representative from Maryland; born in La Plata, Charles County, Md., January 17, 1839; after being tutored at home attended the Charlotte Hall Academy, St. Marys County, Md.; was graduated from St. John's College, Annapolis, Md., in 1858 and from the law department of the University of Virginia at Charlottesville in 1860; moved to Baltimore, Md., in 1860; was admitted to the bar the same year and commenced practice in that city; moved to Port Tobacco, Md., in 1864 and continued the practice of law; also engaged in agricultural pursuits; member of the State house of delegates in 1867, 1868, 1870, 1872, 1879, and 1885; appointed aide and inspector with rank of brigadier general in 1874 on the staff of Governor Groome and reappointed by Governor Carroll; elected as a Democrat to the Forty-seventh Congress (March 4, 1881–March 3, 1883); unsuccessful candidate for reelection in 1882 to the Forty-eighth Congress; resumed the practice of law; appointed deputy collector of internal revenue in 1885 and collector in 1888; delegate to the Democratic National Convention at St. Louis in 1888; died at his home, "Normandy," near La Plata, Md., September 25, 1892; interment in Mount Rest Cemetery, La Plata, Md.

CHAPMAN, Augustus Alexandria, a Representative from Virginia; born in Union, Monroe County, Va. (now West Virginia), March 9, 1803; studied law; was admitted to the bar in 1825 and commenced practice in Union; member of the Virginia Assembly 1841–1843; elected as a Van Buren Democrat to the Twenty-eighth and Twenty-ninth Congresses (March 4, 1843–March 3, 1847); at the outbreak of the Civil War was a brigadier general of the State militia and as such took the field with his command in 1861, serving with the Confederate Army in the Kanawha Valley; resumed the practice of law in Union, W. Va., and also engaged in agricultural pursuits; died in Hinton, Summers County, W. Va., June 7, 1876, while en route to attend the Democratic State convention at Charleston; interment in Green Hill Cemetery, Union, Monroe County, W. Va.

CHAPMAN, Bird Beers, a Delegate from the Territory of Nebraska; born in Salisbury, Litchfield County, Conn., August 24, 1821; attended the public schools; studied law; was admitted to the bar and commenced practice in Elyria, Lorain County, Ohio; moved to the Territory of Nebraska and settled in Omaha;

was editor of the Omaha Nebraskan 1855–1859; elected as a Democrat to the Thirty-fourth Congress (March 4, 1855–March 3, 1857); unsuccessfully contested the election of Fenner Ferguson to the Thirty-fifth Congress; died at Put in Bay, Ottawa County, Ohio, September 21, 1871; interment in Ridgelawn Cemetery, Elyria, Ohio.

CHAPMAN, Charles, a Representative from Connecticut; born in Newtown, Conn., June 21, 1799; pursued academic studies; studied law at the Litchfield (Conn.) Law School; was admitted to the bar in 1820 and commenced practice in New Haven, Conn., in 1827; moved to Hartford in 1832 and became editor of the New England Review; member of the State house of representatives in 1840, 1847, and 1848; United States attorney for the district of Connecticut 1841–1848; unsuccessful candidate in 1848 for election to the Thirty-first Congress; elected as a Whig to the Thirty-second Congress (March 4, 1851–March 3, 1853); unsuccessful candidate for Governor of Connecticut as a Temperance candidate in 1854; elected as a Democrat to the State house of representatives in 1862 and 1864; resumed the practice of law; died in Hartford, Conn., on August 7, 1869; interment in Cedar Hill Cemetery.

CHAPMAN, Henry, a Representative from Pennsylvania; born in Newtown, Pa., February 4, 1804; attended Doylestown Academy and Doctor Gummere's private boys' school near Burlington, N. J.; studied law; was admitted to the bar in 1825 and commenced practice in Doylestown; member of the State senate in 1843; judge of the fifteenth judicial district 1845–1849; elected as a Democrat to the Thirty-fifth Congress (March 4, 1857–March 3, 1859); declined to be a candidate for renomination in 1858; judge of the Bucks County Court in 1861; retired in 1871; died at "Frosterley," near Doylestown, Bucks County, Pa., April 11, 1891; interment in the graveyard of Doylestown Presbyterian Church.

CHAPMAN, John, a Representative from Pennsylvania; born in Wrightstown Township, Bucks County, Pa., October 18, 1740; presumably studied medicine, as he styled himself a "practitioner of physic"; commissioned justice of the peace February 25, 1779, and was one of the justices commissioned judge of the court of common pleas of Bucks County the same year; moved to Upper Makefield, Pa., prior to 1776, his residence having been the headquarters of Col. Alexander Hamilton during the period that Washington's Army was encamped on the west bank of the Delaware just prior to the Battle of Trenton; member of the State assembly 1787–1796; elected as a Federalist to the Fifth Congress (March 4, 1797–March 3, 1799); died in Upper Makefield, January 27, 1800; interment in the Friends' Burying Ground, Wrightstown, Pa.

CHAPMAN, John Grant (father of Andrew Grant Chapman), a Representative from Maryland; born in La Plata, Charles County, Md., July 5, 1798; was tutored at home; attended a college in Pennsylvania in 1812 and 1813 and was graduated from Yale College in 1817; studied law; was admitted to the bar in 1819 and commenced practice at Port Tobacco, Charles County, Md.; also interested in agricultural pursuits; member of the State house of delegates from 1824 to 1832 and from 1843 to 1844, serving as speaker 1826–1829 and again in 1844; member the State senate 1832–1836, serving as president of that body from 1833 to 1836; served in the State militia; unsuccessful candidate for Governor of Maryland in 1844; elected as a Whig to the Twenty-ninth and Thirtieth Congresses (March 4, 1845–March 3, 1849); resumed the practice of law at Port Tobacco, Md.; president of the State constitutional convention in 1851; presi-

dent of the Whig National Convention at Baltimore in 1856; died on his sister's estate, "Waverly," on the Wicomico River, Charles County, Md., on December 10, 1856; interment at St. Johns, a family estate; reinterment in Mount Rest Cemetery, La Plata, Md.

CHAPMAN, Pleasant Thomas, a Representative from Illinois; born on a farm near Vienna, Johnson County, Ill., October 8, 1854; attended the public schools, and was graduated from McKendree College, Lebanon, Ill., in June 1876; taught school; served as superintendent of public schools of Johnson County 1877–1882; studied law; was admitted to the bar at Mount Vernon, Ill., in 1878 and commenced practice in Vienna, Ill.; also engaged in banking and in agricultural pursuits; judge of Johnson County 1882–1890; member of the State senate 1890–1902; elected as a Republican to the Fifty-ninth, Sixtieth, and Sixty-first Congresses (March 4, 1905–March 3, 1911); unsuccessful candidate for reelection in 1910 to the Sixty-second Congress; resumed the practice of law in Vienna, Ill., and also engaged in banking and agricultural pursuits; delegate to the Republican National Convention at Cleveland in 1924; died in Vienna, Ill., January 31, 1931; interment in Fraternal Cemetery.

CHAPMAN, Reuben, a Representative from Alabama; born in Bowling Green, Caroline County, Va., July 15, 1799; attended an academy in Virginia; studied law; was admitted to the bar in 1825 and commenced practice in Somerville, Morgan County, Ala.; member of the State senate 1832–1835; elected as a Democrat to the Twenty-fourth and to the five succeeding Congresses (March 4, 1835–March 3, 1847); was not a candidate for renomination in 1846, having become a gubernatorial candidate; Governor of Alabama 1847–1849; member of the State house of representatives in 1855; delegate to the Baltimore convention held in the interest of peace, in which he used his influence to bring about a reconciliation between northern and southern representatives; retired from public life; was a representative of the Southern Confederacy to France 1862–1865; resumed the practice of law; died in Huntsville, Madison County, Ala., May 16, 1882; interment in Maple Hill Cemetery.

CHAPMAN, Virgil Munday, a Representative and a Senator from Kentucky; born in Middleton, Simpson County, Ky., on March 15, 1895; attended the public schools of Franklin, Ky., and was graduated from Franklin High School in 1913; delegate to all Democratic State conventions since 1915; studied law; was admitted to the bar in 1917; editor in chief of the Kentucky Law Journal in 1917 and 1918; was graduated from the law department of the University of Kentucky at Lexington in 1918 and commenced practice at Irvine, Estill County, Ky., in June 1918; city attorney of Irvine 1918–1920; moved to Paris, Ky., in June 1920 and continued the practice of law, with offices at Lexington, Ky.; assisted in organizing the tobacco growers of Kentucky and nearby States into cooperative marketing associations 1921–1923; elected as a Democrat to the Sixty-ninth and Seventieth Congresses (March 4, 1925–March 3, 1929); unsuccessful candidate for reelection in 1928 to the Seventy-first Congress; elected to the Seventy-second and to the eight succeeding Congresses (March 4, 1931–January 3, 1949); elected as a Democrat to the United States Senate in 1948 and served from January 3, 1949, until his death, due to an automobile accident, in the naval hospital at Bethesda, Md., March 8, 1951; interment in Paris Cemetery, Paris, Ky.

CHAPMAN, William Williams, a Delegate from the Territory of Iowa; born in Clarksburg, Marion County, Va. (now West Virginia), August 11, 1808; attended the common schools; studied law while serving as clerk of the court; was admitted to the bar and commenced practice in Middleton; was one of the first settlers in Burlington, Iowa (then Michigan Territory), in 1835; prosecuting attorney of Michigan Territory in 1836; first district attorney when Wisconsin Territory was organized in July 1836; after the Territory of Iowa was granted representation he was elected as a Democrat to the Twenty-fifth and Twenty-sixth Congresses and served from September 10, 1838, to October 27, 1840, when his term expired by law; moved to Agency City, an Indian village, in Wapello County, Iowa, in 1843; elected from that county as a delegate to the first constitutional convention in Iowa City in 1844; started across the plains to become a pioneer of Oregon in 1847; went to California in 1848; returned to Oregon; member of the Oregon House of Representatives; was one of the founders of the Oregonian, the first newspaper established in the Territory; surveyor general in 1858; died in Portland, Oreg., on October 18, 1892; interment in the Lone Fir Cemetery.

CHAPPELL, Absalom Harris (cousin of Lucius Quintus Cincinnatus Lamar), a Representative from Georgia; born at Mount Zion, Hancock County, Ga., December 18, 1801; attended the local academy at Mount Zion, and was graduated from the law department of the University of Georgia at Athens in 1821; was admitted to the bar the same year and commenced practice in Sandersville, Washington County, Ga.; moved to Forsyth, Ga., in 1824 and practiced; member of the State senate in 1832 and 1833; served in the State house of representatives 1834–1839; moved to Macon, Ga., in 1836 and continued the practice of law; delegate to the Knoxville convention in 1836; promoter of the Monroe Railroad; appointed on the board of commissioners to arrange a State finance system in 1839; elected as a State Rights Whig to the Twenty-eighth Congress to fill the vacancy caused by the resignation of Representative-elect John B. Lamar and served from October 2, 1843, to March 3, 1845; was not a candidate for renomination in 1844 to the Twenty-ninth Congress; member of the State senate in 1845, serving as president; resumed the practice of law; moved to Columbus, Ga., in 1857 and continued the practice of law; also engaged in literary pursuits; affiliated with the Democratic Party; delegate to the State constitutional convention in 1865 and again in 1877; also a delegate to the Conservative convention at Macon in 1867; died in Columbus, Muscogee County, Ga., December 11, 1878; interment in Linwood Cemetery.

CHAPPELL, John Joel, a Representative from South Carolina; born on Little River, near Columbia, Fairfield District, S. C., where the family was on a visit, January 19, 1782; as an infant was taken by his parents to their home on the Congaree River, Richland District, S. C.; attended the common schools and was graduated from the law department of South Carolina College (now the University of South Carolina) at Columbia; was admitted to the bar in 1805 and commenced practice in Columbia, Richland County, S. C.; appointed adjutant of the Thirty-third South Carolina Regiment in 1805 and elected captain and then colonel of the same regiment in 1808; member of the State house of representatives in 1808; appointed trustee of South Carolina College in 1809; served in the War of 1812; elected as a State Rights War Democrat to the Thirteenth and Fourteenth Congresses (March 4, 1813–March 3, 1817); resumed the practice of law until 1837; director of the Columbia branch of the State Bank of South Carolina 1830–1858; moved to Lowndes County, Ala., and became a cotton planter; died in Lowndes County, Ala., May 23, 1871; interment in First Baptist Church Cemetery, Columbia, S. C.

CHARLES, William Barclay, a Representative from New York; born in Glasgow, Scotland, April 3, 1861; attended private schools and high schools in Stirling and Glasgow, Scotland; immigrated to the United States in 1884; spent two years ranching in Texas and Mexico; settled in Amsterdam, N. Y., in 1886 and engaged in textile manufacturing; member of the State assembly 1904–1906; director of the Amsterdam First National Bank; elected as a Republican to the Sixty-fourth Congress (March 4, 1915–March 3, 1917); was not a candidate for renomination in 1916; reengaged in the textile business until his retirement; presidential elector on the Republican ticket of Coolidge and Dawes in 1924; died in Amsterdam, N. Y., November 25, 1950; interment in Green Hill Cemetery.

CHARLTON, Robert Milledge, a Senator from Georgia; born in Savannah, Ga., January 19, 1807; studied law; was admitted to the bar and commenced practice in Savannah; member of the State house of representatives; United States district attorney; elected a judge of the superior court in 1832; resigned to devote himself to his profession; appointed to the United States Senate to fill the vacancy caused by the resignation of John Macpherson Berrien and served from May 31, 1852, to March 3, 1853; mayor of Savannah; died in Savannah, Chatham County, Ga., January 18, 1854; interment in Laurel Grove Cemetery.

CHASE, Dudley (uncle of Salmon Portland Chase and Dudley Chase Denison), a Senator from Vermont; born in Cornish, N. H., December 30, 1771; attended the common schools, and was graduated from Dartmouth College, Hanover, N. H., in 1791; studied law; was admitted to the bar in 1793 and practiced in Randolph, Vt.; prosecuting attorney for Orange County 1803–1812; member of the State house of representatives 1805–1812, and served as speaker 1808–1812; delegate to the State constitutional conventions in 1814 and 1822; elected as a Jeffersonian Democrat to the United States Senate and served from March 4, 1813, to November 3, 1817, when he resigned; chief justice of the supreme court of Vermont 1817–1821; again served in the State house of representatives in 1823 and 1824; elected to the United States Senate and served from March 4, 1825, to March 3, 1831; engaged in agricultural pursuits; died in Randolph Center, Vt., February 23, 1846; interment in Randolph Cemetery.

CHASE, George William, a Representative from New York; born in the town of Maryland, Otsego County, N. Y.; attended the common schools; engaged in agricultural pursuits; also engaged in mercantile and milling pursuits at Schenevus, Otsego County, N. Y.; elected as a Whig to the Thirty-third Congress (March 4, 1853–March 3, 1855); resumed his former agricultural and business pursuits; died in Chaseville, Maryland Township, N. Y., April 17, 1867; interment in the Chase vault in Schenevus Cemetery, Schenevus, N. Y.

CHASE, Jackson Burton, a Representative from Nebraska; born in Seward, Nebr., August 19, 1890; in early life lived in California; moved to Illinois and attended grade school in Chicago and Walnut; worked for the Burlington Railroad; graduated from high school in Omaha, Nebr., in 1907; employed by John Deere Plow Co. 1907–1910; attended the University of Nebraska 1910–1912; graduated from the University of Michigan Law School in 1913; was admitted to the bar the same year and commenced practice in Chicago, Ill.; during the First World War served with the Field Artillery, United States Army; assistant attorney general of Nebraska in 1921 and 1922; engaged in the practice of law in Omaha, Nebr., 1923–1942; legal adviser to Omaha Welfare Board in 1930 and 1931; alternate delegate to the Republican National Convention in 1932; member of the State house of representatives in 1933 and 1934; owner and manager of farmland in Nebraska and Iowa since 1934; during World War II served as a major, Judge Advocate General's Department, 1942–1945; chairman of Nebraska Liquor Control Commission in 1945 and 1946; appointed in July 1946 judge of the fourth judicial district court of Nebraska, elected in 1948 and reelected in 1952, and served until his resignation September 1, 1954, to become a candidate for Congress; elected as a Republican to the Eighty-fourth Congress and served from January 3, 1955, to January 3, 1957; was not a candidate for renomination in 1956; again elected judge of the fourth judicial district court of Nebraska 1956–1960; retired; is a resident of Omaha, Nebr.

CHASE, James Mitchell, a Representative from Pennsylvania; born in Glen Richey, Clearfield County, Pa., December 19, 1891; attended the public schools, the high school at Clearfield, Pa., and was graduated from the law department of Dickinson College, Carlisle, Pa., in 1916; was admitted to the bar in 1919 and commenced practice in Clearfield, Pa.; during the First World War enlisted in the Air Service and served with the American Expeditionary Forces 1917–1919; commander of the American Legion, Department of Pennsylvania, in 1924 and 1925; elected as a Republican to the Seventieth, Seventy-first, and Seventy-second Congresses (March 4, 1927–March 3, 1933); unsuccessful candidate for renomination in 1932; resumed the practice of law; died in Clearfield, Pa., January 1, 1945; interment in Hillcrest Cemetery.

CHASE, Jeremiah Townley, a Delegate from Maryland; born in Baltimore, Md., May 23, 1748; was a member of the committees of observation and correspondence in 1774; delegate to the Maryland constitutional convention of 1776; moved to Annapolis in 1779; member of the Governor's council 1780–1784 and 1786–1788; mayor of Annapolis in 1783; Member of the Continental Congress in 1783 and 1784; an Anti-Federalist member of the convention of ratification of the United States Constitution in 1788; judge of the general court in 1789, and chief justice of the court of appeals until his resignation in 1824; died in Annapolis, Anne Arundel County, Md., May 11, 1828; interment in the City Cemetery.

CHASE, Lucien Bonaparte, a Representative from Tennessee; born in Derby Line, Vt., December 5, 1817; moved to Dover, Tenn., about 1838 and taught school; studied law; was admitted to the bar and commenced practice in Charlotte, Dickson County, Tenn.; moved to Clarksville, Tenn., and resumed the practice of law; elected as a Democrat to the Twenty-ninth and Thirtieth Congresses (March 4, 1845–March 3, 1849); declined to be a candidate for reelection in 1848; moved to New York City in 1849; resumed the practice of law; died in Derby Line, Orleans County, Vt., December 4, 1864; interment in Greenwood Cemetery, Brooklyn, N. Y.

CHASE, Ray P., a Representative from Minnesota; born in Anoka County, Minn., March 12, 1880; attended the public schools; was graduated from the University of Minnesota at Minneapolis in 1903; attended the law department of the University of Minnesota in 1904, 1905, 1915, and 1916; engaged in the publishing and printing business at Anoka, Minn., 1904–1914; municipal judge of Anoka, Minn., 1911–1916; deputy State auditor and land commissioner of Minnesota 1916–1920; was graduated from the St. Paul (Minn.) College of Law in 1919; was admitted to the bar the same year but did not practice; State auditor and land commissioner of Minnesota 1921–1931; unsuccessful Republican candidate for Governor of Minnesota

in 1930; elected as a Republican to the Seventy-third Congress (March 4, 1933–January 3, 1935); unsuccessful candidate for renomination in 1934; practiced law, specializing in legal research, 1935–1943; member of the Minnesota Railroad and Warehouse Commission 1944–1948; died in Anoka, Minn., on September 18, 1948; interment in Forest Hill Cemetery.

CHASE, Salmon Portland (nephew of Dudley Chase and cousin of Dudley Chase Denison), a Senator from Ohio; born in Cornish, N. H., January 13, 1808; attended schools at Windsor, N. H., Worthington, Ohio, and the Cincinnati (Ohio) College; was graduated from Dartmouth College, Hanover, N. H., in 1826; taught school; studied law in Washington, D. C.; was admitted to the bar in 1829; commenced practice in Cincinnati, Ohio, in 1830; elected as a Whig to the Cincinnati City Council in 1840; identified himself in 1841 with the Liberty Party, and was a participant in its national conventions at Buffalo in 1843 and at Cincinnati in 1847; member of the Free-Soil National Convention at Buffalo in 1848, which nominated Van Buren for President; elected to the United States Senate by a fusion of Democrats and Free-Soilers and served from March 4, 1849, to March 3, 1855; elected Governor of Ohio in 1855 as a Free-Soil Democrat and reelected in 1857 as a Republican; elected to the United States Senate in 1860; took his seat March 4, 1861, but resigned two days later to become Secretary of the Treasury under President Lincoln, which position he held until July 1, 1864, when he resigned; member of the peace convention of 1861 held in Washington, D. C., in an effort to devise means to prevent the impending war; appointed Chief Justice of the Supreme Court December 6, 1864; member of the National Peace Convention in 1868; presided at the impeachment trial of President Johnson in 1868; died in New York City May 7, 1873; interment in Oak Hill Cemetery, Washington, D. C.; reinterment in Spring Grove Cemetery, Cincinnati, Ohio.

CHASE, Samuel, a Delegate from Maryland; born in Princess Anne, Somerset County, Md., April 17, 1741; was tutored privately and pursued an academic course; studied law; was admitted to the bar in 1761 and commenced practice in Annapolis, Md.; member of the General Assembly of Maryland 1764–1784; Member of the Continental Congress 1774–1778, 1784, and 1785; sent on a special mission to Canada in 1774 to induce the Canadians to join in the revolution against Great Britain; a signer of the Declaration of Independence; went to England in 1783 as agent for the State of Maryland to recover the stock in the Bank of England which had been purchased when the State was a colony of Great Britain; moved to Baltimore, Md., in 1786; judge of the Baltimore criminal court in 1788; appointed judge of the general court of Maryland in 1791; appointed by President Washington an Associate Justice of the United States Supreme Court in 1796; articles of impeachment were filed against him in 1804 on charges of malfeasance in office five years previous in his conduct of the trials of Fries and Callendar for sedition, and for a more recent address to a Maryland grand jury; tried by the Senate in 1805, he was acquitted of all charges on March 5, 1805; resumed his seat on the bench, and retained it until his death in Washington, D. C., on June 19, 1811; interment in Old St. Paul's Cemetery, Baltimore, Md.

CHASE, Samuel, a Representative from New York; born in Cooperstown, N. Y.; district attorney of Otsego County 1821–1829; elected as an Adams Democrat to the Twentieth Congress (March 4, 1827–March 3, 1829); died in Richfield, Otsego County, N. Y., August 3, 1838.

CHASTAIN, Elijah Webb, a Representative from Georgia; born near Pickens, Pickens County, S. C., September 25, 1813; moved with his parents to Habersham, Ga., in 1821; attended the common schools; served as captain and colonel in the Seminole Indian War; located on a farm in Union County, Ga.; served in the State senate 1840–1850; studied law; was admitted to the bar in 1849 and practiced in Blairsville, Union County, Ga.; elected as a Union Democrat to the Thirty-second and Thirty-third Congresses (March 4, 1851–March 3, 1855); delegate to the secession convention at Milledgeville, Ga., in 1860; during the Civil War served in the Confederate Army as lieutenant colonel of the First Georgia Regiment; State's attorney for the Western & Atlantic Railroad in 1860 and 1861; died near Dalton, Murray County, Ga., April 9, 1874; interment in the family cemetery near Morganton, Fannin County, Ga.

CHATHAM, Richard Thurmond, a Representative from North Carolina; born in Elkin, Surry County, N. C., August 16, 1896; educated in the public schools; attended the University of North Carolina at Chapel Hill in 1915 and 1916 and Yale University, New Haven, Conn., in 1916 and 1917; during the First World War served in the United States Navy from May 1917 until discharged as an ensign in June 1919; in July 1919 started working in the textile mills of Chatham Manufacturing Co. at Winston-Salem, N. C., and retired in 1955 as chairman of the board of directors; also owned and operated a farm near Elkin, N. C.; member of the Woolen Wage and Hour Board, Washington, D. C., in 1939; served as a member of the State Board of Conservation and Development and as county commissioner of Forsyth County; during World War II served in the Navy from February 14, 1942, to November 25, 1945, with combat duty in the Southwest Pacific; awarded the Bronze Star Medal, the Secretary of the Navy's Commendation Medal, American, European, and Asiatic Theater Ribbons with three battle stars, World War I and II Victory Ribbons, and the Royal Order of Nassau with Swords from the Dutch Government; trustee of the University of North Carolina and Woodbury Forest School, Orange, Va.; member of the board of directors of the Hugh Gwyn Chatham Memorial Hospital, Elkin, N. C., and the Methodist Children's Home, Winston-Salem, N. C.; unsuccessful for the Democratic nomination in 1946 to the Eightieth Congress; elected as a Democrat to the Eighty-first and to the three succeeding Congresses (January 3, 1949–January 3, 1957); unsuccessful candidate for renomination in 1956; died in Durham, N. C., February 5, 1957; interment in Salem Cemetery, Winston-Salem, N. C.

CHAVES, Jose Francisco, a Delegate from the Territory of New Mexico; born in Padillas, Mexico (now New Mexico), June 27, 1833; attended schools in St. Louis, Mo.; studied medicine at the New York College of Physicians and Surgeons; engaged in the stock-raising business in the Territory of New Mexico; president of the Territorial council for eight sessions; major of the First New Mexico Infantry in the Union Army during the Civil War; promoted to the rank of lieutenant colonel; took part in the Battle of Valverde in 1862; commanded the escort that accompanied the officials appointed to organize the Territory of Arizona in 1863; elected as a Republican to the Thirty-ninth Congress (March 4, 1865–March 3, 1867); successfully contested the election of Charles P. Clever to the Fortieth Congress; reelected to the Forty-first Congress and served from February 20, 1869, to March 3, 1871; unsuccessful candidate for reelection in 1870 to the Forty-second Congress; engaged in farming and stock raising; district attorney of the second judicial district 1875–1877; member and president of the State constitutional convention in 1889; State superintendent of public instruction from 1903 until his death; appointed State historian of New Mexico in 1903, but died before his term of service began; assassinated in Pinoswells (near Cedar Vale, Torrance County), N. Mex., November 26, 1904; interment in the United States National Cemetery at Santa Fe, N. Mex.; a bronze bust of Colonel Chaves was unveiled in the State Capitol Building at Santa Fe in March 1925.

CHAVEZ, Dennis, a Representative and a Senator from New Mexico; born in Los Chavez, Valencia County, N. Mex., April 8, 1888; attended the public schools; was graduated from the law department of Georgetown University, Washington, D. C., in 1920; served as clerk in the office of the Secretary of the United States Senate 1917–1920; was admitted to the bar in 1920 and commenced practice in Albuquerque, N. Mex.; member of the State house of representatives in 1923 and 1924; member of the Democratic National Committee 1933–1936; elected as a Democrat to the Seventy-second and Seventy-third Congresses (March 4, 1931–January 3, 1935); did not seek renomination in 1934, but was an unsuccessful candidate for United States Senator; appointed on May 11, 1935, and elected on November 3, 1936, to the United States Senate to fill the vacancy in the term ending January 3, 1941, caused by the death of Bronson M. Cutting; reelected in 1940, 1946, 1952, and again in 1958 for the term ending January 3, 1965.

CHEADLE, Joseph Bonaparte, a Representative from Indiana; born in Perrysville, Vermillion County, Ind., August 14, 1842; attended the common schools; entered Asbury (now De Pauw) University, Greencastle, Ind., but upon the organization of the Seventy-first Regiment, Indiana Volunteer Infantry, during the Civil War enlisted as a private in Company K and served until the close of the war; returned home and entered upon the study of law; was graduated from the Indianapolis Law College in 1867; was admitted to the bar and commenced practice in Newport, Ind.; continued in practice until 1873, when he entered upon newspaper work; elected as a Republican to the Fiftieth and Fifty-first Congresses (March 4, 1887–March 3, 1891); unsuccessful candidate for renomination in 1890, 1892, and 1894; affiliated with the Democratic Party in 1896; unsuccessful candidate for election in 1896 and 1898 on the Democratic and Populist tickets; editor of the American Standard in 1896; died in Frankfort, Clinton County, Ind., May 28, 1904; interment in Greenlawn Cemetery.

CHEATHAM, Henry Plummer, a Representative from North Carolina; born near Henderson, Granville (now Vance) County, N. C., December 27, 1857; was of the Negro race; attended the public schools, and was graduated from Shaw University, Raleigh, N. C., in 1883; principal in 1883 and 1884 of the State normal school for colored students at Plymouth, N. C.; moved to Henderson, N. C., and served as register of deeds of Vance County 1884–1888; studied law but did not practice; delegate to the State convention at Raleigh in 1892; delegate to the Republican National Conventions in 1892 and 1900; elected as a Republican to the Fifty-first and Fifty-second Congresses (March 4, 1889–March 3, 1893); unsuccessful candidate for reelection in 1892 to the Fifty-third Congress; recorder of deeds of the District of Columbia 1897–1901; moved to Oxford, N. C., in 1907; superintendent of the North Carolina Colored Orphanage at Oxford from 1907 until his death; one of the founders, incorporators, and directors of the same institution, founded in 1887; president of the Negro Association of North Carolina; also engaged in agricultural pursuits and lecturing; died in Oxford, N. C., November 29, 1935; interment in Harrisburg Cemetery.

CHEATHAM, Richard, a Representative from Tennessee; born in Springfield, Robertson County, Tenn., February 20, 1799; pursued preparatory studies; engaged in mercantile pursuits, stock raising, and operation of a cotton gin; member of the State house of representatives in 1833; member of the State constitutional convention which met at Nashville from May 19 to August 30, 1834; served as general in the State militia; unsuccessful candidate for election to the Twenty-second, Twenty-third, and Twenty-fourth Congresses; elected as a Whig to the Twenty-fifth Congress (March 4, 1837–March 3, 1839); unsuccessful candidate for reelection to the Twenty-sixth and Twenty-seventh Congresses; resumed his former pursuits; died while visiting at White's Creek Springs, near Springfield, Tenn., September 9, 1845; interment in Old City Cemetery.

CHELF, Frank Leslie, a Representative from Kentucky; born on a farm near Elizabethtown, Hardin County, Ky., September 22, 1907; attended the public schools, Elizabethtown High School, Centre College at Danville, Ky., and St. Mary's (Ky.) College; was graduated from the law school of Cumberland University, Lebanon, Tenn., in 1931; was admitted to the bar in 1931 and commenced practice in Lebanon, Ky.; attorney of Marion County, Ky., 1933–1944; took leave of absence from his official duties on August 1, 1942, to volunteer in the United States Army; commissioned a first lieutenant in the Air Corps and saw active service; served as chief code designator, Intelligence Division, Air Transport Command, and later as executive officer, Plans and Liaison Division, and as assistant chief of Air Staff Training; discharged on August 10, 1944, due to physical disability, with rank of major in the Air Corps; delegate to the Democratic National Convention at Philadelphia in 1936; elected as a Democrat to the Seventy-ninth and to the seven succeeding Congresses (January 3, 1945–January 3, 1961). *Reelected to the Eighty-seventh Congress.*

CHENEY, Person Colby, a Senator from New Hampshire; born in Holderness (now Ashland), N. H., February 25, 1828; attended academies in Peterborough and Hancock, N. H., and in Parsonfield, Maine; engaged in the manufacture of paper in Peterborough until 1866; member of the State house of representatives in 1854; during the Civil War was first lieutenant and regimental quartermaster in the Thirteenth Regiment, New Hampshire Volunteer Infantry, from September 12, 1862, until August 6, 1863, when he was forced to resign because of ill health; State railroad commissioner 1864–1867; moved to Manchester, N. H., in 1867 and engaged in business as a dealer in paper stock and continued the manufacture of paper at Goffstown, N. H.; also engaged in agricultural pursuits; elected mayor of Manchester in 1871; Governor of New Hampshire 1875–1877; appointed as a Republican to the United States Senate to fill the vacancy caused by the death of Austin F. Pike and served from November 24, 1886, to June 14, 1887, when a successor was elected and qualified; was not a candidate for election to fill the vacancy; resumed his former manufacturing pursuits; delegate to the Republican National Convention at Chicago in 1888; member of the Republican National Committee 1888–1900; appointed Envoy Extraordinary and Minister Plenipotentiary to Switzerland on December 13, 1892, and served until June 29, 1893; died in Dover, Strafford County, N. H., on June 19, 1901; interment in Pine Grove Cemetery, Manchester, N. H.

CHENOWETH, John Edgar, a Representative from Colorado; born in Trinidad, Las Animas County, Colo., August 17, 1897; attended the public and high schools, and the University of Colorado at Boulder; engaged in railroading and in the mercantile business 1916–1925; studied law; was admitted to the bar in 1925 and commenced practice in Trinidad in 1926; assistant district attorney for the third judicial district 1929–1933; county judge of Las Animas County, Colo., 1933–1941; member of the board of trustees of the Colorado Women's College at Denver; elected as a Republican to the Seventy-seventh and to the three succeeding Congresses (January 3, 1941–January 3, 1949); unsuccessful candidate for reelection in 1948 to the Eighty-first Congress; elected to the Eighty-second and to the four succeeding Congresses (January 3, 1951–January 3, 1961). *Reelected to the Eighty-seventh Congress.*

CHESNEY, Chester Anton, a Representative from Illinois; born in Chicago, Cook County, Ill., March 9, 1916; attended St. Hyacinth and Lane Technical High School; was graduated from De Paul University, Chicago, Ill., in 1938; played professional football with the Chicago Bears in 1939 and 1940; entered the United States Air Force in June 1941 as a private and was discharged as a major in 1946 with service in the Pacific and European Theaters; received honors for encouraging good will among American troops and the people of Calcutta, India, in 1945; assistant chief of special service, Veterans Administration, Hines, Ill., in 1946 and 1947; took graduate work at Northwestern University Graduate Commerce School in 1947; executive with Montgomery Ward & Co. in 1948 and 1949; elected as a Democrat to the Eighty-first Congress (January 3, 1949–January 3, 1951); unsuccessful candidate for reelection in 1950 to the Eighty-second Congress; director of Avondale Savings & Loan Association; resides in Chicago, Ill.

CHESNUT, James, Jr., a Senator from South Carolina; born near Camden, S. C., January 18, 1815; was graduated from the law department of Princeton College in 1837; was admitted to the bar the same year and commenced practice in Camden, S. C.; member of the State house of representatives 1842–1852; delegate to the southern convention at Nashville in 1850; served in the State senate 1854–1858; elected as a State Rights Democrat to the United States Senate to fill the vacancy caused by the death of Josiah J. Evans and served from December 3, 1858, until November 10, 1860, when he withdrew; delegate to the Confederate Provisional Congress in 1861; during the Civil War served as colonel in the Confederate Army, and became aide-de-camp on the staff of President Jefferson Davis in 1861; appointed brigadier general in 1864 and assigned to the command of a brigade on the coast of South Carolina; delegate to the Democratic National Convention at New York City in 1868, which nominated Horatio Seymour and Francis P. Blair; resumed the practice of his profession in Camden, Kershaw County, S. C., and died there February 1, 1885; interment in Knights Hill Cemetery, near Camden, S. C.

CHETWOOD, William, a Representative from New Jersey; born in Elizabeth, N. J., June 17, 1771; was graduated from Princeton College in 1792; studied law; was admitted to the bar in 1796 and commenced practice in Elizabeth, N. J.; served as prosecutor of the pleas for Essex County; member of the State Council of New Jersey; was a major of militia and served in the Whisky Rebellion of 1794 as aide-de-camp to Maj. Gen. Henry Lee; elected as a Jacksonian Democrat to the Twenty-fourth Congress to fill the vacancy caused by the resignation of Philemon Dickerson and served from December 5, 1836, to March 3, 1837; resumed the practice of law; died in Elizabeth, N. J., December 17, 1857; interment in Evergreen Cemetery.

CHEVES, Langdon, a Representative from South Carolina; born September 17, 1776, in Bulltown Fort, near Rocky River, Ninety Six District (now Abbeville County), S. C., where the settlers had taken refuge from the onslaught of the Cherokee Indians; received his early education at his home and Andrew Weed's School near Abbeville, S. C.; joined his father in Charleston, S. C., in 1786 and continued his schooling in that city; studied law; was admitted to the bar October 14, 1797, and commenced practice in Charleston; city alderman in 1802; member of the State house of representatives 1802–1810; presidential elector on the Madison ticket in 1808; elected attorney general of the State in 1808; elected as a Democrat to the Eleventh Congress to fill the vacancy caused by the resignation of Robert Marion, having previously been elected to the Twelfth Congress; reelected to the Thirteenth Congress, and served from December 31, 1810, to March 3, 1815; succeeded Henry Clay as Speaker during the second session of the Thirteenth Congress; served as chairman of the Committee on Ways and Means and of the Naval Committee during the War of 1812; declined to be a candidate for reelection in 1814 to the Fourteenth Congress and also the position of Secretary of the Treasury tendered by President Madison; resumed the practice of law; elected associate justice of law and appeal in December 1816; resigned in 1819; declined to accept an appointment as Associate Justice of the Supreme Court of the United States; elected president of the Bank of the United States March 6, 1819, and held this office until 1822, when he resigned; chief commissioner of claims under the treaty of Ghent; resided in Philadelphia and Washington 1819–1826 and in Lancaster, Pa., 1826–1829; returned to South Carolina in 1829; engaged extensively in the cultivation of rice in South Carolina and Georgia; tendered an appointment by the Governor of South Carolina to the United States Senate to fill the vacancy caused by the death of John C. Calhoun, but declined; delegate to the Southern convention at Nashville, Tenn., in 1850 and to the State convention at Columbia, S. C., in 1852; died in Columbia, S. C., June 26, 1857; interment in Magnolia Cemetery, Charleston, S. C.

CHICKERING, Charles Addison, a Representative from New York; born in Harrisburg, Lewis County, N. Y., November 26, 1843; attended the common schools and Lowville Academy and was for some time a teacher in that institution; engaged in business as a hardware merchant; served as school commissioner of Lewis County 1865–1875; member of the New York Assembly 1879–1881 and as clerk of the Assembly 1884–1890; served as chairman of the Lewis County Republican Committee; member of the Republican State committee, serving as secretary, and as a member of its executive committee; elected as a Republican to the Fifty-third and to the three succeeding Congresses and served from March 4, 1893, until his accidental death from injuries received in a fall from a window of the Grand Union Hotel in New York City while on a business trip February 13, 1900; interment in Riverside Cemetery, Copenhagen, Lewis County, N. Y.

CHILCOTT, George Miles, a Delegate from the Territory of Colorado and a Senator from Colorado; born near Cassville, Huntingdon County, Pa., January 2, 1828; moved with his parents to Jefferson County, Iowa, in 1844; studied medicine until 1850; sheriff of Jefferson County in 1853; moved to the Territory of Nebraska in 1856; member of the Territorial house of representatives in 1856; moved to the Territory of Colorado in 1859; member of the Territorial council in 1861 and 1862; studied law; was admitted to the bar in 1863; register of the United States land office 1863–1867; elected as a Republican a Delegate to the Fortieth Congress (March 4, 1867–March 3, 1869); member of the Territorial council 1872–1874; member of the State house of representatives in 1878; appointed to the United States Senate to fill the vacancy caused by the resignation of Henry M. Teller

and served from April 17, 1882, to January 27, 1883; died in St. Louis, Mo., March 6, 1891; interment in Masonic Cemetery, Pueblo, Colo.

CHILD, Thomas, Jr., a Representative from New York; born in Bakersfield, near St. Albans, Vt., March 22, 1818; attended the common schools and entered the University of Vermont at Burlington at the age of fourteen; member of the State constitutional convention in 1838; studied law; was admitted to the bar in September 1839 and commenced practice in East Berkshire, Vt.; justice of the peace in 1840; moved to New York City about 1848 and engaged in the distilling business; elected as a Democrat to the Thirty-fourth Congress on March 4, 1855, but never qualified or attended a session owing to illness, but by resolution adopted on March 3, 1857, the House resolved that his salary be computed and paid to him from August 18, 1856, to March 3, 1857, as "though he had been in regular attendance at the sittings of the House"; started for Washington to attend the third session of the Thirty-fourth Congress and reached Philadelphia, when he was compelled to return home because of his illness; moved to Port Richmond, Staten Island, N. Y., in 1857 and retired from active business; supervisor of the town of Northfield, N. Y., in 1865 and 1866; member of the State assembly in 1866; died in Port Richmond, Staten Island, N. Y., March 9, 1869; interment in Greenwood Cemetery, Brooklyn, N. Y.

CHILDS, Robert Andrew, a Representative from Illinois; born in Malone, Franklin County, N. Y., March 22, 1845; moved to Illinois with his parents, who settled near Belvidere, Boone County, in 1852; attended the common schools; during the Civil War enlisted in Gen. Stephen A. Hurlbut's company, which subsequently became a part of the Fifteenth Regiment, Illinois Volunteer Infantry, and served throughout the war; after his discharge from the Army entered school, and was graduated from the Illinois State Normal University in 1870; principal and superintendent of the public schools in Amboy 1871–1873; studied law; was admitted to the bar in 1872 and commenced practice in Belvidere, Ill.; settled in Hinsdale, a suburb of Chicago, in July 1873; member of the village board of trustees and president of the school board; presidential elector on the Republican ticket of Blaine and Logan in 1884; elected as a Republican to the Fifty-third Congress (March 4, 1893–March 3, 1895); was not a candidate for renomination in 1894; resumed the practice of law in Chicago, retaining his residence in Hinsdale, Ill.; died in Hinsdale, Ill., December 19, 1915; interment in Bronswood Cemetery.

CHILDS, Timothy, a Representative from New York; born in Pittsfield, Mass., in 1785; moved to Rochester, N. Y.; was graduated from Williams College, Williamstown, Mass., in 1811; studied law; was admitted to the bar and practiced in Rochester, N. Y.; prosecuting attorney of Monroe County 1821–1831; member of the State assembly in 1828 and again in 1833; elected to the Twenty-first Congress (March 4, 1829–March 3, 1831); resumed the practice of law; elected as a Whig to the Twenty-fourth and Twenty-fifth Congresses (March 4, 1835–March 3, 1839); elected to the Twenty-seventh Congress (March 4, 1841–March 3, 1843); died in Santa Cruz, N. Mex., November 8, 1847.

CHILTON, Horace (grandson of Thomas Chilton), a Senator from Texas; born near Tyler, Smith County, Tex., December 29, 1853; received private instructions; attended the local schools in Texas and Lynnland Institute, Glendale, Ky.; learned the printing business and at the age of eighteen published a tri-weekly newspaper in Tyler; studied law; was admitted to the bar in 1872 and commenced practice in Tyler, Tex.; delegate to the Democratic National Conventions in 1888 and 1896; appointed assistant attorney general of Texas by Governor Roberts in 1881 and served until 1883; appointed to the United States Senate to fill the vacancy caused by the resignation of John H. Reagan and served from June 10, 1891, to March 22, 1892, when a successor was elected; unsuccessful candidate for election to this vacancy; elected as a Democrat to the United States Senate and served from March 4, 1895, to March 3, 1901; was a candidate for reelection in 1900 but in April of that year withdrew; after a long illness he resumed the practice of law in Tyler and Beaumont, Tex.; moved to Dallas, Tex., in 1906 and continued the practice of law; died in Dallas, Tex., June 12, 1932; interment in Oakwood Cemetery, Tyler, Tex.

CHILTON, Samuel, a Representative from Virginia; born near Warrenton, Fauquier County, Va., September 7, 1804; moved to Missouri with his parents; attended private school; studied law; was admitted to the bar in 1826 and practiced in Warrenton; elected as a Whig to the Twenty-eighth Congress (March 4, 1843–March 3, 1845); resumed the practice of law in Warrenton, Va., and in Washington, D. C.; delegate to the State constitutional conventions in 1850 and 1851; appointed to defend John Brown at Harpers Ferry, but was dismissed by his client because he advocated that the defendant advance a plea of insanity as his defense; died in Warrenton, Va., January 14, 1867; interment in Warrenton Cemetery.

CHILTON, Thomas (grandfather of Horace Chilton), a Representative from Kentucky; born near Lancaster, Garrard County, Ky., July 30, 1798; attended the common schools in Paris, Ky.; studied law; was admitted to the bar and commenced practice in Owingsville, Bath County, Ky.; member of the State house of representatives in 1819; moved to Elizabethtown, Ky.; was a candidate for election to the Twentieth Congress to fill the vacancy caused by the death of William S. Young, but owing to an irregularity the votes of one county were eliminated and the credentials were issued to his opponent, John Calhoon; subsequently both candidates renounced all claim to the seat and petitioned the Governor for a new election; was duly elected to fill the resulting vacancy; reelected to the Twenty-first Congress and served from December 22, 1827, to March 3, 1831; unsuccessful candidate for reelection in 1830 to the Twenty-second Congress; resumed the practice of law in Elizabethtown; presidential elector in 1832 and voted for Clay and Sergeant; elected as a Whig to the Twenty-third Congress (March 4, 1833–March 3, 1835); declined to be a candidate for renomination in 1834; moved to Talladega, Ala., and resumed the practice of law; was pastor of a church in Hopkinsville, Ky.; president of the Alabama Baptist State Convention in 1841; abandoned the practice of law and became general agent of the Alabama convention; continued his ministerial duties in Montgomery, Greensboro, and Newbern, Ala.; moved to Houston, Tex., in 1851 and served as pastor of a Baptist church; died in Montgomery, Montgomery County, Tex., August 15, 1854; interment in the Old Cemetery.

CHILTON, William Edwin, a Senator from West Virginia; born in Colesmouth (now St. Albans), Kanawha County, W. Va. (then Virginia), March 17, 1858; attended public and private schools and was graduated from Shelton College, St. Albens, W. Va.; taught school; studied law; was admitted to the bar in 1880 and commenced practice in Charleston, W. Va., in 1882; also engaged in the newspaper publishing business; prosecuting attorney of Kanawha County in 1883; chairman of the Democratic State executive committee in 1892; appointed secretary of state by Governor MacCorkle and served from March 4, 1893, to March 3, 1897; colonel in the National Guard of West Virginia in 1897; elected as a Democrat to the United States Senate and served from March 4, 1911, until March 3, 1917; unsuccessfully contested the election of Howard Sutherland to the United States

Senate for the term commencing March 4, 1917; resumed the practice of law and the newspaper publishing business in Charleston, W. Va.; was an unsuccessful candidate for election to the United States Senate in 1924 and again in 1934; died in Charleston, W. Va., November 7, 1939; interment in Teay's Hill Cemetery, St. Albans, W. Va.

CHINDBLOM, Carl Richard, a Representative from Illinois; born in Chicago, Ill., December 21, 1870; attended the public schools; was graduated from Augustana College, Rock Island, Ill., in 1890 and from the Kent College of Law (Lake Forest University) at Chicago in 1898; teacher in Martin Luther College in Chicago 1893–1896; was admitted to the bar in 1900 and commenced the practice of law in Chicago, Ill.; delegate to the Republican State conventions in 1904, 1908, 1912, and 1916; attorney for the Illinois State Board of Health in 1905 and 1906; member of the Cook County Board of Commissioners 1906–1910; county attorney of Cook County 1912–1914; master in chancery of the circuit court of Cook County 1916–1918; elected as a Republican to the Sixty-sixth and to the six succeeding Congresses (March 4, 1919–March 3, 1933); unsuccessful candidate for renomination in 1932; resumed the practice of law in Chicago, Ill., until his death; referee in bankruptcy in the United States District Court for the Northern District of Illinois 1934–1942; died in Chicago, Ill., September 12, 1956; interment in Ridgewood Cemetery, Des Plaines, Ill.

CHINN, Joseph William, a Representative from Virginia; born at "Epping Forest," near Nuttsville, Lancaster County, Va., on November 16, 1798; was graduated from Union College, Schenectady, N. Y., in 1819; studied law at Needham, Va.; was admitted to the bar in 1821 and practiced in Lancaster County, Va.; member of the State house of delegates 1826–1828; served in the State senate 1829–1831; elected as a Democrat to the Twenty-second and Twenty-third Congresses (March 4, 1831–March 3, 1835); moved to Richmond, Va., where he resumed the practice of his profession; died on his estate, "Wilna," near Richmond, Va., on December 5, 1840; interment in the family burying ground at "Wilna."

CHINN, Thomas Withers (cousin of Robert Enoch Withers), a Representative from Louisiana; born near Cynthiana, Harrison County, Ky., November 22, 1791; attended the rural schools of his community and was also tutored by his father; served in the War of 1812 as a private in the First Rifles of the Kentucky Militia Volunteers from August 15, 1812, to October 14, 1812; clerked in a general store in Cynthiana until 1813; moved to Woodville, Miss., and engaged in mercantile pursuits; studied medicine and commenced the practice of his profession in St. Francisville, West Feliciana Parish, La., about 1817; studied law; was admitted to the bar in 1825 and commenced practice in St. Francisville; appointed judge of West Feliciana Parish in 1826; moved to Cypress Hall plantation, near Baton Rouge, in West Baton Rouge Parish, La., in 1831; continued the practice of law and also engaged in sugar-cane planting; elected as a Whig to the Twenty-sixth Congress (March 4, 1839–March 3, 1841); was not a candidate for renomination in 1840 to the Twenty-seventh Congress, preferring to devote his time to the cultivation of sugar cane on his Cypress Hall plantation; appointed by President Taylor as Minister to the Two Sicilies on June 5, 1849, but did not assume his duties because of ill health; returned to his plantation in West Baton Rouge Parish, La., and resumed sugarcane planting until his death there on May 22, 1852; interment at Grosse Tete, La., near Rosedale, La.

CHIPERFIELD, Burnett Mitchell (father of Robert Bruce Chiperfield), a Representative from Illinois; born in Dover,

Bureau County, Ill., June 14, 1870; attended the public schools of Illinois and Hamline University, St. Paul, Minn.; studied law; was admitted to the bar in 1891 and commenced practice at Canton, Ill.; member of the county, State, and American bar associations; prosecuting attorney of Fulton County, Ill., 1896–1900; member of the State house of representatives 1903–1913; secretary and trustee of the Western Illinois State Normal School at Macomb, Ill., 1904–1909; was connected with the Illinois National Guard for twenty years; organized a regiment for service in the Spanish-American War; unsuccessful candidate for election in 1912 to the Sixty-third Congress; elected as a Republican to the Sixty-fourth Congress (March 4, 1915–March 3, 1917); did not seek renomination, having become a candidate for the Republican nomination as United States Senator but was unsuccessful; during the First World War was assigned as division judge advocate of the Thirty-third Division at Camp Logan, Tex., in August 1917; served in France as judge advocate with his division; promoted to lieutenant colonel, Judge Advocate General's Department, October 25, 1918; transferred on December 10, 1918, to the Third Army Corps, with the Army of Occupation in Germany, and served as judge advocate of that corps; transferred on April 29, 1919, to the Thirty-third Division; honorably discharged at Camp Grant, Ill., June 4, 1919; was awarded a meritorious service citation certificate "for exceptionally meritorious and conspicuous services as division judge advocate of the Thirty-third Division," and also cited for gallantry in action; resumed the practice of law and also engaged in banking; delegate to the Republican National Conventions in 1920 and 1936; appointed lieutenant colonel in the Judge Advocate General's Department, Officers' Reserve Corps, February 5, 1921, and served until his retirement in 1934 with the rank of brigadier general; elected to the Seventy-first and Seventy-second Congresses (March 4, 1929–March 3, 1933); unsuccessful candidate for reelection in 1932 to the Seventy-third Congress and for election in 1934 to the Seventy-fourth Congress; reengaged in the practice of law in Canton, Ill., until his death there on June 24, 1940; interment in Greenwood Cemetery.

CHIPERFIELD, Robert Bruce (son of Burnett Mitchell Chiperfield), a Representative from Illinois; born in Canton, Fulton County, Ill., November 20, 1899; educated in the public schools of Canton, Ill., Washington, D. C., and at Phillips Exeter Academy, Exeter, N. H.; served as a private during the First World War; attended Knox College, Galesburg, Ill.; was graduated from Harvard College, Cambridge, Mass., in 1922 and from the law department of Boston University, Boston, Mass., in 1925; was admitted to the bar in 1925 and commenced practice in Canton, Ill.; city attorney of Canton, Ill.; elected as a Republican to the Seventy-sixth and to the ten succeeding Congresses (January 3, 1939–January 3, 1961). *Reelected to the Eighty-seventh Congress.*

CHIPMAN, Daniel (brother of Nathaniel Chipman), a Representative from Vermont; born in Salisbury, Conn., on October 22, 1765; was graduated from Dartmouth College, Hanover, N. H., in 1788; studied law; was admitted to the bar and practiced in Rutland, Vt., 1790–1794; was a member of the State constitutional conventions in 1793, 1814, 1836, 1843, and 1850; moved to Middlebury, Vt., in 1794; member of the State house of representatives 1798–1808, 1812–1814, 1818, and 1821, and served as speaker during the sessions of 1813 and 1814; professor of law at Middlebury College 1806–1818; member of the Governor's council in 1808; elected as a Federalist to the Fourteenth Congress and served from March 4, 1815, to May 5, 1816, when he resigned; appointed reporter of the superior court in 1824; moved to Ripton, Vt., in 1828 and continued the

practice of law; engaged in literary pursuits; died in Ripton, Addison County, Vt., April 23, 1850; interment in West Cemetery, Middlebury, Vt.

CHIPMAN, John Logan (grandson of Nathaniel Chipman), a Representative from Michigan; born in Detroit, Mich., on June 5, 1830; attended the public schools of that city and the University of Michigan at Ann Arbor 1843–1845; engaged in the Lake Superior region as explorer for the Montreal Mining Co. in 1846; assistant clerk of the State house of representatives in 1853; studied law; was admitted to the bar in 1854 and practiced in the Lake Superior region; returned to Detroit; city attorney of Detroit 1857–1860; member of the State house of representatives in 1865 and 1866; unsuccessful Democratic candidate for election in 1866 to the Fortieth Congress; attorney of the police board of Detroit 1867–1879; elected judge of the superior court of Detroit May 1, 1879; reelected in 1885 and served until 1887, when he resigned, having been elected to Congress; elected as a Democrat to the Fiftieth and to the three succeeding Congresses and served from March 4, 1887, until his death in Detroit, Mich., on August 17, 1893; interment in Elmwood Cemetery, Detroit, Mich.

CHIPMAN, John Smith, a Representative from Michigan; born in Shoreham, Addison County, Vt., on August 10, 1800; attended the rural schools and was graduated from Middlebury College in Vermont in 1823; studied law; was admitted to the bar and practiced in Addison County, Vt., and Essex County, N. Y.; moved to Centerville, Mich., in 1838, where he held several local offices; member of the State house of representatives in 1842; elected as a Democrat to the Twenty-ninth Congress (March 4, 1845–March 3, 1847); moved to Niles, Berrien County, Mich., and later, in 1850, to San Francisco, Calif., where he resumed the practice of law; moved to San Jose, Santa Clara County, Calif., in 1869 and lived in retirement until his death there on July 27, 1869; interment in Oak Hill Cemetery.

CHIPMAN, Nathaniel (brother of Daniel Chipman and grandfather of John Logan Chipman), a Senator from Vermont; born in Salisbury, Conn., November 15, 1752; prepared for college under private teacher; entered Yale College in 1773 and received his degree in 1777 while in the Army; served for a time as a lieutenant in the Revolutionary War; was at Valley Forge during the memorable winter of 1777–78 and fought at Monmouth; studied law; was admitted to the bar in 1779 and commenced practice in Tinmouth, Vt.; member of the State house of representatives in 1784 and 1785; elected as judge of the State supreme court in 1786 and chosen chief justice in 1789; appointed judge of the United States District Court in 1791 and served until 1794; again elected chief justice of the State supreme court in 1796; elected to the United States Senate to fill the vacancy caused by the resignation of Isaac Tichenor and served from October 17, 1797, until March 3, 1803; unsuccessful candidate for reelection; again a member of the State house of representatives 1806–1811; chief justice of Vermont 1813–1815; died in Tinmouth, Vt., January 15, 1843; interment in the Tinmouth Cemetery; the State of Vermont caused a monument to be erected to his memory and it was dedicated October 3, 1873.

CHIPMAN, Norton Parker, a Delegate from the District of Columbia; born in Milford Center, Union County, Ohio, March 7, 1836; attended the public schools; moved to Iowa in 1845 and entered Washington College; afterwards attended the law school in Cincinnati; returned to Washington, Iowa; was admitted to the bar and commenced practice in that city; entered the Union Army; commissioned major of the Second

Iowa Infantry September 23, 1861; colonel April 17, 1862; brevetted brigadier general of Volunteers March 13, 1865, "for meritorious services in the Bureau of Military Justice"; mustered out November 30, 1865; settled in Washington, D. C.; upon the establishment of a Territorial form of government for the District of Columbia was appointed secretary, and subsequently was elected as a Republican a Delegate to the Forty-second and Forty-third Congresses and served from April 21, 1871, until March 3, 1875; moved to California in 1876 and engaged in the lumber business; member of the California State Board of Trade and its president 1895–1906; appointed a commissioner of the supreme court of California in April 1897; appointed presiding justice of the district court of appeals for the third district in 1905 and was elected in November 1906 and served until his resignation on December 18, 1922; died in San Francisco, Calif., on February 1, 1924; interment in Cypress Lawn Cemetery.

CHITTENDEN, Martin, a Representative from Vermont; born in Salisbury, Conn., March 12, 1763; moved with his parents to Williston, Vt., in 1776; attended Mares School, and was graduated from Dartmouth College, Hanover, N. H., in 1789; engaged in agricultural and mercantile pursuits in Jericho, Vt.; appointed justice of the peace in October 1789; delegate to the State convention that ratified the Federal Constitution; aide-de-camp to Lieutenant Governor Olcott in 1790; clerk of the county court of Chittenden County 1790–1793; member of the State house of representatives 1790–1796; judge of the Chittenden County Court 1793–1795, and chief justice 1796–1813; captain of the First Militia in Jericho in 1793; lieutenant colonel commanding the First Regiment, Seventh Division, Vermont Militia, in 1794; brigadier general in 1799; major general 1799–1803; first collector of the census for Chittenden County; elected to the Eighth and to the four succeeding Congresses (March 4, 1803–March 3, 1813); Governor of Vermont in 1814 and 1815; judge of probate 1821–1823; died in Williston, Chittenden County, Vt., September 5, 1840; interment in the Old Cemetery.

CHITTENDEN, Simeon Baldwin, a Representative from New York; born in Guilford, New Haven County, Conn., March 29, 1814; attended Guilford Academy; engaged in mercantile pursuits in New Haven 1829–1842; moved to New York City and engaged in mercantile pursuits in 1842; unsuccessful candidate for election in 1866 to the Fortieth Congress; vice president of the New York City Chamber of Commerce 1867–1869; presidential elector on the Republican ticket of Grant and Wilson in 1872; elected as a Republican to the Forty-third Congress to fill the vacancy caused by the resignation of Stewart L. Woodford; reelected to the Forty-fourth, Forty-fifth, and Forty-sixth Congresses and served from November 3, 1874, to March 3, 1881; unsuccessful candidate for reelection in 1880 to the Forty-seventh Congress; retired from public life; died in Brooklyn, N. Y., on April 14, 1889; interment in Greenwood Cemetery.

CHITTENDEN, Thomas Cotton, a Representative from New York; born in Stockbridge, Berkshire County, Mass., on August 30, 1788; moved to Adams, Jefferson County, N. Y.; studied law; was admitted to the bar in 1813 and commenced practice in Adams, N. Y.; elected as a Whig to the Twenty-sixth and Twenty-seventh Congresses (March 4, 1839–March 3, 1843); appointed judge of Jefferson County in 1840, serving for five years; after entering upon his judicial duties, moved to Watertown, N. Y., the county seat; resumed the practice of law in Watertown; also engaged in banking; died in Watertown, N. Y., August 22, 1866; interment in Brookside Cemetery.

CHOATE, Rufus, a Representative and a Senator from Massachusetts; born in Essex, Mass., on October 1, 1799; was graduated from Dartmouth College, Hanover, N. H., in 1819; studied law; was admitted to the bar and commenced practice in Danvers in 1823; member of the State house of representatives in 1825; served in the State senate in 1826; moved to Salem in 1828; elected as a Whig to the Twenty-second and Twenty-third Congresses and served from March 4, 1831, to June 30, 1834, when he resigned; moved to Boston in 1834; elected to the United States Senate to fill the vacancy caused by the resignation of Daniel Webster and served from February 23, 1841, to March 3, 1845; retired from political life to devote his time to his profession; delegate to the Whig National Convention at Baltimore in 1852; member of the State constitutional convention in 1853; attorney general of Massachusetts in 1853; died in Halifax, Nova Scotia, July 13, 1859; interment in Mount Auburn Cemetery, Cambridge, Mass.

CHRISMAN, James Stone, a Representative from Kentucky; born in Monticello, Wayne County, Ky., September 14, 1818; attended the common schools; engaged in agricultural pursuits; studied law; was admitted to the bar in 1849 and commenced practice in Monticello, Wayne County, Ky.; unsuccessful candidate for election to the State house of representatives in 1845 and 1847 and for presidential elector in 1848 and 1852; delegate to the State constitutional convention in 1849; elected as a Democrat to the Thirty-third Congress (March 4, 1853–March 3, 1855); unsuccessfully contested the election of William C. Anderson to the Thirty-sixth Congress; Representative from Kentucky to the First and Second Confederate Congresses 1862–1865; member of the State house of representatives 1869–1871; resumed the practice of law in Monticello, Ky., where he died July 29, 1881; interment in a private cemetery on his farm.

CHRISTGAU, Victor, a Representative from Minnesota; born in Dexter Township, Mower County, near Austin, Minn., September 20, 1894; attended the rural schools and the high school at Austin; was graduated from the school of agriculture of the University of Minnesota at St. Paul in 1917 and from its college of agriculture in 1923; engaged in agricultural pursuits; during the First World War served overseas in the United States Army as a sergeant in the Thirty-third Regiment of Engineers; member of the State senate from 1927 until his resignation in 1929, having been elected to Congress; elected as a Republican to the Seventy-first and Seventy-second Congresses (March 4, 1929–March 3, 1933); unsuccessful candidate for renomination in 1932; resumed agricultural pursuits; appointed executive assistant to the director of production, Division of Agricultural Adjustment Administration, in June 1933, and director of the Production Division and assistant administrator in January 1934, serving until February 1935; was appointed State administrator of the Minnesota Works Progress Administration in June 1935 and served until June 1938; State director of the Minnesota division of employment and security at St. Paul, Minn., 1939–1954; president of the Interstate Conference Employment Security Agencies in 1947 and 1948; Director, Bureau of Old-Age and Survivors Insurance, Social Security Administration, since 1954; resides in Washington, D. C.

CHRISTIANCY, Isaac Peckham, a Senator from Michigan; born near Johnstown, Fulton County, N. Y., March 12, 1812; attended the common schools and Johnstown and Ovid Academies; taught school; studied law; moved to Monroe, Mich., in 1836; was admitted to the bar and practiced in Monroe 1838–1858; prosecuting attorney for Monroe County 1841–1846; delegate to the National Free Soil Convention at Buffalo in 1848;

Free Soil candidate for Governor in 1852; served in the State senate 1850–1852; was a prime mover in the organization of the Republican Party in 1854; delegate to the first Republican National Convention at Philadelphia in 1856; editor and proprietor of the Monroe Commercial in 1857; elected associate judge of the Michigan Supreme Court, with residence in Lansing, in 1857; reelected in 1865 and 1873, and served from January 1, 1858, until his resignation on February 27, 1875, having been elected to the United States Senate; served as chief justice from January 1872 to January 1, 1874; was elected to the United States Senate and served from March 4, 1875, to February 10, 1879, when he resigned owing to ill health; appointed United States Minister to Peru February 11, 1879, and served until August 2, 1881; returned to Lansing and resumed the practice of law; died in Lansing, Mich., September 8, 1890; interment in Woodlawn Cemetery, Monroe, Monroe County, Mich.

CHRISTIANSON, Theodore, a Representative from Minnesota; born on a farm near Lac qui Parle, Lac qui Parle County, Minn., September 12, 1883; attended the rural schools and Dawson (Minn.) High School; was graduated from the arts college of the University of Minnesota at Minneapolis in 1906 and from its law school in 1909; principal of the public school at Robbindale, Minn., 1906–1909; was admitted to the bar in 1909 and commenced practice in Dawson, Lac qui Parle County, Minn.; also owner and publisher of the Dawson Sentinel 1909–1925; president of the village council at Dawson, Minn., in 1910 and 1911; member of the State house of representatives 1915–1925; Governor of Minnesota 1925–1931; manufacturing executive in Minneapolis, Minn., in 1931 and 1932; elected as a Republican to the Seventy-third and Seventy-fourth Congresses (March 4, 1933–January 3, 1937); was not a candidate for renomination, but was an unsuccessful candidate for election to the United States Senate in 1936; served as secretary-manager of the National Association of Retail Grocers, Chicago, Ill., 1937–1939 and as public-relations counsel for the National Association of Retail Druggists, Chicago, Ill., 1939–1945; editor of the National Association of Retail Druggists Journal, Chicago, Ill., from 1945 until his death; died in Dawson, Minn., on December 9, 1948; interment in Sunset Memorial Cemetery, Minneapolis, Minn.

CHRISTIE, Gabriel, a Representative from Maryland; born in Perryman, Harford County, Md., in 1755; during the Revolutionary War was a member of a company of militia organized September 12, 1775, by the provincial convention held at Annapolis on July 26, 1775; member of the State house of delegates; appointed by Gov. William Smallwood one of the commissioners to "straighten and amend the post road from Havre de Grace to Baltimore town" by authority of the act of 1787; elected to the Third and Fourth Congresses (March 4, 1793–March 3, 1797); elected to the Sixth Congress (March 4, 1799–March 3, 1801); one of the commissioners of Havre de Grace in 1800 and 1801, and again in 1806; appointed collector of the port of Baltimore and served until his death in Baltimore, Md., April 1, 1808; interment in Spesutia Churchyard, Perryman, Harford County, Md.

CHRISTOPHER, George Henry, a Representative from Missouri; born on a farm in Bates County, near Butler, Mo., December 9, 1888; attended the public schools of Bates County, Mo.; was graduated from Hill's Business College, Sedalia, Mo., in 1907; lived on a farm in Calhoun County, Ill., and in Craig County, near Vinita, Okla.; owned and operated a nine hundred and seventy-five-acre farm in Bates County, Mo.; elected as a Democrat to the Eighty-first Congress (January 3, 1949–January 3, 1951); unsuccessful candidate for reelection in 1950 to the Eighty-second Congress; assistant to the director, Agricultural

Conservation Program, Department of Agriculture, from January 1951 to September 1952; elected to the Eighty-fourth, Eighty-fifth, and Eighty-sixth Congresses and served from January 3, 1955, until his death in Washington, D. C., January 23, 1959; interment in Oak Hill Cemetery, Butler, Mo.

CHRISTOPHERSON, Charles Andrew, a Representative from South Dakota; born in Amherst Township, Fillmore County, Minn., July 23, 1871; attended the public schools of Amherst Township, Minn., and Sioux Falls (S. Dak.) Business College and Normal School; moved to Sioux Falls, S. Dak., in 1890; studied law; was admitted to the bar in 1893 and commenced practice in Sioux Falls, S. Dak.; member of the board of education of Sioux Falls 1908–1918, serving as president 1911–1915; member of the board of directors of the Union Savings Association in 1912 and was subsequently elected president; member of the State house of representatives 1912–1916, serving as speaker during his last term; elected as a Republican to the Sixty-sixth and to the six succeeding Congresses (March 4, 1919–March 3, 1933); unsuccessful candidate for reelection in 1932 to the Seventy-third Congress and for election in 1934 to the Seventy-fourth Congress; reengaged in the practice of law in Sioux Falls, S. Dak., until September 1936, and was also interested in the banking business; delegate to the Republican State conventions at Pierre, S. Dak., in 1938, 1940, and 1942 and to the Republican National Convention at Chicago in 1944; served as State administrator of the War Savings staff in 1941–1943; executive manager of the State war finance committee; in 1944 became chairman of the Advisory Committee of the United States Savings Bond Division; died in Sioux Falls, S. Dak., November 2, 1951; interment in Woodlawn Cemetery.

CHUDOFF, Earl, a Representative from Pennsylvania; born in Philadelphia, Pa., November 16, 1907; attended the public schools; graduated from the Wharton School, University of Pennsylvania, in economics in 1929 and from the law school of the University of Pittsburgh in 1932; was admitted to the bar in 1933 and commenced the practice of law in Philadelphia, Pa.; building and loan examiner, Pennsylvania State Department of Banking, 1936–1939; served as chief boatswain's mate in the United States Coast Guard Reserve from December 1942 to September 1945; member of the State house of representatives 1941–1948; elected as a Democrat to the Eighty-first and to the four succeeding Congresses and served from January 3, 1949, until his resignation January 5, 1958, having been elected judge of the Philadelphia Court of Common Pleas No. 1 for the term ending in 1968; is a resident of Philadelphia, Pa.

CHURCH, Denver Samuel, a Representative from California; born in Folsom City, Sacramento County, Calif., December 11, 1862; attended the common schools; was graduated from Healdsburg (Calif.) College in 1885; studied law; was admitted to the bar in 1893 and commenced practice in Fresno, Fresno County, Calif.; district attorney of Fresno County 1907–1913; delegate to the Democratic National Convention at St. Louis in 1916; elected as a Democrat to the Sixty-third, Sixth-fourth, and Sixty-fifth Congresses (March 4, 1913–March 3, 1919); was not a candidate for renomination in 1918; resumed the practice of law in Fresno, Calif.; superior judge of Fresno County 1924–1930; elected to the Seventy-third Congress (March 4, 1933–January 3, 1935); was not a candidate for renomination in 1934; resumed the practice of law; died in Fresno, Calif., February 21, 1952; interment in Belmont Memorial Cemetery.

CHURCH, Frank Forrester, a Senator from Idaho; born in Boise, Ada County, Idaho, July 25, 1924; attended the public schools; was graduated from Stanford (Calif.) University in 1947

and from Stanford Law School in 1950; enlisted as a private in the United States Army on December 7, 1942; commissioned an Infantry officer in 1944 and assigned to the Military Intelligence; served in India, Burma, and China and was discharged July 22, 1946; was admitted to the bar in 1950 and commenced the practice of law in Boise, Idaho; selected as temporary chairman and keynoter of Democratic National Convention and also elected Chairman of Idaho delegation in 1960; elected as a Democrat to the United States Senate in 1956 for the term commencing January 3, 1957, and ending January 3, 1963.

CHURCH, Marguerite Stitt (widow of Ralph Edwin Church), a Representative from Illinois; born in New York City, N. Y., September 13, 1892; was graduated from Wellesley (Mass.) College in 1914 and from Columbia University, New York, N. Y., in 1917; teacher at Wellesley College in 1915; consulting psychologist of State Charities Aid Association in New York City during the First World War; lecturer and writer; president of National Alumni Association of Wellesley College 1940–1943; trustee of National College of Education, Evanston, Ill.; participant, through Presidential invitation, in the 1960 White House Conference on children and youth; elected as a Republican to the Eighty-second and to the four succeeding Congresses (January 3, 1951–January 3, 1961). *Reelected to the Eighty-seventh Congress.*

CHURCH, Ralph Edwin (husband of Marguerite Stitt Church), a Representative from Illinois; born on a farm near Catlin, Vermilion County, Ill., on May 5, 1883; attended the public schools; was graduated from the University of Michigan at Ann Arbor in 1907 and from the law department of Northwestern University, Evanston, Ill., in 1909; was admitted to the bar in 1909 and commenced practice in Chicago, Ill.; elected to the State house of representatives in 1916, resigning during the First World War to attend the Reserve Officers' Training Camp; again a member of the State house of representatives 1917–1932; lieutenant commander in the United States Naval Reserve 1938–1941; elected as a Republican to the Seventy-fourth, Seventy-fifth, and Seventy-sixth Congresses (January 3, 1935–January 3, 1941); was not a candidate for renomination in 1940, but was an unsuccessful candidate for the nomination for United States Senator; delegate to the Interparliamentary Conference at Oslo, Norway, in 1939; again elected to the Seventy-eighth and to the three succeeding Congresses and served from January 3, 1943, until his death March 21, 1950, while appearing before the Committee on Expenditures in the Executive Departments, in the House Office Building, Washington, D. C.; interment in Memorial Park, Skokie, Ill.

CHURCHILL, George Bosworth, a Representative from Massachusetts; born in Worcester, Mass., October 24, 1866; attended the grammar and high schools, and was graduated from Amherst (Mass.) College in 1889; taught in the Worcester High School until 1892; moved to Philadelphia and taught in the William Penn Charter School, and at the same time took a postgraduate course at the University of Pennsylvania 1892–1894; went to Europe and studied in the University of Strassburg, Germany, in 1894 and 1895, and then attended the University of Berlin, Germany, 1895–1897; returned to the United States and became assistant editor of the Cosmopolitan Magazine in 1897 and 1898; member of the faculty of Amherst College 1898–1925; moderator of Amherst 1905–1925; member of the State senate 1917–1919; delegate to the State constitutional conventions in 1917 and 1919; elected as a Republican to the Sixty-ninth Congress and served from March 4, 1925, until his death in Amherst, Mass., July 1, 1925; interment in Wildwood Cemetery.

CHURCHILL, John Charles, a Representative from New York; born in Mooers, Clinton County, N. Y., January 17, 1821; attended the Burr Seminary, Manchester, Vt., and was graduated from Middlebury College, Vermont, in 1843; teacher of languages in the Castleton Seminary, Vermont, and a tutor in Middlebury College; attended the Dane Law School of Harvard University; was admitted to the bar in 1847 and commenced practice in Oswego, Oswego County, N. Y., in 1848; member of the Oswego Board of Education 1853–1856; member of the board of supervisors of Oswego County in 1854 and 1855; prosecuting attorney 1857–1860; judge of Oswego County 1860–1864; appointed by Governor Morgan commissioner to superintend the draft for Oswego County in 1862 and 1863; elected as a Republican to the Fortieth and Forty-first Congresses (March 4, 1867–March 3, 1871); delegate to the Republican National Convention at Cincinnati in 1876; unsuccessful candidate for secretary of state of New York in 1877; presidential elector on the Republican ticket of Garfield and Arthur in 1880; again a member of the Oswego Board of Education, and president of the board in 1879 and 1880; appointed associate justice of the supreme court of New York to fill a vacancy January 17, 1881; was subsequently elected, and served until the expiration of his term by age limit December 31, 1891; died in Oswego, N. Y., June 4, 1905; interment in Riverside Cemetery.

CHURCHWELL, William Montgomery, a Representative from Tennessee; born near Knoxville, Knox County, Tenn., February 20, 1826; attended private schools and Emory and Henry College, Emory, Va., 1840–1843; studied law; was admitted to the bar and commenced practice in Knoxville; one of the judges for Knox County; elected as a Democrat to the Thirty-second and Thirty-third Congresses (March 4, 1851–March 3, 1855); provost marshal for the district of east Tennessee; during the administration of President Buchanan was sent on a secret mission to Mexico; during the Civil War served in the Confederate Army as colonel of the Fourth Tennessee Regiment; died in Knoxville, Tenn., August 18, 1862; interment in the Old Gray Cemetery.

CILLEY, Bradbury (uncle of Jonathan Cilley and Joseph Cilley), a Representative from New Hampshire; born in Nottingham, Rockingham County, N. H., on February 1, 1760; attended the common schools; engaged in agricultural pursuits; appointed by President John Adams as United States marshal for the district of New Hampshire on March 19, 1798, and served until May 3, 1802; elected as a Federalist to the Thirteenth and Fourteenth Congresses (March 4, 1813–March 3, 1817); colonel and aide on the staff of Governor Gillman 1814–1816; retired from public life; died in Nottingham, N. H., December 17, 1831; interment in the General Joseph Cilley Burying Ground in Nottingham Square.

CILLEY, Jonathan (nephew of Bradbury Cilley and brother of Joseph Cilley), a Representative from Maine; born in Nottingham, Rockingham County, N. H., July 2, 1802; attended Atkinson Academy, New Hampshire; was graduated from New Hampton Academy and later, in 1825, from Bowdoin College, Brunswick, Maine; studied law; was admitted to the bar in 1828 and commenced practice in Thomaston, Knox County, Maine; editor of the Thomaston Register 1829–1831; member of the State house of representatives 1831–1836 and served as speaker in 1835 and 1836; elected as a Jackson Democrat to the Twenty-fifth Congress and served from March 4, 1837, until February 24, 1838, when he was killed in a duel on the Marlboro Pike, near Washington, D. C., by William J. Graves, a Representative from Kentucky; interment in Cilley Cemetery, Thomaston, Maine.

CILLEY, Joseph (nephew of Bradbury Cilley and brother of Jonathan Cilley), a Senator from New Hampshire; born in Nottingham, Rockingham County, N. H., January 4, 1791; attended the common schools and was graduated from Atkinson Academy, New Hampshire; engaged in agricultural pursuits; commissioned ensign in the Eighteenth New Hampshire Regiment October 17, 1811, and in the Eleventh United States Infantry March 12, 1812; lieutenant in the Twenty-first Infantry March 17, 1814; resigned June 30, 1816, with brevet rank of captain; quartermaster of New Hampshire in 1817; division inspector in 1821; aide-de-camp to Gov. Benjamin Pierce in 1827; elected as a Democrat to the United States Senate to fill the vacancy caused by the resignation of Levi Woodbury and served from June 13, 1846, until March 3, 1847; unsuccessful candidate for reelection in 1846; retired to his farm in Nottingham, N. H., and died there September 12, 1887; interment in the General Joseph Cilley Burying Ground in Nottingham Square.

CITRON, William Michael, a Representative from Connecticut; born in New Haven, Conn., August 29, 1896; moved with his parents to Middletown, Middlesex County, Conn., in 1899; attended the grammar and high schools; was graduated from Wesleyan University, Middletown, Conn., in 1918 and from the law department of Harvard University, Cambridge, Mass., in 1921; during the First World War enlisted on July 5, 1918; was commissioned a second lieutenant of Field Artillery on September 16, 1918, and was in training at Plattsburgh, N. Y., and Camp Taylor, Ky., until discharged on December 14, 1918; was admitted to the bar in 1922 and commenced practice in Middletown, Conn.; delegate to all Democratic State conventions from 1926 to 1940; alternate to the Democratic National Conventions in 1932, 1936, and 1940; member of the State house of representatives 1927–1929 and 1931–1933, serving as minority leader during two sessions; unsuccessful candidate for election in 1928 to the Seventy-first Congress and in 1932 to the Seventy-third Congress; city corporation counsel 1928–1934; served as a member of the Connecticut Old Age Pension Commission in 1932 and 1933; clerk of the State senate 1933–1935; elected as a Democrat to the Seventy-fourth and Seventy-fifth Congresses (January 3, 1935–January 3, 1939); unsuccessful candidate for reelection in 1938 to the Seventy-sixth Congress; chairman of the Housing Authority of Middletown, Conn., 1940–1942; entered the military service of the United States as captain, Corps of Military Police, on July 16, 1942, and was subsequently promoted to major on April 16, 1943; served in Africa from October 1942 until retired for physical incapacity on March 3, 1944; resumed the practice of law; member of the Connecticut Veterans Reemployment and Advisory Commission in 1948 and 1949; unsuccessful candidate in 1952 for election to the Eighty-third Congress; is a resident of Middletown, Conn.

CLAFLIN, William, a Representative from Massachusetts; born in Milford, Mass., March 6, 1818; attended the public schools, and Brown University, Providence, R. I.; engaged in the shoe and leather business in St. Louis, Mo., and afterward in Boston, Mass.; member of the State house of representatives 1849–1852; moved to Newton, Mass., in 1855 and continued his business activity in Boston; served in the State senate in 1860 and 1861, being president of that body in the latter year; member of the Republican National Executive Committee 1864–1875, serving as chairman 1868–1872; Lieutenant Governor of Massachusetts 1866–1868; Governor of Massachusetts 1869–1871; elected as a Republican to the Forty-fifth and Forty-sixth Congresses (March 4, 1877–March 3, 1881); was not a candidate for renomination in 1880; resumed his former business pursuits; died in Newton, Middlesex County, Mass., January 5, 1905; interment in Newton Cemetery, Newtonville, Mass.

CLAGETT, Clifton, a Representative from New Hampshire; born in Portsmouth, N. H., December 3, 1762; studied law; was admitted to the bar and commenced practice in Litchfield in 1787; elected to the Eighth Congress (March 4, 1803–March 3, 1805); appointed a justice of the peace and quorum in 1808; appointed judge of probate for Hillsborough County in 1810 and served until his resignation in 1812, having been appointed to a judicial position; moved to Amherst in 1812; appointed a judge of the supreme court in 1812; member of the State house of representatives in 1816; elected to the Fifteenth and Sixteenth Congresses (March 4, 1817–March 3, 1821); appointed judge of probate August 5, 1823, and held the office until his death in Amherst, Hillsborough County, N. H., January 25, 1829.

CLAGETT, William Horace (uncle of Samuel Barrett Pettengill), a Delegate from the Territory of Montana; born in Upper Marlboro, Prince Georges County, Md., September 21, 1838; moved with his father to Keokuk, Iowa, in 1850; attended the public schools; studied law in Keokuk and later attended the law school at Albany, N. Y.; was admitted to the bar in 1858 and commenced practice in Keokuk; moved to Carson City, Nev., in 1861; moved to Humboldt, Nev., in 1862 and continued the practice of law; member of the Territorial house of representatives in 1862 and 1863 and of the State house of representatives in 1864 and 1865; practiced law in Virginia City, Nev., in 1865 and 1866; moved to Helena, Mont., and later to Deer Lodge, Mont., and practiced law until 1871; elected as a Republican a Delegate from Montana to the Forty-second Congress (March 4, 1871–March 3, 1873); unsuccessful candidate for reelection in 1872 to the Forty-third Congress; resumed the practice of law in Deer Lodge, Mont., and continued until 1877, when he moved to Denver, Colo., where he remained a short time, moving thence to Deadwood, in the Black Hills, and continued his law practice; left Deadwood in 1882 and engaged in mining in Butte, Mont.; shortly afterwards moved to Portland, Oreg., where he opened a law office, but soon moved to Coeur d'Alene, Idaho, and engaged in the practice of law and mining for several years; president of the constitutional convention of Idaho in 1889; unsuccessful candidate for election to the United States Senate from Idaho in 1891 and again in 1895, when he went East for a year or two on account of ill health; moved to Spokane, Wash., resumed the practice of law, and died there August 3, 1901; interment in Greenwood Cemetery.

CLAGUE, Frank, a Representative from Minnesota; born in Warrensville, Cuyahoga County, Ohio, July 13, 1865; attended the common schools; moved to Minnesota in 1881; attended the State normal school at Mankato 1882–1885; taught school at Springfield, Minn., 1886–1890; studied law; was admitted to the bar in 1891 and commenced practice in Lamberton, Redwood County, Minn., the same year; prosecuting attorney of Redwood County, Minn., 1895–1903; member of the State house of representatives from January 1, 1903, to January 1, 1907, serving as speaker in the 1905 session; served in the State senate from January 1, 1907, to December 31, 1915; judge of the ninth judicial district of Minnesota from January 1, 1919, to March 1, 1920, when he resigned; elected as a Republican to the Sixty-seventh and to the five succeeding Congresses (March 4, 1921–March 3, 1933); was not a candidate for renomination in 1932; resumed the practice of law and also engaged in agricultural pursuits until his retirement; died in Redwood Falls, Minn., March 25, 1952; interment in Redwood Falls Cemetery.

CLAIBORNE, James Robert, a Representative from Missouri; born in St. Louis, Mo., June 22, 1882; attended the public schools; was graduated from the law department of the University of Missouri at Columbia in 1907; was admitted to the bar the same year and commenced practice in St. Louis, Mo.; lecturer in the law school at St. Louis University for several years; unsuccessful candidate for judge of the circuit court of the eighth judicial district in 1924, elected as a Democrat to the Seventy-third and Seventy-fourth Congresses (March 4, 1933–January 3, 1937); unsuccessful candidate for renomination in 1936; engaged in the practice of law in St. Louis, Mo., until his death there, February 16, 1944; interment in Oak Grove Cemetery.

CLAIBORNE, John (son of Thomas Claiborne), a Representative from Virginia; born in Brunswick County, Va., in 1777; pursued academic studies; was graduated from the medical department of the University of Pennsylvania at Philadelphia in 1798 and practiced; elected to the Ninth and Tenth Congresses and served from March 4, 1805, until his death in Brunswick County, Va., on October 9, 1808; interment in the family burying ground of Parson Jarratt, Dinwiddie, Va.

CLAIBORNE, John Francis Hamtramck (nephew of William Charles Cole Claiborne and Nathaniel Herbert Claiborne and great-grandfather of Herbert Claiborne Pell, Jr.), a Representative from Mississippi; born in Natchez, Adams County, Miss., April 24, 1809; attended the public schools in Virginia; studied law; was admitted to the bar in 1825 and commenced practice at Natchez, Miss.; member of the State house of representatives 1830–1834; moved to Madison County, Miss.; elected as a Jackson Democrat to the Twenty-fourth Congress (March 4, 1835–March 3, 1837); presented credentials as a Member-elect to the Twenty-fifth Congress and served from July 18, 1837, until February 5, 1838, when the seat was declared vacant; engaged in newspaper work in Natchez, Miss.; moved to New Orleans, La., in 1844 and resumed newspaper interests; appointed United States timber agent for Louisiana and Mississippi in 1853; author of several historical works; returned to his estate, "Dumbarton," near Natchez, Miss., and died there on May 17, 1884; interment in Trinity Churchyard, Natchez, Miss.

CLAIBORNE, Nathaniel Herbert (brother of William Charles Cole Claiborne and uncle of John Francis Hamtramck Claiborne), a Representative from Virginia; born in Chesterfield, Sussex County, Va., November 14, 1777; attended a local academy; engaged in agricultural pursuits; member of the State house of delegates 1810–1812; served in the State senate 1821–1825; an executive councilor; elected as a Republican to the Nineteenth and to the five succeeding Congresses (March 4, 1825–March 3, 1837); unsuccessful candidate in 1836 for reelection to the Twenty-fifth Congress; resumed agricultural pursuits; died near Rocky Mount, Franklin County, Va., August 15, 1859; interment in Claibrook Family Cemetery, near Rocky Mount, Va.

CLAIBORNE, Thomas (father of John Claiborne and Thomas Claiborne), a Representative from Virginia; born in Brunswick County, Va., February 1, 1749; member of the State house of delegates 1783–1788; served as colonel in command of the Brunswick County Militia in 1789; sheriff of Brunswick County 1789–1792; member of the State senate 1790–1792; elected to the Third, Fourth, and Fifth Congresses (March 4, 1793–March 3, 1799); unsuccessful candidate for reelection to the Sixth Congress; again elected to the Seventh and Eighth Congresses (March 4, 1801–March 3, 1805); died on his estate in Brunswick County, Va., in 1812.

CLAIBORNE, Thomas (son of the preceding), a Representative from Tennessee; born near Petersburg, Brunswick County, Va., May 17, 1780; attended the common schools in Virginia; served as major on the staff of Gen. Andrew Jackson

in the Creek War; studied law; was admitted to the bar and commenced practice in Nashville, Tenn., in 1807; served for some years in the General Assembly of Tennessee; elected as a Democrat to the Fifteenth Congress (March 4, 1817–March 3, 1819); resumed the practice of law in Nashville, where he died January 7, 1856; interment in Nashville City Cemetery.

CLAIBORNE, William Charles Cole (brother of Nathaniel Herbert Claiborne and uncle of John Francis Hamtramck Claiborne), a Representative from Tennessee and a Senator from Louisiana; born in Sussex County, Va., in 1775; moved in early youth to New York City; studied law in Richmond, Va.; was admitted to the bar and commenced practice in Sullivan County, Tenn.; delegate to the State constitutional convention from Sullivan County in 1796; appointed judge of the superior court in 1796; elected as a Jeffersonian Democrat to the Fifth and Sixth Congresses (March 4, 1797–March 3, 1801, which service was rendered in contravention of the twenty-five years age requirement of the Constitution); appointed Governor of the Territory of Mississippi in 1801; appointed on October 31, 1803, one of the commissioners to take possession of Louisiana when purchased from France and served as Governor of the Territory of Orleans 1804–1812; Governor of Louisiana 1812–1816; elected as a Democrat from Louisiana to the United States Senate and served from March 4, 1817, until his death, before the assembling of Congress, in New Orleans, La., November 23, 1817; interment in Basin St. Louis Cemetery; reinterment in Metairie Cemetery.

CLANCY, John Michael, a Representative from New York; born in County Queens, Ireland, May 7, 1837; immigrated with his parents to the United States and settled in New York City; attended the public schools of Brooklyn; engaged in the real-estate business; served as an alderman of the city of Brooklyn 1868–1875; member of the State assembly 1878–1881; elected as a Democrat to the Fifty-first, Fifty-second, and Fifty-third Congresses (March 4, 1889–March 3, 1895); was not a candidate for renomination in 1894; resumed the real-estate business in New York City; unsuccessful candidate for election in 1896 to the Fifty-fifth Congress; died in Butte, Mont., while returning from a visit to Yellowstone Park, July 25, 1903; interment in Holy Cross Cemetery, Brooklyn, N. Y.

CLANCY, John Richard, a Representative from New York; born in Syracuse, N. Y., March 8, 1859; attended the public schools; engaged in the manufacture of theatrical rigging in 1885 and later in the manufacture of hardware specialties; vice president of the board of trustees of the New York State College of Forestry; member of the Central New York State Park Commission; director of Salt Spring National Bank and of the Onondaga Provident Loan Association; chairman of the executive committee, board of trustees, Onondaga County Savings Bank; elected as a Democrat to the Sixty-third Congress (March 4, 1913–March 3, 1915); unsuccessful candidate for reelection in 1914 to the Sixty-fourth Congress; resumed manufacturing interests in Syracuse, N. Y.; during the First World War served on the Governor's committee of public safety, on the committee on armories of the State, and had charge of stampings and forgings for five central New York counties under the War Production Board; died in Syracuse, N. Y., April 21, 1932; interment in St. Agnes Cemetery.

CLANCY, Robert Henry, a Representative from Michigan; born in Detroit, Mich., March 14, 1882; attended the public schools; was graduated from the literary department of the University of Michigan at Ann Arbor in 1907; later studied law there one year; reporter on Detroit newspapers for four years; secretary to Congressman Frank E. Doremus 1911–1913; secretary to Assistant Secretary of Commerce E. F. Sweet 1913–1917; United States customs appraiser for Michigan 1917–1922; during the First World War was manager of the War Trade Board at Detroit, chief inspector of purchases in Michigan for the Medical Corps of the War Department, and recruiting officer of the aviation division in Detroit, serving in all three positions without salary; field secretary of the University of Michigan Alumni 1920–1922; elected as a Democrat to the Sixty-eighth Congress (March 4, 1923–March 3, 1925); unsuccessful candidate for reelection in 1924 to the Sixty-ninth Congress; affiliated with the Republican Party in 1926; engaged in the real-estate business; elected as a Republican to the Seventieth, Seventy-first, and Seventy-second Congresses (March 4, 1927–March 3, 1933); unsuccessful candidate for reelection in 1932 to the Seventy-third Congress; engaged in executive capacity with a manufacturing company until his retirement; is a resident of Grosse Pointe Park, Mich.

CLAPP, Asa William Henry, a Representative from Maine; born in Portland, Maine, March 6, 1805; was graduated from the Norwich (Vt.) Military Academy in 1823; engaged as a merchant in foreign and domestic commerce at Portland; elected as a Democrat to the Thirtieth Congress (March 4, 1847–March 3, 1849); was not a candidate for renomination in 1848; delegate to the Democratic National Convention at Baltimore in 1848; resumed his former business pursuits; delegate at large to the convention at Baltimore that nominated Franklin Pierce for President in 1852; served as a director of the Maine General Hospital and of the Portland Public Library until his death in Portland, Maine, on March 22, 1891; interment in Evergreen Cemetery.

CLAPP, Moses Edwin, a Senator from Minnesota; born in Delphi, Carroll County, Ind., May 21, 1851; moved with his parents to Hudson, Wis., in 1857; attended the common schools; was graduated from the law department of the University of Wisconsin at Madison in 1873; was admitted to the bar in 1874 and commenced practice in Hudson, St. Croix County, Wis.; prosecuting attorney of St. Croix County, Wis., 1878–1880; moved to Fergus Falls, Minn., in 1881 and continued the practice of law; attorney general of Minnesota 1887–1893; moved to St. Paul, Minn., in 1891 and continued the practice of law; unsuccessful candidate for the Republican nomination for Governor of Minnesota in 1896; elected as a Republican to the United States Senate in 1901 to fill the vacancy caused by the death of Cushman K. Davis; reelected in 1905 and 1911 and served from January 23, 1901, to March 3, 1917; unsuccessful candidate for renomination in 1916; practiced law in Washington, D. C., 1918–1923; became vice president and general counsel of the North American Development Corporation in Washington, D. C., in 1923; died at his country home "Union Farm," near Accotink, Va., on March 6, 1929; interment in Fort Lincoln Cemetery, Washington, D. C.

CLARDY, John Daniel, a Representative from Kentucky; born in Smith County, Tenn., August 30, 1828; moved with his parents to Christian County, Ky., in 1831; attended the county schools, and was graduated from Georgetown (Ky.) College in 1848; taught school one year; studied medicine at the University of Louisville, Kentucky, for one year, and was graduated from the University of Pennsylvania at Philadelphia in 1851; practiced his profession for a number of years, and then abandoned it to devote his time to scientific agriculture and stock raising; delegate to the State constitutional convention in 1890; appointed as one of the State commis-

sioners to the Columbian Exposition at Chicago in 1893; elected as a Democrat to the Fifty-fourth and Fifty-fifth Congresses (March 4, 1895–March 3, 1899); was not a candidate for renomination in 1898; retired from public life; died at his home, "Oakland," near Hopkinsville, Christian County, Ky., on August 20, 1918; interment in Clardy's County Cemetery, Bells, Christian County, Ky.

CLARDY, Kit Francis, a Representative from Michigan; born in Butler, Bates County, Mo., June 17, 1892; moved with his family to Kansas City and then to a farm near Liberty, Mo., in 1907; attended schools in Butler, Kansas City, and Liberty, Mo., and the William Jewel College, Liberty, Mo.; was graduated from the University of Michigan Law School at Ann Arbor in 1925; admitted to the bar in 1925 and practiced in Ionia, Mich., 1925–1927; assistant attorney general, State of Michigan, 1927–1931; member and chairman of the Michigan Public Utilities Commission 1931–1934; reentered private practice of law in 1934; elected as a Republican to the Eighty-third Congress (January 3, 1953–January 3, 1955); unsuccessful candidate for reelection in 1954 to the Eighty-fourth Congress; in 1956 moved to Palos Verdes Estates, Calif., where he died September 5, 1961; interment in Forest Lawn Memorial Park, Glendale, Calif.

CLARDY, Martin Linn, a Representative from Missouri; born in Ste. Genevieve County, near Farmington, Mo., April 26, 1844; attended the St. Louis University and the University of Mississippi at Oxford; was graduated from the University of Virginia at Charlottesville; served in the Confederate Army until the close of the Civil War and retired with the rank of major; studied law; was admitted to the bar and commenced the practice of law in Farmington, St. Francois County, Mo.; elected as a Democrat to the Forty-sixth and to the four succeeding Congresses (March 4, 1879–March 3, 1889); was an unsuccessful candidate for reelection in 1888 to the Fifty-first Congress; served as a delegate at large to the Democratic National Convention at Chicago in 1884, which nominated Cleveland and Hendricks; resumed the practice of his profession in Farmington, Mo.; moved to St. Louis, Mo., in 1894, having been appointed general attorney for the Missouri Pacific and St. Louis & Iron Mountain Railway companies, and was elected vice president and general solicitor in 1909 and served until his death in St. Louis, Mo., on July 5, 1914; interment in Bellefontaine Cemetery.

CLARK, Abraham, a Delegate and a Representative from New Jersey; born near Elizabethtown (now Elizabeth), N. J., February 15, 1726; attended private schools; studied law but never practiced; sheriff of Essex County; member of the New Jersey Provincial Congress from May 23, 1775, to June 22, 1776, and was appointed assistant secretary October 9, 1775; Member of the Continental Congress from June 22, 1776, to December 1, 1778; reelected in May 1779 but declined; a signer of the Declaration of Independence; delegate to the State conventions of 1786 and 1787; member of the State general assembly in 1776 and 1783–1785; member of the legislative council in 1778; again a Member of the Continental Congress from December 25, 1779, to November 5, 1783, and from November 2, 1787, to March 4, 1789; elected to the Second and Third Congresses and served from March 4, 1791, until his death in Rahway, N. J., on September 15, 1794; interment in Rahway Cemetery.

CLARK, Alvah Augustus (cousin of James Nelson Pidcock), a Representative from New Jersey; born in Lebanon, Hunterdon County, N. J., September 13, 1840; attended public and private schools; studied law; was admitted to the bar in 1863 and commenced practice in New Germantown, N. J.; licensed as counselor in 1867; moved to Somerville, Somerset County, in 1867 and continued the practice of law; elected as a Democrat to the Forty-fifth and Forty-sixth Congresses (March 4, 1877–March 3, 1881); was not a candidate for renomination in 1880; resumed the practice of law; appointed postmaster at Somerville on May 26, 1896, and served until his successor was appointed on June 15, 1899; again resumed the practice of law until his death in Somerville, N. J., on December 27, 1912; interment in Somerville Cemetery.

CLARK, Ambrose Williams, a Representative from New York; born near Cooperstown, N. Y., on February 19, 1810; attended the public schools; publisher of the Otsego Journal 1831–1836, of the Northern Journal in Lewis County 1836–1844, and of the Northern New York Journal at Watertown 1844–1860; surrogate for five years; elected as a Republican to the Thirty-seventh and Thirty-eighth Congresses (March 4, 1861–March 3, 1865); appointed consul at Valparaiso by President Lincoln and served from 1865 to 1869; acted as Chargé d'Affaires in Chile in the absence of the Minister in 1869; died in Watertown, N. Y., October 13, 1887; interment in Brookside Cemetery.

CLARK, Amos, Jr., a Representative from New Jersey; born in Brooklyn, N. Y., November 8, 1828; engaged in business in New York City, with residence in Elizabeth, where he was largely interested in real estate; member of the city council of Elizabeth in 1865 and 1866; served in the State senate 1866–1869; presidential elector on the Republican ticket of Grant and Wilson in 1872; elected as a Republican to the Forty-third Congress (March 4, 1873–March 3, 1875); unsuccessful candidate for reelection in 1874 to the Forty-fourth Congress; retired to his residence in Norfolk County, Mass., but retained business interests in Elizabeth, N. J.; died in Boston, Mass., October 31, 1912; interment in Evergreen Cemetery, Elizabeth, N. J.

CLARK, Charles Benjamin, a Representative from Wisconsin; born in Theresa, Jefferson County, N. Y., August 24, 1844; attended the common schools; moved to Wisconsin in 1855 with his widowed mother, who settled in Neenah, Winnebago County; enlisted in Company I, Twenty-first Regiment, Wisconsin Volunteer Infantry, at its organization, and served with the same during the Civil War; engaged in mercantile pursuits, banking, and the manufacture of paper; mayor of Neenah 1880–1883; member of the city council of Neenah 1883–1885; member of the State assembly in 1885; elected as a Republican to the Fiftieth and Fifty-first Congresses (March 4, 1887–March 3, 1891); unsuccessful candidate for reelection in 1890 to the Fifty-second Congress; died in Watertown, Jefferson County, N. Y., while on a visit to his old home, September 10, 1891; interment in Oak Hill Cemetery, Neenah, Wis.

CLARK, Charles Nelson, a Representative from Missouri; born in Cortland County, N. Y., on August 21, 1827; attended Hamilton College, Clinton, N. Y.; moved to Illinois in 1859; when the Civil War broke out he assisted in raising a company of cavalry, which was made Company G, Third Illinois Cavalry, August 6, 1861, and went directly into service; became disabled and left the Army in 1863; settled in Hannibal, Marion County, Mo., in April 1865; became interested in the Mississippi River bottom lands in Illinois and undertook their reclamation; elected as a Republican to the Fifty-fourth Congress (March 4, 1895–March 3, 1897); engaged in agricultural pursuits; died in Hannibal, Mo., October 4, 1902; interment in Wauseon Cemetery, Wauseon, Fulton County, Ohio.

CLARK, Christopher Henderson (brother of James Clark and uncle of John Bullock Clark), a Representative from Virginia; born in Albemarle County, Va., in 1767; attended Washington College (now Washington and Lee University), Lexington, Va.; studied law in the office of Patrick Henry; was admitted to the bar in 1788 and commenced practice in New London (now Bedford Springs), Va.; member of the State house of delegates in 1790; elected as a Jeffersonian Democrat to the Eighth Congress to fill the vacancy caused by the death of John Trigg; reelected to the Ninth Congress and served from November 5, 1804, to July 1, 1806, when he resigned; resumed the practice of law; died near New London, Va., November 21, 1828; interment in a private cemetery at Old Lawyers Station, near Lynchburg, Va.

CLARK, Clarence Don, a Representative and a Senator from Wyoming; born in Sandy Creek, Oswego County, N. Y., April 16, 1851; attended the common schools and the University of Iowa at Iowa City; studied law; was admitted to the bar in 1874; taught school and practiced law in Manchester, Delaware County, Iowa, until 1881, when he moved to Evanston, Wyo., and continued the practice of law; prosecuting attorney of Uinta County 1882–1884; delegate to the Republican National Conventions in 1888, 1900, 1904, 1908, and 1912; delegate to the State constitutional convention in 1889; upon the admission of Wyoming as a State into the Union was elected as a Republican to the Fifty-first Congress; reelected to the Fifty-second Congress and served from December 1, 1890, to March 3, 1893; unsuccessful candidate for reelection in 1892 to the Fifty-third Congress; elected to the United States Senate in 1895 to fill the vacancy in the term beginning March 4, 1893, caused by the failure of the legislature to elect in 1892–1893; reelected in 1899, 1905, and again in 1911 and served from January 23, 1895, until March 3, 1917; unsuccessful candidate for reelection in 1916; resumed the practice of law in Washington, D. C.; appointed on July 16, 1919, a member of the International Joint Commission, created by treaty, to adjust disputes regarding the use of boundary waters between the United States and Canada, and for other purposes; on April 15, 1923, was elected chairman of the United States section of the commission and served until his resignation on April 25, 1929; retired from active pursuits and resided in Evanston, Wyo., until his death there on November 18, 1930; interment in the Masonic Cemetery.

CLARK, Daniel, a Delegate from the Territory of Orleans; born in Sligo, Ireland, about 1766; educated at Eton and other colleges in England; immigrated to the United States in 1786 and settled in New Orleans, La.; engaged in land speculation and banking; appointed a member of the first legislative council for the Territory of Orleans, but declined; elected to the Ninth and Tenth Congresses and served from December 1, 1806, to March 3, 1809; was an unsuccessful candidate for renomination in 1808; died in New Orleans, La., August 16, 1813; interred in St. Louis Cemetery No. 1.

CLARK, Daniel, a Senator from New Hampshire; born in Stratham, N. H., October 24, 1809; attended the common schools, Hampton Academy, and Union College, Schenectady, N. Y.; was graduated from Dartmouth College, Hanover, N. H., in 1834; studied law; was admitted to the bar in 1837 and commenced practice in Epping, N. H.; moved to Manchester in 1839; member of the State house of representatives in 1842, 1843, 1846, 1854, and 1855; elected as a Republican to the United States Senate to fill the vacancy caused by the death of James Bell; reelected in 1861, and served from June 27, 1857, to July 27, 1866, when he resigned; President pro tempore of the Senate February 9 and April 26, 1864; United

States district judge from July 27, 1866, until his death; president of the New Hampshire constitutional convention in 1876; died in Manchester, N. H., on January 2, 1891; interment in Valley Cemetery.

CLARK, David Worth, a Representative and a Senator from Idaho; born in Idaho Falls, Bonneville County, Idaho, April 2, 1902; attended the public schools; was graduated from the University of Notre Dame, South Bend, Ind., in 1922 and from the law department of Harvard University, Cambridge, Mass., in 1925; was admitted to the bar in 1925 and commenced practice in Pocatello, Idaho; assistant attorney general of Idaho 1933–1935; elected as a Democrat to the Seventy-fourth and Seventy-fifth Congresses (January 3, 1935–January 3, 1939); did not seek renomination in 1938 to the Seventy-sixth Congress, having become a candidate for United States Senator; elected to the United States Senate in 1938 and served from January 3, 1939, to January 3, 1945; unsuccessful candidate for renomination in 1944; resumed the practice of law in Boise, Idaho, and Washington, D. C.; moved to Los Angeles, Calif., in November 1954; held financial interests in radio stations in Van Nuys, Calif., San Francisco, Calif., Honolulu, T. H., and a bank in Las Vegas, Nev.; died in Los Angeles, Calif., June 19, 1955; interment in Holy Cross Cemetery, Culver City, Calif.

CLARK, Ezra, Jr., a Representative from Connecticut; born in Brattleboro, Vt., September 12, 1813; moved with his parents to Hartford, Conn., in 1819; attended the public schools; engaged in business as an iron merchant; member of the common council and the board of aldermen; president of the National Screw Co. of Hartford, later consolidated with the American Screw Co. of Providence, R. I.; director in the Exchange Bank; president of the Spring Grove Cemetery Association; judge of the municipal court; elected as the candidate of the American Party and the Republican Party to the Thirty-fourth and Thirty-fifth Congresses (March 4, 1855–March 3, 1859); unsuccessful candidate for reelection to the Thirty-sixth Congress; president of the Hartford Board of Water Commissioners 1882–1895; president of the Young Men's Institute of Hartford for many years; died in Hartford, Conn., September 26, 1896; interment in Spring Grove Cemetery.

CLARK, Frank, a Representative from Florida; born in Eufaula, Barbour County, Ala., March 28, 1860; attended the common schools of Alabama and Georgia; studied law; was admitted to the bar in 1881 and commenced practice in Newnan, Coweta County, Ga.; moved to Florida in 1884 and settled in Polk County; city attorney of Bartow, Fla., in 1885 and 1886; member of the State house of representatives 1889–1891 and in 1899; assistant United States attorney in 1893; United States attorney for the southern district of Florida 1894–1897; moved to Jacksonville in 1895 and continued the practice of law; delegate to Democratic State conventions in 1888, 1890, 1892, 1896, and 1900; chairman of the Democratic State committee in 1900; delegate to the Democratic National Convention at San Francisco in 1920 and chairman of the delegation; elected as a Democrat to the Fifty-ninth and to the nine succeeding Congresses (March 4, 1905–March 3, 1925); unsuccessful candidate for renomination in 1924; resumed the practice of law in Miami, Fla.; appointed by President Coolidge as a Democratic member of the United States Tariff Commission, serving from April 12, 1928, to September 16, 1930; resumed the practice of law in Washington, D. C.; served as attorney for the Bureau of Internal Revenue, Treasury Department, from November 16, 1933, until his death in Washington, D. C., April 14, 1936; interment in Wildwood Cemetery, Bartow, Fla.

CLARK, Frank Monroe, a Representative from Pennsylvania; born in Bessemer, Lawrence County, Pa., December 24, 1915; attended the public schools and graduated from Bessemer High School; also attended Pittsburgh Institute of Aeronautics; during World War II enlisted in the United States Air Force in 1942 and served in Europe as a flight officer until discharged in 1945; while still in the service was appointed chief of police of Bessemer, serving in that capacity until November 1954; unsuccessful candidate for election to the Eighty-third Congress in 1952; delegate to the North Atlantic Treaty Organization Conference in 1956, to the Interparliamentary Conference in Germany in 1957, to the Christian Leadership for Peace Conference at The Hague in 1958, and to International Roads Conference in 1959; elected as a Democrat to the Eighty-fourth, Eighty-fifth, and Eighty-sixth Congresses (January 3, 1955–January 3, 1961). *Reelected to the Eighty-seventh Congress.*

CLARK, Franklin, a Representative from Maine; born in Wiscasset, Lincoln County, Maine, August 2, 1801; attended the common schools; engaged in the lumber and shipping business in Wiscasset; member of the State senate in 1847; elected as a Democrat to the Thirtieth Congress (March 4, 1847–March 3, 1849); engaged in the manufacture of lumber; an executive councilor in 1855; died in Brooklyn, N. Y., on August 24, 1874; interment in Greenwood Cemetery.

CLARK, Henry Alden, a Representative from Pennsylvania; born in Harborcreek Township, Erie County, Pa., January 7, 1850; attended the common schools and the Erie Academy in 1864, the State normal school, Edinboro, Pa., in 1865 and 1866, and Willoughby Collegiate Institute, Willoughby, Ohio, in 1866 and 1867; taught school; was graduated from the Erie Central High School in 1870, from Harvard University in 1874, and from Harvard Law School in 1877; was admitted to the bar in Fall River, Mass., in March 1878; subsequently associated with the Edison electric light interests in New York; moved to Erie, Pa., in 1882, continuing with the Edison corporation until 1887; was admitted to the Pennsylvania bar May 9, 1884; member of the common council of Erie in 1888; bought and edited the Erie Gazette 1890–1892; chairman of the Republican city and county committees in 1890; delegate to several Republican State conventions; trustee of the Erie Academy in 1893; president of the Erie County Historical Society; director of the Art Club of Erie; city solicitor of Erie from July 11, 1896, until April 30, 1899; served in the State senate in 1911, 1913, and 1915; elected as a Republican to the Sixty-fifth Congress (March 4, 1917–March 3, 1919); was not a candidate for renomination in 1918 to the Sixty-sixth Congress; resumed the practice of his profession; appointed by Governor William C. Sproul presiding judge of the orphans' court for Erie County May 24, 1921, and was elected on November 8, 1921, for a full term of ten years, at the end of which he retired from active professional and political life; died in Erie, Pa., on February 15, 1944; interment in Erie Cemetery.

CLARK, Henry Selby, a Representative from North Carolina; born near Leechville, Beaufort County, N. C., September 9, 1809; attended the common schools, and was graduated from the University of North Carolina at Chapel Hill in 1828; studied law; was admitted to the bar and commenced practice in Washington, Beaufort County, N. C.; member of the State house of commons 1834–1836; solicitor for the district in 1842; elected as a Democrat to the Twenty-ninth Congress (March 4, 1845–March 3, 1847); moved to Greenville, Pitt County, N. C., and resumed the practice of law; died in Greenville, N. C., January 8, 1869; interment at his country home near Leechville, N. C.

CLARK, Horace Francis, a Representative from New York; born in Southbury, Conn., November 29, 1815; was graduated from Williams College, Williamstown, Mass., in 1833; studied law; was admitted to the bar and commenced practice in New York City in 1837, where he was prominent in financial, political, and railroad circles; elected as a Democrat to the Thirty-fifth and Thirty-sixth Congresses (March 4, 1857–March 3, 1861); became director of the New York & Harlem Railroad, and subsequently was president of the Union Pacific, the Michigan Southern, and many other railroads; active manager of the Western Union Telegraph Co. and president of the Union Trust Co.; died in New York City on June 19, 1873; interment in Woodlawn Cemetery.

CLARK, James (brother of Christopher Henderson Clark and uncle of John Bullock Clark), a Representative from Kentucky; born near the Peaks of Otter in Bedford County, Va., January 16, 1770; moved with his parents to Clark County, Ky., in 1794; was educated by private tutors; attended Pisgah Academy, Woodford County, Ky.; studied law; was admitted to the bar and commenced practice in Winchester, Ky., in 1797; member of the State house of representatives in 1807 and 1808; appointed judge of the court of appeals in 1810; elected as a Clay Democrat to the Thirteenth and Fourteenth Congresses and served from March 4, 1813, until his resignation in 1816; judge of the circuit court 1817–1824; elected to the Nineteenth Congress to fill the vacancy caused by the resignation of Henry Clay; reelected to the Twentieth and Twenty-first Congresses and served from August 1, 1825, to March 3, 1831; member of the State senate 1831–1835; elected, as a Whig, Governor of Kentucky in 1836, and served until his death in Frankfort, Ky., September 27, 1839; interment in the private burial ground of the old Clark home at Winchester, Clark County, Ky.

CLARK, James Beauchamp (Champ) (father of Joel Bennett Clark), a Representative from Missouri; born near Lawrenceburg, Anderson County, Ky., March 7, 1850; attended the common schools and Kentucky University at Lexington; was graduated from Bethany (W. Va.) College in 1873 and from Cincinnati Law School in 1875; president of Marshall College, Huntington, W. Va., in 1873 and 1874; admitted to the bar in 1875; edited a country newspaper and practiced law; moved to Bowling Green, Pike County, Mo., in 1876; city attorney of Louisiana, Mo., and Bowling Green, Mo., 1878–1881; presidential elector on the Democratic ticket of Hancock and English in 1880; deputy prosecuting attorney and prosecuting attorney of Pike County 1885–1889; member of the State house of representatives in 1889 and 1891; delegate to the Trans-Mississippi Congress at Denver in May 1891; elected as a Democrat to the Fifty-third Congress (March 4, 1893–March 3, 1895); unsuccessful candidate for reelection in 1894 to the Fifty-fourth Congress; elected to the Fifty-fifth and to the eleven succeeding Congresses and served from March 4, 1897, until his death; unsuccessful candidate for reelection in 1920 to the Sixty-seventh Congress; Democratic minority leader of the House of Representatives in the Sixtieth and Sixty-first Congresses and served as Speaker of the House of Representatives in the Sixty-second, Sixty-third, Sixty-fourth, and Sixty-fifth Congresses; chairman of the Democratic National Convention at St. Louis in 1904; was the leading candidate in the Baltimore Democratic National Convention of 1912 for the Presidential nomination on twenty-nine ballots, and had a clear majority on eight; died in Washington, D. C., on March 2, 1921; funeral services were held in the Hall of the House of Representatives; interment in City Cemetery, Bowling Green, Mo., where a monument was erected to his memory by the State.

CLARK, James West, a Representative from North Carolina; born in Bertie County, N. C., October 15, 1779; was graduated from Princeton College in 1797; member of the State house of commons in 1802, 1803, and 1811; presidential elector on the Madison ticket in 1812; member of the State senate 1812–1814; elected as a Democrat to the Fourteenth Congress (March 4, 1815–March 3, 1817); appointed chief clerk of the Navy Department by Secretary Branch and served from 1829 to 1831; died in Tarboro, Edgecomb County, N. C., December 20, 1843.

CLARK, Jerome Bayard, a Representative from North Carolina; born on Phoebus Plantation near Elizabethtown, Bladen County, N. C., April 5, 1882; attended the public schools, Davidson (N. C.) College, and the University of North Carolina at Chapel Hill; studied law; was admitted to the bar in 1906 and commenced practice in Elizabethtown, N. C.; president of the Bank of Elizabethtown 1910–1922; served in the State house of representatives in 1915; presidential elector in 1916 on the ticket of Wilson and Marshall; moved to Fayetteville, N. C., in 1920 and continued the practice of law; member of the State Democratic committee 1909–1919; member of the North Carolina State Judicial Conference 1924–1928; elected as a Democrat to the Seventy-first and to the nine succeeding Congresses (March 4, 1929–January 3, 1949); was not a candidate for renomination in 1948; resumed the practice of law; died in Fayetteville, N. C., August 26, 1959; interment in Cross Creek Cemetery No. 3.

CLARK, Joel Bennett (Champ) (son of James Beauchamp Clark), a Senator from Missouri; born in Bowling Green, Mo., January 8, 1890; attended the public schools at Bowling Green, Mo., and at Washington, D. C.; was graduated from Eastern High School, Washington, D. C., in 1908, from the University of Missouri at Columbia in 1912, and from the law department of George Washington University, Washington, D. C., in 1914; parliamentarian of the United States House of Representatives 1913–1917; was admitted to the Missouri bar in 1914; during the First World War served as a lieutenant colonel in the One Hundred and Fortieth Infantry, Thirty-fifth Division, and later as a colonel in the Eighty-eighth Division, from August 5, 1917, to May 4, 1919, with overseas service; commenced the practice of law in St. Louis, Mo., in 1919; parliamentarian of the Democratic National Convention in 1916; delegate to the Democratic National Conventions in 1920, 1936, and 1940; author; compiler of several manuals on parliamentary law; member of the Board of Regents, Smithsonian Institution, 1940–1944; elected as a Democrat to the United States Senate in 1932 for the term commencing March 4, 1933, and was subsequently appointed to the Senate to fill the vacancy caused by the resignation of Harry B. Hawes for the term ending March 3, 1933; was sworn in on February 3, 1933, instead of February 4, through a misapprehension of the facts of the case; reelected in 1938 and served from February 4, 1933, to January 3, 1945; unsuccessful candidate for renomination in 1944; appointed, and confirmed by the Senate on September 24, 1945, as an associate justice of the United States Court of Appeals for the District of Columbia, and served until his death at a summer cottage in Gloucester, Mass., July 13, 1954; interment in Arlington National Cemetery, Fort Myer, Va.

CLARK, John Bullock (nephew of Christopher Henderson Clark and James Clark), a Representative from Missouri; born in Madison County, Ky., April 17, 1802; attended the country schools; studied law; was admitted to the bar in 1824 and practiced in Fayette, Mo.; clerk of the Howard County courts 1824–1834; colonel of Missouri Mounted Volunteers in the Black Hawk War in 1832; major general of militia in 1848; member of the

State house of representatives 1850 and 1851; elected as a Democrat to the Thirty-fifth Congress to fill the vacancy caused by the resignation of James S. Green; reelected to the Thirty-sixth and Thirty-seventh Congresses and served from December 7, 1857, until expelled July 13, 1861; a Senator from Missouri in the First Confederate Congress and a Representative in the Second Confederate Congress; brigadier general of Missouri Confederate State troops; practiced law until his death in Fayette, Howard County, Mo., October 29, 1885; interment in Fayette Cemetery.

CLARK, John Bullock, Jr. (son of the preceding), a Representative from Missouri; born in Fayette, Howard County, Mo., January 14, 1831; attended Fayette Academy, and the University of Missouri at Columbia; spent two years in California for travel and adventure; returned to the East, and was graduated from the law department of Harvard University in 1854; was admitted to the bar and practiced in Fayette, Mo., from 1855 until the commencement of the Civil War, when he entered the Confederate Army as a lieutenant; promoted successively to the rank of captain, major, colonel, and brigadier general; resumed the practice of law in Fayette, Mo.; elected as a Democrat to the Forty-third and to the four succeeding Congresses (March 4, 1873–March 3, 1883); unsuccessful candidate for renomination in 1882; clerk of the National House of Representatives 1883–1889; engaged in the practice of law in Washington, D. C., until his death there, September 7, 1903; interment in Rock Creek Cemetery.

CLARK, John Chamberlain, a Representative from New York; born in Pittsfield, Mass., January 14, 1793; pursued preparatory studies; was graduated from Williams College, Williamstown, Mass., in 1811; was admitted to the bar and commenced practice in Hamilton, N. Y.; moved to Bainbridge, Chenango County, about 1818; district attorney 1823–1827; elected as a Democrat to the Twentieth Congress (March 4, 1827–March 3, 1829); elected as a Democrat to the Twenty-fifth Congress (March 4, 1837–March 3, 1839), but changed his politics on the appearance of President Van Buren's message in 1837 favoring an independent Treasury for the safe-keeping and disbursement of the public moneys; reelected as a Whig to the Twenty-sixth and Twenty-seventh Congresses (March 4, 1839–March 3, 1843); served as First Auditor of the Treasury from August 2 to October 31, 1849; moved to Chemung County, N. Y., and engaged in the lumber business; died in Elmira, Chemung County, N. Y., October 25, 1852; interment in St. Peter's Churchyard, Bainbridge, N. Y.

CLARK, Joseph Sill, a Senator from Pennsylvania; born in Philadelphia, Pa., October 21, 1901; attended Chestnut Hill Academy; was graduated from Middlesex School in 1919, Harvard University in 1923, and the University of Pennsylvania Law School in 1926; was admitted to the bar in 1926 and commenced the practice of law in Philadelphia, Pa.; during World War II served with the United States Army Air Force from 1941 until discharged as a colonel in 1945 with service as deputy chief of staff, Eastern Air Command, in the China-Burma-India Theater; city controller of Philadelphia 1950–1952; mayor of Philadelphia 1952–1956; member of board of overseers, Harvard University since 1953; elected as a Democrat to the United States Senate in 1956 for the term commencing January 3, 1957, and ending January 3, 1963.

CLARK, Lincoln, a Representative from Iowa; born in Conway, Franklin County, Mass., August 9, 1800; attended the district and private schools; was graduated from Amherst (Mass.) College in 1825; studied law; was admitted to the bar in 1831 and commenced practice in Pickensville, Pickens County, Ala.; member of the State house of representatives in 1834, 1835, and 1845; moved to Tuscaloosa in 1836; elected attorney general by the legislature in 1839; appointed by Governor Fitzpatrick circuit judge in 1846; moved to Dubuque, Iowa, in 1848; presidential elector on the Democratic ticket of Pierce and King in 1852; elected as a Democrat to the Thirty-second Congress (March 4, 1851–March 3, 1853); unsuccessful candidate in 1852 and 1854 for reelection to the Thirty-third and Thirty-fourth Congresses; resumed the practice of law in Chicago, Ill.; appointed United States register in bankruptcy in 1866; retired from active business and returned to Conway, Mass., in 1869; died in Conway, Mass., September 16, 1886; interment in Howland Cemetery.

CLARK, Linwood Leon, a Representative from Maryland; born in Aberdeen, Harford County, Md., on March 21, 1876; attended the public schools; was graduated from Milton Academy, Baltimore, Md., in 1899, from the American University of Harriman, Tenn., in 1902, and from the law department of the University of Maryland in 1904; was admitted to the bar in 1904 and commenced practice in Baltimore, Md.; completed a LaSalle Extension University course in railway transportation in 1919; unsuccessful candidate for election in 1926 to the Seventieth Congress; elected as a Republican to the Seventy-first Congress (March 4, 1929–March 3, 1931); unsuccessful candidate for reelection in 1930 to the Seventy-second Congress; resumed the practice of law in Baltimore, Md.; appointed judge of the circuit court of Maryland, fifth judicial district, in May 1935 and served until December 20, 1938; practicing law in Annapolis, Md., and is a resident of Horn Point, near Annapolis, Md.

CLARK, Lot, a Representative from New York; born in Hillsdale, Columbia County, N. Y., May 23, 1788; moved with his parents to Otsego County in 1796; pursued academic studies; studied law; was admitted to the bar on June 11, 1816, and practiced in Norwich, N. Y.; district attorney of Chenango County in 1822 and 1823; elected as an old-line Whig to the Eighteenth Congress (March 4, 1823–March 3, 1825); appointed postmaster of Norwich on April 29, 1825, and served until April 12, 1828; again served as district attorney of Chenango County in 1828 and 1829; moved to Lockport, N. Y., in 1829 and continued the practice of law; became president of the Lockport Bank in 1829; member and agent of the so-called Albany Co., owners of all the unsold lands in Niagara and Orleans Counties and in the northern parts of Genesee and Erie Counties; moved to Buffalo, N. Y., in 1835; projector of the first wire-cable bridge over the Niagara chasm; president of the Suspension Bridge Co. until his death; member of the State assembly in 1846; died in Buffalo, N. Y., December 18, 1862; interment in Greenwood Cemetery, Brooklyn, N. Y.

CLARK, Robert, a Representative from New York; born in Washington County, N. Y., on June 12, 1777; was tutored privately; studied medicine in the office of his brother; commenced practice in Galway, Washington County, N. Y., in 1799; moved to Stamford, Delaware County, and later settled near Delhi, Delaware County, where he continued the practice of his profession; member of the State assembly 1812–1815; elected as a Democrat to the Sixteenth Congress (March 4, 1819–March 3, 1821); delegate to the State constitutional convention in 1821; moved to Monroe County, Mich., and settled on a farm near the village of Monroe, where he again engaged in the practice of his profession and was also interested in the scientific cultivation of fruits and grasses and the subject of drainage; appointed register of the land office for the second land district of Michigan Territory on May 26, 1823, and served until March 25, 1831; died October 1, 1837.

CLARK, Rush, a Representative from Iowa; born in Schellsburg, Bedford County, Pa., October 1, 1834; attended the common schools, the local academy at Ligonier, Pa., and was graduated from Jefferson College, Canonsburg, Pa., in 1853; studied law; was admitted to the bar in 1853 and commenced practice in Iowa City, Iowa; member of the Iowa House of Representatives 1860–1864, serving as speaker in 1863 and 1864; served on the staff of the Governor of Iowa in 1861 and 1862, and aided in the organization of volunteer regiments from Iowa during the Civil War; trustee of Iowa University at Iowa City 1862–1866; again served in the State house of representatives in 1876; elected as a Republican to the Forty-fifth and Forty-sixth Congresses and served from March 4, 1877, until his death in Washington, D. C., April 29, 1879; interment in Oakland Cemetery, Iowa City, Iowa.

CLARK, Samuel, a Representative from New York and a Representative from Michigan; born in Clarksville, Cayuga County, N. Y., in January 1800; attended Hamilton College, Clinton, N. Y.; studied law in Auburn, N. Y.; was admitted to the bar and commenced the practice of law in Waterloo, N. Y., in 1826; elected as a Democrat from New York to the Twenty-third Congress (March 4, 1833–March 3, 1835); moved to Kalamazoo, Mich., in 1842 and resumed the practice of law; member of the State constitutional convention in 1850; elected as a Democrat from Michigan to the Thirty-third Congress (March 4, 1853–March 3, 1855); unsuccessful candidate for reelection in 1854 to the Thirty-fourth Congress; assisted in locating and inaugurating a land office at Buchanan, situated at the head of Lake Superior; discontinued the practice of his profession and retired from political activities; became greatly interested in agricultural pursuits; died in Kalamazoo, Kalamazoo County, Mich., on October 2, 1870; interment in Mountain Home Cemetery.

CLARK, Samuel Mercer, a Representative from Iowa; born near Keosauqua, Van Buren County, Iowa, October 11, 1842; attended the public schools and the Des Moines Valley College, West Point, Iowa; studied law; was admitted to the bar in 1864, but did not engage in extensive practice; editor of the Keokuk Daily Gate City for thirty-one years; delegate to the Republican National Conventions in 1872, 1876, and 1880; appointed commissioner of education to the Paris Exposition in 1889; postmaster of Keokuk from January 20, 1879, to November 2, 1885; member of the Keokuk Board of Education 1879–1894, serving as president 1882–1894; elected as a Republican to the Fifty-fourth and Fifty-fifth Congresses (March 4, 1895–March 3, 1899); was not a candidate for renomination in 1898 to the Fifty-sixth Congress; resumed editorial duties; died in Keokuk, Lee County, Iowa, on August 11, 1900; interment in Oakland Cemetery.

CLARK, William, a Representative from Pennsylvania; born in Dauphin, Pa., February 18, 1774; captain of militia in Dauphin County in 1793 and 1795; went to Crawford County, Pa., early in life; was associate judge of Crawford County 1803–1818; participated in the War of 1812; brigade inspector of the western district of Pennsylvania 1800–1817; was on board the flagship *Lawrence* in her first engagement with the British fleet on Lake Erie; secretary of the Pennsylvania land office 1818–1821; State treasurer 1821–1827; Treasurer of the United States from June 4, 1828, to November 1829; elected as a Whig to the Twenty-third and Twenty-fourth Congresses (March 4, 1833–March 3, 1837); member of the State constitutional revision commission in 1837; engaged in agricultural pursuits; died near Dauphin, Pa., March 28, 1851; interment in English Presbyterian Cemetery.

CLARK, William Andrews, a Senator from Montana; born near Connellsville, Fayette County, Pa., January 8, 1839; attended the common schools and the Laurel Hill Academy; in 1856 moved with his parents to Iowa, where he taught school, and while teaching studied law at the Iowa Wesleyan University at Mount Pleasant; worked in the quartz mines near Central City, Gilpin County, Colo., in 1862; went to Montana in 1863 and settled in Bannack, Beaverhead County, and engaged in placer mining for two years; engaged in various mercantile pursuits in Blackfoot and Helena and in banking at Deer Lodge; major of a battalion that pursued Chief Joseph and his band in the Nez Perces invasion of 1877; president of the State constitutional convention in 1884 and of the second constitutional convention in 1889; elected as a Democrat to the United States Senate for the term commencing March 4, 1899, and took his seat December 4, 1899, at which time protests and a memorial were filed requesting that the election be investigated; vacated his seat in the Senate on May 15, 1900, while a resolution declaring his election void was pending, having previously tendered his resignation to the Governor; appointed by the Lieutenant Governor, acting as Governor, to fill the vacancy caused by his own resignation, but did not qualify; again elected to the United States Senate in 1901 and served from March 4, 1901, to March 3, 1907; was not a candidate for reelection; personally superintended his extensive copper mining, banking, and railroad interests in Butte, Mont., with offices and winter residence in New York City; died in New York City, March 2, 1925; interment in Woodlawn Cemetery.

CLARK, William Thomas, a Representative from Texas; born in Norwalk, Conn., June 29, 1831; self-educated; taught school in Norwalk, Conn., in 1846; studied law in New York City; was admitted to the bar in 1855 and commenced practice in Davenport, Iowa, the same year; during the Civil War served in the Union Army; commissioned first lieutenant and adjutant of the Thirteenth Iowa Infantry November 2, 1861; captain and assistant adjutant general March 6, 1862; major and adjutant general November 24, 1862; lieutenant colonel and assistant adjutant general, assigned, February 10, 1863, to April 22, 1865; brevetted brigadier general of volunteers July 22, 1864, "for gallant and distinguished services at the Battle of Atlanta, Ga.," and major general November 24, 1865, "for gallant and meritorious services during the war"; mustered out February 1, 1866; engaged in banking in Galveston, Tex.; upon the readmission of the State of Texas to representation was elected as a Republican to the Forty-first Congress and served from March 31, 1870, to March 3, 1871; presented credentials as a Member-elect to the Forty-second Congress and served from March 4, 1871, to May 13, 1872, when he was succeeded by De Witt C. Giddings, who contested his election; postmaster of Galveston from June 19, 1872, to May 7, 1874; employed in various offices of the Government at Washington from 1876 to April 12, 1880, when he became chief clerk of the Internal Revenue Department, serving until June 30, 1883; moved to Fargo (now in North Dakota) in 1883 and continued the practice of law; also served as assistant editor of the Fargo Daily Argus; moved to Denver, Colo., in 1890 and practiced law; went to Washington, D. C., in 1898 and was employed in the Internal Revenue Service as a special inspector and served until his death in a hospital in New York City, N. Y., October 12, 1905; interment in Arlington National Cemetery, Fort Myer, Va.

CLARKE, Archibald Smith (brother of Staley Nichols Clarke), a Representative from New York; born on a plantation in Prince Georges County, Md., in 1788; attended grammar and high schools; studied law; was admitted to the bar and practiced in Niagara County, N. Y.; surrogate of Niagara County in 1808 and 1809; member of the State assembly 1809–1811; served in the State senate 1813–1816; county clerk in 1815 and 1816; elected to the Fourteenth Congress to fill the vacancy caused by the resignation of Peter B. Porter and served from December 2, 1816, to March 3, 1817; died in Clarence, Erie County, N. Y., December 4, 1821.

CLARKE, Bayard, a Representative from New York; born in New York City March 17, 1815; was graduated from Geneva College in 1835; studied law; was admitted to the bar; attaché to General Cass, United States Minister to France, 1836–1840; student in the Royal Cavalry School; appointed second lieutenant in the Eighth Infantry March 3, 1841; transferred to the Second Dragoons in September 1841, and resigned December 15, 1843; settled in Westchester County, N. Y.; unsuccessful candidate for election in 1852 to the Thirty-third Congress; elected as an American Whig to the Thirty-fourth Congress (March 4, 1855–March 3, 1857); died in Schroon Lake, Essex County, N. Y., June 20, 1884; interment in a vault at Newtown, Long Island, N. Y.

CLARKE, Beverly Leonidas, a Representative from Kentucky; born in Winterfield, Chesterfield County, Va., February 11, 1809; attended the common schools; moved to Kentucky in 1823; studied law in Franklin, Ky., and was graduated from the Lexington Law School in 1831; was admitted to the bar in 1833 and commenced practice in Franklin, Ky.; member of the State house of representatives in 1841 and 1842; delegate to the State constitutional convention in 1849; elected as a Democrat to the Thirtieth Congress (March 4, 1847–March 3, 1849); delegate to the State constitutional convention in 1849; unsuccessful Democratic nominee for Governor in 1855; appointed by President Buchanan Minister to Guatemala, and was also accredited to Honduras, and served from January 7, 1858, until his death in Guatemala, Central America, March 17, 1860; interment in the State Cemetery, Frankfort, Ky.

CLARKE, Charles Ezra, a Representative from New York; born in Saybrook, Conn., April 8, 1790; completed preparatory studies, and was graduated from Yale College in 1809; studied law; was admitted to the bar in 1815 and commenced practice in Watertown, N. Y.; moved to Great Bend, Jefferson County, N. Y., in 1840; member of the State assembly in 1839 and 1840; elected as a Whig to the Thirty-first Congress (March 4, 1849–March 3, 1851); resumed the practice of law; also built and operated a gristmill and engaged in agricultural pursuits; died in Great Bend, N. Y., December 29, 1863; interment in Brookside Cemetery, Watertown, N. Y.

CLARKE, Frank Gay, a Representative from New Hampshire; born in Wilton, Hillsborough County, N. H., September 10, 1850; attended Kimball Union Academy, Meriden, N. H., and Dartmouth College, Hanover, N. H.; studied law; was admitted to the bar in 1876 and commenced practice in Peterboro; member of the State house of representatives in 1885; appointed colonel on the military staff of Governor Hale and served in that capacity from 1885 to 1887; served in the State senate in 1889; elected to the State house of representatives in 1891 and chosen speaker of that body; elected as a Republican to the Fifty-fifth and Fifty-sixth Congresses and served from March 4, 1897, until his death in Peterboro, Hillsborough County, N. H., January 9, 1901; interment in Pine Hill Cemetery.

CLARKE, Freeman, a Representative from New York; born in Troy, N. Y., March 22, 1809; attended the common schools; went into business for himself at the age of fifteen; began his financial career as cashier of the Bank of Orleans, Albion, N. Y.; moved to Rochester, N. Y., in 1845; became director and president of numerous banks, railroads, and telegraph and trust companies of Rochester and New York City; delegate to the Whig National Convention at Baltimore in 1852; vice president of the first Republican State convention of New York in 1854; presidential elector on the Republican ticket of Frémont and Dayton in 1856; appointed Comptroller of the Currency in 1865; delegate to the State constitutional convention in 1867; elected as a Republican to the Thirty-eighth Congress (March 4, 1863–March 3, 1865); was not a candidate for renomination in 1864; Comptroller of the Currency from March 9, 1865, to February 6, 1867; again elected to the Forty-second and Forty-third Congresses (March 4, 1871–March 3, 1875); resumed his former business pursuits; died in Rochester, N. Y., on June 24, 1887; interment in Mount Hope Cemetery.

CLARKE, James Paul, a Senator from Arkansas; born in Yazoo City, Yazoo County, Miss., August 18, 1854; attended the public schools and Professor Tutwilder's Academy, Greenbrier, Ala.; was graduated from the law department of the University of Virginia at Charlottesville in 1878; was admitted to the bar in 1879 and commenced practice in Helena, Phillips County, Ark.; member of the State house of representatives 1886–1888; served in the State senate 1888–1892; was president of that body in 1891 and ex officio Lieutenant Governor; attorney general of Arkansas 1892–1894; declined to be a candidate for renomination; Governor of Arkansas in 1895 and 1896; moved to Little Rock, Ark., in 1897 and resumed the practice of law; elected as a Democrat to the United States Senate in 1903; reelected in 1909 and again in 1915 and served from March 4, 1903, until his death; elected President pro tempore of the Senate in 1913 and again in 1915; member of the Democratic National Committee; died in Little Rock, Ark., October 1, 1916; interment in Oakland Cemetery.

CLARKE, John Blades, a Representative from Kentucky; born near Augusta, Bracken County, Ky., on April 14, 1833; attended the common schools and Augusta (Ky.) College; taught school in the winters of 1851 and 1852; studied law in Augusta, Ky.; was admitted to the bar on April 20, 1854, and commenced practice in Rockport, Ind., in January 1855; moved to Brooksville, Ky., in December 1855 and continued the practice of law; prosecuting attorney of Bracken County 1858–1862; member of the State senate 1867–1870; elected as a Democrat to the Forty-fourth and Forty-fifth Congresses (March 4, 1875–March 3, 1879); declined to be a candidate for renomination in 1878; resumed the practice of his profession; died in Brooksville, Bracken County, Ky., May 23, 1911; interment in Mount Zion Cemetery, near Brooksville, Ky.

CLARKE, John Davenport (husband of Marian Williams Clarke), a Representative from New York; born in Hobart, Delaware County, N. Y., January 15, 1873; attended the common schools, and was graduated from Lafayette College, Easton, Pa., in 1898; took postgraduate courses in economics and history in Colorado College at Colorado Springs; studied law in the New York Law School, and was graduated from the Brooklyn Law School in 1911; was admitted to the bar in 1912 and commenced practice in New York City; engaged in work with the mining department of the Carnegie Steel Co.; assistant to the secretary of mines of the United States Steel Corporation 1901–1907; secretary and treasurer of other mining interests; moved to Delaware County in 1915 and engaged in agricultural pursuits; elected as a Republican to the Sixty-seventh and Sixty-eighth Congresses (March 4, 1921–March 3, 1925); unsuccessful candidate for reelection in 1924 to the Sixty-ninth Congress;

resumed agricultural pursuits; elected to the Seventieth and to the three succeeding Congresses and served from March 4, 1927, until his death, the result of an automobile collision near Delhi, N. Y., November 5, 1933; interment in Locust Hill Cemetery, Hobart, N. Y.

CLARKE, John Hopkins, a Senator from Rhode Island; born in Elizabeth, N. J., April 1, 1789; when quite young he moved to Providence, R. I., where he studied under a private teacher; was graduated from Brown University, Providence, R. I., in 1809; studied law; was admitted to the bar and commenced practice in Providence in 1812; clerk of the supreme court of Providence County in 1813; proprietor of a distillery in Cranston, R. I., until 1824, when he became a cotton manufacturer in Providence, Pontiac, and Woonsocket; member of the State house of representatives 1836–1842 and 1845–1847; elected as a Whig to the United States Senate and served from March 4, 1847, to March 3, 1853; resumed his former manufacturing pursuits; died in Providence, R. I., November 23, 1870; interment in the North Burial Ground.

CLARKE, Marian Williams (wife of John Davenport Clarke), a Representative from New York; born at Standing Stone, Bradford County, Pa., July 29, 1880; moved with her parents to Cheyenne, Wyo., in 1881; attended the public schools and spent one year in the art school of the University of Nebraska at Lincoln; was graduated from Colorado College at Colorado Springs in 1902; resided in seven different States from 1881 to 1918; moved to Delaware County, N. Y., in 1918 and settled on a farm near Fraser; elected as a Republican to the Seventy-third Congress to fill the vacancy caused by the death of her husband, John Davenport Clarke, and served from December 28, 1933, to January 3, 1935; was a candidate for renomination in 1934 to the Seventy-fourth Congress, but withdrew her name before the primary election; alternate delegate to the Republican National Convention at Cleveland in 1936; returned to her farm, "Arbor Hill," near Delhi, N. Y., where she resided until 1950; died in Cooperstown, N. Y., April 8, 1953; interment in Locust Hill Cemetery, Hobart, N. Y.

CLARKE, Reader Wright, a Representative from Ohio; born in Bethel, Ohio, May 18, 1812; learned the art of printing; studied law; was admitted to the bar in 1836 and commenced practice in Batavia, Ohio; published a Whig paper in Shawneetown, Ill., for a few years; returned to Batavia, Ohio; member of the State house of representatives 1840–1842; presidential elector on the Whig ticket of Clay and Frelinghuysen in 1844; clerk of the court of Clermont County 1846–1852; elected as a Republican to the Thirty-ninth and Fortieth Congresses (March 4, 1865–March 3, 1869); third auditor of the Treasury from March 26, 1869, to March 26, 1870; appointed collector of internal revenue in Ohio; died in Batavia, Clermont County, Ohio, May 23, 1872; interment in Union Cemetery.

CLARKE, Richard Henry, a Representative from Alabama; born in Dayton, Marengo County, Ala., February 9, 1843; attended Green Springs Academy, and was graduated from the University of Alabama at Tuscaloosa in July 1861; during the Civil War served in the Confederate Army as a lieutenant in the First Battalion of Alabama Artillery; studied law; was admitted to the bar in 1867 and commenced practice in Dayton, Ala.; moved to Demopolis, Marengo County, Ala., and continued the practice of law; State solicitor (prosecuting attorney) for Marengo County 1872–1876; prosecuting attorney of the seventh judicial circuit in 1876 and 1877; resumed the practice of law in Mobile, Ala.; elected as a Democrat to the Fifty-first and to the three

succeeding Congresses (March 4, 1889–March 3, 1897); was not a candidate for renomination, preferring to be a candidate for Governor; unsuccessful candidate for Governor in 1896; resumed the practice of law; member of the State house of representatives in 1900 and 1901; died in St. Louis, Mo., September 26, 1906; interment in Magnolia Cemetery, Mobile, Ala.

CLARKE, Sidney, a Representative from Kansas; born in Southbridge, Worcester County, Mass., October 16, 1831; attended the public schools; publisher of the Southbridge Press in 1854; settled in Lawrence, Kans., in 1859; enlisted as a volunteer during the Civil War; appointed assistant adjutant general of Volunteers by President Lincoln February 9, 1863; captain and assistant provost marshal general for Kansas, Nebraska, Colorado, and Dakota; elected as a Republican to the Thirty-ninth, Fortieth, and Forty-first Congresses (March 4, 1865–March 3, 1871); unsuccessful candidate in 1870 for reelection to the Forty-second Congress; member of the State house of representatives in 1879 and served as speaker; moved to Oklahoma City, Oklahoma County, Okla., in 1889 and engaged in railroad building; chairman of the statehood executive committee in 1891; member of the Territorial council 1898–1902; died in Oklahoma City, Okla., on June 18, 1909; interment in Fairlawn Cemetery.

CLARKE, Staley Nichols (brother of Archibald Smith Clarke), a Representative from New York; born in Prince Georges County, Md., May 24, 1794; moved to Buffalo, N. Y., in 1815; employed as a clerk in the Bank of Niagara; clerk in the office of the Holland Land Co., Batavia, N. Y., from 1819 to January 1822, when he was transferred as their agent for the county of Cattaraugus to Ellicottville, N. Y.; treasurer of Cattaraugus County for seventeen years; elected as a Whig to the Twenty-seventh Congress (March 4, 1841–March 3, 1843); declined to be a candidate for renomination in 1842; died in Ellicottville, Cattaraugus County, N. Y.. October 14, 1860; interment in Jefferson Street Cemetery.

CLARKSON, Matthew, a Delegate from Pennsylvania; born in New York City in April 1733; moved to Philadelphia, Pa.; was justice of the court of common pleas, quarter sessions of the peace, and of the Philadelphia orphans' court in 1771 and 1772; elected to the Continental Congress in 1785, but did not accompany the other Pennsylvania Delegates to New York and may not have served; member of the board of aldermen in 1789; mayor of Philadelphia 1792–1796; died in Philadelphia, Pa., October 5, 1800; interment in Christ Church Burying Ground.

CLASON, Charles Russell, a Representative from Massachusetts; born in Gardiner, Kennebec County, Maine, September 3, 1890; attended the public schools; was graduated from Bates College, Lewiston, Maine, in 1911, from the law department of Georgetown University, Washington, D. C., in 1914, and from Oxford University, England, in 1917; instructor in law at Northeastern University, Springfield, Mass., 1920–1937; connected with the Interstate Commerce Commission and the Department of Education, Washington, D. C., in 1913 and 1914; member of the commission for relief in Belgium in 1914 and 1915 and was decorated with the Medaille du Roi Albert; was admitted to the bar in 1917 and commenced practice in Boston, Mass.; during the First World War served as a sergeant major in the Coast Artillery, United States Army; assistant district attorney of the western district of Massachusetts 1922–1926 and district attorney 1927–1930; elected as a Republican to the Seventy-fifth and to the five succeeding Congresses (January 3, 1937–January 3, 1949); unsuccessful candidate for reelection in 1948 to the

Eighty-first Congress; resumed the practice of law; delegate to the Republican National Convention in 1952; is a resident of Springfield, Mass.

CLASSON, David Guy, a Representative from Wisconsin; born in Oconto, Oconto County, Wis., September 27, 1870; attended the public schools, and was graduated from the law department of the University of Wisconsin at Madison in 1891; was admitted to the bar the same year and commenced practice in Oconto, Wis.; judge of Oconto County 1894–1898; mayor of Oconto 1898–1900; city attorney 1900–1906; president of the board of education in 1912 and 1913; president of the board of fire and police commissioners in 1915 and 1916; elected as a Republican to the Sixty-fifth, Sixty-sixth, and Sixty-seventh Congresses (March 4, 1917–March 3, 1923); declined to be a candidate for renomination in 1922; resumed the practice of law in Oconto, Wis.; served as circuit judge of the twentieth judicial circuit 1928–1930; died in Oconto, Wis., September 6, 1930; interment in Evergreen Cemetery.

CLAWSON, Isaiah Dunn, a Representative from New Jersey; born in Woodstown, Salem County, N. J., March 30, 1822; attended Delaware College, Newark, N. J., and Lafayette College, Easton, Pa.; was graduated from Princeton College in 1840 and from the medical department of the University of Pennsylvania at Philadelphia in 1843; commenced the practice of medicine in Woodstown, N. J.; member of the State house of assembly in 1854; elected as a Whig to the Thirty-fourth and Thirty-fifth Congresses (March 4, 1855–March 3, 1859); was not a candidate for renomination in 1858; resumed the practice of medicine in Woodstown, N. J., where he died on October 9, 1879; interment in the Baptist Cemetery.

CLAY, Alexander Stephens, a Senator from Georgia; born near Powder Springs, Cobb County, Ga., September 25, 1853; attended the common schools and high school of Palmetto, Ga.; was graduated from Hiawassee (Tenn.) College in 1875; studied law; was admitted to the bar in 1877 and commenced practice in Marietta, Ga.; member of the city council in 1880 and 1881; member of the State house of representatives 1884–1887, 1889, and again in 1890; served as speaker pro tempore in 1886, 1887, 1889, and 1890; member of the State senate 1892–1894 and was president of that body for two years; elected in 1896 as a Democrat to the United States Senate; reelected in 1902 and again in 1908 and served from March 4, 1897, until his death in Atlanta, Ga., on November 13, 1910; interment in the City Cemetery, Marietta, Ga.

CLAY, Brutus Junius, a Representative from Kentucky; born in Richmond, Madison County, Ky., July 1, 1808; attended the common schools and was graduated from Centre College, Danville, Ky.; engaged in agricultural pursuits and stock raising; moved to Bourbon County in 1837 and continued former pursuits; member of State house of representatives in 1840; elected president of Bourbon County Agricultural Association in 1840 and served thirty years; president of the Kentucky Agricultural Association 1853–1861; again a member of the State house of representatives in 1860; elected as a Unionist to the Thirty-eighth Congress (March 4, 1863–March 3, 1865); was not a candidate for reelection; resumed former pursuits; died near Paris, Ky., October 11, 1878; interment in the family burial ground at "Auvergne," near Paris, Ky.

CLAY, Clement Claiborne, Jr. (son of Clement Comer Clay), a Senator from Alabama; born in Huntsville, Ala., December 13, 1816; was graduated from the University of Alabama at Tuscaloosa in 1834 and from the law department of the University of

Virginia at Charlottesville in 1839; was admitted to the bar and commenced practice in Huntsville, Ala., in 1840; member of the State house of representatives in 1842, 1844, and 1845; judge of the county court of Madison County 1846–1848; unsuccessful candidate for election in 1850 to the Thirty-second Congress; presidential elector on the Democratic ticket of Pierce and King in 1852; elected as a Democrat to the United States Senate to fill the vacancy in the term commencing March 4, 1853, caused by the failure of the legislature to elect; reelected in 1858 and served from November 29, 1853, to January 21, 1861, when he withdrew; member of the Confederate Senate 1861–1863; was a diplomatic agent of the Confederate States; arrested and imprisoned in Fortress Monroe in 1865; after the war settled on his plantation in Jackson County, Ala., and devoted himself to agricultural pursuits and to the practice of law; died at "Wildwood," near Gurley, Madison County, Ala., January 3, 1882; interment in Maple Hill Cemetery, Huntsville, Ala.

CLAY, Clement Comer (father of Clement Claiborne Clay, Jr.), a Representative and a Senator from Alabama; born in Halifax County, Va., December 17, 1789; moved with his parents to a farm near Knoxville, Tenn., when a child; attended the public schools and was graduated from the East Tennessee University in 1807; studied law; was admitted to the bar in 1809; moved to Huntsville, Ala., in 1811, and commenced practice; served in the war against the Creek Indians in 1813; member of the Territorial council of Alabama in 1817 and 1818; elected a judge of the circuit court in 1819 and chief justice in 1820; resigned in 1823 and resumed the practice of law; member of the State house of representatives in 1827 and 1828 and served as speaker; elected as a Democrat to the Twenty-first, Twenty-second, and Twenty-third Congresses (March 4, 1829–March 3, 1835); Governor of Alabama in 1836 and 1837; elected to the United States Senate to fill the vacancy caused by the resignation of John McKinley and served from June 19, 1837, until his resignation on November 15, 1841; associate judge of the State supreme court in 1843; codified the laws of Alabama in 1842 and 1843; died in Huntsville, Ala., September 9, 1866; interment in Maple Hill Cemetery.

CLAY, Henry (father of James Brown Clay), a Senator and a Representative from Kentucky; born in the district known as "the Slashes," Hanover County, Va., April 12, 1777; attended the public schools; studied law in Richmond, Va.; was admitted to the bar in 1797 and commenced practice in Lexington, Ky.; member of the State house of representatives in 1803; elected to the United States Senate to fill the vacancy caused by the resignation of John Adair and served from November 19, 1806, to March 3, 1807, which service was rendered in contravention of the thirty-year age requirement of the Constitution; again a member of the State house of representatives in 1808 and 1809 and served as speaker the last year; elected to the United States Senate to fill the vacancy caused by the resignation of Buckner Thruston and served from January 4, 1810, to March 3, 1811; elected to the Twelfth and Thirteenth Congresses and served from March 4, 1811, to January 19, 1814, when he resigned; served as Speaker from November 4, 1811, until his resignation; appointed one of the commissioners to negotiate the treaty of peace with Great Britain in 1814; reelected to the Fourteenth, Fifteenth, and Sixteenth Congresses (March 4, 1815–March 3, 1821); elected Speaker of the House on December 4, 1815, and served until October 28, 1820, when he resigned the office; elected to the Eighteenth and Nineteenth Congresses and served from March 3, 1823, to March 6, 1825, when he resigned; again served as Speaker from December 1, 1823, until the close of the Eighteenth Congress; appointed Secretary of State by President John Quincy Adams and served from March 7, 1825, to March

3, 1829; elected to the United States Senate on November 10, 1831, to fill the vacancy in the term commencing March 4, 1831; reelected in 1836 and served until March 31, 1842, when he resigned; unsuccessful candidate on the Whig ticket for President of the United States in 1824, 1832, and again in 1844; again elected to the United States Senate and served from March 4, 1849, until his death in Washington, D. C., June 29, 1852; interment in Lexington Cemetery, Lexington, Ky.

CLAY, James Brown (son of Henry Clay), a Representative from Kentucky; born in Washington, D. C., November 9, 1817; pursued preparatory studies; attended Transylvania University, Lexington, Ky., and Kenyon College, Gambier, Ohio; clerk in a countinghouse in Boston 1832–1834; studied law at Lexington Law School; was admitted to the bar and practiced with his father in Lexington; Chargé d'Affaires to Portugal from August 1, 1849, to July 19, 1850; was a resident of Missouri in 1851 and 1852, when he returned to Lexington, Ky.; elected as a Democrat to the Thirty-fifth Congress (March 4, 1857–March 3, 1859); was not a candidate for renomination in 1858; declined the appointment by President Buchanan to a mission to Germany; member of the peace convention of 1861 held in Washington, D. C., in an effort to devise means to prevent the impending war; during the Civil War identified himself with the Confederacy; died in Montreal, Canada, January 26, 1864, where he had gone for his health; interment in Lexington Cemetery, Lexington, Ky.

CLAY, James Franklin, a Representative from Kentucky; born in Henderson, Henderson County, Ky., October 29, 1840; attended public and private schools at Henderson; was graduated from Georgetown College, Kentucky, in June 1860; studied law; was admitted to the bar in 1862 and commenced practice in Henderson, Ky.; member of the State senate in 1870; elected as a Democrat to the Forty-eighth Congress (March 4, 1883–March 3, 1885); unsuccessful candidate for renomination in 1884; resumed the practice of his profession in Henderson, Ky.; served as city attorney and as attorney for the St. Louis & Southern Railroad and the Ohio Valley Railway Co.; died in Henderson, Ky., on August 17, 1921; interment in Fernwood Cemetery.

CLAY, Joseph (grandfather of William Henry Stiles), a Delegate from Georgia; born in Beverly, Yorkshire, England, October 16, 1741; immigrated to the United States and in 1760 settled in Savannah, Ga., where he engaged in the general commission business; elected a member of the council of safety June 22, 1775; delegate to the Provisional Congress which met in Savannah July 4, 1775; major in the Georgia Line of the Continental Army during the Revolutionary War; appointed by the Continental Congress deputy paymaster general in Georgia with the rank of colonel August 6, 1777; Member of the Continental Congress in 1778 and 1783; original trustee of Franklin College, Athens, Ga.; elected treasurer of Georgia in July 1782; judge of the United States Court for the District of Georgia 1786–1801; died in Savannah, Ga., November 15, 1804; interment in Colonial Park Cemetery.

CLAY, Joseph, a Representative from Pennsylvania; born in Philadelphia, Pa., July 24, 1769; elected to the Eighth, Ninth, and Tenth Congresses, and served from March 4, 1803, to 1808, when he resigned to engage in banking; one of the managers appointed by the House of Representatives in 1804 to conduct the impeachment proceedings against John Pickering, judge of the United States District Court for New Hampshire; became cashier of the Farmers & Mechanics' Bank of Philadelphia; died in Philadelphia, Pa., on August 27, 1811; interment in Christ Church Burying Ground.

CLAY, Matthew, a Representative from Virginia; born in Halifax County, near Danville, Va., March 25, 1754; during the Revolutionary War entered the Ninth Virginia Regiment October 1, 1776, transferred to the First Virginia Regiment in 1778 and to the Fifth Virginia Regiment in 1781, being successively promoted to first lieutenant, captain, and quartermaster; mustered out 1783; member of the State house of delegates 1790–1794; elected as a Democrat to the Fifth and to the seven succeeding Congresses (March 4, 1797–March 3, 1813); unsuccessful candidate for reelection in 1813 to the Thirteenth Congress; elected to the Fourteenth Congress and served from March 4, 1815, until his death; died at Halifax Court House, Va., May 27, 1815; interment in the old family burying ground in Pittsylvania County, Va.

CLAYPOOL, Harold Kile (son of Horatio Clifford Claypool and cousin of John Barney Peterson), a Representative from Ohio; born in Bainbridge, Ross County, Ohio, June 2, 1886; attended the public schools, and Ohio State University at Columbus; engaged in the publishing business at Columbus, Ohio, and published Hunter and Trader Magazine; deputy probate judge of Ross County, Ohio; elected as a Democrat to the Seventy-fifth, Seventy-sixth, and Seventy-seventh Congresses (January 3, 1937–January 3, 1943); unsuccessful candidate for reelection in 1942 to the Seventy-eighth Congress; resumed the publishing and office supply business; United States marshal for the southern district of Ohio 1944–1953; died in Chillicothe, Ohio, August 2, 1958; interment in Grandview Cemetery.

CLAYPOOL, Horatio Clifford (father of Harold Kile Claypool and cousin of John Barney Peterson), a Representative from Ohio; born in McArthur, Vinton County, Ohio, February 9, 1859; attended the common schools, and was graduated from the normal school at Lebanon, Ohio, in 1880; studied law; was admitted to the bar in 1882 and commenced practice in Chillicothe, Ohio; prosecuting attorney of Ross County 1899–1903; probate judge of the county 1905–1910; elected as a Democrat to the Sixty-second and Sixty-third Congresses (March 4, 1911–March 3, 1915); unsuccessful candidate for reelection in 1914 to the Sixty-fourth Congress; elected to the Sixty-fifth Congress (March 4, 1917–March 3, 1919); unsuccessful candidate for reelection in 1918 to the Sixty-sixth Congress; resumed the practice of law in Chillicothe, Ohio; died in Columbus, Ohio, January 19, 1921; interment in Grandview Cemetery, Chillicothe, Ross County, Ohio.

CLAYTON, Augustin Smith, a Representative from Georgia; born in Fredericksburg, Va., November 27, 1783; moved with his parents to Richmond County, Ga., in 1784; attended Richmond Academy, and was graduated from Franklin College, Athens, Ga., in 1804; studied law; was admitted to the bar in 1806 and commenced practice in Carnesville, Franklin County; moved to Athens; selected by the legislature in 1810 to compile the statutes of Georgia from 1800; member of the State house of representatives 1810–1812; clerk of the State house of representatives 1813–1815; served in the State senate in 1826 and 1827; judge of the superior court 1819–1825 and 1828–1831; presidential elector on the Democratic ticket of Jackson and Calhoun in 1828; elected as a State Rights Democrat to the Twenty-second Congress to fill the vacancy caused by the resignation of Wilson Lumpkin; reelected to the Twenty-third Congress and served from January 21, 1832, to March 3, 1835; resumed the practice of law in Athens, Ga., and died there June 21, 1839; interment in Oconee Cemetery.

CLAYTON, Bertram Tracy (brother of Henry De Lamar Clayton), a Representative from New York; born on the Clayton estate near Clayton, Barbour County, Ala., October 19, 1862; attended the University of Alabama at Tuscaloosa; was graduated from the United States Military Academy at West Point in 1886 and appointed a second lieutenant in the Eleventh Regiment, United States Infantry; served until April 30, 1888, when he resigned to go into business as a civil engineer in Brooklyn; during the Spanish-American War was mustered into the United States volunteer service as captain of Troop C, New York Volunteers, May 20, 1898; was later placed in command of Troops A, B, and C of the New York Cavalry, and served throughout the Puerto Rican campaign; elected as a Democrat to the Fifty-sixth Congress (March 4, 1899–March 3, 1901); unsuccessful candidate in 1900 for reelection to the Fifty-seventh Congress; appointed by President Roosevelt a captain in the United States Regular Army April 17, 1901; quartermaster in the United States Army in the Philippine Islands 1901–1904; quartermaster and disbursing officer of the United States Military Academy, West Point, N. Y., 1911–1914; during the First World War was appointed colonel in the Quartermaster Corps of the American Army March 15, 1918; quartermaster of the First Division in France; killed in action at Noyer, Department of the Oise, France, May 30, 1918; interment in Arlington National Cemetery, Fort Myer, Va.

CLAYTON, Charles, a Representative from California; born in Devonshire, England, October 5, 1825; attended the public schools; immigrated to the United States and settled in Wisconsin in 1842; went to Oregon in 1847 and in the following year to San Francisco, Calif.; alcalde of Santa Clara in 1849 and 1850; built the Santa Clara flour mills in 1852; returned to San Francisco in 1853 and engaged in the grain and flour business; member of the State assembly 1863–1866; member of the board of supervisors of San Francisco, Calif., 1864–1869; appointed surveyor of customs of the port and district of San Francisco by President Grant on March 16, 1870; elected as a Republican to the Forty-third Congress (March 4, 1873–March 3, 1875); was not a candidate for renomination in 1874; State prison director in 1881 and 1882; died in Oakland, Calif., October 4, 1885; interment in Mountain View Cemetery.

CLAYTON, Henry De Lamar (brother of Betram Tracy Clayton), a Representative from Alabama; born near Clayton, Barbour County, Ala., February 10, 1857; attended the common schools; was graduated from the literary department of the University of Alabama at Tuscaloosa in 1877 and from its law department in 1878; was admitted to the bar in the latter year and commenced practice in Clayton, Ala.; moved to Eufaula, Ala., in 1880 and continued the practice of law; presidential elector on the Democratic ticket of Cleveland and Thurman in 1888 and of Cleveland and Stevenson in 1892; member of the State house of representatives in 1890 and 1891; United States district attorney for the middle district of Alabama 1893–1896; permanent chairman of the Democratic National Convention at Denver in 1908; elected as a Democrat to the Fifty-fifth and to the eight succeeding Congresses and served from March 4, 1897, until May 25, 1914, when he resigned and moved to Montgomery, Ala., to accept a commission as United States judge for the middle and northern district of Alabama, in which capacity he served until his death; one of the managers appointed by the House of Representatives in 1905 to conduct the impeachment proceedings against Charles Swayne, judge of the United States District Court for the Northern District of Florida, and in 1912 against Robert W. Archbald, judge of the United States Commerce Court; chevalier of the Legion of Honor tendered by the French Government in 1924; died in Montgomery, Ala., December 21, 1929; interment in Fairview Cemetery, Eufaula, Ala.

CLAYTON, John Middleton (nephew of Joshua Clayton, cousin of Thomas Clayton, and great-grand-uncle of C. Douglass Buck), a Senator from Delaware; born in Dagsboro, Sussex County, Del., July 24, 1796; pursued preparatory studies at academies in Berlin, Md., and Milford, Del., and was graduated from Yale College in 1815; studied law at the Litchfield Law School; was admitted to the bar in 1819 and commenced practice in Dover; member of the State house of representatives in 1824; secretary of state of Delaware 1826–1828; elected as a National Republican to the United States Senate in 1829; reelected in 1835 and served from March 4, 1829, until December 29, 1836, when he resigned; chief justice of Delaware 1837–1839; again elected, as a Whig, to the United States Senate and served from March 4, 1845, until February 23, 1849, when he resigned to accept a Cabinet position; appointed Secretary of State in the Cabinet of President Taylor and served from March 7, 1849, to July 22, 1850; while Secretary of State negotiated the Clayton-Bulwer treaty with Great Britain; reelected as a Whig to the United States Senate and served from March 4, 1853, until his death in Dover, Del., November 9, 1856; interment in Presbyterian Cemetery.

CLAYTON, Joshua (father of Thomas Clayton and uncle of John Middleton Clayton), a Senator from Delaware; born at Bohemia Manor, Cecil County, Md., July 20, 1744; studied medicine in Philadelphia and practiced in Middletown, Del.; during the Revolutionary War served as major in the Bohemia battalion of the Maryland Line and was an aide on the staff of General Washington at the Battle of the Brandywine; delegate to the Provincial Congress 1782–1784; member of the State house of representatives in 1785 and 1787; judge of the court of appeals; elected State treasurer June 24, 1786; President of Delaware from May 30, 1789, to January 13, 1793; was elected the first Governor of Delaware and served from January 13, 1793, to January 13, 1798; elected to the United States Senate to fill the vacancy caused by the resignation of John Vining, and served from January 19, 1798, until his death in Philadelphia, while attending a session of the Senate, August 11, 1798; interment in Bethel Cemetery, Cecil County, Md.

CLAYTON, Powell, a Senator from Arkansas; born in Bethel, Delaware County, Pa., August 7, 1833; attended the common schools and Partridge Military Academy, Bristol, Pa.; studied civil engineering in Wilmington, Del.; moved to Leavenworth, Kans., where he practiced his profession; appointed city engineer in 1857; at the outbreak of the Civil War entered the Union Army as captain of the First Regiment, Kansas Volunteer Infantry; appointed lieutenant colonel of the Fifth Regiment, Kansas Volunteer Cavalry, December 28, 1861, and colonel March 7, 1862; commissioned brigadier general of Volunteers August 1, 1864, and was mustered out on August 24, 1865; moved to Arkansas and became a planter; elected Governor of Arkansas in 1868; elected as a Republican to the United States Senate and served from March 4, 1871, to March 3, 1877; moved to Little Rock, Ark.; member of the Republican National Committee; delegate to the Republican National Convention at Philadelphia in 1872 and at St. Louis in 1896; Ambassador to Mexico 1897–1905; lived in retirement until his death in Washington, D. C., on August 25, 1914; interment in Arlington National Cemetery, Fort Myer, Va.

CLAYTON, Thomas (son of Joshua Clayton and cousin of John Middleton Clayton), a Representative and a Senator from Delaware; born in Masseys Cross Roads, Md., March 9, 1778; received a classical education at Newark Academy; studied law; was admitted to the bar in 1799 and commenced practice in New Castle; clerk of the State house of representatives in 1800, and a member of that body 1802–1806, 1810, 1812, and 1813; secretary of state of Delaware 1808–1810; served in the State senate in 1808; State attorney general 1810–1815; elected as a Federalist to the Fourteenth Congress (March 4, 1815–March 3, 1817); again a member of the State senate in 1821; elected to the United States Senate to fill the vacancy caused by the resignation of Caesar A. Rodney and served from January 8, 1824, to March 3, 1827; chief justice of the court of common pleas of Delaware in 1828; chief justice of the superior court of the State in 1832; again elected as a Whig to the United States Senate to fill the vacancy caused by the resignation of John M. Clayton; reelected in 1841 and served from January 9, 1837, to March 3, 1847; moved to New Castle and retired from public life; died in New Castle, New Castle County, Del., August 21, 1854; interment in Presbyterian Church Cemetery, Dover, Kent County, Del.

CLEARY, William Edward, a Representative from New York; born in Ellenville, Ulster County, N. Y., July 20, 1849; attended the public schools and the Ellenville Academy; moved to Brooklyn in 1879 and engaged in water transportation; vice president of the New York Board of Trade and Transportation; was a founder, and served as president, of the Victory Memorial Hospital; elected as a Democrat to the Sixty-fifth Congress to fill the vacancy caused by the resignation of Daniel J. Griffin; reelected to the Sixty-sixth Congress and served from March 5, 1918, to March 3, 1921; unsuccessful candidate for reelection in 1920 to the Sixty-seventh Congress; elected to the Sixty-eighth and Sixty-ninth Congresses (March 4, 1923–March 3, 1927); was not a candidate for reelection in 1926; resumed his former business interests; died in Brooklyn, N. Y., December 20, 1932; interment in Holy Cross Cemetery.

CLEMENS, Jeremiah, a Senator from Alabama; born in Huntsville, Ala., December 28, 1814; attended La Grange College, and was graduated from the University of Alabama at Tuscaloosa in 1833; studied law at Transylvania University, Lexington, Ky.; was admitted to the bar in 1834 and practiced in Huntsville; appointed United States district attorney for the northern district of Alabama in 1838; member of the State house of representatives 1839–1841; raised a company of riflemen in 1842, and served in the Texas war of independence; again a member of the State house of representatives in 1843 and 1844; served in the Mexican War and appointed major of the Thirteenth United States Infantry March 3, 1847; promoted to lieutenant colonel of the Ninth United States Infantry July 16, 1847; appointed chief of the department of civil and military purchases in Mexico in 1848; discharged from the Army and returned to Alabama; unsuccessful candidate for election in 1848 to the Thirty-first Congress; elected as a Democrat to the United States Senate to fill the vacancy caused by the death of Dixon H. Lewis and served from November 30, 1849, to March 3, 1853; presidential elector on the Democratic ticket of Buchanan and Breckinridge in 1856 and of Breckinridge and Lane in 1860; moved to Memphis, Tenn., in 1858 and became editor of the Memphis Eagle and Enquirer January 1, 1859; returned to Alabama; delegate to the convention in 1861 in which Alabama voted to secede from the Union; held office under the Confederacy, but became a strong Union man in 1864; died in Huntsville, Madison County, Ala., May 21, 1865; interment in Maple Hill Cemetery.

CLEMENS, Sherrard, a Representative from Virginia; born in Wheeling, Va. (now West Virginia), on April 28, 1820; appointed a cadet to the United States Military Academy at West Point, but resigned after six months; was graduated in law from Washington (now Washington and Jefferson) College, Washington, Pa.; was admitted to the bar in 1843 and commenced practice in Wheeling; elected as a Democrat to the

Thirty-second Congress to fill the vacancy caused by the resignation of George W. Thompson and served from December 6, 1852, to March 3, 1853; presidential elector on the Democratic ticket of Buchanan and Breckinridge in 1856; elected to the Thirty-fifth and Thirty-sixth Congresses (March 4, 1857–March 3, 1861); was against secession and therefore was not a candidate for renomination in 1860; resumed the practice of law in Wheeling, W. Va.; moved to St. Louis, Mo., and continued the practice of law; died in St. Louis, Mo., June 30, 1881; interment in Calvary Cemetery.

CLEMENTE, Louis Gary, a Representative from New York; born in New York City, N. Y., June 10, 1908; attended St. Ann's Academy in New York City and LaSalle Military Academy, Oakdale, L. I., N. Y.; received a Reserve officer's certificate at Plattsburg, N. Y., in 1925 and a Reserve commission in 1929; was graduated from Georgetown Law School, Washington, D. C., in 1931; admitted to the District of Columbia bar in 1931 and commenced the practice of law in Washington, D. C.; admitted to the New York State bar and also Supreme Court; during World War II entered the United States Army as a second lieutenant in 1941 and served until released from active duty as a lieutenant colonel in 1946; member of the New York City Council 1946–1949; elected as a Democrat to the Eighty-first and Eighty-second Congresses (January 3, 1949–January 3, 1953); unsuccessful candidate for reelection in 1952 to the Eighty-third Congress; executive vice president of Unexcelled Chemical Corp., Ohio Bronze Corp., Premier Chemical Corp., and Modene Paint Corp.; member of the board of directors of the World's Fair Corp., the Federation Bank and Trust Co., the Mary Immaculate Hospital, the Angel Guardian Home, and Queensboro Council for Social Welfare; resides in Jamaica Estates, N. Y.

CLEMENTS, Andrew Jackson, a Representative from Tennessee; born in Clementsville, Clay County, Tenn., December 23, 1832; attended a private school and Burritt College, Sparta, Tenn.; studied medicine and commenced practice in Lafayette, Tenn.; during the Civil War served as surgeon with the First Regiment, Tennessee Mounted Volunteer Infantry; elected as a Unionist to the Thirty-seventh Congress (March 4, 1861–March 3, 1863); member of the State house of representatives in 1866; resumed the practice of his profession; established a school on his estate for the people of that section of the Cumberland highlands; died in Glasgow, Barren County, Ky.; November 7, 1913; interment in Glasgow Cemetery.

CLEMENTS, Earle C., a Representative and a Senator from Kentucky; born in Morganfield, Union County, Ky., October 22, 1896; attended the public schools and the University of Kentucky at Lexington; during the First World War enlisted in the United States Army as a private and when discharged was a captain of infantry; engaged in agricultural pursuits; sheriff of Union County 1922–1925; clerk of Union County 1926–1933; judge of Union County 1934–1941; member of the State senate 1942–1944, serving as majority floor leader in 1944; elected as a Democrat to the Seventy-ninth and Eightieth Congresses and served from January 3, 1945, until his resignation on January 6, 1948, having been elected Governor; elected Governor of Kentucky in 1947 for the term ending December 1951 but resigned in November 1950 having been elected to the United States Senate to fill the vacancy caused by the resignation of Alben W. Barkley and at the same time was elected for a six-year term and served from November 27, 1950, to January 3, 1957; unsuccessful candidate for reelection in 1956; Highway Commissioner of Kentucky in 1960; Washington consultant for the American Merchant Marine Institute, Inc., since January 1961; resides in Morganfield, Ky.

CLEMENTS, Isaac, a Representative from Illinois; born near Brookville, Franklin County, Ind., March 31, 1837; attended the common schools; was graduated from the Indiana Asbury College (now De Pauw University), Greencastle, Ind., in 1859; studied law in Greencastle; moved to Illinois and taught school; during the Civil War entered the Union Army in July 1861 and served as second lieutenant of Company G, Ninth Regiment, Illinois Volunteer Infantry; remained in the service over three years; was twice promoted; appointed register in bankruptcy in June 1867; elected as a Republican to the Forty-third Congress (March 4, 1873–March 3, 1875); unsuccessful candidate for reelection in 1874 to the Forty-fourth Congress; appointed a United States penitentiary commissioner in 1877; United States pension agent at Chicago, Ill., from March 18, 1890, until November 4, 1893; moved to Normal, Ill., in 1899; superintendent of the Soldiers' Orphans' Home at Normal, Ill.; died in Danville, Vermilion County, Ill., May 31, 1909; interment in Home Cemetery.

CLEMENTS, Judson Claudius, a Representative from Georgia; born near Villanow, Walker County, Ga., February 12, 1846; attended the common schools; served in the Confederate Army during the Civil War as a first lieutenant in the First Regiment, Georgia State Troops, Stovall's brigade; was wounded at Atlanta July 22, 1864; studied law at Cumberland University, Lebanon, Tenn.; was admitted to the bar in 1869 and commenced practice in La Fayette, Walker County, Ga.; served as school commissioner of Walker County in 1871 and 1872; member of the State house of representatives 1872–1876; served in the State senate 1877–1880; elected as a Democrat to the Forty-seventh and to the four succeeding Congresses (March 4, 1881–March 3, 1891); was not a candidate for renomination in 1890; appointed on March 17, 1892, a member, and in 1911 became chairman, of the Interstate Commerce Commission and served until his death in Washington, D. C., June 18, 1917; interment in Cave Hill Cemetery, Louisville, Ky.

CLEMENTS, Newton Nash, a Representative from Alabama; born in Tuscaloosa County, Ala., December 23, 1837; was graduated from the University of Alabama at Tuscaloosa in 1858; entered Harvard University, Cambridge, Mass., in 1859; studied law but never practiced; during the Civil War entered the Confederate Army as a captain in the Twenty-sixth Alabama Regiment, afterward the Fiftieth Alabama Regiment; successively promoted to major, lieutenant colonel, and colonel; member of the State house of representatives 1870–1872 and 1874–1878, serving as speaker in 1876, 1877, and 1878; elected to the Forty-sixth Congress to fill the vacancy caused by the resignation of Burwell B. Lewis and served from December 8, 1880, to March 3, 1881; unsuccessful candidate for renomination in 1880; largely interested in planting and cotton manufactures; died in Tuscaloosa, Ala., February 20, 1900; interment in Evergreen Cemetery.

CLENDENIN, David, a Representative from Ohio; moved from Harford County, Md., to near Struthers in the Mahoning Valley, Ohio, about 1806; was a pioneer in the iron and steel industry, having built the second stack to be constructed in Ohio; lived in Trumbull County, Ohio; served as first lieutenant of Capt. James Hazlep's company of artillery attached to a regiment of the Ohio Militia in the War of 1812; also as lieutenant paymaster in the Second Regiment, Ohio Militia, from August 26, 1812, until January 19, 1813; assistant district paymaster in the United States Army from April 19, 1814, to December 19, 1814; elected to the Thirteenth Congress to fill the vacancy caused by the resignation of Reasin Beall; reelected to the Fourteenth Congress and served from October 11, 1814, to March 3, 1817.

CLEVELAND, Chauncey Fitch, a Representative from Connecticut; born in Canterbury, Conn., February 16, 1799; attended the common schools; taught school from the age of fifteen to twenty; studied law; was admitted to the bar in 1819 and commenced practice in Hampton; member of the State house of representatives 1826–1829, 1832, 1835, 1836, 1838, 1847, and 1848; served as speaker in 1836 and 1838; State's attorney in 1832 and State bank commissioner in 1838; moved to Norwich, Conn., in 1841; Governor of Connecticut in 1842 and 1843; resumed the practice of law in Hampton; elected as a Democrat to the Thirty-first and Thirty-second Congresses (March 4, 1849–March 3, 1853); became affiliated with the Republican Party upon its organization; delegate to the Republican National Convention at Philadelphia in 1856 and at Chicago in 1860; presidential elector on the Republican ticket of Lincoln and Hamlin in 1860; member of the peace convention of 1861 held in Washington, D. C., in an effort to devise means to prevent the impending war; again a member of the State house of representatives in 1863 and 1866 and served as speaker in the former year; engaged in agricultural pursuits and the practice of law; died in Hampton, Windham County, Conn., June 6, 1887; interment in South Cemetery.

CLEVELAND, Jesse Franklin, a Representative from Georgia; born in Greenville, S. C., October 25, 1804; attended the local schools; moved to Georgia; member of the State senate 1831–1834; elected as a Union Democrat to the Twenty-fourth Congress to fill the vacancy caused by the resignation of William Schley; reelected to the Twenty-fifth Congress and served from October 5, 1835, to March 3, 1839; moved to Charleston, S. C., in 1839 and engaged in the mercantile business; served as a director of the Bank of South Carolina until his death; died in Charleston, S. C., on June 22, 1841; interment in St. Michael's Church Burial Ground.

CLEVELAND, Orestes, a Representative from New Jersey; born in Duanesburg, Schenectady County, N. Y., March 2, 1829; attended the common schools; moved to Jersey City, N. J., in 1845, later becoming identified with the Joseph Dixon Crucible Co. in the manufacture of black lead, stove polish, pencils, etc.; member of the board of aldermen of Jersey City in 1861 and 1862, serving as its president in the latter year; mayor of Jersey City 1864–1866; elected as a Democrat to the Forty-first Congress (March 4, 1869–March 3, 1871); unsuccessful candidate for reelection in 1870 to the Forty-second Congress; engaged in business with the Forbes Fibre Co. of Jersey City; unsuccessful candidate for the nomination for Governor on the Democratic ticket in 1880; again mayor of Jersey City 1886–1891; was one of the organizers of the board of trade of Jersey City in 1888 and its first president; moved to Tenafly in 1892 and thence to Engelwood, N. J.; died March 30, 1896, in Norwich, Windsor County, Vt., where he had gone in search of health; interment in Fairview Cemetery.

CLEVENGER, Cliff, a Representative from Ohio; born on a ranch near Long Pine, Brown County, Nebr., August 20, 1885; moved in 1895 with his parents to Lacona, Warren County, Iowa, where he attended the public and high schools; engaged in the mercantile business at Marengo, Iowa, 1901–1903 and at Appleton, Wis., 1904–1914; president of the Clevenger Stores, Bowling Green, Ohio, 1915–1926; manager of the F. W. Uhlman Stores, Bryan, Ohio, 1927–1938; also interested in agricultural pursuits, stock raising, and stock feeding; elected as a Republican to the Seventy-sixth and to the nine succeeding Congresses (January 3, 1939–January 3, 1959); was not a candidate for renomination in 1958; died in Tiffin, Ohio, December 13, 1960; interment in Oak Hill Cemetery, Neenah, Wis.

CLEVER, Charles P., a Delegate from the Territory of New Mexico; born in Cologne, Prussia, February 23, 1830; attended the gymnasium of Cologne and the University of Bonn; immigrated to the United States in 1848 and settled in Santa Fe, N. Mex., in 1850; engaged in trade from 1855 to 1862; appointed United States marshal for New Mexico in 1857; became one of the owners of the Santa Fe Weekly Gazette, a paper published in English and Spanish, in 1858; studied law; was admitted to the bar in 1861 and commenced practice in Santa Fe, N. Mex.; appointed United States marshal and census enumerator in 1861; during the Civil War served as adjutant on the staff of General Canby at the Battle of Valverde; adjutant general of New Mexico 1861–1865 and in 1867 and 1868; attorney general 1862–1867; presented credentials as a Democratic Delegate-elect to the Fortieth Congress and served from September 2, 1867 (date of election), to February 20, 1869, when he was succeeded by J. Francisco Chaves, who contested the election; appointed one of the incorporators of the Centennial Exposition in 1869; served as a commissioner to revise and codify the laws of New Mexico; engaged in the practice of law until his death in Tome, Valencia County, N. Mex., on July 8, 1874; interment in the National Cemetery, Santa Fe, N. Mex.

CLIFFORD, Nathan, a Representative from Maine; born in Rumney, N. H., August 18, 1803; attended the public schools of Rumney, the Haverhill (N. H.) Academy, and New Hampton Literary Institute; taught school and gave vocal lessons; studied law in New York; was admitted to the bar and commenced practice in Newfield, York County, Maine, in 1824; member of the State house of representatives 1830–1834 and served as speaker the last two years; attorney general 1834–1838; elected as a Democrat to the Twenty-sixth and Twenty-seventh Congresses (March 4, 1839–March 3, 1843); was not a candidate for renomination in 1842; Attorney General of the United States in the Cabinet of President Polk and served from October 17, 1846, to March 17, 1848; commissioner to Mexico, with the rank of Envoy Extraordinary and Minister Plenipotentiary, from March 18, 1848, to September 6, 1849; through him the treaty was arranged with the Mexican Government by which California became a part of the United States; resumed the practice of law in Portland, Maine; appointed Associate Justice of the Supreme Court of the United States January 28, 1858, and served until his death; president of the electoral commission convened in 1877; died in Cornish, York County, Maine, on July 25, 1881; interment in Evergreen Cemetery, Portland, Maine.

CLIFT, Joseph Wales, a Representative from Georgia; born in North Marshfield, Plymouth County, Mass., September 30, 1837; attended the common schools and Phillips Exeter Academy, Exeter, N. H.; was graduated from the medical school of Harvard University in 1862; immediately entered the Union Army at the outbreak of the Civil War and was acting surgeon from July 13, 1862, to August 7, 1865; served in the Army of the Potomac until November 18, 1866; practiced medicine in Savannah, Ga.; appointed registrar of the city of Savannah by Major General Pope under the reconstruction acts; upon the readmission of Georgia to representation was elected as a Republican to the Fortieth Congress and served from July 25, 1868, to March 3, 1869; presented credentials as a Member-elect to the Forty-first Congress, but was not permitted to qualify; died in Rock City Falls, Saratoga County, N. Y., May 2, 1908; interment in the cemetery adjoining the Clift estate, North Marshfield, Mass.

CLINCH, Duncan Lamont, a Representative from Georgia; born at "Ard-Lamont," Edgecombe County, N. C., April 6, 1787;

entered the United States Army as first lieutenant of the Third Infantry July 1, 1808; promoted to captain December 31, 1810; appointed lieutenant colonel of the Forty-Third Regiment, United States Infantry, August 4, 1813; appointed colonel of the Eighth Regiment, United States Infantry, April 20, 1819; attained the rank of brigadier general April 20, 1829; commanded at the Battle of Ouithlacoochee against the Seminole Indians December 31, 1835; resigned September 21, 1836, and settled on a plantation near St. Marys, Ga.; elected as a Whig to the Twenty-eighth Congress to fill the vacancy caused by the death of John Millen and served from February 15, 1844, to March 3, 1845; died in Macon, Ga., November 27, 1849; interment in Bonaventure Cemetery, Savannah, Ga.

CLINE, Cyrus, a Representative from Indiana; born near Mansfield, Richland County, Ohio, July 12, 1856; moved to Steuben County, Ind., in 1858 with his parents, who settled near Angola; attended the Angola High School, and was graduated from Hillsdale College, Michigan, in 1876; superintendent of the schools of Steuben County 1877–1883; studied law; was admitted to the bar and began practice in Angola, Steuben County, Ind., in 1884; elected as a Democrat to the Sixty-first and to the three succeeding Congresses (March 4, 1909–March 3, 1917); unsuccessful candidate for reelection in 1916; resumed the practice of law in Angola, Ind., and died there on October 5, 1923; interment in Circle Hill Cemetery.

CLINGAN, William, a Delegate from Pennsylvania; born probably near Wagontown, West Colen Township, Chester County, Pa.; justice of the peace 1757–1786; Member of the Continental Congress 1777–1779; one of the first signers of the Articles of Confederation in 1778; president of the county courts 1780–1786; died on May 9, 1790; interment in Upper Octorara Burial Grounds, Chester County, Pa.

CLINGMAN, Thomas Lanier, a Representative and a Senator from North Carolina; born in Huntsville, N. C., July 27, 1812; educated by private tutors and in the public schools in Iredell County, N. C.; was graduated from the University of North Carolina at Chapel Hill in 1832; studied law; was admitted to the bar in 1834 and began practice in Huntsville, N. C.; elected to the State house of commons in 1835; moved to Asheville, Buncombe County, N. C., in 1836; member of the State senate in 1840; elected as a Whig to the Twenty-eighth Congress (March 4, 1843–March 3, 1845); unsuccessful candidate for reelection to the Twenty-ninth Congress; elected as a Democrat to the Thirtieth and to the five succeeding Congresses and served from March 4, 1847, to May 7, 1858, when he resigned to become Senator; appointed to the United States Senate on May 6, 1858, to fill the vacancy caused by the resignation of Asa Biggs; reelected in 1861 and served from May 7, 1858, to March 28, 1861, when he withdrew; during the Civil War was appointed on May 17, 1862, as a brigadier general in the Confederate service; delegate to the Democratic National Convention at New York in 1868; explored and measured mountain peaks; died in Morganton, Burke County, N. C., on November 3, 1897; interment in Riverside Cemetery, Asheville, N. C.

CLINTON, De Witt (half brother of James Graham Clinton and nephew of George Clinton), a Senator from New York; born in Napanock, Ulster County, N. Y., March 2, 1769; was graduated from Columbia College in 1786; studied law; was admitted to the bar in 1790 and commenced practice in New York City; private secretary to his uncle, Gov. George Clinton, 1790–1795; member of the State assembly from January to April 1798; served in the State senate 1798–1802 and 1806–

1811; delegate to the State constitutional convention in 1801; member of the council of appointments in 1801, 1802, 1806, and 1807; elected as a Democrat to the United States Senate to fill the vacancy caused by the resignation of John Armstrong and served from February 9, 1802, to November 4, 1803, when he resigned; mayor of the city of New York 1803–1807, 1810, 1811, 1813, and 1814; while mayor he organized the Historical Society of New York in 1804 and was its president; also organized the Academy of Fine Arts in 1808; Lieutenant Governor of New York 1811–1813; unsuccessful candidate of the Peace Party for President of the United States in 1812; regent of the University of New York 1808–1825; in 1809 was a member of the commission to explore a route for a canal between Lake Erie and the Hudson River; prepared an elaborate petition to the legislature in 1815 asking for the immediate construction of the canal, which was begun two years later, and while Governor he was the first to break ground for the commencement of work; served several years as canal commissioner; Governor of the State 1817–1821 and 1825–1828; declined the mission to England offered him by President Adams in 1825; died in Albany, N. Y., on February 11, 1828; interment in Clinton Cemetery, Little Britain, Orange County, N. Y.

CLINTON, George (uncle of De Witt Clinton and James Graham Clinton), a Delegate from New York and a Vice President of the United States; born in Little Britain, Ulster (now Orange) County, N. Y., July 26, 1739; completed preparatory studies; served as lieutenant of rangers in the expedition against Fort Frontenac; studied law; was admitted to the bar and commenced practice in Little Britain; clerk of the court of common pleas in 1759 and district attorney in 1765; surveyor of New Windsor; member of the State assembly in 1768; served on the New York Committee of Correspondence in 1774; Member of the Continental Congress from May 15, 1775, to July 8, 1776, when he was ordered by General Washington to take the field as brigadier general of militia; appointed brigadier general by Congress March 25, 1777; Governor of New York 1777–1795; president of the State convention which ratified the Federal Constitution; unsuccessful candidate of the State Rights Democratic Party for Vice President of the United States in 1796; member of the State assembly in 1800 and 1801; again Governor of New York 1801–1804; elected Vice President in 1804 as a State Rights Democrat; reelected in 1808; died in Washington, D. C., April 20, 1812; interment in the Congressional Cemetery; reinterment in the First Dutch Reformed Church Cemetery, Kingston, N. Y., in May 1908.

CLINTON, George (son of the preceding and cousin of De Witt Clinton and James Graham Clinton), a Representative from New York; born in New York City June 6, 1771; delegate to the State constitutional convention in 1801; member of the State assembly 1804 and 1805; elected as a Democrat to the Eighth and Ninth Congresses to fill the vacancies caused by the resignation of Samuel L. Mitchill (who had been reelected to the Ninth Congress); reelected to the Tenth Congress and served from February 14, 1805, to March 3, 1809; died in New York City September 16, 1809.

CLINTON, James Graham (half brother of De Witt Clinton and nephew of George Clinton), a Representative from New York; born in Little Britain, Orange County, N. Y., January 2, 1804; attended the common schools and Newburgh (N. Y.) Academy; studied law; was admitted to the bar in 1823 and practiced in Newburgh; master in chancery of Orange County; judge of the court of common pleas of Orange County; director of the old Newburgh Whaling Co. and of the Delaware & Hudson Railroad project; colonel in the State militia; elected

as a Democrat to the Twenty-seventh and Twenty-eighth Congresses (March 4, 1841–March 3, 1845); was not a candidate for reelection in 1844; died in New York City May 28, 1849; interment in the family cemetery at Little Britain, New Windsor Township, N. Y.

CLIPPINGER, Roy, a Representative from Illinois; born in Fairfield, Wayne County, Ill., January 13, 1886; attended the public schools; learned the printer's trade and engaged in the newspaper business; publisher and editor 1909–1961; founder and president of the Board of Greater Weeklies, New York, N. Y.; president of the Carmi, Ill., Hospital Association 1945–1948; manager of the White County, Ill., Bridge Commission 1941–1961; engaged in the furniture business 1947–1950; elected as a Republican to the Seventy-ninth Congress to fill the vacancy caused by the death of James V. Heidinger; reelected in 1946 to the Eightieth Congress and served from November 6, 1945, to January 3, 1949; was not a candidate for renomination in 1948; resumed his former business pursuits and is a resident of Carmi, Ill.

CLOPTON, David, a Representative from Alabama; born in Putnam County, near Milledgeville, Ga., September 29, 1820; attended the county schools and Edenton (Ga.) Academy; was graduated from Randolph-Macon College, Oakland, Va., in 1840; studied law; was admitted to the bar in 1841 and commenced practice in Milledgeville, Ga.; moved to Tuskegee, Ala., in 1844, and continued the practice of his profession; elected as a State Rights Democrat to the Thirty-sixth Congress and served from March 4, 1859, to January 21, 1861, when he withdrew; during the Civil War enlisted as a private in the Confederate Army in the Twelfth Alabama Infantry for one year; elected as a Representative to the First and Second Confederate Congresses and served from 1862 to 1864; appointed judge of the supreme court of Alabama October 30, 1884, and served until his death; died in Montgomery, Ala., February 5, 1892; interment in Oakwood Cemetery.

CLOPTON, John, a Representative from Virginia; born in St. Peter's parish, near Tunstall, New Kent County, Va., February 7, 1756; was graduated from the College of Philadelphia (now the University of Pennsylvania) in 1776; studied law; was admitted to the bar and practiced; served as first lieutenant and as captain in the Revolutionary War; wounded at the Battle of Brandywine; member of the Virginia House of Delegates 1789–1791; elected as a Democrat to the Fourth and Fifth Congresses (March 4, 1795–March 3, 1799); member of the Virginia Privy Council 1799–1801; elected to the Seventh and to the seven succeeding Congresses and served from March 4, 1801, until his death near Tunstall, New Kent County, Va., September 11, 1816; interment in the family burying ground on his plantation.

CLOUSE, Wynne F., a Representative from Tennessee; born in Goffton, near Cookeville, Putnam County, Tenn., August 29, 1883; attended the public schools; was graduated from Cleveland Hill Academy, Pleasant Hill, Tenn., in 1898 and from Cumberland University, Lebanon, Tenn., in 1911; studied law; was admitted to the bar in 1911 and commenced practice in Cookeville, Tenn., in 1912; delegate to the Republican National Conventions in 1916 and 1924; elected as a Republican to the Sixty-seventh Congress (March 4, 1921–March 3, 1923); unsuccessful candidate for reelection in 1922 to the Sixty-eighth Congress; resumed the practice of law in the city of Nashville; was appointed receiver of the Tennessee Central Railroad Co.; served as special assistant to the Attorney General of the United States in 1924; appointed referee in bankruptcy for the Nashville division of the middle district of Tennessee and served until his resignation in January 1940; died in Franklin, Tenn., February 19, 1944; interment in Mount Hope Cemetery.

CLOVER, Benjamin Hutchinson, a Representative from Kansas; born near Jefferson, Franklin County, Ohio, December 22, 1837; attended the common schools; moved to Kansas in 1871 and located in Cambridge; engaged in agricultural pursuits; member of the board of school commissioners 1873–1888; twice president of the Kansas State Farmers' Alliance and Industrial Union and twice vice president of the national organization of that order; elected as the candidate of the Farmers' Alliance Party to the Fifty-second Congress (March 4, 1891–March 3, 1893); was not a candidate for renomination in 1892; resumed agricultural pursuits; died in Douglas, Butler County, Kans., on December 30, 1899; interment in Douglas Cemetery.

CLOWNEY, William Kennedy, a Representative from South Carolina; born in Union County, S. C., March 21, 1797; attended private schools and an academy; was graduated from South Carolina College at Columbia in 1818; taught in the public schools of Unionville and in the University of South Carolina; member of the State house of representatives; studied law; was admitted to the bar and began practice in Union; commissioner in equity of South Carolina 1830–1833; elected as a Nullifier to the Twenty-third Congress (March 4, 1833–March 3, 1835); elected as a State Rights Democrat to the Twenty-fifth Congress (March 4, 1837–March 3, 1839); member of the State senate in 1840; Lieutenant Governor of South Carolina; died in Union, Union County, S. C., March 12, 1851; interment in Fairforest Cemetery, Union County, S. C.

CLUETT, Ernest Harold, a Representative from New York; born in Troy, N. Y., July 13, 1874; attended the public schools; was graduated from Albany (N. Y.) Academy in 1892 and from Williams College, Williamstown, Mass., in 1896; also studied at Oxford University in England; treasurer of Cluett, Peabody & Co. 1900–1916, vice president 1916–1929, and chairman of the board of directors 1929–1937; head of the employment division of the Watervliet (N. Y.) Government Arsenal in 1918; served on a special mission to France for the Y. M. C. A. in 1918; member of the National War Work Council; presidential elector on the ticket of Taft and Sherman in 1912 and of Hughes and Fairbanks in 1916; unsuccessful candidate for election to the United States Senate in 1934; elected as a Republican to the Seventy-fifth, Seventy-sixth, and Seventy-seventh Congresses (January 3, 1937–January 3, 1943); was not a candidate for renomination in 1942; retired from public life and resided in Palm Beach, Fla., and Troy, N. Y.; died in Troy, N. Y., February 4, 1954; interment in Oakwood Cemetery.

CLUNIE, Thomas Jefferson, a Representative from California; born in St. John's, Newfoundland, March 25, 1852, while his parents were on a visit there from Massachusetts; moved with his parents to California in 1854; returned to the East and settled in Maine, remained a few years, and then went back to California in 1861, where he afterwards resided; attended the public schools; studied law; was admitted to the bar in 1868 and commenced practice in Sacramento in 1870; member of the State assembly in 1875; delegate to the Democratic National Convention at Chicago in 1884; served in the State senate 1887–1889; took an active part in the State militia, and was retired as brigadier general; elected as a Democrat to the Fifty-first Congress (March 4, 1889–March 3, 1891); was an unsuccessful candidate for reelection in 1890 to the Fifty-

second Congress; resumed the practice of his profession; died in San Francisco, Calif., on June 30, 1903; interment in the City Cemetery, Sacramento, Calif.

CLYMER, George, a Delegate and a Representative from Pennsylvania; born in Philadelphia, Pa., March 16, 1739; engaged in mercantile pursuits in Philadelphia; captain of a volunteer company at the outbreak of hostilities with Great Britain and a member of the committee of safety; Member of the Continental Congress 1776–1778 and 1780–1783; a signer of the Declaration of Independence; member of the State house of representatives 1785–1788; delegate to the convention which framed the Federal Constitution in 1787; elected as a Federalist to the First Congress (March 4, 1789–March 3, 1791); was not a candidate for renomination in 1790; appointed collector of excise duties in 1791, but resigned after the Whisky Insurrection; one of the commissioners to negotiate a treaty with the Cherokees and the Creeks June 29, 1796; died at his home, "Sommerseat," Morrisville, Pa., January 23, 1813; interment in Friends Graveyard, Trenton, N. J.

CLYMER, Hiester (nephew of William Hiester and cousin of Isaac Ellmaker Hiester), a Representative from Pennsylvania; born near Morgantown, Caernarvon Township, Berks County, Pa., November 3, 1827; attended primary schools at Reading, and was graduated from Princeton College in 1847; studied law; was admitted to the bar of Berks County April 6, 1849, and practiced in Reading and Berks County until 1851, when he moved to Pottsville, Schuylkill County; returned to Reading in 1856; represented Berks County on the board of revenue commissioners of the State in January 1860; delegate to the Democratic National Conventions at Charleston and at Baltimore in 1860; member of the State senate from October 1860 until March 1866, when he resigned; unsuccessful Democratic candidate for election as Governor in 1866; delegate to the Democratic National Convention at New York in 1868; member of the State board of charities in 1870; president of the Democratic State convention which met in Reading in May 1872; elected as a Democrat to the Forty-third and to the three succeeding Congresses (March 4, 1873–March 3, 1881); was not a candidate for renomination in 1880; after his retirement from Congress was vice president of the Union Trust Co. of Philadelphia and president of the Clymer Iron Co.; also a director of the Reading Fire Insurance Co. and a trustee of the Charles Evans Cemetery; died in Reading, Pa., on June 12, 1884; interment in the Charles Evans Cemetery.

COAD, Merwin, a Representative from Iowa; born in Cawker City, Mitchell County, Kans., September 28, 1924; in 1932 moved with his parents to a farm near Auburn, Nebr.; graduated from high school in Auburn, Nebr., in 1941; student at Peru (Nebr.) State Teachers College in 1941 and 1942, and Phillips University, Enid, Okla., 1942–1944; graduated from Texas Christian University at Fort Worth in 1945; also studied at Drake University, Des Moines, Iowa; ordained to the ministry of Disciples of Christ Church, Boone, Iowa, in 1945; associate minister St. Joseph, Mo., in 1948 and 1949; minister at Lenox, Iowa, 1949–1951, and Boone, Iowa, 1951–1956; elected as a Democrat to the Eighty-fifth and Eighty-sixth Congresses (January 3, 1957–January 3, 1961). *Reelected to the Eighty-seventh Congress.*

COADY, Charles Pearce, a Representative from Maryland; born in Baltimore, Md., February 22, 1868; attended the public schools, and was graduated from Baltimore City College in 1886; engaged in mercantile pursuits; studied law; was admitted to the bar in 1894 and commenced practice in Baltimore, Md., in the same year; member of the State senate for the term 1908–1912;

reelected for the four-year term ending in 1916, but resigned in 1913, having been nominated as a candidate for Congress; elected as a Democrat to the Sixty-third Congress to fill the vacancy caused by the death of George Konig; reelected to the Sixty-fourth, Sixty-fifth, and Sixty-sixth Congresses and served from November 4, 1913, to March 3, 1921; unsuccessful candidate for reelection in 1920 to the Sixty-seventh Congress; resumed the practice of law; Baltimore City collector and manager of the bureau of receipts 1922–1925; died in Baltimore, Md., February 16, 1934; interment in New Cathedral Cemetery.

COBB, Amasa, a Representative from Wisconsin; born in Crawford County, Ill., September 27, 1823; attended the public schools; moved to the Territory of Wisconsin in 1842 and engaged in lead mining; served in the Mexican War as a private in the United States Army; studied law; was admitted to the bar and commenced practice in Mineral Point, Iowa County, Wis.; district attorney 1850–1854; member of the State senate in 1855 and 1856; adjutant general of Wisconsin 1855–1858; member of the State assembly in 1860 and 1861 and served as speaker during the last year; during the Civil War entered the Union Army as colonel of the Fifth Wisconsin Infantry July 12, 1861; became colonel of the Forty-third Wisconsin Infantry on September 29, 1864; brevetted brigadier general March 13, 1865, "for gallant and distinguished services at the Battles of Williamsburg, Goldin's Farm, Va., and Antietam, Md."; mustered out June 24, 1865; elected as a Republican to the Thirty-eighth and to the three succeeding Congresses (March 4, 1863–March 3, 1871); moved to Lincoln, Nebr., and continued the practice of law; appointed mayor of Lincoln, Nebr., in 1873; associate justice of the State supreme court 1878–1892 and served as chief justice for four years; died in Los Angeles, Calif., July 5, 1905; interment in Evergreen Cemetery, Lincoln, Nebr.

COBB, Clinton Levering, a Representative from North Carolina; born in Elizabeth City, Pasquotank County, N. C., August 25, 1842; attended the common schools and was graduated from the University of North Carolina at Chapel Hill; studied law; was admitted to the bar in 1867 and commenced practice in Elizabeth City, N. C.; engaged in the mercantile business; elected as a Republican to the Forty-first, Forty-second, and Forty-third Congresses (March 4, 1869–March 3, 1875); unsuccessful candidate for reelection in 1874 to the Forty-fourth Congress; resumed the practice of law in Elizabeth City, N. C., and died there on April 30, 1879; interment in Episcopal Cemetery.

COBB, David, a Representative from Massachusetts; born in Attleboro, Mass., September 14, 1748; was graduated from Harvard College in 1766; studied medicine in Boston and afterward practiced in Taunton, Mass.; member of the Provincial Congress in 1775; lieutenant colonel of Jackson's regiment in 1777 and 1778, serving in Rhode Island and New Jersey; was aide-de-camp on the staff of General Washington; appointed major general of militia in 1786 and rendered conspicuous service during Shays' Rebellion; judge of the Bristol County court of common pleas 1784–1796; member of the State house of representatives 1789–1793 and served as speaker; elected as a Federalist to the Third Congress (March 4, 1793–March 3, 1795); moved to the district of Maine in 1796 and engaged in agricultural pursuits; elected to the State Senate of Massachusetts from the eastern district of Maine in 1802 and served as president; elected to the State council in 1808; Lieutenant Governor in 1809; member of the board of military defense in 1812; chief justice of the Hancock County Court of Common Pleas; returned to Taunton, Mass., in 1817, where he died April 17, 1830; interment in Plain Cemetery.

COBB, George Thomas, a Representative from New Jersey; born in Morristown, N. J., October 13, 1813; became an orphan when six years of age and received very little schooling; employed at an early age as a clerk in a store at Denville, N. J., and later employed by Capt. William Scott, who owned the iron works at Powerville and Boonton, N. J.; transferred to a store in New York City; engaged in the foreign trade; retired from active business pursuits after having amassed a fortune; returned to New Jersey; elected as a Democrat to the Thirty-seventh Congress (March 4, 1861–March 3, 1863); declined to be a candidate for renomination in 1862; affiliated with the Republican Party in 1863 and as such was elected a member of the State senate in 1865 and again in 1868; mayor of Morristown 1865–1869; became a trustee of Drew Theological Seminary in 1868 and served until his death; unsuccessful candidate for election to the United States Senate in 1869; president of the Sabbath School Association of Morris County; was killed in an accident on the Chesapeake & Ohio Railroad at Jerrys Run, near White Sulphur Springs, Va., August 12, 1870; interment in Evergreen Cemetery, Morristown, N. J.

COBB, Howell (nephew of the preceding), a Representative from Georgia; born at "Cherry Hill," Jefferson County, Ga., September 7, 1815; moved with his father to Athens, Ga., in childhood; was graduated from Franklin College (then a part of the University of Georgia), at Athens in 1834; studied law; was admitted to the bar and commenced practice in Athens, Ga., in 1836; presidential elector on the Van Buren and Johnson ticket in 1836; solicitor general of the western judicial circuit of Georgia 1837–1841; elected as a Democrat to the Twenty-eighth and to the three succeeding Congresses (March 4, 1843–March 3, 1851); served as Speaker of the House of Representatives in the Thirty-first Congress; Governor of Georgia 1851–1853; elected to the Thirty-fourth Congress (March 4, 1855–March 3, 1857); Secretary of the Treasury in the Cabinet of President Buchanan and served from March 6, 1857, to December 10, 1860, when he resigned; chairman of the convention of delegates from the seceded States which assembled in Montgomery, Ala., on February 24, 1861, to form a Confederate Government; during the Civil War was appointed a brigadier general in the Confederate Army February 13, 1862, and promoted to major general September 9, 1863; surrendered at Macon, Ga., April 20, 1864; died in New York City October 9, 1868; interment in Oconee Cemetery, Athens, Clarke County, Ga.

COBB, Howell, a Representative from Georgia; born in Granville County, N. C., August 3, 1772; moved to Georgia and settled near Louisville, Jefferson County, where he engaged in agricultural pursuits; served in the United States Army as ensign and lieutenant in the Second Sub Legion and as captain in the Artillerists and Engineers from February 23, 1793, until January 31, 1806, when he resigned; elected to the Tenth, Eleventh, and Twelfth Congresses and served from March 4, 1807, to 1812, when he resigned; returned to his plantation in Jefferson County, Ga., and resumed agricultural pursuits; died on his plantation, "Cherry Hill," nine miles northwest of Louisville, Jefferson County, Ga., May 26, 1818; interment in the family cemetery on his estate.

COBB, James Edward, a Representative from Alabama; born in Thomaston, Upson County, Ga., October 5, 1835; attended the public schools, and was graduated from Emory College, Oxford, Ga., in June 1856; studied law; was admitted to the bar and practiced; moved to Texas in 1857; during the Civil War entered the Confederate Army in 1861 as lieutenant in Company F, Fifth Texas Regiment, and served in the Army of Northern Virginia until he was made prisoner at the Battle of Gettysburg; after his release settled in Tuskegee, Ala., and practiced law until 1874; circuit judge from 1874 to 1886; reelected in 1886, but before qualifying was elected to Congress; elected to the Fiftieth and to the three succeeding Congresses (March 4, 1887–March 3, 1895); presented credentials as a Member-elect to the Fifty-fourth Congress and served from March 4, 1895, to April 21, 1896, when he was succeeded by Albert T. Goodwyn, who contested his election; resumed the practice of law in Tuskegee, Macon County, Ala.; delegate to the State constitutional convention in 1901; died in East Las Vegas, San Miguel County, N. Mex., June 2, 1903; interment in Evergreen Cemetery, Tuskegee, Ala.

COBB, Seth Wallace, a Representative from Missouri; born near Petersburg, Southampton County, Va., December 5, 1838; attended the common schools; joined a volunteer company from his native county in 1861 and served throughout the Civil War in the Army of Northern Virginia; moved to St. Louis, Mo., in 1867 and was employed as a clerk in a grain commission house for three years; in 1870 became engaged in the same business on his own account; president of the Merchants' Exchange in 1886; president of the corporation which built the Merchants' Bridge across the Mississippi River at St. Louis; elected as a Democrat to the Fifty-second, Fifty-third, and Fifty-fourth Congresses (March 4, 1891–March 3, 1897); was not a candidate for renomination in 1896; resumed the grain commission business in St. Louis; vice president of the Louisiana Purchase Exposition at St. Louis in 1904; died in St. Louis, Mo., May 22, 1909; interment in Calvary Cemetery.

COBB, Stephen Alonzo, a Representative from Kansas; born in Madison, Somerset County, Maine, June 17, 1833; attended the common schools; moved with his father to Minnesota in 1850; studied languages and prepared for college; entered Beloit College, Beloit, Wis., in 1854, where he was a student for two years; was graduated from Brown University, Providence, R. I., in 1858; settled in Wyandotte, Wyandotte County, Kans., in 1859 and commenced the practice of law; during the Civil War entered the Union Army in 1862; became captain and commissary sergeant of Volunteers on May 18, 1864; brevetted major August 16, 1865, "for efficient and meritorious services," and honorably discharged on September 23, 1865; mayor of Wyandotte in 1862 and again in 1868; served in the State senate in 1862, 1869, and 1870; member of the State house of representatives in 1872 and served as speaker; elected as a Republican to the Forty-third Congress (March 4, 1873–March 3, 1875); unsuccessful candidate for reelection in 1874 to the Forty-fourth Congress; died in Wyandotte (now a part of Kansas City), Kans., August 24, 1878; interment in Oak Grove Cemetery, Kansas City, Kans.

COBB, Thomas Reed, a Representative from Indiana; born in Springville, Lawrence County, Ind., July 2, 1828; attended Indiana University, Bloomington, Ind.; studied law; was admitted to the bar in 1851 and commenced practice in Bedford, Ind.; commissioned major of Indiana Militia in 1852; moved to Vincennes, Ind., in 1867; member of the State senate 1858–1866; presidential elector on the Democratic ticket of Seymour and Blair in 1868; president of the Democratic State convention in 1876; delegate to the Democratic National Convention at St. Louis in 1876; elected as a Democrat to the Forty-fifth and to the four succeeding Congresses (March 4, 1877–March 3, 1887); was not a candidate for renomination in 1886; resumed the practice of law and also engaged in agricultural pursuits; retired from public life; died in Vincennes, Knox County, Ind., June 23, 1892; interment in Old Vincennes Cemetery.

COBB, Thomas Willis, a Representative and a Senator from Georgia; born in Columbia County, Ga., in 1784; pursued preparatory studies; studied law; was admitted to the bar and practiced in Lexington, Ga.; moved to Greensboro, Greene County; elected to the Fifteenth and Sixteenth Congresses (March 4, 1817–March 3, 1821); unsuccessful candidate for reelection to the Seventeenth Congress; elected to the Eighteenth Congress and served from March 4, 1823, to December 6, 1824, when he resigned, having been elected Senator; elected to the United States Senate to fill the vacancy caused by the death of Nicholas Ware and served from December 6, 1824, until his resignation in 1828; judge of the superior court of Georgia; died in Greensboro, Ga., February 1, 1830.

COBB, Williamson Robert Winfield, a Representative from Alabama; born in Rhea County, Tenn., June 8, 1807; moved in 1809 to Bellefontaine, Madison County, Ala., with his father, who settled on a plantation and engaged in the raising of cotton; received a very limited education; was a clock peddler for a short time and subsequently entered the mercantile business in Bellefontaine; member of the State house of representatives in 1845 and 1846; located on a plantation in Madison County and engaged in cotton raising; elected as a Democrat to the Thirtieth and to the six succeeding Congresses and served from March 4, 1847, to January 30, 1861, when he withdrew; unsuccessful candidate for election to the Confederate House of Representatives in 1861; resumed agricultural pursuits in Madison County; elected in 1863 to the Confederate House of Representatives, but did not take his seat when the new Congress met, whereupon his fidelity was suspected and subsequently he was expelled by a unanimous vote; was killed by the accidental discharge of his own pistol while putting up a fence on his plantation near Bellefontaine, Ala., November 1, 1864; interment in the plot of the Cobb family estate near Cobb's Bridge over Flint River, on Jackson Highway, in Madison County, Ala.

COBURN, Frank Potter, a Representative from Wisconsin; born on a farm near West Salem, La Crosse County, Wis., December 6, 1858; attended the public schools; engaged in agricultural pursuits near West Salem; also engaged in the banking business in West Salem; was an unsuccessful Democratic candidate for election in 1888 to the Fifty-first Congress; elected as a Democrat to the Fifty-second Congress (March 4, 1891–March 3, 1893); was an unsuccessful candidate for reelection in 1892 to the Fifty-third Congress; resumed banking interests and agricultural pursuits near West Salem, Wis.; member of the county board of supervisors 1894–1903, serving as chairman in 1902 and 1903; jury commissioner 1897–1932; trustee of the county asylum 1907–1932; member of the board of review of income taxes for the county 1912–1926; died in a hospital in La Crosse, Wis., on November 2, 1932; interment in Hamilton Cemetery, West Salem, Wis.

COBURN, John, a Representative from Indiana; born in Indianapolis, Ind., October 27, 1825; attended the public schools, and was graduated from Wabash College, Crawfordsville, Ind., in 1846; studied law; was admitted to the bar in 1849 and commenced practice in Indianapolis; member of the State house of representatives in 1850; judge of the court of common pleas from 1859 to 1861, when he resigned to enter the Union Army; during the Civil War became colonel of the Thirty-third Regiment, Indiana Volunteer Infantry, September 16, 1861, and was mustered out September 20, 1864; brevetted brigadier general of Volunteers March 13, 1865, "for gallant and meritorious services during the war"; appointed as the first secretary of the Territory of Montana in March 1865 but resigned at once; elected judge of the fifth judicial circuit of Indiana in

October 1865 and resigned in July 1866; elected as a Republican to the Fortieth and to the three succeeding Congresses (March 4, 1867–March 3, 1875); was an unsuccessful candidate for reelection in 1874 to the Forty-fourth Congress; was appointed a justice of the supreme court of the Territory of Montana on February 19, 1884, and served until December 1885; returned to Indianapolis, and resumed the practice of law; died in Indianapolis, Ind., on January 28, 1908; interment in Crown Hill Cemetery.

COBURN, Stephen, a Representative from Maine; born in Bloomfield (now Skowhegan), Maine, on November 11, 1817; attended Waterville and China Academies; was graduated from Waterville (now Colby) College, Waterville, Maine, in 1839; taught a plantation school in Tarboro, N. C., in 1839 and 1840; principal of Bloomfield (Maine) Academy 1840–1844; studied law at the Harvard Law School; was admitted to the bar in 1845 and commenced practice in Skowhegan; member of the State board of education in 1849 and 1850; delegate to several Republican State conventions; elected as a Republican to the Thirty-sixth Congress on November 6, 1860, to fill the vacancy caused by the resignation of Israel Washburn, Jr., and served from January 2 to March 3, 1861; was not a candidate for the Thirty-seventh Congress, that election having been held in September 1860, previous to his election to the Thirty-sixth Congress; member of the peace convention of 1861 held in Washington, D. C., in an effort to devise means to prevent the impending war; resumed the practice of law; postmaster of Skowhegan from July 25, 1868, to January 23, 1877; was drowned in the Kennebec River, at Skowhegan, Maine, July 4, 1882; interment in South Cemetery, Skowhegan, Maine.

COCHRAN, Alexander Gilmore, a Representative from Pennsylvania; born in Allegheny City (now a part of Pittsburgh), Pa., March 20, 1846; attended private and public schools of that city, Phillips Academy, Andover, Mass., and Columbia Law School, New York City; was admitted to the bar in 1866 and commenced practice in Pittsburgh, Pa.; elected as a Democrat to the Forty-fourth Congress (March 4, 1875–March 3, 1877); unsuccessful candidate for reelection in 1876 to the Forty-fifth Congress; resumed the practice of law at Pittsburgh; moved to St. Louis, Mo., in 1879, where he continued the practice of law, and for more than twenty years was general solicitor for the Missouri Pacific Railway Co. and head of its legal department in the West; also served as vice president of the Missouri Pacific and Iron Mountain Railway; served as judge advocate with rank of lieutenant colonel in the Missouri National Guard; died in St. Louis, Mo., May 1, 1928; interment in Bellefontaine Cemetery.

COCHRAN, Charles Fremont, a Representative from Missouri; born in Kirksville, Adair County, Mo., September 27, 1846; moved to Atchison, Kans., in 1860; attended public and private schools; apprenticed to the printer's trade; editor and publisher of the Atchison Patriot in 1868 and 1869; studied law; was admitted to the bar in 1873 and practiced until 1885; prosecuting attorney of Atchison County, Kans., 1880–1884; returned to Missouri in 1885 and settled in St. Joseph; engaged in the newspaper business and edited the St. Joseph (Mo.) Gazette; served in the State senate 1890–1894; elected as a Democrat to the Fifty-fifth and to the three succeeding Congresses (March 4, 1897–March 3, 1905); was a contestant for renomination in 1904 but finally withdrew as a candidate; founded the Observer, a weekly newspaper, of which he served as editor until his death in St. Joseph, Mo., on December 19, 1906; interment in Mount Vernon Cemetery, Atchison, Kans.

COCHRAN, James (grandfather of James Cochrane Dobbin), a Representative from North Carolina; born near Mount Tirzah Township, Person County, N. C., about 1767; attended the public schools; engaged in agricultural pursuits near Helena, N. C.; member of the State house of commons 1802–1806; served in the State senate in 1807; elected as a Democrat to the Eleventh and Twelfth Congresses (March 4, 1809–March 3, 1813); died in Roxboro, Person County, N. C., April 7, 1813; interment in the burial ground at Leas Chapel, five miles west of Roxboro, N. C.

COCHRAN, James, a Representative from New York; born in Albany, N. Y., on February 11, 1769; was graduated from Columbia College, New York City, in 1788; studied law; was admitted to the bar; commissioned major in the Army by President John Adams; regent of the University of the State of New York 1796–1820; elected to the Fifth Congress (March 4, 1797–March 3, 1799); member of the State senate 1814–1818; moved to Oswego, N. Y., in 1826; postmaster of Oswego from September 27, 1841, to July 21, 1845; editor of the Oswego Democratic Gazette for several years; died in Oswego, N. Y., November 7, 1848; interment in Riverside Cemetery.

COCHRAN, John Joseph, a Representative from Missouri; born in Webster Groves, St. Louis County, Mo., August 11, 1880; attended the public schools; employed in the editorial department of various St. Louis newspapers for several years; assistant to the election commissioners of St. Louis 1911–1913; secretary to Representative William L. Igoe 1913–1917; private secretary to United States Senator William J. Stone and clerk to the Committee on Foreign Relations of the United States Senate in 1917 and 1918; again secretary to Representative Igoe 1918–1921; studied law; was admitted to the bar in 1921 at St. Louis, Mo., but did not engage in extensive practice; secretary to Representative Harry B. Hawes 1921–1926; elected as a Democrat to the Sixty-ninth Congress to fill the vacancy caused by the resignation of Harry B. Hawes and at the same time was elected to the Seventieth Congress; reelected to the Seventy-first, Seventy-second, and Seventy-third Congresses and served from November 2, 1926, to January 3, 1935; did not seek renomination in 1934, but was an unsuccessful candidate for the Democratic nomination for United States Senator; subsequently was nominated by convention and elected to the Seventy-fourth Congress; reelected to the Seventy-fifth and to the four succeeding Congresses and served from January 3, 1935, to January 3, 1947; was not a candidate for renomination in 1946 to the Eightieth Congress; died in St. Louis, Mo., March 6, 1947; interment in Calvary Cemetery.

COCHRAN, Thomas Cunningham, a Representative from Pennsylvania; born in Sandy Creek Township, near Sheakleyville, Mercer County, Pa., November 30, 1877; moved with his parents to Mercer, Pa., in 1879; attended the public schools; was graduated from the Mercer High School in 1896 and from Westminster College, New Wilmington, Pa., in 1901; member of the faculty of Mercer Academy in 1902 and 1903; studied law; was admitted to the bar in 1903 and commenced practice in Mercer, Pa.; district attorney of Mercer County 1906–1909; trustee of Westminster College; elected as a Republican to the Seventieth and to the three succeeding Congresses (March 4, 1927–January 3, 1935); was not a candidate for renomination in 1934; delegate to the Interparliamentary Union conferences in Paris in 1927, Berlin in 1928, Geneva in 1929, London in 1930, and Istanbul in 1934, and as an observer in Oslo in 1939, Istanbul in 1951, and Washington in 1953; resumed the practice of law; died in Mercer, Pa., December 10, 1957; interment in Mercer Citizens Cemetery.

COCHRANE, Aaron Van Schaick (nephew of Isaac Whitbeck Van Schaick), a Representative from New York; born in Coxsackie, Greene County, N. Y., March 14, 1858; attended the common schools and the Hudson River Institute at Claverack, N. Y.; was graduated from Yale College in 1879; moved to Hudson, N. Y., in 1879; studied law; was admitted to the bar in 1881 and commenced practice in Hudson, N. Y.; city judge of the city of Hudson in 1887 and 1888; district attorney of Columbia County 1889–1892; elected as a Republican to the Fifty-fifth and Fifty-sixth Congresses (March 4, 1897–March 3, 1901); was not a candidate for renomination in 1900, having become a candidate for the judiciary; elected associate justice of the supreme court of New York in 1901; reelected in 1915 for the term ending in 1928, designated by Governor Miller presiding justice of the appellate division of the State supreme court in 1922; retired from the bench in 1928 but served as official referee until 1941; died in Hudson, N. Y., September 7, 1943; interment in Riverside Cemetery, Coxsackie, N. Y.

COCHRANE, Clark Betton, a Representative from New York; born in New Boston, N. H., May 31, 1815; moved to Montgomery County, N. Y.; was graduated from Union College, Schenectady, N. Y., in 1841; studied law; was admitted to the bar in 1841 and practiced in Amsterdam 1841–1851, Schenectady 1851–1855, and Albany, N. Y., from 1855 until his death; elected as a Democrat a member of the State assembly in 1844; trustee of Union College 1853–1867; elected as a Republican to the Thirty-fifth and Thirty-sixth Congresses (March 4, 1857–March 3, 1861); was not a candidate for renomination in 1860; resumed the practice of law in Albany; delegate to the Republican National Convention at Baltimore in 1864; again a member of the State assembly in 1866; died in Albany, N. Y., on March 5, 1867; interment in Green Hill Cemetery, Amsterdam, Montgomery County, N. Y.

COCHRANE, John, a Representative from New York; born in Palatine, N. Y., August 27, 1813; pursued preparatory studies, attended Union College, Schenectady, N. Y., and was graduated from Hamilton College, Clinton, N. Y., in 1831; studied law; was admitted to the bar in 1834 and practiced in Palatine, Oswego, and Schenectady, N. Y.; moved to New York City in 1846; surveyor of the port of New York 1853–1857; elected as a State Rights Democrat to the Thirty-fifth and Thirty-sixth Congresses (March 4, 1857–March 3, 1861); unsuccessful candidate in 1860 for reelection to the Thirty-seventh Congress; delegate to the Democratic National Conventions at Charleston and Baltimore in 1860; during the Civil War entered the Union Army as colonel of the Sixty-fifth New York Infantry June 11, 1861; became brigadier general July 17, 1862, and served until his resignation on February 25, 1863, on account of physical disability; chairman of the Independent Republican National Convention in Cleveland, Ohio, in 1864, which nominated him for Vice President on the ticket with Frémont for President but withdrew, with General Frémont, before the election; attorney general of New York 1863–1865; collector of internal revenue for the sixth district of New York in 1869; declined the position of United States Minister to Uruguay and Paraguay tendered by President Grant in 1869; delegate to the Liberal Republican National Convention at Cincinnati in 1872; member of the board of aldermen and served as president in 1872 and again a member in 1883; appointed police justice of New York May 22, 1889, but resigned after serving a few weeks; died in New York City February 7, 1898; interment in Rural Cemetery, Albany, N. Y.

COCKE, John (son of William Cocke and uncle of William Michael Cocke), a Representative from Tennessee; born in Brunswick, Nottoway County, Va., in 1772; moved with his parents to Tennessee, where he attended the public schools; studied law; was admitted to the bar in 1793 and practiced in Hawkins County; member of the Tennessee House of Representatives in 1796, 1797, 1807, 1809, 1812, and again in 1837, and served as speaker in 1812 and 1837; served in the Tennessee Senate 1799–1801; served as major general of Tennessee Volunteers in the Creek War in 1813 and as colonel of a regiment of Tennessee riflemen, under Gen. Andrew Jackson, at New Orleans; elected to the Sixteenth and to the three succeeding Congresses (March 4, 1819–March 3, 1827); engaged in agricultural pursuits; founded a school for deaf-mutes in Knoxville, Tenn.; again a member of the Tennessee Senate in 1843; died in Rutledge, Grainger County, Tenn., February 16, 1854; interment in the Methodist Church Cemetery.

COCKE, William (father of John Cocke and grandfather of William Michael Cocke), a Senator from Tennessee; born in Amelia County, Va., in 1747; pursued preparatory studies; studied law; was admitted to the bar and practiced; in company with Daniel Boone explored the territory of eastern Tennessee and western Kentucky; led four companies of Virginians against hostile Indians in 1776 and gave them a crushing defeat at Cocke's Fort, Tenn.; member of the Virginia House of Burgesses and a colonel of militia; moved to Tennessee in 1776; member of the State constitutional convention in 1796; upon the admission of Tennessee as a State into the Union was elected to the United States Senate and served from August 2, 1796, to March 3, 1797; was appointed his own successor, as there had been no election by the legislature, and served under this appointment from April 22, 1797, to September 26, 1797, when a successor was elected; again elected to the United States Senate and served from March 4, 1799, to March 3, 1805; appointed judge of the first circuit in 1809; moved to Mississippi, and was elected to the Mississippi Legislature in 1813; served under Gen. Andrew Jackson in the War of 1812; was appointed by President James Madison as Indian agent for the Chickasaw Nation in 1814; died in Columbus, Miss., on August 22, 1828; interment in that city under a tombstone erected to his memory by the State of Mississippi.

COCKE, William Michael (grandson of William Cocke and nephew of John Cocke), a Representative from Tennessee; born in Rutledge, Grainger County, Tenn., July 16, 1815; pursued classical studies and was graduated from the East Tennessee College at Knoxville; studied law; was admitted to the bar and practiced in Rutledge and Nashville; member of the State house of representatives; elected as a Democrat to the Twenty-ninth and Thirtieth Congresses (March 4, 1845–March 3, 1849); was not a candidate for reelection in 1848; held many local and State offices; died in Nashville, Tenn., February 6, 1896; interment in Mount Olivet Cemetery.

COCKERILL, Joseph Randolph, a Representative from Ohio; born in Loudoun County, Va., January 2, 1818; moved to Scott Township, Adams County, Ohio, in 1837 and settled in Youngstown; attended the public schools; taught school; county surveyor in 1840; studied law; was admitted to the bar in 1851 and commenced practice in West Union, Ohio; clerk of the court of common pleas; member of the State house of representatives in 1853 and 1854; elected as a Democrat to the Thirty-fifth Congress (March 4, 1857–March 3, 1859); entered the Union Army during the Civil War and served as colonel of the Seventieth Ohio Volunteer Infantry; brevetted brigadier general of Volunteers March 13, 1865; again a member of the State house of representatives 1868–1871; resumed the practice of law; died in West Union, Adams County, Ohio, October 23, 1875; interment in West Union Cemetery.

COCKRAN, William Bourke, a Representative from New York; born in County Sligo, Ireland, February 28, 1854; was educated in France and in his native country; immigrated to the United States when seventeen years of age; soon after his arrival received an appointment as teacher in a private academy; principal of a public school in Westchester County, N. Y.; while teaching he studied law; was admitted to the bar in 1876 and commenced practice in Mount Vernon, N. Y.; two years later moved to New York City and continued the practice of law; elected as a Democrat to the Fiftieth Congress (March 4, 1887–March 3, 1889); was not a candidate for renomination in 1888 to the Fifty-first Congress; delegate to the Democratic National Conventions in 1884, 1892, 1904, and 1920; member of the commission to revise the judiciary article of the constitution of the State of New York in 1890; elected to the Fifty-second Congress to fill the vacancy caused by the death of Francis B. Spinola; reelected to the Fifty-third Congress and served from November 3, 1891, to March 3, 1895; was not a candidate for renomination in 1896, because of his opposition to the free-silver platform of Bryan and Sewall and campaigned for McKinley; in 1900 on the issue of anti-imperialism returned to the Democratic Party and supported Bryan; elected as a Democrat to the Fifty-eighth Congress to fill the vacancy caused by the resignation of George B. McClellan; reelected to the Fifty-ninth and Sixtieth Congresses and served from February 23, 1904, to March 3, 1909; declined to be a candidate for renomination in 1908 to the Sixty-first Congress; resumed the practice of law in New York City; supported the Progressive Party ticket of Roosevelt and Johnson in 1912; unsuccessful candidate for election in 1912 to the Sixty-third Congress; elected as a Democrat to the Sixty-seventh Congress and served from March 4, 1921, until his death in Washington, D. C., March 1, 1923; had been reelected to the Sixty-eighth Congress; interment in Gate of Heaven Cemetery, Mount Hope, Westchester, N. Y.

COCKRELL, Francis Marion (brother of Jeremiah Vardaman Cockrell), a Senator from Missouri; born in Warrensburg, Johnson County, Mo., October 1, 1834; attended the common schools; was graduated from Chapel Hill College, Lafayette County, Mo., in July 1853; studied law; was admitted to the bar in 1855 and practiced in Warrensburg, Mo.; served in the Confederate Army, and was promoted from the rank of captain to that of brigade commander; appointed brigadier general July 18, 1863; captured at Fort Blakeley, Ala., April 9, 1865; paroled May 14, 1865; at the close of the Civil War resumed the practice of law; elected as a Democrat to the United States Senate; reelected four times and served from March 4, 1875, to March 3, 1905; appointed by President Roosevelt a member of the Interstate Commerce Commission on March 6, 1905, and served until December 31, 1910; appointed in 1911 a United States commissioner to reestablish the boundary line between Texas and New Mexico; civilian member of the board of ordnance in the War Department, which position he held until his death in Washington, D. C., December 13, 1915; interment in Warrensburg Cemetery, Warrensburg, Mo.

COCKRELL, Jeremiah Vardaman (brother of Francis Marion Cockrell), a Representative from Texas; born near Warrensburg, Johnson County, Mo., May 7, 1832; attended the common schools and Chapel Hill College, Lafayette County, Mo.; went to California in 1849; returned to Missouri in 1853; engaged in agricultural pursuits and studied law; entered the Confederate Army as a lieutenant and served throughout the Civil War, attaining the rank of colonel; at the close of the war he settled in Sherman, Grayson County, Tex., and engaged in the practice of law; chief justice of Grayson County in 1872; delegate to the

Democratic State conventions in 1878 and 1880; moved to Jones County; appointed judge of the thirty-ninth judicial district court in 1885, to which position he was elected in 1886 and reelected in 1890; elected as a Democrat to the Fifty-third and Fifty-fourth Congresses (March 4, 1893–March 3, 1897); was not a candidate for renomination in 1896; engaged in farming and stock raising in Jones County, Tex.; died in Abilene, Taylor County, Tex., on March 18, 1915; interment in the Masonic Cemetery.

COCKS, William Willets (brother of Frederick Cocks Hicks), a Representative from New York; born in Old Westbury, Long Island, N. Y., July 24, 1861; attended private schools and Swarthmore College, Swarthmore, Pa.; engaged in agricultural pursuits; elected commissioner of highways of the town of North Hempstead in 1894; reelected in 1896 and again in 1898; served in the State senate in 1901 and 1902; member of the State assembly in 1904; delegate to the Republican National Convention at Chicago in 1908; elected as a Republican to the Fifty-ninth, Sixtieth, and Sixty-first Congresses (March 4, 1905–March 3, 1911); unsuccessful candidate for reelection in 1910 to the Sixty-second Congress; again engaged in agricultural pursuits; member of the board of managers of Swarthmore College; president of the Friends Academy, Locust Valley, Nassau County; vice president of the Roslyn Savings Bank; a director of the Bank of Westbury and the Bank of Hicksville; elected mayor of the village of Old Westbury, Long Island, N. Y., in 1924 and served until his death there on May 24, 1932; interment in Friends Cemetery, Westbury, Long Island, N. Y.

CODD, George Pierre, a Representative from Michigan; born in Detroit, Mich., December 7, 1869; attended the public schools, and was graduated from the University of Michigan at Ann Arbor in 1891; studied law; was admitted to the bar in 1892 and commenced practice in Detroit in 1893; assistant city attorney 1894–1897; member of the board of aldermen 1902–1904; mayor of Detroit in 1905 and 1906; unsuccessful candidate for reelection; delegate to the Republican National Convention at Chicago in 1908; circuit judge of Wayne County 1911–1921; regent of the University of Michigan in 1910 and 1911; elected as a Republican to the Sixty-seventh Congress (March 4, 1921–March 3, 1923); declined to be a candidate for renomination in 1922; resumed the practice of law; again elected circuit judge of Wayne County in 1924 and served until his death in Detroit, Mich., on February 16, 1927; interment in Elmwood Cemetery.

CODDING, James Hodge, a Representative from Pennsylvania; born in Pike Township, Bradford County, Pa., July 8, 1849; moved to Towanda, Pa., in 1854; attended the Susquehanna Collegiate Institute, Towanda, Pa., and Dartmouth College, Hanover, N. H.; engaged in the hardware business at Towanda in 1868; studied law; was admitted to the bar and commenced practice in Towanda, Pa., in 1879; elected as a Republican to the Fifty-fourth Congress to fill the vacancy caused by the death of Myron B. Wright; reelected to the Fifty-fifth Congress and served from November 5, 1895, to March 3, 1899; was not a candidate for reelection in 1898; resumed the practice of law in Towanda; moved to New York City in 1903; grand secretary general of the northern Masonic jurisdiction for the Scottish Rite bodies from 1902 until his death in Brooklyn, N. Y., September 12, 1919; interment in Oak Hill Cemetery, Towanda, Bradford County, Pa.

COFFEE, Harry Buffington, a Representative from Nebraska; born near Harrison, Sioux County, Nebr., March 16, 1890; attended the public schools at Chadron, Nebr., and was graduated from the University of Nebraska at Lincoln in 1913; engaged in the real estate and insurance business in Chadron, Nebr., 1914–1939; during the First World War served as a second lieutenant in the Air Service in 1917 and 1918; organized the Coffee Cattle Co., Inc., in 1915 with extensive ranch holdings in Sioux County, Nebr., and has served as president since its organization; also engaged in agricultural pursuits; elected as a Democrat to the Seventy-fourth and to the three succeeding Congresses (January 3, 1935–January 3, 1943); was not a candidate for renomination in 1942, but was an unsuccessful candidate for the Democratic nomination for United States Senator; president of a stockyard company and also of a terminal railway company since 1943; is a resident of Omaha, Nebr.

COFFEE, John, a Representative from Georgia; born in Prince Edward County, Va., December 3, 1782; received a good schooling; moved with his father to a plantation near Powelton, Hancock County, Ga., in 1800; settled in Telfair County in 1807 and engaged in agricultural pursuits; general of the State militia during the Creek War; cut a road through the State of Georgia (called Coffee Road) to carry munitions of war to Florida Territory to fight the Indians; member of the State senate 1819–1827; elected as a Democrat to the Twenty-third and Twenty-fourth Congresses and served from March 4, 1833, until his death; was reelected to the Twenty-fifth Congress on October 3, 1836, announcement of his death not having been received; died on his plantation near Jacksonville, Telfair County, Ga., on September 25, 1836; interment on his plantation near Jacksonville, Ga.; reinterment in McRae Cemetery, McRae, Ga., in 1921.

COFFEE, John Main, a Representative from Washington; born in Tacoma, Wash., January 23, 1897; attended the public schools; was graduated from the University of Washington at Seattle in 1920 and from the law department of Yale University, New Haven, Conn., in 1921; was admitted to the bar in 1922 and commenced practice in Tacoma, Wash.; secretary to United States Senator C. C. Dill in 1923 and 1924; delegate to the Democratic State conventions in 1932, 1934, 1936, and 1938; secretary of the advisory board of the National Recovery Administration 1933–1935; appraiser and examiner of Pierce County for the Washington State Inheritance Tax and Escheat Division 1933–1936; civil service commissioner for Tacoma, Wash., in 1936; elected as a Democrat to the Seventy-fifth and to the four succeeding Congresses (January 3, 1937–January 3, 1947); unsuccessful candidate for reelection in 1946 to the Eightieth Congress, for election in 1950 to the Eighty-second Congress, and in 1958 to the Eighty-sixth Congress; practicing attorney in Tacoma and Seattle, Wash.; resides in Tacoma, Wash.

COFFEEN, Henry Asa, a Representative from Wyoming; born near Gallipolis, Gallia County, Ohio, February 14, 1841; moved with his parents to Indiana, and thence to Homer, Champaign County, Ill., in 1853; attended the country schools and was graduated from the scientific department of Abingdon College (afterwards consolidated with Eureka College), Illinois; engaged in teaching; member of the faculty of Hiram College, Ohio; moved to Sheridan, Wyo., in 1884; delegate from Wyoming to the World's Fair Congress of Bankers and Financiers at Chicago in June 1893; member of the constitutional convention that framed the constitution of the new State of Wyoming in 1889; elected as a Democrat to the Fifty-third Congress (March 4, 1893–March 3, 1895); unsuccessful candidate for reelection in 1894 to the Fifty-fourth Congress; engaged in literary pursuits until his death in Sheridan, Sheridan County, Wyo., December 9, 1912; interment in Sheridan Cemetery.

COFFEY, Robert Lewis, Jr., a Representative from Pennsylvania; born in Chattanooga, Hamilton County, Tenn., October 21, 1918; moved with his parents in early boyhood to Pennsylvania and graduated from the Ferndale High School in 1935; also attended the University of Pittsburgh and Penn State College; employed in coal mines in all positions from coal loader to engineer; appointed a flying cadet September 23, 1939; commissioned a second lieutenant in June 1940; promoted to first lieutenant November 1, 1941, and served in the United States Army Air Force during World War II; military air attaché, United States Embassy, Santiago, Chile, from October 1945 to April 1948; resigned his commission as a lieutenant colonel September 1, 1948, to pursue political candidacy; commissioned a colonel, Air Force Reserve, September 2, 1948; awarded Distinguished Flying Cross, Air Medal, Purple Heart, Bronze Star, Presidential Citation, and Belgian and French Croix de Guerre; elected as a Democrat to the Eighty-first Congress and served from January 3, 1949, until his death in an airplane accident in Albuquerque, N. Mex., April 20, 1949; interment in Arlington National Cemetery, Fort Myer, Va.

COFFIN, Charles Dustin, a Representative from Ohio; born in Newburyport, Mass., September 9, 1805; attended the public schools; moved with his parents to New Lisbon, Columbiana County, Ohio; studied law; was admitted to the bar in September 1823 and commenced practice in New Lisbon; clerk of the courts of Columbiana County in 1828; was elected as a Whig to the Twenty-fifth Congress to fill the vacancy caused by the resignation of Andrew W. Loomis and served from December 20, 1837, to March 3, 1839; declined to be a candidate for renomination in 1838; resumed the practice of law and engaged in banking; president of the Columbiana Bank of New Lisbon; moved to Cincinnati, Ohio, in 1842 and continued the practice of law; elected judge of the superior court in 1845 and served seven years; was appointed to the same position by Governor Denison in 1861; died in Cincinnati, Ohio, February 28, 1880; interment in Spring Grove Cemetery.

COFFIN, Charles Edward, a Representative from Maryland; born in Boston, Mass., July 18, 1841; attended the Boston grammar and high schools; moved to Maryland in 1863 and settled in Muirkirk, Prince Georges County, where deposits of iron ore were found; took charge of the ironworks erected in 1847 by the Ellicotts and conducted the same; member of the State house of delegates in 1884; served in the State senate 1890–1894; delegate to the Republican National Convention at Minneapolis in 1892; elected as a Republican to the Fifty-third Congress to fill the vacancy caused by the resignation of Barnes Compton; reelected on the same day to the Fifty-fourth Congress and served from November 6, 1894, to March 3, 1897; engaged in the manufacture of charcoal pig iron, and subsequently became the owner of the Muirkirk blast furnaces; died in Muirkirk, Md., May 24, 1912; interment in St. John's Protestant Episcopal Church Cemetery, Beltsville, Md.

COFFIN, Frank Morey, a Representative from Maine; born in Lewiston, Androscoggin County, Maine, July 11, 1919; educated in Lewiston public schools; graduated from Bates College in 1940, from Harvard Business School in 1943, and Harvard Law School in 1947; during World War II served in the Pacific Theater with the United States Navy as an ensign and later as a lieutenant 1943–1946; was admitted to the bar and commenced the practice of law in Lewiston, Maine; law clerk for Federal judge, district of Maine, 1947–1949; chairman Maine Democratic State Committee 1954–1956; elected as a Democrat to the Eighty-fifth and Eighty-sixth Congresses (January 3, 1957–January 3, 1961); was not a candidate for renomination in

1960, but was unsuccessful for election as Governor of Maine; managing director of Development Loan Fund until October 1961 when he became deputy administrator of the Agency for International Development; resides in Washington, D. C.

COFFIN, Howard Aldridge, a Representative from Michigan; born in Middleboro, Plymouth County, Mass., June 11, 1877; attended the Vermont Academy at Saxtons River; was graduated from Brown University, Providence, R. I., in 1901; teacher in Friends School, Providence, R. I., in 1901; representative for Ginn & Co., book publishers, 1901–1911; controller, Warren Motor Car Co., Detroit, Mich., 1911–1913; manager, Firestone Tire & Rubber Co., of Michigan, 1913–1918; secretary, Detroit Pressed Steel Co., 1918–1921; assistant to president, Cadillac Motor Co., of Detroit, 1921–1925; vice president and later president, White Star Refining Co., 1925–1933; general manager, Socony-Vacuum Oil Co., 1933–1946; vice chairman, Appeal Board No. 1, Selective Service, for the State of Michigan; trustee, Grace Hospital, Detroit, Mich., Brown University, and Detroit College of Law; elected as a Republican to the Eightieth Congress (January 3, 1947–January 3, 1949); unsuccessful candidate for reelection in 1948 to the Eighty-first Congress; organized the Industrial Service Bureau in Washington, D. C., and was a business consultant until his retirement in 1954; died in Washington, D. C., February 28, 1956; interment in Woodlawn Cemetery, Detroit, Mich.

COFFIN, Peleg, Jr., a Representative from Massachusetts; born in Nantucket, Mass., November 3, 1756; completed academic studies; president of the New England Marine Insurance Co.; member of the State house of representatives in 1783, 1784, and 1789; served in the State senate in 1785, 1786, 1790–1792, 1795, 1796, and 1802; elected to the Third Congress (March 4, 1793–March 3, 1795); State treasurer 1797–1802; died in Boston, Mass., March 6, 1805; interment probably in Friends Burial Grounds; reinterment in Mount Auburn Cemetery in 1833.

COFFIN, Thomas Chalkley, a Representative from Idaho; born in Caldwell, Canyon County, Idaho, October 25, 1887; moved to Boise, Ada County, Idaho, with his parents in 1898; attended the public schools of Caldwell and Boise, Idaho, and was graduated from the Phillips-Exeter Academy at Exeter, N. H., in 1906; attended Yale Sheffield Scientific School and was graduated from the law department of Yale University in 1910; was admitted to the bar on February 8, 1911, and commenced the practice of law in Boise, Idaho, the same year; served as assistant attorney general of Idaho 1913–1915; moved to Pocatello, Idaho, in 1917 and continued the practice of law; during the First World War served in the aviation branch of the United States Navy; mayor of Pocatello 1931–1933; elected as a Democrat to the Seventy-third Congress and served from March 4, 1933, until his death in Washington, D. C., on June 8, 1934; interment in Mountainview Cemetery, Pocatello, Idaho.

COFFROTH, Alexander Hamilton, a Representative from Pennsylvania; born in Somerset, Somerset County, Pa., May 18, 1828; attended the public schools and Somerset Academy; published a Democratic paper in Somerset for five years; studied law in the law office of Hon. Jeremiah S. Black; was admitted to the bar in February 1851 at Somerset, Pa., where he practiced his profession; delegate to several Democratic State conventions; delegate to the Democratic National Conventions which assembled in Charleston and Baltimore in 1860; an assessor of internal revenue in 1867; delegate to the Democratic National Convention at Baltimore in 1872; elected as a Democrat to the Thirty-eighth Congress (March 4, 1863–March

3, 1865); claimed reelection to the Thirty-ninth Congress; was seated on February 19, 1866, and served until July 18, 1866, when he was succeeded by William H. Koontz, who contested the election; elected to the Forty-sixth Congress (March 4, 1879–March 3, 1881); was not a candidate for renomination in 1880; resumed the practice of law in Somerset, Pa.; he was the last surviving pallbearer who had served at the funeral of President Lincoln; died in Markleton, Somerset County, Pa., September 2, 1906; interment in Union Cemetery, Somerset, Pa.

COGHLAN, John Maxwell, a Representative from California; born in Louisville, Ky., December 8, 1835; moved with his parents to Illinois in 1847, and in 1850 they moved to California and settled in Suisun City; studied law; was admitted to the bar and practiced in Suisun City; member of the State assembly in 1865 and 1866; elected as a Republican to the Forty-second Congress (March 4, 1871–March 3, 1873); unsuccessful candidate for reelection in 1872 to the Forty-third Congress; engaged in the practice of law until his death in Oakland, Calif., March 26, 1879; interment in Mountain View Cemetery.

COGSWELL, William, a Representative from Massachusetts; born in Bradford, Mass., August 23, 1838; attended Phillips Academy, Andover, Mass., and Dartmouth College, Hanover, N. H.; was graduated from the Dane Law School, Harvard University, in 1860; was admitted to the bar and commenced practice in Salem; served in the Union Army throughout the Civil War; was commissioned a captain in the Second Regiment, Massachusetts Volunteer Infantry, May 11, 1861; lieutenant colonel October 23, 1862; colonel June 25, 1863; brevetted brigadier general of Volunteers December 15, 1864; mustered out July 24, 1865; resumed the practice of his profession; mayor of Salem 1867–1869, 1873, and 1874; member of the State house of representatives 1870, 1871, and 1881–1883; served in the State senate in 1885 and 1886; delegate to the Republican National Convention at Minneapolis in 1892; elected as a Republican to the Fiftieth and to the four succeeding Congresses and served from March 4, 1887, until his death in Washington, D. C., May 22, 1895; interment in Harmony Grove Cemetery, Salem, Mass.

COHELAN, Jeffery, a Representative from California; born in San Francisco, Calif., June 24, 1914; attended the public schools; graduated from the University of California School of Economics; Fulbright research scholar at Leeds and Oxford Universities in England in 1953 and 1954; secretary-treasurer Milk Drivers and Dairy Employees, Local 302, Alameda and Contra Costa Counties from 1942 until elected to Congress; consultant, University of California Institute of Industrial Relations; member of Berkeley Welfare Commission 1949–1953, and the Berkeley City Council 1955–1958; former member of San Francisco Council on Foreign Relations; elected as a Democrat to the Eighty-sixth Congress (January 3, 1959–January 3, 1961). *Reelected to the Eighty-seventh Congress.*

COHEN, John Sanford, a Senator from Georgia; born in Augusta, Ga., February 26, 1870; educated at private schools in Augusta, Richmond (Va.) Academy, and Shenandoah Valley Academy at Winchester, Va.; also attended the United States Naval Academy at Annapolis in 1885 and 1886; became a newspaper reporter for the New York World in 1886; secretary to Secretary of the Interior Hoke Smith 1893–1896; member of the press galleries of Congress 1893–1897; during the Spanish-American War served as a war correspondent for the Atlanta Journal, sailing with the fleet of Admiral Robley D. (Fighting Bob) Evans; subsequently enlisted and served as first lieutenant,

Company A, Third Georgia Volunteer Infantry; was later promoted to captain and then to major, and was a member of the army of occupation in Cuba; president and editor of the Atlanta Journal 1917–1935; originator of the plan for the national highway from New York City to Jacksonville, Fla., which was built under joint supervision of the Atlanta Journal and the New York Herald; member of the Democratic national committee for Georgia 1924–1935; vice chairman of the Democratic National Committee 1932–1935; appointed as a Democrat to the United States Senate to fill the vacancy caused by the death of William J. Harris and served from April 25, 1932, to January 11, 1933, when a successor was duly elected and qualified; was not a candidate in 1932 to fill the vacancy; continued in his former business activities until his death in Atlanta, Ga., May 13, 1935; interment in West View Cemetery, Atlanta, Ga.

COHEN, William Wolfe, a Representative from New York; born in Brooklyn, N. Y., September 6, 1874; attended the public schools; became associated with his father in the shoe manufacturing business until 1903, when he engaged in the banking and brokerage business; vice chairman of the Public Schools Athletic League; honorary deputy chief of the New York fire department; member of the New York Stock Exchange and director of the New York Cotton Exchange; a trustee of the Home of the Daughters of Jacob, a director of the Hospital for Joint Diseases, and a director of the New York Guild for Jewish Blind; elected as a Democrat to the Seventieth Congress (March 4, 1927–March 3, 1929); was not a candidate for renomination in 1928; resumed his former business pursuits in New York City until his death there on October 12, 1940; interment in Mount Neboh Cemetery, Brooklyn, N. Y.

COIT, Joshua, a Representative from Connecticut; born in New London, Conn., October 7, 1758; attended the common schools, and was graduated from Harvard College, Cambridge, Mass., in 1776; studied law; was admitted to the bar and commenced practice in New London in 1779; member of the State house of representatives in 1784, 1785, 1789, 1790, 1792, and 1793; served as clerk during several terms and as speaker in 1793; elected as a Federalist to the Third, Fourth, and Fifth Congresses and served from March 4, 1793, until his death in New London, Conn., September 5, 1798; interment in Cedar Grove Cemetery.

COKE, Richard, a Senator from Texas; born in Williamsburg, James City County, Va., March 13, 1829; attended the common schools, and was graduated from William and Mary College, Williamsburg, Va., in 1849; studied law; was admitted to the bar in 1850 and commenced practice in Waco, McLennan County, Tex.; entered the Confederate Army as a private; was promoted to the rank of captain and served throughout the Civil War; appointed district judge in June 1865; elected judge of the State supreme court in 1866; after serving one year was removed by General Sheridan as "an impediment to reconstruction"; resumed the practice of law in Waco, Tex.; elected Governor of Texas in December 1873; reelected in February 1876, and served until December 1, 1877, when he resigned; elected as a Democrat to the United States Senate in 1877; reelected in 1883 and again in 1889 and served from March 4, 1877, to March 3, 1895; was not a candidate for renomination; died in Waco, Tex., May 14, 1897; interment in Oakwood Cemetery.

COKE, Richard, Jr. (uncle of the preceding), a Representative from Virginia; born in Williamsburg, Va., November 16, 1790; completed preparatory studies, and was graduated from William and Mary College, Williamsburg, Va.; studied law;

was admitted to the bar and commenced practice in Gloucester County, Va.; elected as a Jacksonian Democrat to the Twenty-first and Twenty-second Congresses (March 4, 1829–March 3, 1833); died on his plantation, "Abingdon Place," in Gloucester County, Va., March 31, 1851; interment in the family burying ground on the estate.

COLCOCK, William Ferguson, a Representative from South Carolina; born in Beaufort, S. C., November 5, 1804; attended Hulburt's School, Charleston, S. C., and was graduated from South Carolina College (now the University of South Carolina) at Columbia in 1823; studied law; was admitted to the bar in 1825 and commenced practice in Coosawhatchie, Jasper County, S. C.; also engaged in planting; member of the State house of representatives 1831–1848 and served as speaker from 1841 to 1848; elected as a Democrat to the Thirty-first and Thirty-second Congresses (March 4, 1849–March 3, 1853); a Regent of the Smithsonian Institution 1850–1853; collector of the port of Charleston 1853–1865, serving first under the United States Government and subsequently under the Confederate States Government; delegate to the Democratic National Convention at Charleston in 1860; resumed the practice of law; died in McPhersonville, Hampton County, S. C., on June 13, 1889; interment in Stoney Creek Cemetery, Beaufort County, S. C.

COLDEN, Cadwallader David, a Representative from New York; born in Springhill, near Flushing, N. Y., April 4, 1769; prepared for college by a private tutor and pursued classical studies at Jamaica, N. Y., and in London, England; returned to the United States in 1785; studied law; was admitted to the bar in 1791 and commenced practice in New York City; moved to Poughkeepsie in 1793, and in 1796 relocated in New York City; appointed district attorney in 1798 and again in 1810; colonel of Volunteers in the War of 1812; member of the State assembly in 1818; mayor of the city of New York in 1819; successfully contested as a Democrat the election of Peter Sharpe to the Seventeenth Congress and served from December 12, 1821, to March 3, 1823; member of the State senate 1824–1827; moved to Jersey City, N. J.; devoted much time to the completion of the Morris Canal; died in Jersey City, N. J., on February 7, 1834.

COLDEN, Charles J., a Representative from California; born on a farm in Peoria County, Ill., August 24, 1870; moved to Nodaway County, Mo., with his parents in 1880; attended the rural schools, Stanberry (Mo.) Normal School, and Shenandoah College, Shenandoah, Iowa; taught school in Missouri and Iowa 1889–1896; editor and publisher of the Parnell Sentinel 1896–1900 and of the Nodaway Forum, at Maryville, 1900–1908; member of the Missouri House of Representatives 1901–1905; president of the board of regents of Northwest Missouri Teachers College 1905–1908; moved to Kansas City, Mo., in 1908 and engaged in the real-estate business and in the building of residences; moved to San Pedro, Calif., in 1912 and continued in the real estate and building business; president of the San Pedro Chamber of Commerce 1922–1924; member and president of the Los Angeles Harbor Commission 1923–1925; member of the Los Angeles City Council 1925–1929; elected as a Democrat to the Seventy-third, Seventy-fourth, and Seventy-fifth Congresses and served from March 4, 1933, until his death in Washington, D. C., April 15, 1938; interment in Roosevelt Memorial Park Cemetery, Gardena, Calif.

COLE, Albert McDonald, a Representative from Kansas; born in Moberly, Randolph County, Mo., October 13, 1901; moved to Topeka, Kans., in 1909; attended the grade schools of Topeka, Kans., Sabetha (Kans.) High School, and Washburn College, Topeka, Kans.; was graduated from the law department of the University of Chicago, Chicago, Ill., in 1925; was admitted to the bar in 1926 and commenced practice in Holton, Kans.; county attorney of Jackson County 1927–1931; member and president of the Holton School Board 1931–1943; member of the State senate 1941–1944; elected as a Republican to the Seventy-ninth and to the three succeeding Congresses (January 3, 1945–January 3, 1953); unsuccessful candidate for reelection in 1952 to the Eighty-third Congress; Administrator, Housing and Home Finance Agency, Washington, D. C., from March 1953 to January 1959; vice president of Reynolds Aluminum Service Corp. since January 1959; resides in Washington, D. C.

COLE, Cornelius, a Representative and a Senator from California; born in Lodi, Seneca County, N. Y., September 17, 1822; attended the common schools, Ovid Academy at Ovid, Lima Seminary at Lima, and Hobart College at Geneva, N. Y.; was graduated from Wesleyan University, Middletown, Conn., in 1847; studied law; was admitted to the bar in Auburn, Cayuga County, N. Y., May 1, 1848; went to California in 1849, and after working a year in the gold mines commenced the practice of law in San Francisco in 1850; moved to Sacramento in 1851; district attorney of Sacramento City and County 1859–1862; member of the Republican National Committee 1856–1860; moved to Santa Cruz in 1862; during the Civil War was commissioned as a captain in the Union Army in 1863; elected as a Union Republican to the Thirty-eighth Congress (March 4, 1863–March 3, 1865); elected to the United States Senate and served from March 4, 1867, to March 3, 1873; resumed the practice of law; moved to Colegrove, Los Angeles County, Calif., in 1880, and retired from active practice; when he had nearly attained one hundred years of age he came to Washington, D. C., and visited the Capitol, and during a recess of five minutes taken for that purpose by the House of Representatives he addressed that body on June 27, 1922; died in Hollywood, Calif., November 3, 1924; interment in Hollywood Cemetery.

COLE, Cyrenus, a Representative from Iowa; born on a farm near Pella, Marion County, Iowa, January 13, 1863; attended the public schools, and was graduated from Central University, Pella, Iowa, in 1887; engaged in newspaper work, and was connected with the Des Moines Register from 1887 to 1898, serving seven years as editorial writer; acquired an interest in the Cedar Rapids Republican in 1898, and was connected with that paper until 1921, during which period he founded the Times as an evening edition of the Republican; is the author of many publications; elected as a Republican to the Sixty-seventh Congress to fill the vacancy caused by the resignation of James W. Good; reelected to the Sixty-eighth and to the four succeeding Congresses and served from July 19, 1921, to March 3, 1933; was not a candidate for renomination in 1932; engaged as an author and resided in Washington, D. C., until his death there on November 14, 1939; interment in First Dutch Reform Church Cemetery near Pella, Marion County, Iowa.

COLE, George Edward, a Delegate from the Territory of Washington; born in Trenton (now Trenton Falls), Oneida County, N. Y., December 23, 1826; attended the public schools and Hobart Hall Institute; employed as clerk in a country store; moved to Illinois, thence to California in 1849, and later to Oregon in 1850; member of the Oregon House of Representatives in 1852 and 1853; engaged in mercantile pursuits and steamboat transportation on the Willamette River; clerk of the United States District Court of Oregon in 1859 and 1860; moved to Walla Walla, Wash., in 1860; elected as a Democrat to the

Thirty-eighth Congress (March 4, 1863–March 3, 1865); was not a candidate for renomination in 1864; appointed Governor of the Territory by President Johnson in November 1866 and served until March 4, 1867; returned to Portland, Oreg., in 1867; engaged in railroad construction 1869–1872; postmaster of Portland, Oreg., 1873–1881; moved to Spokane, Wash., in 1889; treasurer of Spokane County 1890–1892; had extensive interests in mining, manufacturing, and farming; died in Portland, Oreg., December 3, 1906; interment in Lone Fir Cemetery.

COLE, Nathan, a Representative from Missouri; born in St. Louis, Mo., July 26, 1825; attended the common schools and took a partial course at Shurtleff College, Alton, Ill.; engaged in mercantile pursuits in St. Louis; a director of the Bank of Commerce for forty-three years, most of which time he was vice president; director in a number of insurance and other corporations; mayor of St. Louis 1869–1871; president of the Merchants' Exchange in 1876; elected as a Republican to the Forty-fifth Congress (March 4, 1877–March 3, 1879); unsuccessful candidate for reelection in 1878 to the Forty-sixth Congress; resumed his former business activities in St. Louis, Mo., where his death occurred March 4, 1904; interment in Bellefontaine Cemetery.

COLE, Orsamus, a Representative from Wisconsin; born in Cazenovia, Madison County, N. Y., August 23, 1819; attended the common schools, and was graduated from Union College, Schenectady, N. Y., in 1843; studied law; was admitted to the bar in 1845 and commenced practice in Chicago, Ill.; moved to Potosi, Grant County, Wis., the same year and continued the practice of law; member of the State constitutional convention in 1847; elected as a Whig to the Thirty-first Congress (March 4, 1849–March 3, 1851); unsuccessful candidate for reelection in 1850 to the Thirty-second Congress; resumed the practice of law in Potosi until 1855; associate justice of the State supreme court 1855–1880, and chief justice from April 1881 to January 4, 1892; resumed the practice of law; retired from public life and lived with his son in Milwaukee, Wis., where he died on May 5, 1903; interment in Forest Hill Cemetery, Madison, Wis.

COLE, Ralph Dayton (brother of Raymond Clinton Cole), a Representative from Ohio; born in Vanlue, Hancock County, Ohio, November 30, 1873; attended the common schools; was graduated from Findlay College, Findlay, Ohio, in 1896 and from Ohio Northern University, Ada, Ohio, in 1900; deputy clerk of Hancock County 1897–1899; studied law; was admitted to the bar in 1900 and commenced practice in Findlay, Hancock County, Ohio; member of the State house of representatives 1900–1904; elected as a Republican to the Fifty-ninth, Sixtieth, and Sixty-first Congresses (March 4, 1905–March 3, 1911); unsuccessful candidate for renomination in 1910 to the Sixty-second Congress; resumed the practice of law in Findlay, Toledo, and Columbus, Ohio; legal adviser to the Comptroller of the Currency in 1912 and 1913; chairman of the speakers' bureau, Republican National Committee, in 1916; delegate to many State conventions; delegate to the Republican National Conventions in 1916, 1924, and 1928; during the First World War enlisted in the United States Army June 6, 1917, serving overseas as major and lieutenant colonel in the Thirty-seventh Infantry Division, taking part in many major engagements; was honorably discharged from the service April 6, 1919; one of the founders of the American Legion at Paris February 16, 1919; resumed the practice of his profession; sustained serious injuries in an automobile accident near Parkman, Geauga County, Ohio, from which he died in the local hospital at Warren, Trumbull County, Ohio, on October 15, 1932; interment in Maple Grove Cemetery, Findlay, Ohio.

COLE, Raymond Clinton (brother of Ralph Dayton Cole), a Representative from Ohio; born in Biglick Township, near Findlay, Hancock County, Ohio, August 21, 1870; attended the common schools and Findlay College, Findlay, Ohio; taught school nine years; was graduated from the law department of Ohio Northern University at Ada in 1900; was admitted to the Ohio bar the same year and commenced practice in Findlay, Ohio, in 1901; member of the National Guard 1903–1913; served as city solicitor 1912–1916; elected as a Republican to the Sixty-sixth, Sixty-seventh, and Sixty-eighth Congresses (March 4, 1919–March 3, 1925); was an unsuccessful candidate for reelection in 1924 to the Sixty-ninth Congress; resumed the practice of law; died in Findlay, Ohio, on February 8, 1957; interment in Bright Cemetery.

COLE, William Clay, a Representative from Missouri; born on a farm near Fillmore, Andrew County, Mo., August 29, 1897; attended the public schools; served ten months as a mounted scout on the Mexican border with the Missouri forces in 1916; during the First World War served fourteen months in the war zone on board the U. S. S. *Machias,* doing submarine-patrol and convoy duty; was graduated from St. Joseph (Mo.) Law School in 1928; was admitted to the bar the same year and commenced practice in St. Joseph, Mo.; member of the State house of representatives at a special session in 1942; elected as a Republican to the Seventy-eighth, Seventy-ninth, and Eightieth Congresses (January 3, 1943–January 3, 1949); unsuccessful candidate for reelection in 1948 to the Eighty-first Congress and for election in 1950 to the Eighty-second Congress; elected to the Eighty-third Congress (January 3, 1953–January 3, 1955); unsuccessful candidate for reelection in 1954 to the Eighty-fourth Congress; member, Board of Veterans Appeals, Washington, D. C., from January 21, 1955, to July 31, 1960; resumed the practice of law in St. Joseph, Mo., where he resides.

COLE, William Hinson, a Representative from Maryland; born in Baltimore, Md., January 11, 1837; attended a private school; studied medicine, and then studied law; was admitted to the bar and commenced practice in Baltimore in 1857; moved to Kansas City, Kans., and continued the practice of law; member of the Territorial house of representatives; graduated from the University of Louisiana in 1860; enlisted in the Confederate Army and was appointed surgeon of Bartow's Eighth Georgia Regiment; served in the Battle of Gettysburg, then took charge of the wounded in Longstreet's corps; prisoner in Fort McHenry, Baltimore, for six months; returned South and acted as surgeon on the staff of Gen. Bradley Johnson, of Maryland, until the close of the war; returned to Baltimore; was appointed deputy register of Baltimore in 1870; resigned when elected chief clerk of the first branch of the Baltimore City Council; served as a reading clerk of the Maryland State House of Delegates 1874–1878; became a reporter on the Baltimore Evening Commercial, and later its proprietor; retired, but in a few months became connected with the Baltimore Gazette, and afterward with its successor, The Day, continuing with the press until his election to Congress in 1885; elected as a Democrat to the Forty-ninth Congress and served from March 4, 1885, until his death in Washington, D. C., on July 8, 1886; interment in Bonnie Brae Cemetery, Baltimore, Md.

COLE, William Purington, Jr., a Representative from Maryland; born in Towson, Baltimore County, Md., May 11, 1889; attended the public schools and was graduated from Towson High School in 1907 and as a civil engineer from Maryland Agricultural College (now University of Maryland) in 1910; studied law at the University of Maryland at Baltimore; was admitted to the bar in 1912 and commenced practice the same year; abandoned the practice of law in August 1917 to enter Fort Myer Training Camp, Fort Myer, Va.; commissioned as first lieutenant the following November and was assigned to the Three Hundred and Sixteenth Regiment of Infantry, Seventy-ninth Division, Camp Meade, Md.; served overseas, and was honorably discharged as a captain at Camp Dix, N. J., in June 1919; resumed the practice of law in 1919 at Towson, Md.; elected as a Democrat to the Seventieth Congress (March 4, 1927–March 3, 1929); unsuccessful candidate for reelection in 1928 to the Seventy-first Congress; resumed the practice of law in Towson Md.; again elected to the Seventy-second and to the five succeeding Congresses and served from March 4, 1931, until his resignation on October 26, 1942, to become a judge of the United States Customs Court, in which capacity he served until 1952; member of the Board of Regents of the Smithsonian Institution 1940–1943; named a member of the Board of Regents of the University of Maryland in 1931 and became chairman of the board in 1944; appointed judge of the United States Court of Customs and Patent Appeals by President Truman July 10, 1952, and served until his death in Baltimore, Md., September 22, 1957; interment in Arlington National Cemetery, Fort Myer, Va.

COLE, William Sterling, a Representative from New York; born in Painted Post, Steuben County, N. Y., April 18, 1904; attended the public schools; was graduated from Colgate University, Hamilton, N. Y., in 1925 and from the Albany Law School of Union University, Schenectady, N. Y., in 1929; teacher in the public schools at Corning, N. Y., in 1925 and 1926; was admitted to the bar and commenced practice in Bath, N. Y., in 1930; elected as a Republican to the Seventy-fourth and to the eleven succeeding Congresses and served from January 3, 1935, until his resignation December 1, 1957, to become Director General of the International Atomic Energy Agency with headquarters in Vienna, Austria; resides in Arlington, Va.

COLEMAN, Hamilton Dudley, a Representative from Louisiana; born in New Orleans, La., May 12, 1845; attended public and private schools; enlisted in 1861 as a private in the Washington Artillery, Army of Northern Virginia, and served throughout the Civil War, surrendering at Appomattox with Gen. Robert E. Lee; manufacturer and dealer in plantation machinery at New Orleans; organized and was head of the Coleman Machinery Co. in New Orleans, La.; one of the organizers of the first electric lighting company established in New Orleans in 1880, serving as vice president and in 1881 as president of the company; active in the organization of the World's Industrial and Cotton Centennial Exposition in 1884 and 1885; member of the Republican State central committee in 1884; election commissioner in 1886; president of the New Orleans Chamber of Commerce in 1887 and 1888; one of the vice presidents of the National Board of Trade in 1888 and 1889; vice president of the New Orleans Board of Trade in 1889; elected as a Republican to the Fifty-first Congress (March 4, 1889–March 3, 1891); unsuccessful candidate for reelection in 1890 to the Fifty-second Congress and for election in 1894 to the Fifty-fourth Congress; unsuccessful candidate for Governor in 1890 and 1894 and for Lieutenant Governor in 1892; delegate to the Republican League Convention at Cleveland, Ohio, in 1895; delegate to the Republican State conventions in 1896, 1900, and 1904; appointed melter and refiner of the United States mint at New Orleans in 1899 and served until March 1, 1905; served as a member of the United States Assay Commission in 1912; died in Biloxi, Harrison County, Miss., March 16, 1926; interment in Metairie Cemetery, New Orleans, La.

COLEMAN, Nicholas Daniel, a Representative from Kentucky; born in Cynthiana, Ky., April 22, 1800; attended the grammar and high schools; was graduated from Transylvania College, Lexington, Ky.; studied law; was admitted to the bar and practiced; member of the State house of representatives in 1824 and 1825; elected as a Jacksonian Democrat to the Twenty-first Congress (March 4, 1829–March 3, 1831); moved to Vicksburg, Miss., where he resumed the practice of law; postmaster of Vicksburg 1841–1844; again resumed the practice of law; died in Vicksburg, Warren County, Miss., on May 11, 1874; interment in Cedar Hill Cemetery.

COLEMAN, William Henry, a Representative from Pennsylvania; born in North Versailles Township, Allegheny County, Pa., December 28, 1871; attended the public schools; was graduated from Columbian University (now George Washington University) Law School; mayor of McKeesport, 1906–1909; clerk of courts, Allegheny County, 1909–1915; delegate to the Republican National Convention at Chicago in 1912; was admitted to the bar on November 10, 1913, and commenced practice in Pittsburgh, Pa.; elected as a Republican to the Sixty-fourth Congress (March 4, 1915–March 3, 1917); unsuccessful candidate for reelection in 1916 to the Sixty-fifth Congress; resumed the practice of his profession; died in McKeesport, Pa., June 3, 1943; interment in Richland Cemetery, Dravosburg, Pa.

COLERICK, Walpole Gillespie, a Representative from Indiana; born in Fort Wayne, Ind., August 1, 1845; attended the public schools; studied law; was admitted to the bar in 1872 and commenced practice at Fort Wayne, Ind.; elected as a Democrat to the Forty-sixth and Forty-seventh Congresses (March 4, 1879–March 3, 1883); supreme court commissioner from 1883 to 1885; again engaged in the practice of law at Fort Wayne, Ind., until his death there on January 11, 1911; interment in Lindenwood Cemetery.

COLES, Isaac (father of Walter Coles), a Representative from Virginia; born in Richmond, Va., March 2, 1747; educated at William and Mary College, Williamsburg, Va.; served as a colonel of militia during the Revolutionary War; member of the State house of delegates 1783–1787; member of the convention which met in Richmond, Va., in June 1788 to ratify the new Federal Constitution, which he opposed; during his political career lived on a plantation on Staunton River at Coles Ferry, Halifax County; moved to Pittsylvania County in 1798; elected to the First Congress (March 4, 1789–March 3, 1791); again elected to the Third and Fourth Congresses (March 4, 1793–March 3, 1797); died on his plantation, "Coles Hill," near Chatham, Pittsylvania County, Va., June 3, 1813; interment in the family cemetery on his plantation ten miles northeast of Chatham, Va.

COLES, Walter (son of Isaac Coles), a Representative from Virginia; born at Coles Ferry, Halifax County, Va., December 8, 1790; moved with his parents to Pittsylvania County, Va., in 1798; attended the Hampden-Sidney College, Prince Edward County, Va., and the old Washington College (now Washington and Lee University), Lexington, Va.; served as a second lieutenant in the Second Regiment of Light Dragoons in the War of 1812; promoted to the rank of captain of riflemen on the northern frontier; was honorably discharged in 1815 and returned to Virginia, where he engaged in agricultural pursuits; justice of the peace; member of the State house of delegates 1817, 1818, 1833, and 1834; elected as a Democrat to the Twenty-fourth and to the four succeeding Congresses (March 4, 1835–March 3, 1845); was not a candidate for renomination in 1844; resumed agricultural pursuits; died at his home, "Coles Hill," near Chatham, Va., on November 9, 1857; interment in the family burying ground at "Coles Hill."

COLFAX, Schuyler, a Representative from Indiana and a Vice President of the United States; born in New York City March 23, 1823; attended the common schools; in 1836 moved with his parents to New Carlisle, Ind., where he was appointed deputy auditor of St. Joseph County in 1841 by his stepfather, George W. Mathews, with office in South Bend; became a legislative correspondent in Indianapolis; purchased an interest in the South Bend Free Press and changed its name in 1845 to the St. Joseph Valley Register, the Whig organ of northern Indiana; delegate to the Whig National Conventions in 1848 and 1852; member of the State constitutional convention in 1850; unsuccessful Whig candidate for election to the Thirty-second Congress; elected as a Republican to the Thirty-fourth and to the six succeeding Congresses (March 4, 1855–March 3, 1869); was not a candidate for renomination in 1868, having become the Republican nominee for Vice President; served as Speaker of the House of Representatives in the Thirty-eighth, Thirty-ninth, and Fortieth Congresses; elected Vice President of the United States on the Republican ticket headed by Gen. U. S. Grant in 1868, was inaugurated March 4, 1869, and served until March 3, 1873; unsuccessful candidate for renomination in 1872; declined the chief editorship of the New York Tribune the same year; fully exonerated from charges of corruption brought against Members of Congress in 1873 in connection with the Crédit Mobilier of America; devoted his time to lecturing; died in Mankato, Blue Earth County, Minn., January 13, 1885; interment in City Cemetery, South Bend, Ind.

COLHOUN, John Ewing (cousin of John Caldwell Calhoun and Joseph Calhoun), a Senator from South Carolina; born in Staunton, Augusta County, Va., in 1750; attended the common schools, and was graduated from Princeton College in 1774; member of the State house of representatives 1778–1800; studied law; was admitted to the bar in 1783 and commenced practice in Charleston, S. C., but soon returned to Ninety Six District; farmer; elected a member of the privy council and also a commissioner of confiscated estates in 1785; served in the State senate in 1801; member of the committee which was instructed to report a modification of the judiciary system of the United States; elected as a Democrat to the United States Senate and served from March 4, 1801, until his death in Pendleton, S. C., October 26, 1802; interment in the family cemetery on a high hill between the forks of Twelve Mile Creek and Keowee River, Old Pendleton District, now Pickens County, South Carolina.

COLLAMER, Jacob, a Representative and a Senator from Vermont; born in Troy, N. Y., January 8, 1792; moved with his father to Burlington, Vt.; attended the common schools, and was graduated from the University of Vermont at Burlington in 1810; served in the War of 1812; studied law; was admitted to the bar in 1813 and practiced in Woodstock, Vt., from 1813 to 1833; member of the State house of representatives 1821, 1822, 1827, and 1828; State's attorney for Windsor County 1822–1824; judge of the superior court 1833–1842; elected as a Whig to the Twenty-eighth, Twenty-ninth, and Thirtieth Congresses (March 4, 1843–March 3, 1849); appointed Postmaster General in the Cabinet of President Taylor and served from March 7, 1849, to July 20, 1850; again judge of the superior court of Vermont from November 8, 1850, to October 3, 1854; elected in 1855 as a Republican to the United States Senate; reelected in 1861 and served from March 4, 1855, until his death in Woodstock, Windsor County, Vt., November 9, 1865; interment in River Street Cemetery.

COLLIER, Harold Reginald, a Representative from Illinois; born in Lansing, Ingham County, Mich., December 12, 1915; graduated from J. Sterling Morton High School in 1932; attended Morton Junior College, Cicero, Ill., in 1932 and 1933; entered Lake Forest (Ill.) College in 1934 and left in 1937 to become editor of Berwyn Beacon; editorial department of Life Publications 1938–1941; sales department and personnel manager Match Corp. of America, Chicago, Ill., 1941–1951; alderman Berwyn City Council in 1951; advertising and public relations director McAlear Manufacturing Co., Chicago, Ill., 1952–1956; unsuccessful candidate for nomination for Illinois secretary of state in 1952; township supervisor of Berwyn 1953–1956; secretary-treasurer, Cook County Supervisors Association, 1953–1956; president of Berwyn Public Health Board 1953–1956; chairman first senatorial district Republican committee since 1954; secretary third legislative district Republican committee since 1954; elected as a Republican to the Eighty-fifth and Eighty-sixth Congresses (January 3, 1957–January 3, 1961). *Reelected to the Eighty-seventh Congress.*

COLLIER, James William, a Representative from Mississippi; born in Warren County, Miss., on the Glenwood plantation near Vicksburg September 28, 1872; attended the graded and high schools; was graduated from the law department of the University of Mississippi at Oxford in 1894; was admitted to the bar the same year and commenced practice in Vicksburg; member of the State house of representatives 1896–1899; circuit clerk of Warren County from 1900 until 1909, when he resigned to become a Member of Congress; elected as a Democrat to the Sixty-first and to the eleven succeeding Congresses (March 4, 1909–March 3, 1933); declined to become a candidate for reelection in 1932 to the Seventy-third Congress, after a controversy over whether candidates should run at large or by districts; appointed a member of the United States Tariff Commission by President Franklin D. Roosevelt and served from March 28, 1933, until his death in Washington, D. C., September 28, 1933; interment in Cedar Hill Cemetery, Vicksburg, Miss.

COLLIER, John Allen, a Representative from New York; born in Litchfield, Conn., November 13, 1787; attended Yale College in 1803; studied law in the Litchfield Law School; was admitted to the bar at Troy, N. Y., in 1809 and commenced practice in Binghamton, Broome County, N. Y.; district attorney · of Broome County June 11, 1818, to February 25, 1822; elected as a Clay Democrat to the Twenty-second Congress (March 4, 1831–March 3, 1833); unsuccessful candidate for reelection in 1832 to the Twenty-third Congress; comptroller of the State of New York January 27, 1841, to February 7, 1842; unsuccessful candidate for election in 1844 to the Twenty-ninth Congress; appointed a commissioner to revise the statutes in 1847; presidential elector on the Whig ticket of Taylor and Fillmore in 1848; resumed his law practice; died in Binghamton, N. Y., March 24, 1873; interment in Spring Forest Cemetery.

COLLIN, John Francis, a Representative from New York; born in Hillsdale, N. Y., April 30, 1802; attended the common schools and Lenox Academy, Massachusetts; engaged in agricultural pursuits; member of the State assembly in 1834; supervisor of Hillsdale; elected as a Democrat to the Twenty-ninth Congress (March 4, 1845–March 3, 1847); resumed agricultural pursuits; died in Hillsdale, Columbia County, N. Y., September 16, 1889; interment in Hillsdale Rural Cemetery.

COLLINS, Ela (father of William Collins), a Representative from New York; born in Meriden, Conn., February 14, 1786; attended Clinton Academy; studied law; was admitted to the bar and commenced practice in Lowville, N. Y., in 1807; member of

the State assembly in 1815; district attorney for Lewis, Jefferson, and St. Lawrence Counties 1815–1818, and for Lewis County from June 11, 1818, to March 24, 1840; delegate to the State constitutional convention in 1821; elected as a Democrat to the Eighteenth Congress (March 4, 1823–March 3, 1825); resumed the practice of law; died in Lowville, Lewis County, N. Y., November 23, 1848; interment in Jackson Street Cemetery.

COLLINS, Francis Dolan, a Representative from Pennsylvania; born in Saugerties, Ulster County, N. Y., March 5, 1841; attended St. Joseph's College, near Montrose, Susquehanna County; moved with his parents to Dinsmore, Lackawanna County, Pa.; attended Wyoming Seminary at Kingston, Pa.; studied law; was admitted to the bar in 1866 and commenced practice in Scranton, Pa.; elected district attorney of the mayor's court district in 1869; served in the State senate 1872–1874; elected as a Democrat to the Forty-fourth and Forty-fifth Congresses (March 4, 1875–March 3, 1879); resumed the practice of his profession; died in Scranton, Lackawanna County, Pa., November 21, 1891; interment in Cathedral Cemetery, Hyde Park (Scranton).

COLLINS, John, a Delegate from Rhode Island; born in Newport, R. I., June 8, 1717; member of the committee sent by the general assembly in September 1776 to inform General Washington of the condition of the colony and obtain his views upon the best method to adopt for its defense; Member of the Continental Congress 1778–1783; Governor of Rhode Island 1786–1790; as Governor he cast the deciding vote in the senate, thereby assuring the calling of a convention to decide upon the acceptance of the Constitution of the United States; elected to the First Congress but did not take his seat; died in Newport, R. I., March 4, 1795; interment on his farm, "Brenton Neck," near Newport, R. I.

COLLINS, Patrick Andrew, a Representative from Massachusetts; born near Fermoy, County Cork, Ireland, March 12, 1844; immigrated to the United States with his parents, who settled in Chelsea, Mass., in 1848; attended the common schools; learned the upholstery trade; member of the State house of representatives in 1868 and 1869; served in the State senate in 1870 and 1871; studied law at the Harvard Law School and in Boston; was admitted to the bar in 1871 and practiced in Boston; judge advocate general of Massachusetts in 1875; delegate to the Democratic National Conventions in 1876, 1880, 1888, and 1892; elected as a Democrat to the Forty-eighth, Forty-ninth, and Fiftieth Congresses (March 4, 1883–March 3, 1889); was not a candidate for renomination in 1888; resumed the practice of law; consul general at London from May 6, 1893, to May 17, 1897, under President Cleveland's administration; again engaged in the practice of his profession, served as mayor of Boston 1902–1905; died while on a visit to Hot Springs, Va., on September 13, 1905; interment in Holyhood Cemetery, Brookline, Norfolk County, Mass.

COLLINS, Ross Alexander, a Representative from Mississippi; born in Collinsville, Lauderdale County, Miss., April 25, 1880; attended the public schools of Meridian, Miss., and Mississippi Agricultural and Mechanical College; was graduated from the University of Kentucky at Lexington in 1900 and from the law department of the University of Mississippi at Oxford in 1901; was admitted to the bar in 1901 and commenced practice in Meridian, Lauderdale County, Miss.; attorney general of Mississippi 1912–1920; unsuccessful candidate for Governor of Mississippi in 1919; elected as a Democrat to the Sixty-seventh and to the six succeeding Congresses (March 4, 1921–January 3, 1935); was not a candidate for renomination in 1934, but was an unsuccessful candidate for the Democratic nomination for

United States Senator; elected to the Seventy-fifth, Seventy-sixth, and Seventy-seventh Congresses (January 3, 1937–January 3, 1943); unsuccessful candidate for election to the United States Senate in 1941; was not a candidate for renomination in 1942, but was an unsuccessful candidate for the Democratic nomination for United States Senator; resumed the practice of law and is a resident of Meridian, Miss.

COLLINS, Samuel LaFort, a Representative from California; born in Fortville, Hancock County, Ind., on August 6, 1895; attended the public schools of Indiana and California and was graduated from Chaffey Union High School of Ontario, Calif., in 1915; enlisted as a private in the Hospital Corps, Seventh Infantry, California National Guard, on June 21, 1916, served on the Mexican border, and was discharged on November 11, 1916; during the First World War served in the United States Army from September 18, 1917, until discharged on April 29, 1919, being overseas as a sergeant in Company C, Three Hundred and Sixty-fourth Infantry, Ninety-first Division; studied law; was admitted to the bar in 1921 and commenced practice in Fullerton, Calif.; assistant district attorney of Orange County, Calif., 1926–1930 and district attorney 1930–1932; elected as a Republican to the Seventy-third and Seventy-fourth Congresses (March 4, 1933–January 3, 1937); unsuccessful candidate for reelection in 1936 to the Seventy-fifth Congress; member of the State assembly 1940–1952, serving as speaker 1947–1952; resumed the practice of law; is a resident of Fullerton, Calif.

COLLINS, William (son of Ela Collins), a Representative from New York; born in Lowville, Lewis County, N. Y., February 22, 1818; studied law; was admitted to the bar and commenced practice in Lowville; district attorney for Lewis County 1845–1847; elected as a Democrat to the Thirtieth Congress (March 4, 1847–March 3, 1849); declined to be a candidate for renomination in 1848; moved to Cleveland, Ohio, in 1853 and continued the practice of law; also engaged in banking; served as a director of the Lake Shore Railroad and East Cleveland Railroad; affiliated with the Republican Party upon its organization in 1856; died in Cleveland, Ohio, June 18, 1878; interment in Lake View Cemetery.

COLMER, William Meyers, a Representative from Mississippi; born in Moss Point, Jackson County, Miss., February 11, 1890; attended the public schools and Millsaps College at Jackson, Miss.; taught school at Lumberton, Miss., 1914–1917; studied law; was admitted to the bar in 1917; during the First World War served as a private in the Quartermaster Corps, advancing through the ranks to regimental sergeant major, and served from July 24, 1918, to March 17, 1919; commenced the practice of law in Pascagoula, Miss., in 1919; county attorney of Jackson County, Miss., 1921–1927; district attorney of the second district of Mississippi from 1928 until his resignation in 1933, having been elected to Congress; elected as a Democrat to the Seventy-third and to the thirteen succeeding Congresses (March 4, 1933–January 3, 1961); unsuccessful candidate for the Democratic nomination for United States Senator in 1947. *Reelected to the Eighty-seventh Congress.*

COLQUITT, Alfred Holt (son of Walter Terry Colquitt), a Representative and a Senator from Georgia; born in Monroe, Walton County, Ga., April 20, 1824; attended school in Monroe, and was graduated from Princeton College in 1844; studied law; was admitted to the bar in 1846 and commenced practice in Monroe, Ga.; served as a staff officer with the rank of major during the Mexican War; elected to the Thirty-third Congress (March 4, 1853–March 3, 1855); was not a candidate for renomination in 1854; member of the State house of representa-

tives in 1859; presidential elector on the Democratic ticket of Breckinridge and Lane in 1860; member of the State secession convention in 1861; entered the Confederate service as captain and was later commissioned colonel of the Sixth Georgia Infantry; promoted successively to the rank of brigadier general and major general and served throughout the Civil War; Governor of Georgia 1876–1880; reelected under a new constitution for two years; elected as a Democrat to the United States Senate in 1883; reelected in 1888 and served from March 4, 1883, until his death in Washington, D. C., March 26, 1894; interment in Rose Hill Cemetery, Macon, Bibb County, Ga.

COLQUITT, Walter Terry (father of Alfred Holt Colquitt), a Representative and a Senator from Georgia; born in Halifax County, Va., December 27, 1799; moved with his parents to Mount Zion, Carroll County, Ga.; attended the common schools and Princeton College; studied law; was admitted to the bar in 1820 and commenced practice in Sparta, Hancock County, Ga.; moved to Cowpens, Ga.; elected judge of the Chattahoochee circuit in 1826 and reelected in 1829; was licensed a Methodist preacher in 1827; member of the State senate in 1834 and 1837; elected as a State Rights Whig to the Twenty-sixth Congress and served from March 4, 1839, to July 21, 1840, when he resigned, having refused to support General Harrison for President; elected as a Van Buren Democrat to the Twenty-seventh Congress to fill in part vacancies caused by the resignations of Julius C. Alford, William C. Dawson, and Eugenius A. Nisbet, and served from January 3, 1842, to March 3, 1843; elected to the United States Senate and served from March 4, 1843, until his resignation in February 1848; member of the Nashville convention in 1850; died in Macon, Ga., May 7, 1855; interment in Linnwood Cemetery, Columbus, Ga.

COLSON, David Grant, a Representative from Kentucky; born in Yellow Creek (now Middlesboro), Knox (now Bell) County, Ky., April 1, 1861; attended the common schools and the academies at Tazewell and Mossy Creek, Tenn.; studied law at the University of Kentucky at Lexington in 1879 and 1880; was admitted to the bar and commenced practice in Pineville; examiner and special examiner in the Pension Bureau of the Department of the Interior, Washington, D. C., from September 1882 to June 1886; returned to Kentucky in 1887; member of the State house of representatives in 1887 and 1888; mayor of Middlesboro 1893–1895; elected as a Republican to the Fifty-fourth and Fifty-fifth Congresses (March 4, 1895–March 3, 1899); colonel of a Kentucky regiment during the Spanish-American War: retired; died in Middlesboro, Ky., September 27, 1904; interment in Colson Cemetery.

COLSTON, Edward, a Representative from Virginia; born at "Honeywood," near Martinsburg, Berkeley County, Va. (now West Virginia), December 25, 1786; studied under private teachers, and was graduated from Princeton College, Princeton, N. J., in 1806; studied law; was admitted to the bar and practiced; served in the War of 1812; member of the State house of delegates 1812–1814, 1816, 1817, 1823–1828, and 1833; high sheriff of Berkeley County 1844 and 1845; elected as a Federalist to the Fifteenth Congress (March 4, 1817–March 3, 1819); died at "Honeywood," Berkeley County, Va. (now West Virginia), April 23, 1852; interment in the family burying ground on his estate, "Honeywood," near Hedgesville, Berkeley County, W. Va.

COLT, LeBaron Bradford, a Senator from Rhode Island; born in Dedham, Dedham County, Mass., June 25, 1846; attended the public schools and Williston Seminary; was graduated from Yale University in 1868 and from the law department of Columbia College, New York City, in 1870; devoted a year to

European travel; upon his return to the United States in 1871 was admitted to the bar and commenced practice in Chicago, Ill.; moved to Bristol, R. I., in 1875 and practiced law in Providence, R. I.; member of the State house of representatives 1879–1881; appointed by President Garfield United States district judge for the first judicial district on March 21, 1881, and served until July 1884, when he was appointed by President Arthur presiding judge of the United States Circuit Court of Appeals for the First Circuit; elected in 1913 as a Republican to the United States Senate; reelected in 1919 and served from March 4, 1913, until his death in Bristol, R. I., August 18, 1924; interment in Juniper Hill Cemetery.

COLTON, Don Byron, a Representative from Utah; born near Mona, Juab County, Utah, September 15, 1876; moved with his parents to Uintah County, Utah, in 1879; attended the public schools and the Uintah Academy, Vernal, Utah; was graduated from the commercial department of Brigham Young University, Provo, Utah, in 1896; engaged in teaching in 1898, 1901, and 1902; member of the State house of representatives in 1903; was graduated from the law department of the University of Michigan at Ann Arbor in 1905; was admitted to the bar the same year and commenced practice in Vernal, Utah; also engaged in ranching, sheep raising, and other business enterprises; receiver of the United States land office at Vernal 1905–1914; delegate to the Republican State conventions 1914–1924; member of the State senate 1915–1917; during the First World War served on the county council of national defense, was local food and fuel administrator, and was chairman of the county Red Cross Society; delegate to the Republican National Conventions in 1904, 1924, and 1928; elected as a Republican to the Sixty-seventh and to the five succeeding Congresses (March 4, 1921–March 3, 1933); unsuccessful candidate for reelection in 1932 to the Seventy-third Congress; resumed the practice of law in Vernal, Utah; unsuccessful candidate for United States Senator in 1934; moved to Salt Lake City in 1937 and continued the practice of law; also engaged in farming and stock raising; unsuccessful candidate for Governor in 1940; died in Salt Lake City, Utah, August 1, 1952; interment in Wasatch Lawn Cemetery.

COMBS, George Hamilton, Jr., a Representative from Missouri; born in Kansas City, Mo., May 2, 1899; attended the Kansas City public schools, the University of Missouri at Columbia, and the University of Michigan at Ann Arbor; during the First World War served in the United States Navy in 1918; was graduated from the Kansas City School of Law in 1921; was admitted to the bar the same year and commenced practice in Kansas City, Mo.; assistant prosecuting attorney of Jackson County, Mo., 1922–1924; unsuccessful candidate for election in 1924 to the Sixty-ninth Congress; elected as a Democrat to the Seventieth Congress (March 4, 1927–March 3, 1929); was not a candidate for renomination in 1928; delegate to the Democratic National Convention at Houston, Tex., in 1928; moved to New York City in 1929 and continued the practice of law; vice chairman of the National Speakers Bureau of the Democratic National Committee 1928–1932; special assistant to the attorney general of the State of New York in 1931; attorney for the Triborough Bridge Authority in 1933 and 1934; associate counsel to the New York State Joint Legislative Committee to Investigate Public Utilities 1934–1936; appointed by President Franklin D. Roosevelt as New York State director of the National Emergency Council in 1936; radio news analyst, war correspondent, and writer 1937–1949; foreign correspondent and syndicated columnist 1949–1951; special United States attorney, Office of Price Stabilization for southern district of New York, in 1951 and 1952; television and radio news commentator 1952–1961; lawyer; is a resident of New York, N. Y.

COMBS, Jesse Martin, a Representative from Texas; born in Center, Shelby County, Tex., July 7, 1889; attended the public schools; was graduated from Southwest Texas State Teachers' College in 1912; was admitted to the bar in 1918 and commenced practice in Kountze, Tex.; county judge of Hardin County, Tex., in 1919 and 1920; district judge of the seventy-fifth district 1923–1925; associate justice of the ninth court of civil appeals 1933–1943; member and president of the board of trustees of South Park Schools 1926–1940; president of the board of trustees of Lamar College 1940–1944; elected as a Democrat to the Seventy-ninth and to the three succeeding Congresses (January 3, 1945–January 3, 1953); was not a candidate for renomination in 1952; returned to Beaumont, Tex., where he died August 21, 1953; interment in Magnolia Cemetery.

COMEGYS, Joseph Parsons, a Senator from Delaware; born in "Cherbourg," Kent County, near Dover, Del., December 29, 1813; attended the old academy at Dover; studied law; was admitted to the bar in 1835 and commenced practice in Dover; member of the State house of representatives in 1842 and 1848; member of the commission to revise the State statutes in 1852; declined appointment as associate justice for Kent County tendered by Governor Causey in 1855; appointed as a Whig to the United States Senate to fill the vacancy caused by the death of John M. Clayton and served from November 19, 1856, to January 14, 1857, when a successor was elected; declined renomination; resumed the practice of law in Dover; delegate to the Constitutional Union National Convention at Baltimore in 1860; delegate to the Union National Convention at Philadelphia in 1866; appointed by Governor Cochran chief justice of the supreme court of Delaware May 18, 1876, and served until January 26, 1893, when he resigned owing to ill health; died in Dover, Del., February 1, 1893; interment in the Presbyterian Cemetery.

COMER, Braxton Bragg, a Senator from Alabama; born in Spring Hill, Barbour (now Mobile) County, Ala., November 7, 1848; attended the common schools, the University of Alabama at Tuscaloosa, and the University of Georgia at Athens; was graduated from Emory and Henry College, Emory, Va., in 1869; engaged as a planter, merchant, banker, and cotton manufacturer; member of the commissioners' court of Barbour County, Ala., 1874–1880; moved to Anniston, Ala., and engaged in agricultural pursuits; moved to Birmingham, Ala., in 1890 and became president of the City National Bank and the Birmingham Corn & Flour Mills; later became president of the Avondale Cotton Mills and served in that capacity until his death; president of the Railroad Commission of Alabama in 1905 and 1906; Governor of Alabama 1907–1911; appointed as a Democrat to the United States Senate to fill the vacancy caused by the death of John H. Bankhead and served from March 5 to November 2, 1920, when a successor was elected; resumed his former business pursuits in Birmingham, Jefferson County, Ala., and died there August 15, 1927; interment in Elmwood Cemetery.

COMINGO, Abram, a Representative from Missouri; born near Harrodsburg, Mercer County, Ky., January 9, 1820; attended the common and high schools and was graduated from Centre College, Danville, Ky.; studied law; was admitted to the bar in Harrodsburg, Ky., in 1847; moved to Independence, Mo., in 1848 and commenced the practice of law; delegate to the Missouri State convention in February 1861; appointed provost marshal of the sixth district of Missouri in May 1863; elected recorder of deeds of Jackson County in 1868; elected as a Democrat to the Forty-second and Forty-third Congresses (March 4, 1871–March 3, 1875); was not a candidate for renomination in 1874; resumed the practice of law in Independence, Mo.; appointed by President Grant in 1876 a member of the commission to arbitrate with the Sioux Indians for the possession of Sioux lands in Dakota bordering on the Black Hills; moved to Kansas City, Mo., in 1881; retired from public life; died in Kansas City, Mo., November 10, 1889; interment in Elmwood Cemetery.

COMINS, Linus Bacon, a Representative from Massachusetts; born in Charlton, Mass., November 29, 1817; attended the common schools at Brookfield, Mass., and was graduated from Worcester County Manual Training High School; engaged in manufacturing in Roxbury, Mass.; member of the Roxbury City Council 1846–1848 and served as its president in 1847 and 1848; mayor of Roxbury in 1854; elected by the American Party to the Thirty-fourth Congress and as a Republican to the Thirty-fifth Congress (March 4, 1855–March 3, 1859); resumed manufacturing pursuits; delegate to the Republican National Convention at Chicago in 1860; died in Jamaica Plain, Mass., October 14, 1892; interment in Forest Hills Cemetery, Boston, Mass.

COMPTON, Barnes (great-grandson of Philip Key), a Representative from Maryland; born in Port Tobacco, Charles County, Md., November 16, 1830; attended Charlotte Hall Academy, St. Marys County, Md., and was graduated from Princeton College in June 1851; engaged in agricultural pursuits and as a planter; member of the State house of delegates in 1860 and 1861; member of the State senate in 1867, 1868, 1870, and 1872, and served as president in 1868 and 1870; State tobacco inspector in 1873 and 1874; State treasurer 1874–1885; moved to Laurel, Prince Georges County, Md., in 1880; elected as a Democrat to the Forty-ninth and Fiftieth Congresses (March 4, 1885–March 3, 1889); presented credentials as Member-elect to the Fifty-first Congress and served from March 4, 1889, to March 20, 1890, when he was succeeded by Sydney Mudd, who contested the election; elected to the Fifty-second and Fifty-third Congresses and served from March 4, 1891, until his resignation, effective May 15, 1894; appointed by President Cleveland naval officer at Baltimore, Md., and served from 1894 to 1898; died in Laurel, Md., December 4, 1898; interment in Loudon Park Cemetery, Baltimore, Md.

COMPTON, Ranulf, a Representative from Connecticut; born in Poe, Allen County, Ind., September 16, 1881; attended the public schools at Indianapolis, Ind.; was graduated from the Howe Military School, Howe, Ind., in 1899, and attended Harvard University, Cambridge, Mass.; engaged in banking and finance in New York and Connecticut; served as captain of Infantry, New York National Guard, 1912–1916; captain of Infantry, United States Army, July 1916–March 1918; captain and major in the Tank Corps April 1918–August 1919; went overseas with the A. E. F. on December 12, 1917; captain in the Three Hundred and Sixty-ninth Infantry; assigned to the Tank Corps, Bourg, France, serving as captain and chief instructor in the Tank School; served for a time with French Tank Corps; commanded the Three Hundred and Forty-fifth Battalion, First Brigade, United States Tank Corps, in the Battles of St. Mihiel and the Argonne; decorated with the Purple Heart, the French Legion of Honor, and the New York State Conspicuous Service Cross; retired from the United States Army on August 8, 1919, with rank of major; military secretary to Gov. Nathan L. Miller of New York in 1920; deputy secretary of state of New York in 1921 and 1922; executive secretary and treasurer of the Hudson River Regulating District, Albany, N. Y., 1923–1929; served as aide-de-camp to Gov. Raymond E. Baldwin of Connecticut in 1940 and 1941; elected as a Republican to the Seventy-eighth Congress (January 3, 1943–January 3, 1945); unsuccessful candidate for reelection in 1944 to the Seventy-ninth Congress; president and owner of South Jersey Broadcasting Co. since 1948, operating stations WKDN, Camden, N. J., and WARN, Fort Pierce, Fla.; is a resident of Madison, Conn.

COMSTOCK, Charles Carter, a Representative from Michigan; born in Sullivan, Cheshire County, N. H., March 5, 1818; attended the common schools; moved to Grand Rapids, Mich., in 1853; engaged in agricultural pursuits, lumbering, and the manufacture of furniture and woodenware; mayor of Grand Rapids in 1863 and 1864; unsuccessful Democratic candidate for Governor in 1870; unsuccessful candidate for election in 1873 to the Forty-third Congress; elected as a Fusion Democrat to the Forty-ninth Congress (March 4, 1885–March 3, 1887); declined to be a candidate for renomination in 1886; died in Grand Rapids, Mich., February 20, 1900; interment in Fulton Street Cemetery.

COMSTOCK, Daniel Webster, a Representative from Indiana; born in Germantown, Montgomery County, Ohio, December 16, 1840; attended the common schools, and was graduated from the Ohio Wesleyan University, Delaware, Ohio, in 1860; studied law; was admitted to the bar in 1861 and commenced practice in New Castle, Ind.; district attorney in 1862; during the Civil War enlisted in the Ninth Indiana Cavalry and was successively promoted to regimental sergeant major, first lieutenant, captain, and acting assistant adjutant general in the military division of Mississippi; settled in Richmond, Ind., in 1866; city attorney in 1866; prosecuting attorney of the Wayne circuit court 1872–1874; member of the State senate in 1878; judge of the seventeenth judicial circuit 1886–1895; judge of the appellate court 1896–1911; resumed the practice of law; elected as a Republican to the Sixty-fifth Congress and served from March 4, 1917, until his death in Washington, D. C., May 19, 1917; interment in Earlham Cemetery, Richmond, Wayne County, Ind.

COMSTOCK, Oliver Cromwell, a Representative from New York; born in Warwick, R. I., March 1, 1780; moved with his parents to Schenectady, N. Y., when a child; received a liberal schooling; studied medicine and practiced in Trumansburg, N. Y.; member of the State assembly 1810–1812; first judge of common pleas for Seneca County, N. Y., 1812–1815; elected as a Democrat to the Thirteenth, Fourteenth, and Fifteenth Congresses (March 4, 1813–March 3, 1819); was not a candidate for renomination in 1818; first judge of court of common pleas for Tompkins County in 1817 and 1818; abandoned the practice of medicine and studied theology; was licensed to preach and ordained to the Baptist ministry; installed as pastor of the First Baptist Church, Rochester, N. Y., and served in that capacity from 1825 to 1834; elected Chaplain of the National House of Representatives on December 20, 1836, and served until March 3, 1837; moved to Michigan and resumed ministerial duties at Detroit in 1839; was a regent of the University of Michigan at Ann Arbor 1841–1843; State superintendent of public instruction 1843–1845; died in Marshall, Calhoun County, Mich., January 11, 1860; interment in Oakridge Cemetery.

COMSTOCK, Solomon Gilman, a Representative from Minnesota; born in Argyle, Penobscot County, Maine, May 9, 1842; moved to Passadumkeag, Maine, with his parents in 1845; attended the rural schools, East Corinth (Maine) Academy, Maine Wesleyan Academy at Kents Hill, and Hampden (Maine) Academy; studied law in Bangor, Maine, and later, in 1868 and 1869, continued his studies at the University of Michigan at Ann Arbor; moved to Nebraska in 1869 and settled in Omaha, where he was admitted to the bar the same year and commenced practice; moved to Minneapolis, Minn., in 1870, and to Moorhead, Clay County, Minn., in 1871, where he continued the practice of his profession; prosecuting attorney for Clay County 1872–1878; member of the State house of representatives in 1875, 1876, 1878, and 1881; served in the State senate 1882–1888; unsuccessful candidate for election as State attorney general in 1882 and as Lieutenant Governor in 1884; retired from law practice in 1884 and engaged in the real-estate business; elected as a Republican to the Fifty-first Congress (March 4, 1889–March 3, 1891); unsuccessful candidate for reelection in 1890 to the Fifty-second Congress; delegate to the Republican National Convention at Minneapolis in 1892; resumed the real-estate business in Moorhead, Minn.; also engaged in the manufacture of farm implements in 1893; member of the State normal school board 1897–1905; member of the board of regents of the University of Minnesota at Minneapolis in 1904 and 1905; retired from business pursuits and resided in Moorhead, Minn., until his death there June 3, 1933; interment in Prairie Home Cemetery.

CONARD, John, a Representative from Pennsylvania; born in Chester Valley, Chester County, Pa., in November 1773; educated at the Friends School; moved to Germantown about 1795; studied law; was admitted to the bar and practiced; professor of mathematics at the local academy in Germantown; elected as a Democrat to the Thirteenth Congress (March 4, 1813–March 3, 1815); declined to be a candidate for renomination in 1814; although a member of the Society of Friends, his sympathy for the patriots and his eagerness to repel the British during the War of 1812 acquired for him the soubriquet of "The Fighting Quaker"; after his term in Congress had expired he was made associate judge of the district court; appointed United States marshal for the eastern district of Pennsylvania by President James Monroe; reappointed by President John Quincy Adams and served two years under President Andrew Jackson; retired from public life in 1832; moved to Maryland about 1834 and settled in Cecil County near Port Deposit, where he lived until 1851, when he moved to Philadelphia; did not engage in active pursuits, but lived in retirement until his death in Philadelphia, Pa., May 9, 1857; interment in St. Ann's Protestant Episcopal Churchyard, North East, Cecil County, Md.

CONDICT, Lewis (nephew of Silas Condict), a Representative from New Jersey; born in Morristown, Morris County, N. J., March 3, 1772; attended the common schools; was graduated from the medical department of the University of Pennsylvania at Philadelphia in 1794 and commenced practice in Morristown; sheriff of Morris County, N. J., 1801–1803; member of the commission for adjusting the boundary line between the States of New York and New Jersey in 1804; member of the State house of assembly 1805–1809 and served as speaker the last two years; elected as an Anti-Federalist to the Twelfth, Thirteenth, and Fourteenth Congresses (March 4, 1811–March 3, 1817); president of the State medical society in 1816 and 1819; elected to the Seventeenth and to the five succeeding Congresses (March 4, 1821–March 3, 1833); declined to be a candidate for renomination in 1832; elected trustee of the College of New Jersey (now Princeton University) in 1827, and served in this capacity until 1861, when he resigned; one of the incorporators of the Morris & Essex Railroad Co. and became its first president in 1835; again a member of the State house of assembly in 1837 and 1838 and served as speaker; presidential elector on the Whig ticket of Harrison and Tyler in 1840; died in Morristown, N. J., May 26, 1862; interment in the cemetery of the Presbyterian Church.

CONDICT, Silas (uncle of Lewis Condict and great-grandfather of Augustus William Cutler), a Delegate from New Jersey; born in Morristown, Morris County, N. J., March 7, 1738; completed preparatory studies; was a large landholder in Morristown and vicinity; member of the State council from its organization in 1776 until 1780; member of the committee of safety; Member of the Continental Congress 1781–1784; served in the State general assembly 1791–1794, 1796–1798, and in 1800, and served as speaker 1792–1794 and again in 1797; died in Morristown, N. J., September 6, 1801; interment in the cemetery of the First Presbyterian Church.

CONDIT, John (father of Silas Condit), a Representative and a Senator from New Jersey; born in Orange, N. J., July 8, 1755; attended the public schools; studied medicine and practiced; served as surgeon in the Revolutionary War in Colonel Van Cortlandt's battalion, Heardy brigade; one of the founders and a trustee of the Orange Academy in 1785; member of the State general assembly in 1788 and 1789; elected as a Democrat to the Sixth and Seventh Congresses (March 4, 1799–March 3, 1803); appointed to the United States Senate to fill the vacancy in the term beginning March 4, 1803, caused by the failure of the legislature to elect; subsequently elected and served from September 1, 1803, to March 3, 1809; again appointed to the United States Senate to fill the vacancy caused by the resignation of Aaron Kitchell; subsequently elected and served from March 21, 1809, to March 3, 1817; elected to the Sixteenth Congress and served from March 4 to November 4, 1819, when he resigned to accept a Treasury position; appointed assistant collector of the port of New York, with his office in Jersey City, N. J., and served from November 4, 1819, until January 1830; died in Orange Township, N. J., May 4, 1834; interment in the Old Graveyard, Orange, Essex County, N. J.

CONDIT, Silas (son of John Condit), a Representative from New Jersey; born in Orange, N. J., August 18, 1778; was graduated from Princeton College, New Jersey, in 1795; engaged in mercantile pursuits in Orange; moved to Newark, N. J.; clerk of Essex County 1804–1811; sheriff of Essex County 1813–1816; member of the State general assembly in 1812, 1813, and 1816; served in the State council 1819–1822; president of the Newark Banking Co. 1820–1842; elected as a Clay Democrat to the Twenty-second Congress (March 4, 1831–March 3, 1833); engaged in banking; delegate to the State constitutional convention in 1844; died in Newark, N. J., November 29, 1861; interment in the cemetery of the First Presbyterian Church.

CONDON, Francis Bernard, a Representative from Rhode Island; born in Central Falls, Providence County, R. I., November 11, 1891; attended the public schools; was graduated from Central Falls High School in 1910 and from Georgetown University Law School, Washington, D. C., in 1916; was admitted to the bar in 1916 and commenced practice in Pawtucket, R. I.; during the First World War served as a sergeant in the One Hundred and Fifty-second Regiment, Depot Brigade, Twenty-third Company, from May 1918 to June 1919; member of the State house of representatives 1921–1926, serving as Democratic floor leader 1923–1926; member of the Democratic State committee 1924–1926 and 1928–1930, serving as a member of the executive committee 1928–1930; unsuccessful candidate for Lieutenant Governor of Rhode Island in 1928; Rhode Island department commander of the American Legion in 1927 and 1928; elected as a Democrat to the Seventy-first Congress to fill the vacancy caused by the resignation of Jeremiah E. O'Connell and at the same time was elected to the Seventy-second Congress; reelected to the Seventy-third and Seventy-fourth Congresses and served from November 4, 1930, until his resignation on January 10, 1935, having been appointed an associate justice of the Rhode Island Supreme Court in which capacity he served until January 7, 1958, when he was appointed chief justice, in which office he is now serving; is a resident of Pawtucket, R. I.

CONDON, Robert Likens, a Representative from California; born in Berkeley, Alameda County, Calif., November 10, 1912; attended the public schools; was graduated from the University of California at Berkeley in 1934 and from the law college of the same university in 1938; editor in chief of the California Law Review in 1938; admitted to the California bar in 1938; attorney for National Labor Relations Board 1938–1942; with the Office of Price Administration in 1942 as chief enforcement attorney for northern California and later as regional investigator for five Western States; entered the United States Army as a private in December 1942; served overseas in the European Theater with Company G, Three Hundred and Tenth Infantry Regiment, Seventy-eighth Division, in France, Belgium, and Germany; discharged in February 1946 as a staff sergeant; decorated with two battle stars and the Silver Star; engaged in private practice of law in 1946 in Martinez, Calif.; member of California State Assembly 1948–1952; elected as a Democrat to the Eighty-third Congress (January 3, 1953–January 3, 1955); unsuccessful candidate for reelection in 1954 to the Eighty-fourth Congress; resumed law practice in Martinez, Calif.; is a resident of Walnut Creek, Calif.

CONGER, Edwin Hurd, a Representative from Iowa; born in Knox County, Ill., March 7, 1843; was graduated from Lombard University, Galesburg, Ill., in 1862; during the Civil War enlisted as a private in Company I, One Hundred and Second Regiment, Illinois Volunteer Infantry, and served until the close of the war; attained the rank of captain and received the brevet of major for "gallant and meritorious conduct in the field"; studied law and was graduated from the Albany Law School in 1866; was admitted to the bar and practiced in Galesburg, Ill., until 1868; moved to Dexter, Dallas County, Iowa, in 1868 and engaged in stock growing, banking, and agricultural pursuits; elected treasurer of Dallas County in 1877 and reelected in 1879; elected State treasurer in 1880 and reelected in 1882; elected as a Republican to the Forty-ninth, Fiftieth, and Fifty-first Congresses and served from March 4, 1885, to October 3, 1890, when he resigned to accept a diplomatic mission; Minister to Brazil from September 27, 1890, to September 13, 1893; appointed Minister to China January 19, 1898, and served until his resignation on March 8, 1905, on which day he was appointed as Ambassador to Mexico and served until his resignation on October 18, 1905; died in Pasadena, Los Angeles County, Calif., May 18, 1907; interment in Mountain View Cemetery.

CONGER, Harmon Sweatland, a Representative from New York; born in Freeport, Cortland County, N. Y., April 9, 1816; attended the local academy at Cortland in 1833; studied law; was admitted to the bar in 1844 and commenced practice in Cortland, N. Y.; editor and owner of the Cortland County Whig 1840–1845; elected as a Whig to the Thirtieth and Thirty-first Congresses (March 4, 1847–March 3, 1851); resumed the practice of law in Cortland, N. Y.; moved to Janesville, Wis., in 1855 and continued the practice of law; elected judge of the circuit court in 1870; reelected in 1877 and served until his death in Janesville, Rock County, Wis., October 22, 1882; interment in Oak Hill Cemetery.

CONGER, James Lockwood, a Representative from Michigan; born in Trenton, N. J., February 18, 1805; moved to New York in 1809 with his parents, who settled in Canandaigua, Ontario County; attended the district schools and Canandaigua Academy; studied medicine; moved to Lancaster, Ohio, in 1822; taught school for several years; studied law; was admitted to the bar in 1825 and commenced practice in Lancaster, Ohio; moved to Cleveland, Ohio, and continued the practice of law from 1826 to 1837, when he moved to Macomb County, Mich., and laid out the town of Belvidere; engaged in banking and mercantile pursuits until 1850; moved to Mount Clemens, Mich.; elected as a Free-Soil Whig to the Thirty-second Congress (March 4, 1851–March 3, 1853); declined to be a candidate for renomination in 1852; resumed his former business pursuits; supported Greeley and Brown in 1872; owing to ill health retired from active business pursuits; died in St. Clair, St. Clair County, Mich., April 10, 1876; interment in Green Lawn Cemetery, Columbus, Ohio.

CONGER, Omar Dwight, a Representative and a Senator from Michigan; born in Cooperstown, Otsego County, N. Y., April 1, 1818; moved with his father to Huron County, Ohio, in 1824; pursued academic studies at Huron Institute, Milan, Ohio, and was graduated from Western Reserve College, Hudson, Ohio, in 1841; engaged in mineral explorations of the Lake Superior copper and iron regions in connection with the Michigan State Geological Survey 1845–1847; engaged in the practice of law in Port Huron, Mich., in 1848; elected judge of the St. Clair County Court in 1850; member of the State senate 1855–1859 and served as president pro tempore in 1859; member of the State military board during the Civil War, holding the rank of colonel; delegate to the Republican National Convention at Baltimore in 1864; presidential elector on the Republican ticket of Lincoln and Johnson in 1864; member of the State constitutional convention in 1866; elected as a Republican to the Forty-first and to the five succeeding Congresses and served from March 4, 1869, until March 3, 1881, when he resigned to become Senator; had been reelected to the Forty-seventh Congress; alternate delegate to the Republican National Convention at Philadelphia in 1872; delegate to the Republican National Convention at Chicago in 1880; elected in 1881 to the United States Senate and served from March 4, 1881, to March 3, 1887; unsuccessful candidate for renomination; engaged in the practice of law in Washington, D. C.; died while on a visit in Ocean City, Worcester County, Md., July 11, 1898; interment in Lakeside Cemetery, Port Huron, Mich.

CONKLING, Alfred (father of Frederick Augustus Conkling and Roscoe Conkling), a Representative from New York; born in Amagansett, N. Y., October 12, 1789; was graduated from Union College, Schenectady, N. Y., in 1810; studied law; was admitted to the bar in 1812 and commenced practice in Canajoharie; prosecuting attorney for Montgomery County 1818–1821; elected as an anti-Jackson Democrat to the Seventeenth Congress (March 4, 1821–March 3, 1823); moved to Albany, N. Y., about 1824 and to Auburn, N. Y., in 1839; appointed United States district judge for the northern district of New York and served from 1825 to 1852; appointed United States Minister to Mexico and served from August 6, 1852, to August 17, 1853; settled in Omaha, Nebr., and practiced law until 1861, when he resided successively in Rochester, Geneseo, and Utica, N. Y., moving to the latter city in 1872; devoted much time to literary pursuits; died in Utica, Oneida County, N. Y., on February 5, 1874; interment in Forest Hill Cemetery.

CONKLING, Frederick Augustus (son of Alfred Conkling and brother of Roscoe Conkling), a Representative from New York; born in Canajoharie, Montgomery County, N. Y.,

August 22, 1816; pursued classical studies and attended the Albany Academy; engaged in mercantile pursuits in New York City; member of the State assembly in 1854, 1859, and 1860; during the Civil War organized the Eighty-fourth Regiment, New York Volunteers, in June 1861 and became its colonel; served throughout the Shenandoah campaign, and in 1863 his regiment was on provost-guard duty in Baltimore, Md.; one of the organizers of the West Side Savings Bank of New York City and served as its president for many years; subsequently he became president of the Aetna Fire Insurance Co., of Hartford, Conn., and served until its dissolution in 1880; elected as a Republican to the Thirty-seventh Congress (March 4, 1861–March 3, 1863); unsuccessful candidate for reelection in 1862 to the Thirty-eighth Congress; was an unsuccessful Republican candidate for mayor of New York City in 1868; member of the New York Chamber of Commerce, the New York Historical Society, and the Geographical Society; was the oldest governor of the New York Hospital and a trustee of the College of Physicians and Surgeons; author of numerous pamphlets on political, commercial, and scientific subjects; died in New York City, N. Y., on September 18, 1891; interment in Greenwood Cemetery, Brooklyn, N. Y.

CONKLING, Roscoe (son of Alfred Conkling and brother of Frederick Augustus Conkling), a Representative and a Senator from New York; born in Albany, N. Y., October 3, 1829; moved with his parents to Auburn, N. Y., in 1839; completed an academic course; studied law; was admitted to the bar in 1850 and commenced practice in Utica, N. Y.; district attorney for Oneida County in 1850; mayor of Utica in 1858; elected as a Republican to the Thirty-sixth and Thirty-seventh Congresses (March 4, 1859–March 3, 1863); unsuccessful candidate in 1862 for reelection to the Thirty-eighth Congress; elected to the Thirty-ninth and Fortieth Congresses and served from March 4, 1865, until his resignation, effective March 4, 1867, before the beginning of the Fortieth Congress, to become Senator; had been reelected to the latter Congress; elected in 1867 as a Union Republican to the United States Senate; reelected in 1873 and again in 1879 and served from March 4, 1867, until May 16, 1881, when he resigned as a protest against the Federal appointments made in New York State; was an unsuccessful candidate for reelection to the Senate to fill the vacancy caused by his own resignation; resumed the practice of his profession in New York City; appointed Associate Justice of the Supreme Court of the United States in February 1882 and was confirmed by the Senate, but declined to accept; died in New York City, N. Y., on April 18, 1888; interment in Forest Hill Cemetery, Utica, N. Y.

CONN, Charles Gerard, a Representative from Indiana; born in Phelps, Ontario County, N. Y., January 29, 1844; moved with his parents to Elkhart, Ind., in 1851; attended the common schools; during the Civil War enlisted in the Union Army May 18, 1861, and served as a private in the band of Company B, Fifteenth Regiment, Indiana Volunteer Infantry; discharged September 10, 1862; reenlisted in Company G, First Michigan Sharpshooters, November 18, 1862; served successively as a private, sergeant, second lieutenant, and captain in this company; was wounded and taken prisoner, being released from Columbia (S. C.) prison camp at the close of hostilities; discharged from the service July 28, 1865; awarded the Congressional Medal of Honor; engaged in the grocery and bakery business and, in 1877, in the manufacture of band instruments at Elkhart, Ind.; mayor of Elkhart 1880–1883; member of the State house of representatives in 1889; established the Elkhart Daily Truth in 1890; was owner of the Washington (D. C.) Times during part of his congressional term; elected as a Democrat to the Fifty-third

Congress (March 4, 1893–March 3, 1895); was not a candidate for renomination in 1894; resumed the manufacture of band instruments at Elkhart, Ind., and in 1916 retired from active business pursuits and moved to Los Angeles, Calif.; died in Los Angeles, Calif., on January 5, 1931; interment in Grace Lawn Cemetery, Elkhart, Ind.

CONNALLY, Thomas Terry (Tom), a Representative and a Senator from Texas; born near Hewitt, McLennan County, Tex., August 19, 1877; attended the public schools and Eddy (Tex.) High School; was graduated from Baylor University, Waco, Tex., in 1896 and from the law department of the University of Texas at Austin in 1898; was admitted to the bar in 1898 and commenced practice in Waco, Tex.; moved to Marlin, Falls County, Tex., in 1899 and continued the practice of law; served as sergeant major in the Second Regiment, Texas Volunteer Infantry, during the Spanish-American War; member of the State house of representatives 1901–1904; prosecuting attorney of Falls County, Tex., 1906–1910; during the First World War became captain and adjutant of the Twenty-second Infantry Brigade, Eleventh Division, United States Army, in 1918; delegate to the Democratic National Conventions in 1920, 1932, 1936, 1940, and 1948, serving as chairman of Texas delegation in 1936 and as vice chairman in 1948; permanent chairman of Texas Democratic State convention in 1938; delegate to the Interparliamentary Union at Geneva in 1924, at London in 1930, at Constantinople in 1934, and at Rome 1948; delegate to Empire Parliamentary Association at Ottawa in 1943; special congressional adviser to the United States delegation to the Inter-American conference on Problems of War and Peace at Mexico City in 1945; member and vice chairman of the United States delegation to the United Nations Conference on International Organization at San Francisco in 1945; representative of the United States to the first session of the General Assembly of the United Nations at London and to the second session at New York in 1946; adviser to the Secretary of State at the meetings of the Council of Foreign Ministers at Paris and New York and at the Paris Peace Conference in 1946; delegate to the Inter-American conference for the maintenance of Continental Peace and Security at Rio de Janeiro in 1947; elected as a Democrat to the Sixty-fifth and to the five succeeding Congresses (March 4, 1917–March 3, 1929); did not seek renomination in 1928, having become a candidate for Senator; elected to the United States Senate in 1928; reelected in 1934, 1940, and again in 1946 and served from March 4, 1929, to January 3, 1953; was not a candidate for renomination in 1952; engaged in the practice of law in Washington, D. C.

CONNELL, Charles Robert (son of William Connell), a Representative from Pennsylvania; born in Scranton, Lackawanna County, Pa., September 22, 1864; attended the public schools, and was graduated from Williston Academy, Easthampton, Mass., in 1884; engaged in mercantile pursuits with his father; also engaged in banking; became interested in the Lackawanna Mills and subsequently served as president and treasurer of the Scranton Button Co. from 1888 until his death; also interested in other manufacturing enterprises and banking; elected as a Republican to the Sixty-seventh Congress and served from March 4, 1921, until his death in Scranton, Pa., September 26, 1922; interment in Forest Hill Cemetery.

CONNELL, Richard Edward, a Representative from New York; born in Poughkeepsie, Dutchess County, N. Y., November 6, 1857; attended St. Peter's Parochial School and the public schools of Poughkeepsie; reporter and editor on the Poughkeepsie News Press 1887–1910; police commissioner of Poughkeepsie in 1892; unsuccessful candidate for election to the Fifty-fifth

Congress in 1896; unsuccessful candidate for member of the State assembly in 1898 and 1900; inheritance tax appraiser 1907–1909; delegate to the Democratic National Convention at Kansas City in 1900 and at St. Louis in 1904; elected as a Democrat to the Sixty-second Congress and served from March 4, 1911, until his death; had been nominated in 1912 as the Democratic candidate for reelection to the Sixty-third Congress; died in Poughkeepsie, N. Y., on October 30, 1912; interment in St. Peter's Cemetery.

CONNELL, William (father of Charles Robert Connell), a Representative from Pennsylvania; born in Sidney, Cape Breton, Nova Scotia, September 10, 1827; received a limited schooling; moved with his parents to Hazleton, Luzerne County, Pa., in 1844; in early youth was a driver boy in the coal mines; subsequently became a miner, and in 1856 was appointed superintendent of the mines of the Susquehanna & Wyoming Valley Railroad & Coal Company, with offices in Scranton; upon the expiration of that company's charter in 1870 he purchased its property and became one of the largest independent coal operators in the Wyoming region; one of the founders of the Third National Bank of Scranton in 1872, and in 1879 was chosen its president; was also identified with many other industries and commercial enterprises of Scranton; was a delegate to the Republican National Convention at St. Louis in 1896; member of the Pennsylvania Republican committee; elected as a Republican to the Fifty-fifth, Fifty-sixth, and Fifty-seventh Congresses (March 4, 1897–March 3, 1903); successfully contested the election of George Howell to the Fifty-eighth Congress and served from February 10, 1904, to March 3, 1905; died in Scranton, Lackawanna County, Pa., on March 21, 1909; interment in Forest Hill Cemetery.

CONNELL, William James, a Representative from Nebraska; born in Cowansville, Province of Quebec, Canada, July 6, 1846; moved to Schroon Lake, N. Y., in 1857 and to Vermont in 1862; completed a preparatory course; moved to Omaha, Nebr., in 1867; studied law; was admitted to the bar in 1869 and engaged in practice; district attorney of the third judicial district of Nebraska 1872–1876; city attorney of Omaha 1883–1887; elected as a Republican to the Fifty-first Congress (March 4, 1889–March 3, 1891); unsuccessful candidate for reelection in 1890 to the Fifty-second Congress; reappointed city attorney of Omaha, Nebr., in 1892; resumed the practice of his profession; died in Atlantic City, N. J., August 16, 1924; interment in Prospect Hill Cemetery, Omaha, Douglas County, Nebr.

CONNELLY, John Robert, a Representative from Kansas; born near Mount Sterling, Brown County, Ill., February 27, 1870; moved to Thayer County, Nebr., with his parents in 1883; attended the common schools and Salina (Kans.) Normal University; moved to Thomas County, Kans., in 1888; homesteaded there in 1892; began teaching school when nineteen years of age; superintendent of schools for Thomas County 1894–1898; owner and editor of the Colby Free Press 1897–1919; served as mayor of Colby and as a member of the city council; unsuccessful Democratic candidate for election in 1908 to the Sixty-first Congress; elected as a Democrat to the Sixty-third, Sixty-fourth, and Sixty-fifth Congresses (March 4, 1913–March 3, 1919); unsuccessful candidate for reelection in 1918 to the Sixty-sixth Congress; resumed his former business pursuits; delegate to the Democratic National Conventions in 1908, 1920, and 1928; unsuccessful candidate for election in 1924 to the Sixty-ninth Congress; engaged in the real-estate business at Colby, Thomas County, Kans.; died in Concordia, Kans., while on a visit to receive medical treatment, September 9, 1940; interment in Beulah Cemetery, Colby, Kans.

CONNER, James Perry, a Representative from Iowa; born in Delaware County, Ind., January 27, 1851; attended the Upper Iowa University, Fayette, Iowa, and was graduated from the law department of the University of Iowa at Iowa City in 1873; was admitted to the bar and practiced; district attorney of the thirteenth judicial district of Iowa 1880–1884; circuit judge of the thirteenth judicial district in 1884; district judge of the sixteenth judicial district in 1886; delegate to the Republican National Convention at Minneapolis in 1892; elected as a Republican to the Fifty-sixth Congress to fill the vacancy caused by the resignation of Jonathan P. Dolliver; reelected to the Fifty-seventh and to the three succeeding Congresses and served from December 4, 1900, to March 3, 1909; unsuccessful candidate in 1908 for reelection to the Sixty-first Congress; resumed the practice of law in Denison, Crawford County, Iowa, where he died March 19, 1924; interment in Oakland Cemetery.

CONNER, John Coggswell, a Representative from Texas; born in Noblesville, Hamilton County, Ind., October 14, 1842; attended the Noblesville public schools and Wabash College, Crawfordsville, Ind.; admitted to the United States Naval Academy, Annapolis, Md., September 20, 1861, and remained during the academic year, 1861–1862; during the Civil War was commissioned a second lieutenant in the Sixty-third Regiment, Indiana Volunteer Infantry, on August 30, 1862, and a first lieutenant on September 3, 1862; honorably discharged June 20, 1864; unsuccessful candidate for election to the Indiana House of Representatives in 1866; commissioned a captain in the Forty-first Regiment, United States Infantry, on July 28, 1866, and served in Texas until November 29, 1869, when he resigned, having received the nomination for Congress; upon the readmission of Texas to representation was elected as a Democrat to the Forty-first Congress; reelected to the Forty-second Congress and served from March 31, 1870, to March 3, 1873; owing to failing health was not a candidate for renomination in 1872; died in Washington, D. C., December 10, 1873; interment in the Old Cemetery, Noblesville, Ind.

CONNER, Samuel Shepard, a Representative from Massachusetts; born in Exeter, N. H., about 1783; attended Phillips Exeter Academy, Exeter, N. H., in 1794; was graduated from Yale College in 1806; studied law; was admitted to the bar and commenced practice in Waterville, Maine (at that time a district of Massachusetts), in 1810; served in the War of 1812 as major of the Twenty-first Infantry; promoted to lieutenant colonel of the Thirteenth Infantry March 12, 1813; resigned July 14, 1814; resumed the practice of law in Waterville, Maine; elected to the Fourteenth Congress (March 4, 1815–March 3, 1817); appointed surveyor general of the Ohio land district in 1819; died in Covington, Ky., December 17, 1820.

CONNERY, Lawrence Joseph (brother of William Patrick Connery, Jr.), a Representative from Massachusetts; born in Lynn, Essex County, Mass., October 17, 1895; attended the local parochial and public schools, and St. Mary's College, St. Marys, Kans.; employed as a reporter for the Lynn Item; served on the Mexican border in 1916 with Company A, Ninth Massachusetts Infantry; during the First World War served with Company A, One Hundred and First Regiment, Twenty-sixth Division, from March 25, 1917, until honorably discharged on March 24, 1919, with nineteen months service in France; employed as chief purser aboard the United Fruit Co. liner *Tivives* 1919–1923; secretary to his brother, Congressman William P. Connery, Jr., 1923–1937; was graduated from the law department of Georgetown University, Washington, D. C., in 1926; engaged in the office-supplies and printing business in

1934 in Lynn, Mass.; elected as a Democrat to the Seventy-fifth Congress to fill the vacancy caused by the death of his brother, William P. Connery, Jr.; reelected to the Seventy-sixth and Seventy-seventh Congresses and served from September 28, 1937, until his death in Arlington, Va., October 19, 1941; interment in St. Mary's Cemetery, Lynn, Mass.

CONNERY, William Patrick, Jr. (brother of Lawrence Joseph Connery), a Representative from Massachusetts; born in Lynn, Mass., August 24, 1888; attended St. Mary's School at Lynn, Montreal College in Canada 1902–1904, and Holy Cross College, Worcester, Mass, 1904–1908; entered the theatrical profession as an actor 1908–1916; engaged as a theater manager in 1916 and 1917; during the First World War enlisted as a private in the One Hundred and First Regiment, United States Infantry, and served nineteen months in France; promoted to regimental color sergeant for meritorious service; electric company employee 1919–1921; engaged in the manufacture of candy in 1921; secretary to the mayor of Lynn from January 1, 1922, to February 25, 1923; elected as a Democrat to the Sixty-eighth and to the seven succeeding Congresses and served from March 4, 1923, until his death; studied law; was admitted to the bar October 10, 1934, but did not practice extensively; died in Washington, D. C., June 15, 1937; interment in St. Mary's Cemetery, Lynn, Mass.

CONNESS, John, a Senator from California; born in Abbey, County Galway, Ireland, September 22, 1821; immigrated to the United States in 1833; learned the art of pianoforte making in New York; moved to California in 1849 and engaged in mining and mercantile pursuits; member of the State assembly in 1853 and 1854 and again in 1860 and 1861; unsuccessful candidate for Governor of California in 1861; elected as a Douglass Democrat (afterwards changed to a Union Republican) to the United States Senate and served from March 4, 1863, to March 3, 1869; moved to Boston, Mass., in 1869; retired from active business pursuits; died in Jamaica Plain, Mass., January 10, 1909; interment in Cedar Grove Cemetery, Dorchester, Mass.

CONNOLLY, Daniel Ward, a Representative from Pennsylvania; born in Cochecton, Sullivan County, N. Y., April 24, 1847; moved with his parents to Scranton, Pa., in 1849; attended the public schools; studied law; was admitted to the bar in June 1870 and commenced practice in Scranton; elected president judge of Lackawanna County in 1878 but did not serve because the State supreme court held that there was no vacancy; unsuccessful candidate for election in 1880 to the Forty-seventh Congress; elected as a Democrat to the Forty-eighth Congress (March 4, 1883–March 3, 1885); unsuccessful candidate for reelection in 1884 to the Forty-ninth Congress; appointed postmaster of Scranton, Pa., on May 2, 1885, and served until March 29, 1889; died in Scranton, Pa., December 4, 1894; interment in Forest Hill Cemetery.

CONNOLLY, James Austin, a Representative from Illinois; born in Newark, N. J., March 8, 1843; moved to Chesterville, Ohio, with his parents in 1850; attended the common schools and Selby Academy, Chesterville, Ohio; assistant clerk of the State senate in 1858 and 1859; studied law; was admitted to the bar in 1859 and practiced in Mount Gilead, Ohio; moved to Charleston, Ill., in 1861; during the Civil War enlisted in the Union Army as a private in the One Hundred and Twenty-third Regiment, Illinois Volunteer Infantry, in 1862 and was afterwards captain, major, and brevet lieutenant colonel; member of the State house of representatives 1872–1876; United States attorney for the southern district of Illinois from 1876 to 1885 and again from 1889 to 1893; unsuccessful candidate

for election in 1886 to the Fiftieth Congress; again nominated in 1888 but declined to run; elected as a Republican to the Fifty-fourth and Fifty-fifth Congresses (March 4, 1895–March 3, 1899); was not a candidate for renomination in 1898; resumed the practice of law in Springfield, Ill., where he died December 15, 1914; interment in Oak Ridge Cemetery.

CONNOLLY, James Joseph, a Representative from Pennsylvania; born in Philadelphia, Pa., September 24, 1881; attended the high schools of that city; member of the Republican State committee; served as financial secretary of the Republican city committee of Philadelphia; elected as a Republican to the Sixty-seventh and to the six succeeding Congresses (March 4, 1921–January 3, 1935); unsuccessful candidate for reelection in 1934 to the Seventy-fourth Congress and for election in 1936 to the Seventy-fifth Congress; engaged in the real-estate business; also vice president of Philadelphia Transportation Co. and Transit Investment Corp.; died in Philadelphia, Pa., December 10, 1952; interment in Holy Sepulchre Cemetery, Township of Cheltenham, Montgomery County, Pa.

CONNOLLY, Maurice, a Representative from Iowa; born in Dubuque, Iowa, March 13, 1877; attended the common schools; was graduated from Cornell University, Ithaca, N. Y., in 1897 and from the law department of New York University, New York City, in 1898; was admitted to the bar in 1899; did postgraduate work at Ballio College, Oxford, England, and the University of Heidelberg, Germany; engaged in the insurance business and banking; elected as a Democrat to the Sixty-third Congress (March 4, 1913–March 3, 1915); unsuccessful candidate for election to the United States Senate in 1914; chairman of the Iowa State Democratic convention in 1914; was a delegate to the Democratic National Convention at St. Louis in 1916; major in the Aviation Corps during the First World War; died in an airplane accident near Indianhead, Md., May 28, 1921; interment in Mount Olivet Cemetery, Dubuque, Iowa.

CONNOR, Henry William, a Representative from North Carolina; born near Amelia Court House, Prince George County, Va., August 5, 1793; was graduated from South Carolina College (now the University of South Carolina) at Columbia in 1812; served as aide-de-camp to Brig. Gen. Joseph Graham with rank of major in the expedition against the Creek Indians in 1814; settled in Falls Town, Iredell County, N. C.; engaged in planting; elected as a Democrat to the Seventeenth and to the nine succeeding Congresses (March 4, 1821–March 3, 1841); was not a candidate for renomination in 1840; resumed his former occupation; member of the State senate 1848–1850; died at Beatties Ford, Lincoln County, N. C., January 6, 1866; interment in Rehoboth Methodist Church Cemetery, near Sherrills Ford, Catawba County, N. C.

CONOVER, Simon Barclay, a Senator from Florida; born in Middlesex County, N. J., September 23, 1840; attended an academy in Trenton, N. J.; studied medicine at the University of Pennsylvania at Philadelphia; during the Civil War was appointed acting assistant surgeon in 1863; served in the Union Army of the Cumberland and was stationed at Nashville, Tenn.; was graduated from the medical department of the University of Nashville, Tennessee, in 1864 and the same year was assigned to duty at Haddington Hospital in Philadelphia; transferred to Cincinnati in 1865 in charge of Woodward Military Hospital; resigned in the fall of 1865; was again appointed acting assistant surgeon in 1866, being assigned to Lake City, Fla.; delegate to the State constitutional convention in 1868; resigned from the Medical Department of the Army upon readmission of the State into the Union and was appointed State treasurer by

Gov. Harrison Reed in 1868, serving one term; delegate to the Republican National Convention at Chicago in 1868 and was elected a member of the Republican National Committee, which position he held for four years; member of the State house of representatives in 1873 and served as speaker; elected as a Republican to the United States Senate and served from March 4, 1873, to March 3, 1879; resumed the practice of his profession; was not a candidate for reelection; unsuccessful Republican candidate for Governor in 1880; delegate to the State constitutional convention in 1885; appointed United States surgeon at Port Townsend, Wash., in 1889; became president of the board of regents of the Agricultural College and School of Sciences of the State of Washington in 1891; vice president of the State's commission to the Chicago World's Fair in 1893; practiced medicine in Port Townsend, Wash., until his death, April 19, 1908; interment in the Masonic Cemetery.

CONRAD, Charles Mynn, a Senator and a Representative from Louisiana; born in Winchester, Frederick County, Va., December 24, 1804; moved with his father to Mississippi, and thence to the Teche country in Louisiana; educated in a private school in New Orleans; studied law; was admitted to the bar in 1828 and commenced practice in New Orleans, La.; was a Jackson Democrat, but became a Whig over the bank issue; member of the State house of representatives; elected as a Whig to the United States Senate to fill the vacancy caused by the resignation of Alexander Mouton and served from April 14, 1842, to March 3, 1843; delegate to the State constitutional convention in 1844; elected as a Whig to the Thirty-first Congress and served from March 4, 1849, to August 17, 1850, when he resigned; appointed Secretary of War in the Cabinet of President Fillmore and served from August 15, 1850, to March 7, 1853; delegate from Louisiana to the Provisional Confederate Congress at Montgomery, Ala., in 1861; delegate to the First and Second Confederate Congresses 1862–1864; after the war resumed the practice of law; died in New Orleans, La., February 11, 1878; interment in Girod Street Cemetery.

CONRAD, Frederick, a Representative from Pennsylvania; born near Worcester Township, Montgomery County, Pa., in 1759; attended the common schools; was elected to the State assembly in 1798, 1800, and 1802; paymaster of the Fifty-first Regiment of Pennsylvania Militia in 1804 and 1805; elected as a Federalist to the Eighth and Ninth Congresses (March 4, 1803–March 3, 1807); appointed justice of the peace in 1807; appointed prothonotary and clerk of the courts in 1821, and reappointed in 1824; resided near Center Point and was interested in agricultural pursuits; moved to Norristown, and died there August 3, 1827; interment in Wentz's Reformed Church Cemetery, Center Point, Montgomery County, Pa.

CONRY, Joseph Aloysius, a Representative from Massachusetts; born in Brookline, Mass., September 12, 1868; attended the common schools; studied law; was admitted to the bar and commenced practice in Boston; president of the Boston Common Council in 1896 and 1897; chairman of the board of aldermen in 1898; elected as a Democrat to the Fifty-seventh Congress (March 4, 1901–March 3, 1903); unsuccessful candidate for reelection in 1902 to the Fifty-eighth Congress; resumed the practice of his profession in Boston, Mass.; recognized as consul of Russia in September 1912 and served until 1919; decorated by Nicholas II, the Czar of Russia, and made a member of the Knights of St. Anne; director of the port of Boston, Mass., 1911–1916; resumed the practice of law in Boston; special attorney for the Maritime Commission in Washington, D. C., in 1938 and 1939; practiced law in Washington, D. C., until his death June 22, 1943; interment in Mount Olivet Cemetery.

CONRY, Michael Francis, a Representative from New York; born in Shenandoah, Schuylkill County, Pa., April 2, 1870; employed in the coal mines until crippled for life; attended the public schools; engaged in teaching for seven years; was graduated from the law department of the University of Michigan at Ann Arbor in 1896; was admitted to the bar and commenced practice in Scranton, Pa.; unsuccessful candidate for election in 1900 to the Fifty-seventh Congress; moved to New York City and resumed the practice of law; served two years as assistant corporation counsel of the city of New York; elected as a Democrat to the Sixty-first and to the three succeeding Congresses and served from March 4, 1909, until his death; had been reelected to the Sixty-fifth Congress; died at Providence Hospital, Washington, D. C., March 2, 1917; interment in Calvary Cemetery, New York City, N. Y.

CONSTABLE, Albert, a Representative from Maryland; born near Charlestown, Md., June 3, 1805; studied law; was admitted to the bar in 1829 and settled in Bel Air, Harford County, Md.; moved to Baltimore and practiced law; later moved to Perryville, Cecil County, Md.; elected as a Democrat to the Twenty-ninth Congress (March 4, 1845–March 3, 1847); judge of the circuit court of Maryland in 1851; died in Camden, N. J., September 18, 1855.

CONTE, Silvio Otto, a Representative from Massachusetts; born in Pittsfield, Berkshire County, Mass., November 9, 1921; attended the public schools and graduated from Pittsfield Vocational High School in 1940; machinist at General Electric Co., in Pittsfield, Mass., in 1940 and 1941 and at Berkshire Evening Eagle, Pittsfield, Mass., 1941 and 1942; during World War II joined the Seabees and served from 1942 to 1944, with service in the Southwest Pacific; attended Boston College and Boston College Law School, graduating in 1949; was admitted to the bar in 1949 and commenced the practice of law in Pittsfield, Mass.; member of the Massachusetts State senate from the Berkshire District 1951–1958; in 1954 was selected by Massachusetts Junior Chamber of Commerce as outstanding young man of the year; parliamentarian, Republican State Conventions in 1956 and 1958; delegate to Republican National Convention in 1960; elected as a Republican to the Eighty-sixth Congress (January 3, 1959–January 3, 1961). *Reelected to the Eighty-seventh Congress.*

CONTEE, Benjamin (uncle of Alexander Contee Hanson and granduncle of Thomas Contee Worthington), a Delegate and a Representative from Maryland; born at "Brookefield," near Nottingham, Prince Georges County, Md., in 1755; attended a private school; served in the Revolutionary War as lieutenant and captain in the Third Maryland Battalion; member of the State house of delegates 1785–1787; Member of the Continental Congress in 1787 and 1788; elected to the First Congress (March 4, 1789–March 3, 1791); was not a candidate for renomination in 1790; traveled in various European countries, and studied theology, which he completed on his return to the United States, and was ordained a minister of the Episcopal Church in 1803; was pastor of the Episcopal Church at Port Tobacco, Charles County; was serving as presiding judge of the Charles County Orphans' Court at the time of his death; died in Charles County, Md., November 30, 1815; interment at "Bromont," his former home, near Port Tobacco, Md.

CONVERSE, George Leroy, a Representative from Ohio; born in Georgesville, Franklin County, Ohio, June 4, 1827; attended the common schools and Central College, Ohio, and was graduated from Denison University, Granville, Ohio, in 1849; studied law; was admitted to the bar in 1851 and commenced practice in Columbus, Ohio, in 1852; prosecuting attorney of Franklin

County in 1857; member of the State house of representatives 1860–1863 and 1874–1876 and speaker of the house in 1874; member of the State senate in 1864 and 1865; elected as a Democrat to the Forty-sixth, Forty-seventh, and Forty-eighth Congresses (March 4, 1879–March 3, 1885); was not a candidate for renomination in 1884 to the Forty-ninth Congress; resumed the practice of his profession; delegate to the Nicaraguan Canal Convention in 1892, and made chairman of this and the subsequent convention held in New Orleans; died in Columbus, Ohio, March 30, 1897; interment in Green Lawn Cemetery.

CONWAY, Henry Wharton (cousin of Ambrose Hendley Sevier), a Delegate from the Territory of Arkansas; born near Greeneville, Greene County, Tenn., March 18, 1793; educated by private tutors; enlisted as an ensign in the War of 1812 and was promoted to lieutenant in 1813; clerk in the Treasury Department, Washington, D. C., in 1817; moved to Missouri Territory in 1818 and to Arkansas Territory in 1820; receiver of public moneys in 1820 and 1821; elected as a Democrat a Delegate to the Eighteenth, Nineteenth, and Twentieth Congresses and served from March 4, 1823, until his death near Arkansas Post, Ark., then the Territorial seat of government, November 9, 1827; interment in Arkansas Post Cemetery.

CONWAY, Martin Franklin, a Representative from Kansas; born at "Bretons Hill," near Fallston, Harford County, Md., November 19, 1827; received a liberal schooling; moved to Baltimore, Md., in 1843; learned the art of printing and became an organizer of the National Typographical Union; studied law; was admitted to the bar in 1852 and commenced practice in Baltimore; moved to Kansas in 1853 and continued the practice of law; also an agent in Kansas for the Massachusetts Abolition Society; member of the first legislative council July 2, 1854; member of the Kansas Free State Convention in 1855; chief justice of the supreme court under the Topeka constitution of provisional government in 1856 and 1857; president of the Leavenworth constitutional convention of 1858; upon the admission of Kansas as a State into the Union was elected as a Republican to the Thirty-sixth and Thirty-seventh Congresses and served from January 29, 1861, to March 3, 1863; member of the peace convention of 1861 held in Washington, D. C., in an effort to devise means to prevent the impending war; appointed by President Johnson United States consul at Marseille, France, on June 10, 1866, and served until April 16, 1869, when he retired from public life because of ill health; returned to Washington, D. C., where he died February 15, 1882; interment in Rock Creek Cemetery.

COOK, Burton Chauncey, a Representative from Illinois; born in Pittsford, Monroe County, N. Y., May 11, 1819; attended the Collegiate Institute, Rochester, N. Y.; studied law; in 1835 moved to Ottawa, Ill., where he commenced the practice of law in 1840; elected by the legislature in 1846 State's attorney for the ninth judicial district for two years; reelected by the people in 1848 for four years; member of the State senate 1852–1860; delegate to the Republican National Convention at Chicago in 1860, where he seconded the nomination of Abraham Lincoln for President, and at Baltimore in 1864, where he nominated Abraham Lincoln for President; member of the peace convention of 1861 held in Washington, D. C., in an effort to devise means to prevent the impending war; elected as a Republican to the Thirty-ninth and to the three succeeding Congresses and served from March 4, 1865, to August 26, 1871, when he resigned; resumed the practice of his profession in Evanston, Cook County, Ill., and died there August 18, 1894; interment in Oakwood Cemetery, Chicago, Ill.

COOK, Daniel Pope, a Representative from Illinois; born in Scott County, Ky., in 1794; attended the common schools; studied law; was admitted to the bar and commenced practice in Kaskaskia, Ill., in 1815; moved to Edwardsville, Ill., in 1816 and engaged in newspaper work; editor of the Illinois Intelligencer; auditor of public accounts in 1816; judge of the western circuit; appointed the first attorney general of Illinois and served from March 15 to October 15, 1819; unsuccessful for election in 1818 to the Fifteenth Congress; elected to the Sixteenth and to the three succeeding Congresses (March 4, 1819–March 3, 1827); unsuccessful for reelection in 1826 to the Twentieth Congress; directed in 1827 by President Adams to proceed to Cuba and report on political conditions; a county in Illinois was named in his honor; died in Scott County, Ky., October 16, 1827.

COOK, George Washington, a Representative from Colorado; born in Bedford, Lawrence County, Ind., November 10, 1851; at the age of eleven ran away from home and enlisted in the Fifteenth Regiment, Indiana Volunteer Infantry, in the Union Army and served as a drummer boy; was transferred to the One Hundred and Forty-fifth Regiment, Indiana Volunteer Infantry, and served as chief regimental clerk; at the close of the Civil War attended the public schools, Bedford Academy, and the Indiana University at Bloomington; moved to Chicago in 1880 and entered the employ of the Louisville, New Albany & Chicago Railway; moved to Leadville, Colo., in 1880 and became division superintendent of the Denver & Rio Grande Railroad; mayor of Leadville 1885–1887; moved to Denver in 1888 and became general sales agent for the Colorado Fuel & Iron Co.; department commander of the Grand Army of the Republic for Colorado and Wyoming in 1891 and 1892; became an independent mining operator in 1893; senior vice commander in chief of the Grand Army of the Republic in 1905 and 1906; organized and commanded the famous Cook Drum Corps, of Denver; elected as a Republican to the Sixtieth Congress (March 4, 1907–March 3, 1909); was not a candidate for renomination in 1908; resumed mining operations in Colorado; died in Pueblo, Colo., December 18, 1916; interment in Fairmount Cemetery, Denver, Colo.

COOK, Joel, a Representative from Pennsylvania; born in Philadelphia, Pa., March 20, 1842; attended the public schools and was graduated from the Central High School of Philadelphia in 1859; studied law at the University of Pennsylvania at Philadelphia; was admitted to the bar in 1863 and practiced; correspondent with the Army of the Potomac and a Washington correspondent during the Civil War; on the editorial staff of the Philadelphia Public Ledger from 1865 to 1882; financial editor 1883–1907; president of the board of wardens for the port of Philadelphia 1891–1907; president of the board of trade and of the Vessel Owners and Captains' Association; member of the Union League of Philadelphia; elected as a Republican to the Sixtieth Congress to fill the vacancy caused by the resignation of John E. Reyburn; reelected to the Sixty-first Congress and served from November 5, 1907, until his death in Philadelphia, Pa., December 15, 1910; interment in North Laurel Hill Cemetery.

COOK, John Calhoun, a Representative from Iowa; born in Seneca, Seneca County, Ohio, December 26, 1846; attended the common schools; studied law; was admitted to the bar in 1867 and commenced practice in Newton, Jasper County, Iowa; judge of the sixth judicial district of Iowa in 1878; successfully contested the election of Marsena E. Cutts to the Forty-seventh Congress and took his seat March 3, 1883, the closing day of the Congress; elected as an Independent Democrat to the Forty-eighth Congress to fill the vacancy caused by the death of Marsena E. Cutts and served from October 9, 1883, to March 3, 1885; resumed the practice of law in Newton,

Iowa; moved to Webster City, Iowa, where he became attorney for a railroad company; died in Algona, Kossuth County, Iowa, June 7, 1920; interment in Riverview Cemetery.

COOK, John Parsons, a Representative from Iowa; born in Whitestown, Oneida County, N. Y., August 31, 1817; moved with his father to Davenport, Iowa, in 1836; studied law; was admitted to the bar in 1842 and commenced practice in Tipton, Cedar County, Iowa; member of the Iowa Territorial Council 1842–1845; served in the State senate 1848–1851; returned to Davenport, Iowa, in 1851 and continued the practice of law; unsuccessful candidate in 1850 for election to the Thirty-second Congress; elected as a Whig to the Thirty-third Congress (March 4, 1853–March 3, 1855); was not a candidate for renomination in 1854; continued the practice of law and also engaged in banking in Davenport until his death there April 17, 1872; interment in Oakdale Cemetery.

COOK, Joseph Platt, a Delegate from Connecticut; born in Stratford (now Bridgeport), Conn., on January 4, 1730; was graduated from Yale College, New Haven, Conn., in 1750; from 1763 to 1783 he represented the town in about thirty sessions of the general assembly; justice of the peace in 1764; appointed colonel of the Sixteenth Regiment of Militia in 1771; during the Revolutionary War accompanied General Wolcott's forces to New York in 1776; was in command of Continental forces when the British burned Danbury on April 26 and 27, 1777; resigned his colonelcy early in 1778; member of the council of safety in 1778; member of the State house of representatives in 1776, 1778, 1780–1782, and 1784; Member of the Continental Congress 1784–1788; judge of the probate court for Danbury district 1776–1813; served as one of the Governor's council in 1803; died in Danbury, Conn., on February 3, 1816; interment in Wooster Cemetery.

COOK, Orchard, a Representative from Massachusetts; born in Salem, Mass., March 24, 1763; attended the public schools; engaged in mercantile pursuits; assessor of Pownal Borough in 1786; town clerk of New Milford, district of Maine, 1795–1797; justice of the peace; judge of the court of common pleas for Lincoln County 1799–1810; appointed assistant assessor of the twenty-fifth district in November 1798; overseer of Bowdoin College, Brunswick, Maine, 1800–1805; elected to the Ninth, Tenth, and Eleventh Congresses (March 4, 1805–March 3, 1811); was not a candidate for renomination in 1810; sheriff of Lincoln County in 1811; postmaster of Wiscasset, Lincoln County, Maine, from 1811 until his death there August 12, 1819; interment in Evergreen Cemetery.

COOK, Philip, a Representative from Georgia; born in Twiggs County, Ga., July 30, 1817; was graduated from Oglethorpe University, Georgia, and from the law department of the University of Virginia at Charlottesville in 1840; practiced in Forsyth, Ga., in 1841 and 1842; moved successively to Sumter, Lanier, and Oglethorpe Counties, and continued the practice of law until 1869; served in the State senate in 1859, 1860, 1863, and 1864; entered the Confederate Army in 1861 as a private; was successively commissioned as first lieutenant, lieutenant colonel, colonel, and, in August 1863, brigadier general, and served throughout the Civil War; member of the State convention in 1865; moved to Americus, Sumter County, Ga., in 1885; elected as a Democrat to the Forty-third and to the four succeeding Congresses (March 4, 1873–March 3, 1883); resumed the practice of law in Americus, Ga.; State capitol commissioner 1883–1889; elected secretary of state of Georgia in 1890 and served until his death in Atlanta, Ga., May 24, 1894; interment in Rose Hill Cemetery, Macon, Ga.

COOK, Robert Eugene, a Representative from Ohio; born in Kent, Portage County, Ohio, May 19, 1920; attended Brimfield Elementary School and graduated from Kent State High School in 1938; during World War II served in the United States Air Force as a warrant officer 1942–1946; graduated from Kent State University in 1947 and from William and Mary Law School, Williamsburg, Va., in 1950; was admitted to the Ohio bar in 1950 and commenced the practice of law in Ravenna, Ohio; elected prosecuting attorney of Portage County, Ohio, in 1952, reelected in 1956, and served until January 1, 1959; elected as a Democrat to the Eighty-sixth Congress (January 3, 1959–January 3, 1961). *Reelected to the Eighty-seventh Congress.*

COOK, Samuel Andrew, a Representative from Wisconsin; born in Ontario, Canada, January 28, 1849; moved with his parents to Calumet County, Wis., in 1856; attended the common schools in Fond du Lac and Calumet Counties; enlisted as a private in Company A, Second Wisconsin Cavalry, under General Custer, and served until the end of the Civil War; lived on a farm in Calumet County until 1872, when he located in Marathon County and engaged in business; moved to Neenah, Winnebago County, in 1881; elected mayor of Neenah in 1889; member of the State assembly in 1891 and 1892; delegate to the Republican National Convention at Minneapolis in 1892; elected as a Republican to the Fifty-fourth Congress (March 4, 1895–March 3, 1897); declined renomination in 1896; was an unsuccessful candidate for United States Senator in 1897 and again in 1907; commander of the Grand Army of the Republic for Department of Wisconsin in 1915 and 1916; became a manufacturer of print paper at Menasha, Wis., with residence in Neenah, Wis.; president of the Alexandria Paper Company at Alexandria, Ind.; died in Neenah, Wis., on April 4, 1918; interment in Oak Hill Cemetery.

COOK, Samuel Ellis, a Representative from Indiana; born on a farm in Huntington County, Ind., September 30, 1860; attended the common schools in Whitley County and the normal schools at Columbia City, Ind., and Ada, Ohio; taught school and engaged in agricultural pursuits; studied law; was graduated from the law department of Valparaiso University, Indiana, in 1888; was admitted to the bar the same year and commenced practice in Huntington, Ind.; prosecuting attorney for Huntington County 1892–1894; delegate to the Democratic National Convention at Chicago in 1896; editorial writer for the Huntington News-Democrat 1896–1900; judge of the Huntington Circuit Court for the fifty-sixth judicial district 1906–1918; elected as a Democrat to the Sixty-eighth Congress (March 4, 1923–March 3, 1925); unsuccessful candidate for reelection in 1924 to the Sixty-ninth Congress; resumed the practice of law in Huntington, Ind., where he died February 22, 1946; interment in Mount Hope Cemetery.

COOK, Zadock, a Representative from Georgia; born in Virginia February 18, 1769; moved to Hancock County, Ga., in early life, and was one of the first settlers in Clark County; self-educated, having attended school only three weeks; ensign in the Washington County Militia in 1793; captain of the Eleventh Company, Hancock County Militia, in 1796; member of the State house of representatives in 1806, 1807, and again in 1822; served in the State senate 1810–1814, 1823, and 1824; elected to the Fourteenth Congress to fill the vacancy caused by the resignation of Alfred Cuthbert; reelected to the Fifteenth Congress and served from December 2, 1816, to March 3, 1819; retired from public life and settled on his plantation near Watkinsville, Ga., and engaged in agricultural pursuits until his death on August 3, 1863; interment in Jackson Cemetery, Clark (now Oconee) County, Ga.

COOKE, Bates, a Representative from New York; born in Wallingford, Conn., December 23, 1787; attended the public schools; moved to Lewiston, N. Y.; studied law; was admitted to the bar about 1815 and commenced practice in Lewiston; participated in the War of 1812; supervisor of the town of Cambria in 1814; elected as an Anti-Mason to the Twenty-second Congress (March 4, 1831–March 3, 1833); was not a candidate for renomination in 1832; elected comptroller of the State of New York in February 1839; served as bank commissioner from May 14, 1840, until his death in Lewiston, Niagara County, N. Y., May 31, 1841; interment in Oak Wood Cemetery.

COOKE, Edmund Francis, a Representative from New York; born in Prescott, Yavapai County, Ariz., April 13, 1885; moved with his parents to Alden, N. Y., in 1887; attended the public schools and was graduated from Alden High School in 1900; studied law; was admitted to the bar in 1910 and commenced practice in Alden, N. Y.; served as a member of the New York Assembly 1923–1928; elected as a Republican to the Seventy-first and Seventy-second Congresses (March 4, 1929–March 3, 1933); unsuccessful candidate for reelection in 1932 to the Seventy-third Congress; resumed the practice of law in Buffalo, N. Y.; is a resident of Alden, N. Y.

COOKE, Edward Dean, a Representative from Illinois; born in Cascade, Dubuque County, Iowa, October 17, 1849; attended the common schools, the local academy, and the high school at Dubuque; studied law at Dubuque and in the law department of Columbian (now George Washington) University, Washington, D. C., and was graduated from that institution in 1873; was admitted to the bar in the same year and commenced practice in Chicago, Ill.; member of the State house of representatives in 1883; elected as a Republican to the Fifty-fourth and Fifty-fifth Congresses and served from March 4, 1895, until his death in Washington, D. C., June 24, 1897; interment in Rosehill Cemetery, Chicago, Ill.

COOKE, Eleutheros, a Representative from Ohio; born in Granville, Washington County, N. Y., December 25, 1787; attended the country schools; studied law; was admitted to the bar and commenced practice in Granville; moved to Indiana in 1817, and thence to Sandusky, Erie County, Ohio, in 1819; member of the State house of representatives in 1822, 1823, and 1825; obtained from the Ohio Legislature in 1826 the first charter granted to a railroad in the United States—the Mad River & Lake Erie Railroad—and ground was broken for it in 1832; elected as a National-Republican to the Twenty-second Congress (March 4, 1831–March 3, 1833); was an unsuccessful candidate for reelection to the Twenty-third Congress; resumed the practice of his profession; again a member of the State house of representatives in 1840; died in Sandusky, Ohio, on December 27, 1864; interment on his estate, "Ogontz," near Philadelphia, Pa.

COOKE, Thomas Burrage, a Representative from New York; born in Wallingford, Conn., November 21, 1778; moved to New York about 1802 and settled in Catskill; engaged in mercantile pursuits; elected as a Democrat to the Twelfth Congress (March 4, 1811–March 3, 1813); elected president of what is now the Catskill National Bank in 1813; took the oath of office as justice of the peace September 2, 1818; engaged in the water freighting business in 1823 and also interested in agricultural pursuits; became one of the incorporators of the Catskill & Canajoharie Railway on April 19, 1830; member of the State assembly in 1838 and 1839; died in Catskill, N. Y., on November 20, 1853; interment in the Village Cemetery.

COOLEY, Harold Dunbar, a Representative from North Carolina; born in Nashville, Nash County, N. C., July 26, 1897; attended the public schools, the University of North Carolina at Chapel Hill, and the law school of Yale University, New Haven, Conn.; was admitted to the bar in 1918 and commenced practice in Nashville, N. C.; during the First World War served in the Naval Aviation Flying Corps in 1918; presidential elector in 1932 on the ticket of Roosevelt and Garner; delegate to the Interparliamentary Conferences held at Cairo, Egypt, in 1947 and at Rome, Italy, in 1948; elected as a Democrat to the Seventy-third Congress to fill the vacancy caused by the death of Edward W. Pou; reelected to the Seventy-fourth and to the twelve succeeding Congresses and served from July 7, 1934, to January 3, 1961. *Reelected to the Eighty-seventh Congress.*

COOLIDGE, Calvin, a Vice President and a President of the United States; born in Plymouth, Windsor County, Vt., July 4, 1872; attended the public schools, Black River Academy, Ludlow, Vt., and St. Johnsbury Academy; was graduated from Amherst College, Massachusetts, in 1895; studied law; was admitted to the bar in 1897 and commenced practice in Northampton, Mass.; member of the city council in 1899; city solicitor in 1900 and 1901; clerk of courts in 1904; member of the State house of representatives in 1907 and 1908; resumed the practice of his profession in Northampton; mayor of Northampton in 1910 and 1911; member of the State senate 1912–1915, and served as president of that body in 1914 and 1915; Lieutenant Governor of Massachusetts 1916–1918 and Governor in 1919 and 1920; elected Vice President of the United States on the Republican ticket headed by Warren G. Harding in 1920; was inaugurated on March 4, 1921, and served until August 3, 1923; upon the death of President Warren G. Harding became President of the United States on August 3, 1923; elected President of the United States in 1924 for the term expiring March 3, 1929; was not a candidate for renomination in 1928; served as chairman of the Nonpartisan Railroad Commission and as honorary president of the Foundation of the Blind; died at "The Beeches," Northampton, Mass., January 5, 1933; interment in the family burial ground in Plymouth (Vt.) Cemetery.

COOLIDGE, Frederick Spaulding (father of Marcus Allen Coolidge), a Representative from Massachusetts; born in Westminster, Worcester County, Mass., December 7, 1841; attended the common schools; became manager of the Boston Chair Manufacturing Co. and of the Leominster Rattan Works; selectman of his native town for three years; member of the Democratic State central committee; member of the State house of representatives in 1875; presidential elector on the Democratic ticket of Cleveland and Thurman in 1888; elected as a Democrat to the Fifty-second Congress (March 4, 1891–March 3, 1893); unsuccessful candidate for reelection in 1892 to the Fifty-third Congress; retired from active business pursuits; died in Fitchburg, Mass., on June 8, 1906; interment in Mount Pleasant Cemetery, Westminster, Mass.

COOLIDGE, Marcus Allen (son of Frederick Spaulding Coolidge), a Senator from Massachusetts; born in Westminster, Worcester County, Mass., October 6, 1865; attended the public schools and Bryant & Stratton Commercial College at Boston, Mass.; employed by his father in the manufacture of chairs and rattan; moved to Fitchburg, Mass., in 1895; engaged in the contracting business, building street railways, water works, and bridges, 1883–1905, and in the manufacture of machine tools in 1905; mayor of Fitchburg in 1916; served as chairman and treasurer of the Wilson Advisory Committee in 1916; appointed in 1919 by President Wilson as special envoy to Poland representing the Peace Commission; chairman of the Democratic State convention in 1920; delegate to the Democratic National Conventions in 1920 and 1924; presidential elector on the Democratic ticket of Smith and Robinson in 1928; trustee and president of Cushing Academy at Ashburnham, Mass.; elected as a Democrat to the United States Senate and served from March 4, 1931, to January 3, 1937; was not a candidate for renomination in 1936; resumed his former business pursuits and resided in Fitchburg, Mass.; died at Miami Beach, Fla., January 23, 1947; interment in Mount Pleasant Cemetery, Westminster, Mass.

COOMBS, Frank Leslie, a Representative from California; born in Napa, Napa County, Calif., December 27, 1853; attended the public schools in California; attended the Dorchester High School, Boston, Mass., and was graduated from the law department of Columbian (now George Washington) University, Washington, D. C., in 1875; was admitted to the bar in 1875 and commenced practice in Napa, Calif.; district attorney of Napa County, Calif., 1880–1885; member of the State assembly 1887–1889 and 1891–1897 and served as speaker in 1891 and again in 1897; on the death of John F. Swift was appointed United States Minister to Japan and served from June 1892 to August 1893; State librarian of California from April 1, 1898, to April 1, 1899; United States attorney for the northern district of California from April 1, 1899, to March 1, 1901; elected as a Republican to the Fifty-seventh Congress (March 4, 1901–March 3, 1903); unsuccessful candidate for reelection in 1902; resumed the practice of law in Napa, Calif.; again a member of the State assembly 1921–1923 and 1925–1927; died in Napa, Calif., October 5, 1934; interment in Tulocay Cemetery.

COOMBS, William Jerome, a Representative from New York; born in Jordan, Onondaga County, N. Y., December 24, 1833; attended the Jordan Academy, Jordan, N. Y.; moved to New York City in 1850, and in 1855 took up his residence in Brooklyn; in 1856 entered upon the business of exporting American goods and continued in this business for thirty-seven years, dealing with practically every market in the world; unsuccessful candidate for election in 1888 to the Fifty-first Congress; elected as a Democrat to the Fifty-second and Fifty-third Congresses (March 4, 1891–March 3, 1895); unsuccessful candidate for reelection in 1894 to the Fifty-fourth Congress; appointed a director of the Union Pacific Railroad by President Cleveland in 1894, with special commission to collect the debts due the United States Government from the various Pacific railroads; president of the Manufacturers' Terminal Co., later consolidated with the Title Guarantee & Trust Co. of Brooklyn; in 1904 became president of the South Brooklyn Savings Bank, in which capacity he served until his death in Brooklyn, N. Y., January 12, 1922; interment in Greenwood Cemetery.

COON, Samuel Harrison, a Representative from Oregon; born in Boise, Ada County, Idaho, April 15, 1903; attended public schools in Cambridge and Boise, Idaho; graduated from the University of Idaho at Moscow in 1925; worked as a wool grader, bank clerk, foreman of a sheep ranch, and as office manager for a mining concern; owned and operated a cattle ranch near Keating, Baker County, Oreg., 1929–1950; supervisor Keating Soil Conservation District 1941–1945; engaged in the real-estate business in 1951 and 1952; served in the senate of the Oregon Legislature in 1951 and 1952; elected as a Republican to the Eighty-third and Eighty-fourth Congresses (January 3, 1953–January 3, 1957); was an unsuccessful candidate for reelection in 1956 to the Eighty-fifth Congress; served as Deputy Director for the International Cooperation Administration in Lima, Peru, from February 26, 1957, to March 20, 1959; is a resident of Coronado, Calif.

COONEY, James, a Representative from Missouri; born in County Limerick, Ireland, July 28, 1848; immigrated to the United States in 1852 with his parents, who settled near Troy, N. Y.; moved to Missouri where he attended the public schools and the University of Missouri at Columbia; taught school in Illinois for several years; in 1875 settled in Marshall, Mo.; studied law; was admitted to the bar and engaged in the practice of law; elected probate judge in 1880 and prosecuting attorney of Saline County in 1882 and 1884; elected as a Democrat to the Fifty-fifth, Fifty-sixth, and Fifty-seventh Congresses (March 4, 1897–March 3, 1903); unsuccessful candidate for renomination in 1902; resumed the practice of law; died in Marshall, Saline County, Mo., November 16, 1904; interment in Ridge Park Cemetery.

COOPER, Allen Foster, a Representative from Pennsylvania; born in Franklin Township, Fayette County, Pa., June 16, 1862; attended the public schools of his native township, and was graduated from the State normal school, California, Pa., in 1882; attended Mount Union College, Alliance, Ohio, in 1883; taught school for six years; was graduated from the law department of the University of Michigan at Ann Arbor in 1888; was admitted to the bar December 4, 1888, and commenced practice in Uniontown, Fayette County, Pa.; elected as a Republican to the Fifty-eighth and to the three succeeding Congresses (March 4, 1903–March 3, 1911); resumed business and the practice of law in Uniontown, Pa.; died in Uniontown April 20, 1917; interment in Oak Grove Cemetery.

COOPER, Charles Merian, a Representative from Florida; born in Athens, Clarke County, Ga., January 16, 1856; moved with his parents to Florida in 1864; pursued academic studies at Gainesville Academy; studied law; was admitted to the bar in 1877 and commenced practice in St. Augustine, Fla.; member of the State house of representatives in 1880; served in the State senate in 1884; attorney general of Florida 1885–1889; appointed in 1889 one of the three commissioners to revise the statutes of the State; elected as a Democrat to the Fifty-third and Fifty-fourth Congresses (March 4, 1893–March 3, 1897); was not a candidate for renomination; resumed the practice of law in Jacksonville, Fla., until his death there November 14, 1923; interment in St. Mary's Cemetery.

COOPER, Edmund (brother of Henry Cooper), a Representative from Tennessee; born in Franklin, Williamson County, Tenn., September 11, 1821; was graduated from Jackson (Tenn.) College in 1839; studied law at Harvard University; was admitted to the bar and commenced practice in Shelbyville, Bedford County, Tenn., in 1841; member of the State house of representatives in 1849; presidential elector on the Constitutional Union ticket of Bell and Everett in 1860 and on the Democratic ticket of Tilden and Hendricks in 1876; Union delegate to the State constitutional convention of 1861; again elected to the State house of representatives but in 1865 resigned; upon the readmission of the State of Tennessee to representation was elected as a Conservative to the Thirty-ninth Congress and served from July 24, 1866, to March 3, 1867; appointed by President Johnson Assistant Secretary of the Treasury November 20, 1867, and served until March 20, 1869; resumed the practice of law at Shelbyville and died there July 21, 1911; interment in Willow Mount Cemetery.

COOPER, Edward, a Representative from West Virginia; born in Treverton, Northumberland County, Pa., February 26, 1873; moved with his parents to Fayette County, W. Va., in 1875; attended public and private schools; was graduated from Washington and Lee University, Lexington, Va., in 1892, and subsequently from the law department of the same university; was admitted to the bar in 1894 and practiced law for three years in Bramwell, Mercer County, W. Va.; member of the town council for eight years; on the death of his father abandoned the practice of law and engaged in the development of coal properties in West Virginia; delegate to the Republican National Convention at Chicago in 1912; elected as a Republican to the Sixty-fourth and Sixty-fifth Congresses (March 4, 1915–March 3, 1919); unsuccessful candidate for reelection in 1918 to the Sixty-sixth Congress; again engaged in the production of coal in Mercer and McDowell Counties, W. Va., and served as a director in several coal companies; died in a hospital at Bluefield, W. Va., March 1, 1928; interment in Hollywood Cemetery, Richmond, Va.

COOPER, George Byran, a Representative from Michigan; born at Long Hill, Morris County, N. J., June 6, 1808; attended the public schools; moved to Ann Arbor, Mich., in 1830, and later, in 1835, to Jackson, Mich., where he engaged in mercantile pursuits; postmaster of Jackson from 1836 to 1846; member of the State senate in 1837 and 1838; established an iron foundry at Jackson in 1840; served in the State house of representatives in 1842; State treasurer of Michigan from March 17, 1846, to March 13, 1850; engaged in banking at Jackson in 1851; presented credentials as a Democratic Member-elect to the Thirty-sixth Congress and served from March 4, 1859, to May 15, 1860, when he was succeeded by William A. Howard, who successfully contested his election; resided in New Bedford, Wall Township, Monmouth County, until his death on August 29, 1866; interment probably at Shark River, N. J.

COOPER, George William, a Representative from Indiana; born near Columbus, Bartholomew County, Ind., May 21, 1851; attended the country schools, and was graduated in the academic and law courses from the Indiana University at Bloomington in 1872; was admitted to the bar and commenced practice in Columbus, Ind.; prosecuting attorney of Columbus in 1872; mayor of Columbus in 1877; city attorney of Columbus 1879–1883; elected as a Democrat to the Fifty-first, Fifty-second, and Fifty-third Congresses (March 4, 1889–March 3, 1895); unsuccessful candidate for reelection in 1894 to the Fifty-fourth Congress; resumed the practice of law in Columbus, Ind.; died in Chicago, Ill., November 27, 1899; interment in Garland Brook Cemetery, Columbus, Ind.

COOPER, Henry (brother of Edmund Cooper), a Senator from Tennessee; born in Columbia, Maury County, Tenn., on August 22, 1827; attended Dixon Academy, Shelbyville, Tenn., and was graduated from Jackson (Tenn.) College in 1847; studied law; was admitted to the bar in 1850 and commenced practice in Shelbyville; member of the State house of representatives 1853–1860; delegate to the Democratic National Convention at Baltimore in 1860; appointed judge of the seventh judicial circuit of Tennessee in April 1862 and resigned in January 1866; chosen professor in the law school at Lebanon, Tenn., September 1, 1866; resigned in June 1867 and moved to Nashville, where he resumed the practice of law; member of the State senate in 1869 and 1870; elected as a Democrat to the United States Senate and served from March 4, 1871, to March 3, 1877; was not a candidate for renomination in 1876; was killed by bandits in Tierra Blanca, Guadelupe y Calvo, Mexico, on February 3, 1884, where he was engaged in mining operations; interment where he was killed.

COOPER, Henry Allen, a Representative from Wisconsin; born in Spring Prairie, Walworth County, Wis., September 8, 1850; moved with his parents to Burlington, Wis., in 1851;

attended the common schools; was graduated from Burlington High School in June 1869, from Northwestern University, Evanston, Ill., in 1873, and from Union College of Law (then the legal department of Northwestern University and of the old University of Chicago) in 1875; was admitted to the bar and commenced practice at Burlington, Wis.; elected district attorney of Racine County in November 1880; moved to the city of Racine in January 1881; reelected district attorney without opposition in 1882 and 1884; delegate to the Republican National Conventions in 1884 and 1924; delegate at large to the Republican National Convention at Chicago in 1908; member of the State senate 1887–1889 and author of the bill which became the law first establishing the Australian secret ballot system in the State of Wisconsin; unsuccessful candidate for election in 1890 to the Fifty-second Congress; elected as a Republican to the Fifty-third and to the twelve succeeding Congresses (March 4, 1893–March 3, 1919); unsuccessful candidate for reelection in 1918 to the Sixty-sixth Congress; again elected to the Sixty-seventh and to the four succeeding Congresses and served from March 4, 1921, until his death; had been reelected to the Seventy-second Congress; died in Washington, D. C., March 1, 1931; interment in Mound Cemetery, Racine, Wis.

COOPER, James, a Representative and a Senator from Pennsylvania; born in Frederick County, Md., May 8, 1810; pursued academic studies, and was graduated from Washington (now Washington and Jefferson) College, Washington, Pa., in 1832; studied law; was admitted to the bar in 1834 and commenced practice in Gettysburg, Pa.; elected as a Whig to the Twenty-sixth and Twenty-seventh Congresses (March 4, 1839–March 3, 1843); member of the State house of representatives in 1843, 1844, 1846, and 1848, and served as speaker one term; moved to Pottsville, Pa.; attorney general of Pennsylvania in 1848; elected to the United States Senate and served from March 4, 1849, to March 3, 1855; moved to Philadelphia; authorized by President Lincoln to raise a brigade of loyal Marylanders, and commissioned brigadier general May 7, 1861; served in West Virginia under General Frémont; appointed commandant at Camp Chase, near Columbus, Ohio, and died there March 28, 1863; interment in Mount Olivet Cemetery, Frederick, Md.

COOPER, Jere, a Representative from Tennessee; born on a farm near Dyersburg, Dyer County, Tenn., July 20, 1893; attended the public schools; was graduated from the law department of Cumberland University, Lebanon, Tenn., in 1914; was admitted to the bar in 1915 and commenced practice in Dyersburg, Tenn.; enlisted in the Second Tennessee Infantry, National Guard, in May 1917, and on July 23, 1917, was commissioned a first lieutenant; on October 24, 1917, was transferred with his company to Company K, One Hundred and Nineteenth Infantry, Thirtieth Division, and served with this regiment throughout the First World War, participating in all its engagements in France and Belgium; on July 9, 1918, was promoted to captain and served as regimental adjutant until discharged from the Army on April 2, 1919; after the war resumed the practice of law in Dyersburg, Tenn.; member of city council and city attorney 1920–1928; elected State commander of the American Legion of Tennessee in 1921; elected as a Democrat to the Seventy-first and to the fourteen succeeding Congresses and served from March 4, 1929, until his death in the naval hospital, Bethesda, Md., December 18, 1957; interment in Fairview Cemetery, Dyersburg, Tenn.

COOPER, John, a Delegate from New Jersey; born near Woodbury, Gloucester County, N. J., February 5, 1729; received a liberal education; member of the committee on correspondence for Gloucester County in 1774; member of the Provincial Congress in 1775 and 1776 and served on the committee that drafted the first constitution of New Jersey; appointed by the Provincial Congress treasurer of the western division of New Jersey and served from October 28, 1775, to August 31, 1776; served on the legislative council from Gloucester County 1776–1780 and 1784; Member of the Continental Congress and served from February 14 to June 22, 1776; member of the State council of safety in 1778; elected judge of the pleas for Gloucester County Courts on December 25, 1779; reelected in 1784, and served until his death in Woodbury, N. J., April 1, 1785; interment in Quaker Cemetery.

COOPER, John Gordon, a Representative from Ohio; born in Wigan, England, April 27, 1872; immigrated to the United States in 1880 with his parents, who settled in Youngstown, Ohio; attended the public schools; began work in the steel mills in 1885; entered the service of the Pennsylvania Railroad Company in 1896 and was employed as a locomotive fireman 1896–1900 and as an engineer 1900–1915; member of the Republican county committee in 1906; was a delegate to the Republican State convention in 1910; member of the State house of representatives 1910–1912; elected as a Republican to the Sixty-fourth and to the ten succeeding Congresses (March 4, 1915–January 3, 1937); was an unsuccessful candidate for reelection in 1936 to the Seventy-fifth Congress; served as chairman of the Board of Claims, Ohio Industrial Commission, 1937–1945; retired from public and political activities in 1947 and resided in Youngstown, Ohio; died at the home of his son in Hagerstown, Md., January 7, 1955; interment in Lake Park Cemetery, Youngstown, Ohio.

COOPER, John Sherman, a Senator from Kentucky; born in Somerset, Pulaski County, Ky., August 23, 1901; attended the public schools at Somerset and Centre College, Danville, Ky.; was graduated from Yale College, New Haven, Conn., in 1923; attended Harvard Law School, Cambridge, Mass., 1923–1925; was admitted to the bar in 1928 and commenced practice in Somerset, Ky.; member of the Kentucky House of Representatives 1928–1930; judge of Pulaski County, Ky., 1930–1938; also interested in the banking business; member of the board of trustees of the University of Kentucky 1935–1946; during World War II enlisted as a private in the United States Army in September 1942; commissioned a second lieutenant in 1943; served overseas with the Third Army from July 1944 and was discharged as a captain in February 1946; awarded the Bronze Star and was officially commended for reorganization of the judicial system of Bavaria; elected circuit judge of the twenty-eighth judicial district of Kentucky in 1945 and served until his resignation in November 1946; elected as a Republican to the United States Senate to fill the vacancy caused by the resignation of Albert B. Chandler and served from November 6, 1946, to January 3, 1949; unsuccessful candidate for reelection in 1948; delegate to the Republican National Convention in 1948; resumed the practice of law; delegate to the General Assembly of the United Nations in 1949 and alternate delegate in 1950 and 1951; served as adviser to the Secretary of State at the London and Brussels meetings of the Council of Ministers of the North Atlantic Treaty Organization in 1950; elected to the United States Senate to fill the vacancy caused by the death of Virgil M. Chapman and served from November 5, 1952, to January 3, 1955; unsuccessful candidate for reelection in 1954; Ambassador to India from March 1955 to August 1956; elected to the United States Senate in 1956 to fill the vacancy caused by the death of Alben W. Barkley and served from November 7, 1956, to January 3, 1961. *Reelected in 1960 for the term ending January 3, 1967.*

COOPER, Mark Anthony (cousin of Eugenius Aristides Nisbet), a Representative from Georgia; born near Powellton, Hancock County, Ga., on April 20, 1800; was graduated from South Carolina College (now the University of South Carolina) at Columbia in 1819; studied law; was admitted to the bar in 1821 and commenced practice in Eatonton, Putnam County, Ga.; moved to Columbus, Ga.; served in the campaign against the Seminole Indians in Florida in 1825, and again in 1836; member of the State house of representatives in 1833; elected as a State Rights Whig to the Twenty-sixth Congress (March 4, 1839–March 3, 1841); unsuccessful candidate for reelection in 1840 to the Twenty-seventh Congress but was later elected to fill the vacancy caused by the resignation of William C. Dawson; reelected as a Democrat to the Twenty-eighth Congress and served from January 3, 1842, to June 26, 1843, when he resigned to become a candidate for Governor, but was unsuccessful; president of the Etowah Manufacturing & Mining Co. of Etowah, Ga., in 1859; died at his home, "Glen Holly," near Cartersville, Bartow County, Ga., March 17, 1885; interment on his estate.

COOPER, Richard Matlack, a Representative from New Jersey; born in Gloucester County, N. J., February 29, 1768; completed a preparatory course of studies; engaged in banking; coroner 1795–1799; judge and justice of Gloucester County courts 1803–1823; member of the State general assembly 1807–1810; president of the State Bank of New Jersey at Camden 1813–1842; elected to the Twenty-first and Twenty-second Congresses (March 4, 1829–March 3, 1833); declined to be a candidate for reelection; died in Camden, N. J., March 10, 1843; interment in the Newton Burying Ground.

COOPER, Samuel Bronson, a Representative from Texas; born near Eddyville, Caldwell County, Ky., May 30, 1850; moved with his parents to Texas the same year and located in Woodville, Tyler County; attended the common schools; studied law; was admitted to the bar in 1871 and commenced practice in Woodville in January 1872; prosecuting attorney of Tyler County 1876–1880; member of the State senate 1880–1884; appointed collector of internal revenue for the first district of Texas by President Cleveland in 1885 and served until 1888; unsuccessful candidate for district judge in 1888; elected as a Democrat to the Fifty-third and to the five succeeding Congresses (March 4, 1893–March 3, 1905); unsuccessful candidate for reelection to the Fifty-ninth Congress; again elected to the Sixtieth Congress (March 4, 1907–March 3, 1909); unsuccessful candidate for reelection to the Sixty-first Congress; appointed a member of the United States Board of General Appraisers at the port of New York City by President Taft in 1910; died in New York City August 21, 1918; interment in Magnolia Cemetery, Beaumont, Jefferson County, Tex.

COOPER, Thomas, a Representative from Delaware; born in Little Creek Hundred, Sussex County, Del., in 1764; completed preparatory studies; member of the State house of representatives 1803–1808; studied law; was admitted to the bar in 1805 and practiced; served in the State senate in 1808; elected as a Federalist to the Thirteenth and Fourteenth Congresses (March 4, 1813–March 3, 1817); resumed the practice of law in Georgetown, Del., where he died in 1829; interment in the Cooper family cemetery, near Laurel, Del.

COOPER, Thomas Buchecker, a Representative from Pennsylvania; born in Coopersburg, Pa., December 29, 1823; attended the public schools and Pennsylvania College at Gettysburg; was graduated from the medical department of the University of Pennsylvania at Philadelphia in 1843 and commenced practice in Coopersburg; elected as a Democrat to the Thirty-seventh Congress and served from March 4, 1861, until his death in Coopersburg, Pa., on April 4, 1862; interment in Woodland Cemetery.

COOPER, William, a Representative from New York; born in Philadelphia, Pa., December 2, 1754; moved to Burlington, N. J., in 1786; founded Cooperstown, Otsego County, N. Y., in 1786; appointed first judge of the court of common pleas for Otsego County on February 17, 1791; elected as a Federalist to the Fourth Congress (March 4, 1795–March 3, 1797); again elected to the Sixth Congress (March 4, 1799–March 3, 1801); died in Albany, N. Y., December 22, 1809; interment in Christ Churchyard, Cooperstown, N. Y.

COOPER, William Craig, a Representative from Ohio; born in Mount Vernon, Knox County, Ohio, on December 18, 1832; attended the public schools and Mount Vernon Academy; studied law; was admitted to the bar in 1852 and commenced practice in Mount Vernon, Ohio; prosecuting attorney of Knox County 1859–1863; mayor of Mount Vernon 1862–1864; member of the State house of representatives 1872–1874; judge advocate general of Ohio 1879–1884; member of the board of education of Mount Vernon and president of the board; elected as a Republican to the Forty-ninth, Fiftieth, and Fifty-first Congresses (March 4, 1885–March 3, 1891); was not a candidate for renomination in 1890; resumed the practice of law in Mount Vernon, Ohio, where he died on August 29, 1902; interment in Mound View Cemetery.

COOPER, William Raworth, a Representative from New Jersey; born near Bridgeport, Gloucester County, N. J., February 20, 1793; attended the local schools; engaged in agricultural pursuits; member of the State general assembly 1839–1841; elected as a Democrat to the Twenty-sixth Congress (March 4, 1839–March 3, 1841); resumed agricultural pursuits until his death near Bridgeport, Woolwich Township, N. J., on September 22, 1856; interment in the Cooper family burying ground, near Bridgeport, N. J.

COPELAND, Oren Sturman, a Representative from Nebraska; born on a farm near Huron, Beadle County, S. Dak., March 16, 1887; moved with his parents to Pender, Nebr., in 1891; attended the public schools at Pender and was graduated from the Pender High School in 1903; attended the University of Nebraska at Lincoln 1904–1907; engaged in newspaper work at Lincoln, Nebr., in 1910 and in the fuel business since 1913; served as city commissioner, department of public safety, 1935–1937; mayor of Lincoln from 1937 until his resignation in 1940; elected as a Republican to the Seventy-seventh Congress (January 3, 1941–January 3, 1943); unsuccessful candidate for renomination in 1942; resumed the retail fuel business; died in Lincoln, Nebr., April 10, 1958; interment in Wyuka Cemetery.

COPELAND, Royal Samuel, a Senator from New York; born in Dexter, Washtenaw County, Mich., on November 7, 1868; attended the public schools and Michigan State Normal School, Ypsilanti, Mich.; was graduated from the medical department of the University of Michigan at Ann Arbor in 1889; took postgraduate courses in Europe; was house surgeon in the University of Michigan Hospital in 1889 and 1890; practiced medicine in Bay City, Mich., 1890–1895; professor in the medical school of the University of Michigan 1895–1908; during his residence in Ann Arbor, Mich., was mayor 1901–1903, president of the park board in 1905 and 1906, and president of the board of education in 1907 and 1908; member of the Michigan State tuberculosis board of trustees 1900–1908; moved to New York City in 1908;

dean of the New York Flower Hospital and Medical College 1908–1918; member of the United States pension examining board in 1917; commissioner of public health and president of the New York Board of Health 1918–1923; elected as a Democrat to the United States Senate in 1922; reelected in 1928 and 1934 and served from March 4, 1923, until his death; author of several scientific works, being nationally known for his writings and radio broadcasts on health problems; unsuccessful candidate for nomination as mayor of New York City in 1937; died in Washington, D. C., June 17, 1938; interment in Mahwah Cemetery, Mahwah, N. J.

COPLEY, Ira Clifton (nephew of Richard Henry Whiting), a Representative from Illinois; born near Galesburg, Knox County, Ill., October 25, 1864; moved with his parents to Aurora, Ill., in 1867; attended the public schools and Jennings Seminary at Aurora; was graduated from Yale University in 1887 and from the Union College of Law at Chicago in 1889; became connected with the gas and electric business in Aurora, Ill., in 1889; owner and publisher of the Beacon-News at Aurora in 1905, the Courier-News at Elgin in 1908, and the Herald-News at Joliet in 1913; elected as a Republican (Progressive) to the Sixty-second and to the five succeeding Congresses (March 4, 1911–March 3, 1923); was not a candidate for renomination in 1922; continued the development and publishing of daily newspapers, acquiring the Illinois State Journal at Springfield, the Union and the Tribune at San Diego, Calif., and eleven other dailies in southern California, including the News-Press at Glendale and the News-Pilot at San Pedro; died in Aurora, Ill., November 1, 1947; interment in Spring Lake Cemetery.

CORBETT, Henry Winslow, a Senator from Oregon; born in Westboro, Mass., February 18, 1827; moved with his parents to White Creek, Washington County, N. Y., in 1831; attended the common schools; engaged in mercantile pursuits in Cambridge, N. Y., in 1840 and attended Cambridge Academy; moved to New York City in 1843 and was employed in the mercantile business there until 1851; went with a stock of goods around Cape Horn to Portland, Oreg., in 1851, and engaged in a general merchandising business, later changing to wholesale hardware; became largely interested in banking and investments; city treasurer, member of the city council, and chairman of the Republican State central committee; delegate to the Republican National Convention at Chicago in 1860; elected as a Union Republican to the United States Senate and served from March 4, 1867, to March 3, 1873; was not a candidate for reelection in 1873; resumed business interests; appointed to the United States Senate March 6, 1897, to fill the vacancy in the term beginning March 4, 1897, the legislature having failed to elect, but was not permitted to qualify; unsuccessful candidate for election to the United States Senate in 1901; died in Portland, Oreg., March 31, 1903; interment in Riverview Cemetery.

CORBETT, Robert James, a Representative from Pennsylvania; born in Avalon (Pittsburgh), Pa., August 25, 1905; attended the public schools; was graduated from Allegheny College, Meadville, Pa., in 1927 and from the University of Pittsburgh, Pittsburgh, Pa., in 1929; senior high-school instructor at Coraopolis, Pa., 1929–1938; instructor in the Pittsburgh (Pa.) Academy Evening School in 1938; elected as a Republican to the Seventy-sixth Congress (January 3, 1939–January 3, 1941); unsuccessful candidate for reelection in 1940 to the Seventy-seventh Congress; served on the staff of Senator James J. Davis in Pittsburgh; sheriff of Allegheny County, Pa., 1942–1944; elected to the Seventy-ninth and to the seven succeeding Congresses (January 3, 1945–January 3, 1961). *Reelected to the Eighty-seventh Congress.*

CORDON, Guy, a Senator from Oregon; born in Cuero, De Witt County, Tex., April 24, 1890; moved to Roseburg, Oreg., and attended the public schools of Oregon; deputy assessor 1909–1916; county assessor of Douglas County, Oreg., 1917–1920; during the First World War served as a private in the Field Artillery of the United States Army in 1918; was admitted to the bar in 1920 and commenced practice in Roseburg, Oreg.; district attorney of Douglas County 1923–1935; appointed and subsequently elected as a Republican to the United States Senate to fill the vacancy caused by the death of Charles L. McNary; reelected in 1948 and served from March 4, 1944, to January 3, 1955; unsuccessful candidate for reelection in 1954; engaged in the practice of law in Washington, D. C.

CORKER, Stephen Alfestus, a Representative from Georgia; born near Waynesboro, Burke County, Ga., May 7, 1830; attended the common schools; studied law; was admitted to the bar and commenced practice in Waynesboro, Ga.; also engaged in agricultural pursuits; during the Civil War entered the Confederate Army in 1861, and served as captain of Company A, Third Georgia Regiment; resumed the practice of law in Waynesboro, Ga.; member of the State house of representatives; elected as a Democrat to the Forty-first Congress to fill the vacancy caused by the House declaring Charles H. Prince not entitled to the seat and served from December 22, 1870, to March 3, 1871; resumed the practice of law in Waynesboro, Ga., and died there on October 18, 1879; interment in the Old Cemetery, Waynesboro, Ga.

CORLETT, William Wellington, a Delegate from the Territory of Wyoming; born in Concord, Ohio, April 10, 1842; attended the district schools, and was graduated from the Willoughby (Ohio) Collegiate Institute in 1861; enlisted in the Union Army in 1862 and served in the Twenty-eighth Regiment, Ohio Volunteer Infantry, a short time; transferred to the Eighty-seventh Regiment, Ohio Volunteer Infantry, and was captured with the command at Harpers Ferry September 15, 1862; was paroled; returned to Ohio, where he taught school in Kirkland and Painesville; reentered the Army with the Twenty-fifth Ohio Battery; was later placed on detached service with the Third Iowa Battery and served until the close of the Civil War; returned to Ohio in 1865; attended the law school of the University of Michigan at Ann Arbor, and was graduated from Union Law College, Cleveland, Ohio, in July 1866; was admitted to the bar the same year; professor in elementary law at the State University and Law College and lecturer at several commercial colleges in Cleveland; settled in Cheyenne, Wyo., August 20, 1867, and engaged in the practice of law; unsuccessful Republican candidate for Delegate to the Forty-first Congress in 1869; postmaster of Cheyenne in 1870; member of the Territorial senate in 1871; prosecuting attorney of Laramie County 1872–1876; elected as a Republican a Delegate to the Forty-fifth Congress (March 4, 1877–March 3, 1879); was not a candidate for renomination in 1878; resumed the practice of law; declined the appointment as chief justice of Wyoming Territory in 1879; member of the legislative council 1880–1882; died in Cheyenne, Wyo., July 22, 1890; interment in Lakeview Cemetery.

CORLEY, Manuel Simeon, a Representative from South Carolina; born in Lexington County, S. C., February 10, 1823; was a student in Lexington Academy four years; engaged in business in 1838; opposed the first attempt at secession of South Carolina in 1852, when an effort was made to expel him from the State; editor of the South Carolina Temperance Standard in 1855 and 1856; during the Civil War entered the Confederate Army in 1863; captured by the National troops at Petersburg, Va., April 2, 1865; took the oath of allegiance June 5, 1865; delegate to the constitutional convention of South Carolina in 1867; upon the readmission of South Carolina to representation was elected as a Republican to the Fortieth Congress and served from July 25, 1868, to March 3, 1869; special agent of the United States Treasury in 1869; commissioner of agricultural statistics of South Carolina in 1870; treasurer of Lexington County in 1874; died in Lexington, S. C., November 20, 1902; interment in St. Stephen's Lutheran Cemetery.

CORLISS, John Blaisdell, a Representative from Michigan; born in Richford, Vt., June 7, 1851; attended the common schools and Fairfax (Vt.) Preparatory School; was graduated from the Vermont Methodist University at Montpelier in 1871 and from the law department of Columbian College (now George Washington University), Washington, D. C., in 1875; settled in Detroit, Mich., in 1875; was admitted to the bar the same year and commenced practice in that city; city attorney of Detroit 1882–1886; prepared the first complete charter for Detroit which was passed by the legislature in 1884; elected as a Republican to the Fifty-fourth and to the three succeeding Congresses (March 4, 1895–March 3, 1903); unsuccessful candidate for reelection in 1902 to the Fifty-eighth Congress; served three years as a member of the executive committee of the American Bar Association; member of the board of governors of the American Bar Journal; reengaged in the practice of law in Detroit, Mich., until his death there on December 24, 1929; interment in Woodlawn Cemetery.

CORNELL, Ezekiel, a Delegate from Rhode Island; born in Scituate, R. I., in 1732; attended the public schools; employed as a mechanic; appointed lieutenant colonel in Hitchcock's Rhode Island Regiment in 1775; was present at the siege of Boston; became deputy adjutant general on October 1, 1776; appointed brigadier general of State troops in 1776 and served until March 16, 1780; Member of the Continental Congress 1780–1783; retired to his farm at Scituate; died in Milford, Mass., April 25, 1800.

CORNELL, Thomas, a Representative from New York; born in White Plains, N. Y., January 27, 1814; attended the public schools; engaged in the steamboat transportation business between Rondout and New York City in 1843, and also in the railroad business and banking; commissioned major in the New York Militia during the Civil War; elected as a Republican to the Fortieth Congress (March 4, 1867–March 3, 1869); unsuccessful candidate for reelection in 1868 to the Forty-first Congress; again elected to the Forty-seventh Congress (March 4, 1881–March 3, 1883); was not a candidate for renomination in 1882 to the Forty-eighth Congress; resumed the transportation business and banking in Kingston, N. Y.; delegate to the Republican National Convention at Chicago in 1884; presidential elector on the Republican ticket of Benjamin Harrison and Levi P. Morton in 1888; died in Kingston, N. Y., March 30, 1890; interment in Montrepose Cemetery.

CORNING, Erastus (grandfather of Parker Corning), a Representative from New York; born in Norwich, Conn., December 14, 1794; moved to Troy, N. Y., and thence, in 1814, to Albany, where he established himself in iron manufacturing; served in the State senate 1842–1845; alderman of Albany; mayor 1834–1837; elected as a Democrat to the Thirty-fifth Congress (March 4, 1857–March 3, 1859); unsuccessful candidate for reelection to the Thirty-sixth Congress; member of the peace conference of 1861; elected to the Thirty-seventh and Thirty-eighth Congresses and served from March 4, 1861, to

October 5, 1863, when he resigned; delegate to the State constitutional convention in 1867; died in Albany, N. Y., April 9 1872; interment in Rural Cemetery.

CORNING, Parker (grandson of Erastus Corning), a Representative from New York; born in Albany, N. Y., January 22, 1874; attended the public schools, the Boys' Academy in Albany, and St. Paul's School, Concord, N. H.; was graduated from Yale University in 1895; engaged in the manufacture of steel and woolens; also interested in banking; elected as a Democrat to the Sixty-eighth and to the six succeeding Congresses (March 4 1923–January 3, 1937); was not a candidate for renomination in 1936; resumed his former pursuits; died in Albany, N. Y., May 24, 1943; interment in the Rural Cemetery, Menands, Albany County, N. Y.

CORNISH, Johnston, a Representative from New Jersey; born in Bethlehem Township, Hunterdon County, N. J., June 13, 1858; attended the common schools; moved with his parents to Washington, N. J., in 1870; was graduated from the Easton (Pa.) Business College; engaged in the manufacture of pianos and organs; elected mayor of Washington, N. J., in 1884, and reelected in 1885 and 1886; declined renomination in 1887 and in 1888; member of the State senate 1891–1893; elected as a Democrat to the Fifty-third Congress (March 4, 1893–March 3, 1895); unsuccessful candidate for reelection in 1894; again a member of the State senate 1900–1902 and 1906–1911; president of the Cornish Piano Co. in 1910; member of the Democratic State Committee; president of the First National Bank, the Washington Water Co., the Warren County Bankers' Association, and the Washington Cemetery Association at the time of his death in Washington, N. J., June 26, 1920; interment in the Cornish family plot in Washington Cemetery.

CORWIN, Franklin (nephew of Moses Bledso Corwin and Thomas Corwin), a Representative from Illinois; born in Lebanon, Warren County, Ohio, January 12, 1818; attended private schools; studied law; was admitted to the bar in 1839 and practiced in Wilmington, Ohio; member of the Ohio House of Representatives in 1846 and 1847; served in the State senate 1847–1849; moved to Peru, La Salle County, Ill., in 1857; member of the Illinois House of Representatives and served as speaker; elected as a Republican to the Forty-third Congress (March 4, 1873–March 3, 1875); was an unsuccessful candidate for reelection in 1874 to the Forty-fourth Congress; resumed the practice of his profession in Peru, Ill., until his death there on June 15, 1879.

CORWIN, Moses Bledso (brother of Thomas Corwin and uncle of Franklin Corwin), a Representative from Ohio; born in Bourbon County, Ky., January 5, 1790; spent the early part of his life on a farm; attended the rural schools; studied law; was admitted to the bar in 1812 and commenced practice in Urbana, Champaign County, Ohio; member of the State house of representatives in 1838 and 1839; elected as a Whig to the Thirty-first Congress (March 4, 1849–March 3, 1851); again elected to the Thirty-third Congress (March 4, 1853–March 3, 1855); engaged in the practice of law until his death in Urbana, Ohio, April 7, 1872; interment in Oak Dale Cemetery.

CORWIN, Thomas (brother of Moses Bledso Corwin and uncle of Franklin Corwin), a Representative and a Senator from Ohio; born in Bourbon County, Ky., July 29, 1794; moved with his parents to Lebanon, Warren County, Ohio, in 1798; studied law; was admitted to the bar in 1817 and commenced practice in Lebanon, Ohio; prosecuting attorney of Warren

County 1818–1828; member of the State house of representatives in 1822, 1823, and again in 1829; elected as a Whig to the Twenty-second and to the four succeeding Congresses and served from March 4, 1831, until his resignation, effective May 30, 1840, having become a candidate for Governor; Governor of Ohio 1840–1842; unsuccessful candidate for reelection in 1842 and declined to be a candidate for the nomination in 1844; president of the Ohio Whig convention in 1844; presidential elector on the Whig ticket of Clay and Frelinghuysen in 1844; elected to the United States Senate and served from March 4, 1845, to July 20, 1850, when he resigned to enter the Cabinet; appointed Secretary of the Treasury by President Fillmore and served in that capacity from July 23, 1850, to March 7, 1853; again elected as a Republican to the Thirty-sixth and Thirty-seventh Congresses and served from March 4, 1859, to March 12, 1861, when he again resigned to enter the diplomatic service; appointed by President Lincoln as Minister to Mexico and served from March 22, 1861, until September 1, 1864, when he resigned; settled in Washington, D. C., and practiced law until his death, on December 18, 1865; interment in Lebanon Cemetery, Lebanon, Ohio.

COSDEN, Jeremiah, a Representative from Maryland; born in 1768; presented credentials as a Member-elect to the Seventeenth Congress and served from March 4, 1821, to March 19, 1822, when he was succeeded by Philip Reed, who contested his election; died in Baltimore, Md., December 5, 1824.

COSGROVE, John, a Representative from Missouri; born near Alexandria Bay, Jefferson County, N. Y., September 12, 1839; attended the district schools and the Redwood (N. Y.) School; studied law in Watertown; was admitted to the bar in October 1863 and commenced practice in New York; moved to Boonville, Mo., in 1865 and continued the practice of law; city attorney of Boonville in 1870 and 1871; elected prosecuting attorney of Cooper County in 1872; delegate to the Democratic National Conventions in 1872 and 1920; again city attorney of Boonville from April 1877 to April 1878 and from April 1879 to April 1881; elected as a Democrat to the Forty-eighth Congress (March 4, 1883–March 3, 1885); was renominated in 1884, but withdrew before election day; resumed the practice of law in Boonville, Mo., where his death occurred August 15, 1925; interment in Walnut Grove Cemetery.

COSTELLO, John Martin, a Representative from California; born in Los Angeles, Calif., January 15, 1903; attended the public schools; was graduated from the law department of Loyola University, Los Angeles, Calif., in 1924; was admitted to the bar the same year and commenced practice in Los Angeles; teacher in Los Angeles secondary schools in 1924 and 1925; unsuccessful candidate for election to the Seventy-third Congress in 1932; elected as a Democrat to the Seventy-fourth and to the four succeeding Congresses (January 3, 1935–January 3, 1945); unsuccessful candidate for renomination in 1944; general counsel and manager of the Washington office of the Los Angeles Chamber of Commerce 1945–1947; engaged in the practice of law in Washington, D. C., where he now resides.

COSTELLO, Peter Edward, a Representative from Pennsylvania; born in Boston, Mass., June 27, 1854; attended the public schools of Boston; moved to Philadelphia, Pa., in 1877; engaged in various manufacturing industries, also general construction work and real estate development; member of the common council of Philadelphia 1895–1903; director of the department of public works of Philadelphia 1903–1905; again a member of the common council 1908–1915; elected as a Republican to the Sixty-fourth, Sixty-fifth, and Sixty-sixth Congresses

(March 4, 1915–March 3, 1921); was not a candidate for renomination in 1920; continued in the real-estate and investment brokerage business in Philadelphia, Pa., until his death there October 23, 1935; interment in West Laurel Hill Cemetery.

COSTIGAN, Edward Prentiss, a Senator from Colorado; born near Beaulahville, King William County, Va., July 1, 1874; moved to Colorado in 1877 with his parents, who settled in Ouray, Ouray County; attended the public schools and East Denver High School, Denver, Colo.; studied law; was admitted to the bar in Salt Lake City, Utah, in 1897, and in 1899 was graduated from Harvard University, Cambridge, Mass.; commenced the practice of law in Denver, Colo., in 1900; began his political life as a Republican; one of the founders of the Progressive Party in Colorado in 1912; delegate to the Progressive National Conventions in 1912 and 1916; unsuccessful Progressive candidate for Governor of Colorado in 1912 and 1914; appointed a member of the United States Tariff Commission by President Wilson in March 1917; reappointed in September 1918 and served until his resignation in March 1928; resumed the practice of law in Denver, Colo.; affiliated with the Democratic Party in 1930; delegate to the Democratic State convention in 1930; elected as a Democrat to the United States Senate and served from March 4, 1931, to January 3, 1937; was not a candidate for renomination in 1936; retired from professional and political activities and resided in Denver, Colo., until his death there on January 17, 1939; interment in Fairmount Cemetery.

COTHRAN, James Sproull, a Representative from South Carolina; born near Abbeville, Abbeville County, S. C., August 8, 1830; attended the country schools; was graduated from the University of Georgia at Athens in 1852; studied law; was admitted to the bar in 1853 and commenced practice in Abbeville, S. C.; entered the Confederate service as a private at the beginning of the Civil War and was with his company at the surrender of the Army of Northern Virginia at Appomattox, having attained the rank of captain; resumed the practice of law in Abbeville; elected solicitor of the eighth judicial circuit in 1876 and 1880; appointed to the judgeship of that circuit to fill a vacancy caused by the death of Judge Thomson in 1881; elected by the legislature to the same office the following winter, and reelected in 1885; elected as a Democrat to the Fiftieth and Fifty-first Congresses (March 4, 1887–March 3, 1891); was not a candidate for renomination in 1890; again resumed the practice of law in Abbeville and Greenville, S. C.; died in a sanitarium in New York City, December 5, 1897; interment in Upper Long Cane Cemetery, Abbeville, S. C.

COTTMAN, Joseph Stewart, a Representative from Maryland; born near Allen, Somerset (now Wicomico) County, Md., August 16, 1803; completed preparatory studies; attended Princeton College in 1821 and Yale College in 1822 and 1823; studied law; was admitted to the bar in 1826 and commenced practice in Princess Anne, Md.; member of the State house of delegates in 1831, 1832, and again in 1839; served in the State senate in 1837; presidential elector on the Taylor and Fillmore ticket in 1848; elected as an Independent Whig to the Thirty-second Congress (March 4, 1851–March 3, 1853); unsuccessful candidate for reelection in 1852 to the Thirty-third Congress; resumed the practice of law; also engaged in agricultural and literary pursuits; died on his farm "Mortherton," near Allen, Wicomico County, Md., January 28, 1863; interment in St. Andrew's Episcopal Churchyard, Princess Anne, Md.

COTTON, Aylett Rains, a Representative from Iowa; born in Austintown, Ohio, November 29, 1826; attended the local public schools and Cottage Hill Academy, Ellsworth, Ohio, in 1842 and 1843; taught school; moved to Iowa with his father, who settled near Dewitt, Clinton County, in 1844; attended Allegheny College, Meadville, Pa., in 1845; taught school at Union Academy, Fayette County, Tenn., 1845–1847; returned to Iowa in 1847; studied law; was admitted to the Clinton County bar in 1848 and practiced; went to California in 1849 and engaged in mining on the Feather River; returned to Iowa in 1851 and settled in Lyons; county judge of Clinton County 1851–1853; prosecuting attorney of Clinton County in 1854; mayor of Lyons 1855–1857; member of the State constitutional convention in 1857; member of the State house of representatives 1868–1870, and served as speaker during the last term; elected as a Republican to the Forty-second and Forty-third Congresses (March 4, 1871–March 3, 1875); was not a candidate for renomination in 1874; returned to California in 1883 and engaged in the practice of law in San Francisco, Calif., where he died October 30, 1912; interment in Woodlawn Cemetery, San Mateo County, Calif.

COTTON, Norris, a Representative and a Senator from New Hampshire; born in Warren, Grafton County, N. H., May 11, 1900; attended Phillips Exeter Academy at Exeter, N. H.; was graduated from Wesleyan University, Middletown, Conn., in 1923; attended the law school of George Washington University, Washington, D. C.; was admitted to the bar in 1928 and commenced practice in Concord, N. H., later moving to Lebanon, N. H.; served in the State house of representatives in 1923 and again in 1943 and 1945, serving as speaker in 1945; secretary to United States Senator George H. Moses 1924–1928; clerk of the State senate 1927–1929; prosecuting attorney for Grafton County 1933–1939; judge of the municipal court of Lebanon 1939–1943; delegate to the Republican National Convention at Chicago in 1944; elected as a Republican to the Eightieth and to the three succeeding Congresses and served from January 3, 1947, until his resignation November 7, 1954, having been elected to the United States Senate to fill the vacancy caused by the death of Charles W. Tobey, and served from November 8, 1954, to January 3, 1957; reelected in 1956 for the term ending January 3, 1963.

COTTRELL, James La Fayette, a Representative from Alabama; born near King William, King William County, Va., August 25, 1808; completed preparatory studies; studied law; was admitted to the bar in 1830 and commenced practice in Hayneville, Ala.; member of the Alabama House of Representatives in 1834, 1836, and 1837; served in the State senate 1838–1841, and was president of that body in 1840; elected as a Democrat to the Twenty-ninth Congress to fill the vacancy caused by the resignation of William L. Yancey and served from December 7, 1846, to March 3, 1847; was nominated on the Cass electoral ticket in 1848, but resigned; moved to Florida in 1854; served in the Florida Senate 1865–1885; appointed collector of customs at Cedar Keys, Levy County, Fla., and served until his death in that city September 7, 1885; interment in Old Town Cemetery, Old Town, Dixie County, Fla.

COUDERT, Frederic René, Jr., a Representative from New York; born in New York City, N. Y., May 7, 1898; attended Browning and Morristown Schools in New York City; was graduated from Columbia University in 1918 and from its law school in 1922; awarded a Kent Scholarship and the Columbia University Medal for distinguished public service; during the First World War served as a first lieutenant in the One Hundred and Fifth United States Infantry, Twenty-seventh Division, with overseas service, in 1917 and 1918; was admitted to the bar in 1923 and commenced practice in New York City; assistant United States attorney for the southern district of New York in 1924 and 1925; unsuccessful Republican candidate for district attorney of New York County in 1929; delegate to the Republican State conventions in 1930, 1932, 1934, 1936, 1938, 1940, 1942, 1944, 1946, and 1948; delegate to the Republican National Conventions in 1936, 1940, 1944, and 1948; member of the State senate 1939–1946; elected as a Republican to the Eightieth and to the five succeeding Congresses (January 3, 1947–January 3, 1959); was not a candidate for renomination in 1958; engaged in the practice of law in New York City; member of State Commission on Governmental Operations of the City of New York 1959–1961; is a resident of New York, N. Y.

COUDREY, Harry Marcy, a Representative from Missouri; born in Brunswick, Chariton County, Mo., February 28, 1867; moved with his parents to St. Louis, Mo., in 1878; attended the public schools of Brunswick and St. Louis and was graduated from the Manual Training School at St. Louis in 1886; elected a member of the municipal house of delegates of St. Louis and served from 1897 to 1899, inclusive; became interested in various business enterprises in St. Louis; successfully contested as a Republican the election of Ernest E. Wood to the Fifty-ninth Congress; reelected to the Sixtieth and Sixty-first Congresses and served from June 23, 1906, to March 3, 1911; was not a candidate for renomination in 1910 to the Sixty-second Congress; moved to New York City in 1911; engaged in the real estate, insurance, and publishing businesses; died in Norfolk, Va., July 5, 1930; interment in Bellefontaine Cemetery, St. Louis, Mo.

COUGHLIN, Clarence Dennis, a Representative from Pennsylvania; born in Kingston, Luzerne County, Pa., July 27, 1883; attended the public schools of Wilkes-Barre, Pa., Wesleyan College, Middletown, Conn., and Harvard College; taught in the Wilkes-Barre High School 1906–1910; studied law; was admitted to the bar in 1910 and practiced law in Luzerne County 1910–1920; engaged in manufacturing, banking, and the development of real estate in Wilkes-Barre and Scranton; member of the committee of public safety of the State and county in 1918; served six years as a member of the commission to revise the penal code of Pennsylvania; chairman of the Republican county committee of Luzerne County 1915–1917; elected as a Republican to the Sixty-seventh Congress (March 4, 1921–March 3, 1923); unsuccessful candidate for reelection in 1922 to the Sixty-eighth Congress; resumed the practice of his profession; appointed judge of the court of common pleas of Luzerne County October 6, 1925, to fill an unexpired term caused by the death of Judge Woodward; elected in November 1927 for a ten-year term and served until 1937; died in Wilkes-Barre, Pa., December 15, 1946; interment in Mount Greenwood Cemetery, Trucksville, Pa.

COULTER, Richard, a Representative from Pennsylvania; born in Westmoreland County, Pa., in March 1788; attended Jefferson College; studied law; was admitted to the bar in 1811 and commenced the practice of his profession in Greensburg, Westmoreland County, Pa.; member of the State house of representatives 1816–1820; elected as an Independent to the Twentieth and Twenty-first Congresses and as a Democrat to the Twenty-second and Twenty-third Congresses (March 4, 1827–March 3, 1835); unsuccessful candidate for reelection in 1834 to the Twenty-fourth Congress; elected judge of the supreme court of Pennsylvania and served from 1846 until his death on April 21, 1852, in Greensburg, Pa.; interment in St. Clair Cemetery.

COURTNEY, William Wirt, a Representative from Tennessee; born in Franklin, Williamson County, Tenn., September 7, 1889; was graduated from Battle Ground Academy, Franklin, Tenn., in 1907; attended Vanderbilt University, Nashville, Tenn., and the Faculté de Droit of the Sorbonne, Paris, France; studied law; was admitted to the bar in 1911 and commenced practice in Franklin, Tenn.; city judge 1915–1917; during the First World War enlisted in the United States Army as a private in the One Hundred and Seventeenth Infantry, Thirtieth Division, in September 1917, and was honorably discharged as a first lieutenant in June 1919; resumed the practice of law in Franklin, Tenn.; adjutant general of Tennessee in 1932; member of the Tennessee National Guard in 1933 with rank of brigadier general; served as circuit judge and chancellor of the seventeenth judicial circuit of Tennessee 1933–1939; elected as a Democrat to the Seventy-sixth Congress to fill the vacancy caused by the death of Clarence W. Turner; reelected to the Seventy-seventh and to the three succeeding Congresses and served from May 11, 1939, to January 3, 1949; unsuccessful candidate for renomination in 1948; resumed the practice of law; died in Franklin, Tenn., April 6, 1961; interment in Mount Hope Cemetery.

COUSINS, Robert Gordon, a Representative from Iowa; born on a farm, "Indian Lodge," near Tipton, Cedar County, Iowa, January 31, 1859; attended the common schools, and was graduated from Cornell College, Mount Vernon, Iowa, in 1881; studied law; was admitted to the bar in 1882 and engaged in practice in Tipton, Iowa; member of the State house of representatives in 1886; elected by the State house of representatives as one of the managers to conduct the impeachment proceedings of John L. Brown before the State senate in 1886; prosecuting attorney of Cedar County 1888–1890; presidential elector on the Republican ticket of Harrison and Morton in 1888; elected as a Republican to the Fifty-third and to the seven succeeding Congresses (March 4, 1893–March 3, 1909); declined to be a candidate for renomination in 1908; resumed the practice of law at Tipton, Iowa; also engaged as a writer and as a Chautauqua lecturer; died June 20, 1933, in Iowa City, Iowa, where he had been receiving medical treatment; interment in Red Oak Cemetery, five miles northwest of Tipton, Iowa.

COUZENS, James, a Senator from Michigan; born in Chatham, Province of Ontario, Canada, August 26, 1872; attended the public and high schools of Chatham; moved to Detroit, Mich., in 1890; railroad car checker 1890–1897; clerk in the coal business 1897–1903; was associated with the Ford Motor Co. in the manufacture of automobiles from 1903 until 1919; served as president of the Bank of Detroit and as director of the Detroit Trust Co.; commissioner of street railways 1913–1915; commissioner of the metropolitan police department 1916–1918; during the First World War served as chairman for Wayne County of the United States Fuel Administration; mayor of Detroit 1919–1922; appointed November 29, 1922, as a Republican, to the United States Senate and elected on November 4, 1924, to fill the vacancy caused by the resignation of Truman H. Newberry and on the same day was elected for the term commencing March 4, 1925; reelected in 1930 and served from November 29, 1922, until his death; unsuccessful candidate for renomination in 1936; founded the Children's Fund of Michigan in 1929, with an endowment by him of $12,000,000; died in Detroit, Mich., on October 22, 1936; interment in Woodlawn Cemetery.

COVERT, James Way, a Representative from New York; born at Oyster Bay, Long Island, N. Y., September 2, 1842; attended the public schools and received an academic education in Locust Valley, N. Y.; studied law; was admitted to the bar in 1863 and commenced practice in Flushing, Long Island, N. Y.; district school commissioner 1867–1870; assistant prosecuting attorney of Queens County; surrogate of Queens County 1870–1874; unsuccessful candidate for election in 1872 to the Forty-third Congress; elected as a Democrat to the Forty-fifth and Forty-sixth Congresses (March 4, 1877–March 3, 1881); member of the State senate in 1882 and 1883; elected to the Fifty-first, Fifty-second, and Fifty-third Congresses (March 4, 1889–March 3, 1895); moved to Brooklyn, N. Y., in 1896 and resumed the practice of law; died in Brooklyn, N. Y., May 16, 1910; interment in Mount Olivet Cemetery, Maspeth, N. Y.

COVINGTON, George Washington, a Representative from Maryland; born in Berlin, Worcester County, Md., September 12, 1838; attended the common schools, Buckingham Academy, and the law school of Harvard University; was admitted to the bar in 1861 and practiced in Berlin and Snow Hill, Md.; member of the State constitutional convention in 1867; elected as a Democrat to the Forty-seventh and Forty-eighth Congresses (March 4, 1881–March 3, 1885); was not a candidate for renomination in 1884; resumed the practice of law in Snow Hill, Worcester County, Md.; died in New York City April 6, 1911; interment in All Hallows Cemetery, Snow Hill, Md.

COVINGTON, James Harry, a Representative from Maryland; born in Easton, Talbot County, Md., May 3, 1870; received an academic training in the public schools of Talbot County and the Maryland Military Academy at Oxford; entered the law department of the University of Pennsylvania at Philadelphia in 1891, attending at the same time special lectures in history, literature, and economics, and was graduated from that institution in 1894; commenced the practice of law in Easton, Md.; unsuccessful Democratic nominee for the State senate in 1901; State's attorney for Talbot County 1903–1908; elected as a Democrat to the Sixty-first, Sixty-second, and Sixty-third Congresses and served from March 4, 1909, until his resignation on September 30, 1914, to accept a judicial position; chief justice of the Supreme Court of the District of Columbia from October 1, 1914, to June 1, 1918, when he resigned to practice law in Washington, D. C.; professor of law in Georgetown University, Washington, D. C., 1914–1919; appointed by President Wilson as a member of the United States Railroad Commission in January 1918; practiced law in Washington, D. C., where he died on February 4, 1942; interment in Spring Hill Cemetery, Easton, Md.

COVINGTON, Leonard, a Representative from Maryland; born in Aquasco, Md., October 30, 1768; received a liberal schooling; entered the United States Army as a cornet of Cavalry March 14, 1792; commissioned lieutenant of Dragoons by General Washington in 1793, and joined the Army under General Wayne; distinguished himself at Fort Recovery and the Battle of Miami, and was mentioned in the official report of General Wayne; promoted to a captaincy, and resigned September 12, 1795; engaged in agricultural pursuits; member of the State house of delegates for many years; elected as a Democrat to the Ninth Congress (March 4, 1805–March 3, 1807); appointed by President Jefferson lieutenant colonel of Light Dragoons on January 9, 1809, and colonel February 15, 1809; was in command at Fort Adams on the Mississippi in 1810 and took possession of Baton Rouge and a portion of West Florida; was ordered to the northern frontier in 1813, and appointed brigadier general by President Madison August 1, 1813; mortally wounded at the Battle of Chryslers Field November 11, 1813, and died at Frenchs Mills, N. Y., on November 14, 1813; remains were removed to Sackets Harbor, Jefferson County, N. Y., August 13, 1820; place of burial now known as Mount Covington.

COVODE, John, a Representative from Pennsylvania; born near West Fairfield, Westmoreland County, Pa., March 18, 1808; attended the public schools; engaged in agricultural pursuits, manufacturing, and transportation; largely interested in the coal trade; elected as an Anti-Masonic Whig to the Thirty-fourth Congress and as a Republican to the Thirty-fifth, Thirty-sixth, and Thirty-seventh Congresses (March 4, 1855–March 3, 1863); delegate to the Union National Convention at Philadelphia in 1866; elected to the Fortieth Congress (March 4, 1867–March 3, 1869); contested with Henry D. Foster the election to the Forty-first Congress, neither being sworn pending the contest, as no credentials were issued by the Governor; on February 9, 1870, the House declared him duly elected, whereupon he qualified and served until his death; was not a candidate for reelection in 1870; died in Harrisburg, Pa., January 11, 1871; interment in Methodist Episcopal Cemetery, West Fairfield, Pa.

COWAN, Edgar, a Senator from Pennsylvania; born in Westmoreland County, Pa., September 19, 1815; was graduated from Franklin College, Ohio, in 1839; by turn became a raftsman, boat builder, schoolmaster, and a student of medicine; studied law; was admitted to the bar and commenced practice in Greensburg, Westmoreland County, Pa., in 1842; presidential elector on the Republican ticket of Lincoln and Hamlin in 1860; elected as a Republican to the United States Senate and served from March 4, 1861, to March 3, 1867; he disagreed with his party on the reconstruction policy, and was an unsuccessful candidate for reelection to the Senate; delegate to the Union National Convention at Philadelphia in 1866; appointed by President Johnson as Minister to Austria in January 1867 but was not confirmed by the Senate; resumed the practice of law; died in Greensburg, Pa., August 29, 1885; interment in St. Clair Cemetery.

COWAN, Jacob Pitzer, a Representative from Ohio; born in Florence, Washington County, Pa., March 20, 1823; attended the common schools; moved with his parents to Steubenville, Ohio, in 1835; engaged in the manufacture of woolens until 1843; studied medicine; in 1846 moved to Ashland County, Ohio, where he commenced the practice of his profession; was graduated from Starling Medical College, Columbus, Ohio, March 6, 1855; member of the State house of representatives 1855–1857; resumed the practice of medicine in 1859; elected as a Democrat to the Forty-fourth Congress (March 4, 1875–March 3, 1877); unsuccessful candidate for renomination in 1876; again engaged in the practice of medicine in Ashland, Ashland County, Ohio, where he died July 9, 1895; interment in Ashland Cemetery.

COWEN, Benjamin Sprague, a Representative from Ohio; born in Washington County, N. Y., September 27, 1793; attended the common schools; studied medicine; served in the War of 1812 as a private; in 1820 moved to Moorefield, Ohio, where he practiced medicine and studied law; was admitted to the bar in 1829 and commenced practice in St. Clairsville, Ohio; edited the Belmont Chronicle 1836–1840; delegate to the Whig National Convention at Harrisburg, Pa., in 1839; elected as an antislavery Whig to the Twenty-seventh Congress (March 4, 1841–March 3, 1843); member of the State house of representatives in 1845 and 1846; presiding judge of the court of common pleas in 1847; died in St. Clairsville, Belmont County, Ohio, September 27, 1860.

COWEN, John Kissig, a Representative from Maryland; born near Millersburg, Holmes County, Ohio, October 28, 1844; attended the public schools and the local academies at Fredericksburg and Hayesville, Ohio; was graduated from Princeton College in 1866 and from the law department of the Michigan University at Ann Arbor; was admitted to the bar of Ohio in 1868 and commenced practice in Mansfield, Richland County, Ohio; prosecuting attorney of Holmes County; moved to Baltimore, Md., in February 1872 and was appointed counsel of the Baltimore & Ohio Railroad Co.; from 1876 to 1896 was general counsel of the Baltimore & Ohio Railroad Co.; elected as a Democrat to the Fifty-fourth Congress (March 4, 1895–March 3, 1897); was not a candidate for renomination in 1896 to the Fifty-fifth Congress; president of the Baltimore & Ohio Railroad Co. from January 1896 to June 1901; died in Chicago, Ill., April 26, 1904; interment in Oak Hill Cemetery, Millersburg, Holmes County, Ohio.

COWGILL, Calvin, a Representative from Indiana; born in Clinton County, Ohio, January 7, 1819; attended the common schools; moved with his parents to Indiana in 1836; studied law in Winchester, Randolph County; moved to Wabash County, Ind., in 1846; was admitted to the bar and commenced practice in Wabash; member of the State house of representatives in 1851 and again during the special session of 1865; treasurer of Wabash County 1855–1859; during the Civil War was provost marshal of the eleventh district of Indiana 1862–1865; elected as a Republican to the Forty-sixth Congress (March 4, 1879–March 3, 1881); was not a candidate for renomination in 1880 to the Forty-seventh Congress; resumed the practice of his profession in Wabash, Wabash County, Ind., where he died February 10, 1903; interment in Falls Cemetery.

COWHERD, William Strother, a Representative from Missouri; born near Lees Summit, Jackson County, Mo., September 1, 1860; attended the public schools in the town of Lees Summit, and was graduated from the literary department of the University of Missouri at Columbia in 1881 and from the law department of the same institution in 1882; was admitted to the bar and commenced practice in Kansas City, Mo.; appointed assistant prosecuting attorney of Jackson County in 1885, and served four years; appointed first assistant city counselor of Kansas City in 1890; mayor of Kansas City in 1892; elected as a Democrat to the Fifty-fifth and to the three succeeding Congresses (March 4, 1897–March 3, 1905); unsuccessful candidate for reelection in 1904 to the Fifty-ninth Congress; resumed the practice of law in Kansas City, Mo.; unsuccessful Democratic candidate for Governor in 1908; moved to Pasadena, Los Angles County, Calif., and continued the practice of his profession; died in Pasadena June 20, 1915; interment in Lees Summit Cemetery, near Lees Summit, Mo.

COWLES, Charles Holden (nephew of William Henry Harrison Cowles), a Representative from North Carolina; born in Charlotte, N. C., July 16, 1875; moved with his parents to Wilkesboro, Wilkes County, December 26, 1885; attended Charlotte graded school, private schools, Wilkesboro Academy, and completed a commercial college course; member of the board of aldermen of Wilkesboro in 1897 and again in 1914; deputy clerk of the United States Court at Statesville and Charlotte 1899–1901; private secretary to Representative Edmond S. Blackburn 1901–1903; member of the State house of representatives 1904–1908, 1920–1924, 1928–1930, and 1932–1934; delegate to the Republican National Conventions in 1904, 1908, 1912, and 1916; elected as a Republican to the Sixty-first Congress (March 4, 1909–March 3, 1911); unsuccessful candidate for reelection in 1910 to the Sixty-second Congress; nominated in 1916 by the Roosevelt or Progressive Republicans for the United States Senate but declined the nomination; established and published the Wilkes Patriot, Wilkesboro, N. C., 1906–1919; during the First World War served as a member of the Wilkes County Council of Defense; was a member of the State senate 1938–1940; during World War II served as chairman of War Price and Rationing Board No. 1 for Wilkes County from January 7, 1942, to September 15, 1945, when he

resigned; appointed deputy clerk of the United States Court in Wilkesboro on April 1, 1941, and served until his retirement in October 1956; died in Mocksville, N. C., October 2, 1957; interment in Episcopal Church Cemetery, Wilkesboro, N. C.

COWLES, George Washington, a Representative from New York; born in Otisco, Onondaga County, N. Y., December 6, 1823; attended the common schools, and was graduated from Hamilton College, Clinton, N. Y., in 1845; taught school until 1853; studied law; was admitted to the bar in 1854 and commenced practice in Clyde, Wayne County, N. Y.; judge of the Wayne County Court from January 1, 1864, to October 30, 1869; elected as a Republican to the Forty-first Congress (March 4, 1869–March 3, 1871); was not a candidate for renomination in 1870; resumed the practice of law; again judge of Wayne County Court from January 1, 1874, to January 1, 1880, and from January 1, 1886, until his death in Clyde, N. Y., January 20, 1901; interment in Maple Grove Cemetery.

COWLES, Henry Booth, a Representative from New York; born in Hartford, Conn., March 18, 1798; moved with his father to Dutchess County, N. Y., in 1809; was graduated from Union College, Schenectady, N. Y., in 1816; studied law; was admitted to the bar and commenced practice in Putnam County; member of the State assembly 1826–1828; elected to the Twenty-first Congress (March 4, 1829–March 3, 1831); moved to New York City in 1834 and practiced law until his death there on May 17, 1873; interment in Rhinebeck Cemetery, Rhinebeck, Dutchess County, N. Y.

COWLES, William Henry Harrison (uncle of Charles Holden Cowles), a Representative from North Carolina; born in Hamptonville, Yadkin County, N. C., April 22, 1840; attended the common schools and academies of his native county; during the Civil War entered the Confederate service as a private in Company A, First North Carolina Cavalry, and served from the spring of 1861 to the close of the war with the Army of Northern Virginia, holding successively the ranks of captain, major, and lieutenant colonel of his regiment; twice wounded severely; entered upon the study of law in Richmond Hill, Yadkin County, in 1866; obtained a county court license in January 1867 and a superior court license in January 1868; moved to Wilkesboro, Wilkes County, where he commenced the practice of law; reading clerk of the State senate of North Carolina 1872–1874; elected solicitor of the tenth judicial district in 1874 and served for four years; member of the Democratic State executive committee for eight years; elected as a Democrat to the Forty-ninth and to the three succeeding Congresses (March 4, 1885–March 3, 1893); was not a candidate for renomination in 1892; engaged in agricultural pursuits and also interested in other business activities; died in Wilkesboro, N. C., December 30, 1901; interment in Presbyterian Cemetery.

COX, Edward Eugene, a Representative from Georgia; born near Camilla, Mitchell County, Ga., April 3, 1880; attended the grade schools, Camilla High School, the academic department of Mercer University, Macon, Ga., for nearly four years, and was graduated from the law department of that university in 1902; was admitted to the bar the same year and commenced practice at Camilla, Ga.; mayor of Camilla 1904–1906; delegate to the Democratic National Convention at Denver in 1908; appointed and subsequently elected judge of the superior court of the Albany circuit and served from 1912 until he resigned in 1916, having become a candidate for Congress; unsuccessful candidate for election in 1916 to the Sixty-fifth Congress; elected as a Democrat to the Sixty-ninth and to the thirteen succeeding Congresses and served from March 4, 1925, until his death; had been reelected to the Eighty-third Congress; died in the naval hospital at Bethesda, Md., December 24, 1952; interment in Oakview Cemetery, Camilla, Ga.

COX, Isaac Newton, a Representative from New York; born in Fallsburg, Sullivan County, N. Y., August 1, 1846; moved to Ellenville in 1864 and engaged in the lumber business; supervisor of the town of Wawarsing in 1875 and 1883–1886 and served as chairman of the board during the last year; served four years on the Democratic State committee; delegate to Democratic State and local conventions; appointed by President Cleveland chairman of the commission to examine and report upon the condition of the Northern Pacific Railroad in 1886; elected as a Democrat to the Fifty-second Congress (March 4, 1891–March 3, 1893); unsuccessful candidate for reelection in 1892 to the Fifty-third Congress; appointed a member of the State commission on fisheries, and served from 1894 to 1899; engaged in mercantile pursuits, lumbering, and banking in Ellenville, Ulster County, N. Y., where he died September 28, 1916; interment in Fantinekill Cemetery.

COX, Jacob Dolson, a Representative from Ohio; born in Montreal, Canada, October 27, 1828; moved with his parents to New York City in 1829; attended private schools; moved to Lorain, Ohio, in 1846; was graduated from Oberlin (Ohio) College in 1851; studied law; was admitted to the bar in 1853 and commenced practice in Warren, Trumbull County, Ohio; member of the State senate in 1860 and 1861; during the Civil War entered the Union Army as brigadier general of Ohio Volunteers April 23, 1861; commissioned major general of volunteers October 6, 1862; resigned January 1, 1866, having been elected Governor of Ohio in October 1865; served as Governor 1866–1868; moved to Cincinnati, Ohio, and resumed the practice of law; Secretary of the Interior in the first Cabinet of President Grant and served from March 5, 1869, to November 1, 1870, when he resigned; resumed the practice of law in Cincinnati; president of the Wabash Railroad 1873–1878; moved to Toledo, Ohio, in 1874; elected as a Republican to the Forty-fifth Congress (March 4, 1877–March 3, 1879); declined to be a candidate for renomination in 1878; returned to Cincinnati in 1878; dean of the Cincinnati Law School 1881–1897; president of the University of Cincinnati 1885–1889; was an author and writer on Civil War subjects; died in Magnolia, near Gloucester, Mass., August 4, 1900; interment in Spring Grove Cemetery, Cincinnati, Ohio.

COX, James, a Representative from New Jersey; born in Monmouth, N. J., June 14, 1753; attended the public schools; commanded a company of militia at the Battles of Germantown and of Monmouth and attained the rank of brigadier general; member of the State general assembly 1801–1807, and served as speaker 1804–1807; elected as a Democrat to the Eleventh Congress and served from March 4, 1809, until his death in Monmouth, N. J., September 12, 1810; interment in the Yellow Meeting House Cemetery, Upper Freehold Township, N. J.

COX, James Middleton, a Representative from Ohio; born on a farm near Jacksonburg, Butler County, Ohio, March 31, 1870; attended Butler County schools and Amanda (Ohio) High School; after two years of high school passed teacher's examination and at the age of 16 years began teaching school; commenced newspaper career as reporter on Middletown (Ohio) Signal and in 1892 went to work on the Cincinnati Enquirer; secretary to Congressman Paul Sorg 1894–1897; became owner and publisher of the Dayton Daily News in 1898, of the Springfield Daily News in 1903, of the Miami (Florida) News in 1923, of the Atlanta (Georgia) Journal in 1939, of the Dayton Journal

and Herald in 1949, and of the Atlanta (Georgia) Constitution in 1950; elected as a Democrat to the Sixty-first and Sixty-second Congresses and served from March 4, 1909, until January 12, 1913, when he resigned, having been elected Governor; Governor of Ohio 1913–1915; unsuccessful candidate for election as Governor in 1914; again Governor of Ohio 1917–1921; unsuccessful Democratic candidate for election as President of the United States in 1920; vice chairman of the United States delegation to the World Economic Conference at London in 1933 and president of its monetary commission; declined appointment to the United States Senate by Gov. Frank Lausche in 1946; retired from political life but continued his activities as newspaper publisher and owner of several radio and television stations; died in Dayton, Ohio, July 15, 1957; interment in Woodland Cemetery.

COX, Leander Martin, a Representative from Kentucky; born in Cumberland County, Va., May 7, 1812; completed academic studies; studied law; was admitted to the bar and practiced; moved to Flemingsburg, Fleming County, Ky.; member of the State house of representatives 1843–1845; captain in the Third Kentucky Volunteers in the Mexican War in 1847; presidential elector on the Whig ticket of Scott and Graham in 1852; elected as a Whig to the Thirty-third Congress and by the American Party to the Thirty-fourth Congress (March 4, 1853–March 3, 1857); unsuccessful candidate for reelection in 1856 to the Thirty-fifth Congress; resumed the practice of law; died in Flemingsburg, Ky., March 19, 1865; interment in Fleming County Cemetery.

COX, Nicholas Nichols, a Representative from Tennessee; born in Bedford County, Tenn., January 6, 1837; went to Seguin, Tex., in early childhood; attended the common schools; served on the Mexican frontier; was graduated from Lebanon (Tenn.) Law School in 1858; was admitted to the bar the same year and commenced practice at Linden, Tenn.; was a colonel in the Tenth Tennessee Cavalry of the Confederate Army during the Civil War, serving principally with General Forrest; settled in Franklin, Williamson County, Tenn., in 1866; engaged in agricultural pursuits; presidential elector on the Democratic tickets of Breckinridge and Lane in 1860 and of Greeley and Brown in 1872; elected as a Democrat to the Fifty-second and to the four succeeding Congresses (March 4, 1891–March 3, 1901); declined to be a candidate for renomination in 1900; resumed the practice of law and engaged in banking in Franklin, Tenn., where he died May 2, 1912; interment in Mount Hope Cemetery.

COX, Samuel Sullivan, a Representative from Ohio and from New York; born in Zanesville, Muskingum County, Ohio, September 30, 1824; attended the Ohio University at Athens, and was graduated from Brown University, Providence, R. I., in 1846; studied law; was admitted to the bar and commenced practice in Zanesville in 1849; owner and editor of the Columbus (Ohio) Statesman in 1853 and 1854; appointed secretary of the legation at Lima, Peru, on February 19, 1855, and served until August 11, 1855, when he resigned; delegate to the Democratic National Conventions in 1864 and 1868; elected as a Democrat from Ohio to the Thirty-fifth and to the three succeeding Congresses (March 4, 1857–March 3, 1865); unsuccessful candidate for reelection in 1864 to the Thirty-ninth Congress; moved to New York City on March 4, 1865, and resumed the practice of law; elected from New York to the Forty-first and Forty-second Congresses (March 4, 1869–March 3, 1873); unsuccessful candidate of the Democrats and Liberal Republicans for reelection in 1872 as Representative at large to the Forty-third Congress; subsequently elected to the Forty-third Congress to fill the vacancy caused by the death of James Brooks; reelected to the Forty-fourth and to the five succeeding Congresses and served from November 4, 1873, to May 20, 1885, when he resigned, having accepted a diplomatic position; elected Speaker pro tempore of the House on February 17, May 12, and June 19, 1876, and appointed to that office on May 1 and June 7, 1876; appointed Envoy Extraordinary and Minister Plenipotentiary to Turkey by President Cleveland and served from May 21, 1885, to October 22, 1886, when he resigned; was again elected to the Forty-ninth Congress to fill the vacancy caused by the resignation of Joseph Pulitzer; reelected to the Fiftieth and Fifty-first Congresses and served from November 2, 1886, until his death in New York City September 10, 1889; interment in Greenwood Cemetery, Brooklyn, N. Y.

COX, William Elijah, a Representative from Indiana; born on a farm near Birdseye, Dubois County, Ind., September 6, 1861; attended the common and high schools of Huntingburg and Jasper, Ind.; was graduated from Lebanon University, Tennessee, in 1888 and from the law department of the University of Michigan at Ann Arbor in 1889; was admitted to the bar July 10, 1889, and commenced practice at Rockport, Spencer County, Ind., moving to Jasper, Ind., later in the same year; prosecuting attorney for the eleventh judicial district of Indiana 1892–1898; elected as a Democrat to the Sixtieth and to the five succeeding Congresses (March 4, 1907–March 3, 1919); unsuccessful candidate for reelection in 1918 to the Sixty-sixth Congress; resumed the practice of law and also was engaged with a desk-manufacturing company, serving as president at the time of his death; died in Jasper, Ind., March 11, 1942; interment in Fairmount Cemetery, Huntingburg, Ind.

COX, William Ruffin, a Representative from North Carolina; born in Scotland Neck, Halifax County, N. C., March 11, 1831; attended Vine Hill Academy in his native town; moved with his mother to Nashville, Tenn.; was graduated from Franklin College in 1851 and from the Lebanon College Law School in 1853; was admitted to the bar in 1853 and practiced in Nashville, Tenn., 1853–1857; returned to North Carolina in 1857 and engaged in agricultural pursuits in Edgecombe County; moved to Raleigh, N. C., in 1859; early in the Civil War entered the Confederate Army as major of the Second North Carolina State Troops; became brigadier general and commanded his brigade in the last charge at Appomattox; resumed the practice of law at Raleigh, N. C., in 1865; solicitor of the sixth district 1866–1870; delegate to the Democratic National Convention at New York City in 1868; judge of the superior court for the sixth district in 1877 and 1878, when he resigned; chairman of the Democratic State committee 1875–1877; elected as a Democrat to the Forty-seventh, Forty-eighth, and Forty-ninth Congresses (March 4, 1881–March 3, 1887); unsuccessful candidate for renomination; elected Secretary of the United States Senate April 6, 1893, qualified August 7, 1893, and served until January 31, 1900; resumed agricultural pursuits, with residence at Penelo, Edgecombe County, N. C.; president of the State agricultural society in 1900 and 1901; member of the board of trustees of the University of the South at Sewanee, Tenn.; died in Richmond, Va., on December 26, 1919; interment in Oakwood Cemetery, Raleigh, N. C.

COXE, Tench, a Delegate from Pennsylvania; born in Philadelphia, Pa., May 22, 1755; received a liberal schooling; engaged in mercantile pursuits; resigned from the Pennsylvania Militia in 1776, turned Loyalist, and joined the British Army under Howe in 1777; was arrested, paroled, joined the patriot cause, and began a long political career; commissioner to the Federal Convention at Annapolis in 1786; Member of the Continental Congress in 1787 and 1788; became a Federalist and was appointed Assistant Secretary of the Treasury on September 11, 1789, and served until the office was abolished on May 8, 1792; was

appointed revenue commissioner June 30, 1792, and served until removed by President Adams; joined the Democratic Party and was appointed by President Jefferson purveyor of public supplies and served from 1803 to 1812; was a writer on political and economic subjects; was called the father of the cotton industry in America; died in Philadelphia, Pa., July 17, 1824; interment in Christ Church Burying Ground.

COXE, William, Jr., a Representative from New Jersey; born in Burlington, N. J., May 3, 1762; served as a member of the State general assembly 1796–1804, 1806–1809, and again in 1816 and 1817; served as speaker 1798–1800 and again in 1802; elected as a Federalist to the Thirteenth Congress (March 4, 1813–March 3, 1815); author; died in Burlington, Burlington County, N. J., on February 25, 1831; interment in St. Mary's Churchyard.

COYLE, William Radford, a Representative from Pennsylvania; born in Washington, D. C., July 10, 1878; attended the public schools, and Columbian College (now George Washington University), Washington, D. C., in 1898 and 1899; field assistant in the United States Geological Survey 1896–1899; attended the Naval War College, Newport, R. I., in 1900; served in the United States Marine Corps as second lieutenant, first lieutenant, and captain 1900–1906; attended the law department of the University of Pennsylvania at Philadelphia in 1906 and 1907; moved to Germantown, Pa., in 1906 and to Bethlehem, Pa., in 1908; school director of Bethlehem, Pa., 1912–1918; captain of the Fourth Regiment, National Guard of Pennsylvania, in 1913; during the First World War was commissioned a captain in the United States Marine Corps in 1918, and later the same year, a major; president of the American Wholesale Coal Association in 1921 and 1922; trustee to settle the affairs of the Tidewater Coal Exchange 1922–1925; elected as a Republican to the Sixty-ninth Congress (March 4, 1925–March 3, 1927); unsuccessful candidate for reelection in 1926 to the Seventieth Congress; elected to the Seventy-first and Seventy-second Congresses (March 4, 1929–March 3, 1933); unsuccessful candidate for reelection in 1932 to the Seventy-third Congress, for election in 1936 to the Seventy-fifth Congress, and for election in 1942 to the Seventy-eighth Congress; delegate to the Republican National Conventions in 1936 and 1944 and alternate delegate in 1960; chairman of civilian defense in Bethlehem, Pa., 1941–1945; member of board of the Bethlehem Authority and Redevelopment Authority, serving as chairman until 1959; is a resident of Bethlehem, Pa.

CRABB, George Whitfield, a Representative from Alabama; born in Botetourt County, Va., February 22, 1804; attended the public schools; moved to Tuscaloosa, Ala.; elected assistant secretary of the State senate and comptroller of public accounts in 1829; served in the Florida Indian War of 1836 and was lieutenant colonel of the Alabama Volunteers; member of the State house of representatives in 1836 and 1837; served in the State senate in 1837 and 1838; major general of militia; elected as a Whig to the Twenty-fifth Congress to fill the vacancy caused by the death of Joab Lawler; reelected to the Twenty-sixth Congress and served from September 4, 1838, to March 3, 1841; unsuccessful candidate for reelection to the Twenty-seventh Congress; appointed judge of the county court of Mobile in 1846; died in Philadelphia, Pa., August 15, 1846; interment in Greenwood Cemetery, Tuscaloosa, Ala.

CRABB, Jeremiah, a Representative from Maryland; born in Montgomery County, Md., in 1760; served in the Revolutionary War as second lieutenant in the First Maryland Regiment; promoted to the rank of first lieutenant on December 15,

1777, and served as such until April 1, 1778, when he resigned because of ill health occasioned by the winter hardships endured at Valley Forge; was an extensive landowner in Montgomery County; served as general with Gen. Harry Lee in Pennsylvania during the Whisky Rebellion; elected as a Democrat to the Fourth Congress and served from March 4, 1795, until his resignation in 1796; returned to his home near Rockville, Montgomery County, Md., and died there in 1800; interment in the family burying ground near Derwood, Montgomery County, Md.

CRADDOCK, John Durrett, a Representative from Kentucky; born in Munfordville, Hart County, Ky., October 26, 1881; attended the public and high schools of Hart County; during the Philippine Insurrection and also during the Boxer Uprising in China served as a corporal and sergeant in Troop F, Third United States Cavalry; employed as a railroad engineer with the Isthmian Canal Commission, Panama Canal Zone, 1904–1910; returned to Munfordville, Ky., in 1910 and engaged in banking and agricultural pursuits; member of the board of trustees of Munfordville 1910–1925; assisted in organizing the Burley Tobacco Growers Association in 1922 and served as director from 1922 to 1941; member of the Kentucky Mammoth Cave National Park Commission 1922–1928; elected as a Republican to the Seventy-first Congress (March 4, 1929–March 3, 1931); unsuccessful candidate for reelection in 1930 to the Seventy-second Congress; field man, Federal Farm Board, Washington, D. C., in 1931 and 1932; agent of the Kentucky Blue Grass Cooperative Association, Winchester, Ky., in 1933 and 1934; treasurer of Hart County at Munfordville, Ky., in 1934 and 1935; resumed his former pursuits; served as a member of the State Agricultural Adjustment Administration Committee from 1939 until his death; died in a hospital in Louisville, Ky., May 20, 1942; interment in New Munfordville Cemetery, Munfordville, Ky.

CRADLEBAUGH, John, a Delegate from the Territory of Nevada; born in Circleville, Pickaway County, Ohio, February 22, 1819; attended the common schools, Kenyon College, Gambier, Ohio, and Oxford (Ohio) University; studied law; was admitted to the bar in 1840; appointed United States associate justice for the district of Utah on June 4, 1858; moved to Carson City, Nev.; upon the formation of the Territory of Nevada was elected a Delegate to the Thirty-seventh Congress and served from December 2, 1861, to March 3, 1863; served in the Union Army during the Civil War as colonel of the One Hundred and Fourteenth Regiment, Ohio Volunteer Infantry, and served from April 27, 1862, until honorably discharged October 20, 1863, on tender of resignation; wounded at Vicksburg; returned to Nevada and settled in Eureka; engaged in the mining business until his death in Eureka, Nev., February 22, 1872; interment in Forest Cemetery, Circleville, Ohio.

CRAFTS, Samuel Chandler, a Representative and a Senator from Vermont; born in Woodstock, Conn., October 6, 1768; was graduated from Harvard College in 1790; moved in 1791 to Vermont with his father, who founded the town of Craftsbury; town clerk 1799–1829; was the youngest delegate in the Vermont constitutional convention of 1793; member of the State house of representatives in 1796, 1800, 1801, 1802, 1803, and 1805, and clerk of the house in 1798 and 1799; register of probate 1796–1815; assistant judge of the Orleans County Court 1800–1810 and 1825–1828; made an extensive botanical reconnaissance of the Mississippi Valley in 1802; member of the State council 1809–1813; chief judge of the Orleans County Court 1810–1816; elected to the Fifteenth and to the three succeeding Congresses (March 4, 1817–March 3, 1825); again served as

State councilor in 1825 and 1826; Governor of Vermont 1828–1831; member of the Vermont constitutional convention of 1829 and served as president; clerk of Orleans County 1836–1839; presidential elector on the Whig ticket of Harrison and Tyler in 1840; appointed and subsequently elected to the United States Senate to fill the vacancy caused by the resignation of Samuel Prentiss and served from April 23, 1842, until March 3, 1843; retired to his farm in Craftsbury, Orleans County, Vt., where he died November 19, 1853; interment in North Craftsbury Cemetery, North Craftsbury, Vt.

CRAGIN, Aaron Harrison, a Representative and a Senator from New Hampshire; born in Weston, Windsor County, Vt., February 3, 1821; completed preparatory studies; studied law; was admitted to the bar in Albany, N. Y., in 1847 and commenced practice in Lebanon, N. H.; member of the New Hampshire House of Representatives 1852–1855; elected by the American Party to the Thirty-fourth Congress and as a Republican to the Thirty-fifth Congress (March 4, 1855–March 3, 1859); resumed the practice of law; again a member of the State house of representatives in 1859; delegate to the Republican National Convention at Chicago in 1860; elected by the American Party to the United States Senate; reelected, and served from March 4, 1865, to March 3, 1877; appointed by President Hayes one of the commissioners for the purchase of the Hot Springs Reservation in Arkansas and served as chairman 1877–1879; died in Washington, D. C., May 10, 1898; interment in School Street Cemetery, Lebanon, N. H.

CRAGO, Thomas Spencer, a Representative from Pennsylvania; born in Carmichaels, Greene County, Pa., August 8, 1866; attended Greene Academy and Waynesburg College; was graduated from Princeton College in 1893; studied law; was admitted to the bar of Greene County in 1894 and commenced practice in Waynesburg, Pa.; served as captain of Company K in the Tenth Pennsylvania Volunteer Infantry during the Spanish-American War and the Philippine Insurrection; after the war helped to reorganize the Pennsylvania National Guard and was elected major and later lieutenant colonel of the Tenth Infantry; resigned his commission while in Congress but was later retired with the rank of colonel; presidential elector on the Republican ticket of McKinley and Roosevelt in 1900; delegate to the Republican National Convention at Chicago in 1904; elected as a Republican to the Sixty-second Congress (March 4, 1911–March 3, 1913); unsuccessful candidate for reelection in 1912 to the Sixty-third Congress; commander in chief of the Veterans of Foreign Wars in 1914 and 1915; elected to the Sixty-fourth, Sixty-fifth, and Sixty-sixth Congresses (March 4, 1915–March 3, 1921); was not a candidate for renomination in 1920, but was subsequently elected to the Sixty-seventh Congress to fill the vacancy caused by the death of Mahlon M. Garland and served from September 20, 1921, to March 3, 1923; was not a candidate for renomination in 1922; appointed special assistant to the Attorney General of the United States on March 7, 1923, and assigned to the War Frauds Division, resigned August 15, 1924; member of the board of trustees of Waynesburg College and Waynesburg Hospital; vice president of the Union Deposit & Trust Co. of Waynesburg; died in Waynesburg, Pa., September 12, 1925; interment in Green Mount Cemetery.

CRAIG, Alexander Kerr, a Representative from Pennsylvania; born near Claysville, Buffalo Township, Washington County, Pa., February 21, 1828; attended the common schools and was educated by a private tutor; became a teacher at the age of sixteen; began the study of law, but through the force of adverse circumstances he abandoned his chosen profession and devoted himself to agricultural pursuits; taught school in winter months and subsequently became principal of the Claysville public schools; during the Civil War enlisted in February 1865 in the Eighty-seventh Regiment, Pennsylvania Volunteer Infantry, and was present at the surrender of General Lee at Appomattox; resumed agricultural pursuits near Claysville; school director and justice of the peace; successfully contested as a Democrat the election of Andrew Stewart to the Fifty-second Congress and served from February 26, 1892, until his death in Claysville, Pa., July 29, 1892; interment in Claysville Cemetery.

CRAIG, George Henry, a Representative from Alabama; born in Cahaba, Dallas County, Ala., December 25, 1845; attended the Cahaba Academy; during the Civil War entered the Confederate Army as a private in Colonel Byrd's regiment, Alabama Volunteers, at Mobile, in 1862; at the expiration of his term of enlistment attended the University of Alabama at Tuscaloosa as a cadet in 1863; promoted to first lieutenant of Infantry, and in 1863 again entered the Confederate service and remained until the end of the war; resumed his studies at the University of Alabama in 1865; studied law; was admitted to the bar in December 1867 and commenced practice in Selma, Ala.; elected solicitor of Dallas County in 1868; appointed sheriff of Dallas County in March 1869; elected as judge of the criminal court of Dallas County in March 1870; appointed by the Governor in July 1874 judge of the first judicial circuit to fill an unexpired term and was elected to this position on November 4, 1874, and served until 1880; resumed the practice of law in Selma, Ala.; successfully contested as a Republican the election of Charles M. Shelley to the Forty-eighth Congress and served from January 9, 1885, to March 3, 1885; unsuccessful candidate for reelection in 1884 to the Forty-ninth Congress; appointed United States attorney for the middle and northern districts of Alabama by President Arthur; was appointed by President Cleveland a member of the Board of Visitors to the United States Military Academy at West Point in 1894; resumed the practice of law in Selma, Ala., and died there January 26, 1923; interment in Live Oak Cemetery.

CRAIG, Hector, a Representative from New York; born in Paisley, Scotland, in 1775; immigrated to the United States and settled in Orange County, N. Y., in 1790; founded the town of Craigsville, where he built a paper mill, grist mill, and saw mill; elected as a Jackson Democrat to the Eighteenth Congress (March 4, 1823–March 3, 1825); elected to the Twenty-first Congress and served from March 4, 1829, to July 12, 1830, when he resigned; appointed surveyor of the port of New York by President Jackson in 1830; United States Commissioner of Insolvency in 1832; surveyor of customs in New York 1833–1839; died in Craigsville, N. Y., January 31, 1842; interment in a private cemetery on the Caldwell estate in Blooming Grove, N. Y.

CRAIG, James, a Representative from Missouri; born in Washington County, Pa., February 28, 1818; attended the public schools; moved to Mansfield, Ohio, in 1821; studied law; and was admitted to the bar in New Philadelphia, Ohio, in 1839; moved to St. Joseph, Mo., in 1844, where he commenced the practice of law; captain of a volunteer company in the Mexican War and served until 1848; State's attorney for the twelfth judicial circuit 1852–1856; member of the State house of representatives in 1856 and 1857; elected as a Democrat to the Thirty-fifth and Thirty-sixth Congresses (March 4, 1857–March 3, 1861); unsuccessful candidate for renomination in 1860; resumed the practice of law; during the Civil War was commissioned brigadier general of Volunteers by President Lincoln March 21, 1862; was the first president of the Hannibal & St. Joseph Railroad and the first comptroller of the city of St. Joseph; negotiated the Platt purchase,

which comprised all of northwest Missouri; died in St. Joseph Mo., October 22, 1888; interment in Mount Mora Cemetery.

CRAIG, Robert, a Representative from Virginia; born near Christiansburg, Montgomery County, Va., in 1792; attended the rural schools, Washington College (now Washington and Lee University), Lexington, Va., and was graduated from Lewisburg Academy in Greenbrier County; engaged in planting; served in the State house of delegates in 1817, 1818, and again in 1825–1829; member of the Virginia Board of Public Works 1820–1823; elected as a Democrat to the Twenty-first and Twenty-second Congresses (March 4, 1829–March 3, 1833); unsuccessful candidate for reelection in 1832 to the Twenty-third Congress; resumed agricultural pursuits; elected to the Twenty-fourth, Twenty-fifth, and Twenty-sixth Congresses (March 4, 1835–March 3, 1841); was not a candidate for renomination in 1840; moved to Roanoke County, Va., in 1842 and engaged in agricultural pursuits; again a member of the State house of delegates 1850–1852; died on his estate, "Green Hill," near Salem, Roanoke County, Va., November 25, 1852; interment in the family burying ground at "Green Hill."

CRAIG, Samuel Alfred, a Representative from Pennsylvania; born in Brookville, Jefferson County, Pa., November 19, 1839; attended the common schools of his native town and Washington and Jefferson College, Canonsburg, Pa.; learned the printer's trade and taught school; during the Civil War enlisted in the Union Army as a private April 19, 1861; promoted successively to second lieutenant, first lieutenant, and captain of Company B, One Hundred and Fifth Regiment, Pennsylvania Volunteer Infantry; was severely wounded three times; commissioned captain in the Veteran Reserve Corps, United States Army, and served continuously four years and three months; studied law; was admitted to the bar in 1876 and commenced practice in Brookville, Pa.; elected district attorney of Jefferson County in 1878; elected as a Republican to the Fifty-first Congress (March 4, 1889–March 3, 1891); unsuccessful candidate for renomination in 1890; resumed the practice of law in Brookville, Pa., where he died March 17, 1920; interment in Brookville Cemetery.

CRAIG, William Benjamin, a Representative from Alabama; born in Selma, Dallas County, Ala., November 2, 1877; attended the public and high schools of Selma and was graduated from the law department of Cumberland University, Lebanon, Tenn.; was admitted to the bar in 1898 and commenced practice in Selma, Ala.; served an apprenticeship as a machinist in the shops of the Southern Railway at Selma from 1893 to 1897; served in the Alabama National Guard as a private, noncommissioned officer, and captain; member of the State senate 1903–1907; elected as a Democrat to the Sixtieth and Sixty-first Congresses (March 4, 1907–March 3, 1911); declined to be a candidate for renomination in 1910; resumed the practice of law in Selma, Ala.; president of the Dallas County Bar Association in 1923; died in Selma, Ala., November 27, 1925; interment in Live Oak Cemetery.

CRAIGE, Francis Burton, a Representative from North Carolina; born near Salisbury, Rowan County, N. C., March 13, 1811; attended a private school in Salisbury, and was graduated from the University of North Carolina at Chapel Hill in 1829; editor and proprietor of the Western Carolinian 1829–1831; studied law; was admitted to the bar in 1832 and commenced practice in Salisbury; one of the last borough representatives in the State house of representatives 1832–1834; elected as a Democrat to the Thirty-third and to the three succeeding Congresses (March 4, 1853–March 3, 1861); delegate to the State secession convention in 1861 and introduced the ordinance of secession in the form in which it was adopted;

delegate to the Provisional Congress of the Confederate States which met in Richmond, Va., in July 1861; died in Concord, Cabarrus County, N. C., while attending the courts of that county, December 30, 1875; interment in Old English Cemetery, Salisbury, N. C.

CRAIK, William, a Representative from Maryland; born near Port Tobacco, Md., October 31, 1761; attended Delameve School in Frederick County; studied law; was admitted to the bar and commenced practice in Port Tobacco and Leonardtown; moved to Baltimore; was appointed chief justice of the fifth judicial district of Maryland January 13, 1793, and served until his resignation in 1796; elected to the Fourth Congress to fill the vacancy caused by the resignation of Jeremiah Crabb; reelected to the Fifth and Sixth Congresses and served from December 5, 1796, to March 3, 1801; again appointed chief justice of the fifth judicial district of Maryland and served from October 20, 1801, to January 28, 1802; resided in Frederick, Md.; died prior to 1814.

CRAIL, Joe, a Representative from California; born in Fairfield, Jefferson County, Iowa, December 25, 1877; attended the public schools and was graduated from Drake University, Des Moines, Iowa, in 1898; during the Spanish-American War enlisted as a private in the Twelfth Company, United States Volunteer Signal Corps; promoted to corporal and served in the American Army of Occupation in Cuba until its withdrawal; studied law at Iowa College of Law, Des Moines, Iowa; was admitted to the bar in 1903 and commenced practice in Fairfield, Iowa; moved to California in 1913, settled in Los Angeles, and practiced law until elected to Congress; served as chairman of the Republican State central committee for southern California 1918–1920; elected as a Republican to the Seventieth, Seventy-first, and Seventy-second Congresses (March 4, 1927–March 3, 1933); was not a candidate for renomination in 1932, but was an unsuccessful candidate for nomination as United States Senator; resumed the practice of law; also engaged in banking; died in Los Angeles, Calif., March 2, 1938; interment in Inglewood Park Mausoleum, Inglewood, Calif.

CRAIN, William Henry, a Representative from Texas; born in Galveston, Tex., November 25, 1848; attended the Christian Brothers' School, New York City, until the age of fourteen, and was graduated from St. Francis Xavier's College, New York City, in 1867; returned to Texas and lived on a ranch for two years; studied law in Indianola, Tex., while teaching school; was admitted to the bar in 1871 and commenced practice in Indianola, Tex.; member of the State senate 1876–1878; district attorney of the twenty-third judicial district of Texas 1872–1876; elected as a Democrat to the Forty-ninth and to the five succeeding Congresses and served from March 4, 1885, until his death in Washington, D. C., February 10, 1896; interment in Hillside Cemetery, Cuero, Tex.

CRAMER, John, a Representative from New York; born in Waterford, N. Y., May 17, 1779; attended the rural schools and was graduated from Union College, Schenectady, N. Y., in 1801; studied law; was admitted to the bar and commenced practice in Waterford, N. Y.; presidential elector on the Democratic ticket of Jefferson and Clinton in 1804; appointed a master in chancery in 1805; member of the State assembly in 1806 and 1811; served in the State senate 1823–1825; delegate to the State constitutional convention in 1821; elected as a Democrat to the Twenty-third and Twenty-fourth Congresses (March 4, 1833–March 3, 1837); again a member of the State assembly in 1842; died in Waterford, Saratoga County, N. Y., June 1, 1870; interment in Waterford Rural Cemetery.

CRAMER, William Cato, a Representative from Florida; born in Denver, Colo., August 4, 1922; moved with his parents to St. Petersburg, Fla., in 1925; attended the public schools and St. Petersburg Junior College; enlisted in the Naval Reserve in 1943 and served as a gunnery officer until discharged as a lieutenant in 1946; was cited for his activities during the invasion of southern France; was graduated from the University of North Carolina at Chapel Hill in 1946 and from Harvard Law School, Cambridge, Mass., in 1948; was admitted to the Florida bar in 1948 and commenced the practice of law in St. Petersburg, Fla.; served in the State house of representatives 1950–1952 and was minority leader in 1951; unsuccessful candidate for election in 1952 to the Eighty-third Congress; alternate delegate to the Republican National Convention in 1952 and vice chairman of the Florida delegation to the Republican National Convention in 1956; county attorney for Pinellas County in 1953 and 1954; elected as a Republican to the Eighty-fourth, Eighty-fifth, and Eighty-sixth Congresses (January 3, 1955–January 3, 1961). *Reelected to the Eighty-seventh Congress.*

CRAMTON, Louis Convers, a Representative from Michigan; born in Hadley Township, Lapeer County, Mich., December 2, 1875; attended the common schools of the county; was graduated from the Lapeer High School in 1893 and from the law department of the University of Michigan at Ann Arbor in 1899; was admitted to the bar in 1899 and commenced practice in Lapeer, Mich.; discontinued the practice of his profession in 1905 and published the Lapeer County Clarion 1905–1923; law clerk of the State senate three terms; deputy commissioner of railroads of Michigan in 1907; secretary of the Michigan Railroad Commission from September 1907 to January 1, 1909; member of the State house of representatives in 1909 and 1910; elected as a Republican to the Sixty-third and to the eight succeeding Congresses (March 4, 1913–March 3, 1931); unsuccessful candidate for renomination in 1930; special assistant to the Secretary of the Interior in 1931 and 1932; circuit judge of the fortieth judicial circuit from November 21, 1934, to December 31, 1941; delegate to the Republican National Convention in 1940; resumed the practice of law; elected to the State house of representatives in November 1948; reelected in 1950, 1952, 1954, 1956, and 1958, for the term ending December 31, 1960; retired; resides in Lapeer, Mich.

CRANE, Joseph Halsey (grandson of Stephen Crane), a Representative from Ohio; born in Elizabethtown (now Elizabeth), N. J., August 31, 1782; was a student at Princeton College; studied law; was admitted to the bar of New Jersey in 1802 and practiced; moved to Dayton, Ohio, in 1804 and continued the practice of law; member of the State house of representatives in 1809; prosecuting attorney of Montgomery County 1813–1816; elected president judge of the court of common pleas in 1817; elected as a Whig to the Twenty-first and to the three succeeding Congresses (March 4, 1829–March 3, 1837); declined to be a candidate for renomination in 1836; resumed the practice of his profession in Dayton; associate justice of the supreme court of Ohio at the time of his death in Dayton, Ohio, on November 13, 1851; interment in Woodland Cemetery.

CRANE, Stephen (grandfather of Joseph Halsey Crane), a Delegate from New Jersey; born in Elizabethtown (now Elizabeth), N. J., in July 1709; sheriff of Essex County under George the Third; was chosen by the Elizabethtown Associates to go to England and lay a petition before the King in 1743; member of the town committee in 1750; judge of the court of common pleas during the agitation over the stamp act; member of the State general assembly 1766–1773 and served as speaker in 1771;

mayor of Elizabethtown 1772–1774; was appointed chairman of the county committee of New Brunswick in 1774; Member of the Continental Congress 1774–1776; chairman of the town committee in 1776; member of the State council in 1776, 1777, and 1779; died in Elizabeth, N. J., July 1, 1780; interment in the First Presbyterian Church Cemetery.

CRANE, Winthrop Murray, a Senator from Massachusetts; born in Dalton, Mass., April 23, 1853; attended the public schools of Dalton, Wilbraham Academy, Wilbraham, Mass., and Williston Seminary, Easthampton, Mass.; engaged in the manufacture of paper at Dalton; delegate at large to the Republican National Conventions of 1892, 1896, 1904, 1908, 1916, and 1920; member of the Republican National Committee in 1892, 1896, 1904, and 1908; Lieutenant Governor of Massachusetts 1897–1899; Governor 1900–1902; appointed Secretary of the Treasury by President Theodore Roosevelt in 1902, but declined; appointed and subsequently elected to the United States Senate to fill the vacancy caused by the death of George F. Hoar; reelected in 1907 and served from October 12, 1904, to March 3, 1913; declined to be a candidate for reelection in 1912; resumed his former business pursuits; died in Dalton, Mass., October 2, 1920; interment in Dalton Cemetery.

CRANFORD, John Walter, a Representative from Texas; born near Grove Hill, Clarke County, Ala., in 1862; attended the common and high schools of Alabama and finished preparatory studies under a private tutor; moved to Texas about 1880 and settled at Sulphur Springs; studied law; was admitted to the bar and commenced practice in Texas; member of the State senate 1888–1896; elected president pro tempore of the twenty-second senate; elected as a Democrat to the Fifty-fifth Congress and served from March 4, 1897, until his death in Washington, D. C., March 3, 1899; interment in the City Cemetery, Sulphur Springs, Tex.

CRANSTON, Henry Young (brother of Robert Bennie Cranston), a Representative from Rhode Island; born in Newport, R. I., October 9, 1789; attended the public schools; engaged in mercantile pursuits in New Bedford, Mass.; moved to Newport, R. I., in 1810, and engaged in the commission business until 1815; studied law; was admitted to the bar in 1819 and commenced practice in Newport; clerk of the court of common pleas 1818–1833; member of the State house of representatives 1827–1843; member and vice president of the convention that framed the State constitution in 1842; elected as a Whig to the Twenty-eighth and Twenty-ninth Congresses (March 4, 1843–March 3, 1847); again a member of the State house of representatives 1847–1854 and served three years as speaker; died in Newport, R. I., February 12, 1864; interment in Island Cemetery.

CRANSTON, Robert Bennie (brother of Henry Young Cranston), a Representative from Rhode Island; born in Newport, R. I., January 14, 1791; attended the public schools; employed in the collection of internal revenue 1812–1815; sheriff of Newport County 1818–1827; elected as a Whig to the Twenty-fifth, Twenty-sixth, and Twenty-seventh Congresses (March 4, 1837–March 3, 1843); postmaster of Newport in 1827; member of the State house of representatives 1843–1847, and served one year as speaker; served in the State senate; elected as a Law and Order Whig to the Thirtieth Congress (March 4, 1847–March 3, 1849); was elected the first mayor of Newport on June 9, 1853; resigned the same day; presidential elector on the Republican ticket of Lincoln and Johnson in 1864; died in Newport, R. I., January 27, 1873; interment in Common Burial Ground.

CRAPO, William Wallace, a Representative from Massachusetts; born in Dartmouth, Mass., May 16, 1830; moved with his parents to New Bedford, Mass., in 1832; attended private and public schools of New Bedford, and was graduated from the local high school in 1845; attended Phillips Academy, Andover, Mass., and later the Friends' Academy at New Bedford; was graduated from the latter institution in 1848 and from Yale College in 1852; studied law at Harvard Law School for one year; was admitted to the bar in 1855 and commenced practice in New Bedford; city solicitor of New Bedford 1855–1867; member of the State house of representatives in 1857; elected to the Forty-fourth Congress to fill the vacancy caused by the death of James Buffington; reelected as a Republican to the Forty-fifth, Forty-sixth, and Forty-seventh Congresses and served from November 2, 1875, to March 3, 1883; was not a candidate for renomination in 1882; resumed the practice of law and also engaged in banking and in the manufacture of fine cotton goods; member of the Republican National Committee in 1884; appointed by Governor Wolcott in 1897 a member of the commission to revise street railway regulations; presidential elector on the Republican ticket of Roosevelt and Fairbanks in 1904; died in New Bedford, Mass., February 28, 1926; interment in the Rural Cemetery.

CRARY, Isaac Edwin, a Representative from Michigan; born in Preston, New London County, Conn., October 2, 1804; attended the public schools, and was graduated from Trinity College, Hartford, Conn., in its first class in 1827; studied law; was admitted to the bar and commenced practice in Marshall, Mich., in 1833; delegate to the State constitutional convention in 1835; upon the admission of Michigan as a State into the Union was elected as a Democrat to the Twenty-fourth, Twenty-fifth, and Twenty-sixth Congresses and served from January 26, 1837, to March 3, 1841; regent of Michigan University 1837–1844; founded the public-school system of Michigan; member of the State board of education 1850–1852; editor of the Marshall Expounder for several years; member of the State house of representatives 1842–1846, and speaker of the house in 1846; died in Marshall, Calhoun County, Mich., on May 8, 1854; interment in Oakridge Cemetery.

CRAVENS, James Addison (second cousin of James Harrison Cravens), a Representative from Indiana; born in Rockingham County, Va., November 4, 1818; moved with his father to Indiana in 1820 and settled near Hardinsburg, Madison Township, Washington County; attended the public schools; engaged in agricultural pursuits and stock raising; served in the war with Mexico as major of the Second Indiana Volunteers in 1846 and 1847; member of the State house of representatives in 1848 and 1849; served in the State senate 1850–1853; commissioned brigadier general of militia in 1854; elected as a Democrat to the Thirty-seventh and Thirty-eighth Congresses (March 4, 1861–March 3, 1865); was not a candidate for renomination in 1864; delegate to the Union National Convention of Conservatives at Philadelphia in 1866 and to the Democratic National Convention at New York in 1868; resumed agricultural pursuits; died in Hardinsburg, Washington County, Ind., June 20, 1893; interment in the Hardin Cemetery.

CRAVENS, James Harrison (second cousin of James Addison Cravens), a Representative from Indiana; born in Harrisonburg, Rockingham County, Va., August 2, 1802; studied law; was admitted to the bar in 1823 and commenced practice in Harrisonburg, Va.; moved to Franklin, Pa., in 1823 and resumed the practice of law; moved to Madison, Ind., in 1829 and engaged in agricultural pursuits; member of the State house of representatives in 1831 and 1832; moved to Ripley County, Ind., in 1833, where he practiced law and managed a farm; member of the State senate in 1839; presidential elector on the Whig ticket of Harrison and Tyler in 1840; elected to the Twenty-seventh Congress (March 4, 1841–March 3, 1843); unsuccessful candidate of the Free-Soil Party for Governor of Indiana in 1852, member of the State house of representatives in 1856; unsuccessful candidate for election to the attorney generalship of the State in 1856; lieutenant colonel of the Eighty-third Regiment, Indiana Volunteer Infantry, in the Civil War; during Morgan's raid in Indiana he and his soldiers were taken captive; died in Osgood, Ripley County, Ind., December 4, 1876; interment in Versailles Cemetery, Versailles, Ind.

CRAVENS, Jordan Edgar (cousin of William Ben Cravens), a Representative from Arkansas; born in Fredericktown, Madison County, Mo., November 7, 1830; moved with his father to Arkansas the following year; attended the common schools, and was graduated from the Cane Hill Academy at Boonsboro (now Canehill), Washington County, Ark., in 1850; studied law; was admitted to the bar in 1854 and commenced practice in Clarksville, Ark.; member of the State house of representatives in 1860; entered the Confederate Army in 1861 as a private, promoted to colonel in 1862, and continued in the service until the close of the Civil War; returned to Clarksville; prosecuting attorney of Johnson County in 1865 and 1866; member of the State senate 1866–1868; presidential elector on the Democratic ticket of Greeley and Brown in 1872; elected as a Democrat to the Forty-fifth, Forty-sixth, and Forty-seventh Congresses (March 4, 1877–March 3, 1883); was an unsuccessful candidate for renomination in 1882 to the Forty-eighth Congress; resumed the practice of law in Clarksville, Ark.; judge of the circuit court 1890–1894; died in Fort Smith, Ark., April 8, 1914; interment in Oakland Cemetery, Clarksville, Ark.

CRAVENS, William Ben (father of William Fadjo Cravens and cousin of Jordan Edgar Cravens), a Representative from Arkansas; born in Fort Smith, Sebastian County, Ark., January 17, 1872; attended the common schools, Louisville (Ky.) Military Academy, and Staunton (Va.) Military Academy; was graduated from the law department of the University of Missouri at Columbia in 1893; was admitted to the Arkansas bar the same year and commenced practice in Fort Smith, Ark.; city attorney of Fort Smith 1898–1902; served as prosecuting attorney for the twelfth judicial district of Arkansas 1902–1908; elected as a Democrat to the Sixtieth, Sixty-first, and Sixty-second Congresses (March 4, 1907–March 3, 1913); was not a candidate for reelection in 1912 to the Sixty-third Congress; resumed the practice of law; elected to the Seventy-third and to the three succeeding Congresses and served from March 4, 1933, until his death in Washington, D. C., on January 13, 1939; interment in Oak Cemetery, Fort Smith, Ark.

CRAVENS, William Fadjo (son of William Ben Cravens), a Representative from Arkansas; born in Fort Smith, Sebastian County, Ark., February 15, 1899; attended the public schools, the University of Arkansas at Fayetteville, the University of Pittsburgh, Pittsburgh, Pa., and was graduated from the law school of Washington and Lee University, Lexington, Va., in 1920; was admitted to the bar in 1920 and commenced practice at Fort Smith, Ark.; during the First World War served as a seaman in the United States Navy; city attorney of Fort Smith, Ark., for ten years; elected as a Democrat to the Seventy-sixth Congress to fill the vacancy caused by the death of his father, William Ben Cravens; reelected to the Seventy-seventh and to the three succeeding Congresses and served from September 12, 1939, to January 3, 1949; was not a candidate for renomination in 1948; resumed the practice of law and is a resident of Fort Smith, Ark.

CRAWFORD, Coe Isaac, a Senator from South Dakota; born near Volney, Allamakee County, Iowa, January 14, 1858; attended the common and graded schools and was instructed by a private tutor; was graduated from the law department of the University of Iowa at Iowa City in 1882; was admitted to the bar and commenced practice at Independence, Iowa; moved to Pierre, Territory of Dakota, in 1883 and continued the practice of law; prosecuting attorney of Hughes County in 1887 and 1888; member of the last Territorial council in 1889; upon the admission of South Dakota as a State into the Union was elected as a member of the first State senate; attorney general of South Dakota 1892–1896; unsuccessful Republican candidate in 1896 for Representative at Large to the Fifty-fifth Congress; attorney for the Chicago & North Western Railway Co. for the State of South Dakota in 1897 and served until 1903, when he resigned; moved to Huron in 1897; Governor of South Dakota in 1907 and 1908; delegate to the Republican National Convention at Chicago in 1908; elected as a Republican to the United States Senate and served from March 4, 1909, to March 3, 1915; unsuccessful candidate for renomination in 1914; resumed the practice of law in Huron, S. Dak., until 1934, when he retired from active business and political life; died in Yankton, S. Dak., April 25, 1944; interment in Municipal Cemetery, Iowa City, Iowa.

CRAWFORD, Fred Lewis, a Representative from Michigan; born in Dublin, Erath County, Tex., May 5, 1888; attended the public schools, business college at Peniel, Tex., and the University of Michigan at Ann Arbor; engaged in accountancy at Des Moines, Iowa, and Detroit, Mich., 1914–1917; built, financed, and operated beet sugar mills in various sections of the United States 1917–1935; also engaged in manufacturing, ranching, and overland transportation; director of the Michigan National Bank and the Refiners Transport & Petroleum Corp., of Detroit, Mich., at time of death; elected as a Republican to the Seventy-fourth and to the eight succeeding Congresses and served from January 3, 1935, to January 3, 1953; unsuccessful candidate for renomination in 1952; retired to his farm at Allentown, Prince Georges County, Md.; died in Washington, D. C., April 13, 1957; interment in Cedar Hill Cemetery.

CRAWFORD, George Washington, a Representative from Georgia; born in Columbia County, Ga., December 22, 1798; was graduated from Princeton College in 1820; studied law; was admitted to the bar in 1822 and commenced practice in Augusta, Ga.; attorney general of the State 1827–1831; member of the State house of representatives 1837–1842; elected as a Whig to the Twenty-seventh Congress to fill the vacancy caused by the death of Richard W. Habersham and served from January 7, 1843, to March 3, 1843; Governor of Georgia 1843–1847; appointed Secretary of War in the Cabinet of President Taylor and served from March 8, 1849, to July 23, 1850; presided over the State secession convention in 1861; died on his estate, "Bel Air," near Augusta, Ga., July 22, 1872; interment in Summerville Cemetery.

CRAWFORD, Joel, a Representative from Georgia; born in Columbia County, Ga.; June 15, 1783; completed preparatory studies; studied law at the Litchfield Law School; was admitted to the bar and commenced practice in Sparta in 1808; moved to Milledgeville, Ga., in 1811; served in the war against the Creek Indians as second lieutenant and aide-de-camp to Brigadier General Floyd in 1813 and 1814; resumed the practice of law in Milledgeville; member of the State house of representatives 1814–1817; elected as a Democrat to the Fifteenth and Sixteenth Congress (March 4, 1817–March 3, 1821); returned to Sparta, Hancock County, in 1828; member of the State senate in 1827 and 1828; appointed a commissioner to run the boundary line between Alabama and Georgia in 1826; unsuccessful candidate for Governor of Georgia in 1828 and 1831; delegate to the International Improvement Convention in 1831; elected in 1837 a State commissioner to locate and construct the Western & Atlantic Railroad; died near Blakely, Early County, Ga., April 5, 1858; interment in the family burying ground on his plantation in Early County, Ga.

CRAWFORD, Martin Jenkins, a Representative from Georgia; born in Jasper County, Ga., March 17, 1820; attended Brownwood Institute and Mercer University, Macon, Ga.; studied law; was admitted to the bar in 1839 and practiced in Hamilton, Ga.; also engaged in agricultural pursuits; member of the State house of representatives 1845–1847; moved to Columbus, Ga., in 1849; delegate to the Southern convention at Nashville in May 1850; judge of the superior courts of the Chattahoochee circuit from February 1, 1854, to November 1854; elected as a Democrat to the Thirty-fourth, Thirty-fifth, and Thirty-sixth Congresses and served from March 4, 1855, until January 23, 1861, when he withdrew; elected to the Confederate Provisional Congress and served from January 1861 to February 22, 1862; appointed by President Davis a special commissioner to the Government of the United States at Washington; raised the Third Georgia Cavalry Regiment in May 1862; served with it one year, and was then placed on the staff with Maj. Gen. Howell Cobb, where he served until the close of the Civil War; appointed judge of the superior court of the Chattahoochee circuit to fill a vacancy caused by the resignation of Judge James Johnson on October 1, 1875; reappointed in 1877 and served until February 9, 1880, when he resigned; appointed February 10, 1880, to the supreme court of Georgia to fill a vacancy; reappointed, and served until his death in Columbus, Ga., July 23, 1883; interment in Linnwood Cemetery.

CRAWFORD, Thomas Hartley, a Representative from Pennsylvania; born in Chambersburg, Pa., November 14, 1786; was graduated from Princeton College in 1804; studied law; was admitted to the bar in 1807 and commenced practice in Chambersburg; elected as a Jackson Democrat to the Twenty-first and Twenty-second Congresses (March 4, 1829–March 3, 1833); member of the State house of representatives in 1833 and 1834; appointed a commissioner to investigate alleged frauds in the sale of the Creek Reservation in 1836; appointed by President Van Buren Commissioner of Indian Affairs and served from October 22, 1838, to October 30, 1845; appointed by President Polk as judge of the criminal court of the District of Columbia in 1845 and served until 1861, when the court was reorganized; died in Washington, D. C., on January 27, 1863; interment in the Congressional Cemetery.

CRAWFORD, William, a Representative from Pennsylvania; born in Paisley, Scotland, in 1760; received a liberal schooling; studied medicine at the University of Edinburgh, and in 1781 received his degree; immigrated to the United States and settled near Gettysburg, Pa.; purchased a farm on Marsh Creek in 1785, where he spent the rest of his life practicing medicine; associate judge for Adams County 1801–1808; elected as a Democrat to the Eleventh and to the three succeeding Congresses (March 4, 1809–March 3, 1817); again resumed the practice of medicine near Gettysburg, Adams County, Pa., where he died on October 23, 1823; interment in Evergreen Cemetery, Gettysburg, Pa.

CRAWFORD, William Harris, a Senator from Georgia; born in Nelson County, Va., February 24, 1772; moved with his father to Edgefield District, S. C., in 1779 and to Columbia County, Ga., in 1783; pursued classical studies in a private school and in Richmond Academy, Augusta, Ga.; studied law; was admitted to the bar and commenced practice in Lexington, Ga., in 1799; appointed to prepare a digest of the laws of Georgia in 1799; member of the State house of representatives 1803–1807; elected to the United States Senate to fill the vacancy caused by the death of Abraham Baldwin and served from November 7, 1807, to March 23, 1813, when he resigned; elected President pro tempore of the Senate March 24, 1812; declined the portfolio of Secretary of War tendered by President Madison ni 1813; Minister to France from April 3, 1813, to April 22, 1815; returned home to act as agent for the sale of the land donated by Congress to Lafayette; appointed Secretary of War in the Cabinet of President Madison on August 1, 1815; was transferred to the Treasury October 22, 1816, and served under Presidents Madison and Monroe until March 7, 1825; unsuccessful Democratic candidate for President of the United States in 1824; on account of illness refused the tender of President Adams that he remain Secretary of the Treasury; his course as Secretary of the Treasury was criticized and was made the subject of congressional investigation, but the committee unanimously declared the charges unfounded; returned to Georgia and was appointed judge of the northern circuit court in 1827, which position he held until his death in Oglethorpe County, Ga., September 15, 1834; interment on his estate, "Woodlawn," near Crawford, Oglethorpe County, Ga.

CRAWFORD, William Thomas, a Representative from North Carolina; born near Waynesville, Haywood County, N. C., June 1, 1856; attended the public schools and Waynesville Academy; member of the State house of representatives 1884–1888; presidential elector on the Democratic ticket of Cleveland and Thurman in 1888; engrossing clerk of the State house of representatives in 1889; was graduated from the law department of the University of North Carolina at Chapel Hill in 1890; was admitted to the bar in 1891 and commenced practice in Waynesville; elected as a Democrat to the Fifty-second and Fifty-third Congresses (March 4, 1891–March 3, 1895); delegate to the American Bimetallic League in Washington, D. C., in 1893; unsuccessful candidate for reelection in 1894 to the Fifty-fourth Congress; presented credentials as a Member-elect to the Fifty-sixth Congress and served from March 4, 1899, to May 10, 1900, when he was succeeded by Richmond Pearson, who contested the election; unsuccessful candidate for election in 1900 to the Fifty-seventh Congress; delegate to the Democratic State conventions 1900–1912; presidential elector on the Democratic ticket of Alton B. Parker and Henry G. Davis in 1904; delegate to the gubernatorial convention in 1908; elected as a Democrat to the Sixtieth Congress (March 4, 1907–March 3, 1909); unsuccessful candidate for reelection in 1908 to the Sixty-first Congress; resumed the practice of law in Waynesville, N. C., where he died November 16, 1913; interment in Green Hill Cemetery.

CREAGER, Charles Edward, a Representative from Oklahoma; born near Dayton, Montgomery County, Ohio, April 28, 1873; attended the public schools of Ohio, and Northern Indiana University; engaged in the newspaper business; enlisted as sergeant major in the Fourth Ohio Volunteer Infantry during the Spanish-American War and served under General Miles in the Puerto Rican campaign: city editor of the Columbus Press-Post 1899–1901; editor of the Daily Leader, Marietta, Ohio, 1902–1904; moved to Muskogee, Indian Territory (now Oklahoma) in November 1904 and engaged in the newspaper business, later becoming publisher and editor of several Oklahoma newspapers; elected as a Republican to the Sixty-first Congress (March 4, 1909–March 3, 1911); unsuccessful candidate for reelection in

1910 to the Sixty-second Congress; employed in the United States Indian Service and later engaged in oil production until 1934, when he retired; is a resident of Muskogee, Okla.

CREAL, Edward Wester, a Representative from Kentucky; born in a log house near Mount Sherman, Larue County, Ky., November 20, 1883; attended the public schools of Hart and Larue Counties, Ky.; taught school for nine years in Larue County and between teaching terms attended Southern Normal School at Bowling Green, Ky., and East Lynn College at Buffalo, Ky.; was graduated from the law department of Centre College, Danville, Ky., in 1906; was admitted to the bar in 1904 and commenced practice in Hodgenville, Ky., in 1910; county superintendent of schools of Larue County, Ky., 1910–1918; county attorney 1918–1928; Commonwealth attorney 1929–1936; owner and publisher of a weekly newspaper in Hodgenville, Ky., from 1918 until the time of his death; member of the Democratic State executive committee 1924–1940; elected as a Democrat to the Seventy-fourth Congress to fill the vacancy caused by the death of Cap R. Carden; reelected to the Seventy-fifth and to the three succeeding Congresses and served from November 5, 1935, until his death in Hodgenville, Ky., on October 13, 1943; interment in Red Hill Cemetery.

CREAMER, Thomas James, a Representative from New York; born near Garadice Lake, Ireland, May 26, 1843; immigrated to the United States and took up his residence in New York City; attended the public schools; shipping clerk in a dry-goods house in 1860; studied law; was admitted to the bar and practiced; member of the State assembly 1865–1867; served in the State senate 1868–1871; city tax commissioner for five years; acted as counsel for State commissions to revise the tax laws; elected as a Democrat to the Forty-third Congress (March 4, 1873–March 3, 1875); was not a candidate for renomination in 1874; delegate to three Democratic National Conventions; elected to the Fifty-seventh Congress (March 4, 1901–March 3, 1903); was not a candidate for renomination in 1902; resumed the practice of law in New York City, and died there August 4, 1914; interment in Greenwood Cemetery.

CREBS, John Montgomery, a Representative from Illinois; born in Middleburg, Loudoun County, Va., April 9, 1830; moved to Illinois in 1837 with his parents, who settled in White County; attended the public schools; studied law; was admitted to the bar in 1852 and commenced practice in White County, Ill.; during the Civil War served in the Union Army, and was commissioned lieutenant colonel, Eighty-seventh Regiment, Illinois Infantry, in 1862; took part in the Mississippi, Vicksburg, and Arkansas campaigns; commanded a brigade of Cavalry in the Department of the Gulf; after the close of the war resumed the practice of law; elected as a Democrat to the Forty-first and Forty-second Congresses (March 4, 1869–March 3, 1873); unsuccessful candidate for renomination in 1872; engaged in the practice of his profession until his death in Carmi, White County, Ill., June 26, 1890; interment in Maple Ridge Cemetery.

CREELY, John Vaudain, a Representative from Pennsylvania; born in Philadelphia, Pa., November 14, 1839; received a classical education; studied law; was admitted to the bar in 1862 and practiced in Philadelphia; during the Civil War served with the Union Army as an officer of Light Artillery; member of the Philadelphia City Council for four years; elected as a Republican to the Forty-second Congress (March 4, 1871–March 3, 1873); before his term of service had expired he mysteriously disappeared, and upon the application of his sister, Adelaide G. Creely, to whom was awarded his estate, he was declared legally dead on September 28, 1900, by the orphans' court of Philadelphia.

CREIGHTON, William, Jr., a Representative from Ohio; born in Berkeley County, Va., October 29, 1778; was graduated from Dickinson College, Carlisle, Pa.; studied law; was admitted to the bar in 1798 and commenced practice in Chillicothe, Ohio; secretary of state 1803–1808; member of the State house of representatives in 1810; elected as a Democrat to the Thirteenth Congress to fill the vacancy caused by the resignation of Duncan McArthur; reelected to the Fourteenth Congress and served from May 4, 1813, to March 3, 1817; unsuccessful candidate for election in 1815 to the United States Senate; president of the branch bank of the United States at Chillicothe; elected to the Twentieth Congress and served from March 4, 1827, until his resignation in 1828; was appointed during the recess of Congress and nominated by President John Quincy Adams on December 11, 1828, as a United States judge of the district court, but the Senate on February 16, 1829, passed a resolution that it was "not expedient to fill the vacancy at the present session of Congress"; reelected to the Twenty-first and Twenty-second Congresses (March 4, 1829–March 3, 1833); was not a candidate for renomination in 1832; resumed the practice of law; died in Chillicothe, Ross County, Ohio, October 8, 1851; interment in Grand View Cemetery.

CRESWELL, John Andrew Jackson, a Representative and a Senator from Maryland; born at Creswells Ferry (now Port Deposit), Cecil County, Md., November 18, 1828; attended the local academy at Port Deposit; was graduated from Dickinson College, Carlisle, Pa., in 1848; studied law; was admitted to the bar in Baltimore in 1850 and commenced practice in Elkton, Md.; unsuccessful candidate for election on the Whig ticket in 1850 to the Reform State Convention; delegate to the Democratic National Convention at Cincinnati in 1856; member of the State house of delegates in 1861; affiliated with the Republican Party in 1861; adjutant general of the State in 1862 and 1863; elected as a Republican to the Thirty-eighth Congress (March 4, 1863–March 3, 1865); unsuccessful candidate for reelection in 1864 to the Thirty-ninth Congress; elected to the United States Senate to fill the vacancy caused by the death of Thomas H. Hicks and served from March 9, 1865, to March 3, 1867; delegate to the Republican National Convention at Baltimore in 1864 and at Chicago in 1868; delegate to the Philadelphia Loyalists' Convention in 1866 and to the Border State Convention at Baltimore in 1867; was elected Secretary of the United States Senate in 1868, but declined to serve; appointed Postmaster General in the Cabinet of President Ulysses S. Grant and served from March 5, 1869, until July 3, 1874, when he resigned; served as counsel of the United States before the Alabama Claims Commission 1874–1876; resumed the practice of law; one of the commissioners to close up the affairs of the Freedman's Savings & Trust Company; president of two banks; died near Elkton, Cecil County, Md., December 23, 1891; interment in Elkton Presbyterian Cemetery.

CRETELLA, Albert William, a Representative from Connecticut; born in New Haven, Conn., April 22, 1897; attended the public schools of New Haven; graduated from Yale University in 1917; entered Yale University Law School but interrupted studies and enlisted in the United States Navy June 18, 1918, and was in officers training school when the armistice was signed; reentered Yale Law School and graduated in 1921; was admitted to the Connecticut bar the same year and began practice in New Haven; moved to North Haven in 1926 and served as prosecuting attorney 1931–1945 and town counsel 1931–1952; served as chairman of Draft Board 12–A during World War II; member of the State house of representatives 1947–1952; elected as a Republican to the Eighty-third, Eighty-fourth, and Eighty-fifth Congresses (January 3, 1953–January 3, 1959); unsuccessful candidate for reelection in 1958 to the Eighty-sixth Congress and for election in 1960 to the Eighty-seventh Congress; engaged in the practice of law; is a resident of North Haven, Conn.

CRIPPA, Edward David, a Senator from Wyoming; born in Rock Springs, Sweetwater County, Wyo., April 8, 1899; graduated from Rock Springs High School in 1917; during the First World War served as a private in the United States Army; councilman of Rock Springs, 1926–1928; president of Union Mercantile Co., in 1930; owner and manager of Crippa Motor Co., Rock Springs, Wyo.; president of North Side State Bank and director of Rock Springs Fuel Co. in 1940; Wyoming State Highway Commissioner 1941–1947; delegate to the Republican National Convention in 1944; Republican national committeeman 1948–1960; appointed as a Republican to the United States Senate to fill the vacancy caused by the death of Lester C. Hunt and served from June 24, 1954, to November 28, 1954; was not a candidate for election to fill the vacancy; resumed business activities; died in Rock Springs, Wyo., October 20, 1960; interment in St. Josephs Cemetery.

CRISFIELD, John Woodland, a Representative from Maryland; born near Chestertown, Kent County, Md., November 8, 1806; was educated at Washington College, Chestertown; studied law; was admitted to the bar in 1830 and commenced practice in Princess Anne, Somerset County; member of the State house of representatives in 1836; elected as a Whig to the Thirtieth Congress (March 4, 1847–March 3, 1849); delegate to the State constitutional convention in 1850; member of the peace conference of 1861 held in Washington, D. C., in an effort to devise means to prevent the impending war; elected as a Union Republican to the Thirty-seventh Congress (March 4, 1861–March 3, 1863); unsuccessful candidate for reelection in 1862 to the Thirty-eighth Congress; resumed the practice of law; delegate to the Union National Convention at Philadelphia in 1866; located and founded the town of Crisfield, Somerset County, Md., in 1866; instrumental in building the Eastern Shore Railroad and served as president; died in Princess Anne, Md., on January 12, 1897; interment in Manokin Presbyterian Cemetery.

CRISP, Charles Frederick (father of Charles Robert Crisp), a Representative from Georgia; born in Sheffield, England, January 29, 1845; later in that year his parents immigrated to the United States and settled in Georgia; attended the common schools of Savannah and Macon, Ga.; during the Civil War entered the Confederate Army in May 1861; commissioned lieutenant in Company K, Tenth Regiment, Virginia Infantry, and served with that regiment until May 12, 1864, when he became a prisoner of war; upon his release from Fort Delaware in June 1865 joined his parents at Ellaville, Schley County, Ga.; studied law at Americus, Ga.; was admitted to the bar in 1866 and commenced practice in Ellaville; appointed solicitor general of the southwestern judicial circuit in 1872, and reappointed in 1873 for a term of four years; appointed judge of the superior court of the same circuit in June 1877; elected by the general assembly to the same office in 1878; reelected judge for a term of four years in 1880; resigned that office in September 1882 to accept the Democratic nomination for Congress; permanent president of the Democratic convention which assembled at Atlanta in April 1883 to nominate a candidate for Governor; elected as a Democrat to the Forty-eighth and to the six succeeding Congresses and served from March 4, 1883, until his death; was Speaker of the House of Representatives during the Fifty-second and Fifty-third Congresses; nominated for United States Senator in the State primary of 1896; died in Atlanta, Ga., October 23, 1896; interment in Oak Grove Cemetery.

CRISP, Charles Robert (son of Charles Frederick Crisp), a Representative from Georgia; born in Ellaville, Schley County, Ga., October 19, 1870; attended the public schools of Americus, Ga.; clerk in the Interior Department, Washington, D. C., 1889–1891; parliamentarian of the National House of Representatives 1891–1895; studied law; was admitted to the bar in 1895 and commenced practice in Americus, Sumter County, Ga.; elected as a Democrat to the Fifty-fourth Congress to fill the vacancy caused by the death of his father, Charles F. Crisp, and served from December 19, 1896, to March 3, 1897; was not a candidate for renomination in 1896; resumed the practice of law in Americus, Ga.; judge of the city court of Americus 1900–1912; again parliamentarian of the House of Representatives in the Sixty-second Congress; parliamentarian of the Democratic National Convention at Baltimore in 1912; elected to the Sixty-third and to the nine succeeding Congresses and served from March 4, 1913, until October 7, 1932, when he resigned to become a member of the United States Tariff Commission, in which capacity he served until December 30, 1932; was not a candidate for renomination in 1932, but was an unsuccessful candidate for the nomination for United States Senator to fill the vacancy occasioned by the death of William J. Harris; member of the American World War Debt Funding Commission; resumed the practice of his chosen profession in Washington, D. C.; died in Americus, Ga., February 7, 1937; interment in Oak Grove Cemetery.

CRIST, Henry, a Representative from Kentucky; born in Fredericksburg, Spotsylvania County, Va., October 20, 1764; moved with his father to Pennsylvania, where he attended the public schools; moved to Kentucky and engaged in the surveying of lands; moved to Bullitt County, Ky., in 1788 and engaged in the manufacture of salt; member of the State house of representatives in 1795 and 1806; served in the State senate 1800–1804; elected to the Eleventh Congress (March 4, 1809–March 3, 1811); was a Whig after the organization of that party; died near Shepherdsville, Bullitt County, Ky., August 11, 1844; interment in State Cemetery, Frankfort, Ky.

CRITCHER, John, a Representative from Virginia; born at Oak Grove, Westmoreland County, Va., on March 11, 1820; attended Brent's Preparatory School; was graduated from the University of Virginia at Charlottesville in 1839, and later pursued higher studies in France for three years; studied law; was admitted to the bar in 1842 and commenced practice in Westmoreland County, Va.; served in the State senate 1861 and 1874–1877; member of the State secession convention in 1861; served as lieutenant colonel of Cavalry in the Confederate Army during the Civil War; appointed judge of the eighth judicial circuit of Virginia, but was removed under the resolution of Congress dated February 18, 1869, which provided that anyone who has borne arms against the United States should be dismissed from office within thirty days; elected as a Conservative to the Forty-second Congress (March 4, 1871–March 3, 1873); died in Alexandria, Va., September 27, 1901; interment in the Episcopal Cemetery.

CRITTENDEN, John Jordan (uncle of Thomas Theodore Crittenden), a Senator and a Representative from Kentucky; born near Versailles, Woodford County, Ky., September 10, 1787; completed preparatory studies; attended Pisgah Academy, Woodford County, Ky., Washington College (now Washington and Lee University), Lexington, Va., and was graduated from William and Mary College, Williamsburg, Va., in 1806; studied law; was admitted to the bar and commenced practice in Woodford County, Ky., in 1807; attorney general of Illinois Territory in 1809 and 1810; served in the War of 1812 as aide to Governor Shelby; resumed the practice of law in Russellville, Ky.; member of the State house of representatives 1811–1817, and served as speaker the last term; elected to the United States Senate and served from March 4, 1817, to March 3, 1819, when he resigned; moved to Frankfort, Ky., in 1819; again a member of the State house of representatives in 1825 and 1829–1832; appointed United States district attorney in 1827, confirmed February 8, 1827, but was removed by President Jackson in 1829; nominated in 1828 by President John Quincy Adams as an Associate Justice of the Supreme Court of the United States, but was not confirmed by the Senate; again elected to the United States Senate and served from March 4, 1835, to March 3, 1841; appointed Attorney General of the United States by President Harrison and served from March 5 to September 13, 1841; appointed and subsequently elected to the United States Senate to fill the vacancy caused by the resignation of Henry Clay and served from March 31, 1842, to June 12, 1848, when he resigned; elected Governor of Kentucky in 1848 and served until July 22, 1850, when he resigned; again appointed Attorney General, this time by President Fillmore, and served from July 22, 1850, to March 7, 1853; again elected to the United States Senate and served from March 4, 1855, to March 3, 1861; elected as a Unionist to the Thirty-seventh Congress (March 4, 1861–March 3, 1863); was a candidate for reelection at the time of his death; died in Frankfort, Ky., July 26, 1863; interment in State Cemetery, Frankfort, Ky.

CRITTENDEN, Thomas Theodore (nephew of John Jordan Crittenden), a Representative from Missouri; born near Shelbyville, Shelby County, Ky., January 1, 1832; attended the primary schools at Cloverport, Ky.; was graduated from Centre College, Danville, Ky., in 1855; served as registrar of Franklin County in 1856; studied law in Frankfort, Ky.; was admitted to the bar in 1858 and commenced practice in Lexington, Mo.; served in the Union Army during the Civil War from 1862 to 1864, being commissioned captain and later lieutenant colonel of the Seventh Missouri Cavalry Militia Regiment; was wounded at the Battle of Westport, near Kansas City, Mo., October 23, 1864; moved to Warrensburg in 1865 and continued the practice of law; appointed attorney general of Missouri by Gov. Willard P. Hall in 1864 to fill out the unexpired term of Aikman Welch, deceased; elected as a Democrat to the Forty-third Congress (March 4, 1873–March 3, 1875); was not a candidate for renomination in 1874; again elected to the Forty-fifth Congress (March 4, 1877–March 3, 1879); Governor of Missouri 1881–1885; moved to Kansas City in 1885 and continued the practice of law; United States consul general at the city of Mexico from April 5, 1893, to 1897; referee in bankruptcy from 1898 until his death in Kansas City, Mo., May 29, 1909; interment in Forest Hill Cemetery.

CROCHERON, Henry (brother of Jacob Crocheron), a Representative from New York; born on Staten Island, Richmond County, N. Y., December 26, 1772; attended the common schools; engaged in mercantile pursuits in Northfield; supervisor of Northfield 1808–1814; elected as a Democrat to the Fourteenth Congress (March 4, 1815–March 3, 1817); captain of militia in 1818; died in New Springville, Richmond County, N. Y., on November 8, 1819; interment in St. Andrews' Churchyard, Richmond County, Staten Island, N. Y.

CROCHERON, Jacob (brother of Henry Crocheron), a Representative from New York; born on Staten Island, Richmond County, N. Y., August 23, 1774; engaged in agricultural pursuits; sheriff of Richmond County in 1802, 1811, and again in 1821; elected as a Jackson Democrat to the Twenty-first Congress

(March 4, 1829–March 3, 1831); presidential elector on the Democratic ticket of Van Buren and Johnson in 1836; died in Richmond County, Staten Island, on December 27, 1849; interment in St. Andrew's Churchyard, Staten Island, N. Y.

CROCKER, Alvah, a Representative from Massachusetts; born in Leominster, Mass., October 14, 1801; attended the public schools and Groton Academy; proprietor of paper manufactories at Fitchburg; president of the Boston & Fitchburg Railroad; member of the Hoosac Tunnel Commission; member of the State house of representatives in 1836, 1842, and 1843; served in the State senate for two terms; elected as a Republican to the Forty-second Congress to fill the vacancy caused by the resignation of William B. Washburn; reelected to the Forty-third Congress and served from January 2, 1872, until his death in Fitchburg, Mass., December 26, 1874; interment in Laurel Hill Cemetery.

CROCKER, Samuel Leonard, a Representative from Massachusetts; born in Taunton, Mass., March 31, 1804; was graduated from Brown University, Providence, R. I., in 1822; engaged in manufacturing; member of the executive council of Massachusetts in 1849; elected as a Whig to the Thirty-third Congress (March 4, 1853–March 3, 1855); unsuccessful candidate for reelection in 1854 to the Thirty-fourth Congress; president of the Taunton Copper Manufacturing Co.; died in Boston, Mass., February 10, 1883; interment in Mount Pleasant Cemetery, Taunton, Bristol County, Mass.

CROCKETT, David (father of John Wesley Crockett), a Representative from Tennessee; born at the confluence of Limestone Creek and Noli-Chuckey River in the State of Franklin, which a few years later became Greene County, Tenn., August 17, 1786; attended the common schools for a short time; moved to Lincoln County about 1808 and to what is now Gibson County in 1822; commanded a battalion of mounted riflemen under General Jackson in the Creek campaign in 1813 and 1814; member of the State house of representatives 1821–1823; unsuccessful candidate for election in 1825 to the Nineteenth Congress; elected as a Democrat to the Twentieth and Twenty-first Congresses (March 4, 1827–March 3, 1831); unsuccessful candidate for reelection in 1830 to the Twenty-second Congress; elected as a Whig to the Twenty-third Congress (March 4, 1833–March 3, 1835); unsuccessful candidate for reelection in 1834 to the Twenty-fourth Congress; went to Texas to aid the Texans in their struggle for independence in 1836; joined a band of 186 men in the defense of the Alamo, San Antonio de Bexar, and was among those killed in that battle which terminated on March 6, 1836; his body was buried with all of the Alamo garrison defenders.

CROCKETT, John Wesley (son of David Crockett), a Representative from Tennessee; born in Trenton, Tenn., July 10, 1807; attended the public schools; studied law; was admitted to the bar and commenced practice in Paris, Tenn.; held various local and State offices; was elected as a Whig to the Twenty-fifth and Twenty-sixth Congresses (March 4, 1837–March 3, 1841); elected by the State legislature attorney general for the ninth district of Tennessee and served from 1841 to 1843; moved to New Orleans in 1843 and engaged in business as a commission merchant; became editor of the National May 22, 1848, and established the Crescent in 1850; moved to Memphis, Tenn., in 1852, where he died November 24, 1852; interment in the Old City Cemetery, Paris, Tenn.

CROFT, George William (father of Theodore Gaillard Croft), a Representative from South Carolina; born in Newberry County, S. C., December 20, 1846; attended the common schools in Greenville, S. C.; entered the South Carolina Military Academy at Charleston in 1863; the cadets of that institution were mustered into the Confederate Army in 1864 and served until the close of the Civil War; attended the University of Virginia at Charlottesville in 1866 and 1867; studied law; was admitted to the bar in 1869 and commenced practice in Aiken, S. C., in 1870; president of the State bar association; member of the State house of representatives; served in the State senate; elected as a Democrat to the Fifty-eighth Congress and served from March 4, 1903, until his death in Washington, D. C., on March 10, 1904; interment in St. Thaddeus' Episcopal Churchyard, Aiken, S. C.

CROFT, Theodore Gaillard (son of George William Croft), a Representative from South Carolina; born in Aiken, Aiken County, S. C., November 26, 1874; attended the common schools; was graduated from Bethel Military Academy, Warrenton, Va., in 1895 and from the law department of the University of South Carolina at Columbia in 1897; was admitted to the bar the same year and commenced practice in Aiken, S. C.; elected as a Democrat to the Fifty-eighth Congress to fill the vacancy caused by the death of his father, George W. Croft, and served from May 17, 1904, to March 3, 1905; was not a candidate for renomination in 1904; resumed the practice of law in Aiken, S. C.; member of the State house of representatives in 1907 and 1908; served in the State senate 1909–1912; during the First World War was a member of the draft board for his district from 1917 until he volunteered for service in the United States Army in June 1918; applied for admission to officers' training camp in August 1918; enlisted October 29, 1918; was assigned to duty as a private in the Field Artillery Central Officers' Training School, Camp Zachary Taylor, and served until December 5, 1918, when he was honorably discharged; resumed the practice of law; died in Aiken, S. C., March 23, 1920; interment in St. Thaddeus' Episcopal Churchyard.

CROLL, William Martin, a Representative from Pennsylvania; born in Upper Macungie Township, Lehigh County, Pa., April 9, 1866; attended the public schools and Keystone State Normal School, Kutztown, Pa.; was graduated from Eastman Business College at Poughkeepsie, N. Y.; taught school; moved to Maxatawny in 1889 and engaged in the general merchandise business; moved to Reading, Pa., in 1897 and engaged in the retail clothing business and in banking; treasurer of Berks County 1909–1912; served as naval officer, port of Philadelphia, from 1913 to 1918; delegate to the Democratic National Conventions in 1912 and 1920; elected as a Democrat to the Sixty-eighth Congress (March 4, 1923–March 3, 1925); unsuccessful candidate for reelection in 1924 to the Sixty-ninth Congress; resumed mercantile pursuits; died in Reading, Pa., October 21, 1929; interment in Laureldale Cemetery, Laureldale, Pa.

CROMER, George Washington, a Representative from Indiana; born near Anderson, Madison County, Ind., May 13, 1856; attended the common schools and Wittenberg College, Springfield, Ohio, and was graduated from the Indiana University at Bloomington in 1882; became editor of the Muncie (Ind.) Times in 1883; studied law; was admitted to the bar in 1886 and commenced practice in Muncie, Delaware County, Ind.; prosecuting attorney for the forty-sixth judicial circuit of Indiana 1886–1890; member of the State Republican committee in 1892 and 1894; mayor of Muncie 1894–1898; elected as a Republican to the Fifty-sixth and to the three succeeding Congresses (March 4, 1899–March 3, 1907); unsuccessful candidate for reelection in 1906 to the Sixtieth Congress; resumed the practice of his profession in Muncie, Ind., until his death in that city November 8, 1936; interment in Beech Grove Cemetery.

CROOK, Thurman Charles, a Representative from Indiana; born on a farm near Peru, Miami County, Ind., July 18, 1891; attended the Cass County schools, Logansport High School, Indiana State Normal, Purdue University, Indiana University, and graduated from Valparaiso University in 1930; learned the carpentry and cement trades; taught departmental work and coached athletics at Logansport, Ind., in 1913 and 1914, Reynolds, Ind., High School 1914–1916, Camden, Ind., High School 1916–1918, Plymouth, Ind., High School 1918–1919; supervisor of industrial work at Peru, Ind., High School in 1919 and 1920; drafting instructor, Central High School, South Bend, Ind., 1920–1948; member of the State house of representatives 1939–1943; served in the State senate 1943–1947; fruit grower near Logansport, Ind., 1924–1947; unsuccessful for the Democratic nomination in 1946 to the Eightieth Congress; elected as a Democrat to the Eighty-first Congress (January 3, 1949–January 3, 1951); unsuccessful candidate for reelection in 1950 to the Eighty-second Congress and for election in 1956 to the Eighty-fifth Congress; farmer, horticulturist, and sheep raiser; is a resident of Logansport, Ind.

CROOKE, Philip Schuyler, a Representative from New York; born in Poughkeepsie, N. Y., March 2, 1810; was graduated from Dutchess Academy in Poughkeepsie; studied law; was admitted to the bar in 1831 and commenced practice in Brooklyn, N. Y.; moved to Flatbush (now a part of Greater New York City) in 1838; member of the Board of Supervisors of Kings County 1844–1852 and 1858–1870, and chairman of the board in 1861, 1862, 1864, and 1865; presidential elector on the Democratic ticket of Pierce and King in 1852; elected a member of the general assembly as a Republican in 1863; served forty years in the National Guard of the State of New York, from private to brigadier general, and during the Civil War commanded the Fifth Brigade, National Guard, in Pennsylvania in June and July 1863; elected as a Republican to the Forty-third Congress (March 4, 1873–March 3, 1875); was not a candidate for renomination in 1874; resumed the practice of law; died in Flatbush, N. Y., March 17, 1881; interment in Greenwood Cemetery, Brooklyn, N. Y.

CROSBY, Charles Noel, a Representative from Pennsylvania; born September 29, 1876, in a farming settlement named Cherry Valley, near Andover, Ashtabula County, Ohio; attended preparatory schools, New Lyme (Ohio) Institute, and Allegheny College, Meadville, Pa.; was graduated from Western Reserve University, Cleveland, Ohio, in 1897; moved to Linesville, Pa., in 1901, engaging in the manufacture of silos and in the lumber business; engaged in agricultural pursuits in 1914; member of the Linesville and Meadville (Pa.) Boards of Education 1920–1929; president of the Meadville Chamber of Commerce 1922–1924; elected as a Democrat to the Seventy-third, Seventy-fourth, and Seventy-fifth Congresses (March 4, 1933–January 3, 1939); unsuccessful candidate for renomination in 1938; moved to Montgomery County, Md., in 1940 and operated a large dairy farm near Clarksburg; died in a hospital in Frederick, Md., January 26, 1951; interment in Columbia Gardens Cemetery, Arlington, Va.

CROSBY, John Crawford, a Representative from Massachusetts; born in Sheffield, Berkshire County, Mass., on June 15, 1859; attended the public schools of Pittsfield; was graduated from Eastman Business College, Poughkeepsie, N. Y., and from Boston University Law School, Boston, Mass.; was admitted to the bar in 1882 and commenced practice in Pittsfield, Berkshire County, Mass.; member of the school committee of Pittsfield 1884–1890; served in the State house of representatives in 1886 and 1887; member of the State senate in 1888 and 1889; director of a bank and of fire- and life-insurance companies; elected as a Democrat to the Fifty-second Congress (March 4, 1891–March 3, 1893); unsuccessful candidate for reelection in 1892 to the Fifty-third Congress; mayor of Pittsfield, Mass., in 1894 and 1895; delegate to the Democratic National Convention at Chicago in 1896, which nominated Bryan and Sewall; city solicitor 1896–1900; appointed justice of the superior court on January 25, 1905, and served until December 31, 1913, when he was appointed justice of the Massachusetts Supreme Judicial Court, in which capacity he served until his retirement on October 1, 1937; died in Pittsfield, Mass., on October 14, 1943; interment in Pittsfield Cemetery.

CROSS, Edward, a Representative from Arkansas; born in Hawkins City, Tenn., November 11, 1798; attended the public schools; studied law; was admitted to the bar and practiced; moved to Arkansas in 1826; appointed May 26, 1830, United States judge for the Territory of Arkansas; served as United States surveyor general for Arkansas from April 30, 1836, until September 1, 1838; elected as a Democrat to the Twenty-sixth, Twenty-seventh, and Twenty-eighth Congresses (March 4, 1839–March 3, 1845); was not a candidate for renomination; judge of the State supreme court from July 1845 to 1855; president of the Cairo & Fulton (later the St. Louis, Iron Mountain & Southern) Railway 1855–1862; appointed attorney general of Arkansas in 1874; retired to private life; died at his country residence, "Marlbrook," near Washington, Hempstead County, Ark., April 6, 1887; interment on his estate.

CROSS, Oliver Harlan, a Representative from Texas; born in Eutaw, Greene County, Ala., July 13, 1868; attended the public schools and was graduated from the University of Alabama at Tuscaloosa in 1891; teacher in the public schools at Union Springs, Ala., in 1891 and 1892; studied law; was admitted to the bar in 1893 and commenced practice in Deming, N. Mex.; moved to McGregor, Tex., in 1894 and continued the practice of law; served as city attorney of McGregor in 1895 and 1896; moved to Waco, Tex., in 1896 and continued the practice of law; assistant attorney of McLennan County 1898–1902; member of the State house of representatives in 1900; district attorney of McLennan County 1902–1906; retired from law practice in 1917 and assumed agricultural pursuits; elected as a Democrat to the Seventy-first and to the three succeeding Congresses (March 4, 1929–January 3, 1937); was not a candidate for renomination in 1936; engaged in agricultural pursuits and in real-estate activities; died in Waco, Tex., April 24, 1960; interment in Hearne Cemetery, Hearne, Tex.

CROSSER, Robert, a Representative from Ohio; born in Holytown, Lanarkshire, Scotland, June 7, 1874; immigrated to the United States in 1881 with his parents and settled in Cleveland, Ohio; moved to Salineville, Ohio, the same year and attended the public schools; was graduated from Kenyon College, Gambier, Ohio, in 1897; studied law at Columbia University in New York City and was graduated from Cincinnati Law School in 1901; was admitted to the bar in 1901 and commenced practice in Cleveland, Ohio; taught law at Baldwin-Wallace Law School in 1904 and 1905; member of the State house of representatives in 1911 and 1912; member of the fourth constitutional convention in 1912; elected as a Democrat to the Sixty-third, Sixty-fourth, and Sixty-fifth Congresses (March 4, 1913–March 3, 1919); unsuccessful candidate for renomination in 1918 and for election in 1920; elected to the Sixty-eighth and to the fifteen succeeding Congresses (March 4, 1923–January 3, 1955); unsuccessful candidate for renomination in 1954; resided in Bethesda, Md., until his death there on June 3, 1957; interment in Highland Park Cemetery, Warrensville, Ohio.

CROSSLAND, Edward, a Representative from Kentucky; born in Hickman County, Ky., June 30, 1827; completed preparatory studies; studied law; was admitted to the bar in 1852 and began practice at Clinton, Hickman County, Ky.; sheriff of Hickman County in 1851 and 1852; member of the State house of representatives in 1857 and 1858; during the Civil War enlisted as captain in the First Kentucky Regiment, Confederate Army; was elected colonel of the Seventh Kentucky Regiment and served until the end of the war; elected judge of the court of common pleas of the first judicial district of Kentucky in August 1867 for six years, but resigned November 1, 1870; elected as a Democrat to the Forty-second and Forty-third Congresses (March 4, 1871–March 3, 1875); resumed the practice of law in Mayfield, Graves County, Ky.; elected judge of the circuit court for the first judicial district of Kentucky in August 1880 and served until his death in Mayfield, Ky., September 11, 1881; interment in Maplewood Cemetery.

CROUCH, Edward, a Representative from Pennsylvania; born at Walnut Hill, near Highspire, Paxtang Township, Lancaster (now Dauphin) County, Pa., on November 9, 1764; attended the common schools; at the age of seventeen enlisted during the Revolutionary War; commanded a company in the Whisky Insurrection of 1794; engaged in mercantile pursuits at Walnut Hill; member of the State house of representatives 1804–1806; presidential elector on the Democratic ticket of Madison and Gerry in 1812; appointed associate judge of Dauphin County April 16, 1813, but resigned upon being elected as a Democrat to the Thirteenth Congress to fill the vacancy caused by the resignation of John Gloninger and served from October 12, 1813, until March 3, 1815; was not a candidate for renomination; returned to Walnut Hill, Paxtang Township, Dauphin County, Pa., and resided there until his death, on February 2, 1827; interment in Paxtang Cemetery.

CROUNSE, Lorenzo, a Representative from Nebraska; born in Sharon, Schoharie County, N. Y., January 27, 1834; attended a seminary at Charlotteville, N. Y.; taught school; moved to Fort Plain, N. Y., in 1855; studied law; was admitted to the bar in 1857; during the Civil War raised a battery of light artillery in 1861 and entered the Army as its captain; wounded, and resigned after a year's service; moved to Nebraska Territory in 1864; member of the Territorial house of representatives in 1866; delegate to the State constitutional convention in 1866; elected associate justice of the State supreme court in 1867; at the expiration of his term was elected as a Republican to the Forty-third and Forty-fourth Congresses (March 4, 1873–March 3, 1877); declined to be a candidate for reelection in 1876; collector of internal revenue for the district of Nebraska from March 15, 1879, to March 30, 1883; appointed Assistant Secretary of the United States Treasury on April 27, 1891, and served until his resignation on October 31, 1892; Governor of Nebraska 1892–1895; died in Omaha, Nebr., May 13, 1909; interment in City Cemetery, Fort Calhoun, Washington County, Nebr.

CROUSE, George Washington, a Representative from Ohio; born in Tallmadge, Summit County, Ohio, November 23, 1832; attended the common schools; taught school for five years; moved to Akron, Ohio; deputy in offices of county auditor and treasurer 1855–1858; auditor of Summit County 1858–1863; served as county treasurer in 1863; manager in 1863 of the Akron branch of C. Altman & Co., dealers in farming implements; upon the organization of Altman, Miller & Co. in 1865, as a separate corporation, became secretary and treasurer, and later its president; during the Civil War served as sergeant in Company F, One Hundred and Sixty-fourth Regiment, Ohio Volunteer Infantry, and served in fortifications around Washington in 1864; trustee for the children's home; member and president of the city council for four years and of the board of education of the city of Akron four years; served as commissioner of Summit County in 1874 and 1875; member of the State senate 1885–1887; elected as a Republican to the Fiftieth Congress (March 4, 1887–March 3, 1889); declined to be a candidate for renomination in 1888; resumed former business activities; died in Akron, Ohio, January 5, 1912; interment in Glendale Cemetery.

CROW, Charles Augustus, a Representative from Missouri; born on a farm near Sikeston, Scott County, Mo., March 31, 1873; attended the common schools; moved to a farm near Bernie, Stoddard County, Mo., in August 1896 and engaged in agricultural pursuits; moved to Caruthersville, Pemiscot County, in 1901 and engaged in the real estate and insurance business; postmaster of Caruthersville from May 19, 1902, to January 14, 1909; elected as a Republican to the Sixty-first Congress (March 4, 1909–March 3, 1911); unsuccessful candidate for reelection in 1910 to the Sixty-second Congress; moved to Campbell, Dunklin County, Mo., in 1911 and resumed agricultural pursuits; also engaged in the real estate and insurance business; died in Campbell, Mo., March 20, 1938; interment in Woodlawn Cemetery.

CROW, William Evans (father of William J. Crow), a Senator from Pennsylvania; born in German Township, Fayette County, Pa., March 10, 1870; attended the public schools; was graduated from the Southwestern State Normal School in 1890, and also attended Waynesburg College; engaged in newspaper work for three years; studied law; was admitted to the bar in 1895 and commenced practice in Uniontown, Pa.; appointed assistant district attorney in 1896; was elected district attorney in November 1898 and served three years; chairman of the Republican county committee 1899–1901; delegate to various Republican State conventions; chairman of the Republican State committee in 1913, 1916, and 1918; delegate to the Republican National Conventions at Chicago in 1916 and 1920; member of the State senate from 1907 until October 24, 1921, when he resigned, having been appointed United States Senator; elected President pro tempore in 1909 and 1911; appointed as a Republican to the United States Senate October 17, 1921, to fill the vacancy caused by the death of Philander C. Knox, and served from October 24, 1921, until his death at his home, "Chalk Hill," near Uniontown, Fayette County, Pa., August 2, 1922; interment in Uniontown Cemetery.

CROW, William Josiah (son of William Evans Crow), a Representative from Pennsylvania; born in Uniontown, Fayette County, Pa., January 22, 1902; attended the public schools; was graduated from Pennsylvania Military College at Chester in 1922 and from Dickinson School of Law, Carlisle, Pa., in 1925; was admitted to the bar in 1926 and commenced practice in Uniontown, Pa.; assistant district attorney of Fayette County 1928–1932; elected mayor of Uniontown in 1938 and reelected in 1940 for a four-year term and served until called into active service from the Reserves as major of Ordnance June 4, 1941, being forty-one months overseas, in the Pacific Ocean area; separated from active service January 16, 1946, and returned to the Reserve Corps as a colonel of Ordnance; awarded the Bronze Star for meritorious service; elected as a Republican to the Eightieth Congress (January 3, 1947–January 3, 1949); unsuccessful candidate for reelection in 1948 to the Eighty-first Congress; resumed the practice of law; recalled to active duty with the Ordnance Corps in 1951 and served as chief of legislative coordination branch until 1956; became regional administrator, Securities and Exchange Commission, Washington, D. C., in January 1957; resides in Arlington, Va.

CROWE, Eugene Burgess, a Representative from Indiana; born near Jeffersonville, Clark County, Ind., January 5, 1878; attended the rural schools and Borden (Ind.) Academy; taught in county schools 1894–1896; moved to Bedford, Ind., in 1899 and engaged in the retail furniture business; also interested in real estate and banking; delegate to the Democratic State conventions 1908–1960; delegate to the Democratic National Conventions in 1928, 1944, 1948, 1952, 1956, and 1960; delegate to the Interparliamentary Union Congress at Oslo, Norway, in 1939; elected as a Democrat to the Seventy-second and to the four succeeding Congresses (March 4, 1931–January 3, 1941); unsuccessful candidate for reelection in 1940 to the Seventy-seventh Congress; member of the Anthony Wayne Memorial Commission in 1939 and 1940, serving as chairman in 1940; resumed his former business interests; president of Stone City National Bank and Greystone Hotel; director of Wabash Fire and Casualty Insurance Co.; is a resident of Bedford, Ind.

CROWELL, John, a Delegate from Alabama Territory and a Representative from Alabama; born in Halifax County, N. C., September 18, 1780; attended the public schools; moved to Alabama in 1815, having been appointed as agent of the Government to the Muscogees; settled in St. Stephens, Ala., in 1817; elected as a Delegate to the Fifteenth Congress and served from January 29, 1818, to March 3, 1819; upon the admission of Alabama as a State into the Union was elected as a Representative to the Sixteenth Congress and served from December 14, 1819, until March 3, 1821; in 1821 was appointed agent for the Creek Indians, then inhabiting western Georgia and eastern Alabama, and occupied that position until they were moved to the Indian Territory in 1836; died at Fort Mitchell, Ala., June 25, 1846; interment in a private cemetery at Fort Mitchell, Ala.

CROWELL, John, a Representative from Ohio; born in East Haddam, Middlesex County, Conn., September 15, 1801; moved to Ohio in 1806 with his parents, who settled in Rome, Ashtabula County; attended the district school; moved to Warren, Ohio, in 1822; attended Warren Academy 1822–1825; studied law; was admitted to the bar in 1827 and commenced practice in Warren; was also part owner and editor of the Western Reserve Chronicle at Warren; member of the State senate in 1840; elected as a Whig to the Thirtieth and Thirty-first Congresses (March 4, 1847–March 3, 1851); was not a candidate for renomination in 1850; moved to Cleveland, Ohio, in 1852 and resumed the practice of law; served in the State militia for twenty years, holding the rank of brigadier general and subsequently that of major general; became editor of the Western Law Monthly, published in Cleveland, and a member of the faculty of the Homeopathic Medical College; president of the Ohio State and Union Law College of Cleveland from 1862 to 1876, when he retired to private life owing to failing health; died in Cleveland, Ohio, March 8, 1883; interment in Lake View Cemetery.

CROWLEY, Joseph Burns, a Representative from Illinois; born in Coshocton, Coshocton County, Ohio, July 19, 1858; moved with his parents to a farm near St. Marie, Jasper County, Ill., in 1860 and to Robinson, Ill., in 1872; attended the common schools; engaged in mercantile pursuits 1876–1880; studied law; was admitted to the bar in May 1883 and began practice at Robinson, Crawford County, Ill.; president of the Robinson city school board 1884–1888; master in chancery 1886–1890; elected judge of Crawford County in November 1886, and reelected in 1890; appointed United States special Treasury agent in charge of the seal fisheries of Alaska in April 1893 and served until his resignation in April 1898; elected as a Democrat to the Fifty-sixth, Fifty-seventh, and Fifty-eighth Congresses (March 4,

1899–March 3, 1905); declined to be a candidate for renomination in 1904; resumed the practice of law in Robinson, Ill.; served as State's attorney of Crawford County 1912–1916; died in Robinson, Ill., June 25, 1931; interment in the old Robinson Cemetery.

CROWLEY, Miles, a Representative from Texas; born in Boston, Mass., February 22, 1859; attended the common schools; employed as a longshoreman; moved to Galveston in the seventies; assistant chief of the Galveston Fire Department; studied law; was admitted to the bar in 1892 and commenced practice; member of the State house of representatives in 1892; served in the State senate in 1893 and 1894; elected as a Democrat to the Fifty-fourth Congress (March 4, 1895–March 3, 1897); was not a candidate for reelection in 1896; resumed the practice of law in Galveston, Tex.; prosecuting attorney of Galveston County 1904–1912; elected judge of Galveston County Court in 1920, in which capacity he was serving at the time of his death in Galveston, Tex., on September 22, 1921; interment in Calvary Cemetery.

CROWLEY, Richard, a Representative from New York; born in Pendleton, near Lockport, Niagara County, N. Y., December 14, 1836; attended the public schools and Lockport Union School; studied law; was admitted to the bar in 1860 and commenced practice in Lockport; city attorney of Lockport in 1865 and 1866; admitted to practice before the Supreme Court of the United States in 1865; member of the State senate 1866–1870; appointed by President Grant United States district attorney for the northern district of New York on March 23, 1871; reappointed March 3, 1875, and served in that capacity until March 3, 1879, when he resigned, having been elected to Congress; elected as a Republican to the Forty-sixth and Forty-seventh Congresses (March 4, 1879–March 3, 1883); resumed the practice of law in Lockport, N. Y.; unsuccessful candidate for election in 1888 to the Fifty-first Congress; appointed by Governor Morton in 1896 as counsel for the State of New York in Civil War claims cases, in which capacity he was serving at the time of his death at Olcott Beach, near Lockport, Niagara County, N. Y., July 22, 1908; interment in Glenwood Cemetery.

CROWNINSHIELD, Benjamin Williams (brother of Jacob Crowninshield), a Representative from Massachusetts; born in Salem, Mass., December 27, 1772; prepared for college; engaged in mercantile pursuits in Salem, Mass.; member of the State house of representatives in 1811; served in the State senate in 1812; appointed Secretary of the Navy by President Madison December 19, 1814; reappointed by President Monroe and served in this capacity until October 1, 1818, when he resigned; presidential elector on the Democratic ticket of Monroe and Tompkins in 1820; again a member of the State house of representatives in 1821; elected as a Democrat to the Eighteenth and to the three succeeding Congresses (March 4, 1823–March 3, 1831); unsuccessful candidate for reelection in 1830 to the Twenty-second Congress; again a member of the State house of representatives in 1833; resumed his former business pursuits; died in Boston, Mass., February 3, 1851; interment in Mount Auburn Cemetery, Cambridge, Mass.

CROWNINSHIELD, Jacob (brother of Benjamin Williams Crowninshield), a Representative from Massachusetts; born in Salem, Mass., March 31, 1770; engaged in mercantile pursuits; unsuccessful Democratic candidate for election in 1798 to the Sixth Congress to fill the vacancy caused by the resignation of Dwight Foster; member of the State senate in 1801; was tendered the position of Secretary of the Navy by President Jefferson, but never entered upon his duties on account of ill health; elected as a Democrat to the Eighth, Ninth, and Tenth Congresses and served from March 4, 1803, until his death in Washington, D. C., on April 15, 1808; interment in Harmony Grove Cemetery, Salem, Mass.

CROWTHER, Frank, a Representative from New York; born in Liverpool, England, July 10, 1870; immigrated to the United States in 1872 with his parents, who settled in Canton, Mass.; attended the public schools; was graduated from the Lowell School of Design, a branch of the Massachusetts Institute of Technology, in 1888; designer of fabrics, carpets, and rugs for seven years; was graduated from Harvard Dental School in 1898 and commenced practice in Boston, Mass.; moved to Perth Amboy, N. J., in 1901 and continued the practice of dentistry; member of the New Jersey House of Assembly in 1904 and 1905; member of the Middlesex County Board of Taxation 1906–1909; moved to Schenectady, N. Y., in 1912 and continued the practice of his profession until elected to Congress; president of the common council of Schenectady in 1917 and 1918; elected as a Republican to the Sixty-sixth and to the eleven succeeding Congresses (March 4, 1919–January 3, 1943); was not a candidate for renomination in 1942; moved to Pueblo, Colo., in 1943 and engaged in violin study, landscape painting, and public speaking; died in Pueblo Colo., July 20, 1955; interment in Roselawn Cemetery.

CROWTHER, George Calhoun, a Representative from Missouri; born in Lancashire, England, on January 26, 1849; immigrated to the United States in 1855 with his parents, who settled in Dakota City, Nebr.; attended the public schools until his tenth year, when he became a printer's apprentice at Sioux City, Iowa; during the Civil War entered the Union Army in 1862, and was mustered out of the service July 14, 1865; moved to Kansas in 1866 and engaged in newspaper work until 1873; elected secretary of the Kansas State Senate in January 1869, and reelected in 1871 and 1873; again engaged in the printing and publishing of a newspaper 1875–1886; moved to St. Joseph, Mo., in 1877; appointed deputy sheriff of Buchanan County, Mo., in 1887; elected city treasurer of St. Joseph in 1888 and reelected in 1890; unsuccessful candidate for election in 1892 to the Fifty-third Congress; elected as a Republican to the Fifty-fourth Congress (March 4, 1895–March 3, 1897); unsuccessful candidate for reelection in 1896 to the Fifty-fifth Congress; unsuccessful candidate for mayor of St. Joseph in 1904; engaged in the manufacture of iron and steel in St. Joseph, Mo., until his death there March 18, 1914; interment in Oakland Cemetery.

CROXTON, Thomas, a Representative from Virginia; born in Tappahannock, Essex County, Va., March 8, 1822; attended the primary schools and the Tappahannock and Rappahannock Academies; was graduated from the law department of the University of Virginia at Charlottesville in 1842; was admitted to the bar and commenced practice in Tappahannock, Essex County, Va.; served as attorney for the Commonwealth from 1852 to 1865, when he resigned; during the Civil War served on the staff of Gen. George E. Pickett; presidential elector on the Democratic ticket of Hancock and English in 1880; elected as a Democrat to the Forty-ninth Congress (March 4, 1885–March 3, 1887); unsuccessful candidate for reelection in 1886 to the Fiftieth Congress; resumed the practice of law; also engaged in agricultural pursuits; elected judge of Essex County, Va., and served from 1892 until his resignation in 1901, when he retired from active pursuits; died in Tappahannock, Va., July 3, 1903; interment in St. John's Episcopal Churchyard.

CROZIER, John Hervey, a Representative from Tennessee; born in Knoxville, Tenn., February 10, 1812; attended the public schools; was graduated from the University of Tennessee at Knoxville in 1829; studied law; was admitted to the Tennessee bar and practiced in Knoxville; member of the State house of representatives 1837–1839; presidential elector on the Whig ticket of Clay and Frelinghuysen in 1844; elected as a Whig to the Twenty-ninth and Thirtieth Congresses (March 4, 1845–March 3, 1849); resumed the practice of his profession in Knoxville; affiliated with the Democratic Party in 1856; retired from active practice about 1866 and engaged in literary pursuits and historical research; died in Knoxville, Knox County, Tenn., October 25, 1889; interment in the Old Gray Cemetery.

CROZIER, Robert, a Senator from Kansas; born in Cadiz, Harrison County, Ohio, October 13, 1827; attended the public schools and an academy; studied law in Carrollton, Ohio, and was admitted to the bar October 13, 1848; prosecuting attorney of Carroll County 1848–1850; moved to Leavenworth, Kans., in 1856, where he established the Leavenworth Daily Times and also engaged in the practice of law; member of the Territorial council in 1857 and 1858; appointed United States attorney for the district of Kansas by President Lincoln October 24, 1861, and served until January 1864, when he resigned; elected chief justice of Kansas Supreme Court November 3, 1863, and served from January 5, 1864, until January 14, 1867; cashier and manager of the First National Bank of Leavenworth; appointed as a Republican to the United States Senate to fill the vacancy caused by the resignation of Alexander Caldwell and served from November 24, 1873, to February 12, 1874, when a successor was elected; was not a candidate for election; resumed the practice of his profession in Leavenworth, Kans.; district judge of the first judicial district of Kansas 1876–1892; member of the board of directors of the Kansas Historical Society 1886–1889; died in Leavenworth, Leavenworth County, Kans., October 2, 1895; interment in Mount Muncie Cemetery.

CRUDUP, Josiah, a Representative from North Carolina; born in Wakelon, Wake County, N. C., January 13, 1791; attended a private school in Louisburg, N. C., and Columbian College (now George Washington University), Washington, D. C.; studied theology; was ordained as a Baptist minister and, excepting the service in Congress, continued in the ministry until his death; engaged in farming; served in the State senate in 1820; member of the State house of representatives 1821–1823; elected as a Whig to the Seventeenth Congress (March 4, 1821–March 3, 1823); unsuccessful candidate for reelection in 1822 to the Eighteenth Congress; resumed agricultural pursuits; delegate to the State constitutional convention in 1835; died near Kittrell, Vance County, N. C., May 20, 1872; interment in the family burial ground at his home near Kittrell, N. C.

CRUGER, Daniel, a Representative from New York; born in Sunbury, Pa., December 22, 1780; attended the public schools; learned the printer's trade; published the Owego Democrat at Owego, N. Y.; studied law; was admitted to the bar in 1805, and commenced practice in Bath, N. Y.; served as major in the War of 1812; member of the State assembly 1814–1816 and again in 1826 and served as speaker in 1816; elected as a Democrat to the Fifteenth Congress (March 4, 1817–March 3, 1819); district attorney of the seventh district of New York 1815–1818, and of Steuben County 1818–1821; resumed the practice of law; moved to Wheeling, Va. (now West Virginia); died in Wheeling July 12, 1843; interment in the Stone Church Cemetery.

CRUMP, Edward Hull, a Representative from Tennessee; born on a farm near Holly Springs, Marshall County, Miss., October 2, 1874; attended the public schools; engaged in agricultural pursuits; apprenticed as a printer in 1890; moved to Memphis, Tenn., in 1892; employed as a bookkeeper; engaged in the wholesale mercantile business, the manufacture of harness and buggies, and later in the banking, mortgage-loan, and real-estate businesses; also interested in farming; delegate to the Democratic State conventions in 1902 and 1904; member of the Memphis Board of Public Works in 1905; fire and police commissioner in 1907; mayor of Memphis 1910–1916; delegate to the Democratic National Conventions in 1912, 1924, 1928, 1936, 1940, 1944, and 1948; county treasurer of Shelby County 1917–1923; member of the Democratic State committee 1926–1930 and of the Democratic National Committee 1936–1945; elected as a Democrat to the Seventy-second and Seventy-third Congresses (March 4, 1931–January 3, 1935); was not a candidate for renomination in 1934; Regent of the Smithsonian Institution 1931–1935; again elected mayor of Memphis, in 1939; resumed his activities in the mortgage-loan, investment, real-estate, and insurance businesses; also engaged in farming; died in Memphis, Tenn., October 16, 1954; interment in Elmwood Cemetery.

CRUMP, George William, a Representative from Virginia; born in Powhatan County, Va., September 26, 1786; attended Washington College (now Washington and Lee University), Lexington, Va.; was graduated from Princeton College in 1805; studied medicine at the University of Pennsylvania, Philadelphia, Pa., 1806–1808; member of the State house of delegates 1817–1822 and 1825–1828; elected as a Jackson Democrat to the Nineteenth Congress to fill the vacancy caused by the resignation of John Randolph and served from January 21, 1826, to March 3, 1827; unsuccessful candidate for reelection in 1826 to the Twentieth Congress; was appointed by President Jackson as chief clerk of the Pension Bureau in 1832, which position he held until his death; moved to Powhatan County, Va., where he died on October 1, 1848; interment on his home grounds at "Log Castle" on Swift Creek, Chesterfield County, near Colonial House, Va.

CRUMP, Rousseau Owen, a Representative from Michigan; born in Pittsford, Monroe County, N. Y., May 20, 1843; attended the public schools in Pittsford and Rochester; moved to Plainwell, Mich., in 1869 and engaged in the lumber business in Allegan and Kalamazoo Counties; moved to West Bay City in 1881 and established a sawmill and box factory; member of the board of aldermen 1889–1892; mayor of West Bay City 1893–1895; member of the State house of representatives 1895–1901; elected as a Republican to the Fifty-fourth and to the three succeeding Congresses and served from March 4, 1895, until his death in West Bay City, Mich., May 1, 1901; interment in Elm Lawn Cemetery, Bay City, Bay County, Mich.

CRUMPACKER, Edgar Dean (father of Maurice Edgar Crumpacker and cousin of Shepard J. Crumpacker, Jr.), a Representative from Indiana; born in Westville, La Porte County, Ind., May 27, 1851; attended the common schools and Valparaiso Academy, Valparaiso, Ind.; studied law in the law department of Indiana University at Bloomington; was admitted to the bar in 1876 and commenced practice in Valparaiso, Ind.; prosecuting attorney for the thirty-first judical district of Indiana 1884–1888; served as appellate judge, by appointment of Governor Hovey, from March 1891 to January 1, 1893; elected as a Republican to the Fifty-fifth and to the seven succeeding Congresses (March 4, 1897–March 3, 1913); unsuccessful candidate for reelection in 1912 to the Sixty-third Congress; resumed the practice of law in Valparaiso, Porter County, Ind., where he died May 19, 1920; interment in Graceland Cemetery.

CRUMPACKER, Maurice Edgar (son of Edgar Dean Crumpacker and cousin of Shepard J. Crumpacker, Jr.), a Representative from Oregon; born in Valparaiso, Porter County, Ind., December 19, 1886; attended the public schools of Valparaiso, Ind., and Washington, D. C.; was graduated from the Culver (Ind.) Military Academy in 1905 and from the University of Michigan at Ann Arbor in 1909; studied law at Harvard University; was admitted to the bar in 1912 and commenced practice in Portland, Oreg.; during the First World War was commissioned December 31, 1917, as first lieutenant in the aviation section of the Signal Reserve Corps; accepted appointment as captain in the Air Service (production), National Army, July 8, 1918, and served until December 27, 1918, when he was honorably discharged as captain in the Air Service (aircraft production); special deputy district attorney for Multnomah County, Oreg., in 1921; unsuccessful candidate for the Republican nomination for Congress in 1922; elected as a Republican to the Sixty-ninth and Seventieth Congresses and served from March 4, 1925, until his death in San Francisco, Calif., July 24, 1927; interment in Riverview Cemetery, Portland, Oreg.

CRUMPACKER, Shepard J., Jr. (cousin of Edgar Dean Crumpacker and Maurice Edgar Crumpacker), a Representative from Indiana; born in South Bend, St. Joseph County, Ind., February 13, 1917; attended the public schools; was graduated from Northwestern University, Evanston, Ill., in 1938, and from the law school of the University of Michigan at Ann Arbor in 1941; was admitted to the bar the same year and commenced the practice of law in South Bend, Ind.; entered the United States Army Air Corps as a private September 26, 1941, and advanced through the ranks to flight chief in a fighter squadron; commissioned a lieutenant in 1943 and assigned to heavy-bomber maintenance; relieved from active duty as a first lieutenant March 1, 1946; major in the Air Force Reserve; owns and operates a farm; elected as a Republican to the Eighty-second, Eighty-third, and Eighty-fourth Congresses (January 3, 1951–January 3, 1957); did not seek renomination in 1956; resumed the practice of law; resides in South Bend, Ind.

CRUTCHFIELD, William, a Representative from Tennessee; born in Greeneville, Greene County, Tenn., November 16, 1824; attended the common schools; moved to McMinn County, Tenn., in 1840 and remained there four years; settled in Jacksonville, Ala., in 1844 and engaged in agricultural pursuits; became a permanent resident of Chattanooga in 1850; during the Civil War never enlisted but served in the Union Army as honorary captain in the Chickamauga campaign; was with General Thomas during the siege of Chattanooga, and was an active and important assistant to General Steedman and other commanders until the close of the war; elected as a Republican to the Forty-third Congress (March 4, 1873–March 3, 1875); was not a candidate for renomination in 1874; resumed agricultural pursuits; died in Chattanooga, Tenn., January 24, 1890; interment in the family lot in Old Citizens Cemetery.

CULBERSON, Charles Allen (son of David Browning Culberson), a Senator from Texas; born in Dadeville, Tallapoosa County, Ala., June 10, 1855; moved to Texas with his parents, who settled first in Gilmer and later in Jefferson; attended the common schools, and was graduated from the Virginia Military Institute at Lexington in 1874; studied law at the University of Virginia at Charlottesville in 1876 and 1877; was admitted to the bar in 1877 and commenced practice in Jefferson, Tex.; moved to Dallas, Tex., in 1887; delegate to the Democratic State convention in 1890; attorney general of Texas 1890–1894; Governor of Texas 1894–1898; delegate to all Democratic National Conventions from 1896 to 1916; elected as a Democrat to the United States Senate January 25, 1899; reelected in 1905, 1911, and again in 1916, and served from March 4, 1899, to March 3, 1923; unsuccessful candidate for reelection in 1922; retired from public life, and owing to failing health did not engage in active business pursuits; lived in retirement until his death in Washington, D. C., March 19, 1925; interment in East Oakwood Cemetery, Fort Worth, Tex.

CULBERSON, David Browning (father of Charles Allen Culberson), a Representative from Texas; born in Troup County, Ga., September 29, 1830; pursued preparatory studies in Brownwood College, La Grange, Ga.; studied law; was admitted to the bar in 1851 and commenced practice in Dadeville, Ala.; moved to Texas in 1856; settled in Jefferson, Marion County, in 1861 and continued the practice of law; member of the State house of representatives in 1859; during the Civil War entered the Confederate Army as a private; promoted to the rank of colonel of the Eighteenth Texas Infantry; assigned to duty in 1864 as adjutant general of the State of Texas with the rank of colonel; again a member of the State house of representatives in 1864; elected to the State senate in 1873 and served until his resignation, having been elected to Congress; elected as a Democrat to the Forty-fourth and to the ten succeeding Congresses (March 4, 1875–March 3, 1897); declined to be a candidate for renomination in 1896; appointed by President McKinley on June 21, 1897, as one of the commissioners to codify the laws of the United States and served in this capacity until his death in Jefferson, Tex., May 7, 1900; interment in Oaklawn Cemetery.

CULBERTSON, William Constantine, a Representative from Pennsylvania; born in Edinboro, Erie County, Pa., November 25, 1825; attended the common schools of his native town; engaged in lumbering on the Allegheny River in Jefferson County, Pa.; also operated a mill and a sash, door, and blind factory at Covington, Ky.; moved to Girard, Pa., in 1863; purchased extensive tracts of timberland in Michigan, Wisconsin, and other States; later became interested in agricultural pursuits in Minnesota and in his native county; president of the Citizens' National Bank of Corry, Pa.; elected as a Republican to the Fifty-first Congress (March 4, 1889–March 3, 1891); unsuccessful candidate for renomination in 1890; resumed his former business activities; died in Girard, Erie County, Pa., on May 24, 1906; interment in Girard Cemetery.

CULBERTSON, William Wirt, a Representative from Kentucky; born near Lewistown, Mifflin County, Pa., September 22, 1835; moved with his parents to Kentucky; attended the common schools; engaged in the manufacture of iron; enlisted as a private in the Union Army during the Civil War in Company F, Twenty-seventh Regiment, Ohio Volunteer Infantry, July 16, 1861; promoted to the rank of captain August 2, 1861; resigned March 3, 1864; member of the State house of representatives in 1870; served in the State senate in 1873; delegate to the Republican National Convention at Cincinnati in 1876 and at Chicago in 1880 and 1884; mayor of Ashland, Ky., in 1882 and 1883 when he resigned; elected as a Republican to the Forty-eighth Congress (March 4, 1883–March 3, 1885); died in Oxford, Butler County, Ohio, on October 31, 1911; interment in Ashland Cemetery, Ashland, Ky.

CULBRETH, Thomas, a Representative from Maryland; born in Kent County, Del., eight miles northeast of Greensboro, Md., April 13, 1786; attended the public schools and studied under private tutors; moved to Denton, Caroline County, Md., in 1806; was clerk in a store in Denton; member of the congressional committee at Hillsboro in 1810; member of the State house of delegates in 1812 and 1813; cashier of the State Bank at Denton in

1813; elected as a Democrat to the Fifteenth and Sixteenth Congresses (March 4, 1817–March 3, 1821); declined to be a candidate for reelection in 1820 to the Seventeenth Congress and for election in 1822 to the Eighteenth Congress; appointed chief judge of the Caroline County orphans' court in 1822; clerk of the executive council of Maryland 1825–1838, and resided in Annapolis, Md.; returned to Denton, Md., 1838 and engaged in mercantile pursuits; soon afterward moved to "Orrell Farm," near Greensboro, where he died April 16, 1843; interment in the family cemetery on the farm.

CULKIN, Francis Dugan, a Representative from New York; born in Oswego, Oswego, County, N. Y., November 10, 1874; attended the public schools in Oswego and St. Andrew's College and the University of Rochester in Rochester, N. Y.; newspaper reporter in Rochester, N. Y., 1894–1902; studied law; was admitted to the bar in 1902 and commenced practice in Oswego, N. Y.; served as a private, Company D, Third New York Volunteers, in the Spanish-American War; captain in the New York National Guard 1901–1908; city attorney of Oswego, N. Y., 1906–1910; district attorney of Oswego County, N. Y., 1911–1921; judge of Oswego County 1921–1928; trustee of the Oswego City Library and the Oswego City Hospital; member of the Thomas Jefferson Bicentennial Commission and the Thomas Jefferson Memorial Commission; delegate to several Republican National Conventions; elected as a Republican to the Seventieth Congress to fill the vacancy caused by the death of Thaddeus C. Sweet; reelected to the Seventy-first and to the seven succeeding Congresses and served from November 6, 1928, until his death in Oswego, N. Y., on August 4, 1943; interment in St. Paul's Cemetery.

CULLEN, Elisha Dickerson, a Representative from Delaware; born in Millsboro, Sussex County, Del., April 23, 1799; attended Princeton College; studied law; was admitted to the bar in 1821 and commenced practice in Georgetown, Del.; elected as the candidate of the American Party to the Thirty-fourth Congress (March 4, 1855–March 3, 1857); was an unsuccessful candidate for reelection in 1856 to the Thirty-fifth Congress; resumed the practice of law; died in Georgetown, Del., on February 8, 1862; interment in the Presbyterian Churchyard, Lewes, Del.

CULLEN, Thomas Henry, a Representative from New York; born in Brooklyn, N. Y., March 29, 1868; attended the local parochial schools, and was graduated from St. Francis College, Brooklyn, N. Y., in 1880; became engaged in the marine insurance and shipping business; member of the Senate assembly 1896–1898; served in the State senate 1899–1918; delegate to the Democratic National Conventions in 1912, 1916, 1920, 1924, 1928, 1932, and alternate in 1940; elected as a Democrat to the Sixty-sixth and to the twelve succeeding Congresses and served from March 4, 1919, until his death in Washington, D. C., on March 1, 1944; interment in Holy Cross Cemetery, Brooklyn, N. Y.

CULLEN, William, a Representative from Illinois; born in County Donegal, Ireland, March 4, 1826; immigrated to the United States in 1832 with his parents, who settled in Pittsburgh, Pa.; attended the public schools and the Allegheny Academy at Pittsburgh; moved to Adams Township, La Salle County, Ill., in 1846 and engaged in agricultural pursuits; sheriff of La Salle County in 1864 and 1865; moved to Ottawa, La Salle County, Ill., in 1865; political editor of the Ottawa Republican 1871–1887; elected as a Republican to the Forty-seventh and Forty-eighth Congresses (March 4, 1881–March 3, 1885); unsuccessful

candidate for renomination in 1884; lived in retirement in Ottawa, Ill., until his death there January 17, 1914; interment in Ottawa Avenue Cemetery.

CULLOM, Alvan (brother of William Cullom and uncle of Shelby Moore Cullom), a Representative from Tennessee; born in Monticello, Ky., September 4, 1797; received a liberal schooling; studied law; was admitted to the bar in 1823 and commenced practice in Monroe, Overton County, Tenn.; member of the State house of representatives in 1835 and 1836; elected as a Democrat to the Twenty-eighth and Twenty-ninth Congresses (March 4, 1843–March 3, 1847); resumed the practice of law; circuit judge of the fourth judicial circuit of Tennessee 1850–1852; member of the peace convention of 1861 held in Washington, D. C., in an effort to devise means to prevent the impending war; died in Livingston, Overton County, Tenn., July 20, 1877; interment in Bethlehem Cemetery, near Livingston.

CULLOM, Shelby Moore (nephew of Alvan Cullom and William Cullom), a Representative and a Senator from Illinois; born in Wayne County, Ky., November 22, 1829; moved with his father to Tazewell County, Ill., in 1830; received an academic and university training; moved to Springfield, Ill., in 1853; studied law; was admitted to the bar in 1855 and commenced practice in Springfield; elected city attorney in 1855; presidential elector in 1856; member of the State house of representatives in 1856, 1860, and 1861, and served as speaker of the house during the second year; elected as a Republican to the Thirty-ninth, Fortieth, and Forty-first Congresses (March 4, 1865–March 3, 1871); again a member of the State house of representatives in 1873 and 1874 and served as speaker in 1873; delegate to the Republican National Convention at Philadelphia in 1872 and placed General Grant in nomination for President; also a delegate to the Republican National Convention at Chicago in 1884 and at Minneapolis in 1892; elected Governor of Illinois in 1876 and 1880 and served from January 8, 1877, until February 5, 1883, when he resigned; elected to the United States Senate in 1882; reelected in 1888, 1894, 1900, and 1906 and served from March 4, 1883, to March 3, 1913; Regent of the Smithsonian Institution from March 24, 1885, to March 3, 1913; chairman and resident commissioner of the Lincoln Memorial Commission in 1913 and 1914; member of the commission appointed to prepare a system of laws for the Hawaiian Islands; died in Washington, D. C., January 28, 1914; interment in Oak Ridge Cemetery, Springfield, Ill.

CULLOM, William (brother of Alvan Cullom and uncle of Shelby Moore Cullom), a Representative from Tennessee; born near Monticello, Wayne County, Ky., June 4, 1810; attended the public schools; studied law in Lexington, Ky.; was admitted to the bar and practiced in the courts of Kentucky and Tennessee; moved to Carthage, Tenn.: member of the State house of representatives; served in the State senate; elected as a Whig to the Thirty-second and Thirty-third Congresses (March 4, 1851–March 3, 1855); unsuccessful candidate for reelection in 1854 to the Thirty-fourth Congress; appointed Clerk of the National House of Representatives in the Thirty-fourth Congress and served from February 4, 1856, to December 6, 1857; resumed the practice of law; died in Clinton, Tenn., December 6, 1896; interment in McAdoo Cemetery, Clinton, Tenn., and later reinterred in Mount Olivet Cemetery, Chattanooga, Tenn.

CULLOP, William Allen, a Representative from Indiana; born near Oaktown, Knox County, Ind., March 28, 1853; attended the common schools; was graduated from Hanover (Ind.) College in June 1878; professor for two years in Vincennes (Ind.) University; studied law; was admitted to the bar in 1881 and commenced practice in Vincennes, Ind.; prosecuting attorney of the twelfth judicial circuit 1883–1886; member of the State house of representatives 1891–1893; delegate to the Democratic National Conventions in 1892 and 1896; presidential elector on the Democratic ticket of Bryan and Stevenson in 1900; chairman of the committee on resolutions at the Indiana Democratic State convention in 1904 and reported the platform to the convention; elected as a Democrat to the Sixty-first and to the three succeeding Congresses (March 4, 1909–March 3, 1917); unsuccessful candidate for renomination in 1916; unsuccessful candidate for the Democratic nomination as United States Senator in 1926; resumed the practice of law and was also interested in various business enterprises; died in Vincennes, Ind., October 9, 1927; interment in Greenlawn Cemetery.

CULPEPPER, John, a Representative from North Carolina; born near Wadesboro, Anson County, N. C., in 1761; attended the public schools; became a minister in the Baptist Church; presented credentials as a Federalist Member-elect to the Tenth Congress and served from March 4, 1807, until January 2, 1808, when the seat was declared vacant as the result of a contest on account of alleged irregularities; subsequently reelected to fill the vacancy declared by the House of Representatives and served from February 23, 1808, to March 3, 1809; elected to the Thirteenth and Fourteenth Congresses (March 4, 1813–March 3, 1817); unsuccessful candidate for reelection in 1816 to the Fifteenth Congress; elected to the Sixteenth Congress (March 4, 1819–March 3, 1821); unsuccessful candidate for reelection in 1820 to the Seventeenth Congress; elected to the Eighteenth Congress (March 4, 1823–March 3, 1825); unsuccessful candidate for reelection in 1824 to the Nineteenth Congress; elected to the Twentieth Congress (March 4, 1827–March 3, 1829); declined to be candidate for reelection in 1828 and retired from public life; died at the residence of his son in Darlington County, S. C., in January 1841; interment in the cemetery at Society Hill, S. C.

CULVER, Charles Vernon, a Representative from Pennsylvania; born in Logan, Hocking County, Ohio, September 6, 1830; received a liberal preparatory schooling and attended the Ohio Wesleyan University, Delaware, Ohio; moved to Pennsylvania and settled in Reno, Venango County, and engaged in mercantile pursuits; also became interested in the development of oil in Venango County, Pa., and the establishment of national banks in thirteen cities throughout the East; elected as a Republican to the Thirty-ninth Congress (March 4, 1865–March 3, 1867); was not a candidate for renomination in 1866; while a Member of Congress became bankrupt and was imprisoned in 1866, but after a prolonged trial was acquitted; resumed operations in the oil business, with headquarters in Franklin, Venango County, Pa.; died, while on a business trip, in Philadelphia, Pa., January 10, 1909; interment in Franklin Cemetery, Franklin, Pa.

CULVER, Erastus Dean, a Representative from New York; born in Champlain, Washington County, N. Y., on March 15, 1803; was graduated from the University of Vermont at Burlington in 1826; studied law; was admitted to the bar in 1831 and commenced practice in Fort Ann, N. Y.; moved to Greenwich, N. Y., in 1836; member of the State assembly 1838–1840; elected as a Whig to the Twenty-ninth Congress (March 4, 1845–March 3, 1847); moved to Brooklyn, N. Y., in 1850; judge of the city court of Brooklyn 1854–1861; appointed by President Lincoln as Minister Resident to Venezuela and served in that capacity from 1862 to 1866; died in Greenwich, Washington County, N. Y., October 13, 1889; interment in the Culver vault in Greenwich Cemetery.

CUMBACK, William, a Representative from Indiana; born near Mount Carmel, Franklin County, Ind., March 24, 1829; attended the common schools and was graduated from Miami University, Oxford, Ohio; taught school two years; studied law at the Cincinnati Law School; was admitted to the bar and commenced practice in Greensburg, Ind., in 1853; elected as a Republican to the Thirty-fourth Congress (March 4, 1855–March 3, 1857); unsuccessful candidate for reelection in 1856; resumed the practice of law; presidential elector on the Republican ticket of Lincoln and Hamlin in 1860; appointed a paymaster in the Army and served throughout the Civil War; member of the State senate in 1866; Lieutenant Governor of Indiana in 1868; unsuccessful for election to the United States Senate in 1869; United States revenue collector 1871–1883; trustee of De Pauw University, Greencastle, Ind.; unsuccessful candidate for nomination for Governor in 1896; died in Greensburg, Ind., July 31, 1905; interment in South Park Cemetery.

CUMMING, Thomas William, a Representative from New York; born in Frederick, Md., in 1814 or 1815; moved to Georgia; appointed a midshipman in the United States Navy May 19, 1832; was promoted to passed midshipman June 23, 1838, and served until February 23, 1841, when he resigned; while in the Navy was a member of the Wilkes exploring expedition in 1838; moved to Brooklyn, N. Y.; became a druggist and importer of drugs in New York City and subsequently engaged in mercantile pursuits in Brooklyn, N. Y., 1843–1853; elected as a Democrat to the Thirty-third Congress (March 4, 1853–March 3, 1855); died in Brooklyn, N. Y., October 13, 1855; interment in Greenwood Cemetery.

CUMMING, William, a Delegate from North Carolina; born in Edenton, N. C.; studied law; was admitted to the bar and practiced; member of the North Carolina Provincial Congress in 1776; member of the State house of commons in 1781, 1783, 1784, and 1788; Member of the Continental Congress in 1784–1786; nominated for judge in 1790.

CUMMINGS, Amos Jay, a Representative from New York; born in Conkling, Broome County, N. Y., May 15, 1841; attended the common schools; apprenticed to the printing trade when twelve years of age; was with Walker in the last invasion of Nicaragua in October 1858; during the Civil War served as sergeant major of the Twenty-sixth New Jersey Regiment, Second Brigade, Sixth Corps, Army of the Potomac; filled editorial positions on the New York Tribune under Horace Greeley, the New York Sun, and the New York Express; elected as a Democrat to the Fiftieth Congress (March 4, 1887–March 3, 1889); declined renomination in 1888, but was subsequently elected to the Fifty-first Congress to fill the vacancy caused by the death of Samuel S. Cox; reelected to the Fifty-second and Fifty-third Congresses and served from November 5, 1889, to November 21, 1894, when he resigned; elected to the Fifty-fourth Congress to fill the vacancy caused by the death of Representative-elect Andrew J. Campbell; reelected to the Fifty-fifth, Fifty-sixth, and Fifty-seventh Congresses and served from November 5, 1895, until his death in Baltimore, Md., May 2, 1902; interment in Clinton Cemetery, Irvington, N. J.

CUMMINGS, Fred Nelson, a Representative from Colorado; born on a farm near Groveton, Coos County, N. H., September 18, 1864; in 1865 moved with his parents to Clinton, Iowa, and in 1879 to a farm near West Union, Custer County, Nebr.; attended the rural schools; engaged in agricultural pursuits and the raising of livestock; studied law; was admitted to the bar in 1891 and commenced practice in Custer County, Nebr.; moved to Fort Collins, Colo., in 1906 and resumed agricultural pursuits; member of the city council of Fort Collins 1909–1913; elected as a Democrat to the Seventy-third and to the three succeeding Congresses (March 4, 1933–January 3, 1941); unsuccessful candidate for reelection in 1940 to the Seventy-seventh Congress; resumed his former pursuits; died in Fort Collins, Colo., November 10, 1952; interment in Grandview Cemetery.

CUMMINGS, Henry Johnson Brodhead, a Representative from Iowa; born in Newton, Sussex County, N. J., May 21, 1831; attended the public schools of Muncy, Pa.; edited a newspaper in Schuylkill County, Pa., in 1850; studied law, and was admitted to the bar at Williamsport, Pa., in 1855; moved to Iowa in 1856 and settled in Winterset, Madison County; prosecuting attorney of Madison County 1856–1858; during the Civil War entered the Union Army in July 1861; was made captain of Company F, Fourth Regiment, Iowa Volunteer Infantry, August 15, 1861, to date from July 20, 1861; honorably discharged September 4, 1862, to enable him to accept the commission of colonel of the Thirty-ninth Regiment, Iowa Volunteer Infantry, September 12, 1862, and was honorably discharged December 22, 1864; became editor and proprietor of the Winterset Madisonian in 1869; elected as a Republican to the Forty-fifth Congress (March 4, 1877–March 3, 1879); unsuccessful candidate for reelection in 1878; died in Winterset, Iowa, April 16, 1909; interment in Winterset Cemetery.

CUMMINGS, Herbert Wesley, a Representative from Pennsylvania; born in West Chillisquaque Township, Northumberland County, Pa., July 13, 1873; attended the public schools; was graduated from the Lewisburg (Pa.) High School in 1890; studied law; was admitted to the bar May 7, 1897, and commenced practice in Sunbury, Pa.; district attorney of Northumberland County in 1901 and 1904–1908; elected judge of the common pleas court of Northumberland County in 1911 and served ten years as president judge; elected as a Democrat to the Sixty-eighth Congress (March 4, 1923–March 3, 1925); unsuccessful candidate for reelection in 1924 to the Sixty-ninth Congress; resumed the practice of law until November 18, 1935, when he was appointed judge of Northumberland County; subsequently elected and served until January 7, 1946; resumed the practice of law and is a resident of Sunbury, Pa.

CUMMINS, Albert Baird, a Senator from Iowa; born near Carmichaels, Greene County, Pa., February 15, 1850; attended the public schools, a preparatory academy, and three years at Waynesburg (Pa.) College; moved to Iowa; engaged as a carpenter for a short time; clerked in the office of the recorder of Clayton County; assistant surveyor of Allen County; engaged in railroad building; studied law; was admitted to the bar in 1875 and commenced practice in Chicago; returned to Des Moines, Iowa, in 1878, where he continued the practice of law; delegate to every Republican State and National convention from 1880 until his death; member of the State house of representatives 1888–1890; presidential elector on the Republican ticket of Harrison and Reid in 1892; unsuccessful candidate for election to the United States Senate in 1894 and 1900; member of the Republican National Committee from 1896 to 1900; Governor of Iowa from January 1902 until November 24, 1908, when he resigned, having been elected Senator; unsuccessful candidate for Senator in March 1908; elected as a Republican to the United States Senate in 1908 to fill the vacancy caused by the death of William B. Allison; reelected in 1909, 1914, and again in 1920, and served from November 24, 1908, until his death; President pro tempore of the Senate from May 19, 1919, to March 3, 1925; unsuccessful candidate for renomination in 1926; died in Des Moines, Iowa, July 30, 1926; interment in Woodland Cemetery.

CUMMINS, John D., a Representative from Ohio; born in Pennsylvania in 1791; attended the public schools, and was graduated from Jefferson College, Canonsburg, Pa., in 1834; studied law; was admitted to the bar and commenced practice in New Philadelphia, Ohio; prosecuting attorney of Tuscarawas County 1836–1841; elected as a Democrat to the Twenty-ninth and Thirtieth Congresses (March 4, 1845–March 3, 1849); died in Milwaukee, Wis., while attending a session of the circuit court, September 11, 1849.

CUNNINGHAM, Francis Alanson, a Representative from Ohio; born in Abbeville District, S. C., November 9, 1804; moved to Eaton, Ohio, in 1826; taught school; studied medicine and commenced practice in 1829; clerk of the court of Preble County in 1833; elected as a Democrat to the Twenty-ninth Congress (March 4, 1845–March 3, 1847); unsuccessful candidate for reelection in 1846 to the Thirtieth Congress; studied law; was admitted to the bar in 1847 and began practice in Eaton; appointed additional paymaster of Volunteers by President Polk December 30, 1847; was commissioned paymaster in the Regular Army March 2, 1849, and was retired from active service August 27, 1863; died in Eaton, Preble County, Ohio, August 16, 1864; interment in Mount Hill Cemetery.

CUNNINGHAM, Glenn Clarence, a Representative from Nebraska; born in Omaha, Douglas County, Nebr., September 10, 1912; attended the public schools; was graduated from the University of Omaha in 1935; salesman for Aetna Life Insurance Co., Omaha, Nebr., 1935–1937; executive secretary of Omaha Junior Chamber of Commerce 1936–1940 and president in 1945; manager of the convention bureau, Omaha Chamber of Commerce, in 1940 and 1941; manager of Omaha Safety Council 1942–1947; member of Omaha Board of Education 1946–1948; named Nebraska's outstanding young man in 1946; organized Glenn Cunningham & Co., an insurance agency, in 1947; member of Omaha City Council in 1947 and 1948; mayor of Omaha 1949–1954; appointed Nebraska State Director, Savings Bonds Division, United States Treasury, in 1954 and served until April 1956; delegate to the Republican National Conventions in 1948 and 1952; elected as a Republican to the Eighty-fifth and Eighty-sixth Congresses (January 3, 1957–January 3, 1961). *Reelected to the Eighty-seventh Congress.*

CUNNINGHAM, Paul Harvey, a Representative from Iowa; born on a farm in Indiana County, near Kent, Pa., June 15, 1890; attended the public schools; was graduated from State Teachers College, Indiana, Pa., in 1911, from the literary department of the University of Michigan at Ann Arbor in 1914, and from its law department in 1915; was admitted to the bar in 1915 and commenced practice in Grand Rapids, Mich.; during the First World War served as a first lieutenant of Infantry 1917–1919; moved to Des Moines, Iowa, in 1919 and continued the practice of law; member of the Iowa National Guard 1920–1923; member of the State house of representatives 1933–1937; elected as a Republican to the Seventy-seventh and to the eight succeeding Congresses (January 3, 1941–January 3, 1959); unsuccessful candidate for reelection in 1958 to the Eighty-sixth Congress; resumed the practice of law; died at his summer home on Gull Lake, Brainerd, Minn., July 16, 1961; interment in Masonic Cemetery, Des Moines, Iowa.

CURLEY, Edward Walter, a Representative from New York; born in Easton, Northampton County, Pa., May 23, 1873; moved to New York City, N. Y., with his parents in 1874; attended the public schools and the College of the City of New York; engaged in the building industry 1892–1900, and in the builders' and contractors' machinery and equipment business

1900–1916; member of the New York City Board of Aldermen from January 1, 1916, until November 5, 1935, when he resigned, having been elected to Congress; elected as a Democrat to the Seventy-fourth Congress to fill the vacancy caused by the death of Anthony J. Griffin; reelected to the Seventy-fifth and Seventy-sixth Congresses and served from November 5, 1935, until his death in New York City, N. Y., on January 6, 1940; interment in Kensico Cemetery, Valhalla, Westchester County, N. Y.

CURLEY, James Michael, a Representative from Massachusetts; born in Boston, Mass., November 20, 1874; attended the public, grammar, and high schools of Boston; salesman for Logan, Johnston & Co., a bakers' and confectioners' supply firm; engaged in the real-estate and insurance business; member of the Boston Common Council in 1900 and 1901; served in the State house of representatives in 1902 and 1903; member of the Boston Board of Aldermen 1904–1909; member of the Boston City Council in 1910 and 1911; elected as a Democrat to the Sixty-second and Sixty-third Congresses and served from March 4, 1911, until his resignation, effective February 4, 1914, having been elected mayor of Boston, in which capacity he served from 1914 to 1918; president of Hibernia Savings Bank, Boston, Mass.; again served as mayor, 1922–1926 and 1930–1934; Governor of Massachusetts 1935–1937; unsuccessful Democratic candidate for the United States Senate in 1936; unsuccessful candidate for mayor of Boston in 1938 and again in 1941; member of the Democratic National Committee in 1941 and 1942; elected to the Seventy-eighth and Seventy-ninth Congresses (January 3, 1943–January 3, 1947); was not a candidate for renomination in 1946; again elected mayor of Boston on November 5, 1946, and served until January 1950; unsuccessful candidate for the Democratic nomination for mayor of Boston in 1951 and again in 1955; appointed a member of the State Labor Relations Commission in 1957; died in Boston, Mass., November 12, 1958; interment in Old Calvary Cemetery.

CURRIE, Gilbert Archibald, a Representative from Michigan; born in Midland Township, Midland County, Mich., September 19, 1882; attended the district school, Midland (Mich.) High School, and was graduated from the law department of the University of Michigan at Ann Arbor in 1905; was admitted to the Michigan bar in 1905 and commenced practice in Midland; member of the State house of representatives 1909–1915, serving as speaker in 1913 and 1914; unsuccessful candidate for the Republican nomination in 1914 to the Sixty-fourth Congress; elected as a Republican to the Sixty-fifth and Sixty-sixth Congresses (March 4, 1917–March 3, 1921); unsuccessful candidate for renomination in 1920 to the Sixty-seventh Congress; resumed the practice of law and also engaged in the banking business until his death in Midland, Mich., June 5, 1960; interment in Midland Cemetery.

CURRIER, Frank Dunklee, a Representative from New Hampshire; born in Canaan, Grafton County, N. H., October 30, 1853; attended the common schools, Kimball Union Academy, Meriden, N. H., and Doctor Hixon's School, Lowell, Mass.; studied law; was admitted to the bar in 1874 and commenced practice in Canaan, N. H.; member of the State house of representatives in 1879; secretary of the Republican State committee 1882–1890; clerk of the State senate in 1883 and 1885; delegate to the Republican National Convention at Chicago in 1884; member of the State senate in 1887 and served as president of that body; naval officer of customs at the port of Boston, Mass., 1890–1894; speaker of the State house of representatives in 1899; elected as a Republican to the Fifty-seventh and to the five succeeding Congresses (March 4, 1901–March 3, 1913); unsuccessful candidate for reelection in 1912 to the Sixty-third

Congress; retired from public life and active business pursuits because of failing health; died in Canaan, N. H., November 25, 1921; interment in Canaan Street Cemetery.

CURRY, Charles Forrest, a Representative from California; born in Naperville, Du Page County, Ill., March 14, 1858; attended the common schools and the Episcopal Academy, Mineral Point, Wis.; studied one year at the University of Washington at Seattle, and also was educated by a private tutor; moved with his parents to Seattle, Wash., in 1872, and thence to San Francisco, Calif., in 1873; engaged in agricultural pursuits and the cattle, lumber, and mining businesses; member of the State assembly in 1887 and 1888; was admitted to the bar of San Francisco in 1888; superintendent of Station B post office, San Francisco, 1890–1894; clerk of San Francisco city and county 1894–1898; secretary of state of California 1899–1910; unsuccessful candidate for the Republican nomination for Governor in 1910; appointed building and loan commissioner of California in 1911; representative to the Panama Pacific International Exposition for the Pacific Coast and Intermountain States in 1911; elected as a Republican to the Sixty-third and to the eight succeeding Congresses and served from March 4, 1913, until his death in Washington, D. C., October 10, 1930; interment in Abbey Mausoleum (near Arlington National Cemetery), Arlington, Va.

CURRY, Charles Forrest, Jr. (son of the preceding), a Representative from California; born in San Francisco, Calif., August 13, 1893; attended the public schools, Howe's Academy, Sacramento, Calif., and George Washington University and Georgetown University School of Law, Washington, D. C.; secretary to his father, Congressman Charles F. Curry, 1913–1917; during the First World War enlisted in the Aviation Section, Signal Enlisted Reserve Corps, on August 15, 1917; commissioned a second lieutenant and served until May 22, 1919, with overseas service; clerk to the Committee on the Territories, United States House of Representatives, 1919–1930; was admitted to the bar in 1921; elected as a Republican to the Seventy-second Congress (March 4, 1931–March 3, 1933); unsuccessful candidate for reelection in 1932 to the Seventy-third Congress; engaged in the practice of law, and in mining and other business enterprises; is a resident of Long Beach, Calif.

CURRY, George, a Representative from New Mexico; born on Greenwood plantation, near Bayou Sara, La., April 3, 1863; attended the public schools; moved to the Territory of New Mexico in 1879 and worked on a cattle ranch until 1881; acted as post trader at Fort Stanton; engaged in the mercantile and stock business until 1886; deputy treasurer of Lincoln County in 1886 and 1887; elected county clerk in 1888, county assessor in 1890, and sheriff in 1892; member of the Territorial senate in 1894 and 1896, serving as president the latter year; lieutenant of the First Volunteer Cavalry, known as "Roosevelt's Rough Riders," in the Spanish-American War; appointed first lieutenant May 2, 1898; promoted to captain May 7, 1898; mustered out September 15, 1898; sheriff of Otero County in 1899; resigned to join the Eleventh Volunteer Cavalry; lieutenant, provost marshal, and provost judge, with service in the Philippine Islands from December 16, 1899, to March 20, 1901; Governor of the Province of Camarines, Philippine Islands, in 1901; chief of police of the city of Manila and organized the first police force on August 1, 1901; Governor of the Province of Isabela 1903–1905; Governor of the Province of Samar from 1905 to 1907, when he resigned; Governor of the Territory of New Mexico 1907–1911; upon the admission of New Mexico as a State into the Union was elected as a Republican to the Sixty-second Congress and served from January 8, 1912, to March 3,

1913; declined to be a candidate for renomination in 1912; engaged in the hotel business in Socorro, N. Mex.; delegate to many State conventions; food director and member of the Council of National Defense during the First World War; private secretary to United States Senator Holm O. Bursum of New Mexico in 1921 and 1922; member of the International Boundary Commission, created to carry out the provisions of various treaties dealing with the boundary between the United States and Mexico, from August 11, 1922, until his resignation in 1927, retired and moved to a ranch near Cutter, N. Mex.; during World War II served as chairman of the Sierra County Draft Board; served as State historian for New Mexico from 1945 until his death; died in Albuquerque, N. Mex., November 27, 1947; interment in National Cemetery, Santa Fe, N. Mex.

CURRY, Jabez Lamar Monroe, a Representative from Alabama; born near Double Branches, Lincoln County, Ga., June 5, 1825; moved with his father to Talladega County, Ala., in 1838; was graduated from the University of Georgia at Athens in 1843; studied law at Harvard University; was admitted to the bar and commenced practice in Talladega County in 1845; served in the war with Mexico as a private in the Texas Rangers in 1846, but resigned because of ill health; member of the State house of representatives in 1847, 1853, and 1855; presidential elector on the Democratic ticket of Buchanan and Breckinridge in 1856; elected as a State Rights Democrat to the Thirty-fifth and Thirty-sixth Congresses and served from March 4, 1857, to January 21, 1861, when he withdrew; deputy from Alabama to the Provisional Confederate Congress and a Representative in the First Confederate Congress; during the Civil War served as lieutenant colonel of Cavalry in the Confederate Army; after the war became a Baptist preacher; chosen president of Howard College, Alabama, in 1865; professor in Richmond College, Virginia, 1868–1881; agent of the Peabody and States Funds from 1881 until his death; appointed Envoy Extraordinary and Minister Plenipotentiary to Spain on October 7, 1885, and served until August 6, 1888, when he resigned; appointed Ambassador Extraordinary on special mission to Spain (the coming of age of the King) February 3, 1902; died in Victoria, near Asheville, N. C., February 12, 1903; interment in Hollywood Cemetery, Richmond, Va.

CURTIN, Andrew Gregg, a Representative from Pennsylvania; born in Bellefonte, Pa., April 22, 1817; pursued preparatory studies in Milton (Pa.) Academy, and was graduated from Dickinson College, Carlisle, Pa., in 1837; studied law; was admitted to the bar in 1837 and commenced practice in Bellefonte; supported General Harrison for the Presidency in 1840; presidential elector on the Whig ticket of Taylor and Fillmore in 1848 and of Scott and Graham in 1852; secretary of the Commonwealth of Pennsylvania and superintendent of public instruction; Governor of Pennsylvania from January 15, 1861, to January 15, 1867; was most active in support of the Union Army throughout the period of the Civil War and in raising and equipping 270 regiments, besides a number of detached companies that Pennsylvania furnished for the northern armies; Minister to Russia 1869–1872; delegate to the constitutional convention of Pennsylvania; elected as a Democrat to the Forty-seventh, Forty-eighth, and Forty-ninth Congresses (March 4, 1881–March 3, 1887); was not a candidate for renomination in 1886; resumed the practice of his profession; died in Bellefonte, Centre County, Pa., on October 7, 1894; interment in Union Cemetery.

CURTIN, Willard Sevier, a Representative from Pennsylvania; born in Trenton, Mercer County, N. J., November 28, 1905; moved to Morrisville, Bucks County, Pa., with his parents in

1911; attended the public schools; graduated from Penn State University in 1929 and from the University of Pennsylvania Law School in 1932; was admitted to the bar in 1932 and commenced the practice of law in Morrisville, Pa.; first assistant district attorney of Bucks County 1938–1949; district attorney 1949–1953; county committeeman to the Pennsylvania State Republican Committee 1954–1956; elected as a Republican to the Eighty-fifth and Eighty-sixth Congresses (January 3, 1957; January 3, 1961). *Reelected to the Eighty-seventh Congress.*

CURTIS, Carl Thomas, a Representative and a Senator from Nebraska; born near Minden, Kearney County, Nebr., March 15, 1905; attended the public schools, and Nebraska Wesleyan University and the University of Nebraska at Lincoln; teacher in the Minden, Nebr., schools in 1927; studied law; was admitted to the bar in 1930 and commenced practice in Minden; county attorney of Kearney County, Nebr., 1931–1934; elected as a Republican to the Seventy-sixth and to the seven succeeding Congresses and served from January 3, 1939, until his resignation December 31, 1954; appointed to the United States Senate on January 1, 1955, to fill the vacancy caused by the resignation of Hazel H. Abel in the term ending January 3, 1955; elected in November 1954 for the term beginning January 3, 1955, and ending January 3, 1961. *Reelected in 1960 for the term ending January 3, 1967.*

CURTIS, Carlton Brandaga, a Representative from Pennsylvania; born in Madison County, N. Y., December 17, 1811; pursued an academic course; moved to Mayville, N. Y.; studied law; moved to Erie, Pa., where he continued the study of law; was admitted to the bar in 1834; moved to Warren, Pa., the same year and commenced practice; member of the State house of representatives 1836–1838; elected as a Democrat to the Thirty-second and Thirty-third Congresses (March 4, 1851–March 3, 1855); affiliated with the Republican Party in 1855; during the Civil War entered the Union Army February 13, 1862, as lieutenant colonel of the Fifty-eighth Regiment, Pennsylvania Volunteer Infantry, to take effect from January 29, 1862, for a period of three years; promoted to colonel of that regiment May 23, 1863; because of illness was honorably discharged as colonel July 2, 1863; returned to Warren and practiced law; moved to Erie, Pa., in 1868 and continued the practice of law; also interested in banking and the production of oil, and was one of the originators and builders of the Dunkirk & Venango Railroad; elected as a Republican to the Forty-third Congress (March 4, 1873–March 3, 1875); was an unsuccessful candidate for reelection in 1874 to the Forty-fourth Congress; resumed the practice of law: died in Erie, Erie County, Pa., March 17, 1883; interment in Oakland Cemetery, Warren, Pa.

CURTIS, Charles, a Representative and a Senator from Kansas and a Vice President of the United States; born in Topeka, Kans., January 25, 1860; attended the common schools; studied law; was admitted to the bar in 1881 and commenced practice in Topeka; prosecuting attorney of Shawnee County 1885–1889; elected as a Republican to the Fifty-third and to the six succeeding Congresses and served from March 4, 1893, until January 28, 1907, when he resigned, having been elected Senator; had been reelected to the Sixtieth Congress, but on January 23, 1907, was elected to the United States Senate to fill the vacancy in the term ending March 3, 1907, caused by the resignation of Joseph R. Burton, and on the same day was reelected for the term commencing March 4, 1907, and served from January 29, 1907, to March 3, 1913; unsuccessful candidate for reelection in 1912; was President pro tempore of the Senate December 4–12, 1911; chairman of the Kansas delegation to the Republican

National Convention at Chicago in 1908; delegate to several Republican State conventions; again elected to the United States Senate for the term commencing March 4, 1915; reelected in 1920 and 1926 and served from March 4, 1915, until his resignation on March 3, 1929, having been elected Vice President of the United States; elected Republican whip of the Senate in 1915 and served until 1924; elected majority leader of the Senate in 1924 and served until March 3, 1929; elected Vice President of the United States on the Republican ticket headed by Herbert Hoover in 1928, was inaugurated on March 4, 1929, and served until March 3, 1933; unsuccessful candidate for reelection in 1932 for Vice President; resumed the practice of law in Washington, D. C., where he died on February 8, 1936; interment in Topeka Cemetery, Topeka, Kans.

CURTIS, Edward, a Representative from New York; born in Windsor, Vt., October 25, 1801; was graduated from Union College, Schenectady, N. Y., in 1821; studied law; was admitted to the New York bar in 1824 and commenced the practice of law in New York City; member of the common council in 1834, and was elected president of the board of assistant aldermen; elected as a Whig to the Twenty-fifth and Twenty-sixth Congresses (March 4, 1837–March 3, 1841); was not a candidate for renomination to the Twenty-seventh Congress; appointed collector of the port of New York City March 18, 1841, and served in that office until July 7, 1844; resumed the practice of law in Washington, D. C.; died in New York City on August 2, 1856; place of interment unknown.

CURTIS, George Martin, a Representative from Iowa; born near Oxford, Chenango County, N. Y., April 1, 1844; moved to Ogle County, Ill., in 1856 with his parents, who settled on a farm near Rochelle; attended the common schools and Rock River Seminary, Mount Morris, Ill.; was a clerk in Rochelle, Ill., 1863–1865, and subsequently for two years in Cortland, Ill.; moved to Clinton, Iowa, in 1867 and engaged in the manufacture of lumber; one of the incorporators of the City National Bank of Clinton and served as a director since its organization in 1880; elected vice president of the bank in 1890 and served in that capacity until his death; director in a number of lumber companies; member of the State house of representatives in 1888 and 1889; delegate to the Republican National Convention at Minneapolis in 1892; elected as a Republican to the Fifty-fourth and Fifty-fifth Congresses (March 4, 1895–March 3, 1899); declined to be a candidate for renomination in 1898; resumed his former business activities in Clinton, Clinton County, Iowa, and died there February 9, 1921; interment in Springdale Cemetery.

CURTIS, Laurence, a Representative from Massachusetts; born in Boston, Suffolk County, Mass., September 3, 1893; graduated from Groton School in 1912 and from Harvard University in 1916; served in the Foreign Diplomatic Service for one year; during the First World War entered the United States Navy and after a training crash, resulting in the loss of a leg, served out the rest of the war as a ground officer at Pensacola, Fla.; awarded Silver Star citation for war services; returned to Harvard Law School and graduated in 1921; admitted to the Massachusetts bar the same year and commenced practice in Boston; secretary to United States Supreme Court Justice Oliver Wendell Holmes in 1921 and 1922; assistant United States attorney in Boston 1923–1930; member of Boston City Council 1930–1933; member of the State house of representatives 1933–1936; member of State senate 1936–1941; State treasurer in 1947 and 1948; chairman of Massachusetts division of American Cancer Society drive in 1949; chairman of Suffolk County March of Dimes drive in 1952; delegate to Republican National Convention in 1960; elected as a Republican to the Eighty-third and to the three succeeding Congresses (January 3, 1953–January 3, 1961). *Reelected to the Eighty-seventh Congress.*

CURTIS, Newton Martin, a Representative from New York; born in De Peyster, St. Lawrence County, N. Y., May 21, 1835; attended the common schools and Gouverneur Wesleyan Seminary; during the Civil War entered the Union Army as captain of Company G, Sixteenth Regiment, New York Infantry, May 15, 1861; lieutenant colonel of the One Hundred and Forty-second Regiment, New York Infantry, October 23, 1862; colonel January 21, 1863; brevetted brigadier general of Volunteers October 28, 1864, "for distinguished services on the enemy's works near New Market, Va."; brigadier general January 15, 1865; brevetted major general of Volunteers March 13, 1865, "for gallant and meritorious services at the capture of Fort Fisher, N. C."; awarded the Congressional Medal of Honor "for being the first man at Fort Fisher, N. C., January 15, 1865, to pass through the stockade, and for personally leading each assault on the traverses, where he was wounded several times"; mustered out and honorably discharged as brigadier general of Volunteers January 15, 1866; appointed collector of customs, district of Oswegatchie, N. Y., in 1866; appointed special agent of the United States Treasury Department in 1867, which position he resigned in 1880; employed by the Department of Justice 1880–1882; member of the State assembly 1884–1890; elected as a Republican to the Fifty-second Congress to fill the vacancy caused by the resignation of Leslie W. Russell; reelected to the Fifty-third and Fifty-fourth Congresses and served from November 3, 1891, to March 3, 1897; was not a candidate for renomination in 1896; assistant inspector general of the National Home for Disabled Volunteer Soldiers 1910; died in New York City on January 8, 1910; interment in Ogdensburg Cemetery, Ogdensburg, N. Y.

CURTIS, Samuel Ryan, a Representative from Iowa; born near Champlain, Clinton County, N. Y., February 3, 1805; moved to Ohio, where he attended the public schools; appointed a cadet in the United States Military Academy at West Point in 1827, and was graduated in July 1831, as brevet second lieutenant in the Seventh Infantry; resigned in June 1832; studied law; was admitted to the bar, and commenced practice in Zanesville, Ohio; chief engineer of the Muskingum River improvements from April 1837 to May 1839; served in the war with Mexico as adjutant general of Ohio and colonel of the Third Regiment, Ohio Infantry; honorably discharged June 24, 1847; resumed the practice of law; elected as a Republican to the Thirty-fifth, Thirty-sixth, and Thirty-seventh Congresses and served from March 4, 1857, to August 4, 1861, when he resigned; member of the peace convention of 1861 held in Washington, D. C., in an effort to devise means to prevent the impending war; during the Civil War served in the Union Army; appointed colonel of the Second Regiment, Iowa Volunteer Infantry, June 1, 1861; brigadier general of Volunteers May 17, 1861; major general of Volunteers March 21, 1862; mustered out April 30, 1866; appointed United States peace commissioner to treat with the Indians in 1865; appointed commissioner to examine and report on the condition of the Union Pacific Railroad, and served from November 1865 to April 1866; died in Council Bluffs, Iowa, on December 25, 1866; interment in Oakland Cemetery, Keokuk, Iowa.

CURTIS, Thomas Bradford, a Representative from Missouri; born in St. Louis, Mo., May 14, 1911; attended the public schools of Webster Groves, Mo.; was graduated from Dartmouth College, Hanover, N. H., in 1932, and from the law school of Washington University, St. Louis, Mo., in 1935; was admitted to the bar in

1934 and commenced the practice of law in St. Louis, Mo.; member of the Board of Election Commissioners of St. Louis County in 1942; during World War II served in the United States Navy from April 8, 1942, until discharged as a lieutenant commander December 21, 1945; member of the St. Louis County Republican Central Committee 1946–1950; member of the Missouri State Board of Law Examiners 1948–1950; member board of trustees of Dartmouth College and a member of the board of overseers of Amos Tuck School of Administration; elected as a Republican to the Eighty-second and to the four succeeding Congresses (January 3, 1951–January 3, 1961). *Reelected to the Eighty-seventh Congress.*

CUSACK, Thomas, a Representative from Illinois; born in Kilrush, County Clare, Ireland, October 5, 1858; immigrated to the United States in 1861 with his parents, who settled in New York City; after the death of his parents moved to Chicago, Ill., in 1863; attended private and public schools; learned the sign-painting trade; organized an outdoor advertising company in 1875; member of the board of education 1891–1898 and served as vice president of the board 1896–1898; served as colonel on the staff of Gov. John P. Altgeld 1893–1897; member of the Democratic State central committee 1896–1898; elected as a Democrat to the Fifty-sixth Congress (March 4, 1899–March 3, 1901); was not a candidate for renomination in 1900; resumed his former business pursuits in Chicago, Ill.; retired from political life and active business pursuits in 1924; died in Chicago, Ill., November 19, 1926; interment in Calvary Cemetery.

CUSHING, Caleb, a Representative from Massachusetts; born in Salisbury, Mass., January 17, 1800; was graduated from Harvard University in 1817; studied law; was admitted to the bar at Newburyport in 1823; member of the State house of representatives in 1825; served in the State senate in 1827; again a member of the State house of representatives in 1833 and 1834; elected as a Whig to the Twenty-fourth and to the three succeeding Congresses (March 4, 1835–March 3, 1843); was not a candidate for renomination in 1842; appointed by President Tyler as Envoy Extraordinary and Minister Plenipotentiary to China on May 8, 1843, and also commissioner on the same date; resigned March 4, 1845; while serving as commissioner to China was empowered to negotiate a treaty of navigation and commerce with Japan; again a member of the State house of represetatives in 1845 and 1846; colonel of a Massachusetts regiment which served in the war with Mexico; appointed brigadier general by President Polk April 14, 1847; unsuccessful Democratic candidate for Governor in 1847 and again in 1848; again elected to the State house of representatives in 1850; offered the position as attorney general of Massachusetts in 1851, but declined; mayor of Newburyport, Mass., in 1851 and 1852; appointed judge of the supreme court of Massachusetts in 1852; appointed by President Pierce as Attorney General of the United States on March 7, 1853, and served until March 3, 1857; chairman of the Democratic National Conventions at Baltimore and Charleston in 1860; appointed by President Johnson as a commissioner to codify the laws of the United States and served from 1866 to 1870; instructed on November 25, 1868, in concert with the Minister Resident to Colombia, to negotiate a treaty for a ship canal across the Isthmus; appointed in 1872 by President Grant counsel for the United States before the Geneva Tribunal of Arbitration on the *Alabama* claims; nominated by President Grant in 1874 to be Chief Justice of the Supreme Court of the United States, but was not confirmed by the Senate; Envoy Extraordinary and Minister Plenipotentiary to Spain from January 6, 1874, to April 9, 1877; died in Newburyport, Essex County, Mass., on January 2, 1879; interment in Highland Cemetery.

CUSHING, Thomas, a Delegate from Massachusetts; born in Boston, Mass., March 24, 1725; attended Boston Latin School; was graduated from Harvard College in 1744; studied law; was admitted to the bar and commenced practice in Boston; member of the provincial assembly 1761–1774 and served as speaker; delegate to the Provincial Congress in 1774; Member of the Continental Congress 1774–1776; commissary general of Massachusetts in 1775; declined to be a candidate for election to the Continental Congress in 1779; Lieutenant Governor of Massachusetts 1780–1788 and Acting Governor in 1785; delegate to the State constitutional convention which ratified the Federal Constitution in 1788; one of the founders of the American Academy of Arts and Sciences; died in Boston, Mass., February 28, 1788; interment in Granary Burial Ground.

CUSHMAN, Francis Wellington, a Representative from Washington; born in Brighton, Washington County, Iowa, May 8, 1867; attended the public schools in Brighton and Pleasant Plain Academy in Pleasant Plain, Jefferson County, Iowa; moved to Albany County, Wyo., in 1885; employed as a ranch hand and as a teacher; studied law; was admitted to the bar in 1889 and commenced practice in Bassett, Rock County, Nebr.; moved to Tacoma, Wash., in 1891 and continued the practice of law; member of Troop B, First Cavalry, Washington National Guard, 1896–1903; elected as a Republican to the Fifty-sixth and to the five succeeding Congresses and served from March 4, 1899, until his death in New York City, N. Y., July 6, 1909; the remains were cremated and the ashes interred in Tacoma Cemetery, Tacoma, Wash.

CUSHMAN, John Paine, a Representative from New York; born in Pomfret, Conn., March 8, 1784; attended the common schools and Plainfield Academy, and was graduated from Yale College in 1807; studied law; was admitted to the bar in 1809 and commenced practice in Troy, N. Y.; elected to the Fifteenth Congress (March 4, 1817–March 3, 1819); was not a candidate for renomination in 1818; resumed the practice of law; regent of the State University from April 1830 until April 1834, when he resigned; trustee of Union College, Schenectady, N. Y., from 1833 until his death; recorder of Troy, N. Y., 1834–1838; judge of the circuit court of the third circuit 1838–1844; engaged in the real-estate business and was interested in civic improvements; died in Troy, N. Y., on September 16, 1848; interment in Oakwood Cemetery.

CUSHMAN, Joshua, a Representative from Massachusetts and from Maine; born in Halifax, Mass., April 11, 1761; served in the Revolutionary Army from April 1, 1777, until March 1780; was graduated from Harvard University in 1787; studied theology; was ordained to the ministry and licensed to preach; located in Winslow, Maine (then a district of Massachusetts), and was pastor of the Congregational Church for nearly twenty years; served in the Massachusetts Senate in 1810; member of the Massachusetts House of Representatives in 1811 and 1812; elected as a Democrat from Massachusetts to the Sixteenth Congress (March 4, 1819–March 3, 1821); when the State of Maine was separated from Massachusetts and admitted as a State into the Union was elected a Representative from Maine to the Seventeenth and Eighteenth Congresses (March 4, 1821–March 3, 1825); served in the Maine Senate in 1828; member of the Maine House of Representatives in 1834; died in Augusta, Maine, on January 27, 1834; interment in a tomb on the State grounds, Augusta, Maine.

CUSHMAN, Samuel, a Representative from New Hampshire; born in Portsmouth, N. H., June 8, 1783; attended the common schools; studied law; was admitted to the bar and commenced practice in Portsmouth; served as judge of the Portsmouth police court; county treasurer 1823–1828; member of the State house of representatives 1833–1835; nominated by President Jackson to be United States attorney for the district of New Hampshire but was not confirmed; elected as a Democrat to the Twenty-fourth and Twenty-fifth Congresses (March 4, 1835–March 3, 1839); United States Navy officer at Portsmouth 1845–1849; died in Portsmouth, N. H., on May 20, 1851; interment in Proprietors' Burying Ground.

CUTCHEON, Byron M., a Representative from Michigan; born in Pembroke, Merrimack County, N. H., May 11, 1836; attended the common schools and Pembroke Academy; taught school in Pembroke for several years; moved to Ypsilanti, Mich., in 1855; principal of Birmingham Academy, Oakland County, in 1857; attended Ypsilanti Seminary, and was graduated from the University of Michigan at Ann Arbor in 1861; professor of ancient languages in the Ypsilanti High School 1861 and 1862; during the Civil War enlisted in the Union Army in 1862 and served in the Twentieth Regiment, Michigan Infantry, attaining the rank of lieutenant colonel; brevetted colonel of Volunteers October 18, 1864, "for gallant service in the Battles of the Wilderness and Spotsylvania Court House, Va."; commissioned colonel of the Twenty-seventh Regiment, Michigan Infantry, November 12, 1864; owing to the death of his superior officer he commanded the Second Brigade, Second Division, Ninth Army Corps, from October 16, 1864, until his resignation on March 6, 1865; brevetted brigadier general of United States Volunteers March 13, 1865; was graduated from the University of Michigan Law School in 1866; was admitted to the bar the same year and commenced practice in Ionia, Mich.; president of the Michigan Soldiers' Home Commission in 1866 and 1867; moved to Manistee, Mich., in 1867; member of the board of control of railroads of Michigan 1867–1883; presidential elector on the Republican ticket of Grant and Colfax in 1868; city attorney of Manistee, Mich., 1870–1873; prosecuting attorney of Manistee County, Mich., in 1873 and 1874; regent of Michigan University 1875–1881; postmaster of Manistee, Mich., 1877–1883; elected as a Republican to the Forty-eighth and to the three succeeding Congresses (March 4, 1883–March 3, 1891); unsuccessful candidate for reelection in 1890 to the Fifty-second Congress; awarded a Medal of Honor by Congress June 29, 1891, "for distinguished gallantry at the Battle of Horseshoe Bend, Ky., May 10, 1863"; appointed civilian member of the Board of Ordnance and Fortifications by President Harrison in July 1891 and served until March 25, 1895; editorial writer for the Detroit Daily Tribune and Detroit Journal 1895–1897; resumed the practice of law in Grand Rapids, Mich.; died in Ypsilanti, Washtenaw County, Mich., April 12, 1908; interment in Highland Cemetery.

CUTHBERT, Alfred (brother of John Alfred Cuthbert), a Representative and a Senator from Georgia; born in Savannah, Ga., December 23, 1785; instructed by private tutors, and was graduated from Princeton College in 1803; studied law; was admitted to the bar about 1805 but did not practice; captain of a company of volunteer infantry in 1809; member of the State house of representatives 1810–1813; elected as a Democrat to the Thirteenth Congress to fill the vacancy caused by the resignation of William W. Bibb; reelected to the Fourteenth Congress and served from December 13, 1813, to November 9, 1816, when he resigned; served in the State senate 1817–1819; elected to the Seventeenth, Eighteenth, and Nineteenth Congresses (March 4, 1821–March 3, 1827); was not a candidate for renomination in 1826; member of the State convention in 1832; elected to the United States Senate to fill the vacancy caused by the resignation of John Forsyth; reelected in 1837, and served from January 12, 1835, to March 3, 1843; was not a candidate for reelection in

1843; retired from active business pursuits and lived on his estate near Monticello, Jasper County, Ga., until his death on July 9, 1856; interment in Summerville Cemetery, Augusta, Ga.

CUTHBERT, John Alfred (brother of Alfred Cuthbert), a Representative from Georgia; born in Savannah, Ga., June 3, 1788; was graduated from Princeton College in 1805; studied law; was admitted to the bar in 1809 and commenced practice in Eatonton, Ga.; member of the State house of representatives in 1811, 1813, and 1817; commanded a volunteer company during the War of 1812; served in the State senate in 1814 and 1815; elected as a Democrat to the Sixteenth Congress (March 4, 1819–March 3, 1821); appointed by President Monroe a commissioner to treat with the Creek and Cherokee Indians in 1822; again a member of the State house of representatives in 1822; secretary of the State senate in 1830, 1833, and 1834; editor and subsequently proprietor of the Federal Union at Milledgeville, Ga., 1831–1837; moved to Mobile, Ala., in 1837 and practiced law; elected judge of the county court of Mobile County in 1840, and appointed by the Governor judge of the circuit court of the same county in 1852; retired from the bench and practiced law until his death at "Sans Souci," on Mon Luis Island, near Mobile, Ala., September 22, 1881; interment in a private burying ground on Mon Luis Island.

CUTLER, Augustus William (great-grandson of Silas Condict), a Representative from New Jersey; born in Morristown, Morris County, N. J., October 22, 1827; spent the early part of his life on a farm; attended the common schools and Yale College; studied law; was admitted to the bar in 1849 and commenced practice in Morristown, N. J.; prosecutor of the pleas for Morris County 1856–1861; elected president of the board of education in 1870; member of the State senate 1871–1874; delegate to the State constitutional convention in 1873; elected as a Democrat to the Forty-fourth and Forty-fifth Congresses (March 4, 1875–March 3, 1879); declined to be a candidate for renomination in 1878; resumed the practice of law at Morristown; unsuccessful candidate for election in 1880 to the Forty-seventh Congress and again in 1896 to the Fifty-fifth Congress; died in Morristown, N. J., January 1, 1897; interment in Evergreen Cemetery.

CUTLER, Manasseh, a Representative from Massachusetts; born in Killingly, Conn., May 13, 1742; was prepared for college by private teacher and was graduated from Yale College in 1765; taught school in Dedham, Mass., for a short time; engaged in the whaling business at Edgartown, Marthas Vineyard, Mass.; studied law; was admitted to the bar in 1767 but did not practice; studied theology, and was licensed to preach in 1770; ordained to the ministry by the Congregational Society at Hamilton, Mass., September 11, 1771; appointed chaplain of Colonel Francis' regiment September 5, 1776, and of General Titcomb's brigade in 1778; began the study of medicine the same year and became a skilled physician; taught navigation; held in esteem for his knowledge of botany and astronomy; one of the projectors of the Ohio Company in 1787, formed for the purpose of colonizing the new Territory; drafted the Ordinance of 1787; appointed judge of the United States Court for Ohio in 1795 by President Washington, but declined; member of the State house of representatives in 1800; elected as a Federalist to the Seventh and Eighth Congresses (March 4, 1801–March 3, 1805); was not a candidate for renomination in 1804; engaged in literary pursuits; died in Hamilton, Mass., July 28, 1823; interment in Main Street Cemetery.

CUTLER, William Parker, a Representative from Ohio; born in Marietta, Ohio, July 12, 1812; attended the common schools and Ohio University at Athens; engaged in agricultural pursuits; member of the State house of representatives 1844–1847, serving as speaker during the last term; trustee of Marietta College 1845–1889; delegate to the State constitutional convention in 1850; president of the Marietta & Cincinnati Railroad 1850–1860; elected as a Republican to the Thirty-seventh Congress (March 4, 1861–March 3, 1863); unsuccessful for reelection in 1862 to the Thirty-eighth Congress; resumed agricultural pursuits and also engaged in railroad building; died in Marietta, Ohio, April 11, 1889; interment in Oak Grove Cemetery.

CUTTING, Bronson Murray, a Senator from New Mexico; born in Oakdale, Long Island, N. Y., June 23, 1888; attended the common schools and Groton (Mass.) School; was graduated from Harvard University in 1910; becoming an invalid he moved to Santa Fe, N. Mex., in 1910 to restore his health; became a newspaper publisher in 1912 and published the Santa Fe New Mexican and El Nuevo Mexicano, serving as president of the New Mexican Printing Co. from 1912 to 1918 and of the Santa Fe New Mexican Publishing Corp. from 1920 until his death; treasurer of the Progressive State central committee of New Mexico 1912–1914, and chairman 1914–1916; during the First World War was commissioned captain of Infantry, United States Army, August 5, 1917; served as an assistant military attaché of the American Embassy at London in 1917 and 1918; awarded the British Military Cross; regent of New Mexico Military Institute in 1920; served as chairman of the board of commissioners of the New Mexican State Penitentiary in 1925; national executive committeeman in 1919 and 1920; department commander of the American Legion of New Mexico in 1923 and 1924, and department adjutant 1925–1927; appointed as a Republican to the United States Senate to fill the vacancy caused by the death of Andrieus A. Jones and served from December 29, 1927, until December 6, 1928, when a duly elected successor qualified; was not a candidate for election to this vacancy; elected in 1928 to the United States Senate; reelected in 1934 and served from March 4, 1929, until his death in an airplane crash near Atlanta, Mo., on May 6, 1935; interment in Greenwood Cemetery, Brooklyn, N. Y.

CUTTING, Francis Brockholst, a Representative from New York; born in New York City August 6, 1804; attended Bensel School and was also tutored privately; studied law in the Litchfield (Conn.) Law School; was admitted to the bar in 1827 and commenced practice in New York City; member of the State assembly in 1836 and 1837; was not a candidate for reelection; unsuccessful candidate for election in 1836 to the Twenty-fifth Congress; member of the board of aldermen in 1843; city recorder; elected as a Democrat to the Thirty-third Congress (March 4, 1853–March 3, 1855); was not a candidate for renomination in 1854; resumed the practice of law; died in New York City June 26, 1870; interment in Greenwood Cemetery, Brooklyn, N. Y.

CUTTING, John Tyler, a Representative from California; born in Westport, Essex County, N. Y., September 7, 1844; was left an orphan at ten years of age, when he journeyed westward; resided in Wisconsin and Illinois from 1855 to 1860; worked on a farm; while employed as a clerk in a mercantile establishment attended the public schools of Illinois; enlisted in Taylor's Chicago Battery at the outbreak of the Civil War and served until July 20, 1862; discharged for disability, the result of service in the field; reenlisted January 4, 1864, in the Chicago Mercantile Battery, in which he served until the close of the war; moved to California in 1877 and established a wholesale fruit and commission business; was a member of the National Guard of California, and subsequently assisted in the organization of the Coast Guard, of which he later became brigadier general in command of the Second Brigade; identified himself with State and National politics;

elected as a Republican to the Fifty-second Congress (March 4, 1891–March 3, 1893); declined to be a candidate for renomination in 1892; returned to the East in 1894 and settled in New York City, where he became interested in the automobile industry; retired to his old home in Westport, N. Y., in 1907; died in Toronto, Ontario, Canada, where he had gone to recuperate his health, November 24, 1911; interment in Hillside Cemetery, Westport, N. Y.

CUTTS, Charles, a Senator from New Hampshire; born in Portsmouth, N. H., January 31, 1769; was graduated from Harvard University in 1789; studied law; was admitted to the bar in 1795 and practiced; member of the State house of representatives 1803–1810, serving as speaker in 1807, 1808, and 1810; elected as a Federalist to the United States Senate to fill the vacancy caused by the resignation of Nahum Parker and served from June 21, 1810, to March 3, 1813; subsequently appointed to fill the vacancy occurring at the close of his term and served from April 2, 1813, to June 10, 1813, when a successor was elected; elected Secretary of the United States Senate and served from October 11, 1814, to December 12, 1825; moved to Fairfax County, Va., and settled near Lewinsville, Va., where he died January 25, 1846; interment in a private cemetery near Lewinsville, Fairfax County, Va.

CUTTS, Marsena Edgar, a Representative from Iowa; born in Orwell, Addison County, Vt., May 22, 1833; attended the common schools of his native village and St. Lawrence Academy, Potsdam, N. Y.; moved to Sheboygan Falls, Wis., in 1853; taught school for two years, at the same time studying law; moved to Oskaloosa, Iowa, in June 1855 and completed his law studies; was admitted to the bar in August and commenced practice in Montezuma, Iowa; prosecuting attorney of Poweshiek County in 1857 and 1858; member of the State house of representatives at the extra session in May 1861; served in the State senate from January 1864 until August 1866, when he resigned and returned to Oskaloosa; again a member of the State house of representatives 1870–1872; attorney general of Iowa 1872–1877; presented credentials as a Republican Member-elect to the Forty-seventh Congress and served from March 4, 1881, to March 3, 1883 (the closing day of Congress), when he was succeeded by John C. Cook, who contested the election; elected to the Forty-eighth Congress and served from March 4, 1883, until his death in Oskaloosa, Mahaska County, Iowa, on September 1, 1883, before the assembling of the Congress; interment in Forest Cemetery.

CUTTS, Richard, a Representative from Massachusetts; born on Cutts Island, Saco, Mass. (now Maine), June 28, 1771; attended rural and private schools; was graduated from Harvard University in 1790; studied law; engaged extensively in navigation and commercial pursuits; member of the State house of representatives in 1799 and 1800; elected as a Democrat to the Seventh and to the five succeeding Congresses (March 4, 1801–March 3, 1813); was an unsuccessful candidate for reelection in 1812 to the Thirteenth Congress; appointed superintendent general of military supplies and served from 1813 to 1817; appointed Second Comptroller of the United States Treasury on March 6, 1817, and served in this capacity until March 21, 1829; died in Washington, D. C., April 7, 1845; interment in St. John's Graveyard; reinterment in Oak Hill Cemetery in 1857.

D

DADDARIO, Emilio Quincy, a Representative from Connecticut; born in Newton Center, Suffolk County, Mass., September 24, 1918; attended the public schools in Boston, Mass.; at the age of thirteen years entered Tilton (N. H.) Academy, graduating in 1934; attended Newton (Mass.) Country Day School for one year; graduated from Wesleyan University, Middletown, Conn., in 1939; attended Boston University Law School 1939–1941; transferred to University of Connecticut and graduated in 1942; was admitted to the bar in Connecticut and Massachusetts in 1942 and commenced the practice of law in Middletown, Conn.; in February 1943 enlisted as a private in the United States Army; assigned to the Office of Strategic Services at Fort Meade, Md.; commissioned a second lieutenant and served overseas in the Mediterranean Theater; was separated from the service as a captain in September 1945; awarded the United States Legion of Merit and Italian Medaglia d'Argento medals; member of the Connecticut National Guard; mayor of Middletown, Conn., 1946–1948; appointed judge of the Middletown Municipal Court and served from 1948 to 1950 when he was called into active service with the Forty-third Division of the Connecticut National Guard during the Korean conflict; served as a major with the Far East Liaison Group in Korea and Japan until separated from the service as a major in 1952; resumed the practice of law in Hartford, Conn.; member of the board of directors of Middlesex Hospital and the Long Lane School at Middletown, Conn.; elected as a Democrat to the Eighty-sixth Congress (January 3, 1959–January 3, 1961). *Reelected to the Eighty-seventh Congress.*

DAGGETT, David, a Senator from Connecticut; born in Attleboro, Mass., December 31, 1764; pursued preparatory studies and was graduated from Yale College, New Haven, Conn., in 1783; taught in a private school and also in the Hopkins Grammar School; studied law; was admitted to the bar in 1786 and commenced practice in New Haven, Conn.; member of the State house of representatives 1791–1796, and served as speaker 1794–1796; member of the State council, or upper house, in 1797; Federalist presidential elector in 1804, 1808, and 1812; again a member of the State house of representatives in 1805; again served in the State council from 1809 until 1813, when he was elected a Senator of the United States; State's attorney for New Haven County 1811–1813; elected as a Federalist to the United States Senate to fill the vacancy caused by the resignation of Chauncey Goodrich and served from May 13, 1813, to March 3, 1819; was not a candidate for reelection; resumed the practice of law; became an associate instructor in the New Haven Law School in 1824; was appointed in 1826 to the Kent professorship of law in Yale College, in which capacity he served until 1848; judge of the State supreme court 1826–1832, and then served as chief judge until 1834; mayor of New Haven in 1828, and held other municipal offices; retired from public life; died in New Haven, Conn., on April 12, 1851; interment in Grove Street Cemetery.

DAGGETT, Rollin Mallory, a Representative from Nevada; born in Richville, St. Lawrence County, N. Y., February 22, 1831; moved with his father to northwestern Ohio in 1837; attended school in Defiance, where he also learned the printing business; crossed the plains to the Pacific coast in 1849; followed mining until 1852, and in that year started the Golden Era at San Francisco; with others established the San Francisco Mirror in 1860, and united it with the San Francisco Herald; moved to Nevada in 1862 and settled in Virginia City; elected a member of the Territorial council in 1863; became connected editorially in 1864 with the Territorial Enterprise; clerk of the United States district court 1867–1876; presidential elector on the Republican ticket of Hayes and Wheeler in 1876, and was selected as the messenger to deliver the electoral vote of the State of Nevada; elected as a Republican to the Forty-sixth Congress (March 4, 1879–March 3, 1881); unsuccessful candidate for reelection in 1880 to the Forty-seventh Congress; appointed Minister Resident

to Hawaii July 1, 1882, and served until April 10, 1885, when he resigned; engaged in editorial work in San Francisco, Calif., until his death there November 12, 1901; interment in Laurel Hill Cemetery.

DAGUE, Paul Bartram, a Representative from Pennsylvania; born in Whitford, Chester County, Pa., May 19, 1898; attended the public schools and was graduated from Downingtown High School; took special studies at West Chester State Teachers College and studied electrical engineering at Drexel Institute, Philadelphia, Pa.; during the First World War served as a private in the United States Marine Corps from July 22, 1918, to June 30, 1919; assistant superintendent of the Pennsylvania Department of Highways 1925–1935; served as deputy sheriff of Chester County, Pa., 1936–1943 and as sheriff 1944–1946; elected as a Republican to the Eightieth and to the six succeeding Congresses (January 3, 1947–January 3, 1961). *Reelected to the Eighty-seventh Congress.*

DAHLE, Herman Bjorn, a Representative from Wisconsin; born in Perry, Dane County, Wis., March 30, 1855; attended the public schools, and was graduated from the University of Wisconsin at Madison in 1877; moved to Mount Vernon, Wis., in 1877 and engaged in mercantile pursuits; moved to Mount Horeb in 1887, where he continued in the mercantile business and also, in 1890, engaged in banking; elected as a Republican to the Fifty-sixth and Fifty-seventh Congresses (March 4, 1899–March 3, 1903); unsuccessful candidate for renomination in 1902; resumed mercantile pursuits and banking in Mount Horeb, Dane County, Wis., where he died April 25, 1920; interment in the Lutheran Cemetery.

DAILY, Samuel Gordon, a Delegate from the Territory of Nebraska; born in Trimble County, Ky., in 1823; moved with his parents to Jefferson County, Ind., in 1824; attended the common schools and Hanover (Ind.) College; studied law; was admitted to the bar at Indianapolis and commenced practice in Madison, Ind.; unsuccessful candidate of the Free-Soil Party for election to the State legislature; moved to Indianapolis and engaged in the cooperage business; moved to Nebraska Territory in 1857 and settled in Peru, Nemaha County; built a sawmill on the Missouri River; member of the Territorial house of representatives in 1858; successfully contested as a Republican the election of Experience Estabrook to the Thirty-sixth Congress; reelected to the Thirty-seventh and Thirty-eighth Congresses and served from May 18, 1860, to March 3, 1865; appointed deputy collector of customs in New Orleans at the special request of President Lincoln in March 1865, which position he held until his death in New Orleans, La., August 15, 1866; interment in Mount Vernon Cemetery, Peru, Nebr.

DALE, Harry Howard, a Representative from New York; born in New York City December 3, 1868; moved with his parents to Brooklyn in 1870; attended the public schools of Brooklyn and New York Law School; was admitted to the New York bar May 14, 1891, and commenced practice in Brooklyn, N. Y.; member of the State assembly 1899–1904; served as attorney for the State comptroller in 1911 and 1912; elected as a Democrat to the Sixty-third, Sixty-fourth, and Sixty-fifth Congresses and served from March 4, 1913, to January 6, 1919, when he resigned having been appointed judge of the magistrate's court in 1919; reappointed in 1929 and served from January 7, 1919, to July 21, 1931; appointed judge for the court of special sessions on July 22, 1931, and served until his death in Bellmore, Nassau County, N. Y., on November 17, 1935; remains were cremated and the ashes deposited in an urn and placed in Fresh Pond Road Crematory, Brooklyn, N. Y.

DALE, Porter Hinman, a Representative and a Senator from Vermont; born in Island Pond, Essex County, Vt., March 1, 1867; attended the public schools and Eastman Business College; studied in Philadelphia and Boston and spent two years in study with the Shakespearean scholar and actor, James E. Murdoch; taught school in Green Mountain Seminary, Waterbury, Vt., and Bates College, Lewiston, Maine; studied law; was admitted to the bar in 1896 and commenced practice at Island Pond with his father; was admitted to practice before the United States courts in 1900; chief deputy collector of customs at Island Pond from 1897 to 1910, when he resigned; chairman of the Republican State conventions in 1898 and 1919; appointed judge of the Brighton municipal court by Governor Mead in 1910; member of the State senate 1910–1914; served in the State militia and as colonel on the staff of Governor Grout; before election to Congress was interested in the lumber, electric, and banking businesses; elected as a Republican to the Sixty-fourth and to the four succeeding Congresses and served from March 4, 1915, until August 11, 1923, when he resigned to become a candidate for the United States Senate; elected as a Republican to the United States Senate on November 6, 1923, to fill the vacancy caused by the death of William P. Dillingham during the term ending March 3, 1927; reelected in 1926, and again in 1932, and served from November 7, 1923, until his death at his summer home in Westmore, Vt., October 6, 1933; interment in Lakeside Cemetery, Island Pond, Vt.

DALE, Thomas Henry, a Representative from Pennsylvania; born in Daleville, Lackawanna County, Pa., June 12, 1846; attended the public schools and Wyoming Seminary, Kingston, Pa.; during the Civil War enlisted in the Union Army in 1863; after discharge from the service engaged in business as a coal operator; also engaged in the wholesale beef business; interested in various other business enterprises in Scranton, Pa.; instrumental in organizing the Scranton Board of Trade and was its president for several terms; chairman of the Republican county committee for several years; prothonotary of Lackawanna County 1882–1892; delegate to the Republican National Convention at St. Louis in 1896; elected as a Republican to the Fifty-ninth Congress (March 4, 1905–March 3, 1907); unsuccessful candidate for reelection in 1906 to the Sixtieth Congress; president of the Anthracite Trust Co., Scranton, Pa.; died in Daleville, Pa., August 21, 1912; interment in Dunmore Cemetery, Scranton, Pa.

D'ALESANDRO, Thomas, Jr., a Representative from Maryland; born in Baltimore, Md., August 1, 1903; attended the parochial schools and Calvert Business College, Baltimore, Md.; engaged in the brokerage and insurance business in Baltimore, Md.; member of the State house of delegates in 1926–1933; general deputy collector of internal revenue in 1933 and 1934; member of the Baltimore City Council 1935–1938; delegate to the Democratic National Convention at Chicago in 1944; elected as a Democrat to the Seventy-sixth and to the four succeeding Congresses and served from January 3, 1939, until his resignation on May 16, 1947; mayor of Baltimore, Md., from May 1947 to May 1959; defeated for renomination in the March primary election; unsuccessful candidate for election to the United States Senate in 1958; confirmed as a member of the Renegotiation Board, Washington, D. C., March 27, 1961; resides in Baltimore, Md.

DALLAS, George Mifflin, a Senator from Pennsylvania and a Vice President of the United States; born in Philadelphia, Pa., July 10, 1792; was graduated from Princeton College in 1810; studied law; was admitted to the bar in 1813; private secretary to Albert Gallatin, Minister to Russia; returned in 1814 and commenced the practice of law in New York City; was solicitor of the United States Bank 1815–1817; returned to Philadelphia, and was appointed deputy attorney general in 1817; mayor of Philadelphia in 1829; United States district attorney for the eastern district of Pennsylvania 1829–1831; elected as a Democrat to the United States Senate to fill the vacancy caused by the resignation of Isaac D. Barnard and served from December 13, 1831, to March 3, 1833; declined to be a candidate for reelection in 1832; resumed the practice of law; attorney general of the State 1833–1835; appointed by President Van Buren as Envoy Extraordinary and Minister Plenipotentiary to Russia and served from March 7, 1837, to July 29, 1839; when he was recalled at his own request; elected Vice President of the United States on the Democratic ticket in 1844 with James K. Polk and served from March 4, 1845, to March 3, 1849; appointed Envoy Extraordinary and Minister Plenipotentiary to Great Britain by President Pierce and served from February 4, 1856, to May 16, 1861; returned to Philadelphia, and died there December 31, 1864; interment in St. Peter's Churchyard.

DALLINGER, Frederick William, a Representative from Massachusetts; born in Cambridge, Middlesex County, Mass., October 2, 1871; attended the public schools; was graduated from Cambridge Latin School in 1889, from Harvard University in 1893, and from Harvard University Law School in 1897; was admitted to the bar in 1897 and commenced practice in Boston, Mass.; member of the State house of representatives in 1894 and 1895; served in the State senate 1896–1899; public administrator of Middlesex County 1897–1932; president of the Cambridge Chamber of Commerce; lecturer on government at Harvard University in 1912; elected as a Republican to the Sixty-fourth and to the four succeeding Congresses (March 4, 1915–March 3, 1925); was not a candidate for renomination in 1924, but was an unsuccessful candidate for the Republican nomination for United States Senator; subsequently elected to the Sixty-ninth Congress to fill the vacancy caused by the death of Harry I. Thayer; reelected to the Seventieth, Seventy-first, and Seventy-second Congresses and served from November 2, 1926, until his resignation effective October 1, 1932, having been appointed to the bench; judge of the United States Customs Court from October 2, 1932, until his resignation on October 2, 1942; engaged in agricultural pursuits; retired and resided in Center Lovell, Maine; died in North Conway, N. H., September 5, 1955; interment in Center Lovell Cemetery, Center Lovell, Maine.

DALTON, Tristram, a Senator from Massachusetts; born in Newbury, Mass., May 28, 1738; attended Dummer Academy, Byfield, Mass., and was graduated from Harvard College in 1755; studied law; was admitted to the bar but did not practice; engaged in mercantile pursuits; delegate from Massachusetts to the convention of committees of New England Provinces which met in Providence, R. I., December 25, 1776; member of the State house of representatives 1782–1788 and served as speaker in 1784 and 1785; elected to the United States Senate and served from March 4, 1789, to March 3, 1791; unsuccessful candidate for reelection in 1790; surveyor of the port of Boston from November 10, 1814, until his death in Boston, Mass., May 30, 1817; interment in the churchyard of St. Paul's Episcopal Church, Newburyport, Essex County, Mass.

DALY, John Burrwood, a Representative from Pennsylvania; born in Philadelphia, Pa., February 13, 1872; attended the public schools; was graduated from La Salle College, Philadelphia, Pa., in 1890 and from the University of Pennsylvania at Philadelphia in 1896; studied law; was admitted to the bar in 1896 and commenced practice in Philadelphia, Pa.; assistant city solicitor

1914–1922; member of the faculty of La Salle College 1923–1930; elected as a Democrat to the Seventy-fourth, Seventy-fifth, and Seventy-sixth Congresses and served from January 3, 1935, until his death in Philadelphia, Pa., March 12, 1939; interment in St. Denis Cemetery, South Ardmore, Montgomery County, Pa.

DALY, William Davis, a Representative from New Jersey; born in Jersey City, N. J., June 4, 1851; attended the public schools; from the age of fourteen until he was nineteen was employed as an iron molder; studied law; was admitted to the bar in 1874 and commenced practice in Hudson County, N. J.; assistant United States attorney for New Jersey 1885–1888; member of the State house of assembly 1889–1891; judge of the district court of Hoboken from 1891 until his resignation in 1892; member of the State senate 1892–1898; delegate to the Democratic National Convention at Chicago in 1896; chairman of the Democratic State convention in 1896 and member of the State committee 1896–1898; elected as a Democrat to the Fifty-sixth Congress and served from March 4, 1899, until his death in Hoboken, N. J., July 31, 1900; interment in New York Bay Cemetery.

DALZELL, John, a Representative from Pennsylvania; born in New York City April 19, 1845; moved with his parents to Pittsburgh, Pa., in 1847; attended the common schools and the Western University of Pennsylvania, Pittsburgh, Pa.; was graduated from Yale College with the class of 1865; studied law; was admitted to the bar in 1867 and commenced practice in Pittsburgh, Pa.; elected as a Republican to the Fiftieth and to the twelve succeeding Congresses (March 4, 1887–March 3, 1913); unsuccessful candidate for renomination in 1912; delegate to the Republican National Conventions at Chicago in 1904 and 1908; Regent of the Smithsonian Institution 1906–1913; withdrew from public life and business activities and resided in Washington, D. C.; died while on a visit to Altadena, Los Angeles County, Calif., October 2, 1927; interment in Allegheny Cemetery, Pittsburgh, Pa.

DAMRELL, William Shapleigh, a Representative from Massachusetts; born in Portsmouth, N. H., November 29, 1809; attended the public schools; learned the art of printing and became the proprietor of a large printing establishment in Boston; elected as the candidate of the American Party to the Thirty-fourth Congress and as a Republican to the Thirty-fifth Congress (March 4, 1855–March 3, 1859); suffered a paralytic stroke before the expiration of his term; was not a candidate for re-nomination in 1858; resumed business activities; died in Dedham, Norfolk County, Mass., May 17, 1860; interment in Forest Hills Cemetery.

DANA, Amasa, a Representative from New York; born in Wilkes-Barre, Pa., October 19, 1792; attended private schools and Dana Academy, Wilkes-Barre, Pa.; studied law in Owego, N. Y.; was admitted to the bar in 1817 and practiced; moved to Ithaca, N. Y., in 1821 and continued the practice of law; district attorney of Tompkins County 1823–1837; member of the State assembly in 1828 and 1829; president and trustee of the village of Ithaca in 1835, 1836, and 1839; elected judge of the court of common pleas of Tompkins County in 1837; elected as a Democrat to the Twenty-sixth Congress (March 4, 1839–March 3, 1841); was not a candidate for renomination in 1840; resumed the practice of law; elected to the Twenty-eighth Congress (March 4, 1843–March 3, 1845); resumed the practice of his profession and also engaged in banking; died in Ithaca, Tompkins County, N. Y., on December 24, 1867; interment in Ithaca City Cemetery.

DANA, Francis, a Delegate from Massachusetts; born in Charlestown, Mass., June 13, 1743; was graduated from Harvard College in 1762; studied law; was admitted to the bar and commenced practice in Boston in 1767; delegate to the Provincial Congress in 1774; spent two years in England endeavoring to adjust differences between Great Britain and the American Colonies; State councilor 1776–1780; Member of the Continental Congress 1776–1778 and was one of the signers of the Articles of Confederation July 9, 1778; elected September 28, 1779, secretary to accompany John Adams, who was appointed a commissioner to negotiate a treaty of peace with Great Britain and a treaty of commerce with Holland; appointed December 19, 1780, Minister Resident to Russia, but was never received as such; again a Member of the Continental Congress in 1784; judge of the supreme court of Massachusetts 1785–1791; appointed chief justice November 29, 1791, and served for fifteen years; member of the State convention which adopted the Federal Constitution in 1788; presidential elector in 1788, 1792, 1800, and 1808; a founder of the American Academy of Arts and Sciences; died in Cambridge, Middlesex County, Mass., April 25, 1811; interment in Old Cambridge Cemetery.

DANA, Judah, a Senator from Maine; born in Pomfret, Conn., April 25, 1772; attended the common schools, and was graduated from Dartmouth College, Hanover, N. H., in 1795; studied law; was admitted to the bar in 1798 and practiced in Fryeburg, Maine (at the time a district of Massachusetts); prosecuting attorney of Oxford County 1805–1811 and judge of probate 1811–1822; judge of the court of common pleas 1811–1823; was also a circuit judge; delegate to the State constitutional convention in 1819 at which a committee was appointed to draw up a constitution for Maine; member of the Maine Executive Council in 1834; appointed as a Democrat to the United States Senate to fill the vacancy caused by the resignation of Ether Shepley and served from December 7, 1836, to March 3, 1837, when a successor was elected and qualified; died in Fryeburg, Oxford County, Maine, December 27, 1845; interment in Village Cemetery.

DANA, Samuel, a Representative from Massachusetts; born in Groton, Mass., June 26, 1767; attended the district school; studied law; was admitted to the bar in 1789 and commenced practice in Groton; appointed postmaster of Groton January 1, 1801; member of the State house of representatives in 1803; attorney for Middlesex County 1807–1811; elected as a Democrat to the Thirteenth Congress to fill the vacancy caused by the resignation of William M. Richardson and served from September 22, 1814, to March 3, 1815; unsuccessful candidate for re-election in 1814 to the Fourteenth Congress; member of the State senate 1805–1812 and 1817 and served as its president in 1807, 1811, and 1812; chief justice of the court of common pleas in 1811 and 1812; delegate to the State constitutional convention in 1820; again a member of the State house of representatives 1825–1827; resumed the practice of his profession; died in Charlestown, Mass., November 20, 1835; interment in Groton Cemetery.

DANA, Samuel Whittlesey, a Representative and a Senator from Connecticut; born in Wallingford, Conn., February 13, 1760; pursued academic studies, and was graduated from Yale College in 1775; studied law; was admitted to the bar in 1778 and practiced in Middletown, Conn.; member of the general assembly 1789–1796; elected as a Federalist to the Fourth Congress to fill the vacancy caused by the resignation of Uriah Tracy; reelected to the Fifth and to the six succeeding Congresses and served from January 3, 1797, to May 10, 1810, when he resigned to become Senator; elected in 1810 to the United States Senate to fill the vacancy caused by the resignation of James Hillhouse; reelected in 1815 and served from May 10, 1810, to March 3, 1821; one of the managers appointed by the House of Representatives in 1798 to conduct the impeachment proceedings against William Blount, a Senator from Tennessee; mayor of Middletown, Conn., from 1822 until his death; accepted in 1825 the office of presiding judge of the Middlesex County Court, which he also held until his death in Middletown July 21, 1830; interment in Washington Street Cemetery.

DANAHER, John Anthony, a Senator from Connecticut; born in Meriden, New Haven County, Conn., January 9, 1899; attended parochial schools; during the First World War served in Battery A, First Battalion, Field Artillery, Students' Army Training Corps, at Yale University in 1918; commissioned a second lieutenant, Field Artillery, Officers' Reserve Corps; was graduated from Yale University, New Haven, Conn., in 1920; studied law at Yale Law School and served a law clerkship in New York, N. Y.; was admitted to the bar in 1922 and commenced practice in Hartford, Conn.; assistant United States attorney for the district of Connecticut 1922–1934; secretary of state of Connecticut 1933–1935, member of the State board of finance and control 1933–1935; elected as a Republican in 1938 to the United States Senate and served from January 3, 1939, to January 3, 1945; unsuccessful candidate for reelection in 1944; resumed the practice of law in Hartford, Conn., and Washington, D. C.; appointed a judge of the United States Court of Appeals for the District of Columbia Circuit, by President Eisenhower and took the oath of office November 20, 1953; resides in Washington, D. C.

DANE, Joseph, a Representative from Maine; born in Beverly, Essex County, Mass., October 25, 1778; received his early education in Beverly, Mass.; attended Phillips Academy, Andover, Mass., and was graduated from Harvard University, Cambridge, Mass., in 1799; studied law; was admitted to the bar in 1802 and commenced practice in Kennebunk, Maine (until 1820 a district of Massachusetts); a delegate to the Massachusetts constitutional conventions in 1816 and 1819; chosen a member of the executive council of Massachusetts in 1817, but declined the office; elected as a Federalist to the Sixteenth Congress to fill the vacancy caused by the resignation of John Holmes, a Representative from Massachusetts but residing in the new State of Maine, thus becoming the first Representative from Maine; reelected to the Seventeenth Congress and served from November 6, 1820, to March 3, 1823; was not a candidate for renomination in 1822; member of the Maine House of Representatives in 1824, 1825, 1832, 1833, 1839, and 1840; served in the State senate in 1829; declined to serve as executive councilor of Maine in 1841; died in Kennebunk, York County, Maine, May 1, 1858; interment in Hope Cemetery, Hope, Knox County, Maine.

DANE, Nathan, a Delegate from Massachusetts; born in Ipswich, Mass., December 29, 1752; was graduated from Harvard College in 1778; taught school; studied law; was admitted to the bar and commenced practice in Beverly, Mass., in 1782; member of the State house of representatives 1782–1785; Member of the Continental Congress 1785–1788; served in the State senate in 1790, 1791, and 1794–1797; judge of the court of common pleas for Essex County in 1794; commissioner to codify the laws of Massachusetts in 1795; presidential elector on the Clinton ticket in 1812; was selected the same year to make a new publication of the statutes; member of the Hartford convention of 1814; elected delegate to the State constitutional convention of 1820, but did not serve; died in Beverly, Essex County, Mass., February 15, 1835; interment in Central Cemetery.

DANFORD, Lorenzo, a Representative from Ohio; born in Washington Township, Belmont County, Ohio, on October 18, 1829; attended the common schools and a college at Waynesburg, Pa., for two years; studied law; was admitted to the bar at St. Clairsville, Belmont County, Ohio, in September 1854, and commenced practice there; presidential elector on the American Party ticket of Fillmore and Donelson in 1856; prosecuting attorney of Belmont County from 1857 to 1861, when he resigned to enlist in the Union Army; during the Civil War enlisted in the Fifteenth Regiment, Ohio Volunteer Infantry, as a private; commissioned a lieutenant and later a captain, and served until honorably discharged in August 1864; resumed the practice of his profession in St. Clairsville; presidential elector on the Republican ticket of Lincoln and Johnson in 1864 and of Harrison and Reid in 1892; elected as a Republican to the Forty-third, Forty-fourth, and Forty-fifth Congresses (March 4, 1873–March 3, 1879); was not a candidate for renomination in 1878; resumed the practice of his profession; elected to the Fifty-fourth, Fifty-fifth, and Fifty-sixth Congresses and served from March 4, 1895, until his death in St. Clairsville, Ohio, June 19, 1899; interment in the Methodist Episcopal Cemetery.

DANFORTH, Henry Gold, a Representative from New York; born in the town of Gates (now part of Rochester), Monroe County, N. Y., June 14, 1854; attended private schools in Rochester, N. Y., and Phillips Exeter Academy, Exeter, N. H.; was graduated from the collegiate department of Harvard University in 1877 and from the law department in 1880; was admitted to the bar in 1880 and commenced practice in Rochester; director of the Rochester General Hospital 1889–1918; member of the board of managers of the New York State Reformatory, Elmira, N. Y., 1900–1902; trustee of the Reynolds Library 1906–1918; president of the Rochester Bar Association in 1909; elected as a Republican to the Sixty-second, Sixty-third, and Sixty-fourth Congresses (March 4, 1911–March 3, 1917); unsuccessful candidate for renomination in 1916; resumed the practice of law; died in Rochester, N. Y., April 8, 1918; interment in Mount Hope Cemetery.

DANIEL, Charles Ezra, a Senator from South Carolina; born in Elberton, Elbert County, Ga., November 11, 1895; moved with his family to Anderson, S. C., in 1898 and attended the public schools; student at The Citadel, Charleston, S. C., 1916–1918; during World War I served as a lieutenant in the Fifty-first Infantry, Sixth Division, 1917–1919; organized the Daniel Construction Co. in 1935, serving as president, treasurer, director, and chairman of board of directors; member of the board of directors of Eastern Air Lines, Inc., Georgia-Pacific Corp., Graniteville Co., Liberty Life Insurance Co., Ross Builders Supplies, Inc., Saco-Lowell Shops, South Carolina National Bank, Southern Bell Telephone Co., and J. P. Stevens Co., Inc., life trustee of Clemson College and member of the board of South Carolina Foundation of Independent Colleges; appointed as a Democrat to the United States Senate to fill the vacancy caused by the death of Burnet R. Maybank and served from September 6, 1954, until his resignation December 23, 1954; was not a candidate for election to fill the vacancy; resumed management of his business interests; is a resident of Greenville, S. C.

DANIEL, Henry, a Representative from Kentucky; born in Louisa County, Va., March 15, 1786; attended the public schools; moved to Kentucky; studied law; was admitted to the bar and commenced practice in Mount Sterling, Montgomery County, Ky.; member of the State house of representatives in 1812; served in the War of 1812 as captain of the Eighth Regiment, United States Infantry, 1813–1815; again a member of the

State house of representatives in 1819 and 1826; elected as a Jackson Democrat to the Twentieth, Twenty-first, and Twenty-second Congresses (March 4, 1827–March 3, 1833); unsuccessful candidate for reelection in 1832 to the Twenty-third Congress; resumed the practice of law; died in Mount Sterling, Ky., October 5, 1873; interment in Macphelah Cemetery.

DANIEL, John Reeves Jones, a Representative from North Carolina; born near Halifax, Halifax County, N. C., January 13, 1802; instructed privately at home; was graduated from the University of North Carolina at Chapel Hill in 1821; studied law; was admitted to the North Carolina bar in 1823 and commenced the practice of law in Halifax, N. C.; member of the State house of commons 1832–1834; elected attorney general of North Carolina in 1834; elected as a Democrat to the Twenty-seventh and to the five succeeding Congresses (March 4, 1841–March 3, 1853); was not a candidate for renomination in 1852 to the Thirty-third Congress; resumed the practice of law; moved to Louisiana in 1860 and settled near Shreveport; continued the practice of law and also engaged in planting; died in Shreveport, Caddo Parish, La., June 22, 1868.

DANIEL, John Warwick, a Representative and a Senator from Virginia; born in Lynchburg, Va., September 5, 1842; attended private schools, Lynchburg College, and Dr. Gessner Harrison's University School; during the Civil War entered the Confederate Army in May 1861 as second lieutenant in the Provisional Army of Virginia and drillmaster in the Twenty-seventh Virginia Infantry, Stonewall Brigade; became second lieutenant and later first lieutenant of Company A, Eleventh Virginia Infantry; also adjutant of the same regiment; wounded in the first Battle of Manassas and at Boonsboro, Md.; raised a company of Cavalry and was elected captain in 1862, but the conscription act of the Confederate Congress remanded officers and men to their old regiments; major and chief of staff for Gen. Jubal A. Early until crippled in the Battle of the Wilderness May 6, 1864; studied law at the University of Virginia at Charlottesville; was admitted to the bar in 1866 and commenced practice at Lynchburg, Va.; published his legal work on Attachments in 1869 and on Negotiable Instruments in 1876; member of the State house of delegates 1869–1872; served in the State senate 1875–1881; presidential elector on the Democratic ticket of Tilden and Hendricks in 1876; delegate at large to the Democratic National Conventions in 1880, 1888, 1892, 1896, and 1900; unsuccessful candidate for Governor in 1881; elected as a Democrat to the Forty-ninth Congress (March 4, 1885–March 3, 1887); did not seek renomination in 1886, having been elected Senator; elected in 1885 to the United States Senate; reelected in 1891, 1897, 1904, and 1910, but the credentials of his last election were never presented to the Senate owing to his demise before the commencement of the session; served from March 4, 1887, until his death in Lynchburg, Va., June 29, 1910; interment in Spring Hill Cemetery.

DANIEL, Price Marion, a Senator from Texas; born in Dayton, Liberty County, Tex., October 10, 1910; lived in Liberty and Fort Worth, Tex., as a youth; attended the public schools; reporter, Fort Worth Star-Telegram in 1926 and 1927 and Waco News Tribune 1929–1931; graduated from Baylor University, Waco, Tex., in 1931 and from the law school of the same university in 1932; admitted to the Texas bar in 1932 and began practice in Liberty, Tex.; coowner and publisher of two weekly newspapers, the Liberty Vindicator and the Anahuac Progress; member of the State Democratic executive committee 1939–1941; member of the State house of representatives 1939–1943, serving as speaker in 1943; enlisted as a private in the United States Army in 1943 and served in the Pacific Theater and in Japan until discharged as a captain in June 1946; attorney general of Texas 1946–1953; elected as a Democrat to the United States Senate for the term beginning January 3, 1953, and served until his resignation January 14, 1957; elected Governor of Texas in 1956 for a two-year term beginning January 15, 1957; reelected in 1958 and again in 1960 for the term ending January 15, 1963; is a resident of Austin, Tex.

DANIELL, Warren Fisher, a Representative from New Hampshire; born in Newton Lower Falls, Middlesex County, Mass., June 26, 1826; attended the common schools; moved with his parents to Franklin, Merrimack County, N. H., in 1834; continued his studies until fourteen years of age, when he entered his father's paper mill as an apprentice; constructed a paper mill at Waterville, Maine, in 1852, and in the following year managed a similar mill in Pepperell, Mass.; returned to Franklin, N. H., in 1854 and engaged in the manufacture of paper; also engaged in agricultural pursuits, the breeding of blooded stock, and banking; member of the State house of representatives in 1861, 1862, and 1870–1877; delegate to the Democratic National Convention at Baltimore in 1872; served in the State senate in 1873 and 1874; elected as a Democrat to the Fifty-second Congress (March 4, 1891–March 3, 1893); was not a candidate for renomination in 1892; continued his activities in the manufacture of paper at Franklin, N. H., until 1898, being interested in the Winnepesogee Paper Co.; died in Franklin, N. H., July 30, 1913; interment in Franklin Cemetery.

DANIELS, Charles, a Representative from New York; born in New York City March 24, 1825; at an early age he was taken to Toledo, Ohio, and learned his father's trade of shoemaker; moved to Buffalo, N. Y., in 1842, where he studied law; was admitted to the bar in 1847 and commenced practice in Buffalo; elected an associate justice of the New York Supreme Court in 1863; appointed by Governor Seymour to hold the office of justice of that court until January 1, 1864, when the term to which he had been elected commenced; twice reelected, and served until December 1891, when he reached the age limit and was retired; elected as a Republican to the Fifty-third and Fifty-fourth Congresses (March 4, 1893–March 3, 1897); was not a candidate for renomination in 1896 to the Fifty-fifth Congress; died in Buffalo, N. Y., December 20, 1897; interment in Forest Lawn Cemetery.

DANIELS, Dominick V., a Representative from New Jersey; born in Jersey City, Hudson County, N. J., October 18, 1908; educated in the Jersey City public schools; attended Fordham University, New York City, N. Y.; graduated from Rutgers University Law School, New Brunswick, N. J., in 1929; was admitted to the New Jersey bar in 1930 and commenced the practice of law in Jersey City, N. J.; appointed magistrate of the Jersey City Municipal Court in May 1952, reappointed in 1955, and subsequently was appointed presiding magistrate, in which capacity he served until March 1958; elected as a Democrat to the Eighty-sixth Congress (January 3, 1959–January 3, 1961). *Reelected to the Eighty-seventh Congress.*

DANIELS, Milton John, a Representative from California; born in Cobleskill, Schoharie County, N. Y., April 18, 1838; attended the public schools; when a boy moved to Bradford County, Pa., and engaged with his father in the lumber business; moved to Rochester, Minn., in 1856; appointed deputy postmaster of Rochester in 1859; entered Middlebury Academy, Wyoming County, N. Y., in 1860; left the academy and volunteered April 23, 1861, for service in the Civil War; returned to Minnesota and raised a company in August 1862, and was commissioned second lieutenant of Company F, Ninth Regiment, Minnesota Volunteers; took command of the Third Minnesota Mounted Infantry in the Indian war of 1862; joined his company at St. Louis in 1863, and was commissioned captain; in March 1865 was commissioned captain and commissary of subsistence by President Lincoln and assigned to duty by General Canby at Baton Rouge, La.; commissioned major by brevet by President Johnson in 1865; mustered out and returned home in January 1866; engaged in banking; member of the State house of representatives 1882–1886; served in the State senate 1886–1890; president of the Minnesota State Board of Asylums for the Insane 1882–1888; moved to California in 1889 and located in Riverside; engaged in horticultural pursuits; elected as a Republican to the Fifty-eighth Congress (March 4, 1903–March 3, 1905); was not a candidate for renomination in 1904 to the Fifty-ninth Congress; resumed his occupation as horticulturist in Riverside, Riverside County, Calif., until his death there on December 1, 1914; interment in Evergreen Cemetery.

DANNER, Joel Buchanan, a Representative from Pennsylvania; born in Liberty, Md., in 1804; engaged in the hardware business and carriage building at Gettysburg, Pa.; justice of the peace; elected as a Democrat to the Thirty-first Congress to fill the vacancy caused by the death of Henry Nes and served from December 2, 1850, to March 3, 1851; resumed his former business pursuits in Gettysburg, Pa., where he died July 29, 1885; interment in Evergreen Cemetery.

DARBY, Ezra, a Representative from New Jersey; born in Scotch Plains, N. J., June 7, 1768; attended the common schools; engaged in agricultural pursuits; held offices as chosen freeholder, assessor, and justice of the peace from 1800 to 1804; member of the State house of assembly 1802–1804; elected as a Democrat to the Ninth and Tenth Congresses and served from March 4, 1805, until his death in Washington, D. C., January 27, 1808; interment in Congressional Cemetery.

DARBY, Harry, a Senator from Kansas; born in Kansas City, Wyandotte County, Kans., January 23, 1895; attended the public schools; was graduated from the University of Illinois in 1917 and 1929; with Missouri Boiler Works Co., Kansas City, Kans., as helper, boilermaker, iron worker, and foreman 1911–1915; shop superintendent 1915–1917, and vice president until 1919; during the First World War entered the service in April 1917 and served overseas with the Third Division as a second lieutenant and was discharged as a captain in January 1919; industrialist; farmer-stockman; owner and chairman of the board of the Darby Corp. 1920–; founder and chairman of the board of Leavenworth Steel, Inc.; founder and chairman of the board of Darby Railway Cars, Inc.; director of C. R. I. & P. R. R. (Chicago) in 1948 and 1949 and 1951–; Riverview State Bank, Kansas City, Kans., 1940–1949 and 1951–1956; Commercial National Bank, Kansas City, Kans., 1956–; Central Surety & Insurance Corp., Kansas City, Mo., 1953–; Kansas City Stockyards Co., 1954–; Wyandotte Hotel, Inc., Kansas City, Kans., 1951–; United Utilities, Inc., Abilene, Kans., 1940–1949; Crown Drug Co., 1940–1948; Gas Service Co., 1942–1949 and 1951–; aide-de-camp, lieutenant colonel on Governor's staff, Kansas, in 1928; chairman, State highway commission, 1933–1937; delegate to the Republican National Conventions in 1940, 1944, 1948, 1952, 1956, and 1960; appointed as a Republican to the United States Senate to fill the vacancy caused by the death of Clyde M. Reed and served from December 2, 1949, to November 28, 1950, a successor having been elected; was not a candidate for election to fill the vacancy; resumed business and political activities; resides in Kansas City, Kans.

DARBY, John Fletcher, a Representative from Missouri; born in Person County, N. C., December 10, 1803; attended the public schools; moved with his father to Missouri in 1818, where he worked on a farm; moved to Frankfort, Ky., in 1825; studied law; was admitted to the bar and afterward practiced in St. Louis, Mo.; mayor of St. Louis 1835–1841; member of the Missouri Senate in 1838; elected as a Whig to the Thirty-second Congress (March 4, 1851–March 3, 1853); returned to St. Louis and engaged in banking; died near Pendleton Station, Warren County, Mo., May 11, 1882; interment in Calvary Cemetery, St. Louis, Mo.

DARDEN, Colgate Whitehead, Jr., a Representative from Virginia; born on a farm near Franklin, Southampton County, Va., February 11, 1897; attended the public schools; was graduated from the University of Virginia at Charlottesville in 1922 and from Columbia University, New York City, N. Y., in 1923; awarded a Carnegie Fellowship to Oxford University, England, in 1924; served with the French Army in 1916 and 1917; during the First World War served as a lieutenant in the United States Marine Corps Air Service; studied law; was admitted to the bar in 1922 and commenced practice in Norfolk, Va.; member of the State house of delegates 1930–1933; elected as a Democrat to the Seventy-third and Seventy-fourth Congresses (March 4, 1933–January 3, 1937); unsuccessful candidate for renomination in 1936; again elected to the Seventy-sixth and Seventy-seventh Congresses and served from January 3, 1939, until his resignation in March 1, 1941, to become a candidate for Governor; Governor of Virginia from January 21, 1942, to January 16, 1946; president of the University of Virginia at Charlottesville since June 23, 1947; is a resident of Charlottesville, Va.

DARGAN, Edmund Strother, a Representative from Alabama; born near Wadesboro, Montgomery County, N. C., April 15, 1805; pursued preparatory studies at home; studied law; was admitted to the bar in Wadesboro in 1829; moved to Washington, Ala., where he commenced the practice of law and was for several years a justice of the peace; moved to Montgomery in 1833 and to Mobile in 1841; judge of the circuit court, Mobile district, in 1841 and 1842; served in the State senate in 1844; mayor of Mobile in 1844; elected as a Democrat to the Twenty-ninth Congress (March 4, 1845–March 3, 1847); did not seek renomination in 1846; associate justice of the State supreme court in 1847, and in 1849 became chief justice; resigned in December 1852 and resumed the practice of law; delegate to the State convention in 1861 and voted for the ordinance of secession; Member of the first Confederate House of Representatives; resumed the practice of law in Mobile, Ala., and died there on November 22, 1879; interment in Magnolia Cemetery.

DARGAN, George William (great-grandson of Lemuel Benton), a Representative from South Carolina; born at "Sleepy Hollow," near Darlington, Darlington County, S. C., May 11, 1841; attended the schools of his native county and the South Carolina Military Academy; served in the Confederate Army throughout the Civil War; studied law; was admitted to the bar in 1872 and practiced in Darlington, S. C.; elected to the State house of representatives in 1877; solicitor of the fourth judicial circuit of South Carolina in 1880; elected as a Democrat to the Forty-eighth and to the three succeeding Congresses (March 4, 1883–March 3, 1891); was not a candidate for renomination in 1890; resumed the practice of law; died in Darlington, S. C., June 29, 1898; interment in First Baptist Churchyard.

DARLING, Mason Cook, a Representative from Wisconsin; born in Amherst, Hampshire County, Mass., May 18, 1801; attended the public schools; taught school in the State of New

York; studied medicine; was graduated from the Berkshire Medical College in 1824 and practiced medicine for thirteen years; moved to Wisconsin in 1837 and was one of the original settlers at Fond du Lac; member of the Territorial legislative assembly 1840–1846; member of the Territorial council in 1847 and 1848; upon the admission of Wisconsin as a State into the Union was elected as a Democrat to the Thirtieth Congress and served from June 9, 1848, to March 3, 1849; was not a candidate for renomination in 1848; was elected the first mayor of Fond du Lac in 1852; resumed the practice of medicine and was a dealer in real estate at Fond du Lac until 1864, when he moved to Chicago; died in Chicago, Ill., March 12, 1866; interment in Rienzi Cemetery, Fond du Lac, Wis.

DARLING, William Augustus, a Representative from New York; born in Newark, N. J., December 27, 1817; attended the public schools; moved to New York City, where he was employed as a clerk and afterwards engaged in the wholesale grocery business; director of the Mercantile Library Association; served eleven years as a private and officer in the New York National Guard; deputy receiver of taxes for the city of New York 1847–1854; served as president of the Third Avenue Railroad 1854–1865; presidential elector on the Republican ticket of Lincoln and Hamlin in 1860; elected as a Republican to the Thirty-ninth Congress (March 4, 1865–March 3, 1867); unsuccessful candidate for reelection in 1866 to the Fortieth Congress; unsuccessful candidate for mayor of New York City in 1866; served as collector of internal revenue for the ninth district of New York from April 26, 1869, to April 17, 1871, and as appraiser from April 18, 1871, to April 1, 1876; engaged in banking and served as president of the Murray Hill Bank; died in New York City May 26, 1895; interment in Trinity Cemetery.

DARLINGTON, Edward (cousin of Isaac Darlington and William Darlington), a Representative from Pennsylvania; born in West Chester, Chester County, Pa., September 17, 1795; moved in early youth with his parents to Delaware County; attended the common schools, and was graduated from West Chester Academy; taught school 1817–1820; studied law; was admitted to the bar in 1821 and commenced practice in Chester, Pa.; deputy attorney general 1824–1830; elected as a Whig to the Twenty-third and Twenty-fourth Congresses and as an Anti-Mason to the Twenty-fifth Congress (March 4, 1833–March 3, 1839); was not a candidate for renomination in 1838; resumed the practice of law; attorney for county commissioners 1846–1856; moved to Media, Pa., in 1851; district attorney of Delaware County 1851–1854; died in Media, Delaware County, Pa., November 21, 1884; interment in Chester Rural Cemetery, Chester, Pa.

DARLINGTON, Isaac (cousin of Edward Darlington and William Darlington), a Representative from Pennsylvania; born near West Chester, Chester County, Pa., December 13, 1781; attended Friends School at Birmingham, Chester County, Pa.; taught in the country schools; studied law; was admitted to the bar in 1801 and commenced practice in West Chester, Pa.; member of the State house of representatives 1807–1809; lieutenant and adjutant of the Second Regiment, Pennsylvania Volunteers, in 1814 and 1815; elected as a Federalist to the Fifteenth Congress (March 4, 1817–March 3, 1819); declined to be a candidate for renomination in 1818 to the Sixteenth Congress; was appointed deputy attorney general for Chester County in 1820; president judge of the judicial district comprising the counties of Chester and Delaware from May 1821 until the time of his death in West Chester, Chester County, Pa., April 27, 1839; interment in Friends Burying Ground, Birmingham, Chester County, Pa.

DARLINGTON, Smedley (second cousin of Edward Darlington, Isaac Darlington, and William Darlington), a Representative from Pennsylvania; born in Pocopson Township, Chester County, Pa., December 24, 1827; attended the common schools and the Friends' Central School, Philadelphia; teacher in the latter school for several years; while teaching he made stenographic reports of sermons, lectures, and speeches for the morning dailies of Philadelphia; established a school for boys in Ercildoun in 1851, which he conducted for three years; changed to a girls' school and presided over it for nine years; enlisted in the Civil War as a private and subsequently promoted to the rank of captain in Beaumont's independent company of cavalry, Pennsylvania Volunteer Emergency Militia; discharged with the company September 24, 1862; moved to West Chester in 1864; conducted an extensive banking and brokerage business; delegate to the Liberal Republican National Convention at Cincinnati in 1872 which nominated Horace Greeley for President and the Republican National Convention at St. Louis in 1896; elected as a Republican to the Fiftieth and Fifty-first Congresses (March 4, 1887–March 3, 1891); was not a candidate for renomination in 1890; resumed the brokerage business and banking; died in West Chester, Chester County, Pa., June 24, 1899; interment in Oakland Cemetery near West Chester, Pa.

DARLINGTON, William (cousin of Edward Darlington and Isaac Darlington), a Representative from Pennsylvania; born in Birmingham, Chester County, Pa., April 28, 1782; attended Friends School at Birmingham; spent his youth on a farm; became a botanist at an early age; studied medicine; was graduated from the medical department of the University of Pennsylvania at Philadelphia in 1804; went to the East Indies as ship's surgeon in 1806; returned to West Chester in 1807 and was a practicing physician there for a number of years; raised a company of volunteers at the beginning of the War of 1812 and was major of a volunteer regiment raised after the burning of the Capitol in Washington; elected as a Democrat to the Fourteenth Congress (March 4, 1815–March 3, 1817); elected to the Sixteenth and Seventeenth Congresses (March 4, 1819–March 3, 1823); appointed canal commissioner in 1825; president of the West Chester Railroad; established a natural-history society in West Chester in 1826; became noted as a botanist and was made a corresponding member of some forty literary and scientific societies in Europe and America; published several works on botany and natural history; director and president of the National Bank of Chester County 1830–1863; died in West Chester, Chester County, Pa., on April 23, 1863; interment in Oakland Cemetery.

DARRAGH, Archibald Bard, a Representative from Michigan; born in La Salle Township, Monroe County, Mich., December 23, 1840; attended the common schools and a private academy in Monroe, Mich.; entered the University of Michigan at Ann Arbor in 1857 and pursued a classical course for two years; moved to Claiborne County, Miss., and became a teacher; returned to Michigan upon the outbreak of the Civil War; enlisted in Company H, Eighteenth Regiment, Michigan Volunteer Infantry, in 1862; commissioned second lieutenant, Company D, Ninth Regiment, Michigan Volunteer Cavalry, in 1863; first lieutenant in 1864; promoted to captain June 9, 1865, and honorably discharged July 21, 1865, at Jackson, Mich.; superintendent of the public schools of Jackson in 1867; reentered the University of Michigan and was graduated in 1868; moved to St. Louis, Gratiot County, Mich., in 1870 and engaged in banking; elected treasurer of Gratiot County in 1872; member of the State house of representatives in 1882 and 1883; mayor of St. Louis, Mich., in 1893; member of the board of control of the State asylum; elected as a

Republican to the Fifty-seventh and to the three succeeding Congresses (March 4, 1901–March 3, 1909); was not a candidate for renomination in 1908; again engaged in banking; died in St. Louis, Mich., on February 21, 1927; interment in Oak Grove Cemetery.

DARRAGH, Cornelius, a Representative from Pennsylvania; born in Pittsburgh, Pa., in 1809; attended the Western University of Pennsylvania, and was graduated with the class of 1826; studied law; was admitted to the bar in 1829 and commenced practice in Pittsburgh; member of the State senate 1836–1839; United States district attorney for the western district of Pennsylvania 1841–1844; elected as a Whig to the Twenty-eighth Congress to fill the vacancy caused by the resignation of William Wilkins; reelected to the Twenty-ninth Congress and served from March 26, 1844, to March 3, 1847; attorney general of Pennsylvania from January 4, 1849, to April 28, 1851; died in Pittsburgh, Pa., on December 22, 1854; interment in Allegheny Cemetery.

DARRALL, Chester Bidwell, a Representative from Louisiana; born near Addison, Somerset County, Pa., June 24, 1842; attended the common schools; studied medicine and was graduated from the Albany (N. Y.) Medical College; during the Civil War entered the Union Army as assistant surgeon of the Eighty-sixth Regiment, New York Volunteers, and later was promoted to surgeon; resigned from the Army while on duty in Louisiana in 1867 and engaged in mercantile pursuits and planting in Brashear (now Morgan City), La.; member of the State senate of Louisiana in 1868; delegate to the Republican National Convention at Philadelphia in 1872 and at Cincinnati in 1876; elected as a Republican to the Forty-first and to the three succeeding Congresses (March 4, 1869–March 3, 1877); presented credentials as a Member-elect to the Forty-fifth Congress and served from March 4, 1877, to February 20, 1878, when he was succeeded by Joseph H. Acklen, who contested the election; was not a candidate for renomination in 1878; moved to Morgan City, St. Mary Parish, La.; elected to the Forty-seventh Congress (March 4, 1881–March 3, 1883); unsuccessful candidate for reelection in 1882 to the Forty-eighth Congress; register of the United States land office, New Orleans, La., 1883–1885; engaged in sugarcane planting; unsuccessful candidate for election in 1888 to the Fiftieth Congress; withdrew from public life and moved to Washington, D. C., where he died on January 1, 1908; interment in Glenwood Cemetery.

DARROW, George Potter, a Representative from Pennsylvania; born in Waterford, New London County, Conn., February 4, 1859; attended the common schools of New London, Conn.; was graduated from Alfred University, Alfred, N. Y., in 1880; moved to Philadelphia, Pa., in 1888 and engaged in banking, in the manufacture of paints, and in the insurance business; president of the Twenty-second Sectional School Board of Philadelphia 1906–1909; member of the Philadelphia Common Council 1910–1915; elected as a Republican to the Sixty-fourth and to the ten succeeding Congresses (March 4, 1915–January 3, 1937); unsuccessful candidate for reelection in 1936 to the Seventy-fifth Congress; elected to the Seventy-sixth Congress (January 3, 1939–January 3, 1941); was not a candidate for renomination in 1940; died in Philadelphia, Pa., June 7, 1943; interment in Ivy Hill Mausoleum.

DAUGHERTY, James Alexander, a Representative from Missouri; born in Athens, McMinn County, Tenn., August 30, 1847, attended the common schools; moved to Missouri with his parents, who settled near Carterville, Jasper County, in 1867; active in all civic enterprises of the State and county; engaged in farming, stock raising, and mining; assisted in developing the lead and zinc fields of Missouri; associate judge for the western district of Jasper County 1890–1892, and presiding judge 1892–1896; member of the State house of representatives in 1897; served as president of the First National Bank of Carterville 1907–1920; elected as a Democrat to the Sixty-second Congress (March 4, 1911–March 3, 1913); unsuccessful candidate for renomination in 1912; resumed former business activities; served as fuel administrator for Jasper County during the First World War; appointed May 17, 1919, presiding judge of Jasper County and served until his death; died in Carterville, Jasper County, Mo., on January 26, 1920; interment in Webb City Cemetery, Webb City, Mo.

DAUGHTON, Ralph Hunter, a Representative from Virginia; born in Washington, D. C., September 23, 1885; attended public and private schools in Washington, D. C., and Prince Georges County, Md.; was graduated from the law department of National University, Washington, D. C., in 1905; was admitted to the bar in 1907 and practiced law in Washington, D. C.; joined the investigative agency of the Department of Justice, which later became the Federal Bureau of Investigation in 1910; moved to Norfolk, Va., in 1912, and served as chief of the F. B. I. for Virginia, North Carolina, West Virginia, and part of Maryland until after the First World War; commenced the private practice of law in Norfolk, Va.; served in the State house of delegates 1933–1940; member of the State senate 1940–1944; chairman of the Virginia State Boxing and Wrestling Commission 1934–1944; in 1938 was elected president of the Piedmont Baseball League and served for nine years; elected as a Democrat to the Seventy-eighth Congress to fill the vacancy caused by the resignation of Winder R. Harris and at the same time was elected to the Seventy-ninth Congress and served from November 7, 1944, to January 3, 1947; unsuccessful candidate for renomination in 1946; resumed the practice of law until his death; died in Norfolk, Va., December 22, 1958; interment in Mount Olivet Cemetery, Washington, D. C.

DAVEE, Thomas, a Representative from Maine; born in Plymouth, Mass., December 9, 1797; attended the common schools; moved to Maine, where he engaged in mercantile pursuits; member of the State house of representatives in 1826 and 1827; served in the State senate 1830–1832; high sheriff of Somerset County in 1835; postmaster of Blanchard from November 6, 1833, to March 24, 1837; elected as a Democrat to the Twenty-fifth and Twenty-sixth Congresses (March 4, 1837–March 3, 1841); was not a candidate for renomination in 1840; resumed mercantile pursuits; again a member of the State senate in 1841 and served until his death in Blanchard, Piscataquis County, Maine, December 9, 1841; interment in the Village Cemetery, Monson, Maine.

DAVENPORT, Franklin (nephew of Benjamin Franklin), a Senator and a Representative from New Jersey; born in Philadelphia, Pa., in September 1755; received an academic education; studied law in Burlington, N. J.; was admitted to the bar in 1776 and commenced practice in Gloucester City, N. J.; clerk of Gloucester County Court in 1776; during the Revolutionary War enlisted as a private in Capt. James Sterling's company of New Jersey Militia; was made brigade major on December 22, 1776; participated in the Battles of Trenton and Princeton; appointed brigade quartermaster on February 25, 1778, and in the same year assistant quartermaster for Gloucester County, serving in the latter capacity until the winter of 1778–1779; appointed colonel in the New Jersey Militia in 1779 and subsequently major general, which rank he held until his death; prosecutor of pleas in 1777; moved to Woodbury, N. J., in 1781 and continued the practice of law; appointed first surrogate of Gloucester County in 1785; member of the State general assembly 1786–1789; presidential elector in 1792 and 1812; colonel in the New Jersey Line during the Whisky Insurrection of 1794 and marched with the troops to Pittsburgh, Pa.; appointed brigadier general of Gloucester County Militia in 1796; appointed to the United States Senate to fill the vacancy caused by the resignation of John Rutherfurd and served from December 5, 1798, to March 3, 1799, when a successor was elected and qualified; elected to the Sixth Congress (March 4, 1799–March 3, 1801); was not a candidate for renomination in 1800; resumed the practice of law; appointed master in chancery in 1826; died in Woodbury, Gloucester County, N. J., July 27, 1832; interment in Presbyterian Cemetery, North Woodbury, N. J.

DAVENPORT, Frederick Morgan, a Representative from New York; born in Salem, Essex County, Mass., August 27, 1866; attended the public schools; moved with his parents to Pennsylvania in 1874 and settled in New Milford; moved to Yonkers, N. Y., in 1893; was graduated from Wesleyan University, Middletown, Conn., in 1889 and from Columbia University, New York City, in 1905; member of the faculty of political science of Hamilton College, Clinton, N. Y., 1904–1929; served in the State senate 1909–1911; unsuccessful Progressive candidate for Lieutenant Governor of New York in 1912 and for Governor in 1914; again a member of the State senate 1919–1925; chairman of the New York State Legislative Committee on Taxation and Retrenchment 1919–1925; delegate to the Republican National Convention at Cleveland in 1924; elected as a Republican to the Sixty-ninth and to the three succeeding Congresses (March 4, 1925–March 3, 1933); unsuccessful candidate for reelection in 1932 to the Seventy-third Congress and for election in 1934 to the Seventy-fourth Congress; president of the National Institute of Public Affairs, Washington, D. C., 1934–1949; chairman of the Federal Personnel Council, Washington, D. C., from 1939 until his retirement in 1953; died in Washington, D. C., December 26, 1956; interment in Woodlawn Cemetery, New York City, N. Y.

DAVENPORT, Harry James, a Representative from Pennsylvania; born in Wilmerding, Allegheny County, Pa., August 28, 1902; attended St. Peter's Parochial School and McKeesport High School; newspaper publisher; elected as a Democrat to the Eighty-first Congress (January 3, 1949–January 3, 1951); was an unsuccessful candidate for reelection in 1950 to the Eighty-second Congress and was also unsuccessful for the Democratic nomination in 1960 to the Eighty-seventh Congress; is a resident of Pittsburgh, Pa.

DAVENPORT, Ira, a Representative from New York; born in Hornellsville, Steuben County, N. Y., June 28, 1841; moved with his father to Bath, N. Y., in 1847; attended Haverling Academy, Bath, N. Y., and Russell Collegiate School, New Haven, Conn.; upon the death of his father in 1868 assumed the management of the large estate and business affairs; member of the State senate 1878–1881; comptroller of the State of New York 1881–1883; unsuccessful candidate for reelection in 1883; unsuccessful Republican candidate for Governor of New York in 1885; elected as a Republican to the Forty-ninth and Fiftieth Congresses (March 4, 1885–March 3, 1889); was not a candidate for renomination in 1888; retired from public life and devoted his time to the management of his private affairs; died in Bath, Steuben County, N. Y., October 6, 1904; interment in the family cemetery on his estate, "Riverside," Bath, N. Y.

DAVENPORT, James (brother of John Davenport of Connecticut), a Representative from Connecticut; born in Stamford, Conn., October 12, 1758; was graduated from Yale College, New Haven, Conn., in 1777; served in the commissary department of the Continental Army in the Revolutionary War; judge of the court of common pleas; member of the State house of representatives 1785–1790; served in the State senate 1790–1797; judge of Fairfield County Court from 1792 until 1796; elected to the Fourth Congress to fill the vacancy caused by the resignation of James Hillhouse; reelected to the Fifth Congress and served from December 5, 1796, until his death in Stamford, Conn., August 3, 1797; interment in North Field (now Franklin Street) Cemetery.

DAVENPORT, James Sanford, a Representative from Oklahoma; born on a farm near Gaylesville, Cherokee County, Ala., September 21, 1864; moved with his parents to Conway, Faulkner County, Ark., in 1880; attended the common schools, Vilona (Ark.) High School, and Greenbrier (Ark.) Academy; studied law; was admitted to the bar of Faulkner County February 14, 1890, and commenced practice in Conway; in October of that year moved to Muskogee, Indian Territory (now Oklahoma), and in 1893 to Vinita, where he engaged in the practice of law; member of the Territorial council 1897–1901, serving as speaker the last two years of his term; one of the attorneys for the Cherokee Nation 1901–1907; mayor of Vinita in 1903 and 1904; elected as a Democrat to the Sixtieth Congress on September 17, 1907, and served from November 16, 1907, when Oklahoma was admitted as a State into the Union, until March 3, 1909; unsuccessful candidate for reelection in 1908 to the Sixty-first Congress; elected to the Sixty-second, Sixty-third, and Sixty-fourth Congresses (March 4, 1911–March 3, 1917); unsuccessful candidate for reelection in 1916 to the Sixty-fifth Congress; resumed the practice of law in Vinita; was elected judge of the criminal court of appeals of Oklahoma in November 1926; reelected in 1932 and served until his death in Oklahoma City, Okla., January 3, 1940; interment in Fairview Cemetery, Vinita, Okla.

DAVENPORT, John (brother of James Davenport), a Representative from Connecticut; born in Stamford, Conn., January 16, 1752; pursued academic studies; was graduated from Yale College, New Haven, Conn., in 1770; engaged in teaching there in 1773 and 1774; studied law; was admitted to the bar in 1773 and practiced in Stamford, Conn.; member of the State house of representatives 1776–1796; served in the commissary department of the Continental Army during the Revolutionary War, attaining the rank of major in 1777; elected as a Federalist to the Sixth and to the eight succeeding Congresses (March 4, 1799–March 3, 1817); declined to be a candidate for reelection in 1816 and withdrew from public life; died in Stamford, Fairfield County, Conn., November 28, 1830; interment in North Field (now Franklin Street) Cemetery.

DAVENPORT, John, a Representative from Ohio; born near Winchester, Jefferson County, Va., January 9, 1788; attended the common schools; moved to Ohio in 1818 and engaged in mercantile pursuits; member of the State house of representatives in 1824, 1827, and 1830; member of the State senate in 1825 and 1826; elected as a supporter of John Quincy Adams to the Twentieth Congress (March 4, 1827–March 3, 1829); unsuccessful candidate for reelection in 1828 to the Twenty-first Congress; twice elected by the legislature as judge of the Monroe judicial circuit; died in Woodsfield, Monroe County, Ohio, July 18, 1855; interment in Green Mount Cemetery, Barnesville, Ohio.

DAVENPORT, Samuel Arza, a Representative from Pennsylvania; born near Watkins, Schuyler County, N. Y., January 15, 1834; moved to Pennsylvania with his parents, who settled in Erie, Erie County, in 1839; attended the Erie Academy; studied law; was admitted to the bar in 1854; subsequently, in 1855, was graduated from the Harvard Law School, and commenced the practice of his profession in Erie, Pa., the same year; elected district attorney for the county of Erie in 1860; owner and publisher of the Erie Gazette 1865–1890; delegate to the Republican National Conventions at Chicago in 1888 and at Minneapolis in 1892; elected as a Republican to the Fifty-fifth and Fifty-sixth Congresses (March 4, 1897-March 3, 1901); was not a candidate for renomination in 1900; resumed the practice of law in the county, State, and Federal courts; also interested in the Erie Car Works, and in the manufacture of organs and boots and shoes; died in Erie, Erie County, Pa., on August 1, 1911; interment in Erie Cemetery.

DAVENPORT, Stanley Woodward, a Representative from Pennsylvania; born in Plymouth, Luzerne County, Pa., July 21, 1861; attended the public schools and Wyoming Seminary; was graduated from the Wesleyan University, Middletown, Conn., in 1884; studied law; was admitted to the bar in 1890 and commenced practice in Plymouth, Pa., in 1891; appointed a director of the poor for the central district of Luzerne County in 1893; secretary and treasurer of the poor district; register of wills of Luzerne County 1894–1897; elected as a Democrat to the Fifty-sixth Congress (March 4, 1899-March 3, 1901); unsuccessful candidate for renomination in 1900; resumed the practice of law in Plymouth, Luzerne County, Pa., and died in that city September 26, 1921; interment in Plymouth Cemetery.

DAVENPORT, Thomas, a Representative from Virginia; born in Cumberland County, Va.; completed preparatory studies; studied law; was admitted to the bar and commenced practice in Meadville, Va.; elected as a Federalist to the Nineteenth and to the four succeeding Congresses (March 4, 1825–March 3, 1835); unsuccessful candidate for reelection in 1834 to the Twenty-fourth Congress; died near Meadville, Halifax County, Va., November 18, 1838.

DAVEY, Martin Luther, a Representative from Ohio; born in Kent, Portage County, Ohio, July 25, 1884; attended the public schools; was graduated from Oberlin Academy in 1906 and later attended Oberlin College; associated with his father in tree surgery in 1906; organized and became general manager of the Davey Tree Expert Co. (Inc.) in 1909 and became president in 1923; also became treasurer of the Davey Compressor Co. in 1929; also engaged in the real-estate business; mayor of Kent 1913–1918; elected as a Democrat to the Sixty-fifth Congress to fill the vacancy caused by the death of Ellsworth R. Bathrick; reelected to the Sixty-sixth Congress and served from November 5, 1918, to March 3, 1921; unsuccessful candidate for reelection in 1920 to the Sixty-seventh Congress; resumed his former business pursuits; delegate at large to the Democratic National Conventions at Chicago in 1932 and 1940; elected to the Sixty-eighth, Sixty-ninth, and Seventieth Congresses (March 4, 1923–March 3, 1929); was not a candidate for renomination in 1928 to the Seventy-first Congress; was an unsuccessful candidate for Governor in 1928 and 1940; elected Governor of Ohio and served from January 1935 to January 1939 (two terms); resumed his former business pursuits; died in Kent, Ohio, March 31, 1946; interment in Standing Rock Cemetery.

DAVEY, Robert Charles, a Representative from Louisiana; born in New Orleans, La., October 22, 1853; attended the public schools, and was graduated from St. Vincent's College, Cape Girardeau, Mo., in 1871; engaged in mercantile pursuits; elected to the State senate in 1879, 1884, and again in 1892; served as president pro tempore of the senate during the sessions of 1884 and 1886; judge of the first recorder's court in New Orleans 1880–1888; unsuccessful candidate for mayor of

New Orleans in 1888; elected as a Democrat to the Fifty-third Congress (March 4, 1893–March 3, 1895); declined to be a candidate for renomination in 1894; elected to the Fifty-fifth and to the five succeeding Congresses and served from March 4, 1897, until his death; had been reelected to the Sixty-first Congress, but died in New Orleans, La., December 26, 1908, before the close of the Sixtieth Congress; interment in Metairie Cemetery.

DAVIDSON, Alexander Caldwell, a Representative from Alabama; born near Charlotte, Mecklenburg County, N. C., December 26, 1826; attended the public schools of Marengo County, Ala., and was graduated from the University of Alabama at Tuscaloosa July 11, 1848; studied law in Mobile, Ala., but never practiced; engaged in cotton planting near Uniontown, Perry County, Ala.; member of the State house of representatives in 1880 and 1881; served in the State senate 1882–1885; elected as a Democrat to the Forty-ninth and Fiftieth Congresses (March 4, 1885–March 3, 1889); unsuccessful candidate for renomination in 1888; resumed agricultural pursuits; died at "Westwood," near Uniontown, Ala., November 6, 1897; interment in the Holy Cross Cemetery of Davidson Memorial Church, Uniontown, Perry County, Ala.

DAVIDSON, Irwin Delmore, a Representative from New York; born in New York, N. Y., January 2, 1906; attended the public schools; was graduated from Washington Square College of New York University in 1927 and from New York University Law School in 1928; was admitted to the bar in 1929 and commenced the practice of law in New York City; counsel for Legislative Bill Drafting Commission in 1935 and special counsel to New York State Mortgage Commission in 1936; attended the New York State Constitutional Convention in 1938 and acted as secretary to the Democratic leader; elected to the State assembly in 1936 and resigned in 1948; justice of the Court of Special Sessions in New York City from 1948 until his resignation in 1954 to become a candidate for United States House of Representatives; elected as a Democrat-Liberal to the Eighty-fourth Congress and served from January 3, 1955, until his resignation on December 31, 1956; elected judge of the Court of General Sessions in the county of New York in 1956 for a fourteen-year term; is a resident of New York, N. Y.

DAVIDSON, James Henry, a Representative from Wisconsin; born in Colchester, Delaware County, N. Y., June 18, 1858; attended the public schools and Walton (N. Y.) Academy; taught school in Delaware and Sullivan Counties, N. Y.; was graduated from the Albany Law School in 1884 and was admitted to the bar the same year; moved to Green Lake County, Wis., and commenced practice in Princeton in 1887; also taught school; elected district attorney of Green Lake County in 1888; chairman of the Republican congressional committee for the sixth district of Wisconsin in 1890; moved to Oshkosh, Wis., January 1, 1892, and continued the practice of law; appointed city attorney in May 1895 for two years; elected as a Republican to the Fifty-fifth and to the seven succeeding Congresses (March 4, 1897–March 3, 1913); unsuccessful candidate for reelection in 1912 to the Sixty-third Congress and for election in 1914 to the Sixty-fourth Congress; resumed the practice of his profession; elected to the Sixty-fifth Congress and served from March 4, 1917, until his death in Washington, D. C., August 6, 1918; interment in Riverside Cemetery, Oshkosh, Wis.

DAVIDSON, Robert Hamilton McWhorta, a Representative from Florida; born near Quincy, Gadsden County, Fla., September 23, 1832; attended the common schools and the Quincy Academy in Quincy, Fla.; studied law at the University of

Virginia, Charlottesville, Va.; was admitted to the bar in 1853 and commenced practice in Quincy, Fla.; member of the State house of representatives 1856–1859; served in the State senate 1860–1862; retired from the State senate in 1862 and served during the Civil War in the Confederate Army as captain of Infantry and later with rank of lieutenant colonel; member of the State constitutional convention in 1865; presidential elector on the Democratic ticket of Greeley and Brown in 1872; elected as a Democrat to the Forty-fifth and to the six succeeding Congresses (March 4, 1877–March 3, 1891); unsuccessful candidate for renomination in 1890 to the Fifty-second Congress; member of the State railroad commission in 1897 and 1898; engaged in the practice of his profession until his death in Quincy, Fla., January 18, 1908; interment in Western Cemetery.

DAVIDSON, Thomas Green, a Representative from Louisiana; born at Coles Creek, Jefferson County, Miss., August 3, 1805; completed preparatory studies; studied law; was admitted to the bar and commenced practice in Greensburg, La.; appointed register of the United States land office; member of the State house of representatives 1833–1846; elected as a Democrat to the Thirty-fourth, Thirty-fifth, and Thirty-sixth Congresses (March 4, 1855–March 3, 1861); resumed the practice of his profession; president of the Democratic State convention in 1855; served again in the State house of representatives 1874–1878, 1880, and 1883; died in Springfield, Livingston Parish, La., September 11, 1883; interment in Springfield Cemetery.

DAVIDSON, William, a Representative from North Carolina; born in Charleston, S. C., on September 12, 1778; completed preparatory studies; moved with his parents to North Carolina in early youth and settled in Mecklenburg County; engaged extensively in planting; member of the State senate in 1813, 1815–1819; and 1825; moved to Charlotte, N. C., in 1820; elected as a Federalist to the Fifteenth Congress to fill the vacancy caused by the resignation of Daniel M. Forney; reelected to the Sixteenth Congress and served from December 2, 1818, to March 3, 1821; unsuccessful candidate for reelection in 1820 to the Seventeenth Congress; again elected a member of the State senate and served from 1827 to 1830; retired from political activities and devoted his time to former business pursuits; died in Charlotte, N. C., on September 16, 1857; interment in the Old Cemetery.

DAVIES, Edward, a Representative from Pennsylvania; born in Churchtown, Caernarvon Township, Lancaster County, Pa., in November 1779; attended the rural schools; engaged in agricultural and mercantile pursuits; member of the State house of representatives in 1834 and 1835; elected as a Whig to the Twenty-fifth and Twenty-sixth Congresses (March 4, 1837–March 3, 1841); resumed his former business activities; died in Churchtown, Pa., May 18, 1853; interment in the cemetery at Pottstown, Pa.

DAVIES, John Clay, a Representative from New York; born in Albany, N. Y., May 1, 1920; attended Camden (N. Y.) High School; attended the University of Alabama at Tuscaloosa, Ala., and Hamilton College, Clinton, N. Y.; editor of the Camden (N. Y.) Chronicle in 1940 and 1941; maintained publicity office in Albany 1941–1943; with public relations department, Westinghouse Electric Corp., in New York City 1943–1946; vice president of the Earle Ferris Co., Inc., in New York City 1946–1948; partner in public relations business, Utica, N. Y., 1948–1953; elected as a Democrat to the Eighty-first Congress (January 3, 1949–January 3, 1951); unsuccessful candidate for reelection in 1950 to the Eighty-second Congress; writer; resides in Utica, N. Y., and Washington, D. C.

DAVILA, Felix Cordova, a Resident Commissioner from Puerto Rico; born in Vega Baja, P. R., on November 20, 1878; attended the public schools at Manati; came to Washington, D. C., and was graduated from National University Law School; was admitted to the bar in 1903 and commenced practice in San Juan, P. R.; judge of the municipal court of Caguas in 1904; judge of the municipal court of Manati 1904–1908; renominated as judge, and also as candidate for the Puerto Rico House of Representatives; declined both nominations; district attorney for the district of Aguadilla in 1908; judge of the district court of Guayama 1908–1910; judge of the district court of Arecibo in 1910 and 1911; judge of the district court of San Juan 1911–1917; elected as a Unionist a Resident Commissioner to the United States on July 16, 1917; reelected in 1920, 1924, and 1928 and served from August 7, 1917, until his resignation on April 11, 1932, having been appointed an associate justice of the supreme court of Puerto Rico, in which capacity he served until his death in Condado, San Juan County, P. R., on December 3, 1938; interment in Fournier Cemetery, San Juan, P. R.

DAVIS, Alexander Mathews, a Representative from Virginia; born in Old Mount Airy, Wythe County, Va., near Marion, Smyth County, Va., January 17, 1833; attended the old field schools and was privately tutored; was graduated from Emory and Henry College, Emory, Va.; studied law; was admitted to the bar in 1854 and commenced practice in Wytheville, Va.; moved to Independence, Grayson County, Va.; during the Civil War served in the Confederate Army as captain of Company C, Forty-fifth Virginia Infantry, in 1861; major in 1862; lieutenant colonel in 1864; captured near the close of the war and held prisoner on Johnson's Island, Lake Erie; member of the State senate 1869–1871; presented credentials as a Member-elect to the Forty-third Congress and served from March 4, 1873, to March 5, 1874, when he was succeeded by Christopher Y. Thomas, who contested his election; resumed the practice of law; died in Independence, Grayson County, Va., September 25, 1889; interment in the Davis family burial ground.

DAVIS, Amos (brother of Garrett Davis), a Representative from Kentucky; born in Mount Sterling, Ky., August 15, 1794; completed preparatory studies; studied law; was admitted to the bar and commenced practice in Mount Sterling; was sheriff of Montgomery County, Ky.; member of the State house of representatives in 1819, 1825, 1827, and 1828; unsuccessful candidate for election to the Twentieth and Twenty-second Congresses; elected as a Whig to the Twenty-third Congress (March 4, 1833–March 3, 1835); was a candidate for reelection, but died in Owingsville, Ky., while campaigning, June 11, 1835; interment in the City Cemetery, Mount Sterling, Ky.

DAVIS, Charles Russell, a Representative from Minnesota; born in Pittsfield, Pike County, Ill., September 17, 1849; moved with his father to Le Sueur County, Minn., in 1854; attended the public schools and also instructed by private tutor; was graduated from a business college at St. Paul, Minn.; studied law; was admitted to the bar March 6, 1872, and commenced practice in St. Peter, Minn.; city attorney and city clerk of St. Peter 1878–1898; prosecuting attorney of Nicollet County 1879–1889 and 1901–1903; served as captain in the Minnesota National Guard; member of the State house of representatives in 1889 and 1890; served in the State senate 1891–1895; elected as a Republican to the Fifty-eighth and to the ten succeeding Congresses (March 4, 1903–March 3, 1925); unsuccessful candidate for renomination in 1924; resumed the practice of law in Washington, D. C., and St. Peter, Minn.; died in Washington, D. C., July 29, 1930; interment in Woodlawn Cemetery, St. Peter, Minn.

DAVIS, Clifford, a Representative from Tennessee; born in Hazlehurst, Copiah County, Miss., November 18, 1897; moved with his parents to Memphis, Tenn., in 1911; attended the public schools of Memphis, and was graduated from the law department of the University of Mississippi at Oxford in 1918; was admitted to the bar in 1918 and commenced practice in Memphis, Tenn.; city judge of Memphis 1923–1927; vice mayor and commissioner of public safety of Memphis 1928–1940; elected as a Democrat to the Seventy-sixth Congress to fill the vacancy caused by the resignation of Walter C. Chandler; reelected to the Seventy-seventh and to the nine succeeding Congresses and served from February 15, 1940, to January 3, 1961. *Reelected to the Eighty-seventh Congress.*

DAVIS, Cushman Kellogg, a Senator from Minnesota; born in Henderson, Jefferson County, N. Y., June 16, 1838; moved with his parents to Waukesha, Wis.; attended the public schools, Carroll College in Waukesha, and was graduated from the University of Michigan at Ann Arbor in June 1857; studied law; was admitted to the bar in 1859 and commenced practice in Waukesha; during the Civil War served as first lieutenant in the Twenty-eighth Regiment, Wisconsin Volunteer Infantry, in 1861 and 1862; assistant adjutant general on the staff of Gen. Willis A. Gorman 1862–1864; moved to St. Paul, Minn., in 1865; member of the State house of representatives in 1867; United States district attorney 1868–1873; Governor of Minnesota in 1874 and 1875; elected as a Republican to the United States Senate in 1886; reelected in 1892 and again in 1898 and served from March 4, 1887, until his death; member of the commission which met in Paris, France, in September 1898 to arrange terms of peace after the war between the United States and Spain; died in St. Paul, Minn., November 27, 1900; interment in Arlington National Cemetery, Fort Myer, Va.

DAVIS, David (cousin of Henry Winter Davis), a Senator from Illinois; born near Cecilton, Cecil County, Md., March 9, 1815; attended the public schools of Maryland, and was graduated from Kenyon College, Ohio, in 1832; studied law in Lenox, Mass., and at the law school in New Haven; was admitted to the bar in 1835 and commenced practice in Pekin, Tazewell County, Ill.; moved to Bloomington, Ill., in 1836, and continued the practice of law; member of the State house of representatives in 1844; delegate to the State constitutional convention in 1847; elected judge of the eighth judicial circuit of Illinois in 1848, and held the office by repeated elections until his resignation in October 1862; delegate to the Republican National Convention at Chicago in 1860; appointed by President Lincoln as an Associate Justice of the Supreme Court of the United States in October 1862 and served until March 4, 1877, when he resigned to become a Senator; was a candidate for nomination for President at Cincinnati in 1872 on the Liberal-Republican ticket and received ninety-two and a half votes on the first ballot; elected by the Independents and Democrats to the United States Senate and served from March 4, 1877, until March 3, 1883; was not a candidate for renomination in 1882; elected President pro tempore of the Senate October 13, 1881, and served nearly two years; retired from public life; died in Bloomington, McLean County, Ill., June 26, 1886; interment in Evergreen Cemetery.

DAVIS, Ewin Lamar, a Representative from Tennessee; born in Bedford County, Tenn., February 5, 1876; attended the public schools, Webb School, Bell Buckle, Tenn., Woolwine School, Tullahoma, Tenn., and Vanderbilt University, Nashville, Tenn., 1895–1897; was graduated from Columbian (now George Washington) University Law School, Washington, D. C., in 1899; was admitted to the bar the same year and commenced practice in Tullahoma, Tenn.; delegate to all Democratic State conventions 1900–1910; presidential elector on the Democratic ticket of Parker and Davis in 1904; judge of the seventh judicial circuit of Tennessee 1910–1918; chairman of the district exemption board for the middle district of Tennessee in 1917 and 1918; director of the Traders National Bank of Tullahoma 1903–1940; trustee of Tennessee College for Women 1906–1939; elected as a Democrat to the Sixty-sixth and to the six succeeding Congresses (March 4, 1919–March 3, 1933); was an unsuccessful candidate for renomination in 1932; member of the Federal Trade Commission from May 23, 1933, until his death, serving as chairman in 1935, 1940, and 1945; member of the American National Committee, Third World Power Conference, in 1936; died in Washington, D. C., on October 23, 1949; interment in Oakwood Cemetery, Tullahoma, Tenn.

DAVIS, Garrett (brother of Amos Davis), a Representative and a Senator from Kentucky; born in Mount Sterling, Ky., September 10, 1801; completed preparatory studies; employed in the office of the county clerk of Montgomery County and afterward of Bourbon County; studied law; was admitted to the bar in 1823 and commenced practice in Paris, Ky.; member of the State house of representatives 1833–1835; elected as a Henry Clay Whig to the Twenty-sixth and to the three succeeding Congresses (March 4, 1839–March 3, 1847); declined to be a candidate for reelection in 1846 to the Thirtieth Congress; resumed the practice of law and also engaged in agricultural pursuits; declined to be a candidate for Lieutenant Governor on the ticket headed by John J. Crittenden in 1848; delegate to the State constitutional convention in 1849, but resigned because of his opposition to an elective judiciary; nominated by the American Party as a candidate for President of the United States in 1856, but declined; was opposed to secession; supported the Constitutional Union ticket of Bell and Everett in 1860; elected as an old-line Whig to the United States Senate to fill the vacancy caused by the expulsion of John C. Breckinridge; reelected as a Democrat in 1867 and served from December 10, 1861, until his death in Paris, Bourbon County, Ky., September 22, 1872; interment in Paris Cemetery.

DAVIS, George Royal, a Representative from Illinois; born in Palmer, Hampden County, Mass., January 3, 1840; completed classical studies at Williston Seminary, Easthampton, Mass., and was graduated in 1860; studied law; upon the outbreak of the Civil War entered the Union Army in July 1862 and served as captain in the Eighth Regiment, Massachusetts Volunteer Infantry, and as major in the Third Regiment, Rhode Island Volunteer Cavalry; engaged in manufacturing, the insurance business, and as financial agent at Chicago, Ill.; member of the State militia and senior colonel of the First Regiment, Illinois National Guard; elected as a Republican to the Forty-sixth, Forty-seventh, and Forty-eighth Congresses (March 4, 1879–March 3, 1885); was not a candidate for renomination in 1884; resumed his former business pursuits; served as treasurer of Cook County, Ill., 1886–1890; director general of the World's Columbian Exposition at Chicago in 1893; died in Chicago, Ill., November 25, 1899; interment in Rosehill Cemetery.

DAVIS, George Thomas, a Representative from Massachusetts; born in Sandwich, Mass., January 12, 1810; was graduated from Harvard University in 1829; studied law at Cambridge and Greenfield, Mass.; was admitted to the bar in 1832 and commenced practice in Greenfield, Franklin County; established the Franklin Mercury in 1833; member of the State senate in 1839 and 1840; elected as a Whig to the Thirty-second Congress (March 4, 1851–March 3, 1853); was not a candidate for renomination in 1852; resumed the practice of law in Taunton and Greenfield, Mass.; member of the State house of representatives in 1861; retired to private life; moved to Portland, Maine, where he died June 17, 1877; interment in Green River Cemetery, Greenfield, Mass.

DAVIS, Glenn Robert, a Representative from Wisconsin; born on a farm in Vernon, Waukesha County, Wis., October 28, 1914; attended the rural schools; was graduated from Mukwonago High School in 1930 and from State Teachers College, Platteville, Wis., in 1934; taught high school at Cottage Grove 1934–1936 and at Waupun 1936–1938; was graduated from the University of Wisconsin Law School at Madison in 1940; was admitted to the bar the same year and commenced practice in Waukesha; elected to the State assembly in 1940 and served from January 6, 1941, until his resignation in February 1942 to enlist in the United States Navy; served three and one-half years, with thirty-two months aboard an aircraft carrier in the South Pacific; discharged as a lieutenant on December 12, 1945; resumed the practice of law; elected as a Republican to the Eightieth Congress to fill the vacancy caused by the death of Robert K. Henry; reelected to the Eighty-first and to the three succeeding Congresses and served from April 22, 1947, to January 3, 1957; did not seek renomination in 1956, but was unsuccessful for the Republican nomination for United States Senator; was also unsuccessful for the senatorial nomination in 1957 to fill a vacancy; lawyer; is a resident of Waukesha, Wis.

DAVIS, Henry Gassaway (brother of Thomas Beall Davis and grandfather of Davis Elkins), a Senator from West Virginia; born in Baltimore, Md., November 16, 1823; moved to Howard County, Md., where he attended the country schools; lived and worked upon a farm until 1843; employed by the Baltimore & Ohio Railroad Co. for fourteen years as brakeman and conductor, and later had charge of the Piedmont terminal and shops; commenced the banking business and the mining of coal at Piedmont, W. Va., in 1858; engaged in railroad building and in the lumber business; elected to the House of Delegates of West Virginia in 1865; delegate to the Democratic National Convention at New York City in 1868 and at Baltimore in 1872; served in the State senate in 1868 and 1870; elected as a Democrat to the United States Senate in 1871; reelected in 1877 and served from March 4, 1871, to March 3, 1883; declined to be a candidate for renomination in 1882; settled in Elkins, Randolph County, W. Va., where he resumed banking and became president of the West Virginia Central Railroad and of the Davis Coal & Coke Co.; represented the United States at the Pan American conferences of 1889 and 1901; unsuccessful candidate for Vice President of the United States on the Democratic ticket with Alton B. Parker in 1904; chairman of the permanent Pan American Railway Committee from its organization in 1901 until his death in Washington, D. C., on March 11, 1916; interment in Maplewood Cemetery, Elkins, W. Va.

DAVIS, Henry Winter (cousin of David Davis), a Representative from Maryland; born in Annapolis, Md., August 16, 1817; was tutored privately; upon the removal of his father as president of St. John's College at Annapolis was sent to Alexandria, Va., and resided with his aunt; subsequently went to Wilmington and was instructed under the supervision of his father; returned to Maryland in 1827 with his father, who settled in Anne Arundel County; attended Wilmington College in 1826 and 1827; St. John's College, Annapolis, Md., and Hampden-Sidney College, Virginia; was graduated from Kenyon College, Gambier, Ohio, in 1837; studied law at the University of Virginia, Charlottesville, Va.; was admitted to the bar and commenced practice in Alexandria, Va.; in 1850 moved to Baltimore, Md., where he continued the practice of law and also engaged in literary pursuits; elected as the candidate of the American Party to the Thirty-

fourth Congress and reelected as a Republican to the Thirty-fifth and Thirty-sixth Congresses (March 4, 1855–March 3, 1861); unsuccessful candidate for reelection in 1860 to the Thirty-seventh Congress; elected on the Unconditional Union Party ticket to the Thirty-eighth Congress (March 4, 1863–March 3, 1865); was not a candidate for renomination in 1864; retired from professional and public life; died in Baltimore, Md., on December 30, 1865; interment in Greenmount Cemetery.

DAVIS, Horace, a Representative from California; born in Worcester, Mass., March 16, 1831; attended the public schools of Worcester, and Williams College, Williamstown, Mass.; was graduated from Harvard University in 1849; studied law in the Dane Law School of Harvard University, but did not engage in professional pursuits by reason of failing eyesight; moved to California in 1852 and engaged in mercantile pursuits; moved to San Francisco in 1860 and engaged in the flour-milling business; elected as a Republican to the Forty-fifth and Forty-sixth Congresses (March 4, 1877–March 3, 1881); unsuccessful candidate for reelection in 1880 to the Forty-seventh Congress; resumed his former business pursuits; member of the Republican National Committee 1880–1888; president of the Chamber of Commerce of San Francisco in 1883 and 1884; presidential elector on the Republican ticket of Blaine and Logan in 1884; president of the board of trustees of Leland Stanford Junior University 1885–1916; president of the University of California at Berkeley 1887–1890; died in San Francisco, Calif., July 12, 1916; interment in Cypress Lawn Cemetery.

DAVIS, Jacob Cunningham, a Representative from Illinois; born near Staunton, Augusta County, Va., September 16, 1820; attended the common schools and William and Mary College, Williamsburg Va.; moved to Warsaw, Hancock County, Ill., in 1838; studied law; was admitted to the bar and commenced practice in Warsaw; clerk of Hancock County; appointed circuit clerk in 1841; served in the State senate 1842–1848, and again from 1850 until his resignation in 1856, having been elected to Congress; elected as a Democrat to the Thirty-fourth Congress to fill the vacancy caused by the resignation of William A. Richardson and served from November 4, 1856, to March 3, 1857; was not a candidate to the Thirty-fifth Congress; resumed the practice of law in Clark County, Mo.; died in Alexandria, Clark County, Mo., December 25, 1883; interment in Mitchell Cemetery, near Alexandria, Mo.

DAVIS, Jacob Erastus, a Representative from Ohio; born in Beaver Village, Pike County, Ohio, October 31, 1905; attended the rural schools; was graduated from Beaver (Ohio) High School in 1923, from Ohio State University at Columbus in 1927, and from the law department of Harvard University, Cambridge, Mass., in 1930; was admitted to the bar in 1930 and commenced practice in Waverly, Ohio; prosecuting attorney of Pike County, Ohio, 1931–1935; member of the State house of representatives 1935–1937, serving as speaker pro tempore and majority floor leader in 1937; common pleas judge of Pike County 1937–1940; elected as a Democrat to the Seventy-seventh Congress (January 3, 1941–January 3, 1943); was an unsuccessful candidate for reelection in 1942 to the Seventy-eighth Congress; served as a special assistant to the Secretary of the Navy in 1943 and 1944; became vice president of the Kroger Company in 1945 in Cincinnati, Ohio, where he resides.

DAVIS, James Curran, a Representative from Georgia; born in Franklin, Heard County, Ga., May 17, 1895; attended the public schools, Reinhardt College, Waleska, Ga., and Emory College, Oxford, Ga.; studied law; was admitted to the bar in 1919 and commenced practice in Atlanta, Ga.; during the First

World War enlisted in the United States Marine Corps and served from December 24, 1917, until his discharge on January 11, 1919; served as a first lieutenant and captain in the Judge Advocate General's Department, Officers' Reserve Corps; resumed the practice of law; member of the State house of representatives from De Kalb County 1924–1928; attorney for the Georgia Department of Industrial Relations 1928–1931 and for De Kalb County 1931–1934; judge of superior courts, Stone Mountain judicial circuit, 1934–1947; member of the Reemployment Committee and of Selective Service Board No. 3 of De Kalb County during World War II; elected as a Democrat to the Eightieth and to the six succeeding Congresses (January 3, 1947– January 3, 1961).   *Reelected to the Eighty-seventh Congress.*

DAVIS, James Harvey (Cyclone), a Representative from Texas; born near Walhalla, Pickens District, S. C., December 24, 1853; moved to Texas with his parents, who settled in Wood County, near Winnsboro, in 1857; attended the common schools; taught school from 1875 to 1878; elected judge of Franklin County in 1878; studied law; was admitted to the bar in 1882 and commenced practice in Mount Vernon, Tex.; lecturer for the Farmers' Alliance for three years; engaged in the newspaper-publishing business; president of the Texas Press Association 1886–1888; unsuccessful Populist candidate for attorney general of Texas in 1892; was influential in the formation of the Populist Party and served as organizer and committeeman from 1892 to 1900; unsuccessful Populist candidate for election in 1894 to the Fifty-fourth Congress; declined the appointment as superintendent of agriculture for the Philippine Islands in 1914; elected as a Democrat to the Sixty-fourth Congress (March 4, 1915– March 3, 1917); unsuccessful candidate for renomination in 1916 to the Sixty-fifth Congress; returned to his home in Sulphur Springs, Hopkins County, Tex., and engaged in agricultural pursuits and Chautauqua work; moved to Kaufman, Tex., in 1935, where he died on January 31, 1940; interment in the City Cemetery, Sulphur Springs, Tex.

DAVIS, James John, a Senator from Pennsylvania; was born in Tredegar, South Wales, October 27, 1873; immigrated to the United States in 1881 with his parents, who settled in Pittsburgh, Pa., and later moved to Sharon, Pa.; attended the public schools and Sharon (Pa.) Business College; apprenticed as a puddler in the steel industry when 11 years of age and worked in Sharon, Pa., Pittsburgh, Pa., and Birmingham, Ala.; moved to Elwood, Ind., in 1893 and worked in steel and tin-plate mills; held various offices in the Amalgamated Association of Iron, Steel, and Tin Workers of America; city clerk of Elwood, Ind., 1898–1902; recorder of Madison County, Ind., 1903–1907; moved to Pittsburgh, Pa., in 1907 and engaged in organizational work for the Loyal Order of Moose; chairman of the Loyal Order of Moose War Relief Commission in 1918 and visited the various camps in the United States, Canada, and Europe; appointed Secretary of Labor by President Harding and reappointed by Presidents Coolidge and Hoover and served from March 5, 1921, until his resignation December 2, 1930, having been elected Senator; elected as a Republican to the United States Senate to fill the vacancy caused by the refusal of the Senate to seat William S. Vare; reelected in 1932 and 1938 and served from December 2, 1930, to January 3, 1945; unsuccessful candidate for reelection in 1944; resumed educational and organizational work for the Loyal Order of Moose; died in a hospital at Takoma Park, Md., November 22, 1947; interment in Uniondale Cemetery, Pittsburgh, Pa.

DAVIS, Jeff, a Senator from Arkansas; born near Richmond, Little River County, Ark., May 6, 1862; moved to Dover, Pope County, Ark., with his parents; attended school in Russell-

ville, Ark., and was graduated from Vanderbilt University, Nashville, Tenn., in 1884; studied law; was admitted to the bar in Pope County, Ark., at the age of nineteen years and commenced practice in Russellville, Ark.; prosecuting attorney of the fifth judicial district 1892–1896; attorney general of the State 1898– 1900; Governor of Arkansas 1901–1906; continued the practice of law at Little Rock, Ark., in 1906; delegate to the Democratic National Convention at St. Louis in 1904; elected as a Democrat to the United States Senate and served from March 4, 1907, until his death in Little Rock, Ark., January 3, 1913; interment in Mount Holly Cemetery.

DAVIS, Jefferson, a Representative and a Senator from Mississippi; born in what is now Fairview, Todd (formerly Christian) County, Ky., June 3, 1808; moved with his parents to a plantation near Woodville, Wilkinson County, Miss.; attended the country schools, St. Thomas College, Washington County, Ky., Jefferson College, Adams County, Miss., Wilkinson County Academy, and Transylvania University, Lexington, Ky.; was graduated from the United States Military Academy, West Point, N. Y., in 1828; served in the Black Hawk War in 1830 and 1831; promoted to the rank of first lieutenant in the First Dragoons March 4, 1833, "for gallant service," and served until June 30, 1835, when he resigned; moved to his plantation, "Brierfield," in Warren County, Miss., and engaged in cotton planting; presidential elector on the Democratic ticket of Polk and Dallas in 1844; elected as a Democrat to the Twenty-ninth Congress and served from March 4, 1845, until June 1846, when he resigned to command the First Regiment of Mississippi Riflemen in the war with Mexico; sailed with the regiment from New Orleans July 21, 1846; was with General Taylor in the three days' siege of Monterrey, where he greatly distinguished himself, as he afterward did at Buena Vista; appointed brigadier general May 27, 1847, but declined; appointed to the United States Senate to fill the vacancy caused by the death of Jesse Speight; subsequently was elected and served from August 10, 1847, until September 23, 1851, when he resigned; unsuccessful as a State Rights Democratic candidate for Governor in 1851; appointed Secretary of War by President Pierce and served from March 7, 1853, to March 3, 1857; again elected to the United States Senate and served from March 4, 1857, until January 21, 1861, when he withdrew with other Senators, after explaining his purpose to the Senate; commissioned major general of the State militia January 25, 1861; chosen President of the Confederacy by the Provisional Congress and inaugurated in Montgomery, Ala., February 18, 1861; elected President of the Confederacy for a term of six years and inaugurated in Richmond, Va., February 22, 1862; captured by the Union troops in Irwinsville, Ga., May 10, 1865; imprisoned in Fortress Monroe on May 22, 1865; indicted for treason May 8, 1866, and was paroled in the custody of the court on May 13, 1867; a nolle prosequi was ordered by the Government in December 1868; returned to Mississippi and spent the remaining years of his life writing; died in New Orleans, La., on December 6, 1889; interment in Metairie Cemetery, New Orleans, La.; reinterment on May 31, 1893, in Hollywood Cemetery, Richmond, Va.

DAVIS, John, a Representative and a Senator from Massachusetts; born in Northboro, Mass., January 13, 1787; attended Leicester Academy, and was graduated from Yale College in 1812; studied law; was admitted to the bar and commenced practice in Worcester, Mass., in 1815; elected as a National-Republican to the Nineteenth and to the four succeeding Congresses and served from March 4, 1825, to January 14, 1834, when he resigned, having been elected Governor by the legislature, the popular election having failed; Governor of Massachusetts in 1834 and 1835; elected as a Whig to the United

States Senate and served from March 4, 1835, to January 5, 1841, when he resigned; again Governor of Massachusetts 1841–1843; nominated for Vice President by a Whig mass meeting held in Dayton, Ohio, in 1842, but the action was not ratified by the Whig National Convention at Baltimore in 1844; again elected in 1845 to the United States Senate to fill the vacancy caused by the death of Isaac C. Bates; reelected in 1847 and served from March 24, 1845, to March 3, 1853; declined to be a candidate for renomination in 1852, and retired from public life; died in Worcester, Mass., on April 19, 1854; interment in the Rural Cemetery.

DAVIS, John, a Representative from Pennsylvania; born in Solebury Township, Bucks County, Pa., August 7, 1788; moved to Maryland and settled on a farm at Rock Creek Meeting House in 1795; attended the common schools; returned to Pennsylvania in 1812 and settled in what is now Davisville; engaged in agricultural and mercantile pursuits; served as captain in the War of 1812; rose to the rank of major general of militia; elected as a Democrat to the Twenty-sixth Congress (March 4, 1839–March 3, 1841); unsuccessful candidate for reelection in 1840 to the Twenty-seventh Congress; appointed surveyor of the port of Philadelphia by President Polk and served from March 17, 1845, to March 18, 1849; resumed his former business activities; delegate to several Democratic State and National conventions; died in Davisville, Pa., April 1, 1878; interment in Davisville Baptist Church Cemetery, Bucks County, Pa.

DAVIS, John, a Representative from Kansas; born near Springfield, Sangamon County, Ill., August 9, 1826; moved with his parents to Macon County in 1830; attended the country schools, Springfield Academy, and Illinois College, Jacksonville, Ill.; engaged in agricultural and horticultural pursuits near Decatur, Ill.; moved to Kansas in 1872 and located on a farm near Junction City; secretary of the Central Kansas Horticultural Society for many years; elected president of the first distinctive farmers' convention held in Kansas in 1873, out of which grew the Farmers' Cooperative Association, of which he was the first president; president of the Grange convention in 1874; became proprietor and editor of the Junction City Tribune in 1875; unsuccessful candidate of the Greenback Party for election in 1880 to the Forty-seventh Congress and in 1882 to the Forty-eighth Congress; elected as a candidate of the People's Party to the Fifty-second and Fifty-third Congresses (March 4, 1891–March 3, 1895); unsuccessful candidate for reelection in 1894 to the Fifty-fourth Congress; devoted his time to literary work until his death in Topeka, Kans., August 1, 1901; interment in Topeka Cemetery.

DAVIS, John Givan, a Representative from Indiana; born near Flemingsburg, Fleming County, Ky., October 10, 1810; moved to Indiana with his parents, who settled in Rockville, Parke County, in 1819; attended the country schools; engaged in agricultural pursuits; sheriff of Parke County from 1830 to 1833, when he resigned; clerk of the county court 1833–1850; elected as a Democrat to the Thirty-second and Thirty-third Congresses (March 4, 1851–March 3, 1855); unsuccessful candidate for reelection in 1854 to the Thirty-fourth Congress; reelected as an Anti-Lecompton Democrat to the Thirty-fifth and Thirty-sixth Congresses (March 4, 1857–March 3, 1861); was not a candidate for renomination in 1860 to the Thirty-seventh Congress; engaged in mercantile pursuits and meat packing in Montezuma, Parke County, Ind.; moved to Terre Haute, Ind., and engaged in business as a dry-goods merchant; died in Terre Haute, Ind., on January 18, 1866; interment in Highland Lawn Cemetery.

DAVIS, John James (father of John William Davis), a Representative from West Virginia; born in Clarksburg, Va. (now West Virginia), May 5, 1835; attended the Northwestern Virginia Academy at Clarksburg, and was graduated from the Lexington Law School (now the law department of Washington and Lee University), Lexington, Va., in 1856; was admitted to the bar in 1856 and commenced practice in Clarksburg, Va.; member of the Virginia House of Delegates in 1861; member of the first convention looking toward the formation of a new State loyal to the Union, from counties of western Virginia, held April 22, 1861; delegate from Harrison County to the Wheeling convention June 11, 1861; candidate for presidential elector on the Democratic ticket of McClellan and Pendleton in 1864; delegate at large to the Democratic National Convention at New York in 1868; member of the West Virginia House of Delegates in 1869 and 1870; elected as a Democrat to the Forty-second and Forty-third Congresses (March 4, 1871–March 3, 1875); was not a candidate for renomination in 1874; resumed the practice of law in Clarksburg, W. Va.; delegate to the Democratic National Conventions at St. Louis in 1876 and at Chicago in 1892; presidential elector on the Democratic ticket of Tilden and Hendricks in 1876 and of Cleveland and Hendricks in 1884; president of the State bar association in 1901; died in Clarksburg, Harrison County, W. Va., March 19, 1916; interment in Odd Fellows Cemetery.

DAVIS, John Wesley, a Representative from Indiana; born in New Holland, Lancaster County, Pa., April 16, 1799; moved to Cumberland County, Pa., with his parents, who settled near Shippensburg; completed preparatory studies; studied medicine; was graduated from the Baltimore Medical College in 1821; moved to Carlisle, Ind., in 1823 and practiced medicine; surrogate of Sullivan County 1829–1831; member of the State house of representatives 1831–1833 and served as speaker in 1831; commissioner to negotiate an Indian treaty in 1834; elected as a Democrat to the Twenty-fourth Congress (March 4, 1835–March 3, 1837); declined to be a candidate for renomination in 1836 because of ill health; elected to the Twenty-sixth Congress (March 4, 1839–March 3, 1841); unsuccessful candidate for reelection in 1840 to the Twenty-seventh Congress; again a member of the State house of representatives 1841–1843 and served as speaker in 1841; elected to the Twenty-eighth and Twenty-ninth Congresses (March 4, 1843–March 3, 1847); served as Speaker of the House of Representatives in the Twenty-ninth Congress; was not a candidate for renomination in 1846; appointed by President Polk United States Commissioner to China and served from 1848 to 1851, when his successor was appointed; member of the State house of representatives in 1851, 1852, and again in 1857; delegate to the Democratic National Convention at Baltimore in 1852 which nominated Pierce and King and served as president of the convention; appointed by President Pierce as Governor of Oregon Territory and served in 1853 and 1854; member of the Board of Visitors to the United States Military Academy at West Point in 1858; died in Carlisle, Sullivan County, Ind., August 22, 1859; interment in the City Cemetery.

DAVIS, John William (son of John James Davis), a Representative from West Virginia; born in Clarksburg, Harrison County, W. Va., April 13, 1873; attended various private schools; was graduated from the literary department of Washington and Lee University, Lexington, Va., in 1892; taught school; reentered the university and was graduated from its law department in 1895; was admitted to the bar the same year and commenced practice in Clarksburg, W. Va.; professor of law at Washington and Lee University in 1896 and 1897; resumed the practice of law in Clarksburg, W. Va., in 1897; member of the State house of delegates in 1899; delegate to the Democratic National Convention at St. Louis in 1904; president of the West Virginia Bar Association in 1906; appointed a member of the West Virginia Commission on Uniform State Laws in 1909; elected as a Democrat to the Sixty-second and Sixty-third Congresses and served from March 4, 1911, to August 29, 1913, when he resigned; one of the managers appointed by the House of Representatives in 1912 to conduct the impeachment proceedings against Robert W. Archbald, judge of the United States Commerce Court; Solicitor General of the United States 1913–1918; appointed Ambassador Extraordinary and Plenipotentiary to Great Britain and served from November 21, 1918, to March 31, 1921; member of the American delegation for conference with Germany on the treatment and exchange of prisoners of war, held in Berne, Switzerland, in September 1918; honorary bencher of the Middle Temple, London, England; unsuccessful Democratic candidate for President of the United States in 1924; delegate to the Democratic National Convention in 1932; was a resident of Nassau County, N. Y., and practiced law in New York City until his death; died in Charleston, S. C., March 24, 1955; interment in Locust Valley Cemetery, Glen Cove, Long Island, N. Y.

DAVIS, Joseph Jonathan, a Representative from North Carolina; born near Louisburg, Franklin County, N. C., April 13, 1828; attended Louisburg Academy, Wake Forest (N. C.) College, and William and Mary College, Williamsburg, Va.; was graduated from the law department of the University of North Carolina at Chapel Hill in 1850; was admitted to the bar the same year and practiced in Oxford, N. C., and later in Louisburg, N. C.; served as captain of Company G, Forty-seventh Regiment, Confederate Army, during the Civil War; member of the State house of representatives 1868–1870; elected as a Democrat to the Forty-fourth, Forty-fifth, and Forty-sixth Congresses (March 4, 1875–March 3, 1881); resumed the practice of law; appointed a justice of the State supreme court in 1887, and subsequently elected in 1888; died in Louisburg, N. C., August 7, 1892; interment in Oaklawn Cemetery.

DAVIS, Lowndes Henry, a Representative from Missouri; born in Jackson, Cape Girardeau County, Mo., December 13, 1836; was graduated from Yale College in 1860 and from the Louisville University Law School in 1863; admitted to the bar and commenced practice in Jackson, Mo.; State attorney for the tenth judicial district of Missouri 1868–1872; presidential elector on the Democratic ticket of Greeley and Brown in 1872; member of the State constitutional convention in 1875; member of the State house of representatives 1876–1878; elected as a Democrat to the Forty-sixth, Forty-seventh, and Forty-eighth Congresses (March 4, 1879–March 3, 1885); engaged in agricultural pursuits and in stock raising; died in Cape Girardeau, Mo., February 4, 1920; interment in Maple Hill Cemetery, Huntsville, Ala.

DAVIS, Noah, a Representative from New York; born in Haverhill, N. H., September 10, 1818; moved with his parents to Albion, N. Y., in 1825; attended the common schools and Lima Seminary, Buffalo, N. Y.; studied law in Lewiston; was admitted to the bar and practiced in Gainesville and Buffalo; returned to Albion in February 1844, where he continued the practice of law until May 1858; appointed and subsequently twice elected judge of the supreme court for the eighth judicial district, and served from 1857 to 1868; resumed the practice of law; elected as a Republican to the Forty-first Congress and served from March 4, 1869, until July 15, 1870, when he resigned; appointed by President Grant as United States attorney for the southern district of New York and served from July 20, 1870, until December 31, 1872, when he resigned, having been elected a judge of the su-

preme court of the State, in which position he served until 1887; resumed the practice of law in New York City; member of the council of the University of the City of New York (now New York University); died in New York City March 20, 1902; interment in Mount Albion Cemetery, Albion, Orleans County, N. Y.

DAVIS, Reuben, a Representative from Mississippi; born in Winchester, Tenn., January 18, 1813; moved with his parents to Alabama about 1818; attended the public schools; studied medicine, but practiced only a few years, when he abandoned the profession; studied law; was admitted to the bar in 1834 and commenced practice in Aberdeen, Miss.; prosecuting attorney for the sixth judicial district 1835–1839; judge of the high court of appeals in 1842, but after four months' service resigned; served as colonel of the Second Regiment of Mississippi Volunteers in the war with Mexico; member of the State house of representatives 1855–1857; elected as a Democrat to the Thirty-fifth and Thirty-sixth Congresses and served from March 4, 1857, to January 12, 1861, when he withdrew; during the Civil War served in the Confederate Army as brigadier general; resumed the practice of law; died in Huntsville, Ala., October 14, 1890; interment in Odd Fellows Cemetery, Aberdeen, Monroe County, Miss.

DAVIS, Richard David, a Representative from New York; born at Stillwater, Saratoga County, N. Y., in 1799; was graduated from Yale College in 1818; studied law; was admitted to the bar in 1821 and commenced practice in Poughkeepsie; elected as a Democrat to the Twenty-seventh and Twenty-eighth Congresses (March 4, 1841–March 3, 1845); was not a candidate for renomination in 1844; withdrew from political and professional life; engaged in agricultural pursuits in Waterford, Saratoga County, N. Y., where he died on June 17, 1871; interment in Waterford Rural Cemetery.

DAVIS, Robert Lee, a Representative from Pennsylvania; born in Philadelphia, Pa., October 29, 1893; educated in the public schools and was graduated from South Philadelphia High School in 1910; employed with the Pennsylvania Railroad 1910–1932; during the First World War served as a junior lieutenant in the United States Navy; assistant executive director of the Republican central campaign committee of Philadelphia 1928–1932; director of the Republican city committee 1932–1935; elected as a Republican to the Seventy-second Congress to fill the vacancy caused by the resignation of George A. Welsh and served from November 8, 1932, to March 3, 1933; was not a candidate for election to the Seventy-third Congress in 1932; paymaster and stock analyst with the Dupont Co. at Philadelphia, Pa., 1940–1946; former real-estate broker in Ocean City, N. J.; resides in Cape May, N. J.

DAVIS, Robert Thompson, a Representative from Massachusetts; born in County Down, Ireland, August 28, 1823; immigrated to the United States with his parents, who settled in Amesbury, Essex County, Mass., in 1826; attended the Amesbury Academy and the Friends' School in Providence, R. I.; was graduated from the medical department of Harvard University in 1847; dispensary physician in Boston; practiced medicine in Waterville, Maine; moved to Fall River, Mass., in 1850; member of the State constitutional convention in 1853; served in the State senate 1859–1861; delegate to the Republican National Convention at Chicago in 1860, at Cincinnati in 1876, and at Philadelphia in 1900; member of the State board of charities when organized in 1863; appointed a member of the State board of health upon its organization in 1869; mayor of Fall River in 1873; elected as a Republican to the Forty-eighth, Forty-ninth, and Fiftieth Congresses (March 4, 1883–March 3, 1889); was not a candidate for renomination in 1888; resumed the practice of medicine at Fall River and also engaged in the cotton manufacturing industry; member of the Metropolitan Sewerage Commission of Massachusetts when established in 1891; died at Fall River, Mass., October 29, 1906; interment in Oak Grove Cemetery.

DAVIS, Robert Wyche, a Representative from Florida; born near Albany, Lee County, Ga., March 15, 1849; attended the common schools; during the Civil War enlisted in 1863 at the age of fourteen years in the Fifth Georgia Regiment of the Confederate Army, and served until the surrender of his company, under Gen. Joseph E. Johnston, on April 26, 1865; studied law; was admitted to the bar in 1869 and commenced practice in Blakeley, Ga.; moved to Florida in 1879 and located in Green Cove Springs, Clay County, then in Gainesville, Alachua County, and afterward in Palatka, Putnam County, and continued the practice of law; member of the State house of representatives from Clay County in 1884 and 1885, serving as speaker the latter year; elected as a Democrat to the Fifty-fifth and to the three succeeding Congresses (March 4, 1897–March 3, 1905); was not a candidate for renomination in 1904 to the Fifty-ninth Congress; resumed the practice of law in Palatka, and Tampa, Fla.; moved to Gainesville, Fla., in 1914 and served as register of the United States land office at Gainesville 1914–1922; editor of the Gainesville Sun; served as mayor of Gainesville in 1924 and 1925; resumed the practice of law in 1928; died in Gainesville, Fla., September 15, 1929; interment in Evergreen Cemetery.

DAVIS, Roger, a Representative from Pennsylvania; born in Charlestown Village, Chester County, Pa., October 2, 1762; studied medicine at the University of Pennsylvania and commenced practice about 1785 in Charlestown; member of the State house of representatives 1809–1811; elected as a Democrat to the Twelfth and Thirteenth Congresses (March 4, 1811–March 3, 1815); resumed the practice of medicine in Charlestown, Chester County, Pa., where he died November 20, 1815; interment in Great Valley Presbyterian Churchyard.

DAVIS, Samuel, a Representative from Massachusetts; born in Bath, Maine (until 1820 a district of Massachusetts), in 1774; engaged in mercantile pursuits; became a shipowner in 1801; member of the Massachusetts House of Representatives in 1803 and 1808–1812; overseer of Bowdoin College 1813–1818; president of the Lincoln Bank, Bath, Maine, in 1813; elected as a Federalist to the Thirteenth Congress (March 4, 1813–March 3, 1815); again a member of the Massachusetts House of Representatives in 1815 and 1816; merchant in African and West Indian trade; died in Bath, Maine, April 20, 1831; interment in Maple Grove Cemetery.

DAVIS, Thomas, a Representative from Rhode Island; born in Dublin, Ireland, December 18, 1806; attended private schools; immigrated to the United States and located in Providence, R. I., in 1817; engaged in manufacturing jewelry; member of the State senate 1845–1853; elected as a Democrat to the Thirty-third Congress (March 4, 1853–March 3, 1855); unsuccessful candidate for reelection in 1854 to the Thirty-fourth Congress; resumed his former manufacturing pursuits; unsuccessful candidate for election to the Thirty-sixth, Forty-second, Forty-third, and Forty-sixth Congresses; again served in the State senate in 1877 and 1878; member of the State house of representatives 1887–1890; member of the Providence school committee; died in Providence, R. I., July 26, 1895; interment in Swan Point Cemetery.

DAVIS, Thomas Beall (brother of Henry Gassaway Davis), a Representative from West Virginia; born in Baltimore, Md., April 25, 1828; moved to Howard County, Md., where he attended the common schools; moved to Piedmont, Va. (now West Virginia), in 1854 and entered the employ of the Baltimore & Ohio Railroad Co.; a few years later he moved to Keyser and engaged in the mercantile business, lumbering, banking, mining, and finally the building of railroads; in later years devoted much attention to farming and raising fine stock and race horses; member of the Democratic State executive committee 1876–1907; member of the State house of delegates 1898–1900; elected as a Democrat to the Fifty-ninth Congress to fill the vacancy caused by the resignation of Alston G. Dayton and served from June 6, 1905, to March 3, 1907; was not a candidate for reelection in 1906; resumed agricultural pursuits and coal mining; died in Keyser, Mineral County, W. Va., November 26, 1911; interment in Maplewood Cemetery, Elkins, W. Va.

DAVIS, Thomas Terry, a Representative from Kentucky; studied law; was admitted to the Kentucky bar on June 28, 1789, and commenced the practice of law in Mercer County, Ky.; served as deputy attorney for the Commonwealth and the first prosecuting attorney for his district; member of the State house of representatives 1795–1797; elected to the Fifth, Sixth, and Seventh Congresses (March 4, 1797–March 3, 1803); was appointed United States judge of Indiana Territory February 8, 1803, and served as chancellor of Indiana Territory from March 1, 1806, until his death; died in Jeffersonville, Clark County, Ind., on November 15, 1807.

DAVIS, Thomas Treadwell (grandson of Thomas Tredwell), a Representative from New York; born in Middlebury, Addison County, Vt., August 22, 1810; moved to New York in 1817 with his parents, who settled in Clinton, Oneida County; attended the Clinton (N. Y.) Academy, and was graduated from Hamilton College, Clinton, N. Y., in 1831; moved to Syracuse, Onondaga County, in 1831; studied law; was admitted to the bar in 1833 and commenced practice in Syracuse; was also interested in railroading and coal mining; elected as a Unionist to the Thirty-eighth and Thirty-ninth Congresses (March 4, 1863–March 3, 1867); was not a candidate for renomination in 1866; resumed the practice of law in Syracuse; died in Washington, D. C., May 2, 1872; remains were cremated and the ashes deposited in Oakwood Cemetery.

DAVIS, Timothy, a Representative from Iowa; born in Newark, N. J., March 29, 1794; attended the public schools; moved to Kentucky in 1816; studied law; was admitted to the bar and practiced; moved to Missouri and engaged in the practice of law, and later, in 1837, moved to Dubuque, Iowa, and continued the practice of law; unsuccessful candidate for election in 1848 to the Thirty-first Congress; elected as a Whig to the Thirty-fifth Congress (March 4, 1857–March 3, 1859); resumed the practice of his profession and also engaged in business activities in Dubuque; was also interested in merchant milling at Elkader, Iowa, Galesville, Wis., and Pickwick, Minn.; died in Elkader, Clayton County, Iowa, on April 27, 1872; interment in Elkader Cemetery.

DAVIS, Timothy, a Representative from Massachusetts; born in Gloucester, Mass., April 12, 1821; attended the public schools; served two years in a printing office; engaged in mercantile pursuits in Boston; member of the State house of representatives in 1870 and 1871; elected as the candidate of the American Party to the Thirty-fourth Congress and as a Republican to the Thirty-fifth Congress (March 4, 1855–March 3, 1859); delegate to the Republican National Convention at Chicago in 1860; appointed assistant appraiser in the Boston customhouse in 1861; engaged in the prosecution of claims against the Government; died in Boston, Mass., on October 23, 1888; interment in Oak Grove Cemetery.

DAVIS, Warren Ransom, a Representative from South Carolina; born in Columbia, S. C., May 8, 1793; pursued preparatory studies; was graduated from South Carolina College (now the University of South Carolina) at Columbia in 1810; studied law; was admitted to the bar in 1814 and practiced in Pendleton, S. C.; State solicitor of the western circuit 1818–1824; elected as a State Rights Democrat to the Twentieth and to the three succeeding Congresses and served from March 4, 1827, until his death; had been reelected to the Twenty-fourth Congress; died in Washington, D. C., on January 29, 1835; interment in the Congressional Cemetery.

DAVIS, William Morris, a Representative from Pennsylvania; born in Keene Valley, Essex County, N. Y., August 16, 1815; moved to Pennsylvania and became a sugar refiner in Philadelphia; elected as a Republican to the Thirty-seventh Congress (March 4, 1861–March 3, 1863); died in Keene Valley, N. Y., August 5, 1891; interment in Friends Fair Hill Burial Ground, Germantown, Philadelphia, Pa.

DAVISON, George Mosby, a Representative from Kentucky; born in Stanford, Lincoln County, Ky., March 23, 1855; attended the common schools, Stanford Academy, and Meyers Academy; studied law; was admitted to the bar in 1879 and commenced practice in Stanford, Ky.; appointed collector of internal revenue for the sixth Kentucky district and served from July 20, 1885, to June 30, 1889; appointed master of chancery or commissioner of the Lincoln circuit court in 1886, and served until 1893, when he resigned; member of the State house of representatives 1886–1888; judge of the Lincoln County Court 1894–1896; elected as a Republican to the Fifty-fifth Congress (March 4, 1897–March 3, 1899); unsuccessful candidate for reelection in 1898 to the Fifty-sixth Congress; resumed the practice of law; assistant United States attorney for the eastern district of Kentucky 1900–1910; retired from public life; died in Stanford, Ky., December 18, 1912; interment in Buffalo Springs Cemetery.

DAVY, John Madison, a Representative from New York; born in Ottawa, Ontario, Canada, June 29, 1835; moved to New York with his parents, who settled near Rochester, Monroe County, in 1835; attended the common schools and the Monroe Academy, East Henrietta, N. Y.; served in the Union Army during the Civil War as a first lieutenant in Company G, One Hundred and Eighth Regiment, Volunteer Infantry, in 1862 and 1863; studied law in Rochester; was admitted to the bar in 1863 and commenced practice in Rochester, N. Y.; district attorney of Monroe County 1868–1872; collector of customs for the port of Genesee from 1872 until his resignation in 1875, having been elected to Congress; elected as a Republican to the Forty-fourth Congress (March 4, 1875–March 3, 1877); unsuccessful candidate for reelection in 1876 to the Forty-fifth Congress; resumed the practice of law; elected justice of the supreme court of New York and served from January 1, 1889, until his retirement in 1905; again resumed the practice of law; died while on a week-end visit in Atlantic City, N. J., April 21, 1909; interment in Mount Hope Cemetery, Rochester, N. Y.

DAWES, Beman Gates (son of Rufus Dawes and brother of Vice President Charles Gates Dawes), a Representative from Ohio; born in Marietta, Washington County, Ohio, January 14, 1870; attended the common schools and Marietta Academy and College, Marietta, Ohio; engaged in agricultural pursuits and engineering and became interested in public utilities; elected as a Republican to the Fifty-ninth and Sixtieth Congresses (March 4, 1905–March 3, 1909); after his retirement from Congress became interested in the production of oil and the building of electric railways; founder of the Dawes Arboretum, an endowed

institution dedicated to the education of youth; in 1914 was elected president and chairman of the board of directors of the Pure Oil Co., and was a member of the executive committee at time of death; died in Newark, Ohio, May 15, 1953; interment in Dawes Mausoleum, Dawes Arboretum, Newark, Ohio.

DAWES, Charles Gates (son of Rufus Dawes and brother of Beman Gates Dawes), a Vice President of the United States; born in Marietta, Washington County, Ohio, August 27, 1865; attended the common schools; was graduated from Marietta College in 1884 and from the Cincinnati Law School in 1886; was admitted to the bar in 1886 and practiced in Lincoln, Nebr., 1887–1894; interested in public utilities and banking 1894–1897; Comptroller of the Currency, United States Treasury Department, 1898–1901; during the First World War was commissioned major of the Seventeenth Engineers on June 11, 1917; lieutenant colonel on July 16, 1917; colonel on January 16, 1918; brigadier general on October 15, 1918; appointed to the administrative staff of the commander in chief of the American Expeditionary Forces on September 27, 1917, as chief of supply procurement; member of the military board of Allied supply, American Expeditionary Forces, and of the liquidation commission, War Department; resigned from the Army August 31, 1919; was awarded the Distinguished Service Medal of the United States for "exceptionally meritorious and distinguished services," the French Legion of Honor and the Croix de Guerre with Palm, the Order of the Bath from the British Government, the Order of St. Maurice and St. Lazarus from the Italian Government, and the Order of Leopold from the Belgian Government; brigadier general in the Officers' Reserve Corps 1921–1926; upon the creation of the Bureau of the Budget was appointed its first Director in 1921; appointed by the Reparations Commission as chairman of the first committee of experts in 1923; elected on November 5, 1924, Vice President of the United States on the Republican ticket with President Calvin Coolidge and was inaugurated March 4, 1925, for the term ending March 3, 1929; Ambassador to Great Britain 1929–1932; resumed the banking business and was chairman of the board of the City National Bank and Trust Co., Chicago, Ill., from 1932 until his death in Evanston, Ill., April 23, 1951; interment in Rosehill Cemetery, Chicago, Ill.

DAWES, Henry Laurens, a Representative and a Senator from Massachusetts; born in Cummington, Mass., October 30, 1816; attended the common schools and received private instruction in preparatory studies; was graduated from Yale College in 1839; became a teacher and edited the Greenfield Gazette and the North Adams Transcript; studied law; was admitted to the bar in 1842 and commenced practice in North Adams, Mass.; member of the State house of representatives in 1848, 1849, and 1852; served in the State senate in 1850; member of the State constitutional convention in 1853; district attorney for the western district of Massachusetts 1853–1857; elected to the Thirty-fifth and to the eight succeeding Congresses (March 4, 1857–March 3, 1875); declined to be a candidate for reelection in 1874; elected as a Republican to the United States Senate in 1875; reelected in 1881 and again in 1887, and served from March 4, 1875, to March 3, 1893; declined to be a candidate for reelection in 1893; settled in Pittsfield, Mass.; chairman of the commission created to administer the tribal affairs of the Five Civilized Tribes of Indians in the Indian Territory 1893–1903; died in Pittsfield, Mass., February 5, 1903; interment in Pittsfield Cemetery.

DAWES, Rufus (father of Vice President Charles Gates Dawes and Beman Gates Dawes), a Representative from Ohio; born in Malta, Morgan County, Ohio, July 4, 1838; attended the common schools, and was graduated from Marietta College, Ohio, in 1860; during the Civil War volunteered on April 25, 1861, and was chosen captain of Company K, Sixth Wisconsin Regiment, in the Army of the Potomac; appointed major June 21, 1862, and as such served in the Battles of the Rappahannock, Gainesville, Bull Run (second battle), South Mountain, Antietam, and Fredericksburg; appointed lieutenant colonel March 24, 1863, and took part in the Battles of Fitz Hugh's Crossing, Chancellorsville, Gettysburg, Mine Run, the Wilderness, Spotsylvania, Laurel Hill, Jericho Ford, North Anna, Bethesda Church, and Petersburg; was appointed colonel on July 6, 1864, and brevet brigadier general March 13, 1865; was sixty-two days under fire; commanded his regiment in the Battles of Antietam, Gettysburg, Spotsylvania, Laurel Hill, Jericho Ford, Petersburg, and in the operations thereabout; during the Battle of Antietam sixty-two per cent of his men were killed or wounded, and at Gettysburg he charged and captured the Second Mississippi Regiment, losing 200 men killed and wounded from his own regiment; after the close of the war engaged in the wholesale lumber business in Marietta, Ohio; elected as a Republican to the Forty-seventh Congress (March 4, 1881–March 3, 1883); unsuccessful candidate for reelection in 1882 to the Forty-eighth Congress; resumed the wholesale lumber business in Marietta, Washington County, Ohio, and died there August 2, 1899; interment in Oak Grove Cemetery.

DAWSON, Albert Foster, a Representative from Iowa; born in Spragueville, Jackson County, Iowa, January 26, 1872; attended the public schools and the University of Wisconsin at Madison; engaged in newspaper work at Preston, Iowa, in 1891 and 1892 and at Clinton, Iowa, from 1892 to 1894; secretary to Representative George M. Curtis and Senator William B. Allison of Iowa 1895–1905; studied finance at George Washington University, Washington, D. C.; elected as a Republican to the Fifty-ninth, Sixtieth, and Sixty-first Congresses (March 4, 1905–March 3, 1911); declined the candidacy for renomination in 1910 and also an appointment as private secretary to President William H. Taft tendered in 1910; president of the First National Bank of Davenport, Iowa, 1911–1929; executive secretary of the Republican National Senatorial Committee in 1930; public utility executive 1931–1945; retired from business activities and resided in Highland Park, Ill., until his death March 9, 1949, on a train as it neared Cincinnati, Ohio; interment in Preston Cemetery, Preston, Iowa.

DAWSON, John, a Delegate and a Representative from Virginia; born in that State in 1762; was graduated from Harvard University in 1782; studied law; was admitted to the bar, and practiced; member of the State house of delegates 1786–1789; Member of the Continental Congress in 1788 and 1789; delegate to the State convention in 1788 that ratified the Federal Constitution; elected privy councilor December 16, 1789; presidential elector on the Washington ticket in 1792; elected as a Democrat to the Fifth and to the eight succeeding Congresses and served from March 4, 1797, until his death; was the bearer of dispatches from President John Adams to the Government of France in 1801; served as aide to Gen. Jacob Brown and to Gen. Andrew Jackson in the War of 1812; died in Washington, D. C., March 31, 1814; interment in the Congressional Cemetery.

DAWSON, John Bennett, a Representative from Louisiana; born near Nashville, Tenn., March 17, 1798; attended Centre College, Danville, Ky.; moved to Louisiana and became a planter and was also interested in the newspaper business; unsuccessful candidate for Governor of Louisiana in 1834; member of the State house of representatives; elected brigadier general of militia and a few days afterward was elected major general; judge

of the parish court; while a Member of the House was appointed postmaster at New Orleans, La., April 10, 1843, and served until his successor was appointed December 19, 1843; elected as a Democrat to the Twenty-seventh, Twenty-eighth, and Twenty-ninth Congresses and served from March 4, 1841, until his death in St. Francisville, La., on June 26, 1845; interment in Grace Episcopal Churchyard.

DAWSON, John Littleton, a Representative from Pennsylvania; born in Uniontown, Fayette County, Pa., February 7, 1813; moved with his parents to Brownsville, Pa., in early youth; was graduated from Washington (Pa.) College in 1833; studied law; was admitted to the bar September 9, 1835, and commenced practice in Brownsville, Pa.; deputy attorney general of Fayette County in 1838; delegate to the Democratic National Conventions at Baltimore in 1844, 1848, and 1860, and at New York City in 1868; United States district attorney for the western district of Pennsylvania 1845–1848; unsuccessful candidate for election in 1848 to the Thirty-first Congress; elected as a Democrat to the Thirty-second and Thirty-third Congresses (March 4, 1851–March 3, 1855); declined to be a candidate for renomination in 1854; appointed Governor of Kansas Territory by President Pierce, but declined the office; elected to the Thirty-eighth and Thirty-ninth Congresses (March 4, 1863–March 3, 1867); was not a candidate for renomination; retired from public life and resided on his estate, "Friendship Hill," in Springfield Township, Fayette County, Pa., until his death there on September 18, 1870; interment in Christ Episcopal Churchyard, Brownsville, Fayette County, Pa.

DAWSON, William, a Representative from Missouri; born in New Madrid, New Madrid County, Mo., March 17, 1848; was graduated from Christian Brothers' College, St. Louis, Mo., in 1869; elected sheriff and collector of New Madrid County in 1870 and 1872; served as a member of the State house of representatives 1878–1884; elected as a Democrat to the Forty-ninth Congress (March 4, 1885–March 3, 1887); unsuccessful candidate for renomination in 1886; engaged in the land business in New Madrid, Mo.; served as clerk of the circuit court of New Madrid County 1915–1927; died in New Madrid, Mo., October 12, 1929; interment in Evergreen Cemetery.

DAWSON, William Adams, a Representative from Utah; born in Layton, Davis County, Utah, November 5, 1903; attended the public schools; was graduated from the law department of the University of Utah at Salt Lake City in 1926; was admitted to the bar the same year and commenced practice in Salt Lake City, Utah; county attorney of Davis County 1926–1934; mayor of Layton 1935–1939; member of the State senate 1940–1944; elected as a Republican to the Eightieth Congress (January 3, 1947–January 3, 1949); unsuccessful candidate for reelection in 1948 to the Eighty-first Congress; elected to the Eighty-third, Eighty-fourth, and Eighty-fifth Congresses (January 3, 1953–January 3, 1959); unsuccessful candidate for reelection in 1958 to the Eighty-sixth Congress; resumed the practice of law and is a resident of Salt Lake City, Utah.

DAWSON, William Crosby, a Representative and a Senator from Georgia; born in Greensboro, Greene County, Ga., January 4, 1798; attended the common schools; was graduated from Franklin College, Athens, Ga., in 1816; studied law; was admitted to the bar in 1816 and commenced practice in Greensboro, Ga.; member of the State house of representatives; elected as a State Rights Whig to the Twenty-fourth Congress to fill the vacancy caused by the death of John Coffee; reelected to the Twenty-fifth, Twenty-sixth, and Twenty-seventh Congresses and served from November 7, 1836, to November 13, 1841, when he resigned; was an unsuccessful candidate for Governor of Georgia in 1841; served as a judge of the Ocmulgee circuit court from February 1 to November 11, 1845; elected to the United States Senate and served from March 4, 1849, to March 3, 1855; presided over the Southern convention at Memphis in 1853; died in Greensboro, Ga., on May 6, 1856; interment in Greensboro Cemetery.

DAWSON, William Johnston, a Representative from North Carolina; born near Edenton, Chowan County, N. C.; member of the State house of commons in 1791; served as a member of the committee appointed in 1791 to fix a permanent place for the seat of government of North Carolina; elected to the Third Congress (March 4, 1793–March 3, 1795); died in Bertie County, N. C., in 1798.

DAWSON, William Levi, a Representative from Illinois; born in Albany, Dougherty County, Ga., April 26, 1886; is of the Negro race; attended the public schools and Kent College of Law, Chicago, Ill.; was graduated from Albany (Ga.) Normal School in 1905, Fisk University, Nashville, Tenn., in 1909, and Northwestern University Law School, Evanston, Ill.; during the First World War served overseas as a first lieutenant with the Three Hundred and Sixty-fifth Infantry 1917–1919; was admitted to the bar in 1920 and commenced practice in Chicago, Ill.; State central committeeman for the First Congressional District of Illinois 1930–1932; alderman for the second ward of Chicago 1933–1939 and Democratic committeeman since 1939; elected as a Democrat to the Seventy-eighth and to the eight succeeding Congresses (January 3, 1943–January 3, 1961). *Reelected to the Eighty-seventh Congress.*

DAY, Rowland, a Representative from New York; born in Chester, Mass., March 6, 1779; moved with his parents to Skaneateles, N. Y., in 1805, and from thence to Moravia, N. Y., in 1810; engaged in mercantile pursuits; served in the State assembly in 1816 and 1817; member of the convention to revise the constitution of the State of New York in 1821; held several local offices in Sempronius, where he resided; elected as a Democrat to the Eighteenth Congress (March 4, 1823–March 3, 1825); elected to the Twenty-third Congress (March 4, 1833–March 3, 1835); resumed mercantile pursuits; died in Moravia, Cayuga County, N. Y., December 23, 1853; interment in Indian Mound Cemetery.

DAY, Stephen Albion, a Representative from Illinois; born in Canton, Stark County, Ohio, July 13, 1882; attended the public schools at Canton, the University School at Cleveland, Ohio, and Asheville (N. C.) School; was graduated from the University of Michigan at Ann Arbor in 1905; secretary to Chief Justice Melville W. Fuller of the Supreme Court of the United States 1905–1907; studied law at the University of Michigan; was admitted to the bar in 1907 and commenced practice in Cleveland, Ohio; moved to Evanston, Ill., in 1908 and continued the practice of law in Chicago, Ill.; special counsel to the Comptroller of the Currency 1926–1928; author; elected as a Republican to the Seventy-seventh and Seventy-eighth Congresses (January 3, 1941–January 3, 1945); unsuccessful candidate for reelection in 1944 to the Seventy-ninth Congress; resumed the practice of law in Evanston, Ill., where he died January 5, 1950; interment in Memorial Park, Skokie, Ill.

DAY, Timothy Crane, a Representative from Ohio; born in Cincinnati, Ohio, January 8, 1819; attended the public schools; printer and engraver 1838–1840; engaged in literary pursuits; became one of the editors and proprietors of the Cincinnati Enquirer in 1849; disposed of his interests in that paper in 1852 and

made a tour of Europe; elected as a Republican to the Thirty-fourth Congress (March 4, 1855–March 3, 1857); declined renomination in 1856 because of ill health and retired from active business; died in Cincinnati, Ohio, April 15, 1869; interment in Spring Grove Cemetery.

DAYAN, Charles, a Representative from New York; born in Amsterdam, Montgomery County, N. Y., July 8, 1792; attended the common schools and was tutored privately; was graduated from Lowville Academy, Lewis County, N. Y.; engaged in teaching; commissioned a lieutenant colonel in the War of 1812; studied law; was admitted to the bar in 1817 and practiced in Lowville; member of the State senate in 1827 and 1828 and served as president pro tempore in the latter year; acting Lieutenant Governor from October 17 to December 31, 1828; presidential elector on the Democratic ticket of Jackson and Calhoun in 1828; supreme court commissioner 1830–1838; elected as a Democrat to the Twenty-second Congress (March 4, 1831–March 3, 1833); member of the State assembly in 1835 and 1836; master and examiner in chancery for several years, terminating in 1838; district attorney for Lewis County 1840–1845; retired from public life because of ill health, but continued the practice of law for a number of years; died in Lowville, Lewis County, N. Y., December 25, 1877; interment in Lowville Rural Cemetery.

DAYTON, Alston Gordon, a Representative from West Virginia; born in Philippi, Va. (now West Virginia), October 18, 1857; attended the public schools, and was graduated from the University of West Virginia at Morgantown in June 1878; studied law; was admitted to the bar in 1878 and commenced practice in Philippi; appointed to fill an unexpired term as prosecuting attorney of Upshur County, W. Va., in 1879; prosecuting attorney for Barbour County 1882–1886; elected as a Republican to the Fifty-fourth and to the five succeeding Congresses and served from March 4, 1895, until his resignation March 16, 1905, to accept a judicial position; appointed United States district judge for the northern district of West Virginia on March 5, 1905, and served until his death in Battle Creek, Mich., on July 30, 1920; interment in Fraternity Cemetery, Philippi, Barbour County, W. Va.

DAYTON, Elias (father of Jonathan Dayton), a Delegate from New Jersey; born in Elizabethtown (now Elizabeth), N. J., May 1, 1737; apprenticed as a mechanic; completed preparatory studies; lieutenant of militia March 19, 1756, and captain March 19, 1760; served in the "Jersey Blues" under Wolfe at Quebec and against Pontiac near Detroit; proprietor of a general store at Elizabethtown, N. J.; alderman; member of committee to enforce measures recommended by Continental Congress, and on October 26, 1775, became one of Essex County's four mustermasters; commissioned a colonel of the third battalion of the New Jersey Line on January 10, 1776, and on January 22 led seventy-seven volunteers in three shallops to capture the British supply ship *Blue Mountain Valley;* was with his regiment at Albany, N. Y., in May 1776, and built Fort Schuyler and Fort Dayton (at Herkimer), to ward off Indian raids; returned to Morristown, N. J., in March 1777; saw service at Bound Brook, Staten Island, and Brandywine, and spent the winter of 1777–1778 at Valley Forge; elected to the Continental Congress December 12, 1778, in place of John Neilson, but declined May 25, 1779; led in foiling British sallies against the Continental Army at Morristown; led his brigade to Yorktown, Va., and was in active service until the discharge of the New Jersey Line on November 3, 1783; promoted to brigadier general January 8, 1783; returned to Elizabethtown and operated a general store; major general of militia; recorder of Elizabethtown in 1789; member of State general assembly 1791–1792 and 1794–1796;

mayor of Elizabethtown 1796–1805; president of the New Jersey Society of the Cincinnati; died in Elizabethtown (now Elizabeth), N. J., October 22, 1807; interment in a vault in the First Presbyterian Churchyard.

DAYTON, Jonathan (son of Elias Dayton), a Delegate, a Representative, and a Senator from New Jersey; born in Elizabethtown (now Elizabeth), N. J., October 16, 1760; was graduated from Princeton College in 1776; studied law; was admitted to the bar; during the Revolutionary War entered the Continental Army as ensign in the Third New Jersey Regiment on February 7, 1776; promoted to regimental paymaster August 26, 1776; first lieutenant January 1, 1777; captain,lieutenant April 7, 1779; aide-de-camp to Maj. Gen. John Sullivan May 1, 1779; captain in the Third New Jersey Regiment March 30, 1780; was taken prisoner at Elizabethtown, N. J., on October 5, 1780, and later exchanged; transferred to the Second New Jersey Regiment on January 1, 1781; honorably discharged November 3, 1783; member of the State general assembly in 1786, 1787, and 1790, and served as speaker in the last-named year; delegate to the Federal Constitutional Convention in 1787 and the youngest man to sign the Constitution; elected as a Delegate to the Continental Congress to fill the vacancy caused by the declination of William Paterson; reelected in 1788 and served from November 6, 1787, to March 3, 1789; served in the State council in 1790; elected as a Federalist to the Second and to the three succeeding Congresses (March 4, 1791–March 3, 1799); served as Speaker during the Fourth and Fifth Congresses; was not a candidate for renomination in 1798, having become a candidate for the United States Senate; elected to the United States Senate and served from March 4, 1799, to March 3, 1805; was arrested in 1807 on the charge of conspiring with Aaron Burr in treasonable projects; gave bail and was subsequently released, but never brought to trial; died in Elizabethtown (now Elizabeth), N. J., October 9, 1824; interment in a vault in St. John's Churchyard; the city of Dayton, Ohio, was named for him.

DAYTON, William Lewis, a Senator from New Jersey; born in Basking Ridge, Somerset County, N. J., February 17, 1807; attended Trenton (N. J.) Academy, and was graduated from Princeton College in 1825; studied law; was admitted to the bar in 1830 and commenced practice in Freehold, N. J.; member of the State council in 1837 and 1838; associate judge of the State supreme court from February 28, 1838, to November 1, 1841, when he resigned; appointed and subsequently elected as a Whig to the United States Senate to fill the vacancy caused by the death of Samuel L. Southard; reelected in 1845 and served from July 2, 1842, to March 3, 1851; unsuccessful candidate for reelection; resumed the practice of law; nominated in 1856 by the Republican Party as its candidate for Vice President on the ticket with John C. Frémont; attorney general of New Jersey 1857–1861; appointed Minister to France on March 18, 1861, and served until his death in Paris, December 1, 1864; interment in Riverview Cemetery, Trenton, N. J.

DEAL, Joseph Thomas, a Representative from Virginia; born near Surry, Va., November 19, 1860; attended the public schools; was graduated from Virginia Military Institute at Lexington in 1882; engaged in civil engineering and lumber manufacturing in Surry County in 1883; moved to Norfolk, Va., in 1891; acquired large lumber holdings and was president of important lumber-manufacturing plants; interested in planting and stock raising on the James River; chairman of the Improvement Board of Norfolk 1905–1910; delegate to the Democratic National Convention at Denver in 1908; member of the State house of delegates 1910–1912; served in the State senate in 1919; elected as a Democrat to the Sixty-seventh and to the three succeeding Congresses (March 4, 1921–March 3, 1929); was an unsuccessful candidate for reelection in 1928 to the Seventy-first Congress; resumed his activities in the lumber business until his death in Norfolk, Va., on March 7, 1942; interment in Forest Lawn Cemetery.

DEAN, Benjamin, a Representative from Massachusetts; born in Clitheroe, England, August 14, 1824; immigrated to the United States with his parents, who settled in Lowell, Mass.; attended Lowell schools, and Dartmouth College, Hanover, N. H.; studied law; was admitted to the bar in 1845 and commenced practice in Lowell; moved to Boston in 1852 and continued the practice of law; served in the State senate in 1862, 1863, and 1869; member of the common council 1865–1866 and 1872–1873; successfully contested as a Democrat the election of Walbridge A. Field to the Forty-fifth Congress and served from March 28, 1878, to March 3, 1879; was not a candidate for renomination in 1878 to the Forty-sixth Congress; resumed the practice of law in Boston; member of the board of park commissioners for several years and served as chairman; died in South Boston, Mass., April 9, 1897; interment in Lowell Cemetery, Lowell, Mass.

DEAN, Ezra, a Representative from Ohio; born in Hillsdale, Columbia County, N. Y., April 9, 1795; attended the common schools; in the War of 1812 was appointed ensign in the Eleventh Regiment of United States Infantry April 17, 1814; commissioned lieutenant October 1, 1814, for meritorious conduct at the sortie of Fort Erie; at the close of the war was placed in command of a revenue cutter on Lake Champlain and rendered effective service against smugglers; resigned to study law; was admitted to the bar in Plattsburg, N. Y., in 1823; moved to Ohio in 1824; settled in Wooster and commenced the practice of law; postmaster of Wooster 1828–1832; president judge of the court of common pleas 1834–1841; elected as a Democrat to the Twenty-seventh and Twenty-eighth Congresses (March 4, 1841–March 3, 1845); was not a candidate for renomination in 1844; resumed the practice of law in Wooster; moved to Ironton, Ohio, in 1867, and died there January 25, 1872; interment in Woodland Cemetery.

DEAN, Gilbert, a Representative from New York; born in Pleasant Valley, Dutchess County, N. Y., August 14, 1819; attended the common schools and Amenia Seminary, Dutchess County, N. Y.; was graduated from Yale College in 1841; studied law; was admitted to the bar and commenced practice in Poughkeepsie, N. Y., in 1844; elected as a Democrat to the Thirty-second and Thirty-third Congresses and served from March 4, 1851, to July 3, 1854, when he resigned; appointed justice of the supreme court of New York on June 26, 1854, to fill a vacancy, and served until December 31, 1855; moved to New York City in 1856 and continued the practice of law; died in Poughkeepsie, N. Y., October 12, 1870; interment in the Presbyterian Cemetery, Pleasant Valley, N. Y.; reinterment in Portland Evergreen Cemetery, Brocton, Chautauqua County, N. Y.

DEAN, Josiah, a Representative from Massachusetts; born in Raynham, Mass., March 6, 1748; attended the common schools; engaged in the rolling-mill and shipbuilding business; selectman in 1781; town clerk in 1805; presidential elector on the Jefferson ticket in 1804; served in the State senate 1804–1807; elected as a Democrat to the Tenth Congress (March 4, 1807–March 3, 1809); member of the State house of representatives in 1810 and 1811; resumed his former business pursuits; died in Raynham, Mass., October 14, 1818; interment in Pleasant Street Cemetery.

DEAN, Sidney, a Representative from Connecticut; born in Glastonbury, Conn., November 16, 1818; attended the common schools and Wilbraham and Suffield Academies; minister in the Methodist Episcopal Church from 1843 to 1853, when he retired from the ministry because of impaired health; engaged in manufacturing in Putnam, Conn.; member of the Connecticut House of Representatives in 1854 and 1855; elected as the candidate of the American Party to the Thirty-fourth Congress and as a Republican to the Thirty-fifth Congress (March 4, 1855–March 3, 1859); declined to be a candidate for renomination in 1858; traveled for a short time, and on his return home in 1860 reentered the ministry, with pastorates in Pawtucket, Providence, and finally in Warren, R. I.; took up journalism in 1864; during the period 1865–1880 engaged as editor of the Providence Press, Providence Star, and Rhode Island Press; served in the Rhode Island Senate in 1870 and 1871; engaged in literary pursuits and lecturing; died in Brookline, Norfolk County, Mass., October 29, 1901; interment in South Cemetery, Warren, R. I.

DEANE, Charles Bennett, a Representative from North Carolina; born in Ansonville Township, Anson County, N. C., November 1, 1898; attended Pee Dee Academy, Rockingham, N. C., and Trinity Park School, Durham, N. C., 1918–1920; was graduated from the law department of Wake Forest (N. C.) College in 1923; was admitted to the bar the same year and commenced practice in Rockingham, N. C.; register of deeds of Richmond County 1926–1934; attorney in the Wage and Hour Division, Department of Labor, Washington, D. C., in 1938 and 1939; in 1940 engaged in administrative law and in the general insurance business; served as chairman of the Richmond County Democratic executive committee 1932–1946; trustee of Wake Forest College; elected as a Democrat to the Eightieth and to the four succeeding Congresses (January 3, 1947–January 3, 1957); was an unsuccessful candidate for renomination in 1956 to the Eighty-fifth Congress; lawyer and insurance broker; is a resident of Rockingham, N. C.

DEANE, Silas, a Delegate from Connecticut; born in Groton, Conn., December 24, 1737; received a classical training, and was graduated from Yale College, New Haven, Conn., in 1758; studied law; was admitted to the bar in 1761 and commenced practice in Wethersfield, Conn.: afterward engaged in mercantile pursuits in the same town; deputy of the general assembly 1768–1775; Member of the Continental Congress 1774–1776; ordered to France in March 1776 as a secret political and financial agent, and in September was commissioned as Ambassador with Franklin and Lee; negotiated and signed the treaty between France and the United States in Paris on February 6, 1778; personally secured the services of Lafayette, De Kalb, and other foreign officers, for which he was accused of extravagance, and was recalled in 1777 and investigated by Congress; returned to France to procure transcripts of his transactions there, and found that the publication of some of his confidential dispatches had embittered that Government against him, and he was compelled to go to Holland, and thence to Great Britain, greatly impoverished; died on board ship sailing from Gravesend to Boston September 23, 1789; interment in Deal, on the Kentish coast, England; in 1842 Congress vindicated his memory by deciding that a considerable sum of money was due him, which was paid to his heirs.

DEAR, Cleveland, a Representative from Louisiana; born in Sugartown, Beauregard Parish, La., August 22, 1888; attended the public schools; was graduated from Louisiana State University at Baton Rouge in 1910 and from its law department in 1914; was admitted to the bar in 1914 and commenced practice in Alexandria, Rapides Parish, La.; during the First World War was appointed a second lieutenant of Field Artillery on August 15, 1917; promoted to first lieutenant and served in the ammunition train of the Field Artillery in the Eighty-seventh and One Hundred and Eleventh Divisions until his discharge on December 14, 1918; served as district attorney of the ninth judicial district of Louisiana from 1920 until his resignation in 1933, having been elected to Congress; elected as a Democrat to the Seventy-third and Seventy-fourth Congresses (March 4, 1933–January 3, 1937); was not a candidate for renomination in 1936, but was an unsuccessful candidate for the gubernatorial nomination; resumed the practice of law; appointed judge of the ninth judicial district court of Louisiana in 1941 to fill an unexpired term and was elected in 1942 and again in 1948 and served until his death in Alexandria, La., December 30, 1950; interment in Greenwood Memorial Park, Pineville, La.

DEARBORN, Henry (father of Henry Alexander Scammell Dearborn), a Representative from Massachusetts; born in North Hampton, N. H., February 23, 1751; attended the public schools; studied medicine; commenced practice in Nottingham Square in 1772; during the Revolutionary War was a captain in Stark's Regiment and participated in the Battle of Bunker Hill, where he covered the retreat of the American forces; accompanied Arnold's expedition to Canada and took part in the storming of Quebec; was taken prisoner, but was released on parole in May 1776; fought in the Battles of Stillwater, Saratoga, Monmouth, and Newton; joined Washington's staff in 1781 as deputy quartermaster general with rank of colonel, and served at the siege of Yorktown; moved to Monmouth, Mass. (now Maine), in June 1784; elected brigadier general of militia in 1787 and made major general in 1789; appointed United States marshal for the district of Maine in 1789; elected as a Democrat from a Maine district of Massachusetts to the Third and Fourth Congresses (March 4, 1793–March 3, 1797); appointed Secretary of War by President Jefferson and served from March 4, 1801, to March 7, 1809; appointed collector of the port of Boston by President Madison in 1809, which position he held until January 27, 1812, when he was appointed senior major general in the United States Army; was in command at the capture of York (now Toronto) April 27, 1813, and Fort George May 27, 1813; recalled from the frontier July 6, 1813, and placed in command of the city of New York; appointed Minister Plenipotentiary to Portugal by President Monroe and served from May 7, 1822, to June 30, 1824, when, by his own request, he was recalled; returned to Roxbury, Mass., where he died June 6, 1829; interment in Forest Hills Cemetery, Boston, Mass.

DEARBORN, Henry Alexander Scammell (son of Henry Dearborn), a Representative from Massachusetts; born in Exeter, N. H., March 3, 1783; attended the common schools and Williams College, Williamstown, Mass., for two years; was graduated from William and Mary College, Williamsburg, Va., in 1803; studied law; was admitted to the bar and practiced in Salem, Mass., and Portland, Mass. (now Maine); collector of customs in Boston 1812–1829; served as brigadier general commanding the Volunteers in the defenses of Boston Harbor in the War of 1812; member of the State constitutional convention in 1820; member of the State house of representatives in 1829; served in the State senate in 1830; elected to the Twenty-second Congress (March 4, 1831–March 3, 1833); was an unsuccessful candidate for reelection in 1832 to the Twenty-third Congress; served as adjutant general of Massachusetts 1834–1843; mayor of Roxbury 1847–1851; president of the Massachusetts Horticultural Society; author of many books; died in Portland, Maine, on July 29, 1851; interment in Forest Hills Cemetery, Roxbury, Mass.

DE ARMOND, David Albaugh, a Representative from Missouri; born in Altoona, Blair County, Pa., on March 18, 1844; attended the public schools and Williamsport Dickinson Seminary; moved to Davenport, Iowa, in 1866; studied law; was admitted to the bar in 1867 and commenced practice in Davenport; moved to Missouri in 1869 and settled in Greenfield, Dade County; presidential elector on the Democratic ticket of Cleveland and Hendricks in 1884; member of the State senate 1879–1883; Missouri Supreme Court commissioner in 1884; judge of the twenty-second judicial circuit of Missouri 1886–1890; elected as a Democrat to the Fifty-second and to the nine succeeding Congresses and served from March 4, 1891, until his death; one of the managers appointed by the House of Representatives in 1905 to conduct the impeachment proceedings against Charles Swayne, judge of the United States District Court for the Northern District of Florida; died in Butler, Bates County, Mo., November 23, 1909; interment in Oak Hill Cemetery.

DEBERRY, Edmund, a Representative from North Carolina; born in Lawrenceville (now Mount Gilead), Montgomery County, N. C., August 14, 1787; attended school at High Shoals; engaged in agricultural pursuits and also in the operation of cotton mills and flour mills; member of the State senate 1806–1811, 1813, 1814, 1820, 1821, and 1826–1828; served as justice of the peace; elected to the Twenty-first Congress (March 4, 1829–March 3, 1831); unsuccessful candidate for reelection in 1830 to the Twenty-second Congress; elected as a Whig to the Twenty-third and to the five succeeding Congresses (March 4, 1833–March 3, 1845); was not a candidate for renomination in 1844; elected to the Thirty-first Congress (March 4, 1849–March 3, 1851); was not a candidate for renomination in 1850; resumed his former agricultural and business pursuits; died at his home in Pee Dee Township, Montgomery County, N. C., December 12, 1859; interment in the family cemetery on his plantation near Mount Gilead.

DEBOE, William Joseph, a Senator from Kentucky; born in Crittenden County, Ky., June 30, 1849; attended the public schools of the State, and Ewing College, Illinois; studied law and medicine; was graduated from the medical department of the University of Louisville and practiced a few years, when his health failed; renewed the study of law; was admitted to the bar in 1889 and commenced practice in Marion, Crittenden County, Ky.; served as superintendent of schools of Crittenden County; delegate to the Republican National Convention at Chicago in 1888, at St. Louis in 1896, where he was chairman of the delegation, and at Chicago in 1912; member of the Republican State central committee twelve years; unsuccessful candidate for election in 1892 to the Fifty-third Congress; member of the State senate 1893–1898; elected as a Republican to the United States Senate and served from March 4, 1897, to March 3, 1903; was not a candidate for renomination in 1902; engaged in mining; appointed acting postmaster of Marion on March 28, 1923, and postmaster on June 6, 1924; served until May 23, 1927, when he resigned because of ill health; died in Marion, Crittenden County, Ky., on June 15, 1927; interment in Maple View Cemetery.

DE BOLT, Rezin A., a Representative from Missouri; born near Basil, Fairfield County, Ohio, January 20, 1828; attended the common schools; employed as a tanner; studied law; was admitted to the bar in 1856 and commenced practice in Lancaster, Fairfield County, Ohio; moved to Trenton, Grundy County, Mo., in 1858 and continued the practice of his profession; appointed in 1859 and elected in 1860 commissioner of common schools for Grundy County and served until the Civil War; entered the Union Army as captain in the Twenty-third Regiment, Missouri Volunteers, in 1861; captured at the Battle of Shiloh April 6, 1862, and held as prisoner until the following October; resigned his commission in 1863 because of impaired health; elected judge of the circuit court for the eleventh judicial circuit of Missouri in November 1863, which position he held by reelection until January 1, 1875; in 1864 again entered the United States service as major in the Forty-fourth Regiment, Missouri Volunteer Infantry; mustered out in August 1865; elected as a Democrat to the Forty-fourth Congress (March 4, 1875–March 3, 1877); was not a candidate for renomination in 1876; resumed the practice of law; died in Trenton, Grundy County, Mo., October 30, 1891; interment in Odd Fellows Cemetery.

DECKER, Perl D., a Representative from Missouri; born on a farm near Coolville, Athens County, Ohio, September 10, 1875; moved with his parents to a farm near Hollis, Cloud County, Kans., in 1879; attended the public schools of Cloud County, and Park College, Parkville, Mo., from which he was graduated in 1897; was graduated in law from the University of Kansas at Lawrence in 1899; was admitted to the bar in 1900 and commenced practice at Joplin, Jasper County, Mo.; served as city attorney 1900–1902; elected as a Democrat to the Sixty-third, Sixty-fourth, and Sixty-fifth Congresses (March 4, 1913–March 3, 1919); unsuccessful candidate for reelection in 1918 to the Sixty-sixth Congress; resumed the practice of law in Joplin, Mo.; delegate to the Democratic National Convention at Chicago in 1932; died in Kansas City, Mo., while on a visit for medical treatment, August 22, 1934; interment in Mount Hope Cemetery, Joplin, Mo.

DEEMER, Elias, a Representative from Pennsylvania; born near Durham, Bucks County, Pa., January 3, 1838; attended public and private schools; engaged in mercantile pursuits in Lycoming County and in Philadelphia in 1860; during the Civil War enlisted in July 1861 as a private in Company E, One Hundred and Fourth Regiment, Pennsylvania Volunteers, and served until the middle of May following, when he was discharged because of disabilities; moved to Milford, N. J., in 1862 and engaged in business; moved to Williamsport, Pa., in 1868 and engaged in the manufacture of lumber; president of the common council 1888–1890; president of the Williamsport National Bank 1893–1918; also interested in the publication of several newspapers at Williamsport; delegate to the Republican National Convention at St. Louis in 1896; elected as a Republican to the Fifty-seventh, Fifty-eighth, and Fifty-ninth Congresses (March 4, 1901–March 3, 1907); unsuccessful candidate for reelection in 1906 to the Sixtieth Congress and for election in 1908 to the Sixty-first Congress; resumed lumber operations in Pennsylvania, and at Deemer, Miss., which town he founded and gave his name; died in Williamsport, Pa., March 29, 1918; interment in Wildwood Cemetery.

DEEN, Braswell Drue, a Representative from Georgia; born on a farm near Baxley, Appling County, Ga., June 28, 1893; attended public and high schools and South Georgia College, McRae, Ga.; during the First World War served as a Y. M. C. A. secretary; was graduated from Emory University, Atlanta, Ga., in 1922; superintendent of schools at Tennille, Ga., 1922–1924; president of South Georgia Junior College, McRae, Ga., 1924–1927; engaged in farming and real-estate development in 1927 and 1928; editor and proprietor of the Alma (Ga.) Times; also engaged in banking; elected as a Democrat to the Seventy-third, Seventy-fourth, and Seventy-fifth Congresses (March 4, 1933–January 3, 1939); was not a candidate for renomination in 1938 to the Seventy-sixth Congress; insurance broker; is a resident of Alma, Bacon County, Ga.

DEERING, Nathaniel Cobb, a Representative from Iowa; born in Denmark, Oxford County, Maine, September 2, 1827; attended the common schools and was graduated from North Bridgeton Academy; member of the State house of representatives from Penobscot County in 1855 and 1856; moved to Iowa, and settled in Osage, Mitchell County, in 1857; engaged in the lumber business and built and operated a sawmill; for several years a clerk in the United States Senate, but resigned in 1865; special agent of the Post Office Department for the district of Minnesota, Iowa, and Nebraska from 1865 to 1869, when he resigned; national-bank examiner for the State of Iowa 1872–1877; elected as a Republican to the Forty-fifth, Forty-sixth, and Forty-seventh Congresses (March 4, 1877–March 3, 1883); unsuccessful candidate for renomination in 1882; engaged in agricultural pursuits; also interested in cattle raising in Montana, and at the time of his death served as president of a large cattle company in that territory; died in Osage, Mitchell County, Iowa, December 11, 1887; interment in Osage Cemetery.

DE FOREST, Henry Schermerhorn, a Representative from New York; born in Schenectady, N. Y., February 16, 1847; attended the public schools of his native town and Eastman Business College, Poughkeepsie, N. Y.; engaged in the real-estate, banking, and contracting businesses; city recorder 1883–1885; mayor of Schenectady 1885–1887 and 1889–1891; elected as a Republican to the Sixty-second Congress (March 4, 1911–March 3, 1913); unsuccessful candidate for reelection in 1912 to the Sixty-third Congress; resumed the real-estate business and banking; unsuccessful candidate for nomination in 1914 to the Sixty-fourth Congress and for election in 1916 to the Sixty-fifth Congress; died in Schenectady, N. Y., February 13, 1917; interment in Vale Cemetery.

DE FOREST, Robert Elliott, a Representative from Connecticut; born in Guilford, New Haven County, Conn., February 20, 1845; attended the common schools; was graduated from Guilford Academy in 1863 and from Yale College, New Haven, Conn., in 1867; moved to Royalton, Vt., in 1867 and became an instructor in the Royalton Academy; studied law; was admitted to the bar in 1870 and commenced practice in Bridgeport, Conn.; prosecuting attorney for Bridgeport in 1872; judge of the court of common pleas for Fairfield County in 1874–1877; mayor of Bridgeport in 1878; member of the State house of representatives in 1880; served in the State senate in 1882; corporation counsel for Bridgeport; again elected mayor in 1889 and 1890; elected as a Democrat to the Fifty-second and Fifty-third Congresses (March 4, 1891–March 3, 1895); unsuccessful candidate for reelection in 1894 to the Fifty-fourth Congress; served two terms as judge of the common pleas court; resumed the practice of law in Bridgeport, Conn., where he died October 1, 1924; interment in Mountain Grove Cemetery.

DEFREES, Joseph Hutton, a Representative from Indiana; born in Sparta, White County, Tenn., May 13, 1812; moved to Ohio with his parents, who settled in Piqua in 1819; attended the common schools; apprenticed to the blacksmith trade 1826–1829; learned the art of printing; moved to Indiana and settled in South Bend in 1831, where he established the Northwestern Pioneer; moved to Goshen, Elkhart County, Ind., in 1833 and engaged in mercantile pursuits and later in banking; appointed county agent; sheriff of Elkhart County 1835–1840; member of the State house of representatives in 1849 and again in 1872; served in the State senate 1850–1854; elected as a Republican to the Thirty-ninth Congress (March 4, 1865–March 3, 1867); was not a candidate for renomination in 1866; resumed his former business pursuits; also interested in milling, the manufacture of linseed oil, and the construction of the Goshen Hydraulic Works;

director of the Cincinnati, Wabash & Michigan Railroad and served as its first president; died at Goshen, Ind., December 21, 1885; interment in Oak Ridge Cemetery.

DEGENER, Edward, a Representative from Texas; born in Brunswick, Germany, October 20, 1809; pursued an academic course in Germany and in England; twice a member of the legislative body in Anhalt-Dessau and a member of the first German National Assembly in Frankfort on the Main in 1848; immigrated to the United States in 1850 and located in Sisterdale, Kendall County, Tex.; engaged in agricultural pursuits; during the Civil War was court-martialed and imprisoned by the Confederates because of his devotion to the Union cause; after his release from imprisonment engaged in the wholesale grocery business in San Antonio; member of the Texas constitutional conventions in 1866 and 1868; upon the readmission of the State of Texas to representation was elected as a Republican to the Forty-first Congress and served from March 31, 1870, to March 3, 1871; unsuccessful for reelection in 1870 to the Forty-second Congress; member of the city council of San Antonio, Tex., 1872–1878; died in San Antonio, Tex., September 11, 1890; interment in the City Cemetery.

DEGETAU, Federico, a Resident Commissioner from Puerto Rico; born in Ponce, P. R., December 5, 1862; attended the common schools and Central College of Ponce; completed an academic course at Barcelona, Spain, and was graduated from the law department of Central University of Madrid; was admitted to the bar and commenced practice in Madrid, Spain; returned to Puerto Rico; one of the four commissioners sent by Puerto Rico to ask Spain for autonomy; settled in San Juan and continued the practice of law; member of the municipal council of San Juan in 1897; mayor of San Juan in 1898; deputy to the Spanish Cortes of 1898; appointed by General Henry secretary of the interior of the first American cabinet that was formed in Puerto Rico in 1899; appointed by General Davis a member of the insular board of charities; writer and author; first vice president of the municipal council of San Juan in 1899 and 1900; president of the board of education of San Juan in 1900 and 1901; elected as a Puerto Rican Republican a Resident Commissioner to the United States in 1900; reelected in 1902, and served from March 4, 1901, until March 3, 1905; was not a candidate for renomination in 1904; resumed the practice of law; died in Santurce, Puerto Rico, January 20, 1914; interment in the Cemetery of San Juan.

DE GRAFF, John Isaac, a Representative from New York; born in Schenectady, N. Y., October 2, 1783; attended the common schools, and Union College, Schenectady, N. Y., in 1811; engaged in mercantile pursuits in Schenectady; served in the War of 1812; elected as a Democrat to the Twentieth Congress (March 4, 1827–March 3, 1829); mayor of Schenectady 1832–1834 and again in 1836; elected to the Twenty-fifth Congress (March 4, 1837–March 3, 1839); was not a candidate for renomination; engaged in mercantile pursuits; tendered the portfolio of Secretary of the Treasury in the Cabinet of President Van Buren, but declined the office; interested in the building of the Mohawk & Hudson Railroad; again served as mayor of Schenectady in 1842 and 1845; engaged in banking until his death in Schenectady, N. Y., July 26, 1848; interment in Vale Cemetery.

DE GRAFFENREID, Reese Calhoun, a Representative from Texas; born in Franklin, Williamson County, Tenn., May 7, 1859; attended the common schools of Franklin and the University of Tennessee at Knoxville; was graduated from the law department of Cumberland University, Lebanon, Tenn.; was admitted to the bar in 1879 and commenced practice in Franklin; moved to Chattanooga, Tenn., where he practiced his profession for one year, moving thence to Texas; helped in the construction of the Texas & Pacific Railroad; resumed the practice of law at Longview, Tex., in 1883; elected county attorney and resigned two months afterward; presidential elector on the Democratic ticket of Cleveland and Thurman in 1888; unsuccessful candidate for election in 1890 to the Fifty-second Congress; elected as a Democrat to the Fifty-fifth, Fifty-sixth, and Fifty-seventh Congresses and served from March 4, 1897, until his death in Washington, D. C., August 29, 1902; interment in Greenwood Cemetery, Longview, Gregg County, Tex.

deGRAFFENRIED, Edward, a Representative from Alabama; born in Eutaw, Greene County, Ala., June 30, 1899; attended the public schools in Greensboro, Ala.; was graduated from Gulf Coast Military Academy, Gulfport, Miss., in 1917; during the First World War served as a private in the United States Army and was discharged on December 5, 1918, at Camp Pike, Ark.; graduated from the law school of the University of Alabama at Tuscaloosa in 1921; was admitted to the bar in June 1921 and commenced the practice of law in Tuscaloosa, Ala.; elected solicitor of the sixth judicial circuit of Alabama in 1926 and reelected in 1930 and served from 1927 through 1934; unsuccessful for reelection in 1934 and for election in 1938; again elected solicitor and served from January 1943 to January 1947; was unsuccessful for the Democratic nomination in 1946 to the Eightieth Congress; alternate delegate to the Democratic National Convention in 1932; elected as a Democrat to the Eighty-first and Eighty-second Congresses (January 3, 1949– January 3, 1953); unsuccessful candidate for renomination in 1952; resumed the practice of law; resides in Tuscaloosa, Ala.

DE HART, John, a Delegate from New Jersey; born in Elizabethtown (now Elizabeth), N. J., in 1728; completed preparatory studies; studied law; was admitted to the bar and practiced; was made a sergeant-at-law on September 11, 1770; was one of the signers of the Articles of Association, as the nonimportation agreement was called, in 1774; Member of the Continental Congress and served from July 3, 1774, until his resignation on November 22, 1775; again elected on February 14, 1776, but resigned on June 13, 1776; member of the committee who prepared the draft for the New Jersey State constitution in June 1776; elected chief justice of the State supreme court September 4, 1776, and his declination was accepted February 5, 1777; mayor of Elizabethtown under the revised charter and served from November 1789 until his death; died in Elizabethtown, N. J., June 1, 1795; interment in St. John's Churchyard.

DE HAVEN, John Jefferson, a Representative from California; born in St. Joseph, Buchanan County, Mo., March 12, 1849; moved to California in 1853 with his parents, who settled in Humboldt County; attended the common schools; became a printer, and pursued that vocation for four years; studied law; was admitted to the bar of the district court in Humboldt in 1866 and commenced practice at Eureka; elected district attorney of Humboldt County in 1867; member of the State house of representatives in 1869; served in the State senate 1871–1875; unsuccessful candidate for delegate to the State constitutional convention in 1878; appointed city attorney of Eureka in 1878, and served two years; unsuccessful candidate for election in 1882 to the Forty-eighth Congress; elected judge of the superior court of Humboldt County in 1884; elected as a Republican to the Fifty-first Congress and served from March 4, 1889, until October 1, 1890, when he resigned; elected associate justice of the California Supreme Court to fill an unexpired term of four years; United States district judge for the northern district of California from June 8, 1897, until his death in Yountville, Napa County, Calif., January 26, 1913; interment in Mount Olivet Cemetery, San Francisco, Calif.

DEITRICK, Frederick Simpson, a Representative from Massachusetts; born in New Brighton, Beaver County, Pa., April 9, 1875; attended the public schools; was graduated from Geneva College, Beaver Falls, Pa., in 1895 and from Harvard Law School in 1898; was admitted to the bar in 1899 and commenced practice in Boston, Mass.; member of the board of aldermen of Cambridge in 1908 and 1909; member of the State house of representatives 1902–1905; elected as a Democrat to the Sixty-third Congress (March 4, 1913–March 3, 1915); unsuccessful candidate for reelection in 1914 to the Sixty-fourth Congress; resumed the practice of law in Boston, Mass.; died in Middleton, Mass., May 24, 1948; interment in Mount Auburn Cemetery, Cambridge, Mass.

DE JARNETTE, Daniel Coleman, a Representative from Virginia; born at "Spring Grove Manor," near Bowling Green, Caroline County, Va., October 18, 1822; studied under a private teacher and attended Bethany College, Bethany, Va. (now West Virginia); engaged in agricultural pursuits; served in the State house of representatives 1853–1858; elected as a Democrat to the Thirty-sixth Congress (March 4, 1859–March 3, 1861); reelected to the Thirty-seventh Congress, but did not present his credentials; Representative from Virginia to the First and Second Confederate Congresses 1862–1865; was an arbitrator in 1871 to define the boundary line between Maryland and Virginia; died at White Sulphur Springs, Greenbrier County, W. Va., August 20, 1881; interment in private burying ground on his estate, "Spring Grove," Caroline County, Va.

DE LACY, Emerson Hugh, a Representative from Washington; born in Seattle, King County, Wash., May 9, 1910; attended the Queen Anne public schools; was graduated from the University of Washington at Seattle, in 1932; taught English at the University of Washington 1933–1937; member of the city council of Seattle 1937–1940; employed as a shipyard machinist 1940–1944; elected as a Democrat to the Seventy-ninth Congress (January 3, 1945–January 3, 1947); unsuccessful candidate for reelection in 1946 to the Eightieth Congress; engaged in the newspaper business in Seattle, Wash., as editor of the Machinists' Bulletin; State director of the Progressive Party of Ohio 1948– 1950; general building contractor; resides in Los Angeles, Calif.

DE LA MATYR, Gilbert, a Representative from Indiana; born in Pharsalia, Chenango County, N. Y., July 8, 1825; pursued an academic course; studied theology; was a graduate of the theological course of the Methodist Episcopal Church in 1854; itinerant elder in that church; member of the general conference in 1868, and for one term filled the office of presiding elder; during the Civil War helped enlist the Eighth Regiment of New York Heavy Artillery in 1862, and was its chaplain for three years; after holding pastorates in several large cities he settled in Indianapolis, Ind., and continued his ministerial duties; elected as a National and Democrat to the Forty-sixth Congress (March 4, 1879–March 3, 1881); was not a candidate for renomination in 1880 to the Forty-seventh Congress; moved to Denver, Colo., in 1881 and again engaged in preaching; pastor of the First Methodist Episcopal Church of Akron, Ohio, from 1889 until his death in that city May 17, 1892; interment in Mount Albion Cemetery, Albion, N. Y.

DE LA MONTANYA, James, a Representative from New York; born in New York City March 20, 1798; resided in Haverstraw, Rockland County, N. Y.; supervisor of Haverstraw in 1832 and 1833; member of the State assembly in 1833; elected as a Democrat to the Twenty-sixth Congress (March 4, 1839–March 3, 1841); died in New York City April 29, 1849; interment in the Barnes family burial ground, Stony Point, Rockland County, N. Y.

DELANEY, James Joseph, a Representative from New York; born in New York City, N. Y., March 19, 1901; attended the public and high schools in Long Island City, N. Y.; was graduated from the law department of St. John's College, Brooklyn, N. Y., in 1931; was admitted to the bar in 1933 and commenced practice in New York City, N. Y.; assistant district attorney of Queens County, N. Y., 1936–1944; elected as a Democrat to the Seventy-ninth Congress (January 3, 1945–January 3, 1947); unsuccessful candidate for reelection in 1946 to the Eightieth Congress; resumed the practice of law in New York City; elected to the Eighty-first and to the five succeeding Congress (January 3, 1949–January 3, 1961). *Reelected to the Eighty-seventh Congress.*

DELANEY, John Joseph, a Representative from New York; born in Brooklyn, N. Y., August 21, 1878; attended St. Ann's Parochial School and St. James' Academy, Brooklyn, N. Y., and Manhattan College, New York City; engaged in the diamond business in 1897; was graduated from the Brooklyn Law School of St. Lawrence University in 1914; admitted to the bar in 1915 and commenced practice in New York City; elected as a Democrat to the Sixty-fifth Congress to fill the vacancy caused by the resignation of John J. Fitzgerald and served from March 5, 1918, to March 3, 1919; declined to be a candidate for renomination in 1918; resumed his former business pursuits; delegate to the Democratic State conventions in 1922 and 1924; deputy commissioner of public markets of New York City 1924–1931; elected to the Seventy-second and to the eight succeeding Congresses and served from March 4, 1931, until his death; had been reelected to the Eighty-first Congress; died in Brooklyn, N. Y., November 18, 1948; interment in Holy Cross Cemetery.

DELANO, Charles, a Representative from Massachusetts; born in New Braintree, Worcester County, Mass., June 24, 1820; moved with his parents to Amherst, Mass., in 1833; attended the common schools and was graduated from Amherst College, Amherst, Mass., in 1840; studied law; was admitted to the bar in 1842 and commenced practice in Amherst, Mass.; moved to Northampton, Mass., in 1848 and continued the practice of law; treasurer of Hampshire County 1849–1858; declined the offer of a professorship at the Harvard Law School in 1853; elected as a Republican to the Thirty-sixth and Thirty-seventh Congresses (March 4, 1859–March 3, 1863); was not a candidate for renomination in 1862; resumed the practice of law; trustee of the Clarke School for the Education of the Deaf 1877–1883; appointed by Governor Rice in 1878 to act as special counsel for the Commonwealth of Massachusetts in matters relating to the Hoosac Tunnel and the Troy & Greenfield Railroad, and served in this capacity until his death in Northampton, Mass., January 23, 1883; interment in Bridge Street Cemetery.

DELANO, Columbus, a Representative from Ohio; born in Shoreham, Vt., June 4, 1809; moved with his parents to Mount Vernon, Ohio, in 1817; pursued an academic course; studied law; was admitted to the bar in 1831 and commenced practice in Mount Vernon; elected as a Whig to the Twenty-ninth Congress (March 4, 1845–March 3, 1847); was not a candidate for renomination in 1846; unsuccessful candidate for the nomination for Governor at the Whig State convention in 1847; delegate to the Republican National Convention at Chicago in 1860 and seconded the nomination of Abraham Lincoln as a candidate for President of the United States; served as State commissary general of Ohio in 1861; unsuccessful candidate by two votes for the United States Senate in 1862; member of the State house of representatives in 1863; delegate to the Republican National Convention at Baltimore in 1864; elected as a Republican to the Thirty-ninth Congress (March 4, 1865–March 3, 1867); successfully contested the election of George W. Morgan to the Fortieth

Congress and served from June 3, 1868, to March 3, 1869; was not a candidate for renomination in 1868; Commissioner of Internal Revenue from March 11, 1869, to October 31, 1870; appointed Secretary of the Interior by President Grant on November 1, 1870, which position he held until October 19, 1875, when he resigned; retired to his farm near Mount Vernon, Ohio, and engaged in agricultural pursuits; president of the First National Bank of Mount Vernon until his death in Mount Vernon, Knox County, Ohio, October 23, 1896; interment in Mount View Cemetery.

DE LANO, Milton, a Representative from New York; born in Wampsville, Madison County, N. Y., August 11, 1844; attended the common schools; settled in Canastota, N. Y., and engaged in mercantile pursuits for eight years; town clerk of Lenox 1867–1869; sheriff of Madison County, N. Y., 1873–1875 and 1879–1881; engaged in banking, the real-estate business, and in the manufacture of window glass; member of the Canastota Board of Education 1883–1905 and served as president 1893–1905; aided in the organization of the Canastota Northern Railroad Co.; delegate to the Republican National Convention at Chicago in 1884 when Blaine and Logan were nominated; elected as a Republican to the Fiftieth and Fifty-first Congresses (March 4, 1887– March 3, 1891); declined to be a candidate for renomination in 1890; resumed banking; receiver of the Hudson River Power Co. 1908–1912; became president of the State Bank of Canastota, N. Y., in 1912; died at the Syracuse Memorial Hospital, Syracuse, Onondaga County, N. Y., January 2, 1922; interment in Mount Pleasant Cemetery, Canastota, N. Y.

DELAPLAINE, Isaac Clason, a Representative from New York; born in New York City October 27, 1817; pursued an academic course; was graduated from Columbia College (now Columbia University), New York City, in 1834; studied law; was admitted to the bar about 1840 and commenced practice in New York City; elected as a Fusionist to the Thirty-seventh Congress (March 4, 1861–March 3, 1863); died in New York City July 17, 1866; interment in Greenwood Cemetery, Brooklyn, N. Y.

DE LARGE, Robert Carlos, a Representative from South Carolina; born in Aiken, S. C., March 15, 1842; was of the Negro race; received such an education as was then attainable and was graduated from Wood High School; engaged in agricultural pursuits; delegate to the State constitutional convention in 1868; member of the State house of representatives 1868–1870; was one of the State commissioners of the sinking fund; elected State land commissioner in 1870 and served until elected to Congress; presented credentials as a Republican Member-elect to the Forty-second Congress and served from March 4, 1871, until January 24, 1873, when the seat was declared vacant, the election having been contested by Christopher C. Bowen; local magistrate until his death in Charleston, S. C., February 14, 1874; interment in Brown Fellowship Graveyard.

DELGADO, Francisco A., a Resident Commissioner from the Philippine Islands; born in Bulacan Province, Philippine Islands, January 25, 1886; studied at San Juan de Letran, Ateneo de Manila, Colegio Filipino, Los Angeles (Calif.) High School, and Compton (Calif.) Union High School; was graduated from the law department of Indiana University at Bloomington in 1907 and from Yale University, New Haven, Conn., in 1908; was admitted to the bar in 1908 and commenced practice in Indianapolis, Ind.; returned to the Philippine Islands in 1908 and was employed with the Philippine Government as a law clerk and later as chief of the law division of the executive bureau until 1913, when he returned to the private practice of law; served in the Philippine National Guard in 1918; member of the National

Council of Defense for the Philippines in 1918; served in the Philippine House of Representatives 1931–1934; elected as a Nationalist a Resident Commissioner to the United States and served from January 3, 1935, until February 14, 1936, when a successor qualified in accordance with the new form of government of the Commonwealth of the Philippine Islands; appointed justice of the court of appeals in February 1936; resumed the practice of law; delegate to the International Committee of Jurists at Washington, D. C., and to the United Nations Conference at San Francisco in April 1945; member of the Philippine War Damage Commission from June 4, 1946, to March 31, 1951; Ambassador to the United Nations since September 1958; is a resident of Bulacan, Province of Bulacan, Philippines.

DELLAY, Vincent John, a Representative from New Jersey; born in Union City, Hudson County, N. J., June 23, 1907; educated in West New York High School, New York Evening High School, and the American Institute of Banking; from messenger to bookkeeper, Irving Trust Co., New York City, 1923–1929; assistant comptroller, Sterling National Bank & Trust Co., New York, N. Y., 1929–1936; auditor, New Jersey State Treasury Department, 1936–1956; during World War II served in the United States Navy as a petty officer from February 1944 until December 1945; chief warrant officer New Jersey National Guard 1949–1960; unsuccessful candidate for election in 1954 to the Eighty-fourth Congress; elected as a Republican to the Eighty-fifth Congress (January 3, 1957–January 3, 1959); changed political affiliation from Republican to Democrat during the Eighty-fifth Congress; was unsuccessful for nomination as an Independent candidate to the Eighty-sixth Congress; engaged as supervising field auditor for New Jersey Treasury Department; is a resident of West New York, N. J.

DELLET, James, a Representative from Alabama; born in Camden, N. J., February 18, 1788; moved to Columbia, S. C., with his parents in 1800; was graduated from the University of South Carolina at Columbia in 1810; studied law; was admitted to the bar in 1813 and practiced; moved to Alabama in 1818 and settled in Claiborne and continued the practice of law; elected to the first State house of representatives of Alabama under the State government in 1819 and served as its speaker; reelected in 1821 and 1825; unsuccessful as the Whig candidate for Congress in 1833; elected as a Whig to the Twenty-sixth Congress (March 4, 1839–March 3, 1841); elected to the Twenty-eighth Congress (March 4, 1843–March 3, 1845); resumed the practice of law and also engaged in agricultural pursuits; died in Claiborne, Monroe County, Ala., December 21, 1848; interment in a private cemetery at Claiborne, Ala.

DEMING, Benjamin F., a Representative from Vermont; born in Danville, Caledonia County, Vt., in 1790; pursued an academic course; engaged in mercantile pursuits; member of the Governor's council 1827–1832; clerk of the Caledonia County Court 1817–1833; county judge of probate 1821–1833; elected as a Whig to the Twenty-third Congress and served from March 4, 1833, until his death at Saratoga Springs, N. Y., en route home, July 11, 1834; interment in Danville Green Cemetery, Danville, Caledonia County, Vt.

DEMING, Henry Champion, a Representative from Connecticut; born in Colchester, New London County, Conn., May 23, 1815; pursued classical studies; was graduated from Yale College, New Haven, Conn., in 1836 and from the Harvard Law School in 1839; was admitted to the bar in 1839 and began practice in New York City but devoted his time chiefly to literary work; moved to Hartford, Conn., in 1847; member of the State house of representatives in 1849, 1850, and 1859–1861; member of

the State senate in 1851; mayor of Hartford, Conn., 1854–1858 and 1860–1862; entered the Union Army in September 1861 as colonel of the Twelfth Regiment, Connecticut Volunteers; mayor of New Orleans under martial law from October 1862 to February 1863, when he resigned from the Army; elected as a Republican to the Thirty-eighth and Thirty-ninth Congresses (March 4, 1863–March 3, 1867); unsuccessful candidate for reelection in 1866 to the Fortieth Congress; appointed collector of internal revenue in 1869 and served until his death in Hartford, Conn., October 8, 1872; interment in Spring Grove Cemetery.

DE MOTT, John, a Representative from New York; born in Readington, Hunterdon County, N. J., October 7, 1790; moved to Herkimer County, N. Y., in 1793 with his parents, who settled in what is now the town of Lodi, Seneca County; attended the common schools; pursued an academic course; major general of the Thirty-eighth Brigade of the State militia; supervisor in the town of Covert in 1823 and 1824 and of Lodi in 1826, 1827, 1829, and 1830; engaged in mercantile pursuits in Lodi, N. Y., for more than forty years, and was a prominent merchant and grain buyer; member of the State assembly in 1833; unsuccessful candidate for election in 1840 to the Twenty-seventh Congress; elected as a Democrat to the Twenty-ninth Congress (March 4, 1845–March 3, 1847); was not a candidate for renomination in 1846; resumed his former business pursuits and also engaged in the banking business; died in Lodi, Seneca County, N. Y., July 31, 1870; interment in Evergreen Cemetery, Ovid, N. Y.

DE MOTTE, Mark Lindsey, a Representative from Indiana; born in Rockville, Parke County, Ind., December 28, 1832; pursued preparatory studies; was graduated from the literary department of Indiana Asbury (now De Pauw) University, Greencastle, Ind., in 1853 and from the law department of the same university in 1855; was admitted to the bar and began practice in Valparaiso in 1855; elected prosecuting attorney of the sixty-seventh judicial district in 1856; served in the Union Army during the Civil War with the rank of first lieutenant in 1861; promoted to captain in 1862; at the close of the war moved to Lexington, Mo., and resumed the practice of law; editor and proprietor of the Lexington Register; unsuccessful Republican candidate for election to Congress in 1872 and 1876; delegate to the Republican National Convention at Cincinnati in 1876; returned to Valparaiso, Ind., in 1877 and resumed the practice of law; organized the Northern Indiana Law School in 1879; elected as a Republican to the Forty-seventh Congress (March 4, 1881–March 3, 1883); unsuccessful candidate for reelection in 1882 to the Forty-eighth Congress; member of the State senate 1886–1890; appointed postmaster of Valparaiso March 24, 1890, and served until March 20, 1894; dean of the Northern Indiana Law School 1890–1908; died in Valparaiso, Porter County, Ind., September 23, 1908; interment in Maplewood Cemetery.

DEMPSEY, John Joseph, a Representative from New Mexico; born in White Haven, Luzerne County, Pa., June 22, 1879; attended the grade schools; served as water boy for a railroad contracting crew at thirteen years of age; engaged as a telegrapher; held various positions with the Brooklyn Union Elevator Co.; vice president of the Brooklyn Rapid Transit Co. until 1919; entered the oil business in Oklahoma in 1919 and was vice president of the Continental Oil & Asphalt Co.; moved to Santa Fe, N. Mex., in 1920 and was an independent oil operator; in 1928 became president of the United States Asphalt Co.; in 1932 was appointed a member and later president of the Board of Regents of the University of New Mexico; State director for the National Recovery Administration in 1933, then became

State director of the Federal Housing Administration and the National Emergency Council; elected as a Democrat to the Seventy-fourth, Seventy-fifth, and Seventy-sixth Congresses (January 3, 1935–January 3, 1941); was not a candidate for renomination in 1940, but was an unsuccessful candidate for nomination for United States Senator; appointed a member of the United States Maritime Commission and served from January 3, 1941, until his resignation effective July 7, 1941; Under Secretary of the Interior from July 7, 1941, until his resignation on June 24, 1942; Governor of New Mexico from January 1, 1943, to January 1, 1947; unsuccessful candidate for the Democratic nomination for United States Senator in 1946; elected to the Eighty-second and the three succeeding Congresses and served from January 3, 1951, until his death in Washington, D. C., March 11, 1958; interment in Rosario Cemetery, Santa Fe, N. Mex.

DEMPSEY, Stephen Wallace, a Representative from New York; born in Hartland, Niagara County, N. Y., May 8, 1862; attended the district school of his native town, and was graduated from the De Veaux School, Niagara Falls, N. Y., in 1880; studied law; was admitted to the bar in 1886 and commenced practice in Lockport, Niagara County, N. Y.; assistant United States attorney 1889–1907; special assistant to the Attorney General of the United States 1907–1912, and was in charge of the prosecution of the Standard Oil Co. and certain railroads; elected as a Republican to the Sixty-fourth and to the seven succeeding Congresses (March 4, 1915–March 3, 1931); unsuccessful candidate for renomination in 1930; reengaged in the practice of law in Washington, D. C., until his death on March 1, 1949; interment in Rock Creek Cemetery.

DE MUTH, Peter Joseph, a Representative from Pennsylvania; born in Pittsburgh, Pa., January 1, 1892; attended the public and high schools; was graduated from Carnegie Institute of Technology, Pittsburgh, Pa., in 1914; was a civil engineer from 1914 until his enlistment in the United States Navy as a chief machinist mate during the First World War on July 15, 1918; commissioned engineering ensign and served until honorably discharged May 10, 1919; returned to Pittsburgh, Pa., and was employed as a sales manager 1919–1922; engaged in the real-estate business and as a building contractor in 1922; elected as a Democrat to the Seventy-fifth Congress (January 3, 1937–January 3, 1939); unsuccessful candidate for reelection in 1938 to the Seventy-sixth Congress; senior engineer in Region II of the Federal Public Housing Authority 1940–1944; reengaged in the real-estate and building business in Pittsburgh, Pa., until June 1949; moved to Los Angeles, Calif., and continued the real-estate and building business; is a resident of Los Angeles, Calif.

DENBY, Edwin (grandson of Graham Newell Fitch), a Representative from Michigan; born in Evansville, Vanderburg County, Ind., February 18, 1870; attended the public schools; went to China in 1885 with his father, who was United States Minister; employed in the Chinese imperial maritime customs service 1887–1894; returned to the United States in 1894; was graduated from the law department of the University of Michigan at Ann Arbor in 1896; moved to Detroit, Mich.; was admitted to the bar and commenced practice in 1896; during the war with Spain served as a gunner's mate, third class, United States Navy, on the *Yosemite*; member of the State house of representatives in 1903; elected as a Republican to the Fifty-ninth, Sixtieth, and Sixty-first Congresses (March 4, 1905–March 3, 1911); unsuccessful candidate for reelection in 1910 to the Sixty-second Congress; resumed the practice of law in Detroit; also engaged in banking and various other business enterprises; president of the Detroit Charter Commission in 1913 and

1914; president of the Detroit Board of Commerce in 1916 and 1917; during the First World War enlisted as a private in the United States Marine Corps in 1917; retired as major in the United States Marine Corps Reserve in 1919; appointed chief probation officer in the recorder's court of the city of Detroit and in the circuit court of Wayne County in 1920; appointed Secretary of the Navy by President Harding and served from March 4, 1921, until March 10, 1924, when he resigned; again resumed the practice of law and various business enterprises; died in Detroit, Mich., February 8, 1929; interment in Elmwood Cemetery.

DENEEN, Charles Samuel, a Senator from Illinois; born in Edwardsville, Madison County, Ill., May 4, 1863; raised in Lebanon, St. Clair County, Ill.; attended the public schools, and was graduated from McKendree College, Lebanon, Ill., in 1882; later studied law at the same college and at Union College of Law (later Northwestern University), Chicago, Ill.; was admitted to the bar in 1886 and commenced practice in Chicago; member of the State house of representatives in 1892; attorney for the Chicago Sanitary District in 1895 and 1896; State's attorney for Cook County, Ill., 1896–1904; Governor of Illinois from 1905 to 1913; resumed the practice of his profession in Chicago; appointed as a Republican to the United States Senate on February 26, 1925, to fill the vacancy caused by the death of Medill McCormick in the term ending March 3, 1925; had been previously elected in 1924 for the term commencing March 4, 1925, and served from February 26, 1925, to March 3, 1931; unsuccessful candidate for renomination in 1930; resumed the practice of law; died in Chicago, Ill., February 5, 1940; interment in Oak Woods Cemetery.

DENISON, Charles (nephew of George Denison), a Representative from Pennsylvania; born in Wyoming Valley, Pa., January 23, 1818; received a liberal education, and was graduated from Dickinson College, Carlisle, Pa., in 1838; studied law; was admitted to the bar in 1840 and commenced practice in Wilkes-Barre; elected as a Democrat to the Thirty-eighth, Thirty-ninth, and Fortieth Congresses and served from March 4, 1863, until his death in Wilkes-Barre, Pa., June 27, 1867; interment in Forty Fort Cemetery, Kingston, Pa.

DENISON, Dudley Chase (nephew of Dudley Chase and cousin of Salmon Portland Chase), a Representative from Vermont; born in Royalton, Vt., September 13, 1819; attended Royalton Academy, and was graduated from the University of Vermont at Burlington in 1840; studied law; was admitted to the bar in 1845 and commenced practice in Royalton; member of the State senate in 1853 and 1854; State's attorney 1858–1860; served in the State house of representatives 1861–1863; United States district attorney for the district of Vermont 1865–1869; elected as a Republican to the Forty-fourth and Forty-fifth Congresses (March 4, 1875–March 3, 1879); was not a candidate for renomination in 1878; resumed the practice of law; died in Royalton, Windsor County, Vt., February 10, 1905; interment in North Royalton Cemetery.

DENISON, Edward Everett, a Representative from Illinois; born in Marion, Williamson County, Ill., August 28, 1873; attended the public schools; was graduated from Baylor University, Waco, Tex., in 1895, from Yale University, New Haven, Conn., in 1896, and from Columbian (now George Washington) University Law School, Washington, D. C., in 1899; was admitted to the bar in 1899 and commenced practice in Marion, Ill., in 1900; engaged in the banking business for one year; elected as a Republican to the Sixty-fourth and to the seven succeeding Congresses (March 4, 1915–March 3, 1931); unsuccessful candidate for reelection in 1930 to the Seventy-second Congress and for election in 1932 to the Seventy-third Congress; resumed the general practice of law in Marion, Ill.; unsuccessful candidate for circuit judge of the first judicial circuit of Illinois in 1939; died in Carbondale, Ill., June 17, 1953; interment in Maplewood Cemetery, Marion, Ill.

DENISON, George (uncle of Charles Denison), a Representative from Pennsylvania; born in Kingston, Luzerne County, Pa., February 22, 1790; engaged in mercantile pursuits; attended the Wilkes-Barre Academy; clerk of the Wilkes-Barre Borough Council 1811–1814, and member of the council for many years, serving as president in 1823 and 1824; recorder and registrar of Luzerne County 1812–1815; studied law; was admitted to the bar in 1813 and commenced practice in Luzerne County; member of the State house of representatives in 1815 and 1816; elected as a Democrat to the Sixteenth and Seventeenth Congresses (March 4, 1819–March 3, 1823); was not a candidate for renomination; resumed the practice of law; deputy attorney general for Luzerne County in 1824; again elected to the State house of representatives in 1827, and served until his death; burgess of Wilkes-Barre Borough in 1829 and 1830; died in Wilkes-Barre, Pa., August 20, 1831; interment in Hollenback Cemetery.

DE NIVERNAIS, Edward James, a Representative from California. (*See* LIVERNASH, Edward James.)

DENNING, William, a Representative from New York; born probably in St. John's, Newfoundland, in April 1740; moved to New York City in early youth and engaged in mercantile pursuits; member of the Committee of One Hundred in 1775; deputy to the New York Provincial Congress 1775–1777; member of the convention of State representatives in 1776 and 1777; served in the State assembly 1784–1787 and in the State senate 1798–1808; member of the council of appointment in 1799; elected to the Eleventh Congress and served from March 4, 1809, until his resignation in 1810, never having qualified; devoted himself to private affairs until his death in New York City October 30, 1819; interment in St. Paul's Churchyard.

DENNIS, George Robertson, a Senator from Maryland; born in Whitehaven, Somerset County, Md., April 8, 1822; was graduated from the Rensselaer Polytechnic Institute, Troy, N. Y., and then entered the University of Virginia at Charlottesville; studied medicine at the University of Pennsylvania at Philadelphia; was graduated in 1843 and practiced in Kingston, Md., for many years; later devoted himself to agricultural pursuits; member of the State senate in 1854; delegate to the Whig National Convention at Philadelphia in 1856 and to the Democratic National Convention at New York City in 1868; served in the State house of delegates in 1867; again a member of the State senate in 1871; elected as a Democrat to the United States Senate and served from March 4, 1873, until March 3, 1879; died in Kingston, Somerset County, Md., on August 13, 1882; interment in St. Andrew's Churchyard, Princess Anne, Somerset County, Md.

DENNIS, John (father of John Dennis and uncle of Littleton Purnell Dennis), a Representative from Maryland; born at "Beverly," Worcester County, Md., December 17, 1771; completed preparatory studies in Washington Academy; attended Yale College; studied law; was admitted to the bar in 1793 and commenced practice in Somerset County; served two terms in the State house of delegates; elected as a Federalist to the Fifth and to the three succeeding Congresses (March 4, 1797–March 3, 1805); one of the managers appointed by the House of Representatives in 1798 to conduct the impeachment proceedings

against William Blount, a Senator from Tennessee; died in Philadelphia, Pa., August 17, 1806; interment in Old Christ Church Graveyard.

DENNIS, John (son of the preceding), a Representative from Maryland; born at "Beckford," near Princess Anne, Somerset County, Md., in 1807; completed preparatory studies; studied law; was admitted to the bar and practiced; also engaged in agricultural pursuits; served in the State house of delegates; elected as a Whig to the Twenty-fifth and Twenty-sixth Congresses (March 4, 1837–March 3, 1841); delegate to the State constitutional convention in 1850; died at "Beckford," near Princess Anne, Somerset County, Md., November 1, 1859.

DENNIS, Littleton Purnell (nephew of John Dennis), a Representative from Maryland; born at "Beverly," Worcester County, Md., July 21, 1786; attended Washington Academy, Somerset County, Md.; was graduated from Yale College in 1803; studied law; was admitted to the bar and practiced; member of the State house of delegates in 1815, 1816, and 1819–1827; presidential elector in 1800, 1812, 1816, 1824, and 1828; member of the executive council of Maryland in 1829; an elector of the Maryland State senate in 1831; elected as a Whig to the Twenty-third Congress and served from March 4, 1833, until his death in Washington, D. C., April 14, 1834; interment in the Congressional Cemetery.

DENNISON, David Short, a Representative from Ohio; born in Poland, Mahoning County, Ohio, July 29, 1918; educated in Warren, Ohio, public schools; graduated from Western Reserve Academy, Hudson, Ohio, in 1936, Williams College, Williamston, Mass., in 1940, majoring in government and political science, and Western Reserve University Law School in 1945; admitted to the bar in 1946 and commenced the practice of law in Warren, Ohio; during World War II served as a volunteer ambulance driver with American Field Service and assigned to British Eighth Army in Africa in 1942 and 1943; received the African Star Medal; served as special counsel to the city of Warren in 1950 and 1951; special assistant in Trumbull County to State attorney general 1953–1956; elected as a Republican to the Eighty-fifth Congress (January 3, 1957–January 3, 1959); unsuccessful candidate for reelection in 1958 to the Eighty-sixth Congress; admitted to District of Columbia bar in 1959; served as consultant to Civil Rights Commission, Washington, D. C., in 1959; resumed the practice of law; is a resident of Warren, Ohio.

DENNY, Arthur Armstrong, a Delegate from the Territory of Washington; born in Salem, Washington County, Ind., June 20, 1822; the following year his parents settled near Greencastle, Putnam County, Ind.; attended the public schools; moved to Illinois with his parents, who settled in Knox County in 1834; surveyor of Knox County from 1843 until his resignation in 1851; moved to Oregon Territory in 1851 and settled at Alki Point on Elliott Bay; engaged in cutting timber for market until 1854, when he engaged in mercantile pursuits; served as county commissioner of Thurston County, Oreg., and also of King County, Wash., when the latter was formed; first postmaster of Seattle 1853–1855; upon the organization of Washington Territory in 1853 was elected a member of the Territorial house of representatives and served until 1861; elected speaker in 1857; during the Indian war of 1855 served in the Volunteer Army for six months; register of the land office in Olympia 1861–1865; member of the Territorial council in 1862 and 1863; elected as a Republican a Delegate to the Thirty-ninth Congress (March 4, 1865–March 3, 1867); was not a candidate for renomination in 1866; entered the banking business in 1872 and continued in active business until a few years before his death; also engaged as an author; died in Seattle, Wash., on January 9, 1899; interment in Lakeview Cemetery.

DENNY, Harmar (great-grandfather of Harmar Denny Denny, Jr.), a Representative from Pennsylvania; born in Pittsburgh, Pa., May 13, 1794; was graduated from Dickinson College, Carlisle, Pa., in 1813; studied law; was admitted to the bar in 1816 and commenced practice in Pittsburgh, Pa.; member of the State house of representatives 1824–1829; elected as an Anti-Mason to the Twenty-first Congress to fill the vacancy caused by the resignation of William Wilkins; reelected to the Twenty-second and Twenty-third Congresses and as a Whig to the Twenty-fourth Congress and served from December 15, 1829, to March 3, 1837; was not a candidate for renomination in 1836; resumed the practice of law in Pittsburgh, Pa.; delegate to the State constitutional convention in 1837; presidential elector on the Whig ticket of Harrison and Tyler in 1840; commissioner under act of incorporation of the Pennsylvania Railroad Co. April 13, 1846; incorporator of Ohio & Pennsylvania Railroad Co., act of April 11, 1848; declined the nomination to be a candidate for Congress in 1850; president of the Pittsburgh & Steubenville Railroad Co. in 1851 and 1852; trustee of the Western University of Pennsylvania and director of the Western Theological Seminary; died in Pittsburgh, Pa., January 29, 1852; interment in Allegheny Cemetery.

DENNY, Harmar Denny, Jr. (great-grandson of Harmar Denny), a Representative from Pennsylvania; born in city of Allegheny, Pa., July 2, 1886; attended Allegheny Preparatory School and St. Paul's School, Concord, N. H., in 1904; was graduated from Yale University, New Haven, Conn., in 1908, and from the law school of the University of Pittsburgh in 1911; was admitted to the bar in 1911 and commenced the practice of law in Pittsburgh, Pa.; during the First World War served in the in the United States Army Air Corps as a first lieutenant and bombing pilot; director of public safety, Pittsburgh, Pa., in 1933 and 1934; unsuccessful Republican candidate for mayor of Pittsburgh, Pa., in 1941; during World War II served as a lieutenant colonel in the United States Army Air Corps as assistant air inspector, Eastern Flying Training Command, Maxwell Field, Ala., from February 15, 1942, to December 15, 1945; commissioned lieutenant colonel, Air Force, retired; elected as a Republican to the Eighty-second Congress (January 3, 1951–January 3, 1953); was an unsuccessful candidate for reelection in 1952 to the Eighty-third Congress; served as a member of Civil Aeronautics Board from April 7, 1953, to November 15, 1959; retired and resides in Pittsburgh, Pa.

DENNY, James William, a Representative from Maryland; born in Frederick County, Va., November 20, 1838; attended the academy of the Rev. William Johnson, Berryville, Clarke County, Va.; was graduated from the University of Virginia at Charlottesville; principal of Osage Seminary, Osceola, St. Clair County, Mo.; during the Civil War he returned to his native State and enlisted in Company A, Thirty-ninth Virginia Battalion of Cavalry, Confederate Army, in which he served until 1863, when he was detailed for service at Gen. R. E. Lee's headquarters, where he continued until the surrender at Appomattox Court House; returned to his home in Clarke County, Va., and began the study of law in Winchester, Va.; was admitted to the bar in Baltimore, Md., in 1868 and commenced practice in that city; elected to the first branch of the city council in 1881; reelected in 1882 and became its president; member of the State house of delegates 1888–1890; colonel on the staff of Gov. E. E. Jackson; member of the Baltimore School Board for eight years; elected as a Democrat to the Fifty-sixth Congress (March 4, 1899–March

3, 1901); unsuccessful candidate for reelection in 1900 to the Fifty-seventh Congress; elected to the Fifty-eighth Congress (March 4, 1903–March 3, 1905); engaged in the practice of law until his death in Baltimore, Md., April 12, 1923; interment in Loudon Park Cemetery.

DENNY, Walter McKennon, a Representative from Mississippi; born in Moss Point, Jackson County, Miss., October 28, 1853; attended the common schools and Roanoke College, Salem, Va.; was graduated from the law department of the University of Mississippi at Oxford in 1874; was admitted to the bar and commenced practice in Pascagoula, Jackson County, Miss.; clerk of the circuit and chancery courts of Jackson County, Miss., from November 1883 until January 1, 1895, when he resigned, having been elected to Congress; delegate to the State constitutional convention in 1890; elected as a Democrat to the Fifty-fourth Congress (March 4, 1895–March 3, 1897); unsuccessful candidate for renomination in 1896; joined the Republican Party in 1896; resumed the practice of law at Pascagoula, Miss., and for fifteen years was legal adviser to the Jackson County Board of Supervisors; died in Pascagoula November 5, 1926; interment in Machpelah Cemetery.

DENOYELLES, Peter, a Representative from New York; born in Haverstraw, Rockland County, N. Y., in 1766; completed preparatory studies; engaged in the manufacture of brick; member of the State assembly in 1802 and 1803; held several local offices; elected to the Thirteenth Congress (March 4, 1813–March 3, 1815); resumed his former manufacturing pursuits; died in Haverstraw, Rockland County, N. Y., May 6, 1829; interment in Mount Repose Cemetery.

DENSON, William Henry, a Representative from Alabama; born in Uchee, Russell County, Ala., March 4, 1846; attended the common schools and the University of Alabama at Tuscaloosa; left the University of Alabama in 1863 to join the Confederate Army; worked on his father's farm and studied law; was admitted to the bar in 1868 and commenced practice in Union Springs, Ala.; moved to Lafayette, Chambers County, Ala., in October 1870; mayor of Lafayette in 1874; member of the State house of representatives in 1876; moved to Gadsden, Etowah County, in 1877 and continued the practice of his profession; presidential elector on the Democratic ticket of Cleveland and Hendricks in 1884; appointed by President Cleveland United States district attorney for the northern and middle districts of Alabama and served from June 30, 1885, to June 3, 1889; chairman of the Democratic State convention in 1890; elected as a Democrat to the Fifty-third Congress (March 4, 1893–March 3, 1895); was not a candidate for renomination in 1894; moved to Birmingham, Ala., where he resumed the practice of law; died in Birmingham, Ala., September 26, 1906; interment in Elmwood Cemetery.

DENT, George, a Representative from Maryland; born on his father's estate, "Windsor Castle," on the Mattawoman, Charles County, Md., in 1756; completed preparatory studies; during the Revolutionary War served as first lieutenant of militia of Charles and St. Marys Counties under Capt. Thomas H. Marshall, and as first lieutenant in the Third Battalion of the Flying Camp Regular Troops of Maryland in 1776; captain in the Twenty-sixth Battalion, Maryland Militia, in 1778; member of the Maryland House of Assembly 1782–1790, serving as speaker pro tempore in 1788 and as speaker in 1789; unanimously reelected speaker in 1790; justice of the Charles County Court in 1791 and 1792; member of the State senate in 1791 and 1792, serving as president during the latter year until his resignation on December 21, 1792; elected as a Democrat to the Third and to the three succeeding Congresses (March 4, 1793–March , 13801); Speaker pro tempore of the House at various times from 1797 to 1799; appointed by President Jefferson as United States marshal of the District Court for the Potomac District at Washington, D. C., April 4, 1801; moved to Georgia in 1802 and settled about twelve miles from Augusta, where he died December 2, 1813; interment on his plantation.

DENT, John Herman, a Representative from Pennsylvania; born in Johnetta, Armstrong County, Pa., March 10, 1908; educated in the public schools of Armstrong and Westmoreland Counties, the Great Lakes Naval Aviation Academy, and through correspondence school courses; member of the local council of United Rubber Workers 1923–1937, serving as president of Local 18759 and on the executive council; also member of the international council; served in the United States Marine Air Corps 1924–1928; member of the State house of representatives 1935–1937; elected to the State senate in 1936; reelected in 1940, 1944, 1948, 1952, and 1956, and served until elected to Congress; Democratic floor leader in State senate 1939–1958; operated the Kelden Coal & Coke Co. of Hunkers, Pa., and the Building & Transportation Co. of Trafford and Jeannette, Pa.; elected as a Democrat to the Eighty-fifth Congress to fill the vacancy caused by the death of Augustine B. Kelly; reelected to the Eighty-sixth Congress and served from January 21, 1958, to January 3, 1961. *Reelected to the Eighty-seventh Congress.*

DENT, Stanley Hubert, Jr., a Representative from Alabama; born in Eufaula, Barbour County, Ala., August 16, 1869; attended the common schools, and was graduated from Southern University (later known as Birmingham Southern College), Greensboro, Ala., in 1886; was graduated from the University of Virginia Law School at Charlottesville in 1889; was admitted to the bar the same year and practiced in Eufaula, Ala., until 1899; moved to Montgomery, Ala., in 1899 and continued the practice of his profession; delegate to the State constitutional convention in 1901; prosecuting attorney for Montgomery County 1902–1909; delegate to the Democratic National Convention at Denver in 1908; elected as a Democrat to the Sixty-first and to the five succeeding Congresses (March 4, 1909–March 3, 1921); unsuccessful candidate for renomination in 1920; was chairman of the Committee on Military Affairs of the House of Representatives during the entire period of the First World War; resumed the practice of law in Montgomery, Ala.; served as president of the State constitutional convention for repeal of the Eighteenth Amendment in 1933; died in Montgomery, Ala., on October 6, 1938; interment in Eufaula Cemetery, Eufaula, Ala.

DENT, William Barton Wade, a Representative from Georgia; born in Bryantown, Charles County, Md., September 8, 1806; attended a private school in Charlotte Hall, St. Marys County, Md., and was graduated from Charlotte Hall Military Academy in 1823; moved to Mallorysville, Wilkes County, Ga., in 1824 and taught school; engaged in mercantile pursuits at Bullsboro, Ga., in 1827; took an active part in founding the city of Newnan, Ga., in 1828; subsequently engaged in agricultural pursuits and milling in Coweta, Carroll, and Heard Counties; became interested in large land holdings in Alabama, Georgia, Arkansas, Tennessee, and Texas; served as a colonel in the State militia during the Creek War; member of the State house of representatives in 1843; returned to Newnan in 1849 and served as judge of the inferior court of Coweta County; elected as a Democrat to the Thirty-third Congress (March 4, 1853–March 3, 1855); was not a candidate for renomination in 1854; died in Newnan, Coweta County, Ga., September 7, 1855; interment in Oak Hill Cemetery.

DENTON, George Kirkpatrick, a Representative from Indiana; born near Sebree, Webster County, Ky., November 17, 1864; attended the public schools and Van Horn Institute; was graduated from the Ohio Wesleyan University at Delaware in 1891 and from the law department of Boston (Mass.) University in 1893; was admitted to the bar in 1893 and commenced practice in Evansville, Ind.; served as counsel for the Intermediate Life Insurance Co.; elected as a Democrat to the Sixty-fifth Congress (March 4, 1917–March 3, 1919); unsuccessful candidate for reelection in 1918 to the Sixty-sixth Congress; resumed the practice of law in Evansville, Ind.; unsuccessful candidate in 1924 for judge of the Indiana Supreme Court; candidate for the Democratic nomination for United States Senator in 1926, but died before the primary election; died in Evansville, Ind., January 4, 1926; interment in Oak Hill Cemetery.

DENTON, Winfield Kirkpatrick, a Representative from Indiana; born in Evansville, Vanderburgh County, Ind., October 28, 1896; attended the public schools and De Pauw University, Greencastle, Ind., until the beginning of the First World War when he enlisted as a private; later commissioned a second lieutenant as an aviator in the United States Army Air Corps and served until discharged in 1919 with overseas service; reentered De Pauw University and graduated in 1919; graduated from Harvard Law School, Cambridge, Mass., in 1922; was admitted to the bar in 1920 and commenced the practice of law in Evansville, Ind., in 1922; prosecuting attorney of Vanderburgh County, Ind., 1932–1936; member of the Indiana State Legislature 1937–1942, serving as caucus chairman in 1939 and as minority leader in 1941; member of the State budget committee 1940–1942; during World War II entered the service as a major in 1942; served in the Judge Advocate General's Department, Wright Field, Ohio, and was discharged as a lieutenant colonel in 1945; elected as a Democrat to the Eighty-first and Eighty-second Congresses (January 3, 1949–January 3, 1953); unsuccessful candidate for reelection in 1952 to the Eighty-third Congress; elected to the Eighty-fourth, Eighty-fifth, and Eighty-sixth Congresses (January 3, 1955–January 3, 1961). *Reelected to the Eighty-seventh Congress.*

DENVER, James William (father of Matthew Rombach Denver), a Representative from California; born in Winchester, Va., October 23, 1817; attended the public schools; moved to Ohio in 1830 with his parents, who settled near Wilmington; taught school in Missouri in 1841; was graduated from the Cincinnati Law School in 1844; was admitted to the bar and commenced practice in Xenia, Ohio; also published the Thomas Jefferson; moved to Platte City, Mo., in 1845 and continued the practice of law; served as captain in the Twelfth Regiment, United States Infantry, during the war with Mexico; moved to California in 1850; elected to the State senate in 1851; appointed secretary of state in 1852; elected as an Anti-Broderick Democrat to the Thirty-fourth Congress (March 4, 1855–March 3, 1857); was not a candidate for renomination in 1856; appointed Commissioner of Indian Affairs April 17, 1857; resigned to become Governor of the Territory of Kansas June 17, 1857, and during his administration gold was found on Cherry Creek, and the present capital of Colorado (then Kansas Territory) was founded and named "Denver" for the chief executive; reappointed Commissioner of Indian Affairs November 8, 1858, and served until his resignation on March 31, 1859; during the Civil War was commissioned brigadier general in the Union Army August 14, 1861; resigned from the Army March 5, 1863; resumed the practice of his profession in Washington, D. C., and Wilmington, Ohio; delegate to the Democratic National Conventions in 1876, 1880, and 1884; died in Washington, D.C., August 9, 1892; interment in Sugar Grove Cemetery, Wilmington, Ohio.

DENVER, Matthew Rombach (son of James William Denver), a Representative from Ohio; born in Wilmington, Clinton County, Ohio, December 21, 1870; attended the public schools; was graduated from Georgetown University, Washington, D. C., in 1892; engaged in agricultural pursuits, banking, and the manufacture of furnaces, air compressors, and wood-boring tools; delegate to the Democratic National Conventions in 1896, 1908, 1912, 1920, 1924, 1928, 1932, and 1936; member of the Democratic State committee 1896–1908; elected as a Democrat to the Sixtieth, Sixty-first, and Sixty-second Congresses (March 4, 1907–March 3, 1913); declined to be a candidate for reelection in 1912 to the Sixty-third Congress; returned to Wilmington, Ohio, and resumed banking pursuits; president of the Ohio Bankers' Association in 1918 and 1919; again elected a member of the Democratic State committee for the term 1926–1928; president of the Clinton County National Bank & Trust Co., from 1902 until his death in Wilmington, Ohio, May 13, 1954; interment in Sugar Grove Cemetery.

DEPEW, Chauncey Mitchell, a Senator from New York; born in Peekskill, N. Y., April 23, 1834; attended the private school of a Mrs. Westbrook; was graduated from the Peekskill Military Academy in 1852 and from Yale College in 1856; studied law; was admitted to the bar in 1858 and commenced practice at Peekskill, N. Y., in 1859; member of the State assembly in 1861 and 1862; secretary of state of New York in 1863; refused a renomination; appointed United States Minister to Japan by President Johnson November 11, 1865, and was confirmed by the Senate, but declined; appointed county clerk of Westchester County by Governor Fenton in 1867, and resigned; elected immigration commissioner in 1870, but declined; unsuccessful candidate for election as Lieutenant Governor on the Liberal Republican or Greeley ticket in 1872; colonel and judge advocate of the fifth division of the New York National Guard 1873–1881; appointed a member of the commission to build the State capitol in 1874; appointed boundary commissioner in 1875 for fixing the State line with adjoining States; regent of New York University 1877–1904; unsuccessful Republican candidate for election to the United States Senate in 1881; orator on the occasion of the unveiling of the Statue of Liberty in New York Harbor October 28, 1886; appointed president of the New York Central & Hudson River Railroad Co. in 1885, but resigned in 1899 to become chairman of the board of directors of that railroad system; candidate for the presidential nomination at the Republican National Convention at Chicago in 1888 and received ninety-nine votes; delegate at large to the Republican National Conventions in 1888, 1892, 1896, 1900, and 1904; delegate to all succeeding Republican National Conventions to 1924, inclusive; elected as a Republican to the United States Senate in 1899; reelected in 1905 and served from March 4, 1899, to March 3, 1911; unsuccessful candidate for reelection in 1910; resumed his legal and corporate business pursuits in New York City, where he died on April 5, 1928; interment in Hillside Cemetery, Peekskill, N. Y.

DE PRIEST, Oscar, a Representative from Illinois; born in Florence, Lauderdale County, Ala., March 9, 1871; of the Negro race; moved to Kansas in 1878 with his parents, who settled in Salina; attended the public schools and Salina (Kans.) Normal School; engaged as a painter and decorator; moved to Chicago, Ill., in 1889 and became a real-estate broker; member of the board of commissioners of Cook County, Ill., 1904–1908; member of the city council 1915–1917; elected as a Republican to the Seventy-first, Seventy-second, and Seventy-third Congresses (March 4, 1929–January 3, 1935); unsuccessful candidate for reelection in 1934 to the Seventy-fourth Congress and for election in 1936 to the Seventy-fifth Congress; resumed the

real-estate business; vice chairman of the Cook County Republican central committee 1932–1934; delegate to the Republican National Convention in 1936; again a member of the city council 1943–1947; died in Chicago, Ill., May 12, 1951; interment in Graceland Cemetery.

DE ROUEN, René Louis, a Representative from Louisiana; born on a farm near Ville Platte, St. Landry Parish (now Evangeline Parish), January 7, 1874; attended private and public schools, and St. Charles College, Grand Coteau, La.; was graduated from Holy Cross College, New Orleans, La., in 1892; engaged in mercantile pursuits, banking, and farming; delegate to the State constitutional convention in 1921; elected as a Democrat to the Seventieth Congress to fill the vacancy caused by the death of Ladislas Lazaro; reelected to the Seventy-first and to the five succeeding Congresses and served from August 23, 1927, to January 3, 1941; was not a candidate for renomination in 1940; served in the State banking department in Baton Rouge, La., after his retirement from Congress until his death; died in Baton Rouge, La., March 27, 1942; interment in Catholic Cemetery, Ville Platte, La.

DEROUNIAN, Steven Boghos, a Representative from New York; born in Sofia, Bulgaria, April 6, 1918; brought to the United States at the age of three by his parents who settled in Mineola, N. Y.; attended the public schools; graduated from New York University in 1938 and from the Fordham Law School in 1942; was admitted to the New York bar in 1942 and began practice in Mineola, N. Y., the same year; entered the United States Army as a private in July 1942; graduated from officers school as an Infantry officer and was assigned to the One Hundred and Third Infantry; served overseas from October 1944 to March 1946 and separated from the service as a captain in May 1946; awarded the Purple Heart, Bronze Star, Combat Infantryman's Badge, and foreign service ribbons of the European theater; councilman of town board of North Hempstead, N. Y., from January 1, 1948, to December 30, 1952; alternate delegate to Republican National Conventions in 1956 and 1960; elected as a Republican to the Eighty-third and to the three succeeding Congresses (January 3, 1953–January 3, 1961). *Reelected to the Eighty-seventh Congress.*

DERSHEM, Franklin Lewis, a Representative from Pennsylvania; born near New Columbia, Union County, Pa., March 5, 1865; attended the common schools; was graduated from Palm's National Business College at Philadelphia in 1887; appointed postmaster at Kelly Point, Union County, Pa., on March 9, 1888, and served until January 13, 1891; engaged in agricultural pursuits, and was also interested in the hardware business 1891–1913; member of the board of trustes of Albright College, Myerstown, Pa.; member of the State house of representatives in 1907, 1908, and again in 1911 and 1912; elected as a Democrat to the Sixty-third Congress (March 4, 1913–March 3, 1915); unsuccessful candidate for reelection in 1914 to the Sixty-fourth Congress; appointed as an auditor in the Philadelphia division of the United States Bureau of Internal Revenue October 1, 1915, in which capacity he served until March 31, 1935; was engaged as an auditor and income-tax specialist in Lewisburg, Pa., where he died February 14, 1950; interment in Lewisburg Cemetery.

DERWINSKI, Edward Joseph, a Representative from Illinois; born in Chicago, Ill., September 15, 1926; attended Assumption B. V. M. Grammar School; graduated from Mount Carmel High School in 1944; during World War II served in the United States Army as an infantryman with service in the Pacific Theater and with the Japanese Occupation Forces in 1945 and 1946;

graduated from Loyola University in Chicago in 1951, majoring in history and political science; insurance broker; president of the West Pullman Savings & Loan Association; served one term in the Illinois House of Representatives in 1957 and 1958; elected as a Republican to the Eighty-sixth Congress (January 3, 1959–January 3, 1961). *Reelected to the Eighty-seventh Congress.*

DE SAUSSURE, William Ford, a Senator from South Carolina; born in Charleston, S. C., February 22, 1792; was graduated from Harvard University in 1810; studied law; was admitted to the bar and practiced in Charleston and Columbia, S. C.; member of the State house of representatives in 1846; judge of the chancery court in 1847; delegate to the Democratic National Conventions at Baltimore in 1852 and 1860; appointed and subsequently elected as a Democrat to the United States Senate to fill the vacancy caused by the resignation of R. Barnwell Rhett and served from May 10, 1852, to March 3, 1853; resumed the practice of law in Columbia; trustee of South Carolina College (now the University of South Carolina) at Columbia for many years; died in Columbia, Richland County, S. C., March 13, 1870; interment in Presbyterian Churchyard.

DESHA, Joseph (brother of Robert Desha), a Representative from Kentucky; born in Monroe County, Pa., December 9, 1768; pursued preparatory studies; moved to Kentucky with his parents, who settled in Fayette County in 1779, and later, in 1782, they moved to Tennessee and settled near Gallatin, Sumner County; returned to Kentucky in 1792 and settled in Mason County; served in the Indian wars under Gen. Anthony Wayne and Gen. William H. Harrison in 1794; returned to Kentucky and engaged in agricultural pursuits; member of the State house of representatives in 1797 and 1799–1802; served in the State senate 1803–1807; elected as a Democrat to the Tenth and to the five succeeding Congresses (March 4, 1807–March 3, 1819); was not a candidate for renomination in 1818; unsuccessful candidate for Governor of Kentucky in 1820; was an enthusiastic supporter of the War of 1812 and served as major general of Volunteers under Gen. William H. Harrison at the Battle of the Thames; on his return to civil life he was elected Governor of Kentucky and served from 1824 to 1828; retired from public life and lived on his farm in Harrison County until his death near Georgetown, Ky., October 11, 1842; interment in Georgetown Cemetery.

DESHA, Robert (brother of Joseph Desha), a Representative from Tennessee; born near Gallatin, Sumner County, Tenn., January 14, 1791; attended the public schools; engaged in the mercantile business at Gallatin; appointed on March 12, 1812, a captain in the Twenty-fourth Regiment, United States Infantry, in the War of 1812; also served as brevet major; honorably discharged on June 15, 1815; elected to the Twentieth and Twenty-first Congresses (March 4, 1827–March 3, 1831); declined to be a candidate for renomination in 1830 for the Twenty-second Congress; moved to Mobile, Ala., and continued mercantile pursuits until his death there February 6, 1849; interment in Magnolia Cemetery.

DESTRÉHAN, John Noel, a Senator from Louisiana; born in 1780 in that section of Louisiana fronting the Mississippi River in what was afterward called St. Charles Parish; engaged in mercantile pursuits and as a planter; one of a committee of three Creoles who protested to Congress against the provisions of the first Territorial government, which resulted in the formulation of a second government with more liberal provisions; member of the legislative council of the Territory of Orleans and served as its president from March 25 to May 22, 1806, and from Febru-

ary to April 1811; although opposed to the admission of the Territory to statehood, was a delegate to the convention and helped to draft the constitution of the State of Louisiana; served in the State senate 1812–1817; upon the admission of Louisiana as a State into the Union was elected to the United States Senate on September 3, 1812, but resigned on October 1, 1812, without having qualified; resumed his former occupation as a planter; died in 1824; interment near Destrehan, La.

DEUSTER, Peter Victor, a Representative from Wisconsin; born near Aix la Chapelle, Rhenish Prussia, February 13, 1831; pursued an academic course; immigrated to the United States with his parents, who settled on a farm near Milwaukee, Wis., in May 1847; worked in a printing office; moved to Port Washington, Wis., in 1854 and edited a newspaper; also served simultaneously as postmaster, clerk of the circuit court, clerk of the land office, and notary public; returned to Milwaukee in 1856 and edited the Milwaukee See-Bote, a Democratic daily paper, until 1860, when he became proprietor; member of the State assembly in 1863; served in the State senate in 1870 and 1871 elected as a Democrat to the Forty-sixth, Forty-seventh, and Forty-eighth Congresses (March 4, 1879–March 3, 1885); unsuccessful candidate for reelection in 1884 to the Forty-ninth Congress; resumed newspaper interests; appointed chairman of a commission to diminish the Umatilla Indian Reservation in Oregon in 1887; appointed consul at Crefeld, Germany, February 19, 1896, and served until a successor was appointed October 15, 1897; died in Milwaukee, Wis., December 31, 1904; interment in Calvary Cemetery.

DEVEREUX, James Patrick Sinnott, a Representative from Maryland; born in Cabana, Cuba, February 20, 1903; attended the public schools of Maryland, the Army and Navy Preparatory School in Washington, D. C., the Tome School at Port Deposit, Md., LaVilla in Lausanne, Switzerland, and Loyola College, Baltimore, Md.; enlisted in the United States Marine Corps in 1923; commissioned a second lieutenant in 1925 and advanced through grades to brigadier general in 1948; served in Nicaragua and China; service at Pearl Harbor and Pacific Islands, Wake Island, October 1941; prisoner of war from January 1942 to January 1945; retired from the service in 1948; decorated with Presidential Unit Citation with one star (Wake Island), Navy Cross, Second Nicaraguan Campaign Medal, Yangtze Service Medal, Marine Corps Expeditionary Medal (China), Wake Island with Wake Island clasp and silver wreath, American Defense Service Medal with base clasp and one bronze star, Asiatic-Pacific campaign medal with one bronze star, and World War II Victory Medal; engaged in farming near Stevenson, Md., in 1946; elected as a Republican to the Eighty-second and to the three succeeding Congresses (January 3, 1951–January 3, 1959); was not a candidate for renomination in 1958 but was an unsuccessful candidate for Governor; resides in Stevenson, Md.

DE VEYRA, Jaime Carlos, a Resident Commissioner from the Commonwealth of the Philippine Islands; born in Tanawan, Province of Leyte, Philippine Islands, November 4, 1873; attended public and private schools; was graduated from the College of San Juan de Letran in Manila in 1893; studied law, philosophy, and letters in the University of Santo Tomas at Manila 1895–1897; secretary to the Military Governor of Leyte in 1898 and 1899; engaged in newspaper work; member of the municipal council of Cebu; Governor of Leyte in 1906 and 1907; member of the Philippine House of Representatives 1907–1909; member of the Philippine Commission 1913–1916; executive secretary of the Philippine Islands in 1916 and 1917; elected as a Nationalist a Resident Commissioner to the United States in 1917; reelected in 1920 and served from March 4, 1917, to March 3, 1923; declined to be a candidate for renomination as Resident Commissioner in 1922; engaged in journalistic work during 1923; head of the department of Spanish, University of the Philippines at Manila, 1925–1936; director, Institute of National Language, 1936–1942; served as historical researcher in charge of manuscripts and publications, National Library, until his retirement; is a resident of Manila, Philippine Islands.

DEVINE, Samuel Leeper, a Representative from Ohio; born in South Bend, Saint Joseph County, Ind., December 21, 1915; moved to Columbus, Ohio, in 1920; attended the public schools in Columbus, Grandview, and Upper Arlington, Ohio; attended Colgate University in 1933 and 1934, Ohio State University 1934–1937, and graduated from the University of Notre Dame in 1940; was admitted to the bar in 1940 and practiced law in Columbus, Ohio; in 1940 was appointed special agent, Federal Bureau of Investigation, United States Department of Justice, and served until his resignation October 15, 1945; resumed the private practice of law in Columbus, Ohio; member of the Ohio House of Representatives 1951–1955; prosecuting attorney, Franklin County, Ohio, 1955–1958; former chairman Ohio Un-American Activities Commission; elected as a Republican to the Eighty-sixth Congress (January 3, 1959–January 3, 1961). *Reelected to the Eighty-seventh Congress.*

DEVITT, Edward James, a Representative from Minnesota; born in St. Paul, Ramsey County, Minn., May 5, 1911; attended public and parochial schools; was graduated from St. John's University, Collegeville, Minn., in 1932 and from the law department of the University of North Dakota at Grand Forks in 1935; was admitted to the bar in 1935 and commenced practice in East Grand Forks, Minn.; instructor in the law department of the University of North Dakota 1935–1939; municipal judge at East Grand Forks, Minn., 1935–1939; assistant attorney general of Minnesota 1939–1942; member of faculty of St. Paul College of Law in 1945 and 1946; during World War II served as an intelligence officer in the United States Navy from October 1942 to February 1946, with service in Pacific area; awarded the Purple Heart; elected as a Republican to the Eightieth Congress (January 3, 1947–January 3, 1949); unsuccessful candidate for reelection in 1948 to the Eighty-first Congress; probate judge, Ramsey County, Minn., from January 6, 1950, to December 20, 1954; United States district judge for district of Minnesota since December 20, 1954; is a resident of St. Paul, Minn.

DE VRIES, Marion, a Representative from California; born on a ranch near Woodbridge, San Joaquin County, Calif., August 15, 1865; attended the public schools; was graduated from the San Joaquin Valley College, Woodbridge, Calif., in 1886 and from the law department of the University of Michigan at Ann Arbor in 1888; was admitted to the bar in 1887 and commenced practice in Stockton, Calif., in 1889; assistant district attorney of San Joaquin County from January 1893 to February 1897, when he resigned, having been elected to Congress; elected as a Democrat to the Fifty-fifth and Fifty-sixth Congresses and served from March 4, 1897, to August 20, 1900, when he resigned to accept a court position; appointed on June 9, 1900, a member of the Board of General Appraisers (now United States Customs Court) at New York City and served until his resignation effective April 1, 1910; was president of the board 1906–1910; associate judge of the United States Court of Customs Appeals from April 2, 1910, to June 30, 1921; served as presiding judge from July 1, 1921, until October 31, 1922, when he resigned; reengaged in the practice of law in Washington, D. C., and New York City, until 1939, when he retired to his ranch near Woodbridge, Calif., where he died on September 11, 1939; interment in the family plot on De Vries Ranch.

DEWALT, Arthur Granville, a Representative from Pennsylvania; born in Bath, Northampton County, Pa., October 11, 1854; attended the common schools; was graduated from Keystone State Normal School in 1870 and from Lafayette College, Easton, Pa., in 1874; studied law; was admitted to the bar in 1877 and commenced practice at Allentown, Pa., in 1878; district attorney of Lehigh County 1880–1883; member of the State senate 1902–1910; delegate to the Democratic National Convention at St. Louis in 1904 and delegate at large to the convention at Denver in 1908; chairman of the Democratic State committee in 1909 and 1910; adjutant of the Fourth Regiment of the Pennsylvania National Guard for ten years; elected as a Democrat to the Sixty-fourth, Sixty-fifth, and Sixty-sixth Congresses (March 4, 1915–March 3, 1921); declined to be a candidate for renomination in 1920; unsuccessful candidate for election in 1926 to the Seventieth Congress; resumed the practice of law at Allentown, Pa., where he died on October 26, 1931; interment in Fairview Cemetery.

DEWART, Lewis (father of William Lewis Dewart), a Representative from Pennsylvania; born in Sunbury, Pa., November 14, 1780; attended the common schools; was a clerk in his father's store for several years and later became a coal operator and banker; postmaster at Sunbury 1806–1816; member of the State house of representatives 1812–1820; elected to the State senate in 1823 and served three years; one of the organizers and builders of the Danville & Pottsville Railroad, and served as one of the first directors; elected as a Jackson Democrat to the Twenty-second Congress (March 4, 1831–March 3, 1833); again a member of the State house of representatives 1835–1840 and served as speaker in 1840; chief burgess of Sunbury in 1837; member of the school board; unsuccessful candidate for the Democratic nomination for Governor of Pennsylvania in 1840; retired from public life and active business pursuits in 1840; died in Sunbury, Northumberland County, Pa., on April 26, 1852; interment in Sunbury Cemetery.

D'EWART, Wesley Abner, a Representative from Montana; born in Worcester, Mass., October 1, 1889; attended the grade and high schools of Worcester, Mass., and Washington State College at Pullman; moved to Wilsall, Park County, Mont., in 1910 and engaged in the Forest Service; stockman, farmer, and businessman in Park County, Mont.; served in the State house of representatives 1937–1939; member of the State senate 1941–1945; elected as a Republican to the Seventy-ninth Congress to fill the vacancy caused by the death of James F. O'Connor; reelected to the Eightieth and to the three succeeding Congresses and served from June 5, 1945, to January 3, 1955; was not a candidate for renomination in 1954, but was unsuccessful for election to the United States Senate; assistant to the Secretary of Agriculture, Washington, D. C., from January 1955 to September 1955; assistant secretary, Department of the Interior, from October 1955 to July 1956; special representative to Secretary of Agriculture from August 1956 to October 1958; unsuccessful candidate for the Republican nomination for Governor of Montana in 1960; is a resident of Wilsall, Mont.

DEWART, William Lewis (son of Lewis Dewart), a Representative from Pennsylvania; born in Sunbury, Northumberland County, Pa., June 21, 1821; attended the common schools of Sunbury and Harrisburg, Pa.; was graduated from Dickinson Preparatory School, Carlisle, Pa., and from Princeton College in 1839; studied law; was admitted to the Northumberland County bar on January 3, 1843, and commenced practice in Sunbury, Pa.; chief burgess of Sunbury in 1845 and 1846; president of the school board; delegate to the Democratic National Conventions at Baltimore in 1852 and in 1860, at Cincinnati in 1856, and at

Chicago in 1884; unsuccessful candidate for election in 1854 to the Thirty-fourth Congress; elected as a Democrat to the Thirty-fifth Congress (March 4, 1857–March 3, 1859); unsuccessful candidate for reelection in 1858 to the Thirty-sixth Congress; resumed the practice of his profession in Sunbury, Pa.; presidential elector on the Democratic ticket of Douglas and Johnson in 1860; died in Sunbury, Pa., on April 19, 1888; interment in the family vault in Sunbury Cemetery.

DEWEESE, John Thomas, a Representative from North Carolina; born in Van Buren, Crawford County, Ark., June 4, 1835; his early education was received from his mother; studied law; was admitted to the bar in 1856 and commenced practice in Henderson, Ky.; resident of Denver, Colo., for some years; moved to Pike County, Ind., in 1860; during the Civil War entered the Union Army July 6, 1861, as second lieutenant of Company E, Twenty-fourth Regiment, Indiana Volunteer Infantry, and served with that command until February 15, 1862, when he resigned; mustered in as captain of Company F, Fourth Indiana Cavalry, August 8, 1862; promoted to the rank of major February 12, 1863, and lieutenant colonel May 17, 1863; promoted to the rank of colonel, but never served in that capacity; honorably discharged March 11, 1864; moved to North Carolina; upon the reorganization of the Army was appointed second lieutenant, Eighth United States Infantry, July 24, 1866; resigned August 14, 1867, having been elected to Congress; appointed register in bankruptcy for North Carolina in 1868; upon the readmission of North Carolina to representation was elected as a Democrat to the Fortieth and Forty-first Congresses and served from July 6, 1868, to February 28, 1870, when he resigned, pending the investigation of certain appointments to the United States Military and Naval Academies; delegate to the Democratic National Convention at St. Louis in 1876; resumed the practice of law; died in Washington, D. C., July 4, 1906; interment in Arlington National Cemetery, Fort Myer, Va.

DEWEY, Charles Schuveldt, a Representative from Illinois; born in Cadiz, Harrison County, Ohio, November 10, 1882; moved in infancy to Chicago, Ill.; attended the public schools and St. Paul's School, Concord, N. H.; was graduated from Yale University, New Haven, Conn., in 1904; engaged in the real-estate business in Chicago, Ill., 1905–1917; during the First World War served in the United States Navy 1917–1919 and was honorably discharged with the rank of senior lieutenant; vice president of a trust company in Chicago, Ill., 1920–1924; Assistant Secretary of the Treasury in charge of fiscal affairs 1924–1927; national treasurer of American National Red Cross in 1926 and 1927; served as financial adviser to the Polish Government and as director of the Bank of Poland 1927–1930; decorated Commander, Legion of Honor (France), Grand Commander, Polonia Restituta (Poland), Grand Commander, Crown of Rumania, and Grand Commander, Order of St. Sava (Yugoslavia); returned to Chicago in 1931 and resumed banking; unsuccessful candidate for election in 1938 to the Seventy-sixty Congress; elected as a Republican to the Seventy-seventh and Seventy-eighth Congresses (January 3, 1941–January 3, 1945); unsuccessful candidate for reelection in 1944 to the Seventy-ninth Congress; resumed the banking business; in April 1948 was appointed agent general of the Joint Committee on Foreign Economic Cooperation and served until June 1952; member of Washington National Monument Society since 1953; is a resident of Washington, D. C.

DEWEY, Daniel, a Representative from Massachusetts; born in Sheffield, Mass., January 29, 1766; attended Yale College; studied law; was admitted to the bar in 1787 and commenced practice in Williamstown, Mass.; treasurer of Williams College, Williamstown, Mass., 1798–1814; member of the Governor's council 1809–1812; elected as a Whig to the Thirteenth Congress and served from March 4, 1813, until February 24, 1814, when he resigned, having been assigned to a judicial position; appointed by Governor Strong an associate judge of the supreme court of Massachusetts on February 24, 1814, and served until his death in Williamstown, Mass., May 26, 1815; interment in West Lawn Cemetery.

DE WITT, Alexander, a Representative from Massachusetts; born in New Braintree, Mass., April 2, 1798; pursued an academic course; engaged in textile manufacturing in Oxford; member of the State house of representatives 1830–1836; served in the State senate in 1842, 1844, 1850, and 1851; member of the State constitutional convention in 1853; elected as the candidate of the American Party to the Thirty-third and Thirty-fourth Congresses (March 4, 1853–March 3, 1857); unsuccessful candidate for reelection in 1856 to the Thirty-fifth Congress; resumed the manufacture of textiles; died in Oxford, Worcester County, Mass., January 13, 1879; interment in South Cemetery.

DE WITT, Charles (grandfather of Charles Gerrit De Witt), a Delegate from New York; born in Kingston, Ulster County, N. Y., in 1727; pursued classical studies; colonel of militia; member of the colonial assembly 1768–1776; delegate to the provisional convention in 1775; member of the Provisional Congress which approved the Declaration of Independence 1775–1777; served on the constitutional committee in 1776, and on the committee of safety in 1777; Member of the Continental Congress from February to October 1784; editor of the Ulster Sentinel for several years; member of the State assembly in 1781, 1785, and 1786; member of the committee to draft the State constitution; died in Kingston, N. Y., August 27, 1787; interment in Dutch Reformed Cemetery, Hurley, N. Y.

DE WITT, Charles Gerrit (grandson of Charles De Witt), a Representative from New York; born in Greenhill, Ulster County, N. Y., November 7, 1789; studied law and practiced; clerk in the Navy Department; edited the Ulster Sentinel; elected as a Jackson Democrat to the Twenty-first Congress (March 4, 1829–March 3, 1831); was not a candidate for renomination in 1830; resumed the practice of law; appointed Chargé d'Affaires to Central America January 29, 1833; returned home in February 1839; died on board a river steamer opposite Newburgh, N. Y., April 12, 1839; interment in Dutch Reformed Cemetery, Hurley, N. Y.

DE WITT, David Miller, a Representative from New York; born in Paterson, Passaic County, N. J., November 25, 1837; moved to New York in 1845 with his parents, who settled in Brooklyn; attended the public schools of Brooklyn, a select school at Saugerties, and the local academy at Kingston; was graduated from Rutgers College, New Brunswick, N. J., in 1858; studied law; was admitted to the bar in 1858 and commenced practice in Kingston, N. Y.; principal of New Paltz Academy (later a State normal school) in 1861 and 1862; district attorney of Ulster County 1863–1870; unsuccessful candidate for reelection; elected as a Democrat to the Forty-third Congress (March 4, 1873–March 3, 1875); was not a candidate for renomination; resumed the practice of law and also engaged in literary pursuits; assistant corporation counsel of Brooklyn, N. Y., 1878–1881; member of the State assembly in 1883; corporation counsel of Kingston in 1884; surrogate of Ulster County from November 20, 1885, to December 31, 1886; again engaged in the practice of law; died in Kingston, N. Y., June 23, 1912; interment in Wiltwyck Rural Cemetery.

DE WITT, Francis Byron, a Representative from Ohio; born in Jackson County, Ind., March 11, 1849; moved with his parents in 1854 to a farm in Delaware County, Ohio; during the Civil War enlisted in the Forty-sixth Regiment, Ohio Volunteer Infantry, at the age of twelve and was present during the Battle of Shiloh and the Corinth campaign; mustered out for temporary disability and reenlisted in 1862 in the One Hundred and Twenty-first Regiment, Ohio Volunteer Infantry, and served until the close of the war; prisoner of war in Salisbury, Danville, and Libby Prisons; attended the common schools and high school in Galena, Ohio, National Normal School, Lebanon, Ohio, and Ohio Wesleyan University, Delaware, Ohio; moved to Paulding, Ohio, in 1872 and taught school; studied law; was admitted to the bar in 1875 and practiced his profession in Paulding until 1891, when he engaged in agricultural pursuits; member of the State house of representatives 1892–1895; elected as a Republican to the Fifty-fourth Congress (March 4, 1895–March 3, 1897); unsuccessful candidate for reelection in 1896; resumed agricultural pursuits near Paulding, Ohio; moved to Standish, Arenac County, Mich., in 1903 and resumed the practice of law; served as register of deeds; member of the Michigan House of Representatives 1920–1922; elected prosecuting attorney of Arenac County, Mich., in 1926; reelected in 1928 and served until his death in Standish, Mich., on March 21, 1929; interment in Live Oak Cemetery, Paulding, Ohio.

DE WITT, Jacob Hasbrouck, a Representative from New York; born in Marbletown, Ulster County, N. Y., October 2, 1784; attended the rural schools and Kingston (N. Y.) Academy; engaged in agricultural pursuits; served as adjutant in the War of 1812; elected as a Clinton Democrat to the Sixteenth Congress (March 4, 1819–March 3, 1821); was not a candidate for renomination in 1820; resumed agricultural pursuits; supervisor of Ulster County in 1827 and again in 1840; member of the State assembly in 1839 and again in 1847; died in Kingston, Ulster County, N. Y., January 30, 1867; interment in the Sharpe Cemetery, on Albany Avenue.

DE WOLF, James, a Senator from Rhode Island; born in Bristol, R. I., March 18, 1764; during the Revolutionary War shipped as a sailor boy on a private armed vessel; participated in several naval encounters and was twice captured by the enemy; confined for some time on the island of Bermuda; before he was twenty years old became captain of a ship; engaged in extensive commercial ventures, principally with Cuba and other West Indian islands; member of the State house of representatives 1797–1801 and 1803–1812; fitted out a privateer in the War of 1812; one of the pioneers in cotton manufacturing; built the Arkwright Mills in Coventry, R. I., in 1812; again a member of the State house of representatives 1817–1821 and 1829–1837, and served as speaker 1819–1821; elected as a Democrat to the United States Senate and served from March 4, 1821, to October 31, 1825, when he resigned; died in New York City December 21, 1837; interment in the De Wolf private cemetery, Woodlawn Avenue, Bristol, R. I.

DEXTER, Samuel, a Representative and a Senator from Massachusetts; born in Boston, Mass., on May 14, 1761; was graduated from Harvard University in 1781; studied law; was admitted to the bar in 1784 and commenced practice in Lunenburg, Mass.; member of the State house of representatives 1788–1790; elected as a Federalist to the Third Congress (March 4, 1793–March 3, 1795); elected to the United States Senate and served from March 4, 1799, until May 30, 1800, when he resigned to enter the Cabinet; appointed Secretary of War in the Cabinet of President Adams May 13, 1800; appointed Secretary of the Treasury January 1 and served until May 6,

1801; resumed the practice of law in Washington, D. C.; moved to Boston, Mass., in 1805 and continued the practice of law; declined the appointment of Minister to Spain tendered by President Madison in 1815; unsuccessful candidate for Governor in 1816; died in Athens, Greene County, N. Y., May 3, 1816, where he had gone to attend the marriage of his son; interment in Mount Auburn Cemetery, Boston, Mass.

DEZENDORF, John Frederick, a Representative from Virginia; born in Lansingburg, Rensselaer County, N. Y., August 10, 1834; pursued an academic course; learned the carpenter's trade; studied architecture and civil engineering; engaged in railroad and other building at Toledo and Cleveland, Ohio, 1850–1860, and later, from 1860 to 1862, in mercantile pursuits; moved to Norfolk, Va., in 1863 and engaged in the shipping business until 1866; surveyor of Norfolk City and County 1866–1869; assistant assessor of the United States internal revenue from September 9, 1870, to August 6, 1872; appraiser of merchandise at the Norfolk customhouse from August 7, 1872, until the position was abolished in 1877; delegate to the Republican National Convention at Cincinnati in 1876; unsuccessful Republican candidate for election in 1878 to the Forty-sixth Congress; elected as a Republican to the Forty-seventh Congress (March 4, 1881–March 3, 1883); engaged in the construction business; died in Norfolk, Va., June 22, 1894; interment in Elmwood Cemetery.

DIAL, Nathaniel Barksdale, a Senator from South Carolina; born near Laurens, Laurens County, S. C., April 24, 1862; attended the common schools, Richmond (Va.) College, and Vanderbilt University, Nashville, Tenn.; studied law at the University of Virginia at Charlottesville; was admitted to the bar in 1883 and commenced practice in Laurens, S. C.; mayor of Laurens 1887–1891 and again in 1895; member of the Democratic State executive committee for several terms; delegate to the Democratic National Convention at St. Louis in 1888; declined the office of consul to Zurich, Switzerland, tendered by President Cleveland in 1893; engaged in banking and in various manufacturing enterprises; unsuccessful candidate for election to the United States Senate in 1912; elected in 1918 as a Democrat to the United States Senate and served from March 4, 1919, to March 3, 1925; unsuccessful candidate for reelection in 1924; appointed on March 26, 1925, a member of the commission to report the most practical method of utilizing the nitrate plant at Muscle Shoals, Ala., and served until November 14, 1925, when the commission automatically dissolved, having submitted its conclusions to the President; resumed the practice of law in South Carolina and Washington, D. C., and also his former manufacturing enterprises in South Carolina; died in Washington, D. C., on December 11, 1940; interment in Laurens Cemetery, Laurens, S. C.

DIBBLE, Samuel, a Representative from South Carolina; born in Charleston, S. C., September 16, 1837; pursued an academic course in Bethel, Conn., and Charleston, S. C.; attended the College of Charleston for two years, and was graduated from Wofford College, Spartanburg, S. C., in 1856; engaged in teaching 1856–1858; studied law; was admitted to the bar in 1859 and commenced practice in Orangeburg, S. C.; served in the Confederate Army throughout the Civil War; resumed the practice of law in Orangeburg, S. C.; also edited the Orangeburg News; member of the State house of representatives in 1877 and 1878; trustee of the University of South Carolina at Columbia in 1878; member of the Board of School Commissioners of Orangeburg County; delegate to the Democratic National Convention at Cincinnati in 1880 and presidential elector on the Democratic ticket of Hancock and English the same year;

presented credentials as a Democratic Member-elect to the Forty-seventh Congress to fill a vacancy thought to exist by reason of the death (pending a contest) of Michael P. O'Connor, and served from June 9, 1881, to May 31, 1882, when the seat was awarded to Edmund W. M. Mackey under the original election; elected to the Forty-eighth and to the three succeeding Congresses (March 4, 1883–March 3, 1891); declined to be a candidate for reelection in 1890; engaged in banking and other business interests in Orangeburg, Orangeburg County, S. C.; died near Baltimore, Md., September 16, 1913; interment in Sunny Side Cemetery, Orangeburg, S. C.

DIBRELL, George Gibbs, a Representative from Tennessee; born in Sparta, White County, Tenn., April 12, 1822; attended the public schools, and was graduated from the East Tennessee University, Knoxville, Tenn., in 1843; studied law; was admitted to the bar in 1843 and practiced; engaged in agricultural and mercantile pursuits; member of the State secession convention in 1861; justice of the peace and county court clerk of White County, Tenn., for many years; during the Civil War volunteered in the Confederate Army and served from 1861 to 1865; rose from private to lieutenant colonel of Infantry and colonel of Cavalry, and was discharged as brigadier general; elected as a Democrat to the Forty-fourth and to the four succeeding Congresses (March 4, 1875–March 3, 1885); was not a candidate for renomination in 1884; resumed agricultural and mercantile pursuits; died in Sparta, Tenn., May 9, 1888; interment in the Old Sparta Cemetery.

DICK, Charles William Frederick, a Representative and a Senator from Ohio; born in Akron, Summit County, Ohio, November 3, 1858; attended the public schools; studied law; was admitted to the bar in 1894 and commenced practice in Akron, Ohio; served in the Eighth Regiment, Ohio Volunteer Infantry, in Cuba during the war with Spain; resumed the practice of law; auditor of Summit County, Ohio, 1886–1894; secretary of the Republican National Committee 1896–1900; elected as a Republican to the Fifty-fifth Congress to fill the vacancy caused by the death of Stephen A. Northway; reelected to the Fifty-sixth, Fifty-seventh, and Fifty-eighth Congresses and served from November 8, 1898, to March 23, 1904, when he resigned, having been elected Senator; elected March 2, 1904, to the United States Senate to fill the vacancy caused by the death of Marcus A. Hanna; on the same day also was elected for the ensuing term and served from March 23, 1904, to March 3, 1911; unsuccessful candidate for reelection in 1911; resumed the practice of law in Washington, D. C., and Akron, Ohio; unsuccessful candidate for the Republican nomination for Senator in 1922; died in Akron, Ohio, March 13, 1945; interment in Glendale Cemetery.

DICK, John (father of Samuel Bernard Dick), a Representative from Pennsylvania; born in Pittsburgh, Pa., June 17, 1794; moved with his parents to Meadville, Pa., in December of that year; attended the common schools; major of the First Battalion in 1821; colonel of the First Regiment in 1825; brigadier general Second Brigade, Sixteenth Division, Pennsylvania Militia, in 1831; engaged in mercantile pursuits and banking; presidential elector on the Whig ticket of Harrison and Tyler in 1840; established the banking house of J. & J. R. Dick in 1850; associate judge of Crawford County in 1850; prominent in promoting the Atlantic & Great Western Railroad; trustee of Allegheny College, Meadville, Pa.; president of the Crawford Mutual Insurance Co. and of Greendale Cemetery; elected as a Whig to the Thirty-third Congress and as a Republican to the Thirty-fourth and Thirty-fifth Congresses (March 4, 1853–March 3, 1859); was nominated as a candidate

for reelection in 1858 to the Thirty-sixth Congress, but subsequently withdrew; resumed his former business pursuits; died in Meadville, Crawford County, Pa., May 29, 1872; interment in Greendale Cemetery.

DICK, Samuel, a Delegate from New Jersey; born in Nottingham, Prince Georges County, Md., November 14, 1740; received a classical education; studied medicine in Scotland, and commenced practice in Salem, N. J., in 1770; member of the New Jersey Provincial Congress in 1776; during the Revolutionary War was appointed colonel of the First Battalion, Salem County Militia, in 1776; assistant surgeon in the Continental Army in the Canadian campaign; member of the first State general assembly; appointed collector of customs for the western district of New Jersey in 1778; Member of the Continental Congress in 1783 and 1784; delegate to the New Jersey State convention in 1787 to ratify the Federal Constitution; surrogate of Salem County 1785–1804; died in Salem, Salem County, N. J., November 16, 1812; interment in St. John's Episcopal Churchyard.

DICK, Samuel Bernard (son of John Dick), a Representative from Pennsylvania; born in Meadville, Crawford County, Pa., October 26, 1836; attended the public schools and Allegheny College, Meadville, Pa.; engaged in banking; during the Civil War was in command of Company F, Ninth Regiment, Pennsylvania Reserve Corps; severely wounded in Dranesville, Va., December 20, 1861; subsequently served as colonel of the regiment until February 1863, when he resigned; commanded the Fifth Regiment, Pennsylvania Militia, and proceeded to Newcreek, W. Va., in July 1863; presidential elector on the Republican ticket of Lincoln and Johnson in 1864; mayor of Meadville in 1870; elected as a Republican to the Forty-sixth Congress (March 4, 1879–March 3, 1881); was not a candidate for reelection in 1880 to the Forty-seventh Congress; president of the Pittsburgh, Bessemer & Lake Erie Railroad Co. until April 1900; president of Phoenix Iron Works Co.; trustee of Allegheny College; member of the board of incorporators of Greendale Cemetery; died in Meadville, Pa., May 10, 1907; interment in Greendale Cemetery.

DICKENS, Samuel, a Representative from North Carolina; born near Roxboro, Person County, N. C.; pursued an academic course; member of the State house of commons 1813–1815; elected to the Fourteenth Congress to fill the vacancy caused by the death of Richard Stanford and served from December 2, 1816, to March 3, 1817; again a member of the State house of commons in 1818; moved to Madison County, Tenn., in 1820; died in Madison County in 1840.

DICKERMAN, Charles Heber, a Representative from Pennsylvania; born in Harford, Susquehanna County, Pa., February 3, 1843; attended the public schools of his native village, and was graduated from Harford University, Harford, Pa., in 1860; taught school for several years; studied law, but before qualifying for admission to the bar became bookkeeper for a large coal company at Beaver Meadow, Pa.; interested in the coal commission business and slate quarrying in 1868 at Bethlehem, Pa.; secretary and treasurer of a concern engaged in the manufacture of railroad equipment at Milton, Pa., 1880–1899; chairman of Northumberland County Democratic committee for three years; delegate to the State constitutional convention in 1891; delegate to the Democratic National Convention at Chicago in 1892; interested in banking at Mauch Chunk, Sunbury, and Bethlehem, and in 1897 became president of the First National Bank at Milton, in which capacity he served until his death; elected as a Democrat to the Fifty-eighth Congress (March 4,

1903–March 3, 1905); declined to be a candidate for renomination in 1904; appointed by President Theodore Roosevelt a delegate to the Brussels Peace Congress in 1905; again engaged in banking; died in Milton, Northumberland County, Pa., December 17, 1915; interment in Milton Cemetery.

DICKERSON, Mahlon (brother of Philemon Dickerson), a Senator from New Jersey; born in Hanover, N. J., April 17, 1770; educated by private tutors, and was graduated from Princeton College in 1789; studied law; was admitted to the bar in 1793; during the Whisky Rebellion served as a private in the Second Regiment Cavalry, New Jersey Detached Militia; settled in Philadelphia, Pa., and was admitted to practice in the Pennsylvania courts in 1797; State commissioner of bankruptcy in 1802; adjutant general 1805–1808; recorder of the city 1808–1810; moved to Morris County, N. J., in 1810; member of the State general assembly 1811–1813; law reporter for the State supreme court in 1813 and 1814; justice of the State supreme court 1813–1815; Governor 1815–1817; elected as a Democrat to the United States Senate; reelected in 1823 and served from March 4, 1817, to January 30, 1829, when he resigned; immediately reelected to fill the vacancy caused by the resignation of Ephraim Bateman and served under this election from January 30, 1829, to March 3, 1833; member of the State council in 1833 and served as its vice president; declined appointment as Minister to Russia in 1834; appointed Secretary of the Navy in the Cabinet of President Jackson; reappointed by President Van Buren and served from June 30, 1834, to June 25, 1838; United States district judge for New Jersey in 1840; delegate to the State constitutional convention of 1844; died in Succasunna, Morris County, N. J., October 5, 1853; interment in the Presbyterian Cemetery.

DICKERSON, Philemon (brother of Mahlon Dickerson), a Representative from New Jersey; born in Succasunna, Morris County, N. J., January 11, 1788; pursued classical studies, and was graduated from the University of Pennsylvania at Philadelphia in 1808; studied law; was admitted to the bar in 1813 and commenced practice in Paterson, N. J., the same year; admitted as a counselor in 1817; member of the State general assembly from Essex County in 1821 and 1822; elected as a Democrat to the Twenty-third and Twenty-fourth Congresses and served from March 4, 1833, until November 3, 1836, when he resigned, having been chosen Governor by the legislature; served as Governor and ex officio chancellor from November 3, 1836, to October 27, 1837; appointed sergeant at law in 1834, being the last person in New Jersey to hold that title; elected as a Jackson Democrat to the Twenty-sixth Congress (March 4, 1839–March 3, 1841); unsuccessful candidate for reelection to the Twenty-seventh Congress; appointed judge of the United States District Court for the District of New Jersey on March 2, 1841, and served until his death; president of the city council of Paterson, Passaic County, N. J., in 1851; died in Paterson, N. J., December 10, 1862; interment in Cedar Lawn Cemetery.

DICKERSON, William Worth, a Representative from Kentucky; born in Sherman, Grant County, Ky., November 29, 1851; attended the public schools and the private academy of N. M. Lloyd in Crittenden, Ky.; studied law; was admitted to the bar in 1872 and commenced practice in Williamstown, Ky.; prosecuting attorney of Grant County 1872–1876; member of the State house of representatives 1885–1887; served in the State senate 1887–1891; elected as a Democrat to the Fifty-first Congress to fill the vacancy caused by the resignation of John G. Carlisle; reelected to the Fifty-second Congress and served from June 21, 1890, to March 3, 1893; unsuccessful candidate for renomination in 1892; resumed the practice of law

in Williamstown, Grant County, Ky.; moved to Cincinnati, Ohio, in 1902 and continued the practice of his profession until his death January 31, 1923; remains were cremated and the ashes interred in the City Cemetery, Williamstown, Ky.

DICKEY, Henry Luther, a Representative from Ohio; born in South Salem, Ross County, Ohio, October 29, 1832; moved with his parents to Washington Court House, Ohio, in 1836; moved to Greenfield, Ohio, in 1847; attended Greenfield Academy; pursued the vocation of civil engineer, and in that capacity had charge of the construction of the Marietta & Cincinnati Railroad in Vinton County, Ohio; resigned in 1855; studied law; was admitted to the bar at Chillicothe, Ohio, in 1857; was graduated from the Cincinnati Law School in 1859; commenced practice in Greenfield; member of the State house of representatives in 1861; served in the State senate in 1868 and 1869; elected as a Democrat to the Forty-fifth and Forty-sixth Congresses (March 4, 1877–March 3, 1881); was not a candidate for renomination in 1880; resumed the practice of law; was admitted to practice before the Supreme Court of the United States in 1877; president of the Commercial Bank of Greenfield; died in Greenfield, Ohio, on May 23, 1910; interment in Greenfield Cemetery.

DICKEY, Jesse Column, a Representative from Pennsylvania; born in New Castle, Lawrence County, Pa., February 27, 1808; moved with his parents to New London, Chester County, in 1812; attended the common schools, and was graduated from New London Academy; began teaching school at Hopewell Academy in 1828; engaged in agricultural pursuits; member of the State house of representatives 1842–1845; elected as a Whig to the Thirty-first Congress (March 4, 1849–March 3, 1851), unsuccessful candidate for reelection to the Thirty-second Congress; resumed agricultural pursuits; quartermaster and later paymaster in the United States Army during the Civil War; continued agricultural pursuits; died in New London, Pa., February 19, 1890; interment in Presbyterian Cemetery.

DICKEY, John (father of Oliver James Dickey), a Representative from Pennsylvania; born in Greensburg, Westmoreland County, Pa., June 23, 1794; completed preparatory studies; appointed postmaster of Old Brighton, Pa., on April 11, 1818, and served until May 17, 1821; served as sheriff 1824–1827; member of the State senate in 1835 and 1837; elected as a Whig to the Twenty-eighth Congress (March 4, 1843–March 3, 1845); elected to the Thirtieth Congress (March 4, 1847–March 3, 1849); appointed United States marshal for the western district of Pennsylvania on January 22, 1852; died in Beaver, Beaver County, Pa., on March 14, 1853; interment in the Old Cemetery.

DICKEY, Oliver James (son of John Dickey), a Representative from Pennsylvania; born in Old Brighton, Beaver County, Pa., April 6, 1823; completed preparatory studies; attended Beaver Academy and Dickinson College, Carlisle, Pa.; studied law; was admitted to the bar at Lancaster, Lancaster County, Pa., in 1844 and practiced; district attorney of Lancaster County 1856–1859; during the Civil War served as lieutenant colonel of the Tenth Regiment, Pennsylvania Volunteers; elected as a Republican to the Fortieth Congress to fill the vacancy caused by the death of Thaddeus Stevens and on the same day was elected to the Forty-first Congress; reelected to the Forty-second Congress and served from December 7, 1868, to March 3, 1873; was not a candidate for renomination in 1872; delegate to the State constitutional convention at Harrisburg in 1873; delegate to several Republican National Conventions; resumed the practice of law in Lancaster, Pa., and died there April 21, 1876; interment in Woodward Hill Cemetery.

DICKINSON, Clement Cabell, a Representative from Missouri; born at Prince Edward Court House, Prince Edward County, Va., December 6, 1849; tutored privately and also attended private schools; was graduated from Hampden-Sidney College, Virginia, in June 1869; taught school in Virginia and Kentucky 1869–1872; moved to Clinton, Mo., in September 1872 and continued teaching; also studied law; was admitted to the bar in 1875 and commenced practice in Clinton, Mo.; prosecuting attorney of Henry County, Mo., 1877–1882; city attorney of Clinton 1882–1884; presidential elector on the Democratic ticket of Bryan and Sewall in 1896; member of the State house of representatives 1900–1902; served in the State senate 1902–1906; member of the board of regents of the State Normal School at Warrensburg, Mo., 1907–1913; elected as a Democrat to the Sixty-first Congress to fill the vacancy caused by the death of David A. De Armond; reelected to the Sixty-second and to the four succeeding Congresses and served from February 1, 1910, to March 3, 1921; unsuccessful candidate for reelection in 1920 to the Sixty-seventh Congress; elected to the Sixty-eighth, Sixty-ninth, and Seventieth Congresses (March 4, 1923–March 3, 1929); unsuccessful candidate for reelection in 1928 to the Seventy-first Congress; elected to the Seventy-second and Seventy-third Congresses (March 4, 1931–January 3, 1935); unsuccessful candidate for renomination in 1934; resumed the practice of law at Clinton, Mo., where he died January 14, 1938; interment in Englewood Cemetery.

DICKINSON, Daniel Stevens, a Senator from New York; born in Goshen, Conn., September 11, 1800; moved with his parents to Guilford, Chenango County, N. Y., in 1806; attended the common schools; was apprenticed to a clothier or cloth dresser, and while so engaged studied Latin, mathematics, and some of the sciences; taught school for several years, and subsequently engaged in land surveying; studied law; was admitted to the bar in 1828 and commenced practice in Guilford, N. Y.; appointed postmaster of Guilford on August 20, 1827, and served until February 3, 1832, when he moved to Binghamton, N. Y.; first president of Binghamton in 1834; delegate to the Democratic National Convention at Baltimore in 1835; member of the State senate 1837–1840; Lieutenant Governor and ex officio president of the senate and president of the court of errors 1842–1844; delegate to the Democratic National Convention at Baltimore in 1844; presidential elector on the Democratic ticket of Polk and Dallas in 1844; appointed and subsequently elected as a Democrat to the United States Senate to fill the vacancy caused by the resignation of Nathaniel P. Tallmadge; reelected in 1845 and served from November 30, 1844, to March 3, 1851; unsuccessful candidate for reelection; resumed the practice of law; delegate to the Democratic National Convention at Baltimore in 1848 and 1852; appointed collector of the port of New York, but declined the position; elected attorney general of the State in 1861; delegate to the Republican National Convention at Baltimore in 1864; appointed on June 27, 1864, United States commissioner for the final settlement of the Hudson Bay and Puget Sound Agricultural Cos.' claims; appointed by President Lincoln on April 10, 1865, United States attorney for the southern district of New York and served until his death in New York City on April 12, 1866; interment in Spring Forest Cemetery, Binghamton, Broome County, N. Y.

DICKINSON, David W. (nephew of William Hardy Murfree), a Representative from Tennessee; born in Franklin, Tenn., June 10, 1808; completed preparatory studies and was graduated from the University of North Carolina at Chapel Hill; studied law; was admitted to the bar and practiced; elected as a Democrat to the Twenty-third Congress (March 4, 1833–March 3, 1835); elected as a Whig to the Twenty-eighth Congress (March 4,

1843–March 3, 1845); was unable to attend the last session of Congress on account of his failing health; died at "Grantland," his father's home, near Murfreesboro, Rutherford County, Tenn., on April 27, 1845; interment in the family burying ground on the estate.

DICKINSON, Edward, a Representative from Massachusetts; born in Amherst, Mass., January 1, 1803; attended the public schools and Amherst Academy; was graduated from Yale College in 1823; studied law in the law school of Northampton, Mass.; was admitted to the bar and commenced practice in Amherst in 1826; treasurer of Amherst College 1835–1873; member of the State house of representatives in 1838 and 1839; served in the State senate in 1842 and 1843; member of the Governor's council in 1846 and 1847; elected as a Whig to the Thirty-third Congress (March 4, 1853–March 3, 1855); declined to be a candidate for the Republican nomination of Lieutenant Governor in 1861; again elected a member of the State house of representatives in 1873; died in Boston, Mass., June 16, 1874; interment in West Cemetery, Amherst, Hampshire County, Mass.

DICKINSON, Edward Fenwick, a Representative from Ohio; born in Fremont, Sandusky County, Ohio, January 21, 1829; attended the public schools; was graduated from St. Xavier College, Cincinnati, Ohio; studied law; was admitted to the bar and commenced practice in Fremont, Ohio; prosecuting attorney of Sandusky County, Ohio, from 1852 until his resignation in 1854; during the Civil War served in the Union Army as a lieutenant; promoted to captain and served as regimental quartermaster of Company G, Eighth Regiment, Ohio Volunteer Infantry; served as probate judge of Sandusky County 1866–1869; elected as a Democrat to the Forty-first Congress (March 4, 1869–March 3, 1871); unsuccessful candidate for reelection in 1870 to the Forty-second Congress; resumed the practice of his profession; elected mayor of Fremont in 1871, 1873, and 1875; again served as probate judge of Sandusky County from 1877 to 1879 and from 1885 until his death; died in Fremont, Ohio, August 25, 1891; interment in Oakwood Cemetery.

DICKINSON, John (brother of Philemon Dickinson), a Delegate from Pennsylvania and from Delaware; born on his father's estate, "Crosiadoré," near Trappe, Talbot County, Md., November 8, 1732; moved with his parents in 1740 to Dover, Del., where he studied under a private teacher; studied law in Philadelphia and at the Middle Temple in London; was admitted to the bar 1757 and commenced practice in Philadelphia; member of the Assembly of "Lower Counties," as the State of Delaware was then called, in 1760; member of the Pennsylvania Assembly in 1762 and 1764; delegate to the Colonial Congress in 1765; Member from Pennsylvania to the Continental Congress 1774–1776 and from Delaware in 1776, 1777, 1779, and 1780; brigadier general of Pennsylvania Militia; President of the State of Delaware in 1781; returned to Philadelphia and served as President of Pennsylvania 1782–1785; returned to Delaware; was a member of the Federal convention of 1787 which framed the Constitution and was one of the signers from Delaware; died in Wilmington, New Castle County, Del., on February 14, 1808; interment in the Friends Burial Ground.

DICKINSON, John Dean, a Representative from New York; born in Middletown, Conn., June 28, 1767; completed preparatory studies, and was graduated from Yale College in 1785; moved to Lansingburg, Rensselaer County, N. Y., in 1790; was admitted to the bar in April 1791 and commenced the practice of law in Lansingburg; moved to Troy, N. Y.; served as president of the Farmers' Bank of Troy, N. Y., from its foundation in 1801 until his death; a director and founder of the Rensselaer & Saratoga Insurance Co. in 1814; member of the State assembly from November 1816 to April 1817; first president of the Troy Lyceum of Natural History in 1818; elected as a Federalist to the Sixteenth and Seventeenth Congresses (March 4, 1819–March 3, 1823); one of the original board of trustees of the Rensselaer Polytechnic Institute in 1824; member of the committee which received Lafayette on his visits to Troy in 1824 and 1825; elected as a Whig to the Twentieth and Twenty-first Congresses (March 4, 1827–March 3, 1831); resumed the practice of law in Troy, N. Y., and died there January 28, 1841; interment in Oakwood Cemetery.

DICKINSON, Lester Jesse (cousin of Fred Dickinson Letts), a Representative and a Senator from Iowa; born in Derby, Lucas County, Iowa, October 29, 1873; is a direct descendant of Nathaniel Dickinson, of Hadley, who settled in Massachusetts in 1630; attended the public schools; was graduated from Danbury (Iowa) High School in 1892, from Cornell College, Mount Vernon, Iowa, in 1898, and from the law department of the University of Iowa at Iowa City in 1899; was admitted to the bar in 1899 and commenced practice in Algona, Iowa; second lieutenant in the Fifty-second Infantry, Iowa National Guard, 1900–1902; city clerk of Algona 1900–1904; prosecuting attorney of Kossuth County 1909–1913; member of the Republican State central committee 1914–1918; trustee of Cornell College since 1915; elected as a Republican to the Sixty-sixth and to the five succeeding Congresses (March 4, 1919–March 3, 1931); was not a candidate for renomination in 1930, having become a candidate for Senator; elected to the United States Senate in 1930 and served from March 4, 1931, to January 3, 1937; unsuccessful candidate for reelection in 1936 and for election in 1938; temporary chairman of the Republican National Convention at Chicago in 1932; resumed the practice of law in Des Moines, Iowa, where he resides.

DICKINSON, Philemon (brother of John Dickinson), a Delegate from Delaware and a Senator from New Jersey; born at "Crosiadoré," near Trappe, Talbot County, Md., April 5, 1739; moved with his parents to Dover, Del., in 1740; where he received his education from a private tutor, and was graduated in the first class to emerge from the University of Pennsylvania at Philadelphia in 1757; superintended his father's estates in Delaware until 1760; studied law in Philadelphia and was admitted to the bar, but never practiced; moved to Trenton, N. J., in 1767; delegate to the New Jersey Provincial Congress in 1776; served in the Revolutionary War; was commissioned brigadier general in 1776, and in 1777 major general commanding the New Jersey Militia, serving in the latter capacity throughout the Revolution; was Cadwalader's second in the latter's duel with General Conway; Member of the Continental Congress from Delaware in 1782 and 1783; vice president of the Council of New Jersey in 1783 and 1784; member of the commission to choose a site for the National Capital in 1784; elected to the United States Senate from New Jersey to fill the vacancy caused by the resignation of William Paterson and served from November 23, 1790, to March 3, 1793; was not a candidate for renomination; after leaving the Senate devoted his time to the care of his estates; died at his home, "The Hermitage," near Trenton, N. J., February 4, 1809; interment in the Friends Meeting House Burying Ground, Trenton, N. J.

DICKINSON, Rodolphus, a Representative from Ohio; born in Hatfield, Mass., December 28, 1797; attended the public schools and Williams College, Williamstown, Mass., 1818–1821; studied law; was admitted to the bar and commenced practice in Tiffin, Ohio; appointed prosecuting attorney for Seneca

County in 1824, for Williams County in 1826, and for Sandusky County in 1827; moved to Lower Sandusky, Ohio, in 1826; served as a member of the Board of Public Works of Ohio 1836–1845; elected as a Democrat to the Thirtieth and Thirty-first Congresses and served from March 4, 1847, until his death in Washington, D. C., on March 20, 1849; interment in Washington, D. C.; reinterment in Oakwood Cemetery, Fremont, Sandusky County, Ohio.

DICKSON, David, a Representative from Mississippi; born in Georgia; moved to Mississippi; studied medicine and practiced extensively in Pike County; delegate to the State constitutional convention in 1817; brigadier general of militia in 1818; member of the State senate in 1820 and 1821; Lieutenant Governor of Mississippi in 1821; postmaster of Jackson, Miss., in 1822; unsuccessful candidate for Governor of Mississippi in 1823; delegate to the State constitutional convention in 1832 and was an unsuccessful candidate for president of the convention; secretary of the State senate in 1833; secretary of state in 1835; elected as a Democrat to the Twenty-fourth Congress and served from March 4, 1835, until his death at Hot Springs, Ark., July 31, 1836.

DICKSON, Frank Stoddard, a Representative from Illinois; born in Hillsboro, Montgomery County, Ill., October 6, 1876; attended the public schools, and was graduated from the high school at Decatur, Ill., in 1896; taught school at Ramsey, Ill.; served as a private in the Fourth Regiment, Illinois Infantry, during the war with Spain; again engaged in teaching at Ramsey, Ill.; elected as a Republican to the Fifty-ninth Congress (March 4, 1905–March 3, 1907); unsuccessful candidate for reelection in 1906 to the Sixtieth Congress; assistant adjutant general of Illinois 1908–1910; adjutant general of Illinois from January 1, 1910, to January 1, 1922; assistant to the director of finance, United States Shipping Board and Emergency Fleet Corporation, 1922–1924; secretary to Senator Medill McCormick 1924–1926; associated with the National Board of Fire Underwriters in Chicago, Ill., and was general counsel at time of death; died in Washington, D. C., February 24, 1953; interment in Oak Ridge Cemetery, Springfield, Ill.

DICKSON, John, a Representative from New York; born in Keene, N. H., June 1, 1783; was graduated from Middlebury (Vt.) College in 1808; studied law; was admitted to the bar in 1812 and commenced practice in West Bloomfield, N. Y.; member of the State assembly in 1829 and 1830; elected as a Whig to the Twenty-second and Twenty-third Congresses (March 4, 1831–March 3, 1835); resumed the practice of law in West Bloomfield, Ontario County, N. Y., where he died February 22, 1852; interment in Pioneer Cemetery.

DICKSON, Joseph, a Representative from North Carolina; born in Chester County, Pa., in April 1745; moved with his parents to Rowan County, N. C., and was reared and educated there; engaged in cotton and tobacco planting; member of the committee of safety of Rowan County in 1775; commissioned captain in the Colonial Army the same year; served under Colonel McDowell in 1780, and at the Battle of Kings Mountain as major of the "Lincoln County Men" rendered heroic service; opposed Lord Cornwallis' invasion of the State in 1781, and for brave and efficient conduct was promoted to the rank of colonel, and before the close of the war was made brigadier general; clerk of Lincoln County Court in 1781; member of the State senate 1788–1795, and during this time was appointed one of a commission to establish the University of North Carolina at Chapel Hill; elected as a Federalist to the Sixth Congress (March 4, 1799–March 3, 1801);

moved to Tennessee in 1803 and settled in that portion of Davidson County which subsequently became Rutherford County; member of the State house of representatives 1807–1811 and served as speaker the last two years; died in Rutherford County, Tenn., April 14, 1825; interment on his plantation northeast of Murfreesboro, Tenn.

DICKSON, Samuel, a Representative from New York; born in the town of Bethlehem (now New Scotland), Albany County, N. Y., March 29, 1807; completed preparatory studies; was privately tutored by Dr. O'Donnell; entered Union College, Schenectady, N. Y., at the age of sixteen and was graduated from that institution in 1825; received a diploma from the Censors of the Medical Society of the State of New York in May 1829 and commenced the practice of his chosen profession in New Scotland, N. Y.; elected as a Whig to the Thirty-fourth Congress (March 4, 1855–March 3, 1857); contracted a spinal disease from an accident while attending a session of the House and died in New Scotland, Albany County, N. Y., on May 3, 1858; interment in New Scotland Presbyterian Church Cemetery.

DICKSON, William, a Representative from Tennessee; born in Duplin County, N. C., May 5, 1770; educated at Grove Academy, Kenansville, N. C.; moved with his parents to Tennessee in 1795; studied medicine and practiced in Nashville for many years; member of the State house of representatives 1799–1803 and served as speaker; elected to the Seventh, Eighth, and Ninth Congresses (March 4, 1801–March 3, 1807); trustee of the University of Nashville 1806–1816; died in Nashville, Tenn., in February 1816; interment in a rural cemetery near Nashville.

DICKSON, William Alexander, a Representative from Mississippi; born in Centreville, Wilkinson County, Miss., July 20, 1861; attended private and public schools, Pleasant Grove School, Centenary College, Jackson, La., and Vanderbilt University, Nashville, Tenn.; engaged in agricultural pursuits; studied law but did not practice; supervisor 1886–1888; member of the State house of representatives 1887–1893; school commissioner of Wilkinson County; presidential elector on the Democratic ticket of Parker and Davis in 1904; member of the board of trustees of the Agricultural and Mechanical College, Starkville, Miss., and of Edward Magehee College, Woodville, Miss., for five years; elected as a Democrat to the Sixty-first and Sixty-second Congresses (March 4, 1909–March 3, 1913); engaged in agricultural pursuits; elected supervisor of the third district of Wilkinson County and superintendent of its highways in 1927; died in Centreville, Miss., February 25, 1940; interment in Oaklawn Cemetery.

DICKSTEIN, Samuel, a Representative from New York; born near Vilna, Russia, February 5, 1885; immigrated to the United States in 1887 with his parents, who settled in New York City; attended public and private schools in New York City, the College of the City of New York, and was graduated from the New York City Law School in 1906; was admitted to the bar in 1908 and commenced the practice of law in New York City; special deputy attorney general of the State of New York 1911–1914; member of the board of aldermen in 1917; member of the State assembly 1919–1922; served as a member of the Democratic county committee; elected as a Democrat to the Sixty-eighth and to the eleven succeeding Congresses and served from March 4, 1923, until his resignation on December 30, 1945, to become judge of the New York State Supreme Court, in which capacity he served until his death in New York, N. Y., April 22, 1954; interment in Union Field Cemetery, Queens County, Brooklyn, N. Y.

DIEKEMA, Gerrit John, a Representative from Michigan; born in Holland, Ottawa County, Mich., on March 27, 1859; attended the common schools; was graduated from Hope College, Holland, Mich., in 1881 and from the law department of the University of Michigan at Ann Arbor in 1883; was admitted to the bar and commenced practice in Holland in 1883; city attorney; member of the State house of representatives 1885–1891, serving as speaker in 1889; mayor of Holland in 1895; chairman of the Michigan Republican State central committee 1900–1910; delegate to the Republican National Convention at St. Louis in 1896; member of the Spanish Treaty Claims Commission from 1901 until he resigned in 1907; elected April 27, 1907, as a Republican to the Sixtieth Congress to fill the vacancy caused by the resignation of William Alden Smith; reelected to the Sixty-first Congress and served from March 17, 1908, to March 3, 1911; unsuccessful candidate for reelection in 1910 to the Sixty-second Congress; resumed the practice of law in Holland, Mich.; manager of the Republican Speakers' Bureau in Chicago in 1912; chairman of the Republican State central committee in 1927; appointed United States Minister to the Netherlands by President Hoover on August 20, 1929, and served until his death in The Hague, Netherlands, December 20, 1930; interment in Pilgrim Home Cemetery, Holland, Mich.

DIES, Martin, a Representative from Texas; born in Jackson Parish, La., March 13, 1870; moved with his parents to Freestone County, Tex., in 1876; attended the common schools and was graduated from the law department of the University of Texas at Austin; was admitted to the bar in 1893 and commenced practice in Woodville, Tex.; edited a newspaper in Freestone County; was county marshal; county judge of Tyler County in 1894; district attorney of the first judicial district of Texas 1898–1900; moved to Colorado, Tex., and engaged in the practice of law; moved to Beaumont, Tex., in 1902 and was employed as counsel for the Gulf Refining Co.; elected as a Democrat to the Sixty-first and to the four succeeding Congresses (March 4, 1909–March 3, 1919); was not a candidate for reelection in 1918; retired to his ranch on Turkey Creek, Tyler County, Tex.; moved to Kerrville, Tex., in 1921 and died there July 13, 1922; interment in Glenwood Cemetery, Houston, Tex.

DIES, Martin, Jr. (son of the preceding), a Representative from Texas; born in Colorado, Mitchell County, Tex., November 5, 1900; moved with his parents to Beaumont, Tex., in 1902; attended the public schools, Wesley College, Greenville, Tex., and Cluster Springs Academy, Cluster Springs, Va.; was graduated from the University of Texas at Austin in 1919 and from the law department of National University, Washington, D. C., in 1920; was admitted to the bar in 1920 and commenced practice in Marshall, Tex.; moved to Orange, Tex., in 1922 and continued the practice of law; also interested in ranching and agricultural pursuits at Jasper, Tex.; member of the faculty of East Texas Law School, Beaumont, Tex., in 1930; elected as a Democrat to the Seventy-second and to the six succeeding Congresses (March 4, 1931–January 3, 1945); did not seek renomination in 1944; elected to the Eighty-third, Eighty-fourth and Eighty-fifth Congresses (January 3, 1953–January 3, 1959); did not seek renomination in 1958; while a member of Congress in 1941 and 1957 was defeated for the nomination to fill a vacancy in the United States Senate; resumed the practice of law; resides in Lufkin, Tex.

DIETERICH, William Henry, a Representative and a Senator from Illinois; born on a farm near Cooperstown, Brown County, Ill., March 31, 1876; attended the rural schools; was graduated from Kennedy Normal and Business College, Rushville, Ill., in

1897 and from Northern Indiana Law School, Valparaiso, Ind., in 1901; was admitted to the bar in 1901 and commenced practice in Rushville, Schuyler County, Ill., the same year; during the Spanish-American War served as a corporal in Company K, Anderson's Provisional Regiment; served as city attorney of Rushville, Ill., 1903 to 1907; treasurer of Rushville Union Schools 1906 to 1908; county judge of Schuyler County, Ill., 1906–1910; moved to Chicago, Ill., in 1911, to Beardstown, Ill., in 1912, and continued the practice of law; special inheritance-tax attorney of Illinois 1913–1917; member of the State house of representatives 1917–1921; presidential elector on the Democratic ticket of Alfred E. Smith and Joseph T. Robinson in 1928; elected as a Democrat to the Seventy-second Congress (March 4, 1931–March 3, 1933); did not seek renomination, having become a candidate for the United States Senate; elected to the United States Senate and served from March 4, 1933 to January 3, 1939; was not a candidate for renomination in 1938; resumed the practice of law; died in Springfield, Ill., on October 12, 1940, while on a business trip; interment in Rushville City Cemetery, Rushville, Ill.

DIETRICH, Charles Elmer, a Representative from Pennsylvania; born in Tunkhannock, Wyoming County, Pa., July 30, 1889; attended the public and high schools; was graduated from Wyoming Seminary, Kingston, Pa., in 1907; engaged in motion-picture pursuits and owned and operated a theater 1914–1942; engaged in agricultural pursuits and stock raising 1924–1942, and also was in the memorial-monument business; prothonotary and clerk of the courts of Wyoming County 1920–1935; delegate to the Democratic National Convention at Chicago in 1932; elected as a Democrat to the Seventy-fourth Congress (January 3, 1935–January 3, 1937); unsuccessful candidate for reelection in 1936 to the Seventy-fifth Congress; resumed former business pursuits; died in Tunkhannock, Pa., May 20, 1942; interment in Sunnyside Cemetery.

DIETRICH, Charles Henry, a Senator from Nebraska; born in Aurora, Kane County, Ill., November 26, 1853; attended the public schools; employed as a clerk in a hardware store in St. Joseph, Mo., in 1869; moved to Chicago, Ill., and engaged in the hardware business; moved to Deadwood, Dak. (now South Dakota), in 1875 and engaged in mercantile pursuits, delivering goods on pack animals through the Black Hills until he located the "Aurora" mine; disposed of this property, settled in Hastings, Adams County, Nebr., in 1878, and engaged in mercantile pursuits and in banking; organized the German National Bank in 1887 and was elected its president; elected Governor of Nebraska in 1900 and served from January 3 to May 1, 1901, when he resigned having been elected a Senator; elected as a Republican to the United States Senate to fill the vacancy caused by the death of Monroe L. Hayward and served from March 28, 1901, to March 3, 1905; was not a candidate for reelection in 1904; retired from active business pursuits and public life in 1905; died in Hastings, Nebr., on April 10, 1924; interment in Parkview Cemetery.

DIETZ, William, a Representative from New York; born in Schoharie, N. Y., June 28, 1778; attended the district schools; engaged in agricultural pursuits; town clerk in 1804 and 1805; supervisor of Schoharie in 1812; served in the State assembly in 1814, 1815, and 1823; elected as a Democrat to the Nineteenth Congress (March 4, 1825–March 3, 1827); member of the State senate 1830–1833; resumed agricultural pursuits; presidential elector on the Democratic ticket of Jackson and Van Buren in 1832; colonel of the militia; died in Schoharie, Schoharie County, N. Y., on August 24, 1848; interment in St. Paul's Lutheran Cemetery.

DIFFENDERFER, Robert Edward, a Representative from Pennsylvania; born in Lewisburg, Union County, Pa., June 7, 1849; attended the common schools; worked on a farm in early life and later took up the trade of house painting; studied dentistry and practiced this profession for fourteen years in Lewisburg and Pottsville, Pa.; built and operated the first woolen mill at Tientsin in the Chinese Empire; survived through the Chinese Boxer insurrection in 1900; returned to the United States in August 1900; engaged in the wholesale lumber business and as a contractor at Jenkintown; elected as a Democrat to the Sixty-second and Sixty-third Congresses (March 4, 1911–March 3, 1915); unsuccessful candidate for renomination in 1914, 1916, and 1918; engaged in the retail confectionery business at Jenkintown; died in Philadelphia, Pa., April 27, 1923; interment in Westminster Cemetery.

DIGGS, Charles Coles, Jr., a Representative from Michigan; born in Detroit, Wayne County, Mich., December 2, 1922; is of the Negro race; attended the University of Michigan at Ann Arbor 1940–1942; enrolled at Fisk University, Nashville, Tenn., in the fall of 1942 and while a student entered the United States Army as a private on February 19, 1943, commissioned a second lieutenant in 1944, and was discharged June 1, 1945; in September 1945 enrolled in Wayne University in Detroit, Mich., and graduated in June 1946; subsequently became a licensed mortician and board chairman of the House of Diggs, Inc.; member of the State senate 1951–1954; elected as a Democrat to the Eighty-fourth, Eighty-fifth, and Eighty-sixth Congresses (January 3, 1955–January 3, 1961).   *Reelected to the Eighty-seventh Congress.*

DILL, Clarence Cleveland, a Representative and a Senator from Washington; born near Fredericktown, Knox County, Ohio, September 21, 1884; attended the public schools; engaged in teaching 1901–1903; was graduated from Ohio Wesleyan University, Delaware, Ohio, in 1907; newspaper reporter in Cleveland, Ohio, in 1907; taught in the high schools at Dubuque, Iowa, in 1907 and 1908 and in Spokane, Wash., 1908–1910; studied law; was admitted to the bar in 1910 and commenced practice in Spokane, Wash.; deputy prosecuting attorney of Spokane County 1911–1913; private secretary to Gov. Ernest Lister in 1913; delegate to the Democratic State conventions in 1912, 1916, 1924, 1928, and 1932, serving as chairman in 1912; delegate to the Democratic National Conventions in 1920, 1924, and 1932; elected as a Democrat to the Sixty-fourth and Sixty-fifth Congresses (March 4, 1915–March 3, 1919); unsuccessful candidate for reelection in 1918 to the Sixty-sixth Congress; resumed the practice of law in Spokane, Wash.; elected to the United States Senate in 1922; reelected in 1928 and served from March 4, 1923, to January 3, 1935; was not a candidate for renomination in 1934; engaged in the practice of law in Washington, D. C., and Spokane, Wash., 1935–1939; unsuccessful candidate for Governor in 1940; unsuccessful candidate for election in 1942 to the Seventy-eighth Congress; member of the Columbia Basin Commission of the State of Washington 1945–1948; special assistant to the United States Attorney General from July 31, 1946, until January 31, 1953; resumed the practice of law in Spokane, Wash., where he now resides.

DILLINGHAM, Paul, Jr. (father of William Paul Dillingham), a Representative from Vermont; born in Shutesbury, Mass., August 10, 1799; moved with his father to Waterbury, Vt., in 1805; attended the district school in Waterbury; studied law; was admitted to the bar in March 1823 and commenced practice in Waterbury, Vt.; justice of the peace 1826–1844; town clerk of Waterbury 1829–1844; member of the State house of representatives 1833–1835 and 1837–1840; prosecuting attorney of Washington County 1835–1838; delegate to the State constitutional conventions of 1836, 1857, and again in 1870; served in the State senate in 1841, 1842, and 1861; elected as a Democrat to the Twenty-eighth and Twenty-ninth Congresses (March 4, 1843–March 3, 1847); was not a candidate for renomination in 1846; Lieutenant Governor 1862–1865; Governor of Vermont in 1865 and 1866; resumed the practice of law; retired in 1875; died at his home in Waterbury, Washington County, Vt., July 26, 1891; interment in the Village Cemetery.

DILLINGHAM, William Paul (son of Paul Dillingham, Jr.), a Senator from Vermont; born in Waterbury, Washington County, Vt., December 12, 1843; attended the public schools of Waterbury, Newbury Seminary, and Kimball Union Academy, Meriden, N. H.; studied law; was admitted to the bar in 1867 and commenced practice in Waterbury; prosecuting attorney of Washington County 1872–1876; secretary of civil and military affairs 1874–1876; member of the State house of representatives in 1876 and 1884; served in the State senate in 1878 and 1880; State tax commissioner 1882–1888; Governor of Vermont 1888–1890; president of the Waterbury National Bank 1890–1923; trustee of the University of Vermont at Burlington; president of the board of trustees of Montpelier Seminary; delegate to several Republican National Conventions; chairman of the United States Immigration Commission 1907–1910; elected in 1900 as a Republican to the United States Senate to fill the vacancy caused by the death of Justin S. Morrill; reelected in 1903, 1909. 1914, and 1920, and served from October 18, 1900, until his death in Montpelier, Vt., July 12, 1923; interment in the Village Cemetery, Waterbury, Vt.

DILLON, Charles Hall, a Representative from South Dakota; born near Jasper, Dubois County, Ind., December 18, 1853; attended the public schools; was graduated from the academic department of Indiana Univerity at Bloomington in 1874 and from its law department in 1876; was admitted to the bar in 1876 and commenced practice in Jasper, Ind.; moved to Marion, Iowa, in 1881, to Mitchell, Dakota Territory (now South Dakota), in 1882 and to Yankton in 1894 and continued the practice of law; delegate to the Republican National Conventions in 1900 and 1908; vice president and acting president of the State bar association in 1901; member of the State senate 1903–1911; elected as a Republican to the Sixty-third, Sixty-fourth, and Sixty-fifth Congresses (March 4, 1913–March 3, 1919); was not a candidate for reelection in 1918; resumed the practice of law in Yankton; moved to Vermillion, S. Dak., in 1922, having been elected associate justice of the State supreme court, and served until November 15, 1926, when he resigned; unsuccessful candidate for nomination as United States Senator in 1924; retired in 1926; died in Vermillion, S. Dak., September 15, 1929; interment in Yankton Cemetery, Yankton, S. Dak.

DILWEG, LaVern Ralph, a Representative from Wisconsin; born in Milwaukee, Wis., November 1, 1903; attended the public schools; was graduated from the law department of Marquette University, Milwaukee, Wis., in 1927; was admitted to the bar in 1927 and commenced practice in Green Bay, Wis.; played professional football 1926–1934 and continued his connection with the game as an official in the Big Ten until 1943; connected with a number of business concerns in Green Bay, Wis., but was especially concerned with construction work; in charge of Home Owners Loan Corporation, Green Bay, Wis., area 1934–1942; elected as a Democrat to the Seventy-eighth Congress (January 3, 1943–January 3, 1945); unsuccessful candidate for reelection in 1944 to the Seventy-ninth Congress; resumed the practice of law in Green Bay, Wis., and Washington, D. C.; confirmed as a member of the Foreign Claims Settlement Commission April 13, 1961; resides in Washington, D. C.

DIMMICK, Milo Melankthon (brother of William Harrison Dimmick), a Representative from Pennsylvania; born in Milford, Wayne (now Pike) County, Pa., October 30, 1811; pursued classical studies; studied law; was admitted to the bar in 1834 and commenced practice in Stroudsburg, Pa.; elected as a Democrat to the Thirty-first and Thirty-second Congresses (March 4, 1849–March 3, 1853); was not a candidate for renomination in 1852 to the Thirty-third Congress; resumed the practice of law; unsuccessful candidate for president judge of the twenty-second judicial district of Pennsylvania in 1853; moved to Mauch Chunk, Carbon County, Pa., in 1853 and continued the practice of law; also engaged in the banking business; died in Mauch Chunk, Pa., November 22, 1872; interment in Mauch Chunk Cemetery.

DIMMICK, William Harrison (brother of Milo Melankthon Dimmick), a Representative from Pennsylvania; born in Milford, Wayne (now Pike) County, Pa., December 20, 1815; attended private schools; studied law; was admitted to the bar in 1835 and commenced practice in Bethany, Pa.; moved to Honesdale, Pa., in 1842 and continued the practice of law; prosecuting attorney of Wayne County in 1836 and 1837; member of the State senate 1845–1847; elected as a Democrat to the Thirty-fifth and Thirty-sixth Congresses (March 4, 1857–March 3, 1861); resumed the practice of law; died in Honesdale, Wayne County, Pa., August 2, 1861; interment in Glen Dyberry Cemetery.

DIMOCK, Davis, Jr., a Representative from Pennsylvania; born in Exeter, near Wilkes-Barre, Luzerne County, Pa., September 17, 1801; attended the schools of the pioneer settlement of Montrose, Pa., and the Susquehanna County Academy at Montrose; studied law; was admitted to the bar in 1833 and commenced practice in Montrose, Susquehanna County; also engaged in editorial work; appointed county treasurer in 1834; elected as a Democrat to the Twenty-seventh Congress and served from March 4, 1841, until his death in Montrose, Pa., January 13, 1842; interment in Montrose Cemetery.

DIMOND, Anthony Joseph, a Delegate from the Territory of Alaska; born in Palatine Bridge, Montgomery County, N. Y., November 30, 1881; attended the public schools and St. Mary's Catholic Institute, Amsterdam, N. Y.; taught school in Montgomery County, N. Y., 1900–1903; prospector and miner in Alaska 1904–1912; studied law; was admitted to the bar in 1913 and commenced practice in Valdez, Alaska; United States Commissioner at Chisana, Alaska, in 1913 and 1914; special assistant United States attorney for the third judicial division of Alaska at Valdez in 1917; mayor of Valdez 1920–1922 and 1925–1932; member of the Alaska Territorial senate 1923–1926 and 1929–1932; elected as a Democrat a Delegate to the Seventy-third and to the five succeeding Congresses (March 4, 1933–January 3, 1945); was not a candidate for renomination, having been confirmed as district judge for the third division of Alaska, in which capacity he was serving at the time of death; died in Anchorage, Alaska, May 28, 1953; interment in Anchorage Cemetery.

DINGELL, John David (father of John David Dingell, Jr.), a Representative from Michigan; born in Detroit, Mich., February 2, 1894; newsboy, printer, and newspaperman; engaged in natural-gas pipeline construction; wholesale dealer in beef and pork products; organizer and trustee of Colorado Springs Labor College; elected as a Democrat to the Seventy-third and to the eleven succeeding Congresses and served from March 3, 1933, until his death at Walter Reed Army Medical Center, Washington, D. C., September 19, 1955; interment in Holy Sepulchre Mausoleum, Detroit, Mich.

DINGELL, John David, Jr. (son of the preceding), a Representative from Michigan; born in Colorado Spring, El Paso County, Colo., July 8, 1926; attended Capitol Page School, Washington, D. C., and Georgetown Preparatory School, Garrett Park, Md.; served as a page boy in the United States House of Representatives 1938–1943; was graduated from Georgetown University, Washington, D. C., in 1949 and from Georgetown University Law School in 1952; during World War II served as an infantryman in the Army of the United States from 1944 until discharged as a second lieutenant in 1946; was admitted to the District of Columbia bar in 1952 and to the Michigan bar in 1953; commenced the practice of law in Detroit, Mich., in 1953; served as a research assistant to United States Circuit Judge Theodore Levin in 1952 and 1953; assistant prosecuting attorney of Wayne County, Mich., in 1954 and 1955; delegate to the Democratic National Conventions in 1956 and 1960; elected as a Democrat to the Eighty-fourth Congress to fill the vacancy caused by the death of his father, John D. Dingell, Sr.; reelected to the Eighty-fifth and Eighty-sixth Congresses and served from December 13, 1955, to January 3, 1961. *Reelected to the Eighty-seventh Congress.*

DINGLEY, Nelson, Jr., a Representative from Maine; born in Durham, Androscoggin County, Maine, February 15, 1832; attended the common schools at Unity, Maine, Waterville Seminary, and Waterville College; was graduated from Dartmouth College, Hanover, N. H., in 1855; studied law and was admitted to the bar, but left the profession and became proprietor and editor of the Lewiston (Maine) Journal in 1856; member of the State house of representatives 1862–1865, 1868, and again in 1873, and served as speaker in 1863 and 1864; Governor of Maine in 1874; delegate to the Republican National Convention at Cincinnati in 1876 and at Chicago in 1880; delegate to many Republican State conventions; elected as a Republican to the Forty-seventh Congress to fill the vacancy caused by the resignation of William P. Frye; reelected to the Forty-eighth and to the seven succeeding Congresses and served from September 12, 1881, until his death in Washington, D. C., January 13, 1899, before the close of the Fifty-fifth Congress; had also been reelected to the Fifty-sixth Congress; interment in Oak Hill Cemetery, near Auburn, Maine.

DINSMOOR, Samuel, a Representative from New Hampshire; born in Windham, N. H., July 1, 1766; pursued classical studies; was graduated from Dartmouth College, Hanover, N. H., in 1789; studied law; was admitted to the bar and commenced practice in Keene, N. H.; elected as a War Democrat to the Twelfth Congress (March 4, 1811–March 3, 1813); unsuccessful candidate for reelection in 1812 to the Thirteenth Congress; State councilor in 1821; presidential elector on the Monroe ticket in 1820; judge of probate of Cheshire County 1823–1831; member of the commission to establish the boundary line between the States of New Hampshire and Massachusetts in 1825; Governor of New Hampshire 1831–1833; died in Keene, Cheshire County, N. H., March 15, 1835; interment in Washington Street Cemetery.

DINSMORE, Hugh Anderson, a Representative from Arkansas; born at Cave Springs, Benton County, Ark., on December 24, 1850; attended private schools in Benton and Washington Counties; studied law in Bentonville; appointed clerk of the circuit court for Benton County in 1873; was admitted to the bar in 1874; moved to Fayetteville, Washington County, in 1875 and pursued the practice of law; prosecuting attorney of the fourth judicial district 1878–1884; presidential elector on the Democratic ticket of Cleveland and Hendricks in 1884; in January 1887 was appointed by President Cleveland as Minister Resident and consul general to the Kingdom of Korea and served until May 25, 1890; resumed the practice of law in Fayetteville, Ark.; elected as a Democrat to the Fifty-third and to the five succeeding Congresses (March 4, 1893–March 3, 1905); unsuccessful candidate for renomination in 1904 to the Fifty-ninth Congress; resumed the practice of law in Fayetteville, Ark., and in later years devoted most of his time to the management of his farming interests; member of the board of trustees of the University of Arkansas; died in St. Louis, Mo., where he had gone for medical treatment on May 2, 1930; interment in Evergreen Cemetery, Fayetteville, Ark.

DIRKSEN, Everett McKinley, a Representative and a Senator from Illinois; born in Pekin, Tazewell County, Ill., January 4, 1896; attended grade and high schools and the University of Minnesota College of Law at Minneapolis; during the First World War served overseas as a private and later as a second lieutenant of Field Artillery from January 5, 1918, to October 2, 1919; general manager of a dredging company 1922–1925; commissioner of finance of Pekin, Ill., 1927–1931; studied law; was admitted to the bar in 1936 and commenced practice in Pekin, Ill.; elected as a Republican to the Seventy-third and to the seven succeeding Congresses (March 4, 1933–January 3, 1949); was not a candidate for renomination in 1948; elected as a Republican to the United States Senate in 1950 for the term commencing January 3, 1951; reelected in 1956 for the term ending January 3, 1963.

DISNEY, David Tiernan, a Representative from Ohio; born in Baltimore, Md.; August 25, 1803; moved with his parents to Ohio in 1807; attended the common schools; studied law; was admitted to the bar and commenced practice in Cincinnati; became a writer for a newspaper in 1825; member of the State house of representatives in 1829, 1831, and 1832, and served as speaker in the last-named year; served in the State senate in 1833, 1834, 1843, and 1844, and was president of the senate in 1833; one of the commissioners to adjust the boundary line between the States of Ohio and Michigan in 1834; chairman of the commission to adjust taxes of the counties of Ohio in 1840; delegate to the Democratic National Convention at Baltimore in 1848; elected as a Democrat to the Thirty-first, Thirty-second, and Thirty-third Congresses (March 4, 1849–March 3, 1855); unsuccessful candidate for renomination in 1854; tendered the appointment of Minister to Spain by President Buchanan, but declined; died in Washington, D. C., March 14, 1857; interment in Spring Grove Cemetery, Cincinnati, Ohio.

DISNEY, Wesley Ernest, a Representative from Oklahoma; born in Richland, Shawnee County, Kans., October 31, 1883; attended the public schools of Kansas and was graduated from the law department of the University of Kansas at Lawrence in 1906; was admitted to the Kansas bar in 1906, the Oklahoma bar in 1908, and began practice in Muskogee, Okla., in 1908; county attorney of Muskogee County, Okla., 1911–1915; member of the State house of representatives 1919–1924; chairman of the board of managers in the impeachment trial of Gov. John C. Walton in 1923; delegate to the Kansas State Democratic convention in 1904 and to several Oklahoma State Democratic conventions; elected as a Democrat to the Seventy-second and to the six succeeding Congresses (March 4, 1931–January 3, 1945); was not a candidate for renomination in 1944, but was an unsuccessful candidate for the Democratic nomination for United States Senator; engaged in the practice of law in Washington, D. C., and Tulsa, Okla., until his death in Washington, D. C., March 26, 1961; interment in Memorial Park Cemetery, Tulsa, Okla.

DITTER, John William, a Representative from Pennsylvania; born in Philadelphia, Pa., September 5, 1888; attended the public schools and was graduated from the law department of Temple University, Philadelphia, Pa., in 1913; was admitted to the bar the same year; professor of history and commerce in the Philadelphia (Pa.) high schools 1912-1925; moved to Ambler, Pa., in 1925 and commenced the practice of law; served as workmen's compensation referee for eastern Pennsylvania in 1929; trustee of the Burd Rogers Memorial Home; elected as a Republican to the Seventy-third and to the five succeeding Congresses and served from March 4, 1933, until his death in an airplane crash near Columbia, Lancaster County, Pa., on November 21, 1943; interment in Whitemarsh Memorial Cemetery, Prospectville, Montgomery County, Pa.

DIVEN, Alexander Samuel, a Representative from New York; born in Catharine (later Watkins), N. Y., February 10, 1809; attended the common schools and the academies in Penn Yan and Ovid, N. Y.; studied law; was admitted to the bar in 1831 and commenced practice in Elmira; member of the State senate in 1858; elected as a Republican to the Thirty-seventh Congress (March 4, 1861–March 3, 1863); was not a candidate for renomination in 1862; during the Civil War entered the Army on August 13, 1862, as lieutenant colonel of the One Hundred and Seventh Regiment, New York Volunteer Infantry; promoted to colonel on October 21, 1862; was granted leave of absence from the Army for ninety days to take his seat in Congress; honorably discharged as colonel May 11, 1863; brevetted brigadier general of Volunteers April 30, 1864, for meritorious services during the war; engaged in railroad building and operation 1865-1875; prominently identified with the Erie Railroad; died in Elmira, Chemung County, N. Y., June 11, 1896; interment in Woodlawn Cemetery.

DIX, John Adams (son-in-law of John Jordan Morgan), a Senator from New York; born in Boscawen, N. H., July 24, 1798; completed preparatory studies; during the War of 1812 was appointed a cadet; promoted to ensign in 1813 and took part in the operations on the Canadian frontier; promoted to second lieutenant in March 1814 in the Twenty-first Infantry, stationed at Port Constitution, N. H., and served as adjutant; transferred to the Third Artillery; appointed in 1819 aide-de-camp to General Brown, then in command of the northern military department at Brownsville, where he studied law; later admitted to the bar in Washington, D. C.; resigned his commission in the Army July 29, 1828, having attained the rank of captain; settled in Cooperstown, N. Y., and began the practice of law; moved to Albany in 1830, having been appointed adjutant general of the State by Governor Throop and served from 1831 to 1833; secretary of the Democratic National Convention at Baltimore in 1832; regent of the University of the State of New York, member of the council, and canal commissioner; member of the State house of representatives in 1842; elected as a Democrat to the United States Senate to fill the vacancy caused by the resignation of Silas Wright, Jr., and served from January 27, 1845, to March 3, 1849; was not a candidate for reelection, having become a candidate for Governor; unsuccessful Free-Soil candidate for Governor in 1848; Assistant Treasurer of the United States at New York City from May 20 to November 4, 1853; appointed postmaster of the city of New York May 17, 1860, and served until January 16, 1861; appointed Secretary of the Treasury in the Cabinet of President Buchanan on January 11, 1861, and served until March 3, 1861; served in the Union Army as major general 1861-1865; United States Minister to France from September 24, 1866, to May 23, 1869; served at different times as president of the Mississippi & Missouri Railway Co., the Union Pacific Railroad Co., and the Erie Railroad Co.; elected as a Republican Governor of New York and served from 1873 to 1875; unsuccessful for reelection in 1874 and as the Republican candidate for mayor of New York City in 1876; died in New York City April 21, 1879; interment in Trinity Cemetery, Riverside Drive and One Hundred and Fifty-third Street.

DIXON, Archibald, a Senator from Kentucky; born near Redhouse, Caswell County, N. C., April 2, 1802; moved with his parents to Henderson County, Ky., in 1805; was educated by his mother and attended the common schools for six months; studied law; was admitted to the bar in 1824 and commenced practice in Henderson, Ky.; member of the State house of representatives in 1830 and again in 1841; served in the State senate in 1836; Lieutenant Governor of Kentucky in 1843; member of the State constitutional convention in 1849; elected as a Whig to the United States Senate to fill the vacancy caused by the resignation of Henry Clay and served from September 1, 1852, until March 3, 1855; was not a candidate for reelection in 1854; resumed the practice of law; also engaged as a planter; delegate to the Frankfort peace convention in 1863; was author of the bill to repeal the Missouri Compromise; died in Henderson, Ky., April 23, 1876; interment in Fernwood Cemetery.

DIXON, Henry Aldous, a Representative from Utah; born in Provo, Utah County, Utah, June 29, 1890; attended the public schools; was graduated from Brigham Young University, Provo, Utah, in 1914 from the University of Chicago in 1917, and from the University of Southern California in 1937; instructor at Weber College 1914-1918, president in 1919 and 1920 and 1937-1953; superintendent of Provo city schools 1920-1924 and 1932-1937; managing vice president of Farmers & Merchants Bank 1924-1932; president of Utah Conference of Higher Education in 1938; member of advisory committee, United States Office of Education; member of executive committee, Northwest Accrediting Association; member of President's Commission on Higher Education 1946-1948; member board of directors Salt Lake Branch of Federal Reserve Bank of San Francisco 1945-1951; member of advisory committee, First Security Bank of Utah; director, Association of Junior Colleges, 1950-1954; president of Utah State University at Logan from August 1953 to December 1954; elected as a Republican to the Eighty-fourth, Eighty-fifth, and Eighty-sixth Congresses (January 3, 1955–January 3, 1961); did not seek renomination in 1960; is a resident of Ogden, Utah.

DIXON, James, a Representative and a Senator from Connecticut; born in Enfield, Hartford County, Conn., August 5, 1814; pursued preparatory studies; was graduated from Williams College, Williamstown, Mass., in 1834; studied law; was admitted to the bar in 1834 and commenced practice in Enfield, Conn.; member of the State house of representatives in 1837, 1838, and 1844, and served as speaker in 1837; moved to Hartford, Conn., in 1839 and continued the practice of law; elected as a Whig to the Twenty-ninth and Thirtieth Congresses (March 4, 1845–March 3, 1849); again a member of the State house of representatives in 1854; declined the nomination for Governor of Connecticut in 1854; unsuccessful candidate for United States Senator in 1854; elected as a Republican to the United States Senate in 1856; reelected in 1863, and served from March 4, 1857, to March 3, 1869; unsuccessful Democratic candidate for the United States Senate in 1868 and as a Democratic candidate for election the same year to the Forty-first Congress; delegate from Connecticut to the convention held at Philadelphia, Pa., August 14, 1866, in support of the policies of President Johnson; appointed Minister to Russia in 1869 but declined; engaged in literary pursuits and extensive traveling until his death in Hartford, Conn., March 27, 1873; interment in Cedar Hill Cemetery.

DIXON, Joseph, a Representative from North Carolina; born in Greene County, near Farmville, Pitt County, N. C., April 9, 1828; attended the public schools and was tutored privately; engaged in agricultural pursuits and also in the mercantile business; appointed colonel of the North Carolina State Militia soon after the Civil War; judge of the county court in 1864 and 1865; member of the State house of commons 1865–1867; elected as a Republican to the Forty-first Congress to fill the vacancy caused by the death of David Heaton; took his seat December 5, 1870, and served until March 3, 1871; was not a candidate for renomination in 1870; United States Commissioner of Claims in 1871 and 1872; resumed agricultural pursuits; delegate from Greene County to the State constitutional convention in 1875; died near Fountain Hill, Pitt County, N. C., March 3, 1883; interment in Edwards Chapel Cemetery in Lenoir County.

DIXON, Joseph Andrew, a Representative from Ohio; born in Cincinnati, Ohio, June 3, 1879; attended St. Patrick's School, Hughes High School, and St. Xavier University, Cincinnati, Ohio; clerk in a mercantile store 1893–1900; moved to Anderson, Ind., and engaged in retail clothing business in 1900 and later operated a clothing store in Hartford City, Ind., returning to Cincinnati to engage in the same business; also was manager and owner of amateur and professional baseball teams; honorary member of the executive board, Boy Scouts of America; active in young men's welfare work; elected as a Democrat to the Seventy-fifth Congress (January 3, 1937–January 3, 1939); unsuccessful candidate for reelection in 1938 to the Seventy-sixth Congress and for election in 1940 to the Seventy-seventh Congress; resumed his former business pursuits in Cincinnati, Ohio, until his death there on July 4, 1942; interment in St. Joseph's Cemetery.

DIXON, Joseph Moore, a Representative and a Senator from Montana; born in Snow Camp, Alamance County, N. C., July 31, 1867; attended Earlham College, Richmond, Ind., and was graduated from Guilford College, North Carolina, in May 1889; moved to Missoula, Missoula County, Mont., in 1891; studied law; was admitted to the bar in December 1892; assistant prosecuting attorney of Missoula County 1893–1895; prosecuting attorney 1895–1897; member of the State house of representatives in 1900; delegate to the Republican National Convention at Chicago in 1904; elected as a Republican to the Fifty-eighth and Fifty-ninth Congresses (March 4, 1903–March 3, 1907); delegate at large to the Republican National Conventions in 1904 and 1916; elected to the United States Senate in 1906 and served from March 4, 1907, to March 3, 1913; unsuccessful candidate for reelection in 1912; chairman of the National Progressive Convention in 1912; engaged in newspaper publishing and was also interested in dairy farming; Governor of Montana 1921–1925; unsuccessful candidate for reelection in 1924; unsuccessful candidate for election to the United States Senate in 1928; First Assistant Secretary of the Interior 1929–1933; died at Missoula, Mont., May 22, 1934; interment in Missoula Cemetery.

DIXON, Lincoln, a Representative from Indiana; born in Vernon, Jennings County, Ind., on February 9, 1860; attended Vernon Academy, and was graduated from Indiana University at Bloomington in 1880; employed as a clerk in the Department of the Interior at Washington, D. C., in 1881; returned to Vernon, Ind., and studied law; was admitted to the bar in 1882 and commenced practice in North Vernon; reading clerk of the State house of representatives in 1883; prosecuting attorney for the sixth judicial circuit 1884–1892; member of the Democratic State committee 1897–1904 and 1920–1927; elected as a Democrat to the Fifty-ninth and to the six succeeding Congresses (March 4,

1905–March 3, 1919); unsuccessful candidate for reelection in 1918 to the Sixty-sixth Congress; resumed the practice of law; delegate to the Democratic National Conventions in 1920 and 1924; in charge of the Democratic campaign in the West in 1924; appointed a member of the United States Tariff Commission by President Coolidge in 1927 and retired in 1930; reappointed by President Hoover on June 17, 1931, and served until his death, while on a visit, in Lyndon, Ky., September 16, 1932; interment in Vernon Cemetery, Vernon, Ind.

DIXON, Nathan Fellows, a Senator from Rhode Island; born in Plainfield, Conn., December 13, 1774; attended Plainfield Academy, and was graduated from the College of Rhode Island (now Brown University) in 1799; studied law; was admitted to the bar in 1801 and commenced practice in New London County, Conn.; moved to Westerly, R. I., in 1802 and continued the practice of law; also engaged in banking, serving as president of the Washington Bank of Westerly from 1829 until his death; member of the State house of representatives 1813–1830; served as a colonel in the State militia; elected as a Whig to the United States Senate and served from March 4, 1839, until his death in Washington, D. C., January 29, 1842; interment in River Bend Cemetery, Westerly, Washington County, R. I.

DIXON, Nathan Fellows (son of the preceding), a Representative from Rhode Island; born in Westerly, R. I., May 1, 1812; attended Plainfield (Conn.) Academy, and was graduated from Brown University, Providence, R. I., in 1833; later pursued the study of law at the Cambridge (Mass.) and New Haven (Conn.) Law Schools; was admitted to the bar in 1837 and commenced practice in Westerly, R. I.; also engaged in banking; member of the State house of representatives 1841–1849, 1851–1854, 1858–1862, and 1871–1877; appointed a member of the Governor's council in 1842; presidential elector on the Whig ticket of Clay and Frelinghuysen in 1844; elected as a Whig to the Thirty-first Congress (March 4, 1849–March 3, 1851); was not a candidate for renomination in 1850; elected as a Republican to the Thirty-eighth and to the three succeeding Congresses (March 4, 1863–March 3, 1871); declined to be a candidate for reelection in 1870; delegate to the Union National Convention at Philadelphia in 1866; resumed the practice of law and banking; died in Westerly, Washington County, R. I., April 11, 1881; interment in River Bend Cemetery.

DIXON, Nathan Fellows (son of the preceding), a Representative and a Senator from Rhode Island; born in Westerly, Washington County, R. I., August 28, 1847; attended the common schools of Westerly and Phillips Academy, Andover, Mass.; was graduated from Brown University, Providence, R. I., in 1869 and from Albany (N. Y.) Law School in 1871; was admitted to the bar in 1871 and commenced practice in Westerly, R. I.; United States attorney for the district of Rhode Island 1877–1885; elected as a Republican to the Forty-eighth Congress to fill the vacancy caused by the resignation of Jonathan Chace and served from February 12 to March 3, 1885; was not a candidate for renomination; member of the State senate 1885–1889; elected to the United States Senate to fill the vacancy caused by the resignation of Jonathan Chace and served from April 10, 1889, to March 3, 1895; was not a candidate for reelection; resumed the practice of law and engaged in banking; died in Westerly, R. I., November 8, 1897; interment in River Bend Cemetery.

DIXON, William Wirt, a Representative from Montana; born in Brooklyn, N. Y., June 3, 1838; moved to Illinois in 1843 and to Keokuk, Iowa, in 1849; pursued preparatory studies; studied law in Keokuk and was admitted to the bar in 1858;

moved to Tennessee in 1860, in the same year to Arkansas, then to California in 1862, and thence to Humboldt County, Nev.; in 1866 moved to Montana and resided in Helena and later in Deer Lodge until 1879; member of the Territorial house of representatives in 1871 and 1872; spent two years in the Black Hills; returned to Montana in 1881, settled in Butte, and engaged in the practice of law; delegate to the constitutional conventions of Montana in 1884 and 1889; elected as a Democrat to the Fifty-second Congress (March 4, 1891–March 3, 1893); unsuccessful candidate for reelection to the Fifty-third Congress; resumed the practice of his profession; candidate for election to the United States Senate, but the legislature failed to make a choice; died in Los Angeles, Calif., November 13, 1910; interment in Calvary Cemetery; reinterment in Rock Creek Cemetery, Washington, D. C., March 15, 1911.

DOAN, Robert Eachus, a Representative from Ohio; born near Wilmington, Clinton County, Ohio, July 23, 1831; attended the common schools and completed an academic course; taught school three years in southern Ohio; was graduated from the Cincinnati Law School in 1857; was admitted to the bar the same year and commenced practice in Wilmington, Ohio; editor of the Wilmington Watchman in 1859 and 1860; prosecuting attorney of Clinton County in 1862; presidential elector on the Republican ticket of Garfield and Arthur in 1880; elected as a Republican to the Fifty-second Congress (March 4, 1891–March 3, 1893); unsuccessful candidate for renomination in 1892; resumed the practice of law in Washington, D. C.; died in Wilmington, Ohio, February 24, 1919; interment in Sugar Grove Cemetery.

DOAN, William, a Representative from Ohio; born in Maine April 4, 1792; attended the common schools; moved with his parents in 1812 to Ohio and settled near Lindale, Clermont County; studied medicine at New Richmond and commenced practice in 1818 at Withamsville, Clermont County; was graduated from the Ohio Medical College at Cincinnati in 1827; member of the State house of representatives in 1831 and 1832; served in the State senate in 1833 and 1834; elected as a Democrat to the Twenty-sixth and Twenty-seventh Congresses (March 4, 1839–March 3, 1843); was not a candidate for renomination in 1842; resumed the practice of medicine; died in Withamsville, Clermont County, Ohio, June 22, 1847; interment in Union Township (Mount Moriah) Cemetery, Tobasco, Clermont County, Ohio.

DOBBIN, James Cochrane (grandson of James Cochran of North Carolina), a Representative from North Carolina; born in Fayetteville, N. C., January 17, 1814; attended the Fayetteville Academy and the William Bingham School, Hillsboro, N. C.; was graduated from the University of North Carolina at Chapel Hill in 1832; studied law; was admitted to the bar in 1835 and commenced practice in Fayetteville; elected as a Democrat to the Twenty-ninth Congress (March 4, 1845–March 3, 1847); declined to be a candidate for renomination in 1846; resumed the practice of law; member of the State house of commons in 1848, 1850, and 1852, serving as speaker in 1850; delegate to the Democratic National Convention at Baltimore in 1852; Secretary of the Navy in the Cabinet of President Pierce from March 7, 1853, to March 6, 1857; died in Fayetteville, Cumberland County, N. C., August 4, 1857; interment in Cross Creek Cemetery.

DOBBINS, Donald Claude, a Representative from Illinois; born on a farm near Dewey, Champaign County, Ill., March 20, 1878; attended the public schools, the University of Illinois at Urbana, Dixon (Ill.) Business College, and George Washington University, Washington, D. C.; taught school 1896–1899; stenographer and correspondent 1900–1906; United States post office inspector 1906–1909; studied law; was admitted to the bar in 1909 and commenced practice in Champaign, Ill.; delegate to the Democratic National Convention at Philadelphia in 1936; presidential elector in 1940 on the ticket of Roosevelt and Wallace; elected as a Democrat to the Seventy-third and Seventy-fourth Congresses (March 4, 1933–January 3, 1937); was not a candidate for renomination in 1936; resumed the practice of law; died in Champaign, Ill., February 14, 1943; interment in Mount Hope Cemetery.

DOBBINS, Samuel Atkinson, a Representative from New Jersey; born near Vincentown, Burlington County, N. J., April 14, 1814; attended private and public schools; engaged in agricultural pursuits; moved to Mount Holly, N. J., in 1838 and continued farming; high sheriff of Burlington County 1854–1857; member of the State house of assembly 1859–1861; delegate to the Republican National Convention in 1864; trustee of Pennington (N. J.) Seminary 1866–1886, serving as president of the board of trustees for ten years; elected as a Republican to the Forty-third and Forty-fourth Congresses (March 4, 1873–March 3, 1877); was not a candidate for renomination in 1876; resumed agricultural pursuits; died in Mount Holly, Burlington County, N. J., May 26, 1886; interment in Mount Holly Cemetery.

DOCKERY, Alexander Monroe, a Representative from Missouri; born near Gallatin, Daviess County, Mo., February 11, 1845; attended the common schools and Macon Academy, Macon, Mo.; studied medicine; was graduated from the St. Louis (Mo.) Medical College March 2, 1865, and commenced practice near Linneus, Linn County; attended lectures at Bellevue College, New York City, and Jefferson Medical College, Philadelphia, during the winter of 1865–66; returned to Missouri and settled in Chillicothe, where he continued the practice of his profession for seven years; president of the Board of Education of Chillicothe, Mo., 1870–1872; served as county physician of Livingston County; abandoned medicine in March 1874, and returned to Gallatin, Mo., where he assisted in organizing the Farmers' Exchange Bank, of which he was cashier; one of the curators of the University of Missouri at Columbia 1872–1882; chairman of the congressional committee of his district; member of the city council of Gallatin 1878–1881; mayor 1881–1883; delegate to and chairman of the Democratic State conventions in 1886 and 1901; elected as a Democrat to the Forty-eighth and to the seven succeeding Congresses (March 4, 1883–March 3, 1899); was not a candidate for renomination in 1898; Governor of Missouri 1901–1905; delegate to the Democratic National Convention at St. Louis in 1904; appointed Third Assistant Postmaster General on March 17, 1913, and served until his resignation on March 31, 1921, owing to failing health; died in Gallatin, Mo., December 26, 1926; interment in Edgewood Cemetery, Chillicothe, Livingston County, Mo.

DOCKERY, Alfred (father of Oliver Hart Dockery), a Representative from North Carolina; born near Rockingham, Richmond County, N. C., December 11, 1797; attended the public schools; engaged in planting; member of the State house of commons in 1822; member of the State constitutional convention in 1835; served in the State senate 1836–1844; elected as a Whig to the Twenty-ninth Congress (March 4, 1845–March 3, 1847); declined to be a candidate for reelection in 1846 to the Thirtieth Congress; elected to the Thirty-second Congress (March 4, 1851–March 3, 1853); unsuccessful Whig candidate for Governor of North Carolina in 1854; died near Rockingham, Richmond County, N. C., on December 7, 1875; interment in the family cemetery.

DOCKERY, Oliver Hart (son of Alfred Dockery), a Representative from North Carolina; born near Rockingham, Richmond County, N. C., August 12, 1830; attended the public schools and Wake Forest (N. C.) College; was graduated from the University of North Carolina at Chapel Hill in 1848; studied law, but never practiced; engaged in agricultural pursuits; member of the State house of representatives in 1858 and 1859; served for a short time in the Confederate service, but withdrew and advocated sustaining the Federal Government; upon the readmission of North Carolina to representation was elected as a Republican to the Fortieth Congress; reelected to the Forty-first Congress and served from July 13, 1868, to March 3, 1871; unsuccessful candidate for reelection in 1870 to the Forty-second Congress; again engaged in agricultural pursuits; member of the State constitutional convention in 1875; unsuccessful candidate for Governor in 1888; appointed United States consul general at Rio de Janeiro, Brazil, on June 14, 1889, and served until July 1, 1893; resumed agricultural pursuits; died in a hospital in Baltimore, Md., March 21, 1906; interment in the family cemetery at Mangum, Richmond County, N. C.

DOCKWEILER, John Francis, a Representative from California; born in Los Angeles, Calif., September 19, 1895; attended parochial schools; was graduated from Loyola College, Los Angeles, Calif., in 1918 and from the University of Southern California, Los Angeles, Calif., in 1921; attended the law department of Harvard University, Cambridge, Mass.; was admitted to the bar September 6, 1921, and commenced practice in Los Angeles, Calif., in 1922; elected as a Democrat to the Seventy-third, Seventy-fourth, and Seventy-fifth Congresses (March 4, 1933–January 3, 1939); was not a candidate for renomination in the primaries in 1938, but was an unsuccessful candidate for nomination as Governor; in the general election was an unsuccessful Independent candidate for reelection to the Seventy-sixth Congress; resumed the practice of law; district attorney of Los Angeles County 1940–1943; died in Los Angeles, Calif., January 31, 1943; interment in Calvary Cemetery.

DODD, Edward, a Representative from New York; born in Salem, Washington County, N. Y., August 25, 1805; attended the public schools; engaged in mercantile pursuits; moved to Argyle, N. Y., in 1835; county clerk of Washington County 1835–1844; delegate to the State constitutional convention in 1846; elected as a Whig to the Thirty-fourth and Thirty-fifth Congresses (March 4, 1855–March 3, 1859); United States marshal for the northern district of New York from April 1863 to April 1869; editor of the County Post for thirty years; presidential elector on the Republican ticket of Blaine and Logan in 1884; trustee of the Argyle Academy for fifty-one years; president of the village of Argyle for eight years; member of the Republican State committee for many years; died in Argyle, Washington County, N. Y., March 1, 1891; interment in Prospect Hill Cemetery.

DODD, Thomas Joseph, a Representative and a Senator from Connecticut; born in Norwich, New London County, Conn., May 15, 1907; attended the public schools; graduated from St. Anselm's Preparatory School in 1926, Providence College in 1930, and Yale University Law School in 1933; special agent for Federal Bureau of Investigation in 1933 and 1934; Connecticut director of National Youth Administration 1935–1938; assistant to five successive United States Attorneys General 1938–1945; vice chairman, Board of Review, and later executive trial counsel, Office of the United States Chief of Counsel for the Prosecution of Axis Criminality at Nürnburg, Germany, in 1945 and 1946 and was the recipient of several awards for his work; engaged in private practice of law in Hartford, Conn., since 1947; delegate

to the Democratic National Conventions in 1936, 1948, and 1952; elected as a Democrat to the Eighty-third and Eighty-fourth Congresses (January 3, 1953–January 3, 1957); was not a candidate for renomination in 1956 but was unsuccessful for election to the United States Senate; elected to the United States Senate November 4, 1958, for the term commencing January 3, 1959, and ending January 3, 1965.

DODDRIDGE, Philip, a Representative from Virginia; born in Bedford County, Va., May 17, 1773; reared on a farm; moved to Brooke County, Va. (now West Virginia); attended school in Wellsburg (then Charleston), Va. (now West Virginia); studied law and was admitted to the bar in 1797; member of the House of Delegates of Virginia in 1815, 1816, 1822, 1823, 1828, and 1829; delegate to the Virginia constitutional convention in 1829; unsuccessful candidate for election in 1822 to the Eighteenth Congress and in 1824 to the Nineteenth Congress; elected to the Twenty-first and Twenty-second Congresses and served from March 4, 1829, until his death in Washington, D. C., November 19, 1832; interment in the Congressional Cemetery.

DODDS, Francis Henry, a Representative from Michigan; born on a farm near Waddington, Louisville Township, St. Lawrence County, N. Y., June 9, 1858; attended the local schools; moved with his parents to Isabella County, Mich., in 1866; was graduated from Olivet (Mich.) College; taught school at Farwell and Mount Pleasant; was graduated from the law department of the University of Michigan at Ann Arbor in 1880; was admitted to the bar the same year and commenced the practice of law at Mount Pleasant, Mich.; moved to Bay City, Mich., in 1884 and continued the practice of his profession; returned to Mount Pleasant, Mich., in 1886 and continued the practice of law; served as city attorney of Mount Pleasant 1892–1894; member of the board of education 1894–1897; elected as a Republican to the Sixty-first and Sixty-second Congresses (March 4, 1909–March 3, 1913); unsuccessful candidate for renomination in 1912; resumed the practice of law in Mount Pleasant, Mich., until his death in that city on December 23, 1940; interment in Riverside Cemetery.

DODDS, Ozro John, a Representative from Ohio; born in Cincinnati, Ohio, March 22, 1840; attended the common schools, and Miami University, Oxford, Ohio, for four years; during the Civil War organized Captain Dodd's university company and enlisted on April 18, 1861, as captain of Company B, Twentieth Ohio Volunteer Regiment; captain of Company F, Eighty-first Ohio Volunteer Infantry, and acting assistant quartermaster from September 1, 1861, to January 1, 1863; became lieutenant colonel of the First Alabama Union Cavalry October 18, 1863, and was honorably discharged from the service as such May 2, 1864; at the close of the war was given his graduation degree from Miami University; studied law at Cincinnati Law School; was admitted to the bar in 1866 and commenced practice in Cincinnati; member of the State house of representatives in 1870 and 1871; elected as a Democrat to the Forty-second Congress to fill the vacancy caused by the resignation of Aaron F. Perry and served from October 8, 1872, to March 3, 1873; was not a candidate for renomination in 1872; resumed the practice of law at Cincinnati; died in Columbus, Ohio, April 18, 1882; interment in Spring Grove Cemetery, Cincinnati, Ohio.

DODGE, Augustus Caesar (son of Henry Dodge), a Delegate and a Senator from Iowa; born in Ste. Genevieve, Mo., January 2, 1812; self-educated, having attended school less than six months; moved to Illinois in 1827 with his parents, who settled in Galena; was employed there in various capacities in his father's lead mines; served in the Black Hawk and other Indian wars; moved to Burlington, Iowa, in 1837, where he served as register of the land office from 1838 to 1840; elected as a Democrat a Delegate to the Twenty-sixth Congress to fill the vacancy caused by the act of March 3, 1839; reelected to the Twenty-seventh, Twenty-eighth, and Twenty-ninth Congresses and served from October 28, 1840, to December 28, 1846, when the Territory of Iowa was admitted as a State into the Union; was then elected to the United States Senate; reelected in 1849, and served from December 7, 1848, to February 22, 1855, when he resigned, having previously been appointed Minister to Spain, serving from February 23, 1855, to March 12, 1859; unsuccessful candidate for Governor of Iowa in 1859; delegate to the Democratic National Convention at Chicago in 1864; mayor of Burlington in 1874 and 1875; withdrew from political activities and engaged in lecturing at pioneer gatherings; died in Burlington, Des Moines County, Iowa, November 20, 1883; interment in Aspen Grove Cemetery.

DODGE, Grenville Mellen, a Representative from Iowa; born in Danvers, Essex County, Mass., April 12, 1831; attended the Danvers public schools and Durham Academy, New Hampshire; was graduated as a civil engineer from Norwich University, Vermont, in 1851; moved to Iowa and settled in Council Bluffs; member of the city council of Council Bluffs in 1860; during the Civil War entered the Union Army as colonel of the Fourth Iowa Volunteer Infantry on July 6, 1861; promoted to brigadier general of Volunteers March 21, 1862, and major general June 7, 1864; resigned from the Army May 30, 1866; chief engineer of the Union Pacific Railroad 1866–1870; elected as a Republican to the Fortieth Congress (March 4, 1867–March 3, 1869); declined to be a candidate for renomination in 1868; delegate to the Republican National Convention at Chicago in 1868, at Philadelphia in 1872, and at Cincinnati in 1876; settled in New York City, but retained his residence in Council Bluffs, Pottawattamie County, Iowa; president of the commission to inquire into the management of the war with Spain; extensively interested in western railroad building and management; died in Council Bluffs, Iowa, January 3, 1916; interment in Walnut Hill Cemetery.

DODGE, Henry (father of Augustus Caesar Dodge), a Delegate and a Senator from Wisconsin; born in Vincennes, Ind., October 12, 1782; received a limited schooling; moved to Missouri in 1796 and settled at Ste. Genevieve; sheriff of Cape Girardeau County in 1808; moved to Galena, Ill., and operated a lead mine; moved to Wisconsin in 1827 when it was a part of Michigan Territory, and settled near the present site of Dodgeville; served in the Black Hawk and other Indian wars; was commissioned major of United States Rangers on June 21, 1832; left the Army as colonel of the First United States Dragoons in July 1836; appointed Governor of the Territory of Wisconsin in 1836 and served until 1841; elected as a Democrat a Delegate to the Twenty-seventh and Twenty-eighth Congresses (March 4, 1841–March 3, 1845); was not a candidate for renomination in 1844, having again accepted the appointment of Governor of the Territory of Wisconsin, and served from 1845 until 1848; upon the admission of Wisconsin as a State into the Union in 1848 was elected to the United States Senate; reelected in 1851 and served from June 8, 1848, to March 3, 1857; declined the appointment of Governor of Washington Territory by President Pierce in 1857; retired to private life; died in Burlington, Des Moines County, Iowa, June 19, 1867; interment in Aspen Grove Cemetery.

DODGE, William Earle, a Representative from New York; born in Hartford, Conn., September 4, 1805; completed preparatory studies; moved to New York City in 1818; became a clerk; in 1826 established the house of Phelps, Dodge & Co., of which he was the head for forty years; delegate to the peace convention of 1861 held in Washington, D. C., in an effort to devise means to prevent the impending war; successfully contested as a Republican the election of James Brooks to the Thirty-ninth Congress and served from April 7, 1866, to March 3, 1867; declined to be a candidate for renomination in 1866; resumed business interests; presidential elector on the Republican ticket of Grant and Wilson in 1872; died in New York City February 9, 1883; interment in Woodlawn Cemetery.

DOE, Nicholas Bartlett, a Representative from New York; born in New York City on June 16, 1786; was graduated from Phillips Exeter Academy, Exeter, N. H.; studied law; was admitted to the bar and practiced; settled in Saratoga County, N. Y.; elected as a Whig to the Twenty-sixth Congress to fill the vacancy caused by the death of Anson Brown; took his seat on December 7, 1840, and served until March 3, 1841; resumed the practice of law; trustee of the village of Waterford, Saratoga County, in 1841; died at Saratoga Springs, N. Y., December 6, 1856; interment in Greenridge Cemetery.

DOIG, Andrew Wheeler, a Representative from New York; born in Salem, Washington County, N. Y., July 24, 1799; pursued an academic course; moved to Lowville, N. Y., and engaged in mercantile pursuits; town clerk of Lowville in 1825; county clerk of Lewis County 1825–1831; member of the State assembly in 1832; moved to Martinsburg, N. Y., in 1833; cashier of the Lewis County Bank in 1833 and 1834; returned to Lowville; surrogate of Lewis County 1835–1840; elected as a Democrat to the Twenty-sixth and Twenty-seventh Congresses (March 4, 1839–March 3, 1843); member of the board of directors and vice president of the Bank of Lowville 1843–1847; moved to California in 1849 and engaged in mining; returned in 1850 to Lowville, Lewis County, N. Y., where he resided until late in life; clerk in the customhouse, New York City, 1853–1857; died in Brooklyn, N. Y., July 11, 1875; interment in the Rural Cemetery, Lowville, N. Y.

DOLLINGER, Isidore, a Representative from New York; born in New York, N. Y., November 13, 1903; was graduated from New York University in 1925 and from New York Law School in 1928; was admitted to the bar in 1929 and commenced the practice of law in New York City; served in the State assembly 1937–1944; member of the State senate 1945–1948; elected as a Democrat to the Eighty-first and to the five succeeding Congresses and served from January 3, 1949, until his resignation December 31, 1959; elected district attorney, Bronx County, New York, in November 1959 and took office January 1, 1960, for a four-year term; resides in New York, N. Y.

DOLLIVER, James Isaac (nephew of Jonathan Prentiss Dolliver), a Representative from Iowa; born in Park Ridge, Cook County, Ill., August 31, 1894; attended the public schools and the high school at Hot Springs, S. Dak.; was graduated from Morningside College, Sioux City, Iowa, in 1915; taught school at Alta and Humboldt, Iowa, 1915–1917; during the First World War served in the United States Army as a private in the Third Service Company of the Signal Corps; was graduated from the University of Chicago Law School in 1921; was admitted to the bar the same year and commenced practice in Chicago, Ill.; moved to Fort Dodge, Webster County, Iowa, in 1922; prosecuting attorney of Webster County, Iowa, 1924–1929; member of the school board of Fort Dodge Independent School District 1938–1945; elected as a Republican to the Seventy-ninth and to the five succeeding Congresses (January 3, 1945–January 3, 1957); unsuccessful for reelection in 1956 to the Eighty-fifth Congress; resumed the practice of law; is a resident of Spirit Lake, Iowa.

DOLLIVER, Jonathan Prentiss (uncle of James Isaac Dolliver), a Representative and a Senator from Iowa; born near Kingwood, Preston County, Va. (now West Virginia), February 6, 1858; attended the public schools, and was graduated from the University of West Virginia at Morgantown in 1876; studied law; was admitted to the bar in 1878 and commenced practice in Fort Dodge, Iowa; city solicitor of Fort Dodge 1880–1887; elected as a Republican to the Fifty-first and to the five succeeding Congresses and served from March 4, 1889, to August 22, 1900, when he resigned to become Senator; appointed to the United States Senate in 1900 to fill the vacancy in the term ending March 3, 1901, caused by the death of John H. Gear; reappointed and subsequently elected for the term beginning March 4, 1901; reelected in 1907 and served from August 22, 1900, until his death in Fort Dodge, Iowa, October 15, 1910; interment in Oakland Cemetery.

DOLPH, Joseph Norton (uncle of Frederick William Mulkey), a Senator from Oregon; born in Dolphsburg, Tompkins (now Schuyler) County, N. Y., October 19, 1835; attended the common schools and the Genesee Wesleyan Seminary, Lima, N. Y.; taught school and studied law; was admitted to the bar in Binghamton, N. Y., in November 1861 and commenced practice in Schuyler County, N. Y.; in 1862 enlisted in Capt. M. Crawford's company, known as the Oregon Escort, raised under an act of Congress for the purpose of protecting against hostile Indians emigrants crossing the Plains that year to the Pacific coast; filled the position of orderly sergeant; settled in Portland, Oreg., in October 1862; city attorney in 1864 and 1865; United States district attorney 1865–1868; member of the State senate in 1866, 1868, 1872, and 1874; engaged in various enterprises; elected as a Republican to the United States Senate in 1882; reelected in 1888 and served from March 4, 1883, to March 3, 1895; unsuccessful candidate for reelection in 1894; resumed the practice of law in Portland, Oreg., where he died on March 10, 1897; interment in Riverview Cemetery.

DOMENGEAUX, James, a Representative from Louisiana; born in Lafayette, Lafayette Parish, La., January 6, 1907; attended Mount Carmel Academy, Cathedral High School, Southwestern Louisiana Institute at Lafayette, and Loyola University, New Orleans, La.; was graduated from the law department of Tulane University, New Orleans, La., in 1931; was admitted to the bar the same year and commenced practice in Lafayette, La.; member of the State house of representatives in 1940; elected as a Democrat to the Seventy-seventh Congress; reelected to the Seventy-eighth Congress and served from January 3, 1941, to April 15, 1944, when he resigned to join the armed forces of the United States; served as a private in the Combat Engineers until his medical discharge; was subsequently elected to fill the vacancy in the Seventy-eighth Congress caused by his own resignation; reelected to the Seventy-ninth and Eightieth Congresses and served from November 7, 1944, to January 3, 1949; was not a candidate for renomination in 1948, but was an unsuccessful candidate for the Democratic nomination for United States Senator; resumed the practice of law, and is a resident of Lafayette, La.

DOMINICK, Frederick Haskell, a Representative from South Carolina; born in Peak, Newberry County, S. C., February 20, 1877; attended the public schools of Columbia, Newberry (S. C.) College, South Carolina College at Columbia, and the law school of the University of Virginia at Charlottesville; was admitted to the bar in 1898 and commenced practice in Newberry, S. C.; member of the State house of representatives 1900–1902; delegate to every Democratic State convention since 1900, with the exception of 1914; chairman of the Democratic county committee 1906–1914; assistant attorney general of South Carolina

1913–1916; delegate to the Democratic National Conventions in 1920 and 1924; elected as a Democrat to the Sixty-fifth and to the seven succeeding Congresses (March 4, 1917–March 3, 1933); unsuccessful candidate for renomination in 1932; one of the managers appointed by the House of Representatives in 1926 to conduct the impeachment proceedings against George W. English, judge of the United States District Court for the Eastern District of Illinois; during World War II served as assistant to the Attorney General, Department of Justice, Washington, D. C.; practiced law in Newberry, S. C., until his death there March 11, 1960; interment in Rosemont Cemetery.

DONAHEY, Alvin Victor, a Senator from Ohio; born in Cadwallader, Tuscarawas County, Ohio, July 7, 1873; attended the public schools; learned the printer's trade; employed as a journeyman at New Philadelphia, Ohio, 1893–1905; clerk of Goshen Township, Tuscarawas County, Ohio, 1898–1903; county auditor 1905–1909; member of the board of education of New Philadelphia, Ohio, 1909–1911; delegate to the fourth Ohio constitutional convention in 1912; State auditor 1912; unsuccessful candidate for Governor of Ohio in 1920; elected Governor in 1922 and served three consecutive terms 1923–1929; elected as a Democrat to the United States Senate in 1934 and served from January 3, 1935, to January 3, 1941; was not a candidate for renomination in 1940; engaged in the insurance business and in the manufacture of clay products in Columbus, Ohio; was also interested in banking; died in Columbus, Ohio, April 8, 1946; interment in East Avenue Cemetery, New Philadelphia, Ohio.

DONDERO, George Anthony, a Representative from Michigan; born in Greenfield Township, Wayne County, Mich., on December 16, 1883; attended the public schools; served as village clerk of Royal Oak in 1905 and 1906, as town treasurer in 1907 and 1908, and as village assessor in 1909; was graduated from the Detroit College of Law, Detroit, Mich., in 1910; was admitted to the bar the same year and commenced practice in Royal Oak, Mich.; village attorney 1911–1921; assistant prosecuting attorney for Oakland County, Mich., in 1918 and 1919; mayor of Royal Oak in 1921 and 1922; member of the board of education 1910–1928; elected as a Republican to the Seventy-third and to the eleven succeeding Congresses (March 4, 1933–January 3, 1957); was not a candidate for renomination in 1956; resumed the practice of law; is a resident of Royal Oak, Mich.

DONLEY, Joseph Benton, a Representative from Pennsylvania; born in Mount Morris, Greene County, Pa., on October 10, 1838; completed preparatory studies; was graduated from Waynesburg (Pa.) College in 1859; member of the faculty of Abingdon (Ill.) College 1860–1862; entered the Union Army during the Civil War as a captain in the Eighty-third Regiment, Illinois Volunteer Infantry, in 1862 and served throughout the war; was graduated from the Albany (N. Y.) Law School in 1866; was admitted to the bar in 1867 and commenced practice in Waynesburg, Greene County, Pa.; referee in bankruptcy in 1867 and 1868; elected as a Republican to the Forty-first Congress (March 4, 1869–March 3, 1871); unsuccessful candidate for reelection in 1870 to the Forty-second Congress; resumed the practice of his profession in Waynesburg, Green County, Pa., and died there January 23, 1917; interment in Green Mount Cemetery.

DONNAN, William G., a Representative from Iowa; born in West Charlton, N. Y., June 30, 1834; attended the district schools and Cambridge Academy; was graduated from Union College, New York, in 1856; moved to Independence, Iowa, in 1856; studied law; was admitted to the bar in 1856 and commenced practice at Independence in 1857; treasurer and recorder of Buchanan County 1857–1862; during the Civil War entered the Union Army as a private in Company H, Twenty-seventh Iowa Infantry, in 1862; promoted to the grade of first lieutenant and brevetted captain and major for efficient service in the field; was adjutant on the staff of Gen. James J. Gilbert; member of the State senate in 1868 and 1870; elected as a Republican to the Forty-second and Forty-third Congresses (March 4, 1871–March 3, 1875); declined to be a candidate for reelection in 1874 to the Forty-fourth Congress; resumed the practice of law at Independence; delegate at large to the Republican National Convention at Chicago in 1884; chairman of the Republican State central committee 1884–1886; again a member of the State senate 1884–1886; died in Independence, Buchanan County, Iowa, December 4, 1908; interment in Oakwood Cemetery.

DONNELL, Forrest C., a Senator from Missouri; born in Quitman, Nodaway County, Mo., August 20, 1884; attended the public schools and Maryville (Mo.) High School; was graduated from the University of Missouri at Columbia in 1904 and from its law school in 1907; was admitted to the bar in 1907 and commenced practice in St. Louis, Mo.; city attorney of Webster Groves, Mo.; Governor of Missouri 1941–1945; delegate to the Republican National Convention in 1948; elected as a Republican to the United States Senate and served from January 3, 1945, to January 3, 1951; was an unsuccessful candidate for reelection in 1950; engaged in the practice of law; is a resident of St. Louis, Mo.

DONNELL, Richard Spaight (grandson of Richard Dobbs Spaight), a Representative from North Carolina; born in New Bern, N. C., September 20, 1820; attended New Bern Academy and Yale College; was graduated from the University of North Carolina at Chapel Hill in 1839; studied law; was admitted to the bar in 1840 and commenced practice in New Bern, N. C.; elected as a Whig to the Thirtieth Congress (March 4, 1847–March 3, 1849); was not a candidate for renomination in 1848; resumed the practice of law in Washington, N. C.; delegate to the State secession convention in 1861 and to the State constitutional convention in 1865; member of the State house of commons in 1862 and 1864, and served as speaker; died in New Bern, Craven County, N. C., June 3, 1867; interment in Cedar Grove Cemetery.

DONNELLY, Ignatius, a Representative from Minnesota; born in Philadelphia, Pa., November 3, 1831; attended the public schools and was graduated from the high school of that city; studied law; was admitted to the bar in 1852 and commenced practice in Philadelphia; moved to Minnesota in 1857 and settled in Nininger, Dakota County; engaged in literary pursuits; Lieutenant Governor of Minnesota 1859–1863; elected as a Republican to the Thirty-eighth, Thirty-ninth, and Fortieth Congresses (March 4, 1863–March 3, 1869); unsuccessful candidate for reelection in 1868 to the Forty-first Congress and for election in 1870 to the Forty-second Congress; member of the State senate 1874–1878; resumed the practice of law; also engaged in literary pursuits; was nominated by the People's Party in 1890 for Vice President of the United States; died in Minneapolis, Minn., on January 1, 1901; interment in Calvary Cemetery, St. Paul, Minn.

DONOHOE, Michael, a Representative from Pennsylvania; born in Killeshandra, County Cavan, Ireland, February 22, 1864; attended the schools of Ireland and a private classical school; taught as principal of a national school from January 1885 until October 1886, when he resigned; immigrated to the United States and settled in Philadelphia, Pa., November 8, 1886; real-estate broker; engaged in banking and in the manufacture of glassware; elected as a Democrat to the Sixty-second and Sixty-third Congresses (March 4, 1911–March 3, 1915); unsuccessful candidate for reelection in 1914 to the Sixty-fourth Congress; director of Northwestern General Hospital 1893–1943; trustee of Temple University; real-estate assessor for the city of Philadelphia from April 15, 1919, to March 31, 1946, when he retired; died in Philadelphia, Pa., January 17, 1958; interment in Holy Sepulchre Cemetery.

DONOHUE, Harold Daniel, a Representative from Massachusetts; born in Worcester, Mass., June 18, 1901; attended the public schools; was graduated from Northeastern University School of Law, Worcester, Mass., in 1925; was admitted to the bar in February 1926 and commenced practice in Worcester, Mass.; councilman and alderman of Worcester, Mass., from January 1927 to December 1935; during World War II served with the United States Navy from December 1942 until December 1945, when he was separated from the service with the rank of lieutenant commander; elected as a Democrat to the Eightieth and to the six succeeding Congresses (January 3, 1947–January 3, 1961). *Reelected to the Eighty-seventh Congress.*

DONOVAN, Dennis D., a Representative from Ohio; born near Texas, Henry County, Ohio, January 31, 1859; attended the common schools, and Northern Indiana Normal School, Valparaiso, Ind.; taught school; engaged in the mercantile and timber business; was graduated from the law department of Georgetown University, Washington, D. C., in 1895; was admitted to the bar the same year and commenced practice in Deshler, Ohio; appointed postmaster of Deshler by President Cleveland on July 21, 1885, and served until January 27, 1888; member of the State house of representatives in 1887 and 1889; elected as a Democrat to the Fifty-second and Fifty-third Congresses (March 4, 1891–March 3, 1895); unsuccessful candidate for renomination in 1894 to the Fifty-fourth Congress; resumed the practice of law in Deshler, Ohio; moved to Napoleon, Henry County, Ohio, in 1897 and continued the practice of law; unsuccessful candidate for nomination as Governor of Ohio in 1898; died in Napoleon, Ohio, on April 21, 1941; interment in St. Augustine Cemetery.

DONOVAN, James George, a Representative from New York; born in Clinton, Worcester County, Mass., December 15, 1898; attended Massachusetts Institute of Technology at Cambridge in 1916 and 1917; during the First World War served in the United States Navy as a seaman in 1918; attended Harvard University, Cambridge, Mass., 1919–1921, and was graduated from the law school of Columbia University in New York City, N. Y., in 1924; was admitted to the Massachusetts bar in 1923 and the New York bar in 1925; commenced the practice of law in New York City in 1925; under-sheriff of New York County 1934–1941; member of the State senate in 1943 and 1944; elected on the Democrat-Republican-Liberal ticket to the Eighty-second, Eighty-third, and Eighty-fourth Congresses (January 3, 1951–January 3, 1957); unsuccessful candidate for reelection in 1956 to the Eighty-fifth Congress; engaged in law practice; is a resident of New York City, N. Y.

DONOVAN, Jeremiah, a Representative from Connecticut; born in Ridgefield, Fairfield County, Conn., October 18, 1857; attended the public schools and was graduated from Ridgefield Academy; moved to South Norwalk in 1870 and engaged in the retail liquor business until 1898 when he retired; member of the city council; served as deputy sheriff; delegate to all Democratic National Conventions from 1896 to 1916, inclusive; member of the State house of representatives in 1903 and 1904;

served in the State senate 1905–1909; elected as a Democrat to the Sixty-third Congress (March 4, 1913–March 3, 1915); unsuccessful candidate for reelection in 1914 to the Sixty-fourth Congress; mayor of the city of Norwalk, Conn., 1917–1921; retired from active pursuits; died in Norwalk, Conn., April 22, 1935; interment in St. John's Cemetery.

DONOVAN, Jerome Francis, a Representative from New York; born in New Haven, Conn., February 1, 1872; attended the public schools and Hillhouse High School; was graduated from the law department of Yale University in 1894; was admitted to the bar the same year and commenced practice in New Haven; captain of Company C, Second Regiment of the Connecticut National Guard, 1897–1903; member of the State assembly 1901–1903; auditor of the city of New Haven 1902–1904; secretary of the New Haven Civil Service Commission 1904–1906; moved to New York City in 1910 and was admitted to the New York State bar the same year; special deputy attorney general of New York State 1911–1913; elected as a Democrat to the Sixty-fifth Congress to fill the vacancy caused by the resignation of Murray Hulbert; reelected to the Sixty-sixth Congress and served from March 5, 1918, to March 3, 1921; unsuccessful candidate for reelection in 1920 to the Sixty-seventh Congress; served as deputy attorney general in charge of the legal work of the New York State Labor Department in 1923 and 1924; resumed the practice of law in New York City until his retirement in 1936; moved to Stony Creek, Conn., where he died November 2, 1949; interment in St. Bernard's Cemetery, New Haven, Conn.

DOOLEY, Edwin Benedict, a Representative from New York; born in Brooklyn, Kings County, N. Y., April 13, 1905; graduated from St. John's Prep School, Dartmouth College, Hanover, N. H., in 1927, and Fordham University Law School, New York, N. Y., in 1930; public relations counselor; feature writer New York Sun 1927–1938; vice president Don Spencer Co., an advertising agency, 1938–1942; radio broadcaster, New York, N. Y., 1936–1948; during World War II served on Secretary of the Navy and Secretary of War food committees; director of public relations, General Foods Corp., 1942–1946; trustee, village of Mamaroneck, N. Y., 1942–1946; associated with Institute of Public Relations 1946–1948; member of New York State Sesquicentennial Committee in 1951; director, public relations and advertising, Health Insurance Plan, Greater New York, 1950–1955; mayor of Mamaroneck, N. Y., 1950–1956; director of Mamaroneck Federal Savings & Loan Association 1942–1944; elected as a Republican to the Eighty-fifth and Eighty-sixth Congresses (January 3, 1957–January 3, 1961). *Reelected to the Eighty-seventh Congress.*

DOOLING, Peter Joseph, a Representative from New York; born in New York City, N. Y., February 15, 1857; attended the public schools; engaged in the real-estate business; served as court officer in the court of general sessions 1887–1889; member of the board of aldermen of New York City in 1891 and 1892; deputy clerk of the court of special sessions 1893–1895; member of the aqueduct commission in 1898; deputy commissioner of the department of water supply, gas, and electricity 1898–1901; member of the State senate 1903–1905; clerk of the city and county of New York 1906–1909; elected as a Democrat to the Sixty-third and to the three succeeding Congresses (March 4, 1913–March 3, 1921); unsuccessful candidate for reelection in 1920 to the Sixty-seventh Congress; sheriff of New York County in 1924; commissioner of the department of purchases of New York City in 1926; reengaged in the real-estate business; died in New York City, N. Y., October 18, 1931; interment in Calvary Cemetery.

DOOLITTLE, Dudley, a Representative from Kansas; born at Cottonwood Falls, Chase County, Kans., June 21, 1881; attended the public schools and the University of Kansas at Lawrence, being graduated from its law department in 1903; was admitted to the bar the same year and commenced practice at Cottonwood Falls, Kans., in 1904; prosecuting attorney of Chase County 1908–1912; mayor of Strong City in 1912; elected as a Democrat to the Sixty-third, Sixty-fourth, and Sixty-fifth Congresses (March 4, 1913–March 3, 1919); unsuccessful candidate for reelection in 1918 to the Sixty-sixth Congress; representative of the United States Treasury Department to Italy in 1919; Federal Prohibition Director for Kansas in 1920; engaged in the practice of law in Strong City, Kans., Kansas City, Mo., and Washington, D. C., 1921–1934; elected a member of the Democratic National Committee in 1925; general agent of the ninth district, Farm Credit Administration, 1934–1938; member of the board of directors of the College of Emporia and served as its president 1938–1940; president of the Strong City State Bank and a director of the Exchange National Bank of Cottonwood Falls at time of death; died in Emporia, Kans., November 14, 1957; interment in Prairie Grove Cemetery, Cottonwood Falls, Kans.

DOOLITTLE, James Rood, a Senator from Wisconsin; born in Hampton, N. Y., January 3, 1815; attended the common schools and Middlebury (Vt.) Academy, and was graduated from Hobart College, Geneva, N. Y., in 1834; studied law; was admitted to the bar in 1837 and commenced practice in Rochester, N. Y.; moved to Warsaw, N. Y., in 1841; district attorney of Wyoming County, N. Y., 1847–1850; moved to Racine, Wis., in 1851; elected judge of the first judicial circuit of Wisconsin in 1853, and held the office until 1856, when he resigned; the repeal of the Missouri Compromise caused him to leave the Democratic Party; elected as a Republican to the United States Senate in January 1857; reelected in 1863 and served from March 4, 1857, to March 3, 1869; left the Republican Party and was an unsuccessful candidate for Governor on the Democratic ticket in 1871; resumed the practice of law in Chicago, Ill., but retained his residence in Racine, Wis.; permanent chairman of the Democratic National Convention at Baltimore in 1872; trustee of the University of Chicago, serving one year as its president, and was for many years a professor in its law school; died in Edgewood, Providence, R. I., July 23, 1897; interment in Mound Cemetery, Racine, Wis.

DOOLITTLE, William Hall, a Representative from Washington; born near North East in Erie County, Pa., November 6, 1848; moved with his parents to Portage County, Wis., in 1859; worked in the pineries of that State; attended the district school; early in 1865, during the Civil War, enlisted as a private in the Ninth Wisconsin Battery; discharged the following summer and returned to Wisconsin; went to Pennsylvania in 1867 and pursued an academic course; studied law in Chautauqua County, N. Y., and was admitted to the bar in 1871; moved to Nebraska in 1872 and commenced practice in Tecumseh, Johnson County; member of the State house of representatives 1874–1876; assistant United States district attorney 1876–1880; moved to Washington Territory in 1880 and settled in Colfax, Whitman County; engaged in the practice of law; moved to Tacoma in 1888; elected as a Republican to the Fifty-third and Fifty-fourth Congresses (March 4, 1893–March 3, 1897); unsuccessful for reelection in 1896 to the Fifty-fifth Congress; resumed the practice of law; died in Tacoma, Wash., February 26, 1914; interment in Tacoma Cemetery.

DOREMUS, Frank Ellsworth, a Representative from Michigan; born in Venango County, Pa., August 31, 1865; attended the public schools of Portland, Mich., and was graduated from Detroit (Mich.) College of Law; established the Portland Review in 1885, editing it until 1899; member of the State house of representatives 1890–1892; postmaster of Portland 1895–1899; was admitted to the bar and commenced practice in Detroit in 1899; assistant corporation counsel of Detroit 1903–1907; city comptroller 1907–1910; elected as a Democrat to the Sixty-second and to the four succeeding Congresses (March 4, 1911–March 3, 1921); served as mayor of Detroit, Mich., in 1923 and 1924; resumed the practice of law in Fowlerville, Mich.; died in Howell, Mich., September 4, 1947; interment in Roseland Park, Detroit, Mich.

DORN, Francis Edwin, a Representative from New York; born in Brooklyn, Kings County, N. Y., Aprial 18, 1911; attended St. Augustine and Bishop McLaughlin Memorial High Schools; was graduated from Fordham University in 1932 and from the law school of the same university in 1935; also studied government at New York University in 1936; was admitted to the bar in 1936 and began practice in Brooklyn, N. Y.; elected to the State assembly in 1940 but resigned to enlist in the United States Navy in 1941; served four years overseas and was discharged in 1946 as a lieutenant commander in the Naval Reserve, later being promoted to commander; assistant attorney general, State of New York, 1946–1950; engaged in the private practice of law since 1950; elected as a Republican to the Eighty-third and to the three succeeding Congresses (January 3, 1953–January 3, 1961); unsuccessful candidate for reelection in 1960 to the Eighty-seventh Congress; is a resident of Brooklyn, N. Y.

DORN, William Jennings Bryan, a Representative from South Carolina; born near Greenwood, Greenwood County, S. C., April 14, 1916; attended the public schools; engaged in agricultural pursuits; served in the State house of representatives in 1939 and 1940; member of the State senate in 1941 and 1942; enlisted as a private in the Army Air Forces and served from June 20, 1942, until discharged as a corporal on October 12, 1945, nineteen months of which were in the European Theater; elected as a Democrat to the Eightieth Congress (January 3, 1947–January 3, 1949); was not a candidate for renomination in 1948, but was an unsuccessful candidate for the Democratic nomination for United States Senator; resumed agricultural pursuits; elected to the Eighty-second and to the four succeeding Congresses (January 3, 1951–January 3, 1961). *Reelected to the Eighty-seventh Congress.*

DORR, Charles Philips, a Representative from West Virginia; born in Miltonsburg, Monroe County, Ohio, August 12, 1852; moved with his parents to Woodsfield, Ohio, in 1866; attended the common schools; taught school in Ohio and West Virginia; studied law; was admitted to the bar in 1874 and commenced practice in West Virginia the same year; member of the town council of Webster Springs, W. Va.; elected a member of the State house of delegates in 1884 and 1888; sergeant at arms of that body in 1887; elected as a Republican to the Fifty-fifth Congress (March 4, 1897–March 3, 1899); was not a candidate for renomination in 1898; after retirement from Congress resumed the practice of law at Webster Springs, W. Va.; died on his estate, "Clover Lick Farms," at Clover Lick, near Marlinton, Pocahontas County, W. Va., October 8, 1914; interment in Clover Lick Cemetery.

DORSEY, Clement, a Representative from Maryland; born near Oaklands in Anne Arundel County, Md., in 1778; attended St. John's College, Annapolis, Md.; studied law; was admitted to the bar and commenced practice; major in the Maryland Militia 1812–1818; elected to the Nineteenth, Twentieth, and Twenty-

first Congresses (March 4, 1825–March 3, 1831); resumed the practice of law; unsuccessful candidate for election in 1832 to the Twenty-third Congress; judge of the fifth circuit court of Maryland until his death in Leonardtown, St. Marys County, Md., August 6, 1848; interment in a private burial ground at "Summerseat," near Laurel Grove, Md.

DORSEY, Frank Joseph Gerard, a Representative from Pennsylvania; born in Philadelphia, Pa., April 26, 1891; attended grade and high schools; was graduated from the University of Pennsylvania at Philadelphia in 1917; engaged as an assayer for a watch-case company 1908–1913; served on the faculty of the University of Pennsylvania in 1916 and 1917; during the First World War enlisted as a private in the Ordnance Department, United States Army, in July 1917 and was honorably discharged as a lieutenant on April 18, 1919; engaged in the manufacture of steel tools in 1919; also engaged in banking; elected as a Democrat to the Seventy-fourth and Seventy-fifth Congresses (January 3, 1935–January 3, 1939); unsuccessful candidate for reelection in 1938 to the Seventy-sixth Congress; member of the United States Sesquicentennial Constitution Commission in 1938; director, Region III, Wage and Hours and Public Contracts Division, United States Department of Labor, from 1939 until his death in Philadelphia, Pa., July 13, 1949; interment in St. Dominic's Cemetery.

DORSEY, George Washington Emery, a Representative from Nebraska; born in Loudoun County, Va., January 25, 1842; moved with his parents to Preston County, Va. (now West Virginia), in 1856; attended private schools and Oak Hill Academy; recruited a company and entered the Union Army in August 1861 as first lieutenant in the Sixth Regiment, West Virginia Infantry; promoted to captain and major, and was mustered out with the Army of the Shenandoah in August 1865; moved to Nebraska in 1866; studied law; was admitted to the bar and commenced practice in 1869; engaged in banking; member of the board of trustees of the hospital for the insane; vice president of the State board of agriculture; chairman of the Republican State central committee; elected as a Republican to the Forty-ninth, Fiftieth, and Fifty-first Congresses (March 4, 1885–March 3, 1891); unsuccessful candidate for reelection in 1890 to the Fifty-second Congress; engaged in mining enterprises in Nevada and Utah; died in Salt Lake City, Utah, June 12, 1911; interment in the City Cemetery, Fremont, Dodge County, Nebr.

DORSEY, John Lloyd, Jr., a Representative from Kentucky; born in Henderson, Ky., August 10, 1891; educated in the public schools and at Bethel College, Russellville, Ky.; was graduated from Centre College, Danville, Ky., in 1912; studied law at Centre College; was admitted to the bar in 1913 and commenced practice in Henderson, Ky.; during the First World War served as a private in Headquarters Company, One Hundred and Fifty-ninth Depot Brigade, in 1918; executive Democratic committeeman 1920–1924; city attorney of Henderson in 1926 and 1930; elected as a Democrat to the Seventy-first Congress to fill the vacancy caused by the resignation of David H. Kincheloe and served from November 4, 1930, to March 3, 1931; was not a candidate for election to the Seventy-second Congress in 1930; resumed the practice of law; again served as city attorney of Henderson in 1936 and 1937; is a resident of Henderson, Ky.

DORSEY, Stephen Wallace, a Senator from Arkansas; born in Benson, Rutland County, Vt., February 28, 1842; moved to Ohio and settled in Oberlin; attended the public schools; during the Civil War served in the Union Army under General Grant at Shiloh, General Buell at Perryville, General Rosecrans at Stone River and Chattanooga, and General Thomas at Missionary Ridge; was transferred to the Army of the Potomac in 1864; took part in the Battles of the Wilderness and Cold Harbor, and served until the close of the war; returned to Ohio and settled in Sandusky; was employed by the Sandusky Tool Co. and subsequently became its president; elected president of the Arkansas Railway Co.; moved to Arkansas and settled in Helena; chairman of the Republican county committee; elected as a Republican to the United States Senate and served from March 4, 1873, to March 3, 1879; was not a candidate for reelection; chairman of the Republican State executive committee in 1876 and a member of the Republican National Committee in 1880; after his service in the Senate devoted himself to cattle raising and mining in New Mexico and Colorado, and resided in Colfax County, N. Mex., and later in Denver, Colo.; subsequently moved to Los Angeles, Calif., and resided there until his death on March 20, 1916; interment in Fairmont Cemetery, Denver, Colo.

DORSHEIMER, William, a Representative from New York; born in Lyons, Wayne County, N. Y., February 5, 1832; moved to Buffalo, N. Y., with his parents in 1836; attended the common schools, Phillips Academy, Andover, Mass., and Harvard University; studied law; was admitted to the bar in 1854 and commenced practice in Buffalo, N. Y.; during the Civil War was appointed a major in the United States Army in August 1861 and served as aide-de-camp on the staff of General Frémont; United States attorney for the northern district of New York 1867–1871; delegate to the Liberal Republican Convention at Cincinnati in 1872; member of the first board of park commissioners of Buffalo; Lieutenant Governor of New York 1875–1880; delegate to the Democratic National Convention at St. Louis in 1876; commissioner of the State survey in 1876 and president of the commission in 1883; moved to New York City in 1880 and continued the practice of law; appointed commissioner of the State reservation at Niagara, N. Y., in 1883; elected as a Democrat to the Forty-eighth Congress (March 4, 1883–March 3, 1885); declined to be a candidate for renomination in 1884; appointed United States district attorney for the southern district of New York in 1885; resigned the same year, having become owner of the New York Star; died in Savannah, Ga., March 26, 1888, while en route to Florida for a visit; interment in Forest Lawn Cemetery, Buffalo, N. Y.

DOTY, James Duane (cousin of Morgan Lewis Martin), a Delegate and a Representative from Wisconsin; born in Salem, Washington County, N. Y., November 5, 1799; attended the common schools; studied law; moved to Detroit, Mich., in 1818; was admitted to the bar in 1819 and commenced practice in Detroit; secretary of the legislative council and clerk of court of Michigan Territory; United States judge for northern Michigan 1823–1832; member of the legislative council in 1834 and 1835; assisted in bringing about the division of Michigan Territory into the three Territories of Michigan, Wisconsin, and Iowa; preempted several tracts of Government land in the Territory of Wisconsin; laid out the capital of Wisconsin and named it Madison; successfully contested as a Democrat the election of George W. Jones as a Delegate to the Twenty-fifth Congress; reelected to the Twenty-sixth Congress and served from January 14, 1839, to March 3, 1841; Governor of the Territory of Wisconsin 1841–1844; delegate to the first constitutional convention of 1846; elected as a Democrat a Representative to the Thirty-first Congress and as a Free-Soiler to the Thirty-second Congress (March 4, 1849–March 3, 1853); appointed superintendent of Indian affairs for Utah Territory in 1861; treasurer and Governor of Utah Territory in 1863 and served until his death in Salt Lake City, Utah, June 13, 1865; interment in Fort Douglas Cemetery.

DOUBLEDAY, Ulysses Freeman, a Representative from New York; born in Otsego County, N. Y., December 15, 1792; received a limited schooling; learned the art of printing and worked as a printer in Cooperstown, Utica, and Albany, N. Y.; served at Sackets Harbor in the War of 1812; established the Saratoga Courier at Ballston Spa; moved to Auburn, N. Y., where he published the Cayuga Patriot 1819–1839; elected as a Jackson Democrat to the Twenty-second Congress (March 4, 1831–March 3, 1833); appointed inspector of Auburn Prison in 1834; elected to the Twenty-fourth Congress (March 4, 1835–March 3, 1837); engaged in agricultural pursuits in Scipio, N. Y., 1837–1846; moved to New York City and engaged in mercantile pursuits 1846–1860; died in Belvidere, Boone County, Ill., March 11, 1866; interment probably in the North Street Cemetery, Auburn, N. Y.

DOUGHERTY, Charles, a Representative from Florida; born in Athens, Ga., October 15, 1850; attended the public schools of Athens and the University of Virginia at Charlottesville; followed the sea; moved to Florida in 1871 and settled near Port Orange; engaged in planting; member of the State house of representatives 1877–1885, and served as speaker in 1879; elected as a Democrat to the Forty-ninth and Fiftieth Congresses (March 4, 1885–March 3, 1889); resumed agricultural pursuits; again a member of the State house of representatives in 1891, 1892, 1911, and 1912; served in the State senate 1895–1898; died at Daytona Beach, Volusia County, Fla., on October 11, 1915; interment in Pinewood Cemetery.

DOUGHERTY, John, a Representative from Missouri; born in Iatan, Platte County, Mo., February 25, 1857; moved with his parents the same year to Liberty, Clay County, Mo.; attended the public schools and William Jewell College, Liberty, Mo.; studied law; was admitted to the bar in 1889 and commenced practice at Liberty, Mo.; elected city attorney of Liberty, Mo., in 1881 and served five years; editor and proprietor of the Liberty Tribune 1885–1888; elected prosecuting attorney of Clay County, Mo., in 1888 and served six years; unsuccessful candidate for nomination in 1896 to the Fifty-fifth Congress; elected as a Democrat to the Fifty-sixth, Fifty-seventh, and Fifty-eighth Congresses (March 4, 1899–March 3, 1905); unsuccessful candidate for renomination in 1904; resumed the practice of law; died in Liberty, Mo., August 1, 1905; interment in Fairview Cemetery.

DOUGHTON, Robert Lee, a Representative from North Carolina; born at Laurel Springs, Alleghany County, N. C., on November 7, 1863; was educated in the public schools and the high schools at Laurel Springs and Sparta; engaged in agricultural pursuits and the raising of livestock at Laurel Springs; also interested in banking; member of the State board of agriculture 1903–1909; served in the State senate in 1908 and 1909; director of the State prison board 1909–1911; president of the Deposit & Savings Bank, North Wilkesboro, N. C., since 1911; elected as a Democrat to the Sixty-second and to the twenty succeeding Congresses (March 4, 1911–January 3, 1953); was not a candidate for renomination in 1952; returned to Laurel Springs, N. C., where he died October 1, 1954; interment in Laurel Springs Baptist Church Cemetery.

DOUGLAS, Albert, a Representative from Ohio; born in Chillicothe, Ohio, April 25, 1852; attended the public schools of Chillicothe and a preparatory school; was graduated from Kenyon College, Gambier, Ohio, in 1872 and from the law department of Harvard University in 1874; was admitted to the bar in 1874 and commenced practice in Chillicothe, Ohio; prosecuting attorney of Ross County 1877–1881; presidential elector at large on the Republican ticket of McKinley and Hobart in 1896 and served as president of the electoral college; elected as a Republican to the Sixtieth and Sixty-first Congresses (March 4, 1907–March 3, 1911); unsuccessful candidate for reelection in 1910 to the Sixty-second Congress; resumed the practice of law in Chillicothe, Ohio; appointed Ambassador Extraordinary to represent the United States at the centennial of the independence of Peru in 1921; retired and resided in Washington, D. C., until his death in that city on March 14, 1935; interment in Grand View Cemetery, Chillicothe, Ohio.

DOUGLAS, Beverly Browne, a Representative from Virginia; born at Providence Forge, New Kent County, Va., December 21, 1822; attended Rumford Academy in King William County, William and Mary College, Williamsburg, Va., Yale College, and the University of Edinburgh, Scotland; upon his return to the United States reentered William and Mary College, and was graduated from the law department, under Judge Beverly Tucker, in 1843; was admitted to the bar in 1844 and commenced practice in Norfolk, Va.; moved to King William County in 1846 and continued the practice of his profession; delegate to the State constitutional convention in 1850 and 1851; member of the State senate 1852–1865; presidential elector on the Democratic ticket of Breckinridge and Lane in 1860; during the Civil War entered the Confederate Army as first lieutenant in Lee's Rangers, and was successively promoted to the rank of major of the Fifth Virginia Cavalry; elected as a Conservative to the Forty-fourth Congress and as a Democrat to the Forty-fifth Congress and served from March 4, 1875, until his death in Washington, D. C., December 22, 1878; interment in the family burying ground at "Zoar," near Aylett, King William County, Va.

DOUGLAS, Emily Taft (wife of Senator Paul H. Douglas), a Representative from Illinois; born in Chicago, Cook County, Ill.; was graduated from the University of Chicago, Chicago, Ill., in 1920; engaged in the theatrical profession; organizer for the Illinois League of Women Voters and chairman of department government and foreign policy; secretary of the International Relations Center, Chicago, Ill.; elected as a Democrat to the Seventy-ninth Congress (January 3, 1945–January 3, 1947); unsuccessful candidate for reelection in 1946 to the Eightieth Congress; is a resident of Chicago, Ill.

DOUGLAS, Fred James, a Representative from New York; born in Clinton, Worcester County, Mass., September 14, 1869; moved with his parents to Little Falls, N. Y., in 1874; attended the public schools, and was graduated from the medical department of Dartmouth College, Hanover, N. H., in 1895; moved to Utica, N. Y., the same year and commenced the practice of medicine; interne in Faxton Hospital, Utica, N. Y., 1895–1897; consulting surgeon of the Utica State Hospital 1910–1946; member of the board of education of Utica 1910–1920; mayor of Utica 1922–1924; commissioner of public safety of Utica in 1928 and 1929; unsuccessful candidate for Lieutenant Governor of New York in 1934; elected as a Republican to the Seventy-fifth and to the three succeeding Congresses (January 3, 1937–January 3, 1945); unsuccessful candidate for renomination in 1944; resumed his former profession as a surgeon; died in Utica, N. Y., January 1, 1949; interment in Mount Olivet Cemetery, Whitesboro, N. Y.

DOUGLAS, Helen Gahagan, a Representative from California; born in Boonton, Morris County, N. J., November 25, 1900; attended the public schools, Berkeley School for Girls, Brooklyn, N. Y., Capen School for Girls, Northampton, Mass., and Barnard College, Columbia University, New York City, N. Y.; moved to Los Angeles, Calif., in 1931; engaged in the theatrical profession and also as an opera singer 1922–1938; Democratic

National committeewoman for California 1940–1944; vice chairman of the Democratic State central committee and chairman of the women's division 1940–1944; member of the national advisory committee of the Works Progress Administration and of the State committee of the National Youth Administration in 1939 and 1940; member of the board of governors of the California Housing and Planning Association in 1942 and 1943; appointed by President Franklin D. Roosevelt as a member of the Voluntary Participation Committee, Office of Civilian Defense; appointed by President Harry S. Truman as alternate United States Delegate to the United Nations Assembly; elected as a Democrat to the Seventy-ninth, Eightieth, and Eighty-first Congresses (January 3, 1945–January 3, 1951); was not a candidate for renomination in 1950, but was unsuccessful for election to the United States Senate; lecturer; resides in New York, N. Y.

DOUGLAS, Lewis Williams, a Representative from Arizona; born in Bisbee, Cochise County, Ariz., July 2, 1894; attended the public schools and Montclair (N. J.) Academy; was graduated from Amherst (Mass.) College in 1916; attended the Massachusetts Institute of Technology at Cambridge in 1916 and studied metallurgy and geology; during the First World War attended the first officers' training camp at Presidio, San Francisco, Calif.; commissioned as a second lieutenant on August 15, 1917, and assigned to the Three Hundred and Forty-seventh Regiment, Field Artillery; promoted to first lieutenant and served overseas as assistant, G–3 staff, Ninety-first Division, until discharged on February 18, 1919; cited by General Pershing during the Argonne offensive; decorated with the Croix de Guerre by the Belgian Government during the Lys-Escault offensive; instructor of history at Amherst College in 1920; taught chemistry at Hackley School, Tarrytown, N. Y., in 1921; engaged in mining and general business; member of the Arizona State House of Representatives 1923–1925; elected as a Democrat to the Seventieth and to the three succeeding Congresses and served from March 4, 1927, until his resignation effective March 4, 1933, before the commencement of the Seventy-third Congress; appointed Director of the Budget by President Franklin D. Roosevelt; took the oath of office on March 7, 1933, and served until August 31, 1934, when he resigned; vice president and member of the board of a chemical company 1934–1938; principal and vice chancellor of McGill University, Montreal, Canada, from January 1938 to December 1939; president of an insurance company from January 1940 to March 1947, and later, chairman of the board on leave of absence; deputy administrator of the War Shipping Administration from May 1942 to March 1944; confirmed on March 5, 1947, as United States Ambassador to Great Britain and resigned December 2, 1950; resides in Phoenix, Ariz.

DOUGLAS, Paul Howard (husband of Emily Taft Douglas), a Senator from Illinois; born in Salem, Essex County, Mass., March 26, 1892; attended the public schools of Newport, Maine; graduated from Bowdoin College in 1913, Columbia University in 1915; studied at Harvard University in 1915 and 1916; instructor in economics, University of Illinois, in 1916 and 1917; instructor and assistant professor of economics, Reed College, Portland, Oreg., in 1917 and 1918; industrial relations work with Emergency Fleet Corporation in 1918 and 1919; associate professor of economics, University of Washington in 1919 and 1920; assistant professor, industrial relations, University of Chicago, 1920–1923; associate professor 1923–1925, and professor of economics 1925–1949; visiting professor, Amherst College, 1924–1927; secretary of Pennsylvania Commission on Unemployment and adviser New York Commission on Unemployment in 1930; member of Illinois Housing Commission 1931–1933; member of Consumers' Advisory Board, NRA, 1933–1935; member of Advisory Committee to United States Senate and Social Security Board on Federal social security system in 1938 and 1939; alderman, Chicago City Council, 1939–1942; author of numerous books; during World War II enlisted as a private in the United States Marine Corps in May 1942; served overseas from May 1943 to June 1945, mainly with the First Marine Division, advancing through the ranks to lieutenant colonel; wounded at Pelelieu and Okinawa; awarded the Bronze Star for heroic achievement in action; delegate to the Democratic National Conventions in 1948, 1952, and 1956; elected as a Democrat to the United States Senate in 1948, and again in 1954, and served from January 3, 1949, to January 3, 1961. *Reelected in 1960 for the term ending January 3, 1967.*

DOUGLAS, Stephen Arnold, a Representative and a Senator from Illinois; born in Brandon, Rutland County, Vt., April 23, 1813; educated in the common schools, and completed preparatory studies in Brandon Academy; learned the cabinetmaker's trade; moved to a farm near Clifton Springs, N. Y.; entered Canandaigua Academy in 1832 and studied law; moved to Cleveland, Ohio, in 1833, and finally settled in Winchester, Ill., where he taught school and resumed the study of law; was admitted to the bar in 1834 and commenced practice in Jacksonville, Morgan County, Ill.; elected State's attorney for the Morgan circuit in 1835; member of the State house of representatives in 1836 and 1837; register of the land office at Springfield in 1837; unsuccessful Democratic candidate for election in 1838 to the Twenty-sixth Congress; appointed secretary of state of Illinois during the session of the legislature in 1840 and 1841 and at the same session was elected as one of the judges of the State supreme court; elected as a Democrat to the Twenty-eighth, Twenty-ninth, and Thirtieth Congresses and served from March 4, 1843, until his resignation on March 3, 1847, at the close of the Twenty-ninth Congress, having been elected Senator; elected to the United States Senate in 1847; reelected in 1853 as a Popular Sovereignty Democrat, and again in 1859, defeating Abraham Lincoln, and served from March 4, 1847, until his death; unsuccessful candidate for the nomination for President on the Democratic ticket in 1852 and 1856; nominated for President by the Democratic National Convention at Baltimore in 1860 and received twelve electoral votes for President of the United States; died in Chicago, Ill., June 3, 1861; interment in Douglas Monument Park.

DOUGLAS, William Harris, a Representative from New York; born in New York City December 5, 1853; attended private schools and the College of the City of New York; entered the exporting and importing trade; senior member and president of the firm of Arkell & Douglas (Inc.), having branches in London, England, Sydney and Melbourne, Australia, Cape Town and Port Elizabeth, South Africa, and elsewhere; served as a member of the National and State chambers of commerce, the New York Produce Exchange, Maritime Exchange, Merchants' Association, and various other institutions; elected as a Republican to the Fifty-seventh and Fifty-eighth Congresses (March 4, 1901–March 3, 1905); declined to be a candidate for renomination in 1904; resumed his former business pursuits; delegate to the Republican National Conventions at Chicago in 1908, 1912, and 1916; died in New York City, N. Y., on January 27, 1944; interment in Sleepy Hollow Cemetery, Tarrytown, N. Y.

DOUGLASS, John Joseph, a Representative from Massachusetts; born in East Boston, Suffolk County, Mass., February 9, 1873; attended the public schools; was graduated from East Boston High School in 1889, from Boston College in 1893, and from the law department of Georgetown University, Wash-

ington, D. C., in 1896; was admitted to the bar in 1897 and commenced practice in Boston, Mass.; member of the State house of representatives in 1899, 1900, 1906, and again in 1913; delegate to the Massachusetts constitutional convention in 1917 and 1918; author and playwright; delegate to the Democratic National Conventions in 1928 and 1932; elected as a Democrat to the Sixty-ninth and to the four succeeding Congresses (March 4, 1925–January 3, 1935); unsuccessful candidate for renomination in 1934; resumed the practice of law; served as commissioner of penal institutions of Boston from 1935 until his death in West Roxbury, Suffolk County, Mass., April 5, 1939; interment in St. Joseph's Cemetery.

DOUTRICH, Isaac Hoffer, a Representative from Pennsylvania; born on a farm near Middletown, Dauphin County, Pa., December 19, 1871; moved to Elizabethtown, Pa., with his parents in 1880; attended the rural schools, the public schools in Elizabethtown, Pa., and Keystone State Normal School (now State Teachers College), Kutztown, Pa.; employed as a clerk in a clothing store from 1885 until 1892 when he engaged in the retail clothing business; moved to Middletown, Pa., in 1905 and continued the retail clothing business, operating stores in Orwigsburg, Middletown, Schuylkill Haven, Phoenixville, and Pottsville, Pa.; moved to Harrisburg, Pa., in 1920 and continued in the retail clothing business; also interested in banking and other businesses; member of the city council 1924–1927; elected as a Republican to the Seventieth and to the four succeeding Congresses (March 4, 1927–January 3, 1937); unsuccessful for reelection in 1936 to the Seventy-fifth Congress; reengaged in the retail clothing business in Harrisburg, Pa., until his death May 28, 1941; interment in the East Harrisburg Cemetery.

DOVENER, Blackburn Barrett, a Representative from West Virginia; born in Tays Valley, Cabell County, Va. (now West Virginia), April 20, 1842; attended the common schools; taught school 1858–1861; at the age of nineteen raised a company of loyal Virginians and served as captain of Company A, Fifteenth Regiment, West Virginia Volunteer Infantry, during the Civil War; became captain of an Ohio River steamboat in 1867; studied law; was admitted to the bar in 1873 and commenced practice in Wheeling, W. Va.; member of the State house of delegates in 1883 and 1884; unsuccessful Republican candidate for election to the Fifty-second Congress; elected as a Republican to the Fifty-fourth and to the five succeeding Congresses (March 4, 1895–March 3, 1907); unsuccessful candidate for renomination; resumed the practice of law in Wheeling; moved to Maryland, and lived in retirement with his son at Glen Echo, Md., until his death on May 9, 1914; interment in Arlington National Cemetery, Fort Myer, Va.

DOWD, Clement, a Representative from North Carolina; born at Richland Creek, near Carthage, Moore County, N. C., August 27, 1832; attended the common schools; was graduated from the University of North Carolina at Chapel Hill in 1856; engaged in teaching in 1857 and 1858; studied law; was admitted to the bar in 1859 and commenced practice in Charlotte, N. C.; during the Civil War served in the Confederate Army; after the war resumed the practice of law; mayor of Charlotte 1869–1871; president of the Merchants & Farmers' National Bank 1871–1874; president of the Commercial National Bank of Charlotte, N. C., 1874–1880; delegate to the Democratic State convention in 1881; elected as a Democrat to the Forty-seventh and Forty-eighth Congresses (March 4, 1881–March 3, 1885); was not a candidate for renomination in 1884; State bank examiner in 1885 and 1886; collector of internal revenue for the district of North Carolina in 1886 and 1887; again engaged in the practice of law; died in Charlotte, N. C., April 15, 1898; interment in Elmwood Cemetery.

DOWDELL, James Ferguson, a Representative from Alabama; born near Monticello, Jasper County, Ga., November 26, 1818; completed preparatory studies, and in 1840 was graduated from Randolph-Macon College, Ashland, Va.; studied law; was admitted to the bar in 1841 and commenced practice in Greenville, Ga.; moved to Chambers County, Ala., in 1846 and engaged in agricultural pursuits; unsuccessful candidate for election to the State house of representatives in 1849 and 1851; presidential elector on the Democratic ticket of Pierce and King in 1852; elected as a State Rights Democrat to the Thirty-third, Thirty-fourth, and Thirty-fifth Congresses (March 4, 1853–March 3, 1859); during the Civil War served as colonel of the Thirty-seventh Regiment, Alabama Volunteer Infantry, under General Price from 1862 until the close of the war; president of the East Alabama College at Auburn 1868–1870; died near Auburn, Lee County, Ala., September 6, 1871; interment in City Cemetery, Auburn, Ala.

DOWDNEY, Abraham, a Representative from New York; born in Youghal, Ireland, October 31, 1841; immigrated to the United States with his parents, who settled in New York City; attended private schools; engaged in the building and contracting business; served in the Civil War as captain in the One Hundred and Thirty-second Regiment, New York Volunteer Infantry, in 1862 and 1863; chairman of the public-school trustees of New York City 1882–1885; elected as a Democrat to the Forty-ninth Congress and served from March 4, 1885, until his death in New York City December 10, 1886; interment in Calvary Cemetery, Long Island City, N. Y.

DOWDY, John Vernard, a Representative from Texas; born in Waco, McLennan County, Tex., February 11, 1912; spent early years of his youth in Rusk, Tex.; graduated from high school in Henderson, Tex., in 1928; attended the College of Marshall (now East Texas Baptist College) 1929–1931, then undertook the private study of law and worked as a court reporter 1931–1944; admitted to the bar in 1940 and began practice in Athens, Tex.; district attorney, third judicial district of Texas, 1945–1952; elected as a Democrat to the Eighty-second Congress to fill the vacancy caused by the resignation of Tom Pickett; reelected to the Eighty-third and to the three succeeding Congresses and served from September 23, 1952, to January 3, 1961. *Reelected to the Eighty-seventh Congress.*

DOWELL, Cassius Clay, a Representative from Iowa; born on a farm near Summerset, Warren County, Iowa, February 29, 1864; attended the public schools, Baptist College at Des Moines, Iowa, and Simpson College, Indianola, Iowa; was graduated from the liberal arts department of Drake University, Des Moines, Iowa, in 1886 and from its law department in 1887; was admitted to the bar in 1888 and commenced practice in Des Moines; member of the State house of representatives 1894–1898; served in the State senate 1902–1912; elected as a Republican to the Sixty-fourth and to the nine succeeding Congresses (March 4, 1915–January 3, 1935); unsuccessful candidate for reelection in 1934 to the Seventy-fourth Congress; resumed the practice of law in Des Moines, Iowa; elected to the Seventy-fifth and Seventy-sixth Congresses and served from January 3, 1937, until his death in Washington, D. C., February 4, 1940; interment in Woodland Cemetery, Des Moines, Iowa.

DOWNEY, Sheridan (son of Stephen Wheeler Downey), a Senator from California; born in Laramie, Albany County, Wyo., March 11, 1884; attended the public schools; was graduated from the law department of the University of Michigan at Ann Arbor in 1907; was admitted to the bar the same year and commenced practice in Laramie, Wyo.; moved to Sacramento, Calif., in 1913 and continued the practice of law; elected as a Democrat to the

United States Senate in 1938; reelected in 1944 and served from January 3, 1939, until his resignation November 30, 1950, due to ill health; was not a candidate for renomination in 1950; died in San Francisco, Calif., October 25, 1961; body willed to the University of California Medical Center.

DOWNEY, Stephen Wheeler (father of Sheridan Downey), a Delegate from the Territory of Wyoming; born in Western Port, Allegany County, Md., July 25, 1839; pursued an academic course; during the Civil War enlisted as a private in Company C, Third Regiment, Potomac Home Brigade, Maryland Infantry, October 31, 1861; promoted to first lieutenant January 1, 1862; lieutenant colonel March 1, 1862; colonel September 8, 1862, and was honorably discharged November 6, 1862, on tender of resignation; studied law; was admitted to the bar in Washington, D. C., in 1863; moved to the Territory of Wyoming in 1869 and practiced law in Laramie; prosecuting attorney of Albany County in 1869 and 1870; elected a member of the Territorial council in 1871, 1875, and 1877; treasurer of the Territory 1872–1875; auditor of the Territory 1877–1879; elected as a Republican to the Forty-sixth Congress (March 4, 1879–March 3, 1881); declined to be a candidate for renomination in 1880; elected a member of the Territorial house of representatives in 1886 and again in 1890; trustee of the University of Wyoming at Laramie 1891–1897 and served as its president; member of the State house of representatives in 1893 and 1895 and served as speaker in the latter year; member of the State constitutional convention in 1889; again prosecuting attorney of Albany County from 1899 until his death in Denver, Colo., August 3, 1902; interment in Green Hill Cemetery, Laramie, Albany County, Wyo.

DOWNING, Charles, a Delegate from Florida; born in Virginia; studied law; was admitted to the bar and practiced in St. Augustine, Fla.; member of the legislative council of the Territory of Florida in 1837; elected to the Twenty-fifth and Twenty-sixth Congresses (March 4, 1837–March 3, 1841); died in St. Augustine, Fla., in 1845.

DOWNING, Finis Ewing, a Representative from Illinois; born in Virginia, Cass County, Ill., August 24, 1846; attended public and private schools; engaged as a clerk in mercantile stores at Virginia, Ill., 1864–1869, and at Butler, Mo., 1869–1874; engaged in mercantile pursuits in Virginia, Ill., 1874–1880; member of the board of aldermen 1876–1878; mayor 1878–1880; clerk of the circuit court of Cass County 1880–1892; studied law; was admitted to the bar in December 1887 and commenced practice at Virginia, Ill.; engaged in the newspaper business 1891–1897; secretary of the State senate in 1892 and 1893; presented credentials as a Democratic Member-elect to the Fifty-fourth Congress and served from March 4, 1895, to June 5, 1896, when he was succeeded by John I. Rinaker, who contested his election; unsuccessful candidate for renomination in 1896; unsuccessful Democratic candidate for secretary of state of Illinois in 1896; resumed the practice of law in Virginia, Ill., and also engaged in the real-estate business; died in Virginia, Ill., March 8, 1936; interment in Walnut Ridge Cemetery.

DOWNING, Thomas Nelms, a Representative from Virginia; born in Newport News, Va., February 1, 1919; attended the public schools; graduated from Virginia Military Institute in 1940 and from the University of Virginia in 1948; was admitted to the bar in 1948 and commenced the practice of law in Warwick and Hampton, Va.; during World War II served 1942–1946 as a troop commander of Mechanized Cavalry with Gen. George S. Patton's Third United States Army and commanded the first troops in the Third Army to invade Germany; awarded a Silver Star for gallantry in action in France; former substitute judge of the municipal court for the city of Warwick; elected as a Democrat to the Eighty-sixth Congress (January 3, 1959–January 3, 1961). *Reelected to the Eighty-seventh Congress.*

DOWNS, Le Roy Donnelly, a Representative from Connecticut; born in Danbury, Fairfield County, Conn., April 11, 1900; attended the public and high schools of his native city; during the First World War enlisted on August 27, 1917, and served as a corporal in Detachment No. 11, General Repair Shop, Motor Transport Corps, United States Army, with four months' service in France, being discharged on December 21, 1918; engaged as a newspaper publisher in South Norwalk, Conn., in 1923; member of Connecticut Veterans' Home Commission 1931–1939; chairman and member of the Veterans' Home Building Commission 1931–1938; city clerk of Norwalk, Conn., 1933–1940; elected as a Democrat to the Seventy-seventh Congress (January 3, 1941–January 3, 1943); unsuccessful for reelection in 1942 to the Seventy-eighth Congress; resumed the newspaper publishing business; comptroller of the city of Norwalk, Conn., 1943–1944; War Manpower Director for southwestern Connecticut 1944–1946; vice president of the Norwalk Airconditioning Corp. and secretary of Air Supplies, Inc.; is a resident of South Norwalk, Conn.

DOWNS, Solomon Weathersbee, a Senator from Louisiana; born in Montgomery County, Tenn., in 1801; pursued classical studies, and was graduated from the Transylvania University, Lexington, Ky., in 1823; studied law; was admitted to the bar in 1826 and commenced practice in Bayou Sara, West Feliciana Parish, La.; moved to Ouachita, La., and thence to New Orleans, La., in 1845, where he engaged in the practice of law; United States attorney for the district of Louisiana 1845–1847; member of the State constitutional convention; elected as a Democrat to the United States Senate and served from March 4, 1847, to March 3, 1853; appointed by President Pierce collector of the port of New Orleans in 1853; died at Crab Orchard Springs, Lincoln County, Ky., August 14, 1854; interment in Old City Cemetery, Monroe, Ouachita Parish, La.

DOWSE, Edward, a Representative from Massachusetts; born in Charlestown, Mass., October 22, 1756; moved to Dedham, Mass.; after the Revolution was a shipmaster and engaged in the East Indian and China carrying trade; elected as a Democrat to the Sixteenth Congress and served from March 4, 1819, until May 26, 1820, when he resigned; retired from active business pursuits; died in Dedham, Mass., September 3, 1828; interment in the Old Cemetery.

DOX, Peter Myndert (grandson of John Nicholas), a Representative from Alabama; born in Geneva, Ontario County, N. Y., September 11, 1813; attended Geneva Academy, and was graduated from Hobart College at Geneva in 1833; studied law; was admitted to the bar and commenced practice at Geneva, N. Y.; member of the State assembly in 1842; judge of the Ontario County Courts from November 1855 until his resignation on March 18, 1856; moved to Alabama in the same year and settled in Madison County; engaged in agricultural pursuits; member of the State constitutional convention in 1865; elected as a Democrat to the Forty-first and Forty-second Congresses (March 4, 1869–March 3, 1873); retired from public life; died in Huntsville, Madison County, Ala., April 2, 1891; interment in Maple Hill Cemetery.

DOXEY, Charles Taylor, a Representative from Indiana; born in Tippecanoe County, Ind., July 13, 1841; moved with his mother to Minnesota in 1855 and worked on a farm; later moved to Fairbury, Ill., where he attended the public schools; moved to Anderson, Ind.; during the Civil War entered the service as first sergeant of Company A, Nineteenth Regiment, Indiana Volunteer Infantry, in July 1861; promoted to second lieutenant, subsequently resigned, and then became captain of Company K, Sixteenth Indiana Infantry, in which capacity he served until the close of the war; engaged in the manufacture of staves and headings; member of the State senate in 1876; member of the board of directors in the first natural-gas companies of Anderson; elected as a Republican to the Forty-seventh Congress to fill the vacancy caused by the death of Godlove S. Orth and served from January 17 to March 3, 1883; unsuccessful candidate for election in 1884 to the Forty-ninth Congress; resumed former business activities; died in Anderson, Ind., April 30, 1898; interment in Maplewood Cemetery.

DOXEY, Wall, a Representative and a Senator from Mississippi; born in Holly Springs, Marshall County, Miss., August 8, 1892; attended the public schools; was graduated from the University of Mississippi at Oxford in 1913 and from its law department in 1914; was admitted to the bar in 1914 and commenced practice in Holly Springs, Miss.; prosecuting attorney of Marshall County, Miss., 1915–1923; district attorney for the third judicial district of Mississippi 1923–1929; delegate to the Democratic National Conventions in 1932, 1936, and 1940; elected as a Democrat to the Seventy-first and to the six succeeding Congresses and served from March 4, 1929, until September 28, 1941; elected to the United States Senate on September 23, 1941, to fill the vacancy caused by the death of Pat Harrison and served from September 29, 1941, to January 3, 1943; unsuccessful candidate for renomination to the United States Senate in 1942; elected Sergeant at Arms of the United States Senate and served from January 28, 1943, until January 3, 1947; engaged as a hearing examiner with the United States Department of Agriculture, Washington, D. C., from February 1947 to November 1947; resumed the practice of law until his retirement; resident of Holly Springs, Miss.

DOYLE, Clyde Gilman, a Representative from California; born in Oakland, Alameda County, Calif., July 11, 1887; attended public schools in Oakland, Calif., and Seattle, Wash., and high schools in Los Angeles and Long Beach, Calif.; was graduated from the College of Law of the University of Southern California at Los Angeles in 1917; was admitted to the bar in 1916 and commenced practice in Long Beach, Calif.; member and president of the Board of Freeholders, Long Beach, Calif., in 1921 and 1922; member of the board of trustees of Adelaide Tichenor Hospital-School for Crippled Children; member of the California State Board of Education; received the Meritorious Citizenship Award from the Interallied Council of Service Clubs, Long Beach, Calif., in 1936; elected as a Democrat to the Seventy-ninth Congress (January 3, 1945–January 3, 1947); unsuccessful candidate for reelection in 1946 to the Eightieth Congress; elected to the Eighty-first and to the five succeeding Congresses (January 3, 1949–January 3, 1961). *Reelected to the Eighty-seventh Congress.*

DOYLE, Thomas Aloysius, a Representative from Illinois; born in Chicago, Ill., January 9, 1886; attended the grammar and high schools of his native city; was graduated from McCallister Evening High School, Chicago, Ill., in 1903; engaged in the real-estate and insurance business and, since 1926, in the automobile business; member of the Chicago City Council 1914–1918; member of the State house of representatives 1918–1923; commissioner on the Chicago Board of Local Improvements in 1923; elected as a Democrat to the Sixty-eighth Congress to fill the vacancy caused by the death of John W. Rainey; reelected to the Sixty-ninth, Seventieth, and Seventy-first Congresses and served from November 6, 1923, to March 3,

1931; was not a candidate for renomination in 1930; in 1931 again became a member of the Chicago City Council and served until his death in Chicago, Ill., January 29, 1935; interment in Mount Olivet Cemetery.

DRAKE, Charles Daniel, a Senator from Missouri; born in Cincinnati, Ohio, April 11, 1811; attended St. Joseph's College, Bardstown, Ky., in 1823 and 1824, and Patridge's Military Academy, Middletown, Conn., in 1824 and 1825; appointed midshipman in the United States Navy in 1825 and served four years, when he resigned; studied law; was admitted to the bar in Cincinnati in 1833; moved to St. Louis, Mo., in 1834 and continued the practice of his profession; member of the State house of representatives in 1859 and 1860; presidential elector on the Republican ticket of Lincoln and Johnson in 1864; member of the State constitutional convention in 1865; elected as a Republican to the United States Senate and served from March 4, 1867, to December 19, 1870, when he resigned to accept a judicial position; appointed chief justice of the Court of Claims and served until January 1885, when he retired; died in Washington, D. C., April 1, 1892; remains were cremated and the ashes interred in Bellefontaine Cemetery, St. Louis, Mo.

DRAKE, John Reuben, a Representative from New York; born in Pleasant Valley, Dutchess County, N. Y., November 28, 1782; completed preparatory studies; engaged in mercantile and agricultural pursuits; supervisor of the town of Owego in 1813; first judge of Broome County 1815–1823; member of the State assembly 1817–1819; elected to the Fifteenth Congress (March 4, 1817–March 3, 1819); judge of the court of common pleas for Tioga County 1833–1838; member of the State assembly in 1834; president of Owego village 1841–1845; died in Owego, Tioga County, N. Y., on March 21, 1857; interment in Evergreen Cemetery.

DRANE, Herbert Jackson, a Representative from Florida; born in Franklin, Simpson County, Ky., June 20, 1863; attended the public schools of Louisville, Ky., and Brevards Academy at Franklin, Ky.; moved to Macon, Ga., in 1881, and to Lakeland (of which he was one of the founders), Polk County, Fla., in November 1883; constructed the railway system which operates through that section; engaged in the real-estate and insurance business and in the growing of citrus fruits; mayor of Lakeland 1888–1892; county commissioner of Polk County 1896–1899; chief engrossing clerk of the State house of representatives 1889–1901; member of the State house of representatives 1903–1905; served in the State senate 1913–1917, being its president from 1913 to 1915; elected as a Democrat to the Sixty-fifth and to the seven succeeding Congresses (March 4, 1917–March 3, 1933); unsuccessful candidate for renomination in 1932; member of the Federal Power Commission 1933–1937; voluntarily retired from public life and resumed the real estate and insurance businesses, property management, and the growing of citrus fruits; died in Lakeland, Fla., on August 11, 1947; interment in Roselawn Cemetery.

DRAPER, Joseph, a Representative from Virginia; born in Draper Valley, Wythe (now Pulaski) County, Va., December 25, 1794; attended private schools; studied law; was admitted to the bar in 1818 and commenced practice in Wytheville, Wythe County, Va.; served as a private in the War of 1812; member of the State senate 1828–1830; elected to the Twenty-first Congress to fill the vacancy caused by the death of Alexander Smyth and served from December 6, 1830, to March 3, 1831; unsuccessfully contested the election of Charles C. Johnston to the Twenty-second Congress; subsequently elected to the Twenty-second Congress to fill the vacancy caused by the death of Charles

C. Johnston and served from December 6, 1832, to March 3, 1833; was not a candidate for renomination; resumed the practice of law until his death in Wytheville, Va., June 10, 1834; interment in a private cemetery known as Oglesbies Cemetery, Drapers Valley, Va.

DRAPER, William Franklin, a Representative from Massachusetts; born in Lowell, Mass., April 9, 1842; attended public, private, and high schools; studied mechanical engineering and cotton manufacturing; during the Civil War enlisted as a private in the Twenty-fifth Regiment, Massachusetts Volunteer Infantry, on September 9, 1861; promoted to second lieutenant October 7, 1861; first lieutenant April 15, 1862; captain in the Thirty-sixth Massachusetts Infantry August 27, 1862; major September 1, 1863; lieutenant colonel August 9, 1864; brevetted colonel and brigadier general of Volunteers March 13, 1865, "for gallant and meritorious services in the field during the war"; was shot through the body at the Battle of the Wilderness May 6, 1864, and again slightly wounded at Pegram Farm September 30, 1864; mustered out October 12, 1864; became a manufacturer of cotton machinery at Hopedale, Worcester County, and made and patented many improvements; delegate to the Republican National Convention at Cincinnati in 1876; colonel on the staff of Governor Long from 1880 to 1883; presidential elector at large on the Republican ticket of Harrison and Morton in 1888; elected as a Republican to the Fifty-third and Fifty-fourth Congresses (March 4, 1893–March 3, 1897); was not a candidate for renomination in 1896; president of the Draper Co. upon its incorporation in 1896; Ambassador and Minister Plenipotentiary to Italy 1897–1899; died in Washington, D. C., on January 28, 1910; interment in Village Cemetery, Hopedale, Mass.

DRAPER, William Henry, a Representative from New York; born in Rochdale, Worcester County, Mass., June 24, 1841; moved with his parents to Troy, N. Y., in 1847; attended the public schools until 1856; engaged in mercantile pursuits; trustee of the village of Lansingburgh for ten years; commissioner of jurors for Rensselaer County 1896–1900; elected as a Republican to the Fifty-seventh and to the five succeeding Congresses (March 4, 1901–March 3, 1913); was not a candidate for reelection in 1912; engaged in the manufacture of cordage and twine and was president of the W. H. Draper & Sons (Inc.); died in Troy, N. Y., December 7, 1921; interment in Oakwood Cemetery.

DRAYTON, William, a Representative from South Carolina; born in St. Augustine, Fla., December 30, 1776; attended preparatory schools in England; returned to the United States in 1790 and settled in Charleston, S. C.; studied law; was admitted to the bar December 12, 1797, and commenced practice in Charleston; member of the State house of representatives 1806–1808; during the War of 1812 entered the United States Army as lieutenant colonel of the Tenth Infantry March 12, 1812; became colonel of the Eighteenth Infantry July 25, 1812; inspector general August 1, 1814, and served throughout the war; resumed the practice of law in Charleston, S. C.; recorder of Charleston 1819–1824; elected as a Union Democrat to the Nineteenth Congress to fill the vacancy caused by the resignation of Joel R. Poinsett; reelected to the Twentieth, Twenty-first, and Twenty-second Congresses and served from May 17, 1825, to March 3, 1833; declined the appointment of Secretary of War in the Cabinet of President Jackson and also as Minister to England; opposed nullification in 1830; moved to Philadelphia, Pa., in August 1833; president of the Bank of the United States in 1840 and 1841; died in Philadelphia, Pa., May 24, 1846; interment in Laurel Hill Cemetery.

DRAYTON, William Henry, a Delegate from South Carolina; born at Drayton Hall, on Ashley River, S. C., in September 1742; pursued classical studies; attended Westminster School and Balliol College, Oxford, England; returned to South Carolina in 1764; studied law and was admitted to the bar; visited England again in 1770 and was appointed by King George III privy councilor for the Province of South Carolina; while on his way home was appointed assistant judge, but took such an active part in the pre-Revolutionary movement that he was deprived of both positions; president of the council of safety in 1775, and in 1776 was chief justice; Member of the Continental Congress in 1778 and served until his death in Philadelphia, Pa., on September 3, 1779; interment in Christ Church Cemetery.

DRESSER, Solomon Robert, a Representative from Pennsylvania; born in Litchfield, Hillsdale County, Mich., February 1, 1842; attended the common schools and Hillsdale College; engaged in agricultural pursuits until 1865; became an inventor of oil and gas well equipment; moved to Pennsylvania in 1872 and engaged in the production of oil and gas; founder and president of the S. R. Dresser Manufacturing Co.; elected as a Republican to the Fifty-eighth and Fifty-ninth Congresses (March 4, 1903–March 3, 1907); was not a candidate for renomination in 1906; resumed former business pursuits; died in Bradford, McKean County, Pa., January 21, 1911; interment in Oak Hill Cemetery.

DREW, Ira Walton, a Representative from Pennsylvania; born in Hardwick, Caledonia County, Vt., August 31, 1878; attended the public schools and Hardwick Academy; apprenticed as a printer, becoming a journeyman in 1899; newspaper reporter in Burlington, Vt., 1899–1906; reporter and news editor in Boston, Mass., 1906–1908; was graduated from Philadelphia (Pa.) College of Osteopathy in 1911 and began the practice of osteopathy in Philadelphia the same year; member of the faculty of the Philadelphia College of Osteopathy 1912–1933; elected as a Democrat to the Seventy-fifth Congress (January 3, 1937–January 3, 1939); unsuccessful candidate for reelection in 1938 to the Seventy-sixth Congress; member of the board of trustees, Philadelphia College of Osteopathy; resumed the practice of osteopathy in Philadelphia, Pa., where he now resides.

DREW, Irving Webster, a Senator from New Hampshire; born in Colebrook, Coos County, N. H., January 8, 1845; attended Kimball Union Academy, and was graduated from Dartmouth College, Hanover, N. H., in June 1870; moved to Lancaster, N. H., where he studied law; was admitted to the bar in 1871 and commenced practice in Lancaster; appointed major of the New Hampshire National Guard in 1876 and served three years; delegate to the Democratic National Convention at Cincinnati in 1880 and at Chicago in 1892 and 1896; member of the State senate in 1883 and 1884; left the Democratic Party in 1896, when he refused to accept the free-silver plank, and later became an active member of the Republican Party; delegate to the State constitutional conventions in 1902 and 1912; engaged in banking and the railroad business; elected president of the State bar association in 1899; appointed as a Republican to the United States Senate to fill the vacancy caused by the death of Jacob H. Gallinger and served from September 2 to November 5, 1918, when a successor was elected; was not a candidate for election; retired from active business pursuits; died in Montclair, Essex County, N. J., April 10, 1922; interment in Summer Street Cemetery, Lancaster, Coos County, N. H.

DREWRY, Patrick Henry, a Representative from Virginia; born in Petersburg, Dinwiddie County, Va., May 24, 1875; attended the public schools, Petersburg High School, and McCabe's University School; was graduated from Randolph-Macon College, Ashland, Va., in 1896; studied law at the University of Virginia at Charlottesville; was admitted to the bar in 1901 and commenced practice in Petersburg; director of the Petersburg Savings & American Trust Co., of Petersburg; member of the State senate 1912–1920; delegate to the Democratic State conventions in 1912, 1916, 1920, and 1924; delegate to the Democratic National Convention at St. Louis in 1916; chairman of the Economy and Efficiency Commission of Virginia 1916–1918; chairman of the State auditing committee 1916–1920; chairman of the State advisory board in 1919; member of the Democratic National Congressional Committee 1923–1927; member of the Board of Visitors to the United States Naval Academy at Annapolis in 1925; elected as a Democrat to the Sixty-sixth Congress to fill the vacancy caused by the death of Walter A. Watson; reelected to the Sixty-seventh and to the thirteen succeeding Congresses and served from April 27, 1920, until his death in Petersburg, Va., December 21, 1947; interment in Blandford Cemetery.

DRIGGS, Edmund Hope, a Representative from New York; born in Brooklyn, N. Y., May 2, 1865; attended the public schools and Adelphi Academy in Brooklyn; became engaged in the casualty-insurance business; elected as a Democrat to the Fifty-fifth Congress to fill the vacancy caused by the resignation of Francis H. Wilson; reelected to the Fifty-sixth Congress and served from December 6, 1897, to March 3, 1901; unsuccessful candidate for reelection in 1900 to the Fifty-seventh Congress; resumed the casualty-insurance business and also engaged in safety engineering; died in Brooklyn, N. Y., September 27, 1946; interment in Cypress Hills Cemetery.

DRIGGS, John Fletcher, a Representative from Michigan; born in Kinderhook, N. Y., March 8, 1813; completed preparatory studies; moved with his parents to Tarrytown, N. Y., in 1825; moved to New York City in 1827; was apprenticed to learn the trade of sash, door, and blind manufacturing in 1829; journeyman for two years; commenced business as a master mechanic and continued in it until 1856; superintendent of the New York penitentiary and public institutions on Blackwells Island in 1844; moved to Michigan in 1856; engaged in the real-estate business and salt manufacturing; president of the common council of East Saginaw, Mich., in 1858; member of the State house of representatives in 1859 and 1860; was tendered an appointment as colonel during the Civil War; organized the Twenty-ninth Michigan Infantry July 29, 1864, which was mustered into service October 3, 1864; elected as a Republican to the Thirty-eighth, Thirty-ninth, and Fortieth Congresses (March 4, 1863–March 3, 1869); unsuccessful candidate for election in 1870 to the Forty-second Congress; one of the committee appointed to accompany the body of President Lincoln to Springfield, Ill., for interment; injured by a fall on the ice in the winter of 1875–76, as a result of which he died in East Saginaw, Mich., December 17, 1877; interment in Brady Hill Cemetery, Saginaw, Mich.; reinterment in Forest Lawn Cemetery.

DRISCOLL, Daniel Angelus, a Representative from New York; born in Buffalo, Erie County, N. Y., March 6, 1875; attended the public schools and Central High School; engaged in the undertaking business with his father, and also in other business enterprises; elected as a Democrat to the Sixty-first and to the three succeeding Congresses (March 4, 1909–March 3, 1917); was an unsuccessful candidate for reelection in 1916 to the Sixty-fifth Congress; returned to the active management of the Driscoll Funeral Home in Buffalo, N. Y.; served as postmaster of Buffalo, N. Y., from February 15, 1934, until February 28, 1947; president of the Phoenix Brewery Corp. of Buffalo, N. Y.; died in Buffalo, N. Y., June 5, 1955; interment in Holy Cross Cemetery, Lackawanna, N. Y.

DRISCOLL, Denis Joseph, a Representative from Pennsylvania; born in North Lawrence, St. Lawrence County, N. Y., March 27, 1871; attended the public schools, Lawrenceville (N. Y.) Academy, and State Teachers' College, Potsdam, N. Y.; taught school in Potsdam, N. Y., in 1888 and 1889; moved to St. Marys, Elk County, Pa., in 1890 and continued teaching as a high school teacher in 1890 and 1891 and as a principal of public schools 1892–1897; studied law; was admitted to the bar on April 22, 1898, and on the same day enlisted as a private in the Sixteenth Regiment, Pennsylvania National Guard, which on that day had been called for service in the Spanish-American War, and served under General Miles in Puerto Rico; was honorably discharged as a second lieutenant; after the war commenced the practice of law in St. Marys, Pa.; member of the Democratic State committee 1899–1922, serving as chairman in 1905; chief burgess of St. Marys, Pa., 1903–1906; president of St. Marys School Board 1911–1936; delegate to the Democratic National Conventions in 1916 and 1920 and alternate delegate in 1924 and 1928; United States attorney for the western district of Pennsylvania in 1920 and 1921; elected as a Democrat to the Seventy-fourth Congress (January 3, 1935–January 3, 1937); unsuccessful candidate for reelection in 1936 to the Seventy-fifth Congress; appointed chairman of the Pennsylvania Public Utility Commission for a ten-year term on April 1, 1937, from which position he resigned to accept an appointment on March 2, 1940, by the United States Court for the Southern District of New York, as one of two trustees in the reorganization of the bankrupt Associated Gas and Electric Corporation, and served until August 1946; died in St. Marys, Pa., January 18, 1958; interment in St. Marys Catholic Cemetery.

DRISCOLL, Michael Edward, a Representative from New York; born in Syracuse, N. Y., February 9, 1851; moved with his parents to the town of Camillus, Onondaga County, in 1852; attended the district schools, Monro Collegiate Institute, in Elbridge, Onondaga County, and was graduated from Williams College, Williamstown, Mass., in 1877; studied law; was admitted to the bar in 1879 and commenced practice in Syracuse, N. Y., the same year; appointed one of five commissioners to draft a uniform charter for second-class cities in the State; appointed attorney for the State superintendent of insurance in 1905; member of the Taft party that visited the Philippine Islands and oriental countries in 1905; chairman of the Republican State convention in 1906; elected as a Republican to the Fifty-sixth and to the six succeeding Congresses (March 4, 1899–March 3, 1913); unsuccessful candidate for reelection in 1912 to the Sixty-third Congress; engaged in the practice of law, traveling, and lecturing on his travels; died in Syracuse, N. Y., January 19, 1929; interment in Oakwood Cemetery.

DRIVER, William Joshua, a Representative from Arkansas; born near Osceola, Mississippi County, Ark., March 2, 1873; attended the public schools; studied law; was admitted to the bar in 1894 and commenced practice in Osceola, Ark.; member of the State house of representatives 1897–1899; judge of the second judicial circuit of Arkansas 1911–1918; member of the State constitutional convention in 1918; delegate to the Democratic National Convention at Chicago in 1932; elected as a Democrat to the Sixty-seventh and to the eight succeeding Congresses (March 4, 1921–January 3, 1939); unsuccessful candidate for renomination in 1938; resumed the practice of law and also engaged in the banking business in Osceola, Ark., until his death there on October 1, 1948; interment in Violet Cemetery.

DROMGOOLE, George Coke (uncle of Alexander Dromgoole Sims), a Representative from Virginia; born in Lawrenceville, Brunswick County, Va., May 15, 1797; completed preparatory studies; studied law; was admitted to the bar and practiced; member of the State house of representatives 1823–1826; member of the State senate 1826–1835; delegate to the State constitutional convention in 1829; elected as a Democrat to the Twenty-fourth, Twenty-fifth, and Twenty-sixth Congresses (March 4, 1835–March 3, 1841); declined to be a candidate for reelection in 1840 to the Twenty-seventh Congress; elected to the Twenty-eighth, Twenty-ninth, and Thirtieth Congresses and served from March 4, 1843, until his death on his estate in Brunswick County, Va., April 27, 1847; interment in the family burying ground south of the Meherrin River.

DRUKKER, Dow Henry, a Representative from New Jersey; born in Sneek, Holland, February 7, 1872; immigrated to the United States with his parents, who settled in Grand Rapids, Mich., the same year; attended the public schools of Grand Rapids, Mich.; moved to New Jersey in 1897 and settled in Passaic; member of the Passaic County Board of Chosen Freeholders 1906–1913, serving as director 1908–1912; elected as a Republican to the Sixty-third Congress to fill the vacancy caused by the death of Robert Gunn Bremner; reelected to the Sixty-fourth and Sixty-fifth Congresses and served from April 7, 1914, to March 3, 1919; was not a candidate for renomination in 1918; publisher of the Herald-News of Passaic-Clifton since 1916; president of the Union Building and Investment Co. since 1909; knighted as an Officer of the Order of Orange-Nassau by Queen Juliana for services rendered in the great flood of 1953; resides in Clifton, N. J., and Lake Wales, Fla.

DRUM, Augustus, a Representative from Pennsylvania; born in Greensburg, Pa., November 26, 1815; received private instruction at home and then attended Greensburg Academy; was graduated from Jefferson College (now Washington and Jefferson), Canonsburg, Pa.; studied law; was admitted to the bar in 1836 and commenced practice in Greensburg; member of the State senate in 1852 and 1853; held several local offices; elected as a Democrat to the Thirty-third Congress (March 4, 1853–March 3, 1855); unsuccessful candidate for reelection in 1854 to the Thirty-fourth Congress; resumed the practice of law in Greensburg, Westmoreland County, Pa., and died there September 15, 1858; interment in St. Clair Cemetery.

DRYDEN, John Fairfield, a Senator from New Jersey; born in Temple, Franklin County, Maine, August 7, 1839; moved to Massachusetts in 1846 with his parents, who settled in Worcester; attended Worcester High School and Yale College; made a special study of life insurance, and in 1875, in Newark, N. J., founded the Prudential Insurance Co. of America, becoming its first secretary and in 1881 its president, and served in the latter position until 1911; one of the founders of the Fidelity Trust Co.; identified with the management of various street railways, the establishment of banks, and other financial enterprises in New Jersey, New York, and Pennsylvania; presidential elector on the Republican ticket of McKinley and Hobart in 1896 and of McKinley and Roosevelt in 1900; elected as a Republican to the United States Senate to fill the vacancy caused by the death of William J. Sewell and served from January 29, 1902, to March 3, 1907; was a candidate for reelection, but withdrew because of a deadlock in the legislature; resumed his former business pursuits; died in Newark, N. J., November 24, 1911; interment in Mount Pleasant Cemetery.

DUANE, James, a Delegate from New York; born in New York City February 6, 1733; completed preparatory studies; studied law; was admitted to the bar August 3, 1754; clerk of the chancery court in 1762; attorney general of New York in 1767; boundary commissioner in 1768 and 1784; State Indian commissioner in 1774; delegate to the provincial convention in 1775; member of the Revolutionary Committee of One Hundred in 1775; Member of the Continental Congress 1774–1784; member of the Provincial Congress in 1776 and 1777; served in the State senate 1782–1785 and 1788–1790; chosen a member of the Annapolis Commercial Convention in 1786, but did not attend; mayor of New York City 1784–1789; delegate to the State convention which ratified the Federal Constitution in 1788; United States district judge for the district of New York 1789–1794; died in Duanesburg, Schenectady County, N. Y., February 1, 1797; interment under Christ Church.

DUBOIS, Fred Thomas, a Delegate and a Senator from Idaho; born in Palestine, Crawford County, Ill., May 29, 1851; attended the public schools, and was graduated from Yale College in 1872; secretary of the Board of Railway and Warehouse Commissioners of Illinois 1875 and 1876; moved to Idaho Territory in 1880 and engaged in business; United States marshal of Idaho from August 25, 1882, until September 1, 1886; elected as a Republican a Delegate from the Territory of Idaho to the Fiftieth and Fifty-first Congresses and served from March 4, 1887, to July 3, 1890, having assisted in securing the admission of the Territory of Idaho to the Union on that date; delegate to the Republican National Convention in 1888 and chairman of the first delegation from the new State to the Republican National Convention at Minneapolis in 1892; elected as a Republican to the United States Senate and served from March 4, 1891, to March 3, 1897; unsuccessful Silver Republican candidate for reelection to the United States Senate in 1896; chairman of the Republican delegation from Idaho to the Republican National Convention at St. Louis in 1896, but left the convention and the party when the single gold standard was supported; elected as a Silver Republican to the United States Senate and served from March 4, 1901, to March 3, 1907; shortly after his election to the Senate as a Republican he became a Democrat and served as a delegate to the Democratic National Conventions in 1904, 1908, and 1912; after retirement from Congress took up his residence in Washington, D. C., retaining Blackfoot, Idaho, as his legal residence; appointed civilian member of the Board of Ordnance and Fortifications 1918–1920; appointed by President Coolidge on July 15, 1924, as a Democratic member of the International Joint Commission created to prevent disputes regarding the use of the boundary waters between the United States and Canada, and served until his death in Washington, D. C., February 14, 1930; interment in Grove City Cemetery, Blackfoot, Idaho.

DU BOSE, Dudley McIver, a Representative from Georgia; born in Shelby County, Tenn., October 28, 1834; attended the University of Mississippi at Oxford, and was graduated from the Lebanon (Tenn.) Law School in 1856; was admitted to the bar in 1857 and commenced the practice of law in Memphis, Tenn.; moved to Augusta, Ga., in 1860; served in the Confederate Army during the Civil War as colonel of the Fifteenth Regiment, Georgia Volunteer Infantry, and subsequently became brigadier general in the Western Army; moved to Washington, Wilkes County, Ga.; elected as a Democrat to the Forty-second Congress (March 4, 1871–March 3, 1873); resumed the practice of law; died in Washington, Ga., March 2, 1883; interment in Rest Haven Cemetery.

DUDLEY, Charles Edward, a Senator from New York; born in Johnston Hall, Staffordshire, England, May 23, 1780; immigrated to the United States with his mother, who settled in Newport, R. I., in 1794; entered a counting room as clerk; moved to Albany, N. Y., where he engaged in the mercantile business; presidential elector on the Democratic ticket of Monroe and Tompkins in 1816; member of the State senate 1820–1825; mayor of Albany 1821–1824, 1828, and 1829; elected as a Democrat to the United States Senate to fill the vacancy caused by the resignation of Martin Van Buren and served from January 15, 1829, to March 3, 1833; became interested in astronomical science; died in Albany, N. Y., January 23, 1841; interment in the Rural Cemetery.

DUDLEY, Edward Bishop, a Representative from North Carolina; born near Jacksonville, Onslow County, N. C., December 15, 1769; attended the local academy; member of the State house of commons 1811 and 1813; served in the State senate in 1814; during the War of 1812, as lieutenant colonel of the Onslow Regiment of Volunteers, he was stationed at Wilmington, N. C., to defend that region from an expected attack by Admiral Cockburn; member of the State house of commons from Wilmington in 1816 and 1817; elected as a National Republican to the Twenty-first Congress to fill the vacancy caused by the death of Gabriel Holmes and served from November 10, 1829, to March 3, 1831; declined to be a candidate for reelection in 1830; again a member of the State house of commons in 1834 and 1835; organized the Wilmington & Weldon Railroad Co. and was its first president; Governor of North Carolina 1837–1841, being the first Governor elected by popular vote instead of by the legislature; resumed his former railroad pursuits; died in Wilmington, N. C., October 30, 1855; interment in Oak Dale Cemetery.

DUELL, Rodolphus Holland, a Representative from New York; born in Warren, Herkimer County, N. Y., December 20, 1824; completed preparatory studies; studied law; was admitted to the bar in 1845 and commenced practice in Fabius, N. Y.; moved to Cortland, N. Y., in 1847; district attorney of Cortland County 1850–1855; judge of Cortland County 1855–1859; assessor of internal revenue for the twenty-third district of New York from 1869 to 1871; elected as a Republican to the Thirty-sixth and Thirty-seventh Congresses (March 4, 1859–March 3, 1863); resumed the practice of law in Cortland; elected to the Forty-second and Forty-third Congresses (March 4, 1871–March 3, 1875); appointed by President Grant United States Commissioner of Patents on October 1, 1875, and served until January 30, 1877; resumed the practice of law in Cortland, N. Y., where he died February 11, 1891; interment in Cortland Rural Cemetery.

DUER, William, a Delegate from New York; born in Devonshire, England, March 18, 1747; completed preparatory studies and attended Eton College (England); in 1765 became aide-de-camp to Lord Clive, Governor General of India; immigrated to America in 1768 and settled in Fort Miller, Washington County, N. Y.; appointed justice of the peace, by royal authority, on July 1, 1773; first judge of Charlotte (now Washington) County; built the first saw and grist mills at Fort Miller, and later erected a snuff mill and a powder mill; was prominent in ante-Revolutionary movements; member of the Provincial Congress in 1776 and 1777; served in the State senate in 1777; appointed judge of the court of common pleas in 1777 and reappointed in 1778; moved to Fishkill, N. Y., and later to what is now Paterson, N. J., where he erected the first cotton mill; also built a cotton mill in Westchester County, N. Y.; Member of the Continental Congress in 1777 and 1778; moved to New York City, N. Y., in 1783; served as a member of the State assembly in 1786; assisted Alexander Hamilton in organizing the United States Treasury Department in 1789 and 1790; died in New York City April 18, 1799; interment in the family vault under the old church of St. Thomas; reinterment in Jamaica, Long Island, N. Y.

DUER, William (grandson of the preceding), a Representative from New York; born in New York City May 25, 1805; completed preparatory studies, and was graduated from Columbia College, New York City, in 1824; studied law; was admitted to the bar in 1824 and commenced practice in New York City; unsuccessful candidate for the State assembly in 1832; moved to New Orleans, La., in 1832, where he continued the practice of law; moved to Oswego, N. Y., in 1836 and continued the practice of law; member of the New York State Assembly in 1840 and 1841; unsuccessful candidate i n 1842 for election to the Twenty-eighth Congress; delegate to the Whig National Convention in 1844; district attorney of Oswego County 1845–1847; elected as a Whig to the Thirtieth and Thirty-first Congresses (March 4, 1847–March 3, 1851); appointed by President Fillmore as consul to Valparaiso, Chile, on March 18, 1851, and served until May 23, 1853; on his return to the United States settled in San Francisco, Calif., in 1854 and practiced his profession; served as clerk of San Francisco County in 1858 and 1859; returned to Staten Island, N. Y., in 1859 and lived in retirement until his death in New Brighton, Richmond County, N. Y., August 25, 1879; interment in Silver Mount Cemetery, Thompkinsville, Staten Island, N. Y.

DUFF, James Henderson, a Senator from Pennsylvania; born in Mansfield (now Carnegie), Allegheny County, Pa., January 21, 1883; was graduated from Princeton University in 1904; student at the University of Pennsylvania 1904–1906; graduated from the law school of the University of Pittsburgh in 1907; was admitted to the bar the same year and commenced the practice of law in Pittsburgh, Pa.; attorney general of Pennsylvania 1943–1947; Governor of Pennsylvania from January 21, 1947, to January 15, 1951; member of the Pennsylvania Pardon Board; life trustee Carnegie, Pa., library; delegate to the Republican National Conventions in 1932, 1936, 1940, 1948, and 1952; elected as a Republican to the United States Senate in 1950 for the term commencing January 3, 1951, but did not assume his duties until January 16, 1951, and served until January 3, 1957; unsuccessful candidate for reelection in 1956; engaged in the practice of law in Washington, D. C.; resides on Cedar Lane Farm, Hollywood, Md.

DUFFEY, Warren Joseph, a Representative from Ohio; born in Toledo, Ohio, January 24, 1886; attended the public and high schools; was graduated from St. John's University, Toledo, Ohio, in 1908 and from the law department of Michigan University at Ann Arbor in 1911; was admitted to the bar the same year and commenced the practice of law in Toledo, Ohio; served in the State house of representatives in 1913 and 1914; member of the Toledo City Council in 1917 and 1918; served as chairman of the Lucas County Democratic central committee 1919–1932; delegate to the Democratic National Convention at Chicago in 1932; elected as a Democrat to the Seventy-third and Seventy-fourth Congresses and served from March 4, 1933, until his death; unsuccessful candidate for renomination in 1936; died in Toledo, Ohio, July 7, 1936; interment in Calvary Cemetery.

DUFFY, Francis Ryan, a Senator from Wisconsin; born in Fond du Lac, Fond du Lac County, Wis., June 23, 1888; attended the public and high schools; was graduated from the College of Letters and Science of the University of Wisconsin at Madison in 1910 and from its law department in 1912; was admitted to the bar in 1912 and commenced practice in Fond du Lac, Wis.; during the First World War served in the United States Army from May 9, 1917, until honorably discharged with the rank of major in the Motor Transport Corps on May 24, 1919, serving fourteen months overseas; resumed the practice of law in Fond du Lac, Wis.; elected as a Democrat to the United States Senate and served from March 4, 1933, to January 3, 1939; unsuccessful candidate for reelection in 1938; United States district judge for the eastern district of Wisconsin from July 1, 1939, to February 14, 1949, when he qualified as a United States circuit judge of the court of appeals for the seventh circuit, in which capacity he is now serving; is a resident of Milwaukee, Wis.

DUFFY, James Patrick Bernard, a Representative from New York; born in Rochester, N. Y., November 25, 1878; attended private schools; was graduated from Georgetown University, Washington, D. C., in 1901 and from the law department of Harvard University, Cambridge, Mass., in 1904; was admitted to the bar in 1904 and commenced practice in Rochester, N. Y.; member of the Rochester (N. Y.) School Board 1905–1932; trustee of the Rochester Chamber of Commerce 1912–1952; during the First World War served as a director of the Rochester home unit of the American National Red Cross; served as director and legal adviser of the Rochester chapter of the American National Red Cross 1921–1955, and as director of the Rochester Community Chest 1927–1956; member of the New York State Alcoholic Beverage Control Board in 1933 and 1934; member of the board of commissioners of the Rochester Museum of Arts and Sciences since 1934; member of board of trustees, Rochester Savings Bank, 1935–1959; elected as a Democrat to the Seventy-fourth Congress (January 3, 1935–January 3, 1937); unsuccessful candidate for renomination in 1936; appointed by Governor Lehman justice of the supreme court of the State of New York, seventh judicial district, for term expiring December 31, 1937; member of the State Probation Commission 1938–1944; during World War II was chairman of New York State Appeal Board No. 22, coordinator of Selective Service Appeal Board No. 22, and Washington liaison officer for the United Service Organization; resumed the practice of law; resides in Rochester, N. Y.

DUGRO, Philip Henry, a Representative from New York; born in New York City October 3, 1855; attended the public schools, and was graduated from the school of arts of Columbia College, New York City, in 1876 and from the law department of the same institution in 1878; was admitted to the bar in the latter year and commenced practice in New York City; member of the State assembly in 1879; elected as a Democrat to the Forty-seventh Congress (March 4, 1881–March 3, 1883); was not a candidate for reelection; resumed the practice of law in New York City and also interested in the real-estate business; declined the office of State commissioner of immigration in 1885; judge of the superior court of New York County from 1887 to 1896, when the superior court was merged into the supreme court; associate justice of the New York Supreme Court 1896–1901; reelected in 1901 and again in 1915, and served until his death in New York City March 1, 1920; interment in Woodlawn Cemetery.

DUKE, Richard Thomas Walker, a Representative from Virginia; born near Charlottesville, Albemarle County, Va., June 6, 1822; attended private schools; was graduated from the Virginia Military Institute, Lexington, Va., in 1844; was graduated from the law department of the University of Virginia, Charlottesville, Va., in 1850; elected Commonwealth attorney for the county of Albemarle in 1858 and continued in that office until 1869; during the Civil War entered the Confederate Army; became colonel of the Forty-sixth Regiment, Virginia Infantry; was captured at Sailors Creek, Va., and confined in Johnsons Island Prison, Lake Erie, until July 1865; elected as a Conservative to the Forty-first Congress to fill the vacancy caused by the death of Robert Ridgway; reelected to the Forty-second Congress and served from November 8, 1870, to March 3, 1873; member of the State house of delegates in 1879 and 1880; died at his country estate, "Sunny

Side," near Charlottesville, Albemarle County, Va., on July 2, 1898; interment in Maplewood Cemetery, Charlottesville, Va.

DULLES, John Foster, a Senator from New York; born in Washington, D. C., February 25, 1888; attended the public schools of Watertown, N. Y.; was graduated from Princeton University in 1908; attended the Sorbonne, Paris, in 1908 and 1909; graduated from the law school of George Washington University, Washington, D. C., in 1911; was admitted to the bar and commenced the practice of law in New York, N. Y., in 1911; special agent for Department of State in Central America in 1917; during the First World War served as a captain and a major in the United States Army Intelligence Service in 1917 and 1918; assistant to chairman War Trade Board in 1918; counsel to American Commission to Negotiate Peace in 1918 and 1919; member of Reparations Commission and Supreme Economic Council in 1919; legal adviser, Polish Plan of Financial Stabilization, in 1927; American representative Berlin Debt Conferences in 1933; member, United States delegation, San Francisco Conference on World Organization in 1945; adviser to Secretary of State at Council of Foreign Ministers in London in 1945, Moscow and London in 1947, and Paris in 1949; representative to the General Assembly of the United Nations 1946–1949 and chairman of the United States delegation in Paris in 1948; trustee of Rockefeller Foundation; chairman of the board, Carnegie Endowment for International Peace; member of the New York State Banking Board 1946–1949; appointed as a Republican to the United States Senate to fill the vacancy caused by the resignation of Robert F. Wagner and served from July 7, 1949, to November 8, 1949, when a duly elected successor qualified; unsuccessful for election to the vacancy; United States representative to the Fifth General Assembly of the United Nations in 1950; consultant to the Secretary of State in 1951 and 1952; appointed Secretary of State in the Cabinet of President Dwight D. Eisenhower on January 20, 1953, and served until his resignation, due to illness, April 15, 1959; died in Washington, D. C., May 24, 1959; interment in Arlington National Cemetery, Fort Myer, Va.

DULSKI, Thaddeus J., a Representative from New York; born in Buffalo, Erie County, N. Y., September 27, 1915; attended parochial school, Buffalo Technical High School, Canisius College, Buffalo, N. Y., and the University of Buffalo; with the Bureau of Internal Revenue, Treasury Department, 1940–1947; veteran of World War II; accountant and tax consultant; special agent in the Price Stabilization Administration 1951–1953; in 1953 was elected Walden district councilman for two terms and in 1957 was elected councilman-at-large of the city of Buffalo for a four-year term; elected as a Democrat to the Eighty-sixth Congress (January 3, 1959–January 3, 1961). *Reelected to the Eighty-seventh Congress.*

DUMONT, Ebenezer, a Representative from Indiana; born in Vevay, Ind., November 23, 1814; pursued classical studies; studied law; was admitted to the bar and commenced practice in Vevay; member of the State house of representatives in 1838; treasurer of Vevay 1839–1845; lieutenant colonel of Volunteers in the Mexican War; member of the State house of representatives in 1850 and 1853; presidential elector on the Democratic ticket of Pierce and King in 1852; colonel of the Seventh Regiment, Indiana Volunteer Infantry, during the Civil War; promoted to brigadier general of Volunteers September 3, 1861, and served until February 28, 1863, when he resigned; elected as a Unionist to the Thirty-eighth and Thirty-ninth Congresses (March 4, 1863–March 3, 1867); was not a candidate for renomination in 1866; appointed by President Grant Governor of Idaho Territory, but died in Indianapolis, Ind., April 16, 1871, before taking the oath of office; interment in Crown Hill Cemetery.

DUNBAR, James Whitson, a Representative from Indiana; born in New Albany, Floyd County, Ind., October 17, 1860; attended the public schools, and was graduated from New Albany High School in 1878; engaged in mercantile pursuits; manager of public utilities in New Albany and Jeffersonville; secretary-treasurer of the Western Gas Association 1894–1906; secretary of the American Gas Institute 1906–1909; president of the Indiana Gas Association 1908–1910 and secretary 1914–1919; presidential elector from the State at large on the Republican ticket of Hughes and Fairbanks in 1916; elected as a Republican to the Sixty-sixth and Sixty-seventh Congresses (March 4, 1919–March 3, 1923); was not a candidate for reelection in 1922; elected to the Seventy-first Congress (March 4, 1929–March 3, 1931); unsuccessful candidate for reelection in 1930 to the Seventy-second Congress; resumed his former business pursuits; died in New Albany, Ind., May 19, 1943; interment in Fairview Cemetery.

DUNBAR, William, a Representative from Louisiana; born in Virginia in 1805; completed preparatory studies; moved to Alexandria, Va., and engaged in the practice of law in the early thirties; moved to Louisiana in 1852; appointed associate justice of the supreme court of Louisiana to fill the vacancy caused by the death of Judge Preston and served from September 1, 1852, to May 4, 1853; elected as a Democrat to the Thirty-third Congress (March 4, 1853–March 3, 1855); retired to his sugar plantation in the parish of St. Bernard and resided there until his death on March 18, 1861.

DUNCAN, Alexander, a Representative from Ohio; born in Bottle Hill (now Madison), Morris County, N. J., in 1788; studied and practiced medicine; moved to Ohio and settled in Cincinnati; member of the State house of representatives in 1828, 1829, 1831, and 1832; served in the State senate 1832–1834; elected as a Whig to the Twenty-fifth and Twenty-sixth Congresses (March 4, 1837–March 3, 1841); unsuccessful Whig candidate for reelection in 1840 to the Twenty-seventh Congress; elected to the Twenty-eighth Congress (March 4, 1843–March 3, 1845); was not a candidate in 1844 for reelection to the Twenty-ninth Congress; resumed the practice of his profession; died in Madisonville (now a part of Cincinnati), Hamilton County, Ohio, March 23, 1853; interment in Laurel Cemetery.

DUNCAN, Daniel, a Representative from Ohio; born in Shippensburg, Cumberland County, Pa., July 22, 1806; completed preparatory studies; attended Jefferson College, Canonsburg, Pa., in 1825; moved to Newark, Ohio, in 1828; engaged in mercantile pursuits; member of the State house of representatives in 1843; unsuccessful Whig candidate for election to the State senate in 1844; elected as a Whig to the Thirtieth Congress (March 4, 1847–March 3, 1849); was an unsuccessful candidate for reelection in 1848 to the Thirty-first Congress; died in Washington, D. C., on May 18, 1849; interment in the Newark Graveyard, Newark, Ohio.

DUNCAN, James, a Representative from Pennsylvania; born in Philadelphia, Pa., in 1756; attended the common schools and Princeton College; first prothonotary of Adams County; during the Revolutionary War was appointed on November 3, 1776, a lieutenant in Colonel Hazen's regiment, and on March 25, 1778, was promoted to captain; elected to the Seventeenth Congress but resigned before Congress assembled; died in Mercer County, Pa., June 24, 1844.

DUNCAN, James Henry, a Representative from Massachusetts; born in Haverhill, Mass., December 5, 1793; attended Phillips Exeter Academy, Exeter, N. H., and was graduated from

Harvard University in 1812; studied law; was admitted to the bar in 1815 and commenced practice in Haverhill; an active militia officer, and attained the rank of colonel; president of the Essex Agricultural Society; member of the State house of representatives in 1827, 1837, 1838, and again in 1857; served in the State senate 1828–1831; delegate to the Whig National Convention at Harrisburg, Pa., in 1839; appointed commissioner in bankruptcy in 1841; elected as a Whig to the Thirty-first and Thirty-second Congresses (March 4, 1849–March 3, 1853); engaged in the real-estate business; died in Haverhill, Essex County, Mass., February 8, 1869; interment in Linwood Cemetery.

DUNCAN, Joseph, a Representative from Illinois; born in Paris, Bourbon County, Ky., February 22, 1794; pursued classical studies; during the War of 1812 was commissioned ensign in the Seventeenth Infantry March 12, 1812; second lieutenant March 13, 1813; first lieutenant in the Forty-sixth Infantry July 16, 1814; transferred to the Seventeenth Infantry July 16, 1814; honorably discharged June 15, 1815; received, by resolution of Congress, February 13, 1835, the testimonial of a sword for his part in the defense of Fort Stephenson, Ohio; moved to Illinois in 1818 and settled in Kaskaskia, later in Jackson County; engaged in agricultural pursuits; justice of the peace in Jackson County 1821–1823; appointed major general of State militia in 1822 and commanded Illinois troops in the Black Hawk War in 1831; member of the State senate 1824–1826; elected as a Jackson Democrat to the Twentieth and to the three succeeding Congresses and served from March 4, 1827, until September 21, 1834, when he resigned, having been elected Governor of Illinois; moved to Jacksonville, Ill., in 1829; Governor of Illinois 1834–1838; unsuccessful candidate for Governor in 1842; lived in retirement until his death in Jacksonville, Morgan County, Ill., January 15, 1844; interment in Diamond Grove Cemetery.

DUNCAN, Richard Meloan, a Representative from Missouri; born near Edgerton, Platte County, Mo., November 10, 1889; attended the public schools; was graduated from Christian Brothers College, St. Joseph, Mo., in 1909; deputy circuit clerk of Buchanan County, Mo., 1911–1917; studied law; was admitted to the bar in 1916 and commenced practice in St. Joseph, Mo.; city counselor of St. Joseph 1926–1930; elected as a Democrat to the Seventy-third and to the four succeeding Congresses (March 4, 1933–January 3, 1943); unsuccessful candidate for reelection in 1942 to the Seventy-eighth Congress; appointed judge of the United States District Court for the Eastern and Western Districts of Missouri on July 8, 1943, in which capacity he is now serving; is a resident of Kansas City, Mo.

DUNCAN, William Addison, a Representative from Pennsylvania; born in Cashtown, Franklin Township, Adams County, Pa., February 2, 1836; attended the public schools; was graduated from Franklin and Marshall College, at Lancaster, in 1857; studied law; was admitted to the bar in 1859 and commenced practice in Gettysburg, Pa.; elected district attorney in 1862 and 1868; elected as a Democrat to the Forty-eighth Congress and served from March 4, 1883, until his death; had been reelected to the Forty-ninth Congress; died in Gettysburg, Adams County, Pa., November 14, 1884; interment in Evergreen Cemetery.

DUNCAN, (William) Garnett, a Representative from Kentucky; born in Louisville, Ky., March 2, 1800; completed preparatory studies, and was graduated from Yale College in 1821; studied law; was admitted to the bar in 1822 and commenced practice in Louisville; elected as a Whig to the Thirtieth Congress (March 4, 1847–March 3, 1849); declined to be a candidate for renomination in 1848; moved to Louisiana and settled in New Orleans in 1850, where he continued the practice of law; retired from active law practice in 1860 and traveled in Europe; resided for a while in Paris, France; returned to the United States in 1875 and resided with his son in Louisville, Ky., until his death in that city on May 25, 1875; interment in Cave Hill Cemetery.

DUNGAN, James Irvine, a Representative from Ohio; born in Canonsburg, Washington County, Pa., May 29, 1844; attended the common schools; received an academic education at the local academy at Denmark, Iowa, and at the college at Washington, Iowa; studied law; was admitted to the bar in 1868 and commenced practice in Jackson, Jackson County, Ohio; during the Civil War served as color sergeant in the Nineteenth Regiment, Iowa Volunteer Infantry; was captured and confined ten months in a military prison; superintendent of schools of Jackson, Ohio, and city and county school examiner in 1867 and 1868; mayor of Jackson in 1869; member of the State senate 1877–1879; delegate to the Democratic National Convention at Cincinnati in 1880; delegate to many State conventions; presidential elector on the Democratic ticket of Cleveland and Thurman in 1888; elected as a Democrat to the Fifty-second Congress (March 4, 1891–March 3, 1893); unsuccessful candidate for reelection in 1892 to the Fifty-third Congress; attorney in the Interior Department 1893–1895; returned to Jackson, Ohio, and resumed the practice of law; city solicitor in 1913 to conduct an important case for the city and then resigned; engaged in the practice of his profession until his death in Jackson, Ohio, on December 28, 1931; interment in Fairmont Cemetery.

DUNHAM, Cyrus Livingston, a Representative from Indiana; born in Dryden, Tompkins County, N. Y., January 16, 1817; attended the common schools; taught school; studied law and was admitted to the bar; moved to Salem, Washington County, Ind., in 1841 and commenced practice; elected prosecuting attorney of Washington County in 1845; member of the State house of representatives in 1846 and 1847; presidential elector on the Democratic ticket of Cass and Butler in 1848; elected as a Democrat to the Thirty-first, Thirty-second, and Thirty-third Congresses (March 4, 1849–March 3, 1855); unsuccessful candidate for reelection in 1854 to the Thirty-fourth Congress; appointed by Governor Willard secretary of state and served in 1859 and 1860; served in the Union Army during the Civil War as colonel of the Fiftieth Regiment, Indiana Volunteer Infantry, 1861–1863; resumed the practice of law in New Albany, Floyd County, Ind.; elected a member of the State house of representatives in 1864 and 1865; moved to Jeffersonville, Ind., in 1871; judge of Clark County Criminal Court 1871–1874; resumed the practice of law; died in Jeffersonville, Clark County, Ind., November 21, 1877; interment in Walnut Ridge Cemetery.

DUNHAM, Ransom Williams, a Representative from Illinois; born in Savoy, Berkshire County, Mass., March 21, 1838; attended the common schools and the high school in Springfield, Mass.; engaged as a clerk for a life insurance company 1855–1857; moved to Chicago in 1857; became a grain and provision commission merchant; president of the Board of Trade of Chicago in 1882; elected as a Republican to the Forty-eighth, Forty-ninth, and Fiftieth Congresses (March 4, 1883–March 3, 1889); retired from active business pursuits; died in Springfield, Hampden County, Mass., on August 19, 1896, while en route to attend the centennial celebration of his native town, Savoy; interment in Mount Hope Cemetery, Chicago, Ill.

DUNLAP, George Washington, a Representative from Kentucky; born at Walnut Hills, near Lexington, Fayette County, Ky., February 22, 1813; pursued preparatory studies; was graduated from Transylvania University, Lexington, Ky., in 1834; studied law; was admitted to the bar and commenced practice in Lancaster, Ky.; commissioner of the circuit court 1843–1874; member of the State house of representatives in 1853; elected as a Unionist to the Thirty-seventh Congress (March 4, 1861–March 3, 1863); member of the border State convention in 1861; one of the managers appointed by the House of Representatives in 1862 to conduct the impeachment proceedings against West H. Humphreys, United States judge for the several districts of Tennessee; presidential elector on the Democratic ticket of George B. McClellan and George H. Pendleton in 1864; resumed the practice of law; died in Lancaster, Garrard County, Ky., on June 6, 1880; interment in Lancaster Cemetery.

DUNLAP, Robert Pinckney, a Representative from Maine; born in Brunswick, Maine, August 17, 1794; educated by private tutors; was graduated from Bowdoin College, Brunswick, Maine, in 1815; studied law; was admitted to the bar in 1818 and commenced practice in Brunswick; member of the State house of representatives 1821–1823; president of the board of overseers of Bowdoin College from 1821 until his death; member of the State militia, and was delegated to receive General Lafayette when he visited in Maine in 1824; served in the State senate 1824–1828 and 1831–1833; president of the State senate for four years; executive councilor 1829–1833; Governor of Maine 1834–1838; elected as a Democrat to the Twenty-eighth and Twenty-ninth Congresses (March 4, 1843–March 3, 1847); collector of customs in Portland, Maine, in 1848 and 1849; postmaster of Brunswick 1853–1857; died in Brunswick, Maine, October 20, 1859; interment in Pine Grove Cemetery.

DUNLAP, William Claiborne, a Representative from Tennessee; born in Knoxville, Tenn., February 25, 1798; attended the Ebenezer Academy and Maryville College, Maryville, Tenn., 1813–1817; studied law; was admitted to the bar and commenced practice in Knoxville in 1819; served in the Indian campaign in 1818 and 1819; moved to Bolivar, Hardeman County, Tenn., in 1828; held a commission in the United States Volunteers in 1830; elected as a Democrat to the Twenty-third and Twenty-fourth Congresses (March 4, 1833–March 3, 1837); unsuccessful candidate for reelection in 1836 to the Twenty-fifth Congress; judge of the Eleventh Circuit Court of Tennessee from 1840 to 1849, when he resigned and resumed the practice of law; member of the State senate in 1851, 1853, and 1857; served in the State house of representatives 1857–1859; died near Memphis, Shelby County, Tenn., November 16, 1872; interment in Elmwood Cemetery, Memphis, Tenn.

DUNN, Aubert Culberson, a Representative from Mississippi; born in Meridian, Lauderdale County, Miss., November 20, 1896; attended the public schools, the University of Mississippi at Oxford, and the University of Alabama at Tuscaloosa; reporter on the Cincinnati Enquirer in 1917; during the First World War served in the United States Navy from December 7, 1917, to June 16, 1919; studied law; was admitted to the bar in 1924 and commenced practice in Meridian, Miss.; district attorney for the tenth judicial district of Mississippi 1931–1934; elected as a Democrat to the Seventy-fourth Congress (January 3, 1935–January 3, 1937); was not a candidate for renomination in 1936; served as expert to the United States Senate Committee on Finance in 1938 and as attorney for the Social Security Board in 1939; engaged in the practice of law in Gulfport, Miss., where he now resides.

DUNN, George Grundy, a Representative from Indiana; born in Washington County, Ky., December 20, 1812; moved to Monroe County, Ind.; completed preparatory studies and attended the Indiana University at Bloomington; moved to Bedford, Lawrence County, Ind., in 1833, where he taught school; studied law; was admitted to the bar in 1835 and commenced practice in Bedford, Ind.; prosecuting attorney of Lawrence County in 1842; elected as a Whig to the Thirtieth Congress (March 4, 1847–March 3, 1849); unsuccessful candidate for reelection in 1848; served in the State senate from 1850 until 1852, when he resigned; elected as a Republican to the Thirty-fourth Congress (March 4, 1855–March 3, 1857); was not a candidate for renomination in 1856; died in Bedford, Ind., September 4, 1857; interment in Green Hill Cemetery.

DUNN, George Hedford, a Representative from Indiana; born in New York City, N. Y., November 15, 1794; moved to Lawrenceburg, Dearborn County, Ind., in 1817; studied law; was admitted to the bar in 1822 and commenced practice in Lawrenceburg; member of the State house of representatives in 1828, 1832, and 1833; promoter of the first railway in Indiana; unsuccessful candidate for election to the Twenty-fourth Congress; elected as a Whig to the Twenty-fifth Congress (March 4, 1837–March 3, 1839); unsuccessful candidate for reelection; resumed the practice of law; State treasurer 1841–1844; judge of Dearborn County, Ind.; president of the Cincinnati & Indianapolis Railroad at the time of his death in Lawrenceburg, Ind., January 12, 1854; interment in New Town Cemetery.

DUNN, John Thomas, a Representative from New Jersey; born in Tipperary, Ireland, June 4, 1838; immigrated to the United States with his father, who settled in New Jersey in 1845; owing to the death of his mother when only four years of age he was placed with a farmer for rearing and private tutoring, but being unable to endure the hardship and abuse he ran away at the age of eleven and shipped as a cabin boy on a vessel trading with the West Indies; two years later his older brother took him to Gloucester City, where he became engaged as a bobbin boy in a silk factory; learned iron molding at the age of sixteen and subsequently learned brass turning and silver burnishing and was also apprenticed as a painter; completed elementary studies at home; engaged in business in 1862 and acquired a competency; elected a member of the board of aldermen of Elizabeth in 1878; member of the State house of assembly 1879–1882 and speaker of the house in 1882; studied law; was admitted to the bar in 1882 and commenced practice in Elizabeth, N. J.; again elected a member of the city council; elected as a Democrat to the Fifty-third Congress (March 4, 1893–March 3, 1895); unsuccessful candidate for reelection in 1894 to the Fifty-fourth Congress; resumed the practice of law; died in Elizabeth, N. J., February 22, 1907; interment in Mount Olivet Cemetery, Newark, N. J.

DUNN, Matthew Anthony, a Representative from Pennsylvania; born in Braddock, Allegheny County, Pa., August 15, 1886; attended the public schools in Pittsburgh and Meyersdale; by accidents, lost the sight of his left eye at the age of twelve and that of his right eye at the age of twenty; attended the school for the blind in Pittsburgh and was graduated from Overbrook (Philadelphia) School for the Blind in 1909; engaged in the sale of periodicals and newspapers 1907 and 1908, and in the insurance brokerage business 1920–1924; member of the State house of representatives 1926–1932; elected as a Democrat to the Seventy-third and to the three succeeding Congresses (March 4, 1933–January 3, 1941); was not a candidate for renomination in 1940 due to ill health and retired from active business; died in Pittsburgh, Pa., February 13, 1942; interment in Homewood Cemetery.

DUNN, Poindexter, a Representative from Arkansas; born near Raleigh, Wake County, N. C., November 3, 1834; moved with his father to Limestone County, Ala., in 1837; attended the country schools, and was graduated from Jackson College, Columbia, Tenn., in 1854; studied law; moved to St. Francis County, Ark., in 1856; elected to the State house of representatives in 1858; engaged in cotton growing until 1861; served as a captain in the Confederate Army during the Civil War; was admitted to the bar in 1867 and commenced the practice of law in Forrest City, Ark.; presidential elector on the Democratic ticket of Greeley and Brown in 1872 and of Tilden and Hendricks in 1876; elected as a Democrat to the Forty-sixth and to the four succeeding Congresses (March 4, 1879–March 3, 1889); was not a candidate for renomination in 1888; moved to Los Angeles, Calif., in 1888 and continued the practice of law; appointed a special commissioner for the prevention of frauds on the customs revenue, New York City, in 1893; moved to Baton Rouge, La., in 1895 and engaged in the construction of railroads; settled in Texarkana, Bowie County, Tex., in 1905, and died there on October 12, 1914; interment in Rose Hill Cemetery.

DUNN, Thomas Byrne, a Representative from New York; born in Providence, R. I., March 16, 1853; moved with his parents to Rochester, N. Y., in 1858; attended the public schools and the De Graff Military Institute of Rochester; engaged in the manufacture of perfumes and extracts; president of the chamber of commerce in 1905 and 1906; member of the State senate in 1907; chief commissioner for New York to the Jamestown Tercentennial Exposition, Jamestown, Va., in 1907; State treasurer in 1908; elected as a Republican to the Sixty-third and to the four succeeding Congresses (March 4, 1913–March 3, 1923); was not a candidate for reelection in 1922 to the Sixty-eighth Congress; retired to private life; died in Rochester, N. Y., July 2, 1924; interment in Mount Hope Cemetery.

DUNN, William McKee, a Representative from Indiana; born in Hanover, Jefferson County, Territory of Indiana, December 12, 1814; attended school in the first schoolhouse in Hanover; was graduated from Indiana State College in 1832 and from Yale College in 1835; studied law; was admitted to the bar in 1837 and practiced; member of the State house of representatives in 1848; delegate to the State constitutional convention in 1850; elected as a Republican to the Thirty-sixth and Thirty-seventh Congresses (March 4, 1859–March 3, 1863); unsuccessful candidate for reelection in 1862 to the Thirty-eighth Congress; during the Civil War served in the Union Army as a volunteer aide-de-camp to General McClellan from June 19, 1861, to August 1861, in the campaign in western Virginia; major and judge advocate of Volunteers, Department of the Missouri, from March 13, 1863, to July 6, 1864; appointed lieutenant colonel and Assistant Judge Advocate General of the United States Army June 22, 1864, and brigadier general and Judge Advocate General December 1, 1875; brevetted brigadier general March 13, 1865, for faithful, meritorious, and distinguished services in his department; retired January 22, 1881; died at his summer residence, "Maplewood," Dunn Loring, Fairfax County, Va., July 24, 1887; interment in Oak Hill Cemetery, Washington, D. C.

DUNNELL, Mark Hill, a Representative from Minnesota; born in Buxton, York County, Maine, July 2, 1823; completed preparatory studies, and was graduated from Waterville College (now Colby University), Waterville, Maine, in 1849; for five years was principal of Norway and Hebron Academies; member of the Maine House of Representatives in 1854; served in the State senate in 1855; State superintendent of common schools in 1855 and 1857–1859; delegate to the Republican National Convention at Philadelphia in 1856; studied law; was admitted to the bar in 1856 and commenced practice in Portland, Maine, in 1860; during the Civil War entered the Union Army as colonel of the Fifth Regiment, Maine Volunteer Infantry, May 6, 1861; mustered out August 31, 1861; United States consul at Vera Cruz, Mexico, in 1861 and 1862; trustee of Waterville College for ten years; declined the appointment as secretary of Montana Territory in 1864; moved to Minnesota and settled in Winona in 1865, and later, in 1867, in Owatonna; member of the Minnesota House of Representatives in 1867; State superintendent of public instruction from April 2, 1867, to August 1870, when he resigned, having been elected to Congress; elected as a Republican to the Forty-second and to the five succeeding Congresses (March 4, 1871–March 3, 1883); unsuccessful candidate for Speaker of the Forty-seventh Congress; was not a candidate for renomination in 1882; unsuccessful candidate for election to the United States Senate in 1883; elected to the Fifty-first Congress (March 4, 1889–March 3, 1891); unsuccessful candidate for reelection in 1890 to the Fifty-second Congress; delegate to the Republican National Convention at Minneapolis in 1892 at which Harrison and Reid were nominated; one of the founders and a member of the board of trustees of Pillsbury Academy; died in Owatonna, Steele County, Minn., August 9, 1904; interment in Forest Hill Cemetery.

DUNPHY, Edward John, a Representative from New York; born in New York City May 12, 1856; attended the public schools and St. Francis Xavier College, New York City; was graduated from Mount St. Mary's College, Emmitsburg, Md., in 1876; studied law; was admitted to the bar in 1878 and commenced practice in New York City; connected with the law department of the New York Central & Hudson River Railroad Co.; elected as a Democrat to the Fifty-first, Fifty-second, and Fifty-third Congresses (March 4, 1889–March 3, 1895); was not a candidate for reelection in 1894; continued the practice of law in New York City until his death there on July 29, 1926; interment in Calvary Cemetery.

DUNWELL, Charles Tappan, a Representative from New York; born in Newark, Wayne County, N. Y., February 13, 1852; moved with his parents to Lyons, Wayne County, N. Y., in 1854; attended the Lyons Union School; entered Cornell University, Ithaca, N. Y., in the class of 1873; at the close of his junior year entered Columbia College Law School in the city of New York, and was graduated in 1874; was admitted to the bar in 1874 and commenced practice in New York City; general agent for the New York Life Insurance Co. in 1889; unsuccessful candidate for comptroller of the city of Brooklyn in 1890; member of the New York Republican State committee in 1891 and 1892; elected as a Republican to the Fifty-eighth, Fifty-ninth, and Sixtieth Congresses and served from March 4, 1903, until his death in Brooklyn, N. Y., June 12, 1908; interment in Evergreen Cemetery.

DU PONT, Henry Algernon (cousin of Thomas Coleman du Pont), a Senator from Delaware; born at Eleutherean Mills, New Castle County, Del., July 30, 1838; attended private schools; entered the University of Pennsylvania in Philadelphia in 1855, where he spent a year in the sophomore and junior classes; was graduated from the United States Military Academy, West Point, N. Y., May 6, 1861; during the Civil War was commissioned second lieutenant, Corps of Engineers; first lieutenant, Fifth Regiment, United States Artillery, May 14, 1861; adjutant July 6, 1861, to March 24, 1864; captain March 24, 1864; brevetted major September 19, 1864, "for gallant service at the Battles of Opequan and Fishers Hill, Va.," and lieutenant colonel October 19, 1864, "for distinguished service at the Battle of Cedar Creek, Va."; awarded a medal of honor March 22, 1898, "for gallant conduct" at the last-named battle (October 19, 1864), "while chief of artillery, Army of West Virginia, by his brave bearing, most distinguished gallantry, and voluntary exposure to the enemy's guns at a critical moment, when the Union line had been broken and defeated, he encouraged his men to stand to their guns, checked the advance of the enemy, and brought off the most of his guns"; resigned March 1, 1875; was president and general manager of the Wilmington & Northern Railroad Co. from 1879 to 1899; retired from active business and engaged in agricultural pursuits; elected on June 13, 1906, as a Republican to the United States Senate to fill the vacancy in the term beginning March 4, 1905, caused by the failure of the legislature to elect; reelected in 1911 and served until March 3, 1917; unsuccessful candidate for reelection in 1916; retired from public life and engaged in literary pursuits; died at Winterthur, near Wilmington, Del., December 31, 1926; interment in the du Pont Cemetery, Christiana Hundred, New Castle County, Del.

DU PONT, Thomas Coleman (cousin of Henry Algernon du Pont), a Senator from Delaware; born in Louisville, Ky., December 11, 1863; attended the public schools, Urbana University, Urbana, Ohio, Chauncy Hall School, Boston, Mass., and Massachusetts Institute of Technology, Boston, Mass.; engaged in engineering, later being interested in coal mining, street railways, steel manufacturing, explosives, hotels, office buildings, and road building; moved to Central City, Ky., in 1883 and was engaged as a mining engineer; moved to Johnstown, Pa., in 1893 and engaged in steel manufacturing; moved to Wilmington, Del., in 1900, from whence he conducted his vast business enterprises; retired from business activities in 1915; member of the Republican National Committee 1908–1930 and had the longest continuous service thereon; appointed as a Republican to the United States Senate to fill the vacancy caused by the resignation of Josiah O. Wolcott and served from July 7, 1921, to November 7, 1922, when a successor was elected; unsuccessful candidate for election to this vacancy in the Senate in 1922, and also for election to the full term; elected to the United States Senate in 1924 and served from March 4, 1925, until his resignation on December 9, 1928; retired from active business pursuits; died in Wilmington, Del., November 11, 1930; the remains were cremated, placed in a bronze urn, and committed to a grave in the family burial ground near Christ Church in Christiana Hundred.

DUPRÉ, Henry Garland, a Representative from Louisiana; born in Opelousas, St. Landry Parish, La., July 28, 1873; attended the public schools, and was graduated from Tulane University, New Orleans, La., in 1892; was subsequently graduated from the law school of the same university; was admitted to the bar and commenced practice in New Orleans in 1895; assistant city attorney of New Orleans 1900–1910; member of the State house of representatives 1900–1910 and served as speaker 1908–1910; chairman of the Democratic State convention in 1908; elected as a Democrat to the Sixty-first Congress to fill the vacancy caused by the death of Samuel L. Gillmore; reelected to the Sixty-second and to the six succeeding Congresses and served from November 8, 1910, until his death in Washington, D. C., February 21, 1924; interment in the Catholic Cemetery, Opelousas, La.

DURAND, George Harman, a Representative from Michigan; born in Cobleskill, Schoharie County, N. Y., February 21, 1838; attended the common schools and Genesee Wesleyan Seminary at Lima, N. Y.; moved to Oxford, Oakland County, Mich., in 1856; taught school; studied law; was admitted to the bar and commenced practice at Flint, Genesee County, Mich., in 1858; member of the board of education; member of the board of aldermen 1862–1867; mayor of Flint in 1873 and 1874; elected as a Democrat to the Forty-fourth Congress (March 4, 1875–March

3, 1877); unsuccessful candidate for reelection in 1876 to the Forty-fifth Congress; resumed the practice of his profession; appointed temporarily justice of the Michigan Supreme Court in 1892; presidential elector on the Democratic ticket of Cleveland and Stevenson in 1892; president of the Michigan State Bar Association in 1893; president of the State board of law examiners for many years; appointed special assistant United States attorney in Chinese and opium smuggling cases in Oregon and served from 1893 to 1896; died in Flint, Mich., June 8, 1903; interment in Glenwood Cemetery.

DURBOROW, Allan Cathcart, Jr., a Representative from Illinois; born in Philadelphia, Pa., November 10, 1857; moved to Indiana in 1862 with his parents, who settled in Williamsport, Warren County; attended the public schools; entered Wabash College, Crawfordsville, Ind., in the fall of 1872; was graduated from Indiana University at Bloomington in 1877; after residing in Indianapolis moved to Chicago in 1880, and in 1887 became business manager of the Western Electrician, a trade magazine; elected as a Democrat to the Fifty-second and Fifty-third Congresses (March 4, 1891–March 3, 1895); was not a candidate for renomination in 1894; engaged in the insurance business; unsuccessful candidate for election in 1902 to the Fifty-eighth Congress; died in Chicago, Ill., March 10, 1908; interment in Graceland Cemetery.

DURELL, Daniel Meserve, a Representative from New Hampshire; born in Lee, N. H., July 20, 1769; was graduated from Dartmouth College, Hanover, N. H., in 1794; studied law; was admitted to the bar in 1797 and commenced practice in Dover, N. H.; elected to the Tenth Congress (March 4, 1807–March 3, 1809); member of the State house of representatives in 1816; chief justice of the district court of common pleas 1816–1821; United States attorney for the district of New Hampshire 1830–1834; resumed the practice of law; died in Dover, Strafford County, N. H., April 29, 1841; interment in Pine Hill Cemetery.

DUREY, Cyrus, a Representative from New York; born in Caroga, Fulton County, N. Y., May 16, 1864; attended the common schools and Johnstown Academy; was supervisor's clerk; supervisor of Caroga in 1889 and 1890; engaged in the lumber and real-estate business; appointed postmaster of Johnstown on August 19, 1898, and served until February 28, 1907; member of the Republican State committee 1904–1906; elected as a Republican to the Sixtieth and Sixty-first Congresses (March 4, 1907–March 3, 1911); unsuccessful candidate for reelection in 1910 to the Sixty-second Congress; appointed on March 20, 1911, collector of internal revenue, fourteenth district of New York, and served until September 30, 1914; delegate to the Republican National Conventions at Chicago in 1912 and 1920; again appointed collector of internal revenue on September 30, 1921, and served until his death at Albany, N. Y., January 4, 1923; interment in North Bush Cemetery, near Johnstown, N. Y.

DURFEE, Job, a Representative from Rhode Island; born in Tiverton, R. I., September 20, 1790; attended the common schools, and was graduated from Brown University, Providence, R. I., in 1813; studied law; was admitted to the bar at Newport, R. I., in 1817 and commenced practice in Tiverton; member of the State house of representatives 1816–1820; elected as the People's candidate to the Seventeenth Congress and as a Democrat to the Eighteenth Congress (March 4, 1821–March 3, 1825); unsuccessful candidate for reelection in 1824 to the Nineteenth Congress and for election in 1828 to the Twenty-first Congress; again a member of the State house of representatives 1826–

1829, and served as speaker 1827–1829; declined to be a candidate for reelection; resumed the practice of law; elected associate justice of the State supreme court in 1833; chief justice of the State supreme court from June 1835 until his death in Tiverton, Newport County, R. I., July 26, 1847; interment in the family burying ground at Quaket Neck, near Tiverton, R. I.

DURFEE, Nathaniel Briggs, a Representative from Rhode Island; born in Tiverton, R. I., September 29, 1812; completed preparatory studies; engaged in agricultural pursuits and conducted a fruit orchard; member of the Rhode Island House of Representatives for eleven years; elected by the American Party to the Thirty-fourth Congress and as a Republican to the Thirty-fifth Congress (March 4, 1855–March 3, 1859); resumed his former pursuits; was serving as county clerk at the time of his death in Tiverton, Newport County, R. I., on November 9, 1872; interment in the family burial ground near Tiverton, R. I.

DURGAN, George Richard, a Representative from Indiana; born in Westpoint, Tippecanoe County, Ind., January 20, 1872; attended the village school in Westpoint; moved to La Fayette, Ind., in 1892 and was employed as a clerk and later as a traveling salesman; engaged in mercantile pursuits; mayor of La Fayette 1904–1913 and 1917–1925; delegate to the Democratic National Convention at Baltimore in 1912; elected as a Democrat to the Seventy-third Congress (March 4, 1933–January 3, 1935); unsuccessful candidate for reelection in 1934 to the Seventy-fourth Congress; resumed mercantile pursuits; appointed to the Indiana Public Service Commission in 1941 and moved to Indianapolis, Ind.; died in Indianapolis January 13, 1942; interment in Springvale Cemetery, La Fayette, Ind.

DURHAM, Carl Thomas, a Representative from North Carolina; born in Bingham Township, Orange County, at White Cross, N. C., August 28, 1892; attended the public schools of Orange County, Mandale Private School, Saxapahaw, N. C., and the University of North Carolina at Chapel Hill; pharmacist at Chapel Hill 1912–1938; during the First World War served as a pharmacist's mate in the United States Navy in 1918; member of the city council of Chapel Hill, N. C., 1924–1932, and of the Orange County Board of Commissioners 1932–1938; member of the school board of Chapel Hill, N. C., 1924–1938; trustee of the University of North Carolina; elected as a Democrat to the Seventy-sixth and to the ten succeeding Congresses (January 3, 1939–January 3, 1961); was not a candidate for renomination in 1960; is a resident of Chapel Hill, N. C.

DURHAM, Milton Jameson, a Representative from Kentucky; born near Perryville, Mercer County (now Boyle County), Ky., May 16, 1824; attended the common schools; was graduated from Indiana Asbury (now De Pauw) University, Greencastle, Ind., in 1844; taught school for several years: was graduated from the Louisville (Ky.) Law School in 1850; was admitted to the bar in the same year and commenced practice in Danville, Boyle County, Ky.; circuit judge of the eighth judicial district in 1861 and 1862; elected as a Democrat to the Forty-third, Forty-fourth, and Forty-fifth Congresses (March 4, 1873–March 3, 1879); unsuccessful candidate for renomination in 1878; resumed the practice of law in Danville, Ky.; appointed First Comptroller of the Treasury of the United States on March 20, 1885, and served until the office was discontinued on April 22, 1889; moved to Lexington, Ky., in 1890 and engaged in banking; appointed deputy clerk, Internal Revenue Service, at Lexington, Ky., in 1901 and served until his death in that city on February 12, 1911; interment in Belleview Cemetery Danville, Ky.

DURKEE, Charles, a Representative and a Senator from Wisconsin; born in Royalton, Windsor County, Vt., December 10, 1805; attended the common schools and the Burlington (Vt.) Academy; engaged in mercantile pursuits; moved to Wisconsin in 1836 and was one of the founders of Southport, now Kenosha; engaged in agricultural pursuits and lumbering; member of the Territorial Legislature 1836–1838 and again elected in 1847 and 1848; elected as a Free-Soiler to the Thirty-first and Thirty-second Congresses (March 4, 1849–March 3, 1853); delegate to the World's Peace Convention in Paris; elected as a Republican to the United States Senate and served from March 4, 1855, to March 3, 1861; appointed Governor of Utah Territory July 15, 1865, and served until failing health compelled him to resign; died in Omaha, Nebr., January 14, 1870; interment in Green Ridge Cemetery, Kenosha, Wis.

DUVAL, Isaac Harding, a Representative from West Virginia; born in Wellsburg, Brooke County, Va. (now West Virginia), September 1, 1824; attended the common schools; as a youth he went to Fort Smith, Ark., and joined an elder brother, who was conducting a trading post; became a scout on the Western Plains; crossed the Plains in 1849 for the gold fields of California; was a member of the historic Lopez expedition to Cuba in an attempt to aid the Cubans in gaining national independence; returned to Virginia in 1853 and engaged in mercantile pursuits at Wellsburg; during the Civil War was commissioned major of the First Regiment, West Virginia Volunteer Infantry, June 1, 1861; promoted to the colonelcy of the Ninth Regiment, West Virginia Volunteer Infantry, September 6, 1862; promoted to brigadier general October 20, 1864, and subsequently brevetted major general; member of the State senate 1867–1869; adjutant general of West Virginia 1867–1869; elected as a Republican to the Forty-first Congress (March 4, 1869–March 3, 1871); declined to be candidate for renomination in 1870; United States assessor of internal revenue in 1871 and 1872; collector of internal revenue for the first district of West Virginia 1872–1884; member of the State house of delegates 1887–1889; died in Wellsburg, Brooke County, W. Va., July 10, 1902; interment in Brooke Cemetery.

DUVAL, William Pope, a Representative from Kentucky; born in Mount Comfort, near Richmond, Va., in 1784; completed preparatory studies; moved to Kentucky; studied law; was admitted to the bar about 1804 and practiced; during the Indian hostilities of 1812 commanded a company of mounted Volunteers; elected as a Democrat to the Thirteenth Congress (March 4, 1813–March 3, 1815); resumed the practice of law in Bardstown, Ky.; appointed on May 18, 1821, United States judge, east Florida district; Governor of the Territory of Florida under Presidents Monroe, Adams, and Jackson, serving from April 17, 1822, to 1834; appointed on November 4, 1841, law agent in Florida; moved to Texas in 1848; was the original of "Ralph Ringwood" of Washington Irving and "Nimrod Wildfire" of James K. Paulding; died in Washington, D. C., March 19, 1854; interment in the Congressional Cemetery.

DUVALL, Gabriel, a Representative from Maryland; born in Prince Georges County, Md., December 6, 1752; completed preparatory studies; studied law; was admitted to the bar and practiced; member of the Governor's council in 1783 and 1784; elected as a Democrat to the Third Congress to fill the vacancy caused by the resignation of John F. Mercer; reelected to the Fourth Congress and served from November 11, 1794, to March 28, 1796, when he resigned; appointed chief justice of the general court of Maryland on April 2, 1796, and resigned in 1802; presidential elector in 1796 and 1800; appointed First Comptroller of the Treasury December 15, 1802, and served until his resignation November 18, 1811, having been appointed to a judicial position; elected judge of the court of appeals of Maryland on January 16, 1806, but declined to serve; appointed by President James Madison on November 15, 1811, an Associate Justice of the Supreme Court of the United States, confirmed by the Senate on November 18, 1811, took his seat on February 3, 1812, and served until his resignation on January 15, 1835, because of deafness; died near Glenn Dale, in Prince Georges County, Md., on March 6, 1844; interment in the private burying ground on his estate.

DWIGHT, Henry Williams, a Representative from Massachusetts; born in Stockbridge, Mass., February 26, 1788; attended Williams College, Williamstown, Mass.; studied law; was admitted to the Massachusetts bar in 1809 and commenced practice in Stockbridge; during the War of 1812 served as aide-de-camp with the rank of colonel on the staff of General Whiton; member of the State house of representatives in 1818; elected to the Seventeenth and to the four succeeding Congresses (March 4, 1821–March 3, 1831); was not a candidate for renomination in 1830 to the Twenty-second Congress; again a member of the State house of representatives in 1834; interested in the breeding of purebred sheep and cattle; died in New York City February 21, 1845; interment in Stockbridge Cemetery, Stockbridge, Berkshire County, Mass.

DWIGHT, Jeremiah Wilbur (father of John Wilbur Dwight), a Representative from New York; born in Cincinnatus, Cortland County, N. Y., April 17, 1819; moved with his parents in 1830 to Caroline, and in 1836 to Dryden, Tompkins County, N. Y.; attended the district schools and the Burhan's School in Dryden; engaged in mercantile pursuits, farming, real-estate business, and in the manufacture and sale of lumber; chairman of the board of supervisors of the town of Dryden in 1857 and 1858; member of the State assembly in 1860 and 1861; appointed by Governor Morgan a member of the senatorial district war committee in 1861; delegate to the Republican National Conventions in 1868, 1872, 1876, 1880, and 1884; director, member of the executive committee, and vice president of the Southern Central Railroad for many years; elected as a Republican to the Forty-fifth, Forty-sixth, and Forty-seventh Congresses (March 4, 1877–March 3, 1883); declined to be a candidate for renomination in 1882; resumed former business activities; died in Dryden, Tompkins County, N. Y., November 26, 1885; interment in Green Hills Cemetery.

DWIGHT, John Wilbur (son of Jeremiah Wilbur Dwight), a Representative from New York; born in Dryden, Tompkins County, N. Y., May 24, 1859; attended the public schools and the Dryden High School; pursued further studies at New Haven, Conn., in preparation for entering Yale College, but abandoned this plan to engage in the lumber business at Clinton, Iowa, in 1879; shortly thereafter moved to northern Wisconsin, where he continued in the lumber business and also engaged in farming; returned to Dryden, N. Y., in 1884; upon the death of his father in 1885 became president of the Dwight Farm & Land Co.; delegate to the Republican National Conventions in 1888, 1892, 1900, 1904, and 1920; acquired extensive land holdings in Minnesota and South Dakota; elected as a Republican to the Fifty-seventh Congress to fill the vacancy caused by the resignation of George W. Ray; reelected to the Fifty-eighth and to the four succeeding Congresses and served from November 2, 1902, to March 3, 1913; retired voluntarily from political life and resided in Washington, D. C.; became president of the Virginia Blue Ridge Railway Co. in 1913, in which capacity he served until his death in Washington, D. C., January 19, 1928; interment in Rock Creek Cemetery.

DWIGHT, Theodore (cousin of Aaron Burr), a Representative from Connecticut; born in Northampton, Mass., December 15, 1764; completed preparatory studies; studied law; was admitted to the bar in 1787 and began practice in Haddam, Conn.; moved to Hartford, Conn., in 1791 and continued the practice of law; editor of the Hartford Courant and of the Connecticut Mirror; member of the State council 1809–1815; elected as a Federalist to the Ninth Congress to fill the vacancy caused by the resignation of John Cotton Smith and served from December 1, 1806, to March 3, 1807; declined to be a candidate for renomination in 1806; secretary of the Hartford Convention in 1814; moved to Albany, N. Y., in 1815; published the Albany Daily Advertiser 1815–1817; moved to New York City in 1817 and established the New York Daily Advertiser, with which he was connected until the great fire of 1835; returned to Hartford, Conn., and resided there until about three years before his death, when he returned to New York City; died in New York City, June 12, 1846; interment in Greenwood Cemetery, Brooklyn, N. Y.

DWIGHT, Thomas, a Representative from Massachusetts; born in Springfield, Mass., October 29, 1758; pursued preparatory studies; was graduated from Harvard College in 1778; studied law; was admitted to the bar and commenced practice in Springfield, Mass.; member of the State house of representatives in 1794 and 1795; served in the State senate 1796–1803; elected as a Federalist to the Eighth Congress (March 4, 1803–March 3, 1805); selectman of the town of Springfield 1806–1809 and in 1811; member of the Governor's council in 1808 and 1809; retired from political life and engaged in the practice of his profession in Springfield, Hampden County, until his death January 2, 1819; interment in Peabody Cemetery.

DWINELL, Justin, a Representative from New York; born in Shaftsbury, Vt., October 28, 1785; attended a local private school and Williams College, Williamstown, Mass.; was graduated from Yale College in 1808; studied law; was admitted to the bar in 1811 and commenced practice in Cazenovia, N. Y., the same year; member of the State assembly in 1821 and 1822; elected to the Eighteenth Congress (March 4, 1823–March 3, 1825); was not a candidate for renomination; resumed the practice of law; judge of the common pleas court of Madison County, N. Y., 1828–1833; district attorney of Madison County 1837–1845; died in Cazenovia, Madison County, N. Y., September 17, 1850; interment in Evergreen Cemetery.

DWORSHAK, Henry Clarence, a Representative and a Senator from Idaho; born in Duluth, Minn., August 29, 1894; attended the public schools; worked at the printing trade 1909–1918; during the First World War served overseas as a sergeant in the Fourth Antiaircraft Machine Gun Battalion in 1918 and 1919; manager of printers' supply business in Duluth, Minn., 1920–1924; editor and publisher of the Burley Bulletin in Burley, Idaho, 1924–1944; elected as a Republican to the Seventy-sixth and to the three succeeding Congresses and served from January 3, 1939, to November 5, 1946, when he resigned; elected to the United States Senate on November 5, 1946, to fill the vacancy caused by the death of John Thomas and served from November 6, 1946, to January 3, 1949; unsuccessful candidate for reelection in 1948; appointed to the United States Senate and subsequently elected to fill the vacancy caused by the death of Bert H. Miller and served from October 14, 1949, to January 3, 1955; again elected in 1954 for the term ending January 3, 1961. *Reelected in 1960 for the term ending January 3, 1967.*

DWYER, Florence Price, a Representative from New Jersey; born in Reading, Berks County, Pa., July 4, 1902; State legislation chairman of New Jersey Business and Professional Women;

moved to Elizabeth, Union County, N. J.; delegate to the Republican National Convention in 1944; member of the State house of assembly 1950–1956; elected as a Republican to the Eighty-fifth and Eighty-sixth Congresses (January 3, 1957–January 3, 1961). *Reelected to the Eighty-seventh Congress.*

DYER, David Patterson (uncle of Leonidas Carstarphen Dyer), a Representative from Missouri; born in Henry County, Va., February 12, 1838; moved with his parents to Lincoln County, Mo., in 1841; completed preparatory studies; studied law in Bowling Green, Pike County, Mo., and was admitted to the bar in March 1859; elected prosecuting attorney for the third judicial circuit in 1860; during the Civil War enlisted as a private in Captain Hardin's company, Pike County Regiment, Missouri Home Guard, June 17, 1861, and was discharged September 2, 1861; commissioned lieutenant colonel of the Forty-ninth Regiment, Missouri Volunteer Infantry, September 20, 1864; promoted to colonel February 9, 1865, and honorably discharged August 5, 1865; member of the State house of representatives 1862–1865; secretary of the State senate in 1866; delegate to the Republican National Convention at Chicago in 1868 which nominated the presidential ticket of Grant and Colfax; elected as a Republican to the Forty-first Congress (March 4, 1869–March 3, 1871); unsuccessful candidate for reelection in 1870 to the Forty-second Congress; resumed the practice of his profession in St. Louis, Mo.; unsuccessful Republican candidate for Governor in 1880; appointed by President Theodore Roosevelt United States attorney for the eastern district of Missouri; reappointed, and served from March 9, 1902, to March 31, 1907, when he resigned, having been appointed judge; served as United States judge for the eastern district of Missouri from April 1, 1907, to November 3, 1919, when he retired; died in St. Louis, Mo., April 29, 1924; interment in Bellefontaine Cemetery.

DYER, Eliphalet, a Delegate from Connecticut; born in Windham, Conn., September 14, 1721; pursued preparatory studies, and was graduated from Yale College, New Haven, Conn., in 1740; served as town clerk; appointed captain in the militia in 1745; studied law; was admitted to the bar in 1746 and commenced practice in Windham; justice of the peace in 1746; elected a deputy to the general assembly in 1747, 1749, 1752, and 1753, and was advanced to the rank of major in the last-named year; was active in the project of establishing a Connecticut colony in the Susquehanna Valley, being an original member of the Susquehanna Co. formed in 1753, and served as a member of the committee to purchase the Indian title to the lands selected for the proposed colony at Wyoming, which were then believed to be within the charter limits of Connecticut; in 1755, during the French and Indian War, was appointed a lieutenant colonel of one of the regiments sent by Connecticut to assist in the reduction of Crown Point, and later, in 1758, was made colonel of a regiment sent against Canada; again a member of the general assembly 1756–1784, serving as deputy from 1756 to 1762 and as assistant from 1762 to 1784; went to England in 1763 to obtain confirmation of the Susquehanna Co.'s title to the Wyoming region, but was unsuccessful; appointed comptroller of the port of New London in 1764; delegate to the Stamp-Act Congress in 1765; judge of the superior court 1766–1793, and served as chief judge from 1789 until 1793; Member of the Continental Congress 1774–1779 and 1780–1783; member of the committee of safety in 1775; retired from public life in 1793; died in Windham, Conn., May 13, 1807; interment in Windham Cemetery.

DYER, Leonidas Carstarphen (nephew of David Patterson Dyer), a Representative from Missouri; born near Warrenton, Warren County, Mo., June 11, 1871; attended the common schools, Central Wesleyan College, Warrenton, Mo., and Washington University, St. Louis, Mo.; studied law; was admitted to the bar in 1893 and commenced practice in St. Louis, Mo.; served in the Spanish-American War; was a member of the staff of Governor Hadley of Missouri, with the rank of colonel; commander in chief of the Spanish War Veterans in 1915 and 1916; elected as a Republican to the Sixty-second Congress (March 4, 1911–March 3, 1913); presented credentials as a Member-elect to the Sixty-third Congress and served from March 4, 1913, to June 19, 1914, when he was succeeded by Michael J. Gill, who contested his election; elected to the Sixty-fourth and to the eight succeeding Congresses (March 4, 1915–March 3, 1933); unsuccessful candidate for reelection in 1932 to the Seventy-third Congress and for election in 1934 to the Seventy-fourth Congress and in 1936 to the Seventy-fifth Congress; resumed the practice of law; died in St. Louis, Mo., December 15, 1957; interment in Oak Grove Cemetery.

E

EAGAN, John Joseph, a Representative from New Jersey; born in Hoboken, N. J., January 22, 1872; was graduated from public, parochial, and private schools; in 1894 founded and was president of the Eagan Schools of Business in Hoboken, Union Hill, and Hackensack, N. J., and Brooklyn, N. Y.; first vice president of the Merchants & Manufacturers' Trust Co.; collector of taxes of Union, N. J., 1896–1899; elected as a Democrat to the Sixty-third and to the three succeeding Congresses (March 4, 1913–March 3, 1921); delegate to the Democratic National Convention at San Francisco in 1920; unsuccessful candidate for reelection in 1920 to the Sixty-seventh Congress; again elected to the Sixty-eighth Congress (March 4, 1923–March 3, 1925); unsuccessful candidate for renomination in 1924; resumed his former business pursuits; member and president of the Board of Education, Weehawken, N. J., 1932–1940; appointed collector of taxes and custodian of school moneys of Weehawken in 1940; elected collector of taxes in November 1941; reelected in 1943, 1947, and 1951, and served until his retirement in 1955; resided in Weehawken, N. J., until his death in Paramus, N. J., June 13, 1956; interment in Rosendale Cemetery, Tillson, N. Y.

EAGER, Samuel Watkins, a Representative from New York; born in Neelytown, Orange County, N. Y., on April 8, 1789; attended Montgomery Academy, Montgomery, N. Y., and was graduated from Princeton College in 1809; studied law; was admitted to the bar in 1811 and commenced practice in Newburgh, N. Y.; moved to Montgomery, N. Y., in 1826, and continued the practice of his profession; elected as a Republican to the Twenty-first Congress to fill the vacancy caused by the resignation of Hector Craig and served from November 2, 1830, to March 3, 1831; was not a candidate at the election held the same day for the Twenty-second Congress; returned to Newburgh in 1836 and engaged in literary pursuits; died in Newburgh, N. Y., December 23, 1860; interment in St. George Cemetery.

EAGLE, Joe Henry, a Representative from Texas; born in Tompkinsville, Monroe County, Ky., January 23, 1870; was graduated from the local high school in 1883 and obtained a first-grade teacher's certificate in 1884; was also graduated from Burritt College, Spencer, Tenn., in 1887; moved to Texas; taught school 1887–1893 and served as superintendent of the city schools of Vernon, Tex., 1889–1891; studied law at night and during vacations; was admitted to the bar in 1893 and commenced practice in Wichita Falls, Tex.; city attorney of Wichita Falls in 1894 and 1895; moved to Houston in 1895 and continued the practice of law; elected as a Democrat to the Sixty-third and to the three succeeding Congresses (March 4, 1913–March 3, 1921);

was not a candidate for renomination in 1920; elected on January 28, 1933, to both the Seventy-second and Seventy-third Congresses to fill the vacancies caused by the death of Daniel E. Garrett, who had been reelected in 1932; reelected to the Seventy-fourth Congress and served from January 28, 1933, to January 3, 1937; was not a candidate for renomination in 1936, but was an unsuccessful candidate for the Democratic nomination for United States Senator; resumed the practice of his profession; is a resident of Houston, Tex.

EAMES, Benjamin Tucker, a Representative from Rhode Island; born in Dedham, Norfolk County, Mass., June 4, 1818; attended the common schools of Providence, R. I., and some of the leading academies of Massachusetts and Connecticut; employed as a bookkeeper for several years; was graduated from Yale College in 1843; engaged as a teacher in the academy at North Attleboro, studying law at the same time; was admitted to the bar in 1845 and commenced practice in Providence, R. I.; recording and reading clerk of the State house of representatives 1845–1850; member of the State senate 1854–1857, 1863, and again in 1864; one of the commissioners on the revision of the public laws of the State of Rhode Island in 1857; served in the State house of representatives in 1859, 1860, 1868, and 1869; elected as a Republican to the Forty-second and to the three succeeding Congresses (March 4, 1871–March 3, 1879); was not a candidate for renomination; again a member of the State house of representatives 1879–1881; again served in the State senate in 1884 and 1885; died in East Greenwich, R. I., October 6, 1901; interment in Swan Point Cemetery, Providence, R. I.

EARHART, Daniel Scofield, a Representative from Ohio; born in Columbus, Franklin County, Ohio, May 28, 1907; attended the public grade and high schools, and the College of Engineering of Ohio State University at Columbus; was graduated from the College of Law of Ohio State University in 1928; was admitted to the bar the same year and commenced practice in Columbus, Ohio; served as counsel for the select committee to investigate attempted bribery of members of the State house of representatives in 1933; special counsel for the Ohio Tax Commission in 1935 and 1936; elected as a Democrat to the Seventy-fourth Congress to fill the vacancy caused by the death of Charles V. Truax and served from November 3, 1936, to January 3, 1937; was not a candidate for election in 1936 to the Seventy-fifth Congress; resumed the practice of law; presidential elector on the Democratic ticket of Roosevelt and Wallace in 1940; member of the Officers' Reserve Corps 1928–1941; during World War II was ordered to active service in the Infantry with rank of captain on May 26, 1941; transferred to the Army Air Forces with rank of major; served in the Pacific Theater of Operations; promoted to lieutenant colonel and was relieved of active duty on February 24, 1946; commissioned lieutenant colonel in the Ohio Air National Guard in 1948; recalled to active Federal military service September 2, 1951, and served until September 7, 1953, as commanding officer, deputy commander, and operations officer of the One Hundred and Fifty-fifth Tactical Control Group, United States Air Force, building up NATO tactical air control facilities in western Europe; resumed the practice of law in Columbus, Ohio, where he now resides.

EARLE, Elias (uncle of Samuel Earle and John Baylis Earle and great-grandfather of John Laurens Manning Irby and Joseph Haynsworth Earle), a Representative from South Carolina; born in Frederick County, Va., June 19, 1762; attended private school; moved to Greenville County, S. C., in September 1787; was one of the earliest ironmasters of the South, and prospected and negotiated in the iron region of Georgia; member of the State senate in 1800; elected as a Democrat to the Ninth Congress (March 4, 1805–March 3, 1807); elected to the Twelfth and Thirteenth Congresses (March 4, 1811–March 3, 1815); again elected to the Fifteenth and Sixteenth Congresses (March 4, 1817–March 3, 1821); died in Centerville, S. C., May 19, 1823; interment in Old Earle Cemetery, Buncombe Road, Greenville, S. C.

EARLE, John Baylis (nephew of Elias Earle and cousin of Samuel Earle), a Representative from South Carolina; born on the North Carolina side of the North Pacolet River, near Landrum, Spartanburg County, S. C., October 23, 1766; moved to South Carolina; completed preparatory studies; served as a drummer boy and soldier during the Revolutionary War; engaged in agricultural pursuits; elected to the Eighth Congress (March 4, 1803–March 3, 1805); declined to be a candidate for reelection in 1804; resumed agricultural pursuits; adjutant and inspector general of South Carolina for sixteen years; served throughout the War of 1812; member of the nullification convention of 1832 and 1833; died in Anderson County, S. C., February 3, 1863; interment in the cemetery on his plantation, "Silver Glade," in Anderson County, S. C.

EARLE, Joseph Haynsworth (great-grandson of Elias Earle, cousin of John Laurens Manning Irby, and nephew of William Lowndes Yancey), a Senator from South Carolina; born in Greenville, Greenville County, S. C., April 30, 1847; was left an orphan at an early age and was reared by his aunt at "Engleside," Sumter County; attended private schools in Sumter, S. C.; at the outbreak of the Civil War enlisted in the service of the Confederate Army at the age of fifteen years; at the close of the war returned home, and was graduated from Furman University, Greenville, S. C., in 1867; engaged in teaching for two years; studied law; was admitted to the bar in 1870 and commenced practice in Anderson, S. C.; returned to Sumter, S. C., in 1875 and continued the practice of law; also interested in the logging business and in agricultural pursuits; member of the State house of representatives 1878–1882; served in the State senate 1882–1886; delegate to the Democratic National Convention at Cincinnati in 1880 and at Chicago in 1884; attorney general of South Carolina 1886–1890; declined the nomination for Governor in 1888; unsuccessful candidate for Governor in 1890; returned to Greenville in 1892; elected circuit judge in 1894; elected as a Democrat to the United States Senate and served from March 4, 1897, until his death in Greenville, S. C., May 20, 1897; interment in Christ Churchyard.

EARLE, Samuel (nephew of Elias Earle and cousin of John Baylis Earle), a Representative from South Carolina; born in Frederick County, Va., November 28, 1760; moved to South Carolina in 1774; participated in the Revolutionary War, entering the service as an ensign in 1777 and leaving as captain of a company of rangers in 1782; member of the State house of representatives 1784–1788; delegate to the State convention that ratified the Federal Constitution May 12, 1788; delegate to the State constitutional convention in 1790; elected to the Fourth Congress (March 4, 1795–March 3, 1797); died in Pendleton District, S. C., November 24, 1833; interment in Beaverdam Cemetery, Oconee County, S. C.

EARLL, Jonas, Jr. (cousin of Nehemiah Hezekiah Earll), a Representative from New York; born in 1786; resided in Onondaga County, N. Y., and attended the common schools; sheriff of Onondaga County 1815–1819; member of the State assembly in 1820 and 1821; served in the State senate from January 1823 to January 1827; elected as a Democrat to the Twentieth and Twenty-first Congresses (March 4, 1827–March 3, 1831); elected a canal commissioner and served from January 1832 to February 1840; postmaster of Syracuse, N. Y., from June 26,

1840, until March 10, 1842; again elected a canal commissioner and served from February 8, 1842, until his death in Syracuse, N. Y., October 28, 1846; interment in Walnut Grove Cemetery, Onondaga Hill, Onondaga County, N. Y.

EARLL, Nehemiah Hezekiah (cousin of Jonas Earll, Jr.), a Representative from New York; born in Whitehall, Washington County, N. Y., October 5, 1787; moved with his parents to Onondaga Valley in 1793; nine months later moved to Onondaga County and resided in Skaneateles until 1804; attended the public schools and Fairfield Academy for two years; studied law; was admitted to the bar in 1809 and commenced practice in Salina (which in 1848 became a part of Syracuse), Onondaga County; adjutant in the Army during the War of 1812 at Oswego; resumed the practice of law at Onondaga Hill, N. Y., in 1814; postmaster of Onondaga Hill in 1816; justice of the peace 1816–1820; master in chancery for six years; appointed first judge of Onondaga County and served from 1823 until his resignation in 1831; superintendent of the Onondaga Salt Springs 1831–1836, with residence in Syracuse, N. Y.; resigned, and engaged in the milling business in Jordan; returned to Syracuse, N. Y., in 1838; elected as a Democrat to the Twenty-sixth Congress (March 4, 1839–March 3, 1841); unsuccessful candidate for reelection in 1840 to the Twenty-seventh Congress; retired to private life, being blind for many years; died in Mottville, Onondaga County, N. Y., August 26, 1872; interment in Oakwood Cemetery, Syracuse, N. Y.

EARLY, Peter, a Representative from Georgia; born near Madison, Madison County, Va., June 20, 1773; attended the Lexington Academy (later Washington College) in Rockbridge County; was graduated from Princeton College in 1792; studied law in Philadelphia, Pa.; was admitted to the bar and commenced practice in Wilkes County, Ga., in 1796; moved to Greene County in 1801 and continued the practice of law; elected to the Seventh Congress to fill the vacancy caused by the resignation of John Milledge; reelected to the Eighth and Ninth Congresses and served from January 10, 1803, to March 3, 1807; one of the managers appointed by the House of Representatives in January 1804 to conduct the impeachment proceedings against John Pickering, judge of the United States District Court for New Hampshire, and in December of the same year against Samuel Chase, Associate Justice of the Supreme Court of the United States; declined to be a candidate for reelection; first judge of the superior court of the Ocmulgee circuit 1807–1813; Governor of Georgia 1813–1815; elected to the State senate in 1815 and served until his death near Scull Shoals, Greene County, Ga., August 15, 1817; interment on the west bank of the Oconee River near his mansion; reinterment in City Cemetery, Greensboro, Ga.

EARNSHAW, Manuel, a Resident Commissioner from the Philippine Islands; born in Cavite, Philippine Islands, November 19, 1862; attended the Ateneo de Manila and the Nauti School, Manila, Philippine Islands; became engaged in engineering and in the drydocking business in 1884; founder, president, and general manager of the Earnshaw Slipways & Engineering Co.; elected as an Independent candidate a Resident Commissioner to the United States and served from March 4, 1913, to March 3, 1917; was not a candidate for renomination in 1916; discontinued his former business pursuits in 1921 and lived in retirement with residence in Cavite; died in Manila, Philippine Islands, February 13, 1936; interment in Cementerio del Norte.

EARTHMAN, Harold Henderson, a Representative from Tennessee; born in Murfreesboro, Rutherford County, Tenn., April 13, 1900; attended the public schools, Webb School at Bell Buckle, Tenn., Southern Methodist University at Dallas, Tex., and the University of Texas at Austin; during the First World War served in the United States Army as a private and was assigned to the Student's Army Training Corps; moved to Nashville, Tenn., and engaged in the banking business 1921–1925; was admitted to the bar in 1926 and commenced the practice of law in Murfreesboro, Tenn.; also engaged in agricultural pursuits; resumed the study of law and was graduated from the law department of Cumberland University, Lebanon, Tenn., in 1927; served in the State house of representatives in 1931 and 1932; judge of Rutherford County, Tenn., 1942–1945; associate administrator of war bonds for the State of Tennessee 1940–1946; elected as a Democrat to the Seventy-ninth Congress (January 3, 1945–January 3, 1947); unsuccessful candidate for renomination in 1946; engaged in the practice of law; is owner of Earthman Enterprises; is a resident of Murfreesboro, Tenn.

EASTLAND, James Oliver, a Senator from Mississippi; born in Doddsville, Sunflower County, Miss., November 28, 1904; moved with his parents to Forest, Miss., in 1905; attended the public schools, the University of Mississippi at Oxford, Vanderbilt University, Nashville, Tenn., and the University of Alabama at Tuscaloosa; studied law; was admitted to the bar in 1927 and commenced practice in Forest, Miss.; also engaged in agricultural pursuits; member of the State house of representatives 1928–1932; moved to Ruleville, Miss., in 1934; appointed as a Democrat to the United States Senate to fill the vacancy caused by the death of Pat Harrison and served from June 30, 1941, to September 28, 1941; was not a candidate for election to the vacancy; elected to the United States Senate in 1942, 1948, and again in 1954, and served from January 3, 1943, to January 3, 1961. *Reelected in 1960 for the term ending January 3, 1967.*

EASTMAN, Ben C., a Representative from Wisconsin; born in Strong, Maine, October 24, 1812; attended the public schools; studied law; was admitted to the bar in 1840 and practiced in Green Bay, Wis.; moved to Platteville, Wis., the same year and continued the practice of law; secretary of the legislative council of Wisconsin Territory 1843–1846; district attorney of Grant County; elected as a Democrat to the Thirty-second and Thirty-third Congresses (March 4, 1851–March 3, 1855); declined to be a candidate for renomination in 1854; resumed the practice of law; died in Platteville, Grant County, Wis., February 2, 1856; interment in Forest Hill Cemetery, Madison, Wis.

EASTMAN, Ira Allen (nephew of Nehemiah Eastman), a Representative from New Hampshire; born in Gilmanton, N. H., January 1, 1809; attended the local schools; was graduated from Dartmouth College, Hanover, N. H., in 1829; studied law; was admitted to the bar in 1832 and commenced practice in Troy, N. H.; returned to Gilmanton in 1834 and continued the practice of law; clerk of the State house of representatives in 1835; member of the State house of representatives 1836–1838, and served as speaker in 1837 and 1838; register of probate from 1836 to 1839, when he resigned, having been elected to Congress; elected as a Democrat to the Twenty-sixth and Twenty-seventh Congresses (March 4, 1839–March 3, 1843); was not a candidate for renomination in 1842; judge of the court of common pleas 1844–1849; associate judge of the supreme court 1849–1855; judge of the superior judicial court from 1855 to 1859, when he retired; chosen trustee of Dartmouth College in 1859; unsuccessful Democratic candidate for Governor in 1863 and for United States Senator in 1866; resumed the practice of law; died in Manchester, N. H., March 21, 1881; interment in Valley Cemetery.

EASTMAN, Nehemiah (uncle of Ira Allen Eastman), a Representative from New Hampshire; born in Gilmanton, Belknap County, N. H., June 16, 1782; attended the local academy in

Gilmanton; studied law; was admitted to the bar in 1807 and practiced in Farmington, N. H.; member of the State house of representatives in 1813; served in the State senate 1820–1825; elected as a Democrat to the Nineteenth Congress (March 4, 1825–March 3, 1827); resumed the practice of law; died in Farmington, N. H., January 11, 1856; interment in Farmington Cemetery.

EASTON, Rufus, a Delegate from the Territory of Missouri; born in Litchfield, Conn., May 4, 1774; completed an academic course; studied law; was admitted to the bar and commenced practice in Rome, N. Y.; started west and settled in Vincennes, Indiana Territory, in 1804; moved to St. Louis, Mo. (then the District of Louisiana), and was appointed judge of the District of Louisiana in 1805; appointed the first postmaster of St. Louis and served from January 1, 1805, to January 1, 1815; elected as a Democrat a Delegate from the Territory of Missouri on September 17, 1814, and served until August 5, 1816; unsuccessfully contested the election of John Scott for the succeeding term; upon the organization of the State government in 1821 was appointed attorney general and served until 1826; engaged in the practice of law and in the real-estate business; died in St. Charles, Mo., July 5, 1834; interment in Lindenwood College Cemetery.

EATON, Charles Aubrey (uncle of William Robb Eaton), a Representative from New Jersey; born in Nova Scotia March 29, 1868; attended the public schools; was graduated from Acadia University, Nova Scotia, in 1890 and from Newton Theological Institution, Newton Center, Mass., in 1893; pastor of the First Baptist Church, Natick, Mass., 1892–1895, of the Bloor Street Church, Toronto, Canada, 1895–1901, and of the Euclid Avenue Church, Cleveland Ohio, 1901–1909; moved to Watchung, Somerset County, N. J., in 1909; pastor of the Madison Avenue Church, New York City, 1909–1919; sociological editor of the Toronto Globe, Toronto, Canada, 1896–1901; associate editor, Westminster, Toronto, Canada, 1899–1901; head of the national service section of the United States Shipping Board Emergency Fleet Corporation from November 1917 to January 1919; editor of Leslie's Weekly in 1919 and 1920; elected as a Republican to the Sixty-ninth and to the thirteen succeeding Congresses (March 4, 1925–January 3, 1953); was not a candidate for renomination in 1952; died in Washington, D. C., January 23, 1953; interment in Hillside Cemetery, Plainfield, N. J.

EATON, John Henry, a Senator from Tennessee; born near Scotland Neck, Halifax County, N. C., June 18, 1790; attended the common schools and the University of North Carolina at Chapel Hill in 1803 and 1804; studied law; was admitted to the bar and commenced practice in Franklin, Tenn.; member of the State house of representatives in 1815 and 1816; appointed in 1818 and subsequently elected as a Democrat to the United States Senate to fill the vacancy caused by the resignation of George W. Campbell and served from September 5, 1818, to March 3, 1821; reelected in September 1821, and again in 1826, and served from September 27, 1821, until March 9, 1829, when he resigned to accept a Cabinet position; appointed Secretary of War in the Cabinet of President Jackson and served from March 9, 1829, to June 18, 1831, when he resigned; Governor of the Territory of Florida 1834–1836; Envoy Extraordinary and Minister Plenipotentiary to Madrid, Spain, 1836–1840; declined to support Van Buren for President in 1840; died in Washington, D. C., November 17, 1856; interment in Oak Hill Cemetery.

EATON, Lewis, a Representative from New York; born in that State; sheriff of Schenectady County in 1821 and 1822; resided in Duanesburg; elected to the Eighteenth Congress (March 4, 1823–March 3, 1825); member of the State senate 1829–1832.

EATON, Thomas Marion, a Representative from California; born on a farm near Edwardsville, Madison County, Ill., August 3, 1896; attended the country schools and Edwardsville High School; was graduated from the State Normal School, Normal, Ill., in 1917; served as principal of the Lincoln grade school, Clinton, Ill., in 1917 and 1918; during the First World War served in the United States Navy as an ensign; moved to Long Beach, Calif., in 1921 and engaged in the automobile sales business; elected to the city council in 1934; reelected in 1936, and was unanimously chosen mayor by the council; elected as a Republican to the Seventy-sixth Congress and served from January 3, 1939, until his death in Long Beach, Calif., September 16, 1939; interment in Sunnyside Mausoleum.

EATON, William Robb (nephew of Charles Aubrey Eaton), a Representative from Colorado; born in Pugwash, Province of Nova Scotia, Canada, December 17, 1877; immigrated to the United States with his parents who settled in Boston, Mass., in 1878, and in Denver, Colo., in 1881; attended public and private schools; employed as a bank clerk 1889–1901; engaged as a jobber and wholesaler and in the warehouse business 1901–1909; served in Troop B, First Squadron Cavalry, National Guard of Colorado, 1898–1904; was graduated from the law department of the University of Denver at Denver in 1909; was admitted to the bar the same year and commenced practice in Denver, Colo.; served as deputy district attorney of the second judicial district 1909–1913; member of the State senate 1915–1918 and 1923–1926; elected as a Republican to the Seventy-first and Seventy-second Congresses (March 4, 1929–March 3, 1933); unsuccessful candidate for reelection in 1932 to the Seventy-third Congress and for election in 1934 to the Seventy-fourth Congress; resumed the practice of law in Denver, Colo., until his death there on December 16, 1942; interment in Fairmount Cemetery.

EATON, William Wallace, a Senator and a Representative from Connecticut; born in Tolland, Conn., October 11, 1816; educated in the schools of his native town, supplemented by private instruction; moved to Columbia, S. C., and engaged in mercantile pursuits for four years; returned to Tolland, Conn.; studied law; was admitted to the bar in 1837 and commenced practice in Tolland; clerk of courts of Tolland County in 1846 and 1847; member of the State house of representatives in 1847, 1848, 1853, 1863, 1868, 1870, 1871, 1873, and 1874; served as speaker in 1853 and 1873; served in the State senate in 1850; moved to Hartford, Conn., in 1851; clerk of courts of Hartford County in 1851 and 1854; city attorney in 1857 and 1858; unsuccessful Democratic candidate for United States Senator in 1860; chief judge of the city court of Hartford in 1863, 1864, and 1867–1872; appointed as a Democrat to the United States Senate to fill the vacancy caused by the death of William A. Buckingham and served from February 5, 1875, to March 3, 1875; elected for the term beginning March 4, 1875, and ending March 3, 1881; elected as a Democrat to the Forty-eighth Congress (March 4, 1883–March 3, 1885); unsuccessful candidate for reelection in 1884 to the Forty-ninth Congress; resumed the practice of his profession; died in Hartford, Conn., September 21, 1898; interment in Spring Grove Cemetery.

EBERHARTER, Herman Peter, a Representative from Pennsylvania; born in Pittsburgh, Pa., April 29, 1892; attended Holy Trinity parish school, Morehead School and Fifth Avenue High School; during the First World War served in the United States Army as a private in the Twentieth Infantry; attended officers training school at Camp Meade, Md., and was commissioned as a second lieutenant; was graduated from Duquesne University Law School, Pittsburgh, Pa., in 1925; was admitted to the bar the same year and commenced practice in Pittsburgh, Pa.; was a member of the Officers' Reserve Corps with rank of captain; member of the State house of representatives in 1935 and 1936; elected as a Democrat to the Seventy-fifth and to the ten succeeding Congresses and served from January 3, 1937, until his death; had been renominated to the Eighty-sixth Congress; died in Arlington, Va., September 9, 1958; interment in Mount Carmel Cemetery, Pittsburgh, Pa.

ECHOLS, Leonard Sidney, a Representative from West Virginia; born in Madison, Boone County, W. Va., October 30, 1871; attended the public schools; was graduated from the commercial department of the University of Kentucky at Lexington in 1894, from the Concord State Normal School, Athens, W. Va., in 1898, and from the law department of the Southern Normal University, Huntingdon, Tenn., in 1900; was admitted to the bar in 1900 and commenced practice in Point Pleasant, W. Va., in 1903; prosecuting attorney of Mason County 1904–1909; assistant State tax commissioner for West Virginia 1909–1919; elected as a Republican to the Sixty-sixth and Sixty-seventh Congresses (March 4, 1919–March 3, 1923); unsuccessful candidate for reelection in 1922 to the Sixty-eighth Congress and for election in 1924 to the Sixty-ninth Congress; member of the committee on appeals and review of the United States Treasury Department from May 1, 1923, to September 15, 1924; delegate to the Republican State convention in 1924; postmaster at Charleston, W. Va., 1925–1928; resumed the practice of law; served as referee in bankruptcy and as special master in the United States District Court, Charleston, W. Va.; died in Charleston, W. Va., May 9, 1946; interment in Sunset Memorial Park, South Charleston, W. Va.

ECKERT, Charles Richard, a Representative from Pennsylvania; born in Pittsburgh, Allegheny County, Pa., January 20, 1868; attended the public schools, Piersol's Academy at West Bridgewater, Pa., and Geneva College at Beaver Falls, Pa.; studied law; was admitted to the bar in 1894 and commenced practice in Beaver, Pa., the same year; delegate to the Democratic National Convention at Houston in 1928; elected as a Democrat to the Seventy-fourth and Seventy-fifth Congresses (January 3, 1935–January 3, 1939); unsuccessful candidate for reelection in 1938 to the Seventy-sixth Congress; member of board of directors of Beaver Trust Co.; resumed the practice of law until his death as the result of an automobile accident in Rochester, Pa., October 26, 1959; interment in Beaver Cemetery, Beaver, Pa.

ECKERT, George Nicholas, a Representative from Pennsylvania; born in Womelsdorf, Berks County, Pa., July 4, 1802; was graduated from the medical department of the University of Pennsylvania at Philadelphia in 1824 and commenced practice in Reading, Pa.; one of the organizers of Berks County Medical Society in 1824; moved to Pine Grove, Schuylkill County, Pa., and engaged in the coal and iron trade; elected as a Whig to the Thirtieth Congress (March 4, 1847–March 3, 1849); appointed Director of the United States Mint at Philadelphia by President Millard Fillmore and served from June 1851 to June 6, 1853; died in Philadelphia, Pa., on June 28, 1865; interment in Laurel Hill Cemetery.

ECKLEY, Ephraim Ralph, a Representative from Ohio; born near Mt. Pleasant, Jefferson County, Ohio, December 9, 1811; moved with his parents to Hayesville, Ohio, in 1816; attended the common schools and was graduated from Vermillion Institute, Hayesville, Ohio; moved to Carrollton, Carroll County, Ohio, in 1833 and taught school; studied law; was admitted to the bar in 1836 and commenced practice in Carrollton; member of the State senate 1843–1846, 1849, and 1850; unsuccessful candidate for

Lieutenant Governor of Ohio in 1851; served in the State house of representatives 1853–1857; unsuccessful candidate for election in 1853 to the United States Senate; delegate to the first Republican National Convention at Philadelphia in 1856; during the Civil War served in the Union Army as colonel of the Twenty-sixth Regiment, Ohio Volunteer Infantry, and also of the Eighteenth Regiment, Ohio Volunteer Infantry; brevetted brigadier general "for gallant and meritorious services"; elected as a Republican to the Thirty-eighth, Thirty-ninth, and Fortieth Congresses (March 4, 1863–March 3, 1869); was not a candidate for renomination in 1868; resumed the practice of law in Carrollton, Carroll County, Ohio, where he died March 27, 1908; interment in Grand View Cemetery.

ECTON, Zales Nelson, a Senator from Montana; born in Weldon, McCone County, Iowa, April 1, 1898; moved to Gallatin County, Mont., in 1907; attended the public schools of Gallatin County, Montana State College at Bozeman, and the University of Chicago Law School; during the First World War served as a private in the Infantry, Student Army Training Corps; engaged as a rancher (grain and livestock) 1921–1946; member of the State house of representatives from Gallatin County 1933–1937; served as a State senator from Gallatin County 1937–1946; chairman of the State Republican central committee 1940–1944; elected as a Republican to the United States Senate November 5, 1946, and served from January 3, 1947, to January 3, 1953; unsuccessful candidate for reelection in 1952; resumed farming activities; died at Bozeman, Mont., March 3, 1961; interment in Sunset Hills Cemetery.

EDDY, Frank Marion, a Representative from Minnesota; born in Pleasant Grove, Olmsted County, Minn., April 1, 1856; with his parents moved to Iowa in 1860, returned in 1863 to Olmsted County, Minn., and settled near Elmira, and in 1867 moved to Sauk Centre, Stearns County, Minn.; attended the common schools; taught school in a rural district; employed by the Northern Pacific Railroad Co. as a land examiner in 1881 and 1882; moved to Glenwood, Minn., and served as clerk of the district court of Pope County 1884–1893; was the first Representative from Minnesota who was a native of that State; elected as a Republican to the Fifty-fourth and to the three succeeding Congresses (March 4, 1895–March 3, 1903); declined to be a candidate for renomination in 1902; editor and owner of the Sauk Centre Herald 1901–1907; engaged in writing and lecturing 1907–1915; member of the Minnesota Immigration Bureau in 1916; became engaged in journalism in St. Paul; employed as a clerk in the automobile department in the office of the secretary of state of Minnesota in 1918, in which capacity he served until his death in St. Paul, Minn., January 13, 1929; interment in Greenwood Cemetery, Sauk Centre, Minn.

EDDY, Norman, a Representative from Indiana; born in Scipio, N. Y., December 10, 1810; attended the common schools, and was graduated from the medical department of the University of Pennsylvania at Philadelphia in 1835; moved to Indiana, settled in Mishawaka, and practiced medicine until 1847; studied law; was admitted to the bar in 1847 and commenced practice in South Bend, Ind.; member of the State senate in 1850; held several local offices; elected as a Democrat to the Thirty-third Congress (March 4, 1853–March 3, 1855); unsuccessful candidate for reelection in 1854 to the Thirty-fourth Congress; appointed by President Pierce attorney general of the Territory of Minnesota in 1855; colonel of the Forty-eighth Indiana Volunteer Infantry during the Civil War; collector of internal revenue 1865–1870; secretary of state of Indiana 1870–1872; died in Indianapolis, Ind., January 28, 1872; interment in the City Cemetery, South Bend, Ind.

EDDY, Samuel, a Representative from Rhode Island; born in Johnston, near Providence, R. I., March 31, 1769; completed preparatory studies; was graduated from Brown University, Providence, R. I., in 1787; studied law; was admitted to the bar in 1790 and practiced a short time in Providence; clerk of the Rhode Island Supreme Court 1790–1793; secretary of state 1798–1819; elected as a Democrat to the Sixteenth, Seventeenth, and Eighteenth Congresses (March 4, 1819–March 3, 1825); unsuccessful candidate for reelection in 1824 to the Nineteenth Congress and for election in 1828 to the Twenty-first Congress; associate justice of the State supreme court in 1826 and 1827, and served as chief justice 1827–1835; died in Providence, R. I., February 3, 1839; interment in North End Cemetery.

EDELSTEIN, Morris Michael, a Representative from New York; born in Meseritz, Poland, February 5, 1888; at three years of age immigrated to the United States with his parents, who settled in New York City, N. Y.; attended the public schools and Cooper Union College in New York City; was graduated from the Brooklyn Law School of St. Lawrence University, New York City, in 1909; was admitted to the bar in 1910 and commenced the practice of law in New York City; elected as a Democrat to the Seventy-sixth Congress to fill the vacancy caused by the death of William I. Sirovich; reelected to the Seventy-seventh Congress and served from February 6, 1940, until his death on June 4, 1941, in the cloakroom of the House of Representatives, Washington, D. C., after completing the delivery of a speech on the floor of the House; interment in Mount Zion Cemetery, Maspeth, Long Island, N. Y.

EDEN, John Rice, a Representative from Illinois; born in Bath County, Ky., February 1, 1826; moved with his parents to Indiana; attended the public schools; studied law; was admitted to the bar in 1853 and commenced practice in Sullivan, Ill.; prosecuting attorney for the seventeenth judicial district of Illinois 1856–1860; elected as a Democrat to the Thirty-eighth Congress (March 4, 1863–March 3, 1865); unsuccessful candidate for reelection in 1864 to the Thirty-ninth Congress; unsuccessful Democratic nominee for Governor of Illinois in 1868; elected to the Forty-third, Forty-fourth, and Forty-fifth Congresses (March 4, 1873–March 3, 1879); unsuccessful candidate for renomination in 1878; resumed the practice of law in Sullivan, Ill.; elected to the Forty-ninth Congress (March 4, 1885–March 3, 1887); unsuccessful candidate for renomination in 1886; again engaged in the practice of law; died in Sullivan, Moultrie County, Ill., June 9, 1909; interment in Greenhill Cemetery.

EDGE, Walter Evans, a Senator from New Jersey; born in Philadelphia, Pa., November 20, 1873; moved with his parents to Pleasantville, N. J., in 1877; attended the public schools; employed in a printing office in Atlantic City, N. J., 1890–1894; journal clerk of the State senate 1897–1899; during the Spanish-American War served as second lieutenant; after the war was commissioned lieutenant colonel and made chief of the ordnance department of the staff of the major general commanding the New Jersey National Guard; secretary of the State senate 1901–1904; presidential elector on the Republican ticket of Roosevelt and Fairbanks in 1904; served in the State house of assembly in 1910; member of the State senate 1911–1916, serving as president of that body in 1915; Governor of New Jersey from January 16, 1917, to May 16, 1919, when he resigned, having been elected United States Senator; delegate at large to eleven Republican National Conventions 1916–1956; elected as a Republican to the United States Senate in 1918; reelected in 1924 and served from March 4, 1919, until his resignation on November 21, 1929, having been appointed Ambassador to France by President

Hoover, in which capacity he served until March 4, 1933; again Governor of New Jersey from January 18, 1944, to January 20, 1947; died in New York, N. Y., October 29, 1956; interment in Northbrook Cemetery, Downingtown, Pa.

EDGERTON, Alfred Peck (brother of Joseph Ketchum Edgerton), a Representative from Ohio; born in Plattsburg, N. Y., January 11, 1813; was graduated from Plattsburg Academy; engaged in newspaper work for a brief period, and later in commercial pursuits in New York City; moved to Hicksville, Ohio, in 1837; manager of the American Land Co., and engaged in opening new land for settlement in northwestern Ohio, near Hicksville, 1837–1852; member of the State senate in 1845 and 1846; elected as a Democrat to the Thirty-second and Thirty-third Congresses (March 4, 1851–March 3, 1855); financial agent of the Board of State Fund Commissioners of Ohio in 1853, with residence in New York City; moved to Fort Wayne, Ind., in 1857; general manager of the Wabash & Erie Canal 1859–1868; unsuccessful candidate for Lieutenant Governor of Ohio in 1868; chairman of the United States Civil Service Commission in 1885; served in many important positions in his later years, including that of member of the Fort Wayne School Board; died in Hicksville, Defiance County, Ohio, May 14, 1897; interment in Lindenwood Cemetery, Fort Wayne, Ind.

EDGERTON, Alonzo Jay, a Senator from Minnesota; born in Rome, Oneida County, N. Y., June 7, 1827; pursued preparatory studies; was graduated from Wesleyan University, Middletown, Conn., in 1850; settled in Mantorville, Minn., in 1855; studied law; was admitted to the bar in 1855 and commenced practice in Mantorville, Minn.; prosecuting attorney of Dodge County; member of the State senate in 1858 and 1859; during the Civil War was commissioned a captain in 1862 in the Tenth Minnesota Volunteer Regiment; promoted to colonel in 1864; brevetted brigadier general in 1865, and was mustered out in March 1867; served as railroad commissioner 1871–1875; presidential elector on the Republican ticket of Hayes and Wheeler in 1876; again a member of the State senate 1877–1879; moved to Kasson, Minn., in 1878; appointed as a Republican to the United States Senate to fill the vacancy caused by the resignation of William Windom and served from March 12 to October 30, 1881, when a successor was elected; appointed chief justice of the Territorial Supreme Court of Dakota; upon the admission of South Dakota as a State into the Union was made United States judge of that district; served as president of the constitutional convention of South Dakota; died at Sioux Falls, S. Dak., on August 9, 1896; interment in Evergreen Cemetery, Mantorville, Minn.

EDGERTON, Joseph Ketchum (brother of Alfred Peck Edgerton), a Representative from Indiana; born in Vergennes, Addison County, Vt., February 16, 1818; attended the public schools of Clinton County, N. Y.; studied law in Plattsburg (N. Y.) Academy; was admitted to the bar and commenced practice in New York City in 1839; moved to Fort Wayne, Ind., in 1844 and continued the practice of law; director of the Fort Wayne & Chicago Railroad Co. in 1854 and later its president; president of the Grand Rapids & Indiana Railroad Co. in 1855; director of the Ohio & Indiana Railroad Co. in 1856 and a leader in the movement to consolidate the properties which now comprise the Pennsylvania system west of Pittsburgh, of which he was made vice president; elected as a Democrat to the Thirty-eighth Congress (March 4, 1863–March 3, 1865); unsuccessful for reelection in 1864 to the Thirty-ninth Congress; financially interested in many leading manufacturing and banking institutions of the Middle West; died in Boston, Mass., August 25, 1893; interment in Lindenwood Cemetery, Fort Wayne, Ind.

EDGERTON, Sidney, a Representative from Ohio; born in Cazenovia, N. Y., August 17, 1818; attended the country schools and the academy at Lima, N. Y., where he was later an instructor; moved to Ohio in 1844; taught in the academy at Tallmadge, Ohio, in 1844; studied law; was graduated from the Cincinnati Law School in 1845; was admitted to the bar and commenced practice in Akron, Ohio, in 1846; delegate to the convention that formed the Free-Soil Party in 1848; prosecuting attorney of Summit County 1852–1856; delegate to the first Republican National Convention, which was held in Philadelphia in 1856; elected as a Republican to the Thirty-sixth and Thirty-seventh Congresses (March 4, 1859–March 3, 1863); was not a candidate for renomination in 1862; served as colonel of the Squirrel Hunters during the Civil War; appointed United States judge for the Territory of Idaho in 1863; Governor of Montana Territory in 1865 and 1866; resumed the practice of law in Akron, Ohio, where he died July 19, 1900; interment in Tallmadge Cemetery, Tallmadge, Ohio.

EDIE, John Rufus, a Representative from Pennsylvania; born in Gettysburg, Adams County, Pa., January 14, 1814; attended the public schools, Emmitsburg (Md.) College, and the United States Military Academy at West Point, N. Y.; principal of the Gettysburg schools for several years; studied law; was admitted to the bar in 1840 and commenced practice in Somerset, Pa.; member of the State senate in 1845 and 1846; appointed deputy attorney general in 1847 and served until 1850; district attorney 1850–1854; elected as a Whig to the Thirty-fourth and Thirty-fifth Congresses (March 4, 1855–March 3, 1859); was not a candidate for renomination in 1858; during the Civil War was commissioned a major of the Fifteenth Regiment, United States Infantry, May 14, 1861; promoted to the rank of lieutenant colonel in 1863 and served with the Fifteenth and Eighth Regiments, United States Infantry, until January 1871, when he was honorably discharged; brevetted colonel September 1, 1864, "for gallant and meritorious services" during the Atlanta campaign; resumed the practice of law in Somerset, Pa., and died there August 27, 1888; interment in Union Cemetery.

EDMANDS, John Wiley, a Representative from Massachusetts; born in Boston, Mass., March 1, 1809; completed preparatory studies, and was graduated from the English High School at Boston; interested in woolen mills in Dedham, Mass., and the Pacific Mills Co. in Lawrence, Mass.; elected as a Whig to the Thirty-third Congress (March 4, 1853–March 3, 1855); declined to be a candidate for renomination in 1854; treasurer of the Pacific Mills at Lawrence in 1855; presidential elector on the Republican ticket of Grant and Colfax in 1868; died in Newton, Mass., on January 31, 1877; interment in Mount Auburn Cemetery, Cambridge, Mass.

EDMISTON, Andrew, a Representative from West Virginia; born in Weston, Lewis County, W. Va., November 13, 1892; attended the Friends' Select School, Washington, D. C., Kentucky Military Institute at Lyndon, and the University of West Virginia at Morgantown; engaged in agricultural pursuits 1915–1917 and in the manufacture of glass at Weston, W. Va., since 1925; during the First World War served overseas as a second lieutenant with the Thirty-ninth Infantry, Fourth Division, 1917–1919; awarded the Distinguished Service Cross, the Purple Heart with Oak Leaf Cluster, and the Distinguished Service Medal of West Virginia; editor of the Weston (W. Va.) Democrat 1920–1935; mayor of Weston, W. Va., 1924–1926; delegate to the Democratic National Conventions in 1928 and 1952; State chairman of the Democratic executive committee 1928–1932; elected as a Democrat to the Seventy-third Congress to fill the vacancy caused by the death of Lynn S. Horner; reelected to the Seventy-fourth and to the three succeeding Congresses and served from November 28, 1933, to January 3, 1943; unsuccessful candidate for reelection in 1942 to the Seventy-eighth Congress; resumed his former business pursuits; appointed State director of War Manpower for West Virginia on June 28, 1943, and served until his resignation on June 30, 1945, to return to private business; is a resident of Weston, W. Va.

EDMOND, William, a Representative from Connecticut; born in Woodbury, Conn., September 28, 1755; attended the common schools, and was graduated from Yale College, New Haven, Conn., in 1778; served in the Revolutionary Army and was wounded at the Battle of Danbury in 1777, when that village was burned by the British; studied law; was admitted to the bar in 1780 and commenced practice in Newtown, Conn.; member of the State house of representatives 1791–1797, 1801, and 1802; served in the State senate 1797–1799; elected as a Federalist to the Fifth Congress to fill the vacancy caused by the death of James Davenport; reelected to the Sixth Congress and served from November 13, 1797, to March 3, 1801; declined to be a candidate for renomination in 1800; resumed the practice of law in Newtown; associate judge of the State supreme court 1805–1819; retired to private life and continued the practice of law; died in Newtown, Fairfield County, Conn., on August 1, 1838; interment in Newtown Cemetery.

EDMONDS, George Washington, a Representative from Pennsylvania; born in Pottsville, Schuylkill County, Pa., February 22, 1864; attended the public schools and Central High School; was graduated from the Philadelphia College of Pharmacy in 1887 and practiced pharmacy for several years; engaged in the coal business; member of the common council of Philadelphia 1896–1902; elected as a Republican to the Sixty-third and to the five succeeding Congresses (March 4, 1913–March 3, 1925); unsuccessful candidate for renomination in 1924; engaged in the wholesale coal and lumber business; elected manager of the Port of Philadelphia Ocean Traffic Bureau in September 1927 and served until 1933; again elected to the Seventy-third Congress (March 4, 1933–January 3, 1935); unsuccessful candidate for reelection in 1934 to the Seventy-fourth Congress; resumed the wholesale coal business in Philadelphia, Pa.; died in Philadelphia on September 28, 1939; interment in West Laurel Hill Cemetery.

EDMONDSON, Edmond Augustus, a Representative from Oklahoma; born in Muskogee, Okla., April 7, 1919; attended the public schools; graduated from Muskogee Junior College in 1938 and from the University of Oklahoma in 1940; special agent with the Federal Bureau of Investigation, Washington, D. C., 1940–1943, while attending Georgetown University; interrupted studies there and served in the United States Navy 1943–1946 with service in the South Pacific and discharged as a lieutenant; returned to Georgetown University and graduated in 1947; was admitted to the bar the same year and commenced practice in Muskogee, Okla.; county attorney of Muskogee County, Okla.; elected as a Democrat to the Eighty-third and to the three succeeding Congresses (January 3, 1953–January 3, 1961). *Reelected to the Eighty-seventh Congress.*

EDMUNDS, George Franklin, a Senator from Vermont; born in Richmond, Chittenden County, Vt., February 1, 1828; attended the common schools and was privately tutored; studied law; was admitted to the bar in 1849 and commenced practice in Burlington, Vt.; served in the State house of representatives 1854–1859, serving three years as speaker; member of the State senate, serving as its presiding officer pro tempore in 1861 and 1862; appointed on April 3, 1866, and elected on October 24,

1866, as a Republican to the United States Senate to fill the vacancy caused by the death of Solomon Foote; reelected in 1868, 1874, 1880, and 1886 and served from April 3, 1866, until his resignation, effective November 1, 1891; President pro tempore of the Senate from March 3, 1883, to March 3, 1885; appointed a member of the Electoral Commission created by act of Congress approved January 29, 1877, to decide the contests in various States in the presidential election of 1876; resumed the practice of law in Philadelphia, Pa.; subsequently moved to Pasadena, Calif., where he died February 27, 1919; interment in Green Mount Cemetery, Burlington, Vt.

EDMUNDS, Paul Carrington, a Representative from Virginia; born at "Springwood," the country estate, near Halifax Court House, Halifax County, Va., November 1, 1836; studied under a private teacher; was graduated from the University of Virginia at Charlottesville in 1855, and from the law department of William and Mary College, Williamsburg, Va., in 1857; was admitted to the bar the same year and commenced practice in Jefferson City, Mo.; returned to Virginia in 1859 and engaged in agricultural pursuits on his farm in Halifax County; served as first lieutenant, Company A, Montague's battalion, in the Confederate Army during the Civil War; member of the Virginia State senate 1881–1888; delegate to the Democratic National Convention at Chicago in 1884; elected as a Democrat to the Fifty-first, Fifty-second, and Fifty-third Congresses (March 4, 1889–March 3, 1895); declined to be a candidate for renomination in 1894; retired to his farm and discontinued active pursuits; died in Houston, Halifax County, Va., March 12, 1899; interment in St. John's Churchyard, Halifax, Va.

EDMUNDSON, Henry Alonzo, a Representative from Virginia; born in Blacksburg, Montgomery County, Va., June 14, 1814; attended private schools, and was graduated from Georgetown University, Washington, D. C.; studied law; was admitted to the bar in 1838 and commenced practice in Salem, Va.; elected as a Democrat to the Thirty-first and to the five succeeding Congresses (March 4, 1849–March 3, 1861); during the Civil War served in the Confederate Army as lieutenant colonel of the Fifty-fourth Virginia Regiment until 1862, when he was assigned to the command of the Twenty-seventh Virginia Cavalry; at the close of hostilities he resumed the practice of law, and subsequently, in 1880, engaged in agricultural pursuits; died at his home, "Falling Waters," Shawsville, Montgomery County, Va., December 16, 1890; interment in Fotheringay Cemetery, Montgomery County, Va.

EDSALL, Joseph E., a Representative from New Jersey; born in Rudeville, near Hamburg, Sussex County, N. J., in 1789; attended the common schools; engaged in mercantile pursuits; operated a distillery and a tannery; served as county clerk; member of the New Jersey House of Assembly; served as judge of the court of common pleas; elected as a Democrat to the Twenty-ninth and Thirtieth Congresses (March 4, 1845–March 3, 1849); died in Hamburg, N. J., in 1865; interment in the Baptist Burying Ground.

EDWARDS, Benjamin (father of Ninian Edwards), a Representative from Maryland; born in Stafford County, Va., August 12, 1753; attended the common schools; engaged in agricultural and mercantile pursuits in Montgomery County, Md.; member of the State house of delegates for several years; delegate to the State convention which ratified the Federal Constitution in 1788; elected to the Third Congress to fill the vacancy caused by the resignation of Uriah Forrest and served from January 2 to March 3, 1795; moved to Todd County, Ky.; died in Elkton, Ky., November 13, 1829; interment on his estate at Elkton, Ky.

EDWARDS, Caldwell, a Representative from Montana; born in Sag Harbor, Suffolk County, N. Y., January 8, 1841; was educated in the district schools; salesman and bookkeeper in dry-goods stores for several years; moved to Bozeman, Territory of Montana, in 1864 and became engaged in agricultural pursuits; member of the State house of representatives 1901–1905; elected on the Democratic-Populist ticket to the Fifty-seventh Congress (March 4, 1901–March 3, 1903); was not a candidate for renomination in 1902; at the expiration of his term returned to his ranch in Montana; died in Sag Harbor, N. Y., July 23, 1922; interment in Oakland Cemetery.

EDWARDS, Charles Gordon, a Representative from Georgia; born in Daisy, Tattnall (now Evans) County, Ga., July 2, 1878; attended the public schools, Gordon Institute, Barnesville, Ga., and Florida State College (now part of the University of Florida) at Lake City; was graduated from the law department of the University of Georgia at Athens in 1898; was admitted to the bar the same year and commenced practice in Reidsville; moved to Savannah in 1900 and continued the practice of law; also interested in agricultural pursuits; served as a sergeant in the Savannah Volunteer Guards, Company B, Coast Artillery, in 1902 and 1903 and as a second lieutenant in the Oglethorpe Light Infantry of the First Georgia Regiment of Infantry in 1903 and 1904; elected as a Democrat to the Sixtieth and to the four succeeding Congresses (March 4, 1907–March 3, 1917); voluntarily retired to resume the practice of law in Savannah, Ga.; president of the Savannah Board of Trade in 1919 and 1920; trustee of the Southern Methodist College, McRae, Ga.; member of the Harbor Commission of Savannah, Ga., 1920–1924; elected to the Sixty-ninth and to the three succeeding Congresses and served from March 4, 1925, until his death in Atlanta, Ga., July 13, 1931; interment in Bonaventure Cemetery, Savannah, Ga.

EDWARDS, Don Calvin, a Representative from Kentucky; born in Moulton, Appanoose County, Iowa, on July 13, 1861; moved to Erie, Neosho County, Kans., with his parents in 1869; attended the common schools of Iowa and Kansas, and Campbell University, Holton, Kans.; engaged in banking and in the insurance business in Erie, Kans., in 1883; moved to London, Laurel County, Ky., in 1892 and engaged in the manufacture of staves and in the wholesale lumber business; president of the National Bank of London, Ky.; clerk and master commissioner of the Laurel circuit court from 1898 to 1904; chairman of the Kentucky State Republican convention in 1908; elected as a Republican to the Fifty-ninth, Sixtieth, and Sixty-first Congresses (March 4, 1905–March 3, 1911); unsuccessful candidate for reelection in 1910 to the Sixty-second Congress; resumed the lumber and banking business in London, Ky.; delegate to the Republican National Convention at Chicago in 1912, which nominated the presidential ticket of Taft and Sherman; during the First World War was a member of the State council of national defense; chairman of five Liberty Loan campaigns; fuel administrator for Laurel County in 1917 and 1918; unsuccessful candidate for nomination in 1918 to the Sixty-sixth Congress; died in London, Ky., September 19, 1938; interment in Pine Grove Cemetery.

EDWARDS, Edward Irving, a Senator from New Jersey; born in Jersey City, N. J., December 1, 1863; attended the Jersey City public schools, and New York University, New York City, in 1884; studied law; engaged in banking and in the general contracting business; president and chairman of the board of directors of the First National Bank of Jersey City; comptroller of the treasury of New Jersey 1911–1917; member of the State senate from November 5, 1918, to January 1, 1920; elected Governor of New Jersey and served from 1920 to 1923; elected as a Democrat to the United States Senate and served from March 4, 1923, to March 3, 1929; unsuccessful candidate for reelection in 1928; died in Jersey City, N. J., January 26, 1931; interment in New York Bay Cemetery.

EDWARDS, Francis Smith, a Representative from New York; born in Windsor, Broome County, N. Y., May 28, 1817; completed preparatory studies; attended Hamilton (N. Y.) College (now Colgate University), but did not graduate; studied law; was admitted to the bar in New York City May 20, 1840, and practiced in Sherburne and Albany; moved to Fredonia in 1851 and continued the practice of law; appointed master and examiner in chancery for Chenango County in 1842; appointed special county surrogate of Chautauqua County in 1853, and served until November 1, 1855; elected as the candidate of the American Party to the Thirty-fourth Congress and served from March 4, 1855, to February 28, 1857, when he resigned; unsuccessful candidate for reelection in 1856 to the Thirty-fifth Congress; settled in Dunkirk, N. Y., in 1859, and resumed the practice of his profession; city attorney for nine years; retired from the practice of law in 1892; elected police justice in 1895 and served until ten days before his death; died in Dunkirk, N. Y., on May 20, 1899; interment in Forest Hill Cemetery, Fredonia, N. Y.

EDWARDS, Henry Waggaman (son of Pierrepont Edwards), a Representative and a Senator from Connecticut; born in New Haven, Conn., in October 1779; was graduated from Princeton College in 1797; studied law at the Litchfield Law School; was admitted to the bar and commenced practice in New Haven, Conn.; elected as a Democrat to the Sixteenth and Seventeenth Congresses (March 4, 1819–March 3, 1823); appointed to the United States Senate to fill the vacancy caused by the death of Elijah Boardman; subsequently elected and served from October 8, 1823, to March 3, 1827; served in the State senate 1827–1829; member of the State house of representatives in 1830 and served as speaker; elected Governor of Connecticut in 1833; was an unsuccessful candidate for reelection in 1834; again elected Governor in 1835, 1836, and 1837; resumed the practice of law; died in New Haven, Conn., on July 22, 1847; interment in Grove Street Cemetery.

EDWARDS, John, a Senator from Kentucky; born in Stafford County, Va., in 1748; attended the common schools; moved to Fayette County, Ky. (then a part of Virginia), in 1780; member of the Virginia House of Delegates 1781–1783, 1785, and 1786; delegate to the eighth convention called to define the limits of the proposed State of Kentucky 1785–1788; member of the convention of 1792 that framed the State constitution of Kentucky; upon the admission of Kentucky as a State into the Union was elected to the United States Senate and served from June 18, 1792, to March 3, 1795; member of the State house of representatives in 1795; served in the State senate 1796–1800; died on his plantation near Paris, Bourbon County, Ky., in 1837; interment in the family cemetery on a farm subsequently owned by Benjamin Ardery, near Paris, Ky.

EDWARDS, John, a Representative from New York; born in Beekmans precinct, Dutchess County, near Poughkeepsie, N. Y., on August 6, 1781; attended the common schools; sheriff of Montgomery County and keeper of Johnstown Jail 1806–1812; moved to Fulton County and settled in the village of Ephratah; elected as a Democrat to the Twenty-fifth Congress (March 4, 1837–March 3, 1839); engaged in the mercantile business and also interested in manufacturing pursuits; died in Johnstown, Fulton County, N. Y., December 28, 1850; interment in Johnstown Cemetery.

EDWARDS, John (granduncle of John Edwards Leonard), a Representative from Pennsylvania; born in Ivy Mills, Delaware County, Pa., in 1786; studied law; was admitted to the bar in 1807 and commenced practice in Chester, Delaware County, Pa.; deputy attorney general for Delaware County in 1811; moved to Philadelphia, Pa.; returned to Delaware County; counsel for the defense in the trial of Wellington for the murder of Bonsall in 1824; moved to West Chester in 1825 and shortly thereafter engaged in the manufacture of iron and later of nails near Glen Mills, Delaware County; elected as a Whig to the Twenty-sixth and Twenty-seventh Congresses (March 4, 1839–March 3, 1843); resumed his former manufacturing pursuits; died on his estate near Glen Mills June 26, 1843; interment in the Friends' (Hicksite) Cemetery of the Middletown Meeting House, Middletown Township, Delaware County, Pa.

EDWARDS, John, a Representative from Arkansas; born in Louisville, Jefferson County, Ky., October 24, 1805; received a limited schooling; studied law and was admitted to the bar; moved to Indiana, where he served in the State house of representatives in 1845 and 1846; moved to California, and in 1849 was elected an alcalde; returned to Indiana in 1852; member of the State senate in 1853; moved to Chariton, Iowa, in 1855; member of the Iowa constitutional convention; served in the State house of representatives 1856–1860, the last two years as speaker of the house; founder in 1857 of the Patriot, a newspaper; during the Civil War was appointed lieutenant colonel May 21, 1861, on the staff of the Governor of Iowa; colonel of the Eighteenth Regiment, Iowa Volunteer Infantry, August 8, 1862; brigadier general of Volunteers September 26, 1864; honorably mustered out January 15, 1866; at the close of the war settled in Fort Smith, Ark.; appointed by President Johnson as United States assessor of internal revenue and served from August 15, 1866, to May 31, 1869; presented credentials of election as a Liberal Republican to the Forty-second Congress and served from March 4, 1871, to February 9, 1872, when he was succeeded by Thomas Boles, who contested the election; was not a candidate for renomination; settled in Washington, D. C., and died there April 8, 1894; interment in Arlington National Cemetery, Fort Myer, Va.

EDWARDS, John Cummins, a Representative from Missouri; born in Frankfort, Franklin County, Ky., June 24, 1804; completed preparatory studies and was graduated from Black's College, Kentucky; studied law; was admitted to the bar in 1825 and practiced in Murfreesboro, Tenn., and later in Jefferson City, Mo.; secretary of state of Missouri 1830–1835 and in 1837; district judge of Cole County, Mo., 1832–1837; member of the State house of representatives in 1836; judge of the State supreme court 1837–1839; elected as a Democrat to the Twenty-seventh Congress (March 4, 1841–March 3, 1843); did not seek renomination, having become a candidate for the gubernatorial office; Governor of Missouri 1844–1848; moved to Stockton, Calif., in 1849 and continued the practice of his profession; mayor of Stockton in 1851; engaged in cattle raising, mercantile pursuits, and the real-estate business; died in Stockton, Calif., October 14, 1888; interment in the Rural Cemetery.

EDWARDS, Ninian (son of Benjamin Edwards), a Senator from Illinois; born on the Edwards farm, "Mount Pleasant," Montgomery County, Md., March 17, 1775; attended private schools; was graduated from Dickinson College, Carlisle, Pa., in 1792; studied law; moved with his parents to Bardstown, Ky., in 1795; was elected to the legislature before reaching his majority; member of the State house of representatives in 1796 and 1797; was admitted to the bar in 1798 and commenced practice in Russellville, Ky.; judge of the general court of Kentucky in 1803; judge of the circuit court in 1804;

presidential elector in 1804 on the Democratic ticket of Jefferson and Clinton; judge of the court of appeals in 1806 and chief justice of the State in 1808; Governor of the Territory of Illinois 1809–1818; upon the admission of Illinois as a State into the Union was elected as a Democrat to the United States Senate and served from December 3, 1818, to March 4, 1824, when he resigned; appointed Minister to Mexico March 4, 1824, but while en route was recalled to testify before a select committee of the House of Representatives appointed to investigate charges made by him against William H. Crawford, Secretary of the Treasury; resumed the practice of law; was also interested in saw and grist mills and engaged in mercantile pursuits; elected Governor of Illinois and served from 1826 to 1831; died in Belleville, Ill., on July 20, 1833; interment in that city; reinterment in 1855 in Oak Ridge Cemetery, Springfield, Ill.

EDWARDS, Pierrepont (father of Henry Waggaman Edwards), a Delegate from Connecticut; born in Northampton, Mass., April 8, 1750; was graduated from Princeton College in 1768; studied law; was admitted to the bar and began practice in New Haven, Conn., in 1771; served in the Revolutionary Army; when Benedict Arnold was found guilty of treason was made administrator of his estate; Member of the Continental Congress in 1787 and 1788; member of the State house of representatives in 1789 and 1790 and served as speaker; appointed United States district judge for the district of Connecticut in 1806; member of the Federal constitutional convention and of the constitutional convention which framed the constitution of Connecticut in 1818; died in Bridgeport, Conn., April 5, 1826; interment in Grove Street Cemetery, New Haven, Conn.

EDWARDS, Samuel, a Representative from Pennsylvania; born in Chester Township, Delaware County, Pa., March 12, 1785; attended the common schools; studied law; was admitted to the bar in 1806 and commenced practice in Chester; served in the War of 1812; member of the State house of representatives 1814–1816; elected as a Federalist to the Sixteenth and to the three succeeding Congresses (March 4, 1819–March 3, 1827); resumed the practice of his profession in Chester; inspector of customs 1838–1842; died in Chester, Pa., November 21, 1850; interment in Chester Rural Cemetery.

EDWARDS, Thomas McKey, a Representative from New Hampshire; born in Keene, Cheshire County, N. H., December 16, 1795; tutored privately; was graduated from Dartmouth College, Hanover, N. H., in 1813; studied law; was admitted to the bar in 1817 and commenced practice in Keene, N. H.; postmaster of Keene, N. H., from June 30, 1818, to July 23, 1829; served in the State house of representatives in 1834, 1836, 1838, and 1839; abandoned his law practice in 1845 and superintended the construction of the Cheshire Railroad, serving as its first president; also served as president of a bank and a fire-insurance company; presidential elector on the Republican ticket of Frémont and Dayton in 1856; elected as a Republican to the Thirty-sixth and Thirty-seventh Congresses (March 4, 1859–March 3, 1863); was not a candidate for renomination in 1862 to the Thirty-eighth Congress; resumed his former business pursuits; died in Keene, N. H., May 1, 1875; interment in Woodlawn Cemetery.

EDWARDS, Thomas Owen, a Representative from Ohio; born in Williamsburg, Ind., March 29, 1810; completed preparatory studies; studied medicine at the University of Maryland, Baltimore, Md.; moved to Lancaster, Ohio, in 1836 and engaged in the practice of medicine; elected as a Whig to the Thirtieth

Congress (March 4, 1847–March 3, 1849); unsuccessful candidate for reelection in 1848 to the Thirty-first Congress; attended former President John Quincy Adams, who was then a Congressman, when he was stricken with apoplexy while making a speech in the Hall of the House of Representatives, and who died in his arms in the United States Capitol, Washington, D. C.; served as inspector of marine hospitals; moved to Cincinnati, Ohio, and engaged in the drug business; member and president of the city council; professor in the Ohio Medical College, Cincinnati, Ohio; moved to Madison, Wis., and thence to Dubuque, Iowa; during the Civil War served as surgeon in the Third Regiment, Iowa Volunteer Infantry; returned to Lancaster, Ohio, about 1870 and resumed the practice of medicine; moved to Wheeling, W. Va., in 1875 and continued the practice of his profession; died in Wheeling, W. Va., February 5, 1876; interment in Mount Wood Cemetery.

EDWARDS, Weldon Nathaniel, a Representative from North Carolina; born in Gaston, Northampton County, N. C., January 25, 1788; attended Warrenton Academy; studied law; was admitted to the bar in 1810 and commenced practice in Warrenton, N. C.; member of the State house of representatives in 1814 and 1815; elected as a Democrat to the Fourteenth Congress to fill the vacancy caused by the resignation of Nathaniel Macon; reelected to the Fifteenth and to the four succeeding Congresses and served from February 7, 1816, to March 3, 1827; declined to be a candidate for reelection in 1826; returned to his plantation; member of the State senate 1833–1844; member of the State constitutional convention in 1835; again elected to the State senate in 1850 and chosen its president; president of the State secession convention in 1861; died in Warren County, N. C., December 18, 1873; interment in a private cemetery at his home, "Poplar Mount," about twelve miles from Warrenton, Warren County, N. C.

EDWARDS, William Posey, a Representative from Georgia; born near Talbotton, Talbot County, Ga., November 9, 1835; attended the common schools, and was graduated from Collinsworth Institute, Talbotton, Ga., in 1856; studied law; was admitted to the bar in 1857 and commenced practice in Butler, Ga.; member of the State constitutional convention in 1857 and 1858; served during the Civil War in the Confederate Army as captain of Company F, Twenty-seventh Georgia Volunteer Infantry; subsequently promoted to colonel of the regiment; upon the readmission of Georgia to representation was elected as a Republican to the Fortieth Congress and served from July 25, 1868, to March 3, 1869; presented credentials as a Member-elect to the Forty-first Congress, but was not permitted to qualify; resumed the practice of his profession at Butler, Ga., and died there June 28, 1900; interment in the Methodist Cemetery.

EFNER, Valentine, a Representative from New York; born in Blenheim Hill, near Blenheim, Schoharie County, N. Y., May 5, 1776; completed preparatory studies; engaged in agricultural pursuits; commissioned as major in the War of 1812; member of the State house of representatives in 1829; elected as a Democrat to the Twenty-fourth Congress (March 4, 1835–March 3, 1837); resumed agricultural pursuits; died in Blenheim Hill, N. Y., November 20, 1865; interment in Blenheim Hill Cemetery.

EGBERT, Albert Gallatin, a Representative from Pennsylvania; born near Sandy Lake, Mercer County, Pa., on April 13, 1828; attended the public schools and Austinburg Academy, Ohio; was graduated from the medical department of the Western Reserve University, Cleveland, Ohio, in 1856 and commenced the practice of medicine in Clintonville, Pa.; moved to Cherrytree, Pa., and practiced his profession until 1861, when he retired in order to devote his entire time to the production of oil and to agricultural pursuits; served during the Civil War as a volunteer surgeon; elected as a Democrat to the Forty-fourth Congress (March 4, 1875–March 3, 1877); declined to be a candidate for renomination in 1876; resumed his former business pursuits; died in Franklin, Venango County, Pa., March 28, 1896; interment in Franklin Cemetery.

EGBERT, Joseph, a Representative from New York; born near Bull Head, Staten Island, N. Y., April 10, 1807; attended the common schools; engaged in agricultural pursuits; elected as a Democrat to the Twenty-seventh Congress (March 4, 1841–March 3, 1843); was not a candidate for renomination in 1842; resumed agricultural pursuits; supervisor of Southfield, Richmond County, in 1855 and 1856; county clerk of Richmond County in 1869; died at his home near New Dorp, N. Y., July 7, 1888; interment in the Moravian Cemetery, New Dorp, Staten Island, N. Y.

EGE, George, a Representative from Pennsylvania; born near Womelsdorf, Berks County, Pa., March 9, 1748; attended the common schools; engaged in land and iron interests; member of the State house of representatives in 1783; appointed one of the first associate judges of Berks County under the constitution in 1790, and served from 1791 until 1818, when he resigned; resumed his extensive business interests; elected to the Fourth Congress to fill the vacancy caused by the resignation of Daniel Hiester; reelected to the Fifth Congress and served from December 8, 1796, until October 1797, when he resigned; resumed business interests; built and operated Schuylkill County Forge, near Port Clinton, Pa., in 1804; died at his residence, "Charming Forge," Marion Township, Berks County, Pa., December 14, 1829; interment in Zion's Church Cemetery, Womelsdorf, Pa.

EGGLESTON, Benjamin, a Representative from Ohio; born in Corinth, Saratoga County, N. Y., January 3, 1816; completed preparatory studies; moved with his parents to Hocking County, Ohio, in 1831; moved to Cleveland and worked on a canal boat, later becoming an owner of boats and interested in several companies; settled in Cincinnati in 1845 and engaged in mercantile pursuits; presiding officer of the city council of Cincinnati; delegate to the Republican National Convention at Chicago in 1860; presidential elector on the Republican ticket of Lincoln and Hamlin in 1860; member of the State senate 1862–1865; elected as a Republican to the Thirty-ninth and Fortieth Congresses (March 4, 1865–March 3, 1869); unsuccessful candidate for reelection in 1868 to the Forty-first Congress; again served in the State senate in 1880 and 1881; resumed mercantile pursuits; died in Cincinnati, Ohio, February 9, 1888; interment in Spring Grove Cemetery.

EGGLESTON, Joseph (uncle of William Segar Archer), a Representative from Virginia; born in Middlesex County, Va., November 24, 1754; when four years old was taken to his father's plantation "Egglestetton," near Amelia Court House, Va.; studied under private teachers; was graduated from William and Mary College, Williamsburg, Va., in 1776; captain and major in Lee's Lighthorse Cavalry in the Revolutionary Army; won special distinction in the Battle of Guilford Court House, March 15, 1781, and the capture of Augusta, Ga., June 5, 1781; member of the State house of delegates 1785–1788 and 1791–1799; elected a member of the Virginia Privy Council on November 7, 1787; elected as a Democrat to the Fifth Congress to fill the vacancy caused by the resignation of William B. Giles; reelected to the Sixth Congress and served from December 3, 1798, to March 3, 1801; was not a candidate for renomination in 1800; engaged in

agricultural pursuits; justice of the peace from 1801 until his death in Amelia County, Va., February 13, 1811; interment in the Old Grubhill Church Cemetery, near Amelia Court House, Amelia County, Va.

EICHER, Edward Clayton, a Representative from Iowa; born on a farm near Noble, Washington County, Iowa, December 16, 1878; attended the public schools, Washington (Iowa) Academy, and Morgan Park (Ill.) Academy; was graduated from the University of Chicago, Chicago, Ill., in 1904; studied law; was admitted to the bar in 1906 and commenced practice in Washington, Iowa; served as assistant registrar of the University of Chicago 1907–1909; moved to Burlington, Iowa, in 1909 and served as assistant attorney for a railroad company 1909–1918; returned to Washington, Iowa, in 1918 and continued the practice of law; member of Governor's commission to take Iowa soldiers' vote in 1918; delegate to the Democratic National Convention at Chicago in 1932; elected as a Democrat to the Seventy-third, Seventy-fourth, and Seventy-fifth Congresses and served from March 4, 1933, to December 2, 1938, when he resigned to accept a Presidential appointment; was renominated in 1938 but later withdrew and was not a candidate for reelection; appointed by President Franklin D. Roosevelt on December 2, 1938, as a commissioner of the Securities and Exchange Commission in Washington, D. C., and served until February 2, 1942, being chairman of the Commission at the time; appointed chief justice of the District Court of the United States for the District of Columbia on February 2, 1942, in which capacity he served until his death in Alexandria, Va., on November 29, 1944; interment in Woodlawn Cemetery, Washington, Iowa.

EICKHOFF, Anthony, a Representative from New York; born in Westphalia, Prussia, September 11, 1827; taught school in Prussia; immigrated to the United States in 1847; settled in St. Louis, Mo., where he studied law; became an editor; edited papers in St. Louis, Dubuque, Louisville, and finally in New York in 1852; appointed commissary general of subsistence for the State of New York in 1863; member of the State assembly in 1864; city coroner in 1874; elected as a Democrat to the Forty-fifth Congress (March 4, 1877–March 3, 1879); unsuccessful candidate for reelection in 1878 to the Forty-sixth Congress; Fifth Auditor in the United States Treasury Department from August 1, 1885, to May 17, 1889; appointed fire commissioner in New York City in 1889; reappointed in 1891; at the time of his death he was auditor of the fire department; died in New York City November 5, 1901; interment in Greenwood Cemetery.

EINSTEIN, Edwin, a Representative from New York; born in Cincinnati, Ohio, November 18, 1842; moved with his parents to New York City in 1846; worked as clerk in a store; received a collegiate training in the College of the City of New York, and entered Union College, but did not graduate; engaged in mercantile pursuits; elected as a Republican to the Forty-sixth Congress (March 4, 1879–March 3, 1881); was not a candidate for renomination in 1880; unsuccessful Republican candidate for mayor of New York City in 1892; dock commissioner of New York City in 1895; was prominently identified with a number of investment companies and woolen factories; died in New York City January 24, 1905; interment in Shearith Israel Cemetery, Brooklyn, N. Y.

EKWALL, William Alexander, a Representative from Oregon; born in Ludington, Mason County, Mich., June 14, 1887; moved to Klamathon, Calif., with his parents in 1893, and to Portland, Oreg., in 1906; attended the public schools; was graduated in 1912 from the Oregon Law School at Portland; was admitted to the bar the same year and commenced practice in Portland,

Oreg.; during the First World War served in the United States Army as a private in the Infantry, Central Officers Training School, in 1918; municipal judge of Portland 1922–1927; judge of the circuit court, fourth judicial district (Multnomah County), department 8, from 1927 until elected to Congress; elected as a Republican to the Seventy-fourth Congress (January 3, 1935–January 3, 1937); unsuccessful candidate for reelection in 1936 to the Seventy-fifth Congress; resumed the practice of law at Portland, Oreg., 1937–1942; delegate to the Republican National Convention at Philadelphia in 1940; appointed judge of the United States Customs Court, New York, N. Y., on February 13, 1942, and served until his death in Portland, Oreg., October 16, 1956; interment in Portland Memorial Cemetery.

ELA, Jacob Hart, a Representative from New Hampshire; born in Rochester, N. H., July 18, 1820; attended the village school in Rochester; at fourteen years of age was apprenticed in a woolen manufactory and subsequently learned the printer's trade; member of the State house of representatives in 1857 and 1858; United States marshal from July 1861 to October 1866; elected as a Republican to the Fortieth and Forty-first Congresses (March 4, 1867–March 3, 1871); appointed by President Grant as Fifth Auditor of the Treasury on January 1, 1872, and served until June 2, 1881; on June 3, 1881, was appointed Auditor of the Treasury for the Post Office Department and served in that position until his death in Washington, D. C., on August 21, 1884; interment in North Side Cemetery, Rochester, N. H.

ELAM, Joseph Barton, a Representative from Louisiana; born near Hope, Hempstead County, Ark., June 12, 1821; moved with his father to Natchitoches, La., in 1826; studied law; was admitted to the bar in 1843 and commenced practice in Alexandria, La.; moved to the parish of De Soto in 1851; member and speaker of the State house of representatives 1851–1861; elected a delegate to the State constitutional convention in 1861 and signed the ordinance of secession; elected as a Democrat to the Forty-fifth and Forty-sixth Congresses (March 4, 1877–March 3, 1881); unsuccessful candidate for reelection in 1880 to the Forty-seventh Congress; resumed the practice of law in Mansfield, De Soto Parish, La., where he died July 4, 1885; interment in Mansfield Cemetery.

ELBERT, Samuel, a Delegate from Georgia; born in Prince William Parish, S. C., in 1743; engaged in mercantile business in Savannah, Ga.; captain of a grenadier company in 1774; member of the council on safety in 1775; lieutenant colonel in 1776 and later the same year made a colonel of a battalion of Continental troops; commanded a brigade under General Ashe at the battle of Briar Creek, S. C.; taken prisoner but was exchanged and took part in the battle of Yorktown; promoted to brigadier general in 1783; elected as a Delegate to the Continental Congress in 1784; Governor of Georgia in 1785 and appointed major general of militia; died in Savannah, Ga., November 2, 1788.

ELDER, James Walter, a Representative from Louisiana; born in Grand Prairie, Dallas County, Tex., October 5, 1882; attended the public schools, and Baylor University, Waco, Tex., 1895–1901; studied law; was admitted to the bar in 1903 and commenced practice in Farmerville, Union Parish, La.; mayor of Farmerville, La.; moved to Monroe, Ouachita Parish, and continued the practice of his profession; member of the State senate 1908–1912; elected as a Democrat to the Sixty-third Congress (March 4, 1913–March 3, 1915); unsuccessful candidate for renomination in 1914; reengaged in the practice of law in Farmerville, La., until January 1, 1925; moved to Ruston, La., and continued the practice of law until his death on December 16, 1941; interment in Greenwood Cemetery.

ELDREDGE, Charles Augustus, a Representative from Wisconsin; born in Bridport, Vt., February 27, 1820; moved with his parents to Canton, St. Lawrence County, N. Y., in 1825; attended the common schools; studied law; was admitted to the bar in 1846 and commenced practice in Canton, N. Y.; moved to Fond du Lac, Wis., in 1848 and continued the practice of his profession; member of the State senate 1854–1856; elected as a Democrat to the Thirty-eighth and to the five succeeding Congresses (March 4, 1863–March 3, 1875); unsuccessful candidate for renomination in 1874; resumed the practice of law; died in Fond du Lac, Wis., October 26, 1896; interment in Rienzi Cemetery.

ELDREDGE, Nathaniel Buel, a Representative from Michigan; born in Auburn, N. Y., March 28, 1813; attended the common schools; appointed as a cadet to the United States Military Academy at West Point in 1829, but was financially unable to accept; attended Fairfield Medical College; engaged in the practice of medicine in Commerce, Oakland County, Mich.; clerk of the Michigan Senate in 1845; member of the State house of representatives in 1848; judge of probate 1852–1856; studied law; was admitted to the bar and commenced practice in 1854; held several minor offices; during the Civil War was enrolled as captain of Company G, Seventh Regiment, Michigan Volunteers, June 19, 1861; promoted to major August 7, 1861, and to lieutenant colonel April 1, 1862; was honorably discharged January 7, 1863; elected sheriff of Lenawee County in 1874; elected as a Democrat to the Forty-eighth and Forty-ninth Congresses (March 4, 1883–March 3, 1887); died in Adrian, Mich., on November 27, 1893; interment in Oakwood Cemetery.

ELIOT, Samuel Atkins (great-grandfather of Thomas Hopkinson Eliot), a Representative from Massachusetts; born in Boston, Mass., March 5, 1798; attended the Boston Latin School; was graduated from Harvard University in 1817 and from the divinity school in 1820; member of the State house of representatives 1834–1837; mayor of Boston 1837–1839; served in the State senate in 1843–1844; elected as a Whig to the Thirty-first Congress to fill the vacancy caused by the resignation of Robert C. Winthrop and served from August 22, 1850, to March 3, 1851; declined to be a candidate for renomination in 1850; treasurer of Harvard University 1842–1853; died in Cambridge, Mass., January 29, 1862; interment in Mount Auburn Cemetery

ELIOT, Thomas Dawes, a Representative from Massachusetts; born in Boston, on Mass., March 20, 1808; attended the public schools of Washington, D. C., and was graduated from Columbian College (now George Washington University), in that city, in 1825; was admitted to the bar in 1831 and commenced practice in New Bedford, Mass.; member of the State house of representatives in 1839; served in the State senate in 1846; elected as a Whig to the Thirty-third Congress to fill the vacancy caused by the resignation of Zeno Scudder and served from April 17, 1854, to March 3, 1855; declined to be a candidate for renomination in 1854; delegate to the Free-Soil Convention in Worcester, Mass., in 1855; declined to be a candidate for nomination by the Republican Party for attorney general of Massachusetts in 1857; elected as a Republican to the Thirty-sixth and to the four succeeding Congresses (March 4, 1859–March 3, 1869); declined to be a candidate for renomination in 1868; resumed the practice of law in New Bedford, Mass., where he died on June 14, 1870; interment in Oak Grove Cemetery.

ELIOT, Thomas Hopkinson (great-grandson of Samuel Atkins Eliot), a Representative from Massachusetts; born in Cambridge, Middlesex County, Mass., June 14, 1907; attended

Browne and Nichols School; was graduated from Harvard University, Cambridge, Mass., in 1928; student at Emmanuel College, Cambridge, England, in 1928 and 1929; was graduated from the law school of Harvard University in 1932; newspaper reporter in Boston, Mass., in 1923 and 1924; was admitted to the bar in 1933 and commenced practice in Buffalo, N. Y.; served as assistant solicitor in the United States Department of Labor 1933–1935; general counsel for the Social Security Board 1935–1938; lecturer on government at Harvard University in 1937 and 1938; regional director of the Wage and Hour Division in the Department of Labor in 1939 and 1940; unsuccessful candidate for election in 1938 to the Seventy-sixth Congress; elected as a Democrat to the Seventy-seventh Congress (January 3, 1941–January 3, 1943); unsuccessful candidate for renomination in 1942 and for nomination in 1944 to the Seventy-ninth Congress; director of the British Division, Office of War Information, London, England, and special assistant to the United States Ambassador, January to November 1943; chairman of the appeals committee, National War Labor Board, November 1943 to March 1944; served with the Office of Strategic Services in 1944; served as chief counsel, Division of Power, Department of the Interior, from November 1944 to November 1945; engaged in the practice of law in Boston, Mass., 1945–1950; executive director, Massachusetts Reorganization Commission, 1950–1952; professor of political science, Washington University, St. Louis, Mo., since 1952, and of constitutional law since 1958, and dean of the College of Liberal Arts since 1961; consultant, Missouri Reorganization Commission, in 1953 and 1954; codirector, metropolitan St. Louis survey in 1956 and 1957; is a resident of University City, Mo.

ELIZALDE, Joaquin Miguel, a Resident Commissioner from the Commonwealth of the Philippines; born in Manila, Philippine Islands, August 2, 1896; attended St. Joseph's College at London, England, and Dr. Schmidt's Institute at St. Gallen, Switzerland; industrialist and financier; economic adviser to President Manuel L. Quezon in 1937 and 1938; member of the National Economic Council 1937–1941 and 1952 and 1953, and of the Joint Preparatory Committee on Philippine Affairs in 1936 and 1937; member of the Council of State 1936–1941 and 1952 and 1953; served as major, Cavalry reserve, Philippine Army; appointed as a Resident Commissioner to the United States on September 29, 1938, to fill the vacancy caused by the resignation of Quintin Paredes and served until his resignation on August 9, 1944; member of the war cabinet of President Manuel L. Quezon 1941–1944; representative of the Republic of the Philippines to international organization conferences; member of the board of governors of the International Monetary Fund and of the International Bank for Reconstruction and Development 1946–1950; appointed Ambassador Extraordinary and Plenipotentiary of the Republic of the Philippines to the United States on July 6, 1946, in which capacity he served until January 1952; Minister of Foreign Affairs of the Republic of the Philippines 1952 and 1953; economic adviser to the United Nations 1956–; resides in Washington, D. C.

ELKINS, Davis (son of Stephen Benton Elkins and grandson of Henry Gassaway Davis), a Senator from West Virginia; born in Washington, D. C., January 24, 1876; attended the Lawrenceville (N. J.) School, Phillips Academy, Andover, Mass., and Harvard University; enlisted May 16, 1898, during the war with Spain, as a private in Company E, First West Virginia Volunteer Infantry; promoted to first lieutenant and battalion adjutant May 23, 1898, and to captain and assistant adjutant general June 16, 1898; served on the staff of Brigadier General Schawan in Cuba and Puerto Rico until November 15, 1898; former president of Morgantown & Kingwood Railroad Co., Elkins Coal & Coke Co., Union Utility Co., of Morgantown, W. Va., and Kingwood National Bank, Kingwood, W. Va.; appointed as a Republican to the United States Senate to fill the vacancy caused by the death of his father, Stephen B. Elkins, and served from January 9 to January 31, 1911, when a successor was elected; during the First World War was commissioned major in the Officers' Reserve Corps on December 14, 1917, and subsequently served as adjutant of the Thirteenth Infantry Brigade, Seventh Division, in France; honorably discharged December 27, 1918; elected as a Republican to the United States Senate and served from March 4, 1919, to March 3, 1925; was not a candidate for renomination in 1924; owner of the Washington & Old Dominion Railroad Company, 1936–1956; died in Richmond, Va., on January 5, 1959; interment in Maplewood Cemetery, Elkins, W. Va.

ELKINS, Stephen Benton (father of Davis Elkins), a Delegate from the Territory of New Mexico and a Senator from West Virginia; born in Perry County, Ohio, September 26, 1841; moved with his parents to Westport, Mo.; attended the public schools, and was graduated from the law department of the University of Missouri at Columbia in 1860; during the Civil War enlisted in the Union Army as a captain in the Kansas Militia; moved to the Territory of New Mexico in 1864; was admitted to the bar in 1864 and commenced practice in Messila, N. Mex.; member of the Territorial house of representatives in 1864 and 1865; district attorney for the Territory of New Mexico in 1866 and 1867; appointed attorney general of the Territory January 14, 1867, and served until March 1 of that year; United States district attorney for the Territory 1867–1870; elected as a Republican a Delegate to the Forty-third and Forty-fourth Congresses (March 4, 1873–March 3, 1877); was not a candidate for renomination in 1876; moved to New York City and resumed the practice of law; appointed Secretary of War December 17, 1891, and served until the close of the administration of President Harrison; moved to Elkins, W. Va., and resumed the practice of law; elected to the United States Senate in February 1895; reelected in 1901 and 1907 and served from March 4, 1895, until his death in Washington, D. C., January 4, 1911; interment in Maplewood Cemetery, Elkins, W. Va.

ELLENBOGEN, Henry, a Representative from Pennsylvania; born in Vienna, Austria, April 3, 1900; attended the Vienna public schools and the University of Vienna Law School, Austria; immigrated to the United States and settled in Pittsburgh, Pa.; was graduated from Duquesne University, Pittsburgh, Pa., in 1921 and from its law department in 1924; was admitted to the bar in 1926 and commenced practice in Pittsburgh, Pa.; appointed as arbitrator and public panel chairman by the National War Labor Board and the Third Regional War Labor Board in cases involving labor disputes; writer of articles on economic, social, and legal problems; elected as a Democrat to the Seventy-third, Seventy-fourth, and Seventy-fifth Congresses and served from March 4, 1933, to January 3, 1938, when he resigned, having been elected judge of the common pleas court of Allegheny County, Pa.; reelected in November 1947 and again in 1957 for a ten-year term, in which capacity he is now serving; is a resident of Pittsburgh, Pa.

ELLENDER, Allen Joseph, a Senator from Louisiana; born in Montegut, Terrebonne Parish, La., September 24, 1891; attended the public schools; was graduated from St. Aloysius College, New Orleans, La., in 1909 and from the law department of Tulane University, New Orleans, La., in 1913; was admitted to the bar in 1913 and commenced practice in Houma, La.; city attorney of Houma 1913–1915; district attorney of Terrebonne Parish in 1915 and 1916; during the First World War served as a sergeant in the Artillery Corps, United States Army, in 1917 and 1918; delegate to the constitutional convention of Louisiana in 1921; member of the Louisiana House of Representatives 1924–1936, serving as floor leader 1928–1932 and as speaker of the house 1932–1936; elected as a Democrat to the United States Senate in 1936, 1942, 1948, and again in 1954, and served from January 3, 1937, to January 3, 1961. *Reelected in 1960 for the term ending January 3, 1967.*

ELLERBE, James Edwin, a Representative from South Carolina; born in Sellers, Marion County, S. C., January 12, 1867; attended Pine Hill Academy and the University of South Carolina at Columbia; was graduated from Wofford College, Spartanburg, S. C., in 1887; engaged in agricultural pursuits; member of the State house of representatives 1894–1896; delegate to the State constitutional convention in 1895; elected as a Democrat to the Fifty-ninth and to the three succeeding Congresses (March 4, 1905–March 3, 1913); unsuccessful candidate for renomination in 1912; resumed his agricultural pursuits; died in Asheville, N. C., October 24, 1917; interment in the family burial ground near Sellers, S. C.

ELLERY, Christopher (nephew of William Ellery), a Senator from Rhode Island; born in Newport, R. I., November 1, 1768; was graduated from Yale College in 1787; studied law; was admitted to the bar and commenced practice in Newport; clerk of the superior court of Newport County 1794–1798; elected as a Democrat to the United States Senate to fill the vacancy caused by the resignation of Ray Greene and served from May 6, 1801, to March 3, 1805; unsuccessful candidate for reelection in 1804; appointed by President Jefferson as United States commissioner of loans at Providence, R. I., in 1806; appointed collector of customs at Newport and served from May 1, 1820, to July 7, 1834; died in Middletown, R. I., on December 2, 1840; interment in Island Cemetery, Newport, R. I.

ELLERY, William (uncle of Christopher Ellery), a Delegate from Rhode Island; born in Newport, R. I., on December 22, 1727; taught by private teachers; was graduated from Harvard College in 1747; naval officer of Rhode Island in 1754; clerk of the court of common pleas of Newport County in 1768 and 1769; studied law; was admitted to the bar in 1770 and commenced practice in Newport, R. I.; elected a Member of the Continental Congress to fill the vacancy caused by the death of Samuel Ward and served from May 14, 1776, to 1781; one of the signers of the Declaration of Independence; chosen to the newly constituted board of admiralty in 1779, with full oversight of the marine affairs of the Nation; again a Member of the Continental Congress 1783–1785; appointed chief justice of Rhode Island in 1785; appointed by the Continental Congress commissioner of the Continental Loan Office in 1786; collector of the port of Newport from 1790 until his death in Newport, R. I., February 15, 1820; interment in the Old Cemetery.

ELLETT, Henry Thomas, a Representative from Mississippi; born in Salem, N. J., March 8, 1812; attended the Latin School in Salem and Princeton College; studied law; was admitted to the bar in 1833 and commenced practice in Bridgeton, Cumberland County, N. J.; moved to Port Gibson, Claiborne County, Miss., in 1837 and continued the practice of law; elected as a Democrat to the Twenty-ninth Congress to fill the vacancy caused by the resignation of Jefferson Davis and served from January 26 to March 3, 1847; declined to be a candidate for reelection in 1846; resumed the practice of law; member of the State senate 1853–1865; presidential elector on the Democratic ticket of Buchanan and Breckinridge in 1856; code commissioner in 1857; member of the State secession convention in

1861, and member of the committee that framed and reported the ordinance of secession of Mississippi; appointed Postmaster General of the Confederacy in February 1861 but declined; elected judge of the State supreme court on October 2, 1865, and served until January 1868, when he resigned; moved to Memphis, Tenn., in 1868 and resumed the practice of law; elected chancellor of the twelfth division of Tennessee in 1886; died while delivering an address of welcome to President Grover Cleveland in Memphis, Tenn., October 15, 1887; interment in Elmwood Cemetery.

ELLETT, Tazewell, a Representative from Virginia; born in Richmond, Va., January 1, 1856; attended private schools in Richmond; cadet in the Virginia Military Institute at Lexington and was graduated from that institution in 1876; studied law; was graduated from the University of Virginia at Charlottsville in 1878 and immediately commenced practice in Richmond; member of the board of visitors of the Virginia Military Institute; presidential elector on the Democratic ticket of Cleveland and Thurman in 1888; elected as a Democrat to the Fifty-fourth Congress (March 4, 1895–March 3, 1897); was an unsuccessful candidate for reelection in 1896 to the Fifty-fifth Congress; resumed the practice of law in Richmond, Va., and New York City, N. Y.; died in Summerville, Dorchester County, S. C., May 19, 1914; interment in Hollywood Cemetery, Richmond, Va.

ELLICOTT, Benjamin, a Representative from New York; born at Ellicotts Mills, near Baltimore, Md., April 17, 1765; accompanied his brothers in 1789 to upper Canada on the survey to determine the western boundary of the State of New York; employed as a surveyor and draftsman for the Holland Land Co. in New York and Pennsylvania; one of the first judges of the court of common pleas of Genesee County, N. Y., in 1803, with residence in Batavia; was also an extensive landowner; elected as a Democrat to the Fifteenth Congress (March 4, 1817–March 3, 1819); unsuccessful candidate for election in 1820 to the Seventeenth Congress; retired from active life, and in 1826 moved to Williamsville, Erie County, N. Y., where he died December 10, 1827; interment in the graveyard at Williamsville; reinterment in Batavia Cemetery, Batavia, N. Y., in 1849.

ELLIOTT, Alfred James, a Representative from California; born in Guinda, Yolo County, Calif., June 1, 1895; moved with his parents to Winters, Calif., in 1901 and to Tulare, Calif., in 1910; attended the public schools; engaged in farming and livestock raising; secretary-manager of the Tulare County Fair since 1929; owner and publisher of a newspaper; chairman of the board of supervisors of Tulare County 1933–1937; served on the California State Safety Council in 1936; member of the California Supervisor Association of the State welfare board in 1935 and 1936; elected as a Democrat to the Seventy-fifth Congress to fill the vacancy caused by the death of Henry E. Stubbs; reelected to the Seventy-sixth and to the four succeeding Congresses and served from May 4, 1937, to January 3, 1949; was not a candidate for renomination in 1948 to the Eighty-first Congress; president of Tulare Daily News; farmer and livestock breeder; is a resident of Tulare, Calif.

ELLIOTT, Carl Atwood, a Representative from Alabama; born in Vina, Franklin County, Ala., December 20, 1913; attended the public schools of Franklin County and Vina High School; was graduated from the University of Alabama at Tuscaloosa in 1933 and from its law school in 1936; was admitted to the bar the same year and commenced the practice of law in Russellville, Ala.; in December 1936 moved to Jasper, Ala., and continued the practice of law; served as judge of Recorders Court, Jasper, Ala., in 1942 and 1946; city attorney at various times for Dora, Parrish, Cordova, Carbon Hill, and Oakman, Ala.; during World War II served with the Seventy-ninth Division, Three Hundred and Thirteenth Infantry, United States Army, 1942–1944; member of Alabama State Democratic Executive Committee 1942–1950; compiler of Annals of Northwest Alabama Volume I in 1958 and volume II in 1959; elected as a Democrat to the Eighty-first and to the five succeeding Congresses (January 3, 1949–January 3, 1961). *Reelected to the Eighty-seventh Congress.*

ELLIOTT, Douglas Hemphill, a Representative from Pennsylvania; born in Philadelphia, Pa., June 3, 1921; attended the schools of Philadelphia, Pa., and graduated from Haverford School in 1938; attended the University of Virginia at Charlottesville 1938–1940; during World War II served in the United States Navy from 1941 until discharged as a chief petty officer in 1945 with service in the Southwest Pacific; sales representative, Phoenix Mutual Life Insurance Co. and Guardian Life Insurance Co., 1945–1948; manager of public relations, Lumberman's Mutual Casualty Co. 1948–1952; director of public relations of the Franklin Institute, Philadelphia, Pa., 1950–1952; vice president of Wilson College, Chambersburg, Pa., 1952–1960; elected in November 1956 to the State senate and served until elected to Congress; elected as a Republican to the Eighty-sixth Congress to fill the vacancy caused by the death of Richard M. Simpson and served from April 26, 1960, until his death in Horse Valley, Franklin County, Pa., June 19, 1960; interment in Falling Spring Presbyterian Church Cemetery, Chambersburg, Pa.

ELLIOTT, James, a Representative from Vermont; born in Gloucester, Mass., August 18, 1775; during his early years worked on a farm and clerked in a store; educated by his mother, by his employer, and by reading and travel; moved to Guilford, Vt., in 1790; served as a sergeant in the Indian war of 1793 in Ohio; published several works of poems and essays in 1798; clerk of the State house of representatives 1801–1803; studied law; was admitted to the bar in 1803 and commenced practice in Brattleboro, Vt.; elected as a Federalist to the Eighth, Ninth, and Tenth Congresses (March 4, 1803–March 3, 1809); published a newspaper in Philadelphia, Pa., on his retirement from Congress; served in the War of 1812 for a short time as captain; resumed the practice of law in Brattleboro, Vt.; clerk of the Windham County Court 1817–1835; member of the State house of representatives in 1818 and 1819; moved to Newfane, Vt.; register of the probate court 1822–1834; again served in the State house of representatives in 1837 and 1838; State's attorney of Windham County 1837–1839; died in Newfane, Vt., November 10, 1839; interment in Prospect Hill Cemetery, Brattleboro, Vt.

ELLIOTT, James Thomas, a Representative from Arkansas; born in Columbus, Monroe County, Ga., April 22, 1823; attended the common schools; studied law; was admitted to the bar in 1854 and commenced practice in Camden, Ark.; chosen president of the Mississippi, Ouachita & Red River Railroad in 1858; circuit judge of the sixth judicial district of Arkansas from October 2, 1865, to September 15, 1866; established and edited the South Arkansas Journal in 1867; elected as a Republican to the Fortieth Congress to fill the vacancy caused by the death of James Hinds and served from January 13, 1869, to March 3, 1869; unsuccessful candidate for reelection in 1868 to the Forty-first Congress; elected to the State senate in 1870; appointed judge of the ninth judicial district in 1872 and served until the adoption of the State constitution in 1874; died in Camden, Ouachita County Ark., on July 28, 1875; interment in Oakland Cemetery.

ELLIOTT, John, a Senator from Georgia; born in St. Johns Parish, now Liberty County, Ga., October 24, 1773; completed preparatory studies; was graduated from Yale College in 1794; studied law; was admitted to the bar and commenced practice in Sunbury, Liberty County, Ga., in 1797; held several important local offices; elected to the United States Senate and served from March 4, 1819, to March 3, 1825; died in Sunbury, Ga., August 9, 1827; interment in Old Midway Cemetery in Liberty County.

ELLIOTT, John Milton, a Representative from Kentucky; born on the banks of Clinch River in Scott County, Va., May 20, 1820; moved to Morgan County (now Elliott County), Ky., and attended the common schools; was graduated from Emory and Henry College, Emory, Va., in 1841; studied law; was admitted to the bar in 1843 and commenced practice in Prestonsburg, Floyd County, Ky.; member of the State house of representatives in 1847; elected as a Democrat to the Thirty-third, Thirty-fourth, and Thirty-fifth Congresses (March 4, 1853–March 3, 1859); was not a candidate for renomination in 1858; resumed the practice of law; again a member of the State house of representatives in 1861; elected a Representative from Kentucky to the First and Second Confederate Congresses; circuit judge 1868–1874; judge of the court of appeals 1876–1879; assassinated at Frankfort, Ky., March 26, 1879; interment in the State Cemetery at Frankfort.

ELLIOTT, Mortimer Fitzland, a Representative from Pennsylvania; born in Cherry Flats, near Wellsboro, Tioga County, Pa., September 24, 1839; attended the common schools, Wellsboro Academy, and Alfred University, Allegheny County, Pa.; studied law; was admitted to the bar in 1860 and commenced practice in Wellsboro; member of the convention to revise the constitution of Pennsylvania in 1873; elected as a Democrat to the Forty-eighth Congress (March 4, 1883–March 3, 1885); unsuccessful candidate for reelection in 1884 to the Forty-ninth Congress; resumed the practice of law; general solicitor for the Standard Oil Co. in New York City; died in Mansfield, Tioga County, Pa., August 5, 1920; interment in Wellsboro Cemetery, Wellsboro, Pa.

ELLIOTT, Richard Nash, a Representative from Indiana; born near Connersville, Fayette County, Ind., April 25, 1873; attended the common schools; taught school three years; studied law; was admitted to the bar in 1896 and commenced practice in Connersville, Ind.; county attorney of Fayette County 1897–1906; member of the State house of representatives 1905–1909; city attorney of Connersville 1905–1909; delegate to the Republican National Convention at Chicago in 1916; chairman of the Republican State convention in 1930; elected as a Republican to the Sixty-fifth Congress to fill the vacancy caused by the death of Daniel W. Comstock; reelected to the Sixty-sixth and to the five succeeding Congresses and served from June 26, 1917, to March 3, 1931; unsuccessful candidate for reelection in 1930 to the Seventy-second Congress; served as assistant comptroller general of the United States from March 6, 1931, to April 30, 1943, when he retired; resided in Washington, D. C., until his death on March 21, 1948; interment in Dale Cemetery, Connersville, Ind.

ELLIOTT, Robert Brown, a Representative from South Carolina; born in Boston, Mass., August 11, 1842; was of the Negro race; attended High Hollow Academy, London, England, in 1853, and was graduated from Eton College, England, in 1859; studied law; was admitted to the bar and practiced in Columbia, S. C.; member of the State constitutional convention in 1868; member of the State house of representatives from

July 6, 1868, to October 23, 1870; assistant adjutant general of South Carolina 1869–1871; elected as a Republican to the Forty-second and Forty-third Congresses and served from March 4, 1871, until his resignation, effective November 1, 1874; again a member of the State house of representatives 1874–1876, and served as speaker; unsuccessful candidate for election as attorney general of South Carolina in 1876; moved to New Orleans, La., in 1881 and practiced law until his death there on August 9, 1884; interment in St. Louis Cemetery No. 2.

ELLIOTT, William, a Representative from South Carolina; born in Beaufort, Beaufort County, S. C., September 3, 1838; attended Beaufort College and Harvard University; studied law at the University of Virginia at Charlottesville, and was admitted to the bar in Charleston, S. C., in 1861; upon the outbreak of the Civil War entered the Confederate Army as a lieutenant and served throughout the war, attaining the rank of lieutenant colonel; at the close of the war commenced the practice of law in Beaufort, S. C.; member of the State house of representatives 1866 and 1867; intendant of Beaufort in 1866; delegate to the Democratic National Convention at St. Louis in 1876; presidential elector on the Democratic ticket of Hancock and English in 1880; unsuccessful Democratic candidate for election in 1884 to the Forty-ninth Congress; elected as a Democrat to the Fiftieth Congress (March 4, 1887–March 3, 1889); presented credentials as a Member-elect to the Fifty-first Congress and served from March 4, 1889, until September 23, 1890, when he was succeeded by Thomas E. Miller, who contested the election; elected to the Fifty-second Congress (March 4, 1891–March 3, 1893); was not a candidate for renomination in 1892; presented credentials as a Member-elect to the Fifty-fourth Congress and served from March 4, 1895, until June 4, 1896, when he was succeeded by George W. Murray, who contested the election; elected to the Fifty-fifth, Fifty-sixth, and Fifty-seventh Congresses (March 4, 1897–March 3, 1903); was not a candidate for renomination in 1902, having become a candidate for election to the United States Senate, in which he was unsuccessful; appointed by President Theodore Roosevelt in 1906 as commissioner of the United States to mark the graves of Confederate dead in the North and served in this capacity until his death in Beaufort, S. C., on December 7, 1907; interment in St. Helena Churchyard.

ELLIS, Caleb, a Representative from New Hampshire; born in Walpole, Mass., April 16, 1767; was graduated from Harvard University in 1793; studied law and was admitted to the bar; moved to Newport, N. H., and then to Claremont; elected to the Ninth Congress (March 4, 1805–March 3, 1807); member of the New Hampshire House of Representatives in 1803; member of the Governor's council 1809 and 1810; served in the State senate in 1811; presidential elector on the Clinton and Ingersoll ticket in 1812; appointed judge of the superior court of New Hampshire in 1813, which office he held until his death in Claremont, N. H., May 6, 1816; interment in Broad Street Cemetery.

ELLIS, Chesselden, a Representative from New York; born in New Windsor, Vt., in 1808; completed preparatory studies and was graduated from Union College, Schenectady, N. Y., in 1823; studied law; was admitted to the bar in 1829 and commenced practice in Waterford, N. Y.; elected prosecuting attorney of Saratoga County, N. Y., and served from April 25, 1837, until September 11, 1843, when he resigned to take his seat in Congress; elected as a Democrat to the Twenty-eighth Congress (March 4, 1843–March 3, 1845); unsuccessful candidate for reelection in 1844 to the Twenty-ninth Congress; resumed the practice of law in Waterford; moved to New York City in 1845 and continued the practice of his profession until his death there on May 10, 1854; interment in Albany Cemetery, Albany, N. Y.

ELLIS, Clyde Taylor, a Representative from Arkansas; born on a farm near Garfield, Benton County, Ark., December 21, 1908; attended the public schools, University High School, Fayetteville, Ark., the University of Arkansas College of Arts and Sciences and School of Law at Fayetteville, and George Washington University Law School at Washington, D. C.; teacher in the rural schools at Garfield, Ark., in 1927 and 1928; superintendent of schools at Garfield, Ark., 1929–1934; was admitted to the bar in 1933 and commenced practice at Bentonville, Ark.; served in the State house of representatives 1932–1934; member of the State senate 1934–1938; delegate to the Democratic National Convention at Chicago in 1940; elected as a Democrat to the Seventy-sixth and Seventy-seventh Congresses (January 3, 1939–January 3, 1943); was not a candidate for renomination in 1942 but was an unsuccessful candidate for the Democratic nomination for United States Senator; during World War II served as combat officer in the United States Navy 1943–1945; executive manager of the National Rural Electric Cooperative Association, Washington, D. C., since January 3, 1943; is a legal resident of Bentonville, Ark.

ELLIS, Edgar Clarence, a Representative from Missouri; born in Vermontville, Eaton County, Mich., October 2, 1854; attended Olivet (Mich.) College, and was graduated from Carleton College, Northfield, Minn., in 1881; intructor in Latin at Carleton College in 1881 and 1882; superintendent of the public schools at Fergus Falls, Minn., 1882–1885; in the meantime studied law; was admitted to the bar and commenced practice in Beloit, Kans., in 1885; moved to Kansas City, Mo., in 1888 and continued the practice of his profession; elected as a Republican to the Fifty-ninth and Sixtieth Congresses (March 4, 1905–March 3, 1909); unsuccessful candidate for reelection in 1908 to the Sixty-first Congress; resumed the practice of law in Kansas City, Mo.; appointed a member of the Missouri Waterway Commission and served in 1911 and 1912; elected to the Sixty-seventh Congress (March 4, 1921–March 3, 1923); unsuccessful candidate for reelection in 1922 to the Sixty-eighth Congress; elected to the Sixty-ninth Congress (March 4, 1925–March 3, 1927); unsuccessful candidate for reelection in 1926 to the Seventieth Congress; elected to the Seventy-first Congress (March 4, 1929–March 3, 1931); unsuccessful candidate for reelection in 1930 to the Seventy-second Congress; retired from law practice and political life; died in St. Petersburg, Fla., March 15, 1947; remains were cremated and the ashes interred in Kansas City, Mo.

ELLIS, Ezekiel John, a Representative from Louisiana; born in Covington, St. Tammany Parish, La., October 15, 1840; attended private schools in Covington and Clinton, La., and Centenary College, Jackson, La., 1855–1858; was graduated from the law department of the Louisiana State University at Pineville (now at Baton Rouge), La., in 1861; during the Civil War joined the Confederate Army and was commissioned a first lieutenant; was promoted to captain in the Sixteenth Regiment, Louisiana Infantry, and served two years, when he was captured and made prisoner at the Battle of Missionary Ridge, Tennessee; held as a prisoner of war on Johnsons Island in Lake Erie until the end of the war; was admitted to the bar of Louisiana in 1866 and commenced practice in Covington, La.; member of the State senate 1866–1870; elected as a Democrat to the Forty-fourth and to the four succeeding Congresses (March 4, 1875–March 3, 1885); declined to be a candidate for renomination in 1884; resumed the practice of his profession in Washington, D. C., where he died April 25, 1889; interment in the Ellis family cemetery at "Ingleside," near Amite, Tangipahoa Parish, La.

ELLIS, Hubert Summers, a Representative from West Virginia; born in Hurricane, Putnam County, W. Va., July 6, 1887; attended the public schools and Marshall College, Huntington, W. Va.; engaged in banking and as a salesman 1910–1917 and in the general insurance business in 1920; during the First World War served overseas as a first lieutenant in the One Hundred and Fiftieth Field Artillery, Forty-second Division, 1917–1919; elected as a Republican to the Seventy-eighth, Seventy-ninth, and Eightieth Congresses (January 3, 1943–January 3, 1949); unsuccessful candidate for reelection in 1948 to the Eighty-first Congress, and for election in 1950 to the Eighty-second Congress; appointed West Virginia director for the Federal Housing Administration February 2, 1954, and resigned February 10, 1958; died in Huntington, W. Va., December 3, 1959; interment in Woodmere Cemetery.

ELLIS, Powhatan, a Senator from Mississippi; born at "Red Hill," Amherst County, Va., January 17, 1790; was graduated from Washington Academy (now Washington and Lee University), Lexington, Va., in 1809; attended Dickinson College, Carlisle, Pa., in 1809 and 1810; studied law at William and Mary College, Williamsburg, Va., in 1813 and 1814; was admitted to the bar and commenced practice in Lynchburg, Va.; moved to Natchez, Miss., in April 1816 and continued the practice of law; judge of the State supreme court 1823–1825; appointed as a Democrat to the United States Senate to fill the vacancy caused by the resignation of David Holmes and served from September 28, 1825, to January 28, 1826, when a successor was elected and qualified; unsuccessful candidate for election to fill this vacancy; elected to the United States Senate for the term commencing March 4, 1827, and served until July 16, 1832, when he resigned to accept a judicial position; judge of he United States court for the district of Mississippi 1832–1836; appointed by President Jackson Chargé d'Affaires of the United States to Mexico January 5, 1836, and closed the Legation December 28, 1836; United States Minister Plenipotentiary to Mexico from February 15, 1839, to April 21, 1842; moved to Richmond, Va., where he died on March 18, 1863; interment in Shockoe Cemetery.

ELLIS, William Cox, a Representative from Pennsylvania; born in Fort Muncy, Pa., May 5, 1787; attended the public schools, and was graduated from the Friends' School near Pennsdale, Lycoming County, Pa., in 1803; deputy surveyor general 1803–1810; cashier of the Union and Northumberland County Bank 1810–1818; studied law; was admitted to the bar in 1817 and commenced practice in Muncy, Pa.; elected as a Federalist in 1820 to the Seventeenth Congress, but resigned before the Congress assembled; unsuccessful candidate for reelection to fill the vacancy caused by his own resignation; elected to the Eighteenth Congress (March 4, 1823–March 3, 1825); member of the State house of representatives in 1825 and 1826; became affiliated with the Republican Party in 1856; resumed the practice of law in Muncy, Pa., and died there December 13, 1871; interment in Muncy Cemetery.

ELLIS, William Russell, a Representative from Oregon; born near Waveland, Montgomery County, Ind., April 23, 1850; moved with his parents to Guthrie County, Iowa, in 1855; attended the district schools and the Iowa State Agricultural College at Ames; was graduated from the law department of the University of Iowa at Iowa City in 1874; was admitted to the bar and commenced practice in Panora, Iowa; mayor of Panora for one term; moved to Hamburg, Iowa, where he continued the practice of law, and also engaged in newspaper work; served two years as city attorney; mayor of Hamburg in 1880 and 1881; moved to Heppner, Oreg., in 1884; superintendent of schools of Morrow County in 1885 and 1886; district attorney of the seventh judicial district of Oregon 1886–1892; elected as a Republican to the Fifty-third, Fifty-fourth, and Fifty-fifth Congresses (March 4, 1893–March 3, 1899); unsuccessful candidate for renomination in 1898; circuit judge of the sixth judicial district of Oregon from July 10, 1900, to July 1, 1906; moved to Pendleton in 1901 and practiced law; elected to the Sixtieth and Sixty-first Congresses (March 4, 1907–March 3, 1911); unsuccessful candidate for renomination in 1910; resumed the practice of law in Pendleton, Oreg.; moved to Portland, Oreg., in July 1914, where he died January 18, 1915; interment in a mausoleum in Portland Crematorium.

ELLIS, William Thomas, a Representative from Kentucky; born near Knottsville, Daviess County, Ky., on July 24, 1845; attended the common schools; enlisted in 1861, at the age of sixteen, in the First Kentucky Confederate Cavalry, which became a part of the celebrated Orphan Brigade, and served with his regiment continuously until April 21, 1865; attended Pleasant Valley Seminary, Daviess County; principal of Mount Etna Academy, Ohio County, in 1867 and 1868; studied law and was admitted to the bar in 1868; was graduated from the Harvard Law School, Cambridge, Mass., in 1870 and commenced practice in Owensboro, Ky., the same year; elected county attorney in 1870 and 1874; presidential elector on the Democratic ticket of Tilden and Hendricks in 1876; unsuccessful candidate for election in 1886 to the Fiftieth Congress; elected as a Democrat to the Fifty-first, Fifty-second, and Fifty-third Congresses (March 4, 1889–March 3, 1895); declined to be a candidate for renomination in 1894; delegate to the Democratic National Convention at Chicago in 1896 which nominated Bryan and Sewall; resumed the practice of law; also engaged in literary pursuits; died in Owensboro, Ky., January 8, 1925; interment in Elmwood Cemetery.

ELLISON, Andrew, a Representative from Ohio; born in West Union, Adams County, Ohio, in 1812; attended the public schools; studied law; was admitted to the bar in Adams County, Ohio, in August 1835 and commenced practice in Georgetown, Brown County, Ohio, the same year; elected prosecuting attorney of Brown County and served from 1840 to 1843; member of the State house of representatives in 1846; elected as a Democrat to the Thirty-third Congress (March 4, 1853–March 3, 1855); unsuccessful candidate for reelection in 1854 to the Thirty-fourth Congress; resumed the practice of law; died about 1860.

ELLISON, Daniel, a Representative from Maryland; born in Russia, February 14, 1886; as an infant, was brought to the United States by his parents; attended the public schools of Baltimore, Md.; was graduated from Johns Hopkins University, Baltimore, Md., in 1907 and from the law department of the University of Maryland at Baltimore in 1909; was admitted to the bar the same year and commenced practice in Baltimore, Md.; served as a member of the Baltimore City Council 1923–1942; elected as a Republican to the Seventy-eighth Congress (January 3, 1943–January 3, 1945); unsuccessful candidate for reelection in 1944 to the Seventy-ninth Congress; resumed the practice of law in Baltimore, Md.; member of the State senate 1946–1950; died in Baltimore, Md., August 20, 1960, interment in Hebrew Friendship Cemetery.

ELLMAKER, Amos, a Representative from Pennsylvania; born at "Walnut Bottom" farm, Leacock Township, Lancaster County, Pa., February 2, 1787; attended the common schools; was graduated from Princeton College; studied law in Lancaster, Pa., and Litchfield, Conn.; was admitted to the bar and commenced practice in Harrisburg, Pa.; deputy attorney general for Dauphin County 1809–1815; member of the State house of representatives in 1813 and 1814; elected to the Fourteenth Congress, but did not qualify, having been appointed and commissioned president judge of the twelfth judicial district on July 3, 1815, and served until his resignation on December 21, 1816; attorney general of Pennsylvania 1816–1819; declined the appointment of Secretary of War in the Cabinet of President Monroe; moved to Lancaster, Pa., in 1821 and resumed the practice of law; again attorney general of the State in 1828 and 1829; unsuccessful candidate for Vice President of the United States on the Anti-Masonic ticket in 1832 and for the United States Senate in 1833; continued the practice of law until his death in Lancaster, Pa., November 28, 1851; interment in St. James' Episcopal Churchyard.

ELLSBERRY, William Wallace, a Representative from Ohio; born in New Hope, Brown County, Ohio, December 18, 1833; attended the public schools of Brown County and a private academy in Clermont County; taught school two years; began the study of medicine with his father; attended medical lectures and was graduated from the Cincinnati College of Medicine and Surgery, and later from the Ohio Medical College; engaged in the practice of his profession at Georgetown, Ohio, until his election to Congress; appointed superintendent of the Central Insane Asylum at Columbus in 1878, but declined to serve; county auditor; delegate to the Democratic National Convention at Cincinnati in 1880; elected as a Democrat to the Forty-ninth Congress (March 4, 1885–March 3, 1887); was not a candidate for renomination in 1886; resumed the practice of medicine until his death in Georgetown, Brown County, Ohio, September 7, 1894; interment in Confidence Cemetery.

ELLSWORTH, Charles Clinton, a Representative from Michigan; born in West Berkshire, Franklin County, Vt., January 29, 1824; attended the common schools of West Berkshire and the academy at Bakersfield, Vt.; taught school in Vermont one winter; moved to Howell, Livingston County, Mich.; taught school one term; studied law; was admitted to the bar in 1848 and commenced practice in Howell, Mich.; prosecuting attorney of Livingston County in 1849; moved to Montcalm County and settled in Greenville in 1851; served as the first president of the village; member of the State house of representatives 1852–1854; prosecuting attorney of Montcalm County in 1853; during the Civil War served in the Union Army as paymaster with the rank of major in 1862; elected as a Republican to the Forty-fifth Congress (March 4, 1877–March 3, 1879); was not a candidate for renomination in 1878; resumed the practice of law; died in Greenville, Mich., June 25, 1899; interment in Forest Home Cemetery.

ELLSWORTH, Franklin Fowler, a Representative from Minnesota; born in St. James, Watonwan County, Minn., July 10, 1879; attended the grade and high schools; enlisted as a private in Company H, Twelfth Regiment, Minnesota Volunteer Infantry, during the Spanish-American War; attended the law department of the University of Minnesota at Minneapolis; was admitted to the bar in 1901 and commenced practice in St. James, Minn.; city attorney of St. James in 1904 and 1905; prosecuting attorney of Watonwan County 1905–1909; elected as a Republican to the Sixty-fourth, Sixty-fifth, and Sixty-sixth Congresses (March 4, 1915–March 3, 1921); was not a candidate for renom-

ination in 1920, having become a gubernatorial candidate; unsuccessful candidate for Governor of Minnesota in 1920 and 1924; moved to Minneapolis, Minn., in 1921 and resumed the practice of his profession; died in Minneapolis, Minn., December 23, 1942; interment in Lakewood Cemetery.

ELLSWORTH, Mathew Harris, a Representative from Oregon; born in Hoquiam, Grays Harbor County, Wash., September 17, 1899; moved with his parents to Eugene and later to Wendling, Oreg.; attended the public and high schools; served in the Student Army Training Corps during the First World War; was graduated in journalism from the University of Oregon at Eugene in 1922; advertising manager of a newspaper in Eugene, Oreg., in 1923; engaged in the lumber business 1923–1925; manager of a lumber-industry publication 1926–1928; associate professor in journalism at the University of Oregon in 1928 and 1929; publisher and part owner of the Roseburg (Oreg.) News-Review since 1929; member of the Oregon Educational Policies Commission; served by appointment in the State senate in 1941; elected as a Republican to the Seventy-eighth and to the six succeeding Congresses (January 3, 1943–January 3, 1957); unsuccessful candidate for reelection in 1956 to the Eighty-fifth Congress; appointed by President Eisenhower as chairman of the Civil Service Commission for a two-year term and served from April 18, 1957, to February 28, 1959; retired and resides in Roseburg, Oreg.

ELLSWORTH, Oliver (father of William Wolcott Ellsworth), a Delegate and a Senator from Connecticut; born in Windsor, Conn., April 29, 1745; pursued preparatory studies; attended Yale College, New Haven, Conn., and was graduated from Princeton College, Princeton, N. J., in 1766; studied law; was admitted to the bar in 1771 and commenced practice in Windsor; moved to Hartford, Conn., in 1775; representative in the general assembly in 1775 and 1776; appointed State attorney in 1777; Member of the Continental Congress 1777–1784; from 1780 to 1785 he was a member of the Governor's council, which with the lower house before 1784 and alone from 1784 to 1807 constituted a supreme court of errors; declined appointment in 1784 as Commissioner of the Treasury, tendered by the Continental Congress; judge of the Connecticut Superior Court 1785–1789; delegate to the convention which framed the Federal Constitution in 1787; elected as a Federalist to the United States Senate; reelected and served from March 4, 1789, to March 8, 1796, when he resigned, having been appointed Chief Justice of the United States Supreme Court on March 4, 1796; retired from the bench in 1799; appointed Envoy Extraordinary and Minister Plenipotentiary to France February 26, 1799, to negotiate a treaty, and served until November 3, 1799; returned to the United States in 1801; again a member of the Governor's council 1801–1807; died in Windsor, Conn., November 26, 1807; interment in the Old Cemetery.

ELLSWORTH, Samuel Stewart, a Representative from New York; born in Pownal, Vt., October 13, 1790; attended the common schools; moved to Penn Yan, N. Y., in 1819 and engaged in mercantile pursuits; supervisor of Milo, Yates County, 1824–1828; judge of Yates County 1824–1829; served in the State assembly in 1840; elected as a Democrat to the Twenty-ninth Congress (March 4, 1845–March 3, 1847); died in Penn Yan, N. Y., June 4, 1863; interment in Lake View Cemetery.

ELLSWORTH, William Wolcott (son of Oliver Ellsworth), a Representative from Connecticut; born in Windsor, Conn., November 10, 1791; completed preparatory studies, and was graduated from Yale College, New Haven, Conn., in 1810; studied law in Litchfield, Conn.; was admitted to the bar in 1813 and practiced; appointed professor of law at Trinity College,

Hartford, Conn., in 1827, which he held until his death; elected as a Whig to the Twenty-first, Twenty-second, and Twenty-third Congresses and served from March 4, 1829, to July 8, 1834, when he resigned; Governor of Connecticut 1838–1842; judge of the State supreme court from 1847 to 1861, when, by the constitutional provision relative to age, he was retired; twice declined to accept the nomination to the United States Senate; retired from public life; died in Hartford, Conn., January 15, 1868; interment in the Old North Cemetery.

ELLWOOD, Reuben, a Representative from Illinois; born in Minden, Montgomery County, N. Y., February 21, 1821; attended the public schools and Cherry Valley Seminary, New York; manufacturer of agricultural implements; member of the New York State Assembly in 1851; moved to Sycamore, Ill., about 1854; resumed manufacturing interests and engaged in the hardware business; elected as a Republican to the Forty-eighth and Forty-ninth Congresses and served from March 4, 1883, until his death, before the assembling of the Forty-ninth Congress, in Sycamore, Ill., July 1, 1885; interment in Elmwood Cemetery.

ELLZEY, Lawrence Russell, a Representative from Mississippi; born on a farm near Wesson, Copiah County, Miss., March 20, 1891; attended the rural schools and was graduated from Mississippi College at Clinton in 1912; attended the University of Chicago, Chicago, Ill., in 1927; engaged as a teacher in the consolidated county schools of Mississippi 1912–1917; during the First World War volunteered his services as a private in the Quartermaster Corps on December 13, 1917; was commissioned a second lieutenant on July 22, 1918; promoted to a first lieutenant, Army Service Corps, on February 20, 1919, and was honorably discharged on May 21, 1919, serving nine months overseas; served as superintendent of education of Lincoln County, Miss., 1919–1922; teacher in the agricultural high school, Wesson, Miss., 1922–1928; served as president of Copiah-Lincoln Junior College, Wesson, Miss., 1928–1932; elected as a Democrat to the Seventy-second Congress to fill the vacancy caused by the death of Percy E. Quin; reelected to the Seventy-third Congress and served from March 15, 1932, to January 3, 1935; unsuccessful candidate for renomination in 1934; engaged in the life-insurance business; executive secretary for the Mississippi Salvage Campaign in 1942 and 1943; is a resident of Jackson, Miss.

ELMENDORF, Lucas Conrad, a Representative from New York; born in Kingston, N. Y., in 1758; was graduated from Princeton College in 1782; studied law; was admitted to the bar in 1785 and practiced; unsuccessful candidate in 1794 for election to the Fourth Congress; elected as a Democrat to the Fifth, Sixth, and Seventh Congresses (March 4, 1797–March 3, 1803); declined to be a candidate for renomination in 1802; member of the State assembly in 1804 and 1805; served in the State senate 1814–1817; first judge of the court of common pleas (now county court) of Ulster County and served from 1815 to 1821; surrogate of Ulster County 1835–1840; died in Kingston, N. Y., August 17, 1843; interment in the crypt of the First Dutch Church.

ELMER, Ebenezer (brother of Jonathan Elmer and father of Lucius Quintius Cincinnatus Elmer), a Representative from New Jersey; born in Cedarville, Cumberland County, N. J., August 23, 1752; pursued an academic course; studied medicine and practiced in Cedarville; served in the Revolutionary Army as ensign, lieutenant, surgeon's mate, and regimental surgeon; practiced medicine in Bridgeton, N. J., 1783–1789; member of the State general assembly 1789–1795, serving as speaker in 1791 and 1795; elected as a Democrat to the Seventh, Eighth,

and Ninth Congresses (March 4, 1801–March 3, 1807); was not a candidate for renomination in 1806; member of the State council in 1807, and was chosen vice president of that body; collector of customs of Bridgeton from 1808 until 1817, when he resigned; reappointed in 1822 and served until 1832, when he again resigned; served in the War of 1812; adjutant general of the New Jersey Militia and brigadier general of the Cumberland brigade; vice president of Burlington College 1808–1817 and 1822–1832; retired from public life; was the last survivor of the Society of the Cincinnati of New Jersey; died in Bridgeton, N. J., on October 18, 1843; interment in the Presbyterian Cemetery.

ELMER, Jonathan (brother of Ebenezer Elmer and uncle of Lucius Quintius Cincinnatus Elmer), a Delegate and a Senator from New Jersey; born in Cedarville, Cumberland County, N. J., November 29, 1745; completed preparatory studies; was graduated from the first medical class of the University of Pennsylvania at Philadelphia in 1769 and practiced in Bridgeton, N. J.; high sheriff of Cumberland County in 1772; was chosen captain of a light infantry company in 1775; Member of the Continental Congress 1776–1778, 1781–1784, 1787, and 1788; member of the State council in 1780 and 1784; trustee of the College of New Jersey 1782–1795; surrogate of Cumberland County 1784–1802; president of the State medical society in 1787; elected as a Federalist to the United States Senate and served from March 4, 1789, to March 3, 1791; appointed presiding judge of the county court of common pleas in 1802 and served until his resignation in 1804; again appointed to the same office in the winter of 1813, but in the following term, in February 1814, declined to serve further because of impaired health; died in Bridgeton, N. J., September 3, 1817; interment in the Old Presbyterian Cemetery.

ELMER, Lucius Quintius Cincinnatus (son of Ebenezer Elmer and nephew of Jonathan Elmer), a Representative from New Jersey; born in Bridgeton, N. J., February 3, 1793; attended the private schools and was graduated from the University of Pennsylvania at Philadelphia; during the War of 1812 served in the militia as a lieutenant of artillery, and was promoted to the rank of brigade major and inspector; studied law; was admitted to the bar in 1815 and commenced practice in Bridgeton, N. J.; prosecuting attorney for the State in 1824; member of the State general assembly 1820–1823, serving the last year as speaker; prosecutor of the pleas for Cumberland County in 1824; United States district attorney for the district of New Jersey 1824–1829; elected as a Democrat to the Twenty-eighth Congress (March 4, 1843–March 3, 1845); unsuccessful for reelection in 1844 to the Twenty-ninth Congress; attorney general of New Jersey 1850–1852; justice of the State supreme court from 1852 until 1869 when he retired; died in Bridgeton, N. J., on March 11, 1883; interment in Bridgeton Cemetery.

ELMER, William Price, a Representative from Missouri; born in Robertsville, Franklin County, Mo., March 2, 1871; attended the public and high schools and Wingo Law School, Salem, Mo.; was admitted to the bar in 1892 and commenced practice in Salem, Mo.; prosecuting attorney for Dent County, Mo., in 1895 and 1896 and again in 1905 and 1906; member of the State house of representatives in 1903, 1904, 1921, 1922, and 1929–1933, serving as temporary speaker and floor leader in 1929; city attorney of Salem, Mo., 1920–1930; delegate or alternate to the Republican National Conventions in 1904, 1908, 1912, and 1920; chairman of the Republican county committee 1908–1944; member of the 1929 commission to revise Missouri laws; originator of old-age pensions in Missouri; unsuccessful candidate for Lieutenant Governor in 1940; elected as a Republican to the Seventy-eighth Congress (January 3, 1943–January 3, 1945); unsuccessful candidate for reelection in 1944 to the Seventy-ninth Congress; unsuccessful candidate for the Republican nomination for United States Senator in 1946; resumed the practice of law; director of First National Bank of Salem; member of board of curators of University of Missouri 1949–1955; member of board of trustees of State Historical Society of Missouri from 1955 until his death; died in Salem, Mo., May 11, 1956; interment in Cedar Grove Cemetery.

ELMORE, Franklin Harper, a Representative and a Senator from South Carolina; born in Laurens District, S. C., October 15, 1799; was graduated from the South Carolina College at Columbia in 1819; studied law; was admitted to the bar in 1821 and commenced practice in Walterboro, S. C.; was solicitor for the southern circuit 1822–1836; colonel on the staff of Governor Manning 1824–1826; elected as a State Rights Democrat to the Twenty-fourth Congress to fill the vacancy caused by the resignation of James H. Hammond; reelected to the Twenty-fifth Congress and served from December 10, 1836, to March 3, 1839; president of the Bank of the State of South Carolina 1839–1850; declined appointment by President Polk as Minister to Great Britain; appointed to the United States Senate to fill the vacancy caused by the death of John C. Calhoun and served from April 11, 1850, until his death in Washington, D. C., May 28, 1850; interment in First Presbyterian Churchyard, Columbia, S. C.

ELSAESSER, Edward Julius, a Representative from New York; born in Buffalo, Erie County, N. Y., March 10, 1904; attended the public schools; was graduated from the law department of the University of Buffalo, Buffalo, N. Y., in 1926; was admitted to the bar in 1927 and commenced practice in Buffalo, N. Y.; Republican State committeeman 1937–1945; elected as a Republican to the Seventy-ninth and Eightieth Congresses (January 3, 1945–January 3, 1949); unsuccessful candidate for reelection in 1948 to the Eighty-first Congress; resumed the practice of law; is a resident of Buffalo, N. Y.

ELSTON, Charles Henry, a Representative from Ohio; born in Marietta, Washington County, Ohio, August 1, 1891; attended the public and high schools of Marietta and Cincinnati, Ohio; was graduated from the Y. M. C. A. Law School, Cincinnati, Ohio, in 1914; was admitted to the bar the same year and commenced practice in Cincinnati, Ohio; assistant prosecuting attorney of Hamilton County, Ohio, 1915–1922; member of the faculty of the Y. M. C. A. Law School 1916–1936; during the First World War served as an aviation cadet in the aviation service of the United States Army; member of the Hamilton County Charter Commission; elected as a Republican to the Seventy-sixth and to the six succeeding Congresses (January 3, 1939–January 3, 1953); was not a candidate for renomination in 1952; resumed the practice of law in Cincinnati, Ohio.

ELSTON, John Arthur, a Representative from California; born in Woodland, Yolo County, Calif., February 10, 1874; attended the public schools; was graduated from Hesperian College, Woodland, Calif., in 1892 and the University of California at Berkeley in 1897; engaged in educational work; studied law; was admitted to the bar in 1901 and commenced practice in Berkeley, Calif.; executive secretary to the Governor of California 1903–1907; member of the board of trustees of the State Institution for the Deaf and Blind 1911–1914; elected as a Progressive Republican to the Sixty-fourth and to the three succeeding Congresses and served from March 4, 1915, until his death in Washington, D. C., December 15, 1921; remains were cremated in Oakland, Calif., and the ashes placed in the California Crematorium at Oakland.

ELTSE, Ralph Roscoe, a Representative from California; born in Oskaloosa, Mahaska County, Iowa, September 13, 1885; attended the public schools; was graduated from Penn College, Oskaloosa, Iowa, in 1909 and from Haverford (Pa.) College in 1910; moved to Berkeley, Alameda County, Calif., in 1912; attended the law department of the University of California at Berkeley; was admitted to the bar in 1915 and commenced practice in Berkeley, Calif.; member of the Republican State committee 1932–1935; delegate to the Republican State conventions in 1932, 1934, and 1940; elected as a Republican to the Seventy-third Congress (March 4, 1933–January 3, 1935); unsuccessful candidate for reelection in 1934 to the Seventy-fourth Congress and for election in 1940 to the Seventy-seventh Congress; resumed the practice of law and is a resident of Berkeley, Calif.

ELVINS, Politte, a Representative from Missouri; born in French Village, St. Francois County, Mo., March 16, 1878; attended the public schools; was graduated from Carleton College, Farmington, Mo., in 1897 and from the law department of the University of Missouri at Columbia in 1899; was admitted to the bar the same year and commenced practice in Elvins, Mo.; presidential elector on the Republican ticket of Roosevelt and Fairbanks in 1904; elected as a Republican to the Sixty-first Congress (March 4, 1909–March 3, 1911); unsuccessful candidate for reelection in 1910 to the Sixty-second Congress; resumed the practice of law in Elvins, Mo.; delegate to the Republican National Convention at Chicago in 1912; chairman of the State Republican committee 1912–1914; moved to Bonne Terre, Mo., in 1917 and continued the practice of law; member and chairman of the committee on rules and order of business for the Missouri constitutional convention in 1922 and 1923; moved to Pharr, Hidalgo County, Tex., in 1936; unsuccessful candidate to the United States Senate in 1940; died at McAllen, Tex., January 14, 1943; remains cremated at McAllen, Tex., and the ashes retained by his family.

ELY, Alfred, a Representative from New York; born in Lyme, New London County, Conn., February 15, 1815; attended the common schools and Bacon Academy at Colchester, Conn.; moved to Rochester, N. Y., in 1835; studied law; was admitted to the bar in 1841 and commenced practice in Rochester; elected as a Republican to the Thirty-sixth and Thirty-seventh Congresses (March 4, 1859–March 3, 1863); was not a candidate for renomination in 1862; while witnessing the Battle of Bull Run was taken a prisoner by the Confederates, and imprisoned in Richmond for nearly six months; resumed the practice of law; died in Rochester, N. Y., May 18, 1892; interment in the Ely vault in Mount Hope Cemetery.

ELY, Frederick David, a Representative from Massachusetts; born in Wrentham, Norfolk County, Mass., September 24, 1838; attended Day's Academy, Wrentham, and was graduated from Brown University, Providence, R. I., in 1859; studied law; was admitted to the bar and commenced practice at Dedham, Mass., in 1862; trial justice 1867–1885; member of the State house of representatives in 1873; served in the State senate in 1878 and 1879; member of the school committee of Dedham 1882–1894; elected as a Republican to the Forty-ninth Congress (March 4, 1885–March 3, 1887); unsuccessful candidate for reelection in 1886 to the Fiftieth Congress; resumed the practice of law; justice of the municipal court of Boston 1888–1914; died in Dedham, Mass., August 6, 1921; interment in Old Parish Cemetery.

ELY, John, a Representative from New York; born in Saybrook, Conn., October 8, 1774; completed preparatory studies; studied medicine, and practiced in Coxsackie, N. Y.; member of the State assembly in 1806 and 1812; one of the organizers of the New York State and Greene County Medical Societies in 1807 and also of the Albany Female Academy; elected as a Democrat to the Twenty-sixth Congress (March 4, 1839–March 3, 1841); resumed the practice of medicine; died in Coxsackie, N. Y., August 20, 1849; interment in Old Coxsackie Cemetery.

ELY, Smith, Jr., a Representative from New York; born in Hanover, Morris County, N. J., April 17, 1825; completed preparatory studies; was graduated from the New York University Law School, New York City, in 1846; was admitted to the bar the same year, but never practiced his profession; engaged in mercantile pursuits in New York City; served as school commissioner 1856–1860; served in the State senate in 1858 and 1859; county supervisor in 1860, retaining the latter office until 1870, when it was abolished; commissioner of public instruction in 1867; elected as a Democrat to the Forty-second Congress (March 4, 1871–March 3, 1873); was not a candidate for renomination in 1872; elected to the Forty-fourth Congress and served from March 4, 1875, to December 11, 1876, when he resigned; mayor of New York City in 1877 and 1878; appointed commissioner of parks in 1895 and served until 1897, when he resigned and retired from public life; died in Livingston, Essex County, N. J., July 1, 1911; interment in a private cemetery on his farm at Livingston.

ELY, William, a Representative from Massachusetts; born in Longmeadow, Mass., August 14, 1765; completed preparatory studies; was graduated from Yale College in 1787; studied law; was admitted to the bar in 1791 and commenced practice in Springfield, Mass.; member of the State house of representatives 1801–1803; elected as a Federalist to the Ninth and to the four succeeding Congresses (March 4, 1805–March 3, 1815); again a member of the State house of representatives in 1815 and 1816; died in Springfield, Mass., October 9, 1817, and was buried there.

EMBREE, Elisha, a Representative from Indiana; born in Lincoln County, Ky., September 28, 1801; moved to Indiana in 1811 with his father, who settled in Knox (now Gibson) County, near where Princeton was subsequently located; received a very meager schooling and was practically self-educated; engaged in agricultural pursuits; studied law; was admitted to the bar in 1836 and commenced practice in Princeton, Gibson County, Ind.; circuit judge for the fourth circuit of Indiana 1835–1845; was nominated as the Whig candidate for Governor of Indiana in 1849, but declined, preferring to run for Congress; elected as a Whig to the Thirtieth Congress (March 4, 1847–March 3, 1849); unsuccessful candidate for reelection in 1848 to the Thirty-first Congress; resumed the practice of law and also interested in farming; died in Princeton, Ind., February 28, 1863; interment in Warnock Cemetery.

EMERICH, Martin, a Representative from Illinois; born in Baltimore, Md., April 27, 1846; attended the public schools; engaged in the importing business; appointed ward commissioner of the poor of Baltimore in 1870; member of the State house of delegates 1881–1883; aide-de-camp to Gov. William T. Hamilton 1880–1884, and to Gov. Elihu E. Jackson 1884–1887; moved to Chicago, Ill., in 1887 and engaged in mercantile pursuits until 1896, when he engaged in the manufacture of bricks; member of the Board of Commissioners of Cook County 1892–1894; assessor of South Chicago 1897; elected as a Democrat to the Fifty-eighth Congress (March 4, 1903–March 3, 1905); was not a candidate for renomination in 1904; discontinued active business pursuits in 1907 and lived in retirement until his death; died while on a visit in New York City September 27, 1922; interment in Rosehill Cemetery, Chicago, Ill.

EMERSON, Henry Ivory, a Representative from Ohio; born in Litchfield, Kennebec County, Maine, March 15, 1871; moved with his parents to Lewiston, Maine, where he attended the public schools and studied law; moved to Cleveland, Ohio, in 1892 and was graduated from the Cincinnati Law School in 1893; was admitted to the bar the same year and commenced practice in Cleveland, Ohio; member of the Cleveland City Council in 1902 and 1903; elected as a Republican to the Sixty-fourth, Sixty-fifth, and Sixty-sixth Congresses (March 4, 1915–March 3, 1921); unsuccessful candidate for renomination in 1920; resumed the practice of law; died in East Cleveland, Ohio, October 28, 1953; interment in Lakeview Cemetery, Cleveland, Ohio.

EMERSON, Louis Woodard, a Representative from New York; born in Warrensburg, Warren County, N. Y., July 25, 1857; attended the district school and was graduated from Warrensburg Academy; engaged in the lumber, banking, and manufacturing business; delegate to the Republican National Conventions in 1888, 1892, and 1896; member of the State senate 1890–1893; elected as a Republican to the Fifty-sixth and Fifty-seventh Congresses (March 4, 1899–March 3, 1903); resumed former business activities in Warrensburg, N. Y., and died there June 10, 1924; interment in the City Cemetery.

EMOTT, James, a Representative from New York; born in Poughkeepsie, N. Y., March 9, 1771; completed preparatory studies; studied law; was admitted to the bar in 1790 and commenced practice in Ballson Center, N. Y.; land commissioner to settle disputes of titles to military reservations in Onondaga County in 1797; moved to Albany, N. Y., in 1800; member of the State assembly from Albany County in 1804, and served as speaker; elected as a Federalist to the Eleventh and Twelfth Congresses (March 4, 1809–March 3, 1813); member of the State assembly from Dutchess County 1814–1817, and served as speaker the first year; judge of the court of common pleas of Dutchess County from April 8, 1817, to February 3, 1823; appointed judge for the second judicial circuit February 21, 1827, and held that office until February 1831, when he retired; died in Poughkeepsie, Dutchess County, N. Y., April 7, 1850; interment in Poughkeepsie Rural Cemetery.

EMRIE, Jonas Reece, a Representative from Ohio; born in Hillsboro, Highland County, Ohio, April 25, 1812; pursued preparatory studies; studied law; was admitted to the bar and commenced practice in Hillsboro, Ohio; editor and publisher of the Hillsboro Gazette 1839–1848 and 1854–1856; leader in organizing the Hillsboro Female College; appointed postmaster of Hillsboro April 8, 1839, and served until February 23, 1841; member of the State senate in 1847 and 1848; first probate judge of Highland County 1851–1854; elected as a Republican to the Thirty-fourth Congress (March 4, 1855–March 3, 1857); unsuccessful candidate for reelection in 1856 to the Thirty-fifth Congress; moved to Mound City, Pulaski County, Ill., in 1857; engaged in mercantile pursuits, conducted a newspaper, and practiced law; police magistrate of the city in 1858; township treasurer of schools; master in chancery of Pulaski County, Ill.; died in Mound City, Ill., June 5, 1869; interment in Beech Grove Cemetery.

ENGEL, Albert Joseph, a Representative from Michigan; born in New Washington, Crawford County, Ohio, January 1, 1888; attended the public schools in Grand Traverse County, Mich., and the Central Y. M. C. A., Chicago, Ill.; was graduated from the law department of Northwestern University, Evanston, Ill., in 1910; was admitted to the bar the same year and commenced practice in Lake City, Mich.; prosecuting attorney of Missaukee County, Mich., in 1916 and 1917 and in 1919 and 1920; during the First World War served as a first lieutenant in the War

Department, Washington, D. C., later being promoted to captain and served overseas for twenty-three months, 1917–1919; served in the State senate in 1921, 1922, and 1927–1932; elected as a Republican to the Seventy-fourth and to the seven succeeding Congresses (January 3, 1935–January 3, 1951); was not a candidate for renomination in 1950 but was an unsuccessful candidate for the Republican gubernatorial nomination; operated a 1,400-acre tree plantation near Lake City, Mich.; died in Grand Rapids, Mich., December 2, 1959; interment in Lake City Cemetery, Lake City, Mich.

ENGLAND, Edward Theodore, a Representative from West Virginia; born in Gay, Jackson County, W. Va., September 29, 1869; attended the public schools; was graduated from the Concord Normal School, Athens, W. Va., in 1892; taught school for several years; was graduated from the law department of Southern Normal University, Huntingdon, Tenn., in 1898; was admitted to the bar the same year and commenced practice in Oceana, W. Va.; moved to Logan, W. Va., in 1901 and continued the practice of law; elected mayor of Logan in 1903; member of the State senate 1908–1916; elected president of the State senate in 1915 and by virtue of this office was Lieutenant Governor in 1915 and 1916; presided over the first meeting of all Lieutenant Governors of the United States at Rhea Springs, Tenn., in 1915; elected attorney general of the State and served from 1917 to 1925; as attorney general had charge of and on behalf of the State of West Virginia made the argument before the Supreme Court of the United States in the celebrated Virginia debt controversy; elected president of the Attorney Generals' Association of the United States at Minneapolis, Minn., in 1923; was an unsuccessful candidate for the Republican nomination for Governor in 1924; elected as a Republican to the Seventieth Congress (March 4, 1927–March 3, 1929); unsuccessful candidate for reelection in 1928 to the Seventy-first Congress; resumed the practice of law in Charleston, W. Va.; died in Cleveland, Ohio, where he had gone to receive medical treatment, on September 9, 1934; interment in Sunset Memorial Park, Charleston, W. Va.

ENGLE, Clair, a Representative and a Senator from California; born in Bakersfield, Kern County, Calif., September 21, 1911; attended the public schools; was graduated from Chico (Calif.) State College in 1930 and from the University of California Hastings College of Law in 1933; was admitted to the bar in 1933 and commenced practice in Corning, Calif.; district attorney of Tehama County, Calif., 1934–1942; member of the State senate in 1943; elected as a Democrat to the Seventy-eighth Congress to fill the vacancy caused by the death of Harry L. Englebright; reelected to the Seventy-ninth and to the six succeeding Congresses and served from August 31, 1943, to January 3, 1959; was not a candidate for renomination in 1958 having become a candidate for United States Senator; delegate to the Democratic National Convention in 1948; elected to the United States Senate in 1958 for the term commencing January 3, 1959, and ending January 3, 1965.

ENGLEBRIGHT, Harry Lane (son of William F. Englebright), a Representative from California; born in Nevada City, Nevada County, Calif., January 2, 1884; was graduated from the grammar and high schools; attended the University of California at Berkeley; was graduated as a mining engineer, and followed his profession; mineral inspector for the field division of the General Land Office, and also engineer for the State Conservation Commission of California 1911–1914; actively connected with various mining enterprises in California; member of the American Mining Congress; elected as a Republican to the Sixty-ninth Congress to fill the vacancy caused by the death of John E. Raker;

reelected to the Seventieth and to the eight succeeding Congresses and served from August 31, 1926, until his death; Republican whip from the Seventy-third to the Seventy-eighth Congresses; died in Naval Medical Center, Bethesda, Md., May 13, 1943; interment in Pine Grove Cemetery, Nevada City, Calif.

ENGLEBRIGHT, William Fellows (father of Harry Lane Englebright), a Representative from California; born in New Bedford, Mass., November 23, 1855; moved with his parents to Vallejo, Calif.; attended private and public schools; entered the service of the United States at the navy yard, Mare Island, as joiner's apprentice and completed his studies in engineering; established himself in Nevada City, Calif., as a mining engineer; member of the Nevada City Board of Education; elected as a Republican to the Fifty-ninth Congress to fill the vacancy caused by the resignation of James N. Gillett; reelected to the Sixtieth and Sixty-first Congresses and served from November 6, 1906, to March 3, 1911; unsuccessful candidate for reelection in 1910 to the Sixty-second Congress; resumed his occupation as a mining engineer; died in Oakland, Calif., February 10, 1915; interment in Pine Grove Cemetery, Nevada City, Calif.

ENGLISH, James Edward, a Representative and a Senator from Connecticut; born in New Haven, Conn., March 13, 1812; attended the common schools; engaged in the lumber business, banking, and manufacturing; member of the New Haven Board of Selectmen 1847–1861; member of the common council in 1848 and 1849; member of the State house of representatives in 1855; served in the State senate 1856–1858; declined to be a candidate for reelection; unsuccessful candidate for Lieutenant Governor in 1860; elected as a Democrat to the Thirty-seventh and Thirty-eighth Congresses (March 4, 1861–March 3, 1865); was not a candidate for renomination in 1864; delegate to the National Union Convention at Philadelphia in 1866; unsuccessful candidate for election as Governor in 1866; elected Governor of Connecticut in 1867 and 1868; unsuccessful candidate for reelection as Governor in 1869; again elected Governor in 1870; again a member of the State house of representatives in 1872; unsuccessful candidate for election in 1872 to the Forty-third Congress; appointed as a Democrat to the United States Senate to fill the vacancy caused by the death of Orris S. Ferry and served from November 27, 1875, to May 17, 1876, when a successor was elected; was an unsuccessful candidate for election in 1876 to fill the vacancy; engaged in manufacturing and commercial activities; presidential elector on the Democratic tickets of Tilden and Hendricks in 1876 and Cleveland and Hendricks in 1884; died in New Haven, Conn., on March 2, 1890; interment in Evergreen Cemetery.

ENGLISH, Thomas Dunn, a Representative from New Jersey; born in Philadelphia, Pa., June 29, 1819; attended the Friends' Academy, Burlington, N. J., and was graduated from the medical department of the University of Pennsylvania at Philadelphia in 1839; studied law; was admitted to the Philadelphia bar in 1842, but mainly pursued journalism; wrote the song Ben Bolt in 1843, and was the author of many poems, ballads, and lyrics; moved to Virginia in 1852; prominent opponent of Know-Nothingism; moved to New York City in 1857, and to Newark, N. J., a year later; member of the State house of assembly in 1863 and 1864; elected as a Democrat to the Fifty-second and Fifty-third Congresses (March 4, 1891–March 3, 1895); unsuccessful candidate for reelection in 1894 to the Fifty-fourth Congress; resumed his former literary pursuits in Newark, N. J., until his death on April 1, 1902; interment in Fairmont Cemetery.

ENGLISH, Warren Barkley, a Representative from California; born in Charles Town, Va. (now West Virginia), May 1, 1840; attended the public schools and Charles Town Academy until June 1861; served in the Confederate Army; moved to Oakland, Calif., and attended the California Military Academy; elected a member of the board of supervisors of Contra Costa County in 1877 and served four years; elected State senator in 1882; delegate to the Democratic National Convention at Chicago in 1884; successfully contested as a Democrat the election of Samuel G. Hilborn to the Fifty-third Congress and took his seat April 4, 1894, serving until March 3, 1895; unsuccessful candidate for reelection in 1894 to the Fifty-fourth Congress; engaged in the real-estate business in Oakland, Calif.; in 1905 moved to Sonoma County, Calif., where he engaged in viticulture; died in Santa Rosa, Calif., January 9, 1913; interment in Mountain View Cemetery, Oakland, Calif.

ENGLISH, William Eastin (son of William Hayden English) a Representative from Indiana; born at "Englishton Park," near Lexington, Scott County, Ind., November 3, 1850; moved to Indianapolis in 1865; attended public and private schools; was graduated from the law department of the Northwestern Christian (now Butler) University at Indianapolis in 1873; was admitted to the bar the same year and practiced in Indianapolis until 1882; member of the State house of representatives in 1880; successfully contested as a Democrat the election of Stanton J. Peelle to the Forty-eighth Congress and served from May 22, 1884, to March 3, 1885; declined to be a candidate for renomination in 1884 and resumed his former business pursuits at Indianapolis; delegate to the Democratic National Conventions at Chicago in 1892 and 1896, and chairman of the committee on rules and order of business in the former; left the Democratic Party in 1900 and became active in the Republican Party; served without pay as captain and aide-de-camp on the staff of Gen. Joseph Wheeler in the Spanish-American War; was dangerously wounded in the bombardment of El Pozo Hill, at the Battle of Santiago; was the first elected commander in chief of the United Spanish War Veterans of the United States; president of the board of park commissioners of Indianapolis 1898–1900; president of the board of safety of Indianapolis 1904–1906; delegate to the Republican National Convention at Chicago in 1912; elected a member of the State senate in 1916; reelected in 1920 and again in 1924 and served until his death in Indianapolis, Ind., April 29, 1926; interment in Crown Hill Cemetery.

ENGLISH, William Hayden (father of William Eastin English), a Representative from Indiana; born in Lexington, Scott County, Ind., August 27, 1822; pursued classical studies at Hanover (Ind.) College; studied law; was admitted to the bar in 1846 and commenced practice at Lexington, Ind.; principal clerk of the State house of representatives in 1843; clerk in the United States Treasury Department at Washington, D. C., 1844–1848; secretary of the Indiana State constitutional convention in 1850; member of the State house of representatives in 1851 and 1852 and served as speaker; elected as a Democrat to the Thirty-third and to the three succeeding Congresses (March 4, 1853–March 3, 1861); Regent of the Smithsonian Institution 1853–1861; moved to Indianapolis, Ind., at the end of his congressional term; unsuccessful candidate for Vice President of the United States on the Democratic ticket of Hancock and English in 18 0; author of several books; died at his home in Indianapolis, Ind., February 7, 1896; interment in Crown Hill Cemetery.

ENLOE, Benjamin Augustine, a Representative from Tennessee; born near Clarksburg, Carroll County, Tenn., January 18, 1848; attended the public schools, Bethel College, McKenzie,

Tenn., and the Cumberland University, Lebanon, Tenn.; while a student at the latter institution in 1869 was elected a member of the State house of representatives; reelected under the new constitution in 1870; was graduated from the law department of Cumberland University in 1872; was admitted to the bar in 1873 and commenced practice in Jackson, Tenn.; delegate to the Democratic National Convention in Baltimore in 1872; presidential elector on the Democratic ticket of Tilden and Hendricks in 1876; appointed a commissioner by Governor Marks in 1878 to negotiate a settlement of the State debt; served on the State executive committee 1878–1880; delegate to the Democratic National Convention at Cincinnati in 1880; edited the Jackson Tribune and Sun 1874–1886; elected as a Democrat to the Fiftieth and to the three succeeding Congresses (March 4, 1887–March 3, 1895); unsuccessful candidate for reelection in 1894 to the Fifty-fourth Congress; edited the Daily Sun at Nashville, Tenn., for two years; moved to Louisville, Ky., and edited the Louisville Dispatch for two years; secretary of the State fair commission and director of exhibits from Tennessee at St. Louis World's Fair in 1903; elected railroad commissioner of Tennessee and served from 1904 until his death in Nashville, Tenn., July 8, 1922; interment in Mount Olivet Cemetery.

ENOCHS, William Henry, a Representative from Ohio; born near Middleburg, Noble County, Ohio, March 29, 1842; attended the common schools and Ohio University at Athens; during the Civil War enlisted as a private in Company B, Second Regiment, Ohio Infantry, April 17, 1861; commissioned first lieutenant, Fifth Regiment, West Virginia Infantry, September 15, 1861; captain April 19, 1862; lieutenant colonel September 29, 1863; colonel First Regiment, West Virginia Infantry, December 23, 1864; brevetted brigadier general of Volunteers March 13, 1865; mustered out July 21, 1865; was graduated from the Cincinnati Law School in 1866; was admitted to the bar and commenced practice in Ironton, Ohio; member of the State house of representatives in 1870 and 1871; elected as a Republican to the Fifty-second and Fifty-third Congresses and served from March 4, 1891, until his death in Ironton, Lawrence County, Ohio, July 13, 1893; interment in Arlington National Cemetery, Fort Myer, Va.

EPES, James Fletcher (cousin of Sydney Parham Epes), a Representative from Virginia; born near Blackstone, Nottoway County, Va., May 23, 1842; attended private schools and the University of Virginia at Charlottesville; during the Civil War served in the Confederate Army in Company E, Third Virginia Cavalry, and was wounded at Reams Station, Va.; was graduated from the law department of Washington and Lee University, Lexington, Va., in 1867; was admitted to the bar the same year and commenced practice at Nottoway Court House, Va.; also engaged in agricultural pursuits; prosecuting attorney for Nottoway County 1870–1883; elected as a Democrat to the Fifty-second and Fifty-third Congresses (March 4, 1891–March 3, 1895); was not a candidate for renomination in 1894; retired to his plantation, "The Old Place," near Blackstone, Nottoway County, Va., and engaged in agricultural pursuits until his death there August 24, 1910; interment in Lake View Cemetery, Blackstone, Va.

EPES, Sydney Parham (cousin of James Fletcher Epes and William Bacon Oliver), a Representative from Virginia; born near Nottoway Court House, Nottoway County, Va., August 20, 1865; moved with his parents to Kentucky and settled near Franklin, Ky.; attended the public schools; returned to Virginia in 1884 and edited and published a Democratic newspaper at Blackstone, Va.; delegate to all State conventions from 1890 until his death; member of the house of delegates in 1891 and 1892;

register of the Virginia land office 1895–1897; presented credentials as a Member-elect to the Fifty-fifth Congress and served from March 4, 1897, until March 23, 1898, when he was succeeded by Robert T. Thorp, who contested the election; elected as a Democrat to the Fifty-sixth Congress and served from March 4, 1899, until his death in Washington, D. C., March 3, 1900; interment in Lake View Cemetery, Blackstone, Va.

EPPES, John Wayles, a Representative and a Senator from Virginia; born in Chesterfield County, near Petersburg, Va., April 7, 1773; attended the University of Pennsylvania at Philadelphia; was graduated from Hampden-Sydney College in Virginia in 1786; studied law; was admitted to the bar in 1794 and commenced practice in Richmond, Va.; member of the State house of delegates 1801–1803; elected as a Democrat to the Eighth and to the three succeeding Congresses (March 4, 1803–March 3, 1811); unsuccessful candidate for reelection to the Twelfth Congress; engaged in agricultural pursuits; elected to the Thirteenth Congress (March 4, 1813–March 3, 1815); unsuccessful candidate for reelection to the Fourteenth Congress; elected to the United States Senate and served from March 4, 1817, until December 4, 1819, when he resigned because of ill health; retired to his estate, "Millbrook," in Buckingham County, Va., where he died September 13, 1823; interment in the private cemetery of the Eppes family at Millbrook, near Curdsville, Va.

ERDMAN, Constantine Jacob (grandson of Jacob Erdman), a Representative from Pennsylvania; born in Upper Saucon Township, near Allentown, Lehigh County, Pa., September 4, 1846; attended the common schools of the district and a classical school in Quakerstown, Pa.; was graduated from Pennsylvania College, Gettysburg, Pa., in 1865; studied law; was admitted to the bar in 1867 and practiced in Allentown, Pa.; elected district attorney in 1874; adjutant of the Fourth Regiment, National Guard of Pennsylvania, during the riots at Reading in 1877; elected as a Democrat to the Fifty-third and Fifty-fourth Congresses (March 4, 1893–March 3, 1897); was not a candidate for reelection in 1896; resumed the practice of law in Allentown; trustee of Muhlenberg College at Allentown; president of the Coplay Cement Manufacturing Co., the Allentown & Coopersburg Turnpike Co., and the Allen Fire Insurance Co. for many years; died in Allentown, Pa., January 15, 1911; interment in Fairview Cemetery.

ERDMAN, Jacob (grandfather of Constantine Jacob Erdman), a Representative from Pennsylvania; born in Coopersburg, Lehigh County, Pa., February 22, 1801; attended the common schools; engaged in agricultural pursuits; member of the State house of representatives 1834–1836; elected as a Democrat to the Twenty-ninth Congress (March 4, 1845–March 3, 1847); unsuccessful candidate for reelection in 1846 to the Thirtieth Congress; discontinued agricultural pursuits and lived in retirement; elected associate judge of Lehigh County Court November 9, 1866, and served until his death in Coopersburg, Pa., July 20, 1867; interment in Blue Church Cemetery near Coopersburg, Pa.

ERICKSON, John Edward, a Senator from Montana; born in Stoughton, Dane County, Wis., March 14, 1863; moved with his parents to Eureka, Greenwood County, Kans., where he attended the public schools; was graduated from Washburn College, Topeka, Kans., in 1890; studied law; was admitted to the bar in 1891 at Eureka, Kans., and commenced practice in Choteau, Teton County, Mont., in 1893; county attorney of Teton County 1897–1905; judge of the eleventh judicial district of Montana 1905–1915; resumed the practice of law at Kalispell, Mont., in

1916; delegate to the Democratic National Convention at San Francisco in 1920; chairman of the Democratic State central committee 1920–1924; Governor of Montana 1925–1933; appointed as a Democrat to the United States Senate to fill the vacancy caused by the death of Thomas J. Walsh and served from March 13, 1933, until November 6, 1934, when a successor was elected; unsuccessful candidate for nomination in 1934 to fill this vacancy; resumed the practice of law in Helena, Mont., where he died on May 25, 1946; interment in Conrad Memorial Cemetery, Kalispell, Mont.

ERK, Edmund Frederick, a Representative from Pennsylvania; born in Allegheny City (now North Side, Pittsburgh), Pa., April 17, 1872; attended the public schools; engaged extensively in newspaper work in Pittsburgh, Pa.; served as secretary to Congressman Stephen G. Porter 1911–1919 and as clerk of the Committee on Foreign Affairs of the United States House of Representatives from June 1, 1919, to November 3, 1930, when he resigned, having been elected to Congress; secretary of the American delegation to the League of Nations Conference at Geneva in 1924 and 1925; elected as a Republican to the Seventy-first Congress to fill the vacancy caused by the death of Stephen G. Porter, at the same time being elected to the Seventy-second Congress, and served from November 4, 1930, to March 3, 1933; unsuccessful candidate for reelection in 1932 to the Seventy-third Congress and for election in 1934 to the Seventy-fourth Congress; secretary to Congressman Michael J. Muldowney from March 4, 1933, to January 2, 1935; also an author and compiler; clerk to United States Senator James J. Davis of Pennsylvania from February 6, 1939, to January 3, 1945; retired and resided in Bethesda, Md., until his death there, December 14, 1953; interment in St. John's Cemetery, Pittsburgh, Pa.

ERMENTROUT, Daniel, a Representative from Pennsylvania; born in Reading, Pa., January 24, 1837; attended the public and classical schools, Franklin and Marshall College, Lancaster, Pa., and Elmwood Institute, Norristown, Pa.; studied law; was admitted to the bar in 1859 and commenced practice in Reading, Pa.; elected district attorney in 1862 for three years; solicitor for the city of Reading 1867–1870; member of the board of school control of Reading 1868–1876; delegate to the Democratic National Convention at New York in 1868 and at Cincinnati in 1880; chairman of the standing committee of Berks County in 1869, 1872, and 1873; member of the State senate 1873–1880; appointed in October 1877 by Governor Hartranft as a member of the Pennsylvania Statuary Commission; elected as a Democrat to the Forty-seventh and to the three succeeding Congresses (March 4, 1881–March 3, 1889); unsuccessful candidate for renomination in 1888; delegate to the Democratic State conventions 1895–1899; elected to the Fifty-fifth and Fifty-sixth Congresses and served from March 4, 1897, until his death in Reading, Pa., on September 17, 1899; interment in Charles Evans Cemetery.

ERNST, Richard Pretlow, a Senator from Kentucky; born in Covington, Ky., February 28, 1858; attended the public schools of Covington; was graduated from Chickerings Academy, Cincinnati, Ohio, in 1874, from Centre College, Danville, Ky., in 1878, and from the law school of the University of Cincinnati in 1880; was admitted to the bar in 1880 and practiced in Covington and Cincinnati; member of the Covington City Council 1888–1892; trustee of Centre College, the University of Kentucky at Lexington, Pikeville College, and Western College for Women, Oxford, Ohio; delegate to several Republican National Conventions; unsuccessful candidate for election in 1896 to the Fifty-fifth Congress; elected as a Republican to the United States

Senate in 1920 and served from March 4, 1921, to March 3, 1927; unsuccessful candidate for reelection in 1926; resumed the practice of law in Cincinnati, Ohio; also engaged in banking in Covington, Ky.; while en route from Colon, Panama, on the liner *California,* he suffered a paralytic stroke, and on arrival in this country was taken to Johns Hopkins Hospital, Baltimore, Md., where he died on April 13, 1934; interment in Highland Cemetery, Covington, Ky.

ERRETT, Russell, a Representative from Pennsylvania; born in New York City, November 10, 1817; self-instructed; moved to Pittsburgh, Pa., in 1829; engaged in newspaper work; elected comptroller of Pittsburgh in 1860; served as clerk of the Pennsylvania Senate in 1860, 1861, and 1872–1876; during the Civil War was appointed additional paymaster in the United States Army in 1861 and served until mustered out in 1866; member of the State senate in 1867; appointed assessor of internal revenue in 1869, and served until 1873; elected as a Republican to the Forty-fifth, Forty-sixth, and Forty-seventh Congresses (March 4, 1877–March 3, 1883); unsuccessful candidate for reelection in 1882 to the Forty-eighth Congress; appointed by President Arthur as United States pension agent at Pittsburgh in 1883 and served in this capacity until May 1887; died in Carnegie, Pa., April 7, 1891; interment in Chartiers Cemetery.

ERVIN, James, a Representative from South Carolina; born in Williamsburg District, S. C., October 17, 1778; was graduated from Rhode Island College (now Brown University), Providence, R. I., in 1797; studied law; was admitted to the bar in 1800 and commenced practice in Peedee, S. C.; member of the State house of representatives 1800–1804; solicitor of the northern judicial circuit 1804–1816; trustee of South Carolina College 1809–1817; again a member of the State house of representatives in 1810 and 1811; elected as a Protectionist to the Fifteenth and Sixteenth Congresses (March 4, 1817–March 3, 1821); declined to be a candidate for renomination in 1820; engaged in agricultural pursuits; member of the State senate 1826–1829; served as a delegate to the State convention in 1832; died in Darlington, S. C., July 7, 1841; interment in the garden in the rear of his home.

ERVIN, Joseph Wilson (brother of Samuel James Ervin, Jr.), a Representative from North Carolina; born in Morganton, Burke County, N. C., March 3, 1901; attended the public schools; was graduated from the University of North Carolina at Chapel Hill in 1921 and from its law school in 1923; was admitted to the bar in 1923 and commenced practice in Charlotte, N. C.; elected as a Democrat to the Seventy-ninth Congress and served from January 3, 1945, until his death in Washington, D. C., December 25, 1945; interment in Forest Hill Cemetery, Morganton, N. C.

ERVIN, Samuel James, Jr. (brother of Joseph Wilson Ervin), a Representative and a Senator from North Carolina; born in Morganton, Burke County, N. C., September 27, 1896; attended the public schools; was graduated from the University of North Carolina at Chapel Hill in 1917 and from the law school of Harvard University, Cambridge, Mass., in 1922; during the First World War served in France with the First Division 1917–1919; awarded the French Fourragère, the Purple Heart with Oak Leaf Cluster, the Silver Star, and the Distinguished Service Cross; was admitted to the bar in 1919 and commenced practice in Morganton, N. C., in 1922; member of the North Carolina General Assemblies of 1923, 1925, and 1931; member of the North Carolina State Democratic executive committee 1930–1937; judge of the Burke County Criminal Court 1935–1937; judge of the North Carolina Superior Court 1937–1943; member of the North Carolina State Board of Law Examiners

1944–1946; trustee of the Morganton graded schools 1927–1930 and of the University of North Carolina 1932–1935 and 1945–1946; elected as a Democrat to the Seventy-ninth Congress to fill the vacancy caused by the death of his brother, Joseph W. Ervin, and served from January 22, 1946, to January 3, 1947; was not a candidate for renomination in 1946; resumed the practice of law; appointed associate justice of the North Carolina Supreme Court on February 3, 1948, for the term ending December 31, 1950; appointed and subsequently elected to the United States Senate to fill the vacancy caused by the death of Clyde R. Hoey and served from June 5, 1954, to January 3, 1957; reelected in 1956 for the term ending January 3, 1963.

ESCH, John Jacob, a Representative from Wisconsin; born near Norwalk, Monroe County, Wis., March 20, 1861; moved with his parents to Milwaukee in 1865 and thence to Sparta, Wis., in 1871; attended the public schools; was graduated from the University of Wisconsin at Madison in 1882 and from its law department in 1887; was admitted to the bar in 1887 and commenced practice at La Crosse, Wis.; assistant principal of Sparta High School 1883–1886; city treasurer of Sparta in 1885; organized the Sparta Rifles (afterward known as Company I, Third Regiment, Wisconsin National Guard) in 1883 and was commissioned captain, retaining the office until 1887; also assisted in the organization of Company M of the same regiment, serving as first lieutenant and afterward as captain; was commissioned acting judge advocate general with the rank of colonel by Gov. W. H. Upham in January 1894 and held the position for two years; delegate to the Republican State conventions in 1894 and 1896; elected as a Republican to the Fifty-sixth and to the ten succeeding Congresses (March 4, 1899–March 3, 1921); unsuccessful candidate for renomination in 1920; appointed as a member of the Interstate Commerce Commission on March 11, 1921; elected chairman on January 1, 1927, and served until May 31, 1928; resumed the practice of law in Washington, D. C., until he retired in 1938; returned to La Crosse, Wis., where he died on April 27, 1941; interment in Oak Grove Cemetery.

ESLICK, Edward Everett (husband of Willa McCord Eslick), a Representative from Tennessee; born near Pulaski, Giles County, Tenn., April 19, 1872; attended the public schools and Bethel College, Russellville, Ky.; studied law; was admitted to the bar in 1893 and commenced practice in Pulaski; also engaged in banking and agricultural pursuits; presidential elector on the Democratic tickets of Bryan and Sewall in 1896, of Bryan and Stevenson in 1900, and of Parker and Davis in 1904; served as Government appeal agent for Giles County during the First World War; elected as a Democrat to the Sixty-ninth and to the three succeeding Congresses and served from March 4, 1925, until his death in the Capitol, at Washington, D. C., on June 14, 1932, while addressing the House of Representatives; interment in Maplewood Cemetery, Pulaski, Tenn.

ESLICK, Willa McCord Blake (wife of Edward Everett Eslick), a Representative from Tennessee; born in Fayetteville, Lincoln County, Tenn., September 8, 1878; attended private schools, Dick White College and Milton College, Fayetteville, Tenn., Winthrop Model School and Peabody College, Nashville, Tenn., and Metropolitan College of Music and Synthetic School of Music, New York City, N. Y.; during the First World War served as chairman of the Giles County Council of National Defense; member of the State Democratic committee; elected as a Democrat to the Seventy-second Congress to fill the vacancy caused by the death of her husband, Edward E. Eslick, and served from August 4, 1932, to March 3, 1933; was not eligible for reelection to the Seventy-third Congress, not having qualified for nomination as required by the State law; died in Pulaski, Tenn., February 18, 1961; interment in Maplewood Cemetery.

ESSEN, Frederick, a Representative from Missouri; born near Pond, St. Louis County, Mo., April 22, 1863; attended the public schools; engaged in agricultural pursuits; recorder of deeds of St. Louis County 1894–1902; engaged in newspaper business at Clayton, Mo., becoming the owner of two papers which he combined under the name of the Watchman-Advocate; delegate to the Republican National Conventions at Chicago in 1904, 1908, and 1912; member of the board of education of Clayton and served as president 1909–1919; elected as a Republican to the Sixty-fifth Congress to fill the vacancy caused by the death of Jacob E. Meeker and served from November 5, 1918, until March 3, 1919; was not a candidate for renomination in 1918; resumed newspaper activities; also interested in banking; died in Creve Coeur, Mo., August 18, 1946; interment in Bethel Cemetery, Pond, Mo.

ESTABROOK, Experience, a Delegate from the Territory of Nebraska; born in Lebanon, N. H., April 30, 1813; moved with his parents to Clarence, Erie County, N. Y., in 1822; attended the public schools and Dickinson College, Carlisle, Pa.; was graduated from the Chambersburg (Pa.) Law School; was admitted to the bar in Brooklyn, N. Y., in 1839; worked as a clerk at the navy yard in Brooklyn and later commenced the practice of law in Buffalo; moved to Geneva, Wis., in 1840 and continued the practice of law; delegate to the second State constitutional convention in 1848; member of the State house of representatives in 1851; attorney general of Wisconsin in 1852 and 1853; appointed by President Pierce attorney general of the Territory of Nebraska and served from 1855 to 1859; presented credentials as a Delegate-elect to the Thirty-sixth Congress and served from March 4, 1859, to May 18, 1860, when he was succeeded by Samuel G. Daily, who contested his election; appointed by the Governor to codify the Nebraska State laws in 1866; prosecuting attorney for Douglas County in 1867 and 1868; member of the State constitutional convention in 1871; died in Omaha, Nebr., March 26, 1894; interment in Forest Lawn Cemetery.

ESTEP, Harry Allison, a Representative from Pennsylvania; born in Pittsburgh, Pa., February 1, 1884; attended the public schools and the high school in Marion, Ind., and Purdue University, Lafayette, Ind.; was graduated from the law department of the University of Pittsburgh, Pittsburgh, Pa., in 1913; was admitted to the bar in 1914 and commenced practice in Pittsburgh, Pa.; assistant district attorney of Allegheny County, Pa., 1917–1927, serving the last five years as first assistant district attorney; elected as a Republican to the Seventieth, Seventy-first, and Seventy-second Congresses (March 4, 1927–March 3, 1933); unsuccessful candidate for reelection in 1932 to the Seventy-third Congress; resumed the practice of law and is a resident of Pittsburgh, Pa.

ESTERLY, Charles Joseph, a Representative from Pennsylvania; born in Reading, Pa., February 8, 1888; attended the public schools; employed with an electric company until 1916 and later in the sales department of a knitting mill; also engaged in the breeding of Ayrshire cattle and Berkshire hogs; served as president and director of a water company, and as a director of a knitting mill and bottle-stopper company; during the First World War served as chairman of the Red Cross roll calls in Reading and Berks Counties; member of the board of school directors of Wyomissing, Pa., 1914–1920; committeeman of Wyomissing Borough 1917–1921; delegate to the Republican

National Convention at Chicago in 1920; member of the Republican State committee 1922–1924; elected as a Republican to the Sixty-ninth Congress (March 4, 1925–March 3, 1927); declined to be a candidate for renomination in 1926; again elected to the Seventy-first Congress (March 4, 1929–March 3, 1931); was not a candidate for renomination in 1930; resumed former business interests; died in Wernersville, Pa., September 3, 1940; interment in Charles Evans Cemetery, Reading, Pa.

ESTIL, Benjamin, a Representative from Virginia; born in Hansonville (now Russell County), Va., March 13, 1780; received an academic education, and attended Washington Academy (now Washington and Lee University), Lexington, Va.; studied law; was admitted to the bar and commenced practice in Abingdon, Va.; prosecuting attorney for Washington County; member of the State house of delegates 1814–1817; elected to the Nineteenth Congress (March 4, 1825–March 3, 1827); judge of the fifteenth judicial circuit from 1831 until 1852, when he resigned; retired to a farm in Oldham County, Ky., where he died July 14, 1853.

ESTOPINAL, Albert, a Representative from Louisiana; born in St. Bernard Parish, La., January 30, 1845; attended the public and private schools; left school in January 1862 to enlist in the Confederate Army and served in Company G, Twenty-eighth Regiment, Louisiana Infantry, being several times in charge of the guard to conduct Federal prisoners to Richmond; made sergeant of Company G, Twenty-second Louisiana Heavy Artillery, and served throughout the Civil War; engaged in the commission business at New Orleans for several years but most of his life was spent at his home, "Kenilworth Plantation," near New Orleans; sheriff of St. Bernard Parish 1872–1876; member of the State house of representatives 1876–1880; member of the constitutional conventions in 1879 and 1898; served in the State senate 1880–1900; Lieutenant Governor 1900–1904; chairman of the Democratic State central committee in 1908; elected as a Democrat to the Sixtieth Congress to fill the vacancy caused by the death of Adolph Meyers; reelected to the Sixty-first and to the five succeeding Congresses and served from November 3, 1908, until his death in New Orleans, La., April 28, 1919; interment in St. Louis Cemetery No. 3, New Orleans, La.

ESTY, Constantine Canaris, a Representative from Massachusetts; born in Framingham, Middlesex County, Mass., December 26, 1824; attended the local academies of Framingham and Leicester; was graduated from Yale College in 1845; studied law; was admitted to the bar and commenced practice in Framingham, Mass., in 1847; served in the State senate in 1857 and 1858; member of the State house of representatives in 1867; appointed assessor of internal revenue by President Lincoln in 1862 and served until he was removed for political reasons by President Johnson in 1866; reappointed by him in 1867; resigned in 1872; elected as a Republican to the Forty-second Congress to fill the vacancy caused by the resignation of George M. Brooks and served from December 2, 1872, to March 3, 1873; was not a candidate for renomination in 1872; continued the practice of his profession in Framingham, Mass., until his death there December 27, 1912; interment in Edgell Grove Cemetery.

ETHERIDGE, Emerson, a Representative from Tennessee; born in Currituck, N. C., September 28, 1819; moved with his parents to Tennessee in 1831; completed preparatory studies; studied law; was admitted to the bar in 1840 and commenced practice in Dresden, Tenn.; member of the State house of representatives 1845–1847; elected as a Whig to the Thirty-third and Thirty-fourth Congresses (March 4, 1853–March 3, 1857); unsuccessful candidate for reelection in 1856 to the Thirty-fifth Congress; elected as a Whig to the Thirty-sixth Congress (March

4, 1859–March 3, 1861); Clerk of the National House of Representatives 1861–1863; unsuccessful candidate for Governor in 1867; member of the State senate in 1869 and 1870; surveyor of customs in Memphis 1891–1894; died in Dresden, Tenn., October 21, 1902; interment in Mount Vernon Cemetery, near Sharon, Tenn.

EUSTIS, George, Jr. (brother of James Biddle Eustis), a Representative from Louisiana; born in New Orleans, La., September 28, 1828; was graduated from Jefferson College, Convent, La., and from the law department of Harvard University; was admitted to the bar and commenced practice in New Orleans; elected as the American Party candidate to the Thirty-fourth and Thirty-fifth Congresses (March 4, 1855–March 3, 1859); secretary to John Slidell and was taken prisoner with him from the British mail steamer *Trent* in 1861; secretary of the Confederate mission at Paris; remained in Paris after the close of the war; commissioned by Elihu B. Washburne, United States Minister at Paris, to negotiate a postal treaty with the French Government; died in Cannes, France, March 15, 1872; interment in Oak Hill Cemetery, Washington, D. C.

EUSTIS, James Biddle (brother of George Eustis, Jr.), a Senator from Louisiana; born in New Orleans, La., August 27, 1834; pursued classical studies; attended the Harvard Law School in 1853 and 1854; was admitted to the bar in 1856 and commenced practice in New Orleans; served as judge advocate during the Civil War in the Confederate Army on the staffs of General Magruder and Gen. Joseph E. Johnston; resumed the practice of law in New Orleans; elected a member of the State house of representatives prior to the reconstruction acts; one of the committee sent to Washington to confer with President Johnson on Louisiana affairs; member of the State house of representatives in 1872; served in the State senate 1874–1878; elected as a Democrat to the United States Senate to fill the vacancy in the term commencing March 4, 1873, caused by the action of the Senate in declining to seat certain claimants and served from January 12, 1876, to March 3, 1879; unsuccessful candidate for reelection; professor of civil law in the University of Louisiana 1877–1884; again elected to the United States Senate and served from March 4, 1885, to March 3, 1891; was not a candidate for reelection; practiced law in Washington, D. C., in 1891; Ambassador Extraordinary and Plenipotentiary to France 1893–1897; settled in New York City; died in Newport, R. I., on September 9, 1899; interment in Cave Hill Cemetery, Louisville, Ky.

EUSTIS, William, a Representative from Massachusetts; born in Cambridge, Mass., June 10, 1753; attended the Boston public schools, and was graduated from Harvard College in 1772; studied medicine and served in the Revolutionary Army as surgeon; resumed practice in Boston; was a surgeon in the expedition sent to suppress Shays' Rebellion in 1786 and 1787; member of the State house of representatives 1788–1794; elected as a Democrat to the Seventh and Eighth Congresses (March 4, 1801–March 3, 1805); unsuccessful candidate for reelection in 1804 to the Ninth Congress; one of the managers appointed by the House of Representatives in 1804 to conduct the impeachment proceedings against John Pickering, judge of the United States District Court for New Hampshire; appointed Secretary of War in the Cabinet of President Madison and served from March 7, 1809, to January 19, 1813; appointed Envoy Extraordinary and Minister Plenipotentiary to the Netherlands and served from December 19, 1814, to May 5, 1818; elected to the Sixteenth Congress to fill the vacancy caused by the resignation of Edward Dowse; reelected to the Seventeenth Congress and served from August 21, 1820, to March 3, 1823; did not seek renomination, having become a gubernatorial candidate; elected Governor of Massachusetts and served from May 31, 1823, until his death in Boston, Mass., February 6, 1825; interment in the Old Burying Ground, Lexington, Mass.

EVANS, Alexander, a Representative from Maryland; born in Elkton, Cecil County, Md., September 13, 1818; received a public-school education; was a civil engineer's assistant; attended the local academy at Elkton; studied law; was admitted to the bar in 1845 and commenced practice in his native city; elected as a Whig to the Thirtieth, Thirty-first, and Thirty-second Congresses (March 4, 1847–March 3, 1853); engaged in the practice of his profession until his death in Elkton, Md., December 5, 1888; interment in Elkton Presbyterian Cemetery.

EVANS, Alvin, a Representative from Pennsylvania; born in Ebensburg, Cambria County, Pa., October 4, 1845; attended the public schools and the Iron City Business College, Pittsburgh, Pa.; engaged in lumbering; during the Civil War served in a volunteer company organized to repel the expected invasion of Pennsylvania by the Confederates under General Lee; studied law; was admitted to the bar in 1873 and commenced practice in Ebensburg, Pa.; later practiced in the superior and supreme courts of the State and in the Federal courts; served one term as burgess of Ebensburg Borough; solicitor for the Pennsylvania Railroad in Cambria County for several years; one of the incorporators and president of the board of directors of the First National Bank of Ebensburg; for a number of years served on the school board and in the common council of his native town; elected as a Republican to the Fifty-seventh and Fifty-eighth Congresses (March 4, 1901–March 3, 1905); declined to be a candidate for renomination in 1904; resumed the practice of his profession; died in Ebensburg, Pa., June 19, 1906; interment in Lloyd Cemetery.

EVANS, Charles Robley, a Representative from Nevada; born in Breckenridge, Sangamon County, Ill., August 9, 1866; attended the common schools; engaged in mining in Manhattan, Nev., in 1905; moved to Goldfield, Esmeralda County, Nev., in 1908 and continued mining operations; delegate to the Democratic National Convention at Denver in 1908; elected as a Democrat to the Sixty-sixth Congress (March 4, 1919–March 3, 1921); unsuccessful candidate for reelection in 1920 to the Sixty-seventh Congress; guide at the United States Capitol from 1934 until his retirement in 1948; died in Kearney, Nebr., November 30, 1954; interment in Waco Cemetery, Waco, Nebr.

EVANS, David Ellicott, a Representative from New York; born in Ellicotts Upper Mills, Md., March 19, 1788; attended the common schools; moved to New York in 1803 and settled in Batavia; employed as a clerk and afterward as an accounting clerk with the Holland Land Co.; member of the State senate 1819–1822; member of the council of appointment in 1820 and 1821; elected as a Democrat to the Twentieth Congress and served from March 4, 1827, until his resignation May 2, 1827, before the assembling of Congress; appointed resident agent of the Holland Land Co., in 1827 and served until his resignation in 1837; also engaged in banking; delegate to the convention held at Albany, N. Y., in 1827 to advocate a protective tariff; retired from active business pursuits in 1837 to devote his attention to his extensive land interests; died in Batavia, Genesee County, N. Y., May 17, 1850; interment in Batavia Cemetery.

EVANS, David Reid, a Representative from South Carolina; born in Westminster, England, February 20, 1769; immigrated to the United States in 1784 with his father, who settled in

South Carolina; attended Mount Zion College; studied law; was admitted to the bar in 1796 and commenced practice in Winnsboro; member of the State house of representatives 1800–1804; solicitor of the middle judicial circuit 1804–1811; elected as a Democrat to the Thirteenth Congress (March 4, 1813–March 3, 1815); declined to be a candidate for reelection and returned to his plantation; member of the State senate 1818–1826; first president of the Fairfield Bible Society; died in Winnsboro, Fairfield County, S. C., March 8, 1843; interment in a plot in the rear of a residence on North Main Street, formerly occupied by Mr. Harvey Flenniken.

EVANS, George, a Representative and a Senator from Maine; born in Hallowell, Maine, January 12, 1797; was graduated from Bowdoin College, Brunswick, Maine, in 1815; studied law; was admitted to the bar and practiced in Gardiner, Maine, 1818–1847; member of the State house of representatives, and served as speaker in 1829; elected to the Twenty-first Congress to fill the vacancy caused by the resignation of Peleg Sprague; reelected to the Twenty-second and five succeeding Congresses and served from July 20, 1829, until his resignation, effective March 3, 1841, at the close of the Twenty-sixth Congress; elected as a Whig to the United States Senate and served from March 4, 1841, until March 3, 1847; unsuccessful candidate for reelection in 1846; resumed the practice of law in Portland, Maine; member of the commission to ascertain the claims against Mexico in 1849 and 1850; elected attorney general of Maine in 1850, 1854, and 1856; died in Portland, Cumberland County, Maine, April 6, 1867; interment in the Evans tomb, Oak Grove Cemetery, Gardiner, Maine.

EVANS, Henry Clay, a Representative from Tennessee; born in Juniata County, Pa., June 18, 1843; moved to Wisconsin in 1844, with his parents, who settled in Platteville, Grant County; attended the common schools and a business school in Madison; was graduated from a business training school at Chicago in 1861; during the Civil War enlisted on May 6, 1864, as a corporal in Company A, Forty-first Regiment, Wisconsin Volunteer Infantry; appointed quartermaster sergeant June 8, 1864; honorably discharged September 24, 1864; settled in Chattanooga, Tenn., in 1870; engaged in the manufacture of freight cars at Chattanooga, Tenn.; elected mayor in 1881, serving two terms; organized the public-school system of Chattanooga and served as first school commissioner; elected as a Republican to the Fifty-first Congress (March 4, 1889–March 3, 1891); unsuccessful candidate for reelection in 1890 to the Fifty-second Congress; First Assistant Postmaster General 1891–1893; elected Governor of Tennessee in 1894 on the face of the returns, but a legislative recount rejected certain votes and declared his Democratic opponent, Peter Turney, elected; appointed Commissioner of Pensions April 1, 1897, and served until May 13, 1902, when he resigned to enter the diplomatic service; appointed United States consul general to London, England, May 9, 1902, retiring in 1905; chosen commissioner of health and education of Chattanooga in 1911; delegate to several Republican National Conventions from 1892 to 1912; died in Chattanooga, Tenn., December 12, 1921; interment in Forest Hill Cemetery, St. Elmo, Chattanooga, Tenn.

EVANS, Hiram Kinsman, a Representative from Iowa; born in Walnut Township, Wayne County, Iowa, March 17, 1863; attended the country schools and Seymour and Allerton (Iowa) High Schools; was graduated from the law department of the University of Iowa at Iowa City in 1886; was admitted to the bar in 1886 and commenced practice in Holdrege, Nebr.; moved to Seymour, Iowa, in 1887, and to Corydon, Iowa, in 1889 and continued the practice of law; prosecuting attorney for Wayne County 1891–1895; member of the State house of representatives in 1896 and 1897; member of the board of regents of the University of Iowa 1897–1904; mayor of Corydon 1901–1903; judge of the third judicial district of Iowa from 1904 until 1923, when he resigned; elected as a Republican to the Sixty-eighth Congress to fill the vacancy caused by the resignation of Horace M. Towner and served from June 4, 1923, to March 3, 1925; declined to be a candidate for renomination in 1924; resumed the practice of law in Corydon, Iowa; appointed by the Governor of Iowa as a member of the State board of parole on July 1, 1927, and served to July 1, 1933; died in Corydon, Iowa, July 9, 1941; interment in Corydon Cemetery.

EVANS, Isaac Newton, a Representative from Pennsylvania; born near Westchester, East Nantmeal Township, Chester County, Pa., July 29, 1827; attended the common schools; was graduated from the medical department of Bowdoin College, Brunswick, Maine, in 1851 and from Jefferson Medical College, Philadelphia, in 1852; commenced the practice of medicine in Johnsville, Bucks County, Pa., in 1852; moved to Hatboro, Montgomery County, Pa., in 1856 and continued the practice of medicine; president of the Hatboro National Bank; elected as a Republican to the Forty-fifth Congress (March 4, 1877–March 3, 1879); was not a candidate for renomination; elected to the Forty-eighth and Forty-ninth Congresses (March 4, 1883–March 3, 1887); declined to be a candidate for renomination; engaged in the practice of medicine, the real-estate business, and banking; died in Hatboro, Pa., December 3, 1901; interment in Friends Cemetery, Horsham, Montgomery County, Pa.

EVANS, James La Fayette, a Representative from Indiana; born in Clayville, Harrison County, Ky., March 27, 1825; attended the public schools; moved to Indiana, with his parents, who settled in Hancock County in 1837; moved to Marion, Ind., in 1845 and engaged in mercantile pursuits; moved to Hamilton County, Ind.; settled in Noblesville in 1850 and continued mercantile pursuits; also engaged in the grain-elevator business and in the pork-packing business; elected as a Republican to the Forty-fourth and Forty-fifth Congresses (March 4, 1875–March 3, 1879); was not a candidate for renomination in 1878; resumed the grain-elevator business; died in Noblesville, Ind., May 28, 1903; interment in Crownland Cemetery.

EVANS, John, a Delegate from Delaware; member of the Delaware Assembly in 1774, 1775, and 1776; deputy to the convention to formulate the State constitution in 1776; elected as a Delegate to the Continental Congress on November 10, 1776, but declined to serve on account of ill health; his credentials were presented December 2, 1776, and he was permitted to withdraw April 4, 1777, without having been present; justice of the State supreme court in 1777.

EVANS, John Morgan, a Representative from Montana; born in Sedalia, Pettis County, Mo., January 7, 1863; attended the common schools, the United States Military Academy, West Point, N. Y., in 1884 and 1885, and was graduated from the University of Missouri at Columbia in 1887; studied law; was admitted to the bar in 1888 and commenced practice in Missoula, Mont.; judge of the police court 1889–1894; register of the United States land office 1894–1898; mayor of Missoula under the first city commission government established in the State in 1911 and 1912; elected as a Democrat to the Sixty-third and to the three succeeding Congresses (March 4, 1913–March 3, 1921); unsuccessful candidate for reelection in 1920 to the Sixty-seventh Congress; resumed the practice of law in Missoula, Mont.; elected to the Sixty-eighth and to the four succeeding Congresses (March 4, 1923–March 3, 1933); unsuccessful candidate for renomination in 1932; alternate delegate to the Democratic National Convention at Chicago in 1932; retired from active practice and resided in Washington, D. C., until his death March 12, 1946; interment in Missoula Cemetery, Missoula, Mont.

EVANS, Joshua, Jr., a Representative from Pennsylvania; born in Paoli, Chester County, Pa., January 20, 1777; attended the common schools; hotel keeper and also engaged in agricultural pursuits; member of the State house of representatives in 1820; appointed the first postmaster of Paoli December 9, 1826, and served until February 13, 1830; president of the Tredyffrin Township school board 1836–1846; brigadier general of State militia; elected as a Democrat to the Twenty-first and Twenty-second Congresses (March 4, 1829–March 3, 1833); was not a candidate for renomination in 1832; resumed his former business pursuits; died in Paoli, Pa., October 2, 1846; interment in the cemetery of the Great Valley Baptist Church, New Centerville, Pa.

EVANS, Josiah James, a Senator from South Carolina; born in Marlboro District, S. C., November 27, 1786; was graduated from South Carolina College at Columbia in 1808; studied law; was admitted to the bar and began practice in Marlboro District in 1811; member of the State house of representatives in 1812 and 1813; moved to Darlington District in 1816; again a member of the State house of representatives; State solicitor for the northern district of South Carolina 1816–1829; judge of the circuit court 1829–1835; judge of the State supreme court 1829–1852; elected as a State Rights Democrat to the United States Senate and served from March 4, 1853, until his death in Washington, D. C., May 6, 1858; interment in a private cemetery within the grounds of his ancestral home at Society Hill, Darlington County, S. C.

EVANS, Lemuel Dale, a Representative from Texas; born in Tennessee January 8, 1810; studied law and was admitted to the bar; moved to Marshall, Tex., in 1843 and engaged in the practice of law; member of the State convention that annexed the State of Texas to the Union in 1845; elected as the candidate of the American Party to the Thirty-fourth Congress (March 4, 1855–March 3, 1857); unsuccessful candidate for reelection in 1856 to the Thirty-fifth Congress; collector of internal revenue in 1867; member of the reconstruction convention in 1868; chief justice of the supreme court in 1870 and 1871; associate justice and presiding judge from 1872 to 1873, when he resigned; United States marshal for the eastern judicial district of Texas in 1875; died in Washington, D. C., on July 1, 1877; interment in the Congressional Cemetery.

EVANS, Lynden, a Representative from Illinois; born in La Salle, La Salle County, Ill., June 28, 1858; attended the public schools and was graduated from Knox College, Galesburg, Ill., in 1882; taught in the schools of La Salle and Evanston, Ill.; studied law; was admitted to the bar in 1885 and commenced practice at Chicago, Ill.; member of the Illinois, Chicago, and American Bar Associations; author of Illinois Citations and Overruled Cases published in 1900; lecturer on corporation law in the John Marshall Law School in 1907 and 1908; elected as a Democrat to the Sixty-second Congress (March 4, 1911–March 3, 1913); unsuccessful candidate for reelection in 1912 to the Sixty-third Congress; resumed the practice of law in Chicago, Ill., until his death there on May 6, 1926; interment in Graceland Cemetery.

EVANS, Marcellus Hugh, a Representative from New York; born in Brooklyn, N. Y., September 22, 1884; attended St. John the Baptist School and St. James Academy, Brooklyn, N. Y.; was graduated from the law department of Fordham University in 1910; was admitted to the bar in 1910 and commenced practice in Brooklyn; member of the State assembly 1922–1926; served in the State senate 1927–1934; elected as a Democrat to the Seventy-fourth, Seventy-fifth, and Seventy-sixth Congresses (January 3, 1935–January 3, 1941); unsuccessful candidate in 1940 for renomination as a Democrat and for election as a Republican to the Seventy-seventh Congress; resumed the practice of law; died in Brooklyn, N. Y., November 21, 1953; interment in Calvary Cemetery, Long Island City, N. Y.

EVANS, Nathan, a Representative from Ohio; born in Belmont County, Ohio, June 24, 1804; attended a country school in winter and worked on his father's farm in summer; county clerk of Belmont County in 1827 and 1828; taught school; studied law; was admitted to the bar in 1831 and commenced practice in Hillsboro, Ohio; moved to Cambridge, Ohio, in 1832; mayor of Cambridge in 1841; prosecuting attorney of Guernsey County 1842–1846; elected as a Whig to the Thirtieth and Thirty-first Congresses (March 4, 1847–March 3, 1851); was not a candidate for renomination in 1850; resumed the practice of law in Cambridge; again mayor of Cambridge 1855–1857; judge of the court of common pleas 1859–1864; resumed the practice of law; died in Cambridge, Ohio, September 27, 1879; interment in South Cemetery.

EVANS, Robert Emory, a Representative from Nebraska; born in Coalmont, Huntingdon County, Pa., July 15, 1856; attended the public schools, the State normal school at Millersville, Pa., and the Indiana (Pa.) Normal School; employed in Colorado as a machinist 1877–1883; was graduated from the law department of the University of Michigan at Ann Arbor in 1886; was admitted to the bar and practiced; moved to Dakota City, Nebr., in 1887; superintendent of Winnebago Industrial School 1889–1891; prosecuting attorney of Dakota County in 1895; resigned to become judge of the eighth judicial district, in which capacity he served from 1895 to 1899; delegate to the Republican National Convention at Chicago in 1912; president of the Nebraska State Bar Association in 1919; elected as a Republican to the Sixty-sixth and Sixty-seventh Congresses (March 4, 1919–March 3, 1923); unsuccessful candidate for reelection in 1922 to the Sixty-eighth Congress; resumed the practice of law in Dakota City, Nebr.; elected judge of the supreme court from the third district of Nebraska in 1924; moved to Lincoln, Nebr., where he died July 8, 1925; interment in Graceland Park Cemetery, Sioux City, Iowa.

EVANS, Thomas, a Representative from Virginia; born in Accomac County, Va.; attended the public schools and William and Mary College at Williamsburg; studied law and was admitted to the bar; member of the State house of delegates in 1780, 1781, and 1794–1796; elected to the Fifth and Sixth Congresses (March 4, 1797–March 3, 1801); one of the managers appointed by the House of Representatives in 1798 to conduct the impeachment proceedings against William Blount, a Senator from Tennessee; moved to Wheeling, Va. (now West Virginia), in 1802; member of the State house of representatives in 1805 and 1806.

EVANS, Walter (nephew of Burwell Clark Ritter), a Representative from Kentucky; born near Glasgow, Barren County, Ky., September 18, 1842; attended the public schools near Harrodsburg, Ky.; moved to Hopkinsville, Christian County; deputy county clerk in 1859; served as a captain in the Union Army 1861–1863; served as deputy and later as chief clerk of the circuit court; studied law; was admitted to the bar in 1864 and commenced practice in Hopkinsville; delegate to the Republican National Conventions in 1868, 1872, 1880, and 1884; elected to the State house of representatives in 1871 and to the State senate in 1873; moved to Louisville, Ky., in 1874 and continued the practice of law; unsuccessful candidate for election in 1876 to the Forty-fifth Congress; Republican nominee for Governor in 1879; appointed by President Arthur as Commissioner of Internal Revenue May 21, 1883, and served until April 20, 1885, when he returned to Louisville and resumed the practice of law; elected as a Republican to the Fifty-fourth and Fifty-fifth Congresses (March 4, 1895–March 3, 1899); unsuccessful candidate for reelection in 1898 to the Fifty-sixth Congress; appointed by President McKinley judge of the District Court of the United States for the District of Kentucky March 4, 1899, and served until his death at his home in Louisville, Ky., December 30, 1923; interment in Cave Hill Cemetery.

EVANS, William Elmer, a Representative from California; born near London, Laurel County, Ky., December 14, 1877; attended the public schools and Sue Bennett Memorial College, London, Ky.; studied law; was admitted to the bar in 1902 and commenced practice in London, Ky.; moved to Glendale, Calif., in 1910 and engaged in the practice of law and in banking; city attorney of Glendale, Calif., 1911–1921; delegate to the Republican National Convention at Cleveland in 1924; elected as a Republican to the Seventieth and to the three succeeding Congresses (March 4, 1927–January 3, 1935); unsuccessful candidate for reelection 1934 to the Seventy-fourth Congress; resumed the practice of law, real-estate development, and ranching until his death in Los Angeles, Calif., November 12, 1959; interment in Forest Lawn Cemetery, Glendale, Calif.

EVARTS, William Maxwell (grandson of Roger Sherman), a Senator from New York; born in Boston, Mass., February 6, 1818; attended the Boston Latin School, and was graduated from Yale College in 1837; was one of the four founders of the Yale Literary Magazine in 1836; studied for a year in Harvard Law School; was admitted to the bar in New York City in 1841 and practiced; assistant United States district attorney 1849–1853; chairman of the New York delegation to the Republican National Convention at Chicago in 1860; unsuccessful Republican candidate for the United States Senate in 1861; member of the State constitutional convention in 1867 and 1868; Attorney General of the United States in the Cabinet of President Grant from July 15, 1868, to March 3, 1869; chief counsel for President Johnson in the impeachment proceedings in 1868; counsel for the United States before the tribunal of arbitration on the *Alabama* claims at Geneva, Switzerland, in 1872; counsel for President Hayes, in behalf of the Republican Party, before the Electoral Commission; Secretary of State of the United States in the Cabinet of President Hayes from March 12, 1877, to March 3, 1881; delegate to the International Monetary Conference at Paris in 1881; elected as a Republican to the United States Senate and served from March 4, 1885, to March 3, 1891; voluntarily retired from public life due to ill health; died in New York City February 28, 1901; interment in Ascutney Cemetery, Windsor, Vt.

EVELEIGH, Nicholas, a Delegate from South Carolina; born in Charleston, S. C., about 1748; moved with his parents to Bristol, England, about 1755; was educated in England; returned to Charleston, S. C., in 1774; during the Revolutionary War was appointed captain in the Second South Carolina Regiment (Continentals) June 17, 1775; engaged in the battle with the British fleet and forces at Fort Moultrie on June 28, 1776; was promoted to colonel and appointed deputy adjutant general for South Carolina and Georgia on April 3, 1778; served in the Georgia campaign at Fort Tonyn in July 1778; resigned August 24, 1778; engaged in agricultural pursuits; member of the State house of representatives in 1781; Member of the Continental Congress in 1781 and 1782; member of the State legislative council in 1783;

appointed First Comptroller of the United States Treasury on September 11, 1789, and served until his death in Philadelphia, Pa., April 16, 1791; interment probably in Philadelphia.

EVERETT, Edward (father of William Everett), a Representative and a Senator from Massachusetts; born in Dorchester, Mass., April 11, 1794; was graduated from Harvard University in 1811; tutor in that university 1812–1814; studied theology, and was ordained pastor of the Brattle Street Unitarian Church, Boston, February 9, 1814; professor of Greek literature in Harvard University 1815–1820; Eliot professor of Greek literature 1820–1826; overseer of Harvard University 1827–1847, 1849–1854, and 1862–1865; elected as a National-Republican to the Nineteenth and to the four succeeding Congresses (March 4, 1825–March 3, 1835); declined to be a candidate for renomination in 1834; Governor of Massachusetts 1836–1840; appointed United States Envoy Extraordinary and Minister Plenipotentiary to Great Britain and served from September 13, 1841, to August 8, 1845; declined a diplomatic commission to China in 1843; elected president of Harvard University and served from 1846 to 1849; appointed Secretary of State in the Cabinet of President Fillmore to fill the vacancy caused by the death of Daniel Webster and served from November 6, 1852, to March 3, 1853; elected to the United States Senate and served from March 4, 1853, until his resignation, effective June 1, 1854; unsuccessful candidate for Vice President in 1860 on the Constitutional-Union ticket with John Bell of Tennessee; delivered the address of dedication of the national cemetery at Gettysburg, Pa., November 19, 1863; presidential elector on the Republican ticket of Lincoln and Johnson in 1864; died in Boston, Mass., January 15, 1865; interment in Mount Auburn Cemetery, Cambridge, Mass.

EVERETT, Horace, a Representative from Vermont; born in Foxboro, Mass., July 17, 1779; was graduated from Brown University, Providence, R. I., in 1797; studied law; was admitted to the bar in 1801 and commenced practice in Windsor, Vt.; prosecuting attorney for Windsor County 1813–1818; member of the State house of representatives in 1819, 1820, 1822, 1824, and again in 1834; delegate to the State constitutional convention in 1828; elected as a Whig to the Twenty-first and to the six succeeding Congresses (March 4, 1829–March 3, 1843); died in Windsor, Vt., January 30, 1851; interment in Old South Burying Ground.

EVERETT, Robert Ashton, a Representative from Tennessee; born on a farm near Union City, Obion County, Tenn., February 24, 1915; attended the public schools in Obion County; was graduated from Union City High School in 1932 and from Murray (Ky.) State College in 1936; elected a member of Obion County Court in 1936 and in 1938 was elected circuit court clerk of Obion County; during World War II served in the United States Army 1942–1945; administrative assistant to Senator Tom Stewart 1945–1949; administrative assistant to Gov. Gordon Browning 1950–1952; executive secretary of Tennessee County Services Association 1954–1958; elected as a Democrat to the Eighty-fifth Congress to fill the vacancy caused by the death of Jere Cooper; reelected to the Eighty-sixth Congress and served from February 1, 1958, to January 3, 1961. *Reelected to the Eighty-seventh Congress.*

EVERETT, Robert William, a Representative from Georgia; born near Hayneville, Houston County, Ga., March 3, 1839; attended the village schools and Hayneville Academy; was graduated from Mercer University, Macon, Ga., in 1859; taught school in Polk and Houston Counties for two years; settled in Polk County, Ga., in 1860; entered the Confederate Army as a sergeant in Captain Gartrell's company, Gen. N. B. Forrest's escort squadron, and served until the close of the Civil War;

again engaged in teaching school in Houston County and also in Cedartown, Ga., until 1872, when he abandoned the profession for agricultural pursuits; commissioner of roads and revenue of Polk County 1875–1880; member of the Board of Education of Polk County 1880–1891 and served as president of the board 1882–1891; member of the State house of representatives 1882–1885; elected as a Democrat to the Fifty-second Congress (March 4, 1891–March 3, 1893); was not a candidate for renomination in 1892; resumed agricultural pursuits; again a member of the State house of representatives in 1898 and 1899; discontinued active pursuits and lived in retirement until his death in Rockmart, Polk County, Ga., on February 27, 1915; interment in Cedartown Cemetery, Cedartown, Ga.

EVERETT, William (son of Edward Everett), a Representative from Massachusetts; born in Watertown, Middlesex County, Mass., October 10, 1839; attended the public schools of Cambridge and Boston; was graduated from Harvard University in 1859, from Trinity College, Cambridge, England, in 1863, and from the law department of Harvard University in 1865; was admitted to the bar in 1866; studied for the ministry, and was licensed to preach in 1872 by the Suffolk Association of Unitarian Ministers; tutor in Harvard University 1870–1873; assistant professor of Latin 1873–1877; master of Adams Academy, Quincy, Mass., 1878–1893; elected as a Democrat to the Fifty-third Congress to fill the vacancy caused by the resignation of Henry Cabot Lodge and served from April 25, 1893, to March 3, 1895; was not a candidate for renomination in 1894; unsuccessful candidate for Governor of Massachusetts in 1897; master of school at Quincy, Mass., where he died February 16, 1910; interment in Mount Auburn Cemetery, Cambridge, Mass.

EVERHART, James Bowen (son of William Everhart), a Representative from Pennsylvania; born in the Boot, near West Chester, West Whiteland Township, Chester County, Pa., July 26, 1821; attended Bolmar's Academy, West Chester, Pa., and was graduated from Princeton College in 1842; studied law at Harvard University and in Philadelphia, Pa.; was admitted to the bar in 1845; went abroad and spent two years in study at the Universities of Berlin and Edinburgh; returned to West Chester, Pa., and engaged in the practice of law; during the Civil War served in Company B, Tenth Regiment, Pennsylvania Militia, in the volunteer army called by Gov. Andrew G. Curtin to repel Lee's invasion in 1862 and 1863, and was promoted to major the latter year; member of the State senate from 1876 to 1882, when he resigned, having been elected to Congress; elected as a Republican to the Forty-eighth and Forty-ninth Congresses (March 4, 1883–March 3, 1887); unsuccessful candidate for renomination in 1886; resumed the practice of law; died in West Chester, Pa., August 23, 1888; interment in Oakland Cemetery, near West Chester.

EVERHART, William (father of James Bowen Everhart), a Representative from Pennsylvania; born in Chester County, Pa., May 17, 1785; attended the common schools and became a civil engineer; served in the War of 1812 as captain of a company of riflemen; was the only passenger saved from the packet ship *Albion*, wrecked off the coast of Ireland in 1822; upon his return to Pennsylvania he platted a large addition to the city of West Chester; was elected as a Whig to the Thirty-third Congress (March 4, 1853–March 3, 1855); was not a candidate for renomination; engaged in mercantile pursuits; died in West Chester, Pa., October 30, 1868; interment in Oakland Cemetery.

EVINS, John Hamilton, a Representative from South Carolina; born in Spartanburg District, S. C., July 18, 1830; attended the common schools, and was graduated from South Carolina College at Columbia in 1853; studied law; was admitted to the bar in 1856 and commenced practice in Spartanburg, S. C.; entered the Confederate Army as a lieutenant and served until the close of the Civil War, attaining the rank of lieutenant colonel; resumed the practice of law in Spartanburg; member of the State house of representatives in 1863 and 1864; delegate to the Democratic National Convention at St. Louis in 1876; elected as a Democrat to the Forty-fifth and to the three succeeding Congresses and served from March 4, 1877, until his death in Spartanburg, S. C., October 20, 1884; interment in Magnolia Street Cemetery.

EVINS, Joseph Landon (Joe), a Representative from Tennessee; born on a farm near Liberty, DeKalb County, Tenn., October 24, 1910; attended the public schools; was graduated from Vanderbilt University, Nashville, Tenn., in 1933 and from Cumberland University School of Law, Lebanon, Tenn., in 1934; postgraduate student of law at George Washington University, Washington, D. C., 1938–1940; was admitted to the bar in 1934 and commenced practice in Smithville, Tenn.; attorney for Federal Trade Commission in Washington, D. C., 1935–1938; assistant secretary of the Federal Trade Commission 1938–1940; during World War II served in the United States Army on the staff of the Judge Advocate General, War Department, from March 1942 until discharged as a major in March 1946, with two years' service overseas in England and France; resumed the practice of law in Smithville, Tenn.; chairman of the DeKalb County Democratic Executive Committee in 1946; elected as a Democrat to the Eightieth and to the six succeeding Congresses (January 3, 1947–January 3, 1961). *Reelected to the Eighty-seventh Congress.*

EWART, Hamilton Glover, a Representative from North Carolina; born in Columbia, Richland County, S. C., October 23, 1849; attended private schools; moved to Hendersonville, Henderson County, N. C., with his parents in 1862; was graduated from the literary and law departments of the University of South Carolina at Columbia; was admitted to the bar in 1870 and commenced practice in Hendersonville, N. C.; appointed register in bankruptcy for the ninth congressional district in 1872; delegate to the Republican National Convention at Cincinnati in 1876; presidential elector on the Republican ticket of Hayes and Wheeler in 1876; elected mayor of Hendersonville in 1877; member of the State house of representatives 1887–1889, 1895–1897, and 1911–1913; elected as a Republican to the Fifty-first Congress (March 4, 1889–March 3, 1891); unsuccessful candidate for reelection in 1890 to the Fifty-second Congress and for election in 1904; resumed the practice of law in Hendersonville, N. C.; judge of the criminal court in 1895; judge of the circuit court in 1897; served as judge of the United States District Court for the Western District of North Carolina from July 16, 1898, to March 4, 1899, and April 14, 1899, to June 7, 1900; moved to Chicago, Ill., in 1916 and continued the practice of law; died in Chicago, Ill., April 28, 1918; interment in Oakdale Cemetery, Hendersonville, N. C.

EWING, Andrew (brother of Edwin Hickman Ewing), a Representative from Tennessee; born in Nashville, Tenn., June 17, 1813; completed preparatory studies, and was graduated from the University of Nashville in 1832; studied law; was admitted to the bar in 1835 and commenced practice in Nashville, Tenn.; chosen trustee of the University of Nashville in 1833, and served in that office until his death; elected as a Democrat to the Thirty-first Congress (March 4, 1849–March 3, 1851); declined to be a candidate for renomination in 1850; resumed the practice of law in Nashville, Tenn.; delegate to the Democratic National Convention at Baltimore in 1860; during the Civil War served as judge of Gen. Braxton Bragg's military court; died in Atlanta, Ga., June 16, 1864; interment in Nashville City Cemetery, Nashville, Tenn.

EWING, Edwin Hickman (brother of Andrew Ewing), a Representative from Tennessee; born in Nashville, Tenn., December 2, 1809; completed preparatory studies, and was graduated from the University of Nashville in 1827; studied law; was admitted to the bar in 1831 and commenced practice in Nashville, Tenn.; became a trustee of the University of Nashville in 1831, and served until his death; member of the State house of representatives in 1841 and 1842; elected as a Whig to the Twenty-ninth Congress (March 4, 1845–March 3, 1847); was not a candidate for renomination; resumed the practice of law in Nashville; after the Civil War was appointed president of the University of Nashville; died in Murfreesboro, Tenn., April 24, 1902; interment in Murfreesboro City Cemetery.

EWING, John, a Representative from Indiana; born in Cork, Ireland, May 19, 1789; immigrated to the United States with his parents, who settled in Baltimore, Md.; attended the public schools; moved to Vincennes, Ind., in 1813 and engaged in commercial pursuits; established the Wabash Telegraph; associate judge of the circuit court of Knox County from 1816 to 1820, when he resigned; unsuccessful candidate for the State senate in 1816 and 1821; appointed lieutenant colonel of the State militia in 1825; member of the State senate 1825–1833; elected as a Whig to the Twenty-third Congress (March 4, 1833–March 3, 1835); elected to the Twenty-fifth Congress (March 4, 1837–March 3, 1839); unsuccessful candidate for reelection in 1838 to the Twenty-sixth Congress; again a member of the State senate 1842–1844; retired from public life and active business pursuits; died in Vincennes, Ind., April 6, 1858; interment in the City Cemetery.

EWING, John Hoge, a Representative from Pennsylvania; born near Brownsville, Fayette County, Pa., October 5, 1796; attended the common schools, and was graduated from Washington (now Washington and Jefferson) College, Washington, Pa., in 1814; studied law; was admitted to the bar in 1818 and commenced practice in Washington, Pa.; engaged in agricultural pursuits; trustee of Washington College 1834–1887 and of Washington Female Seminary 1846–1887; member of the State house of representatives in 1835 and 1836; served in the State senate 1838–1842; elected as a Whig to the Twenty-ninth Congress (March 4, 1845–March 3, 1847); resumed agricultural pursuits; delegate to the Republican National Convention at Chicago in 1860; died in Washington, Pa., June 9, 1887; interment in Washington Cemetery.

EWING, Presley Underwood, a Representative from Kentucky; born in Russellville, Ky., September 1, 1822; attended the public schools; completed preparatory studies; was graduated from Centre College, Danville, Ky., in 1840 and from the law school of Transylvania University, Lexington, Ky., in 1843; studied theology at the Baptist Seminary at Newton, Mass., in 1845 and 1846; traveled in Germany for a while; returned to Kentucky and practiced law in Russellville; member of the State house of representatives in 1848 and 1849; elected as a Whig to the Thirty-second and Thirty-third Congresses and served from March 4, 1851, until his death in the town of Mammoth Cave, Ky., September 27, 1854; interment in Maple Grove Cemetery, Russellville, Ky.

EWING, Thomas, a Senator from Ohio; born near West Liberty, Ohio County, Va. (now West Virginia), December 28, 1789; moved to Ohio with his parents, who settled on a farm near the mouth of Olive Green Creek in 1792 and on Federal Creek, in Athens County, in 1797; pursued preparatory studies; was graduated from Ohio University at Athens in 1816; studied law; was admitted to the bar in 1816 and commenced practice in Lancaster, Ohio; elected as a Whig to the United States Senate and served from March 4, 1831, to March 3, 1837; unsuccessful candidate for reelection in 1836; appointed Secretary of the Treasury by President Harrison and served from March 5 to September 13, 1841; appointed Secretary of the Interior by President Taylor and served from March 8, 1849, to July 23, 1850; appointed to the United States Senate to fill the vacancy caused by the resignation of Thomas Corwin and served from July 20, 1850, to March 3, 1851; unsuccessful candidate for election to the United States Senate in 1851; resumed the practice of law in Lancaster; delegate to the peace convention held in Washington, D. C., in 1861 in an effort to devise means to prevent the impending war; delegate to the Union National Convention in 1865; appointed Secretary of War by President Johnson on February 22, 1868, but the Senate refused to confirm the appointment; advocated National Government control of the flood waters of the Mississippi River by using the Atchafalaya as waste weirs in 1870; died in Lancaster, Ohio, October 26, 1871; interment in St. Mary's Cemetery.

EWING, Thomas (son of the preceding), a Representative from Ohio; born in Lancaster, Fairfield County, Ohio, August 7, 1829; pursued preparatory studies; private secretary to President Taylor in 1849 and 1850; was graduated from Brown University, Providence, R. I., in 1854; studied law; was admitted to the bar in 1855 and commenced practice in Cincinnati, Ohio; moved to Leavenworth, Kans., in 1856; member of the Leavenworth constitutional convention of 1858; delegate to the peace convention held in Washington, D. C., in 1861 in an effort to devise means to prevent the impending war; chief justice of the supreme court of Kansas in 1861 and 1862, when he resigned; during the Civil War served in the Union Army; recruited the Eleventh Regiment, Kansas Volunteer Cavalry, and was commissioned its colonel on September 15, 1862; brigadier general of Volunteers March 13, 1863; brevetted major general of Volunteers for meritorious services at the Battle of Pilot Knob, Missouri; resigned February 23, 1865; practiced law in Washington, D. C., until 1871, when he returned to Lancaster, Ohio; member of the Ohio State constitutional convention in 1873 and 1874; elected as a Democrat to the Forty-fifth and Forty-sixth Congresses (March 4, 1877–March 3, 1881); declined to be a candidate for renomination in 1880; unsuccessful candidate for Governor of Ohio in 1879; moved to New York City in 1881, where he engaged in the practice of law until his death there on January 21, 1896; interment in Oakland Cemetery, Yonkers, N. Y.

EWING, William Lee Davidson, a Senator from Illinois; born in Paris, Ky., August 31, 1795; pursued academic studies; studied law; was admitted to the bar and commenced practice in Shawneetown, Ill.; appointed by President Monroe receiver of the land office at Vandalia in 1820; brigadier general of State militia; colonel of the "Spy Battalion" during the Black Hawk War; clerk of the State house of representatives 1826–1828; member of the State house of representatives in 1830 and served as speaker; served in the State senate 1832–1834, and was chosen president pro tempore of that body in 1832; commissioned acting Lieutenant Governor March 1, 1833, caused by the resignation of Zadoc Casey; became Governor of Illinois in November 1834 as successor to John Reynolds, who had resigned, but served only fifteen days; appointed as a Jackson Democrat to the United States Senate to fill the vacancy caused by the death of Elias K. Kane and served from December 30, 1835, to March 3, 1837; unsuccessful candidate for election in 1837; again a member of the

State house of representatives in 1838 and 1840 and at both sessions was chosen speaker over Abraham Lincoln; elected clerk of the State house of representatives in 1842; appointed auditor of public accounts in March 1843; died in Vandalia, Ill., March 25, 1846; interment in Oak Ridge Cemetery, Springfield, Ill.

F

FADDIS, Charles I., a Representative from Pennsylvania; born in Loudonville, Ashland County, Ohio, June 13, 1890; moved with his parents to Waynesburg, Greene County, Pa., in 1891; attended the public schools and Waynesburg (Pa.) College; was graduated from the agricultural department of Pennsylvania State College at State College in 1915; served as a sergeant in the Tenth Infantry, Pennsylvania National Guard, on the Mexican border in 1916; entered an officers' training camp in August 1917; commissioned captain of Infantry in November 1917; served during the First World War with the Forty-seventh Regiment, United States Infantry, and the Fourth Ammunition Train; saw service in all major offenses in France; rose to rank of lieutenant colonel of Infantry; served in the Army of Occupation in Germany; awarded the Purple Heart Medal; engaged in the general contracting business in Waynesburg, Pa., 1919–1926; broker of oil and gas properties 1926–1933; elected as a Democrat to the Seventy-third and to the four succeeding Congresses and served from March 4, 1933, until his resignation on December 4, 1942, to enter the United States Army; unsuccessful candidate for renomination in 1942; during World War II was a colonel in the United States Army, serving in northern Africa, Tunisia, Central Africa, Italy, France, and Germany; wounded in Tunisia; awarded the Purple Heart and Bronze Star; discharged on December 15, 1945; engaged in raising Hereford cattle, producing oil and gas, and operating coal mines; is a resident of Waynesburg, Pa.

FAIR, James Graham, a Senator from Nevada; born near Belfast, County Tyrone, Ireland, December 3, 1831; immigrated to the United States in 1843 with his parents, who settled in Illinois; received a thorough business training; moved to California in 1849 and engaged in mining until 1860, when he moved to Virginia City, Nev.; again engaged extensively in mining and eventually formed a partnership with John W. Mackay, J. C. Flood, and William S. O'Brien in 1867; this firm purchased control of the Bonanza properties and various other well-known mines, from which the yield of gold and silver, while under the superintendency of Mr. Fair, was estimated at about $200,000,000; also engaged in the real-estate business in San Francisco and was largely interested in various manufactures of the Pacific coast; elected as a Democrat to the United States Senate and served from March 4, 1881, to March 3, 1887; unsuccessful candidate for reelection in 1886; died in San Francisco, Calif., December 28, 1894; interment in Laurel Hill Cemetery.

FAIRBANKS, Charles Warren, a Senator from Indiana and a Vice President of the United States; born near Unionville Center, Union County, Ohio, May 11, 1852; attended the common schools, and was graduated from the Ohio Wesleyan University, Delaware, Ohio, in 1872; agent of the Associated Press in Pittsburgh, Pa., and in Cleveland, Ohio; studied law; was admitted to the bar by the supreme court of Ohio in 1874; moved to Indianapolis, Ind., the same year and commenced practice; trustee of the Ohio Wesleyan University in 1885; chairman of the Indiana Republican State conventions in 1892 and 1898; unsuccessful candidate for election to the United States Senate in 1893; delegate at large to the Republican National Conventions in 1896 and 1900; appointed a member of the United States and British Joint High Commission which met in Quebec in 1898

for the adjustment of Canadian questions; elected as a Republican to the United States Senate in 1896; reelected in 1902 and served from March 4, 1897, until his resignation March 3, 1905, having been elected Vice President of the United States; delegate to the Republican National Convention at Chicago in 1904; elected Vice President of the United States in 1904 on the Republican ticket with Theodore Roosevelt as the nominee for President and served from March 4, 1905, to March 3, 1909; unsuccessful candidate for Vice President of the United States on the Republican ticket with Charles E. Hughes for President in 1916; resumed the practice of law in Indianapolis, Ind., where he died June 4, 1918; interment in Crown Hill Cemetery.

FAIRCHILD, Benjamin Lewis, a Representative from New York; born in Sweden (near Rochester), Monroe County, N. Y., January 5, 1863; attended the public schools of Washington, D. C., and a business college; was graduated from the law department of Columbian (now George Washington) University at Washington, D. C., in 1885; was admitted to the bar in 1885 and commenced practice in New York City; employed in the draftsman division of the United States Patent Office 1877–1879; clerk in the Bureau of Engraving and Printing 1879–1885; elected as a Republican to the Fifty-fourth Congress (March 4, 1895–March 3, 1897); unsuccessfully contested the election of William L. Ward to the Fifty-fifth Congress; resumed the practice of law in New York City; elected to the Sixty-fifth Congress (March 4, 1917–March 3, 1919); unsuccessful candidate for reelection in 1918 to the Sixty-sixth Congress; again elected to the Sixty-seventh Congress (March 4, 1921–March 3, 1923); unsuccessful candidate for reelection in 1922 to the Sixty-eighth Congress, but was subsequently elected to that Congress to fill the vacancy caused by the death of James V. Ganly; reelected to the Sixty-ninth Congress and served from November 6, 1923, to March 3, 1927; unsuccessful candidate for reelection in 1926 to the Seventieth Congress; resumed the practice of law in New York City; died in Pelham Manor, N. Y., October 25, 1946; interment in Woodlawn Cemetery, New York, N. Y.

FAIRCHILD, George Winthrop, a Representative from New York; born in Oneonta, Otsego County, N. Y., May 6, 1854; completed preparatory studies; engaged in agricultural pursuits and apprenticed as a printer; owner of the Oneonta Herald Publishing Co. 1890–1912; also interested in banking and in the manufacture of time recorders; elected as a Republican to the Sixtieth and to the five succeeding Congresses (March 4, 1907–March 3, 1919); elected vice president of the International Peace Conference; appointed by President Taft on August 10, 1910, as special commissioner to the First Centenary of Mexico at Mexico City, with the rank of Minister; resumed his former business pursuits; president and director of the White Plains Development Co., White Plains, N. Y.; died in New York City December 31, 1924; interment in Glenwood Cemetery, Oneonta, N. Y.

FAIRFIELD, John, a Representative and a Senator from Maine; born in Saco, York County, Maine, January 30, 1797; attended the Saco schools, Thornton Academy, and Bowdoin College, Brunswick, Maine; engaged in trade; studied law; was admitted to the bar in 1826 and commenced practice in Biddleford and Saco, Maine; trustee of Thornton Academy in 1826; appointed reporter of the State supreme court in 1832; elected as a Democrat to the Twenty-fourth and Twenty-fifth Congresses and served from March 4, 1835, to December 24, 1838, when he resigned, having been elected Governor; served as Governor of Maine from 1839 to 1843, when he resigned, having been elected Senator; elected to the United States Senate to fill the vacancy caused by the resignation of Reuel Williams; reelected, and served from March 3, 1843, until his death;

president of the Thornton board of trustees 1845–1847; died in Washington, D. C., December 24, 1847; interment in Laurel Hill Cemetery, Saco, Maine.

FAIRFIELD, Louis William, a Representative from Indiana; born in a log cabin near Wapakoneta, Auglaize County, Ohio, October 15, 1858; moved to Allen County, Ohio, in 1866 and resided on a farm near Lima; attended the public schools; moved to Middle Point, Van Wert County, Ohio, in 1872; by working on a farm and on the fencing gang of the Pennsylvania Railroad, was able to attend winter school; attended a select school in 1875; taught school for six months, and then attended the Ohio Northern University at Ada in 1876; continued teaching and attending school until 1888; editor of the Hardin County Republican at Kenton, Ohio, in 1881 and 1882; taught school in Middle Point in 1883 and 1884; moved to Angola, Steuben County, Ind., in 1885, being selected to assist in the building of Tri-State College, Angola, Ind.; vice president of and teacher at Tri-State College 1885–1917; unsuccessful candidate for the State senate in 1912; elected as a Republican to the Sixty-fifth and to the three succeeding Congresses (March 4, 1917–March 3, 1925); unsuccessful candidate for renomination in 1924; retired from active pursuits; occasionally engaged as a lecturer and resided in Angola, Ind.; died in Joilet, Ill., while on a visit, February 20, 1930; interment in Circle Hill Cemetery, Angola, Ind.

FAISON, John Miller, a Representative from North Carolina; born near Faison, Duplin County, N. C., April 17, 1862; attended Faison Male Academy, and was graduated from Davidson College, North Carolina, in 1883; studied medicine at the University of Virginia at Charlottesville; completed a postgraduate medical course at New York Polyclinic in 1885, and commenced practice at Faison, N. C., the same year; also engaged in agricultural pursuits; member of the State and county Democratic executive committee 1898–1906; member of the North Carolina Jamestown Exposition Commission; elected as a Democrat to the Sixty-second and Sixty-third Congresses (March 4, 1911–March 3, 1915); was not a candidate for reelection in 1914; died in Faison, N. C., April 21, 1915; interment in Faison Cemetery.

FALCONER, Jacob Alexander, a Representative from Washington; born in Ontario, Canada, January 26, 1869; moved with his parents to Saugatuck, Mich., in 1873; attended the public schools; moved to Washburn, Wis.; was graduated from Beloit (Wis.) Academy in 1890 and later took college work at Beloit College; moved to Everett, Wash., in 1894; engaged in the lumber business; mayor of Everett in 1897 and 1898; member of the State house of representatives 1904–1908, serving as speaker during the 1907 session; member of the State senate 1909–1912; elected as a Progressive to the Sixty-third Congress (March 4, 1913–March 3, 1915); unsuccessful candidate for the nomination for United States Senator on the Progressive ticket in 1914; engaged in the ship-brokerage business in New York City 1915–1919; moved to Fort Worth, Tex., in 1919 and engaged in road-construction contracting; moved to Farmington, N. Mex., in 1925 and engaged in the oil and gas industry; died in Wingdale, Dutchess County, N. Y., July 1, 1928; interment in Saugatuck Cemetery, Saugatuck, Mich.

FALL, Albert Bacon, a Senator from New Mexico; born in Frankfort, Franklin County, Ky., November 26, 1861; attended the country schools; principally self-taught; taught school; studied law; was admitted to the bar in 1891 and commenced practice at Las Cruces, N. Mex.; made a specialty of Mexican law; became interested in mines, lumber, land, railroads, farming, and stock raising in New Mexico and mining in Mexico;

member of the Territorial house of representatives in 1891 and 1892; appointed judge of the third judicial district in 1893; associate justice of the supreme court of New Mexico in 1893; Territorial attorney general in 1897 and again in 1907; member of the Territorial council in 1897; served as captain of Company H in the First Territorial Infantry during the Spanish-American War; upon the admission of New Mexico as a State into the Union was elected in 1912 as a Republican to the United States Senate for the term ending March 3, 1913; reelected in June 1912, but as the Governor did not sign the credentials, he was again elected in January 1913; reelected in 1918, and served from March 27, 1912, until March 4, 1921, when he resigned to accept a portfolio in the Cabinet of President Harding; appointed Secretary of the Interior and served from March 5, 1921, until March 4, 1923, when he resigned; resumed his former business pursuits in Three Rivers, N. Mex.; died in El Paso, Tex., November 30, 1944; interment in Evergreen Cemetery.

FALLON, George Hyde, a Representative from Maryland; born in Baltimore, Md., July 24, 1902; attended the public schools, Calvert Business College, and Johns Hopkins University, Baltimore, Md.; engaged in the advertising sign business; chairman of the Democratic State central committee of Baltimore, Md., in 1938; member of the Baltimore City Council 1939–1944; elected as a Democrat to the Seventy-ninth and to the seven succeeding Congresses (January 3, 1945–January 3, 1961). *Reelected to the Eighty-seventh Congress.*

FARAN, James John, a Representative from Ohio; born in Cincinnati, Ohio, on December 29, 1808; attended the common schools, and was graduated from Miami University, Oxford, Ohio, in 1831; studied law; was admitted to the bar in 1833 and commenced practice in Cincinnati; elected as a Democrat a member of the State house of representatives 1835–1839 and served as speaker in 1838 and 1839; served in the State senate 1839–1843, and was its presiding officer 1841–1843; associate editor and proprietor of the Cincinnati Enquirer 1844–1881; elected as a Democrat to the Twenty-ninth and Thirtieth Congresses (March 4, 1845–March 3, 1849); was not a candidate for renomination in 1848; appointed by Governor Medill one of the commissioners to supervise the erection of the State capitol in 1854; mayor of Cincinnati 1855–1857; appointed by President Buchanan postmaster of Cincinnati June 4, 1855, and served until October 21, 1859; delegate to the Democratic National Convention at Baltimore in 1860; engaged in newspaper work until shortly before his death; died in Cincinnati, Ohio, December 12, 1892; interment in Spring Grove Cemetery.

FARBSTEIN, Leonard, a Representative from New York; born in the Borough of Manhattan, New York, N. Y., October 12, 1902; attended public schools and graduated from High School of Commerce; studied in evening classes at City College of New York and entered New York University Law School, graduating in 1924; was admitted to the bar in 1925 and commenced the practice of law in New York City; member of the State assembly 1932–1956; during World War II served in the United States Coast Guard Reserve; vice chairman of East River Day Camp, a philanthropic organization; elected as a Democrat to the Eighty-fifth and Eighty-sixth Congresses (January 3, 1957–January 3, 1961). *Reelected to the Eighty-seventh Congress.*

FARIS, George Washington, a Representative from Indiana; born near Rensselaer, Jasper County, Ind., June 9, 1854; attended the public schools; was graduated from Asbury (now De Pauw) University, Greencastle, Ind., in 1877; studied law; was admitted to the bar in 1877 and commenced practice in Indianapolis, Ind.; resided in Colorado for the benefit of his health in 1879; returned to Terre Haute, Ind., in 1880 and continued the practice of law; unsuccessful Republican candidate for judge of the circuit court in 1884; elected as a Republican to the Fifty-fourth, Fifty-fifth, and Fifty-sixth Congresses (March 4, 1895–March 3, 1901); declined to be a candidate for renomination in 1900; resumed the practice of law in Terre Haute, Ind., and shortly thereafter moved to Washington, D. C., and continued the practice of law until his death in that city on April 17, 1914; interment in Highland Lawn Cemetery, Terre Haute, Ind.

FARLEE, Isaac Gray, a Representative from New Jersey; born at White House, Hunterdon County, N. J., May 18, 1787; attended the public schools; engaged in mercantile pursuits in Flemington; member of the State general assembly in 1819, 1821, 1828, and 1830; clerk of Hunterdon County 1830–1840; brigadier general of the State militia; elected to the Twenty-eighth Congress (March 4, 1843–March 3, 1845); unsuccessful candidate for reelection in 1844 to the Twenty-ninth Congress; member of the State senate 1847–1849; judge of the court of common pleas 1852–1855; died in Flemington, N. J., January 12, 1855; interment in Presbyterian Cemetery.

FARLEY, Ephraim Wilder, a Representative from Maine; born in Newcastle, Maine, August 29, 1817; attended the common schools and was graduated from Bowdoin College, Brunswick, Maine, in 1836; studied law; was admitted to the bar and commenced practice in Newcastle; member of the State house of representatives in 1843 and 1851–1853; elected as a Whig to the Thirty-third Congress (March 4, 1853–March 3, 1855); unsuccessful candidate for reelection in 1854 to the Thirty-fourth Congress; member of the State senate in 1856; died in Newcastle, Maine, April 3, 1880; interment in a tomb on the family estate.

FARLEY, James Indus, a Representative from Indiana; born on a farm near Hamilton, Steuben County, Ind., on February 24, 1871; attended the public schools and Tri-State College, Angola, Ind., and Simpson College, Indianola, Iowa; taught in the public schools of Steuben and De Kalb Counties, Ind., 1890–1894; engaged as a salesman for the Auburn Automobile Co. in 1906, later becoming sales manager, vice president, and president of the company, retiring in 1926; delegate to the Democratic National Convention at Houston in 1928; elected as a Democrat to the Seventy-third, Seventy-fourth, and Seventy-fifth Congresses (March 4, 1933–January 3, 1939); unsuccessful candidate for reelection in 1938 to the Seventy-sixth Congress; engaged in agricultural pursuits; died in a hospital at Bryn Mawr, Pa., on June 16, 1948; interment in Woodlawn Cemetery, Auburn, Ind.

FARLEY, James Thompson, a Senator from California; born in Albemarle County, Va., August 6, 1829; attended the common schools; moved when quite young to Missouri and thence to California in 1850 and settled in Jackson; studied law; was admitted to the bar in 1854 and commenced practice in Amador County; member of the State assembly in 1855 and 1856 and served as speaker in the latter year; member of the State senate 1869–1876 and served as president pro tempore in 1871 and 1872; elected as a Democrat to the United States Senate and served from March 4, 1879, until March 3, 1885; was not a candidate for renomination in 1884; resumed the practice of law; died in Jackson, Amador County, Calif., on January 22, 1886; interment in the City Cemetery.

FARLEY, Michael Francis, a Representative from New York; born in Birr, Ireland, March 1, 1863; immigrated to the United States in 1881 and settled in Brooklyn, N. Y.; attended the public schools of New York City; engaged in the liquor business; elected as a Democrat to the Sixty-fourth Congress (March 4, 1915–March 3, 1917); unsuccessful candidate for reelection in 1916 to the Sixty-fifth Congress; engaged in his former business pursuits until his death in New York City October 8, 1921; interment in Calvary Cemetery.

FARLIN, Dudley, a Representative from New York; born in Norwich, New London County, Conn., September 2, 1777; moved to Dutchess County, N. Y., in early youth, and later to Warren County; engaged in the lumber and grain business; supervisor of the town of Warrensburg 1818–1820, 1827, and 1828; sheriff of Warren County in 1821, 1822, and again in 1828; member of the State assembly in 1824; presidential elector on the Democratic ticket of Jackson and Van Buren in 1832; elected as a Democrat to the Twenty-fourth Congress (March 4, 1835–March 3, 1837); resumed his former business pursuits; died in Warrensburg, Warren County, N. Y., on September 26, 1837; interment in Warrensburg Cemetery.

FARNSWORTH, John Franklin, a Representative from Illinois; born in Eaton, Canada, March 27, 1820; completed preparatory studies; settled in Ann Arbor, Mich.; studied law; was admitted to the bar in 1841 and commenced practice at St. Charles, Ill.; moved to Chicago, Ill.; elected as a Republican to the Thirty-fifth and Thirty-sixth Congresses (March 4, 1857–March 3, 1861); was not a candidate for renomination in 1860; served in the Union Army during the Civil War; commissioned colonel of the Eighth Regiment, Illinois Volunteer Cavalry, September 18, 1861; brigadier general of Volunteers December 5, 1862; resigned March 4, 1863, to take up his duties as Congressman; elected to the Thirty-eighth and to the four succeeding Congresses (March 4, 1863–March 3, 1873); unsuccessful candidate for renomination in 1872; resumed the practice of law in Chicago, Ill.; moved to Washington, D. C., in 1880 and continued the practice of law until his death on July 14, 1897; interment in North Cemetery, St. Charles, Ill.

FARQUHAR, John Hanson, a Representative from Indiana; born in Union Bridge, Carroll County, Md., December 20, 1818; attended the public schools; moved to Indiana with his parents, who settled in Richmond in 1833; employed as an assistant engineer on the White River Canal until 1840; studied law; was admitted to the bar and commenced practice in Brookville, Ind.; secretary of the State senate in 1842 and 1843; chief clerk of the State house of representatives in 1844; unsuccessful candidate for election in 1852 to the Thirty-third Congress; presidential elector on the Republican ticket of Lincoln and Hamlin in 1860; served as captain in the Nineteenth Infantry of the Regular Army in the Civil War; elected as a Republican to the Thirty-ninth Congress (March 4, 1865–March 3, 1867); was not a candidate for renomination in 1866; moved to Indianapolis in 1870 and engaged in banking; appointed secretary of state by Gov. Conrad Baker; died in Indianapolis, Ind., October 1, 1873; interment in Crown Hill Cemetery.

FARQUHAR, John McCreath, a Representative from New York; born near Ayr, Scotland, April 17, 1832; attended Ayr Academy; immigrated to the United States when a boy and settled in Buffalo, N. Y.; was a printer, editor, and publisher for thirty-three years; president of the International Typographical Union 1860–1862; during the Civil War enlisted in the Union Army August 9, 1862, as a private in Company B, Eighty-ninth Regiment, Illinois Volunteer Infantry; was promoted to sergeant major August 13, 1862, captain February 24, 1863, and major April 25, 1863; served as judge advocate and as inspector on the staffs of Generals Willich, Beatty, and Wood in the Fourth Army Corps; was awarded the Congressional Medal of Honor for distinguished bravery and skill on the battlefield of Stone River, Tenn.; after the close of the war returned to Buffalo, N. Y., and resumed business activities; elected as a Republican to the Forty-ninth, Fiftieth, and Fifty-first Congresses (March 4, 1885–March 3, 1891); was not a candidate for renomination in 1890 to the Fifty-second Congress; member of the United States Industrial Commission 1898–1902; retired from public life and active business pursuits; died in Buffalo, N. Y., on April 24, 1918; interment in Forest Lawn Cemetery.

FARR, Evarts Worcester, a Representative from New Hampshire; born in Littleton, Grafton County, N. H., October 10, 1840; attended the common schools and Dartmouth College, Hanover, N. H.; during the Civil War entered the Union Army as first lieutenant of Company G, Second Regiment, New Hampshire Volunteer Infantry; was promoted to captain of that company and mustered into the service on January 1, 1862; honorably discharged as captain of Company G on September 22, 1862, to accept appointment as major in the Eleventh Regiment, New Hampshire Volunteer Infantry, on September 23, 1862; honorably discharged as major in that regiment on June 4, 1865; assistant assessor of internal revenue 1865–1869; studied law; was admitted to the bar in 1867 and commenced practice in Littleton; assessor of internal revenue 1869–1873; solicitor for Grafton County 1873–1879; member of the executive council of New Hampshire in 1876; elected as a Republican to the Forty-sixth and Forty-seventh Congresses and served from March 4, 1879, until his death in Littleton, N. H., November 30, 1880; interment in Glenwood Cemetery.

FARR, John Richard, a Representative from Pennsylvania; born in Scranton, Lackawanna County, Pa., July 18, 1857; attended the public schools, School of the Lackawanna, Scranton, Pa., and Phillips Academy, Andover, Mass.; was graduated from Lafayette College, Easton, Pa.; newsboy, printer, and publisher; active in the real-estate business; served four years on the Scranton School Board; member of the State house of representatives in 1891, 1893, 1895, 1897, and 1899, serving as speaker of the 1899 session; unsuccessful candidate for election in 1908 to the Sixty-first Congress; elected as a Republican to the Sixty-second and to the three succeeding Congresses (March 4, 1911–March 3, 1919); successfully contested the election of Patrick McLane to the Sixty-sixth Congress and served from February 25 to March 3, 1921; unsuccessful candidate for renomination in 1920 to the Sixty-seventh Congress; resumed the real-estate business in Scranton, Pa.; unsuccessful candidate for the Republican nomination in 1930 to the Seventy-second Congress and in 1932 to the Seventy-third Congress; died in Scranton, Pa., on December 11, 1933; interment in Shady Lane Cemetery, Chinchilla (near Scranton), Lackawanna County, Pa.

FARRELLY, John Wilson (son of Patrick Farrelly), a Representative from Pennsylvania; born in Meadville, Crawford County, Pa., July 7, 1809; received a limited schooling; was graduated from Allegheny College at Meadville in 1826; studied law; was admitted to the bar in 1828 and commenced practice in Meadville; member of the State senate in 1828; served in the State house of representatives in 1837; again a member of the State senate 1838–1842; elected as a Whig to the Thirtieth Congress (March 4, 1847–March 3, 1849); was not a candidate for renomination in 1848; appointed Sixth Auditor of the Treasury by President Taylor and served from November 5, 1849, until April 9, 1853, when he resigned; engaged in the practice of law in Meadville, Pa., until his death, December 20, 1860; interment in Greendale Cemetery.

FARRELLY, Patrick (father of John Wilson Farrelly), a Representative from Pennsylvania; born in Ireland in 1770, where he completed his education; immigrated to the United States in 1798; studied law; was admitted to the bar July 11, 1803, and commenced practice in Meadville, Pa.; member of the State house of representatives in 1811 and 1812; served in the War of 1812 as a major of militia; elected as a Democrat to the Seventeenth, Eighteenth, and Nineteenth Congresses and served from March 4, 1821, until his death in Meadville, Crawford County, Pa., January 12, 1826; interment in Greendale Cemetery.

FARRINGTON, James, a Representative from New Hampshire; born in Conway, Carroll County, N. H., October 1, 1791; attended the common schools; was graduated from Fryeburg Academy, Fryeburg, Maine, in 1814; studied medicine and engaged in practice in Rochester, N. H., in 1818; member of the State house of representatives 1828–1831; served in the State senate in 1836; elected as a Democrat to the Twenty-fifth Congress (March 4, 1837–March 3, 1839); appointed one of the trustees of the New Hampshire Insane Asylum in 1845; resumed the practice of medicine; was one of the organizers of the Rochester Bank, and served as president until his death in Rochester, N. H., October 29, 1859; interment in the Old Cemetery.

FARRINGTON, Joseph Rider (husband of Mary Elizabeth Pruett Farrington), a Delegate from the Territory of Hawaii; born in Washington, D. C., October 15, 1897, and while still an infant moved with his parents to Hawaii; attended Punahou Academy, Honolulu, T. H., and the University of Wisconsin at Madison; during the First World War left college at the close of his junior year in June 1918 and enlisted in the United States Army; commissioned a second lieutenant of Field Artillery in September and was discharged in December 1918; returned to the University of Wisconsin and graduated in 1919; reporter on the staff of the Public Ledger in Philadelphia in 1919 and in Washington, D. C., 1920–1923; returned to Honolulu to become associated with the Honolulu Star-Bulletin, Ltd., and was president and general manager from 1939 until his death; secretary to the Hawaii Legislative Commission in 1933; member of the Territorial senate 1934–1942; elected as a Republican a Delegate to the Seventy-eighth and to the five succeeding Congresses and served from January 3, 1943, until his death in Washington, D. C., June 19, 1954; interment in Nuuanu Cemetery, Honolulu, T. H.

FARRINGTON, Mary Elizabeth Pruett (widow of Joseph Rider Farrington), a Delegate from the Territory of Hawaii; born in Tokyo, Japan, May 30, 1898; attended Tokyo Foreign School and grammar schools of Nashville, Tenn., El Paso, Tex., Los Angeles, Calif., and Hollywood (Calif.), High School; graduated from Ward-Belmont Junior College, Nashville, Tenn., in 1916 and from the University of Wisconsin in Madison in 1918; graduate work at the University of Hawaii; newspaper correspondent 1918–1957; president of League of Republican Women in Washington, D. C., 1946–1948; president of National Federation of Women's Republican Clubs 1949–1953; delegate to the Republican National Convention in 1952; elected as a Republican a Delegate to the Eighty-third Congress to fill the vacancy caused by the death of her husband, Joseph Rider Farrington; reelected to the Eighty-fourth Congress and served from July 31, 1954, to January 3, 1957; unsuccessful candidate for reelection in 1956 to the Eighty-fifth Congress; publisher of the Honolulu Star-Bulletin; is a resident of Honolulu, Hawaii.

FARROW, Samuel, a Representative from South Carolina; born in Virginia in 1759; moved to South Carolina with his father's family, who settled in Spartanburg District in 1765; served in the

Revolutionary War and was wounded in the face by a saber; studied law; was admitted to the bar in 1793 and commenced practice in Spartanburg, S. C.; also engaged in agricultural pursuits near Cross Anchor; Lieutenant Governor of South Carolina 1810–1812; elected as a War Democrat to the Thirteenth Congress (March 4, 1813–March 3, 1815); was not a candidate for renomination in 1814; resumed the practice of law; also engaged in agricultural pursuits; member of the State house of representatives 1816–1821; died in Columbia, S. C., November 18, 1824; interment in the family burial ground on his plantation, near the battlefield of Musgrove Mill, Spartanburg County, S. C.

FARWELL, Charles Benjamin, a Representative and a Senator from Illinois; born in Painted Post, Steuben County, N. Y., July 1, 1823; attended Elmira Academy; moved to Illinois in 1838 and settled in Mount Morris; employed in Government surveying and in farming until 1844, when he engaged in the real-estate business and banking in Chicago; clerk of Cook County 1853–1861; engaged in the wholesale dry-goods business; member of the State board of equalization in 1867; chairman of the Board of Supervisors of Cook County in 1868; national-bank-examiner in 1869; elected as a Republican to the Forty-second and Forty-third Congresses (March 4, 1871–March 3, 1875); presented credentials as a Member-elect to the Forty-fourth Congress and served from March 4, 1875, until May 6, 1876, when he was succeeded by John V. Le Moyne, who contested his election; declined to be a candidate for renomination in 1876; resumed mercantile pursuits; elected to the Forty-seventh Congress (March 4, 1881–March 3, 1883); declined to be a candidate for renomination in 1882; elected to the United States Senate to fill the vacancy caused by the death of John A. Logan and served from January 19, 1887, until March 3, 1891; was not a candidate for reelection in 1891; resumed mercantile pursuits; died in Lake Forest, Ill., September 23, 1903; interment in Rosehill Cemetery, Chicago, Ill.

FARWELL, Nathan Allen (cousin of Owen Lovejoy), a Senator from Maine; born in Unity, Waldo County, Maine, on February 24, 1812; attended the common schools; taught school in 1832 and 1833; moved to East Thomaston in 1834 and engaged in the manufacture of lime and in ship building; subsequently became a master mariner and trader; studied law but was never admitted to the bar; moved to Rockland, Maine, where he founded the Rockland Marine Insurance Co., and served as president; served in the State senate in 1853, 1854, 1861, and 1862, the last year as presiding officer; member of the State house of representatives in 1860, 1863, and 1864; delegate to the Republican National Convention at Baltimore in 1864; appointed and subsequently elected as a Republican to the United States Senate to fill the vacancy caused by the resignation of William Pitt Fessenden and served from October 27, 1864, to March 3, 1865; was not a candidate for reelection in 1865; resumed his activities in the insurance business; delegate to the Southern Loyalists Convention at Philadelphia in 1866; died in Rockland, Maine, December 9, 1893; interment in Achorn Cemetery.

FARWELL, Sewall Spaulding, a Representative from Iowa; born in Keene, Coshocton County, Ohio, April 26, 1834; attended the common schools and an academy in Cleveland, Ohio; moved to Iowa in 1852 and engaged in agricultural pursuits; during the Civil War enlisted in the Union Army in 1862 as captain of Company H, Thirty-first Regiment, Iowa Volunteer Infantry; promoted to major in 1864, and served until the close of the war; member of the State senate 1865–1869; assessor of internal revenue 1869–1873; collector of internal revenue 1875–1881; elected as a Republican to the Forty-seventh Congress

(March 4, 1881–March 3, 1883); unsuccessful candidate for reelection in 1882 to the Forty-eighth Congress; president of the Monticello State Bank; died in Monticello, Iowa, September 21, 1909; interment in Oakwood Cemetery.

FASCELL, Dante Bruno, a Representative from Florida; born in Bridgehampton, Long Island, N. Y., March 9, 1917; moved with his parents to Miami, Fla., in 1925; graduated from Ponce de Leon High School, Coral Gables, Fla., in 1933 and from the law school of the University of Miami in 1938; was admitted to the bar in 1938 and commenced the practice of law in Miami, Fla.; during World War II entered the Federal service with the Florida National Guard on January 6, 1941; commissioned a second lieutenant May 23, 1942; served in the African, Sicilian, and Italian campaigns, and separated from the service as a captain January 20, 1946; legal attaché to the State legislative delegation from Dade County 1947–1950; member of the State house of representatives 1950–1954; delegate to the Democratic National Convention in 1956; elected as a Democrat to the Eighty-fourth, Eighty-fifth, and Eighty-sixth Congresses (January 3, 1955–January 3, 1961). *Reelected to the Eighty-seventh Congress.*

FASSETT, Jacob Sloat, a Representative from New York; born in Elmira, Chemung County, N. Y., November 13, 1853; attended the public schools, and was graduated from the University of Rochester in 1875; studied law; was admitted to the bar in 1878 and commenced practice in Elmira; district attorney of Chemung County in 1878 and 1879; proprietor of the Elmira Daily Advertiser 1879–1896; was a student in Heidelberg University, Germany; returned to Elmira, N. Y., in 1882 and resumed the practice of law; member of the State senate 1884–1891, and served as president pro tempore 1889–1891; delegate to the Republican National Convention at Chicago in 1880 and at Minneapolis in 1892, and served as temporary chairman in the latter year; secretary of the Republican National Committee 1888–1892; unsuccessful candidate for Governor of New York in 1891; appointed by President Harrison collector of customs of the port of New York, and served from August 1 to September 15, 1891; delegate to the State constitutional convention in 1904; elected to the Fifty-ninth, Sixtieth, and Sixty-first Congresses (March 4, 1905–March 3, 1911); unsuccessful candidate for reelection in 1910 to the Sixty-second Congress; delegate to the Republican National Convention at Chicago in 1916; chairman of the Republican advisory convention in 1918; engaged in the banking and lumber business in Elmira, N. Y.; died in Vancouver, British Columbia, on April 21, 1924, while returning from a business trip to Japan and the Philippine Islands; interment in Woodlawn Cemetery, Elmira, N. Y.

FAULKNER, Charles James, a Representative from Virginia and from West Virginia; born in Martinsburg, Va. (now West Virginia), July 6, 1806; was graduated from Georgetown University, Washington, D. C., in 1822; studied law; was admitted to the bar in 1829 and practiced; member of the Virginia House of Delegates 1829–1834, 1848, and 1849; commissioner of Virginia on the disputed boundaries between that State and Maryland; member of the State senate from 1838 to 1842, when he resigned; member of the State constitutional convention in 1850; elected from Virginia to the Thirty-second and to the three succeeding Congresses (March 4, 1851–March 3, 1859); appointed United States Minister to France by President Buchanan in 1859; returned to the United States in August 1861 and was detained as a prisoner of state, but exchanged in December 1861 for Alfred Ely, Member of the United States House of Representatives from New York; during the Civil War entered the Confederate Army and was assistant adjutant general on the staff of Gen. Thomas J. (Stonewall) Jackson; engaged in railroad enterprises; member of the State constitutional convention of West Virginia in 1872; elected as a Democrat from West Virginia to the Forty-fourth Congress (March 4, 1875–March 3, 1877); resumed the practice of law; died on the family estate, "Boydville," near Martinsburg, W. Va., November 1, 1884; interment in the family lot on the estate.

FAULKNER, Charles James (son of the preceding), a Senator from West Virginia; born on the family estate, "Boydville," near Martinsburg, Va. (now West Virginia), September 21, 1847; accompanied his father, who was United States Minister to France, to that country in 1859; attended school in Paris and Switzerland; returned to the United States in August 1861; during the Civil War entered the Virginia Military Institute at Lexington in 1862; served with the cadets in the Battle of New Market; served as aide to Gen. John C. Breckinridge, and afterward to Gen. Henry A. Wise, and surrendered with the latter at Appomattox; was graduated from the law department of the University of Virginia at Charlottesville in June 1868; was admitted to the bar in September 1868 and commenced practice in Martinsburg, W. Va.; elected judge of the thirteenth judicial circuit in 1880; elected as a Democrat to the United States Senate in 1887; reelected in 1893 and served from March 4, 1887, to March 3, 1899; permanent chairman of the Democratic State convention of West Virginia in 1888, and both temporary and permanent chairman of the Democratic State convention in 1892; appointed a member of the International Joint High Commission of the United States and Great Britain in 1898; member of the American Society of International Law; member of the committee of one hundred of the American Association for the Advancement of Science; trustee of the Alumni endowment fund of the University of Virginia; retired from public life and devoted his time to the practice of law in Martinsburg, W. Va., and Washington, D. C., and to the management of his agricultural interests in West Virginia; died at "Boydville," near Martinsburg, W. Va., January 13, 1929; interment in the Old Norbourne Cemetery, Martinsburg, W. Va.

FAUST, Charles Lee, a Representative from Missouri; born near Bellefontaine, Logan County, Ohio, April 24, 1879; moved with his parents to a farm near Highland, Doniphan County, Kans.; attended the public schools and Highland University; engaged in teaching in a country school near Highland 1898–1900; was graduated from the law department of the University of Kansas at Lawrence in 1903, was admitted to the bar the same year, and commenced the practice of his profession in St. Joseph, Mo.; city counselor of St. Joseph 1915–1919; elected as a Republican to the Sixty-seventh and to the three succeeding Congresses and served from March 4, 1921, until his death; had been reelected to the Seventy-first Congress; died December 17, 1928, at the United States Naval Hospital, Washington, D. C.; interment in Highland Cemetery, Highland, Kans.

FAVROT, George Kent, a Representative from Louisiana; born in Baton Rouge, East Baton Rouge Parish, La., November 26, 1868; attended the public schools and was graduated from Louisiana State University at Baton Rouge in 1888 and from the law department of Tulane University, New Orleans, La., in 1890; was admitted to the bar in 1890 and commenced practice in Baton Rouge, La.; served as district attorney of the twenty-second judicial district of Louisiana 1892–1896; unsuccessful candidate for reelection in 1896; delegate at large to the State constitutional convention in 1898; again served as district attorney 1900–1904; district judge 1904–1906; elected as a Democrat to the Sixtieth Congress (March 4, 1907–March 3,

1909); unsuccessful candidate for renomination in 1908; member of the State house of representatives 1912–1916; resumed the practice of law in Baton Rouge, La.; elected to the Sixty-seventh and Sixty-eighth Congresses (March 4, 1921–March 3, 1925); unsuccessful candidate for reelection in 1924 to the Sixty-ninth Congress; again engaged in the practice of law in Baton Rouge, La.; elected judge of division B of the nineteenth judicial district court in 1926 and served until his death in Baton Rouge, La., December 26, 1934; interment in Roselawn Memorial Park.

FAY, Francis Ball, a Representative from Massachusetts; born in Southboro, Worcester County, Mass., June 12, 1793; received a limited education; engaged in mercantile pursuits; postmaster of Southboro from September 15, 1817, to March 29, 1832; deputy sheriff of Worcester County 1824–1830; member of the Massachusetts General Court in 1830 and 1831; moved to Chelsea, which he represented in the Massachusetts General Court from 1834 to 1836 and in 1840; served in the State senate 1843–1845 and again in 1848; elected as a Whig to the Thirty-second Congress to fill the vacancy caused by the death of Robert Rantoul, Jr., and served from December 13, 1852, to March 3, 1853; was not a candidate for the Thirty-third Congress; mayor of Chelsea in 1857; founded the public library in Southboro, Mass.; settled in Lancaster in 1858; founded the State reform school in Lancaster; again a member of the State senate in 1868; died in South Lancaster, Mass., October 6, 1876; interment in Woodlawn Cemetery, Everett, Mass.

FAY, James Herbert, a Representative from New York; born in New York City, N. Y., April 29, 1899; attended the public schools and De La Salle Institute; during the First World War enlisted April 3, 1917, and served overseas as a private, first class, with the Sixty-ninth Regiment, One Hundred and Sixty-fifth Infantry, and was discharged October 11, 1919; wounded in action; awarded the Purple Heart Medal; was graduated from Brooklyn (N. Y.) Law School in 1929; served as deputy and acting commissioner of hospitals of New York City 1929–1934; chief field deputy, United States Bureau of Internal Revenue, 1935–1938; elected as a Democrat to the Seventy-sixth Congress (January 3, 1939–January 3, 1941); unsuccessful candidate for reelection in 1940 to the Seventy-seventh Congress; elected to the Seventy-eighth Congress (January 3, 1943–January 3, 1945); was not a candidate for renomination in 1944; engaged in the advertising and insurance business in New York City until his death September 10, 1948; interment in Pinelawn National Cemetery, Farmingdale, N. Y.

FAY, John, a Representative from New York; born in Hardwick, Worcester County, Mass., February 10, 1773; attended the common schools for a period of only six months; moved to New York with his parents, who settled in Montgomery County, and later in Galway, Saratoga County; moved to Northampton, Fulton County, in 1804; became a land surveyor and later engaged in agricultural pursuits, milling, and manufacturing; held various local offices and was postmaster of Northampton several years; member of the State assembly in 1808, 1809, and 1812; elected as a Democrat to the Sixteenth Congress (March 4, 1819–March 3, 1821); resumed his former activities; served as sheriff of Jefferson County from 1828 to 1831; presidential elector on the Democratic ticket of Polk and Dallas in 1844; died in Northampton, N. Y., June 21, 1855; interment in the Old Presbyterian Church Cemetery.

FEARING, Paul, a Delegate from the Territory Northwest of the River Ohio; born in Wareham, Plymouth County, Mass., February 28, 1762; prepared for college by tutors; was graduated from Harvard University in 1785; studied law in Windham, Conn., and was admitted to the bar in 1787; moved to the Northwest Territory in May 1788 and engaged in the practice of law at Fort Harmer, now a part of Marietta, Ohio; appointed United States counsel for Washington County in 1788; probate judge in 1797; member of the Territorial legislature 1799–1801; elected as a Federalist to the Seventh Congress (March 4, 1801–March 3, 1803); was not a candidate for renomination in 1802; resumed the practice of law and engaged in fruit and stock raising; appointed associate judge of the court of common pleas in 1810 and served seven years; appointed master in chancery in 1814; died at his home, below the mouth of the Muskingum River, near Marietta, Ohio, August 21, 1822; interment in Harmer Cemetery, Marietta, Ohio.

FEATHERSTON, Winfield Scott, a Representative from Mississippi; born near Murfreesboro, Rutherford County, Tenn., August 8, 1820; completed preparatory studies; moved to Mississippi and settled in Houston; studied law; was admitted to the bar in 1840 and commenced practice in Houston, Miss.; elected as a Democrat to the Thirtieth and Thirty-first Congresses (March 4, 1847–March 3, 1851); unsuccessful candidate for reelection in 1850 to the Thirty-second Congress; resumed the practice of law at Houston, Miss.; moved to Holly Springs in 1856; served in the Confederate Army during the Civil War; commissioned brigadier general March 4, 1862; paroled in Greensboro, N. C., May 1, 1865; unsuccessful candidate for United States Senator in 1865; member of the State house of representatives in 1876 and 1880; delegate to the Democratic National Convention at Cincinnati in 1880; member of the State constitutional convention in 1890; died in Holly Springs, Miss., May 28, 1891; interment in Hill Crest Cemetery.

FEATHERSTONE, Lewis Porter, a Representative from Arkansas; born in Oxford, Lafayette County, Miss., July 28, 1851; attended the common schools and the law department of Cumberland University, Lebanon, Tenn.; engaged in planting in Shelby County, Tenn., 1872–1881; moved to St. Francis County, Ark., and continued as a planter; member of the State house of representatives in 1887 and 1888; elected president of the State Wheel (a farmers' organization) in 1887 and reelected in 1888; successfully contested as an independent Union Laborite the election of William H. Cate to the Fifty-first Congress and served from March 5, 1890, until March 3, 1891; unsuccessful candidate on the Union Labor ticket for reelection in 1890 to the Fifty-second Congress; engaged in railroad building and in development of iron resources of Texas; was commissioned captain in the First Regiment, United States Volunteers (Immune), in 1898; died in Longview, Tex., March 14, 1922; interment in Mission Cemetery, San Antonio, Tex.

FEAZEL, William Crosson, a Senator from Louisiana; born near Farmerville, Union Parish, La., June 10, 1895; attended the public schools; engaged as an independent oil and gas producer since 1916; member of the State house of representatives 1932–1936; appointed as a Democrat to the United States Senate to fill the vacancy caused by the death of John H. Overton and served from May 18, 1948, to December 30, 1948; was not a candidate for election to the vacancy in 1948; resumed the oil and gas business in Monroe and Shreveport, La.; is a resident of West Monroe, La.

FEELY, John Joseph, a Representative from Illinois; born on a farm near Wilmington, Will County, Ill., August 1, 1875; attended the public schools; was graduated from Niagara (N. Y.) University in 1895 and from the law department of Yale University in 1897; was admitted to the bar in Connecticut in 1897; moved to Chicago, Ill., in 1898 and engaged in the practice of law; elected as a Democrat to the Fifty-seventh Congress (March 4, 1901–March 3, 1903); was not a candidate for renomination in 1902; engaged in the practice of his profession until his death in Chicago, Ill., February 15, 1905; interment in Mount Olivet Cemetery, Joilet, Ill.

FEIGHAN, Michael Aloysius, a Representative from Ohio; born in Lakewood, Cuyahoga County, Ohio, February 16, 1905; attended the public and parochial schools; was graduated from St. Ignatius High School and attended John Carroll University, Cleveland, Ohio, for two years; was graduated from Princeton University, Princeton, N. J., in 1927 and from Harvard Law School, Cambridge, Mass., in 1931; was admitted to the bar in 1931 and commenced practice in Cleveland, Ohio; member of the Ohio House of Representatives 1937–1940, serving as Democratic floor leader in 1939 and 1940; elected as a Democrat to the Seventy-eighth and to the eight succeeding Congresses (January 3, 1943–January 3, 1961). *Reelected to the Eighty-seventh Congress.*

FELCH, Alpheus, a Senator from Michigan; born in Limerick, York County, Maine, September 28, 1804; prepared for college in Phillips Exeter Academy, Exeter, N. H., and was graduated from Bowdoin College, Brunswick, Maine, in 1827; studied law; was admitted to the bar and practiced in Houlton, Maine, from 1830 to 1833; moved to Monroe, Mich., in 1833 and continued the practice of law; represented Monroe County in the State house of representatives 1835–1837; State bank commissioner in 1838 and 1839 and rendered great service in stamping out the so-called "wildcat" banks; auditor general of the State in 1842; appointed associate justice of the Michigan Supreme Court in 1842 and served until his resignation in 1845, having been elected Governor; moved to Ann Arbor, Mich., in 1843; served as Governor from January 5, 1846, to March 3, 1847, when he resigned, having been elected as a Democrat a United States Senator in February 1847 and served from March 4, 1847, to March 3, 1853; president of the commission to settle Spanish and Mexican war claims 1853–1856; died in Ann Arbor, Mich., June 13, 1896; interment in Forest Hill Cemetery.

FELDER, John Myers, a Representative from South Carolina; born in Orangeburg District, S. C., July 7, 1782; was graduated from Yale College, New Haven, Conn., in 1804; studied law in the Litchfield (Conn.) Law School; was admitted to the bar in 1808 and commenced practice in Orangeburg, S. C.; major of drafted militia in the War of 1812; elected a trustee of South Carolina College in 1812; member of the State house of representatives 1812–1816 and 1822–1824; served in the State senate 1816–1820; elected as a Democrat to the Twenty-second and Twenty-third Congresses (March 4, 1831–March 3, 1835); declined to be a candidate for renomination in 1834; engaged extensively in agricultural pursuits and in the lumber business; member of the State senate from 1840 until his death in Union Point, Ga., September 1, 1851; interment in the family burial ground on his former plantation, "Midway," near Orangeburg, S. C.

FELL, John, a Delegate from New Jersey; born in New York City February 5, 1721; attended the public schools; engaged in overseas commerce and also in agricultural pursuits; moved to Bergen County, N. J.; appointed judge of the court of common pleas on September 30, 1766, and served until October 1, 1774; member of the Provincial Congress which met in Trenton in May, June, and August 1775; chairman of the committee of safety of Bergen County, N. J.; member of the provincial council in 1776; a zealous patriot for his country throughout the Revolution, as a result of which he was captured and held as a political prisoner from April 23, 1777, until January 1778, when he was released;

Member of the Continental Congress 1778–1780; member of the State council in 1782 and 1783; moved to New York City in 1793, and subsequently to Coldenham, N. Y., where he resided with his son John until his death on May 15, 1798; interment in Colden Cemetery.

FELLOWS, Frank, a Representative from Maine; born in Bucksport, Hancock County, Maine, on November 7, 1889; attended the public schools, East Maine Conference Seminary, Bucksport, Maine, and the University of Maine at Orono; was graduated from the University of Maine Law School; was admitted to the bar in 1911 and commenced practice in Portland, Maine; clerk of the United States District Court of Maine 1917–1920; elected as a Republican to the Seventy-seventh and to the five succeeding Congresses and served from January 3, 1941, until his death in Bangor, Maine, August 27, 1951; interment in Silver Lake Cemetery, Bucksport, Maine.

FELLOWS, John R., a Representative from New York; born in Troy, N. Y., July 29, 1832; moved to Saratoga County, N. Y., with his parents, who settled near Mechanicville; attended the country schools; moved to Camden, Ark., in 1850; studied law; was admitted to the bar in 1855 and commenced practice in Camden; presidential elector on the Constitutional-Union ticket of Bell and Everett in 1860; delegate to the State secession convention in 1861; delegate to the Democratic National Convention at New York City in 1868; during the Civil War entered the Confederate Army in the First Arkansas Regiment; after the Battle of Shiloh was assigned to staff duties as assistant adjutant and inspector general, and ordered to report to General Van Dorn at Vicksburg; assigned to the staff of Brig. Gen. W. N. R. Bell, commanding a district in General Van Dorn's department; captured at the surrender of Port Hudson, La., July 9, 1863, and released June 10, 1865; returned to Camden, Ark., and resumed the practice of law; member of the State senate in 1866 and 1867; moved to New York City in 1868 and continued the practice of law; assistant district attorney 1869–1872 and 1885–1887; elected district attorney and served from 1888 to 1890; elected as a Democrat to the Fifty-second and Fifty-third Congresses and served from March 4, 1891, until his resignation, effective December 31, 1893, having again been elected district attorney; district attorney of New York City from January 1, 1894, until his death; died in New York City December 7, 1896; interment in Trinity Church Cemetery.

FELTON, Charles Norton, a Representative and a Senator from California; born in Buffalo, N. Y., January 1, 1828; attended Syracuse (N. Y.) Academy; studied law; was admitted to the bar but never practiced; went to California in 1849; engaged in mercantile pursuits and afterward in banking; sheriff of Yuba County in 1853; subsequently tax collector; appointed treasurer of the United States Mint at San Francisco and Assistant Treasurer of the United States, and served from September 4, 1868, to April 23, 1877; member of the State assembly 1878–1882; elected as a Republican to the Forty-ninth and Fiftieth Congresses (March 4, 1885–March 3, 1889); was not a candidate for renomination; elected to the United States Senate to fill the vacancy caused by the death of George Hearst and served from March 19, 1891, to March 3, 1893; was not a candidate for reelection; State prison director 1903–1907; presidential elector on the Republican ticket of Taft and Butler in 1912; died at his home in Menlo Park, Calif., September 13, 1914; interment in Cypress Lawn Cemetery, Lawndale, San Mateo County, Calif.

FELTON, Rebecca Latimer (wife of William Harrell Felton), a Senator from Georgia; born near Decatur, De Kalb County, Ga., June 10, 1835; attended the common schools, and was graduated from the Madison Female College in 1852; moved to Bartow County, Ga., in 1854; taught school and engaged as a writer and lecturer; served as secretary to her husband while he was a Member of Congress 1875–1881; delegate from the Georgia Agricultural Department to the Tennessee Centennial Exposition in 1887; served on the board of lady managers of the Chicago Exposition 1890–1894; chairman of the woman's executive board of the Cotton States and International Exposition, Atlanta, Ga., in 1894 and 1895; juror on general agriculture at the Louisiana Purchase Exposition at St. Louis, Mo., in 1904; delegate to the Progressive Republican National Convention at Chicago in 1912; appointed by Gov. Thomas W. Hardwick as a Democrat to the United States Senate on October 3, 1922, to fill the vacancy caused by the death of Thomas E. Watson and attended two sessions of the Senate, November 21 and 22, 1922, a successor having been elected; was not a candidate for election to fill this vacancy; has the distinction of being the first woman to occupy a seat in the United States Senate; engaged as a writer and lecturer and resided in Cartersville, Bartow County, Ga.; died in Atlanta, Ga., while on a visit, January 24, 1930; interment in Oak Hill Cemetery, Cartersville, Ga.

FELTON, William Harrell (husband of Rebecca Latimer Felton), a Representative from Georgia; born near Lexington, Oglethorpe County, Ga., June 19, 1823; attended the common and primary schools; was graduated from the University of Georgia at Athens in 1843 and from the Medical College of Georgia at Augusta in 1844; practiced medicine, taught school, and also engaged in agricultural pursuits near Cartersville, Ga.; member of the State house of representatives from Cass (now Bartow) County in 1851; ordained as a Methodist minister in 1857; served as a surgeon during the Civil War; elected as a Democrat to the Forty-fourth, Forty-fifth, and Forty-sixth Congresses (March 4, 1875–March 3, 1881); unsuccessful candidate for reelection in 1880 to the Forty-seventh Congress; resumed his activity as a minister and again followed agricultural pursuits; again served in the State house of representatives 1884–1890; trustee from the State at large for the University of Georgia 1886–1892; died in Cartersville, Ga., September 24, 1909; interment in Oak Hill Cemetery.

FENERTY, Clare Gerald, a Representative from Pennsylvania; born in Philadelphia, Pa., July 25, 1895; attended the parochial schools; was graduated from St. Joseph's College, Philadelphia, Pa., in 1916 and from the law department of the University of Pennsylvania at Philadelphia in 1921; during the First World War served in the United States Navy in 1917 and 1918; reentered the naval service as a lieutenant, senior grade, in 1933; was admitted to the bar in 1921 and commenced practice in Philadelphia, Pa.; member of the law faculty at the Wharton School, University of Pennsylvania, 1924–1929; member of the Philadelphia Board of Law Examiners 1928–1940; assistant district attorney at Philadelphia, Pa., 1928–1935; elected as a Republican to the Seventy-fourth Congress (January 3, 1935–January 3, 1937); unsuccessful candidate for reelection in 1936 to the Seventy-fifth Congress; resumed the practice of law; appointed judge of Common Pleas Court No. 5 of Philadelphia in November 1939 and was elected for a ten-year term in November 1941; reelected in November 1951 and served until his death in Philadelphia, Pa., July 1, 1952; interment in Holy Sepulchre Cemetery, Wyndmoor, Montgomery County, Pa.

FENN, Edward Hart, a Representative from Connecticut; born in Hartford, Conn., September 12, 1856; attended private schools, Hartford High School, and Yale University, New Haven, Conn.; engaged in newspaper work in 1878; associated with the Hartford Post and the Hartford Courant as reporter, city editor,

State editor, and special and editorial writer; reported sessions of the Connecticut Legislature from 1878 to 1908; member of the State house of representatives in 1907 and 1915; served in the State senate in 1909 and 1911; fish and game commissioner 1912–1916; served five years in the First Regiment of the Connecticut National Guard; elected as a Republican to the Sixty-seventh and to the four succeeding Congresses (March 4, 1921–March 3, 1931); was not a candidate for renomination in 1930; retired from public life and lived in Washington, D. C., in the winter and Wethersfield, Conn., in the summer; died in Washington, D. C., February 23, 1939; interment in Spring Grove Cemetery, Hartford, Conn.

FENN, Stephen Southmyd, a Delegate from the Territory of Idaho; born in Watertown, Conn., March 28, 1820; moved with his parents to Niagara County, N. Y., in 1824; attended the public schools; moved in 1841 to Jackson County, Iowa, where he held several local offices; moved to California in 1850 and engaged in mining and ranching; studied law; was admitted to the bar in 1862 and commenced practice in that part of Washington Territory which became a part of the Territory of Idaho upon its organization in 1863, where he also engaged in mining; member of the Idaho Territorial council 1864–1867; district attorney for the first judicial district in 1869; member of the Territorial house of representatives in 1872 and served as speaker of the house; engaged in agricultural pursuits; successfully contested as a Democrat the election of Thomas W. Bennett to the Forty-fourth Congress; reelected to the Forty-fifth Congress and served from June 23, 1876, to March 3, 1879; was not a candidate for renomination in 1878; continued his former pursuits until July 1891; died in Blackfoot, Idaho, on April 13, 1892; interment in Asylum Cemetery.

FENNER, James, a Senator from Rhode Island; born in Providence, R. I., January 22, 1771; received a classical education, and was graduated from Brown University, Providence, R. I., in 1789; elected as a Democrat to the United States Senate and served from March 4, 1805, to September 1807, when he resigned to become Governor; Governor of Rhode Island 1807–1811, 1824–1831, and 1843–1845; presidential elector on the Democratic ticket of Monroe and Tompkins in 1816 and 1820 and of Van Buren and Johnson in 1836; president of the Rhode Island Historical Society in 1822 and 1823 and served as its first presiding officer; delegate to the State constitutional convention in 1842 and served as president; retired to his estate, "What Cheer," near Providence, R. I.; resided there until his death on April 17, 1846; interment in North Burial Ground, Providence, R. I.

FENTON, Ivor David, a Representative from Pennsylvania; born in Mahanoy City (Buck Mountain), Schuylkill County, Pa., August 3, 1889; attended the public schools, and Bucknell University, Lewisburg, Pa.; was graduated from Jefferson Medical College, Philadelphia, Pa., in 1912; served an internship at Ashland (Pa.) State Hospital in 1912 and 1913; commenced the practice of medicine in Mahanoy City, Pa., in 1914; enlisted in the United States Army Medical Corps and was commissioned a lieutenant August 8, 1917, rising later to the rank of captain; served twenty months (eleven overseas) with the Three Hundred and Fifteenth Infantry, Seventy-ninth Division; discharged on June 6, 1919, and returned to Mahanoy City to resume his medical practice; elected as a Republican to the Seventy-sixth and to the ten succeeding Congresses (January 3, 1939–January 3, 1961). *Reelected to the Eighty-seventh Congress.*

FENTON, Lucien Jerome, a Representative from Ohio; born in Winchester, Ohio, May 7, 1844; attended the public schools, Lebanon Normal School, and Ohio University at Athens; during the Civil War enlisted as a private in Company I, Ninety-first Regiment, Ohio Volunteer Infantry, August 11, 1862, and was dangerously wounded at the Battle of Winchester, Va., September 19, 1864; discharged because of wounds on May 29, 1865; taught school from 1865 to 1881; unsuccessful candidate for clerk of the courts of Adams County in 1880; clerk in the United States Treasury Department, Washington, D. C., 1881–1884; returned to Ohio and organized the Winchester Bank, becoming its cashier and manager in 1884; appointed a trustee of the Ohio University at Athens by Governor McKinley in 1892; delegate to the Republican National Convention at Minneapolis in 1892; elected as a Republican to the Fifty-fourth and Fifty-fifth Congresses (March 4, 1895–March 3, 1899); unsuccessful candidate for renomination in 1898; resumed banking in Winchester, Ohio; president of the Winchester School Board 1912–1922; president of the Adams County School Board 1918–1922; died in Winchester, Ohio, June 28, 1922; interment in Winchester Cemetery.

FENTON, Reuben Eaton, a Representative and a Senator from New York; born in Carroll, Chautauqua County, N. Y., on July 4, 1819; completed preparatory studies; studied law; engaged in mercantile pursuits; supervisor of Carroll 1846–1852; one of the founders of the Republican Party and chairman of its first State convention in New York; elected as a Republican to the Thirty-third Congress (March 4, 1853–March 3, 1855); unsuccessful candidate for reelection in 1854 to the Thirty-fourth Congress; elected to the Thirty-fifth and to the three succeeding Congresses and served from March 4, 1857, until his resignation, effective December 20, 1864, having been elected Governor of New York; Governor of New York 1865–1868; elected to the United States Senate and served from March 4, 1869, to March 3, 1875; appointed chairman of the United States commission to the International Monetary Conference held at Paris in 1878; engaged in banking; died in Jamestown, N. Y., on August 25, 1885; interment in Lakeview Cemetery.

FERDON, John William, a Representative from New York; born in Piermont, Rockland County, N. Y., December 13, 1826; was graduated from Rutgers College, New Brunswick, N. J., in 1847; studied law; was admitted to the bar and practiced; member of the State assembly in 1855; served in the State senate in 1856 and 1857; delegate to the Republican National Convention at Baltimore in 1864 and at Cincinnati in 1876; elected as a Republican to the Forty-sixth Congress (March 4, 1879–March 3, 1881); died in Monmouth Beach, N. J., on August 5, 1884; interment in private cemetery on the Ferdon estate in Piermont, N. Y.

FERGUSON, Fenner, a Delegate from the Territory of Nebraska; born in Nassau, Rensselaer County, N. Y., April 25, 1814; attended the common schools; studied law; was admitted to the bar in 1840 and commenced practice in Albany, N. Y.; moved to Albion, Mich., in 1846 and continued the practice of law; served successively as master in chancery, district attorney, and member of the State house of representatives 1854–1859; appointed by President Pierce as chief justice of the Territory of Nebraska in 1854; moved to Bellevue, Nebr., in October 1854; organized the first district and supreme courts of Nebraska; assisted the first Territorial legislature in drafting the first code of laws enacted for the government of the Territory; resigned as chief justice, having been elected as a Democrat to the Thirty-fifth Congress (March 4, 1857–March 3, 1859); was not a candidate for renomination in 1858; died in Bellevue, Nebr., on October 11, 1859; interment in Bellevue Cemetery.

FERGUSON, Homer, a Senator from Michigan; born in Harrison City, Westmoreland County, Pa., February 25, 1889; attended the public schools, and the University of Pittsburgh, Pittsburgh, Pa.; was graduated from the University of Michigan at Ann Arbor in 1913; was admitted to the bar the same year and commenced practice in Detroit, Mich.; served as circuit judge of the circuit court for Wayne County, Mich., 1929–1942; professor of law at Detroit (Mich.) College of Law 1929–1939; sat as a one-man grand jury of Wayne County, Mich., from August 1939 to May 1942; elected as a Republican to the United States Senate in 1942, reelected in 1948 and served from January 3, 1943, to January 3, 1955; unsuccessful candidate for reelection in 1954; Ambassador to the Philippines from March 1955 to February 1956; confirmed February 17, 1956, as a judge on the Military Court of Appeals at Washington, D. C., for an unexpired term ending May 1, 1956, and for a full term of fifteen years ending May 1, 1971; resides in Washington, D. C.

FERGUSON, Phillip Colgan, a Representative from Oklahoma; born in Wellington, Sumner County, Kans., August 15, 1903; attended the public schools; was graduated from the University of Kansas at Lawrence in 1926; moved to Oklahoma and settled on a ranch near Woodward, Woodward County, in 1926; engaged in agricultural pursuits and cattle raising; elected as a Democrat to the Seventy-fourth, Seventy-fifth, and Seventy-sixth Congresses (January 3, 1935–January 3, 1941); unsuccessful candidate for reelection in 1940 to the Seventy-seventh Congress and for election in 1944 to the Seventy-ninth Congress; resumed his former pursuits; commissioned a major in the United States Marine Corps in World War II, was wounded in action in the South Pacific, and served from March 2, 1942, to August 1, 1944; received the Silver Star Medal for gallantry in action; resumed his former pursuits; unsuccessful Republican candidate for Governor of Oklahoma in 1958; is a resident of Woodward, Okla.

FERGUSSON, Harvey Butler, a Delegate from the Territory of New Mexico and a Representative from New Mexico; born near Pickensville, Pickens County, Ala., September 9, 1848; attended the public schools of Alabama; was graduated from Washington and Lee University, Lexington, Va., in 1873 and from the law department of that university in 1874; taught in the Shenandoah Valley Academy, Winchester, Va.; was admitted to the bar in 1875 and commenced the practice of law in Wheeling, W. Va.; moved to White Oaks, Lincoln County, N. Mex., in 1882, and to Albuquerque, N. Mex., in 1883; engaged in the practice of law; special United States attorney in 1893 and 1894; member of the Democratic National Committee 1896–1904; elected as a Democrat a Delegate to the Fifty-fifth Congress (March 4, 1897–March 3, 1899); unsuccessful candidate for reelection in 1898 to the Fifty-sixth Congress and for election in 1902 to the Fifty-eighth Congress; upon the admission of New Mexico as a State into the Union was elected to the Sixty-second Congress; reelected to the Sixty-third Congress and served from January 8, 1912, to March 3, 1915; unsuccessful candidate for reelection in 1914 to the Sixty-fourth Congress; died in Albuquerque, N. Mex., June 10, 1915; remains were cremated and the ashes sent to Los Angeles, Calif., and retained by relatives.

FERNALD, Bert Manfred, a Senator from Maine; born in West Poland, Androscoggin County, Maine, April 3, 1858; attended the public schools, Hebron Academy, and a business and preparatory school in Boston; taught school; elected supervisor of schools in 1878; large landowner and agriculturist; extensive packer of canned goods from 1888 to his death; member of the board of trustees of Hebron Academy for many years; president of the Poland Telephone Co. and the Poland Dairy Co.; chairman of the Poland centennial committee in 1895; member of the State house of representatives 1896–1898; served in the State senate 1898–1902; Governor of Maine 1909–1911; president of the National Canners' Association in 1910; director of the Fidelity Trust Co. of Portland; elected as a Republican to the United States Senate in 1916 to fill the vacancy caused by the death of Edwin C. Burleigh; reelected in 1918 and 1924 and served from September 12, 1916, until his death in West Poland, Maine, August 23, 1926; interment in Highland Cemetery.

FERNANDEZ, Antonio Manuel, a Representative from New Mexico; born in Springer, Colfax County, N. Mex., January 17, 1902; attended the public schools, and Highlands University, Las Vegas, N. Mex.; received law training at Cumberland University, Lebanon, Tenn.; court reporter for the eighth judicial district of New Mexico 1925–1930; was admitted to the bar in 1931 and commenced practice in Raton, Colfax County, N. Mex.; assistant district attorney of the eighth judicial district in 1933; practiced law in Santa Fe, N. Mex., in 1934; served in the State house of representatives in 1935; chief tax attorney for the State Tax Commission in 1935 and 1936; first assistant attorney general 1937–1941; member of the first New Mexico Public Service Commission in 1941 and 1942; elected as a Democrat to the Seventy-eighth and to the six succeeding Congresses and served from January 3, 1943, until his death; had been reelected on November 6, 1956, to the Eighty-fifth Congress; died in Albuquerque, N. Mex., November 7, 1956; interment in Rosario Catholic Cemetery, Santa Fe, N. Mex.

FERNANDEZ, Joachim Octave, a Representative from Louisiana; born in New Orleans, La., August 14, 1896; attended the public schools and Cecil Barrois School in New Orleans, La.; demurrage and storage tariff expert from 1921; delegate to the State constitutional convention in 1921; member of the State house of representatives 1924–1928; served in the State senate 1928–1930; elected as a Democrat to the Seventy-second and to the four succeeding Congresses (March 4, 1931–January 3, 1941); unsuccessful candidate for renomination in 1940; called to active duty as a lieutenant commander in the United States Naval Reserve on January 8, 1941, and served until placed on the inactive duty list on September 30, 1943; appointed collector of internal revenue for the district of Louisiana in September 1943 and served until his resignation in October 1946; engaged in the general tax business and as a tax consultant; revenue examiner for department of revenue, State of Louisiana, 1951–, and head of income tax section; is a resident of New Orleans, La.

FERNÓS-ISERN, Antonio, a Resident Commissioner from Puerto Rico; born in San Lorenzo, P. R., May 10, 1895; attended elementary and high schools in Puerto Rico and Pennsylvania State Normal School at Bloomsburg; was graduated from the University of Maryland, College of Physicians and Surgeons and School of Medicine, in May 1915; engaged in the practice of medicine in Caguas, P. R., 1916–1918; health officer of the city of San Juan and Chief of the Bureau of Transmissible Diseases, Insular Department of Health, in 1919; assistant commissioner of health of Puerto Rico in 1920, 1921, and 1923–1931; director of school hygiene in city of San Juan in 1922; commissioner of health of Puerto Rico 1931–1933 and 1942–1946; professor at the Public Health School of Tropical Medicine of Puerto Rico 1931–1935; resumed the private practice of medicine in San Juan, P. R., 1933–1942; unsuccessful candidate as a Popular Democrat for Resident Commissioner in 1940; director of civilian defense, metropolitan area of Puerto Rico, in 1942; Acting Governor of Puerto Rico at various times from 1943 to 1946; appointed as a Popular Democrat Resident Commissioner of Puerto Rico to the United States to fill the vacancy in the term ending January 3, 1949, caused by the resignation of Jesus T. Pinero; elected in 1948, 1952, and again in 1956, and served from September 11, 1946, to January 3, 1961. *Reelected in 1960 for a four-year term.*

FERRELL, Thomas Merrill, a Representative from New Jersey; born in Glassboro, Gloucester County, N. J., June 20, 1844; attended the common schools and completed an academic course; elected a member of the township committee in 1872 and 1873; president of Hollow Ware Glassworkers' Association 1878–1883; member of the school board 1885–1890, serving as its president in 1887; member of the State house of assembly in 1879 and 1880; member of the State senate in 1880 and 1881; elected as a Democrat to the Forty-eighth Congress (March 4, 1883–March 3, 1885); unsuccessful candidate for reelection in 1884 to the Forty-ninth Congress; employed as a glassware salesman; died in Glassboro, N. J., October 20, 1916; interment in Methodist Episcopal Cemetery.

FERRIS, Charles Goadsby, a Representative from New York; born at "The Homestead," Throgs Neck, the Bronx, N. Y., about 1796; received a limited education; studied law; was admitted to the bar and practiced in New York City; member of the board of aldermen in 1832 and 1833; elected as a Jackson Democrat to the Twenty-third Congress to fill the vacancy caused by the resignation of Dudley Selden and served from December 1, 1834, to March 3, 1835; elected to the Twenty-seventh Congress (March 4, 1841–March 3, 1843); was largely instrumental in securing an appropriation through Congress to build the first telegraph line; died in New York City June 4, 1848.

FERRIS, Scott, a Representative from Oklahoma; born in Neosho, Newton County, Mo., November 3, 1877; attended the public schools, and was graduated from Newton County High School in 1897 and from the Kansas City School of Law in 1901; was admitted to the bar in 1901 and commenced practice in Lawton, Okla., the same year; member of the State house of representatives in 1904 and 1905; upon the admission of Oklahoma as a State into the Union was elected as a Democrat to the Sixtieth Congress; reelected to the Sixty-first and to the five succeeding Congresses and served from November 16, 1907, until March 3, 1921; did not seek renomination as a Representative, having become a candidate for Senator; delegate to the Democratic National Conventions in 1912 and 1916; unsuccessful candidate for election to the United States Senate in 1920; moved to New York City and engaged in the oil business 1921–1924; returned to Pauls Valley, Okla., in 1925; moved to Oklahoma City in 1928; Democratic national committeeman from Oklahoma 1924–1940; resumed the practice of law; engaged in the oil business and also in agricultural pursuits; died in Oklahoma City, Okla., June 8, 1945; interment in Rosehill Cemetery.

FERRIS, Woodbridge Nathan, a Senator from Michigan; born in Spencer, Tioga County, N. Y., January 6, 1853; attended the academies of Spencer, Candor, and Owego, N. Y., the Oswego (N. Y.) Normal Training School 1870–1873, and the medical department of the University of Michigan at Ann Arbor in 1873 and 1874; principal of Spencer Academy in 1874 and 1875; principal of the Business College and Academy of Freeport, Ill., in 1875 and 1876, of Dixon (Ill.) Business College and Academy 1877–1879, and superintendent of schools in Pittsfield, Ill., 1879–1884; settled in Big Rapids, Mich., where he established the Ferris Industrial School (now the Ferris Institute) in 1884, and served as president until his death; president of the Big Rapids Savings Bank; unsuccessful Democratic candidate for election in 1892 to the Fifty-third Congress and for Governor of Michigan in 1904;

Governor of Michigan 1913–1916; unsuccessful candidate for Governor in 1920; elected as a Democrat to the United States Senate in 1922 and served from March 4, 1923, until his death in Washington, D. C., March 23, 1928; interment in Highland View Cemetery, Big Rapids, Mich.

FERRISS, Orange, a Representative from New York; born at Glens Falls, Warren County, N. Y., November 26, 1814; completed preparatory studies; attended the University of Vermont at Burlington; studied law; was admitted to the bar in 1840 and commenced practice in Glens Falls, N. Y.; justice of the peace 1838–1841 and 1845–1848; inspector of public schools in 1839 and 1840; corporation clerk 1839–1842; county judge and surrogate of Warren County 1851–1863; elected as a Republican to the Fortieth and Forty-first Congresses (March 4, 1867–March 3, 1871); was not a candidate for renomination in 1870; appointed by President Grant as commissioner of southern claims and served from 1871 to 1877; Second Auditor of the Treasury from May 12, 1880, until his resignation on June 19, 1885; retired to private life, and resided in Glens Falls, N. Y., where he died April 11, 1894; interment in Glens Falls Cemetery.

FERRY, Orris Sanford, a Representative and a Senator from Connecticut; born in Bethel, Fairfield County, Conn., August 15, 1823; pursued preparatory studies, and was graduated from Yale College, New Haven, Conn., in 1844; studied law; was admitted to the bar in 1846 and practiced; appointed judge of probate in 1849; member of the State senate in 1855 and 1856; prosecuting attorney for Fairfield County 1856–1859; unsuccessful candidate for election in 1856 to the Thirty-fifth Congress; elected as a Republican to the Thirty-sixth Congress (March 4, 1859–March 3, 1861); unsuccessful candidate for reelection in 1860 to the Thirty-seventh Congress; entered the Union Army on July 23, 1861, as colonel of the Fifth Regiment, Connecticut Volunteer Infantry; was mustered out April 12, 1862, to enable him to accept an appointment as brigadier general of United States Volunteers; served in the latter capacity until June 15, 1865, when he was honorably discharged on tender of resignation; elected as a Republican to the United States Senate in 1866 and was reelected in 1873 by a combination of Independent Republicans and Democrats and served from March 4, 1867, until his death in Norwalk, Conn., November 21, 1875; interment in Norwalk Cemetery.

FERRY, Thomas White, a Representative and a Senator from Michigan; born in the old mission house of the Astor Fur Co. on Mackinac Island, Mich., June 10, 1827; moved with his parents to Grand Haven, Mich.; attended the public schools; engaged in mercantile pursuits in Grand Haven; member of the State house of representatives 1850–1852; member of the State senate in 1856; delegate to the Republican National Convention at Chicago in 1860; appointed in 1864 to represent Michigan on the board of managers of the Gettysburg National Cemetery and reappointed in 1867; delegate to the Loyalist Convention at Philadelphia in 1866; elected as a Republican to the Thirty-ninth, Fortieth, and Forty-first Congresses (March 4, 1865–March 3, 1871); reelected to the Forty-second Congress, but resigned, having been elected Senator; elected to the United States Senate in 1871, reelected in 1877 and served from March 4, 1871, to March 3, 1883; unsuccessful candidate for reelection in 1882; President pro tempore of the Senate March 9 and March 19 to 24, 1875, and at the death of Vice President Wilson became presiding officer of the Senate, serving from December 6, 1875, to March 3, 1877; designated by the President to represent him at the Centennial Exposition in Philadelphia July 4, 1876; presided over the high court of impeachment of Secretary of War Belknap and over the sixteen joint meetings of the two Houses during the Hayes-

Tilden contest in 1877; reelected President pro tempore of the Senate March 5, 1877, February 26, April 17, 1878, and March 3, 1879; died in Grand Haven, Mich., October 13, 1896; interment in Lake Forest Cemetery.

FESS, Simeon Davison, a Representative and a Senator from Ohio; born on a farm near Harrod, Allen County, Ohio, December 11, 1861; attended the country schools; was graduated from the Ohio Northern University at Ada in 1889; occupied the chair of American history at Ohio Northern University 1889–1896 and was graduated from its law department in 1894; dean of the College of Law 1896–1900; vice president of the university 1900–1902; graduate student and lecturer at the University of Chicago 1902–1907; president of Antioch College, Yellow Springs, Ohio, 1907–1917; editor and author; delegate to the fourth State constitutional convention in 1912; elected as a Republican to the Sixty-third and to the four succeeding Congresses (March 4, 1913–March 3, 1923); did not seek renomination, having become a candidate for Senator; elected to the United States Senate in 1922; reelected in 1928 and served from March 4, 1923, to January 3, 1935; unsuccessful candidate for reelection in 1934; chairman of the Republican National Congressional Committee 1918–1922; delegate to the Republican National Convention in 1924; temporary chairman of the Republican National Convention in 1928 and made the keynote address; chairman of the Republican National Committee 1930–1932; engaged in literary pursuits; served as executive secretary of the George Rogers Clark Sesquicentennial Commission from 1935 until his death, while on a visit in Washington, D. C., December 23, 1936; interment in Glen Forest Cemetery, Yellow Springs, Ohio.

FESSENDEN, Samuel Clement (brother of Thomas Amory Deblois Fessenden and William Pitt Fessenden), a Representative from Maine; born in New Gloucester, Cumberland County, Maine, March 7, 1815; pursued classical studies and was graduated from Bowdoin College, Brunswick, Maine, in 1834 and from Bangor (Maine) Theological Seminary in 1837; was ordained and installed as pastor of the Second Congregational Church, Thomaston (now Rockland), Maine, 1837–1856; studied law; was admitted to the bar and commenced practice in 1858; judge of the Rockland municipal court; elected as a Republican to the Thirty-seventh Congress (March 4, 1861–March 3, 1863); was not a candidate for renomination in 1862 to the Thirty-eighth Congress; examiner in the United States Patent Office 1865–1879; United States consul at St. John, New Brunswick, 1879–1881; died in Stamford, Conn., on April 18, 1882; interment in Woodland Cemetery.

FESSENDEN, Thomas Amory Deblois (brother of Samuel Clement Fessenden and William Pitt Fessenden), a Representative from Maine; born in Portland, Maine, January 23, 1826; attended North Yarmouth Academy and Dartmouth College, Hanover, N. H.; was graduated from Bowdoin College, Brunswick, Maine, in 1845; studied law; was admitted to the bar in April 1848 and commenced practice in Mechanic Falls, Maine; moved to Auburn, Maine, in 1850 and continued the practice of law; delegate to the Republican National Convention at Philadelphia in 1856 and at Chicago in 1868; member of the State house of representatives in 1860 and 1868; prosecuting attorney for Androscoggin County in 1861 and 1862; elected as a Republican to the Thirty-seventh Congress to fill the vacancy caused by the resignation of Charles W. Walton and served from December 1, 1862, to March 3, 1863; was not a candidate for renomination in 1862; resumed the practice of law; presidential elector on the Republican ticket of Grant and Colfax 1868; died in Auburn, Maine, September 28, 1868; interment in Riverside Cemetery, Lewiston, Maine.

FESSENDEN, William Pitt (brother of Samuel Clement Fessenden and Thomas Amory Deblois Fessenden), a Representative and a Senator from Maine; born in Boscawen, Merrimack County, N. H., October 16, 1806; attended the common schools; was graduated from Bowdoin College, Brunswick, Maine, in 1827; studied law; was admitted to the bar in 1827 and practiced in Bridgeton, Bangor, and Portland, Maine; member of the State house of representatives in 1832 and 1840; delegate to the Whig National Conventions in 1840, 1848, and 1852; elected as a Whig to the Twenty-seventh Congress (March 4, 1841–March 3, 1843); declined to be a candidate for reelection in 1842; again a member of the State house of representatives in 1845 and 1846; unsuccessful Whig candidate for election to the Thirty-second Congress; again a member of the State house of representatives in 1853 and 1854; elected as a Whig to the United States Senate to fill the vacancy in the term beginning March 4, 1853, caused by the failure of the legislature to elect; reelected in 1859 and served from February 10, 1854, to July 1, 1864, when he resigned to accept the appointment of Secretary of the Treasury in the Cabinet of President Lincoln, in which capacity he served until March 3, 1865; member of the peace convention of 1861 held in Washington, D. C., in an effort to devise means to prevent the impending war; author of the plan for issuing Government bonds; again elected to the United States Senate and served from March 4, 1865, until his death in Portland, Maine, September 9, 1869; interment in Evergreen Cemetery.

FEW, William, a Delegate and a Senator from Georgia; born near Baltimore, Md., June 8, 1748; moved with his parents to Orange County, N. C., in 1758; completed preparatory studies; studied law; was admitted to the bar and commenced practice in Augusta, Ga., in 1776; member of the State house of representatives in 1777, 1779, 1783, and 1793; member of the executive council in 1777 and 1778; engaged in the expedition for the subjugation of east Florida in 1778; presiding judge of the Richmond County Court and surveyor general in 1778; served as lieutenant colonel of the Richmond County Militia in 1779; Member of the Continental Congress 1780–1788; original trustee for establishing the University of Georgia in 1785; delegate to the convention which revised the Federal Constitution in 1787; delegate to the Georgia convention that ratified the Federal Constitution in 1788; elected as a Democrat to the United States Senate and served from March 4, 1789, to March 3, 1793; unsuccessful candidate for election to the United States Senate in 1795; judge of the circuit court of Georgia 1794–1797; moved to New York City in 1799; member of the State assembly 1802–1805; State prison inspector 1802–1810; United States commissioner of loans in 1804; director of the Manhattan Bank 1804–1814, and president in 1814; served as alderman in 1813 and 1814; died in Fishkill, N. Y., July 16, 1828; interment in Reformed Dutch Church Cemetery, Fishkill Landing, Dutchess County, N. Y.

FICKLIN, Orlando Bell, a Representative from Illinois; born in Scott County, Ky., December 16, 1808; attended the common schools; was graduated from Transylvania Law School, Lexington, Ky., in 1830; was admitted to the bar in 1830 and commenced practice in Mount Carmel, Ill.; served in the Black Hawk War as quartermaster in 1832; colonel of the militia of Wabash County in 1833; State's attorney for the Wabash circuit in 1835; member of the State house of representatives in 1835, 1838, and 1842; moved to Charleston, Ill., in 1837; elected as a Democrat to the Twenty-eighth, Twenty-ninth, and Thirtieth Congresses (March 4, 1843–March 3, 1849); elected to the Thirty-second Congress (March 4, 1851–March

3, 1853); resumed the practice of law in Charleston; presidential elector on the Democratic ticket of Buchanan and Breckinridge in 1856; delegate to the Democratic National Convention at Cincinnati in 1856, at Charleston, S. C., in 1860, and at Chicago in 1864; delegate to the State constitutional convention in 1869 and 1870; again served in the State house of representatives in 1878; presidential elector on the Democratic ticket of Cleveland and Hendricks in 1884; died in Charleston, Ill., May 5, 1886; interment in Mound Cemetery.

FIEDLER, William Henry Frederick, a Representative from New Jersey; born in New York City August 25, 1847; moved to New Jersey with his parents, who settled in Newark; attended the public and high schools; apprenticed to the hat-finishing trade at the age of fifteen; employed as clerk and engaged in the retail hat and later in the men's clothing business; elected an alderman of Newark in 1876 and 1878; member of the State house of assembly in 1878 and 1879; mayor of Newark 1880–1882; unsuccessful candidate for reelection in 1881; again a member of the State house of assembly in 1882; elected as a Democrat to the Forty-eighth Congress (March 4, 1883–March 3, 1885); unsuccessful candidate for reelection; appointed postmaster of Newark, N. J., March 29, 1886, and served until October 1, 1889; resumed his former business pursuits until 1905, when he engaged in the real-estate business and in banking; unsuccessful candidate for mayor in 1904; died in Newark, N. J., January 1, 1919; interment in Fairmount Cemetery.

FIELD, David Dudley, a Representative from New York; born in Haddam, Middlesex County, Conn., February 13, 1805; educated by private tutors; was graduated from Williams College, Williamstown, Mass., in 1825; studied law in Albany, N. Y., and New York City; was admitted to the bar in 1828 and commenced practice in New York City; author of many works on political, civil, and criminal procedure; unsuccessful candidate for election to the State assembly in 1841; member of the commission on legal practice and procedure 1847–1850; member of a State commission to prepare a political, penal, and civil code 1857–1865; member of the peace convention of 1861 held in Washington, D. C., in an effort to devise means to prevent the impending war; elected as a Democrat to the Forty-fourth Congress to fill the vacancy caused by the resignation of Smith Ely, Jr., and served from January 11 to March 3, 1877; resumed the practice of law; died in New York City April 13, 1894; interment in Stockbridge Cemetery, Stockbridge, Mass.

FIELD, Moses Whelock, a Representative from Michigan; born in Watertown, Jefferson County, N. Y., February 10, 1828; moved with his parents to Cato, Cayuga County, N. Y.; attended the public schools, and was graduated from the academy in Victor, N. Y.; moved to Detroit, Mich., in 1844 and engaged in mercantile and agricultural pursuits; alderman of Detroit 1863–1865; elected as a Republican to the Forty-third Congress (March 4, 1873–March 3, 1875); unsuccessful for reelection in 1874 to the Forty-fourth Congress; instrumental in organizing the Independent Greenback Party, having called the national convention at Indianapolis, Ind., May 17, 1876; gave fifty acres of land to Detroit for a park (Linden Park) in 1875; regent of the University of Michigan in 1888; lived on his farm, "Linden Lawn," in the township of Hamtramck, a suburb of Detroit, where he died March 14, 1889; interment in Woodmere Cemetery.

FIELD, Richard Stockton (grandson of Richard Stockton), a Senator from New Jersey; born in Princeton, N. J., December 31, 1803; pursued an academic course, and was graduated from Princeton College in 1821; studied law; was admitted to the bar in 1825 and commenced practice in Salem, N. J.; moved to Prince-

ton, N. J., in 1832; member of the State house of assembly in 1837; attorney general of the State 1838–1841; member of the State constitutional convention in 1844; elected professor in the Princeton Law School in 1847; appointed as a Republican to the United States Senate to fill the vacancy caused by the death of John R. Thomson and served from November 21, 1862. to January 14, 1863, when a successor was elected; was not a candidate for election in 1863; appointed by President Lincoln judge of the United States District Court for the District of New Jersey and served from January 21, 1863, until his death in Princeton, N. J., May 25, 1870; interment in Princeton Cemetery

FIELD, Scott, a Representative from Texas; born in Canton, Madison County, Miss., January 26, 1847; attended the McKee School in Madison County; during the Civil War enlisted in the Confederate Army as a member of the Harvey Scouts; later served in Maj. Gen. W. H. Jackson's division, Forrest's corps; saw active service in northern Alabama and through the Georgia and Tennessee campaigns under Generals Johnston and Hood; after the war resumed his studies, and was graduated from the University of Virginia at Charlottesville in 1868; taught school for two years; studied law; was admitted to the bar in 1872; moved to Calvert, Tex., in 1872 and practiced law; prosecuting attorney of Robertson County 1878–1882; served in the State senate 1887–1891; delegate to the Democratic National Convention at Chicago in 1892; elected as a Democrat to the Fifty-eighth and Fifty-ninth Congresses (March 4, 1903–March 3, 1907); was not a candidate for reelection in 1906; resumed the practice of law until 1913, when he engaged in extensive agricultural pursuits; died in Calvert, Tex., December 20, 1931; interment in Calvert Cemetery.

FIELD, Walbridge Abner, a Representative from Massachusetts; born in North Springfield, Windsor County, Vt., April 26, 1833; was graduated from Dartmouth College, Hanover, N. H., in 1855; tutor at Dartmouth College in 1856, 1857, and 1859; studied law in Boston in 1858 and at the Harvard Law School in 1859; was admitted to the bar in 1860 and commenced practice in Boston, Mass.; member of the school committee of Boston in 1863 and 1864; served in the common council 1865–1867; appointed assistant attorney of the United States in 1865, serving in this capacity until April 1869, when he was appointed Assistant Attorney General of the United States, holding this office until August 1870, when he resigned; resumed the practice of law in Boston; presented credentials as a Member-elect to the Forty-fifth Congress and served from March 4, 1877, to March 28, 1878, when he was succeeded by Benjamin Dean, who contested his election; elected as a Republican to the Forty-sixth Congress (March 4, 1879–March 3, 1881); declined to be a candidate for renomination in 1880; appointed by Governor Long to the bench of the supreme judicial court on February 21, 1881; promoted to the position of chief justice on September 4, 1890, and served until his death in Boston, Mass., July 15, 1899; interment in Forest Hills Cemetery, West Roxbury, Mass.

FIELDER, George Bragg, a Representative from New Jersey; born in Jersey City, N. J., July 24, 1842; attended private and public schools in his native town, and was graduated from the Dickinson Lyceum in Jersey City and from Selleck's Academy, Norwalk, Conn.; engaged in banking, and, in company with his father, built the New Jersey Southern and New York, New Hampshire & Willimantic Railroads; enlisted as a private in the Union Army in 1862 and served throughout the Civil War, being promoted to sergeant major and lieutenant; elected register of Hudson County in 1884, and reelected in 1889; elected as a Democrat to the Fifty-third Congress (March 4, 1893–March 3, 1895); declined to be a candidate for renomination in 1894;

elected county register for a third time in 1895; died in Windham, N. Y., August 14, 1906; interment in Bay View Cemetery, Jersey City, N. J.

FIELDS, William Craig, a Representative from New York; born in New York City February 13, 1804; attended the common schools; moved to Laurens, Otsego County, N. Y., in 1836 and engaged in mercantile pursuits and in 1847 engaged in the manufacture of cotton and linen goods; justice of the peace for sixteen years; clerk of Otsego County 1852–1855; supervisor of Otsego County in 1865 and 1866; elected as a Republican to the Fortieth Congress (March 4, 1867–March 3, 1869); retired from public life; died in Laurens, Otsego County, N. Y., October 27, 1882; interment in Laurens Cemetery.

FIELDS, William Jason, a Representative from Kentucky; born in Willard, Carter County, Ky., December 29, 1874; attended the public schools, and the University of Kentucky at Lexington; studied law; engaged in agricultural pursuits and also in the real-estate business at Olive Hill, Ky.; was a commercial traveler 1899–1910; elected as a Democrat to the Sixty-second and to the six succeeding Congresses and served from March 4, 1911, to December 11, 1923, when he resigned, having been elected Governor; Governor of Kentucky from December 1923 to December 1927; returned to Olive Hill and was admitted to the bar in 1927; Commonwealth's attorney for the thirty-seventh judicial district of Kentucky from July 1, 1932, to January 1, 1935; appointed a member of the State Workmen's Compensation Board January 20, 1936, and served until his retirement on August 8, 1944; coowner of an insurance agency 1940–1945; died in Grayson, Ky., October 21, 1954; interment in Olive Hill Cemetery, Olive Hill, Ky.

FIESINGER, William Louis, a Representative from Ohio; born in Willard, Huron County, Ohio, October 25, 1877; educated in the public schools of Norwalk, Ohio; was graduated from the law department of Baldwin-Wallace University, Berea, Ohio, in 1901; was admitted to the bar the same year and commenced practice in Sandusky, Ohio; served as city solicitor of Sandusky 1903–1909; judge of the common pleas court of Erie County 1925–1931; elected as a Democrat to the Seventy-second, Seventy-third, and Seventy-fourth Congresses (March 4, 1931–January 3, 1937); unsuccessful candidate for renomination in 1936; resumed the practice of law in Sandusky, Ohio; died in Cleveland, Ohio, September 11, 1953; interment in Oakland Cemetery, Sandusky, Ohio.

FILLMORE, Millard, a Representative from New York and a Vice President and a President of the United States; born in Locke Township (now Summerhill), Cayuga County, N. Y., January 7, 1800; reared on a farm; attended the primitive schools and was self-instructed under adverse conditions; was apprenticed to a clothier at fifteen years of age; taught school in Buffalo while studying law; was admitted to the bar in 1823 and commenced practice in East Aurora, N. Y.; moved to Buffalo, N. Y., in 1830; member of the State assembly 1829–1831; elected as a Whig to the Twenty-third Congress (March 4, 1833–March 3, 1835); elected to the Twenty-fifth, Twenty-sixth, and Twenty-seventh Congresses (March 4, 1837–March 3, 1843); declined to be a candidate for renomination in 1842; unsuccessful Whig candidate for Governor in 1844; elected State comptroller in 1847 and served until his resignation on February 20, 1849; elected Vice President of the United States on the Whig ticket headed by Zachary Taylor in 1848, and was inaugurated March 4, 1849; became President upon the death of President Taylor and served from July 9, 1850, to March 3, 1853; unsuccessful Whig candidate for President in 1852 and as the National

American candidate in 1856; president of the Buffalo Historical Society; commanded a corps of home guards during the Civil War; traveled extensively; died in Buffalo, N. Y., March 8, 1874; interment in Forest Hill Cemetery.

FINCH, Isaac, a Representative from New York; born in Stillwater, Saratoga County, N. Y., October 13, 1783; moved with his parents to Peru, Clinton County, N. Y., in 1787; attended the public schools; studied law, but did not engage in extensive practice; settled near Jay, Essex County, N. Y., and became interested in agricultural pursuits; served as major in the Twenty-sixth Regiment of Infantry during the War of 1812; member of the State assembly 1822–1824; elected as a Democrat to the Twenty-first Congress (March 4, 1829–March 3, 1831); was not a candidate for renomination in 1830; resumed agricultural pursuits; died in Jay, N. Y., June 23, 1845; interment in Central Cemetery.

FINCK, William Edward, a Representative from Ohio; born in Somerset, Perry County, Ohio, September 1, 1822; attended the public schools and St. Joseph's College; studied law; was admitted to the bar in 1843 and commenced practice in Somerset, Ohio; unsuccessful candidate for election in 1850 to the Thirty-second Congress; member of the State senate in 1851; delegate to the Whig National Convention at Baltimore in 1852 which nominated Scott and Graham; again a member of the State senate in 1861; elected as a Democrat to the Thirty-eighth and Thirty-ninth Congresses (March 4, 1863–March 3, 1867); unsuccessful Democratic candidate for judge of the supreme court of Ohio in 1868; elected as a Democrat to the Forty-third Congress to fill the vacancy caused by the resignation of Hugh J. Jewett and served from December 7, 1874, to March 3, 1875; resumed the practice of law; died in Somerset, Ohio, January 25, 1901; interment in Holy Trinity Cemetery.

FINDLAY, James (brother of John Findlay and William Findlay), a Representative from Ohio; born in Mercersburg, Franklin County, Pa., October 12, 1770; attended the public schools; moved to Cincinnati, Ohio, in 1793; studied law; was admitted to the bar and practiced; member of the Territorial legislative council in 1798; United States receiver of public moneys at Cincinnati in 1800; United States marshal of Ohio in 1802; member of the State house of representatives in 1803; mayor of Cincinnati in 1805 and 1806, and again in 1810 and 1811; served in the War of 1812 as colonel of the Second Ohio Volunteer Infantry, and was commissioned brigadier general of the State militia for gallant service in that war; elected as a Jackson Democrat to the Nineteenth and to the three succeeding Congresses (March 4, 1825–March 3, 1833); was not a candidate for renomination in 1832; unsuccessful Democratic candidate for Governor of Ohio in 1834; died in Cincinnati, Ohio, December 28, 1835; interment in Spring Grove Cemetery.

FINDLAY, John (brother of James Findlay and William Findlay), a Representative from Pennsylvania; born in Mercersburg, Franklin County, Pa., March 31, 1766; received a limited schooling; prothonotary 1809–1821; served as captain in the War of 1812; moved to Chambersburg, Pa.; register and recorder of deeds; clerk of the orphans' court; clerk of the court of quarter sessions 1809–1818; elected as a Democrat to the Seventeenth Congress to fill the vacancy caused by the resignation of James Duncan; reelected to the Eighteenth and Nineteenth Congresses and served from October 9, 1821, to March 3, 1827; was not a candidate for renomination in 1826; appointed postmaster of Chambersburg, Pa., March 20, 1829, and held the office until his death there November 5, 1838; interment in Falling Spring Presbyterian Church Cemetery at Chambersburg.

FINDLAY, John Van Lear, a Representative from Maryland; born at Mount Tammany, near Williamsport, Washington County, Md., December 21, 1839; was privately tutored and pursued classical studies; was graduated from Princeton College in 1858; member of the State house of delegates in 1861 and 1862; studied law; was admitted to the bar and commenced practice in Baltimore, Md., in 1869; collector of internal revenue for the third district of Maryland at Baltimore in 1865 and 1866; appointed city solicitor for Baltimore in 1876 and served two years; elected as a Democrat to the Forty-eighth and Forty-ninth Congresses (March 4, 1883–March 3, 1887); resumed the practice of law; appointed a member of the Venezuelan Claims Commission in 1889; nominated as arbitrator on the Chilean Claims Commission in 1893, but the Senate rejected the nomination; died in Baltimore, Md., April 19, 1907: interment in Greenmount Cemetery.

FINDLAY, William (brother of James Findlay and John Findlay), a Senator from Pennsylvania; born in Mercersburg, Franklin County, Pa., June 20, 1768; attended the public schools; engaged in agricultural pursuits; served as brigade inspector in the State militia; studied law; was admitted to the bar and commenced practice in Franklinton, Pa.; member of the State house of representatives 1797 and 1804–1807; State treasurer 1807–1817; Governor of Pennsylvania 1817–1820; unsuccessful candidate for reelection in 1820; elected as a Democrat to the United States Senate to fill the vacancy in the term commencing March 4, 1821, caused by the failure of the legislature to elect and served from December 10, 1821, to March 3, 1827; was not a candidate for reelection in 1826; Director of the United States Mint from 1827 to 1841, when he resigned on account of illness; died in Harrisburg, Pa., November 12, 1846; interment in Harrisburg Cemetery.

FINDLEY, William, a Representative from Pennsylvania; born in Ireland in 1741 or 1742; attended the parish schools; immigrated to the United States and settled in Philadelphia, Pa., in 1762; enlisted as a private, rose to the rank of captain, and served during the Revolution; moved to Westmoreland County, Pa.; tailor; member of the council of censors in 1783; member of the general assembly 1785 and 1786; member of the State supreme executive council 1789 and 1790; served in the State house of representatives 1790 and 1791; delegate to the State constitutional convention in 1790; elected as a Democrat to the Second and to the three succeeding Congresses (March 4, 1791–March 3, 1799); engaged in agricultural pursuits; was in opposition to the Government during the Whisky Insurrection in 1794 and wrote a book defending his course; again a member of the State senate 1799–1802; elected to the Eighth and to the six succeeding Congresses (March 4, 1803–March 3, 1817); died near Greensburg, Pa., on April 4, 1821; interment in Unity Meeting House Cemetery, near Latrobe, Pa.

FINE, John, a Representative from New York; born in New York City August 26, 1794; received private instructions; was graduated from Columbia College at New York City in 1809; studied law in the Litchfield (Conn.) Law School; was admitted to the bar in 1815 and commenced practice in Ogdensburg, St. Lawrence County, N. Y.; treasurer of St. Lawrence County 1821–1833; judge of the court of common pleas for St. Lawrence County from 1824 until his resignation in March 1839; elected as a Democrat to the Twenty-sixth Congress (March 4, 1839–March 3, 1841); again judge of the court of common pleas from February 16, 1843, until the court was abolished in 1847; unsuccessful candidate for judge of the State supreme court in 1847 and again in 1849; member of the State senate in 1848; resumed the practice of law; died in Odgensburg, N. Y., January 4, 1867; interment in Ogdensburg Cemetery.

FINE, Sidney Asher, a Representative from New York; born in New York, N. Y., September 14, 1903; attended Public School 53 in the Bronx and Townsend Harris Hall High School; was graduated from College of the City of New York in 1923 and from the law school of Columbia University in 1926; was admitted to the bar in 1926 and commenced practice in New York, N. Y.; member of the State assembly in 1945 and 1946 and the State senate 1947–1950; elected as a Democrat to the Eighty-second, Eighty-third, and Eighty-fourth Congresses and served from January 3, 1951, until his resignation January 2, 1956; elected a justice of the New York State Supreme Court for a fourteen-year term commencing January 3, 1956, and ending December 31, 1969; resides in New York, N. Y.

FINERTY, John Frederick, a Representative from Illinois; born in Galway, Ireland, September 10, 1846; completed preparatory studies; immigrated to the United States in 1864; enlisted in the Union Army during the Civil War and served in the Ninety-ninth Regiment, New York State Militia; correspondent for the Chicago Times in the Sioux War of 1876, with General Crook; in the Northern Indian (Sioux) War of 1879, with General Miles; in the Ute campaign of 1879, with General Merritt, and afterward in the Apache campaign of 1881, with General Carr; correspondent in Washington during the sessions of the Forty-sixth Congress 1879–1881; established the Citizen, a weekly newspaper, in Chicago in 1882; elected as an Independent Democrat to the Forty-eighth Congress (March 4, 1883–March 3, 1885); member of the board of local improvements 1906–1908; engaged in journalism; died in Chicago, Ill., June 10, 1908; interment in Calvary Cemetery.

FINKELNBURG, Gustavus Adolphus, a Representative from Missouri; born near Cologne, Germany, April 6, 1837; immigrated to the United States in 1848 with his parents, who settled in St. Charles, Mo.; attended St. Charles College, Missouri, and was graduated from the Cincinnati (Ohio) Law School in 1859; was admitted to the bar in 1860 and commenced practice in St. Louis, Mo.; served in the Union Army during the Civil War; member of the State house of representatives 1864–1868, and served as speaker pro tempore in 1868; elected as a Republican to the Forty-first Congress and as a Liberal Republican to the Forty-second Congress (March 4, 1869–March 3, 1873); appointed United States judge for the eastern district of Missouri in 1905, and served until March 31, 1907, when he resigned; died in Denver, Colo., May 18, 1908; interment in Bellefontaine Cemetery, St. Louis, Mo.

FINLEY, Charles (son of Hugh Franklin Finley), a Representative from Kentucky; born in Williamsburg, Whitley County, Ky., March 26, 1865; attended the common and subscription schools, and Milligan College, Milligan, Tenn.; engaged in business as a coal operator, banker, and publisher; member of the State house of representatives 1894–1896; delegate to the Republican State convention in 1895; served as secretary of state of Kentucky 1896–1900; chairman of the Republican executive committee of the Eleventh Kentucky Congressional District 1912–1928; elected as a Republican to the Seventy-first Congress to fill the vacancy caused by the resignation of John M. Robsion; reelected to the Seventy-second Congress and served from February 15, 1930, to March 3, 1933; was not a candidate for renomination in 1932; retired from business activities; died in Williamsburg, Ky., March 18, 1941; interment in Highland Cemetery, Williamsburg, Ky.

FINLEY, David Edward, a Representative from South Carolina; born in Trenton, Phillips County, Ark., February 28, 1861; attended the public schools of Rock Hill and Ebenezer,

S. C., and was graduated from the law department of South Carolina College (now the University of South Carolina) at Columbia in 1885; was admitted to the bar in 1886 and commenced practice in York, S. C.; member of the State house of representatives 1890–1892; served in the State senate 1892–1896; trustee of the University of South Carolina 1890–1896; elected as a Democrat to the Fifty-sixth and to the eight succeeding Congresses and served from March 4, 1899, until his death; had been reelected to the Sixty-fifth Congress; died in Charlotte, N. C., on January 26, 1917; interment in Rose Hill Cemetery, York, S. C.

FINLEY, Ebenezer Byron (nephew of Stephen Ross Harris), a Representative from Ohio; born in Orrville, Wayne County, Ohio, July 31, 1833; attended the public schools; studied law at Bucyrus, Ohio, from 1859 until the outbreak of the Civil War; was active in recruiting Company K, Twenty-fourth Ohio Volunteer Infantry, in which he served as a first lieutenant; was honorably discharged in 1862 on account of wounds; resumed the study of law; was admitted to the bar in 1862, and commenced practice in Bucyrus, Crawford County, Ohio; elected as a Democrat to the Forty-fifth and Forty-sixth Congresses (March 4, 1877–March 3, 1881); was not a candidate for renomination in 1880; adjutant general of Ohio in 1884; served as circuit judge of the third circuit of Ohio; resumed the practice of law in Bucyrus, Ohio, where he died August 22, 1916; interment in Oakwood Cemetery.

FINLEY, Hugh Franklin (father of Charles Finley), a Representative from Kentucky; born at Tyes Ferry, Whitley County, Ky., January 18, 1833; attended the common schools; engaged in agricultural pursuits; studied law; was admitted to the bar in 1859 and commenced practice in Williamsburg, Ky.; member of the State house of representatives from 1861 to August 1862, when he resigned; elected Commonwealth attorney in 1862, and served until 1866, when he resigned; again elected in 1867, and reelected in 1868 for six years; unsuccessful candidate for election in 1870 to the Forty-second Congress; served in the State senate in 1875 and 1876, when he resigned; appointed in 1876 by President Grant as United States district attorney for Kentucky, and served until 1877; resumed the practice of law; judge of the fifteenth judicial circuit 1880–1886; elected as a Republican to the Fiftieth and Fifty-first Congresses (March 4, 1887–March 3, 1891); unsuccessful candidate for renomination in 1890; resumed the practice of law and also engaged in the coal-mining business; died in Williamsburg, Ky., October 16, 1909; interment in Woodlawn Cemetery.

FINLEY, Jesse Johnson, a Representative from Florida; born near Lebanon, Wilson County, Tenn., November 18, 1812; pursued an academic course; captain of mounted volunteers in the Seminole War in 1836; studied law and was admitted to the bar in 1838; moved to Mississippi County, Ark., in 1840 and practiced his profession; served in the State senate in 1841; returned to Tennessee in 1842, settled in Memphis, and continued the practice of law; mayor of Memphis in 1845; moved to Mariana, Fla., in November 1846; elected to the State senate of Florida in 1850; presidential elector on the Whig ticket of Scott and Graham in 1852; appointed judge of the western circuit of Florida in 1853; was elected to the same office in 1855 and again in 1859; appointed judge of the Confederate States court for the district of Florida in 1861; resigned and volunteered as a private in the Confederate Army in March 1862, and was successively promoted to the rank of brigadier general November 16, 1863; settled in Lake City, Fla., in 1865, and continued the practice of law; moved to Jacksonville, Fla., in 1871; successfully contested as a Democrat the election of Josiah J. Walls to the Forty-fourth

Congress and served from April 19, 1876, to March 3, 1877; successfully contested the election of Horatio Bisbee, Jr., to the Forty-fifth Congress and served from February 20 to March 3, 1879; presented credentials as a Member-elect to the Forty-Seventh Congress and served from March 4, 1881, to June 1, 1882, when he was succeeded by Horatio Bisbee, Jr., who contested his election; presented credentials on December 5, 1887, as a Senator-designate to the United States Senate for the term commencing March 4, 1887, but was not permitted to qualify for the reason that the appointment was made before the vacancy occurred; died in Lake City, Fla., November 6, 1904; interment in Evergreen Cemetery, Gainesville, Fla.

FINNEY, Darwin Abel, a Representative from Pennsylvania; born in Shrewsbury, Rutland County, Vt., August 11, 1814; attended the public schools and was graduated from the military academy at Rutland, Vt.; moved with his parents to Meadville, Pa.; clerk in a law office in Kingsbury, N. Y., in 1834 and 1835; was graduated from Allegheny College, Meadville, Pa., in 1840; studied law; was admitted to the bar in 1842 and commenced practice in Meadville, Pa.; member of the State senate 1856–1861; elected as a Republican to the Fortieth Congress and served from March 4, 1867, until his death, while traveling in Europe, at Brussels, Belgium, August 25, 1868; interment in Greendale Cemetery, Meadville, Pa.

FINO, Paul Albert, a Representative from New York; born in New York, N. Y., December 15, 1913; attended the public schools; graduated from the law school of St. John's University, New York, N. Y., in 1937; was admitted to the New York State bar in 1938 and began practice in New York City; served as an assistant attorney general in the State government from March 1943 to December 1944, first in the Labor Bureau and later in the Criminal Division of the Education Bureau; member of the State senate from January 1945 to May 1950; member of the New York City Civil Service Commission from June 1, 1950, to December 31, 1952; elected as a Republican to the Eighty-third and to the three succeeding Congresses (January 3, 1953–January 3, 1961). *Reelected to the Eighty-seventh Congress.*

FISCHER, Israel Frederick, a Representative from New York; born in New York City August 17, 1858; moved to Brooklyn in September 1887; attended the public schools and Cooper Institute, New York City; employed as a clerk in a law office; studied law; was admitted to the bar in 1879 and commenced practice in New York City; member of the executive committee of the Republican State committee 1888–1890; chairman of the executive committee of Kings County during the same period and chairman of the campaign committee in 1888; elected as a Republican to the Fifty-fourth and Fifty-fifth Congresses (March 4, 1895–March 3, 1899); unsuccessful candidate for reelection in 1898 to the Fifty-sixth Congress; appointed on May 2, 1899, by President McKinley as a member of the United States Board of General Appraisers (now the United States Customs Court); appointed chief justice of that court by President Coolidge on April 16, 1927, and served until his retirement on March 31, 1933; delegate to the International Customs Congress held in New York City in 1903; died in New York, N. Y., March 16, 1940; interment in Maimonides Cemetery, Brooklyn, N. Y.

FISH, Hamilton (grandfather of Hamilton Fish, Jr.), a Representative and a Senator from New York; born in New York City August 3, 1808; attended Doctor Bancel's French School, New York City; was graduated from Columbia College, New York City, in 1827; studied law; was admitted to the bar in 1830 and practiced in New York City; commissioner of deeds for the city and county of New York 1832–1833; elected as a Whig to the Twenty-eighth Congress (March 4, 1843–March 3, 1845); unsuccessful candidate for reelection in 1844 to the Twenty-ninth Congress; resumed the practice of law; Lieutenant Governor of New York from November 1848 to January 1, 1849; Governor in 1849 and 1850; elected to the United States Senate and served from March 4, 1851, to March 3, 1857; was not a candidate for reelection; president general of the Society of the Cincinnati from 1854 until his death; appointed by President Lincoln as one of the board of commissioners for the relief and exchange of Union prisoners of war in the South; president of the New York Historical Society 1867–1869; appointed by President Grant as Secretary of State on March 11, 1869; reappointed on March 17, 1873, and served until March 12, 1877; member of the joint high commission which settled the differences between the United States and Great Britain in 1871 and negotiated the treaty of Washington in 1873, and in the same year he negotiated with the Spanish Minister the settlement of the *Virginius* question; resumed the practice of law and managed his large real-estate holdings in New York City; died in Garrison, N. Y., September 7, 1893; interment in St. Philip's Cemetery.

FISH, Hamilton (son of the preceding), a Representative from New York; born in Albany, N. Y., April 17, 1849; attended private schools in this country and in Switzerland, and was graduated from Columbia College, New York City, in 1869; private secretary to his father, who was Secretary of State in the Cabinet of President Grant, 1869–1871; was graduated from Columbia Law School in 1873; was admitted to the bar the same year and commenced practice in New York City; member of the State assembly 1874–1896, serving as speaker in 1895 and 1896; appointed by President Theodore Roosevelt in 1903 as assistant treasurer of the United States at New York City; reappointed in 1907 and served until October 1908, when he resigned; elected as a Republican to the Sixty-first Congress (March 4, 1909–March 3, 1911); unsuccessful candidate for reelection in 1910 to the Sixty-second Congress; retired from public life and active pursuits and resided in Garrison, N. Y.; died while on a visit in Aiken, S. C., January 15, 1936; interment in the cemetery of St. Philip's Church-in-the-Highlands, Garrison, N. Y.

FISH, Hamilton, Jr. (son of the preceding and grandson of Hamilton Fish), a Representative from New York; born in Garrison, Putnam County, N. Y., December 7, 1888; attended St. Marks School; was graduated from Harvard University, Cambridge, Mass., in 1910; served in the State assembly 1914–1916; during the First World War was commissioned on July 15, 1917, captain of Company K, Fifteenth New York National Guard (colored), which subsequently became the Three Hundred and Sixty-ninth Infantry; took an active part in the capture of Sechault, and was discharged as a major on May 14, 1919; decorated with the Croix de Guerre and the American Silver Star and also cited in War Department general orders; colonel in the Officers' Reserve Corps; elected as a Republican to the Sixty-sixth Congress to fill the vacancy caused by the resignation of Edmund Platt; reelected to the Sixty-seventh and to the eleven succeeding Congresses and served from November 2, 1920, to January 3, 1945; unsuccessful candidate for reelection in 1944 to the Seventy-ninth Congress; author; engaged in the oil-development business; is a resident of New York, N. Y.

FISHBURNE, John Wood (cousin of Maury Maverick), a Representative from Virginia; born near Charlottesville, Albemarle County, Va., March 8, 1868; attended private schools, Pantop's Academy, near Charlottesville, Va., and Washington and Lee University, Lexington, Va.; taught at Fishburne Military Academy, Waynesboro, Va., in 1886 and 1887; was graduated from the law department of the University of Virginia at Charlottesville in 1890; was admitted to the bar the same year and commenced practice in Charlottesville, Va.; also engaged in agricultural pursuits; served in the State house of delegates 1895–1897; member of the Virginia State Library Board 1904–1913; appointed judge of the eighth judicial circuit in 1913 by Gov. W. H. Mann; subsequently elected by the legislature and served from 1913 until his resignation in 1930, having become a candidate for Representative in Congress; elected as a Democrat to the Seventy-second Congress (March 4, 1931–March 3, 1933); was not a candidate for renomination in 1932; resumed the practice of law; presidential elector on the Democratic ticket of Roosevelt and Garner in 1936; died in Ivy Depot, near Charlottesville, Va., June 24, 1937; interment in Riverview Cemetery, Charlottesville, Va.

FISHER, Charles, a Representative from North Carolina; born near Salisbury, Rowan County, N. C., October 20, 1789; educated by private tutors in Raleigh, N. C.; studied law; was admitted to the bar but did not practice to any extent; member of the State senate in 1818; elected as a Democrat to the Fifteenth Congress to fill the vacancy caused by the death of George Mumford; reelected to the Sixteenth Congress and served from February 11, 1819, to March 3, 1821; declined to be a candidate for renomination in 1820; member of the State house of commons 1821–1836 and served as speaker in 1831 and 1832; member of the State constitutional convention in 1835; elected to the Twenty-sixth Congress (March 4, 1839–March 3, 1841); was not a candidate for renomination in 1840; unsuccessful candidate for election in 1844 to the Twenty-ninth Congress; declined to be a candidate for the Democratic nomination for Governor of North Carolina in 1846; died in Hillsboro, Miss., while on a visit, May 7, 1849.

FISHER, David, a Representative from Ohio; born in Somerset County, Pa., December 3, 1794; moved with his parents to Point Pleasant, Clermont County, Ohio, in 1799; pursued preparatory studies; was a lay preacher and newspaper contributor; member of the State house of representatives in 1834; unsuccessful candidate for Governor in 1844; editor and proprietor of a newspaper in Wilmington, Ohio, in 1846; elected as a Whig to the Thirtieth Congress (March 4, 1847–March 3, 1849); was not a candidate for renomination in 1848; while in Congress he occupied a seat next to John Quincy Adams, who fell into his arms when stricken with paralysis while delivering a speech; returned to Cincinnati, Ohio; city magistrate in 1849 and 1850; resumed newspaper activities; died near Mount Holly, Ohio, May 7, 1886; interment in Wesleyan Cemetery, Cincinnati, Ohio.

FISHER, George, a Representative from New York; born in Franklin, Mass., March 17, 1788; attended the common schools and Brown University, Providence, R. I.; studied law; was admitted to the bar in Oswego County, N. Y., in 1816 and commenced practice in Oswego, N. Y.; appointed inspector of schools in 1818; trustee of the village of Oswego in 1828 and 1833; presented credentials as a Member-elect to the Twenty-first Congress and served from March 4, 1829, to February 5, 1830, when the seat was awarded to Silas Wright, Jr., who contested the election; trustee of schools in 1830; continued the practice of law in Oswego, N. Y., until 1833; took his family to France, where he spent five years for the education of his children; returned to Oswego and engaged in real-estate operations; served as president of the Northwestern Insurance Co. for several years; moved to New York City about 1856 and died there March 26, 1861.

FISHER, George Purnell, a Representative from Delaware; born in Milford, Sussex County, Del., October 13, 1817; attended the public schools of Kent County and Mount St. Mary's College,

Emmitsburg, Md.; was graduated from Dickinson College, Carlisle, Pa., in 1838; studied law; was admitted to the bar in 1841 and commenced practice in Dover, Del.; member of the State house of representatives in 1843 and 1844; secretary of state in 1846; confidential clerk to Secretary Clayton in the Department of State at Washington in 1849; appointed by President Taylor a commissioner to adjudicate claims against Brazil, and served from 1850 to 1852; attorney general of Delaware 1857–1860; elected as a Union Republican to the Thirty-seventh Congress (March 4, 1861–March 3, 1863); unsuccessful candidate for reelection in 1862 to the Thirty-eighth Congress; appointed by President Lincoln on March 11, 1863, a judge of the Supreme Court of the District of Columbia, which position he resigned when appointed district attorney for the District of Columbia, serving until 1875, when he resigned; returned to Dover; appointed by President Harrison on May 31, 1889, First Auditor of the Treasury Department and served until March 23, 1893; died in Washington, D. C., February 10, 1899; interment in Oak Hill Cemetery; reinterment in the Methodist Cemetery, Dover, Del.

FISHER, Horatio Gates, a Representative from Pennsylvania; born in Huntingdon, Huntingdon County, Pa., April 21, 1838; attended public and private schools; was graduated from Lafayette College, Easton, Pa., in July 1855; engaged in mining, shipping, and the wholesale coal business; member of the borough council 1862–1865; auditor of Huntingdon County 1865–1868; burgess of the borough of Huntingdon 1874–1876; member of the State senate 1876–1879; elected as a Republican to the Forty-sixth and Forty-seventh Congresses (March 4, 1879–March 3, 1883); declined to be a candidate for renomination; resumed his former business pursuits; appointed by Governor Beaver a member of the board of managers of Huntingdon Reformatory in 1888; died in Punxsutawney, Pa., May 8, 1890; interment in River View Cemetery, Huntingdon, Pa.

FISHER, Hubert Frederick, a Representative from Tennessee; born in Milton, Santa Rosa County, Fla., October 6, 1877; attended the common schools and was graduated from the University of Mississippi at Oxford in 1898; took a postgraduate course at Princeton University in 1900 and 1901; studied law; was admitted to the bar in 1904 and commenced practice in Memphis, Tenn.; delegate to the Democratic National Convention at Baltimore in 1912; member of the State senate in 1913 and 1914; United States attorney for the western district of Tennessee 1914–1917; elected as a Democrat to the Sixty-fifth and to the six succeeding Congresses (March 4, 1917–March 3, 1931); was not a candidate for renomination in 1930; due to deafness retired from active legal and political activities and moved to Germantown, Tenn., where he engaged in nursery pursuits, specializing in flowers and plants; died June 16, 1941, while on a visit in New York City, N. Y.; interment in Old Gray Cemetery, Knoxville, Tenn.

FISHER, John, a Representative from New York; born in Londonderry, Rockingham County, N. H., March 13, 1806; attended the common schools; engaged in mercantile pursuits; managed an iron manufacturing establishment in Hamilton, Canada, 1836–1856; member of the city council of Hamilton 1848 and 1849 and served as mayor in 1850; returned to New York State and settled in Batavia in 1856; acted as State commissioner in the erection of the institution for the blind in Batavia 1866–1868; president of a fire insurance company; elected as a Republican to the Forty-first Congress (March 4, 1869–March 3, 1871); unsuccessful candidate for reelection in 1870 to the Forty-second Congress; engaged in the fire insurance business; died in Batavia, N. Y., on March 28, 1882; interment in Batavia Cemetery.

FISHER, Ovie Clark, a Representative from Texas; born near Junction, Kimble County, Tex., November 22, 1903; attended the public schools at Junction, Tex., and the University of Texas at Austin; was graduated from the law department of Baylor University, Waco, Tex., in 1929; was admitted to the bar the same year and commenced practice in San Angelo, Tex.; county attorney of Tom Green County, Tex., 1931–1935; member of the State house of representatives 1935–1937; district attorney, fifty-first judicial district, 1937–1943; elected as a Democrat to the Seventy-eighth and to the eight succeeding Congresses (January 3, 1943–January 3, 1961). *Reelected to the Eighty-seventh Congress.*

FISHER, Spencer Oliver, a Representative from Michigan; born in Camden, Hillsdale County, Mich., February 3, 1843; attended the public schools and Albion and Hillsdale Colleges in Michigan; engaged in lumbering and banking in West Bay City, Mich.; mayor of West Bay City 1881–1884; delegate to the Democratic National Convention at Chicago in 1884; elected as a Democrat to the Forty-ninth and Fiftieth Congresses (March 4, 1885–March 3, 1889); unsuccessful candidate for reelection in 1888 to the Fifty-first Congress; resumed his former business pursuits in Bay City, Mich., where he died June 1, 1919; interment in Elmlawn Cemetery.

FISK, James, a Representative and a Senator from Vermont; born in Greenwich, Hampshire County, Mass., October 4, 1763; self-educated; served in the Revolutionary War 1779–1782; member of the General Assembly of Massachusetts in 1785; entered the Universalist ministry and preached occasionally; moved to Barre, Vt., in 1798; studied law; was admitted to the bar and commenced practice in Barre; member of the Vermont House of Representatives 1800–1805, 1809, 1810, and 1815; judge of the Orange County Court 1802–1809 and in 1816; selected as the member from Orange County to locate the capital in 1803; chairman of the committee that endeavored to get a settlement of the northern boundary with Canada in 1804; elected as a Democrat to the Ninth and Tenth Congresses (March 4, 1805–March 3, 1809); unsuccessful candidate for reelection in 1808 to the Eleventh Congress; elected to the Twelfth and Thirteenth Congresses (March 4, 1811–March 3, 1815); unsuccessful candidate for reelection in 1814 to the Fourteenth Congress; appointed United States judge for the Territory of Indiana in 1812, but declined; judge of the supreme court of Vermont in 1815 and 1816; elected to the United States Senate to fill the vacancy caused by the resignation of Dudley Chase and served from November 4, 1817, to January 8, 1818, when he resigned; collector of customs for the district of Vermont 1818–1826; moved to Swanton, Vt., in 1819, and died there November 17, 1844; interment in Church Street Cemetery.

FISK, Jonathan, a Representative from New York; born in Amherst, N. H., September 26, 1778; attended the public schools; taught school; moved to Newburgh, N. Y., in 1800; studied law; was admitted to the bar in 1802 and commenced practice in Newburgh; elected as a Democrat to the Eleventh Congress (March 4, 1809–March 3, 1811); elected to the Thirteenth and Fourteenth Congresses and served from March 4, 1813, until March 1815, when he resigned to accept the position of United States attorney for the southern district of New York, to which he was appointed by President Madison and which position he held until June 30, 1819; resumed the practice of law; died in Newburgh, N. Y., July 13, 1832; interment in Old Town Cemetery.

FITCH, Asa, a Representative from New York; born in Groton, Conn., November 10, 1765; received a limited schooling; during the Revolutionary War served as a sergeant in Captain

Livingston's company; studied medicine and practiced in Duanesburg and Salem, N. Y.; justice of the peace 1799–1810; president of the Washington County Medical Society 1806–1826; county judge 1810–1821; elected as a Federalist to the Twelfth Congress (March 4, 1811–March 3, 1813); declined to be a candidate for renomination in 1812; resumed the practice of medicine; died in Salem, N. Y., August 24, 1843; interment in Evergreen Cemetery.

FITCH, Ashbel Parmelee, a Representative from New York; born in Moores, Clinton County, N. Y., October 8, 1848; attended the public schools of New York, Williston Seminary, East Hampton, Mass., the Universities of Jena and Berlin, Germany, and Columbia College Law School in New York City; was admitted to the bar in November 1869 and commenced practice in New York City; elected as a Republican to the Fiftieth Congress and as a Democrat to the Fifty-first, Fifty-second, and Fifty-third Congresses and served from March 4, 1887, until December 26, 1893, when he resigned; comptroller of New York City 1893–1897; president of the Trust Company of America in 1899; died in New York City on May 4, 1904; interment in Woodlawn Cemetery.

FITCH, Graham Newell (grandfather of Edwin Denby), a Representative and a Senator from Indiana; born in Le Roy, Genesee County, N. Y., December 5, 1809; attended Middlebury Academy and Geneva (N. Y.) College; studied medicine and completed his medical course at the College of Physicians and Suregons; commenced practice in Logansport, Ind., in 1834; member of the State house of representatives in 1836 and 1839; professor of anatomy at the Rush Medical College, Chicago, Ill., 1844–1848 and at the Indianapolis (Ind.) Medical College in 1878; Democratic presidential elector in 1844, 1848, and 1856; elected as a Democrat to the Thirty-first and Thirty-second Congresses (March 4, 1849–March 3, 1853); was not a candidate for renomination in 1852; resumed the practice of medicine; elected to the United States Senate to fill a vacancy in the term beginning March 4, 1855, and served from February 4, 1857, to March 3, 1861; was not a candidate for reelection in 1860; raised the Forty-sixth Regiment, Indiana Volunteer Infantry, during the Civil War and served as its colonel from November 1, 1861, to August 2, 1862, when he resigned because of injuries received in action; commanded a brigade at the capture of Fort Thompson, Mo., and Island No. 10; also participated in the capture of Forts Pillow and Charles; resumed the practice of medicine in Logansport, Ind.; delegate to the Democratic National Convention at New York City in 1868, which nominated the presidential ticket of Seymour and Blair; died in Logansport, Ind., November 29, 1892; interment in Mount Hope Cemetery.

FITCH, Thomas, a Representative from Nevada; born in New York City January 27, 1838; attended the public schools; moved to Chicago, Ill., in 1855, and to Milwaukee, Wis., in 1856; employed as a clerk; local editor of the Milwaukee Free Democrat in 1859 and 1860; moved to California in 1860; editor of the San Francisco Times and Placerville Republican; studied law; was admitted to the bar and practiced; member of the California Assembly in 1862 and 1863; moved to Nevada in June 1863; elected a member of the convention which framed the State constitution in 1864; Union nominee for Territorial Delegate to Congress in 1864; district attorney of Washoe County in 1865 and 1866; elected as a Republican to the Forty-first Congress (March 4, 1869–March 3, 1871); unsuccessful candidate for reelection in 1870 to the Forty-second Congress; continued the practice of law; moved to Los Angeles, Calif., in 1909 and was employed as a writer on the Times; died in Decoto, Calif., November 12, 1923; interment in Cypress Cemetery.

FITE, Samuel McClary, a Representative from Tennessee; born near Alexandria, Smith County, Tenn., June 12, 1816; attended the common and private schools and was graduated from Clinton College, Tennessee; studied law in Lebanon; was admitted to the bar and commenced practice in Carthage, Tenn.; member of the State senate in 1850; presidential elector on the Whig ticket of Scott and Graham in 1852; judge of the sixth judicial district 1858–1861; resumed the practice of law in Carthage, Tenn.; appointed on July 24, 1869, judge of the sixth judicial district to fill a vacancy; elected to the same office on January 8, 1870, and served until 1874; elected as a Democrat to the Forty-fourth Congress to fill the vacancy caused by the death of John W. Head and served from March 4, 1875, until his death, at Hot Springs, Ark., October 23, 1875, before the assembling of Congress; interment in Carthage Cemetery, Carthage, Tenn.; reinterment in Mount Olivet Cemetery, Nashville, Tenn., in 1908.

FITHIAN, George Washington, a Representative from Illinois; born near Willow Hill, Jasper County, Ill., July 4, 1854; attended the common schools; learned the printer's trade in Mount Carmel, Ill.; studied law; was admitted to the bar in 1875 and commenced practice in Newton, Jasper County, Ill.; prosecuting attorney of Jasper County 1876–1884; elected as a Democrat to the Fifty-first, Fifty-second, and Fifty-third Congresses (March 4, 1889–March 3, 1895); unsuccessful candidate for reelection in 1894 to the Fifty-fourth Congress; railroad and warehouse commissioner of Illinois 1895–1897; resumed the practice of law and engaged in agricultural pursuits and stock raising in Newton, Ill.; was also the owner of an extensive cotton plantation near Falcon, Miss., where he contracted pneumonia; died in a hospital at Memphis, Tenn., January 21, 1921; interment in Riverside Cemetery, Newton, Ill.

FITZGERALD, Frank Thomas, a Representative from New York; born in New York City May 4, 1857; was graduated from the College of St. Francis Xavier, New York City, from St. Mary's College, Niagara Falls, N. Y., in 1876, and from the Columbia Law School, New York City, in 1878; was admitted to the bar the same year and commenced the practice of his profession in New York City in 1879; elected as a Democrat to the Fifty-first Congress and served from March 4, 1889, until November 4, 1889, when he resigned; register of New York County in 1891 and 1892; delegate to the State constitutional convention in 1893; elected surrogate of New York County in 1892 for a term of fourteen years; reelected in 1906 and served in this capacity until his death in New York City November 25, 1907; interment Calvary Cemetery, Long Island City, N. Y.

FITZGERALD, John Francis (grandfather of John F. Kennedy), a Representative from Massachusetts; born in Boston, Mass., February 11, 1863; was graduated from the Eliot Grammar School and from the Boston Latin School; attended Harvard Medical School for one year; held a position in the Boston customhouse from 1886 to 1891; member of the Boston Common Council in 1892; member of the State senate in 1893 and 1894; elected as a Democrat to the Fifty-fourth, Fifty-fifth, and Fifty-sixth Congresses (March 4, 1895–March 3, 1901); was not a candidate for renomination in 1900; mayor of Boston in 1906, 1907, and 1910–1914; engaged in the insurance and investment business; also owner of a weekly newspaper; chairman of the Massachusetts delegation to the Democratic National Convention in Baltimore in 1912; unsuccessful candidate for election to the United States Senate in 1916; presented credentials as a Democratic Member-elect to the Sixty-sixth Congress and served from March 4, 1919, until October 23, 1919, when he was succeeded by Peter F. Tague, who contested his election; resumed his newspaper activities and also engaged as an investment banker; unsuccessful candidate for Governor in 1922; presidential elector in 1924, 1936, 1940, and 1944; member of the Port of Boston Authority 1934–1948; retired to private life; died in Boston, Mass., October 2, 1950; interment in St. Joseph's Cemetery, West Roxbury, Boston, Mass.

FITZGERALD, John Joseph, a Representative from New York; born in Brooklyn, N. Y., March 10, 1872; attended the public schools, La Salle Military Academy (formerly Sacred Heart Academy), and was graduated from Manhattan College, New York City, in 1891; studied law in the New York Law School; was admitted to the bar in 1893 and commenced practice in New York City; delegate to the Democratic National Conventions from 1900 to 1928; trustee of Manhattan College in New York City; elected as a Democrat to the Fifty-sixth and to the nine succeeding Congresses and served from March 4, 1899, until December 31, 1917, when he resigned to resume the practice of law; appointed county judge of Kings County in March 1932, elected in November 1932, and served until his retirement, due to age limitation, on December 31, 1942; resumed the private practice of law; died in Brooklyn, N. Y., May 13, 1952; interment in St. John's Cemetery, Middle Village, N. Y.

FITZGERALD, Roy Gerald, a Representative from Ohio; born in Watertown, Jefferson County, N. Y., August 25, 1875; moved to Ohio in 1890 with his parents, who settled in Dayton; attended the common schools; was graduated from the Dayton High School in 1893; was privately tutored in modern languages; studied law; was admitted to the bar in 1896 and commenced practice in Dayton, Ohio; during the First World War served as captain in the Three Hundred and Twenty-ninth Infantry, Headquarters Company, American Expeditionary Forces, 1917–1919; commissioned lieutenant colonel of Infantry, United States Army Reserve Corps, in 1928; delegate to conferences of the Interparliamentary Union at Paris, Berlin, Geneva, and London; elected as a Republican to the Sixty-seventh and to the four succeeding Congresses (March 4, 1921–March 3, 1931); unsuccessful candidate for reelection in 1930 to the Seventy-second Congress; resumed the practice of law; chairman of the local Red Cross 1931–1946; in 1939 became president of the Dayton Public Library and Museum; president of the Dayton and Montgomery County Historical Societies; is a resident of Dayton, Ohio.

FITZGERALD, Thomas, a Senator from Michigan; born in Germantown, Herkimer County, N. Y., April 10, 1796; pursued an academic course; served under General Harrison in the War of 1812 in the Fifth Regiment, New York Militia; severely wounded; taught school in Marcellus, N. Y.; in 1819 moved to Boonville, Warrick County, Ind., where he taught school; studied law; was admitted to the bar March 22, 1821, and commenced practice in Boonville; member of the State house of representatives in 1821; appointed keeper of the lighthouse, just then established at the mouth of the St. Joseph River, in 1832, and moved to St. Joseph, Mich.; clerk of Berrien County in 1834; regent of the University of Michigan in 1837; appointed bank commissioner in 1838; elected to the State house of representatives in 1839; unsuccessful candidate for Lieutenant Governor in 1839; appointed as a Democrat to the United States Senate to fill the vacancy caused by the resignation of Lewis Cass and served from June 8, 1848, until March 3, 1849; moved to Niles, Mich., in 1851; elected probate judge of Berrien County in 1852 and served until his death in Niles, Mich., March 25, 1855; interment in Silverbrook Cemetery.

FITZGERALD, William, a Representative from Tennessee; born at Port Tobacco, Charles County, Md., August 6, 1799; received a thorough English training; studied law; was admitted to the bar at Dover, Stewart County, Tenn., in 1821; clerk of the circuit court of Stewart County 1822–1825; member of the Tennessee Legislature in 1825–1827; served as attorney general of the sixteenth judicial circuit of Tennessee in 1826; elected as a Jackson Democrat to the Twenty-second Congress (March 4, 1831–March 3, 1833); unsuccessful candidate for reelection in 1832 to the Twenty-third Congress; moved to Paris, Tenn.; served as judge of the ninth judicial circuit of Tennessee 1845–1861; died at Paris, Tenn., in March 1864; interment in Fitzgerald Cemetery, near Paris, Tenn.

FITZGERALD, William Joseph, a Representative from Connecticut; born in Norwich, New London County, Conn., March 2, 1887; attended St. Patrick's Parochial School in Norwich, Conn.; employed in a foundry as a molder and later served as superintendent 1904–1930; served on the State commission to investigate widows' aid in 1916; member of the State senate 1931–1935; deputy State commissioner of labor 1931–1936; elected as a Democrat to the Seventy-fifth Congress (January 3, 1937–January 3, 1939); unsuccessful candidate for reelection in 1938 to the Seventy-sixth Congress; mayor of Norwich, Conn., in 1940 and 1941; elected to the Seventy-seventh Congress (January 3, 1941–January 3, 1943); unsuccessful candidate for reelection in 1942 to the Seventy-eighth Congress; appointed on March 1, 1943, as area director and later as State director of the War Manpower Commission of Connecticut and served until October 1, 1945; appointed State director of the United States Employment Service and served until his resignation in January 1947; died at Norwich, Conn., May 6, 1947; interment in St. Joseph's Cemetery.

FITZGERALD, William Thomas, a Representative from Ohio; born in Greenville, Darke County, Ohio, October 13, 1858; attended the rural schools and the Greenville High School; member of the National Guard of Ohio 1875–1882, and saw service during the Newark riots in 1877; was graduated from the National Normal University, Lebanon, Ohio, in 1887; taught in the Greenville High School 1886–1889; was graduated from the medical department of the University of Wooster, Cleveland, Ohio, in 1891 and commenced practice in Greenville in 1891; member of the board of education 1906–1914; mayor of Greenville 1921–1925; president of the Ocean-to-Ocean Highway Association, Ohio division, in 1926 and 1927; elected as a Republican to the Sixty-ninth and Seventieth Congresses (March 4, 1925–March 3, 1929); was not a candidate for renomination in 1928 to the Seventy-first Congress; resumed the practice of medicine in Greenville, Ohio, where he died on January 12, 1939; interment in Greenville Cemetery.

FITZGIBBONS, John, a Representative from New York; born in Glenmore, Oneida County, N. Y., July 10, 1868; moved to Oswego, Oswego County, N. Y., in 1870; attended the public schools; employed as a railway trainman in 1885; served as legislative representative of the Brotherhood of Railroad Trainmen of New York State 1896–1914 and again from February 1915 until January 1, 1933; served as referee for the New York State Labor Bureau in 1914 and 1915; alderman of Oswego in 1908 and 1909; mayor of Oswego in 1910, 1911, and 1918–1921; delegate to several Democratic State conventions; delegate to the Democratic National Conventions at San Francisco in 1920, at New York in 1924, and at Chicago in 1932; elected as a Democrat to the Seventy-third Congress (March 4, 1933–January 3, 1935); was not a candidate for renomination in 1934 to the Seventy-fourth Congress; engaged as legislative representative for the Railroad Brotherhoods in Albany, N. Y., until his death in a Buffalo, N. Y., hospital on August 4, 1941; interment in St. Peter's Cemetery, Oswego, N. Y.

FITZHENRY, Louis, a Representative from Illinois; born in Bloomington, McLean County, Ill., June 13, 1870; attended the public and high schools of Bloomington; engaged in journalism; was graduated from the law department of Illinois Wesleyan University at Bloomington in 1897; was admitted to the bar in 1897 and commenced practice in Bloomington, Ill.; city attorney of Bloomington 1907–1911; unsuccessful candidate for election in 1910 to the Sixty-second Congress; elected as a Democrat to the Sixty-third Congress (March 4, 1913–March 3, 1915); unsuccessful candidate for reelection in 1914 to the Sixty-fourth Congress; resumed the practice of law in Bloomington; unsuccessful candidate for election as a justice of the State supreme court in 1915; appointed United States district judge for the southern district of Illinois July 1, 1918, serving until October 3, 1933, when he was appointed a judge of the United States Circuit Court of Appeals for the Seventh District, in which capacity he served until his death in Normal, Ill., November 18, 1935; interment in Bloomington Cemetery, Bloomington, Ill.

FITZHUGH, William, a Delegate from Virginia; born in Eagles Nest, King George County, Va., August 24, 1741; pursued classical studies with private teachers; engaged in agricultural pursuits; delegate to the State constitutional convention in 1776; member of the State house of delegates in 1776 and 1777; Member of the Continental Congress in 1779 and 1780; again a member of the State house of delegates in 1780, 1781, 1787, and 1788; served in the State senate 1781–1785; engaged in agricultural pursuits; died in Ravensworth, Fairfax County, Va., June 6, 1809; interment in the private cemetery on the Ravensworth estate.

FITZPATRICK, Benjamin, a Senator from Alabama; born in Greene County, Ga., June 30, 1802; left an orphan, he was taken by his brother to Alabama in 1815; attended the public schools; studied law; was admitted to the bar in 1821 and commenced practice in Montgomery, Ala.; solicitor of the Montgomery circuit in 1822 and 1823; moved to his plantation in Autauga County in 1829 and engaged in planting; Governor of Alabama 1841–1845; appointed as a State Rights Democrat to the United States Senate to fill the vacancy caused by the death of Dixon H. Lewis and served from November 25, 1848, to November 30, 1849, when a successor was elected; again appointed and subsequently elected to the United States Senate to fill the vacancy caused by the resignation of William R. King and served from January 14, 1853, to March 3, 1855; elected to the United States Senate to fill the vacancy in the term commencing March 4, 1855, caused by the failure of the legislature to elect and served from November 26, 1855, until January 21, 1861, when he withdrew; served as President pro tempore of the Senate on various occasions during the Thirty-fifth and Thirty-sixth Congresses; nominated for Vice President of the United States on the ticket with Stephen A. Douglas at the Charleston-Baltimore Democratic National Convention in 1860, but declined; served as president of the constitutional convention of Alabama in 1865; died on his plantation near Wetumpka, Ala., November 25, 1869; interment in Oakwood Cemetery, Montgomery, Ala.

FITZPATRICK, James Martin, a Representative from New York; born in West Stockbridge, Berkshire County, Mass., June 27, 1869; attended the public schools; worked in the iron-ore mines in West Stockbridge, Mass.; moved to New York City in 1891 and worked in the various departments of the Metropolitan Street Railroad Company and the Interborough Rapid Transit Company until 1925, when he became engaged in the real-estate business; served as a commissioner of street openings in New York City in 1919; member of the board of aldermen of New York City 1919–1927; elected as a Democrat to the Seventieth and to the eight succeeding Congresses (March 4, 1927–

January 3, 1945); was not a candidate for renomination in 1944, retired from public and political activities in 1944; died in New York City, N. Y., April 10, 1949; interment in St. Raymond's Cemetery.

FITZPATRICK, Morgan Cassius, a Representative from Tennessee; born near Carthage, Smith County, Tenn., October 29, 1868; attended the common schools and Lebanon (Ohio) University in 1887; was graduated from the law department of Cumberland University, Lebanon, Tenn., in 1891; was admitted to the bar the same year and commenced practice in Hartsville, Tenn.; edited a newspaper at Hartsville; member of the State house of representatives 1895–1897, serving as speaker in 1897; State superintendent of public instruction 1899–1901; chairman of the Democratic State executive committee; elected as a Democrat to the Fifty-eighth Congress (March 4, 1903–March 3, 1905); was not a candidate for renomination in 1904; resumed the practice of law; died in Nashville, Tenn., June 25, 1908; interment in Gallatin Cemetery, Gallatin, Tenn.

FITZPATRICK, Thomas Young, a Representative from Kentucky; born near Prestonsburg, Floyd County, Ky., September 20, 1850; attended the common schools; studied law; was admitted to the bar in 1877 and practiced; county judge in 1874 and 1875; member of the State house of representatives in 1876 and 1877; county attorney 1880–1884; presidential elector on the Democratic ticket of Cleveland and Hendricks in 1884; elected as a Democrat to the Fifty-fifth and Fifty-sixth Congresses (March 4, 1897–March 3, 1901); died in Frankfort, Ky., January 21, 1906; interment in Frankfort Cemetery.

FITZSIMONS, Thomas, a Delegate and a Representative from Pennsylvania; born in County Tubber, Wicklow, Ireland, in 1741; immigrated to the United States and entered a counting-house in Philadelphia, Pa., as clerk; commanded a company of volunteer home guards during the Revolutionary War; Member of the Continental Congress in 1782 and 1783; member of the State house of representatives in 1786 and 1787; delegate to the United States Constitutional Convention in 1787; elected as a Federalist to the First, Second, and Third Congresses (March 4, 1789–March 3, 1795); unsuccessful candidate for reelection in 1794 to the Fourth Congress; president of the Philadelphia Chamber of Commerce; trustee of the University of Pennsylvania; founder and director of the Bank of North America; died in Philadelphia, Pa., on August 26, 1811; interment in St. Mary's Roman Catholic Churchyard.

FJARE, Orvin Benonie, a Representative from Montana; born on a ranch near Big Timber, Sweet Grass County, Mont., April 16, 1918; attended the rural schools and Sweet Grass County High School; employed as a clerk in a clothing store at Big Timber, Mont., and later became part owner; during World War II enlisted as a private in the United States Army in 1940; commissioned a second lieutenant of Artillery in 1942; learned to fly and received his wings in 1944; served as a pilot in the South Pacific and was discharged as a captain in 1946; member of the Montana Public Welfare Commission 1952–1954; member of board of trustees of Big Timber Public Schools 1951–1954; elected as a Republican to the Eighty-fourth Congress (January 3, 1955–January 3, 1957); unsuccessful candidate for reelection in 1956 to the Eighty-fifth Congress; member of State house of representatives in 1959; engaged in the life insurance business; unsuccessful candidate for election to the United States Senate in 1960; is a resident of Big Timber, Mont.

FLACK, William Henry, a Representative from New York; born in Franklin Falls, Franklin County, N. Y., March 22, 1861; attended the public schools; became interested in lumbering and tanning; supervisor of the town of Waverly for seven years and chairman of the board for two years; county clerk of Franklin County in 1897, and reelected in 1900; chairman of the Republican county committee 1898–1902; served as trustee of the village of Malone and elected president of said village in 1902; elected as a Republican to the Fifty-eighth and Fifty-ninth Congresses and served from March 4, 1903, until his death in Malone, N. Y., February 2, 1907; interment in Morningside Cemetery.

FLAGLER, Thomas Thorn, a Representative from New York; born in Pleasant Valley, Dutchess County, N. Y., October 12, 1811; attended the common schools; learned the printer's trade and became one of the owners and publishers of the Chenango Republican, Oxford, N. Y.; moved to Lockport in 1836 and published the Niagara Courier until 1842, when he engaged in the hardware business; member of the State assembly in 1842 and 1843; treasurer of Niagara County 1849–1852; elected as a Whig to the Thirty-third and Thirty-fourth Congresses (March 4, 1853–March 3, 1857); was not a candidate for renomination in 1856; resumed former business pursuits; again a member of the State assembly in 1860; member of the State constitutional convention in 1867 and 1868; organized and became president of the Holly Manufacturing Co. in 1859, and for many years was the head of eight such organizations; died in Lockport, N. Y., on September 6, 1897; interment in Glenwood Cemetery.

FLAHERTY, Lawrence James, a Representative from California; born in San Mateo, San Mateo County, Calif., July 4, 1878; moved with his parents to San Francisco in 1888; attended the public schools; learned the trade of cement mason; member of the board of police commissioners of San Francisco 1911–1915; served in the State senate 1915–1922; president of the San Francisco Building Trades 1921–1926; appointed United States surveyor of customs for the port of San Francisco on November 1, 1921, and served until March 3, 1925, when he resigned, having been elected to Congress; elected as a Republican to the Sixty-ninth Congress and served from March 4, 1925, until his death in New York City June 13, 1926; interment in Holy Cross Cemetery, near San Mateo, Calif.

FLAHERTY, Thomas Aloysius, a Representative from Massachusetts; born in Boston, Mass., December 21, 1898; attended the public schools and Northeastern University Law School, Boston, Mass.; during the First World War served as a private in the United States Army in 1918; employed with the United States Veterans' Administration at Boston, Mass., 1920–1934; member of the State house of representatives 1935–1937; elected as a Democrat to the Seventy-fifth Congress to fill the vacancy caused by the resignation of John P. Higgins; reelected to the Seventy-sixth and Seventy-seventh Congresses and served from December 14, 1937, to January 3, 1943; was not a candidate for renomination in 1942; served as transit commissioner of the city of Boston 1943–1945; chairman of the Department of Public Utilities of Massachusetts 1946–1953, serving as commissioner 1953–1955; chairman, Board of Review, Assessing Department, city of Boston, 1956–1960; real-estate broker and appraiser; resides in Charlestown, Mass.

FLANAGAN, De Witt Clinton, a Representative from New Jersey; born in New York City December 28, 1870; attended the Callison and Woodbridge private schools and Columbia College, New York City; pursued a commercial career, being interested in a number of industrial enterprises; elected as a Democrat to the Fifty-seventh Congress to fill the vacancy caused by the death of Joshua S. Salmon and served from June 18, 1902, to March 3, 1903; delegate to the Democratic National Convention at St. Louis in 1904; organized the Boston, Cape Cod & New York

Canal Co., which built and operated the Cape Cod Canal; engaged in the agricultural and civic development of Baldwin County, Ala.; died in Utica, N. Y., January 15, 1946; interment in the family mausoleum, Woodlawn Cemetery, New York, N. Y.

FLANAGAN, James Winright, a Senator from Texas; born in Gordonsville, Orange County, Va., September 5, 1805; attended the common schools and received private instruction; moved to Cloverport, Ky., in 1816, and engaged in mercantile pursuits; justice of the peace 1823–1833; studied law; was admitted to the bar in 1825 and practiced in the Breckenridge County circuit from 1833 to 1843; moved to Henderson, Rusk County, Tex., in 1843 and continued the practice of law; also engaged in mercantile and agricultural pursuits; member of the State house of representatives in 1851 and 1852; served in the State senate in 1855 and 1856; member of the State constitutional conventions in 1866 and 1868; elected Lieutenant Governor of Texas in 1869 and served until his resignation in 1870 to become Senator; upon the readmission of Texas to representation was elected as a Republican to the United States Senate and served from March 30, 1870, to March 3, 1875; was the caucus nominee of his party, which was in the minority in 1875; delegate to the Republican National Conventions at Philadelphia in 1872, at Cincinnati in 1876, and at Chicago in 1880; died in Longview, Gregg County, Tex., September 28, 1887; interment in the family burying ground in East Henderson, Tex.

FLANDERS, Alvan, a Delegate from the Territory of Washington; born in Hopkinton, Merrimack County, N. H., August 2, 1825; attended the public schools; learned the machinist trade in Boston; moved to Humboldt County, Calif., in 1851, and there engaged in the lumber business until 1858, when he moved to San Francisco; one of the founders and proprietors of the San Francisco Daily Times; member of the State house of representatives in 1861; officer of the United States branch mint in 1861; was commissioned on June 20, 1862, by President Lincoln as register of the United States land office at Humboldt, but never served; moved to the Territory of Washington in 1863 and engaged in mercantile pursuits in Wallula; first postmaster of Wallula 1865–1867; elected as a Republican to the Fortieth Congress (March 4, 1867–March 3, 1869); was not a candidate for renomination in 1868; appointed by President Grant as Governor of the Territory of Washington on April 5, 1869, and served until 1870; moved to San Francisco, Calif., at the expiration of his term and died there March 14, 1884; interment in Laurel Hill Cemetery.

FLANDERS, Benjamin Franklin, a Representative from Louisiana; born in Bristol, Grafton County, N. H., January 26, 1816; attended New Hampton (N. H.) Academy, and was graduated from Dartmouth College, Hanover, N. H., in 1842; moved to New Orleans in 1843; studied law, but never practiced; edited the New Orleans Tropic in 1845; elected alderman of New Orleans in 1847; superintendent of public schools in 1850; reelected alderman in 1852; assisted in organizing the New Orleans, Opelousas & Great Western Railroad Co.; secretary and treasurer of the company 1852–1861; appointed city treasurer by General Butler July 20, 1862, and served until December 10 of the same year; mustered into the Federal military service July 13, 1863, at New Orleans, La., as captain of Company C, Fifth Regiment of Louisiana Volunteer Infantry, and was mustered out and honorably discharged from the service on August 12, 1863; elected as a Unionist to the Thirty-seventh Congress and served from December 3, 1862, to March 3, 1863; was not a candidate for renomination in 1862; appointed in 1863 special agent of the Treasury Department for the southern district, comprising the States of Louisiana, Texas, Mississippi,

Alabama, and western Florida; unsuccessful candidate for election as Governor of Louisiana in 1864; first president of the First National Bank of New Orleans in 1864; reappointed special Treasury agent in 1866; Military Governor of Louisiana in 1867 and 1868; mayor of New Orleans 1870–1872; Assistant Treasurer of the United States at New Orleans 1873–1882; unsuccessful Republican candidate for State treasurer in 1888; died on his estate, "Ben Alva," near Youngsville, Lafayette Parish, La., March 13, 1896; interment in Metairie Cemetery, New Orleans, La.

FLANDERS, Ralph Edward, a Senator from Vermont; born in Barnet, Caledonia County, Vt., September 28, 1880; moved with his parents to Pawtucket, R. I., in 1886; attended the common schools at Pawtucket and Lincoln, R. I.; was graduated from high school in Central Falls, R. I., in 1896; engaged as a machinist apprentice at Providence, R. I., on January 14, 1897, and has since been in machine tool industry, serving in various capacities as journeyman, draftsman, designer, editor, and executive; moved to Springfield, Vt., in 1910 and continued his profession; served as president of the Federal Reserve Board of Boston from May 1944 to March 1946; appointed as a Republican to the United States Senate to fill the vacancy in the term ending January 3, 1947, caused by the resignation of Warren R. Austin; elected in 1946 and again 1952 and served from November 1, 1946, to January 3, 1959; was not a candidate for renomination in 1958; retired, and is a resident of Springfield, Vt.

FLANNAGAN, John William, Jr., a Representative from Virginia; born on a farm near Trevilians, Louisa County, Va., February 20, 1885; attended the public schools and was graduated from the law department of Washington and Lee University, Lexington, Va., in 1907; was admitted to the bar the same year and commenced practice in Appalachia, Wise County, Va.; served as Commonwealth's attorney for Buchanan County, Va., in 1916 and 1917; moved to Clintwood, Va., in 1917, and to Bristol, Va., in 1925, and continued the practice of law; also engaged in banking 1917–1930; congressional adviser to the first session of the Food and Agriculture Organization of the United Nations at Quebec in 1945; elected as a Democrat to the Seventy-second and to the eight succeeding Congresses (March 4, 1931–January 3, 1949); was not a candidate for renomination in 1948; resumed the practice of law in Bristol, Va., until his death there April 27, 1955; interment in Mountain View Cemetery.

FLANNERY, John Harold, a Representative from Pennsylvania; born in Pittston, Luzerne County, Pa., April 19, 1898; attended the public schools; was graduated from Wyoming Seminary, Kingston, Pa., in 1917 and from Dickinson School of Law, Carlisle, Pa., in 1920; during the First World War served as a private in the United States Army and was honorably discharged on December 14, 1918; was admitted to the bar in 1921 and commenced practice in Pittston, Pa.; solicitor for Pittston City, Pa., 1926–1930; served as assistant district attorney of Luzerne County, Pa., 1932–1936; elected as a Democrat to the Seventy-fifth, Seventy-sixth, and Seventy-seventh Congresses and served from January 3, 1937, until his resignation on January 3, 1942, to become judge of the common pleas court of Luzerne County, Pa.; reelected in 1951 for a ten-year term and served until his death; delegate to the Democratic National Conventions in 1944 and in 1960; died in Bethesda, Md., June 3, 1961; interment in Mount Olivet Catholic Cemetery, Pittston, Pa.

FLEEGER, George Washington, a Representative from Pennsylvania; born in Concord Township, Butler County, Pa., March 13, 1839; attended the common schools and West Sunbury Academy; during the Civil War enlisted in the Union Army on June 10, 1861, as a private in Company C, Eleventh Regiment, Pennsylvania Reserves, and was commissioned a first lieutenant in June 1862; afterward brevetted captain, and served until March 13, 1865; studied law; was admitted to the bar in 1866 and commenced practice in Butler; member of the State house of representatives in 1871 and 1872; chairman of the Republican State central committee; delegate to the Republican State conventions in 1882 and 1890; elected as a Republican to the Forty-ninth Congress (March 4, 1885–March 3, 1887); resumed the practice of law in Butler, Pa., and died there June 25, 1894; interment in the North Cemetery.

FLEETWOOD, Frederick Gleed, a Representative from Vermont; born in St. Johnsbury, Caledonia County, Vt., September 27, 1868; attended the common schools of St. Johnsbury, and was graduated from St. Johnsbury Academy in 1886; also attended the University of Vermont at Burlington, and was graduated from Harvard University, Cambridge, Mass., in 1891; secretary of the commission on revision of Vermont statutes in 1893 and 1894; studied law; was admitted to the bar and commenced practice in Morrisville, Vt., in 1894; prosecuting attorney for Lmaoille County 1896–1898; town clerk and treasurer of Morrisville, Vt., 1896–1900; presidential elector on the Republican ticket of McKinley and Roosevelt in 1900; member of the State house of representatives 1900–1902; secretary of state and insurance commissioner of Vermont 1902–1908; again secretary of state 1917–1919; elected as a Republican to the Sixty-eighth Congress (March 4, 1923–March 3, 1925); was not a candidate for renomination in 1924; resumed the practice of law; also engaged in banking; died in Morrisville, Vt., January 28, 1938; interment in Pleasant View Cemetery.

FLEGER, Anthony Alfred, a Representative from Ohio; born in Austria-Hungary October 21, 1900; in 1903 immigrated to the United States with his parents, who settled in Cleveland, Cuyahoga County, Ohio; attended the public and high schools and was graduated from John Marshall School of Law, Cleveland, Ohio, in 1926; was admitted to the bar the same year and commenced practice in Cleveland, Ohio; moved to Parma, Cuyahoga County, Ohio, and continued the practice of law; served as justice of the peace in Parma, Ohio, 1930–1932; elected a member of the State house of representatives in 1932 and served from January 1, 1933, to December 31, 1933, when he resigned, having been elected mayor of Parma; served as mayor from January 1, 1934, to December 31, 1935; elected as a Democrat to the Seventy-fifth Congress (January 3, 1937–January 3, 1939); unsuccessful candidate for reelection in 1938 to the Seventy-sixth Congress and for election in 1940 to the Seventy-seventh Congress; resumed the practice of law in Cleveland, Ohio; served as special assistant to the Attorney General, Washington, D. C., from March 3, 1941, to July 9, 1950, and as an attorney in the Department of Justice from July 10, 1950, to May 9, 1953; engaged in the practice of law in Washington, D. C., and resides in Oxon Hill, Md.

FLEMING, William, a Delegate from Virginia; born in Cumberland County, Va., July 6, 1736; was graduated from William and Mary College, Williamsburg, Va., in 1763; studied law; was admitted to the bar and practiced; member of the State house of burgesses 1772–1775; delegate to the Revolutionary conventions in 1775 and 1776; member of the committee of independence in 1776; served in the house of delegates 1776–1778; Member of the Continental Congress 1779–1781; judge of the general court in 1788; elected a member of the first supreme court of appeals in 1789 and served in this capacity until his death; became president of the court in 1809; died at his country home, "Summerville," Chesterfield County, Va., February 15, 1824; interment in the family cemetery on his estate.

FLEMING, William Bennett, a Representative from Georgia; born on a plantation near Flemington, Liberty County, Ga., October 29, 1803; attended the common schools, and was graduated from Yale College in 1825; studied law; was admitted to the bar and practiced in Savannah, Ga.; judge of the superior court of Chatham County, Ga., 1847–1849 and 1853–1868; resumed the practice of law in Savannah; recorder of the city of Savannah from 1868 until the office was abolished; elected as a Democrat to the Forty-fifth Congress to fill the vacancy caused by the death of Julian Hartridge and served from February 10, 1879, to March 3, 1879; was not a candidate for renomination; again judge of the superior court from 1879 until 1881, when he resigned on account of ill health; retired to Walthourville, Liberty County, Ga., and died there August 19, 1886; interment in Laurel Grove Cemetery, Savannah, Ga.

FLEMING, William Henry, a Representative from Georgia; born in Augusta, Richmond County, Ga., October 18, 1856; attended Summerville Academy and Academy of Richmond County; was graduated from the University of Georgia at Athens in 1874; superintendent of the public schools of Augusta and Richmond County, Ga., from 1877 to 1880, when he resigned; studied law; was admitted to the bar in 1880 and commenced practice in Augusta, Ga.; member of the State house of representatives 1888–1896, and served as speaker of the house in 1894 and 1895; president of the State bar association in 1894 and 1895; elected as a Democrat to the Fifty-fifth, Fifty-sixth, and Fifty-seventh Congresses (March 4, 1897–March 3, 1903); unsuccessful candidate for renomination in 1902; resumed the practice of law and engaged in literary pursuits; died in Augusta, Ga., June 9, 1944; interment in Summerville Cemetery.

FLETCHER, Charles Kimball, a Representative from California; born in San Diego, Calif., December 15, 1902; attended the public schools; was graduated from Stanford University of California in 1924; also attended Pembroke College, Oxford University, England in 1934; engaged in the savings and loan business; during World War II served as a lieutenant with the United States Naval Reserve from 1943 to 1945; elected as a Republican to the Eightieth Congress (January 3, 1947–January 3, 1949); unsuccessful candidate for reelection in 1948 to the Eighty-first Congress; president and manager of the Home Federal Savings & Loan Association 1934–1959 and chairman of board of directors 1959– ; member of California Commission on Correctional Facilities and Services, 1955–1957; is a resident of San Diego, Calif.

FLETCHER, Duncan Upshaw, a Senator from Florida; born near Americus, Sumter County, Ga., January 6, 1859; moved with his parents to Monroe County in 1860; attended the common schools and Gordon Institute, Barnesville, Ga.; was graduated from Vanderbilt University, Nashville, Tenn., in 1880; studied law at the same institution; was admitted to the bar in July 1881 and commenced practice in Jacksonville, Fla.; member of the city council in 1887; served in the State house of representatives in 1893; mayor of Jacksonville 1893–1895 and 1901–1903; chairman of the board of public instruction of Duval County 1900–1907; president of the Gulf Coast Inland Waterways Association in 1908, and, later, of the Mississippi to Atlantic Waterway Association; appointed and subsequently elected as a Democrat to the United States Senate for the term commencing March 4, 1909; reelected in 1914, 1920, 1926, and 1932 and served from March 4, 1909, until his death; president of the Southern Commercial Congress 1912–1918; appointed by President Wilson in 1913 as chairman of the United States commission to investigate and study cooperative land-mortgage banks, cooperative rural credit unions, and similar organizations devoting their attention to the promotion of agriculture and the betterment of rural

conditions in European countries; elected in 1913 as chairman of the American commission, composed of delegates from different States in the United States and different Provinces in Canada, appointed to investigate cooperative agricultural finance, production, distribution, and rural life in European countries; delegate from the United States to the International High Commission to promote substantial uniformity in commercial law and administrative regulations of the American Republics and more stable financial regulations between Latin America and the United States, held at Buenos Aires, Argentina, in 1916; died in Washington, D. C., on June 17, 1936; interment in Evergreen Cemetery, Jacksonville, Fla.

FLETCHER, Isaac, a Representative from Vermont; born in Dunstable, Middlesex County, Mass., November 22, 1784; pursued classical studies, and was graduated from Dartmouth College, Hanover, N. H., in 1808; taught in the academy at Chesterfield, N. H.; studied law; was admitted to the bar in December 1811 and commenced practice at Lyndon, Vt., in 1812; member of the State house of representatives 1819–1824, and served one term as speaker; prosecuting attorney of Caledonia County, Vt., 1820–1829; member of the State constitutional convention in 1822; was graduated from the University of Vermont at Burlington in 1825; elected as an Anti-Masonic Democrat to the Twenty-fifth and Twenty-sixth Congresses (March 4, 1837–March 3, 1841); unsuccessful candidate for reelection in 1840 to the Twenty-seventh Congress; adjutant general on the staff of Governor Van Ness; died in Lyndon, Vt., October 19, 1842; interment in Lyndon Town Cemetery.

FLETCHER, Loren, a Representative from Minnesota; born in Mount Vernon, Kennebec County, Maine, April 10, 1833; attended the public schools and Maine Wesleyan Seminary, Kents Hill, Maine; moved to Bangor in 1853; was a stonecutter, clerk in a store, and an employee of a lumber company; moved to Minneapolis, Minn., in 1856 and engaged in manufacturing and mercantile pursuits, largely in the manufacture of lumber and flour; member of the board of directors of the First National Bank upon its establishment in 1864; member of the State house of representatives 1872–1886 and served as speaker from 1880 to 1886; elected as a Republican to the Fifty-third and to the four succeeding Congresses (March 4, 1893–March 3, 1903); unsuccessful candidate for reelection in 1902 to the Fifty-eighth Congress; elected to the Fifty-ninth Congress (March 4, 1905–March 3, 1907); declined to be a candidate for reelection; retired from active business and traveled; died in Atlanta, Ga., April 15, 1919; interment in Lakewood Cemetery, Minneapolis, Minn.

FLETCHER, Richard, a Representative from Massachusetts; born in Cavendish, Windsor County, Vt., January 8, 1788; pursued classical studies and was graduated from Dartmouth College, Hanover, N. H., in 1806; taught school at Salisbury, N. H., 1806–1808; studied law; was admitted to the bar and commenced practice at Salisbury, N. H., in 1809; moved to Boston, Mass., in 1819; elected as a Whig to the Twenty-fifth Congress (March 4, 1837–March 3, 1839); was not a candidate for renomination in 1838 to the Twenty-sixth Congress; judge of the supreme court of Massachusetts 1848–1853; died in Boston, Mass., on June 21, 1869; interment Mount Auburn Cemetery, Cambridge, Mass.

FLETCHER, Thomas, a Representative from Kentucky; born in Westmoreland County, Pa., October 21, 1779; settled in Montgomery County, Ky.; member of the State house of representatives in 1803, 1805, and 1806; served in the War of 1812 as major of Kentucky Volunteers under General Harrison and distinguished himself at Fort Meigs May 15, 1813; elected to the Fourteenth Congress to fill the vacancy caused by the resignation of James Clark and served from December 2, 1816, to March 3, 1817; declined to be a candidate for renomination in 1816; again elected a member of the State house of representatives and served in 1817, 1820, 1821, 1823, and 1825; died near Sharpsburg, Bath County, Ky.; interment in a private burial ground near Sharpsburg, Ky.

FLETCHER, Thomas Brooks, a Representative from Ohio; born in Mechanicstown, Carroll County, Ohio, October 10, 1879; attended the grade schools, Carrollton (Ohio) High School, a private school at Augusta, Ohio, and the Richard School of Dramatic Art in Cleveland; was graduated from the business department of Mount Union College, Alliance, Ohio, in 1900; editor of the Daily Leader, Alliance, Ohio, from 1903 until 1905; resigned to join the staff of the Morning News, Canton, Ohio, and served from 1905 to 1906; became a Redpath lecturer in 1906; editor and publisher of the Daily Tribune at Marion, Ohio, 1910–1922; elected as a Democrat to the Sixty-ninth and Seventieth Congresses (March 4, 1925–March 3, 1929); unsuccessful candidate for reelection in 1928 to the Seventy-first Congress; elected to the Seventy-third, Seventy-fourth, and Seventy-fifth Congresses (March 4, 1933–January 3, 1939); unsuccessful candidate for reelection in 1938 to the Seventy-sixth Congress and for election in 1942 to the Seventy-eighth Congress; resumed lecturing and chautauqua work; died in Washington, D. C., July 1, 1945; interment in Mechanicstown Cemetery, Mechanicstown, Ohio.

FLICK, James Patton, a Representative from Iowa; born in Bakerstown, Allegheny County, Pa., August 28, 1845; moved with his parents to Wapello County, Iowa, in 1852 and to Taylor County in 1857; attended the common schools; during the Civil War enlisted in Company K, Fourth Regiment, Iowa Volunteer Infantry, as a private soldier and served from April 3, 1862, to September 4, 1864; recorder of Taylor County in 1869 and 1870; studied law; was admitted to the bar in 1870 and commenced practice in Bedford, Iowa; member of the State house of representatives in 1878 and 1879; district attorney of the third judicial district of Iowa 1880–1886; elected as a Republican to the Fifty-first and Fifty-second Congresses (March 4, 1889–March 3, 1893); was not a candidate for renomination in 1892 to the Fifty-third Congress; resumed the practice of his profession in Bedford, Iowa, until his death there on February 25, 1929; interment in Bedford Cemetery.

FLINT, Frank Putnam, a Senator from California; born in North Reading, Middlesex County, Mass., July 15, 1862; moved with his parents to San Francisco, Calif., in 1869; attended the public schools; moved to Los Angeles in 1887; served as deputy United States marshal 1888–1892; appointed clerk in the district attorney's office in 1892; meanwhile studied law; was admitted to the bar on October 10, 1892, and commenced practice in Los Angeles; assistant United States attorney in 1892 and 1893; judge of the superior court of Los Angeles County 1895–1897; United States district attorney for the southern district of California from April 8, 1897, to September 5, 1901; elected as a Republican to the United States Senate and served from March 4, 1905, to March 3, 1911; was not a candidate for reelection; resumed the practice of law in Los Angeles, Calif.; also engaged in banking; appointed a member of the State land settlement board in 1917; reappointed in 1926; served as president of the National Boulder Dam Association and as a trustee of Occidental College; died February 11, 1929, on board the steamer *President Polk* in Philippine waters, while on a tour of the world; interment Forest Lawn Mausoleum, Glendale, Calif.

FLOOD, Daniel John, a Representative from Pennsylvania; born in Hazleton, Luzerne County, Pa., November 26, 1903; attended the public schools of Wilkes-Barre, Pa., and St. Augustine, Fla.; was graduated from Syracuse (N. Y.) University in 1924; attended Harvard Law School, Cambridge, Mass., and was graduated from Dickinson School of Law, Carlisle, Pa., in 1929; was admitted to the bar in 1930 and commenced practice in Wilkes-Barre, Pa.; attorney for the Home Owners' Loan Corporation in 1934 and 1935; deputy attorney general for the Commonwealth of Pennsylvania and counsel for the Pennsylvania Liquor Control Board 1935–1939; director of the State Bureau of Public Assistance Disbursements and executive assistant to the State treasurer 1941–1944; national committeeman for Pennsylvania, Young Democratic Clubs of America, in 1942 and 1943; elected as a Democrat to the Seventy-ninth Congress (January 3, 1945–January 3, 1947); unsuccessful candidate for reelection in 1946 to the Eightieth Congress; elected to the Eighty-first and Eighty-second Congresses (January 3, 1949–January 3, 1953); unsuccessful candidate for reelection in 1952 to the Eighty-third Congress; elected to the Eighty-fourth, Eighty-fifth, and Eighty-sixth Congresses (January 3, 1955–January 3, 1961). *Reelected to the Eighty-seventh Congress.*

FLOOD, Henry De La Warr (brother of Joel West Flood and uncle of Harry Flood Byrd), a Representative from Virginia; born in "Eldon," Appomattox County, Va., September 2, 1865; attended the public schools of Appomattox and Richmond, Washington and Lee University, Lexington, Va., and the University of Virginia at Charlottesville; studied law; was admitted to the bar in 1886 and commenced practice in Appomattox, Va.; member of the State house of delegates 1887–1891; served in the State senate 1891–1903; elected prosecuting attorney for Appomattox County in 1891, 1895, and 1899; presidential elector on the Democratic ticket of Cleveland and Stevenson in 1892; unsuccessful candidate for election to the Fifty-fifth Congress; elected as a Democrat to the Fifty-seventh and to the nine succeeding Congresses and served from March 4, 1901, until his death; chairman of the Committee on Foreign Affairs from January 1913 to March 4, 1919, and was author of the resolution declaring a state of war to exist between the United States and the Imperial German Government and with the Imperial Austro-Hungarian Government; died in Washington, D. C., December 8, 1921; interment in a mausoleum on the courthouse green at Appomattox, Va.

FLOOD, Joel West (brother of Henry De La Warr Flood and uncle of Harry Flood Byrd), a Representative from Virginia; born near Appomattox, Appomattox County, Va., August 2, 1894; attended the public schools, Appomattox Agricultural High School, Washington and Lee University, Lexington, Va., the University of Virginia at Charlottesville, and Oxford University, Oxford, England; studied law; was admitted to the bar in 1917 and commenced practice in Appomattox, Va.; also engaged in agricultural pursuits; during the First World War served from March 29, 1918, until his discharge July 18, 1919, as a private in Company A, Three Hundred and Fifth Engineers, Eightieth Division; served as colonel on the staff of Gov. E. Lee Trinkle of Virginia 1922–1926; elected Commonwealth attorney of Appomattox County in 1919 and served until November 8, 1932, having been elected to Congress; special assistant to the attorney general of Virginia from April 1, 1928, to July 1, 1932; elected as a Democrat to the Seventy-second Congress to fill the vacancy caused by the death of Henry St. George Tucker and served from November 8, 1932, to March 3, 1933; was not a candidate for election to the Seventy-third Congress; resumed the practice of law and agricultural pursuits; delegate to the Democratic National Convention at Philadelphia in 1936; appointed assistant United States attorney for the western district of Virginia and served from June 1, 1939, to January 28, 1940; elected in January 1940 and reelected in January 1946 as a judge of the fifth judicial circuit of Virginia, in which capacity he is now serving; is a resident of Appomattox, Va.

FLOOD, Thomas Schmeck, a Representative from New York; born in Lodi, Seneca County, N. Y., April 12, 1844; attended the common schools and Elmira Free Academy; studied medicine, but did not practice; engaged in the drug business; sent to Pennsylvania by his wife's uncle, he built railroads and mines and founded the town of Dubois; first postmaster of Dubois and its first express and railroad agent; returned to Elmira, N. Y.; member of the Board of Aldermen of Elmira in 1882 and 1883; president of the Chemung County Agricultural Society in 1884 and 1885; engaged in agricultural pursuits, lumbering, and the breeding of high-grade horses; elected as a Republican to the Fiftieth and Fifty-first Congresses (March 4, 1887–March 3, 1891); was not a candidate for renomination in 1890; engaged in the real-estate business; died, while on a visit, in Pittsburgh, Pa., on October 28, 1908; interment in Woodlawn Cemetery, Elmira, N. Y.

FLORENCE, Elias, a Representative from Ohio; born in Fauquier County, Va., February 15, 1797; attended the public schools; engaged in agricultural pursuits; moved to Ohio and settled in Circleville, Pickaway County; member of the State house of representatives in 1829, 1830, 1834, and 1840; served in the State senate in 1835; elected as a Whig to the Twenty-eighth Congress (March 4, 1843–March 3, 1845); member of the State constitutional convention in 1850; resumed agricultural pursuits and was also engaged in the purchase and shipment of cattle; died in Muhlenberg Township, Pickaway County, Ohio, November 21, 1880.

FLORENCE, Thomas Birch, a Representative from Pennsylvania; born in Philadelphia, Pa., January 26, 1812; attended the public schools; learned the hatter's trade and engaged in that business in 1833; proprietor of a hat store; engaged in the newspaper business; captain of a volunteer rifle company, and asked for his company's acceptance for service in the war with Mexico; unsuccessful Democratic candidate for election in 1846 to the Thirtieth Congress and in 1848 to the Thirty-first Congress; elected as a Democrat to the Thirty-second and to the four succeeding Congresses (March 4, 1851–March 3, 1861); after leaving Congress edited and published the Constitutional Union in Washington, D. C., and subsequently became the proprietor of the Sunday Gazette; unsuccessful candidate in his old district for election in 1868 to the Forty-first Congress and in 1874 to the Forty-fourth Congress; died in Washington, D. C., July 3, 1875; interment in Monument Cemetery, Philadelphia, Pa.

FLOURNOY, Thomas Stanhope, a Representative from Virginia; born in Prince Edward County, Va., December 15, 1811; was educated at Hampden-Sidney (Va.) College; engaged as a private teacher; studied law; was admitted to the bar and commenced practice in Halifax, Va., in 1834; elected as a Whig to the Thirtieth Congress (March 4, 1847–March 3, 1849); unsuccessful candidate for reelection in 1848 to the Thirty-first Congress and for election in 1850 to the Thirty-second Congress; unsuccessful candidate of the American Party for Governor in 1855; member of the convention in 1861 which met at Richmond to consider the question of secession; entered the Confederate Army, raised a company of Cavalry, and served as captain; promoted to colonel of the Sixth Virginia Cavalry; engaged in many battles, and

was wounded in June 1864; again an unsuccessful candidate for Governor in 1863; after the war settled in Danville, Va., and practical law; delegate to the Democratic National Convention at St. Louis in 1876 which nominated Tilden and Hendricks; died at his home in Halifax County, Va., March 12, 1883; interment in the family plot on his estate.

FLOWER, Roswell Pettibone, a Representative from New York; born in Theresa, Jefferson County, N. Y., August 7, 1835; attended the public schools, and was graduated from the Theresa High School in 1851; engaged in mercantile and manufacturing pursuits in 1851; assistant postmaster of Watertown, N. Y., 1854–1860; moved to New York City in 1869 and engaged in banking; elected as a Democrat to the Forty-seventh Congress to fill the vacancy caused by the resignation of Levi P. Morton and served from November 8, 1881, to March 3, 1883; elected to the Fifty-first and Fifty-second Congresses and served from March 4, 1889, to September 16, 1891, when he resigned, having been elected Governor; elected Governor of New York in 1891 and served until 1895; died in Eastport, N. Y., May 12, 1899; interment in Brookside Cemetery, Watertown, N. Y.

FLOYD, Charles Albert, a Representative from New York; born in Smithtown, Suffolk County, N. Y., in 1791; attended the common schools: engaged in agricultural pursuits; county clerk in 1820 and 1821; studied law; was admitted to the bar and practiced; district attorney in 1830; member of the State assembly in 1836 and 1838; president of the board of trustees of Huntington 1837–1840; elected as a Democrat to the Twenty-seventh Congress (March 4, 1841–March 3, 1843); county judge of Suffolk County 1843–1865; supervisor of the town of Huntington 1843–1865; resumed agricultural pursuits; died in Commack, Long Island, N. Y., February 20, 1873; interment in the Methodist Church Cemetery.

FLOYD, John, a Representative from Georgia; born in Beaufort, Beaufort County, S. C., October 3, 1769; learned the carpenter's trade; moved in 1791 with his father to Camden County, Ga., and engaged in boat building; served in the War of 1812 as brigadier general in the First (Floyd's) Brigade of Georgia Militia from August 30, 1813, to March 8, 1814, and from October 17, 1814, to March 10, 1815, having participated in expeditions against the Creek Indians; member of the State house of representatives 1820–1827; elected to the Twentieth Congress (March 4, 1827–March 3, 1829); died near Jefferson, Ga., June 24, 1839.

FLOYD, John, a Representative from Virginia; born at Floyds Station, near the present city of Louisville, Jefferson County, Ky. (then a part of Virginia), April 24, 1783; pursued an academic course; attended Dickinson College, Carlisle, Pa., and was graduated from the medical department of the University of Pennsylvania at Philadelphia in 1806; settled in Lexington, Va., the same year, and soon thereafter moved to Christiansburg, Montgomery County, Va., where he practiced his profession; justice of the peace in 1807; major of Virginia State Militia 1807–1812: served as surgeon with rank of major in the War of 1812; subsequently became brigadier general of militia; member of the State house of delegates in 1814 and 1815; elected as a Democrat to the Fifteenth and to the five succeeding Congresses (March 4, 1817–March 3, 1829); was not a candidate for renomination in 1828; Governor of Virginia 1830–1834; received the electoral vote of North Carolina for President in 1832; died near Sweetsprings, Monroe County, Va. (now West Virginia), August 17, 1837; interment in an unmarked grave in the cemetery at Sweetsprings.

FLOYD, John Charles, a Representative from Arkansas; born in Sparta, White County, Tenn., April 14, 1858; moved to Benton County, Ark., in 1869 with his parents, who settled near Bentonville; attended the common and high schools, and was graduated from the Arkansas Industrial University (later the University of Arkansas) at Fayetteville in 1879; taught school at Springdale, Ark., in 1880 and 1881; studied law; was admitted to the bar in 1882 and commenced practice in Yellville, Ark.; served in the State house of representatives 1889–1891; prosecuting attorney of the fourteenth judicial circuit 1890–1894; elected as a Democrat to the Fifty-ninth and to the four succeeding Congresses (March 4, 1905–March 3, 1915); one of the managers appointed by the House of Representatives in 1912 to conduct the impeachment proceedings against Robert W. Archbald, judge of the United States Commerce Court; was not a candidate for renomination in 1914; resumed the practice of law in Yellville, Ark.; unsuccessful candidate for nomination as Governor of Arkansas in 1920; died in Yellville, Ark., November 4, 1930; interment in Layton Cemetery.

FLOYD, John Gelston, a Representative from New York; born in Mastic, near Moriches, Long Island, N. Y., February 5, 1806; attended the common schools, and was graduated from Hamilton College, Clinton, N. Y., in 1824; studied law; was admitted to the bar in 1825 and commenced practice in Utica, N. Y.; clerk and prosecuting attorney of Utica, N. Y., 1829–1833; founded the Utica Democrat (later the Observer-Dispatch) in 1836; appointed judge of Suffolk County; member of the State assembly 1839–1843; elected as a Democrat to the Twenty-sixth and Twenty-seventh Congresses (March 4, 1839–March 3, 1843); returned to Mastic, Long Island, about 1842; member of the State senate in 1848 and 1849; elected to the Thirty-second Congress (March 4, 1851–March 3, 1853); joined the Republican Party upon its formation in 1856; retired from public life; died in Mastic, Long Island, N. Y., October 5, 1881; interment in the family cemetery.

FLOYD, William, a Delegate and a Representative from New York; born in Brookhaven, Long Island, N. Y., December 17, 1734; pursued an academic course; served as major general in the State militia; was prominent in the ante-Revolutionary movements; Member of the Continental Congress 1774–1777; signed the Declaration of Independence; served in the State senate in 1777 and 1778; again a Member of the Continental Congress 1778–1783; again served in the State senate 1784–1788; elected to the First Congress (March 4, 1789–March 3, 1791); unsuccessful candidate for reelection in 1790 to the Second Congress; presidential elector in 1792; moved in 1794 to Westernville, Oneida County; again presidential elector in 1800, 1804, and 1820; delegate to the State constitutional convention in 1801; again a member of the State senate in 1808; died in Westernville, N. Y., August 4, 1821; interment in Presbyterian Church Cemetery.

FLYE, Edwin, a Representative from Maine; born in Newcastle, Lincoln County, Maine, March 4, 1817; attended the common schools and Lincoln Academy, Newcastle, Maine; engaged in mercantile pursuits and shipbuilding; member of the State house of representatives in 1858; served for many years as president of the First National Bank of Damariscotta, Maine; during the Civil War served as paymaster with the rank of major in the Union Army; delegate to the Republican National Convention at Cincinnati in 1876; elected as a Republican to the Forty-fourth Congress to fill the vacancy caused by the resignation of James G. Blaine and served from December 4, 1876, to March 3, 1877; was not a candidate for renomination in 1876; resumed shipbuilding and also engaged in banking; died while on a visit to the home of his daughter at Ashland, Ky., July 12, 1886; interment in Congregational Cemetery, Newcastle, Maine.

FLYNN, Dennis Thomas, a Delegate from the Territory of Oklahoma; born in Phoenixville, Chester County, Pa., February 13, 1861; moved with his mother to Buffalo, N. Y., in 1863; became an orphan when three years of age; was raised in a Catholic orphanage where he remained until 1880; attended the common schools and Canisius College, Buffalo, N. Y.; moved to Riverside, Iowa, established and edited the Riverside Leader; studied law; was admitted to the bar in 1882 and commenced practice in Kiowa, Barber County, Kans.; also engaged in the publication of the Kiowa Herald; first postmaster of New Kiowa (later Kiowa), and served from December 5, 1884, to July 17, 1885; city attorney 1886–1889; moved to Oklahoma; postmaster of Guthrie from April 4, 1889, to December 20, 1892; was the first Republican member of the national committee from Oklahoma; unsuccessful candidate for election in 1890 to the Fifty-second Congress; elected as a Republican to the Fifty-third and Fifty-fourth Congresses (March 4, 1893–March 3, 1897); unsuccessful candidate for reelection in 1896 to the Fifty-fifth Congress; elected to the Fifty-sixth and Fifty-seventh Congresses (March 4, 1899–March 3, 1903); was nominated but declined to be a candidate for reelection in 1902 to the Fifty-eighth Congress; resumed the practice of law in Oklahoma City, Okla., in 1904; unsuccessful Republican candidate for election to the United States Senate in 1908; delegate to the Republican National Convention at Chicago in 1912; died in Oklahoma City, Okla., June 19, 1939; interment in Fairlawn Cemetery.

FLYNN, Gerald Thomas, a Representative from Wisconsin; born on a farm in Racine County near Racine, Wis., October 7, 1910; attended a rural one-room grade school and Racine (Wis.) High School; graduated from Marquette Law School in 1933; was admitted to the bar in 1933 and commenced the practice of law in Racine, Wis.; delegate to Democratic National Conventions in 1940, 1944, 1948, 1952, 1956, and 1960; member of the Wisconsin State senate 1950–1954; elected as a Democrat to the Eighty-sixth Congress (January 3, 1959–January 3, 1961); unsuccessful candidate for reelection in 1960 to the Eighty-seventh Congress; is a resident of Racine, Wis.

FLYNN, Joseph Vincent, a Representative from New York; born in Brooklyn, N. Y., September 2, 1883; attended the public schools and the Boys' High School of Brooklyn; was graduated from the College of the City of New York in 1904 and from the Brooklyn Law School of St. Lawrence University in 1906; was admitted to the bar in the latter year and commenced the practice of law in New York City; elected as a Democrat to the Sixty-fourth and Sixty-fifth Congresses (March 4, 1915–March 3, 1919); was not a candidate for renomination in 1918; resumed the practice of law in New York City; delegate to the Democratic State conventions in 1925 and 1927; resided in Brooklyn, N. Y., until his death there February 6, 1940; interment in Calvary Cemetery, Long Island City, N. Y.

FLYNT, John James, Jr., a Representative from Georgia; born in Griffin, Spalding County, Ga., November 8, 1914; attended the public schools and Georgia Military Academy; was graduated from the University of Georgia at Athens in 1936; served as second lieutenant in Sixth Cavalry, United States Army, in 1936 and 1937; attended Emory University Law School in 1937 and 1938, and graduated from George Washington University Law School, Washington, D. C., in 1940; was admitted to the bar in 1938 and commenced the practice of law in Griffin, Ga.; during World War II served as a lieutenant in the United States Army from March 22, 1941, until discharged as a lieutenant colonel December 12, 1945; was awarded the Bronze Star Medal for meritorious service in northern France; colonel in the Army Reserve Corps; assistant United States attorney for northern district of Georgia 1939–1941 and in 1945 and 1946; member of the State house of representatives in 1947 and 1948; solicitor general for Griffin Judicial Circuit from January 1, 1949, to November 2, 1954; elected as a Democrat to the Eighty-third Congress to fill the vacancy caused by the death of A. Sidney Camp and at the same time was elected to the Eighty-fourth Congress; reelected to the Eighty-fifth and Eighty-sixth Congresses and served from November 2, 1954, to January 3, 1961. *Reelected to the Eighty-seventh Congress.*

FOCHT, Benjamin Kurtz, a Representative from Pennsylvania; born in New Bloomfield, Perry County, Pa., March 12, 1863; attended the public schools, Bucknell University, Lewisburg, Pa., Pennsylvania State College at State College, and Susquehanna University, Selinsgrove, Pa.; established the Lewisburg (Pa.) Saturday News in 1881, serving as editor and publisher until his death; delegate to the Republican State convention in 1889; served as an officer of the National Guard of Pennsylvania; member of the State house of representatives 1893–1897; served in the State senate 1901–1905; water supply commissioner of Pennsylvania 1912–1914; elected as a Republican to the Sixtieth, Sixty-first, and Sixty-second Congresses (March 4, 1907–March 3, 1913); unsuccessful candidate for reelection in 1912 to the Sixty-third Congress; elected to the Sixty-fourth and to the three succeeding Congresses (March 4, 1915–March 3, 1923); unsuccessful candidate for renomination in 1922 to the Sixty-eighth Congress and for nomination in 1924, 1926, 1928, and 1930, and also in 1932 for the unexpired term of Edward M. Beers in the Seventy-second Congress; resumed business activities in Lewisburg, Pa.; served as deputy secretary of the Commonwealth in 1928 and 1929; elected to the Seventy-third, Seventy-fourth, and Seventy-fifth Congresses and served from March 4, 1933, until his death in Washington, D. C., March 27, 1937; interment in Lewisburg Cemetery, Lewisburg, Pa.

FOELKER, Otto Godfrey, a Representative from New York; born in the city of Mainz, Germany, December 29, 1875; immigrated to the United States in 1888 with his parents, who settled in Troy, N. Y.; attended the public schools; moved to Brooklyn in December 1895; studied law in the New York Law School; was admitted to the bar in 1908 and commenced practice in Brooklyn; member of the State assembly in 1905 and 1906; served in the State senate in 1907 and 1908; elected as a Republican to the Sixtieth Congress to fill the vacancy caused by the death of Charles T. Dunwell; reelected to the Sixty-first Congress and served from November 3, 1908, to March 3, 1911; declined to be a candidate for renomination in 1910; traveled in Europe in 1912; returned to this country and moved to California; resumed the practice of law in Oakland, Calif., where he died on January 18, 1943; interment in Evergreen Cemetery.

FOERDERER, Robert Hermann, a Representative from Pennsylvania; born in Frankenhausen, Germany, May 16, 1860, while his parents were sojourning in Europe; attended public and private schools in Philadelphia, Pa.; engaged in the manufacture of leather and in various other business enterprises; elected as a Republican to the Fifty-seventh and Fifty-eighth Congresses and served from March 4, 1901, until his death in Torresdale, Pa., July 26, 1903; interment in South Laurel Hill Cemetery, Philadelphia, Pa.

FOGARTY, John Edward, a Representative from Rhode Island; born in Providence, R. I., March 23, 1913; attended La Salle Academy and Providence College; apprenticed as a bricklayer in 1930; moved to Harmony, R. I., and was employed as a bricklayer; served as president of Bricklayers Union No. 1 of Rhode Island; elected as a Democrat to the Seventy-seventh and Seventy-eighth Congresses and served from January 3, 1941,

until his resignation on December 7, 1944, to enlist in the United States Army; reelected to the Seventy-ninth and to the seven succeeding Congresses (January 3, 1945–January 3, 1961). *Reelected to the Eighty-seventh Congress.*

FOGG, George Gilman, a Senator from New Hampshire; born in Meredith Center, Belknap County, N. H., May 26, 1813; pursued classical studies, and was graduated from Dartmouth College, Hanover, N. H., in 1839; studied law at Meredith and at the Harvard Law School; was admitted to the bar in 1842 and commenced practice at Gilmanton Iron Works, N. H.; moved to Concord in 1846; member of the State house of representatives in 1846; secretary of state of New Hampshire in 1846; newspaper publisher from 1847 to 1861; reporter of the State supreme court 1856–1860; delegate to the Republican National Convention at Chicago in 1860; secretary of the Republican National Executive Committee in 1860; appointed by President Lincoln as Minister Resident to Switzerland and served from March 28, 1861, to October 16, 1865; appointed as a Republican to the United States Senate to fill the vacancy caused by the resignation of Daniel Clark and served from August 31, 1866, to March 3, 1867; was not a candidate for election to the Senate in 1866; editor of the Concord Daily Monitor; died in Concord, N. H., October 5, 1881; interment in Blossom Hill Cemetery.

FOLEY, James Bradford, a Representative from Indiana; born near Dover, Mason County, Ky., October 18, 1807; received a limited schooling; employed on a flatboat on the Mississippi River in 1823; moved to Greensburg, Ind., in 1834; engaged in mercantile pursuits 1834–1837, and afterwards in farming; treasurer of Decatur County 1841–1843; member of the State constitutional convention in 1850; appointed commander of the Fourth Brigade of State militia in 1852; elected as a Democrat to the Thirty-fifth Congress (March 4, 1857–March 3, 1859); resumed agricultural pursuits in Decatur County; died in Greensburg, Ind., December 5, 1886; interment in South Park Cemetery.

FOLEY, John Robert, a Representative from Maryland; born in Wabasha, Minn., October 16, 1917; graduated from St. Felix High School in Wabasha in 1935 and St. Thomas College, St. Paul, Minn., in 1940; entered the Army of the United States as a private at Fort Snelling, Minn., July 15, 1941; commissioned a second lieutenant, Quartermaster Corps, Camp Lee, Va., July 15, 1942; served overseas in Australia, New Guinea, and the Philippine Islands with the Four Hundred and Seventy-third Quartermaster Group from November 1943 to November 1945; discharged in February 1946 with rank of major; graduated from Georgetown University Law School, Washington, D. C., in 1947 and from Catholic University Law School, Washington, D. C., in 1950; was admitted to the District of Columbia bar in 1947 and commenced the practice of law; admitted to the Maryland bar in 1953; instructor of administrative law, Catholic University Law School, 1953–1957; elected judge of the Orphan's (Probate) Court, Montgomery County, Md., in November 1954 for a four-year term and served until December 1958; unsuccessful Democratic candidate for election to the Eighty-fifth Congress in 1956; elected as a Democrat to the Eighty-sixth Congress (January 3, 1959–January 3, 1961); unsuccessful candidate for reelection in 1960 to the Eighty-seventh Congress; resides in Kensington, Md.

FOLGER, Alonzo Dillard (brother of John Hamlin Folger), a Representative from North Carolina; born in Dobson, Surry County, N. C., July 9, 1888; attended the public schools; was graduated from the University of North Carolina at Chapel Hill in 1912 and from its law department in 1914; was admitted to the bar in 1914 and commenced practice in Dobson, N. C.; moved to Mount Airy, N. C., and continued the practice of law;

also interested in banking; trustee of the University of North Carolina 1932–1938; served as judge of the State superior court in 1937, resigning after two months' service to become a Democratic national committeeman; member of the Democratic National Committee 1936–1941; elected as a Democrat to the Seventy-sixth and Seventy-seventh Congresses and served from January 3, 1939, until his death in an automobile accident in Mount Airy, N. C., April 30, 1941; interment in Dobson Cemetery, Dobson, N. C.

FOLGER, John Hamlin (brother of Alonzo D. Folger), a Representative from North Carolina; born in Rockford, Surry County, N. C., December 18, 1880; attended the public and high schools, Guilford College, Greensboro, N. C., and studied law at the University of North Carolina at Chapel Hill; was admitted to the bar in 1901 and commenced practice in Dobson, Surry County, N. C.; mayor of Mount Airy, N. C., 1908–1912; member of the State house of representatives in 1927 and 1928; served in the State senate in 1931 and 1932; delegate to the Democratic State conventions 1924–1940; delegate to the Democratic National Conventions at Chicago in 1932 and 1944; elected as a Democrat to the Seventy-seventh Congress in a special election to fill the vacancy caused by the death of his brother, Alonzo D. Folger; reelected to the Seventy-eighth, Seventy-ninth, and Eightieth Congresses and served from June 14, 1941, to January 3, 1949; was not a candidate for renomination in 1948; resumed the practice of law until his retirement in 1959; is a resident of Mount Airy, N. C.

FOLGER, Walter, Jr., a Representative from Massachusetts; born in Nantucket, Nantucket County, Mass., June 12, 1765; attended the public schools; studied law; was admitted to the bar and practiced; member of the State senate 1809–1815 and in 1822; elected as a Democrat to the Fifteenth and Sixteenth Congresses (March 4, 1817–March 3, 1821); resumed the practice of law; died in Nantucket, Mass., September 8, 1849; interment in Friends Burying Ground.

FOLLETT, John Fassett, a Representative from Ohio; born near Enosburg, Franklin County, Vt., February 18, 1831; moved to Ohio in 1837 with his parents, who settled in Licking County; pursued classicial studies, and was graduated from Marietta (Ohio) College in 1855; taught school two years; studied law; was admitted to the bar in 1858 and practiced; member of the State house of representatives 1866–1868; served as speaker in 1868; moved to Cincinnati in 1868 and engaged in the practice of law; presidential elector at large on the Democratic ticket of Hancock and English in 1880; elected as a Democrat to the Forty-eighth Congress (March 4, 1883–March 3, 1885); unsuccessful candidate for reelection in 1884 to the Forty-ninth Congress; resumed the practice of law; unsuccessful candidate for election in 1898 to the Fifty-sixth Congress; died in Cincinnati, Ohio, April 15, 1902; interment in Spring Grove Cemetery.

FOLSOM, Nathaniel, a Delegate from New Hampshire; born in Exeter, Rockingham County, N. H., September 18, 1726; attended the public schools; served in the French and Indian Wars as a captain in Colonel Blanchard's regiment; successively major, lieutenant colonel, and colonel of the Fourth Regiment of New Hampshire Militia, which he commanded at the beginning of the Revolutionary War; brigadier general of the New Hampshire troops sent to Massachusetts and served during the siege of Boston; appointed major general and planned the details of troops sent from New Hampshire to Ticonderoga; Member of the Continental Congress in 1774, 1775, and 1777–1780; executive councilor in 1778; a delegate to the State constitutional convention of 1783, serving as its president; chief justice of the court of common pleas; died in Exeter, N. H., on May 26, 1790; interment in Winter Street Cemetery.

FONG, Hiram Leong, a Senator from Hawaii; born in Honolulu, Hawaii, October 1, 1907; attended Kalihiwaena Grammar School, St. Louis College, and McKinley High School; graduated from the University of Hawaii in 1930 and from Harvard Law School in 1935; was admitted to the bar in 1935 and commenced the practice of law in Honolulu; during World War II served as judge advocate of the Seventh Fighter Command of the Seventh Air Force with rank of major 1942–1945; member of the Territorial legislature for fourteen years, serving six years as speaker and four years as vice speaker; vice president of the Territorial Constitutional Convention in 1950; corporation president of Finance Factors, Grand Pacific Life Insurance, Finance Realty, Finance Home Builders, Finance Investment, Finance Factors Building, Finance Factors Foundation, and Market City; operates a banana farm in Honolulu; delegate to the Republican National Conventions in 1952 and 1956; elected as a Republican to the United States Senate on July 28, 1959, and upon the admission of Hawaii as a State into the Union on August 21, 1959, in the classification of Senators from that State, drew the six-year term beginning on that day and ending January 3, 1965.

FOOT, Solomon, a Representative and a Senator from Vermont; born in Cornwall, Addison County, Vt., November 19, 1802; pursued classical studies, and was graduated from Middlebury (Vt.) College in 1826; studied law; was admitted to the bar in 1831 and commenced practice in Rutland, Vt.; member of the State house of representatives in 1833 and 1836–1838, serving as speaker the last two sessions; delegate to the State constitutional convention in 1836; prosecuting attorney 1836–1842; elected as a Whig to the Twenty-eighth and Twenty-ninth Congresses (March 4, 1843–March 3, 1847); unsuccessful candidate for Clerk of the National House of Representatives in December 1849; elected as a Whig to the United States Senate; twice reelected as a Republican, and served from March 4, 1851, until his death; served several times as president pro tempore of the Senate; died in Washington, D. C., March 28, 1866; funeral services were held in the Chamber of the United States Senate; interment in Evergreen Cemetery, Rutland, Vt.

FOOTE, Charles Augustus, a Representative from New York; born in Newburgh, Orange County, N. Y., April 15, 1785; attended private schools in Newburgh and Kingston, N. Y., and was graduated from Union College, Schenectady, N. Y., in 1805; studied law; was admitted to the bar in 1808 and practiced in New York City and later in Delhi, Delaware County, N. Y.; colonel in the New York State Militia, Sixth Division; trustee of Delaware Academy; president of the village of Delhi; elected as a Democrat to the Eighteenth Congress (March 4, 1823–March 3, 1825); resumed the practice of law in Delhi, N. Y., where he died August 1, 1828; interment in the private burying ground at "Arbor Hill," the estate of his father.

FOOTE, Ellsworth Bishop, a Representative from Connecticut; born in North Branford, New Haven County, Conn., January 12, 1898; attended the public schools; was graduated from Yale Business College of New Haven in 1916 and from Georgetown University Law School, Washington, D. C., in 1923; was admitted to the bar in 1924 and commenced practice in New Haven, Conn.; corporation counsel of North Branford 1924–1946; special assistant to the attorney general, Department of Justice, Washington, D. C., February 1925 to July 1926; chairman of the board of finance of North Branford 1934–1946;

judge of probate, North Branford District, 1938–1946; acting judge of probate, New Haven Probate Court, November 1944 to July 1945; attorney for the county of New Haven 1942–1946; elected as a Republican to the Eightieth Congress (January 3, 1947–January 3, 1949); unsuccessful candidate for reelection in 1948 to the Eighty-first Congress; resumed the practice of law and is a resident of North Branford, Conn.

FOOTE, Henry Stuart, a Senator from Mississippi; born in Fauquier County, Va., February 28, 1804; pursued classical studies; was graduated from Washington College (now Washington and Lee University), Lexington, Va., in 1819; studied law; was admitted to the bar in 1823 and commenced practice in Tuscumbia, Ala., in 1825; moved to Mississippi in 1826 and practiced his profession in Jackson, Natchez, Vicksburg, and Raymond; presidential elector on the Democratic ticket of Polk and Dallas in 1844; elected as a Unionist to the United States Senate, and served from March 4, 1847, until January 8, 1852, when he resigned to become Governor; Governor of Mississippi 1852–1854; while serving in the latter capacity was unsuccessful candidate for United States Senator, lacking but one vote necessary for election; moved to California in 1854; unsuccessful candidate of the Reform Party for election to the United States Senate in 1856, again lacking but one vote; returned to Vicksburg, Miss., in 1858; member of the Southern convention held at Knoxville in 1859; moved to Tennessee and settled near Nashville; elected to the First and Second Confederate Congresses; afterwards moved to Washington, D. C., and practiced law; supported the Republican presidential ticket of Hayes and Wheeler in 1876; appointed by President Hayes superintendent of the mint at New Orleans and served from December 18, 1878, until his death; author of several books; died in Nashville, Tenn., on May 19, 1880; interment in Mount Olivet Cemetery.

FOOTE, Samuel Augustus, a Representative and a Senator from Connecticut; born in Cheshire, Conn., November 8, 1780; pursued an academic course; was graduated from Yale College, New Haven, Conn., in 1797; attended the Litchfield Law School; discontinued law studies on account of ill health and engaged in the shipping trade at New Haven; returned to Cheshire in 1813 and engaged in agricultural pursuits; member of the State house of representatives in 1817 and 1818; elected to the Sixteenth Congress (March 4, 1819–March 3, 1821); again a member of the State house of representatives 1821–1823, 1825, and 1826, and served as speaker in 1825 and 1826; elected to the Eighteenth Congress (March 4, 1823–March 3, 1825); elected to the United States Senate and served from March 4, 1827, to March 3, 1833; unsuccessful candidate for reelection in 1832; elected as a Whig to the Twenty-third Congress, and served from March 4, 1833, to May 9, 1834, when he resigned to become Governor of Connecticut, and served in 1834 and 1835; unsuccessful Whig candidate for Governor in 1836; presidential elector on the Whig ticket of Clay and Frelinghuysen in 1844; died in Cheshire, Conn., on September 15, 1846; interment in Hillside Cemetery.

FOOTE, Wallace Turner, Jr., a Representative from New York; born in Port Henry, Essex County, N. Y., April 7, 1864; attended the Port Henry Union School and Williston Seminary, Easthampton, Mass., and was graduated as a civil engineer from Union College, Schenectady, N. Y., in 1885; elected alumni trustee of that university in 1896; assistant superintendent of the Cedar Point Furnace in Port Henry 1885–1887; attended Columbia Law School, New York City; was admitted to the bar in 1889 and commenced practice in Port Henry; elected as a Republican to the Fifty-fourth and Fifty-fifth

Congresses (March 4, 1895–March 3, 1899); was not a candidate for renomination in 1898; resumed the practice of law and also engaged in mining; died in New York City December 17, 1910; interment in Union Cemetery, Port Henry, N. Y.

FORAKER, Joseph Benson, a Senator from Ohio; born near Rainsboro, Highland County, Ohio, on July 5, 1846; pursued preparatory studies; enlisted July 14, 1862, as a private in Company A, Eighty-ninth Regiment, Ohio Volunteer Infantry, and served until the close of the Civil War, retiring with the rank of first lieutenant and brevet captain; was graduated from Cornell University, Ithaca, N. Y., July 1, 1869; studied law; was admitted to the bar in 1869 and commenced practice in Cincinnati, Ohio; judge of the superior court of Cincinnati from 1879 until his resignation in 1882; unsuccessful Republican candidate for Governor of Ohio in 1883; delegate to the Republican National Conventions at Chicago in 1884 and 1888, at Minneapolis in 1892, at St. Louis in 1896, and at Philadelphia in 1900; chairman of the Ohio delegation in the conventions of 1884 and 1888; Governor of Ohio 1885–1889; unsuccessful candidate for Governor in 1889; chairman of the Republican State conventions in 1886, 1890, 1896, and 1900; elected on January 14, 1896, as a Republican to the United States Senate; reelected in 1903 and served from March 4, 1897, to March 3, 1909; unsuccessful candidate for reelection in 1909; resumed the practice of law in Cincinnati, Ohio, where he died May 10, 1917; interment in Spring Grove Cemetery.

FORAN, Martin Ambrose, a Representative from Ohio; born in Choconut, Susquehanna County, Pa., November 11, 1844; attended the public schools and St. Joseph's College; taught school three years; spent two years in Ireland; during the Civil War served as a private in the Fourth Regiment, Pennsylvania Volunteer Cavalry, from April 1864 to July 1865; member of the State constitutional convention of Ohio in 1873; studied law; was admitted to the bar in 1874 and commenced practice in Cleveland; prosecuting attorney for the city of Cleveland 1875–1877; elected as a Democrat to the Forty-eighth, Forty-ninth, and Fiftieth Congresses (March 4, 1883–March 3, 1889); was not a candidate for reelection; resumed the practice of law in Cleveland, Ohio; judge of the court of common pleas from January 1911 until his death in Cleveland, Ohio, June 28, 1921; interment in Lake View Cemetery.

FORAND, Aime Joseph, a Representative from Rhode Island; born in Fall River, Bristol County, Mass., May 23, 1895; attended the public and parochial schools, Magnus Commercial School, Providence, R. I., and Columbia University, New York, N. Y.; during the First World War served in France as sergeant, first class, from May 1918 to July 1919, in the Motor Transport Corps; newspaper reporter at Pawtucket and Woonsocket, R. I., 1924–1930; member of the State house of representatives 1923–1926; served as secretary to Representative Jeremiah E. O'Connell in 1929 and 1930 and to Representative Francis B. Condon 1930–1935; chief of the Rhode Island State division of soldiers' relief and commandant of the Rhode Island Soldiers' Home in 1935 and 1936; elected as a Democrat to the Seventy-fifth Congress (January 3, 1937–January 3, 1939); unsuccessful candidate for reelection in 1938 to the Seventy-sixth Congress; elected to the Seventy-seventh and to the nine succeeding Congresses (January 3, 1941–January 3, 1961); was not a candidate for renomination in 1960; is a resident of Cumberland, R. I.

FORBES, James, a Delegate from Maryland; born near Benedict, Charles County, Md., about 1731; appointed justice of the peace of Charles County, Md., April 1, 1777; tax commissioner of Charles County and also member of the State general assembly in 1777; Member of the Continental Congress 1778–1780; died in Philadelphia, Pa., March 25, 1780; interment in the yard surrounding Christ Protestant Episcopal Church.

FORD, Aaron Lane, a Representative from Mississippi; born in Potts Camp, Marshall County, Miss., December 21, 1903; attended public schools in Mississippi and the law department of Cumberland University, Lebanon, Tenn.; was admitted to the bar in 1927 and commenced practice in Aberdeen, Miss.; moved to Ackerman, Miss., the same year and continued the practice of law; district attorney of the fifth circuit court district 1932–1934; elected as a Democrat to the Seventy-fourth and to the three succeeding Congresses (January 3, 1935–January 3, 1943); unsuccessful candidate for renomination in 1942 to the Seventy-eighth Congress; delegate to the Interparliamentary Union Conference at The Hague, Netherlands, in 1938; resumed the practice of law in Washington, D. C., and Jackson, Miss.; is a resident of Jackson, Miss.

FORD, George, a Representative from Indiana; born in South Bend, St. Joseph County, Ind., January 11, 1846; attended the common schools; engaged in the cooper's trade in early youth; entered the law department of the University of Michigan at Ann Arbor, and was graduated from that institution in 1869; was immediately admitted to the bar and commenced practice in South Bend, Ind.; prosecuting attorney of St. Joseph County in 1873 and 1875–1884, when he retired, having been elected to Congress; elected as a Democrat to the Forty-ninth Congress (March 4, 1885–March 3, 1887); declined to be a candidate for reelection in 1866 to the Fiftieth Congress; became the head of the legal department of an implement concern, but subsequently resumed the private practice of his profession in South Bend, Ind.; elected judge of the superior court of St. Joseph County in 1914 and served until failing health compelled him to retire; died in South Bend, Ind., on August 30, 1917; interment in Riverview Cemetery.

FORD, Gerald R., Jr., a Representative from Michigan; born in Omaha, Douglas County, Nebr., July 14, 1913; moved to Grand Rapids, Kent County, Mich., in 1914 and attended the public schools; was graduated from the University of Michigan at Ann Arbor in 1935 and from Yale University Law School, New Haven, Conn., in 1941; was admitted to the bar in 1941 and commenced the practice of law in Grand Rapids, Mich.; during World War II served in the United States Navy from 1942 until discharged as a lieutenant commander in 1946; received the Grand Rapids Junior Chamber of Commerce Distinguished Service Award in 1947 and the United States Junior Chamber of Commerce Distinguished Service Award in 1949; elected as a Republican to the Eighty-first and to the five succeeding Congresses (January 3, 1949–January 3, 1961). *Reelected to the Eighty-seventh Congress.*

FORD, James, a Representative from Pennsylvania; born in Perth Amboy, Middlesex County, N. J., May 4, 1783; attended the common schools; moved to New York City in 1797 and to Lindsley Town (later Lindley), Steuben County, N. Y., in 1803; entered an office as a clerk and subsequently moved with his employer to Tioga County, Pa.; purchased land on the banks of the Cowanesque River and built a home in 1816; called the place Lawrence (later Lawrenceville), after Captain Lawrence, of the War of 1812; member of the State house of representatives in 1824 and 1825; elected as a Jackson Democrat to the Twenty-first and Twenty-second Congresses (March 4, 1829–March 3, 1833); operated a sawmill and a gristmill at Lawrenceville, Tioga County, Pa., until his death at that place on August 18, 1859; interment in the old Lindsley family cemetery at Lindley, N. Y

FORD, Leland Merritt, a Representative from California; born in Eureka, Eureka County, Nev., March 8, 1893; attended the public and high schools; also took various courses at the University of Arizona at Tucson, Virginia Polytechnic Institute at Blackburg, Sheldon Science of Business, Chicago, Ill., and the University of Southern California at Los Angeles; instructor in real estate at the University of Southern California in 1923 and 1924; surveyor for Southern Sierras Power Co., in 1909 and 1910; employee of the Southern Pacific Railroad in California in 1911 and in New York in 1912 and 1913; moved to Los Angeles, Calif., in 1915 and was employed by the Union Pacific Railroad; moved to Lynchburg, Va., and engaged in farming and livestock breeding 1915–1919; moved to Santa Monica, Calif., in 1919 and engaged in the real-estate business; member of the planning commission, Santa Monica, Calif., 1923–1927; county supervisor of Los Angeles County, Calif., 1936–1939; elected as a Republican to the Seventy-sixth and Seventy-seventh Congresses (January 3, 1939–January 3, 1943); unsuccessful candidate for reelection in 1942 to the Seventy-eighth Congress; resumed the real-estate business; builder, subdivider, developer, and owner of a shopping center in Los Angeles County, Calif., and is a resident of Pacific Palisades, Calif.

FORD, Melbourne Haddock, a Representative from Michigan; born in Salem, Washtenaw County, Mich., June 30, 1849; moved to Lansing with his parents in 1859; attended the common schools and the Michigan State College of Agriculture at East Lansing; enlisted in the United States Navy in 1864, and in 1867 was appointed a midshipman at the United States Naval Academy, Annapolis, Md.; resigned the following year and returned to Lansing; moved to Grand Rapids in 1873 and was engaged as official stenographer of several municipal, State, and Federal courts; studied law and was admitted to the bar in 1878; member of the State house of representatives in 1885 and 1886; elected as a Democrat to the Fiftieth Congress (March 4, 1887–March 3, 1889); unsuccessful candidate for reelection in 1888 to the Fifty-first Congress; commenced the practice of law at Grand Rapids in 1889; chairman of the Democratic State convention in 1890; elected to the Fifty-second Congress and served from March 4, 1891, until his death in Grand Rapids, Mich., April 20, 1891; interment in Oak Hill Cemetery.

FORD, Nicholas, a Representative from Missouri; born in Wicklow, Ireland, June 21, 1833; attended the village school and Maynooth College, Dublin, Ireland; immigrated to the United States in 1848 with his parents, who settled in Chicago, Ill.; moved to St. Joseph, Mo., in 1859 and later to Colorado and Montana, in which States he engaged in mining; returned to Missouri and settled in Rochester, Andrew County, and engaged in mercantile pursuits; elected a member of the State house of representatives in 1875; elected as a Liberal Republican to the Forty-sixth and Forty-seventh Congresses (March 4, 1879–March 3, 1883); unsuccessful candidate for reelection in 1882 to the Forty-eighth Congress and for election in 1890 to the Fifty-second Congress; unsuccessful Republican candidate for Governor of Missouri in 1884; moved to Virginia City, Nev.; member of the first city council; retired from active business and moved to Miltonvale, Kans., where he died June 18, 1897; interment in the Catholic Cemetery, Aurora, Cloud County, Kans.

FORD, Thomas Francis, a Representative from California; born in St. Louis, Mo., February 18, 1873; attended public and private schools; served in the United States Postal Service 1896–1903; studied law at Toledo, Ohio; engaged in newspaper work in Washington, Idaho, California, and Washington, D. C., 1913–1929; magazine and literary editor in Los Angeles 1919–1929; lecturer on international trade at the University of Southern California at Los Angeles in 1920 and 1921; publicity director of the Los Angeles water and power department 1929–1931; member of the Los Angeles City Council 1931–1933; author of "The Foreign Trade of the United States"; elected as a Democrat to the Seventy-third and to the five succeeding Congresses (March 4, 1933–January 3, 1945); was not a candidate for renomination in 1944; assumed the management of his rental properties; died in South Pasadena, Calif., December 26, 1958; interment in Forest Lawn Memorial Park, Glendale, Calif.

FORD, William D., a Representative from New York; born in Herkimer County, N.Y., in 1779; educated at Fairfield Seminary, Herkimer County, N. Y.; studied law; was admitted to the bar in 1809 and commenced practice in Fairfield, N. Y.; member of the State assembly in 1816 and 1817; appointed commissioner to perform duties of judge of the supreme court in 1817; moved to Watertown, Jefferson County, N. Y., in 1817 and continued the practice of law; elected as a Democrat to the Sixteenth Congress (March 4, 1819–March 3, 1821); was not a candidate for reelection in 1820 to the Seventeenth Congress; resumed the practice of his profession in Watertown, N. Y.; served as district attorney of Jefferson County and also as master of chancery; trustee of the village of Watertown in 1827; moved to Sackets Harbor, N. Y., about 1830, and died there October 1, 1833; interment in the Village Cemetery.

FORDNEY, Joseph Warren, a Representative from Michigan; born on a farm near Hartford City, Blackford County, Ind., November 5, 1853; attended the common schools; moved to Saginaw, Saginaw County, Mich., in June 1869 and engaged in the lumber industry, being employed as a chore boy, cook, chopper, driver, etc., and afterward became the owner of extensive lumber enterprises; vice president of the Saginaw Board of Trade; member of the board of aldermen of Saginaw 1896–1900; elected as a Republican to the Fifty-sixth and to the eleven succeeding Congresses (March 4, 1899–March 3, 1923); voluntarily retired and declined to be a candidate for renomination in 1922; delegate to the Republican National Convention in 1908 which nominated the presidential ticket of Taft and Sherman; engaged in the lumber business in Saginaw, Mich.; also interested in banking and agricultural pursuits; died in Saginaw, Mich., on January 8, 1932; interment in St. Andrew's Cemetery.

FORESTER, John B., a Representative from Tennessee; born in McMinnville, Warren County, Tenn.; received a limited schooling; studied law; was admitted to the bar and practiced; elected to the Twenty-third and Twenty-fourth Congresses (March 4, 1833–March 3, 1837); died August 31, 1845.

FORKER, Samuel Carr, a Representative from New Jersey; born in Mount Holly, Burlington County, N. J., March 16, 1821; completed preparatory studies; moved to Bordentown and engaged in banking; director and cashier of the Bordentown Banking Co.; elected as a Democrat to the Forty-second Congress (March 4, 1871–March 3, 1873); unsuccessful candidate for reelection in 1872 to the Forty-third Congress; again engaged in banking; moved to Delanco, Burlington County, N. J., in 1890; lived in retirement with his son until his death in Edgewater Park, Burlington County, N. J., February 10, 1900; interment in Mount Holly Cemetery, Mount Holly, N. J.

FORMAN, William St. John, a Representative from Illinois; born in Natchez, Adams County, Miss., January 20, 1847; moved with his father to Nashville, Washington County, Ill., in 1851; attended the public schools, and Washington Seminary, Richview, Ill.; studied law; was admitted to the bar in 1870 and commenced practice in Nashville, Ill.; mayor 1878–1884; delegate to all State and National Democratic Conventions from 1876 to 1896; member of the State senate 1884–1888; elected as a Democrat to the Fifty-first, Fifty-second, and Fifty-third Congresses (March 4, 1889–March 3, 1895); moved to East St. Louis, Ill., in 1895; unsuccessful candidate as a Gold Standard Democrat for election as Governor in 1896; resumed the practice of his profession; appointed by President Cleveland as Commissioner of Internal Revenue and served from 1895 to 1899; died in Champaign, Ill., June 10, 1908, while en route from a visit at Urbana, Ill.; interment in Masonic Cemetery, Nashville, Ill.

FORNANCE, Joseph, a Representative from Pennsylvania; born in Lower Merion Township, Montgomery County, Pa., October 18, 1804; attended the public schools and the Old Academy at Lower Merion; studied law; was admitted to the bar in 1832 and commenced practice in Norristown, Pa.; president of the council of the borough of Norristown; member of the State house of representatives in 1834; appointed Winfield Scott Hancock as a cadet to the United States Military Academy at West Point; elected as a Democrat to the Twenty-sixth and Twenty-seventh Congresses (March 4, 1839–March 3, 1843); was not a candidate for renomination in 1842; resumed the practice of his profession; died in Norristown, Montgomery County, Pa., on November 24, 1852; interment in Montgomery Cemetery.

FORNES, Charles Vincent, a Representative from New York; born on a farm near Williamsville, Erie County, N. Y., January 22, 1844; attended the public schools, and was graduated from Union Academy, Lockport, N. Y., in 1864; moved to Buffalo, N. Y., in 1866; taught school in a district school and then served as principal of a Buffalo public school for three years; employed as a clerk for a wholesale woolen merchant in Buffalo and later established a similar business for himself; moved to New York City in 1877 and engaged in business as an importer and jobber of woolens; president of the board of aldermen of New York City 1902–1907; trustee and director of several banks and corporations; elected as a Democrat to the Sixtieth, Sixty-first, and Sixty-second Congresses (March 4, 1907–March 3, 1913); declined to be a candidate for renomination in 1912; resumed his former business pursuits in New York City; retired from active business in 1926 and returned to Buffalo, N. Y., where he died on May 22, 1929; interment in United German and French Roman Catholic Cemetery, Pine Hill, Buffalo, N. Y.

FORNEY, Daniel Munroe (son of Peter Forney), a Representative from North Carolina; born near Lincolnton, Lincoln County, N. C., in May 1784; attended the public schools and the University of North Carolina at Chapel Hill; engaged in agricultural pursuits; served as a major in the War of 1812; held several local offices; elected to the Fourteenth and Fifteenth Congresses and served from March 4, 1815, until his resignation in 1818; appointed by President Monroe a commissioner to treat with the Creek Indians in 1820; served as a member of the State senate 1823–1826; moved to Alabama in 1834 and settled in Lowndes County; resumed agricultural pursuits and became interested in various business enterprises; died in Lowndes County, Ala., October 15, 1847; interment in family burying ground, Lowndes County, Ala.

FORNEY, Peter (father of Daniel Munroe Forney), a Representative from North Carolina; born near Lincolnton, Lincoln County, N. C., April 21, 1756; attended the public schools; served as a captain during the Revolutionary War; engaged in the manufacture of iron; member of the State house of commons

1794–1796; served in the State senate in 1801 and 1802; presidential elector on the Democratic ticket of Jefferson and Clinton in 1804, of Madison and Clinton in 1808, of Monroe and Tompkins in 1816, and of Jackson and Calhoun in 1824 and 1828; elected as a Democrat to the Thirteenth Congress (March 4, 1813–March 3, 1815); declined to be a candidate in 1814 for reelection to the Fourteenth Congress; retired from public life; died at his country home, "Mount Welcome," in Lincoln County, N. C., on February 1, 1834; interment in the private burying ground on his estate.

FORNEY, William Henry (grandson of Peter Forney), a Representative from Alabama; born in Lincolnton, Lincoln County, N. C., November 9, 1823; pursued classical studies, and was graduated from the University of Alabama at Tuscaloosa in 1844; served in the war with Mexico as a first lieutenant in the First Regiment of Alabama Volunteers; studied law; was admitted to the bar in 1848 and commenced practice in Jacksonville, Calhoun County, Ala.; trustee of the University of Alabama 1851–1860; member of the State house of representatives in 1859 and 1860; during the Civil War entered the Confederate Army in 1861 as a captain, and was successively promoted to major, lieutenant colonel, colonel, and brigadier general; surrendered at Appomattox Court House; member of the State senate in 1865 and 1866; elected as a Democrat to the Forty-fourth and to the eight succeeding Congresses (March 4, 1875–March 3, 1893); was not a candidate for renomination in 1892; appointed by President Cleveland a member of the Gettysburg Battlefield Commission and served until his death in Jacksonville, Ala., January 16, 1894; interment in the City Cemetery.

FORREST, Thomas, a Representative from Pennsylvania; born in Philadelphia, Pa., in 1747; attended the common schools; during the Revolutionary War was commissioned a captain in Col. Thomas Proctor's Pennsylvania Artillery October 5, 1776, promoted to major March 3, 1777, and lieutenant colonel December 2, 1778; resigned October 7, 1781; elected to the Sixteenth Congress (March 4, 1819–March 3, 1821); elected to the Seventeenth Congress to fill the vacancy caused by the resignation of William Milnor and served from October 8, 1822, to March 3, 1823; unsuccessful candidate for reelection in 1822 to the Eighteenth Congress; died in Germantown (now a part of Philadelphia), Pa., March 20, 1825.

FORREST, Uriah, a Delegate and a Representative from Maryland; born near Leonardtown, St. Marys County, Md., in 1756; received a limited schooling; served as a first lieutenant, captain, and major in Maryland forces in the Revolutionary War; wounded at the Battle of Germantown and lost a leg at the Battle of Brandywine; Member of the Continental Congress in 1786 and 1787; elected as a Federalist to the Third Congress and served from March 4, 1793, to November 8, 1794, when he resigned; commissioned major general of Maryland Militia in 1795; clerk of the circuit court of the District of Columbia 1800–1805; died at his home, "Rosedale," near Georgetown, D. C., July 6, 1805; interment in Oak Hill Cemetery, Washington, D. C.

FORRESTER, Elijah Lewis, a Representative from Georgia; born on a farm near Leesburg, Lee County, Ga., August 16, 1896; attended the Leesburg public schools; studied law and passed the State bar examination in 1917; during the First World War served as a private in the United States Army; commenced the practice of law in 1919 in Leesburg, Ga.; solicitor, City Court, Leesburg, Ga., 1920–1933; mayor of Leesburg 1922–1931; county attorney of Lee County 1928–1937; solicitor general, southwestern judicial circuit, 1937–1950; delegate to Democratic National Conventions in 1948 and 1952; elected as a Democrat to the Eighty-second and to the four succeeding Congresses (January 3, 1951–January 3, 1961). *Reelected to the Eighty-seventh Congress.*

FORSYTH, John, a Representative and a Senator from Georgia; born in Fredericksburg, Va., October 22, 1780; was graduated from Princeton College in 1799; moved to Augusta, Ga., with his father; studied law; was admitted to the bar in 1802 and commenced practice in Augusta; elected attorney general of Georgia in 1808; elected as a Democrat to the Thirteenth, Fourteenth, and Fifteenth Congresses, and served from March 4, 1813, until his resignation, effective November 23, 1818; elected to the United States Senate on November 7, 1818, to fill the vacancy caused by the resignation of George M. Troup, and served from November 23, 1818, to February 17, 1819, when he resigned to accept an appointment as Minister to Spain, serving in that capacity until March 2, 1823; elected to the Eighteenth, Nineteenth, and Twentieth Congresses and served from March 4, 1823, until his resignation, effective November 7, 1827; Governor of Georgia 1827–1829; again elected to the United States Senate to fill the vacancy caused by the resignation of John Macpherson Berrien and served from November 9, 1829, to June 27, 1834, when he resigned to accept a Cabinet portfolio; appointed Secretary of State in the Cabinet of President Jackson; reappointed by President Van Buren and served from July 1, 1834, to March 4, 1841; died in Washington, D. C., October 21, 1841; interment in Congressional Cemetery.

FORSYTHE, Albert Palaska, a Representative from Illinois; born in New Richmond, Clermont County, Ohio, May 24, 1830; attended the common schools and Asbury University (now De Pauw University), Greencastle, Ind.; admitted into the Indiana conference of the Methodist Church as a traveling preacher in 1853 and served eight years; during the Civil War served in the Union Army as first lieutenant of Company I, Ninety-seventh Regiment, Indiana Volunteer Infantry; discharged in August 1864 by reason of disability incurred in service; moved to Illinois in 1865 and settled on a farm thirteen miles west of Paris, Edgar County; took an active part in the Grange movement and served six years as master of the State Grange of Illinois; elected as a Republican to the Forty-sixth Congress (March 4, 1879–March 3, 1881); unsuccessful candidate for reelection in 1880 to the Forty-seventh Congress; moved to Kansas in 1882 and engaged in agricultural pursuits near Liberty, Independence County; regent of the Kansas State Agricultural College 1886–1892; moved to Independence, Kans., where he died September 2, 1906; interment in Liberty Cemetery, Liberty, Kans.

FORT, Franklin William, a Representative from New Jersey; born in Newark, N. J., March 30, 1880; moved in 1888 with his parents to East Orange, N. J.; attended the public schools and Newark Academy; was graduated from Lawrenceville School in 1897 and from Princeton University in 1901; attended New York Law School 1901–1903; was admitted to the bar in 1903 and commenced practice in Newark; recorder of East Orange, N. J., in 1907 and 1908; during the First World War served as a volunteer on the staff of the United States Food Administrator, Washington, D. C., 1917–1919; engaged in the insurance business in 1919 at Newark, N. J., and was also interested in banking; elected as a Republican to the Sixty-ninth, Seventieth, and Seventy-first Congresses (March 4, 1925–March 3, 1931); was not a candidate for renomination, but was an unsuccessful candidate for nomination as United States Senator in 1930; served as secretary of the Republican National Committee 1928–1930;

resumed the practice of law; served as chairman of the Federal Home Loan Bank Board from January 1932 to March 1933; died on June 20, 1937, in Rochester, Minn., where he had gone to receive medical treatment; interment in Bloomfield Cemetery, Bloomfield, N. J.

FORT, Greenbury Lafayette, a Representative from Illinois; born in French Grant, Scioto County, Ohio, October 17, 1825; moved with his parents to Marshall County, Ill., in April 1834; completed preparatory studies and attended Rock River Seminary; studied law; was admitted to the bar in 1847 and commenced practice in Lacon, Ill.; elected sheriff in 1850; clerk of Marshall County in 1852; county judge in 1857; served in the Union Army during the Civil War; was appointed a second lieutenant in the Eleventh Regiment, Illinois Volunteer Infantry, on April 30, 1861; first lieutenant with the rank of quartermaster May 22, 1861; captain September 1, 1861; lieutenant colonel and quartermaster July 21, 1864; brevetted major and lieutenant colonel of Volunteers March 13, 1865, "for faithful and meritorious services during the war"; mustered out March 20, 1866; member of the State senate in 1866; elected as a Republican to the Forty-third and to the three succeeding Congresses (March 4, 1873–March 3, 1881); was not a candidate for renomination in 1880; retired from public life; died in Lacon, Ill., January 13, 1883; interment in Lacon Cemetery.

FORT, Tomlinson, a Representative from Georgia; born in Warrenton, Warren County, Ga., July 14, 1787; completed preparatory studies; studied medicine; was graduated from the Philadelphia Medical College, and commenced practice in 1810; captain of a volunteer company in the War of 1812; member of the State house of representatives 1818–1826; elected as a Democrat to the Twentieth Congress (March 4, 1827–March 3, 1829); resumed the practice of medicine in Milledgeville, Ga.; president of the State Bank of Georgia in 1832, which position he held until his death in Milledgeville, Ga., May 11, 1859; interment in the City Cemetery.

FORWARD, Chauncey (brother of Walter Forward), a Representative from Pennsylvania; born in Old Granby, Conn., February 4, 1793; moved with his father to Ohio in 1800, and a short time afterward to Greensburg, Pa.; pursued classical studies; studied law; was admitted to the bar in Pittsburgh, Pa., in 1817 and began practice in Somerset, Pa.; member of the State house of representatives 1820–1822; elected as a Democrat to the Nineteenth Congress to fill the vacancy caused by the resignation of Alexander Thomson; reelected to the Twentieth and Twenty-first Congresses and served from December 4, 1826, to March 3, 1831; appointed prothonotary and recorder of Somerset County in 1831; died in Somerset, Somerset County, Pa., October 19, 1839; interment in Aukeny Square Cemetery.

FORWARD, Walter (brother of Chauncey Forward), a Representative from Pennsylvania; born in East Granby, Conn., January 24, 1783; attended the common schools; moved with his father to Aurora, Ohio; settled in Pittsburgh, Pa., in 1803; studied law; was admitted to the bar in 1806 and commenced practice in Pittsburgh; also served for several years as editor of the Tree of Liberty, a Democratic paper published in that city; elected as a Democrat to the Seventeenth Congress to fill the vacancy caused by the resignation of Henry Baldwin; reelected to the Eighteenth Congress, and served from October 8, 1822, to March 3, 1825; unsuccessful candidate for reelection in 1824 to the Nineteenth Congress; member of the State constitutional convention in 1837; declined the appointment of United States district attorney for the western district of New York tendered by President Harrison in 1841; appointed by President Harrison as First Comptroller of the Treasury on April 6, 1841, and served until September 13, 1841, when he was appointed Secretary of the Treasury in the Cabinet of President Tyler, which position he held until March 1, 1843; resumed the practice of law in Pittsburgh; appointed by President Taylor Chargé d'Affaires to Denmark and served from November 8, 1849, to October 10, 1851; returned to the United States to serve as president judge of the district court of Allegheny County; died in Pittsburgh, Pa., November 24, 1852; interment in Allegheny Cemetery.

FOSDICK, Nicoll, a Representative from New York; born in New London, Conn., November 9, 1785; completed preparatory studies; moved to Norway, N. Y.; presidential elector on the Monroe ticket in 1816; member of the State assembly in 1818 and 1819; elected as a Whig to the Nineteenth Congress (March 4, 1825–March 3, 1827); returned to New London, Conn., in 1843; collector of customs 1849–1853; engaged in mercantile pursuits; died in New London, Conn., May 7, 1868; interment in Cedar Grove Cemetery.

FOSS, Eugene Noble (brother of George Edmund Foss), a Representative from Massachusetts; born in West Berkshire, near St. Albans, Franklin County, Vt., on September 24, 1858; attended the public schools, Franklin County Academy at St. Albans, Vt., and the University of Vermont; settled in Boston, Mass., in 1882; engaged in the manufacture of iron and steel products; elected as a Democrat to the Sixty-first Congress to fill the vacancy caused by the death of William C. Lovering and served from March 22, 1910, until his resignation, effective January 4, 1911, having been elected Governor of Massachusetts, in which capacity he served from 1911 to 1913; unsuccessful candidate for reelection as Governor in 1912; resumed his former manufacturing pursuits, and managed his large real-estate holdings in Boston, Mass.; died in Jamaica Plain (Boston) Mass., September 13, 1939; interment in Forest Hill Cemetery.

FOSS, Frank Herbert, a Representative from Massachusetts; born in Augusta, Kennebec County, Maine, September 20, 1865; attended the public schools, and was graduated from Kent Hill (Maine) Seminary in 1886; moved to Fitchburg, Mass., in 1893; member of a firm engaged as general contractors in the construction of industrial plants, and also interested in banking; member of the Fitchburg city council 1906–1912; water commissioner 1913–1915; mayor of Fitchburg 1917–1920; member of the Republican State committee 1915–1946, and served as chairman 1921–1924; delegate to the Republican State conventions from 1915 to 1946; elected as a Republican to the Sixty-ninth and to the four succeeding Congresses (March 4, 1925–January 3, 1935); unsuccessful candidate for reelection in 1934 to the Seventy-fourth Congress; resumed management in the contracting business and resided in Fitchburg, Mass., until his death there on February 15, 1947; interment in Forest Hill Cemetery.

FOSS, George Edmund (brother of Eugene Noble Foss), a Representative from Illinois; born in West Berkshire, Franklin County, Vt., July 2, 1863; attended the common schools, and was graduated from Harvard University in 1885; attended Columbia Law School and the School of Political Science in New York City; was graduated from Union College of Law at Chicago, Ill., in 1889; was admitted to the bar the same year and commenced the practice of law in Chicago; elected as a Republican to the Fifty-fourth and to the eight succeeding Congresses (March 4, 1895–March 3, 1913); unsuccessful candidate for reelection in 1912; elected to the Sixty-fourth and Sixty-fifth Congresses (March 4, 1915–March 3, 1919); was not a candidate for renomination in 1918, but was an unsuccessful candidate for nomination to the United States Senate; resumed the practice of law; unsuccessful candidate for nomination in 1932 to the Seventy-third Congress; died in Chicago, Ill., March 15, 1936; interment in Graceland Cemetery.

FOSTER, A. Lawrence, a Representative from New York; attended the public schools; studied law in Vernon; was admitted to the bar and commenced practice in Morrisville about 1827; elected as a Whig to the Twenty-seventh Congress (March 4, 1841–March 3, 1843); settled permanently in Virginia.

FOSTER, Abiel, a Delegate and a Representative from New Hampshire; born in Andover, Mass., August 8, 1735; was graduated from Harvard College in 1756; studied theology; licensed to preach; was ordained and installed as pastor in Canterbury, N. H., in 1761 and served until 1779; deputy to the Provincial Congress at Exeter in 1775; Member of the Continental Congress 1783–1785; judge of the court of common pleas of Rockingham County 1784–1788; elected to the First Congress (March 4, 1789–March 3, 1791); member of the State senate 1791–1794, and served as its president in 1793; elected to the Fourth and to the three succeeding Congresses (March 4, 1795–March 3, 1803); died in Canterbury, N. H., February 6, 1806; interment in Center Cemetery.

FOSTER, Addison Gardner, a Senator from Washington; born in Belchertown, Hampshire County, Mass., January 28, 1837; moved to Oswego, Kendall County, Ill., and attended the common schools; moved to Wabasha County, Minn., and engaged in the grain and real-estate business; auditor and surveyor of Wabasha County; moved to St. Paul, Minn., in 1873 and engaged in the lumber business; moved to Tacoma, Wash., in 1888 and continued in the lumber business; also engaged in coal-mine operations and railroad construction; elected as a Republican to the United States Senate and served from March 4, 1899, to March 3, 1905; was not a candidate for reelection; resumed the lumber business at Tacoma, Wash.; retired from active business pursuits in 1914, and resided in Tacoma until his death January 16, 1917; interment in Tacoma Cemetery.

FOSTER, Charles, a Representative from Ohio; born near Tiffin, Seneca County, Ohio, April 12, 1828; moved with his father to Rome, now the city of Fostoria, Seneca County, Ohio; attended the common schools until he was twelve years old; engaged in the dry-goods business and later banking; elected as a Republican to the Forty-second and to the three succeeding Congresses (March 4, 1871–March 3, 1879); unsuccessful candidate for reelection in 1878 to the Forty-sixth Congress; Governor of Ohio 1880–1884; unsuccessful candidate for election in 1890 to the Fifty-second Congress; Secretary of the Treasury in the Cabinet of President Harrison from February 25, 1891, to March 3, 1893; resumed his former business pursuits; died in Springfield, Ohio, January 9, 1904; interment in Fountain Cemetery, Fostoria, Ohio.

FOSTER, David Johnson, a Representative from Vermont; born in Barnet, Caledonia County, Vt., June 27, 1857; attended the public schools of his native city and was graduated from the St. Johnsbury (Vt.) Academy in 1876 and from Dartmouth College, Hanover, N. H., in 1880; studied law; was admitted to the bar in 1883 and commenced practice in Burlington, Vt.; prosecuting attorney of Chittenden County 1886–1890; member of the State senate 1892–1894; commissioner of State taxes 1894–1898; chairman of the board of railroad commissioners 1898–1900; chairman of the commission representing the United States at the first Centennial of the Independence of Mexico at Mexico City in 1910; chairman of the United States delega-

tion to the general assembly of the International Institute of Agriculture at Rome in May 1911; elected as a Republican to the Fifty-seventh and to the five succeeding Congresses and served from March 4, 1901, until his death in Washington, D. C., March 21, 1912; interment in Lakeview Cemetery, Burlington, Vt.

FOSTER, Dwight (brother of Theodore Foster), a Representative and a Senator from Massachusetts; born in Brookfield, Worcester County, Mass., December 7, 1757; completed preparatory studies, and was graduated from Brown University, Providence, R. I., in 1774; studied law; was admitted to the bar in 1778 and commenced practice in Providence, R. I.; justice of the peace for Worcester County 1781–1823; special justice of the court of common pleas in 1792; sheriff of Worcester County in 1792; member of the State house of representatives in 1791 and 1792; elected as a Federalist to the Third and to the three succeeding Congresses and served from March 4, 1793, to June 6, 1800, when he resigned; delegate to the State constitutional convention in 1799; elected to the United States Senate to fill the vacancy caused by the resignation of Samuel Dexter and served from June 6, 1800, to March 2, 1803, when he resigned; served as chief justice of the court of common pleas 1801–1811; again a member of the State house of representatives in 1808 and 1809; member of the Governor's council and held other State and local offices; died in Brookfield, Mass., April 29, 1823; interment in Brookfield Cemetery.

FOSTER, Ephraim Hubbard, a Senator from Tennessee; born near Bardstown, Nelson County, Ky., September 17, 1794; moved to Tennessee with his parents, who settled near Nashville, Davidson County, in 1797; completed preparatory studies, and was graduated from Cumberland College (later the University of Nashville) in 1813; studied law; was admitted to the bar in 1820 and commenced practice in Nashville, Tenn.; served in the Creek War and was private secretary to Gen. Andrew Jackson 1813–1815; member of the State house of representatives 1829–1831 and 1835–1837, and served as speaker during that time; appointed as a Whig to the United States Senate to fill the vacancy caused by the resignation of Felix Grundy and served from September 17, 1838, to March 3, 1839; was reelected for the term beginning March 4, 1839, but resigned, not wishing to obey instructions given him by the State legislature; presidential elector on the Whig ticket of Harrison and Tyler in 1840; elected to the United States Senate to fill the vacancy caused by the death of his successor, Felix Grundy, and served from October 17, 1843, to March 3, 1845; unsuccessful Whig candidate for Governor in 1845; resumed the practice of law; died in Nashville, Tenn., September 14, 1854; interment in the City Cemetery.

FOSTER, George Peter, a Representative from Illinois; born in Dover, Morris County, N. J., April 3, 1858; moved to Chicago in 1867; attended the public schools and the University of Chicago; was graduated from Union College of Law at Chicago in 1882; was admitted to the bar the same year and commenced practice in Chicago, Ill.; justice of the peace for the town of South Chicago 1891–1899; acting police magistrate of the principal police court of the city 1893–1899; presidential elector on the Democratic ticket of Bryan and Sewall in 1896, but resigned in order to permit a fusion between the Democratic and People's Parties; elected as a Democrat to the Fifty-sixth, Fifty-seventh, and Fifty-eighth Congresses (March 4, 1899–March 3, 1905); unsuccessful candidate for reelection in 1904; resumed the practice of law; assistant corporation counsel of Chicago, Ill., 1912–1922; retired from active pursuits in 1928 and moved to Wheaton, Ill., where he died November 11, 1928; interment in Calvary Cemetery, Chicago, Ill.

FOSTER, Henry Allen, a Representative and a Senator from New York; born in Hartford, Conn., May 7, 1800; moved to Cazenovia, N. Y., when a boy; attended the common schools; studied law; was admitted to the bar in 1822 and commenced practice in Oneida County, N. Y.; surrogate to Oneida County 1827–1831 and 1835–1839; supervisor of the town of Rome, N. Y., in 1829 and 1830, and again in 1833 and 1834; member of the State senate 1831–1834 and 1841–1844; elected as a Democrat to the Twenty-fifth Congress (March 4, 1837–March 3, 1839); resumed the practice of law in Rome; appointed to the United States Senate to fill the vacancy caused by the resignation of Silas Wright, Jr., and served from November 30, 1844, to January 27, 1845, when a successor was elected and qualified; delegate to the Democratic National Convention at New York in 1848; elected judge of the supreme court for the fifth district November 3, 1863, and served from January 1, 1864, to January 1, 1872; senior member and president of the board of trustees of Hamilton College; vice president of the American Colonization Society; died in Rome, N. Y., May 11, 1889; interment in Rome Cemetery.

FOSTER, Henry Donnel (cousin of John Cabell Breckinridge), a Representative from Pennsylvania; born in Mercer, Mercer County, Pa., December 19, 1808; pursued classical studies; was graduated from the College of Meadville; studied law; was admitted to the bar in 1829 and commenced practice in Greensburg, Pa.; elected as a Democrat to the Twenty-eighth and Twenty-ninth Congresses (March 4, 1843–March 3, 1847); member of the State house of representatives in 1857 and 1858; unsuccessful candidate for election in 1858 to the Thirty-sixth Congress; unsuccessful candidate for Governor in 1860; unsuccessfully contested the election of John Covode to the Forty-first Congress; elected to the Forty-second Congress (March 4, 1871–March 3, 1873); unsuccessful candidate for reelection in 1872 to the Forty-third Congress; resumed the practice of law in Greensburg, Pa.; moved to Irwin, Westmoreland County, Pa., in 1879 and died there October 16, 1880; interment in St. Clair Cemetery, Greensburg, Pa.

FOSTER, Israel Moore, a Representative from Ohio; born in Athens, Athens County, Ohio, January 12, 1873; attended the public schools, and was graduated from the Ohio University at Athens in 1895; studied law at the Harvard Law School in 1895 and 1896; was graduated from the Ohio State Law School in 1898 and commenced practice the same year in Athens, Ohio; prosecuting attorney of Athens County 1902–1910; member and secretary of the board of trustees of the Ohio University twenty-four years; secretary of the Republican State central committee in 1912; elected as a Republican to the Sixty-sixth, Sixty-seventh, and Sixty-eighth Congresses (March 4, 1919–March 3, 1925); unsuccessful candidate for renomination in 1924; appointed a commissioner of the court of claims April 1, 1925, and served until April 1, 1942, when he retired; died in Washington, D. C., June 10, 1950; interment in Rock Creek Cemetery.

FOSTER, John Hopkins, a Representative from Indiana; born in Evansville, Vanderburg County, Ind., January 31, 1862; attended the common schools of his native city and was graduated from Indiana University at Bloomington in 1882 and from the law department of Columbian University (now George Washington University), Washington, D. C., in 1884; was admitted to the bar in 1885 and commenced the practice of his profession in Evansville, Ind.; member of the State house of representatives in 1893; judge of the superior court of Vanderburg County 1896–1905; elected as a Republican to the Fifty-ninth Congress to fill the vacancy caused by the resignation of James A. Hemenway; reelected to the Sixtieth Congress and served from May 16, 1905, to March 3, 1909; unsuccessful candidate for reelection in 1908 to the Sixty-first Congress; resumed the practice of law in Evansville, Ind., where he died September 5, 1917; interment in Oak Hill Cemetery.

FOSTER, Lafayette Sabine, a Senator from Connecticut; born in Franklin, New London County, Conn., November 22, 1806; attended the common schools; received preparatory instruction at Hartford and Windham, and was graduated from Brown University, Providence, R. I., in 1828; taught school in Providence and commenced the study of law in Norwich; took charge of an academy at Centerville, Md., and while there was admitted to the Maryland bar in 1830; returned to Norwich, Conn., and completed his law studies; was admitted to the bar in 1831 and commenced the practice of his profession; moved to Hampton, Conn., in 1833, but returned to Norwich in 1835 and became editor of the Republican, a Whig newspaper; member of the State house of representatives in 1839, 1840, 1846–1848, and again in 1854, and served three years as speaker of the house; unsuccessful Whig candidate for Governor of Connecticut in 1850 and again in 1851; mayor of Norwich in 1851 and 1852; elected in 1854 as a Republican to the United States Senate; reelected in 1860, and served from March 4, 1855, to March 3, 1867; unsuccessful candidate for reelection; President pro tempore of the Senate and served from March 7, 1865, to March 2, 1867, when he resigned; professor of law in Yale College in 1869; again a member of the State house of representatives in 1870 and was elected speaker but resigned June 16, 1870, to accept a judicial position; appointed associate justice of the Connecticut Supreme Court in 1870 and served until 1876, when he retired; unsuccessful Democratic candidate for election to the Forty-fourth Congress; died in Norwich, Conn., September 19, 1880; interment in Yantic Cemetery.

FOSTER, Martin David, a Representative from Illinois; born near West Salem, Edwards County, Ill., September 3, 1861; attended the public schools and Eureka (Ill.) College; was graduated from the Eclectic Medical Institute, Cincinnati, Ohio, in 1882 and from the Hahnemann Medical College, Chicago, Ill., in 1884; commenced the practice of medicine in Olney, Richland County, Ill., in 1884; served as a member of a board of United States examining surgeons in 1885–1889, and again from 1893 to 1897; mayor of Olney, Ill., in 1895 and 1902; was elected surgeon of Colonel Knopf's regiment, raised for service in the Spanish-American War, but the regiment was never called into active service; elected as a Democrat to the Sixtieth and to the five succeeding Congresses (March 4, 1907–March 3, 1919); unsuccessful candidate for reelection in 1918; engaged in the practice of medicine until his death in Olney, Ill., October 20, 1919; interment in Haven Hill Cemetery.

FOSTER, Murphy James, a Senator from Louisiana; born in Franklin, St. Mary Parish, La., January 12, 1849; received his education under private tutors and attended a preparatory school at Whites Creek, near Nashville, Tenn., and the Washington and Lee University, Lexington, Va., in 1867 and 1868; was graduated from Cumberland University, Lebanon, Tenn., in 1870 and from the law school of the University of Louisiana (now Tulane University) at New Orleans in 1871; was admitted to the bar in 1871 and commenced practice in Franklin, La.; member of the John McEnery Democratic legislature in 1872, but, owing to the fact that this government was never recognized by the Federal Government and the Kellogg government was, did not take his seat; member of the State senate 1879–1895, and served as president pro tempore 1888–1890; was leader of the antilottery fight in the State legislature in 1890; was nominated by the antilottery convention as a candidate for Governor of Louisiana; was elected and reelected and served from May 18, 1892, to May 21, 1900; elected as a Democrat to the United States Senate in 1901; reelected in 1907 and served from March 4, 1901, to March 3, 1913; appointed by President Wilson collector of the port of New Orleans and served from August 1, 1914, until his death at Dixie plantation, near Franklin, La., on June 12, 1921; interment in Franklin Cemetery.

FOSTER, Nathaniel Greene, a Representative from Georgia; born near Madison, Greene (now Morgan) County, Ga., on August 25, 1809; attended private schools, and was graduated from the University of Georgia at Athens in 1830; studied law; was admitted to the bar in 1831 and commenced practice in Madison, Ga.; captain of a company in the Seminole War; elected solicitor general of the Ocmulgee circuit and served from March 3, 1838, to October 3, 1840, when he resigned; member of the State house of representatives in 1840; served in the State senate 1841–1843 and again in 1851 and 1852; elected as a candidate by the American Party to the Thirty-fourth Congress (March 4, 1855–March 3, 1857); affiliated with the Democratic Party; pastor of the Baptist Church at Madison 1855–1869; elected judge of the Ocmulgee circuit and served from September 30, 1867, until his resignation in 1868 on account of ill health; died in Madison, Ga., October 19, 1869; interment in Madison Cemetery.

FOSTER, Stephen Clark, a Representative from Maine; born in Machias, Maine, December 24, 1799; attended the common schools; learned the blacksmith's trade and subsequently became a shipbuilder; member of the State house of representatives 1834–1837; member of the State senate in 1840, and served as president; again elected to the State house of representatives in 1847; elected as a Republican to the Thirty-fifth and Thirty-sixth Congresses (March 4, 1857–March 3, 1861); member of the peace convention of 1861 held in Washington, D. C., in an effort to devise means to prevent the impending war; died in Pembroke, Washington County, Maine, October 5, 1872; interment in Forest Hill Cemetery.

FOSTER, Theodore (brother of Dwight Foster), a Senator from Rhode Island; born in Brookfield, Worcester County, Mass., April 29, 1752; pursued classical studies and was graduated from Rhode Island College (now Brown University), Providence, R. I., in 1770; studied law; was admitted to the bar about 1771 and commenced practice in Providence, R. I.; town clerk of Providence 1775–1787; member of the State house of representatives 1776–1782; appointed judge of the court of admiralty in May 1785; elected as a Law and Order candidate to the United States Senate in 1790; reelected in 1791 and again in 1797 and served from June 7, 1790, to March 3, 1803; was not a candidate for reelection in 1802; retired from public life and engaged in writing and historical research; again a member of the State house of representatives 1812–1816; trustee of Brown University 1794–1822; died in Providence, R. I., January 13, 1828; interment in Swan Point Cemetery.

FOSTER, Thomas Flournoy, a Representative from Georgia; born in Greensboro, Ga., November 23, 1790; pursued preparatory studies, and was graduated from Franklin College in 1812; studied law at the Litchfield (Ga.) Law School; was admitted to the bar in 1816 and commenced practice in Greensboro; member of the State house of representatives 1822–1825; elected as a Democrat to the Twenty-first, Twenty-second, and Twenty-third Congresses (March 4, 1829–March 3, 1835); unsuccessful candidate for reelection in 1834 to the Twenty-fourth Congress; member of the State convention from Greene County in 1833 to reduce membership of the general assembly; moved to Columbus, Muscogee County, Ga., in 1835 and continued the practice of his profession; delegate to a convention at Tuscaloosa, Ala., in the interest of Gen. William H. Harrison's candidacy for President of the United States; elected to the Twenty-seventh Congress (March 4, 1841–March 3, 1843); died in Columbus, Ga., September 14, 1848; interment in Linwood Cemetery.

FOSTER, Wilder De Ayr, a Representative from Michigan; born in Orange County, N. Y., January 8, 1819; attended the common schools of his native county; moved to Michigan in 1837, and engaged in the hardware business at Grand Rapids in 1845; city treasurer and member of the board of aldermen; mayor of Grand Rapids in 1854; member of the State senate in 1855 and 1856; again elected mayor of Grand Rapids and served in 1865 and 1866; elected as a Republican to the Forty-second Congress to fill the vacancy caused by the resignation of Thomas White Ferry; reelected to the Forty-third Congress and served from December 4, 1871, until his death in Grand Rapids, Mich., September 20, 1873; interment in Fulton Street Cemetery.

FOUKE, Philip Bond, a Representative from Illinois; born in Kaskaskia, Ill., January 23, 1818; attended the public schools and became a civil engineer; established and published the Belleville Advocate in 1841; studied law; was admitted to the bar in 1845 and commenced practice in Belleville; prosecuting attorney for the Kaskaskia district (second circuit) 1846–1850; member of the State house of representatives in 1851; unsuccessfully contested the election of Lyman Trumbull to the Thirty-fourth Congress; elected as a Democrat to the Thirty-sixth and Thirty-seventh Congresses (March 4, 1859–March 3, 1863); was not a candidate for renomination in 1862; during the Civil War served as colonel of the Thirtieth Regiment, Illinois Volunteer Infantry, and was wounded at the Battle of Belmont; engaged in the practice of law in Washington, D. C., and died there October 3, 1876; interment in Congressional Cemetery.

FOULKES, George Ernest, a Representative from Michigan; born in Chicago, Ill., December 25, 1878; attended the public schools of Chicago; was graduated from the law department of Lake Forest University, Chicago, Ill., in 1900; was admitted to the bar the same year and commenced practice in the United States Treasury Department; special agent of the United States Treasury Department in charge of field service at New York City, El Paso, Tex., St. Paul, Minn., and Minneapolis, Minn., 1900–1919; moved to Hartford, Mich., in 1920 and engaged in agricultural pursuits and as an author; delegate to the Democratic State conventions in 1924, 1926, and 1928; elected as a Democrat to the Seventy-third Congress (March 4, 1933–January 3, 1935); nominated for Governor by the Farmer-Labor Party in 1934, but declined; unsuccessful candidate for reelection in 1934 to the Seventy-fourth Congress; resumed agricultural pursuits, having extensive acreage in North Dakota, Minnesota, and Michigan; also engaged as an author and in farm-organization work; died in Hartford, Mich., December 13, 1960; interment in Hartford Cemetery.

FOULKROD, William Walker, a Representative from Pennsylvania; born in Frankford, Philadelphia, Pa., November 22, 1846; attended public and private schools in Philadelphia; engaged in the wholesale dry-goods business and the manufacture of hosiery; president of the Philadelphia Trades League; interested in plans for the improvement of the Delaware River and Channel; a trustee of the Philadelphia Commercial Museum; member of the Pennsylvania Historical Society; elected as a Republican to the Sixtieth and Sixty-first Congresses and served from March 4, 1907, until his death; unsuccessful candidate for reelection in 1910; died in Frankford, Philadelphia, Pa., November 13, 1910; interment in Cedar Hill Cemetery.

FOUNTAIN, Lawrence H., a Representative from North Carolina; born in the village of Leggett, Edgecombe County, N. C., April 23, 1913; attended the public schools; graduated from the University of North Carolina at Chapel Hill in 1934 and from the law school of the same university in 1936; was admitted to the bar the same year and has practiced law since then in Tarboro, N. C.; during World War II enlisted as a private in the United States Army on March 4, 1942; was promoted through the ranks and released from the service as a major from the Judge Advocate General's Office on March 4, 1946; eastern organizer of Young Democratic Clubs of North Carolina in 1941 and former chairman of the Second Congressional District Executive Committee; reading clerk in the State senate 1936–1941; member of the State senate 1947–1951; secretary-treasurer, Coastal Plains Broadcasting Co., Tarboro, N. C., 1949–; elected as a Democrat to the Eighty-third and to the three succeeding Congresses (January 3, 1953–January 3, 1961).   *Reelected to the Eighty-seventh Congress.*

FOWLER, Charles Newell, a Representative from New Jersey; born in Lena, Stephenson County, Ill., November 2, 1852; attended the public schools in Lena, Ill., and Beloit College, Beloit, Wis.; was graduated from Yale College in 1876 and from Chicago Law School in 1878; was admitted to the bar in 1878 and commenced the practice of law in Beloit, Kans.; moved to Cranford, N. J., in 1883 and to Elizabeth in 1891 and engaged in banking, serving as president of a mortgage company; elected as a Republican to the Fifty-fourth and to the seven succeeding Congresses (March 4, 1895–March 3, 1911); unsuccessful candidate for nomination for election to the United States Senate in 1910; member of the Republican State committee 1898–1907; resumed banking activities at Elizabeth, N. J.; also engaged in literary pursuits and operated a group of marble quarries in Vermont; moved to Orange, N. J., in 1930 and retired from active business pursuits; died in Orange, N. J., May 27, 1932; interment in Fairview Cemetery, Westfield, N. J.

FOWLER, Hiram Robert, a Representative from Illinois; born near Eddyville, Pope County, Ill., February 7, 1851; attended the public schools of his native city, and was graduated from the Illinois Normal University at Normal in 1880; studied law at the University of Michigan at Ann Arbor and was graduated in 1884; was admitted to the bar in 1884 and commenced the practice of his profession in Elizabethtown, Ill.; State's attorney of Hardin County 1888–1892; served in the State house of representatives 1893–1895; member of the State senate 1900–1904; elected as a Democrat to the Sixty-second and Sixty-third Congresses (March 4, 1911–March 3, 1915); unsuccessful candidate for reelection in 1914; resumed the practice of law in Elizabethtown, Ill.; moved to Harrisburg, Ill., in 1915 and continued practice until his death on January 5, 1926; interment in Sunset Hill Cemetery.

FOWLER, John, a Representative from Kentucky; born in Virginia in 1755; attended the common schools; served as captain in the Revolutionary War; member of the convention held in Danville, Fayette County, Va. (now Kentucky), in 1787; served in the Virginia House of Delegates in 1787; member of the Virginia convention which ratified the Constitution; moved to Lexington, Ky.; elected to the Fifth and to the four succeeding Congresses (March 4, 1797–March 3, 1807); postmaster of Lexington 1814–1822; died in Lexington, Fayette County, Ky., August 22, 1840; interment in the Old Episcopal Cemetery.

FOWLER, John Edgar, a Representative from North Carolina; born in Honeycutt's Township, near Clinton, Sampson County, N. C., September 8, 1866; attended the common schools and Wake Forest (N. C.) College; studied law at the University of North Carolina at Chapel Hill; was admitted to the bar in 1894 and commenced the practice of his chosen profession at Clinton, N. C.; trustee of State Normal College for Women, Greensboro, N. C., 1895–1903; member of the State senate in 1895 and 1896; elected as a Populist to the Fifty-fifth Congress (March 4, 1897–March 3, 1899); resumed the practice of law in Clinton, N. C.; also engaged in agricultural pursuits; member of the State house of representatives in 1905 and 1906; retired from active pursuits in 1927 because of ill health; died in Clinton, N. C., July 4, 1930; interment in Clinton Cemetery.

FOWLER, Joseph Smith, a Senator from Tennessee; born in Steubenville, Jefferson County, Ohio, August 31, 1820; two years later moved with his parents to a nearby farm; attended the common schools and Grove Academy, Steubenville, Ohio; was graduated from Franklin College, New Athens, Ohio, in 1843; taught school in Shelby County, Ky., in 1844; professor of mathematics at Franklin College, Davidson County, Tenn., 1845–1849; studied law in Bowling Green, Ky.; was admitted to the bar and practiced in Tennessee until 1861; president of Howard Female College, Gallatin, Tenn., 1856–1861; moved to Springfield, Ill., in 1861, but returned to Nashville, Tenn., in 1862; appointed by Governor Johnson comptroller of Tennessee and served until 1865; took an active part in the reconstruction of the State government; delegate to the Republican National Convention at Philadelphia in 1864 which nominated Lincoln and Johnson; upon the readmission of the State of Tennessee to representation was elected as a Union Republican to the United States Senate and served from July 24, 1866, to March 3, 1871; was not a candidate for reelection; presidential elector on the Democratic ticket of Greeley and Brown in 1872; engaged in the practice of law in Washington, D. C., until his death in that city April 1, 1902; interment in Lexington Cemetery, Lexington, Ky.

FOWLER, Orin, a Representative from Massachusetts; born in Lebanon, Conn., July 19, 1791; pursued classical studies and attended Williams College, Williamstown, Mass., and was graduated from Yale College in 1814; studied theology and pursued extensive missionary work in the Valley of the Mississippi; finally settled as a minister in Plainfield, Conn., in 1820; moved to Fall River, Mass., in 1829, where he was installed as pastor of the Congregational Church in 1831; wrote a history of Fall River in 1841; served in the State senate in 1848; elected as a Free-Soil Whig to the Thirty-first and Thirty-second Congresses and served from March 4, 1849, until his death in Washington, D. C., September 3, 1852; interment in the North Burial Ground, Fall River, Mass.

FOWLER, Samuel, a Representative from New Jersey; born in Newburgh, Orange County, N. Y., October 30, 1779; attended the Montgomery Academy; studied medicine at the Pennsylvania Medical College, Philadelphia, Pa., and commenced practice in Hamburg, N. J., in 1800; moved to Franklin, N. J.; member of the State council in 1827; elected as a Jackson Democrat to the Twenty-third and Twenty-fourth Congresses (March 4, 1833–March 3, 1837); was the discoverer of Fowlerite, a rare mineral named in his honor, and of franklinite, named by him; owned and developed the zinc mines at Franklin, Sussex County; owned and conducted the Franklin Furnace Iron Works; was a frequent contributor to numerous scientific publications; died in Franklin, N. J., February 20, 1844; interment in North Church Cemetery, Hardyston Township, near Hamburg, N. J.

FOWLER, Samuel (grandson of the preceding), a Representative from New Jersey; born in Port Jervis, Orange County, N. Y., March 22, 1851; attended the Newton (N. J.) Academy, Princeton College, and Columbia College (now Columbia University)

Law School in New York City; was admitted to the bar of New York in 1873 and of New Jersey in 1876 and practiced law in Newark and Newton, N. J.; elected as a Democrat to the Fifty-first and Fifty-second Congresses (March 4, 1889–March 3, 1893); was not a candidate for reelection to the Fifty-third Congress; resumed the practice of his profession in Ogdensburg, N. J.; died in Newark, N. J., March 17, 1919; interment in North Church Cemetery, Hardyston Township, near Hamburg, N. J.

FOX, Andrew Fuller, a Representative from Mississippi; born in Reform, Pickens County, Ala., April 26, 1849; moved to Calhoun County, Miss., with his parents in 1853; attended private schools, and was graduated from Mansfield (Tex.) College in 1872; studied law in Grenada, Miss.; was admitted to the bar in 1877 and commenced practice in Calhoun and Webster Counties; moved to West Point, Miss., in 1883; delegate to the Democratic National Convention at St. Louis in 1888; member of the State senate from 1891 until 1893, when he resigned to accept the office of United States attorney for the northern district of Mississippi; resigned the latter office on September 1, 1896; elected as a Democrat to the Fifty-fifth, Fifty-sixth, and Fifty-seventh Congresses (March 4, 1897–March 3, 1903); was not a candidate for renomination in 1902; president of Mississippi State Bar Association in 1911; engaged in the practice of law in West Point, Miss., until 1914, when he retired; died in West Point, Miss., August 29, 1926; interment in West Point Cemetery.

FOX, John, a Representative from New York; born in Frederickton, New Brunswick, Canada, June 30, 1835; moved to New York City, N. Y., with his parents in 1840; attended teh public schools; engaged in mechanical pursuits; employed as a master block maker in the Brooklyn Navy Yard in 1857; member of the board of aldermen and supervisor of New York City in 1863 and 1864; supervisor of New York County in 1864; elected as a Democrat to the Fortieth and Forty-first Congresses (March 4, 1867–March 3, 1871); declined to be a candidate for renomination in 1870; member of the State senate 1874–1878; president of the National Democratic Club 1894–1910; engaged in business as an iron merchant, with residence in New York City, where he died January 17, 1914; interment in Calvary Cemetery.

FRANCE, Joseph Irvin, a Senator from Maryland; born in Cameron, Clinton County, Mo., October 11, 1873; attended the common schools; prepared for college at Canandaigua Academy, Canandaigua, N. Y.; was graduated from Hamilton College, Clinton, N. Y., in 1895; awarded the Elihu Root scholarship and attended the University of Leipzig, Germany; was graduated from the medical department of Clark University, Worcester, Mass., in 1897; elected head of the department of natural science, Jacob Tome Institute, Port Deposit, Md., in 1897; resigned to enter the College of Physicians and Surgeons, Baltimore, Md., from which he was graduated in 1903; commenced the practice of medicine in Baltimore in 1903; member of the State senate 1906–1908; engaged in finance in 1908; delegate to the Republican National Convention at Chicago in 1908; secretary to the medical and chirurgical faculty of Maryland in 1916 and 1917; elected as a Republican to the United States Senate in 1916 and served from March 4, 1917, until March 3, 1923; went to Russia in the summer of 1921 to study economic conditions in that country; unsuccessful candidate for reelection in 1922 to the United States Senate; trustee of Hamilton College; president of the Republic International Corporation; resumed the practice of medicine in Port Deposit, Cecil County, Md.; unsuccessful candidate for election in 1934 to the United States Senate; died in Port Deposit, Md., January 26, 1939; interment in Hopewell Cemetery, near Port Deposit.

FRANCHOT, Richard, a Representative from New York; born in Morris, Otsego County, N. Y., June 2, 1816; attended the public schools and the Hartwick and Cherry Valley Academies; studied civil engineering at the Polytechnic Institute, Troy, N. Y.; became interested in agricultural pursuits and subsequently in the construction of railroads; served for some years as president of the Albany & Susquehanna Railroad Co.; elected as a Republican to the Thirty-seventh Congress (March 4, 1861–March 3, 1863); was not a candidate for renomination in 1862; moved to Schenectady, N. Y.; during the Civil War raised the One Hundred and Twenty-first Regiment, New York Volunteer Infantry, and was commissioned colonel August 23, 1862; brevetted brigadier general United States Volunteers March 13, 1865; associated with the Central Pacific Railroad Co.; died in Schenectady, N. Y., November 23, 1875; interment in Vale Cemetery.

FRANCIS, George Blinn, a Representative from New York; born in Cranston (now a part of Providence), R. I., August 12, 1883; attended the University School in Providence, R. I.; was graduated from Brown University, Providence, R. I., in 1904 and from the law department of Harvard University in 1907; was admitted to the bar in 1907 and commenced practice in New York City; elected as a Republican to the Sixty-fifth Congress (March 4, 1917–March 3, 1919); was not a candidate for renomination in 1918; resumed the practice of law in New York City; was special assistant United States attorney in Minnesota in 1926 and 1927 in connection with elevator litigation growing out of the activities of the United States Grain Corporation in that State; elected a member of the board of water commissioners of Tarrytown, N. Y., and served as its president; retired in October 1953; resides at Delray Beach, Fla.

FRANCIS, John Brown (grandson of John Brown, of Rhode Island), a Senator from Rhode Island; born in Philadelphia, Pa., May 31, 1791; upon the death of his father was raised by his grandfather, John Brown, of Providence, R. I.; attended the common schools, and was graduated from Brown University, Providence, R. I., in 1808; engaged in mercantile pursuits; attended the Litchfield (Conn.) Law School; was admitted to the bar but never practiced; member of the State house of representatives 1821–1829; declined to be a candidate for reelection; member of the board of trustees of Brown University 1828–1857; member of the State senate in 1831 and 1842; Governor of Rhode Island 1833–1838; chancellor of Brown University 1841–1854; elected as a Law and Order candidate to the United States Senate to fill the vacancy caused by the resignation of William Sprague and served from January 25, 1844, to March 3, 1845; was not a candidate for reelection; served again in the State senate 1845–1856; retired from public life and engaged in agricultural pursuits until his death at "Spring Green," Warwick, R. I., August 9, 1864; interment in North Burial Ground, Providence, R. I.

FRANCIS, William Bates, a Representative from Ohio; born near Updegraff, Jefferson County, Ohio, October 25, 1860; attended the public schools; studied law; was admitted to the bar in 1889 and commenced practice in Martins Ferry, Belmont County, Ohio; city solicitor in 1897, 1898, and 1900; member of the board of school examiners of Martins Ferry 1903–1908; delegate to the Democratic National Convention at St. Louis in 1904; member of the board of education of Martins Ferry 1908–1914; elected as a Democrat to the Sixty-second and Sixty-third Congresses (March 4, 1911–March 3 1915); unsuccessful candidate for reelection in 1914 to the Sixty-fourth Congress; resumed the practice of his profession; chairman of the Ohio State Civil Service 1931–1935; supervisor of properties for aid to aged, until his retirement; resided in Martins Ferry and later in St. Clairsville, Ohio, until his death in Wheeling, W. Va., December 5, 1954; interment in Mount Pleasant Cemetery, Mount Pleasant, Ohio.

FRANK, Augustus (nephew of William Patterson, of New York), a Representative from New York; born in Warsaw, Wyoming County, N. Y., July 17, 1826; attended the common schools; engaged in mercantile pursuits; director and vice president of the Buffalo & New York City Railroad Co.; delegate to the Republican National Convention at Philadelphia in 1856; elected as a Republican to the Thirty-sixth, Thirty-seventh, and Thirty-eighth Congresses (March 4, 1859–March 3, 1865); was not a candidate for renomination in 1864; director of Wyoming County National Bank in 1865; member of the State constitutional convention in 1867 and 1868; one of the managers of the Buffalo State Hospital for the Insane at Buffalo, N. Y., 1870–1882; organized the Bank of Warsaw in 1871 and served as president until his death; director of the Rochester Trust & Safe Deposit Co.; presidential elector on the Republican ticket of Harrison and Morton in 1888; State commissioner for the preservation of public parks; member of the board of directors of the Buffalo, Rochester & Pittsburgh Railroad; delegate at large to the State constitutional convention in 1894; died in New York City April 29, 1895; interment in Warsaw Cemetery, Warsaw, N. Y.

FRANK, Nathan, a Representative from Missouri; born in Peoria, Ill., February 23, 1852; attended the public schools of Peoria and St. Louis and Washington University, St. Louis, Mo.; was graduated from Harvard Law School in 1871; was admitted to the bar and commenced practice in St. Louis in 1872; unsuccessfully contested the election of John M. Glover to the Fiftieth Congress in 1886; elected as a Republican and Union Labor candidate to the Fifty-first Congress (March 4, 1889–March 3, 1891); declined to be a candidate for renomination in 1890; founder and owner of the St. Louis Star; delegate to the Republican National Convention at St. Louis in 1896; vice president of the Louisiana Purchase Exposition at St. Louis in 1904; unsuccessful candidate for nomination for United States Senator in 1910, 1916, and 1928; retired from the active practice of law; died at St. Louis, Mo., April 5, 1931; interment in Mount Sinai Cemetery.

FRANKHAUSER, William Horace, a Representative from Michigan; born in Wood County, Ohio, March 5, 1863; moved with his parents to Monroe, Mich., in 1875; attended the public schools, Michigan State Normal School at Ypsilanti, and Oberlin College, Ohio; taught school for several years; studied law; was admitted to the bar in 1891 and commenced practice in Hillsdale, Mich.; city attorney and prosecutor of Hillsdale County 1896–1903; elected as a Republican to the Sixty-seventh Congress and served from March 4, 1921, until his death in Battle Creek, Mich., on May 9, 1921; interment in Oak Grove Cemetery, Hillsdale, Mich.

FRANKLIN, Benjamin (uncle of Franklin Davenport), a Delegate from Pennsylvania; born in Boston, Mass., January 17, 1706; attended the Boston Grammar School one year; was instructed in elementary branches by a private tutor; employed in a tallow chandlery for two years; learned the art of printing, and after working at his trade in Boston, Philadelphia, and London established himself in Philadelphia as a printer and publisher; founded the Pennsylvania Gazette in 1728, and in 1732 began the publication of Poor Richard's Almanac; State printer; clerk of the Pennsylvania General Assembly 1736–1750; postmaster of Philadelphia in 1737; a member of the provincial assembly 1744–1754; a member of several Indian commissions; elected a member of the Royal Society on account of his scientific discoveries; deputy postmaster general of the British North American Colonies 1753–1774; agent of Pennsylvania in London 1757–1762 and 1764–1775; Member of the Continental Congress in 1775 and 1776; signed the Declaration of Independence; president of the Pennsylvania constitutional convention of 1776; sent as a diplomatic commissioner to France by the Continental Congress and, later, Minister to France 1776–1785; one of the negotiators of the treaty of peace with Great Britain; Governor of Pennsylvania 1785–1788; president of the trustees of the University of Pennsylvania; a delegate to the convention which framed the Federal Constitution in May 1787; died in Philadelphia, Pa., April 17, 1790; interment in Christ Church Burial Ground.

FRANKLIN, Benjamin Joseph, a Representative from Missouri; born in Maysville, Mason County, Ky., in March 1839; attended private schools, and Bethany College, Bethany, Va. (now West Virginia), 1849–1851; taught school; studied law; was admitted to the bar in 1859 and commenced practice in Leavenworth, Kans.; elected to the State senate of Kansas in 1861, but due to the outbreak of the Civil War never served; entered the Confederate Army as a private; was promoted to the rank of captain and served throughout the Civil War; moved to Columbia, Mo., and engaged in agricultural pursuits; moved to Kansas City, Mo., in 1868 and resumed the practice of law; prosecuting attorney for Jackson County, Mo., 1871–1875; elected as a Democrat to the Forty-fourth and Forty-fifth Congresses (March 4, 1875–March 3, 1879); was a candidate for renomination, but withdrew; again engaged in the practice of law in Kansas City, Mo.; appointed United States consul at Hankow, China, in 1885; returned to the United States in 1890 and settled in Phoenix, Ariz., and engaged in the practice of law; appointed Governor of the Territory of Arizona and served from April 18, 1896, to July 29, 1897; died in Phoenix, Ariz., May 18, 1898; interment in Rosedale Cemetery.

FRANKLIN, Jesse (brother of Meshack Franklin), a Representative and a Senator from North Carolina; born in Orange County, Va., March 24, 1760; moved with his parents to North Carolina in 1774; served as major during the Revolutionary War; fought in the Battle of Kings Mountain and at Guilford Court House in 1780; member of the State house of commons in 1793, 1794, 1797, and 1798; served in the State senate in 1805 and 1806; elected as a Democrat to the Fourth Congress (March 4, 1795–March 3, 1797); elected to the United States Senate and served from March 4, 1799, until March 3, 1805, serving as President pro tempore from March 10, 1804; trustee of the University of North Carolina in 1805; again elected to the United States Senate in 1806 and served from March 4, 1807, until March 3, 1813; was not a candidate for reelection; appointed a commissioner to treat with the Chickasaw Indians in 1817; Governor of North Carolina in 1820 and 1821; died in Surry County, N. C., August 31, 1823; interment in the old National Park at Guilford battleground, near Greensboro, N. C.

FRANKLIN, John Rankin, a Representative from Maryland; born near Berlin, Worcester County, Md., May 6, 1820; pursued classical studies, and was graduated from Jefferson College in 1836; studied law; was admitted to the bar in 1841 and commenced practice in Snow Hill, Md.; member of the State house of delegates 1840–1843, and served as speaker one term; president of the State board of public works in 1851; elected as a Whig to the Thirty-third Congress (March 4, 1853–March 3, 1855); again a member of the State house of delegates in 1859; judge of the first judicial circuit of Maryland from 1867 until his death in Snow Hill, Worcester County, Md., January 11, 1878; interment in the churchyard of Makemie Memorial Presbyterian Church.

FRANKLIN, Meshack (brother of Jesse Franklin), a Representative from North Carolina; born in Surry County, N. C., in 1772; member of the State house of commons in 1800 and 1801; served in the State senate in 1828, 1829, and 1838; elected as a Democrat to the Tenth and to the three succeeding Congresses (March 4, 1807–March 3, 1815); died in Surry County, N. C., December 18, 1839.

FRAZIER, James Beriah, a Senator from Tennessee; born in Pikeville, Bledsoe County, Tenn., October 18, 1856; attended the common schools, and Franklin College near Nashville, Tenn.; was graduated from the University of Tennessee at Knoxville in June 1878; read law with his father, Judge Thomas N. Frazier, in Nashville, Tenn.; was admitted to the bar in 1881 and commenced practice in Chattanooga, Tenn.; presidential elector at large on the Democratic ticket of Bryan and Stevenson in 1900; elected Governor of Tennessee in 1902; reelected in 1904 and served until his resignation, having been elected a United States Senator; elected as a Democrat to the United States Senate March 21, 1905, to fill the vacancy caused by the death of William B. Bate and served from March 21, 1905, to March 3, 1911; unsuccessful candidate for reelection to the Senate in 1910; resumed the practice of law; died in Chattanooga, Tenn., March 28, 1937; interment in Forest Hill Cemetery.

FRAZIER, James Beriah, Jr. (son of the preceding), a Representative from Tennessee; born in Chattanooga, Hamilton County, Tenn., June 23, 1890; educated in the public schools and Baylor Preparatory School in Chattanooga, Tenn., and the University of Virginia at Charlottesville; was graduated from Chattanooga College of Law in 1914; was admitted to the bar in 1914 and commenced the practice of law in Chattanooga, Tenn.; during the First World War volunteered for service on April 21, 1917; commissioned a second lieutenant at First Officers Training School, Fort Oglethorpe, Ga., on August 1, 1917; recommissioned a first lieutenant of Field Artillery on November 1, 1917; promoted to captain and served as instructor, Field Officers Training School, Eighty-first Division, and later assigned as instructor, Field Artillery, Officers Training School, Camp Taylor, Ky., and was discharged as a major in March 1919; appointed United States attorney for the eastern district of Tennessee on September 25, 1933; reappointed in 1934, 1938, 1942, and 1946, and served until his resignation on April 12, 1948, having become a candidate for the Democratic nomination for Congress; elected as a Democrat to the Eighty-first and to the five succeeding Congresses (January 3, 1949–January 3, 1961). *Reelected to the Eighty-seventh Congress.*

FRAZIER, Lynn Joseph, a Senator from North Dakota; born near Medford, Steele County, Minn., December 21, 1874; moved to Dakota Territory (now North Dakota) in 1881 with his parents, who homesteaded in Pembina County, near the present town of Hoople; attended the country schools; was graduated from Mayville State Normal School, North Dakota, in 1895, and from the University of North Dakota at Grand Forks in 1901; engaged in agricultural pursuits in Pembina County; Governor of North Dakota 1917–1921; elected as a Republican to the United States Senate in 1922; reelected in 1928 and in 1934 and served from March 4, 1923, to January 3, 1941; unsuccessful candidate for renomination in 1940; resumed his agricultural pursuits in Pembina County, near Hoople, N. Dak.; died January 11, 1947, in Riverdale, Md., while visiting there; interment in Park Cemetery, Hoople, N. Dak.

FREAR, James Archibald, a Representative from Wisconsin; born in Hudson, St. Croix County, Wis., October 24, 1861; attended the public schools, and Laurence University, Appleton, Wis., in 1878; moved with his parents to Washington, D. C., in 1879; served in the Signal Service, United States Army, 1879–1884; was graduated from the National Law University, Washington, D. C., in 1884; was admitted to the bar the same year and commenced practice in Hudson, Wis.; city attorney of Hudson in 1894 and 1895; served eleven years with the Wisconsin National Guard, retiring with the rank of colonel and judge advocate; district attorney of St. Croix County 1896–1901; member of the State assembly in 1903; served in the State senate in 1905; secretary of state of Wisconsin 1907–1913; elected as a Republican to the Sixty-third and to the ten succeeding Congresses (March 4, 1913–January 3, 1935); was not a candidate for renomination in 1934; resumed the practice of law in Washington, D. C., where he died May 28, 1939; interment in Arlington National Cemetery, Fort Myer, Va.

FREAR, Joseph Allen, Jr., a Senator from Delaware; born on a farm near Rising Sun, Kent County, Del., March 7, 1903; attended the Rising Sun rural school and Caesar Rodney High School; graduated from the University of Delaware in 1924; president and owner of a retail business in Dover, Del.; commissioner of Delaware State College 1936–1941 and Delaware Old Age Welfare Commission 1938–1948; director, Federal Land Bank Board, Baltimore, Md., 1938–1947, being chairman of the board the last two years; director of the Farmer's Bank of Dover and the Baltimore Trust Co. of Camden, Del.; president of Kent General Hospital, Dover, Del., 1947–1951; during World War II served in the United States Army as a major, with overseas service in the European Theater of Operations with the Military Government, 1944–1946; delegate to Democratic National Conventions in 1948, 1952, and 1956; elected as a Democrat to the United States Senate in 1948 for the term commencing January 3, 1949; reelected in 1954 for the term ending January 3, 1961; unsuccessful candidate for reelection in 1960; appointed to the Securities and Exchange Commission March 15, 1961, for an unexpired term ending June 5, 1965; resides in Washington, D. C.

FREDERICK, Benjamin Todd, a Representative from Iowa; born in Fredericktown, Columbiana County, Ohio, October 5, 1834; attended the district schools; completed preparatory studies; engaged in the foundry and machine business at Marshalltown, Iowa, 1865–1888; went to Marysville, Calif., in 1857 and engaged in placer mining; returned to Marshalltown, Iowa, in 1859; member of the city council of Marshalltown 1874–1877; member of the school board three terms; successfully contested as a Democrat the election of James Wilson to the Forty-eighth Congress and took his seat the last day of that Congress, March 3, 1885; reelected to the Forty-ninth Congress (March 4, 1885–March 3, 1887); was not a candidate for renomination in 1886; moved to San Diego, Calif., in 1887 and engaged in the real-estate business; collector of internal revenue 1893–1902; died in San Diego, Calif., November 3, 1903; interment in Mount Hope Cemetery.

FREDERICKS, John Donnan, a Representative from California; born in Burgettstown, Washington County, Pa., September 10, 1869; attended the public schools and Washington and Jefferson College, Washington, Pa.; studied law; was admitted to the bar in 1896 and commenced practice in Los Angeles, Calif.; served as an adjutant in the Seventh Regiment, California Volunteer Infantry, during the Spanish-American War in 1898; district attorney of Los Angeles County 1903–1915; unsuccessful Republican candidate for Governor of California in 1915;

elected as a Republican to the Sixty-eighth Congress to fill the vacancy caused by the death of Henry Z. Osborne; reelected to the Sixty-ninth Congress and served from May 1, 1923, to March 3, 1927; was not a candidate for renomination in 1926; resumed the practice of law at Los Angeles, Calif., where he died August 26, 1945; interment in Forest Lawn Memorial Park.

FREE, Arthur Monroe, a Representative from California; born in San Jose, Calif., January 15, 1879; attended the public and high schools of Santa Clara and the University of the Pacific, Stockton, Calif.; was graduated from the academic department of Leland Stanford Junior University, Palo Alto, Calif., in 1901 and from its law department in 1903; was admitted to the bar in 1903 and commenced practice in San Jose; moved to Mountain View and was city attorney 1904–1910; district attorney of Santa Clara County 1907–1919; voluntarily retired and resumed the practice of law at San Jose; delegate to the Republican State conventions in 1914 and from 1920 to 1936; elected as a Republican to the Sixty-seventh and to the five succeeding Congresses (March 4, 1921–March 3, 1933); unsuccessful candidate for reelection in 1932 to the Seventy-third Congress; resumed the practice of law in San Jose, Calif., where he died April 1, 1953; interment in Oak Hill Memorial Park.

FREEDLEY, John, a Representative from Pennsylvania; born in Norristown, Pa., May 22, 1793; attended the public schools and Norristown Academy; assistant to his father, who operated a brickyard; studied law; was admitted to the bar in 1820 and commenced practice in Norristown; also became interested in marble and soapstone quarries; elected as a Whig to the Thirtieth and Thirty-first Congresses (March 4, 1847–March 3, 1851); died in Norristown, Montgomery County, Pa., December 8, 1851.

FREEMAN, Chapman, a Representative from Pennsylvania; born in Philadelphia, Pa., October 8, 1832; was educated at public and private schools and was graduated from the Philadelphia High School in 1850; commenced the study of law, but became engaged in mercantile pursuits until the outbreak of the Civil War, when he entered the United States Navy as acting assistant paymaster in 1863 and was attached to the East Gulf and North Atlantic Squadrons and subsequently was on the United States steamer *Iron Age* at the time of its destruction at Lockwood's Folly Inlet, off the coast of North Carolina; afterward on special duty in eastern Carolina; on account of impaired health resigned in 1864 and resumed the study of law; was admitted to the bar in 1867 and commenced practice in Philadelphia; one of the commissioners on behalf of the Centennial from the city of Philadelphia to Vienna, Austria, in 1873; elected as a Republican to the Forty-fourth and Forty-fifth Congresses (March 4, 1875–March 3, 1879); declined to be a candidate for renomination in 1878; died in Strafford, Pa., March 22, 1904.

FREEMAN, James Crawford, a Representative from Georgia; born in Clinton (later Gray), Jones County, Ga., April 1, 1820; attended the common schools; engaged in agricultural pursuits; moved to Griffin, Ga., in 1865 and continued in farming operations; engaged in mercantile pursuits and in banking; elected as a Republican to the Forty-third Congress (March 4, 1873–March 3, 1875); moved to Atlanta, Ga., and again engaged in mercantile pursuits; died in Atlanta, Ga., September 3, 1885; interment in Oakland Cemetery.

FREEMAN, John D., a Representative from Mississippi; born in Cooperstown, N. Y.; attended the common schools; moved to Mississippi and located in Grand Gulf; studied law; was admitted to the bar and practiced; district attorney; moved to Natchez, Miss.; attorney general of Mississippi 1841–1851;

author of the first volume of reports of decisions of the Chancery Court of Mississippi published in 1844; elected as a Unionist to the Thirty-second Congress (March 4, 1851–March 3, 1853); served as attorney general; member of the Democratic State central committee and served as chairman; moved to Colorado and settled in Canon City in 1882; resumed the practice of his profession; died in Canon City, Colo., January 17, 1886; interment in Jackson, Miss.

FREEMAN, Jonathan (uncle of Nathaniel Freeman, Jr.), a Representative from New Hampshire; born in Mansfield, Conn., March 21, 1745; attended the public schools; moved to New Hampshire in 1769, and settled in Hanover; engaged in agricultural pursuits; was town clerk and also justice of the peace; executive councilor 1789–1797; member of the State house of representatives 1787–1789; served in the State senate 1789–1794; delegate to the Constitutional Convention of 1791; member of the State council; overseer of Dartmouth College, Hanover, N. H., 1793–1808; treasurer of Dartmouth College for more than forty years; elected as a Federalist to the Fifth and Sixth Congresses (March 4, 1797–March 3, 1801); resumed agricultural pursuits; died in Hanover, N. H., August 20, 1808; interment in Hanover Center Cemetery.

FREEMAN, Nathaniel, Jr. (nephew of Jonathan Freeman), a Representative from Massachusetts; born in Sandwich, Barnstable County, Mass., on May 1, 1766; attended the common schools; was graduated from Harvard University in 1787; studied law; was admitted to the bar about 1791 and commenced practice in Sandwich and the Cape Cod district; served as brigade major in the Massachusetts Militia for sixteen years; justice of the peace in 1793; elected to the Fourth and Fifth Congresses (March 4, 1795–March 3, 1799); died in Sandwich, Mass., August 22, 1800; interment in the Old Burial Ground.

FREEMAN, Richard Patrick, a Representative from Connecticut; born in New London, New London County, Conn., April 24, 1869; attended the public schools; was graduated from Bulkeley High School at New London in 1887, from Noble and Greenough's Preparatory School, Boston, Mass., in 1888, from Harvard University, Cambridge, Mass., in 1891, and from the law department of Yale University, New Haven, Conn., in 1894; was admitted to the bar in 1894 and commenced practice in New London, Conn.; special agent for the Department of the Interior in the States of Oregon and Washington 1896–1898; during the war with Spain served as regimental sergeant major in the Third Regiment, Connecticut Volunteer Infantry, and afterward became major and judge advocate of the Connecticut National Guard; prosecuting attorney of the city of New London 1898–1901; unsuccessful candidate for the Republican nomination to Congress in 1912; elected as a Republican to the Sixty-fourth and to the eight succeeding Congresses (March 4, 1915–March 3, 1933); unsuccessful candidate for renomination in 1932; resumed the practice of law in New London, Conn.; died in a veteran's hospital at Newington, Conn., July 8, 1944; interment in Cedar Grove Cemetery, New London, Conn.

FREER, Romeo Hoyt, a Representative from West Virginia; born in Bazetta, Trumbull County, Ohio, November 9, 1846; attended the common schools of Ashtabula County, Ohio, where his parents had moved when he was three years old; during the Civil War served in the Union Army as a private; settled in Charleston, W. Va., in March 1866; taught school; studied law; was admitted to the bar in 1868 and practiced; assistant prosecuting attorney of Kanawha County 1868–1871; prosecuting attorney of the same county 1871–1873; presidential elector on the Republican ticket of Grant and Wilson in 1872; appointed commercial agent to San Juan del Norte, Nicaragua, January 15, 1873, and served until January 1877; moved to Harrisville, Ritchie County, W. Va., in 1882; presidential elector on the Republican ticket of Blaine and Logan in 1884; member of the State house of delegates in 1891; prosecuting attorney of Ritchie County 1892–1897; judge of the fourth circuit of West Virginia 1896–1899; elected as a Republican to the Fifty-sixth Congress (March 4, 1899–March 3, 1901); unsuccessful candidate for reelection; attorney general of West Virginia 1901–1905; appointed postmaster of Harrisville, W. Va., on October 4, 1907, and served until his death, May 9, 1913; interment in Harrisville Cemetery.

FRELINGHUYSEN, Frederick (father of Theodore Frelinghuysen and great-great-great-grandfather of Peter Hood Ballantine Frelinghuysen, Jr.), a Delegate and a Senator from New Jersey; born near Somerville, Somerset County, N. J., April 13, 1753; was graduated from Princeton College in 1770; studied law; was admitted to the bar in 1774 and commenced practice in Somerset County, N. J.; member of the Provincial Congress of New Jersey in 1775 and 1776; served in the Revolutionary War; was commissioned first major in the Minutemen February 15, 1776; captain of the Eastern Company of Artillery, New Jersey State Troops, March 1, 1776; colonel of the First Battalion, Somerset County Militia, February 28, 1777; served as aide-de-camp to Brig. Gen. Philemon Dickinson; Member of the Continental Congress in 1778, 1779, 1782, and 1783; clerk of the common pleas court, Somerset County, from 1781 to 1789, when he resigned; member of the State general assembly in 1784 and 1800–1804; member of the New Jersey convention that ratified the Federal Constitution in 1787; member of the State council 1790–1792; appointed by President Washington brigadier general in 1790 in the campaign against the western Indians; elected as a Federalist to the United States Senate and served from March 4, 1793, to November 12, 1796, when he resigned; commissioned major general in 1794 during the Whisky Insurrection; trustee of Princeton College 1802–1804; died in Millstone, N. J., April 13, 1804; interment in the Old Cemetery, Weston, N. J.

FRELINGHUYSEN, Frederick Theodore (nephew and adopted son of Theodore Frelinghuysen, uncle of Joseph Sherman Frelinghuysen, and great-grandfather of Peter Hood Ballantine Frelinghuysen, Jr.), a Senator from New Jersey; born in Millstone, N. J., August 4, 1817; was graduated from Rutgers College, New Brunswick, N. J., in 1836; studied law; was admitted to the bar in 1839 and commenced practice in Newark, N. J.; city attorney in 1849; member of the city council in 1850; trustee of Rutgers 1851–1885; member of the peace convention of 1861 held in Washington, D. C., in an effort to devise means to prevent the impending war; appointed attorney general of New Jersey in 1861; reappointed in 1866 and resigned the same year; appointed and subsequently elected as a Republican to the United States Senate to fill the vacancy caused by the death of William Wright and served from November 12, 1866, to March 3, 1869; unsuccessful candidate for reelection in 1868; appointed United States Minister to England by President Grant in July 1870; confirmed after considerable opposition from Senators Sumner and Wilson, but declined the appointment; again elected to the United States Senate and served from March 4, 1871, to March 3, 1877; appointed a member of the Electoral Commission created by act of Congress approved January 29, 1877, to decide the contests in various States in the presidential election of 1876; unsuccessful candidate for reelection; resumed the practice of law in Newark, N. J.; appointed Secretary of State in the Cabinet of President Arthur and served from December 19, 1881, to March 6, 1885; president of the American Bible Society in 1884 and 1885; died in Newark, N. J., May 20, 1885; interment in Mount Pleasant Cemetery.

FRELINGHUYSEN, Joseph Sherman (nephew of Frederick Theodore Frelinghuysen and cousin of Peter Hood Ballantine Frelinghuysen, Jr.), a Senator from New Jersey; born in Raritan, Somerset County, N. J., March 12, 1869; attended the public schools; interested in insurance companies; served in the Spanish-American War in 1898 as second lieutenant, first lieutenant, and ordnance officer; chairman of the Somerset County Republican executive committee 1902–1905; member of the State senate 1906–1912; president of the senate in 1909 and 1910 and Acting Governor of New Jersey ad interim; member of the Republican State committee 1914–1916; member of the New York Chamber of Commerce 1912–1926 and of the New Jersey Chamber of Commerce 1914–1925; president of the State board of agriculture 1912–1925; president of the State board of education 1915–1919; elected as a Republican to the United States Senate and served from March 4, 1917, to March 3, 1923; unsuccessful Republican candidate for reelection to the United States Senate in 1922; trustee of Rutgers College, New Brunswick, N. J., 1918–1928; delegate to the Republican National Conventions in 1916, 1920, 1924, 1928, 1936, and 1944; reengaged in the insurance business until his death in Tucson, Ariz., where he had gone for his health, February 8, 1948; interment in St. Bernard's Cemetery, Bernardsville, N. J.

FRELINGHUYSEN, Peter Hood Ballantine, Jr. (cousin of Joseph Sherman Frelinghuysen, great-grandson of Frederick T. Frelinghuysen, great-great-great-nephew of Theodore Frelinghuysen, and great-great-great-grandson of Frederick Frelinghuysen), a Representative from New Jersey; born in New York, N. Y., January 17, 1916; attended St. Mark's School, Southboro, Mass.; graduated from Princeton University in 1938 and from Yale Law School in 1941; admitted to the bar the same year and practiced law in New York City from December 1941 to April 1942; during World War II served in Office of Naval Intelligence from September 1942 to December 1945 and was released to inactive duty with a commission as lieutenant; took postgraduate work in history at Columbia University in 1946 and 1947; on staff of Foreign Affairs Task Force of the Hoover Commission from May to October 1948; engaged in investment business in New York, N. Y.; director of Trust Company of Morris County, N. J., since 1949; elected as a Republican to the Eighty-third and to the three succeeding Congresses (January 3, 1953–January 3, 1961). *Reelected to the Eighty-seventh Congress.*

FRELINGHUYSEN, Theodore (son of Frederick Frelinghuysen and great-great-great-uncle of Peter Hood Ballantine Frelinghuysen, Jr.), a Senator from New Jersey; born in Millstone, N. J., March 28, 1787; pursued classical studies and was graduated from Princeton College in 1804; studied law; was admitted to the bar in 1808 and commenced practice in Newark, N. J.; served as captain of volunteer militia in the War of 1812; attorney general of New Jersey from 1817 to 1829, when he resigned; declined the office of justice of the supreme court in 1826; vice president of the American Sunday School Union 1826–1860; unsuccessful candidate for election to the United States Senate in 1826; elected as an Adams Democrat to the United States Senate and served from March 4, 1829, to March 3, 1835; resumed the practice of law in Newark, N. J.; mayor of Newark in 1837 and 1838; chancellor of New York University 1839–1850; president of the American Board of Commissioners for Foreign Missions 1841–1857; president of the American Tract Society 1842–1848; vice president of the American Colonization Society; unsuccessful Whig candidate for Vice President on the ticket with Henry Clay in 1844; president of the American Bible Society 1846–1861; president of Rutgers College, New Brunswick, N. J., from 1850 until his death in New Brunswick, N. J., April 12, 1862; interment in First Reformed Church Cemetery.

FRÉMONT, John Charles, a Senator from California; born in Savannah, Ga., January 21, 1813; pursued classical studies and attended Charleston College 1828–1830; instructor in mathematics in the United States Navy 1833–1835; civil engineer assistant of Nicollet in 1838 and 1839, exploring the territory between the Missouri River and the northern boundary of the United States; appointed second lieutenant of Topographical Engineers of the United States Army July 7, 1838; commenced in 1842 his explorations and surveys for an overland route from the Mississippi to the Pacific Ocean; major of a battalion of California Volunteers in 1846; appointed lieutenant colonel of United States Mounted Rifles in 1846 and ordered to act as Governor of California by Commodore Stockton; General Kearny, United States Army, revoked this order and placed him under arrest for mutiny; tried by court martial in Washington, found guilty, and pardoned by President Polk, but resigned; crossed the continent in 1848; located in California on the Mariposa grant; commissioner to run the boundary line between United States and Mexico in 1849; upon the admission of California as a State into the Union was elected as a Free-Soil Democrat to the United States Senate and served from September 9, 1850, to March 3, 1851; crossed the continent in 1853 for the fifth time; unsuccessful as the first Republican candidate for President of the United States in 1856; appointed major general in the United States Army by President Lincoln May 14, 1861, and placed in command of the western military district; was removed December 2, 1861; appointed to command the mountain department February 10, 1862; resigned June 4, 1864; again nominated for President by the Cleveland convention in 1864; Governor of Arizona Territory 1878–1881; appointed a major general in the United States Army on the retired list April 28, 1890; died in New York City July 13, 1890; interment in Trinity Church Cemetery; reinterment in Rockland Cemetery, Nyack, N. Y., March 17, 1891.

FRENCH, Burton Lee, a Representative from Idaho; born near Delphi, Carroll County, Ind., August 1, 1875; moved with his parents to Kearney, Nebr., in 1880, and thence to Idaho in 1882; attended the public schools; was graduated from the University of Idaho at Moscow in 1901; fellow in the University of Chicago 1901–1903; studied law; was admitted to the bar and commenced practice in Moscow, Idaho; member of the State house of representatives 1898–1902; elected as a Republican to the Fifty-eighth, Fifty-ninth, and Sixtieth Congresses (March 4, 1903–March 3, 1909); unsuccessful candidate for reelection in 1908 to the Sixty-first Congress; elected to the Sixty-second and Sixty-third Congresses (March 4, 1911–March 3, 1915); was not a candidate for renomination in 1914, but was an unsuccessful candidate for the Republican nomination for United States Senator; elected to the Sixty-fifth and to the seven succeeding Congresses (March 4, 1917–March 3, 1933); unsuccessful candidate for reelection in 1932 to the Seventy-third Congress and for election in 1934 to the Seventy-fourth Congress; delegate to the Interparliamentary Union Conventions, at London in 1930, and at Bucharest in 1931; professor of government at Miami University, Oxford, Ohio, from 1935 until his retirement in 1947; appointed by President Truman in 1947 a member of the Federal Loyalty Review Board and served until 1953; died in Hamilton, Ohio, September 12, 1954; interment in Moscow Cemetery, Moscow, Idaho.

FRENCH, Carlos, a Representative from Connecticut; born in Humphreysville (later Seymour), Conn., August 6, 1835; attended the common schools of Seymour and General Russell's Military School, New Haven, Conn.; engaged in manufacturing; invented the spiral steel car spring and the corrugated volute spring; member of the State house of representatives in 1860 and again in 1868; president and treasurer of the Fowler Nail Co.

from 1869 until his death; vice president of the H. A. Matthews Manufacturing Co.; director of the Union Horse Shoe Nail Co. of Chicago, of the Second National Bank of New Haven, of the Colonial Trust Co. of Waterbury, Conn., and of the New York, New Haven & Hartford Railroad Co.; member of the Democratic National Committee; elected as a Democrat to the Fiftieth Congress (March 4, 1887–March 3, 1889); was not a candidate for renomination in 1888; resumed his former manufacturing pursuits and corporate connections; died in Seymour, New Haven County, Conn., April 14, 1903; interment in Union Cemetery.

FRENCH, Ezra Bartlett, a Representative from Maine; born in Landaff, Grafton County, N. H., September 23, 1810; attended the common schools and pursued an academic course; studied law in Bath, N. H., and Plymouth, N. H.; was admitted to the bar in 1833 and commenced practice in Portland and Waldoboro, Maine; moved to Noblesboro (later Damariscotta), Maine, and continued practice; member of the State house of representatives 1838–1840; served in the State senate 1842–1845; secretary of state of Maine 1845–1850; bank commissioner; newspaper editor in 1856; assisted in organizing the Republican Party in 1856; elected as a Republican to the Thirty-sixth Congress (March 4, 1859–March 3, 1861); was not a candidate for renomination in 1860; member of the peace convention of 1861 held in Washington, D. C., in an effort to devise means to prevent the impending war; appointed Second Auditor of the Treasury August 3, 1861, by President Lincoln, and continued during the administrations of Presidents Johnson, Grant, and Hayes, serving until his death in Washington, D. C., April 24, 1880; interment in Hillside Cemetery, Damariscotta, Maine.

FRENCH, John Robert, a Representative from North Carolina; born in Gilmanton, Belknap County, N. H., May 28, 1819; received an academic education in Gilmanton and Concord, N. H.; learned the printer's trade; publisher and associate editor of the New Hampshire Statesman at Concord for five years; editor of the Eastern Journal at Biddeford, Maine, two years; moved to Lake County, Ohio, in 1854; editor of the Telegraph, the Press, and, in 1856, of the Cleveland Morning Leader; member of the State house of representatives in 1858 and 1859; appointed by Secretary Chase to a position in the Treasury Department, Washington, D. C., in 1861; appointed by President Lincoln in 1864 a member of the board of direct-tax commissioners for the State of North Carolina; settled in Edenton, N. C., at the close of the Civil War; delegate to the State constitutional convention in 1867; upon the readmission of the State of North Carolina to representation was elected as a Republican to the Fortieth Congress and served from July 6, 1868, to March 3, 1869; was not a candidate for renomination in 1868; elected Sergeant at Arms of the United States Senate March 22, 1869, and served in that capacity until March 24, 1879; appointed secretary of the Ute Commission in July 1880; returned to Washington, D. C.; moved to Omaha, Nebr., and thence to Boise City, Idaho, where he was editor of the Boise City Sun until his death October 2, 1890; interment in Boise City Cemetery.

FRENCH, Richard, a Representative from Kentucky; born near Boonesborough, Madison County, Ky., June 20, 1792; attended private schools; studied law; was admitted to the bar in 1820 and commenced practice in Winchester, Ky.; member of the State house of representatives 1820–1826; presidential elector on the Democratic ticket of Jackson and Calhoun in 1828; judge of the circuit court in 1829; elected as a Democrat to the Twenty-fourth Congress (March 4, 1835–March 3, 1837); unsuccessful candidate for reelection in 1836 to the Twenty-fifth Congress; unsuccessful Democratic candidate for Governor of Kentucky in 1840; elected to the Twenty-eighth

Congress (March 4, 1843–March 3, 1845); again elected to the Thirtieth Congress (March 4, 1847–March 3, 1849); resumed the practice of law; died in Covington, Ky., on May 1, 1854; interment in the family burial ground near Mount Sterling, Montgomery County, Ky.

FREY, Oliver Walter, a Representative from Pennsylvania; born near Quakertown, Richland Township, Bucks County, Pa., September 7, 1887; moved to Ohio with his parents in 1891 and to Allentown, Pa., in 1893; attended the public schools of Allentown; was graduated from the College of William and Mary, Williamsburg, Va., in 1915; attended the University of Pennsylvania at Philadelphia until the outbreak of the First World War, when he enlisted in the United States Army and served from April 1917 until honorably discharged in June 1919; was commissioned a first lieutenant in the Three Hundred and Fourteenth Infantry, serving overseas in the Seventy-ninth Division; resumed his studies at the University of Pennsylvania and graduated from its law department in 1920; was admitted to the bar the same year and commenced practice in Allentown, Pa.; elected as a Democrat to the Seventy-third Congress to fill the vacancy caused by the death of Henry W. Watson; reelected to the Seventy-fourth and Seventy-fifth Congresses and served from November 7, 1933, to January 3, 1939; unsuccessful for reelection in 1938 to the Seventy-sixth Congress; general counsel for the Farm Credit Administration in Baltimore, Md., from April 1939 until his death in Allentown, Pa., August 26, 1939; interment in Grandview Cemetery.

FRICK, Henry, a Representative from Pennsylvania; born in Northumberland, Pa., March 17, 1795; attended the public schools; apprenticed to a printer in Philadelphia; served in the War of 1812; settled in Milton, Pa., in 1816; established the Miltonian, a political journal, with which he was connected for over twenty years; member of the State house of representatives 1828–1831; elected as a Whig to the Twenty-eighth Congress and served from March 4, 1843, until his death in Washington, D. C., March 1, 1844; interment in the Congressional Cemetery.

FRIEDEL, Samuel Nathaniel, a Representative from Maryland; born in Washington, D. C., April 18, 1898; moved with his family to Baltimore, Md., when six months of age; attended the public schools and Strayer Business College; mailing clerk in a Baltimore store 1919–1923; founder and president of Industrial Loan Co., 1926–1956; member of the State house of delegates 1935–1939; member of the city council of Baltimore 1939–1952, representing the first and later the fifth district; elected as a Democrat to the Eighty-third and to the three succeeding Congresses (January 3, 1953–January 3, 1961). *Reelected to the Eighty-seventh Congress.*

FRIES, Frank William, a Representative from Illinois; born in Hornsby, Macoupin County, Ill., May 1, 1893; moved with his parents to Gillespie, Ill., in 1904; attended the public schools; coal miner 1915–1917; during the First World War served as a sergeant in the Thirty-seventh Company, One Hundred and Fifty-third Depot Brigade, United States Army, from April 1918 to December 1918; coal mine operator in 1920 and 1921; engaged in the insurance business 1922–1927; moved to Carlinville, Ill., in 1930 and engaged in the wholesale produce business; sheriff of Macoupin County 1930–1934; member of the State house of representatives 1934–1936; elected as a Democrat to the Seventy-fifth and Seventy-sixth Congresses (January 3, 1937–January 3, 1941); unsuccessful candidate for reelection in 1940 to the Seventy-seventh Congress; is an arbitrator in the coal industry and resides at Gillespie, Ill.

FRIES, George, a Representative from Ohio; born in Pennsylvania in 1799; attended the common schools; studied medicine and commenced practice in Hanoverton, Ohio, in 1833; elected as a Democrat to the Twenty-ninth and Thirtieth Congresses (March 4, 1845–March 3, 1849); declined to be a candidate for renomination in 1848; moved to Cincinnati, Ohio, and resumed the practice of medicine; treasurer of Hamilton County 1860–1862; died in Cincinnati, Ohio, on November 13, 1866; interment in the Catholic Cemetery.

FROMENTIN, Eligius, a Senator from Louisiana; born in France; pursued classical studies; ordained a Catholic priest; exercised his ministry at Etampes, France; fled from France during the Reign of Terror and immigrated to the United States, settling in Pennsylvania; moved to Maryland, where he taught school; studied law; subsequently left the church and moved to Louisiana; was admitted to the bar and commenced practice in New Orleans; clerk to house of representatives of Orleans Territory 1807–1811; secretary of the State constitutional convention in 1812; secretary of the State senate in 1812 and 1813; elected to the United States Senate and served from March 4, 1813, to March 3, 1819; appointed judge of the criminal court of New Orleans in 1821; appointed United States judge for west Florida and for that part of east Florida westward of the cape, to reside at Pensacola, Fla., on May 18, 1821, but soon resigned; resumed the practice of law in New Orleans, and died there October 6, 1822.

FROST, George, a Delegate from New Hampshire; born in Newcastle, N. H., April 26, 1720; entered business in Kittery Point, near Portsmouth; followed the sea as captain for twenty years; returned to Newcastle in 1760; moved to Durham, N. H., in 1770; judge of the court of common pleas of Strafford County 1773–1791; served as chief justice several years; Member of the Continental Congress 1777–1779; executive councilor 1781–1784; died in Durham, N. H., June 21, 1796; interment in Pine Hill Cemetery, Dover, N. H.

FROST, Joel, a Representative from New York; born in Westchester County, N. Y.; attended the public schools; member of the State assembly 1806–1808; surrogate of Putnam County in 1812, 1813, 1815–1819, 1821, and 1822; member of the State constitutional convention in 1821; moved to Schenectady; elected to the Eighteenth Congress (March 4, 1823–March 3, 1825).

FROST, Richard Graham, a Representative from Missouri; born in St. Louis, Mo., December 29, 1851; attended St. John's College, New York City, the University of London, England, and the St. Louis (Mo.) Law School; was admitted to the bar and practiced in St. Louis, Mo.; unsuccessfully contested as a Democrat the election in 1876 of Lyne S. Metcalfe to the Forty-fifth Congress; elected as a Democrat to the Forty-sixth Congress (March 4, 1879–March 3, 1881); presented credentials as a Member-elect to the Forty-seventh Congress and served from March 4, 1881, until March 2, 1883, when he was succeeded by Gustavus Sessinghaus, who contested his election; resumed the practice of law; died in St. Louis, Mo., February 1, 1900; interment in Calvary Cemetery.

FROST, Rufus Smith, a Representative from Massachusetts; born in Marlboro, Cheshire County, N. H., July 18, 1826; moved to Boston, Mass., in 1833; attended the public schools; engaged in mercantile pursuits; mayor of Chelsea, Mass., in 1867 and 1868; member of the State senate in 1871 and 1872 and of the Governor's council in 1873 and 1874; presented credentials as a Republican Member-elect to the Forty-fourth Congress and served from March 4, 1875, until July 28, 1876, when he was succeeded by Josiah G. Abbott, who contested his election; unsuccessful candidate for election in 1876 to the Forty-fifth Congress; president of the National Association of Woolen Manufacturers 1877–1884; president of the Boston Board of Trade 1878–1880; president of the New England Conservatory of Music; one of the founders of the New England Law and Order League and of the Boston Art Club; delegate to the Republican National Convention at Minneapolis in 1892; died in Chicago, Ill., March 6, 1894; interment in Woodlawn Cemetery, Chelsea, Mass.

FROTHINGHAM, Louis Adams, a Representative from Massachusetts; born in Jamaica Plain, Mass., July 13, 1871; attended the public schools and Adams Academy; was graduated from Harvard University in 1893 and from Harvard Law School in 1896; admitted to the bar in 1896 and commenced practice in Boston; second lieutenant, United States Marine Corps, in the Spanish-American War in 1898; member of the State house of representatives 1901–1905, and served as speaker in 1904 and 1905; Lieutenant Governor 1909–1911; unsuccessful candidate for Governor in 1911; lecturer at Harvard University 1913–1916; moved to North Easton, Mass., in 1916 and continued the practice of law; delegate to the Republican National Convention at Chicago in 1916; major in the United States Army during the First World War; member of the commission to visit the soldiers and sailors from Massachusetts in France in 1918; first vice commander of the Massachusetts branch of the American Legion in 1919; overseer of Harvard University for eighteen years; elected as a Republican to the Sixty-seventh and to the three succeeding Congresses and served from March 4, 1921, until his death on board the yacht *Winsome*, at North Haven, Maine, August 23, 1928; interment in Village Cemetery, North Easton, Mass.

FRY, Jacob, Jr., a Representative from Pennsylvania; born in Trappe, Montgomery County, Pa., June 10, 1802; attended the public schools; taught school in Trappe, Pa.; clerk of courts of Montgomery County 1830–1833; elected as a Democrat to the Twenty-fourth and Twenty-fifth Congresses (March 4, 1835–March 3, 1839); was not a candidate for renomination in 1838; engaged in mercantile business in Trappe, Pa.; member of the State house of representatives in 1853 and 1854; auditor general of Pennsylvania 1857–1860; resumed mercantile pursuits; died in Trappe, Pa., November 28, 1866; interment in Lutheran Cemetery.

FRY, Joseph, Jr., a Representative from Pennsylvania; born in Upper Saucon Township, Northampton (later Lehigh) County, Pa., August 4, 1781; attended the rural schools; engaged in mercantile pursuits in Fryburg (later Coopersburg), Lehigh County, Pa.; member of the State house of representatives in 1816 and 1817; served in the State senate 1817–1821; served in the State militia and attained the rank of colonel; elected as a Democrat to the Twentieth and Twenty-first Congresses (March 4, 1827–March 3, 1831); was not a candidate for renomination in 1830; resumed business activities; member of the State constitutional convention in 1837 and 1838; died in Allentown, Pa., August 15, 1860; interment in Union Cemetery.

FRYE, William Pierce (grandfather of Wallace Humphrey White, Jr.), a Representative and a Senator from Maine; born in Lewiston, Androscoggin County, Maine, September 2, 1830; attended the public schools in Lewiston, and was graduated from Bowdoin College, Brunswick, Maine, in 1850; studied law; was admitted to the bar and commenced practice in Rockland, Maine, in 1853; returned to Lewiston, Maine, and practiced law; member of the State house of representatives in 1861,

1862, and 1867; mayor of Lewiston in 1866 and 1867; attorney general of the State of Maine 1867–1869; elected a trustee of Bowdoin College in June 1880; presidential elector on the Republican ticket of Lincoln and Johnson in 1864; delegate to the Republican National Convention at Philadelphia in 1872, at Cincinnati in 1876, and at Chicago in 1880; elected chairman of the Republican State committee of Maine in November 1881; elected as a Republican to the Forty-second and to the five succeeding Congresses and served from March 4, 1871, to March 17, 1881, when he resigned, having been elected Senator; elected to the United States Senate on March 15, 1881, to fill the vacancy caused by the resignation of James G. Blaine; reelected in 1883, 1889, 1895, 1901, and 1907 and served from March 18, 1881, until his death; elected President pro tempore of the Senate February 7, 1896; reelected March 7, 1901, and December 5, 1907, and served as such until his death; member of the commission which met in Paris in September 1898 to adjust terms of peace between the United States and Spain; died in Lewiston, Maine, August 8, 1911; interment in Riverside Cemetery.

FUGATE, Thomas Bacon, a Representative from Virginia; born near Tazewell, Claiborne County, Tenn., April 10, 1899; attended the public schools of Tennessee; student at the University of Tennessee at Knoxville in 1917 and at the Lincoln Memorial University, Harrogate, Tenn., in 1918; moved to Rose Hill, Va., in 1921 and engaged in the mercantile business; engaged in the hardware business at Ewing, Va., 1936–1940; also engaged in agricultural pursuits; member of the Virginia House of Delegates 1928–1930; president of the Peoples Bank of Ewing since 1935; director, Virginia-Tennessee Farm Bureau, Inc., since 1936; president of Ewing Live Stock Co., Inc., since 1938; member of Virginia Board of Public Welfare 1937–1947; delegate to the Democratic National Convention in 1944; member of Constitutional Convention of Virginia in 1945; vice president of Grace Nettleton Home for Girls, Harrogate, Tenn., since 1948; member of the board of trustees and vice president of Lincoln Memorial University; elected as a Democrat to the Eighty-first and Eighty-second Congresses (January 3, 1949–January 3, 1953); was not a candidate for renomination in 1952; banker and farmer; is a resident of Ewing, Va.

FULBRIGHT, James Franklin, a Representative from Missouri; born near Millersville, Cape Girardeau County, Mo., January 24, 1877; attended the public schools, and was graduated from the State Normal School, Cape Girardeau, Mo., in 1900; taught school in Cape Girardeau and Ripley Counties for several years; attended the Washington Law School, St. Louis, Mo., for a short time; was admitted to the bar in 1903 and commenced practice in Doniphan, Mo., in 1904; appointed and subsequently elected prosecuting attorney of Ripley County in 1906; reelected in 1908 and 1910; member of the State house of representatives 1913–1919, serving as speaker pro tempore 1915–1919; mayor of Doniphan, Mo., 1919–1921; elected as a Democrat to the Sixty-eighth Congress (March 4, 1923–March 3, 1925); unsuccessful candidate for reelection in 1924 to the Sixty-ninth Congress; elected to the Seventieth Congress (March 4, 1927–March 3, 1929); unsuccessful candidate for reelection in 1928 to the Seventy-first Congress; elected to the Seventy-second Congress (March 4, 1931–March 3, 1933); unsuccessful candidate for renomination in 1932; resumed the practice of law; delegate to the Democratic National Convention at Houston in 1928; permanent chairman of the Democratic State convention in 1936; elected judge of the Springfield Court of Appeals in 1936 and served from January 1, 1937, until his death in Springfield, Mo., April 5, 1948; interment in Doniphan Cemetery, Doniphan, Mo.

FULBRIGHT, James William, a Representative and a Senator from Arkansas; born in Sumner, Chariton County, Mo., April 9, 1905; moved with his parents to Fayetteville, Ark., in 1906; attended the public schools; was graduated from the University of Arkansas at Fayetteville in 1925, as a Rhodes scholar from Oxford University, England, in 1928, and from the law department of George Washington University, Washington, D. C., in 1934; was admitted to the District of Columbia bar in 1934; attorney, United States Department of Justice, Antitrust Division, in 1934 and 1935; instructor in law, George Washington University, in 1935, and lecturer in law, University of Arkansas, 1936–1939; president of the University of Arkansas 1939–1941; also engaged in the newspaper business, in the lumber business, in banking, and in farming; elected as a Democrat to the Seventy-eighth Congress (January 3, 1943–January 3, 1945); was not a candidate for renomination in 1944; chairman of the American delegation to the London Conference of the Allied Ministers of Education in 1944; delegate to the Democratic National Conventions in 1948, 1952, and 1956; elected to the United States Senate in 1944 for the term commencing January 3, 1945; reelected in 1950 and again in 1956 for the term ending January 3, 1963.

FULKERSON, Abram, a Representative from Virginia; born in Washington County, Va., May 13, 1834; was graduated from the Virginia Military Institute at Lexington in 1857; taught school in Palmyra, Va., and Rogersville, Tenn., until the beginning of the Civil War; entered the Confederate service in June 1861 as captain; promoted to major in the Nineteenth Tennessee Regiment; lieutenant colonel and colonel of the Sixty-third Tennessee Regiment; participated in many battles; at the close of the war studied law; was admitted to the bar and commenced practice in Goodson (later Bristol), Va., in 1866; member of the Virginia House of Delegates 1871–1873; served in the State senate of Virginia 1877–1879; elected as a Readjuster to the Forty-seventh Congress (March 4, 1881–March 3, 1883); was a Democrat, but assisted in organizing the Readjuster Party, after which he returned to the Democratic Party; resumed the practice of law after leaving Congress; elected to the State house of delegates in 1888; delegate to the Democratic National (Gold) Convention in 1896; died in Bristol, Va., on December 17, 1902; interment in East Hill Cemetery.

FULKERSON, Frank Ballard, a Representative from Missouri; born near Edinburg, Grundy County, Mo., March 5, 1866; eight months later moved with his parents to a farm near Higginsville, Lafayette County, Mo.; attended the common schools and was graduated from Westminster College, Fulton, Mo., in 1888; taught school for two years; attended the law department of the University of Michigan at Ann Arbor; was graduated from the law department of the University of Missouri at Columbia in 1892; was admitted to the bar the same year and commenced practice in Warrensburg, Mo.; city attorney of Warrensburg 1893–1895; prosecuting attorney of Johnson County in 1895 and 1896; moved to Holden, Mo., in 1897 and to St. Joseph, Mo., in 1900 and continued the practice of law; city attorney of Holden in 1899 and 1900; elected as a Republican to the Fifty-ninth Congress (March 4, 1905–March 3, 1907); unsuccessful candidate for reelection in 1906 to the Sixtieth Congress; unsuccessful Republican candidate for attorney general of Missouri in 1908; unsuccessful candidate for mayor of St. Joseph, Mo., in 1908; resumed the practice of law in St. Joseph, Mo.; delegate to several Republican State conventions; delegate to the Republican National Convention at Chicago in 1908 which nominated Taft and Sherman; president of the city police board in 1909; city counselor in 1913 and 1914; returned to Lafayette County, Mo., in 1918 and continued the practice of law; also engaged in agricultural pursuits near Higginsville; prosecuting attorney of Lafayette County 1921–1925; died near Higginsville, Mo., August 30, 1936; interment in Higginsville City Cemetery.

FULLER, Alvan Tufts, a Representative from Massachusetts; born in Boston, Mass., February 27, 1878; attended the public schools; engaged in the bicycle business in 1896; founder and owner of the Packard Motor Car Co. of Boston, a pioneer in the automobile business; member of the State house of representatives in 1915; delegate to the Republican National Convention at Chicago in 1916; elected as a Republican to the Sixty-fifth and Sixty-sixth Congresses and served from March 4, 1917, to January 5, 1921, when he resigned, having been elected Lieutenant Governor; Lieutenant Governor of Massachusetts 1921–1924; elected Governor of Massachusetts in 1924 and assumed his duties January 7, 1925; reelected in 1926 for the term expiring January 1, 1929; chairman of the board of Cadillac-Oldsmobile Co., of Boston; did not accept compensation for services while in public office; died in Boston, Mass., April 30, 1958; remains were cremated and interred in East Cemetery, Rye Beach, N. H.

FULLER, Benoni Stinson, a Representative from Indiana; born near Boonville, Warrick County, Ind., November 13, 1825; attended the common schools; taught school in Warrick County; sheriff of Warrick County in 1856 and 1858; served in the State senate in 1862, 1870, and 1872; member of the State house of representatives 1866–1868; elected as a Democrat to the Forty-fourth and Forty-fifth Congresses (March 4, 1875–March 3, 1879); was not a candidate for renomination in 1878; engaged in agricultural pursuits in Warrick County; died in Boonville, Ind., April 14, 1903; interment in Old Boonville Cemetery.

FULLER, Charles Eugene, a Representative from Illinois; born near Belvidere, Boone County, Ill., March 31, 1849; attended the common schools; studied law; was admitted to the bar in 1870 and commenced practice in Belvidere, Ill.; city attorney of Belvidere in 1875 and 1876; prosecuting attorney for Boone County 1876–1878; served in the State senate 1878–1882; member of the State house of representatives 1882–1888; again a member of the State senate 1888–1892; raised a provisional regiment for the war with Spain and was commissioned colonel of the Thirteenth Illinois Infantry by Governor Tanner; judge of the seventeenth judicial circuit 1897–1903; vice president of the People's Bank of Belvidere for many years; elected as a Republican to the Fifty-eighth and to the four succeeding Congresses (March 4, 1903–March 3, 1913); unsuccessful candidate for reelection in 1912 to the Sixty-third Congress; elected to the Sixty-fourth and to the five succeeding Congresses and served from March 4, 1915, until his death at a hospital in Rochester, Minn., June 25, 1926; interment in Belvidere Cemetery, Belvidere, Ill.

FULLER, Claude Albert, a Representative from Arkansas; born in Prophetstown, Whiteside County, Ill., January 20, 1876; in 1885 moved to Arkansas with his parents, who settled on a farm near Eureka Springs; attended the public schools in Eureka Springs, Ark., and Kent College of Law, Chicago, Ill.; was admitted to the bar in 1898 and commenced practice in Eureka Springs the same year; city clerk of Eureka Springs 1898–1902; member of the State house of representatives 1903–1905; mayor of Eureka Springs 1906–1910 and 1920–1928; prosecuting attorney of the fourth Arkansas judicial district 1910–1914; president of the Eureka Springs School Board 1916–1928; delegate to all Democratic State conventions 1903–1943; delegate to the Democratic National Conventions in 1908, 1912, and others 1924–1960; elected as a Democrat to the Seventy-first and to the four succeeding Congresses (March 4, 1929–January 3,

1939); unsuccessful candidate for renomination in 1938; resumed the practice of law, also engaged in banking and agricultural pursuits; is a resident of Eureka Springs, Ark.

FULLER, George, a Representative from Pennsylvania; born in Norwich, Conn., November 7, 1802; attended the public schools; moved to Pennsylvania and resided in Montrose; engaged in mercantile pursuits; elected as a Democrat to the Twenty-eighth Congress to fill the vacancy caused by the death of Almon H. Read and served from December 2, 1844, to March 3, 1845; editor of the Montrose (Pa.) Democrat, the Montrose Gazette, and the Susquehanna Register; treasurer of Susquehanna County; member of the Republican Party during the last twenty-five years of his life; died in Scranton, Lackawanna County, Pa., on November 24, 1888; interment in Montrose, Pa.

FULLER, Hadwen Carlton, a Representative from New York; born in West Monroe, Oswego County, N. Y., August 28, 1895; attended the public schools and Central Square (N. Y.) High School; engaged as bank clerk and later as assistant cashier of the First National Bank of Central Square, N. Y., 1912–1918; during the First World War served in the United States Army; organized the State Bank of Parish, N. Y., in 1919 and has served as a director since that date; organizer of the Parish Oil Co., Inc., in 1926, serving as president since 1937; chairman of the Oswego County Republican Committee in 1942; chairman of Pulaski, N. Y., Draft Board No. 486, 1940–1943; member of the Oswego County War Council 1941–1944; served in the State assembly in 1942 and 1943; elected as a Republican to the Seventy-eighth Congress to fill the vacancy caused by the death of Francis D. Culkin; reelected to the Seventy-ninth and Eightieth Congresses and served from November 2, 1943, to January 3, 1949; unsuccessful candidate for reelection in 1948 to the Eighty-first Congress; delegate to the Republican National Convention at Philadelphia in 1948; resumed his former business pursuits and is a resident of Parish, N. Y.

FULLER, Henry Mills, a Representative from Pennsylvania; born in Bethany, Wayne County, Pa., January 3, 1820; pursued classical studies and was graduated from Princeton College in 1839; studied law; was admitted to the bar January 3, 1842, and commenced practice in Wilkes-Barre, Luzerne County, Pa.; member of the State house of representatives in 1848 and 1849; elected as a Whig to the Thirty-second Congress (March 4, 1851–March 3, 1853); unsuccessful candidate for reelection in 1852 to the Thirty-third Congress; elected to the Thirty-fourth Congress (March 4, 1855–March 3, 1857); was not a candidate for renomination in 1856; resumed the practice of law; died in Philadelphia, Pa., December 26, 1860; interment in Hollenback Cemetery, Wilkes-Barre, Pa.

FULLER, Philo Case, a Representative from New York; born near Marlboro, Mass., August 14, 1787; attended the common schools; studied law and was admitted to the bar in 1813; served in the War of 1812; honorably discharged February 15, 1815; private secretary to General Wadsworth at Geneseo, N. Y.; practiced law in Albany, N. Y.; member of the State assembly in 1829 and 1830; served in the State senate in 1831 and 1832; elected as a Whig to the Twenty-third and Twenty-fourth Congresses and served from March 4, 1833, until September 2, 1836, when he resigned; moved to Adrian, Mich., in 1836; engaged in banking; president of the Erie & Kalamazoo Railroad Co.; member of the State assembly in 1841 and served as speaker; unsuccessful Whig candidate for Governor of Michigan in 1841; returned to Geneseo, N. Y.; appointed Second Assistant Postmaster General in 1841; appointed comptroller of the State of New York December 18, 1850, and served until November

4, 1851; died near Geneva, Ontario County, N. Y., August 16, 1855; interment in Temple Hill Cemetery, Geneseo, Livingston County, N. Y.

FULLER, Thomas James Duncan, a Representative from Maine; born in Hardwick, Caledonia County, Vt., March 17, 1808; attended the common schools; studied law; was admitted to the bar and commenced practice in Calais, Maine; elected as a Democrat to the Thirty-first and to the three succeeding Congresses (March 4, 1849–March 3, 1857); was not a candidate for renomination in 1856; appointed by President Buchanan as Second Auditor of the Treasury and served from April 15, 1857, to August 3, 1861; engaged in the practice of law before the United States Supreme Court and the Court of Claims in Washington, D. C.; died, while on a visit to his son, near Upperville, Fauquier County, Va., February 13, 1876; interment in Oak Hill Cemetery, Washington, D. C.

FULLER, Timothy, a Representative from Massachusetts; born in Chilmark, Dukes County, Mass., July 11, 1778; received a classical education and was graduated from Harvard University in 1801; taught at Leicester Academy; studied law; was admitted to the bar and commenced practice in Boston in 1804; served in the State senate 1813–1817; elected as a Democrat to the Fifteenth and to the three succeeding Congresses (March 4, 1817–March 3, 1825); member of the State house of representatives 1825–1828; State councilor in 1828; again elected to the State house of representatives in 1831; died in Groton, Middlesex County, Mass., October 1, 1835; interment in Mount Auburn Cemetery, Cambridge, Mass.

FULLER, William Elijah, a Representative from Iowa; born in Howard, Center County, Pa., March 30, 1846; moved with his parents to West Union, Fayette County, Iowa, in 1853; attended the common schools, the Upper Iowa University at Fayette, and the State University of Iowa at Iowa City; was graduated from the law department of the latter university in June 1870; was admitted to the bar the same year and commenced practice in West Union; held a position in the Office of Indian Affairs, Department of the Interior, in 1866 and 1867; member of the West Union Board of Education for six years; member of the Iowa House of Representatives in 1876 and 1877; member of the Republican State and congressional committees; elected as a Republican to the Forty-ninth and Fiftieth Congresses (March 4, 1885–March 3, 1889); declined to be a candidate for renomination in 1888; Assistant Attorney General, Spanish Treaty Claims Commission, 1901–1907; resumed the practice of law in West Union; died in Washington, D. C., April 23, 1918; interment in West Union Cemetery, West Union, Iowa.

FULLER, William Kendall, a Representative from New York; born in Schenectady, N. Y., November 24, 1792; attended the common schools, and was graduated from Union College in 1810; studied law; was admitted to the bar in 1814 and commenced practice in Schenectady; adjutant general of New York in 1823; district attorney of Madison County 1821–1829; member of the State assembly in 1829 and 1830; elected as a Democrat to the Twenty-third and Twenty-fourth Congresses (March 4, 1833–March 3, 1837); resumed the practice of law; died in Schenectady, N. Y., on November 11, 1883; interment in Vale Cemetery.

FULLERTON, David (uncle of David Fullerton Robison), a Representative from Pennsylvania; born in the Cumberland Valley, near Greencastle, Franklin County, Pa., October 4, 1772; attended the public schools; served as major in the War of 1812; settled in Greencastle and engaged in mercantile pursuits and banking; elected to the Sixteenth Congress and served from March 4, 1819, until May 15, 1820, when he resigned; was not a candidate for renomination; resumed mercantile pursuits and banking; member of the State senate 1827–1839; died in Greencastle, Pa., February 1, 1843; interment in Cedar Hill Cemetery.

FULMER, Hampton Pitts (husband of Willa L. Fulmer), a Representative from South Carolina; born near Springfield, Orangeburg County, S. C., June 23, 1875; attended the public schools, and was graduated from Massey's Business College, Columbus, Ga., in 1897; engaged in agricultural and mercantile pursuits in Norway, S. C.; also engaged in banking; member of the State house of representatives 1917–1920; elected as a Democrat to the Sixty-seventh and to the eleven succeeding Congresses and served from March 4, 1921, until his death; had been nominated for reelection to the Seventy-ninth Congress; died in Washington, D. C., October 19, 1944; interment in Memorial Park Cemetery, Orangeburg, S. C.

FULMER, Willa Lybrand (widow of Hampton P. Fulmer), a Representative from South Carolina; born in Wagener, Aiken County, S. C., February 3, 1884; attended the Wagener (S. C.) public schools and Greenville (S. C.) Female College; elected as a Democrat to the Seventy-eighth Congress to fill the vacancy caused by the death of her husband, Hampton P. Fulmer, and served from November 7, 1944, to January 3, 1945; was not a candidate for election to the Seventy-ninth Congress; engaged in agricultural pursuits until her retirement; resides in Washington, D. C.

FULTON, Andrew Steele (brother of John H. Fulton), a Representative from Virginia; born near Waynesboro, Augusta County, Va., on September 29, 1800; attended the common schools and Hampden-Sidney College, Hampden-Sidney, Va.; studied law in Staunton, Va.; was admitted to the bar in 1825 and commenced practice in Abingdon, Va., in 1826; moved to Wytheville in 1828; elected a member of the State house of delegates in 1840 and 1845; prosecuting attorney for Wythe County; elected as a Whig to the Thirtieth Congress (March 4, 1847–March 3, 1849); was not a candidate for renomination in 1848; resumed the practice of law; judge of the fifteenth judicial circuit of Virginia 1852–1869; died near Austinville, Wythe County, Va., on November 22, 1884; interment in the family cemetery on New River, near Austinville, Va.

FULTON, Charles William (brother of Elmer Lincoln Fulton), a Senator from Oregon; born in Lima, Allen County, Ohio, August 24, 1853; moved to Iowa in 1855 with his parents, who settled in Magnolia; attended the common schools; moved to Pawnee City, Nebr., in 1870; studied law; was admitted to the bar in 1875 and practiced; moved to Oregon and settled in Astoria in 1875; member of the State senate in 1878; city attorney 1880–1882; presidential elector on the Republican ticket of Harrison and Morton in 1888, and was the messenger selected to carry the electoral vote of Oregon to Washington, D. C.; again a member of the State senate in 1890, 1898, and 1902, and was its president in 1893 and 1901; elected as a Republican to the United States Senate and served from March 4, 1903, to March 3, 1909; unsuccessful candidate for reelection; tendered the position of Minister to China by President Taft in 1909, but declined; continued the practice of law in Portland, Oreg., where he died January 27, 1918; interment in Ocean View Cemetery, Astoria, Oreg.

FULTON, Elmer Lincoln (brother of Charles William Fulton), a Representative from Oklahoma; born in Magnolia, Harrison County, Iowa, April 22, 1865; moved to Nebraska in 1870 with his parents, who settled in Pawnee City; attended the public schools and Tabor College, Tabor, Iowa; studied law; was admitted to the bar in 1895 and commenced practice at Pawnee City, Nebr.; moved to Stillwater, in the Territory of Oklahoma, in 1901 and continued the practice of law; elected as a Democrat to the Sixtieth Congress September 17, 1907, and served from November 16, 1907, when Oklahoma was admitted as a State into the Union, until March 3, 1909; unsuccessful candidate for reelection in 1908 to the Sixty-first Congress; resumed the practice of law in Oklahoma City, Okla.; appointed assistant attorney general of Oklahoma in 1919 and served until 1922, when he resigned and again resumed the practice of his profession; died in Oklahoma City, Okla., October 4, 1939; interment in Valhalla Cemetery, St. Louis, Mo.

FULTON, James Grove, a Representative from Pennsylvania; born in Dormont Borough, Allegheny County, Pa., March 1, 1903; attended the public schools in South Hills and the Fine Arts Department of Carnegie Institute of Technology, Pittsburgh, Pa.; was graduated from Pennsylvania State College at State College in 1924 and from Harvard Law School, Cambridge, Mass., in 1927; was admitted to the bar in 1928 and commenced practice in Pittsburgh, Pa.; also engaged in agricultural pursuits; member of the Allegheny County Board of Law Examiners 1934–1942; served in the State senate in 1939 and 1940; solicitor for Dormont Borough in 1942; publisher of the Mount Lebanon (Pa.) News and several other newspapers; during World War II enlisted in the United States Naval Reserve in 1942 and served in the South Pacific as a lieutenant until discharged in 1945; in 1944 while still in the service was elected to the Seventy-ninth Congress but did not take his seat until February 2, 1945; reelected to the Eightieth and to the six succeeding Congresses (January 3, 1945–January 3, 1961); delegate to the United Nations Conference on Trade and Employment at Habana in 1947 and 1948, and to the fourteenth General Assembly of United Nations in 1959. *Reelected to the Eighty-seventh Congress.*

FULTON, John Hall (brother of Andrew Steele Fulton), a Representative from Virginia; born in Augusta County, Va.; attended the common schools and was graduated from Hampden-Sidney College, Hampden-Sidney, Va.; studied law; was admitted to the bar and commenced practice in Abingdon, Va.; member of the State house of delegates in 1823 and 1824; served in the State senate 1829–1831; elected as a Whig to the Twenty-third Congress (March 4, 1833–March 3, 1835); unsuccessful candidate for reelection in 1834 to the Twenty-fourth Congress; also was a candidate for election to the Twenty-fifth Congress at the time of his death in Abingdon, Washington County, Va., January 28, 1836; interment in Sinking Spring Cemetery.

FULTON, William Savin, a Senator from Arkansas; born in Cecil County, Md., June 2, 1795; pursued classical studies, and was graduated from Baltimore College in 1813; commenced the study of law, but during the War of 1812 enlisted in a company of Volunteers at Fort McHenry; after the war moved to Tennessee and resumed the study of law; was admitted to the bar in 1817 and commenced practice in Gallatin, Tenn.; military secretary to General Jackson in his Florida campaign in 1818; moved to Alabama in 1820 and settled in Florence; elected judge of the county court in 1822; appointed by President Jackson secretary of the Territory of Arkansas in 1829; appointed Governor of Arkansas March 9, 1835, and served until its admission into the Union in 1836; upon the admission of Arkansas as a State was elected as a Democrat to the United States Senate; reelected in 1840 and served from September 18, 1836, until his death in Little Rock, Ark., August 15, 1844; interment Mount Holly Cemetery.

FUNK, Benjamin Franklin (father of Frank Hamilton Funk), a Representative from Illinois; born in Funks Grove Township, McLean County, Ill., October 17, 1838; attended the public schools and Wesleyan University in Bloomington; left school in 1862 to enlist in the Sixty-eighth Regiment, Illinois Volunteer Infantry, as a private, and served five months during the Civil War; returned to the university and finished the course; engaged in agricultural pursuits; moved to Bloomington, Ill., in 1869; mayor of Bloomington 1871–1876 and 1884–1886; trustee of the asylum for the blind at Jacksonville; president of the board of trustees of Wesleyan University for twenty years; delegate to the Republican National Convention at Chicago in 1888; elected as a Republican to the Fifty-third Congress (March 4, 1893–March 3, 1895); unsuccessful candidate for renomination in 1894; resumed agricultural pursuits; died in Bloomington, Ill., February 14, 1909; interment in Bloomington Cemetery.

FUNK, Frank Hamilton (son of Benjamin Franklin Funk), a Representative from Illinois; born in Bloomington, McLean County, Ill., April 5, 1869; attended the public schools and the Illinois Normal School at Normal, Ill.; was graduated from the Lawrenceville School, Lawrenceville, N. J., in 1888 and from Yale University in 1891; engaged in agricultural pursuits and livestock production in Bloomington, Ill.; member of the Illinois Republican State central committee 1906–1912; member of the State senate 1909–1911; unsuccessful candidate of the Progressive Party for Governor of Illinois in 1912; chairman of the Illinois delegation to the Progressive National Conventions in 1912 and 1916; unsuccessful Progressive nominee for United States Senator in 1913; commissioner on the Illinois Public Utilities Commission 1914–1921; delegate to the Republican National Convention at St. Louis in 1920; elected as a Republican to the Sixty-seventh, Sixty-eighth, and Sixty-ninth Congresses (March 4, 1921–March 3, 1927); unsuccessful candidate for renomination in 1926; retired from public life and active business pursuits; resided at Bloomington, Ill., until his death there on November 24, 1940; interment in Funk's Grove Cemetery, Funk's Grove, Ill.

FUNSTON, Edward Hogue, a Representative from Kansas; born near New Carlisle, Clark County, Ohio, September 16, 1836; attended the country schools, Lindle Hill Academy, New Carlisle, Ohio, and Marietta (Ohio) College; taught school; during the Civil War entered the Union Army in 1861 as lieutenant, Sixteenth Ohio Battery; participated in the principal engagements along the Mississippi River; mustered out in 1865; located on a prairie farm near Carlyle, Allen County, Kans., in 1867; member of the State house of representatives 1873–1876, and served as speaker in 1875; member of the State senate 1880–1884, and served as president pro tempore in 1880; elected as a Republican to the Forty-eighth Congress to fill the vacancy caused by the death of Dudley C. Haskell; reelected to the Forty-ninth and to the three succeeding Congresses and served from March 21, 1884, to March 3, 1893; presented credentials as a Member-elect to the Fifty-third Congress and served from March 4, 1893, until August 2, 1894, when he was succeeded by Horace L. Moore, who contested the election; resumed agricultural pursuits; died in Iola, Kans., on September 10, 1911; interment in Iola Cemetery.

FURCOLO, Foster, a Representative from Massachusetts; born in New Haven, Conn., July 29, 1911; attended the public schools of New Haven, Conn., and Springfield, Mass.; was graduated from Yale University, New Haven, Conn., in 1933 and from its law school in 1936; was admitted to the Massachusetts bar in 1937 and commenced the practice of law in Springfield, Mass., the same year; during World War II served in the

United States Navy with service in the Pacific Theater; elected as a Democrat to the Eighty-first and Eighty-second Congresses and served from January 3, 1949, until his resignation September 30, 1952; elected State treasurer on November 4, 1952, and served until 1954; unsuccessful candidate for election in 1954 to the United States Senate; elected Governor of Massachusetts in 1956 for the term commencing January 1957; reelected in 1958 for the term ending January 1961; unsuccessful for the Democratic nomination for United States Senator in 1960; resides in Longmeadow, Mass.

FURLONG, Robert Grant, a Representative from Pennsylvania; born in Roscoe, Washington County, Pa., January 4, 1886; attended the public schools at Roscoe, Pa.; was graduated from State Teachers College, California, Pa., in 1904 and from Jefferson Medical College, Philadelphia, Pa., in 1909; taught school at Roscoe, Pa., in 1904 and 1905; practiced medicine in Donora, Pa., 1912–1942; during the First World War served from September 27, 1918, as a first lieutenant with the Two Hundred and Eightieth Ambulance Company, Twentieth Division, until his discharge January 25, 1919; burgess of Donora, Pa., 1922–1926 and in 1941 and 1942; postmaster of Donora, Pa., 1933–1938; inheritance tax appraiser for Washington County, Pa., in 1938; elected as a Democrat to the Seventy-eighth Congress (January 3, 1943–January 3, 1945); unsuccessful candidate for renomination in 1944; resumed the practice of medicine; elected sheriff of Washington County, Pa., in 1945, 1949, 1953, 1957, and again in 1961 for a four-year term; is a resident of Donora, Pa.

FURLOW, Allen John, a Representative from Minnesota; born in Rochester, Olmsted County, Minn., November 9, 1890; attended the public schools; was graduated from Rochester High School in 1910; during the First World War enlisted October 1, 1917, as a private; served overseas as a pilot in the aviation branch of the Army; promoted to first lieutenant; honorably discharged February 21, 1919; after the war resumed his studies, and was graduated from the law department of George Washington University, Washington, D. C., in 1920; was admitted to the bar in 1920 and commenced practice in Rochester, Minn.; member of the Minnesota State senate 1923–1925; elected as a Republican to the Sixty-ninth and Seventieth Congresses (March 4, 1925–March 3, 1929); unsuccessful candidate for renomination in 1928; employed in the legal department of the Curtiss-Wright Corporation, Washington, D. C., in 1929 and 1930; in 1933 was appointed by the United States Attorney General as a special assistant in cases assigned under the petroleum code; was in the legal department of the Veterans Administration, Washington, D. C., 1934–1937; returned to Rochester, Minn., and practiced law until his death, January 29, 1954; interment in Oakwood Cemetery.

FYAN, Robert Washington, a Representative from Missouri; born in Bedford Springs, Bedford County, Pa., March 11, 1835; attended the common schools; studied law; was admitted to the bar in 1858 and commenced practice in Marshfield, Webster County, Mo.; county attorney in 1859; during the Civil War entered the Union Army in June 1861 as lieutenant colonel in Colonel Hampton's regiment, Webster County Home Guards, which was disbanded; in the same year was a captain and major in the Twenty-fourth Regiment, Missouri Volunteer Infantry, and colonel of the Forty-sixth Regiment, Missouri Volunteer Infantry; circuit attorney in 1865 and 1866; circuit judge of the fourteenth judicial circuit of Missouri from April 1866 to January 1883, having four years to serve when elected to Congress; member of the State constitutional convention in 1875; elected as a Democrat to the Forty-eighth Congress

(March 4, 1883–March 3, 1885); elected to the Fifty-second and Fifty-third Congressses (March 4, 1891–March 3, 1895); resumed the practice of law; died in Marshfield, Mo., July 28, 1896; interment in Lebanon Cemetery, Lebanon, Mo.

G

GABALDON, Isauro, a Resident Commissioner from the Philippine Islands; born in San Isidoro, Nueva Ecija, Philippine Islands, December 8, 1875; attended the public schools in Tebar, Spain, and the Colleges Quintanar del Rey and Villa Nueva de la Jara, Cuenca, Spain; studied law in the Universidad Central, Madrid, Spain, and was graduated from the Universidad Santo Tomas, Manila, Philippine Islands, in 1900; practiced law from 1903 to 1906; Governor of the Province of Nueva Ecija in 1906 and 1912–1916; member of the Philippine House of Representatives 1907–1911; served in the Philippine Senate 1916–1919; elected as a Nationalist a Resident Commissioner to the United States in 1920; reelected in 1923 and 1925, and served from March 4, 1920, until his resignation effective July 16, 1928, having been nominated for election to the Philippine House of Representatives; had also been elected in 1925 as a member of the Philippine House of Representatives, but did not qualify, preferring to continue as Commissioner; died in Manila, Philippine Islands, December 21, 1942; interment in North Cemetery in Manila.

GADSDEN, Christopher, a Delegate from South Carolina, born in Charleston, S. C., February 16, 1723; attended preparatory and classical schools in England; employed in a commercial house in Philadelphia, Pa., 1742–1745; delegate to the Colonial Congress that met in New York in 1765; Member of the First Continental Congress in Philadelphia, Pa., 1774–1776; served as an officer in the Continental Army 1776–1783, and participated in the defense of Charleston in 1780; entered the service as colonel and subsequently attained the rank of brigadier general; was a framer of the State constitution in 1778; Lieutenant Governor 1778–1780; elected Governor of South Carolina in 1781, but declined; died in Charleston, S. C., September 15, 1805; interment in St. Philip's Churchyard.

GAGE, Joshua, a Representative from Massachusetts; born in Harwich, Mass., on August 7, 1763; completed preparatory studies; in 1795 moved to Augusta, Maine (until 1820 a district of Massachusetts); was a master mariner, and subsequently became engaged in mercantile pursuits; member of the Massachusetts House of Representatives in 1805 and 1807; served in the State senate in 1813 and 1815; treasurer of Kennebec County, Maine, 1810–1831; elected as a Democrat to the Fifteenth Congress (March 4, 1817–March 3, 1819); member of the Maine Executive Council in 1822 and 1823; died in Augusta, Maine, January 24, 1831; interment in Augusta, Maine.

GAHN, Harry Conrad, a Representative from Ohio; born in Elmore, Ottawa County, Ohio, April 26, 1880; attended the public and high schools; taught school three years; was graduated from the law department of the University of Michigan at Ann Arbor in 1904; was admitted to the bar and commenced practice in Cleveland, Ohio; attorney for the Cleveland Legal Aid Society 1909–1911; member of the city council 1910–1921, serving as its president in 1918 and 1919; member of the Cleveland River and Harbor Commission 1911–1921; treasurer of the American Association of Port Authorities 1912–1919; was in charge of Liberty Loan campaigns in his district during the First World War; elected as a Republican to the Sixty-seventh Congress (March 4, 1921–March 3, 1923); unsuccessful candidate for reelection in 1922 to the Sixty-eighth Congress and for election in 1936 to the Seventy-fifth Congress; resumed the practice of his profession; solicitor for Independence, Ohio, 1936–1956; during World War II served on Selective Service Board No. 32 of Cleveland, Ohio, 1940–1946; is a resident of Cleveland, Ohio.

GAILLARD, John (uncle of Theodore Gaillard Hunt), a Senator from South Carolina; born in St. Stephens District, S. C., September 5, 1765; educated for the legal profession in England; member of the State house of representatives; served in the State senate in 1804; elected as a Democrat to the United States Senate to fill the vacancy caused by the resignation of Pierce Butler; reelected in 1806, 1812, 1818, and 1824 and served from December 6, 1804, until his death; chosen President pro tempore of the Senate on February 28 and April 17, 1810, April 18, 1814, and again upon the death of Vice President Gerry and served from November 25, 1814, to March 4, 1817; again chosen on March 6, 1817, January 25, 1820, February 1, 1822, February 19, 1823, May 21, 1824, and March 9, 1825; died in Washington, D. C., February 26, 1826; interment in the Congressional Cemetery.

GAINES, John Pollard, a Representative from Kentucky; born in Augusta, Va. (now West Virginia), September 22, 1795; moved to Boone County, Ky., in early youth; received a thorough English training; studied law; was admitted to the bar and commenced practice in Walton, Ky.; volunteered for service in the War of 1812; was in the Battle of the Thames and other engagements; represented Boone County for several years in the Kentucky Legislature; served in the Mexican War as major in Gen. Thomas Marshall's Kentucky Cavalry Brigade and also as aide-de-camp on the staff of Gen. Winfield Scott; captured at Incarnacion in January 1847 and was confined for several months in the City of Mexico; while in captivity was elected as a Whig to the Thirtieth Congress (March 4, 1847–March 3, 1849); unsuccessful candidate for reelection; appointed Governor of Oregon Territory in 1850 and served until the expiration of his term in 1853; resumed agricultural pursuits; died near Salem, Marion County, Oreg., December 9, 1857; interment in Odd Fellows Cemetery, Salem, Oreg.

GAINES, John Wesley, a Representative from Tennessee; born in Wrencoe, near Nashville, Davidson County, Tenn., August 24, 1860; attended private and public schools, in which he also taught; studied law at home; studied medicine, and was graduated from the University of Nashville and from Vanderbilt University, Nashville, Tenn., in 1882; never practiced medicine, but the day after graduation resumed the study of law; was admitted to the bar in 1884 and commenced practice in Nashville in 1885; presidential elector on the Democratic ticket of Cleveland and Stevenson in 1892; elected as a Democrat to the Fifty-fifth and to the five succeeding Congresses (March 4, 1897–March 3, 1909); unsuccessful for reelection in 1908 to the Sixty-first Congress; practiced law in Nashville, Tenn., where he died July 4, 1926; interment in Mount Olivet Cemetery.

GAINES, Joseph Holt, a Representative from West Virginia; born in Washington, D. C., September 3, 1864; moved with his parents to Fayette County, W. Va., in 1867; attended the University of West Virginia at Morgantown and was graduated from Princeton College in 1886; was admitted to the bar in 1887 and commenced practice in Fayetteville, W. Va.; appointed United States district attorney for West Virginia by President McKinley in 1897; resigned in 1901; elected as a Republican to the Fifty-seventh and to the four succeeding Congresses (March 4, 1901–March 3, 1911); unsuccessful candidate for reelection in 1910 to the Sixty-second Congress; resumed the practice of law in Charleston, W. Va.; died in Montgomery, W. Va., April 12, 1951; interment in Spring Hill Cemetery, Charleston, W. Va.

GAINES, William Embre, a Representative from Virginia; born near Charlotte Court House, Charlotte County, Va., August 30, 1844; attended the common schools; during the Civil War enlisted as a private in Company K, Eighteenth Virginia Regiment (Pickett's division); reenlisted in the Army of the Cape Fear, and surrendered with Johnston, near Greensboro, N. C., in April 1865, having attained the rank of adjutant of Manly's artillery battalion; studied law; was admitted to the bar and practiced; engaged in the tobacco business and banking at Burkeville, Va.; member of the State senate from 1883 to 1887, when he resigned; delegate to the Republican National Convention at Chicago in 1884; mayor of Burkeville; delegate to several State conventions; elected as a Republican to the Fiftieth Congress (March 4, 1887–March 3, 1889); was not a candidate for renomination in 1888; died in Washington, D. C., May 4, 1912; interment in Glenwood Cemetery.

GAITHER, Nathan, a Representative from Kentucky; born near Mocksville, Davie County, N. C., September 15, 1788; completed preparatory studies; attended Bardstown College; studied medicine; was graduated from Jefferson Medical College and began practice in Columbia, Ky.; served as assistant surgeon in the War of 1812; member of the State house of representatives 1815–1818; presidential elector on the Democratic ticket of Jackson and Calhoun in 1829; elected as a Democrat to the Twenty-first and Twenty-second Congresses (March 4, 1829–March 3, 1833); unsuccessful candidate for reelection 1832 to the Twenty-third Congress; delegate to the State constitutional convention in 1849; again a member of the State house of representatives 1855–1857; resumed the practice of medicine; died in Columbia, Ky., August 12, 1862; interment in Columbia Cemetery.

GALBRAITH, John, a Representative from Pennsylvania; born in Huntingdon, Pa., on August 2, 1794; moved with his parents in 1796 to Allegheny Township, Huntingdon County, Pa., and subsequently, in 1802, to Centre Township, Butler County; attended the common schools; served an apprenticeship at the printer's trade; taught school; studied law; was admitted to the bar in 1817 and commenced practice in Butler, Pa.; moved to Franklin, Venango County, Pa., in 1822 and continued the practice of his profession; member of the State house of representatives 1829–1832; elected as a Democrat to the Twenty-third and Twenty-fourth Congresses (March 4, 1833–March 3, 1837); unsuccessful candidate for renomination in 1836; moved to Erie, Pa., in 1837; resumed the practice of law; elected to the Twenty-sixth Congress (March 4, 1839–March 3, 1841); was not a candidate for renomination in 1840; again engaged in the practice of law; elected president judge of the sixth judicial district in 1851 and served until his death in Erie, Pa., June 15, 1860; interment in Erie Cemetery.

GALE, George (father of Levin Gale), a Representative from Maryland; born in Somerset County, Md., June 3, 1756; attended the common schools; served during the Revolutionary War; member of the Maryland convention which ratified the Federal Constitution in 1788; elected to the First Congress (March 4, 1789–March 3, 1791); appointed by President Washington on March 4, 1791, supervisor of distilled liquors for the district of Maryland; died at "Brookland," Cecil County, Md., January 2, 1815; interment in the family burying ground on his estate.

GALE, Levin (son of George Gale), a Representative from Maryland; born in Elkton, Cecil County, Md., April 24, 1784; attended the common schools; studied law; was admitted to the bar and practiced in Elkton, Md.; member of the State senate in 1816; elected to the Twentieth Congress (March 4, 1827–March 3, 1829); declined to be a candidate for renomination in 1828; resumed the practice of law; died in Elkton, Md., December 18, 1834.

GALE, Richard Pillsbury, a Representative from Minnesota; born in Minneapolis, Minn., October 30, 1900; attended the public schools and Minnesota Farm School, University of Minnesota at Minneapolis; was graduated from Yale University, New Haven, Conn., in 1922; engaged in agricultural pursuits since 1923; member of the State house of representatives in 1939 and 1940; member of the Mound (Minn.) School Board for eight years; trustee of Blake School at Hopkins, Minn.; elected as a Republican to the Seventy-seventh and Seventy-eighth Congresses (January 3, 1941–January 3, 1945); unsuccessful candidate for reelection in 1944 to the Seventy-ninth Congress; resumed agricultural pursuits; is a resident of Mound, Minn.

GALLAGHER, Cornelius Edward, a Representative from New Jersey; born in Bayonne, N. J., March 2, 1921; attended the local schools of Bayonne; was graduated from John Marshall College, Jersey City, N. J., in 1946 and from John Marshall Law School in 1948; additional studies at New York University in 1948 and 1949; during World War II commanded an Infantry rifle company in General Patton's Third Army in Europe and served from September 1941 until discharged as a captain in November 1946; wounded three times; awarded eight decorations; served one year during the Korean War; was admitted to the bar in 1949 and commenced the practice of law in Bayonne, N. J.; served on faculty of Rutgers University in 1945 and 1946; director of the Broadway National Bank; elected to the Hudson County Board of Freeholders in 1953 and resigned in 1956; appointed commissioner of New Jersey Turnpike Authority in 1956, presently serving as vice chairman; delegate to the Democratic National Conventions in 1952, 1956, and 1960; elected as a Democrat to the Eighty-sixth Congress (January 3, 1959–January 3, 1961). *Reelected to the Eighty-seventh Congress.*

GALLAGHER, James A., a Representative from Pennsylvania; born in Philadelphia, Pa., January 16, 1869; attended the public schools and Pierce Business College, Philadelphia, Pa., 1891–1893; engaged in merchandise warehousing and transportation since 1886; also engaged in banking; elected as a Republican to the Seventy-eighth Congress (January 3, 1943–January 3, 1945); unsuccessful candidate for reelection in 1944 to the Seventy-ninth Congress; elected in 1946 to the Eightieth Congress (January 3, 1947–January 3, 1949); unsuccessful candidate for renomination in 1948; returned to merchandise warehousing and transportation business; died in Philadelphia, Pa., December 8, 1957; interment in Holy Cross Cemetery, Yeadon, Pa.

GALLAGHER, Thomas, a Representative from Illinois; born in Concord, Merrimack County, N. H., July 6, 1850; moved to Chicago in 1866; attended the public schools; learned the trade of iron molder; entered the hat business in Chicago in 1878; director of the Cook County State Savings Bank; member of the city council of Chicago 1893–1897; member of the board of education 1897–1903; chairman of the Democratic central committee of Cook County in 1902; president of the Democratic county committee in 1906 and 1907 and a member of the executive committee in 1909, 1911, and 1913; elected as a Democrat to the Sixty-first and to the five succeeding Congresses (March 4, 1909–March 3, 1921); unsuccessful candidate for reelection in 1920 to the Sixty-seventh Congress; retired from active pursuits and resided in Chicago, Ill.; died February 24, 1930, in San Antonio, Tex., while on a visit; interment in St. Boniface Cemetery, Chicago, Ill.

GALLAGHER, William James, a Representative from Minnesota; born in Minneapolis, Hennepin County, Minn., May 13, 1875; attended the public schools, and was graduated from North High School in 1894; engaged as an editorial employee and proofreader in Minneapolis, Minn., in 1895 and 1896; moved to Spokane, Wash., in 1897 and continued his former pursuits with a labor journal until 1899; returned to Minneapolis, Minn., and engaged as a trucker and clerk in freight houses until 1919; employed as a street sweeper for Hennepin County 1919–1927 and for the city of Minneapolis, Minn., from 1927 until his retirement in 1942; was elected as a Democrat to the Seventy-ninth Congress and served from January 3, 1945, until his death; had been renominated to the Eightieth Congress in 1946; died in a hospital at Rochester, Minn., August 13, 1946; interment in Crystal Lake Cemetery, Minneapolis, Minn.

GALLATIN, Albert, a Senator and a Representative from Pennsylvania; born in Geneva, Switzerland, January 29, 1761; was graduated from the University of Geneva in 1779; immigrated to the United States and settled in Boston, Mass., in 1780; served in the Revolutionary Army; instructor of French in Harvard University in 1782; moved to Virginia in 1785 and settled on a tract of land in Fayette County (now in Pennsylvania) which he purchased; his estate becoming a portion of Pennsylvania, he was made a member of the Pennsylvania constitutional convention in 1789; member of the State house of representatives 1790–1792; presented credentials as a Senator-elect on February 28, 1793; no action was taken during the Second Congress, but on December 2, 1793, he took his seat, at which time a petition was presented alleging he had not been a citizen of the United States the term of years required by the Constitution, and on February 28, 1794, the Senate declared the election void; elected a member of the State house of representatives, but declined; elected as a Democrat to the Fourth, Fifth, and Sixth Congresses (March 4, 1795–March 3, 1801); was not a candidate for renomination in 1800; appointed Secretary of the Treasury by President Jefferson January 26, 1802; reappointed by President Madison, and held the position until February 9, 1814, when appointed one of the commissioners to negotiate the Treaty of Ghent, which was signed December 24, 1814; one of the commissioners which negotiated a commercial convention with Great Britain in 1816; appointed United States Envoy Extraordinary and Minister Plenipotentiary to France by President Madison in 1815 and served until 1823; Minister Plenipotentiary to Great Britain from May 10, 1826, to October 4, 1827; returned to New York City and became president of the National Bank of New York; died in Astoria, N. Y., August 12, 1849; interment in Trinity Churchyard, New York City, N. Y.

GALLEGOS, José Manuel, a Delegate from the Territory of New Mexico; was born in what is now Rio Arriba County, N. Mex., October 30, 1815; attended parochial schools; studied theology at the College of Durango, Republic of Mexico, and was graduated in 1840; member of the legislative assembly of what was then the Department of New Mexico, Republic of Mexico, 1843–1846; member of the first Territorial council of the Territory of New Mexico in 1851; elected as a Democrat to the Thirty-third Congress (March 4, 1853–March 3, 1855); presented credentials as a Delegate-elect to the Thirty-fourth Congress and served from March 4, 1855, to July 23, 1856, when he was succeeded by Miguel A. Otero, who contested his election; member of the Territorial house of representatives 1860–1862 and served as speaker; unsuccessful candidate for election in 1862 to the Thirty-eighth Congress; made a prisoner of war by the Texas Confederate troops in 1862; treasurer of the Territory in 1865 and 1866; superintendent of Indian affairs in New

Mexico in 1868; elected as a Democrat to the Forty-second Congress (March 4, 1871–March 3, 1873); unsuccessful candidate for reelection in 1872 to the Forty-third Congress; died in Santa Fe, N. Mex., April 21, 1875; interment in the Catholic Cemetery.

GALLINGER, Jacob Harold, a Representative and a Senator from New Hampshire; born in Cornwall, Ontario, Canada, March 28, 1837; attended the common schools and completed an academic course; became a printer in early life; studied medicine, and was graduated from the Cincinnati (Ohio) Medical Institute in 1858; studied abroad for two years; returned to the United States and engaged in the practice of medicine and surgery in Concord, N. H., in April 1862; member of the State house of representatives in 1872, 1873, and 1891; member of the State constitutional convention in 1876; served in the State senate 1878–1880, and was president of that body the last two years; was surgeon general of New Hampshire, with the rank of brigadier general, in 1879 and 1880; chairman of the Republican State committee from 1882 to 1890, when he resigned; again elected to the position in 1898, 1900, 1902, 1904, and 1906; resigned in 1908; chairman of the delegation from New Hampshire to the Republican National Conventions in 1888, 1900, 1904, and 1908; chairman of the Merchant Marine Commission in 1904 and 1905; elected as a Republican to the Forty-ninth and Fiftieth Congresses (March 4, 1885–March 3, 1889); declined to be a candidate for reelection in 1888 to the Fifty-first Congress; elected as a Republican to the United States Senate in 1891; reelected in 1897, 1903, 1909, and 1914, and served from March 4, 1891, until his death in Franklin, N. H., August 17, 1918; interment in Blossom Hill Cemetery, Concord, N. H.

GALLIVAN, James Ambrose, a Representative from Massachusetts; born in Boston, Mass., October 22, 1866; attended the public schools; was graduated from the Boston Latin School (the first public school in the United States) in 1884 and from Harvard University in 1888; engaged in newspaper work in 1888; member of the State house of representatives in 1895 and 1896; served in the State senate in 1897 and 1898; street commissioner of Boston 1900–1914; elected as a Democrat to the Sixty-third Congress to fill the vacancy caused by the resignation of James M. Curley; reelected to the Sixty-fourth and to the six succeeding Congresses and served from April 7, 1914, until his death in Arlington, Mass., April 3, 1928; interment in St. Joseph's Cemetery (West Roxbury), Boston, Mass.

GALLOWAY, Joseph, a Delegate from Pennsylvania; born at West River, Anne Arundel County, Md., about 1729; moved with his father to Pennsylvania in 1740; received a liberal schooling; studied law; was admitted to the bar and began practice in Philadelphia, Pa.; member of the Pennsylvania Colonial House of Representatives 1757–1775, and served as speaker 1766–1774; Member of the Continental Congress in 1775; signed the nonimportation agreement, but was opposed to independence of the Colonies and remained loyal to the King; in December 1776 joined the British Army of General Howe in New York; moved to England in 1778; the same year the General Assembly of Pennsylvania convicted him of high treason and confiscated his estates, valued at about £40,000; died in Watford, Herts, England, August 29, 1803.

GALLOWAY, Samuel, a Representative from Ohio; born in Gettysburg, Pa., March 20, 1811; attended the public schools; moved to Ohio and settled in Highland County in 1830; graduated from Miami University, Oxford, Ohio, in 1833; attended Princeton Theological Seminary in 1835 and 1836; taught school in Hamilton, Ohio, 1836 and 1837, in Miami University in 1837 and 1838, and in Hanover College, Indiana, in 1839 and 1840;

studied law; was admitted to the bar in 1843 and commenced practice in Chillicothe, Ohio; secretary of state in 1844; moved to Columbus in 1844; delegate to the Whig National Convention at Philadelphia in 1848; elected as a Republican to the Thirty-fourth Congress (March 4, 1855–March 3, 1857); unsuccessful candidate for reelection in 1856 to the Thirty-fifth Congress and for election in 1858 to the Thirty-sixth Congress; resumed the practice of law; during the Civil War appointed judge advocate of Camp Chase, Columbus, Ohio, by President Lincoln; appointed by President Johnson to investigate conditions in the South during the period of reconstruction; died in Columbus, Ohio, April 5, 1872; interment in Greenlawn Cemetery.

GALLUP, Albert, a Representative from New York; born in East Berne, Albany County, N. Y., January 30, 1796; received a limited schooling; studied law; was admitted to the bar and practiced in Albany; sheriff of Albany County 1831–1834; elected as a Democrat to the Twenty-fifth Congress (March 4, 1837–March 3, 1839); unsuccessful candidate for reelection in 1838 to the Twenty-sixth Congress; appointed by President Polk collector of customs at Albany; died in Providence, R. I., November 5, 1851; interment in Swan Point Cemetery.

GAMBLE, James, a Representative from Pennsylvania; born in Jersey Shore, Lycoming County, Pa., on January 28, 1809; attended the common schools and Jersey Shore (Pa.) Academy; studied law; was admitted to the bar in December 1833 and commenced practice in Jersey Shore, Pa.; county treasurer 1834–1836; resumed the practice of law in Jersey Shore; member of the State house of representatives in 1841 and 1842; elected as a Democrat to the Thirty-second and Thirty-third Congresses (March 4, 1851–March 3, 1855); president judge of Clearfield County in 1859 and 1860; president judge of the court of common pleas of Lycoming County 1868–1878; retired from public life; died in Williamsport, Lycoming County, Pa., February 22, 1883; interment in Wildwood Cemetery.

GAMBLE, John Rankin (brother of Robert Jackson Gamble and uncle of Ralph Abernethy Gamble), a Representative from South Dakota; born in Alabama, Genesee County, N. Y., January 15, 1848; attended the common schools; moved with his parents to Fox Lake, Wis., in 1862; was graduated from Lawrence University, Appleton, Wis., in 1872; studied law; was admitted to the bar in 1873 and commenced practice in Yankton, Territory of Dakota (now South Dakota); district attorney for Yankton County 1876–1878; United States attorney for Dakota Territory in 1878; member of the Territorial house of representatives 1877–1879; served in the Territorial council 1881–1885; elected as a Republican to the Fifty-second Congress and served from March 4, 1891, until his death in Yankton, S. Dak., August 14, 1891, before the assembling of the Congress; interment in Yankton Cemetery.

GAMBLE, Ralph Abernethy (son of Robert Jackson Gamble and nephew of John Rankin Gamble), a Representative from New York; born in Yankton, S. Dak., May 6, 1885; attended the public schools of Yankton, S. Dak., and Washington, D. C.; was graduated from Tome Prep School, Port Deposit, Md., in 1905, from Princeton University, Princeton, N. J., in 1909, from George Washington Law School, Washington, D. C., in 1911, and from Columbia University Law School, New York, N. Y., in 1912; was admitted to the bar in 1913 and commenced practice in New York City; counsel for the town of Mamaroneck, N. Y., 1918–1933, and for Larchmont, N. Y., 1926–1928; member of the State assembly 1931–1937; elected as a Republican to the Seventy-fifth Congress to fill the vacancy caused by the resignation of Charles D. Millard; reelected to the Seventy-sixth and

to the eight succeeding Congresses and served from November 2, 1937, to January 3, 1957; was not a candidate for renomination in 1956; retired and resided in St. Michaels, Md., until his death there on March 4, 1959; interment in Hopewell Cemetery, Port Deposit, Md.

GAMBLE, Robert Jackson (brother of John Rankin Gamble and father of Ralph Abernethy Gamble), a Representative and a Senator from South Dakota; born in Genesee County, near Akron, Erie County, N. Y., February 7, 1851; moved with his parents to Fox Lake, Wis., in 1862; was graduated from Lawrence University, Appleton, Wis., in 1874; studied law; was admitted to the bar in 1875 and commenced practice in Yankton, Territory of Dakota (now South Dakota); district attorney for the second judicial district of the Territory of Dakota in 1880; city attorney of Yankton in 1881 and 1882; member of the Territorial council in 1885; chairman of the Republican State conventions in 1892 and 1893; elected as a Republican to the Fifty-fourth Congress (March 4, 1895–March 3, 1897); unsuccessful candidate for reelection in 1896 to the Fifty-fifth Congress; elected to the Fifty-sixth Congress (March 4, 1899–March 3, 1901); elected as a Republican to the United States Senate in 1901; reelected in 1906, and served from March 4, 1901, to March 3, 1913; unsuccessful candidate for renomination in 1912; moved to Sioux Falls, S. Dak., in 1915; resumed the practice of law; referee in bankruptcy, southern district of South Dakota, 1916–1924; member of the National Executive Committee of the League to Enforce Peace and chairman of the South Dakota branch; director of the American Red Cross for South Dakota in 1917; member of the American Bar Association, National Institute of Social Science, and the State Historical Society; died in Sioux Falls, S. Dak., September 22, 1924; interment in Yankton Cemetery, Yankton, S. Dak.

GAMBLE, Roger Lawson, a Representative from Georgia; born near Louisville, Jefferson County, Ga., in 1787; completed preparatory studies; studied law; was admitted to the bar about 1815 and commenced practice in Louisville, Ga.; cotton planter; served in the War of 1812 as a commissioned officer; member of the State house of representatives in 1814 and 1815; elected as a Democrat to the Twenty-third Congress (March 4, 1833–March 3, 1835; unsuccessful candidate for reelection in 1834 to the Twenty-fourth Congress; elected as a Whig to the Twenty-seventh Congress (March 4, 1841–March 3, 1843); unsuccessful candidate for reelection in 1842 to the Twenty-eighth Congress; judge of the superior court of Georgia 1845–1847; died in Augusta, Ga., December 20, 1847; interment in Old Capitol Cemetery, Louisville, Ga.

GAMBRILL, Stephen Warfield, a Representative from Maryland; born near Savage, Howard County, Md., October 2, 1873; attended the common schools and Maryland Agricultural College (now Maryland University); was graduated from the law department of Columbian College (now George Washington University), Washington, D. C., in 1896; was admitted to the bar in 1897 and practiced in Baltimore, Md.; member of the State house of delegates 1920–1922; served in the State senate in 1924; elected as a Democrat to the Sixty-eighth Congress to fill the vacancy caused by the death of Sidney E. Mudd; reelected to the Sixty-ninth and to the six succeeding Congresses and served from November 4, 1924, until his death; had been reelected to the Seventy-sixth Congress; died in Washington, D. C., on December 19, 1938; interment in Cedar Hill Cemetery.

GANDY, Harry Luther, a Representative from South Dakota; born in Churubusco, Whitley County, Ind., August 13, 1881; attended the public schools; was graduated from Tri-State

College, Angola, Ind., in 1901; moved to Rapid City, Pennington County, S. Dak., in 1907; publisher of the Wasta (S. Dak.) Gazette 1910–1918; United States commissioner at Wasta, S. Dak., 1910–1913; member of the State senate in 1911; appointed by President Wilson as receiver of public moneys of the United States land office at Rapid City and served from July 16, 1913, to March 3, 1915; elected as a Democrat to the Sixty-fourth, Sixth-fifth, and Sixty-sixth Congresses (March 4, 1915–March 3, 1921); unsuccessful candidate for reelection in 1920 to the Sixty-seventh Congress; engaged in agricultural pursuits and in the raising of livestock near Wasta, S. Dak., 1910–1945; executive secretary of the National Coal Association, Washington, D. C., 1923–1930; connected with subsidiary companies of the Pittston Co., 1930–1937; chairman Bituminous Coal Producers Board, Cincinnati, Ohio, 1937–1940; assistant to the president, Elk River Coal & Lumber Co. and Buffalo Creek & Gauley Railroad Co., Widen, W. Va., from 1944 until his retirement; died in Los Gatos, Calif., August 15, 1957; interment in Mountain View Cemetery, Rapid City, S. Dak.

GANLY, James Vincent, a Representative from New York; born in New York City September 13, 1878; attended the public schools and Packard Business College; engaged in the oil, real estate, and automobile businesses; member of the State assembly in 1907; was the first county clerk of Bronx County 1914–1918; elected as a Democrat to the Sixty-sixth Congress (March 4, 1919–March 3, 1921); unsuccessful candidate for reelection in 1920 to the Sixty-seventh Congress; elected to the Sixty-eighth Congress and served from March 4, 1923, until his death in an automobile accident in New York City September 7, 1923, before the convening of Congress; interment in St. Raymond's Cemetery, Borough of the Bronx, New York City.

GANNETT, Barzillai, a Representative from Massachusetts; born in Bridgewater, Mass., June 17, 1764; was graduated from Harvard University in 1785; studied theology, but did not enter the ministry; selectman of Pittston, Maine (then a district of Massachusetts), in 1793, 1794, 1796–1798, 1801, and 1802; town clerk in 1794; moderator 1797–1802; selectman and assessor, Gardiner, Maine, 1803–1808; appointed as the first postmaster of Gardiner and served from September 30, 1804, to October 1, 1809; moderator 1804–1806, 1808, 1809, and 1811; member of the Massachusetts House of Representatives in 1805 and 1806; served in the Massachusetts Senate in 1807 and 1808; elected as a Democrat to the Eleventh and Twelfth Congresses and served from March 4, 1809, until his resignation in 1812; died in New York City in 1832.

GANSEVOORT, Leonard, a Delegate from New York; born in Albany, N. Y., July 14, 1751; studied law; was admitted to the bar in 1771 and commenced practice in Albany, N. Y.; colonel of Light Cavalry in the Revolutionary War; member of the Provincial Congress in 1775 and 1776; president of New York from April 18 to May 14, 1777; clerk of Albany County in 1777 and 1778; member of the State assembly in 1778, 1779, and 1788; member of the commercial convention in Annapolis, Md., in 1786; Member of the Continental Congress in 1787 and 1788; served in the State senate 1791–1793; judge of Albany County 1794–1797; member of the council of appointment in 1797; judge of the probate court from 1799 until his death in Albany, N. Y., August 26, 1810; interment in Albany Rural Cemetery.

GANSON, John, a Representative from New York; born in Le Roy, Genesee County, N. Y., January 1, 1818; attended the public schools and Le Roy Academy; was graduated from Harvard University in 1839; studied law; was admitted to the bar in 1846 and commenced practice in Canandaigua, Ontario County,

N. Y.; moved to Buffalo the same year; member of the State senate in 1862 and 1863; elected as a Democrat to the Thirty-eighth Congress (March 4, 1863–March 3, 1865); was not a candidate for renomination in 1864; resumed the practice of law at Buffalo, N. Y.; railroad director; delegate to the Democratic National Convention at Chicago in 1864; died in Buffalo, N. Y., September 28, 1874; interment in Forest Lawn Cemetery.

GANTZ, Martin Kissinger, a Representative from Ohio; born in Bethel Township, Miami County, Ohio, January 28, 1862; attended the common schools and Lebanon (Ohio) College; was graduated from the Cincinnati Law College in 1883; was admitted to the bar in 1883 and commenced practice in Troy, Ohio; mayor of the city of Troy in 1889; elected as a Democrat to the Fifty-second Congress (March 4, 1891–March 3, 1893); unsuccessful candidate for reelection in 1892 to the Fifty-third Congress; resumed the practice of law in Troy; commissioner from the State of Ohio to the Louisiana Purchase Exposition in 1904; delegate to all Democratic State conventions from 1892 to 1906, inclusive; delegate to the Democratic National Convention at Denver in 1908; represented the Department of State on the directorate of El Banco Nacional de Nicaragua y El Ferrocarril del Pacífico de Nicaragua in 1914 and 1915; died in Troy, Ohio, February 10, 1916; interment in Riverside Cemetery.

GARBER, Harvey Cable, a Representative from Ohio; born in Hill Grove, Darke County, Ohio, July 6, 1866; moved to Greenville, Ohio, with his parents in 1872; attended the public schools; employed as a telegraph operator; manager of the Western Union Telegraph Co.; superintendent of the Central Union Telephone Co. for Ohio, and served four years as assistant general solicitor; member of the State house of representatives 1890–1893; vice chairman of the Democratic State central committee in 1900; chairman of the Democratic State committee in 1901 and chairman of the Democratic State executive committee 1902–1908; elected as a Democrat to the Fifty-eighth and Fifty-ninth Congresses (March 4, 1903–March 3, 1907); was not a candidate for renomination; moved to Columbus, Ohio, in 1910 and served as assistant to the president of the Bell Telephone Co. in Ohio, Indiana, and Illinois 1910–1915; engaged in manufacturing ignition products in 1915; also studied law; was admitted to the bar in 1921 and commenced practice in Columbus, Ohio; died at his winter home in Naples, Fla., March 23, 1938; interment in Greenville Cemetery, Greenville, Ohio.

GARBER, Jacob Aaron, a Representative from Virginia; born near Harrisonburg, Rockingham County, Va., January 25, 1879; attended the public schools of Rockingham County, and Bridgewater (Va.) College; principal of Brentsville Academy in 1904 and 1905; was graduated from Emerson College, Boston, Mass., in 1907; taught in Well's Memorial Institute, Boston, Mass., in 1906 and 1907; secretary of Emerson College in 1907 and 1908; moved to Timberville, Va., in 1908 and was employed as a bank cashier until 1924; served as treasurer of Rockingham County 1924–1929; member of the State house of delegates 1920–1922; interested in various orchard and canning organizations; elected as a Republican to the Seventy-first Congress (March 4, 1929–March 3, 1931); unsuccessful candidate for reelection in 1930 to the Seventy-second Congress; served as chief of the field and processing-tax divisions, Internal Revenue Office, Richmond, Va., 1931–1935; delegate to the Republican National Convention at Chicago in 1932; unsuccessful candidate for election in 1940 to the Seventy-seventh Congress; served in the State senate 1945–1947; from 1935 until his death devoted his time to the operation of commerical orchards and in the handling of grain and other farm products; died in Harrisonburg, Va., December 2, 1953; interment in Church of the Brethren Cemetery, Timberville, Va.

GARBER, Milton Cline, a Representative from Oklahoma; born in Humboldt, Calif., November 30, 1867; was reared on a farm in Iowa; attended the common schools, Upper Iowa University at Fayette 1887–1890, and the law department of the University of Iowa at Iowa City 1891–1893; settled in Oklahoma upon the opening of the Cherokee Strip; was admitted to the bar in 1893 and commenced the practice of law in Guthrie, Okla.; in company with his father and brother founded the town of Garber in 1893 and opened up the Garber oil fields; appointed probate judge of Garfield County in 1902 and subsequently elected in 1904; appointed associate justice of the supreme court of the Territory of Oklahoma and trial judge of the fifth judicial district by President Theodore Roosevelt in 1906, serving in these capacities until Oklahoma became a State; elected judge of the twentieth judicial district in 1908 and served until 1912, when he resigned; resumed the practice of law; mayor of Enid, Okla., 1919–1921; engaged in the newspaper business and in agricultural pursuits; elected as a Republican to the Sixty-eighth and to the four succeeding Congresses (March 4, 1923–March 3, 1933); unsuccessful candidate for reelection in 1932 to the Seventy-third Congress; co-publisher and editor of two daily papers in Enid, Okla.; died at a summer camp in Alexandria, Minn., September 12, 1948; interment in Memorial Park Cemetery, Enid, Okla.

GARD, Warren, a Representative from Ohio; born in Hamilton, Butler County, Ohio, July 2, 1873; attended the public schools, and was graduated from the Cincinnati Law School in 1894; was admitted to the bar in 1894 and commenced practice in Hamilton, Ohio; prosecuting attorney of Butler County 1898–1903; judge of the court of common pleas 1907–1912; elected as a Democrat to the Sixty-third and to the three succeeding Congresses (March 4, 1913–March 3, 1921); was not a candidate for renomination in 1920; resumed the practice of law in Hamilton, Ohio, where he died November 1, 1929; interment in Greenwood Cemetery.

GARDENIER, Barent, a Representative from New York; born in Kingston, Ulster County, N. Y.; completed preparatory studies; studied law; was admitted to the bar and practiced; held several local offices; elected as a Federalist to the Tenth and Eleventh Congresses (March 4, 1807–March 3, 1811); declined to be a candidate for renomination in 1810; engaged in the practice of law in Ulster and Columbia Counties; district attorney of the first district from March 1813 to April 1815; died in Kingston, N. Y., January 10, 1822; interment beneath the First Reformed Dutch Church of that city.

GARDINER, John, a Delegate from Rhode Island; born in South Kingstown, R. I., in 1747; engaged in agricultural pursuits in Narragansett, R. I.; served in the Revolutionary War; captain of the "Kingstown Reds" in 1775 and 1776; representative to the general assembly by the Paper Money Party in 1786 and 1787; Member of the Continental Congress in 1789; justice of the peace for South Kingstown in 1791; died in South Kingstown, R. I., October 18, 1808.

GARDINER, Sylvester, a Delegate from Rhode Island; born in South Kingstown, R. I., about 1730; admitted a freeman from West Greenwich, Kent County, R. I., in 1757; commissioned major for Kings County in 1769 and again in 1770; justice of the peace for North Kingstown in 1774; deputy from North Kingstown in 1775; appointed one of the men to take account of the powder, arms, and ammunition in 1775; appointed on the committee to cause the removal of livestock in 1775; again a deputy from North Kingstown 1776–1778, 1780, and 1781; appointed major in Kings County Militia in 1780; made sixth assistant in 1781 and again in 1782; justice of the court of common pleas for

Washington County 1781–1788; again made assistant in 1783; elected a Delegate to the Continental Congress in 1787, but did not take his seat; deputy from North Kingstown in 1790; chief justice of the court of common pleas in 1792; died in North Kingstown, R. I., in 1803.

GARDNER, Augustus Peabody, a Representative from Massachusetts; born in Boston, Mass., November 5, 1865; attended St. Paul's School, Concord, N. H., and was graduated from Harvard University in 1886; studied law in Harvard Law School, but never practiced, devoting himself to the management of his estate; captain and assistant adjutant general on the staff of Gen. James H. Wilson during the Spanish-American War; member of the State senate 1900 and 1901; elected as a Republican to the Fifty-seventh Congress to fill the vacancy caused by the resignation of William H. Moody; reelected to the Fifty-eighth and to the seven succeeding Congresses and served from November 3, 1902, until May 15, 1917, when he resigned to enter the Army; during the First World War served at Governors Island and in Macon, Ga., as colonel in the Adjutant General's Department, and later was transferred at his own request to the One Hundred and Thirty-first Regiment, United States Infantry, with the rank of major; died at Camp Wheeler, Macon, Ga., January 14, 1918; interment in Arlington National Cemetery, Fort Myer, Va.

GARDNER, Edward Joseph, a Representative from Ohio; born in Hamilton, Butler County, Ohio, August 7, 1898; attended the parochial schools; was graduated from the College of Commerce and Finance of St. Xavier University, Cincinnati, Ohio, in 1920; took post-graduate work at Wharton School of Business of the University of Pennsylvania at Philadelphia and at the University of Cincinnati, Cincinnati, Ohio; during the First World War served as a private in the United States Army in 1918; district controller of a food distributing company at Philadelphia, Pa., 1920–1924; public accountant, Hamilton, Ohio, 1924–1950; president of Hamilton City Council and vice mayor 1926–1928; member of the State house of representatives in 1937, 1938, 1941, and 1942; elected as a Democrat to the Seventy-ninth Congress (January 3, 1945–January 3, 1947); unsuccessful candidate for reelection in 1946 to the Eightieth Congress; continued his profession as an accountant; died in Hamilton, Ohio, December 7, 1950; interment in St. Mary's Cemetery.

GARDNER, Francis, a Representative from New Hampshire; born in Leominster, Mass., on December 27, 1771; was graduated from Harvard University in 1793; studied law; was admitted to the bar in Cheshire County, N. H., in 1796 and commenced practice at Walpole, N. H.; moved to Keene, N. H., in 1806; solicitor of Cheshire County 1807–1820; elected to the Tenth Congress (March 4, 1807–March 3, 1809); was not a candidate for reelection in 1808; died at the home of his son in Roxbury, Mass., June 25, 1835.

GARDNER, Frank, a Representative from Indiana; born on a farm in Finley Township, near Scottsburg, Scott County, Ind., May 8, 1872; attended the rural schools; was graduated from Borden Institute, Clark County, Ind., in 1896 and from the law department of the University of Indiana at Bloomington in 1900; was admitted to the bar in 1900 and commenced the practice of law in Scottsburg, Ind.; auditor of Scott County 1903–1911; county attorney 1911–1917; member of the Democratic county committee and served as chairman 1912–1922; served as field examiner for the State board of accounts 1911–1920; elected as a Democrat to the Sixty-eighth, Sixty-ninth, and Seventieth Congresses (March 4, 1923–March 3, 1929); unsuccessful candidate for reelection in 1928 to the Seventy-first Congress; resumed the practice of law in Scottsburg, Ind.; elected judge of the sixth judicial circuit of Indiana in 1930; reelected in 1936 and served until his death in Scottsburg, Ind., February 1, 1937; interment in Scottsburg Cemetery.

GARDNER, Gideon, a Representative from Massachusetts; born in Nantucket, Mass., May 30, 1759; received a limited schooling; was a successful shipmaster, and later became a shipowner; also engaged in mercantile pursuits; elected to the Eleventh Congress (March 4, 1809–March 3, 1811); resumed his former business pursuits; was the bearer of a petition from the citizens of Nantucket to Congress for tax relief in 1813; died in Nantucket, Mass., March 22, 1832; interment in Friends Burying Ground.

GARDNER, John James, a Representative from New Jersey; born in Atlantic County, N. J., October 17, 1845; attended the common schools and the law school of the University of Michigan at Ann Arbor in 1866 and 1867; served in the Sixth New Jersey Volunteers 1861–1865 and one year in the United States Veteran Volunteers; engaged in the real-estate and insurance business; elected alderman of Atlantic City, N. J., in 1867; mayor of Atlantic City 1868–1872, 1874, and 1875; member of the common council and coroner of Atlantic County in 1876; member of the State senate 1878–1893, serving as its president in 1883; engaged in agricultural pursuits; delegate to the Republican National Convention at Chicago in 1884; elected as a Republican to the Fifty-third and to the nine succeeding Congresses (March 4, 1893–March 3, 1913); unsuccessful candidate for reelection in 1912 to the Sixty-third Congress; resumed agricultural pursuits; died in Indian Mills, Burlington County, N. J., February 7, 1921; interment in Atlantic City Cemetery, Pleasantville, N. J.

GARDNER, Joseph, a Delegate from Pennsylvania; born in Honeybrook Township, Chester County, Pa., in 1752; studied medicine and practiced; raised a company of Volunteers in 1776 and commanded the Fourth Battalion of militia from Chester County; member of the committee of safety in 1776 and 1777; member of the State assembly 1776–1778 and of the supreme executive council in 1779; Member of the Continental Congress in 1784 and 1785; resumed the practice of medicine in Philadelphia, Pa., 1785–1792, and in Elkton, Md., 1792–1794; died in Elkton, Md., in 1794.

GARDNER, Mills, a Representative from Ohio; born in Russellville, Brown County, Ohio, January 30, 1830; attended the common schools of Highland County and Rankins Academy at Ripley, Ohio; moved to Fayette County in 1854; studied law; was admitted to the bar in 1855 and commenced practice at Washington Court House, Ohio; prosecuting attorney of Fayette County 1855–1859; member of the Ohio State Senate in 1862 and 1863; presidential elector on the Republican ticket of Lincoln and Johnson in 1864; member of the State house of representatives in 1866 and 1867; member of the State constitutional convention in 1872; elected as a Republican to the Forty-fifth Congress (March 4, 1877–March 3, 1879); was not a candidate for renomination in 1878; resumed the practice of law until his death; died at Washington Court House, Ohio, February 20, 1910; interment in Washington Cemetery.

GARDNER, Obadiah, a Senator from Maine; born in Grant (formerly Burchville), St. Clair County, Mich., September 13, 1850; moved to Union, Maine, with his parents in 1864; attended the common schools, Eastman's Business College, Poughkeepsie, N. Y., and Coburn Classical Institute, Waterville, Maine; engaged in the lumber, lime, and creamery business in Rockland,

Maine, and also in agricultural pursuits and in cattle raising; member of the city government in 1872; member of the State board of agriculture; master of the Maine State Grange 1897–1907; delegate to all Democratic State conventions from 1902 to 1910, inclusive; delegate to the Democratic National Convention at Baltimore in 1912; unsuccessful candidate for Governor of Maine in 1908; appointed chairman of the board of State assessors April 1, 1911, for six years, but resigned, having been appointed Senator; appointed and subsequently elected as a Democrat to the United States Senate to fill the vacancy caused by the death of William P. Frye and served from September 23, 1911, until March 3, 1913; unsuccessful candidate for reelection in 1913; appointed a member of the International Joint Commission created to prevent disputes regarding the use of the boundary waters between the United States and Canada October 1, 1913, and served as chairman of the United States section from December 1, 1914, to February 28, 1921, and from March 23, 1921, to April 5, 1923; returned to Rockland, Maine, and retired from public life and active business pursuits; moved to Augusta, Maine, where he died July 24, 1938; interment in Achorn Cemetery, Rockland, Maine.

GARDNER, Washington, a Representative from Michigan; born in Morrow County, Ohio, February 16, 1845; when sixteen years of age entered the Union Army during the Civil War, and served in Company D, Sixty-fifth Regiment, Ohio Volunteer Infantry, from October 1861 to December 1865; severely wounded in action at Resaca, Ga.; attended school at Berea. Ohio, the Hillsdale College, Hillsdale, Mich., and was graduated from the Ohio Wesleyan University, Delaware, Ohio, in 1870; studied in the school of theology, Boston University, Boston, Mass., in 1870 and 1871; was graduated from the Albany Law School in 1876; was admitted to the bar and commenced practice in Grand Rapids, Mich., and then entered the ministry of the Methodist Episcopal Church, in which he served twelve years; commander of the Department of Michigan, Grand Army of the Republic, in 1888; professor in Albion College 1889–1894; appointed secretary of state of Michigan in March 1894 and served until 1899; elected as a Republican to the Fifty-sixth and to the five succeeding Congresses (March 4, 1899–March 3, 1911); unsuccessful candidate for reelection in 1910 to the Sixty-second Congress; commander in chief of the Grand Army of the Republic in 1913 and 1914; Commissioner of Pensions from March 22, 1921, to March 4, 1925, when he resigned; retired from public life and died in Albion, Mich., March 31, 1928; interment in Riverside Cemetery.

GARFIELD, James Abram, a Representative from Ohio and a President of the United States; born in Orange, Cuyahoga County, Ohio, November 19, 1831; his boyhood was spent working on a farm, aiding in the support of his widowed mother; attended district school about three months each winter; at the age of seventeen was driver and helmsman on the Ohio Canal; entered Geauga Seminary, Chester, Ohio, in March 1849, and at the close of the fall term taught a district school; attended the Eclectic Institute, Hiram, Ohio, 1851–1854; was graduated from Williams College, Williamstown, Mass., in 1858; professor of ancient languages and literature in Hiram College, Hiram, Ohio; president of Hiram College 1857–1861; member of the State senate in 1859; studied law and was admitted to the bar in 1860; during the Civil War entered the Union Army; commissioned lieutenant colonel of the Forty-second Regiment, Ohio Volunteer Infantry, August 21, 1861; colonel November 27, 1861; brigadier general of Volunteers January 11, 1862; major general September 19, 1863; resigned December 5, 1863; elected as a Republican to the Thirty-eighth and to the eight succeeding Congresses and served from March 4, 1863, until November 8,

1880, when he resigned, having been elected President of the United States; appointed a member of the Electoral Commission created by act of Congress approved January 29, 1877, to decide the contests in various States in the presidential election of 1876; elected to the United States Senate on January 13, 1880, for the term beginning March 4, 1881, but declined to accept on December 23, 1880, having been elected President of the United States on November 4, 1880, to which office he had been nominated on June 8, 1880, in the Republican National Convention at Chicago; was inaugurated March 4, 1881; on the morning of July 2, 1881, while passing through the Pennsylvania Railroad Depot in Washington, D. C., was shot by Charles J. Guiteau; died from the effects of the wound, in Elberon, N. J., September 19, 1881; interment in Lake View Cemetery, Cleveland, Ohio.

GARFIELDE, Selucius, a Delegate from the Territory of Washington; born in Shoreham, Addison County, Vt., December 8, 1822; moved to Gallipolis, Ohio, and later to Paris, Ky., where he engaged in newspaper work; pursued an academic course; member of the State constitutional convention in 1849; immigrated to California in 1851; member of the State house of representatives in 1852; elected by the legislature to codify the laws of the State in 1853; studied law; was admitted to the bar in 1854 and commenced practice in San Francisco, Calif.; returned to Kentucky in 1855; delegate to the Democratic National Convention at Cincinnati in 1856; moved to the Territory of Washington in 1857; receiver of public moneys 1857–1860; unsuccessful Democratic candidate for election in 1860 to the Thirty-seventh Congress; surveyor general of the Territory of Washington 1866–1869; elected as a Republican to the Forty-first and Forty-second Congresses (March 4, 1869–March 3, 1873); unsuccessful candidate for reelection in 1872 to the Forty-third Congress; appointed collector of customs for the Puget Sound district in 1873; moved to Seattle, Wash., where he engaged in the practice of law; also practiced in Washington, D. C.; died in Washington, D. C., April 13, 1881; interment in Glenwood Cemetery.

GARLAND, Augustus Hill, a Senator from Arkansas; born in Tipton County, Tenn., June 11, 1832; moved with his parents to Hempstead County, Ark., in 1833; attended St. Mary's College, and was graduated from St. Joseph's College in Kentucky in 1849; studied law; was admitted to the bar in 1853 and commenced practice in Washington, Ark.; moved to Little Rock in 1856; presidential elector on the Constitutional Union ticket of Bell and Everett in 1860; Union delegate to the State convention that passed the ordinance of secession in 1861; member of the provisional congress that met in Montgomery, Ala., in May 1861 and subsequently of the Confederate Congress and served in both houses; elected to the United States Senate for the term beginning March 4, 1867, but was not permitted to take his seat, as Arkansas had not been readmitted to representation; argued the test-oath case as to lawyers in the Supreme Court of the United States and won it; followed the practice of law until the fall of 1874; Governor of Arkansas 1874–1876; elected as a Democrat to the United States Senate in 1876; reelected in 1883, and served from March 4, 1877, to March 6, 1885, when he resigned, having been appointed Attorney General in the Cabinet of President Cleveland, and served from March 9, 1885, to March 5, 1889; resumed the practice of law in Little Rock; died in Washington, D. C., January 26, 1899; interment in Mount Holly Cemetery, Little Rock, Ark.

GARLAND, David Shepherd, a Representative from Virginia; born near New Glasgow (now Clifford), Amherst County, Va., September 27, 1769; pursued an academic course; studied law; was admitted to the bar and commenced practice in Virginia; member of the State house of delegates 1799–1802 and 1805–1809; served in the State senate 1809–1811; elected as a Democrat to the Eleventh Congress to fill the vacancy caused by the resignation of Wilson C. Nicholas and served from January 17, 1810, to March 3, 1811; again a member of the State house of delegates in 1814, 1815, 1819–1826, and 1832–1836; died in Clifford, Va., October 7, 1841; interment in the Meredith and Garland families' graveyard, Clifford, Va.

GARLAND, James, a Representative from Virginia; born at Ivy Depot, Albemarle County, Va., June 6, 1791; pursued preparatory studies; studied law; was admitted to the bar and commenced practice in Lovingston, Va.; served in the War of 1812; resumed the practice of law; served in the State house of delegates 1829–1831; elected as a Democrat to the Twenty-fourth, Twenty-fifth, and Twenty-sixth Congresses (March 4, 1835–March 3, 1841); unsuccessful candidate for reelection in 1840 to the Twenty-seventh Congress; resumed the practice of law; moved to Lynchburg, Va., in 1841; Commonwealth attorney for Lynchburg 1849–1872; elected judge of the corporation court in 1841, and served until December 31, 1882; withdrew from public life and lived in retirement until his death in Lynchburg, Va., August 8, 1885; interment in Spring Hill Cemetery.

GARLAND, Mahlon Morris, a Representative from Pennsylvania; born in Pittsburgh, Pa., May 4, 1856; moved with his parents to Alexandria, Huntingdon County, Pa.; attended the common schools; having learned the trade of puddling and heating, joined the Amalgamated Association of Iron, Steel and Tin Workers, of which he became president; member of the select council of Pittsburgh in 1886 and 1887; appointed by President McKinley United States collector of customs (then called surveyor of customs) at Pittsburgh on April 7, 1898; reappointed by President Roosevelt in 1902 and 1906 and by President Taft in 1910, and served until March 3, 1915; served as vice president of the American Federation of Labor; member of the Pittsburgh School Board; member of the borough council of Edgewood, Pa.; elected as a Republican to the Sixty-fourth, Sixty-fifth, and Sixty-sixth Congresses and served from March 4, 1915, until his death; had been reelected to the Sixty-seventh Congress; died in Washington, D. C., November 19, 1920; interment in Woodlawn Cemetery, Pittsburgh, Pa.

GARLAND, Rice, a Representative from Louisiana; born in Lynchburg, Va., about 1795; pursued an academic course; studied law; was admitted to the bar and commenced practice; moved to Opelousas, La., in 1820 and continued the practice of his profession; elected as a Whig to the Twenty-third Congress to fill the vacancy caused by the resignation of Henry A. Bullard; reelected to the Twenty-fourth, Twenty-fifth, and Twenty-sixth Congresses and served from April 28, 1834, to July 21, 1840, when he resigned to accept an appointment as judge of the supreme court of Louisiana, in which capacity he served, with residence in New Orleans, La., until 1846; moved to Brownsville, Tex., in 1846 and continued the practice of law until his death in that city in 1861; interment in a cemetery at Brownsville.

GARMATZ, Edward Alexander, a Representative from Maryland; born in Baltimore, Md., February 7, 1903; attended the public schools and Polytechnic Institute; engaged in the electrical business 1920–1942; associated with the Maryland State Racing Commission 1941–1944; served as police magistrate 1944–1947; elected as a Democrat to the Eightieth Congress to fill the vacancy caused by the resignation of Thomas D'Alesandro; reelected to the Eighty-first and to the five succeeding Congresses and served from July 15, 1947, to January 3, 1961. *Reelected to the Eighty-seventh Congress.*

GARNER, Alfred Buckwalter, a Representative from Pennsylvania; born in Ashland, Schuylkill County, Pa., March 4, 1873; attended the public schools; studied law; was admitted to the bar in 1897 and commenced practice in Ashland, Pa.; member of the State house of representatives 1901–1907; elected as a Republican to the Sixty-first Congress (March 4, 1909–March 3, 1911); again a member of the State house of representatives 1915–1917; resumed the practice of law in Ashland, Pa.; taxing officer, auditor general's department, Harrisburg, Pa., from May 1917, until his death; died in Harrisburg July 30, 1930; interment in Fountain Spring Cemetery, Fountain Spring, Pa.

GARNER, John Nance, a Representative from Texas and a Vice President of the United States; born near Detroit, Red River County, Tex., November 22, 1868; had limited elementary educational advantages; studied law in Clarksville, Tex.; was admitted to the bar in 1890 and commenced practice in Uvalde, Uvalde County, Tex.; judge of Uvalde County, Tex., 1893–1896; member of the State house of representatives 1898–1902; delegate to the Democratic National Conventions in 1900, 1916, and 1924; elected as a Democrat to the Fifty-eighth and to the fourteen succeeding Congresses (March 4, 1903–March 3, 1933); served as minority floor leader in the Seventy-first Congress and as Speaker in the Seventy-second Congress; reelected to the Seventy-third Congress on November 8, 1932, and on the same day was elected Vice President of the United States on the ticket headed by Franklin D. Roosevelt; resigned from the Seventy-third Congress on March 3, 1933; reelected Vice President in 1936 and served in that office from March 4, 1933, to January 20, 1941; retired to private life and is a resident of Uvalde, Tex.

GARNETT, James Mercer (brother of Robert Selden Garnett and grandfather of Muscoe Russell Hunter Garnett), a Representative from Virginia; born at "Mount Pleasant," near Loretto, Essex County, Va., June 8, 1770; studied under private teachers; engaged in planting; member of the State house of delegates in 1800 and 1801; elected as a Democrat to the Ninth and Tenth Congresses (March 4, 1805–March 3, 1809); member of the grand jury that indicted Aaron Burr, former Vice President, for treason in 1807; was not a candidate for renomination in 1808; again engaged in planting, and during the later years of his life conducted a school for boys on his plantation; president of the Fredericksburg Agricultural Society 1817–1837; again a member of the State house of delegates in 1824 and 1825; member of the antitariff conventions of 1821 and 1831; one of the founders of the Virginia State Agricultural Society; vice president of the Virginia Colonization Society; delegate to the State constitutional convention in 1829; died on his estate, "Elmwood," near Loretto, Va., April 23, 1843; interment in the family burying ground on his estate.

GARNETT, Muscoe Russell Hunter (grandson of James Mercer Garnett), a Representative from Virginia; born at "Elmwood," near Loretto, Essex County, Va., July 25, 1821; tutored at home and was graduated from the University of Virginia at Charlottesville (literary department in 1839 and the law department in 1842); was admitted to the bar in 1842 and commenced the practice of his profession in Loretto, Va.; delegate to the State constitutional convention in 1850 and 1851; delegate to the Democratic National Convention at Baltimore in 1852 which nominated Pierce and King and at Cincinnati in 1856 which nominated Buchanan and Breckinridge; member of the State house of delegates 1853–1856; member of the board of visitors of the University of Virginia 1855–1859; elected as a Democrat to the Thirty-fourth Congress to fill the vacancy caused by the death of Thomas H. Bayly; reelected to the Thirty-fifth and Thirty-sixth Congresses and served from December 1, 1856, to March 3, 1861; delegate to the Virginia secession convention and to the State constitutional convention in 1861; member from Virginia of the First Confederate Congress 1862–1864; died at "Elmwood," near Loretto, Va., on February 14, 1864; interment in the family cemetery on his estate.

GARNETT, Robert Selden (brother of James Mercer Garnett and cousin of Charles Fenton Mercer), a Representative from Virginia; born at "Mount Pleasant," near Loretto, Essex County, Va., April 26, 1789; attended the College of New Jersey (now Princeton University); studied law; was admitted to the bar and commenced practice in Lloyds, Va.; member of the State house of delegates in 1816 and 1817; elected as a Democrat to the Fifteenth and to the four succeeding Congresses (March 4, 1817–March 3, 1827); was not a candidate for renomination in 1826; resumed the practice of law in Lloyds; died on his estate, "Champlain," near Lloyds, Essex County, Va., August 15, 1840; interment in the family burying ground on his estate.

GARNSEY, Daniel Greene, a Representative from New York; born in Canaan, Columbia County, N. Y., June 17, 1779; attended private schools; member of the State militia in 1805; brigade inspector in Saratoga County, N. Y., in 1810 and 1811; studied law in Norwich, Chenango County, N. Y.; was admitted to the bar in 1811 and practiced in Rensselaer and Saratoga Counties; served in the War of 1812 as aide-de-camp to major general with rank of major; moved to Pomfret in 1816 and labored to promote the building up of the village of Dunkirk; commissioner to perform certain duties of a judge of the supreme court at chambers; surrogate of Chautauqua County 1813–1831; brigade inspector, Chautauqua County, N. Y., in 1817; district attorney of Chautauqua County from June 11, 1818, to March 4, 1826; elected as a Jackson Democrat to the Nineteenth and Twentieth Congresses (March 4, 1825–March 3, 1829); moved to Michigan in 1831 and settled in the vicinity of Battle Creek; appointed postmaster and Government superintendent of public works near Detroit and Ypsilanti; served with General Scott in the Black Hawk War in 1836; moved to Rock Island, Ill.; appointed on March 22, 1841, by President William Henry Harrison, receiver of public moneys at the land office in Dixon, Ill., and served until removed by President Tyler on August 25, 1843; president of the Harrison celebration in Galena, Ill., July 4, 1840; upon returning from a visit to his daughter in Philadelphia and while en route to attend a celebration at Dunkirk, N. Y., of the completion of the Erie Railroad he stopped at Gowanda, N. Y., where he was taken violently ill and died May 11, 1851; interment in Pine Hill Cemetery.

GARRETT, Abraham Ellison, a Representative from Tennessee; born near Livingston, Overton County, Tenn., March 6, 1830; attended the public schools and Poplar Springs College, Kentucky; studied law; was admitted to the bar and commenced practice in Livingston, Tenn.; also engaged in agricultural pursuits; served as lieutenant colonel of the First Regiment, Tennessee Mounted Infantry, in the Union Army during the Civil War; delegate to the State constitutional convention in 1865; member of the State house of representatives in 1865 and 1866; served in the State senate in 1867; elected as a Democrat to the Forty-second Congress (March 4, 1871–March 3, 1873); unsuccessful candidate for reelection in 1872; resumed the practice of law in Carthage, Tenn., where he died February 14, 1907; interment in Carthage Cemetery.

GARRETT, Clyde Leonard, a Representative from Texas; born on a farm near Gorman, Eastland County, Tex., December 16, 1885; attended the public schools and Hankins' Normal

College in his native city; raised on a farm; worked as a railroad section hand; taught school at Sweetwater, Nolan County, Tex., in 1906 and 1907; deputy in the office of the tax collector 1907–1912; county clerk of Eastland County, Tex., 1913–1919; engaged in the real estate, insurance, and banking businesses 1920–1922; city manager of the city of Eastland, Tex., in 1922 and 1923; county judge 1929–1936; elected as a Democrat to the Seventy-fifth and Seventy-sixth Congresses (January 3, 1937–January 3, 1941); unsuccessful candidate for renomination in 1940; administrative officer in the office of the Secretary of Commerce from January 15, 1941, to May 1, 1942, at which time he became staff specialist in the Office of War Information and served until October 15, 1943; unsuccessful candidate for Democratic nomination to the Seventy-ninth Congress in 1944; technical assistant, Veterans Administration, Washington, D. C., and Dallas, Tex., 1949–1950; manager, Veterans Administration regional office, Waco, Tex., from 1951 until retirement on January 1, 1956; was an unsuccessful candidate for Eastland County judgeship in 1958; died in Eastland, Tex., December 18, 1959; interment in Eastland Cemetery.

GARRETT, Daniel Edward, a Representative from Texas; born near Springfield, Robertson County, Tenn., April 28, 1869; attended the common schools of his native county; studied law; was admitted to the bar and commenced practice in Springfield, Tenn., in 1893; member of the State house of representatives 1892–1896; elected to the State senate in 1902 and again in 1904; moved to Houston, Tex., in 1905 and continued the practice of law; elected as a Democrat to the Sixty-third Congress (March 4, 1913–March 3, 1915); unsuccessful candidate for reelection in 1914 to the Sixty-fourth Congress; resumed the practice of law in Houston, Tex.; elected to the Sixty-fifth Congress (March 4, 1917–March 3, 1919); was not a candidate for renomination in 1918; elected to the Sixty-seventh and to the five succeeding Congresses and served from March 4, 1921, until his death; had been reelected to the Seventy-third Congress; died in Washington, D. C., on December 13, 1932; interment in Forest Park Cemetery, Houston, Tex.

GARRETT, Finis James, a Representative from Tennessee; born near Ore Springs, Weakley County, Tenn., August 26, 1875; attended the common schools and Clinton (Ky.) College; was graduated from Bethel College, McKenzie, Tenn., in 1897; editor of country newspapers at Dresden and McKenzie, Tenn., before completing his college course; engaged in teaching at Como and Milan, Tenn.; studied law; was admitted to the bar in 1899 and commenced practice in Dresden, Tenn.; appointed master in chancery September 14, 1900, and served until January 24, 1905; delegate to all Democratic State conventions from 1896 to 1925; delegate to the Democratic National Convention in New York in 1924; elected as a Democrat to the Fifty-ninth and to the eleven succeeding Congresses (March 4, 1905–March 3, 1929); was not a candidate for renomination in 1928 but was an unsuccessful candidate for the Democratic nomination for United States Senator; nominee of his party for Speaker of the House in the Sixty-eighth, Sixty-ninth, and Seventieth Congresses and as such became the minority floor leader for those terms; appointed judge of the United States Court of Customs and Patent Appeals by President Coolidge, taking office on March 5, 1929, and became presiding judge of the court on December 9, 1937, by appointment of President Franklin D. Roosevelt, and served until his retirement September 15, 1955; died in Washington, D. C., May 25, 1956; interment in Sunset Cemetery, Dresden, Tenn.

GARRISON, Daniel, a Representative from New Jersey; born in Lower Penns Neck Township, near Salem, N. J., April 3, 1782; pursued an academic course; engaged in agricultural pursuits; member of the State general assembly 1806–1808; surrogate of Salem County 1809–1823; elected as a Democrat to the Eighteenth and Nineteenth Congresses (March 4, 1823–March 3, 1827); was not a candidate for renomination in 1826; appointed by President Jackson inspector of the revenue and collector of the customs at the port of Bridgeton, N. J., in 1834 and served until 1838; died in Salem, N. J., February 13, 1851; interment in St. John's Episcopal Cemetery.

GARRISON, George Tankard, a Representative from Virginia; born in Accomack County, Va., January 14, 1835; was graduated from Dickinson College, Carlisle, Pa., in 1853 and from the law department of the University of Virginia, Charlottesville, Va., in 1857; was admitted to the bar and commenced practice in Accomac; served as a private in the Confederate Army during the Civil War; member of the State house of delegates 1861–1863; served in the State senate 1863–1865; resumed the practice of law and also engaged in agricultural pursuits; elected judge of the eighth Virginia circuit in 1870 and subsequently judge of the seventeenth circuit; elected as a Democrat to the Forty-seventh Congress (March 4, 1881–March 3, 1883); successfully contested the election of Robert M. Mayo to the Forty-eighth Congress and served from March 20, 1884, to March 3, 1885; resumed the practice of law; elected judge of the county court of Accomack County, Va.; died at Accomac, Va., November 14, 1889; interment in Edge Hill Cemetery.

GARROW, Nathaniel, a Representative from New York; born in Barnstable, Barnstable County, Mass., April 25, 1780; attended the public schools; followed the sea; moved to Auburn, N. Y., in 1796; appointed justice of the peace in 1809; sheriff of Cayuga County 1815–1819 and 1821–1825; elected as a Democrat to the Twentieth Congress (March 4, 1827–March 3, 1829); presidential elector on the Democratic ticket of Jackson and Van Buren in 1832; United States marshal of the northern district of New York from February 1837 to March 1841; died in Auburn, Cayuga County, N. Y., March 3, 1841; interment in the family burying ground on his estate; reinterment in Fort Hill Cemetery, Auburn, N. Y.

GARTH, William Willis, a Representative from Alabama; born in Morgan County, Ala., October 28, 1828; pursued classical studies in Lagrange, Va., and at Emory and Henry College, Emory, Va.; studied law at the University of Virginia at Charlottesville; was admitted to the Alabama bar and commenced the practice of law in Huntsville, Ala.; during the Civil War was lieutenant colonel on the staff of General Longstreet in the Confederate Army; elected as a Democrat to the Forty-fifth Congress (March 4, 1877–March 3, 1879); was an unsuccessful candidate for reelection in 1878 to the Forty-sixth Congress; resumed the practice of law; died in Huntsville, Ala., on February 25, 1912; interment in Maple Hill Cemetery.

GARTNER, Fred Christian, a Representative from Pennsylvania; born in Philadelphia, Pa., March 14, 1896; attended the public schools and Brown Preparatory School in Philadelphia; during the First World War served as a yeoman in the United States Naval Reserve in 1918 and 1919; was graduated from the law department of Temple University, Philadelphia, Pa., in 1920; was admitted to the bar the same year and commenced practice in Philadelphia, Pa.; member of the State civil service commission at Philadelphia 1928–1932; served in the State house of representatives in 1933 and 1934; elected as a Republican to the Seventy-sixth Congress (January 3, 1939–January 3, 1941); was an unsuccessful candidate for reelection in 1940 to the Seventy-seventh Congress; resumed the practice of law and is a resident of Philadelphia, Pa.

GARTRELL, Lucius Jeremiah (uncle of Choice Boswell Randell), a Representative from Georgia; born near Washington, Wilkes County, Ga., January 7, 1821; attended private schools, Randolph-Macon College, Lynchburg, Va., and Franklin College, Georgia; studied law; was admitted to the bar in 1842 and practiced in Washington, Ga.; moved to Atlanta, Ga.; elected solicitor general of the northern judicial circuit in 1843; resigned in 1847; member of the State house of representatives 1847–1850; presidential elector on the Democratic ticket of Buchanan and Breckinridge in 1856; elected as a Democrat to the Thirty-fifth and Thirty-sixth Congresses and served from March 4, 1857, to January 23, 1861, when he retired, giving his adherence to the Southern Confederacy; organized the Seventh Regiment, Georgia Volunteer Infantry, of which he was elected colonel; participated in the first Battle of Bull Run; resigned his commission January 3, 1862, having been elected to the Confederate Congress and served until 1864; appointed in 1864 brigadier general in the Confederate service; resumed the practice of law; member of the State constitutional convention in 1877; died in Atlanta, Ga., April 7, 1891; interment in Oakland Cemetery.

GARVIN, William Swan, a Representative from Pennsylvania; born in Mercer, Mercer County, Pa., on July 25, 1806; pursued an academic course; editor of the Western Press, in Mercer, for fifty years; appointed postmaster of Mercer January 3, 1837, and served until June 12, 1841; elected as a Democrat to the Twenty-ninth Congress (March 4, 1845–March 3, 1847) flour inspector in Pittsburgh, Pa.; again appointed postmaster of Mercer April 10, 1867, and served until June 23, 1869; engaged in journalism; died in Mercer, Pa., February 20, 1883; interment in the Citizens' Cemetery.

GARY, Frank Boyd, a Senator from South Carolina; born in Cokesbury, Abbeville County, S. C., March 9, 1860; attended the Cokesbury Conference School and Union College, Schenectady, N. Y.; studied law; was admitted to the bar and commenced practice in Abbeville, S. C., in 1881; member of the State house of representatives 1890–1900, and served as speaker 1895–1900; delegate to the State constitutional convention in 1895; Democratic chairman of Abbeville County for a number of years; again elected a member of the State house of representatives in 1906; elected as a Democrat to the United States Senate to fill the vacancy caused by the death of Asbury C. Latimer and served from March 6, 1908, to March 3, 1909; was not a candidate for reelection in 1908; again served in the State house of representatives in 1910; delegate to the Democratic National Convention at Baltimore in 1912; elected judge of the eighth judicial circuit in 1912, and served in this capacity until his death in Charleston, S. C., December 7, 1922; interment in Long Cane Cemetery, Abbeville, S. C.

GARY, Julian Vaughan, a Representative from Virginia; born in Richmond, Henrico County, Va., February 25, 1892; attended the public schools; was graduated from the University of Richmond in 1912 and from its law department in 1915; taught at Blackstone Academy for Boys in 1912 and 1913; was admitted to the bar in 1915 and commenced practice in Richmond, Va.; during the First World War served in the United States Army; counsel and executive assistant of the Virginia Tax Board 1919–1924; served in the State house of delegates 1926–1934; member of the board of trustees of the University of Richmond; elected as a Democrat to the Seventy-ninth Congress to fill the vacancy caused by the resignation of Dave E. Satterfield, Jr.; reelected to the Eightieth and to the six succeeding Congresses and served from March 6, 1945, to January 3, 1961. *Reelected to the Eighty-seventh Congress.*

GASQUE, Allard Henry (husband of Bessie Hawley Gasque), a Representative from South Carolina; born on Friendfield plantation, near Hyman, Marion (now Florence) County, S. C., March 8, 1873; attended the public schools; worked on a farm and taught in the country schools for several years; was graduated from the University of South Carolina at Columbia in 1901; principal of Waverly Graded School, Columbia, S. C., in 1901 and 1902; elected superintendent of education of Florence County in 1902 and served by reelection until 1923, when he resigned, having been elected to Congress; president of the county superintendents' association of the State in 1911 and 1912 and of the State teachers' association in 1914 and 1915; member of the Democratic State executive committee 1912–1920; chairman of the Democratic county committee 1919–1923; elected as a Democrat to the Sixty-eighth and to the seven succeeding Congresses and served from March 4, 1923, until his death in Washington, D. C., on June 17, 1938; interment in Mount Hope Cemetery, Florence, S. C.

GASQUE, Elizabeth Hawley (widow of Allard Henry Gasque (now Mrs. A. J. Van Exem)), a Representative from South Carolina; born near Blythewood, on Rice Creek Plantation, Richland County, S. C.; attended private schools and Greenville (S. C.) Woman's College; moved to Florence, S. C., in 1908; elected as a Democrat to the Seventy-fifth Congress to fill the vacancy caused by the death of her husband, Allard H. Gasque, and served from September 13, 1938, to January 3, 1939; was not a candidate for election to the Seventy-sixth Congress; active in dramatics; author and lecturer; is a resident of Cedar Tree Plantation, Ridgeway, S. C.

GASSAWAY, Percy Lee, a Representative from Oklahoma; born in Waco, McLennan County, Tex., August 30, 1885; moved to Fort Sill, Okla. (then Indian Territory), with his parents in 1899; attended the public schools in Fort Sill and Oklahoma City, Okla.; employed as a clerk in a law office; studied law; was admitted to the bar in 1918 and commenced practice in Coalgate, Okla.; also engaged in agricultural and ranching pursuits; appointed county judge of Coal County, Okla., in 1923, elected in 1924, and served until 1926; district judge of the twenty-sixth judicial district 1926–1934; elected as a Democrat to the Seventy-fourth Congress (January 3, 1935–January 3, 1937); unsuccessful candidate for renomination in 1936; resumed the practice of law and also engaged as a rancher near Coalgate, Coal County, Okla.; died in Coalgate, Okla., May 15, 1937; interment in Coalgate Cemetery.

GASTON, Athelston, a Representative from Pennsylvania; born in Castile, Wyoming County, N. Y., April 24, 1838; moved with his parents to Crawford County, Pa., in 1854; attended the common schools; engaged in agricultural pursuits until he was thirty-five years old, when he became a dealer in and manufacturer of lumber; mayor of Meadville, Pa., 1891–1895; elected as a Democrat to the Fifty-sixth Congress (March 4, 1899–March 3, 1901); unsuccessful candidate for reelection in 1900 to the Fifty-seventh Congress; resumed the lumber business; killed while on a hunting trip along Lake Edward in northern Quebec, Canada, September 23, 1907; interment in Greendale Cemetery, Meadville, Pa.

GASTON, William, a Representative from North Carolina; born in New Bern, N. C., September 19, 1778; entered Georgetown College, Washington, D. C., at the age of thirteen; later returned to his native State and became a student in the Academy of New Bern; was graduated from Princeton College in 1796; studied law; was admitted to the bar in 1798 and commenced practice in New Bern, N. C.; member of the State senate in 1800; served in the State house of representatives 1807–1809, and as speaker in 1808; presidential elector on the Federalist ticket of Pinckney and King in 1808; again a member of the State senate in 1812, 1818, and 1819; elected as a Federalist to the Thirteenth and Fourteenth Congresses (March 4, 1813–March 3, 1817); was not a candidate for renomination in 1816; again served in the State house of representatives in 1824, 1827, 1828, 1829, and 1831; appointed judge of the supreme court of North Carolina in 1833, holding the position until his death; member of the State constitutional convention in 1835; declined a nomination for election to the United States Senate in 1840; died in Raleigh, N. C., January 23, 1844; interment in Cedar Grove Cemetery, New Bern, N. C.

GATES, Seth Merrill, a Representative from New York; born in Winfield, Herkimer County, N. Y., October 10, 1800; moved with his parents to Sheldon, Genesee (now Wyoming) County, N. Y., in 1806; attended the common schools and Middleburg Academy, Wyoming, N. Y.; inspector of common schools and deputy sheriff of Le Roy about 1825; studied law; was admitted to the bar in 1827 and commenced practice in Le Roy, N. Y.; supervisor of Le Roy in 1830; member of the State assembly in 1832; declined to be a candidate for reelection; purchased the Le Roy Gazette in 1838, editing it for nine months; elected as an Anti-Slavery Whig to the Twenty-sixth and Twenty-seventh Congresses (March 4, 1839–March 3, 1843); unsuccessful candidate for reelection; moved to Warsaw, Wyoming County, N. Y., in 1843 and continued the practice of law; also engaged in the lumber trade and as a hardware and dry-goods merchant; unsuccessful Free-Soil candidate for Lieutenant Governor of New York in 1848; secretary of the Wyoming County Insurance Co. 1851–1865; appointed postmaster at Warsaw on May 28, 1861, and served until July 9, 1870, when his successor was appointed; vice president of the Genesee County Pioneer Association in 1872; died in Warsaw, N. Y., August 24, 1877; interment in Warsaw Cemetery.

GATHINGS, Ezekiel Candler, a Representative from Arkansas; born in Prairie, Monroe County, Miss., November 10, 1903; attended the public schools, Earl (Ark.) High School, and the University of Alabama at Tuscaloosa; was graduated from the law department of the University of Arkansas at Fayetteville in 1929; was admitted to the bar the same year and commenced practice in Helena, Ark.; moved to West Memphis, Ark., in 1932 and continued the practice of law; served in the State senate 1935–1939; elected as a Democrat to the Seventy-sixth and to the ten succeeding Congresses (January 3, 1939–January 3, 1961). *Reelected to the Eighty-seventh Congress.*

GATLIN, Alfred Moore, a Representative from North Carolina; born in Edenton, N. C., April 20, 1790; pursued classical studies at New Bern, N. C., and was graduated from the University of North Carolina at Chapel Hill in 1808; studied law; was admitted to the bar in 1823 and commenced practice in Camden, Camden County, N. C., in the same year; elected to the Eighteenth Congress (March 4, 1823–March 3, 1825); unsuccessful candidate for reelection in 1824 to the Nineteenth Congress; moved to the Territory of Florida.

GAUSE, Lucien Coatsworth, a Representative from Arkansas; born near Wilmington, Brunswick County, N. C., December 25, 1836; moved to Lauderdale County, Tenn.; studied under a private tutor; was graduated from the University of Virginia at Charlottesville; studied law and was graduated from Cumberland University, Lebanon, Tenn.; was admitted to the bar and commenced practice in Jacksonport, Ark., in 1859; during the Civil War entered the Confederate service as lieutenant, attaining the rank of colonel; resumed the practice of law in Jacksonport

in 1865; member of the State house of representatives in 1866; commissioner to represent the State government at Washington; unsuccessfully contested the election of Asa Hodges to the Forty-third Congress; elected as a Democrat to the Forty-fourth and Forty-fifth Congresses (March 4, 1875–March 3, 1879); was not a candidate for renomination in 1878; resumed the practice of law; died in Jacksonport, Ark., November 5, 1880; interment in the private burying ground near Jacksonport.

GAVAGAN, Joseph Andrew, a Representative from New York; born in New York City, N. Y., August 20, 1892; attended the public and parochial schools; was graduated from the law department of Fordham University, New York City, N. Y., in 1920; during the First World War enlisted as a private and later was promoted to second lieutenant in the Quartermaster Corps and served from August 20, 1917, to October 13, 1919; first lieutenant in the Quartermaster Reserve Corps from April 3, 1920, to February 16, 1925; was admitted to the bar in 1920 and commenced practice in New York City; member of the State assembly 1923–1929; elected as a Democrat to the Seventy-first Congress to fill the vacancy caused by the death of Royal H. Weller; reelected to the Seventy-second and to the six succeeding Congresses and served from November 5, 1929, until December 30, 1943, when he resigned, having been elected a justice of the New York Supreme Court; reelected for term ending December 31, 1962; is a resident of New York City, N. Y.

GAVIN, Leon Harry, a Representative from Pennsylvania; born in Buffalo, Erie County, N. Y., February 25, 1893; veteran of the First World War; elected as a Republican to the Seventy-eighth and to the eight succeeding Congresses (January 3, 1943–January 3, 1961). *Reelected to the Eighty-seventh Congress.*

GAY, Edward James, a Representative from Louisiana; born in Liberty, Bedford County, Va., February 3, 1816; moved with his parents to Illinois in 1820, and thence to St. Louis, Mo., in 1824; spent several years under a private instructor in Belleville, Ill., and attended Augusta College, Kentucky, in 1833 and 1834; engaged in commercial affairs in St. Louis 1838–1860; moved to Louisiana and engaged in commercial manufacturing, and agricultural pursuits; first president of the Louisiana Sugar Exchange in New Orleans; elected as a Democrat to the Forty-ninth, Fiftieth, and Fifty-first Congresses and served from March 4, 1885, until his death on his St. Louis plantation, Iberville Parish, La., May 30, 1889; interment in Bellefontaine Cemetery, St. Louis, Mo.

GAY, Edward James (grandson of the preceding), a Senator from Louisiana; born on Union plantation, Iberville Parish, La., May 5, 1878; attended Pantops Academy, Charlottesville, Va., the Lawrenceville (N. J.) School, and Princeton (N. J.) University; engaged in sugar production and the cultivation of various agricultural products; member of the State house of representatives 1904–1918; delegate to the Democratic National Convention at St. Louis in 1904; elected as a Democrat to the United States Senate to fill the vacancy caused by the death of Robert F. Broussard and served from November 6, 1918, to March 3, 1921; declined to be a candidate for reelection in 1920; delegate at large to the Democratic National Convention at San Francisco in 1920; president of the Edward J. Gay Planting & Manufacturing Co. (Ltd.) and of the Lake Long Drainage District, Iberville Parish; member of the board of supervisors of Louisiana State University and chairman of the building committee for the new university 1921–1928; member at large to the electoral college in 1941 and 1945; died in New Orleans, La., December 1, 1952; interment in Metairie Cemetery.

GAYLE, John, a Representative from Alabama; born in Sumter District, S. C., September 11, 1792; pursued classical studies and was graduated from South Carolina College at Columbia; studied law; was admitted to the bar and commenced practice in Mobile, Ala., in 1813; member of the Territorial council in 1817; solicitor of the first judicial district in 1819; member of the State house of representatives in 1822 and 1823; judge of the State supreme court in 1823; member and speaker of the State house of representatives in 1829; Governor of Alabama 1831–1835; candidate for presidential elector on the Whig ticket in 1836 and 1840; elected as a Whig to the Thirtieth Congress (March 4, 1847–March 3, 1849); appointed United States district judge of Alabama on March 13, 1849; died near Mobile, Ala., July 28, 1859; interment in Magnolia Cemetery, Mobile, Ala.

GAYLE, June Ward, a Representative from Kentucky; born in New Liberty, Owen County, Ky., February 22, 1865; attended Concord College, New Liberty, Ky., and Georgetown College, Georgetown, Ky.; deputy sheriff; delegate to Democratic National Conventions at St. Louis and at San Francisco; member of the Democratic State central committee and of the State executive committee; high sheriff of Owen County 1892–1896; unsuccessful candidate for State auditor in 1899; engaged in banking and in the tobacco business; elected as a Democrat to the Fifty-sixth Congress to fill the vacancy caused by the death of Evan E. Settle and served from January 15, 1900, to March 3, 1901; resumed his former business activities; died in Owenton, Ky., on August 5, 1942; interment in New Liberty Cemetery, New Liberty, Ky.

GAYLORD, James Madison, a Representative from Ohio; born in Zanesville, Ohio, May 29, 1811; moved to McConnelsville, Ohio, in 1818; attended the common schools and the University of Ohio at Athens; studied law; was admitted to the bar and practiced; appointed clerk of the court of common pleas in 1834; elected to the Thirty-second Congress (March 4, 1851–March 3, 1853); at the expiration of his term in Congress he was elected probate judge; appointed deputy United States marshal in 1860; elected justice of the peace in 1865, and by successive reelections was continued in that office until his death in McConnelsville, Ohio, June 14, 1874; interment in McConnelsville Cemetery.

GAZLAY, James William, a Representative from Ohio; born in New York City, N. Y., July 23, 1784; moved with his parents to Dutchess County, N. Y., in 1789; attended the common schools, after which he pursued an academic course; studied law in Poughkeepsie, N. Y.; was admitted to the bar in 1809 and practiced; moved to Cincinnati, Ohio, in 1813 and continued the practice of law; elected as a Jackson Free-Statesman to the Eighteenth Congress (March 4, 1823–March 3, 1825); unsuccessful candidate for reelection in 1824 to the Nineteenth Congress; edited a weekly paper called the Western Tiller in 1826 and 1827; engaged in literary pursuits; died in Cincinnati, Ohio, June 8, 1874; interment in Spring Grove Cemetery.

GEAR, John Henry, a Representative and a Senator from Iowa; born in Ithaca, Tompkins County, N. Y., April 7, 1825; attended the common schools; moved to Galena, Ill., in 1836, to Fort Snelling, Iowa, in 1838, and to Burlington in 1843, where he engaged in mercantile pursuits; he was one of the first citizens of Iowa to join the Republican Party, and was chosen by it mayor of the city of Burlington in 1863; member of the State house of representatives 1871–1873 and served as speaker two terms; Governor of Iowa 1878–1881; delegate to the Republican National Convention at Minneapolis in 1892 which nominated Harrison and Reid and at St. Louis in 1896 which nominated McKinley and Hobart; elected as a Republican to the Fiftieth and Fifty-first Congresses (March 4, 1887–March 3, 1891); unsuccessful candidate for reelection in 1890 to the Fifty-second Congress; appointed by President Harrison as Assistant Secretary of the Treasury and served from November 22, 1892, to March 3, 1893; elected to the Fifty-third Congress (March 4, 1893–March 3, 1895); elected to the United States Senate and served from March 4, 1895, until his death; had been reelected for the term beginning March 4, 1901; died in Washington, D. C., July 14, 1900; interment in Aspen Grove Cemetery, Burlington, Iowa.

GEARHART, Bertrand Wesley, a Representative from California; born in Fresno, Calif., May 31, 1890; attended the public schools; was graduated from Boones University School, Berkeley, Calif., in 1910 and from the law department of the University of Southern California at Los Angeles in 1914; was admitted to the California bar in 1913 and commenced the practice of law in Fresno, Calif., in 1914; during the First World War served overseas as a second lieutenant in the Six Hundred and Ninth Aero Squadron 1917–1919; assistant district attorney and district attorney of Fresno County, Calif., 1917–1923; member of the State Athletic Commission in 1931; served as a member of the board of directors of the California Veterans' Home in 1932; delegate to the California Constitutional Convention in 1933; elected as a Republican to the Seventy-fourth and to the six succeeding Congresses (January 3, 1935–January 3, 1949); was an unsuccessful candidate for reelection in 1948 to the Eighty-first Congress; resumed the practice of law in Fresno, Calif.; died in San Francisco, Calif., October 11, 1955; interment in Mountain View Cemetery, Fresno, Calif.

GEARIN, John McDermeid, a Senator from Oregon; born near Pendleton, Umatilla County, Oreg., August 15, 1851; attended the country schools, St. Mary's College, San Francisco, and was graduated from Notre Dame University, Indiana, in 1871; studied law; was admitted to the bar in 1873 and commenced practice in Portland, Oreg.; member of the State house of representatives in 1874; city attorney of Portland in 1875; unsuccessful Democratic candidate for election in 1878 to the Forty-sixth Congress; district attorney for Multnomah County 1884–1886; when the celebrated opium frauds were unearthed in 1893 was appointed by President Cleveland as special prosecutor for the Government in the cases; appointed as a Democrat to the United States Senate to fill the vacancy caused by the death of John H. Mitchell and served from December 13, 1905, until January 23, 1907, when a successor was elected; was not a candidate for election in 1907 to fill the vacancy in the Senate; resumed the practice of law in Portland, Oreg., until his death there November 12, 1930; interment in Mount Calvary Cemetery.

GEARY, Thomas J., a Representative from California; born in Boston, Mass., January 18, 1854; moved with his parents to San Francisco, Calif., in April 1863; attended the public schools; studied law at St. Ignatius College; was admitted to the bar in 1877 and commenced practice in Petaluma, Calif., moving to Santa Rosa, Calif., in 1882; district attorney of Sonoma County, Calif., in 1883 and 1884; resumed the practice of law; elected as a candidate of the Democratic and American Parties to the Fifty-first Congress to fill the vacancy caused by the resignation of John J. De Haven; reelected to the Fifty-second and Fifty-third Congresses and served from December 9, 1890, to March 3, 1895; unsuccessful candidate for reelection in 1894 to the Fifty-fourth Congress; resumed the practice of law; moved to Nome, Alaska, in 1900, to San Francisco, Calif., in 1902, and returned to Santa Rosa, Calif., in 1903, continuing the practice of law; city attorney in 1906; retired from active pursuits in 1923; died in Santa Rosa, Calif., July 6, 1929; interment in Rural Cemetery.

GEBHARD, John, a Representative from New York; born in Claverack, Columbia County, N. Y., February 22, 1782; attended the public schools; studied law; was admitted to the bar and practiced; surrogate of Schoharie County 1811–1813, and again from 1815 to 1822; elected to the Seventeenth Congress (March 4, 1821–March 3, 1823); resumed the practice of law; died in Schoharie, N. Y., January 3, 1854; interment in St. Paul's Lutheran Cemetery.

GEDDES, George Washington, a Representative from Ohio; born in Mount Vernon, Knox County, Ohio, July 16, 1824; attended the common schools; studied law; was admitted to the bar in July 1845 and practiced; judge of the court of common pleas of the sixth judicial district in 1856; reelected in 1861; again elected in 1868, and served until 1873; resumed the practice of law; unsuccessful Democratic candidate for judge of the State supreme court in 1872; resumed the practice of law in Mansfield; elected as a Democrat to the Forty-sixth and to the three succeeding Congresses (March 4, 1879–March 3, 1887); declined to be a candidate for reelection in 1886 to the Fiftieth Congress; resumed the practice of his profession; died in Mansfield, Richland County, Ohio, November 9, 1892; interment in Mansfield Cemetery.

GEDDES, James, a Representative from New York; born near Carlisle, Pa., July 22, 1763; attended the public schools; moved to Onondaga County, N. Y., in 1794, and began the manufacture of salt at Liverpool, N. Y.; justice of the peace in 1800; member of the State assembly in 1804; associate justice of the county court in 1809; judge of the court of common pleas in 1809; elected as a Federalist to the Thirteenth Congress (March 4, 1813–March 3, 1815); again a member of the State assembly in 1822; appointed chief engineer of the Ohio Canal in 1822; engineer on the Chesapeake & Ohio Canal in 1827; died in Geddes, N. Y., August 19, 1838; interment in Oakwood Cemetery, Syracuse, N. Y.

GEELAN, James Patrick, a Representative from Connecticut; born in New Haven, Conn., August 11, 1901; attended the public schools of New Haven, Conn., and was graduated from St. Anthony's College, San Antonio, Tex., in 1922; engaged in the retail cigar business 1922–1941; member of the State senate in 1939, 1941, and 1943; assistant clerk of the New Haven City Court 1941–1943; vice president of the New Haven Central Labor Council in 1942; engaged in the insurance business since 1943; elected as a Democrat to the Seventy-ninth Congress (January 3, 1945–January 3, 1947); unsuccessful candidate for reelection in 1946 to the Eightieth Congress; resumed his former business pursuits and is a resident of New Haven, Conn.

GEHRMANN, Bernard John, a Representative from Wisconsin; born in Gnesen, near Koenigsberg, East Prussia, Germany, February 13, 1880; attended the common schools in Germany; in 1893 immigrated to the United States with his parents, who settled in Chicago, Ill.; employed in a packing plant in Chicago and later learned the printing trade on a German-language daily newspaper; attended night school; moved to Wisconsin and settled on a farm near Neillsville, Clark County, in 1896 and engaged in agricultural pursuits; moved to a farm near Mellen, Ashland County, in 1915; clerk of the school board 1916–1934, town assessor 1916–1921, and chairman of the town board 1921–1932; conducted farmers' institutes throughout the State for the University of Wisconsin College of Agriculture 1920–1933;

served in the State assembly 1927–1933; delegate to the Republican National Convention at Chicago in 1932; member of the State senate in 1933 and 1934; elected as a Progressive to the Seventy-fourth and to the three succeeding Congresses (January 3, 1935–January 3, 1943); unsuccessful candidate for reelection in 1942 to the Seventy-eighth Congress; engaged in work for the United States Department of Agriculture from January 1943 until April 1945; elected to the Wisconsin Assembly in 1946, 1948, 1950, and 1952; elected to the State senate in 1954 for the term ending in January 1957; died in Mellen, Wis., July 12, 1958; interment in Mellen Union Cemetery.

GEISSENHAINER, Jacob Augustus, a Representative from New Jersey; born in New York City August 28, 1839; attended private schools, and was graduated from Columbia College at New York City in 1858; studied law at Yale College, and at the New York University, where he was graduated; also a student in the University of Berlin; was admitted to the bar and commenced practice in New York City in 1862; elected as a Democrat to the Fifty-first, Fifty-second, and Fifty-third Congresses (March 4, 1889–March 3, 1895); unsuccessful candidate for reelection in 1894 to the Fifty-fourth Congress; resumed the practice of law; died at Mount Pocono, Monroe County, Pa., on July 20, 1917; interment in West Laurel Hill Cemetery, Philadelphia, Pa.

GELSTON, David, a Delegate from New York; born in Bridgehampton, Suffolk County, N. Y., July 4, 1744; signed the articles of association in 1775; delegate to the Second, Third, and Fourth Provincial Congresses of New York 1775–1777; member of the State constitutional convention in 1777; elected a member of the State assembly under the constitution of 1777, and served from 1777 to 1785; was speaker in 1784 and 1785; appointed one of the commissioners on specie in 1780; Member of the last Continental Congress in 1789; member of the council of appointment in 1792 and 1793; served in the State senate 1791–1794, 1798, and 1802; canal commissioner in 1792; surrogate of the county of New York 1787–1801; collector of the port of New York 1801–1820; engaged in mercantile pursuits in New York City, where he died August 21, 1828; interment in First Presbyterian Church Cemetery.

GENSMAN, Lorraine Michael, a Representative from Oklahoma; born near Wichita, Sedgwick County, Kans., August 26, 1878; attended the district schools, the Garden Plain Graded School, Wichita Commercial College, Lewis Academy, and the Kansas State Normal School at Emporia; principal of the Andale (Kans.) schools in 1896 and 1897; was graduated from the law department of the University of Kansas at Lawrence in 1901; was admitted to the bar the same year and commenced practice in Lawrence, Kans.; moved to Lawton, Okla., in 1901; served as referee in bankruptcy 1902–1907; prosecuting attorney of Comanche County in 1918 and 1919; elected as a Republican to the Sixty-seventh Congress (March 4, 1921–March 3, 1923); unsuccessful candidate for reelection in 1922 to the Sixty-eighth Congress and for election in 1936 to the Seventy-fifth Congress; delegate to the Republican National Convention at Cleveland in 1924; engaged in the oil business; resumed the practice of law until his retirement in 1953; died in Lawton, Okla., May 27, 1954; interment in Highland Cemetery.

GENTRY, Brady Preston, a Representative from Texas; born in Colfax, Van Zandt County, Tex., March 25, 1896; attended the public schools and East Texas State College, Commerce, Tex.; graduated from Cumberland University, Lebanon, Tenn.; studied law; was admitted to the bar and began practice in Tyler, Tex.; during the First World War enlisted in the United States Army in 1918; served in Europe and rose to the rank of captain of Infantry; was gassed during combat; discharged in 1919; county attorney of Smith County 1921–1924; county judge of Smith County 1931–1939; chairman of the Texas State Highway Commission 1939–1945; elected as a Democrat to the Eighty-third and Eighty-fourth Congresses (January 3, 1953–January 3, 1957); was not a candidate for renomination in 1956 to the Eighty-fifth Congress; resumed the practice of law; is a resident of Tyler, Tex.

GENTRY, Meredith Poindexter, a Representative from Tennessee; born in Rockingham County, N. C., September 15, 1809; moved with his parents to Williamson County, Tenn., in 1813; completed preparatory studies; studied law; was admitted to the bar and commenced practice in Franklin, Tenn.; member of the State house of representatives 1835–1839; elected as a Whig to the Twenty-sixth and Twenty-seventh Congresses (March 4, 1839–March 3, 1843); on account of the death of his wife refused to be a candidate for renomination in 1842; again elected to the Twenty-ninth and to the three succeeding Congresses (March 4, 1845–March 3, 1853); was not a candidate for renomination in 1852; unsuccessful candidate for Governor of Tennessee in 1855; retired to his plantation in Tennessee, where he remained until 1861; member of the First and Second Confederate Congresses 1862–1863; died in Nashville, Tenn., November 2, 1866; interment in Mount Olivet Cemetery.

GEORGE, Henry, Jr., a Representative from New York; born in Sacramento, Calif., November 3, 1862; attended the common schools; at the age of sixteen entered a printing office where he was employed for one year; moved with his parents to Brooklyn, N. Y., in 1880; reporter on the Brooklyn Eagle in 1881; in 1884 accompanied his father as his secretary on a lecture tour of Great Britain, at the close of which he joined the staff of the London Truth; shortly thereafter he returned to this country and became a member of the staff of the North American Review; managing editor of the Standard 1887–1891; served as correspondent in Washington, D. C., for a syndicate of Western papers in 1891; correspondent in England for the same syndicate in 1892; returned to the United States in 1893 and became managing editor of the Florida Citizen at Jacksonville; resigned this position in 1895 and returned to New York City; on the death of his father in 1897 was nominated to succeed him as the candidate of the Jefferson Party for mayor of New York City, but was unsuccessful; in 1900 he made a tour as a special newspaper correspondent to study economic conditions in the countries through which he passed; special correspondent in Japan in 1906; had written extensively on labor, single tax, socialism, and other topics for many newspapers; elected as a Democrat to the Sixty-second and Sixty-third Congresses (March 4, 1911–March 3, 1915); was not a candidate for reelection in 1914; engaged in literary pursuits until his death in Washington, D. C., on November 14, 1916; interment in Greenwood Cemetery, Brooklyn, N. Y.

GEORGE, James Zachariah, a Senator from Mississippi; born in Monroe County, Ga., October 20, 1826; moved to Mississippi with his mother when a lad; attended the "old field" schools; joined the Mississippi Rifles, commanded by Col. Jefferson Davis, in 1846 and served in Mexico until discharged on account of ill health; studied law; was admitted to the bar in 1847 and commenced practice in Carrollton, Miss.; reporter of the Mississippi Supreme Court in 1854 and compiled ten volumes of supreme court reports; member of the Mississippi secession convention; voted for and signed the ordinance of secession; served in the Confederate Army during the Civil War as a captain in the

Twentieth Regiment, Mississippi Infantry, colonel of the Fifth Regiment, Mississippi Cavalry, and brigadier general of State troops; resided in Jackson, Miss., from 1872 to 1887, when he returned to Carrollton; chairman of the Democratic State executive committee in 1875 and 1876; appointed judge of the State supreme court in 1879 and was elected chief justice by his associates; elected as a Democrat to the United States Senate in 1880; reelected in 1886, and again in 1892, and served from March 4, 1881, until his death; member of the constitutional convention of the State of Mississippi in 1890; died in Mississippi City, Miss., where he had gone in search of health, August 14, 1897; interment in Evergreen Cemetery, Carrollton, Miss.

GEORGE, Melvin Clark, a Representative from Oregon; born near Caldwell, Noble County, Ohio, May 13, 1849; moved with his parents over the Old Oregon Trail in 1851 and settled on a homestead near Lebanon, Linn County, Oreg.; attended the country schools, Santiam Academy, and Willamette University, Oregon; studied law; was admitted to the bar and commenced practice in Portland, Oreg., in 1875; member of the State senate from Multnomah district 1876–1880; received the votes of all the Republican senators for president of the State senate in the session of 1878; elected as a Republican to the Forty-seventh and Forty-eighth Congresses (March 4, 1881–March 3, 1885); declined to be a candidate for renomination in 1884; resumed the practice of law in Portland, Oreg.; judge of the State circuit court 1897–1907; appointed by the circuit judges to superintend the construction of the Burnside Bridge over the Willamette River at Portland; director of the Portland public schools for five years; presidential elector on the Republican ticket of Harding and Coolidge in 1920 and Coolidge and Dawes in 1924, and was selected as the messenger to deliver the electoral vote of Oregon in 1925; died in Portland, Oreg., February 22, 1933; interment in Lone Fir Cemetery.

GEORGE, Myron Virgil, a Representative from Kansas; born in Erie, Neosho County, Kans., January 6, 1900; attended the grade schools and graduated from Labette County High School at Altamont, Kans.; during the First World War enlisted in April 1917 and served in the United States Army with rank of corporal until discharged in May 1919; learned the printing trade on the Altamont Journal, published by his father; owner and publisher of the Edna Sun from 1924–1941; right-of-way agent, Kansas State Highway Commission, 1939–1942, executive secretary 1942–1945, and acting director from May 1945 to September 1945; director of Kansas Secondary Roads Department from October 1945 to December 1946; executive secretary of Kansas State Highway Commission from December 1946 until his resignation in October 1950, having become a candidate for Congress; elected as a Republican to the Eighty-first Congress to fill the vacancy caused by the death of Herbert A. Meyer and at the same time was elected to the Eighty-second Congress; reelected to the Eighty-third, Eighty-fourth, and Eighty-fifth Congresses, and served from November 7, 1950, to January 3, 1959; unsuccessful candidate for reelection in 1958 to the Eighty-sixth Congress; engaged in public relations in the transportation and construction fields; is a resident of Chanute, Kans.

GEORGE, Newell A., a Representative from Kansas; born in Kansas City, Mo., September 24, 1904; attended Hawthorne Grade School, Wyandotte High School, Kansas City, Kans., Wentworth Military Academy, Lexington, Mo., Park College, Parkville, Mo., and University of Kansas City School of Law; graduated from National University, Washington, D. C., in 1935; was admitted to the District of Columbia bar in 1935 and to the Kansas bar in 1941; commenced the practice of law in

Kansas City, Kans.; member of the staff of United States Senator George McGill of Kansas in 1933 and 1934; regional attorney, Bureau of Employment Security, 1941–1945, and Federal Security Agency 1947–1953; chief legal counsel, Regional War Manpower Commission, during World War II; first assistant Wyandotte County attorney 1953–1958; delegate to the Democratic National Convention in 1960; elected as a Democrat to the Eighty-sixth Congress (January 3, 1959–January 3, 1961); unsuccessful candidate for reelection in 1960 to the Eighty-seventh Congress; appointed United States attorney for the district of Kansas March 28, 1961, for a four-year term; is a resident of Kansas City, Kans.

GEORGE, Walter Franklin, a Senator from Georgia; born on a farm near Preston, Webster County, Ga., January 29, 1878; attended the common schools; was graduated from the scientific department of Mercer University, Macon, Ga., in 1900 and from its law department in 1901; was admitted to the bar in 1901 and commenced practice in Vienna, Ga.; solicitor general of the Cordele judicial circuit 1907–1912 and judge of the superior court 1912–1917; judge of the State court of appeals from January 1, 1917, to October 1, 1917, when he resigned; associate justice of the State supreme court from 1917 until his resignation in 1922; elected as a Democrat to the United States Senate on November 7, 1922, to fill the vacancy caused by the death of Thomas E. Watson and took his seat November 22, 1922, for the term ending March 3, 1927; reelected in 1926, 1932, 1938, 1944, and again in 1950 for the term ending January 3, 1957; was not a candidate for renomination in 1956; President Eisenhower's special ambassador to the North Atlantic Treaty Organization until his death; died in Vienna, Ga., August 4, 1957; interment in Vienna Cemetery.

GERAN, Elmer Hendrickson, a Representative from New Jersey; born in Matawan, Monmouth County, N. J., October 24, 1875; attended the public schools and Glenwood Military Academy; was graduated from Peddie Institute, Hightstown, N. J., in 1895, from Princeton University in 1899, and from New York Law School in 1901; was admitted to the New Jersey bar in 1901 and commenced practice in Jersey City, N. J.; member of the State house of assembly in 1911 and 1912; member of the New Jersey State Water Supply Commission 1912–1915; assistant prosecutor of the pleas of Monmouth County 1915–1917; again a member of the State house of assembly in 1916 and 1917 and served as minority leader; sheriff of Monmouth County 1917–1920; appointed United States district attorney for New Jersey by President Wilson in 1920; resigned in 1921 and resumed the practice of law in Asbury Park, N. J.; elected as a Democrat to the Sixty-eighth Congress (March 4, 1923–March 3, 1925); unsuccessful candidate for reelection in 1924 to the Sixty-ninth Congress; resumed the practice of his profession until September 22, 1927; in 1927 became associated with the New Jersey Gravel & Sand Co. at Farmington, and was serving as vice president and treasurer at time of death; died in Marlboro Township, Morganville, N. J., January 12, 1954; interment in Old Tennent Cemetery, Tennent, N. J.

GERLACH, Charles Lewis, a Representative from Pennsylvania; born in Bethlehem, Northampton County, Pa., September 14, 1895; attended the public schools of Bethlehem, Pa.; moved to Allentown, Pa., in 1914; organizer, and later president, of the Allentown Supply Co., dealers in wholesale and retail fuels, burners, heat conditioners, and appliances since 1920; Republican State committeeman in 1936 and 1937; elected as a Republican to the Seventy-sixth and to the four succeeding Congresses and served from January 3, 1939, until his death in Allentown, Pa., May 5, 1947; interment in Greenwood Cemetery.

GERMAN, Obadiah, a Senator from New York; born in Amenia, Dutchess County, N. Y., April 22, 1766; attended the district schools; studied law; was admitted to the bar in 1792 and commenced practice in Norwich, N. Y.; member of the State assembly 1798, 1804, 1805, and 1807–1809; elected as a Democrat to the United States Senate and served from March 4, 1809, to March 3, 1815; judge of Chenango County 1815–1819; appointed commissioner of public works in 1817; again elected a member of the State assembly in 1819 and served as speaker; affiliated with the Whig Party on its organization; died in Norwich, N. Y., September 24, 1842; interment in Riverside Cemetery, North Norwich, N. Y.

GERNERD, Fred Benjamin, a Representative from Pennsylvania; born in Allentown, Lehigh County, Pa., November 22, 1879; attended the public schools; was graduated from Franklin and Marshall College, Lancaster, Pa., in 1901, from the school of political science of Columbia University, New York City, in 1903, and from the law school of Columbia University in 1904; was admitted to the bar in 1904 and commenced practice in Buffalo, N. Y.; returned to Allentown, Pa., in 1905; district attorney of Lehigh County 1908–1912; presidential elector on the Republican ticket of Taft and Butler in 1912; Pennsylvania Republican State committeeman 1912–1920; member of the American Bar Association and those of Lehigh County and Pennsylvania; trustee of Franklin and Marshall College and of Cedar Crest College, Allentown, Pa.; president of the Allentown Hospital Association; honorary president of the Allentown Council of the Boy Scouts of America and of the John Hay Republican Association; elected as a Republican to the Sixty-seventh Congress (March 4, 1921–March 3, 1923); unsuccessful candidate for reelection in 1922 to the Sixty-eighth Congress; resumed the practice of law in Allentown, Pa.; delegate to the Republican National Convention at Kansas City, Mo., in 1928; died in Allentown, Pa., August 7, 1948; interred in Trexlertown Cemetery, Trexlertown, Pa.

GERRY, Elbridge (great-grandfather of Peter Goelet Gerry), a Delegate and a Representative from Massachusetts and a Vice President of the United States; born in Marblehead, Mass., July 17, 1744; pursued classical studies, and was graduated from Harvard College in 1762; engaged in commercial pursuits; member of the colonial house of representatives 1772–1775; Member of the Continental Congress 1776–1781 and 1782–1785; a signer of the Declaration of Independence; delegate to the constitutional convention of the United States held in Philadelphia in 1787; refused to sign the instrument, insisting it gave the President too much power, but subsequently gave it his support; elected as an Anti-Federalist to the First and Second Congresses (March 4, 1789–March 3, 1793); sent to France with Marshall and Pinckney on a diplomatic mission in 1797; unsuccessful Democratic candidate for Governor of Massachusetts in 1801 and again in 1812; Governor of Massachusetts in 1810 and 1811; elected Vice President of the United States as a Democrat on the ticket with James Madison in 1812 and served from March 4, 1813, until his death in Washington, D. C., on November 23, 1814; interment in the Congressional Cemetery.

GERRY, Elbridge (grandson of the preceding), a Representative from Maine; born in Waterford, Oxford County, Maine, December 6, 1813; pursued an academic course and attended Bridgton Academy; studied law; was admitted to the bar in 1839 and commenced practice in Waterford; clerk of the State house of representatives in 1840; appointed United States commissioner in bankruptcy in 1841; prosecuting attorney for Oxford County 1842–1845; member of the State house of representatives in 1846; elected as a Democrat to the Thirty-first Congress (March 4, 1849–

March 3, 1851); was not a candidate for renomination in 1850; moved to Portland, Maine, where he resumed the practice of law; died in Portland, Maine, April 10, 1886; interment in Evergreen Cemetery.

GERRY, James, a Representative from Pennsylvania; born near Rising Sun, Cecil County, Md., August 14, 1796; pursued an academic course and was graduated from West Nottingham Academy; studied medicine at the University of Maryland, Baltimore, Md., and commenced practice in Shrewsbury, Pa., in 1824; elected as a Democrat to the Twenty-sixth and Twenty-seventh Congresses (March 4, 1839–March 3, 1843); continued the practice of medicine until 1870, when he retired; died in Shrewsbury, York County, Pa., July 19, 1873; interment in Lutheran Cemetery.

GERRY, Peter Goelet (great-grandson of Elbridge Gerry), a Representative and a Senator from Rhode Island; born in New York City September 18, 1879; attended the public schools; was graduated from Harvard University, Cambridge, Mass., in 1901; studied law; was admitted to the Rhode Island bar in 1906; member of the representative council of Newport in 1912; delegate to the Democratic National Conventions in 1912, 1916, and 1932; vice president of the American Humane Association; member of the Democratic National Committee 1932–1936; elected as a Democrat to the Sixty-third Congress (March 4, 1913–March 3, 1915); unsuccessful candidate for reelection in 1914 to the Sixty-fourth Congress; elected to the United States Senate in 1916; reelected in 1922 and served from March 4, 1917, to March 3, 1929; unsuccessful candidate for renomination in 1928; elected to the United States Senate in 1934; reelected in 1940 and served from January 3, 1935, to January 3, 1947; was not a candidate for renomination in 1946; resumed the practice of law; died in Providence, R. I., October 31, 1957; interment in St. James Cemetery, Hyde Park, N. Y.

GERVAIS, John Lewis, a Delegate from South Carolina; born, it is said, in France, of Huguenot parents, refugees to Hanover, Germany; attended schools and colleges in Hanover; immigrated to England and later to the United States, arriving in Charleston, S. C., on June 27, 1764; merchant, planter, and landowner; delegate to the provincial convention and Provincial Congress in 1775 and 1776; member of the council of safety in 1775, 1776, and 1781; appointed by Congress deputy postmaster general for South Carolina in 1778; served in the Revolutionary War, in organizing the Army and in the defense of Charleston in 1780; member of the State senate in 1781 and 1782 and served as president; Member of the Continental Congress in 1782 and 1783; member of the committee to which were referred letters from United States representatives abroad in April 1783; commissioner of public accounts for South Carolina in 1794 and 1795; died in Charleston, S. C., August 18, 1798; interment in St. Philip's Churchyard.

GEST, William Harrison, a Representative from Illinois; born in Jacksonville, Morgan County, Ill., January 7, 1838; moved with his parents to Rock Island in 1842; was graduated from Williams College, Williamstown, Mass., in 1860; studied law; was admitted to the bar in 1862 and commenced practice in Rock Island, Ill.; elected as a Republican to the Fiftieth and Fifty-first Congresses (March 4, 1887– March 3, 1891); unsuccessful candidate for reelection in 1890 to the Fifty-second Congress; circuit judge of the fourteenth judicial district of Illinois from June 1897 until his death in Rock Island, Ill., August 9, 1912; interment in Chippiannock Cemetery.

GETZ, James Lawrence, a Representative from Pennsylvania; born in Reading, Berks County, Pa., September 14, 1821; pursued an academic course; one of the founders of the Reading Gazette in 1840; having become sole owner of that paper, some years later he purchased the Jefferson Democrat and merged the two papers under the name of the Reading Gazette and Democrat, disposing of his interests in 1868; studied law; was admitted to the bar in 1846 but never practiced; member of the State house of representatives in 1856 and 1857 and served as speaker of the house during the latter year; elected as a Democrat to the Fortieth, Forty-first, and Forty-second Congresses (March 4, 1867–March 3, 1873); was not a candidate for renomination in 1872; again engaged in the newspaper business; city comptroller of Reading, Pa., from 1888 until his death in that city December 25, 1891; interment in Charles Evans Cemetery.

GEYER, Henry Sheffie, a Senator from Missouri; born in Frederick, Frederick County, Md., December 9, 1790; was instructed privately by an uncle; studied law; was admitted to the bar in 1811 and practiced in Fredericktown until May 2, 1813; during the War of 1812 was commissioned first lieutenant in the Thirty-sixth Regiment, Maryland Infantry, May 20, 1813, and served until June 15, 1815; settled in St. Louis, Mo., in 1815 and resumed the practice of his profession; member of the Territorial assembly in 1818; delegate to the State constitutional convention in 1820; member of the State house of representatives 1820–1824, and served as speaker in 1820, 1822, and 1824; declined the portfolio of Secretary of War tendered by President Fillmore in 1850; elected as a Democrat to the United States Senate and served from March 4, 1851, to March 3, 1857; was not a candidate for reelection; resumed the practice of law in St. Louis, and was one of the counsel in the Dred Scott case; died in St. Louis, Mo., March 5, 1859; interment in Bellefontaine Cemetery.

GEYER, Lee Edward, a Representative from California; born in Wetmore, Nemaha County, Kans., September 9, 1888; attended the public schools; was graduated from Wetmore (Kans.) High School in 1908 and from Baker University, Baldwin City, Kans., in 1922 and afterwards did post-graduate work at the University of Wisconsin at Madison and the University of Southern California at Los Angeles; teacher in the rural schools in Nemaha County, Kans., 1908–1912; principal of Hamlin (Kans.) High School 1916–1918; during the First World War served as a private in the Third Company, First Battalion, Central Officers' Training School, Camp Grant, Ill.; principal of Corning (Kans.) High School 1919–1923 and of Duncan (Ariz.) High School 1923– 1925; football coach of David Starr Jordan High School, Los Angeles, Calif., 1925–1927 and of Bell High School, Los Angeles, 1927–1929; teacher of social sciences in Gardena (Calif.) High School 1929–1938; member of the State house of representatives 1934–1936; unsuccessful candidate for election in 1936 to the Seventy-fifth Congress; elected as a Democrat to the Seventy-sixth and Seventy-seventh Congresses and served from January 3, 1939, until his death; delegate to the Democratic National Convention at Chicago in 1940; died in Washington, D. C., October 11, 1941; interment in Wetmore Cemetery, Wetmore, Nemaha County, Kans.

GHOLSON, James Herbert, a Representative from Virginia; born in Gholsonville, Brunswick County, Va., in 1798; pursued an academic course, and was graduated from Princeton College in 1820; studied law; was admitted to the bar and commenced practice in Percivals, Va.; member of the State house of delegates 1824–1828 and 1830–1833; elected as a Democrat to the Twenty-third Congress (March 4, 1833– March 3, 1835); served as judge of the circuit court for the Brunswick circuit for many years; died in Brunswick County, Va., July 2, 1848.

GHOLSON, Samuel Jameson, a Representative from Mississippi; born near Richmond, Madison County, Ky., May 19, 1808; moved with his father to Franklin County, Ala., in 1817; attended the common schools; studied law; was admitted to the bar at Russellville, Ala., in 1829; moved to Athens, Monroe County, Miss., and commenced the practice of law; member of the State house of representatives in 1835, 1836, and 1839; elected as a Democrat to the Twenty-fourth Congress to fill the vacancy caused by the death of David Dickson and served from December 1, 1836, to March 3, 1837; presented credentials as a Member-elect to the Twenty-fifth Congress and served from July 18, 1837, until February 5, 1838, when the seat was declared vacant; appointed United States district judge in 1839 and served until 1861, when Mississippi seceded from the Union; member of the State secession convention in 1861; during the Civil War served in the Confederate Army as a private, captain, colonel, brigadier general, and major general of State troops; became brigadier general of the Confederate States Army in June 1863, and was placed in command of a brigade of Cavalry; lost an arm at Egypt during Grierson's raid in Mississippi; again a member of the State house of representatives in 1865, 1866, and 1878; continued the practice of law in Aberdeen, Miss., until his death there October 16, 1883; interment in Odd Fellows Cemetery.

GHOLSON, Thomas, Jr., a Representative from Virginia; born in Brunswick, Brunswick County, Va.; pursued an academic course; studied law; was admitted to the bar and commenced practice in Brunswick County, Va.; member of the State house of delegates 1806–1809; elected as a Democrat to the Tenth Congress to fill the vacancy caused by the death of John Claiborne; reelected to the Eleventh and to the three succeeding Congresses and served from November 7, 1808, until his death in Brunswick County, Va., July 4, 1816.

GIAIMO, Robert Nicholas, a Representative from Connecticut; born in New Haven, Conn., October 15, 1919; attended North Haven public schools; graduated from Hillhouse High School at New Haven in 1937, Fordham College, New York City, in 1941, and University of Connecticut in 1943; during World War II served in the United States Army from 1943 until separated from the service as a first lieutenant in 1946; captain, Judge Advocate General Corps, United States Army Reserve; former branch director, Judge Advocate School, and Army Reserve Service School, New Haven, Conn.; was admitted to the bar in 1947 and commenced the practice of law in New Haven, Conn.; member of North Haven Board of Education 1949–1955, serving as secretary 1953–1955, and Board of Finance 1952–1955; assistant clerk, Probate Court, New Haven, Conn., 1952–1954; chairman, Connecticut Personnel Appeals Board 1955–1958; third selectman, North Haven, 1955–1957; member of board of directors Grace-New Haven Community Hospital; unsuccessful Democratic candidate for election in 1956 to the Eighty-fifth Congress; elected as a Democrat to the Eighty-sixth Congress (January 3, 1959–January 3, 1961). *Reelected to the Eighty-seventh Congress.*

GIBBONS, William, a Delegate from Georgia; born at Bear Bluff, S. C., April 8, 1726; studied law in Charleston, S. C.; was admitted to the bar and practiced in Savannah, Ga.; member of the colonial assembly 1760–1762; joined the Sons of Liberty in 1774, and on May 11, 1775, was one of the party that broke open the magazine in Savannah and removed 600 pounds of the King's powder; delegate to the Provincial Congress of July 1775, and was chosen a member of the committee of safety on December 11, 1775; member of the executive council 1777–1781; associate justice of Chatham County in 1781 and 1782; Member of

the Continental Congress in 1784 and 1785; member of the State house of representatives in 1783, 1785–1789, and 1791–1793, and served as speaker in 1783, 1786, and 1787; president of the State constitutional convention in 1789; justice of the inferior court of Chatham County 1790–1792; died in Savannah, Ga., September 27, 1800; interment probably in Colonial Park, formerly called the Old Cemetery, or Christ Church Cemetery.

GIBBS, Florence Reville (widow of Willis Benjamin Gibbs), a Representative from Georgia; born in Thomson, McDuffie County, Ga., April 4, 1890; attended the public schools; was graduated from Brenau College, Gainesville, Ga.; elected as a Democrat to the Seventy-sixth Congress to fill the vacancy caused by the death of her husband, Willis Benjamin Gibbs, and served from October 1, 1940, to January 3, 1941; was not a candidate for reelection in 1940 to the Seventy-seventh Congress; retired from public life and is a resident of Jesup, Ga.

GIBBS, Willis Benjamin (husband of Florence Reville Gibbs), a Representative from Georgia; born in Dupont, Clinch County, Ga., April 15, 1889; attended the public schools and Mercer University, Macon, Ga.; was graduated from the Atlanta (Ga.) Law School in 1911; admitted to the bar and commenced practice in Folkston, Ga., the same year; moved to Jesup, Ga., in 1912 and continued the practice of law; served as solicitor (prosecuting attorney) of the city court of Jesup 1913–1924, and solicitor general (prosecuting attorney) of the Brunswick judicial circuit 1925–1939; county attorney for Wayne County, Ga., 1922–1938; lieutenant colonel on staff of Gov. Clifford Walker in 1924 and 1925; served on the State Board of Control of Eleemosynary Institutions 1931–1937; elected as a Democrat to the Seventy-sixth Congress and served from January 3, 1939, until his death in Washington, D. C., on August 7, 1940; interment in Jesup Cemetery, Jesup, Ga.

GIBSON, Charles Hopper (cousin of Henry Richard Gibson), a Representative and a Senator from Maryland; born near Centerville, Queen Annes County, Md., January 19, 1842; attended Centerville Academy and the Archer School in Harford County; was graduated from Washington College, Chestertown, Md.; studied law; was admitted to the bar in 1864 and commenced practice in Easton, Md.; appointed by President Johnson in 1867 collector of internal revenue for the Eastern Shore district, but his nomination was rejected by a majority of one vote; appointed in 1869 auditor and commissioner in chancery, which offices he resigned in 1870 to accept the appointment of State's attorney for Talbot County; elected to that office in 1871 and 1875; elected as a Democrat to the Forty-ninth, Fiftieth, and Fifty-first Congresses (March 4, 1885–March 3, 1891); was not a candidate for reelection in 1890; appointed and subsequently elected as a Democrat to the United States Senate to fill the vacancy caused by the death of Ephraim K. Wilson and served from November 19, 1891, to March 3, 1897; resumed the practice of law; died in Washington, D. C., March 31, 1900; interment in Chesterfield Cemetery, Centerville, Md.

GIBSON, Ernest Willard (father of Ernest William Gibson), a Representative and a Senator from Vermont; born in Londonderry, Windham County, Vt., December 29, 1872; attended the common schools and Black River Academy, Ludlow, Vt.; was graduated from Norwich University, Northfield, Vt., in 1894; principal of Chester (Vt.) High School 1894–1898; attended the law department of the University of Michigan at Ann Arbor in 1899; was admitted to the bar the same year and commenced practice in Brattleboro, Vt.; register of probate and deputy clerk of the United States district court; served in the State house of representatives in 1906; member of the State senate, serving as president pro tempore in 1908; delegate to the Republican National Convention at Chicago in 1912; enlisted in the Vermont National Guard in 1899 and retired as a colonel in 1908; returned to the service in 1915 as a captain of Infantry; served during the Mexican border troubles and two years during the First World War; was overseas with the Fifty-seventh Pioneer Infantry as captain; promoted to rank of major in the One Hundred and Seventy-second Regiment of Infantry, National Guard, and later served as colonel from August 5, 1921, to November 1, 1923; State's attorney 1919–1921; secretary of civil and military affairs for Vermont in 1921 and 1922; chairman of the board of commissioners of Brattleboro, Vt., for eight years; vice president of Norwich University; elected as a Republican to the Sixty-eighth Congress to fill the vacancy caused by the resignation of Porter H. Dale; reelected to the Sixty-ninth and to the four succeeding Congresses and served from November 6, 1923, to October 19, 1933, when he resigned; appointed to the United States Senate and subsequently elected to fill the vacancy caused by the death of Porter H. Dale; reelected in 1938 and served from November 21, 1933, until his death in Washington, D. C., June 20, 1940; interment in Morningside Cemetery, Brattleboro, Vt.

GIBSON, Ernest William (son of Ernest Willard Gibson), a Senator from Vermont; born in Brattleboro, Windham County, Vt., March 6, 1901; attended the public schools; graduated from Norwich University, Northfield, Vt., in 1923 and commissioned a Reserve second lieutenant in Cavalry and has served continuously since that time; member of the faculty of New York Military Academy, Cornwall, N. Y., in 1923 and 1924; computer in the Coast and Geodetic Survey 1924–1927; attended night classes at George Washington University Law School, Washington, D. C.; was admitted to the bar in 1926 and commenced practice in Brattleboro, Vt., in 1927; State's attorney of Windham County, Vt., 1929–1933; assistant secretary of the Vermont State Senate 1931–1933 and secretary 1933–1940; member of Vermont Railroad Tax Commission from April 1939 to June 1940; appointed as a Republican to the United States Senate to fill the vacancy caused by the death of his father, Ernest W. Gibson, and served from June 24, 1940, to January 3, 1941; was not a candidate for election to fill the vacancy; during World War II entered the armed services as a captain in May 1941 and served in the South Pacific as G–2, Forty-third Infantry Division, being discharged as a colonel in December 1945; received the Silver Star, Legion of Merit, Purple Heart, and the War Department citation; elected Governor of Vermont in 1946 and again in 1948 and served until his resignation January 15, 1950, having been appointed a United States district judge for the district of Vermont, in which capacity he is still serving; is a resident of Brattleboro, Vt.

GIBSON, Eustace, a Representative from West Virginia; born in Culpeper County, Va., October 4, 1842; attended the common schools; studied law; was admitted to the bar and commenced practice in 1861; during the Civil War enlisted in the Confederate Army in June 1861 as first lieutenant; promoted to captain in 1863 and retired on account of wounds; member of the constitutional convention of Virginia in 1867 and 1868; settled in Huntington, W. Va., in 1871; member of the State house of delegates in 1877 and 1878, and served as speaker in 1877; presidential elector on the Democratic ticket of Hancock and English in 1880; elected as a Democrat to the Forty-eighth and Forty-ninth Congresses (March 4, 1883–March 3, 1887); unsuccessful candidate for renomination in 1886 and for nomination in 1888; again resumed the practice of law; died in Clifton Forge, Va., on December 10, 1900; interment in Spring Hill Cemetery, Huntington, W. Va.

GIBSON, Henry Richard (cousin of Charles Hopper Gibson), a Representative from Tennessee; born on Kent Island, Queen Annes County, Md., December 24, 1837; attended the common schools on Kent Island and at Bladensburg, Md.; was graduated from Decker's Academy at Bladensburg in 1858 and from Hobart College, Geneva, N. Y., in 1862; during the Civil War served in the commissary department of the Union Army from March 1863 to July 1865; entered Albany (N. Y.) Law School in September 1865; was admitted to the bar in December 1865 and commenced practice in Knoxville, Tenn., in January 1866; moved to Jacksboro, Campbell County, Tenn., in October 1866; appointed commissioner of claims by Gov. William G. Brownlow in 1868; delegate to the State constitutional convention in 1870; member of the State senate in 1871 and 1872; served as a member of the State house of representatives in 1874 and 1875; returned to Knoxville in 1876; founded the Knoxville Republican in 1879 and became its editor; appointed post-office inspector in 1881; became editor of the Knoxville Daily Chronicle in 1882; appointed United States pension agent at Knoxville on June 22, 1883, and served until June 9, 1885; chancellor of the second chancery division of Tennessee 1886–1894; professor of medical jurisprudence in the Tennessee Medical College 1889–1906; author of "Gibson's Suits in Chancery" in 1891; elected as a Republican to the Fifty-fourth and to the four succeeding Congresses (March 4, 1895–March 3, 1905); declined to be a candidate for renomination in 1904; associate editor in 1896 and associate reviser in 1918 of the "Code of Tennessee"; retired from public life and resided in Washington, D. C., being engaged as a writer and author and as a consulting editor of the American and English Encyclopedia of Law and Practice; died in Washington, D. C., May 25, 1938; remains were cremated and the ashes deposited in the Old Gray Cemetery, Knoxville, Tenn.

GIBSON, James King, a Representative from Virginia; born in Abingdon, Washington County, Va., February 18, 1812; attended the common schools; moved to Huntsville, Limestone County, Ala., in 1833; returned to Abingdon, Va., the following year and engaged in mercantile pursuits; deputy sheriff of Washington County in 1834 and 1835; appointed postmaster of Abingdon on December 19, 1837, and served until July 26, 1849, when a successor was appointed; upon the readmission of the State of Virginia to representation was elected as a Democrat to the Forty-first Congress and served from January 28, 1870, to March 3, 1871; declined to be a candidate for renomination in 1870; engaged in agricultural pursuits and banking; died in Abingdon, Va., March 30, 1879; interment in Sinking Spring Cemetery.

GIBSON, John Strickland, a Representative from Georgia; born near Folkston, Charlton County, Ga., January 3, 1893; attended the common schools; studied law by correspondence from La Salle Extension University, Chicago, Ill.; was admitted to the bar in 1922 and commenced practice in Douglas, Ga., in 1923; solicitor (prosecuting attorney) of the city court of Douglas, Ga., 1928–1934; solicitor general (prosecuting attorney), Waycross judicial circuit, 1934–1940; elected as a Democrat to the Seventy-seventh, Seventy-eighth, and Seventy-ninth Congresses (January 3, 1941–January 3, 1947); unsuccessful candidate for renomination in 1946; resumed the practice of law; died in Douglas, Ga., October 19, 1960; interment in City Cemetery.

GIBSON, Paris, a Senator from Montana; born in Brownfield, Oxford County, Maine, July 1, 1830; attended the common schools and the Fryeburg Academy, Fryeburg, Maine; was graduated from Bowdoin College, Brunswick, Maine, in 1851; engaged in the real-estate business; member of the State house of representatives in 1852; settled in Minneapolis, Minn., in 1858, and in conjunction with W. W. Eastman built the first flour mill in that city; later built and operated the North Star woolen mill in the same place; moved to Fort Benton, Mont., in 1879 and was financially interested in the first flocks of sheep driven into northern Montana; founded the city of Great Falls in 1882, of which he was the first mayor; delegate to the State constitutional convention in 1889; elected to the State senate in 1890; elected as a Democrat to the United States Senate to fill the vacancy caused by the resignation of William A. Clark and served from March 7, 1901, to March 3, 1905; was not a candidate for reelection; engaged in the real-estate business; died in Great Falls, Mont., December 16, 1920; interment in Highland Cemetery.

GIBSON, Randall Lee, a Representative and a Senator from Louisiana; born September 10, 1832, at Spring Hill, near Versailles, Woodford County, Ky., while his parents were on a visit from their home in Terrebonne Parish, La.; was educated by a private tutor at "Live Oak," his father's plantation; was graduated from Yale College in 1853 and from the law department of the University of Louisiana (later Tulane University) New Orleans, La., in 1855; traveled in Europe for several years; engaged in planting until the outbreak of the Civil War; enlisted in the Confederate Army and was appointed aide-de-camp on the staff of Governor Moore; commissioned captain in the First Regiment, Louisiana Artillery, in March 1861, and colonel of the Thirteenth Regiment, Louisiana Infantry, on August 13, 1861; promoted to the rank of brigadier general January 11, 1864; after the war was admitted to the bar and practiced in New Orleans, La.; also resumed agricultural pursuits; served as administrator of the Howard Memorial Library, trustee of the Peabody Fund, Regent of the Smithsonian Institution, and as president of the board of administrators of Tulane University, New Orleans, La.; unsuccessful candidate for election in 1872 to the Forty-third Congress; elected as a Democrat to the Forty-fourth and to the three succeeding Congresses (March 4, 1875–March 3, 1883); elected as a Democrat to the United States Senate; reelected in 1889 and served from March 4, 1883, until his death at Hot Springs, Ark., December 15, 1892; interment Lexington Cemetery, Lexington, Ky.

GIDDINGS, De Witt Clinton, a Representative from Texas; born in Susquehanna County, Pa., July 18, 1827; pursued an academic course; studied law in Honesdale, Pa.; was admitted to the bar in Texas in 1852 and commenced practice in Brenham, Tex.; served in the Confederate Army throughout the Civil War; member of the State constitutional convention in 1866; successfully contested as a Democrat the election of William T. Clark to the Forty-second Congress; reelected to the Forty-third Congress and served from May 13, 1872, to March 3, 1875; again elected to the Forty-fifth Congress (March 4, 1877–March 3, 1879); engaged in the banking business in Brenham, Tex.; delegate to the Democratic National Conventions in 1884, 1888, and 1892; died in Brenham, Tex., on August 19, 1903; interment in Prairie Lea Cemetery.

GIDDINGS, Joshua Reed, a Representative from Ohio; born in Tioga Point (later Athens), Bradford County, Pa., October 6, 1795; moved with his parents to Canandaigua, N. Y., in 1795; received a common-school education; again moved with his parents to Ashtabula County, Ohio, in 1806; completed preparatory studies; served in the War of 1812; taught school; studied law; was admitted to the bar in February 1821 and commenced practice in Jefferson, Ohio; member of the State house of representatives in 1826; elected as an Anti-Slavery Whig to the Twenty-fifth Congress to fill the vacancy caused by the resignation of Elisha Whittlesey; reelected to the Twenty-sixth and Twenty-seventh Congresses and served from December 3, 1838, until March 22, 1842, when he resigned, after a vote of censure had been passed upon him by the House; subsequently elected to

the Twenty-seventh Congress to fill the vacancy caused by his own resignation; reelected to the Twenty-eighth and to the seven succeeding Congresses and served from December 5, 1842, until March 3, 1859; declined to be a candidate for reelection; appointed consul general to the British North American Provinces by President Lincoln on March 25, 1861, and served until his death; died in Montreal, Canada, May 27, 1864; interment in Oakdale Cemetery, Jefferson, Ohio.

GIDDINGS, Napoleon Bonaparte, a Delegate from the Territory of Nebraska; born near Boonsborough, Clark County, Ky., January 2, 1816; moved with his parents to Fayette, Howard County, Mo., in 1828; attended the common schools; during the Texas war of independence enlisted in the army in 1836 and became sergeant major of his regiment; when Texas had gained her independence he was appointed chief clerk in the auditor's office of the Republic of Texas; served as acting auditor until his resignation in 1838; returned to Fayette, Mo., studied law; was admitted to the bar in 1841 and commenced practice in Fayette, Mo.; commissioned as captain of Company A, Second Regiment, Missouri Mounted Volunteers, in the Mexican War July 22, 1846, and served until March 3, 1847, when he resigned; after the close of the war he edited the Union Flag, the first paper published in Franklin County, Mo.; went to California and engaged in gold mining; returned to Missouri, settled in Savannah, and practiced law; moved to Nebraska City, Nebr., and continued the practice of law; when the Territory of Nebraska was formed was elected as a Democrat to the Thirty-third Congress and served from January 5, to March 3, 1855; was not a candidate for renomination in 1854; resumed the practice of law in Savannah, Mo.; was commissioned lieutenant colonel of the Fifty-first Regiment, Missouri Volunteer Infantry, during the Civil War and served from April 11, 1865, to August 31, 1865, when he was honorably discharged; died in Savannah, Mo., August 3, 1897; interment in the City Cemetery.

GIFFORD, Charles Laceille, a Representative from Massachusetts; born in Cotuit, Barnstable County, Mass., March 15, 1871; attended the common schools; taught school in Massachusetts and Connecticut from 1890 to 1900; engaged in the real-estate business in 1900 on Cape Cod and later became interested in the propagation of oysters and the raising of cranberries; member of the State house of representatives in 1912 and 1913; served in the State senate 1914–1919; elected as a Republican to the Sixty-seventh Congress to fill the vacancy caused by the resignation of Joseph Walsh and on the same day was elected to the Sixty-eighth Congress; reelected to the Sixty-ninth and to the eleven succeeding Congresses and served from November 7, 1922, until his death at Cotuit, Mass., August 23, 1947; interment in Mosswood Cemetery.

GIFFORD, Oscar Sherman, a Delegate from the Territory of Dakota and a Representative from South Dakota; born in Watertown, Jefferson County, N. Y., October 20, 1842; moved with his parents to Wisconsin, who settled in Rock County, thence to Brown County, Ill., in 1853; attended the common schools and the local academy at Beloit, Wis.; during the Civil War served in the Union Army as a private in the Elgin (Ill.) Battery 1863–1865; studied law; was admitted to the bar in 1871 and commenced practice in Canton, Territory of Dakota (now South Dakota); district attorney for Lincoln County in 1874; mayor of Canton in 1881 and 1882; member of the State constitutional convention of South Dakota which convened at Sioux Falls September 7, 1883; elected as a Republican a Delegate to the Forty-ninth and Fiftieth Congresses (March 4, 1885–March 3, 1889); upon the admission of South Dakota as a State into the Union was elected as a Representative to the Fifty-first Congress and served from November 2, 1889, to March 3, 1891; was not a candidate for renomination in 1890; resumed the practice of law in Canton, S. Dak., where he died on January 16, 1913; interment in Forest Hill Cemetery.

GILBERT, Abijah, a Senator from Florida; born in Gilbertsville, Otsego County, N. Y., June 18, 1806; attended Gilbertsville Academy, and was graduated from Hamilton College, Clinton, N. Y., in 1822; engaged in mercantile pursuits in New York City 1822–1850; moved to St. Augustine, Fla., in 1865; elected as a Republican to the United States Senate and served from March 4, 1869, to March 3, 1875; retired from business and political life; died in Gilbertsville, N. Y., November 23, 1881; interment in Brookside Cemetery.

GILBERT, Edward, a Representative from California; born in Cherry Valley, Otsego County, N. Y., about 1819; attended the public schools; was a compositor on the Albany Argus in 1839, and later an associate editor; during the war with Mexico served as first lieutenant of Company H in Col. J. D. Stevenson's New York Volunteer Regiment; arrived with his company in San Francisco in March 1847; was in command of the detachment and deputy collector of the port of San Francisco in 1847 and 1848, when the regiment was disbanded; became founder and editor of the Alta California in 1849; member of the State constitutional convention in 1849; upon the admission of California as a State into the Union was elected as a Democrat to the Thirty-first Congress and served from September 11, 1850, to March 3, 1851; was not a candidate for renomination in 1850; killed in a duel with Gen. James W. Denver, near Sacramento, Calif., August 2, 1852; interment in Lone Mountain (now Laurel Hill) Cemetery, San Francisco, Calif.

GILBERT, Ezekiel, a Representative from New York; born in Middletown, Middlesex County, Conn., March 25, 1756; pursued classical studies, and was graduated from Yale College in 1778; studied law; was admitted to the bar and commenced practice in Hudson, N. Y.; member of the State assembly in 1789 and 1790; elected to the Third and Fourth Congresses (March 4, 1793–March 3, 1797); resumed the practice of law; again a member of the State assembly in 1800 and 1801; clerk of Columbia County 1813–1815; died in Hudson, N. Y., July 17, 1841.

GILBERT, George Gilmore (father of Ralph Waldo Emerson Gilbert), a Representative from Kentucky; born in Taylorsville, Spencer County, Ky., December 24, 1849; attended the common schools, Cecilian College in 1868 and 1869, and Lyndland Institute in Kentucky; taught school; was graduated from the law department of the University of Louisville, Kentucky, in 1873; was admitted to the bar and began practice in Taylorsville, Ky., in 1874; prosecuting attorney of Spencer County 1876–1880; member of the State senate 1885–1889; delegate to the Democratic National Convention at Chicago in 1896; elected as a Democrat to the Fifty-sixth and to the three succeeding Congresses (March 4, 1899–March 3, 1907); was not a candidate for reelection; resumed the practice of law; died in Louisville, Ky., November 9, 1909; interment in Cave Hill Cemetery.

GILBERT, Jacob H., a Representative from New York; born in New York City, N. Y., June 17, 1920; attended the public schools and James Monroe High School; was graduated from St. John's College and from St. John's Law School; was admitted to the bar in 1944 and commenced the practice of law in New York City, N. Y.; appointed an assistant corporation counsel of the city of New York and served from January 1949 to December 1950; served in the State assembly 1951–1954; member of the State senate from 1955 to March 1960; elected as a Democrat to the

Eighty-sixth Congress to fill the vacancy caused by the resignation of Isidore Dollinger and served from March 8, 1960, to January 3, 1961. *Reelected to the Eighty-seventh Congress.*

GILBERT, Newton Whiting, a Representative from Indiana; born in Worthington, Franklin County, Ohio, May 24, 1862; moved with his parents to Steuben County, Ind., in 1875; attended the common schools of Ohio and Indiana and Ohio State University at Columbus; studied law; was admitted to the bar in 1885 and commenced practice in Angola, Ind.; appointed surveyor of Steuben County, Ind., in 1886 and elected to the office in 1888; member of the State senate 1896–1900; Lieutenant Governor of Indiana 1900–1904; captain of Company H, One Hundred and Fifty-seventh Indiana Volunteer Infantry, during the war with Spain; elected as a Republican to the Fifty-ninth Congress and served from March 4, 1905, to November 6, 1906, when he resigned; judge of the court of first instance at Manila, Philippine Islands, 1906–1908, by appointment of President Theodore Roosevelt; member of the Philippine Commission in 1908 and 1909; president of the board of regents, Philippine University, in 1908 and 1909; served as secretary of public instruction of the Philippine Islands in 1909; Vice Governor of the Philippine Islands 1909–1913; moved to New York City, N. Y., in 1916 and resumed the practice of law; delegate to the Republican National Convention at Chicago in 1916; retired in 1937 and moved to Santa Ana, Calif.; died in Santa Ana on July 5, 1939; interment in Circle Hill Cemetery, Angola, Ind.

GILBERT, Ralph Waldo Emerson (son of George Gilmore Gilbert), a Representative from Kentucky; born in Taylorsville, Spencer County, Ky., January 17, 1882; attended the public schools, and the University of Virginia at Charlottesville; was graduated from the law school of the University of Louisville in 1901; was admitted to the bar the same year and commenced practice in Shelbyville, Ky.; elected judge of the Shelby County Court in 1910; reelected in 1914 and served until his resignation in 1917; elected as a Democrat to the Sixty-seventh and to the three succeeding Congresses (March 4, 1921–March 3, 1929); unsuccessful candidate for reelection in 1928 to the Seventy-first Congress; member of the State house of representatives in 1929; elected to the Seventy-second Congress (March 4, 1931–March 4, 1933); was not a candidate for renomination in 1932; resumed the practice of law in Shelbyville, Ky.; again served in the State house of representatives in 1933; elected a member of the State senate in 1936 and served until his death in Louisville, Ky., July 30, 1939; interment in Grove Hill Cemetery, Shelbyville, Ky.

GILBERT, Sylvester, a Representative from Connecticut; born in Hebron, Tolland County, Conn., October 20, 1755; pursued classical studies, and was graduated from Dartmouth College, Hanover, N. H., in 1775; studied law; was admitted to the bar in November 1777 and commenced practice in Hebron; member of the State house of representatives 1780–1812; State's attorney for Tolland County 1786–1807; chief judge of the county court and judge of the probate court 1807–1818; principal of a law school 1810–1818; member of the State senate in 1815 and 1816; elected to the Fifteenth Congress to fill the vacancy caused by the resignation of Uriel Holmes and served from November 16, 1818, to March 3, 1819; resumed the practice of law in Hebron; again judge of the county court 1820–1825; again a member of the State house of representatives in 1826; died in Hebron, Conn., January 2, 1846; interment in Old Cemetery.

GILBERT, William Augustus, a Representative from New York; born in Gilead, Conn., January 25, 1815; moved with his parents to Champion, N. Y.; attended the public schools;

studied law; was admitted to the New York bar in 1843 and commenced the practice of law in Adams, N. Y.; member of the State assembly in 1851 and 1852; elected as a Whig to the Thirty-fourth Congress and served from March 4, 1855, until his resignation February 27, 1857; served as president of Adams village in 1859 and 1860; engaged in the banking business; died in Adams, Jefferson County, N. Y., on May 25, 1875; interment in the Rural Cemetery.

GILCHRIST, Fred Cramer, a Representative from Iowa; born in California, Washington County, Pa., June 2, 1868; moved with his parents to Cedar Falls, Iowa, in 1871; attended the public schools; was graduated from State Teachers' College, Cedar Falls, Iowa, in 1886; teacher and superintendent of schools in Laurens and Rolfe, Iowa, 1886–1890; superintendent of schools of Pocahontas County, Iowa, 1890–1892; was graduated from the law department of the State University of Iowa at Iowa City in 1893; was admitted to the bar in 1893 and commenced practice in Laurens, Iowa; member of the State house of representatives 1902–1904; president of the board of education of Laurens, Iowa, 1905–1928; served in the State senate 1923–1931; elected as a Republican to the Seventy-second and to the six succeeding Congresses (March 4, 1931–January 3, 1945); unsuccessful candidate for renomination in 1944; resumed the practice of law; died in Laurens, Iowa, March 10, 1950; interment in Laurens Cemetery.

GILDEA, James Hilary, a Representative from Pennsylvania; born in Coaldale, Schuylkill County, Pa., October 21, 1890; attended the public schools; apprenticed to the printing trade in 1905; engaged in the newspaper publishing business since 1910, when he founded the Coaldale (Pa.) Observer, being editor and publisher since that date; received the American Legion Distinguished Service Certificate in 1930 for community and Legion service; chairman of the Coaldale Relief Society 1930–1933, and of the Panther Valley Miners' Equalization Committee; elected as a Democrat to the Seventy-fourth and Seventy-fifth Congresses (January 3, 1935–January 3, 1939); unsuccessful candidate for reelection in 1938 to the Seventy-sixth Congress, for election in 1940 to the Seventy-seventh Congress, and in 1950 to the Eighty-second Congress; superintendent of Coaldale State Hospital; is a resident of Coaldale, Pa.

GILES, William Branch, a Representative and a Senator from Virginia; born near Amelia Court House, Amelia County, Va., August 12, 1762; pursued classical studies, and was graduated from Princeton College in 1781; studied law; was admitted to the bar and practiced in Petersburg, Va., 1784–1789; elected as an Anti-Federalist to the First Congress to fill the vacancy caused by the death of Theodorick Bland; reelected to the Second and to the three succeeding Congresses and served from December 7, 1790, to October 2, 1798, when he resigned; presidential elector on the Democratic ticket of Jefferson and Burr in 1800; member of the State house of delegates 1798–1800; elected as a Democrat to the Seventh Congress (March 4, 1801–March 3, 1803); appointed to the United States Senate to fill the vacancy in the term beginning March 4, 1803, caused by the resignation of Abraham B. Venable; while holding the office of Senator-designate was elected on December 4, 1804, to fill the vacancy in the term beginning March 4, 1799, caused by the resignation of Wilson C. Nicholas; was reelected in 1804 and 1811 and served successively in the two classes from August 11, 1804, to March 3, 1815, when he resigned; again a member of the State house of delegates in 1816, 1817, 1826, and 1827; unsuccessful candidate for election to the United States Senate in 1825; served as Governor of Virginia from March 4, 1827, to March 4, 1830, was a member of the State constitutional convention in

1829 and 1830; again elected Governor in 1830, but declined; died on his estate, "Wigwam," near Amelia Court House, Amelia County, Va., December 4, 1830; interment in a private cemetery on his estate.

GILES, William Fell, a Representative from Maryland; born in Harford County, Md., April 8, 1807; attended a private academy and the Bel Air Academy; studied law; was admitted to the bar in 1829 and commenced practice in Baltimore, Md.; member of the State house of delegates 1838–1840; elected as a Democrat to the Twenty-ninth Congress (March 4, 1845–March 3, 1847); declined to be a candidate for renomination; United States district judge for the district of Maryland from July 18, 1853, until his death; officer of the American Colonization Society for more than thirty years, and for more than twenty years one of the commissioners of the State of Maryland for removing its free Negroes to Liberia; died in Baltimore, Md., March 21, 1879; interment in Greenmount Cemetery.

GILFILLAN, Calvin Willard, a Representative from Pennsylvania; born near East Brook, Mercer (now Lawrence) County, Pa., February 20, 1832; attended the common schools and was graduated from Westminster College, New Wilmington, Pa.; superintendent of schools of Mercer County for two terms; clerk of the State house of representatives in 1859; studied law; was admitted to the bar in 1859 and commenced practice in Mercer, Pa.; appointed prosecuting attorney for Venango County in 1861, and elected in 1862 for three years; elected as a Republican to the Forty-first Congress (March 4, 1869–March 3, 1871); unsuccessful candidate for reelection in 1870 to the Forty-second Congress; resumed the practice of law, in which he continued until 1873; later engaged in banking; delegate to the Republican National Convention at Philadelphia in 1872; presidential elector on the Republican ticket of Garfield and Arthur in 1880; died in Franklin, Pa., December 2, 1901; interment in the Franklin Cemetery.

GILFILLAN, John Bachop, a Representative from Minnesota; born in Barnet, Caledonia County, Vt., February 11, 1835; attended the common schools; was graduated from the Caledonia County Academy in 1855; moved to Minneapolis, Minn.; taught school; studied law; was admitted to the bar in July 1860 and commenced practice in Minneapolis, Minn.; member of the board of education 1860–1868; city prosecuting attorney 1861–1864; prosecuting attorney of Hennepin County 1863–1867 and 1869–1873; alderman of the city of Minneapolis 1865–1869; member of the State senate 1875–1885; regent of the University of Minnesota at Minneapolis 1880–1888; elected as a Republican to the Forty-ninth Congress (March 4, 1885–March 3, 1887); unsuccessful candidate for reelection in 1886 to the Fiftieth Congress; resumed the practice of law; died in Minneapolis, Minn., August 19, 1924; interment in Lakewood Cemetery.

GILHAMS, Clarence Chauncey, a Representative from Indiana; born in Brighton, Lagrange County, Ind., April 11, 1860; attended the common schools and the State normal school at Terre Haute, Ind.; taught school; was employed as a salesman; auditor of Lagrange County 1894–1902; engaged in the life insurance business; elected as a Republican to the Fifty-ninth Congress to fill the vacancy caused by the resignation of Newton W. Gilbert; reelected to the Sixtieth Congress and served from November 6, 1906, to March 3, 1909; unsuccessful candidate for reelection in 1908 to the Sixty-first Congress; studied law; was admitted to the bar in 1910; resumed the life insurance business; died in Lagrange, Ind., June 5, 1912; interment in Greenwood Cemetery.

GILL, John, Jr., a Representative from Maryland; born in Baltimore, Md, June 9, 1850; pursued an academic course in Hampden-Sidney College, Virginia; was graduated from the University of Maryland at Baltimore in 1870; studied law; was admitted to the bar in 1871 and commenced practice in Baltimore, Md.; member of the State house of delegates 1874–1877; examiner of titles in the Baltimore city legal department 1879–1884; served in the State senate 1882–1886, 1904, and 1905; delegate to all Democratic State conventions from 1880 to 1908; delegate to the Democratic National Conventions in 1884, 1888, and 1892; police commissioner 1888–1897; elected as a Democrat to the Fifty-ninth, Sixtieth, and Sixty-first Congresses (March 4, 1905–March 3, 1911); was not a candidate for reelection in 1910; judge of the appeal tax court of the city of Baltimore 1912–1918; died in Baltimore, Md., January 27, 1918; the remains were cremated at Loudon Park Crematorium and the ashes scattered to the winds.

GILL, Joseph John, a Representative from Ohio; born in Barnesville, Belmont County, Ohio, September 21, 1846; moved with his parents to Mount Pleasant, Jefferson County, in 1848; pursued an academic course, and was graduated from the law department of the University of Michigan at Ann Arbor in 1868; was admitted to the bar and commenced practice in Jefferson County, Ohio; subsequently engaged in banking, and later in manufacturing and iron mining; elected as a Republican to the Fifty-sixth Congress to fill the vacancy caused by the death of Lorenzo Danford; reelected to the Fifty-seventh and Fifty-eighth Congresses and served from December 4, 1899, until October 31, 1903, when he resigned; died in Steubenville, Ohio, May 22, 1920; interment in Union Cemetery.

GILL, Michael Joseph, a Representative from Missouri; born in Covington, Kenton County, Ky., December 5, 1864; attended the common schools and Oberlin (Ohio) College; engaged in the glass manufacturing business; chairman of the advisory board of the National Bottle Blowers' Association of the United States and Canada in 1889; executive member of the National Bottle Blowers' Association 1892–1912; member of the State house of representatives 1892–1896; delegate to the Democratic National Convention at Baltimore in 1912; successfully contested as a Democrat the election of Leonidas C. Dyer to the Sixty-third Congress and served from June 19, 1914, to March 3, 1915; unsuccessful candidate for reelection; served as Government labor conciliator from March 31 to May 31, 1916, and from July 1 to October 2, 1916; died in St. Louis, Mo., November 1, 1918; interment in Calvary Cemetery.

GILL, Patrick Francis, a Representative from Missouri; born in Independence, Jackson County, Mo., August 16, 1868; moved with his widowed mother to St. Louis, Mo., in 1871; attended the parochial schools and St. Louis University in 1890; engaged in the grocery business; clerk of the circuit court 1904–1908; unsuccessful candidate for sheriff in 1906; elected as a Democrat to the Sixty-first Congress (March 4, 1909–March 3, 1911); successfully contested the election of Theron E. Catlin to the Sixty-second Congress and served from August 12, 1912, to March 3, 1913; unsuccessful candidate for renomination; served as mediator in the Bureau of Mediation and Conciliation, Department of Labor, from July 13, 1918, to September 11, 1922; died in St. Louis, Mo., May 21, 1923; interment in Calvary Cemetery.

GILLEN, Courtland Craig, a Representative from Indiana; born in Roachdale, Putnam County, Ind., July 3, 1880; attended the rural schools; was graduated from Fincastle High School in 1897; taught common and high schools for five years 1897–1904; attended De Pauw University at Greencastle, Ind., 1901–1903; was graduated from the law department of the University of Indianapolis (Indiana Law School) in 1905; was admitted to the bar in 1904 and commenced practice in Greencastle, Putnam County, Ind.; served as county attorney 1909–1914 and as prosecuting attorney of the sixty-fourth judicial circuit in 1917 and 1918; delegate to the Democratic State convention in 1924; alternate delegate to the Democratic National Convention at Philadelphia in 1936; elected as a Democrat to the Seventy-second Congress (March 4, 1931–March 3, 1933); unsuccessful candidate for renomination in 1932; elected judge of the sixty-fourth judicial circuit (Putnam Circuit Court) in 1934 and served from January 1, 1935, until his resignation on April 15, 1939; resumed the private practice of law; died in Greencastle, Ind., September 1, 1954; interment in Forest Hill Cemetery.

GILLESPIE, Dean Milton, a Representative from Colorado; born in Salina, Saline County, Kans., May 3, 1884; attended the public schools and Salina Normal University; engaged in agricultural pursuits and cattle raising in Clay County, Kans., 1900–1904; moved to Denver, Colo., in 1905 and worked as grocery clerk, sign painter, and salesman; engaged in the automobile and oil business since 1905; elected as a Republican to the Seventy-eighth Congress to fill the vacancy caused by the death of Lawrence Lewis, reelected to the Seventy-ninth Congress, and served from March 7, 1944, to January 3, 1947; unsuccessful candidate for reelection in 1946 to the Eightieth Congress; reengaged in his former business pursuits until his death, while on a business trip, in Baltimore, Md., February 2, 1949; interment in Fairmount Cemetery, Denver, Colo.

GILLESPIE, Eugene Pierce, a Representative from Pennsylvania; born in Greenville, Mercer County, Pa., September 24, 1852; attended the public schools, Allegheny College, Meadville, Pa., and St. Michael's College, Toronto, Canada; studied law; was admitted to the bar in August 1874 and commenced practice in Greenville, Pa.; elected as a Democrat to the Fifty-second Congress (March 4, 1891–March 3, 1893); unsuccessful candidate for reelection in 1892 to the Fifty-third Congress; returned to Greenville, Pa., and continued the practice of law until his death December 16, 1899; interment in Shenango Valley Cemetery.

GILLESPIE, James, a Representative from North Carolina; born in Kenansville, Duplin County, N. C.; pursued classical studies; member of the State constitutional convention in 1776; member of the State house of commons 1779–1783; served in the State senate 1784–1786; elected to the Third, Fourth, and Fifth Congresses (March 4, 1793–March 3, 1799); elected to the Eighth Congress and served from March 4, 1803, until his death in Washington, D. C., January 11, 1805; interment in Congressional Cemetery.

GILLESPIE, James Frank, a Representative from Illinois; born in White Sulphur Springs, Greenbrier County, W. Va., April 18, 1869; attended the graded schools and Concord (W. Va.) Normal School; taught in the public schools at White Sulphur Springs, W. Va., in 1891 and 1892; principal of White Sulphur Springs High School in 1891; studied law at Central College, Danville, Ind.; was admitted to the bar in 1892 and commenced practice in Charleston, W. Va.; moved to Bloomington, McLean County, Ill., in 1894 and continued the practice of law; also engaged in agricultural pursuits; served in the State house of representatives in 1913 and 1914; elected as a Democrat to the Seventy-third Congress (March 4, 1933–January 3, 1935); unsuccessful candidate for reelection in 1934 to the Seventy-fourth Congress and for election in 1936 to the Seventy-fifth Congress; resumed the practice of law in Bloomington, Ill., until his death there on November 26, 1954; interment in Park Hill Cemetery.

GILLESPIE, Oscar William, a Representative from Texas; born near Quitman, Clarke County, Miss., June 20, 1858; attended private schools, and was graduated from Mansfield College, Texas, in 1885; studied law; was admitted to the bar in 1886 and commenced practice in Fort Worth, Tex., assistant attorney of Tarrant County 1886–1888; prosecuting attorney of Tarrant County 1890–1894; elected as a Democrat to the Fifty-eighth and to the three succeeding Congresses (March 4, 1903–March 3, 1911); unsuccessful candidate for renomination in 1910; resumed the practice of law in Fort Worth, Tex., where he died August 23, 1927; interment in Mansfield Cemetery, Mansfield, Tex.

GILLET, Charles William, a Representative from New York; born in Addison, Steuben County, N. Y., November 26, 1840; attended the public schools and the Delaware Literary Institute, Franklin, N. Y.; was graduated from Union College, Schenectady, N. Y., in 1861; during the Civil War enlisted as a private in the Eighty-sixth Regiment, New York Volunteer Infantry, in August 1861; promoted to adjutant of the regiment in November 1861; was wounded and honorably discharged for physical disability in 1863; engaged in the manufacture of sash, doors, and blinds in Addison; appointed postmaster of Addison on June 15, 1878, and served until July 26, 1886; elected as a Republican to the Fifty-third and to the five succeeding Congresses (March 4, 1893–March 3, 1905); declined to be a candidate for renomination in 1904; engaged in the management of his financial affairs; died at the home of his daughter in New York City December 31, 1908; interment in the Rural Cemetery, Addison, N. Y.

GILLET, Ransom Hooker, a Representative from New York; born in New Lebanon, Columbia County, N. Y., January 27, 1800; pursued an academic course; studied law in Canton, N. Y.; was admitted to the bar and commenced practice in Ogdensburg; postmaster of Ogdensburg, N. Y., 1830–1833; delegate to the Democratic National Convention at Baltimore in 1832; elected as a Democrat to the Twenty-third and Twenty-fourth Congresses (March 4, 1833–March 3, 1837); was not a candidate for renomination in 1836; commissioner to treat with the New York Indians 1837–1839; delegate to the Democratic National Convention at Baltimore in 1840; appointed Register of the Treasury and served from April 1, 1845, to May 27, 1847, when he was appointed Solicitor of the Treasury, and continued in this office until October 31, 1849; appointed Assistant Attorney General and served from 1855 to 1858; appointed solicitor of the court of claims and served from 1858 to 1861; retired from public life in 1867 and engaged in literary pursuits; died in Washington, D. C., October 24, 1876; interment in Glenwood Cemetery.

GILLETT, Frederick Huntington, a Representative and a Senator from Massachusetts; born in Westfield, Hampden County, Mass., October 16, 1851; attended the public schools; was graduated from Amherst College, Amherst, Mass., in 1874 and from the law department of Harvard University in 1877; was admitted to the bar at Springfield, Mass., in 1877 and commenced practice in that city; assistant attorney general of Massachusetts 1879–1882; member of the State house of representatives in 1890 and 1891; elected as a Republican to the Fifty-third and to the fifteen succeeding Congresses, and served from March 4, 1893, to March 3, 1925; Speaker in the Sixty-sixth, Sixty-seventh, and Sixty-eighth Congresses; was not a candidate for renomination to the Sixty-ninth Congress, having become a candidate of the Republican Party for United States Senator; elected to the United States Senate in 1924 and served from March 4, 1925 to March 3, 1931; was not a candidate for

renomination in 1930; engaged in literary pursuits; died in Springfield, Mass., July 31, 1935; interment in Pine Hill Cemetery, Westfield, Mass.

GILLETT, James Norris, a Representative from California; born in Viroqua, Vernon County, Wis., September 20, 1860; moved with his parents to Sparta, Wis., in 1865; attended the grammar and high schools; studied law; was admitted to the bar in 1881 and commenced practice in Sparta, Wis.; moved to Eureka, Humboldt County, Calif., in 1883 and continued the practice of law; city attorney 1889–1895; member of the State senate 1897–1899; elected as a Republican to the Fifty-eighth and Fifty-ninth Congresses and served from March 4, 1903, to November 4, 1906, when he resigned, having been elected Governor; served as Governor of California 1907–1911; resumed the practice of law in San Francisco, Calif., and resided in Berkeley, Calif., until his death there on April 20, 1937; interment in Oakland Columborium, Oakland, Calif.

GILLETTE, Edward Hooker (son of Francis Gillette), a Representative from Iowa; born in Bloomfield, Hartford County, Conn., October 1, 1840; attended the public schools at Hartford, Conn., and the New York State Agricultural College, Ovid, N. Y.; moved to Des Moines, Iowa, in 1863 and engaged in agricultural pursuits, building, and manufacturing; editor of the Iowa Tribune; chairman of the national committee of the Greenback Party; delegate to the Greenback National Convention at Indianapolis in 1876 which nominated Peter Cooper, of New York, for President; elected as the candidate of the Greenback Party to the Forty-sixth Congress (March 4, 1879–March 3, 1881); unsuccessful candidate for reelection in 1880 to the Forty-seventh Congress; retired from public life and resided on his farm, "Clover Hills Place," near Valley Junction, Iowa, where he died August 14, 1918; interment in Glendale Cemetery.

GILLETTE, Francis (father of Edward Hooker Gillette), a Senator from Connecticut; born in that portion of Old Windsor now included in the town of Bloomfield, Hartford County, Conn., December 14, 1807; moved with his parents to Ashfield, Mass., where he fitted himself for college; was graduated from Yale College in 1829; commenced the study of law, but his health becoming impaired he engaged in agricultural pursuits in Bloomfield; member of the State house of representatives in 1832, 1836, and 1838; unsuccessful candidate for Governor in 1841 and several times subsequently as the candidate of the Liberty and Free-Soil Parties; chairman of the board of education of Connecticut 1849–1865; moved to Hartford in 1852; elected as a Free-Soil Whig to the United States Senate to fill the vacancy caused by the resignation of Truman Smith and served from May 24, 1854, to March 3, 1855; was not a candidate for reelection in 1854; engaged in lecturing on agriculture and total abstinence; trustee of the State normal school and served as its president for many years; aided in the formation of the Republican Party and for several years was a silent partner in the Evening Press, the first distinctive organ of that party; engaged in the real-estate business in Hartford, Conn; died in Hartford, Conn., on September 30, 1879; interment in Riverside Cemetery, Farmington, Conn.

GILLETTE, Guy Mark, a Representative and a Senator from Iowa; born in Cherokee, Cherokee County, Iowa, February 3, 1879; attended the public schools; was graduated from the law department of Drake University, Des Moines, Iowa, in 1900; was admitted to the bar in 1900 and commenced practice in Cherokee; during the Spanish-American War served as a sergeant in the Fifty-second Iowa Regiment, United States Army, from May 25, 1898, until discharged October 30, 1898; engaged in agricultural pursuits; city attorney of Cherokee in 1906 and 1907; prosecuting attorney of Cherokee County 1907–1909; member of the State senate 1912–1916; during the First World War served from November 27, 1917, as a captain in the Forty-ninth Regulars, United States Army, with five months overseas, and was discharged March 10, 1919; elected as a Democrat to the Seventy-third and Seventy-fourth Congresses and served from March 4, 1933, until his resignation on November 3, 1936, having been elected to the United States Senate to fill the vacancy caused by the death of Richard Louis Murphy during the term ending January 3, 1939; reelected in 1938 and served from November 4, 1936, to January 3, 1945; unsuccessful candidate for reelection in 1944; appointed on January 18, 1945, as chairman of the Surplus Property Board and served until his resignation on July 15, 1945, to become president of the American League for a Free Palestine, in which capacity he served from August 1, 1945, until January 1, 1948; elected to the United States Senate and served from January 3, 1949, to January 3, 1955; unsuccessful candidate for reelection in 1954; engaged as counsel with the Senate Post Office and Civil Service Committee from March 1955 to July 1956 and with the Judiciary Committee until June 1961; is a resident of Cherokee, Iowa.

GILLETTE, Wilson Darwin, a Representative from Pennsylvania; born on a farm near Sheshequin, Bradford County, Pa., July 1, 1880; attended the public schools, Ulster (Pa.) High School, and Susquehanna Collegiate Institute, Towanda, Pa.; engaged in agricultural pursuits, clerked in a general store, and has been a dealer and distributor of automobiles since 1913; member of the State house of representatives 1930–1941; elected as a Republican to the Seventy-seventh Congress to fill the vacancy caused by the death of Albert G. Rutherford; reelected to the Seventy-eighth and to the four succeeding Congresses and served from November 4, 1941, until his death in Towanda, Pa., August 7, 1951; interment in Oak Hill Cemetery.

GILLIE, George W., a Representative from Indiana; born in Berwickshire, Scotland, August 15, 1880; moved to the United States with his parents, who settled in Kankakee, Ill., in 1882 and in Fort Wayne, Ind., in 1884; attended the public schools, International Business College, Fort Wayne, Ind., in 1898, and Purdue University, Lafayette, Ind., 1899–1901; was graduated from Ohio State University at Columbus in 1907 as doctor of veterinary surgery; meat and dairy inspector of Allen County, Ind., 1908–1914; began the practice of veterinary medicine in Fort Wayne, Ind., in 1914; sheriff of Allen County 1917–1920, 1929–1930, and 1935–1937; elected as a Republican to the Seventy-sixth and to the four succeeding Congresses (January 3, 1939–January 3, 1949); unsuccessful candidate for reelection in 1948 to the Eighty-first Congress; engaged in agricultural pursuits; president of Allen County Historical Society and Allen County Tax Adjustment Board; Chairman of Allen County Fort Wayne Humane Commission; resides in Fort Wayne, Ind.

GILLIS, James Lisle, a Representative from Pennsylvania; born in Hebron, Washington County, N. Y., October 2, 1792; attended the public schools; became a tanner; served in the War of 1812; moved to Ridgway, Pa., in 1822; appointed associate judge of Jefferson County by Governor Porter; member of the State house of representatives in 1840 and 1851; one of the judges of Jefferson County in 1842; member of the State senate in 1845; served as a mail agent in San Francisco, Calif., under President Pierce; elected as a Democrat to the Thirty-fifth Congress (March 4, 1857–March 3, 1859); appointed agent for the Pawnee Tribe of Indians; died in Mount Pleasant, Henry County, Iowa, July 8, 1881; interment in Forest Home Cemetery.

GILLON, Alexander, a Representative from South Carolina; born in Rotterdam, Holland, in 1741; pursued an academic course; immigrated to London, England, and engaged in commerce; was master of merchant vessels that entered the port of Charleston, S. C., in 1765 and 1766; about the end of the latter year settled in Charleston, and established and carried on for many years a large and profitable business; delegate to the Second Provincial Congress of South Carolina in 1775 and 1776; member of the first general assembly in 1776; was elected captain of the newly organized German Fusiliers of Charleston, a company of the militia of South Carolina, in May 1775; commodore of the South Carolina Navy in 1778 and was sent to France to procure vessels; purchased *L'Judieu,* a powerful frigate, for the South Carolina Navy, changed its name to *South Carolina,* with which he joined the fleet of Spanish vessels, and together they captured the Bahama Islands May 8, 1782; delegate to the State convention which adopted the Constitution of the United States in 1788; elected to the Third Congress and served from March 4, 1793, until his death at his plantation, "Gillon's Retreat," Orangeburg District, S. C., October 6, 1794; interment in the family burial ground at "Gillon's Retreat," Calhoun County, S. C.

GILMAN, Charles Jervis (grandnephew of John Taylor Gilman and Nicholas Gilman), a Representative from Maine; born in Exeter, Rockingham County, N. H., February 26, 1824; attended Phillips Exeter Academy, Exeter, N. H., and pursued classical studies; was graduated from Harvard Law School; was admitted to the bar in 1850 and commenced practice in Exeter, N. H.; member of the house of representatives of New Hampshire in 1851 and 1852; moved to Brunswick, Maine, and continued the practice of law; member of the house of representatives of Maine in 1854 and 1855; member of the State Whig committee; elected as a Republican to the Thirty-fifth Congress (March 4, 1857–March 3, 1859); declined to be a candidate for renomination in 1858; delegate to the Republican National Convention at Chicago in 1860 which nominated the presidential ticket of Lincoln and Hamlin; interested in introducing waterworks and other public improvements; died in Brunswick, Maine, on February 5, 1901; interment in Pine Grove Cemetery.

GILMAN, John Taylor (brother of Nicholas Gilman and granduncle of Charles Jervis Gilman), a Delegate from New Hampshire; born in Exeter, Rockingham County, N. H., December 19, 1753; received a limited education; engaged in shipbuilding and also in agricultural pursuits; one of the Minutemen of 1775; selectman in 1777 and 1778; member of the State house of representatives in 1779 and 1781; delegate to the convention of the States in Hartford, Conn., in October 1780; Member of the Continental Congress in 1782 and 1783; State treasurer in 1791; moderator 1791–1794, 1806, 1807, 1809–1811, 1817, 1818, and 1820–1825; Governor of New Hampshire 1794–1805; unsuccessful candidate for reelection in 1805; again a member of the State house of representatives in 1810 and 1811; presidential elector on the Peace Party ticket of Clinton and Ingersoll in 1812; again an unsuccessful candidate for Governor in 1812; elected Governor and served from 1813 to 1816; declined to be a candidate for renomination for Governor in 1816; ex officio trustee of Dartmouth College, Hanover, N. H., 1794–1805 and 1813–1816, and trustee by election 1817–1819; president of the board of trustees of Phillips Exeter Academy, Exeter, N. H., 1795–1827, and donor of the property upon which the older buildings stand; died in Exeter, N. H., September 1, 1828; interment in Exeter Cemetery.

GILMAN, Nicholas (brother of John Taylor Gilman and granduncle of Charles Jervis Gilman), a Delegate, a Representative, and a Senator from New Hampshire; born in Exeter,

Rockingham County, N. H., August 3, 1755; pursued an academic course; employed as a clerk in his father's countinghouse; served as adjutant in Colonel Scammell's regiment during the Revolutionary War; Member of the Continental Congress 1786–1788; member of the Constitutional Convention in 1787; elected as a Federalist to the First and to the three succeeding Congresses (March 4, 1789–March 3, 1797); declined to be a candidate for renomination in 1796; presidential elector in 1793 and in 1797; elected in 1805 as a Democrat to the United States Senate; reelected in 1811 and served from March 4, 1805, until his death in Philadelphia, Pa., May 2, 1814; interment in Exeter Cemetery, Exeter, N. H.

GILMER, George Rockingham, a Representative from Georgia; born near Lexington, Wilkes (now Oglethorpe) County, Ga., April 11, 1790; attended a classical school and an academy at Abbeville, S. C.; taught a private school while studying law; served as first lieutenant in the Forty-third Regiment, United States Infantry, from 1813 to 1815 in the campaign against the Creek Indians and built a fort on the Chattahoochie River at Standing Peachtree, which became the town of Marthasville and later the city of Atlanta, Ga.; resumed the study of law and began practice in Lexington in 1818; member of the State house of representatives in 1818, 1819, and 1824; elected as a Democrat to the Seventeenth Congress (March 4, 1821–March 3, 1823); resumed the practice of law; trustee of the University of Georgia at Athens 1826–1857; elected to the Twentieth Congress to fill the vacancy caused by the resignation of Edward F. Tatnall and served from October 1, 1827, to March 3, 1829; reelected to the Twenty-first Congress, but failing to signify his acceptance, the Governor announced a vacancy and ordered a new election; Governor of Georgia 1829–1831; elected to the Twenty-third Congress (March 4, 1833–March 3, 1835); presidential elector in 1836 and voted for White and Tyler; again Governor of Georgia 1837–1839; presidential elector on the Whig ticket of Harrison and Tyler in 1840; author and historian; died in Lexington, Ga., November 16, 1859; interment in Presbyterian Cemetery.

GILMER, John Adams, a Representative from North Carolina; born near Greensboro, Guilford County, N. C., November 4, 1805; attended the public schools and an academy in Greensboro, N. C.; taught school; studied law; was admitted to the bar in 1832 and began practice in Greensboro, N. C.; county solicitor; member of the State senate 1846–1856; defeated as the Whig candidate for Governor of North Carolina in 1856; elected as the candidate of the American Party to the Thirty-fifth and Thirty-sixth Congresses (March 4, 1857–March 3, 1861); member of the Second Confederate Congress in 1864; delegate to the Union National Convention of Conservatives at Philadelphia in 1866; died in Greensboro, N. C., May 14, 1868; interment in Presbyterian Church Cemetery.

GILMER, Thomas Walker, a Representative from Virginia; born in Gilmerton, Albemarle County, Va., April 6, 1802; attended the common schools; studied law; was admitted to the bar and commenced practice in Charlottesville, Va.; member of the State house of delegates 1829–1836 and again in 1839 and 1840, serving as speaker the last two years; elected Governor of Virginia and served from March 31, 1840, until his resignation on March 20, 1841; elected as a Whig to the Twenty-seventh Congress and as a Democrat to the Twenty-eighth Congress and served from March 4, 1841, until February 16, 1844, when he resigned; appointed Secretary of the Navy in the Cabinet of President Tyler February 15, 1844, and served until he was killed by the bursting of a gun on board the U. S. S. *Princeton* on the Potomac River, near Washington, D. C., February 28, 1844; interment in Mount Air Cemetery, Albemarle County, Va.

GILMER, William Franklin (Dixie), a Representative from Oklahoma; born in Mount Airy, Surry County, N. C., June 7, 1901; moved with his parents to Oklahoma; attended the public schools of Oklahoma City, Okla.; served as a page boy in the National House of Representatives, Washington, D. C., when Champ Clark was Speaker 1911–1919; graduated from the law school of Oklahoma University at Norman in 1923; was admitted to the bar in 1923 and commenced the practice of law in Oklahoma; member of the State house of representatives; moved to Tulsa, Okla., in 1929; assistant county attorney of Tulsa County, Okla., 1931–1933; county attorney of Tulsa County 1936–1946; unsuccessful for the Democratic nomination for Governor in 1946; elected as a Democrat to the Eighty-first Congress (January 3, 1949–January 3, 1951); unsuccessful candidate for reelection in 1950 to the Eighty-second Congress; State safety commissioner until his death in Oklahoma City, Okla., June 9, 1954; interment in Memorial Park.

GILMORE, Alfred (son of John Gilmore), a Representative from Pennsylvania; born in Butler, Butler County, Pa., June 9, 1812; attended the public schools, and was graduated from Washington College, Washington, Pa., in 1833; studied law; was admitted to the bar in 1836 and commenced practice in Butler, Pa.; elected as a Democrat to the Thirty-first and Thirty-second Congresses (March 4, 1849–March 3, 1853); was not a candidate for reelection in 1852; resumed the practice of law in Philadelphia, Pa.; moved to Lenox, Mass., in 1866, and continued the practice of his profession; died while on a visit in New York City, June 29, 1890; interment in Lenox Cemetery, Lenox, Mass.

GILMORE, Edward, a Representative from Massachusetts; born in Brockton, Plymouth County, Mass., January 4, 1867; attended the graded schools, the high school, and Massachusetts State University extension classes; engaged in mercantile pursuits; member of the Democratic State committee 1896–1903; delegate to the Democratic National Conventions in 1900 and 1904; president of the Brockton Board of Aldermen 1901–1906; member of the State house of representatives in 1907 and 1908; elected as a Democrat to the Sixty-third Congress (March 4, 1913–March 3, 1915); postmaster of Brockton 1915–1923; city assessor in 1923 and 1924; died in Boston, Mass., April 10, 1924; interment in Calvary Cemetery, Brockton, Mass.

GILMORE, John (father of Alfred Gilmore), a Representative from Pennsylvania; born in Somerset County, Pa., February 18, 1780; moved with his parents to Washington, Pa., in 1780; attended the common schools; studied law; was admitted to the bar in 1801 and commenced practice in Washington; moved to Butler, Butler County, Pa., in 1803; appointed deputy district attorney for Butler County in 1803; member of the State house of representatives 1816–1821 and served as speaker in 1821; elected as a Jackson Democrat to the Twenty-first and Twenty-second Congresses (March 4, 1829–March 3, 1833); elected State treasurer by the legislature of Pennsylvania in 1841; died in Butler, Pa., May 11, 1845; interment in North Cemetery.

GILMORE, Samuel Louis, a Representative from Louisiana; born in New Orleans, La., July 30, 1859; instructed by private tutors; was graduated from the Central High School of New Orleans in 1874, from Seton Hall College, South Orange, N. J., in 1877, and from the law department of the University of Louisiana (now Tulane University) at New Orleans in 1879; was admitted to the bar in 1880 and commenced practice in New Orleans, La.; assistant city attorney 1888–1896; presidential elector on the Democratic ticket of Cleveland and Stevenson in 1892; city attorney from 1896 until March 15, 1909, when he resigned; delegate to the Democratic National Convention at

Denver in 1908; elected as a Democrat to the Sixty-first Congress to fill the vacancy caused by the death of Robert C. Davey and served from March 30, 1909, until his death in Abita Springs, La., on July 18, 1910; interment in Metairie Cemetery, New Orleans, La.

GINGERY, Don, a Representative from Pennsylvania; born in Woodland, Clearfield County, Pa., February 19, 1884; moved to Clearfield, Pa., in 1892; attended the public schools of Clearfield, Pa., Mercersburg (Pa.) Academy, and Ohio Northern University at Ada; was engaged in the hardware and mine-supply business from 1902 to 1934; also engaged as a civil engineer in 1903; member of the State house of representatives in 1915 and 1916; served in the Pennsylvania National Guard, in grades from private to captain, 1902–1906; chairman of the Clearfield County Democratic Committee in 1916 and 1917; member of the Democratic State committee in 1919 and 1920; member of the official delegation attending the inauguration of President Manuel Quezon of the Philippine Republic at Manila, in 1935; elected as a Democrat to the Seventy-fourth and Seventy-fifth Congresses (January 3, 1935–January 3, 1939); unsuccessful candidate for reelection in 1938 to the Seventy-sixth Congress; manager of the office of the Bituminous Coal Division, regional coal manager of the Coal Mines Administration, and later associate area distribution manager of the Solid Fuels Administration for War of the United States Department of the Interior, at Altoona, Pa., 1939–1946; is a resident of Clearfield, Pa.

GIST, Joseph, a Representative from South Carolina; born near the mouth of Fair Forest Creek, Union District, S. C., January 12, 1775; moved to Charleston with his parents in 1788; attended the common schools; was graduated from Charleston College, South Carolina; studied law; was admitted to the bar in 1799 and began practice in Pinckneyville, S. C., in 1800; member of the State house of representatives 1801–1819; member of the board of trustees of South Carolina College at Columbia 1809–1821; elected as a Democrat to the Seventeenth, Eighteenth, and Nineteenth Congresses (March 4, 1821–March 3, 1827); was not a candidate for renomination; resumed the practice of law; died in Pinckneyville, S. C., on March 8, 1836; interment in the family burial ground.

GITTINS, Robert Henry, a Representative from New York; born in Oswego, Oswego County, N. Y., December 14, 1869; attended St. Paul's Academy, Oswego, N. Y.; engaged in the lumber, grain, and coal business; was graduated from the law department of the University of Michigan at Ann Arbor in 1900; was admitted to the bar in the States of Michigan and New York in 1900 and commenced the practice of law at Niagara Falls, N. Y., in 1901; member of the State senate 1911–1913; delegate to the Democratic National Convention at Baltimore in 1912 which nominated Wilson and Marshall; elected as a Democrat to the Sixty-third Congress (March 4, 1913–March 3, 1915); unsuccessful candidate for reelection in 1914 to the Sixty-fourth Congress; owner and publisher of the Niagara Falls Journal 1914–1918; postmaster of Niagara Falls, N. Y., from October 16, 1916, to January 21, 1920; resumed the practice of his profession; appointed commissioner of the State reservation at Niagara Falls in 1918 and served until 1940; moved to New York City in 1923 and continued the practice of law; is a resident of Sloatsburg, Rockland County, N. Y.

GLASCOCK, John Raglan, a Representative from California; born in Panola County, Miss., August 25, 1845; in 1856 moved to California with his parents, who settled in San Francisco; attended the public schools, and was graduated from the University of California at Berkeley in 1865; studied law at the University of Virginia at Charlottesville; was admitted to the bar by the supreme court of California in 1868 and commenced practice in Oakland, Calif.; admitted to practice before the Supreme Court of the United States in 1882; district attorney of Alameda County, Calif., 1875–1877; elected as a Democrat to the Forty-eighth Congress (March 4, 1883–March 3, 1885); unsuccessful candidate for reelection in 1884 to the Forty-ninth Congress; mayor of Oakland, Calif., 1887–1890; resumed the practice of law in Oakland, Calif.; died at his country home in Woodside, Calif., November 10, 1913; interment in Mountain View Cemetery, Oakland, Calif.

GLASCOCK, Thomas, a Representative from Georgia; born in Augusta, Ga., October 21, 1790; attended the public schools; studied law; was admitted to the bar and commenced practice in Augusta; delegate to the constitutional convention in 1798; captain of Volunteers in the War of 1812; served with the rank of brigadier general in the Seminole War in 1817; member of the State house of representatives 1821, 1823, 1831, 1834, 1839, serving as speaker in 1833 and 1834; elected as a Union Democrat to the Twenty-fourth Congress to fill the vacancy caused by the resignation of John W. A. Sanford; reelected to the Twenty-fifth Congress and served from October 5, 1835, to March 3, 1839; retired from public life; moved to Decatur, Ga., and lived in retirement until his death there May 19, 1841; interment in the City Cemetery, Augusta, Ga.

GLASGOW, Hugh, a Representative from Pennsylvania; born in Nottingham, Chester County, Pa., September 8, 1769; attended the public schools; engaged in agricultural pursuits; studied law; was admitted to the bar and practiced; judge of York County from July 1, 1800, to March 29, 1813; elected to the Thirteenth and Fourteenth Congresses (March 4, 1813–March 3, 1817); died at Peach Bottom, York County, Pa., January 31, 1818; interment in Slate Ridge Burying Ground.

GLASS, Carter, a Representative and a Senator from Virginia; born in Lynchburg, Campbell County, Va., January 4, 1858; attended private and public schools; served eight years in the mechanical department of a printing office, and afterward was successively reporter, city editor, and editor; owner of the Lynchburg Daily News and of the Daily Advance; member of the board of visitors of the University of Virginia at Charlottesville 1898–1906; member of the State senate from 1899 until 1903, when he resigned; delegate to the State constitutional convention in 1901; elected as a Democrat to the Fifty-seventh Congress to fill the vacancy caused by the death of Peter J. Otey; reelected to the Fifty-eighth and to the eight succeeding Congresses and served from November 4, 1902, until his resignation on December 16, 1918, before the close of the Sixty-fifth Congress, having been appointed Secretary of the Treasury in the Cabinet of President Wilson; member of the Democratic National Committee 1916–1928; resigned from the Cabinet February 2, 1920, having previously been appointed Senator; appointed to the United States Senate on November 18, 1919, and subsequently elected to fill the vacancy caused by the death of Thomas S. Martin in the term ending March 3, 1925, but did not qualify until February 2, 1920, preferring to retain his Cabinet portfolio; reelected in 1924, 1930, 1936, and again in 1942, and served from February 2, 1920, until his death; declined an appointment as Secretary of the Treasury in the Cabinet of President Franklin D. Roosevelt; died in Washington, D. C., May 28, 1946; interment in Spring Hill Cemetery, Lynchburg, Va.

GLASS, Presley Thornton, a Representative from Tennessee; born in Houston, Halifax County, Va., October 18, 1824; in 1828 moved with his parents to Weakley County, Tenn., where he attended Dresden Academy; elected colonel of militia when eighteen years of age; studied law; attended one course at Lexington (Ky.) Law School; was admitted to the bar in 1847 and commenced practice in Ripley, Tenn.; member of the State house of representatives in 1848 and again in 1882; during the Civil War served as commissary with the rank of major in the Confederate service; elected as a Democrat to the Forty-ninth and Fiftieth Congresses (March 4, 1885–March 3, 1889); unsuccessful candidate for renomination in 1888; retired from public life; died in Ripley, Tenn., on October 9, 1902; interment in Maplewood Cemetery.

GLATFELTER, Samuel Feiser, a Representative from Pennsylvania; born near Loganville, Springfield Township, York County, Pa., April 7, 1858; attended the public schools, York County Academy, and Pennsylvania College at Gettysburg, Pa.; engaged in teaching for several years; later became a building contractor and also interested in banking; elected as a Democrat to the Sixty-eighth Congress (March 4, 1923–March 3, 1925); unsuccessful candidate for reelection in 1924 to the Sixty-ninth Congress; resumed his business as a building contractor; died in York, Pa., on April 23, 1927; interment in Prospect Hill Cemetery.

GLEN, Henry, a Representative from New York; born in Schenectady, N. Y., July 13, 1739; appointed clerk of Schenectady County February 27, 1767, and served until March 11, 1809; served as a deputy quartermaster general in the Revolutionary War; Member of the First, Second, and Third Provincial Congresses 1774–1776; served as a member of the State assembly in 1786 and 1787; elected to the Third and to the three succeeding Congresses (March 4, 1793–March 3, 1801); member of the State assembly in 1810; died in Schenectady, N. Y., on January 6, 1814.

GLENN, Milton Willits, a Representative from New Jersey; born in Atlantic City, N. J., June 18, 1903; attended the public schools in Atlantic City; attended Georgetown University, Washington, D. C., in 1921 and 1922 and graduated from Dickinson Law School, Carlisle, Pa., in 1924; was admitted to the bar in 1925 and commenced practice in Atlantic City, N. J.; during World War II was commissioned a lieutenant in the United States Navy and served from November 1943 to June 1946; municipal magistrate in Margate City, N. J., from January 1940 to November 1943; Atlantic County Freeholder from June 1946 to January 1951; lieutenant commander in the United States Naval Reserve; elected to the State house of assembly for an unexpired term in 1950; reelected in 1951, 1953, and 1955; elected as a Republican to the Eighty-fifth Congress to fill the vacancy caused by the death of T. Millet Hand; reelected to the Eighty-sixth Congress and served from November 5, 1957, to January 3, 1961. *Reelected to the Eighty-seventh Congress.*

GLENN, Otis Ferguson, a Senator from Illinois; born in Mattoon, Coles County, Ill., August 27, 1879; attended the public schools; was graduated from the law department of the University of Illinois at Urbana in 1900; was admitted to the bar in 1900 and commenced practice in Murphysboro, Ill.; served as State's attorney of Jackson County 1906–1908 and 1916–1920; member of the State senate 1920–1924; elected as a Republican to the United States Senate to fill the vacancy caused by the resignation of Frank L. Smith and served from December 3, 1928, to March 3, 1933; unsuccessful candidate for reelection in 1932 and for election in 1936; resumed the practice of law in Chicago, Ill.; died in Portage Point, near Onekama, Mich., March 11, 1959; interment in Onekama Cemetery, Onekama, Mich.

GLENN, Thomas Louis, a Representative from Idaho; born near Bardwell, Ballard (now Carlisle) County, Ky., February 2, 1847; attended the public schools and the Commercial College, Evansville, Ind.; during the Civil War served in Company F, Second Regiment, Kentucky Cavalry (John H. Morgan's brigade), Confederate Army; was wounded in action at Mount Sterling, Ky., June 9, 1864; captured, and imprisoned in Transylvania University, Lexington, Ky., until September 9, 1864, when he was paroled; clerk of Ballard County 1874–1882; member of the State senate 1887–1891; studied law; was admitted to the bar in 1890 and commenced practice in Montpelier, Idaho; elected as a Populist to the Fifty-seventh Congress (March 4, 1901–March 3, 1903); was not a candidate for renomination in 1902; mayor of Montpelier in 1904; served as prosecuting attorney; resumed the practice of law in Montpelier, Idaho, where he died November 18, 1918; interment in the City Cemetery.

GLONINGER, John, a Representative from Pennsylvania; born in Lebanon Township, Lancaster County, Pa., September 19, 1758; attended the common schools; served as a subaltern officer in the Associaters during the Revolutionary War and later was in command of a battalion of militia; upon the organization of Dauphin County was appointed by the supreme executive council a lieutenant May 6, 1785; member of the State house of representatives in 1790; resigned, and served in the State senate from 1790 until 1792, when he resigned; appointed by Governor Mifflin justice of the peace of Dauphin County on September 8, 1790; commissioned as associate judge August 17, 1791, and upon the formation of Lebanon County in 1813, was commissioned on September 11, 1813, one of the associate judges for that county; elected as a Democrat to the Thirteenth Congress and served from March 4, 1813, until August 2, 1813, when he resigned; again appointed associate judge of Lebanon County; died in Lebanon, Pa., January 22, 1836; interment in First Reformed Churchyard.

GLOSSBRENNER, Adam John, a Representative from Pennsylvania; born in Hagerstown, Washington County, Md., August 31, 1810; learned the art of printing; publisher of the Western Telegraph in Hamilton, Ohio, in 1827 and 1828; moved to York, Pa., in 1829; established the York County Farmer in 1831; became a partner in the York Gazette in 1835, and continued his connection with that paper until 1860; clerk in the State house of representatives in 1836; clerk in the National House of Representatives during the Twenty-eighth and Twenty-ninth Congresses 1843–1847, and in the Department of State at Washington, D. C., in 1848 and 1849; Sergeant at Arms of the House of Representatives 1850–1860; private secretary to President Buchanan in 1860 and 1861; established the Philadelphia Age in 1862, although residing in York; elected as a Democrat to the Thirty-ninth and Fortieth Congresses (March 4, 1865–March 3, 1869); unsuccessful candidate for reelection in 1868 to the Forty-first Congress; engaged in banking in York, Pa., in 1872; moved to Philadelphia in 1880, and was in the employ of the Pennsylvania Railroad Co. until his death in that city on March 1, 1889; interment in Prospect Hill Cemetery, York, Pa.

GLOVER, David Delano, a Representative from Arkansas; born in Prattsville, Grant County, Ark., January 18, 1868; attended the public schools of Prattsville and Sheridan, Ark.; was graduated from Sheridan High School in 1886; engaged in agricultural pursuits and in the mercantile business; taught in the public schools of Hot Spring County, Ark., 1898–1908; studied law; was admitted to the bar in 1910 and commenced practice in Malvern, Ark.; member of the State house of representatives in 1909 and 1911; delegate to several State conventions; served as prosecuting attorney of the seventh judicial circuit of Arkansas 1913–1917; elected as a Democrat to the Seventy-first, Seventy-second, and Seventy-third Congresses (March 4, 1929–January 3, 1935); unsuccessful candidate for renomination in 1934; resumed the practice of law in Malvern, Ark., until his death April 5, 1952; interment in Shadowlawn Cemetery.

GLOVER, John Milton (nephew of John Montgomery Glover), a Representative from Missouri; born in St. Louis, Mo., June 23, 1852; attended the public schools of his native city and Washington University, St. Louis, Mo.; studied law; was admitted to the bar and commenced practice in St. Louis; elected as a Democrat to the Forty-ninth and Fiftieth Congresses (March 4, 1885–March 3, 1889); was not a candidate for renomination in 1888, having become a candidate for the Democratic gubernatorial nomination, in which he was unsuccessful; reengaged in the practice of law in St. Louis, Mo., until 1909, when he moved to Denver, Colo., and continued the practice of his profession until incapacitated by ill health in 1926; died in Pueblo, Colo., October 20, 1929; interment in Bellefontaine Cemetery, St. Louis, Mo.

GLOVER, John Montgomery (uncle of John Milton Glover), a Representative from Missouri; born in Harrodsburg, Mercer County, Ky., September 4, 1822; attended the public schools in Kentucky; moved to Missouri in 1836 with his parents, who settled in Knox County, near Newark, and continued his schooling; attended Marion and Masonic Colleges, Philadelphia, Mo.; studied law; was admitted to the bar and commenced practice in St. Louis, Mo.; moved to California in 1850 and continued the practice of his profession; returned to Knox County, Mo., in 1855 to take charge of his father's affairs; during the Civil War served as colonel of the Third Regiment, Missouri Volunteer Cavalry, from September 4, 1861, until February 23, 1864, when he resigned on account of impaired health; collector of internal revenue for the third district of Missouri from December 1, 1866, until March 3, 1867, when his successor was appointed; elected as a Democrat to the Forty-third, Forty-fourth, and Forty-fifth Congresses (March 4, 1873–March 3, 1879); unsuccessful candidate for renomination in 1878; engaged in agricultural pursuits; died near Newark, Knox County, Mo., November 15, 1891; interment on his farm near Newark, Mo.; reinterment in Woodland Cemetery, Quincy, Ill.

GLYNN, James Peter, a Representative from Connecticut; born in Winsted, Litchfield County, Conn., November 12, 1867; attended the public schools; studied law; was admitted to the bar in 1895 and commenced practice in Winsted, Conn.; town clerk 1892–1902; prosecuting attorney of the town court 1899–1902; postmaster of Winsted 1902–1914; elected as a Republican to the Sixty-fourth and to the three succeeding Congresses (March 4, 1915–March 3, 1923); unsuccessful candidate for reelection in 1922 to the Sixty-eighth Congress; elected to the Sixty-ninth, Seventieth, and Seventy-first Congresses and served from March 4, 1925, until his death on a train near Washington, D. C., March 6, 1930, while returning from the funeral of former Representative James A. Hughes of West Virginia; interment in the new St. Joseph's Cemetery, Winsted, Conn.

GLYNN, Martin Henry, a Representative from New York; born in Kinderhook, Columbia County, N. Y., September 27, 1871; attended the public schools, and was graduated from St. John's College, Fordham, N. Y., in 1894; studied law; was admitted to the bar in 1897 and commenced practice in Albany; engaged in journalistic work on several papers until he became managing editor and publisher of the Albany Times-Union; elected as a Democrat to the Fifty-sixth Congress (March 4, 1899–March 3, 1901); unsuccessful candidate for reelection in

1900 to the Fifty-seventh Congress; vice president of the National Commission of the Louisiana Purchase Exposition 1901–1905; comptroller of New York State 1906–1908; elected Lieutenant Governor of New York in 1912; became Governor on removal of William Sulzer from office October 17, 1913, and served until December 31, 1914; unsuccessful candidate for election as Governor; delegate to and temporary chairman of the Democratic State conventions in 1912 and 1916; temporary chairman of the Democratic National Convention at St. Louis in 1916; appointed a member of the Federal Industrial Commission in 1919; member of the New York Bar Association; died in Albany, N. Y., December 14, 1924; interment in St. Agnes Cemetery.

GODDARD, Calvin, a Representative from Connecticut; born in Shrewsbury, Worcester County, Mass., July 17, 1768; attended Plainfield (Conn.) Academy, where he pursued classical studies, and was graduated from Dartmouth College, Hanover, N. H., in 1786; studied law; was admitted to the bar in 1790 and commenced practice in Plainfield, Conn.; member of the State house of representatives 1795–1801; elected as a Federalist to the Seventh Congress to fill the vacancy caused by the resignation of Elizur Goodrich; reelected to the Eighth and Ninth Congresses and served from May 14, 1801, until his resignation in 1805 before the convening of the Ninth Congress; again elected to the State house of representatives in 1807 and served as speaker; moved to Norwich, Conn., in 1807 and resumed the practice of his profession; member of the executive council 1808–1815; presidential elector on the Peace Party ticket of Clinton and Ingersoll in 1812; delegate to the Hartford Convention in 1814; judge of the superior court in 1815 and 1818; mayor of Norwich 1814–1834; died in Norwich, Conn., May 2, 1842; interment in the City Cemetery.

GODSHALK, William, a Representative from Pennsylvania; born in East Nottingham, Chester County, Pa., October 25, 1817; moved with his parents to Bucks County in 1818; attended the common schools and Union Academy, Doylestown, Pa.; learned the miller's trade and in 1847 engaged in milling in Doylestown Township; served in the Union Army during the Civil War as a private in Company K, One Hundred and Fifty-third Regiment, Pennsylvania Volunteer Infantry, from October 11, 1862, to July 23, 1863; unsuccessful candidate for election to the State senate in 1864; elected associate judge of Bucks County in October 1871 and served five years; elected as a Republican to the Forty-sixth and Forty-seventh Congresses (March 4, 1879–March 3, 1883); engaged in milling; died in New Britain, Bucks County, Pa., February 6, 1891; interment in the Presbyterian Church Cemetery, Doylestown, Pa.

GODWIN, Hannibal Lafayette, a Representative from North Carolina; born on a farm near Dunn, Harnett County, N. C., November 3, 1873; attended the common schools and Trinity College (now Duke University), Durham, N. C.; studied law at the University of North Carolina at Chapel Hill; was admitted to the bar in 1896 and commenced practice in Dunn, N. C.; elected mayor of Dunn in 1897; member of the State senate in 1903; presidential elector on the Democratic ticket of Parker and Davis in 1904; member of the Democratic State executive committee 1904–1906; elected as a Democrat to the Sixtieth and to the six succeeding Congresses (March 4, 1907–March 3, 1921); unsuccessful candidate for renomination in 1920; engaged in the practice of his profession until his death in Dunn, N. C., June 9, 1929; interment in Greenwood Cemetery.

GOEBEL, Herman Philip, a Representative from Ohio; born in Cincinnati, Ohio, April 5, 1853; attended the public schools; employed as a messenger boy for a law firm; was graduated from the Cincinnati Law College in 1872; was admitted to the bar in 1874 and commenced practice in Cincinnati, Ohio; member of the State house of representatives in 1875 and 1876; judge of the probate court of Hamilton County 1884–1890; elected as a Republican to the Fifty-eighth and to the three succeeding Congresses (March 4, 1903–March 3, 1911); unsuccessful candidate for reelection in 1910 to the Sixty-second Congress; engaged in the practice of his profession until his death in Cincinnati, Ohio, May 4, 1930; interment in Spring Grove Cemetery.

GOEKE, John Henry, a Representative from Ohio; born near Minster, Auglaize County, Ohio, October 28, 1869; attended the common schools, and was graduated from Pio Nono College, St. Francis, Wis., in 1888; studied law at Cincinnati Law School and was graduated in 1891; was admitted to the bar in 1891 and commenced practice in St. Marys, Ohio; city solicitor of St. Marys 1892–1894; prosecuting attorney of Auglaize County 1894–1900; resumed the practice of law in Wapakoneta, Ohio, in 1900; also served as a director of several banks and manufacturing concerns; chairman of the Democratic State convention in 1903; elected as a Democrat to the Sixty-second and Sixty-third Congresses (March 4, 1911–March 3, 1915); unsuccessful candidate for renomination in 1914 to the Sixty-fourth Congress; delegate to the Democratic National Conventions in 1912, 1920, 1924, and 1928; resumed the practice of law in Wapakoneta, Ohio; moved to Lima, Ohio, in 1921 and continued the practice of law; died in Lima, Ohio, March 25, 1930; interment in Gethsemane Cemetery.

GOFF, Abe McGregor, a Representative from Idaho; born in Colfax, Whitman County, Wash., December 21, 1899; attended the public schools; during the First World War served as a private in the United States Army; was graduated from the College of Law of the University of Idaho in 1924; was admitted to the bar the same year and commenced practice in Moscow, Idaho; prosecuting attorney of Latah County, Idaho, 1926–1934; special lecturer at the University of Idaho Law School 1933–1941; member of the State senate in 1941; during World War II was called to active duty from the Reserves as a major in August 1941 and served until his discharge as a colonel in September 1946; was among the first American officers to go overseas; was decorated with the Legion of Merit; elected as a Republican to the Eightieth Congress (January 3, 1947–January 3, 1949); unsuccessful candidate for reelection in 1948 to the Eighty-first Congress; solicitor and later general counsel, Post Office Department, 1954–1958; appointed a commissioner of the Interstate Commerce Commission January 30, 1958; reappointed in 1959 for term ending December 31, 1966; resides in Washington, D. C., and Moscow, Idaho.

GOFF, Guy Despard (son of Nathan Goff and father of Mrs. Louise Goff Reece), a Senator from West Virginia; born in Clarksburg, Harrison County, W. Va., September 13, 1866; attended the common schools, and William and Mary College, Williamsburg, Va.; was graduated from Kenyon College at Gambier, Ohio, in 1888 and from the law department of Harvard University in 1891; was admitted to the bar the same year and commenced practice in Boston, Mass.; moved to Milwaukee, Wis., in 1893 and continued the practice of law; elected prosecuting attorney of Milwaukee County, Wis., in 1895; appointed by President Taft as United States district attorney for the eastern district of Wisconsin on July 6, 1911, and served until August 4, 1915; appointed special assistant to the Attorney General of the United States on June 28, 1917, and served until September 15, 1917; during the First World War was commissioned a colonel in the Judge Advocate

General's Department, United States Army, and served in France and Germany in 1918 and 1919; appointed by President Woodrow Wilson on May 21, 1920, as general counsel of the United States Shipping Board, and on November 10, 1920, became a member of the Board and served until March 4, 1921, when his term expired; again appointed special assistant to the Attorney General on December 2, 1920, and served until December 7, 1921; assistant to the Attorney General of the United States from March 16, 1921, until November 9, 1922, when he resigned; again special assistant to the Attorney General of the United States from November 10, 1922, until his resignation on July 31, 1923; returned to Clarksburg, W. Va., in 1923; elected as a Republican to the United States Senate and served from March 4, 1925, to March 3, 1931; was not a candidate for renomination in 1930; established his residence in Washington, D. C., in 1931 and retired from public life; died at his winter home in Thomasville, Ga., January 7, 1933; interment in Arlington National Cemetery, Fort Myer, Va.

GOFF, Nathan (father of Guy Despard Goff and grandfather of Mrs. Louise Goff Reece), a Representative and a Senator from West Virginia; born in Clarksburg, Harrison County, Va. (now West Virginia), February 9, 1843; attended the Northwestern Academy, Clarksburg, W. Va., and Georgetown University, Washington, D. C.; studied law and was graduated from the University of the City of New York; during the Civil War enlisted in the Union Army in June 1861 in the Third Regiment of Virginia Volunteer Infantry; served as lieutenant of Company G, as adjutant of the same regiment and as major in the Fourth Regiment, Virginia Volunteer Cavalry; was admitted to the bar in 1865 and practiced; member of the State house of delegates in 1867 and 1868; appointed United States attorney for West Virginia in 1868 and served until his resignation in 1881; appointed Secretary of the Navy in the Cabinet of President Hayes on January 6, 1881, and served until March 5, 1881, when a successor was appointed; reappointed United States attorney for West Virginia by President Garfield in 1881, which position he again resigned in July 1882; delegate to the Republican National Conventions in 1872, 1876, and 1880; unsuccessful Republican candidate for election to Congress in 1870 and 1874; unsuccessful candidate for Governor of West Virginia in 1876 and 1888; elected as a Republican to the Forty-eighth, Forty-ninth, and Fiftieth Congresses (March 4, 1883–March 3, 1889); was not a candidate for renomination, having become a candidate for the gubernatorial office in 1888; the returns showed his election as Governor by one hundred and thirty votes, but in a contest by his Democratic opponent, A. B. Fleming, the legislature declared, by a party vote, the election of the latter; appointed by President Harrison United States circuit judge for the fourth judicial circuit on March 17, 1892, and served until March 31, 1913, when he resigned, having been elected Senator; elected to the United States Senate for the term commencing March 4, 1913, but did not take his seat until later, preferring to remain on the bench; served from April 1, 1913, to March 3, 1919; died in Clarksburg, W. Va., April 24, 1920; interment in Odd Fellows Cemetery.

GOGGIN, William Leftwich, a Representative from Virginia; born near Bunker Hill, Bedford County, Va., May 31, 1807; attended the country schools, and was graduated from Tucker's Law School, Winchester, Va.; was admitted to the bar in 1828 and commenced practice in Liberty (now Bedford), Va.; also engaged in agricultural pursuits; member of the State house of delegates in 1836 and 1837; elected as a Whig to the Twenty-sixth and Twenty-seventh Congresses (March 4, 1839–March 3, 1843); unsuccessfully contested the election of Thomas W. Gilmer to the Twenty-eighth Congress; subsequently elected to the Twenty-eighth Congress to fill the vacancy caused by the resignation of Thomas W. Gilmer and served from April 25, 1844, to March 4, 1845; was not a candidate for renomination in 1844; elected to the Thirtieth Congress (March 4, 1847–March 3, 1849); was not a candidate for renomination in 1848; unsuccessful Whig candidate for Governor in 1859; delegate to the State constitutional convention in 1861; captain of Home Guards, Confederate Army, during the Civil War; resumed the practice of law; died on his estate near Liberty (now Bedford City), Bedford County, Va., January 3, 1870; interment in Goggin Cemetery on the family estate near Bunker Hill, Va.

GOLD, Thomas Ruggles, a Representative from New York; born in Cornwall, Conn., November 4, 1764; pursued classical studies, and was graduated from Yale College in 1786; studied law; was admitted to the bar and commenced practice in Goshen, Conn.; settled in Whitesboro, Oneida County, N. Y., in 1792; assistant attorney general of New York 1797–1801; member of the State senate 1796–1802; unsuccessful candidate for election in 1804 to the Ninth Congress; served in the State assembly in 1808; elected as a Federalist to the Eleventh and Twelfth Congresses (March 4, 1809–March 3, 1813); unsuccessful candidate for reelection in 1812 to the Thirteenth Congress; elected to the Fourteenth Congress (March 4, 1815–March 3, 1817); was not a candidate for renomination in 1816; resumed the practice of law in Whitesboro, N. Y., where he died October 24, 1827; interment in Grand View Cemetery.

GOLDEN, James Stephen, a Representative from Kentucky; born in Barbourville, Knox County, Ky., September 20, 1891; attended the grade schools in Barbourville and high school at Union College, Barbourville, Ky.; was graduated from the University of Kentucky at Lexington in 1912 and from the law school of the University of Michigan at Ann Arbor in 1916; was admitted to the bar in 1916 and commenced the practice of law in Barbourville, Ky., the same year; elected county attorney of Knox County, Ky., in 1918 and served until 1922; delegate to Republican National Convention in 1952; elected as a Republican to the Eighty-first, Eighty-second, and Eighty-third Congresses (January 3, 1949–January 3, 1955); was not a candidate for renomination in 1954; resumed the practice of law; is a resident of Pineville, Bell County, Ky.

GOLDER, Benjamin Martin, a Representative from Pennsylvania; born in Alliance, near Vineland, Cumberland County, N. J., December 23, 1891; moved with his parents to Philadelphia, Pa., in 1893; attended the public schools, and was graduated from the law department of the University of Pennsylvania at Philadelphia in 1913; was admitted to the bar in 1914 and commenced practice in Philadelphia; enlisted in the Naval Aviation Service during the First World War, and was honorably discharged as ensign after the armistice; member of the State house of representatives 1916–1924; elected as a Republican to the Sixty-ninth and to the three succeeding Congresses (March 4, 1925–March 3, 1933); unsuccessful candidate for renomination in 1932 and for election in 1940 to the Seventy-seventh Congress; resumed the practice of law in Philadelphia, Pa.; during World War II was commissioned a captain in the Army of the United States on February 5, 1943, and served until discharged as a lieutenant colonel July 1, 1945; resumed the practice of law and also engaged in the banking business; died December 30, 1946, at Philadelphia, Pa.; interment in Mount Sinai Cemetery.

GOLDFOGLE, Henry Mayer, a Representative from New York; born in New York City May 23, 1856; attended the public schools and Townsend College; studied law; was admitted to the bar in 1877 and commenced practice in New York City; justice of the fifth district court in New York in 1887 and 1893;

judge of the municipal court of New York City 1888–1900; resumed the practice of law; delegate to the Democratic National Conventions in 1892 and 1896; elected as a Democrat to the Fifty-seventh and to the six succeeding Congresses (March 4, 1901–March 3, 1915); unsuccessful candidate for reelection to the Sixty-fourth and Sixty-fifth Congresses; again elected to the Sixty-sixth Congress (March 4, 1919–March 3, 1921); unsuccessful candidate for reelection in 1920 to the Sixty-seventh Congress; resumed the practice of law; appointed president of the New York City Board of Taxes and Assessments in July 1921 and served until his death in New York City, N. Y., June 1, 1929; interment in Union Hills Cemetery, Long Island, N. Y.

GOLDSBOROUGH, Charles (great-grandfather of Thomas Alan Goldsborough and Winder Laird Henry), a Representative from Maryland; born at "Hunting Creek," near Cambridge, Dorchester County, Md., July 15, 1765; pursued an academic course, and was graduated from the University of Pennsylvania at Philadelphia in 1784; studied law; was admitted to the bar in 1790; held several local offices; member of the State senate 1791–1795 and 1799–1801; elected as a Federalist to the Ninth and to the five succeeding Congresses (March 4, 1805–March 3, 1817); Governor of Maryland in 1818 and 1819; retired from public life in 1820, and resided on his estate near Cambridge, Md.; died at "Shoal Creek," near Cambridge, Md., December 13, 1834; interment in Christ Protestant Episcopal Church Cemetery, Cambridge, Md.

GOLDSBOROUGH, Phillips Lee, a Senator from Maryland; born in Princess Anne, Somerset County, Md., August 6, 1865; educated in public and private schools; studied law; was admitted to the bar in 1886 and commenced practice in Cambridge, Md.; also interested in banking; State's attorney for Dorchester County 1892–1898; served as comptroller of the treasury of Maryland in 1898 and 1899; collector of internal revenue, district of Maryland, 1902–1911; Governor of Maryland 1912–1915; elected as a Republican to the United States Senate and served from March 4, 1929, to January 3, 1935; was not a candidate for reelection in 1934, but was an unsuccessful candidate for nomination as Governor of Maryland; member of the Republican National Committee 1932–1936; resumed the practice of law; appointed a director of the Federal Deposit Insurance Corporation by President Franklin D. Roosevelt on April 24, 1935, in which capacity he served until his death; died in Baltimore, Md., October 22, 1946; interment in the old churchyard of Christ Protestant Episcopal Church, Cambridge, Md.

GOLDSBOROUGH, Robert (great-great-great-grandfather of Thomas Alan Goldsborough), a Delegate from Maryland; born at "Horns Point," Dorchester County, Md., December 3, 1733; pursued an academic course; studied law at the Inner Temple, London, England; was admitted to the bar in 1754 and commenced practice in London; barrister of the Inner Temple, London, 1755–1759; returned to the United States; was graduated from the Philadelphia College (now the University of Pennsylvania) in 1760; continued the practice of law at Cambridge, Md.; high sheriff of Dorchester County 1761–1765; burgess to the Maryland Assembly in 1765; attorney general of Maryland in 1766; prominent in ante-Revolutionary movements; Member of the Continental Congress in 1774 and 1775; member of the council of safety in 1775 and of the convention of the Province of Maryland, August 14, 1776, called to frame a constitution; member of the State senate in 1777; retired from public life to his estate near Cambridge, Md.; died at "Horns Point," near Cambridge, Md., on December 22, 1788; interment in Christ Protestant Episcopal Church Cemetery, Cambridge, Md.

GOLDSBOROUGH, Robert Henry (great-grandfather of Winder Laird Henry), a Senator from Maryland; born at "Myrtle Grove," near Easton, Talbot County, Md., January 4, 1779; was educated by private tutors and was graduated from St. John's College, Annapolis, in 1795; engaged in agricultural pursuits; member of the State house of delegates in 1804; commanded a troop of horsemen in the Maryland Militia during the War of 1812; elected as a Federalist to the United States Senate to fill the vacancy in the term commencing March 4, 1813, caused by the failure of the legislature to elect, and served from May 21, 1813, to March 3, 1819; resumed agricultural pursuits; instrumental in establishing the Easton Gazette in 1817; again a member of the State house of delegates in 1825; presidential elector on the National-Republican ticket of Clay and Sergeant in 1832; again elected as a Whig to the United States Senate to fill the vacancy caused by the resignation of Ezekiel F. Chambers and served from January 13, 1835, until his death; member of the board of public works of the Eastern Shore of Maryland in 1836; died at "Myrtle Grove," near Easton, Md., October 5, 1836; interment at "Ashby," the original seat of the family in Talbot County, Md.

GOLDSBOROUGH, Thomas Alan (great-great-great-grandson of Robert Goldsborough and great-grandson of Charles Goldsborough), a Representative from Maryland; born in Greensboro, Caroline County, Md., September 16, 1877; attended the public schools and the local academy at Greensboro; was graduated from Washington College, Chestertown, Md., in 1899 and from the law department of the University of Maryland at Baltimore in 1901; was admitted to the bar in 1901 and commenced practice in Denton, Md.; prosecuting attorney for Caroline County 1904–1908; elected as a Democrat to the Sixty-seventh and to the nine succeeding Congresses and served from March 4, 1921, to April 5, 1939, when he resigned, having been appointed an associate justice of the District Court of the United States for the District of Columbia and served until his death; Regent of the Smithsonian Institution 1932–1939; died in Washington, D. C., June 16, 1951; interment in Denton Cemetery, Denton, Md.

GOLDTHWAITE, George Thomas, a Senator from Alabama; born in Boston, Mass., December 10, 1809; attended the public schools; studied at the United States Military Academy, West Point, N. Y., 1823–1826; moved to Alabama in 1826; studied law; was admitted to the bar the same year and commenced practice in Monticello, Pike County, Ala.; judge of the circuit court 1843–1852; associate justice of the State supreme court 1852–1856; appointed chief justice in 1856, but resigned, and resumed the practice of law; served as adjutant general of Alabama during the Civil War; elected judge of the circuit court in 1868, but was disqualified from serving under the provision of an act of Congress; elected as a Democrat to the United States Senate and served from March 4, 1871, to March 3, 1877; was not a candidate for reelection; retired from public life; died in Tuscaloosa, Ala., on March 18, 1879; interment in Oakwood Cemetery, Montgomery, Ala.

GOLDWATER, Barry Morris, a Senator from Arizona; born in Phoenix, Maricopa County, Ariz., January 1, 1909; attended the public schools, Staunton Military Academy, and one year at the University of Arizona at Tucson in 1928; began merchandising career in 1929 in family mercantile business, starting in the receiving and shipping departments and rising to presidency of the firm; also a partner in Rainbow Lodge and Trading Post on the Navajo Indian Reservation, Tonalea, Ariz.; commissioned a second lieutenant of Infantry in 1930; during World War II entered active service in August 1941 in the United States Air Force, serving in the Asiatic Theater in India, and was dis-

charged in November 1945 as a lieutenant colonel with rating as pilot; served with the Arizona National Guard as a colonel 1945–1952; chief of staff, Arizona Air National Guard, 1946–1952; brigadier general in Air Force Reserve in 1959; member of advisory committee, Indian Affairs, Department of the Interior, 1948–1950; member of the city council of Phoenix 1949–1952; elected as a Republican to the United States Senate in 1952 for the term commencing January 3, 1953; reelected in 1958 for the term ending January 3, 1965.

GOLDZIER, Julius, a Representative from Illinois; born in Vienna, Austria, January 20, 1854; attended the public schools of Vienna; immigrated to the United States in 1866 and settled in New York; studied law and was admitted to the bar; moved to Chicago in 1872 and commenced the practice of law; member of the city council of Chicago 1890–1892; elected as a Democrat to the Fifty-third Congress (March 4, 1893–March 3, 1895); unsuccessful for reelection in 1894 to the Fifty-fourth Congress; practiced law in Chicago, Ill.; again a member of the Chicago City Council in 1899; died in Chicago, Ill., January 20, 1925; interment in Graceland Cemetery.

GOLLADAY, Edward Isaac (brother of Jacob Shall Golladay), a Representative from Tennessee; born in Lebanon, Wilson County, Tenn., September 9, 1830; attended the common schools and was graduated from the literary department of Cumberland University, Lebanon, Tenn., in 1848 and from the law department of the same institution in 1849; was admitted to the bar in 1849 and commenced practice in Lebanon; member of the State house of representatives in 1857 and 1858; presidential elector on the Constitutional-Union ticket of Bell and Everett in 1860; served in the Confederate Army as a colonel during the entire Civil War; elected as a Democrat to the Forty-second Congress (March 4, 1871–March 3, 1873); unsuccessful candidate for reelection in 1872 to the Forty-third Congress; resumed the practice of law in Lebanon and Nashville; died in Columbia, S. C., while on a visit to his daughter, July 11, 1897; interment in Cedar Grove Cemetery, Lebanon, Tenn.

GOLLADAY, Jacob Shall (brother of Edward Isaac Golladay), a Representative from Kentucky; born in Lebanon, Wilson County, Tenn., January 19, 1819; attended the public schools; moved to Nashville, Tenn., in 1838 and thence to Kentucky in 1845; member of the State house of representatives 1851–1853; member of the State senate 1853–1855; elected as a Democrat to the Fortieth Congress to fill the vacancy caused by the death of Elijah Hise; reelected to the Forty-first Congress and served from December 5, 1867, until February 28, 1870, when he resigned; resumed the practice of his profession at Allensville, Ky.; died near Russellville, Logan County, Ky., May 20, 1887; interment in Maple Grove Cemetery, Russellville, Ky.

GOOCH, Daniel Linn, a Representative from Kentucky; born in Rumsey, McLean County, Ky., October 28, 1853; attended a private school; entered the drug business at the age of seventeen, and subsequently became president of a large wholesale drug and chemical company; deputy governor general of the Society of Sons of Colonial Wars; governor of the Order of Descendants of Colonial Governors; elected as a Democrat to the Fifty-seventh and Fifty-eighth Congresses (March 4, 1901–March 3, 1905); unsuccessful candidate for renomination in 1904; retired from public life; died in Covington, Ky., April 12, 1913; interment in Woodlawn Cemetery, Dayton, Ohio.

GOOCH, Daniel Wheelwright, a Representative from Massachusetts; born in Wells, York County, Maine, January 8, 1820; attended the public schools and Phillips Academy, Andover,

Mass., and was graduated from Dartmouth College, Hanover, N. H., in 1843; studied law; was admitted to the bar and commenced practice in Boston in 1846; member of the Massachusetts House of Representatives in 1852; member of the State constitutional convention in 1853; elected as a Republican to the Thirty-fifth Congress to fill the vacancy caused by the resignation of Nathaniel P. Banks; reelected to the four succeeding Congresses and served from January 31, 1858, to September 1, 1865, when he resigned; appointed Navy agent of the port of Boston in 1865; removed by President Johnson in 1866; again elected to the Forty-third Congress (March 4, 1873–March 3, 1875); unsuccessful candidate for reelection in 1874 to the Forty-fourth Congress; pension agent in Boston 1876–1886; resumed the practice of law and also engaged in literary pursuits; died in Melrose, Mass., November 11, 1891; interment in Wyoming Cemetery.

GOOD, James William, a Representative from Iowa; born near Cedar Rapids, Linn County, Iowa, September 24, 1866; attended the common schools, and was graduated from Coe College, Cedar Rapids, Iowa, in 1892 and from the law department of the University of Michigan at Ann Arbor in 1893; was admitted to the bar in 1893 and commenced practice in Indianapolis, Ind., the same year; moved to Cedar Rapids, Iowa, in 1896 and continued the practice of law; served as city attorney 1906–1908; elected as a Republican to the Sixty-first and to the six succeeding Congresses and served from March 4, 1909, until his resignation on June 15, 1921; moved to Evanston, Ill., in 1921 and engaged in the practice of law in Chicago, Ill.; appointed Secretary of War in the Cabinet of President Hoover and served from March 5, 1929, until his death in Washington, D. C., November 18, 1929; interment in Oak Hill Cemetery, Cedar Rapids, Iowa.

GOODALL, Louis Bertrand, a Representative from Maine; born in Winchester, Cheshire County, N. H., September 23, 1851; moved to Troy, N. H., with his parents in 1852; attended the common schools of Troy, N. H., a private school in Thompson, Conn., in 1862 and 1863, Vermont Episcopal Institute at Burlington 1863–1866, a private school in England in 1866 and 1867, and Kimball Union Academy at Meridian, N. H., in 1870; entered his father's mills at Sanford, Maine, in 1874 and afterward engaged extensively in the wool-manufacturing industry and in the railroad business; established the Goodall Worsted Co., which originated Palm Beach cloth; president of the Sanford National Bank from its organization in 1896; chairman of the Maine commission to the Louisiana Purchase Exposition, St. Louis, Mo., in 1904; lieutenant colonel on the staff of Governor Fernald in 1909; elected as a Republican to the Sixty-fifth and Sixty-sixth Congresses (March 4, 1917–March 3, 1921); was not a candidate for renomination in 1920; resumed manufacturing interests and banking in Sanford, Maine, until his death there June 26, 1935; interment in Oakdale Cemetery.

GOODE, John, Jr., a Representative from Virginia; born near Liberty (now Bedford), Bedford County, Va., May 27, 1829; attended the New London Academy, and was graduated from Emory and Henry College, Emory, Va., in 1848; studied law; was admitted to the bar in April 1851 and commenced practice in Liberty, Va.; member of the State house of delegates in 1852; presidential elector on the Democratic ticket in 1852, 1856, and again in 1884; served as president of the Electoral College in 1884; member of the State constitutional convention which passed the ordinance of secession in 1860; served as a colonel in the Confederate Army during the Civil War; twice elected a member of the Confederate Congress; moved to Norfolk, Va., in 1865 and continued the practice of his profession; again served in the State house of delegates in 1866 and 1867; member of the Democratic National Executive Committee 1868–1876; delegate to the Democratic National Conventions in 1868, 1872, 1884, and 1892; elected as a Democrat to the Forty-fourth, Forty-fifth, and Forty-sixth Congresses (March 4, 1875–March 3, 1881); unsuccessful candidate for reelection in 1880 to the Forty-seventh Congress; appointed Solicitor General of the United States by President Cleveland in May 1885 and served until August 1886; member of the United States and Chilean Claims Commission in 1893; president of the Virginia State Bar Association in 1898; member and president of the State constitutional convention in 1901 and 1902; resumed the practice of law in Washington, D. C.; died in Norfolk, Va., July 14, 1909; interment in Longwood Cemetery, Bedford, Va.

GOODE, Patrick Gaines, a Representative from Ohio; born in Cornwall parish, Charlotte County, Va., May 10, 1798; moved with his parents early in life to Wayne County, Ohio; attended Xenia (Ohio) Academy and the public schools in Philadelphia, Pa.; studied law; was admitted to the bar in 1821 and practiced in Madison, Ind., and then in Shelby County, Ohio; member of the Ohio House of Representatives 1833–1835; elected as a Whig to the Twenty-fifth, Twenty-sixth, and Twenty-seventh Congresses (March 4, 1837–March 3, 1843); was not a candidate for renomination in 1842; was a local preacher nearly all his life and occupied a pulpit almost every Sunday while in Washington during his congressional career; subsequently joined the Methodist Episcopal clergy in the central Ohio conference and preached until near the close of his life; judge of the court of common pleas 1844–1851; retired from public life and active business pursuits; died in Sidney, Ohio, on October 17, 1862; interment in Graceland Cemetery.

GOODE, Samuel, a Representative from Virginia; born in "Whitby," Chesterfield County, Va., March 21, 1756; completed preparatory studies; studied law; was admitted to the bar and practiced; during the Revolutionary War served as a lieutenant in the Chesterfield Troop of Horse and later as a colonel of militia; member of the Virginia House of Delegates 1778–1785; elected to the Sixth Congress (March 4, 1799–March 3, 1801); died in Invermay, Mecklenburg County, Va., November 14, 1822; interment on his estate near Invermay, Mecklenburg County, Va.

GOODE, William Osborne, a Representative from Virginia; born in Inglewood, Mecklenburg County, Va., September 16, 1798; completed preparatory studies, and was graduated from William and Mary College, Williamsburg, Va., in 1819; studied law; was admitted to the bar in 1821 and commenced practice in Boydton, Mecklenburg County, Va.; served in the State house of delegates in 1822 and 1824–1832; member of the State constitutional convention in 1829 and 1830; unsuccessful candidate for election in 1832 to the Twenty-third Congress; again served in the State house of delegates in 1839, 1840, 1845, 1846, and 1852; served as speaker three terms; elected as a Democrat to the Twenty-seventh Congress (March 4, 1841–March 3, 1843); was not a candidate for renomination; delegate to the State constitutional convention in 1850; again elected to the Thirty-third and three succeeding Congresses and served from March 4, 1853, until his death in Boydton, Va., July 3, 1859; interment on his estate, "Wheatland," near Boydton, Va.

GOODELL, Charles Ellsworth, a Representative from New York; born in Jamestown, Chautauqua County, N. Y., March 16, 1926; attended the public schools of Jamestown; graduated from Williams College, Williamstown, Mass., in 1948; during World War II served in the United States Navy as a seaman second-class 1944–1946, and in the United States Air Force as a first lieutenant during the Korean conflict in 1952 and 1953; graduated from Yale University School of Law in 1951; received master's degree from Yale University Graduate School of Government in 1952; teacher in Quinnipiac College, New Haven, Conn., in 1952; was admitted to the Connecticut bar in 1951, the New York bar in 1954, and commenced practice in Jamestown, N. Y.; congressional liaison assistant for the Department of Justice in 1954 and 1955; chairman of the Governmental Affairs Committee and member of the board of directors of the Jamestown Area Chamber of Commerce 1957–1959; elected as a Republican to the Eighty-sixth Congress to fill the vacancy caused by the death of Daniel A. Reed and served from May 26, 1959, to January 3, 1961. *Reelected to the Eighty-seventh Congress.*

GOODENOW, John Milton, a Representative from Ohio; born in Westmoreland, Cheshire County, N. H., in 1782; attended the public schools; engaged in mercantile pursuits; studied law; was admitted to the bar and commenced practice in Steubenville, Ohio, in 1813; appointed collector of direct taxes and internal duties for the sixth collection district of Ohio in 1817; member of the State house of representatives in 1823; elected as a Jackson Democrat to the Twenty-first Congress and served from March 4, 1829, until April 9, 1830, when he resigned, having been chosen a judge of the supreme court of Ohio; resigned in the summer of 1830 on account of ill health; moved to Cincinnati in 1832; appointed presiding judge of the court of common pleas in 1833; died in Cincinnati, Ohio, July 20, 1838; interment in Spring Grove Cemetery.

GOODENOW, Robert (brother of Rufus King Goodenow), a Representative from Maine; born in Henniker, Merrimack County, N. H., on April 19, 1800; moved with his parents to Bownfield, Maine, in 1802; attended the common schools at that place, and at Sanford in 1815 and 1816; studied medicine; went to Paris, Maine, and served as clerk of the courts during his brother's illness; studied law; was admitted to the bar in 1822 and commenced practice in Wilton, Maine; county attorney 1828–1834; moved to Farmington, Maine, in 1832 and continued the practice of law; elected as a Whig to the Thirty-second Congress (March 4, 1851–March 3, 1853); unsuccessful candidate for renomination; appointed State bank commissioner in 1857; county treasurer of Franklin County 1866–1868; again county attorney in 1869 and 1870; treasurer of the Franklin County Savings Bank 1868–1874; died in Farmington, May 15, 1874; interment in Riverside Cemetery.

GOODENOW, Rufus King (brother of Robert Goodenow), a Representative from Maine; born in Henniker, Merrimack County, N. H., April 24, 1790; moved with his parents to Brownfield, Maine, in 1802; received a limited schooling; engaged in agricultural pursuits; also followed the sea, having made several voyages to European ports; served as a captain in the Thirty-third Regiment, United States Infantry, in the War of 1812; moved to Paris, Maine, in 1821; clerk of the Oxford County Courts 1821–1837; member of the State house of representatives in 1837 and 1838; delegate to the Whig National Convention at Harrisburg, Pa., in 1839; presidential elector on the Whig ticket of Harrison and Tyler in 1840; studied law; was admitted to the bar and practiced in the courts of Maine; elected as a Whig to the Thirty-first Congress (March 4, 1849–March 3, 1851); died in Paris, Maine, March 24, 1863; interment in Riverside Cemetery, South Paris, Maine.

GOODHUE, Benjamin, a Representative and a Senator from Massachusetts; born in Salem, Mass., September 20, 1748; was graduated from Harvard College in 1766; served in the State house of representatives 1780–1782; member of the State senate

1786–1788; member of the State constitutional convention in 1779 and 1780; elected to the First and to the three succeeding Congresses and served from March 4, 1789, until his resignation in June 1796; elected to the United States Senate to fill the vacancy caused by the resignation of George Cabot; reelected and served from June 11, 1796, to November 8, 1800, when he resigned; died in Salem, Mass., on July 28, 1814; interment in Broad Street Cemetery.

GOODIN, John Randolph, a Representative from Kansas; born in Tiffin, Seneca County, Ohio, December 14, 1836; moved with his father to Kenton, Ohio, in 1844; attended the Kenton High School and Geneva College; studied law; was admitted to the bar in 1857 and commenced practice in Kenton; moved to Humboldt, Kans., in 1859; elected to the State house of representatives in 1866; judge of the seventh judicial district of Kansas 1868–1876; elected as a Democrat to the Forty-fourth Congress (March 4, 1875–March 3, 1877); unsuccessful candidate for reelection; editor of the Inter State in Humboldt, Kans.; moved to Kansas City, Kans., in 1883, where he died December 18, 1885; interment in Oak Grove Cemetery.

GOODING, Frank Robert, a Senator from Idaho; born in Tiverton, England, September 16, 1859; immigrated in 1867 to the United States with his parents, who settled on a farm near Paw Paw, Mich.; attended the common schools; moved to Shasta, Calif., in 1877 and engaged in farming and mining; moved to Idaho in 1881 and settled in Ketchum, where he worked as a mail carrier, and subsequently engaged in the firewood and charcoal business; in 1888 settled near the present site of Gooding, which is named for him; engaged in farming and stock raising; member of the State senate 1900–1904; chairman of the Republican State central committee in 1902; Governor of Idaho 1905–1909; unsuccessful candidate for election in 1918 to the United States Senate; elected as a Republican in 1920 to the United States Senate for the term commencing March 4, 1921; was subsequently appointed to the Senate on January 8, 1921, to become effective January 15, 1921, to fill the vacancy in the term ending March 3, 1921, caused by the resignation of John F. Nugent; reelected in 1926, and served from January 15, 1921, until his death in Gooding, Idaho, June 24, 1928; interment in Elmwood Cemetery.

GOODNIGHT, Isaac Herschel, a Representative from Kentucky; born near Scottsville, Allen County, Ky., January 31, 1849; attended the common schools; moved to Franklin, Ky., in 1870; was graduated from Cumberland University, Lebanon, Tenn., in 1872, and afterwards attended the law department of the same university; was admitted to the bar in 1873 and commenced practice in Franklin; member of the State house of representatives in 1877 and 1878; chairman of the Democratic State convention at Louisville, Ky., in 1891; elected as a Democrat to the Fifty-first, Fifty-second, and Fifty-third Congresses (March 4, 1889–March 3, 1895); was not a candidate for renomination in 1894; elected judge of the seventh Kentucky circuit in 1897 and served until his death in Franklin, Ky., July 24, 1901; interment in Green Lawn Cemetery.

GOODRICH, Chauncey (brother of Elizur Goodrich), a Representative and a Senator from Connecticut; born in Durham, Middlesex County, Conn., October 20, 1759; pursued preparatory studies; was graduated from Yale College in 1776; taught in the Hopkins Grammar School in 1777 and 1778 and in Yale College from May 1778 to February 1781; studied law; was admitted to the bar in 1781 and began practice in Hartford, Conn.; member of the State house of representatives in 1793 and 1794; elected as a Federalist to the Fourth, Fifth, and Sixth Congresses (March 4, 1795–March 3, 1801); resumed the practice of law in Hartford; member of the State executive council 1802–1807; elected to the United States Senate to fill the vacancy caused by the death of Uriah Tracy; reelected, and served from October 25, 1807, until May 1813, when he resigned to become Lieutenant Governor; elected mayor of Hartford in June 1812 and Lieutenant Governor of Connecticut in 1813, holding both offices at the time of his death; delegate to the Hartford Convention in 1814; died in Hartford, Conn., August 18, 1815; interment in the Old North Cemetery.

GOODRICH, Elizur (brother of Chauncey Goodrich), a Representative from Connecticut; born in Durham, Middlesex County, Conn., March 24, 1761; pursued preparatory studies, and was graduated from Yale College in 1779; studied law; was admitted to the bar and commenced practice in New Haven in 1783; member of the State house of representatives 1795–1802, during which time he served as clerk of the house for six sessions and as speaker in two; Federalist presidential elector in 1796; elected as a Federalist to the Sixth Congress (March 4, 1799–March 3, 1801); had been reelected to the Seventh Congress, but resigned, effective March 3, 1801, having been appointed by President John Adams on February 19, 1801, collector of customs at New Haven; elected in 1803 to the Governor's council, which office he held until the change in the State constitution in 1818; professor of law in Yale College 1801–1810; judge of the probate court 1802–1818; also chief judge of the county court 1805–1818; member of the city council and board of aldermen for several years; served as mayor of New Haven 1803–1822; member of the corporation of Yale College 1809–1818 and secretary of the same until 1846; died in New Haven, Conn., November 1, 1849; interment in Grove Street Cemetery

GOODRICH, John Zacheus, a Representative from Massachusetts; born in Sheffield, Berkshire County, Mass., September 27, 1804; attended the common schools and Lenox Academy, Lenox, Mass.; studied law; was admitted to the bar and practiced; engaged in manufacturing; presidential elector on the Whig ticket of Harrison and Tyler in 1840; served in the State senate in 1848 and 1849; elected as a Whig to the Thirty-second and Thirty-third Congresses (March 4, 1851–March 3, 1855); presidential elector on the Republican ticket of Lincoln and Hamlin in 1860; member of the peace convention of 1861 held in Washington, D. C., in an effort to devise means to prevent the impending war; elected, as a Republican, Lieutenant Governor of Massachusetts in 1860 and served from January 1, 1861, until his resignation on March 29, 1861; appointed collector of customs at Boston March 13, 1861, and served until March 11, 1865; retired from public life, and died in Stockbridge, Mass., April 19, 1885; interment in Stockbridge Cemetery.

GOODRICH, Milo, a Representative from New York; born in East Homer, Cortland County, N. Y., January 3, 1814; moved with his parents to Cortlandville, N. Y., in 1816; attended the South Cortland district school, Cortland Academy, Homer, N. Y., and Oberlin College, Ohio; taught school in New York, Pennsylvania, and Ohio; studied law; was admitted to the bar in Worcester, Mass., in 1840, and practiced for two years in Beloit, Wis.; returned to New York and settled in Dryden in 1844; postmaster of Dryden from October 2, 1849, to June 25, 1853; member of the State constitutional convention in 1867 and 1868; elected as a Republican to the Forty-second Congress (March 4, 1871–March 3, 1873); unsuccessful candidate for reelection in 1872 to the Forty-third Congress; resumed the practice of law; moved to Auburn, N. Y., in 1875 and continued the practice of law; died in Auburn, N. Y., April 15, 1881; interment in Green Hills Cemetery, Dryden, N. Y.

GOODWIN, Angier Louis, a Representative from Massachusetts; born in Fairfield, Somerset County, Maine, January 30, 1881; attended the public schools; was graduated from Colby College, Waterville, Maine, in 1902; attended Harvard Law School, Cambridge, Mass., in 1905; was admitted to the Maine bar in 1905, the Massachusetts bar in 1906, and commenced the practice of law in Boston, Mass.; trustee of the Melrose Public Library in 1915; member of the Melrose Board of Aldermen 1912–1914 and 1916–1920, serving as president in 1920; mayor of Melrose, Mass., 1921–1923; member of the Massachusetts State Guard and legal adviser to aid draft registrants during the First World War; member of the Planning Board and chairman of the Board of Appeal, Melrose, Mass., 1923–1925; served in the State house of representatives 1925–1928; member of the State senate 1929–1941, serving as president in 1941; chairman of the Massachusetts Commission on Participation in New York World's Fair, in 1939 and 1940; chairman of the State Commission on Administration and Finance in 1942; elected as a Republican to the Seventy-eighth and to the five succeeding Congresses (January 3, 1943–January 3, 1955); unsuccessful candidate for reelection in 1954 to the Eighty-fourth Congress; member of the Massachusetts State Board of Appeals 1955–1960; retired; is a resident of Melrose, Mass.

GOODWIN, Forrest, a Representative from Maine; born in Skowhegan, Somerset County, Maine, June 14, 1862; attended the common schools; was graduated from Skowhegan High School and Bloomfield Academy, and later, in 1887, from Colby College, Waterville, Maine, and Boston University Law School in 1890; was admitted to the bar in 1889 and commenced practice in Skowhegan, Maine, in 1891; member of the State house of representatives in 1889; clerk at the Speaker's table under Speaker Reed in the Fifty-first Congress 1889–1891; member of the State senate 1903–1905 and served as president in 1905; elected as a Republican to the Sixty-third Congress and served from March 4, 1913, until his death in Portland, Maine, May 28, 1913; interment in South Side Cemetery, Skowhegan, Maine.

GOODWIN, Godfrey Gummer, a Representative from Minnesota; born near St. Peter, Nicollet County, Minn., January 11, 1873; moved with his mother to St. Paul, Minn., in 1882; attended the public schools and was graduated from the academic department of the University of Minnesota at Minneapolis in 1895 and from the law department of that university in 1896; was admitted to the bar in 1896 and commenced practice in Cambridge, Minn.; prosecuting attorney of Isanti County 1898–1907; again elected as prosecuting attorney of Isanti County in November 1913 and served until February 15, 1925, when he resigned, having been elected to Congress; president of the Cambridge (Minn.) Board of Education 1914–1917; served without compensation during the First World War as a Government intervenor and appeal agent for draft board of Isanti County from June 1917 to March 1919; elected as a Republican to the Sixty-ninth and to the three succeeding Congresses and served from March 4, 1925, until his death; unsuccessful candidate for renomination in 1932; died in Washington, D. C., on February 16, 1933; interment in Lakewood Cemetery, Minneapolis, Minn.

GOODWIN, Henry Charles, a Representative from New York; born in De Ruyter, Madison County, N. Y., June 25, 1824; completed preparatory studies; studied law; was admitted to the bar in 1846 and commenced practice in Hamilton, N. Y.; district attorney of Madison County 1847–1850; elected as a Republican to the Thirty-third Congress to fill the vacancy caused by the resignation of Gerrit Smith and served from November 7, 1854, to March 3, 1855; elected to the Thirty-fifth Congress (March 4, 1857–March 3, 1859); resumed the practice of law; died in Hamilton, N. Y., November 12, 1860; interment in Madison Street Cemetery.

GOODWIN, John Noble, a Representative from Maine and a Delegate from the Territory of Arizona; born in South Berwick, York County, Maine, October 18, 1824; attended public schools and the local academy at Berwick, Maine; graduated from Dartmouth College in 1844; studied law; admitted to the bar in 1848, commencing practice in South Berwick; member of State senate in 1854; elected as a Republican from Maine to the Thirty-seventh Congress (March 4, 1861–March 3, 1863); unsuccessful candidate for reelection in 1862; appointed March 6, 1863, by President Lincoln as chief justice of Arizona Territory and on August 21, 1863, as the first Governor of the Territory; entered the Territory and formally proclaimed its organization at Navajo Springs, December 29, 1863; elected as a Republican a Delegate from Arizona Territory to the Thirty-ninth Congress (March 4, 1865–March 3, 1867); was not a candidate for reelection and did not return to Arizona; resumed the practice of law in New York City; died in Paraiso Springs, Calif., April 29, 1887; interment in Forest Grove Cemetery, Augusta, Maine.

GOODWIN, Philip Arnold, a Representative from New York; born in Athens, Greene County, N. Y., January 20, 1882; attended the public schools; moved to Coxsackie, N. Y., with his parents in 1896; was graduated from the high school at Coxsackie, N. Y., in 1900, and from Albany (N. Y.) Business College in 1902; engaged in the steel bridge construction business at Albany, N. Y., 1902–1916; owner and operator of a lumber business at Coxsackie, N. Y., from 1916 until his death; also interested in banking, in a milling and supply company, and in a securities company; served as president of the Greene County Historical Society in 1931; trustee of the Heermance Memorial Library; elected as a Republican to the Seventy-third, Seventy-fourth, and Seventy-fifth Congresses and served from March 4, 1933, until his death in Coxsackie, N. Y., June 6, 1937; interment in Riverside Cemetery.

GOODWIN, Robert Kingman, a Representative from Iowa; born in Des Moines, Iowa, May 23, 1905; attended the public schools; was graduated from Drake University, Des Moines, Iowa, in 1928 and later attended the law school of George Washington University, Washington, D. C.; moved to Redfield, Dallas County, Iowa, in 1929 and engaged in the brick and tile manufacturing business and farming 1934–1949; mayor of Redfield, Iowa, 1938–1940; county chairman of the Young Republicans 1934–1938; delegate to the Republican State conventions in 1936 and 1938; vice president of the Dallas County Farm Bureau in 1939 and 1940; elected as a Republican to the Seventy-sixth Congress to fill the vacancy caused by the death of Cassius C. Dowell and served from March 5, 1940, to January 3, 1941; was not a candidate for renomination in 1940; director of the Central National Bank & Trust Co. since 1941; during World War II was commissioned a lieutenant in the United States Naval Reserve in June 1942 and reported for active duty on July 1, 1942, promoted to lieutenant commander and served until November 2, 1945; delegate to the Republican National Convention in 1952; member of the Republican National Committee 1952–1956; civilian aide to the Secretary of the Army 1952–1956; trustee and vice president of Herbert Hoover Foundation, Inc.; resumed his manufacturing business; is a resident of Des Moines, Iowa.

GOODWIN, William Shields, a Representative from Arkansas; born in Warren, Bradley County, Ark., on May 2, 1866; attended the public schools, the Farmers' Academy near Duluth,

Ga., Cooledge's Preparatory School, Moore's College, Atlanta, Ga., and the Universities of Arkansas and Mississippi; studied law; was admitted to the bar in 1894 and commenced practice in Warren, Ark.; member of the State house of representatives in 1895; presidential elector on the Democratic ticket of Bryan and Stevenson in 1900; served in the State senate 1905–1909; member of the board of trustees of the University of Arkansas at Fayetteville 1907–1911; elected as a Democrat to the Sixty-second and to the four succeeding Congresses (March 4, 1911–March 3, 1921); unsuccessful candidate for renomination in 1920; reengaged in the practice of law in Warren, Ark., until his death there August 9, 1937; interment in Oak Lawn Cemetery.

GOODWYN, Albert Taylor, a Representative from Alabama; born at Robinson Springs, Montgomery County, Ala., December 17, 1842; attended Robinson Springs Academy and South Carolina College at Columbia; during the Civil War enlisted in the Confederate Army and served until June 1865; mustered out at the close of the war as captain of a company of sharpshooters and was decorated with the Confederate Cross of Honor; was graduated from the University of Virginia at Charlottesville in 1867; engaged in agricultural pursuits near Robinson Springs; State inspector of convicts 1874–1880; member of the State house of representatives in 1886 and 1887; served in the State senate 1892–1896; successfully contested as a Democrat the election of James E. Cobb to the Fifty-fourth Congress and served from April 22, 1896, until March 3, 1897; was an unsuccessful candidate for reelection in 1896 to the Fifty-fifth Congress; elected commander in chief of the United Confederate Veterans May 8, 1928; resumed agricultural pursuits near Robinson Springs, Ala.; died while on a visit in Birmingham, Ala., on July 2, 1931; interment in Oakwood Cemetery, Montgomery, Ala.

GOODWYN, Peterson, a Representative from Virginia; born at "Martins," near Petersburg, Dinwiddie County, Va., in 1745; received his education from private tutors; completed preparatory studies; engaged in planting; studied law; was admitted to the bar in 1776 and commenced practice in Petersburg, Va., and surrounding counties; during the Revolutionary War equipped his own company and rose from captain to major; was promoted to colonel for gallantry at the battles of Smithfield and Great Bridge; member of the State house of delegates 1789–1802; elected as a Democrat to the Eighth and to the seven succeeding Congresses and served from March 4, 1803, until his death at his home, "Sweden," in Dinwiddie County, Va., February 21, 1818; interment in the family burying ground on his estate.

GOODYEAR, Charles, a Representative from New York; born in Cobleskill, Schoharie County, N. Y., April 26, 1804; attended the Hartwick Academy in Otsego County; was graduated from Union College, Schenectady, N. Y., in 1824; studied law; was admitted to the bar in 1826 and commenced practice in Schoharie, N. Y.; appointed first judge of Schoharie County in February 1838 and served until July 1847; member of the State assembly in 1840; elected as a Democrat to the Twenty-ninth Congress (March 4, 1845–March 3, 1847); continued the practice of law in Schoharie until 1852, when he established the Schoharie County Bank and served as its president; elected to the Thirty-ninth Congress (March 4, 1865–March 3, 1867); was not a candidate for renomination in 1866; resumed the practice of law; delegate to the Union National Convention of Conservatives at Philadelphia in 1866 and to the Democratic National Convention at New York City in 1868; retired in 1869 and moved to Charlottesville, Va.; served as judge of the Albemarle County Court; died in Charlottesville, Va., on April 9, 1876; interment in Maplewood Cemetery.

GOODYKOONTZ, Wells, a Representative from West Virginia; born near Newbern, Pulaski County, Va., June 3, 1872; educated under private tutors and attended Oxford Academy at Floyd, Va., and the law department of Washington and Lee University, Lexington, Va.; was admitted to the bar in 1893 and commenced practice at Williamson, W. Va., in 1894; also engaged in banking; member of the State house of delegates in 1911 and 1912; member of the State senate 1914–1918 and served as president of the senate and Lieutenant Governor ex officio of the State from 1917 to December 1, 1918; president of the West Virginia Bar Association in 1917 and 1918; chairman of the central legal advisory board for West Virginia during the First World War; elected as a Republican to the Sixty-sixth and Sixty-seventh Congresses (March 4, 1919–March 3, 1923); unsuccessful candidate for reelection in 1922 to the Sixty-eighth Congress; resumed the practice of law and banking interests in Williamson, W. Va.; also engaged in literary work; died in a hospital in Cincinnati, Ohio, on March 2, 1944; interment in Fairview Cemetery, Williamson, W. Va.

GORDON, George Washington, a Representative from Tennessee; born in Pulaski, Giles County, Tenn., October 5, 1836; received a collegiate training and was graduated from the Western Military Institute, Nashville, Tenn., in 1859; practiced civil engineering until the beginning of the Civil War; enlisted in the military service of the Confederacy; was drillmaster of the Eleventh Regiment, Tennessee Infantry; was successively a captain, lieutenant colonel, colonel, and brigadier general, and served until the close of the war; studied law; was admitted to the bar and practiced in Memphis, Tenn., until 1883; appointed one of the railroad commissioners of Tennessee; received an appointment in the Department of the Interior July 14, 1887, as special Indian agent in Arizona and Nevada and served until February 15, 1890; returned to Memphis, Tenn.; resumed the practice of law; superintendent of the Memphis city schools 1889–1907; elected as a Democrat to the Sixtieth, Sixty-first, and Sixty-second Congresses and served from March 4, 1907, until his death in Memphis, Tenn., on August 9, 1911; interment in Elmwood Cemetery.

GORDON, James, a Representative from New York; born in the parish of Killead, County Antrim, Ireland, October 31, 1739; attended the local schools; immigrated to the United States in 1758; settled in Schenectady, N. Y., where he engaged in Indian trading; served as a lieutenant colonel in the Militia Regiment of Albany County, N. Y., during the Revolutionary War; captured and taken prisoner to Canada; returned to Albany, N. Y.; member of the State assembly 1777–1780, 1786, and 1790; moved to Ballston Spa, N. Y.; elected as a Federalist to the Second and Third Congresses (March 4, 1791–March 3, 1795); member of the board of trustees of Union College, Schenectady, N. Y., 1795–1809; served in the State senate 1797–1804; died in Ballston Spa, N. Y., January 17, 1810; interment in Briggs Cemetery.

GORDON, James, a Senator from Mississippi; born in Cotton Gin Port, Monroe County, Miss., December 6, 1833; moved with his parents to Pontotoc County in 1834; attended the public schools, St. Thomas Hall, Holly Springs, Miss., and La Grange College, Alabama; was graduated from the University of Mississippi at Oxford in 1855; became a planter and was also a newspaper and magazine writer; member of the State house of representatives in 1857 and 1859; located in Okolona, Miss., in 1859; during the Civil War served as colonel in the Confederate Army with Cavalry regiments he had raised and organized; special commissioner of the Confederacy to visit European countries in 1864; captured in the harbor of Wilmington, N. C., on his return in January 1865, but escaped February 22, 1865, and fled to Canada; surrendered to General Dix in New York City and received a passport to his home; again a member of the State house of representatives in 1876 and 1886; member of the State senate 1904–1906; appointed to the United States Senate to fill the vacancy caused by the death of Anselm J. McLaurin and served from December 27, 1909, to February 22, 1910; was not a candidate for election in 1910; resumed agricultural pursuits and literary activities; died in Okolona, Chickasaw County, Miss., November 28, 1912; interment in Odd Fellows Cemetery.

GORDON, John Brown, a Senator from Georgia; born in Upson County, Ga., February 6, 1832; attended private schools and the University of Georgia at Athens; studied law; was admitted to the bar in 1853 and commenced practice in Atlanta, Ga.; upon the outbreak of the Civil War entered the Confederate Army as captain of Infantry, and served successively as major, lieutenant colonel, colonel, brigadier general, major general, and lieutenant general; commanded the Second Army Corps and one wing of General Lee's army at Appomattox and led the last charge at Appomattox, taking the Union breastworks and capturing artillery; resumed the practice of law in Atlanta, Ga.; delegate to the Union National Convention at Philadelphia in 1866; unsuccessful Democratic candidate for Governor in 1868; member of the Democratic National Convention at New York City in 1868 and at Baltimore in 1872; presidential elector on the Democratic ticket of Seymour and Blair in 1868 and of Greeley and Brown in 1872; elected as a Democrat to the United States Senate in 1873; reelected in 1879 and served from March 4, 1873, until May 26, 1880, when he resigned to promote the building of the Georgia Pacific Railroad; Governor of Georgia 1886–1890; again elected to the United States Senate and served from March 4, 1891, to March 3, 1897; declined to be a candidate for reelection; engaged in lecturing and literary work; died in Miami, Fla., January 9, 1904; interment in Oakland Cemetery, Atlanta, Ga.

GORDON, Robert Bryarly, a Representative from Ohio; born at St. Marys, Auglaize County, Ohio, August 6, 1855; attended the public schools; postmaster of St. Marys 1885–1889; auditor of Auglaize County 1890–1896; delegate to the Democratic National Convention at Chicago in 1896; elected as a Democrat to the Fifty-sixth and Fifty-seventh Congresses (March 4, 1899–March 3, 1903); engaged in the flour and grain business at St. Marys, Ohio; superintendent of the document room of the National House of Representatives 1911–1913; Sergeant at Arms of the House of Representatives 1913–1919; died in Washington, D. C., January 3, 1923; interment in Elm Grove Cemetery, St. Marys, Ohio.

GORDON, Samuel, a Representative from New York; born at Wattle's Ferry, Delaware County, N. Y., April 28, 1802; attended the public schools; engaged in agricultural pursuits until attaining the age of twenty-five; studied law in Delhi, N. Y.; was admitted to the bar in 1829 and commenced practice in Delhi; appointed postmaster of Delhi, N. Y., September 14, 1831, and served until August 16, 1841; member of the State assembly in 1834; district attorney of Delaware County 1841–1844; supervisor of the town of Delhi for several terms; elected as a Democrat to the Twenty-seventh Congress (March 4, 1841–March 3, 1843); owing to a realignment of the districts in the State was not a candidate for renomination; elected to the Twenty-ninth Congress (March 4, 1845–March 3, 1847); was not a candidate for renomination in 1846; resumed the practice of his legal profession; upon the breaking out of the Civil War was appointed provost marshal for the nineteenth district of New York 1863–1865; owing to ill health discontinued active business pursuits and lived in retirement until his death in Delhi, Delaware County, N. Y., October 28, 1873; interment in Woodland Cemetery.

GORDON, Thomas Sylvy, a Representative from Illinois; born in Chicago, Ill., December 17, 1893; attended the parochial schools and was graduated from St. Stanislaus College, Chicago, Ill., in 1912; engaged in the banking business 1916–1920; associated with a Polish-language daily newspaper 1921–1942, starting as a clerk and advancing to head cashier and office manager; commissioner of Chicago West Parks 1933–1936 and of public vehicle licenses 1936–1939; delegate to the Democratic National Convention at Philadelphia in 1936; city treasurer of Chicago, Ill., 1939–1942; elected as a Democrat to the Seventy-eighth and to the seven succeeding Congresses (January 3, 1943–January 3, 1959); was not a candidate for renomination in 1958; died in Chicago, Ill., January 22, 1959; interment in St. Adalbert Cemetery (Niles), Chicago, Ill.

GORDON, William, a Representative from New Hampshire; born near Boston, Mass., April 12, 1763; was graduated from Harvard College in 1779; studied law; was admitted to the bar in 1787 and commenced practice in Amherst, N. H.; appointed register of probate in 1793; member of the State senate in 1794 and 1795; solicitor of Hillsborough County 1794–1801; elected to the Fifth and Sixth Congresses and served from March 4, 1797, until June 12, 1800, when he resigned to accept the office of attorney general of New Hampshire, which be held until his death; while a Member of the House was one of the managers appointed by the House of Representatives in 1798 to conduct the impeachment proceedings against William Blount, a Senator from Tennessee; died in Boston, Mass., May 8, 1802; interment in Amherst Cemetery, Amherst, N. H.

GORDON, William, a Representative from Ohio; born on a farm near Oak Harbor, Ottawa County, Ohio, December 15, 1862; attended the public schools and Toledo (Ohio) Business College; taught school; deputy county treasurer 1887–1891; member of the board of school examiners of Ottawa County 1890–1896; was graduated from the law department of the University of Michigan at Ann Arbor in 1893; was admitted to the bar the same year and commenced practice in Oak Harbor, Ohio; prosecuting attorney for Ottawa County 1895–1901; delegate to the Democratic National Convention at Chicago in 1896; member of the Democratic State committee in 1903 and 1904; founder of the Gordon Lumber Co.; moved to Cleveland, Ohio, in 1906; unsuccessful candidate for election in 1910 to the Sixty-second Congress; elected as a Democrat to the Sixty-third, Sixty-fourth, and Sixty-fifth Congresses (March 4, 1913–March 3, 1919); was an unsuccessful candidate for reelection in 1918 to the Sixty-sixth Congress; reengaged in the practice of law until his death in Cleveland, Ohio, January 16, 1942; interment in Oak Harbor Cemetery, Oak Harbor, Ohio.

GORDON, William Fitzhugh, a Representative from Virginia; born on Germanna plantation, near Fredericksburg, Spotsylvania County, Va., January 13, 1787; attended the country schools and Spring Hill Academy; studied law; was admitted to the bar in 1808 and commenced practice at Orange Court House, Va.; moved to Charlottesville, Va., in 1809 and continued the practice of law; Commonwealth attorney in 1812; served in the War of 1812; later attained the rank of major general in the Virginia Militia; member of the State house of delegates 1818–1829; member of the State constitutional convention in 1829 and 1830; elected as a Democrat to the Twenty-first Congress to fill the vacancy caused by the resignation of William C. Rives; reelected to the Twenty-second and Twenty-third Congresses and served from January 25, 1830, to March 3, 1835; unsuccessful candidate for reelection in 1834 to the Twenty-fourth Congress; engaged in agricultural pursuits; delegate to the Southern Convention at Nashville, Tenn., in 1850; died on his plantation, "Edgeworth," Albemarle County, Va., August 28, 1858; interment in the family burying ground at Springfield, near Gordonsville, Va.

GORE, Albert Arnold, a Representative and a Senator from Tennessee; born in Granville, Jackson County, Tenn., December 26, 1907; attended the public schools; was graduated from State Teachers' College, Murfreesboro, Tenn., in 1932 and from Nashville (Tenn.) Y. M. C. A. night law school in 1936; taught in the rural schools of Overton County, Tenn.; taught in the schools of Smith County, Tenn., 1926–1930; served as county superintendent of education of Smith County 1932–1936; was admitted to the bar in 1936 and commenced practice in Carthage, Tenn.; Tennessee commissioner of labor in 1936 and 1937; elected as a Democrat to the Seventy-sixth, Seventy-seventh, and Seventy-eighth Congresses and served from January 3, 1939, until his resignation on December 4, 1944, to enter the United States Army; reelected to the Seventy-ninth and to the three succeeding Congresses (January 3, 1945–January 3, 1953); was not a candidate for renomination in 1952, having received the Democratic nomination for Senator; elected to the United States Senate in 1952 for the term commencing January 3, 1953; reelected in 1958 for the term ending January 3, 1965.

GORE, Christopher, a Senator from Massachusetts; born in Boston, Mass., September 21, 1758; was graduated from Harvard College in 1776; studied law; was admitted to the bar and commenced practice in Boston; member of the State constitutional convention in 1788; member of the State house of representatives in 1788, 1789, and 1808; United States attorney for the district of Massachusetts 1789–1796; commissioner to England 1796–1803; Chargé d'Affaires at London in 1803 and 1804; served in the State senate in 1806 and 1807; Governor of Massachusetts in 1809; appointed and subsequently elected to the United States Senate to fill the vacancy caused by the resignation of James Lloyd and served from May 5, 1813, until May 30, 1816, when he resigned; presidential elector on the Federalist ticket of King and Howard in 1816; overseer of Harvard University 1810–1815 and a fellow 1812–1820; died in Waltham, Mass., March 1, 1827; interment in Granary Burying Ground, Boston, Mass.

GORE, Thomas Pryor, a Senator from Oklahoma; born near Embry, Webster County, Miss., December 10, 1870; by accidents lost the sight of his left eye at the age of eight and that of his right eye at the age of eleven; attended the public schools; was graduated from the normal school at Walthall, Miss., in 1890; taught school in 1890 and 1891; was graduated from the law department of Cumberland University, Lebanon, Tenn., in 1892; was admitted to the bar in 1892 and commenced practice in Walthall, Miss.; moved to Corsicana, Tex., in 1895; delegate to the Populist National Convention at St. Louis in 1896; unsuccessful candidate for election as a Populist in 1898 to the Fifty-sixth Congress; moved to Lawton, Okla., in 1901 and continued the practice of law; member of the Territorial council 1903–1905; upon the admission of Oklahoma as a State into the Union was elected as a Democrat to the United States Senate for the term ending March 3, 1909; reelected in 1908 and again in 1914 and served from December 11, 1907, to March 3, 1921; unsuccessful candidate for renomination in 1920; delegate to the Democratic National Convention at Baltimore in 1912; member of the Democratic National Committee 1912–1916; appointed by President Wilson in 1913 as a member of the Commission to Investigate and Study Rural Credits and Agricultural Cooperative Organizations in European Countries; entered the practice of law in

Washington, D. C., in 1921; again elected to the United States Senate in 1930 and served from March 4, 1931, to January 3, 1937; unsuccessful candidate for renomination in 1936; reengaged in the practice of law in Washington, D. C., until his death on March 16, 1949; interment in Rose Hill Cemetery, Oklahoma City, Okla.

GORHAM, Benjamin (son of Nathaniel Gorham), a Representative from Massachusetts; born in Charlestown, Mass., February 13, 1775; pursued preparatory studies; was graduated from Harvard University in 1795; studied law; was admitted to the bar and commenced practice in Boston, Mass.; member of the State house of representatives 1814–1818; served in the State senate from May 26, 1819, to January 10, 1821, when he resigned; elected to the Sixteenth Congress to fill the vacancy caused by the resignation of Jonathan Mason; reelected to the Seventeenth Congress and served from November 6, 1820, to March 3, 1823; again a member of the State senate for one term beginning May 28, 1823; elected to the Twentieth Congress to fill the vacancy caused by the resignation of Daniel Webster; reelected to the Twenty-first Congress and served from July 23, 1827, to March 3, 1831; again elected to the Twenty-third Congress (March 4, 1833–March 3, 1835); again a member of the State house of representatives in 1841; resumed the practice of law; died in Boston, Mass., September 27, 1855; interment in the old burial ground of Phipps Street Cemetery, Charlestown, Mass.

GORHAM, Nathaniel (father of Benjamin Gorham), a Delegate from Massachusetts; born in Charlestown, Mass., May 27, 1738; attended the public schools; engaged in mercantile pursuits; member of the provincial legislature 1771–1775; delegate to the Provincial Congress in 1774 and 1775; member of the board of war 1778–1781; delegate to the State constitutional convention in 1779; served in the State senate in 1780 and 1781; Member of the Continental Congress in 1782, 1783, and 1785–1787, and was its president from June 6, 1786, to February 2, 1787; delegate to the Federal constitutional convention at Philadelphia in 1787; delegate to the State constitutional convention which ratified the Federal Constitution in 1788; judge of the court of common pleas from July 1, 1785, until his resignation on May 31, 1796; interested in the purchase and settlement of lands in the Genesee Valley, N. Y.; died in Charlestown, Mass., June 11, 1796; interment in Phipps Street Cemetery.

GORMAN, Arthur Pue, a Senator from Maryland; born in Woodstock, Howard County, Md., March 11, 1839; attended the public schools; appointed page in the National House of Representatives in 1852; transferred to the Senate side through the influence of Stephen A. Douglas and served the Senate as page, messenger, assistant postmaster, and postmaster; removed September 1, 1866, and immediately appointed collector of internal revenue for the fifth district of Maryland and served until March 1869; appointed a director in the Chesapeake & Ohio Canal Co. in June 1869; member of the State house of delegates 1869–1873 and served as speaker for one session; elected president of the Chesapeake & Ohio Canal Co. in 1872; served in the State senate from 1875 to 1881, when he resigned; elected as a Democrat to the United States Senate; reelected in 1886 and 1892 and served from March 4, 1881, to March 3, 1899; unsuccessful candidate for reelection; was again elected to the United States Senate in 1902 and served from March 4, 1903, until his death in Washington, D. C., June 4, 1906; interment in Oak Hill Cemetery.

GORMAN, George Edmund, a Representative from Illinois; born in Chicago, Ill., April 13, 1873; attended the public schools of his native city; was graduated in law from Georgetown University at Washington, D. C., in 1895; was admitted to the bar in 1895 and commenced the practice of law in Chicago the following year; assistant prosecuting attorney of Chicago 1897–1900; elected as a Democrat to the Sixty-third Congress (March 4, 1913–March 3, 1915); declined to be a candidate for reelection in 1914; resumed the practice of law in Chicago, Ill.; assistant State's attorney 1920–1928; served as master in chancery of the circuit court from 1930 until his death in Chicago, Ill., January 13, 1935; interment in Holy Sepulchre Cemetery.

GORMAN, James Sedgwick, a Representative from Michigan; born in Lyndon Township, near Chelsea, Washtenaw County, Mich., December 28, 1850; attended the common schools and the Union School of Chelsea, and was graduated from the law department of the University of Michigan at Ann Arbor in 1876; was admitted to the bar and commenced practice in Jackson, Mich.; assistant prosecuting attorney of Jackson County for two years; moved to Dexter, Mich., in 1879; member of the State house of representatives in 1880; served in the State senate in 1886 and 1888; elected as a Democrat to the Fifty-second and Fifty-third Congresses (March 4, 1891–March 3, 1895); was not a candidate for renomination; engaged in farming near Chelsea, Mich., and resumed the practice of law; died in Detroit, Mich., May 27, 1923; interment in Mount Olivet Cemetery, Chelsea, Mich.

GORMAN, John Jerome, a Representative from Illinois; born in Minneapolis, Minn., June 2, 1883; attended the common schools and the Bryant and Stratton Business College at Chicago, Ill.; clerk and letter carrier in the Chicago city post office 1902–1918; studied law at Loyola University in Chicago, and was graduated in 1914; was admitted to the bar in 1914 and commenced practice in Chicago; delegate to the State constitutional convention in 1920; elected as a Republican to the Sixty-seventh Congress (March 4, 1921–March 3, 1923); unsuccessful candidate for reelection; resumed the practice of law at Chicago, Ill.; elected to the Sixty-ninth Congress (March 4, 1925–March 3, 1927); unsuccessful candidate for reelection; resumed the practice of law in Chicago, Ill., where he now resides.

GORMAN, Willis Arnold, a Representative from Indiana; born near Flemingsburg, Ky., January 12, 1816; pursued an academic course; moved to Bloomington, Ind., in 1835; was graduated from the law department of the Indiana University at Bloomington in 1845; was admitted to the bar the same year and commenced practice in Bloomington; clerk of the State senate in 1837 and 1838; major and colonel of Indiana Volunteers in the Mexican War; elected as a Democrat to the Thirty-first and Thirty-second Congresses (March 4, 1849–March 3, 1853); was not a candidate for renomination in 1852; moved to Minnesota in 1853; Territorial Governor of Minnesota 1853–1857; delegate to the constitutional convention of Minnesota in 1857; practiced law in St. Paul, Minn., 1857–1861; member of the State house of representatives in 1858; during the Civil War entered the Union Army in 1861 and was colonel of the First Regiment, Minnesota Volunteer Infantry; was mustered out as brigadier general in 1864; resumed the practice of law; prosecuting attorney of St. Paul 1869–1875; died in St. Paul, Minn., May 20, 1876; interment in Oakland Cemetery.

GORSKI, Chester Charles, a Representative from New York; born in Buffalo, Erie County, N. Y., June 22, 1906; attended Sts. Peter and Paul Parochial School and Technical High School; member of the Erie County Board of Supervisors 1941–1945, serving as minority leader 1942–1945; member of the Buffalo Common Council 1946–1948, serving as minority leader 1946–1947 and majority leader in 1948; delegate to Democratic National Conventions in 1948, 1952, and 1956; elected as a

Democrat to the Eighty-first Congress (January 3, 1949–January 3, 1951); unsuccessful candidate for reelection in 1950 to the Eighty-second Congress and for election in 1952 to the Eighty-third Congress; industrial analyst, United States Department of Commerce, from May 16, 1951, to November 5, 1951; assistant director, Buffalo office, United States Department of Commerce, from February 1, 1952, to October 1, 1952; again elected to Buffalo Common Council and served from January 1, 1954, to February 1, 1956, and was majority leader; appointed to the New York State Building Code Commission on February 1, 1956, and served until April 1, 1959; elected president of the Buffalo Common Council and took office January 1, 1960; is a resident of Buffalo, N. Y.

GORSKI, Martin, a Representative from Illinois; born in Poland, October 30, 1886; immigrated in 1889 to the United States with his parents, who settled in Chicago, Ill.; attended the public and high schools; was graduated from business college and from Chicago (Ill.) Law School in 1917; was admitted to the bar in 1917 and commenced practice in Chicago, Ill.; assistant State's attorney 1918–1920; master in chancery of the superior court of Cook County, Ill., 1929–1942; elected as a Democrat to the Seventy-eighth, Seventy-ninth, and Eightieth Congresses and served from January 3, 1943, until his death; had been reelected to the Eighty-first Congress; died in Chicago, Ill., December 4, 1949; interment in Resurrection Cemetery (Village of Justice).

GOSS, Edward Wheeler, a Representative from Connecticut; born in Waterbury, Conn., April 27, 1893; attended the public schools and was graduated from Hill School, Pottstown, Pa.; during the First World War entered the military service September 6, 1918, was assigned to the Fortieth Company, Tenth Battalion, One Hundred and Sixty-sixth Depot Brigade, and served until his discharge as a sergeant on December 4, 1918; engaged in the manufacture of brass 1912–1930; delegate to the Republican National Conventions in 1924, 1928, and 1932; served in the State senate 1926–1928; elected as a Republican to the Seventy-first Congress to fill the vacancy caused by the death of James P. Glynn and at the same time was elected to the Seventy-second Congress; reelected to the Seventy-third Congress and served from November 4, 1930, to January 3, 1935; unsuccessful for reelection in 1934 to the Seventy-fourth Congress; statistical and research work in Washington, D. C., 1935–1939; during World War II enlisted in the United States Coast Guard Reserve May 25, 1942, as chief bosun mate, promoted to lieutenant, and served until discharged February 15, 1948; distributor for Investors Diversified Services, Inc., of Minneapolis, Minn.; retired; resides in Fort Lauderdale, Fla.

GOSS, James Hamilton, a Representative from South Carolina; born in Union, Union County, S. C., August 9, 1820; attended the common schools and the Union Male Academy; engaged in mercantile pursuits; served with the South Carolina Militia during the Civil War; delegate to the State constitutional convention in 1867; upon the readmission of the State of South Carolina to representation was elected as a Republican to the Fortieth Congress and served from July 18, 1868, to March 3, 1869; was not a candidate for renomination in 1868; member of the board of commissioners of Union County 1871–1874; appointed postmaster of Union August 12, 1875, and served until September 23, 1884; died in Union, S. C., October 31, 1886; interment in the Presbyterian Cemetery.

GOSSETT, Charles Clinton, a Senator from Idaho; born in Pricetown, Highland County, Ohio, September 2, 1888; attended the public schools at Pricetown, Highland County, Ohio; moved to Cunningham, Wash., in 1907, to Ontario, Oreg., in 1910, and to Nampa, Canyon County, Idaho, in 1922 and engaged in agricultural pursuits and in the livestock, feed, and shipping businesses; member of the State house of representatives 1933–1937; delegate to several State conventions; Lieutenant Governor 1937–1939 and 1941–1943; served as Governor of Idaho from January 1945 until his resignation on November 16, 1945; appointed as a Democrat to the United States Senate to fill the vacancy caused by the death of John Thomas and served from November 17, 1945, to January 3, 1947; unsuccessful candidate for nomination to fill the vacancy in 1946; resumed his former business pursuits and is a resident of Nampa, Idaho.

GOSSETT, Ed Lee, a Representative from Texas; born in a sawmill camp known as Yellow Pine, near Many, Sabine Parish, La., January 27, 1902; moved to Texas in 1908 with his parents, who settled on a farm near Henrietta, Clay County; attended the rural schools of Clay and Garza Counties, Tex.; was graduated from the University of Texas at Austin in 1924 and from the law school of the same university in 1927; was admitted to the bar the latter year and commenced practice in Vernon, Tex.; moved to Wichita Falls, Tex., in 1937 and continued the practice of law; served as district attorney of the forty-sixth judicial district 1933–1937; elected as a Democrat to the Seventy-sixth and to the six succeeding Congresses and served from January 3, 1939, until his resignation July 31, 1951; resumed the practice of law and is general attorney for the Texas Southwestern Bell Telephone Co., Dallas, Tex.

GOTT, Daniel, a Representative from New York; born in Hebron, near New London, Conn., July 10, 1794; attended the public schools; at the age of sixteen taught school; moved to Pompey, N. Y., in 1817; studied law; was admitted to the bar in 1819 and commenced practice in Pompey, N. Y.; elected as a Whig to the Thirtieth and Thirty-first Congresses (March 4, 1847–March 3, 1851); moved to Syracuse, N. Y., in 1853 and resumed the practice of his profession; died in Syracuse, N. Y., July 6, 1864; interment in Pompey Hill Cemetery, Pompey, N. Y.

GOULD, Arthur Robinson, a Senator from Maine; born in East Corinth, Penobscot County, Maine, March 16, 1857; attended the common schools and East Corinth Academy; in early life engaged in commercial enterprises; moved to Presque Isle, Maine, in 1887 and engaged in the lumber business, operating mills at Fort Fairfield and Presque Isle; was the builder of the Maine & New Brunswick Co. power plant and also of an electric railroad from Presque Isle to Caribou, linking it with the Canadian Pacific Railway; president of the Aroostook Valley Railroad Co. 1902–1946; served in the State senate in 1921 and 1922; elected on November 29, 1926, as a Republican to the United States Senate to fill the vacancy caused by the death of Bert M. Fernald and served from November 30, 1926, to March 3, 1931; was not a candidate for renomination in 1930; engaged in the railroad and lumber businesses; died in Presque Isle, Maine, July 24, 1946; interment in Mount Hope Cemetery, Bangor, Maine.

GOULD, Herman Day, a Representative from New York; born in Sharon, Litchfield County, Conn., January 16, 1799; pursued an academic course; engaged in mercantile pursuits; president of the Delhi National Bank 1839–1849; unsuccessful candidate for election in 1840 to the Twenty-seventh Congress and in 1844 to the Twenty-ninth Congress; elected as a Whig to the Thirty-first Congress (March 4, 1849–March 3, 1851); was not a candidate for renomination in 1850; resumed business interests in Delhi, N. Y., and died there January 26, 1852; interment in Woodland Cemetery.

GOULD, Norman Judd (grandson of Norman Buel Judd), a Representative from New York; born at Seneca Falls, Seneca County, N. Y., March 15, 1877; attended school at Seneca Falls, N. Y., and at Lawrenceville, N. J., was graduated from Cornell University in 1899; specialized in mechanical engineering; engaged in the manufacture of pumps; delegate to the Republican National Conventions in 1908 and 1916; chairman of the Seneca County Republican committee 1912–1923; member of the New York State committee 1914–1922; elected as a Republican to the Sixty-fourth Congress to fill the vacancy caused by the death of Sereno E. Payne; reelected to the Sixty-fifth, Sixty-sixth, and Sixty-seventh Congresses and served from November 2, 1915, to March 3, 1923; declined to be a candidate for renomination in 1922; resumed his former manufacturing pursuits; is a resident of Seneca Falls, N. Y.

GOULD, Samuel Wadsworth, a Representative from Maine; born in Porter, Oxford County, Maine, January 1, 1852; moved with his parents to Hiram, Maine; attended the public schools and North Parsonsfield Seminary; was graduated from the University of Maine at Orono in 1877; studied law; was admitted to the bar and commenced practice in Skowhegan, Maine in 1879; postmaster of Skowhegan 1896–1900; attended all Democratic State conventions for more than forty years; secretary of the Democratic State committee 1882–1890; delegate to the Democratic National Conventions in 1900, 1908, and 1912; unsuccessful candidate for Governor of Maine in 1902 and for election to the Sixty-first Congress in 1908; elected as a Democrat to the Sixty-second Congress (March 4, 1911–March 3, 1913); unsuccessful candidate for reelection in 1912; resumed the practice of law in Skowhegan, Maine; interested in various business enterprises; president of the board of trustees of the University of Maine; died in Skowhegan, Maine, December 19, 1935; interment in Southside Cemetery.

GOULDEN, Joseph Aloysius, a Representative from New York; born in Littlestown, Adams County, Pa., August 1, 1844; attended the common schools; served in the Marine Corps of the Navy in 1864 and 1865; member of the board of managers at the State reformatory, Morganza, Pa.; moved to New York City; commissioner and trustee of public schools for ten years; member of board of trustees of the soldiers' home, Bath, N. Y.; secretary and member of the New York City commission that erected the soldiers' and sailors' monument on Riverside Drive; elected as a Democrat to the Fifty-eighth and to the three succeeding Congresses (March 4, 1903–March 3, 1911); declined to be a candidate for reelection; engaged in the insurance business in New York City; elected to the Sixty-third and Sixty-fourth Congresses and served from March 4, 1913, until his death in Philadelphia, Pa., May 3, 1915; interment in St. Joseph's Cemetery, Taneytown, Md.

GOURDIN, Theodore, a Representative from South Carolina; born near Kingstree, Williamsburg County, S. C., March 20, 1764; was educated in Charleston, S. C., and in Europe; engaged in planting; elected as a Democrat to the Thirteenth Congress (March 4, 1813–March 3, 1815); resumed agricultural pursuits; died in Pineville, S. C., January 17, 1826; interment in Episcopal Cemetery, St. Stephen, S. C.

GOVAN, Andrew Robison, a Representative from South Carolina; born in Orange Parish, Orangeburg District, S. C., January 13, 1794; pursued classical studies at a private school in Willington, S. C., and was graduated from South Carolina College at Columbia in 1813; member of the State house of representatives 1820–1822; elected to the Seventeenth Congress to fill the vacancy caused by the death of James Overstreet;

reelected to the Eighteenth and Nineteenth Congresses and served from December 4, 1822, to March 3, 1827; moved to Mississippi in 1828 and devoted the remainder of his life to planting; died in Marshall County, Miss., June 27, 1841; interment in the family cemetery on the estate, "Snowdown" plantation, Marshall County, Miss.

GOVE, Samuel Francis, a Representative from Georgia; born in Weymouth, Norfolk County, Mass., March 9, 1822; attended the common schools; moved to Georgia in 1835 with his parents, who settled in Twiggs County; engaged in mercantile and agricultural pursuits; was also a missionary; upon the readmission of the State of Georgia to representation was elected as a Republican to the Fortieth Congress and served from June 25, 1868, to March 3, 1869; presented credentials as a Member-elect to the Forty-first Congress, but was not permitted to qualify; ordained as a Baptist minister in 1877 and was a traveling missionary from 1879 until his death in St. Augustine, Fla., December 3, 1900; interment in Rose Hill Cemetery, Macon, Ga.

GRADY, Benjamin Franklin, a Representative from North Carolina; born near Sarecta, Duplin County, N. C., October 10, 1831; attended private and public schools, and was graduated from the University of North Carolina at Chapel Hill in 1857; professor of mathematics and natural sciences in Austin College, Huntsville, Tex., 1858–1862; enlisted during the Civil War in Company K, Twenty-fifth Regiment, Texas Cavalry; promoted to orderly sergeant in Granbury's brigade, Cleburne's division; became ill with typhoid fever and remained in Peace Institute Hospital at Raleigh until the end of the war; settled in Clinton, N. C., at the close of the war and engaged in teaching in Clinton and La Grange, N. C.; in 1877 returned to Duplin County, where he continued to teach and also engaged in agricultural pursuits; superintendent of public instruction for Duplin County 1881–1890; justice of the peace 1878–1889; elected as a Democrat to the Fifty-second and Fifty-third Congresses (March 4, 1891–March 3, 1895); retired to a farm near Turkey, Sampson County, N. C., where he again taught school for several years; returned to Clinton, N. C., and died there March 6, 1914; interment in Clinton Cemetery.

GRAFF, Joseph Verdi, a Representative from Illinois; born in Terre Haute, Vigo County, Ind., July 1, 1854; was graduated from the Terre Haute High School, and attended Wabash College, Crawfordsville, Ind., one year; moved to Delavan, Ill., in 1873 and engaged in mercantile pursuits; studied law; was admitted to the bar in 1879 and commenced practice in Delavan, Ill.; moved to Pekin, Ill., and continued the practice of law; elected as an inspector of the Pekin public schools in 1891 and served as president of the board of education; delegate to the Republican National Convention at Minneapolis in 1892; elected as a Republican to the Fifty-fourth and to the seven succeeding Congresses (March 4, 1895–March 3, 1911); unsuccessful candidate for reelection in 1910 to the Sixty-second Congress; continued the practice of law in Peoria, Ill., where he had moved in 1899; also engaged in banking; died in Peoria, Ill., November 10, 1921; interment in Glendale Cemetery, Washington, Tazewell County, Ill.

GRAHAM, Frank Porter, a Senator from North Carolina; born in Fayetteville, Cumberland County, N. C., October 14, 1886; attended the public schools of Charlotte and Warrenton, N. C.; was graduated from the University of North Carolina in 1909; studied law for two years at the University of North Carolina and received license to practice in 1910; studied at University of Chicago; received master's degree at Columbia University, New York City, N. Y., in 1916; instructor in English at Raleigh (N. C.) High School 1910–1912; instructor, assistant professor, and professor of history 1915–1930; during the First World War enlisted as a private in the United States Marine Corps in June 1917 and served with the First and Tenth Regiments until discharged in July 1919 as a first lieutenant; in 1919 returned to the University of North Carolina as assistant professor and was president 1930–1949; served as vice chairman of Consumers Board of National Recovery Administration and chairman of National Advisory Council to the Cabinet Committee on Economic Security in 1934; member of President's Committee on Education; chairman, Industries Committee of American Railroads; member of National Defense Mediation Board in 1941 and 1942; public member National War Labor Board 1942–1945; member of Maritime War Emergency Board 1942–1946; United States representative on Good Offices Committee of the Security Council of the United Nations on Indonesia in 1947 and 1948; adviser to the Secretary of State on Indonesian Affairs in 1948; appointed as a Democrat to the United States Senate to fill the vacancy caused by the death of J. Melville Broughton and served from March 29, 1949, to November 26, 1950; unsuccessful candidate for the nomination in 1950 to fill the vacancy; member of panel, United Nations mediators, and United Nations representative to India and Pakistan in the Kashmir dispute 1951–1957; with the United Nations and resides in New York City, N. Y.

GRAHAM, George Scott, a Representative from Pennsylvania; born in Philadelphia, Pa., September 13, 1850; attended the public schools, and was privately tutored; was graduated from the law department of the University of Pennsylvania at Philadelphia in 1870; was admitted to the bar in 1871 and commenced practice in Philadelphia; member of the select council of Philadelphia 1877–1880; unsuccessful candidate for district attorney of Philadelphia County in 1877; district attorney of Philadelphia County 1880–1899; declined to be a candidate for further election and resumed the practice of law in Philadelphia and New York City; professor of criminal law and procedure in the University of Pennsylvania 1887–1898; delegate to the Republican National Conventions in 1892 and 1924; elected as a Republican to the Sixty-third and to the nine succeeding Congresses and served from March 4, 1913, until his death at his summer home in Islip, N. Y., July 4, 1931; interment in Woodlawn Cemetery, New York City, N. Y.

GRAHAM, James (brother of William Alexander Graham), a Representative from North Carolina; born in Lincoln County, N. C., January 7, 1793; pursued classical studies, and was graduated from the University of North Carolina at Chapel Hill in 1814; studied law; was admitted to the bar in 1818 and commenced practice in Rutherford County; member of the State house of representatives in 1822, 1823, 1824, 1828, and 1829; elected to the Twenty-third Congress (March 4, 1833–March 3, 1835); presented credentials as a Member-elect to the Twenty-fourth Congress and served from March 4, 1835, to March 29, 1836, when the seat was declared vacant; subsequently elected to the same Congress; elected to the Twenty-fifth, Twenty-sixth, and Twenty-seventh Congresses and served from December 5, 1836, to March 3, 1843; unsuccessful candidate for reelection in 1842 to the Twenty-eighth Congress; elected as a Whig to the Twenty-ninth Congress (March 4, 1845–March 3, 1847); was not a candidate for renomination in 1846; engaged in agricultural pursuits near Rutherfordton, Rutherford County, N. C., where he died September 25, 1851.

GRAHAM, James Harper, a Representative from New York; born in Bovina, Delaware County, N. Y., September 18, 1812; attended the public schools; supervisor of the town of Delhi,

N. Y.; chairman of the board of supervisors of Delaware County; engaged in agricultural pursuits; elected as a Republican to the Thirty-sixth Congress (March 4, 1859–March 3, 1861); was not a candidate for renomination in 1860; presidential elector on the Republican ticket of Grant and Colfax in 1868; member of the State assembly in 1871; served in the State senate in 1872 and 1873; engaged in agricultural and mercantile pursuits; died in Delhi, N. Y., June 23, 1881; interment in Woodland Cemetery.

GRAHAM, James McMahon, a Representative from Illinois; born in Castleblayney, County Monaghan, Ireland, April 14, 1852; immigrated with his family to the United States and settled in Sangamon County, Ill., in 1868; attended the common schools, the University of Illinois at Urbana, and Valparaiso University, Indiana; taught school for seven years; studied law; was admitted to the bar in 1885 and commenced practice in Springfield, Ill.; member of the State house of representatives in 1885 and 1886; prosecuting attorney for Sangamon County 1892–1896; member of the board of education of Springfield 1891–1894; elected as a Democrat to the Sixty-first, Sixty-second, and Sixty-third Congresses (March 4, 1909–March 3, 1915); unsuccessful candidate for reelection in 1914 to the Sixty-fourth Congress; member of the National Conference of Commissioners on Uniform State Laws 1916–1928; member of the board of directors of Lincoln Library 1936–1945; resumed the practice of law in Springfield, Ill., where he died on October 23, 1945; interment in Calvary Cemetery.

GRAHAM, John Hugh, a Representative from New York; born in Belfast, Ireland, April 1, 1835; immigrated in 1836 to the United States with his parents, who settled in Brooklyn, N. Y.; attended the public schools of Brooklyn; during the Civil War recruited Company A, Fifth Regiment, Heavy Artillery, New York Volunteers, and served three years as its captain; for gallant and meritorious services at Harpers Ferry and in the Shenandoah Valley, Va., was commissioned major and brevetted lieutenant colonel; after the war engaged in the hardware business in Brooklyn, N. Y.; nominated as presidential elector in 1892, but subsequently resigned; elected as a Democrat to the Fifty-third Congress (March 4, 1893–March 3, 1895); was not a candidate for renomination in 1894; died in Brooklyn, N. Y., on July 11, 1895; interment in Greenwood Cemetery.

GRAHAM, Louis Edward, a Representative from Pennsylvania; born in New Castle, Lawrence County, Pa., August 4, 1880; moved with his parents to Beaver, Pa., in 1893; attended preparatory school and Beaver (Pa.) High School; was graduated from Washington and Jefferson College, Washington, Pa., in 1901; served as deputy sheriff of Beaver County, Pa., 1903–1906; studied law; was admitted to the bar in 1906 and commenced practice in Beaver, Pa.; district attorney of Beaver County 1912–1924 and deputy attorney general of Pennsylvania 1924–1927; chief legal adviser of the former sixth Federal prohibition district 1927–1929; served as United States attorney for the western district of Pennsylvania November 7, 1929, to September 1, 1933; special assistant to the Attorney General of the United States in the Pittsburgh, Pa., vote-fraud cases 1934–1936; elected as a Republican to the Seventy-sixth and to the seven succeeding Congresses (January 3, 1939–January 3, 1955); unsuccessful candidate for reelection in 1954 to the Eighty-fourth Congress; resumed the practice of law; is a resident of Beaver, Pa.

GRAHAM, William, a Representative from Indiana; born at sea March 16, 1782; settled with his parents in Harrodsburg, Mercer County, Ky.; attended the public schools; moved to Vallonia, Ind., in 1811; engaged in agricultural pursuits;

member of the Territorial house of representatives in 1812; delegate to the State constitutional convention in 1816; member of the State house of representatives 1816–1821 and served as speaker; served in the State senate 1821–1833; elected as a Whig to the Twenty-fifth Congress (March 4, 1837–March 3, 1839); unsuccessful candidate for reelection in 1838 to the Twenty-sixth Congress; resumed agricultural pursuits; died near Vallonia, Ind., August 17, 1858; interment in the White Church Cemetery, Vallonia, Ind.

GRAHAM, William Alexander (brother of James Graham), a Senator from North Carolina; born at Vesuvius Furnace, near Lincolnton, Lincoln County, N. C., September 5, 1804; pursued classical studies, and was graduated from the University of North Carolina at Chapel Hill in 1824; studied law; was admitted to the bar in 1825 and commenced practice in Hillsboro, N. C.; member of the State house of commons in 1836, 1838, and 1840; served as speaker during the sessions of 1838 and 1840; elected as a Whig to the United States Senate to fill the vacancy caused by the resignation of Robert Strange and served from November 25, 1840, to March 3, 1843; Governor of North Carolina 1845–1849; declined the mission to Spain in 1849; Secretary of the Navy in the Cabinet of President Fillmore from July 22, 1850, to July 25, 1852; Whig candidate for Vice President of the United States in 1852; member of the State senate in 1854, 1862, and 1865; served in the Senate in the Second Confederate Congress; elected to the United States Senate in 1866, but his credentials were not presented; delegate to the Philadelphia Union Convention in 1866; member of the board of Peabody trustees 1867–1875; arbitrator selected by Virginia on the disputed boundary line between that State and Maryland 1873–1875; died at Saratoga Springs, N. Y., August 11, 1875; interment in the Presbyterian Church Cemetery, Hillsboro, N. C.

GRAHAM, William Harrison, a Representative from Pennsylvania; born in Allegheny (now part of Pittsburgh), Pa., August 3, 1844; attended the public schools; during the Civil War enlisted on April 5, 1861, in the Second Regiment, Virginia Infantry (Union Army), which, after a service of two years, was mounted and became the Fifth Regiment, West Virginia Cavalry; mustered out June 14, 1864; engaged in the leather business in Allegheny, Pa.; member of the State house of representatives 1875–1878; recorder of deeds of Allegheny County 1882–1891; engaged in banking; elected as a Republican to the Fifty-fifth Congress to fill the vacancy caused by the resignation of William A. Stone; reelected to the Fifty-sixth and Fifty-seventh Congresses and served from November 29, 1898, to March 3, 1903; unsuccessful candidate for reelection in 1902 to the Fifty-eighth Congress; elected to the Fifty-ninth, Sixtieth, and Sixty-first Congresses (March 4, 1905–March 3, 1911); unsuccessful candidate in the Republican primaries for renomination; member of the Allegheny County Board of Viewers 1911–1923; died in Pittsburgh, Pa., March 2, 1923; interment in Highwood Cemetery.

GRAHAM, William Johnson, a Representative from Illinois; born near New Castle, Lawrence County, Pa., February 7, 1872; moved to Illinois with his parents, who settled near Aledo, Mercer County, in 1879; attended the public schools; was graduated from the law department of the University of Illinois at Urbana in 1893; was admitted to the bar in 1895 and commenced practice in Aledo, Ill.; prosecuting attorney of Mercer County 1901–1909; delegate to the Republican National Convention at Chicago in 1912; member of the State house of representatives in 1915 and 1916; elected as a Republican to the Sixty-fifth and to the three succeeding Congresses and served

from March 4, 1917, to June 7, 1924, when he resigned; appointed by President Coolidge on May 29, 1924, as presiding judge of the United States Court of Customs Appeals, Washington, D. C., and served from June 8, 1924, until his death in Washington, D. C., November 10, 1937; remains were cremated and the ashes interred in Aledo Cemetery, Aledo, Ill.

GRAMMER, Elijah Sherman, a Senator from Washington; born in Quincy, Hickory County, Mo., April 3, 1868; attended the common schools and Bentonville (Ark.) College; moved to the State of Washington in 1887, where he was engaged in manual labor and as general manager in logging camps near Tacoma; returned to Bentonville (Ark.) College in 1892; went to Alaska in 1897 as general manager of logging camps and was in charge of the construction of the tramway at Chilcoot Pass; returned to the State of Washington in 1901 and located in Seattle; engaged as owner-logger in many companies; served as president of the Employers' Association of Washington in 1916 and 1917; during the First World War was appointed a major in the United States Army, assigned to the spruce-production division at Grays and Willapa Harbors, and served from 1918 to 1919; appointed as a Republican to the United States Senate to fill the vacancy caused by the death of Wesley L. Jones and served from November 22, 1932, to March 3, 1933; was not a candidate for election to the full term; resumed his interests in the logging business; also served as president and manager of an investment company and vice president and treasurer of a railway company; died in Seattle, Wash., on November 19, 1936; interment in Lakeview Cemetery.

GRANAHAN, Kathryn Elizabeth (widow of William Thomas Granahan), a Representative from Pennsylvania; born in Easton, Northampton County, Pa.; educated in Easton public schools; graduate of Easton High School and Mount St. Joseph College, Philadelphia, Pa.; supervisor of public assistance in the State Auditor General's Department, and liaison officer between that department and Department of Public Assistance, Commonwealth of Pennsylvania, 1940–1943; member of national board, Woman's Medical College of Pennsylvania; delegate to the Democratic National Convention in 1960; elected as a Democrat to the Eighty-fourth Congress to fill the vacancy caused by the death of her husband, William T. Granahan, and at the same time was elected to the Eighty-fifth Congress; reelected to the Eighty-sixth Congress and served from November 6, 1956, to January 3, 1961. *Reelected to the Eighty-seventh Congress.*

GRANAHAN, William Thomas (husband of Kathryn Elizabeth Granahan), a Representative from Pennsylvania; born in Philadelphia, Pa., July 26, 1895; attended parochial schools, and La Salle Extension University at Chicago, Ill.; during the First World War served as a private in the Fourth Army Corps and served in the Army of Occupation in Germany in 1918 and 1919; engaged in the building business 1925–1929; member of the State Democratic committee 1938–1942; State supervisor of inheritance tax in 1940 and 1941; chief disbursing officer of the State treasury 1941–1944; elected as a Democrat to the Seventy-ninth Congress (January 3, 1945–January 3, 1947); unsuccessful candidate for reelection in 1946 to the Eightieth Congress; engaged in the building business; elected to the Eighty-first and to the three succeeding Congresses and served from January 3, 1949, until his death in Darby, Pa., May 25, 1956; had been renominated in the April 1956 primary election; interment in Saint Bernard Cemetery, Easton, Pa.

GRANATA, Peter Charles, a Representative from Illinois; born in Chicago, Ill., October 28, 1898; attended the public and high schools of his native city; was graduated from Bryant and

Stratton Business College at Chicago in 1912; engaged in the coal business in 1917; chief clerk to the prosecutor of the city of Chicago 1926–1928 and chief deputy coroner 1928–1930; elected to the State house of representatives in 1930 to fill a vacancy; presented credentials as a Republican Member-elect to the Seventy-second Congress and served from March 3, 1931, to April 5, 1932, when he was succeeded by Stanley H. Kunz, who successfully contested the election; unsuccessful candidate for election in 1932 to the Seventy-third Congress; engaged in the coal and oil business in Chicago until May 1933; member of the State house of representatives 1932–1941; assistant director of finance of the State of Illinois 1941–1943; again a member of the State house of representatives 1944–1948; vice president of a glass company in Chicago, Ill., 1948–; is a resident of Chicago, Ill.

GRANFIELD, William Joseph, a Representative from Massachusetts; born in Springfield, Mass., December 18, 1889; attended the grammar and high schools; was graduated from Williston Academy, Easthampton, Mass., in 1910 and from the law school of the University of Notre Dame, South Bend, Ind., in 1913; member of the common council in 1915 and 1916; was admitted to the bar in 1916 and commenced practice in Springfield, Mass.; served in the State house of representatives 1917–1919; delegate to the State constitutional convention of 1918 and 1919; delegate to the Democratic National Conventions in 1924 and 1928 and delegate at large in 1932, 1936, and 1940; elected as a Democrat to the Seventy-first Congress to fill the vacancy caused by the death of William K. Kaynor; reelected to the Seventy-second, Seventy-third, and Seventy-fourth Congresses and served from February 11, 1930, to January 3, 1937; was not a candidate for renomination in 1936; appointed for life as presiding justice of the district court, Springfield, Mass., in 1936, and served until his retirement July 27, 1949, due to illness; died in Springfield, Mass., May 28, 1959; interment in St. Michael's Cemetery.

GRANGER, Amos Phelps (cousin of Francis Granger), a Representative from New York; born in Suffield, Conn., June 3, 1789; attended the public schools; in 1811 moved to Manlius, N. Y., where he was president of the town for several years; served as captain in the War of 1812 at Sackets Harbor and on the Canadian border; moved to Syracuse, N. Y., in 1820 and engaged in numerous business enterprises; trustee of the city of Syracuse 1825–1830; delivered the address of welcome to General Lafayette when he visited Syracuse in 1825; delegate to the Whig National Convention at Baltimore in 1852; elected as a Whig to the Thirty-fourth and Thirty-fifth Congresses (March 4, 1855–March 3, 1859); was not a candidate for renomination in 1858; retired from active business pursuits; died in Syracuse, N. Y., on August 20, 1866; interment in Oakwood Cemetery.

GRANGER, Bradley Francis, a Representative from Michigan; born in Lowville, Lewis County, N. Y., March 12, 1825; attended the public schools; studied law; was admitted to the bar in 1847 and commenced practice in Tecumseh, Mich.; moved to Ann Arbor, Mich., and resumed practice; elected as a Democrat to the Thirty-seventh Congress (March 4, 1861–March 3, 1863); engaged in the practice of law until his death in Ann Arbor, Mich., November 4, 1882; interment in Forest Hill Cemetery.

GRANGER, Daniel Larned Davis, a Representative from Rhode Island; born in Providence, R. I., May 30, 1852; attended the common schools; was graduated from Brown University, Providence, R. I., in 1874 and from the law department of Boston University in 1877; was admitted to the bar in 1877 and com-

menced practice in Providence, R. I.; reading clerk of the State house of representatives 1887–1890; treasurer of Providence from January 1890 to January 1901; mayor in 1901 and 1902; elected as a Democrat to the Fifty-eighth, Fifty-ninth, and Sixtieth Congresses and served from March 4, 1903, until his death in Washington, D. C., February 14, 1909; interment in Swan Point Cemetery, Providence, R. I.

GRANGER, Francis (cousin of Amos Phelps Granger), a Representative from New York; born in Suffield, Conn., December 1, 1792; pursued classical studies, and was graduated from Yale College in 1811; moved with his father to Canandaigua, N. Y., in 1814; studied law; was admitted to the bar in 1816 and commenced practice in Canandaigua, N. Y.; member of the State assembly 1826–1828 and 1830–1832; unsuccessful candidate for Lieutenant Governor of New York in 1828; unsuccessful candidate of the National Republicans for Governor of New York in 1830 and 1832; delegate to the Anti-Masonic National Convention at Philadelphia September 11, 1830; unsuccessful Whig and Anti-Masonic candidate for Vice President in 1836; elected as a Whig to the Twenty-fourth Congress (March 4, 1835–March 3, 1837); unsuccessful Whig candidate for election in 1836 to the Twenty-fifth Congress; again elected to the Twenty-sixth and Twenty-seventh Congresses and served from March 4, 1839, to March 5, 1841, when he resigned; appointed Postmaster General in the Cabinet of President William Henry Harrison and served from March 6 to September 18, 1841; again elected to the Twenty-seventh Congress to fill the vacancy caused by the resignation of John Greig and served from November 27, 1841, to March 3, 1843; was not a candidate for reelection in 1842; member of the peace convention of 1861 held in Washington, D. C., in an effort to devise means to prevent the impending war; died in Canandaigua, N. Y., on August 31, 1868; interment in Woodlawn Cemetery.

GRANGER, Miles Tobey, a Representative from Connecticut; born in New Marlboro, Berkshire County, Mass., August 12, 1817; moved with his parents to Canaan, Conn., in 1819; pursued common-school, academic, and collegiate studies, and was graduated from Wesleyan University, Middletown, Conn., in 1842; moved to Louisiana in 1843; studied law; was admitted to the bar of Wilkinson County, Miss., in April 1845; returned to Canaan, Conn.; was admitted to the bar in Litchfield County in October 1845 and practiced law in Canaan 1847–1867; member of the State house of representatives in 1857; served in the senate in 1866 and 1867; judge of probate court 1849–1867; judge of the superior court of Connecticut 1867–1876; elected judge of the supreme court in 1876 and served until March 1, 1887, when he resigned; elected as a Democrat to the Fiftieth Congress (March 4, 1887–March 3, 1889); was not a candidate for renomination in 1888; elected State referee in 1893 and served until his death in North Canaan, Litchfield County, Conn., October 21, 1895; interment in the Lower Cemetery.

GRANGER, Walter Kiel, a Representative from Utah; born in St. George, Washington County, Utah, October 11, 1888; moved with his parents to Cedar City, Utah, in 1894; attended the public schools; was graduated from a branch of the University of Utah at Cedar City in 1909 and later attended the Branch Agricultural College at Cedar City, Utah; engaged in agricultural pursuits and livestock raising; member of the board of trustees of Utah State Agricultural College; during the First World War served overseas as a sergeant in the Eleventh Regiment, United States Marines, in 1918 and 1919; mayor of Cedar City, Utah, 1923–1926 and 1930–1932; member of the State house of representatives 1932–1937, serving as speaker in 1935; member of the Public Service Commission of Utah 1937–1940; elected as a

Democrat to the Seventy-seventh and to the five succeeding Congresses (January 3, 1941–January 3, 1953); was not a candidate for renomination in 1952 but was an unsuccessful candidate for election to the United States Senate; unsuccessful candidate for election in 1954 to the Eighty-fourth Congress; resumed his farming interests; is a resident of Cedar City, Utah.

GRANT, Abraham Phineas, a Representative from New York; born in New Lebanon, Columbia County, N. Y., April 5, 1804; attended the public schools and was graduated from Hamilton College, Clinton, N. Y.; studied law; was admitted to the bar in 1828 and commenced practice in Oswego, N. Y.; district attorney of Oswego County in 1835; elected as a Democrat to the Twenty-fifth Congress (March 4, 1837–March 3, 1839); resumed the practice of law; died in Oswego, N. Y., December 11, 1871; interment in Riverside Cemetery.

GRANT, George McInvale, a Representative from Alabama; born in Louisville, Barbour County, Ala., July 11, 1897; attended the public schools; was graduated from the law department of the University of Alabama at Tuscaloosa in 1922; was admitted to the bar the same year and commenced practice at Troy, Ala.; during the First World War served as a private and aviation cadet in the aviation section of the Signal Corps of the United States Army in 1918 and 1919; county solicitor of Pike County, Ala., 1927–1937; elected as a Democrat to the Seventy-fifth Congress to fill the vacancy caused by the resignation of Lister Hill; reelected to the Seventy-sixth and to the ten succeeding Congresses and served from June 14, 1938, to January 3, 1961. *Reelected to the Eighty-seventh Congress.*

GRANT, John Gaston, a Representative from North Carolina; born in Edneyville Township, Henderson County, N. C., January 1, 1858; received a limited schooling; engaged in agricultural pursuits; member of the State house of representatives in 1889; declined a renomination; sheriff of Henderson County 1892–1896; refused a renomination in 1896; presidential elector on the Republican ticket of McKinley and Hobart in 1896; elected as a Republican to the Sixty-first Congress (March 4, 1909–March 3, 1911); unsuccessful candidate for reelection in 1910 to the Sixty-second Congress; resumed agricultural pursuits; died in Hendersonville, N. C., June 21, 1923; interment in Oak Dale Cemetery.

GRANT, Robert Allen, a Representative from Indiana; born near Bourbon, Marshall County, Ind., July 31, 1905; moved to Hamlet, Ind., in 1912 and to South Bend, Ind., in 1922; attended the public schools; was graduated from the University of Notre Dame at South Bend, Ind., in 1928 and from its law department in 1930; was admitted to the bar in 1930 and commenced practice in South Bend; deputy prosecuting attorney of St. Joseph County, Ind., in 1935 and 1936; elected as a Republican to the Seventy-sixth and to the four succeeding Congresses (January 3, 1939–January 3, 1949); unsuccessful candidate for reelection in 1948 to the Eighty-first Congress; resumed the practice of law in South Bend, Ind.; United States district judge, northern district of Indiana, 1957–; is a resident of South Bend, Ind.

GRANTLAND, Seaton, a Representative from Georgia; born in New Kent County, Va., on June 8, 1782; pursued an academic course; studied law; was admitted to the bar and commenced practice in Milledgeville, Ga.; elected as a Union candidate on a general ticket to the Twenty-fourth and Twenty-fifth Congresses (March 4, 1835–March 3, 1839); presidential elector on the Whig ticket of Harrison and Tyler in 1840; died at his home, "Woodville," near Milledgeville, Ga., October 18, 1864; interment in Milledgeville Cemetery.

GRAVELY, Joseph Jackson, a Representative from Missouri; born near Leatherwood, Henry County, Va., September 25, 1828; attended the public schools; engaged in agricultural pursuits and taught school; studied law; was admitted to the bar and practiced; member of the State house of representatives in 1853 and 1854; moved to Missouri in 1854; delegate to the State constitutional convention in 1860; served in the State senate in 1862 and 1864; during the Civil War served in the Union Army as colonel of the Eighth Regiment, Missouri Volunteer Cavalry; elected as a Republican to the Fortieth Congress (March 4, 1867–March 3, 1869); Lieutenant Governor of Missouri in 1871 and 1872; died in Stockton, Cedar County, Mo., April 28, 1872; interment in Lindley Prairie Cemetery, near Bear Creek, Mo.

GRAVES, Alexander, a Representative from Missouri; born in Mount Carmel, Covington County, Miss., August 25, 1844; attended Centre College, Danville, Ky.; at the outbreak of the Civil War joined the Confederate Army and served under Gen. N. B. Forrest; paroled with him at Gainesville, Ala., in May 1865; after being mustered out returned to college, and was graduated from Oakland (later Alcorn) University, Mississippi, in July 1867; studied law; was graduated from the University of Virginia at Charlottesville in June 1869; was admitted to the bar and practiced law in Lexington, Mo.; city attorney in 1872; prosecuting attorney of Lafayette County, Mo., in 1874; elected as a Democrat to the Forty-eighth Congress (March 4, 1883–March 3, 1885); unsuccessful candidate for reelection in 1884 to the Forty-ninth Congress; continued the practice of law until his death in Lexington, Mo., on December 23, 1916; interment in Machpelah Cemetery.

GRAVES, Dixie Bibb, a Senator from Alabama; born on a plantation near Montgomery, Montgomery County, Ala., July 26, 1882; attended the public schools and was graduated from Montgomery High School in 1900; trustee of Alabama Boys' Industrial School, Birmingham, Ala.; president of the Alabama Division, United Daughters of the Confederacy, 1915–1917; vice president of the Alabama Federation of Women's Clubs in 1929; appointed as a Democrat to the United States Senate to fill the vacancy caused by the resignation of Hugo L. Black and served from August 19, 1937, until her resignation January 10, 1938; was not a candidate for election to fill the vacancy; retired from public life and is a resident of Montgomery, Ala.

GRAVES, William Jordan, a Representative from Kentucky; born in New Castle, Ky., in 1805; pursued an academic course; studied law; was admitted to the bar and practiced; member of the State house of representatives in 1834; elected as a Whig to the Twenty-fourth, Twenty-fifth, and Twenty-sixth Congresses (March 4, 1835–March 3, 1841); was not a candidate for renomination in 1840; engaged in a duel on the Marlboro Road in Maryland with Jonathan Cilley in 1838, in which the latter was killed; again a member of the State house of representatives in 1843; presidential elector on the Whig ticket of Clay and Frelinghuysen in 1844; died in Louisville, Ky., September 27, 1848; interment in the private burial grounds at his former residence in Henry County, Ky.

GRAY, Edward Winthrop, a Representative from New Jersey; born in Jersey City, N. J., August 18, 1870; attended the public schools; newspaper reporter in New York City 1894–1896; owner and publisher of the Summit (N. J.) Herald in 1897 and 1898; city editor and managing editor of the Newark Daily Advertiser 1898–1902; president and general manager of the Newark Daily Advertising Publishing Co. 1902–1904; secretary to Gov. Edward C. Stokes 1904–1907; appointed by

Governor Murphy a commissioner to investigate tenement-house conditions in 1902; member of the board of tenement-house supervision 1900–1908; secretary of the Republican State committee 1908–1913; organized the Commercial Casualty Insurance Co., Newark, N. J., in 1909; elected as a Republican to the Sixty-fourth and Sixty-fifth Congresses (March 4, 1915–March 3, 1919); unsuccessful candidate for election in 1918 to the United States Senate; unsuccessful candidate for nomination for Representative in 1924 and for Senator in 1928; writer, publisher, and lecturer; died in Newark, N. J., June 10, 1942; interment in Mount Pleasant Cemetery.

GRAY, Edwin, a Representative from Virginia; born in Southampton County, Va., July 18, 1743; educated at William and Mary College, Williamsburg, Va.; served in the State house of burgesses 1769–1775; member of the State conventions in 1774, 1775, and 1776; member of the State house of delegates in 1776, 1779, 1787, 1788, and 1791; served in the State senate 1777–1779; elected to the Sixth and to the six succeeding Congresses (March 4, 1799–March 3, 1813); died in Nansemond County, Va.

GRAY, Finly Hutchinson, a Representative from Indiana; born near Orange, Fayette County, Ind., July 21, 1863; attended the common schools; studied law; was admitted to the bar in 1892 and commenced practice in Connersville, Ind.; mayor of Connersville 1904–1910; elected as a Democrat to the Sixty-second, Sixty-third, and Sixty-fourth Congresses (March 4, 1911–March 3, 1917); unsuccessful candidate for reelection in 1916 to the Sixty-fifth Congress and for election in 1917 to fill the vacancy in the same Congress caused by the death of Daniel W. Comstock; resumed the practice of law and also engaged in lecturing; again elected to the Seventy-third, Seventy-fourth, and Seventy-fifth Congresses (March 4, 1933–January 3, 1939); unsuccessful candidate for reelection in 1938 to the Seventy-sixth Congress; reengaged in the practice of law in Connersville, Ind.; until his death there on May 8, 1947; interment in Dale Cemetery.

GRAY, George, a Senator from Delaware; born in New Castle, New Castle County, Del., May 4, 1840; attended the common schools and was graduated from Princeton College in 1859; studied law with his father and one year in the Harvard Law School; was admitted to the bar in 1863 and commenced practice in New Castle; appointed attorney general of Delaware in 1879; reappointed in 1884 and served until his resignation in March 1885, having been elected Senator; delegate to the Democratic National Conventions in 1876, 1880, 1884, 1892, and 1896; moved to Wilmington, Del., in 1881; elected as a Democrat to the United States Senate to fill the vacancy caused by the resignation of Thomas F. Bayard; reelected in 1887 and 1893 and served from March 18, 1885, to March 3, 1899; unsuccessful candidate for reelection in 1899; member of the commission which met in Quebec in August 1898 to settle differences between the United States and Canada; member of the commission which met in Paris in September 1898 to arrange terms of peace between the United States and Spain; appointed judge of the United States Circuit Court of Appeals for the Third Circuit by President McKinley March 29, 1899, and served until June 1, 1914, when he retired; appointed in October 1902 as chairman of the commission to investigate conditions of the coal strike in Pennsylvania; appointed by President McKinley to the Permanent Court of Arbitration at The Hague in 1900; reappointed in 1906 by President Theodore Roosevelt, in 1912 by President Taft, and in 1920 by President Wilson; member of said court in the North Atlantic coast fisheries arbitration, under the special agreement between the United States and Great Britain of

January 27, 1909; appointed on June 1, 1915, as the American member of the international commission provided for in the treaty between the United States and Great Britain for the advancement of peace; appointed on August 31, 1916, one of the three special commissioners of the President of the United States to discuss with the commissioners of the de facto Government of Mexico the settlement of questions arising out of the Mexican situation; member of the Board of Regents of the Smithsonian Institution for thirty-five years; vice president and trustee of the Carnegie Endowment for International Peace; died in Wilmington, Del., August 7, 1925; interment in Presbyterian Cemetery, New Castle, Del.

GRAY, Hiram, a Representative from New York; born in Salem, Washington County, N. Y., July 10, 1801; attended Salem Academy; was graduated from Union College in 1821; studied law; was admitted to the bar in 1823 and practiced in Elmira, N. Y., 1825–1828; elected as a Democrat to the Twenty-fifth Congress (March 4, 1837–March 3, 1839); appointed by Gov. Silas Wright circuit judge and vice chancellor of the sixth judicial district of New York in 1846; elected justice of the supreme court of New York in 1847; reelected in 1851 and served until 1860; commissioner of appeals 1870–1875; resumed the practice of law; died in Elmira, N. Y., May 6, 1890; interment in Woodlawn Cemetery.

GRAY, John Cowper, a Representative from Virginia; born in Southampton County, Va., in 1783; pursued an academic course; member of the State house of delegates 1804–1806 and 1821–1823; elected to the Sixteenth Congress to fill the vacancy caused by the resignation of James Johnson and served from August 28, 1820, to March 3, 1821; unsuccessful candidate in 1820 for reelection to the Seventeenth Congress; died May 18, 1823.

GRAY, Joseph Anthony, a Representative from Pennsylvania; born in Susquehanna Township (now Spangler Borough), Cambria County, Pa., February 25, 1884; attended the public schools and St. Benedict's School, Carrolltown, Pa.; was graduated from Eastman College at Poughkeepsie, N. Y., in 1905; served in the Spanish-American War as a private in Company H, Fifth Infantry, United States Army, 1900–1902 and in the United States Signal Corps in 1902 and 1903; studied law; was admitted to the bar in 1910 and commenced practice in Ebensburg, Pa.; member of the State house of representatives in 1913 and 1914; served as president of the board of health 1916–1920; became a motion-picture exhibitor at Spangler, Pa., in 1920; school director of Spangler, Pa., 1930–1934 and councilman 1939–1943; elected as a Democrat to the Seventy-fourth and Seventy-fifth Congresses (January 3, 1935–January 3, 1939); unsuccessful candidate for reelection in 1938 to the Seventy-sixth Congress and for election in 1940 to the Seventy-seventh Congress; resumed the practice of law and also publisher of "The Conservative" a weekly newspaper; is a resident of Spangler, Pa.

GRAY, Kenneth James, a Representative from Illinois; born in West Frankfort, Franklin County, Ill., November 14, 1924; attended the West Frankfort and Pope County elementary schools and graduated from West Frankfort Community High School; owner of Gray Motors, West Frankfort, Ill., 1942–1954; also operated an air service at Benton, Ill., 1948 to 1952; licensed pilot; during World War II served from January 1943 as a crew chief with the Twelfth Air Force in North Africa; wounded during a battle over Corsica and later served with the combat engineers of the Fifth Army in Italy; returned to the Twelfth Air Force and participated in combat over southern France and central Europe until discharged as a first sergeant in December 1945; one of the founders of the Walking Dog Foundation for the Blind; licensed auctioneer; elected as a Democrat to the

Eighty-fourth, Eighty-fifth, and Eighty-sixth Congresses (January 3, 1955–January 3, 1961). *Reelected to the Eighty-seventh Congress.*

GRAY, Oscar Lee, a Representative from Alabama; born in Mississippi July 2, 1865; attended the common schools of Choctaw County, and was graduated from the University of Alabama at Tuscaloosa in 1885; taught school for several years; studied law; was admitted to the bar and commenced practice in March 1919 in Alabama; superintendent of education for Choctaw County; solicitor for the first judicial circuit 1904–1910; delegate to the Democratic National Convention at Baltimore in 1912; elected as a Democrat to the Sixty-fourth and Sixty-fifth Congresses (March 4, 1915–March 3, 1919); resumed the practice of law; elected judge of the first judicial circuit of Alabama in November 1934; died at Shreveport, La., January 2, 1936; interment in Forest Park Cemetery.

GRAYSON, William (father of William John Grayson and uncle of Alexander Dalrymple Orr), a Delegate and a Senator from Virginia; born in Prince William County, Va., in 1740; attended the University of Pennsylvania at Philadelphia; pursued classical studies in England, and was graduated from the University of Oxford; studied law at the Temple in London; returned to Virginia and practiced law in Dumfries; during the Revolutionary War was appointed aide-de-camp to General Washington August 24, 1776; commissioned colonel of a Virginia regiment January 1, 1777; distinguished himself at the Battle of Monmouth in 1778; member of the board of war in 1780 and 1781; Member of the Continental Congress 1784–1787; delegate to the Virginia convention of 1788 for the adoption of the Federal Constitution, which he opposed; elected to the United States Senate and served from March 4, 1789, until his death in Dumfries, Va., March 12, 1790; interment on the old family estate at Belle Air, near Dumfries, Va.

GRAYSON, William John (son of William Grayson and cousin of Alexander Dalrymple Orr), a Representative from South Carolina; born in Beaufort, S. C., November 2, 1788; pursued classical studies, and was graduated from South Carolina College at Columbia in 1809; studied law; was admitted to the bar in 1822 and commenced practice in Beaufort, S. C.; member of the State house of representatives 1822–1826; served in the State senate 1826–1831; elected commissioner in equity for Beaufort District in 1831 and resigned from the senate; elected as a Whig to the Twenty-third and Twenty-fourth Congresses (March 4, 1833–March 3, 1837); collector of customs at Charleston from August 9, 1841, to March 19, 1853; retired to his plantation; was a frequent contributor to the Southern Quarterly Review; died in Newberry, S. C., on October 4, 1863; interment in Magnolia Cemetery, Charleston, S. C.

GREELEY, Horace, a Representative from New York; born in Amherst, N. H., February 3, 1811; attended the public schools; apprenticed to the art of printing in East Poultney, Vt., 1826–1830; worked as a journeyman printer in Erie, Pa., in 1831, and later in New York City; commenced the publication of the Morning Post January 1, 1833, but it was soon discontinued; published the New Yorker 1834–1841; edited the Log Cabin in 1840; founded the New York Tribune April 10, 1841, and edited it until his death; elected as a Whig to the Thirtieth Congress to fill the vacancy caused by the unseating of David S. Jackson and served from December 4, 1848, to March 3, 1849; was not a candidate for reelection in 1848; visited Europe in 1851 and was chairman of one of the juries at the World's Fair in London; commissioner to the Paris Exposition in 1855; delegate to the Republican National Convention at Chicago in 1860 from Oregon, being denied a place on the New York delegation; unsuccessful candidate for Senator in 1861; presidential elector on the Republican ticket of Lincoln and Johnson in 1864; delegate to the State constitutional convention in 1867; at the close of the Civil War advocated universal amnesty, and in May 1867 offered bail for Jefferson Davis, former President of the Southern Confederacy; in November 1867 was appointed United States Minister to Austria, but declined; unsuccessful Republican candidate for election in 1870 to the Forty-second Congress; nominated by the Liberal Republicans in Cincinnati in 1872 and by the Democrats in Baltimore for the Presidency, but was defeated by General Grant; died near New York City November 29, 1872; interment in Greenwood Cemetery, Brooklyn, N. Y.

GREEN, Byram, a Representative from New York; born in East Windsor, Berkshire County, Mass., April 15, 1786; attended the public schools, and was graduated from Williams College, Williamstown, Mass., in 1808; professor in a college at Beaufort, S. C., in 1810; studied law; was admitted to the bar and practiced; judge of the circuit court of Wayne County in 1814; fought in the Battle of Sodus Point during the War of 1812; member of the State assembly 1816–1822; served in the State senate in 1823 and 1824; elected to the Twenty-eighth Congress (March 4, 1843–March 3, 1845); died in Sodus, N. Y., October 18, 1865; interment in the Rural Cemetery.

GREEN, Edith, a Representative from Oregon; born in Trent, Moody County, S. Dak., January 17, 1910; moved with her parents to Oregon, in 1916; attended the schools of Salem, Oreg., and Willamette University 1927–1929; was graduated from the University of Oregon at Eugene in 1939; graduate work at Stanford (Calif.) University in 1944; taught school in Salem, Oreg., 1930–1941; staff member of Portland Radio Station KPOJ and with station KALE 1943–1947; legislative representative of the State Parent-Teachers Association to the State legislature in 1951; director of public relations and legislative representative of the Oregon Education Association for the 1953 legislature; Democratic candidate for secretary of state of Oregon in 1952; delegate to the Democratic National Convention in 1956; United States delegate to Interparliamentary conference in Switzerland in 1958; Congressional delegate to NATO conference in London in 1959; elected as a Democrat to the Eighty-fourth, Eighty-fifth, and Eighty-sixth Congresses (January 3, 1955–January 3, 1961). *Reelected to the Eighty-seventh Congress.*

GREEN, Frederick William, a Representative from Ohio; born in Fredericktown (now Frederick), Md., February 18, 1816; settled in Tiffin, Ohio, in 1833; pursued an academic course; studied law; was admitted to the bar and commenced practice in Tiffin, Ohio; auditor of Seneca County for six years; elected as a Democrat to the Thirty-second and Thirty-third Congresses (March 4, 1851–March 3, 1855); was not a candidate for renomination; moved to Cleveland, Ohio, and served as clerk of the United States District Court for the Northern District of Ohio 1855–1866; Ohio commissioner to the Philadelphia Centennial Exposition; editor of the Cleveland Plain Dealer 1866–1874; State oil inspector in 1878 and 1879; died in Cleveland, Ohio, on June 18, 1879; interment in Woodland Cemetery.

GREEN, Henry Dickinson, a Representative from Pennsylvania; born in Reading, Berks County, Pa., May 3, 1857; attended the public schools, and was graduated from the Reading High School in 1872 and Yale College in 1877; studied law; was admitted to the bar in 1879 and commenced practice in Reading, Pa.; member of the State house of representatives 1883–1886; served in the State senate 1889–1896; captain of

Company G, Ninth Regiment, Pennsylvania Volunteers, in the war with Spain in 1898; delegate to the Democratic National Convention at Kansas City in 1900; elected as a Democrat to the Fifty-sixth Congress to fill the vacancy caused by the death of Daniel Ermentrout; reelected to the Fifty-seventh Congress and served from November 7, 1899, to March 3, 1903; was not a candidate for renomination; editor of the Reading Telegram 1903–1912 and of the Reading Times 1911–1913; resumed the practice of law in Reading, Pa.; also admitted to the bar in Texas in 1920; engaged in oil operation in the midcontinent oil field; died in Reading, Pa., on December 29, 1929; interment in Arlington National Cemetery, Fort Myer, Va.

GREEN, Innis, a Representative from Pennsylvania; born in Hanover Township, Pa., February 26, 1776; pursued an academic course; studied law; was admitted to the bar and practiced; appointed associate judge of Dauphin County by Governor Findlay August 10, 1818, and resigned October 23, 1827; elected as a Democrat to the Twentieth and Twenty-first Congresses (March 4, 1827–March 3, 1831); reappointed associate judge of Dauphin County and served until his death in Dauphin, Pa., August 4, 1839; interment in Dauphin Cemetery.

GREEN, Isaiah Lewis, a Representative from Massachusetts; born in Barnstable, Barnstable County, Mass., December 28, 1761; pursued classical studies, and was graduated from Harvard University in 1781; studied law; was admitted to the bar and practiced; elected to the Ninth and Tenth Congresses (March 4, 1805–March 3, 1809); elected to the Twelfth Congress (March 4, 1811–March 3, 1813); appointed by President Madison collector of customs for the district of Barnstable, Mass., in 1814 and served until 1837; resumed the practice of law; died in Cambridge, Mass., on December 5, 1841; interment in the Old Cambridge Cemetery.

GREEN, James Stephen, a Representative and a Senator from Missouri; born near Rectortown, Fauquier County, Va., February 28, 1817; attended the common schools; moved to Alabama and thence to Missouri about 1838; studied law; was admitted to the bar in 1840 and commenced practice in Canton, Mo.; presidential elector on the Democratic ticket of Polk and Dallas in 1844; delegate to the State constitutional convention in 1845; elected as a Democrat to the Thirtieth and Thirty-first Congresses (March 4, 1847–March 3, 1851); was not a candidate for renomination in 1850; Chargé d'Affaires to Colombia from May 24, 1853, to August 13, 1854; appointed Minister Resident June 29, 1854, but did not present his credentials; elected as a Democrat to the Thirty-fifth Congress, but did not take his seat, having been elected to the United States Senate to fill the vacancy in the term commencing March 4, 1855, and served from January 12, 1857, to March 3, 1861; died in St. Louis, Mo., January 19, 1870; interment in the Old Cemetery, Canton, Mo.

GREEN, Robert Alexis, a Representative from Florida; born near New River, Bradford County, Fla., February 10, 1892; attended the rural schools; commenced teaching in Liberty Public School at the age of 16; was graduated from the high school at Lake Butler in 1913; messenger in the State house of representatives 1913–1915; assistant chief clerk of the State house of representatives 1915–1917 and chief clerk in 1917 and 1918; was graduated from the University of Florida at Gainesville in 1916; principal of Suwannee High School in 1916 and 1917; vice president of the Florida Educational Association in 1918; member of the State house of representatives 1918–1920, serving as speaker pro tempore in 1918; studied law at Yale University; was admitted to the bar in 1921 and com-

menced practice in Starke, Fla.; elected judge of Bradford County Fla., in 1920 and served until 1924, when he resigned, having been elected to Congress; elected as a Democrat to the Sixty-ninth and to the nine succeeding Congresses and served from March 4, 1925, until his resignation on November 25, 1944, to enter the United States Navy; was not a candidate for renomination in 1944, but was an unsuccessful candidate for the Florida gubernatorial nomination; served as a lieutenant commander in the United States Navy from November 25, 1944, to November 2, 1945; resumed the practice of law at Starke, Fla., and served as county prosecuting attorney and as city attorney for the city of Starke; operates an automobile agency; is a resident of Starke, Fla.

GREEN, Robert Stockton, a Representative from New Jersey; born in Princeton, Mercer County, N. J., March 25, 1831; attended the common schools, and was graduated from the College of New Jersey (now Princeton University) at Princeton in 1850; studied law; was admitted to the bar in 1853 and commenced practice in Elizabeth, N. J.; prosecutor of the borough courts in 1857; city attorney of Elizabeth 1857–1868; delegate to the Democratic National Conventions in 1860, 1880, and 1888; surrogate of Union County 1862–1867; member of the city council 1863–1873; presiding judge of Union County Court of Common Pleas 1868–1873; member of the commission to suggest amendments to the constitution of New Jersey in 1873; admitted to the bar of New York in 1874; elected as a Democrat to the Forty-ninth Congress and served from March 4, 1885, until his resignation on January 17, 1887; Governor of New Jersey 1887–1889; vice chancellor of the State 1890–1895; judge of the court of errors and appeals in 1894 and 1895; died in Elizabeth, N. J., May 7, 1895; interment in Greenwood Cemetery, Brooklyn, N. Y.

GREEN, Theodore Francis (grandnephew of Samuel Greene Arnold, great-grandnephew of Tristam Burges, great-grandson of James Burrill, Jr., great-great-grandson of Jonathan Arnold, and great-great-nephew of Lemuel Hastings Arnold), a Senator from Rhode Island; born in Providence, R. I., October 2, 1867; attended private schools and Providence (R. I.) High School; was graduated from Brown University, Providence, R. I., in 1887; attended Harvard University Law School, Cambridge, Mass., and the Universities of Bonn and Berlin in Germany, was admitted to the bar in 1892 and commenced practice in Providence, R. I.; instructor in Roman law at Brown University, Providence, R. I., 1894–1897; received a commission as lieutenant during the Spanish-American War and commanded Provisional Company A, R. I. M.; trustee of Butler Hospital, Providence, R. I., 1900–1919; chairman of the city plan commission of Providence 1917–1919; member of the State house of representatives in 1907; unsuccessful Democratic candidate for Governor in 1912, 1928, and 1930; delegate to the Democratic National Conventions 1912–1944; presidential elector in 1912 on the Democratic ticket of Wilson and Marshall; chairman of the Democratic State conventions in 1914, 1924, and 1926; unsuccessful candidate for election in 1920 to the Sixty-seventh Congress; Governor of Rhode Island 1933–1936; national committeeman from Rhode Island 1936–1946; financially interested in numerous corporations and business enterprises and served as officer and director; elected as a Democrat to the United States Senate in 1936, 1942, 1948, and again in 1954, and served from January 3, 1937, to January 3, 1961; was not a candidate for renomination in 1960; is a resident of Providence, R. I.

GREEN, Wharton Jackson (grandson of Jesse Wharton and cousin of Matt Whitaker Ransom), a Representative from North Carolina; born in St. Marks, Wakula County, Fla., February

28, 1831; was instructed by private tutors; attended Georgetown College, Lovejoy's Academy, Raleigh, N. C., and the United States Military Academy, West Point, N. Y.; studied law in the University of Virginia at Charlottesville and in Cumberland University, Lebanon, Tenn.; was admitted to the bar in 1854 and commenced practice in Washington, D. C.; engaged in agricultural pursuits in Warren County, N. C., in 1859; during the Civil War enlisted in the Confederate service in 1861; commissioned as a lieutenant colonel, in the Second North Carolina Battalion; afterward served on General Daniel's staff; wounded and taken prisoner at the Battle of Gettysburg; settled at "Tokay Vineyard," near Fayetteville, N. C., and became interested in viticulture; delegate to the Democratic National Conventions in 1868, 1872, 1876, and 1888; first president of the Society of Confederate Soldiers and Sailors in North Carolina; elected as a Democrat to the Forty-eighth and Forty-ninth Congresses (March 4, 1883–March 3, 1887); unsuccessful candidate for renomination in 1886; devoted his time to the cultivation of his vineyard and to literary pursuits; died at "Tokay," near Fayetteville, N. C., August 6, 1910; interment in Cross Creek Cemetery, Fayetteville, N. C.

GREEN, William Joseph, Jr., a Representative from Pennsylvania; born in Philadelphia, Pa., March 5, 1910; attended the parochial schools and was graduated from St. Joseph's Prep School; attended St. Joseph's College, Philadelphia, Pa.; engaged as an insurance broker in Philadelphia, Pa., since 1937; during World War II served in the United States Army as a private in the Quartermaster Corps from March 22, 1944, to December 4, 1944; elected as a Democrat to the Seventy-ninth Congress (January 3, 1945–January 3, 1947); unsuccessful for reelection in 1946 to the Eightieth Congress; elected to the Eighty-first and to the five succeeding Congresses (January 3, 1949–January 3, 1961). *Reelected to the Eighty-seventh Congress.*

GREEN, William Raymond, a Representative from Iowa; born in Colchester, New London County, Conn., November 7, 1856; attended the public schools in Malden, Ill., and Princeton (Ill.) High School; was graduated from Oberlin College at Oberlin, Ohio, in 1879; studied law; was admitted to the bar in 1882 and commenced practice in Dow City, Iowa; moved his office to Audubon, Iowa, in 1884; judge of the district court in the fifteenth judicial district of Iowa from 1894 until 1911, when he resigned; elected as a Republican to the Sixty-second Congress to fill the vacancy caused by the resignation of Walter I. Smith; reelected to the Sixty-third and to the seven succeeding Congresses and served from June 5, 1911, until March 31, 1928, when he resigned; appointed a judge of the Court of Claims of the United States and served from April 1, 1928, until May 29, 1940, when he resigned, but was recalled and continued to serve until June 1942; retired from active pursuits and resided at Bellport, N. Y., until his death there on June 11, 1947; interment in Rock Creek Cemetery, Washington, D. C.

GREEN, Willis, a Representative from Kentucky; born in the Shenandoah Valley of Virginia; attended the public schools; settled in that part of Virginia which is now the State of Kentucky; clerk of court of Lincoln County in 1783; served as a member of the State constitutional convention in 1792; surveyor for locating land warrants; member of the State house of representatives in 1836 and 1837; elected as a Whig to the Twenty-sixth, Twenty-seventh, and Twenty-eighth Congresses (March 4, 1839–March 3, 1845).

GREENE, Albert Collins, a Senator from Rhode Island; born in East Greenwich, R. I., April 15, 1791; was graduated from Kent Academy in his native town; studied law; was admitted to

the bar in 1812 and commenced practice in East Greenwich, R. I.; member of the State house of representatives 1815–1825 and served as speaker from October 1821 to May 1822, and from October 1822 to May 1825; brigadier general of the Fourth Brigade of State Militia 1816–1821; major general 1821–1823; attorney general of Rhode Island 1825–1843; member of the State senate in 1843 and 1844; elected as a Whig to the United States Senate and served from March 4, 1845, to March 3, 1851; was not a candidate for reelection; again elected to the State senate in 1851 and 1852; again a member of the State house of representatives in 1857; retired from public life; died in Providence, R. I., January 8, 1863; interment in Grace Church Cemetery.

GREENE, Frank Lester, a Representative and a Senator from Vermont; born in St. Albans, Franklin County, Vt., February 10, 1870; moved to Cleveland, Ohio, with his parents in 1873, and to St. Albans, Vt., in 1878; attended the public schools; employed by the Central Vermont Railway Co. in various capacities 1883–1891; served in the Vermont National Guard 1888–1900, rising from private to captain; recruited Company B, First Regiment, Vermont Volunteer Infantry, for the war with Spain, serving as captain; mustered out and commissioned colonel on the staff of the Governor; reporter in 1891 and editor 1899–1912 of the St. Albans Daily Messenger; president of the Vermont Press Association in 1904 and 1905; member of the commission to prepare and propose amendments to the State constitution in 1908; delegate to the Republican National Convention at Chicago in 1908; delegate to the Republican State conventions in 1910 and 1914, serving as chairman in 1914; elected as a Republican to the Sixty-second Congress to fill the vacancy caused by the death of David J. Foster; reelected to the Sixty-third and to the five succeeding Congresses and served from July 30, 1912, until March 3, 1923; Regent of the Smithsonian Institution 1917–1923; trustee of the Vermont Soldiers' Home and Lyndon Institute; elected in 1922 to the United States Senate; reelected in 1928 and served from March 4, 1923, until his death in St. Albans, Vt., December 17, 1930; interment in Greenwood Cemetery.

GREENE, George Woodward, a Representative from New York; born in Mount Hope, Orange County, N. Y., July 4, 1831; pursued classical studies and was graduated from the University of Pennsylvania at Philadelphia; taught school; studied law; was admitted to the bar in 1860 and commenced practice in Goshen, N. Y.; school commissioner for Orange County; judge of the Orange County Courts 1861–1864; presented credentials as a Democratic Member-elect to the Forty-first Congress and served from March 4, 1869, to February 17, 1870, when he was succeeded by Charles H. Van Wyck, who contested his election; member of the State assembly 1885–1888; died in New York City July 21, 1895; interment in "The Plains" Cemetery, Otisville, N. Y.

GREENE, Ray, a Senator from Rhode Island; born in Warwick, R. I., February 2, 1765; pursued classical studies, and was graduated from Yale College in 1784; studied law; was admitted to the bar and commenced practice in Providence, R. I.; attorney general of Rhode Island 1794–1797; elected to the United States Senate to fill the vacancy caused by the resignation of William Bradford; reelected in 1799 and served from November 13, 1797, to March 5, 1801, when he resigned, having been nominated for a judicial position; designated a district judge of Rhode Island by President John Adams, but through some informality connected with this appointment, which was discovered too late to be corrected by Mr. Adams, was not appointed, and when the matter was referred to his successor, President Jefferson, he refused to rectify it and appointed instead another to that office; died in Warwick, R. I., January 11, 1829; interment in the family burying ground on his estate at Warwick.

GREENE, Thomas Marston, a Delegate from Mississippi Territory; born in James City County, Va., February 26, 1758; moved with his parents to Natchez District, Mississippi Territory, in 1780; moved to Bruinsburg; engaged in planting; member of the first general assembly of the Territory; elected a Delegate to the Seventh Congress to fill the vacancy caused by the death of Narsworthy Hunter and served from December 6, 1802, to March 3, 1803; died February 7, 1813.

GREENE, William Laury, a Representative from Nebraska; born near Ireland, Pike County, Ind., October 3, 1849; moved with his parents to Dubois County, in the same State; attended the common schools and was graduated from Ireland Academy, Indiana; taught school; studied law; was admitted to the bar in 1876 and commenced practice in Bloomington, Ind.; moved with his family to Kearney, Nebr., in 1883 and continued the practice of his profession; unsuccessful candidate for election to the United States Senate in 1893; judge of the twelfth judicial district of Nebraska 1895–1897; elected as a Populist to the Fifty-fifth and Fifty-sixth Congresses and served from March 4, 1897, until his death in Omaha, Nebr., March 11, 1899; interment in Kearney Cemetery, Kearney, Nebr.

GREENE, William Stedman, a Representative from Massachusetts; born in Tremont, Tazewell County, Ill., April 28, 1841; moved with his parents to Fall River, Mass., in 1844; attended the public schools; engaged in the real-estate and insurance business; member of the common council 1876–1879, and served as president of that body 1877–1879; mayor of Fall River in 1880; reelected mayor in 1881, but resigned the same year; alternate delegate to the Republican National Convention at Chicago in 1880; appointed postmaster of Fall River on March 22, 1881, and served until March 30, 1885; again served as mayor 1886 and 1895–1897; declined to be a candidate for reelection in 1898; general superintendent of State prisons 1888–1893; appointed postmaster of Fall River and served from March 9, to July 1, 1898, when he resigned; elected as a Republican to the Fifty-fifth Congress to fill the vacancy caused by the death of John Simpkins; reelected to the Fifty-sixth and to the twelve succeeding Congresses and served from May 31, 1898, until his death at Fall River, Mass., September 22, 1924; interment in Oak Grove Cemetery.

GREENHALGE, Frederic Thomas, a Representative from Massachusetts; born in Clitheroe, England, July 19, 1842; immigrated with his parents to the United States in early childhood; attended the public schools of Lowell, Mass., and Harvard University 1859–1862; taught school and studied law; during the Civil War was with the Union Army in New Bern, N. C., for five months; was admitted to the bar in Lowell, Mass., in 1865; served in the common council of Lowell in 1868 and 1869; member of the school committee 1871–1873; mayor of Lowell in 1880 and 1881; unsuccessful candidate for election to the State senate in 1881; delegate to the Republican National Convention at Chicago in 1884; member of the State house of representatives in 1885; unsuccessful candidate for reelection; city solicitor in 1888; practiced law in Middlesex and other counties; elected as a Republican to the Fifty-first Congress (March 4, 1889–March 3, 1891); unsuccessful candidate for reelection in 1890 to the Fifty-second Congress; elected Governor of Massachusetts and served from January 1894 until his death in Lowell, Mass., on March 5, 1896; interment in Lowell Cemetery.

GREENLEAF, Halbert Stevens, a Representative from New York; born in Guilford, Windham County, Vt., April 12, 1827; attended the common schools and completed an academic course; moved to Shelburne Falls, Mass., and engaged in the manufac-

ture of locks; appointed justice of the peace in 1856; captain of Massachusetts Militia in 1857; organized the Yale & Greenleaf Lock Co.; during the Civil War enlisted as a private in the Union Army in August 1862; commissioned captain of Company E, Fifty-second Regiment, Massachusetts Volunteers, September 12, 1862; elected colonel of the regiment October 23, 1862; employed in a salt works near New Orleans, La., for several years; settled in Rochester, N. Y., in 1867 and resumed the manufacture of locks; elected as a Democrat to the Forty-eighth Congress (March 4, 1883–March 3, 1885); unsuccessful candidate for reelection in 1884 to the Forty-ninth Congress; elected to the Fifty-second Congress (March 4, 1891–March 3, 1893); was not a candidate for renomination in 1892; resumed his former business activities; retired from active business life in 1896; died at his summer home in the town of Greece, near Charlotte, N. Y., on August 25, 1906; interment in Mount Hope Cemetery, Rochester, N. Y.

GREENMAN, Edward Whitford, a Representative from New York; born in Berlin, Rensselaer County, N. Y., January 26, 1840; attended the common schools and De Ruyter Academy, Alfred, N. Y.; engaged in mercantile and manufacturing pursuits in Berlin, N. Y.; supervisor of Berlin 1866–1868; clerk of Rensselaer County 1868–1871; deputy county clerk for ten years; moved to Troy, N. Y., in 1874; elected as a Democrat to the Fiftieth Congress (March 4, 1887–March 3, 1889); was not a candidate for renomination in 1888; cashier of the Central National Bank of Troy, N. Y., 1888–1905; cashier of the National City Bank of Troy 1906–1908; died in Troy, N. Y., on August 3, 1908; interment in Oakwood Cemetery.

GREENUP, Christopher, a Representative from Kentucky; born in Westmoreland County, Va., in 1750; completed academic studies; studied law; was admitted to the bar in 1783 and commenced practice in Fayette County, Ky. (then a part of Virginia); clerk of the district court at Harrodsburg 1785–1792; served in the Revolutionary War and attained the rank of colonel; took part afterwards in various fights with the Indians; member of the Virginia House of Delegates in 1785; member of the conventions at Danville, Ky., in 1785 and 1788 to consider separation from Virginia; moved to Frankfort, Ky., in 1792; upon the admission of Kentucky as a State into the Union was elected to the Second, Third, and Fourth Congresses and served from November 9, 1792, to March 3, 1797; member of the State house of representatives in 1798; clerk of the State senate 1799–1802; appointed judge of the circuit court in 1802; Governor of Kentucky 1804–1808; presidential elector on the Madison and Clinton ticket in 1808; justice of the peace in Franklin County in 1812; one of the original trustees of Transylvania University, Lexington, Ky.; died in Frankfort, Ky., April 27, 1818; interment in State Cemetery.

GREENWAY, Isabella Selmes (later Mrs. Harry Orland King), a Representative from Arizona; born in Boone County, Ky., March 22, 1886; attended the public schools and Miss Chapin's School, in New York City, N. Y.; homesteaded near Tyrone, N. Mex., in 1910; served as chairman of the Women's Land Army of New Mexico in 1918; moved to Tucson, Ariz., in 1923; Democratic National committeewoman from Arizona; owner and operator of a cattle ranch; owner of Gilpin Air Lines, Los Angeles, Calif., 1929–1934; in 1929 established the Arizona Inn (a hotel resort) in Tucson; elected as a Democrat to the Seventy-third Congress to fill the vacancy caused by the resignation of Lewis W. Douglas; reelected to the Seventy-fourth Congress and served from October 3, 1933, to January 3, 1937; was not a candidate for renomination in 1936; member of the Mount Rushmore National Memorial Commission; retired from political activities; died in Tucson, Ariz., December 18, 1953; interment in the family cemetery on the Selmes farm in Boone County, Ky., twenty miles from Covington, Ky.

GREENWOOD, Alfred Burton, a Representative from Arkansas; born in Franklin County, Ga., July 11, 1811; pursued classical studies at Lawrenceville, Ga.; was graduated from the University of Georgia at Athens; studied law; was admitted to the bar in 1832 and commenced practice in Bentonville, Ark; member of the State house of representatives 1842–1845; State prosecuting attorney 1845–1851; circuit judge of Arkansas 1851–1853; elected as a Democrat to the Thirty-third, Thirty-fourth, and Thirty-fifth Congresses (March 4, 1853–March 3, 1859); Commissioner of Indian Affairs from May 13, 1859, to April 13, 1861; served in the Confederate House of Representatives 1862–1865; died in Bentonville, Ark., October 4, 1889; interment in Odd Fellows Cemetery.

GREENWOOD, Arthur Herbert, a Representative from Indiana; born near Plainville, Daviess County, Ind., January 31, 1880; attended the country schools of Daviess County; was graduated from the high school of Washington, Ind., from the law department of the University of Indiana at Bloomington, Ind., in 1905, and from George Washington University, Washington, D. C., in 1925; was admitted to the bar in 1905 and commenced practice in Washington, Ind.; member of the board of education 1910–1916; county attorney of Daviess County 1911–1915; prosecuting attorney for the forty-ninth judicial circuit 1916–1918; member of George Rogers Clark Memorial Commission, Vincennes, Ind.; member of the official delegation attending the inauguration of President Manuel Quezon of the Philippine Republic at Manila, P. I., in 1935; elected as a Democrat to the Sixty-eighth and to the seven succeeding Congresses (March 4, 1923–January 3, 1939); unsuccessful candidate for reelection in 1938 to the Seventy-sixth Congress and for election in 1944 to the Seventy-ninth Congress; served as majority whip in the Seventy-second Congress; lawyer, farmer, and banker in Washington, Ind., until his retirement; resides in Bradenton, Fla., and Bethesda, Md.

GREENWOOD, Ernest, a Representative from New York; born in Yorkshire, England, November 25, 1884; attended the public schools of Halifax, England, and the Evening Technical Institute and College, working as an apprentice engineer during the day; employed with engineering firms in Sheffield, England, in 1905 and 1906, and Halifax, England, 1907–1910; immigrated to the United States in 1910 and worked for the General Electric Co., Schenectady, N. Y., 1910–1914; took courses in education at City College of New York and Columbia University; teacher in public schools of Schenectady 1914–1916; head of vocational department of Islip (N. Y.) High School 1916–1920; member of committee on Census and Inventory of Military Resources during the First World War; supervisor, Federal Board of Vocational Education, 1920–1922; associate head master, Dwight School for Boys and New York Preparatory School for Adults 1922–1927, headmaster 1927–1946, and chairman board of trustees 1946–1955; member of Civil Defense Council, World War II; director, First National Bank, Islip, N. Y.; chairman of planning commission, Board of Education, Bay Shore, N. Y., in 1947 and 1948, and treasurer 1947–1950; in 1949 was an unsuccessful Republican candidate from Islip for representative on the Suffolk County Board of Supervisors; elected as a Democrat to the Eighty-second Congress (January 3, 1951–January 3, 1953); unsuccessful candidate for reelection in 1952 to the Eighty-third Congress and for election in 1954 to the Eighty-fourth Congress; retired; died in Bay Shore, N. Y., June 15, 1955; interment in Oakwood Cemetery.

GREEVER, Paul Ranous, a Representative from Wyoming; born in Lansing, Leavenworth County, Kans., September 28, 1891; attended public and high schools, and was graduated from the law department of the University of Kansas at Lawrence in 1917; during the First World War served as a first lieutenant in the Three Hundred and Fourteenth Trench Mortar Battery, Eighty-ninth Division, from April 1917 to March 1919; was admitted to the bar in 1917 and commenced practice in Pine Bluffs, Wyo., and in Cody, Park County, Wyo., in 1921; served as mayor of Cody 1930–1932; trustee of the University of Wyoming 1933–1934; also engaged in banking; elected as a Democrat to the Seventy-fourth and Seventy-fifth Congresses (January 3, 1935–January 3, 1939); unsuccessful candidate for reelection in 1938 to the Seventy-sixth Congress; resumed the practice of law; accidentally shot himself while cleaning a shotgun and died in Cody, Wyo., on February 16, 1943; interment in Riverside Cemetery.

GREGG, Alexander White, a Representative from Texas; born in Centerville, Leon County, Tex., January 31, 1855; attended the common schools of Texas, and was graduated from King College, Bristol, Tenn., in 1874; studied law at the University of Virginia at Charlottesville; was admitted to the bar in 1878 and commenced practice in Palestine, Tex.; member of the State senate 1886–1888; resumed the practice of law; elected as a Democrat to the Fifty-eighth and to the seven succeeding Congresses (March 4, 1903–March 3, 1919); was not a candidate for renomination; died in Palestine, Anderson County, Tex., April 30, 1919; interment in East Hill Cemetery.

GREGG, Andrew (grandfather of James Xavier McLanahan), a Representative and a Senator from Pennsylvania; born in Carlisle, Pa., June 10, 1755; attended Rev. John Steel's Latin School in Carlisle, and completed his education in Newark, Del.; while at the latter place served several tours in the militia of the Revolution; tutor in the University of Pennsylvania at Philadelphia 1779–1783; moved to Middletown, Dauphin County, Pa., in 1783 and engaged in mercantile pursuits; moved to Pennvalley (now in Bucks County), Pa., in 1789 and engaged in agricultural pursuits; elected to the Second and to the seven succeeding Congresses (March 4, 1791–March 3, 1807); elected to the United States Senate and served from March 4, 1807, to March 3, 1813; elected President pro tempore of the Senate June 26, 1809; moved to Bellefonte, Pa., in 1814 and engaged in banking; secretary of state of Pennsylvania from December 19, 1820, to December 16, 1823; unsuccessful candidate for Governor in 1823; died in Bellefonte, Pa., May 20, 1835; interment in Union Cemetery.

GREGG, Curtis Hussey, a Representative from Pennsylvania; born in Adamsburg, Westmoreland County, Pa., August 9, 1865; attended the common schools and Greensburg (Pa.) Seminary; engaged in teaching; associate editor of the Greensburg (Pa.) Evening Press 1883–1887; studied law; was admitted to the bar in 1888, and commenced practice in Greensburg, Pa.; district attorney of Westmoreland County in 1891; member of the school board of Greensburg 1892–1896; delegate to the Democratic State conventions in 1892, 1894, and 1896; served as chairman of the Democratic county committee 1896–1913; unsuccessful candidate in 1900 for election to the Fifty-seventh Congress and in 1904 for election to the State senate; member of the council of the borough of Greensburg 1901–1905; delegate to the Democratic National Conventions in 1908, 1928, and 1932; elected as a Democrat to the Sixty-second Congress (March 4, 1911–March 3, 1913); unsuccessful candidate for renomination in 1912; reengaged in the practice of law at Greensburg, Pa., until his death there on January 18, 1933; interment in St. Clair Cemetery.

GREGG, James Madison, a Representative from Indiana; born in Patrick County, Va., June 26, 1806; attended the public schools; studied law; was admitted to the bar in 1830 and began practice in Danville, Ind.; county surveyor of Hendricks County 1834–1837; clerk of the circuit court 1837–1845; elected as a Democrat to the Thirty-fifth Congress (March 4, 1857–March 3, 1859); unsuccessful candidate for reelection in 1858 to the Thirty-sixth Congress; resumed the practice of law in Danville, Ind.; member of the State house of representatives in 1862; died in Danville, Ind., on June 16, 1869; interment in South Cemetery.

GREGORY, Dudley Sanford, a Representative from New Jersey; born in Redding, Fairfield County, Conn., February 5, 1800; moved with his father to Albany, N. Y., in 1805; attended the public schools; was a member of the guard of honor to receive General Lafayette on his visit to the United States in 1824; moved to New York City in 1824 and to Jersey City in 1834; served three terms as a freeholder of Hudson County; elected first mayor of Jersey City in 1838 and held the office three terms; was at one time a director of sixteen different railroads; elected as a Whig to the Thirtieth Congress (March 4, 1847–March 3, 1849); declined to be a candidate for renomination in 1848; engaged in banking; died in Jersey City, N. J., December 8, 1874; interment in Greenwood Cemetery.

GREGORY, Noble Jones (brother of William Voris Gregory), a Representative from Kentucky; born in Mayfield, Graves County, Ky., August 30, 1897; attended private and public schools and was graduated from Mayfield (Ky.) High School in 1915 and from Mayfield Business College; served as bookkeeper, cashier, and trust officer of the First National Bank of Mayfield, Ky., 1917–1936; served as secretary-treasurer of the Mayfield Board of Education 1923–1936; elected as a Democrat to the Seventy-fifth and to the ten succeeding Congresses (January 3, 1937–January 3, 1959); unsuccessful candidate for renomination in 1958; engaged in banking and general investments; is a resident of Mayfield, Ky.

GREGORY, William Voris (brother of Noble J. Gregory), a Representative from Kentucky; born near Farmington, Graves County, Ky., October 21, 1877; attended private and public schools and was graduated from West Kentucky College, Mayfield, Ky., in 1896; taught school and served as superintendent of schools, Mayfield, 1898–1900; attended the law department of Cumberland University, Lebanon, Tenn.; was admitted to the bar in 1902 and commenced practice in Mayfield; county surveyor 1902–1910; judge of the Graves County Court 1913–1919; United States attorney for the western district of Kentucky 1919–1923; appointed chairman of the Kentucky State Tax Commission in 1924 but declined; elected professor of law at Cumberland University in 1925 but declined; member of the board of trustees of Presbyterian Theological Seminary, Louisville, Ky., 1920–1927, serving as president 1925–1927; served as vice president of the Jefferson Davis Memorial Commission; elected as a Democrat to the Seventieth and to the four succeeding Congresses and served from March 4, 1927, until his death; was renominated in 1936 for election to the Seventy-fifth Congress but died before the election; died in Mayfield, Ky., October 10, 1936; interment in Maplewood Cemetery.

GREIG, John, a Representative from New York; born in Moffat, Dumfriesshire, Scotland, August 6, 1779; attended the Edinburgh High School; immigrated to the United States in 1797; studied law; was admitted to the bar in 1804 and commenced practice in Canandaigua, N. Y.; president of the Ontario Bank 1820–1856; regent of the University of the State of New York from 1825 and vice chancellor of the same institution from 1845, serving in both capacities until his death; one of the founders of the Ontario Female Seminary; elected as a Whig to the Twenty-seventh Congress to fill the vacancy caused by the resignation of Francis Granger and served from May 21, 1841, to September 25, 1841, when he resigned; president of the Ontario Agricultural Society; died in Canandaigua, N. Y., April 9, 1858; interment in West Avenue Cemetery.

GRENNELL, George, Jr., a Representative from Massachusetts; born in Greenfield, Mass., December 25, 1786; attended Deerfield Academy, and was graduated from Dartmouth College, Hanover, N. H., in 1808; was admitted to the bar in 1811; prosecuting attorney for Franklin County 1820–1828; member of the State senate 1825–1827; elected to the Twenty-first and to the four succeeding Congresses (March 4, 1829–March 3, 1839); was not a candidate for renomination in 1838; presidential elector on the Whig ticket of Harrison and Tyler in 1840; trustee of Amherst College, Massachusetts, 1838–1859; judge of probate 1849–1853; clerk of Franklin County Courts 1853–1865; first president of the Troy & Greenfield Railroad; died in Greenfield, Mass., November 19, 1877; interment in Green River Cemetery.

GRESHAM, Walter, a Representative from Texas; born at "Woodlawn," near Newtown, King and Queen County, Va., July 22, 1841; attended Stevensville Academy and Edge Hill Academy, and was graduated from the University of Virginia at Charlottesville in 1863; served as a private in the Confederate Army during the Civil War; studied law; was admitted to the bar in 1867 and commenced practice in Galveston, Tex.; district attorney for the Galveston judicial district in 1872; member of the State house of representatives 1886–1891; elected as a Democrat to the Fifty-third Congress (March 4, 1893–March 3, 1895); unsuccessful candidate for reelection in 1894 to the Fifty-fourth Congress; resumed the practice of law in Galveston, Tex.; died in Washington, D. C., November 6, 1920; interment in Lakeview Cemetery, Galveston, Tex.

GREY, Benjamin Edwards (grandson of Benjamin Edwards), a Representative from Kentucky; born at "Shiloh," near Bardstown, Nelson County, Ky.; pursued an academic course; studied law; was admitted to the bar and began practice in Hopkinsville, Ky.; member of the State house of representatives in 1838 and 1839; served in the State senate 1847–1851; presiding officer of the senate and Acting Lieutenant Governor in 1850; elected as a Whig to the Thirty-second and Thirty-third Congresses (March 4, 1851–March 3, 1855); unsuccessful candidate for reelection in 1854 to the Thirty-fourth Congress; died in Selma, Ala.

GRIDER, Henry, a Representative from Kentucky; born in Garrard County, Ky., July 16, 1796; pursued an academic course; studied law; was admitted to the bar and commenced practice in Bowling Green, Ky.; served in the War of 1812; member of the State house of representatives in 1827 and 1831; served in the State senate 1833–1837; elected as a Whig to the Twenty-eighth and Twenty-ninth Congresses (March 4, 1843–March 3, 1847); elected to the Thirty-seventh, Thirty-eighth, and Thirty-ninth Congresses and served from March 4, 1861, until his death in Bowling Green, Ky., September 7, 1866; interment in Old College Street Cemetery.

GRIEST, William Walton, a Representative from Pennsylvania; born in Christiana, Lancaster County, Pa., September 22, 1858; attended the common schools, and was graduated from the Millersville State Normal School in 1876; engaged in teaching; member of the city school board of Lancaster, Pa., for twenty-four years; director and an incorporator of the Pennsylvania

Public School Memorial Association; engaged in newspaper work; editor of the Inquirer, Lancaster, Pa., 1882–1888; chief clerk in the county commissioner's office 1887–1899; member of the Pennsylvania Tax Commission; delegate to several Republican State conventions and to every Republican National Convention 1896–1928, inclusive; secretary of state of Pennsylvania 1899–1903; member of the State sinking fund commission and of the board of pardons; president of lighting and street railway companies 1903–1927; elected as a Republican to the Sixty-first and to the ten succeeding Congresses and served from March 4, 1909, until his death at Mount Clemens, Mich., December 5, 1929; interment in Woodward Hill Cemetery, Lancaster, Pa.

GRIFFIN, Anthony Jerome, a Representative from New York; born in New York City April 1, 1866; attended the public schools, City College, Cooper Union, and the New York University Law School; was admitted to the bar in 1892 and commenced practice in New York City; organized and commanded Company F, Sixty-ninth Regiment, New York Volunteer Infantry, in the Spanish-American War in 1898 and 1899; founded and edited the Bronx Independent 1905–1907; member of the State senate 1911–1915; member of the New York State constitutional convention in 1915; elected as a Democrat to the Sixty-fifth Congress to fill the vacancy caused by the resignation of Henry Bruckner; reelected to the Sixty-sixth and to the eight succeeding Congresses and served from March 5, 1918, until his death in New York City, January 13, 1935; interment in Arlington National Cemetery, Fort Myer, Va.

GRIFFIN, Cyrus, a Delegate from Virginia; born in Farnham, Richmond County, Va., July 16, 1748; sent to England to be educated; studied law at the University of Edinburgh and at the Temple in London; returned to Virginia; prominent in pre-Revolutionary movements; member of the colonial house of burgesses in 1777, 1778, 1786, and 1787; Member of the Continental Congress 1778–1781, 1787, and 1788, and served as its president in 1788; president of the supreme court of admiralty; commissioner to the Creek Nation in 1789; judge of the United States District Court of Virginia from December 1789 until his death in Yorktown, Va., December 14, 1810; interment in Bruton Churchyard, Williamsburg, Va.

GRIFFIN, Daniel Joseph, a Representative from New York; born in Brooklyn, N. Y., March 26, 1880; attended the parochial schools, St. Laurent College, near Montreal, Canada, and St. Peter's College, Jersey City; was graduated in law from the New York Law School; was admitted to the bar in 1902 and commenced practice in Brooklyn; commissioner of licenses for the Borough of Brooklyn 1903–1906; head of the administration and guardianship departments of the surrogate's court of Kings County 1906–1912; delegate to the Democratic National Convention at Baltimore in 1912 which nominated Wilson and Marshall; elected as a Democrat to the Sixty-third, Sixty-fourth, and Sixty-fifth Congresses and served from March 4, 1913, to December 31, 1917, when he resigned; served as sheriff of Kings County in 1918 and 1919; resumed the practice of law; died in Brooklyn, N. Y., on December 11, 1926; interment in Holy Cross Cemetery.

GRIFFIN, Isaac (great-grandfather of Eugene McLanahan Wilson), a Representative from Pennsylvania; born in Kent County, Del., February 27, 1756; attended the public schools; moved to Fayette County, Pa., and engaged in agricultural pursuits; commissioned a captain during the Revolutionary War; appointed justice of the peace in 1794; elected a member of the Pennsylvania House of Representatives in 1807 and served four terms; elected as a Democrat to the Thirteenth Congress to fill the vacancy caused by the death of John Smilie; reelected to the Fourteenth Congress and served from February 16, 1813, to March 3, 1817; unsuccessful candidate for reelection in 1816 to to the Fifteenth Congress; died from the effects of a fall from a wagon, on his estate in Nicholson Township, Pa., October 12, 1827; interment on what was known as the old Woods farm, Nicholson Township, Pa.

GRIFFIN, John King, a Representative from South Carolina; born near Clinton, Laurens County, S. C., August 13, 1789; pursued an academic course; engaged as a planter; served in the State house of representatives 1816–1818; member of the State senate 1820–1824 and again in 1828; elected as a State Rights Whig to the Twenty-second and to the four succeeding Congresses (March 4, 1831–March 3, 1841); died near Clinton, S. C., August 1, 1841; interment in Little River Church Cemetery.

GRIFFIN, Levi Thomas, a Representative from Michigan; born in Clinton, Oneida County, N. Y., May 23, 1837; moved with his parents to Rochester, Oakland County, Mich., in 1848; was graduated from the University of Michigan at Ann Arbor in 1857; studied law; was admitted to the bar in 1858 and commenced practice in Detroit, Mich.; during the Civil War entered the United States Army in August 1862 as second lieutenant, and served as first lieutenant, adjutant, captain, brigade inspector, acting assistant adjutant general of the Cavalry division, and acting assistant adjutant general of the Cavalry corps, Military Division of Mississippi, and brevetted major; at the close of the war resumed the practice of law in Detroit; Fletcher professor of law in the University of Michigan 1886–1897; unsuccessful candidate for judge of the State supreme court in 1887; elected as a Democrat to the Fifty-third Congress to fill the vacancy caused by the death of John Logan Chipman and served from December 4, 1893, to March 3, 1895; unsuccessful candidate for reelection in 1894 to the Fifty-fourth Congress; resumed the practice of his profession; pension agent in 1896 and 1897; died in Detroit, Mich., March 17, 1906; interment in Woodmere Cemetery.

GRIFFIN, Michael, a Representative from Wisconsin; born in County Clare, Ireland, September 9, 1842; immigrated with his parents to Canada in 1847 and to Ohio in 1851; moved to Wisconsin in 1856 and settled in Newport, Sauk County; attended the common schools of Ohio and Wisconsin; during the Civil War enlisted in the Union Army September 11, 1861, as a private in Company E, Twelfth Regiment, Wisconsin Volunteer Infantry, and served until the close of the war, attaining the rank of first lieutenant; mustered out July 16, 1865; moved to Kilbourn City, Wis., in 1865; studied law; was admitted to the bar in 1868 and commenced practice in Kilbourn City; cashier of the Bank of Kilbourn 1871–1876; member of the County Board of Columbia County, Wis., in 1874 and 1875; member of the State assembly in 1876; moved to Eau Claire, Wis., in 1876; city attorney of Eau Claire in 1878 and 1879; served in the State senate in 1880 and 1881; department commander of the Grand Army of the Republic in 1887 and 1888; elected as a Republican to the Fifty-third Congress to fill the vacancy caused by the death of George B. Shaw and at the same election to the Fifty-fourth Congress; reelected to the Fifty-fifth Congress and served from November 5, 1894, to March 3, 1899; was not a candidate for renomination in 1898; appointed chairman of the State tax commission by Governor Schofield May 28, 1899; died in Eau Claire, Wis., December 29, 1899; interment in Forest Hill Cemetery.

GRIFFIN, Robert Paul, a Representative from Michigan; born in Detroit, Wayne County, Mich., November 6, 1923; attended grade school in Garden City, Mich., and in 1941 graduated from Fordson High School, Dearborn, Mich.; during World War II served as an enlisted man in the Seventy-first Infantry Division, as forward observer in the Field Artillery, with fourteen months overseas in Europe; awarded two battle stars; graduated from Central Michigan College at Mount Pleasant in 1947; attended The Citadel, Charleston, S. C., and Shrivenham University, England; graduated from the University of Michigan Law School in 1950; was admitted to the bar in 1950 and commenced the practice of law in Traverse, Mich.; elected as a Republican to the Eighty-fifth and Eighty-sixth Congresses (January 3, 1957–January 3, 1961). *Reelected to the Eighty-seventh Congress.*

GRIFFIN, Samuel, a Representative from Virginia; born in Richmond County, Va.; pursued classical studies; studied law; was admitted to the bar and practiced; colonel in the Revolutionary War; was wounded at Harlem Heights October 12, 1776; served on the State board of war; member of the State house of delegates 1786–1788; elected to the First, Second, and Third Congresses (March 4, 1789–March 3, 1795); died November 3, 1810.

GRIFFIN, Thomas, a Representative from Virginia; born in Yorktown, Va., in 1773; pursued classical studies; studied law; was admitted to the bar and practiced; also engaged in agricultural pursuits; member of the State house of delegates 1793–1800; appointed justice of the court of oyer and terminer on October 17, 1796, and served in this capacity until 1810; elected to the Eighth Congress (March 4, 1803–March 3, 1805); appointed chief justice of the court of quarter sessions September 1, 1805, holding court at Yorktown, Va., and served until 1810; justice of the York County Court 1810–1812; served in the War of 1812 as major of Infantry; again justice of the court of oyer and terminer (chairman of the court) 1814–1820; again a member of the State house of delegates 1819–1823 and 1827–1830; died at "The Mansion," near Yorktown, Va., October 7, 1837.

GRIFFITH, Francis Marion, a Representative from Indiana; born in Moorefield, Switzerland County, Ind., August 21, 1849; attended the country schools of the county, the high school in Vevay, Ind., and Franklin College, Franklin, Ind.; taught school; appointed school superintendent of Switzerland County in 1873; studied law; was admitted to the bar in 1875 and commenced practice in Vevay; county treasurer 1875–1877; delegate to the Democratic National Convention at Cincinnati in 1880; member of the State senate 1886–1894 and served as Acting Lieutenant Governor 1891–1894; unsuccessful candidate for attorney general of Indiana in 1894; elected as a Democrat to the Fifty-fifth Congress to fill the vacancy caused by the death of William S. Holman; reelected to the Fifty-sixth, Fifty-seventh, and Fifty-eighth Congresses and served from December 6, 1897, to March 3, 1905; declined to be a candidate for renomination in 1904; resumed the practice of law in Vevay, Ind.; city attorney 1912–1916; judge of the circuit court of the fifth judicial district 1916–1922; again engaged in the practice of his profession; died in Vevay, Ind., February 8, 1927; interment in Vevay Cemetery.

GRIFFITH, John Keller, a Representative from Louisiana; born in Port Hudson, East Baton Rouge Parish, La., October 16, 1882; attended the public schools and Louisiana State University at Baton Rouge; was graduated from the medical department of Tulane University, New Orleans, La., in 1907; assistant superintendent, East Louisiana Hospital for the Insane, Jackson, La., in 1909 and 1910; practicing physician in Slidell, La., 1910–1937; also interested in banking; during the First World War served as a first lieutenant in the Medical Corps; elected as a Democrat to the Seventy-fifth and Seventy-sixth Congresses (January 3, 1937–January 3, 1941); unsuccessful candidate for renomination in

1940; served with the Milk Marketing Service of the Department of Agriculture at Slidell, La., until his death there on September 25, 1942; interment in Greenwood Cemetery.

GRIFFITH, Samuel, a Representative from Pennsylvania; born in Merthyr Tydfil, South Wales, Great Britain, February 14, 1816; instructed in elementary subjects by a private teacher; was graduated from Allegheny College, Meadville, Pa.; studied law; was admitted to the bar in 1846 and commenced practice in Mercer, Pa.; delegate to the Democratic National Convention at Baltimore; elected as a Democrat to the Forty-second Congress (March 4, 1871–March 3, 1873); unsuccessful candidate for reelection in 1872 to the Forty-third Congress; resumed the practice of law in Mercer, Pa.; died in Mercer, Pa., October 1, 1893; interment in Mercer Cemetery.

GRIFFITHS, Martha Wright, a Representative from Michigan; born in Pierce City, Lawrence County, Mo., January 29, 1912; attended the public schools; was graduated from the University of Missouri at Columbia in 1934 and from the University of Michigan Law School at Ann Arbor in 1940; was admitted to the bar in 1941; member of the legal department of the American Automobile Insurance Co. in 1941 and 1942; during World War II joined the Detroit Ordnance District as a contract negotiator and served from 1942 to 1946; commenced the private practice of law in Detroit, Mich., in 1946; elected to the State house of representatives in 1948, reelected in 1950, and served from 1948 to 1952; appointed in April 1953 as recorder and judge of Recorders Court in Detroit and in November was elected as judge and served until 1954; unsuccessful candidate for election in 1952 to the Eighty-third Congress; elected as a Democrat to the Eighty-fourth, Eighty-fifth, and Eighty-sixth Congresses (January 3, 1955–January 3, 1961). *Reelected to the Eighty-seventh Congress.*

GRIFFITHS, Percy Wilfred, a Representative from Ohio; born in Taylor, Lackawanna County, Pa., March 30, 1893; attended the public schools and Bloomsburg (Pa.) Normal School 1913–1916; was graduated from Pennsylvania State College at State College in 1921 and from Columbia University, New York, N. Y., in 1930; served in the United States Navy 1910–1913 and during the First World War 1917–1919; director of athletics at Marietta (Ohio) College 1921–1927; football coach at various colleges 1927–1936; in 1922 engaged as an automobile dealer in Marietta, Ohio; mayor of Marietta in 1938 and 1939; elected as a Republican to the Seventy-eighth, Seventy-ninth, and Eightieth Congresses (January 3, 1943–January 3, 1949); unsuccessful candidate for reelection in 1948 to the Eighty-first Congress; resumed the automobile business until his retirement in June 1961; is a resident of Marietta, Ohio.

GRIGGS, James Mathews, a Representative from Georgia; born in Lagrange, Troup County, Ga., March 29, 1861; attended the common schools, and was graduated from the Peabody Normal College, Nashville, Tenn., in 1881; taught school and studied law; was admitted to the bar in 1883 and commenced the practice of law in Alapaha, Berrien County, Ga.; engaged in the newspaper business; moved to Dawson, Ga., in 1885; elected by the legislature solicitor general of the Pataula judicial circuit in 1888; reelected in 1892 and served until his resignation in 1893 to accept appointment by the Governor as judge of the Pataula judicial circuit; elected to the same office by the legislature; reelected and served until his resignation in 1896 to accept the Democratic nomination for Congress; delegate to the Democratic National Convention at Chicago in 1892 which nominated Cleveland and Stevenson; chairman of the Democratic Congressional Campaign Committee 1904–1908; elected as a Democrat to the Fifty-fifth and to the six succeeding Congresses and served from March 4, 1897, until his death in Dawson, Ga., January 5, 1910; interment in Cedar Hill Cemetery.

GRIGSBY, George Barnes, a Delegate from the Territory of Alaska; born in Sioux Falls, Dak. (now South Dakota), December 2, 1874; attended the public schools, State University, Vermillion, S. Dak., and Sioux Falls (S. Dak.) University; studied law; was admitted to the bar in 1896 and commenced practice in Sioux Falls, S. Dak.; delegate to the State Democratic Convention in 1896; during the Spanish-American War served as a lieutenant in the Third Regiment, United States Volunteer Cavalry; moved to Nome, Alaska, in 1902; assistant United States attorney 1902–1908; United States attorney 1908–1910; city attorney of Nome in 1911; mayor in 1914; member of the board of commissioners for the promotion of uniform legislation in 1915; elected the first attorney general in 1916 and resigned in 1919; presented credentials as a Democratic Delegate-elect to the Sixty-sixth Congress to fill the vacancy caused by the death of Charles A. Sulzer and served from June 3, 1920, until March 1, 1921, when he was succeeded by James Wickersham, who contested the election of Mr. Sulzer in the first instance and continued the contest against Mr. Grigsby; delegate to the Democratic National Conventions in 1920 and 1924; resumed the practice of law and is a resident of Anchorage, Alaska.

GRIMES, James Wilson, a Senator from Iowa; born in Deering, N. H., October 20, 1816; was graduated from Hampton Academy, and from Dartmouth College, Hanover, N. H., in 1836; studied law; was admitted to the bar in 1836 and commenced practice in the "Black Hawk Purchase," Wisconsin Territory, afterward the site of Burlington, Iowa; member of the Iowa Territorial House of Representatives in 1838 and 1845; Governor of Iowa 1854–1858; elected as a Republican to the United States Senate in 1859; reelected in 1865 and served from March 4, 1859, until December 6, 1869, when he resigned; member of the peace convention of 1861 held in Washington, D. C., in an effort to devise means to prevent the impending war; died in Burlington, Iowa, February 7, 1872; interment in Aspen Grove Cemetery.

GRIMES, Thomas Wingfield, a Representative from Georgia; born in Columbus, Muscogee County, Ga., December 18, 1844; attended private schools, and was graduated from the University of Georgia at Athens in 1863; studied law; was admitted to the bar and commenced practice in Columbus, Ga.; served in the Confederate Army during the Civil War for eighteen months with Nelson's rangers, Gen. S. D. Lee's escort company; member of the State house of representatives in 1868, 1869, 1875, and 1876; member of the State senate in 1878 and 1879; delegate to the Democratic National Convention at Cincinnati in 1880; solicitor general of the Chattahoochee circuit from 1880 to 1888, when he resigned; elected as a Democrat to the Fiftieth and Fifty-first Congresses (March 4, 1887–March 3, 1891); unsuccessful candidate for reelection in 1890 to the Fifty-second Congress; resumed the practice of law in Columbus, Ga., and died there on October 28, 1905; interment in Linwood Cemetery.

GRINNELL, Joseph (brother of Moses Hicks Grinnell), a Representative from Massachusetts; born in New Bedford, Mass., November 17, 1788; completed preparatory studies; moved to New York City in 1809; engaged in mercantile pursuits; traveled in Europe, and returned to New Bedford; president of the First National Bank of New Bedford in 1832; president of the New Bedford & Taunton Railroad in 1839; member of the Governor's council 1839–1841; in 1840 he became a director of the Boston & Providence Railroad, the following year its president, resigning that position in 1846, but remaining a director until 1863; president of the Wamsutta Cotton Mills in 1847; elected as a Whig to the Twenty-eighth Congress to fill the vacancy caused by the death of Barker Burnell; reelected to the Twenty-ninth, Thirtieth, and Thirty-first Congresses and served from December 7, 1843, to March 3, 1851; declined to be a candidate for renomination in 1850; resumed his former business activities; died in New Bedford, Mass., February 7, 1885; interment in Oak Grove Cemetery.

GRINNELL, Josiah Bushnell, a Representative from Iowa; born in New Haven, Addison County, Vt., December 22, 1821; attended the common schools and Oneida Institute; pursued classical studies; was graduated from Auburn Theological Seminary in 1847; ordained a Presbyterian clergyman; held pastorates in Union Village, N. Y., Washington, D. C., and in the Congregational Church of New York City; moved to Iowa in 1854 and founded the town of Grinnell, Poweshiek County, and also Grinnell University; member of the State senate 1856–1860; studied law; was admitted to the bar in 1858 and practiced; delegate to the Republican National Convention at Chicago in 1860 which nominated Lincoln and Hamlin; special agent for the Post Office Department for two years; elected as a Republican to the Thirty-eighth and Thirty-ninth Congresses (March 4, 1863–March 3, 1867); was not a candidate for renomination in 1866; resumed the practice of law; interested in building of railroads; director of the Rock Island Railroad; receiver of the Iowa Central Railroad (later the St. Louis & St. Paul Railroad); president of the State Horticultural Society and of the First National Bank in Grinnell; died in Grinnell, Iowa, March 31, 1891; interment in Hazelwood Cemetery.

GRINNELL, Moses Hicks (brother of Joseph Grinnell), a Representative from New York; born in New Bedford, Mass., March 3, 1803; pursued an academic course; entered a counting-room in New York City in 1818; subsequently engaged in mercantile pursuits; elected as a Whig to the Twenty-sixth Congress (March 4, 1839–March 3, 1841); unsuccessful candidate for reelection in 1840 to the Twenty-seventh Congress; presidential elector on the first Republican ticket of Frémont and Dayton in 1856; president of the chamber of commerce and of the Merchants Clerks' Savings Bank; commissioner of charities and corrections; Central Park commissioner; one of the Union defense committee; collector of the port of New York from March 1869 to July 1870; appointed naval officer of customs and served from July 1870 to April 1871; died in New York City November 24, 1877; interment in Sleepy Hollow Burying Ground, Tarrytown, N. Y.

GRISWOLD, Dwight Palmer, a Senator from Nebraska; born in Harrison, Nebr., November 27, 1893; attended the high school at Gordon, Nebr.; graduated from Kearney (Nebr.) Military Academy in 1910; attended the Nebraska Wesleyan University 1910–1912 and graduated from the University of Nebraska in 1914; served as a sergeant in the Fourth Nebraska Infantry on the Mexican border in 1916 and during the First World War served as a first lieutenant and later as a captain of the One Hundred and Twenty-seventh Field Artillery in 1917 and 1918; cashier of the First National Bank of Gordon 1919–1922 and a director 1919–1954; also president of Gering National Bank 1951–1954; editor and publisher of the Gordon Journal 1922–1940; served in the State house of representatives in 1921; member of the State senate 1925–1929; Republican nominee for Governor in 1932, 1934, and 1936; elected Governor in 1940, 1942, and 1944; unsuccessful candidate for the Republican nomination for United States Senator in 1946; Director, Division of Internal

Affairs and Communications, Military Government of Germany, from January to June 1947; chief, American Mission for Aid to Greece, from June 1947 to September 1948; member, Nebraska University Board of Regents 1950–1954; elected as a Republican to the United States Senate for the term ending January 3, 1955, to fill the vacancy caused by the death of Kenneth S. Wherry, and served from November 5, 1952, until his death in the naval hospital at Bethesda, Md., April 12, 1954; interment in Fairview Cemetery, Scottsbluff, Nebr.

GRISWOLD, Gaylord, a Representative from New York; born in Windsor, Hartford County, Conn., December 18, 1767; pursued classical studies, and was graduated from Yale College in 1787; studied law; was admitted to the bar in 1790 and commenced practice in Windsor, Conn.; moved to Herkimer, N. Y., in 1792 and was the first lawyer in Herkimer County; member of the State assembly 1796–1798; elected as a Federalist to the Eighth Congress (March 4, 1803–March 3, 1805); resumed the practice of law in Herkimer, N. Y., and died there March 1, 1809; interment in Oak Hill Cemetery.

GRISWOLD, Glenn Hasenfratz, a Representative from Indiana; born in New Haven, Franklin County, Mo., January 20, 1890; attended the public schools; moved to Peru, Miami County, Ind., in 1911; attended Valparaiso (Ind.) Law School; was admitted to the bar in 1917 and commenced practice in Peru, Ind.; during the First World War served in the United States Army as a private in Company B, Fourth Regiment Casual Detachment, at Camp Zachary Taylor, Kentucky; city attorney of Peru, Ind., 1921–1925; prosecuting attorney of Miami County, Ind., in 1925 and 1926; member of the Indiana Railroad Commission in 1930; elected as a Democrat to the Seventy-second and to the three succeeding Congresses (March 4, 1931–January 3, 1939); unsuccessful candidate for reelection in 1938 to the Seventy-sixth Congress; reengaged in the practice of law in Peru, Ind., until his death there on December 5, 1940; interment in Mount Hope Cemetery.

GRISWOLD, Harry Wilbur, a Representative from Wisconsin; born on a farm near West Salem, La Crosse County, Wis., May 19, 1886; attended the West Salem public and high schools, and the college of agriculture of the University of Wisconsin at Madison; engaged in agricultural pursuits, specializing in the breeding of cattle; member of the La Crosse County Guernsey Breeders Association, serving as secretary 1907–1930 and as president 1930–1936; member of the West Salem School Board 1912–1929 and of the Wisconsin Board of Vocational Education 1930–1936; served in the State senate 1932–1936; delegate to the Republican State convention at La Crosse in 1934; elected as a Republican to the Seventy-sixth Congress and served from January 3, 1939, until his death in Washington, D. C., July 4, 1939; interment in Hamilton Cemetery, West Salem, Wis.

GRISWOLD, John Ashley, a Representative from New York; born in Cairo, Greene County, N. Y., November 18, 1822; attended the common schools, and the academies in Prattsville and Catskill, N. Y.; studied law; was admitted to the bar in 1848 and commenced practice in Greene County; district attorney of Greene County 1856–1859; county judge 1863–1867; elected as a Democrat to the Forty-first Congress (March 4, 1869–March 3, 1871); declined to be a candidate for renomination in 1870; resumed the practice of his profession; elected supervisor of Catskill, N. Y., in 1871; member of the State constitutional convention in 1894; died in Catskill, Greene County, N. Y., February 22, 1902; interment in Catskill Village Cemetery.

GRISWOLD, John Augustus, a Representative from New York; born in Nassau, Rensselaer County, N. Y., November 11, 1822; received an academic training; engaged in mercantile pursuits and in steel manufacture; mayor of Troy in 1855; engaged in banking and also served as president of the Troy & Lansingburgh Railroad Co., of the Troy & Cohoes Railroad Co., and of the New Orleans, Mobile & Texas Railroad Co.; was also a director and stockholder in the Port Henry Iron Ore Co. and Fall Creek Bituminous Coal Co.; besides these positions of honor and responsibility was greatly interested in the Rensselaer Polytechnic Institute and also in the Troy Female Seminary; was an unsuccessful candidate for election in 1860 to the Thirty-seventh Congress; elected as a Democrat to the Thirty-eighth Congress (March 4, 1863–March 3, 1865); reelected as a Republican to the Thirty-ninth and Fortieth Congresses (March 4, 1865–March 3, 1869); was not a candidate for renomination in 1868; unsuccessful Republican candidate for Governor of New York in 1868; elected regent of the University of the State of New York April 29, 1869; died in Troy, N. Y., on October 31, 1872; interment in Oakwood Cemetery.

GRISWOLD, Matthew (grandson of Roger Griswold), a Representative from Pennsylvania; born in Lyme, New London County, Conn., June 6, 1833; attended the common schools and pursued an academic course; engaged in teaching and in agricultural pursuits for a number of years; elected to various local offices; member of the Connecticut House of Representatives in 1862 and 1865; moved to Erie, Pa., in 1866; engaged in manufacturing; elected a trustee of Erie Academy for four successive terms; elected as a Republican to the Fifty-second Congress (March 4, 1891–March 3, 1893); was not a candidate for renomination in 1892; elected to the Fifty-fourth Congress (March 4, 1895–March 3, 1897); was not a candidate for renomination in 1896; resumed manufacturing pursuits; died in Erie, Pa., May 19, 1919; interment in Erie Cemetery.

GRISWOLD, Roger (grandfather of Matthew Griswold), a Representative from Connecticut; born in Lyme, New London County, Conn., May 21, 1762; pursued classical studies, and was graduated from Yale College in 1780; studied law; was admitted to the bar in 1783 and commenced practice in Norwich; returned to Lyme in 1794; elected as a Federalist to the Fourth and to the five succeeding Congresses and served from March 4, 1795, until his resignation in 1805 before the convening of the Ninth Congress; declined the portfolio of Secretary of War tendered by President Adams in 1801; served as a judge of the supreme court of Connecticut in 1807; presidential elector on the Pinckney and King ticket; Lieutenant Governor of Connecticut 1809–1811; Governor of the State from 1811 until his death in Norwich, Conn., on October 25, 1812; interment in Griswold Cemetery at Black Hall, in the town of Lyme (now Old Lyme), Conn.

GRISWOLD, Stanley, a Senator from Ohio; born in Torrington, Litchfield County, Conn., November 14, 1763; pursued classical studies, and was graduated from Yale College in 1786; studied theology; pastor in Milford, Conn., 1790–1802, and also in Greenfield, Mass.; editor of a Democratic paper in Walpole, N. H., in 1804; appointed secretary of Michigan Territory and served from March 1, 1805, to March 18, 1808; appointed collector and inspector of the port of Detroit; moved to Ohio; appointed to the United States Senate to fill the vacancy caused by the resignation of Edward Tiffin and served from May 18 to December 11, 1809, when a successor was elected; appointed a United States judge for Illinois Territory and served from March 16, 1810, until his death in Shawneetown, Ill., August 21, 1815.

GROESBECK, William Slocum, a Representative from Ohio; born in Kinderhook, Rensselaer County, N. Y., July 24, 1815; moved with his parents to Cincinnati, Ohio, in 1816; attended the common schools and Augusta (Ky.) College; was graduated from Miami University, Oxford, Ohio, in 1835; studied law; was admitted to the bar in 1836 and commenced practice in Cincinnati, Ohio; member of the State constitutional convention in 1851; commissioner to codify the laws of Ohio in 1852; elected as a Democrat to the Thirty-fifth Congress (March 4, 1857–March 3, 1859); unsuccessful candidate for reelection in 1858 to the Thirty-sixth Congress; member of the peace convention of 1861 held in Washington, D. C., in an effort to devise means to prevent the impending war; served in the State senate 1862–1864; delegate to the Union National Convention at Philadelphia in 1866; one of President Johnson's counsel in his impeachment trial in 1868; delegate to the International Monetary Conference in Paris, France, in 1878; died in Cincinnati, Ohio, July 7, 1897; interment in Spring Grove Cemetery.

GRONNA, Asle Jorgenson, a Representative and a Senator from North Dakota; born in Elkader, Clayton County, Iowa, December 10, 1858; moved with his parents to Houston County, Minn.; attended the public schools and the Caledonia Academy; taught school in Wilmington, Minn.; moved to Dakota Territory in 1879 and engaged in farming and teaching; in 1880 moved to Buxton, Traill County, and engaged in business; moved to Lakota, Nelson County, in 1887; member of the Territorial house of representatives in 1889; served as president of the village board of trustees and president of the board of education several terms; chairman of the Nelson County Republican central committee 1902–1906; appointed a member of the board of regents of the University of North Dakota by Gov. Frank White in 1902; elected as a Republican to the Fifty-ninth, Sixtieth, and Sixty-first Congresses and served from March 4, 1905, until February 2, 1911, when he resigned, having been elected Senator; elected in 1911 to the United States Senate to fill the vacancy caused by the death of Martin N. Johnson; reelected in 1914 and served from February 2, 1911, to March 3, 1921; unsuccessful candidate for reelection in 1920 to the United States Senate; resumed agricultural pursuits; died in Lakota, N. Dak., May 4, 1922; interment in Lakota Cemetery.

GROOME, James Black, a Senator from Maryland; born in Elkton, Cecil County, Md., April 4, 1838; completed preparatory studies in the Tennant School, Hartsville, Pa.; studied law; was admitted to the bar in 1861 and commenced practice in Elkton, Md.; member of the convention which framed the new constitution of Maryland in 1867; member of the State house of delegates in 1871 and 1872; presidential elector on the Democratic ticket of Greeley and Brown in 1872; again elected a member of the State house of delegates in 1873; resigned February 4, 1874, having been elected Governor to fill the vacancy caused by the resignation of William Pinckney Whyte; served as Governor from March 4, 1874, to January 12, 1876; resumed the practice of law; elected as a Democrat to the United States Senate and served from March 4, 1879, to March 3, 1885; collector of customs for the port of Baltimore 1889–1893; died in Baltimore, Md., October 5, 1893; interment in Elkton Presbyterian Cemetery, Elkton, Md.

GROSS, Chester Heilman, a Representative from Pennsylvania; born on a farm in East Manchester Township, York County, Pa., October 13, 1888; attended the rural schools, a business college in York, Pa., and Pennsylvania State College at State College; engaged in agricultural pursuits; served as township supervisor 1918–1922; member of the State house of representatives in 1929 and 1930; school board director 1931–1940; president of the State School Directors Association in 1939 and 1940; elected as a Republican to the Seventy-sixth Congress (January 3, 1939–January 3, 1941); unsuccessful candidate for reelection in 1940 to the Seventy-seventh Congress; resumed agricultural pursuits near Manchester, Pa.; elected to the Seventy-eighth, Seventy-ninth, and Eightieth Congresses (January 3, 1943–January 3, 1949); unsuccessful for reelection in 1948 to the Eighty-first Congress and for the Republican nomination in 1954 and 1956; real-estate salesman; is a resident of York, Pa.

GROSS, Ezra Carter, a Representative from New York; born in Hartford, Windsor County, Vt., July 11, 1787; pursued classical studies; was graduated from the University of Vermont at Burlington in 1806; studied law; was admitted to the bar in 1810 and practiced in Elizabethtown, N. Y., and later in Keeseville, N. Y.; was admitted as a master in chancery in 1812; served in the War of 1812, and took part in several engagements; held a commission in the New York Militia 1814–1821; surrogate of Essex County 1815–1819; supervisor of Elizabethtown in 1818 and again in 1823 and 1824; elected as a Democrat to the Sixteenth Congress (March 4, 1819–March 3, 1821); resumed the practice of law; member of the New York State Assembly in 1828 and 1829; died in Albany, N. Y., April 9, 1829; interment in Evergreen Cemetery, Keeseville, N. Y.

GROSS, Harold Royce, a Representative from Iowa; born in Arispe, Union County, Iowa, June 30, 1899; educated in the rural schools; served with the First Iowa Field Artillery in the Mexican border campaign in 1916; during the First World War served in the United States Army, with overseas service, 1917–1919; attended the University of Missouri School of Journalism at Columbia; newspaper reporter and editor for various newspapers 1921–1935; radio news commentator 1935–1948; elected as a Republican to the Eighty-first and to the five succeeding Congresses (January 3, 1949–January 3, 1961). *Reelected to the Eighty-seventh Congress.*

GROSS, Samuel, a Representative from Pennsylvania; born in Upper Providence, Montgomery County, Pa., in 1774; attended the public schools; engaged in agricultural pursuits; member of the State house of representatives 1803–1807; served in the State senate 1811–1815; elected as a Democrat to the Sixteenth and Seventeenth Congresses (March 4, 1819–March 3, 1823); retired from public life; died in Trappe, Pa., March 19, 1844; interment in Augustus Lutheran Cemetery.

GROSVENOR, Charles Henry (uncle of Charles Grosvenor Bond), a Representative from Ohio; born in Pomfret, Windham County, Conn., September 20, 1833; moved with his parents to Ohio in 1838; attended school in Athens County; taught school; studied law; was admitted to the bar in 1857 and practiced; during the Civil War served in the Union Army; major in the Eighteenth Regiment, Ohio Volunteer Infantry, September 25, 1861; lieutenant colonel June 9, 1863; colonel April 19, 1865; brevetted colonel and brigadier general of Volunteers March 13, 1865, "for gallant and meritorious services during the war"; mustered out October 9, 1865; held divers township and village offices; presidential elector in 1872 and 1880; member of the State house of representatives 1874–1878 and served as speaker two years; member of the board of trustees of the Ohio Soldiers and Sailors Orphans' Home in Xenia from April 1880 until 1888, and president of the board for five years; delegate at large to the Republican National Convention at St. Louis in 1896 and at Philadelphia in 1900; elected as a Republican to the Forty-ninth, Fiftieth, and Fifty-first Congresses (March 4, 1885–March 3, 1891); unsuccessful candidate for renomination in 1890; elected to the Fifty-third and to the six succeeding Congresses

(March 4, 1893–March 3, 1907); unsuccessful candidate for renomination in 1906; resumed the practice of law in Athens, Ohio; appointed chairman of the Chickamauga and Chattanooga National Park Commission and served from 1910 until his death in Athens, Ohio, October 30, 1917; interment in Union Street Cemetery.

GROSVENOR, Thomas Peabody, a Representative from New York; born in Pomfret, Windham County, Conn., December 20, 1778; pursued classical studies; was graduated from Yale College in 1800; studied law; was admitted to the bar in 1803 and commenced practice in Hudson, N. Y.; member of the State assembly 1810–1812; district attorney of Essex County in 1810 and 1811; elected as a Federalist to the Twelfth Congress to fill the vacancy caused by the resignation of Robert Le Roy Livingston; reelected to the Thirteenth and Fourteenth Congresses and served from January 29, 1813, to March 3, 1817; engaged in the practice of law in Baltimore, Md.; died in Waterloo, near Baltimore, Md., April 24, 1817; interment in Hudson, N. Y.

GROUT, Jonathan, a Representative from Massachusetts; born in Lunenburg, Worcester County, Mass., July 23, 1737; served in the expedition against Canada 1757–1760; studied law; was admitted to the bar and commenced practice in Petersham, Mass.; served in the Revolutionary War; member of the State house of representatives in 1781, 1784, and 1787; served in the State senate in 1788; member of the State constitutional convention in 1788; elected as a Democrat to the First Congress (March 4, 1789–March 3, 1791); returned to Lunenburg, Mass. (now Vermont), in 1803; died in Dover, N. H., September 8, 1807; interment in Pine Hill Cemetery.

GROUT, William Wallace, a Representative from Vermont; born in Compton, Province of Quebec, May 24, 1836; pursued an academic course, and was graduated from the Poughkeepsie (N. Y.) Law School in 1857; was admitted to the bar in December of the same year and practiced in Barton, Vt.; served as lieutenant colonel of the Fifteenth Regiment, Vermont Volunteer Infantry, in the Union Army during the Civil War; prosecuting attorney of Orleans County in 1865 and 1866; served in the State house of representatives 1868–1870 and in 1874; member of the State senate in 1876 and served as president pro tempore of that body; elected as a Republican to the Forty-seventh Congress (March 4, 1881–March 3, 1883); unsuccessful candidate for reelection in 1882 to the Forty-eighth Congress; elected to the Forty-ninth and to the seven succeeding Congresses (March 4, 1885–March 3, 1901); engaged in agricultural pursuits; died in Kirby, Vt., October 7, 1902; interment in Pine Grove Cemetery.

GROVE, William Barry, a Representative from North Carolina; born in Fayetteville, Cumberland County, N. C., January 15, 1764; studied law; was admitted to the bar and practiced; member of the State house of commons in 1786, 1788, and 1789; delegate to the convention in 1788 called to consider the ratification of the Constitution of the United States and voted against postponement; delegate to the constitutional convention of 1789 when the Constitution was finally ratified; trustee of the University of North Carolina; president of the Fayetteville Branch of the Bank of the United States; elected as a Federalist to the Second and to the five succeeding Congresses (March 4, 1791–March 3, 1803); unsuccessful candidate for reelection in 1802 to the Eighth Congress; died in Fayetteville, N. C., March 30, 1818; interment in Grove Creek Cemetery.

GROVER, Asa Porter, a Representative from Kentucky; born near Phelps, Ontario County, N. Y., February 18, 1819; attended the common schools; moved to Kentucky in 1837; attended Centre College, Danville, Ky.; taught school in Woodford and Franklin Counties; studied law; was admitted to the bar in 1843 and commenced practice in Owenton, Ky.; member of the State senate 1857–1865; member of the Democratic State convention in 1863; elected as a Democrat to the Fortieth Congress (March 4, 1867–March 3, 1869); resumed the practice of law; moved to Georgetown, Scott County, Ky., in 1881 and continued the practice of law until his death in that city on July 20, 1887; interment in Georgetown Cemetery.

GROVER, La Fayette, a Representative and a Senator from Oregon; born in Bethel, Oxford County, Maine, November 29, 1823; attended the common schools, Gould's Academy, Bethel, and Bowdoin College, Brunswick, Maine, 1844–1846; studied law in Philadelphia, Pa., and was admitted to the bar in 1850; moved to Oregon in August 1851 and entered upon the practice of law in Salem; elected by the Territorial legislature prosecuting attorney for the second judicial district, and as auditor of public accounts for the Territory in 1851 and 1852; member of the Territorial house of representatives in 1853; appointed by the Department of the Interior as a commissioner to audit the spoliation claims growing out of the Rogue River Indian War in 1854; reelected a member of the Territorial house of representatives in 1855 and was speaker of the house; appointed by the Secretary of War a member of the board of commissioners to audit the Indian war expenses of Oregon and Washington in 1856; delegate to the convention which framed the constitution of Oregon in 1857; upon the admission of Oregon as a State into the Union was elected as a Democrat to the Thirty-fifth Congress and served from February 15, 1859, to March 3, 1859; was not a candidate for renomination in 1858; resumed the practice of law; one of the organizers of the Willamette Woolen Manufacturing Co. and was manager from 1867 to 1871; Governor of Oregon from 1870 to 1877, when he resigned, having been elected to the United States Senate; elected to the United States Senate and served from March 4, 1877, to March 3, 1883; was not a candidate for reelection; retired from public life and resumed the practice of law; died in Portland, Multnomah County, Oreg., May 10, 1911; interment in Riverview Cemetery.

GROVER, Martin, a Representative from New York; born in Hartwick, Otsego County, N. Y., October 20, 1811; attended the common schools; studied law; was admitted to the bar and commenced practice in Angelica, N. Y.; elected as a Native American Democrat to the Twenty-ninth Congress (March 4, 1845–March 3, 1847); elected justice of the supreme court of New York in November 1857 and reelected in 1859; elected judge of the court of appeals in 1867; after the reorganization of the court of appeals in 1869 was elected an associate judge in 1870 for a term of fourteen years and served until his death in Angelica, Allegany County, N. Y., August 23, 1875; interment in Angelica Cemetery.

GROW, Galusha Aaron, a Representative from Pennsylvania; born in Ashford (now Eastford), Windham County, Conn., August 31, 1823; moved to Glenwood, Susquehanna County, Pa., in May 1834; attended the common schools and Franklin Academy, Susquehanna County; was graduated from Amherst College, Amherst, Mass., in 1844; studied law; was admitted to the bar of Susquehanna County in 1847 and practiced; elected as a Free-Soil Democrat to the Thirty-second, Thirty-third, and Thirty-fourth Congresses and as a Republican to the Thirty-fifth, Thirty-sixth, and Thirty-seventh Congresses (March 4, 1851–March 3, 1863); unsuccessful Republican nominee for Speaker in 1857; served as Speaker of the House of Representatives in the Thirty-seventh Congress; delegate to the Republican National Conventions in 1864, 1884, and 1892; president of the Houston & Great Northern Railroad Co. of Texas 1871–1876; returned to Pennsylvania and engaged in lumber, oil, and soft-coal pursuits; elected to the Fifty-third Congress to fill the vacancy caused by the death of William Lilly; reelected to the Fifty-fourth and to the three succeeding Congresses and served from February 26, 1894, to March 3, 1903; declined a renomination in 1902; died in Glenwood, near Scranton, Pa., March 31, 1907; interment in Harford Cemetery, Harford, Pa.

GRUENING, Ernest, a Senator from Alaska; born in New York City, N. Y., February 6, 1887; attended Disler School and Sachs School; graduated from Hotchkiss School in 1903, Harvard College in 1907, and Harvard Medical School in 1912; gave up practice of medicine to enter journalism; reporter for Boston American in 1912; copy desk editor and rewrite man for Boston Evening Herald in 1912 and 1913; editorial writer for Boston Herald in 1913 and 1914; managing editor of the Boston Evening Traveler 1914–1916, and New York Tribune in 1917; served in the Field Artillery Corps in 1918; editor of The Nation 1920–1923; editor, New York Post, in 1932 and 1933; appointed adviser to the United States delegation to the Seventh Inter-American Conference, Montevideo, in 1933; director of the Division of Territories and Island Possessions of the Department of the Interior 1934–1939; administrator of the Puerto Rico Reconstruction Administration 1935–1937; member of Alaska International Highway Commission 1938–1942; appointed Governor of Alaska in 1939 and twice reappointed, serving until 1953; delegate to the Democratic National Conventions in 1952, 1956, and 1960; United States Senator-elect under Alaska-Tennessee Plan, Washington, D. C., provisional basis, pending statehood, in 1957 and 1958; elected as a Democrat to the United States Senate on November 25, 1958, and upon admission of Alaska as a State into the Union on January 3, 1959, in the classification of Senators from that State, drew the four-year term beginning on that day and ending January 3, 1963.

GRUNDY, Felix, a Representative and a Senator from Tennessee; born in Berkeley County, Va., on September 11, 1777; moved with his parents to Brownsville, Pa., and in 1780 to Kentucky; pursued an academic course at Bardstown, Ky.; first studied medicine, then studied law; was admitted to the bar and commenced practice in Bardstown, Ky., in 1797; member of the Kentucky constitutional convention in 1799; member of the State house of representatives 1800–1805; chosen judge of the supreme court of Kentucky in 1806, and was soon afterward, in 1807, made chief justice, which office he resigned in the winter of the same year; moved to Nashville, Tenn., in 1807 and resumed the practice of his profession; elected as a War Democrat to the Twelfth and Thirteenth Congresses and served from March 4, 1811, until his resignation in 1814; was an active factor in bringing about the War of 1812; member of the Tennessee House of Representatives 1815–1819; in 1820 was associated with Judge W. L. Brown in effecting an amicable adjustment of the State line between Tennessee and Kentucky; elected to the United States Senate to fill the vacancy caused by the resignation of John H. Eaton and served from October 19, 1829, to July 4, 1838, when he resigned to accept the position of Attorney General of the United States to which he was appointed by President Van Buren July 5, 1838; resigned December 1, 1839, having been elected to the United States Senate on November 19, 1839, to fill the vacancy in the term commencing March 4, 1839, caused by the resignation of Ephraim Foster; the question of his eligibility to election as Senator while holding the office of Attorney General of the United States having been raised, he resigned from the Senate on December 14, 1839, and was reelected the same day, serving from December 14, 1839, until his death in Nashville, Tenn., December 19, 1840; interment in Mount Olivet Cemetery.

GRUNDY, Joseph Ridgway, a Senator from Pennsylvania; born in Camden, N. J., on January 13, 1863; attended private and public schools and Swarthmore College, Swarthmore, Pa.; engaged in the textile industry and in banking at Bristol, Pa., and became president of a large woolen manufacturing concern in 1920; served as president of the Pennsylvania Manufacturers Association 1909–1930; delegate to the Republican National Conventions in 1924 and 1928; appointed as a Republican to the United States Senate to fill the vacancy caused by the refusal of the Senate to seat William S. Vare and served from December 11, 1929, to December 1, 1930, when a duly elected successor qualified; was an unsuccessful candidate for nomination to the United States Senate in 1930 to fill this vacancy; engaged in the textile industry and banking in Bristol, Pa.; died in Nassau, Bahamas, March 3, 1961; interment in Beechwood Cemetery, Hulmeville, Pa.

GUBSER, Charles Samuel, a Representative from California; born in Gilroy, Santa Clara County, Calif., February 1, 1916; attended the public schools; graduated from San Jose State Junior College in 1934, the University of California in 1937, and then took two years of graduate work; taught in Gilroy Union High School 1939–1943; engaged in farming since 1940; member of the State assembly in 1951 and 1952; elected as a Republican to the Eighty-third and to the three succeeding Congresses (January 3, 1953–January 3, 1961). *Reelected to the Eighty-seventh Congress.*

GUDGER, James Madison, Jr. (father of Katherine Gudger Langley), a Representative from North Carolina; born near Marshall, Madison County, N. C., October 22, 1855; attended the common schools at Sand Hill, N. C., and Emory and Henry College, Emory, Va.; studied law in Pearson's Law School, Asheville, N. C.; was admitted to the bar and commenced practice in Marshall, N. C., in 1872; member of the State senate in 1900; State solicitor of the sixteenth district in 1901 and 1902; elected as a Democrat to the Fifty-eighth and Fifty-ninth Congresses (March 4, 1903–March 3, 1907); resumed the practice of law at Asheville, N. C.; elected to the Sixty-second and Sixty-third Congresses (March 4, 1911–March 3, 1915); unsuccessful candidate for reelection in 1914 to the Sixty-fourth Congress; again resumed the practice of his profession; died in Asheville, N. C., February 29, 1920; interment in Riverside Cemetery.

GUENTHER, Richard William, a Representative rom Wisconsin; born in Potsdam, Prussia, on November 30, 1845; received a collegiate training; studied pharmacy and was graduated from the Royal Pharmacy in Potsdam; immigrated to the United States in July 1866 and settled in New York City; moved to Oshkosh, Wis., in 1867 and engaged in the drug business; State treasurer of Wisconsin 1878–1882; elected as a Republican to the Forty-seventh and to the three succeeding Congresses (March 4, 1881–March 3, 1889); appointed by President Harrison consul general at Mexico City January 28, 1890, and served until May 21, 1893, when he resigned; appointed by President McKinley consul general at Frankfort on the Main, Germany, November 11, 1898, and served until July 21, 1910; appointed by President Taft consul general at Cape Town, Africa, May 4, 1910, and served until his death in Oshkosh, Wis., April 5, 1913; interment in Riverside Cemetery.

GUERNSEY, Frank Edward, a Representative from Maine; born in Dover, Piscataquis County, Maine, October 15, 1866; attended the common schools, Foxcroft Academy, Eastern Maine Conference Seminary, Bucksport, Maine, Wesleyan Seminary, Kents Hill, Maine, and Eastman's College, Poughkeepsie,

N. Y.; studied law; was admitted to the bar in 1890 and commenced practice in Dover, Maine; treasurer of Piscataquis County 1890–1896; member of the State house of representatives 1897–1899; served in the State senate in 1903; delegate to the Republican National Convention at Chicago in 1908; elected as a Republican to the Sixtieth Congress to fill the vacancy caused by the death of Llewellyn Powers; reelected to the Sixty-first and to the three succeeding Congresses and served from November 3, 1908, to March 3, 1917; declined renomination to the Sixty-fifth Congress in order to enter the Republican primaries for nomination to the United States Senate, but was unsuccessful; president of the Piscataquis Savings Bank and trustee of the University of Maine at Orono; also engaged in the practice of law; died in Boston, Mass., January 1, 1927; interment in Dover Cemetery, Dover-Foxcroft, Maine.

GUEVARA, Pedro, a Resident Commissioner from the Philippine Islands; born in Santa Cruz, Laguna Province, Philippine Islands, February 23, 1879; attended the Ateneo Municipal, and was graduated from San Juan de Letran, Manila, in 1896; joined the forces fighting against Spain and assisted in promoting the peace agreement of Biakna-bato in 1897; rejoined the Filipino forces and took part in the revolution, serving throughout the Spanish-American War and the Philippine Insurrection and attaining the rank of lieutenant colonel; after the signing of the peace agreement was a member of the organization to maintain peace; engaged in journalism as an editor and special correspondent; municipal councilor of San Felipe Neri in 1907; studied law at La Jurisprudencia, and was admitted to the bar in 1909; member of the Philippine House of Representatives 1909–1912; served in the Philippine Senate 1916–1922; chairman of the Philippine delegation to the Far Eastern Bar Conference at Pekin, China, in 1921; elected as a Nationalist a Resident Commissioner to the United States in 1922; reelected in 1925, 1928, 1931, and again in 1934 and served from March 4, 1923, until February 14, 1936, when a successor qualified in accordance with the new form of government of the Commonwealth of the Philippine Islands; died in Manila, Philippine Islands, January 19, 1937; interment in Cemetario del Norte.

GUFFEY, Joseph F., a Senator from Pennsylvania; born at Guffey's Station, Westmoreland County, Pa., December 29, 1870; attended the public schools in Greensburg, Pa., Princeton (N. J.) Preparatory School, and Princeton (N. J.) University; employed in the United States Postal Service at Pittsburgh, Pa., 1894–1899; secretary of a public utilities company 1899–1901 and general manager 1901–1918; also financially interested in the production of oil; during the First World War served as a member of the War Industries Board, Petroleum Service Division, and as a director in the Bureau of Sales in the Alien Property Custodian's Office; member of the Democratic National Committee 1920–1932; elected as a Democrat to the United States Senate in 1934; reelected in 1940 and served from January 3, 1935, to January 3, 1947; unsuccessful candidate for reelection in 1946; retired and resided in Washington, D. C., until his death there on March 6, 1959; interment in West Newton Cemetery, West Newton, Westmoreland County, Pa.

GUGGENHEIM, Simon, a Senator from Colorado; born in Philadelphia, Pa., December 30, 1867; was graduated from the public schools of Philadelphia; studied languages in Europe for two years; engaged in the mining and smelting business in the United States and Mexico; moved to Pueblo, Colo., in 1888 and became associated with his brothers in the management of the Philadelphia Smelting & Refining Co.; moved to Denver in 1892; presidential elector on the Republican ticket of Roosevelt and Fairbanks in 1904; elected as a Republican

to the United States Senate and served from March 4, 1907, to March 3, 1913; was not a candidate for reelection; donor of the Simon Guggenheim Buildings at the State School of Mines in Golden, the University of Colorado in Boulder, the State Agricultural College in Fort Collins, and the State normal school in Greeley; moved to New York in April 1913; chairman of the board of the American Smelting & Refining Co. and elected president of that company in January 1919; established jointly with his wife, in 1925, in memory of their son who died in 1922, the John Simon Guggenheim Memorial Foundation for scholarships for advanced study abroad, without regard to sex, race, creed, or color, making a preliminary gift of $3,500,000; continued active in financial interests until his death in New York City, November 2, 1941; interment in Woodlawn Cemetery.

GUILL, Ben Hugh, a Representative from Texas; born in Smyrna, Rutherford County, Tenn., September 8, 1909; moved to Hereford, Deaf Smith County, Tex., in 1918; attended the public schools of Hereford, El Paso, and Canyon, Tex.; was graduated from West Texas State College at Canyon in 1933; taught in the public schools of Amarillo, Pampa, Panhandle, and Hopkins, Tex., 1929–1936; president of the Royal Crown Bottling Co., Amarillo, Tex., 1939–1942; during World War II served in the United States Navy as a lieutenant commander 1942–1945; engaged in seven amphibious landings on shore gunnery control duty and was wounded in action; awarded Bronze Star and Purple Heart Medal; returned to Pampa, Tex., in September 1945 and engaged in the real-estate business; elected as a Republican to the Eighty-first Congress to fill the vacancy caused by the resignation of Eugene Worley, and served from May 6, 1950, to January 3, 1951; unsuccessful candidate for reelection in 1950 to the Eighty-second Congress; delegate to Republican National Convention in 1952; executive assistant to the Postmaster General, Washington, D. C., from February 1953 to January 1955; was appointed a member of the Federal Maritime Board in 1955; reappointed in 1957 and served as vice chairman until his resignation December 31, 1959; engaged as a public relations consultant; resides in Washington, D. C.

GUION, Walter, a Senator from Louisiana; born near Thibodaux, Lafourche Parish, La., April 3, 1849; tutored at home until 1863; attended Jefferson College, Convent, St. James Parish; moved to Assumption Parish in 1866; deputy clerk of the court in 1870 and 1871; studied law; was admitted to the bar in 1870 and commenced practice in the Parishes of Assumption, Lafourche, and Ascension; judge of the twentieth district 1888–1892 and of the twenty-seventh district 1892–1900; attorney general of the State 1900–1912; appointed by President Wilson United States attorney for the eastern district of Louisiana in July 1913 and served until March 15, 1917, when he resigned; resumed the practice of law in Napoleonville and Convent, La.; chairman of the district exemption board, division No. 2, eastern district of Louisiana, and a member of the State council of defense during the First World War; appointed as a Democrat to the United States Senate to fill the vacancy caused by the death of Robert F. Broussard and served from April 22, 1918, until November 5, 1918, when a successor was elected; reengaged in the practice of law in New Orleans, La., until his death in that city on February 7, 1927; interment in Metairie Cemetery.

GUNCKEL, Lewis B., a Representative from Ohio; born in Germantown, Montgomery County, Ohio, October 15, 1826; pursued preparatory studies; was graduated from Farmer's College in 1848 and from the law school of Cincinnati College in 1851; was admitted to the bar and commenced practice in Dayton, Ohio, in 1851; delegate to the Republican National Convention at Philadelphia in 1856; member of the State senate 1862–1865; presidential elector on the Republican ticket of Lincoln and Johnson in 1864; appointed by Congress a member of the Board of Managers of the National Homes for Disabled Volunteer Soldiers in 1864; reappointed in 1870 to serve six years; in 1871 appointed United States commissioner to investigate frauds practiced on the Cherokee, Chickasaw, and Creek Indians; elected as a Republican to the Forty-third Congress (March 4, 1873–March 3, 1875); unsuccessful candidate for reelection in 1874 to the Forty-fourth Congress; resumed the practice of his profession; died in Dayton, Montgomery County, Ohio, October 3, 1903; interment in Woodland Cemetery.

GUNN, James, a Delegate and a Senator from Georgia; born in Virginia, March 13, 1753; attended the common schools; studied law; was admitted to the bar and commenced practice in Savannah, Ga.; served during the Revolutionary War, and as a captain of dragoons participated in the relief of Savannah, Ga., in 1782; colonel of the First Regiment of Chatham County Militia, and subsequently was promoted to the grade of brigadier general of Georgia Militia; elected to the Continental Congress in 1788 and 1789 but did not serve; elected to the United States Senate in 1789; reelected in 1795 and served from March 4, 1789, to March 3, 1801; died in Louisville, Jefferson County, Ga., July 30, 1801; interment in Old Capitol Cemetary.

GUNN, James, a Representative from Idaho; born in County Fermanagh, Ireland, March 6, 1843; immigrated to the United States with his parents, who settled in Wisconsin; attended the common schools and Notre Dame Academy, Indiana; taught school; studied law, but did not practice; during the Civil War volunteered as a private in Company G, Twenty-seventh Regiment, Wisconsin Volunteer Infantry, in 1862 and served until October 1865; was mustered out with the rank of captain; in 1866 moved to Colorado, where he resided nine years in the counties of Gilpin and Clear Creek; mayor of Georgetown, Colo., three years; moved to Virginia City, Nev., in 1875, later to California, and to Hailey, Idaho, in Wood River Valley, in 1881, and was editor of the Sentinel; member of the State senate of the first State legislature in 1890; delegate to the Trans-Mississippi Congress in Denver, Colo.; editor of the Boise Sentinel 1892–1897; unsuccessful Populist candidate for election in 1892 to the Fifty-third Congress and in 1894 to the Fifty-fourth Congress; elected to the Fifty-fifth Congress (March 4, 1897–March 3, 1899); unsuccessful candidate for reelection in 1898 to the Fifty-sixth Congress; commandant of the Idaho Soldiers' Home 1901–1903; died in Boise, Idaho, November 5, 1911; interment in St. John's Cemetery.

GUNTER, Thomas Montague, a Representative from Arkansas; born near McMinnville, Warren County, Tenn., September 18, 1826; pursued classical studies, and was graduated from Irving College in 1850; studied law; was admitted to the bar in 1853 and commenced practice in Fayetteville, Washington County, Ark., in 1853; during the Civil War served in the Confederate Army as colonel of the Thirteenth Regiment, Arkansas Volunteers; prosecuting attorney for the fourth judicial circuit 1866–1868; successfully contested as a Democrat the election of William W. Wilshire to the Forty-third Congress; reelected to the Forty-fourth and to the three succeeding Congresses and served from June 16, 1874, to March 3, 1883; was not a candidate for renomination in 1882; resumed the practice of law in Fayetteville, Ark., and died there January 12, 1904; interment in Evergreen Cemetery.

GURLEY, Henry Hosford, a Representative from Louisiana; born in Lebanon, New London County, May 20, 1788; pursued classical studies; attended Williams College, Williamstown, Mass., 1805–1808; studied law; was admitted to the bar and commenced practice in Baton Rouge, La.; elected as a Whig to the Eighteenth and to the three succeeding Congresses (March 4, 1823–March 3, 1831); served as judge of the district court at Baton Rouge until his death in that city March 16, 1833.

GURLEY, John Addison, a Representative from Ohio; born in East Hartford, Hartford County, Conn., on December 9, 1813; attended the district schools and received academic instruction; learned the hatter's trade; studied theology; pastor of the Universalist Church in Methuen, Mass., 1835–1838; moved to Cincinnati, Ohio, in 1838 and became owner and editor of the Star and Sentinel, later called the Star in the West, and also served as pastor in that city; retired from the ministry in 1850; sold his newspaper in 1854 and retired to his farm near Cincinnati; unsuccessful Republican candidate for election in 1856 to the Thirty-fifth Congress; elected as a Republican to the Thirty-sixth and Thirty-seventh Congresses (March 4, 1859–March 3, 1863); unsuccessful candidate for reelection in 1862 to the Thirty-eighth Congress; during the Civil War served as colonel and aide-de-camp on the staff of Gen. John C. Frémont at St. Louis, Mo., from August 6, 1861, until October 1, 1861, when he resigned; appointed Governor of Arizona by President Lincoln, but died in Green Township, near Cincinnati, Ohio, on the eve of his departure to assume his duties, August 19, 1863; interment in Spring Grove Cemetery, Cincinnati, Ohio.

GURNEY, Chan (John Chandler), a Senator from South Dakota; born in Yankton, S. Dak., May 21, 1896; attended the public schools and was graduated from the high school at Yankton, S. Dak., in 1914; during the First World War served as a sergeant in Company A, Thirty-fourth Engineers, United States Army, with service overseas from August 1918 to April 1919; engaged in the seed and nursery business 1914–1926; operator of a radio station at Yankton, S. Dak., 1926–1932; moved to Sioux Falls, S. Dak., and engaged in the wholesale gasoline and oil business 1932–1936; unsuccessful candidate for election to the United States Senate in 1936; elected as a Republican in 1938 to the United States Senate; reelected in 1944 and served from January 3, 1939, to January 3, 1951; unsuccessful candidate for renomination in 1950; appointed a member of the Civil Aeronautics Board March 9, 1951, reappointed in 1958 for term ending December 31, 1964; resides in Arlington, Va.

GUSTINE, Amos, a Representative from Pennsylvania; born in 1789; member of the board of managers of Mifflin Bridge Co., Mifflin County, in 1828; sheriff of Juniata County 1831–1834; awarded the contract for the first courthouse erected at Mifflintown in 1832; member of the first town council of Mifflintown in 1833; engaged in mercantile pursuits in that borough the same year; elected treasurer of Juniata County in 1837; elected as a Democrat to the Twenty-seventh Congress to fill the vacancy caused by the death of William S. Ramsey and served from May 4, 1841, to March 3, 1843; engaged in agricultural pursuits and milling; died in Jericho Mills, Juniata County, Pa., on March 3, 1844; interment in the Presbyterian Cemetery, Mifflintown, Pa.

GUTHRIE, James, a Senator from Kentucky; born near Bardstown, Nelson County, Ky., December 5, 1792; attended McAllister's Academy, Bardstown, Ky.; engaged in transporting merchandise to New Orleans in 1812; studied law; was admitted to the bar in 1817 and commenced practice in Bardstown, Ky.; appointed Commonwealth attorney in 1820 and moved to Louisville; member of the State house of representatives 1827–1829; served in the State senate 1831–1840; unsuccessful candidate for election to the United States Senate in 1835; delegate to and president of Kentucky constitutional convention in 1849; president of the University of Louisville; appointed Secretary of the Treasury in the Cabinet of President Pierce and served from March 7, 1853, to March 5, 1857; vice president and then president of the Louisville & Nashville Railroad Co. and president of the Louisville & Portland Canal Co.; member of the peace convention of 1861 held in Washington, D. C., to devise means to prevent the impending war; delegate to the Democratic National Convention at Chicago in 1864; elected as a Democrat to the United States Senate and served from March 4, 1865, to February 7, 1868, when he resigned because of failing health; delegate to the Union National Convention at Philadelphia in 1866; died in Louisville, Ky., March 13, 1869; interment in Cave Hill Cemetery.

GUYER, Ulysses Samuel, a Representative from Kansas; born near Pawpaw, Lee County, Ill., December 13, 1868; attended the public schools, Lane University at Lecompton, Kans., and the University of Kansas School of Law at Lawrence, Kans.; principal of St. John (Kans.) High School and superintendent of the city schools of St. John 1896–1901; was admitted to the bar in 1902 and commenced practice in Kansas City, Kans.; judge of the first division city court of Kansas City, Kans., 1907–1909; mayor of Kansas City, Kans., 1909–1910; elected as a Republican to the Sixty-eighth Congress to fill the vacancy caused by the death of Edward C. Little and served from November 4, 1924, to March 3, 1925; was not a candidate for election for the full term in 1924; resumed the practice of law in Kansas City, Kans.; again elected to the Seventieth and to the eight succeeding Congresses and served from March 4, 1927, until his death; one of the managers appointed by the House of Representatives in 1933 to conduct the impeachment proceedings against Harold Louderback, judge of the United States District Court for the Northern District of California; died at the Naval Medical Center, Bethesda, Md., June 5, 1943; interment in Fairview Cemetery St. John, Kans.

GUYON, James, Jr., a Representative from New York; born in Richmond, Richmond County, N. Y., December 24, 1778; pursued an academic course; appointed captain of the Second Squadron, First Division of Cavalry, in 1807; member of the State assembly 1812–1814; promoted to the rank of major in 1814, and in 1819 colonel of the First Regiment of Horse Artillery; successfully contested as a Federalist the election of Ebenezer Sage to the Sixteenth Congress and served from January 14, 1820, to March 3, 1821; was not a candidate for renomination; engaged in farming; died in Richmond, N. Y., March 9, 1846; interment in St. Andrew's Cemetery.

GWIN, William McKendree, a Representative from Mississippi and a Senator from California; born near Gallatin, Sumner County, Tenn., October 9, 1805; pursued classical studies; was graduated from the medical department of Transylvania University, Lexington, Ky., in 1828 and commenced practice in Clinton, Miss.; United States marshal of Mississippi in 1833; elected as a Democrat from Mississippi to the Twenty-seventh Congress (March 4, 1841–March 3, 1843); declined to be a candidate for renomination in 1842; moved to California in June 1849; member of the State constitutional convention in 1849; upon the admission of California as a State into the Union was elected as a Democrat to the United States Senate and served from September 9, 1850, to March 3, 1855; reelected to the United States Senate to fill the vacancy occurring at the expiration of his term, caused by the failure of the legislature to elect, and served from January 13, 1857, to March 3, 1861; connected with the Southern Confederacy and with the Mexican Imperial Government of Maximilian; returned to California and engaged in agricultural pursuits; died in New York City September 3, 1885; interment in Mountain View Cemetery, Oakland, Calif.

GWINN, Ralph Waldo, a Representative from New York; born in Noblesville, Hamilton County, Ind., March 29, 1884; attended the public schools and the preparatory school of Taylor University, Upland, Ind.; was graduated from DePauw University, Greencastle, Ind., in 1905 and from the law school of Columbia University, New York, N. Y., in 1908; was admitted to the bar in 1908 and commenced practice in New York City; during the First World War served as special counsel for the War Shipping Board and as a special representative of the Secretary of War in the European Theater; engaged in agricultural pursuits at Pawling, N. Y., in 1928; member and president of the board of education, Bronxville, N. Y., 1920–1930; trustee of DePauw University since 1923 and of Asheville (N. C.) School for Boys since 1930; author of numerous articles on agriculture and religious education; elected as a Republican to the Seventy-ninth and to the six succeeding Congresses (January 3, 1945–January 3, 1959); was not a candidate for renomination in 1958; retired to his farm, Ravenwood, Pawling, N. Y.

GWINNETT, Button, a Delegate from Georgia; born in Down Hatherly, Gloucestershire, England, in 1732; pursued an academic course; engaged in mercantile pursuits in Bristol, England; immigrated to the United States and settled in Charleston, S. C.; engaged in commercial pursuits; moved to Savannah, Ga., in 1765 and entered business as a general trader; moved to St. Catherines Island, Ga., in 1770 and engaged in planting; delegate to the Provincial Congress at Savannah in 1776; Member of the Continental Congress in 1776 and 1777; a signer of the Declaration of Independence; member of the State constitutional convention in February 1777; Acting President and commander in chief of Georgia from February to March 1777; unsuccessful candidate for Governor of Georgia; engaged in a duel May 16, 1777, with Gen. Lachlan McIntosh, which resulted in his death, near Savannah, Ga., May 19, 1777; interment probably in the Old Colonial Cemetery (later called Colonial Park), Savannah, Ga.

GWYNNE, John Williams, a Representative from Iowa; born in Victor, Iowa County, Iowa, October 20, 1889; attended the public schools and was graduated from the law department of the State University of Iowa at Iowa City in 1914; was admitted to the bar the same year and commenced practice in Waterloo, Black Hawk County, Iowa; also engaged in agricultural pursuits; during the First World War served as a second lieutenant in the Three Hundred and Thirteenth Trench Mortar Battery, Eighty-eighth Division, United States Army, 1917–1919; judge of the municipal court of Waterloo, Iowa, 1920–1926; county attorney of Black Hawk County, Iowa, 1929–1934; elected as a Republican to the Seventy-fourth and to the six succeeding Congresses (January 3, 1935–January 3, 1949); unsuccessful candidate for renomination in 1948 to the Eighty-first Congress; member of the Federal Trade Commission, Washington, D. C., 1953–1959, serving as chairman 1955–1959; retired; is a resident of Waterloo, Iowa.

H

HABERSHAM, John (brother of Joseph Habersham and uncle of Richard Wylly Habersham), a Delegate from Georgia; born at "Beverly," near Savannah, Ga., December 23, 1754; completed preparatory studies, and later attended Princeton College; engaged in mercantile pursuits; served in the Revolutionary War as first lieutenant and brigade major of the First Georgia Continental Regiment; twice a prisoner of war; Member of the Continental Congress in 1785; appointed Indian agent by General Washington; appointed commissioner to the Beaufort convention to adjust the Georgia-South Carolina boundary; member of the first board of trustees to establish the University of Georgia; secretary of the Georgia branch of the Society of the Cincinnati upon its organization; collector of customs at Savannah from 1789 until his death near Savannah, Ga., December 17, 1799; interment in Colonial Park Cemetery.

HABERSHAM, Joseph (brother of John Habersham and uncle of Richard W. Habersham), a Delegate from Georgia; born in Savannah, Ga., July 28, 1751; attended preparatory schools and Princeton College; member of the council of safety and the Provincial Council in 1775; major of a battalion of Georgia militiamen and subsequently a colonel in the Continental Army; Delegate to the Continental Congress in 1783 and 1784; member of the convention in 1788 which ratified the Federal Constitution; mayor of the city of Savannah in 1792; appointed Postmaster General of the United States by President Washington in 1795 and served until 1801; returned to Savannah and engaged in the mercantile business; president of the branch bank of the United States at Savannah, Ga., from 1802 until his death on November 17, 1815.

HABERSHAM, Richard Wylly (nephew of John Habersham and Joseph Habersham), a Representative from Georgia; born in Savannah, Ga., in Decemb r 1786; attended private schools, and was graduated from Princeton College in 1810; studied law; was admitted to the bar and commenced practice in Savannah, Ga.; appointed United States attorney and served until 1825, when he resigned, owing to a disagreement between the administration of John Quincy Adams and Gov. George M. Troup; attorney general of Georgia; moved to Clarksville, Habersham County, in 1835; elected as a State Rights Democrat to the Twenty-sixth and Twenty-seventh Congresses and served from March 4, 1839, until his death; while he lay dying, a message was received that the Democratic and Whig Parties had united to make him Governor of Georgia; died in Clarksville, Ga., December 2, 1842; interment in the Old Cemetery.

HACKETT, Richard Nathaniel, a Representative from North Carolina; born in Wilkesboro, Wilkes County, N. C., December 4, 1866; attended the Wilkesboro High School, and was graduated from the University of North Carolina at Chapel Hill in 1887; studied law; was admitted to the bar in 1888 and commenced practice in Wilkesboro, N. C.; chairman of the Wilkes County Democratic executive committee 1890–1923; member of the Democratic State executive committee 1890–1923; mayor of Wilkesboro 1894–1896; represented North Carolina at the centennial of Washington's inauguration in New York in 1889; unsuccessful candidate for election in 1896 to the Fifty-fifth Congress; elected as a Democrat to the Sixtieth Congress (March 4, 1907–March 3, 1909); unsuccessful candidate for reelection in 1908 to the Sixty-first Congress; resumed the practice of law in North Wilkesboro, N. C.; died in Statesville, N. C., November 22, 1923; interment in the St. Paul's Espiscopal Churchyard, Wilkesboro, N. C.

HACKETT, Thomas C., a Representative from Georgia; born in that State; attended the common schools; solicitor general of the Cherokee circuit 1841–1843; served in the State senate in 1845; elected as a Democrat to the Thirty-first Congress (March 4, 1849–March 3, 1851); died in Marietta, Ga., October 8, 1851.

HACKLEY, Aaron, Jr., a Representative from New York; born in Wallingford, New Haven County, Conn., May 6, 1783; attended the public schools, and was graduated from Williams College, Williamstown, Mass., in 1805; moved to Herkimer, N. Y.; elected county clerk in 1812 and again in 1815; judge advocate in the War of 1812; member of the State assembly in 1814, 1815, and 1818; elected to the Sixteenth Congress (March 4, 1819–March 3, 1821); district attorney of Herkimer County 1828–1833; again a member of the State assembly in 1837; justice of the county court of St. Lawrence County, N. Y., in 1823 and 1824; master in chancery; recorder of Utica, N. Y.; died in New York City on December 28, 1868; interment in Trinity Church Cemetery.

HACKNEY, Thomas, a Representative from Missouri; born near Campbellsville, Giles County, Tenn., December 11, 1861; moved with his parents to Jackson County, Ill., in 1864; attended the common schools of Jackson County, the Southern Illinois Normal University at Carbondale, and the University of Missouri at Columbia; studied law; was admitted to the bar September 18, 1886, and commenced practice in Carthage, Mo.; also interested in zinc and lead mines in the Joplin district; member of the State house of representatives in 1901; elected as a Democrat to the Sixtieth Congress (March 4, 1907–March 3, 1909); unsuccessful candidate for reelection in 1908 to the Sixty-first Congress; resumed the practice of law in Carthage, Mo.; delegate to the Democratic National Convention at Baltimore in 1912 which nominated Wilson and Marshall; moved to Kansas City, Mo., in 1914 and continued the practice of law; general counsel for the Missouri Pacific Railroad 1914–1932; retired from public life and resided in Kansas City, Mo., until his death there on December 24, 1946; interment in Elmwood Cemetery.

HADLEY, Lindley Hoag, a Representative from Washington; born near Sylvania, Parke County, Ind., June 19, 1861; attended the common schools of his native city, Bloomingdale (Ind.) Academy, and Illinois Wesleyan University, Bloomington, Ill.; taught school in Rockville, Ind., 1884–1889; studied law; was admitted to the bar in 1889; moved to the State of Washington in 1890 and settled in Whatcom (now Bellingham), where he practiced law until elected to Congress; elected as a Republican to the Sixty-fourth and to the eight succeeding Congresses (March 4, 1915–March 3, 1933); unsuccessful candidate for reelection in 1932 to the Seventy-third Congress; reengaged in the practice of law in Washington, D. C., until 1940, when he retired from active life and moved to Wilton, Conn.; died in Wallingford, Conn., November 1, 1948; interment in St. Matthew's Cemetery, Wilton, Conn.

HADLEY, William Flavius Lester, a Representative from Illinois; born near Collinsville, Madison County, Ill., June 15, 1847; attended the common schools; was graduated from McKendree College, Lebanon, Ill., in June 1867, and from the law department of the University of Michigan at Ann Arbor in 1871; was admitted to the bar in 1871 and commenced practice at Edwardsville, Ill.; member of the State senate in 1886; delegate to the Republican National Convention at Chicago in 1888; elected as a Republican to the Fifty-fourth Congress to fill the vacancy caused by the death of Frederick Remann and served from December 2, 1895, to March 3, 1897; unsuccessful candidate for reelection in 1896; engaged in banking; died while on a visit for his health in Riverside, Calif., April 25, 1901; interment in Woodlawn Cemetery, Edwardsville, Ill.

HAGANS, John Marshall, a Representative from West Virginia; born in Brandonville, Preston County, Va. (now West Virginia), August 13, 1838; attended the public schools; studied law at Harvard University; was admitted to the bar in 1859 and commenced practice in Morgantown; elected prosecuting attorney for Monongahela County in 1862, 1863, 1864, and 1870; law reporter for the supreme court of appeals from January 1864 to March 4, 1873; mayor of Morgantown 1866, 1867, and 1869; Republican presidential elector in 1868; member of the

State constitutional convention in 1871; elected as a Republican to the Forty-third Congress (March 4, 1873–March 3, 1875); unsuccessful candidate for renomination; member of the State house of delegates 1879–1883; elected judge of the second judicial district in 1888 and served until his death in Morgantown, W. Va., June 17, 1900; interment in Oak Grove Cemetery.

HAGEN, Harlan Francis, a Representative from California; born in Lawton, Ramsey County, N. Dak., October 8, 1914; attended the public schools of Lawton, N. Dak., and Long Beach, Calif.; moved to Long Beach, Calif., at the age of fifteen; was graduated from Long Beach (Calif.) Junior College in 1933, the University of California at Berkeley in 1937, and from the law school of the same university in 1940; was admitted to the bar in 1940 and commenced the practice of law in Hanford, Calif.; during World War II served in the United States Army from February 1943 to April 1946 as counterintelligence agent and later as head of the Denver, Colo., office of the Security Intelligence Corps; holds Reserve commission as major in Army Military Intelligence; member of the city council of Hanford in 1948; member of the State assembly 1949–1952; alternate delegate to the Democratic National Convention in 1956 and a delegate in 1960; elected as a Democrat to the Eighty-third and to the three succeeding Congresses (January 3, 1953–January 3, 1961). *Reelected to the Eighty-seventh Congress.*

HAGEN, Harold Christian, a Representative from Minnesota; born in Crookston, Polk County, Minn., November 10, 1901; attended the public and high schools; was graduated from St. Olaf College, Northfield, Minn., in 1917; engaged in railroading, in agricultural pursuits, and as reporter, editor, and publisher of a Norwegian-language newspaper 1920–1928; taught history and civics at Mandan (N. Dak.) High School in 1928; publisher and editor of the Polk County Leader, Crookston, Minn., 1928–1932; secretary to Hon. Richard T. Buckler 1934–1942; delegate to the National Rivers and Harbors Congress, Washington, D. C., in 1937; member of the Minnesota Tri-State Waters Commission in 1937; elected as a Farmer-Laborite to the Seventy-eighth Congress and as a Republican to the Seventy-ninth and to the four succeeding Congresses (January 3, 1943–January 3, 1955); unsuccessful candidate for reelection in 1954 to the Eighty-fourth Congress and for election in 1956 to the Eighty-fifth Congress; engaged in public relations work until his death in Washington, D. C., March 19, 1957; interment in Oakdale Cemetery, Crookston, Minn.

HAGER, Alva Lysander, a Representative from Iowa; born near Jamestown, Chautauqua County, N. Y., on October 29, 1850; moved in 1859 to Iowa with his parents, who settled near Cottonville, Jackson County; moved to Jones County in 1863; attended the public schools of Monticello and Anamosa; was graduated from the law department of the University of Iowa at Iowa City in 1875; was admitted to the bar in 1875 and commenced practice in Greenfield, Iowa; member of the State senate in 1891; chairman of the Iowa Republican State convention in 1892; elected as a Republican to the Fifty-third, Fifty-fourth, and Fifty-fifth Congresses (March 4, 1893–March 3, 1899); unsuccessful candidate for reelection; resumed the practice of law; moved to Des Moines in 1901 and continued the practice of his profession; engaged in banking 1911–1918; died in Des Moines, Iowa, January 29, 1923; interment in Harbach Funeral Home vault.

HAGER, John Sharpenstein, a Senator from California; born near Morristown, in German Valley, Morris County, N. J., March 12, 1818; completed preparatory studies, and was graduated from Princeton College in 1836; studied law; was admitted to the bar in 1840 and practiced in Morristown, N. J.; moved to California in 1849 and engaged in mining; practiced law in San Francisco; member of the State constitutional convention in 1849; served in the State senate 1852–1854 and 1865–1871; elected State district judge for the district of San Francisco in 1855 and served six years; elected a regent of the University of California in 1871; elected as an Anti-Monopoly Democrat to the United States Senate to fill the vacancy caused by the resignation of Eugene Casserly and served from December 23, 1873, to March 3, 1875; was not a candidate for renomination; member of the State constitutional convention in 1879; collector of customs of the port of San Francisco 1885–1889; died in San Francisco on March 19, 1890; interment in Bellefontaine Cemetery, St. Louis, Mo.

HAGGOTT, Warren Armstrong, a Representative from Colorado; born near Sidney, Shelby County, Ohio, May 18, 1864; attended the common schools, Sidney Grammar School, and Xenia (Ohio) College; was graduated from Valparaiso (Ind.) College in 1886; taught school in Dallas County, Tex., in 1886 and 1887; moved to Idaho Springs, Colo., in 1887; taught school in Russell Gulch, Gilpin County, in 1887 and 1888; school principal in Black Hawk in 1888 and 1889; superintendent of public schools at Idaho Springs, Colo., 1890–1899; studied law; was admitted to the bar in 1892 and commenced practice in 1899 at Idaho Springs, Colo.; Lieutenant Governor of Colorado 1903–1905; chairman of the Republican State convention in 1904; elected as a Republican to the Sixtieth Congress (March 4, 1907–March 3, 1909); unsuccessful candidate in 1908 for reelection to the Sixty-first Congress; moved to Denver, Colo., in 1911; judge of the district court of the second judicial district of Colorado in 1921 and 1922; president of Vermillion Oil Co., 1925–1944; resumed the practice of law until his retirement in 1951; died in Denver, Colo., April 29, 1958; interment in Fairmount Cemetery.

HAHN, John, a Representative from Pennsylvania; born in New Hanover Township, Montgomery County, Pa., October 30, 1776; attended the common schools; studied medicine and practiced; elected as a Democrat to the Fourteenth Congress (March 4, 1815–March 3, 1817); resumed the practice of medicine and also engaged in agricultural pursuits; died in New Hanover Township February 26, 1823; interment in Falkner Swamp Graveyard.

HAHN, Michael, a Representative from Louisiana; born in Bavaria, Germany, November 24, 1830; immigrated to the United States with his parents, who settled in New York City; moved to New Orleans, La., about 1840; attended the graded and high schools, and was graduated from the law department of the University of Louisiana in 1850; was admitted to the bar in 1851 and commenced practice in New Orleans, La.; elected as a Unionist to the Thirty-seventh Congress and served from December 3, 1862, to March 3, 1863; returned to New Orleans and engaged in newspaper work; appointed prize commissioner of New Orleans; elected Governor of Louisiana on February 22, 1864, and served until March 4, 1865, when he resigned; manager and editor of the New Orleans Daily Republican 1867–1871; retired to his plantation in St. Charles Parish and founded the village of Hahnville; member of the State house of representatives 1872–1876 and served as speaker in 1875; appointed State register of voters on August 15, 1876; superintendent of the United States Mint at New Orleans in 1878; district judge of the twenty-sixth district from 1879 until March 3, 1885, when he resigned; elected as a Republican to the Forty-ninth Congress and served from March 4, 1885, until his death in Washington, D. C., March 15, 1886; interment in Metairie Cemetery, New Orleans, La.

HAIGHT, Charles, a Representative from New Jersey; born at Colts Neck, Monmouth County, N. J., January 4, 1838; attended private schools in Freehold, N. J., and was graduated from Princeton College in 1857; studied law; was admitted to the bar in 1861 and commenced practice in Freehold, N. J.; member of the State house of assembly 1860–1862, and served as speaker in 1861 and 1862; commissioned a brigadier general of militia on May 27, 1861; during the Civil War was in command of Camp Vredenburgh from August 22, 1862, until the close of the war; organized, equipped, and sent to the seat of war the Fourteenth, Twenty-eighth, and Twenty-ninth Regiments; elected as a Democrat to the Fortieth and Forty-first Congresses (March 4, 1867–March 3, 1871); was not a candidate for renomination in 1870; resumed the practice of law; delegate to the Democratic National Convention at Baltimore in 1872, and served as chairman of the State delegation; appointed prosecutor of the pleas; appointed prosecuting attorney of Monmouth County in 1873 and served until his death in Freehold, N. J., August 1, 1891; interment in Maplewood Cemetery.

HAIGHT, Edward, a Representative from New York; born in New York City on March 26, 1817; attended the common schools; employed in a countinghouse early in life; later engaged in the wholesale dry-goods business and in banking; moved to Westchester, N. Y., in 1850; a director of the National Bank of New York; organized the Bank of the Commonwealth of New York City in 1856 and was its president until 1870; elected as a Democrat to the Thirty-seventh Congress (March 4, 1861–March 3, 1863); unsuccessful candidate of the Republican-Union Party for reelection to the Thirty-eighth Congress; member of the board of directors of several banks and insurance companies; died in Westchester, N. Y., September 15, 1885; interment in Trinity Church Cemetery, New York City.

HAILE, William, a Representative from Mississippi; born in 1797; moved to Mississippi and settled in Woodville, Wilkinson County; member of the State house of representatives in 1826; elected to the Nineteenth Congress to fill the vacancy caused by the death of Christopher Rankin; reelected to the Twentieth Congress and served from July 10, 1826, to September 12, 1828, when he resigned; unsuccessful candidate for reelection in 1828 to the Twenty-first Congress; delegate to the State constitutional convention in 1832; died near Woodville, Miss., March 7, 1837.

HAILEY, John, a Delegate from the Territory of Idaho; born in Smith County, Tenn., August 29, 1835; attended the common schools; moved in 1848 to Missouri with his parents, who settled in Dade County; crossed the plains to Oregon in 1853; enlisted as a private on the outbreak of the Rogue River Indian War in 1855 and subsequently promoted to lieutenant; moved to Idaho in 1862; engaged in agricultural pursuits, stock raising, and mining; elected as a Democrat to the Forty-third Congress (March 4, 1873–March 3, 1875); declined to be a candidate for renomination in 1874; member of the Territorial council of Idaho in 1880 and served as its president; elected to the Forty-ninth Congress (March 4, 1885–March 3, 1887); unsuccessful candidate for reelection in 1886 to the Fiftieth Congress; appointed warden of the Idaho Penitentiary in 1899; died in Boise, Idaho, April 10, 1921; interment in the Masonic Cemetery.

HAINER, Eugene Jerome, a Representative from Nebraska; born in Funfkirchen, Hungary, August 16, 1851; immigrated to the United States with his parents, who settled in Columbia, Mo., in 1854, and in New Buda, Iowa, in 1861; spent his boyhood on a farm near Garden Grove, Iowa, until 1873; attended the public schools of Decatur County, Garden Grove Seminary, and Iowa Agricultural College; was graduated from the law depart-

ment of Simpson Centenary College, Indianola, Iowa, in 1876; was admitted to the bar the same year and commenced practice at Aurora, Nebr., in 1877; became interested in banking and in a group of creameries in southern Nebraska; elected as a Republican to the Fifty-third and Fifty-fourth Congresses (March 4, 1893–March 3, 1897); unsuccessful candidate for reelection in 1896 to the Fifty-fifth Congress; resumed the practice of law in Aurora; moved to Lincoln, Nebr., in 1904 and continued the practice of his profession; also interested in farming and in the manufacture of creamery products; retired from active pursuits in July 1928 and moved to Omaha, Nebr., where he resided until his death on March 17, 1929; interment in Wyuka Cemetery, Lincoln, Nebr.

HAINES, Charles Delemere, a Representative from New York; born in Medusa, Albany County, N. Y., June 9, 1856; moved with his parents to Coxsackie; attended the common schools; studied telegraphy and became a train dispatcher; was assistant superintendent and superintendent of a railroad; at the age of twenty-six he turned his attention to building railways and, associated with his four brothers under the firm name of Haines Bros., built, controlled, and operated twenty-eight street, interurban, and short-line railroads in eleven States, Mexico, and Canada; settled in Kinderhook, N. Y., in 1888 and built the Kinderhook & Hudson Railroad; elected as a Democrat to the Fifty-third Congress (March 4, 1893–March 3, 1895); unsuccessful candidate for reelection in 1894 to the Fifty-fourth Congress; resumed his former business activities; president of the American Patriots; founder of the International Press Foundation in Florida in 1926; resided at Altamonte Springs, Fla., until his death there April 11, 1929; interment in Hudson Falls Cemetery, Hudson Falls, N. Y.

HAINES, Harry Luther, a Representative from Pennsylvania; born in Red Lion, York County, Pa., February 1, 1880; attended the public schools, the State normal school at Lock Haven, Pa., and Patrick's Business College at York, Pa.; engaged in the manufacture and brokerage of cigars 1906–1934; burgess of Red Lion 1921–1930; delegate to the Democratic State convention at Harrisburg in 1918; elected as a Democrat to the Seventy-second and to the three succeeding Congresses (March 4, 1931–January 3, 1939); unsuccessful candidate for reelection in 1938 to the Seventy-sixth Congress; served in the office of the State treasurer in 1939 and 1940; elected to the Seventy-seventh Congress (January 3, 1941–January 3, 1943); unsuccessful candidate for reelection in 1942 to the Seventy-eighth Congress; editor of the plant magazine of the York Safe & Lock Co. from 1943 to 1944, when he retired due to physical disability; died at Red Lion, Pa., March 29, 1947; interment in Red Lion Cemetery.

HALDEMAN, Richard Jacobs, a Representative from Pennsylvania; born in Harrisburg, Pa., May 19, 1831; pursued an academic course, and was graduated from Yale College in 1851; attended Heidelberg and Berlin Universities; United States attaché of the legation at Paris in 1853 and later occupied similar positions at St. Petersburg and Vienna; returned to Harrisburg and purchased the Daily and Weekly Patriot and Union and was its editor until 1860; delegate to the Democratic National Conventions at Baltimore and Charleston in 1860; elected as a Democrat to the Forty-first and Forty-second Congresses (March 4, 1869–March 3, 1873); was not a candidate for renomination in 1872; retired from active pursuits; died in Harrisburg, Pa., October 1, 1886; interment in Harrisburg Cemetery.

HALE, Artemas, a Representative from Massachusetts; born in Winchendon, Worcester County, Mass., October 20, 1783; received a limited education and worked on a farm; taught school in Hingham, Mass., 1804–1814; became interested in the manufacture of cotton gins in Bridgewater; member of the State house of representatives 1824, 1825, 1827, and 1828; served in the State senate 1833 and 1834; again a member of the State house of representatives 1838–1842; delegate to the State constitutional convention in 1853; elected as a Whig to the Twenty-ninth and Thirtieth Congresses (March 4, 1845–March 3, 1849); engaged in agricultural pursuits; presidential elector on the Republican ticket of Lincoln and Johnson in 1864; died in Bridgewater, Mass., August 3, 1882; interment in Mount Prospect Cemetery.

HALE, Eugene (father of Frederick Hale), a Representative and a Senator from Maine; born in Turner, Oxford County, Maine, June 9, 1836; received an academic education; studied law in Portland, Maine; was admitted to the bar in 1857 and commenced practice in Ellsworth, Maine; prosecuting attorney for Hancock County 1858–1866; member of the State house of representatives in 1867, 1868, and again in 1880; elected as a Republican to the Forty-first and to the four succeeding Congresses (March 4, 1869–March 3, 1879); unsuccessful candidate for reelection in 1878 to the Forty-sixth Congress; chairman of the Republican Congressional Committee; tendered the appointment of Postmaster General in the Cabinet of President Grant in 1874, but declined; delegate to the Republican National Conventions in 1868, 1876, and 1880; declined the appointment as Secretary of the Navy in the Cabinet of President Hayes; elected as a Republican to the United States Senate; reelected in 1887, 1893, 1899, and 1905 and served from March 4, 1881, to March 3, 1911, a longer continuous service than any other Member then in the Senate; was not a candidate for renomination; member of the National Monetary Commission; retired from public life and was a resident of Washington, D. C., until his death on October 28, 1918; interment in Woodbine Cemetery, Ellsworth, Hancock County, Maine.

HALE, Fletcher, a Representative from New Hampshire; born in Portland, Maine, January 22, 1883; attended the public schools; was graduated from English High School, Boston, Mass., in 1900 and from Dartmouth College, Hanover, N. H., in 1905; studied law; was admitted to the bar in 1908 and commenced practice in Littleton, N. H.; moved to Laconia, N. H., in 1912 and continued the practice of his profession; city solicitor of Laconia in 1915; solicitor for Belknap County 1915–1920; member of the board of education 1916–1925, serving as chairman 1918–1925; delegate to the State constitutional convention in 1918; member of the State tax commission 1920–1925; trustee of the New Hampshire Orphans' Home at Franklin in 1923; elected as a Republican to the Sixty-ninth and to the three succeeding Congresses and served from March 4, 1925, until his death in Brooklyn (N. Y.) Naval Hospital on October 22, 1931; interment in Union Cemetery, Laconia, N. H.

HALE, Frederick (son of Eugene Hale, grandson of Zachariah Chandler, and cousin of Robert Hale), a Senator from Maine; born in Detroit, Mich., October 7, 1874; attended preparatory schools in Lawrenceville, N. J., and Groton, Mass., and was graduated from Harvard University, Cambridge, Mass., in 1896; attended Columbia Law School, New York City, N. Y., in 1896 and 1897; was admitted to the bar and commenced the practice of law in Portland, Maine, in 1899; member of the State house of representatives in 1904; member of the Republican National Committee 1912–1918; elected as a Republican to the United States Senate in 1916; reelected in 1922, 1928, and again in 1934, and served from March 4, 1917, to January 3, 1941; was not a candidate for renomination in 1940; retired to private life and is a resident of Portland, Maine.

HALE, James Tracy, a Representative from Pennsylvania; born in Towanda, Bradford County, Pa., October 14, 1810; attended the public schools; studied law; was admitted to the bar in 1832 and commenced practice in Bellefonte, Pa.; appointed president judge of the twentieth judicial district in 1851; elected as a Republican to the Thirty-sixth, Thirty-seventh, and Thirty-eighth Congresses (March 4, 1859–March 3, 1865); died in Bellefonte, Pa., April 6, 1865; interment in City Cemetery.

HALE, John Blackwell, a Representative from Missouri; born in Brooks (now Hancock) County, Va. (now West Virginia), February 27, 1831; attended the common schools; studied law; was admitted to the bar in 1849 and commenced practice in Brunswick, Mo.; member of the State house of representatives 1856–1858; presidential elector on the Democratic ticket of Douglas and Johnson in 1860; colonel of the Sixty-fifth Regiment, Missouri Militia, and of the Fourth Provisional Regiment, Missouri Militia, in the United States service during the Civil War; delegate to the Democratic National Convention at Chicago in 1864 which nominated McClellan and Pendleton and at New York in 1868 which nominated Seymour and Blair; presidential elector on the Democratic ticket of Greeley and Brown in 1872; member of the Missouri constitutional convention in 1875; elected as a Democrat to the Forty-ninth Congress (March 4, 1885–March 3, 1887); unsuccessful candidate for renomination on the Democratic ticket and defeated for reelection as an Independent; resumed the practice of law; died in Carrollton, Mo., on February 1, 1905; interment in Oak Hill Cemetery.

HALE, John Parker, a Representative and a Senator from New Hampshire; born in Rochester, Strafford County, N. H., March 31, 1806; received preparatory education at Phillips Exeter Academy, Exeter, N. H.; was graduated from Bowdoin College, Brunswick, Maine, in 1827; studied law; was admitted to the bar in 1830 and commenced practice in Dover, N. H.; member of the State house of representatives in 1832; appointed by President Jackson United States attorney in 1834, and was removed by President Tyler in 1841; elected as a Democrat to the Twenty-eighth Congress (March 4, 1843–March 3, 1845); refused to vote for the annexation of Texas, although instructed to do so by the legislature; member of the State house of representatives in 1846 and served as speaker; accepted the nomination in January 1848 by the Liberty Party for President of the United States but withdrew as a candidate in August of that year; elected as the first antislavery candidate to the United States Senate and served from March 4, 1847, to March 3, 1853; unsuccessful candidate for President of the United States on the Free-Soil ticket with Julian in 1852; again elected to the Senate in 1855 to fill the vacancy caused by the death of Charles G. Atherton; reelected in 1859 and served from July 30, 1855, to March 3, 1865; appointed Minister to Spain and served from March 1865 to July 1869; returned to Dover, N. H., and died there November 19, 1873; interment in Pine Hill Cemetery.

HALE, Nathan Wesley, a Representative from Tennessee; born near Gate City, Scott County, Va., February 11, 1860; attended the common schools of Nicholasville, Va., and Kingsley Academy near Kingsport, Tenn.; taught school at Hale's Mill, Va., in 1876; moved to Knoxville, Tenn., in 1878 and engaged in the nursery business; also engaged in the wholesale dry goods business, banking, and farming; member of the State house of representatives in 1890 and 1891; served in the State senate in 1892 and 1893; unsuccessful candidate for the Republican nomination in 1902 as a Representative to the Fifty-eighth Congress; elected as a Republican to the Fifty-ninth and Sixtieth Congresses (March 4, 1905–March 3, 1909); unsuccessful candidate for reelection in 1908 to the Sixty-first Congress; delegate to the

Republican National Convention at Chicago in 1908; member of the Republican National Committee 1908–1912; moved to Los Angeles, Calif., in 1909 and engaged in the oil and real-estate business until his death in Alhambra, Calif., September 16, 1941; interment in Rose Hills Memorial Park, Whittier, Calif.

HALE, Robert (cousin of Frederick Hale), a Representative from Maine; born in Portland, Cumberland County, Maine, November 29, 1889; attended the public schools; was graduated from Portland High School in 1906, from Bowdoin College, Brunswick, Maine, in 1910, and from Oxford University, Oxford, England, in 1912; attended Harvard Law School in 1913 and 1914; was admitted to the Massachusetts bar in 1914, the Maine bar in 1917, and the District of Columbia bar in 1959; practiced in Portland, Maine, 1917–1942; during the First World War served in the United States Army in grades up to second lieutenant, with overseas service, 1917–1919; member of the State house of representatives 1923–1930, serving as speaker in 1929 and 1930; elected as a Republican to the Seventy-eighth and to the seven succeeding Congresses (January 3, 1943–January 3, 1959); unsuccessful candidate for reelection in 1958 to the Eighty-sixth Congress; resumed the practice of law in Washington, D. C., where he now resides.

HALE, Robert Safford, a Representative from New York; born in Chelsea, Orange County, Vt., September 24, 1822; attended South Royalton (Vt.) Academy, and was graduated from the University of Vermont at Burlington in 1842; studied law; was admitted to the bar and commenced practice in Elizabethtown, N. Y., in 1847; judge of Essex County 1856–1864; appointed a regent of the University of New York, New York City, in 1859; presidential elector on the Republican ticket of Lincoln and Hamlin in 1860; special counsel of the United States charged with the defense of the "abandoned and captured property claims" 1868–1870; agent and counsel for the United States before the American and British Mixed Commission under the treaty of Washington 1871–1873; elected as a Republican to the Thirty-ninth Congress to fill the vacancy caused by the death of Orlando Kellogg and served from December 3, 1866, to March 3, 1867; elected to the Forty-third Congress (March 4, 1873–March 3, 1875); was not a candidate for reelection in 1874; appointed a commissioner of the State survey April 29, 1876, in which capacity he was serving when he died in Elizabethtown, N. Y., on December 14, 1881; interment in Riverside Cemetery.

HALE, Salma, a Representative from New Hampshire; born in Alstead, Cheshire County, N. H., March 7, 1787; became a printer and in 1805 edited the Walpole Political Observatory; studied law; appointed clerk of the court of common pleas of Cheshire County; moved to Keene in 1813; elected as a Democrat to the Fifteenth Congress (March 4, 1817–March 3, 1819); was not a candidate for renomination in 1818; clerk of the supreme court of New Hampshire 1817–1834; member of the State house of representatives in 1823, 1828, and again in 1844; served in the State senate in 1824, 1825, and again in 1845 and 1846; was admitted to the bar in October 1834; secretary to the commission appointed under the treaty of Ghent for determining the northeastern boundary line of the United States; died in Somerville, Mass., November 19, 1866; interment in Woodland Cemetery, Keene, N. H.

HALE, William, a Representative from New Hampshire; born in Portsmouth, N. H., August 6, 1765; attended the public schools; was a merchant and shipowner; served in the State senate 1796–1800; member of the Governor's council 1803–1805; elected as a Federalist to the Eleventh Congress (March 4, 1809–March 3, 1811); again elected to the Thirteenth and Fourteenth Congresses (March 4, 1813–March 3, 1817); died in Dover, N. H., November 8, 1848; interment in Pine Hill Cemetery.

HALEY, Elisha, a Representative from Connecticut; born in Groton, New London County, Conn., January 21, 1776; attended the common schools; engaged in agricultural pursuits; served in the State house of representatives in 1820, 1824, 1826, 1829, 1833, and 1834; member of the State senate in 1830; captain in the State militia; elected as a Democrat to the Twenty-fourth and Twenty-fifth Congresses (March 4, 1835–March 3, 1839); engaged in civil engineering; died in Groton, Conn., January 22, 1860; interment in Crary Cemetery.

HALEY, James Andrew, a Representative from Florida; born in Jacksonville, Calhoun County, Ala., January 4, 1899; attended the public schools; during the First World War enlisted in Troop A, Second Cavalry, in April 1917; served overseas in campaigns of Chateau-Thierry, St. Mihiel, the Argonne Forest, and in the Army of Occupation; was discharged in August 1919; accountant, Sarasota, Fla., 1920–1933; general manager of John Ringling estate 1933–1943; first vice president of Ringling Circus 1943–1945 and president and director of Ringling Brothers, Barnum & Bailey Circus, Sarasota, Fla., 1946–1948; engaged in newspaper publishing and later in general printing business as president of the Halcoe Printing Co., Inc., Sarasota, Fla.; chairman of the Democratic executive committee of Sarasota County 1935–1952; member of the State house of representatives 1948–1950; delegate to the Democratic National Conventions in 1952 and 1960; elected as a Democrat to the Eighty-third and to the three succeeding Congresses (January 3, 1953–January 3, 1961). *Reelected to the Eighty-seventh Congress.*

HALL, Albert Richardson, a Representative from Indiana; born near West Baden, Orange County, Ind., August 27, 1884; attended the district school and the Paoli (Ind.) High School; was graduated from Indiana Central Business College at Indianapolis in 1906 and from Earlham College, Richmond, Ind., in 1912; principal of the high school at French Lick 1909–1911; superintendent of schools of Fairmount 1913–1917, of Waterloo in 1917 and 1918, and of Grant County 1921–1925; elected as a Republican to the Sixty-ninth, Seventieth, and Seventy-first Congresses (March 4, 1925–March 3, 1931); unsuccessful candidate for reelection in 1930 to the Seventy-second Congress and for election in 1934 to the Seventy-fourth Congress; engaged in commercial printing 1932–1942; secretary and treasurer of Driveways Contractors, Inc.; engaged in the real-estate business in Marion, Ind., where he resides.

HALL, Augustus, a Representative from Iowa; born in Batavia, Genesee County, N. Y., April 29, 1814; attended the common schools and Middleburg (N. Y.) Academy; studied law; was admitted to the bar in 1836 and commenced practice in Mount Vernon, Ohio; assistant United States marshal in 1839; prosecuting attorney of Union County 1840–1842; moved to Keosauqua, Iowa, in 1844; presidential elector on the Democratic ticket of Pierce and King in 1852; elected as a Democrat to the Thirty-fourth Congress (March 4, 1855–March 3, 1857); unsuccessful candidate for reelection in 1856 to the Thirty-fifth Congress; appointed by President Buchanan as chief justice of Nebraska Territory in 1858 and served until his death in Bellevue, Nebr., February 1, 1861; interment in Prospect Hill Cemetery.

HALL, Benton Jay, a Representative from Iowa; born in Mount Vernon, Knox County, Ohio, January 13, 1835; moved with his parents to Iowa in December 1840; attended Knox College,

Galesburg, Ill., and was graduated from Miami University, Oxford, Ohio, in 1855; studied law; was admitted to the bar in 1857 and practiced; member of the State house of representatives in 1872 and 1873; served in the State senate 1882–1886; elected as a Democrat to the Forty-ninth Congress (March 4, 1885–March 3, 1887); was an unsuccessful candidate for reelection in 1886 to the Fiftieth Congress; appointed Commissioner of Patents by President Cleveland and served from April 12, 1887, to March 31, 1889; resumed the practice of law; died in Burlington, Iowa, January 5, 1894; interment in Aspen Grove Cemetery.

HALL, Bolling, a Representative from Georgia; born in Dinwiddie County, Va., December 25, 1767; pursued classical studies; served in the Revolutionary War at the age of 16; moved to Hancock County, Ga., in 1792; held several local offices; member of the State house of representatives 1800–1802 and 1804–1806; elected as a War Democrat to the Twelfth, Thirteenth, and Fourteenth Congresses (March 4, 1811–March 3, 1817); retired to private life; moved to Alabama in 1808 and engaged in planting near Montgomery; chairman of the reception committee to welcome General Lafayette in 1824; died on his plantation, "Ellerslie," in Autauga (now Elmore) County, Ala., February 25, 1836; interment on his estate.

HALL, Chapin, a Representative from Pennsylvania; born in Busti, Chautauqua County, N. Y., July 12, 1816; attended the common schools and the Jamestown (N. Y.) Academy; moved to Pine Grove (now Russell), Warren County, Pa., about 1841 and engaged in the lumber business and mercantile pursuits; moved to Warren, Pa., in 1851 and engaged in banking; elected as a Republican to the Thirty-sixth Congress (March 4, 1859–March 3, 1861); was not a candidate for renomination in 1860; interested in the manufacture of lumber products at Louisville, Ky., Fond du Lac, Wis., and Newark, N. J., and in the manufacture of worsted goods at Jamestown, N. Y.; died in Jamestown, N. Y., September 12, 1879; interment in Lake View Cemetery.

HALL, Darwin Scott, a Representative from Minnesota; born in Mound Prairie, Wheatland Township, Kenosha County, Wis., January 23, 1844; moved with his parents to Waukaw, Winnebago County, in 1847, thence to Grand Rapids, Wis., in 1856; attended the common schools, the local academy at Elgin, Ill., and Markham's Academy, Milwaukee, Wis.; served as a private in Company K, Forty-second Regiment, Wisconsin Volunteer Infantry, during the Civil War; at the close of the war settled near Birch Cooley, Renville County, Minn., in 1866 and engaged in agricultural pursuits until 1868; auditor of Renville County 1869–1873; clerk of the district court 1873–1878; member of the State house of representatives in 1876; editor of the Renville Times, which he founded in 1876; register of the United States land office at Benson, Minn., 1878–1886; served in the State senate in 1886; elected as a Republican to the Fifty-first Congress (March 4, 1889–March 3, 1891); unsuccessful candidate for reelection in 1890 to the Fifty-second Congress; appointed chairman of the Chippewa Indian Commission by President Harrison in 1891 and served until 1893; delegate to the Republican National Convention at Minneapolis in 1892, which nominated Harrison and Reid; again appointed chairman of the Chippewa Indian Commission in 1897; member of the board of managers of the Minnesota State Agricultural Society 1905–1910; again a member of the State senate in 1906; engaged in agricultural pursuits near Olivia, Renville County, Minn., until his death there on February 23, 1919; interment in Olivia Cemetery.

HALL, David McKee, a Representative from North Carolina; born in Sylva, Jackson County, N. C., May 16, 1918; attended the public schools in Jackson County, N. C.; special student at the University of North Carolina, receiving a certificate of law in 1947 and a law degree in 1948; was admitted to the bar and in 1948 commenced the practice of law in Sylva, N. C.; served as attorney for the towns of Sylva, Dillsboro, Webster, and Jackson County; in 1952 was appointed to the Twentieth Judicial District Committee; organized the Jackson County Savings & Loan Association and served as secretary; in 1953 organized Jackson County Industries, Inc., and served as president; member of the State senate in the 1955 session; member of North Carolina Board of Water Commissioners 1955–1958; paraplegic and confined to wheelchair since fifteen years of age; farmer and cattle raiser; elected as a Democrat to the Eighty-sixth Congress and served from January 3, 1959, until his death in Sylva, N. C., January 29, 1960; interment in Webster Methodist Church Cemetery, Webster, N. C.

HALL, Edwin Arthur, a Representative from New York; born in Binghamton, Broome County, N. Y., February 11, 1909; attended the public schools, and Cornell University, Ithaca, N. Y.; engaged in the building and banking business and in agricultural pursuits; member of the Broome County Republican committee in 1935; delegate to the New York State Republican convention in 1936; member of the city council of Binghamton, N. Y., 1937–1939, resigning after his election to Congress; elected as a Republican to the Seventy-sixth Congress to fill the vacancy caused by the death of Bert Lord; reelected to the Seventy-seventh and to the five succeeding Congresses and served from November 7, 1939, to January 3, 1953; was an unsuccessful candidate for renomination in 1952; administrative aide to Hon. Richard H. Knauf, member of the State legislature, in 1953 and 1954; employed by the New York State Civil Service Commission in Syracuse, N. Y., in 1955 and 1956 and with the New York State Soil Conservation Service in 1957 and 1958; engaged in agricultural pursuits on his estate, Indian Mountain, Brackney, Pa.

HALL, George, a Representative from New York; born in Cheshire New Haven County, Conn., May 12, 1770; attended the common schools; studied law; was admitted to the bar and practiced in Onondaga County, N. Y.; moved to Onondaga, N. Y., in 1802 and continued the practice of law; postmaster of Onondaga Hollow in 1802; surrogate of Onondaga County 1800–1822; supervisor in 1811 and 1812; justice of the peace 1818–1822; member of the State assembly in 1816 and 1817; elected as a Democrat to the Sixteenth Congress (March 4, 1819–March 3, 1821); unsuccessful candidate in 1820 to the Seventeenth Congress; resumed the practice of law; died in Onondaga Valley, Onondaga County, N. Y., March 20, 1840; interment in Onondaga Valley Cemetery.

HALL, Hiland, a Representative from Vermont; born in Bennington, Vt., July 20, 1795; attended the common schools; studied law; was admitted to the bar in 1819 and commenced practice in Bennington; member of the State house of representatives in 1827; clerk of Benton County in 1828 and 1829; State's attorney 1828–1831; elected as a Whig to the Twenty-second Congress to fill the vacancy caused by the death of Jonathan Hunt; reelected to the Twenty-third and to the four succeeding Congresses and served from January 1, 1833, to March 3, 1843; was not a candidate for renomination in 1842; State bank commissioner 1843–1846; judge of the State supreme court 1846–1850; Second Comptroller of the Treasury from November 27, 1850, to September 10, 1851; United States land commissioner for California 1851–1854; returned to Vermont; Governor of Vermont 1858–1860; member of the peace convention of 1861 held in Washington, D. C., in an effort to devise means to prevent the impending war; vice president of the

Bennington Battle Monument Association; died in Springfield, Mass., December 18, 1885; interment in Bennington Center Cemetery, Bennington, Vt.

HALL, Homer William, a Representative from Illinois; born in Shelbyville, Shelby County, Ill., July 22, 1870; moved with his parents to Bloomington, Ill., in 1876; attended the public schools, and Illinois Wesleyan University at Bloomington; studied law; was admitted to the bar in 1892 and commenced practice in Bloomington, Ill.; engaged in banking and was also interested in agricultural pursuits; county judge of McLean County 1909–1914, probate judge 1909–1914, and master in chancery 1916–1918; delegate to the Republican National Convention at Chicago in 1916; elected as a Republican to the Seventieth, Seventy-first, and Seventy-second Congresses (March 4, 1927–March 3, 1933); unsuccessful candidate for reelection in 1932 to the Seventy-third Congress; resumed the practice of law and agricultural pursuits; again elected as county judge of McLean County, in 1934, and served until his retirement in 1942; died in Bloomington, Ill., September 22, 1954; interment in Park Hill Cemetery.

HALL, James Knox Polk, a Representative from Pennsylvania; born in Milesburg, Center County, Pa., September 30, 1844; educated in Pittsburgh, Pa.; studied law; was admitted to the bar November 8, 1866; elected district attorney of Elk County in 1867; reelected in 1870 and 1873; retired from practice in 1883 to engage in the coal, lumber, and railroad business and also in banking; elected as a Democrat to the Fifty-sixth and Fifty-seventh Congresses and served from March 4, 1899, to November 29, 1902, when he resigned; member of the State senate in 1902–1914; died in Tampa, Fla., January 5, 1915; interment in Pine Grove Cemetery, Ridgway, Pa.

HALL, John, a Delegate from Maryland; born near Annapolis, Anne Arundel County, Md., November 27, 1729; completed preparatory studies; studied law; was admitted to the bar and commenced practice at Annapolis; declined the office of judge of the admiralty; member of the council of safety; delegate to the Maryland convention in 1775; Member of the Continental Congress in 1775, 1777, 1780, 1783, and 1784; continued the practice of law; died on his plantation, "The Vineyard" (now known as "Iglehart"), near Annapolis, Md., March 8, 1797; interment in the family burial ground on his estate.

HALL, Joseph, a Representative from Maine; born in Methuen, Essex County, Mass., June 26, 1793; attended the common schools and Andover Academy, Andover, Mass.; moved to Camden, Maine, in 1809 and engaged in mercantile pursuits; during the War of 1812 served as ensign in 1814 in Colonel Forte's regiment, Massachusetts Militia, and was subsequently appointed colonel; deputy sheriff in 1821; sheriff in 1827; postmaster of Camden 1830–1833; elected as a Democrat to the Twenty-third and Twenty-fourth Congresses (March 4, 1833–March 3, 1837); again postmaster in 1837 and 1838; appointed measurer in the Boston customhouse in 1838 and served until 1846; naval agent at Boston 1846–1849; unsuccessful candidate for mayor of Boston in 1849; engaged in agricultural pursuits 1850–1857; clerk in the Boston (Mass.) customhouse from 1857 until his death in that city on December 31, 1859; interment in Mountain Cemetery, Camden, Maine.

HALL, Joshua Gilman, a Representative from New Hampshire; born in Wakefield, Carroll County, N. H., November 5, 1828; attended Gilmanton Academy, and was graduated from Dartmouth College, Hanover, N. H., in 1851; studied law; was admitted to the bar in 1855 and practiced in Wakefield and Dover, N. H.; solicitor of the county of Strafford 1862–1874; mayor of Dover in 1866 and 1867; member of the State senate 1871 and 1872; served in the State house of representatives in 1874; attorney of the United States for the district of Hampshire from April 1874 to February 1879; elected as a Republican to the Forty-sixth and Forty-seventh Congresses (March 4, 1879–March 3, 1883); resumed the practice of his profession; died in Dover, Strafford County, N. H., on October 31, 1898; interment in Pine Hill Cemetery.

HALL, Lawrence Washington, a Representative from Ohio; born in Lake County, Ohio, in 1819; was graduated from Hudson College in 1839; studied law; was admitted to the bar in 1843 and commenced practice in Bucyrus, Ohio, in 1844; prosecuting attorney of Crawford County 1845–1851; judge of the court of common pleas 1852–1857; elected as a Democrat to the Thirty-fifth Congress (March 4, 1857–March 3, 1859); unsuccessful candidate for reelection in 1858 to the Thirty-sixth Congress; resumed the practice of his profession; imprisoned for alleged disloyalty to the Union in 1862; died in Bucyrus, Crawford County, Ohio, on January 18, 1863; interment in Oakwood Cemetery.

HALL, Leonard Wood, a Representative from New York; born in Oyster Bay, Nassau County, N. Y., October 2, 1900; attended the public schools; was graduated from the law department of Georgetown University, Washington, D. C., in 1920; was admitted to the bar in 1921 and commenced practice in New York City; member of the State assembly in 1927 and 1928 and 1934–1938; sheriff of Nassau County, N. Y., 1929–1931; delegate to the Republican State conventions 1930–1958 and to the Republican National Conventions in 1948, 1952, and 1956; elected as a Republican to the Seventy-sixth and to the six succeeding Congresses and served from January 3, 1939, until his resignation December 31, 1952; did not seek renomination in 1952; elected surrogate of Nassau County, N. Y., in November 1952, resigning to become chairman of the Republican National Committee, serving from 1952 to 1957; President Eisenhower's personal representative at opening of the Brussels World Fair in April 1958; resumed the practice of law in Garden City, N. Y., and New York City; is a resident of Locust Valley, N. Y.

HALL, Lyman, a Delegate from Georgia; born in Wallingford, New Haven County, Conn., April 12, 1724; was graduated from Yale College in 1747; studied theology for a short time and in 1749 began preaching; later studied medicine and commenced practice in Wallingford; moved to Dorchester, S. C., in 1752, and, a few years later, to the "Midway District," Liberty County, Ga., where he continued the practice of his profession and also engaged in the cultivation of rice; member of the conventions of 1774 and 1775 held in Savannah; was a strong influence in promoting revolutionary sentiments in his State; Member of the Continental Congress 1775–1778 and in 1780; a signer of the Declaration of Independence; upon the fall of Savannah in 1778 and the capture of Sunbury, when his property was despoiled, went north with his family; resumed residence in Savannah in 1782 and again practiced medicine; Governor of Georgia in 1783; judge of the inferior court of Chatham County, which office he resigned upon moving to Burke County; died in Burke County, Ga., October 19, 1790; interment on his plantation near Shell Bluff, Burke County, Ga.; reinterment in 1848 beneath the monument in front of the courthouse on Greene Street, Augusta, Ga.

HALL, Nathan Kelsey, a Representative from New York; born in Marcellus, Onondaga County, N. Y., March 28, 1810; moved to Erie County in early youth with his parents; attended the district school; became engaged as a shoemaker and also in agricultural pursuits; studied law in Buffalo with Millard Fillmore; was admitted to the bar in 1832 and practiced in Buffalo; from 1831 to 1837 held various local county and town offices in Erie County, including deputy clerk of the county, clerk of the board of supervisors, and city attorney; member of the board of aldermen; appointed by Governor Seward in 1839 master in chancery; judge of Erie County from January 1841 to January 1845; member of the State assembly in 1846; elected as a Whig to the Thirtieth Congress (March 4, 1847–March 3, 1849); was not a candidate for renomination in 1848; appointed Postmaster General in the Cabinet of President Fillmore and served from July 23, 1850, to August 31, 1852; appointed United States district judge for the western district of New York August 31, 1852, and held the position until his death in Buffalo, N. Y., March 2, 1874; interment in Forest Lawn Cemetery.

HALL, Norman, a Representative from Pennsylvania; born on the Muncy Farms, near Halls Station, Lycoming County, Pa., November 17, 1829; was graduated from Dickinson College, Carlisle, Pa., in 1847; engaged in the iron business; elected as a Democrat to the Fiftieth Congress (March 4, 1887–March 3, 1889); engaged in banking in Sharon, Pa.; member of the commission to select a site and erect an institution for the feebleminded children of western Pennsylvania; retired from active business; died in Sharon, Pa., September 29, 1917; interment in Hall's Burying Ground, Halls Station, Pa.

HALL, Obed, a Representative from New Hampshire; born in Raynham, Bristol County, Mass., December 23, 1757; moved to Madbury, N. H., and thence to Upper Bartlett and engaged in agricultural pursuits; subsequently became an innkeeper; surveyor of highways in 1790; member of the board of selectmen 1791, 1798, 1800, 1802–1810, 1814–1819, and 1823; member of the State house of representatives in 1801 and 1802; appointed judge of the court of common pleas by Gov. John Taylor Gilman; elected as a Democrat to the Twelfth Congress (March 4, 1811–March 3, 1813); member of the State senate in 1819; died in Bartlett, Carroll County, N. H., April 1, 1828; interment in Garland Ridge Cemetery, about two miles south of Bartlett; reinterment in Evergreen Cemetery, Portland, Maine.

HALL, Osee Matson, a Representative from Minnesota; born in Conneaut, Ashtabula County, Ohio, September 10, 1847; attended the common schools; was graduated from Hiram (Ohio) College and Williams College, Williamstown, Mass., in 1868; studied law; was admitted to the bar and commenced practice in Red Wing, Minn.; member of the State senate 1885–1887; elected as a Democrat to the Fifty-second and Fifty-third Congresses (March 4, 1891–March 3, 1895); unsuccessful candidate for reelection in 1894 to the Fifty-fourth Congress; resumed the practice of law; member of the Minnesota State Tax Commission from 1907 until his death in St. Paul, Minn., November 26, 1914; interment in Oakwood Cemetery, Red Wing, Minn.

HALL, Philo, a Representative from South Dakota; born in Wilton, Waseca County, Minn., December 31, 1865; attended the common schools; studied law; was admitted to the bar in 1887 and commenced practice in Brookings, Dak. (now South Dakota); prosecuting attorney for Brookings County 1892–1898; member of the State senate 1901–1903; attorney general of South Dakota 1902–1906; elected as a Republican to the Sixtieth Congress (March 4, 1907–March 3, 1909); unsuccessful candidate for renomination in 1908 to the Sixty-first Congress; resumed the practice of law; delegate to the Republican State convention in 1923; died in Brookings, S. Dak., October 7, 1938; interment in Greenwood Cemetery.

HALL, Robert Bernard, a Representative from Massachusetts; born in Boston, Mass., January 28, 1812; entered the Boston Latin School in 1822; studied theology in New Haven in 1833 and 1834 and was ordained to the ministry, first as a Congregationalist and then as an Episcopalian; was one of the twelve original members of Garrison's Anti-Slavery Society in 1832; moved to Plymouth, Mass.; served in the State senate in 1855; elected as the candidate of the American Party to the Thirty-fourth Congress and as a Republican to the Thirty-fifth Congress (March 4, 1855–March 3, 1859); delegate to the Union Convention at Philadelphia in 1866; died in Plymouth, Mass., April 15, 1868; interment in Oak Grove Cemetery.

HALL, Robert Samuel, a Representative from Mississippi; born in Williamsburg, Covington County, Miss., March 10, 1879; attended the common schools of Williamsburg and Hattiesburg, Miss.; taught school in Hancock County, Miss., in 1894; was graduated from Millsaps College, Jackson, Miss., in 1898; owned and edited the Hattiesburg Citizen 1895–1900 and 1920–1925; was graduated from the law department of Millsaps College in 1900; was admitted to the bar the same year and commenced practice in Hattiesburg; member of the State senate 1906–1908; delegate to the Democratic National Convention at Denver, Colo., in 1908; prosecuting attorney of Forrest County 1910–1912; district attorney of the twelfth judicial district from 1912 to 1918 and circuit judge of that district from 1918 to 1929; elected as a Democrat to the Seventy-first and Seventy-second Congresses (March 4, 1929–March 3, 1933); unsuccessful candidate for renomination in 1932; employed in the legal division of the Federal Trade Commission, Washington, D. C., from 1933 until his death in Arlington, Va., June 10, 1941; interment in the Old City Cemetery, Hattiesburg, Miss.

HALL, Thomas, a Representative from North Dakota; born in Cliff Mine, Keweenaw County, Mich., June 6, 1869; moved with his parents to a homestead near Jamestown, Stutsman County, N. Dak., in 1883; attended the public schools and Concordia College, Moorehead, Minn.; construction worker for Aberdeen, Bismarck, and Northwestern Railroad, and clerk for Northern Pacific Railroad at Mandan and Fargo, N. Dak., 1887–1894; newspaper reporter at Fargo, N. Dak., 1896–1907; also engaged in agricultural pursuits; city assessor of Fargo, N. Dak., 1903–1907; member of Company B, North Dakota National Guard, 1893–1898 and 1903–1906; secretary of the Progressive Republican committee of North Dakota 1906–1912; secretary of the board of railroad commissioners 1910–1914; secretary of state of North Dakota 1912–1924; elected as a Republican to the Sixty-eighth Congress to fill the vacancy caused by the resignation of George M. Young; reelected to the Sixty-ninth and to the three succeeding Congresses and served from November 4, 1924, to March 3, 1933; unsuccessful candidate for renomination in 1932; engaged in ranching and farming in Oliver County, N. Dak.; secretary of state of North Dakota from 1942 until his retirement in 1954; died in Bismarck, N. Dak., December 4, 1958; interment in Fairview Cemetery.

HALL, Thomas H., a Representative from North Carolina; born in Prince George County, Va., in June 1773; studied medicine and practiced in Tarboro, Edgecombe County, N. C.; elected as a Democrat to the Fifteenth and to the three succeeding Congresses (March 4, 1817–March 3, 1825); unsuccessful candidate for reelection in 1824 to the Nineteenth Congress; elected to the Twentieth and to the three succeeding Congresses (March 4, 1827–March 3, 1835); resumed the practice of medicine and also engaged in agricultural pursuits; member of the State senate in 1836; died in Tarboro, N. C., on June 30, 1853; interment in Macnail-Hall Cemetery, near Tarboro, N. C.

HALL, Uriel Sebree (son of William Augustus Hall and nephew of Willard Preble Hall), a Representative from Missouri; born near Huntsville, Randolph County, Mo., April 12, 1852; was tutored privately, and was graduated from Mount Pleasant College, Huntsville, Mo., in 1873; served as superintendent of schools at Moberly, Mo.; founded an academy at Prairie Hill, Mo., and served as its president; studied law; was admitted to the bar in 1879 and practiced in Moberly, Randolph County, Mo., until 1885, when he engaged in agricultural pursuits near Hubbard, Mo.; elected as a Democrat to the Fifty-third and Fifty-fourth Congresses (March 4, 1893–March 3, 1897); declined to be a candidate for renomination in 1896; president of Pritchett College, Glasgow, Mo., 1897–1901; moved to Columbia, Mo., in 1918 and founded the Hall West Point-Annapolis Coaching School, serving as its president and supervisor from 1918 to 1930, when he retired; died in Columbia, Mo., December 30, 1932; interment in Oakland Cemetery, Moberly, Mo.

HALL, Willard, a Representative from Delaware; born in Westford, Middlesex County, Mass., on December 24, 1780; attended the public schools and Westford Academy; was graduated from Harvard University in 1799; studied law; was admitted to the bar in 1803 and commenced practice in Dover, Del.; secretary of state of Delaware 1811–1814; elected as a Democrat to the Fifteenth and Sixteenth Congresses and served from March 4, 1817, until January 22, 1821, when he resigned; unsuccessful candidate in 1820 for reelection to the Seventeenth Congress; again secretary of state in 1821; member of the State senate in 1822; appointed United States district judge for Delaware and served from May 6, 1823, until December 6, 1871, when he resigned; moved to Wilmington, Del., in 1825; compiler of the Revised Code of Delaware in 1829; delegate to the State constitutional convention in 1821; president of the Wilmington School Board 1852–1870; died in Wilmington, Del., May 10, 1875; interment in Wilmington and Brandywine Cemetery.

HALL, Willard Preble (brother of William Augustus Hall and uncle of Uriel Sebree Hall), a Representative from Missouri; born at Harpers Ferry, Jefferson County, Va. (now West Virginia), May 9, 1820; attended a private school in Baltimore, Md.; was graduated from Yale College in 1839; accompanied his father to Randolph County, Mo., in 1840; studied law; was admitted to the bar at Huntsville, Mo., in 1841 and commenced practice in Sparta, Mo., in 1842; appointed circuit attorney in 1843 and served several years; presidential elector on the Democratic ticket of Polk and Dallas in 1844; during the Mexican War enlisted as a private in the First Missouri Cavalry under Col. Alexander Doniphan, and later promoted to lieutenant; was appointed by General Kearny, together with Colonel Doniphan, to construct the code of civil laws known as the "Kearny Code" in English and Spanish for the territory taken from Mexico; elected as a Democrat to the Thirtieth, Thirty-first, and Thirty-second Congresses (March 4, 1847–March 3, 1853); moved to St. Joseph, Mo., in 1854 and continued the practice of law; unsuccessful candidate for election to the United States Senate in 1856; member of the constitutional convention of Missouri in 1861 that determined the relations of Missouri to the Union and the other States and decided in favor of the Union; provisional Lieutenant Governor of Missouri 1861–1864; as brigadier general, Missouri Militia, commanded the northwestern Missouri district until 1863; Governor of Missouri in 1864 and 1865; resumed the practice of law; died in St. Joseph, Mo., November 2, 1882; interment in Mount Moriah Cemetery.

HALL, William, a Representative from Tennessee; born in Surry County, N. C., February 11, 1775; attended the country schools; moved with his parents to New River, N. C., in 1779 and to Sumner County, Tenn., in 1785 and engaged in agricultural pursuits; served in the State house of representatives 1797–1805; brigadier general in the War of 1812; served under Jackson in the Creek War and against the British; member of the State senate 1821–1829, and served as speaker 1827–1829; served as Governor of Tennessee in 1829, succeeding Gov. Sam Houston, resigned; major general of militia; elected as a Democrat to the Twenty-second Congress (March 4, 1831–March 3, 1833); resumed agricultural pursuits; died on his farm, "Locust Land," near Castalian Springs, Sumner County, Tenn., October 7, 1856; interment in the family cemetery on his farm.

HALL, William Augustus (father of Uriel Sebree Hall and brother of Willard Preble Hall), a Representative from Missouri; born in Portland, Maine, October 15, 1815; moved with his parents to Harpers Ferry, Va.; attended the public schools and Yale College; accompanied his father to Randolph County, Mo., in 1840; studied law; was admitted to the bar in 1841 and commenced practice in Huntsville, Mo.; moved to Fayette, Mo., and continued the practice of law; presidential elector on the Democratic ticket of Polk and Dallas in 1844; judge of the circuit court 1847–1861; during the Mexican War served as captain; delegate to the State constitutional convention in 1861; elected as a Democrat to the Thirty-seventh Congress to fill the vacancy caused by the expulsion of John B. Clark; reelected to the Thirty-eighth Congress and served from January 20, 1862, to March 3, 1865; was not a candidate for renomination in 1864; delegate to the Democratic National Convention at Chicago in 1864; resumed the practice of law and also engaged in agricultural pursuits; died near Darkville, Randolph County, Mo., December 15, 1888; interment in the family private cemetery.

HALL, Wilton Earle, a Senator from South Carolina; born in Starr, Hall Township, Anderson County, S. C., March 11, 1901; attended the public schools, Starr (S. C.) High School, and Furman University, Greenville, S. C.; founded a morning newspaper in Anderson, S. C., in 1924, and in 1929 acquired an evening newspaper; in 1935 established a radio station, which serves Anderson College and Clemson College; was awarded the University of Missouri School of Journalism Silver Plaque in 1941, and again in 1944, for having rendered the greatest community service in the United States; chairman of the South Carolina Planning Board 1934–1938; chairman of the Anderson County Democratic convention in 1936; delegate to several Democratic State conventions; presidential elector in 1944 on the Democratic ticket of Roosevelt and Truman; appointed as a Democrat to the United States Senate to fill the vacancy caused by the death of Ellison D. Smith and served from November 20, 1944, to January 3, 1945; was not a candidate for election to the full term; resumed the newspaper publishing business; founded television station WAIM in 1953; is a resident of Anderson, S. C.

HALLECK, Charles Abraham, a Representative from Indiana; born in Demotte, Jasper County, Ind., August 22, 1900; attended the public schools; during the First World War served in the Infantry of the United States Army; was graduated from Indiana University at Bloomington in 1922 and from the law department of the same university in 1924; was admitted to the bar in 1924 and commenced practice in Rensselaer, Ind.; prosecuting attorney for the thirtieth judicial circuit 1924–1934; elected as a Republican to the Seventy-fourth Congress to fill the vacancy caused by the death of Congressman-elect Frederick Landis; reelected to the Seventy-fifth and to the eleven succeeding Congresses and served from January 29, 1935, to January 3, 1961; majority leader in the Eightieth and Eighty-third Congresses; minority leader in the Eighty-sixth Congress. *Reelected to the Eighty-seventh Congress and again elected minority leader.*

HALLOCK, John, Jr., a Representative from New York; born in Oxford, Orange County, N. Y., in July 1783; member of the State assembly 1816–1821; member of the State constitutional convention in 1821; elected as a Democrat to the Nineteenth and Twentieth Congresses (March 4, 1825–March 3, 1829); died in Ridgebury, N. Y., December 6, 1840; interment in the Hallock family cemetery near Ridgebury, N. Y.

HALLOWAY, Ransom, a Representative from New York; born in Beekman, Dutchess County, N. Y., about 1793; engaged in agricultural pursuits; brigade paymaster of the New York Militia in 1818; elected as a Whig to the Thirty-first Congress (March 4, 1849–March 3, 1851); died in Mount Pleasant, N. Y., April 6, 1851.

HALLOWELL, Edwin, a Representative from Pennsylvania; born near Willow Grove, Abington Township, Montgomery County, Pa., April 2, 1844; attended the public schools; engaged in agricultural pursuits; member of the State house of representatives 1876–1879; chairman of the Democratic county committee of Montgomery County in 1886; delegate to the Democratic National Convention at St. Louis in 1888; elected as a Democrat to the Fifty-second Congress (March 4, 1891–March 3, 1893); unsuccessful candidate for reelection in 1892 to the Fifty-third Congress; resumed agricultural pursuits; died in Abington, Pa., September 13, 1916; interment in Abington Friends Burying Ground, Jenkintown, Pa.

HALPERN, Seymour, a Representative from New York; born in New York City, N. Y., November 19, 1913; graduate of Richmond Hill High School; attended Seth Low College of Columbia University; reporter, Long Island Daily Press, in 1931 and 1932; feature writer, Chicago Herald Examiner, in 1932 and 1933; engaged in the insurance business; assistant to president of New York City Council, 1938–1940; member, State senate, 1941–1954; member, Temporary State Commission to Revise the Civil Service Laws, 1952–1954; impartial chairman, moving and storage industry of New York City in 1955; member, Mayor's Committee on Courts, 1956–1958; chairman of the board, The Insurist Corporation of America in 1957, and the Riverside Hospital of New York City; delegate to the President's Highway Safety Conference at the White House in 1952; unsuccessful Republican candidate from the Sixth Congressional District in 1954; elected as a Republican from the Fourth District to the Eighty-sixth Congress (January 3, 1959–January 3, 1961). *Reelected to the Eighty-seventh Congress.*

HALSELL, John Edward, a Representative from Kentucky; born near Bowling Green, Warren County, Ky., September 11, 1826; attended the common schools at Rich Pond, Ky., and Cumberland University, Lebanon, Tenn.; studied law; was admitted to the bar in 1856 and commenced practice in Bowling Green; prosecuting attorney of Warren County for four years; elected circuit judge of the fourth judicial district of Kentucky in 1870; elected as a Democrat to the Forty-eighth and Forty-ninth Congresses (March 4, 1883–March 3, 1887); unsuccessful candidate for renomination; resumed the practice of law; mayor of Bowling Green from December 5, 1888, to December 5, 1889; moved to Fort Worth, Tex., and continued the practice of law; died in Fort Worth December 26, 1899; interment in Fair View Cemetery, Bowling Green, Ky.

HALSEY, George Armstrong, a Representative from New Jersey; born in Springfield, Union County, N. J., December 7, 1827; attended the local schools and Springfield Academy; engaged in the manufacture of leather at Newark in 1844 and later in the wholesale clothing business; resumed the leather business in 1866; member of the State House of Assembly of New Jersey in 1861 and 1862; United States assessor of internal revenue 1862–1866; elected as a Republican to the Fortieth Congress (March 4, 1867–March 3, 1869); unsuccessful candidate for reelection in 1868 to the Forty-first Congress; elected to the Forty-second Congress (March 4, 1871–March 3, 1873); was not a candidate for renomination in 1872; resumed his former manufacturing pursuits; president of an insurance company; died in Newark, N. J., April 1, 1894; interment in Mount Pleasant Cemetery.

HALSEY, Jehiel Howell (son of Silas Halsey), a Representative from New York; born in Southampton, Suffolk County, Long Island, N. Y., October 7, 1788; moved to Herkimer County in 1793 with his parents, who settled in what is now the town of Lodi, Seneca County; attended the common schools; engaged in agricultural pursuits; county clerk of Seneca County 1819–1821; elected as a Jacksonian Democrat to the Twenty-first Congress (March 4, 1829–March 3, 1831); resumed agricultural pursuits; member of the State senate 1832–1835; surrogate of Seneca County 1837–1843; supervisor of the town of Lodi 1845–1846; died in Lodi, Seneca County, N. Y., December 5, 1867; interment in West Lodi Cemetery.

HALSEY, Nicoll (son of Silas Halsey), a Representative from New York; born in Southampton, Suffolk County, Long Island, N. Y., March 8, 1782; moved to Herkimer County in 1793 with his parents, who settled in what is now the town of Lodi, Seneca County; attended the common schools; moved to Tompkins County and settled near Trumansburg in 1808; engaged in agricultural pursuits and milling; supervisor for Ulysses in 1812, 1814, 1815, 1818, 1821, and 1826; member of the State assembly in 1816 and again in 1824; sheriff of Tompkins County 1819–1821; foreman of the grand jury that indicted one Hyde in a famous slave case; elected as a Democrat to the Twenty-third Congress (March 4, 1833–March 3, 1835); was not a candidate for renomination in 1834; appointed judge of the Tompkins County Court on February 11, 1834; resumed the milling business; died while on a visit in Marshall, Calhoun County, Mich., March 3, 1865; interment in Grove Cemetery, Trumansburg, N. Y.

HALSEY, Silas (father of Jehiel Howell Halsey and Nicoll Halsey), a Representative from New York; born in Southampton, Long Island, N. Y., October 6, 1743 (old style); attended the public schools; studied medicine at Elizabethtown (later Elizabeth), N. J.; returned to Southampton and practiced medicine from 1764 to 1776; resided three years in Killingsworth, Conn., during the Revolutionary War, when he again returned to Southampton, N. Y.; undersheriff of Suffolk County 1784–1787; sheriff 1787–1792; moved to Herkimer County in 1793 and settled in what is now the town of Lodi, Seneca County, and continued the practice of medicine; also erected and operated a grist mill; supervisor of the town of Ovid 1794–1804; member of the State assembly from Onondaga County in 1797 and 1798 and from Cayuga County in 1800, 1801, 1803, and 1804; member of the State constitutional convention in 1801; clerk of Seneca County 1804–1813 and 1815; elected as a Democrat to the Ninth Congress (March 4, 1805–March 3, 1807); served in the State senate in 1808 and 1809; engaged in farming; died at Lodi, Seneca County, N. Y., November 19, 1832; interment in Old Halsey Cemetery, South Lodi, N. Y.

HALSEY, Thomas Jefferson, a Representative from Missouri; born in Dover, Morris County, N. J., May 4, 1863; in 1878 moved to Missouri with his parents, who settled on a farm near Holden, Johnson County; attended public and private schools, Home Academy at Holden, Mo., Holden (Mo.) College, the State normal school at Warrensburg, Mo., and the University of Missouri at Columbia; taught school in 1880 and 1881; engaged in the mercantile business at Holden, Mo., in 1882; member of the State Republican committee 1896–1898; delegate to the Republican State conventions in 1896, 1908, and 1912; mayor of Holden 1902–1904; moved to Sedalia, Mo., in 1904 and engaged in the wholesale tea and coffee business; member of the executive committee of the Missouri State Roads Commission 1906–1910; moved to Glendale, Calif., in 1910 and engaged in the mercantile business; returned to Holden, Mo., in 1911 and engaged in the milling and grain business; member of the Holden Board of Education in 1911 and 1912; member of the board of regents, Central Missouri Teachers College at Warrensburg, 1928–1932; elected as a Republican to the Seventy-first Congress (March 4, 1929–March 3, 1931); unsuccessful candidate for reelection in 1930 to the Seventy-second Congress; returned to former business activities in Holden, Mo.; died in Westfield, N. J., March 17, 1951; interment in Holden Cemetery, Holden, Mo.

HALSTEAD, William, a Representative from New Jersey; born in Elizabeth, N. J., June 4, 1794; was graduated from Princeton College in 1812; studied law; was admitted to the bar in 1816 and commenced practice in Trenton, N. J.; appointed State supreme court reporter November 23, 1821, and served until 1832; published seven volumes of Halstead's Law Reports; prosecuting attorney of Hunterdon County 1824–1829 and 1833–1837; elected as a Whig to the Twenty-fifth Congress (March 4, 1837–March 3, 1839); presented credentials as a Member-elect to the Twenty-sixth Congress but the House declined to seat him; elected to the Twenty-seventh Congress (March 4, 1841–March 3, 1843); appointed by President Taylor United States district attorney for New Jersey and served from 1849 to 1853; raised the First Regiment of Volunteer Cavalry of New Jersey for the Civil War and served as colonel until February 18, 1862; retired from public life and died in Trenton, Mercer County, N. J., March 4, 1878; interment in Riverview Cemetery.

HALTERMAN, Frederick, a Representative from Pennsylvania; born in Vegesack on the Weser, part of the old Hanse town of Bremen, Germany, on October 22, 1831; attended high school; immigrated to the United States and settled in Philadelphia in September 1849; engaged in the grocery business, from which he retired in 1891; elected a member of the select council in 1880 for a term of three years; elected as a Republican to the Fifty-fourth Congress (March 4, 1895–March 3, 1897); was an unsuccessful candidate for reelection in 1896 to the Fifty-fifth Congress; elected president of the twelfth sectional school board of Philadelphia, Pa., in 1898 and served until his death; died in Philadelphia, Pa., March 22, 1907; interment in Laurel Hill Cemetery.

HALVORSON, Kittel, a Representative from Minnesota; born in Telemarken, Norway, December 15, 1846; in 1848 immigrated to the United States with his parents, who settled near White Water, Walworth County, Wis.; moved to Columbia County and then to Winnebago County; attended the public schools in Winchester, Wis.; during the Civil War enlisted in Company C, First Regiment, Wisconsin Heavy Artillery, in 1863, and served until the close of the war; moved to Minnesota in November 1865 and settled near Belgrade, Stearns County; engaged in agricultural pursuits and stock raising; justice of the peace 1870–1875; chairman of the board of supervisors 1870–1880; township assessor in 1880; town clerk 1880–1891; member of the State house of representatives 1886–1888; elected as the candidate of the Farmers' Alliance and the Prohibitionists to the Fifty-second Congress (March 4, 1891–March 3, 1893); un-

successful candidate for reelection in 1892 to the Fifty-third Congress; resumed agricultural pursuits near Brooten, Stearns County, Minn.; alternate delegate to the People's Party National Convention in 1896; moved to Tewaukon Township, Sargent County, N. Dak., in 1900 and engaged in agricultural pursuits; returned to Minnesota in 1910 and resumed farming in North Fork until 1924, when he retired from active pursuits; died in Havana, N. Dak., on July 12, 1936, while on a visit with his daughter; interment in Big Grove Church Cemetery, North Fork Township, near Brooten, Minn.

HAMBLETON, Samuel, a Representative from Maryland; born at "Waterloo" farm, Talbot County, Md., January 8, 1812; educated by private tutors and attended Easton Academy; studied law; was admitted to the bar in 1833 and commenced practice in Easton, Talbot County, Md.; member of the State house of delegates in 1834 and 1835; State's attorney for Talbot County 1836–1844; served in the State senate 1844–1850; presidential elector on the Democratic ticket of Polk and Dallas in 1844; president of the Chesapeake & Ohio Canal in 1853 and 1854; again a member of the State house of delegates in 1853; elected as a Democrat to the Forty-first and Forty-second Congresses (March 4, 1869–March 3, 1873); died in Easton, Md., December 9, 1886; interment in Spring Hill Cemetery.

HAMER, Thomas Lyon (uncle of Thomas Ray Hamer), a Representative from Ohio; born in Northumberland County, Pa., in July 1800; attended the public schools; moved to Ohio in 1817 and taught school; studied law; was admitted to the bar in 1821 and commenced practice in Georgetown, Brown County, Ohio; member of the State house of representatives in 1825, 1828, and 1829, and served as speaker in 1829; elected as a Democrat to the Twenty-third, Twenty-fourth, and Twenty-fifth Congresses (March 4, 1833–March 3, 1839); nominated Ulysses S. Grant to be a cadet at the United States Military Academy at West Point; volunteered as a private for the Mexican War and received the next day, July 1, 1846, the commission of brigadier general; had been elected to the Thirtieth Congress, but died in the service at Monterey, Mexico, December 2, 1846; on March 2, 1847, Congress passed a resolution of sorrow and as an expression of their deep regret presented his nearest male relative with a sword; interment near Monterey, Mexico; reinterment in Georgetown Cemetery, Georgetown, Ohio.

HAMER, Thomas Ray (nephew of Thomas Lyon Hamer), a Representative from Idaho; born in Vermont, Fulton County, Ill., May 4, 1864; attended the public schools, Hedding College, and Bloomington Law School; was admitted to the bar and commenced practice in St. Anthony, Idaho, in 1893; engaged in agricultural pursuits in Fremont County, Idaho; member of the State house of representatives in 1896; enlisted in April 1898 as a private in the First Regiment, Idaho Volunteer Infantry, during the war with Spain; served as captain and lieutenant colonel in that regiment and was wounded at the Battle of Caloocan, Philippine Islands, February 11, 1899; Military Governor of the island of Cebu; associate justice of the supreme court of the Philippine Islands; mustered out at San Francisco, Calif., as lieutenant colonel of the Thirty-seventh Regiment, United States Volunteer Infantry, on May 27, 1901, when he returned to St. Anthony, Idaho; delegate to the Republican State conventions in 1908 and 1912; elected as a Republican to the Sixty-first Congress (March 4, 1909–March 3, 1911); unsuccessful candidate for renomination in 1910; resumed the practice of law in St. Anthony, Idaho; engaged in banking at St. Anthony and Boise, Idaho, 1912–1921; served as major and lieutenant colonel, Judge Advocate General's Department, during the First World War; reengaged in the practice of law at Portland,

Oreg., until 1943, when he retired and moved to Los Angeles, Calif.; died in a rest home at Phoenix, Ariz., December 22, 1950; interment in Greenwood Memorial Park.

HAMILL, James Alphonsus, a Representative from New Jersey; born in Jersey City, N. J., March 30, 1877; attended St. Bridget's Academy; was graduated from St. Peter's College, Jersey City, N. J., in 1897 and from the New York Law School in 1899; was admitted to the bar in 1900 and commenced practice in Jersey City, N. J.; member of the State house of assembly 1902–1905; delegate to the Democratic National Convention at Denver in 1908, which nominated Bryan and Kern; elected as a Democrat to the Sixtieth and to the six succeeding Congresses (March 4, 1907–March 3, 1921); was not a candidate for renomination in 1920; resumed the practice of law in New Jersey and New York; represented the Ukrainian people of the United States at the Peace Conference in Paris in 1919; decorated Chevalier of the French Legion of Honor for work in French literature; corporation counsel of Jersey City 1932–1941; died in Jersey City, December 15, 1941; interment in Holy Name Cemetery.

HAMILL, Patrick, a Representative from Maryland; born in Allegany County, near Altamont, Md., April 28, 1817; attended the common schools in Westernport; engaged in the real-estate business and mercantile pursuits; collector of taxes in 1841 and 1842; member of the State house of delegates in 1843 and 1844; judge of the orphans' court of Allegany County 1854–1869 and elected chief judge in 1867; elected as a Democrat to the Forty-first Congress (March 4, 1869–March 3, 1871); was not a candidate for renomination in 1870; engaged in the real-estate business until his death in Oakland, Garrett County, Md., January 15, 1895; interment in Odd Fellows Cemetery.

HAMILTON, Alexander, a Delegate from New York; born on the island of Nevis, British West Indies, January 11, 1757; immigrated to the United States in 1772, where he received educational training in the schools of Elizabethtown, N. J., and King's College (now Columbia University), New York City; entered the Continental Army in New York in 1776 as captain of Artillery; appointed aide-de-camp to General Washington March 1, 1777, and served in that capacity until February 16, 1781; led a storming party in the Battle of Yorktown; Member of the Continental Congress in 1782, 1783, 1787, and 1788; member of the Annapolis Convention of 1786; served in the New York State assembly in 1787; member of the Philadelphia Constitutional Convention in 1787 which adopted the Constitution of the United States; member of the State constitutional convention in 1788; studied law; was admitted to the bar and practiced in New York City; Secretary of the Treasury in the Cabinet of President Washington 1789–1795; returned to New York and resumed the practice of law; mortally wounded in a duel with Aaron Burr at Weehawken on the Hudson, and died in New York City the following day, July 12, 1804; interment in Trinity Churchyard.

HAMILTON, Andrew Holman, a Representative from Indiana; born in Fort Wayne, Ind., June 7, 1834; attended the common schools, and was graduated from Wabash College, Crawfordsville, Ind., in 1854; studied law at Harvard University; was admitted to the bar in 1859 and commenced practice in Fort Wayne, Ind.; elected as a Democrat to the Forty-fourth and Forty-fifth Congresses (March 4, 1875–March 3, 1879); resumed the practice of law; died in Fort Wayne, Ind., May 9, 1895; interment in Lindenwood Cemetery.

HAMILTON, Andrew Jackson (brother of Morgan Calvin Hamilton), a Representative from Texas; born in Huntsville, Madison County, Ala., January 28, 1815; attended the common schools; studied law; was admitted to the bar in Talladega, Ala., in 1841; moved to Texas and commenced the practice of law in Lagrange, Fayette County, in 1846; attorney general of the State in 1850; member of the State house of representatives 1851–1853; presidential elector on the Democratic ticket of Buchanan and Breckinridge in 1856; elected as an Independent Democrat to the Thirty-sixth Congress (March 4, 1859–March 3, 1861); was not a candidate for renomination in 1860; moved to New Orleans, La., in 1862; during the Civil War was commissioned brigadier general of Volunteers November 14, 1862; appointed by President Lincoln Military Governor of Texas in 1862; appointed provisional Governor by President Johnson in 1865; justice of the supreme court of Texas in 1866; delegate to the Loyalist convention at Philadelphia in 1866; unsuccessful candidate for Governor of Texas in 1869; died in Austin, Tex., April 11, 1875; interment in Oakwood Cemetery.

HAMILTON, Charles Mann, a Representative from New York; born in Ripley, Chautauqua County, N. Y., January 23, 1874; attended the Ripley High School, the Fredonia (N. Y.) Normal School, and the Pennsylvania Military College at Chester; interested in agricultural pursuits and in oil production; member of the State assembly 1906–1908; served in the State senate 1908–1912; represented the senate in 1911 on the New York State Factory Commission; delegate to the Republican National Convention at Chicago in 1912; elected as a Republican to the Sixty-third, Sixty-fourth, and Sixty-fifth Congresses (March 4, 1913–March 3, 1919); was not a candidate for renomination in 1918; engaged in agricultural pursuits in Ripley, N. Y., and in the production of oil and gas in Kansas; died in Miami Beach, Fla., on January 3, 1942; interment in Quincy Rural Cemetery, Ripley, N. Y.

HAMILTON, Charles Memorial, a Representative from Florida; born in Pine Creek Township, Clinton County, Pa., November 1, 1840; attended the public schools and was graduated from the Columbia Law School, Columbia, Pa.; during the Civil War entered the Union Army as a private in 1861 and served in Company A, Fifth Regiment, Pennsylvania Reserve Corps; captured at Fredericksburg and confined in Libby Prison, Richmond, Va., until February 1863, when he was exchanged; was made ensign and transferred to the Veterans' Reserve Corps; promoted to the rank of first lieutenant and later to captain; appointed judge advocate of the general court martial and general pass officer for the Army of the Potomac; served on the staff of the Military Governor of Washington, D. C., until transferred to Marianna, Fla., in 1865; was admitted to the bar in 1867 and commenced practice in Marianna, Fla.; upon the readmission of the State of Florida to representation was elected as a Republican to the Fortieth and Forty-first Congresses and served from July 1, 1868, to March 3, 1871; unsuccessful candidate for renomination in 1870; appointed senior major general of the Florida Militia in February 1871; postmaster of Jacksonville, Fla., from July 27, 1871, to March 1, 1872; appointed collector of customs at Key West, Fla., in February 1873; resigned on account of ill health; died in Pine Creek Township, Clinton County, Pa., October 22, 1875; interment in Jersey Shore Cemetery.

HAMILTON, Cornelius Springer, a Representative from Ohio; born in Gratiot, Muskingum County, Ohio, January 2, 1821; attended the common schools and Granville (Ohio) College; moved with his parents to Union County in 1839; engaged in agricultural pursuits with his father; studied law; was admitted to the bar in 1845 and commenced practice in Marysville, Ohio; land appraiser and assessor in 1845; delegate to the State constitutional convention 1850–1851; editor and proprietor of the Marysville Tribune 1850–1853; member of the State senate in

1856 and 1857; appointed by President Lincoln assessor of the eighth congressional district of Ohio in 1862 and served until 1866; elected as a Republican to the Fortieth Congress and served from March 4, 1867, until killed by an insane son in Marysville, Union County, Ohio, December 22, 1867; interment in Oakdale Cemetery.

HAMILTON, Daniel Webster, a Representative from Iowa; born near Dixon, Ogle County, Ill., December 20, 1861; moved to Miami County, Kans., with his parents in 1868 and to Prairie Township, Keokuk County, Iowa, in 1874; attended the country schools, and was graduated from the law department of the University of Iowa at Iowa City in June 1884; was admitted to the bar in 1884 and commenced practice in Sigourney, Iowa; postmaster of Sigourney 1894–1898; elected as a Democrat to the Sixtieth Congress (March 4, 1907–March 3, 1909; unsuccessful candidate for reelection in 1908 to the Sixty-first Congress; resumed the practice of law in Sigourney, Iowa; moved to Grinnell, Iowa, when elected judge of the district court of the sixth judicial district of Iowa in 1918, in which capacity he served until his death in a hospital in Rochester, Minn., August 21, 1936; interment in No. 16 Cemetery, near Thornburg, in Keokuk County, Iowa.

HAMILTON, Edward La Rue, a Representative from Michigan; born in Niles Township, Berrien County, Mich., December 9, 1857; attended the graded schools, and was graduated from the Niles High School in 1876; studied law; was admitted to the bar in 1884 and commenced practice in Niles, Mich.; elected as a Republican to the Fifty-fifth and to the eleven succeeding Congresses (March 4, 1897–March 3, 1921); was not a candidate for renomination in 1920; engaged in the practice of law until his death in St. Joseph, Berrien County, Mich., November 2, 1923; interment in Silverbrook Cemetery, Niles, Mich.

HAMILTON, Finley, a Representative from Kentucky; born in Vincent, Owsley County, Ky., June 19, 1886; attended the public schools and Berea (Ky.) College; studied law; was admitted to the bar in 1915 and commenced practice in London, Laurel County, Ky.; was with the Signal Corps, United States Army, with service in the Philippine Islands and Alaska, from 1907 to 1915, and during the First World War enlisted on March 18, 1916; commissioned a first lieutenant and later a captain and served in Company D, Three Hundred and Fifteenth Field Signal Battalion, Ninetieth Division, with service in France, until discharged on July 31, 1919; elected as a Democrat to the Seventy-third Congress (March 4, 1933–January 3, 1935); was not a candidate for renomination in 1934; resumed the practice of law; died in London, Ky., January 10, 1940; interment in Pine Grove Cemetery.

HAMILTON, James, Jr., a Representative from South Carolina; born in Charleston, S. C., May 8, 1786; completed academic studies; studied law; was admitted to the bar and commenced practice in Charleston; served in the War of 1812 as major; mayor of Charleston; member of the State house of representatives; elected as a State Rights Free Trader to the Seventeenth Congress to fill the vacancy caused by the resignation of William Lowndes; reelected to the Eighteenth, Nineteenth, and Twentieth Congresses and served from December 13, 1822, to March 3, 1829; Governor of South Carolina 1830–1832; moved to Texas; was drowned on November 15, 1857, while on his way from New Orleans to Galveston.

HAMILTON, John, a Representative from Pennsylvania; born in York (now Adams) County, Pa., November 25, 1754; moved to Washington County, Pa., in 1783; commissioned lieutenant

colonel of militia in 1786 and brigadier general in 1800; major general of the Fourteenth Division of Militia of Washington and Greene Counties in 1807; appointed high sheriff of Washington County by Governor Mifflin in 1793 and served until November 1, 1796; member of the State senate 1796–1805; associate judge of Washington County 1802–1805; member of the first board of trustees of Jefferson (now Washington and Jefferson) College, Washington, Pa., 1802–1831; presidential elector on the Jefferson ticket in 1804 and on the Monroe ticket in 1820; elected as a Democrat to the Ninth Congress (March 4, 1805–March 3, 1807); again appointed associate judge of Washington County on May 31, 1820, and served until his death at his home near Ginger Hill, Washington County, Pa., August 22, 1837; interment in Mingo Cemetery, near Monongahela, Pa.

HAMILTON, John M., a Representative from West Virginia; born in Weston, Lewis County, Va. (now West Virginia), March 16, 1855; attended the public schools; recorder of the town of Weston in 1876; studied law; was admitted to the bar in 1877 and commenced practice in Grantsville, Calhoun County, W. Va.; committee clerk in the State senate 1881 and 1882; assistant clerk of the senate 1883–1887; resumed the practice of law in 1887; member of the State house of delegates 1887 and 1888; clerk of the house of delegates 1888–1890; also engaged in banking and served as president of the Calhoun County Bank 1901–1916; elected as a Democrat to the Sixty-second Congress (March 4, 1911–March 3, 1913); unsuccessful candidate for reelection in 1912 to the Sixty-third Congress and for election in 1914 to the Sixty-fourth Congress; resumed the practice of law; served as president of the Calhoun County High School Board; died in Grantsville, W. Va., on December 27, 1916; interment in Odd Fellows Cemetery, Old Bethlehem, W. Va.

HAMILTON, John Taylor, a Representative from Iowa; born near Geneseo, Henry County, Ill., October 16, 1843; attended the common schools and the Geneseo Academy; moved to Cedar Rapids, Iowa, in 1868, and engaged in the wholesale farm-implement and seed business; mayor of Cedar Rapids in 1878; member of the Linn County Board of Supervisors 1882–1884; president of Cedar Rapids Savings Bank and director of the electric light company; member of the State house of representatives 1885–1891 and served as speaker for one term; elected as a Democrat to the Fifty-second Congress (March 4, 1891–March 3, 1893); unsuccessful candidate for reelection in 1892 to the Fifty-third Congress; resumed his former business pursuits in Cedar Rapids; member of the board of control of State institutions; unsuccessful candidate for Governor of Iowa in 1914; died in Cedar Rapids, Iowa, January 25, 1925; interment in Oak Hill Cemetery.

HAMILTON, Morgan Calvin (brother of Andrew Jackson Hamilton), a Senator from Texas; born near Huntsville, Madison County, Ala., February 25, 1809; attended the public schools; engaged in mercantile pursuits in Elyton, Ala.; moved to the Republic of Texas in 1837; clerk in the War Department of the Republic of Texas 1839–1845 and acted as Secretary of War and Marine ad interim of that Republic from December 9, 1844, to March 10, 1845; appointed comptroller of the treasury of Texas in 1867; delegate to the State constitutional convention in 1868; upon the readmission of the State of Texas to representation was elected on February 22, 1870, as a Republican to the United States Senate to fill the vacancy in the term ending March 3, 1871; subsequently elected for the term commencing March 4, 1871, and served from March 30, 1870, to March 3, 1877; retired from public life and traveled extensively; was a resident of Brooklyn, N. Y., until his death; died in San Diego, Calif., where he had been visiting, November 21, 1893; interment to Oakwood Cemetery, Austin, Travis County, Tex.

HAMILTON, Norman Rond, a Representative from Virginia; born in Portsmouth, Norfolk County, Va., November 13, 1877; attended the public and high schools; newspaper reporter in Norfolk 1895–1914; publisher of the Portsmouth (Va.) Star from 1917 until merged with Norfolk Ledger in 1955; presidential elector on the Democratic ticket of Wilson and Marshall in 1912; collector of customs of Virginia 1914–1922; chairman of the Port War Board of Hampton Roads 1916–1918; served as neutrality enforcement officer prior to the entrance of the United States in the First World War and interned the German ships *Prinz Eitel Friedrich, Kronprinz Wilhelm,* and *Appam;* commended by President Wilson for services during neutrality; delegate to the Democratic National Conventions in 1924, 1928, 1932, 1952, and 1960; trustee of Virginia State Teachers' College 1922–1926; appointed in 1933 as receiver at Washington, D. C., of five District of Columbia insolvent banks, resigning in June 1936 to become a candidate for Congress; elected as a Democrat to the Seventy-fifth Congress (January 3, 1937–January 3, 1939); unsuccessful candidate for renomination in 1938 and for election in 1941 to fill a vacancy in the Seventy-seventh Congress; executive of the Norfolk-Portsmouth Newspapers, Inc.; member of Virginia State Ports Authority 1956– ; member of Virginia State Committee 350th Anniversity Festival Landing of First Permanent English Settlers at Jamestown, Va., in 1957; is a resident of Portsmouth, Va.

HAMILTON, Robert, a Representative from New Jersey; born in Hamburg, Sussex County, N. J., December 9, 1809; attended the common schools; moved to Newton, N. J., in 1831; studied law; was admitted to the bar in 1836 and commenced practice in Newton; prosecutor of pleas of Sussex County 1848–1858, 1868, and 1869; delegate to the Democratic National Conventions at Charleston and Baltimore in 1860; member of the State house of assembly 1863 and 1864 and served as speaker; president of the Merchant's National Bank 1865–1878; elected as a Democrat to the Forty-third and Forty-fourth Congresses (March 4, 1873–March 3, 1877); resumed the practice of law; director of the Morris & Essex Railroad Co.; died in Newton, Sussex County, N. J., March 14, 1878; interment in Newton Cemetery.

HAMILTON, William Thomas, a Representative and a Senator from Maryland; born in Boonsboro, Washington County, Md., September 8, 1820; attended Brown's School, Boonsboro, Md., and Jefferson College, Canonsburg, Pa.; studied law; was admitted to the bar in 1843 and commenced practice in Hagerstown; member of the State house of delegates in 1848; presidential elector on the Democratic ticket of Cass and Butler in 1848; elected as a Democrat to the Thirty-first, Thirty-second, and Thirty-third Congresses (March 4, 1849–March 3, 1855); was not a candidate for renomination in 1854; resumed the practice of his profession in Hagerstown, Md.; elected to the United States Senate and served from March 4, 1869, to March 3, 1875; was not a candidate for reelection in 1874; Governor of Maryland 1879–1883; continued the practice of law until his death in Hagerstown, Md., October 26, 1888; interment in Rose Hill Cemetery.

HAMLIN, Courtney Walker (cousin of William Edward Barton), a Representative from Missouri; born in Brevard, Transylvania County, N. C., October 27, 1858; in 1869 moved to Missouri with his parents, who settled in Leasburg, Crawford County; attended the common schools and Salem (Mo.) Academy; studied law; was admitted to the bar in 1882 and commenced practice in Bolivar, Polk County, Mo.; elected as a Democrat to the Fifty-eighth Congress (March 4, 1903–March 3, 1905); unsuccessful candidate for reelection in 1904 to the Fifty-ninth

Congress; elected to the Sixtieth and to the five succeeding Congresses (March 4, 1907–March 3, 1919); unsuccessful candidate for renomination in 1918; resumed the practice of law in Springfield, Greene County, Mo., until November 1935, when he retired and moved to Santa Monica, Calif., where he died February 16, 1950; interment in East Lawn Cemetery, Springfield, Mo.

HAMLIN, Edward Stowe, a Representative from Ohio; born in Hillsdale, Columbia County, N. Y., July 6, 1808; attended the district school of Hillsdale, N. Y., and a private school in Stockbridge, Mass.; pursued an academic course in Hudson, N. Y.; studied law; was admitted to the bar in 1831 and commenced practice in Elyria, Ohio; prosecuting attorney of Lorain County 1833–1835; elected as a Whig to the Twenty-eighth Congress to fill the vacancy caused by the death of Henry R. Brinkerhoff and served from October 8, 1844, to March 3, 1845; was not a candidate for renomination in 1844; moved to Cleveland, Ohio, in 1844; engaged in the newspaper business; established the True Democrat (now the Cleveland Plain Dealer) in 1846; member of the Free-Soil Convention at Buffalo in 1848; president of the board of public works 1849–1852; attorney for the State to arrange the water leases of canals and to collect and readjust water rents; declined the appointment of attorney general of Ohio in 1855; moved to Cincinnati in 1856; attorney for the Cincinnati, Indianapolis & Lafayette Railroad for many years; moved to Williamsburg, James City County, Va., in 1884 to supervise his extensive land holdings at Newport News; died in Washington, D. C., November 23, 1894; interment in Cedar Grove Cemetery, Williamsburg, Va.

HAMLIN, Hannibal, a Representative and a Senator from Maine and a Vice President of the United States; born in Paris, Oxford County, Maine, August 27, 1809; attended the district schools and Hebron Academy; took charge of his home farm until he was of age; employed as a compositor in a printing office for a year; studied law; was admitted to the bar in 1833 and practiced in Hampden, Penobscot County, until 1848; member of the State house of representatives 1836–1840 and in 1847 and served as speaker in 1837, 1839, and 1840; unsuccessful Democratic candidate for election in 1840 to the Twenty-seventh Congress; elected as a Democrat to the Twenty-eighth and Twenty-ninth Congresses (March 4, 1843–March 3, 1847); unsuccessful Anti-slavery Democratic candidate for election to the United States Senate in 1846; elected to the United States Senate to fill the vacancy caused by the death of John Fairfield; reelected in 1850 and served from June 8, 1848, to January 7, 1857, when he resigned to become Governor; left the Democratic Party in 1856; was elected, as a Republican, Governor of Maine and served from January 8, 1857, until February 20, 1857, when he resigned; reelected to the United States Senate and served from March 4, 1857, until his resignation, effective January 17, 1861; elected Vice President of the United States on the ticket with Abraham Lincoln and served from March 4, 1861, to March 3, 1865; enlisted as a private in the Maine State Guards July 7, 1864, for a period of sixty days; appointed collector of the port of Boston in 1865 but resigned in 1866; again elected to the United States Senate in 1869; reelected in 1875 and served from March 4, 1869, until March 3, 1881; was not a candidate for renomination; chosen a Regent of the Smithsonian Institution in 1870; United States Minister to Spain from 1881 to 1882, when he resigned; devoted the remainder of his life to agricultural pursuits; died in Bangor, Maine, July 4, 1891; interment in Mount Hope Cemetery.

HAMLIN, Simon Moulton, a Representative from Maine; born in Standish (Richville), Cumberland County, Maine, August 10, 1866; attended the public schools, Gorham (Maine)

Normal School, and Bridgton (Maine) Academy; taught school at the Frederick Robie, Standish, Windham, and Raymond High Schools and at Greeley Institute and Bridgton Academy; was graduated from Bowdoin College, Brunswick, Maine, in 1900; superintendent of the South Portland and Cape Elizabeth schools 1901–1925; city clerk of South Portland, Maine, in 1913; engaged in the real-estate business at South Portland in 1925; also interested in farming; member of the board of registration 1926–1932; served as mayor in 1933 and 1934; elected as a Democrat to the Seventy-fourth Congress (January 3, 1935–January 3, 1937); unsuccessful candidate for reelection in 1936 to the Seventy-fifth Congress; resumed the real-estate business and farming in South Portland, Maine, until his death there July 27, 1939; interment in Hamlin Cemetery, Standish (Richville), Maine.

HAMMER, William Cicero, a Representative from North Carolina; born near Asheboro, Randolph County, N. C., March 24, 1865; attended private and common schools; studied at Yadkin Institute and Western Maryland College, Westminster, Md.; taught school and was principal of two academies; was graduated in law from the University of North Carolina at Chapel Hill in 1891; was admitted to the bar in September 1891 and commenced practice in Asheboro, N. C.; mayor of Asheboro, member of the city council, and school commissioner 1895–1899; superintendent of public instruction 1891–1895 and again in 1899–1901; solicitor in the superior court 1901–1914; for more than forty years was owner and editor of the Asheboro Courier; appointed United States attorney on February 24, 1914, and served until September 20, 1920; elected as a Democrat to the Sixty-seventh and to the four succeeding Congresses and served from March 4, 1921, until his death in Asheboro, N. C., September 26, 1930; interment in City Cemetery.

HAMMETT, William H., a Representative from Mississippi; born in Virginia; studied theology; chaplain of the University of Virginia at Charlottesville 1832–1834 and of the State house of delegates; moved to Princeton, Miss.; elected as a Democrat to the Twenty-eighth Congress (March 4, 1843–March 3, 1845)

HAMMOND, Edward, a Representative from Maryland; born at "Font Hill," near Ellicott City, Anne Arundel (now Howard) County, Md., March 17, 1812; attended the common schools, Rockhill Academy, and was graduated from Yale College in 1830; studied law in New Haven, Conn., and in Baltimore, Md.; was admitted to the bar in 1833 and commenced practice in Annapolis, Md.; served in the State house of delegates from Anne Arundel County in 1839, 1841, and 1842; member of the State senate in 1848; elected as a Democrat to the Thirty-first and Thirty-second Congresses (March 4, 1849–March 3, 1853); was not a candidate for renomination in 1852; elected to the State house of delegates from Howard County in 1861 and 1867; elected associate judge of the fifth judicial district in 1867 and was serving in that position when he died at "Font Hill," near Ellicott City, Md., October 19, 1882; interment in St. John's Cemetery, near Ellicott City, Md.

HAMMOND, Jabez Delno, a Representative from New York; born in New Bedford, Mass., August 2, 1778; attended preparatory schools; studied medicine; commenced practice in Reading, Vt., in 1799; studied law; was admitted to the bar and commenced practice in Cherry Valley, N. Y., in 1805; elected a trustee of the village of Cherry Valley in 1812; member of the council of appointment; elected as a Democrat to the Fourteenth Congress (March 4, 1815–March 3, 1817); resumed the practice of law in Cherry Valley; served in the State senate 1817–1821; moved to Albany, N. Y., in 1822 and continued the practice of law; returned to Cherry Valley in 1838 and practiced law; also

engaged in literary pursuits; elected judge of Otsego County, N. Y., in 1838 and served five years; served as county superintendent of schools; appointed a member of the State board of regents May 10, 1845, and served until his death; died in Cherry Valley, Otsego County, N. Y., August 18, 1855; interment in Cherry Valley Cemetery.

HAMMOND, James Henry, a Representative and a Senator from South Carolina; born in Newberry District, S. C., November 15, 1807; was graduated from the South Carolina College (now the University of South Carolina) at Columbia in 1825; studied law; was admitted to the bar in 1827 and practiced; appointed a member of the Governor's staff in 1833; elected as a State Rights Free Trader to the Twenty-fourth Congress and served from March 4, 1835, until February 26, 1836, when he resigned because of ill health; spent two years in Europe; returned to South Carolina and engaged in agricultural pursuits; Governor of South Carolina 1842–1844; elected as a State Rights Democrat to the United States Senate to fill the vacancy caused by the resignation of Andrew P. Butler and served from December 7, 1857, to November 11, 1860, when he retired; died at "Redcliffe," Beach Island, S. C., November 13, 1864.

HAMMOND, John, a Representative from New York; born at Crown Point, Essex County, N. Y., August 17, 1827; attended the public schools and St. Albans Academy, St. Albans, Vt.; was graduated from Rensselaer Polytechnic Institute in Troy, N. Y.; pioneer in California in 1849; volunteered as a private in the Civil War; promoted to captain of Cavalry and advanced to brigadier general; a manufacturer of iron for twenty-five years; president of the Crown Point Iron Co.; elected as a Republican to the Forty-sixth and Forty-seventh Congresses (March 4, 1879–March 3, 1883); was not a candidate for renomination; retired from business; died at Crown Point, N. Y., May 28, 1889; interment in Forest Dale Cemetery.

HAMMOND, Nathaniel Job, a Representative from Georgia; born in Elbert County, Ga., December 26, 1833; attended the common schools and was graduated from the University of Georgia at Athens in 1852; studied law, was admitted to the bar in 1853 and commenced practice in Atlanta, Ga.; solicitor general of the Atlanta circuit 1861–1865; reporter of the supreme court 1867–1872; attorney general 1872–1877; member of the State constitutional conventions in 1865 and 1877; elected a trustee of the University of Georgia in 1872; elected as a Democrat to the Forty-sixth and to the three succeeding Congresses (March 4, 1879–March 3, 1887); unsuccessful candidate for renomination in 1886; resumed the practice of law in Atlanta, Ga., and died there April 20, 1899; interment in Oakland Cemetery

HAMMOND, Peter Francis, a Representative from Ohio; born in Lancaster, Fairfield County, Ohio, June 30, 1887; attended the parochial schools and St. Mary's High School, Lancaster, Ohio; was graduated from Josephinum College, Columbus, Ohio, in 1910; became engaged in the men's clothing business at Lancaster, Ohio, in 1913; elected as a Democrat to the Seventy-fourth Congress to fill the vacancy caused by the resignation of Mell G. Underwood and served from November 3, 1936, to January 3, 1937; was not a candidate for election in 1936 to the Seventy-fifth Congress; resumed the retail clothing business until 1938; postmaster of Lancaster, Ohio, from December 17, 1938, to May 31, 1954; retired; is a resident of Lancaster, Ohio.

HAMMOND, Robert Hanna, a Representative from Pennsylvania; born in Milton, Northumberland County, Pa., April 28, 1791; attended the academies at Milton; engaged in mercantile pursuits; member of the State militia, with the rank of brigadier general; enlisted in the United States Army as a lieutenant in 1817; resigned and returned to Milton, Pa.; was register and recorder of Northumberland County; postmaster of Milton 1833–1837; elected as a Van Buren Democrat to the Twenty-fifth and Twenty-sixth Congresses (March 4, 1837–March 3, 1841); reentered the Army and was commissioned paymaster during the Mexican War; was wounded and ordered home on sick leave; sailed on the steamship *Orleans* for New Orleans but died on the high seas before reaching port on June 2, 1847; interment in Milton Cemetery, Milton, Pa.

HAMMOND, Samuel, a Representative from Georgia; born in Farnham Parish, Richmond County, Va., September 21, 1757; attended the common schools; served as a volunteer under Governor Dunmore against the Indians; during the Revolutionary War served in the Continental Army with great distinction; promoted to assistant quartermaster at the siege of Savannah; member of the "council of capitulation" at Charleston; shortly after the war settled in Savannah, Ga.; surveyor general of Georgia in 1796; served in the Creek War and commanded a corps of Georgia Volunteers in 1793; member of the house of representatives of Georgia 1796–1798; one of the early Governors of the State; member of the State senate 1799 and 1800; elected as a Democrat to the Eighth Congress and served from March 4, 1803, until February 2, 1805, when he became Civil and Military Governor of upper Louisiana Territory and served from 1805 to 1824; receiver of public moneys in Missouri; president of the Bank of St. Louis; moved to South Carolina in 1824; member of the house of representatives of South Carolina; surveyor general in 1825; secretary of state of South Carolina 1831–1835; retired from public life and died at "Varello Farm," on the South Carolina side of the Savannah River, near Augusta, Ga., September 11, 1842; interment in Hammond Cemetery, New Richmond, S. C.

HAMMOND, Thomas, a Representative from Indiana; born in Fitchburg, Worcester County, Mass., February 27, 1843; attended the common schools; engaged in carpentry and contracting work until twenty-one years of age; moved to Detroit, Mich., and engaged in the packing-house business; moved to Hammond, Lake County, Ind., in 1876 and assisted in the establishment of the dressed-beef industry; mayor of Hammond 1888–1893; president of the Commercial Bank of Hammond 1892–1907; elected as a Democrat to the Fifty-third Congress (March 4, 1893–March 3, 1895); was not a candidate for renomination in 1894; resumed his former business pursuits; also engaged in the real-estate business and banking; member of the city council; appointed by Governor Hanly a member of the metropolitan police board; died in Hammond, Ind., September 21, 1909; interment in Oak Hill Cemetery.

HAMMOND, Winfield Scott, a Representative from Minnesota; born in Southboro, Worcester County, Mass., November 17, 1863; attended the public schools and was graduated from Dartmouth College, Hanover, N. H., in 1884; moved to Minnesota and settled in Madelia, Watonwan County; principal in the public schools; studied law; was admitted to the bar in 1891 and commenced practice in St. James, Minn.; prosecuting attorney of Watonwan County in 1895 and 1896 and again from 1900 to 1905; member of the State board of normal school directors 1896–1900; elected as a Democrat to the Sixtieth and to the three succeeding Congresses and served from March 4, 1907, until January 6, 1915, when he resigned to become Governor; Governor of Minnesota from January 7, 1914, until his death while on a visit to Clinton, La., December 30, 1915; interment in Mount Hope Cemetery, St. James, Minn.

HAMMONS, David, a Representative from Maine; born in Cornish, Maine, May 12, 1808; attended the common schools; studied law; was admitted to the bar in 1836 and commenced practice in Lovell, Oxford County, Maine; member of the State senate in 1840 and 1841; elected as a Democrat to the Thirtieth Congress (March 4, 1847–March 3, 1849); continued the practice of law until his death in Bethel, Oxford County, Maine, on November 7, 1888; interment in Woodland Cemetery.

HAMMONS, Joseph, a Representative from New Hampshire; born in Cornish, York County, Maine, March 3, 1787; educated by private tutors and in the common schools; studied medicine in Ossipee, N. H., and commenced practice in Farmington, N. H., in 1817; member of the New Hampshire Medical Society; elected as a Jacksonian Democrat to the Twenty-first and Twenty-second Congresses (March 4, 1829–March 3, 1833); postmaster at Dover, N. H., from June 1833 until his death in Farmington, N. H., March 29, 1836; interment in the old family cemetery.

HAMPTON, James Giles, a Representative from New Jersey; born in Bridgeton, Cumberland County, N. J., June 13, 1814; attended the common schools and was graduated from Princeton College in 1835; studied law; was admitted to the bar in 1839 and commenced practice in Bridgeton, N. J.; collector of the port of Bridgeton, N. J., 1841–1844; elected as a Whig to the Twenty-ninth and Thirtieth Congresses (March 4, 1845–March 3, 1849); was not a candidate for renomination in 1848; resumed the practice of law in Bridgeton, N. J.; solicitor of the board of chosen freeholders of Cumberland County in 1852; died in Bridgeton, N. J., on September 22, 1861; interment in Broad Street Presbyterian Cemetery.

HAMPTON, Moses, a Representative from Pennsylvania; born in Beaver, Beaver County, Pa., October 28, 1803; moved with his parents to Trumbull County, Ohio; pursued classical studies, and was graduated from Washington College (now Washington and Jefferson University), Washington, Pa., in 1827; studied law in Uniontown; was admitted to the bar in 1829 and commenced practice in Somerset; moved to Pittsburgh in 1838 and continued the practice of law; elected as a Whig to the Thirtieth and Thirty-first Congresses (March 4, 1847–March 3, 1851); was not a candidate for renomination in 1850; president judge of the Allegheny County District Court 1853–1873; died at his home, "Hampton Place," adjoining the village of Wilkinsburg, Allegheny County, Pa., June 27, 1878; interment in Allegheny Cemetery, Pittsburgh, Pa.

HAMPTON, Wade, a Representative from South Carolina; born in Virginia in 1752; received a thorough education; engaged in agricultural pursuits; moved to South Carolina; served in the Revolutionary War as lieutenant colonel of the regiment of light dragoons in General Sumter's brigade of State troops; elected as a Democrat to the Fourth Congress (March 4, 1795–March 3, 1797); unsuccessful candidate for reelection; presidential elector on the Jefferson and Burr ticket in 1801; elected to the Eighth Congress (March 4, 1803–March 3, 1805); unsuccessful candidate for reelection; colonel in the United States Army in 1808; appointed brigadier general in February 1809 and major general March 2, 1813; served in the War of 1812 until April 6, 1814, when he resigned; reputed the wealthiest planter in the United States and the owner of 3,000 slaves in 1830; died in Columbia, S. C., on February 4, 1835; interment in Trinity Churchyard, Columbia, S. C.

HAMPTON, Wade (grandson of the preceding), a Senator from South Carolina; born in Charleston, S. C., March 28, 1818; received private instructions, was graduated from the South Carolina College (now the University of South Carolina) at

Columbia in 1837; studied law but never practiced; engaged as a planter; served in the State senate 1858–1862; served in the Confederate Army during the Civil War; raised and commanded "Hampton's Legion"; made brigadier general of Cavalry May 23, 1862, and promoted to the rank of major general August 3, 1863; promoted to the rank of lieutenant general February 14, 1865, commanding the Cavalry of the Army of Northern Virginia; Governor of South Carolina 1876–1879; elected in 1878 as a Democrat to the United States Senate; reelected in 1884 and served from March 4, 1879, until March 3, 1891; unsuccessful candidate for reelection; United States railroad commissioner 1893–1897; died in Columbia, S. C., April 11, 1902; interment in Trinity Churchyard.

HANBACK, Lewis, a Representative from Kansas; born in Winchester, Scott County, Ill., March 27, 1839; attended the common schools, and Cherry Grove Seminary in Knox County, Ill., for three years; taught school in Morgan County, Ill., in 1860 and 1861; during the Civil War enlisted as a private in the Union Army, first in Company B, Tenth Regiment, Illinois Volunteer Infantry, and then in Company K, Twenty-seventh Regiment, Illinois Volunteer Infantry; promoted to captain August 20, 1861; brigade inspector from November 1862 to September 20, 1864, when he was mustered out; studied law in Albany, N. Y.; returned to Illinois and from there moved to Topeka, Kans.; was admitted to the bar in 1865 and practiced; elected justice of the peace in 1867; probate judge of Shawnee County 1868–1872; assistant chief clerk of the State house of representatives; assistant secretary of the State senate in 1877; assistant United States district attorney of Kansas 1877–1879; receiver of public moneys at Salina; elected as a Republican to the Forty-eighth and Forty-ninth Congresses (March 4, 1883–March 3, 1887); unsuccessful candidate for reelection to the Fiftieth Congress; resumed the practice of law; died in Kansas City, Kans., September 7, 1897; interment in Topeka Cemetery, Topeka, Kans.

HANBURY, Harry Alfred, a Representative from New York; born in Bristol, England, January 1, 1863; immigrated to the United States with his parents at an early age; attended the public schools and was graduated from the Boys' High School in New York City; entered mercantile life and established ironworks; delegate to State conventions in 1896, 1898, 1900, 1902, 1906, and 1914; elected as a Republican to the Fifty-seventh Congress (March 4, 1901–March 3, 1903); United States shipping commissioner, port of New York, from March 1903 to November 1909; established a foundry and machine works in Brooklyn, N. Y.; engaged in mechanical engineering and ship reconstruction in Brooklyn, N. Y.; died in Methuen, Mass., August 22, 1940; interment in Greenwood Cemetery, Brooklyn, N. Y.

HANCHETT, Luther, a Representative from Wisconsin; born in Middlebury, Portage County, Ohio, October 25, 1825; attended the common schools; studied law; was admitted to the bar in 1846 and commenced practice in Fremont, Ohio; moved to Portage County, Wis., in 1849; engaged in lumber and mining enterprises; county attorney two years; member of the State senate 1856–1860; elected as a Republican to the Thirty-seventh Congress and served from March 4, 1861, until his death in Plover, Portage County, Wis., November 24, 1862; interment in Plover Cemetery.

HANCOCK, Clarence Eugene, a Representative from New York; born in Syracuse, N. Y., February 13, 1885; attended the public schools; was graduated from Wesleyan University, Middletown, Conn., in 1906 and from New York (N. Y.) Law School in 1908; was admitted to the bar in 1908 and commenced practice in Syracuse, N. Y.; served as a sergeant in the First New York Cavalry on the Mexican border in 1916; during the First World War served overseas as a captain with the One Hundred and Fourth Machine Gun Battalion, Twenty-seventh Division, 1917–1919; corporation counsel of Syracuse, N. Y., 1926–1927; trustee of Wesleyan University, Middletown, Conn.; elected as a Republican to the Seventieth Congress to fill the vacancy caused by the death of Walter W. Magee; reelected to the Seventy-first and to the eight succeeding Congresses and served from November 8, 1927, to January 3, 1947; was not a candidate for renomination in 1946; resumed the practice of law in Syracuse, N. Y.; died January 3, 1948, in a hospital in Washington, D. C.; interment in Woodlawn Cemetery, Syracuse, N. Y.

HANCOCK, Franklin Wills, Jr., a Representative from North Carolina; born in Oxford, Granville County, N. C., November 1, 1894; attended the public schools, Horner Military Academy, Oxford, N. C., and the University of North Carolina at Chapel Hill; in 1915 and 1916 served as secretary to a special assistant to the Attorney General of the United States; studied law; was admitted to the bar in 1916 and commenced practice in Oxford, N. C.; also interested in insurance and real estate; during the First World War attended the officers' training camp at Fort Oglethorpe, Ga., and was honorably discharged shortly thereafter; chairman of the Granville County Democratic Executive Committee in 1924; presidential elector on the Democratic ticket of Davis and Bryan in 1924; served in the State senate 1926–1928; member of the State house of representatives 1928–1930; trustee of the Colored Orphanage of North Carolina at Oxford 1920–1937; delegate to the Democratic National Convention at Chicago in 1940; elected as a Democrat to the Seventy-first Congress to fill the vacancy caused by the death of Charles M. Stedman and on the same day was elected to the Seventy-second Congress; reelected to the Seventy-third, Seventy-fourth, and Seventy-fifth Congresses and served from November 4, 1930, to January 3, 1939; did not seek renomination, but was an unsuccessful candidate for the Democratic nomination for United States Senator in 1938; appointed a member of the Federal Home Loan Bank Board by President Franklin D. Roosevelt and served from January 4, 1939, to April 24, 1942, when the board was abolished by Executive order; appointed special representative of the Reconstruction Finance Corporation with special duties incident to the prosecution of the war and served until June 1943; administrator of the Farm Security Administration from November 1943 to November 1945 and also president of the Commodity Credit Corporation from December 1944 to August 1945; resumed the general practice of law at Oxford, N. C., where he now resides.

HANCOCK, George, a Representative from Virginia; born in Chesterfield County, Va., on June 13, 1754; pursued classical studies; served in the Revolutionary War as colonel of Infantry, Virginia Line, and, according to tradition, was a member of the staff of Count Pulaski, whom he caught in his arms, mortally wounded, at the siege of Savannah, Ga.; was taken prisoner in this engagement, paroled, and returned to Virginia; studied law; was admitted to the bar in June 1774 and commenced practice in Chesterfield County; appointed ensign in Chesterfield County, Va., in 1776 and later promoted to captain; admitted to the practice of law in the courts of Powhatan County, Va., July 20, 1780, and later moved to Botetourt County, Va., where, on April 12, 1782, he was admitted to the practice of law; appointed colonel of militia of Botetourt County, Va., on August 10, 1785; served as Commonwealth's attorney of Botetourt County from March 4, 1787, to October 11, 1789, and as deputy State's attorney from 1789 to 1793; elected as a Democrat to the Third and Fourth Congresses (March 4, 1793–March 3, 1797); engaged in the management of his estate, "Fotheringay," Elliston Valley, Montgomery County, Va., where he died July 18, 1820; interment in a tomb on his estate.

HANCOCK, John, a Delegate from Massachusetts; born in Quincy, Norfolk County, Mass., January 12, 1737; pursued classical studies; was graduated from Harvard College in 1754; a selectman of Boston several terms; member of the provincial legislature 1766–1772; president of the Provincial Congress in 1774; active in pre-Revolutionary movements and, with Samuel Adams, was exempted from pardon in Governor Gage's proclamation of June 12, 1775; Member of the Continental Congress 1775–1780, 1785, and 1786, and served as President of the Congress from May 24, 1775, to October 1777; first signer of the Declaration of Independence; served as senior major general of Massachusetts Militia during the Revolutionary War; member of the Massachusetts constitutional convention in 1780; Governor of Massachusetts 1780–1785; was again elected President of the Continental Congress on November 23, 1785, but resigned May 29, 1786, not having served on account of illness; again Governor of Massachusetts from 1787 until his death in Quincy, Mass., October 8, 1793; interment in Old Granary Burying Ground, Boston, Mass.

HANCOCK, John, a Representative from Texas; born near Bellefonte, Jackson County, Ala., October 24, 1824; attended the public schools and the University of Tennessee at Knoxville; studied law; was admitted to the bar in 1846; settled in Austin, Tex., in 1847 and practiced his profession there until August 1851; served as judge of the second judicial district of Texas from 1851 to 1855, when he resigned; resumed the practice of law and engaged in planting and stock raising; member of the State house of representatives in 1860 and 1861; refused to take the oath of allegiance to the Confederate States and was expelled from the legislature; took up his residence in the North until the conclusion of the war, when he returned to Texas; member of the State constitutional convention in 1866; elected as a Democrat to the Forty-second, Forty-third, and Forty-fourth Congresses (March 4, 1871–March 3, 1877); unsuccessful candidate for renomination; elected to the Forty-eighth Congress (March 4, 1883–March 3, 1885); was not a candidate for renomination; resumed the practice of law; died in Austin, Tex., July 19, 1893; interment in Oakwood Cemetery.

HAND, Augustus Cincinnatus, a Representative from New York; born in Shoreham, Addison County, Vt., September 4, 1803; pursued academic studies; studied law in Litchfield, Conn.; was admitted to the bar in 1828 and commenced practice at Crown Point, N. Y.; moved to Elizabethtown, N. Y., in 1831; surrogate of Essex County 1831–1839; elected as a Democrat to the Twenty-sixth Congress (March 4, 1839–March 3, 1841); elected a member of the State senate in 1844 and served several years; associate justice of the State supreme court 1847–1855; delegate to the Democratic National Convention at New York in 1868; resumed the practice of his profession; died in Elizabethtown, Essex County, N. Y., March 8, 1878; interment in Riverside Cemetery.

HAND, Edward, a Delegate from Pennsylvania; born in Clyduff, County Kings, Ireland, December 31, 1744; accompanied the Eighteenth Royal Irish Regiment to the United States as surgeon's mate in 1774, but resigned; settled in Pennsylvania and practiced medicine; during the Revolution was commissioned lieutenant colonel June 25, 1775; promoted colonel March 7, 1776, and brigadier general April 1, 1777; succeeded Gen. John Stark in command at Albany in 1778 and served in the expedition against the Indians of the Six Nations; took command of a brigade of the Light Infantry Corps in August 1780; adjutant general of the Army from January 1781 to November 1783; brevetted major general September 30, 1783; mustered out November 3, 1783; Member of the Continental Congress in 1784 and 1785; major general in the United States Army June 19, 1798; honorably discharged June 15, 1800; died in Rockford, Lancaster County, Pa., September 3, 1802; interment in St. James's Episcopal Cemetery.

HAND, Thomas Millet, a Representative from New Jersey; born in Cape May, N. J., July 7, 1902; attended the public schools; was graduated from Cape May High School in 1919 and from Dickinson School of Law, Carlisle, Pa., in 1922; was admitted to the bar in 1924 and commenced practice in Cape May City, N. J.; clerk of the Board of Chosen Freeholders of Cape May County, N. J., 1924–1928; prosecutor of the pleas of Cape May County 1928–1933; mayor of Cape May, N. J., 1937–1944; publisher of the Cape May Star and Wave from 1940 until his death; also a partner in the Mecray-Hand Co., a real-estate and insurance business; elected as a Republican to the Seventy-ninth and to the five succeeding Congresses and had been reelected November 6, 1956, to the Eighty-fifth Congress; served from January 3, 1945, until his death in Cold Spring, N. J., December 26, 1956; remains were cremated at Ewing Cemetery, Trenton, N. J., and interred in Cold Spring Cemetery.

HANDLEY, William Anderson, a Representative from Alabama; born at Liberty Hill, near Franklin, Heard County, Ga., December 15, 1834; moved to Alabama; attended the public schools; moved to Roanoke, Randolph County, Ala.; during the Civil War served in the Confederate Army as captain of the Twenty-fifth Regiment; engaged in mercantile pursuits; elected as a Democrat to the Forty-second Congress (March 4, 1871–March 3, 1873); served in the State senate 1888–1892; delegate to the State constitutional convention in 1901; member of the State house of representatives 1903–1907; resumed his former mercantile activities; died in Roanoke, Ala., June 23, 1909; interment in the City Cemetery.

HANDY, Levin Irving (nephew of William Campbell Preston Breckenridge), a Representative from Delaware; born in Berlin, Worcester County, Md., December 24, 1861; attended the public schools in Maryland and New York; taught school at Damos Quarter, Somerset County, Md.; elected principal of the high school at Smyrna, Del., in 1881; superintendent of free schools in Kent County 1887–1890; principal of Old Newark Academy, Newark, Del., 1890–1892; chairman of the Democratic State central committee 1892–1896; editorial writer on the Wilmington Every Evening in 1894 and 1895; unsuccessful candidate for election in 1894 to the Fifty-fourth Congress; studied law; was admitted to the bar in 1899 and practiced in Wilmington, Del.; elected as a Democrat to the Fifty-fifth Congress (March 4, 1897–March 3, 1899); unsuccessful candidate for reelection to the Fifty-sixth Congress; unsuccessful candidate for attorney general in 1904; unsuccessful candidate for election to the Sixty-first Congress; delegate to the Democratic National Conventions in 1900, 1904, and 1908; resumed the practice of law in Wilmington, Del., and died there February 3, 1922; interment in Glenwood Cemetery, Smyrna, Del.

HANKS, James Millander, a Representative from Arkansas; born in Helena, Phillips County, Ark., February 12, 1833; attended the public schools, the college at New Albany, Ind., and Jackson College, Columbia, Tenn.; studied law; was graduated from the University of Louisville in 1855; was admitted to the bar and commenced practice in Helena; judge of the first judicial district of Arkansas 1864–1868; elected as a Democrat to the Forty-second Congress (March 4, 1871–March 3, 1873); was not a candidate for renomination in 1872; engaged in agricultural pursuits; died in Helena, Ark., May 24, 1909; interment in Maple Hill Cemetery.

HANLY, James Franklin, a Representative from Indiana; born near St. Joseph, Champaign County, Ill., April 4, 1863; attended the common schools and the Eastern Illinois Normal School at Danville, Ill., 1879–1881; moved to Warren County, Ind., in 1879; taught in the public schools of the State 1881–1889; studied law; was admitted to the bar in 1889 and commenced practice in Williamsport, Warren County, Ind.; member of the State senate in 1890 and 1891; elected as a Republican to the Fifty-fourth Congress (March 4, 1895–March 3, 1897); unsuccessful candidate for renomination in 1896; moved to Lafayette, Ind., in 1896; Governor of Indiana 1905–1909; prohibition lecturer throughout the United States 1910–1920 and in France in 1919; organized and was editor of the Enquirer Publishing Co. and the Indianapolis Commercial in 1915; resumed the practice of law in Indianapolis; unsuccessful candidate of the Prohibition Party for President of the United States in 1916; died as the result of an automobile accident near Dennison, Tuscarawas County, Ohio, August 1, 1920; interment in Hillside Cemetery, near Williamsport, Ind.

HANNA, John, a Representative from Indiana; born near Indianapolis, Ind., September 3, 1827; pursued classical studies; was graduated from the Indiana Asbury (now De Pauw) University, Greencastle, Ind., in 1850; studied law; was admitted to the bar and commenced practice in Greencastle; mayor of Greencastle 1851–1854; moved to Kansas; was a member of its Territorial legislature in 1857 and 1858; returned to Indiana; presidential elector on the Republican ticket of Lincoln and Hamlin in 1860; United States district attorney 1861–1869; elected as a Republican to the Forty-fifth Congress (March 4, 1877–March 3, 1879); died in Plainfield, Ind., October 24, 1882; interment in Forest Hill Cemetery, Greencastle, Ind.

HANNA, John Andre (grandfather of Archibald McAllister), a Representative from Pennsylvania; born in Flemington, Hunterdon County, N. J., in 1762; received a classical education; was graduated from Princeton College in 1782; studied law; was admitted to the bar of Lancaster County in 1783 and commenced practice in Lancaster, Pa.; upon the formation of the county of Dauphin moved to Harrisburg, and was admitted to the Dauphin County bar in 1785; delegate to the State convention to ratify Federal Constitution in 1787; secretary of the anti-Federal conference in 1788; member of the State house of representatives in 1791; was elected lieutenant colonel of the Third Battalion of Dauphin County December 29, 1792; appointed brigadier general of Dauphin County Brigade April 19, 1793, and was in command during the Whisky Insurrection of that year; appointed major general of the Sixth Division of Dauphin and Berks Counties April 23, 1800; elected as an Anti-Federalist to the Fifth and to the four succeeding Congresses and served from March 4, 1797, until his death in Harrisburg, Pa., July 23, 1805; interment in Mount Kalmia Cemetery.

HANNA, Louis Benjamin, a Representative from North Dakota; born in New Brighton, Beaver County, Pa., August 9, 1861; attended the common schools of Ohio, Massachusetts, and New York; moved to Dakota Territory in 1881 and settled near what is now Hope, N. Dak.; moved to Page, Cass County, in 1882 and engaged in the lumber business and in mercantile pursuits; member of the State house of representatives 1895–1897; moved to Fargo in 1899 to become vice president of the First National Bank of Fargo; served in the State senate 1897–1901 and 1905–1909; chairman of the Republican State central committee 1902–1908; trustee of Fargo College since 1898; delegate to the Republican National Convention at Chicago in 1904; elected as a Republican to the Sixty-first and Sixty-second Congresses and served from March 4, 1909, to January 7, 1913,

when he resigned, having been elected Governor; Governor of North Dakota 1913–1917; unsuccessful candidate for the Republican nomination for United States Senator in 1916 and 1926; chairman of the State Liberty Loan Committee in 1917 and 1918; served as captain in the American Red Cross in France during the First World War and was decorated with the Grand Cross of St. Olaf by the King of Norway and cited an officer of the French Legion of Honor by the French Government; chairman of the Republican State campaign committee in 1924; engaged in agricultural pursuits and banking until his retirement; died in Fargo, N. Dak., on April 23, 1948; interment in Riverside Cemetery.

HANNA, Marcus Alonzo (father of Ruth Hanna McCormick), a Senator from Ohio; born in New Lisbon (now Lisbon), Columbiana County, Ohio, September 24, 1837; moved with his parents to Cleveland in 1852; attended the common schools of that city and Western Reserve College, Hudson, Ohio; engaged in the wholesale grocery business and later in the iron and coal business; was identified with the lake carrying trade; director of the Union Pacific Railway in 1885 by appointment of President Cleveland; delegate to the Republican National Conventions in 1884, 1888, and 1896; chairman of the Republican National Committee in 1896; appointed and subsequently elected as a Republican to the United States Senate to fill the vacancy caused by the resignation of John Sherman; reelected in January 1898 and also was elected for the succeeding full term and served from March 5, 1897, until his death in Washington, D. C., February 15, 1904; funeral services were held in the Chamber of the United States Senate; interment in Lake View Cemetery, Cleveland, Ohio.

HANNA, Robert, a Senator from Indiana; born near Fountainius, Laurens District, S. C., April 6, 1786; settled in Brookville, Ind., in 1802; sheriff of the common pleas court 1811–1820; member of the State constitutional convention in 1816; brigadier general of State militia; register of the land office 1820–1830; moved to Indianapolis in 1825; appointed as a Whig to the United States Senate to fill the vacancy caused by the death of James Noble and served from August 19, 1831, to January 3, 1832; served in the State house of representatives 1832, 1833, and 1836–1839; contractor for national roads in 1835; member of the State senate 1842–1846; killed by a train while walking upon the track in Indianapolis, Ind., November 16, 1858; interment in Crown Hill Cemetery.

HANNEGAN, Edward Allen, a Representative and a Senator from Indiana; born in Hamilton County, Ohio, June 25, 1807; moved with his parents to Bourbon County, Ky., the same year; attended the public schools; studied law; was admitted to the bar in 1827; moved to Indiana and settled in Terre Haute, where he commenced the practice of law in 1827; moved to Crawfordsville in 1830, and after a few months to Covington, and continued the practice of his profession; member of the State house of representatives in 1832, 1833, 1841, and 1842; elected as a Democrat to the Twenty-third and Twenth-fourth Congresses (March 4, 1833–March 3, 1837); was not a candidate for renomination in 1836; resumed the practice of law; register of the land office at Laporte, Ind., in 1839; unsuccessful candidate in 1840 for election to fill a vacancy in the Twenty-sixth Congress; resumed the practice of law in Covington; elected to the United States Senate and served from March 4, 1843, to March 3, 1849; unsuccessful candidate for renomination in 1848 to the United States Senate; United States Minister to Prussia from March 22, 1849, to January 13, 1850; resumed the practice of law in Covington; moved to St. Louis, Mo., in 1857 and continued the practice of law until his death there on February 25, 1859; interment in Woodlawn Cemetery, Terre Haute, Ind.

HANSBROUGH, Henry Clay, a Representative and a Senator from North Dakota; born near Prairie du Rocher, Randolph County, Ill., January 30, 1848; attended the common schools; moved to San Jose, Calif., with his parents in 1867; learned the art of printing, and worked at the trade in San Jose, Calif., and later at Baraboo, Wis.; moved to Dakota Territory and established the Grand Forks News in 1881 and the Inter Ocean, at Devils Lake, in 1883; mayor of Devils Lake 1885–1888; delegate to the Republican National Conventions in 1888, 1892, and 1900; member of the Republican National Committee 1888–1896; upon the admission of North Dakota as a State into the Union was elected as a Republican to the Fifty-first Congress and served from November 2, 1889, until March 3, 1891; did not seek renomination in 1891, having become a candidate for Senator; elected to the United States Senate in 1891; reelected in 1897 and again in 1903 and served from March 4, 1891, to March 3, 1909; unsuccessful candidate for reelection in 1909; resumed his former business pursuits in Devils Lake, N. Dak., from which he retired and moved to St. Petersburg, Fla., in 1919; moved to Water Mill, Long Island, N. Y., in 1925 and thence to Washington, D. C., in 1927, where he died on November 16, 1933; remains cremated and the ashes scattered under an elm tree in the United States Capitol Grounds, Washington, D. C.

HANSEN, Julia Butler, a Representative from Washington; born in Portland, Multnomah County, Oreg., June 14, 1907; attended the public schools of Washington and graduated from the University of Washington at Seattle in 1930; member of Cathlamet, Wash., city council 1938–1946; chairman of Western Interstate Committee on Highway Policies 1951–1961; manager of a title and casualty insurance business 1958–1961; writer; member of the State house of representatives from January 1939 until November 1960, serving as speaker pro tempore 1955–1960; chairman and member of board of trustees of Century 21, State of Washington, since 1958; elected as a Democrat to the Eighty-sixth Congress to fill the vacancy caused by the death of Russell V. Mack and served from November 8, 1960, to January 3, 1961. *Reelected to the Eighty-seventh Congress.*

HANSON, Alexander Contee (grandson of John Hanson and grandnephew of Benjamin Contee), a Representative and a Senator from Maryland; born in Annapolis, Md., February 27, 1786; attended local private schools, and was graduated from St. John's College, Annapolis, in 1802; studied law; was admitted to the bar and commenced practice in Annapolis, Md.; member of the State house of delegates 1811–1815; established and edited the Federal Republican in Baltimore, and on June 18, 1812, two days after war was declared, a mob, irritated by his articles denouncing the administration, destroyed the office; he issued the paper from another building one week later and escaped serious injury from a mob only by seeking police protection; moved the paper to Georgetown, D. C., where he published it unmolested; moved to Rockville, Md.; elected as a Federalist to the Thirteenth and Fourteenth Congresses and served from March 4, 1813, until his resignation in 1816; unsuccessful candidate in 1816 for election to the State house of delegates; elected to the United States Senate to fill the vacancy caused by the resignation of Robert G. Harper and served from December 20, 1816, until his death on his estate, "Belmont," near Elkridge, Howard County, Md., April 23, 1819; interment in the family burial ground.

HANSON, John (grandfather of Alexander Contee Hanson), a Delegate from Maryland; born at Mulberry Grove, near Port Tobacco, Charles County, Md., April 3, 1715; pursued an academic course; engaged in agricultural pursuits; member of the State house of delegates for nine terms; member of the State senate 1757–1773; moved to Frederick County in 1773; active in pre-Revolutionary matters; Delegate to the General Congress at Annapolis in 1774; treasurer of Frederick County in 1775; member of the Maryland convention of 1775 which issued its declaration known as the "Association of Freemen of Maryland"; Member of the Continental Congress 1780–1783; elected President of the Continental Congress on November 5, 1781; served one year, and in that capacity tendered General Washington on November 28, 1781, the thanks of the Congress for the victory at Yorktown; signer of the Articles of Confederation of the United States; retired from public life and sought seclusion and rest; died at the residence of his nephew at Oxon Hill, Prince Georges County, Md., November 15, 1783, and is interred there.

HARALSON, Hugh Anderson, a Representative from Georgia; born near Penfield, Greene County, Ga., November 13, 1805; attended the common schools and was also instructed by private tutors; was graduated from Franklin College (now the University of Georgia) in 1825; studied law; was admitted to the bar in 1825 and commenced practice in Monroe, Walton County, Ga.; moved to Lagrange, Troup County, Ga., in 1828, and continued the practice of law; also engaged in agricultural pursuits; member of the State house of representatives in 1831 and 1832; served in the State senate in 1837 and 1838; served in the State militia as a major general 1838–1850; elected as a Democrat to the Twenty-eighth, Twenty-ninth, Thirtieth, and Thirty-first Congresses (March 4, 1843–March 3, 1851); was not a candidate for renomination in 1850; resumed the practice of law; died in Lagrange, Troup County, Ga., September 25, 1854; interment in Hill View Cemetery.

HARALSON, Jeremiah, a Representative from Alabama; born on a plantation near Columbus, Muscogee County, Ga., April 1, 1846; was of the Negro race and raised as a slave; self-educated; moved to Alabama and engaged in agricultural pursuits; became a minister of the gospel; member of the State house of representatives in 1870; served in the State senate in 1872; unsuccessful candidate for election in 1868 to the Forty-first Congress; elected as a Republican to the Forty-fourth Congress (March 4, 1875–March 3, 1877); appointed to a Federal position in the United States customhouse in Baltimore, Md.; later employed as a clerk in the Interior Department; appointed August 12, 1882, to the Pension Bureau in Washington, D. C., and resigned August 21, 1884; moved to Louisiana, where he engaged in agricultural pursuits, and thence to Arkansas in 1904; served as pension agent for a short time; returned to Alabama and settled in Selma in 1912; moved to Texas and later to Oklahoma and Colorado and engaged in coal mining in the latter State; killed by wild beasts near Denver, Colo., about 1916.

HARD, Gideon, a Representative from New York; born in Arlington, Bennington County, Vt., April 29, 1797; was graduated from Union College, Schenectady, N. Y., in 1822; taught school; studied law; was admitted to the bar in 1825 and commenced practice in Newport (now Albion), N. Y., in 1826; elected as a Whig to the Twenty-third and Twenty-fourth Congresses (March 4, 1833–March 3, 1837); commissioner of schools for Barre Township, Orleans County, N. Y., 1841–1848; served in the State senate 1841–1848; canal appraiser in 1849 and 1850; resumed the practice of law until 1850; county judge and surrogate for Orleans County 1856–1860; retired to private life; died in Albion, Orleans County, N. Y., April 27, 1885; interment in Mount Albion Cemetery.

HARDEMAN, Thomas, Jr., a Representative from Georgia; born in Eatonton, Putnam County, Ga., January 12, 1825; was graduated from Emory College in 1845; studied law; was admitted to the bar in 1847; abandoned his profession and engaged in the warehouse and commission business; served in the State house of representative in 1853, 1855, and 1857; elected as a Democrat to the Thirty-sixth Congress and served from March 4, 1859, until January 23, 1861, when he withdrew; captain of the Floyd Rifles; during the Civil War was major of the Second Georgia Battalion and, later, colonel of the Forty-fifth Georgia Infantry of the Confederate Army; again served in the State house of representatives, in 1863, 1864, and 1874, and was speaker during these sessions; delegate to the Democratic National Convention at Baltimore in 1872, which nominated Greeley and Brown; president of the State convention and chairman of the Democratic State executive committee for four years; elected as a Democrat to the Forty-eighth Congress (March 4, 1883–March 3, 1885); died in Macon, Ga., March 6, 1891; interment in Oak Hill Cemetery.

HARDEN, Cecil Murray, a Representative from Indiana; born in Covington, Fountain County, Ind., November 21, 1894; graduated from the public schools of Covington, Ind., in 1912, and attended the University of Indiana at Bloomington; taught all grades in Troy township schools, Fountain County, Ind., and Covington (Ind.) public schools 1912–1914; Republican national committeewoman from Indiana 1944–1959; delegate at large to the Republican National Conventions in 1948, 1952, and 1956; elected as a Republican to the Eighty-first and to the four succeeding Congresses (January 3, 1949–January 3, 1959); unsuccessful candidate for reelection in 1958 to the Eighty-sixth Congress; special assistant for women's affairs to Postmaster General, Washington, D. C., March 1959 to January 1961; is a resident of Covington, Ind.

HARDENBERGH, Augustus Albert, a Representative from New Jersey; born in New Brunswick, Middlesex County, N. J., May 18, 1830; attended Rutgers College, New Brunswick, N. J., in 1844; took up his residence in Jersey City in 1846 and was employed in a banking house in New York City; clerk in the Hudson County National Bank in 1852; member of the State house of assembly in 1853 and 1854; member of the board of education in 1855 and 1856; member of the common council of Jersey City 1857–1863, serving as president in 1860; moved to Bergen, N. J., in 1863; member of the city council of Bergen; elected State director of railroads in 1868; moved to Demarest, N. J., the same year; delegate to the Democratic National Convention at Baltimore in 1872; moved to Jersey City in 1873; elected president of the Northern Railroad of New Jersey in 1874; elected as a Democrat to the Forty-fourth and Forty-fifth Congresses (March 4, 1875–March 3, 1879); declined to be a candidate for renomination in 1878; elected president of the Hudson County National Bank in 1878; elected to the Forty-seventh Congress (March 4, 1881–March 3, 1883); was not a candidate for renomination in 1882; appointed a member of the Jersey City Board of Finance and Taxation in 1883 and served until 1889, when the board was abolished; appointed by Governor Abbett as a trustee of the State reform school in 1884; presidential elector on the Democratic ticket of Cleveland and Hendricks in 1884; died in Jersey City, N. J., on October 5, 1889; interment in Mount Pleasant Cemetery, Newark, N. J.

HARDIN, Benjamin (cousin of Martin Davis Hardin), a Representative from Kentucky; born at the Georges Creek settlement on the Monongahela River, Westmoreland County, Pa., February 29, 1784; moved with his parents to Washington County, Ky., in 1788; attended the schools of Nelson and Washington Counties, Ky.; studied law; was admitted to the bar in 1806 and commenced practice in Elizabethtown and Bardstown, Nelson County, Ky.; settled in Bardstown in 1808; member of the State house of representatives in 1810, 1811, 1824, and 1825; served in the State senate 1828–1832; elected to the Fourteenth Congress (March 4, 1815–March 3, 1817); elected to the Sixteenth and Seventeenth Congresses (March 4, 1819–March 3, 1823); elected to the Twenty-third Congress and, as a Whig, to the Twenty-fourth Congress (March 4, 1833–March 3, 1837); secretary of state of Kentucky 1844–1847; member of the State constitutional convention in 1849; died in Bardstown, Ky., September 24, 1852; interment in the family burying ground near Springfield, Ky.

HARDIN, John J. (son of Martin Davis Hardin), a Representative from Illinois; born in Frankfort, Ky., January 6, 1810; pursued classical studies and was graduated from Transylvania University, Lexington, Ky.; studied law; was admitted to the bar in Kentucky in 1831 and commenced practice in Jacksonville, Morgan County, Ill.; served in the Illinois Militia during the Black Hawk War 1831–1832; was brigadier general in command during the Mormon trouble in Hancock County in 1844 and later attained the rank of major general; appointed prosecuting attorney of Morgan County in 1832; member of the State house of representatives 1836–1842; elected as a Whig to the Twenty-eighth Congress (March 4, 1843–March 3, 1845); was not a candidate for renomination in 1844; during the Mexican War recruited the First Regiment, Illinois Volunteer Infantry, of which he was commissioned colonel; was killed at the Battle of Buena Vista, Mexico, February 23, 1847; interment in City Cemetery (East), Jacksonville, Ill.

HARDIN, Martin Davis (cousin of Benjamin Hardin and father of John J. Hardin), a Senator from Kentucky; born on the Monongahela River, western Pennsylvania, June 21, 1780; moved with his parents to Kentucky in April 1786; pursued an academic course; attended Transylvania University, Lexington, Ky.; studied law; was admitted to the bar and practiced in Richmond and Frankfort, Ky.; member of the State house of representatives in 1812, 1818, and 1819, serving as speaker in 1819; secretary of state of Kentucky 1812–1816; served as major in the War of 1812; appointed and subsequently elected as a Democrat to the United States Senate to fill the vacancy caused by the resignation of William T. Barry and served from November 13, 1816, to March 3, 1817; presidential elector on the Democratic ticket of Monroe and Tompkins in 1820; died in Frankfort, Ky., October 8, 1823; interment on his farm in Franklin County; reinterment in State Cemetery, Frankfort, Ky.

HARDING, Aaron, a Representative from Kentucky; born near Campbellsville, Taylor County (now a part of Green County), Ky., February 20, 1805; attended the rural schools; became familiar with the classics; studied law; was admitted to the bar in 1833 and commenced practice in Greensburg, Ky.; elected prosecuting attorney of Green County in 1833; member of the State house of representatives in 1840; declined to be a candidate for the State senate; elected as a Union Democrat to the Thirty-seventh, Thirty-eighth, and Thirty-ninth Congresses (March 4, 1861–March 3, 1867); delegate to the Union National Convention at Philadelphia in 1866; resumed the practice of law in Danville, Ky.; died in Georgetown, Scott County, Ky., December 24, 1875; interment in Georgetown Cemetery.

HARDING, Abner Clark, a Representative from Illinois; born in East Hampton, Middlesex County, Conn., February 10, 1807; attended Hamilton Academy, Clinton, N. Y.; studied law; was admitted to the bar and commenced practice in Oneida County, N. Y., about 1827; moved to Monmouth, Warren County, Ill., in 1838 and continued the practice of law; member of the State constitutional convention in 1848; member of the State house of representatives 1848–1850; during the Civil War enlisted as a private in the Union Army in the Eighty-third Regiment, Illinois Volunteer Infantry, later was commissioned colonel, and in 1863 was promoted to brigadier general for gallantry in action; elected as a Republican to the Thirty-ninth and Fortieth Congresses (March 4, 1865–March 3, 1869); was not a candidate for renomination in 1868; engaged in banking and railroad building; died in Monmouth, Ill., July 19, 1874; interment in Monmouth Cemetery.

HARDING, Benjamin Franklin, a Senator from Oregon; born near Tunkhannock, Wyoming County, Pa., on January 4, 1823; attended the public schools; studied law; was admitted to the bar in 1847 and commenced practice in Joliet, Ill., in 1849; moved to California, and thence to Oregon in 1850; clerk of the Territorial legislature in 1850 and 1851; member of that body and served as its speaker in 1852; United States district attorney in 1853; secretary of the Territory 1854–1859; member of the State house of representatives 1858–1862 and served as speaker in 1860 and 1861; elected as a Republican to the United States Senate to fill the vacancy caused by the death of Edward D. Baker and served from September 12, 1862, to March 3, 1865; retired to his farm near Salem, Marion County, Oreg., and a few years later moved to Cottage Grove, Lane County, where he died June 16, 1899; interment in Cottage Grove Cemetery.

HARDING, John Eugene, a Representative from Ohio; born in Excello, Butler County, Ohio, June 27, 1877; attended the Amanda public schools and Pennsylvania Military Academy at Chester; was graduated from the University of Michigan at Ann Arbor in 1900; engaged in business in Middletown, Ohio, and in industrial enterprises; member of the State senate in 1902; elected as a Republican to the Sixtieth Congress (March 4, 1907–March 3, 1909); delegate to the Republican State convention in 1910; engaged in the paper business in Chicago, Ill., until he moved to New York City, N. Y., where he was associated with the Pure Oil Co., 1921–1926; engaged in industrial enterprises until retirement in 1949; died in New Haven, Conn., July 26, 1959; interment in Woodside Cemetery, Middletown, Ohio.

HARDING, Warren Gamaliel, a Senator from Ohio and a President of the United States; born in Blooming Grove, Morrow County, Ohio, November 2, 1865; attended the public schools in and near Caledonia, Ohio, and Ohio Central College at Iberia; studied law for a short time; taught school; engaged in the insurance business; became editor and publisher of the Marion Star in 1884; member of the State senate 1899–1903; served as Lieutenant Governor of Ohio in 1904 and 1905; unsuccessful Republican candidate for Governor in 1910; elected as a Republican to the United States Senate and served from March 4, 1915, until his resignation, effective January 13, 1921, having been elected President; elected President of the United States on the Republican ticket with Calvin Coolidge as Vice President, was inaugurated March 4, 1921, and served until his death in San Francisco, Calif., while on a tour of the Western States and Alaska, August 2, 1923; interment in Marion Cemetery, Marion, Ohio; reinterment in Harding Memorial Tomb.

HARDWICK, Thomas William, a Representative and a Senator from Georgia; born in Thomasville, Thomas County, Ga., on December 9, 1872; attended the common schools and Mercer University, Macon, Ga.; was graduated from the law department of the University of Georgia at Athens in 1893; was admitted to the bar the same year and commenced practice in Sandersville, Ga.; member of the State house of representatives 1890–1899, 1901, and 1902; prosecuting attorney for Washington County from March 1895 until January 1897, when he resigned; captain of Company D, Sixth Regiment Infantry, Georgia State Troops (Washington Rifles), in 1900 and 1901;

elected as a Democrat to the Fifty-eighth and to the five succeeding Congresses and served from March 4, 1903, to November 2, 1914, when he resigned; elected to the United States Senate to fill the vacancy caused by the death of Augustus O. Bacon and served from November 4, 1914, to March 3, 1919; unsuccessful candidate for renomination in 1918; Governor of Georgia 1921–1923; special assistant to the Attorney General of the United States from July 1, 1923, to May 15, 1924, when he resigned; unsuccessful candidate for nomination to the United States Senate in 1924; resumed the practice of law, with offices in Washington, D. C., and Atlanta, Ga., in 1924, moved to Sandersville, Ga., in 1927 and continued the practice of law; died in Sandersville, Ga., January 31, 1944; interment in the Old City Cemetery.

HARDY, Alexander Merrill, a Representative from Indiana; born in Simcoe, Norfolk County, Ontario, Canada, December 16, 1847; pursued a college course and studied law; came to the United States in 1864, taking a commercial course at Eastman College, Poughkeepsie, N. Y.; went to New Orleans in 1869, where he engaged in newspaper work until 1873, when he moved to Natchez, Miss.; conducted a Republican newspaper until 1877; collector of the port of Natchez under appointment of President Grant; moved to Washington, Daviess County, Ind., in 1884; was admitted to the bar in 1884 and commenced practice in Terre Haute, Ind.; elected as a Republican to the Fifty-fourth Congress (March 4, 1895–March 3, 1897); unsuccessful candidate for reelection in 1896 to the Fifty-fifth Congress; resumed the practice of law in Washington, Ind.; moved to Los Angeles, Calif., in 1904 and continued the practice of law; moved to Searchlight, Nev., thence to Salt Lake City, Utah, and finally settled in Tonopah, Nev., in 1914 and engaged in the practice of his profession; was also interested in mining; died in Tonopah, Nev., on August 31, 1927; interment in Tonopah Cemetery.

HARDY, Guy Urban, a Representative from Colorado; born in Abingdon, Knox County, Ill., April 4, 1872; attended the public schools, Albion Normal College, Albion, Ill., and Transylvania University, Lexington, Ky.; taught school in Illinois and Florida 1890–1893; moved to Canon City, Colo., in 1894; editor and publisher of the Canon City Daily and Weekly Records since 1895; postmaster of Canon City from June 5, 1900, to July 30, 1904; president of the National Editorial Association in 1918 and 1919; elected as a Republican to the Sixty-sixth and to the six succeeding Congresses (March 4, 1919–March 3, 1933); unsuccessful candidate for reelection in 1932 to the Seventy-third Congress; resumed his former publishing pursuits in Canon City, Colo., and resided there until his death on January 26, 1947; interment in Greenwood Cemetery.

HARDY, John, a Representative from New York; born in Scotland September 19, 1835; immigrated to the United States in 1839 with his parents, who settled in New York City; attended the public schools, and was graduated from the College of the City of New York in 1853; studied law; was admitted to the bar in 1861 and commenced practice in New York City; member of the State assembly in 1861; member of the board of aldermen of New York City in 1863, 1864, and 1867–1869; clerk of the common council in 1870 and 1871; chief clerk in the office of the mayor in 1877 and 1878; elected as a Democrat to the Forty-seventh Congress to fill the vacancy caused by the death of Fernando Wood; reelected to the Forty-eighth Congress and served from December 5, 1881, until March 3, 1885; unsuccessful candidate for reelection in 1884 to the Forty-ninth Congress; resumed the practice of law in New York City and died there December 9, 1913; interment in Greenwood Cemetery, Brooklyn, N. Y.

HARDY, Porter, Jr., a Representative from Virginia; born in Bon Air, Chesterfield County, Va., June 1, 1903; attended the public schools, and Randolph-Macon Academy, Bedford, Va.; was graduated from Boykins (Va.) High School in 1918 and from Randolph-Macon College, Ashland, Va., in 1922; attended the Graduate School of Business Administration at Harvard University in 1923 and 1924; accountant and warehouse manager at New York, N. Y., and Norfolk, Va., 1924–1927; wholesaler of electrical equipment, Salisbury, Md., 1927–1932; moved to Churchland, Va., in 1932 and engaged in agricultural pursuits; elected as a Democrat to the Eightieth and to the six succeeding Congresses (January 3, 1947–January 3, 1961). *Reelected to the Eighty-seventh Congress.*

HARDY, Rufus, a Representative from Texas; born near Aberdeen, Monroe County, Miss., December 16, 1855; attended private schools in Texas and Somerville Institute in Mississippi; was graduated from the law department of the University of Georgia at Athens in 1875; was admitted to the bar the same year and commenced practice in Navasota, Tex.; moved to Corsicana, Navarro County, Tex., in 1878; prosecuting attorney of Navarro County 1880–1884; district attorney for the thirteenth judicial district 1884–1888; district judge from 1888 to December 1896, when he retired; chairman of the Texas Sound Money Democracy in 1896; resumed the practice of law in Corsicana, Tex.; elected as a Democrat to the Sixtieth and to the seven succeeding Congresses (March 4, 1907–March 3, 1923); was not a candidate for renomination in 1922; resumed the practice of his profession; died in Corsicana, Tex., March 13, 1943; interment in Oakwood Cemetery.

HARDY, Samuel, a Delegate from Virginia; born in Isle of Wight County, Va., about 1758; completed preparatory studies, and was graduated from William and Mary College, Williamsburg, Va., in 1781; studied law; was admitted to the bar and commenced the practice of law; member of the State house of delegates in 1778 and 1780–1782; appointed a member of the executive council in June 1781; Lieutenant Governor of Virginia from May 29 to October 11, 1782; Member of the Continental Congress 1783–1785; died while attending Congress in Philadelphia, Pa., on October 17, 1785; interment in Christ Church Cemetery.

HARE, Butler Black (father of James Butler Hare), a Representative from South Carolina; born on a farm in Edgefield (now Saluda) County, near Leesville, S. C., November 25, 1875; attended the public schools; was graduated from Newberry (S. C.) College in 1899; taught in the public schools 1900–1903; secretary to Representative George W. Croft in 1904 and to his successor, Representative Theodore G. Croft, in 1905; professor of history and economics in Leesville (S. C.) College 1906–1908; special agent in the woman and child labor investigation conducted by the United States Bureau of Labor in 1908 and 1909; was graduated from George Washington University, Washington, D. C., in 1910, and from its law department in 1913; was admitted to the bar in 1913 and commenced practice in Saluda, S. C., in 1915; assistant in agricultural education, editor in rural economics, and agricultural statistician in the United States Department of Agriculture 1911–1924, and prepared an outline plan for a system of rural credits in the United States; engaged in agricultural pursuits; resumed the practice of law in Saluda, S. C., in 1924 and 1925; elected as a Democrat to the Sixty-ninth and to the three succeeding Congresses (March 4, 1925–March 3, 1933); was not a candidate for renomination in 1933; resumed his former pursuits; elected to the Seventy-sixth and to the three succeeding Congresses (January 3, 1939–January 3, 1947); unsuccessful candidate for renomination in 1946; resumed the practice of law and his agricultural pursuits; is a resident of Saluda, S. C.

HARE, Darius Dodge, a Representative from Ohio; born near Adrian, Seneca County, Ohio, January 9, 1843; attended the common schools; entered the military service as a private in the Signal Corps, United States Army, in March 1864, and served during the remainder of the Civil War; after the war was assigned to special duty at the headquarters of Major General Canby and afterward was with Major General Sheridan at New Orleans; remained on duty with the latter until discharged February 17, 1866; attended the law department of the University of Michigan at Ann Arbor; was admitted to the bar in September 1867 and commenced practice in Carey, Ohio; moved to Upper Sandusky, Ohio, in May 1868; mayor of Upper Sandusky 1872–1882; elected as a Democrat to the Fifty-second and Fifty-third Congresses (March 4, 1891–March 3, 1895); declined to be a candidate for renomination in 1894; continued the practice of law until his death in Upper Sandusky, Ohio, February 10, 1897; interment in Oak Hill Cemetery.

HARE, James Butler (son of Butler Black Hare), a Representative from South Carolina; born in Saluda, S. C., September 4, 1918; attended the public schools; was graduated from Newberry College in 1939; postgraduate work at Erskin College, Due West, S. C., in 1941; enlisted in the United States Navy in August 1940 and released to inactive duty in the Naval Reserve as a lieutenant commander in January 1946 with thirty-two months in the Pacific Theater; participated in the battles of Midway, Guadalcanal, Munda, Bougainville, Philippines, and Okinawa; was graduated from the law school of the University of South Carolina in 1947; was admitted to the bar the same year and commenced the practice of law in Saluda, S. C.; member of the board of trustees of the University of South Carolina; elected as a Democrat to the Eighty-first Congress (January 3, 1949–January 3, 1951); unsuccessful candidate for renomination in 1950; recalled to active duty in the United States Navy January 1, 1950, and served as law specialist until released to inactive duty as a commander in May 1952; resumed the practice of law; resides in Saluda, S. C.

HARE, Silas, a Representative from Texas; born in Ross County, Ohio, November 13, 1827; moved to Hamilton County, Ind., in 1840 with his parents, who settled near Noblesville; attended the common and private schools; served during the war with Mexico as a private in Captain Drake's company, First Regiment, Indiana Volunteers, 1846 and 1847; studied law; was admitted to the bar in 1850 and commenced practice in Noblesville, Ind.; moved to Belton, Tex., in 1853 and continued the practice of law; chief justice of New Mexico in 1862 under the Confederate Government; during the Civil War served as a captain in the Confederate Army; settled in Sherman, Tex., in 1865 and resumed the practice of law; district judge of the criminal court 1873–1876; delegate to the Democratic National Convention at Chicago in 1884; presidential elector for the State at large on the Democratic ticket of Cleveland and Hendricks in 1884; elected as a Democrat to the Fiftieth and Fifty-first Congresses (March 4, 1887–March 3, 1891); unsuccessful candidate for renomination in 1890; resumed the practice of law in Washington, D. C., where he died November 26, 1907; interment in West Hill Cemetery, Sherman, Grayson County, Tex.

HARGIS, Denver David, a Representative from Kansas; born in Key West, Fla., July 22, 1921; parents moved to Coffeyville, Montgomery County, Kans., in 1922; attended Coffeyville schools; enlisted in the United States Navy in January 1941 as an apprentice seaman and served until discharged as a signalman, second class, in October 1943 due to disability suffered while serving in the Pacific Theater; graduated from Washburn University, Topeka, Kans., in 1946 and from the law department in

1948; was admitted to the bar in 1948 and commenced the practice of law in Coffeyville, Kans.; in February 1949 was appointed district supervisor of the Census Bureau for the third district of Kansas; promoted to administrative officer for Kansas, Missouri, and Nebraska, and later promoted to regional assistant and served until December 1950; defeated for election as mayor of Coffeyville in 1951; elected mayor in 1953, reelected in 1955 and 1957 and served until elected to Congress; member of Library Board, Memorial Hall Board, Hospital Board, and Police Pension Board; appointed by Governor Docking as a member of the Arkansas River Basin Committee 1956–1959; delegate to Democratic State Conventions from 1952 to 1958 and delegate at large to Democratic National Convention in 1960; unsuccessful candidate for election in 1956 to the Eighty-fifth Congress; elected as a Democrat to the Eighty-sixth Congress (January 3, 1959–January 3, 1961); unsuccessful candidate for reelection in 1960 to the Eighty-seventh Congress; consultant with the Department of Defense, Installations and Logistics, in 1961; is a resident of Coffeyville, Kans.

HARING, John, a Delegate from New York; born in Tappan, Rockland County, N. Y., September 28, 1739; attended school in New York City; studied law; was admitted to the bar and practiced in New York City and Rockland County; Member of the Continental Congress in 1774, 1775, and 1785–1788; judge of Orange County in 1774, 1775, and 1778–1788; member of the provincial convention of April 1775 and of the four New York Provincial Congresses 1775–1777, serving as president pro tempore of the Second and Third Provincial Congresses; served in the State senate 1781–1789; member of the council of appointment in 1781 and 1782; member of the State board of regents in 1784; member of the State convention in 1788 to consider the Federal Constitution and voted to reject it; member of the State assembly in 1806; died in Blauveltville, Rockland County, N. Y., April 1, 1809; interment in Tappan Church Cemetery, Tappan, N. Y.

HARLAN, Aaron (cousin of Andrew Jackson Harlan), a Representative from Ohio; was born in Warren County, Ohio, September 8, 1802; attended the public schools; studied law; was admitted to the bar and commenced practice in Xenia, Ohio, in 1825; member of the State house of representatives in 1832 and 1833; served in the State senate in 1838, 1839, and 1849; moved to a farm near Yellow Springs, Ohio, in 1841 and continued the practice of law; presidential elector on the Polk and Dallas ticket in 1844; delegate to the State constitutional convention in 1850; member of the board of trustees of Antioch College in 1852; elected as a Whig to the Thirty-third, Thirty-fourth, and Thirty-fifth Congresses (March 4, 1853–March 3, 1859); unsuccessful candidate for reelection in 1858 to the Thirty-sixth Congress and in 1861 to fill a vacancy in the Thirty-seventh Congress; resumed the practice of law and engaged in agricultural pursuits near Yellow Springs; lieutenant colonel of the Ninety-fourth Regiment of Minutemen of Ohio in 1862 during the Civil War; moved to San Francisco, Calif., in 1864 and resided there until his death on January 8, 1868; interment in Laurel Hill Cemetery.

HARLAN, Andrew Jackson (cousin of Aaron Harlan), a Representative from Indiana; born near Wilmington, Clinton County, Ohio, March 29, 1815; attended the public schools; studied law; was admitted to the bar in 1839 and commenced practice in Richmond, Ind.; moved to Marion, Ind., in 1839; clerk of the State house of representatives in 1842 and a member 1846–1848; presidential elector on the Democratic ticket of Cass and Butler in 1848; elected as a Democrat to the Thirty-first Congress (March 4, 1849–March 3, 1851); elected to the

Thirty-third Congress (March 4, 1853–March 3, 1855); in a Democratic congressional convention at Marion, Ind., in 1854 he was publicly read out of the Democratic Party for voting against the repeal of the Missouri Compromise; declined the nomination from the People's Party in 1854 for the Thirty-fourth Congress; afterward allied himself with the Republican Party; moved to Dakota Territory in 1861; member of the Territorial house of representatives in 1861 and served as speaker; driven from the Territory by the Indians in September 1862 and settled in Savannah, Mo., where he resumed the practice of law; member of the State house of representatives 1864–1868, serving as speaker the last two years; moved to Wakeeney, Kans., in 1885 and practiced law; appointed by President Harrison as postmaster of Wakeeney and served from 1890 to 1894; removed to Savannah, Andrew County, Mo., in 1894; retired from practice of law; died in Savannah, Mo., May 19, 1907; interment in Savannah Cemetery.

HARLAN, Byron Berry, a Representative from Ohio; born in Greenville, Darke County, Ohio, October 22, 1886; moved with his parents to Dayton, Ohio, in 1894; attended the public schools; was graduated from the Law College of the University of Michigan at Ann Arbor in 1909 and from its College of Arts and Sciences in 1911; was admitted to the bar in 1909 and commenced practice in Dayton, Ohio, in 1911; assistant prosecuting attorney of Montgomery County, Ohio, 1912–1916; president of the Ohio Federated Humane Societies 1928–1943 and honorary vice president of the American Humane Association in 1938; elected as a Democrat to the Seventy-second and to the three succeeding Congresses (March 4, 1931–January 3, 1939); unsuccessful candidate for reelection in 1938 to the Seventy-sixth Congress; resumed the practice of law; delegate to the Democratic National Convention at Chicago in 1940; United States district attorney for the southern district of Ohio from May 1944 until March 1946; appointed judge of the Tax Court of the United States in 1946 and served until his death in Williamsport, Pa., November 11, 1949; interment in Woodland Cemetery, Dayton, Ohio.

HARLAN, James, a Representative from Kentucky; born in Mercer County, Ky., June 22, 1800; attended the public schools; engaged in mercantile pursuits from 1817 to 1821; studied law; was admitted to the bar in 1823 and commenced practice in Harrodsburg, Ky.; prosecuting attorney 1829–1844; elected as a Whig to the Twenty-fourth and Twenty-fifth Congresses (March 4, 1835–March 3, 1839); secretary of state of Kentucky 1840–1844; presidential elector on the Whig ticket of Harrison and Tyler in 1840; member of the State house of representatives in 1845; attorney general of Kentucky from 1850 until his death in Frankfort, Franklin County, Ky., February 18, 1863.

HARLAN, James, a Senator from Iowa; born in Clark County, Ill., August 26, 1820; when four years of age moved with his family to Indiana; attended the rural schools and assisted his father until 1841, when he entered college; was graduated from Indiana Asbury (now De Pauw) University, Greencastle, Ind., in 1845; moved to Iowa City, Iowa, in 1845; superintendent of public instruction in 1847; studied law; was admitted to the bar in 1848 and commenced practice in Iowa City; declined the Whig nomination for Governor of Iowa in 1850; president of Iowa Wesleyan University, Mount Pleasant, Iowa, 1853–1855; presented credentials as a Whig Senator-elect to the United States Senate and took his seat December 31, 1855; owing to irregularities in the legislative proceedings the Senate declared the seat vacant on January 12, 1857; reelected as a Republican in 1857 to fill the vacancy thus created; reelected in 1861 and served from January 29, 1857, until May 15, 1865, when he resigned to accept a Cabinet portfolio; Secretary of the Interior in the Cabinet of President Andrew Johnson from May 15, 1865, until July 27, 1866, when he resigned; again elected to the United States Senate and served from March 4, 1867, to March 3, 1873; delegate to the peace convention held in Washington, D. C., in 1861, in an effort to devise means to prevent the impending war; delegate to the Philadelphia Loyalist Convention in 1866; presiding judge of the court of commissioners of Alabama claims 1882–1885; died in Mount Pleasant, Henry County, Iowa, on October 5, 1899; interment in Forest Home Cemetery.

HARLESS, Richard Fielding, a Representative from Arizona; born in Kelsey, Upshur County, Tex., August 6, 1905; moved to Thatcher, Ariz., in 1917 and attended the grade and high schools; was graduated from University of Arizona at Tucson in 1928; taught school at Marana, Ariz., 1928–1930; was graduated from the law school of the University of Arizona in 1933; was admitted to the bar the same year and commenced practice in Phoenix, Ariz.; assistant city attorney of Phoenix, Ariz., in 1935; assistant attorney general of Arizona in 1936; county attorney of Maricopa County, Ariz., 1938–1942; elected as a Democrat to the Seventy-eighth, Seventy-ninth, and Eightieth Congresses (January 3, 1943–January 3, 1949); did not seek renomination in 1948 but was unsuccessful for the gubernatorial nomination; unsuccessful for the Democratic nomination in 1954 for the Eighty-fourth Congress; Democratic nominee in 1960 for the Eighty-seventh Congress; resumed the practice of law; is a resident of Phoenix, Ariz.

HARMANSON, John Henry, a Representative from Louisiana; born in Norfolk, Va., January 15, 1803; pursued classical studies and was graduated from Jefferson College, Washington, Miss.; moved to Avoyelles Parish, La., in 1830 and engaged in agricultural pursuits; studied law; was admitted to the bar and practiced; member of the State senate in 1844; elected as a Democrat to the Twenty-ninth, Thirtieth, and Thirty-first Congresses and served from March 4, 1845, until his death in New Orleans, La., October 24, 1850; interment in Moreau Plantation Cemetery, Pointe Coupee Parish, La.

HARMER, Alfred Crout, a Representative from Pennsylvania; born in Germantown, Pa., August 8, 1825; attended the public schools and Germantown Academy; commenced business as a shoe manufacturer; was a wholesale dealer until 1860; identified with railroad enterprises, shipping, and the wholesale coal business; member of the city council of Philadelphia 1856–1860; recorder of deeds for Philadelphia 1860–1863; delegate to the Republican National Convention at Chicago in 1865; elected as a Republican to the Forty-second and Forty-third Congresses (March 4, 1871–March 3, 1875); was an unsuccessful candidate for reelection in 1874 to the Forty-fourth Congress; elected to the Forty-fifth and to the eleven succeeding Congresses and served from March 4, 1877, until his death in Germantown, Philadelphia, Pa., on March 6, 1900; interment in West Laurel Hill Cemetery.

HARMON, Randall S., a Representative from Indiana; born in North Vernon, Jennings County, Ind., July 19, 1903; graduated from North Vernon High School; took extension courses in law and tool engineering; employed as a tool engineer with Delco Battery Operations in Muncie, Ind., 1933–1959; elected as a Democrat to the Eighty-sixth Congress (January 3, 1959–January 3, 1961); unsuccessful candidate for reelection in 1960 to the Eighty-seventh Congress; is a resident of Muncie, Ind.

HARNESS, Forest Arthur, a Representative from Indiana; born in Kokomo, Howard County, Ind., June 24, 1895; attended the public schools and was graduated from the law department of Georgetown University, Washington, D. C., in 1917; during the First World War served overseas as a first lieutenant, Three Hundred and Nineteenth Infantry, 1917–1919; wounded in action and was awarded Purple Heart Decoration; captain, Infantry Reserve, United States Army, 1920–1949; admitted to the District of Columbia bar in 1917, to the Indiana bar in 1919, and commenced practice in Kokomo, Ind.; prosecuting attorney of Howard County, Ind., 1920–1924; special assistant to the Attorney General of the United States from 1931 to 1935 when he resigned to resume private practice; elected as a Republican to the Seventy-sixth and to the four succeeding Congresses (January 3, 1939–January 3, 1949); unsuccessful candidate for reelection in 1948 to the Eighty-first Congress; resumed the practice of law; Sergeant at Arms of the United States Senate from January 3, 1953, to January 3, 1955; member of American Battle Monuments Commission 1955–1961; is a resident of Kokomo, Ind.

HARNETT, Cornelius, a Delegate from North Carolina; born near Edenton, Chowan County, N. C., April 20, 1723; moved with his parents to Brunswick in 1726 and later to Wilmington N. C.; engaged in mercantile pursuits; appointed by Governor Johnston as justice of the peace for New Hanover County in April 1750; elected town commissioner in August 1750 and served at different times for eleven years; member of the colonial assembly 1754–1775; chairman of the Sons of Liberty of North Carolina and leader in the resistance to the Stamp Act in 1765 and 1766; member of the committee of correspondence in 1773 and 1774; chairman of the Wilmington Committee of Safety in 1774 and 1775; member of the Second, Third, Fourth and Fifth Provincial Congresses in 1775 and 1776, serving as president in the Fifth; delegate to the provincial council in 1775 and 1776, and served as president of the council, thus becoming chief executive of the new government; excepted by Sir Henry Clinton from his proclamation of general amnesty in 1776; councilor of state in 1777; Member of the Continental Congress 1777–1780; captured by the British upon their occupation of Wilmington, N. C., in January 1781, and died as a prisoner in Wilmington on April 20, 1781; interment in St. James' Churchyard.

HARPER, Alexander, a Representative from Ohio; born near Belfast, Ireland, February 5, 1786; immigrated to the United States and settled in Zanesville, Muskingum County, Ohio; pursued preparatory studies; studied law; was admitted to the bar in 1813 and commenced practice in Zanesville, Ohio; member of the State house of representatives in 1820 and 1821; president judge of the court of common pleas 1822–1836; elected as a Whig to the Twenty-fifth Congress (March 4, 1837–March 3, 1839); elected to the Twenty-eighth and Twenty-ninth Congresses (March 4, 1843–March 3, 1847); again elected to the Thirty-second Congress (March 4, 1851–March 3, 1853); resumed the practice of law; died in Zanesville, Ohio, on December 1, 1860; interment in Greenwood Cemetery.

HARPER, Francis Jacob, a Representative from Pennsylvania; born in Frankford, Philadelphia County, Pa., March 5, 1800; member of the State house of representatives in 1832; served in the State senate in 1834 and 1835; elected as a Democrat to the Twenty-fifth Congress, but died in Frankford, Pa., March 18, 1837, before the assembling of Congress; interment in Frankford Cemetery; reinterment in December 1848 in the Congressional Cemetery, Washington, D. C.

HARPER, James, a Representative from Pennsylvania; born in Castlederg, County Tyrone, Ireland, March 28, 1780; immigrated to the United States and settled in Philadelphia, Pa.; attended the public schools; engaged in the manufacture of brick and from 1820 to 1830 in the wholesale grocery trade;

elected as a Clay Democrat to the Twenty-third Congress and as a Whig to the Twenty-fourth Congress (March 4, 1833–March 3, 1837); was not a candidate for renomination in 1836; resumed the manufacture of brick until he retired in 1869; member of the board of guardians of the poor and of the board of prison inspectors; died in Philadelphia, Pa., March 31, 1873; interment in Laurel Hill Cemetery.

HARPER, James Clarence, a Representative from North Carolina; born in Cumberland County, Pa., December 6, 1819; moved with his father to Darke County, Ohio, in 1831; attended the common schools; moved to Lenoir, Caldwell County, N. C., in 1840; land surveyor, civil engineer, and draftsman; laid out the town of Lenoir, N. C., in 1841; engaged in mercantile pursuits and subsequently became interested in the manufacture of cotton and woolen goods; held several local offices; colonel in the State militia; member of the State house of commons in 1865 and 1866; elected as a Conservative to the Forty-second Congress (March 4, 1871–March 3, 1873); was not a candidate for renomination in 1872; engaged in agricultural pursuits and in road building; died near Patterson, Caldwell County, N. C., January 8, 1890; interment in the Cemetery at Harpers Chapel, Patterson, N. C.

HARPER, John Adams, a Representative from New Hampshire; born in Derryfield, N. H., November 2, 1779; attended Phillips Exeter Academy, Exeter, N. H., in 1794; studied law; was admitted to the bar about 1802 and commenced practice in Sanbornton, N. H.; first postmaster of Sanbornton, N. H.; moved to Meredith Bridge (now Laconia, Belknap County) in 1806; clerk of the State senate 1805–1808; member of the State house of representatives in 1809 and 1810; served in the State militia 1809–1812; elected as a War Democrat to the Twelfth Congress (March 4, 1811–March 3, 1813); unsuccessful candidate for reelection in 1812 to the Thirteenth Congress; died at Meredith Bridge, N. H., June 18, 1816; interment in Union Cemetery.

HARPER, Joseph Morrill, a Representative from New Hampshire; born in Limerick, York County, Maine, June 21, 1787; attended the district school and the Fryeburg Academy; studied medicine; commenced practice in Sanbornton, N. H., in 1810; moved to Canterbury, N. H., in 1811 and continued the practice of medicine; served as assistant surgeon in the Fourth Infantry in the War of 1812; member of the State house of representatives in 1826 and 1827; justice of the peace in Canterbury 1826–1865; served in the State senate in 1829 and 1830, the last year as president of the senate and as ex officio Governor from February until June 1831; elected as a Democrat to the Twenty-second and Twenty-third Congresses (March 4, 1831–March 3, 1835); resumed the practice of medicine; justice of the peace and quorum in the State 1835–1865; president of Mechanics' Bank of Concord 1847–1856; retired from his profession; died in Canterbury, N. H., January 15, 1865; interment in the Village Cemetery.

HARPER, Robert Goodloe, a Representative from South Carolina and a Senator from Maryland; born near Fredericksburg, Va., in January 1765; moved with his parents to Granville, N. C., about 1769; received his early education at home and later attended grammar school; joined a volunteer corps of Cavalry when only fifteen years of age and served under Gen. Nathanael Greene in the Revolutionary Army until the British left the State; made a surveying tour through Kentucky and Tennessee in 1783; was graduated from Princeton College in 1785; studied law in Charleston, S. C., teaching school at the same time; was admitted to the bar in 1786 and commenced practice in Ninety Six District, S. C.; moved to Charleston,

S. C., in 1789; member of the State house of representatives 1790–1795; elected as a Federalist from South Carolina to the Third Congress to fill the vacancy caused by the death of Alexander Gillon; reelected to the Fourth, Fifth, and Sixth Congresses and served from February 5, 1795, to March 3, 1801; unsuccessful candidate for reelection in 1800 to the Seventh Congress; one of the managers appointed by the House of Representatives in 1798 to conduct the impeachment proceedings against William Blount, a Senator from Tennessee; Federalist leader of the House during the Fifth and Sixth Congresses; moved to Baltimore, Md., and engaged in the practice of law; served in the War of 1812, attaining the rank of major general; assisted in organizing the Baltimore Exchange Co. in 1815 and was a member of the first board of directors; member of the State Senate of Maryland; elected from Maryland to the United States Senate for the term beginning March 4, 1815, and served from January 29, 1816, until December 6, 1816, when he resigned; traveled extensively in England, France, and Italy in 1819 and 1820; took a prominent part in the ceremonies on the occasion of Lafayette's visit to Baltimore in 1824; died in Baltimore, Md., January 14, 1825; interment in the family burial ground on his estate, "Oakland"; reinterment in Greenmount Cemetery, Baltimore, Md.

HARPER, William, a Senator from South Carolina; born on the island of Antigua, West Indies, January 17, 1790; immigrated to the United States with his parents, who settled in Charleston, S. C., in 1791; moved to Columbia, S. C., and attended the common schools; was graduated from South Carolina College (now the University of South Carolina) at Columbia in 1808; studied medicine for a time in Charleston and later studied law; was admitted to the bar in 1813 and commenced the practice of law in Columbia; trustee of South Carolina College in 1813; member of the State house of representatives for the Richland District 1816–1818; moved to Missouri in 1818; chancellor of the State of Missouri 1819–1823; member of the State constitutional convention in 1821; returned to Columbia, S. C., in 1823; State reporter 1823–1825; appointed as a State Rights Democrat to the United States Senate to fill the vacancy caused by the death of John Gaillard and served from March 8 to November 29, 1826, when a successor was elected; returned to Charleston, S. C., in 1827 and practiced law; again a member of the State house of representatives for the Richland District in 1827 and 1828, serving as speaker in the latter year; chancellor of the State of South Carolina in 1828; returned to Columbia, S. C.; appointed judge of the court of appeals in 1830; member of the State convention in 1832 and 1833 (known as the Nullification Convention); again chancellor of the State from 1834 until his death in Fairfield District, S. C., October 10, 1847.

HARRELD, John William, a Representative and a Senator from Oklahoma; born near Morgantown, Butler County, Ky., January 24, 1872; attended the public schools, the normal school at Lebanon, Ohio, and Bryant and Stratton Business College of Louisville, Ky., where he taught while studying law; was admitted to the bar in 1889 and commenced practice in Morgantown, Ky.; prosecuting attorney of Butler County 1892–1896; moved to Ardmore, Okla., in 1906 and continued the practice of law; referee in bankruptcy 1908–1915, when he resigned to become an executive with an oil corporation; moved to Oklahoma City, Okla., in 1917 and engaged in the production of oil and continued the practice of law; elected as a Republican to the Sixty-sixth Congress to fill the vacancy caused by the death of Joseph B. Thompson and served from November 8, 1919, to March 3, 1921; was not a candidate for renomination, having become a candidate for the Republican nomination for United States Senator; elected as a Republican to the United States

Senate in 1920 and served from March 4, 1921, to March 3, 1927; unsuccessful candidate for reelection in 1926, and for election in 1940 to the Seventy-seventh Congress; returned to Oklahoma City and continued the practice of law and his interest in the oil business; died in Oklahoma City, Okla., December 26, 1950; interment in Fairlawn Cemetery.

HARRIES, William Henry, a Representative from Minnesota; born near Dayton, Montgomery County, Ohio, January 15, 1843; moved to La Crosse, Wis.; during the Civil War enlisted as a private in Company B, Second Regiment, Wisconsin Volunteer Infantry, April 18, 1861; commissioned captain of Company F, Third Regiment, United States Veteran Volunteers, General Hancock's corps, December 21, 1864; honorably discharged April 17, 1866; was graduated from the law school of the University of Michigan at Ann Arbor in 1868; was admitted to the bar May 6, 1868, and commenced practice in Hokah, Minn.; afterwards practiced in Caledonia, Houston County, Minn.; prosecuting attorney of Houston County 1874–1878; elected as a Democrat to the Fifty-second Congress (March 4, 1891–March 3, 1893); unsuccessful candidate for reelection in 1892 to the Fifty-third Congress; appointed by President Cleveland as collector of internal revenue for Minnesota and served from 1894 to 1898, residing in St. Paul, Minn.; returned to Caledonia, Minn., and resumed the practice of his profession in 1898; department commander of the Minnesota department of the Grand Army of the Republic in 1901; member of the board of trustees of the Minnesota Soldiers' Home in 1903, secretary of the board 1907–1911, and commandant of the home 1911–1918; died in Seattle, Wash., July 23, 1921; interment in Evergreen Cemetery, Caledonia, Minn.

HARRINGTON, Henry William, a Representative from Indiana; born near Cooperstown, Otsego County, N. Y., September 12, 1825; attended the common schools and in 1845 entered Temple Hill Academy, Livingston County, N. Y., where he remained for three years; studied law in Geneseo; was admitted to the bar in 1848 and commenced practice in Nunda, N. Y.; moved to Madison, Ind., in 1856 and continued the practice of law; moved to St. Louis, Mo., in 1872; returned to Indiana in 1874, settled in Indianapolis, and resumed the practice of law; delegate to the Democratic National Conventions in 1860, 1868, and 1872; elected as a Democrat to the Thirty-eighth Congress (March 4, 1863–March 3, 1865); unsuccessful candidate for reelection in 1864 to the Thirty-ninth Congress; collector of internal revenue for the third district of Indiana from October 27, 1866, to March 3, 1867; again engaged in the practice of law; died in Indianapolis, Ind., March 20, 1882; interment in Evergreen Cemetery, Alpena, Mich.

HARRINGTON, Vincent Francis, a Representative from Iowa; born in Sioux City, Woodbury County, Iowa, May 16, 1903; attended the public schools and Trinity College of his native city; was graduated from the University of Notre Dame, South Bend, Ind., in 1925; instructor in history and economics and athletic director at the University of Portland, Portland, Oreg., 1926–1927; returned to Sioux City, Iowa, in 1927 and became vice president and general manager of a mortgage company; member of the State senate 1933–1937; was nominated as a candidate for Lieutenant Governor of Iowa in 1936, but withdrew to accept a nomination for the House of Representatives; elected as a Democrat to the Seventy-fifth, Seventy-sixth, and Seventy-seventh Congresses and served from January 3, 1937, until his resignation on September 5, 1942, to accept a commission as major in the Air Corps, United States Army; died at Rutlandshire, England, on November 29, 1943, while on active duty in England; was posthumously awarded the Legion of Merit

for outstanding performance as special services officer of a Troop Carrier Command; interment in the United States Military Cemetery at Brookwood, thirty miles southwest of London, England.

HARRIS, Benjamin Gwinn, a Representative from Maryland; born near Leonardtown, St. Marys County, Md., December 13, 1805; attended Yale College and Cambridge (Mass.) Law School; studied law; was admitted to the bar in 1840; member of the State house of delegates in 1833 and 1836; elected as a Democrat to the Thirty-eighth and Thirty-ninth Congresses (March 4, 1863–March 3, 1867); was tried by a military court in Washington, D. C., in May 1865 for harboring two paroled Confederate soldiers, and sentenced to three years imprisonment and forever disqualified from holding any office under the United States Government, but President Andrew Johnson subsequently remitted the sentence; died on his estate, "Ellenborough," near Leonardtown, Md., April 4, 1895; interment in the family burying ground on his estate.

HARRIS, Benjamin Winslow (father of Robert Orr Harris), a Representative from Massachusetts; born in East Bridgewater, Mass., November 10, 1823; pursued an academic course, and was graduated from Dane Law School, Harvard University, in 1849; was admitted to the bar in Boston in 1850 and commenced practice in East Bridgewater; served in the State senate in 1857; member of the State house of representatives in 1858; district attorney for the southeastern district of Massachusetts from July 1, 1858, to June 30, 1866; collector of internal revenue for the second district of Massachusetts from June 30, 1866, to March 1, 1873, when he resigned, having been elected to Congress; elected as a Republican to the Forty-third and to the four succeeding Congresses (March 4, 1873–March 3, 1883); was not a candidate for renomination in 1882; resumed the practice of law in East Bridgewater, Plymouth County; judge of probate for the county of Plymouth 1887–1906; died in East Bridgewater, Mass., on February 7, 1907; interment in Union Cemetery.

HARRIS, Charles Murray, a Representative from Illinois; born in Munfordsville, Hart County, Ky., April 10, 1821; attended the common schools; studied law; was admitted to the bar; moved to Illinois and located in Oquawka, where he commenced the practice of his profession; elected as a Democrat to the Thirty-eighth Congress (March 4, 1863–March 3, 1865); unsuccessful candidate for reelection in 1864 to the Thirty-ninth Congress; died in Chicago, Ill., September 20, 1896; interment in Oquawka, Ill.

HARRIS, Christopher Columbus, a Representative from Alabama; born near Mount Hope, Lawrence County, Ala., January 28, 1842; educated in the common schools, and also by private tutors; during the Civil War enlisted in the Confederate Army in 1861 as a private in Company F, Sixteenth Alabama Infantry; was subsequently promoted to the rank of lieutenant; slightly wounded at Shiloh, Chickamauga, and Jonesboro, and desperately wounded at Franklin; taken as a prisoner to Camp Chase, Ohio, where he remained until the close of the war; clerk of the circuit court of Lawrence County 1865–1867; studied law; was admitted to the bar and commenced practice in Moulton, Ala., in 1868; moved to Decatur, Ala., in 1872 and continued the practice of law; in 1887 assisted in organizing the First National Bank of Decatur, of which he served as president until January 1913; organized the Bank of Commerce in 1913 and became its president; chairman of the Democratic executive committee of the eighth congressional district; elected as a Democrat to the Sixty-third Congress to fill the vacancy caused by the death of William Richardson and served from May 11, 1914, to March 3, 1915; was not a candidate for renomination in 1914; became president of the City National Bank of Decatur, Ala.; elected chairman of the board of directors on January 10. 1928; died in Decatur, Ala., December 28, 1935; interment in Decatur Cemetery.

HARRIS, George Emrick, a Representative from Mississippi; born in Orange County, N. C., January 6, 1827; moved to Tennessee and thence to Mississippi; attended the common schools; studied law; was admitted to the bar in 1854 and practiced; entered the Confederate Army and served as lieutenant colonel until the close of the Civil War; elected district attorney in 1865 and reelected in 1866; upon the readmission of the State of Mississippi to representation was elected as a Republican to the Forty-first and Forty-second Congresses and served from February 23, 1870, to March 3, 1873; attorney general of the State of Mississippi 1873–1877; Lieutenant Governor 1877–1879; engaged as an author of books on legal subjects; died in Washington, D. C., March 19, 1911; interment in Oak Hill Cemetery.

HARRIS, Henry Richard, a Representative from Georgia; born in Sparta, Hancock County, Ga., February 2, 1828; moved to Greenville, Meriwether County, Ga., in 1833; attended Professor Beeman's School for Boys, Mount Zion, Hancock County, Ga., and was graduated from Emory College at Oxford, Ga., in 1847; member of the State constitutional convention in 1861; during the Civil War served in the Confederate Army as colonel; elected as a Democrat to the Forty-third, Forty-fourth, and Forty-fifth Congresses (March 4, 1873–March 3, 1879); unsuccessful candidate for reelection in 1878 to the Forty-sixth Congress; elected to the Forty-ninth Congress (March 4, 1885–March 3, 1887); was not a candidate for renomination in 1886; appointed by President Cleveland as Third Assistant Postmaster General of the United States and served from April 1, 1887, to March 18, 1889; engaged in agricultural pursuits; died in Odessadale, Meriwether County, Ga., October 15, 1909; interment in Greenville Cemetery, Greenville, Ga.

HARRIS, Henry Schenck, a Representative from New Jersey; born in Belvidere, Warren County, N. J., December 27, 1850; attended the common schools, and was graduated from Princeton College in 1870; studied law; was admitted to the bar in 1873 and commenced practice in Belvidere, N. J.; appointed prosecutor of the pleas for Warren County in March 1877; elected as a Democrat to the Forty-seventh Congress (March 4, 1881–March 3, 1883); unsuccessful candidate for reelection in 1882 to the Forty-eighth Congress; resumed the practice of law; died in Belvidere, N. J., May 2, 1902; interment in Belvidere Cemetery.

HARRIS, Ira (grandfather of Henry Riggs Rathbone), a Senator from New York; born in Charleston, Montgomery County, N. Y., May 31, 1802; attended the district school and Homer (N. Y.) Academy; was graduated from Union College, Schenectady, N. Y., in 1824; studied law in Albany; was admitted to the bar in 1832 and commenced practice in Albany; member of the State assembly in 1845 and 1846; delegate to the State constitutional convention in 1846; served in the State senate in 1847; upon the organization of the Albany Law School in 1850 was engaged as lecturer on equity jurisprudence; justice of the State supreme court 1847–1859; elected as a Republican to the United States Senate and served from March 4, 1861, to March 3, 1867; unsuccessful candidate for reelection; delegate to the State constitutional convention in 1867; professor in the Albany Law School from 1867 until his death; died in Albany, N. Y., December 2, 1875; interment in Rural Cemetery, Colonie, near Watervliet, Albany County, N. Y.

HARRIS, Isham Green, a Representative and a Senator from Tennessee; born near Tullahoma, Franklin County, Tenn., February 10, 1818; attended the common schools and Winchester Academy; moved with his father to Paris, Tenn.; studied law; was admitted to the bar and commenced practice in Paris, Henry County, Tenn., in 1841; member of the State senate in 1847; presidential elector on the Democratic ticket in 1848; elected as a Democrat to the Thirty-first and Thirty-second Congresses (March 4, 1849–March 3, 1853); declined to be a candidate for renomination in 1852; moved to Memphis in 1853 and resumed the practice of law; presidential elector at large for the State in 1856; elected Governor of Tennessee in 1857, 1859, and 1861; volunteer aide on the staff of Gen. Albert Sidney Johnston until the latter's death and then served in the Confederate Army at headquarters of the Army of the West for the last three years of the Civil War; resumed the practice of law in Memphis, Tenn.; elected as a Democrat to the United States Senate in 1877; reelected in 1883, 1889, and 1895 and served from March 4, 1877, until his death; elected President pro tempore of the Senate March 22, 1893, and served until March 3, 1895, excepting three days in January of the latter year; died in Washington, D. C., July 8, 1897; funeral services were held in the Chamber of the United States Senate; interment in Elmwood Cemetery, Memphis, Tenn.

HARRIS, James Morrison, a Representative from Maryland; born in Baltimore, Md., November 20, 1817; educated at private institutions in Baltimore; entered Lafayette College, Easton, Pa., in 1833, but in 1835, owing to an eye affection, was obliged to leave before graduation; studied law; was admitted to the bar in 1843 and commenced practice in Baltimore; elected by the American Party to the Thirty-fourth, Thirty-fifth, and Thirty-sixth Congresses (March 4, 1855–March 3, 1861); declined to be a candidate for renomination in 1860; resumed the practice of law and also engaged in educational and religious work; trustee of Lafayette College 1865–1872; died in Baltimore, Md., on July 16, 1898; interment in Westminster Presbyterian Burying Ground.

HARRIS, John (cousin of Robert Harris), a Representative from New York; born at Harris Ferry (now Harrisburg), Pa., September 26, 1760; moved to Aurelias (now in Cayuga County), Onondaga County, N. Y., in 1789; operated the first ferry across Cayuga Lake; acted as an Indian interpreter, and opened the first store and tavern in Cayuga County in 1789; appointed a colonel in the New York State Militia in 1806; elected to the Tenth Congress (March 4, 1807–March 3, 1809); commanded the One Hundred and Fifty-eighth New York Regiment in the War of 1812; died in Bridgeport, near Seneca Falls, N. Y., in November 1824; interment in the local cemetery.

HARRIS, John Spafford, a Senator from Louisiana; born in Truxton, Cortland County, N. Y., on December 18, 1825; attended the common schools; moved to Du Page County, Ill., in the spring of 1846, and in December of the same year to Milwaukee, Wis.; employed as clerk in a mercantile establishment 1846–1849; studied the higher branches of education; engaged in mercantile pursuits 1849–1863; moved to Natchez, La., in 1863 and at the close of the Civil War was one of the largest cotton planters in the State; member of the State constitutional convention in 1868, being chosen one of a committee of seven to conduct the affairs of the State until the constitution should be adopted; served in the State senate in 1868; upon the readmission of Louisiana to representation was elected as a Republican to the United States Senate and served from July 9, 1868, to March 3, 1871; appointed surveyor general for Montana by President Arthur on November 21, 1881; died in Butte, Mont., January 25, 1906; interment in Forestvale Cemetery, Helena, Mont.

HARRIS, John Thomas (cousin of John Hill, of Virginia), a Representative from Virginia; born at Browns Gap, Albemarle County, Va., May 8, 1823; completed academic studies; studied law; was admitted to the bar in 1845 and commenced practice in Harrisonburg; Commonwealth attorney for Rockingham County, Va., 1852–1859; presidential elector on the Democratic ticket of Buchanan and Breckinridge in 1856; elected as a Democrat to the Thirty-sixth Congress (March 4, 1859–March 3, 1861); was nominated for reelection in 1860 but no election was held, Virginia having seceded from the Union on April 17, 1861; member of the State house of delegates 1863–1865; judge of the twelfth judicial circuit 1866–1869; on the readmission of Virginia to representation was an unsuccessful candidate for Congress at a special election held in July 1869; elected as a Democrat to the Forty-second and to the four succeeding Congresses (March 4, 1871–March 3, 1881); declined a unanimous renomination; chairman of the Virginia Democratic convention in 1884; presidential elector on the Democratic ticket of Cleveland and Thurman in 1888; commissioner to the World's Fair at Chicago; died in Harrisonburg, Va., October 14, 1899; interment in Woodbine Cemetery.

HARRIS, Mark, a Representative from Maine; born in Ipswich, Essex County, Mass., January 27, 1779; attended the common schools; moved to Portland, Maine (then a district of Massachusetts), in 1800; engaged in mercantile pursuits; member of the Massachusetts State Senate in 1816; held several local offices; elected to the Seventeenth Congress to fill the vacancy caused by the resignation of Ezekiel Whitman and served from December 2, 1822, to March 3, 1823; resumed mercantile pursuits; member of the State house of representatives in 1830; treasurer of Cumberland County 1824–1832 and 1834–1840; State treasurer 1828 and 1832–1834; moved to New York City in 1842 and engaged in mercantile pursuits; died in New York City March 2, 1843; interment probably in Old Eastern Cemetery, Portland, Maine.

HARRIS, Oren, a Representative from Arkansas; born in Belton, Hempstead County, Ark., December 20, 1903; attended the public schools; was graduated from Henderson College, Arkadelphia, Ark., in 1929 and from the Cumberland University Law School, Lebanon, Tenn., in 1930; was admitted to the bar in 1930 and commenced practice in El Dorado, Union County, Ark.; deputy prosecuting attorney of Union County, Ark., 1933–1936; prosecuting attorney of the thirteenth judicial circuit of Arkansas 1936–1940; delegate to the Democratic State conventions in 1936 and 1940 and to the Democratic National Convention at Chicago in 1944; elected as a Democrat to the Seventy-seventh and to the nine succeeding Congresses (January 3, 1941–January 3, 1961). *Reelected to the Eighty-seventh Congress.*

HARRIS, Robert (cousin of John Harris), a Representative from Pennsylvania; born at Harris Ferry (now Harrisburg), Pa., September 5, 1768; was reared on a farm; attended the public schools; assisted in establishing various enterprises, including building of the bridge over the Susquehanna River, the organization of the Harrisburg Bank, and the construction of the Middletown Turnpike Road; surveyor to lay off the road from Chambersburg to Pittsburgh, and also for improving the Susquehanna River; appointed commissioner to choose the location of the capitol building in Harrisburg; paymaster in the Army during the War of 1812; was a member of the party on the steamboat of John Fitch when it made the trial trip across the Delaware River; elected to the Eighteenth and Nineteenth Congresses (March 4, 1823–March 3, 1827); prothonotary of Dauphin County; died in Harrisburg, Pa., September 3, 1851; interment in Harrisburg Cemetery.

HARRIS, Robert Orr (son of Benjamin Winslow Harris), a Representative from Massachusetts; born in Boston, Mass., November 8, 1854; attended the common schools and Phillips Exeter Academy, Exeter, N. H.; was graduated from Harvard University in 1877; studied law; was admitted to the bar in 1879 and practiced in Boston and Brockton, Mass., 1879–1902; member of the State house of representatives in 1889; district attorney for the southeastern district of Massachusetts 1891–1901; associate judge of the superior court of Massachusetts from June 4, 1902, to March 1, 1911; elected as a Republican to the Sixty-second Congress (March 4, 1911–March 3, 1913); was not a candidate for renomination in 1912; resumed the practice of law; appointed United States district attorney for the Massachusetts district by President Harding in 1921 and served until removed by President Coolidge in December 1924; died in Brockton, Mass., June 13, 1926; interment in Central Cemetery, East Bridgewater, Mass.

HARRIS, Sampson Willis, a Representative from Alabama; born in Elbert County, Ga., February 23, 1809; obtained his early education from his mother, and was graduated from the University of Georgia at Athens in 1828; studied law; was admitted to the bar in 1830 and commenced practice in Athens, Ga.; member of the State house of representatives in 1834 and 1835; moved to Wetumpka, Ala., in 1838; elected solicitor of the eighth circuit in 1841; member of the State senate in 1844 and 1845; elected as a Democrat to the Thirtieth and to the four succeeding Congresses (March 4, 1847–March 3, 1857); declined to be a candidate for renomination in 1856; died in Washington, D. C., April 1, 1857; interment in Oconee Cemetery, Athens, Ga.

HARRIS, Stephen Ross (uncle of Ebenezer Byron Finley), a Representative from Ohio; born near Massillon, Stark County, Ohio, May 22, 1824; attended the common and select schools, Washington (Pa.) College, Norwalk (Ohio) Seminary, and Western Reserve College, then at Hudson, Ohio; studied law; was admitted to the bar in 1849 and commenced practice in Columbus, Ohio; moved to Bucyrus, Ohio, the same year and continued the practice of law; mayor of Bucyrus 1852, 1853, 1861, and 1862; deputy United States marshal in 1861; president of the State bar association in 1893 and 1894; elected as a Republican to the Fifty-fourth Congress (March 4, 1895–March 3, 1897); unsuccessful candidate for reelection in 1896 to the Fifty-fifth Congress; engaged in the practice of law in Bucyrus, Crawford County, Ohio, until his death there January 15, 1905; interment in Oakwood Cemetery.

HARRIS, Thomas K., a Representative from Tennessee; studied law; was admitted to the bar and practiced in Sparta and McMinnville, Tenn.; trustee of Priestly Academy, Sparta, Tenn.; member of the State senate 1809–1811; elected as a Democrat to the Thirteenth Congress (March 4, 1813–March 3, 1815); died from wounds received in an encounter with Col. John W. Simpson March 18, 1816, on the old Kentucky Road at Shells Ford of Collins River, between Sparta and McMinnville, Tenn.

HARRIS, Thomas Langrell, a Representative from Illinois; born in Norwich, Conn., October 29, 1816; pursued classical studies, and was graduated from Washington (now Trinity) College, Hartford, Conn., in 1841; studied law; was admitted to the bar in 1842 and commenced practice in Petersburg, Menard County, Ill.; school commissioner for Menard County in 1845; during the Mexican War raised and commanded a company and joined the Fourth Regiment, Illinois Volunteer Infantry; subsequently elected major of the regiment; while absent and with the Army was elected a member of the State senate in 1846; was presented with a sword by the State of

Illinois for gallantry at the Battle of Cerro Gordo, Mexico; elected as a Democrat to the Thirty-first Congress (March 4, 1849–March 3, 1851); unsuccessful candidate for reelection in 1850 to the Thirty-second Congress; was not a candidate in 1852; elected to the Thirty-fourth and Thirty-fifth Congresses and served from March 4, 1855, until his death; had been reelected to the Thirty-sixth Congress; died in Springfield, Ill., November 24, 1858; interment in Rose Hill Cemetery, Petersburg, Ill.

HARRIS, Wiley Pope, a Representative from Mississippi; born near Holmesville, Pike County, Miss., November 9, 1818; attended the common schools and the University of Virginia at Charlottesville; was graduated from the law department of Transylvania College, Lexington, Ky., in 1840; was admitted to the bar in 1840 and commenced practice in Gallatin, Copiah County, Miss.; circuit judge of the second district 1844–1850; member of the State constitutional conventions in 1850, 1861, and 1890; elected as a Democrat to the Thirty-third Congress (March 4, 1853–March 3, 1855); declined to be a candidate for renomination in 1854; resumed the practice of law in Jackson, Miss., Member of the Provisional Congress of the Confederate States in 1861; continued the practice of law in Jackson, Miss., and died there on December 3, 1891; interment in Greenwood Cemetery.

HARRIS, William Alexander, a Representative from Virginia; born near Warrenton, Fauquier County, Va., August 24, 1805; completed an academic course; studied law; was admitted to the bar and commenced practice in Luray; member of the State house of delegates in 1830 and 1831; presidential elector on the Democratic ticket of Van Buren and Johnson in 1840; elected as a Democrat to the Twenty-seventh Congress (March 4, 1841–March 3, 1843); editor of the Spectator and the Constitution in Washington, D. C.; Chargé d'Affaires to the Argentine Republic 1846–1851; moved to Missouri, and later returned to Washington, D. C.; editor of the Washington Union and printer to the United States Senate 1857–1859; died in Pike County, Mo., March 28, 1864; interment in Riverview Cemetery, Louisiana, Mo.

HARRIS, William Alexander (son of the preceding), a Representative and a Senator from Kansas; born near Luray, Loudon County, Va., October 29, 1841; attended the common schools, and was graduated from Columbian College (later George Washington University), Washington, D. C., in 1859 and from the Virginia Military Institute at Lexington in 1861; during the Civil War served three years in the Confederate Army as adjutant general of Gen. C. M. Wilcox's brigade and as ordnance officer of Gen. D. H. Hill's and General Rodes' divisions, Army of Northern Virginia; moved to Kansas in 1865 and was employed as a civil engineer in the construction of the Union Pacific Railroad until 1868; moved to Lawrence, Kans., in 1868; appointed agent for the railroad companies in the sale of the Delaware Reservation and other lands; moved to Linwood, Leavenworth County, in 1884 and engaged in agricultural pursuits and stock raising; elected as a Populist to the Fifty-third Congress (March 4, 1893–March 3, 1895); unsuccessful candidate for reelection in 1894 to the Fifty-fourth Congress; member of the State senate in 1896; elected as a Democrat to the United States Senate and served from March 4, 1897, to March 3, 1903; unsuccessful candidate for reelection; resumed his agricultural pursuits; unsuccessful candidate for Governor of Kansas in 1906; died in Chicago, Ill., on December 20, 1909; interment in Oak Hill Cemetery, Lawrence, Kans.

HARRIS, William Julius (great-grandson of Charles Hooks), a Senator from Georgia; born in Cedartown, Polk County, Ga., February 3, 1868; attended the common schools and was grad-

uated from the University of Georgia at Athens in 1890; engaged in the general insurance business and banking at Cedartown; served as private secretary to United States Senator Alexander S. Clay 1904–1909; member of the State senate in 1911 and 1912; chairman of the Democratic State committee in 1912 and 1913; appointed Director of the United States Census Bureau on July 1, 1913, and served until March 15, 1915, when he resigned to become a member of the Federal Trade Commission; Acting Secretary of the Department of Commerce 1913–1915; appointed a member of the Federal Trade Commission on March 16, 1915, and served until May 31, 1918, when he resigned to become a candidate for United States Senator; served as chairman of the commission from February 1, 1917, to May 6, 1918; elected as a Democrat to the United States Senate in 1918; reelected in 1924 and in 1930 and served from March 4, 1919, until his death; member of the National Forest Reservation Commission 1929–1932; died in Washington, D. C., April 18, 1932; funeral services were held in the Chamber of the United States Senate; interment in Greenwood Cemetery, Cedartown, Ga.

HARRIS, Winder Russell, a Representative from Virginia; born in Wake County (now a part of Raleigh), N. C., December 3, 1888; attended the public schools and St. Mary's College (now Belmont Abbey College), Belmont, N. C.; served in various editorial positions on newspapers in North Carolina and Virginia 1908–1918; member of the staff of Universal Service in Washington, D. C., 1918–1925, during which period was a member of the Press Galleries in the Capitol; assistant secretary to the American delegation to the International Narcotics Congress in Geneva, Switzerland, in 1924 and 1925; managing editor of the Virginian-Pilot, Norfolk, Va., 1925–1941; elected as a Democrat to the Seventy-seventh Congress to fill the vacancy caused by the resignation of Colgate W. Darden, Jr.; reelected to the Seventy-eighth Congress and served from April 8, 1941, until his resignation on September 15, 1944; engaged as vice president, Shipbuilders' Council of America, in Washington, D. C., until his resignation December 31, 1958; editor of the Alexandria Journal, the Arlington Journal, and the Fairfax County Journal-Standard; is a resident of Alexandria, Va.

HARRISON, Albert Galliton, a Representative from Missouri; born in Mount Sterling, Ky., June 26, 1800; completed preparatory studies, and was graduated from Transylvania University, Lexington, Ky., in 1820; studied law; was admitted to the bar and commenced practice in Mount Sterling; moved to Fulton, Mo., in 1827 and continued the practice of law; member of the Board of Visitors to the United States Military Academy at West Point in 1828; member of the commission to adjust land titles growing out of Spanish grants 1829–1835; elected as a Van Buren Democrat to the Twenty-fourth and Twenty-fifth Congresses (March 4, 1835–March 3, 1839); died in Fulton, Mo., September 7, 1839; interment in Congressional Cemetery, Washington, D. C.

HARRISON, Benjamin (father of Carter Bassett Harrison and William Henry Harrison), a Delegate from Virginia; born on the plantation "Berkeley," Charles City County, Va., April 5, 1726; pursued classical studies and attended William and Mary College, Williamsburg, Va.; member of the colonial house of burgesses 1749–1775 and was a member of the committee which drew up the address to the King and the remonstrance to Parliament on the passage of the declaratory act of 1764; member of the Virginia revolutionary convention in March, July, and December, 1775; Member of the Continental Congress 1774–1778; as chairman of the Committee of the Whole House he reported the resolution on June 10, 1776, offered three days before by Richard Henry Lee, declaring the independence of the American Colonies, and reported the Declaration of Independence, of which he was one of the signers, on July 4, 1776; resigned in 1778; member of the State house of delegates 1776–1782 and 1787–1791 and served as speaker 1778–1782, 1785, and 1786; Governor of Virginia 1782–1784; delegate to the State convention for the ratification of the Federal Constitution in 1788; died at his home, "Berkeley," Charles City County, Va., April 24, 1791; interment thought to be in the old "Westover" plantation family burial grounds on the north side of the James River.

HARRISON, Benjamin (great-grandson of Benjamin Harrison of Virginia, grandson of President William Henry Harrison, son of John Scott Harrison of Ohio, and grandfather of William Henry Harrison of Wyoming), a Senator from Indiana and a President of the United States; born in North Bend, Hamilton County, Ohio, August 20, 1833; was graduated from Miami University, Oxford, Ohio, in 1852; studied law in Cincinnati; moved to Indianapolis in March 1854; was admitted to the bar and practiced; reporter of the decisions of the supreme court of the State; during the Civil War was commissioned second lieutenant of Indiana Volunteers in July 1862; raised Company A of the Seventieth Regiment, Indiana Volunteer Infantry, was made its captain, and on the organization of the regiment was commissioned colonel; went with the regiment to Kentucky in August and served until mustered out in June 1865; brevetted brigadier general January 23, 1865; while in the field in October 1864 was reelected reporter of the State supreme court and served four years; unsuccessful Republican candidate for Governor of Indiana in 1876; appointed a member of the Mississippi River Commission in 1879; delegate to the Republican National Conventions at Chicago in 1880 and 1884; elected as a Republican to the United States Senate and served from March 4, 1881, to March 3, 1887; elected President of the United States in 1888, was inaugurated on March 4, 1889, and served until March 3, 1893; renominated for a second term but was defeated by Grover Cleveland; attorney for the Republic of Venezuela in the boundary dispute between Venezuela and Great Britain, which was arbitrated at Paris in 1900; died in Indianapolis, Ind., March 13, 1901; interment in Crown Hill Cemetery.

HARRISON, Burr Powell (son of Thomas Walter Harrison), a Representative from Virginia; born in Winchester, Frederick County, Va., July 2, 1904; attended the public schools, Woodberry Forest School, Virginia Military Institute, Hampden-Sydney College, and the University of Virginia; was graduated from Georgetown University Law School, Washington, D.C., in 1926; was admitted to the bar the same year and commenced practice in Winchester, Va.; attorney for Frederick County 1932–1940; served in State senate 1940–1942; judge of the seventeenth judicial circuit and the corporation court of Winchester 1942–1946; elected on November 5, 1946, as a Democrat to the Seventy-ninth Congress to fill the vacancy caused by the resignation of A. Willis Robertson and at the same time was elected to the Eightieth Congress, reelected to the Eighty-first and to the five succeeding Congresses and served from November 6, 1946, to January 3, 1961. *Reelected to the Eighty-seventh Congress.*

HARRISON, Byron Patton (Pat), a Representative and a Senator from Mississippi; born at Crystal Springs, Copiah County, Miss., August 29, 1881; attended the public schools, and the University of Louisiana at Baton Rouge; taught school at Leakesville, Miss., and also studied law; was admitted to the bar in 1902 and commenced practice in Leakesville, Miss.; district attorney for the second district of Mississippi from 1905 to 1910, when he resigned; moved to Gulfport, Miss., in 1908; chairman of the Democratic State convention in 1916; delegate to the Democratic National Conventions in 1908 and 1920; also delegate to and temporary chairman of the Democratic

National Convention at New York City in 1924; elected as a Democrat to the Sixty-second and to the three succeeding Congresses (March 4, 1911–March 3, 1919); was not a candidate for renomination in 1918, having become a candidate for Senator; elected to the United States Senate in 1918; reelected in 1924, 1930, and again in 1936 and served from March 4, 1919, until his death; was elected President pro tempore of the Senate January 6, 1941; died in Washington, D. C., June 22, 1941; services were held in the Chamber of the United States Senate; interment in Evergreen Cemetery, Gulfport, Miss.

HARRISON, Carter Bassett (son of Benjamin Harrison of Virginia and brother of William Henry Harrison), a Representative from Virginia; born in Charles City County, Va.; pursued classical studies; attended William and Mary College, Williamsburg, Va.; member of the State house of delegates 1784–1786; elected to the Third, Fourth, and Fifth Congresses (March 4, 1793–March 3, 1799); again a member of the State house of delegates 1805–1808; died at the Maycock plantation, Prince George County, Va., April 18, 1808.

HARRISON, Carter Henry, a Representative from Illinois; born near Lexington, Fayette County, Ky., February 15, 1825; educated by private tutors; was graduated from Yale College in 1845; traveled and studied in Europe 1851–1853; was graduated from the law department of Transylvania College, Lexington, Ky., in 1855; was admitted to the bar in 1855 and commenced practice in Chicago, Ill.; also engaged in the real-estate business; unsuccessful candidate in 1872 for election to the Forty-third Congress; member of the board of commissioners of Cook County 1874–1876; elected as a Democrat to the Forty-fourth and Forty-fifth Congresses (March 4, 1875–March 3, 1879); was not a candidate for renomination in 1878; mayor of Chicago 1879–1887 and declined a renomination; unsuccessful candidate for Governor of Illinois in 1884; delegate to the Democratic National Conventions in 1880 and 1884; delegate to the Democratic State convention at Peoria in 1884; owner and editor of the Chicago Times 1891–1893; again elected mayor of Chicago in 1893 and served until his death in Chicago by assassination October 28, 1893; interment in Graceland Cemetery, Chicago, Ill.

HARRISON, Francis Burton, a Representative from New York; born in New York City December 18, 1873; was graduated from Cutler School at New York City, from Yale University in 1895, and from the New York Law School in 1897; instructor in the New York Night Law School 1897–1899; was admitted to the bar in 1898; served during the war with Spain in Troop A, New York Volunteer Cavalry, from May 19 to June 20, 1898, and was captain and assistant adjutant general, United States Volunteers, from June 20, 1898, to January 31, 1899; elected as a Democrat to the Fifty-eighth Congress (March 4, 1903–March 3, 1905); did not seek renomination in 1904, having become a candidate for Lieutenant Governor of New York, but was unsuccessful; elected to the Sixtieth and to the three succeeding Congresses and served from March 4, 1907, until his resignation, effective September 1, 1913; Governor General of the Philippine Islands 1913–1921; resided in Scotland 1921–1934; appointed adviser to the president of the Philippine Commonwealth in November 1935 and served for ten months; in May 1942 was again appointed to the same position; United States Commissioner of Claims in the civil service of the United States Army in Manila from November 1946 to February 1947; served as an adviser to the first four presidents of the Philippine Republic after their independence in 1946; resided in Spain for six years, returning to Califon, Hunterdon County, N. J., in August 1957; died in Flemington, N. J., November 21, 1957; interment in Manila Cemetery, Manila, Philippines.

HARRISON, George Paul, a Representative from Alabama; born at "Monteith Plantation," near Savannah, Ga., March 19, 1841; attended Effingham Academy and the Georgia Military Institute at Marietta; during the Civil War entered the Confederate Army as second lieutenant of the First Georgia Regulars and was successively promoted to first lieutenant, major, colonel, and brigadier general; moved to Alabama in 1865; studied law; was admitted to the bar and commenced practice in Auburn, Ala.; member of the constitutional convention of Alabama in 1875; served in the State senate 1876–1884 and was its president 1882–1884; delegate to the Democratic National Convention at Chicago in 1892; elected as a Democrat to the Fifty-third Congress to fill the vacancy caused by the resignation of William C. Oates; reelected to the Fifty-fourth Congress and served from November 6, 1894, to March 3, 1897; resumed the practice of law in Opelika, Lee County, Ala.; delegate to the State constitutional convention in 1901; general counsel for the Western Railway of Alabama; division counsel for the Central of Georgia Railway; died in Opelika, Ala., July 17, 1922; interment in Rosemere Cemetery.

HARRISON, Horace Harrison, a Representative from Tennessee; born in Lebanon, Wilson County, Tenn., on August 7, 1829; attended Carroll Academy and completed the course in the ancient classics under a private instructor; moved with his parents to McMinnville in 1841; clerk of the county court; master of the chancery court; register of deeds; clerk of the State senate in 1851 and 1852; studied law; was admitted to the bar in 1857 and commenced practice in McMinnville; moved to Nashville in 1859 and continued the practice of law; United States district attorney 1863–1866; chancellor in the Nashville division in 1866; judge of the State supreme court in 1867 and 1868; presidential elector on the Republican ticket of Grant and Colfax in 1868; again United States district attorney in 1872 and 1873; elected as a Republican to the Forty-third Congress (March 4, 1873–March 3, 1875); unsuccessful candidate for reelection; delegate to the Republican National Convention in 1880; member of the State legislature in 1880 and 1881; presidential elector on the Republican ticket of Blaine and Logan in 1884; died in Nashville, Tenn., December 20, 1885; interment in Mount Olivet Cemetery.

HARRISON, John Scott (son of President William Henry Harrison of Ohio, grandson of Benjamin Harrison of Virginia, and father of President Benjamin Harrison of Indiana), a Representative from Ohio; born in Vincennes, Knox County, Ind., October 4, 1804; completed preparatory studies; studied medicine but abandoned the profession; engaged in agricultural pursuits; elected as a Whig to the Thirty-third and Thirty-fourth Congresses (March 4, 1853–March 3, 1857); unsuccessful candidate for reelection; retired to his estate "Point Farm," near North Bend, Ohio, and died there May 25, 1878; interment in the Harrison Tomb, North Bend, Ind.

HARRISON, Richard Almgill, a Representative from Ohio; born in Thirsk, Yorkshire, England, April 8, 1824; immigrated to the United States in 1832 with his parents, who settled in Ohio; attended the public schools and was graduated from the Cincinnati Law School in 1846; was admitted to the bar in 1846 and commenced practice in London, Madison County, Ohio; member of the State house of representatives 1858 and 1859; served in the State senate 1860 and 1861; elected as a Union Democrat to the Thirty-seventh Congress to fill the vacancy caused by the resignation of Thomas Corwin and served from July 4, 1861, to March 4, 1863; continued the practice of law in Columbus, Ohio, until his death there July 30, 1904; interment in Kirkwood Cemetery, London, Ohio.

HARRISON, Robert Dinsmore, a Representative from Nebraska; born on a farm near Panama, Lancaster County, Nebr., January 26, 1897; attended the public schools of Lancaster County; was graduated from Peru State Teachers College in 1926, University of California in 1928, and University of Nebraska in 1934; during the First World War served as a sergeant in the Twenty-second Engineers in 1918 and 1919; superintendent of schools in Bradshaw, Nebr., 1926–1929, and in De Witt, Nebr., 1929–1937; member of the Norfolk, Nebr., School Board 1942–1951, and the Governor's Highway Advisory Committee; owner and operator of an oil business in Norfolk, Nebr.; also operates a farm in Cedar County, Nebr.; elected as a Republican to the Eighty-second Congress to fill the vacancy caused by the death of Karl Stefan; reelected to the Eighty-third, Eighty-fourth, and Eighty-fifth Congresses and served from December 4, 1951, to January 3, 1959; unsuccessful for reelection in 1958 to the Eighty-sixth Congress; adviser to Board of Directors of the Commodity Credit Corporation, Department of Agriculture from January 6, 1959 to April 1, 1960; appointed Nebraska State director, Federal Crop Insurance Corporation, April 1, 1960; resides in Norfolk, Nebr.

HARRISON, Samuel Smith, a Representative from Pennsylvania; born in Virginia in 1780; completed preparatory studies; studied law; was admitted to the bar and practiced; moved to Kittanning, Armstrong County, Pa.; elected as a Democrat to the Twenty-third and Twenty-fourth Congresses (March 4, 1833–March 3, 1837); resumed the practice of law; died in Kittanning, Pa., April 1853; interment in Old Kittanning Cemetery.

HARRISON, Thomas Walter (father of Burr Powell Harrison), a Representative from Virginia; born in Leesburg, Loudoun County, Va., August 5, 1856; attended local academies at Leesburg, Middleburg, and Hanover; was graduated from the academic and law departments of the University of Virginia at Charlottesville in 1879; was admitted to the bar in 1879 and commenced practice in Winchester, Va.; member of the State senate 1887–1894; judge of the circuit court for the seventeenth judicial district of Virginia from 1895 until September 1, 1916, when he resigned to make the canvass for the congressional nomination; editor of the Winchester Times; member of the State constitutional convention in 1901 and 1902; elected as a Democrat to the Sixty-fourth Congress to fill the vacancy caused by the resignation of James Hay; reelected to the Sixty-fifth and Sixty-sixth Congresses and served from November 7, 1916, to March 3, 1921; presented credentials as a Member-elect to the Sixty-seventh Congress and served from March 4, 1921, to December 15, 1922, when he was succeeded by John Paul, who contested his election; elected to the Sixty-eighth, Sixty-ninth, and Seventieth Congresses (March 4, 1923–March 3, 1929); unsuccessful candidate for reelection in 1928 to the Seventy-first Congress; practiced law in Winchester, Va., until his death there on May 9, 1935; interment in Mount Hebron Cemetery.

HARRISON, William, Jr., a Delegate from Maryland; born in that State; member of the Continental Congress 1785–1787; engaged in shipbuilding at St. Michaels, Talbot County, Md., in 1810; served as first lieutenant in Capt. Robert H. Goldsborough's Troop of Horse, called the Independent Light Dragoons, Ninth Regiment of Cavalry, Maryland Militia, in 1812; later commanded this troop as captain; served as justice of the court at St. Michaels in 1813.

HARRISON, William Henry (son of Benjamin Harrison of Virginia, father of John Scott Harrison, brother of Carter

Basset Harrison, grandfather of Benjamin Harrison, and great-great-grandfather of William Henry Harrison of Wyoming) a, Delegate from the Territory Northwest of the River Ohio, a Representative and a Senator from Ohio, and a President of the United States; born in Berkeley, Charles City County, Va., February 9, 1773; pursued classical studies; attended Hampden-Sidney College, Virginia; studied medicine; commissioned by President Washington ensign in the First Infantry August 16, 1791, and served in the Indian wars; in May 1797 was made captain and given command of Fort Washington; resigned June 1, 1798, with the rank of captain; secretary of the Northwest Territory 1798–99; elected as a Delegate from the Territory Northwest of the River Ohio to the Sixth Congress and served from March 4, 1799, to May 14, 1800, when he resigned; Territorial Governor of Indiana 1801–1813 and also Indian commissioner; defeated the Indians at Tippecanoe November 7, 1811; major general in the United States Army in the War of 1812; again defeated the British and Indians in the Battle of the Thames, October 5, 1813; resigned from the Army in 1814; head commissioner to treat with the Indians; elected as a Whig to the Fourteenth Congress to fill the vacancy caused by the resignation of John McLean; reelected to the Fifteenth Congress and served from October 8, 1816, to March 3, 1819; member of the State senate 1819–1821; elected to the United States Senate and served from March 4, 1825, to May 20, 1828, when he resigned; Minister to Colombia May 24, 1828, to September 26, 1829; unsuccessful Whig candidate for President in 1836; elected President of the United States and served from March 4, 1841, until his death in Washington, D. C., April 4, 1841; interment in the Harrison Tomb, opposite Congress Green Cemetery, North Bend, Ohio.

HARRISON, William Henry (great-great-grandson of President William Henry Harrison and grandson of President Benjamin Harrison and Alvin Saunders), a Representative from Wyoming; born in Terre Haute, Vigo County, Ind., August 10, 1896; attended the public schools of Omaha, Nebr., the Sidwell Friends School, Washington, D. C., and the College of Agriculture at the University of Nebraska in 1919 and 1920; during the First World War served in the United States Army as a private in the Signal Enlisted Air Corps; was admitted to the Indiana bar in 1925 and practiced in Indianapolis 1925–1936; member of the Indiana House of Representatives 1927–1929; was admitted to the Wyoming bar in 1937 and practiced in Sheridan, Wyo.; member of the Wyoming House of Representatives 1945–1950; secretary to the Wyoming Interim Committee 1947–1950; elected as a Republican to the Eighty-second and Eighty-third Congresses (January 3, 1951–January 3, 1955); was not a candidate for renomination in 1954, but was an unsuccessful candidate for election to the United States Senate; regional administrator, Housing and Home Finance Agency, from April 1955 to August 31, 1956; liaison officer, Housing and Home Finance Agency, Washington, D. C., from April 1, 1957, to November 15, 1958. *Elected to the Eighty-seventh Congress.*

HART, Alphonso, a Representative from Ohio; born in Vienna, Trumbull County, Ohio, July 4, 1830; attended the common schools and Grand River Institute, Austinburg, Ohio; studied law in Warren, Ohio; was admitted to the bar August 12, 1851, and commenced practice in Ravenna, Ohio; prosecuting attorney for Portage County 1861 to 1864, when he resigned; member of the State senate 1865, 1872, and 1873; presidential elector at large on the Republican ticket of Grant and Wilson in 1872; Lieutenant Governor of Ohio 1873–1875; elected as a Republican to the Forty-eighth Congress (March 4, 1883–March 3, 1885); unsuccessful candidate for election to the Forty-ninth Congress; served as Solicitor of Internal Revenue, Treasury

Department, 1888–1892; resumed the practice of law in Washington, D. C., and died there December 23, 1910; interment in Maple Grove Cemetery, Ravenna, Portage County, Ohio.

HART, Archibald Chapman, a Representative from New Jersey; born in Lennoxville, Province of Quebec, Canada, February 27, 1873; moved with his parents to New York City in 1882 and to Hackensack, N. J., in 1884; attended the common schools; studied law; was admitted to the New Jersey bar in 1896 and commenced practice in Hackensack, N. J.; served in the Second Regiment, New Jersey Volunteer Infantry, during the Spanish-American War; served four years in the Twenty-third Regiment of the New York National Guard; banker, publisher, and real-estate operator; delegate to the Democratic National Convention at Denver in 1908; elected as a Democrat to the Sixty-second Congress to fill the vacancy caused by the resignation of William Hughes and served from November 5, 1912, to March 3, 1913; unsuccessful candidate for the Democratic nomination in 1912 to the Sixty-third Congress but was later elected to this Congress to fill the vacancy caused by the death of Lewis J. Martin; reelected to the Sixty-fourth Congress and served from July 22, 1913, to March 3, 1917; declined to be a candidate for renomination in 1916; resumed the practice of law and his former business pursuits in Hackensack and resided in Teaneck, N. J.; prosecuting attorney for Bergen County 1920–1930; died in Teaneck, N. J., July 24, 1935; interment in Hackensack Cemetery, Hackensack, N. J.

HART, Edward Joseph, a Representative from New Jersey; born in Jersey City, N. J., March 25, 1893; attended the public and parochial schools; was graduated from St. Peter's College, Jersey City, N. J., in 1913 and from the law department of Georgetown University, Washington, D. C., in 1924; secretary to the Excise Commission, Washington, D. C., 1913–1917; chief field deputy, Internal Revenue Bureau, 1916–1921; admitted to the District of Columbia bar in 1924 and to the New Jersey bar in 1925; practiced law in Jersey City since 1927; assistant corporation counsel of Jersey City 1930–1934; chairman of the Democratic State Committee of New Jersey 1944–1949; alternate delegate at large to the Democratic National Convention in 1940 and delegate at large in 1944; elected as a Democrat to the Seventy-fourth and to the nine succeeding Congresses (January 3, 1935–January 3, 1955); was not a candidate for renomination in 1954; member of State Board of Public Utility Commissioners 1955–1960; died in West Allenhurst, Ocean Township, Monmouth County, N. J., April 20, 1961; interment in St. Catharine's Cemetery, Sea Girt, N. J.

HART, Elizur Kirke, a Representative from New York; born in Albion, Orleans County, N. Y., April 8, 1841; attended the Albion Academy; engaged in banking; member of the State assembly in 1872; director Niagara Falls International Bridge Co.; elected as a Democrat to the Forty-fifth Congress (March 4, 1877–March 3, 1879); was not a candidate for renomination in 1878; resumed his former business pursuits; founder and president of the Rochester (N. Y.) Post-Express in 1882; president of Orleans County National Bank 1890–1893; died in Albion, N. Y., February 18, 1893; interment in Mount Albion Cemetery.

HART, Emanuel Bernard, a Representative from New York; born in New York City October 27, 1809; attended the public schools and prepared for college; engaged in mercantile pursuits; colonel in the militia; member of the board of aldermen in 1845; elected as a Democrat to the Thirty-second Congress (March 4, 1851–March 3, 1853); appointed by President Buchanan surveyor of the port of New York and served from

1857 to 1861; member of the city board of assessors; studied law; was admitted to the bar in 1868 and practiced; presidential elector on the Democratic ticket of Seymour and Blair in 1868; president of Mount Sinai Hospital 1870–1876; commissioner of immigration 1870–1873; excise commissioner in 1879; treasurer of the Society for the Relief of Poor Hebrews; died in New York City August 29, 1897; interment in Cypress Hills Cemetery, Brooklyn, N. Y.

HART, John, a Delegate from New Jersey; born in Stonington, Conn., about 1707; moved with his parents to Hopewell Township, Hunterdon County, N. J.; attended private school; engaged in agricultural pursuits; member of the Provincial Assembly of New Jersey 1761–1771; judge of Hunterdon County courts 1768–1775; member of the New Jersey Provincial Congress from May 23, 1775, to June 22, 1776, and was elected vice president on June 16, 1776; member of the committee of safety from August 17 to October 4, 1775, and again from October 28, 1775, to January 31, 1776; Member of the Continental Congress from June 22 to August 30, 1776; a signer of the Declaration of Independence; elected to the first State general assembly under the State constitution in August 1776 and reelected in 1777 and 1778; served as speaker 1776–1778; chairman of the New Jersey Council of Safety in 1777 and 1778; when the British troops invaded New Jersey his estate was devastated, and he was forced to flee to the forests to save his life; returned to his home after the capture of the Hessians by General Washington; died on his estate near Hopewell, Hunterdon County, N. J., on May 11, 1779; interment in the First Baptist Church Cemetery, Hopewell, N. J.

HART, Joseph Johnson, a Representative from Pennsylvania; born in Nyack, Rockland County, N. Y., April 18, 1859; attended the schools of Nyack, and was graduated from the Charlier Institute, New York City, in 1876; conducted and owned City and Country, a Democratic newspaper of Nyack, until 1883, when he moved to Pike County, Pa., where he engaged in the real-estate, lumber, and insurance businesses; school director of Milford; conducted and owned the Milford Dispatch 1890–1900; elected as a Democrat to the Fifty-fourth Congress (March 4, 1895–March 3, 1897); was not a candidate for renomination in 1896; resumed his newspaper interests in Milford; moved to New York City in 1900 and engaged in clerical work; deputy tax commissioner of the city of New York from 1907 until his death; died in Brooklyn, N. Y., July 13, 1926; interment in Oak Hill Cemetery, Nyack, N. Y.

HART, Michael James, a Representative from Michigan; born in Waterloo, Quebec Province, Canada, July 16, 1877; immigrated to the United States with his parents in 1880 and settled in James Township, Saginaw County, Mich.; attended the district schools of Jamestown and Saginaw, Mich., and a business college; teacher in the public schools of Saginaw County, Mich., 1896–1898; engaged in agricultural pursuits and in 1920 also engaged in the packing and shipping of farm products; unsuccessful candidate for election in 1930 to the Seventy-second Congress, but was later elected as a Democrat to the Seventy-second Congress to fill the vacancy caused by the death of Bird J. Vincent; reelected to the Seventy-third Congress and served from November 3, 1931, to January 3, 1935; unsuccessful candidate for reelection in 1934 to the Seventy-fourth Congress and for election in 1936 to the Seventy-fifth Congress and in 1942 to the Seventy-eighth Congress; was a delegate to the Democratic National Convention in 1932; returned to Saginaw, Mich., and former business activities; president of a brewing company, 1935–1937; died in Saginaw, Mich., February 14, 1951; interment in St. Andrews Cemetery.

HART, Philip A., a Senator from Michigan; born in Bryn Mawr, Montgomery County, Pa., December 10, 1912; attended Waldron Academy and West Philadelphia Catholic High School; graduated from Georgetown University, Washington, D. C., in 1934 and from the University of Michigan Law School at Ann Arbor in 1937; was admitted to the Michigan bar in 1938 and commenced the practice of law in Detroit, Mich.; during World War II served in the United States Army from 1941 until discharged in 1946 as a lieutenant colonel of Infantry; while serving with the Fourth Infantry Division was wounded during the D-Day assault on Utah Beach in Normandy; Michigan Corporation Securities Commissioner from 1949 until his resignation in 1951; State director of the Office of Price Stabilization in 1951 and 1952; United States district attorney of the Eastern Michigan District in 1952 and 1953; trustee and former president of Michigan State Bar Foundation; legal adviser to Governor Williams in 1953 and 1954; Lieutenant Governor 1955–1958; delegate at large to the Democratic National Conventions in 1956 and 1960; elected as a Democrat to the United States Senate for the term commencing January 3, 1959, and ending January 3, 1965.

HART, Roswell, a Representative from New York; born in Rochester, N. Y., August 4, 1824; completed preparatory studies, and was graduated from Yale College in 1843; studied law; was admitted to the bar in 1847; engaged in commercial pursuits; elected as a Republican to the Thirty-ninth Congress (March 4, 1865–March 3, 1867); unsuccessful candidate for reelection in 1866 to the Fortieth Congress; superintendent of the Railway Mail Service for the States of New York and Pennsylvania 1869–1876; died in Rochester, N. Y., on April 20, 1883; interment in Mount Hope Cemetery.

HART, Thomas Charles, a Senator from Connecticut; born in Davison, Genesee County, Mich., June 12, 1877; attended various public schools in Michigan; was graduated from the United States Naval Academy, Annapolis, Md., in 1897; served in the Regular Navy from graduation until February 14, 1945, when placed on the inactive list as an admiral (retired); his naval career covered service afloat during the Spanish-American War and both World Wars; received the Distinguished Service Medal; appointed as a Republican to the United States Senate to fill the vacancy caused by the death of Francis T. Maloney and served from February 15, 1945, to November 5, 1946; was not a candidate for election to the vacancy in 1946; retired; resides in Sharon, Conn.

HARTER, Dow Watters, a Representative from Ohio; born in Akron, Summit County, Ohio, January 2, 1885; attended the Akron public schools; received preparatory education at the University of Michigan at Ann Arbor and was graduated from the law department of the same university in 1907; was admitted to the Michigan and Ohio bars in 1907; commenced practice in Akron, Ohio, in 1911; first assistant prosecuting attorney of Summit County, Ohio, 1914–1916; member of the State house of representatives in 1919 and 1920; United States commissioner at Akron, Ohio, 1918–1926; elected as a Democrat to the Seventy-third and to the four succeeding Congresses (March 4, 1933–January 3, 1943); unsuccessful candidate for reelection in 1942 to the Seventy-eighth Congress; admitted to practice of law in the District of Columbia in 1943; is a resident of Washington, D. C.

HARTER, John Francis, a Representative from New York; born in Perry, Wyoming County, N. Y., September 1, 1897; attended the public schools; during the First World War served in the United States Army at Officers' Training Camp, Camp Lee, Va.; was graduated from the law department of the University of

Buffalo, Buffalo, N. Y., in 1919; was admitted to the bar in 1920 and commenced practice in Buffalo, N. Y.; elected as a Republican to the Seventy-sixth Congress (January 3, 1939–January 3, 1941); unsuccessful candidate for reelection in 1940 to the Seventy-seventh Congress; resumed the practice of law in Buffalo, N. Y., and resided in Eggertsville, N. Y., until his death there on December 20, 1947; interment in Forest Lawn Cemetery, Buffalo, N. Y.

HARTER, Michael Daniel (grandson of Robert Moore), a Representative from Ohio; born in Canton, Ohio, April 6, 1846; attended the public schools; engaged in mercantile pursuits and banking; moved to Mansfield, Ohio, in 1869; at the age of twenty-three became treasurer and manager of the Aultman & Taylor Co. upon its organization; elected as a Democrat to the Fifty-second and Fifty-third Congresses (March 4, 1891–March 3, 1895); declined to be a candidate for renomination in 1894; retired from public life; moved to Philadelphia, Pa., but spent his summers in Mansfield; died in Fostoria, Ohio, February 22, 1896; interment in Mansfield Cemetery, Mansfield, Ohio.

HARTKE, Rupert Vance, a Senator from Indiana; born in Stendal, Pike County, Ind., May 31, 1919; attended the public schools of Stendal; graduated from Evansville College in 1940 and Indiana University Law School in 1948; during World War II served in the United States Coast Guard and Navy as a seaman and through the ranks to lieutenant from 1942–1946, including supply and purchasing duties at Underwater Sound Laboratory at New London, Conn.; was admitted to the Indiana bar in 1948 and commenced the practice of law in Evansville, Ind.; deputy prosecuting attorney of Vandenburgh County, Ind., in 1950 and 1951; mayor of Evansville, Ind., from 1956 until his resignation December 5, 1958; elected as a Democrat to the United States Senate for the term commencing January 3, 1959, and ending January 3, 1965.

HARTLEY, Fred Allan, Jr., a Representative from New Jersey; born in Harrison, Hudson County, N. J., February 22, 1902; attended the public schools, Rutgers Prep, and Rutgers University, New Brunswick, N. J.; library commissioner of Kearny, N. J., in 1923 and 1924; police and fire commissioner 1924–1928; elected as a Republican to the Seventy-first and to the nine succeeding Congresses (March 4, 1929–January 3, 1949); was not a candidate for renomination in 1948; engaged as a business consultant; is a resident of Milford, N. J.

HARTLEY, Thomas, a Representative from Pennsylvania; born in Reading, Pa., September 7, 1748; completed preparatory studies; studied law; was admitted to the bar and commenced practice in York, Pa., in 1789; member of the provincial convention at Philadelphia in 1775; served in the Revolutionary War as lieutenant colonel of Irvine's regiment, and as colonel of the Sixth Pennsylvania Regiment in 1776; commanded an expedition against the Indians in 1778; member of the State house of representatives in 1778; member of the council of censors in 1783; member of the State convention which adopted the Constitution of the United States in 1787; elected to the First and to the five succeeding Congresses and served from March 4, 1789, until his death in Yorktown (later York), Pa., December 21, 1800; interment in St. John's Churchyard.

HARTMAN, Charles Sampson, a Representative from Montana; born in Monticello, White County, Ind., March 1, 1861; attended the public schools and Wabash College, Crawfordsville, Ind.; moved to Bozeman, Mont., in January 1882; studied law; was admitted to the bar in 1884 and commenced practice in Bozeman, Mont.; probate judge of Gallatin County 1884–1886;

member of the State constitutional convention in 1889; delegate to numerous State conventions; elected as a Republican to the Fifty-third and Fifty-fourth Congresses; reelected as a Silver Republican to the Fifty-fifth Congress and served from March 4, 1893 to March 3, 1899; declined to be a candidate for renomination in 1898; delegate to the Republican National Convention at St. Louis in 1896; resumed the practice of law; became affiliated with the Democratic Party in 1900; delegate to the Democratic National Convention at Kansas City in 1900; unsuccessful candidate for election as a Democrat in 1910 to the Sixty-second Congress; appointed Envoy Extraordinary and Minister Plenipotentiary to Ecuador in July 1913 and served until May 14, 1922, when he returned to Bozeman, Mont.; moved to Great Falls, Mont., in 1926 and resumed the practice of law; moved to Fort Benton, Mont., in 1927, having been appointed judge of the twelfth judicial district of Montana on March 3, 1927; elected to the same office in 1928, and served until his death in Great Falls, Mont., on August 3, 1929; interment in Riverside Cemetery, Fort Benton, Mont.

HARTMAN, Jesse Lee, a Representative from Pennsylvania; born at Cottage, Huntingdon County, Pa., June 18, 1853; attended public and private schools and Hollidaysburg (Pa.) Seminary; employed as a clerk in a general store in Hollidaysburg, Pa., 1872–1878; manager of a blast furnace at McKees Gap, Pa., 1878–1891; returned to Hollidaysburg, Pa., being elected prothonotary of Blair County, Pa., in 1891; reelected in 1894 and in 1897; extensively engaged in the quarrying and shipping of ganister; president of the Hollidaysburg Trust Co., 1898–1930; elected as a Republican to the Sixty-second Congress (March 4, 1911–March 3, 1913); unsuccessful candidate for reelection in 1912 to the Sixty-third Congress and for election in 1914 to the Sixty-fourth Congress; resumed his former mining and banking pursuits at Hollidaysburg, Pa.; delegate to the Republican National Conventions in 1908, 1924, and 1928; died in Hollidaysburg, Pa., February 17, 1930; interment in Presbyterian Cemetery.

HARTRIDGE, Julian, a Representative from Georgia; born in Savannah, Ga., September 9, 1829; attended Chatham Academy and Montpelier Institute; was graduated from Brown University, Providence, R. I., in 1848, and from Harvard Law School in 1850; was admitted to the bar in 1851 and commenced practice in Savannah, Ga.; solicitor general of the eastern judicial circuit of Georgia 1854–1858; member of the State house of representatives in 1858 and 1859; delegate to the Democratic National Convention at Charleston in 1860; during the Civil War served one year in the Confederate Army as a lieutenant in the Chatham Artillery; member of the First and Second Confederate Congresses 1862–1865; delegate to the Democratic National Conventions in 1872 and 1876; presidential elector at large on the Democratic ticket of Greeley and Brown in 1872; elected as a Democrat to the Forty-fourth and Forty-fifth Congresses and served from March 4, 1875, until his death in Washington, D. C., January 8, 1879; interment in Laurel Grove Cemetery, Savannah, Ga.

HARTZELL, William, a Representative from Illinois; born in Canton, Stark County, Ohio, February 20, 1837; moved with his parents to Danville, Ill., in 1840, and later, in 1844, to the Republic of Mexico, where he remained until 1853; returned to Randolph County, Ill.; was graduated from McKendree College, Lebanon, Ill., in 1859; settled in Chester, Randolph County, Ill.; studied law; was admitted to the bar in 1864 and commenced practice in Chester, Ill.; elected as a Democrat to the Forty-fourth and Forty-fifth Congresses (March 4, 1875–March 3, 1879); was not a candidate for renomination in

1878; resumed the practice of law in Chester; judge of the third judicial circuit of Illinois 1897–1903; died in Chester, Ill., August 14, 1903; interment in Evergreen Cemetery.

HARVEY, David Archibald, a Delegate from the Territory of Oklahoma; born in Stewiack, Province of Nova Scotia, Canada, March 20, 1845; moved with his parents to Clermont County, Ohio, in 1852; attended the public schools at Isabel, Ohio; enlisted in Company B, Fourth Regiment, Ohio Volunteer Cavalry, in September 1861 and served throughout the Civil War; attended Miami University, Oxford, Ohio; studied law; was admitted to the bar in 1868 and commenced practice in Topeka, Kans., in 1869; city attorney of Topeka 1871–1881; judge of the probate court 1881–1889; moved to Wyandotte, Okla., in 1889; elected as a Republican to the Fifty-first and Fifty-second Congresses and served from November 4, 1890, to March 3, 1893; unsuccessful candidate for reelection in 1892 to the Fifty-third Congress; resumed the practice of law, representing Indian tribes in northeast Oklahoma and the Cayugas in New York, with residence in Wyandotte, Okla.; died in Hope, Eddy County, N. Mex., on May 24, 1916; interment in Seneca Cemetery, Seneca, Jasper County, Mo.

HARVEY, James Madison, a Senator from Kansas; born near Salt Sulphur Springs, Monroe County, Va. (now West Virginia), September 21, 1833; attended the common schools in Indiana, Illinois, and Iowa; became a civil engineer; moved to Kansas in 1859 and engaged in agricultural pursuits; served with the Union Army during the Civil War as captain in the Fourth and Tenth Regiments of Kansas Volunteer Infantry 1861–1864; member of the State house of representatives 1865 and 1866; served in the State senate 1867 and 1868; Governor of Kansas 1868–1872; elected as a Republican to the United States Senate to fill the vacancy caused by the resignation of Alexander Caldwell and served from February 2, 1874, to March 3, 1877; Government surveyor in New Mexico, Utah, Nevada, and Oklahoma; resumed agricultural pursuits; died near Junction City, Kans., April 15, 1894; interment in Highland Cemetery, Junction City, Kans.

HARVEY, Jonathan (brother of Matthew Harvey), a Representative from New Hampshire; born in Sutton, Merrimack County, N. H., February 25, 1780; attended the common schools; engaged in agricultural pursuits; member of the State house of representatives 1811–1816, 1831–1834, and 1838–1840; served in the State senate 1816–1823, and was president of that body 1817–1823; member of the executive council 1823–1825; elected to the Nineteenth, Twentieth, and Twenty-first Congresses (March 4, 1825–March 3, 1831); was not a candidate for renomination in 1830; retired to his farm at North Sutton, N. H., where he died on August 23, 1859; interment in North Sutton Cemetery.

HARVEY, Matthew (brother of Jonathan Harvey), a Representative from New Hampshire; born in Sutton, Merrimack County, N. H., June 21, 1781; studied under private tutors; graduated from Dartmouth College in 1806; studied law; was admitted to the bar and commenced practice in Hopkinton, N. H., in 1809; served in the State house of representatives 1814–1820 and as speaker three terms; elected as a Democrat to the Seventeenth and Eighteenth Congresses (March 4, 1821–March 3, 1825); member of the State senate 1825–1827 and served as its president; member of the executive council 1828 and 1829; Governor of New Hampshire in 1830; appointed by President Jackson judge of the United States District Court for New Hampshire in 1831 and served until his death in Concord, N. H., April 7, 1866; interment in Old North Cemetery.

HARVEY, Ralph, a Representative from Indiana; born on a farm near Mount Summit, Henry County, Ind., August 9, 1901; attended the public schools; was graduated from Mount Summit High School in 1918 and from Purdue University, Lafayette, Ind., in 1923; engaged as an agricultural instructor 1923–1928; also engaged in agricultural pursuits; served as county councilman 1932–1942; member of the State house of representatives 1942–1947; elected as a Republican to the Eightieth Congress to fill the vacancy caused by the death of Raymond S. Springer; reelected to the Eighty-first and to the four succeeding Congresses and served from November 4, 1947, to January 3, 1959; unsuccessful candidate for reelection in 1958 to the Eighty-sixth Congress. *Elected to the Eighty-seventh Congress.*

HARVIE, John, a Delegate from Virginia; born in Albemarle County, Va., in 1742; studied law; was admitted to the bar and practiced; appointed commissioner to treat with the western Indians in 1774; member of the Virginia conventions of 1775 and 1776; Member of the Continental Congress 1777–1779 and one of the signers of the Articles of Confederation; purchasing agent for the State, with provisional rank of colonel; register of the land office 1780–1791; secretary of the Commonwealth 1788; engaged in building operations in Richmond, Va; died as the result of an accident in Richmond, Va., on February 6, 1807; interment in Hollywood Cemetery.

HASBROUCK, Abraham Bruyn (cousin of Abraham Joseph Hasbrouck), a Representative from New York; born in Kingston, Ulster County, N. Y., on November 29, 1791; attended Kingston Academy, and was graduated from Yale College, New Haven, Conn., in 1810; studied law in Hudson, N. Y., and in Litchfield, Conn.; was admitted to the bar in 1813 and commenced law practice in Kingston, N. Y., in 1814; elected as a National Republican to the Nineteenth Congress (March 4, 1825–March 3, 1827); resided in New Brunswick, N. J., while president of Rutgers College, 1840–1850; moved to Kingston, N. Y., in 1850; president of the Kingston Bank; founded the Ulster County Historical Society; died in Kingston, N. Y., on February 24, 1879; interment in Pine Street Cemetery.

HASBROUCK, Abraham Joseph (cousin of Abraham Bruyn Hasbrouck), a Representative from New York; born at "Guilford," Ulster County, N. Y., October 16, 1773; was privately tutored; moved to Kingston in 1795 and engaged in mercantile pursuits; one of the incorporators of the Delaware & Hudson Canal; appointed by Governor Jay as first lieutenant of Cavalry; organizer and director of the Middle District Bank of Kingston; served in the State assembly in 1811; elected as a Clintonian Democrat to the Thirteenth Congress (March 4, 1813–March 3, 1815); was not a candidate for renomination in 1814; engaged in freighting goods to New York City by water; member of the State senate in 1822; died in Kingston, N. Y., January 12, 1845; interment in Albany Avenue Cemetery.

HASBROUCK, Josiah, a Representative from New York; born in New Paltz, Ulster County, N. Y., March 5, 1755; completed preparatory studies; conducted a general merchandising business; second lieutenant in the Third Regiment of Ulster County Militia in 1780; supervisor of New Paltz 1784–1786, 1793, 1794, and 1799–1805; member of the State assembly 1796, 1797, 1802, and 1806; elected to the Eighth Congress to fill the vacancy caused by the resignation of John Cantine and served from April 28, 1803, to March 3, 1805; engaged in agricultural pursuits; elected to the Fifteenth Congress (March 4, 1817–March 3, 1819); died near Plattekill, Ulster County, N. Y., March 19, 1821; interment in the family burial ground; reinterment in New Paltz Rural Cemetery, New Paltz, N. Y.

HASCALL, Augustus Porter, a Representative from New York; born in Hinsdale, Berkshire County, Mass., June 24, 1800; moved to Le Roy, N. Y., in 1815; attended public and private schools; engaged in surveying; studied law; was admitted to the bar and commenced practice in Le Roy, N. Y.; justice of the peace and supervisor; judge of the court of common pleas; presidential elector on the Whig ticket of Taylor and Fillmore in 1848; elected as a Whig to the Thirty-second Congress (March 4, 1851–March 3, 1853); resumed the practice of law; trustee of the village of Le Roy in 1858; died in Le Roy, Genesee County, N. Y., June 27, 1872; interment in Myrtle Street Cemetery.

HASKELL, Dudley Chase (grandfather of Otis Halbert Holmes), a Representative from Kansas; born in Springfield, Windsor County, Vt., March 23, 1842; moved with his parents to Lawrence, Kans., in 1855; attended school at Springfield, Vt., in 1857 and 1858; engaged in businesss as a shoe merchant; followed the gold rush to Pikes Peak, Colo., in 1859 and resided there until 1861; during the Civil War was assistant to the quartermaster of the Union Army in Missouri, Arkansas, Kansas, and the Indian Territory in 1861 and 1862; left the service and entered Williston's Seminary, Easthampton, Mass., in 1863; was graduated from Yale College in 1865; returned to Lawrence, Kans., and engaged in the shoe business 1865–1867; member of the State house of representatives in 1872, 1875, and 1876, and served as speaker in 1876; elected as a Republican to the Forty-fifth and to the three succeeding Congresses and served from March 4, 1877, until his death in Washington, D. C., December 16, 1883; interment in Oak Hill Cemetery, Lawrence, Douglas County, Kans.

HASKELL, Harry Garner, Jr., a Representative from Delaware; born in Wilmington, New Castle County, Del., May 27, 1921; educated at Tower Hill School, Wilmington, Del., and St. Mark's School, Southboro, Mass.; attended Princeton University 1940–1942; personnel manager of Speakman Co. in 1947 and 1948; president of Greenhill Dairies, Inc., 1948–1953; interests in firms of Garrett Miller & Co. and Brown & Scott Packing Co.; director in Wilmington Trust Co. and Abercrombie & Fitch Co.; during World War II enlisted in the United States Coast Guard Reserve September 8, 1942, made an ensign in 1943, and was discharged as a lieutenant (jg) in 1946; participated in invasions of Ie Shima and Okinawa; awarded Asiatic-Pacific theater campaign ribbon with battle star and Philippine Liberation Campaign Ribbon; secretary of the Departmental Council of the Department of Health, Education, and Welfare in 1953 and 1954; consultant to special assistant to President Eisenhower in 1955; owner and operator of Hill Girt Farm, Chadds Ford, Pa.; treasurer of University of Delaware Research Foundation; trustee of Fisk University and Hobart and William Smith Colleges; delegate to the Republican National Convention in 1952; elected as a Republican to the Eighty-fifth Congress (January 3, 1957–January 3, 1959); unsuccessful candidate for reelection in 1958 to the Eighty-sixth Congress; resumed former business interests; is a resident of Wilmington, Del.

HASKELL, Reuben Locke, a Representative from New York; born in Brooklyn, N. Y., October 5, 1878; was graduated from Hempstead High School, Long Island, N. Y., in 1894; attended Ithaca High School in 1894 and 1895, New York Law School in 1896 and 1897 and was graduated from the law department of Cornell University, Ithaca, N. Y., in 1898; was admitted to the bar in 1899 and commenced practice in New York City; served with the Twenty-second Regiment of New York Volunteers during the Spanish-American War; served in the Thirteenth Regiment of the National Guard, Company I and Company G, as private, corporal, and sergeant 1899–1902; delegate to the Republican National Conventions at Chicago in 1908 and 1920; counsel to the county clerk of Kings County 1908 and 1909; secretary for the Borough of Brooklyn 1910–1913; deputy commissioner of public works for the Borough of Brooklyn 1913–1915; member of the Republican State committee 1907–1913 and 1914–1919; unsuccessful candidate for election in 1914 to the Sixty-third Congress; elected as a Republican to the Sixty-fourth, Sixty-fifth, and Sixty-sixth Congresses and served from March 4, 1915, to December 31, 1919, when he resigned; judge of the Kings County Court 1920–1925; defeated for reelection to that office; resumed the practice of law in New York City; transit commissioner, State of New York, 1932–1942; is a resident of Hillsdale, N. J.

HASKELL, William T. (nephew of Charles Ready), a Representative from Tennessee; born in Murfreesboro, Rutherford County, Tenn., July 21, 1818; privately tutored; also attended the public schools of Murfreesboro and the University of Nashville, Tennessee; fought in the Seminole War in 1836; studied law; was admitted to the bar in 1838 and commenced practice in Jackson, Tenn.; member of the State house of representatives in 1840 and 1841; served in the Mexican War; appointed on May 13, 1846, as colonel of the First Brigade, Second Regiment, Tennessee Volunteers; elected as a Whig to the Thirtieth Congress (March 4, 1847–March 3, 1849); resumed the practice of his profession; died in an asylum in Hopkinsville, Christian County, Ky., March 12, 1859; interment in Riverside Cemetery, Jackson, Tenn.

HASKIN, John Bussing, a Representative from New York; born in Fordham (now a part of New York City), N. Y., August 27, 1821; attended the public schools; studied law; was admitted to the bar in 1843 and commenced practice in New York City in 1845; civil justice of New York City 1847–1849; supervisor of Fordham 1850–1853; corporation attorney 1853–1856; elected as a Democrat to the Thirty-fifth and Thirty-sixth Congresses (March 4, 1857–March 3, 1861); resumed the practice of law; supervisor of the town of West Farms, Westchester County, N. Y., in 1863; delegate to several Democratic conventions; died at Friends Lake, N. Y., September 18, 1895; interment in Woodlawn Cemetery, New York City.

HASKINS, Kittredge, a Representative from Vermont; born in Dover, Vt., April 8, 1836; attended the public schools and received instruction from a private tutor; studied law; was admitted to the bar in 1858 and commenced practice in Wilmington, Vt.; moved to Williamsville in 1861 and continued the practice of law; during the Civil War enlisted as a private in Company I, Sixteenth Regiment, Vermont Volunteers, August 23, 1862; was commissioned first lieutenant September 20, 1862, and served until March 19, 1863, when he resigned and was honorably discharged on account of disabilities; returned to Vermont and settled in Brattleboro; entered the Government service as a civil employee in the office of the assistant quartermaster of Volunteers and served in that capacity until the close of the war; resumed the practice of law; appointed colonel and chief of staff to Gov. Peter T. Washburn in 1869; member of the Republican State committee 1869–1872; State's attorney 1870–1872; member of the State house of representatives 1872–1874 and 1896–1900; speaker of the house 1898–1900; United States attorney for the district of Vermont from October 1880 to July 1887; served in the State senate 1892–1894; chairman of the Vermont board of commissioners to establish the boundary line between that State and Massachusetts 1892–1900; elected as a Republican to the Fifty-seventh and to the three succeeding Congresses (March 4, 1901–March 3,1909); unsuccessful candidate for renomination in

1908; judge of the municipal court in Brattleboro, Vt., in 1910; postmaster of Brattleboro 1912–1915; died in Brattleboro, Windham County, Vt., August 7, 1916; interment in Prospect Hill Cemetery.

HASTINGS, Daniel Oren, a Senator from Delaware; born near Princess Anne, Somerset County, Md., March 5, 1874; was educated under private tutorship; moved to Wilmington, Del., in 1894; attended the law department of Columbian (now George Washington) University, Washington, D. C.; was admitted to the bar in 1902 and commenced practice in Wilmington, Del.; served as deputy attorney general of Delaware 1904–1909; appointed secretary of state on January 18, 1909, and served until his resignation on June 16, 1909, having been appointed an associate justice of the State supreme court, in which capacity he served until his resignation on January 17, 1911; special counsel for the State legislature in 1911; city solicitor of Wilmington 1911–1917; judge of the municipal court of Wilmington 1920–1929; served as proxy on the Republican National Committee at the Kansas City Convention in 1928 and was subsequently a member of the Republican National Committee, serving until June 1943, when he resigned; appointed as a Republican on December 10, 1928, and elected on November 4, 1930, to the United States Senate to fill the vacancy in the term ending March 3, 1931, caused by the resignation of T. Coleman du Pont; on the same day was also elected for the term commencing March 4, 1931, and served from December 10, 1928, to January 3, 1937; unsuccessful candidate for reelection in 1936; resumed the practice of law in Wilmington, Del.

HASTINGS, George, a Representative from New York; born in Clinton, Oneida County, N. Y., March 13, 1807; attended the public schools; was graduated from Hamilton College, Clinton, N. Y., in 1826; studied law; in 1830 was admitted to the bar and commenced practice in Mount Morris, Livingston County; district attorney 1839–1848; elected as a Democrat to the Thirty-third Congress (March 4, 1853–March 3, 1855); elected judge of the county court of Livingston County and served from November 1855 until his death in Mount Morris, Livingston County, N. Y., August 29, 1866; interment in the City Cemetery.

HASTINGS, John, a Representative from Ohio; born in Ireland in 1778; engaged in agricultural pursuits; studied law in Lisbon, Ohio; was admitted to the bar and practiced in Mississippi; engaged in various business enterprises; returned to Ohio and settled in Hanover Township, Columbiana County; engaged in agricultural pursuits; elected as a Jackson Democrat to the Twenty-sixth and Twenty-seventh Congresses (March 4, 1839–March 3, 1843); resumed agricultural pursuits; died near Hanoverton, Ohio, December 8, 1854; interment in Grove Hill Cemetery, Hanoverton, Ohio.

HASTINGS, Serranus Clinton, a Representative from Iowa; born in Watertown, Jefferson County, N. Y., November 14, 1813; completed a preparatory course at Gouverneur Academy and was graduated from Hamilton College; principal of Norwich Academy in 1834; moved to Lawrenceburg, Ind., in 1835; edited the Indiana Signal in 1836; studied law; was admitted to the bar in 1837 and commenced practice in what is now Burlington, Iowa; when Iowa was made a separate Territory served as a member of the Territorial council 1838–1846 and was president of the council one session; upon the admission of Iowa as a State into the Union was elected as a Democrat to the Twenty-ninth Congress and served from December 28, 1846, to March 3, 1847; was not a candidate for renomination; chief justice of the supreme court of Iowa in 1848; resigned in 1849 and moved to Benicia, Calif.; chief justice of the supreme court of California 1849–1851; attorney

general of the State in 1851; at the end of his term of two years retired to private life; founded and endowed Hastings College of Law in the University of California in 1878; engaged in the real-estate business; died in San Francisco, Calif., February 18, 1893; interment in St. Helena Cemetery, St. Helena, Calif.

HASTINGS, Seth (father of William Soden Hastings), a Representative from Massachusetts; born in Cambridge, Mass., on April 8, 1762; was graduated from Harvard University in 1782; studied law; was admitted to the bar in 1786 and commenced practice in Mendon, Mass.; town treasurer in 1794 and 1795; elected one of the first school commissioners in 1796; elected as a Federalist to the Seventh Congress to fill the vacancy caused by the resignation of Levi Lincoln; reelected to the Eighth and Ninth Congresses and served from August 24, 1801, to March 3, 1807; declined to be a candidate for renomination in 1806; member of the State senate 1810 and 1814; chief justice of the court of sessions for Worcester County 1819–1828; died in Mendon, Mass., on November 19, 1831; interment in the Old Cemetery.

HASTINGS, William Soden (son of Seth Hastings), a Representative from Massachusetts; born in Mendon, Worcester County, Mass., June 3, 1798; completed preparatory studies, and was graduated from Harvard University in 1817; studied law; was admitted to the bar in 1820 and commenced practice in Mendon; member of the State house of representatives in 1828; served in the State senate 1829–1833; elected as a Democrat to the Twenty-fifth, Twenty-sixth, and Twenty-seventh Congresses and served from March 4, 1837, until his death in Red Sulphur Springs, Monroe County, Va. (now West Virginia), June 17, 1842; interment in Old Cemetery, Mendon, Mass.

HASTINGS, William Wirt, a Representative from Oklahoma; born on a farm in Benton County, Ark., near the Indian Territory boundary, December 31, 1866; was of the Indian (Cherokee) race; moved with his parents to a farm at Beatties Prairie, Delaware County (then part of the Cherokee Nation in Indian Territory), Okla., and attended the Cherokee tribal school; was graduated from Cherokee Male Seminary, at Tahlequah, in 1884; teacher in the Cherokee tribal schools 1884–1886 and 1889–1891; was graduated from the law department of Vanderbilt University, Nashville, Tenn., in 1889; was admitted to the bar the same year and commenced practice in Tahlequah, Okla.; attorney general for the Cherokee Nation 1891–1895; national attorney for the Cherokee tribe 1907–1914; delegate to the Democratic State convention at Oklahoma City in 1912; delegate to the Democratic National Convention at Baltimore in 1912; presidential elector on the Democratic ticket of Wilson and Marshall in 1912; elected as a Democrat to the Sixty-fourth, Sixty-fifth, and Sixty-sixth Congresses (March 4, 1915–March 3, 1921); unsuccessful candidate for reelection in 1920 to the Sixty-seventh Congress; elected to the Sixty-eighth and to the five succeeding Congress (March 4, 1923–January 3, 1935); was not a candidate for renomination in 1934; resumed the practice of law in Tahlequah, Okla.; commissioned by President Franklin D. Roosevelt on January 22, 1936, as chief of the Cherokees for one day to sign certain papers; died April 8, 1938, in Muskogee, Okla.; interment in City Cemetery, Tahlequah, Okla.

HATCH, Carl Atwood, a Senator from New Mexico; born in Kirwin, Phillip County, Kans., November 27, 1889; attended the public schools of Kansas and Oklahoma; was graduated from the law department of Cumberland University, Lebanon, Tenn., in 1912; was admitted to the bar the same year and began practice in Eldorado, Okla.; moved to Clovis, N. Mex., in 1916 and continued the practice of law; assistant attorney general of New

Mexico in 1917 and 1918; collector of internal revenue 1919–1922; district judge of the ninth judicial district of New Mexico 1923–1929; chairman of the Democratic State Committee in 1930; member of the State board of bar examiners 1930–1933; presidential elector for New Mexico in 1932; appointed as a Democrat to the United States Senate on October 10, 1933, and elected on November 6, 1934, to fill the vacancy caused by the resignation of Sam G. Bratton; reelected in 1936 and again in 1942 and served from October 10, 1933, to January 3, 1949; was not a candidate for renomination in 1948; appointed United States district judge for the district of New Mexico and has served since February 3, 1949; is a resident of Albuquerque, N. Mex.

HATCH, Herschel Harrison, a Representative from Michigan; born in Morrisville, Madison County, N. Y., February 17, 1837; attended the common schools, and was graduated from Hamilton College Law School, Clinton, N. Y., in 1857; was admitted to the bar, and practiced in Morrisville, N. Y., 1858–1863; moved to Bay City, Mich.; elected alderman of Bay City at its first organization in 1865; judge of probate of Bay County 1868–1872; member of the constitutional commission of Michigan in 1873; member of the tax commission in 1881; elected as a Republican to the Forty-eighth Congress (March 4, 1883–March 3, 1885); declined to be a candidate for renomination in 1884; resumed the practice of law; moved to Detroit, Mich., in 1895 and practiced law until 1910, when he retired; died in Detroit, Mich., November 30, 1920; interment in Elm Lawn Cemetery, Bay City, Mich.

HATCH, Israel Thompson, a Representative from New York; born in Johnstown, Fulton County, N. Y., June 30, 1808; pursued preparatory studies; was graduated from Union College, Schenectady, N. Y., in 1829; studied law; was admitted to the bar in 1828; moved to Buffalo the same year and practiced law; assistant secretary of state 1829–1831; practiced law in Buffalo 1831–1840; member of the State assembly 1833, 1834, and 1851; surrogate of Erie County 1833–1836; president of the Commercial Bank of Buffalo 1840–1842; grain merchant; elected as a Democrat to the Thirty-fifth Congress (March 4, 1857–March 3, 1859); unsuccessful candidate for reelection in 1858 to the Thirty-sixth Congress; appointed by President Buchanan as postmaster of Buffalo, N. Y., and served from November 11, 1859, to March 27, 1861; resumed the practice of law; also engaged in banking and was prominently connected with elevator and dock enterprises; member of the State constitutional convention 1867–68; commissioner to negotiate a reciprocity treaty between the United States and the Dominion of Canada in 1869 and 1870; built the Marine and Empire elevators in Buffalo; died in Buffalo, N. Y., September 24, 1875; interment in Forest Lawn Cemetery.

HATCH, Jethro Ayers, a Representative from Indiana; born in Pitcher, Chenango County, N. Y., June 18, 1837; settled in Sugar Grove, Kane County, Ill.; attended the common schools and the institute in Batavia, Ill.; was graduated from Rush Medical College, Chicago, Ill., in February 1860 and commenced practice at Kentland, Ind., in July 1860; served as city health officer of Kentland and county health officer of Newton County, Ind., for several years; during the Civil War was commissioned assistant surgeon of the Thirty-sixth Regiment, Illinois Volunteer Infantry, on December 11, 1862, and promoted to surgeon of the same regiment; mustered out of service February 8, 1865, and returned to Kentland, Ind.; secretary and later president of the pension examining board 1865–1907; member of the State house of representatives 1872 and 1873; alternate delegate to the Republican National Convention at Chicago

in 1888; elected as a Republican to the Fifty-fourth Congress (March 4, 1895–March 3, 1897); was not a candidate for renomination in 1896; returned to Kentland, Ind., and resumed the practice of medicine; member of board of the hospital for the insane at Logansport, Ind.; physician and surgeon for the Logansport division of the Pennsylvania Railroad for many years; physician and surgeon for the Chicago and Cairo division of the New York Central Railroad from the time it was built until 1907; moved to Victoria, Tex., in 1907 and engaged in the real-estate business; died in Victoria, Tex., August 3, 1912; interment in Fair Lawn Cemetery, Kentland, Ind.

HATCH, William Henry, a Representative from Missouri; born near Georgetown, Scott County, Ky., September 11, 1833; attended the schools of Lexington, Ky.; studied law; was admitted to the bar in September 1854 and practiced; circuit attorney 1858 and 1860; during the Civil War served in the Confederate Army; commissioned captain and assistant adjutant general December 1862, and in March 1863 was assigned to duty as assistant commissioner of exchange of prisoners under the cartel, and continued in this position until the close of the war; elected as a Democrat to the Forty-sixth and to the seven succeeding Congresses (March 4, 1879–March 3, 1895); unsuccessful candidate for reelection in 1894 to the Fifty-fourth Congress; engaged in agricultural pursuits; died near Hannibal, Marion County, Mo., December 23, 1896; interment in Riverside Cemetery.

HATCHER, Robert Anthony, a Representative from Missouri; born in Buckingham County, Va., February 24, 1819; attended private schools in Lynchburg, Va.; studied law; was admitted to the bar in Kentucky and commenced practice at New Madrid, Mo., in 1847; circuit attorney for several years; member of the State house of representatives 1850 and 1851; during the Civil War enlisted in the Confederate Army and attained the rank of major; delegate to the State convention in 1862; member of the Confederate Congress 1864 and 1865; elected as a Democrat to the Forty-third, Forty-fourth, and Forty-fifth Congresses (March 4, 1873–March 3, 1879); resumed the practice of law; died in Charleston, Mo., December 4, 1886; interment in Odd Fellows Cemetery.

HATFIELD, Henry Drury, a Senator from West Virginia; born at Sydney post office, Logan County, W. Va., September 15, 1875; attended the local schools and Franklin College at New Athens, Ohio; was graduated in medicine from the University of Louisville, Louisville, Ky., in 1895 and from New York University, New York, N. Y., in 1904; also studied at Poli Clinic Medical School and Hospital, New York Post Graduate School and Hospital, and Cornell University Medical College; commissioner of health of Mingo County, W. Va., 1895–1900; commissioner of district roads of McDowell County 1900–1905; surgeon for the Norfolk and Western Railway 1895–1913; surgeon in chief of West Virginia State Hospital No. 1 at Welsh, W. Va., 1899–1913; member of the county court of McDowell 1906–1912; member of the State senate 1908–1912, serving as president in 1911; Governor of West Virginia from March 4, 1913, to March 3, 1917; during the First World War was a major in the Medical Corps of the United States Army and served from July 7, 1917, to January 13, 1919; was chief of the Surgical Service at Base Hospital No. 36, at Detroit, Mich.; appointed lieutenant colonel in the Medical Officers Reserve Corps of the United States Army on January 15, 1925, and reappointed January 15, 1935; delegate to the Republican National Convention at Chicago in 1916; elected as a Republican to the United States Senate in 1928 and served from March 4, 1929, to January 3, 1935; unsuccessful candidate for reelection in 1934; resumed the practice of medicine and also manages a hospital and several farms; is a resident of Huntington, W. Va.

HATHAWAY, Samuel Gilbert, a Representative from New York; born in Freetown, Bristol County, Mass., July 18, 1780; attended the public schools; worked at various occupations and made one sea voyage; moved to Chenango County, N. Y., in 1803 and two years later to Cincinnatus, Cortland County, and engaged in agricultural pursuits; justice of the peace 1810–1858; member of the State assembly in 1814 and 1818; moved to Solon, N. Y., in 1819; served in the State senate in 1822; major general in the New York Militia 1823–1858; elected as a Democrat to the Twenty-third Congress (March 4, 1833–March 3, 1835); presidential elector on the Democratic ticket of Pierce and King in 1852; delegate to the Democratic National Convention at Charleston, S. C., in 1860; died in Solon, Cortland County, N. Y., May 2, 1867; interment in the family cemetery near Solon.

HATHORN, Henry Harrison, a Representative from New York; born in Greenfield, Ulster County, N. Y., November 28, 1813; attended the common schools, and was graduated from the public schools of Greenfield; discoverer of the "Hathorn Mineral Spring"; sheriff of Saratoga County 1853–1856 and 1862–1865; engaged in mercantile pursuits in Saratoga Springs 1839–1849; supervisor of Saratoga Springs 1858, 1860, 1866, and 1867; elected as a Republican to the Forty-third and Forty-fourth Congresses (March 4, 1873–March 3, 1877); again became engaged in the mineral-water business; died at Saratoga Springs, Saratoga County, N. Y., February 20, 1887; interment in Greenridge Cemetery.

HATHORN, John, a Representative from New York; born in Wilmington, Del., January 9, 1749; completed preparatory studies; surveyor by profession and a school teacher; captain of the Colonial Militia; colonel of the Fourth Orange County (N. Y.) Regiment February 7, 1776, and served throughout the Revolutionary War; brigadier general of the Orange County Militia September 26, 1786; major general of State militia October 8, 1793; member of the State assembly 1778, 1780, 1782–1785, 1795, and 1805, and served as speaker in 1783 and 1784; served in the State senate 1786–1790 and 1799–1803; member of the council of appointment in 1787 and 1789; elected to the Continental Congress in December 1788 but no further sessions were held; elected as a Federalist to the First Congress (March 4, 1789–March 3, 1791); unsuccessful candidate for reelection in 1790 to the Second Congress and for election in 1792 to the Third Congress; elected to the Fourth Congress (March 4, 1795–March 3, 1797); unsuccessful candidate for reelection in 1796 to the Fifth Congress; engaged in mercantile pursuits; died in Warwick, Orange County, N. Y., February 19, 1825; interment in the cemetery on the family estate; reinterment in Warwick Cemetery.

HATTON, Robert Hopkins, a Representative from Tennessee; born in Steubenville, Jefferson County, Ohio, November 2, 1826; attended the common schools and was graduated from the Cumberland University, Lebanon, Tenn., in 1847; was a tutor in Cumberland University in 1847 and 1848; attended the law school of Cumberland University in 1848 and 1849; principal of Woodland Academy, Sumner County, Tenn., in 1849 and 1850; was admitted to the bar in 1850 and commenced practice in Lebanon, Tenn.; trustee of Cumberland University from 1854 until his death; member of the State house of representatives 1855–1857; unsuccessful candidate for Governor in 1857; elected by the American Party to the Thirty-sixth Congress (March 4, 1859–March 3, 1861); colonel of the

Seventh Regiment, Tennessee Volunteer Infantry, May 26, 1861; made brigadier general in the Confederate Army May 23, 1862; assigned to the command of the Fifth Brigade, First Corps, Army of Virginia; killed in the Battle of Seven Pines, near Richmond, Va., on May 31, 1862; interment in Cedar Grove Cemetery, Lebanon, Tenn.

HAUGEN, Gilbert Nelson, a Representative from Iowa; born near Orfordville, Rock County, Wis., April 21, 1859; attended the rural schools; moved to Decorah, Winneshiek County, Iowa, in 1873 and engaged in agricultural pursuits; attended Breckenridge College, Decorah, Iowa, and Academic and Commercial College, Janesville, Wis.; engaged in various enterprises, principally real estate and banking; moved to Northwood, Iowa, in 1886 and engaged in banking; treasurer of Worth County, Iowa, 1887–1893; in 1890 organized the Northwood Banking Co. and became its president; member of the State house of representatives 1894–1898; elected as a Republican to the Fifty-sixth and to the sixteen succeeding Congresses (March 4, 1899–March 3, 1933); unsuccessful candidate for reelection in 1932 to the Seventy-third Congress; died at Northwood, Iowa, July 18, 1933; interment in Sunset Rest Cemetery, Northwood, Iowa.

HAUGEN, Nils Pederson, a Representative from Wisconsin; born in Modum, Norway, March 9, 1849; immigrated to the United States in 1854 with his parents, who settled in Pierce County, Wis., in 1855; attended the common schools and Luther College, Decorah, Iowa; was graduated from the law department of the University of Michigan at Ann Arbor in 1874; was admitted to the bar the same year and commenced practice in River Falls, Wis.; member of the State assembly in 1879 and 1880; State railroad commissioner 1882–1887; elected as a Republican to the Fiftieth Congress to fill the vacancy caused by the death of William T. Price; reelected to the Fifty-first, Fifty-second, and Fifty-third Congresses and served from March 4, 1887, to March 3, 1895; did not seek renomination in 1894, having become a candidate for the nomination for Governor, for which he was unsuccessful; member of the State tax commission 1901–1921; president of the National Tax Association in 1919 and 1920; adviser to the board of equalization of Montana 1921–1923; retired from public life; moved to Madison, Wis., and engaged in literary pursuits; died in Madison, Wis., April 23, 1931; interment in Forest Hill Cemetery.

HAUGHEY, Thomas, a Representative from Alabama; born in Glasgow, Scotland, in 1826; received a limited education; immigrated to the United States with his father, who settled in New York City; moved to Jefferson County, Ala., in 1841; while teaching in St. Clair County, studied medicine; was granted a diploma by the New Orleans Medical College and engaged in practice at Elyton, Jefferson County; during the Civil War served as a surgeon in the Third Regiment, Tennessee Volunteer Infantry, in the Union Army 1862–1865; resumed the practice of his profession in Decatur, Ala.; delegate to the State constitutional convention in 1867; upon the readmission of the State of Alabama to representation was elected as a Republican to the Fortieth Congress and served from July 21, 1868, to March 3, 1869; was a candidate for renomination and while making a political speech was assassinated in Courtland, Ala., in August 1869; interment in Green Cemetery, near Pinson, Jefferson County, Ala.

HAUN, Henry Peter, a Senator from California; born near Newtown, Scott County, Ky., January 18, 1815; attended the common schools and Transylvania University, Lexington, Ky.; studied law; was admitted to the bar in 1839 and began practice in Lexington, Ky.; prosecuting attorney of Scott County in 1845;

moved to Clinton County, Iowa, and settled in Hauntown in 1845; practiced law and with his brother formed a partnership in a distillery, sawmill, and store; delegate to the Iowa constitutional convention in 1846; moved to Yuba County, Calif., in 1849 and settled in Marysville; continued the practice of law; also engaged in agricultural pursuits; county judge 1851–1854; appointed as a Democrat to the United States Senate to fill the vacancy caused by the death of David C. Broderick and served from November 3, 1859, to March 4, 1860; unsuccessful candidate for reelection; died in Marysville, Yuba County, Calif., June 6, 1860; interment in Marysville Cemetery.

HAVEN, Nathaniel Appleton, a Representative from New Hampshire; born in Portsmouth, N. H., July 19, 1762; pursued classical studies, and was graduated in medicine from Harvard College in 1779; practiced his profession in Portsmouth, N. H., and also engaged in mercantile pursuits; served as a ship's surgeon in the latter part of the Revolutionary War; elected as a Federalist to the Eleventh Congress (March 4, 1809–March 3, 1811); died in Portsmouth, N. H., March 13, 1831; interment in Proprietors' Burying Ground.

HAVEN, Solomon George, a Representative from New York; born in Chenango County, N. Y., November 27, 1810; attended the common schools and was instructed by a private tutor in the classics; pursued a course in medicine; studied law; was admitted to the bar in 1835 and commenced practice in Buffalo, N. Y.; commissioner of deeds; district attorney of Erie County 1844–1846; mayor of Buffalo, N.Y., 1846 and 1847; elected as a Whig to the Thirty-second, Thirty-third, and Thirty-fourth Congresses (March 4, 1851–March 3, 1857); unsuccessful candidate for reelection in 1856 to the Thirty-fifth Congress and for election in 1860 to the Thirty-seventh Congress; engaged in the practice of his profession until his death in Buffalo, N. Y., December 24, 1861; interment in Forest Lawn Cemetery.

HAVENNER, Franck Roberts, a Representative from California; born in Sherwood, Baltimore County, Md., September 20, 1882; attended the public schools, Columbian College (now George Washington University), Washington, D. C., and Stanford University, California; newspaper writer in San Francisco, Calif., 1907–1917; member of the board of supervisors, San Francisco, 1926–1936; elected as a Progressive to the Seventy-fifth Congress and as a Democrat to the Seventy-sixth Congress (January 3, 1937–January 3, 1941); unsuccessful candidate for reelection in 1940 to the Seventy-seventh Congress; member of California Railroad Commission 1941–1944; elected as a Democrat to the Seventy-ninth and to the three succeeding Congresses (January 3, 1945–January 3, 1953); unsuccessful candidate for reelection in 1952 to the Eighty-third Congress; director of Union Labor Party, AFL; is a resident of San Francisco, Calif.

HAVENS, Harrison Eugene, a Representative from Missouri; born in Franklin County, Ohio, December 15, 1837; attended the common schools; studied law; was admitted to the bar and commenced practice in Ohio; served as captain of Company H, Forty-seventh Regiment, Iowa Volunteer Infantry, in the Union Army during the Civil War; moved to Illinois, thence to Iowa, and from there to Springfield, Mo., in 1867, becoming editor of the Springfield Patriot; elected as a Republican to the Forty-second and Forty-third Congresses (March 4, 1871–March 3, 1875); unsuccessful candidate for reelection in 1874 to the Forty-fourth Congress and also to the State senate in 1878; superintendent of the Springfield & Western Missouri Railway Co. in 1881; resumed the practice of his profession in Springfield, Mo.; prosecuting attorney in 1893 and 1894; moved to Enid, Garfield County, Okla., and engaged in newspaper pursuits 1901–1906; moved to Herradura,

Cuba, and engaged in planting; died in Habana, Cuba, where he had been taken on account of illness, August 16, 1916; interment in Colon Cemetery.

HAVENS, James Smith, a Representative from New York; born in Weedsport, Cayuga County, N. Y., May 28, 1859; attended the public schools and Monroe Collegiate Institute, Elbridge, N. Y.; was graduated from Yale College in 1884; moved to Rochester, N. Y., the same year; studied law; was admitted to the bar in 1887 and commenced practice in Rochester, N. Y.; delegate to the Democratic National Convention at St. Louis in 1904; elected as a Democrat to the Sixty-first Congress to fill the vacancy caused by the death of James B. Perkins and served from April 19, 1910, to March 3, 1911; was not a candidate for renomination in 1910; resumed the practice of his profession in Rochester, N.Y.; declined the Democratic nomination for mayor of Rochester in 1913; vice president and secretary of the Eastman Kodak Co., and head of its legal department from 1919 until his death in Rochester, N. Y., February 27, 1927; interment in Mount Hope Cemetery.

HAVENS, Jonathan Nicoll, a Representative from New York; born on Shelter Island, Suffolk County, N. Y., June 18, 1757; pursued classical studies and was graduated from Yale College in 1777; member of the State assembly 1786–1795; town clerk 1783–1787; elected to the State convention which ratified the Federal Constitution January 8, 1788; took a great interest in popular education and was chairman of the committee for establishing public schools in New York in 1795; justice of the peace of Suffolk County in 1795; elected as a Democrat to the Fourth, Fifth, and Sixth Congresses and served from March 4, 1795, until his death on Shelter Island, N. Y., October 25, 1799; interment in the south burial ground of the Presbyterian Church.

HAWES, Albert Gallatin (brother of Richard Hawes, nephew of Aylett Hawes, granduncle of Harry Bartow Hawes, and cousin of Aylett Hawes Buckner), a Representative from Kentucky; born near Bowling Green, Caroline County, Va., April 1, 1804; moved to Kentucky in 1810 with his parents, who settled in Fayette County near Lexington; pursued classical studies at Transylvania University, Lexington, Ky.; moved to Hancock County and settled near Hawesville; engaged in agricultural pursuits; elected as a Jackson Democrat to the Twenty-second, Twenty-third, and Twenty-fourth Congresses (March 4, 1831–March 3, 1837); resumed agricultural pursuits; moved to Daviess County and settled near Yelvington and continued agricultural pursuits; died near Yelvington, Daviess County, Ky., March 14, 1849; interment in the Hawes family burial ground on the old "Richard Hawes Place" on the Owensboro and Yelvington Road.

HAWES, Aylett (uncle of Richard Hawes, Albert Gallatin Hawes, and Aylett Hawes Buckner), a Representative from Virginia; born in Culpeper County, Va., April 21, 1768; pursued classical studies; studied medicine and finished his education in Edinburg, Scotland; returned to Virginia and practiced medicine; also engaged as a planter; member of the State house of delegates 1802–1806; elected as a Democrat to the Twelfth, Thirteenth, and Fourteenth Congresses (March 4, 1811–March 3, 1817); resumed the practice of medicine and was also an extensive landowner; died on his farm in Rappahannock County, Va., August 31, 1833; interment on a farm near Sperryville, Rappahannock County, Va.

HAWES, Harry Bartow (grandnephew of Albert Gallatin Hawes), a Representative and a Senator from Missouri; born in Covington, Kenton County, Ky., November 15, 1869; attended preparatory schools; moved to St. Louis, Mo., in 1887

and studied law; was graduated from Washington University Law School at St. Louis in 1896 and commenced practice in that city; represented the Republic of Hawaii during its annexation to the United States; president of the St. Louis police board 1898–1904; member of the State house of representatives 1916–1917; served during the First World War with the Military Intelligence Department of the General Staff, and later was assigned to the United States Embassy in Madrid, Spain; resigned in 1919; chief organizer of the Lakes-to-the-Gulf Deep Waterways Association; president of the Missouri Good Roads Federation and of the Federated Roads Council of St. Louis 1917–1920; served on the Democratic notification committee in 1904 and 1916; elected as a Democrat to the Sixty-seventh, Sixty-eighth, and Sixty-ninth Congresses and served from March 4, 1921, to October 15, 1926, when he resigned; elected on November 2, 1926, to the United States Senate to fill the vacancy caused by the death of Selden P. Spencer and on the same day was also elected for the full term commencing March 4, 1927; served from December 6, 1926, until his resignation effective February 3, 1933, to devote his time to the wildlife conservation movement and to the practice of law; was not a candidate for renomination in 1932; joint author of the Hawes-Cutting bill granting independence to the Philippine Islands; served as counsel for the Philippine Commonwealth; engaged in the practice of law in Washington, D. C., until his death there on July 31, 1947; remains were cremated and the ashes scattered in the Current River near Doniphan, Mo.

HAWES, Richard (brother of Albert Gallatin Hawes, nephew of Aylett Hawes, and cousin of Aylett Hawes Buckner), a Representative from Kentucky; born near Bowling Green, Caroline County, Va., February 6, 1797; moved to Kentucky in 1810 with his parents, who settled in Fayette County, near Lexington; pursued classical studies at Transylvania University, Lexington, Ky.; studied law; was admitted to the bar in 1824 and commenced practice in Winchester; served in the Black Hawk War; member of the State house of representatives 1828, 1829, and 1834; unsuccessful candidate for election in 1834 to the Twenty-fourth Congress; elected as a Whig to the Twenty-fifth and Twenty-sixth Congresses (March 4, 1837–March 3, 1841); moved to Paris, Ky., in 1843 and continued the practice of law; was installed by Confederate sympathizers Provisional Governor October 4, 1862, and served until 1865; county judge in 1866, and later, in the same year, chosen master commissioner of the circuit and common pleas courts; served in this capacity until his death in Paris, Bourbon County, Ky., May 25, 1877; interment in Paris Cemetery.

HAWK, Robert Moffett Allison, a Representative from Illinois; born near Rushville, Hancock County, Ind., April 23, 1839; moved with his parents to Freedom Township, Carroll County, Ill., in 1844; attended the common and select schools of Carroll County, Ill., and Eureka (Ill.) College; studied law but never practiced; entered the Union Army during the Civil War as first lieutenant September 4, 1862; promoted to captain on January 1, 1863; brevetted major April 10, 1865; moved to Mount Carroll, Ill., in 1865 and engaged in agricultural pursuits; clerk of the court of Carroll County, Ill., from December 13, 1865, to February 27, 1879; elected as a Republican to the Forty-sixth and Forty-seventh Congresses and served from March 4, 1879, until his death in Washington, D. C., June 29, 1882; interment in Oak Hill Cemetery, Mount Carroll, Ill.

HAWKES, Albert Wahl, a Senator from New Jersey; born in Chicago, Ill., November 20, 1878; attended the public and high schools; was graduated from Chicago College of Law (night school) in 1900 and was admitted to the bar the same year;

studied chemistry at Lewis Institute (now the Illinois Institute of Technology), Chicago, Ill., for two years; engaged in the chemical business at the age of 15, serving in various positions from office boy to executive vice president 1894–1926; during the First World War served as director of the Chemical Alliance, Washington, D. C., in 1917 and 1918; president of Congoleum-Nairn, Inc., at Kearny, N. J., 1927–1942, becoming chairman of the board in 1937; president and director of the Chamber of Commerce of the United States in 1941 and 1942; member of the Newark Labor Board and later appointed by Governor Edison to the five-man Board to Maintain Industrial Peace in New Jersey in 1941 aad 1942; member of the National War Labor Board, Washington, D. C., in 1942; appointed chairman to organize the New Jersey State Committee for the sale of war stamps and bonds in 1942; elected as a Republican to the United States Senate in 1942 for the term commencing January 3, 1943, and ending January 3, 1949; was not a candidate for renomination in 1948; resumed former business activities in Montclair, N. J., until 1961 when he moved to Pasadena, Calif., where he now resides.

HAWKES, James, a Representative from New York; born in Petersham, Worcester County, Mass., December 13, 1776; moved with his parents to Richfield, N. Y., in 1789; attended the common schools; taught school in Richfield and later in Burlington, N. Y.; returned to Richfield and served as sheriff of Otsego County 1815–1819; member of the State assembly in 1820; elected to the Seventeenth Congress (March 4, 1821–March 3, 1823); died in Rochester, N. Y., on October 2, 1865; interment in Mount Hope Cemetery.

HAWKINS, Benjamin (uncle of Micajah Thomas Hawkins), a Delegate and a Senator from North Carolina; born in what was then Granville, later Bute, and now Warren County, N. C., August 15, 1754; attended the county schools; student in the senior class at Princeton College when the Revolutionary War began; acquired a knowledge of French, left the school, and was appointed on the staff of George Washington and acted as his interpreter; member of the State house of commons in 1778, 1779, and 1784; chosen by the North Carolina Legislature in 1780 to procure arms and munitions of war to defend the State; Member of the Continental Congress 1781–1784, 1786, and 1787; appointed by Congress to negotiate treaties with the Creek and Cherokee Indians in 1785; delegate to the State constitutional convention which ratified the Federal Constitution November 21, 1789; elected as a Federalist to the United States Senate and served from November 27, 1789, to March 3, 1795; appointed Indian agent for all the tribes south of the Ohio River by President Washington in 1796 and held the office until his death in Crawford County, Ga., on June 6, 1816; interment on a plantation near Roberta, Crawford County, overlooking the Flint River.

HAWKINS, George Sydney, a Representative from Florida; born in Kingston, Ulster County, N. Y., in 1808; attended the common schools and was graduated from Columbia University, New York City; studied law; was admitted to the bar and practiced; moved to Florida and settled in Pensacola; served as captain in the Indian war of 1837; member of the Legislative Council of the Territory of Florida; appointed district attorney in 1841; appointed United States district attorney for the Apalachicola district in Florida in 1842; associate justice of the State supreme court 1846–1850; elected judge of the circuit court in January 1851; member of the State house of representatives; served in the State senate; collector of customs for the port of Apalachicola; elected as a Democrat to the Thirty-fifth and Thirty-sixth Congresses and served from March 4,

1857, to January 21, 1861, when he withdrew; judge of the district court under the Confederate Government 1862–1865; commissioned by the legislature of 1877 to prepare a digest of the State laws of Florida; died in Marianna, Fla., March 15, 1878; interment in St. Luke's Episcopal Cemetery.

HAWKINS, Isaac Roberts, a Representative from Tennessee; born near Columbia, Maury County, Tenn., May 16, 1818; moved with his parents to Carroll County in 1828; attended the common schools; engaged in agricultural pursuits; studied law; was admitted to the bar in 1843 and commenced practice in Huntingdon, Carroll County, Tenn.; served as a lieutenant in the Mexican War; resumed the practice of law; delegate from Tennessee to the peace conference held in Washington, D. C., in 1861 in an effort to devise means to prevent the impending war; elected to the convention for the consideration of Federal relations; judge of the circuit court in 1862; entered the Union Army as lieutenant colonel of the Seventh Regiment, Tennessee Volunteer Cavalry, in 1862; captured with his regiment at Union City, Tenn., in 1864 and imprisoned at Mobile, Ala., Macon, Ga., and Camp Oglethorpe, and was one of the fifty officers who were placed under fire at Charleston; exchanged in August 1864 and resumed active service, being in command of the Cavalry force in western Kentucky until the close of the Civil War; commissioned by Governor Brownlow as one of the chancellors of Tennessee in July 1865 but declined to qualify; delegate to the Republican National Convention at Chicago in 1868; upon the readmission of Tennessee to representation was elected as a Republican to the Thirty-ninth, Fortieth, and Forty-first Congresses and served from July 24, 1866, to March 3, 1871; died in Huntingdon, Tenn., August 12, 1880; interment in the Hawkins family burial ground near Huntingdon, Tenn.

HAWKINS, Joseph, a Representative from New York; born in that State on November 14, 1781; completed preparatory studies; studied law; was admitted to the bar and commenced practice in Henderson, N. Y., and also engaged in agricultural pursuits; elected as an Adams Democrat to the Twenty-first Congress (March 4, 1829–March 3, 1831); died in Henderson, Jefferson County, N. Y., April 20, 1832; interment in Clark Cemetery.

HAWKINS, Joseph H., a Representative from Kentucky; born in Lexington, Ky.; pursued an academic course; studied law; was admitted to the bar and practiced; member of the State house of representatives 1810–1813 and served two years as speaker; elected as a Federalist to the Thirteenth Congress to fill the vacancy caused by the resignation of Henry Clay and served from March 29, 1814, to March 3, 1815; was not a candidate for renomination in 1814; resumed the practice of law; also engaged in mercantile pursuits; moved to New Orleans, La., in 1819 and died in that city in 1823.

HAWKINS, Micajah Thomas (nephew of Benjamin Hawkins and Nathaniel Macon), a Representative from North Carolina; born near Warrenton, Warren County, N. C., May 20, 1790; attended the Warrenton (N. C.) Academy and the University of North Carolina at Chapel Hill; engaged in agricultural pursuits; member of the State house of commons in 1819 and 1820; served in the State senate 1823–1827; served in the State militia, attaining the rank of major general; elected as a Democrat to the Twenty-second Congress to fill the vacancy caused by the resignation of Robert Potter; reelected to the Twenty-third and to the three succeeding Congresses and served from December 15, 1831, to March 3, 1841; declined to be a candidate for renomination in 1840; resumed agricultural pur-

suits; again elected to the State senate in 1846; member of the council of state 1854 and 1855; died near Warrenton, Warren County, N. C., December 22, 1858; interment in the family burying ground near Warrenton.

HAWKS, Charles, Jr., a Representative from Wisconsin; born in Horicon, Dodge County, Wis., July 7, 1899; attended the public and high schools and the commerce school of the University of Wisconsin at Madison; during the First World War served as a yeoman, first class, in the United States Navy 1917–1919; employed as a salesman 1922–1925; engaged in the insurance business at Horicon, Wis., 1925–1928 and in insurance and investments 1928–1943; delegate to the Republican State conventions since 1933; member of the Board of Supervisors of Dodge County, Wis., 1935–1939; elected as a Republican to the Seventy-sixth Congress (January 3, 1939–January 3, 1941); unsuccessful candidate for reelection in 1940 to the Seventy-seventh Congress and for election in 1942 to the Seventy-eighth Congress; insurance and investment broker; moved to Wynnewood, Pa., in 1943 and engaged in research on public relations work; vice president of General Grinding Wheel Corp., Philadelphia, Pa.; died in Bryn Mawr, Pa., January 6, 1960; interment in Oak Hill Cemetery, Horicon, Wis.

HAWLEY, John Baldwin, a Representative from Illinois; born in Hawleyville, Fairfield County, Conn., February 9, 1831; moved with his parents to Carthage, Hancock County, Ill., in 1833; attended the public schools and Jacksonville College, Jacksonville, Ill.; studied law; was admitted to the bar in 1854 and commenced practice at Rock Island, Ill.; elected State's attorney in 1856 and served four years; enlisted in the Union Army during the Civil War and served as captain of Company H, Forty-fifth Regiment, Illinois Volunteer Infantry, until forced to retire from the Army on account of injuries in 1862; appointed postmaster of Rock Island, Ill., in 1865, and was removed the year following by President Johnson; elected as a Republican to the Forty-first, Forty-second, and Forty-third Congresses (March 4, 1869–March 3, 1875); unsuccessful candidate for renomination in 1874; Assistant Secretary of the Treasury from December 6, 1877, until April 1880, when he resigned; moved to Chicago, Ill., in 1880 and resumed the practice of law; moved to Omaha, Nebr., in 1886; general attorney for the western branches of the Northwestern Railroad Co.; died at Hot Springs, S. Dak., May 24, 1895; interment in Prospect Hill Cemetery, Omaha, Nebr.

HAWLEY, Joseph Roswell, a Representative and a Senator from Connecticut; born in Stewartsville, Richmond County, N. C., October 31, 1826; completed preparatory studies, and was graduated from Hamilton College, Clinton, N. Y., in 1847; studied law; was admitted to the bar in 1850 and commenced practice in Hartford, Conn.; delegate to the Free-Soil National Convention in 1852; editor of the Hartford Evening Press in 1857, which in 1867 was consolidated with the Hartford Courant, of which he became editor; during the Civil War enlisted in the Union Army and was commissioned a captain in the First Regiment, Connecticut Volunteer Infantry, on April 22, 1861; lieutenant colonel of the Seventh Regiment, Connecticut Volunteer Infantry, September 17, 1861; colonel June 20, 1862; brigadier general of Volunteers September 13, 1864; brevetted major general of Volunteers September 28, 1865, "for gallant and meritorious services during the war"; mustered out January 15, 1866; Governor of Connecticut in 1866; chairman of the Republican National Convention at Chicago in 1868; presidential elector on the Republican ticket of Grant and Colfax in 1868; delegate to the Republican National Conventions in 1872, 1876, and 1880; president of the United States Centennial

Commission from its organization in March 1873 to the completion of the work of the Centennial Exposition; elected as a Republican to the Forty-second Congress to fill the vacancy caused by the death of Julius L. Strong; reelected to the Forty-third Congress and served from December 2, 1872, to March 3, 1875; unsuccessful candidate for reelection in 1874 to the Forty-fourth Congress; again elected to the Forty-sixth Congress (March 4, 1879–March 3, 1881); was not a candidate for reelection in 1880, elected to the United States Senate in 1881; reelected in 1887, 1893, and 1899 and served from March 4, 1881, to March 3, 1905; declined to be a candidate for renomination in 1904; appointed a brigadier general in the United States Army on the retired list March 4, 1905; died in Washington, D. C., on March 17, 1905; interment in Cedar Hill Cemetery, Hartford, Conn.

HAWLEY, Robert Bradley, a Representative from Texas; born in Memphis, Tenn., October 25, 1849; attended the public schools and the Christian Brothers' College, Memphis, Tenn.; moved to Galveston, Tex., in 1875; was a merchant, importer, and manufacturer in the city of Galveston for twenty years; president of the Galveston Board of Education 1889–1893; temporary chairman of the Republican State convention at San Antonio September 4, 1890; delegate to several Republican National Conventions; elected as a Republican to the Fifty-fifth and Fifty-sixth Congresses (March 4, 1897–March 3, 1901); was not a candidate for renomination in 1900; organized and became president of the Cuban-American Sugar Co. in 1900; died in New York City November 28, 1921; interment in Lake View Cemetery, Galveston, Tex.

HAWLEY, Willis Chatman, a Representative from Oregon; born on a farm in the old Belknap settlement near Monroe, Benton County, Oreg., May 5, 1864; attended the country schools, and was graduated from the academic and law departments of Willamette University, Salem, Oreg., in 1888; principal of the Umpqua Academy, Wilbur, Oreg., 1884–1886; president of the Oregon State Normal School at Drain 1888–1891; was admitted to the bar in Oregon in 1893; president of Willamette University 1893–1902 and was professor of history and economics for sixteen years; engaged in numerous business and educational enterprises; member of the National Forest Reservation Commission; member of the Special Committee on Rural Credits created by Congress in 1915; member of the Commission for the Celebration of the Two Hundredth Anniversary of the Birth of George Washington; elected as a Republican to the Sixtieth and to the twelve succeeding Congresses (March 4, 1907–March 3, 1933); unsuccessful candidate for renomination in 1932; returned to Salem and resumed the practice of law: died in Salem, Oreg., July 24, 1941; interment in City View Cemetery.

HAWS, John Henry Hobart, a Representative from New York; born in New York City in 1809; was graduated from Columbia College, New York City, in 1827; studied law; was admitted to the bar and commenced practice; elected as a Whig to the Thirty-seventh Congress (March 4, 1851–March 3, 1853); unsuccessful for reelection in 1852; died in New York City January 27, 1858; interment in St. Stephen's Cemetery; reinterment in Greenwood Cemetery, Brooklyn, N. Y., in 1866.

HAY, Andrew Kessler, a Representative from New Jersey; born near Lowell, Mass., January 19, 1809; completed preparatory studies; was employed in the manufacture of window glass; moved to Waterford Works, N. J., in 1829 and later to Winslow, N. J., and engaged in the manufacture of glass; was also largely interested in real estate and agriculture; elected as a Whig to the Thirty-first Congress (March 4, 1849–March 3,

1851); declined to be a candidate for renomination; resumed his business interests; presidential elector on the Republican ticket of Grant and Wilson in 1872; president of the Camden & Atlantic Railroad Co. 1872–1876; died in Winslow, Camden County, N. J., February 7, 1881; interment in Colestown Cemetery, near Haddonfield, N. J.

HAY, James, a Representative from Virginia; born in Millwood, Clark County, Va., January 9, 1856; attended private schools and the University of Pennsylvania at Philadelphia; was graduated from the law department of Washington and Lee University, Lexington, Va., in 1877; was admitted to the bar and commenced practice in Harrisonburg, Va., in 1877; moved to Madison, Va., in June 1879 and continued the practice of law; Commonwealth attorney 1883–1896; member of the State house of delegates 1885–1889; served in the State senate 1893–1897; member of the Democratic State committee in 1888; delegate to the Democratic National Convention at St. Louis in 1888; elected as a Democrat to the Fifty-fifth and to the nine succeeding Congresses and served from March 4, 1897, until his resignation on October 1, 1916, to accept the appointment as judge of the United States Court of Claims, in which position he served until December 1, 1927, when he resigned; died in Madison, Va., June 12, 1931; interment in Cedar Hill Cemetery.

HAY, John Breese, a Representative from Illinois; born in Belleville, St. Clair County, Ill., January 8, 1834; received a limited schooling; learned the art of printing; studied law; was admitted to the bar in 1851 and commenced practice in Belleville, Ill.; prosecuting attorney for the twenty-fourth judicial district of Illinois 1860–1868; delegate to the Republican State convention in 1860; served in the Union Army during the Civil War in the One Hundred and Thirtieth Regiment, Illinois Volunteer Infantry; elected as a Republican to the Forty-first and Forty-second Congresses (March 4, 1869–March 3, 1873); unsuccessful candidate for reelection in 1872 to the Forty-third Congress and for election in 1880 to the Forty-seventh Congress; resumed the practice of law in Belleville; postmaster of Belleville, Ill., 1881–1885; judge of St. Clair County Court 1886–1900; served as mayor of Belleville from 1901 to 1905, when he resigned, having been again elected county judge, and served until 1914; died in Belleville, Ill., on June 16, 1916; interment in Green Mount Cemetery.

HAYDEN, Carl, a Representative and a Senator from Arizona; born in Hayden's Ferry (now Tempe), Maricopa County, Ariz., October 2, 1877; attended the public schools; graduated from the Normal School of Arizona at Tempe in 1896; attended Leland Stanford Junior University, California, 1896–1900; engaged in mercantile pursuits and in the flour-milling business at Tempe 1900–1904; member, Tempe Town Council, 1902–1904; delegate to the Democratic National Convention at St. Louis in 1904; treasurer of Maricopa County 1904–1906; sheriff of Maricopa County 1907–1912; upon the admission of Arizona as a State into the Union was elected as a Democrat to the Sixty-second and to the seven succeeding Congresses and served from February 19, 1912, to March 3, 1927; did not seek renomination, having become a candidate for United States Senator; during the First World War was commissioned a major of Infantry in the United States Army; elected to the United States Senate in 1926 for the term commencing March 4, 1927; reelected in 1932, 1938, 1944, 1950, and again in 1956 for the term ending January 3, 1963.

HAYDEN, Edward Daniel, a Representative from Massachusetts; born in Cambridge, Mass., December 27, 1833; attended the Lawrence Academy, Groton, Mass., and was graduated from

Harvard University in 1854; studied law; was admitted to the bar in 1857 and commenced practice in Woburn, Mass.; entered the United States Navy as assistant paymaster in 1861, and served in the Mississippi Squadron under Admiral Porter in the Vicksburg and Red River campaigns; returned to Woburn, Mass., in 1866 and engaged in mercantile pursuits; president of the First National Bank 1874–1900; member of the State house of representatives 1880–1882; elected as a Republican to the Forty-ninth and Fiftieth Congresses (March 4, 1885–March 3, 1889); was not a candidate for renomination in 1888; delegate to the Republican National Convention at Chicago in 1888; served for more than thirty years on the directorate of the Boston & Albany Railroad, and at the time of his death had been vice president for many years; served as selectman and later as alderman; director of the Shawmut National Bank of Boston; died in Woburn, Mass., November 15, 1908; interment in Mount Auburn Cemetery, Cambridge, Mass.

HAYDEN, Moses, a Representative from New York; born near Westfield, Hampden County, Mass., in 1786; completed preparatory studies, and was graduated from Williams College, Williamstown, Mass., in 1804; studied law; was admitted to the bar and commenced practice in York, Livingston County, N. Y.; was first judge of the court of common pleas of Livingston County 1821–1823; elected to the Eighteenth and Nineteenth Congresses (March 4, 1823–March 3, 1827); member of the State senate from January 6, 1829, until his death in Albany, N. Y., February 13, 1830; interment in Mount Pleasant Cemetery, York, near Fowlerville, N. Y.

HAYES, Everis Anson, a Representative from California; born in Waterloo, Jefferson County, Wis., March 10, 1855; attended the public schools; was graduated from the Waterloo High School in 1873 and from the literary and law departments of the University of Wisconsin at Madison in 1879; was admitted to the bar in 1879 and commenced practice in Madison, Wis.; moved to Ashland, Wis., in 1883 and subsequently, in 1886, to Hurley, Wis., and continued the practice of his profession; moved to Ironwood, Mich., in 1886 and engaged in the mining of ore; moved to San Jose, Santa Clara County, Calif., in 1887 and engaged in fruit raising and mining; with his brother became publisher and proprietor of the San Jose Daily Mercury Herald in 1901; elected as a Republican to the Fifty-ninth and to the six succeeding Congresses (March 4, 1905–March 3, 1919); unsuccessful candidate for reelection in 1918 to the Sixty-sixth Congress; resumed his newspaper activities in San Jose, Calif., with mining interests in Ironwood, Mich., and Sierra City, Calif.; died in San Jose, Calif., June 3, 1942; interment in Oak Hill Memorial Park Cemetery.

HAYES, Philip Cornelius, a Representative from Illinois; born in Granby, Hartford County, Conn., February 3, 1833; moved with his father's family to La Salle County, Ill.; attended the country schools; was graduated from Oberlin (Ohio) College in 1860 and from the Theological Seminary, Oberlin, Ohio, in 1863; served in the Union Army during the Civil War and commissioned captain in the One Hundred and Third Regiment, Ohio Volunteer Infantry, July 16, 1862; lieutenant colonel November 18, 1864; brevetted colonel and brigadier general March 13, 1865, "for gallant and meritorious services during the war"; mustered out June 12, 1865; superintendent of schools of Mount Vernon, Ohio, in 1866; moved to Circleville, Ohio, in 1867, to Bryan, Ohio, in 1869, and to Morris, Grundy County, Ill., in 1874; delegate to the Republican National Convention at Philadelphia in 1872; elected as a Republican to the Forty-fifth and Forty-sixth Congresses (March 4, 1877–March 3, 1881);

was not a candidate for renomination in 1880; moved to Joliet, Ill., in 1892, where he resumed journalism; died in Joilet July 13, 1916; interment in Elmhurst Cemetery.

HAYES, Rutherford Birchard, a Representative from Ohio and a President of the United States; born in Delaware, Delaware County, Ohio, October 4, 1822; attended the common schools, the Methodist Academy in Norwalk, Ohio, and the Webb Preparatory School in Middletown, Conn.; was graduated from Kenyon College, Gambier, Ohio, in August 1842 and from the Harvard Law School in January 1845; was admitted to the bar May 10, 1845, and commenced practice in Lower Sandusky (now Fremont); moved to Cincinnati in 1849 and resumed the practice of law; city solicitor 1857–1859; during the Civil War entered the Union Army; commissioned major of the Twenty-third Regiment, Ohio Volunteer Infantry, June 27, 1861; lieutenant colonel October 24, 1861; colonel October 24, 1862; brigadier general of Volunteers October 9, 1864; brevetted major general of Volunteers March 3, 1865, "for gallant and distinguished services during the campaign of 1864 in West Virginia, and particularly at the Battles of Fishers Hill and Cedar Creek, Va."; resigned June 8, 1865; elected as a Republican to the Thirty-ninth and Fortieth Congresses and served from March 4, 1865, to July 20, 1867, when he resigned, having been nominated for Governor of Ohio; Governor 1868–1872; unsuccessful candidate for election to the Forty-third Congress; declined appointment as United States treasurer at Cincinnati, Ohio; again elected Governor and served from January 1876 to March 2, 1877, when he resigned, having been elected President of the United States in 1876; was inaugurated March 4, 1877, and served until March 3, 1881; president and trustee of many educational funds, colleges, and historical societies and commander of several military orders; died in Fremont, Sandusky County, Ohio, January 17, 1893; interment in Oakwood Cemetery; following the gift of his home to the State of Ohio for the Spiegel Grove State Park was reinterred there in 1915.

HAYES, Walter Ingalls, a Representative from Iowa; born in Marshall, Calhoun County, Mich., December 9, 1841; attended the common schools, and was graduated from the law department of Michigan University at Ann Arbor in 1863; was admitted to the bar in 1863 and commenced practice in Marshall, Mich.; city attorney 1864 and 1865; United States commissioner for the eastern district of Michigan 1864 and 1865 and of Iowa 1865–1875; city solicitor of Clinton, Iowa, in 1870; district judge of the seventh judicial district of Iowa 1875–1887; delegate to the Democratic National Conventions at Chicago in 1884 and 1892; elected as a Democrat to the Fiftieth and to the three succeeding Congresses (March 4, 1887–March 3, 1895); unsuccessful candidate for reelection in 1894 to the Fifty-fourth Congress; resumed the practice of law in Clinton, Iowa; member of the State house of representatives in 1897 and 1898; died in Marshall, Mich., March 14, 1901; interment in Springdale Cemetery, Clinton, Iowa.

HAYMOND, Thomas Sherwood, a Representative from Virginia; born near Fairmont, Monongalia County, Va. (now West Virginia), January 15, 1794; attended private schools and William and Mary College, Williamsburg, Va.; served as a private in the War of 1812; studied law; was admitted to the bar in 1815 and commenced practice in Morgantown, Va. (now West Virginia); president of the county court of Marion County in 1842; elected as a Whig to the Thirty-first Congress to fill the vacancy caused by the death of Alexander Newman and served from November 8, 1849, to March 3, 1851; brigadier general of the State militia prior to 1861; entered the Confederate Army as a colonel in 1861 and served throughout the Civil War; died in Richmond, Va., April 5, 1869; interment in Palatine Cemetery, near Fairmont, Marion County, W. Va.

HAYMOND, William Summerville, a Representative from Indiana; born near Clarksburg, Harrison County, Va. (now West Virginia), February 20, 1823; attended the common schools and was graduated from Bellevue Hospital Medical College, New York City; commenced the practice of his profession at Monticello, Ind., in 1852; during the Civil War entered the Union Army as a surgeon in 1862 and served one year; unsuccessful candidate for the State senate in 1866; president of the Indianapolis, Delphi & Chicago Railroad Co. 1872–1874; elected as a candidate of both Democrats and Liberals to the Forty-fourth Congress (March 4, 1875–March 3, 1877); unsuccessful candidate for reelection in 1876 to the Forty-fifth Congress; resumed his former professional and business activities; organized the Central Medical College in Indianapolis in 1877 and was dean until his death; published in 1879 a history of Indiana; died in Indianapolis, Ind., December 24, 1885; interment in Crown Hill Cemetery.

HAYNE, Arthur Peronneau (brother of Robert Young Hayne), a Senator from South Carolina; born in Charleston, S. C., March 12, 1790; pursued classical studies; engaged in business; served in the War of 1812 as first lieutenant at Sackets Harbor, major of Cavalry on the St. Lawrence, and inspector general in 1814; brevetted lieutenant colonel for gallant conduct at New Orleans; studied law; was admitted to the bar and practiced; served in the Florida War as commander of the Tennessee Volunteers and retired in 1820; member of the State house of representatives; Democratic presidential elector in 1828; United States naval agent in the Mediterranean for five years; declined the Belgian mission; appointed to the United States Senate to fill the vacancy caused by the death of Josiah J. Evans and served from May 11, 1858, to December 2, 1858; was not a candidate to succeed himself; died in Charleston, S. C., January 7, 1867; interment in St. Michael's Churchyard.

HAYNE, Robert Young (brother of Arthur Peronneau Hayne), a Senator from South Carolina; born on Pon Pon plantation, St. Paul's Parish, Colleton District, S. C., November 10, 1791; on his mother's death he was confided to the care of his aunt in Beaufort until he was nine years of age, when he entered private schools in Charleston; studied law; was admitted to the bar in October 1812 and commenced practice in Charleston, S. C.; during the War of 1812 served in the Third South Carolina Regiment and as lieutenant of the Charleston Cadet Infantry; captain of the Charleston Cadet Riflemen in 1814; appointed by Governor Alston quartermaster general of the State in December 1814; member of the State house of representatives 1814–1818, and served as speaker in 1818; attorney general 1818–1822; elected as a Tariff-for-Revenue Democrat to the United States Senate; reelected in 1828 and served from March 4, 1823, to December 13, 1832, when he resigned to become Governor; participated in 1830 in a notable debate with Daniel Webster upon the principles of the Constitution, the authority of the General Government, and the rights of the States; colonel of militia in Charleston; member of the South Carolina nullification convention in 1832; Governor of South Carolina from December 13, 1832, to 1834; mayor of Charleston 1835–1837; president of the Knoxville convention in 1836; chairman of the committee appointed for promotion of the Louisville, Cincinnati & Charleston Railroad in 1836 and president of same 1836–1839; died in Asheville, N. C., September 24, 1839; interment in St. Michael's Churchyard, Charleston, S. C.

HAYNES, Charles Eaton, a Representative from Georgia; born in Brunswick, Mecklenburg County, Va., April 15, 1784; moved to Sparta, Ga.; completed preparatory studies; was graduated in medicine from the University of Pennsylvania at Philadelphia and practiced; elected as a Democrat to the Nineteenth, Twentieth, and Twenty-first Congresses (March 4, 1825–March 3, 1831); unsuccessful candidate for reelection in 1830 to the Twenty-second Congress and for election in 1832 to the Twenty-third Congress; elected as a Unionist to the Twenty-fourth and Twenty-fifth Congresses (March 4, 1835–March 3, 1839); died August 29, 1841; interment in Sparta, Ga.

HAYNES, Martin Alonzo, a Representative from New Hampshire; born in Springfield, Sullivan County, N. H., July 30, 1842; moved with his parents to Manchester, N. H., in 1846; attended the common schools; apprenticed to the printer's trade; during the Civil War enlisted in June 1861 in the Union Army as a private in the Second New Hampshire Regiment and served three years; was wounded in the first Battle of Bull Run, the Battle of Glendale, near Richmond, and in the second Battle of Bull Run; moved to Lakeport, Belknap County, N. H., in 1868, where he established the Lake Village Times, which he conducted for twenty years; member of the State house of representatives in 1872 and 1873; clerk of the supreme court for Belknap County 1876–1883; president of the New Hampshire Veterans' Association in 1881 and 1882; department commander of the Grand Army of the Republic in 1881 and 1882; elected as a Republican to the Forty-eighth and Forty-ninth Congresses (March 4, 1883–March 3, 1887); unsuccessful candidate for reelection in 1886 to the Fiftieth Congress; internal-revenue agent of the Treasury 1890–1893 and 1898–1912; established internal-revenue service in the Philippine Islands; died in Lakeport, N. H., November 28, 1919; interment in Bayside Cemetery.

HAYNES, William Elisha (cousin of George William Palmer), a Representative from Ohio; born in Hoosick Falls, Rensselaer County, N. Y., October 19, 1829; moved to Ohio with his parents, who settled in Lower Sandusky (now Fremont) in 1839; attended the common schools; apprenticed as a printer; clerk on a steamer on Lake Superior in 1848 and 1849; engaged in mercantile pursuits at Fremont 1850–1856; auditor of Sandusky County, Ohio, 1856–1860; during the Civil War enlisted in the Union Army as a private April 16, 1861, in the Eighth Regiment, Ohio Volunteer Infantry; commissioned captain, and served in western Virginia, the Shenandoah Valley, and in the Army of the Potomac until November 1862, when he was commissioned lieutenant colonel of the Tenth Regiment, Ohio Volunteer Cavalry, and served with it in the Army of the Cumberland until 1864, when he was honorably discharged; by appointment of President Johnson served as collector of internal revenue for the ninth district of Ohio in 1866 and 1867; again engaged in mercantile pursuits 1866–1873; engaged in banking 1873–1914, serving as cashier, vice president, and president; member of the board of trustees of the Toledo Insane Asylum 1884–1888; delegate to the Democratic National Convention at Cincinnati in 1880, which nominated Hancock and English, and at Chicago in 1884, which nominated Cleveland and Hendricks; elected as a Democrat to the Fifty-first and Fifty-second Congresses (March 4, 1889–March 3, 1893); declined to be a candidate for renomination in 1892; resumed banking in Fremont, Sandusky County, Ohio, in which he continued until his death there on December 5, 1914; interment in Oakwood Cemetery.

HAYS, Charles, a Representative from Alabama; born at "Hays Mount," near Boligee, Greene County, Ala., February 2, 1834; completed preparatory studies under private teachers;

attended the University of Georgia at Athens and the University of Virginia at Charlottesville; was a cotton planter and also engaged in other agricultural pursuits; was a delegate to the Democratic National Convention at Baltimore in 1860; during the Civil War was a major in the Confederate Army; member of the constitutional convention of Alabama in 1867; served in the State senate in 1868; elected as a Republican to the Forty-first and to the three succeeding Congresses (March 4, 1869–March 3, 1877); died at his home, "Myrtle Hall," in Greene County, Ala., June 24, 1879; interment in the family cemetery, "Hays Mount" plantation.

HAYS, Edward Dixon, a Representative from Missouri; born on a farm near Oak Ridge, Cape Girardeau County, Mo., April 28, 1872; attended the public schools; was graduated from the Oak Ridge High School in 1889 and from the Cape Girardeau State Normal School in 1893; taught school until 1895; moved to Jackson, Mo., in 1895; studied law; was admitted to the bar in 1896 and commenced practice in Jackson, Cape Girardeau County, Mo.; mayor of Jackson 1903–1907; probate judge of Cape Girardeau County 1907–1918; unsuccessful Republican nominee for circuit judge in 1916; moved to Cape Girardeau, Mo., in 1915 and continued the practice of law; elected as a Republican to the Sixty-sixth and Sixty-seventh Congresses (March 4, 1919–March 3, 1923); unsuccessful candidate for reelection in 1922 to the Sixty-eighth Congress; resumed the practice of his profession in Cape Girardeau, Mo.; trial lawyer for the Department of Justice in the Court of Claims 1923–1925; appointed valuation attorney for the Interstate Commerce Commission in 1925 and served until 1933; continued the practice of law in Washington, D. C., and resided in Bethesda, Md., where he died on July 25, 1941; interment in Cedar Hill Cemetery, Washington, D. C.

HAYS, Edward Retilla, a Representative from Iowa; born near Fostoria, Wood County, Ohio, May 26, 1847; attended rural schools near Fostoria and Heidelberg College, Tiffin, Ohio; during the Civil War served as a private in the First Regiment, Ohio Heavy Artillery, 1862–1865; studied law; was admitted to the bar in 1869 and commenced practice in Knoxville, Iowa; elected as a Republican to the Fifty-first Congress to fill the vacancy caused by the resignation of Edwin H. Conger and served from November 4, 1890, to March 3, 1891; was not a candidate for renomination in 1890; resumed the practice of law; died in Knoxville, Marion County, Iowa, February 28, 1896; interment in Graceland Cemetery.

HAYS, Lawrence Brooks, a Representative from Arkansas; born in London, Pope County, Ark., August 9, 1898; attended the public schools in Russellville, Ark.; was graduated from the University of Arkansas at Fayetteville in 1919 and from the law school of George Washington University, Washington, D. C., in 1922; was admitted to the bar in 1922 and commenced practice in Russellville, Ark.; during the First World War served in the United States Army from September 30, 1918, to December 6, 1918; served as assistant attorney general of Arkansas 1925–1927; Democratic national committeeman for Arkansas 1932–1939; NRA labor compliance officer for Arkansas in 1934; assistant to the administrator of resettlement in 1935; held administrative and legal positions in the Farm Security Administration 1936–1942; member of the board of trustees of George Peabody College; elected as a Democrat to the Seventy-eighth and to the seven succeeding Congresses (January 3, 1943–January 3, 1959); unsuccessful candidate for reelection in 1958 to the Eighty-sixth Congress; appointed a member of the Board of Directors of the Tennessee Valley Authority for a short term and later reappointed for a ten-year term and served from July 1, 1959, until

his resignation February 27, 1961; confirmed as Assistant Secretary of State for Congressional Relations on February 20, 1961, and took the oath of office on February 28, 1961; resides in Washington, D. C.

HAYS, Samuel, a Representative from Pennsylvania; born in County Donegal, Ireland, September 10, 1783; immigrated to the United States with his mother, who settled in Franklin, Venango County, Pa., in 1792; treasurer of Venango County in 1808; elected sheriff of Venango County in 1808, 1820, 1829, and in 1833; member of the State house of representatives in 1813, 1816, 1823, and 1825; served in the State senate in 1822 and 1839; member of the board of trustees of Allegheny College, Meadville, Pa., 1837–1861; served as brigadier general, commanding the First Brigade, Seventeenth Division, Pennsylvania State Militia, 1841–1843; elected as a Democrat to the Twenty-eighth Congress (March 4, 1843–March 3, 1845); was not a candidate for renomination in 1844; engaged in iron manufactures, operating furnaces on French Creek, near Franklin; appointed in 1847 marshal for the western district of Pennsylvania; associate judge of the district court in 1856; died in Franklin, Pa., July 1, 1868; interment in Old Town Cemetery; reinterment in New Franklin Cemetery.

HAYS, Samuel Lewis, a Representative from Virginia; born near Clarksburg, Harrison County, Va. (now West Virginia), October 20, 1794; moved to Lewis County, Va., and to Stewarts Creek, Lewis County, Va. (now Glenville, Gilmer County, W. Va.), in 1833 and engaged in agricultural pursuits; member of the State assembly of Virginia; elected as a Democrat to the Twenty-seventh Congress (March 4, 1841–March 3, 1843); unsuccessful candidate for reelection to the Twenty-eighth Congress in 1842; presidential elector on the Democratic ticket of Polk and Dallas in 1844, of Pierce and King in 1852, and of Buchanan and Breckinridge in 1856; delegate to the State constitutional convention in 1850; appointed receiver of public moneys at Sauk Rapids, Minn., April 28, 1857, by President Buchanan and served until June 10, 1860; resumed agricultural pursuits; died at Sauk Rapids, Benton County, Minn., March 17, 1871; interment in the original Old Benton County Cemetery.

HAYS, Wayne Levere, a Representative from Ohio; born in Bannock, Belmont County, Ohio, May 13, 1911; attended the public schools of Bannock and St. Clairsville, Ohio; was graduated from Ohio State University at Columbus in 1933; student at Duke University, Durham, N. C., in 1935; teacher of history and public speaking in Flushing, Ohio, 1934–1937 and Findlay, Ohio, in 1937 and 1938; also engaged in agricultural pursuits; mayor of Flushing, Ohio, 1939–1945; served in the State senate in 1941 and 1942; member of the Officers' Reserve Corps, United States Army, from 1933 until called to active duty during World War II as a second lieutenant on December 8, 1941; was separated from service with medical discharge in August 1942; Belmont County commissioner 1945–1949; chairman, board of directors, Citizens National Bank, Flushing, Ohio, since December 1953; delegate to Democratic National Convention in 1960; elected as a Democrat to the Eighty-first and to the five succeeding Congresses (January 3, 1949–January 3, 1961). *Reelected to the Eighty-seventh Congress.*

HAYWARD, Monroe Leland, a Senator from Nebraska; born in Willsboro, Essex County, N. Y., December 22, 1840; served during the Civil War in the Twenty-second Regiment, New York Volunteer Infantry, and in the Fifth Regiment, New York Volunteer Cavalry; was graduated from Fort Edward Collegiate Institute, New York, in 1865; studied law in Whitewater, Wis.; was admitted to the bar in 1867 and commenced practice in

Nebraska City, Nebr.; member of the constitutional convention in 1873; judge of the district court of Nebraska in 1886; chairman of the Republican State conventions in 1885 and 1896; elected as a Republican to the United States Senate to fill the vacancy in the term beginning March 4, 1899, and served from March 8, 1899, until his death in Nebraska City, Otoe County, Nebr., December 5, 1899; interment in Wyuka Cemetery.

HAYWARD, William, Jr., a Representative from Maryland; born at "Shipshead," near Easton, Talbot County, Md., in 1787; attended Easton Academy, and was graduated from Princeton College in 1808; studied law; was admitted to the bar in 1809 and commenced practice in Easton; member of the State house of delegates 1818–1820; delegate to the Democratic State convention in 1818; elected as a Democrat to the Eighteenth Congress (March 4, 1823–March 3, 1825); continued the practice of law in Easton, Md., until his death there October 19, 1836; interment in the family burial ground on his estate, "Shipshead," near Easton, Md.

HAYWOOD, William Henry, Jr., a Senator from North Carolina; born in Raleigh, N. C., October 23, 1801; attended the Raleigh Male Academy, and was graduated from the University of North Carolina, at Chapel Hill, in 1819; studied law; was admitted to the bar in 1822 and commenced practice in Raleigh, N. C.; member of the State house of commons 1831 and 1834–1836, serving the last year as speaker; appointed Chargé d'Affaires to Belgium by President Van Buren, but declined; elected as a Democrat to the United States Senate and served from March 4, 1843, until July 25, 1846, when he resigned, having refused to be instructed by the legislature; resumed the practice of law in Raleigh, N. C., and died there on October 7, 1852; interment in the Old City Cemetery, Raleigh, N. C.

HAYWORTH, Donald, a Representative from Michigan; born in Toledo, Tama County, Iowa, January 13, 1898; boyhood spent on a farm in southeastern Iowa; attended a country school in Mahaska County and high school in New Sharon, Iowa; was graduated from Grinnell (Iowa) College in 1918; during the First World War served as a private in the United States Army; was graduated from the University of Chicago in 1921; teacher in Oskaloosa (Iowa) High School 1921–1923; head of the department of speech at Penn College, Oskaloosa, Iowa, 1923–1927, at the University of Akron, Akron, Ohio, 1928–1937, at Michigan State College, East Lansing, Mich., 1937–1942, and professor of speech 1946–1954; chairman of Michigan Victory Speakers Bureau in 1941 and 1942; in charge of speakers bureau, Office of Civil Defense, Washington, D. C., in 1942 and 1943; directed speakers' activities for fund raising with the American Red Cross in 1944; in charge of relations with the States on fuel conservation for the Department of the Interior 1944–1946; owner of Plastics Manufacturing Co. since 1950; unsuccessful candidate for election to the Eighty-third Congress in 1952; elected as a Democrat to the Eighty-fourth Congress (January 3, 1955–January 3, 1957); unsuccessful candidate for reelection in 1956 to the Eighty-fifth Congress and for election in 1958 to the Eighty-sixth Congress; author of magazine articles and books; is a resident of East Lansing, Mich.

HAZARD, Jonathan J., a Delegate from Rhode Island; born in Newport, R. I., in 1744; completed preparatory studies; member of the State house of representatives in 1776; paymaster in the Continental Battalion from Rhode Island in 1777 and joined General Washington's Army in New Jersey that year; again elected a member of the State house of representatives and a member of the council of war in 1778; Member of the Continental Congress 1787–1789; again a member of the State house of repre-

sentatives 1790–1805; moved to New York in 1805 and located upon an estate in the Friends' settlement at Verona, Oneida County, N. Y., where he died later than 1824.

HAZARD, Nathaniel, a Representative from Rhode Island; born in Newport, R. I., in 1776; was graduated from Brown University, Providence, R. I., in 1792; member of the State house of representatives in 1818 and 1819 and served as speaker; elected as a Democrat to the Sixteenth Congress and served from March 4, 1819, until his death in Washington, D. C., December 17, 1820; interment in the Congressional Cemetery.

HAZELTINE, Abner, a Representative from New York; born in Wardsboro, Windham County, Vt., June 10, 1793; attended the common schools; fitted for college under the instruction of his pastor; was graduated from Williams College, Williamstown, Mass., in 1815; moved to Jamestown, N. Y., November 2, 1815; taught school; studied law; was admitted to the bar in 1819 and commenced practice in Chautauqua County, N. Y.; moved to Warren, Pa., and was the first located lawyer in the county; moved to Jamestown, Chautauqua County, N. Y., and resumed the practice of law in 1823; editorial writer on the Jamestown Journal 1826–1829; member of the State assembly in 1829 and 1830; elected as a Whig to the Twenty-third and Twenty-fourth Congresses (March 4, 1833–March 3, 1837); was not a candidate for renomination in 1836; prosecuting attorney of Chautauqua County 1847–1850; judge of Chautauqua County 1859–1863; appointed special county judge of Chautauqua County in 1873 but did not qualify; United States commissioner for the northern district of New York until his death; died in Jamestown, N. Y., on December 20, 1879; interment in Lakeview Cemetery.

HAZELTINE, Ira Sherwin, a Representative from Missouri; born in Andover, Windsor County, Vt., July 13, 1821; attended the common schools and pursued an academic course; moved to Richland Center, Wis., in 1842; taught school in Natchez, Miss., for three years; studied law; was admitted to the bar and commenced practice in Richland Center, Wis.; delegate to the Republican National Convention in 1860; member of the State house of representatives 1867–1869; engaged in farming near Springfield, Greene County, Mo., in 1870; elected as a Greenback Republican to the Forty-seventh Congress (March 4, 1881–March 3, 1883); unsuccessful for reelection in 1882; laid out and named the city of Richland Center, Wis., in 1851 and practiced law there; died near Springfield, Mo., January 13, 1899; interment in Hazelwood Cemetery, Springfield, Mo.

HAZELTON, George Cochrane (brother of Gerry Whiting Hazelton and nephew of Clark Beaton Cochrane), a Representative from Wisconsin; born in Chester, Rockingham County, N. H., January 3, 1832; attended the district schools; prepared for college at Pinkerton Academy in New Hampshire and Dummer Academy in Massachusetts; was graduated from Union College, Schenectady, N. Y., in 1858; studied law; was admitted to the bar at Malone, N. Y., in 1858; settled in Boscobel, Wis., in 1863 and practiced his profession; prosecuting attorney of Grant County 1864–1868; member of the State senate 1867–1869; was reelected in 1869 and served as president pro tempore of the senate 1869–1871; elected as a Republican to the Forty-fifth, Forty-sixth, and Forty-seventh Congresses (March 4, 1877–March 3, 1883); unsuccessful candidate for renomination in 1882; settled in Washington, D. C., and practiced law; attorney for the District of Columbia during the Harrison administration; compiled and edited the Dedicatory Proceedings of the Soldiers' Monument at Chester, N. H., August 22, 1904; died in Chester, N. H., while on a visit, September 4, 1922; interment in Vale Cemetery, Schenectady, N. Y.

HAZELTON, Gerry Whiting (brother of George Cochrane Hazelton and nephew of Clark Beaton Cochrane), a Representative from Wisconsin; born in Chester, Rockingham County, N. H., on February 24, 1829; attended the common schools, Pinkerton Academy, Derry, N. H., and received instruction from a private tutor; taught school; studied law; was admitted to the bar in 1852 and commenced practice in Amsterdam, N. Y.; moved to Wisconsin in 1856 and settled in Columbus; served in the State senate in 1860 and was chosen president pro tempore; delegate to the Republican National Convention at Chicago in 1860; district attorney for Columbia County in 1864; appointed collector of internal revenue for the second district of Wisconsin in 1866 and removed by President Johnson the same year; elected as a Republican to the Forty-second and Forty-third Congresses (March 4, 1871–March 3, 1875); was not a candidate for renomination in 1874; moved to Milwaukee in 1876; United States attorney for the eastern district of Wisconsin 1876–1885; continued the practice of law; appointed special master in chancery in 1912; United States court commissioner and commissioner for Milwaukee County for many years; engaged in the practice of law at Milwaukee, Wis., until his death September 29, 1920; interment in Forest Home Cemetery.

HAZELTON, John Wright, a Representative from New Jersey; born in Mullica Hill, Gloucester County, N. J., December 10, 1814; attended the common schools; engaged in agricultural pursuits; delegate to the Republican National Convention at Philadelphia in 1856 and at Chicago in 1868; presidential elector on the Republican ticket of Grant and Colfax in 1868; elected as a Republican to the Forty-second and Forty-third Congresses (March 4, 1871–March 3, 1875); unsuccessful candidate for reelection in 1874 to the Forty-fourth Congress; retired from public life and resumed agricultural pursuits; died near Mullica Hill, N. J., December 20, 1878; interment in Friends Cemetery, Mullica Hill, N. J.

HAZLETT, James Miller, a Representative from Pennsylvania; born in Londonderry, Ireland, October 14, 1864; when two years of age immigrated to the United States with his parents who settled in South Philadelphia, Pa.; attended the public schools of Philadelphia; began working in his father's blacksmith shop in 1881 and was engaged as a farrier until 1915; nominated and elected to the Philadelphia Common Council in 1896, and served in councils for sixteen years, resigning as president of the select council in 1911; served as president of the Philadelphia Board of Road Viewers 1911–1916; elected recorder of deeds of Philadelphia in 1915 and served until elected to Congress; elected as a Republican to the Seventieth Congress and served from March 4, 1927, until his resignation on October 20, 1927, before the convening of Congress; again became a candidate for recorder of deeds and was elected, serving from 1927 to 1936; elected chairman of the Republican Central Campaign Committee in May 1928 and served until 1934; delegate to the Republican National Conventions in 1928 and 1932; member of the Board of Road Viewers from November 7, 1935, until he retired on February 23, 1937; died at Philadelphia, Pa., November 8, 1940; interment in West Laurel Hill Cemetery.

HEALD, William Henry, a Representative from Delaware; born in Wilmington, Del., August 27, 1864; was graduated from the public and high schools of Wilmington, from the University of Delaware at Newark in 1883, and from the law department of George Washington University, Washington, D. C., in 1888; national bank examiner for the States of Montana, Idaho, Washington, and Oregon 1888–1892; was admitted to the bar and commenced practice in Wilmington, Del., in 1897; post-

master of Wilmington 1901–1905; elected as a Republican to the Sixty-first and Sixty-second Congresses (March 4, 1909–March 3, 1913); was not a candidate for renomination in 1912; resumed the practice of law in Wilmington, Del.; also engaged in banking; member of the board of trustees of the University of Delaware 1915–1939 and served as president from 1936 until his death; presidential elector on the Republican ticket of Hughes and Fairbanks in 1916; died in Wilmington, Del., June 3, 1939; interment in Wilmington and Brandywin Cemetery.

HEALEY, Arthur Daniel, a Representative from Massachusetts; born in Somerville, Middlesex County, Mass., on December 29, 1889; attended the public schools; was graduated from Somerville (Mass.) Latin School in 1908; attended Dartmouth College, Hanover, N. H., in 1909 and 1910 and was graduated from the law department of Boston (Mass.) University in 1913; was admitted to the bar in 1914 and commenced practice in Boston, Mass.; during the First World War enlisted on August 9, 1917, and served through the ranks to second lieutenant in the Quartermaster Corps, being discharged on March 6, 1919; elected as a Democrat to the Seventy-third and to the four succeeding Congresses and served from March 4, 1933, until his resignation on August 3, 1942, to accept an appointment as judge of the United States District Court for Massachusetts, in which capacity he served until his death in Somerville, Mass., September 16, 1948; interment in Oak Grove Cemetery, Medford, Mass.

HEALEY, James Christopher, a Representative from New York; born in the Bronx, New York City, N. Y., December 24, 1909; attended the public schools of New York City; graduated from the Wharton School of the University of Pennsylvania at Philadelphia in 1933; attended Fordham and St. John's Law School, graduating in 1936; was admitted to the bar in 1937; attorney for the New York State Labor Relations Board 1938–1940; assistant United States attorney for the southern district of New York 1941–1943; during World War II served as a lieutenant in the United States Navy 1943–1946; assistant corporation counsel for the city of New York 1946–1949; counsel to the borough president of the Bronx 1949–1956; elected as a Democrat to the Eighty-fourth Congress to fill the vacancy caused by the resignation of Sidney A. Fine; reelected to the Eighty-fifth and Eighty-sixth Congresses and served from February 7, 1956, to January 3, 1961. *Reelected to the Eighty-seventh Congress.*

HEALY, Joseph, a Representative from New Hampshire; born in Newton, Middlesex County, Mass., August 21, 1776; completed preparatory studies; was a hotel keeper and also engaged in agricultural pursuits; member of the State senate in 1824; elected as a Democrat to the Nineteenth and Twentieth Congresses (March 4, 1825–March 3, 1829); member of the State executive council 1829–1832; resumed agricultural pursuits and the hotel business; died in Washington, Sullivan County, N. H., October 10, 1861; interment in the Old Cemetery.

HEALY, Ned R., a Representative from California; born in Milwaukee, Wis., August 9, 1905; attended the public schools, Marquette University, Milwaukee, Wis., and the University of Wisconsin at Madison; stock and bond salesman at Milwaukee, Wis., 1929–1932; moved to Los Angeles, Calif., in 1932 and engaged in merchandising and office management; production manager of the Avery Adhesives manufacturing business at Los Angeles, Calif., 1940–1943; director of the Hollywood office of the California State Relief Administration in 1939 and 1940; member of the Los Angeles City Council in 1943 and 1944; delegate to the Democratic State conventions in 1944, 1946, and

1948; elected as a Democrat to the Seventy-ninth Congress (January 3, 1945–January 3, 1947); unsuccessful candidate for reelection in 1946 to the Eightieth Congress and for election in 1948 to the Eighty-first Congress; dealer in auto parts and accessories; is a resident of Los Angeles, Calif.

HEARD, John Thaddeus, a Representative from Missouri; born in Georgetown, Pettis County, Mo., October 29, 1840; attended the public schools and was graduated from the University of Missouri at Columbia in 1860; studied law; was admitted to the bar in 1862 and practiced several years in Sedalia, Pettis County, Mo.; member of the State house of representatives 1872–1875; served in the State senate 1880–1884; employed in 1881 by the fund commissioners of the State to prosecute and adjust all claims of the State against the General Government; elected as a Democrat to the Forty-ninth and to the four succeeding Congresses (March 4, 1885–March 3, 1895); unsuccessful candidate for reelection in 1894 to the Fifty-fourth Congress; delegate to the Democratic National Convention at St. Louis in 1904; engaged in banking; retired from active business in 1922; died while on a visit to Los Angeles, Calif., January 27, 1927; interment in Crown Hill Cemetery, Sedalia, Mo.

HEARST, George (father of William Randolph Hearst), a Senator from California; born near Sullivan, Franklin County, Mo., September 3, 1820; attended the public schools, and was graduated from the Franklin County Mining School in 1838; moved to California in 1850 and settled in Eldorado County, later moving to Nevada County; engaged in mining, stock raising, and farming; moved to San Francisco in 1862; member of the State assembly in 1865 and 1866; became the owner of the San Francisco Examiner in 1880; unsuccessful Democratic candidate for Governor of California in 1882; appointed as a Democrat to the United States Senate to fill the vacancy caused by the death of John F. Miller and served from March 23, 1886, to August 4, 1886, when a successor was elected; engaged in agricultural pursuits in California; elected in 1887 to the United States Senate and served from March 4, 1887, until his death in Washington, D. C., February 28, 1891; interment in Cypress Lawn Cemetery.

HEARST, William Randolph (son of George Hearst), a Representative from New York; born in San Francisco, Calif., April 29, 1863; attended the public schools and Harvard University; became editor and proprietor of the San Francisco Examiner in 1886, since which time he established a chain of newspapers extending from coast to coast; also owner and publisher of many magazines; elected as a Democrat to the Fifty-eighth and Fifty-ninth Congresses (March 4, 1903–March 3, 1907); did not seek renomination in 1906, having become a gubernatorial candidate; was the Municipal Ownership candidate for mayor of Greater New York in November 1905; unsuccessful Democratic candidate for Governor of New York in 1906; organized the Independence League Party in 1908; resumed his publishing business; died in Beverly Hills, Calif., August 14, 1951; interment in Cypress Lawn Cemetery, San Francisco, Calif.

HEATH, James P., a Representative from Maryland; born in Delaware, December 21, 1777; completed preparatory studies; served in the Regular Army as lieutenant of Engineers 1799–1802; register in chancery in Annapolis, Md.; served throughout the War of 1812 as aide-de-camp to General Winder; elected as a Democrat to the Twenty-third Congress (March 4, 1833–March 3, 1835); unsuccessful candidate for reelection in 1834 to the Twenty-fourth Congress; died in Georgetown, D. C., June 12, 1854; interment in Oak Hill Cemetery, Washington, D. C.

HEATH, John, a Representative from Virginia; born in Wicomico Parish, Northumberland County, Va., May 8, 1758; prepared for college under competent tutors; attended William and Mary College, Williamsburg, Va.; one of the students who organized the Phi Beta Kappa on December 5, 1776, the first "Greek letter" society to be established in an American college, and was elected its president; served in the Revolutionary War; studied law; was admitted to the bar and practiced in Northumberland County; served as Commonwealth's attorney from September 10, 1781, to May 12, 1784, and from November 15, 1787, to May 13, 1793; member of the privy council for several years; moved to a new residence in 1791 near the present town of Heathsville, Northumberland County, Va., and settled upon an estate which he named "Springfield"; served in the State house of delegates in 1782 but declined reelection, having again been appointed Commonwealth's attorney; elected as a Republican to the Third and Fourth Congresses (March 4, 1793–March 3, 1797); declined to be a candidate for renomination; resumed the practice of law in Heathsville; moved to Richmond, Va., in 1803, having been appointed a member of the Virginia Privy Council on December 30, 1803, and served until his death; was also engaged in the practice of law; died in Richmond, Va., October 13, 1810.

HEATON, David, a Representative from North Carolina; born in Hamilton, Butler County, Ohio, March 10, 1823; completed preparatory studies; studied law; was admitted to the bar; elected to the State senate in 1855; moved to St. Anthony Falls, Minn., in 1857; member of the State Senate of Minnesota 1858–1863; appointed special agent of the Treasury Department and the United States depository in New Bern, N. C., in 1863; appointed Third Auditor of the Treasury in 1864, but declined; served as a member of the constitutional convention of North Carolina in 1867; upon the readmission of North Carolina to representation was elected as a Republican to the Fortieth Congress; reelected to the Forty-first Congress and served from July 15, 1868, until his death; had been nominated as a Republican candidate for reelection to the Forty-second Congress; died in Washington, D. C., on June 25, 1870; interment in the National Cemetery, New Bern, N. C.

HEATON, Robert Douglas, a Representative from Pennsylvania; born in Raven Run, Schuylkill County, Pa., July 1, 1873; moved to Ashland, Pa., with his parents in 1886; attended the common schools, the Canandaigua Academy, Canandaigua, N. Y., the New York Military Academy, at Cornwall on the Hudson, N. Y., and the University of Pennsylvania at Philadelphia; identified with many business enterprises of the State and county; unsuccessful candidate for election in 1910 to the Sixty-second Congress; elected as a Republican to the Sixty-fourth and Sixty-fifth Congresses (March 4, 1915–March 3, 1919); did not seek renomination in 1918, having become a candidate for State senator; member of the State senate 1919–1932; resumed his former business activities; member of the board of trustees of the Ashland State Hospital; died at Ashland, Pa., June 11, 1933; interment in the family cemetery at Mauch Chunk, Pa.

HEATWOLE, Joel Prescott, a Representative from Minnesota; born at Waterford Mills, Elkhart County, Ind., August 22, 1856; attended the public schools; learned the printer's trade; taught school and later became superintendent of the Millersburg (Ind.) School; employed by the Millersburg newspaper in 1876 and afterward became editor and proprietor; moved to Minnesota in 1882 and settled in Glencoe; in 1884, after being employed by various newspapers, he settled in Northfield, Minn., and published the Northfield News; delegate to the Republican State conventions in 1886 and 1888· elected secretary of the

Republican State central committee in 1886 and 1888 and served as chairman in 1890; delegate to the Republican National Convention at Chicago in 1888; appointed a member of the board of regents of the State university in 1890; member of the State Editorial Association and served as president for three terms; unsuccessful candidate for election in 1892 to the Fifty-third Congress; elected mayor of Northfield in 1894; elected as a Republican to the Fifty-fourth and the three succeeding Congresses (March 4, 1895–March 3, 1903); was not a candidate for renomination in 1902; resumed his former newspaper pursuits; unsuccessful candidate for nomination for Governor of Minnesota in 1908; died in Northfield, Minn., April 4, 1910; interment in Oaklawn Cemetery.

HEBARD, William, a Representative from Vermont; born in Windham, Conn., November 29, 1800; attended the common schools, and was fitted for college at the Orange County Grammar School in Randolph, Vt.; studied law; was admitted to the bar in 1827 and commenced practice in East Randolph, Vt.; prosecuting attorney of Orange County 1832–1836; member of the State house of representatives in 1835; served in the State senate in 1836 and 1838; judge of probate of Randolph district in 1838, 1840, and 1841; again a member of the State house of representatives 1840–1842, 1858, 1859, 1864, 1865, and 1872; elected associate judge of the State supreme court in 1842 and 1844; moved to Chelsea, Vt., in 1845; elected as a Whig to the Thirty-first and Thirty-second Congresses (March 4, 1849–March 3, 1853); delegate to the constitutional convention in 1857; again a member of the general assembly in 1858, 1859, 1864, 1865, and 1872; resumed the practice of law; delegate to the Republican National Convention at Chicago in 1860; died in Chelsea, Orange County, Vt., October 20, 1875; interment in the Old Cemetery, Randolph Center, Vt.

HÉBERT, Felix, a Senator from Rhode Island; born near St. Hyacinthe, Province of Quebec, Canada, December 11, 1874, during a temporary stay of his parents there; came to the United States when his parents returned in 1880 and resumed their residence in the town of Coventry, R. I.; attended the public schools of Coventry, R. I., the parish school of St. Jean Baptiste, West Warwick, R. I., and La Salle Academy, Providence, R. I.; employed as a railroad freight billing clerk 1893–1896 and as a private secretary 1896–1898; deputy insurance commissioner of Rhode Island 1898–1906; studied law; was admitted to the bar in 1907 and commenced practice in Providence, R. I.; justice of the district court of the fourth judicial district of Rhode Island 1908–1928; trustee of the Nathanael Green Homestead Association of Rhode Island 1924–1934; member and secretary of the Providence County Courthouse Commission 1925–1934; member of the executive committee of the Republican State central committee 1926–1944; elected as a Republican to the United States Senate and served from March 4, 1929, to January 3, 1935; unsuccessful candidate for reelection in 1934; resumed the practice of law; member of the Republican National Committee since 1944; is a resident of Coventry Centre, R. I.

HÉBERT, Felix Edward, a Representative from Louisiana; born in New Orleans, La., October 12, 1901; attended public and parochial schools, Jesuit High School, New Orleans, La., and Tulane University, New Orleans, La., 1920–1924; engaged in newspaper and editorial work in New Orleans, La., 1918–1940; colonel on staff of the Governor of Louisiana in 1936; served as personal representative of the Governor in Washington, D. C., in 1940; elected as a Democrat to the Seventy-seventh and to the nine succeeding Congresses (January 3 1941–January 3, 1961). *Reelected to the Eighty-seventh Congress.*

HECHLER, Kenneth, a Representative from West Virginia; born in Nassau County, near Roslyn, Long Island, N. Y., September 20, 1914; attended the public schools; graduated from Swarthmore (Pa.) College in 1935, Columbia University in 1936 and 1940; taught political science at Columbia, Princeton, and Marshall College; research assistant to Judge Samuel I. Rosenman and President Franklin D. Roosevelt on Roosevelt's public papers; teacher at Barnard College in 1939 and 1940; administrative analyst, United States Bureau of the Budget, in 1941 and 1946; entered the United States Army in 1942 as a private in the Infantry; commissioned a second lieutenant, Armored Force, in 1943; assigned to European Theater of Operations as combat historian in 1944; discharged as a major in 1946; lieutenant colonel in Army Reserve; awarded five battle stars from Normandy to the Elbe; special assistant to President Truman 1949–1953; associate director of American Political Science Association at Washington, D. C., 1953–1956; administrative aide to Senator John A. Carroll of Colorado in 1957; moved to Huntington, W. Va., in 1957; television commentator, WHTN–TV, Huntington, W. Va., in 1957 and 1958; elected as a Democrat to the Eighty-sixth Congress (January 3, 1959–January 3, 1961). *Reelected to the Eighty-seventh Congress.*

HEDGE, Thomas, a Representative from Iowa; born in Burlington, Iowa, June 24, 1844; attended the common schools and Denmark (Iowa) Academy; was graduated from Phillips Academy, Andover, Mass., in 1861, Yale College in 1867, and Columbia College Law School, New York City, in 1869; was admitted to the bar in New York in 1869 and commenced practice in Burlington, Iowa; served as a private during the Civil War in Company E and as second lieutenant in Company G, One Hundred and Sixth Regiment, New York Volunteer Infantry, in 1864 and 1865; resumed the practice of law in Burlington, Iowa; elected as a Republican to the Fifty-sixth and to the three succeeding Congresses (March 4, 1899–March 3, 1907); was not a candidate for renomination in 1906; resumed the practice of law; died in Burlington, Iowa, November 28, 1920; interment in Aspen Grove Cemetery.

HEDRICK, Erland Harold, a Representative from West Virginia; born in Barn, Mercer County, W. Va., August 9, 1894; attended the public schools and Beckley (W. Va.) Institute; was graduated from the medical school of the University of Maryland at Baltimore in 1917; served in the United States Army Medical Corps as a first lieutenant 1917–1919; engaged in the practice of medicine in Beckley, W. Va., 1919–1944; medical examiner for the Veterans' Administration 1919–1944; city and county health officer 1927–1932; superintendent of Pinecrest Tuberculosis Sanitarium, Beckley, W. Va., 1943–1944; elected as a Democrat to the Seventy-ninth and to the three succeeding Congresses (January 3, 1945–January 3, 1953); was not a candidate for renomination in 1952 but was unsuccessful for the Democratic gubernatorial nomination; resumed business and professional interests; died in Beckley, W. Va., September 20, 1954; interment in Sunset Memorial Park.

HEFFERNAN, James Joseph, a Representative from New York; born in Brooklyn, Kings County, N. Y., November 8, 1888; attended private and public schools; was graduated from Bryant Stratton College, Brooklyn, N. Y., in 1906 and from Pratt Institute, Brooklyn, N. Y., in 1908; engaged in architectural pursuits in 1908; commissioner of highways, Brooklyn, N. Y., 1926–1933; delegate to the State constitutional convention in 1938; elected as a Democrat to the Seventy-seventh and to the five succeeding Congresses (January 3, 1941–January 3, 1953); was not a candidate for renomination in 1952; architect; is a resident of Brooklyn, N. Y.

HEFLIN, James Thomas (nephew of Robert Stell Heflin), a Representative and a Senator from Alabama; born in Louina, Randolph County, Ala., April 9, 1869; attended the common schools of Randolph County, Southern University, Greensboro, Ala., and the Agricultural and Mechanical College, Auburn, Ala.; was admitted to the bar in 1893 and commenced practice in Lafayette, Ala.; mayor of Lafayette in 1893 and 1894; register in chancery from 1894 to 1896, when he resigned; member of the State house of representatives 1896–1900; member of the Democratic State executive committee 1896–1902; member of the State constitutional convention in 1901; elected secretary of state in 1902 and served until May 1, 1904, when he resigned; delegate to the State Democratic convention at Montgomery, Ala., in 1900 and to the Democratic National Convention at Denver, Colo., in 1908; elected as a Democrat to the Fifty-eighth Congress to fill the vacancy caused by the death of Charles W. Thompson; reelected to the Fifty-ninth and to the seven succeeding Congresses and served from May 10, 1904, until November 1, 1920, when he resigned, having become a candidate for Senator; elected to the United States Senate November 2, 1920, to fill the vacancy caused by the death of John H. Bankhead 1st, in the term ending March 3, 1925; reelected in 1924 and served from November 3, 1920, to March 3, 1931; unsuccessful candidate for reelection in 1930; special assistant to the United States Attorney General in Alabama from August 20, 1936, to September 18, 1937; appointed special representative of the Federal Housing Administration effective July 12, 1935, and served until his resignation March 31, 1936; reappointed on April 20, 1936, and served until June 23, 1936, when he resigned; reappointed July 1, 1939, and served until March 31, 1942, when he retired; died in Lafayette, Ala., April 22, 1951; interment in Lafayette Cemetery.

HEFLIN, Robert Stell (uncle of James Thomas Heflin), a Representative from Alabama; born near Madison, Morgan County, Ga., April 15, 1815; pursued academic studies; served in the Creek War in 1836; clerk of the superior court of Fayette County, Ga., 1836–1840; studied law; was admitted to the bar in 1840 and practiced in Fayetteville, Ga., and Wedowee, Ala.; served in the State senate of Georgia in 1840 and 1841; moved to Randolph County, Ala., in 1844; member of the Alabama House of Representatives in 1849 and 1860; served in the State senate in 1860; judge of probate of Randolph County, Ala., in 1865 and 1866; presidential elector on the Republican ticket of Grant and Colfax in 1868; elected as a Republican to the Forty-first Congress (March 4, 1869–March 3, 1871); died near Wedowee, Randolph County, Ala., January 24, 1901; interment in Masonic Cemetery.

HEIDINGER, James Vandaveer, a Representative from Illinois; born on a farm near Mount Erie, Wayne County, Ill., July 17, 1882; attended the rural schools, Northern Illinois Normal School, De Kalb, Ill., and Valparaiso (Ind.) University; taught in the rural schools of Wayne County, Ill.; was graduated from Northern Illinois College of Law, Dixon, Ill., in 1908; was admitted to the bar the same year and commenced practice in Fairfield, Ill.; county judge of Wayne County, Ill., 1914–1926; assistant attorney general of Illinois 1927–1933; delegate to the Republican National Convention at Kansas City, Mo., in 1928; unsuccessful candidate for election to the Seventy-second and Seventy-fourth Congresses; elected as a Republican to the Seventy-seventh, Seventy-eighth, and Seventy-ninth Congresses and served from January 3, 1941, until his death in Phoenix, Ariz., where he had gone for his health, on March 22, 1945; interment in Maple Hill Cemetery, Fairfield, Ill.

HEILMAN, William (great-grandfather of Charles Marion LaFollette), a Representative from Indiana; born in Albig, Duchy of Hesse-Darmstadt, Germany, October 11, 1824; immigrated to the United States in 1843 and settled on a farm in Vanderburg County, Ind.; moved to Evansville, Ind., and entered the employ of a manufacturing company and subsequently became president of a cotton mill; founded a machine shop for the manufacture of drills in 1847; member of the city council 1852–1865; member of the State house of representatives 1870–1876; delegate to the Republican National Convention at Cincinnati in 1876; served in the State senate from 1876 until March 3, 1879, when he resigned, having been elected to Congress; elected as a Republican to the Forty-sixth and Forty-seventh Congresses (March 4, 1879–March 3, 1883); unsuccessful candidate for reelection in 1882 to the Forty-eighth Congress; resumed his former business activities; died in Evansville, Ind., September 22, 1890; interment in Oak Hill Cemetery.

HEINER, Daniel Brodhead, a Representative from Pennsylvania; born in Kittanning, Armstrong County, Pa., December 30, 1854; attended the public schools at Kittanning, Dayton (Pa.) Academy, and Dickinson Law School at Carlisle, Pa.; was graduated from Allegheny College, Meadville, Pa., in 1879; was admitted to the bar of Armstrong County, Pa., in 1882 and commenced practice in Kittanning; also engaged in banking; elected district attorney of Armstrong County, Pa., in 1885, reelected in 1888, and served until January 1, 1892; chairman of the Republican county executive committee 1884–1888; elected as a Republican to the Fifty-third and Fifty-fourth Congresses (March 4, 1893–March 3, 1897); was not a candidate for renomination in 1896; appointed by President McKinley as United States district attorney for the western district of Pennsylvania and served from 1897 to 1902; appointed on February 2, 1902, as internal-revenue collector for the twenty-third district of Pennsylvania by President Theodore Roosevelt and served until November 1, 1913; delegate to the Republican National Convention at Chicago in 1920; again served as internal-revenue collector 1921–1933; retired from active business pursuits and political life; died at Kittanning, Pa., on February 14, 1944; interment in Kittanning Cemetery.

HEINKE, George Henry, a Representative from Nebraska; born on a farm near Dunbar, Otoe County, Nebr., July 22, 1882; moved with his parents to Douglas, Nebr., in 1889, to San Angelo, Tex., in 1891, and to Talmage, Nebr., in 1894; attended the public schools; was graduated from the law department of the University of Nebraska at Lincoln in 1908; was admitted to the bar the same year and commenced practice in Nebraska City, Nebr.; prosecuting attorney of Otoe County, Nebr., 1919–1923 and 1927–1935; elected as a Republican to the Seventy-sixth Congress and served from January 3, 1939, until his death in a hospital at Morrilton, Ark., January 2, 1940, as a result of injuries received in an automobile accident near there while en route to Washington, D. C., to attend the opening session of Congress; interment in Wyuka Cemetery, Nebraska City, Nebr.

HEINTZ, Victor, a Representative from Ohio; born on a farm near Grayville, White County, Ill., November 20, 1876; attended the public schools; was graduated from the University of Cincinnati in 1896 and from its law department in 1899; was admitted to the bar in 1898 and commenced practice in Cincinnati, Ohio; served six years in the Cavalry and Infantry of the Ohio National Guard; elected as a Republican to the Sixty-fifth Congress (March 4, 1917–March 3, 1919); was not a candidate for renomination in 1918; during the First World War absented himself from the House and was commissioned a captain in the One Hundred and Forty-seventh Regiment, United States Infantry, on August 4, 1917; went overseas June 22, 1918, and served until the end of the war; was wounded and decorated with the Distinguished Service Cross with Oak Leaf Cluster,

Silver Star Medal, Purple Heart, and the Croix de Guerre; founded the Cincinnatus Association of Cincinnati, Ohio; resumed the practice of law until his retirement in 1950; is a resident of Cincinnati, Ohio.

HEISKELL, John Netherland, a Senator from Arkansas; born in Rogersville, Hawkins County, Tenn., on November 2, 1872; attended the public and private schools of Memphis; was graduated from the University of Tennessee at Knoxville in 1893; after leaving college engaged in newspaper work; became editor of the Arkansas Gazette and president of the Gazette Publishing Co. in 1902 at Little Rock, Ark.; appointed as a Democrat to the United States Senate to fill the vacancy caused by the death of Jeff Davis and served from January 6 to January 29, 1913, when a successor was elected; was not a candidate for election in 1913; president of board of trustees of Little Rock Public Library; resumed his former newspaper pursuits and resides in Little Rock, Ark.

HEITFELD, Henry, a Senator from Idaho; born in St. Louis, Mo., January 12, 1859; attended public and private schools; moved with his parents to Seneca, Kans., in 1870, to Pomeroy, Wash., in 1882, and to Lewiston, Idaho, in 1883; engaged in agricultural pursuits and stock raising; member of the State senate 1894–1897; delegate to several State conventions between the years 1894 and 1906; elected as a Populist to the United States Senate January 28, 1897, and served from March 4, 1897, to March 3, 1903; was not a candidate for reelection in 1902; unsuccessful candidate for Governor of Idaho in 1904; mayor of Lewiston 1905–1909; register of the United States land office at Lewiston 1914–1922; engaged in fruit growing in Lewiston, Idaho; member of the board of county commissioners 1930–1936, serving two terms as chairman; retired in 1938 and resided in Spokane, Wash., until his death in that city on October 21, 1938; interment in Norman Hill Cemetery, Lewiston, Idaho.

HELGESEN, Henry Thomas, a Representative from North Dakota; born near Decorah, Iowa, June 26, 1857; attended the public schools, and the John Breckenridge Normal Institute and the J. R. Slack Business College at Decorah; moved to Milton, Dakota Territory (now North Dakota), in 1887; engaged in the mercantile and lumber business and also in agricultural pursuits; State commissioner of agriculture and labor 1889–1892; member of the board of education of Milton, N. Dak., 1893–1896, and served as president in 1893 and 1894; member of the board of regents of the University of North Dakota 1897–1901 and 1907–1913; unsuccessful candidate for election to the Sixty-first Congress in 1910; elected as a Republican to the Sixty-second and to the three succeeding Congresses and served from March 4, 1911, until his death in Washington, D. C., April 10, 1917; interment in Phelps Cemetery, Decorah, Iowa.

HELLER, Louis Benjamin, a Representative from New York; born in Manhattan, New York City, N. Y., February 10, 1905; attended the public schools; was graduated from Fordham University School of Law in New York City in 1926; was admitted to the bar in 1927 and commenced the practice of law in Brooklyn, N. Y.; served as special deputy assistant attorney general in election fraud cases in New York 1936–1946; appeal agent, United States Selective Service, in New York in 1941 and 1942; member of the State senate in 1943 and 1944; appointed by Gov. Thomas E. Dewey as secretary of the New York State Temporary Commission Against Discrimination in 1944 and 1945; Democratic State committeeman and executive member (leader) of the sixth assembly district of Kings County, N. Y., 1944–1954; elected as a Democrat to the Eighty-first Congress to fill the vacancy caused by the death of John J. Delaney; reelected to the Eighty-second

and Eighty-third Congresses and served from February 15, 1949, until his resignation July 21, 1954; appointed a judge of the Court of Special Sessions of New York City and served from July 22, 1954, to December 1958, when elected a justice of the city court of the city of New York for a ten-year term ending in 1969; is a resident of Brooklyn, N. Y.

HELM, Harvey, a Representative from Kentucky; born in Danville, Boyle County, Ky., December 2, 1865; attended the Stanford Male Academy, and was graduated from the Central University of Kentucky in 1887; studied law; was admitted to the bar in 1890 and began practice in Stanford, Ky.; member of the State house of representatives in 1894; county attorney of Lincoln County 1897–1905; delegate to the Democratic National Convention at Kansas City in 1900; elected as a Democrat to the Sixtieth and to the six succeeding Congresses and served from March 4, 1907, until his death before the commencement of the Sixty-sixth Congress; died in Columbus, Miss., March 3, 1919; interment in Buffalo Spring Cemetery, Stanford, Ky.

HELMICK, William, a Representative from Ohio; born near Canton, Stark County, Ohio, September 6, 1817; attended the public schools; studied law; was admitted to the bar in 1845 and commenced practice in New Philadelphia, Tuscarawas County, Ohio; prosecuting attorney of Tuscarawas County in 1851; elected as a Republican to the Thirty-sixth Congress (March 4, 1859–March 3, 1861); unsuccessful candidate for reelection in 1860 to the Thirty-seventh Congress; appointed by President Lincoln chief clerk of the Pension Office on May 3, 1861, and served until January 31, 1865; resumed the practice of law in Washington, D. C.; appointed justice of the peace by President Hayes in 1877; died in Washington, D. C., March 31, 1888; interment in the Congressional Cemetery.

HELMS, William, a Representative from New Jersey; born in Sussex County, N. J.; served during the Revolutionary War as second lieutenant, first lieutenant, and captain, and was brevetted major on September 30, 1783; member of the State house of assembly in 1791 and 1792; elected as a Democrat to the Seventh and to the four succeeding Congresses (March 4, 1801–March 3, 1811); moved to Hamilton County, Ohio; died in 1813.

HELVERING, Guy Tresillian, a Representative from Kansas; born in Felicity, Clermont County, Ohio, January 10, 1878; moved to Kansas in 1887 with his parents, who settled in Beattie, Marshall County; attended the public schools; during the Spanish-American War enlisted as a corporal in Company M, Twenty-second Regiment, Kansas Infantry, and served from May 12 to November 3, 1898, when he was honorably discharged; attended the University of Kansas at Lawrence; was graduated from the law department of the University of Michigan at Ann Arbor in 1906; was admitted to the bar in the same year and commenced practice in Marysville, Kans.; prosecuting attorney of Marshall County 1907–1911; unsuccessful Democratic candidate for election in 1910 to the Sixty-second Congress; elected as a Democrat to the Sixty-third, Sixty-fourth, and Sixty-fifth Congresses (March 4, 1913–March 3, 1919); unsuccessful candidate for reelection in 1918 to the Sixty-sixth Congress; moved to Salina, Saline County, Kans., and became engaged in banking; Democratic State chairman 1930–1934; mayor of Salina, Kans., from February 15, 1926, until his resignation on December 8, 1930, to become State highway director; State highway director in 1931 and 1932; appointed Commissioner of Internal Revenue by President Franklin D. Roosevelt in 1933 and served until his appointment as a Federal district judge for Kansas in 1943, in which capacity he was serving at the time of his death in Washington, D. C., on July 4, 1946; interment in Marysville Cemetery, Marysville, Kans.

HEMENWAY, James Alexander, a Representative and a Senator from Indiana; born in Boonville, Warrick County, Ind., March 8, 1860; attended the common schools; studied law; was admitted to the bar and commenced practice in Boonville in 1885; prosecuting attorney for the second judicial circuit of Indiana 1886–1890; member of the Republican State committee in 1890; elected as a Republican to the Fifty-fourth and to the five succeeding Congresses and served from March 4, 1895, until his resignation, effective March 3, 1905, at the close of the Fifty-eighth Congress, having been elected Senator; elected to the United States Senate to fill the vacancy caused by the resignation of Charles W. Fairbanks and served from March 4, 1905, to March 3, 1909; was the candidate of his party, which was in the minority, for reelection; resumed the practice of his profession in Boonville, Ind.; died, while on a visit for the benefit of his health, in Miami, Dade County, Fla., February 10, 1923; interment in Maple Grove Cemetery, Boonville, Warrick County, Ind.

HEMPHILL, John (uncle of John James Hemphill and great-great-uncle of Robert Witherspoon Hemphill), a Senator from Texas; born in Chester District, S. C., December 18, 1803; was graduated from Jefferson College in 1825; studied law; was admitted to the bar in 1829 and commenced practice in Sumter, S. C.; edited a nullification paper in 1832 and 1833; second lieutenant in the war with the Seminole Indians in 1836; moved to Texas in 1838; elected judge of the fourth judicial district of Texas in 1840 and served until 1842, when he resigned; adjutant general in the Mier expedition in 1842; chief justice of the supreme court of Texas 1846–1858; elected as a State Rights Democrat to the United States Senate and served from March 4, 1859, until expelled by resolution of July 11, 1861; he was one of the fourteen Senators who met on January 6, 1861, and recommended immediate secession of their States; deputy in the Provisional Congress of the Confederacy in Montgomery, Ala., in 1861; died in Richmond, Va., January 7, 1862; interment in State Cemetery, Austin, Tex.

HEMPHILL, John James (cousin of William Huggins Brawley, nephew of John Hemphill and great-uncle of Robert Witherspoon Hemphill), a Representative from South Carolina; born in Chester, Chester County, S. C., August 25, 1849; attended the public schools and was graduated from the University of South Carolina at Columbia in 1869; studied law; was admitted to the bar in 1870 and practiced in Chester, S. C.; unsuccessful candidate for the State legislature in 1874; member of the State house of representatives 1876–1882; elected as a Democrat to the Forty-eighth and to the four succeeding Congresses (March 4, 1883–March 3, 1893); unsuccessful candidate for reelection in 1892 to the Fifty-third Congress; resumed the practice of law in Washington, D. C., while retaining his residence in South Carolina; unsuccessful candidate for election as United States Senator from South Carolina in 1902; died in Washington, D. C., May 11, 1912; interment in Oak Hill Cemetery.

HEMPHILL, Joseph, a Representative from Pennsylvania; born in Thornburg Township, Chester County, Pa., January 7, 1770; completed a preparatory course; was graduated from the University of Pennsylvania at Philadelphia in 1791; studied law; was admitted to the bar in 1793 and commenced practice in West Chester, Pa.; member of the State house of representatives 1797–1800; elected as a Federalist to the Seventh Congress (March 4, 1801–March 3, 1803); moved to Philadelphia in 1803; again a member of the State house of representatives in 1805; appointed

the first president judge of the district court of the city and county of Philadelphia; elected to the Sixteenth and to the three succeeding Congresses and served from March 4, 1819, until his resignation in 1826; elected as a Jackson Democrat to the Twenty-first Congress (March 4, 1829–March 3, 1831); member of the State house of representatives in 1831 and 1832; died in Philadelphia, Pa., May 29, 1842; interment in Laurel Hill Cemetery.

HEMPHILL, Robert Witherspoon (great-great-nephew of John Hemphill, great-nephew of John J. Hemphill, great-nephew of William Huggins Brawley, and great-great-grandson of Robert Witherspoon), a Representative from South Carolina; born in Chester, S. C., May 10, 1915; attended the public schools; graduated from the University of South Carolina in 1936 and from the law school of the same university in 1938; was admitted to the bar in 1938 and commenced the practice of law in Chester; volunteered in 1941 as a flying cadet in the United States Air Force and after graduation from cadet school served as a bomber pilot until December 1945; chairman of Chester County Democratic Conventions in 1946 and 1947; member of State house of representatives 1946–1948; solicitor of the Sixth South Carolina Judicial Circuit 1951–1956; delegate to the North Atlantic Treaty Organization Congress in London in 1959; elected as a Democrat to the Eighty-fifth and Eighty-sixth Congresses (January 3, 1957–January 3, 1961). *Reelected to the Eighty-seventh Congress.*

HEMPSTEAD, Edward, a Delegate from the Territory of Missouri; born in New London, Conn., June 3, 1780; pursued academic studies; studied law; was admitted to the bar in 1801 and commenced practice in Rhode Island; moved to St. Louis, Mo. (then District of Louisiana), in 1805; attorney general of the Territory of Upper Louisiana 1809–1811; served in several expeditions against the Indians north of the Missouri River; member of the third Territorial general assembly in 1812 and served as speaker; elected as a Delegate to the Thirteenth Congress on November 9, 1812, and served until September 17, 1814; declined to be a candidate for renomination; was thrown from a horse August 4, 1817, which resulted in his death August 10, 1817, at St. Louis, Mo.; interment on Hempstead Farm, now a part of Bellefontaine Cemetery.

HEMSLEY, William, a Delegate from Maryland; born at "Clover Fields Farm," near Queenstown, Queen Annes County, Md., in 1737; engaged in planting; provincial treasurer of Eastern Shore, Md., in 1773; surveyor of Talbot County, Md.; colonel of the Twentieth Battalion, Queen Annes County Militia, in 1777; justice of the peace of Queen Annes County in 1777; member of the State senate 1779–1781; Member of the Continental Congress 1782–1784; again served in the State senate in 1786, 1790, and 1800; resumed agricultural pursuits; died in Queen Annes County, June 5, 1812; interment in Clover Fields Farm Cemetery, Queen Annes County, Md.

HENDEE, George Whitman, a Representative from Vermont; born in Stowe, Lamoille County, Vt., November 30, 1832; attended the common schools of Morrisville, Vt., and People's Academy; studied law; was admitted to the bar in 1855 and commenced practice in Morrisville, Vt.; prosecuting attorney of Lamoille County in 1858 and 1859; member of the State house of representatives in 1861 and 1862; during the Civil War served as deputy provost marshal; served in the State senate 1866–1868; Lieutenant Governor of Vermont in 1869 and acted as Governor after the death of Governor Washburn; elected as a Republican to the Forty-third, Forty-fourth, and Forty-fifth Congresses (March 4, 1873–March 3, 1879); unsuccessful candidate for renomination in 1878; resumed the practice of law; national-bank examiner 1879–1885; interested in the breeding of Morgan horses; died in Morrisville, Vt., on December 6, 1906; interment in Pleasant View Cemetery.

HENDERSON, Archibald, a Representative from North Carolina; born near Williamsborough, Granville County, N. C., August 7, 1768; attended the common schools and was graduated from Springer College; moved to Salisbury, N. C., about 1790; studied law; was admitted to the bar and commenced practice in Salisbury; clerk and master in equity 1795–1798; elected as a Federalist to the Sixth and Seventh Congresses (March 4, 1799–March 3, 1803); member of the State house of commons 1807–1809, 1814, 1819, and 1820; resumed the practice of law in Salisbury, N. C., and died there October 21, 1822; interment in the City Cemetery.

HENDERSON, Bennett H., a Representative from Tennessee; born in Bedford, Bedford County, Va., September 5, 1784; moved to Tennessee; elected to the Fourteenth Congress (March 4, 1815–March 3, 1817); died in Summitville, Tenn.

HENDERSON, Charles Belknap, a Senator from Nevada; born in San Jose, Calif., June 8, 1873; moved with his parents to Nevada in 1876; attended the public schools in Elko, Nev., the University of the Pacific, and Leland Stanford Junior University in California; graduated in law from the University of Michigan in 1895; was admitted to the bar in 1896 and commenced practice in Elko, Nev.; district attorney of Elko County 1901–1905; member of the State house of representatives 1905–1907; regent of the University of Nevada 1907–1917; served as lieutenant in Torrey's Rough Riders during the Spanish-American War; appointed and subsequently elected as a Democrat to the United States Senate to fill the vacancy caused by the death of Francis G. Newlands and served from January 12, 1918, to March 3, 1921; unsuccessful for reelection in 1920; appointed a member of the board of directors of the Reconstruction Finance Corporation in 1934; elected chairman in 1941 and served until April 1947; resigned July 15, 1947; retired from political activities; president and director of the Elko Telephone & Telegraph Co. and a director of the Western Pacific Railroad; died in San Francisco, Calif., November 8, 1954; interment in Elko Cemetery, Elko, Nev.

HENDERSON, David Bremner, a Representative from Iowa; born in Old Deer, Scotland, March 14, 1840; immigrated to the United States with his parents, who settled in Winnebago County, Ill., in 1846; moved to Fayette County, Iowa, in 1849; attended the common schools and the Upper Iowa University at Fayette; during the Civil War enlisted in the Union Army September 15, 1861, as a private in Company C, Twelfth Regiment, Iowa Volunteer Infantry; was elected and commissioned first lieutenant of that company and served with it until discharged, owing to the loss of a leg, February 26, 1863; commissioner of the board of enrollment of the third district of Iowa from May 1863 to June 1864; entered the Army as colonel of the Forty-sixth Regiment, Iowa Volunteer Infantry, and served until the close of the war; studied law; was admitted to the bar in 1865 and commenced practice in Dubuque, Iowa; collector of internal revenue for the third district of Iowa from November 1865 to June 1869 when he resigned; assistant United States district attorney for the northern district of Iowa 1869–1871; elected as a Republican to the Forty-eighth and to the nine succeeding Congresses (March 4, 1883–March 3, 1903); declined to be a candidate for renomination in 1902; Speaker of the House in the Fifty-sixth and Fifty-seventh Congresses; died in Dubuque, Iowa, February 25, 1906; interment in Linwood Cemetery.

HENDERSON, James Henry Dickey, a Representative from Oregon; born near Salem, Ky., July 23, 1810; moved to Missouri Territory in 1817; attended the public schools; learned the art of printing; entered the ministry and was pastor of a church in Washington County, Pa., 1843–1851; returned to Missouri and published a literary magazine; moved to Oregon in 1852 and settled in Yamhill County; by land claim acquired a homestead, and lived on it four years; moved to Eugene, Lane County, and engaged in agricultural pursuits, specializing in the raising of fruits; superintendent of the public schools of Lane County in 1859; elected as a Union Republican to the Thirty-ninth Congress (March 4, 1865–March 3, 1867); unsuccessful candidate for renomination in 1866; returned to Eugene, Oreg., and engaged in agricultural pursuits; also preached, lectured, and wrote for periodicals; died in Eugene, Oreg., December 13, 1885; interment in Odd Fellows Cemetery.

HENDERSON, James Pinckney, a Senator from Texas; born in Lincolnton, Lincoln County, N. C., March 31, 1808; pursued academic studies in Lincolnton; was graduated from the University of North Carolina at Chapel Hill; served as aide-de-camp to Major General Dorrett of the Carolina Militia in 1830 and subsequently was elected colonel; studied law; was admitted to the bar in 1828 and commenced practice in Lincolnton, N. C.; moved to Mississippi in 1835 and recruited a company for service in behalf of the Republic of Texas; preceded his company to Austin, Tex., in 1836; was commissioned brigadier general and returned to the United States to recruit volunteers; raised a company at his own expense; appointed by President Houston as Attorney General of the Republic of Texas in 1836, and as Secretary of State in 1837; visited Europe as the diplomatic representative of the Republic of Texas in 1838, and in 1844 visited the United States as special minister to negotiate annexation; member of the State constitutional convention in 1845; elected as the first Governor of the State of Texas in 1846; commissioned major general in the United States Army and served in the Mexican War; received from Congress a vote of thanks and a sword for bravery in action; completed his term of office as Governor; declined to be a candidate for reelection; appointed as a State Rights Democrat to the United States Senate to fill the vacancy caused by the death of Thomas J. Rusk and served from November 9, 1857, until his death in Washington, D. C., June 4, 1858; interment in Congressional Cemetery; reinterred in 1930 in the State Cemetery, Austin, Tex.

HENDERSON, John, a Senator from Mississippi; born in a northern State in 1795; pursued an academic course; studied law; was admitted to the bar and commenced practice in Woodville, Wilkinson County, Miss., in 1820; brigadier general of State militia; moved to Pass Christian, Harrison County; member of the State house of representatives in 1835; elected as a Whig to the United States Senate and served from March 4, 1839, to March 3, 1845; resumed the practice of his profession in New Orleans, La.; in 1851 was tried in the United States district court in New Orleans for violation of the neutrality laws of 1818 for complicity with the Lopez expedition against Cuba, was acquitted, and retired from public life; died in Pass Christian, Miss., September 13, 1866; interment in Live Oak Cemetery.

HENDERSON, John Brooks, a Senator from Missouri; born near Danville, Pittsylvania County, Va., November 16, 1826; moved with his parents to Lincoln County, Mo., in 1832; pursued academic studies; studied law; was admitted to the bar in 1848 and practiced; member of the State house of representatives 1848–1856; presidential elector on the Democratic ticket of Buchanan and Breckinridge in 1856 and of Douglas and Johnson in 1860; delegate to the Democratic National

Convention at Charleston in 1860; member of the State convention in 1861; commissioned a brigadier general in the State militia in 1861; appointed and subsequently elected to the United States Senate to fill the vacancy caused by the expulsion of Trusten Polk; reelected in 1863 and served from January 17, 1862, to March 3, 1869; special United States attorney for prosecution of a whisky ring at St. Louis in 1865; appointed a commissioner to treat with hostile tribes of Indians in 1867; moved to Washington, D. C., in 1891, and resided there until his death, April 12, 1913; interment in Greenwood Cemetery, Brooklyn, N. Y.

HENDERSON, John Earl, a Representative from Ohio; born in Crafton, Allegheny County, Pa., January 4, 1917; moved to Cambridge, Ohio, in 1920 and to a dairy farm in Guernsey County, near Cambridge, Ohio, in 1922; attended the county schools of Guernsey County and high school at Cambridge; was graduated from Ohio Wesleyan University at Delaware in 1939, and from the University of Michigan Law School at Ann Arbor in 1942; was admitted to the Ohio bar in 1942; entered the United States Army as a private in 1942 and advanced to the rank of captain of Infantry after combat service in Europe; following hostilities was assigned to the historical division of the European Theater and was discharged in 1946; commenced the practice of law in Cambridge, Ohio, in 1946; member of the State house of representatives 1951–1954; elected as a Republican to the Eighty-fourth, Eighty-fifth, and Eighty-sixth Congresses (January 3, 1955–January 3, 1961); was not a candidate for renomination in 1960 to the Eighty-seventh Congress; is a resident of Cambridge, Ohio.

HENDERSON, John Steele, a Representative from North Carolina; born near Salisbury, Rowan County, N. C., January 6, 1846; attended a private school in Melville, N. C.; entered the University of North Carolina at Chapel Hill in January 1862, and left in November 1864 to enter the Confederate Army as a private in Company B, Tenth Regiment, North Carolina State Troops; served throughout the Civil War; was graduated from the University of North Carolina in 1865 without reentering; studied law; obtained a county court license in June 1866 and a superior court license in June 1867; appointed in June 1866 register of deeds for Rowan County and served until September 1868, when he resigned; delegate to the State constitutional convention in 1875; member of the State house of representatives in 1876; served in the State senate in 1878; elected by the general assembly in 1881 one of the three commissioners to codify the statute laws of the State; elected presiding justice of the inferior court of Rowan County in June 1884; elected as a Democrat to the Forty-ninth and to the four succeeding Congresses (March 4, 1885–March 3, 1895); resumed the practice of law in Salisbury, N. C.; elected to the State senate in 1900 and 1902; member of the board of aldermen in 1900; died in Salisbury, N. C., on October 9, 1916; interment in Chestnut Hill Cemetery.

HENDERSON, Joseph, a Representative from Pennsylvania; born in Shippensburg, Cumberland County, Pa., August 2, 1791; moved with his parents to Center County, Pa., in 1802; attended the public schools and was graduated from the Jefferson Medical College at Philadelphia in 1813; during the War of 1812 was commissioned first lieutenant in the Twenty-second Regiment, Pennsylvania Volunteers, in the spring of 1813; promoted to captain in the fall of the same year; brevetted major and given command of a regiment in 1814; participated in the Battles of Chippewa and Lundys Lane and in the siege of Fort Erie; settled at Browns Mills, Pa., at the close of the war and engaged in the practice of medicine; elected to the Twenty-third

and Twenty-fourth Congresses (March 4, 1833–March 3, 1837); was not a candidate for renomination in 1836; moved to Lewistown, Pa., in 1850 and continued the practice of medicine; died in Lewistown, Pa., December 25, 1863; interment in St. Mark's Cemetery.

HENDERSON, Samuel, a Representative from Pennsylvania; born in England November 27, 1764; attended school in England; immigrated to the United States in 1782 and settled in Montgomery, Pa.; owned and operated the Henderson Marble Quarries in Montgomery County, Pa.; elected as a Republican to the Thirteenth Congress to fill the vacancy caused by the resignation of Jonathan Roberts and served from October 11, 1814, to March 3, 1815; retired from public life and resumed former business pursuits; died on his estate at Upper Merion, Montgomery County, Pa., November 17, 1841; interment in the family burying ground, Montgomery County, Pa.

HENDERSON, Thomas, a Representative from New Jersey; born in Freehold, Monmouth County, N. J., August 15, 1743; attended the public schools, and was graduated from Princeton College in 1761; studied medicine; practiced first in Freneau and afterwards in Freehold, N. J., about 1765; member of the committee of safety in 1774; served as a lieutenant in the New Jersey Militia in 1775; appointed second major in Col. Charles Stewart's Battalion of Minutemen February 15, 1776; brigade major, Monmouth County Militia, April 19, 1776; major of Col. Nathaniel Heard's battalion June 14, 1776, and later lieutenant colonel and brigadier major at Monmouth; surrogate of Monmouth County in 1776; member of the provincial council in 1777; elected as a Delegate to the Continental Congress, November 17, 1779, but declined December 25, 1779; served in the State general assembly 1780–1784; master in chancery in 1790; member of the State council in 1793 and 1794, serving as vice president of that body; Acting Governor of New Jersey in 1794; elected to the Fourth Congress (March 4, 1795–March 3, 1797); judge of the court of common pleas 1783–1799; one of the commissioners appointed to settle the boundary line between New Jersey and Pennsylvania; again a member of the State council in 1812 and 1813; died in Freehold, N. J., December 15, 1824; interment in Old Tennent Cemetery, Tennent, N. J.

HENDERSON, Thomas Jefferson, a Representative from Illinois; born in Brownsville, Haywood County, Tenn., November 29, 1824; moved with his parents to Illinois at the age of eleven; pursued academic studies; clerk of the Board of Commissioners of Stark County, Ill., 1847–1849; clerk of the court of Stark County 1849–1853; studied law; was admitted to the bar in 1852 and commenced practice in Toulon, Ill.; member of the State house of representatives in 1855 and 1856; served in the State senate 1857–1860; during the Civil War entered the Union Army in 1862 as colonel of the One Hundred and Twelfth Regiment, Illinois Volunteer Infantry; commanded Third Brigade, Third Division, Twenty-third Army Corps, from August 12, 1864, to the close of the war; was brevetted brigadier general in January 1865 for gallant service; resumed the practice of law; moved to Princeton, Ill., in 1867 and continued the practice of law; presidential elector on the Republican ticket of Grant and Colfax in 1868; appointed collector of internal revenue for the fifth district of Illinois in 1871; elected as a Republican to the Forty-fourth and to the nine succeeding Congresses (March 4, 1875–March 3, 1895); unsuccessful candidate for renomination in 1894; appointed member of the board of managers for the National Home for Disabled Volunteer Soldiers in 1896; appointed civilian member on the Board of Ordnance and Fortifications in 1900 and served until his death in Washington, D. C., February 6, 1911; interment in Oakland Cemetery, Princeton, Ill.

HENDRICK, John Kerr, a Representative from Kentucky; born in Caswell County, N. C., October 10, 1849; moved with his parents to Logan County and later to Todd County, Ky.; attended private schools and Bethel College, Russellville, Ky.; moved to Crittenden County, Ky., in 1869 and engaged in teaching school; studied law; was admitted to the bar in 1874 and commenced practice in Smithland, Ky.; prosecuting attorney of Livingston County 1878–1886; member of the State senate 1887–1891; delegate to the Democratic National Convention at St. Louis in 1888; elected as a Democrat to the Fifty-fourth Congress (March 4, 1895–March 3, 1897); unsuccessful candidate for renomination in 1896; resumed the practice of law in Paducah, Ky., where he died June 20, 1921; interment in Maplelawn Cemetery.

HENDRICKS, Joseph Edward, a Representative from Florida; born at Lake Butler, Union County, Fla., September 24, 1903; attended the rural schools and Montverde (Fla.) School; was graduated from John B. Stetson University, De Land, Fla., in 1930 and from its law department in 1934; was admitted to the bar in 1934 and commenced practice in De Land, Fla.; attorney for the legal tax survey of the State in 1934; elected as a Democrat to the Seventy-fifth and to the five succeeding Congresses (January 3, 1937–January 3, 1949); was not a candidate for renomination in 1948; lawyer; president of Hendricks Homes, Inc.; resides in Plant City, Fla.

HENDRICKS, Thomas Andrews (nephew of William Hendricks), a Representative and a Senator from Indiana and a Vice President of the United States; born near Zanesville, Ohio, September 7, 1819; moved with his parents to Madison, Ind., and thence, in 1832, to Shelby County; pursued classical studies, and was graduated from Hanover (Ind.) College in 1841; studied law in Chambersburg, Pa.; was admitted to the bar in 1843 and commenced practice in Shelbyville, Ind.; member of the State house of representatives in 1848; served in the State senate in 1849; member of the State constitutional convention in 1851; elected as a Democrat to the Thirty-second and Thirty-third Congresses (March 4, 1851–March 3, 1855); unsuccessful candidate for reelection in 1854 to the Thirty-fourth Congress; Commissioner of the General Land Office 1855–1859; unsuccessful Democratic candidate for Governor of Indiana in 1860; moved to Indianapolis in 1860 and practiced law; elected to the United States Senate and served from March 4, 1863, to March 3, 1869; Governor of Indiana in 1872; unsuccessful candidate for Vice President of the United States on the Democratic ticket with Tilden in 1876; elected Vice President of the United States in 1884 and served from March 4, 1885, until his death in Indianapolis, Ind., November 25, 1885; interment in Crown Hill Cemetery.

HENDRICKS, William (uncle of Thomas Andrew Hendricks), a Representative and a Senator from Indiana; born in Ligonier Valley, Westmoreland County, Pa., November 12, 1782; attended the common schools, and was graduated from the Washington and Jefferson College, Washington, Pa., in 1810; taught school 1810–1812; studied law in Cincinnati, Ohio; was admitted to the bar and practiced; moved to Madison, Indiana Territory, in 1812; became a printer; owner of the second printing press set up in the Territory; proprietor of the Western Eagle; secretary of the general assembly at Vincennes in 1814 and 1815; secretary of the first State constitutional convention in 1816; upon the admission of Indiana as a State into the Union was elected as a Democrat to the Fourteenth Congress; reelected to the Fifteenth, Sixteenth, and Seventeenth Congresses and served from December 11, 1816, until his resignation July 25, 1822; Governor of Indiana from December 5, 1822, to February 12, 1825, when he resigned; elected to the United States Senate in 1824; reelected in 1830 and served from March 4, 1825, to March 3, 1837; unsuccessful

candidate for reelection in 1836; resumed the practice of law in Madison, Ind.; trustee of Indiana University at Bloomington 1829–1840; died in Madison, Ind., May 16, 1850; interment in Fairmount Cemetery.

HENDRICKSON, Robert Clymer, a Senator from New Jersey; born in Woodbury, Gloucester County, N. J., August 12, 1898; attended elementary and high schools; during the First World War enlisted in the United States Army in April 1918 and served overseas in the Aisne-Marne, St. Mihiel, Champagne, and Meuse-Argonne offensives; awarded Medal of Verdun, Unit Citations, and Letters of Commendation; graduated from Temple University Law School, Philadelphia, Pa., in 1922; was admitted to the New Jersey bar in 1922 and commenced the practice of law in Woodbury, N. J.; county supervisor, inheritance tax, 1929–1934; solicitor, city of Woodbury, since 1931; elected in 1934 to fill an unexpired term as State senator from Gloucester County; reelected in 1938 and again in 1941, serving as president of the senate in 1939; Republican nominee for Governor in 1940; elected State treasurer in 1942 and reelected in 1946; member of board of managers, Council of State Governments, in 1940 and chairman in 1941; vice chairman of Commission on Delaware River Basin 1936–1951; during World War II enlisted on May 31, 1943; commissioned a major and reported for active duty on July 24, 1943, with the American Military Government in the Mediterranean Theater of Operations in North Africa, Italy, and Upper Austria; entered Rome with the Fifth Army as senior legal officer; promoted to lieutenant colonel in 1944 and separated from the service on February 10, 1946; awarded World War II Medal, European-African-Middle Eastern Theater Service Medal with four bronze stars, Army Commendation Ribbon, and Military Government Medal (Fifth Army); elected as a Republican to the United States Senate in 1948 for the term commencing January 3, 1949, and ending January 3, 1955; was not a candidate for renomination in 1954; delegate to the Republican National Convention in 1952; appointed Ambassador to New Zealand by President Eisenhower and served in 1955 and 1956; lawyer; is a resident of Woodbury, N. J.

HENDRIX, Joseph Clifford, a Representative from New York; born in Fayette, Howard County, Mo., May 25, 1853; attended private schools and Central College at Fayette and Cornell University, Ithaca, N. Y., 1870–1873; moved to New York City in 1873, and until 1883 was a reporter, night city editor, and writer on the New York Sun; moved to Brooklyn, N. Y., in 1873; appointed a member of the Board of Education of Brooklyn in 1882; unsuccessful Democratic candidate for mayor of Brooklyn in 1883; appointed trustee of the New York and Brooklyn Bridge in 1884; elected secretary of the board of bridge trustees in 1885; appointed postmaster of Brooklyn by President Cleveland in 1886 and served until July 1, 1890; elected president of the board of education of Brooklyn in 1887; appointed rapid transit commissioner in 1889 but declined the office; president of the Kings County Trust Co. 1889–1893; president of the National Union Bank of New York City 1893–1900; elected as a Democrat to the Fifty-third Congress (March 4, 1893–March 3, 1895); was not a candidate for renomination in 1894; president of the National Bank of Commerce in 1900; trustee of the Brooklyn Institute of Arts and Sciences; trustee of Cornell University; died in Brooklyn, N. Y., November 9, 1904; interment in Greenwood Cemetery.

HENKLE, Eli Jones, a Representative from Maryland; born in Westminster, Carroll County, Md., November 24, 1828; completed an academic course; taught school in Anne Arundel County; studied medicine, and was graduated from the University of Maryland at Baltimore in 1850; practiced his profession in

Brooklyn, Md.; trustee, and also professor of anatomy, physiology, and hygiene, Maryland Agricultural College at College Park; member of the State house of delegates in 1863; member of the State constitutional convention in 1864; served in the State senate in 1867, 1868, and 1870; again a member of the State house of delegates 1872–1875; delegate to the Democratic National Convention at Baltimore in 1872; elected as a Democrat to the Forty-fourth, Forty-fifth, and Forty-sixth Congresses (March 4, 1875–March 3, 1881); unsuccessful candidate for reelection in 1880 to the Forty-seventh Congress; superintendent of vaccination in Baltimore in 1883; moved to Chicago, Ill., in 1889, and later returned to Baltimore, Md., where he died November 1, 1893; interment in Druid Ridge Cemetery, Baltimore, Md.

HENLEY, Barclay (son of Thomas Jefferson Henley), a Representative from California; born in Charlestown, Clark County, Ind., March 17, 1843; moved with his parents to San Francisco, Calif., in 1853; returned to Indiana in 1858; attended the common schools and Hanover (Ind.) College; returned to San Francisco in 1861; studied law; was admitted to the bar in 1864 and commenced practice in Santa Rosa, Calif.; member of the State assembly in 1869 and 1870; district attorney of Sonoma County in 1875 and 1876; presidential elector on the Democratic ticket of Tilden and Hendricks in 1876 and Hancock and English in 1880; elected as a Democrat to the Forty-eighth and Forty-ninth Congresses (March 4, 1883–March 3, 1887); again settled in San Francisco and continued the practice of law until his death in that city on February 15, 1914; remains were cremated at Cypress Lawn Crematory, San Mateo County, Calif., and the ashes interred in the Santa Rosa Cemetery, Santa Rosa, Calif.

HENLEY, Thomas Jefferson (father of Barclay Henley), a Representative from Indiana; born in Richmond, Ind., April 2, 1810; attended Indiana University at Bloomington; studied law; was admitted to the bar in 1828 and commenced practice in Richmond, Ind.; engaged in banking; member of the State house of representatives 1832–1842 and served as speaker in 1840; elected as a Democrat to the Twenty-eighth, Twenty-ninth, and Thirtieth Congresses (March 4, 1843–March 3, 1849); moved to California in 1849 and engaged in banking in Sacramento; member of the first State house of representatives 1851–1853; superintendent of Indian affairs of California 1855–1858; postmaster of San Francisco 1860–1864; died in San Francisco, Calif., January 2, 1865; interment in Santa Rosa Cemetery, Santa Rosa, Calif.

HENN, Bernhart, a Representative from Iowa; born in Cherry Valley, N. Y., in 1817; attended the common schools; moved to Burlington, Iowa, in 1838; studied law; was admitted to the bar in Burlington, Iowa; moved to Fairfield, Iowa, when appointed register of the United States land office in 1845 by President Polk; elected as a Democrat to the Thirty-second and Thirty-third Congresses (March 4, 1851–March 3, 1855); engaged in banking and dealing in real estate; died in Fairfield, Iowa, August 30, 1865; interment in Evergreen Cemetery.

HENNEY, Charles William Francis, a Representative from Wisconsin; born on a farm near Dunlap, Harrison County, Iowa, February 2, 1884; attended the district school and Denison (Iowa) Normal School; taught in a district school in Crawford County, Iowa, 1902–1905; was graduated from the pharmacy department of Fremont (Nebr.) Normal School in 1906 and from the medical department of Northwestern University, Chicago, Ill., in 1910; served as an interne in Cook County Hospital, Chicago, Ill., 1910–1912; moved to Portage, Columbia County, Wis., in 1912 and commenced the practice of medicine; delegate to all Democratic State Conventions from 1920 to 1936; delegate to Democratic National Conventions in 1936, 1940, 1944, and

1948; member of the Portage City Park Commission 1925–1933; chief of staff of St. Savior's Hospital, Portage City, Wis., in 1926 and 1927; admitted to fellowship in the American College of Surgeons in 1927 and attended clinics in Europe the same year; president of the Columbia County Medical Society 1928–1930; elected as a Democrat to the Seventy-third Congress (March 4, 1933–January 3, 1935); unsuccessful candidate for reelection in 1934 to the Seventy-fourth Congress; resumed the practice of medicine and surgery; chief of surgical staff, Divine Savior Hospital, 1936–1946; presidential elector, Wisconsin Electoral College, 1940; elected to fellowship in International College of Surgeons in 1954; resides in Portage, Wis.

HENNINGS, Thomas Carey, Jr., a Representative and a Senator from Missouri; born in St. Louis, Mo., June 25, 1903; attended the grade schools and Soldan High School of St. Louis, Mo.; was graduated from Cornell University, Ithaca, N. Y., in 1924 and from the law department of Washington University, St. Louis, Mo., in 1926; was admitted to the bar in 1926 and commenced practice in St. Louis; served as assistant circuit attorney for St. Louis 1929–1934; served as a colonel on the Governor's staff 1932–1936; lecturer on criminal jurisprudence at the Benton College of Law, St. Louis, Mo., 1934–1938; elected as a Democrat to the Seventy-fourth, Seventy-fifth, and Seventy-sixth Congresses and served from January 3, 1935, until his resignation on December 31, 1940; did not seek renomination to the Seventy-seventh Congress; circuit attorney for the city of St. Louis 1941–1944; served as a lieutenant commander in the United States Naval Reserve during World War II from August 15, 1941, until he received a medical discharge on April 7, 1943, after service in the Pacific-Asiatic area; resumed the practice of law; elected as a Democrat to the United States Senate in 1950, reelected in 1956, and served from January 3, 1951, until his death in Washington, D. C., September 13, 1960; interment in Arlington National Cemetery, Fort Myer, Va.

HENRY, Charles Lewis, a Representative from Indiana; born in Green Township, Hancock County, Ind., July 1, 1849; moved with his parents to Pendleton, Ind.; attended the common schools and Asbury (now De Pauw) University, Greencastle, Ind.; was graduated from the law department of Indiana University at Bloomington in 1872; was admitted to the bar and commenced practice in Pendleton; moved to Anderson, Ind., in 1875; member of the State senate in 1880, 1881, and 1883; elected as a Republican to the Fifty-fourth and Fifty-fifth Congresses (March 4, 1895–March 3, 1899); declined to be a candidate for renomination in 1898; interested in the development and operation of electric interurban railways; at the time of his death was president and receiver of the Indianapolis & Cincinnati Traction Co., which he had managed for twenty-three years; died in Indianapolis, Ind., May 2, 1927; interment in Maplewood Cemetery, Anderson, Ind.

HENRY, Daniel Maynadier, a Representative from Maryland; born near Cambridge, Dorchester County, Md., February 19, 1823; attended Cambridge Academy and St. John's College, Annapolis, Md.; studied law; was admitted to the bar in 1844 and practiced in Cambridge; member of the house of delegates in 1846 and 1849; served in the State senate in 1869; elected as a Democrat to the Forty-fifth and Forty-sixth Congresses (March 4, 1877–March 3, 1881); resumed the practice of law; died in Cambridge, Md., August 31, 1899; interment in Christ Protestant Episcopal Church Cemetery.

HENRY, Edward Stevens, a Representative from Connecticut; born in the town of Gill, Franklin County, Mass., February 10, 1836; moved to Rockville, Conn.; attended the public schools; engaged in the dry-goods business; treasurer of the People's Saving Bank, Rockville, 1870–1921; member of the State house of representatives in 1883; served in the State senate in 1887 and 1888; delegate at large to the Republican National Convention at Chicago in 1888; treasurer of the State of Connecticut 1889–1893; mayor of Rockville in 1894 and 1895; elected as a Republican to the Fifty-fourth and to the eight succeeding Congresses (March 4, 1895–March 3, 1913); declined to be a candidate for renomination in 1912; resumed his former mercantile pursuits in Rockville, Tolland County, Conn., where he died October 10, 1921; interment in Grove Hill Cemetery.

HENRY, James, a Delegate from Virginia; born in Accomac County, Va., in 1731; pursued classical studies; studied law at the University of Edinburgh; was admitted to the bar and practiced; member of the house of burgesses 1772–1774; member of the State house of delegates in 1776, 1777, and 1779; Member of the Continental Congress in 1780 and 1781; judge of the State court of admiralty 1782–1788; judge of the general court from December 24, 1788, to January 1800, when he resigned; died at his home, "Fleet Bay," in Northumberland County, Va., December 9, 1804.

HENRY, John, a Delegate and a Senator from Maryland; born at "Weston," on the Nanticoke River, near Vienna, Dorchester County, Md., in November 1750; attended West Nottingham Academy, Cecil County, Md., and was graduated from Princeton College in 1769; studied law in the Temple in London; returned to the United States in 1775 and practiced his profession in Dorchester County, Md.; Member of the Continental Congress 1778–1781 and 1784–1787; was a member of the committee to prepare the ordinance for the government of the Northwest Territory; elected as a Democrat to the United States Senate; reelected in 1790 and 1796 and served from March 4, 1789, until December 10, 1797, when he resigned, having been elected Governor; Governor of Maryland in 1797 and 1798; died at his country estate, "Weston," Dorchester County, Md., December 16, 1798; interment in Christ Protestant Episcopal Church Cemetery, Cambridge, Md.

HENRY, John, a Representative from Illinois; born near Stanford, Lincoln County, Ky., November 1, 1800; attended the public schools; served as a private in Captain Arnett's company of Illinois volunteers in the Black Hawk War; member of the State house of representatives 1832–1840; was prominently identified with the construction of the first railway in Illinois in 1838; member of the State senate 1840–1847; elected as a Whig to the Twenty-ninth Congress to fill the vacancy caused by the resignation of Edward D. Baker and served from February 5, 1847, to March 3, 1847; was not a candidate for the Thirtieth Congress; superintendent of the State insane asylum at Jacksonville, Ill., 1850–1855; during the Civil War was connected with the Quartermaster's Department at Jackson, Tenn., from August 25, 1862, to April 30, 1863; died in St. Louis, Mo., April 28, 1882; interment in Bellefontaine Cemetery.

HENRY, John Flournoy, a Representative from Kentucky; born at Henrys Mill, Scott County, Ky., on January 17, 1793; attended Georgetown Academy, Kentucky, and Jefferson Medical College, Philadelphia, Pa.; was graduated from the College of Physicians and Surgeons in 1817; served at Fort Meigs in 1813 as surgeon's mate of Kentucky troops; engaged in agricultural pursuits and the practice of medicine; elected to the Nineteenth Congress to fill the vacancy caused by the death of Robert P. Henry and served from December 11, 1826, to March 3, 1827; unsuccessful candidate for reelection in 1827 to the Twentieth Congress; professor in the Medical College of Ohio at Cincinnati in 1831; moved to Bloomington, Ill., in 1834 and to Burlington, Iowa, in 1845 and resumed the practice of medicine; died in Burlington, Iowa, November 12, 1873; interment in Aspen Grove Cemetery.

HENRY, Lewis, a Representative from New York; born in Elmira, Chemung County, N. Y., June 8, 1885; attended the public schools; was graduated from Elmira (N. Y.) Academy in 1904, from Cornell University, Ithaca, N. Y., in 1909, and from the law department of Columbia University, New York City, in 1911; was admitted to the bar in 1912 and commenced practice in Elmira, N. Y.; supervisor of the first ward of that city 1914–1920; delegate to the Republican State convention at Saratoga in 1920; elected as a Republican to the Sixty-seventh Congress to fill the vacancy caused by the resignation of Alanson B. Houghton and served from April 11, 1922, to March 3, 1923; unsuccessful candidate for renomination; resumed the practice of law at Elmira, N. Y.; president of the Oriental Consolidated Mining Company until 1939; died at Boston, Mass., on July 23, 1941; interment in Woodlawn Cemetery, Elmira, N. Y.

HENRY, Patrick (grandfather of William Henry Roane, cousin of Isaac Coles, and great-great-great-grandfather of Robert Lee Henry), a Delegate from Virginia; born in Studley, Hanover County, Va., May 29, 1736; pursued classical studies; engaged in mercantile pursuits; studied law; was admitted to the bar in 1760; moved to Louisa County in 1764; served as a member of the colonial house of burgesses in 1765; was foremost in the movement to call a Continental Congress; Member of the Continental Congress 1774–1776; Governor of Virginia 1776–1779 and 1784–1786; member of the State convention which ratified the Constitution in 1788; declined the appointment of United States Senator in 1794, the Cabinet portfolio of Secretary of State in 1795, the appointment of Chief Justice of the United States tendered by President Washington, and of Minister to France offered by President Adams; elected to the State senate in 1799, but did not take the seat; died in Red Hill, Va., June 6, 1799; interment in Red Hill Cemetery.

HENRY, Patrick, a Representative from Mississippi; born near Cynthia, Madison County, Miss., February 12, 1843; attended the common schools, Mississippi College, Clinton, Miss., Madison College, Sharon, Miss., and the Nashville (Tenn.) Military College; moved to Brandon, Miss., in 1858; enlisted in the Confederate service as a first lieutenant in Company B, Sixth Mississippi Infantry Regiment, in 1861; served throughout the Civil War and surrendered at Greensboro, N. C., April 26, 1865, as major of the Fourteenth (Consolidated) Mississippi Regiment; engaged in agricultural pursuits in Hinds and Rankin Counties until 1873; studied law; was admitted to the bar in 1873 and commenced practice in Brandon, Miss.; member of the State house of representatives 1878–1890; delegate to the State constitutional convention in 1890; assistant United States district attorney in 1896; elected as a Democrat to the Fifty-fifth and Fifty-sixth Congresses (March 4, 1897–March 3, 1901); unsuccessful candidate for renomination in 1900; resumed the practice of law in Brandon, Miss.; member of the State senate 1904–1908; served as mayor of Brandon from 1916 until his death in Brandon, Miss., May 18, 1930; interment in Brandon Cemetery.

HENRY, Patrick (nephew of the preceding), a Representative from Mississippi; born near Helena, Phillips County, Ark., February 15, 1861; moved with his parents to Vicksburg, Miss., in 1865; attended the public schools and was graduated from the

University of Mississippi, Oxford, Miss.; attended the United States Military Academy; studied law; was admitted to the bar in 1882 and commenced practice in Vicksburg, Miss.; city attorney 1884–1888; member of the State senate from 1888 until he resigned to become district attorney in 1890; district attorney for the ninth judicial district 1890–1900; delegate to the Democratic National Convention at Chicago in 1896; appointed circuit judge of the ninth judicial district in 1900 and served until 1901, when he resigned, having been elected as a Democrat to the Fifty-seventh Congress (March 4, 1901–March 3, 1903); unsuccessful candidate for renomination in 1902; resumed the practice of law in Vicksburg, Miss., until his death there on December 28, 1933; interment in Cedar Hill Cemetery.

HENRY, Robert Kirkland, a Representative from Wisconsin; born in Jefferson, Jefferson County, Wis., February 9, 1890; attended the public schools of his native city and the University of Wisconsin at Madison; engaged in the banking business; served as State treasurer 1931–1935; member of the Jefferson Municipal Water and Light Commission from November 7, 1939, to December 1, 1944; member of the State Banking Commission 1940–1944; elected as a Republican to the Seventy-ninth Congress and served from January 3, 1945, until his death; had been reelected to the Eightieth Congress; died in Madison, Wis., November 20, 1946; interment in Greenwood Cemetery, Jefferson, Wis.

HENRY, Robert Lee (great-great-great-grandson of Patrick Henry 1736–1799), a Representative from Texas; born in Linden, Cass County, Tex., May 12, 1864; attended the common schools; moved to Bowie County in 1878 and to McLennan County in 1895; was graduated from the Southwestern University of Texas at Georgetown in 1885; studied law; was admitted to the bar in 1886 and practiced for a short time in Texarkana, Tex.; was graduated from the University of Texas at Austin in 1887; elected mayor of Texarkana in 1890 but resigned in 1891; first office assistant to the attorney general of Texas 1891–1893; assistant attorney general 1893–1896; settled in Waco, McLennan County, Tex., in 1895 and practiced law; elected as a Democrat to the Fifty-fifth and to the nine succeeding Congresses (March 4, 1897–March 3, 1917); was not a candidate for renomination in 1916, but was an unsuccessful candidate for the Democratic nomination for United States Senator; engaged in the practice of law in Waco, Tex.; again an unsuccessful candidate for the Democratic nomination for United States Senator in 1922 and 1928; moved to Houston, Tex., in 1923 and resumed the practice of his profession; died in Houston, Tex., July 9, 1931, from a gunshot wound; interment in Rose Hill Cemetery, Texarkana, Tex.

HENRY, Robert Pryor, a Representative from Kentucky; born in Henrys Mills, Scott County, Ky. (then a part of Virginia), November 24, 1788; pursued classical studies and was graduated from Transylvania College, Lexington, Ky.; studied law; was admitted to the bar in 1809 and commenced practice in Georgetown, Ky.; prosecuting attorney in 1819; served in the War of 1812; moved to Hopkinsville in 1817; elected as a Clay Democrat to the Eighteenth and Nineteenth Congresses and served from March 4, 1823, until his death in Hopkinsville, Ky., August 25, 1826; interment in Pioneer Cemetery.

HENRY, Thomas, a Representative from Pennsylvania; born in County Down, Ireland, in 1779; immigrated to America and settled in Beaver, Pa., in 1798; appointed justice of the peace by Governor Snyder December 24, 1808; elected county commissioner in 1810; captain of a company that went from Beaver to help defend the northern frontier from a threatened British in-

vasion in 1814; elected a member of the State house of representatives in 1815; prothonotary and clerk of courts 1816–1821; elected sheriff of the county in 1821; proprietor and editor of the Western Argus 1821–1831; county treasurer in 1828 and 1829; elected as a Whig to the Twenty-fifth, Twenty-sixth, and Twenty-seventh Congresses (March 4, 1837–March 3, 1843); died in Beaver, Pa., July 20, 1849; interment in Old Beaver Cemetery.

HENRY, William, a Delegate from Pennsylvania; born near Downington, Chester County, Pa., May 19, 1729; attended the common schools; justice of the court of common pleas of Lancaster County in 1770, 1773, and 1777; canal commissioner of Pennsylvania in 1771; member of the State assembly in 1776; assistant commissary general with the rank of colonel for the district of Lancaster, Pa., during the whole period of the Revolutionary War; member of the council of safety 1777; treasurer of Lancaster County 1777–1785; president judge of the court of common pleas in 1780; inventor of the screw auger and the first to suggest steam as a motive power; first gave encouragement and patronage to Benjamin West, the American painter; Member of the Continental Congress 1784–1786; died in Lancaster, Pa., December 15, 1786; interment in the Moravian Cemetery; reinterment in Greenwood Cemetery.

HENRY, William, a Representative from Vermont; born in Charlestown, N. H., March 22, 1788; attended the common schools; engaged in business in Chester, Vt., and later engaged in manufacturing in Vermont, New York, and Jaffery, N. H.; moved to Bellows Falls, Vt., in 1831; engaged in banking; member of the State house of representatives in 1834 and 1835; served in the State senate in 1836; a director of the Rutland & Burlington Railroad Co.; delegate to the Whig National Convention at Harrisburg, Pa., in 1839; presidential elector on the Whig ticket of Harrison and Tyler in 1840; elected as a Whig to the Thirtieth and Thirty-first Congresses (March 4, 1847–March 3, 1851); unsuccessful candidate for election in 1852 to the Thirty-third Congress; resumed banking; presidential elector on the Republican ticket of Lincoln and Hamlin in 1860; died in Bellows Falls, Vt., April 16, 1861; interment in South Street Cemetery, Chester, Vt.

HENRY, Winder Laird (great-grandson of Charles Goldsborough and Robert Henry Goldsborough), a Representative from Maryland; born near Cambridge, Dorchester County, Md., December 20, 1864; attended the public schools; engaged in mercantile pursuits; purchased an interest in and became editor of the Cambridge Chronicle; elected as a Democrat to the Fifty-third Congress to fill the vacancy caused by the death of Robert F. Bratton and served from November 6, 1894, to March 3, 1895; was not a candidate for renomination in 1894; resumed newspaper work until 1898; studied law; was admitted to the bar of Dorchester County in 1898 and engaged in practice in Cambridge; colonel on the staff of Gov. John Walter Smith 1899–1903; commissioner of the land office of Maryland April 1 to May 1, 1908; appointed chief judge of the first judicial circuit in May 1908 and served until October 1, 1909; resumed the practice of law in Cambridge, Md., and also engaged in banking; member of the Public Service Commission of Maryland from August 1, 1914, to June 1, 1916; died in Cambridge, Md., July 5, 1940; interment in Christ Church Cemetery.

HENSLEY, Walter Lewis, a Representative from Missouri; born near Pevely, Jefferson County, Mo., September 3, 1871; attended the public schools, and the law department of the University of Missouri at Columbia; was admitted to the bar in 1894 and commenced practice in Wayne County, Mo.;

moved to Bonne Terre, St. Francois County, Mo., and continued the practice of law; prosecuting attorney of St. Francois County 1898–1902; moved to Farmington, Mo., and practiced law; elected as a Democrat to the Sixty-second and to the three succeeding Congresses (March 4, 1911–March 3, 1919); was not a candidate for renomination in 1918; United States district attorney from March 1919 until he resigned in May 1920; reengaged in the private practice of law in St. Louis, Mo., until 1936, when he retired and moved to near Pevely; died at his summer home in Ludington, Mich., July 18, 1946; interment in Sandy Baptist Cemetery, near Pevely, Mo.

HEPBURN, William Peters (great-grandson of Matthew Lyon), a Representative from Iowa; born in Wellsville, Columbiana County, Ohio, November 4, 1833; moved to Iowa with his mother and stepfather (George S. Hampton), who settled near Iowa City in April 1841; attended the common schools of Iowa City and the academy conducted by James F. Harlan (later a Senator); served an apprenticeship in a printing office; studied law in Iowa City and Chicago; was admitted to the Illinois bar in 1854 and commenced practice in Iowa City, Iowa; settled in Marshalltown, Marshall County, in February 1856; prosecuting attorney of Marshall County in 1856; district attorney of the eleventh judicial district 1856–1861; clerk of the house of representatives at the first session that convened in Des Moines in January 1858; delegate to the Republican National Convention at Chicago in 1860; during the Civil War served in the Second Iowa Cavalry as captain, major, and lieutenant colonel; resident of Memphis, Tenn., 1865–1867; moved to Clarinda, Iowa, in 1867; resumed the practice of law until 1881; presidential elector on the Republican tickets of Hayes and Wheeler in 1876 and Harrison and Morton in 1888; elected as a Republican to the Forty-seventh, Forty-eighth, and Forty-ninth Congresses (March 4, 1881–March 3, 1887); delegate to the Republican National Convention at Chicago in 1888 and at St. Louis in 1896; served as Solicitor of the Treasury during the administration of President Benjamin Harrison; unsuccessful candidate for reelection in 1886 to the Fiftieth Congress; elected to the Fifty-third and to the seven succeeding Congresses (March 4, 1893–March 3, 1909); unsuccessfully contested the election of William D. Jamieson to the Sixty-first Congress; engaged in the practice of law in Clarinda, Iowa, and Washington, D. C.; died in Clarinda, Iowa, February 7, 1916; interment in Clarinda Cemetery.

HERBERT, Hilary Abner, a Representative from Alabama; born in Laurens, Laurens County, S. C., March 12, 1834; moved with his parents to Greenville, Butler County, Ala., in 1846; attended the University of Alabama at Tuscaloosa in 1853 and 1854 and the University of Virginia at Charlottesville in 1855 and 1856; studied law; was admitted to the bar in 1857 and commenced practice in Greenville, Ala.; entered the Confederate service as captain of the Greenville Guards; promoted to the rank of colonel of the Eighth Regiment, Alabama Infantry; disabled at the Battle of the Wilderness May 6, 1864; resumed the practice of law in Greenville, Ala., until 1872, when he moved to Montgomery, Ala.; elected as a Democrat to the Forty-fifth and to the seven succeeding Congresses (March 4, 1877–March 3, 1893); served in the Cabinet of President Cleveland as Secretary of the Navy 1893–1897; located in Washington, D. C., and practiced law until his death; died in Tampa, Fla., March 5, 1919; interment in Oakwood Cemetery, Montgomery, Ala.

HERBERT, John Carlyle, a Representative from Maryland; born in Alexandria, Va., August 16, 1775; received private instruction, and was graduated from St. John's College, Annapolis, Md., in 1794; studied law; was admitted to the bar and commenced practice in Richmond, Va., about 1795; member of the Virginia House of Delegates in 1798 and 1799; settled in Prince Georges County, Md., in 1805; member of the Maryland House of Delegates 1808–1813 and served as speaker in 1812 and 1813; served as captain of the Bladensburg Troop of Horse in the War of 1812; elected as a Federalist to the Fourteenth and Fifteenth Congresses (March 4, 1815–March 3, 1819); retired to his estate, "Walnut Grange," Beltsville, Md., in 1820 and resumed the practice of law; presidential elector at large from Maryland in 1824 and 1832; died in Buchanan, Botetourt County, Va., while returning from a visit to Hot Springs, Va., September 1, 1846; interment in Greenmount Cemetery, Baltimore, Md.

HERBERT, Philemon Thomas, a Representative from California; born in Pine Apple, Wilcox County, Ala., November 1, 1825; attended the common schools and the University of Alabama at Tuscaloosa; moved to Mariposa City, Calif., about 1850; member of the State assembly in 1853 and 1854; elected as a Democrat to the Thirty-fourth Congress (March 4, 1855–March 3, 1857); was not a candidate for renomination in 1856; moved to El Paso, Tex., about 1859 and practiced law; during the Civil War served with the Confederate Army as lieutenant colonel of the Seventh Texas Cavalry; was wounded at the Battle of Mansfield April 8, 1864, and died in Kingston, La., July 23, 1864, from the effects of his wounds; interment in Evergreen Cemetery.

HEREFORD, Frank, a Representative and a Senator from West Virginia; born near Warrenton, Fauquier County, Va., July 4, 1825; completed preparatory studies, and was graduated from McKendree College, Lebanon, Ill., in 1845; studied law; was admitted to the bar and practiced; moved to California in 1849; district attorney of Sacramento County from October 1855 to October 1857; moved to West Virginia; elected as a Democrat to the Forty-second, Forty-third, and Forty-fourth Congresses and served from March 4, 1871, until January 31, 1877, when he resigned; elected to the United States Senate on January 26, 1877, to fill the vacancy caused by the death of Allen Taylor Caperton and served from January 31, 1877, to March 3, 1881; resumed the practice of law; presidential elector on the Democratic ticket of Cleveland and Thurman in 1888; died in Union, Monroe County, W. Va., December 21, 1891; interment in Green Hill Cemetery.

HERKIMER, John, a Representative from New York; born in what is now Herkimer (then Tryon and later Montgomery) County, N. Y., in 1773; attended the public schools; member of the State house of representatives in 1800, 1804, and 1806; member of the State constitutional convention in 1801; moved to Danube, Herkimer County, N. Y.; major in the War of 1812 and commanded a battalion of New York Volunteers in the defense of Sackets Harbor May 29, 1813; judge of the circuit court for several years; elected as a Democrat to the Fifteenth Congress (March 4, 1817–March 3, 1819); moved to Meriden, N. Y.; elected to the Eighteenth Congress (March 4, 1823–March 3, 1825); returned to Danube, where he died June 8, 1848; interment in General Herkimer Cemetery, Danube, N. Y.

HERLONG, Albert Sydney, Jr., a Representative from Florida; born in Manistee, Monroe County, Ala., February 14, 1909; moved with his parents to Marion County, Fla., in 1912; attended the public schools of Sumter and Lake Counties and Leesburg High School; was graduated from the University of Florida at Gainesville in 1930; was admitted to the bar in 1930 and commenced the practice of law in Leesburg, Lake County, Fla.; elected county judge of Lake County, Fla., and served from 1937 to 1949; city attorney of Leesburg from 1946 to 1948; held Reserve commission as captain in the United

States Army and was called to active duty in the Judge Advocate General's Department in August 1941; was discharged in 1942 due to physical disability; served two enlistments in the Florida State Guard; president of the Florida State Baseball League in 1947 and 1948; elected as a Democrat to the Eighty-first and to the five succeeding Congresses (January 3, 1949–January 3, 1961). *Reelected to the Eighty-seventh Congress.*

HERMANN, Binger, a Representative from Oregon; born in Lonaconing, Allegany County, Md., February 19, 1843; attended rural schools and was graduated from the Independent Academy, Manchester, Md., later known as Irving College; moved to Oregon in 1859, where he taught school; studied law; was admitted to the bar in 1866 and commenced practice in Oakland, Oreg.; member of the State house of representatives 1866–1868; served in the State senate 1868–1870; deputy collector of internal revenue for southern Oregon 1868–1871; receiver of public moneys at the United States land office in Roseburg, Oreg., 1871–1873; colonel Oregon State Militia 1882–1884; appointed by President McKinley Commissioner of the General Land Office and served from March 27, 1897, until February 1, 1903, when he resigned; elected as a Republican to the Forty-ninth and to the five succeeding Congresses (March 4, 1885–March 3, 1897); was not a candidate for renomination in 1896; again elected to the Fifty-eighth Congress to fill the vacancy caused by the death of Thomas H. Tongue; reelected to the Fifty-ninth Congress and served from June 1, 1903, to March 3, 1907; was not a candidate for renomination in 1906; resumed the practice of law and engaged in literary pursuits in Roseburg, Oreg., where he died April 15, 1926; interment in the Masonic Cemetery.

HERNANDEZ, Benigno Cardenas, a Representative from New Mexico; born in Taos, N. Mex., February 13, 1862; attended common and private schools; clerk in a general merchandise establishment in Taos County from 1880 to 1889; engaged in general merchandising and stock raising; moved to Lumberton in 1896 and engaged in mercantile pursuits; probate clerk and ex officio recorder of deeds for Rio Arriba County 1900–1904; moved to Tierra Amarilla in 1901; sheriff of Rio Arriba County 1904–1906; county treasurer and ex officio collector of taxes from 1908 until 1912; delegate to numerous State Republican conventions; receiver of the land office at Sante Fe, N. Mex., in 1912 and 1913, when he resigned; again engaged in mercantile pursuits and stock raising; delegate to the Republican National Conventions in 1912 and 1916; member of the State exemption board during the First World War; elected as a Republican to the Sixty-fourth Congress (March 4, 1915–March 3, 1917); unsuccessful candidate for reelection in 1916 to the Sixty-fifth Congress; elected to the Sixty-sixth Congress (March 4, 1919–March 3, 1921); was not a candidate for renomination in 1920; appointed collector of internal revenue for the district of New Mexico by President Harding on April 22, 1921, and served until 1933; member of the Selective Service Board 1940–1947; died in Los Angeles, Calif., on October 18, 1954; interment in Inglewood Park Cemetery, Inglewood, Calif.

HERNANDEZ, Joseph Marion, a Delegate from the Territory of Florida; born in St. Augustine, Fla. (then a Spanish colony), August 4, 1793; transferred his allegiance to the United States; upon the formation of Florida Territory was elected as a Delegate to the Seventeenth Congress and served from September 30, 1822, to March 3, 1823; member and presiding officer of the Territorial house of representatives; appointed brigadier general of Volunteers in the war against the Florida Indians; entered the United States service and served from 1835 to 1838; commanded the expedition in 1837 that captured the Indian chief Oceola; appointed brigadier general of Mounted Volunteers in July 1837;

unsuccessful candidate of the Whig Party for the United States Senate in 1845; moved to Cuba and engaged as a planter in the District of Coliseo, near Matanzas; died at the family's sugar estate, "Audaz," in the District of Coliseo, Matanzas Province, Cuba, June 8, 1857; interment in the Junco family vault in San Carlos Cemetery, Matanzas, Cuba.

HERNDON, Thomas Hord, a Representative from Alabama; born in Erie, Greene (now Hale) County, Ala., July 1, 1828; attended a private school; was graduated from the University of Alabama at Tuscaloosa in 1847; attended the law school of Harvard University in 1848; was admitted to the bar in 1849 and commenced practice in Eutaw, Ala.; editor of the Eutaw Democrat in 1850; moved to Mobile, Ala., in 1853 and resumed the practice of law; member of the State house of representatives in 1857 and 1858; trustee of the University of Alabama in 1858 and 1859; returned to Greene County in 1859; member of the State secession convention in 1861; during the Civil War served as major, lieutenant colonel, and colonel of the Thirty-sixth Regiment, Alabama Infantry, in the Confederate Army and was wounded twice in battle; paroled May 13, 1865; after the war he volunteered to command the troops at the evacuation of Spanish Fort, performing that duty in such a manner that he is credited with saving the lives of hundreds of his comrades; engaged in literary pursuits; again moved to Mobile and resumed the practice of his profession; unsuccessful Democratic candidate for Governor of Alabama in 1872; member of the State constitutional convention which met September 6, 1875; member of the State house of representatives in 1876 and 1877; elected as a Democrat to the Forty-sixth, Forty-seventh, and Forty-eighth Congresses and served from March 4, 1879, until his death in Mobile, Ala., March 28, 1883, before the convening of the Forty-eighth Congress; interment in Magnolia Cemetery.

HERNDON, William Smith, a Representative from Texas; born in Rome, Floyd County, Ga., November 27, 1835; moved to Wood County, Tex., in May 1852; attended the common schools, and was graduated from McKenzie College in 1859; studied law; was admitted to the bar in 1860 and commenced practice in Tyler, Smith County, Tex.; during the Civil War served in the Confederate Army from 1861 to 1865 and attained the rank of captain; resumed the practice of law in Tyler; attorney, executive adviser, and general solicitor for numerous railroad companies 1868–1881; elected as a Democrat to the Forty-second and Forty-third Congresses (March 4, 1871–March 3, 1875); unsuccessful candidate for reelection in 1874 to the Forty-fourth Congress; again engaged in the practice of law in Tyler, Tex.; delegate to many Democratic State and National conventions; engaged in railroad construction; died in Albuquerque, N. Mex., October 11, 1903; interment in Oakwood Cemetery, Tyler, Tex.

HEROD, William, a Representative from Indiana; born in Bourbon County, Ky., March 31, 1801; completed preparatory studies; studied law and was admitted to the bar in Bracken County, Ky.; later moved to Columbus, Ind.; was admitted to the bar in Bartholomew County in 1825 and began practice in Columbus, Ind.; member of the State house of representatives in 1829, 1830, and 1844; served in the State senate 1831–1834, 1845, and 1846; elected prosecuting attorney of Bartholomew County and served from 1833 until 1837, when he resigned; elected as a Whig to the Twenty-fourth Congress to fill the vacancy caused by the death of George L. Kinnard; reelected to the Twenty-fifth Congress and served from January 25, 1837, to March 3, 1839; unsuccessful candidate for reelection in 1838 to the Twenty-sixth Congress; resumed the practice of his profession in Columbus, Ind.; clerk of the circuit court of Bartholomew County in 1853; became a Republican upon the formation of that party; engaged in the practice of law until his death at Columbus, Ind., October 20, 1871; interment in City Cemetery.

HERRICK, Anson (son of Ebenezer Herrick), a Representative from New York; born in Lewiston, Androscoggin County, Maine, January 21, 1812; attended the public schools; learned the art of printing; established the Citizen at Wiscasset, Maine, in 1833; moved to New York City in 1836; established the New York Atlas in 1838, which he continued until his death; member of the board of aldermen 1854–1856; naval storekeeper for the port of New York 1857–1861; elected as a Democrat to the Thirty-eighth Congress (March 4, 1863–March 3, 1865); unsuccessful candidate for reelection in 1864 to the Thirty-ninth Congress; resumed his journalistic pursuits; delegate to the Union National Convention at Philadelphia in 1866; died in New York City February 6, 1868; interment in Greenwood Cemetery, Brooklyn, N. Y.

HERRICK, Ebenezer (father of Anson Herrick), a Representative from Maine; born in Lewiston, Androscoggin County, Maine (then a district of Massachusetts), October 21, 1785; attended the common schools; studied law; was admitted to the bar and commenced practice in Bowdoinham, Lincoln County, Maine; engaged in mercantile pursuits 1814–1818; member of the Massachusetts House of Representatives in 1819; member of the convention which formed the first constitution of the State of Maine in 1820; secretary of the Maine Senate in 1821; elected to the Seventeenth, Eighteenth, and Nineteenth Congresses (March 4, 1821–March 3, 1827); declined to be a candidate for reelection in 1826; member of the Maine Senate in 1828 and 1829; died in Lewiston, Maine, May 7, 1839; interment in the Old Herrick Burying Ground.

HERRICK, Joshua, a Representative from Maine; born in Beverly, Mass., March 18, 1793; attended the common schools; moved to the district of Maine in 1811 and engaged in the lumber business; served in the War of 1812; moved to Brunswick, Maine, and became connected with the first cotton factory of Maine; deputy sheriff of Cumberland County for many years; deputy collector and inspector of customs at Kennebunkport, Maine, 1829–1841; town clerk of Kennebunkport 1832–1842; also selectman, assessor, and overseer of the poor of Kennebunkport 1839–1842; county commissioner of York County in 1842 and 1843; elected as a Democrat to the Twenty-eighth Congress (March 4, 1843–March 3, 1845); unsuccessful candidate for renomination in 1844 to the Twenty-ninth Congress; again deputy collector at Kennebunkport 1847–1849; register of probate of York County 1849–1855; retired from active life; died in Alfred, Maine, August 30, 1874; interment in Village Cemetery, Kennebunkport, Maine.

HERRICK, Manuel, a Representative from Oklahoma; born in Perry, Tuscarawas County, Ohio, September 20, 1876; moved with his parents to Greenwood County, Kans., in 1877; was self-educated; engaged in agricultural pursuits; settled in the "Cherokee Strip," Oklahoma, in 1893; moved to Perry, Okla., and became interested in agriculture and stock raising; elected as a Republican to the Sixty-seventh Congress (March 4, 1921–March 3, 1923); unsuccessful candidate in 1922 for renomination; became a resident of California in 1933 and of Plumas County, Calif., in 1937; disappeared during a Sierra blizzard January 11, 1952, while on a trip to his mining claim eight miles northeast of Quincy, Calif., and was found dead in a snowbank two miles from his cabin on February 29, 1952; remains were cremated in Sacramento, Calif., and the ashes interred in Quincy Cemetery, Quincy, Calif.

HERRICK, Richard Platt, a Representative from New York; born in Greenbush (now Rensselaer), Rensselaer County, N. Y., March 23, 1791; member of the State assembly in 1839; elected as a Whig to the Twenty-ninth Congress and served from March 4, 1845, until his death in Washington, D. C., June 20, 1846; interment in Greenbush Cemetery, Greenbush (now Rensselaer), N. Y.

HERRICK, Samuel, a Representative from Ohio; born in Amenia, Dutchess County, N. Y., April 14, 1779; pursued an academic course; studied law in Carlisle, Pa.; was admitted to the bar in 1805 and commenced practice in St. Clairsville, Ohio; moved to Zanesville, Ohio, in 1810; appointed prosecuting attorney of Guernsey County in 1810 and also United States district attorney; in 1814 appointed prosecuting attorney of Licking County and commissioned brigadier general of the Ohio Militia; elected as a Democrat to the Fifteenth and Sixteenth Congresses (March 4, 1817–March 3, 1821); was not a candidate for reelection in 1820; continued the practice of law; presidential elector on the Jackson and Calhoun ticket in 1828; appointed United States district attorney for Ohio in 1829 but resigned June 30, 1830; died in Zanesville, Ohio, June 4, 1852; interment in City (now Greenwood) Cemetery.

HERRING, Clyde LaVerne, a Senator from Iowa; born in Jackson, Jackson County, Mich., May 3, 1879; attended the public schools; moved to Detroit, Mich., in 1897; served as a private in Company D, Third Michigan Regiment, in the Spanish-American War; moved to Colorado Springs, Colo., and engaged in ranching 1902–1906; moved to Massena, Iowa, and engaged in agricultural pursuits 1906–1908; entered the automobile business in Atlantic, Iowa, 1908–1910; moved to Des Moines, Iowa, in 1910 and continued in the automobile business; during the First World War served with the Iowa National Guard on the Mexican border; unsuccessful candidate for Governor of Iowa in 1920; unsuccessful candidate for election to the United States Senate in 1922; member of the Democratic National Committee of Iowa 1924–1928; served as Governor of Iowa 1933–1937; delegate at large to the Democratic National Convention at Chicago in 1940; elected as a Democrat to the United States Senate for the term beginning January 3, 1937, but did not qualify until the expiration of his term as Governor, and served from January 15, 1937, to January 3, 1943; unsuccessful candidate for reelection in 1942; senior assistant administrator in the Office of Price Administration from March 2, 1943, until his resignation on November 3, 1943; resumed the automobile and accessory business in Des Moines, Iowa; died in Washington, D. C., September 15, 1945; interment in Glendale Cemetery, Des Moines, Iowa.

HERSEY, Ira Greenlief, a Representative from Maine; born in Hodgdon, Aroostook County, Maine, March 31, 1858; attended the public schools, and Ricker Classical Institute, Houlton, Maine; studied law; was admitted to the bar in 1880 and commenced practice in Houlton, Maine; unsuccessful candidate for Governor of Maine in 1886; member of the State house of representatives 1909–1912; served in the State senate 1913–1916 and was president of that body in 1915 and 1916; elected as a Republican to the Sixty-fifth and to the five succeeding Congresses (March 4, 1917–March 3, 1929); one of the managers appointed by the House of Representatives in 1926 to conduct the impeachment proceedings against George W. English, judge of the United States District Court for the Eastern District of Illinois; unsuccessful candidate for renomination in 1928 to the Seventy-first Congress; judge of probate for Aroostook County, Maine, 1934–1942, when he retired and moved to Washington, D. C., where he died on May 6, 1943; interment in Evergreen Cemetery, Houlton, Maine.

HERSEY, Samuel Freeman, a Representative from Maine; born in Sumner, Oxford County, Maine, April 12, 1812; attended the common schools of Sumner and Buckfield; taught school 1828–1831; was graduated from Hebron Academy in 1831; removed to Bangor the same year; engaged in the merchandise business in Lincoln in 1833 and in Milford in 1837; engaged in the lumber business in Stillwater, Maine, in 1842 and in Bangor in 1850; extended his business to Minnesota, Wisconsin, and Iowa, and continued in business until September 1863; member of the State house of representatives in 1842, 1857, and 1865; member of the executive council 1852–1854; delegate to the Republican National Convention at Chicago in 1860; member of the Republican National Committee 1864–1868; member of the State senate in 1868 and 1869; unsuccessful candidate for Governor of Maine in 1870; elected as a Republican to the Forty-third and Forty-fourth Congresses and served from March 4, 1873, until his death in Bangor, Maine, February 3, 1875, before the close of the Forty-third Congress; interment in Mount Hope Cemetery.

HERSMAN, Hugh Steel, a Representative from California; born in Port Deposit, Cecil County, Md., July 8, 1872; moved to California with his parents, who settled in Berkeley in 1881; attended the public schools in California; was graduated from the Southwestern Presbyterian University, Tennessee, in 1893; studied at the University of California at Berkeley in 1897 and 1898; president of the First National Bank, Gilroy, Calif., 1914–1918; officer and director of various corporations; elected as a Democrat to the Sixty-sixth Congress (March 4, 1919–March 3, 1921); unsuccessful for reelection in 1920 to the Sixty-seventh Congress; member of the board of directors of the American Trust Co., Gilroy, Calif.; died in San Francisco, Calif., March 7, 1954; interment in Nottingham Cemetery, Colora, Cecil County, Md.

HERTER, Christian Archibald, a Representative from Massachusetts; born in Paris, France, March 28, 1895, of American parents; attended school in Paris 1901–1904 and Browning School of New York City 1904–1911; was graduated from Harvard University, Cambridge, Mass., in 1915; attaché of the American Embassy in Berlin, Germany, in 1916 and for two months was in charge of the American Legation in Brussels, Belgium; served in the State Department, Washington, D. C., 1917–1919; assistant commissioner and secretary of a diplomatic mission to draw up a prisoner-of-war agreement with Germany, and secretary of the American Peace Commission in 1918; executive secretary of the European Relief Council in 1920; personal assistant to the Secretary of Commerce, Washington, D. C., 1921–1924; engaged in the publishing business as an associate editor, editor, and vice president at Boston, Mass., 1924–1937; visiting lecturer on government at Harvard University in 1929 and 1930; overseer, Harvard University, 1940–1944 and 1946–1952; member of the State house of representatives 1931–1943, serving as speaker 1939–1943; trustee of many philanthropic and charitable organizations; deputy director of the Office of Facts and Figures, Washington, D. C., in 1941 and 1942; elected as a Republican to the Seventy-eighth and to the four succeeding Congresses (January 3, 1943–January 3, 1953); was not a candidate for renomination in 1952; delegate to the Republican National Convention in 1948; was Governor of Massachusetts from January 1953 to January 1957; was not a candidate for reelection as Governor in 1956; Under Secretary of State from February 21, 1957, and Secretary of State from April 22, 1959, to January 20, 1961; resides in Millis, Mass.

HESELTON, John Walter, a Representative from Massachusetts; born in Gardiner, Kennebec County, Maine, March 17, 1900; attended the public schools of Gardiner, Maine, Amherst (Mass.) College, and Harvard Law School, Cambridge, Mass.; during the First World War served in the United States Army from October 10, 1918, to December 12, 1918; was admitted to the bar in 1926 and commenced practice in Greenfield, Mass.; also interested in banking; secretary of the board of trustees of Deerfield Academy; selectman of Deerfield, Mass., 1932–1935; president of the Massachusetts Selectmen's Association 1935–1938; secretary of the Deerfield Republican Town Committee 1928–1938; member of the Republican State Committee 1936–1938; district attorney of the northwestern district of Massachusetts 1939–1944; elected as a Republican to the Seventy-ninth and to the six succeeding Congresses (January 3, 1945–January 3, 1959); was not a candidate for renomination in 1958; engaged in practice of law; is a resident of Fort Pierce, Fla.

HESS, William Emil, a Representative from Ohio; born in Cincinnati, Ohio, February 13, 1898; attended the public schools, the University of Cincinnati, Cincinnati, Ohio, and Cincinnati (Ohio) Law School; during the First World War served in the United States Army as a private; was admitted to the bar in 1919 and commenced the practice of law in Cincinnati, Ohio, the same year; member of the Cincinnati City Council 1922–1926; elected as a Republican to the Seventy-first and to the three succeeding Congresses (March 4, 1929–January 3, 1937); unsuccessful candidate for reelection in 1936 to the Seventy-fifth Congress; resumed the practice of law; elected to the Seventy-sixth and to the four succeeding Congresses (January 3, 1939–January 3, 1949); unsuccessful candidate for reelection in 1948 to the Eighty-first Congress; elected to the Eighty-second and to the four succeeding Congresses (January 3, 1951–January 3, 1961); was not a candidate for renomination in 1960; resumed the practice of law; is a resident of Cincinnati, Ohio.

HEWES, Joseph, a Delegate from North Carolina; born in Kingston, N. J., January 23, 1730; pursued classical studies and attended Princeton College; engaged in business in Philadelphia, Pa., for a time; settled in Wilmington, N. C., and engaged in mercantile pursuits; moved to Edenton, N. C., in 1756; member of the State house of commons 1766–1775; member of the committee of correspondence in 1773; delegate to the Provincial Congress; Member of the Continental Congress 1774–1777; again served in the State house of commons in 1778 and 1779; member of the committee to report upon the rights of the Colonies; was a signer of the Declaration of Independence; again a Member of the Continental Congress in 1779 and served until his death in Philadelphia, Pa., on November 10, 1779; interment in Christ Churchyard.

HEWITT, Abram Stevens, a Representative from New York; born in Haverstraw, N. Y., July 31, 1822; attended the public schools of New York City, and was graduated from Columbia College in 1842; studied law; and was admitted to practice in October 1845; his eyesight failing, he engaged in the iron business with Peter Cooper and established works in New Jersey and Pennsylvania; appointed one of the ten United States scientific commissioners to visit the French Exposition Universelle of 1867 and made a report on iron and steel, which was published by Congress; organized and managed the Cooper Union for the advancement of science and art; elected as a Democrat to the Forty-fourth and Forty-fifth Congresses (March 4, 1875–March 3, 1879); was not a candidate for renomination in 1878; elected to the Forty-seventh, Forty-eighth, and Forty-ninth Congresses and served from March 4, 1881, until December 30, 1886, when he resigned, mayor of New York City in 1887 and 1888; appointed member of the Palisades Interstate Park Commission in 1900; elected a trustee of Columbia University in 1901; died in New York City January 18, 1903; interment in Greenwood Cemetery.

HEWITT, Goldsmith Whitehouse, a Representative from Alabama; born near Elyton (now Birmingham), Jefferson County, Ala., February 14, 1834; attended the country schools; during the Civil War entered the Confederate Army in June 1861 as a private in Company B, Tenth Regiment, Alabama Infantry; was promoted to captain of Company G, Twenty-eighth Regiment, Alabama Infantry, in 1862; participated in several battles and was severely wounded on the field of Chickamauga; was graduated from the law department of Cumberland University, Lebanon, Tenn., in 1866; was admitted to the bar the same year and commenced practice in Birmingham, Ala.; member of the State house of representatives in 1870 and 1871; served in the State senate from 1872 to 1874 and resigned in the latter year; elected as a Democrat to the Forty-fourth and Forty-fifth Congresses (March 4, 1875–March 3, 1879); elected to the Forty-seventh and Forty-eighth Congresses (March 4, 1881–March 3, 1885); was not a candidate for renomination in 1884; resumed the practice of law; again a member of the State house of representatives 1886–1888; died in Birmingham, Ala., on May 27, 1895; interment in Oak Hill Cemetery.

HEYBURN, Weldon Brinton, a Senator from Idaho; born near Chadds Ford, Delaware County, Pa., May 23, 1852; attended the public schools, Maplewood Institute, Concordville, Pa., and the University of Pennsylvania at Philadelphia; studied law; was admitted to the bar in 1876 and commenced practice in Media, Pa.; moved to Shoshone County, Idaho, in the winter of 1883 and continued the practice of law in Wallace; was a member of the convention that framed the constitution of the State of Idaho in 1889; delegate to the Republican National Convention at Chicago in 1888, at Minneapolis in 1892, at Philadelphia in 1900, and at Chicago in 1904; National committeeman for Idaho 1904–1908; unsuccessful Republican candidate for election in 1898 to the Fifty-sixth Congress; elected in 1903 as a Republican to the United States Senate; reelected in 1908 and served from March 4, 1903, until his death in Washington, D. C., October 17, 1912; interment in Lafayette Cemetery, near Chadds Ford, Pa.

HEYWARD, Thomas, Jr., a Delegate from South Carolina; born on his father's plantation; settled in that part of St. Helena's Parish which later became St. Luke's Parish, South Carolina, July 28, 1746; pursued academic studies; studied law in the Middle Temple at London; returned to South Carolina in 1771; was admitted to the bar and established himself in the practice of law; member of the Commons House of Assembly of South Carolina in 1772; delegate to the provincial convention in 1774; member of the council of safety in 1775 and 1776; signer of the Declaration of Independence; member of the general assembly 1776–1778; Member of the Continental Congress 1776–1778; member of the State constitutional committee in 1776; served in the State house of representatives 1778–1784; served in the Revolutionary War as captain; taken prisoner at the capture of Charlestown May 12, 1780, and was a prisoner at St. Augustine one year; judge of the circuit court 1779–1789; founder and first president of the Agricultural Society of South Carolina in 1785; engaged in agricultural pursuits; member of the State constitutional convention in 1790; died on his plantation, "White Hall," in St. Luke's Parish, South Carolina, March 6, 1809; interment in the family burial ground on his father's plantation, "Old House."

HIBBARD, Ellery Albee (cousin of Harry Hibbard), a Representative from New Hampshire; born in St. Johnsbury, Caledonia County, Vt., July 31, 1826; pursued academic studies; studied law in Haverhill and Exeter, N. H.; was admitted to the bar in 1849 and practiced in Plymouth, N. H., until 1853, and subsequently in Laconia; clerk of the State house of representatives 1852–1854; moderator of Laconia in 1862 and 1863; member of the State house of representatives in 1865 and 1866; elected as a Democrat to the Forty-second Congress (March 4, 1871–March 3, 1873); unsuccessful candidate for reelection in 1872 to the Forty-third Congress; appointed judge of the supreme court of New Hampshire in March 1873 and served until 1874, when he resigned and continued the practice of law; director of the Laconia National Bank; member of board of education of Laconia; declined a reappointment under the revised judiciary system; died in Laconia, N. H., July 24, 1903; interment in Union Cemetery.

HIBBARD, Harry (cousin of Ellery Albee Hibbard), a Representative from New Hampshire; born in Concord, Essex County, Vt., June 1, 1816; pursued classical studies, and was graduated from Dartmouth College, Hanover, N. H., in 1835; studied law; was admitted to the bar in 1838 and commenced practice in Bath, Grafton County, N. H.; assistant clerk and clerk of the State house of representatives 1840–1842; member of the State house of representatives 1843–1845 and speaker in 1844 and 1845; served in the State senate in 1845, 1847, and 1848 and as president of that body in 1847 and 1848; delegate to the Democratic National Conventions in 1848 and 1856; elected as a Democrat to the Thirty-first, Thirty-second, and Thirty-third Congresses (March 4, 1849–March 3, 1855); was not a candidate for renomination in 1854; declined an appointment to the State supreme court; died in a sanatorium in Sommerville, Mass., on July 28, 1872; interment in the Village Cemetery, Bath, N. H.

HIBSHMAN, Jacob, a Representative from Pennsylvania; born on a farm near Ephrata, Lancaster County, Pa., January 31, 1772; attended the common schools and a private school in Harrisburg, Pa.; engaged in agricultural pursuits; associate judge of Lancaster County 1810–1819; elected as a Republican to the Sixteenth Congress (March 4, 1819–March 3, 1821); unsuccessful candidate for reelection in 1820 to the Seventeenth Congress; deputy surveyor of Lancaster County for twenty years; justice of the peace under the old constitution, and after the adoption of the new constitution was continued in office by the suffrage of the people; chairman of the board of canal appraisers; major general of Pennsylvania Militia for twelve years; organized the Northern Mutual Insurance Co., in 1844 and served as its first president; died at his residence near Ephrata, Pa., May 19, 1852; interment in the Hibshman Cemetery on the farm near Ephrata, Pa.

HICKENLOOPER, Bourke Blakemore, a Senator from Iowa; born in Blockton, Taylor County, Iowa, July 21, 1896; attended the public schools at Blockton, Iowa, and Iowa State College at Ames until April 6, 1917, when he enrolled in the officer's training camp at Fort Snelling, Minn.; commissioned a second lieutenant and assigned to the Three Hundred and Thirty-ninth Field Artillery, Eighty-eighth Division; embarked overseas in August 1918 and served in France as battalion orientation officer with the Third Battalion, Three Hundred and Thirty-ninth Field Artillery; returned to the United States in February 1919 and was honorably discharged in March 1919; reentered Iowa State College and was graduated in June 1919; was also graduated from the College of Law of the State University of Iowa at Iowa City in 1922; was admitted to the bar in 1922 and commenced practice in Cedar Rapids, Iowa; member of the State house of representatives 1934–1937; Lieutenant Governor of Iowa 1939–1942 and Governor in 1943 and 1944; elected as a Republican to the United States Senate in 1944 for the term commencing January 3, 1945; reelected in 1950 and again in 1956 for the term ending January 3, 1963.

HICKEY, Andrew James, a Representative from Indiana; born in Albion, Orleans County, N. Y., August 27, 1872; attended the grade and high schools of his native city and Buffalo

(N. Y.) Law School; was admitted to the New York bar in 1896 and commenced practice in La Porte, Ind., in 1897; member of the Indiana State and La Porte County Bar Associations; elected as a Republican to the Sixty-sixth and to the five succeeding Congresses (March 4, 1919–March 3, 1931); unsuccessful candidate for reelection in 1930 to the Seventy-second Congress, for election in 1934 to the Seventy-fourth Congress, and in 1936 to the Seventy-fifth Congress; resumed the practice of law; died in Buffalo, Erie County, N. Y., August 20, 1942, while on a motor trip; interment in Pine Lake Cemetery, La Porte, Ind.

HICKMAN, John, a Representative from Pennsylvania; born in West Bradford Township, Chester County, Pa., September 11, 1810; pursued English and classical studies under private tutors; began the study of medicine but abandoned it for the study of law; was admitted to the bar in 1833 and commenced practice in West Chester; delegate to the Democratic convention at Baltimore in 1844; district attorney for Chester County in 1845 and 1846; elected as a Democrat to the Thirty-fourth and Thirty-fifth Congresses, as a Douglas Democrat to the Thirty-sixth Congress, and as a Republican to the Thirty-seventh Congress (March 4, 1855–March 3, 1863); declined to be a candidate for renomination in 1862; one of the managers appointed by the House of Representatives in 1862 to conduct the impeachment proceedings against West H. Humphreys, United States judge for the several districts of Tennessee; resumed the practice of law; member of the State house of representatives in 1869; died in West Chester, Pa., March 23, 1875; interment in Oaklands Cemetery, near West Chester, Pa.

HICKS, Frederick Cocks (original name, Frederick Hicks Cocks, brother of William Willets Cocks), a Representative from New York; born in Westburg, Long Island, N. Y., March 6, 1872; attended the public schools, Swarthmore (Pa.) College, and Harvard University; engaged in banking; unsuccessful candidate for election in 1912 to the Sixty-third Congress; elected as a Republican to the Sixty-fourth and to the three succeeding Congresses (March 4, 1915–March 3, 1923); was not a candidate for renomination in 1922; declined a diplomatic position to Uruguay, tendered by President Harding; was eastern director of the Republican National Committee campaign in 1924; appointed by President Coolidge, as a member of the commission to represent the United States at the celebration of the Centennial of the Battle of Aracucho, held at Lima, Peru, during December 1924; appointed Alien Property Custodian April 10, 1925, and served until his death in Washington, D. C., December 14, 1925; interment in Quaker Cemetery, Westbury, Long Island, N. Y.

HICKS, Josiah Duane, a Representative from Pennsylvania; born in Machen, Wales, August 1, 1844; immigrated to the United States with his parents, who settled in Chester County, Pa., in 1847, and in the same year moved to Duncansville, Pa.; attended the common schools of Blair and Huntingdon Counties; moved to Altoona, Pa., in 1861; during the Civil War enlisted in the One Hundred and Twenty-fifth Regiment, Pennsylvania Volunteer Infantry, as a private in 1862 and served nearly eighteen months; reentered civil life as a clerk on the Pennsylvania Railroad; studied law; was admitted to the bar in 1875 and commenced practice in Tyrone, Pa.; elected district attorney of Blair County in 1880; reelected in 1883; elected as a Republican to the Fifty-third, Fifty-fourth, and Fifty-fifth Congresses (March 4, 1893–March 3, 1899); was not a candidate for renomination in 1898; resumed the practice of law; member of the Altoona Board of Education 1911–1919; State commander of the Grand Army of the Republic in 1921; died in Altoona, Pa., May 9, 1923; interment in Fairview Cemetery.

HICKS, Thomas Holliday, a Senator from Maryland; born near East New Market, Dorchester County, Md., September 2, 1798; attended the local subscription schools; sheriff of Dorchester County in 1824; member of the State electoral college in 1836 and while a member of the college was elected to the State house of delegates in 1836; member of the Governor's council in 1837; register of wills of Dorchester County 1838–1851; member of the Maryland constitutional convention in 1851; again appointed register of wills 1855–1861; Governor of Maryland in 1862; declined the appointment by President Lincoln as brigadier general in July 1862; took a firm stand against secession; appointed and subsequently elected as a Republican to the United States Senate to fill the vacancy caused by the death of James A. Pearce and served from December 29, 1862, until his death in Washington, D. C., February 14, 1865; interment in the Cambridge Cemetery, Cambridge, Md.

HIESTAND, Edgar Willard, a Representative from California; born in Chicago, Ill., December 3, 1888; attended the public schools; was graduated from Dartmouth College in 1910; during the First World War served as a civilian executive with Committee on Education and Special Training, War Plans Division, Army General Staff, in 1917 and 1918; director and president of Better Business Bureau; member and president of board of education, San Marino, Calif.; engaged in merchandising as a career, starting at the bottom as stock clerk and rising to manager of several of the Nation's leading department stores 1912–1931; executive of a large mail-order house 1931–1949; elected as a Republican to the Eighty-third and to the three succeeding Congresses (January 3, 1953–January 3, 1961). *Reelected to the Eighty-seventh Congress.*

HIESTAND, John Andrew, a Representative from Pennsylvania; born in East Donegal Township, Lancaster County, Pa., October 2, 1824; attended the common schools and an academy in Marietta, Pa., and Pennsylvania College at Gettysburg; studied law; was admitted to the bar in 1849 and commenced practice in Lancaster, Pa.; elected as a Whig to the State house of representatives in 1852, 1853, and 1856; purchased an interest in the Lancaster Examiner printing establishment in 1858 and relinquished the practice of law; served in the State senate in 1860; presidential elector on the Republican ticket of Lincoln and Johnson in 1864 and selected as the messenger to carry the electoral vote of the State to Washington, D. C.; unsuccessful candidate in 1868 to Congress to fill the unexpired term of Thaddeus Stevens; appointed by President Grant in 1871 naval officer at the port of Philadelphia; reappointed in 1875 and served until 1879; elected as a Republican to the Forty-ninth and Fiftieth Congresses (March 4, 1885–March 3, 1889); unsuccessful candidate for reelection in 1888 to the Fifty-first Congress; died in Lancaster, Pa., December 13, 1890; interment in Marietta Cemetery, Marietta, Pa.

HIESTER, Daniel (brother of John Hiester, cousin of Joseph Hiester, and uncle of William Hiester), a Representative from Pennsylvania and from Maryland; born in Berks County, Pa., June 25, 1747; attended the public schools; engaged in business in Montgomery County; colonel and brigadier general of militia and served in the Revolutionary War; member of the supreme executive council of Pennsylvania 1784–1786; commissioner of the Connecticut land claims in 1787; elected from Pennsylvania to the First and to the three succeeding Congresses and served from March 4, 1789, to July 1, 1796, when he resigned and moved to Hagerstown, Md.; elected from Maryland to the Seventh and Eighth Congresses and served from March 4, 1801, until his death in Washington, D. C., March 7, 1804; interment in Zion Reformed Graveyard, Hagerstown, Md.

HIESTER, Daniel (son of John Hiester and nephew of the preceding), a Representative from Pennsylvania; born in Chester County, Pa., in 1774; prothonotary and clerk of the courts of Chester County 1800–1809; elected to the Eleventh Congress (March 4, 1809–March 3, 1811); was instrumental in establishing the Bank of Chester County and was its first cashier 1814–1817; burgess of West Chester 1815–1817; appointed register of wills and recorder of deeds February 28, 1821; died in Hagerstown, Md., March 8, 1834; interment in Congressional Cemetery, Washington, D. C.

HIESTER, Isaac Ellmaker (son of William Hiester and cousin of Hiester Clymer), a Representative from Pennsylvania; born in New Holland, Earl Township, Lancaster County, Pa., May 29, 1824; pursued classical studies; was graduated from Yale College in 1842; studied law; was admitted to the bar in 1845 and commenced practice in Lancaster; district attorney for Lancaster County 1848–1851; elected as a Whig to the Thirty-third Congress (March 4, 1853–March 3, 1855); unsuccessful candidate for reelection in 1854 to the Thirty-fourth Congress and for election in 1856 to the Thirty-fifth Congress; resumed the practice of law; delegate to the Democratic National Convention at New York in 1868; died in Lancaster, Pa., February 6, 1871; interment in Lancaster Cemetery.

HIESTER, John (brother of Daniel Hiester, cousin of Joseph Hiester, and uncle of William Hiester), a Representative from Pennsylvania; born in Goshenhoppen, Montgomery (formerly Philadelphia) County, Pa., April 9, 1745; attended the common schools; engaged with his father in the lumbering business in Berne Township, Berks County, Pa.; served in the Revolutionary War as captain in the Pennsylvania Militia; elected to the Tenth Congress (March 4, 1807–March 3, 1809); died in Goshenhoppen, Pa., October 15, 1821; interment in Union Church Cemetery, Parker Ford, Pa.

HIESTER, Joseph (cousin of John Hiester and Daniel Hiester and grandfather of Henry Augustus Muhlenberg), a Representative from Pennsylvania; born in Berne Township, Berks County, Pa., November 18, 1752; attended the common schools; engaged in mercantile pursuits; served in the Revolutionary Army as captain and colonel; taken prisoner and confined on the prison ship *Jersey*; member of the State conference in 1776 which assumed the government of the colony; member of the State constitutional convention which ratified the Federal Constitution December 12, 1787, and of the State constitutional convention of 1790; member of the State house of representatives 1787–1790; served in the State senate 1790–1794; elected as a Federalist to the Fifth Congress to fill the vacancy caused by the resignation of George Ege; reelected to the Sixth, Seventh, and Eighth Congresses and served from December 1, 1797, to March 3, 1805; major general of Pennsylvania Militia in 1807; elected to the Fourteenth, Fifteenth, and Sixteenth Congresses and served from March 4, 1815, until his resignation in December 1820, having been elected chief executive of the State; Governor of Pennsylvania 1820–1824; retired from public life; died in Reading, Pa., June 10, 1832; interment in the burying ground of the Reformed Church; reinterment in Charles Evans Cemetery.

HIESTER, William (father of Isaac Ellmaker Hiester, uncle of Hiester Clymer, and nephew of John Hiester and Daniel Hiester), a Representative from Pennsylvania; born in Berne Township, near Reading, Berks County, Pa., October 10, 1790; attended the common schools; served as a lieutenant during the War of 1812; engaged in agricultural and mercantile pursuits in Lancaster County; justice of the peace 1823–1828; was an un-successful Anti-Masonic candidate for reelection to the Twenty-first Congress; elected as a Whig to the Twenty-second, Twenty-third, and Twenty-fourth Congresses (March 4, 1831–March 3, 1837); delegate to the State constitutional convention in 1837; member of the State senate 1840–1842 and served as speaker in 1842; retired from public life; died in New Holland, Lancaster County, Pa., on October 13, 1853; interment in Lancaster Cemetery, Lancaster, Pa.

HIGBY, William, a Representative from California; born in Willsboro, N. Y., on August 18, 1813; attended a preparatory school in Westport, N. Y., and was graduated from the University of Vermont at Burlington in 1840; studied law; was admitted to the bar in 1847 and commenced practice in Elizabethtown, N. Y.; moved to California in 1850 and settled in Calaveras County; resumed the practice of law; district attorney 1853–1859; served in the State senate in 1862 and 1863; elected as a Republican to the Thirty-eighth, Thirty-ninth, and Fortieth Congresses (March 4, 1863–March 3, 1869); unsuccessful candidate for renomination in 1868; editor of the Calaveras Chronicle for several years; was collector of internal revenue 1877–1881; devoted himself to horticulture until his death; died in Santa Rosa, Calif., November 27, 1887; interment in Mountain View Cemetery, Oakland, Calif.

HIGGINS, Anthony, a Senator from Delaware; born in Red Lion Hundred, New Castle County, Del., October 1, 1840; attended Newark Academy and Delaware College, and was graduated from Yale College in 1861; studied law at the Harvard Law School; was admitted to the bar in 1864 and commenced practice in Wilmington, Del.; served in Company B, Seventh Regiment, Delaware State Militia, from July 11 to August 12, 1864; appointed deputy attorney general in September 1864; United States attorney for Delaware from May 1869 until 1876; unsuccessful Republican candidate for election to the Forty-ninth Congress in 1884; elected as a Republican to the United States Senate and served from March 4, 1889, to March 3, 1895; was a candidate for reelection in 1894 but owing to a deadlock in the State legislature was unsuccessful; resumed the practice of his profession in Wilmington, Del.; delegate to the Republican National Convention at St. Louis in 1896; served as one of the attorneys for the respondent in the impeachment proceedings of United States District Judge Charles Swayne, of Florida, in 1904 and 1905; died in New York City on June 26, 1912; interment in St. Georges Cemetery, near St. Georges, New Castle County, Del.

HIGGINS, Edwin Werter, a Representative from Connecticut; born in Clinton, Middlesex County, Conn., July 2, 1874; attended Norwich Free Academy; was graduated from Yale Law School in 1897; was admitted to the bar in 1897 and commenced practice in Norwich, Conn.; member of the State house of representatives in 1899 and 1900; member of the Republican State central committee 1900–1905; health officer of New London County 1900–1905; corporation counsel of Norwich 1901, 1902, and 1919–1922; prosecuting attorney of Norwich in 1905; delegate to the Republican National Conventions in 1904 and 1916; elected as a Republican to the Fifty-ninth Congress to fill the vacancy caused by the resignation of Frank B. Brandegee; reelected to the Sixtieth, Sixty-first, and Sixty-second Congresses and served from October 2, 1905, to March 3, 1913; was not a candidate for renomination in 1912; resumed the practice of law; served in the Connecticut State National Guard during the First World War; prosecuting attorney, Court of Common Pleas, New London County, Conn., 1932–1946; resumed the general practice of law; died in Norwich, Conn., September 24, 1954; interment in Maplewood Cemetery.

HIGGINS, John Patrick, a Representative from Massachusetts; born in Boston, Mass., February 19, 1893; attended the public schools and was graduated from Harvard University, Cambridge, Mass., in 1917; during the First World War served as an ensign in the United States Navy 1917–1919; employed as a chemist 1919–1922; student in Boston University Law School and Northeastern College of Law, Boston, Mass., in 1925 and 1926; was admitted to the bar in 1927 and commenced practice in Boston; member of the State house of representatives 1929–1934; elected as a Democrat to the Seventy-fourth and Seventy-fifth Congresses and served from January 3, 1935, until his resignation on September 30, 1937, having been appointed by Gov. Charles F. Hurley on October 1, 1937, as chief justice of the superior court of Massachusetts, in which capacity he served until his death; suspended his bench career in February 1945 to accept appointment by Gen. Douglas MacArthur as a judge on the International Military Tribunal for the Far East at Tokyo, Japan, and resigned in June 1946; died in Boston, Mass., August 2, 1955; interment in St. Joseph Cemetery, West Roxbury, Mass.

HIGGINS, William Lincoln, a Representative from Connecticut; born in Chesterfield, Hampshire County, Mass., March 8, 1867; attended the public schools of Chesterfield and Northampton, Mass., and Deerfield (Mass.) Academy; was graduated from the medical department of the University of the City of New York in 1890 and commenced the practice of medicine in Willington, Conn., the same year; moved to South Coventry, Conn., in 1891; served in the State house of Representatives 1905–1907, 1917, 1919–1921, 1925, and 1927; member of the State senate 1909–1911; first selectman of Coventry, Conn., 1917–1932; county commissioner of Tolland County, Conn., 1921–1932; secretary of state 1928–1932; delegate to the Republican National Conventions in 1928, 1932, and 1936; elected as a Republican to the Seventy-third and Seventy-fourth Congresses (March 4, 1933–January 3, 1937); unsuccessful candidate for reelection in 1936 to the Seventy-fifth Congress; resumed the practice of medicine in South Coventry, Conn.; died in Norwich, Conn., November 19, 1951; remains were cremated and interred in Chesterfield Center Cemetery, Chesterfield, Mass.

HIGGINSON, Stephen, a Delegate from Massachusetts; born in Salem, Mass., November 28, 1743; attended the common schools; engaged in mercantile pursuits and was an active and successful shipmaster 1765–1775; Member of the Continental Congress in 1782 and 1783; naval officer at the port of Boston 1797–1808; was a Federalist in politics and a supporter of the administrations of Washington and Adams; prominent in putting down Shays' Rebellion; served as lieutenant colonel of the Boston regiment; died in Boston, Mass., November 22, 1828; interment in Central Burying Ground.

HILBORN, Samuel Greeley, a Representative from California; born in Minot, Androscoggin (then Cumberland) County, Maine, December 9, 1834; attended the common schools, Hebron Academy, and Gould's Academy, Bethel, Maine, and was graduated from Tufts College, Medford, Mass., in 1859; studied law and was admitted to the bar in 1861; moved to California; located in Vallejo, Solano County, and engaged in the practice of law; served in the State senate 1875–1879; member of the constitutional convention in 1879; moved to San Francisco, Calif., in 1883; appointed by President Arthur United States district attorney for the district of California and served from 1883 to 1886; moved to Oakland in 1887 and continued the practice of his profession; elected as a Republican to the Fifty-second Congress to fill the vacancy caused by the resignation of Joseph McKenna; presented credentials as a Member-elect to the Fifty-third Congress and served from December 5, 1892, until April 4, 1894, when he was succeeded by Warren B. English, who contested his election; elected to the Fifty-fourth and Fifty-fifth Congresses (March 4, 1895–March 3, 1899); unsuccessful candidate for renomination in 1898; lived in retirement until his death in Washington, D. C., April 19, 1899; interment in Rock Creek Cemetery.

HILDEBRANDT, Fred Herman, a Representative from South Dakota; born in West Bend, Washington County, Wis., August 2, 1874; moved with his parents to Waupun, Wis., in 1888, where he attended the public and high schools; subsequently moved to Watertown, S. Dak., in 1900 and was employed as a railroad freight brakeman 1903–1906, as a freight conductor 1906–1911, and as a passenger conductor 1911–1932; member of the State house of representatives in 1922 and 1923; served as chairman of the South Dakota Game and Fish Commission 1927–1931; elected as a Democrat to the Seventy-third, Seventy-fourth, and Seventy-fifth Congresses (March 4, 1933–January 3, 1939); was not a candidate for renomination in 1938, but was an unsuccessful candidate for the Democratic nomination for United States Senator; unsuccessful candidate for election in 1942 to the Seventy-eighth Congress; delegate to the Democratic National Convention at Chicago in 1944; retired from active business life and resided in Watertown, S. Dak.; died in Bradenton, Fla., January 26, 1956; interment in Mount Hope Cemetery, Watertown, S. Dak.

HILDEBRANT, Charles Quinn, a Representative from Ohio; born in Wilmington, Clinton County, Ohio, October 17, 1864; attended the public schools and Ohio State University at Columbus; clerk of the court of Clinton County in 1890 and reelected in 1893 and 1896; elected as a Republican to the Fifty-seventh and Fifty-eighth Congresses (March 4, 1901–March 3, 1905); unsuccessful candidate for reelection in 1904 to the Fifty-ninth Congress; resumed his business and agricultural pursuits; delegate to the Republican National Convention at Chicago in 1908 which nominated Taft and Sherman; secretary of state of Ohio 1915–1917; mayor of Wilmington, Ohio, from November 1927 until his retirement December 31, 1941; died in Wilmington, Ohio, March 31, 1953; interment in Sugar Grove Cemetery.

HILL, Benjamin Harvey (cousin of Hugh Lawson White Hill), a Representative and a Senator from Georgia; born in Hillsborough, Jasper County, Ga., September 14, 1823; pursued classical studies, and was graduated from the University of Georgia at Athens in 1844; studied law; was admitted to the bar in 1845 and commenced practice in Lagrange, Troup County, Ga.; member of the State house of representatives in 1851; served in the State senate in 1859 and 1860; nominated as a presidential elector on the American Party ticket of Fillmore and Donelson in 1856 and on the Constitutional Union ticket of Bell and Everett in 1860; delegate to the State convention in 1861 and advocated the Union until the secession ordinance had been adopted; delegate to the Confederate Provisional Congress in 1861; Senator in the Confederate Congress 1861–1865; resumed the practice of law; elected as a Democrat to the Forty-fourth Congress to fill the vacancy caused by the death of Representative-elect Garnett McMillan; reelected to the Forty-fifth Congress and served from May 5, 1875, until his resignation, effective March 3, 1877; elected to the United States Senate and served from March 4, 1877, until his death in Atlanta, Ga., August 16, 1882; interment in Oakland Cemetery.

HILL, Charles Augustus, a Representative from Illinois; born in Truxton, Cortland County, N. Y., August 23, 1833; attended the common schools and a select school at Griffins Mills; in 1853 taught school in Hamburg, Erie County, N. Y., and in the spring of 1854 moved to Will County, Ill., and taught school for two years; attended Bell's Commercial College, Chicago, in 1856; studied law; was admitted to the bar in Indianapolis, Ind.; returned to Will County, Ill., in 1860 and practiced; during the Civil War enlisted in Company F, Eighth Regiment, Illinois Volunteer Cavalry, in August 1862; appointed first lieutenant in the First Regiment, United States Colored Troops; commissioned in 1865 captain of Company C of that regiment; after the war served for some time on detached duty as a member of a court martial sitting in New Bern, N. C.; commanded a separate post at Elizabeth City, N. C., and mustered out September 29, 1865; returned to Will County, Ill., in 1865 and resumed the practice of law in Joliet; elected prosecuting attorney in 1868 for the counties of Will and Grundy and served four years; declined a renomination; elected as a Republican to the Fifty-first Congress (March 4, 1889–March 3, 1891); unsuccessful candidate for reelection in 1890 to the Fifty-second Congress; resumed the practice of law in Joliet, Ill.; assistant attorney general of Illinois 1897–1900; died in Joliet, Ill., May 29, 1902; interment in Oakwood Cemetery.

HILL, Clement Sidney, a Representative from Kentucky; born near Lebanon, Marion County, Ky., February 13, 1813; pursued academic studies; attended St. Mary's College, St. Mary, Ky.; studied law; was admitted to the bar in 1837 and commenced practice in Lebanon, Ky.; member of the State house of representatives in 1839; elected as an Independent Democrat to the Thirty-third Congress (March 4, 1853–March 3, 1855); resumed the practice of law in Lebanon, Ky., where he died January 5, 1892; interment in St. Augustine's Cemetery.

HILL, David Bennett, a Senator from New York; born in Havana (now Montour Falls), Chemung (now Schuyler) County, N. Y., August 29, 1843; attended the public schools and was graduated from Havana Academy; studied law; was admitted to the bar in 1864 and commenced practice in Elmira, N. Y.; city attorney the same year; member of the State assembly in 1871 and 1872; president of the Democratic State conventions in 1877 and 1881; mayor of Elmira in 1882; delegate to the Democratic National Conventions in 1884, 1896, 1900, and 1904; president of the New York State Bar Association in 1886 and 1887; chosen Lieutenant Governor of the State in November 1882; became Governor upon the resignation of Grover Cleveland in January 1885; elected Governor in November 1885; reelected in 1888 and served until January 1892; elected as a Democrat to the United States Senate on January 1, 1891, for the term beginning March 4, 1891, but did not assume these duties until later, preferring to continue as Governor, and served from January 7, 1892, to March 3, 1897; was not a candidate for reelection in 1896; while Senator was nominated for Governor of New York in 1894 but was defeated; resumed the practice of law; died in Albany, N. Y., October 20, 1910; interment in Montour Cemetery, Montour Falls, N. Y.

HILL, Ebenezer J., a Representative from Connecticut; born in Redding, Fairfield County, Conn., August 4, 1845; attended the public schools, Center Academy, and Yale College in 1865 and 1866; during the Civil War enlisted in the Union Army in 1863 and served until the close of the war; engaged in business and banking in Norwalk; burgess of Norwalk; chairman of the board of school visitors; delegate to the Republican National Convention at Chicago in 1884; member of the State senate in 1886 and 1887; served one term on the Republican State central committee; elected as a Republican to the Fifty-fourth and to the eight succeeding Congresses (March 4, 1895–March 3, 1913); unsuccessful candidate in 1912 for reelection to the Sixty-third Congress; elected to the Sixty-

fourth and Sixty-fifth Congresses and served from March 4, 1915, until his death in Norwalk, Conn., September 27, 1917; interment in Riverside Cemetery.

HILL, Hugh Lawson White (cousin of Benjamin Harvey Hill), a Representative from Tennessee; born near McMinnville, Warren County, Tenn., March 1, 1810; attended private schools and the Carroll Male Academy at McMinnville; was graduated from Cumberland College, Nashville, Tenn.; taught school for a short time; engaged in agricultural pursuits and fruit growing; member of the State house of representatives 1837–1839 and in 1841; elected as a Democrat to the Thirtieth Congress (March 4, 1847–March 3, 1849); was not a candidate for renomination in 1848; resumed agricultural pursuits; member of the State constitutional convention in 1870; died at Hills Creek, Warren County, Tenn., January 18, 1892; interment in Hill Graveyard, near McMinnville, Tenn.

HILL, Isaac, a Senator from New Hampshire; born in West Cambridge, near Arlington, Mass., on April 6, 1788; attended the common schools; moved with his parents to Ashburnham, Mass., in 1798; apprenticed to a printer in Amherst, N. H.; moved to Concord in 1809; purchased and for twenty years edited the New Hampshire Patriot; served in the State senate 1820–1822 and in 1827; member of the State house of representatives in 1826; Second Comptroller of the United States Treasury in 1829 and 1830; elected as a Democrat to the United States Senate and served from March 4, 1831, to May 30, 1836, when he resigned; Governor of New Hampshire 1836–1839; United States subtreasurer at Boston in 1840 and 1841; returned to newspaper publishing 1840–1847; died in Washington, D. C., March 22, 1851; interment in Blossom Hill Cemetery, Concord, N. H.

HILL, John, a Representative from North Carolina; born near Germanton, Stokes County, N. C., April 9, 1797; completed preparatory studies, and was graduated from the University of North Carolina at Chapel Hill in 1816; was a planter; clerk of court of Stokes County for thirty years; member of the State house of commons 1819–1823; served in the State senate 1823–1825, 1830, and 1831; elected as a Democrat to the Twenty-sixth Congress (March 4, 1839–March 3, 1841); reading clerk in the State senate in 1850; delegate to the State constitutional convention at Raleigh, N. C., in 1861; died in Raleigh, N. C., April 24, 1861; interment in Old Hill Burying Ground, near Germanton, N. C.

HILL, John (cousin of John Thomas Harris), a Representative from Virginia; born in New Canton, Buckingham County, Va., July 18, 1800; completed preparatory studies and was graduated from Washington Academy (now Washington and Lee University), Lexington, Va., in 1818; studied law; was admitted to the bar in 1821 and practiced; elected as a Whig to the Twenty-sixth Congress (March 4, 1839–March 3, 1841); unsuccessful candidate for reelection in 1840 to the Twenty-seventh Congress; resumed the practice of law: member of the Virginia constitutional convention 1850–1851; Commonwealth attorney for several years; county judge of Buckingham County 1870–1879; died at Buckingham Court House, Va., April 19, 1880; interment in the Presbyterian Cemetery.

HILL, John, a Representative from New Jersey; born in Catskill, Greene County, N. Y., June 10, 1821; attended private schools; employed as a bank clerk and learned bookkeeping in Catskill, N. Y.; moved to Boonton, N. H., in 1845; was employed as a bookkeeper and paymaster, and later engaged in mercantile pursuits; served as postmaster from November 1849 to May 1853; member of the township committee 1852–1856 and 1863–1867;

justice of the peace 1856–1861; member of the State house of assembly in 1861, 1862, and 1866, serving as speaker during the last year; unsuccessful candidate for election to the State senate in 1862; took an active part in raising troops during the Civil War; elected as a Republican to the Fortieth, Forty-first, and Forty-second Congresses (March 4, 1867–March 3, 1873); resumed mercantile pursuits until 1876, when he retired; delegate to the Republican National Convention at Chicago in 1868; member of the State senate 1875–1877; elected as a Republican to the Forty-seventh Congress (March 4, 1881–March 3, 1883); was not a candidate for renomination in 1882; died in Boonton, N. J., July 24, 1884; interment in Boonton Cemetery.

HILL, John Boynton Philip Clayton, a Representative from Maryland; born in Annapolis, Anne Arundel County, Md., May 2, 1879; attended the common schools; was graduated from Johns Hopkins University in 1900 and from the law department of Harvard University in 1903; was admitted to the bar the same year and commenced practice in Boston, Mass.; returned to Baltimore, Md., in 1904 and continued the practice of law; enlisted in the National Guard in 1904; served as lieutenant and captain of the Fourth Maryland Infantry 1905–1910 and as major 1910–1918; unsuccessful candidate for election to the Sixty-first Congress in 1908; United States attorney for the district of Maryland 1910–1915; military observer Eleventh German Army Corps maneuvers in 1911; observer with the Tenth Cavalry, Connecticut maneuvers, in 1912; unsuccessful candidate for mayor of Baltimore in 1915; delegate to the Republican National Convention at Chicago in 1916; judge advocate for the Fifteenth Division, and attached to the Fourteenth Cavalry, Mexican border service, from August 26 to December 15, 1916; during the First World War was major and lieutenant colonel in the United States Army in 1918 and 1919; judge advocate and acting division inspector of the Twenty-ninth Division, American Expeditionary Forces; judge advocate and assistant, G–3, General Staff, Eighth Army Corps, American Expeditionary Forces, until its dissolution; liaison officer to Fifth United States Corps during the Meuse-Argonne offensive and to Seventeenth French Army Corps during offensive north of Verdun in October 1918; promoted to lieutenant colonel October 22, 1918; received a Distinguished Service Medal, Mexican Border Service Medal, and Victory Medal from the United States Government, Croix de Guerre and Legion of Honor from the Republic of France, and the Medal de la Solidaridad of Panama; recommended for the Distinguished Service Cross; member of the American Battle Monuments Commission; was honorably discharged from the Army May 9, 1919; elected as a Republican to the Sixty-seventh, Sixty-eighth, and Sixty-ninth Congresses (March 4, 1921–March 3, 1927); unsuccessful candidate for the Senate in 1926; unsuccessful candidate for election in 1928 to the Seventy-first Congress and in 1936 to the Seventy-fifth Congress; moved to New York City in 1937 and continued the practice of law; returned in 1940 to Annapolis, Md.; died in Washington, D. C., May 23, 1941; interment in Arlington National Cemetery, Fort Myer, Va.

HILL, Joshua, a Representative and a Senator from Georgia; born in Abbeville District, S. C., January 10, 1812; attended the common schools; studied law; was admitted to the bar and commenced practice in Monticello, Jasper County, Ga.; delegate to the Whig National Convention at Baltimore in 1844; elected by the American Party to the Thirty-fifth and Thirty-sixth Congresses and served from March 4, 1857, to January 23, 1861, when he resigned; unsuccessful candidate for Governor in 1863; appointed collector of customs at Savannah in 1866 and register in bankruptcy in 1867 but declined both offices; upon the readmission of the State of Georgia to representation was

elected as a Union Republican to the United States Senate on July 28, 1868; qualified on February 1, 1871, and served until March 3, 1873; was not a candidate for reelection; returned to Madison, Ga., and resumed the practice of law; member of the State constitutional convention in 1877; died in Madison, Ga., March 6, 1891; interment in Madison Cemetery.

HILL, Knute, a Representative from Washington; born on a farm near Creston, Ogle County, Ill., July 31, 1876; moved to De Forest, Wis., in 1877 and to Red Wing, Minn., in 1889; attended the public schools, Red Wing (Minn.) Seminary, and the University of Minnesota at Minneapolis; was graduated from the law department of the University of Wisconsin at Madison in 1906; was admitted to the bar the same year and practiced law in Milwaukee and Eau Claire, Wis., 1908–1910; moved to Prosser, Wash., in 1911 and taught in the public and high schools of Benton County, Wash., 1911–1922; lecturer, State Grange, 1922–1932; also engaged in agricultural pursuits; member of the State house of representatives 1927–1933; elected as a Democrat to the Seventy-third and to the four succeeding Congresses (March 4, 1933–January 3, 1943); unsuccessful candidate for reelection in 1942 to the Seventy-eighth Congress; superintendent of the Uintah-Ouray Indian agency at Fort Duchesne, Utah, from August 16, 1943, until his resignation on March 31, 1944; commentator for radio station KGA–KHQ in Spokane, Wash., 1944–1946; unsuccessful Independent Progressive candidate for election in 1946 to the Eightieth Congress; consulting appraiser and information clerk in the Bureau of Reclamation, Columbia Basin Project, Ephrata, Wash., from March 1949 until his retirement in 1951; is a resident of Ephrata, Wash.

HILL, Lister, a Representative and a Senator from Alabama; born in Montgomery, Ala., December 29, 1894; attended the public schools; was graduated from Starke University School at Montgomery, Ala., in 1911, from the literary department of the University of Alabama at Tuscaloosa in 1914, and from its law department in 1915; took special law courses at the University of Michigan at Ann Arbor in 1915 and at Columbia University, New York City, in 1916; was admitted to the Alabama bar in 1916 and commenced practice at Montgomery, Ala.; president of the Montgomery Board of Education 1917–1922; served in the Army with the Seventeenth and Seventy-first United States Infantry Regiments during the First World War 1917–1919; elected as a Democrat to the Sixty-eighth Congress to fill the vacancy caused by the death of John R. Tyson; reelected to the Sixty-ninth and to the six succeeding Congresses and served from August 14, 1923, to January 11, 1938, when he resigned, having been appointed to the United States Senate on January 10, 1938; was subsequently elected on April 26, 1938, to fill the vacancy caused by the resignations of Hugo L. Black and Mrs. Dixie Bibb Graves for the term ending January 3, 1939; reelected in 1938, 1944, 1950, and again in 1956 for the term ending January 3, 1963.

HILL, Mark Langdon, a Representative from Massachusetts and from Maine; born in Biddeford, York County, Maine (then a district of Massachusetts), June 30, 1772; attended the public schools; merchant and shipbuilder at Phippsburg, Maine; overseer and trustee of Bowdoin College, Brunswick, Maine, 1796–1842; member of the State house of representatives 1797–1808, 1810, 1813, and 1814; served in the State senate in 1804 and 1815–1817; judge of the court of common pleas in 1810; served on the General Court of Massachusetts; elected from Massachusetts to the Sixteenth Congress (March 4, 1819–March 3, 1821); when Maine was separated from Massachusetts and admitted as a State into the Union was elected to the

Seventeenth Congress from that State (March 4, 1821–March 3, 1823); postmaster of Phippsburg, Maine, 1819–1824; appointed as a collector of customs at Bath, Maine, in 1824; died in Phippsburg, Sagadahoc County, November 26, 1842; interment in the churchyard of the Congregational Church, Phippsburg Center, Maine.

HILL, Nathaniel Peter, a Senator from Colorado; born in Montgomery, Orange County, N. Y., February 18, 1832; attended Montgomery Academy and was graduated from Brown University in Providence, R. I., in 1856; professor of chemistry in Brown University 1860–1864; visited Colorado in the spring of 1865 to investigate mineral resources of the "Gilpin grant"; spent a portion of 1865 and 1866 in Swansea, Wales, and Freiberg, Saxony, studying metallurgy; took up a permanent residence in Black Hawk, Colo., in 1867 as manager of the Boston & Colorado Smelting Co.; mayor of Black Hawk in 1871; member of the Territorial council in 1872 and 1873; moved to Denver, Colo., in 1873 and engaged in smelting and in the real-estate business; elected as a Republican to the United States Senate and served from March 4, 1879, to March 3, 1885; engaged in mining; owner and publisher of the Denver Republican; member of the commission appointed by President Benjamin Harrison in 1891 to consider the question of an international metal currency; died in Denver, Colo., on May 22, 1900; interment in Fairmount Cemetery.

HILL, Ralph, a Representative from Indiana; born in Trumbull County, Ohio, October 12, 1827; worked on a farm until he was sixteen years old, attending the district school in the winter; attended the Kinsman Academy and the Grand River Institute, Austinburg, Ohio; taught school in 1846, 1847, 1849, and 1850; studied law at the New York State and National Law School, Ballston, N. Y., and was admitted to the bar in Albany, N. Y., in 1851; returned to Jefferson, Ohio, in August 1851 and practiced; established a select school at Austinburg, Ohio, in November 1851; resumed the practice of law in Jefferson, Ohio, in March 1852; moved to Columbus, Ind., in August 1852 and continued the practice of law; elected as a Republican to the Thirty-ninth Congress (March 4, 1865–March 3, 1867); was not a candidate for renomination in 1866; collector of internal revenue for the third district of Indiana 1869–1875; moved to Indianapolis, Ind., in 1879 and resumed the practice of law; died in Indianapolis, Ind., August 20, 1899; interment in Crown Hill Cemetery.

HILL, Robert Potter, a Representative from Illinois and from Oklahoma; born near Ewing, Franklin County, Ill., April 18, 1874; attended the public schools, and Ewing College in 1889; taught school in Franklin County 1891–1893; reentered Ewing College and was graduated in 1896; moved to Marion, Williamson County, Ill., in 1896; justice of the peace in 1899; studied law; was admitted to the bar in 1902 and commenced practice in Marion; police magistrate of Marion in 1903; city attorney of Marion 1908–1910; member of the State house of representatives 1910–1912; elected as a Democrat from Illinois to the Sixty-third Congress (March 4, 1913–March 3, 1915); unsuccessful candidate for reelection in 1914 to the Sixty-fourth Congress; resumed the practice of law; moved to Oklahoma City, Okla., in 1918 and continued the practice of law; appointed assistant county attorney, Oklahoma County, in 1925 and served until 1929; served as district judge of the thirteenth judicial district from 1931 until his resignation on December 15, 1936, having been elected to Congress; elected as a Democrat from Oklahoma to the Seventy-fifth Congress and served from January 3, 1937, until his death in Oklahoma City, Okla., October 29, 1937; interment in Memorial Park Cemetery.

HILL, Samuel Billingsley, a Representative from Washington; born in Franklin, Izard County, Ark., April 2, 1875; attended the common schools, the University of Arkansas at Fayetteville, and was graduated from its law department in 1898; was admitted to the bar the same year and commenced practice in Danville, Ark.; moved to Waterville, Wash., in 1904 and continued the practice of law; prosecuting attorney of Douglas County 1907–1911; judge of the superior court for Douglas and Grant Counties 1917–1924; elected as a Democrat to the Sixty-eighth Congress to fill the vacancy caused by the resignation of J. Stanley Webster; reelected to the Sixty-ninth and to the five succeeding Congresses and served from September 25, 1923, until his resignation, effective June 25, 1936, having been confirmed as a member of the United States Board of Tax Appeals (now the Tax Court of the United States) on May 21, 1936, serving as a judge on the court until his retirement November 30, 1953; died in Bethesda, Md., March 16, 1958; interment in Rock Creek Cemetery, Washington, D. C.

HILL, Whitmel, a Delegate from North Carolina; born in Bertie County, N. C., February 12, 1743; attended the common schools, and was graduated from the University of Pennsylvania at Philadelphia in 1760; prominently connected with the early Revolutionary movements; served in the Revolutionary War, attaining the rank of colonel; engaged in agricultural pursuits; delegate to the assembly of freemen at Hillsboro in 1775; member of the State congress at Halifax in 1776; delegate to the State constitutional convention in 1776; member of the State house of commons in 1777; Member of the Continental Congress 1778–1781; served in the State senate 1778–1780, 1784, and 1785; died on his plantation at Hills Ferry, near Hamilton, Martin County, N. C., September 26, 1797; interment in the family cemetery on his estate; reinterment in 1887 in Trinity Cemetery, near Scotland Neck, N. C.

HILL, William David, a Representative from Ohio; born in Nelson County, Va., October 1, 1833; attended the country schools and Antioch College; moved to Springfield, Ohio, and published the Ohio Press in 1858; studied law; was admitted to the bar in 1859 and commenced practice in Springfield, Ohio; mayor of Springfield 1861–1863; member of the State house of representatives 1866–1870; member of the Board of Education of Defiance, Ohio; superintendent of insurance 1875–1878; delegate to the Democratic National Convention at Cincinnati, Ohio, in 1880, which nominated the presidential ticket of Hancock and English; elected as a Democrat to the Forty-sixth Congress (March 4, 1879–March 3, 1881); elected to the Forty-eighth and Forty-ninth Congresses (March 4, 1883–March 3, 1887); unsuccessful candidate for reelection in 1886 to the Fiftieth Congress; delegate to the Democratic National Convention at St. Louis in 1888 which nominated Grover Cleveland for a second term; resumed the practice of law in Defiance, Ohio; moved to Kalispell, Mont., in 1891; returned to Defiance in 1896 and continued the practice of law; city solicitor of Defiance 1903–1905; died near Litchfield, Ill., while en route to Los Angeles, Calif., December 26, 1906; interment in Riverside Cemetery, Defiance, Ohio.

HILL, William Henry, a Representative from North Carolina; born in Brunswick, Columbus County, N. C., on May 1, 1767; attended the public schools in Boston, Mass.; engaged in agricultural pursuits; studied law in Boston; was admitted to the bar and practiced; appointed United States district attorney for North Carolina by President Washington in 1790; member of the State senate in 1794; elected as a Federalist to the Sixth and Seventh Congresses (March 4, 1799–March 3, 1803); appointed judge of the United States District Court for the District of North Carolina by President John Adams at the close of his term but the designation was withdrawn by President Jefferson; returned to his estate near Wilmington, N. C., where he engaged in agricultural pursuits until his death there in 1809; interment in the family burial ground on his estate, "Hilton," near Wilmington, N. C.

HILL, William Henry, a Representative from New York; born in Plains, Luzerne County, Pa., March 23, 1877; attended the public schools; was graduated from the high school at Binghamton, N. Y.; mayor of Lestershire (now Johnson City), N. Y., 1898–1901; postmaster of Lestershire 1902–1910; editor and publisher of the Record at Johnson City 1898–1921; member of the State senate 1914–1918; elected as a Republican to the Sixty-sixth Congress (March 4, 1919–March 3, 1921); was not a candidate for renomination in 1920; delegate to the Republican National Conventions in 1924, 1928, 1932, 1940, and 1944; appointed as a member of the New York State Parks Commission by Governor Smith in 1925 and elected chairman in 1933; chairman of the New York Hoover-for-President Committee in 1928; vice chairman of the Republican Campaign Committee in the East in 1932; trustee of Syracuse University; member of the Republican executive committee of the State of New York; president and majority stockholder of Johnson City Publishing Co., Inc.; is a resident of Johnson City, N. Y.

HILL, William Luther, a Senator from Florida; born in Gainesville, Alachua County, Fla., October 17, 1873; attended private and public schools and the East Florida Seminary at Gainesville, Fla.; engaged in banking and insurance; was graduated from the law college of the University of Florida at Gainesville in 1914; was admitted to the bar the same year and commenced practice in Gainesville, Fla.; secretary to United States Senator Duncan U. Fletcher from May 1917 to June 1936, and also served as clerk to the Senate Committee on Commerce 1917–1921 and to the Senate Committee on Banking and Currency 1933–1936; appointed as a Democrat to the United States Senate to fill the vacancy caused by the death of Duncan U. Fletcher and served from July 1 to November 3, 1936, when a successor was elected; was not a candidate for election to fill this vacancy; resumed the practice of law until his retirement in 1947; died in Gainesville, Fla., January 5, 1951; interment in Evergreen Cemetery.

HILL, William Silas, a Representative from Colorado; born in Kelly, Nemaha County, Kans., January 20, 1886; attended the public schools, Kansas State Normal at Emporia, and Colorado State College of Agriculture at Fort Collins; homesteaded near Cheyenne Wells, Colo., 1907–1915; superintendent of Cache la Poudre Consolidated School of Larimer County, Colo., 1919–1922; secretary of the Colorado State Farm Bureau in 1923; served in the State house of representatives 1924–1926; engaged in the mercantile business at Fort Collins, Colo., 1927–1953; elected as a Republican to the Seventy-seventh and the eight succeeding Congresses (January 3, 1941–January 3, 1959); was not a candidate for renomination in 1958 to the Eighty-sixth Congress; retired; is a resident of Fort Collins, Colo.

HILL, Wilson Shedric, a Representative from Mississippi; born near Lodi, Choctaw County, Miss., January 19, 1863; attended the common schools and the University of Mississippi at Oxford; was graduated from the law department of Cumberland University, Lebanon, Tenn., in 1884; was admitted to the bar in 1884 and commenced practice in Winona, Miss.; member of the State house of representatives in 1885; district attorney for the fifth judicial district of Mississippi 1891–1903; member of the city council of Winona 1892–1894; elected as a Democrat to the Fifty-eighth, Fifty-ninth, and Sixtieth Congresses (March 4, 1903–March 3, 1909); unsuccessful candidate for renomination in 1908; resumed the practice of law in Greenwood, Miss.; delegate to the

Democratic National Convention at Baltimore in 1912; district attorney for the northern judicial district 1914–1921; died in Greenwood, Miss., February 14, 1921; interment in Oakwood Cemetery, Winona, Miss.

HILLELSON, Jeffrey Paul, a Representative from Missouri; born in Springfield, Clark County, Ohio, March 9, 1919; moved with his parents to St. Joseph, Mo., when two years of age; attended the public schools; moved to Kansas City, Mo., in 1940; attended the University of Kansas City Law School but gave up his studies to enlist in the United States Army as a private April 25, 1942; served in the Transportation Corps in the United States, Europe, and Alaska, and was discharged as a captain May 26, 1946, retaining his commission in the Reserve; returned to his studies and was graduated from the University of Kansas City in 1947; engaged in the grocery business 1947–1952; unsuccessful candidate for the State house of representatives in 1948; chairman of the Republican City Central Committee of Independence, Mo., in 1949; elected as a Republican to the Eighty-third Congress (January 3, 1953–January 3, 1955); unsuccessful candidate for reelection in 1954 to the Eighty-fourth Congress; executive assistant to the Postmaster General, Washington, D. C., from January 3, 1955, until his resignation September 22, 1955; unsuccessful candidate for election in 1956 to the Eighty-fifth Congress; delegate to Republican State Conventions in 1948, 1952, and 1956; delegate to the Republican National Convention in 1956; appointed acting postmaster of Kansas City, Mo., May 1, 1957; resides in Kansas City, Mo.

HILLEN, Solomon, Jr., a Representative from Maryland; born on the family estate, Hillen Road, near Baltimore, Md., July 10, 1810; was graduated from Georgetown College; studied law; was admitted to the bar and commenced practice in Baltimore; member of the State house of representatives 1834–1838; elected as a Democrat to the Twenty-sixth Congress (March 4, 1839–March 3, 1841); resumed the practice of law; mayor of Baltimore 1842–1845; died in New York City on June 26, 1873; interment in Greenmount Cemetery, Baltimore, Md.

HILLHOUSE, James (son of William Hillhouse), a Representative and a Senator from Connecticut; born in Montville, Conn., October 21, 1754; attended the Hopkins Grammar School, New Haven, Conn., and was graduated from Yale College in 1773; studied law; was admitted to the bar in 1775 and commenced practice in New Haven, Conn.; served in the Revolutionary War and in 1779 was captain of the Governor's foot guards when New Haven was invaded by the British under Tryon; member of the State house of representatives 1780–1785; member of the council in 1789 and 1790; elected as a Federalist to the Second, Third, and Fourth Congresses and served from March 4, 1791, until his resignation in the fall of 1796, having been elected to the United States Senate on May 12, 1796, to fill the vacancy caused by the resignation of Oliver Ellsworth; reelected in 1797, 1803, and 1809; took his seat December 6, 1796, and served until June 10, 1810, when he resigned to become commissioner of the school fund, which position he held until 1825; was elected President pro tempore of the Senate February 28, 1801; member of the Hartford convention; treasurer of Yale College 1782–1832; died in New Haven, Conn., December 29, 1832; interment in Grove Street Cemetery.

HILLHOUSE, William (father of James Hillhouse), a Delegate from Connecticut; born in Montville, Conn., August 25, 1728; received a liberal schooling; studied law; was admitted to the bar and practiced; served in the State house of representatives 1756–1760 and 1763–1785; major in the Second

Regiment of the Connecticut Cavalry in the Revolutionary War; Member of the Continental Congress 1783–1786; judge of the court of common pleas 1784–1806; member of the State senate 1785–1808; judge of probate for New London district 1786–1807; died in Montville, Conn., January 12, 1816; interment in Raymond Hill Cemetery.

HILLIARD, Benjamin Clark, a Representative from Colorado; born near Osceola, Clarke County, Iowa, January 9, 1868; attended the public schools of Iowa and Kansas; taught school in Kansas; was graduated from the law department of the University of Iowa at Iowa City in 1891; was admitted to the bar the same year and commenced practice in Kansas City, Mo.; moved to Denver, Colo., in 1893; city attorney of Highlands, Colo., in 1896 and 1897; county attorney of Elbert County, Colo., 1897–1907; county attorney of Grand County 1909–1913; member of the State house of representatives in 1902; member of the Denver Board of Education 1900–1902, 1904–1909, and 1913–1917; elected as a Democrat to the Sixty-fourth and Sixty-fifth Congresses (March 4, 1915–March 3, 1919); was not a candidate for renomination in 1918; resumed the practice of law; elected justice of the supreme court of Colorado in 1930 and served as chief justice in 1939 and 1940; reelected in 1940 and again in 1950; again became chief justice in January 1949; died in Denver, Colo., August 7, 1951; interment in Crown Hill Cemetery.

HILLIARD, Henry Washington, a Representative from Alabama; born in Fayetteville, Cumberland County, N. C., on August 4, 1808; was graduated from South Carolina College (now the University of South Carolina) at Columbia in 1826; studied law; moved to Athens, Ga., where he was admitted to the bar in 1829; professor in the University of Alabama at Tuscaloosa from 1831 to 1834, when he resigned to practice law in Montgomery, Ala.; member of the State house of representatives 1836–1838; member of the Whig National Convention at Harrisburg, Pa., in 1839; Whig presidential elector in 1840; unsuccessful candidate for election to the Twenty-seventh Congress in 1840; Chargé d'Affaires to Belgium from May 12, 1842, to August 15, 1844; elected as a Whig to the Twenty-ninth, Thirtieth, and Thirty-first Congresses (March 4, 1845–March 3, 1851); was not a candidate for renomination in 1850; presidential elector on the National American ticket of Fillmore and Donelson in 1856; during the Civil War served as brigadier general in the Confederate Army; moved to Augusta, Ga., in 1865 and resumed the practice of his profession; appointed by Jefferson Davis Confederate commissioner to Tennessee; unsuccessful Republican candidate for election in 1876 to the Forty-fifth Congress; resumed the practice of law in Augusta, Ga., moving later to Atlanta; Minister to Brazil 1877–1881; died in Atlanta, Ga., December 17, 1892; interment in Oakwood Cemetery, Montgomery, Ala.

HILLINGS, Patrick Jerome, a Representative from California; born in Hobart Mills, Nevada County, Calif., February 19, 1923; attended El Monte Union High School, El Monte, Calif. and Benjamin Franklin High School, Los Angeles, Calif.; attended the University of Southern California until March 1943; during World War II served as a sergeant in the Signal Corps Intelligence Service from March 1943 to February 1946 with service in the South Pacific; returned to the University of Southern California and graduated from its law school in 1949; was admitted to the bar in 1949 and commenced the practice of law in Arcadia, Calif.; delegate to the Republican National Conventions in 1952, 1956, and 1960; elected as a Republican to the Eighty-second and to the three succeeding Congresses (January 3, 1951–January 3, 1959); was not a candidate for renomination in 1958; resumed the practice of law in Los Angeles in January 1959; elected chairman of the Republican Central Committee of Los Angeles County in February 1960; radio commentator for station KMPC; resides in Arcadia, Calif.

HILLYER, Junius, a Representative from Georgia; born in Wilkes County, Ga., April 23, 1807; was graduated from the University of Georgia at Athens in 1828; studied law; was admitted to the bar and commenced practice in Athens; elected solicitor general for the western district of Georgia in 1834; circuit judge 1841–1845; elected as a Democrat to the Thirty-second and Thirty-third Congresses (March 4, 1851–March 3, 1855); Solicitor of the United States Treasury from December 1, 1857, to February 13, 1861, when he resigned; died in Decatur, Ga., June 21, 1886; interment in Oakland Cemetery, Atlanta, Ga.

HIMES, Joseph Hendrix, a Representative from Ohio; born in New Oxford, Adams County, Pa., August 15, 1885; attended the public schools, Gettysburg College, and Pennsylvania State College; employed in the steel industry in various capacities from cinder pitman to general manager; engaged as banker; elected as a Republican to the Sixty-seventh Congress (March 4, 1921–March 3, 1923); unsuccessful candidate in 1922 for reelection to the Sixty-eighth Congress; trustee of Mount Union College, Alliance, Ohio; member of the board of visitors of Maryland State School for the Deaf; member of board of trustees of Frederick (Md.) Memorial Hospital; member of board of directors in 1929 and later president of Columbia Hospital, Washington, D. C.; founder, president, and chairman of the board of directors of Group Hospitalization, Inc., Washington, D. C.; engaged in various business interests in Washington, D. C., New York City, and elsewhere; died in Washington, D. C., September 9, 1960; interment in Fort Lincoln Cemetery.

HINDMAN, Thomas Carmichael, a Representative from Arkansas; born in Knoxville, Tenn., January 28, 1828; moved with his parents to Jacksonville, Calhoun County, Ala., in 1832 and to Ripley, Tippah County, Miss., in 1841; attended public and private schools; was graduated from the Lawrenceville Classical Institute near Princeton, N. J., in 1846; raised a company in Tippah County in 1846 for the Second Mississippi Regiment under Colonel Clark in the war with Mexico; served throughout the war as lieutenant and later as captain of his company; returned to Ripley, Miss.; studied law; was admitted to the bar in 1851 and commenced practice in Ripley, Miss.; member of the State house of representatives in 1852; moved to Helena, Ark., in 1853 and continued the practice of law; elected as a Democrat to the Thirty-sixth Congress (March 4, 1859–March 3, 1861); reelected to the Thirty-seventh Congress in 1860 but declined to take his seat and raised and commanded "Hindman's legion" in 1861 for the Confederate Army; commissioned brigadier general September 28, 1861, and major general April 18, 1862, for "gallant conduct in the Battle of Shiloh"; was wounded twice and served throughout the war; moved to the city of Mexico after the war and engaged in literary pursuits; returned to Helena, Ark., in 1868 and resumed the practice of law; was assassinated in that city on September 27, 1868; interment in Maple Hill Cemetery.

HINDMAN, William, a Delegate, a Representative, and a Senator from Maryland; born in Dorchester County, Md., April 1, 1743; pursued classical studies; was graduated from the University of Pennsylvania in 1761, and from the Inns of Court, London, England, in 1765; returned to the United States; was admitted to the bar in 1765 and commenced practice in Talbot County, Md.; was secretary of the Talbot (Md.) County committee of observation in 1775 and was designated to carry out the declarations of the council of safety; sat in the State convention of 1775; treasurer of the Eastern Shore 1775–1777; member of the State senate 1777–1784; Member of the Continental Congress 1784–1788; member of the executive council 1789–1792; elected to the Second Congress to fill the vacancy caused by the resignation of Joshua Seney; reelected to the Third, Fourth, and Fifth Congresses and served from January 30, 1793, to March 3, 1799; member of the State house of delegates in 1799 and 1800; elected to the United States Senate to fill the vacancy caused by the resignation of James Lloyd; at expiration of the term was appointed to fill the vacancy caused by the failure to elect his successor; served from December 12, 1800, to November 19, 1801; was not a candidate for reelection; engaged in agricultural pursuits on his estate near Wyes Landing; died in Baltimore, Md., January 19, 1822; interment in St. Paul's Burial Ground.

HINDS, Asher Crosby, a Representative from Maine; born in Benton, Kennebec County, Maine, February 6, 1863; attended the public schools and Coburn Classical Institute; was graduated from Colby College, Waterville, Maine, in 1883; began newspaper work in Portland in 1884; clerk to the Speaker, United States House of Representatives, 1889–1891; clerk at the Speaker's table, United States House of Representatives, 1895–1911; editor of the Rules, Manual, and Digest of the House of Representatives in 1899 and of Hinds' Precedents of the House of Representatives 1908; elected as a Republican to the Sixty-second, Sixty-third, and Sixty-fourth Congresses (March 4, 1911–March 3, 1917); voluntarily retired from public life and resided in Washington, D. C., until his death on May 1, 1919; interment in Evergreen Cemetery, Portland, Maine.

HINDS, James, a Representative from Arkansas; born in the town of Hebron, near Salem, N. Y., December 5, 1833; attended the common schools and the State normal school at Albany, N. Y.; moved to what was then the Far West; attended law school at St. Louis, Mo., and was graduated from the Cincinnati Law College in 1856; was admitted to the bar and commenced practice in St. Peter, Minn.; district attorney for three years and served for some time as United States district attorney for the State of Minnesota; joined an expedition under Governor Sibley against the Indians on the western frontier in 1862; although a member of the Democratic Party, was a supporter of President Lincoln; moved to Little Rock, Ark., in 1865 and continued the practice of law; delegate from Pulaski County to the State constitutional convention in 1867; served as a commissioner to codify the State laws; upon the readmission of Arkansas to representation was elected as a Republican to the Fortieth Congress and served from June 22, 1868, until assassinated near Indian Bay, Ark., October 22, 1868; interment in East Norwich, N. Y.

HINDS, Thomas, a Representative from Mississippi; born in Berkeley County, Va., January 9, 1780; moved to Greenville, Miss.; served in the War of 1812 as major of Cavalry; distinguished himself at the Battle of New Orleans and was brevetted brigadier general for gallantry; unsuccessful candidate for Governor in 1820; elected as a Democrat to the Twentieth Congress to fill the vacancy caused by the resignation of William Haile; reelected to the Twenty-first Congress and served from October 21, 1828, to March 3, 1831; died in Greenville, Miss., August 23, 1840.

HINEBAUGH, William Henry, a Representative from Illinois; born near Marshall, Calhoun County, Mich., December 16, 1867; attended the common schools, Litchfield High School, the State normal school at Ypsilanti, Mich., and the University of Michigan at Ann Arbor; moved to Illinois and settled in Ottawa in 1891; studied law; was admitted to the bar in 1893 and commenced practice in Ottawa; appointed assistant prosecuting

attorney of La Salle County in December 1900; judge of the La Salle County Court 1902–1912; president of the State Association of County Judges of Illinois 1908–1910; elected and reelected chairman of the Republican county central committee, but resigned in July 1912 to join the Progressive Party; elected as a Progressive to the Sixty-third Congress (March 4, 1913–March 3, 1915); unsuccessful candidate for reelection in 1914 to the Sixty-fourth Congress; resumed the practice of law in Ottawa, Ill.; assistant attorney general of Illinois 1916–1922; president and general counsel of the Central Life Insurance Co., of Illinois, and resided in Chicago; moved to Albion, Mich., in 1933 and continued the practice of law until his death there September 22, 1943; interment in Mount Hope Cemetery, Litchfield, Mich.

HINES, Richard, a Representative from North Carolina; born in Tarboro, Edgecombe County, N. C.; studied law; was admitted to the bar in 1816 and practiced in Raleigh, N. C.; member of the State house of commons in 1824; elected as a Democrat to the Nineteenth Congress (March 4, 1825–March 3, 1827); unsuccessful candidate for reelection in 1826 to the Twentieth Congress; resumed the practice of law in Raleigh, N. C., and died there November 20, 1851; interment in the Old City Cemetery, Raleigh, N. C.

HINES, William Henry, a Representative from Pennsylvania; born in Brooklyn, N. Y., March 15, 1856; moved to Pennsylvania in 1865 with his parents, who settled in Hanover Township, near Wilkes-Barre, Luzerne County, Pa.; attended the public schools in Brooklyn, N. Y., and Wyoming Seminary, Kingston, Pa.; studied law; was admitted to the bar in Luzerne County in 1881 and practiced; member of the State house of representatives in 1879, 1880, 1883, and 1884; served in the State senate 1888–1892; elected as a Democrat to the Fifty-third Congress (March 4, 1893–March 3, 1895); unsuccessful candidate for reelection in 1894 to the Fifty-fourth Congress; resumed the practice of law in Wilkes-Barre, Pa.; died there January 17, 1914; interment in St. Mary's Cemetery, Hanover Township, Luzerne County, Pa.

HINRICHSEN, William Henry, a Representative from Illinois; born in Franklin, Morgan County, Ill., May 27, 1850; attended the public schools and the Illinois Industrial University (now the University of Illinois) at Champaign; engaged in newspaper work; elected justice of the peace in 1871 and reelected in 1873; appointed deputy sheriff of Morgan County in 1874 and served three terms in that position, residing at Jacksonville; sheriff 1880–1882; editor of the Illinois Courier in 1882; moved to Quincy in 1887; editor of the Quincy Herald 1887–1890; returned to Jacksonville and elected clerk of the house of representatives of Illinois in 1891; secretary of state of Illinois 1892–1896; delegate to the Democratic National Convention at Chicago in 1896; chairman of the Democratic State committee in 1895 and 1896; elected as a Democrat to the Fifty-fifth Congress (March 4, 1897–March 3, 1899); engaged in literary pursuits; died in Alexander, Ill., December 18, 1907; interment in Diamond Grove Cemetery, Jacksonville, Ill.

HINSHAW, Edmund Howard (cousin of Edwin Bruce Brooks), a Representative from Nebraska; born in Greensboro, Henry County, Ind., December 8, 1860; attended the common schools, and was graduated from Butler College, Indianapolis, in 1885; moved to Fairbury, Nebr., in 1887; superintendent of the public schools in 1887 and 1888; studied law; was admitted to the bar in 1888 and commenced practice in Fairbury; city clerk and attorney of Fairbury in 1889 and 1890; attorney of Jefferson County 1895–1899; unsuccessful candidate for election in 1898 to the Fifty-sixth Congress and in 1901 to the United States Senate; elected as a Republican to the Fifty-eighth and to the three succeeding Congresses (March 4, 1903–March 3, 1911); was not a candidate for renomination in 1910; resumed the practice of law in Fairbury, Nebr.; moved to Los Angeles, Calif., in 1912 and continued the practice of his profession; also engaged in the operation of a chain of motion-picture theaters, serving as president of the company from 1922 until his death in Los Angeles, Calif., on June 15, 1932; interment in Forest Lawn Cemetery, Glendale, Calif.

HINSHAW, John Carl Williams, a Representative from California; born in Chicago, Ill., July 28, 1894; attended the public schools and Valparaiso (Ind.) University; was graduated from Princeton (N. J.) University in 1916; pursued a postgraduate course in business administration at the University of Michigan at Ann Arbor; during the First World War served overseas as a first lieutenant in the Sixteenth Railroad Engineers from May 1917 to September 1919, when he was discharged as a captain in the Corps of Engineers; served as laborer, salesman, and manager in automotive manufacturing in Chicago 1920–1926; engaged in investment banking in 1927 and 1928; moved to Pasadena, Calif., in 1929 and engaged in the real estate and insurance business; unsuccessful candidate for election in 1936 to the Seventy-fifth Congress; elected as a Republican to the Seventh-sixth and to the eight succeeding Congresses and served from January 3, 1939, until his death in the naval hospital at Bethesda, Md., August 5, 1956; had been renominated in the June 1956 primary election; interment in Rock Creek Cemetery, Washington, D. C.

HIRES, George, a Representative from New Jersey; born in Elsinboro Township, Salem County, N. J., January 26, 1835; attended the common schools and the Friends' School and received a commercial training; engaged in mercantile and manufacturing pursuits; sheriff of Salem County 1867–1869; member of the State senate 1881–1884; elected as a Republican to the Forty-ninth and Fiftieth Congresses (March 4, 1885–March 3, 1889); was not a candidate for renomination in 1888; resumed mercantile pursuits; also engaged in banking; delegate to the State constitutional convention in 1894; delegate to the Republican National Convention at St. Louis in 1896; member of the Republican State committee for twelve years; died in Atlantic City, N. J., February 16, 1911; interment in the First Presbyterian Cemetery, Salem, N. J.

HISCOCK, Frank, a Representative and a Senator from New York; born in Pompey, Onondaga County, N. Y., September 6, 1834; was graduated from Pompey Academy; studied law; was admitted to the bar in 1855 and commenced practice in Tully, Onondaga County; elected district attorney of Onondaga County and served from 1860 to 1863; member of the State constitutional convention in 1867; delegate to the Republican National Convention at Cincinnati in 1876; elected as a Republican to the Forty-fifth and to the five succeeding Congresses and served from March 4, 1877, until his resignation on March 3, 1887, at the close of the Forty-ninth Congress, having been elected Senator; elected to the United States Senate and served from March 4, 1887, to March 3, 1893; unsuccessful candidate for reelection; resumed the practice of law in Syracuse, N. Y.; died in Syracuse, N. Y., June 18, 1914; interment in Oakwood Cemetery.

HISE, Elijah, a Representative from Kentucky; born in Allegheny County, Pa., July 4, 1802; moved with his parents to Russellville, Logan County, Ky., when young; completed preparatory studies; attended Transylvania University, Lexington, Ky.; studied law; was admitted to the bar and commenced practice; member of the State house of representatives in 1829; unsuccessful Democratic candidate for Lieutenant Governor in 1836; Chargé d'Affaires to Guatemala March 31, 1848, to June 21, 1849; presidential elector on the Democratic ticket of Buchanan and Breckinridge in 1856; chief justice of the court of appeals of Kentucky; elected as a Democrat to the Thirty-ninth Congress to fill the vacancy caused by the death of Henry Grider; reelected to the Fortieth Congress and served from December 3, 1866, until his death in Russellville, Ky., May 8, 1867; interment in Maple Grove Cemetery.

HITCHCOCK, Gilbert Monell (son of Phineas Warren Hitchcock), a Representative and a Senator from Nebraska; born in Omaha, Nebr., September 18, 1859; attended the public schools of Omaha and the more advanced schools of Baden-Baden, Germany; was graduated from the law department of the University of Michigan at Ann Arbor in 1881; was admitted to the bar and commenced practice in Omaha, Nebr., in 1882; continued the practice of law until August 1885, when he established and edited the Omaha Evening World; purchased the Morning Herald in 1889 and consolidated the two into the Morning and Evening World-Herald; unsuccessful candidate for election in 1898 to the Fifty-sixth Congress; elected as a Democrat to the Fifty-eighth Congress (March 4, 1903–March 3, 1905); unsuccessful candidate for reelection in 1904 to the Fifty-ninth Congress; elected to the Sixtieth and Sixty-first Congresses (March 4, 1907–March 3, 1911); did not seek renomination in 1910, having become a candidate for the United States Senate; elected to the United States Senate January 18, 1911; reelected in 1916 and served from March 4, 1911, to March 3, 1923; unsuccessful candidate for reelection in 1922 and for election in 1930; resumed newspaper work in Omaha, Nebr.; delegate to the Democratic National Convention at Chicago in 1932; retired from active business in 1933 and moved to Washington, D. C., where he died on February 3, 1934; interment in Forest Lawn Cemetery, Omaha, Nebr.

HITCHCOCK, Herbert Emery, a Senator from South Dakota; born in Maquoketa, Jackson County, Iowa, August 22, 1867; attended the public schools, the high schools at Anamosa, Iowa, and San Jose, Calif., a business college at Davenport, Iowa, Iowa State College at Ames, and the College of Law, Chicago, Ill.; moved to Mitchell, S. Dak., in 1884 and attended school and worked as a stenographer; was admitted to the South Dakota bar in 1896 and commenced practice in Mitchell, S. Dak., the same year; also engaged in banking; served as State's attorney 1902–1906; member of the State senate in 1909, 1911, and 1929; served as vice president of the selective draft board for South Dakota during the First World War; became a trustee of Yankton (S. Dak.) College in 1936; president of Mitchell School Board 1924–1934; chairman of the Democratic State executive committee 1934–1937; delegate to the Democratic National Conventions in 1908, 1928, 1932, 1936, and 1940; appointed as a Democrat to the United States Senate to fill the vacancy caused by the death of Peter Norbeck and served from December 29, 1936, to November 8, 1938, when a successor was elected; unsuccessful candidate for the nomination to fill the vacancy in 1938; resumed the practice of law until his death; died in Mitchell, S. Dak., February 17, 1958; interment in Graceland Cemetery.

HITCHCOCK, Peter, a Representative from Ohio; born in Cheshire, Conn., October 19, 1781; pursued classical studies, and was graduated from Yale College in 1801; studied law; was admitted to the bar in 1804 and commenced practice in Cheshire; moved to Geauga County, Ohio, in 1806; member of the State house of representatives in 1810; member of the State senate 1812–1815 and served as speaker in 1815; commissioned lieutenant colonel of the Fourth Regiment, Ohio State Militia, in 1814; tendered seat on State supreme bench in 1815 but declined; commissioned major general, Fourth Division, Ohio State Militia, in 1816; elected to the Fifteenth Congress (March 4, 1817–March 3, 1819); was not a candidate for renomination in 1818; judge of the supreme court of Ohio 1819–1832 and served a portion of that time as chief justice; again a member of the State senate in 1833 and 1834; delegate to the State constitutional convention in 1850; died in Painesville, Lake County, Ohio, March 4, 1854; interment in Welton Cemetery, Burton, Ohio.

HITCHCOCK, Phineas Warren (father of Gilbert Monell Hitchcock), a Delegate and a Senator from Nebraska; born in New Lebanon, Columbia County, N. Y., November 30, 1831; was graduated from Williams College, Massachusetts, in 1855; studied law; was admitted to the bar and commenced practice in Omaha, Nebr., in 1857; delegate to the Republican National Convention at Chicago in 1860; appointed United States marshal in 1861; resigned in 1864; elected as a Republican a Delegate to the Thirty-ninth Congress and served from March 4, 1865, to March 1, 1867, when the Territory was admitted as a State into the Union; surveyor general of Nebraska and Iowa 1867–1869; elected to the United States Senate and served from March 4, 1871, to March 3, 1877; unsuccessful candidate for reelection; died in Omaha, Nebr., July 10, 1881; interment in Prospect Hill Cemetery.

HITT, Robert Roberts, a Representative from Illinois; born in Urbana, Champaign County, Ohio, January 16, 1834; moved to Ogle County, Ill., in 1837 with his parents, who settled in Mount Morris; attended the Rock River Seminary (later Mount Morris College), and De Pauw University, Greencastle, Ind.; reported the Lincoln-Douglas debates in 1858; first secretary of legation and Chargé d'Affaires ad interim in Paris from December 1874 until March 1881; Assistant Secretary of State in 1881; elected as a Republican to the Forty-seventh Congress to fill the vacancy caused by the death of Robert M. A. Hawk; reelected to the Forty-eighth and to the eleven succeeding Congresses and served from November 7, 1882, until his death; Regent of the Smithsonian Institution from August 11, 1893, until his death; appointed by President McKinley in July 1898 as a member of the commission to establish government in the Hawaiian Islands; died at Narragansett Pier, R. I., September 19, 1906; interment in Oakwood Cemetery, Mount Morris, Ogle County, Ill.

HOAG, Truman Harrison, a Representative from Ohio; born in Manlius, Onondaga County, N. Y., April 9, 1816; attended the public schools; moved to Syracuse, N. Y., in 1832 and was employed as a clerk in a store and later in the canal collector's office; moved to Oswego, N. Y., in 1839 and was employed for a commission merchants company, moving to Toledo, Ohio, in 1849 as agent of the same firm; later became engaged in transportation and in mercantile pursuits; also engaged in the manufacture of illuminating gas and of coke; unsuccessful candidate for mayor in 1867; elected as a Democrat to the Forty-first Congress and served from March 4, 1869, until his death in Washington, D. C., on February 5, 1870; interment in Forest Cemetery, Toledo, Ohio.

HOAGLAND, Moses, a Representative from Ohio; born near Baltimore, Md., June 19, 1812; attended the public schools; studied law; was admitted to the bar in 1842 and commenced practice in Millersburg, Ohio; served in the Mexican War and was promoted to the rank of major for bravery in action; elected as a Democrat to the Thirty-first Congress (March 4, 1849–March 3, 1851); unsuccessful candidate for reelection in 1850 to the Thirty-second Congress; resumed the practice of

law; appointed associate justice for the Territory of Washington on June 21, 1853, but declined to accept; died in Millersburg, Ohio, April 16, 1865; interment in Oak Hill Cemetery.

HOAR, Ebenezer Rockwood (son of Samuel Hoar, brother of George Frisbie Hoar, and father of Sherman Hoar), a Representative from Massachusetts; born in Concord, Mass., February 21, 1816; pursued classical studies and was graduated from Harvard University in 1835; was admitted to the bar in 1840 and commenced practice in Concord and Boston, Mass.; served in the State senate in 1846 as an anti-slavery Whig; judge of the court of common pleas 1849–1855; judge of the State supreme court 1859–1869; Attorney General of the United States from March 1869 until his resignation in June 1870; nominated in 1869 by President Grant as an Associate Justice of the Supreme Court but was not confirmed by the Senate; member of the joint high commission which framed the treaty of Washington in 1871 under which the tribunal was provided for to settle the *Alabama* claims; elected as a Republican to the Forty-third Congress (March 4, 1873–March 3, 1875); was not a candidate for renomination in 1874; resumed the practice of his profession in Concord and Boston, Mass.; member of the board of overseers of Harvard University 1868–1882; died in Concord, Mass., January 31, 1895; interment in Sleepy Hollow Cemetery.

HOAR, George Frisbie (son of Samuel Hoar, brother of Ebenezer Rockwood Hoar, and father of Rockwood Hoar), a Representative and a Senator from Massachusetts; born in Concord, Mass., August 29, 1826; attended Concord Academy, and was graduated from Harvard University in 1846; studied law; was graduated from the Dane Law School, Harvard University, in 1849; was admitted to the bar the same year and commenced practice in Worcester, Mass.; city solicitor in 1860; member of the State house of representatives in 1852; served in the State senate in 1857; elected as a Republican to the Forty-first and to the three succeeding Congresses (March 4, 1869–March 3, 1877); was not a candidate for renomination in 1876; one of the managers appointed by the House of Representatives in 1876 to conduct the impeachment proceedings against William W. Belknap, ex-Secretary of War; appointed a member of the Electoral Commission created by act of Congress approved January 29, 1877, to decide the contests in various States in the presidential election of 1876; overseer of Harvard University 1874–1880 and from 1896 until his death; presided over the Massachusetts State Republican conventions in 1871, 1877, 1882, and 1885; delegate to the Republican National Conventions in 1876, 1880, 1884, and 1888, presiding over the convention of 1880, and was chairman of the Massachusetts delegation in 1880, 1884, and 1888; Regent of the Smithsonian Institution in 1880; elected as a Republican to the United States Senate in 1877; reelected in 1883, 1889, 1895, and 1901 and served from March 4, 1877, until his death in Worcester, Mass., September 30, 1904; interment in Sleepy Hollow Cemetery, Concord, Mass.

HOAR, Rockwood (son of George Frisbie Hoar), a Representative from Massachusetts; born in Worcester, Mass., August 24, 1855; attended the Worcester public schools, and was graduated from Harvard University in 1876; member of Company C, Fifth Massachusetts Infantry, 1875–1879; studied law; was admitted to the bar in 1879 and commenced practice in Worcester; assistant district attorney for the middle district of Massachusetts 1884–1887; member of the common council of Worcester 1887–1891; aide-de-camp with rank of colonel on the staff of Gov. Oliver Ames 1887–1890; judge advocate general with rank of brigadier general on the staff of Gov. Roger Wolcott 1897–1900; district attorney from January 1899 to January 1905; trustee of Clark University, Worcester, Mass., and trustee of the Worcester Insane Hospital; elected as a Republican to the Fifty-ninth Congress and served from March 1, 1905, until his death in Worcester, Mass., November 1, 1906; interment in the Rural Cemetery.

HOAR, Samuel (father of Ebenezer Rockwood Hoar and George Frisbie Hoar), a Representative from Massachusetts; born in Lincoln, Middlesex County, Mass., May 18, 1778; pursued classical studies, and was graduated from Harvard University in 1802; studied law; was admitted to the bar in 1805 and commenced practice in Concord, Mass.; delegate to the State constitutional convention in 1820; served in the State senate in 1826, 1832, and 1833; elected as a Whig to the Twenty-fourth Congress (March 4, 1835–March 3, 1837); unsuccessful candidate for reelection in 1836 to the Twenty-fifth Congress; resumed the practice of law in Concord, Mass.; sent by the State legislature to South Carolina to test the constitutionality of acts prohibiting free Negroes from coming into the State and on his arrival, December 5, 1844, the Legislature of South Carolina passed resolutions expelling him from the city of Charleston; member of the State house of representatives in 1850; State chairman of the State convention in 1855 which formed the Republican Party in Massachusetts; died in Concord, Mass., November 2, 1856; interment in Sleepy Hollow Cemetery.

HOAR, Sherman (son of Ebenezer Rockwood Hoar), a Representative from Massachusetts; born in Concord, Mass., July 30, 1860; attended the public schools and Phillips Exeter Academy, Exeter, N. H.; was graduated from Harvard University in 1882 and from the law department of the university in 1884; president of the Young Men's Democratic Club of Massachusetts in 1884; was admitted to the bar of Middlesex County in 1885 and commenced practice in Concord; trustee of Phillips Exeter Academy and director of the American Unitarian Association; elected as a Democrat to the Fifty-second Congress (March 4, 1891–March 3, 1893); United States district attorney for Massachusetts 1893–1897; director of the Massachusetts Volunteer Aid Association in the war with Spain and served in Army hospitals in the South; died in Concord, Mass., October 7, 1898; interment in Sleepy Hollow Cemetery.

HOARD, Charles Brooks, a Representative from New York; born in Springfield, Windsor County, Vt., June 5, 1805; attended the public schools; moved to Antwerp, N. Y., where he was postmaster during the administrations of Jackson and Van Buren; member of the State assembly in 1837; moved to Watertown, N. Y., in January 1844; clerk of Jefferson County 1844–1846; elected as a Republican to the Thirty-fifth and Thirty-sixth Congresses (March 4, 1857–March 3, 1861); engaged in the manufacture of portable engines, but in 1861, during the Civil War, converted his factory into an armory for the manufacture of arms for the Government; moved to West Virginia in 1870; died in Ceredo, W. Va., November 20, 1886; interment in Spring Hill Cemetery, Huntington, W. Va.

HOBART, Aaron, a Representative from Massachusetts; born in Abington, Mass., June 26, 1787; pursued classical studies, and was graduated from Brown University, Providence, R. I., in 1805; studied law; was admitted to the bar in 1809 and commenced practice in Abington; moved to Hanover in 1811; member of the State house of representatives in 1814 and served in the State senate in 1819; moved to East Bridgewater in 1824; elected as a Democrat to the Sixteenth Congress to fill the vacancy caused by the resignation of Zabdiel Sampson; reelected to the Seventeenth, Eighteenth, and Nineteenth Congresses and served from November 24, 1820, to March 3, 1827; declined to be a candidate for renomination in 1826; executive councilor 1827–1831; judge of probate 1843–1858; died in East Bridgewater, Mass., September 19, 1858; interment in Central Cemetery.

HOBART, Garret Augustus, a Vice President of the United States; born near Long Branch, Monmouth County, N. J., June 3, 1844; attended the common schools, and was graduated from Rutgers College, New Brunswick, N. J., in 1863; taught school for a brief period; clerk for the grand jury of Passaic County, N. J., in 1865; studied law; was admitted to the bar in 1869 and commenced practice at Paterson, N. J.; city counsel of Paterson in 1871 and 1872; elected counsel for the board of freeholders in May 1872; member of the State house of assembly 1872–1876 and served as speaker in 1874; member of the State senate 1876–1882 and served as president of that body in 1881 and 1882; delegate at large to the Republican National Conventions in 1876 and 1880; was the nominee of his party for the United States Senate in 1883; member of the Republican National Committee from 1884 until 1896, when he was nominated as a candidate for Vice President at the Republican National Convention held in St. Louis, Mo.; elected, as a Republican, Vice President of the United States in 1896 and served from March 4, 1897, until his death in Paterson, N. J., on November 21, 1899; interment in Cedar Lawn Cemetery.

HOBART, John Sloss, a Delegate and a Senator from New York; born in Fairfield, Fairfield County, Conn., May 6, 1738; was graduated from Yale College in 1757; studied law; was admitted to the bar and commenced practice in the State of New York; deputy to the provincial convention in 1775; delegate to the Provincial Congress 1775–1777; member of the council of safety in 1777; a puisne justice of the supreme court 1777–1798; member of the Hartford convention in 1780; member of the State convention in 1788 which ratified the Federal Constitution; elected to the United States Senate to fill the vacancy caused by the resignation of Philip Schuyler and served from January 11 to April 16, 1798, when he resigned to accept the appointment as judge of the United States District Court of New York; died in New York City on February 4, 1805; interment in Trinity Churchyard.

HOBBIE, Selah Reeve, a Representative from New York; born in Newburgh, Orange County, N. Y., March 10, 1797; studied law; was admitted to the bar and commenced practice in Delhi, N. Y.; district attorney of Delaware County 1823–1827; member of the State house of representatives 1827–1829; served in the militia as brigade major and inspector; elected as a Jackson Democrat to the Twentieth Congress (March 4, 1827–March 3, 1829); was appointed Assistant Postmaster General and served from 1829 until 1851, when he resigned on account of ill health; appointed First Assistant Postmaster General and served from March 22, 1853, until his death in Washington, D. C., March 23, 1854.

HOBBS, Samuel Francis (Sam), a Representative from Alabama; born in Selma, Dallas County, Ala., October 5, 1887; attended the public schools, Callaway's Preparatory School, Selma, Ala., Marion (Ala.) Military Institute, Vanderbilt University at Nashville, Tenn., and was graduated from the law department of the University of Alabama at Tuscaloosa in 1908; was admitted to the bar in 1908 and commenced practice in Selma, Ala.; appointed judge of the fourth judicial circuit of Alabama in 1921; elected to the same office in 1923 and served until his resignation in 1926; resumed the practice of law; chairman of the Muscle Shoals Commission in 1931 and of the Alabama National Recovery Administration Committee in 1933; elected as a Democrat to the Seventy-fourth and to the seven succeeding Congresses (January 3, 1935–January 3, 1951); one of the managers appointed by the House of Representatives in 1936 to conduct the impeachment proceedings against Halstead L. Ritter, judge of the United States District Court for the Southern District of Florida; did not seek renomination in 1950; returned to Selma, Ala., and reestablished his law practice; died in Selma, Ala., May 31, 1952; interment in Live Oak Cemetery.

HOBLITZELL, Fetter Schrier, a Representative from Maryland; born in Cumberland, Md., October 7, 1838; attended the primary schools and was graduated from the Allegany Academy, Cumberland, Md.; studied law; was admitted to the bar in 1859 and commenced practice in Baltimore, Md.; during the Civil War served as a private in the First Maryland Regiment of Infantry, Confederate Army; resumed the practice of law; member of the State house of delegates in 1870 and 1876; reelected in 1878 and served as speaker; elected as a Democrat to the Forty-seventh and Forty-eighth Congresses (March 4, 1881–March 3, 1885); city counselor of Baltimore in 1888 and 1889; resumed the practice of law; died in Baltimore, Md., May 2, 1900; interment in Loudon Park Cemetery.

HOBLITZELL, John Dempsey, Jr., a Senator from West Virginia; born in Parkersburg, Wood County, W. Va., December 30, 1912; attended the public schools; graduated from the University of West Virginia in 1934; partner, Blackford-Beckner Insurance Co., 1935–1937; president of Parkersburg Realty Co. 1937–1958, Hoblitzell-Reagle, Inc., 1948–1957, and Colonial Builders, Inc., 1956–1958; appointed to the board of governors of West Virginia University in 1937 and served until 1944; served in the United States Naval Reserve 1942–1946, retiring as a lieutenant; member, Wood County School Board 1950–1956; delegate, White House Conference on Education, in 1954; chairman, Governor's West Virginia Commission on State and Local Finance in 1954; president, West Virginia School Board Association in 1954; member, National Citizens Committee on Higher Education in 1955; executive vice president of Jackson County Bank, Ravenswood, W. Va., 1957–1960; appointed as a Republican to the United States Senate to fill the vacancy caused by the death of Matthew M. Neely and served from January 25, 1958, to November 4, 1958; unsuccessful candidate for election to the vacancy; on February 1, 1960, became executive vice president of First National Bank, Bluefield, W. Va., where he now resides.

HOBSON, Richmond Pearson, a Representative from Alabama; born in Greensboro, Hale County, Ala., August 17, 1870; attended private schools and Southern University; was graduated from the United States Naval Academy in 1889 and from the French National School of Naval Design at Paris in 1893; served in the United States Navy from 1885 until 1903, when he resigned; during the Spanish-American War commanded the collier *Merrimac*, and with a crew of seven volunteers sank her in Santiago Harbor; special representative of the Navy Department to the Buffalo Exposition in 1901 and to the Charleston Exposition in 1901 and 1902; naval architect, author, and lecturer; presidential elector on the Democratic ticket of Parker and Davis in 1904; elected as a Democrat to the Sixtieth and to the three succeeding Congresses (March 4, 1907–March 3, 1915); unsuccessful candidate for nomination in 1916 to the Sixty-fifth Congress; moved to Los Angeles, Calif., and later to New York City, N. Y.; resumed literary pursuits and lecturing; organized the American Alcohol Education Association in 1921 and served as general secretary; organized the International Narcotic Education Association in 1923 and served as president; organized the World Conference on Narcotic Education in 1926 and served as secretary general and as chairman of the board of

governors; founder of the World Narcotic Defense Association in 1927, serving as president; awarded the Congressional Medal of Honor in 1933 for sinking the collier *Merrimac* in 1898; was made a rear admiral by act of Congress in 1934; founder and president of the Constitutional Democracy Association in 1935; died in New York City, N. Y., March 16, 1937; interment in Arlington National Cemetery, Fort Myer, Va.

HOCH, Daniel Knabb, a Representative from Pennsylvania; born on a farm near Reading, Oley Township, Berks County, Pa., January 31, 1866; attended the public schools; served a printing apprenticeship on a Reading, Pa., newspaper; worked in every department of a newspaper, as pressman, compositor, reporter, editor, advertising manager, and circulation manager; active in the promotion and maintenance of the Appalachian Trail, a mountain path extending from Maine to Georgia; member of the State house of representatives 1899–1901; delegate to the Democratic National Convention at Denver in 1908; controller of Berks County, Pa., 1912–1916; trustee of St. Matthew's Lutheran Church since 1937; elected as a Democrat to the Seventy-eighth and Seventy-ninth Congresses (January 3, 1943–January 3, 1947); unsuccessful candidate for reelection in 1946 to the Eightieth Congress; engaged in historical research; died in Reading, Pa., October 11, 1960; interment in Charles Evans Cemetery.

HOCH, Homer, a Representative from Kansas; born in Marion, Marion County, Kans., July 4, 1879; attended the public schools, and was graduated from Baker University, Baldwin, Kans., in 1902; attended George Washington Law School, Washington, D. C., and Washburn Law School, Topeka, Kans., from which he was graduated in 1909; clerk and chief of the Appointment Division, Post Office Department, Washington, D. C., 1903–1905; private secretary to the Governor of Kansas in 1907 and 1908; engaged in the practice of law in Marion, Kans., 1909–1919; editor of the Marion (Kans.) Record; delegate to the Republican National Convention at Kansas City, Mo., in 1928; elected as a Republican to the Sixty-sixth and to the six succeeding Congresses (March 4, 1919–March 3, 1933); unsuccessful candidate for reelection in 1932 to the Seventy-third Congress; member and chairman of the State Corporation Commission of Kansas 1933–1939; elected a member of the supreme court of Kansas in 1938; reelected in 1944, and served until his death in Topeka, Kans., January 30, 1949; interment in Marion Cemetery, Marion, Kans.

HODGES, Asa, a Representative from Arkansas; born near Moulton, Lawrence County, Ala., January 22, 1822; moved to Marion, Ark.; attended La Grange College; studied law; was admitted to the bar in 1848 and practiced until 1860; delegate to the State constitutional convention in 1867; served in the State house of representatives in 1868; member of the State senate 1870–1873; elected as a Republican to the Forty-third Congress (March 4, 1873–March 3, 1875); was not a candidate for reelection in 1874 to the Forty-fourth Congress; engaged in agricultural pursuits; died near Marion, Ark., June 6, 1900; interment in Elmwood Cemetery, Memphis, Tenn.

HODGES, Charles Drury, a Representative from Illinois; born in Queen Anne, Talbot County, Md., February 4, 1810; attended the public schools, and was graduated from Trinity College, Hartford, Conn., in 1829; studied law in Annapolis, Md.; was admitted to the bar in 1831 and commenced practice in Annapolis; moved to Carrollton, Ill., in 1833 and resumed the practice of law; also engaged in the mercantile business for a short time; member of the State house of representatives 1851–1853; elected judge of Greene County in

1854; reelected for a four-year term in 1858 but resigned in 1859 having been elected to Congress; secretary and treasurer of the St. Louis, Jacksonville & Chicago Railroad in 1858; afterward director for many years; elected as a Democrat to the Thirty-fifth Congress to fill the vacancy caused by the death of Thomas L. Harris and served from January 4 to March 3, 1859; was not a candidate for election to fill the vacancy in the Thirty-sixth Congress, caused also by the death of Mr. Harris; resumed the practice of law in Carrollton, Ill.; circuit judge 1867–1873; member of the State senate 1873–1877; again practiced law in Carrollton, Ill., until his death, April 1, 1884; interment in the City Cemetery.

HODGES, George Tisdale, a Representative from Vermont; born in Clarendon, Vt., July 4, 1789; attended the common schools; engaged in business in Rutland, Vt.; member of the State house of representatives 1827–1829, 1839, and 1840; served in the State senate 1845–1847 and was president pro tempore of that body in 1846 and 1847; presidential elector in 1848; president of the Bank of Rutland for over twenty-five years; elected as a Republican to the Thirty-fourth Congress to fill the vacancy caused by the death of James Meacham and served from December 1, 1856, to March 3, 1857; was not a candidate for renomination in 1856; died in Rutland, Vt., August 9, 1860; interment in Evergreen Cemetery.

HODGES, James Leonard, a Representative from Massachusetts; born in Taunton, Bristol County, Mass., April 24, 1790; attended the common schools; studied law; was admitted to the bar and practiced; bank cashier; postmaster of Taunton; member of the State constitutional convention in 1820; served in the senate in 1823 and 1824; elected to the Twentieth, Twenty-first, and Twenty-second Congresses (March 4, 1827–March 3, 1833); declined to be a candidate for renomination; died in Taunton, Bristol County, Mass., March 8, 1846; interment in Plain Burying Ground.

HOEPPEL, John Henry, a Representative from California; born near Tell City, Perry County, Ind., February 10, 1881; attended the grammar school in Evansville, Ind.; enlisted in the United States Army on July 27, 1898, and served successively as private, corporal, and sergeant; went to France in June 1917, as a member of Outpost Company C, of the Second Field Battalion, Signal Corps, First Division; commissioned a second lieutenant, Aviation Section, Officers' Reserve Corps, February 1, 1918, served as a first lieutenant in the Air Service from February 21, 1919, to October 29, 1919, and was discharged by reason of demobilization of forces with twenty-eight months' overseas service; reenlisted on October 30, 1919, and served until retired as master sergeant on August 16, 1921; moved to Arcadia, Los Angeles County, Calif., in 1919; postmaster at Arcadia, Calif., 1923–1931; in 1928 became editor of National Defense magazine; elected as a Democrat to the Seventy-third and Seventy-fourth Congresses (March 4, 1933–January 3, 1937); unsuccessful candidate for renomination in 1936; resumed his editorial interests; unsuccessful Prohibition candidate for election in 1946 to the Eightieth Congress; is a resident of Arcadia, Calif.

HOEVEN, Charles Bernard, a Representative from Iowa; born in Hospers, Sioux County, Iowa, March 30, 1895; attended the public schools and Alton (Iowa) High School; was graduated from the State University of Iowa at Iowa City in 1920 and from its law department in 1922; was admitted to the bar in 1922 and commenced practice in Alton, Iowa; during the First World War served as a sergeant, Company D, Three Hundred and Fiftieth Infantry, Eighty-eighth Division, and with the Intelligence Service, First Battalion, in England and France; county attorney of Sioux County, Iowa, 1925–1937; member of the State senate 1937–1941, serving as president pro tempore 1939–1941; permanent chairman of the Iowa Republican State convention in 1940; temporary and permanent chairman of the Iowa Republican State Judicial Convention in 1942; elected as a Republican to the Seventy-eighth and to the eight succeeding Congresses (January 3, 1943–January 3, 1961). *Reelected to the Eighty-seventh Congress.*

HOEY, Clyde Roark, a Representative and a Senator from North Carolina; born in Shelby, Cleveland County, N. C., on December 11, 1877; attended the public schools and was graduated from the law department of the University of North Carolina at Chapel Hill; worked in a printing office and later became editor and publisher of the Cleveland Star; was admitted to the bar in 1899 and commenced the practice of law in Shelby, N. C.; member of the State house of representatives 1898–1902; served in the State senate 1902–1904; assistant United States attorney for the western district of North Carolina 1913–1919; member of the State Democratic executive committee for a number of years and served as chairman several times; elected as a Democrat to the Sixty-sixth Congress to fill the vacancy caused by the resignation of Edwin Y. Webb and served from December 16, 1919, to March 3, 1921; declined to be a candidate for renomination in 1920; resumed the practice of law; Governor of North Carolina 1937–1941; State Democratic National committeeman 1941–1944; elected as a Democrat to the United States Senate in 1944; reelected in 1950 and served from January 3, 1945, until his death in Washington, D. C., May 12, 1954; interment in Sunset Cemetery, Shelby, N. C.

HOFFECKER, John Henry (father of Walter Oakley Hoffecker), a Representative from Delaware; born at Mansion House, near Smyrna, Del., September 12, 1827; attended public and private schools; was graduated in civil engineering, and engaged in his profession in Smyrna in 1853; delegate to the Republican National Convention at Cincinnati in 1876 and at Chicago in 1884; member of the State house of representatives in 1888, and on January 1, 1889, was chosen speaker of the house; president of the town council in 1878 and served continuously by reelection until 1898; unsuccessful candidate for Governor in 1896; elected as a Republican to the Fifty-sixth Congress and served from March 4, 1899, until his death in Smyrna, Del., June 16, 1900; interment in Glenwood Cemetery.

HOFFECKER, Walter Oakley (son of John Henry Hoffecker), a Representative from Delaware; born near Smyrna, Kent County, Del., September 20, 1854; attended the public schools in Smyrna, and was graduated from Smyrna Seminary in 1872; in September 1873 entered Lehigh University, Bethlehem, Pa.; studied civil engineering and followed that profession; president of the Philadelphia & Smyrna Transportation Co.; engaged in the general insurance business in 1884; also engaged in the canning industry and in banking; elected as a Republican to the Fifty-sixth Congress to fill the vacancy caused by the death of his father and served from November 6, 1900, until March 3, 1901; was not a candidate for renomination in 1900; resumed business activities in Smyrna, Del.; delegate to the Republican National Convention at Chicago in 1908; member of the State highway commission; died in Smyrna, Del., January 23, 1934; interment in Glenwood Cemetery.

HOFFMAN, Carl Henry, a Representative from Pennsylvania; born in Bangor, Northampton County, Pa., August 12, 1896; attended the public schools, and was graduated from Juniata College, Huntingdon, Pa., in 1922; served during the First

World War as a candidate in Officers' Training School for Infantry; taught school and was a coach of athletics at Juniata College in 1922; engaged in the lumber, oil, and banking businesses in Somerset, Pa., in 1923; elected as a Republican to the Seventy-ninth Congress to fill the vacancy caused by the death of J. Buell Snyder and served from May 21, 1946, to January 3, 1947; was not a candidate for renomination in 1946 to the Eightieth Congress; resumed his former business pursuits at Somerset, Pa., where he now resides.

HOFFMAN, Clare Eugene, a Representative from Michigan; born in Vicksburg, Union County, Pa., September 10, 1875; attended the public schools and was graduated from the law department of Northwestern University, Evanston, Ill., in 1895; was admitted to the Michigan bar in 1896 and commenced practice in Allegan, Mich.; prosecuting attorney for Allegan County, Mich., 1904–1910; elected as a Republican to the Seventy-fourth and to the twelve succeeding Congresses (January 3, 1935–January 3, 1961). *Reelected to the Eighty-seventh Congress.*

HOFFMAN, Elmer Joseph, a Representative from Illinois; born on a farm in Du Page County, near Wheaton, Ill., July 7, 1899; attended the public schools of Wheaton; enlisted in the Artillery Corps during the First World War and served in France; helped operate his father's farm as well as his own trucking firm 1919–1930; employed in Du Page County sheriff's office 1930–1938; sheriff of Du Page County 1939–1942; chief deputy sheriff 1943–1946; again sheriff 1947–1950; in 1951 was probation officer of Du Page County's circuit and county courts; elected State treasurer in 1952, reelected in 1956 and served until elected to Congress; elected as a Republican to the Eighty-sixth Congress (January 3, 1959–January 3, 1961). *Reelected to the Eighty-seventh Congress.*

HOFFMAN, Harold Giles, a Representative from New Jersey; born in South Amboy, N. J., February 7, 1896; attended the public schools, and was graduated from the South Amboy High School in 1913; engaged in newspaper work; during the First World War enlisted on July 25, 1917, as a private in Company H, Third Regiment, New Jersey Infantry, and successive promotions made him in 1918 a captain, commanding Headquarters Company, One Hundred and Fourteenth Regiment Infantry, Twenty-ninth Division, while north of Verdun in the Meuse-Argonne engagements; was discharged June 4, 1919; secretary-treasurer of South Amboy Trust Co., 1919–1926 and executive vice president 1926–1942; city treasurer of South Amboy 1920–1925; served in the State house of assembly in 1923 and 1924; mayor of South Amboy in 1925 and 1926; president of the Middlesex County Bankers' Association in 1925 and 1926; delegate to the Republican State conventions in 1934, 1935, 1936, and 1937, and to the Republican National Convention in 1936; elected as a Republican to the Seventieth and Seventy-first Congresses (March 4, 1927–March 3, 1931); was not a candidate for renomination in 1930, having been appointed motor vehicle commissioner of New Jersey, and served until 1935; Governor of New Jersey from January 15, 1935, to January 18, 1938; became executive director of the New Jersey Unemployment Compensation Commission in 1938, and served until granted military leave to reenter the United States Army on June 15, 1942, as a major in the Transportation Corps; was advanced to the rank of lieutenant colonel on December 15, 1942, and served until June 24, 1946, when he was discharged with the rank of colonel; resumed his former occupation as executive director of the New Jersey Unemployment Compensation Commission; died in New York City, N. Y., June 4, 1954; interment in Christ Church Cemetery, South Amboy, N. J.

HOFFMAN, Henry William, a Representative from Maryland; born in Cumberland, Allegany County, Md., November 10, 1825; attended the public schools and Allegany County Academy; was graduated from Jefferson College, Pennsylvania, in 1846; studied law; was admitted to the bar in 1848; elected by the American Party to the Thirty-fourth Congress (March 4, 1855–March 3, 1857); unsuccessful candidate for reelection in 1856 to the Thirty-fifth Congress and for election in 1858 to the Thirty-sixth Congress; treasurer of the Chesapeake & Ohio Canal Co. 1858–1860; elected Sergeant at Arms of the House of Representatives in the Thirty-sixth Congress and served from February 3, 1860, to July 5, 1861; appointed by President Lincoln as collector of customs at Baltimore, Md., and served from 1861 to 1866; resumed the practice of law in Cumberland, Md.; elected associate judge of the sixth Maryland circuit court in 1883 and served until his death in Cumberland, Allegany County, Md., July 28, 1895; interment in Rose Hill Cemetery.

HOFFMAN, Josiah Ogden, a Representative from New York; born in New York City May 3, 1793; pursued classical studies, and was graduated from Columbia College in 1812; served for three years in the Navy and was warranted a midshipman in 1814; studied law; was admitted to the bar in 1818 and commenced practice in Goshen, Orange County; district attorney of that county 1823–1826; returned to New York City; member of the State assembly in 1825, 1826, and 1828; district attorney of the city and county of New York 1829–1835; elected as a Whig to the Twenty-fifth and Twenty-sixth Congresses (March 4, 1837–March 3, 1841); United States district attorney at New York 1841–1845; attorney general of the State November 8, 1853, to November 7, 1855; died in New York City May 1, 1856; interment in St. Mark's Church vault.

HOFFMAN, Michael, a Representative from New York; born in Half Moon, Saratoga County, N. Y., October 11, 1787; completed academic studies; studied medicine and law; was admitted to the bar and commenced practice in Herkimer, Herkimer County, N. Y.; district attorney 1823–1825; elected as a Democrat to the Nineteenth and to the three succeeding Congresses (March 4, 1825–March 3, 1833); judge of Herkimer County 1830–1833; canal commissioner of New York 1833–1835; register of the land office at Saginaw, Mich., in 1836; returned to Herkimer, N. Y.; member of the State assembly in 1841, 1842, and 1844; delegate to the State constitutional convention in 1846; naval officer of New York City from May 3, 1845, until his death in Brooklyn, N. Y., September 27, 1848.

HOFFMAN, Richard William, a Representative from Illinois; born in Chicago, Ill., December 23, 1893; veteran of the First World War; engaged in the printing and publishing business; owner and operator of radio stations WHFC and WEHS–FM in Chicago, Ill.; president of the board of education of J. Sterling Morton High School and Junior College 1933–1936 and 1939–1948; elected as a Republican to the Eighty-first and to the three succeeding Congresses (January 3, 1949–January 3, 1957); was not a candidate for renomination in 1956; resumed former business activities; is a resident of Riverside, Ill.

HOGAN, Earl Lee, a Representative from Indiana; born in Hope, Bartholomew County, Ind., March 13, 1920; attended the public schools of Burney; also attended Indiana University and the University of Kentucky; during World War II served from 1940 in the Air Force as a bombardier on a B–17; completed twenty-five combat missions over Europe; was also on Caribbean submarine-air patrol for eighteen months, and was discharged June 5, 1945; awarded the Distinguished Flying Cross, Purple Heart, and Air Medal with three Oak Leaf Clusters; deputy sheriff of Bartholomew County, Ind., 1946–1950 and sheriff 1950–1958; delegate to the Democratic State convention in 1952; elected as a Democrat to the Eighty-sixth Congress (January 3, 1959–January 3, 1961); unsuccessful candidate for reelection in 1960 to the Eighty-seventh Congress; owns and operates a farm; is a resident of Hope, Ind.

HOGAN, John, a Representative from Missouri; born in Mallow, County Cork, Ireland, January 2, 1805; immigrated to the United States in 1817 and settled in Baltimore, Md.; apprenticed to learn the shoemaker's trade; received a limited schooling; became a licensed Methodist preacher before twenty years of age; went West in 1826 and preached in the Illinois conference; entered general merchandise business in Madison, Ill., in 1831; president of the Illinois Board of Public Works 1834–1837; member of the State house of representatives in 1836; unsuccessful Whig candidate for Congress in 1838; register of the land office at Dixon, Ill., 1841–1845; moved to St. Louis, Mo., and engaged in the wholesale grocery business; postmaster of St. Louis 1857–1861; elected as a Democrat to the Thirty-ninth Congress (March 4, 1865–March 3, 1867); unsuccessful candidate in 1866 for reelection to the Fortieth Congress; maintained his ministerial authority and preached his last sermon a few months before he died in St. Louis, Mo., February 5, 1892; interment in Bellefontaine Cemetery.

HOGAN, Michael Joseph, a Representative from New York; born in New York City April 22, 1871; attended the parochial and public schools; member of the Thirteenth Regiment, New York National Guard, 1889–1898; served on the board of aldermen of New York City 1914–1920; declined a renomination; elected as a Republican to the Sixty-seventh Congress (March 4, 1921–March 3, 1923); unsuccessful candidate for reelection in 1922 to the Sixty-eighth Congress; delegate to the Republican State conventions in 1914, 1918, 1920, 1922, 1924, and 1926; engaged in the management of transportation business in New York City; died in Rockville Centre, N. Y., May 7, 1940; interment in Greenwood Cemetery, Brooklyn, N. Y.

HOGAN, William, a Representative from New York; born in the parish of St. Paul's Covent Garden, London, England, July 17, 1792; as a young man went with his father to Cape Colony, where he learned the Dutch language; immigrated to the United States in 1803 with his parents, who settled in New York City; pursued classical studies, and was graduated from Columbia College, New York City, in 1811; served in the War of 1812 and fought in the Battle of Plattsburg on Clinton's staff; studied law; was admitted to the bar but did not engage in practice; became largely interested in undeveloped lands in Franklin County; member of the State assembly in 1822 and 1823; county judge of Franklin County 1829–1837; elected as a Jackson Democrat to the Twenty-second Congress (March 4, 1831–March 3, 1833); unsuccessful candidate for reelection in 1832 to the Twenty-third Congress; was appointed examiner of claims on March 30, 1855, and subsequently became a translator in the Department of State at Washington, D. C., serving until October 8, 1869, when he retired to private life; died in Washington, D. C., November 25, 1874; interment in Trinity Church Cemetery, New York City, N. Y.

HOGE, John (brother of William Hoge), a Representative from Pennsylvania; born near Hogestown, Pa., September 10, 1760; pursued English studies; served in the Revolutionary War as ensign in the Ninth Pennsylvania Regiment; moved to what is now Washington, Pa., in 1782, which he and his brother William founded; delegate to the State constitutional convention in 1790; member of the State senate 1790–1795;

elected as a Democrat to the Eighth Congress to fill the vacancy caused by the resignation of his brother, William Hoge, and served from November 2, 1804, to March 3, 1805; died at Meadow Lands, near Washington, Pa., August 4, 1824; interment in the City Cemetery, Washington, Pa.

HOGE, John Blair, a Representative from West Virginia; born in Richmond, Va., on February 2, 1825; studied law; was admitted to the bar in April 1845 and commenced practice in Martinsburg; chosen president of the Bank of Berkeley, Virginia (now West Virginia), in 1853; served in the Virginia House of Delegates 1855–1859; delegate to the Democratic National Conventions at Charleston and Baltimore in 1860; during the Civil War served in the Confederate Army in line and staff until paroled in 1865; engaged in journalism; resumed the practice of law in Martinsburg, W. Va., in 1870; delegate to the State constitutional convention in 1872; member of the Democratic National Committee 1872–1876; judge of the third judicial circuit in 1872, which office he resigned in August 1880; elected as a Democrat to the Forty-seventh Congress (March 4, 1881–March 3, 1883); United States district attorney for the District of Columbia 1885–1889; died in Martinsburg, W. Va., March 1, 1896; interment in Norborne Cemetery.

HOGE, Joseph Pendleton, a Representative from Illinois; born in Steubenville, Ohio, December 15, 1810; attended the common schools and was graduated from Jefferson College; studied law; was admitted to the bar in 1836; moved to Illinois and located in Galena in 1836 and practiced law; held several local offices; elected as a Democrat to the Twenty-eighth and Twenty-ninth Congresses (March 4, 1843–March 3, 1847); was not a candidate for renomination in 1846; resumed the practice of law in Galena; moved to California in 1853 and continued the practice of his profession; unsuccessful candidate for election to the United States Senate in 1869; president of the State constitutional convention in 1878 and of the board of freeholders in 1880; judge of the superior court from January 1, 1889, until his death in San Francisco, Calif., August 14, 1891; interment in Laurel Hill Cemetery.

HOGE, Solomon Lafayette, a Representative from South Carolina; born in Pickreltown, Logan County, Ohio, July 11, 1836; attended Bellefontaine (Ohio) public schools and Northwood College, Northwood, Ohio (now Geneva College, Beaver Falls, Pa.); received a classical education, and was graduated from the Cincinnati Law School in 1859; was admitted to the bar in 1859 and commenced practice in Bellefontaine, Ohio; during the Civil War entered the Union Army in 1861 as first lieutenant in the Ohio Volunteer Infantry and was subsequently promoted to the rank of captain; moved to Columbia, S. C. in 1868; associate justice of the State supreme court 1868–1870; successfully contested as a Republican the election of J. P. Reed to the Forty-first Congress and served from April 8, 1869, to March 3, 1871; comptroller general of South Carolina in 1874 and 1875; elected to the Forty-fourth Congress (March 4, 1875–March 3, 1877); was not a candidate for renomination in 1876; moved to Kenton, Ohio, in September 1877 and practiced law until 1882; president of the First National Bank of Kenton; died in Battle Creek, Mich., February 23, 1909; interment in Grove Cemetery, Kenton, Ohio.

HOGE, William (brother of John Hoge), a Representative from Pennsylvania; born near Hogestown, Cumberland County, Pa., in 1762; received a limited schooling; moved to western Pennsylvania in 1782, where he and his brother John founded the town of Washington, Pa.; member of the State house of representatives in 1796 and 1797; elected as a Federalist to the Seventh and Eighth Congresses and served from March 4, 1801, until his resignation on October 15, 1804; elected to the Tenth Congress (March 4, 1807–March 3, 1809); retired to his farm near Washington, Pa., where he died September 25, 1814; interment in the "Old Graveyard."

HOGEBOOM, James Lawrence, a Representative from New York; born in Ghent, Columbia County, N. Y., August 25, 1766; moved to Pittstown, Rensselaer County, N. Y., in 1794; moved to Castleton, N. Y., in April 1802; merchant; member of the State house of representatives in 1804, 1805, and 1808; judge of Rensselaer County 1805–1808; member of the State constitutional convention in 1821; elected as a Whig to the Eighteenth Congress (March 4, 1823–March 3, 1825); engaged in the mercantile business; died in Castleton, N. Y., December 23, 1839; interment in Castleton Cemetery.

HOGG, Charles Edgar (father of Robert Lynn Hogg), a Representative from West Virginia; born on a farm near Point Pleasant, Mason County, Va. (now West Virginia), December 21, 1852; attended the common schools at Locust Grove, Carleton College, Racine, Ohio, and was graduated from Oldham & Hawe's Business College, Pomeroy, Ohio, in 1869; taught school and was employed as a bookkeeper 1870–1873; studied law; was admitted to the bar in 1875 and commenced practice in Point Pleasant, W. Va.; county superintendent of free schools of Mason County 1875–1879; presidential elector on the Democratic ticket of Cleveland and Hendricks in 1884; elected as a Democrat to the Fiftieth Congress (March 4, 1887–March 3, 1889); unsuccessful candidate for renomination in 1888; resumed the practice of law in Point Pleasant, W. Va.; became affiliated with the Republican Party in 1900; dean of the College of Law of West Virginia University at Morgantown 1906–1913; author of several works on legal procedure; died in Point Pleasant, W. Va., June 14, 1935; interment in Lone Oak Cemetery.

HOGG, David, a Representative from Indiana; born near Crothersville, Jackson County, Ind., August 21, 1886; attended the common schools; was graduated from Indiana University College of Liberal Arts at Bloomington in 1909 and from the law department of Indiana University in 1912; was admitted to the bar in 1913 and commenced practice in Fort Wayne, Ind.; chairman of the Allen County Republican Committee 1922–1924; elected as a Republican to the Sixty-ninth and to the three succeeding Congresses (March 4, 1925–March 3, 1933); unsuccessful candidate for reelection in 1932 to the Seventy-third Congress and for election in 1934 to the Seventy-fourth Congress and in 1936 to the Seventy-fifth Congress; resumed the practice of law; organized a mutual life insurance company in 1939; president of Goodwill Industries of Fort Wayne 1940–1943; co-publisher of an interdenominational newspaper since 1941; is a resident of Fort Wayne, Ind.

HOGG, Herschel Millard, a Representative from Colorado; born in Youngstown, Mahoning County, Ohio, November 21, 1853; attended the common schools, and was graduated from Monmouth College, Monmouth, Ill., in June 1876; studied law; was admitted to the bar in 1878 and commenced practice in Indianola, Iowa; moved to Gunnison, Colo., in 1881 and resumed the practice of law; city attorney of Gunnison in 1882 and 1883; district attorney of the seventh judicial district of Colorado 1885–1893; moved to Telluride, Colo., in 1888; city attorney 1890–1898; county attorney of San Miguel County, Colo., 1890–1902; elected as a Republican to the Fifty-eighth and Fifty-ninth Congresses (March 4, 1903–March 3, 1907); was not a candidate for renomination in 1906; resumed

the practice of law in Cortez, Colo.; retired from political life in 1915; engaged in mining; resided in Denver, Colo., until his death there August 27, 1934; interment in Crown Hill Cemetery.

HOGG, Robert Lynn (son of Charles Edgar Hogg), a Representative from West Virginia; born in Point Pleasant, Mason County, W. Va., December 30, 1893; attended the public schools and West Virginia Preparatory School; was graduated from the University of West Virginia at Morgantown in 1914 and from its law department in 1916; was admitted to the bar in 1916 and commenced practice in Point Pleasant, W. Va.; during the First World War was commissioned a second lieutenant, Coast Artillery Corps; transferred to the Air Service and commissioned a first lieutenant, and served from April 1917 to July 1919, with overseas service; resumed the practice of law in Point Pleasant, W. Va.; prosecuting attorney of Mason County 1921–1924; member of the State senate 1925–1929; elected as a Republican to the Seventy-first Congress to fill the vacancy caused by the death of James A. Hughes; reelected to the Seventy-second Congress and served from November 4, 1930, to March 3, 1933; unsuccessful candidate for reelection in 1932 to the Seventy-third Congress; resumed the practice of law in Point Pleasant, W. Va.; assistant general counsel of the Association of Life Insurance Presidents, New York City, N. Y., 1935–1942, and associate general counsel 1942–1944; executive and vice president of American Life Convention, Chicago, Ill., 1944–1954; senior vice president, advisory counsel, and vice chairman of the board, Equitable Life Assurance Society of United States, from 1954 until retirement in 1960, continuing to serve as a member of its board and executive committee; counsel to a law firm in Charleston, W. Va.; resides in Millwood (Douglass Farm), W. Va.

HOGG, Samuel, a Representative from Tennessee; born in Halifax, N. C., April 18, 1783; attended the public schools in Caswell County; taught school for a short time; studied medicine in Gallatin, Sumner County, Tenn., about 1804; moved to Lebanon County, Tenn., after a short time; surgeon in the First Regiment of Tennessee Volunteer Infantry from November 21, 1812, to April 22, 1813; hospital surgeon on the staff of Maj. Gen. Andrew Jackson in the expedition against the Creek Indians from February 22 to May 25, 1814; also hospital surgeon on the staff of Maj. Gen. William Carroll from November 13, 1814, to May 13, 1815; member of the State house of representatives; elected as a Democrat to the Fifteenth Congress (March 4, 1817–March 3, 1819); engaged in the practice of medicine in Lebanon, Tenn., until 1828, in Nashville 1828–1836 and 1838–1840, and in Natchez 1836–1838; president of the State Medical Society of Tennessee in 1840; died in Rutherford County, Tenn., May 28, 1842; interment in Nashville City Cemetery.

HOIDALE, Einar, a Representative from Minnesota; born in Tromso, Norway, August 17, 1870; immigrated in 1879 to the United States with his parents, who settled near Dawson, Lac qui Parle County, Minn.; attended the common schools; was graduated from the law department of the University of Minnesota at Minneapolis in 1898; was admitted to the bar the same year and commenced practice in New Ulm, Minn.; prosecuting attorney of Brown County 1900–1906; also engaged as a newspaper publisher at Dawson and Madison, Minn., 1900–1904; judge advocate of the State militia 1900–1908; moved to Minneapolis, Minn., in 1907 and continued the practice of law; delegate to the Democratic National Conventions in 1920, 1932, and 1936; unsuccessful Democratic candidate for election to the United States Senate in 1930; elected as a Democrat to the Seventy-third Congress (March 4, 1933–January 3, 1935); was not a candidate for renomination in 1934, but was an unsuccessful candidate for election to the United States Senate; returned to Minneapolis, Minn., and practiced law; died in St. Petersburg, Fla., December 5, 1952; interment in Lakewood Cemetery, Minneapolis, Minn.

HOLADAY, William Perry, a Representative from Illinois; born near Ridgefarm, Vermilion County, Ill., on December 14, 1882; attended the common schools, Vermilion Grove (Ill.) Academy, Penn College, Oskaloosa, Iowa, and the University of Missouri at Columbia; was graduated from the law department of the University of Illinois at Urbana in 1905; was admitted to the bar the same year and commenced practice in Danville, Vermilion County, Ill.; assistant prosecuting attorney of Vermilion County 1905–1907; member of the State house of representatives 1909–1923; elected as a Republican to the Sixty-eighth and to the four succeeding Congresses (March 4, 1923–March 3, 1933); unsuccessful candidate for reelection in 1932 to the Seventy-third Congress; resumed the practice of law in Danville, Ill.; died in Georgetown, Vermilion County, Ill., January 29, 1946; interment in Georgetown Cemetery.

HOLBROCK, Greg John, a Representative from Ohio; born in Hamilton, Butler County, Ohio, June 21, 1906; attended the parochial schools and Notre Dame University, South Bend, Ind.; was graduated from Xavier University, Cincinnati, Ohio, in 1928, and from the law school of the University of Cincinnati, Cincinnati, Ohio, in 1932; was admitted to the bar in 1932 and commenced practice in Hamilton, Ohio; delegate to the Democratic State conventions in 1938, 1939, and 1940; elected as a Democrat to the Seventy-seventh Congress (January 3, 1941–January 3, 1943); unsuccessful candidate for reelection in 1942 to the Seventy-eighth Congress; during World War II served in the United States Navy from 1943 to January 18, 1946; resumed law practice; delegate to the Democratic National Conventions in 1948 and 1960; is a resident of Hamilton, Ohio.

HOLBROOK, Edward Dexter, a Delegate from Idaho; born in Elyria, Lorain County, Ohio, May 6, 1836; attended the common schools and Oberlin (Ohio) College; studied law; was admitted to the bar in 1859 and commenced practice in Elyria; moved to the Pacific coast in 1859 and practiced law for a short time at Weaverville, Calif.; moved to Placerville, Idaho, in 1863 and resumed the practice of law; elected as a Democrat to the Thirty-ninth and Fortieth Congresses (March 4, 1865–March 3, 1869); was not a candidate for reelection; shot by Charles H. Douglas in Idaho City, Idaho, on June 17, 1870, and died from his wounds in that city the next day, June 18, 1870; interment in the Masonic Burial Ground.

HOLCOMBE, George, a Representative from New Jersey; born in West Amwell (now Lambertsville), Hunterdon County, N. J., in March 1786; completed preparatory studies, and was graduated from Princeton College in 1805; attended the medical department of the University of Pennsylvania at Philadelphia; later studied medicine in Trenton, N. J., and was granted a license by the Medical Society of New Jersey; practiced medicine in Allentown, N. J., 1808–1815; held several local offices; member of the State general assembly in 1815 and 1816; elected as a Democrat to the Seventeenth and to the three succeeding Congresses and served from March 4, 1821, until his death in Allentown, N. J., January 14, 1828; interment in the Congressional Cemetery, Washington, D. C.

HOLIFIELD, Chet, a Representative from California; born in Mayfield, Graves County, Ky., December 3, 1903; moved with his family to Springfield, Ark., in 1905; attended the public

schools; moved to Montebello, Calif., in 1920 and engaged in the manufacture and selling of men's apparel 1920–1943; chairman of the Los Angeles County Democratic Central Committee of the Fifty-first District 1934–1938; chairman of the California State Central Committee of the Twelfth Congressional District 1938–1940; delegate to the Democratic National Convention at Chicago in 1940; elected as a Democrat to the Seventy-eighth and to the eight succeeding Congresses (January 3, 1943–January 3, 1961). *Reelected to the Eighty-seventh Congress.*

HOLLADAY, Alexander Richmond, a Representative from Virginia; born in Prospect Hill, Spotsylvania County, Va., September 18, 1811; attended the public schools, received special training under John Lewis of Spotsylvania County, and attended the University of Virginia at Charlottesville; studied law; was admitted to the bar and practiced in Spotsylvania, Orange, and Louisa Counties; member of the State house of delegates 1845–1847; held several local offices; elected as a Democrat to the Thirty-first and Thirty-second Congresses (March 4, 1849–March 3, 1853); declined to be a candidate for renomination; moved to Richmond, Va., in 1853 and practiced law; president of the Virginia Board of Public Works 1857–1861; died in Richmond, Va., January 29, 1877; interment in family burial ground called "Prospect Hill" in Spotsylvania County, Va.

HOLLAND, Cornelius, a Representative from Maine; born in Sutton, Mass., July 9, 1783; attended the common schools; studied medicine and commenced practice in Livermore, Maine, in 1814; moved to Canton, Maine, in 1815; also engaged in agricultural pursuits; delegate to the Maine constitutional convention in 1819; member of the Maine House of Representatives in 1821 and 1822; served in the State senate in 1822, 1825, and 1826; justice of the peace 1826–1855; elected as a Democrat to the Twenty-first Congress to fill the vacancy caused by the resignation of James W. Ripley; reelected to the Twenty-second Congress and served from December 6, 1830, to March 3, 1833; resumed the practice of medicine and engaged in agricultural pursuits; died in Canton Point, Maine, June 2, 1870; interment in Hillside Cemetery.

HOLLAND, Edward Everett, a Representative from Virginia; born near Suffolk, Nansemond County, Va., February 26, 1861; attended private schools, Richmond (Va.) College, and was graduated from the University of Virginia at Charlottesville; studied law; was admitted to the bar in 1882 and commenced practice in Suffolk, Va.; mayor of Suffolk 1885–1887; Commonwealth attorney for Nansemond County 1887–1907; elected president of the Farmers Bank of Nansemond in 1892; member of the State senate 1907–1911; elected as a Democrat to the Sixty-second and to the four succeeding Congresses (March 4, 1911–March 3, 1921); was not a candidate for renomination in 1920; resumed his banking pursuits; delegate to the Democratic National Convention at San Francisco in 1920, and at New York in 1924; member of the State senate 1930–1941; died in Suffolk, Va., on October 23, 1941; interment in Cedar Hill Cemetery, Suffolk, Va.

HOLLAND, Elmer Joseph, a Representative from Pennsylvania; born in Pittsburgh, Pa., January 8, 1894; attended the public schools, Duquesne University, Pittsburgh, Pa., and the University of Montpelier, France; was graduated from Samaur Cavalry School, France, in 1919; served with the American Expeditionary Forces during the First World War as a second lieutenant of Field Artillery; engaged as sales and advertising manager for a glass manufacturer 1915–1933; member of the State house of representatives 1934–1942; superintendent of highways and sewers, Pittsburgh, Pa., 1940–1942; elected as a Democrat to the Seventy-seventh Congress to fill the vacancy caused by the resignation of Joseph A. McArdle and served from May 19, 1942, to January 3, 1943; was not a candidate for renomination in 1942; served as a major in the European Theater of Operations during World War II; member of the State senate 1943–1956; elected to the Eighty-fourth Congress to fill the vacancy caused by the death of Vera Buchanan; reelected to the Eighty-fifth and Eighty-sixth Congresses and served from January 24, 1956, to January 3, 1961. *Reelected to the Eighty-seventh Congress.*

HOLLAND, James, a Representative from North Carolina; born in Anson County, near the present town of Rutherfordton, N. C., in 1754; received a very limited education; was a major in the State militia and also saw service in the Continental line 1775–1783; sheriff of Tryon County from July 1777 to July 1778; justice of the peace of Rutherford County 1780–1800; comptroller of Rutherford County from July 1782 to January 1785; member of the State senate in 1783; served in the State house of commons in 1786 and again in 1789; delegate to the second State constitutional convention in 1789 that adopted the Federal Constitution; member of the first board of trustees of the University of North Carolina 1789–1795; studied law; was admitted to the bar on October 15, 1793, and commenced practice in Rutherfordton, N. C.; elected as an Anti-Federalist to the Fourth Congress (March 4, 1795–March 3, 1797); declined to be a candidate for reelection, preferring to serve in the State senate; again a member of the State senate in 1797; resumed the practice of his profession and also engaged in agricultural pursuits; elected to the Seventh and to the four succeeding Congresses (March 4, 1801–March 3, 1811); was not a candidate for renomination in 1810; retired from public life and in 1811 moved to what is now Maury County, Tenn., engaging in agricultural pursuits near Columbia; justice of the peace 1812–1818; died on his estate in Maury County, Tenn., May 19, 1823; interment in the Holland Family (now known as Watson) Cemetery, nine miles east of Columbia, Tenn., in District Four, Maury County, Tenn.

HOLLAND, Spessard Lindsey, a Senator from Florida; born in Bartow, Polk County, Fla., July 10, 1892; attended the public schools; was graduated from Emory College (now Emory University) near Atlanta, Ga., in 1912 and from the University of Florida College of Law at Gainesville in 1916; taught in public schools of Warrenton, Ga., 1912–1914; was admitted to the bar in 1916 and commenced practice in Bartow, Fla.; during the First World War served in the Coast Artillery Corps, United States Army, all grades through captain and as aerial observer, Twenty-fourth Squadron, Army Air Corps, in France from March 1918 to January 1919; awarded the Distinguished Service Cross; prosecuting attorney of Polk County, Fla., in 1919 and 1920; county judge of Polk County 1921–1929; member of the Florida State senate 1932–1940; Governor of Florida 1941–1945; trustee of Southern College 1932–1935; trustee of Emory University 1943–1946; appointed as a Democrat to the United States Senate on September 25, 1946, to fill the vacancy caused by the death of Charles O. Andrews for the term ending January 3, 1947; elected in 1946, 1952, and again in 1958 for the term ending January 3, 1965.

HOLLEMAN, Joel, a Representative from Virginia; born near Smithfield, Isle of Wight County, Va., October 1, 1799; completed preparatory studies; was graduated from Chapel Hill College, Wake Forest, N. C.; studied law; was admitted to the bar and commenced practice at Burwell Bay; member of the State house of delegates 1832–1836; member of the State senate 1836–1839;

elected as a Van Buren Democrat to the Twenty-sixth Congress and served from March 4, 1839, until 1840, when he resigned; again a member of the State house of delegates 1841–1844, and served as speaker; resumed the practice of law; died in Smithfield, Va., August 5, 1844; interment in Ivy Hill Cemetery.

HOLLEY, John Milton, a Representative from New York; born in Salisbury, Conn., November 10, 1802; was graduated from Yale College in 1822; studied law; was admitted to the bar and commenced practice at Black Rock, N. Y., in 1825; moved to Lyons, N. Y., in 1826 and continued the practice of law; member of the State assembly 1838–1841; district attorney of Wayne County 1842–1845; unsuccessful candidate for election in 1844 to the Twenty-ninth Congress; elected as a Whig to the Thirtieth Congress and served from March 4, 1847, until his death in Jacksonville, Fla., March 8, 1848; interment in the Rural Cemetery, Lyons, N. Y.

HOLLIDAY, Elias Selah, a Representative from Indiana; born in Aurora, Dearborn County, Ind., March 5, 1842; spent the early part of his life on farms in Indiana, Missouri, and Iowa; attended the common schools and taught in the public schools in Iowa; during the Civil War enlisted in the Fifth Kansas Regiment and served until August 12, 1864, when he was mustered out with the rank of first sergeant; attended Hartsville College, Bartholomew County, Ind.; engaged in teaching in Jennings County, Ind.; studied law at Mount Vernon, Ind.; was admitted to the bar in 1873 and commenced practice in Carbon, Clay County, Ind.; moved to Brazil, Ind., in 1874; mayor of Brazil, Ind., 1877–1880, 1887, and 1888; city attorney in 1884; presidential elector on the Republican ticket of Blaine and Logan in 1884; member of the city council 1892–1896; elected as a Republican to the Fifty-seventh and to the three succeeding Congresses (March 4, 1901–March 3, 1909); was not a candidate for renomination in 1908; reengaged in the practice of law in Brazil, Ind., until 1922, when he retired from active pursuits; died in Brazil, Ind., March 13, 1936; interment in Cottage Hill Cemetery.

HOLLINGSWORTH, David Adams, a Representative from Ohio; born in Belmont, Belmont County, Ohio, November 21, 1844; moved with his parents to Flushing, Ohio; attended the public schools; during the Civil War served in the Union Army in Company B, Twenty-fifth Regiment, Ohio Volunteer Infantry, 1861–1863; studied law at Mount Union College, Alliance, Ohio; was admitted to the bar in St. Clairsville, Ohio, on September 17, 1867, and commenced practice in Flushing; mayor of Flushing in 1867; moved to Cadiz, Ohio, in 1869 and continued the practice of law; elected prosecuting attorney of Harrison County in 1873 and reelected in 1875; member of the State senate in 1879 and reelected in 1881; admitted to practice before the United States Supreme Court in 1880; chairman of the Republican State convention in 1882; attorney general of Ohio in 1883 and 1884; resumed the practice of law in Cadiz; one of the organizers of the Ohio State Bar Association, serving as chairman in 1908; elected as a Republican to the Sixty-first Congress (March 4, 1909–March 3, 1911); unsuccessful candidate for reelection in 1910 to the Sixty-second Congress; resumed the practice of law in Cadiz; elected to the Sixty-fourth and Sixty-fifth Congresses (March 4, 1915–March 3, 1919); declined to be a candidate for renomination in 1918; resumed the practice of law until his death in Cadiz, Ohio, December 3, 1929; interment in Cadiz Cemetery.

HOLLIS, Henry French, a Senator from New Hampshire; born in Concord, N. H., August 30, 1869; attended the public schools and studied under private tutors; engaged in civil engineering for the Chicago, Burlington & Quincy Railroad in 1886 and 1887; was graduated from Harvard University in 1892; studied law; was admitted to the bar in 1893 and commenced practice in Concord; unsuccessful candidate for election in 1900 to the Fifty-seventh Congress; unsuccessful Democratic candidate for Governor in 1902 and 1904; elected as a Democrat to the United States Senate for the term beginning March 4, 1913, and served from March 13, 1913, until March 3, 1919; declined to be a candidate for renomination in 1918; Regent of the Smithsonian Institution 1914–1919; delegate to the Democratic National Convention at St. Louis in 1916; representative of the United States Treasury in Europe with the Interallied War Finance Council from July to December 1918; appointed a member of the United States Liquidation Commission for France and England in February 1919, with residence in Paris, France; commenced the practice of international law in 1919; appointed to the International Bank of Bulgaria December 2, 1922; died in Paris, France, July 7, 1949; interment in Blossom Hill Cemetery, Concord, N. H.

HOLLISTER, John Baker, a Representative from Ohio; born in Cincinnati, Ohio, November 7, 1890; attended the public schools, and St. Paul's School, Concord, N. H.; was graduated from Yale University, New Haven, Conn., in 1911; attended the University of Munich, Germany, in 1911 and 1912, and was graduated from Harvard University Law School, Cambridge, Mass., in 1915; was admitted to the bar the same year and commenced practice in Cincinnati, Ohio; during the First World War attended reserve officers' training camp and taught at the Heavy Artillery School, Fort Monroe, Va.; appointed on August 15, 1917, a first lieutenant in the United States Army and served overseas as captain of Battery B, Forty-sixth Artillery Corps, later being in command of the Third Battalion of his regiment; on detached service with American Relief Administration under Herbert Hoover, January to June 1919, in Poland and Lithuania, from which he was discharged June 15, 1919, at Gievres, France; after the war resumed the practice of law in Cincinnati, Ohio; director of various financial and manufacturing corporations; member of the Cincinnati Board of Education 1921–1929; served as trustee of the Cincinnati Art Museum, the Cincinnati Natural History Museum, and the Cincinnati Orphan Asylum; chairman of the Colored Industrial School; elected as a Republican to the Seventy-second Congress to fill the vacancy caused by the death of Nicholas Longworth; reelected to the Seventy-third and Seventy-fourth Congresses and served from November 3, 1931, to January 3, 1937; was an unsuccessful candidate for reelection in 1936 to the Seventy-fifth Congress; resumed the practice of his profession; delegate to the Republican National Conventions in 1940, 1948, and 1952; executive director, Hoover Commission, from October 1953 to July 1955; Director, International Cooperation Administration, from June 15, 1955, until his resignation September 13, 1957; returned to law practice in Cincinnati, Ohio.

HOLLOWAY, David Pierson, a Representative from Indiana; born in Waynesville, Warren County, Ohio, December 7, 1809; moved with his parents to Cincinnati in 1813; attended the common schools; learned the printing business and served four years in the office of the Cincinnati Gazette; moved to Richmond, Ind., in 1823; purchased the Richmond Palladium in 1832 and was its editor and proprietor until he died; member of the State house of representatives in 1843 and 1844; served in the State senate 1844–1850; appointed in 1849 examiner of land offices; elected by the People's Party to the Thirty-fourth Congress (March 4, 1855–March 3, 1857); appointed Commissioner of Patents and served from 1861 to 1865; engaged as a patent attorney in Washington, D. C., until his death, September 9, 1883; interment in Maple Grove Cemetery, Richmond, Ind.; reinterment in Earlham Cemetery.

HOLMAN, Rufus Cecil, a Senator from Oregon; born in Portland, Oreg., October 14, 1877; attended the public schools; district school teacher at Meadowbrook, Clackamas County, Oreg., 1896–1898; engaged in agricultural pursuits, steamboating, bookkeeping, accounting, and auditing 1899–1910; in 1910 engaged in the manufacture of record books and paper boxes, and in the ice and cold storage business in Portland, Oreg.; member of the Portland Charter Commission in 1912; member and chairman of the Multnomah County Commission 1913–1921; member and chairman of the Columbia River Interstate Bridge Commission 1913–1921; president of the Mount Hood Loop Road Association 1913–1921; member of the board of directors of the Portland Library Association 1913–1921, vice president of the West Side Pacific Highway Association 1913–1921, and member of the Port of Portland Commission in 1931; State treasurer of Oregon 1931–1939; elected as a Republican to the United States Senate and served from January 3, 1939, to January 3, 1945; unsuccessful candidate for renomination in 1944; resumed management of Portland Paper Box Co., Portland, Oreg., and of a farm near Molalla, Oreg.; died in Portland, Oreg., November 27, 1959; interment in Riverview Cemetery.

HOLMAN, William Steele, a Representative from Indiana; born near Aurora, Dearborn County, Ind., September 6, 1822; attended the common schools and Franklin College, Franklin, Ind.; taught in the public schools; studied law; was admitted to the bar and practiced; judge of the probate court 1843–1846; prosecuting attorney 1847–1849; member of the State constitutional convention in 1850; member of the State house of representatives in 1851 and 1852; judge of the court of common pleas 1852–1856; elected as a Democrat to the Thirty-sixth, Thirty-seventh, and Thirty-eighth Congresses (March 4, 1859–March 3, 1865); not a candidate for reelection to the Thirty-ninth Congress; elected to the Fortieth and to the four succeeding Congresses (March 4, 1867–March 3, 1877); not a candidate for election to the Forty-fifth Congress; elected to the Forty-seventh and to the six succeeding Congresses (March 4, 1881–March 3, 1895); unsuccessful candidate for reelection to the Fifty-fourth Congress; again elected to the Fifty-fifth Congress and served from March 4, 1897, until his death in Washington, D. C., April 22, 1897; interment in Veraestau Cemetery, Aurora, Ind.

HOLMES, Adoniram Judson, a Representative from Iowa; born in Wooster, Wayne County, Ohio, March 2, 1842; moved with his parents to Palmyra, Wis., in 1853; attended the common schools; entered Milton College, Milton, Wis., but left in 1862 to enter the Union Army, where he served as a private in the Twenty-fourth Regiment, Wisconsin Volunteer Infantry, and as first lieutenant in the Thirty-seventh Regiment, Wisconsin Volunteer Infantry, until the close of the Civil War; completed his studies in Milton College and was graduated from the law department of the University of Michigan at Ann Arbor in 1867; was admitted to the bar and commenced practice in Boone, Iowa, in 1868; mayor in 1880 and 1881; member of the State house of representatives in 1882 and 1883; elected as a Republican to the Forty-eighth, Forty-ninth, and Fiftieth Congresses (March 4, 1883–March 3, 1889); unsuccessful candidate for renomination in 1888; Sergeant at Arms of the National House of Representatives in the Fifty-first Congress; resumed the practice of law in Boone, Iowa; county attorney 1896–1899; died in Clarinda, Iowa, January 21, 1902; interment in Linwood Cemetery, Boone, Iowa.

HOLMES, Charles Horace, a Representative from New York; born in Albion, Orleans County, N. Y., October 24, 1827; attended the public schools, Albion (N. Y.) Academy and was graduated from the Albany Law School; was admitted to the bar in 1855 and commenced practice in Albion; elected as a Republican to the Forty-first Congress to fill the vacancy caused by the resignation of Noah Davis and served from December 6, 1870, to March 3, 1871; was not a candidate for renomination; resumed the practice of law in Albion, N. Y., where he died October 2, 1874; interment in Mount Albion Cemetery.

HOLMES, David, a Representative from Virginia and a Senator from Mississippi; born at Mary Ann Furnace, near Hanover, York County, Pa., March 10, 1769; attended Winchester Academy, Winchester, Va.; studied law; was admitted to the bar in 1791 and commenced practice in Winchester, Va.; held several local offices; elected to the Fifth and to the five succeeding Congresses (March 4, 1797–March 3, 1809); was not a candidate for renomination in 1808; Governor of the Territory of Mississippi 1809–1817; Governor of the State of Mississippi from October 7, 1817, to January 5, 1820; appointed to the United States Senate to fill the vacancy caused by the resignation of Walter Leake; subsequently elected and served from August 30, 1820, to September 25, 1825, when he resigned; returned to Winchester, Va., in 1827; died at Jordan's Sulphur Springs, near Winchester, Va., on August 20, 1832; interment in Mount Hebron Cemetery, Winchester, Va.

HOLMES, Elias Bellows, a Representative from New York; born in Fletcher, Vt., May 22, 1807; attended the district schools and St. Albans Academy; taught school; studied law at Pittsford, N. Y.; was admitted to the bar in 1830; moved to Brockport, N. Y., in 1831, and commenced the practice of law; engaged in agricultural pursuits and transportation; engaged in running canal packets between Rochester and Buffalo 1840–1855; one of the promoters and constructors of the Rochester & Niagara Falls Railroad and was a director until it merged with the New York Central Railroad; elected as a Whig to the Twenty-ninth and Thirtieth Congresses (March 4, 1845–March 3, 1849); was not a candidate for renomination; resumed agricultural pursuits; died in Brockport, N. Y., July 31, 1866; interment in the City Cemetery.

HOLMES, Gabriel, a Representative from North Carolina; born near Clinton, Sampson County, N. C., in 1769; attended Zion Parnassus Academy in Rowan County and Harvard University; studied law in Raleigh, N. C.; was admitted to the bar in 1790 and commenced practice in Clinton, N. C.; served in the State house of commons 1794 and 1795; member of the State senate 1797–1802, 1812, and 1813; Governor of North Carolina 1821–1824; elected to the Nineteenth, Twentieth, and Twenty-first Congresses and served from March 4, 1825, until his death near Clinton, Sampson County, N. C., September 26, 1829; interment in the family burial plot on his estate.

HOLMES, Isaac Edward, a Representative from South Carolina; born in Charleston, S. C., April 6, 1796; attended the common schools, received private tuition, and was graduated from Yale College in 1815; studied law; was admitted to the bar in 1818 and commenced practice in Charleston; member of the city council; served in the State house of representatives 1826–1833; elected as a Democrat to the Twenty-sixth and to the five succeeding Congresses (March 4, 1839–March 3, 1851); practiced law in San Francisco, Calif., 1851–1854, when he returned to Charleston, S. C.; again resided in San Francisco 1857–1861; returned to South Carolina in 1861 and was appointed a commissioner of the State to confer with the Federal Government; died in Charleston, S. C., February 24, 1867; interment in Circular Churchyard.

HOLMES, John, a Representative from Massachusetts and a Senator from Maine; born in Kingston, Mass., March 14, 1773; attended private schools at Kingston and Plymouth; was graduated from Brown University, Providence, R. I., in 1796; studied law; was admitted to the bar in 1799 and commenced practice in Alfred, Maine (then a district of Massachusetts); also engaged in literary pursuits; elected as a Federalist a member of the Massachusetts State House of Representatives in 1802 and 1803; elected as a Democrat a member of the State senate in 1813 and 1814; one of the commissioners under the treaty of Ghent in 1814 and 1815 to divide the islands of Passamaquoddy Bay between the United States and Great Britain; elected as a Democrat from Massachusetts to the Fifteenth and Sixteenth Congresses and served from March 4, 1817, to March 15, 1820, when he resigned; delegate to the Maine constitutional convention; upon separation from Massachusetts and the admission of the State into the Union was elected to the United States Senate from Maine and served from June 13, 1820, to March 3, 1827; again elected to the United States Senate to fill the vacancy caused by the resignation of Albion K. Parris and served from January 15, 1829, to March 3, 1833; resumed law practice; member of State house of representatives 1835–1838; appointed United States attorney in 1841 and served until his death in Portland, Maine, July 7, 1843; interment in private tomb of Cotton Brooks, Eastern Cemetery.

HOLMES, Otis Halbert (Hal) (grandson of Dudley Chase Haskell), a Representative from Washington; born in Cresco, Howard County, Iowa, February 22, 1902; moved in 1915 to Walla Walla, Wash., where he attended the public schools; was graduated from Whitman College, Walla Walla, Wash., in 1923 and from Columbia University, New York City, in 1927; teacher of economics at Ellensburg (Wash.) High School in 1924; member of the faculty of Central Washington College of Education at Ellensburg in 1925 and 1930–1942; taught at Columbia University, New York City, in 1928 and 1929; was livestock rancher and operator; elected as a Republican to the Seventy-eighth and to the seven succeeding Congresses (January 3, 1943–January 3, 1959); was not a candidate for renomination in 1958; retired; is a resident of Ellensburg, Wash.

HOLMES, Pehr Gustaf, a Representative from Massachusetts; born in Mölnbacka, Värmland, Sweden, April 9, 1881; in 1886 immigrated to the United States with his parents, who settled in Worcester, Mass.; attended the public schools; engaged in manufacturing; organizer and owner of Holmes Electrotype Foundry in 1909; also engaged in the banking and insurance business; member of the common council of Worcester, Mass., 1908–1911; member of the board of aldermen 1913–1916, serving as president in 1915 and 1916; mayor of Worcester 1917–1919; member of the Governor's council, seventh Massachusetts district 1925–1928; elected as a Republican to the Seventy-second and to the seven succeeding Congresses (March 4, 1931–January 3, 1947); unsuccessful candidate for reelection in 1946 to the Eightieth Congress; returned to Worcester, Mass., and his electrotype business; died in Venice, Fla., December 19, 1952; interment in Old Swedish Cemetery, Worcester, Mass.

HOLMES, Sidney Tracy, a Representative from New York; born in Schaghticoke, Rensselaer County, N. Y., August 14, 1815; moved with his parents to Morrisville, Madison County, N. Y., in 1819; attended the public schools and was graduated from Morrisville (N. Y.) Academy; taught school; was engaged in civil engineering on the Chenango and Black River Canals for five years; studied law; was admitted to the bar in 1841 and commenced practice in Morrisville, N. Y.; loan commissioner for Madison County 1848–1851; judge and surrogate for Madison County 1851–1864; elected as a Republican to the Thirty-ninth Congress (March 4, 1865–March 3, 1867); was not a candidate for renomination in 1866; resumed the practice of law in Morrisville, N. Y., for a short time, and in Utica, N. Y., until 1872, when he moved to Bay City, Bay County, Mich., continuing the practice of law; died in Bay City, Mich., January 16, 1890; interment in Cedar Street Cemetery, Morrisville, N. Y.

HOLMES, Uriel, a Representative from Connecticut; born in East Haddam, Middlesex County, Conn., August 26, 1764; moved with his parents to Hartland, Conn.; attended the common schools; and was graduated from Yale College in 1784; studied law; was admitted to the bar in 1798 and commenced practice in Litchfield, Conn.; member of the State house of representatives 1803–1805; prosecuting attorney of Litchfield County 1807–1814; judge of the Litchfield County court 1814–1817; elected as a Federalist to the Fifteenth Congress and served from March 4, 1817, until his resignation in 1818; died in Canton, Conn., May 18, 1827; interment in East Cemetery, Litchfield, Conn.

HOLSEY, Hopkins, a Representative from Georgia; born near Lynchburg, Campbell County, Va., August 25, 1779; received a good English training and attended the University of Virginia at Charlottesville; was graduated from a law school in Litchfield, Conn.; was admitted to the bar and commenced practice in Hamilton, Ga.; held several local offices and represented Hancock County several years in the State house of representatives; moved to Harris County; elected as a Union Democrat to the Twenty-fourth Congress to fill the vacancy caused by the resignation of James C. Terrell; reelected to the Twenty-fifth Congress and served from October 5, 1835, to March 3, 1839; moved to Athens, Ga., and engaged in newspaper work as publisher of the Southern Banner; unsuccessful candidate for election in 1852 to the Thirty-third Congress; relinquished the newspaper business and resumed the practice of law, in Butler, Ga.; died at his home, "Brightwater," near Butler, Ga., March 31, 1859; interment on the side of a high hill on his estate.

HOLT, Hines, a Representative from Georgia; born near Milledgeville, Baldwin County, Ga., April 27, 1805; completed preparatory studies; was graduated from Franklin College (now the University of Georgia) at Athens in 1824; studied law; was admitted to the bar and commenced practice in Columbus, Ga.; elected as a Whig to the Twenty-sixth Congress to fill the vacancy caused by the resignation of Walter T. Colquitt and served from February 1 to March 3, 1841; resumed the practice of law; member of the State senate in 1859; Member of the House of Representatives of the First Confederate Congress 1862–1864; died while attending as a delegate the State constitutional convention at Milledgeville, Ga., on November 4, 1865; interment in Linwood Cemetery, Columbus, Ga.

HOLT, Joseph Franklin, 3d, a Representative from California; born in Springfield, Hampden County, Mass., July 6, 1924; moved to Los Angeles, Calif., with his parents when one year of age; attended the public schools; enrolled at the University of Southern California but interrupted studies to enlist as a private in the United States Marine Corps; was called to active duty in July 1943 and rose through the ranks until discharged as a second lieutenant in October 1945; returned to the University of Southern California and graduated in 1947; engaged in the insurance business and then entered the public relations field; State president of the Young Republicans of California; in January 1951 was recalled to active duty with the Marine Corps and assigned to the Second Marine Division as an Infantry company commander; volunteered for duty in Korea and arrived there in October 1951; wounded by the explosion of an enemy booby trap while on

combat patrol, causing serious leg injury, and was discharged in May 1952; was awarded the Purple Heart; elected as a Republican to the Eighty-third and to the three succeeding Congresses (January 3, 1953–January 3, 1961); was not a candidate for renomination in 1960; is a resident of Van Nuys, Calif.

HOLT, Orrin, a Representative from Connecticut; born in Willington, Conn., March 13, 1792; received a limited schooling; engaged in agricultural pursuits; member of the State house of representatives 1830–1832; served in the State senate in 1835 and 1836; resigned in the latter year; elected as a Democrat to the Twenty-fourth Congress to fill the vacancy caused by the resignation of Andrew T. Judson; reelected to the Twenty-fifth Congress and served from December 5, 1836, to March 3, 1839; resumed agricultural pursuits; interested in military organizations of the State and held official ranks up to inspector general; died in East Willington, Conn., June 20, 1855; interment in Old Cemetery, Willington Hill, Tolland County, Conn.

HOLT, Rush Dew, a Senator from West Virginia; born in Weston, Lewis County, W. Va., June 19, 1905; attended the public schools, and West Virginia University at Morgantown; was graduated from Salem (W. Va.) College in 1924; became a teacher in Bedford City (Va.) High School and later an instructor in Salem (W. Va.) College; athletic director of St. Patrick's School in West Virginia 1925–1928; instructor in Glenville (W. Va.) State Teachers' College in 1927 and 1928; served in the State house of delegates 1931–1935; member of the United States delegation to the Interparliamentary Conference, Oslo, Norway, in 1939; elected as a Democrat to the United States Senate on November 6, 1934, for the term beginning January 3, 1935, but not having reached the age qualification required by the Constitution did not take his seat until June 21, 1935, and served until January 3, 1941; unsuccessful candidate for renomination in 1940; elected to the State house of delegates in 1942, 1944, 1946, and again in 1948 for a two-year term; unsuccessful for the Democratic gubernatorial nomination in 1944 and for the Democratic nomination in 1948 for United States Senator; engaged in research work; affiliated with the Republican Party in 1949 and was an unsuccessful Republican candidate for election to the Eighty-second Congress in 1950, and for election as Governor of West Virginia in 1952; elected to the State house of delegates in 1954 and served until his death; died in Bethesda, Md., February 8, 1955; interment in Macpelah Cemetery, Weston, W. Va.

HOLTEN, Samuel, a Delegate and a Representative from Massachusetts; born in Danvers, Mass., June 9, 1738; completed preparatory studies; studied medicine and practiced in Gloucester, Mass., for a short time; returned to Danvers and continued the practice of medicine; member of the State house of representatives in 1787; served in the State senate 1780–1782, 1784, 1786, 1789, and 1790; member of the Governor's council 1780–1782, 1784, 1786, 1789–1792, 1795, and 1796; Member of the Provincial Congress 1774–1775; member of the committee of safety in 1775; Member of the Continental Congress 1778–1780 and 1782–1787; elected President pro tempore August 17, 1785; member of the State constitutional convention in 1779; one of the signers of the Articles of Confederation in 1788; elected to the Third Congress (March 4, 1793–March 3, 1795); appointed judge of the probate court for Essex County in 1796 and served until his resignation in 1815; died in Danvers, Mass., on January 2, 1816; interment in the Holten Cemetery.

HOLTON, Hart Benton, a Representative from Maryland; born near Elkton, Cecil County, Md., October 13, 1835; attended the common schools and Hopewell Academy, Chester, Pa.; moved to Baltimore, Md., in 1857; taught school in Alberton, Howard County, Md., 1857–1873; served in the State senate 1862–1867; moved to Woodlawn, Md., in 1873; engaged in the raising of blooded horses; elected as a Republican to the Forty-eighth Congress (March 4, 1883–March 3, 1885); unsuccessful candidate for reelection in 1884 to the Forty-ninth Congress; retired from public life and became interested in stock raising; died in Woodlawn, Md., January 4, 1907; interment in Loudon Park Cemetery, Baltimore, Md.

HOLTZMAN, Lester, a Representative from New York; born in New York City, N. Y., June 1, 1913; attended the public schools; graduated from St. John's Prelaw School (evenings) and St. John's Law School, Brooklyn, N. Y., in 1935; was admitted to the bar in 1935 and began practice in Middle Village, Queens County, N. Y.; continued the general practice of law there, in Jamaica, N. Y., and in Kew Gardens, N. Y.; elected as a Democrat to the Eighty-third and to the three succeeding Congresses (January 3, 1953–January 3, 1961). *Reelected to the Eighty-seventh Congress.*

HONEYMAN, Nan Wood, a Representative from Oregon; born in West Point, Orange County, N. Y., July 15, 1881; moved with her parents to Portland, Oreg., in 1884; attended private schools, was graduated from St. Helens Hall, Portland, Oreg., in 1898, and later attended Finch School, New York, N. Y.; delegate to the State constitutional convention in 1933 which ratified the Twenty-first amendment to the Constitution of the United States and served as president; member of the State house of representatives 1935–1937; delegate to the Democratic National Conventions in 1936 and 1940; elected as a Democrat to the Seventy-fifth Congress (January 3, 1937–January 3, 1939); unsuccessful candidate for reelection in 1938 to the Seventy-sixth Congress and for election in 1940 to the Seventy-seventh Congress; senior representative of the Pacific Coast Office of Price Administration from August 1941 to May 1942; appointed by the Multnomah County Commissioners to the State senate in 1941 to fill a vacancy and served until her resignation in 1942; collector of customs, twenty-ninth district, Portland, Oreg., from May 1, 1942, to July 13, 1953; member of board of Doernbecher Hospital Guild of Portland, Oreg., 1925– ; is a resident of Portland, Oreg.

HOOD, George Ezekial, a Representative from North Carolina; born near Goldsboro, Wayne County, N. C., January 25, 1875; attended the public schools; studied telegraphy and became a telegraph operator; studied law; was admitted to the bar of the supreme court of North Carolina in 1896 and commenced practice in Goldsboro, N. C.; treasurer of Wayne County 1898–1900; served in the State house of representatives 1899–1901; mayor of Goldsboro 1901–1907; presidential elector on the Democratic ticket of Wilson and Marshall in 1912; secretary of the Wayne County Democratic executive committee 1896–1900; captain in the Second Regiment of the North Carolina National Guard and subsequently promoted to colonel 1899–1909; name presented as a candidate for Congress in 1912, but lost out at the nominating convention by less than ten votes; elected as a Democrat to the Sixty-fourth and Sixty-fifth Congresses (March 4, 1915–March 3, 1919); was not a candidate for renomination in 1918; practicing attorney in Goldsboro, N. C., until his death there March 8, 1960; interment in Willow Dale Cemetery.

HOOK, Enos, a Representative from Pennsylvania; born in Waynesburg, Greene County, Pa., December 3, 1804; received a limited schooling; studied law; was admitted to the bar in 1826 and commenced practice in Waynesburg, Pa.; member of the State house of representatives in 1837 and 1838; elected as a Dem-

ocrat to the Twenty-sixth and Twenty-seventh Congresses and served from March 4, 1839, to April 18, 1841, when he resigned; died in Waynesburg, Pa., July 15, 1841; interment in Green Mount Cemetery.

HOOK, Frank Eugene, a Representative from Michigan; born in L'Anse, Baraga County, Mich., May 26, 1893; graduated from L'Anse High School in 1912; attended College of Law of the University of Detroit, Detroit, Mich.; was graduated from the law department of Valparaiso (Ind.) University in 1918; during the First World War served in the Infantry, United States Army, from July 1918 until discharged to accept a commission as second lieutenant in February 1919; employed in lumber woods and as an iron ore miner and also as a law clerk at Wakefield, Mich., 1919–1924; member of the board of supervisors of Gogebic County, Mich., 1921–1923; was admitted to the bar in 1924 and commenced practice in Wakefield, Mich.; admitted to practice before the United States Supreme Court in 1936; served as city commissioner of Wakefield 1921–1923; municipal judge of Wakefield in 1924 and 1925; moved to Ironwood, Mich., in 1925 and continued the practice of law; president of WJMS Radio Station in Ironwood 1930–1933; delegate to Democratic National Conventions in 1936, 1940, 1944, and 1948; elected as a Democrat to the Seventy-fourth and to the three succeeding Congresses (January 3, 1935–January 3, 1943); unsuccessful candidate for reelection in 1942 to the Seventy-eighth Congress; elected to the Seventy-ninth Congress (January 3, 1945–January 3, 1947); unsuccessful candidate for reelection in 1946 to the Eightieth Congress and for election in 1948 to the United States Senate; member of President's Fair Employment Practices Committee in 1943 and 1944; appointed a member of Motor Carrier Claims Commission October 1, 1949, and served until his resignation August 22, 1950; unsuccessful candidate for election in 1954 to the Eighty-fourth Congress; resumed the practice of law in Detroit, Mich.; in 1953 moved to Ironwood, Mich., where he reestablished his law practice.

HOOKER, Charles Edward, a Representative from Mississippi; born in Union, Union County, S. C., in 1825; upon the death of his mother was reared in the home of his grandfather in Laurens District, S. C.; attended the common schools, and was graduated from the Harvard Law School in 1846; was admitted to the bar in 1848 and commenced practice in Jackson, Miss.; district attorney of the river district 1850–1854; member of the State house of representatives in 1859; resigned to enter the Confederate Army as a private during the Civil War; became lieutenant and later captain in the First Regiment of Mississippi Light Artillery; lost an arm during the siege of Vicksburg; promoted to the rank of colonel of Cavalry, assigned to duty on the military court attached to General Polk's command, and served until the close of the Civil War; elected attorney general of Mississippi in 1865 and the same year was removed with the other officers of the State by the military authorities; again elected in 1868; resumed the practice of law in Jackson, Miss.; elected as a Democrat to the Forty-fourth and to the three succeeding Congresses (March 4, 1875–March 3, 1883); delegate to the Democratic National Convention at Chicago in 1884 which nominated Cleveland and Hendricks; elected to the Fiftieth and to the three succeeding Congresses (March 4, 1887–March 3, 1895); again elected to the Fifty-seventh Congress (March 4, 1901–March 3, 1903); continued the practice of law in Jackson, Miss., where he died January 8, 1914; interment in Greenwood Cemetery.

HOOKER, James Murray, a Representative from Virginia; born in Buffalo Ridge, Patrick County, Va., October 29, 1873; attended the public schools; was graduated from William and

Mary College, Williamsburg, Va., and from the law department of Washington and Lee University, Lexington, Va., in 1896; was admitted to the bar in 1896 and commenced practice in Stuart, Va.; Commonwealth attorney for Patrick County; delegate to the Virginia constitutional convention in 1901 and 1902; member of the board of visitors to the Virginia Military Institute at Lexington 1901–1906; member of the Virginia Fisheries Commission 1908–1914; elected as a Democrat to the Sixty-seventh Congress to fill the vacancy caused by the death of Rorer A. James; reelected to the Sixty-eighth Congress and served from November 8, 1921, to March 3, 1925; was not a candidate for renomination in 1924; delegate to the Democratic National Convention at New York City in 1924 which nominated Davis and Bryan; chairman of the Democratic State committee in 1925; resumed the practice of his profession at Stuart, Patrick County, Va., where he died August 6, 1940; interment in Stuart Cemetery.

HOOKER, Warren Brewster, a Representative from New York; born in Perrysburg, Cattaraugus County, N. Y., November 24, 1856; attended the public schools and Forestville Free Academy, Forestville, N. Y.; studied law; was admitted to the bar in 1879 and commenced practice in Forestville; special surrogate of Chautauqua County 1878–1881; moved to Tacoma, Wash., and practiced there 1882–1884; returned to Fredonia, Pomfret Township, N. Y., and resumed his profession 1884–1898; supervisor of the town of Pomfret in 1889 and 1890; elected as a Republican to the Fifty-second and to the four succeeding Congresses and served from March 4, 1891, until his resignation on November 10, 1898, before the close of the Fifty-fifth Congress, having been appointed a justice of the supreme court of New York on that date; elected to that office in 1899 for the term ending 1913; member of the appellate division 1902–1909; resumed the practice of law in Fredonia, Chautauqua County, N. Y., in 1914; appointed official referee of the State supreme court in 1919; died in Fredonia, N. Y., March 5, 1920; interment in Forest Hill Cemetery.

HOOKS, Charles (great-grandfather of William Julius Harris), a Representative from North Carolina; born in Bertie County, N. C., February 20, 1768; when he was two years old his parents moved to Duplin County and settled on a plantation near Kenansville; became a planter; member of the State house of commons 1801–1805; served in the State senate in 1810 and 1811; elected as a Democrat to the Fourteenth Congress to fill the vacancy caused by the resignation of William R. King and served from December 2, 1816, to March 3, 1817; elected to the Sixteenth, Seventeenth, and Eighteenth Congresses (March 4, 1819–March 3, 1825); moved to Alabama in 1826, settled near Montgomery, and again engaged in planting; died near Montgomery, Ala., October 18, 1843; interment in the Molton family cemetery on Laurel Hill near Montgomery, Ala.

HOOPER, Benjamin Stephen, a Representative from Virginia; born near Buckingham, Buckingham County, Va., March 6, 1835; attended the common schools; engaged in mercantile pursuits and the manufacture of tobacco; served in the Confederate Army during the Civil War; elected as a Readjuster to the Forty-eighth Congress (March 4, 1883–March 3, 1885); resumed mercantile pursuits at Farmville, Va.; delegate to the Republican National Convention at Chicago in 1888; died in Farmville, Prince Edward County, Va., on January 17, 1898; interment in the Farmville Cemetery.

HOOPER, Joseph Lawrence, a Representative from Michigan; born in Cleveland, Ohio, December 22, 1877; moved to Michigan with his parents, who settled in Battle Creek in 1891; attended the graded and high schools; studied law; was admitted to the bar in 1899 and commenced practice in Battle Creek; circuit court commissioner of Calhoun County 1901–1903; prosecuting attorney of Calhoun County 1903–1907; city attorney of Battle Creek 1916–1918; elected as a Republican to the Sixty-ninth Congress to fill the vacancy caused by the death of Arthur B. Williams; reelected to the Seventieth and to the three succeeding Congresses and served from August 18, 1925, until his death in Washington, D. C., February 22, 1934; interment in Oak Hill Cemetery, Battle Creek, Mich.

HOOPER, Samuel, a Representative from Massachusetts; born in Marblehead, Mass., February 3, 1808; attended the common schools; employed as agent for an importing firm and traveled extensively in foreign countries until 1832, when he engaged in the importing business in Boston, Mass., and later in the iron business; member of the State house of representatives 1851–1853; served in the State senate in 1858; elected as a Republican to the Thirty-seventh Congress to fill the vacancy caused by the resignation of William Appleton; reelected to the Thirty-eighth and to the five succeeding Congresses and served from December 2, 1861, until his death; declined to be a candidate for renomination in 1874; died in Washington, D. C., February 14, 1875; interment in Oak Hill Cemetery.

HOOPER, William, a Delegate from North Carolina; born in Boston, Mass., June 17, 1742; attended the Boston Latin School, and was graduated from Harvard College in 1760; studied law; was admitted to the bar; moved to Wilmington, N. C., in 1767, where he began practice; member of the Colonial Assembly of North Carolina 1773–1776; published a series of articles against the Crown which aroused the people to the issues involved, and he was disbarred for one year; Member of the Continental Congress 1774–1777; a signer of the Declaration of Independence; mover for the first Provincial Congress in 1774; prominent in Revolutionary movements; member of the State assembly in 1777 and 1778; member of the commission to settle a boundary dispute between Massachusetts and New York in 1786; died in Hillsboro, N. C., October, 1790; interment in Guilford Battle Ground, N. C.

HOOPER, William Henry, a Delegate from the Territory of Utah; born in Cambridge, Dorchester County, Md., December 25, 1813; attended the common schools; engaged in mercantile pursuits; moved to Illinois in 1835 and settled in Galena; engaged in trade on the Mississippi River; moved to Utah in 1850 and settled in Salt Lake City; secretary of the Territory in 1857 and 1858; elected as a Democrat to the Thirty-sixth Congress (March 4, 1859–March 3, 1861); unsuccessful candidate for reelection in 1860 to the Thirty-seventh Congress; member of the State senate in 1862; elected to the Thirty-ninth and to the three succeeding Congresses (March 4, 1865–March 3, 1873); was not a candidate for renomination in 1872; engaged in mercantile pursuits and mining operations in Salt Lake City; superintendent of Zion's Cooperative Mercantile Institution 1873–1877, and its president 1877–1882; president of the Deseret National Bank, Salt Lake City, from 1872 until his death in Salt Lake City, Utah, December 30, 1882; interment in Salt Lake City Cemetery.

HOPE, Clifford Ragsdale, a Representative from Kansas; born in Birmingham, Van Buren County, Iowa, June 9, 1893; attended the public schools and Nebraska Wesleyan University, Lincoln, Nebr.; was graduated from Washburn Law School, Topeka, Kans., in 1917 and was admitted to the bar the same year; during the First World War served as a second lieutenant with the Thirty-fifth and Eighty-fifth Divisions in the United States and France 1917–1919; commenced practice of law in Garden City, Kans., in 1919; member of the State house of representatives

1921–1927, serving as speaker pro tempore in 1923 and as speaker in 1925; elected as a Republican to the Seventieth and to the fourteen succeeding Congresses (March 4, 1927–January 3, 1957); was not a candidate for renomination in 1956; president, Great Plains Wheat, Inc., of Garden City, Kans., where he now resides.

HOPKINS, Albert Cole, a Representative from Pennsylvania; born in Villanovia, near Jamestown, Chautauqua County, N. Y., September 15, 1837; attended the public schools; was graduated from Alfred University, Alfred, N. Y.; taught school; engaged in mercantile pursuits in Troy, Pa., where he remained until 1867; moved to Lock Haven, Clinton County, Pa., and engaged in the lumber business; elected as a Republican to the Fifty-second and Fifty-third Congresses (March 4, 1891–March 3, 1895); was not a candidate for renomination in 1894; resumed lumber manufacturing pursuits; State forestry commissioner 1899–1904; died in Lock Haven, Pa., June 9, 1911; interment in Highland Cemetery.

HOPKINS, Albert Jarvis, a Representative and a Senator from Illinois; born near Cortland, De Kalb County, Ill., August 15, 1846; attended the public schools, and was graduated from Hillsdale (Mich.) College in June 1870; studied law; was admitted to the bar in 1871 and commenced practice in Aurora, Ill.; prosecuting attorney of Kane County 1872–1876; member of the Republican State central committee 1878–1880; presidential elector on the Republican ticket of Blaine and Logan in 1884; elected as a Republican to the Forty-ninth Congress to fill the vacancy caused by the death of Reuben Ellwood; reelected to the Fiftieth and to the seven succeeding Congresses and served from December 7, 1885, to March 3, 1903; did not seek renomination, having become a candidate for Senator; elected to the United States Senate and served from March 4, 1903, to March 3, 1909; unsuccessful candidate for reelection; delegate to the Republican National Conventions at Chicago in 1904 and in 1908; resumed the practice of law in Aurora and Chicago, Ill.; died in Aurora, Ill., August 23, 1922; interment in Spring Lake Cemetery.

HOPKINS, Benjamin Franklin, a Representative from Wisconsin; born in Hebron, N. Y., April 22, 1829; attended the common schools and became a telegraph operator; moved to Madison, Wis., in 1849; private secretary to Governor Bashford in 1856 and 1857; served in the State senate in 1862 and 1863; member of the State assembly in 1866; elected as a Republican to the Fortieth and Forty-first Congresses and served from March 4, 1867, until his death in Madison, Dane County, Wis., January 1, 1870; interment in Forest Hill Cemetery.

HOPKINS, David William, a Representative from Missouri; born in Troy, Doniphan County, Kans., on October 31, 1897; moved in 1899 to Missouri with his parents, who settled in St. Joseph; attended the public schools, and was graduated from Graceland Academy, Lamoni, Iowa, in 1916; during the First World War served as a sergeant in Company F, Student Training Corps, from October 1918 until honorably discharged in December 1918; was graduated from Iowa State University at Iowa City in 1920 and from the University of Missouri at Columbia in 1926; taught in the high schools of St. Joseph from 1922 until elected to Congress; served as superintendent of schools of St. Joseph in 1928 and 1929; elected as a Republican to both the Seventieth and Seventy-first Congresses to fill the vacancies caused by the death of Charles L. Faust, who had been reelected in 1928; reelected to the Seventy-second Congress and served from February 5, 1929, to March 3, 1933; unsuccessful candidate for reelection in 1932 to the Seventy-third Congress; engaged in the insurance business; member of St. Joseph Board of Education; is a resident of St. Joseph, Mo.

HOPKINS, Francis Alexander (Frank), a Representative from Kentucky; born in Jeffersonville, Tazewell County, Va., May 27, 1853; attended the public schools and the Tazewell High School; studied law; was admitted to the bar in November 1874 and commenced practice in Prestonsburg, Floyd County, Ky.; also engaged in agricultural pursuits; commissioner of common schools 1882–1884; member of the State constitutional convention in 1890; elected as a Democrat to the Fifty-eighth and Fifty-ninth Congresses (March 4, 1903–March 3, 1907); unsuccessful candidate for reelection in 1906 to the Sixtieth Congress; delegate to the Democratic National Convention at St. Louis in 1916 which nominated the presidential ticket of Wilson and Marshall; presidential elector on the Democratic ticket of Wilson and Marshall in 1916; resumed agricultural pursuits and the practice of law in Prestonsburg, Ky., and died there on June 5, 1918; interment in Davidson Cemetery.

HOPKINS, George Washington, a Representative from Virginia; born near Goochland Court House, Goochland County, Va., February 22, 1804; attended the common schools; taught school; studied law; was admitted to the bar in 1834 and commenced practice in Lebanon, Va.; member of the State house of delegates 1833–1835; elected as a Democrat to the Twenty-fourth and to the five succeeding Congresses (March 4, 1835–March 3, 1847); was not a candidate for reelection in 1846 to the Thirtieth Congress; appointed by President Polk Chargé d'Affaires to Portugal and served from March 3, 1847, to October 18, 1849; again a member of the State house of delegates in 1850 and 1851; member of the State constitutional convention of 1850 and 1851; judge of the circuit court of Washington and other counties; elected to the Thirty-fifth Congress (March 4, 1857–March 3, 1859); was not a candidate for renomination in 1858 to the Thirty-sixth Congress; resumed the practice of law in Abingdon, Va.; again elected to State house of delegates and served from 1859 until his death in Richmond, Henrico County, Va., March 1, 1861; interment in Sinking Springs Cemetery, Abingdon, Va.

HOPKINS, James Herron, a Representative from Pennsylvania; born in Washington, Washington County, Pa., November 3, 1832; attended the common schools, and was graduated from Washington College (now Washington and Jefferson University), Washington, Pa., in 1850; studied law; was admitted to the bar in 1852 and practiced in Pittsburgh, Pa., for twenty years; also engaged in banking, manufacturing, and mining; for several years vice president of the Pittsburgh Chamber of Commerce; unsuccessful candidate for election in 1872 to the Forty-third Congress; elected as a Democrat to the Forty-fourth Congress (March 4, 1875–March 3, 1877); unsuccessful candidate for reelection in 1876 to the Forty-fifth Congress; elected to the Forty-eighth Congress (March 4, 1883–March 3, 1885); unsuccessful candidate for reelection in 1884 to the Forty-ninth Congress; engaged in the practice of law in Washington, D. C.; died at his summer home at North Hatley, Quebec, Canada, June 17, 1904; interment in Oak Hill Cemetery, Washington, D. C.

HOPKINS, Nathan Thomas, a Representative from Kentucky; born in Ashe County, N. C., October 27, 1852; moved to Pike County, Ky.; attended the common schools; engaged in agricultural pursuits; ordained to the ministry in the Baptist Church in 1876 and actively engaged in ministerial work for half a century; county tax assessor of Floyd County 1878–1890; member of the State house of representatives in 1893 and 1894; successfully contested as a Republican the election of Joseph M. Kendall to the Fifty-fourth Congress and served from

February 18 to March 3, 1897; became a merchant, timberman, lumberman, and farmer in Pike County, Ky.; unsuccessful candidate for election in 1900 to the Fifty-seventh Congress; again a member of the State house of representatives in 1923 and 1924; engaged in agricultural pursuits near Yeager, Pike County, Ky.; died in Pikesville, Ky., February 11, 1927; interment in Potter Cemetery, Yeager, Ky.

HOPKINS, Samuel, a Representative from Kentucky; born in Albemarle County, Va., April 9, 1753; educated by private tutors; served in the Revolutionary War for a while on the staff of General Washington and later as lieutenant colonel and colonel of the Tenth Virginia Regiment; moved to Kentucky in 1796 and settled on the Ohio River in 1797 at a point then called Red Banks; studied law; was admitted to the bar and practiced; appointed chief justice of the first court of criminal common law and chancery jurisdiction in 1799 and served until his resignation in 1801; member of the State house of representatives in 1800, 1801, and 1803–1806; presidential elector on the Democratic ticket of Madison and Clinton in 1809; served in the State senate 1809–1813; appointed in 1812 commander in chief, with title of major general, of the western frontier (Illinois and Indiana Territory); in October 1812 led 2,000 mounted volunteers in the campaign against the Kickapoo villages on the Illinois River, and later up the Wabash River; elected as a Democrat to the Thirteenth Congress (March 4, 1813–March 3, 1815); was not a candidate for renomination in 1814; retired to his country estate, "Spring Garden," near Henderson, Ky., and died there September 16, 1819; interment in the family burying ground at "Spring Garden."

HOPKINS, Samuel Isaac, a Representative from Virginia; born near Owensville, Prince Georges County, Md., December 12, 1843; moved to Anne Arundel County with his parents, who settled near Annapolis; attended the common schools and was graduated from Owensville Academy; enlisted in Company A, Second Regiment, Maryland Confederate Infantry, in the Civil War and served until he was severely wounded at the Battle of Gettysburg; after the war settled in Lynchburg, Va., and engaged in mercantile pursuits; elected as a Democrat to the Fiftieth Congress (March 4, 1887–March 3, 1889); declined to be a candidate for renomination in 1888; resumed mercantile pursuits in Lynchburg, Campbell County, Va., and died there January 15, 1914; interment in Spring Hill Cemetery.

HOPKINS, Samuel Miles, a Representative from New York; born in Salem, Conn., May 9, 1772; was graduated from Yale College in 1791; studied law; was admitted to the bar and commenced practice in Le Roy, Genesee County, N. Y., in 1793; moved to New York City in 1794 and continued the practice of law; elected to the Thirteenth Congress (March 4, 1813–March 3, 1815); member of the State assembly in 1820 and 1821; moved to Albany in 1821; served in the State senate in 1822; reporter of the New York Court of Chancery 1823–1826; member of the commission to superintend the construction of Sing Sing Prison 1825–1830; judge of the State circuit court 1832–1836; died in Geneva, Ontario County, N. Y., March 9, 1837; interment in Washington Street Cemetery.

HOPKINS, Stephen, a Delegate from Rhode Island; born in Providence, R. I., March 7, 1707; attended the public schools; was raised on a farm in the town of Scituate, Providence County; member of the general assembly 1732–1752 and 1770–1775; served as speaker 1738–1744 and 1749; chief justice of the court of common pleas in 1739; moved to Providence in 1742 and engaged in surveying and mercantile pursuits; chief justice of the superior court 1751–1754; delegate to the Colonial Congress which met in Albany in 1754; Colonial Governor of Rhode Island in 1755, 1756, 1758–1761, 1763, 1764, and 1767; again appointed chief justice of the superior court in 1773; held three important offices at the same time—member of the assembly, Member of the Continental Congress, and chief justice; Member of the Continental Congress 1774–1780; a signer of the Declaration of Independence; died in Providence, R. I., July 13, 1785; interment in the North Burial Ground.

HOPKINS, Stephen Tyng, a Representative from New York; born in New York City March 25, 1849; attended the Anthon Grammar School in New York City; was an iron merchant and broker; moved to Catskill, N. Y.; member of the State assembly in 1885 and 1886; connected with several coal and iron syndicates in West Virginia and Tennessee; elected as a Republican to the Fiftieth Congress (March 4, 1887–March 3, 1889); watchman in the customhouse in New York City from April 9 to August 15, 1890, when he resigned; was found dead by a train crew alongside the railroad tracks near Pleasantville, adjacent to Atlantic City, N. J., March 3, 1892; interment in Greenwood Cemetery, Brooklyn, N. Y.

HOPKINSON, Francis (father of Joseph Hopkinson), a Delegate from New Jersey; born in Philadelphia, Pa., September 21, 1737; was graduated from the University of Pennsylvania at Philadelphia in 1757; the first native American composer of a secular song in 1759; studied law; was admitted to the bar in 1761 and commenced practice in Philadelphia; secretary of a commission of the Provincial Council of Pennsylvania which made a treaty between the Province and certain Indian tribes in 1761; appointed collector of customs at the port of Salem, N. J., in 1763, and at New Castle, Del., in 1772; settled in Bordentown, N. J., in 1774 and resumed the practice of law; member of the Provincial Council of New Jersey 1774–1776; member of the executive council from January 13 to November 15, 1775; was admitted to practice before the bar of the supreme court of New Jersey on May 8, 1775; elected an associate justice of that court in 1776 but declined the office; Member of the Continental Congress from June 22 to November 30, 1776; a signer of the Declaration of Independence; elected on November 18, 1776, to serve on the Navy Board at Philadelphia; returned to Philadelphia in 1777; treasurer of the Continental Loan Office in 1778; judge of the Admiralty Court of Pennsylvania in 1779 and reappointed in 1780 and 1787; member of the constitutional convention in 1787 which ratified the Constitution of the United States; judge of the United States District Court for the Eastern District of Pennsylvania 1789–1791; died in Philadelphia, Pa., May 9, 1791; interment in Christ Church Burial Ground.

HOPKINSON, Joseph (son of Francis Hopkinson), a Representative from Pennsylvania; born in Philadelphia, Pa., on November 12, 1770; was graduated from the University of Pennsylvania at Philadelphia in 1786; studied law; was admitted to the bar in Philadelphia in 1791 where he practiced his profession, except for the period of one year at Easton, Pa.; wrote the patriotic anthem "Hail Columbia!" in 1798; became a distinguished lawyer; was associated with Daniel Webster in the Dartmouth College case; counsel for Justice Samuel Chase in his impeachment trial before the United States Senate in 1804 and 1805; elected as a Federalist to the Fourteenth and Fifteenth Congresses (March 4, 1815–March 3, 1819); was not a candidate for renomination in 1818; moved to Bordentown, N. J., in 1820; member of the New Jersey House of Assembly; returned to Philadelphia, Pa., in 1823; judge of the United States District Court for the Eastern District of Pennsylvania 1828–1842; chairman of the State constitutional convention in 1837; secretary of the board of trustees of the

University of Pennsylvania in 1790 and 1791; trustee 1806–1819 and 1822–1842; died in Philadelphia, Pa., January 15, 1842; interment in the old Borden-Hopkinson Burial Ground, Bordentown, N. J.

HOPWOOD, Robert Freeman, a Representative from Pennsylvania; born in Uniontown, Fayette County, Pa., July 24, 1856; attended public schools; studied under private teachers; studied law; was admitted to the bar in 1879 and commenced practice in Uniontown; president of the Fayette County Bar Association; chairman of the Republican county committee; attorney for Uniontown Borough 1881–1891; solicitor of Fayette County 1894–1912; president of the Uniontown Hospital 1905–1920; elected as a Republican to the Sixty-fourth Congress (March 4, 1915–March 3, 1917); unsuccessful candidate for reelection in 1916 to the Sixty-fifth Congress; resumed the practice of law in Uniontown; died at his winter home in St. Petersburg, Fla., on March 1, 1940; interment in Oak Grove Cemetery, Uniontown, Pa.

HORAN, Walter Franklin, a Representative from Washington; born in Wenatchee, Chelan County, Wash., October 15, 1898; attended the public schools; was graduated from the high school at Wenatchee, Wash., and from Washington State College at Pullman in 1925; during the First World War served as gunner's mate, third class, in the United States Navy from April 5, 1917, to November 24, 1919; in 1925 engaged in fruit growing, packing, storing, and shipping; elected as a Republican to the Seventy-eighth and to the eight succeeding Congresses (January 3, 1943–January 3, 1961). *Reelected to the Eighty-seventh Congress.*

HORN, Henry, a Representative from Pennsylvania; born in Philadelphia, Pa., in 1786; completed preparatory studies; studied law; was admitted to the bar and practiced law in Philadelphia, Pa.; elected as a Jackson Democrat to the Twenty-second Congress (March 4, 1831–March 3, 1833); unsuccessful candidate for reelection to the Twenty-third Congress in 1832; resumed the practice of law in Philadelphia; collector of customs at Philadelphia, Pa., from May 12, 1845, until August 4, 1846; died in Flourtown, a suburb of Philadelphia, Montgomery County, Pa., January 12, 1862; interment in Woodlands Cemetery, Philadelphia, Pa.

HORNBECK, John Westbrook, a Representative from Pennsylvania; born in Montague, Sussex County, N. J., January 24, 1804; completed preparatory studies, and was graduated from Union College, Schenectady, N. Y., in 1827; studied law; was admitted to the bar of Northampton County, Pa., in 1829 and commenced practice in Allentown, Pa., in 1830; commissioned deputy attorney general of the State of Pennsylvania for the county of Lehigh in 1836 and served three years; elected as a Whig to the Thirtieth Congress and served from March 4, 1847, until his death in Allentown, Pa., January 16, 1848; interment in Allentown Cemetery.

HORNBLOWER, Josiah, a Delegate from New Jersey; born in Staffordshire, England, February 23, 1729; completed preparatory studies and became a civil engineer; immigrated to the United States in 1753 and settled in Belleville, N. J.; captain of a company engaged in the defense of New Jersey during the French and Indian wars; member of the State general assembly in 1779 and 1780 and served as speaker in the latter year; Member of the Continental Congress in 1785 and 1786; judge of the Essex County court 1798–1809; died in Newark, N. J., January 21, 1809; interment in Dutch Reformed Churchyard, Belleville, N. J.

HORNOR, Lynn Sedwick, a Representative from West Virginia; born in Clarksburg, Harrison County, W. Va., November 3, 1874; attended the public schools and was graduated from Towers High School at Clarksburg; was employed as a bank clerk in 1892 and served successively as cashier and director until his death; president and manager of a number of coal, oil- and gas-development, and land companies; president of the West Virginia Natural Gas Association in 1917 and 1918; during the First World War served as a member of the advisory State council of defense; elected as a Democrat to the Seventy-second and Seventy-third Congresses and served from March 4, 1931, until his death in Washington, D. C., September 23, 1933; interment in Odd Fellows Cemetery, Clarksburg, W. Va.

HORR, Ralph Ashley, a Representative from Washington; born in Saybrook, McLean County, Ill., August 12, 1884; attended the public schools, and the University of Illinois at Urbana; moved to the State of Washington in 1908 and settled in Seattle; was graduated from the law department of the University of Washington at Seattle in 1911; was admitted to the bar the same year and commenced practice in Seattle; chief deputy county treasurer of King County in 1911 and 1912; graduate manager of athletics at the University of Washington in 1912 and 1913; served as chairman of the Republican county committee of King County; unsuccessful candidate for mayor of Seattle in 1918; during the First World War served from August 31, 1918, as a lieutenant and battalion adjutant in the Twenty-sixth Infantry Regiment with overseas service and was discharged March 8, 1920; elected as a Republican to the Seventy-second Congress (March 4, 1931–March 3, 1933); unsuccessful candidate for renomination in 1932, for the nomination for United States Senator in 1934, for Governor of Washington in 1936, and for mayor of Seattle in 1948; practiced law until 1957; died in Seattle, Wash., January 26, 1960; remains were cremated and interred in Hillcrest Burial Park, Kent, Wash.

HORR, Roswell Gilbert, a Representative from Michigan; born in Waitsfield, Washington County, Vt., November 26, 1830; moved with his parents to Lorain County, Ohio, in 1834; attended the public schools; was graduated from Antioch College, Yellow Springs, Ohio, in 1857; clerk of the court of common pleas of Lorain County 1857–1862 and reelected in 1860; studied law; was admitted to the bar in 1862 and commenced practice in Elyria, Lorain County, Ohio; moved to southeastern Missouri in 1866 and engaged in mining for six years; moved to East Saginaw, Mich., in 1872; elected as a Republican to the Forty-sixth, Forty-seventh, and Forty-eighth Congresses (March 4, 1879–March 3, 1885); unsuccessful candidate for reelection in 1884; delegate to the Republican National Convention at Chicago in 1884; unsuccessful candidate for election in 1886 to the Fiftieth Congress; moved to New York City in 1890; associate editor on the staff of the New York Tribune until his death in Plainfield, N. J., December 19, 1896; interment in Greenwood Cemetery, Wellington, Ohio.

HORSEY, Outerbridge, a Senator from Delaware; born near Laurel, Sussex County, Del., March 5, 1777; received a liberal education; studied law; was admitted to the bar in 1807 and commenced practice in Wilmington, Del.; member of the State house of representatives 1800–1802; attorney general of Delaware 1806–1810; elected in 1810 as a Federalist to the United States Senate to fill the vacancy caused by the death of Samuel White; reelected in 1815 and served from January 12, 1810, to March 3, 1821; was not a candidate for reelection; retired to his wife's estate, "Needwood," near Petersville, Frederick County, Md., and died there June 9, 1842; interment in St. John's Cemetery, Frederick, Md.

HORSFORD, Jerediah, a Representative from New York; born in Charlotte, Chittenden County, Vt., March 8, 1791; attended the common schools; engaged in agricultural pursuits; served during the War of 1812; missionary to the Seneca Indians at Moscow, N. Y., in 1815; held several local offices; member of the State assembly in 1831; elected as a Whig to the Thirty-second Congress (March 4, 1851–March 3, 1853); served as colonel of light infantry in the State militia; moved to Livonia, N. Y., in 1863; resumed agricultural pursuits; died in Livonia, Livingston County, N. Y., January 14, 1875; interment in Moscow Cemetery, Moscow (now Leicester), N. Y.

HORTON, Frank Ogilvie, a Representative from Wyoming; born in Muscatine, Muscatine County, Iowa, October 18, 1882; attended the public schools; was graduated from Morgan Park (Ill.) Military Academy in 1899 and from the University of Chicago, Chicago, Ill., in 1903; during the Spanish-American War served as a private in Company C, Fiftieth Iowa Regiment, in 1898; moved to Saddlestring, Wyo., in 1905 and engaged in livestock raising; member of the State house of representatives 1921–1923; served in the State senate 1923–1931, being president in 1931; delegate to the Republican National Conventions in 1928 and 1936; Republican National committeeman 1937–1948; elected as a Republican to the Seventy-sixth Congress (January 3, 1939–January 3, 1941); unsuccessful candidate for reelection in 1940 to the Seventy-seventh Congress; resumed his former pursuits in Saddlestring, Wyo.; died in Sheridan, Wyo., August 17, 1948; interment in Willowgrove Cemetery, Buffalo, Wyo.

HORTON, Thomas Raymond, a Representative from New York; born in Fultonville, Montgomery County, N. Y., in April 1822; attended the public schools; studied law; was admitted to the bar and practiced; member of the board of trustees of Fultonville in 1848; clerk of the board of supervisors of Montgomery County for six years; justice of the peace eight years; editor and publisher of the Amsterdam (N. Y.) Recorder 1841–1857; elected as a Republican to the Thirty-fourth Congress (March 4, 1855–March 3, 1857); was not a candidate for renomination in 1856; delegate to the Republican National Convention at Chicago in 1860; during the Civil War served as adjutant of the One Hundred and Fifteenth Regiment, New York Volunteer Infantry, 1862–1864; editor and publisher of the Montgomery County Republican; died in Fultonville, N. Y., July 26, 1894; interment in the Village Cemetery.

HORTON, Valentine Baxter, a Representative from Ohio; born in Windsor, Vt., January 29, 1802; attended the Partridge Military School and afterward became one of its tutors; studied law in Middletown, Conn.; was admitted to the bar in 1830; moved to Pittsburgh, Pa., where he practiced; moved to Cincinnati, Ohio, in 1833, and to Pomeroy, Ohio, in 1835; engaged in the sale and transportation of coal and the development of the salt industry; member of the State constitutional convention in 1860; elected as a Whig to the Thirty-fourth and Thirty-fifth Congresses (March 4, 1855–March 3, 1859); was not a candidate for renomination in 1858; elected as a Republican to the Thirty-seventh Congress (March 4, 1861–March 3, 1863); was not a candidate for renomination in 1862; member of the peace convention of 1861 held in Washington, D. C., in an effort to devise means to prevent the impending war; engaged in coal mining; died in Pomeroy, Ohio, January 14, 1888; interment in Beach Grove Cemetery.

HOSKINS, George Gilbert, a Representative from New York; born in Bennington, N. Y., December 24, 1824; completed preparatory studies; engaged in mercantile pursuits; for a number of years town clerk of Bennington and justice of the peace; postmaster of Bennington, N. Y., 1849–1853 and 1861–1866; member of the State assembly in 1860, 1865, and 1866, and served as speaker in 1865; removed to Attica, N. Y., in 1867; commissioner of public accounts 1868–1870; appointed collector of internal revenue for the twenty-ninth district of New York May 1, 1871, and served until March 4, 1873, when he resigned; elected as a Republican to the Forty-third and Forty-fourth Congresses (March 4, 1873–March 3, 1877); unsuccessful candidate for reelection in 1876 to the Forty-fifth Congress; Lieutenant Governor of New York 1880–1883; delegate to the Republican National Convention at Chicago in 1880; died in Attica, N. Y., June 12, 1893; interment in Forest Hill Cemetery.

HOSMER, Craig, a Representative from California; born in Brea, Orange County, Calif., May 6, 1915; attended the public schools; graduated from the University of California in 1937; attended the University of Michigan Law School in 1938 and was graduated from the University of Southern California in 1940; was admitted to the bar in 1940 and began practice in Long Beach, Calif.; enlisted in the United States Navy in July 1940 and advanced to the rank of commander of an assault transport; participated in the invasions of Iwo Jima and Okinawa and in the occupation of Japan; released from active service in September 1946; captain, Naval Reserve; attorney with the Atomic Energy Commission at Los Alamos, N. Mex., and special assistant United States district attorney for New Mexico in 1948; returned to Long Beach, Calif., to specialize in Federal tax laws; unsuccessful Republican candidate for election in 1950 to the Eighty-second Congress; elected as a Republican to the Eighty-third and to the three succeeding Congresses (January 3, 1953–January 3, 1961). *Reelected to the Eighty-seventh Congress*

HOSMER, Hezekiah Lord, a Representative from New York; born June 7, 1765; studied law; was admitted to practice in the mayor's court of Hudson, N. Y., in 1785; recorder of Hudson in 1793 and 1794; elected to the Fifth Congress (March 4, 1797–March 3, 1799); one of the managers appointed by the House of Representatives in 1798 to conduct the impeachment proceedings against William Blount, a Senator from Tennessee; again served as recorder of Hudson in 1810, 1811, 1813, and 1814; died in Hudson, N. Y., June 9, 1814.

HOSMER, Titus, a Delegate from Connecticut; born in what is now West Hartford, Hartford County, Conn., in 1736; was graduated from Yale College in 1757; studied law; was admitted to the bar in 1760 and commenced practice in Middletown, Conn.; held several local offices; member of the State house of representatives 1773–1778, serving as speaker in 1776 and 1778; member of the council of safety in 1776 and 1777; served in the State senate from May 1778 until his death; Member of the Continental Congress in 1775, 1776, and 1777–1779; resumed the practice of law; judge of the United States Maritime Court of Appeals in 1780; died in Middletown, Conn., August 4, 1780; interment in Mortimer Cemetery.

HOSTETLER, Abraham Jonathan, a Representative from Indiana; born in Washington County, Ind., November 22, 1818; attended the common schools; apprenticed to learn the blacksmith's trade; later engaged in agricultural pursuits; member of the State senate 1854–1858; elected as a Democrat to the Forty-sixth Congress (March 4, 1879–March 3, 1881); unsuccessful candidate for reelection in 1880 to the Forty-seventh Congress; engaged in mercantile pursuits; delegate to the Democratic National Convention at Cincinnati in 1880; died near Bedford, Ind., November 24, 1899; interment in the Leatherwood Church Cemetery, near Bedford, Ind.

HOSTETTER, Jacob, a Representative from Pennsylvania; born near York, Pa., May 9, 1754; attended the common schools; pioneer in the manufacture of the tall eight-day clock; member of the general assembly of Pennsylvania 1797–1802; elected as a Democrat to the Fifteenth Congress to fill the vacancy caused by the resignation of Jacob Spangler; reelected to the Sixteenth Congress and served from November 16, 1818, until March 3, 1821; moved to Ohio and settled in Columbiana, where he died June 29, 1831.

HOTCHKISS, Giles Waldo, a Representative from New York; born in Windsor, Broome County, N. Y., October 25, 1815; attended the common schools, Windsor Academy, and Oxford Academy; studied law; was admitted to the bar in 1837 and began practice in Binghamton, N. Y.; one of the founders of the Republican Party; delegate to the Republican National Convention at Chicago in 1860; elected as a Republican to the Thirty-eighth and Thirty-ninth Congresses (March 4, 1863–March 3, 1867); unsuccessful candidate for renomination in 1866; was a close friend and supporter of President Lincoln; elected to the Forty-first Congress (March 4, 1869–March 3, 1871); was not a candidate for renomination; resumed the practice of law in Binghamton, where he died July 5, 1878; interment in Spring Forest Cemetery.

HOTCHKISS, Julius, a Representative from Connecticut; born in Waterbury, Conn., July 11, 1810; attended the common schools; engaged in manufacturing pursuits; mayor of Waterbury in 1852; member of the State house of representatives in 1851 and 1858; elected as a Republican to the Fortieth Congress (March 4, 1867–March 3, 1869); Lieutenant Governor of Connecticut in 1870; retired from public life and active business pursuits; died in Middletown, Conn., December 23, 1878; interment in Pine Grove Cemetery.

HOUCK, Jacob, Jr., a Representative from New York; born in Schoharie, N. Y., January 14, 1801; attended the common schools; was graduated from Union College, Schenectady, N. Y., in 1822; studied law; was admitted to the bar and practiced in Schoharie; district attorney of Schoharie County 1831–1836; elected as a Democrat to the Twenty-seventh Congress (March 4, 1841–March 3, 1843); resumed the practice of law; died in Schoharie, N. Y., October 2, 1857; interment in Lutheran Cemetery.

HOUGH, David, a Representative from New Hampshire; born in Norwich, Conn., March 13, 1753; attended the common schools; ship carpenter; moved to Lebanon, N. H., in 1778; member of the State house of representatives in 1788, 1789, and 1794; justice of the peace; colonel of militia; delegate to the State constitutional convention in 1783; commissioner of valuation in 1798; elected to the Eighth and Ninth Congresses (March 4, 1803–March 3, 1807); engaged in agricultural pursuits; died in Lebanon, N. H., April 18, 1831; interment in the cemetery in the southern vicinity of Lebanon.

HOUGH, William Jervis, a Representative from New York; born in Cazenovia, N. Y., March 20, 1795; completed preparatory studies; moved to Madison County; studied law; practiced in Syracuse, N. Y.; member of the State assembly in 1835 and 1836; general in the State militia; elected as a Democrat to the Twenty-ninth Congress (March 4, 1845–March 3, 1847); resumed the practice of law in Syracuse, N. Y., where he died October 4, 1869; interment in Oakwood Cemetery.

HOUGHTON, Alanson Bigelow, a Representative from New York; born in Cambridge, Mass., October 10, 1863; moved to Corning, N. Y., with his parents in 1868; attended the public

schools, Corning (N. Y.) Free Academy, and St. Paul's School, Concord, N. H.; was graduated from Harvard University in 1886; took postgraduate courses at Gottingen, Berlin, and Paris from 1886 to 1889; commenced the manufacture of glass at Corning N. Y., in 1889; vice president of the Corning Glass Works from 1902 to 1910, when he was elected president of the company; president of the board of education of Corning; presidential elector on the Republican ticket of Roosevelt and Fairbanks in 1904, of Hughes and Fairbanks in 1916, and of Coolidge and Dawes in 1924; became trustee of Hobart College in 1917; elected as a Republican to the Sixty-sixth and Sixty-seventh Congresses and served from March 4, 1919, to February 28, 1922, when he resigned, having been appointed on February 10, 1922, by President Harding, as Ambassador to Germany, in which capacity he served until April 6, 1925; appointed by President Coolidge as Ambassador to Great Britain on February 24, 1925, and served in that capacity until April 27, 1929; unsuccessful candidate for election to the United States Senate in 1928; resumed his interests in the glass manufacturing industry; also financially interested in various other concerns; trustee of Stephens College; president of the Board of Religious Education of Western New York; treasurer of the Carnegie Foundation; director of the Bamberger Foundation; chairman of the Princeton Institute; died at his summer home in South Dartmouth, Mass., September 15, 1941; interment in Hope Cemetery Annex, Corning, N. Y.

HOUGHTON, Sherman Otis, a Representative from California; born in New York City on April 10, 1828; completed preparatory studies and attended Collegiate Institute, New York; during the Mexican War enlisted in the First Regiment, New York Volunteers, in June 1846; honorably discharged at Monterey, Calif.; in October 1848; proceeded to the gold mines and thence to San Jose; deputy clerk of the State supreme court in 1854; mayor of San Jose, Calif., in 1855 and 1856; studied law; was admitted to the bar in 1857 and commenced practice in San Jose; during the Civil War was commissioned captain and promoted to lieutenant colonel, and served successively as inspector and ordnance officer; elected as a Republican to the Forty-second and Forty-third Congresses (March 4, 1871–March 3, 1875); unsuccessful candidate for reelection in 1874 to the Forty-fourth Congress; appointed commissioner to investigate the affairs of the United States Mint at San Francisco in 1881; moved to Los Angeles in 1886 and continued the practice of law; retired from active practice in 1903; died in Compton, Los Angeles County, Calif., August 31, 1914; interment in Rosedale Cemetery, Los Angeles, Calif.

HOUK, George Washington, a Representative from Ohio; born near Mount Holly Springs, Cumberland County, Pa., on September 25, 1825; moved to Ohio with his parents, who settled in Dayton in 1827; attended the common schools and the E. E. Barney Academy at Dayton; studied law; was admitted to the bar in 1847 and commenced practice in Dayton; member of the State house of representatives in 1852 and 1853; delegate to the Democratic National Conventions in 1860 and 1876; presidential elector on the Democratic ticket of Cleveland and Hendricks in 1884; elected as a Democrat to the Fifty-second and Fifty-third Congresses and served from March 4, 1891, until his death in Washington, D. C., February 9, 1894; interment in Woodland Cemetery, Dayton, Ohio.

HOUK, John Chiles (son of Leonidas Campbell Houk), a Representative from Tennessee; born in Clinton, Anderson County, Tenn., February 26, 1860; attended the local schools; moved with his parents to Knoxville in 1871; was graduated from the University of Tennessee at Knoxville; employed as a clerk in the Pension Bureau at Washington, D. C., 1881–1883; studied law at Columbian (now George Washington University), Washington, D. C.; was admitted to the bar in 1884 and commenced practice in Knoxville; secretary of the State Republican committee for four years; Assistant Doorkeeper of the National House of Representatives in the Fifty-first Congress; elected as a Republican to the Fifty-second Congress to fill the vacancy caused by the death of his father, Leonidas C. Houk; reelected to the Fifty-third Congress and served from December 7, 1891, to March 3, 1895; unsuccessful candidate for reelection in 1894; elected to the State senate in 1896; 1910, 1916, 1918, and again in 1920; resumed the practice of law in Knoxville, Tenn.; died in Fountain City, Knox County, Tenn., June 3, 1923; interment in Greenwood Cemetery, Knoxville, Tenn.

HOUK, Leonidas Campbell (father of John Chiles Houk), a Representative from Tennessee; born near Boyds Creek, Sevier County, Tenn., June 8, 1836; attended the common schools less than three months; learned the trade of cabinet-making; studied law; was admitted to the bar October 13, 1859, and practiced; during the Civil War enlisted in the Union Army as a private August 9, 1861; promoted to lieutenant in the First Regiment, Tennessee Volunteer Infantry; mustered in as colonel of the Third Regiment, Tennessee Volunteer Infantry February 2, 1862, and served until his resignation on account of ill health April 23, 1863; presidential elector on the Republican ticket of Lincoln and Johnson in 1864; member of the State constitutional convention in 1865; judge of the circuit court of Tennessee 1866–1870; moved to Knoxville and resumed the practice of law; delegate to the Republican National Conventions in 1868, 1880, 1884, and 1888; presidential elector on the Republican ticket of Grant and Wilson in 1872 and of Hayes and Wheeler in 1876: member of the State house of representatives 1873–1875; elected as a Republican to the Forty-sixth and to the six succeeding Congresses and served from March 4, 1879, until his death in Knoxville, Tenn., May 25, 1891; interment in the Old Gray Cemetery.

HOUSE, John Ford, a Representative from Tennessee; was born near Franklin, Williamson County, Tenn., on January 9, 1827; attended the local academy and the Transylvania University, Lexington, Ky., and was graduated from the Lebanon Law School in 1850; was admitted to the bar and commenced practice in Franklin, Tenn.; moved to Montgomery County, Tenn.; member of the State house of representatives in 1853; presidential elector on the Constitutional Union ticket of Bell and Everett in 1860; member of the Provisional Congress of the Confederacy from Tennessee; during the Civil War enlisted in the Confederate Army and served until paroled in Columbus, Miss., in June 1865; delegate to the Democratic National Convention at New York City in 1868; member of the State constitutional convention in 1870; elected as a Democrat to the Forty-fourth and to the three succeeding Congresses (March 4, 1875–March 3, 1883); was not a candidate for renomination in 1882; resumed the practice of law; died in Clarksville, Tenn., June 28, 1904; interment in Greenwood Cemetery.

HOUSEMAN, Julius, a Representative from Michigan; born in Zeckendorf, Bavaria, Germany, December 8, 1832; attended the common schools in Zeckendorf and the commercial school at Munich, Bavaria; immigrated to the United States in 1848 and settled in Battle Creek, Mich.; moved to Grand Rapids, Mich., in 1852; engaged in the mercantile and lumber business for forty years; member of the board of aldermen of Grand Rapids 1861–1870; served in the State house of representatives in 1871 and 1872; mayor of Grand Rapids 1873–1875; unsuccessful candidate for Lieutenant Governor in 1876; elected as

a Democrat to the Forty-eighth Congress (March 4, 1883–March 3, 1885); was not a candidate for renomination in 1884; resumed his former business pursuits; died in Grand Rapids, Mich., February 8, 1891; interment in Oak Hill Cemetery.

HOUSTON, Andrew Jackson (son of Samuel Houston), a Senator from Texas; born in Independence, Washington County, Tex., June 21, 1854; attended the common schools, Baylor University, Waco, Tex., Bastrop (Tex.) Military Academy, Texas Military Institute at Austin, and Old Salado (Tex.) College; appointed to West Point (N. Y.) Military Academy in June 1871 and was honorably discharged due to physical disability in 1873; employed as a clerk in the State school department 1873–1875 and in the General Land Office, Washington, D. C., in 1875; one of the organizers of the Travis Rifles at Austin during the reconstruction period in 1874; studied law; was admitted to the bar on April 21, 1876, and practiced in Tyler, Tex., 1876–1879; clerk of the United States district court at Dallas, Tex., 1879–1889; served in the Texas National Guard 1884 to 1893 with the rank of colonel; practiced law in Dallas, Tex., 1889–1901 and in Beaumont, Tex., in 1901 and 1902; during the Spanish-American War formed a troop of Cavalry for the Rough Riders of Theodore Roosevelt but was not a member thereof; appointed United States marshal for the eastern district of Texas at Beaumont by President Theodore Roosevelt and served from 1902 to 1910; unsuccessful Prohibition Party candidate for Governor of Texas in 1910 and 1912; professor of military science and tactics at St. Mary's University in 1917 and 1918; retired from active business pursuits in 1918 and lived near La Porte, Tex., and was engaged as a writer and author; appointed by Governor Neff in 1924 as superintendent of the State park at the San Jacinto battleground and served until appointed to the Senate; appointed as a Democrat to the United States Senate to fill the vacancy in the term ending January 3, 1943, caused by the death of Morris Sheppard and served from April 21, 1941, until his death; died in a hospital in Baltimore, Md., June 26, 1941; interment in the Abbey Mausoleum, Arlington, Va.

HOUSTON, George Smith, a Representative and a Senator from Alabama; born near Franklin, Williamson County, Tenn., January 17, 1808; moved with his parents to Lauderdale County, Ala., and attended an academy there; studied law in Florence, Ala., and Harrodsburg, Ky.; was admitted to the bar in 1831; commenced practice in Florence, Ala.; member of the State house of representatives in 1832; settled in Athens, Ala., in 1835; State's attorney for the Florence judicial district in 1836; elected as a Democrat to the Twenty-seventh and to the three succeeding Congresses (March 4, 1841–March 3, 1849); declined to be a candidate for renomination in 1848; elected to the Thirty-second and to the four succeeding Congresses and served from March 4, 1851, until January 21, 1861, when he withdrew; presented credentials as a Senator-elect to the United States Senate on February 9, 1866, for the term ending March 3, 1867, but was not permitted to take his seat; delegate to the Union National Convention at Philadelphia in 1866; Governor of Alabama 1874–1878; elected to the United States Senate and served from March 4, 1879, until his death in Athens, Ala., December 31, 1879; interment in Athens City Cemetery.

HOUSTON, Henry Aydelotte, a Representative from Delaware; born in Dagsboro Hundred, Sussex County, Del., July 10, 1847; attended the public schools and Newark Academy; engaged in agricultural pursuits; moved to Missouri in 1872; returned to Delaware and settled in Millsboro in 1875 and taught school for five years; engaged in mercantile pursuits; member of the Sussex County School Commission; elected as a Democrat to the Fifty-eighth Congress (March 4, 1903–

March 3, 1905); was not a candidate for renomination in 1904; engaged in lumber manufacturing and banking in Millsboro, Del.; died in Milford, Del., April 5, 1925; interment in Brotherhood Cemetery, Millsboro, Del.

HOUSTON, John Mills, a Representative from Kansas; born on a farm near Formosa, Jewell County, Kans., September 15, 1890; attended the public schools of Wichita, Kans., St. John's Military School, Salina, Kans., and Fairmount University, Wichita, Kans.; engaged in the theatrical business 1912–1917; during the First World War served as a noncommissioned officer in the United States Marine Corps 1917–1919; engaged in the retail lumber business at Newton, Kans., 1919–1934; mayor of Newton 1927–1931; secretary of the Democratic State central committee in 1934 and 1935; elected as a Democrat to the Seventy-fourth and to the three succeeding Congresses (January 3, 1935–January 3, 1943); unsuccessful candidate for reelection in 1942 to the Seventy-eighth Congress; appointed a member of the National Labor Relations Board on March 15, 1943, and served until his retirement on August 27, 1953; resides in Laguna Beach, Calif.

HOUSTON, John Wallace (uncle of Robert Griffith Houston), a Representative from Delaware; born in Concord, Sussex County, Del., May 4, 1814; attended the country schools and Newark Academy, and was graduated from Yale College in 1834; studied law in Dover, Del.; was admitted to the bar in 1837; moved to Georgetown, Del., in 1839 and commenced the practice of law; secretary of state of Delaware 1841–1844; elected as a Whig to the Twenty-ninth, Thirtieth, and Thirty-first Congresses (March 4, 1845–March 3, 1851); was not a candidate for renomination in 1850; appointed associate judge of the superior court of Delaware May 4, 1855; member of the peace conference of 1861, held in Washington, D. C., in an effort to devise means to prevent the impending war; retired from the bench in 1893; died in Georgetown, Del., April 26, 1896; interment in the Presbyterian Cemetery, Lewes, Del.

HOUSTON, Robert Griffith (nephew of John Wallace Houston), a Representative from Delaware; born in Milton, Sussex County, Del., October 13, 1867; attended the public schools at Lewes, Del., 1872–1882; engaged in agricultural pursuits; studied law; was admitted to the bar in 1888 and commenced practice in Georgetown, Sussex County, Del.; member of the Delaware National Guard 1890–1895, serving successively as first lieutenant, captain of Company G, and assistant adjutant general; owner and publisher of the Sussex Republican 1893–1934; continued its publication under the name of the Sussex Countian 1934–1946; collector of customs for the district of Delaware 1900–1904; president of the First National Bank of Georgetown 1901–1903; member of the first State Anti-Tuberculosis Commission 1911–1914 and of the Delaware Commission for the Feeble Minded 1918–1936; member of the citizens' committee which drafted the Delaware school law enacted in 1921; assistant attorney general of the State 1920–1924 and 1933–1935; employed in the Bureau of Law, Office of the Alien Property Custodian, 1922–1925, serving as chief of that bureau 1923–1925; elected as a Republican to the Sixty-ninth and to the three succeeding Congresses (March 4, 1925–March 3, 1933); was not a candidate for renomination in 1932; resumed the publishing business and also the practice of law at Georgetown, Del.; died in a hospital at Lewes, Del., January 29, 1946; interment in the Presbyterian Cemetery, Lewes, Del.

HOUSTON, Samuel (father of Andrew Jackson Houston and cousin of David Hubbard), a Representative from Tennessee and a Senator from Texas; born at Timber Ridge Church, near Lexington, Va., March 2, 1793; moved about 1806 with his widowed mother to Blount County, Tenn., where he was adopted into the Cherokee tribe of Indians by Chief Jolly; attended Maryville Academy (now Maryville College), Maryville, Tenn., for a short time; employed as clerk in a store in Kingston, Tenn.; enlisted as a private in the Thirty-ninth Regiment, United States Infantry; promoted to ensign July 29, 1813; served under General Jackson in the Creek War as a sergeant in the Seventh Regiment, United States Infantry, and as lieutenant in May 1814; studied law in Nashville, Tenn.; was admitted to the bar in 1818 and commenced practice in Lebanon, Tenn.; district attorney in 1819; adjutant general of the State in 1820; major general in 1821; elected as a Democrat to the Eighteenth and Nineteenth Congresses (March 4, 1823–March 3, 1827); Governor of Tennessee from 1827 until April 16, 1829, when he resigned; moved to the territory of the Cherokee Nation, now a part of Oklahoma, and subsequently to Texas in 1833; member of the convention of 1833 at San Felipe de Austin, the purpose of which was to establish separate statehood for Texas; member of the constitutional convention in 1835; commander in chief of the Texas Army; led the Texans against Santa Ana and his Mexicans in the famous Battle of San Jacinto, and completely routed them April 21, 1836; first President of the Republic of Texas 1836–1838; member of the Texas Congress 1838–1840; again President of the Republic 1841–1844; upon the admission of Texas as a State into the Union was elected as a Democrat to the United States Senate; reelected in 1847 and 1853 and served from February 21, 1846, to March 3, 1859; Governor of Texas 1859–1861; deposed March 18, 1861, because he refused to take the oath of allegiance to the Confederate States; died in Huntsville, Tex., July 26, 1863; interment in Oakwood Cemetery.

HOUSTON, Victor Stewart Kaleoaloha, a Delegate from the Territory of Hawaii; born in San Francisco, Calif., July 22, 1876; received a preparatory education, and attended Real Schule in Dresden, Saxony, Cantonal College, Lausanne, Switzerland, Force School, Washington, D. C., and Werntz Preparatory School, Annapolis, Md.; was graduated from the United States Naval Academy, Annapolis, Md., in 1897 and served in the United States Navy in various grades, retiring as commander in 1926; moved to Honolulu, T. H., in 1909; elected as a Republican a Delegate to the Seventieth, Seventy-first, and Seventy-second Congresses (March 4, 1927–March 3, 1933); unsuccessful candidate for reelection in 1932 to the Seventy-third Congress; delegate to the Republican National Conventions in 1928 and 1932; retired from active business and political life until recalled to active duty in the United States Navy on December 7, 1941, and served until March 1, 1945; promoted to the rank of captain on the retired list on June 9, 1943; appointed on April 26, 1945, by Governor Stainback, as a member of the Hawaiian Homes Commission and served until October 1951; trustee of the Liliuokalani Trust; died in Honolulu, Hawaii, July 31, 1959; interment in Oahu Cemetery.

HOUSTON, William Cannon, a Representative from Tennessee; born near Shelbyville, Bedford County, Tenn., March 17, 1852; moved with his mother to Woodbury, Cannon County, Tenn., in 1858; attended the schools of Woodbury and Sweetwater, Tenn.; engaged in agricultural pursuits and later in the publication of a newspaper; member of the State house of representatives 1877–1879, 1881–1885, and 1879; studied law; was admitted to the bar in 1878 and commenced practice in Woodbury, Tenn.; member of the Democratic State executive committee in 1888; chairman of the Democratic State convention in 1888; presidential elector on the Democratic ticket of Cleveland and Thurman in 1888; elected judge of the eighth judicial circuit in 1894, was reelected in 1902, and served until elected to Congress; elected as a Democrat to the Fifty-ninth and to the six succeeding Congresses (March 4, 1905–March 3, 1919); was not a candidate for renomination in 1918; retired from public life in 1919 and engaged in agricultural pursuits near Woodbury, Tenn.; delegate to the Democratic National Convention at San Francisco in 1920; died on his plantation, "Beaver Dam," near Woodbury, Tenn., August 30, 1931; interment in Riverside Cemetery, near Woodbury, Tenn.

HOUSTON, William Churchill, a Delegate from New Jersey; born in the Poplar Tent neighborhood of Cabarrus County, N. C., in 1745 or 1746; pursued classical studies; was graduated from Princeton College in 1768; professor in the same college from 1769 to 1783, when he resigned; served as captain in the Second Regiment, Somerset Militia, during the Revolutionary War; deputy secretary of the Continental Congress in 1775 and 1776; member of the New Jersey Provincial Congress in 1776; member of the New Jersey House of Assembly 1777–1779; member of the council of safety in 1778; Member of the Continental Congress 1779–1781; studied law; was admitted to the bar in 1781 and commenced practice in Trenton, N. J., in 1783; elected as the first Comptroller of the Treasury in 1781, but declined to serve; receiver of Continental taxes 1782–1785; clerk of the supreme court of New Jersey 1781–1788; again a Member of the Continental Congress in 1784 and 1785; member of the Annapolis Convention in 1786; delegate to the Philadelphia Constitutional Convention in 1787; died in Frankford, Pa., August 12, 1788; interment in the Second Presbyterian Churchyard, Philadelphia, Pa.

HOUSTOUN, John, a Delegate from Georgia; born in Waynesboro, Ga., August 31, 1744; attended the common schools; studied law; was admitted to the bar and commenced practice in Savannah, Ga.; prominent in early Revolutionary movements; one of the four originators of the "Sons of Liberty"; delegate to the Provincial Congress of Georgia in 1775; Member of the Continental Congress 1775–1777 and in 1779; was absent in Georgia when the Declaration of Independence was signed; member of the executive council in 1777; Governor of Georgia in 1778 and 1784; member of the commission to establish the boundary line between Georgia and South Carolina; chief justice of Georgia in 1786; unsuccessful candidate for Governor in 1787; justice for Chatham County in 1787; mayor of Savannah in 1789 and 1790; judge of the State superior court in 1792; died at "White Bluff," near Savannah, Ga., July 20, 1796.

HOUSTOUN, William, a Delegate from Georgia; born in Savannah, Ga., in 1755; completed preparatory studies and attended higher schools in England; studied law; was admitted to the Inner Temple, London, in 1776; returned to Savannah at the beginning of the Revolution and took an active part in the cause of liberty for the Colonies; Member of the Continental Congress 1783–1786; one of the agents on the part of Georgia to settle the boundary between that Commonwealth and South Carolina in 1785; delegate to the constitutional convention which framed the Federal Constitution in 1787, but declined to sign the instrument; was one of the original trustees for the establishment of the University of Georgia, at Athens; died in Savannah, Ga., March 17, 1813; interment in St. Paul's Chapel, New York City, N. Y.

HOVEY, Alvin Peterson, a Representative from Indiana; born near Mount Vernon, Posey County, Ind., September 6, 1821; attended the common schools of Mount Vernon; studied law; was admitted to the bar September 25, 1842, and practiced; commissioned first lieutenant in June 1846 for service in the war with Mexico; delegate to the State constitutional convention in 1850; circuit judge 1851–1854; judge of the supreme court in 1854; district attorney of the United States in 1856; removed by President Buchanan in 1858; during the Civil War served in the Union Army; commissioned colonel of the Twenty-fourth Regiment, Indiana Volunteers, July 31, 1861; brigadier general of Volunteers April 28, 1862; brevetted major general of Volunteers July 4, 1864, "for meritorious and distinguished services during the war"; resigned October 7, 1865; commissioned United States Minister to the Republic of Peru in 1865; resigned in 1870; elected as a Republican to the Fiftieth Congress and served from March 4, 1887, until January 17, 1889, when he resigned; elected Governor in 1888; inaugurated in January 1889 and served until his death in Indianapolis, Ind., November 23, 1891; interment in Bellefontaine Cemetery.

HOWARD, Benjamin, a Representative from Kentucky; born in Lexington, Ky. (then a part of Virginia), in 1760; completed preparatory studies; studied law; was admitted to the bar and commenced practice in Lexington; member of the Kentucky House of Representatives in 1800; elected to the Tenth and Eleventh Congresses and served from March 4, 1807, to April 10, 1810, when he resigned; Governor of the Territory of Louisiana 1810–1812; appointed a brigadier general in the United States Army March 12, 1813, and given command of the Eighth Military Department, embracing the territory west of the Mississippi River; died in St. Louis, Mo., September 18, 1814; interment in Old Grace Church Graveyard; reinterment in Bellefontaine Cemetery.

HOWARD, Benjamin Chew (son of John Eager Howard), a Representative from Maryland; born at "Belvedere," near Baltimore, Md., November 5, 1791; pursued classical studies, and was graduated from Princeton College in 1809; studied law; was admitted to the bar and commenced practice in Baltimore; served in the War of 1812, and at the Battle of North Point, in 1814, was captain of the Baltimore Mechanical Volunteers; was promoted to command of the Fifth Regiment, subsequently becoming brigadier general, and continued for many years prominently identified with the State military organization; member of the city council of Baltimore in 1820; member of the State house of delegates in 1824; elected as a Democrat to the Twenty-first and Twenty-second Congresses (March 4, 1829–March 3, 1833); declined the mission to Russia tendered by President Van Buren; commissioned by President Jackson in 1835, with Richard Rush, of Philadelphia, as peace emissary of the National Government in the controversy over the boundary line between Ohio and Michigan; elected to the Twenty-fourth and Twenty-fifth Congresses (March 4, 1835–March 3, 1839); reporter of the decisions of the Supreme Court of the United States 1843–1862; member of the peace conference of 1861, held in Washington, D. C., in an effort to devise means to prevent the impending war; unsuccessful Democratic candidate for Governor of Maryland in 1861; withdrew from public life and business activities; died in Baltimore, Md., March 6, 1872; interment in Greenmount Cemetery.

HOWARD, Edgar, a Representative from Nebraska; born in Osceola, Clarke County, Iowa, September 16, 1858; attended the common schools, Western Collegiate Institute, and Iowa College of Law; reporter and city editor of various newspapers until 1884; editor of the Papillion (Nebr.) Times 1884–1900; was admitted to the bar in 1886 and commenced practice in Papillion, Nebr.; member of the State house of representatives 1894–1896; probate judge of Sarpy County 1896–1900; delegate to the Democratic National Convention at Chicago in 1896; purchased the Weekly Telegram of Columbus, Nebr., in 1900 and made it a daily publication in 1922; Lieutenant Governor of Nebraska 1917–1919; elected as a Democrat to the Sixty-eighth and to the five succeeding Congresses (March 4, 1923–January 3, 1935); unsuccessful candidate for reelection in 1934 to the Seventy-fourth Congress and for election in 1938 to the Seventy-sixth Congress; resumed the newspaper publishing business in Columbus, Nebr., where he died July 19, 1951; interment in Columbus Cemetery.

HOWARD, Everette Burgess, a Representative from Oklahoma; born in Morgantown, Butler County, Ky., September 19, 1873; attended the public schools; learned the art of printing and engaged in newspaper work in Kentucky, Oklahoma, and Missouri; moved to Tulsa, Okla., in 1905 and engaged in the manufacture of brick and in the production of oil and gas; member of the State board of public affairs 1911–1915; State auditor of Oklahoma 1915–1919; elected as a Democrat to the Sixty-sixth Congress (March 4, 1919–March 3, 1921); unsuccessful candidate for reelection in 1920 to the Sixty-seventh Congress; elected to the Sixty-eighth Congress (March 4, 1923–March 3, 1925); was not a candidate for renomination in 1924, but was an unsuccessful candidate for the Democratic nomination for United States Senator; elected to the Seventieth Congress (March 4, 1927–March 3, 1929); unsuccessful candidate for reelection in 1928 to the Seventy-first Congress; engaged in the production of oil and gas in Oklahoma and Texas in 1930; died in Midland, Tex., April 3, 1950; interment in Memorial Park, Oklahoma City, Okla.

HOWARD, Guy Victor, a Senator from Minnesota; born in Minneapolis, Minn., November 28, 1879; attended the public schools, Minneapolis (Minn.) School of Business, and Georgetown University, Washington, D. C.; served as a clerk in the post office in the United States House of Representatives 1897–1901; engaged in the insurance business at Minneapolis in 1901; served as first assistant sergeant at arms of the 1908, 1912, 1916, and 1920 Republican National Conventions; deputy registrar of motor vehicles for Hennepin County, Minn., 1912–1934; presidential elector on the Republican ticket of Hughes and Fairbanks in 1916; elected as a Republican to the United States Senate to fill the vacancy caused by the death of Thomas D. Schall and served from November 4, 1936, to January 3, 1937; was not a candidate for election for the full term in 1936; resumed the insurance business; died in Minneapolis, Minn., August 20, 1954; interment in Lakewood Cemetery.

HOWARD, Jacob Merritt, a Representative and a Senator from Michigan; born in Shaftsbury, Bennington County, Vt., July 10, 1805; attended the district schools and the academies of Bennington and Brattleboro; was graduated from Williams College, Williamstown, Mass., in 1830; studied law in Ware, Mass.; moved to Detroit, Mich., in July 1832; was admitted to the bar in 1833 and commenced practice in Detroit, Mich.; city attorney of Detroit in 1834; member of the State house of representatives in 1838; elected as a Whig to the Twenty-seventh Congress (March 4, 1841–March 3, 1843); was not a candidate for renomination in 1842; drew up the platform of the first convention ever held by the Republican Party and christened that party in 1854; member of the first Republican informal national convention held at Pittsburgh, Pa., on February 22, 1856, for the purpose of perfecting the national organization and to provide for a national delegate convention at some subsequent date; attorney general of Michigan 1855–1861; elected as a Republican to the United States Senate to fill the vacancy caused by the death of Kinsley S. Bingham; reelected in 1865 and served from January 17, 1862, to March 3, 1871; died in Detroit, Mich., April 2, 1871; interment in Elmwood Cemetery.

HOWARD, John Eager (father of Benjamin Chew Howard), a Delegate and a Senator from Maryland; born near Baltimore, Md., June 4, 1752; was instructed by private tutors; served in the Revolutionary War; commanded a company at the Battle of White Plains October 28, 1776; was commissioned major, lieutenant colonel, and was a colonel when peace was declared; was voted a medal and the thanks of Congress for gallantry at the Cowpens January 17, 1781; Member of the Continental Congress 1784–1788; Governor of Maryland 1789–1791; served in the State senate 1791–1795; elected as a Federalist to the United States Senate to fill the vacancy caused by the resignation of Richard Potts; reelected in 1797 and served from November 30, 1796, to March 3, 1803; was offered by President Washington a seat in his Cabinet, also a commission as brigadier general in the expected war with France in 1798; died at "Belvedere," near Baltimore, Md., October 12, 1827; interment in Old St. Paul's Cemetery, Baltimore, Md.

HOWARD, Jonas George, a Representative from Indiana; born on a farm near New Albany, Floyd County, Ind., May 22, 1825; attended private school, Indiana Asbury College (now De Pauw University), Greencastle, Ind., and Louisville (Ky.) Law School; was graduated from the law department of Indiana University at Bloomington in 1851; was admitted to the bar in 1852 and commenced the practice of law in Jeffersonville, Clark County, Ind.; city attorney of Jeffersonville in 1854, 1865, 1871–1873, and 1877–1879; member of the city council 1859–1863; member of the State house of representatives 1863–1866; presidential elector on the Democratic ticket of Seymour and Blair in 1868, of Tilden and Hendricks in 1876, and of Cleveland and Hendricks in 1884; elected as a Democrat to the Forty-ninth and Fiftieth Congresses (March 4, 1885–March 3, 1889); unsuccessful candidate for renomination in 1888; returned to Jeffersonville, Ind., where he resumed the practice of law; also engaged in agricultural pursuits; died in Jeffersonville, Ind., October 5, 1911; interment in Walnut Ridge Cemetery.

HOWARD, Milford Wriarson, a Representative from Alabama; born near Rome, Floyd County, Ga., December 18, 1862; attended the common schools; studied law in Cedartown, Ga.; moved to Fort Payne, De Kalb County, Ala., in 1880; was admitted to the bar in 1881 and commenced practice in Fort Payne; elected as a Populist to the Fifty-fourth and Fifty-fifth Congresses (March 4, 1895–March 3, 1899); was not a candidate for renomination in 1898; resumed the practice of law in Fort Payne in 1904; moved to Montrose, near Los Angeles, Calif., in 1918 and engaged in literary pursuits; returned to Fort Payne in 1923; established the Master Schools for underprivileged mountain boys and girls; elected president of the Lookout Mountain Scenic Highway Association in 1926; resumed literary pursuits and also engaged in educational work; died in Los Angeles, Calif. December 28, 1937; interment in His Shrine Chapel, atop Lookout Mountain, near Mentone, Ala.

HOWARD, Tilghman Ashurst, a Representative from Indiana; born near Pickensville, S. C., November 14, 1797; attended the public schools; moved to Knoxville, Tenn., in 1816; studied law; was admitted to the bar in 1818 and commenced practice in Knoxville; member of the State senate in 1824; presidential elector on the Democratic ticket of Jackson and Calhoun in 1828; moved to Bloomington, Ind., in 1830 and resumed the practice of law; moved to Rockville, Ind., in 1833 and continued the practice of law; appointed by President Jackson district attorney for Indiana and served from 1833 to 1837; unsuccessful candidate for election to the United States Senate in 1838; elected as a Democrat to the Twenty-sixth Congress on August 5,

1839, and served until his resignation on July 1, 1840; unsuccessful candidate for election as Governor of Indiana in 1840, and for United States Senator in 1843; appointed Chargé d'Affaires to the Republic of Texas on June 11, 1844; died in Washington, Tex., August 16, 1844; interment in Rockville Cemetery, Rockville, Parke County, Ind.

HOWARD, Volney Erskine, a Representative from Texas; born in Norridgewock, Somerset County, Maine, October 22, 1809; completed preparatory studies; attended Bloomfield Academy and Waterville College; studied law; was admitted to the bar in 1832 and commenced practice in Brandon, Miss.; member of the State house of representatives in 1836; chosen by the legislature to carry the electoral vote for Van Buren to Washington, D. C.; reporter of the supreme court of the State of Mississippi; unsuccessful Democratic candidate for election in 1840 to the Twenty-seventh Congress; editor of the Mississippian; fought duels with Sergeant S. Prentiss and Alexander G. McNutt; moved to New Orleans, La., and was admitted to the bar there; moved to San Antonio, Tex., in 1847; member of the first State constitutional convention; elected as a Democrat to the Thirty-first and Thirty-second Congresses (March 4, 1849–March 3, 1853); unsuccessful candidate for reelection in 1852 to the Thirty-third Congress; sent on a special mission to California by the President; resigned, and engaged in the practice of law in San Francisco, Calif.; moved to Los Angeles in 1861 and continued the practice of law; district attorney 1861–1870; declined the nomination for judge of the supreme court; delegate to the State constitutional convention in 1878 and 1879; elected judge of the superior court of Los Angeles in 1879; retired at the end of one term on account of ill health; died in Santa Monica, Calif., May 14, 1889; interment in Fort Hill Cemetery, Los Angeles, Calif.

HOWARD, William, a Representative from Ohio; born in Jefferson County, Va., December 31, 1817; attended the common schools; studied law; was admitted to the bar in 1840 and practiced; moved to Batavia, Ohio; prosecuting attorney 1845–1849; served in the war with Mexico and was made second lieutenant of Company C, Second Regiment, Ohio Volunteer Infantry, on August 10, 1847; honorably mustered out July 25, 1848; member of the State senate 1850–1852; elected as a Democrat to the Thirty-sixth Congress (March 4, 1859–March 3, 1861); during the Civil War was commissioned major of the Fifty-ninth Regiment, Ohio Volunteer Infantry, on August 11, 1861, and served until February 24, 1863, when he was honorably discharged; resumed the practice of law; died in Batavia, Ohio, June 1, 1891; interment in Union Cemetery.

HOWARD, William Alanson, a Representative from Michigan; born in Hinesburg, Chittenden County, Vt., April 8, 1813; attended the public schools; moved to Albion, N. Y., in 1827 and was apprenticed as a cabinet maker until 1832; was graduated from Wyoming (N. Y.) Academy in 1835 and from Middlebury (Vt.) College in 1839; moved to Detroit, Mich., in 1840 and was a tutor in the branch of Michigan University; also studied law; was admitted to the bar in 1842 and commenced practice in Detroit; city treasurer 1848–1850; elected as a Republican to the Thirty-fourth and Thirty-fifth Congresses (March 4, 1855–March 3, 1859); successfully contested the election of George B. Cooper to the Thirty-sixth Congress and served from May 15, 1860, until March 3, 1861; was not a candidate for renomination in 1860; chairman of the Republican State central committee in 1860 and 1861; postmaster of Detroit 1861–1866; tendered the appointment of Minister to China in 1869, but declined; delegate to the Republican National Conventions in 1868, 1872, and 1876; moved to Grand Rapids, Mich., to assume duties

as land commissioner of the Grand Rapids & Indiana Railway 1869–1871 and of the Northern Pacific Railway 1872–1878; was an unsuccessful candidate for election to the United States Senate in 1871; member of the Republican National Committee 1872–1876; appointed Territorial Governor of Dakota by President Rutherford B. Hayes in 1878 and served until his death in Washington, D. C., on April 10, 1880; interment in Elmwood Cemetery, Detroit, Mich.

HOWARD, William Marcellus, a Representative from Georgia; born in Berwick City, St. Mary Parish, La., December 6, 1857; moved to Georgia with his parents at an early age; attended the common schools and Martin's Institute, Jefferson, Ga.; was graduated from the University of Georgia at Athens in 1877; studied law; was admitted to the bar in 1880 and commenced practice in Lexington, Ga.; solicitor general of the northern circuit of Georgia 1884–1896; elected as a Democrat to the Fifty-fifth and to the six succeeding Congresses (March 4, 1897–March 3, 1911); unsuccessful candidate for renomination in 1910; member of the Board of Regents of the Smithsonian Institution 1905–1912; one of the original trustees of the Carnegie Endowment for International Peace in 1910; appointed by President Taft as a member of the United States Tariff Board and served from 1911 to 1913; moved to Augusta, Ga., in 1913 and resumed the practice of law; died in Augusta, Ga., July 5, 1932; interment in Clarke Cemetery, Lexington, Ga.

HOWARD, William Schley (cousin of Augustus O. Bacon), a Representative from Georgia; born in Kirkwood, De Kalb County, Ga., June 29, 1875; attended Neel's Academy; was a page in the State house of representatives in 1888 and 1889; calendar clerk of the Georgia House of Representatives in 1890 and 1891; private secretary to United States Senator Patrick Walsh, of Georgia, from August 8, 1894, to February 18, 1895; studied law; was admitted to the bar in 1897 and commenced practice in Wrightsville, Ga.; enlisted in the Third Regiment, Georgia Volunteer Infantry, on July 2, 1898, and served as sergeant during the Spanish-American War; returned to De Kalb County and resumed the practice of his profession; member of the State house of representatives in 1900 and 1901; solicitor general of the Stone Mountain judicial circuit 1905–1911; elected as a Democrat to the Sixty-second and to the three succeeding Congresses (March 4, 1911–March 3, 1919); unsuccessful candidate in 1918 for nomination for the United States Senate; resumed the practice of law in Atlanta, Ga., until his death there on August 1, 1953; interment in Decatur Cemetery, Decatur, Ga.

HOWE, Albert Richards, a Representative from Mississippi; born in Brookfield, Worcester County, Mass., January 1, 1840; pursued classical studies; during the Civil War enlisted in the Union Army in 1861 as a private in the Forty-seventh Regiment, Massachusetts Volunteer Infantry, and served successively as sergeant, second and first lieutenant, and acting adjutant, participating in the campaign in North Carolina; upon the expiration of the nine months' service of the regiment was commissioned second lieutenant in the Fifth Regiment, Massachusetts Volunteer Cavalry, and was subsequently promoted to first lieutenant, captain, and major and served in Virginia and Texas until November 30, 1865, when he was honorably mustered out; settled in Como, Panola County, Miss., in 1865 and engaged in cotton planting; member of the Mississippi constitutional convention in 1868; delegate to the Republican National Convention at Chicago in 1868 which nominated Grant and Colfax; appointed treasurer of Panola County in 1869; member of the State house of representatives 1870–1872; elected as a Republican to the Forty-third Congress

(March 4, 1873–March 3, 1875); unsuccessful candidate for reelection in 1874 to the Forty-fourth Congress; moved to Illinois in 1875 and engaged in the brokerage business in Chicago, where he died June 1, 1884; interment in Brookfield Cemetery, Brookfield, Mass.

HOWE, James Robinson, a Representative from New York; born in the Borough of Manhattan, New York City, January 27, 1839; attended the common schools; employed as a clerk in a dry-goods store; moved to Brooklyn in 1870 and engaged in the dry-goods business; trustee in a number of public institutions in the city; elected as a Republican to the Fifty-fourth and Fifty-fifth Congresses (March 4, 1895–March 3, 1899); declined to be a candidate for renomination in 1898; register of Kings County 1900–1902; director of several banks; died in North Salem, N. Y., on September 21, 1914; interment in Greenwood Cemetery, Brooklyn, N. Y.

HOWE, John W., a Representative from Pennsylvania; born in Maine in 1801; studied law; was admitted to the bar; moved to Smethport, Pa., and then to Franklin, Pa., in 1829 and commenced the practice of law; justice of the peace; elected as a Free-Soil Whig to the Thirty-first and Thirty-second Congresses (March 4, 1849–March 3, 1853); moved to Meadville, Pa., and later to Rochester, N. Y., where he died December 1, 1873; interment in Greendale Cemetery, Meadville, Crawford County, Pa.

HOWE, Thomas Marshall (father-in-law of James W. Brown), a Representative from Pennsylvania; born in Williamstown, Orange County, Vt., April 20, 1808; moved with his parents to Bloomfield, Ohio, in 1817; attended private schools and was graduated from Warren (Ohio) Academy; moved to Pittsburgh, Pa., in 1829; served as clerk in a wholesale dry-goods establishment; commenced business for himself in 1833; was cashier and president of the Exchange National Bank of Pittsburgh 1839–1859; engaged in copper mining, copper and steel manufacturing, commercial pursuits, and banking; elected as a Whig to the Thirty-second and Thirty-third Congresses (March 4, 1851–March 3, 1855); was not a candidate for renomination in 1854; resumed former business pursuits; delegate to the Republican National Convention at Chicago in 1860 which nominated the presidential ticket of Lincoln and Hamlin; presidential elector on the Republican ticket of Lincoln and Hamlin in 1860; assistant adjutant general on the staff of Governor Curtin and chairman of the Allegheny County committee for recruiting Union soldiers during the Civil War; one of the organizers and first president of the Pittsburgh Chamber of Commerce; died in Pittsburgh, Pa., July 20, 1877; interment in Allegheny Cemetery.

HOWE, Thomas Y., Jr., a Representative from New York; born in Auburn, N. Y., in 1801; completed preparatory studies; inspector of Auburn Prison 1834–1838; elected surrogate of Cayuga County and served from March 18, 1836, to April 14, 1840; elected as a Democrat to the Thirty-second Congress (March 4, 1851–March 3, 1853); mayor of Auburn, N. Y., from March 1853 to March 1854; died in Auburn, N. Y., July 15, 1860; interment in Fort Hill Cemetery.

HOWE, Timothy Otis, a Senator from Wisconsin; born in Livermore, Androscoggin County, Maine, February 24, 1816; attended the common schools and was graduated from the Readfield (Maine) Seminary; studied law; was admitted to the bar in 1839 and commenced practice in Readfield, Maine; member of the State house of representatives in 1845; moved to Wisconsin in 1845 and settled in Green Bay; judge of the circuit

and supreme courts of Wisconsin from 1850 until 1855, when he resigned; elected as a Union Republican to the United States Senate in 1860; reelected in 1866 and 1872 and served from March 4, 1861, to March 3, 1879; unsuccessful candidate for reelection; served as a commissioner for the purchase of the Black Hills territory from the Indians; appointed one of the delegates to the International Monetary Conference held at Paris in 1881; appointed Postmaster General in the Cabinet of President Arthur December 20, 1881; entered upon duties of the office January 5, 1882, and served until his death in Kenosha, Wis., on March 25, 1883; interment in Woodlawn Cemetery, Green Bay, Wis.

HOWELL, Benjamin Franklin, a Representative from New Jersey; born in Cedarville, Cumberland County, N. J., January 27, 1844; attended the common schools; was graduated from Fort Edward Institute, New York; enlisted in the Twelfth Regiment, New Jersey Volunteers, in 1862 and served until the close of the war; engaged in mercantile pursuits in South Amboy, N. J., 1865; surrogate of Middlesex County 1882–1892; president of the People's National Bank of New Brunswick and vice president of the New Brunswick Savings Institution; elected as a Republican to the Fifty-fourth and to the seven succeeding Congresses (March 4, 1895–March 3, 1911); unsuccessful candidate for reelection in 1910 to the Sixty-second Congress; delegate to the Republican National Convention at St. Louis in 1896; member of the United States Immigration Commission 1907–1910; retired from active business; died at New Brunswick, N. J., February 1, 1933; interment in Christ Cemetery, South Amboy, N. J.

HOWELL, Charles Robert, a Representative from New Jersey; born in Trenton, Mercer County, N. J., April 23, 1904; attended Trenton public schools and graduated from Hoosac School, Hoosick, N. Y.; student at Princeton University in 1923 and 1924 and took special courses at the University of Pennsylvania in 1936 and 1937; insurance broker in Trenton, N. J., 1928–1954; elected to the New Jersey House of Assembly in 1944, reelected in 1945, and served until 1947; elected as a Democrat to the Eighty-first, Eighty-second, and Eighty-third Congresses (January 3, 1949–January 3, 1955); was not a candidate for renomination in 1954 but was an unsuccessful candidate for election to the United States Senate; appointed New Jersey State Commissioner of Banking and Insurance in February 1955; delegate at large to the Democratic National Convention in 1956; is a resident of Pennington, N. J.

HOWELL, David (father of Jeremiah Brown Howell), a Delegate from Rhode Island; born in Morristown, Morris County, N. J., January 1, 1747; attended Eaton's Academy, Hopewell, N. J., and was graduated from Princeton College in 1766; studied law; was admitted to the bar in 1768 and commenced practice in Providence, R. I.; tutor in Brown University, Providence, R. I., 1766–1769 and professor of natural philosophy 1769–1779; fellow of Brown University 1773–1824; justice of the peace in 1779; justice of the court of common pleas in 1780; Member of the Continental Congress 1782–1785; justice of the State supreme court in 1786 and 1787; attorney general of the State in 1789; appointed by the general assembly to prepare an address to be presented to the President of the United States in 1790; secretary of Brown University 1780–1806, professor of law 1790–1824, and acting president of the university in 1791 and 1792; commissioner for settling the boundaries of the United States; district attorney of Rhode Island; judge of the United States District Court for Rhode Island from 1812 until his death in Providence, R. I., July 21, 1824; interment in North Burial Ground.

HOWELL, Edward, a Representative from New York; was born in Newburgh, Orange County, N. Y., October 16, 1792; attended the public schools; moved to Sidney, N. Y., in 1808, and in the following year to Unadilla, N. Y., where he taught school; moved to Bath, N. Y., in 1811; appointed postmaster of Bath December 30, 1817, and served until August 13, 1821; county clerk of Steuben County 1818–1821; studied law; was admitted to the bar in 1823 and commenced practice in Bath; district attorney of Steuben County 1829–1834; member of the State assembly in 1832; elected as a Democrat to the Twenty-third Congress (March 4, 1833–March 3, 1835); was not a candidate for renomination in 1834; again district attorney of Steuben County 1836–1840; resumed the practice of law; died in Bath, N. Y., January 30, 1871; interment in Grove Cemetery.

HOWELL, Elias (father of James Bruen Howell), a Representative from Ohio; born in New Jersey in 1792; attended the public schools; moved to Newark, Ohio, in 1819; member of the State senate 1830–1832; elected as a Whig to the Twenty-fourth Congress (March 4, 1835–March 3, 1837); was not a candidate for renomination; died near Newark, Ohio, in May 1844.

HOWELL, Evan (George), a Representative from Illinois; born in Marion, Williamson County, Ill., September 21, 1905; attended the public schools at Villa Grove, Douglas County, Ill.; graduated from the University of Illinois College of Commerce at Urbana in 1927 and from the College of Law in 1930; taught school at the Harvard Community High School, McHenry County, Ill., in 1927 and 1928; member of the faculty of the College of Commerce, University of Illinois, 1928–1930; was admitted to the bar in 1930 and commenced practice in Springfield, Ill.; member of the Officers' Reserve Corps since 1933; referee in bankruptcy, United States District Court, southern division of Illinois, 1937–1941; elected as a Republican to the Seventy-seventh and to the three succeeding Congresses and served from January 3, 1941, until his resignation on October 5, 1947; judge of the United States Court of Claims from October 6, 1947, until his resignation on September 30, 1953; chairman of the Illinois Toll Highway Commission 1953–1955; resumed the practice of law; is a resident of Springfield, Ill.

HOWELL, George, a Representative from Pennsylvania; born in Scranton, Lackawanna County, Pa., June 28, 1859; attended the public schools, Pennington (N. J.) Seminary, Newton (Pa.) Collegiate Institute, and Lafayette College, Easton, Pa.; was graduated from the Illinois State Normal University at Normal, Ill.; taught school fourteen years in Illinois, New Jersey, and Pennsylvania, and served seven years as superintendent of the public schools of Scranton, Pa.; studied law; was admitted to the bar in 1904 and commenced practice in Scranton; presented credentials as a Republican Member-elect to the Fifty-eighth Congress and served from March 4, 1903, to February 10, 1904, when he was succeeded by William Connell, who contested the election; assistant principal of the Scranton Technical High School 1906–1908; superintendent of schools from 1908 until his death in Scranton, Pa., November 19, 1913; interment in Forest Hill Cemetery.

HOWELL, James Bruen (son of Elias Howell), a Senator from Iowa; born near Morristown, Morris County, N. J., July 4, 1816; moved with his parents to Newark, Ohio, in 1819; was graduated from the Newark High School in 1833 and from Miami University, Oxford, Ohio, in 1839; studied law; was admitted to the bar in 1839 and commenced practice in Newark; moved to Keosauqua, Iowa, in 1841, where he practiced for several years; engaged in newspaper work; moved to Keokuk, Iowa, in 1849; postmaster of Keokuk from April 8, 1861,

until August 27, 1866; published and edited the Daily Gate City; delegate to the Republican National Convention at Philadelphia in 1856; elected as a Republican to the United States Senate to fill the vacancy caused by the resignation of James W. Grimes and served from January 18, 1870, to March 3, 1871; was not a candidate for reelection to the Senate; one of three commissioners appointed by President Grant in 1871 to adjust claims for stores and supplies under the act of March 3, 1871, and served until March 10, 1880; died in Keokuk, Iowa, June 17, 1880; interment in Oakland Cemetery.

HOWELL, Jeremiah Brown (son of David Howell), a Senator from Rhode Island; born in Providence, R. I., August 28, 1771; attended private schools; pursued classical studies, and was graduated from Brown University, Providence, R. I., in 1789; studied law; was admitted to the bar in 1793 and commenced practice in Providence; brigadier general in the State militia; elected as a Federalist to the United States Senate and served from March 4, 1811, to March 3, 1817; was not a candidate for reelection; died in Providence, R. I., February 5, 1822; interment in North Burial Ground.

HOWELL, Joseph, a Representative from Utah; born in Brigham City, Boxelder County, Utah, February 17, 1857; moved with his parents to Wellsville, Utah, in 1863; attended the common schools and the University of Utah at Salt Lake City; taught school; engaged in mercantile pursuits; mayor of Wellsville 1882–1884; served in the Territorial house of representatives 1886–1892; regent of the University of Utah 1896–1900; member of the State senate 1896–1900; moved to Logan, Utah, in 1901; elected as a Republican to the Fifty-eighth and to the six succeeding Congresses (March 4, 1903–March 3, 1917); was not a candidate for renomination; engaged in banking and the real-estate business; died in Logan, Utah, July 18, 1918; interment in the City Cemetery.

HOWELL, Nathaniel Woodhull, a Representative from New York; born in Blooming Grove, Orange County, N. Y., January 1, 1770; was graduated from Princeton College in 1788; taught school in Montgomery, N. Y., 1789–1792; studied law; was admitted to the bar and practiced in New York City and in Tioga County 1794–1796, and in Canandaigua, N. Y., 1796–1851; attorney general for western New York 1799–1802; member of the State assembly in 1804; elected to the Thirteenth Congress (March 4, 1813–March 3, 1815); appointed a member of the commission to appraise the Western Inland Lock Navigation Co. in 1817; was the first judge of Ontario County 1819–1832; died in Canandaigua, N. Y., October 15, 1851; interment in West Avenue Cemetery.

HOWELL, Robert Beecher, a Senator from Nebraska; born in Adrian, Lenawee County, Mich., January 21, 1864; attended the public schools; appointed cadet midshipman in the United States Navy in 1881 and was graduated from the United States Naval Academy, Annapolis, Md., in 1885; moved to Omaha, Nebr., in 1888; attended the Detroit School of Law, class of 1893; served as State engineer of Nebraska in 1895 and 1896; city engineer of Omaha in 1896 and 1897; lieutenant in the United States Navy during the Spanish-American War; member of the State senate in 1902, 1903, and 1904; member of the Omaha Water Board and its successor, board of directors of Metropolitan Utilities District, 1904–1923; elected Republican national committeeman in 1912, 1916, and 1920; unsuccessful Republican candidate for Governor of Nebraska in 1914; general manager of the Metropolitan Utilities District, operating public water, gas, and ice plants, 1912–1923; lieutenant in the United States Naval Reserve Force 1917–1923;

chairman of the radio commission, United States Post Office Department, in 1921; elected as a Republican to the United States Senate in 1922; reelected in 1928, and served from March 4, 1923, until his death in Washington, D. C., March 11, 1933; interment in Forest Lawn Cemetery, Omaha, Nebr.

HOWEY, Benjamin Franklin (nephew of Charles Creighton Stratton), a Representative from New Jersey; born in Pleasant Meadows, near Swedesboro, Gloucester County, N. J., March 17, 1828; instructed by private tutors at Pleasant Meadows and the academies in Swedesboro and Bridgeton, N. J.; engaged in business in Philadelphia as a flour and grain commission merchant in 1847 and later in quarrying and manufacturing slate; during the Civil War served as captain of Company G, Thirty-first Regiment, New Jersey Volunteers, from September 3, 1862, to June 26, 1863; sheriff of Warren County, N. J., from November 13, 1878, to November 15, 1881; elected as a Republican to the Forty-eighth Congress (March 4, 1883–March 3, 1885); died in Columbia, N. J., February 6, 1895; interment in Trinity Church Cemetery, Swedesboro, N. J.

HOWLAND, Benjamin, a Senator from Rhode Island; born in Tiverton, R. I., July 27, 1755; attended the common schools; engaged in agricultural pursuits; collector of taxes in 1801; town auditor in 1802; town moderator in 1805; member of the State house of representatives in 1810; general in the State militia during the War of 1812; elected as a Democrat to the United States Senate to fill the vacancy caused by the death of Samuel J. Potter and served from October 29, 1804, until March 3, 1809; died in Tiverton, R. I., May 1, 1821; interment in the family lot on his estate.

HOWLAND, Leonard Paul, a Representative from Ohio; born in Jefferson, Ashtabula County, Ohio, December 5, 1865; completed preparatory studies; was graduated from Oberlin (Ohio) College in 1887 and from the law department of Harvard University in 1890; was admitted to the bar in 1890 and commenced practice in Jefferson, Ohio; moved to Cleveland in 1894 and continued the practice of law; served as second lieutenant, squadron adjutant, First Regiment, Ohio Volunteer Cavalry, during the Spanish-American War; elected as a Republican to the Sixtieth, Sixty-first, and Sixty-second Congresses (March 4, 1907–March 3, 1913); unsuccessful candidate for reelection in 1912 to the Sixty-third Congress; one of the managers appointed by the House of Representatives in 1912 to conduct the impeachment proceedings against Robert W. Archbald, judge of the United States Commerce Court; resumed the practice of law; delegate to the Republican National Conventions in 1916, 1920, and 1924; died in Cleveland, Ohio, December 23, 1942; interment in Lake View Cemetery.

HOWLEY, Richard, a Delegate from Georgia; born in Liberty County, Ga., in 1740; pursued an academic course; studied law; was admitted to the bar and commenced practice in St. John's Parish, Georgia; also engaged in the planting of rice; moved to St. Paul's Parish in 1779; member of the State house of representatives 1779–1783; member of the executive council of Liberty County in 1779 and 1780; Governor of Georgia in 1780; Member of the Continental Congress in 1780 and 1781; practiced law in Sunbury, Ga.; chosen chief justice of Georgia and served from October 1, 1782, to January 3, 1783; moved to Savannah, Ga., and died there in December 1784.

HOXWORTH, Stephen Arnold, a Representative from Illinois; born in Maquon Township, near Maquon, Knox County, Ill., May 1, 1860; attended the public schools and was graduated from Maquon High School; moved to Blue Springs, Gage County,

Nebr., in 1880; engaged in banking and in the grain and implement business; member of the Nebraska State Militia; returned to Illinois in 1885 and engaged in agricultural pursuits near Rapatee, Knox County; served as supervisor of Maquon Township 1907–1912; elected as a Democrat to the Sixty-third Congress (March 4, 1913–March 3, 1915); was not a candidate for renomination in 1914; resumed agricultural pursuits; died in Rapatee, Ill., January 25, 1930; interment in Lyons Cemetery near Rapatee, Ill.

HRUSKA, Roman Lee, a Representative and a Senator from Nebraska; born in David City, Butler County, Nebr., August 16, 1904; attended the public schools; took a prelegal course at the University of Omaha 1923–1925; attended the University of Chicago Law School in 1927 and 1928; graduated from Creighton University College of Law, Omaha, Nebr., in 1929; was admitted to the bar in 1929 and commenced practice in Omaha, Nebr.; member of Board of Douglas County Commissioners 1944–1952 and chairman 1945–1952; member of Advisory Committee to Nebraska Board of Control 1947–1952; president Nebraska Association of County Officials in 1950 and 1951; vice president of National Association of County Officials in 1951 and 1952; vice chairman of Nebraska Civil Defense in 1951 and 1952; member of Board of Regents of the University of Omaha 1950–1957; delegate at large to the Republican National Convention in 1960; elected as a Republican to the Eighty-third Congress and served from January 3, 1953, until his resignation November 8, 1954, having been elected to the United States Senate to fill the vacancy caused by the death of Hugh Butler, and served from November 8, 1954, to January 3, 1959; reelected in 1958 for the term ending January 3, 1965.

HUBARD, Edmund Wilcox, a Representative from Virginia; born near Farmville, Buckingham County, Va., February 20, 1806; attended private schools and the University of Virginia at Charlottesville; engaged in agricultural pursuits; justice of the peace; elected as a Democrat to the Twenty-seventh, Twenty-eighth, and Twenty-ninth Congresses (March 4, 1841–March 3, 1847); was not a candidate for renomination in 1846; resumed agricultural pursuits; colonel of a militia regiment in 1864; appraiser of the Confederate Government to regulate the value of the Confederate dollar; died at his home near Farmville, Buckingham County, Va., December 9, 1878; interment in the family cemetery near his home.

HUBBARD, Asahel Wheeler (father of Elbert Hamilton Hubbard), a Representative from Iowa; born in Haddam, Conn., January 19, 1819; worked on his father's farm in the summer time and in winter attended the public schools; engaged as a stonecutter; subsequently pursued his studies at a select school in Middletown, Conn.; moved to Rushville, Ind., in 1838, where he was employed as a book agent and taught school; studied law; was admitted to the bar in 1841 and commenced practice in Rushville; member of the Indiana House of Representatives 1847–1849; moved to Sioux City, Iowa, in 1857 and engaged in the real-estate business; judge of the fourth judicial district 1859–1862; elected as a Republican to the Thirty-eighth, Thirty-ninth, and Fortieth Congresses (March 4, 1863–March 3, 1869); was not a candidate for renomination in 1868; withdrew from political life; one of the organizers of the First National Bank of Sioux City in 1871 and served as its president until January 15, 1879; was also interested in railroad building in Iowa and in mining property in Leadville, Colo.; died in Sioux City, Iowa, September 22, 1879; interment in Floyd Cemetery.

HUBBARD, Chester Dorman (father of William Pallister Hubbard), a Representative from West Virginia; born in Hamden, Middlesex County, Conn., November 25, 1814; moved with his parents in 1819 to Wheeling, Va. (now West Virginia); was graduated from the Wesleyan University, Middletown, Conn., in 1840; engaged in banking and in the manufacture of iron and lumber; member of the house of delegates of Virginia in 1852 and 1853; delegate to the Virginia convention in Richmond in 1861 and opposed secession; delegate to the West Virginia convention in Wheeling the same year; served in the senate of West Virginia in 1863 and 1864; delegate to the Republican National Convention at Baltimore in 1864 which nominated Lincoln and Johnson and at Chicago in 1880 which nominated Garfield and Arthur; elected as a Republican to the Thirty-ninth and Fortieth Congresses (March 4, 1865–March 3, 1869); resumed banking and manufacturing pursuits; died in Wheeling, W. Va., August 23, 1891; interment in Greenwood Cemetery.

HUBBARD, David (cousin of Samuel Houston), a Representative from Alabama; born near the town of Old Liberty (now Bedford), Bedford County, Va., in 1792; attended the county schools and an academy; during the War of 1812 entered the Army as a volunteer under General Jackson at New Orleans and served as major in the Quartermaster Corps; was severely wounded, captured by the British, and placed on a warship, but subsequently released; moved to Huntsville, Ala., where he worked as a carpenter; studied law; was admitted to the bar about 1820 and commenced practice in Huntsville; moved to Florence and served as solicitor 1823–1826; moved to Moulton in 1827 and entered the mercantile business; member of the State senate in 1827 and 1828; member of the board of trustees of the University of Alabama 1828–1835; moved to Courtland in 1829, where he engaged in buying and selling Chickasaw Indian land; member of the State house of representatives in 1831, 1842, 1843, 1845, and 1853; elected as a State Rights Democrat to the Twenty-sixth Congress (March 4, 1839–March 3, 1841); unsuccessful candidate for reelection in 1840 to the Twenty-seventh Congress; resumed the practice of law; presidential elector on the Democratic ticket of Polk and Dallas in 1844; elected to the Thirty-first Congress (March 4, 1849–March 3, 1851); unsuccessful candidate for reelection in 1850 to the Thirty-second Congress; delegate to the Southern Commercial Congress at Savannah, Ga., in 1859; presidential elector on the Breckinridge and Lane ticket in 1860; member of the Confederate States House of Representatives 1861–1863; first Confederate States Commissioner of Indian Affairs 1863–1865; built one of the first railroads in the United States, from Tuscumbia to Decatur, Ala.; moved to Spring Hill, Tenn.; died at the home of his son in Pointe Coupee Parish, La., January 20, 1874; interment in Trinity Episcopal Churchyard, Rosedale, Iberville Parish, La.

HUBBARD, Demas, Jr., a Representative from New York; born in Winfield, Herkimer County, N. Y., January 17, 1806; attended the public schools and pursued an academic course; studied law; was admitted to the bar and commenced practice in Smyrna, N. Y., in 1835; member of the State assembly 1838–1840; supervisor of Smyrna 1859–1864; elected chairman of the board of supervisors of Chenango County, N. Y.; elected as a Republican to the Thirty-ninth Congress (March 4, 1865–March 3, 1867); was not a candidate for renomination in 1866; resumed the practice of his profession; died in Smyrna, Chenango County, N. Y., September 2, 1873; interment in Smyrna East Cemetery.

HUBBARD, Elbert Hamilton (son of Asahel Wheeler Hubbard), a Representative from Iowa; born in Rushville, Rush County, Ind., August 19, 1849; attended the public schools and was instructed by a private tutor; was graduated from Yale College in 1872; studied law; was admitted to the bar in 1874

and commenced practice in Sioux City, Iowa; member of the State house of representatives in 1882; served in the State senate 1900–1902; elected as a Republican to the Fifty-ninth and to the three succeeding Congresses and served from March 4, 1905, until his death in Sioux City, Iowa, June 4, 1912; interment in Floyd Cemetery.

HUBBARD, Henry, a Representative and a Senator from New Hampshire; born in Charlestown, Sullivan County, N. H., May 3, 1784; pursued classical studies under private tutors and was graduated from Dartmouth College, Hanover, N. H., in 1803; studied law in Portsmouth, N. H.; was admitted to the bar about 1806 and commenced practice in Charlestown, Sullivan County, N. H.; in 1810 he was chosen moderator, which office he held sixteen times; first selectman in 1819, 1820, and 1828; member of the State house of representatives 1812–1815, 1819, 1820, and 1823–1827, and served three years as speaker; State solicitor for Cheshire County 1823–1828; probate judge of Sullivan County 1827–1829; elected as a Democrat to the Twenty-first, Twenty-second, and Twenty-third Congresses (March 4, 1829–March 3, 1835); served as Speaker pro tempore for one day, May 16, 1834; elected as a Democrat to the United States Senate and served from March 4, 1835, to March 3, 1841; was not a candidate for reelection; Governor of New Hampshire 1841–1843; United States subtreasurer at Boston, Mass., 1846–1849; died in Charlestown, N. H., June 5, 1857; interment in Forest Hill Cemetery.

HUBBARD, Joel Douglas, a Representative from Missouri; born near Marshall, Saline County, Mo., November 6, 1860; attended the public schools and Central College, Fayette, Mo.; was graduated from the Missouri Medical College at St. Louis in 1882; practiced medicine in Syracuse, Morgan County, Mo., until 1886; county clerk 1886–1894; elected as a Republican to the Fifty-fourth Congress (March 4, 1895–March 3, 1897); was an unsuccessful candidate for reelection in 1896 to the Fifty-fifth Congress; studied law; was admitted to the Missouri bar in 1899 and commenced practice in Versailles, Mo.; also engaged in the banking business; practiced medicine in Sedalia, Mo., in 1904 and 1905; returned to Versailles and resumed the practice of law and his banking interests; moved to El Paso, Tex., in 1917 and continued the practice of law; died in Tampa, Fla., on May 26, 1919; interment in Versailles Cemetery, Versailles, Mo.

HUBBARD, John Henry, a Representative from Connecticut; born in Salisbury, Litchfield County, Conn., March 24, 1804; attended the public schools; studied law; was admitted to the bar in 1828 and commenced practice in Lakeville; member of the State senate 1847–1849; prosecuting attorney 1849–1852; moved to Litchfield in 1855 and continued the practice of law; elected as a Republican to the Thirty-eighth and Thirty-ninth Congresses (March 4, 1863–March 3, 1867); unsuccessful candidate for renomination in 1866; resumed the practice of law; died in Litchfield, Conn., on July 30, 1872; interment in the East Cemetery.

HUBBARD, Jonathan Hatch, a Representative from Vermont; born in Tolland, Tolland County, Conn., May 7, 1768; at the age of eleven moved with his parents to Claremont, N. H.; was instructed by a private tutor; studied law; was admitted to the bar in 1790 and commenced practice in Windsor, Vt.; elected as a Federalist to the Eleventh Congress (March 4, 1809–March 3, 1811); unsuccessful candidate in 1810 for reelection to the Twelfth Congress; judge of the State supreme court 1813–1815; resumed the practice of law; died in Windsor, Vt., September 20, 1849; interment in the Old South Cemetery.

HUBBARD, Levi, a Representative from Massachusetts; born in Worcester, Mass., December 19, 1762; attended the common schools; moved to Paris, Maine (then a district of Massachusetts), in 1785; engaged in agricultural pursuits; was prominent in State military organizations; member of the Massachusetts House of Representatives in 1804, 1805, and 1812; served in the Massachusetts Senate 1806–1811; elected as a Democrat to the Thirteenth Congress (March 4, 1813–March 3, 1815); again served in the Massachusetts Senate in 1816; resumed agricultural pursuits; member of Maine Executive Council in 1829; died in Paris, Maine, February 18, 1836; interment in a tomb on his farm.

HUBBARD, Richard Dudley, a Representative from Connecticut; born in Berlin, Hartford County, Conn., September 7, 1818; pursued preparatory studies at East Hartford; was graduated from Yale College in 1839; studied law; was admitted to the bar in 1842 and commenced practice in Hartford, Conn.; member of the State house of representatives in 1842, 1855, and again in 1858; prosecuting attorney for Hartford County 1846–1868; elected as a Democrat to the Fortieth Congress (March 4, 1867–March 3, 1869); declined to be a candidate for renomination in 1868; resumed the practice of law in Hartford; Governor of Connecticut in 1878 and 1879; unsuccessful candidate for reelection in 1879; engaged in the practice of law from 1877 until his death in Hartford, Conn., February 28, 1884; interment in Cedar Hill Cemetery.

HUBBARD, Samuel Dickinson, a Representative from Connecticut; born in Middletown, Conn., August 10, 1799; pursued classical studies; was graduated from Yale College in 1819; studied law; was admitted to the bar and practiced in Middletown, Conn., 1823–1837; also engaged in manufacturing; elected as a Whig to the Twenty-ninth and Thirtieth Congresses (March 4, 1845–March 3, 1849); served as Postmaster General of the United States in the Cabinet of President Fillmore from August 31, 1852, to March 7, 1853; died in Middletown, Conn., October 8, 1855; interment in Indian Hill Cemetery.

HUBBARD, Thomas Hill, a Representative from New York; born in New Haven, Conn., December 5, 1781; pursued classical studies; was graduated from Yale College in 1799; studied law; was admitted to the bar in 1804 and commenced practice in Hamilton, N. Y.; surrogate of Madison County 1806–1816; presidential elector on the Clinton and Ingersoll ticket in 1812; district attorney of the sixth district 1816–1818 and of Madison County 1818–1821; elected as a Democrat to the Fifteenth Congress (March 4, 1817–March 3, 1819); elected to the Seventeenth Congress (March 4, 1821–March 3, 1823); moved to Utica, N. Y., in 1823; appointed the first clerk of the court of chancery of Oneida County in 1823; clerk of the supreme court 1825–1835; retired from public activities in 1835; one of the founders of Hamilton College, Clinton, N. Y., and Hamilton (N. Y.) Academy; served as a trustee of Utica (N. Y.) Academy; presidential elector on the Democratic ticket of Polk and Dallas in 1844 and of Pierce and King in 1852; died in Utica, N. Y., May 21, 1857; interment in Forest Hill Cemetery.

HUBBARD, William Pallister (son of Chester Dorman Hubbard), a Representative from West Virginia; born in Wheeling, Va. (later West Virginia), December 24, 1843; attended the public schools and Linsly Institute of Wheeling; was graduated from Wesleyan University, Middletown, Conn., in 1863; studied law; was admitted to the bar in 1864; enlisted in the Union Army as a private in 1865 in the Third West Virginia Cavalry, being a first lieutenant when honorably discharged; returned to Wheeling and commenced the practice of law in 1866; clerk of the

West Virginia House of Delegates 1866–1870; member of the house of delegates in 1881 and 1882; delegate to the Republican National Convention at Chicago in 1888; unsuccessful Republican candidate for attorney general of West Virginia in 1888; unsuccessful Republican candidate for election in 1890 to the Fifty-second Congress; chairman of the commission to revise the tax laws of West Virginia 1901–1903; elected as a Republican to the Sixtieth and Sixty-first Congresses (March 4, 1907–March 3, 1911); declined to be a candidate for renomination in 1910; resumed the practice of law in Wheeling, W. Va.; delegate to the Republican National Convention at Chicago in 1912; died in Wheeling, W. Va., December 5, 1921; interment in Greenwood Cemetery.

HUBBELL, Edwin Nelson, a Representative from New York; born in Coxsackie, Greene County, N. Y., August 13, 1815; pursued an academic course; several years supervisor of Greene County; elected as a Democrat to the Thirty-ninth Congress (March 4, 1865–March 3, 1867); moved to East Saginaw, Mich., and was employed as a clerk for a lumber company 1883–1887; served as assistant city treasurer 1887–1890 and as deputy city treasurer 1894–1896.

HUBBELL, James Randolph, a Representative from Ohio; born in Lincoln Township, Delaware County, Ohio, July 13, 1824; attended the common schools; taught school at Woodbury, Ohio; studied law; was admitted to the bar in 1845 and commenced practice at London, Ohio; moved to Delaware, Ohio, and continued the practice of law; member of the State house of representatives in 1849, 1858, 1859, 1862, and 1863 and served as speaker in 1863; presidential elector on the Republican ticket of Frémont and Dayton in 1856; elected as a Republican to the Thirty-ninth Congress (March 4, 1865–March 3, 1867); appointed by President Johnson as Minister to Portugal, but his nomination was not confirmed; resumed the practice of law; served in the State senate in 1869; resigned for the purpose of accepting the Democratic nomination for Congress; unsuccessful Democratic candidate for election in 1870 to the Forty-second Congress; died at the home of his son in Bellville, Ohio, on November 26, 1890; interment in Oak Grove Cemetery, Delaware, Ohio.

HUBBELL, Jay Abel, a Representative from Michigan; born in Avon, Mich., September 15, 1829; attended the district schools; was graduated from the University of Michigan at Ann Arbor in 1853; studied law; was admitted to the bar in 1855; moved to Ontonagon, Mich., in November 1855 and engaged in the practice of law; elected district attorney of the Upper Peninsula in 1857 and 1859; moved to Houghton, Mich., in February 1860 and continued the practice of law until 1870; prosecuting attorney of Houghton County 1861–1867; identified with the development of the mineral interests of the Upper Peninsula; appointed by the Governor of Michigan in 1876, State commissioner to the Centennial Exhibition and collected and prepared the State exhibit of minerals; elected as a Republican to the Forty-third and to the four succeeding Congresses (March 4, 1873–March 3, 1883); member of the State senate 1885–1887; served as circuit judge of the twelfth judicial circuit from January 1, 1894, to December 31, 1899, when he resigned; died in Houghton, Mich., October 13, 1900; interment in Forest Hill Cemetery.

HUBBELL, William Spring, a Representative from New York; born in Painted Post, Steuben County, N. Y., January 17, 1801; attended the public schools; postmaster of Bath, N. Y., in 1829; town clerk in 1831; later engaged in banking; member of the State house of representatives in 1841; elected as a Democrat to the Twenty-eighth Congress (March 4, 1843–March 3, 1845); delegate to the Democratic National Convention at Charleston, S. C., in 1860; banker; died in Bath, N. Y., November 16, 1873; interment in Grove Cemetery.

HUBBS, Orlando, a Representative from North Carolina; born in Commack, Suffolk County, N. Y., February 18, 1840; attended the district schools and the local academy at Commack; went to Northport in 1856 and learned the trade of a carriage and wagon builder and subsequently became employed as a ship's joiner at Hunters Point, N. Y.; moved to New Bern, N. C., in 1865 and became engaged in mercantile pursuits; took an active part in organizing the Republican Party in North Carolina; sheriff of Craven County 1871–1881; elected as a Republican to the Forty-seventh Congress (March 4, 1881–March 3, 1883); was not a candidate for renomination in 1882; presidential elector on the Republican ticket of Blaine and Logan in 1884; returned to New York in 1890 and settled in Central Islip; engaged in agricultural pursuits; member of the New York Assembly 1902–1908; served in the State senate in 1910 and 1911; retired from public life; resided in Smithtown Branch, Suffolk County, N. Y., until his death on December 5, 1930; interment in Commack Cemetery, Commack, N. Y.

HUBER, Walter B., a Representative from Ohio; born in Akron, Summit County, Ohio, June 29, 1903; associated with the Summit County prosecuting attorney 1936–1944; elected as a Democrat to the Seventy-ninth, Eightieth, and Eighty-first Congresses (January 3, 1945–January 3, 1951); unsuccessful candidate for reelection in 1950 to the Eighty-second Congress and for election in 1952 to the Eighty-third Congress; investigator for the United States Senate Committee on the Judiciary, Subcommittee on Patents, Trademarks, and Copyrights, from October 20, 1955, to April 30, 1958; administrative assistant with House Subcommittee on Legislative Oversight from May 1, 1958, to January 3, 1959; consultant with House Un-American Activities Committee January 4, 1959– ; resides in Riverside, Md.

HUBLEY, Edward Burd, a Representative from Pennsylvania; born in Reading, Pa., in 1792; attended the public schools; studied law; was admitted to the bar in 1820 and commenced practice in Reading; afterwards moved to Orwigsburg, the county seat of Schuylkill County; elected as a Jackson Democrat to the Twenty-fourth and Twenty-fifth Congresses (March 4, 1835–March 3, 1839); canal commissioner of Pennsylvania 1839–1842; appointed on November 8, 1842, a commissioner to adjust and settle certain claims under the treaty with the Cherokee Indians of 1835; resumed the practice of law in Reading, Pa.; moved to Philadelphia, Pa., where he died February 23, 1856; interment in Charles Evans Cemetery, Reading, Pa.

HUCK, Winnifred Sprague Mason (daughter of William Ernest Mason), a Representative from Illinois; born in Chicago, Ill., September 14, 1882; attended the public schools of Chicago and also at Washington, D. C., while her father was a Member of Congress; elected as a Republican to the Sixty-seventh Congress to fill the vacancy caused by the death of her father, William E. Mason, and served from November 7, 1922, to March 3, 1923; unsuccessful candidate for renomination in 1922; engaged in journalism and lecturing; died in Chicago, Ill., August 24, 1936; remains were cremated and the ashes deposited in Oakwood Cemetery, Waukegan, Ill.

HUDD, Thomas Richard, a Representative from Wisconsin; born in Buffalo, N. Y., October 2, 1835; moved with his mother to Chicago, Ill., in 1842 and to Appleton, Wis., in 1853; attended the common schools and Lawrence University, Appleton, Wis.; studied law; was admitted to the bar in 1856 and commenced practice in Appleton, Wis.; district attorney of Outagamie County in 1856 and 1857; served in the State senate in 1862, 1863, 1876–1879, 1882, 1883, and 1885; moved to Green Bay in 1868 and continued the practice of law; member of the State assembly in 1868 and 1875; city attorney of Green Bay in 1873 and 1874; delegate to the Democratic National Convention at Cincinnati in 1880; elected as a Democrat to the Forty-ninth Congress to fill the vacancy caused by the death of Joseph Rankin; reelected to the Fiftieth Congress and served from March 8, 1886, to March 3, 1889; did not seek renomination in 1888; resumed the practice of law; died in Green Bay, Wis., on June 22, 1896; interment in Woodlawn Cemetery.

HUDDLESTON, George, a Representative from Alabama; born on a farm near Lebanon, Wilson County, Tenn., November 11, 1869; attended the common schools; studied law at Cumberland University, Lebanon, Tenn.; was admitted to the bar in 1891 and practiced in Birmingham, Ala., until 1911, when he retired from practice; during the Spanish-American War served as a private in the First Regiment, Alabama Volunteer Infantry; elected as a Democrat to the Sixty-fourth and to the ten succeeding Congresses (March 4, 1915–January 3, 1937); unsuccessful candidate for renomination in 1936; retired from active business and political life; died in Birmingham, Ala., February 29, 1960; interment in Elmwood Cemetery.

HUDDLESTON, George, Jr. (son of the preceding), a Representative from Alabama; born in Birmingham, Jefferson County, Ala., March 19, 1920; attended the public schools and graduated from Eastern High School, Washington, D. C.; attended George Washington University, Washington, D. C., for one year; was graduated from Birmingham (Ala.) Southern College in 1941, majoring in economics and political science; coeditor of an index to the official proceedings of the Alabama Constitutional Convention of 1901; during World War II served as a lieutenant commander in the United States Navy 1942–1946, with thirty-two months overseas in the Pacific Theater; awarded eight battle stars; commander in the Naval Reserve; graduated from the University of Alabama Law School in 1948; was admitted to the bar in 1948; deputy circuit solicitor for the tenth judicial circuit of Alabama in 1948 and 1949; assistant United States attorney for the northern district of Alabama 1949–1952; engaged in the practice of law in Birmingham, Ala., 1952–1954; elected as a Democrat to the Eighty-fourth, Eighty-fifth, and Eighty-sixth Congresses (January 3, 1955–January 3, 1961). *Reelected to the Eighty-seventh Congress.*

HUDSON, Charles, a Representative from Massachusetts; born in Marlboro, Middlesex County, Mass., November 14, 1795; attended the common schools and later an academy; taught school; served in the War of 1812; studied theology; was ordained as a Universalist minister in 1819 and located in Westminster in 1824; author of religous textbooks and sacred memoirs; member of the State house of representatives 1828–1833; served in the State senate 1833–1839; member of the Massachusetts State Board of Education 1837–1845; executive councilor 1839–1841; elected as a Whig to the Twenty-seventh Congress to fill the vacancy caused by the resignation of Levi Lincoln; reelected to the Twenty-eighth, Twenty-ninth, and Thirtieth Congresses and served from May 3, 1841, to March 3, 1849; unsuccessful for reelection in 1848 to the Thirty-first Congress; moved to Lexington, Mass., in 1849; naval officer of the port of Boston 1849–1853; edited the Boston Daily Atlas; assessor of internal revenue 1864–1868; selectman of Lexington, Mass., 1868–1875; died in Lexington, Mass., May 4, 1881; interment in Munroe Cemetery.

HUDSON, Grant Martin, a Representative from Michigan; born in Eaton Township, Lorain County, Ohio, July 23, 1868; attended the common schools; was graduated from Kalamazoo (Mich.) College and also attended the University of Chicago; minister of the gospel at Dowagiac, Mich., 1894–1896; became engaged in mercantile pursuits in Schoolcraft, Mich., in 1896; member of the State house of representatives 1905–1909; president of the village of Schoolcraft, Mich., 1909–1911; member of the State industrial accident compensation commission in 1920 and 1921; elected as a Republican to the Sixty-eighth and to the three succeeding Congresses (March 4, 1923–March 3, 1931); unsuccessful candidate for renomination in 1930; engaged in the insurance business in Lansing, Mich.; State purchasing agent in 1939; State tax commissioner in 1940; died in Kalamazoo, Mich., October 26, 1955; interment in Mount Hope Cemetery, Lansing, Mich.

HUDSON, Thomas Jefferson, a Representative from Kansas; born near Jamestown, Boone County, Ind., October 30, 1839; attended a neighborhood private school, Lebanon (Ind.) Academy, and Wabash College, Crawfordsville, Ind.; moved to Nodaway, Mo., in 1854; moved to Coysville, Wilson County, Kans., in 1866 and taught in the first county school; studied law; was admitted to the bar in Iola, Kans., in June 1869; moved to Fredonia Kans., in 1869 and commenced practice; aided in the adoption of the fifteenth amendment; treasurer and member of the first Fredonia school board in the early seventies; member of the State house of representatives in 1870; mayor of Fredonia in 1871; organized the Wilson County Bank in Fredonia in 1871; was graduated from the law department of the University of Cincinnati, Ohio, in 1874; prosecuting attorney for Wilson County 1884–1886; delegate to the Democratic National Conventions in 1884, 1888, 1896; elected as a Populist to the Fifty-third Congress (March 4, 1893–March 3, 1895); was not a candidate for renomination in 1894; resumed the practice of law in Fredonia; regent of the State college of agriculture in 1897 and 1898; died in Wichita, Kans., on January 4, 1923; interment in Fredonia Cemetery, Fredonia, Kans.

HUDSPETH, Claude Benton, a Representative from Texas; born in Medina, Bandera County, Tex., May 12, 1877; attended the country schools; learned the printing trade; moved to Ozona, Tex., in 1893 and published the Ozona Kicker for a few years; employed as a cowboy; engaged in the cattle trading business and later in ranching, owning ranches in Brewster, Val Verde, Crockett, and Terrell Counties, Tex.; member of the State house of representatives 1902–1906; served in the State senate 1906–1918 and was elected president of that body four times; studied law; was admitted to the bar in 1909 and commenced practice in El Paso, Tex.; director of the Texan Oil & Land Co.; elected as a Democrat to the Sixty-sixth and to the five succeeding Congresses (March 4, 1919–March 3, 1931); was not a candidate for renomination in 1930; retired from active political and business pursuits in 1930 and resided in San Antonio, Tex., until his death there on March 19, 1941; interment in Mission Burial Park.

HUFF, George Franklin, a Representative from Pennsylvania; born in Norristown, Montgomery County, Pa., July 16, 1842; attended the public schools in Middletown and later in Altoona; at the age of eighteen entered the Pennsylvania Railroad car shops in Altoona, where he learned the trade of car finisher; moved to Westmoreland County in 1867 and engaged in banking in Greensburg, Pa., later becoming largely identified with the industrial and mining interests of western Pennsylvania; delegate to the Republican National Convention at Chicago in 1880; president of the Keystone Coal & Coke Co.; member of the State senate 1884–1888; elected as a Republican to the Fifty-second Congress (March 4, 1891–March 3,

1893); elected to the Fifty-fourth Congress (March 4, 1895–March 3, 1897); was not a candidate for renomination in 1896; again elected to the Fifty-eighth and to the three succeeding Congresses (March 4, 1903–March 3, 1911); was not a candidate for renomination in 1910; died in Washington, D. C., on April 18, 1912; interment in St. Clair Cemetery, Greensburg, Pa.

HUFFMAN, James Wylie, a Senator from Ohio; born in Chandlersville, Muskingum County, Ohio, September 13, 1894; attended the public schools of Rich Hill Township, Muskingum County, and of Ashland County, Ohio, and also Ohio Wesleyan University, Ohio State University, and the University of Chicago, graduating in 1922; admitted to the bar in Ohio and Illinois in 1922 and commenced practice in Chicago, Ill.; taught high school for three years; during the First World War served as a machine gun officer, Three Hundred and Twenty-ninth Infantry, Eighty-third Division, and with the One Hundred and Twentieth Machine Gun Battalion, Thirty-second Division, participating in four major offensives and spending six months beyond the Rhine with the Army of Occupation; assistant attorney general of Illinois in 1923; returned to Ohio in 1924 and was executive secretary to the Governor of Ohio 1924–1926; member of the Public Utilities Commission of Ohio 1927–1929; engaged in the practice of law at Columbus, Ohio, since 1929; served as director of commerce of Ohio from January 8, 1945, to October 8, 1945; appointed as a Democrat to the United States Senate to fill the vacancy caused by the resignation of Harold H. Burton and served from October 8, 1945, to November 5, 1946, when a successor was elected; was not a candidate for nomination to fill the the vacancy in 1946, but was an unsuccessful candidate for election to the full term; vice president and director, Logan Clay Products Co., Logan, Ohio, since 1950; director and later president, Motorists Mutual Insurance Co. of Columbus, Ohio, since 1946; member of board of trustees, Ohio State University, 1951–1957; is a resident of Columbus, Ohio.

HUFTY, Jacob, a Representative from New Jersey; born in New Jersey; was a blacksmith by trade; served as a private in the State militia; freeholder for Salem Township in 1792; elected overseer of the poor and collector of Salem Township in 1793; county justice of Salem County, N. J., in 1797, county judge in 1798, and county justice and judge in 1804; served as sheriff 1801–1804; freeholder of Salem Township 1800–1804; a director of the board of chosen freeholders in 1801; member of the State council in 1804, 1806, and 1807; county collector 1805–1808; judge of Orphans Court 1805–1808; surrogate in 1808; elected as a Democrat to the Eleventh, Twelfth, and Thirteenth Congresses and served from March 4, 1808, until his death in Salem, N. J., May 20, 1814; interment in St. John's Episcopal Churchyard.

HUGER, Benjamin, a Representative from South Carolina; born at or near Charleston, S. C., in 1768; pursued an academic course; engaged in the cultivation of rice on the Waccamaw River; member of the State house of representatives in 1798 and 1799; elected to the Sixth, Seventh, and Eighth Congresses (March 4, 1799–March 3, 1805); again a member of the State house of representatives 1808–1812; elected to the Fourteenth Congress (March 4, 1815–March 3, 1817); member of the State senate 1818–1823 and served as president 1819–1822; died on his estate on Waccamaw River, near Georgetown, S. C., July 7, 1823; interment in All Saints' Churchyard.

HUGER, Daniel (father of Daniel Elliott Huger), a Delegate and a Representative from South Carolina; born on Limerick plantation in St. John's parish, Berkeley County, S. C., February 20, 1742; educated at home and in the schools of Charleston, S. C.; also studied in England; justice of the peace in 1775; prominent in the Revolutionary War; member of the State house of representatives in 1778 and 1779; member of the Governor's council in 1780; present in Charleston during the siege; left the town with Governor Rutledge to continue the defense of the State; narrowly escaped capture by General Tarleton; later surrendered and was paroled; Member of the Continental Congress 1786–1788; elected to the First and Second Congresses (March 4, 1789–March 3, 1793); on retiring from Congress resided in Charleston and on his Wateree plantation; engaged in the management of his extensive estates; died in Charleston, S. C., July 6, 1799; interment in the western churchyard of St. Philip's Church, Charleston, S. C., with a memorial tablet in the Huguenot church there.

HUGER, Daniel Elliott (son of Daniel Huger), a Senator from South Carolina; born on Limerick plantation, near Charleston, S. C., June 28, 1779; pursued classical studies in Charleston; was graduated from Princeton College in 1798; studied law; was admitted to the bar in 1799 and began practice in Charleston, S. C.; secretary to the Governor in 1808; member of the State house of representatives 1804–1819; brigadier general of State troops in 1814; judge of the circuit court 1819–1830; again served in the State house of representatives in 1830; member of the State nullification convention in 1832 and also of the State Rights Unionist Party Convention of the same year; elected as a State Rights Democrat to the United States Senate to fill the vacancy caused by the resignation of John C. Calhoun and served from March 4, 1843, to March 3, 1845, when he resigned; delegate to the Nashville convention in 1852 to discuss the question of secession; died on Sullivans Island, S. C., August 21, 1854; interment in Magnolia Cemetery, Charleston, S. C.

HUGHES, Charles, a Representative from New York; born in New Orleans, La., February 27, 1822; completed preparatory studies; studied law; was admitted to the bar in 1846 and commenced practice in Sandy Hill, N. Y.; elected as a Democrat to the Thirty-third Congress (March 4, 1853–March 3, 1855); clerk of the court of appeals 1860–1862; provost marshal for the sixteenth district of New York in 1862; member of the Governor's staff and judge advocate general of State militia 1875–1879; member of the State senate in 1878 and 1879; resumed the practice of his profession; died in Sandy Hill, N. Y., August 10, 1887; interment in Union Cemetery, between Fort Edward and Sandy Hill (now Hudson Falls).

HUGHES, Charles James, Jr., a Senator from Colorado; born in Kingston, Caldwell County, Mo., February 16, 1853; attended the common schools; was graduated from Richmond (Mo.) College in 1871 and from the law department of the University of Missouri at Columbia in 1873; was admitted to the bar in 1877 and commenced practice at Richmond, Mo.; moved to Denver in 1879; presidential elector on the Democratic ticket of Bryan and Stevenson in 1900; delegate to the Democratic National Convention at St. Louis in 1904 which nominated Parker and Davis and at Denver in 1908 which nominated Bryan and Kern; for many years professor of mining law in the law school of the University of Denver, Colorado, and Harvard University, Cambridge, Mass.; elected as a Democrat to the United States Senate and served from March 4, 1909, until his death in Denver, Colo., January 11, 1911; interment in Fairmont Cemetery.

HUGHES, Dudley Mays, a Representative from Georgia; born in Jeffersonville, Twiggs County, Ga., October 10, 1848; attended the country schools; was graduated from the University of Georgia at Athens in 1870; engaged in agricultural pursuits in 1871; member of the State senate in 1882 and 1883; president of the Georgia State Agricultural Society 1904–1906; commissioner general of Georgia at the World's Fair, St. Louis, Mo., in 1904; trustee of the Danville School, the State Normal Institute, the University of Georgia, and the Georgia State Agricultural College; president of the Georgia Fruit Growers' Association; one of the original projectors and builders of the Macon, Dublin & Savannah Railroad and served as president and director; elected as a Democrat to the Sixty-first and to the three succeeding Congresses (March 4, 1909–March 3, 1917); unsuccessful candidate for renomination in 1916; engaged in agricultural pursuits in Danville, Ga.; died in Macon, Bibb County, Ga., January 20, 1927; interment in Evergreen Cemetery, Perry, Houston County, Ga.

HUGHES, George Wurtz, a Representative from Maryland; born in Elmira, N. Y., September 30, 1806; received a liberal schooling; was graduated from the United States Military Academy at West Point in 1827; became a civil engineer in New York City; reappointed to the Army July 7, 1838, as captain of topographical engineers; served in the Mexican War; lieutenant colonel of Maryland and District of Columbia Volunteers August 4, 1847; colonel October 1, 1847; honorably mustered out of the volunteer service July 24, 1848; brevetted major April 18, 1847, "for gallant and meritorious conduct" in the Battle of Cerro Gordo, Mexico; commissioned lieutenant colonel on May 30, 1848, "for meritorious conduct" while serving in the enemy's country; resigned August 4, 1851; became president of the Northern Central Railroad; elected as a Democrat to the Thirty-sixth Congress (March 4, 1859–March 3, 1861); consulting engineer and planter thereafter at West River, Md., until his death there on September 3, 1870; interment in the family burying ground of the Galloway family, "Tulip Hill," West River, Md.

HUGHES, James, a Representative from Indiana; born in Baltimore County, Md., November 24, 1823; attended the common schools and Indiana University at Bloomington; studied law; was admitted to the bar in 1842 and commenced practice in Indiana; served in the Mexican War; served as judge of the sixth judicial circuit of Indiana from 1852 until 1856, when he resigned; professor of law in Indiana University 1853–1856; elected as a Democrat to the Thirty-fifth Congress (March 4, 1857–March 3, 1859); unsuccessful candidate for reelection in 1858 to the Thirty-sixth Congress; appointed judge of the Court of Claims and served from January 18, 1860, to December 1864, when he resigned; member of the State house of representatives 1864–1866; cotton agent of the Treasury Department 1866–1868; died in Wattsville, Md., on October 24, 1873; interment in Rose Hill Cemetery, Bloomington, Ind.

HUGHES, James Anthony, a Representative from West Virginia; born near Corunna, Ontario, Canada, February 27, 1861; attended the public schools; moved with his parents to Ashland, Ky., in July 1873; completed preparatory studies; was graduated from Duff's Business College at Pittsburgh, Pa., in 1875; employed as a bank messenger 1879–1881 and as a traveling salesman in 1881 and 1882; moved to Louisa, Ky., in 1883 and engaged in the dry goods business; member of the Kentucky House of Representatives 1888–1890; moved to Ceredo, W. Va., in 1891 and engaged in the timber business; moved to Huntington, W. Va., in 1892 and engaged in the real-estate business; served in the State senate 1894–1898; delegate to the Republican State conventions in 1896 and 1898; delegate to all the Republican National Conventions from 1892 to 1924, inclusive;

served as postmaster of Huntington 1896–1900; elected as a Republican to the Fifty-seventh and to the six succeeding Congresses (March 4, 1901–March 3, 1915); was not a candidate for renomination in 1914; resumed the real-estate business in Huntington, W. Va.; elected to the Seventieth and Seventy-first Congresses and served from March 4, 1927, until his death in a sanitarium at Marion, Ohio, on March 2, 1930; interment in Spring Hill Cemetery, Huntington, W. Va.

HUGHES, James Frederic, a Representative from Wisconsin; born in Green Bay, Brown County, Wis., August 7, 1883; attended the public schools and was graduated from West Green Bay High School in 1901; moved to De Pere, Brown County, Wis., in 1901 and was employed as a salesman until 1905, when he became western sales manager for a foundry supply company; member of the De Pere Board of Education 1914–1937; delegate to the Democratic National Conventions in 1920 and 1928; member of the Democratic State central committee 1920–1924; served as chairman of the eighth Wisconsin Democratic congressional committee 1928–1932; elected as a Democrat to the Seventy-third Congress (March 4, 1933–January 3, 1935); was not a candidate for renomination in 1934; resumed his former pursuits as sales manager in De Pere, Wis.; died in a hospital at Rochester, Minn., August 9, 1940; interment in Cady Cemetery, Lawrence, near De Pere, Wis.

HUGHES, James Hurd, a Senator from Delaware; born on a farm near Felton, Kent County, Del., January 14, 1867; attended the public schools and Collegiate Institute in Dover, Del., and also received instruction from private tutors; taught school in Kent County, Del., 1885–1889; studied law; was admitted to the bar in 1890 and commenced practice at Dover, Del.; also engaged in agricultural pursuits and banking; secretary of state of Delaware 1897–1901; presidential elector on the ticket of Wilson and Marshall in 1912; unsuccessful candidate for Governor of Delaware in 1916; elected as a Democrat in 1936 to the United States Senate and served from January 3, 1937, to January 3, 1943; unsuccessful candidate for renomination in 1942; returned to Dover, Del., and continued the practice of law; director of the Farmers Bank, Dover, Del., from 1905 until his death; died in Lewes, Del., August 29, 1953; interment in Lakeside Cemetery, Dover, Del.

HUGHES, James Madison, a Representative from Missouri; born in Bourbon County, Ky., April 7, 1809; received a liberal schooling; studied law; was admitted to the bar and practiced in Liberty, Clay County, Mo.; also engaged in mercantile pursuits in Liberty; member of the State house of representatives in 1839; elected as a Democrat to the Twenty-eighth Congress (March 4, 1843–March 3, 1845); moved to St. Louis, Mo., in 1855 and engaged in the banking business; died in Jefferson City, Mo., on February 26, 1861; interment in Bellefontaine Cemetery, St. Louis, Mo.

HUGHES, Thomas Hurst, a Representative from New Jersey; born in Cold Spring, Cape May County, N. J., January 10, 1769; attended the public schools; moved to Cape May City in 1800 and engaged in the mercantile business; in 1816 he built Congress Hall, a hotel which he conducted for many summer seasons; sheriff of Cape May County 1801–1804; member of the State general assembly 1805–1807, 1809, 1812, and 1813; member of the State council 1819–1823 and in 1824 and 1825; elected as a Whig to the Twenty-first and Twenty-second Congresses (March 4, 1829–March 3, 1833); was not a candidate for renomination in 1832; resumed the hotel business; died in Cold Spring, N. J., November 10, 1839; interment in Cold Spring Cemetery.

HUGHES, William, a Representative and a Senator from New Jersey; born in Drogheda, Ireland, April 3, 1872; immigrated to the United States in 1880 with his parents, who settled in Paterson, N. J.; attended the common schools; as a youth was employed in the silk mills of his home city; studied stenography at Columbia Business College at Paterson and was employed as a stenographer in New York City and subsequently became a court reporter at Paterson; upon the beginning of the Spanish-American War enlisted as a private in Company A, Second Regiment, New Jersey Volunteer Infantry, and served throughout the war; studied law; was admitted to the bar in 1900 and commenced practice in Paterson, N. J.; elected as a Democrat to the Fifty-eighth Congress (March 4, 1903–March 3, 1905); unsuccessful candidate for reelection in 1904 to the Fifty-ninth Congress; elected to the Sixtieth, Sixty-first, and Sixty-second Congresses and served from March 4, 1907, until September 27, 1912, when he resigned, having been appointed to a position on the judicial bench; appointed judge of the court of common pleas of Passaic County by Gov. Woodrow Wilson on April 1, 1912, and served until March 12, 1913, when he resigned, having been elected Senator; elected as a Democrat to the United States Senate and served from March 4, 1913, until his death in Trenton, N. J., January 30, 1918; interment in Cedar Lawn Cemetery, Paterson, N. J.

HUGHSTON, Jonas Abbott, a Representative from New York; born in Sidney, Delaware County, N. Y., in 1808; completed preparatory studies; studied law; was admitted to the bar in 1839 and commenced practice at Delhi, N. Y.; district attorney of Delaware County 1842–1845; resumed the practice of law; elected as a Whig to the Thirty-fourth Congress (March 4, 1855–March 3, 1857); appointed by President Lincoln marshal of the consular court at Shanghai, China, on March 26, 1862, and served until his death in Shanghai, China, on November 10, 1862; interment in Poo-ting Cemetery.

HUGUNIN, Daniel, Jr., a Representative from New York; born in Montgomery County, N. Y., February 6, 1790; pursued classical studies; served in the War of 1812; successfully contested the election of Egbert Ten Eyck to the Nineteenth Congress and served from December 15, 1825, until March 3, 1827; appointed on March 15, 1841, United States marshal for the Territory of Wisconsin; died in Kenosha, Wis., June 21, 1850; interment in Green Ridge Cemetery.

HUKRIEDE, Theodore Waldemar, a Representative from Missouri; born near New Truxton, Warren County, Mo., on November 9, 1878; attended the public schools, Central Wesleyan College, Warrenton, Warren County, Mo., and the University of Missouri at Columbia; studied law; was admitted to the bar in 1903 and commenced practice in Warrenton, Mo., in 1903; elected prosecuting attorney of Warren County in 1904, 1906, and 1908; probate judge of Warren County 1910–1920; delegate to the Missouri State conventions in 1900, 1908, 1912, 1916, 1936, and 1940; delegate to the Republican National Conventions in 1916 and 1936; president of the Warrenton School Board 1916–1920; chairman of the Republican State committee 1916–1918; elected as a Republican to the Sixty-seventh Congress (March 4, 1921–March 3, 1923); unsuccessful for reelection in 1922 to the Sixty-eighth Congress; appointed United States Marshal for the eastern district of Missouri May 12, 1923, and served until March 1933; resumed the practice of law; served on the Warren County Draft Board during World War I and as appeal agent for Selective Service of Warren County in World War II; elected to the State General Assembly in 1942; reelected in 1944 and served until his death; died at Warrenton, Mo., April 14, 1945; interment in Warrenton Memorial Society Cemetery.

HULBERT, George Murray, a Representative from New York; born in Rochester, N. Y., May 14, 1881; moved to Waterloo, N. Y., where he attended the public schools; was graduated from the New York Law School; was admitted to the bar in 1902 and practiced law in New York City; elected as a Democrat to the Sixty-fourth and Sixty-fifth Congresses and served from March 4, 1915, to January 1, 1918, when he resigned to become commissioner of docks and director of the port of New York City; elected president of the Board of Aldermen of New York City in November 1921 and served as acting mayor during the long illness of Mayor Hylan; president of the Boston, Cape Cod & New York Canal Co.; resumed the practice of law until June 1934, when he was appointed by President Franklin D. Roosevelt as United States district judge of the southern district of New York, in which capacity he served until his death in Bayport, L. I., April 26, 1950; interment in Gate of Heaven Cemetery, Valhalla, N. Y.

HULBERT, John Whitefield, a Representative from Massachusetts; born in Alford, Mass., June 1, 1770; completed preparatory studies; was graduated from Harvard University in 1795; studied law; was admitted to the bar and commenced practice in Alford, Mass., in 1797; director of Berkshire Bank, Pittsfield, Mass.; elected as a Federalist to the Thirteenth Congress to fill the vacancy caused by the resignation of Daniel Dewey; reelected to the Fourteenth Congress and served from September 26, 1814, to March 3, 1817; was not a candidate for renomination in 1816; moved to Auburn, Cayuga County, N. Y., in 1817; member of the State house of representatives in 1825; resumed the practice of his profession; died in Auburn, N. Y., October 19, 1831; interment in North Street Cemetery.

HULBURD, Calvin Tilden, a Representative from New York; born in Stockholm, St. Lawrence County, N. Y., June 5, 1809; completed preparatory studies; was graduated from Middlebury College, Vermont; attended Yale College Law School; was admitted to the bar in 1833; member of the New York Assembly 1842–1844 and in 1862; elected as a Republican to the Thirty-eighth, Thirty-ninth, and Fortieth Congresses (March 4, 1863–March 3, 1869); superintendent of construction of the New York post office; died in Brasher Falls, N. Y., on October 25, 1897; interment in Fairview Cemetery.

HULICK, George Washington, a Representative from Ohio; born in Batavia, Clermont County, Ohio, June 29, 1833; attended the public schools; was graduated from Farmer's College, near Cincinnati; took charge of Pleasant Hill Academy and taught two years; studied law; was admitted to the bar in 1857 and commenced practice in Batavia; during the Civil War enlisted as a private in Company E, Twenty-second Regiment, Ohio Volunteer Infantry, April 14, 1861; appointed orderly sergeant and afterward elected captain of the company; discharged August 16, 1861; probate judge of Clermont County 1864–1867; served nine years on the board of education; delegate to the Republican National Convention at Chicago in 1868; presidential elector on the Republican ticket of Hayes and Wheeler in 1876; elected as a Republican to the Fifty-third and Fifty-fourth Congresses (March 4, 1893–March 3, 1897); unsuccessful candidate for renomination in 1896; resumed the practice of law in Batavia, Ohio; died in Batavia, Ohio, August 13, 1907; interment in Union Cemetery.

HULING, James Hall, a Representative from West Virginia; born in Williamsport, Lycoming County, Pa., March 24, 1844; attended the public schools and Dickinson Seminary in Williamsport, Pa.; served in the Pennsylvania Cavalry in 1863; engaged in the lumber business; moved to West Virginia in 1870, where he continued in the lumber business until 1874; mayor of Charleston, W. Va., 1884–1888; declined a renomination; elected as a Republican to the Fifty-fourth Congress (March 4, 1895–March 3, 1897); resumed business in Charleston, W. Va., where he died April 23, 1918; interment in Pleasant View Cemetery.

HULINGS, Willis James, a Representative from Pennsylvania; born in Rimersburg, Clarion County, Pa., July 1, 1850; attended the public schools and Kittanning Academy; studied law; was admitted to practice in Pennsylvania, West Virginia, and Arizona; became a civil engineer and engaged in mining and the petroleum business; elected as a Republican to the State house of representatives and served from 1881 to 1887; member of the National Guard of Pennsylvania 1876–1912, serving in the various grades from private to brigadier general; served in the war with Spain and was mentioned for meritorious conduct in action at the Battle of Coamo August 9, 1898; member of the State senate 1906–1910; elected as a Progressive to the Sixty-third Congress (March 4, 1913–March 3, 1915); unsuccessful candidate for reelection in 1914 to the Sixty-fourth Congress; elected as a Republican to the Sixty-sixth Congress (March 4, 1919–March 3, 1921); unsuccessful candidate for reelection in 1920 to the Sixty-seventh Congress; died in Oil City, Pa., August 8, 1924; interment in Grove Hill Cemetery.

HULL, Cordell, a Representative and a Senator from Tennessee; born in Olympus, Overton (now Pickett) County, Tenn., October 2, 1871; attended the common schools, and was graduated from the law department of Cumberland University, Lebanon, Tenn., in 1891; was admitted to the bar the same year and commenced practice in Celina, Tenn.; delegate to the Democratic State convention in 1890; member of the State house of representatives 1893–1897; during the Spanish-American War served in the Fourth Regiment, Tennessee Volunteer Infantry, with the rank of captain; judge of the fifth judicial circuit of Tennessee 1903–1906; elected as a Democrat to the Sixtieth and to the six succeeding Congresses (March 4, 1907–March 3, 1921); unsuccessful candidate for reelection in 1920 to the Sixty-seventh Congress; chairman of the Democratic National Executive Committee 1921–1924; again elected to the Sixty-eighth and to the three succeeding Congresses (March 4, 1923–March 3, 1931); was not a candidate for renomination in 1930, having become a candidate for Senator; elected to the United States Senate in 1930 and served from March 4, 1931, to March 3, 1933, when he resigned to become Secretary of State; appointed Secretary of State in the cabinet of President Franklin D. Roosevelt March 4, 1933, serving until his resignation December 1, 1944; awarded the Nobel Peace Prize in 1945; retired and resided in Washington, D. C., until his death in the naval hospital at Bethesda, Md., July 23, 1955; interment in the Central Burial Vault of the Chapel of St. Joseph of Arimathea in the Washington Cathedral, Washington, D. C.

HULL, Harry Edward, a Representative from Iowa; born near Belvidere, Allegany County, N. Y., on March 12, 1864; moved with his parents to Cedar Rapids, Iowa, in 1873; attended the grammar and high schools; employed as a clerk and bookkeeper for a grain company; moved to Palo, Iowa, in 1883, and to Williamsburg, Iowa, in 1884 and engaged in the grain business; also engaged in the manufacture of brick and tile; president of the Williamsburg Telephone Co.; alderman of Williamsburg 1887–1889; mayor 1889–1901; postmaster 1901–1914; president of the Williamsburg Fair Association 1900–1915; elected as a Republican to the Sixty-fourth and to the four succeeding Congresses (March 4, 1915–March 3, 1925); unsuccessful candidate for renomination in 1924; appointed by President Coolidge on May 15, 1925, as Commissioner General of Immigration and served until 1933 when he retired from active pursuits; continued to reside in Washington, D. C., until his death there January 16, 1938; interment in Oak Hill Cemetery, Williamsburg, Iowa.

HULL, John Albert Tiffin, a Representative from Iowa; born in Sabina, Clinton County, Ohio, May 1, 1841; moved with his parents to Iowa in 1849; attended the public schools, Indiana Asbury (now De Pauw) University, Greencastle, Ind., and Iowa Wesleyan College at Mount Pleasant; was graduated from the Cincinnati (Ohio) Law School in the spring of 1862; was admitted to the bar the same year and commenced practice in Des Moines, Iowa; during the Civil War enlisted in the Twenty-third Regiment, Iowa Volunteer Infantry, in July 1862; first lieutenant and captain; wounded in the charge on intrenchments at Black River May 17, 1863; resigned on account of wounds in October 1863; secretary of the Iowa Senate in 1872 and reelected in 1874, 1876, and 1878; secretary of state in 1878 and reelected in 1880 and 1882; Lieutenant Governor in 1885 and reelected in 1887; engaged in agricultural pursuits and banking; elected as a Republican to the Fifty-second and to the nine succeeding Congresses (March 4, 1891–March 3, 1911); unsuccessful candidate for renomination; resumed the practice of law in Washington, D. C.; retired in 1916, and died in Clarendon, Arlington County, Va., September 26, 1928; interment in Arlington National Cemetery, Fort Myer, Va.

HULL, Merlin, a Representative from Wisconsin; born in Warsaw, Kosciusko County, Ind., December 18, 1870; attended Gale College, Galesville, Wis., De Pauw University, Greencastle, Ind., and Columbian (now George Washington) University, Washington, D. C.; studied law; was admitted to the bar in 1894 and commenced practice in Black River Falls, Wis.; publisher of the Jackson County Journal 1904–1926 and of the Banner-Journal 1926–1953; also engaged in agricultural pursuits; district attorney of Jackson County 1907–1909; member of the Wisconsin Assembly 1909–1915, serving as speaker in 1913; secretary of state of Wisconsin 1917–1921; elected as a Republican to the Seventy-first Congress (March 4, 1929–March 3, 1931); unsuccessful candidate for renomination in 1930 and unsuccessful Independent candidate for reelection to the Seventy-second Congress; resumed former business pursuits; elected as a Progressive to the Seventy-fourth and to the five succeeding Congresses, and as a Republican to the Eightieth and to the three succeeding Congresses and served from January 3, 1935, until his death in La Crosse, Wis., May 17, 1953; interment in Oak Grove Cemetery.

HULL, Morton Denison, a Representative from Illinois; born in Chicago, Ill., January 13, 1867; attended the public schools and Phillips Exeter Academy, Exeter, N. H., in 1885; was graduated from Harvard University in 1892; was admitted to the bar in 1892 and commenced the practice of law in Chicago, Ill.; also financially interested in various manufacturing concerns; member of the State house of representatives 1906–1914; member of the State senate 1915–1922; unsuccessful candidate for nomination for Governor in 1916; delegate to the Republican National Convention at Chicago in 1916 which nominated Hughes and Fairbanks; served as trustee of the Meadville (Pa.) Theological Seminary; delegate to the State constitutional convention in 1920; elected as a Republican to the Sixty-eighth Congress to fill the vacancy caused by the death of James R. Mann; reelected to the Sixty-ninth and to the three succeeding Congresses and served from April 3, 1923, to March 3, 1933; was not a candidate for renomination in 1932; resumed his former pursuits; died at his summer home in Bennington, Vt., August 20, 1937; remains were cremated in Troy, N. Y., and the ashes placed in a crypt in the First Unitarian Church, Chicago, Ill.

HULL, Noble Andrew, a Representative from Florida; born in Little York, Camden County, Ga., March 11, 1827; attended the county schools and Chatham Academy, Savannah, Ga.; engaged in mercantile pursuits in Savannah in 1845; moved to Florida in 1851 and engaged in business in Columbia County; when Suwanee County was formed was elected sheriff; member of the Florida House of Representatives in 1860 and 1861; during the Civil War served as captain of Company H, First Florida Cavalry, in the Confederate Army; engaged in mercantile pursuits in Jacksonville and Sanford, Seminole County; Lieutenant Governor of Florida 1877–1879; resigned to take his seat in Congress; presented credentials as a Democratic Member-elect to the Forty-sixth Congress and served from March 4, 1879, to January 22, 1881, when he was succeeded by Horatio Bisbee, Jr., who contested his election; resumed business activities in Jacksonville; assistant postmaster of Jacksonville 1884–1888; clerk of Duval County circuit court 1888–1900; declined to be a candidate for reelection; died in Jacksonville, Fla., January 28, 1907; interment in Evergreen Cemetery.

HULL, William Edgar, a Representative from Illinois; born in Lewistown, Fulton County, Ill., January 13, 1866; attended the common schools, Lewistown High School, and Illinois College at Jacksonville, Ill.; president of the Manito Chemical Co.; postmaster of Peoria, Ill., 1898–1906; delegate to the Republican National Conventions at Chicago in 1916 which nominated Hughes and Fairbanks and in 1920 which nominated Harding and Coolidge; member of the board of directors of the Illinois Highway Improvement Association; elected as a Republican to the Sixty-eighth and to the four succeeding Congresses (March 4, 1923–March 3, 1933); unsuccessful candidate for renomination in 1932; resumed his former pursuits in Peoria, Ill.; died in a hospital in Toronto, Canada, May 30, 1942, while on a visit; interment in Oak Hill Cemetery, Lewistown, Ill.

HULL, William Raleigh, Jr., a Representative from Missouri; born in Weston, Platte County, Mo., April 17, 1906; attended the public schools and graduated from Weston High School; engaged in farming; coowner of Hull's Tobacco Warehouse, Weston, Mo.; director of First National Bank, Leavenworth, Kans.; mayor of Weston, Mo., in 1939 and 1940; elected as a Democrat to the Eighty-fourth, Eighty-fifth, and Eighty-sixth Congresses (January 3, 1955–January 3, 1961). *Reelected to the Eighty-seventh Congress.*

HUMPHREY, Augustin Reed, a Representative from Nebraska; born near Madison, Jefferson County, Ind., February 18, 1859; moved with his parents to Drakesville, Davis County, Iowa, in 1864; attended the public schools; was graduated from the State normal school at Bloomfield in 1881 and from the law department of the University of Iowa at Iowa City in 1882; was admitted to the bar in 1882 and commenced practice at Broken Bow, Custer County, Nebr., in 1885; homesteaded in Custer County in 1886; delegate to every Republican State convention 1887–1936; engaged in agricultural and stock-raising pursuits and in the practice of law at Broken Bow; commissioner of public lands and buildings of Nebraska 1891–1895; president of the board of education 1898–1914; judge of probate 1906–1910; mayor in 1916 and 1917; moved to his ranch on the South Loup River in 1920; elected as a Republican to the Sixty-seventh Congress to fill the vacancy caused by the death of Moses P. Kinkaid and served from November 7, 1922, to March 3, 1923; declined to be a candidate for renomination in 1922; resumed the practice of law in Broken Bow; presidential elector on the Republican ticket of Coolidge and Dawes in 1924; died in Fort Collins, Colo., while on a visit, December 10, 1937; interment in Broken Bow Cemetery, Broken Bow, Nebr.

HUMPHREY, Charles, a Representative from New York; born in Little Britain, Orange County, N. Y., February 14, 1792; moved to Newburgh, N. Y., at an early age and attended the Newburgh Academy; commenced the study of law; entered the United States Army at the beginning of the War of 1812 as first sergeant of Newburgh Company Number Five; commissioned captain in the Forty-first Regiment, United States Infantry, on August 15, 1813; resumed the study of law; was admitted to the bar in Newburgh, N. Y., January 11, 1816; moved to Ithaca, N. Y., in 1818 and engaged in the practice of law; elected as a Democrat to the Nineteenth Congress (March 4, 1825–March 3, 1827); president of the village of Ithaca in 1828 and 1829; elected surrogate of Tompkins County and served from March 4, 1831, to January 8, 1834; member of the State assembly 1834–1836 and in 1842; speaker of the assembly in 1835 and 1836; appointed clerk of the New York Supreme Court in 1843 and held that position with residence in Albany until the court was superseded by the court of appeals under the constitution of 1847; died in Albany, N. Y., April 17, 1850; interment in City Cemetery, Ithaca, Tompkins County, N. Y.

HUMPHREY, Herman Leon, a Representative from Wisconsin; born in Candor, Tioga County, N. Y., March 14, 1830; attended the common schools and also the Cortland Academy for one year; became a clerk in Ithaca, N. Y.; after several years in business he studied law; was admitted to the bar in July 1854 and in January 1855 moved to Hudson, Wis., where he commenced the practice of his chosen profession; appointed district attorney of St. Croix County; appointed county judge to fill a vacancy in the fall of 1860 and in the spring of 1861 was elected for the full term of four years, but resigned that office in February 1862; served in the State senate in 1862 and 1863; mayor of Hudson one year; elected in the spring of 1866 judge of the eighth judicial circuit of Wisconsin and reelected in 1872; elected as a Republican to the Forty-fifth, Forty-sixth, and Forty-seventh Congresses (March 4, 1877–March 3, 1883); unsuccessful candidate for renomination; resumed the practice of law in Hudson, St. Croix County, Wis.; member of the State assembly in 1887; died in Hudson, Wis., June 10, 1902; interment in Willow River Cemetery.

HUMPHREY, Hubert Horatio, Jr., a Senator from Minnesota; born in Wallace, Codington County, S. Dak., May 27, 1911; attended the public schools of Doland, S. Dak., where his family had moved; graduated from Denver (Colo.) College of Pharmacy, the University of Minnesota, and the University of Louisiana; pharmacist with Humphrey Drug Co., Huron, S. Dak., 1933–1937; assistant instructor of political science at the University of Louisiana in 1939 and 1940 and University of Minnesota in 1940 and 1941; State director of war production training and reemployment and State chief of Minnesota war service program in 1942; assistant director, War Manpower Commission, in 1943; professor in political science at Macalester College in 1943 and 1944; assigned as instructor, United States Army Air Corps, Three Hundred and Forty-seventh Training Detachment; radio news commentator in 1944 and 1945; mayor of Minneapolis 1945–1948; United States delegate to the United Nations General Assembly in 1956; elected as a Democrat to the United States Senate in 1948 and again in 1954, and served from January 3, 1949, to January 3, 1961. *Reelected in 1960 for the term ending January 3, 1967.*

HUMPHREY, James, a Representative from New York; born in Fairfield, Fairfield County, Conn., on October 9, 1811; pursued classical studies; was graduated from Amherst (Mass.) College in 1831; studied law; was admitted to the bar and practiced; moved to Louisville, Ky., in 1837 and one year later to Brooklyn, N. Y.; elected as a Republican to the Thirty-sixth Congress (March 4, 1859–March 3, 1861); unsuccessful candidate for reelection in 1860 to the Thirty-seventh Congress and for election in 1862 to the Thirty-eighth Congress; elected to the Thirty-ninth Congress and served from March 4, 1865, until his death in Brooklyn, N. Y., June 16, 1866; interment in Greenwood Cemetery.

HUMPHREY, James Morgan, a Representative from New York; born in Holland, Erie County, N. Y., September 21, 1819; attended the common schools; studied law; was admitted to the bar in 1847 and commenced practice in East Aurora, Erie County, N. Y.; district attorney for Erie County 1857–1859; member of the State senate in 1863 and 1864; elected as a Democrat to the Thirty-ninth and Fortieth Congresses (March 4, 1865–March 3, 1869); was not a candidate in 1869 for renomination; resumed the practice of law; appointed to the superior court of Buffalo, N. Y., in 1871 and served until January 1, 1873; practiced his profession in Buffalo from 1873 to 1894, when he retired; died in Buffalo, N. Y., February 9, 1899; interment in Forest Lawn Cemetery.

HUMPHREY, Reuben, a Representative from New York; born in West Simsbury, Hartford County, Conn., September 2, 1757; completed preparatory studies; enlisted in the Revolutionary War as a private; mustered out as captain; held several local offices; keeper of Newgate State Prison in Simsbury, Conn., for five years; located near Marcellus, Onondaga County, N. Y., in 1801; first county judge 1804–1807; elected to the Tenth Congress (March 4, 1807–March 3, 1809); was not a candidate for renomination in 1808; member of the State senate 1811–1815; engaged in agricultural pursuits; died near Marcellus, August 10, 1832; interment in the Old City Cemetery.

HUMPHREY, William Ewart, a Representative from Washington; born near Alamo, Montgomery County, Ind., March 31, 1862; attended the common schools; was graduated from Wabash College, Crawfordsville, Ind., in 1887; studied law; was admitted to the bar in 1887 and commenced practice in Crawfordsville; moved to Seattle, Wash., in 1893 and continued the practice of law; corporation counsel of the city of Seattle 1898–1902; elected as a Republican to the Fifty-eighth and to the six succeeding Congresses (March 4, 1903–March 3, 1917); did not seek renomination in 1916, having become a Senatorial aspirant; resumed the practice of law in Seattle; appointed February 25, 1925, by President Coolidge as a member of the Federal Trade Commission and served until September 1933; died in Washington, D. C., February 14, 1934; interment in Oak Hill Cemetery, Crawfordsville, Ind.

HUMPHREYS, Andrew, a Representative from Indiana; born near Knoxville, Tenn., March 30, 1821; moved with his parents to Owen County, Ind., in 1829; afterwards moved to Putnam County and located near Manhattan; attended the common schools; moved to Greene County in 1842; member of the State house of representatives 1849–1852 and from January 8 to March 9, 1857; appointed Indian agent for Utah by President Buchanan in 1857; delegate to the Democratic National Convention at Baltimore in 1872 and at St. Louis in 1888; served in the State senate 1874–1876, 1878–1882, and 1896–1900; elected as a Democrat to the Forty-fourth Congress to fill the vacancy caused by the resignation of James D. Williams and served from December 5, 1876, to March 3, 1877; resumed agricultural pursuits in Greene County, Ind.; attended almost every Democratic State convention during his political life; died in Linton, Ind., June 14, 1904; interment in Moss Cemetery.

HUMPHREYS, Benjamin Grubb (father of William Yerger Humphreys), a Representative from Mississippi; born in Claiborne County, Miss., August 17, 1865; attended the public schools at Lexington, Miss., and the University of Mississippi at Oxford; engaged in mercantile pursuits; studied law; was admitted to the bar in 1891 and commenced practice in Greenwood, Miss.; superintendent of education for Leflore County 1892–1896; district attorney for the fourth district of Mississippi 1895–1903; raised a company in April 1898 for service in the Spanish-American War and was its first lieutenant, serving under Maj. Gen. Fitzhugh Lee in Florida during the entire war; elected as a Democrat to the Fifty-eighth and to the ten succeeding Congresses and served from March 4, 1903, until his death; delegate to the Democratic National Convention at San Francisco in 1920; died in Greenville, Miss., October 16, 1923; interment in Greenville Cemetery.

HUMPHREYS, Charles, a Delegate from Pennsylvania; born in Haverford, Delaware County, Pa., September 19, 1714; completed preparatory studies; engaged in milling; member of the Provincial Congress 1764–1774; Member of the Continental Congress 1774–1776; voted against the Declaration of Independence as he was a Quaker and opposed to war; died in Haverford, Pa., March 11, 1786; interment in Old Haverford Meeting House Cemetery.

HUMPHREYS, Parry Wayne, a Representative from Tennessee; born in Staunton, Va., in 1778; with his family moved to Kentucky in 1789, and later settled in Tennessee; completed preparatory studies; studied law; was admitted to the bar in 1801 and commenced practice in Nashville, Tenn.; judge of the superior court of Tennessee 1807–1809; judge of the State judicial circuit 1809–1813; elected as a Democrat to the Thirteenth Congress (March 4, 1813–March 3, 1815); unsuccessful Whig candidate for election to the United States Senate in 1817; again judge of the State judicial circuit 1818–1836; moved to Hernando, De Soto County, Miss., and engaged in banking until his death there February 12, 1839; interment in the Methodist Cemetery.

HUMPHREYS, Robert, a Senator from Kentucky; born in Fulgham, Hickman County, Ky., August 20, 1893; educated in public schools and graduated from Marvin College, Clinton, Ky., in 1914; attended the University of Wisconsin; during the First World War served in the Eighty-fourth Division from July 1917 to June 1919 with overseas service and was discharged as a first sergeant; registered pharmacist in the retail drug business in Mayfield, Ky., and later at Frankfort, Ky.; member of Kentucky House of Representatives in 1920; member Kentucky Senate 1932–1936; president pro tempore of State senate in 1934 and clerk of three senate sessions 1936–1942; delegate to five Democratic National Conventions; Kentucky highway commissioner 1936–1940; served as a captain in the Medical Corps in World War II from January 1943 to November 1945, with overseas service under General Patton; appointed State highway commissioner in 1955 and served until his resignation to accept appointment as a Democrat to the United States Senate to fill the vacancy caused by the death of Alben W. Barkley and served from June 21, 1956, to November 6, 1956; was not a candidate for election to the vacancy; resumed retail drug business; is a resident of Frankfort, Ky.

HUMPHREYS, William Yerger (son of Benjamin Grubb Humphreys), a Representative from Mississippi; born in Greenville, Washington County, Miss., September 9, 1890; attended the public schools and Sewanee Grammar School, Sewanee,
Tenn.; studied law at George Washington University, Washington, D. C., 1911–1914, while in the employ of the United States House of Representatives as assistant superintendent of the House document room; was admitted to the bar on June 1, 1914, and commenced practice in Greenville, Miss.; served as first lieutenant in the Chemical Warfare Service of the United States Army during the First World War; elected as a Democrat to the Sixty-eighth Congress to fill the vacancy caused by the death of his father, Benjamin G. Humphreys, and served from November 27, 1923, to March 3, 1925; was not a candidate for renomination in 1924; resumed the practice of law in Greenville, Miss.; elected prosecuting attorney of Washington County in 1928 and served until his death in Greenville, Miss., on February 26, 1933; interment in Greenville Cemetery.

HUNGERFORD, John Newton, a Representative from New York; born in Vernon, Oneida County, N. Y., December 31, 1825; completed preparatory studies; was graduated from Hamilton College at Clinton, N. Y., in 1846; settled in Corning, N. Y., in 1848 and engaged in the banking business; delegate to the Republican National Convention at Philadelphia in 1872; elected as a Republican to the Forty-fifth Congress (March 4, 1877–March 3, 1879); resumed banking business; died in Corning, N. Y., April 2, 1883; interment in Glenwood Cemetery, Watkins Glen, N. Y.

HUNGERFORD, John Pratt, a Representative from Virginia; born in Leeds, Westmoreland County, Va., January 2, 1761; received an elementary education under private teachers; studied law; was admitted to the bar, and practiced; served in the Revolutionary War; member of the house of delegates 1797–1801; member of the State senate 1801–1809; presented credentials as a Democratic Member-elect to the Twelfth Congress and served from March 4 to November 29, 1811, when he was succeeded by John Taliaferro, who contested his election; elected to the Thirteenth and Fourteenth Congresses (March 4, 1813–March 3, 1817); served in the War of 1812 as brigadier general of militia; again a member of the State house of delegates 1823–1830; died at "Twiford," Westmoreland County, Va., December 21, 1833; interment in Hungerford Cemetery, Leedstown, Va.

HUNGERFORD, Orville, a Representative from New York; born in Farmington, Hartford County, Conn., October 29, 1790; attended the public schools; moved with his father to Watertown, N. Y., in 1804; clerked in a store at Burrville, N. Y., and subsequently engaged in mercantile pursuits at Watertown; cashier of the Jefferson County National Bank at Watertown 1820–1833; served as its president 1834–1845, and was a director at the time of his death; presidential elector in 1836 on the Democratic ticket of Van Buren and Johnson; elected as a Democrat to the Twenty-eighth and Twenty-ninth Congresses (March 4, 1843–March 3, 1847); unsuccessful candidate for reelection in 1846 to the Thirtieth Congress; unsuccessful Democratic candidate for State comptroller in 1847; elected president of the Watertown & Rome Railroad Co. in 1847, in which capacity he served until his death in Watertown, N. Y., April 6, 1851; interment in Brookside Cemetery.

HUNT, Carleton (nephew of Theodore Gaillard Hunt), a Representative from Louisiana; born in New Orleans, La., January 1, 1836; attended the University Grammar School at New Orleans; was graduated from Harvard University in 1856 and from the law department of the University of Louisiana (now Tulane University) at New Orleans in 1858; was admitted to the bar the same year and practiced in New Orleans, La.; member of the convention of the Constitutional Union Party which met in Baton Rouge, La., in 1860; appointed in April 1861 first lieutenant in the Louisiana Regiment of Artillery, Confederate Army, during the Civil War; administrator of the University of Louisiana in 1866; appointed professor of admiralty and international law in the University of Louisiana in 1869 and later professor of civil law; dean of the law school of the university for ten years; chairman of the committee formed for the purpose of organizing the American Bar Association in 1878; professor of civil law in the University of Louisiana in 1879; elected as a Democrat to the Forty-eighth Congress (March 4, 1883–March 3, 1885); resumed the practice of his profession in New Orleans, La.; city attorney 1888–1892; died in New Orleans, La., August 14, 1921; interment in St. Louis Cemetery No. 2.

HUNT, Hiram Paine, a Representative from New York; born in Pittstown, Rensselaer County, N. Y., May 23, 1796; attended the public schools, and was graduated from Union College, Schenectady, N. Y., in 1816; studied law at the Litchfield Law School; was admitted to the bar in May 1819 and commenced practice in Pittstown, N. Y.; served as town clerk of Pittstown in 1822; moved to Lansingburgh, N. Y., in 1825 and to Troy, N. Y., in 1831, where he continued the practice of law; elected as a Whig to the Twenty-fourth Congress (March 4, 1835–March 3, 1837); unsuccessful candidate for reelection in 1836 to the Twenty-fifth Congress; elected to the Twenty-sixth and Twenty-seventh Congresses (March 4, 1839–March 3, 1843); was not a candidate for renomination in 1842; resumed the practice of his profession in Troy, Rensselaer County, N. Y.; moved to New York City and continued the practice of law until his death on August 14, 1865.

HUNT, James Bennett, a Representative from Michigan; born in Demerara, British Guiana, South America, August 13, 1799; returned with his father to New York City in 1803; pursued an academic course; studied law; was admitted to the bar in 1824 and commenced practice in New York City; moved to Pontiac, Mich., in 1836; judge of the probate court in 1836; appointed commissioner of internal improvement by Governor Mason in March 1837 and had charge of the Michigan Central Railroad from Detroit to Ann Arbor; also supervised the construction of that portion of the Clinton & Kalamazoo Canal from Mount Clemens to Rochester; served as prosecuting attorney of Oakland County 1841–1843; elected as a Democrat to the Twenty-eighth and Twenty-ninth Congresses (March 4, 1843–March 3, 1847); appointed register of the land office at Sault Ste. Marie January 1848 and served until June 1849; returned to Pontiac and held the office of circuit court commissioner of Oakland County; moved to Washington, D. C., and died there on August 15, 1857; interment in Oak Hill Cemetery, Pontiac, Oakland County, Mich.

HUNT, John Thomas, a Representative from Missouri; born in St. Louis, Mo., February 2, 1860; attended the common schools; in his youth was a professional ball player and umpire; became a stonecutter and later a stone contractor; elected as a Democrat to the Fifty-eighth and Fifty-ninth Congresses (March 4, 1903–March 3, 1907); unsuccessful candidate for renomination in 1906 and for nomination in 1908; resumed the business of stone contractor; died in St. Louis, Mo., November 30, 1916; interment in Calvary Cemetery.

HUNT, Jonathan, a Representative from Vermont; born in Vernon, Windham County, Vt., August 12, 1787; was graduated from Dartmouth College, Hanover, N. H., in 1807; studied law; was admitted to the bar and commenced practice in Brattleboro, Vt., in 1812; first president of the Old Brattleboro Bank in 1821; member of the State house of representatives in 1811, 1816, 1817, and 1824; elected as a National-Republican to the Twentieth,

Twenty-first, and Twenty-second Congresses, and served from March 4, 1827, until his death in Washington, D. C., May 15, 1832; interment in Brattleboro, Vt.

HUNT, Lester Callaway, a Senator from Wyoming; born in Isabel, Edgar County, Ill., July 8, 1892; attended the public schools; student at Wesleyan University, Bloomington, Ill., in 1912 and 1913; was graduated from the St. Louis University College of Dentistry in 1917; moved to Wyoming in 1917 and commenced the practice of dentistry in Lander; during the First World War served as a lieutenant, captain, and major in the United States Army Dental Corps 1917–1919; after postgraduate study at Northwestern University in 1920 resumed the practice of dentistry in Lander, Wyo; president of the Wyoming State Board of Dental Examiners 1924–1928; served in the State house of representatives in 1933 and 1934; secretary of state of Wyoming 1935–1943; Governor of Wyoming 1943–1949; chairman of the Governors' Conference held in Portsmouth, N. H., in June 1948; elected as a Democrat to the United States Senate in 1948 for the term commencing January 3, 1949, and served until his death in Washington, D. C., June 19, 1954; interment in Beth El Cemetery, Cheyenne, Wyo.

HUNT, Samuel, a Representative from New Hampshire; born in Charlestown, Sullivan County, N. H., July 8, 1765; completed preparatory studies; studied law; was admitted to the bar in 1790 and commenced practice in Alstead, N. H.; moved to Keene, N. H., the same year and in 1795 abandoned the practice of law; moved to Charlestown, N. H., and engaged in agricultural pursuits; member of the State house of representatives in 1802 and 1803; elected to the Seventh Congress to fill the vacancy caused by the resignation of Joseph Peirce; reelected to the Eighth Congress and served from December 6, 1802, to March 3, 1805; unsuccessful candidate for renomination in 1804; founded a colony in Ohio; died in Gallipolis, Ohio, July 7, 1807; interment in Mound Cemetery, Marietta, Ohio.

HUNT, Theodore Gaillard (nephew of John Gaillard and uncle of Carleton Hunt), a Representative from Louisiana; born in Charleston, S. C., October 23, 1805; completed preparatory studies; was graduated from the law department of Columbia College, New York City; was admitted to the bar and commenced practice in Charleston, S. C.; moved to New Orleans, La., about 1830; district attorney for New Orleans; member of the State house of representatives from 1837 until his election to Congress; elected as a Whig to the Thirty-third Congress (March 4, 1853–March 3, 1855); judge of the first Louisiana district (then the criminal court of New Orleans) in 1859; colonel of the Fifth Louisiana Regiment, Confederate Army, in 1861 and 1862; appointed by Governor Allen adjutant general of Louisiana with the rank of brigadier general and remained in active service until the close of the Civil War; died in New Orleans, La., November 15, 1893; interment in Metairie Cemetery.

HUNT, Washington, a Representative from New York; born in Windham, Greene County, N. Y., August 5, 1811; moved with his parents to Portage, Livingston County, N. Y., in 1818; completed preparatory studies; studied law; was admitted to the bar in 1834 and commenced practice in Lockport, N. Y.; unsuccessful candidate for election in 1836 to the Twenty-fifth Congress; appointed judge of the court of common pleas of Niagara County and served from January 30, 1836, to February 4, 1841; elected as a Whig to the Twenty-eighth, Twenty-ninth, and Thirtieth Congresses (March 4, 1843–March 3, 1849); was not a candidate for renomination in 1848; comptroller of New York in 1849 and 1850; Governor of the State 1850–1852; unsuccessful candidate for reelection; retired to his farm near Lockport; temporary chairman of the last Whig National Convention at Baltimore in 1856 which adopted the nominees of the American Party, Fillmore and Donelson; was tendered the Democratic nomination for Vice President in 1860 but declined; delegate to the Democratic National Convention at Chicago in 1864, which nominated McClellan and Pendleton; died in New York City February 2, 1867; interment in Glenwood Cemetery, Lockport, N. Y.

HUNTER, Allan Oakley, a Representative from California; born in Los Angeles, Calif., June 15, 1916; attended the public schools of Fresno, Calif.; was graduated from Fresno State College in 1937 and from the law school of the University of California in 1940; was admitted to the bar in 1940; special agent for the Federal Bureau of Investigation 1940–1944; during World War II served in the United States Naval Reserve, assigned to the Office of Strategic Services in France and Germany with a special counter-intelligence unit attached to the Sixth Army Group 1944–1946; commenced the practice of law in Fresno, Calif., in 1946; elected as a Republican to the Eighty-second and Eighty-third Congresses (January 3, 1951–January 3, 1955); unsuccessful candidate for reelection in 1954 to the Eighty-fourth Congress; general counsel with Housing and Home Finance Agency, Washington, D. C., from January 1955 to July 1957, when he resigned to return to the practice of law; delegate to the Republican National Conventions in 1952 and 1960; is a resident of Fresno, Calif.

HUNTER, Andrew Jackson, a Representative from Illinois; born in Greencastle, Putnam County, Ind., December 17, 1831; moved with his parents to Paris, Edgar County, Ill., in 1832; attended the common schools and Edgar Academy; engaged as a civil engineer 1852–1856; studied law; was admitted to the bar in 1856 and commenced practice in Paris; member of the State senate 1864–1868; member of the board of investigation of State institutions; unsuccessful candidate in 1870 to the Forty-second Congress and again, in 1882, to the Forty-eighth Congress; judge of the Edgar County court 1886–1892; elected as a Democrat to the Fifty-third Congress (March 4, 1893–March 3, 1895); unsuccessful candidate for reelection in 1894 to the Fifty-third Congress; elected to the Fifty-fifth Congress (March 4, 1897–March 3, 1899); unsuccessful candidate for reelection in 1898 to the Fifty-sixth Congress; delegate to the Democratic National Convention at Denver in 1908; retired from public life; died in Paris, Ill., January 12, 1913; interment in Edgar Cemetery.

HUNTER, John, a Representative and a Senator from South Carolina; born in that State in 1732; completed preparatory studies; engaged in agricultural pursuits near Newberry, S. C.; member of the State house of representatives 1786–1792; presidential elector in 1792 on the Federalist ticket of Washington and Adams; elected as a Federalist to the Third Congress (March 4, 1793–March 3, 1795); elected to the United States Senate to fill the vacancy caused by the resignation of Pierce Butler and served from December 8, 1796, to November 26, 1798, when he resigned; resumed agricultural pursuits on his plantation; died in 1802; interment in the family plot in the Presbyterian Church Cemetery, at Little River, S. C.

HUNTER, John Feeney, a Representative from Ohio; born in Ford City, Armstrong County, Pa., October 19, 1896; moved with his parents in 1907 to Toledo, Ohio, where he attended the public schools; was graduated from the law department of St. John's University, Toledo, Ohio, in 1918; was admitted to the bar the same year and commenced practice in Toledo; during the First World War enlisted in the United States Army on March 6, 1918, and served as a private first class in the Replacement Troops, Infantry, Central Officers' Training School, at

Camp Grant, Ill., until honorably discharged on November 26, 1918; delegate to the Democratic State conventions in 1932, 1934, 1936, and 1938; alternate to the Democratic National Conventions in 1932 and 1936; member of the State house of representatives in 1933 and 1934; served in the State senate in 1935 and 1936; elected as a Democrat to the Seventy-fifth, Seventy-sixth, and Seventy-seventh Congresses (January 3, 1937–January 3, 1943); unsuccessful candidate for reelection in 1942 to the Seventy-eighth Congress and for election in 1944 to the Seventy-ninth Congress; resumed the practice of law in Toledo, Ohio, and Washington, D. C.; in 1953 was appointed a representative on the Virginia National Capital Park Authority; president of Hunter Motors in Alexandria, Va., at the time of his death; died in Alexandria, Va., December 19, 1957; interment in Calvary Cemetery, Toledo, Ohio.

HUNTER, John Ward, a Representative from New York; born in Bedford (now a part of Brooklyn), N. Y., October 15, 1807; received a liberal schooling; clerk in a wholesale grocery store in New York City in 1824; clerk in the United States customhouse at New York City 1831–1836; assistant auditor of the customhouse 1836–1865; engaged in banking as treasurer of the Dime Savings Bank in Brooklyn; elected to the Thirty-ninth Congress to fill the vacancy caused by the death of James Humphrey and served from December 4, 1866, to March 3, 1867; was not a candidate for renomination in 1866; mayor of Brooklyn in 1875 and 1876; resumed banking; died in Brooklyn, N. Y., April 16, 1900; interment in Greenwood Cemetery.

HUNTER, Morton Craig, a Representative from Indiana; born in Versailles, Ripley County, Ind., on February 5, 1825; completed a preparatory course; was graduated from the law department of Indiana University at Bloomington in 1849; was admitted to the bar and practiced; member of the State house of representatives in 1858; presidential elector on the Republican ticket of Lincoln and Hamlin in 1860; during the Civil War enlisted in the Union Army August 27, 1862; commanded the First Brigade, Third Division, Fourteenth Army Corps; was with Sherman in his march to the sea; brevetted brigadier general of Volunteers; honorably discharged June 24, 1865; elected as a Republican to the Fortieth Congress (March 4, 1867–March 3, 1869); elected to the Forty-third, Forty-fourth, and Forty-fifth Congresses (March 4, 1873–March 3, 1879); operated a quarry in the Indiana limestone district; died in Bloomington, Ind., October 25, 1896; interment in Rose Hill Cemetery.

HUNTER, Narsworthy, a Delegate from Mississippi Territory; born in Virginia; captain in the militia organization of the district formed in 1793; commissioned inspector of the military posts on the east side of the Mississippi River; elected to the Seventh Congress and served from March 4, 1801, until his death in Washington, D. C., March 11, 1802; interment in the Congressional Cemetery.

HUNTER, Richard Charles, a Senator from Nebraska, born on a farm near Westpoint, Cuming County, Nebr., December 3, 1884; moved with his parents to Omaha, Nebr., in 1885; attended the public and high schools of Omaha; was graduated from the University of Nebraska at Lincoln in 1909; attended the law school of Harvard University, Cambridge, Mass., in 1909 and 1910; was graduated from the law department of Columbia University, New York City, N. Y., in 1911; was admitted to the bar the same year and commenced practice in Lincoln, Nebr.; moved to Omaha, Nebr., in 1912 and continued the practice of law; delegate to the Democratic State conventions from 1912 to 1936; member of the State house of representatives

1915–1917; judge of the municipal court of Omaha 1915–1917; unsuccessful candidate for election as attorney general of Nebraska in 1920 and as State railway commissioner in 1928; elected as a Democrat to the United States Senate to fill the vacancy caused by the death of Robert B. Howell and served from November 7, 1934, to January 3, 1935; was not a candidate for election in 1934 to the full term; resumed the practice of law; attorney general of Nebraska in 1937 and 1938; died in Tucson, Ariz., January 23, 1941; interment in West Lawn Memorial Park, Omaha, Nebr.

HUNTER, Robert Mercer Taliaferro, a Representative and a Senator from Virginia; was born at "Mount Pleasant," near Loretto, Essex County, Va., April 21, 1809; tutored at home; was graduated from the University of Virginia at Charlottesville; studied law; was admitted to the bar in 1830 and commenced practice at Lloyds; member of the State house of delegates in 1833; served in the State senate 1835–1837; elected as a Democrat to the Twenty-fifth, Twenty-sixth, and Twenty-seventh Congresses (March 4, 1837–March 3, 1843); served as Speaker of the House in the Twenty-sixth Congress; unsuccessful candidate for reelection to the Twenty-eighth Congress; elected to the Twenty-ninth Congress (March 4, 1845–March 3, 1847); elected to the United States Senate and served from March 4, 1847, to March 28, 1861, when he withdrew; author of the tariff act of 1857; candidate for the presidential nomination in 1860; declined the position of Secretary of State tendered him by Presidents Pierce and Buchanan; delegate from Virginia to the Confederate Provincial Congress at Richmond; Confederate Secretary of State from July 25, 1861, to February 18, 1862; served in the Confederate Senate from Virginia in the First and Second Congresses 1862–1865 and was President pro tempore on various occasions; was one of the peace commissioners that met with President Lincoln and his party in Hampton Roads in February 1865; elected State treasurer of Virginia in 1877; collector at Tappahannock, Va., in 1885; died on his estate "Fonthill," near Lloyds, Va., on July 18, 1887; interment in "Elmwood," the old family burial ground, near Loretto, Va.

HUNTER, Whiteside Godfrey, a Representative from Kentucky; born near Belfast, Ireland, December 25, 1841; completed preparatory studies; immigrated to the United States in 1858 and settled in New Castle, Pa.; studied medicine in Philadelphia and was admitted to practice; surgeon in the Union Army during the Civil War; moved to Burkesville, Cumberland County, Ky., at the close of the war; member of the State house of representatives 1874–1878; delegate to the Republican National Convention at Chicago in 1880 and at Minneapolis in 1892; United States Minister to Guatemala and Honduras from November 8, 1897, to December 8, 1902; elected as a Republican to the Fiftieth Congress (March 4, 1887–March 3, 1889); unsuccessful candidate for reelection in 1888 to the Fifty-first Congress and for election in 1892 to the Fifty-third Congress; elected to the Fifty-fourth Congress (March 4, 1895–March 3, 1897); unsuccessful candidate for reelection in 1896 to the Fifty-fifth Congress; elected to the Fifty-eighth Congress to fill the vacancy caused by the death of Vincent S. Boreing and served from November 10, 1903, to March 3, 1905; was not a candidate for renomination in 1904; interested in public utilities and the development of oil lands; resided in Louisville, Ky., until his death there on November 2, 1917; interment in Cave Hill Cemetery.

HUNTER, William, a Representative from Vermont; born in Sharon, Litchfield County, Conn., January 3, 1754; attended the common schools; resided near Fort Edward, N. Y., from 1763 until 1775, when he moved to Windsor, Vt.; served in the Revolutionary War as a sergeant and lieutenant under General

Montgomery; member of the State house of representatives in 1795, 1807, and 1808; register of probate 1798–1801; judge of probate for the district of Windsor 1801–1816; presidential elector on the Democratic ticket of Jefferson and Clinton in 1804; assistant judge of the county court 1805–1816; member of the Vermont council of censors in 1806 and 1820; member of the executive council 1810–1813 and in 1815; elected as a Republican to the Fifteenth Congress (March 4, 1817–March 3, 1819); was not a candidate for reelection in 1818 to the Sixteenth Congress; died in Windsor, Windsor County, Vt., November 30, 1827; interment in Sheddsville Cemetery, West Windsor, Vt.

HUNTER, William, a Senator from Rhode Island; born in Newport, R. I., November 26, 1774; attended Rogers School in Newport and was graduated from Brown University, Providence, R. I., in 1791; went abroad and studied law at the Inner Temple, London; returned to Newport, R. I.; was admitted to the bar in 1796 and commenced practice in Newport; member of the State house of representatives 1799–1811; elected as a Federalist to the United States Senate to fill the vacancy caused by the resignation of Christopher G. Champlin; reelected and served from October 28, 1811, to March 3, 1821; again a member of the State house of representatives 1822–1826; resumed the practice of his profession in Newport; appointed by President Jackson Chargé d'Affaires to Brazil June 28, 1834, and by President Tyler Envoy Extraordinary and Minister Plenipotentiary September 13, 1841; served until December 9, 1843; died in Newport, R. I., December 3, 1849; interment in Trinity Church Graveyard.

HUNTER, William Forrest, a Representative from Ohio; born in Alexandria, Va., December 10, 1808; received a common-school training; studied law; was admitted to the bar and commenced practice in Woodsfield, Ohio; elected as a Whig to the Thirty-first and Thirty-second Congresses (March 4, 1849–March 3, 1853); was not a candidate for renomination in 1852; died in Woodsfield, Ohio, on March 30, 1874; interment in Woodsfield Cemetery.

HUNTER, William H., a Representative from Ohio; born in Frankfort, Franklin County, Ky.; completed preparatory studies; studied law; was admitted to the bar and commenced practice in Tiffin, Ohio; moved to Norwalk, Huron County, Ohio, about 1825 and continued the practice of his profession for several years; moved to Sandusky, Ohio; appointed collector of customs at Sandusky in 1835; elected as a Democrat to the Twenty-fifth Congress (March 4, 1837–March 3, 1839); died under mysterious circumstances near Sandusky, Ohio, in 1842; interment in the Old Burial Ground.

HUNTINGTON, Abel, a Representative from New York; born in Norwich, Conn., February 21, 1777; received a liberal schooling; moved to East Hampton, Long Island, N. Y., where he practiced medicine; presidential elector in 1820; member of the State senate in 1822; supervisor of East Hampton 1829–1832 and in 1844; elected as a Democrat to the Twenty-third and Twenty-fourth Congresses (March 4, 1833–March 3, 1837); member of the State constitutional convention in 1846; collector of customs at Sag Harbor, N. Y., 1845–1849; died in East Hampton, Long Island, N. Y., May 18, 1858; interment in South End Cemetery.

HUNTINGTON, Benjamin, a Delegate and a Representative from Connecticut; born in Norwich, Conn., April 19, 1736; pursued academic studies; was graduated from Yale College in 1761; appointed surveyor of lands for Windham County in October 1764; studied law; was admitted to the bar in 1765 and commenced practice in Norwich; member of the State house of representatives 1771–1780 and served as speaker in 1778 and 1779; clerk of the State house of representatives in 1776 and 1777; delegate to the Provincial Congress at New Haven in January 1778; Member of the Continental Congress 1780–1784, 1787, and 1788; member of the State senate 1781–1790 and 1791–1793; mayor of Norwich from 1784 to 1796, when he resigned; elected to the First Congress (March 4, 1789–March 3, 1791); judge of the superior court of the State 1793–1798; died in Rome, N. Y., October 16, 1800; interment in Norwichtown Cemetery, Norwich, Conn.

HUNTINGTON, Ebenezer, a Representative from Connecticut; born in Norwich, Conn., December 26, 1754; pursued academic studies; was graduated from Yale College in 1775; served in the Revolutionary Army, first in the Lexington alarm in April 1775; lieutenant in Col. Samuel Wyllis's regiment, and was made captain in May 1776; brigade major and adjutant general to General Heath in August 1776; major in Colonel Webb's additional Continental regiment January 1, 1777; lieutenant colonel October 10, 1778; transferred to the Third Connecticut Regiment January 1, 1781, and to the First Connecticut January 1, 1783; brigadier general, United States Army, July 19, 1798, when war with France was threatened; honorably discharged June 15, 1800; elected as a Whig to the Eleventh Congress to fill the vacancy caused by the resignation of Samuel W. Dana and served from October 11, 1810, to March 3, 1811; elected to the Fifteenth Congress (March 4, 1817–March 3, 1819); died in Norwich, Conn., June 17, 1834; interment in Norwichtown Cemetery.

HUNTINGTON, Jabez Williams, a Representative and a Senator from Connecticut; born in Norwich, Conn., November 8, 1788; pursued classical studies; was graduated from Yale College in 1806; taught in the Litchfield South Farms Academy one year; studied law; was admitted to the bar and commenced practice in Litchfield; member of the State house of representatives in 1829; elected to the Twenty-first, Twenty-second, and Twenty-third Congresses and served from March 4, 1829, to August 16, 1834, when he resigned to accept the appointment of judge of the State supreme court of errors; moved to Norwich in October 1834; elected as a Whig to the United States Senate to fill the vacancy caused by the death of Thaddeus Betts; reelected, and served from May 4, 1840, until his death in Norwich, Conn., November 1, 1847; interment in Norwichtown Cemetery.

HUNTINGTON, Samuel, a Delegate from Connecticut; born in Windham, Conn., July 3, 1731; attended the common schools; learned the trade of cooper; studied law; was admitted to the bar in 1758 and commenced practice in Norwich, Conn., in 1758; executive councilor in 1763; member of the colonial assembly in 1764; appointed Crown attorney in 1765; judge of the superior court from 1774 to 1784 and served as chief justice in the last-named year; Member of the Continental Congress 1776–1784 and served as President from September 28, 1779, to July 6, 1781, when he retired, receiving the thanks of the Congress, but was returned again for a short period in 1783; a signer of the Declaration of Independence; Lieutenant Governor of the State in 1785, and Governor from 1786 until his death in Norwich, Conn., January 5, 1796; interment in Norwichtown Cemetery.

HUNTON, Eppa, a Representative and a Senator from Virginia; born near Warrenton, Fauquier County, Va., September 24, 1822; his early schooling was limited; taught school three years; studied law; was admitted to the bar in 1843 and commenced practice in Brentsville, Va.; served as colonel of the Prince William Regiment, and later promoted to the rank of general; Commonwealth attorney for the county of Prince William from 1849 until 1861, when he resigned; member of the Vir-

ginia convention at Richmond in February 1861; served through its first session and then entered the Confederate Army as colonel of the Eighth Regiment, Virginia Infantry; promoted after the Battle of Gettysburg and served through the remainder of the Civil War as brigadier general, succeeding Brigadier General Garnett; captured at Sailors Creek April 6, 1865, and released from Fort Warren in July 1865; resumed the practice of law; elected as a Democrat to the Forty-third and to the three succeeding Congresses (March 4, 1873–March 3, 1881); was not a candidate for renomination in 1880; appointed a member of the so-called Florida Electoral Commission created by act of Congress approved January 29, 1877, to decide the contests in various States in the presidential election of 1876; resumed the practice of law; appointed and subsequently elected to the United States Senate to fill the vacancy caused by the death of John S. Barbour and served from May 28, 1892, to March 3, 1895; was not a candidate for renomination in 1894; resumed the practice of law in Warrenton, Va.; died in Richmond, Va., October 11, 1908; interment in Hollywood Cemetery.

HUNTSMAN, Adam, a Representative from Tennessee; born in Virginia; moved to Jackson, Tenn.; elected as a Jackson Democrat to the Twenty-fourth Congress (March 4, 1835–March 3, 1837); unsuccessful candidate for reelection in 1836 to the Twenty-fifth Congress.

HURD, Frank Hunt, a Representative from Ohio; born in Mount Vernon, Knox County, Ohio, December 25, 1840; was graduated from Kenyon College, Gambier, Ohio, in 1858; studied law; was admitted to the bar in 1861 and practiced; prosecuting attorney of Knox County in 1863; member of the State senate in 1866; appointed to codify the criminal laws of Ohio in 1868; moved to Toledo, Ohio, in 1869; city solicitor of Toledo 1871–1873; unsuccessful Democratic candidate for election in 1872 to the Forty-third Congress; elected as a Democrat to the Forty-fourth Congress (March 4, 1875–March 3, 1877); unsuccessful candidate for reelection in 1876 to the Forty-fifth Congress; elected to the Forty-sixth Congress (March 4, 1879–March 3, 1881); unsuccessful candidate for reelection in 1880 to the Forty-seventh Congress; elected to the Forty-eighth Congress (March 4, 1883–March 3, 1885); unsuccessfully contested the election of Jacob Romeis to the Forty-ninth Congress; resumed the practice of law; unsuccessful Democratic candidate for election in 1886 to the Fiftieth Congress; continued the practice of law in Toledo, until his death on July 10, 1896; interment in Mound View Cemetery, Mount Vernon, Ohio.

HURLBUT, Stephen Augustus, a Representative from Illinois; born in Charleston, S. C., November 29, 1815, completed preparatory studies; studied law; was admitted to the bar in 1837 and practiced; served as adjutant of a South Carolina regiment in the Florida War; moved to Belvidere, Ill., in 1845; Whig delegate to the State constitutional convention in 1847; presidential elector on the Whig ticket in 1848 and on the Republican ticket of Grant and Colfax in 1868; member of the State house of representatives in 1859, 1861, and 1867; during the Civil War served in the Union Army 1861–1865; appointed brigadier general of Volunteers May 17, 1861, and major general September 17, 1862; mustered out June 20, 1865; one of the founders of the Grand Army of the Republic, and served as commander in chief 1866–1868; Minister Resident to the United States of Colombia 1869–1872; elected as a Republican to the Forty-third and Forty-fourth Congresses (March 4, 1873–March 3, 1877); unsuccessful candidate for reelection as an independent Republican to the Forty-fifth Congress in 1876; appointed Minister to Peru in 1881 and served until his death in Lima, Peru, March 27, 1882; interment in Belvidere Cemetery, Belvidere, Ill.

HURLEY, Denis Michael, a Representative from New York born in the city of Limerick, Ireland, March 14, 1843; immigrated to the United States in 1850 with his parents, who settled in Brooklyn, N. Y.; moved to New York City in 1854; was educated in the public schools; returned to Brooklyn in 1866; learned the carpenter's trade; engaged in the building contractors' business; delegate to the Republican State conventions from 1879 to 1899; unsuccessful Republican candidate for member of the State assembly in 1880; elected as a Republican to the Fifty-fourth and Fifty-fifth Congresses and served from March 4, 1895, until his death; unsuccessful in 1898 for reelection to the Fifty-sixth Congress; died at Hot Springs, Va., February 26, 1899; interment in Holy Cross Cemetery, Brooklyn, N. Y.

HUSTED, James William, a Representative from New York; born in Peekskill, Westchester County, N. Y., March 16, 1870; attended private schools, the Peekskill Military Academy, and Cutler's School, New York City; was graduated from Phillips Academy, Andover, Mass., in 1888, from Yale University in 1892, and from the New York Law School in 1894; was admitted to the bar in 1894 and commenced practice in Peekskill, N. Y.; member of the State assembly 1895–1897; declined a renomination; moved to White Plains in 1897 and continued the practice of law; returned to Peekskill in 1902 and again practiced law; president of the village of Peekskill in 1903 and 1904; member and treasurer of the board of park commissioners from 1909 to 1920; unsuccessful candidate for election in 1912 to the Sixty-third Congress; elected as a Republican to the Sixty-fourth and to the three succeeding Congresses (March 4, 1915–March 3, 1923); was not a candidate for renomination in 1922; resumed the practice of law in Peekskill; also engaged in banking and served as president of the Peekskill Bank; died at the New York Hospital in New York City, while on a business trip, January 2, 1925; remains were cremated; interment of ashes in Hillside Cemetery, Peekskill, N. Y.

HUSTING, Paul Oscar, a Senator from Wisconsin; born in Fond du Lac, Fond du Lac County, Wis., April 25, 1866; moved with his parents to Mayville, Wis., in 1876; attended the public schools and the University of Wisconsin at Madison; studied law; was admitted to the bar in 1895 and commenced practice in Mayville, Wis.; district attorney of Dodge County 1902–1906; served in the State senate 1907–1913; elected as a Democrat to the United States Senate in 1914 and served from March 4, 1915, until his accidental death while duck hunting on Rush Lake, near Picketts, Wis., on October 21, 1917; interment in Graceland Cemetery, Mayville, Wis.

HUTCHESON, Joseph Chappell, a Representative from Texas; born near Boydton, Mecklenburg County, Va., May 18, 1842; attended the common schools; was graduated from Randolph-Macon College, Ashland, Va., in 1861; enlisted as a private in the Twenty-first Virginia Regiment during the Civil War; served in the Valley of Virginia under Stonewall Jackson and surrendered at Appomattox, at which time he was in command of Company E, Fourteenth Virginia Regiment; was graduated from the law department of the University of Virginia at Charlottesville in 1866; was admitted to the bar in 1866 and commenced practice in Anderson, Grimes County, Tex.; moved to Houston, Tex., in 1874 and continued the practice of law; member of the State house of representatives in 1880; elected as a Democrat to the Fifty-third and Fifty-fourth Congresses (March 4, 1893–March 3, 1897); was not a candidate for renomination in 1896; resumed the practice of law in Houston, Tex.; died at his summer home on Signal Mountain, near Chattanooga, Tenn., May 25, 1924; interment in Glenwood Cemetery, Houston, Tex.

HUTCHINS, John (cousin of Wells Andrews Hutchins), a Representative from Ohio; born in Vienna, Trumbull County, Ohio, July 25, 1812; attended the district schools and Western Reserve College, Cleveland, Ohio; studied law; was admitted to the bar in 1837 and commenced practice in Warren, Trumbull County; clerk of the common pleas court for Trumbull County 1838–1843; member of the State house of representatives in 1849 and 1850; mayor of Warren two years; member of the Warren Board of Education six years; elected as a Republican to the Thirty-sixth and Thirty-seventh Congresses (March 4, 1859–March 3, 1863); unsuccessful candidate for renomination in 1862; resumed the practice of law in Warren; moved to Cleveland, Ohio, in 1868 and continued the practice of law; died in Cleveland, Ohio, November 20, 1891; interment in Lakeview Cemetery.

HUTCHINS, Waldo, a Representative from New York; born in Brooklyn, Windham County, Conn., September 30, 1822; was graduated from Amherst (Mass.) College in 1842; studied law; was admitted to the bar in 1845 and commenced practice in New York City; member of the State assembly in 1852; offered the Democratic nomination for judge of the supreme court when thirty-three years old, but declined; delegate to the State constitutional convention in 1867; park commissioner 1857–1869; elected as a Democrat to the Forty-sixth Congress to fill the vacancy caused by the death of Alexander Smith; reelected to the Forty-seventh and Forty-eighth Congresses and served from November 4, 1879, to March 3, 1885; was not a candidate for renomination in 1884; resumed the practice of law in New York City; appointed in 1887 member of the park commission and served until his death, February 8, 1891, in New York City; interment in Woodlawn Cemetery.

HUTCHINS, Wells Andrews (cousin of John Hutchins), a Representative from Ohio; born in Hartford, Trumbull County, Ohio, October 8, 1818; attended the public schools; taught school; studied law; was admitted to the bar in 1841 and commenced practice in Warren, Trumbull County, Ohio; moved to Portsmouth, Ohio, in 1842; member of the State house of representatives in 1852 and 1853; city solicitor of Portsmouth 1857–1861; United States provost marshal for Ohio in 1862; unsuccessful candidate in 1860 to the Thirty-seventh Congress; elected as a Democrat to the Thirty-eighth Congress (March 4, 1863–March 3, 1865); unsuccessful candidate in 1864 for reelection to the Thirty-ninth Congress and again in 1880 to the Forty-seventh Congress; resumed the practice of law in Portsmouth, Ohio, and died there January 25, 1895; interment in Greenlawn Cemetery.

HUTCHINSON, Elijah Cubberley, a Representative from New Jersey; born in Windsor, Mercer County, N. J., August 7, 1855; attended the public schools and Riders Business College, Trenton, N. J.; became a merchant miller, having a large flour mill and grain elevator situated in Hamilton Township; also interested in banking and in the manufacture of fertilizer; served as township clerk for three years; member of the State house of assembly in 1895 and 1896; served in the State senate 1899–1904 and was president of that body in 1903; State road commissioner 1905–1908; elected as a Republican to the Sixty-fourth and to the three succeeding Congresses (March 4, 1915–March 3, 1923); unsuccessful for reelection in 1922 to the Sixty-eighth Congress; retired; resided in Trenton, N. J., until his death there June 25, 1932; interment in Greenwood Cemetery.

HUTSON, Richard, a Delegate from South Carolina; born in Prince William parish, South Carolina, July 9, 1748; pursued classical studies and was graduated from Princeton College (Nassau Hall) in 1765; studied law; was admitted to the bar and practiced in Charleston, S. C.; member of the State house of representatives 1776–1779, 1781, 1782, 1785, and 1788; Member of the Continental Congress in 1778 and 1779 and signed the Articles of Confederation; captured at the fall of Charleston and was confined as a prisoner at St. Augustine, Fla., in 1780 and 1781 by Lord Cornwallis, who, being incensed at the late revolt, suspected him of being one of those fomenting the spirit of rebellion; member of the Legislative Council of South Carolina 1780–1782; Lieutenant Governor in 1782 and 1783; first intendant of Charleston in 1783 and 1784; chancellor of the court of chancery of South Carolina 1784–1791; member of the State constitutional convention in 1788 which adopted the Federal Constitution; senior judge of the chancery court 1791–1795; died in Charleston, S. C., April 12, 1795; interment in the Perrineau family vault in Independent Congregational Church Cemetery.

HUTTON, John Edward, a Representative from Missouri; born in Polk County, Tenn., March 28, 1828; moved with his parents to Troy, Lincoln County, Mo., in 1831; attended the common schools; taught school and at the same time studied medicine; attended lectures at Pope's Medical College, St. Louis, Mo.; was graduated in medicine and began practice in Warrenton, Mo., in 1860; during the Civil War entered the Union Army and was commissioned colonel of the Fifty-ninth Regiment, Missouri Volunteer Infantry; studied law; was admitted to the bar in 1864 and commenced practice in Warrenton, Mo.; moved to Mexico, Mo., in 1865 and continued to practice law until 1873, when he became the owner and publisher of the Intelligencer, a Democratic newspaper; elected as a Democrat to the Forty-ninth and Fiftieth Congresses (March 4, 1885–March 3, 1889); was not a candidate for renomination in 1888; resumed his activities as a physician and also engaged in the practice of law; died in Mexico, Mo., December 28, 1893; interment in Elmwood Cemetery.

HUYLER, John, a Representative from New Jersey; born in New York City April 9, 1808; attended the common schools at Tenafly, N. J.; apprenticed as a mason and later engaged in contracting and building in New York City until 1846; moved to New Jersey and engaged in agricultural pursuits at Pollifly, Lodi Township; settled in the village of Hackensack, N. J., about 1855; engaged in the mercantile and lumber business; president of the board of freeholders of Bergen County; member of the State house of assembly 1849–1851, and served as speaker in 1851; judge of the court of appeals 1854–1857; elected as a Democrat to the Thirty-fifth Congress (March 4, 1857–March 3, 1859); unsuccessful candidate as a Lecompton Democrat for reelection in 1858 to the Thirty-sixth Congress; resumed the lumber business; assassinated in Hackensack, N. J., January 9, 1870; interment in New York Cemetery at Hackensack.

HYDE, DeWitt Stephen, a Representative from Maryland; born in Washington, D. C., March 21, 1909; attended the public schools; graduated from George Washington University in 1935; with the Farm Credit Administration for three years; admitted to the bar in 1935 and commenced the practice of law in Washington, D. C.; moved to Maryland in 1938 and continued law work; entered the United States Navy as a lieutenant (jg) in March 1943, served in the South Pacific, and was separated from the service as a lieutenant commander in May 1946; instructor of law, Benjamin Franklin University, Washington, D. C., 1946–1951; served in the State house of delegates 1947–1950; member of the State senate in 1951 and 1952; elected as a Republican to the Eighty-third, Eighty-fourth, and Eighty-

fifth Congresses (January 3, 1953–January 3, 1959); unsuccessful candidate for reelection in 1958 to the Eighty-sixth Congress; engaged in the practice of law; in 1959 was appointed an associate judge of the Municipal Court for the District of Columbia for a ten-year term; is a resident of Bethesda, Md.

HYDE, Ira Barnes, a Representative from Missouri; born near Guilford, Chenango County, N. Y., January 18, 1838; attended the public schools and the Norwich Academy; when fifteen years of age moved with his parents to East Cleveland, Cuyahoga County, Ohio, and later entered Oberlin (Ohio) College; studied law; was admitted to the bar by the Minnesota Supreme Court in 1861 and commenced practice in St. Paul, Minn., in 1862; during the Civil War served in the Union Army; enlisted as a private in Company F, First Regiment of Minnesota Mounted Rangers, and served until the regiment was mustered out; also served in the campaigns against the Sioux Indians along the northwestern frontier; moved to Washington, D. C., in 1865 and resumed the practice of law; moved to Princeton, Mo., in 1866; appointed prosecuting attorney of Mercer County in 1872; delegate to many State conventions; elected as a Republican to the Forty-third Congress (March 4, 1873–March 3, 1875); unsuccessful candidate for reelection in 1874 to the Forty-fourth Congress; delegate to the Republican National Convention at Chicago in 1884 which nominated James G. Blaine for President; resumed the practice of law in Princeton, Mo.; also engaged in banking; died in Princeton, Mo., December 6, 1926; interment in Princeton Cemetery.

HYDE, Samuel Clarence, a Representative from Washington; born in Fort Ticonderoga, Essex County, N. Y., April 22, 1842; moved to Wisconsin; attended the common schools; served in the Seventeenth Regiment, Wisconsin Volunteer Infantry, during the Civil War; spent several years as surveyor in northern Wisconsin and Michigan; studied law at the University of Iowa at Iowa City; was admitted to the bar in 1876 and commenced practice at Rock Rapids, Iowa; moved to the Territory of Washington in 1877 and practiced law at Puget Sound; moved to Spokane in 1880 and continued the practice of law; prosecuting attorney of Spokane County 1880–1886; elected as a Republican to the Fifty-fourth Congress (March 4, 1895–March 3, 1897); unsuccessful candidate for reelection in 1896 to the Fifty-fifth Congress; justice of the peace from 1904 until his death in Spokane, Wash., March 7, 1922; interment in Fairmount Cemetery.

HYMAN, John Adams, a Representative from North Carolina; born a slave near Warrenton, Warren County, N. C., July 23, 1840; was of the Negro race; was sold and sent to Alabama; returned to North Carolina in 1865 and engaged in agricultural pursuits; pursued elementary studies; delegate to the State equal rights convention in 1865 and to the State constitutional convention in 1868; member of the State senate 1868–1874; elected as a Republican to the Forty-fourth Congress (March 4, 1875–March 3, 1877); unsuccessful candidate for renomination in 1876; resumed agricultural pursuits; special deputy collector of internal revenue for the fourth district of North Carolina from July 1, 1877, to June 30, 1878; died in Washington, D. C., on September 14, 1891; interment in Harmony Cemetery.

HYNEMAN, John M., a Representative from Pennsylvania; born in Reading, Berks County, Pa., about April 25, 1771; received a common-school education; member of the State house of representatives in 1809; clerk of the orphans' court 1810–1816; elected as a Democrat to the Twelfth and Thirteenth Congresses and served from March 4, 1811, until his resignation August 2, 1813; was not a candidate for renomination in 1814; commissioned a brigadier general in the Pennsylvania Militia; surveyor of Berks County in 1816; died in Reading, Berks County, Pa., April 16, 1816; interment in the Trinity Lutheran Cemetery.

HYNES, William Joseph, a Representative from Arkansas; born in County Clare, Ireland, March 31, 1843; immigrated to the United States in 1854 and settled in New York; attended the public schools of Massachusetts; learned the art of printing; studied law; was admitted to the bar in 1870 and commenced practice in Little Rock, Ark.; elected as a Democrat to the Forty-third Congress (March 4, 1873–March 3, 1875); unsuccessful candidate for reelection in 1874 to the Forty-fourth Congress; moved to Chicago in 1876 and resumed the practice of his profession; retired from the practice of law in 1910 and moved to Los Angeles, Calif., where he remained until his death, April 2, 1915; interment in Calvary vault.

I

IGLESIAS, Santiago (formerly Santiago Iglesias Pantin), a Resident Commissioner from Puerto Rico; born in La Coruña, Spain, February 22, 1872; attended the common schools; apprenticed as a cabinet maker; moved to Cuba and was secretary of the Workingmen Trades Circle in Habana 1889–1896; moved to Puerto Rico and was the founder and editor of three labor papers: Porvenir Social 1898–1900, Union Obrera 1903–1906, Justicia 1914–1925; appointed general organizer of the American Federation of Labor for the districts of Puerto Rico and Cuba in 1901; member of the Puerto Rican Senate 1917–1933; served as secretary of the Pan American Federation of Labor 1925–1933; elected as a Coalitionist, a Resident Commissioner to the United States on November 8, 1932; reelected in 1936 for the term ending January 3, 1941, and served from March 4, 1933, until his death in Washington, D. C., December 5, 1939; interment in San Juan Cemetery, San Juan, P. R.

IGOE, James Thomas, a Representative from Illinois; born in Chicago, Cook County, Ill., October 23, 1883; attended the Holden School, Bryant and Stratton College, and St. Ignatius College, all in Chicago, Ill.; became engaged in the printing and publishing business in Chicago, Ill., in 1907; president of a printing and lithographing company in 1912; served as city clerk of Chicago 1917–1923; delegate to the Democratic National Conventions in 1920, 1928, and 1936; elected as a Democrat to the Seventieth, Seventy-first, and Seventy-second Congresses (March 4, 1927–March 3, 1933); unsuccessful candidate for renomination in 1932; president of a building corporation in 1931; chairman of Illinois delegation to Golden Gate International Exposition in San Francisco in 1939 and 1940; organized James T. Igoe and Associates, Realtors, in 1942; director and later chairman of executive committee of Mercantile National Bank of Chicago since 1955; is a resident of Chicago, Ill.

IGOE, Michael Lambert, a Representative from Illinois; born in St. Paul, Ramsey County, Minn., April 16, 1885; educated in the parochial schools and De La Salle Institute, Chicago, Ill.; was graduated from the law department of Georgetown University, Washington, D. C., in 1908; was admitted to the bar the same year and commenced practice in Chicago, Ill.; member of the State house of representatives 1913–1930; served as chief assistant in the United States attorney's office in Chicago 1915–1917; member of the board of South Park Commissioners 1924–1934; delegate to the Democratic National Convention at Houston in 1928; member of the Democratic National Committee 1930–1932; elected as a Democrat to the Seventy-fourth Congress, serving from January 3, 1935, until his resignation effective June 2, 1935, having been appointed a United States attorney for the northern district of Illinois on May 16, 1935, and served until his appointment as United States district judge on March 4, 1939, in which capacity he is now serving; is a resident of Chicago, Ill.

IGOE, William Leo, a Representative from Missouri; born in St. Louis, Mo., on October 19, 1879; attended the public and parochial schools of his native city and was graduated from the law department of Washington University at St. Louis in 1902; was admitted to the bar in the same year and commenced the practice of law in St. Louis, Mo.; member of the municipal assembly of St. Louis from 1909 until March 3, 1913, when he resigned to enter Congress; elected as a Democrat to the Sixty-third and to the three succeeding Congresses (March 4, 1913–March 3, 1921); declined to become a candidate for renomination in 1920; resumed the practice of law; unsuccessful Democratic nominee for mayor of St. Louis in 1925; chairman of the St. Louis Board of Police Commissioners 1933–1937; died in St. Louis, Mo., April 20, 1953; interment in Calvary Cemetery.

IHRIE, Peter, Jr., a Representative from Pennsylvania; born in Easton, Pa., February 3, 1796; completed preparatory studies; was graduated from Dickinson College, Carlisle, Pa., in 1815; studied law; was admitted to the bar in 1818 and commenced practice in Easton, Pa.; charter member of the board of trustees of Lafayette College in 1826; member of the State house of representatives in 1826 and 1827; brigadier general of State militia in 1845; elected as a Jackson Democrat to the Twenty-first Congress to fill in part the vacancies caused by the resignation of George Wolf and Samuel D. Ingraham; reelected to the Twenty-second Congress and served from October 13, 1829, to March 3, 1833; member of the board of directors of the Easton Bank; died in Easton, Pa., on March 29, 1871; interment in Easton Cemetery.

IKARD, Frank Neville, a Representative from Texas; born in Henrietta, Clay County, Tex., January 30, 1914; attended the public schools and Shriner Institute, Kerrville, Tex.; was graduated from the law school of the University of Texas in 1937; was admitted to the bar in 1937 and commenced the practice of law in Wichita Falls, Tex.; during World War II enlisted in the United States Army in January 1944 and served with Company K, One Hundred and Tenth Infantry, Twenty-eighth Division; prisoner of war in Germany in 1944 and 1945; awarded the Purple Heart Medal; was discharged from the service in December 1945; chairman of Veterans Affairs Commission of Texas in 1948 and 1949; Democratic presidential elector in 1948; appointed by Gov. Beauford Jester in November 1948 judge of the Thirtieth District Court, subsequently elected in 1950, and served until September 8, 1951; delegate to the Democratic National Convention in 1956; elected as a Democrat to the Eighty-second Congress to fill the vacancy caused by the resignation of Ed Gossett; reelected to the Eighty-third and to the four succeeding Congresses and served from September 8, 1951, to December 15, 1961, when he resigned; executive vice president of American Petroleum Institute; is a resident of Wichita Falls, Tex.

IKIRT, George Pierce, a Representative from Ohio; born near West Beaver, Columbiana County, Ohio, November 3, 1852; attended the public schools of New Lisbon, Ohio; taught school and studied law, but on account of ill health was compelled to abandon both; attended the Columbus Medical College; moved to Cincinnati; was graduated from the Cincinnati College of Medicine and Surgery in 1877 and practiced five years; went to New York City in 1882 and was graduated from the Bellevue Hospital Medical College in 1883; again resumed practice in East

Liverpool, Ohio; unsuccessful candidate for election in 1888 to the Fifty-first Congress; elected as a Democrat to the Fifty-third Congress (March 4, 1893–March 3, 1895); declined to be a candidate for renomination in 1894; resumed the practice of medicine in East Liverpool, Ohio, and died there February 12, 1927; interment in Riverview Cemetery.

ILSLEY, Daniel, a Representative from Massachusetts; born in Falmouth, Cumberland County, Maine (then a part of Massachusetts), May 30, 1740; received a liberal schooling; became a distiller and was also interested in shipping; member of the committee of correspondence and safety; major and mustering officer at Falmouth, Maine, during the Revolutionary War; delegate to the Massachusetts State convention in 1788 that adopted the Federal Constitution; member of the Massachusetts House of Representatives in 1793 and 1794; elected as a Democrat to the Tenth Congress (March 4, 1807–March 3, 1809); unsuccessful candidate for reelection in 1808 to the Eleventh Congress; died in Portland, Maine, May 10, 1813; interment in the Eastern Cemetery.

IMHOFF, Lawrence E., a Representative from Ohio; born at Round Bottom, Monroe County, Ohio, December 28, 1895; moved to St. Clairsville, Ohio, in 1907; attended the rural schools and St. Clairsville High School; during the First World War enlisted as a private in the Fifth Regiment, United States Marines, and served from August 9, 1917, until honorably discharged on April 1, 1919; was wounded three times in the second battle of the Marne; received the French Fourragère decoration and two citations and the Purple Heart Medal; after the war attended Ohio State University at Columbus; clerk of courts of Belmont County, Ohio, 1921–1925; studied law and was admitted to the bar in January 1930; served as probate judge of Belmont County 1925–1933; elected as a Democrat to the Seventy-third, Seventy-fourth, and Seventy-fifth Congresses (March 4, 1933–January 3, 1939); unsuccessful candidate for reelection in 1938 to the Seventy-sixth Congress; special assistant to the United States Attorney General in 1939 and 1940; again elected to the Seventy-seventh Congress (January 3, 1941–January 3, 1943); unsuccessful candidate for reelection in 1942 to the Seventy-eighth Congress; during World War II was commissioned as a lieutenant commander in the United States Naval Reserve on January 21, 1943; was promoted to rank of commander and released from active duty on November 8, 1945; appointed on November 9, 1945, a member of the Board of Veterans' Appeals, Washington, D. C., in which capacity he is now serving; resides in Washington, D. C., and is a legal resident of St. Clairsville, Ohio.

IMLAY, James Henderson, a Representative from New Jersey; was born in Imlaystown, Upper Freehold, Monmouth County, N. J., November 26, 1764; pursued classical studies; was graduated from Princeton College in 1786, where he was also a tutor; studied law; was admitted to the bar in 1791 and practiced; major in the Monmouth County Militia, and served in the Revolutionary War; counselor in 1796; member of the State general assembly 1793–1796 and served as speaker in 1796; elected to the Fifth and Sixth Congresses (March 4, 1797–March 3, 1801); one of the managers appointed by the House of Representatives in 1798 to conduct the impeachment proceedings against William Blount, a Senator from Tennessee; postmaster of Allentown, N. J., 1804–1805; resumed the practice of law in Allentown, N. J., where he died March 6, 1823; interment in the Presbyterian Church Cemetery.

INGALLS, John James, a Senator from Kansas; born in Middleton, Essex County, Mass., December 29, 1833; attended the public schools in Haverhill, Mass., and was graduated from Williams College, Williamstown, Mass., in 1855; studied law; was admitted to the bar in 1857; moved to Sumner, Kans., in 1858; member of the State constitutional convention held at Wyandotte (now a part of Kansas City) in 1859; secretary of the Territorial Council in 1860; secretary of the State senate in 1861; during the Civil War served as judge advocate, with the rank of major and lieutenant colonel, to Gen. George Deitzler, of the Kansas Volunteers; member of the State senate in 1862; unsuccessful candidate for Lieutenant Governor of Kansas in 1862 and 1864; edited the Atchison Champion 1863–1865 and aided in founding the Kansas Magazine; elected as a Republican to the United States Senate in 1872; reelected in 1879 and again in 1885 and served from March 4, 1873, to March 3, 1891; President pro tempore of the Senate from February 25, 1887, to February 19, 1891, when he resigned that office; unsuccessful candidate for reelection to the United States Senate in 1890; devoted his time to journalism, literature, and farming until his death in East Las Vegas, N. Mex., August 16, 1900; interment in Mount Vernon Cemetery, Atchison, Kans.

INGE, Samuel Williams (nephew of William Marshall Inge), a Representative from Alabama; born in Warren County, N. C., on February 22, 1817; moved to Greene County, Ala.; attended the public schools; studied law; was admitted to the bar and commenced the practice of law in Livingston, Sumter County, Ala.; member of the Alabama House of Representatives in 1844 and 1845; elected as a Democrat to the Thirtieth and Thirty-first Congresses (March 4, 1847–March 3, 1851); participated in a duel with Edward Stanly, a Representative from North Carolina, in Bladensburg, near Washington, D. C., but neither was seriously injured; resumed the practice of law; was appointed by President Franklin Pierce a United States attorney for the northern district of California on April 1, 1853; died in San Francisco, Calif., on June 10, 1868; interment in Mount Calvary Cemetery.

INGE, William Marshall (uncle of Samuel Williams Inge), a Representative from Tennessee; born in Granville County, N. C., in 1802; attended the schools of North Carolina; moved to Tennessee and continued his school studies; studied law; was admitted to the bar and practiced; elected as a Democrat to the Twenty-third Congress (March 4, 1833–March 3, 1835); moved to Livingston, Sumter County, Ala., in 1836; resumed the practice of his profession; member of the State house of representatives in 1840, 1844, and 1845; died in Livingston, Sumter County, Ala., in 1846; interment in Livingston Cemetery.

INGERSOLL, Charles Jared (son of Jared Ingersoll and brother of Joseph Reed Ingersoll), a Representative from Pennsylvania; born in Philadelphia, Pa., October 3, 1782; received an academic training; studied law; was admitted to the bar in 1802 and commenced practice in Philadelphia, Pa.; elected as a Democrat to the Thirteenth Congress (March 4, 1813–March 3, 1815); was not a candidate for renomination in 1814, having been appointed United States district attorney for Pennsylvania; United States district attorney for Pennsylvania 1815–1829; member of the State improvement convention in 1825; member of the State house of representatives in 1830; member of the State constitutional convention in 1837; appointed secretary of the legation to Prussia March 8, 1837; unsuccessful candidate in 1837 for election to fill the vacancy caused by the death of Francis J. Harper in the Twenty-fifth Congress; unsuccessful candidate for election in 1838 to the Twenty-sixth Congress; elected to the Twenty-seventh and to the three succeeding Congresses (March 4, 1841–March 3, 1849); was not a candidate for renomination in 1848; appointed

Minister to France in 1847 but was not confirmed by the Senate; appointed United States judge for the district of Connecticut April 8, 1853; died in Philadelphia, Pa., May 14, 1862; interment in the Woodlands Cemetery.

INGERSOLL, Colin Macrae (son of Ralph Isaacs Ingersoll), a Representative from Connecticut; born in New Haven, Conn., March 11, 1819; pursued academic studies and later attended Trinity College, Hartford, Conn.; was graduated from the law department of Yale College in 1839; was admitted to the bar in the same year and commenced practice in New Haven, Conn.; clerk of the State senate in 1843; secretary of the legation at St. Petersburg, by appointment of President Polk, in 1847 and 1848 and was Acting Chargé d'Affaires in 1848; elected as a Democrat to the Thirty-second and Thirty-third Congresses (March 4, 1851–March 3, 1855); resumed the practice of law; adjutant general of Connecticut 1867–1871; died in New Haven, Conn., September 13, 1903; interment in the Grove Street Cemetery.

INGERSOLL, Ebon Clark, a Representative from Illinois; born in Dresden, Yates County, N. Y., on December 12, 1831; moved to Wisconsin Territory in 1843 and subsequently to Illinois; pursued classical studies in Peoria, Ill., and in Paducah, Ky.; studied law; was admitted to the bar in 1854 and commenced practice in Peoria, Ill.; member of the State house of representatives in 1856; elected as a Republican to the Thirty-eighth Congress to fill the vacancy caused by the death of Owen Lovejoy; reelected to the Thirty-ninth, Fortieth, and Forty-first Congresses and served from May 20, 1864, to March 3, 1871; unsuccessful candidate for reelection in 1870 to the Forty-second Congress; settled in Washington, D. C., and engaged in the practice of law until his death there on May 31, 1879; interment in Oak Hill Cemetery.

INGERSOLL, Jared (father of Charles Jared Ingersoll and Joseph Reed Ingersoll), a Delegate from Pennsylvania; born in New Haven, Conn., October 24, 1749; received a classical education; was graduated from Yale College in 1766; settled in Philadelphia, Pa., in 1771; studied law, and was admitted to the bar in 1773; finished his legal education at the Middle Temple, London, England, in 1774, and then went to Paris in 1776; returned to Philadelphia in 1778 and commenced practice; Member of the Continental Congress in 1780 and 1781; delegate to the convention that framed the Federal Constitution in 1787; was the first attorney general of Pennsylvania 1790–1799 and served again from 1811 to 1817; United States district attorney for the eastern district of Pennsylvania; declined the appointment as judge of the Federal court in 1801; unsuccessful Federalist candidate for Vice President of the United States in 1812; presiding judge of the district court of Philadelphia County until his death in Philadelphia, Pa., October 31, 1822; interment in the First Presbyterian Church Cemetery, Fourth and Pine Streets.

INGERSOLL, Joseph Reed (son of Jared Ingersoll and brother of Charles Jared Ingersoll), a Representative from Pennsylvania; born in Philadelphia, Pa., June 14, 1786; pursued a classical course, and was graduated from Princeton College in 1804; studied law; was admitted to the bar and commenced practice in Philadelphia, Pa.; elected as a Whig to the Twenty-fourth Congress (March 4, 1835–March 3, 1837); declined to be a candidate for renomination in 1836; resumed the practice of law; elected to the Twenty-seventh Congress to fill the vacancy caused by the resignation of John Sergeant; reelected to the Twenty-eighth, Twenty-ninth, and Thirtieth Congresses and served from October 12, 1841, to March 3,

1849; declined to accept the nomination as a candidate for reelection in 1848 to the Thirty-first Congress; appointed Minister to Great Britain by President Fillmore and served from August 21, 1852, to August 23, 1853; retired from public life and engaged in literary pursuits; died in Philadelphia, Pa., February 20, 1868; interment in St. Peter's Protestant Episcopal Churchyard.

INGERSOLL, Ralph Isaacs (father of Colin Macrae Ingersoll), a Representative from Connecticut; born in New Haven, Conn., February 8, 1789; pursued classical studies, and was graduated from Yale College in 1808; studied law; was admitted to the bar in 1810 and commenced practice in New Haven; member of the State house of representatives 1820–1825 and served as speaker during the last two years; elected as a Democrat to the Nineteenth and to the three succeeding Congresses (March 4, 1825–March 3, 1833); was not a candidate for renomination in 1832; resumed the practice of law; appointed State's attorney for New Haven County in 1833; declined the appointment as United States Senator tendered by Governor Edwards upon the death of Senator Nathan Smith in 1835; Minister to Russia from August 8, 1846, until July 1, 1848, when he resigned; again engaged in the practice of law; mayor of New Haven in 1851; retired to private life in 1864; died in New Haven, Conn., August 26, 1872; interment in Grove Street Cemetery.

INGHAM, Samuel, a Representative from Connecticut; born in Hebron, Conn., September 5, 1793; attended the common schools in Vermont; studied law; was admitted to the bar in 1815 and commenced practice in Canaan, Vt.; moved to Jewett City, Conn., and subsequently, in 1819, to Essex (then part of Saybrook), Conn., and continued the practice of his profession; State's attorney for Middlesex County 1827–1835 and again in 1843 and 1844; member of the State house of representatives in 1828, 1834, 1851, and 1852 and served as speaker in 1851 and 1852; judge of probate 1829–1833; judge of the Middlesex County Court 1849–1853; elected as a Democrat to the Twenty-fourth and Twenty-fifth Congresses (March 4, 1835–March 3, 1839); unsuccessful candidate for reelection in 1838 to the Twenty-sixth Congress; served in the State senate 1843–1850; unsuccessful Democratic candidate for the United States Senate in 1854; United States commissioner of customs from December 5, 1857, to May 14, 1861; resumed the practice of law; died in Essex, Middlesex County, Conn., November 10, 1881; interment in River View Cemetery.

INGHAM, Samuel Delucenna, a Representative from Pennsylvania; born at Great Spring, near New Hope, Bucks County, Pa., September 16, 1779; pursued classical studies; engaged in the manufacture of paper; member of the State house of representatives 1806–1808; elected as a Jefferson Democrat to the Thirteenth, Fourteenth, and Fifteenth Congresses and served from March 4, 1813, until July 6, 1818, when he resigned; prothonotary of the courts of Bucks County in 1818 and 1819; served as secretary of the Commonwealth of Pennsylvania from October 1819 to December 1820; again elected to the Seventeenth Congress to fill the vacancy caused by the resignation of Samuel Moore; reelected to the Eighteenth and to the three succeeding Congresses and served from October 8, 1822, until his resignation in 1829, before the convening of the Twenty-first Congress; Secretary of the Treasury in the Cabinet of President Andrew Jackson from March 6, 1829, to June 21, 1831, when he resigned; resumed the manufacture of paper; also engaged in the development of anthracite coal fields; died in Trenton, N. J., on June 5, 1860; interment in the Solebury Presbyterian Churchyard, Solebury, Pa.

INOUYE, Daniel Ken, a Representative from Hawaii; born in Honolulu, Hawaii, September 7, 1924; attended the public schools of Honolulu; during World War II volunteered as a private in 1943 with the Four Hundred and Forty-second Infantry Regimental Combat Team; received a battlefield commission as a second lieutenant in 1944 and retired as a captain in 1947; awarded the Distinguished Service Cross, Bronze Star Medal, Purple Heart with Oak Leaf Cluster, Good Conduct Medal, Victory Medal, Asiatic Pacific Theater Medal, American Theater Medal, European Theater Medal with five battle stars, Occupation Medal (Japan), Combat Infantryman's Badge, Distinguished Unit Citation Ribbon with four clusters; graduated from the University of Hawaii in 1950 and from George Washington University Law School, Washington, D. C., in 1952; was admitted to the bar in 1953 and commenced practice in Honolulu; assistant public prosecutor in Honolulu in 1953 and 1954; served as majority leader in the Territorial house of representatives 1954–1958; member of the Territorial senate in 1958 and 1959; director, Central Pacific Bank, 1956–1960; delegate to the Democratic National Convention in 1956; upon the admission of Hawaii as a State into the Union was elected as a Democrat to the Eighty-sixth Congress for the term commencing August 21, 1959, and ending January 3, 1961. *Reelected to the Eighty-seventh Congress.*

IRBY, John Laurens Manning (great-grandson of Elias Earle), a Senator from South Carolina; born in Laurens, Laurens County, S. C., September 10, 1854; attended Laurensville Male Academy, Laurens, S. C., Princeton College, Princeton, N. J., in 1870 and 1871, and the University of Virginia at Charlottesville 1871–1873; studied law; was admitted to the bar in 1875 and commenced practice at Cheraw, Chesterfield County, S. C., but soon returned to Laurens; appointed lieutenant colonel of the South Carolina Militia in 1877; intendant of Laurens in 1877; member of the State house of representatives in 1886, 1888, and 1890, serving as speaker in 1890; chairman of the State Democratic executive committee in 1890; elected as a Democrat to the United States Senate and served from March 4, 1891, to March 3, 1897; was not a candidate for reelection; subsequently an unsuccessful candidate for election to the United States Senate in August 1897 to fill the vacancy caused by the death of Senator Joseph H. Earle; delegate at large from South Carolina to the Democratic National Convention at Chicago in 1892; delegate to the State constitutional convention in 1895; resumed the practice of law in Laurens, S. C., and also engaged in agricultural pursuits; died in Laurens, S. C., on December 9, 1900; interment in the City Cemetery.

IREDELL, James, a Senator from North Carolina; born in Edenton, Chowan County, N. C., November 2, 1788; attended Edenton Academy, and was graduated from Princeton College in 1806; studied law; was admitted to the bar in 1809 and commenced practice in Edenton; during the War of 1812 served as captain of a company of Volunteers and went to the defense of Norfolk, Va.; member of the State house of commons in 1813 and 1816–1828 and served as speaker 1817–1828; appointed judge of the superior court of North Carolina in March and resigned in May 1819; Governor of North Carolina in 1828; elected as a Democrat to the United States Senate to fill the vacancy caused by the resignation of Nathaniel Macon and served from December 15, 1828, to March 3, 1831; was not a candidate for reelection; moved to Raleigh in 1830; resumed the practice of law; reporter of the supreme court of North Carolina 1840–1852; commissioner to revise the State laws in 1836 and 1837; died while on a visit to Edenton, N. C., April 13, 1853; interment in the Johnston Burial Ground on the Hayes plantation at Edenton.

IRELAND, Clifford Cady, a Representative from Illinois; born in Washburn, Woodford County, Ill., February 14, 1878; attended the common schools, Cheltenham Military Academy, Ogontz, Pa., and Knox College, Galesburg, Ill.; was graduated from the University of Wisconsin at Madison in 1901 and from the Illinois College of Law at Chicago in 1908; was admitted to the bar in 1909 and commenced practice in Peoria; served as a private in the Illinois National Guard during the Spanish-American War; member of the Illinois Bar Association; president of the Western Live Stock Insurance Co.; elected as a Republican to the Sixty-fifth, Sixty-sixth, and Sixty-seventh Congresses (March 4, 1917–March 3, 1923); unsuccessful candidate for renomination in 1922; resumed the practice of law at Peoria; appointed a director of the department of trade and commerce of Illinois in 1923, serving until his resignation in 1926; died while on a visit in Chicago, Ill., May 24, 1930; interment in Linn-Mount Vernon Cemetery, Washburn, Ill.

IRION, Alfred Briggs, a Representative from Louisiana; born near Evergreen, Avoyelles Parish, La., February 18, 1833; attended the common schools, Franklin College, Opelousas, La., and was graduated from the University of North Carolina at Chapel Hill in 1855; studied law; was admitted to the bar in 1857 and commenced practice in Marksville, La.; delegate to the State secession convention in 1860 and was opposed to secession; during the Civil War served in the Confederate Army, being attached to General Walker's division under Colonel Randall; member of the State house of representatives in 1864 and 1865; resumed the practice of his profession; editor of a local newspaper in Marksville, La., 1866–1874; moved to Evergreen, La., in 1870 and engaged in planting; continued the practice of law and also engaged in literary pursuits; member of the State constitutional convention in 1879; judge of the third circuit court of appeals of Louisiana 1880–1884; elected as a Democrat to the Forty-ninth Congress (March 4, 1885–March 3, 1887); unsuccessful candidate for renomination; discontinued active pursuits and lived on his plantation near Eola, La.; died at the home of his son in New Orleans, La., May 21, 1903; interment in the Baptist Cemetery, Evergreen, La.

IRVIN, Alexander, a Representative from Pennsylvania; born in Penns Valley, Center County, Pa., January 18, 1800; attended the public schools; moved to Curwensville in 1820 and to Clearfield, Pa., in 1826; engaged in mercantile and lumbering pursuits; treasurer of Clearfield County 1828–1830; member of the State senate in 1837 and 1838; prothonotary of the court of common pleas in 1842; clerk of the several courts; recorder of deeds and register of wills of Clearfield County 1842–1844; elected as a Whig to the Thirtieth Congress (March 4, 1847–March 3, 1849); was not a candidate for renomination; United States marshal for the western district of Pennsylvania from January 17 to September 3, 1850, when he resigned, being succeeded by his brother, William Irvin; delegate to the Republican National Convention at Cincinnati in 1872; engaged in mercantile pursuits at Clearfield, Clearfield County, Pa., until his death on March 20, 1874; interment in the Reed addition to the Old Graveyard.

IRVIN, James, a Representative from Pennsylvania; born in Linden Hall, Center County, Pa., February 18, 1800; attended the common schools; became engaged in mercantile pursuits, milling, mining, and manufacturing in Oak Hill, Milesburg, and Bellefonte, Pa.; elected as a Whig to the Twenty-seventh and Twenty-eighth Congresses (March 4, 1841–March 3, 1845); unsuccessful Whig candidate for Governor of Pennsylvania in 1847; United States naval storekeeper at Philadelphia in 1857; died in Hecla, Schuylkill County, Pa., on November 28, 1862; interment in the Union Cemetery, Bellefonte, Pa.

IRVIN, William W., a Representative from Ohio; born near Charlottesville, Albemarle County, Va., about 1778; pursued an academic course; studied law; was admitted to the bar in 1800 and commenced practice in his native county; moved to Lancaster, Ohio, about 1801 and continued the practice of his profession; appointed an associate judge of the court of common pleas for Fairfield County by the first general assembly in 1803; was impeached in 1804 by the State house of representatives and subsequently removed from office by the decision of the senate; member of the State house of representatives in 1806 and 1807; justice of the State supreme court 1810–1815; again a member of the State house of representatives 1825–1827 and served as speaker in 1825 and 1826; elected as a Democrat to the Twenty-first and Twenty-second Congresses (March 4, 1829–March 3, 1833); was an unsuccessful candidate for reelection in 1832 to the Twenty-third Congress; returned to his farm near Lancaster, Ohio, and engaged in agricultural pursuits until his death March 28, 1842.

IRVINE, William, a Delegate and a Representative from Pennsylvania; born in County Fermanagh, Ulster, Ireland, on November 3, 1741; pursued classical studies and was graduated from the Dublin University; studied medicine and was admitted to practice; served as surgeon on a British man-of-war; immigrated to the United States and settled in Carlisle, Pa., in 1763; delegate to the State Revolutionary conventions 1764–1766; colonel of the Sixth Pennsylvania Regiment in the Revolutionary Army; captured in Canada June 16, 1776, and remained a prisoner of war until exchanged May 6, 1778; appointed brigadier general May 12, 1779, and served until the close of the war; Member of the Continental Congress 1786–1788; commanded the State troops during the Whisky Rebellion in 1794; elected to the Third Congress (March 4, 1793–March 3, 1795); moved to Philadelphia, where he was superintendent of military stores 1801–1804; died in Philadelphia, Pa., July 29, 1804.

IRVINE, William, a Representative from New York; born in Whitneys Point, Broome County, N. Y., February 14, 1820; attended the common schools; moved to Greene County, N. Y., in 1841; studied law; was admitted to the bar in 1849 and commenced practice in Corning, Steuben County, N. Y.; elected as a Republican to the Thirty-sixth Congress (March 4, 1859–March 3, 1861); during the Civil War assisted in raising the Tenth Regiment, New York Volunteer Cavalry, of which he became lieutenant colonel November 25, 1861; was wounded at the Battle of Beverly Ford, Virginia, where he was taken prisoner and confined in Libby Prison for several months; honorably discharged on December 6, 1864; brevetted colonel and brigadier general of Volunteers March 13, 1865, "for faithful and meritorious service"; adjutant general on the staff of Governor Fenton in 1865 and 1866; moved to California and continued the practice of his profession until his death in San Francisco, Calif., November 12, 1882; interment in the Elmira Cemetery, Elmira, N. Y.

IRVING, Theodore Leonard, a Representative from Missouri; born in St. Paul, Ramsey County, Minn., March 24, 1898; moved with his parents to a farm in North Dakota; attended the public schools of North Dakota; started working at the age of thirteen, during summer vacation, as a railroad call boy and advanced to position of assistant passenger agent; served as a key transportation official during the First World War; left the railroad to become manager of a theater in Montana; moved to California and was manager of a hotel; moved to Jackson County, Mo., in 1934 and was employed as a construction worker and later became a representative of the American Federation of Labor; elected as a Democrat to the Eighty-first and Eighty-second Congresses (January 3, 1949–January 3, 1953); unsuccessful candidate for reelection in 1952 to the Eighty-third Congress; defeated for Democratic nomination in 1954 to the Eighty-fourth Congress; labor organizer; is a resident of Independence, Mo.

IRVING, William, a Representative from New York; born in New York City August 15, 1766; completed preparatory studies; engaged in mercantile pursuits and also in fur trade with the Indians along the Mohawk River, residing at Johnstown and Caughnawaga, N. Y.; returned to New York City in 1793; elected as a Democrat to the Thirteenth Congress to fill the vacancy caused by the resignation of Egbert Benson; reelected to the Fourteenth and Fifteenth Congresses and served from January 22, 1814, to March 3, 1819; contributed several essays and poems to Salmagundi, published by his brother, Washington Irving; died in New York City on November 9, 1821.

IRWIN, Donald J., a Representative from Connecticut; born of American parents in Argentina September 7, 1926; came to the United States in 1945 to attend Yale University; entered the United States Army and served with the Joint Brazil-United States Military Commission in Rio de Janeiro; reentered Yale University and graduated in 1951 and also from Yale Law School in 1954; was admitted to the bar and commenced the practice of law in Connecticut; taught Spanish at Yale University while a student there; member of Norwalk Board of Education; adviser to Roodner Public Court Housing Development; received distinguished service award of United States Chamber of Commerce in 1957; elected as a Democrat to the Eighty-sixth Congress (January 3, 1959–January 3, 1961); unsuccessful candidate for reelection in 1960 to the Eighty-seventh Congress; appointed general counsel, United States Information Agency, in February 1961; resides in Washington, D. C.

IRWIN, Edward Michael, a Representative from Illinois; born near Leasburg, Crawford County, Mo., on April 14, 1869; attended the public schools of his native city; taught school in Leasburg, Mo.; attended the University of Missouri at Columbia; was graduated from Missouri Medical College at St. Louis in 1892; moved to New Athens, St. Clair County, Ill., in the same year and commenced the practice of medicine; chairman of the Republican county central committee 1898–1924; moved to Belleville, St. Clair County, Ill., in 1903 and continued the practice of medicine; coroner of St. Clair County 1904–1908; elected president of the Belleville Bank & Trust Co. in 1910; in 1917 and 1918, during the First World War, served as medical member of the draft board for district No. 2 in St. Clair County, Ill.; delegate to the Republican National Convention at Chicago in 1920; elected as a Republican to the Sixty-ninth, Seventieth, and Seventy-first Congresses (March 4, 1925–March 3, 1931); unsuccessful candidate for reelection in 1930 to the Seventy-second Congress; resumed the practice of his profession; died in Belleville, Ill., January 30, 1933; interment in Green Mount Cemetery.

IRWIN, Harvey Samuel, a Representative from Kentucky; born in Highland County, Ohio, December 10, 1844; attended the public schools; was graduated from the high school of Greenfield, Ohio; studied law, but abandoned the same to enlist in the Union Army during the Civil War; assisted in raising a regiment of Artillery and was commissioned a lieutenant; transferred to a special corps in the Regular Army, in which he served until the close of the war; settled in Louisville, Ky.; resumed the study of law; was admitted to the bar and practiced; appointed successively assistant internal-revenue assessor, deputy clerk of the United States district court, and chief deputy collector of the fifth internal-revenue district of Kentucky; railroad commissioner in 1895; elected as a Republican to the Fifty-seventh Congress (March 4, 1901–March 3, 1903); unsuccessful candidate for reelection in 1902; resumed the practice of law in Washington, D. C.; was licensed as an evangelist in Washington, D. C., in 1913; had a charge in Idylwood and Vienna, Va.; died in Vienna, Va., September 3, 1916; interment in Cave Hill Cemetery, Louisville, Ky.

IRWIN, Jared, a Representative from Pennsylvania; born in Georgia on January 19, 1768; appointed commissioner for valuation of lands and dwellings and enumeration of slaves for the second division of Georgia on July 17, 1798; engaged in mercantile pursuits at Milton, Pa.; served as postmaster of Milton, Pa., from June 1, 1802, to June 29, 1803; sheriff of Northumberland County 1808–1812; member of the State house of representatives in 1811; served as colonel of the Fifth Rifle Regiment in the War of 1812; elected as a Democrat to the Thirteenth and Fourteenth Congresses (March 4, 1813–March 3, 1817); moved to South America.

IRWIN, Thomas, a Representative from Pennsylvania; born in Philadelphia, Pa., February 22, 1785; attended the common schools and Franklin College, Lancaster, Pa.; became editor of the Philadelphia Repository in 1804; studied law; was admitted to the bar in 1808 and commenced practice in Uniontown, Pa.; appointed Indian agent at Natchitoches, La., where he also engaged in the practice of law for two years; returned to Uniontown, Pa., in 1811 and resumed the practice of law; member of the State house of representatives 1824–1828; elected as a Democrat to the Twenty-first Congress (March 4, 1829–March 3, 1831); was not a candidate for renomination in 1830; appointed a United States judge for the western district of Pennsylvania April 14, 1831, and served until February 8, 1859, when a successor was appointed; lived in retirement until his death in Pittsburgh, Pa., May 14, 1870; interment in Allegheny Cemetery.

IRWIN, William Wallace, a Representative from Pennsylvania; born in Pittsburgh, Pa., in 1803; attended a private school in Pittsburgh and Allegheny College, Meadville, Pa.; studied law; was admitted to the bar in 1828 and commenced practice in Pittsburgh; mayor of Pittsburgh in 1840; elected as a Whig to the Twenty-seventh Congress (March 4, 1841–March 3, 1843); was not a candidate for reelection in 1842; Chargé d'Affaires to Denmark from March 3, 1843, to June 12, 1847; died in Pittsburgh, Pa., September 15, 1856; interment in Allegheny Cemetery.

ISACKS, Jacob C., a Representative from Tennessee; born in Montgomery County, Pa.; moved to Winchester, Tenn.; elected to the Eighteenth and to the four succeeding Congresses (March 4, 1823–March 3, 1833); unsuccessful candidate for reelection in 1832; died in Winchester, Tenn.

ISACSON, Leo, a Representative from New York; born in New York City, N. Y., April 20, 1910; attended the public schools; was graduated from New York University in 1931 and from the law department of the same university in 1933; was admitted to the bar in 1934 and commenced practice in New York City; member of the State assembly in 1945 and 1946; elected as an American Laborite to the Eightieth Congress to fill the vacancy caused by the resignation of Benjamin J. Rabin and served from February 17, 1948, to January 3, 1949; unsuccessful candidate for reelection in 1948 to the Eighty-first Congress; resumed the practice of law; is a resident of New York City, N. Y.

ITTNER, Anthony Friday, a Representative from Missouri; born in Lebanon, Warren County, Ohio, October 8, 1837; moved to St. Louis, Mo., with his parents in 1844; attended the common

schools for twelve months; went to work at the age of nine; learned the bricklaying trade and at the age of twenty-one started in that business; later engaged in the manufacture of brick; member of the Enrolled Missouri Militia; member of the city council of St. Louis, Mo., in 1867 and 1868; member of the State house of representatives 1868–1870; served in the State senate from 1870 until November 1876, when he resigned; elected as a Republican to the Forty-fifth Congress (March 4, 1877–March 3, 1879); declined to be a candidate for renomination in 1878; resumed the manufacture of brick; president of the National Association of Builders and of the National Brick Manufacturers' Association; retired from active business in 1917 and resided in St. Louis, Mo., until his death there on February 22, 1931; interment in Bellefontaine Cemetery.

IVERSON, Alfred, Sr., a Representative and a Senator from Georgia; born in Waynesboro, Burke County, Ga., December 3, 1798; attended private schools in Burke and Putnam Counties, Ga., and was graduated from Princeton College in 1820; studied law; was admitted to the bar in 1822 and commenced practice in Clinton, Jones County, Ga.; member of the State house of representatives 1827–1830; moved to Columbus, Muscogee County, Ga., in 1830 and continued the practice of law; served as judge of the State superior court 1835–1837; member of the State senate in 1843 and 1844; presidential elector on the Democratic ticket of Polk and Dallas in 1844; elected as a Democrat to the Thirtieth Congress (March 4, 1847–March 3, 1849); again served as judge of the State superior court 1849–1853; elected to the United States Senate and served from March 4, 1855, to January 28, 1861, when he withdrew; resumed the practice of law in Columbus, Ga., until 1868, when he purchased a plantation in East Macon, Ga., and engaged in agricultural pursuits until his death there on March 5, 1873; interment in Linwood Cemetery, Columbus, Ga.

IVES, Irving McNeil, a Senator from New York; born in Bainbridge, Chenango County, N. Y., January 24, 1896; attended the public schools; was graduated from Hamilton College, Clinton, N. Y., in 1920; during the First World War served with the United States Army 1917–1919, with overseas service in France and Germany; discharged as first lieutenant, Infantry; engaged in the banking business in New York 1920–1930, and general insurance at Norwich, N. Y., since 1933; member New York State Assembly 1930–1946, minority leader in 1935, speaker in 1936, and majority leader 1937–1946; chairman of New York State Temporary Commission Against Discrimination in 1944 and 1945; member of the board of trustees of Hamilton College and Cornell University; member of the board of temporary trustees New York State School of Industrial and Labor Relations in 1944 and 1945, and dean of school 1945–1947; elected as a Republican to the United States Senate in 1946, reelected in 1952, and served from January 3, 1947, to January 3, 1959; was not a candidate for renomination in 1958; unsuccessful candidate for election as Governor of New York in 1954; retired; resides in Norwich, N. Y.

IVES, Willard, a Representative from New York; born in Watertown, Jefferson County, N. Y., July 7, 1806; attended the common schools, also Belleville (N. Y.) Academy, and Lowville (N. Y.) Academy; engaged in agricultural pursuits and was also interested in banking; member of the State house of representatives in 1829 and 1830; delegate to the world convention of Methodists held in London, England, in 1846; unsuccessful candidate for election to the Thirtieth Congress in 1848; elected as a Democrat to the Thirty-second Congress (March 4, 1851–March 3, 1853); president of Ives Seminary, Antwerp, N. Y., which he endowed; one of the originators and organizers of

Syracuse University and served on the board of trustees 1870–1886; resumed agricultural pursuits; died in Watertown, N. Y., April 19, 1896; interment in Brookside Cemetery.

IZAC, Edouard Victor Michel, a Representative from California; born in Cresco, Howard County, Iowa, December 18, 1891; attended the School of the Assumption, Cresco, Iowa, the high school at South St. Paul, Minn., and Werntz Preparatory School, Annapolis, Md.; was graduated from the United States Naval Academy at Annapolis, Md., in 1915; served in the United States Navy as ensign, lieutenant (jg), and senior lieutenant until forced to retire in 1921 on account of wounds received while a prisoner of war in Germany; awarded Congressional Medal of Honor, the Croce di Guerra of Italy, and the Cross of Montenegro; located in San Diego, Calif., and engaged in newspaper work and writing 1922–1928; unsuccessful candidate for election in 1934 to the Seventy-fourth Congress; delegate to the Democratic National Conventions in 1940 and 1944; elected as a Democrat to the Seventy-fifth and to the four succeeding Congresses (January 3, 1937–January 3, 1947); unsuccessful candidate for reelection in 1946 to the Eightieth Congress; interested in lumbering and the raising of thoroughbred cattle; retired; resides in Washington, D. C.

IZARD, Ralph, a Delegate and a Senator from South Carolina; born at "The Elms," near Charleston, S. C., January 23, 1742; pursued classical studies in Hackney, England, and was graduated from Christ College, Cambridge, England; returned to America, but went abroad to reside, taking up his residence in London in 1771; moved to Paris, France, in 1776; appointed commissioner to the Court of Tuscany by the Continental Congress on December 30, 1776, but was recalled in 1779; pledged his large estate in South Carolina for the payment of warships to be used in the Revolutionary War; Member of the Continental Congress in 1782 and 1783; elected to the United States Senate and served from March 4, 1789, to March 3, 1795; President pro tempore of the Senate from May 31, 1794, to February 20, 1795; founded the College of Charleston; retired from public life to the care of his estates; died near Charleston, Charleston County, S. C., May 30, 1804; interment in the churchyard of St. James Goose Creek Episcopal Church, near Charleston, S. C.

IZLAR, James Ferdinand, a Representative from South Carolina; born near Orangeburg, Orangeburg County, S. C., November 25, 1832; attended the common schools; was graduated from Emory College, Oxford, Ga., in 1855; studied law; was admitted to the bar in 1858 and commenced practice in South Carolina; served as an officer in the Confederate Army during the Civil War; resumed the practice of law in Orangeburg, S. C.; member of the State senate 1880–1890; elected by the general assembly judge of the first judicial circuit in 1889; delegate to the Democratic National Convention at Chicago in 1884; elected as a Democrat to the Fifty-third Congress to fill the vacancy caused by the resignation of William H. Brawley and served from April 12, 1894, to March 3, 1895; was not a candidate for renomination in 1894; again engaged in the practice of law in Orangeburg until 1907, when he retired; died in Orangeburg, S. C., May 26, 1912; interment in the Episcopal Cemetery.

J

JACK, Summers Melville, a Representative from Pennsylvania; born in Summersville, Jefferson County, Pa., July 18, 1852; attended the public and private schools of Jefferson County and the Indiana Normal School (now State Teachers College) of Pennsylvania; taught school for six years; studied law; was ad-

mitted to the bar in 1879 and commenced practice in Indiana, Pa.; district attorney for Indiana County 1884–1890; appointed member of the board of trustees of the Indiana Normal School in 1886 and by reappointment served more than forty years; chairman of the congressional conference for the twenty-first district in 1896; elected as a Republican to the Fifty-sixth and Fifty-seventh Congresses (March 4, 1899–March 3, 1903); was not a candidate for renomination in 1902; member of the delegation of Senators and Representatives sent to the Philippine Islands in 1901 to inquire into the advisability of establishing civil government; resumed the practice of law; delegate to the Republican National Convention at Chicago in 1908; died in Indiana, Pa., September 16, 1945; interment in the Oakland Cemetery, Indiana, Pa.

JACK, William, a Representative from Pennsylvania; born in Greensburg, Westmoreland County, Pa., July 29, 1788; studied law; was admitted to the bar and practiced; moved to Brookville, Jefferson County, Pa., in 1831 and engaged in mercantile pursuits; division inspector of militia for Westmoreland and Fayette Counties 1830–1835; sheriff of Brookville in 1833; was a contractor and builder in Mississippi and assisted in the construction of a canal in that State; returned to Pennsylvania; county judge of Jefferson County about 1840; elected as a Democrat to the Twenty-seventh Congress (March 4, 1841–March 3, 1843); engaged in agricultural pursuits; returned to Greensburg, Pa., in 1846 and died there on February 28, 1852; interment in the Old Cemetery of the St. Clair Cemetery Association.

JACKSON, Alfred Metcalf, a Representative from Kansas; born in South Carrollton, Muhlenberg County, Ky., July 14, 1860; attended the common schools and West Kentucky College; studied law; was admitted to the bar and practiced; moved to Howard, Elk County, Kans., in 1881 and engaged in the practice of law; prosecuting attorney of Elk County in 1890; judge of the thirteenth judicial district of Kansas in 1892; moved to Winfield, Kans., in 1898; elected as a Democrat to the Fifty-seventh Congress (March 4, 1901–March 3, 1903); unsuccessful candidate for reelection in 1902; resumed the practice of law in Winfield, Kans., and died there on June 11, 1924; interment in the Highland Mausoleum.

JACKSON, Amos Henry, a Representative from Ohio; born near Franklin, Delaware County, N. Y., May 10, 1846; moved with his parents to Gibson, Steuben County, N. Y., in 1854 and to a farm near Corning, Steuben County, N. Y., in 1862; attended the common schools; moved to Ohio in 1866; employed as a carpenter for several years and then engaged in selling notions from a wagon; settled in Fremont, Sandusky County, Ohio, in 1882 and engaged in the retail dry goods and shoe business and later engaged in the manufacture of muslin and flannelette garments and knives and shears; mayor of Fremont 1897–1901; elected as a Republican to the Fifty-eighth Congress (March 4, 1903–March 3, 1905); was not a candidate for renomination in 1904; resumed manufacturing interests in Fremont, Ohio, until 1922 when he retired from active business pursuits; died in Fremont, Ohio, on August 30, 1924; interment in Oakwood Cemetery.

JACKSON, Andrew, a Representative and a Senator from Tennessee and a President of the United States; born in such obscurity on March 15, 1767, that two States have claimed his birthplace, though he himself stated that he had been told it was in the Waxhaw settlement in South Carolina; attended the "old field" school and the academy of Doctor Humphries; during the Revolution was captured by the British and confined in the stockade at Camden, S. C.; left an orphan at fourteen years of age; worked for a time in a saddler's shop and afterward taught school; studied law in Salisbury, N. C.; was admitted to the bar in 1787 and commenced practice in McLeanville, Guilford County, N. C.; appointed solicitor of the western district of North Carolina, comprising what is now the State of Tennessee, in 1788 and located in Nashville, Tenn., in October 1788; delegate to the convention to frame a constitution for the new State, held in Knoxville in January 1796; upon the admission of Tennessee as a State into the Union was elected as a Democrat to the Fourth Congress and served from December 5, 1796, to March 3, 1797; elected to the United States Senate for the term commencing March 4, 1797, and served from September 26, 1797, until his resignation in April 1798; elected judge of the State supreme court of Tennessee and served from 1798 to July 24, 1804; moved to the "Hermitage," near Nashville, and engaged in planting and in mercantile pursuits; served in the Creek War of 1813; major general of Volunteers 1812–1814; commissioned brigadier general in the United States Army April 19, 1814; major general May 1, 1814; led his army to New Orleans, where he defeated the British January 8, 1815; received the thanks of Congress and a gold medal by resolution of February 27, 1815; commanded an expedition which captured Florida in 1817; Governor of Florida from March 10 to July 18, 1821; declined the position of Minister to Mexico; again elected to the United States Senate and served from March 4, 1823, to October 14, 1825, when he resigned; unsuccessful Democratic candidate for President in 1824; elected President of the United States in 1828; reelected in 1832 and served from March 4, 1829, to March 3, 1837; retired to his country home, the "Hermitage," near Nashville, Tenn., where he died June 8, 1845; interment in the garden on his estate.

JACKSON, David, a Delegate from Pennsylvania; born in Newtown-Limavady, County Londonderry, Ireland, about 1730; immigrated to the United States and settled in Edenton, Chester County, Pa.; attended Nottingham Academy at West Nottingham Township; was graduated from the medical department of the University of Pennsylvania in 1768 and was an apothecary and physician in Philadelphia, Pa., 1768–1801; during the Revolutionary War was appointed paymaster of the Second Battalion of Philadelphia Militia December 3, 1776; quartermaster of militia in the field October 23, 1779; hospital physician and surgeon September 30, 1780; lost an arm at the Battle of Trenton; was present at the surrender of Lord Cornwallis, Yorktown, Va., October 19, 1781; Member of the Continental Congress in 1785 and 1786; resumed the profession of apothecary, in addition to the practice of medicine; died in Oxford, Pa., September 17, 1801; interment in the Oxford Cemetery.

JACKSON, David Sherwood, a Representative from New York; born in New York City in 1813; attended the public schools; alderman in the common council of New York City 1843–1846; engaged in mercantile pursuits; presented credentials as a Democratic Member-elect to the Thirtieth Congress and served from March 4, 1847, until April 19, 1848, when the House declared the seat vacant, the election having been contested by James Monroe; resumed his former business pursuits; again an alderman in the common council in 1856 and 1857; died in New York City January 20, 1872; interment in the Marble Cemetery.

JACKSON, Donald Lester, a Representative from California; born in Ipswich, Edmunds County, S. Dak., January 23, 1910; attended the public schools of South Dakota and California; served as a private in the United States Marine Corps 1927–1931 and again during World War II from 1940 until discharged as a major in 1945 with two years' combat service overseas; engaged in public relations as a profession in Santa Monica, Calif.;

reporter and editor, Santa Monica, 1938–1940; director of publicity, city of Santa Monica, Calif., in 1939 and 1940; congressional adviser at ninth conference of American States at Bogotá, Colombia, in 1948; elected as a Republican to the Eightieth and to the six succeeding Congresses (January 3, 1947–January 3, 1961); was not a candidate for renomination in 1960; is a resident of Pacific Palisades, Calif.

JACKSON, Ebenezer, Jr., a Representative from Connecticut; born in Savannah, Ga., January 31, 1796; pursued academic studies; was graduated from St. Mary's College, near Baltimore, Md., in 1814; studied law at the Litchfield Law School, Connecticut; was admitted to the bar and commenced practice in Philadelphia, Pa., in 1821; moved to Middletown, Conn., in 1826; member of the State house of representatives 1829–1832; elected as a Whig to the Twenty-third Congress to fill the vacancy caused by the resignation of Samuel A. Foote and served from December 1, 1834, to March 3, 1835; unsuccessful candidate for reelection in 1834 to the Twenty-fourth Congress; again a member of the State house of representatives in 1849; withdrew from political life; died in Middletown, Middlesex County, Conn., August 17, 1874; interment in Indian Hill Cemetery.

JACKSON, Edward Brake (son of George Jackson and brother of John George Jackson), a Representative from Virginia; born in Clarksburg, Harrison County, Va. (now West Virginia), January 25, 1793; attended Randolph Academy at Clarksburg; studied medicine and commenced practice in Clarksburg; during the War of 1812 was detailed surgeon's mate, Third Regular Virginia Militia, at Fort Meigs, Ohio; member of the State house of delegates 1815–1818; clerk of the United States district court in 1819; elected as a Democrat to the Sixteenth Congress to fill the vacancy caused by the resignation of James Pindall; reelected to the Seventeenth Congress and served from October 23, 1820, to March 3, 1823; declined to be a candidate for renomination in 1822; died at Bedford Springs, near Bedford, Pa., September 8, 1826; interment near Bedford, Pa.

JACKSON, Fred Schuyler, a Representative from Kansas; born in Stanton, Miami County, Kans., April 19, 1868; moved to Greenwood County, Kans., with his parents in 1881; attended the public schools of Miami and Greenwood Counties; taught school in Kansas 1885–1890; was graduated in law from the University of Kansas at Lawrence in 1892; was admitted to the bar and commenced practice in Eureka, Kans.; prosecuting attorney of Greenwood County 1893–1897; assistant State attorney general in 1906 and 1907; attorney general 1907–1911; elected as a Republican to the Sixty-second Congress (March 4, 1911–March 3, 1913); unsuccessful candidate for reelection in 1912 to the Sixty-third Congress; resumed the practice of law in Eureka and Topeka, Kans.; moved to Topeka, Kans., in 1915, having been appointed attorney for the Public Utilities Commission of Kansas and served until 1924; resumed the practice of law in Topeka, Kans.; also was an extensive land owner and engaged in agricultural pursuits and stock raising in Greenwood, Wabaunsee, and Jefferson Counties; died in Topeka, Kans., November 21, 1931; interment in Greenwood Cemetery, Eureka, Kans.

JACKSON, George (father of John George Jackson and Edward Brake Jackson), a Representative from Virginia; born in Cecil County, Md., January 9, 1757; moved with his parents to Moorefield, Va. (now West Virginia), and in 1769 to Jacksons Fort, Va. (now Buckhannon, W. Va.); served in the Revolution, attaining the rank of colonel; studied law; was admitted to the bar in 1784 and commenced practice in Clarksburg, Va. (now

West Virginia); justice of the peace in 1784; member of the State house of delegates 1785–1791 and again in 1794; member of the State convention which ratified the United States Constitution in 1788; elected to the Fourth Congress (March 4, 1795–March 3, 1797); elected to the Sixth and Seventh Congresses (March 4, 1799–March 3, 1803); was not a candidate for reelection; moved to Zanesville, Ohio, about 1806 and engaged in agricultural pursuits; member of the State house of representatives 1809–1812; member of the State senate 1817–1819; died in Zanesville, Ohio, May 17, 1831; interment on an estate once owned by him in Falls Township, near Zanesville.

JACKSON, Henry Martin, a Representative and a Senator from Washington; born in Everett, Snohomish County, Wash., May 31, 1912; attended the public schools and Stanford University, Stanford, Calif.; was graduated from the law school of the University of Washington at Seattle in 1935; was admitted to the bar the same year and commenced practice in Everett, Wash.; prosecuting attorney of Snohomish County 1938–1940; attended the International Maritime Conference in Copenhagen, Denmark, in November 1945 as adviser to the American delegation; elected president of the International Maritime Conference, held in Seattle, Wash., in June 1946; elected as a Democrat to the Seventy-seventh and to the five succeeding Congresses (January 3, 1941–January 3, 1953); did not seek renomination in 1952, but was elected to the United States Senate for the term commencing January 3, 1953; reelected in 1958 for the term ending January 3, 1965; chairman of the Democratic National Committee in 1960.

JACKSON, Howell Edmunds, a Senator from Tennessee; born in Paris, Henry County, Tenn., April 8, 1832; moved with his parents to Jackson, Tenn., in 1840; pursued classical studies, and was graduated from West Tennessee College in 1849, from the University of Virginia at Charlottesville in 1854, and from the law department of Cumberland University, Lebanon, Tenn., in 1856; was admitted to the bar and commenced practice in Jackson; moved to Memphis, Tenn., in 1859 and engaged in the practice of law; returned to Jackson in 1874 and served on the court of arbitration for west Tennessee by appointment on two occasions; member of the State house of representatives in 1880; elected as a Democrat to the United States Senate and served from March 4, 1881, until April 14, 1886, when he resigned; appointed United States circuit judge for the sixth Federal circuit April 12, 1886, and served until February 4, 1893; appointed Associate Justice of the United States Supreme Court to fill the vacancy caused by the death of Lucius Q. C. Lamar; took his seat March 4, 1894, and served until his death in West Meade, Tenn., August 8, 1895; interment in Mount Olivet Cemetery, Nashville, Tenn.

JACKSON, Jabez Young (son of Senator James Jackson and uncle of Representative James Jackson), a Representative from Georgia; born in Savannah, Ga., in July 1790; resided at Clarkesville; elected as a Union Democrat to the Twenty-fourth Congress to fill the vacancy caused by the resignation of James M. Wayne; reelected to the Twenty-fifth Congress and served from October 5, 1835, to March 3, 1839; retired from public life; died in Clarkesville, Habersham County, Ga.

JACKSON, James (father of Jabez Y. Jackson and grandfather of James Jackson), a Representative and a Senator from Georgia; born in Moreton-Hampstead, Devonshire, England, September 21, 1757; came to Georgia in 1772 and located in Savannah; clerk of the court, by election of the Provincial Congress, in 1776 and 1777; member of the first constitutional convention of Georgia in 1777; elected Governor in 1778 but declined;

entered the Revolutionary Army as captain and commander of the Georgia Legionary Forces in 1781; received the keys to Savannah from the British July 12, 1782; presented with a house in Savannah by the Assembly of the State of Georgia; elected to the First Congress (March 4, 1789–March 3, 1791); contested the election of Anthony Wayne in the Second Congress and the seat was declared vacant by the House March 21, 1792; elected to the United States Senate and served from March 4, 1793, until his resignation in 1795; Democratic presidential elector in 1797 and voted for Jefferson and Clinton; Governor of Georgia 1798–1801; was again elected to the United States Senate and served from March 4, 1801, until his death in Washington, D. C., March 19, 1806; interment in the Congressional Cemetery.

JACKSON, James (grandson of the preceding and nephew of Jabez Y. Jackson), a Representative from Georgia; born in Jefferson County, Ga., on October 18, 1819; pursued classical studies, and was graduated from the University of Georgia at Athens in 1837; studied law; was admitted to the bar in 1839 and commenced practice in Athens, Ga.; secretary of the State senate in 1842; elected to the State house of representatives in 1845 and 1847; judge of the superior court 1846–1859; resigned in June 1859; elected as a Democrat to the Thirty-fifth and Thirty-sixth Congresses and served from March 4, 1857, until January 23, 1861, when he retired from the House; judge advocate on the staff of Gen. Thomas J. (Stonewall) Jackson 1861–1865; moved to Macon, Ga., and practiced law from 1865 until 1875, when he moved to Atlanta; appointed an associate justice of the State supreme court in 1875; elected to the position by the legislature in 1880 to fill an unexpired term; reelected in 1887; chief justice of Georgia from 1879 until his death in Atlanta, Ga., January 13, 1887; interment in Rose Hill Cemetery, Macon, Ga.

JACKSON, James Monroe (cousin of William Thomas Bland), a Representative from West Virginia; born in Parkersburg, Wood County, Va. (now West Virginia), December 3, 1825; pursued an academic course, and was graduated from Princeton College in 1845; studied law; was admitted to the bar in 1847 and commenced practice in Parkersburg, W. Va.; elected prosecuting attorney for Wood County in 1856 and 1860; member of the State house of delegates in 1870 and 1871; member of the State constitutional convention in 1872; elected judge of the fifth judicial circuit and served from 1873 to 1888, when he resigned; presented credentials as a Democratic Member-elect to the Fifty-first Congress and served from March 4, 1889, until February 3, 1890, when he was succeeded by Charles B. Smith, who contested the election; judge of the criminal court for Wood County, W. Va., from 1891 until his death in Parkersburg, W. Va., February 14, 1901; interment in Riverview Cemetery.

JACKSON, James Streshly, a Representative from Kentucky; born in Fayette County, Ky., September 27, 1823; pursued classical studies in Centre College, Danville, Ky.; was graduated from Jefferson College, Canonsburg, Pa., in 1844, and from the law department of Transylvania University, Lexington, Ky., in 1845; was admitted to the bar; commenced practice in Greenupsburg, Ky., in 1845; during the Mexican War enlisted as a private in the First Kentucky Cavalry June 9, 1846; commissioned third lieutenant July 9, 1846; resigned October 10, 1846; moved to Hopkinsville in 1859; elected as a Unionist to the Thirty-seventh Congress and served from March 4 to December 13, 1861, when he resigned to enter the Union Army during the Civil War; raised a troop of cavalrymen and was commissioned colonel of the Third Regiment, Kentucky Volunteer Cavalry, December 13, 1861; brigadier general of Volunteers July 16, 1862; killed in the Battle of Perryville October 8, 1862; interment in Riverside Cemetery, Hopkinsville, Christian County, Ky.

JACKSON, John George (son of George Jackson, brother of Edward Brake Jackson, and grandfather of William Thomas Bland), a Representative from Virginia; born in Buckhannon, Va. (now West Virginia), September 22, 1777; moved with his parents to Clarksburg in 1784; received an English training and became a civil engineer; appointed surveyor of public lands of what is now the State of Ohio in 1793; member of the Virginia House of Burgesses 1798–1801; elected as a Democrat to the Eighth and to the three succeeding Congresses and served from March 4, 1803, to September 28, 1810, when he resigned; while in Congress fought a duel with Joseph Pearson, of North Carolina, and on the second fire was wounded in the hip; member of the State house of delegates in 1811 and 1812; brigadier general of Virginia Militia in 1812; elected as a Democrat to the Thirteenth and Fourteenth Congresses (March 4, 1813–March 3, 1817); declined to be a candidate for reelection in 1816 to the Fifteenth Congress; appointed United States district judge for the western district of Virginia in 1819 and served until his death in Clarksburg, Va. (now West Virginia), March 28, 1825; interment in the Old Jackson Cemetery.

JACKSON, Jonathan, a Delegate from Massachusetts; born in Boston, Mass., June 4, 1743; pursued classical studies, and was graduated from Harvard College in 1761; engaged in mercantile pursuits in Newburyport; member of the Provincial Congress in 1775; member of the State house of representatives in 1777; Member of the Continental Congress in 1782; elected to the State senate in 1789; United States marshal, district of Massachusetts, 1789–1791; treasurer of the Commonwealth 1802–1806; inspector and supervisor of internal revenue; president of the State bank and of the Harvard corporation; died in Boston, Mass., March 5, 1810; interment in the Granary Burying Ground.

JACKSON, Joseph Webber, a Representative from Georgia; born at Cedar Hill, near Savannah, Ga., December 6, 1796; attended the common schools; studied law; was admitted to the bar and practiced; member of the municipal council of Savannah; mayor of Savannah; member of the State house of representatives; served in the State senate; elected as a Democrat to the Thirty-first Congress to fill the vacancy caused by the resignation of Thomas Butler King; reelected to the Thirty-second Congress and served from March 4, 1850, to March 3, 1853; declined to be a candidate for renomination in 1852; captain of the Savannah Volunteer Guards and colonel of the First Georgia Regiment of Militia; judge of the superior court of Georgia; died in Savannah, Ga., September 29, 1854.

JACKSON, Oscar Lawrence, a Representative from Pennsylvania; born in Shenango Township, Lawrence County, Pa., September 2, 1840; attended the common schools, Tansy Hill Select School, and Darlington Academy; taught school in Hocking County, Ohio; during the Civil War served in the Union Army from 1861 to 1865; entered as captain of Company H, Sixty-third Regiment, Ohio Volunteer Infantry, and received promotions of major, lieutenant colonel, and colonel by brevet; severely wounded in the Battle of Corinth, Miss., October 4, 1862; studied law; was admitted to the bar in 1867 and commenced practice in New Castle, Pa.; district attorney 1868–1871; member of the commission to codify laws and devise a plan for the government of cities of Pennsylvania in 1877 and 1878; elected as a Republican to the Forty-ninth and Fiftieth Congresses (March 4, 1885–March 3, 1889); unsuccessful candidate for renomination in 1888 to the Fifty-first Congress; resumed the practice of law in New Castle, Pa.; delegate to the Republican National Convention at St. Louis in 1896; died in New Castle, Pa., on February 16, 1920; interment in Greenwood Cemetery.

JACKSON, Richard, Jr., a Representative from Rhode Island; born in Providence, R. I., July 3, 1764; completed preparatory studies in the schools of Providence and Pomfret, Conn.; entered the mercantile and cotton manufacturing businesses; president of the Washington Insurance Co., Providence, R. I., 1800–1838; elected as a Federalist to the Tenth Congress to fill the vacancy caused by the death of Nehemiah Knight; reelected to the Eleventh, Twelfth, and Thirteenth Congresses and served from November 11, 1808, to March 3, 1815; was not a candidate for renomination in 1814; trustee of Brown University 1809–1838; died in Providence, R. I., on April 18, 1838.

JACKSON, Samuel Dillon, a Senator from Indiana; born near Zanesville, Allen County, Ind., May 28, 1895; attended the public schools of Fort Wayne, Ind.; was graduated from the Indiana Law School at Indianapolis in 1917, and was admitted to the bar the same year; during the First World War attended the first officers training camp at Fort Benjamin Harrison, Ind., and served as a captain of Infantry from May 1917 to April 1919; engaged in the practice of law at Fort Wayne, Ind., in 1919; prosecuting attorney of Allen County, Ind., 1924–1928; unsuccessful Democratic candidate for election in 1928 to the Seventy-first Congress; served as chairman of the Indiana Democratic State Speakers' Bureau in 1934 and as permanent chairman of the Democratic State convention in 1936; appointed attorney general of Indiana to fill an unexpired term and served from June 1940 to January 1941; appointed as a Democrat to the United States Senate to fill the vacancy caused by the death of Frederick Van Nuys and served from January 28, 1944, to November 13, 1944, when a duly elected successor qualified; was not a candidate for election to fill the vacancy, but was an unsuccessful Democratic candidate for Governor of Indiana in 1944; permanent chairman of the Democratic National Convention in 1944; resumed the practice of law; died in Fort Wayne, Ind., March 8, 1951; interment in Lindenwood Cemetery.

JACKSON, Thomas Birdsall, a Representative from New York; born in Jerusalem, Long Island, N. Y., March 24, 1797; attended the public schools; engaged in agricultural pursuits; studied law; was admitted to the bar and practiced in Jerusalem, Hempstead, and Newtown, N. Y.; elected county judge in 1832; member of the State assembly 1833–1835; moved to Newtown, Long Island, N. Y., in 1835; justice of the peace; elected as a Democrat to the Twenty-fifth and Twenty-sixth Congresses (March 4, 1837–March 3, 1841); was not a candidate for renomination in 1840; resumed agricultural pursuits; died in Newtown (now Elmhurst Station), Flushing, Long Island, N. Y., April 23, 1881; interment in Flushing Cemetery.

JACKSON, William, a Representative from Massachusetts; born in Newton, Middlesex County, Mass., September 2, 1783; attended the district school; member of the board of selectmen; served on the school board committee of Newton; chief founder of Newton Temperance Society; engaged in the manufacture of soap and candles; became interested in railroads 1826–1836; member of the State house of representatives 1829–1832; secretary of the Newton Female Academy in 1831; first president of the Newton Savings Bank 1831–1835; again president 1848–1855; elected as a Whig to the Twenty-third and Twenty-fourth Congresses (March 4, 1833–March 3, 1837); declined to be a candidate for renomination in 1836 to the Twenty-fifth Congress; resumed his manufacturing pursuits; one of the founders of the Liberty Party in 1846; president of the American Missionary Society 1846–1854; publisher of a newspaper; died in Newton, Mass., on February 26, 1855; interment in the Old Burial Ground.

JACKSON, William Humphreys (father of William Purnell Jackson), a Representative from Maryland; born near Salisbury, Wicomico County, Md., October 15, 1839; received a common-school training; engaged in agricultural pursuits; moved to Salisbury, Md., in 1864 and engaged in the manufacture of lumber; gave the land and furnished the funds for the construction of the Peninsula General Hospital at Salisbury in 1901; elected as a Republican to the Fifty-seventh and Fifty-eighth Congresses (March 4, 1901–March 3, 1905); unsuccessful candidate for reelection in 1904 to the Fifty-ninth Congress; elected to the Sixtieth Congress (March 4, 1907–March 3, 1909); unsuccessful candidate for reelection in 1908 to the Sixty-first Congress; resumed lumber manufacturing in Salisbury, Md., and died there on April 3, 1915; interment in Parsons Cemetery.

JACKSON, William Purnell (son of William Humphreys Jackson), a Senator from Maryland; born in Salisbury, Wicomico County, Md., January 11, 1868; attended the public schools of Wicomico County and the Wilmington Conference Academy, Dover, Del.; engaged in the lumber business in 1887; member of the Republican National Committee 1908–1932; appointed as a Republican to the United States Senate to fill the vacancy caused by the death of Isidor Rayner and served from November 29, 1912, until January 28, 1914, when a duly elected successor qualified; was not a candidate for election to the vacancy in 1913; resumed his former business pursuits; treasurer of the State 1918–1920; president of the Salisbury National Bank and a director of the Baltimore, Chesapeake & Atlantic Railway Co.; died in Salisbury, Md., March 7, 1939; interment in Parsons Cemetery.

JACKSON, William Terry, a Representative from New York; born in Chester, Orange County, N. Y., December 29, 1794; attended the common schools and later studied surveying; taught school in Goshen 1813–1815; employed as a surveyor and later engaged in mercantile pursuits in Chester and Owego, N. Y., and Bermerville, Sussex County, N. J.; moved to Havana, Chemung County (now township of Montour, Schuyler County), N. Y., in 1825 and engaged in mercantile pursuits; justice of the peace 1836–1838; judge of the court of common pleas and general sessions of Chemung County 1839–1846; justice of the peace, town of Catherine, Chemung County; elected as a Whig to the Thirty-first Congress (March 4, 1849–March 3, 1851); resumed mercantile pursuits; died in Montour Falls, N. Y., September 15, 1882; interment in Montour Falls Cemetery.

JACOBS, Andrew, Sr., a Representative from Indiana; born near Gerald, Perry County, Ind., February 22, 1906; attended the public schools in Gerald, Ind., and St. Benedict's College, Atchison, Kans.; was graduated from Ben Harrison Law School, Indianapolis, Ind., in 1928; was admitted to the bar in June 1927 and commenced the practice of law in Indianapolis, Ind.; public defender in Marion County Felony Court 1930–1933; elected as a Democrat to the Eighty-first Congress (January 3, 1949–January 3, 1951); was an unsuccessful candidate for reelection in 1950 to the Eighty-second Congress; delegate to the Democratic National Conventions in 1952 and 1956; resumed the practice of law; resides in Indianapolis, Ind.

JACOBS, Ferris, Jr., a Representative from New York; born in Delhi, Delaware County, N. Y., March 20, 1836; attended Delaware Academy, Delhi, N. Y., and Delaware Literary Institute, Franklin, N. Y.; was graduated from Williams College, Williamstown, Mass., in 1856; studied law; was admitted to the bar in 1859 and commenced practice in Delhi;

during the Civil War served in the Union Army; commissioned captain of the Third New York Cavalry August 26, 1861; major June 13, 1863; lieutenant colonel July 22, 1864; honorably mustered out October 12, 1864; lieutenant colonel of the Twenty-sixth New York Cavalry March 15, 1865; brevetted brigadier general of Volunteers March 13, 1865, "for gallant and meritorious service during the war"; mustered out July 1, 1865; resumed law practice in Delhi, N. Y.; elected district attorney in 1865 and 1866; delegate to the Republican National Convention at Chicago in 1880; elected as a Republican to the Forty-seventh Congress (March 4, 1881–March 3, 1883); was not a candidate for renomination in 1882; resumed the practice of law; died in White Plains, N. Y., August 30, 1886; interment in Woodland Cemetery, Delhi, N. Y.

JACOBS, Israel, a Representative from Pennsylvania; born near Perkiomen Creek, Providence Township, Montgomery County, Pa., June 9, 1726; attended the public schools; engaged in agricultural and mercantile pursuits; member of the colonial assembly 1770–1774; one of the first to advocate the union of the Colonies; appointed by the council of safety to distribute aid to the families of poor soldiers during the Revolutionary War; elected to the Second Congress (March 4, 1791–March 3, 1793); resumed agricultural pursuits; died in Providence Township about December 10, 1796; interment probably in graveyard of the Friends Meeting House.

JACOBS, Orange, a Delegate from the Territory of Washington; born near Geneseo, Livingston County, N. Y., May 2, 1827; moved with his parents to Michigan Territory in 1831; attended the common schools, Albion (Mich.) College, and the University of Michigan at Ann Arbor; studied law; was admitted to the Michigan bar in 1851 and commenced practice in Sturgis, Mich.; moved to the Territory of Oregon in 1852 and settled in Jacksonville, Jackson County, and continued the practice of law; edited and published the Jacksonville Sentinel until 1859, when he moved to the Territory of Washington; associate justice of the supreme court of the Territory of Washington in 1869; chief justice of the supreme court 1871–1875; elected as a Republican to the Forty-fourth and Forty-fifth Congresses (March 4, 1875–March 3, 1879); was not a candidate for renomination in 1878; resumed the practice of law in Seattle; mayor of Seattle in 1880; member of the Territorial council 1885–1887; member of the Seattle charter revision commission in 1889; corporation counsel for the city of Seattle in 1890; judge of the superior court of King County 1896–1900; died in Seattle, Wash., May 21, 1914; interment in Mount Pleasant Cemetery.

JACOBSEN, Bernhard Martin (father of William Sebastian Jacobsen), a Representative from Iowa; born in Töendren, Schleswig-Holstein, Germany, March 26, 1862; attended the public schools; immigrated in 1876 to the United States with his parents, who settled in Clinton, Iowa; employed as a clerk in a dry goods store until 1886, when he engaged in the mercantile business; served as postmaster of Clinton 1914–1923; retired from the mercantile business in 1927 and engaged in the industrial finance business; elected as a Democrat to the Seventy-second, Seventy-third, and Seventy-fourth Congresses and served from March 4, 1931, until his death; had been renominated for reelection to the Seventy-fifth Congress at the time of his death; went to Rochester, Minn., for medical treatment and died there on June 30, 1936; interment in Springdale Cemetery, Clinton, Iowa.

JACOBSEN, William Sebastian (son of Bernhard Martin Jacobsen), a Representative from Iowa; born in Clinton, Clinton County, Iowa, January 15, 1887; attended the public schools and the Normal College of American Gymnastics Union, Indianapolis, Ind.; director of physical education of the Turner Society and Y. M. C. A., Clinton, Iowa, 1910–1915; manager and part owner of a mercantile store in Clinton, Iowa, 1915–1927; secretary, treasurer, manager, and organizer of Clinton Thrift Co., 1927–1937; also manager of business property and farm interests; delegate to Democratic State conventions 1932–1944; delegate to the Democratic National Conventions in 1936 and 1944; elected as a Democrat to the Seventy-fifth, Seventy-sixth, and Seventy-seventh Congresses (January 3, 1937–January 3, 1943); unsuccessful candidate for reelection in 1942 to the Seventy-eighth Congress; president of Clinton Broadcasting Corp., Credit Bureau of Clinton, and Clinton Thrift Co.; liaison officer, War Assets Administration, Washington, D. C., July 1945 to January 1947; acting postmaster, Clinton, Iowa, August 1, 1951, to January 1954; died in Dubuque, Iowa, April 10, 1955; interment in Springdale Cemetery, Clinton, Iowa.

JACOBSTEIN, Meyer, a Representative from New York; born in New York City, N. Y., January 25, 1880; moved with his parents to Rochester, N. Y., in 1882; attended the public schools and the University of Rochester, Rochester, N. Y.; was graduated from Columbia University, New York City, N. Y., in 1904; pursued postgraduate courses at the same university in economics and political science; special agent in the Bureau of Corporations, Department of Commerce, Washington, D. C., in 1907; assistant professor of economics, University of North Dakota at Grand Forks 1909–1913; professor of economics in the University of Rochester 1913–1918; during the First World War was a director in emergency employment management at the University of Rochester under the auspices of the War Industry Board 1916–1918; elected as a Democrat to the Sixty-eighth, Sixty-ninth, and Seventieth Congresses (March 4, 1923–March 3, 1929); was not a candidate for renomination in 1928; delegate to the Democratic National Conventions in 1924 and 1932; declined the nomination of mayor of Rochester, N. Y., in 1925; engaged in banking in Rochester, N. Y., 1929–1936; in 1936 became chairman of the board of the Rochester Business Institute; member of the Brookings Institution staff 1939–1946; economic counsel in the legislative reference service of the Library of Congress from 1947 until his retirement May 31, 1952; resides in Rochester, N. Y.

JACOWAY, Henderson Madison, a Representative from Arkansas; born in Dardanelle, Yell County, Ark., November 7, 1870; attended the common schools; was graduated from the Dardanelle High School in 1887, from the Winchester Normal College, Winchester, Tenn., in 1892, and from the law department of Vanderbilt University, Nashville, Tenn., in 1898; was admitted to the bar in 1898 and commenced practice in Dardanelle; secretary of the so-called Dawes Commission, engaged in distributing the estates of the Five Civilized Tribes of Indians in the then Indian Territory, during Cleveland's administration; prosecuting attorney of the fifth judicial district 1904–1908; member of the State Democratic central committee 1910–1912; elected as a Democrat to the Sixty-second and to the five succeeding Congresses (March 4, 1911–March 3, 1923); was not a candidate for renomination in 1922; member of the special committee appointed by Speaker Clark to investigate the so-called Sugar Trust; voluntarily withdrew from political life; moved to Little Rock, Ark., in 1922 and served as vice president of the People's Savings Bank 1923–1929; resumed the practice of law; regional counsel of the Social Security Board for the States of Arkansas, Missouri, Oklahoma, and Kansas, 1936–1945; died in Little Rock, Ark., August 4, 1947; interment in Roselawn Cemetery.

JADWIN, Cornelius Comegys, a Representative from Pennsylvania; born in Carbondale, Lackawanna County, Pa., March 27, 1835; attended the common schools; taught school for four years; studied civil engineering and pharmacy; engaged as a civil and mining engineer 1857–1861; entered the drug business and located in Honesdale, Pa., in 1862; nine successive years a member and for three years president of the board of education of his district; delegate to the Republican National Convention at Chicago in 1880; elected as a Republican to the Forty-seventh Congress (March 4, 1881–March 3, 1883); was an unsuccessful Independent candidate for reelection in 1882 to the Forty-eighth Congress; continued the drug business in Honesdale, Pa., until his death there on August 17, 1913; interment in Glen Dyberry Cemetery.

JAMES, Addison Davis (grandfather of John Albert Whitaker), a Representative from Kentucky; born near Morgantown, Butler County, Ky., February 27, 1850; attended the public schools; began the study of medicine in 1870; was graduated from the University of Louisville, Louisville, Ky., in 1873; member of the State constitutional convention in 1890; member of the State house of representative 1891–1893; commissioner to the World's Fair at Chicago representing the State of Kentucky in 1892 and 1893; member of the State senate in 1895; appointed United States marshal for the district of Kentucky on July 6, 1897; reappointed on December 17, 1901, and served until December 31, 1905; elected as a Republican to the Sixtieth Congress (March 4, 1907–March 3, 1909); unsuccessful candidate for reelection; resumed the practice of medicine; died in Penrod, Ky., June 10, 1947; interment in cemetery on the family estate.

JAMES, Amaziah Bailey, a Representative from New York; born in Stephentown, Rensselaer County, N. Y., July 1, 1812; moved with his father to Sweden, Monroe County, N. Y., in 1814; pursued an academic course; at the age of fourteen was apprenticed to the printer's trade in Batavia, N. Y.; moved to Ogdensburg, St. Lawrence County, N. Y., in 1831 and established the Northern Light, a weekly newspaper; later became part owner of the Times and Advertiser, the Whig paper of the county; captain of the Ogdensburg Artillery in 1836; afterward promoted to major general of militia; studied law; was admitted to the bar in 1838 and commenced practice in Ogdensburg; elected justice of the State supreme court in 1853; reelected in 1861 and again in 1869 and served until 1876, when he resigned, having been elected a Member of Congress; member of the peace convention of 1861 held in Washington, D. C., in an effort to devise means to prevent the impending war; elected as a Republican to the Forty-fifth and Forty-sixth Congresses (March 4, 1877–March 3, 1881); while serving his second term in Congress was stricken with paralysis, from which he partially recovered; died in Ogdensburg, N. Y., July 6, 1883; interment in the City Cemetery.

JAMES, Benjamin Franklin, a Representative from Pennsylvania; born in Philadelphia, Pa., August 1, 1885; attended the public schools of Philadelphia and continued education extensively in graphic arts; moved to Radnor Township, Delaware County, Pa., in 1910; during the First World War enlisted in the United States Army and was assigned to the Central Officers Training School; honorably discharged in November 1918 as second lieutenant, United States Army Reserves; former president and chairman of the board of directors of the Franklin Printing Co., Philadelphia, Pa. (founded in 1728 by Benjamin Franklin); member of the Radnor Township Board of Commissioners 1929–1936; served in the State house of representatives 1939–1947; elected as a Republican to the Eighty-first and to the four succeeding Congresses (January 3, 1949–January 3, 1959); was not a candidate for renomination in 1958; died in Bryn Mawr, Pa., January 26, 1961; interment in Arlington Cemetery, Drexel Park, Upper Darby Township, Pa.

JAMES, **Charles Tillinghast**, a Senator from Rhode Island; born in West Greenwich Center, Kent County, R. I., September 15, 1805; attended the common schools; in early youth moved to Providence, R. I., and learned the trade of a carpenter; subsequently became an expert machinist; erected a cotton mill in Newburyport and another in Salem and afterward superintended the construction of several cotton mills in New York, Pennsylvania, Indiana, and Tennessee; served as major general of the Rhode Island Militia; elected as a Protective Tariff Democrat to the United States Senate and served from March 4, 1851, to March 3, 1857; was not a candidate for reelection in 1856; devoted his time to perfecting a rifled cannon and an explosive projectile, which he had invented; died of wounds that he received from the explosion of a shell of his own manufacture with which he was experimenting at Sag Harbor, N. Y., on October 17, 1862; interment in Swan Point Cemetery, Providence, R. I.

JAMES, **Darwin Rush**, a Representative from New York; born in Williamsburg, Hampshire County, Mass., May 14, 1834; pursued an academic course in the Mount Pleasant Boarding School, Amherst, Mass.; moved with his parents to Williamsburg, N. Y., in 1847; entered the mercantile business in New York City in 1850 and became an importer of indigo, spices, and other commodities from the East Indies in 1858; secretary of the New York Board of Trade and Transportation; park commissioner of Brooklyn 1876–1882; elected as a Republican to the Forty-eighth and Forty-ninth Congresses (March 4, 1883–March 3, 1887); declined a renomination; chairman of United States Board of Indian Commissioners in 1890; member of New York Canal Commission in 1898; resumed mercantile pursuits; died in Brooklyn, N. Y., November 19, 1908; interment in the City Cemetery, Williamsburg, Mass.

JAMES, **Francis**, a Representative from Pennsylvania; born in Thornbury Township, Chester County, Pa., April 4, 1799; attended the public schools and Gauses' Academy; studied law; was admitted to the bar of Chester County in 1825 and commenced practice in West Chester, Pa.; member of the State senate 1834–1836; elected as a Whig to the Twenty-sixth and Twenty-seventh Congresses (March 4, 1839–March 3, 1841); resumed the practice of his profession in West Chester, Chester County, Pa.; chief burgess in 1850; died in West Chester, Pa., January 4, 1886; interment in Oakland Cemetery.

JAMES, **Hinton**, a Representative from North Carolina; born in Laurinburg, Richmond County (now Scotland County), N. C., April 24, 1884; attended public and private schools and Davidson College, Davidson, N. C.; engaged in agricultural pursuits and as a cotton merchant in Laurinburg, N. C.; also interested in banking; member of the city council 1917–1919; mayor of Laurinburg 1919–1921; elected as a Democrat to the Seventy-first Congress to fill the vacancy caused by the death of William C. Hammer and served from November 4, 1930, to March 3, 1931; was not a candidate for election in 1930 to the Seventy-second Congress; resumed his former business pursuits; member of the Laurinburg school board 1941–1944; State commissioner of game and inland fisheries 1941–1945; member of the county Democratic executive committee; engaged as a cotton and produce merchant; resident of Laurinburg, N. C., until his death November 3, 1948; interment in Hillside Cemetery.

JAMES, **Ollie Murray**, a Representative and a Senator from Kentucky; born near Marion, Crittenden County, Ky., July 27, 1871; attended the common schools; page in the Kentucky Legislature in 1887; studied law; was admitted to the bar in 1891 and practiced; one of the attorneys for Governor Goebel in his celebrated contest for Governor of the State of Kentucky; delegate to the Democratic National Conventions in 1896, 1904, and 1908, and seconded the nomination of William J. Bryan for President in 1908; permanent chairman of the Democratic National Convention held at Baltimore in 1912 which nominated Woodrow Wilson for President and was chairman of the committee appointed to notify him of his nomination; served as chairman of the State convention in Kentucky in 1900; elected as a Democrat to the Fifty-eighth and to the four succeeding Congresses (March 4, 1903–March 3, 1913); did not seek renomination in 1912, having become a candidate for Senator; elected to the United States Senate and served from March 4, 1913, until his death in a hospital at Baltimore, Md., August 28, 1918; interment Mapleview Cemetery, Marion, Ky.

JAMES, **Rorer Abraham**, a Representative from Virginia; born near Brosville, Pittsylvania County, Va., March 1, 1859; instructed by private tutors; attended Roanoke College; was graduated from the Virginia Military Institute at Lexington in 1882 and from the law department of the University of Virginia at Charlottesville in 1887; was admitted to the bar in 1887 and commenced practice in Danville, Va.; became owner and editor of the Danville Register in 1899 and later purchased the Danville Bee; member of the State house of delegates 1889–1892; served in the State senate 1893–1901; delegate to the Democratic National Convention at San Francisco in 1920 which nominated Cox and Roosevelt; chairman of the fifth district Democratic committee; chairman of the Democratic State committee; elected as a Democrat to the Sixty-sixth Congress to fill the vacancy caused by the resignation of Edward W. Saunders; reelected to the Sixty-seventh Congress and served from June 15, 1920, until his death in Danville, Va., August 6, 1921; interment in Green Hill Cemetery.

JAMES, **William Francis (Frank)**, a Representative from Michigan; born in Morristown, Morris County, N. J., May 23, 1873; moved with his parents to Hancock, Mich., in 1876; attended the public schools; was graduated from Hancock (Mich.) High School in 1890; student at local college in Albion, Mich., in 1890 and 1891; treasurer of Houghton County, Mich., 1900–1904; engaged in real estate and insurance business; served as a private in Company F of the Thirty-fourth Regiment, Michigan Volunteer Infantry, during the Spanish-American War; member of the board of aldermen of Hancock 1906–1908; mayor of Hancock, Mich., 1908 and 1909; member of the State senate 1910–1914; elected as a Republican to the Sixty-fourth and to the nine succeeding Congresses (March 4, 1915–January 3, 1935); unsuccessful candidate for reelection in 1934 to the Seventy-fourth Congress and for election in 1936 to the Seventy-fifth Congress; retired from active business pursuits and political life; died in Arlington, Va., November 17, 1945; interment in Arlington National Cemetery, Fort Myer, Va.

JAMESON, **John**, a Representative from Missouri; born near Mount Sterling, Montgomery County, Ky., March 6, 1802; attended the common schools; moved to Callaway County, Mo., in 1825; studied law; was admitted to the bar in 1826 and commenced practice in Fulton, Mo.; held several local offices; member of the State house of representatives 1830–1836 and served as speaker in 1834 and 1836; elected as a Democrat to the Twenty-sixth Congress to fill the vacancy caused by the death of Albert G. Harrison and served from December 12, 1839, to March 3, 1841; was not a candidate for renomination in 1840; elected to the Twenty-eighth Congress (March 4, 1843–March 3, 1845); was not a candidate for renomination in 1844; elected to the Thirtieth Congress (March 4, 1847–March 3, 1849); was not a candidate for renomination in 1848;

ordained as a minister in the Christian Church; also engaged in agricultural pursuits; served as a captain in the Black Hawk War; died in Fulton, Mo., January 24, 1857; interment in the Jameson family cemetery near Fulton, Mo.

JAMIESON, William Darius (great-grandson of James R. Gillis), a Representative from Iowa; born near Wapello, Louisa County, Iowa, November 9, 1873; attended the common schools and the University of Iowa at Iowa City; studied law at the National University Law School, Washington, D. C.; edited and published the Ida Grove Pioneer in 1893 and 1894, the Columbus Junction Gazette 1899–1901, the Shenandoah World 1901–1916, and was also editor of the Hamburg Democrat; member of the State senate from January 1, 1907, until March 3, 1909, when he resigned to enter Congress; elected as a Democrat to the Sixty-first Congress (March 4, 1909–March 3, 1911); declined to be a candidate for renomination in 1910; resumed newspaper activities in Shenandoah, Iowa; postmaster of Shenandoah from May 29, 1915, until September 1, 1916, when he resigned; assistant treasurer of the Democratic National Committee in 1916 and its director of finance 1917–1920; delegate at large to the Democratic National Convention at San Francisco in 1920; engaged in the practice of law in Washington, D. C.; editor of the Window Seat, a weekly syndicate letter for country newspapers, from 1925 until his death in Washington, D. C., November 18, 1949; interment in Fort Lincoln Cemetery.

JANES, Henry Fisk, a Representative from Vermont; born in Brimfield, Hampden County, Mass., October 10, 1792; moved with his parents to Calais, Vt.; pursued an academic course; served in the War of 1812 and participated in the Battle of Plattsburg; studied law in Montpelier, Vt.; was admitted to the bar and commenced practice in Waterbury, Vt., in 1817; postmaster 1820–1830; member of the State legislative council 1830–1834; elected as a Whig and Anti-Mason to the Twenty-third Congress to fill the vacancy caused by the death of Benjamin F. Deming; reelected to the Twenty-fourth Congress and served from December 2, 1834, to March 3, 1837; unsuccessful Anti-Masonic candidate for reelection in 1836 to the Twenty-fifth Congress; State treasurer 1838–1841; member of the State council of censors in 1848; town representative in 1854, 1861, and 1862; member of the State house of representatives in 1855; died in Waterbury, Vt., June 6, 1879; interment in the Village Cemetery.

JARMAN, John, a Representative from Oklahoma; born in Sallisaw, Sequoyah County, Okla., July 17, 1915; attended the public schools of Oklahoma City, Okla., and Westminster Presbyterian College, Fulton, Mo., 1932–1934; graduated from Yale University in 1937 and from Harvard Law School in 1941; was admitted to the bar in 1941 and commenced the practice of law in Oklahoma City, Okla.; during World War II enlisted as a private in the United States Army on January 12, 1942, and served in the Security Intelligence Corps, assigned to the United Nations Conference in California; was discharged as a master sergeant on December 11, 1945; member of the State house of representatives in 1947 and 1948; served in the State senate in 1949 and 1950; elected as a Democrat to the Eighty-second and to the four succeeding Congresses (January 3, 1951–January 3, 1961). *Reelected to the Eighty-seventh Congress.*

JARMAN, Pete, a Representative from Alabama; born in Greensboro, Hale County, Ala., on October 31, 1892; attended the public schools, the Normal College, Livingston, Ala., and Southern University, Greensboro, Ala.; was graduated from the University of Alabama at Tuscaloosa in 1913, and attended the University of Montpellier, France, in 1919; clerk in probate office

in Sumter County, Ala., 1913–1917; during the First World War served overseas as second and first lieutenant in the Three Hundred and Twenty-seventh Infantry, and was wounded in action; served in the Alabama National Guard as inspector general with rank of major 1922–1924, and as division inspector of the Thirty-first Infantry Division with rank of lieutenant colonel 1924–1940; assistant State examiner of accounts 1919–1930; secretary of state of Alabama 1931–1934; assistant State comptroller in 1935 and 1936; member of the State Democratic Executive Committee of Alabama 1927–1930; department commander of the American Legion of Alabama in 1927 and 1928; elected as a Democrat to the Seventy-fifth and to the five succeeding Congresses (January 3, 1937–January 3, 1949); unsuccessful candidate for renomination in 1948; appointed by President Harry S. Truman as Ambassador to Australia and confirmed by the United States Senate June 7, 1949, and served until 1953; retired from public and political activities; died in Washington, D. C., February 17, 1955; interment in Arlington National Cemetery, Fort Myer, Va.

JARNAGIN, Spencer, a Senator from Tennessee; born in Grainger County, Tenn., in 1792; pursued classical studies, and was graduated from Greenville College in 1813; studied law; was admitted to the bar in 1817 and commenced practice in Knoxville; member of the State senate 1833–1835; trustee of the East Tennessee College 1836–1851; moved to Athens, Tenn., in 1837 and continued the practice of his profession; presidential elector on the Whig ticket of Harrison and Tyler in 1840; Whig nominee for United States Senator in 1841 but the general assembly met and adjourned without electing a Senator; elected as a Whig to the United States Senate and served from October 17, 1843, to March 3, 1847; unsuccessful Whig candidate for reelection to the United States Senate and for member of the supreme court of Tennessee; moved to Memphis and continued the practice of law; died in Memphis, Tenn., June 25, 1853; interment in Elmwood Cemetery.

JARRETT, Benjamin, a Representative from Pennsylvania; born in Sharon, Mercer County, Pa., July 18, 1881; attended the public schools of Wheatland, Pa.; worked as a telegraph operator and later as foreman in a steel mill; studied law; was admitted to the bar in 1907 and commenced practice in Farrell, Mercer County, Pa.; city solicitor of Farrell, Pa., 1910–1930; served in the State senate 1911–1913; member of the Pennsylvania State Workmen's Compensation Board 1919–1923; served as chairman of Mercer County Republican committee; elected as a Republican to the Seventy-fifth, Seventy-sixth, and Seventy-seventh Congresses (January 3, 1937–January 3, 1943); was not a candidate for renomination in 1942; resumed the practice of law; died, while on a visit, in Zanesville, Ohio, July 20, 1944; interment in Oakwood Cemetery, Sharon, Pa.

JARRETT, William Paul, a Delegate from the Territory of Hawaii; born in Honolulu, Hawaii, August 22, 1877; attended St. Louis College, Honolulu; deputy sheriff and sheriff of the city and county of Honolulu 1906–1914; high sheriff of the Territory of Hawaii and warden of Oahu Prison 1914–1922; member of the Board of Industrial Schools from May 1919 to January 1922; elected as a Democrat a Delegate to the Sixty-eighth and Sixty-ninth Congresses (March 4, 1923–March 3, 1927); unsuccessful candidate for reelection in 1926 to the Seventieth Congress; served as manager of the Lunalilo Home for Aged Hawaiians from 1927 until his death at Honolulu, T. H., November 10, 1929; interment in Diamond Head Memorial Park.

JARVIS, Leonard, a Representative from Maine; born in Boston, Mass., October 19, 1781; attended the common schools;

was graduated from Harvard University, Cambridge, Mass., in 1800; moved to Surey, Maine; sheriff of Hancock County, Maine, 1821–1829; collector of customs for the Penobscot district 1829–1831; elected as a Democrat to the Twenty-first and to the three succeeding Congresses (March 4, 1829–March 3, 1837); Navy agent for the port of Boston 1838–1841; returned to Surry, Maine, where he died October 18, 1854; interment in Hillside Cemetery.

JARVIS, Thomas Jordan, a Senator from North Carolina; born in Jarvisburg, Currituck County, N. C., January 18, 1836; received his early schooling from his father, who was a Methodist minister; was graduated from Randolph-Macon College, Virginia, in 1860; served in the Confederate Army during the Civil War; permanently disabled in the right arm in 1864; member of the State constitutional convention in 1865; moved to Tyrrell County in 1866; studied law; was admitted to the bar in 1867 and commenced practice in Columbia, Tyrrell County, N. C., in 1867; member of the State house of representatives in 1868 and 1870 and served as speaker in 1870; moved to Greenville, N. C., in 1872; member of the State constitutional convention in 1875; elected Lieutenant Governor of North Carolina in 1876; became Governor February 5, 1879, by the resignation of Zebulon B. Vance and was elected Governor for a full term in 1880, thus serving for six consecutive years; United States Minister to Brazil 1885–1889; appointed as a Democrat to the United States Senate to fill the vacancy caused by the death of Zebulon B. Vance and served from April 19, 1894, until January 23, 1895, when a successor was qualified; delegate to the Democratic National Convention at Chicago in 1896; trustee of the University of North Carolina; chairman of the executive committee of the board of trustees of East Carolina Teachers College at Greenville, N. C.; resumed the practice of law in Greenville, N. C., and died there June 17, 1915; interment in Cherry Hill Cemetery.

JAVITS, Jacob Koppel, a Representative and a Senator from New York; born in New York, N. Y., May 18, 1904; attended the public schools; moved to Washington Heights, N. Y., in 1918; was graduated from the George Washington High School in 1920 and continued his schooling at night classes at Columbia University; was graduated from the New York University Law School in 1926; was admitted to the bar in 1927 and commenced practice in New York, N. Y.; lecturer and author of articles on economic problems; served as special assistant to the Chief of Chemical Warfare Service from February 1941 to March 1942, when he was commissioned a major; assistant to the Chief of Operations, Chemical Warfare Service, with overseas service in the European Theater in 1943 and the Pacific Theater in 19 4 awarded the Legion of Merit and the Army Commendation Ribbon; discharged as a lieutenant colonel in June 1945; resumed the practice of law; elected as a Republican to the Eightieth and to the three succeeding Congresses and served from January 3, 1947, until his resignation December 31, 1954; had been renominated in 1954 to the Eighty-fourth Congress but withdrew; elected attorney general of New York in 1954 for a four-year term and served until his resignation January 9, 1957; elected to the United States Senate in 1956 for the term commencing January 3, 1957, and ending January 3, 1963, but did not assume his duties until January 9, 1957.

JAY, John, a Delegate from New York; born in New York City December 12, 1745; attended a boarding school in New Rochelle, N. Y., and was graduated from Kings College (now Columbia University) in 1764; studied law; was admitted to the bar in 1768; served on the New York committee of correspondence; Member of the Continental Congress 1774–1777, 1778, and 1779; while attending the Congress in Phila-

delphia in 1776 the Convention of the Representatives of the State of New York (formerly the New York Provincial Congress), meeting at White Plains, N. Y., requested his presence and counsel and it was upon his motion, as a member of the convention, July 9, 1776, that the Declaration of Independence was unanimously approved; recalled some months in 1777 to aid in forming the New York State constitution; appointed chief justice of the State of New York in May 1777 but resigned December 1778 to become President of the Continental Congress and served in that capacity from December 10, 1778, to September 28, 1779; appointed Minister Plenipotentiary to Spain September 27, 1779; appointed one of the ministers to negotiate peace with Great Britain June 14, 1781, and signed the treaty of Paris; appointed one of the ministers to negotiate treaties with the European powers May 1, 1783; returned to New York in 1784; appointed Secretary of Foreign Affairs July 1784, which position he held until the establishment of the Federal Government in 1789; appointed the first Chief Justice of the United States by President Washington September 26, 1789, and served until June 29, 1795, when he resigned; unsuccessful Federal candidate for Governor of New York in 1792; appointed Envoy Extraordinary and Minister Plenipotentiary to Great Britain April 19, 1794, and served until April 8, 1795, still retaining his position as Chief Justice of the United States; Governor of New York 1795–1801; declined reelection and also a reappointment as Chief Justice of the United States; retired to his farm at Bedford, near New York City, where he died May 17, 1829; interment in the family burying ground at Rye, N. Y.

JAYNE, William, a Delegate from the Territory of Dakota; born in Springfield, Ill., October 8, 1826; completed preparatory studies at Illinois College, Jacksonville, Ill., and was graduated from the medical department of the University of Missouri at Columbia in 1849; commenced the practice of medicine in Springfield; mayor of Springfield 1859–1861; member of the State senate in 1860 but resigned in 1861 to accept the appointment of Governor of Dakota Territory from President Lincoln; served as Governor 1861–1863; presented credentials as a Delegate-elect to the Thirty-eighth Congress and served from March 4, 1863, to June 17, 1864, when he was succeeded by John B. S. Todd, who contested his election; returned to Springfield and continued the practice of medicine; served three terms as mayor of Springfield during the period 1865 to 1880; appointed by President Grant pension agent at Springfield and served from 1869 to 1873; resumed the practice of medicine; died in Springfield, Ill., on March 20, 1916; interment in Oak Ridge Cemetery.

JEFFERIS, Albert Webb, a Representative from Nebraska; born near Embreeville, Chester County, Pa., December 7, 1868; attended the public schools in Romansville, Pa., and the State normal school at West Chester; taught school in West Bradford Township three years; was graduated from the law department of the University of Michigan, at Ann Arbor, in 1893; was admitted to the bar the same year and commenced practice in Omaha, Nebr.; member of various Republican State and county committees; assistant county attorney 1896–1898; unsuccessful candidate for election in 1908 to the Sixty-first Congress; chairman of the Republican State convention in 1910; elected as a Republican to the Sixty-sixth and Sixty-seventh Congresses (March 4, 1919–March 3, 1923); unsuccessful candidate for election to the United States Senate in 1922; resumed the practice of law; was elected delegate at large to the Republican National Convention at Cleveland in 1923 and placed Charles G. Dawes in nomination for Vice President; was chosen by the Republican National Committee to make the notification address to General Dawes at

Evanston, Ill., August 19, 1924; was manager of the Coolidge-Dawes automobile caravan from Plymouth, Vt., to Bellingham, Wash.; resumed the practice of law in Omaha, Nebr.; unsuccessful candidate for nomination as United States Senator in 1940; died at Omaha, Nebr., on September 14, 1942; interment in Forest Lawn Cemetery.

JEFFERS, Lamar, a Representative from Alabama; born in Anniston, Calhoun County, Ala., April 16, 1888; attended the public schools and the Alabama Presbyterian College at Anniston; served with the Alabama National Guard 1904–1914; clerk of the circuit court of Calhoun County, taking office in January 1917; resigned that office in May 1917 to enter officers' training camp, Fort McPherson, Ga.; was graduated August 14, 1917, as captain of Infantry; assigned to the Eighty-second Division, commanding Company G, Three Hundred and Twenty-sixth Infantry, during the First World War; served until twice wounded on October 11, 1918, before St. Juvin, France; was awarded the Distinguished Service Cross by the United States Government; promoted to rank of major of Infantry; elected as a Democrat to the Sixty-seventh Congress to fill the vacancy caused by the death of Fred L. Blackmon; reelected to the Sixty-eighth and to the five succeeding Congresses and served from June 7, 1921, to January 3, 1935; unsuccessful candidate for renomination in 1934; resides in Miami, Fla.

JEFFERSON, Thomas, a Delegate from Virginia and a Vice President and a President of the United States; born in Old Shadwell, Va., April 13, 1743; attended a preparatory school conducted by the Rev. Mr. Maury; was graduated from William and Mary College, Williamsburg, Va., in 1762; studied law; was admitted to the bar and commenced practice in 1767; member of the colonial house of burgesses 1769–1774; prominent in pre-Revolutionary movements; Member of the Continental Congress in 1775 and 1776; chairman of the committee that drew up the Declaration of Independence; made and presented the first draft of the Declaration that was submitted to the Congress July 2, 1776; signed the Declaration of Independence August 2, 1776; resigned soon after and returned to his estate, "Monticello"; Governor of Virginia 1779–1781; member of the State house of delegates in 1782; again a Member of the Continental Congress 1783–1785; appointed a Minister Plenipotentiary to France May 7, 1784, and then sole Minister to the King of France March 10, 1785, for three years; appointed Secretary of State of the United States September 26, 1789, and served until December 3, 1793; elected Vice President of the United States and served from March 4, 1797, to March 3, 1801; elected President of the United States in 1801 by the House of Representatives on the thirty-sixth ballot; reelected in 1805 and served from March 4, 1801, to March 3, 1809; retired to his estate, "Monticello," in Virginia; active in founding the University of Virginia at Charlottesville; died at "Monticello," Albemarle County, Va., July 4, 1826; interment in the grounds of "Monticello."

JEFFORDS, Elza, a Representative from Mississippi; born in Ironton, Lawrence County, Ohio, May 23, 1826; attended the common schools in Portsmouth, Ohio; studied law; was admitted to the bar in 1847 and commenced practice in Portsmouth, Ohio; during the Civil War served in the Army of the Tennessee from June 1862 to December 1863 as clerk in the Quartermaster's Department (land transportation); judge of the high court of errors and appeals in Mississippi 1868 and 1869; delegate to the Republican National Convention at Philadelphia in 1872; elected as a Republican to the Forty-eighth Congress (March 4, 1883–March 3, 1885); unsuccessful candidate for reelection in 1884; died in Vicksburg, Miss., on March 19, 1885; interment in Cedar Hill Cemetery, near Vicksburg.

JEFFREY, Harry Palmer, a Representative from Ohio; born in Dayton, Ohio, December 26, 1901; attended the public schools; was graduated from the Steele High School, Dayton, Ohio, from Ohio State University at Columbus in 1924, and from the College of Law of the same university in 1926; was admitted to the bar in 1926 and commenced practice in Columbus, Ohio; moved to Dayton, Ohio, in 1927, and continued the practice of law; special assistant attorney general of Ohio 1933–1936; elected as a Republican to the Seventy-eighth Congress (January 3, 1943–January 3, 1945); unsuccessful candidate for reelection in 1944 to the Seventy-ninth Congress; resumed the practice of law in Dayton, Ohio, where he resides.

JEFFRIES, Walter Sooy, a Representative from New Jersey; born in Atlantic City, Atlantic County, N. J., October 16, 1893; attended the public schools and was graduated from the Atlantic City (N. J.) Business College in 1909; was also graduated in celestial navigation from Franklin Institute, Philadelphia, Pa., in 1943; engaged in the manufacture of paint 1910–1934; mayor of Margate City, N. J., 1931–1935; served as sheriff of Atlantic County, N. J., 1935–1938; became engaged in the hotel business at Atlantic City in 1938; elected as a Republican to the Seventy-sixth Congress (January 3, 1939–January 3, 1941); unsuccessful candidate for reelection in 1940 to the Seventy-seventh Congress; treasurer of Atlantic County 1941–1944; president of Jeffries & Co., Inc., a painting and decorating firm; died in Margate City, N. J., October 11, 1954; interment in Laurel Memorial Cemetery, Egg Harbor Township, Atlantic County, N. J.

JENCKES, Thomas Allen, a Representative from Rhode Island; born in Cumberland, R. I., November 2, 1818; attended the public schools; was graduated from Brown University, Providence, R. I., in 1838; studied law; was admitted to the bar in 1840 and commenced practice in Providence, R. I.; clerk in the State legislature 1840–1844; secretary of the State constitutional convention in 1842; adjutant general 1845–1855; member of the State house of representatives 1854–1857; commissioner to revise the laws of the State in 1855; elected as a Republican to the Thirty-eighth and to the three succeeding Congresses (March 4, 1863–March 3, 1871); unsuccessful candidate for reelection in 1870; resumed the practice of law; died in Cumberland, R. I., on November 4, 1875; interment in Swan Point Cemetery, Providence, R. I.

JENCKES, Virginia Ellis, a Representative from Indiana; born in Terre Haute, Vigo County, Ind., November 6, 1882; attended the public and high schools; engaged in agricultural pursuits in 1912; secretary of Wabash Maumee Valley Improvement Association 1926–1932; elected as a Democrat to the Seventy-third, Seventy-fourth, and Seventy-fifth Congresses (March 4, 1933–January 3, 1939); unsuccessful candidate for reelection in 1938 to the Seventy-sixth Congress; United States delegate to the Interparliamentary Union in Paris, France, in 1937; is a resident of Terre Haute, Ind.

JENIFER, Daniel, of St. Thomas, a Delegate from Maryland; born in Charles County, Md., in 1723; member of the provincial court in 1766; active in pre-Revolutionary movements; member of the Governor's council in 1773; member and president of the council of safety 1775–1777; president of the State senate 1777–1780; Member of the Continental Congress 1778–1782, also of the convention that framed the Federal Constitution, and a signer of that instrument on September 17, 1778; unsuccessful candidate for Governor of Maryland in 1782 and 1785; died in Annapolis, Anne Arundel County, Md., November 16, 1790.

JENIFER, Daniel (nephew of the preceding), a Representative from Maryland; born in Charles County, Md., April 15, 1791; completed preparatory studies; studied law; served in the State house of delegates; elected as a National-Republican to the Twenty-second Congress (March 4, 1831–March 3, 1833); unsuccessful candidate for reelection in 1832 to the Twenty-third Congress; elected to the Twenty-fourth, Twenty-fifth, and Twenty-sixth Congresses (March 4, 1835–March 3, 1841); appointed Minister to Austria on August 27, 1841, and served until July 7, 1845; register of wills for Charles County 1846–1851; died in Mulberry Grove, near Port Tobacco, Md., December 18, 1855; interment on a farm, "Charleston," between the Wicomico River and Charleston Creek in the southern part of Charles County, Md.

JENISON, Edward Halsey, a Representative from Illinois; born in Fond du Lac, Wis., July 27, 1907; attended the public schools and the University of Wisconsin at Madison; engaged in newspaper work 1925–1937, and as a publisher in 1938 in Paris, Ill.; during World War II served as a lieutenant commander in the United States Navy, attached to the Deputy Chief of Naval Operations for Air, with service in the Pacific and Atlantic forces, from April 1943 to September 1946; elected as a Republican to the Eightieth, Eighty-first, and Eighty-second Congresses (January 3, 1947–January 3, 1953); unsuccessful candidate for reelection in 1952 to the Eighty-third Congress and for election in 1954 to the Eighty-fourth Congress; resumed the publishing business; delegate to the Republican National Convention in 1956; director, Department of Finance, State of Illinois, from June 15, 1960, to January 20, 1961; is a resident of Paris, Ill.

JENKINS, Albert Gallatin, a Representative from Virginia; born in Cabell County, Va., November 10, 1830; was graduated from Jefferson College, Canonsburg, Pa., in 1848 and from Harvard Law School in 1850; was admitted to the bar in 1850, but engaged in agricultural pursuits; delegate to the Democratic National Convention at Cincinnati in 1856; elected as a Democrat to the Thirty-fifth and Thirty-sixth Congresses (March 4, 1857–March 3, 1861); delegate to the Confederate Provisional Congress in 1861; during the Civil War enlisted in the Confederate Army; appointed brigadier general August 1, 1862; mortally wounded in the Battle of Cloyds Mountain, near Dublin, Va., May 9, 1864, and died May 21, 1864; interment in New Dublin Presbyterian Cemetery; reinterred after the close of the war at his home in Green Valley, near Huntington, W. Va.; again reinterred in the Confederate plot in Spring Hill Cemetery, Huntington, W. Va.

JENKINS, John James, a Representative from Wisconsin; born in Weymouth, England, August 24, 1843; attended the common schools; immigrated to the United States with his parents, who settled in Baraboo, Wis., in June 1852; served in the Civil War as a member of Company A, Sixth Regiment, Wisconsin Volunteer Infantry, 1861–1865; clerk of the circuit court of Sauk County 1867–1870; moved to Chippewa Falls, Wis., in 1870; studied law; was admitted to the bar and practiced; city clerk and city attorney of Chippewa Falls; member of the State assembly in 1872; county judge of Chippewa County 1872–1876; appointed United States attorney for the Territory of Wyoming in March 1876 and served until 1880, when he returned to Chippewa Falls, Wis., and resumed the practice of law; elected as a Republican to the Fifty-fourth and to the six succeeding Congresses (March 4, 1895–March 3, 1909); unsuccessful candidate for renomination in 1908; appointed judge of Puerto Rico by President Taft in May 1910 and served until his death in Chippewa Falls, Wis., June 8, 1911; interment in Forest Hill Cemetery.

JENKINS, Lemuel, a Representative from New York; born in Bloomingburg, Sullivan County, N. Y., October 20, 1789; completed preparatory studies; studied law; was admitted to the Sullivan County bar in October 1815 and practiced in Bloomingburg, N. Y.; master in chancery; the first district attorney of Sullivan County and served from June 1818 to March 1819; elected as a Democrat to the Eighteenth Congress (March 4, 1823–March 3, 1825); moved to Albany, N. Y., and resumed the practice of law; died in Albany, N. Y., August 18, 1862; interment in Albany Rural Cemetery.

JENKINS, Mitchell, a Representative from Pennsylvania; born in Forty Fort, Luzerne County, Pa., January 24, 1896; attended the Kingston public schools and the Wyoming Seminary, Kingston, Pa.; was graduated from Wesleyan University, Middletown, Conn., in June 1919 and New York University Law School, New York, N. Y., in June 1923; was admitted to the New York bar in December 1923 and the Pennsylvania bar in January 1924 and commenced practice in Wilkes-Barre, Pa.; assistant district attorney of Luzerne County 1938–1946; during the First World War enlisted as a private in the United States Army in April 1917, and was discharged as a first lieutenant January 2, 1919; enlisted in the Pennsylvania National Guard as a private in January 1926 and rose through the ranks to lieutenant colonel prior to induction into Federal service on February 17, 1941; served four and a half years during World War II, promoted to colonel and was placed on inactive status October 5, 1945; awarded Victory Medal in World Wars I and II, American Defense Ribbon, Asiatic Theater Ribbon with one Battle Star, and American Theater Ribbon; elected as a Republican to the Eightieth Congress (January 3, 1947–January 3, 1949); was not a candidate for renomination in 1948; assistant district attorney of Luzerne County, Pa., in 1949 and in 1950; resumed the practice of law in Wilkes-Barre, Pa.; resides in Dallas, Pa.

JENKINS, Robert, a Representative from Pennsylvania; born in Windsor Forges, Lancaster County, Pa., July 10, 1769; attended the common schools and the select school of Dr. Robert Smith of Pequea; was an ironmaster in Caernarvon Township; member of the State house of representatives in 1804 and 1805; elected to the Tenth and Eleventh Congresses (March 4, 1807–March 3, 1811); member of a Group of Horse, and took an active part in suppressing the Whisky Insurrection in Pennsylvania; died in Windsor Forges, Pa., April 18, 1848; interment in the Caernarvon Presbyterian Churchyard, Churchtown, Lancaster County, Pa.

JENKINS, Thomas Albert, a Representative from Ohio; born at Oak Hill, Jackson County, Ohio, October 28, 1880; attended the grade and high schools; was graduated from Providence University, Oak Hill, Ohio, in 1901 and from the law department of the Ohio State University at Columbus in 1907; was admitted to the bar the same year and commenced practice in Ironton, Ohio; prosecuting attorney of Lawrence County, Ohio, 1916–1920; served in the State senate in 1923 and 1924; delegate to the Republican State conventions in 1920 and 1924; elected as a Republican to the Sixty-ninth and to the sixteen succeeding Congresses (March 4, 1925–January 3, 1959); was not a candidate for renomination in 1958; died in Worthington, Ohio, December 21, 1959; interment in Woodland Cemetery, Ironton, Ohio.

JENKINS, Timothy, a Representative from New York; born in Barre, Worcester County, Mass., January 29, 1799; located in Washington County, N. Y., in 1817; pursued an academic course; studied law; was admitted to the bar in 1825 and commenced practice in Oneida Castle, N. Y.; moved to Vernon,

N. Y., in 1832; was attorney for the Oneida Indians in their dealings with the State of New York 1838–1845; district attorney for Oneida County 1840–1845; elected as a Democrat to the Twenty-ninth and Thirtieth Congresses (March 4, 1845–March 3, 1849); unsuccessful candidate for reelection in 1848 to the Thirty-first Congress; elected to the Thirty-second Congress (March 4, 1851–March 3, 1853); unsuccessful candidate for reelection in 1852 to the Thirty-third Congress; delegate to the Republican National Convention at Philadelphia in 1856 and was thereafter a Republican; died in Martinsburg, N. Y., December 24, 1859; interment in the City Cemetery, Oneida Castle, N. Y.

JENKS, Arthur Byron, a Representative from New Hampshire; born in West Dennis, Barnstable County, Mass., October 15, 1866; attended the public schools; employed as a shoe worker in 1881; engaged in the shoe manufacturing business at Manchester, N. H., 1902–1930; also became engaged in the banking business in 1917 at Manchester, N. H.; unsuccessful candidate for election in 1934 to the Seventy-fourth Congress; delegate to the Republican National Conventions in 1936 and 1940; presented his credentials as a Republican Member-elect to the Seventy-fifth Congress and served from January 3, 1937, until June 9, 1938, when he was succeeded by Alphonse Roy, who contested his election; elected as a Republican to the Seventy-sixth and Seventy-seventh Congresses (January 3, 1939–January 3, 1943); unsuccessful candidate for renomination in 1942; resumed the banking business in Manchester, N. H., until his death there on December 14, 1947; interment in Pine Grove Cemetery.

JENKS, George Augustus, a Representative from Pennsylvania; born in Punxsutawney, Jefferson County, Pa., on March 26, 1836; attended the public school; learned the carpenter's trade; taught school; was graduated from Jefferson College, Canonsburg, Pa., in 1858; studied law; was admitted to the bar in 1859 and commenced practice in Brookville, Pa.; elected as a Democrat to the Forty-fourth Congress (March 4, 1875–March 3, 1877); one of the managers appointed by the House of Representatives in 1876 to conduct the impeachment proceedings against William W. Belknap, ex-Secretary of War; unsuccessful Democratic candidate for the State supreme bench in 1880; Assistant Secretary of the Department of the Interior in 1885 and 1886; Solicitor General of the United States 1886–1889; unsuccessful Democratic candidate for Governor of Pennsylvania in 1898; unsuccessful Democratic candidate for United States Senator in the joint legislative convention of 1899; resumed the practice of law; died in Brookville, Pa., February 10, 1908; interment in the Brookville Cemetery.

JENKS, Michael Hutchinson, a Representative from Pennsylvania; born at Bridgetown Mills, Bucks County, near Middletown, Pa., May 21, 1795; pursued an academic course; engaged in agricultural pursuits; commissioner of Bucks County 1830–1833; treasurer 1833–1835; moved to Newtown, Pa., in 1837; associate judge of the court of common pleas of Bucks County 1838–1843; elected as a Whig to the Twenty-eighth Congress (March 4, 1843–March 3, 1845); unsuccessful candidate for reelection in 1844 to the Twenty-ninth Congress; engaged in the real-estate business and as general business agent 1845–1865; chief burgess of Newtown 1848–1853; died in Newtown, Bucks County, Pa., on October 16, 1867; interment in the Newtown Friends Meeting Cemetery.

JENNER, William Ezra, a Senator from Indiana; born in Marengo, Crawford County, Ind., July 21, 1908; attended the public schools; was graduated from Indiana University at Bloomington in 1930 and from the law department of the same university in 1932; was admitted to the bar in 1930 and commenced practice in Paoli, Ind., in 1932; member of the State senate from 1934 to June 1942, serving as minority leader 1937–1939 and majority leader and president pro tempore 1939–1941; resigned his seat in June 1942 to serve in World War II as a lieutenant; served overseas and was retired for physical disability as a captain in the Army Air Corps October 7, 1944; Republican State chairman 1945 to 1946; elected as a Republican to the United States Senate on November 7, 1944, to fill the vacancy caused by the death of Frederick Van Nuys and served from November 14, 1944, to January 3, 1945; was not a candidate for election to the full term; elected to the United States Senate in 1946 for the term commencing January 3, 1947, and ending January 3, 1953; reelected in 1952 for the term ending January 3, 1959; was not a candidate for renomination in 1958; resumed the practice of law; is a resident of Bedford, Ind.

JENNESS, Benning Wentworth, a Senator from New Hampshire; born in Deerfield, Rockingham County, N. H., July 14, 1806; attended Bradford Academy, Massachusetts; engaged in mercantile pursuits in Strafford, N. H., 1826–1856; held several local offices; member of the State house of representatives; judge of probate of Strafford County 1841–1845; appointed to the United States Senate to fill the vacancy caused by the resignation of Levi Woodbury and served from December 1, 1845, to June 13, 1846; unsuccessful Democratic candidate for election in 1846 to the Thirtieth Congress; member of the State constitutional convention in 1850; delegate to the Democratic National Convention at Baltimore in 1852; nominated for Governor of New Hampshire but withdrew in favor of Gen. George Starke in 1861; moved to Ohio and engaged in lumbering and banking; died in Cleveland, Ohio, November 16, 1879; interment in the family cemetery, Strafford, N. H.

JENNINGS, David, a Representative from Ohio; born in Readington Township, Hunterdon County, N. J., in 1787; attended the public schools; moved to St. Clairsville, Ohio, in 1812; studied law; was admitted to the bar in 1813 and commenced practice in St. Clairsville; prosecuting attorney of Belmont County 1815–1825; held several local offices; member of the State senate 1819–1824; elected to the Nineteenth Congress and served from March 4, 1825, until his resignation, May 25, 1826; died in Baltimore, Md., in 1834.

JENNINGS, John, Jr., a Representative from Tennessee; born in Jacksboro, Campbell County, Tenn., June 6, 1880; attended the public schools and American Temperance University, Harriman, Tenn.; was graduated from U. S. Grant University, Athens, Tenn., in 1906; studied law; was admitted to the bar in 1903 and commenced practice in Jellico, Campbell County, Tenn.; served as county superintendent of public instruction, Campbell County, Tenn., in 1903 and 1904; county attorney of Campbell County 1911–1918; delegate to the Republican National Conventions in 1912, 1936, and 1944; special assistant to the Attorney General of the United States in 1918 and 1919; served as judge of the second chancery division of Tennessee from September 1, 1918, until his resignation July 1, 1923; moved to Knoxville, Tenn., in 1923 and continued the practice of law; elected as a Republican to the Seventy-sixth Congress to fill the vacancy caused by the death of J. Will Taylor; reelected to the Seventy-seventh and to the four succeeding Congresses and served from December 30, 1939, to January 3, 1951; unsuccessful candidate for renomination in 1950 to the Eighty-second Congress; resumed the practice of law; died in Knoxville, Tenn., February 27, 1956; interment in Highland Memorial Cemetery.

JENNINGS, Jonathan, a Delegate from the Territory of Indiana and a Representative from Indiana; born in Hunterdon County, N. J., in 1784; moved about the year 1790 to Fayette County, Pa., with his parents, who settled near Dunlap's Creek; acquired a common school education; attended a grammar school conducted by Rev. John McMillin at Canonsburg, Pa.; studied law; moved to Indiana Territory in 1806 and settled at Jeffersonville; completed his legal studies and commenced the practice of law; moved to Vincennes in 1807; was admitted to the bar and continued his legal profession; clerk to the receiver of public money; became assistant to the clerk of the house of representatives of the Territorial government in 1807; engaged in newspaper work in 1808; moved to Clark County in 1809 and settled in Charlestown; elected a Delegate to the Eleventh and to the three succeeding Congresses and served from November 27, 1809, to December 11, 1816, when the Territory was admitted as a State into the Union; delegate to the State constitutional convention in 1816 and served as president; elected Governor of Indiana in December 1816 and served until 1822; member of the commission to negotiate a treaty with the Indians for lands in 1818; elected as a Democrat to the Seventeenth Congress to fill the vacancy caused by the resignation of William Hendricks; reelected to the Eighteenth and to the three succeeding Congresses and served from December 2, 1822, to March 3, 1831; unsuccessful candidate for reelection in 1830; retired to his farm and engaged in agricultural pursuits; in 1832 served as a commissioner to negotiate with the Indians for the purchase of lands in northern Indiana and southern Michigan; died near Charlestown, Ind., July 26, 1834; interment in Charlestown Cemetery.

JENNINGS, William Pat, a Representative from Virginia; born on a farm in Camp, Smyth County, Va., August 20, 1919; attended the public schools and Sugar Grove High School; graduated from Virginia Polytechnic Institute at Lexington in 1941; entered the United States Army July 1, 1941; served in the United States for two years and in the European Theater of Operations for two and a half years with the Twenty-ninth Infantry as platoon leader, company commander, and operations officer; participated in five major battles; returned to the United States in 1945; instructor in ROTC at the University of Illinois; discharged as a major in May 1946; awarded five battle stars; automobile and farm implement dealer in Marion, Va., since 1946; cattle farmer; elected sheriff of Smyth County, Va., in 1947, reelected in 1951, and served until 1954; elected as a Democrat to the Eighty-fourth, Eighty-fifth, and Eighty-sixth Congresses (January 3, 1955–January 3, 1961). *Reelected to the Eighty-seventh Congress.*

JENSEN, Benton Franklin (Ben), a Representative from Iowa; born in Marion, Linn County, Iowa, December 16, 1892; attended the rural and high schools; employed by a lumber company as yardman and assistant auditor 1914–1917; during the First World War served as a second lieutenant in 1918; manager of a lumber company 1919–1938; student of government science; elected as a Republican to the Seventy-sixth and to the ten succeeding Congresses (January 3, 1939–January 3, 1961). *Reelected to the Eighty-seventh Congress.*

JETT, Thomas Marion, a Representative from Illinois; born near Greenville, Bond County, Ill., May 1, 1862; attended the common schools and the Northern Indiana Normal School, Valparaiso, Ind., for two years; taught school in Bond and Montgomery Counties, Ill.; studied law; was admitted to the bar in 1887 and commenced practice in Nokomis, Ill.; moved to Hillsboro, Ill., and served as prosecuting attorney of Montgomery County 1889–1896; elected as a Democrat to the Fifty-fifth, Fifty-sixth, and Fifty-seventh Congresses (March 4, 1897–March

3, 1903); was not a candidate for renomination in 1902; resumed the practice of law in Hillsboro, Ill.; also interested in agricultural pursuits; delegate to the Democratic National Conventions in 1900 and 1908; was elected as a judge of the circuit court, fourth judicial district of Illinois, in 1909; reelected in 1915, 1921, 1927, and 1935 and served until his death; was a member of the appellate court of the second district of Illinois 1922–1936; died in Litchfield, Ill., January 10, 1939; interment in Oak Grove Cemetery, Hillsboro, Ill.

JEWETT, Daniel Tarbox, a Senator from Missouri; born in Pittston, Kennebec County, Maine, September 14, 1807; completed preparatory studies; attended Colby College; was graduated from Columbia College, New York City, N. Y., in 1830 and from the Harvard Law School; was admitted to the bar and practiced in Bangor, Maine; city solicitor of Bangor 1834–1837; engaged with his brother, Albert G. Jewett, in operating a steamboat line upon the Chagres River, Isthmus of Panama, 1850–1853; moved to California and engaged in gold mining for two years; returned to Bangor, Maine, and practiced law; moved to St. Louis, Mo., in 1857 and continued the practice of law; member of the State house of representatives in 1866; appointed as a Republican to the United States Senate to fill the vacancy caused by the resignation of Charles D. Drake and served from December 19, 1870, to January 20, 1871, when a successor was elected; declined to be a candidate for election to the Senate to fill this vacancy; resumed the practice of law; died in St. Louis, Mo., October 7, 1906; interment in Bellefontaine Cemetery.

JEWETT, Freeborn Garrettson, a Representative from New York; born in Sharon, Litchfield County, Conn., August 4, 1791; pursued an academic course; moved to Skaneateles, N. Y., in 1815; justice of the peace in 1817; studied law; was admitted to the bar in 1818 and commenced practice in Skaneateles; surrogate of Onondaga County 1824–1831; member of the State assembly in 1826; presidential elector on the Democratic ticket of Jackson and Calhoun in 1828; elected as a Jackson Democrat to the Twenty-second Congress (March 4, 1831–March 3, 1833); was not a candidate for renomination in 1832; inspector of Auburn Prison in 1838 and 1839; district attorney for Onondaga County in 1839; appointed associate justice of the State supreme court March 5, 1845; elected a judge of the State court of appeals in 1847; reelected in 1849 and served until June 1853, when he resigned on account of ill health; served as chief justice of the court 1847–1850; died in Skaneateles, N. Y., January 27, 1858; interment in Lake View Cemetery.

JEWETT, Hugh Judge (brother of Joshua Husband Jewett), a Representative from Ohio; born at Deer Creek, near Darlington, Md., on July 1, 1817; completed preparatory studies and attended Hopewell Academy, Chester County, Pa.; studied law in Elkton, Cecil County, Md.; was admitted to the bar in 1838 and commenced practice in St. Clairsville, Ohio; moved to Columbus, Ohio, and thence to Zanesville, Ohio, in 1848; president of the branch State bank in 1852; presidential elector on the Democratic ticket of Pierce and King in 1852; United States attorney for the southern district of Ohio in 1854; member of the State senate in 1853; member of the State house of representatives in 1855; president of the Central Ohio Railroad Co. in 1857; organized the Pittsburgh, Cincinnati & St. Louis Railroad Co.; one of the organizers of the Pennsylvania Railroad; unsuccessful Democratic candidate for Governor of Ohio in 1861 and for United States Senator in 1863; member of the State house of representatives in 1868 and 1869; general counsel of the Pennsylvania Railway system in 1871; elected as a Democrat to the Forty-third Congress and served from March 4, 1873, until June 23, 1874, when he resigned to become president of the Erie Railroad Co.; retired from public life and resided in New York City; died while on a visit in Augusta, Ga., March 6, 1898; interment in Woodlawn Cemetery, Zanesville, Ohio.

JEWETT, Joshua Husband (brother of Hugh Judge Jewett), a Representative from Kentucky; born at Deer Creek, Harford County, Md., September 30, 1815; attended the common schools; studied law; was admitted to the bar in 1836 and commenced practice in Elizabethtown, Ky.; prosecuting attorney of Hardin County; elected as a Democrat to the Thirty-fourth and Thirty-fifth Congresses (March 4, 1855–March 3, 1859); unsuccessful candidate for reelection in 1858 to the Thirty-sixth Congress; resumed the practice of law; died in Elizabethtown, Hardin County, Ky., July 14, 1861; interment in the City Cemetery.

JEWETT, Luther, a Representative from Vermont; born in Canterbury, Windham County, Conn., December 24, 1772; was graduated from Dartmouth College, Hanover, N. H., in 1795; studied medicine and practiced in Putney, Vt.; member of the State house of representatives; elected as a Federalist to the Fourteenth Congress (March 4, 1815–March 3, 1817); moved to St. Johnsbury, Caledonia County, Vt.; studied theology; was ordained as a minister and officiated in Newbury, Vt., 1821–1828; returned to St. Johnsbury and published the Farmer's Herald 1828–1832 and the Free Mason's Friend 1830–1832; died in St. Johnsbury, Vt., March 8, 1860; interment in Mount Pleasant Cemetery.

JOHANSEN, August Edgar, a Representative from Michigan; born in Philadelphia, Pa., July 21, 1905; was reared in Battle Creek, Mich., by his grandparents after his mother died when he was an infant; attended the public schools in Battle Creek; attended Olivet (Mich.) College in 1922 and 1923, and Western Michigan College of Education in Kalamazoo in 1923 and 1924; graduated from the University of Chicago in 1926; reporter with the Battle Creek Moon-Journal during the summers 1922–1927; minister of the Seventh-day Baptist Church in Chicago, Ill., and Congregational Church, Bedford, Mich., 1924–1934; manager of industrial relations of the Kellogg Co., Battle Creek, Mich., 1934–1944; editorial writer for the Battle Creek Enquirer-News 1944–1948; editor of the Lakeview News and news editor of Radio Station WBCK 1944–1951; member of the Calhoun County Tax Allocation Board in 1949 and 1950; administrative assistant to Representative Paul W. Shafer 1951–1954; elected as a Republican to the Eighty-fourth, Eighty-fifth, and Eighty-sixth Congresses (January 3, 1955–January 3, 1961). *Reelected to the Eighty-seventh Congress.*

JOHNS, Joshua Leroy, a Representative from Wisconsin; born in the town of Eagle, Richland County, Wis., February 27, 1881; attended the public schools; engaged in banking in Richland Center, Wis., 1902–1905; was graduated from the law department of the University of Chattanooga, Chattanooga, Tenn., in 1906 and from Yale University, New Haven, Conn., in 1907; was admitted to the Tennessee bar in 1906 and commenced practice in Chattanooga, Tenn., in 1907; was admitted to the Wisconsin bar in 1910 and commenced practice in Richland Center, Wis.; moved to Appleton, Wis., in 1920 and continued the practice of law; also interested in various business enterprises; colonel in the Wisconsin National Guard 1928–1929; elected as a Republican to the Seventy-sixth and Seventy-seventh Congresses (January 3, 1939–January 3, 1943); unsuccessful candidate for reelection in 1942 to the Seventy-eighth Congress; resumed the practice of law in Green Bay, Wis., and also served as president of the Plumbers Woodwork Co.,

the Norcor Manufacturing Co., and the Northland Lumber Co., of Summit Lake; died at Green Bay, Wis., March 16, 1947; interment in Fort Howard Cemetery.

JOHNS, Kensey, Jr., a Representative from Delaware; born in New Castle, New Castle County, Del., December 10, 1791; pursued classical studies, and was graduated from Princeton College in 1810; studied law; was admitted to the bar in 1813 and commenced practice in New Castle; elected as a Federalist to the Twentieth Congress to fill the vacancy caused by the resignation of Louis McLane; reelected to the Twenty-first Congress and served from October 2, 1827, to March 3, 1831; was not a candidate for renomination in 1830 to the Twenty-second Congress; appointed chancellor of Delaware in 1832 and served until his death in New Castle, Del., on March 28, 1857; interment in the Presbyterian Cemetery.

JOHNSON, Adna Romulus, a Representative from Ohio; born in Sweet Springs, Saline County, Mo., December 14, 1860; moved with his mother to a farm in Lawrence County, Ohio, in 1864; attended the common schools; taught school seven years; studied law; was admitted to the bar in 1886; was graduated from the law department of the University of Michigan at Ann Arbor in 1887 and practiced his profession in Ironton, Ohio; prosecuting attorney of Lawrence County in 1889; elected as a Republican to the Sixty-first Congress (March 4, 1909–March 3, 1911); was renominated without opposition in 1910 but declined to accept; resumed the practice of law in Ironton, Ohio; also engaged in banking and was financially interested in various manufacturing concerns; served as president of the Ohio State Bar Association in 1933; died in Ironton, Ohio, June 11, 1938; interment in Woodland Cemetery.

JOHNSON, Albert, a Representative from Washington; born in Springfield, Sangamon County, Ill., March 5, 1869; attended the public and high schools at Atchison and Hiawatha, Kans.; reporter on the St. Joseph (Mo.) Herald and the St. Louis (Mo.) Globe-Democrat 1888–1891; managing editor of the New Haven Register in 1896 and 1897; news editor of the Washington (D. C.) Post in 1898; moved to Tacoma, Wash., in 1898; editor of the Tacoma News 1898–1906; became editor and publisher of Grays Harbor Washingtonian (Hoquiam, Wash.) in 1907; elected as a Republican to the Sixty-third and to the nine succeeding Congresses (March 4, 1913–March 3, 1933); unsuccessful candidate for reelection in 1932 to the Seventy-third Congress; while a Member of Congress was commissioned a captain in the Chemical Warfare Service, during the First World War, receiving an honorable discharge on November 29, 1918; retired from the newspaper business in 1934; died in a veterans hospital at American Lake, Wash., January 17, 1957; interment in Sunset Memorial Park, Hoquiam, Wash.

JOHNSON, Andrew, a Representative and a Senator from Tennessee and a Vice President and a President of the United States; was born in Raleigh, N. C., on December 29, 1808; self-educated, never having attended school a day in his life; at the age of ten was apprenticed to a tailor; ran away and worked as a tailor at Laurens Court House, S. C., until 1825; returned and endeavored to make settlement with his former employer; moved to Greeneville, Tenn., in September 1826, where he received instruction in elementary English branches from the young woman he married May 27, 1826; moved to Rutledge, Grainger County, Tenn., where he was employed as a tailor for a short time; returned to Greeneville, Tenn., in 1827; organized a workingman's party in 1828 and became its leader; alderman of Greeneville 1828–1830; mayor 1830–1834; member of the State house of representatives 1835–1837 and 1839–1841;

unsuccessful candidate for presidential elector on the Democratic ticket of Van Buren and Johnson in 1840; served in the State senate in 1841; elected as a Democrat to the Twenty-eighth and to the four succeeding Congresses (March 4, 1843–March 3, 1853); did not seek renomination, having become a gubernatorial candidate; Governor of Tennessee 1853–1857; elected to the United States Senate and served from October 8, 1857, to March 4, 1862, when he resigned; appointed by President Lincoln Military Governor of Tennessee, with the rank of brigadier general of Volunteers, March 4, 1862; was nominated as a War Democrat and elected Vice President of the United States on the Republican ticket headed by Abraham Lincoln in 1864 and was inaugurated March 4, 1865; became President of the United States April 15, 1865, upon the death of Abraham Lincoln; wide differences arising between the President and the Republican Congress, a resolution for his impeachment passed the House of Representatives February 24, 1868; eleven articles were set out in the resolutions and the trial before the Senate lasted three months, at the conclusion of which he was acquitted (May 16, 1868) by a vote of thirty-five for conviction to nineteen for acquittal, the necessary two-thirds vote for impeachment not having been obtained; retired to his home in Tennessee upon the expiration of the presidential term, March 3, 1869; unsuccessful candidate for election to the United States Senate before the legislature in 1869; unsuccessful as an independent candidate for election in 1872 to the Forty-third Congress; elected to the United States Senate and served from March 4, 1875, until his death at the home of his daughter near Elizabethton, Carter County, Tenn., July 31, 1875; interment in the Andrew Johnson National Cemetery, Greeneville, Greene County, Tenn.

JOHNSON, Anton Joseph, a Representative from Illinois; born in Peoria, Ill., October 20, 1878; attended the public schools and the School of Agriculture of the University of Missouri at Columbia; served as first sergeant, Fifth Infantry, Company G, Illinois National Guard, 1898–1901; letter carrier, Peoria, Ill., 1900–1913; engaged in agricultural pursuits near Peoria, Ill., 1913–1921; engaged in dairy-products manufacturing in Macomb, Ill., 1926–1938; president of the Illinois Milk Dealers' Association 1931–1936; president of the Illinois Dairy Products Association in 1937; elected as a Republican to the Seventy-sixth and to the four succeeding Congresses (January 3, 1939–January 3, 1949); was not a candidate for renomination in 1948 to the Eighty-first Congress; elected mayor of Macomb, Ill., in 1949 for a four-year term but resigned after serving two years; died in Macomb, Ill., on April 16, 1958; interment in Springdale Cemetery, Peoria, Ill.

JOHNSON, Ben, a Representative from Kentucky; born near Bardstown, Nelson County, Ky., May 20, 1858; pursued preparatory studies; was graduated from St. Mary's College, Marion County, Ky., in June 1878 and from the Louisville Law University in 1882; was admitted to the bar in 1882 and commenced practice in Bardstown; member of the State house of representatives in 1885 and 1887, serving as speaker in the latter year; appointed by President Cleveland collector of internal revenue for the fifth Kentucky district on July 10, 1893, and served until August 10, 1897; member of the State senate from 1905 until his resignation on November 5, 1906; elected as a Democrat to the Sixtieth and to the nine succeeding Congresses (March 4, 1907–March 3, 1927); declined to be a candidate for renomination in 1926; delegate at large to the Democratic National Conventions in 1912 and 1920; resumed the practice of law; member of the Kentucky Highway Commission 1927–1936; died in Bardstown, Ky., June 4, 1950; interment in St. Joseph's Cemetery.

JOHNSON, Byron Lindberg, a Representative from Colorado; born in Chicago, Ill., October 12, 1917; moved to Oconomowoc, Wis., in 1927 and attended the public schools; graduated from the University of Wisconsin in 1940 in economics, public administration, and constitutional law; statistician and economist, State of Wisconsin, 1938–1942; Bureau of the Budget, 1942–1944, and Social Security Administration, Washington, D. C., 1944–1947; professor of economics, University of Denver, 1947–1956; member of the Colorado House of Representatives in 1955 and 1956; unsuccessful candidate for election in 1956 to the Eighty-fifth Congress; assistant to Gov. Steve McNichols of Colorado in 1957 and 1958; elected as a Democrat to the Eighty-sixth Congress (January 3, 1959–January 3, 1961); unsuccessful candidate for reelection in 1960 to the Eighty-seventh Congress; appointed consultant for International Cooperation Administration in February 1961; resides in Bethesda, Md.

JOHNSON, Calvin Dean, a Representative from Illinois; born in Fordsville, Ohio County, Ky., November 22, 1898; moved with his parents to St. Clair County, Ill., in 1904, where he was educated in the graded schools and the East St. Louis (Ill.) High School; engaged in the general contracting business 1922–1944; member of the St. Clair County, Ill., Board of Supervisors 1930–1934; served in the State house of representatives 1935–1940; elected as a Republican to the Seventy-eighth Congress (January 3, 1943–January 3, 1945); unsuccessful candidate for reelection in 1944 to the Seventy-ninth Congress and for election in 1946 to the Eightieth Congress; executive assistant to vice president of Remington-Rand, Inc., in Washington, D. C., since 1952; resides in Upper Marlboro, Md.

JOHNSON, Cave, a Representative from Tennessee; born in Robertson County, Tenn., January 11, 1793; pursued an academic course and attended Cumberland College, Nashville, Tenn.; studied law; was admitted to the bar in 1814 and commenced practice in Clarksville, Tenn.; prosecuting attorney of Montgomery County in 1817; elected as a Democrat to the Twenty-first and to the three succeeding Congresses (March 4, 1829–March 3, 1837); unsuccessful candidate for reelection in 1836 to the Twenty-fifth Congress; elected to the Twenty-sixth, Twenty-seventh, and Twenty-eighth Congresses (March 4, 1839–March 3, 1845); appointed Postmaster General of the United States and served from March 5, 1845, to March 5, 1849; judge of the seventh judicial circuit court in 1850 and 1851; president of the Bank of Tennessee 1854–1860; United States commissioner in settling the affairs of the United States and Paraguay Navigation Co. in 1860; during the Civil War was elected to the State senate but was not permitted to take his seat; died in Clarksville, Tenn., November 23, 1866; interment in Greenwood Cemetery.

JOHNSON, Charles, a Representative from North Carolina; born in Chowan County, N. C.; pursued an academic course; engaged as a planter; served in the State senate 1781–1784, 1788–1790, and 1792; elected to the Seventh Congress and served from March 4, 1801, until his death in Bandon, near Edenton, Chowan County, N. C., July 23, 1802; interment in Edenton Cemetery.

JOHNSON, Charles Fletcher, a Senator from Maine; born in Winslow, Kennebec County, Maine, February 14, 1859; attended the common schools and the Waterville Classical Institute; was graduated from Bowdoin College, Brunswick, Maine, in 1879; principal of the high school of Machias, Washington County, Maine, 1881–1886; studied law; was admitted to the bar in 1886 and commenced practice in Waterville, Maine; unsuccessful candidate for Governor of Maine in 1892 and

1894; mayor of Waterville in 1893; member of the State house of representatives in 1905 and 1907; delegate to the Democratic National Conventions in 1904 and 1912; elected as a Democrat to the United States Senate in 1910 and served from March 4, 1911, until March 3, 1917; unsuccessful candidate for reelection in 1916; served as judge of the United States Circuit Court of Appeals for the first circuit from 1917 until his retirement in May 1929; died while on a visit in St. Petersburg, Fla., February 15, 1930; interment in Pine Grove Cemetery, Waterville, Maine.

JOHNSON, Dewey William, a Representative from Minnesota; born in Minneapolis, Minn., March 14, 1899; attended the public schools, the University of Minnesota at Minneapolis, and the Y. M. C. A. Law School; engaged in the insurance business; member of the State house of representatives 1929–1935; unsuccessful candidate for election in 1934 to the Seventy-fourth Congress; served as deputy commissioner of insurance and State fire marshal in 1935 and 1936; elected as a Farmer-Laborite to the Seventy-fifth Congress (January 3, 1937–January 3, 1939); unsuccessful candidate for reelection in 1938 to the Seventy-sixth Congress and for election in 1940 to the Seventy-seventh Congress; resumed insurance business in Minneapolis, Minn., and also engaged in retail radio sales business; died in Minneapolis, Minn., September 18, 1941; interment in Lakewood Cemetery.

JOHNSON, Edwin Carl, a Senator from Colorado; born in Scandia, Republic County, Kans., January 1, 1884; moved with his parents to a cattle ranch near Elsie, Nebr., in 1884; attended the rural schools and was graduated from the Lincoln High School in 1903; employed as railroad laborer, telegrapher, and train dispatcher 1901–1909; homesteaded on Government land in Colorado in 1910; operated the Farmers' Cooperative Milling Elevator and also engaged in the produce business 1920–1930; member of the State house of representatives 1923–1931; Lieutenant Governor of Colorado 1931–1933 and Governor 1933–1937; elected as a Democrat to the United States Senate in 1936; reelected in 1942 and again in 1948 and served from January 3, 1937, to January 3, 1955; was not a candidate for reelection in 1954; elected Governor of Colorado in 1954 for a two-year term ending January 1957; was not a candidate for the gubernatorial nomination in 1956; resides in Denver, Colo.

JOHNSON, Edwin Stockton, a Senator from South Dakota; born near Spencer, Owen County, Ind., February 26, 1857; moved with his parents to Osceola, Iowa, in 1857; attended the public schools; engaged in the mercantile business; moved to Wheeler County, Nebr., in 1880; homesteaded and engaged in agricultural pursuits; returned to Osceola, Iowa, in 1881 and was employed as a bank cashier; established the Citizens' Bank of Grand View, S. Dak., in 1884; moved to Armour, Douglas County, S. Dak., in 1886 and engaged in banking; also engaged in agricultural pursuits; later established a number of banks in South Dakota, Minnesota, and Iowa; studied law; was admitted to the bar in 1888 and practiced; prosecuting attorney of Douglas County in 1892 and 1893; served as a Republican in the State senate in 1894 and 1895; affiliated with the Democratic Party in 1896; chairman of the Democratic State central committee 1902–1904; retired from the banking business in 1902 and engaged in the real estate and loan business at Platte, S. Dak.; member of the Democratic National Committee 1904–1916; unsuccessful Democratic candidate for Governor in 1912; elected as a Democrat to the United States Senate in 1914 and served from March 4, 1915, to March 3, 1921; declined to be a candidate for renomination in 1920; resumed his activities in the real estate and loan business; died in Platte, S. Dak., July 19, 1933, interment in Pleasant Ridge Cemetery, Armour, S. Dak.

JOHNSON, Francis, a Representative from Kentucky; born in Caroline County, Va., June 19, 1776; pursued preparatory studies; studied law; was admitted to the bar and practiced; moved to Woodford County, Ky., in 1796 and to Bowling Green in 1807; member of the State house of representatives in 1812, 1813, and 1815; elected as an Adams Democrat to the Sixteenth Congress to fill the vacancy caused by the death of David Walker; reelected to the Seventeenth, Eighteenth, and Nineteenth Congresses and served from November 13, 1820, to March 3, 1827; moved to Louisville, Ky., in 1829 and resumed the practice of law; served as Commonwealth attorney for the fifth district; unsuccessful Republican candidate for Governor; died in Louisville, Ky., May 16, 1842; interment in the old family burial ground, later a municipal playground.

JOHNSON, Frederick Avery, a Representative from New York; born in Fort Edward, Warren County, N. Y., January 2, 1833; attended the common schools and was graduated from the Glens Falls Academy; engaged in banking and in the wool business in New York City and later in banking in Glens Falls; president of the village of Glens Falls; elected to the Forty-eighth and Forty-ninth Congresses (March 4, 1883–March 3, 1887); was not a candidate for renomination in 1886; retired from public life; executor of several large estates; died at Glens Falls, Warren County, N. Y., on July 17, 1893; interment in the Bay Street Cemetery.

JOHNSON, Fred Gustus, a Representative from Nebraska; born on a farm near Dorchester, Saline County, Nebr., October 16, 1876; attended the country schools; was graduated from Dorchester (Nebr.) High School in 1893, and from the law department of the University of Nebraska at Lincoln in 1903; was admitted to the bar in 1903 and commenced practice in Dorchester, Nebr.; also engaged in agricultural pursuits; represented Saline County in the State legislature 1907–1909; moved to Oxford, Nebr., in 1909 and to Hastings, Nebr., in 1911, and continued the practice of law; served in the State house of representatives 1917–1919; member of the State senate in 1919 and 1920; Lieutenant Governor of Nebraska in 1923 and 1924; delegate to the Republican State conventions 1900–1938; elected as a Republican to the Seventy-first Congress (March 4, 1929–March 3, 1931); unsuccessful candidate for reelection in 1930 to the Seventy-second Congress and for election in 1932 to the Seventy-third Congress; engaged in the practice of law and the real-estate business 1931–1933, and in an agricultural-industrial enterprise in Hastings, Nebr., 1934–1938, and Charleston, Miss., 1941–1943; elected judge of the county court of Adams County, Nebr., for the term commencing January 4, 1945; reelected in 1948 and served until his death in Hastings, Nebr., April 30, 1951; interment in Parkview Cemetery.

JOHNSON, George William, a Representative from West Virginia; born near Charles Town, Jefferson County, W. Va., on November 10, 1869; attended the common schools and Shepherd College State Normal School, Shepherdstown, W. Va.; was graduated from the University of West Virginia at Morgantown in 1894 and from the law department of the same university in 1896; was admitted to the bar and commenced practice in Martinsburg, W. Va.; city attorney of Martinsburg, W. Va.; moved to Parkersburg, W. Va., in 1900 and continued the practice of law; member of the board of regents of the State Normal School 1897–1900; served as referee in bankruptcy for the United States District Court of West Virginia; general counsel to the West Virginia Public Service Commission; engaged in fruit growing and stock raising; elected as a Democrat to the Sixty-eighth Congress (March 4, 1923–March 3, 1925); unsuccessful candidate for reelection in 1924 to the Sixty-ninth Congress; elected to the Seventy-third and to the four succeeding Congresses (March 4, 1933–January 3, 1943); unsuccessful candidate for reelection in 1942 to the Seventy-eighth Congress; engaged in agricultural pursuits and fruit growing at Charles Town, Jefferson County, W. Va.; died in a hospital at Martinsburg, W. Va., February 24, 1944; interment in Edgehill Cemetery, Charles Town, W. Va.

JOHNSON, Glen Dale, a Representative from Oklahoma; born in Melbourne, Izard County, Ark., September 11, 1911; moved to Paden, Okla., in 1920; attended the public schools; graduated from Paden High School at Paden, Okla., in 1930, and from the University of Oklahoma Law School at Norman in 1939; was admitted to the bar the same year and commenced practice at Okemah, Okla.; member of the State house of representatives 1940–1942; resigned his membership in the house in January 1942 and enlisted in the United States Army as a private; promoted through the ranks and served in Military Intelligence Service and Judge Advocate General's Department with two years overseas, and was discharged as a captain in May 1946; resumed the practice of law; elected as a Democrat to the Eightieth Congress (January 3, 1947–January 3, 1949); was not a candidate for renomination in 1948, but was an unsuccessful candidate for the Democratic nomination for United States Senator; neutral arbitrator for National Mediation Board in 1949 and 1950; head of National Production Authority for State of Oklahoma 1950–1952; resumed the practice of law; appointed an attorney in the Office of the Solicitor, Department of the Interior, Washington, D. C., in 1961; is a resident of Oklahoma City, Okla.

JOHNSON, Grove Lawrence (father of Hiram Warren Johnson), a Representative from California; born in Syracuse, N. Y., March 27, 1841; attended the common schools; studied law; was admitted to the bar April 2, 1862; school commissioner of Syracuse in 1862 and 1863; moved to California in October 1863; during the Civil War served as quartermaster clerk in the States of California, Arizona, and Washington, and was honorably discharged in April 1865; moved to Sacramento in May 1865; swamp-land clerk of Sacramento County 1866–1879; commenced the practice of law in Sacramento May 1, 1873; member of the California Assembly 1878 and 1879; served in the State senate 1880–1882; delegate to the Republican State conventions in 1884, 1888, 1892, and 1908; delegate to the Republican National Convention at St. Louis in 1896; elected as a Republican to the Fifty-fourth Congress (March 4, 1895–March 3, 1897); unsuccessful candidate for reelection in 1896 to the Fifty-fifth Congress; resumed the practice of law in Sacramento, Calif.; again a member of the State assembly 1901–1903 and 1907–1909; traveled extensively in Europe in 1911 and 1912, and upon his return lectured frequently on the European countries; appointed receiver of public moneys of the United States land office at Sacramento July 19, 1921, and served until the discontinuance of the office on June 30, 1925; died at his home in Sacramento, Calif., February 1, 1926; interment in the City Cemetery.

JOHNSON, Harold Terry, a Representative from California; born in Yolo County, Calif., December 2, 1907; attended the public schools of Roseville, Calif., and the University of Nevada; supervisor of Pacific Fruit Express Co.; district chairman of Brotherhood of Railway Clerks; served as school trustee, city councilman, and mayor of Roseville for eight years; president of American River Development League; member of the California State Senate from 1949 until elected to Congress; elected as a Democrat to the Eighty-sixth Congress (January 3, 1959–January 3, 1961). *Reelected to the Eighty-seventh Congress.*

JOHNSON, Harvey Hull, a Representative from Ohio; born in West Rutland, Rutland County, Vt., September 7, 1808; attended the common schools and Middlebury Academy; studied law; was admitted to the bar in 1833 and commenced practice in Akron, Ohio; postmaster of Akron in 1837; moved to Ashland, Ohio, about 1848; elected as a Democrat to the Thirty-third Congress (March 4, 1853–March 3, 1855); unsuccessful candidate for reelection in 1854; moved to Minnesota in 1855 and settled in Winona; resumed the practice of law; president of the Winona & St. Peter Railroad during its construction to Rochester; moved to Owatonna, Steele County, Minn., in 1865 and engaged in the practice of law; mayor and city justice 1867–1870; died in Owatonna, Minn., February 4, 1896; interment in Forest Hill Cemetery.

JOHNSON, Henry, a Senator and a Representative from Louisiana; born in Virginia September 14, 1783; pursued an academic course; studied law; was admitted to the bar; moved to the Territory of Orleans in 1809 and became clerk of the second superior court of the Territory; district judge of the Parish Court in 1811; delegate to the first State constitutional convention in 1812; unsuccessful candidate for election in 1812 to the Thirteenth Congress; practiced law in Donaldsonville, La.; elected to the United States Senate to fill the vacancy caused by the death of William C. C. Claiborne; reelected in 1823 and served from January 12, 1818, to May 27, 1824, when he resigned to become a gubernatorial candidate; Governor of Louisiana 1824–1828; unsuccessful candidate for election to the United States Senate in 1829; elected as a Whig to the Twenty-third Congress to fill the vacancy caused by the resignation of Edward D. White; reelected to the Twenty-fourth and Twenty-fifth Congresses and served from September 25, 1834, to March 3, 1839; unsuccessful Whig candidate for Governor in 1838 and 1842; again elected to the United States Senate to fill the vacancy caused by the death of Alexander Porter and served from February 12, 1844, to March 3, 1849; unsuccessful candidate for election in 1850 to the Thirty-second Congress; moved to New River, La., and continued the practice of law; died in the Parish of Pointe Coupee, La., September 4, 1864; interment on his plantation where the Grosse Tete and Maringoin Bayous meet.

JOHNSON, Henry Underwood, a Representative from Indiana; born in Cambridge City, Wayne County, Ind., October 28, 1850; attended the Centerville Collegiate Institute and Earlham College, Richmond, Ind.; studied law; was admitted to the bar in 1872 and commenced practice in Centerville, Wayne County, Ind.; moved to Richmond, Ind., in 1876 and continued the practice of his profession; prosecuting attorney of Wayne County 1876–1880; member of the State senate 1887–1889; elected as a Republican to the Fifty-second and to the three succeeding Congresses (March 4, 1891–March 3, 1899); was not a candidate for renomination in 1898; affiliated with the Democratic Party upon the expiration of his congressional career; moved to St. Louis, Mo., in 1899 and continued the practice of law until 1900 when he returned to Richmond, Ind., to resume his former law practice; died in Richmond, Ind., June 4, 1939; interment in Earlham Cemetery.

JOHNSON, Herschel Vespasian, a Senator from Georgia; born near Farmer's Bridge, across Brier Creek, in Burke County, Ga., September 18, 1812; attended private schools and Monaghan Academy near Warrenton; was graduated from Franklin College (now the University of Georgia) at Athens, in 1834; studied law; was admitted to the bar in 1834 and commenced practice in Augusta, Ga.; moved to a plantation, "Sandy Grove," in Jefferson County, in 1839 and practiced law in Louisville, delegate to the Democratic State convention at Milledgeville in

1841; declined to become a candidate in 1841 for election to the Twenty-seventh Congress; unsuccessful Democratic candidate in 1843 for election to fill a vacancy in the Twenty-eighth Congress; presidential elector on the Democratic ticket of Polk and Dallas in 1844; moved to Milledgeville, Ga., in 1844 and continued the practice of law; unsuccessful candidate for nomination as Governor in 1847; appointed as a Democrat to the United States Senate to fill the vacancy caused by the resignation of Walter T. Colquitt and served from February 4, 1848, to March 3, 1849; was not a candidate for election to fill this vacancy; delegate to the Democratic National Conventions in 1848, 1852, and 1856; judge of the superior court of the Ocmulgee circuit from November 1849 to August 1853; presidential elector on the Democratic ticket of Pierce and King in 1852; Governor of Georgia 1853–1857; returned to his plantation near Louisville, Jefferson County, in 1857; was an unsuccessful candidate for Vice President of the United States on the Douglas Democratic ticket in 1860; delegate to the State secession convention at Milledgeville in 1861; a Senator from Georgia in the Second Confederate Congress 1862–1865; president of the State constitutional convention in October 1865; presented credentials in 1866 as a Senator-elect to the United States Senate but was not permitted to qualify; resumed the practice of law in Louisville; appointed judge of the middle circuit of Georgia in 1873 and served until his death on his plantation near Louisville, Ga., August 16, 1880; interment in the Old Louisville Cemetery.

JOHNSON, Hiram Warren (son of Grove Lawrence Johnson), a Senator from California; born in Sacramento, Calif., September 2, 1866; attended the public schools, and the University of California at Berkeley; studied law; was admitted to the bar in 1888 and commenced practice in Sacramento; moved to San Francisco in 1902; one of the founders of the Progressive Party in 1912 and nominee for Vice President of the United States on the Progressive ticket in 1912 with Theodore Roosevelt, who headed the ticket; elected Governor of California in 1910; reelected in 1914 and served from January 2, 1911, until his resignation on March 15, 1917, having previously been elected Senator; elected as a Republican to the United States Senate on November 7, 1916, for the term beginning March 4, 1917, but, preferring to continue as Governor, did not assume his senatorial duties until March 16, 1917; reelected in 1922, 1928, 1934 and again in 1940 and served from March 16, 1917, until his death in the naval hospital at Bethesda, Md., August 6, 1945; interment in Cyprus Lawn Cemetery, San Francisco, Calif.

JOHNSON, Jacob, a Representative from Utah; born in Aalborg, Denmark, November 1, 1847; immigrated to the United States in 1854 and was admitted to citizenship in California in 1868; attended common and private schools of California; studied law; was admitted to the bar in 1877 and commenced practice in Spring City, Utah; also engaged in agricultural pursuits; United States district attorney 1880–1888; United States commissioner for Utah 1881–1893; probate judge of Sanpete County 1888–1890; prosecuting attorney of Sanpete County 1892–1894; member of the Territorial house of representatives 1893–1895; judge of the seventh judicial district for the State of Utah 1896–1905; delegate to the Republican National Convention at Chicago in 1912; elected as a Republican to the Sixty-third Congress (March 4, 1913–March 3, 1915); unsuccessful candidate for renomination in 1914; resumed the practice of law in Salt Lake City, Utah, and died there August 15, 1925; interment in Wasatch Lawn Cemetery.

JOHNSON, James, a Representative from Virginia; born in Virginia; completed preparatory studies; was graduated from William and Mary College, Williamsburg, Va., about 1795;

studied law; was admitted to the bar and practiced in Williamsburg; delegate to the State constitutional convention in 1788; member of the State house of delegates 1797–1804, 1806, 1807, and 1809–1813; moved to Isle of Wight County in 1807 and continued the practice of law; elected as a Democrat to the Thirteenth and to the three succeeding Congresses and served from March 4, 1813, until February 1, 1820, when he resigned, having been appointed collector of customs at Norfolk, in which capacity he served until his death in that city on December 7, 1825.

JOHNSON, James (brother of Richard Mentor Johnson and John Telemachus Johnson and uncle of Robert Ward Johnson), a Representative from Kentucky; born in Orange County, Va., January 1, 1774; moved with his father to Kentucky in 1779; pursued preparatory studies; a member of the State senate in 1808; served as lieutenant colonel in the War of 1812 and commanded the right wing in the Battle of the Thames; contractor for furnishing supplies to troops on the western frontier in 1819 and 1820; presidential elector on the Democratic ticket of Monroe and Tompkins in 1820; elected as a Democrat to the Nineteenth Congress and served from March 4, 1825, until his death in Washington, D. C., August 14, 1826; interment in the family cemetery, Great Crossings, Ky.

JOHNSON, James, a Representative from Georgia; born in Robeson County, N. C., February 12, 1811; was graduated from the University of Georgia at Athens in 1832; taught school; studied law; was admitted to the bar in 1835 and commenced practice in Columbus, Ga., in 1836; prosecuting attorney of Muscogee County; elected as a Unionist to the Thirty-second Congress (March 4, 1851–March 3, 1853); unsuccessful candidate for reelection; appointed Provisional Governor of Georgia in 1865 and served from June 17 to December 19 of that year; unsuccessful candidate for election to the United States Senate in 1866; collector of customs at Savannah 1866–1869; presidential elector on the Republican ticket of Grant and Colfax in 1868; judge of the superior court of Georgia from July 1, 1869, until October 1, 1875, when he resigned and resumed the practice of law; died on his plantation in Chattahoochee County, November 20, 1891; interment in Linwood Cemetery, Columbus, Ga.

JOHNSON, James Augustus, a Representative from California; born in Spartanburg, S. C., May 16, 1829; moved with his parents to Arkansas when quite young; attended the common schools; moved to California in 1853; studied medicine and was graduated from Jefferson Medical College, Philadelphia, Pa.; studied law; was admitted to the bar in 1859 and commenced the practice of law in Downieville, Calif.; member of the general assembly in 1859 and 1860; elected as a Democrat to the Fortieth and Forty-first Congresses (March 4, 1867–March 3, 1871); Lieutenant Governor of California 1875–1880; moved to San Francisco; registrar of voters in 1883 and 1884; engaged in the practice of his profession until his death in San Francisco, Calif., May 11, 1896; interment in the Masonic Cemetery.

JOHNSON, James Hutchins, a Representative from New Hampshire; born in Bath, Grafton County, N. H., June 3, 1802; attended the public schools; owned and operated a lumber mill; deputy sheriff of Grafton County in 1824 and 1825; served as paymaster of the Thirty-second Regiment Militia in 1826, later as adjutant and colonel; member of the State senate in 1839; State councilor in 1842 and 1845; elected to the Twenty-ninth and Thirtieth Congresses (March 4, 1845–March 3, 1849); died in Bath, N. H., September 2, 1887; interment in the Village Cemetery.

JOHNSON, James Leeper, a Representative from Kentucky; born near Smithland, Livingston County, Ky., October 30, 1818;

attended private schools; moved to Owensboro, Ky., in 1836; studied law; was admitted to the bar in 1841 and commenced practice in Owensboro; member of the State house of representatives in 1844; presidential elector on the Whig ticket of Taylor and Fillmore in 1848; elected as a Whig to the Thirty-first Congress (March 4, 1849–March 3, 1851); was nominated for reelection in 1850 but declined to accept; resumed the practice of law in Owensboro and also engaged in agricultural pursuits; appointed judge of the Daviess County circuit court May 4, 1867, and served until September 2 of that year; died in Owensboro, Ky., February 12, 1877; interment in Elmwood Cemetery.

JOHNSON, Jed Joseph, a Representative from Oklahoma; born on a farm near Waxahachie, Ellis County, Tex., July 31, 1888; attended the public schools in Texas and Oklahoma; was graduated from the law department of the University of Oklahoma at Norman in 1915, and postgraduate work at l'Université de Clermont at Clermont-Ferrand, France; was admitted to the bar in 1918 and commenced practice at Walters, Okla.; during the First World War served overseas as a private in Company L of the Thirty-sixth Division in 1918 and 1919; editor of a newspaper in Cotton County, Okla., 1920–1922; member of the State senate 1920–1927; delegate to the annual peace conference of the Interparliamentary Union at Paris, France, in 1927 and 1937, and at Geneva, Switzerland, in 1929; chairman of the speakers' bureau, Democratic National Congressional Committee; elected as a Democrat to the Seventieth and to the nine succeeding Congresses (March 4, 1927–January 3, 1947); was an unsuccessful candidate for renomination in 1946; appointed by President Franklin D. Roosevelt to the United States Customs Court in 1945, which position he declined; was appointed by President Harry S. Truman to the United States Customs Court in 1947, in which capacity he is now serving; is a resident of Chickasha, Okla.

JOHNSON, Jeromus, a Representative from New York; born in Wallabout, Kings County, N. Y., November 2, 1775; attended the public schools; moved to New York City; engaged in mercantile pursuits; member of the State assembly in 1822; elected as a Democrat to the Nineteenth and Twentieth Congresses (March 4, 1825–March 3, 1829); appointed appraiser of merchandise for the port of New York May 26, 1830, and served until 1840 when he retired from active business and moved to Goshen, Orange County, N. Y.; died in Goshen, N. Y., September 7, 1846; interment in a private cemetery on his estate in Goshen.

JOHNSON, John, a Representative from Ohio; born near Dungannon, County Tyrone, Ireland, in 1805; immigrated with his mother to the United States in 1818; settled in Coshocton, Ohio, in 1819; received a limited schooling; learned the tanner's trade; later engaged in merchandising and banking; member of the State senate in 1843 and 1844; delegate to the State constitutional convention in 1849 and 1850; elected as an Independent to the Thirty-second Congress (March 4, 1851–March 3, 1853); was not a candidate for renomination in 1852; retired from political life and resided in Washington, D. C., for several years; returned to Coshocton, Coshocton County, Ohio, and engaged in banking and also interested in agricultural pursuits until his death there February 5, 1867; interment in Oakbridge Cemetery.

JOHNSON, John Telemachus (brother of James Johnson and Richard Mentor Johnson and uncle of Robert Ward Johnson), a Representative from Kentucky; born at Great Crossings, Scott County, Ky., October 5, 1788; pursued preparatory studies; attended Transylvania University, Lexington, Ky.; studied law; was admitted to the bar in 1809 and commenced practice in Georgetown, Ky.; served in the War of 1812 as an aide to Gen. William H. Harrison; member of the State house of representatives and served five terms; elected as a Jackson Democrat to the Seventeenth and Eighteenth Congresses (March 4, 1821–March 3, 1825); was not a candidate for renomination in 1824; appointed judge of the court of appeals April 20, 1826, and served until December 30, 1826; minister of the Christian Church for a number of years; became editor of the Christian Messenger in 1832, the Gospel Advocate in 1835, and the Christian in 1837; was instrumental in establishing the old Bacon College at Georgetown, Ky., in 1836; died in Lexington, Mo., while engaged in evangelistic work there on December 17, 1856; interment in Lexington Cemetery, Lexington, Ky.

JOHNSON, Joseph (uncle of Waldo Porter Johnson), a Representative from Virginia; born in Orange County, N. Y., December 19, 1785; moved with his mother to Belvidere, N. J., in 1791 and thence to Bridgeport, Va. (now West Virginia), in 1801; acquired a knowledge of rudimentary studies by personal effort; engaged in agricultural pursuits; served in the War of 1812 as captain of a company of Virginia riflemen; member of the State house of delegates in 1815, 1816, and 1818–1822; elected as a Democrat to the Eighteenth and Nineteenth Congresses (March 4, 1823–March 3, 1827); unsuccessful candidate for reelection in 1826 to the Twentieth Congress; elected to the Twenty-second Congress to fill the vacancy caused by the death of Philip Doddridge and served from January 21 to March 3, 1833; was not a candidate for renomination in 1832; elected to the Twenty-fourth, Twenty-fifth, and Twenty-sixth Congresses (March 4, 1835–March 3, 1841); declined to be a candidate for renomination in 1840; delegate to the Democratic National Convention at Baltimore in 1844 which nominated James K. Polk, of Tennessee, for President of the United States; elected to the Twenty-ninth Congress (March 4, 1845–March 3, 1847); declined to be a candidate for renomination in 1846; again a member of the State house of delegates in 1847 and 1848; resumed agricultural pursuits; delegate to the Virginia constitutional convention of 1850 and 1851; elected Governor of Virginia in 1851, serving a short term, reelected and entered upon the duties of the office January 1, 1852, and served four years; presidential elector in 1860; died in Bridgeport, Harrison County, W. Va., February 27, 1877; interment in the old Brick Church Cemetery.

JOHNSON, Joseph Travis, a Representative from South Carolina; born in Brewerton, Laurens County, S. C., February 28, 1858; attended the common schools and was graduated from Erskine College, Due West, S. C., in 1879; taught school for several years; studied law; was admitted to the bar in 1883; practiced law in Laurens and later in Spartanburg; elected as a Democrat to the Fifty-seventh and to the seven succeeding Congresses and served from March 4, 1901, until April 19, 1915, when he resigned; Federal judge of the western district of South Carolina from 1915 until his death in Spartanburg, S. C., May 8, 1919; interment in Oakwood Cemetery.

JOHNSON, Justin Leroy, a Representative from California; born in Wausau, Marathon County, Wis., April 8, 1888; attended the public schools and was graduated from the University of Wisconsin at Madison in 1911 and from the law department of the University of California at Berkeley in 1915; was admitted to the bar in 1915; during the First World War served as a pilot in the One Hundred and Fourth Aero Squadron 1917–1919, participating in the St. Mihiel and Argonne drives; awarded the Silver Star Medal; located in Stockton, Calif., in 1919 and commenced the practice of law; deputy district attorney of San Joaquin County, Calif., in 1920 and 1921; city attorney of Stockton, Calif., 1923–1933; member of the Planning Commission of Stockton 1934–1941; referee in bankruptcy in 1922 and 1923; delegate to the Republican National Conventions in 1936 and 1948; elected as a Republican to the Seventy-eighth and to the six succeeding Congresses (January 3, 1943–January 3, 1957); unsuccessful candidate for reelection in 1956 to the Eighty-fifth Congress; died in Stockton, Calif., March 26, 1961; interment in Casa Bonita Crematorium.

JOHNSON, Lester R., a Representative from Wisconsin; born in Brandon, Wis., June 16, 1901; attended the public schools and Lawrence College 1919–1921; graduated from the University of Wisconsin School of Commerce in 1924; was associated with his father in the lumber, feed, and coal business 1924–1938; entered the University of Wisconsin Law School in 1938 and graduated in February 1941; was admitted to the Wisconsin bar and commenced practice in Black River Falls, Wis., the same year; chief clerk of the Wisconsin Assembly 1936–1939; with State banking commission in 1942; district attorney of Jackson County 1943–1946 and again in 1953; delegate to the Democratic National Conventions in 1952 and 1960; elected as a Democrat to the Eighty-third Congress to fill the vacancy caused by the death of Merlin Hull; reelected to the Eighty-fourth, Eighty-fifth, and Eighty-sixth Congresses, and served from October 13, 1953, to January 3, 1961. *Reelected to the Eighty-seventh Congress.*

JOHNSON, Luther Alexander, a Representative from Texas; born in Corsicana, Navarro County, Tex., October 29, 1875; attended the public schools, and was graduated from the law department of Cumberland University, Lebanon, Tenn., in 1896; was admitted to the bar the same year and commenced practice in Corsicana, Tex.; prosecuting attorney of Navarro County 1898–1902; district attorney of the thirteenth judicial district of Texas 1904–1910; delegate to the Democratic National Convention at St. Louis in 1916; chairman of the Democratic State convention at Fort Worth in 1920; elected as a Democrat to the Sixty-eighth and to the eleven succeeding Congresses and served from March 4, 1923, until his resignation on July 17, 1946; judge of the Tax Court of the United States from July 1946 until his retirement in September 1956; is a resident of Corsicana, Tex.

JOHNSON, Lyndon Baines, a Representative and a Senator from Texas and a Vice President of the United States; born on a farm near Stonewall, Gillespie County, Tex., on August 27, 1908; moved with his parents to Johnson City, in 1913; attended the public schools of Blanco County, Tex.; was graduated from the Johnson City (Tex.) High School in 1924 and from the Southwest Texas State Teachers College at San Marcos in 1930; attended the Georgetown University Law School, Washington, D. C.; teacher in Houston, Tex., public schools and high school 1930–1932; served as secretary to Congressman Richard M. Kleberg 1932–1935; State director of the National Youth Administration of Texas 1935–1937; elected as a Democrat to the Seventy-fifth Congress to fill the vacancy caused by the death of James P. Buchanan; reelected to the Seventy-sixth and to the four succeeding Congresses and served from April 10, 1937, to January 3, 1949; served as lieutenant commander in the United States Navy from December 9, 1941, to July 27, 1942; delegate to the Democratic National Conventions in 1940, 1944, and 1948; was an unsuccessful candidate for election to the United States Senate in 1941; was not a candidate for renomination to the Eighty-first Congress in 1948; elected to the United States Senate in 1948 for the term commencing January 3, 1949; reelected in 1954 and again in 1960 for the term ending January 3, 1967; nominated for the office of Vice President of the United States by the Demo-

cratic Party at the convention in Los Angeles in 1960; elected Vice President of the United States on November 8, 1960, for the term beginning January 20, 1961; resigned from the United States Senate January 3, 1961.

JOHNSON, Magnus, a Senator and a Representative from Minnesota; born near Karlstad in Ed Parish, Varmland, Sweden, September 19, 1871; attended the rural schools of his native country; employed as a glass blower 1888–1891; immigrated to the United States in 1891 and settled in La Crosse, Wis., where he was engaged as a lumberjack; moved to Meeker County, Minn., in 1893 and engaged in agricultural pursuits; president of the State Union of the American Society of Equity 1911–1914; vice president of the Equity Cooperative Exchange 1912–1926; also served as school clerk and assessor of Kingston, Minn.; member of the State house of representatives 1915–1919; delegate to the Republican National Convention at Chicago in 1916; served in the State senate 1919–1923; unsuccessful candidate for Governor of Minnesota on the Farmer-Labor ticket in 1922 and again in 1926; elected on the Farmer-Labor ticket to the United States Senate to fill the vacancy caused by the death of Knute Nelson and served from July 16, 1923, to March 3, 1925; unsuccessful candidate for reelection in 1924; resumed agricultural pursuits near Kimball, Minn.; elected as a Farmer-Laborite to the Seventy-third Congress (March 4, 1933–January 3, 1935); unsuccessful candidate for reelection in 1934 to the Seventy-fourth Congress; resumed agricultural pursuits; served as State supervisor of public stockyards 1934–1936; unsuccessful candidate for the Farmer-Labor nomination for Governor of Minnesota in 1936; died in Litchfield, Minn., where he had gone for medical treatment, on September 13, 1936; interment in Dassel Cemetery, Dassel, Minn.

JOHNSON, Martin Nelson, a Representative and a Senator from North Dakota; born in Racine County, Wis., March 3, 1850; moved with his parents to Decorah, Iowa, the same year; was taught at home and attended the country schools; was graduated from the law department of the University of Iowa at Iowa City in 1873; taught two years in the California Military Academy at Oakland, Calif.; returned to Iowa in 1875; was admitted to the bar in 1876 and commenced practice in Decorah; member of the State house of representatives in 1877; served in the State senate 1878–1882; presidential elector on the Republican ticket of Hayes and Wheeler in 1876; moved to Dakota Territory in 1882; engaged in agricultural pursuits; prosecuting attorney of Nelson County 1886–1890; member of the constitutional convention of North Dakota in 1889; chairman of the first Republican State convention in 1889; unsuccessful candidate for election to the United States Senate in 1889; elected as a Republican to the Fifty-second and to the three succeeding Congresses (March 4, 1891–March 3, 1899); was not a candidate for renomination in 1898, having become a candidate for Senator; unsuccessful candidate for election to the United States Senate in 1899; elected to the United States Senate and served from March 4, 1909, until his death in Fargo, N. Dak., October 21, 1909; interment in the City Cemetery, Petersburg, N. Dak.

JOHNSON, Noadiah, a Representative from New York; born in Connecticut in 1795; completed preparatory studies; moved to Delaware County, N. Y., in 1817; studied law; was admitted to the bar and commenced practice in Delhi, N. Y.; district attorney for Delaware County from June 1825 to November 1833; one of the publishers of the Delaware Gazette; elected as a Democrat to the Twenty-third Congress (March 4, 1833–March 3, 1835); member of the State senate from 1837 until his death in Albany, N. Y., April 4, 1839; interment in the cemetery at Delhi, Delaware County, N. Y.

JOHNSON, Noble Jacob, a Representative from Indiana; born in Terre Haute, Vigo County, Ind., August 23, 1887; attended the grade and high schools of Terre Haute; studied law; was admitted to the bar in 1911 and commenced practice in Terre Haute; deputy prosecuting attorney for the forty-third judicial circuit of Indiana in 1917 and 1918; prosecuting attorney for the same judicial circuit 1921–1924; elected as a Republican to the Sixty-ninth, Seventieth, and Seventy-first Congresses (March 4, 1925–March 3, 1931); unsuccessful candidate for reelection in 1930 to the Seventy-second Congress, and for election in 1936 to the Seventy-fifth Congress; elected to the Seventy-sixth and to the four succeeding Congresses and served from January 3, 1939, until his resignation on July 1, 1948; appointed a judge of the United States Court of Customs and Patent Appeals and served from July 2, 1948, to July 19, 1956, and as chief judge from July 20, 1956, until his retirement August 7, 1958; resides in Washington, D. C.

JOHNSON, Paul Burney, a Representative from Mississippi; born in Hillsboro, Scott County, Miss., March 23, 1880; attended the public schools, Harpersville College, and Millsaps College; studied law; was admitted to the bar in 1903, and commenced practice in Hattiesburg, Forrest County, Miss.; judge of the city court in 1907 and 1908; circuit judge of the twelfth judicial district 1910–1919; elected as a Democrat to the Sixty-sixth and Sixty-seventh Congresses (March 4, 1919–March 3, 1923); declined to be a candidate for renomination in 1922; resumed the practice of his profession and also engaged in agricultural pursuits; served as Governor from 1939 until his death at Hattiesburg, Miss., December 26, 1943; interment in the City Cemetery.

JOHNSON, Perley Brown, a Representative from Ohio; born in the blockhouse in Marietta, Ohio, September 8, 1798; attended the public schools; studied medicine; commenced practice in Marietta in 1822; moved to McConnelsville, Morgan County, Ohio, in 1823 and continued practice; clerk of the court of common pleas in 1825; member of the State house of representatives 1833–1835; Whig presidential elector on the Harrison and Tyler ticket in 1840; elected as a Whig to the Twenty-eighth Congress (March 4, 1843–March 3, 1845); unsuccessful candidate for reelection in 1844 to the Twenty-ninth Congress; resumed the practice of medicine in McConnelsville, Ohio; discontinued the practice of his profession in 1847 on account of ill health and lived in retirement until his death in McConnelsville, Ohio, February 9, 1870; interment in McConnelsville Cemetery.

JOHNSON, Philip, a Representative from Pennsylvania; born in Polkville, Knowlton Township, Warren County, N. J., January 17, 1818; moved to Mount Bethel, Pa., in 1839; attended the common schools and Lafayette College, Easton, Pa., 1842–1844; was a plantation tutor in Mississippi 1844–1846; returned to Pennsylvania; studied law; attended Union Law School in Easton, Pa.; was admitted to the bar in 1848 and commenced practice in Easton; county court clerk 1848–1853; member of the State house of representatives in 1853 and 1854; revenue commissioner of the third judicial district in 1859 and 1860; elected as a Republican to the Thirty-seventh, Thirty-eighth, and Thirty-ninth Congresses and served from March 4, 1861, until his death in Washington, D. C., January 29, 1867; interment in Easton Cemetery, Easton, Pa.

JOHNSON, Reverdy (brother-in-law of Thomas Fielder Bowie), a Senator from Maryland; born in Annapolis, Md., May 21, 1796; attended St. John's College, Annapolis, Md.; studied law; was admitted to the bar in 1816 and commenced practice in Upper Marlboro; deputy attorney general of Maryland in 1816 and 1817; moved to Baltimore in 1817; appointed chief commissioner of insolvent debtors of Maryland in 1817; member of the State senate 1821–1826; reelected in 1826 to serve five years; resigned in 1829 and resumed the practice of law in Baltimore; elected to the United States Senate as a Whig and served from March 4, 1845, to March 7, 1849, when he resigned; appointed by President Taylor Attorney General of the United States March 8, 1849, and served until July 20, 1850; member of the peace convention of 1861 held in Washington, D. C., in an effort to devise means to prevent the impending war; again served in the State senate in 1860 and 1861; elected as a Democrat to the United States Senate and served from March 4, 1863, to July 10, 1868, when he resigned; United States Minister to England in 1868 and 1869; returned to Baltimore, Md., where he resumed the practice of his profession; compiler of the reports of decisions of the Maryland Court of Appeals; died suddenly in Annapolis, Md., while on business, February 10, 1876; interment in Greenmount Cemetery, Baltimore, Md.

JOHNSON, Richard Mentor (brother of James Johnson and John Telemachus Johnson and uncle of Robert Ward Johnson), a Representative and a Senator from Kentucky and a Vice President of the United States; born at Bryants Station, Ky., October 17, 1781; attended the common schools and Transylvania University, Lexington, Ky.; studied law; was admitted to the bar in 1802 and commenced practice in Great Crossings, Ky.; member of the State house of representatives 1804–1807 and again in 1819; elected as a Democrat to the Tenth and to the five succeeding Congresses (March 4, 1807–March 3, 1819); during his term of congressional service was commissioned colonel of Kentucky Volunteers and commanded a regiment under Gen. William H. Harrison in the expedition and engagements in lower Canada in 1813; participated in the Battle of the Thames October 5, 1813; Congress by resolution of April 4, 1818, presented him a sword in recognition of "the daring and distinguished valor displayed by himself and the regiment of volunteers under his command in charging and essentially contributing to vanquish the combined British and Indian forces" in the battle; elected as a Jackson Democrat to the United States Senate to fill the vacancy caused by the resignation of John J. Crittenden; reelected and served from December 10, 1819, to March 3, 1829; elected as a Representative to the Twenty-first and to the three succeeding Congresses (March 4, 1829–March 3, 1837); was chosen Vice President of the United States by the Senate on February 8, 1837, no candidate having received a majority of the electoral vote, and served from March 4, 1837, to March 3, 1841; unsuccessful Democratic candidate for Vice President in 1840; member of the State house of representatives in 1841 and 1842; died in Frankfort, Ky., November 19, 1850; interment in the State Cemetery.

JOHNSON, Robert Davis, a Representative from Missouri; born on a farm near Slater, Saline County, Mo., August 12, 1883; educated in the rural graded schools of his native county, and was graduated from the Portland (Ind.) High School in 1901; attended the Missouri Valley College, Marshall, Mo.; taught school in Saline Valley and Orearville, Mo., 1901–1907; served as clerk of the circuit court of Saline County 1915–1923; while serving as clerk also studied law; was admitted to the bar in 1917 and commenced practice in Marshall, Mo., in 1923; served as prosecuting attorney of Saline County 1925–1928; elected as a Democrat to the Seventy-second Congress to fill the vacancy caused by the death of Samuel C. Major and served from September 29, 1931, to March 3, 1933; unsuccessful candidate for renomination in 1932; resumed the practice of law in Marshall, Mo.; elected judge of the State circuit court of the fifteenth judicial circuit of Missouri on November 5, 1940, and served until January 1, 1947; again resumed the practice of law, and is a resident of Marshall, Mo.

JOHNSON, Robert Ward (nephew of James Johnson, John Telemachus Johnson and Richard Mentor Johnson), a Representative and a Senator from Arkansas; born in Scott County, Ky., July 22, 1814; attended the common schools in Scott County; moved with his father to Arkansas in 1821; attended the Indian Academy near Frankfort, Ky., and was graduated from St. Joseph's College, Bardstown, Ky., in 1833, and from the Yale Law School in 1835; was admitted to the bar the same year and practiced in Little Rock, Ark., 1835–1847; prosecuting attorney for the Little Rock circuit 1840–1842 and State attorney general ex officio; elected as a Democrat to the Thirtieth, Thirty-first, and Thirty-second Congresses (March 4, 1847–March 3, 1853); declined to be a candidate for renomination in 1852; appointed and subsequently elected to the United States Senate to fill the vacancy caused by the resignation of Solon Borland; reelected in 1855 and served from July 6, 1853, to March 3, 1861; was not a candidate for reelection in 1870; delegate to the Provisional Government of the Confederate States in 1862; member of the Confederate Senate; engaged in the practice of law in Washington, D. C.; unsuccessful candidate for election to the United States Senate from Arkansas in 1877; died in Little Rock, Ark., July 26, 1879; interment in Mount Holly Cemetery.

JOHNSON, Royal Cleaves, a Representative from South Dakota; born in Cherokee, Cherokee County, Iowa, October 3, 1882; moved with his parents to Highmore, Hyde County, S. Dak., March 19, 1883; attended the public schools; was graduated from the law department of the University of South Dakota at Vermilion in 1906; was admitted to the bar in 1906 and commenced practice in Highmore, S. Dak.; assistant State's attorney of Hyde County in 1906 and 1907 and State's attorney of the same county in 1908 and 1909; moved to Aberdeen, S. Dak., in 1913 and resumed the practice of law; attorney general of South Dakota 1910–1914; elected as a Republican to the Sixty-fourth and to the eight succeeding Congresses (March 4, 1915–March 3, 1933); was not a candidate for renomination in 1932; during the First World War tendered his resignation to Speaker Champ Clark, which was not entertained, whereupon he absented himself from the House and on January 5, 1918, enlisted in the Army; served in the Three Hundred and Thirteenth Infantry as private, sergeant, second lieutenant, and first lieutenant; was wounded at Mont Faucon, in the Meuse-Argonne attack, on September 27, 1918, and was honorably discharged December 20, 1918; was awarded the Distinguished Service Cross by the United States Government and the Croix de Guerre with gold star by the Republic of France; continued to practice law in Washington, D. C., until his death there on August 2, 1939; interment in Arlington National Cemetery, Fort Myer, Va.

JOHNSON, Thomas, a Delegate from Maryland; born near the mouth of St. Leonards Creek, Calvert County, Md., November 4, 1732; at an early age moved to Annapolis, Md., and became a writer in the office of the clerk of the provincial court; studied law; was admitted to the bar; entered the provincial assembly as a delegate from Anne Arundel County in 1762; member of the committee of correspondence and of the council of safety; assisted in organizing the Potomac Co. for improving the navigation of the Potomac River; a member of the Annapolis Convention of June 1774; Member of the Continental Congress 1774–1777; nominated George Washington as commander in chief of the American forces June 15, 1775; delegate to the first constitutional convention of Maryland in 1776; served in the Revolutionary War as senior brigadier general of Maryland Militia and led the western Maryland forces that went to Washington's relief during his retreat

through New Jersey; first Governor of Maryland 1777–1779; moved to Frederick County, Md.; member of the Maryland House of Delegates in 1780, 1786, and 1787; member of the Maryland convention for ratification of the Federal Constitution in 1788; chief judge of the general court of Maryland in 1790 and 1791; appointed by President Washington the first United States judge for the district of Maryland in September 1789 but declined; appointed Associate Justice of the United States Supreme Court in 1791 to fill the vacancy caused by the death of John Rutledge and served until February 1793, when he resigned on account of ill health; declined a Cabinet portfolio of Secretary of State tendered by President Washington August 24, 1795; appointed by President John Adams chief judge of the Territory of Columbia February 28, 1801; as a member of the Board of Commissioners of the Federal City assisted in laying out the streets and designating sites for public buildings and named the capital city "Washington"; died at "Rose Hill," Frederick, Md., October 26, 1819; interment in All Saints' Episcopal Churchyard; reinterment in Mount Olivet Cemetery, Frederick, Md.

JOHNSON, Thomas F., a Representative from Maryland; born in Worcester County, Md., June 26, 1909; attended the schools in Worcester County, Md.; graduated from Staunton (Va.) Military Academy in 1926, St. John's College, University of Virginia, and University of Maryland; was admitted to the bar and commenced the practice of law in Snow Hill, Md.; in 1932 was elected chairman of the board of Commercial National Bank of Snow Hill, Md.; elected State's attorney in 1934; elected to the State senate in 1938, reelected in 1942 and again in 1946 and served until 1951; specialized in international law with practice in the Far East, Middle East, and continental Europe; owns and operates a 300-acre farm in Maryland; elected as a Democrat to the Eighty-sixth Congress (January 3, 1959–January 3, 1961). *Reelected to the Eighty-seventh Congress.*

JOHNSON, Tom Loftin, a Representative from Ohio; born in Georgetown, Scott County, Ky., July 18, 1854; moved to Indiana in boyhood; attended the public schools; employed in a rolling mill; clerk in a street-railway office in Louisville, Ky., 1869–1875; later became secretary of the company; invented several street-railway devices; purchased a street railway in Indianapolis, Ind.; later acquired large street-railway interests in Cleveland, Detroit, and Brooklyn; settled in Cleveland, Ohio; became interested in rolling mills and iron manufacturing; unsuccessful Democratic candidate for election in 1888 to the Fifty-first Congress; elected as a Democrat to the Fifty-second and Fifty-third Congresses (March 4, 1891–March 3, 1895); unsuccessful candidate for reelection in 1894 to the Fifty-fourth Congress; retired from active business pursuits; mayor of Cleveland, Ohio, 1899–1909; unsuccessful candidate for reelection in 1909; unsuccessful Democratic candidate for Governor of Ohio in 1903; died in Cleveland, Ohio, April 10, 1911; interment in Greenwood Cemetery.

JOHNSON, Waldo Porter (nephew of Joseph Johnson), a Senator from Missouri; born in Bridgeport, Harrison County, Va., September 16, 1817; attended public and private schools; was graduated from Rector College, Pruntytown, Taylor County, Va., in 1839; studied law; was admitted to the bar and commenced practice in Harrison County, Va., in 1841; moved to Osceola, St. Clair County, Mo., in 1842 and continued the practice of law; served in the war with Mexico as a member of the First Missouri Regiment of Mounted Volunteers; member of the State house of representatives in 1847; elected circuit attorney in 1848 and judge of the seventh judicial circuit in 1851; resigned in 1852 and resumed the practice of law;

member of the peace convention of 1861 held in Washington, D. C., in an effort to devise means to prevent the impending war; elected as a Democrat to the United States Senate and served from March 17, 1861, to January 10, 1862, when he was expelled from the Senate; served in the Confederate Army during the Civil War; attained the rank of lieutenant colonel of the Fourth Missouri Infantry; was twice wounded in the Battle of Pea Ridge, March 8, 1862; engaged in recruiting and organizing troops for General Price's army; appointed a Member of the Senate of the Confederate States to fill a vacancy; resided in Hamilton, Canada, from August 1865 to April 1866; returned to Osceola, Mo., and resumed the practice of his profession; president of the State constitutional convention in 1875; died in Osceola, Mo., on August 14, 1885; interment in Forest Hill Cemetery, Kansas City, Mo.

JOHNSON, William Cost, a Representative from Maryland; born near Jefferson, Frederick County, Md., January 14, 1806; completed preparatory studies; studied law; was admitted to the bar in 1831 and commenced practice in Jefferson, Frederick County, Md.; member of the State house of representatives in 1831 and 1832; elected as a Whig to the Twenty-third Congress (March 4, 1833–March 3, 1835); delegate to the State constitutional convention in 1836; again elected to the Twenty-fifth, Twenty-sixth, and Twenty-seventh Congresses (March 4, 1837–March 3, 1843); continued the practice of his profession until his death in Washington, D. C., on April 14, 1860; interment in the Reformed Church Cemetery, Jefferson, Md.

JOHNSON, William Richard, a Representative from Illinois; born in Rock Island, Ill., May 15, 1875; moved with his parents to Freeport, Ill., in 1879; attended the public schools and the College of Commerce at Freeport; served from 1890 to 1894 as an apprentice and from 1894 to 1899 as a locomotive blacksmith in the Illinois Central Railroad shops at Freeport; appointed a member of the United States Capitol police force on January 1, 1901, and served as private, sergeant, lieutenant, and captain until he became a member of the clerical staff of the House; appointed superintendent of the folding room of the National House of Representatives on June 18, 1919, and served until March 3, 1925, when he resigned, having been elected to Congress; elected as a Republican to the Sixty-ninth and to the three succeeding Congresses (March 4, 1925–March 3, 1933); unsuccessful candidate for renomination in 1932; returned to Freeport, Ill., having retired from active political and business pursuits; died in Freeport, Ill., on January 2, 1938; interment in Oakland Cemetery.

JOHNSON, William Samuel, a Delegate and a Senator from Connecticut; born in Stratford, Conn., on October 7, 1727; was tutored privately by his father; was graduated from Yale College in 1744 and from Harvard College in 1747; commenced the study of law in 1747; was admitted to the bar and practiced in Stratford; member of the colonial house of representatives in 1761 and 1765; served as a delegate to the Stamp Act Congress held in New York City in October 1765; was Connecticut agent extraordinary to the court of England 1767–1771 to determine the State title to Indian lands; member of the upper house, or Governor's council, in 1766 and 1771–1775; judge of Connecticut Supreme Court 1772–1774; elected a Member of the Continental Congress in 1774 but declined to serve; member of the Continental Congress 1784–1787; delegate to the constitutional convention in 1787; elected to the United States Senate and served from March 4, 1789, to March 4, 1791, when he resigned; served as the first president of Columbia College of New York City 1787–1800; died in Stratford, Conn., on November 14, 1819; interment in the Episcopal Cemetery.

JOHNSON, William Ward, a Representative from California; born in Brighton, Washington County, Iowa, March 9, 1892; attended the public schools at Brighton, Iowa, and Twin Falls, Idaho, and the University of California at Berkeley in 1913 and 1914; was graduated from the law school of the University of Southern California at Los Angeles in 1925; member of the Idaho National Guard in 1910 and 1911; bookkeeper, stenographer, and manager of an automobile company at Montpelier, Idaho, and Price, Utah, 1912–1918; engaged in the mercantile business in Idaho and Utah, 1918–1922; also engaged in the banking and oil business at Twin Falls, Idaho, and Long Beach, Calif.; admitted to the bar in 1925 and commenced practice in Long Beach, Calif.; elected as a Republican to the Seventy-seventh and Seventy-eighth Congresses (January 3, 1941–January 3, 1945); unsuccessful candidate for reelection in 1944 to the Seventy-ninth Congress; resumed the practice of law in Long Beach, Calif., where he now resides.

JOHNSTON, Charles, a Representative from New York; born in Salisbury, Conn., on February 14, 1793; attended the common schools; moved to Poughkeepsie, N. Y.; studied law; was admitted to the bar and practiced; elected as a Whig to the Twenty-sixth Congress (March 4, 1839–March 3, 1841); unsuccessful candidate for reelection in 1840 to the Twenty-seventh Congress; engaged in the practice of law until his death in Poughkeepsie, N. Y., September 1, 1845; interment in the burying ground of Christ Episcopal Church; reinterment in 1861 in the Rural Cemetery.

JOHNSTON, Charles Clement (brother of Joseph Eggleston Johnston and uncle of John Warfield Johnston), a Representative from Virginia; born in Longwood, near Farmville, Prince Edward County, Va., April 30, 1795; was educated at home; moved with his parents to Panicello, near Abingdon, Va., in 1811; studied law; was admitted to the bar in 1818 and commenced practice in Abingdon, Va.; elected as a State Rights Democrat to the Twenty-second Congress and served from March 4, 1831, until his death by drowning near one of the docks in Alexandria, Va., on June 17, 1832; interment in the Congressional Cemetery, Washington, D. C.

JOHNSTON, David Emmons, a Representative from West Virginia; born near Pearisburg, Giles County, Va., April 10, 1845; attended the common schools; enlisted in the Confederate Army in April 1861 and served four years in the Seventh Virginia Regiment of Infantry, Kemper's brigade of Pickett's division; twice wounded at Williamsburg, Va., May 5, 1862, and in the charge of Pickett's division at Gettysburg July 3, 1863; studied law; was admitted to the bar in Giles County, Va., in 1867 and commenced practice in Pearisburg, Va.; moved to Mercer County, W. Va., in 1870; prosecuting attorney 1872–1876; member of the State senate in 1878; resigned; judge of the ninth judicial circuit 1880–1888; presidential elector on the Democratic ticket of Bryan and Sewall in 1896; elected as a Democrat to the Fifty-sixth Congress (March 4, 1899–March 3, 1901); unsuccessful candidate for reelection in 1900 to the Fifty-seventh Congress; moved to Portland, Oreg., in 1908 and resumed the practice of law; died in that city July 7, 1917; interment in Mount Scott Park Cemetery.

JOHNSTON, James Thomas, a Representative from Indiana; born near Greencastle, Putnam County, Ind., January 19, 1839; attended the common schools; studied law; during the Civil War enlisted as a private in Company C, Sixth Indiana Cavalry, in July 1862; transferred to Company A, Eighth Tennessee Cavalry, in September 1863 and commissioned as second lieutenant, serving until January 1864, when he resigned; afterwards served as commissary sergeant of the One Hundred and Thirty-third Regiment, Indiana Volunteer Infantry; commissioned lieutenant and assistant quartermaster of the One Hundred and Forty-ninth Regiment, Indiana Volunteer Infantry, and mustered out in September 1865; was admitted to the bar in March 1866 and commenced practice in Rockville, Parke County, Ind.; prosecuting attorney 1866–1868; member of the State house of representatives in 1868; served in the State senate 1874–1878; elected as a Republican to the Forty-ninth and Fiftieth Congresses (March 4, 1885–March 3, 1889); unsuccessful candidate for reelection; resumed the practice of law; commander of the Grand Army of the Republic, Department of Indiana, in 1893; died in Rockville, Ind., July 19, 1904; interment in the Rockville Cemetery.

JOHNSTON, John Brown, a Representative from New York; born in Glasgow, Scotland, July 10, 1882; immigrated to America in 1886 with his parents, who settled in Brooklyn, N. Y.; attended the public schools in Long Island City and Brooklyn and the New York Law School; was admitted to the bar and commenced the practice of law in Brooklyn; elected as a Democrat to the Sixty-sixth Congress (March 4, 1919–March 3, 1921); was not a candidate for renomination; resumed the practice of his profession in New York City; delegate to the Democratic National Conventions in 1920 and 1924; elected a justice of the supreme court for the second district of New York and assumed his duties on January 1, 1928, and on January 1, 1935, was designated an associate justice of the appellate division and served until his retirement December 31, 1952; on January 1, 1953, was appointed an official referee of the supreme court and continued until July 4, 1955, and then assumed the office of State Administrator of the Judicial Conference of the State of New York until his death; died in Brooklyn, N. Y., January 11, 1960; interment in Green Wood Cemetery.

JOHNSTON, John Warfield (uncle of Henry Bowen and nephew of Charles Clement Johnston and Joseph Eggleston Johnston), a Senator from Virginia; born in Panicello, near Abingdon, Va., September 9, 1818; attended Abingdon Academy, South Carolina College at Columbia, and the law department of the University of Virginia at Charlottesville; was admitted to the bar in 1839 and commenced practice in Tazewell, Tazewell County, Va.; Commonwealth attorney for Tazewell County 1844–1846; State senator 1846–1848; judge of the circuit court of Virginia 1866–1870; upon the readmission of the State of Virginia to representation was elected as a Conservative to the United States Senate and served from January 26, 1870, to March 3, 1871; elected on March 15, 1871, for the term beginning March 4, 1871; reelected in 1877 and served until March 3, 1883; unsuccessful candidate for reelection; resumed the practice of his profession; died in Richmond, Va., February 27, 1889; interment in St. Mary's Cemetery, Wytheville, Va.

JOHNSTON, Joseph Eggleston (brother of Charles Clement Johnston and uncle of John Warfield Johnston), a Representative from Virginia; born in Longwood, Prince Edward County, Va., February 3, 1807; moved with his parents to Panicello, near Abingdon, Va., in 1811; attended the Abingdon Academy; was graduated from the United States Military Academy, West Point, N. Y., in 1829 in the class with Robert E. Lee; was assigned to the Fourth United States Artillery as second lieutenant and was garrisoned in New York and Fort Monroe, Va., 1829–1832; first lieutenant July 31, 1836; resigned May 31, 1837; commissioned first lieutenant of topographical engineers July 7, 1838; captain September 21, 1846; lieutenant colonel of voltigeurs April 9, 1847, to August 28, 1848; lieutenant colonel First Cavalry March 3, 1855; brigadier general and quartermaster general June 28, 1860; brevetted captain July 7, 1838, "for gallantry on several occa-

sions in the war against the Florida Indians"; major and colonel April 12, 1847, "for gallantry and meritorious conduct at Cerro Gordo, Mexico, where he was severely wounded under the enemy's works while on reconnoitering duty"; lieutenant colonel September 13, 1847, "for gallantry and meritorious conduct in the Battle of Chapultepec, Mexico"; quartermaster general June 28, 1860; resigned April 22, 1861, to enter the Confederate service; during the Civil War was appointed major general of the Virginia State forces on April 26, 1861; commissioned brigadier general, Confederate States Army, May 14, 1861, and general on August 31, 1861, in which capacity he served until April 26, 1865, when the terms of surrender of his army were agreed upon; settled in Savannah, Ga.; was president of a railroad company in Arkansas; and engaged in the general insurance business in 1868 and 1869; returned to Virginia and settled in Richmond in 1877 and became president of an express company; elected as a Democrat to the Forty-sixth Congress (March 4, 1879–March 3, 1881); was not a candidate for renomination in 1880; was appointed Commissioner of Railroads by President Grover Cleveland in 1887 and served until 1891; died in Washington, D. C., March 21, 1891; interment in Greenmount Cemetery, Baltimore, Md.

JOHNSTON, Joseph Forney, a Senator from Alabama; born near Lowesville, Lincoln County, N. C., March 23, 1843; attended the country schools in Lincoln County; while attending a military school in Alabama at the outbreak of the Civil War enlisted as a private in the Confederate Army in March 1861 and served in the Eighteenth Alabama and Twelfth North Carolina Regiments; was wounded four times; rose to the rank of captain; studied law; was admitted to the bar in 1866 and practiced in Selma, Ala., 1866–1884; moved to Birmingham, Ala., in 1884 and became president of the Alabama National Bank, resigning in 1894; became president of the Sloss Iron & Steel Co. in 1887; Governor of Alabama 1896–1900; elected as a Democrat to the United States Senate to fill the vacancy in the term ending March 3, 1909, caused by the death of Edmund W. Pettus; on the same day was elected for the term commencing March 4, 1909, and served from August 6, 1907, until his death in Washington, D. C., August 8, 1913; interment Elmwood Cemetery, Birmingham, Ala.

JOHNSTON, Josiah Stoddard, a Representative and a Senator from Louisiana; born in Salisbury, Litchfield County, Conn., November 24, 1784; moved with his father to Kentucky in 1790; sent to New Haven, Conn., in 1796 to attend primary school; was graduated from Transylvania University, Lexington, Ky., in 1805; studied law; was admitted to the bar and commenced practice in Alexandria, La. (then the Territory of Orleans); elected to the first Territorial legislature in 1805 and served until the adoption of the State constitution in 1812; appointed major in the Territorial militia June 6, 1809; colonel of militia in 1814 and organized a regiment for the defense of New Orleans, but reached the city after the battle; engaged in agricultural pursuits; member of the State house of representatives in 1812; State district judge 1812–1821; elected as a Democrat to the Seventeenth Congress (March 4, 1821–March 3, 1823); unsuccessful candidate for reelection in 1822 to the Eighteenth Congress; appointed to the United States Senate to fill the vacancy caused by the resignation of James Brown; elected and reelected and served from January 15, 1824, until his death, caused by an explosion on the steamboat *Lioness,* on the Red River in Louisiana, May 19, 1833; interment in Rapides Cemetery, Pineville, La.

JOHNSTON, Olin DeWitt Talmadge, a Senator from South Carolina; born near Honea Path, Anderson County, S. C., November 18, 1896; attended the public schools; was graduated from Textile Industrial Institute, Spartanburg, S. C., in 1915;

attended Wofford College, Spartanburg, S. C., until 1917 when he enlisted in the United States Army, serving eighteen months overseas as a sergeant in Company C, One Hundred and Seventeenth Engineers, Forty-second Division; received a regimental citation and was discharged in June 1919; reentered Wofford College and was graduated in 1921; was graduated from the law school of the University of South Carolina at Columbia in 1924; was admitted to the bar the same year and commenced practice in Spartanburg, S. C.; member of the State house of representatives in 1923, 1924, and 1927–1930; Democratic National executive committeeman 1934–1940 and 1944–1948; Governor of South Carolina 1935–1939 and from 1943 until his resignation on January 3, 1945; elected as a Democrat to the United States Senate in 1944 for the term commencing January 3, 1945; reelected in 1950 and again in 1956 for the term ending January 3, 1963.

JOHNSTON, Rienzi Melville (cousin of Benjamin Edward Russell), a Senator from Texas; born in Sandersville, Washington County, Ga., September 9, 1849; attended the public schools; during the Civil War served in the Confederate Army; moved to Austin, Tex., in 1878 and engaged in journalism; moved to Houston in 1883 and established the Houston Post; member of the Democratic National Committee 1900–1912; appointed as a Democrat to the United States Senate to fill the vacancy caused by the resignation of Joseph W. Bailey and served from January 4 to February 2, 1913, when a successor was elected and qualified; resumed his former activities as editor and president of the Houston Post; relinquished the active management of his newspaper business in 1919 and lived in retirement until his death in Houston, Tex., February 28, 1926; interment in Glenwood Cemetery.

JOHNSTON, Rowland Louis, a Representative from Missouri; born in Louisiana, Pike County, Mo., April 23, 1872; attended the public schools; studied law; was admitted to the bar in 1894 and commenced practice in St. Louis, Mo.; member of the State house of representatives 1892–1896; served as prosecuting attorney of St. Louis County 1904–1908; delegate to the Republican National Convention at Chicago in 1908; assistant circuit attorney for the city of St. Louis 1920–1926; member of the State militia; during the Spanish-American War served as a recruiting officer; moved to Rolla, Mo., in 1926 and continued the practice of law; elected as a Republican to the Seventy-first Congress (March 4, 1929–March 3, 1931); unsuccessful candidate for reelection in 1930 to the Seventy-second Congress and for election in 1932 to the Seventy-third Congress; resumed the practice of law in Rolla, Mo., until his death there on September 22, 1939; remains were cremated and the ashes deposited in the mausoleum at Oak Grove Cemetery, St. Louis, Mo.

JOHNSTON, Samuel, a Delegate and a Senator from North Carolina; born in Dundee, Scotland, December 15, 1733; immigrated to the United States in 1736 with his parents, who settled in Chowan County, N. C.; attended school in New England; studied law; was admitted to the bar and practiced; member of the State assembly in 1760; provincial treasurer of the northern division; moderator of the Revolutionary convention in 1775; member of the State senate in 1779; Member of the Continental Congress 1780–1782 and elected first president after the Articles of Confederation were signed, but declined to serve; presided over the State conventions of 1788 and 1789; elected as a Federalist to the United States Senate and served from November 27, 1789, to March 3, 1793; judge of the superior court of North Carolina 1800–1803; died near Edenton, Chowan County, N. C., August 18, 1816; interment in the Johnston Burial Ground on the Hayes plantation, near Edenton, N. C.

JOHNSTON, Thomas Dillard, a Representative from North Carolina; born in Waynesville, Haywood County, N. C., April 1, 1840; attended the common schools and Col. Stephen Lee's Preparatory School, Asheville, N. C.; entered the University of North Carolina at Chapel Hill in 1858, but left in the spring of 1859 on account of failing health; studied law; during the Civil War entered the Confederate Army in the spring of 1861; received three serious wounds at Malvern Hill; was admitted to the bar in 1867 and commenced practice in Asheville; mayor of Asheville in 1869; member of the State house of representatives 1870–1874; declined to be a candidate for reelection; served in the State senate in 1876; elected as a Democrat to the Forty-ninth and Fiftieth Congresses (March 4, 1885–March 3, 1889); was an unsuccessful candidate for reelection in 1888 to the Fifty-first Congress; resumed the practice of law; died in Asheville, N. C., on June 22, 1902; interment in Riverside Cemetery.

JOHNSTON, William, a Representative from Ohio; born in Ireland in 1819; immigrated to the United States and settled in Ohio; attended the public schools; studied law; was admitted to the bar and practiced in Mansfield, Ohio, from 1859 to 1863; elected as a Democrat to the Thirty-eighth Congress (March 4, 1863–March 3, 1865); unsuccessful candidate for reelection in 1864 to the Thirty-ninth Congress; resumed the practice of law; died in Mansfield, Ohio, May 1, 1866; interment in Mansfield Cemetery.

JOHNSTONE, George, a Representative from South Carolina; born in Newberry, S. C., April 18, 1846; attended the common schools; entered the State Military Academy, from which he enlisted in the Confederate Army as a member of the battalion of State cadets and served until the close of the Civil War; attended the University of Edinburgh, Scotland, 1866–1869; returned to the United States; studied law; was admitted to the bar in 1871 and commenced practice in Newberry, S. C.; declined a nomination to the State house of representatives in 1874; member of the State house of representatives 1877–1884; declined to be a candidate for reelection; member of the commission that revised the tax laws and suggested amendments to the State constitution in 1881; member of the State executive committee of the Democratic Party 1880–1884; elected as a Democrat to the Fifty-second Congress (March 4, 1891–March 3, 1893); unsuccessful candidate for renomination in 1892; resumed the practice of law in Newberry, S. C.; member of the State constitutional convention in 1895; died in Newberry, S. C., March 8, 1921; interment in Johnstone Cemetery.

JOLLEY, John Lawlor, a Representative from South Dakota; born in Montreal, Quebec, Canada, July 14, 1840; attended the common schools; graduated from Eastman Business College; moved to Wisconsin in 1857; during the Civil War enlisted as a private in Company C, Twenty-third Regiment, Wisconsin Volunteer Infantry, August 22, 1862; was mustered out as second lieutenant July 4, 1865; studied law; was admitted to the bar in 1866 and commenced practice in Vermilion, Dakota Territory; member of the Territorial house of representatives in 1867 and 1868; president of the Territorial council in 1875 and 1881; mayor of Vermilion in 1877 and 1885; delegate to the Republican National Convention at Chicago in 1884; member of the constitutional convention in 1889; member of the State senate in 1889 and 1890; elected as a Republican to the Fifty-second Congress to fill the vacancy caused by the death of John R. Gamble and served from December 7, 1891, to March 3, 1893; was not a candidate for renomination; resumed the practice of law; died in Vermilion, S. Dak., December 14, 1926; interment in Bluff View Cemetery.

JONAS, Benjamin Franklin, a Senator from Louisiana; born in Williamsport, Grant County, Ky., July 19, 1834; moved with his parents to Adams County, Ill.; attended the public schools; moved to New Orleans, La., in 1853; was graduated from the law department of the University of Louisiana at Pineville in 1855; was admitted to the bar the same year and commenced practice in New Orleans; enlisted as a private in the Confederate Army in 1862 and served in the Washington Artillery until 1863, when Captain Fenner's battery joined Hood's corps of the Army of the Tennessee; appointed sergeant major and later adjutant of the Artillery regiment commanded by Col. Robert F. Beckham and served throughout the Civil War; member of the State house of representatives 1865–1868; chairman of the Louisiana delegation to the Democratic National Convention at New York City in 1868; elected to the State senate in 1872 but declined to take the seat; city attorney of New Orleans 1875–1879; delegate to the Democratic National Conventions in 1876 and 1884; member of the State house of representatives in 1876 and 1877; elected as a Democrat to the United States Senate and served from March 4, 1879, to March 3, 1885; unsuccessful Democratic candidate for reelection to the United States Senate in 1884; collector of the port of New Orleans 1885–1889; resumed the practice of law; died in New Orleans, La., on December 21, 1911; interment in Dispersed of Judah Cemetery.

JONAS, Charles Andrew (father of Charles Raper Jonas), a Representative from North Carolina; born on a farm near Lincolnton, Lincoln County, N. C., August 14, 1876; attended the public schools, Ridge Academy, Henry, N. C., and Fallston (N. C.) Institute; was graduated from the University of North Carolina at Chapel Hill in 1902; taught school 1902–1906; studied law; was admitted to the bar in 1906 and commenced practice in Lincolnton, N. C.; postmaster at Lincolnton 1907–1910 and later editor of a newspaper which he helped to establish in 1906; city attorney of Lincolnton 1908–1912; member of the State senate 1915–1919; delegate to the Republican National Conventions in 1916, 1928, 1932, and 1936; member of the board of trustees of the University of North Carolina since 1917; assistant United States attorney for the western district of North Carolina 1921–1925; served in the State house of representatives 1927–1929 and 1935–1937; member of the Republican National Committee; elected as a Republican to the Seventy-first Congress (March 4, 1929–March 3, 1931); unsuccessful candidate for reelection in 1930 to the Seventy-second Congress and for election in 1932 to the Seventy-third Congress; served as United States attorney for the western district of North Carolina from April 1, 1931, to July 1, 1932; unsuccessful candidate for election to the United States Senate in 1938; unsuccessful candidate for election in 1942 to the Seventy-eighth Congress; resumed the general practice of law at Lincolnton, N. C.; died in a nursing home near Charlotte, N. C., May 25, 1955; interment in Hollybrook Cemetery, Lincolnton, N. C.

JONAS, Charles Raper (son of Charles Andrew Jonas), a Representative from North Carolina; born near Lincolnton, Lincoln County, N. C., December 9, 1904; graduated from Lincolnton High School in 1921, from the University of North Carolina at Chapel Hill in 1925, and from the same university law school in 1928; was admitted to the bar in 1927 and commenced practice in Lincolnton, N. C., in 1928; assistant United States attorney for the western district of North Carolina 1931–1933; member of the North Carolina National Guard since 1927; entered active duty in the Army of the United States as a captain September 21, 1940, and was separated from the service April 20, 1946, as a lieutenant colonel in the Judge Advocate General's Corps; commissioned a colonel in the North Carolina National Guard; resumed the practice of law; delegate to the Republican

National Convention in 1952; elected as a Republican to the Eighty-third and to the three succeeding Congresses (January 3, 1953–January 3, 1961). *Reelected to the Eighty-seventh Congress.*

JONAS, Edgar Allan, a Representative from Illinois; born in Mishicot, Manitowoc County, Wis., October 14, 1885; attended the public schools and graduated from the Manitowoc County Normal School; taught in the rural schools of Manitowoc County 1903–1907; was graduated from Chicago Law School in June 1910; was admitted to the bar in 1909 and commenced the practice of law in Chicago, Ill.; served as trustee of the Chicago Public Library 1916–1918; assistant corporation counsel of Chicago, Ill., in 1919 and 1920; first assistant State's attorney of Cook County, Ill., 1921–1923; president of board of directors of the Municipal Tuberculosis Sanitarium of the city of Chicago 1921–1923; judge of the Municipal Court of Chicago 1923–1937; judge of the Superior Court of Cook County in 1941 and 1942; associate member of Board of Pardons and Paroles of Illinois 1945–1947; delegate to the Republican National Convention in 1948; elected as a Republican to the Eighty-first, Eighty-second, and Eighty-third Congresses (January 3, 1949–January 3, 1955); unsuccessful candidate for reelection in 1954 to the Eighty-fourth Congress and for election in 1956 to the Eighty-fifth Congress; resumed the practice of law; is a resident of Chicago, Ill.

JONES, Alexander Hamilton, a Representative from North Carolina; born in Buncombe County, N. C., July 21, 1822; completed preparatory studies; engaged in mercantile pursuits; during the Civil War enlisted in the Union Army in 1863; was captured in east Tennessee while raising a regiment of Union Volunteers and imprisoned in Asheville, also at Camp Vance, at Camp Holmes, and in Libby Prison at Richmond, Va.; conscripted; made his escape November 14, 1864; again joined the Union forces in Cumberland, Md.; after the war returned to North Carolina; member of the State convention in 1865; elected as a Republican to the Thirty-ninth Congress but was not permitted to qualify; upon the readmission of North Carolina to representation was elected to the Fortieth and Forty-first Congresses and served from July 6, 1868, to March 3, 1871; unsuccessful candidate for reelection in 1870 to the Forty-second Congress; resided in Washington, D. C., until 1876, in Maryland until 1884, in Asheville, N. C., until 1890, and in Oklahoma until 1897, when he moved to California; died in Long Beach, Calif., January 29, 1901; interment in Signal Hill Cemetery.

JONES, Allen, a Delegate from North Carolina; born in Edgecombe (now Halifax) County, N. C., December 24, 1739; attended Eton College, England; was a member of the colonial assembly 1773–1775; delegate to the five Provincial Congresses 1774–1776; served throughout the Revolutionary War, attaining the rank of brigadier general; served in the State senate 1777–1779, 1783, 1784, and 1787; Member of the Continental Congress in 1779 and 1780; member of the convention that rejected the proposed Constitution of the United States at Halifax, N. C., in 1788; died on his plantation, "Mount Gallant," near Roanoke Rapids, Northampton County, N. C., on November 10, 1798; interment in the private burial ground on his estate.

JONES, Andrieus Aristieus, a Senator from New Mexico; born near Union City, Abion County, Tenn., May 16, 1862; attended the common schools and Bethel College, McKenzie, Tenn.; was graduated from the Valparaiso University, Indiana, in 1885; taught school in Tennessee; moved to Las Vegas, N. Mex., where he was principal of the public schools from 1885 to 1887; studied law while teaching school; was admitted to the bar in 1888 and commenced practice in Las Vegas; president of the New Mexico Bar Association in 1893; mayor of Las Vegas in 1893 and 1894; was admitted to practice before the Supreme Court of the United States in 1894; special United States district attorney 1894–1898; delegate to the Democratic National Convention at Chicago in 1896; chairman of the Democratic State committee 1906–1908 and again in 1911; member of the Democratic National Committee 1908–1922; unsuccessful candidate for election to the United States Senate in 1912; served as First Assistant Secretary of the Interior from June 1, 1913, to August 31, 1916, when he resigned; elected as a Democrat to the United States Senate in 1916; reelected in 1922 and served from March 4, 1917, until his death in Washington, D. C., on December 20, 1927; interment in the Masonic Cemetery, Las Vegas, N. Mex.

JONES, Benjamin, a Representative from Ohio; born in Winchester, Frederick County, Va., on April 13, 1787; moved with his parents to Washington, Pa.; received a limited schooling; learned the trade of cabinetmaking; moved to Wooster, Ohio, in 1812 and engaged in mercantile pursuits; justice of the peace in 1815; commissioner for Wayne County in 1818; member of the State house of representatives in 1821 and 1822; presidential elector on the Democratic ticket of Jackson and Calhoun in 1824; member of the State senate 1829–1832; elected as a Democrat to the Twenty-third and Twenty-fourth Congresses (March 4, 1833–March 3, 1837); was not a candidate for renomination; resumed business interests in Wooster, Ohio, and died there April 24, 1861; interment in Oak Hill Cemetery.

JONES, Burr W., a Representative from Wisconsin; born near Evansville, Rock County, Wis., March 9, 1846; attended the common schools and the Evansville (Wis.) Seminary; taught school for several years; was graduated from the literary department of the University of Wisconsin at Madison in 1870 and from the law department in 1871; was admitted to the bar in 1871 and commenced practice in Portage, Wis.; moved to Madison, Wis., in 1872 and continued the practice of law; prosecuting attorney of Dane County in 1872 and 1874; elected as a Democrat to the Forty-eighth Congress (March 4, 1883–March 3, 1885); unsuccessful candidate for reelection in 1884 to the Forty-ninth Congress; professor of law at the University of Wisconsin 1885–1915; served as city attorney in 1891; chairman of the Democratic State convention in 1892; delegate to the national convention (gold standard) at Indianapolis in 1896 which nominated Palmer and Buckner for President and Vice President; member of the Wisconsin Tax Commission in 1897 and 1898 and served as chairman; appointed associate justice of the State supreme court September 6, 1920, to fill a vacancy; elected to the same office April 4, 1922, and served until his retirement on January 1, 1926; resumed the practice of law; died in Madison, Wis., January 7, 1935; interment in Forest Hill Cemetery.

JONES, Charles William, a Senator from Florida; born in Balbriggan, Ireland, on December 24, 1834; immigrated to the United States in 1844 with his mother and settled in New York City, where he attended the public schools; moved to Louisiana in 1848 and later to Mississippi; moved thence to Santa Rosa County, Fla., in 1854; worked as a carpenter, and studied law at night; was admitted to the bar in 1857 and commenced practice in Pensacola, Fla.; delegate to the Democratic National Convention at Baltimore in 1872; unsuccessful Democratic candidate for election in 1872; member of the State house of representatives in 1874; elected as a Democrat to the United States Senate in 1875; reelected in 1881 and served from March 4, 1875, to March 3, 1887; was not a candidate for reelection; moved to Detroit, Mich., in 1885; died at St. Joseph's Retreat, Dearborn, Mich., October 11, 1897; interment in St. Michael's Cemetery, Pensacola, Fla.

JONES, Daniel Terryll, a Representative from New York; born in Hebron, Tolland County, Conn., August 17, 1800; received a liberal schooling; was graduated from the medical department of Yale College in 1826 and was licensed to practice medicine in Connecticut and New York; began the practice of his profession in Amboy, Oswego County, N. Y.; moved to Baldwinsville, N. Y., in 1841; elected as a Democrat to the Thirty-second and Thirty-third Congresses (March 4, 1851–March 3, 1855); was not a candidate for renomination in 1854; chairman of the Republican State convention at Syracuse, N. Y., in 1858; resumed the practice of medicine; died in Baldwinsville, Onondaga County, N. Y., March 29, 1861; interment in Riverside Cemetery.

JONES, Evan John, a Representative from Pennsylvania; born in Shamokin, Northumberland County, Pa., October 23, 1872; attended the public schools; was graduated from Clarion Normal School, Clarion, Pa., in 1892; taught school; was graduated from the Dickinson Law School in 1896; was admitted to the bar in 1896 and commenced practice at St. Marys, Pa.; elected as a Republican to the Sixty-sixth and Sixty-seventh Congresses (March 4, 1919–March 3, 1923); unsuccessful candidate for renomination in 1922; resumed the practice of law at Bradford, McKean County, Pa.; vice president and general manager of the Emporium Forestry Co., director and general counsel of the Grasse River Railroad Corp.; died in Bradford, Pa., January 9, 1952; interment in Willow Dale Cemetery.

JONES, Francis, a Representative from Tennessee; received a limited schooling; studied law; was admitted to the bar and commenced practice in Winchester, Tenn.; solicitor general of the third Tennessee district in 1815; elected to the Fifteenth, Sixteenth, and Seventeenth Congresses (March 4, 1817–March 3, 1823); resumed the practice of his profession in Winchester, Franklin County, Tenn., and died there.

JONES, Frank, a Representative from New Hampshire; born in Barrington, N. H., September 15, 1832; attended the public schools; moved to Portsmouth in 1849 and became a merchant and brewer; owned establishments in Portsmouth and South Boston, Mass.; mayor of Portsmouth in 1868 and 1869; elected as a Democrat to the Forty-fourth and Forty-fifth Congresses (March 4, 1875–March 3, 1879); was not a candidate for renomination in 1878; unsuccessful Democratic candidate for Governor of New Hampshire in 1880; affiliated with the Republican Party; interested in railroads; presidential elector on the Republican ticket of McKinley and Roosevelt in 1900; died in Portsmouth, N. H., October 2, 1902; interment in Harmony Grove Cemetery.

JONES, George (son of Noble Wymberley Jones), a Senator from Georgia; born in Savannah, Ga., February 25, 1766; received an academic training; studied medicine with his father and practiced for a number of years; participated in the Revolutionary War and during 1780 and 1781 was imprisoned upon an English ship; member of the State house of representatives; served in the State senate; during the War of 1812 served as captain of a company of Savannah reserves; member of the board of aldermen in 1793, 1794, 1802, 1803, 1814, and 1815; mayor of Savannah 1812–1814; appointed judge of the eastern judicial circuit of Georgia by Governor Milledge on July 27, 1804, and served until appointed Senator; appointed to the United States Senate to fill the vacancy caused by the death of Abraham Baldwin and served from August 27 to November 7, 1807, when a successor was elected; died in Savannah, Chatham County, Ga., on November 13, 1838; interment in Bonaventure Cemetery.

JONES, George Wallace, a Delegate from the Territory of Michigan and the Territory of Wisconsin and a Senator from Iowa; born in Vincennes, Ind., April 12, 1804; was graduated from the Transylvania University, Lexington, Ky., in 1825; studied law; was admitted to the bar; clerk of the United States courts in Missouri in 1826; served as aide-de-camp to Gen. Henry Dodge in the Black Hawk War; moved to Michigan Territory and located in Sinsinawa Mound; judge of the county court; elected as a Delegate from Michigan Territory to the Twenty-fourth Congress and served from March 4, 1835, until the Territory of Wisconsin was formed from a portion of Michigan Territory, when, his residence being in the new Territory, he was elected and qualified as a Delegate from the Territory of Wisconsin, serving until March 3, 1837; presented credentials as a Delegate-elect from the Territory of Wisconsin to the Twenty-fifth Congress and served from March 4, 1837, to January 14, 1839, when he was succeeded by James D. Doty, who contested his election; appointed surveyor of public lands for the Territories of Wisconsin and Iowa by President Van Buren January 29, 1840; removed by President Tyler July 4, 1841; reappointed by President Polk January 3, 1846, and served, with headquarters in Dubuque, Iowa, until December 1848, when he resigned; elected to the United States Senate as one of the first Senators from the State of Iowa and served from December 7, 1848, to March 3, 1859; unsuccessful candidate for renomination in 1858; appointed Minister Resident of the United States to New Granada by President Buchanan March 8, 1859, and served in Bogota until recalled by President Lincoln in July 1861; on his return to the United States was arrested in New York City by order of Secretary Seward on the charge of disloyalty, based on a friendly letter to his former college mate, Jefferson Davis; was imprisoned in Fort Lafayette, New York Harbor, for sixty-four days, when he was released by order of President Lincoln; retired from public life; returned to Dubuque, Dubuque County, Iowa, and died there July 22, 1896; interment in Mount Olivet Cemetery at Key West, Dubuque, Iowa.

JONES, George Washington, a Representative from Tennessee; born in King and Queen County, Va., March 15, 1806; moved to Tennessee with his parents, who settled in Fayetteville; received a common-school and academical education; apprenticed to the saddler's trade; justice of the peace 1832–1835; member of the State house of representatives 1835–1839; served in the State senate 1839–1841; clerk of Lincoln County Court 1840–1843; elected as a Democrat to the Twenty-eighth and to the seven succeeding Congresses (March 4, 1843–March 3, 1859); delegate to the peace convention of 1861 held in Washington, D. C., in an effort to devise means to prevent the impending war, but did not attend; elected from Tennessee a Member of the House of Representatives in the First Confederate Congress and served from February 18, 1862, to February 18, 1864; was not a candidate for reelection; delegate to the State constitutional convention in 1870; appointed a member of the board of trustees of the Tennessee Hospital for the Insane in 1871 and reappointed in 1877; died in Fayetteville, Lincoln County, Tenn., November 14, 1884; interment in Rose Hill Cemetery.

JONES, George Washington, a Representative from Texas; born in Marion County, Ala., September 5, 1828; moved with his parents to Tipton County, Tenn., and shortly afterward to Bastrop, Tex., in 1848; attended the common schools; studied law; was admitted to the bar in 1851 and commenced practice in Bastrop, Tex.; elected district attorney in 1856; during the Civil War enlisted in the Confederate Army as a private; commissioned lieutenant colonel and afterward promoted to the colonelcy of the Seventeenth Texas Infantry; returned to Bastrop County; member of the State constitutional convention in 1866; elected Lieutenant Governor of Texas in 1866; removed by General Sheridan as "an impediment to reconstruction" in 1867; elected on the Greenback Party ticket to the Forty-sixth and Forty-seventh Congresses (March 4, 1879–March 3, 1883); was not a candidate for reelection in 1882 to the Forty-eighth Congress; resumed the practice of his profession in Bastrop, Tex., and died there July 11, 1903; interment in Fairview Cemetery.

JONES, Hamilton Chamberlain, a Representative from North Carolina; born in Charlotte, Mecklenburg County, N. C., September 26, 1884; attended the schools of Charlotte, N. C., Central High School, Washington, D. C., and Horners Military School, Oxford, N. C.; was graduated from the University of North Carolina at Chapel Hill in 1906 and Columbia University, New York, N. Y., in 1907; studied law at both institutions; was admitted to the bar in 1906 and commenced practice in Charlotte, N. C., in 1910; also engaged in agricultural pursuits; judge of City Recorder's Court and Juvenile Court of Charlotte, N. C., 1913–1919; assistant United States district attorney for the western district of North Carolina 1919–1921; served in the State senate 1925–1927; trustee of the University of North Carolina; elected as a Democrat to the Eightieth, Eighty-first, and Eighty-second Congresses (January 3, 1947–January 3, 1953); unsuccessful candidate for reelection in 1952 to the Eighty-third Congress; resumed the practice of law; died in Charlotte, N. C., August 10, 1957; interment in Evergreen Cemetery.

JONES, Homer Raymond, a Representative from Washington; born in Martinsburg, Audrain County, Mo., September 3, 1893; moved to Bremerton, Wash., in 1901; attended the public schools and studied business administration at Seattle Business College; during the First World War served as an enlisted man in the United States Navy 1917–1919; engaged as a sheet-metal worker, Navy Yard, Bremerton, Wash., 1919–1921; city councilman of Charleston, Wash., 1922–1924 and mayor 1924–1927; treasurer of Kitsap County, Wash., 1926–1929; assistant State treasurer of Washington 1929–1933; treasurer of Bremerton, Wash., 1933–1937; mayor of Bremerton, Wash., 1939–1941; during World War II served as an officer in the United States Naval Reserve from 1941 until his discharge as a captain in 1946; awarded Bronze Star Medal; elected as a Republican to the Eightieth Congress (January 3, 1947–January 3, 1949); unsuccessful candidate for reelection in 1948 to the Eighty-first Congress; superintendent of the Washington State Veterans' Home at Retsil 1949–1953; assistant State treasurer 1953–1957; real-estate salesman; is a resident of Bremerton, Wash.

JONES, Isaac Dashiell, a Representative from Maryland; born on the family homestead, "Wetcpquin," Somerset County, Md., November 1, 1806; completed preparatory studies; was graduated from Washington Academy, Somerset County, where he became assistant tutor before his studies were completed; studied law; was admitted to the bar and commenced practice in Princess Anne, Somerset County, Md.; member of the State house of delegates in 1832, 1835, 1840, and 1866; elected as a Whig to the Twenty-seventh Congress (March 4, 1841–March 3, 1843); took an active part in the State constitutional conventions of 1864 and 1867; elected attorney general of the State in 1867; elected judge of the court of arbitration of Baltimore in 1877; member of the Maryland Historical Society and the Maryland Bible Society; director of the Maryland State School for the Deaf, Frederick, Md., 1867–1893 and of the Maryland School for the Colored Blind and Deaf at Baltimore 1872–1893; died in Baltimore, Md., July 5, 1893; interment in Greenmount Cemetery.

JONES, James, a Representative from Georgia; born in Maryland; moved to Georgia with his uncle, Colonel Marbury, in 1740; attended the academy in Augusta; studied law; was admitted to the bar and practiced in Savannah; first lieutenant of East Company, Chatham County Regiment of Militia, in 1790; member of the State house of representatives 1796–1798; member of the State constitutional convention in May 1798; elected as a Republican to the Sixth Congress and served from March 4, 1799, until his death in Washington, D. C., January 11, 1801; interment in the Congressional Cemetery.

JONES, James, a Representative from Virginia; born in Nottoway Parish, Amelia (now Nottoway) County, Va., on December 11, 1772; attended Hampden-Sidney College, Virginia, from which he graduated in 1791, and the Jefferson Medical College, Philadelphia, Pa.; was graduated in medicine from the University of Edinburgh, Scotland, in 1796; returned to Amelia County, where he practiced medicine and also engaged in agricultural pursuits; member of the State house of delegates 1804–1809; privy councilor of Virginia from 1809 to 1811, when he resigned; served in the War of 1812; director general of hospital and medical stores and rations from April 17 to May 22, 1813; member of the State house of delegates in 1818; a presidential elector in 1824, 1828, 1832, 1836, and 1840; unsuccessful candidate for election to the Fifteenth Congress to fill the vacancy caused by the death of Peterson Goodwin; elected as a Democrat to the Sixteenth and Seventeenth Congresses (March 4, 1819–March 3, 1823); again a member of the State house of delegates 1827–1829; resumed agricultural pursuits; died at his home, "Mountain Hall," near Nottoway, Nottoway County, Va., April 25, 1848; interment in the family burying ground on his estate.

JONES, James Chamberlain, a Senator from Tennessee; born near the line between Davidson and Wilson Counties, within two miles of the "Hermitage," Tennessee, April 20, 1809; attended the public schools; member of the State house of representatives in 1839; Governor of Tennessee 1841–1845; presidential elector on the Whig ticket of Taylor and Fillmore in 1848; elected as a Whig to the United States Senate and served from March 4, 1851, to March 3, 1857; was not a candidate for reelection; retired to his farm near Memphis, Tenn., where he died October 29, 1859; interment in Elmwood Cemetery, Memphis.

JONES, James Henry, a Representative from Texas; born in Shelby County, Ala., September 13, 1830; moved with his parents to Talladega County, Ala., in early youth; pursued an academic course; studied law; was admitted to the bar in 1851 and commenced practice in Henderson, Tex.; during the Civil War enlisted in the Confederate Army and served as captain, lieutenant colonel, and colonel of the Eleventh Texas Infantry; presidential elector on the Democratic ticket of Hancock and English in 1880; elected as a Democrat to the Forty-eighth and Forty-ninth Congresses (March 4, 1883–March 3, 1887); resumed the practice of law in Henderson, Tex., and died there March 22, 1904; interment in the New Cemetery.

JONES, James Kimbrough, a Representative and a Senator from Arkansas; born in Marshall County, Miss., September 29, 1839; moved with his parents to Dallas County, Ark., in 1848; pursued classical studies under a private tutor; served in the Confederate Army during the Civil War; returned to his plantation in Arkansas; studied law; was admitted to the bar in 1874 and commenced practice in Washington, Hempstead County, Ark.; member of the State senate 1873–1879 and served as president of that body in 1877; delegate to the Democratic National Convention at Chicago in 1896 and at Kansas

City in 1900; chairman of the Democratic National Committee in 1896 and 1900; elected as a Democrat to the Forty-seventh and Forty-eighth Congresses (March 4, 1881–March 3, 1885); had been reelected to the Forty-ninth Congress but tendered his resignation February 19, 1885, having been elected Senator; elected to the United States Senate in 1885; reelected in 1891 and 1897 and served from March 4, 1885, to March 3, 1903; unsuccessful candidate for reelection; resumed the practice of law in Washington, D. C., and died there June 1, 1908; interment in Rock Creek Cemetery.

JONES, James Taylor, a Representative from Alabama; born in Richmond, Va., July 20, 1832; moved with his father to Marengo County, Ala., in 1834; pursued classical studies; was graduated from Princeton College in 1852 and from the law school of the University of Virginia at Charlottesville in 1855; was admitted to the bar in 1856 and commenced practice in Demopolis, Ala.; during the Civil War enlisted in the Confederate Army as a private in the Fourth Alabama Regiment; elected captain of Company D in this regiment in 1862; appointed judge advocate in the Confederate War Department in 1864 and served until the close of the war; delegate to the State constitutional convention in 1865; member of the State senate in 1872 and 1873; unsuccessful candidate for election in 1874 to the Forty-fourth Congress; elected as a Democrat to the Forty-fifth Congress (March 4, 1877–March 3, 1879); unsuccessful candidate for reelection in 1878 to the Forty-sixth Congress; elected to the Forty-eighth Congress to fill the vacancy caused by the death of Thomas H. Herndon; reelected to the Forty-ninth and Fiftieth Congresses and served from December 3, 1883, to March 3, 1889; was not a candidate for renomination in 1888; resumed the practice of law in Demopolis, Ala.; circuit judge of the first judicial circuit of Alabama from 1890 until his death in Demopolis, Marengo County, Ala., February 15, 1895; interment in Lyon Cemetery.

JONES, Jehu Glancy, a Representative from Pennsylvania; born in Caernarvon Township, Berks County, Pa., October 7, 1811; attended Kenyon College; studied theology; was ordained to the ministry of the Episcopal Church in 1835 and withdrew in 1841; studied law; was admitted to the bar in Georgia in 1841 and commenced practice at Easton, Pa.; district attorney for Berks County 1847–1849; delegate to the Democratic State conventions in 1848, 1849, and 1855, and served as president in 1855; delegate to the Democratic National Convention at Baltimore in 1848 and at Cincinnati in 1856 and served as vice president in 1848; elected as a Democrat to the Thirty-second Congress (March 4, 1851–March 3, 1853); declined to be a candidate for renomination in 1852; elected to the Thirty-third Congress to fill the vacancy caused by the death of Henry A. Muhlenberg; reelected to the Thirty-fourth and Thirty-fifth Congresses and served from February 4, 1854, to October 30, 1858, when he resigned; unsuccessful candidate for election in 1858 to the Thirty-sixth Congress; was tendered the position of United States Minister to Berlin in 1857 but declined; appointed Minister to Austria by President Buchanan December 7, 1858, and served from December 15, 1858, to November 14, 1861; resumed the practice of law; died in Reading, Pa., March 24, 1878; interment in the Charles Evans Cemetery.

JONES, John James, a Representative from Georgia; born near Waynesboro, Burke County, Ga., on November 13, 1824; attended the Waynesboro Academy and was graduated from Emory College, Oxford, Ga., in 1845; studied law; was admitted to the bar in 1848 and practiced in Waynesboro, Ga.; elected as a Democrat to the Thirty-sixth Congress and served from March 4, 1859, to January 23, 1861, when he withdrew; served as a lieutenant in the Confederate Army during the Civil

War; resumed the practice of law in Burke County, Ga.; died in Waynesboro, Ga., on October 19, 1898; interment in the City Cemetery.

JONES, John Percival, a Senator from Nevada; born at "The Hay," Herefordshire, England, January 27, 1829; immigrated the same year to the United States with his parents, who settled in the northern part of Ohio; attended the public schools in Cleveland, Ohio, and received instruction from private teachers; moved to California and engaged in mining and various other enterprises in Trinity County; sheriff of the county; member of the State senate 1863–1867; moved to Gold Hill, Nev., in 1868; engaged in the development of the mineral resources of that State; elected as a Republican to the United States Senate in 1873, 1879, 1885, 1891, and 1897 and served from March 4, 1873, to March 3, 1903; declined to be a candidate for reelection, having had a continuous service of thirty years; resumed his former business activities and devoted his time to the care of his mining investments; retired to his home in Santa Monica, Calif.; died in Los Angeles, Calif., November 27, 1912; interment in Laurel Hill Cemetery, San Francisco, Calif.

JONES, John Sills, a Representative from Ohio; born near St. Paris, Champaign County, Ohio, February 12, 1836; attended the public schools; was graduated from Ohio Wesleyan University, Delaware, Ohio, in 1855; studied law; was admitted to the bar in 1857 and commenced practice in Delaware, Ohio; prosecuting attorney for Delaware County in 1860 and 1861; served during the Civil War as first lieutenant and captain in the Union Army 1861–1864; reenlisted to command the One Hundred and Seventy-fourth Regiment, Ohio Volunteer Infantry, in September 1864; mustered out July 7, 1865; resumed the practice of law; mayor of Delaware, Ohio, in 1866; again prosecuting attorney for Delaware County 1866–1872; presidential elector on the Republican ticket of Grant and Wilson in 1872; elected as a Republican to the Forty-fifth Congress (March 4, 1877–March 3, 1879); was not a candidate for renomination in 1878; member of the State house of representatives 1879–1884; again resumed the practice of law in Delaware, Ohio, and died there April 11, 1903; interment in Oak Grove Cemetery.

JONES, John William, a Representative from Georgia; born in Rockville, Montgomery County, Md., April 14, 1806; moved to Kentucky in 1810 with his parents, who settled in Nicholas (now Bourbon) County, near Carlisle; attended the common schools and Carlisle Seminary; studied medicine; commenced practice in Washington, Tenn., in 1826; appointed regimental surgeon of the Ninety-sixth Regiment, Tennessee Militia, in 1827; moved to Monroe, Walton County, Ga., and thence to Campbellton, Ga., in 1829 and practiced his profession; attended the University of Pennsylvania at Philadelphia in 1830 and 1831; appointed regimental surgeon of the Seventy-third Regiment, Georgia Militia, in 1830; moved to Culloden, Ga., in 1833; was graduated from Jefferson Medical College and Therapeutic Institute at Philadelphia in 1836; member of the State house of representatives in 1837; moved to Griffin, Pike County, Ga., in 1841 and continued the practice of medicine; president of the Griffin (Ga.) Medical Society; elected as a Whig to the Thirtieth Congress (March 4, 1847–March 3, 1849); declined to be a candidate for renomination in 1848; was tendered an appointment as consul at Habana, Cuba, by President Taylor but declined; resumed the practice of medicine in Oak Bowery, Ala.; trustee of the Oak Bowery Female College in 1850; moved to Auburn, Ala., in 1851; one of the founders of the Auburn Masonic Female College (now Auburn College); moved to Atlanta, Ga., in 1856; professor in the Atlanta Medical College (now Emory University) 1856–1862; during the Civil War served as surgeon in the Confederate Army; again

professor in the Atlanta Medical College 1865–1870; moved to Decatur, Ga., where he died April 27, 1871; interment in Oakland Cemetery, Atlanta, Ga.

JONES, John Winston, a Representative from Virginia; born near Amelia Court House, Amelia County, Va., November 22, 1791; attended private schools; was graduated from the law department of William and Mary College, Williamsburg, Va., in 1813; was admitted to the bar the same year and commenced practice in Chesterfield County, Va.; prosecuting attorney for the fifth Virginia circuit in 1818; member of the State constitutional convention in 1829 and 1830; elected as a Democrat to the Twenty-fourth and to the four succeeding Congresses (March 4, 1835–March 3, 1845); served as Speaker of the House of Representatives in the Twenty-eighth Congress; declined to be a candidate for renomination in 1844; resumed the practice of law and also engaged in agricultural pursuits; member of the State house of delegates in 1846 and served as speaker; reelected in 1847 but resigned on account of ill health; died at his residence, "Dellwood," in Chesterfield County, Virginia, January 29, 1848; interment in the family cemetery on his estate, "Dellwood," northwest of Petersburg, Va.

JONES, Joseph (uncle of James Monroe), a Delegate from Virginia; born in King George County, Va., in 1727; member of the State house of burgesses; served on the committee of safety in 1775; delegate to the State constitutional convention of 1776; served in the State house of delegates in 1776, 1777, 1780, 1781, and 1783–1785; Member of the Continental Congress in 1777, 1778, and 1780–1783; appointed judge of the Virginia General Court January 23, 1778, and resigned in October 1779; reappointed to the same court November 19, 1789; member of the State convention in 1788 which ratified the Federal Constitution; major general of State militia; died in Fredericksburg, Va., October 28, 1805.

JONES, Marvin, a Representative from Texas; born near Valley View, Cooke County, Tex., February 26, 1886; attended the common schools; was graduated from Southwestern University, Georgetown, Tex., in 1905, and from the law department of the University of Texas at Austin in 1907; was admitted to the bar the same year and commenced practice in Amarillo, Tex.; appointed a member of the board of legal examiners for the seventh supreme judicial district of Texas in 1913; member of the Democratic National Congressional Campaign Committee; served during the First World War as a private in Company A, Three Hundred and Eighth Battalion of the Tank Corps, in 1918; elected as a Democrat to the Sixty-fifth and to the eleven succeeding Congresses and served from March 4, 1917, until his resignation on November 20, 1940, to become a judge of the United States Court of Claims, having been appointed to that office by President Franklin D. Roosevelt; on leave from the Court of Claims beginning January 15, 1943, served as adviser and assistant to the Director of Economic Stabilization until June 29, 1943, when he was appointed administrator of the United States War Food Administration and served until July 1, 1945, when he resumed his duties as judge of the United States Court of Claims, serving as chief judge since July 10, 1947; is a legal resident of Amarillo, Tex.

JONES, Morgan, a Representative from New York; born in London, England, February 26, 1830; immigrated in 1833 to the United States with his parents, who settled in New York City; attended the public schools; engaged in the plumbing business in 1850; member of the board of councilmen 1859–1863 and president of that body in 1860, 1861, and 1863; member of the board of aldermen in 1864 and 1865, serving as president of the board in 1865; elected as a Democrat to the Thirty-ninth Congress

(March 4, 1865–March 3, 1867); resumed business interests in New York City until 1887, when he retired; died in that city July 13, 1894; interment in Greenwood Cemetery, Brooklyn, N. Y.

JONES, Nathaniel, a Representative from New York; born in Warwick, Orange County, N. Y., February 17, 1788; completed preparatory studies and later taught school; member of the State assembly in 1827 and 1828; engaged in banking in 1834; elected as a Democrat to the Twenty-fifth and Twenty-sixth Congresses (March 4, 1837–March 3, 1841); moved to Newburgh, N. Y., in 1841; surveyor general of New York from February 1842 to November 1844; State canal commissioner 1844–1847; superintendent of schools and clerk of the Board of Education of Newburgh in 1851; member of the State senate in 1852 and 1853; died in Newburgh, Orange County, N. Y., July 20, 1866.

JONES, Noble Wymberley (father of George Jones), a Delegate from Georgia; born in Lambeth, near London, England, in 1723; immigrated to the United States with his parents, who settled in Savannah, Ga., in 1733; studied medicine and practiced in Savannah 1756–1774; member of the colonial assembly in 1755, 1756, 1760–1762, 1764, 1768, 1769, 1771, and 1772, and served as speaker in 1768 and 1769; member of the council of safety and the Provincial Congress in 1775; Member of the Continental Congress in 1775; member of the State house of representatives in 1777 and 1778; moved to Charleston, S. C., in 1778; captured at the fall of Charleston in 1780 and imprisoned at St. Augustine, Fla.; exchanged in 1781; moved to Philadelphia, Pa., in 1781 and engaged in the practice of medicine; again a Member of the Continental Congress, accredited to Georgia, in 1781 and 1782; returned to Savannah, Ga., in 1782 and resumed his profession; again a member of the State house of representatives in 1783; member of reception committee upon the occasion of President Washington's visit to Savannah in 1791; president of State constitutional convention in 1795; died in Savannah, Ga., January 9, 1805; interment in Bonaventure Cemetery.

JONES, Owen, a Representative from Pennsylvania; born near Ardmore, Montgomery County, Pa., December 29, 1819; attended the public schools and was graduated from the University of Pennsylvania at Philadelphia; studied law in Philadelphia; was admitted to the bar of Montgomery County May 19, 1842, and commenced practice in Ardmore, Pa.; elected as a Democrat to the Thirty-fifth Congress (March 4, 1857–March 3, 1859); unsuccessful candidate for reelection in 1858 to the Thirty-sixth Congress; during the Civil War raised a troop of Cavalry (Troop B, First Pennsylvania Cavalry); captain August 5, 1861; major January 3, 1862; lieutenant colonel and colonel May 1863; resumed the practice of law; died near Ardmore, Pa., December 25, 1878; interment in Laurel Hill Cemetery, Philadelphia, Pa.

JONES, Paul Caruthers, a Representative from Missouri; born in Kennett, Dunklin County, Mo., March 12, 1901; attended the Kennett, Mo., public schools; was graduated from the University of Missouri at Columbia in 1923; member of the city council 1931–1933 and mayor of Kennett, Mo., 1933–1935; member and president of the board of education 1934–1946; served in the State house of representatives 1935–1937; member of the State senate 1937–1944; copublisher of the Dunklin Democrat since 1923; general manager of radio station KBOA since 1947; chairman of the State highway commission from August 1945 to May 1948; elected as a Democrat to the Eightieth Congress to fill the vacancy caused by the death of Orville Zimmerman and at the same time was elected to the Eighty-first Congress; reelected to the Eighty-second and to the four succeeding Congresses and served from November 2, 1948, to January 3, 1961. *Reelected to the Eighty-seventh Congress.*

JONES, Phineas, a Representative from New Jersey; born in Spencer, Worcester County, Mass., April 18, 1819; attended the common schools; moved to Elizabeth (then called Elizabethtown), N. J., in 1855; member of the city council of Elizabeth 1856–1860; moved to Newark in 1860; engaged in manufacturing and mercantile pursuits; vice president of the New Jersey State Agricultural Society; member of the State house of assembly in 1873 and 1874; elected as a Republican to the Forty-seventh Congress (March 4, 1881–March 3, 1883); declined to be a candidate for renomination in 1882; retired from active life and died in Newark, N. J., April 19, 1884; interment in Evergreen Cemetery, Elizabeth, N. J.

JONES, Robert Emmett, Jr., a Representative from Alabama; born in Scottsboro, Jackson County, Ala., June 12, 1912; attended the public schools and was graduated from the law department of the University of Alabama, Tuscaloosa, January 7, 1937; was admitted to the bar the same year and commenced practice in Scottsboro, Ala.; elected judge of Jackson County Court in July 1940; reelected in absentia in May 1945 and served until October 1946; during World War II served in the United States Navy as a gunnery officer in both the Atlantic and Pacific theaters from December 1943 until February 1946; elected as a Democrat to the Eightieth Congress to fill the vacancy caused by the resignation of John J. Sparkman; reelected to the Eighty-first and to the five succeeding Congresses and served from January 28, 1947, to January 3, 1961. *Reelected to the Eighty-seventh Congress.*

JONES, Robert Franklin, a Representative from Ohio; born in Cairo, Allen County, Ohio, June 25, 1907; attended the village school in Cairo, Ohio; was graduated from the Lima Central High School, Lima, Ohio, in 1924 and from Ohio Northern University College of Law at Ada in 1929; was admitted to the bar the same year and commenced practice in Lima, Ohio; prosecuting attorney of Allen County, Ohio, 1935–1939; elected as a Republican to the Seventy-sixth and to the four succeeding Congresses and served from January 3, 1939, until his resignation on September 2, 1947; member of the Federal Communications Commission from September 1947 until his resignation on September 19, 1952; resumed the practice of law in Washington, D. C.; resides in Silver Spring, Md.

JONES, Roland, a Representative from Louisiana; born in Salisbury, N. C., November 18, 1813; attended private schools; taught school in Wilkesboro, N. C., 1830–1835; was graduated from Cambridge (Mass.) Law School in 1838; was admitted to the bar and commenced practice in Brandon, Miss.; editor of the Brandon Republican 1838–1840; moved to Shreveport, La., in 1840 and continued the practice of law; member of the State house of representatives 1844–1848; district judge of Caddo Parish in 1851 and 1852; elected as a Democrat to the Thirty-third Congress (March 4, 1853–March 3, 1855); was not a candidate for renomination in 1854; resumed the practice of law; again elected district judge in 1860 and served until 1868; died in Shreveport, La., February 5, 1869; interment in Oakland Cemetery.

JONES, Samuel, a Delegate from New York; born in Oyster Bay, Long Island, N. Y., July 26, 1734; elected as a Delegate to the Continental Congress in 1789 and presented his credentials on January 30, 1789; died November 21, 1819.

JONES, Seaborn, a Representative from Georgia; born in Augusta, Ga., February 1, 1788; attended Princeton College; studied law; by a special act of the legislature was admitted to the bar in 1808; commenced practice in Milledgeville, Ga.;

appointed solicitor general of the Ocmulgee circuit in September 1817; solicitor general of Georgia in 1823; one of the commissioners appointed to investigate the disturbances in the Creek Nation; moved to Columbus, Ga., in 1827; elected as a Democrat to the Twenty-third Congress (March 4, 1833–March 3, 1835); elected to the Twenty-ninth Congress (March 4, 1845–March 3, 1847); died in Columbus, Ga., March 18, 1864; interment in Linnwood Cemetery.

JONES, Thomas Laurens, a Representative from Kentucky; born in White Oak, Rutherford County, N. C., January 22, 1819; attended private schools; was graduated from Princeton College and from the law department of Harvard University; was admitted to the bar in Columbia, S. C., in 1846 and commenced practice in New York City in 1847; moved to Newport, Ky., in 1849 and continued the practice of law; member of the State house of representatives from Campbell County 1853–1855; elected as a Democrat to the Fortieth and Forty-first Congresses (March 4, 1867–March 3, 1871); was not a candidate for renomination in 1870; elected to the Forty-fourth Congress (March 4, 1875–March 3, 1877); was not a candidate for renomination; resumed the practice of law; died in Newport, Ky., June 20, 1887; interment in Evergreen Cemetery.

JONES, Walter, a Representative from Virginia; born in Williamsburg, Va., December 18, 1745; was graduated from William and Mary College, Williamsburg, Va., in 1760; studied medicine in Edinburgh, Scotland, and received the degree of doctor of medicine in 1770; returned to Virginia and located in Northumberland County; physician general of the middle military department in 1777; member of the State house of delegates 1785–1787; delegate to the State constitutional convention in 1788; elected as a Democrat to the Fifth Congress (March 4, 1797–March 3, 1799); again a member of the house of delegates in 1802 and 1803; elected to the Eighth and to the three succeeding Congresses (March 4, 1803–March 3, 1811); died in Westmoreland County, Va., December 31, 1815; interment in the family burial ground at "Hayfield," a few miles from what is now Callo, Northumberland County, Va.

JONES, Wesley Livsey, a Representative and a Senator from Washington; born near Bethany, Moultrie County, Ill., October 9, 1863; attended the common schools; taught school; was graduated from the Southern Illinois College at Enfield in 1885; studied law; was admitted to the bar in 1886 and commenced practice in Decatur, Ill.; moved to North Yakima, Wash., in 1889, and continued the practice of his profession; elected as a Republican to the Fifty-sixth and to the four succeeding Congresses (March 4, 1899–March 3, 1909); did not seek renomination in 1908, having become a candidate for Senator; elected to the United States Senate in 1909; reelected in 1914, 1920, and 1926, and served from March 4, 1909, until his death; was an unsuccessful candidate for reelection in 1932; died in Seattle, Wash., November 19, 1932; remains were cremated and the ashes placed in the Bonney-Watson Mortuary, Seattle, Wash.

JONES, William, a Representative from Pennsylvania; born in Philadelphia, Pa., in 1760; completed academic studies; served in the Revolutionary War, joining a company of volunteers at the age of sixteen and participated in the Battles of Trenton and Princeton; later served as third lieutenant on the Pennsylvania private armed ship *St. James* under Captain (later Commodore) Truxton and was promoted to first lieutenant for gallantry during an engagement in 1781 between that vessel and a British sloop of war, in which he was injured; was twice wounded and twice taken prisoner; moved to Charleston, S. C.; returned to Pennsylvania; elected as a Democrat to the Seventh Congress (March 4, 1801–March 3, 1803); appointed Secretary of the Navy in the Cabinet of President Madison and served from January 12, 1813, to December, 2, 1814; president of the Bank of the United States 1816–1819; collector of customs in Philadelphia, Pa., 1827–1829; died in Bethlehem, Pa., September 6, 1831; interment in St. Peter's Churchyard, Philadelphia, Pa.

JONES, William Atkinson, a Representative from Virginia; born in Warsaw, Richmond County, Va., on March 21, 1849; entered the Virginia Military Institute at Lexington in 1864 and served in the defense of Richmond, Va., until its evacuation; attended Coleman's School in Fredericksburg, and was graduated from the law department of the University of Virginia at Charlottesville in 1870; was admitted to the bar in 1870 and commenced practice in Warsaw, Va.; Commonwealth attorney for several years; delegate to the Democratic National Conventions in 1880, 1896, and 1900; elected as a Democrat to the Fifty-second and to the thirteen succeeding Congresses and served from March 4, 1891, until his death in Warsaw, Richmond County, Va., on April 17, 1918; interment in St. John's Episcopal Church Cemetery.

JONES, William Carey, a Representative from Washington; born in Remsen, Oneida County, N. Y., April 5, 1855; attended the public schools, the West Salem (Wis.) Seminary, and was graduated from the law department of the University of Wisconsin at Madison in 1876; was admitted to the bar the same year and practiced in Madelia, Minn., until 1883; city attorney of Madelia in 1882 and 1883; moved to the Territory of Washington in 1883 and settled in Cheney; city attorney of Cheney 1884–1889; moved to Spokane, Wash., in 1887; prosecuting attorney for the twelfth district of the Territory of Washington 1886–1889; upon the admission of Washington into the Union was elected attorney general of the State and served from 1889 to 1897; delegate to every Territorial and State Republican convention from 1884 to 1894; chairman of the State central committee of the Free Coinage Republican Party in 1896; elected as a Free Silver Republican to the Fifty-fifth Congress (March 4, 1897–March 3, 1899); unsuccessful candidate for reelection in 1898 to the Fifty-sixth Congress; affiliated with the Democratic Party; delegate to all Democratic State conventions from 1904 to 1924; resumed the practice of his profession; died in Spokane, Wash., June 14, 1927; remains were cremated and the ashes scattered over Liberty Lake, near Spokane, Wash.

JONES, William Theopilus, a Delegate from the Territory of Wyoming; born in Corydon, Harrison County, Ind., February 20, 1842; received a liberal schooling; studied law; was admitted to the bar in 1865 and commenced practice in Corydon, Ind.; during the Civil War served in the Union Army as major of the Seventeenth Regiment, Indiana Volunteer Infantry; presidential elector on the Republican ticket of Grant and Colfax in 1868; appointed associate justice of the supreme court of the Territory of Wyoming in 1869; settled in Cheyenne, Wyo., in 1869; elected as a Republican a Delegate to the Forty-second Congress (March 4, 1871–March 3, 1873); unsuccessful candidate for reelection in 1872 to the Forty-third Congress; resumed the practice of law in Corydon, Ind., where he died October 9, 1882; interment in Cedar Hill Cemetery.

JONES, Willie, a Delegate from North Carolina; born in Northampton County, N. C., December 24, 1740; attended Eton College, England; engaged in agricultural pursuits; member of the Provincial Congress in 1774 and 1776; president of the North Carolina Committee of Safety in 1776 and first Governor ex officio of the new State; member of the first constitutional convention in 1776; member of the State house of commons

1776–1778; Member of the Continental Congress in 1780 and 1781; elected to the United States Constitutional Convention in 1787 but declined to accept; member of the State constitutional convention called to ratify the Constitution of the United States July 21, 1788; resumed agricultural pursuits; died at his summer home in Raleigh, N. C., June 18, 1801; interment in the family burying ground on his plantation near Raleigh, N. C.

JONES, Woodrow Wilson, a Representative from North Carolina; born in Green Hill Township, Rutherford County, N. C., January 26, 1914; attended the public schools of Rutherford County; graduated from Mars Hill (N. C.) College in 1934 and from Wake Forest Law School in 1937; was admitted to the bar in 1937 and commenced the practice of law in Rutherfordton, N. C.; during World War II served in the United States Navy from November 1943 until discharged as a lieutenant (jg) in January 1946; city attorney of Rutherfordton, N. C., 1940–1943; served as prosecuting attorney of Rutherford County Recorder's Court 1941–1943; member of the State house of representatives 1947–1949; elected as a Democrat to the Eighty-first Congress to fill the vacancy caused by the death of Alfred L. Bulwinkle; reelected to the Eighty-second, Eighty-third, and Eighty-fourth Congresses and served from November 7, 1950, to January 3, 1957; was not a candidate for renomination in 1956; delegate to all Democratic State Conventions 1940–1960 and delegate to Democratic National Convention in 1960; resumed the practice of law; is a resident of Rutherfordton, N. C.

JONKMAN, Bartel John, a Representative from Michigan; born in Grand Rapids, Mich., April 28, 1884; attended the public schools and was graduated from the law department of the University of Michigan at Ann Arbor in 1914; was admitted to the bar the same year and commenced practice in Grand Rapids, Mich.; assistant prosecutor of Kent County, Mich., 1915–1920 and prosecuting attorney 1929–1936; elected as a Republican to the Seventy-sixth Congress to fill the vacancy caused by the death of Carl E. Mapes; reelected to the Seventy-seventh and to the three succeeding Congresses and served from February 19, 1940, to January 3, 1949; unsuccessful candidate for renomination in 1948; resumed the practice of law; died in Grand Rapids, Mich., June 13, 1955; interment in Woodlawn Cemetery.

JORDAN, B. Everett, a Senator from North Carolina; born in Ramseur, Randolph County, N. C., September 8, 1896; attended the public schools, Rutherford (N. C.) College Preparatory School in 1912 and 1913, and Trinity College in 1914 and 1915; during the First World War served with the Tank Corps, United States Army, in France in 1918 and with the occupation forces in Germany in 1919; organized Sellers Manufacturing Co. in 1927 and served as secretary-treasurer and general manager; interested in several textile manufacturing companies; chairman, North Carolina Democratic Executive Committee, 1949–1954; Democratic national committeeman 1954–1958; member of North Carolina Peace Officers Benefit and Retirement Commission 1943–1958; member of North Carolina Medical Care Commission 1945–1951; chairman, Board of Trustees, Alamance County General Hospital; trustee of Duke University and Elon College; vice president of Board of Methodist Colleges 1952–1956; appointed as a Democrat to the United States Senate April 19, 1958, and elected November 4, 1958, to fill the vacancy caused by the death of W. Kerr Scott in the term ending January 3, 1961. *Reelected in 1960 for the term ending January 3, 1967.*

JORDAN, Isaac M., a Representative from Ohio; born in Mifflinburg, Union County, Pa., May 5, 1835; moved with his parents to Springfield, Ohio, in 1837; attended Northwood (Ohio) Institute for two years, and was graduated from Miami University, Oxford, Ohio, in 1857; studied law; was admitted to the bar in 1858 and commenced practice in Dayton, Ohio; moved to Cincinnati in 1859 and continued the practice of law; elected as a Democrat to the Forty-eighth Congress (March 4, 1883–March 3, 1885); declined to be a candidate for renomination in 1884; engaged in the practice of law in Cincinnati; died from injuries received in an elevator accident in Cincinnati, Ohio, December 3, 1890; interment in the family vault in Spring Grove Cemetery.

JORDEN, Edwin James, a Representative from Pennsylvania; born in Spring Hill, near Towanda, Bradford County, Pa., August 30, 1863; attended the common schools and Keystone Academy; was graduated from the State Normal School at Mansfield, Pa.; studied law; was admitted to the bar in 1888 and commenced practice in Tunkhannock, Pa.; elected as a Republican to the Fifty-third Congress to fill the vacancy caused by the death of Myron B. Wright and served from February 23 until March 4, 1895; was not a candidate for renomination in 1894; resumed the practice of his profession; died in Tunkhannock, Wyoming County, Pa., September 7, 1903; interment in Sunnyside Cemetery.

JORGENSEN, Joseph, a Representative from Virginia; born in Philadelphia, Pa., February 11, 1844; was graduated from the medical department of the University of Pennsylvania at Philadelphia; cadet surgeon, United States Army, March 17, 1864, to March 23, 1865; acting assistant surgeon April 10 to September 10, 1865, and June 5, 1867, to February 21, 1870; member of the Virginia House of Delegates from Prince Edward County 1871–1873; moved to Petersburg, Va.; appointed postmaster of Petersburg, Va., May 21, 1874, and served until June 8, 1877, when he resigned, having been elected to Congress; elected as a Republican to the Forty-fifth, Forty-sixth, and Forty-seventh Congresses (March 4, 1877–March 3, 1883); delegate to the Republican National Convention at Chicago in 1880; appointed register of the land office at Walla Walla, Wash., by President Arthur February 27, 1883, and served until removed by President Cleveland in 1886; died in Portland, Oreg., January 21, 1888; interment in Mountain View Cemetery, Walla Walla, Wash.

JOSEPH, Antonio, a Delegate from the Territory of New Mexico; born in Taos, N. Mex., August 25, 1846; attended Lux's Academy in Taos, Bishop Lammy's School in Santa Fe, N. Mex., Webster College in St. Louis County, Mo., and Bryant and Stratton's Commercial College, St. Louis, Mo.; engaged in mercantile pursuits; county judge of Taos County, N. Mex., 1878–1880; delegate to all State and National conventions during his life; moved to Ojo Caliente, N. Mex., in 1880; member of the Territorial house of representatives in 1882; elected as a Democrat to the Forty-ninth and to the four succeeding Congresses (March 4, 1885–March 3, 1895); unsuccessful candidate for reelection in 1894 to the Fifty-fourth Congress; served in the Territorial senate 1896–1898, serving as president of that body in 1898; again engaged in the mercantile business; owner of hotels and extensive lands; died in Ojo Caliente, N. Mex., April 19, 1910; interment in Fairmount Cemetery, Santa Fe, N. Mex.

JOST, Henry Lee, a Representative from Missouri; born in New York City December 6, 1873; moved to Hopkins, Nodaway County, Mo., in 1881; attended the common schools; studied law; was admitted to the bar in 1898; afterward attended the Kansas City Law School in 1898 and 1899 and commenced the practice of law in Kansas City, Mo., in 1899; associate city counselor in 1909; first assistant prosecuting attorney 1910–

1912; mayor of Kansas City 1912–1916; lecturer on criminal law at Kansas City School of Law 1917–1936; elected as a Democrat to the Sixty-eighth Congress (March 4, 1923–March 3, 1925); was not a candidate for renomination in 1924; resumed law practice in Kansas City, Mo., where he died July 13, 1950; interment in Mount Moriali Cemetery, near Kansas City, Mo.

JOY, Charles Frederick, a Representative from Missouri; born in Jacksonville, Morgan County, Ill., December 11, 1849; attended the public schools; was graduated from Yale College in 1874; studied law; was admitted to the bar and commenced practice in St. Louis, Mo., in 1876; presented credentials as a Republican Member-elect to the Fifty-third Congress and served until April 3, 1894, when he was succeeded by John J. O'Neill, who contested the election; elected to the Fifty-fourth and to the three succeeding Congresses (March 4, 1895–March 3, 1903); unsuccessful candidate for renomination in 1902; resumed the practice of his profession in St. Louis; served as recorder of deeds from 1907 until March 22, 1921, when he resigned; died in St. Louis, Mo., on April 13, 1921; the remains were cremated and placed in Elks Rest in Bellefontaine Cemetery.

JOYCE, Charles Herbert, a Representative from Vermont; born near Andover, England, January 30, 1830; immigrated to the United States in 1836 with his parents, who settled in Waitsfield, Vt.; attended Northfield Academy and Newbury Seminary; studied law; was admitted to the bar in 1852 and commenced practice in Northfield, Vt.; State librarian for two years; district attorney for Washington County in 1857 and 1858; during the Civil War served in the Union Army as major and lieutenant colonel of the Second Vermont Volunteers; resumed the practice of law in Rutland, Vt.; member of the State house of representatives 1869–1871 and served as speaker in 1870 and 1871; elected as a Republican to the Forty-fourth and to the three succeeding Congresses (March 4, 1875–March 3, 1883); was not a candidate for renomination in 1882; resumed the practice of his profession in Rutland, Vt.; later retired and resided in Pittsfield, Vt., until his death, November 22, 1916; interment in Greenwood Cemetery, Rutland, Vt.

JOYCE, James, a Representative from Ohio; born in Cumberland, Guernsey County, Ohio, July 2, 1870; attended the common schools; taught school in Cumberland and Pleasant City, Ohio, and also studied law; entered the senior class of the Cincinnati Law School in 1891 and was graduated in 1892; was admitted to the bar at Columbus, Ohio, on March 3, 1892; superintendent of the Senecaville (Ohio) High School 1893–1895; began the active practice of law in Cambridge, Ohio, in 1895; member of the State house of representatives 1896–1900; delegate to the Republican National Convention at Chicago in 1904; elected as a Republican to the Sixty-first Congress (March 4, 1909–March 3, 1911); unsuccessful candidate for reelection in 1910 to the Sixty-second Congress; resumed the practice of law in Cambridge, Ohio; unsuccessful candidate for election as associate justice of the supreme court of Ohio in 1916; died in Cambridge, Ohio, March 25, 1931; interment in the mausoleum in Northwood Cemetery.

JUDD, Norman Buel (grandfather of Norman Judd Gould), a Representative from Illinois; born in Rome, N. Y., January 10, 1815; received a liberal schooling; studied law; was admitted to the bar in 1836 and commenced practice in Rome, N. Y.; moved to Chicago, Ill., in 1836 and continued the practice of his profession; city attorney 1837–1839; member of the State senate 1844–1860; delegate to the Republican National Convention at Chicago in 1860 and nominated Abraham Lincoln as a candidate for President of the United States; appointed Minister Plenipotentiary to Berlin by President Lincoln March 6, 1861, and

served until 1865; elected as a Republican to the Fortieth and Forty-first Congresses (March 4, 1867–March 3, 1871); declined to be a candidate for reelection in 1870; appointed collector at the port of Chicago by President Grant December 5, 1872, and served until his death in Chicago, Ill., November 10, 1878; interment in Graceland Cemetery.

JUDD, Walter Henry, a Representative from Minnesota; born in Rising City, Butler County, Nebr., on September 25, 1898; attended the public schools; was graduated from the University of Nebraska at Lincoln in 1920 and from the medical department of the same university in 1923; during the First World War enlisted in the United States Army in 1918 as a private and was discharged as a second lieutenant, Field Artillery, in 1919; second lieutenant, Field Artillery, Officers Reserve Corps, 1919–1924; instructor of zoology, University of Omaha, 1920–1924; traveling secretary, Student Volunteer Movement in Colleges and Universities in 1924 and 1925; fellowship in surgery, Mayo Foundation, Rochester, Minn., 1932–1934; medical missionary and hospital superintendent in China, under auspices of American Board of Commissioners for Foreign Missions, 1925–1931 and 1934–1938; returned from China in 1938, speaking throughout the United States in an attempt to arouse Americans to menace of Japan's military expansion and to get embargo on sale and shipment of war materials to Japan in 1939 and 1940; engaged in private medical practice in Minneapolis, Minn., in 1941 and 1942; elected as a Republican to the Seventy-eighth and to the eight succeeding Congresses (January 3, 1943–January 3, 1961). *Reelected to the Eighty-seventh Congress.*

JUDSON, Andrew Thompson, a Representative from Connecticut; born in Eastford, Windham County, Conn., November 29, 1784; received a limited schooling; studied law; was admitted to the bar in 1806; moved to Montpelier, Vt., where he began the practice of law; returned to Connecticut and settled in Canterbury in 1809; State's attorney for Windham County 1819–1833; member of the State house of representatives 1822–1825; elected as a Democrat to the Twenty-fourth Congress and served from March 4, 1835, until July 4, 1836, when he resigned; appointed by President Jackson United States judge for the district of Connecticut June 28, 1836, and served until his death in Canterbury, Conn., March 17, 1853; interment in Hyde Cemetery.

JULIAN, George Washington, a Representative from Indiana; born near Centerville, Wayne County, Ind., on May 5, 1817; attended the common schools; studied law; was admitted to the bar in 1840 and commenced practice in Greenfield, Ind.; member of the State house of representatives in 1845; delegate to the Buffalo Free-Soil Convention in 1848; presidential elector on the Free-Soil ticket of Van Buren and Adams in 1848; elected as a Free-Soiler to the Thirty-first Congress (March 4, 1849–March 3, 1851); unsuccessful candidate for election in 1850 to the Thirty-second Congress; unsuccessful candidate for Vice President of the United States on the Free-Soil ticket in 1852; delegate to the Republican National Convention at Pittsburgh, Pa., in 1856 and chairman of its committee on organization; elected as a Republican to the Thirty-seventh and to the four succeeding Congresses (March 4, 1861–March 3, 1871); appointed by President Cleveland surveyor general of New Mexico and served from July 1885 until September 1889; returned to Indiana and settled in Irvington; engaged in literary pursuits; died in Irvington, a suburb of Indianapolis, Ind., July 7, 1899; interment in Crown Hill Cemetery, Indianapolis, Ind.

JUNKIN, Benjamin Franklin, a Representative from Pennsylvania; born near Carlisle, Cumberland County, Pa., November 12, 1822; attended private schools and was graduated from

Lafayette College, Easton, Pa.; studied law; was admitted to the bar in 1844 and commenced practice in New Bloomfield, Pa.; district attorney for Perry County 1850–1853; elected as a Republican to the Thirty-sixth Congress (March 4, 1859–March 3, 1861); unsuccessful candidate for reelection in 1860 to the Thirty-seventh Congress; resumed the practice of his profession in New Bloomfield; president judge of the ninth judicial district 1871–1881; presidential elector on the Republican ticket of Blaine and Logan in 1884; solicitor of the Pennsylvania Railroad Co. from 1886 until his death in New Bloomfield, Perry County, Pa., October 9, 1908; interment in New Bloomfield Cemetery.

JUUL, Niels, a Representative from Illinois; born in Randers, Denmark, April 27, 1859; attended the Real (Royal) School, Randers, Denmark; immigrated to the United States and settled in Chicago, Ill., in 1880; engaged in the publishing business; studied law; was graduated from the law department of Lake Forest University in 1898; was admitted to the bar in 1899 and commenced practice in Chicago, Ill.; member of the State senate 1898–1914; assistant attorney of the Sanitary District of Chicago 1907–1911; elected as a Republican to the Sixty-fifth and Sixty-sixth Congresses (March 4, 1917–March 3, 1921); unsuccessful candidate for renomination in 1920; appointed by President Harding United States collector of customs for the port of Chicago January 1, 1921, and served until December 31, 1922, when he resigned; resumed the practice of law until his death in Chicago, Ill., on December 4, 1929; interment in Mount Olive Cemetery.

K

KADING, Charles August, a Representative from Wisconsin; born in Lowell, Dodge County, Wis., January 14, 1874; attended the country schools, Lowell graded school, Horicon High School, and the University of Wisconsin at Madison; was graduated from the law department of Valparaiso University, Valparaiso, Ind., in 1900; was admitted to the bar the same year and commenced practice in Watertown, Wis.; also interested in agricultural pursuits; city attorney of Watertown 1905–1912; district attorney for Dodge County, Wis., 1906–1912; mayor of Watertown 1914–1916; elected as a Republican to the Seventieth, Seventy-first, and Seventy-second Congresses (March 4, 1927–March 3, 1933); unsuccessful candidate for renomination in 1932; resumed the practice of law; died in Watertown, Wis., June 19, 1956; interment in Oak Hill Cemetery.

KAHN, Florence Prag (wife of Julius Kahn), a Representative from California; born in Salt Lake City, Utah, November 9, 1868; moved to California in 1869 with her parents, who settled in San Francisco; attended the public schools of San Francisco; was graduated from the Girls' High School in 1883 and from the University of California at Berkeley in 1887; elected as a Republican to the Sixty-ninth Congress on February 17, 1925, to fill the vacancy caused by the death of her husband, Representative-elect Julius Kahn; reelected to the Seventieth and to the four succeeding Congresses and served from March 4, 1925, to January 3, 1937; unsuccessful candidate for reelection in 1936 to the Seventy-fifth Congress; retired to private life and resided in San Francisco, Calif., until her death on November 16, 1948; interment in Home of Peace Cemetery, Colma, Calif.

KAHN, Julius (husband of Florence Prag Kahn), a Representative from California; born in Kuppenheim, Grand Duchy of Baden, Germany, February 28, 1861; immigrated to the United States with his parents, who settled in California in 1866; attended the public schools of San Francisco; followed the theatrical profession for ten years, playing with Edwin Booth, Joseph Jefferson, Tomasso Salvini, Mr. and Mrs. W. J. Florence, Clara Morris, and other well-known stars; returned to San Francisco in 1890; studied law; member of the State assembly in 1892; was admitted to the bar in January 1894 and commenced practice in San Francisco; elected as a Republican to the Fifty-sixth and Fifty-seventh Congresses (March 4, 1899–March 3, 1903); unsuccessfully contested the election of Edward J. Livernash to the Fifty-eighth Congress; elected to the Fifty-ninth and to the nine succeeding Congresses and served from March 4, 1905, until his death; had been reelected to the Sixty-ninth Congress; member of the House Committee on Military Affairs during the entire period of the First World War and assisted in securing the passage of the selective draft act of 1917; died in San Francisco, Calif., December 18, 1924; interment in the Home of Peace Cemetery, Colma, Calif.

KALANIANAOLE, Jonah Kuhio, a Delegate from the Territory of Hawaii; born in Koloa, island of Kauai, Hawaii, March 26, 1871; attended the Royal School and Punahou College, Honolulu; studied four years in St. Matthew's College, California; was a student at the Royal Agricultural College in England and was graduated from a business college in England; created a prince by royal proclamation in 1884; occupied a position in the Department of the Interior of the Hawaiian Government; took part in the revolution of the Hawaiians in 1895 and was sentenced to one year's imprisonment; visited Africa during the years 1899–1902 and fought in the British Army in the Boer War; elected as a Republican to the Fifty-eighth and to the nine succeeding Congresses and served from March 4, 1903, until his death in Waikiki, near Honolulu, Hawaii, on January 7, 1922; interment in Royal Mausoleum, Nuuanu.

KALBFLEISCH, Martin, a Representative from New York; born in Flushing, Holland, on February 8, 1804; attended the public schools; studied chemistry; immigrated to the United States and settled in New York City in 1826; engaged in the manufacture and sale of paints; health warden in 1832; school trustee in 1836; established a chemical factory at Greenpoint, N. Y., in 1844; supervisor of Bushwick 1852–1854; unsuccessful candidate for mayor of Brooklyn in 1854; alderman in Brooklyn 1855–1861; mayor 1862–1864; elected as a Democrat to the Thirty-eighth Congress (March 4, 1863–March 3, 1865); delegate to the Union National Convention at Philadelphia in 1866; again mayor of Brooklyn 1867–1871; unsuccessful independent candidate for reelection; retired from active pursuits; died in Brooklyn, N. Y., February 12, 1873; interment in Greenwood Cemetery.

KANE, Elias Kent, a Senator from Illinois; born in New York City on June 7, 1794; attended the public schools; was graduated from Yale College in 1813; studied law; was admitted to the bar and commenced practice in Nashville, Tenn.; moved to Kaskaskia, Ill., in 1814; appointed judge of the Territory of Illinois; delegate to the first State constitutional convention in 1818; unsuccessful candidate for election in 1820 to the Seventeenth Congress; appointed the first secretary of state of Illinois in 1820 and served until 1824; member of the State house of representatives in 1824; elected as a Democrat to the United States Senate in 1824; reelected in 1831 and served from March 4, 1825, until his death in Washington, D. C., December 12, 1835; interment in the family cemetery on the old Kane farm, near Fort Gage, Ill.

KANE, Nicholas Thomas, a Representative from New York; born in County Waterford, Ireland, September 12, 1846; immigrated to the United States when a boy and settled near Albany, N. Y.; attended the common schools; during the Civil War enlisted in the Union Army in 1863 and served until 1865; engaged in mercantile pursuits; represented Watervliet on the Albany County Board of Supervisors 1883–1885; elected as a Democrat to the Fiftieth Congress and served from March 4, 1887, until his death in Albany, N. Y., September 14, 1887, before the assembling of the Congress; interment in St. Agnes Cemetery, Colonie, Albany County, N. Y.

KARCH, Charles Adam, a Representative from Illinois; born on a farm in Engleman Township, St. Clair County, Ill., March 17, 1875; attended the public schools; was graduated from Northern Illinois Normal University (now the Illinois State Normal University), at Normal, Ill., in 1894; taught school 1895–1900; was graduated from the law department of Wesleyan College, Bloomington, Ill., in 1898; was admitted to the bar in 1898 and commenced practice in Belleville, Ill.; served as secretary to Congressman Fred J. Kern 1901–1903; member of the Illinois House of Representatives 1904–1906 and 1910–1914; moved to East St. Louis in 1914 and continued the practice of law; served as United States attorney for the eastern judicial district of Illinois 1914–1918; elected as a Democrat to the Seventy-second Congress and served from March 4, 1931, until his death; had been nominated for reelection to the Seventy-third Congress; died in St. Mary's Hospital, St. Louis, Mo., on November 6, 1932; interment in Mount Hope Cemetery, Belleville, Ill.

KARST, Raymond Willard, a Representative from Missouri; born in South St. Louis, Mo., December 31, 1902; attended Wyman grade school and St. Louis Academy; was graduated from the law school of St. Louis University in 1927; was admitted to the bar in 1926 and commenced the practice of law in St. Louis, Mo.; member of the State house of representatives in 1935 and 1936; provisional city judge and judge of Court of Criminal Correction 1936–1940; during World War II served as a captain, Ordnance Department, United States Army, 1942–1945; elected as a Democrat to the Eighty-first Congress (January 3, 1949–January 3, 1951); was an unsuccessful candidate for reelection in 1950 to the Eighty-second Congress; resumed the practice of law in Clayton, Mo.; resides in city of Frontenac, St. Louis, Mo.

KARSTEN, Frank Melvin, a Representative from Missouri; born in San Antonio, Bexar County, Tex., January 7, 1913; moved to St. Louis, Mo., with his family in 1925; attended Benton and Cupples Elementary Schools and Beaumont High School in St. Louis, Mo.; served as secretary to Congressman John Joseph Cochran 1934–1946; was graduated from National University, Washington, D. C., in 1940; was admitted to the District of Columbia bar in 1946, but did not practice; elected as a Democrat to the Eightieth and to the six succeeding Congresses (January 3, 1947–January 3, 1961). *Reelected to the Eighty-seventh Congress.*

KARTH, Joseph Edward, a Representative from Minnesota; born in New Brighton, Ramsey County, Minn., August 26, 1922; attended elementary schools in Ramsey County and North St. Paul High School, also the University of Nebraska School of Engineering; interrupted his education during World War II to serve in the United States Army, with service in the European Theater of Operations; received a recommendation for battlefield commission; returned to the University of Nebraska and graduated; employed by the Minnesota Mining & Manufacturing Company; international representative of OCAW–AFL–CIO 1947–1958; served as a member of the Minnesota House of Representatives 1950–1958; elected as a Democrat to the Eighty-sixth Congress (January 3, 1959–January 3, 1961). *Reelected to the Eighty-seventh Congress.*

KASEM, George Albert, a Representative from California; born in Drumright, Creek County, Okla., April 6, 1919; attended the public schools in Holdenville, Okla., Oklahoma City, Okla., Borger, Tex., Hobbs, N. Mex., and high school in Las Vegas, Nev.; graduated from John H. Francis Polytechnic High School, Los Angeles, Calif., in 1938; during World War II entered the service in 1941 and while in the Army Air Force attended Weather Observer School, Macon, Ga., and Air Force Weather Forecaster School, Grand Rapids, Mich.; later stationed in Anglo-Egyptian Sudan, Egypt, and Iraq, and was discharged in 1945; graduated from the University of Southern California in 1949 and from the law department of the same university in 1951; was admitted to the bar in 1951 and practiced law in Los Angeles; moved to Baldwin Park, Calif., in 1953 and associated with the law firm of Kasem & Trench; elected as a Democrat to the Eighty-sixth Congress (January 3, 1959–January 3, 1961); unsuccessful candidate for reelection in 1960 to the Eighty-seventh Congress; resides in West Covina, Calif.

KASSON, John Adam, a Representative from Iowa; born in Charlotte, Chittenden County, Vt., January 11, 1822; attended the local school; was graduated from the University of Vermont at Burlington in 1842; studied law; was admitted to the bar and practiced in St. Louis, Mo., until 1857; moved to Des Moines, Iowa, and resumed the practice of law; delegate to the Republican National Convention at Chicago in 1860; First Assistant Postmaster General in President Lincoln's administration in 1861 and resigned in 1862; United States commissioner to the International Postal Congress at Paris in 1863; elected as a Republican to the Thirty-eighth and Thirty ninth Congresses (March 4, 1863–March 3, 1867); unsuccessful candidate for renomination in 1866; commissioner from the United States in 1867 to negotiate postal conventions with Great Britain, France, Belgium, Holland, Germany, Switzerland, and Italy; member of the State house of representatives 1868–1872; elected to the Forty-third and Forty-fourth Congresses (March 4, 1873–March 3, 1877); was not a candidate for renomination in 1876; appointed Minister to Austria-Hungary October 17, 1877, and served until 1881; elected to the Forty-seventh and Forty-eighth Congresses and served from March 4, 1881, until his resignation on July 13, 1884; appointed Minister to Germany July 4, 1884, and served one year; special envoy to the Congo International Conference at Berlin in 1885 and to the Samoan International Conference in 1889; United States special commissioner plenipotentiary to negotiate reciprocity treaties in 1897; member of the United States and British Joint High Commission in 1898 to adjust differences with Canada; died in Washington, D. C., May 19, 1910; interment in Woodland Cemetery, Des Moines, Iowa.

KASTENMEIER, Robert William, a Representative from Wisconsin; born in Beaver Dam, Dodge County, Wis., January 24, 1924; attended the public schools of Beaver Dam, also Carleton College, Northfield, Minn.; graduated from the University of Wisconsin in 1952; was admitted to the bar the same year and commenced the practice of law in Watertown, Wis.; entered the United States Army as a private in February 1943; served in the Philippines and was discharged as a first lieutenant on August 15, 1946; War Department branch office director, claims service, in the Philippines 1946–1948; elected justice of the peace for Jefferson and Dodge counties in 1955 and served until 1959; delegate to the Democratic National Convention in 1956; elected as a Democrat to the Eighty-sixth Congress (January 3, 1959–January 3, 1961). *Reelected to the Eighty-seventh Congress.*

KAUFMAN, David Spangler, a Representative from Texas; born in Boiling Springs, Cumberland County, Pa., December 18,

1813; pursued classical studies, and was graduated from Princeton College in 1833; studied law; was admitted to the bar in Natchez, Miss., and commenced practice in Natchitoches, La.; moved to Nacogdoches, Republic of Texas, in 1837; served against the Indians; member of the Texas House of Representatives 1839–1843; served in the Texas Senate 1843–1845; appointed Chargé d'Affaires of Texas to the United States in 1845; moved to Lowes Ferry, Tex.; upon the admission of Texas as a State into the Union was elected as a Democrat to the Twenty-ninth Congress; reelected to the Thirtieth and Thirty-first Congresses and served from March 30, 1846, until his death in Washington, D. C., on January 31, 1851; interment in the Congressional Cemetery; reinterment in the State Cemetery at Austin, Tex., in 1932.

KAVANAGH, Edward, a Representative from Maine; born in Newcastle, Lincoln County, Maine, April 27, 1795; attended Montreal Seminary, Montreal, Canada, and Georgetown College, Georgetown, D. C.; was graduated from St. Mary's College, Baltimore, Md., in 1813; traveled abroad for two years; studied law; was admitted to the bar and commenced practice in Damariscotta, Maine; member of the State house of representatives 1826–1828; secretary of the State senate in 1830; elected as a Democrat to the Twenty-second and Twenty-third Congresses (March 4, 1831–March 3, 1835); unsuccessful candidate for reelection in 1834 to the Twenty-fourth Congress; appointed Chargé d'Affaires to Portugal on March 3, 1835, and served until his resignation in June 1841; one of the joint commission on the northeastern boundary in 1842; member of the State senate in 1842 and 1843 and served as president of that body; became Governor of Maine upon the resignation of Governor Fairfield on March 7, 1843, and served until the end of the term in 1844; died in Newcastle, Maine, January 20, 1844; interment in St. Patrick's Catholic Cemetery, Damariscotta Mills, Maine.

KAVANAUGH, William Marmaduke, a Senator from Arkansas; born near Eutaw, Green County, Ala., March 3, 1866; attended the common schools in Kentucky; was graduated from the Kentucky Military Institute at Farmdale, Ky., in 1885; moved to Arkansas and settled in Little Rock; engaged in newspaper work, first as reporter and subsequently became editor and manager of the Arkansas Gazette; sheriff and tax collector of Pulaski County 1896–1900; county and probate judge 1900–1904; engaged in banking, street railway, and gas supply interests; member of the Democratic National Committee 1912–1915; elected as a Democrat to the United States Senate to fill the vacancy caused by the death of Jeff Davis and served from January 29 until March 3, 1913; director of the Lakes to Gulf Deep Waterways Association; died in Little Rock, Ark., February 21, 1915; interment in Oakland Cemetery.

KAYNOR, William Kirk, a Representative from Massachusetts; born in Sanborn, O'Brien County, Iowa, November 29, 1884; attended the common schools of Spencer and Clear Lake, Iowa; in his early youth was employed as a drug clerk in Clear Lake; moved to Gann Valley, Buffalo County, S. Dak., and herded cattle; moved to the East in the fall of 1903; was graduated from Hotchkiss School, Lakeville, Conn., in 1908 and from Yale University in 1912; moved to Springfield, Mass., in 1912 and engaged in the real estate and insurance business; during the First World War attended the officers' training school at Camp Lee, Va., from July to November 1918; member of the common council of Springfield 1920–1924; postmaster of Springfield 1923–1928; elected as a Republican to the Seventy-first Congress and served from March 4, 1929, until his death in an airplane accident near Washington, D. C., on December 20, 1929; interment in Oak Grove Cemetery, Springfield, Mass.

KEAN, Hamilton Fish (father of Robert Winthrop Kean, brother of John Kean of New Jersey, and great-grandson of John Kean of South Carolina), a Senator from New Jersey; born at "Ursino," his ancestral estate near Elizabeth, in Union Township, Union County, N. J., February 27, 1862; attended the public schools of Elizabeth, N. J.; was graduated from St. Paul's School, Concord, N. H.; engaged in banking and agricultural pursuits; secretary and treasurer of the Union County Republican committee 1884–1906, serving as chairman 1900–1906; member of the Republican State committee 1905–1919 and of the Republican National Committee 1919–1928; delegate to the Republican National Conventions at Chicago in 1916 and 1932; unsuccessful candidate for the Republican nomination for United States Senator in 1924; elected as a Republican to the United States Senate and served from March 4, 1929, to January 3, 1935; unsuccessful candidate for reelection in 1934; engaged in banking until his death in New York City, N. Y., December 27, 1941; interment in Greenwood Cemetery, Brooklyn, N. Y.

KEAN, John (great-grandfather of Hamilton Fish Kean, and John Kean of New Jersey, and great-great-grandfather of Robert Winthrop Kean), a Delegate from South Carolina; born in Charleston, S. C., in 1756; engaged in mercantile pursuits; taken prisoner at the capture of Charleston in 1780 by General Clinton and was confined aboard a prison ship for several months; appointed by General Washington a member of the commission to audit accounts of the Revolutionary Army; Member of the Continental Congress 1785–1787; appointed by President Washington cashier of the Bank of the United States in Philadelphia and served from its organization until his death in Philadelphia, Pa., on May 4, 1795; interment in St. John's Churchyard.

KEAN, John (brother of Hamilton Fish Kean, great-grandson of John Kean of South Carolina, and uncle of Robert Winthrop Kean), a Representative and a Senator from New Jersey; born in Ursino, near Elizabeth, N. J., December 4, 1852; studied in private schools and attended Yale College; was graduated from the Columbia Law School, New York City, in 1875, and was admitted to the New Jersey bar in 1877, but did not engage in extensive practice; engaged in banking and interested in manufacturing; elected as a Republican to the Forty-eighth Congress (March 4, 1883–March 3, 1885); unsuccessful candidate for reelection in 1884; elected to the Fiftieth Congress (March 4, 1887–March 3, 1889); unsuccessful candidate for reelection in 1888; chairman of the Republican State committee in 1891 and 1892; unsuccessful Republican candidate for Governor in 1892; member of the committee to revise the judiciary system of New Jersey; elected to the United States Senate in 1899 and 1905, and served from March 4, 1899, to March 3, 1911; engaged in banking in Elizabeth, N. J.; died in Ursino, N. J., on November 4, 1914; interment in Evergreen Cemetery, Elizabeth, N. J.

KEAN, Robert Winthrop (son of Hamilton Fish Kean, nephew of Senator John Kean, and great-great-grandson of Delegate John Kean), a Representative from New Jersey; born in Elberon, Monmouth County, N. J., September 28, 1893; was graduated from St. Mark's School, Southboro, Mass., in 1911 and from Harvard University, Cambridge, Mass., in 1915; bank clerk in Carteret, N. J., and New York City, N. Y., 1915–1917; served with Squadron A in the New York National Guard on the Mexican border in 1916; during the First World War served overseas as a first lieutenant with the Fifteenth Field Artillery, Second Division, in 1917 and 1918; decorated with the Silver Star Medal and the Distinguished Service Cross; engaged in the investment and banking business in Livingston,

N. J., Newark, N. J., and New York City, N. Y., since 1920; delegate to the Republican National Convention at Cleveland in 1936; elected as a Republican to the Seventy-sixth and to the nine succeeding Congresses (January 3, 1939–January 3, 1959); was not a candidate for renomination in 1958 but was unsuccessful as the Republican candidate for election to the United States Senate; resumed his investment and banking interests; delegate at large to the Republican National Convention in 1960; chairman of the National Advisory Committee of the White House Conference on Aging May 1959–April 1961; chairman of Essex County Republican Committee since 1959; is a resident of Livingston, N. J.

KEARNEY, Bernard William, a Representative from New York; born in Ithaca, N. Y., May 23, 1889; attended the public schools; was graduated from Schenectady (N. Y.) High School and from Union University Albany Law School in 1914; was admitted to the bar the same year and commenced practice in Albany, N. Y.; member of the New York National Guard 1909–1917, serving on the Mexican border in 1916 and 1917; attended officers' training school at Niagara Falls, N. Y., in 1917 and was commissioned a captain; served overseas in the First World War in various outfits and took part in numerous engagements, including St. Mihiel and Meuse-Argonne; returned to the United States in 1919; continued active in the New York National Guard, retiring in 1940, due to physical disability, with rank of major general, having risen from the ranks through all noncommissioned and commissioned grades; decorated with the French Legion of Honor and the Croix de Guerre; city judge of Gloversville, N. Y.; 1920–1924; assistant district attorney of Hamilton County, N. Y., 1924–1929, and of Fulton County, N. Y., 1929–1931; district attorney of Fulton County, N. Y., 1931–1942; elected as a Republican to the Seventy-eighth and to the seven succeeding Congresses (January 3, 1943–January 3, 1959); was not a candidate for renomination in 1958; resides in Lake Pleasant, N. Y., and Venice Gardens, Venice, Fla.

KEARNEY, Dyre, a Delegate from Delaware; born in Kent County, Del.; studied law; was admitted to the bar of New Castle County in 1784 and commenced practice in Dover, Del.; Member of the Continental Congress 1787–1788; resumed the practice of his profession in Dover, Del., where he died about November 1, 1791.

KEARNS, Carroll Dudley, a Representative from Pennsylvania; born in Youngstown, Mahoning County, Ohio, May 7, 1900; moved with his parents to New Castle, Lawrence County, Pa., in 1901; attended the public schools; student in the Army Training Corps at the University of Pittsburgh in 1918; engaged in railroading as yard clerk, leverman, telegraph operator, and in the car-service department in New Castle, Pa., and Chicago, Ill., while going to college 1919–1924; was graduated from Chicago Musical College in Chicago, Ill., in 1923, Westminster College, New Wilmington, Pa., in 1933, University of Pittsburgh, Pittsburgh, Pa., in 1938, and took special studies at Pennsylvania State College at State College in 1932 and 1933; engaged in the construction business in Chicago, Ill., 1925–1929; taught school and engaged in educational work in supervisory and administrative positions in Illinois and Pennsylvania 1924–1947; also pursued a musical career as a concert artist and conductor of instrumental and choral groups; elected as a Republican to the Eightieth and to the six succeeding Congresses (January 3 1947–January 3, 1961). *Reelected to the Eighty-seventh Congress,*

KEARNS, Charles Cyrus, a Representative from Ohio; born in Tonica, La Salle County, Ill., February 11, 1869; moved with his parents to Georgetown, Brown County, Ohio, in 1874; at-

tended the public schools in Georgetown, Ohio Northern College at Ada, and Lebanon (Ohio) College; taught school in Brown County; was graduated from the Cincinnati Law School in 1894; was admitted to the bar the same year and commenced practice in Batavia, Clermont County; managing editor of the Las Vegas (N. Mex.) Daily Record in 1900 and 1901 and of the Daily Record, Hot Springs, Ark., in 1901 and 1902; returned to Ohio in 1903 and practiced law in Batavia; prosecuting attorney of Clermont County, Ohio, 1906–1909; elected as a Republican to the Sixty-fourth and to the seven succeeding Congresses (March 4, 1915–March 3, 1931); unsuccessful candidate for reelection in 1930 to the Seventy-second Congress; engaged in the practice of law at Cincinnati, Ohio, in 1930; died in Amelia, Ohio, on December 17, 1931; interment in Mount Moriah Cemetery, Tobasco, Ohio.

KEARNS, Thomas, a Senator from Utah; born near Woodstock, Oxford County, Ontario, Canada, April 11, 1862; moved with his parents to Holt County, Nebr., and attended the public schools; worked on a farm four years; engaged in the freighting business; moved to Salt Lake City, and afterward to Park City, Utah; interested in mining and operated several mines; served in the City Council of Park City in 1895; member of the State constitutional convention in 1895; delegate to the Republican National Convention at St. Louis in 1896 which nominated McKinley and Hobart, and at Philadelphia in 1900 which nominated McKinley and Roosevelt; elected as a Republican to the United States Senate to fill the vacancy in the term commencing March 4, 1899, caused by the failure of the legislature to elect and served from January 23, 1901, to March 3, 1905; was not a candidate for reelection in 1904; resumed the mining business and resided in Salt Lake City, Utah, until his death on October 18, 1918; interment in Mount Calvary Cemetery.

KEATING, Edward, a Representative from Colorado; born on a small farm near Kansas City, Kans., on July 9, 1875; his father having died, he moved with his mother to Pueblo, Colo., in 1880; moved to Denver in 1889; attended the public schools; engaged in newspaper work as copyholder, reporter, city editor, and managing editor; city auditor of Denver 1899–1901; member of the first convention elected to draft a charter for the city of Denver in 1903; editor of the Rocky Mountain News 1906–1911; president of the International League of Press Clubs in 1906 and 1907; president of the Colorado State Board of Land Commissioners 1911–1913; purchased the Pueblo Leader and moved to Pueblo in 1912; elected as a Democrat to the Sixty-third, Sixty-fourth, and Sixty-fifth Congresses (March 4, 1913–March 3, 1919); unsuccessful for reelection in 1918 to the Sixty-sixth Congress; editor and manager of Labor, official weekly newspaper of the associated railroad labor organizations, published in Washington, D. C., until his retirement in 1953; resides in Washington, D. C.

KEATING, Kenneth Barnard, a Representative and a Senator from New York; born in Lima, Livingston County, N. Y., May 18, 1900; attended the public schools; was graduated from Genesee Wesleyan Seminary, Lima, N. Y., in 1915, from the University of Rochester, Rochester, N. Y., in 1919, and from Harvard Law School, Cambridge, Mass., in 1923; was admitted to the bar in 1923 and commenced practice in Rochester, N. Y.; during the First World War served as a sergeant in the United States Army and in World War II served as a colonel, with three years' service overseas; promoted to brigadier general in 1948; awarded the Legion of Merit with Oak Leaf Cluster, American, European, and Asiatic Theater Ribbons with three battle stars, and the Order of the British Empire; resumed the practice of law; delegate to the Republican National Conventions in 1940 and 1948; elected as a Republican to the Eightieth and to the five succeeding Congresses (January 3, 1947–January 3, 1959); was not a candidate for renomination in 1958; elected to the United States Senate in 1958 for the term commencing January 3, 1959, and ending January 3, 1965.

KEE, John (husband of Maude Elizabeth Kee), a Representative from West Virginia; born in Glenville, Gilmer County, W. Va., August 22, 1874; attended the public schools, Glenville (W. Va.) State Normal School, and West Virginia University at Morgantown; studied law; was admitted to the bar in 1897 and commenced practice in Glenville, W. Va.; with South Penn Oil Co., 1900–1902; served as counsel for the Virginia Railway Co. 1902–1910; moved to Bluefield, Mercer County, W.Va., in 1910 and continued the practice of law; engaged in special legal work in Mexico 1916–1918; returned to Bluefield, W. Va., in 1918 and resumed the practice of law; member of the State senate 1923–1927; elected as a Democrat to the Seventy-third and to the nine succeeding Congresses and served from March 4, 1933, until his death in Washington, D. C., May 8, 1951; interment in Monte Vista Cemetery, Bluefield, W. Va.

KEE, Maude Elizabeth (widow of John Kee), a Representative from West Virginia; born in Radford, Montgomery County, Va.; attended public and private schools of Montgomery County, Roanoke, Va., and Bluefield, W. Va.; graduated from Roanoke Business College, Roanoke, Va.; author of a weekly column in West Virginia newspapers; sponsor of library for physically handicapped at Woodrow Wilson Rehabilitation Center, Fishersville, Va.; served as executive secretary to her husband, John Kee, from November 1932 until his death; elected as a Democrat to the Eighty-second Congress to fill the vacancy caused by the death of her husband, John Kee; reelected to the Eighty-third and to the three succeeding Congresses and served from July 17, 1951, to January 3, 1961. *Reelected to the Eighty-seventh Congress.*

KEEFE, Frank Bateman, a Representative from Wisconsin; born in Winneconne, Winnebago County, Wis., September 23, 1887; attended the public schools; was graduated from Oshkosh (Wis.) State Normal School in 1906 and from the law department of the University of Michigan at Ann Arbor in 1910; teacher in the schools at Viroqua, Vernon County, Wis., in 1906 and 1907; was admitted to the bar in 1910 and commenced practice in Oshkosh, Wis.; prosecuting attorney of Winnebago County, Wis., 1922–1928; vice president and director of Oshkosh National Bank and Oshkosh Savings and Loan Association; president of Lakeview Memorial Association; elected as a Republican to the Seventy-sixth and to the five succeeding Congresses (January 3, 1939–January 3, 1951); was not a candidate for renomination in 1950; resumed the practice of law; died in Neenah, Wis., February 5, 1952; interment in Lakeview Memorial Park, Oshkosh, Wis.

KEENEY, Russell Watson, a Representative from Illinois; born in Pittsfield, Pike County, Ill., December 29, 1897; attended grade and high schools in Naperville, Du Page County, Ill.; graduated from De Paul University, Chicago, Ill., in 1919 and in 1921; during the First World War served as a private in the S. A. T. C., De Paul University; was admitted to the bar in 1919 and commenced the practice of law in Naperville, Ill.; in 1920 became justice of the peace of Lisle Township and in 1924 town clerk; assistant State's attorney until 1935; State's attorney of Du Page County 1936–1939; county judge of Du Page County 1940–1952; circuit judge of the sixteenth judicial district of Illinois 1953–1956; elected as a Republican to the Eighty-fifth Congress and served from January 3, 1957, until his death in the naval hospital at Bethesda, Md., January 11, 1958; interment in Naperville (Ill.) Protestant Cemetery.

KEESE, Richard, a Representative from New York; born in Peru (now Ausable) Township, Clinton County, N. Y., on November 23, 1794; attended the common schools and Keeseville Academy; engaged in agricultural pursuits; elected as a Democrat to the Twentieth Congress (March 4, 1827–March 3, 1829); engaged in auctioneering; judge of the Clinton County court of common pleas in 1835 and 1836; died in Keeseville, Ausable Township, Clinton County, N. Y., February 7, 1883; interment in Evergreen Cemetery.

KEFAUVER, Carey Estes, a Representative and a Senator from Tennessee; born on a farm near Madisonville, Monroe County, Tenn., July 26, 1903; attended the public schools; was graduated from the University of Tennessee at Knoxville in 1924 and from the law department of Yale University, New Haven, Conn., in 1927; was admitted to the bar in 1926 and commenced practice in Chattanooga, Tenn., in 1927; served as State commissioner of finance and taxation from January to May 1939; elected as a Democrat to the Seventy-sixth Congress to fill the vacancy caused by the death of Sam D. McReynolds; reelected to the Seventy-seventh and to the three succeeding Congresses and served from September 13, 1939, to January 3, 1949; did not seek renomination in 1948; elected to the United States Senate in 1948 and again in 1954 for the term commencing January 3, 1949, and ending January 3, 1961; Democratic nominee for Vice President of the United States in 1956. *Reelected in 1960 for the term ending January 3, 1967.*

KEHOE, James Nicholas, a Representative from Kentucky; born in Maysville, Mason County, Ky., July 15, 1862; attended public and private schools; engaged in the printing business until 1884; studied law in Louisville, Ky.; was admitted to the bar November 1, 1888, and engaged in practice in Maysville; served as precinct, county, and district chairman of the Democratic executive committee; city attorney of Maysville; master in chancery of the Mason County Circuit Court; elected as a Democrat to the Fifty-seventh and Fifty-eighth Congresses (March 4, 1901–March 3, 1905); unsuccessful candidate for reelection in 1904 to the Fifty-ninth Congress; delegate to the Democratic National Convention at Baltimore in 1912; chairman of the local Liberty bond committee and president of the local Red Cross society during the First World War; engaged in banking; vice president of the Ohio Valley Improvement Association and of the Burley Tobacco Growers' Cooperation Association; ex-president of the Kentucky Bankers' Association; died in Cincinnati, Ohio, June 16, 1945; interment in Maysville Cemetery, Maysville, Ky.

KEHOE, James Walter, a Representative from Florida; born in Eufaula, Barbour County, Ala., April 25, 1870; attended the common schools; moved to Florida in 1883; studied law; was admitted to the bar in 1889 and, being a minor, was authorized by a special act of the State legislature to commence practice in Milton, Fla.; member of the State house of representatives in 1900 but resigned before the legislature convened; member of the Democratic congressional executive committee; State's attorney for the first judicial circuit of Florida 1900–1909; elected as a Democrat to the Sixty-fifth Congress (March 4, 1917–March 3, 1919); unsuccessful candidate for reelection to the Sixty-sixth Congress in 1918; again State's attorney from June 1925 until March 1926, when he resigned; resumed the practice of law in Miami, Fla.; died in Coral Gables, Fla., on August 20, 1938; interment in Graceland Park Cemetery, Miami, Fla.

KEHR, Edward Charles, a Representative from Missouri; born in St. Louis, Mo., November 5, 1837; pursued an academic course; studied law; was admitted to the bar in 1858 and commenced practice in St. Louis; elected as a Democrat to the Forty-fourth Congress (March 4, 1875–March 3, 1877); unsuccessful candidate for reelection in 1878 to the Forty-fifth Congress; engaged in the practice of law in St. Louis, Mo., until his death in that city on April 20, 1918; the remains were cremated and the ashes deposited in the columbarium of the Missouri Crematory.

KEIFER, Joseph Warren, a Representative from Ohio; born near Springfield, Bethel Township, Clark County, Ohio, January 30, 1836; attended the common schools, and Antioch College, Yellow Springs, Ohio; studied law; was admitted to the bar and began practice in Springfield, Ohio, January 12, 1858; during the Civil War enlisted in the Union Army on April 19, 1861; commissioned major in the Third Ohio Volunteer Infantry April 27, 1861; lieutenant colonel February 12, 1862; colonel of the One Hundred and Tenth Ohio Volunteer Infantry September 30, 1862; brevetted brigadier general of Volunteers October 19, 1864, "for gallant and meritorious services in the Battles of Opequon, Fishers Hill, and Cedar Creek, Virginia"; severely wounded in the Battle of the Wilderness May 5, 1864; promoted to major general April 9, 1865, "for gallant and distinguished services during the campaign ending in the surrender of the Confederate Army under Gen. Robert E. Lee"; mustered out June 27, 1865; resumed the practice of law in July 1865; member of the State senate in 1868 and 1869; commander of the Ohio Department of the Grand Army of the Republic in 1871 and 1872; trustee of the Ohio Soldiers and Sailors Orphans Home from April 16, 1870, to March 5, 1878, and again in 1903 and 1904; trustee of Antioch College; delegate to the Republican National Convention in 1876; elected as a Republican to the Forty-fifth and to the three succeeding Congresses (March 4, 1877–March 3, 1885); served as Speaker of the House in the Forty-seventh Congress; unsuccessful candidate for renomination in 1884; was a major general of Volunteers in the Spanish-American War from June 9, 1898, to May 12, 1899; first commander in chief of the Spanish War Veterans in 1900 and 1901; elected to the Fifty-ninth, Sixtieth, and Sixty-first Congresses (March 4, 1905–March 3, 1911); unsuccessful candidate for reelection in 1910 to the Sixty-second Congress; addressed the Conference on Universal Peace in Brussels in 1911 and had reached Berlin, Germany, in 1914, on his way to Stockholm to address the conference of that year when the First World War began; president of the Perry's Victory Memorial Commission; resumed his law practice; president of the Lagonda National Bank of Springfield, Ohio, for more than fifty years; died in Springfield, Ohio, April 22, 1932; interment in Ferncliff Cemetery.

KEIGHTLEY, Edwin William, a Representative from Michigan; born on a farm near Scott, Lagrange County, Ind., August 7, 1843; attended the common schools; Lagrange Academy, and Valparaiso Collegiate Institute; was graduated from the law department of the University of Michigan at Ann Arbor in 1865; was admitted to the bar in 1865 and commenced practice at White Pigeon, St. Joseph County, Mich.; prosecuting attorney of St. Joseph County in 1873 and 1874; appointed and subsequently elected judge of the fifteenth judicial circuit of Michigan in 1876 and served until 1877, having been elected to Congress; elected as a Republican to the Forty-fifth Congress (March 4, 1877–March 3, 1879); appointed by President Hayes Third Auditor of the United States Treasury Department and served from April 30, 1879, to April 30, 1885, when he resigned; resumed the practice of his profession in Chicago; moved to Constantine, Mich., in 1899 and engaged in agricultural pursuits; died there May 4, 1926; interment in Constantine Cemetery.

KEIM, George May (uncle of William High Keim), a Representative from Pennsylvania; born in Reading, Pa., March 23, 1805; pursued classical studies; attended Princeton College; studied law; was admitted to the bar in 1826 and commenced practice in Reading; major general of militia; delegate to the State constitutional convention of 1837 and 1838; elected as a Democrat to the Twenty-fifth Congress to fill the vacancy caused by the resignation of Henry A. P. Muhlenberg; reelected to the Twenty-sixth and Twenty-seventh Congresses and served from March 17, 1838, to March 3, 1843; appointed by President Tyler United States marshal for the eastern district of Pennsylvania December 18, 1843; reappointed by President Polk January 3, 1848, and served until 1850; mayor of Reading in 1852; presidential elector on the Democratic ticket of Douglas and Johnson in 1860; died in Reading, Pa., June 10, 1861; interment in Charles Evans Cemetery.

KEIM, William High (nephew of George May Keim), a Representative from Pennsylvania; born near Reading, Pa., on June 13, 1813; attended Mount Airy Military School, and attained the rank of major general of militia; mayor of Reading in 1848; elected as a Democrat to the Thirty-fifth Congress to fill the vacancy caused by the resignation of J. Glancy Jones and served from December 7, 1858, to March 3, 1859; was not a candidate for renomination in 1858; surveyor general of Pennsylvania 1860–1862; during the Civil War enlisted in the Union Army and was commissioned a major general of Pennsylvania Volunteers on April 20, 1861; honorably mustered out on July 21, 1861; commissioned brigadier general of Volunteers December 20, 1861; died in the military service at Harrisburg, Pa., May 18, 1862; interment in Charles Evans Cemetery, Reading, Berks County, Pa.

KEISTER, Abraham Lincoln, a Representative from Pennsylvania; born in Upper Tyrone Township, Fayette County, Pa., near the present borough of Scottdale, Westmoreland County, Pa., September 10, 1852; attended the public schools; was graduated from Otterbein University, Westerville, Ohio, in 1874; studied law; was admitted to the bar by the supreme court of Ohio in 1878 and commenced practice in Columbus, Ohio; moved to Fayette County, Pa., in 1882; engaged in the manufacture of coke; organized the First National Bank of Scottdale, Pa., in 1889 and served continuously as its president for twenty-eight years; organized the Scottdale Savings & Trust Co. in 1901, with which he was connected until the time of his death; member of the Scottdale Board of Education for more than twenty years; founded and donated the Scottdale Free Public Library; was elected as a Republican to the Sixty-third and Sixty-fourth Congresses (March 4, 1913–March 3, 1917); unsuccessful candidate for renomination in 1916; resumed his former business pursuits; died at his home in Scottdale, Westmoreland County, Pa., on May 26, 1917; interment in Scottdale Cemetery.

KEITH, Hastings, a Representative from Massachusetts; born in Brockton, Plymouth County, Mass., November 22, 1915; graduated from Brockton High School, Deerfield Academy, and the University of Vermont at Burlington in 1938; graduate work at Harvard University in 1938; member of the faculty of the Boston University Evening College of Commerce in 1948 and 1949; in 1933 was a student in the Citizens Military Training Camps; served as battery officer in Massachusetts National Guard; during World War II served in the United States Army with eighteen months overseas service in Europe; graduate of the Command and General Staff School; lieutenant colonel in the Army Reserve; salesman and later district manager for the Equitable Life Assurance Society in Boston, Mass., 1946–1952;

member of the State senate 1953–1956; partner in the firm of Roger Keith & Sons, general insurance, Brockton, Mass.; unsuccessful candidate for the Republican nomination for Congress in 1956; elected as a Republican to the Eighty-sixth Congress (January 3, 1959–January 3, 1961). *Reelected to the Eighty-seventh Congress.*

KEITT, Laurence Massillon, a Representative from South Carolina; born in Orangeburg District, S. C., October 4, 1824; pursued classical studies, and was graduated from South Carolina College (now the University of South Carolina) at Columbia in 1843; studied law; was admitted to the bar in 1845 and commenced practice in Orangeburg; elected as a Democrat to the Thirty-third and Thirty-fourth Congresses and served from March 4, 1853, to July 16, 1856, when he resigned after the House adopted a resolution disapproving his action in regard to the assault made upon Senator Charles Sumner on May 22, 1856; again elected to the Thirty-fourth Congress to fill the vacancy caused by his own resignation; reelected to the Thirty-fifth and Thirty-sixth Congresses and served from August 6, 1856, until his retirement in December 1860; delegate to the secession convention of South Carolina; member of the Provisional Congress of the Confederacy in Montgomery, Ala., in February 1861 and in Richmond, Va., in July 1861; during the Civil War raised the Twentieth South Carolina Regiment of Volunteers and was commissioned its colonel on January 11, 1862; subsequently promoted to the rank of brigadier general; wounded in the Battle of Cold Harbor, near Richmond, Va., and died as a result of his wounds the following day, June 4, 1864; interment in the family cemetery, near St. Matthews, S. C.

KELIHER, John Austin, a Representative from Massachusetts; born in Boston, Mass., November 6, 1866; attended the public schools; engaged in the real-estate business in Boston, Mass.; member of the State house of representatives in 1896 and 1897; served in the State senate in 1899 and 1900; elected as a Democrat to the Fifty-eighth and to the three succeeding Congresses (March 4, 1903–March 3, 1911); unsuccessful candidate for reelection in 1910 to the Sixty-second Congress; chairman of the Massachusetts Statehouse Building Commission in 1915 and 1916; member of the Massachusetts constitutional convention 1917–1919; elected sheriff of Suffolk County in 1917; reelected in 1920, 1926, and 1932, and served in that capacity until his death at Boston, Mass., on September 20, 1938; interment in Mount Calvary Cemetery, West Roxbury, Mass.

KELLER, Kent Ellsworth, a Representative from Illinois; born on a farm near Campbell Hill, Jackson County, Ill., June 4, 1867; attended the public schools in Ava, Ill.; was graduated from Southern Illinois Normal University at Carbondale in 1890; engaged as an editor and in the newspaper business in 1890 and 1891; taught school in Ava Township, Ill., in 1893 and 1894, and at Duckwater, Nye County, Nev., in 1884 and 1885; founded the Ava Community High School in 1889 and 1890; attended Heidelberg University, Germany, in 1891 and 1892; was graduated from St. Louis (Mo.) Law School in 1896; was admitted to the bar the same year and commenced practice in Ava, Ill.; because of ill health went to Mexico in 1899, where he later engaged in mining; returned to Ava, Ill., in 1912 and engaged in literary work and politics; served in the State senate 1913–1917; delegate to the Democratic National Convention at St. Louis in 1916; elected as a Democrat to the Seventy-second and to the four succeeding Congresses (March 4, 1931–January 3, 1941); unsuccessful candidate for reelection in 1940 to the Seventy-seventh Congress and for election in 1942 to the Seventy-eighth Congress and in 1944 to the Seventy-ninth Congress;

engaged in literary work and lecturing; served as special adviser to the United States Ambassador at Mexico City from June 1945 to August 1946; unsuccessful candidate for election in 1948 to the Eighty-first Congress and in 1950 to the Eighty-second Congress; died in Ava, Ill., September 3, 1954; interment in Ava Evergreen Cemetery.

KELLER, Oscar Edward, a Representative from Minnesota; born in Helenville, Jefferson County, Wis., July 30, 1878; attended the public schools, high school, and the University of Wisconsin at Madison; moved to Minnesota in 1901 and settled in St. Paul; employed as a billing clerk and later engaged in mercantile pursuits; member of the city council of St. Paul 1910–1914; city commissioner 1914–1919; commissioner of public utilities from 1914 until July 1, 1919, when he resigned, having been elected to Congress; elected as an Independent Republican to the Sixty-sixth Congress to fill the vacancy caused by the death of Carl C. Van Dyke; reelected to the Sixty-seventh, Sixty-eighth, and Sixty-ninth Congresses and served from July 1, 1919, to March 3, 1927; unsuccessful candidate for renomination in 1926; engaged in the real-estate business; died in St. Paul, Minn., November 21, 1927; interment in Elmhurst Cemetery.

KELLEY, Augustine Bernard, a Representative from Pennsylvania; born in New Baltimore, Somerset County, Pa., July 9, 1883; attended a parochial school, Greensburg (Pa.) High School, and the United States Military Academy, West Point, N. Y., in 1904 and 1905; studied mining engineering with International Correspondence School 1907–1912; began business career in 1905 as clerk with the Pennsylvania Railroad Co., and later became superintendent of the H. C. Frick Coke Co., and was also associated with the Hillman Coal & Coke Co.; owner and president of the Mammoth Coal & Coke Co. at time of death; receiver of the Fairfield Coal Co. 1923–1925; member of the Greensburg (Pa.) Board of Education in 1935 and 1936; elected as a Democrat to the Seventy-seventh and to the eight succeeding Congresses and served from January 3, 1941, until his death in Bethesda, Md., November 20, 1957; interment in Arlington National Cemetery, Fort Myer, Va.

KELLEY, Harrison, a Representative from Kansas; born in Montgomery Township, Wood County, Ohio, May 12, 1836; attended the common schools; moved to Coffey County, Kans., in March 1858; during the Civil War enlisted in the Fifth Regiment, Kansas Volunteer Cavalry, and served through all grades to captain; captain of Company B, Fifth Cavalry, for over two years; returned to Burlington, Kans., in 1865; brigadier general of Kansas State Militia in 1865; member of the State house of representatives 1868–1870; director of the State penitentiary 1868–1873; receiver of the United States land office at Topeka in 1877 and 1878; served in the State senate 1880–1884; deputy collector of internal revenue; chairman of the livestock sanitary commission of the State; treasurer of the State board of charities in 1889; elected as a Republican to the Fifty-first Congress to fill the vacancy caused by the resignation of Thomas Ryan and served from December 2, 1889, to March 3, 1891; died in Burlington, Coffey County, Kans., July 24, 1897; interment in Bowman Cemetery, Ottumwa, near Burlington, Kans.

KELLEY, John Edward, a Representative from South Dakota; born near Portage City, Columbia County, Wis., March 27, 1853; attended the public schools; moved to Moody County, Dak. (now South Dakota), in 1878 and engaged in agricultural pursuits; engaged in the newspaper business at Flandreau; member of the State house of representatives in 1890 and 1891; unsuccessful candidate of the People's Party for election to the

Fifty-third and Fifty-fourth Congresses; elected as the candidate of the Democratic Party and the People's Party to the Fifty-fifth Congress (March 4, 1897–March 3, 1899); unsuccessful candidate for reelection in 1898; resumed agricultural pursuits near Coleman, S. Dak.; delegate to the Democratic National Convention at Baltimore in 1912; register of the United States land office at Pierre 1915–1918; moved to St. Paul, Minn., and became editor of the Cooperative Herald; died in Minneapolis, Minn., August 5, 1941; interment in St. Mary's Cemetery.

KELLEY, Patrick Henry, a Representative from Michigan; born near Dowagiac, Silver Creek Township, Cass County, Mich., October 7, 1867; moved to Berrien County with his parents, who settled in Watervliet in 1875; attended the district and village schools; was graduated from the Valparaiso (Ind.) Normal School in 1887; taught school at Fair Plain for several years; attended the Michigan Normal College at Ypsilanti, and was graduated from the law department of the University of Michigan at Ann Arbor in 1900; was admitted to the bar the same year and commenced practice in Lansing, Mich.; member of the State board of education 1901–1905; State superintendent of public instruction 1905–1907; Lieutenant Governor of Michigan 1907–1911; elected as a Republican to the Sixty-third and to the four succeeding Congresses (March 4, 1913–March 3, 1923); did not seek renomination, having announced his candidacy for Senator; unsuccessful candidate for election to the United States Senate in 1922; resumed the practice of law in Lansing, Mich.; died while on a visit to Washington, D. C., September 11, 1925; interment in Mount Hope Cemetery, Lansing, Mich.

KELLEY, William Darrah, a Representative from Pennsylvania; born in Philadelphia, Pa., April 12, 1814; pursued classical studies; apprentice in a jewelry establishment 1828–1835; moved to Boston, Mass., in 1835 and was engaged as a journeyman jeweler; returned to Philadelphia in 1840; studied law; was admitted to the bar in 1841 and practiced in Philadelphia, Pa.; deputy prosecuting attorney for the city and county of Philadelphia in 1845 and 1846; judge of the court of common pleas for Philadelphia 1846–1856; unsuccessful candidate for election in 1856 to the Thirty-fifth Congress; delegate to the Republican National Convention at Chicago in 1860 which nominated Lincoln and Hamlin; elected as a Republican to the Thirty-seventh and to the fourteen succeeding Congresses and served from March 4, 1861, until his death in Washington, D. C., January 9, 1890; interment in Laurel Hill Cemetery, Philadelphia, Pa.

KELLOGG, Charles, a Representative from New York; born in Sheffield, Berkshire County, Mass., October 3, 1773; attended the common schools; moved to Cayuga County, N. Y., in 1798 and founded Kelloggsville; engaged in mercantile pursuits; also operated a gristmill at New Hope; studied law; was admitted to the bar and practiced; county judge; member of the State assembly 1808–1810; justice of the peace for Sempronius Township; appointed postmaster of Kelloggsville on July 1, 1814, and served until September 6, 1825; again a member of the State assembly 1820–1822; elected to the Nineteenth Congress (March 4, 1825–March 3, 1827); engaged in agricultural pursuits; moved to Ann Arbor, Mich., in 1839; died in Ann Arbor, Washtenaw County, Mich., May 11, 1842; interment in Fairview Cemetery.

KELLOGG, Francis William, a Representative from Michigan and from Alabama; born in Worthington, Mass., May 30, 1810; attended the common schools; moved to Columbus, Ohio, in 1833; thence to Grand Rapids, Mich., in 1855 and engaged in the lumber business at Kelloggville, Kent County; member of the State house of representatives in 1857 and

1858; elected from Michigan as a Republican to the Thirty-sixth, Thirty-seventh, and Thirty-eighth Congresses (March 4, 1859–March 3, 1865); during the Civil War organized the Second, Third, and Sixth Regiments by authority of the War Department and was appointed colonel of the Third Regiment; appointed by President Johnson collector of internal revenue for the southern district of Alabama April 30, 1866; was confirmed by the Senate July 26, 1866, and served until July 1868, residing in Mobile, Ala.; upon the readmission of Alabama to representation was elected from Alabama as a Republican to the Fortieth Congress and served from July 22, 1868, to March 3, 1869; moved to New York City and later to Alliance, Stark County, Ohio, where he died January 13, 1879; interment in Fulton Street Cemetery, Grand Rapids, Mich.

KELLOGG, Frank Billings, a Senator from Minnesota; born in Potsdam, St. Lawrence County, N. Y., December 22, 1856; in 1865 moved with his parents to Viola, Olmsted County, Minn., and in 1872 to a farm near Elgin, Minn.; attended the public and rural schools; worked on the farm until 1875 and then studied law in Rochester, Minn., until December 1877, when he was admitted to the bar; commenced practice in Rochester, Minn., the same year; city attorney of Rochester 1878–1881; county attorney for Olmsted County 1882–1887; moved to St. Paul, Minn., in October 1887 and resumed the practice of law; Government delegate to the Universal Congress of Lawyers and Jurists at St. Louis in 1904; member of the Republican National Committee 1904–1912; delegate to the Republican National Conventions in 1904, 1908, and 1912; special counsel for the Government to prosecute antitrust suits; president of the American Bar Association in 1912 and 1913; elected as a Republican to the United States Senate and served from March 4, 1917, to March 3, 1923; unsuccessful candidate for reelection in 1922; delegate to the Fifth International Conference of American States, Santiago, Chile, 1923; appointed Ambassador Extraordinary and Plenipotentiary to Great Britain and served from December 11, 1923, until his resignation effective March 4, 1925; appointed Secretary of State in the Cabinet of President Coolidge and served from March 5, 1925, to March 4, 1929; coauthor of the Kellogg-Briand Peace Pact signed in 1928; resumed the practice of law in St. Paul, Minn.; elected associate judge of the Permanent Court for International Justice in 1930 and served until 1935; awarded the Nobel Peace Prize in 1930; died in St. Paul, Minn., December 21, 1937; interment in the Chapel of St. Joseph of Arimathea in Washington Cathedral, Washington, D. C.

KELLOGG, Orlando, a Representative from New York; born in Elizabethtown, Essex County, N. Y., June 18, 1809; pursued an academic course; engaged in the carpenter's trade in early youth; studied law; was admitted to the bar in 1838 and commenced practice in Elizabethtown; surrogate of Essex County 1840–1844; elected as a Whig to the Thirtieth Congress (March 4, 1847–March 3, 1849); was not a candidate for renomination in 1848; resumed the practice of his profession in Elizabethtown, N. Y.; delegate to the Republican National Convention at Chicago in 1860; elected as a Republican to the Thirty-eighth and Thirty-ninth Congresses and served from March 4, 1863, until his death in Elizabethtown, N. Y., August 24, 1865; interment in Riverside Cemetery.

KELLOGG, Stephen Wright, a Representative from Connecticut; born in Shelburne, Mass, April 5, 1822; attended an academy at Shelburne Falls, Mass., and Amherst (Mass.) College; was graduated from Yale College in 1846; studied law; was admitted to the bar in 1848 and commenced practice in Naugatuck, Conn.; clerk in the State senate in 1851; member of the State senate in 1853; moved to Waterbury, Conn., in 1854; resumed the practice of law; judge of the New Haven County Court in 1854 and of the probate court 1854–1860; served in the State house of representatives in 1856; delegate to the Republican National Conventions at Chicago in 1860 and 1868 and at Cincinnati in 1876; served as colonel of the Second Regiment, Connecticut National Guard, 1863–1866; brigadier general of the regiment 1866–1870; city attorney of Waterbury, Conn., 1866–1869 and 1877–1883; elected as a Republican to the Forty-first and Forty-second Congresses (March 4, 1869–March 3, 1873); unsuccessful candidate for election in 1874 to the Forty-fourth Congress and in 1876 to the Forty-fifth Congress; resumed the practice of his profession; presidential elector on the Republican ticket of McKinley and Roosevelt in 1900; died in Waterbury, New Haven County, Conn., on January 27, 1904; interment in Riverside Cemetery.

KELLOGG, William, a Representative from Illinois; born in Kelloggsville, Ashtabula County, Ohio, July 8, 1814; attended the public schools; studied law; was admitted to the bar and commenced practice in Canton, Fulton County, Ill.; member of the State house of representatives in 1849 and 1850; judge of the State circuit court 1850–1855; elected as a Republican to the Thirty-fifth, Thirty-sixth, and Thirty-seventh Congresses (March 4, 1857–March 3, 1863); moved to Peoria, Ill., in 1864; appointed by President Lincoln as Minister Resident to Guatemala April 21, 1864, but declined; appointed by President Johnson chief justice of Nebraska Territory December 20, 1865, and served until 1867; collector of internal revenue for the Peoria (Ill.) district 1867–1869; moved to Mississippi in 1869, having been appointed to a judgeship under the prevailing provisional government; upon the readmission of Mississippi to representation he was an unsuccessful candidate to the Forty-first Congress in 1869 and shortly afterward returned to Illinois; died in Peoria, Peoria County, Ill., on December 20, 1872; interment in Springdale Cemetery.

KELLOGG, William Pitt, a Senator and a Representative from Louisiana; born in Orwell, Addison County, Vt., December 8, 1831; attended Norwich University, Vermont; moved to Peoria, Ill., in 1848; taught school for several years, studying law in the meantime; was admitted to the bar in 1853 and commenced practice in Canton, Fulton County, Ill.; presidential elector on the Republican ticket of Lincoln and Hamlin in 1860; appointed by President Lincoln chief justice of the supreme court of the Territory of Nebraska March 27, 1861; reappointed April 17, 1865, but resigned upon the outbreak of the Civil War; returned to Illinois and accepted the colonelcy of the Seventh Regiment, Illinois Volunteer Cavalry; served under General Pope in Missouri and commanded General Granger's cavalry brigade until the evacuation of Corinth; resigned on account of ill health; appointed by President Lincoln collector of the port of New Orleans April 13, 1865, and served until July 1868, when he resigned, having been elected Senator; delegate to every Republican National Convention from 1868 to 1896 and served as chairman of his delegation in five of them; upon the readmission of Louisiana to representation was elected as a Republican to the United States Senate and served from July 9, 1868, until November 1, 1872, when he resigned, having been elected Governor; elected Governor of Louisiana and served from January 5, 1873, to January 5, 1877; again elected to the United States Senate and served from March 4, 1877, to March 3, 1883; declined to be a candidate for reelection to the Senate; elected to the Forty-eighth Congress (March 4, 1883–March 3, 1885); withdrew from active political life and lived in retirement in Washington, D. C., where he died on August 10, 1918; interment in Arlington National Cemetery, Fort Myer, Va.

KELLY, Edna Flannery, a Representative from New York; born in East Hampton, Suffolk County, N. Y., August 20, 1906; attended the public schools of East Hampton; graduated from Hunter College, New York City, N. Y., in 1928; elected a member of the executive committee of the Democratic Party of Kings County, N. Y., from the Eighteenth Assembly District in 1944; reelected in 1946 and again in 1948; appointed associate research director of the Democratic Party in the New York State Legislature in 1943; designated chief research director in 1944 and served in that capacity until elected to Congress; elected as a Democrat to the Eighty-first Congress to fill the vacancy caused by the death of Andrew L. Somers; reelected to the Eighty-second and to the four succeeding Congresses and served from November 8, 1949, to January 3, 1961. *Reelected to the Eighty-seventh Congress.*

KELLY, Edward Austin, a Representative from Illinois; born in Chicago, Cook County, Ill., April 3, 1892; attended Longfellow School and Lake High School; was graduated from Orr's Business College, Chicago, Ill., in 1911; played professional baseball 1912–1916; employed as an accountant with a steel corporation 1916–1920; during the First World War served as a sergeant in Battery D of the Three Hundred and Thirty-second Field Artillery 1917–1919, with nine months' service overseas; engaged in the real-estate and insurance brokerage business in 1920; elected as a Democrat to the Seventy-second and to the five succeeding Congresses (March 4, 1931–January 3, 1943); unsuccessful candidate for reelection in 1942 to the Seventy-eighth Congress; assistant to the chief justice of the municipal court of Chicago, Ill., 1943–1945; member of the Chicago Planning Committee 1944–1946; elected to the Seventy-ninth Congress (January 3, 1945–January 3, 1947); unsuccessful candidate for reelection in 1946 to the Eightieth Congress; resumed his former business pursuits and is a resident of Chicago, Ill.

KELLY, George Bradshaw, a Representative from New York; born in Waterloo, Seneca County, N. Y., December 12, 1900; attended parochial and high schools and the University of Rochester, Rochester, N. Y.; employed by a railway signal company as clerk and later as timekeeper 1915–1919; salesman for a candy company in 1920; production manager for a clothing manufacturer 1921–1933; member of the State assembly in 1933 and 1934; served in the State senate in 1935 and 1936; elected as a Democrat to the Seventy-fifth Congress (January 3, 1937–January 3, 1939); unsuccessful candidate for reelection in 1938 to the Seventy-sixth Congress and for election in 1940 to the Seventy-seventh Congress; regional director of the Wage-Hour Division of the United States Department of Labor for New York and Connecticut in 1939 and 1940; member of the State board of mediation in 1941 and 1942; manager of an industrial alcohol plant for war production during World War II; associated with a brewing company and also interested in radio broadcasting companies; insurance broker; resides in Rochester, N. Y.

KELLY, James, a Representative from Pennsylvania; born in York County, Pa., July 17, 1760; pursued classical studies, and was graduated from the University of Pennsylvania at Philadelphia in 1782; was a tutor at the University of Pennsylvania in 1782 and 1783; studied law; was admitted to the bar and practiced in Philadelphia 1785–1819; member of the State house of representatives in 1793, 1794, 1797, and 1798; elected to the Ninth and Tenth Congresses (March 4, 1805–March 3, 1809); resumed the practice of law in York, Pa., where he died on February 4, 1819.

KELLY, James Kerr, a Senator from Oregon; born in Center County, Pa., February 16, 1819; attended the country schools and Milton and Lewisburg Academies; was graduated from Princeton College in 1839; studied law at Carlisle, Pa.; was admitted to the bar in 1842 and commenced practice in Lewistown, Mifflin County, Pa.; deputy attorney general for Mifflin County, Pa.; went to the California gold fields in 1849, and later, in 1851, to Oregon Territory and settled in Portland, where he engaged in the practice of law; one of three commissioners for the codification of the Territorial laws in 1852; served in the Territorial legislature 1853–1857 and was twice its president; lieutenant colonel of the First Regiment, Oregon Mounted Volunteers, in the Yakima Indian War in 1855 and 1856; a member of the State constitutional convention in 1857 and a framer of the Oregon constitution; served in the State senate 1860–1864; appointed by President Buchanan in 1860 United States district attorney for Oregon, but declined to accept the position; unsuccessful candidate for election in 1864 to the Thirty-ninth Congress; unsuccessful candidate for election in 1866 for Governor of Oregon; elected as a Democrat to the United States Senate and served from March 4, 1871, to March 3, 1877; was not a candidate for reelection; chief justice of the State supreme court 1878–1882; resumed the practice of his profession in Portland, Oreg.; moved to Washington, D. C., in 1890 and continued the practice of his profession until his death there on September 15, 1903; interment in Rock Creek Cemetery.

KELLY, John, a Representative from New York; born in New York City April 21, 1821; attended the common schools; apprenticed to the mason's trade and engaged in that business for himself in 1845; elected city alderman in 1854; elected as a Democrat to the Thirty-fourth and Thirty-fifth Congresses and served from March 4, 1855, to December 25, 1858, when he resigned; served as sheriff of the city and county of New York 1859–1862 and 1865–1867; was an unsuccessful candidate for mayor of New York City in 1868; appointed comptroller of New York in 1876 and served for three years; delegate to the Democratic National Conventions in 1864, 1868, 1872, 1876, 1880, and 1884; at the time of his death and for many years previous was head of Tammany Hall; died in New York City, N.Y., on June 1, 1886; interment in Old St. Patrick's Cathedral on Mott Street.

KELLY, Melville Clyde, a Representative from Pennsylvania; born in Bloomfield, Muskingum County, Ohio, August 4, 1883; attended the public schools, and Muskingum College, New Concord, Ohio; engaged in newspaper publishing at Braddock, Pa., in 1903 and established the Braddock Leader in 1904; in 1907 purchased the Daily News and the Evening Herald and consolidated them into the Daily News-Herald; member of the State house of representatives 1910–1913; elected as a Republican to the Sixty-third Congress (March 4, 1913–March 3, 1915); unsuccessful candidate in 1914 for reelection to the Sixty-fourth Congress; continued his newspaper work; elected to the Sixty-fifth and to the eight succeeding Congresses (March 4, 1917–January 3, 1935); unsuccessful candidate for reelection in 1934 to the Seventy-fourth Congress; resumed his former business pursuits; accidentally shot while cleaning a rifle and died in a local hospital at Punxsutawney, Pa., on April 29, 1935; interment in Mahoning Union Cemetery, near Marchand, Pa.

KELLY, William, a Senator from Alabama; born in Tennessee in 1770; received a classical education; studied law; was admitted to the bar and commenced practice in Huntsville, Ala.; elected to the United States Senate to fill the vacancy caused by the resignation of John W. Walker and served from December 12, 1822, to March 3, 1825; moved to New Orleans, La., and died there in 1832.

KELSEY, William Henry, a Representative from New York; born in Smyrna, Chenango County, N. Y., October 2, 1812; attended the common schools; studied law; was admitted to the bar in 1843 and commenced practice in Geneseo, N. Y.; surrogate of Livingston County 1840–1844; district attorney of Livingston County 1850–1853; elected as a Whig to the Thirty-fourth and Thirty-fifth Congresses (March 4, 1855–March 3, 1859); was not a candidate for renomination in 1858 to the Thirty-sixth Congress; resumed the practice of his profession; elected as a Republican to the Fortieth and Forty-first Congresses (March 4, 1867–March 3, 1871); voluntarily retired from political life and resumed the practice of law in Geneseo, N. Y., where he died on April 20, 1879; interment in Temple Hill Cemetery.

KELSO, John Russell, a Representative from Missouri; born near Columbus, Franklin County, Ohio, March 23, 1831; received a classical training, and was graduated from Pleasant Ridge College, Missouri, in June 1859; during the Civil War served in the Union Army as a member of the Twenty-fourth Missouri Infantry, the Fourteenth Missouri Cavalry, and the Eighth Missouri Cavalry, and was captain of Company M; brevetted major, lieutenant colonel, and colonel "for gallant and meritorious services"; mustered out April 18, 1865; elected as an Independent Radical to the Thirty-ninth Congress (March 4, 1865–March 3, 1867); was not a candidate for renomination in 1866; principal of Kelso Academy, Springfield, Mo., 1867–1869; moved to Modesto, Calif., in 1872 and to Longmont, Colo., in July 1885; author and lecturer; died in Longmont, Boulder County, Colo., January 26, 1891; interment on his estate near Longmont; subsequently the remains were cremated at the Riverside Cemetery, Denver, Denver County, Colo., and the ashes scattered.

KEM, James Preston, a Senator from Missouri; born in Macon, Mo., April 2, 1890; attended Blees Military Academy; was graduated from the University of Missouri at Columbia in 1910, and from Harvard Law School, Cambridge, Mass., in 1913; was admitted to the bar in 1913 and commenced practice in Kansas City, Mo.; during the First World War served in the Infantry of the United States Army from 1917 until discharged as a first lieutenant in 1919; resumed the general practice of law in Kansas City, Mo.; chairman of the Jackson County Republican committee in 1944; delegate to the Republican National Conventions in 1944 and 1948; vice chairman of the board of trustees of the University of Kansas City; director of St. Luke's Hospital, Kansas City, Mo.; elected as a Republican to the United States Senate in 1946 and served from January 3, 1947, to January 3, 1953; was unsuccessful for reelection in 1952; resumed the practice of law in Washington, D. C., until retirement in 1961; resides at "Sherwood," The Plains, Va., and engaged in the breeding of Angus cattle.

KEM, Omer Madison, a Representative from Nebraska; born in Hagerstown, Wayne County, Ind., on November 13, 1855; attended the public schools; moved to Custer County, Nebr., in 1882, thence to Broken Bow in 1890 and engaged in agricultural pursuits; deputy treasurer of Custer County in 1890 and 1891; elected as a Populist to the Fifty-second, Fifty-third, and Fifty-fourth Congresses (March 4, 1891–March 3, 1897); was not a candidate for renomination in 1896; engaged in fruit growing and cattle raising near Montrose, Colo.; member of the Colorado State House of Representatives in 1907; moved to Cottage Grove, Oreg., in 1908 and became interested in electric light and power enterprises; retired in 1922; died in Cottage Grove, Oreg., February 13, 1942; remains were cremated and the ashes scattered.

KEMBLE, Gouverneur, a Representative from New York; born in New York City January 25, 1786; completed preparatory studies and was graduated from Columbia College, New York City, in 1803; engaged in mercantile pursuits; visited Spain in 1816 and while there studied the process of casting cannon; after his return to the United States he established a cannon foundry at Cold Spring, N. Y., where cannon were for the first time cast in this county with any degree of perfection; sent to the Mediterranean as a naval agent during the war with Tripoli; elected as a Democrat to the Twenty-fifth and Twenty-sixth Congresses (March 4, 1837–March 3, 1841); declined the nomination for reelection in 1840; delegate to the State constitutional convention in 1846; delegate to the Democratic National conventions in 1844 and 1860; interested in the promotion of the Hudson River and Panama Railroads; died at Cold Spring, Putnam County, N. Y., September 16, 1875; interment in Cold Spring Cemetery.

KEMP, Bolivar Edwards, a Representative from Louisiana; born on the Kemp homestead near Amite, St. Helena Parish, La., December 28, 1871; was privately tutored and also attended the public schools of Amite, La., and the University of Louisiana at Baton Rouge; was graduated in law from Tulane University at New Orleans in 1897; was admitted to the bar the same year and commenced practice at Amite, La.; was active in the development of agricultural and trucking industries and also interested in banking; member of the board of supervisors of the University of Louisiana since 1910; elected as a Democrat to the Sixty-ninth and to the four succeeding Congresses and served from March 4, 1925, until his death in Amite, La., on June 19, 1933; interment in Amite Cemetery.

KEMPSHALL, Thomas, a Representative from New York; born in England about 1796; attended the common schools; immigrated to the United States with his father, who settled in Pittsford, N. Y., in 1806; moved to Rochester, N. Y., in 1813; employed as a carpenter; engaged in mercantile pursuits and later became engaged in milling; member of the board of aldermen in 1834 and again in 1844; mayor of Rochester, N. Y., in 1837; elected as a Whig to the Twenty-sixth Congress (March 4, 1839–March 3, 1841); resumed milling; unsuccessful candidate for mayor in 1852; died in Rochester, N. Y., January 14, 1865; interment in Mount Hope Cemetery.

KENAN, Thomas, a Representative from North Carolina; born in Kenansville, Duplin County, N. C., February 26, 1771; educated by private tutors; member of the State house of commons 1799–1803; served in the State senate in 1804; elected as a Democrat to the Ninth, Tenth, and Eleventh Congresses (March 4, 1805–March 3, 1811); was not a candidate for renomination; moved to Selma, Dallas County, Ala., in 1833 and engaged in planting; member of the Alabama House of Representatives for several years; died near Selma, Ala., October 22, 1843; interment in Valley Creek Cemetery, near Selma.

KENDALL, Charles West, a Representative from Nevada; born in Searsmont, Waldo County, Maine, April 22, 1828; attended Phillips Academy, Andover, Mass., and Yale College, New Haven, Conn.; moved to California in 1849 and engaged in mining; editor and proprietor of the San Jose Tribune 1855–1859; studied law; was admitted to the bar in 1859 and commenced practice in Sacramento, Calif.; member of the State assembly in 1861 and 1862; moved to Hamilton, Nev., in 1862 and resumed the practice of law; elected as a Democrat to the Forty-second and Forty-third Congresses (March 4, 1871–March 3, 1875); declined to be a candidate for renomination in 1874; moved to Denver, Colo., and practiced law; assistant

librarian in the Interstate Commerce Commission, Washington, D. C., from 1892 until his death; orator and writer on political and economic subjects; died in Mount Rainier, Md., June 25, 1914; interment in Congressional Cemetery, Washington, D. C.

KENDALL, Elva Roscoe, a Representative from Kentucky; born near Carlisle, Nicholas County, Ky., February 14, 1893; attended the public schools, the Young Men's Christian Association School of Accountancy at New York City, having private instruction in higher accounting, and National University at Washington, D. C.; engaged as a public accountant and tax consultant; also interested in agricultural pursuits; during the First World War served in the personnel office of the Sixty-first Division; employed as a field auditor for the United States Treasury Department 1922–1927; elected as a Republican to the Seventy-first Congress (March 4, 1929–March 3, 1931); unsuccessful candidate for reelection in 1930 to the Seventy-second Congress; resumed agricultural pursuits and his profession as a public accountant; also engaged in the real-estate business; is a resident of Carlisle, Ky.

KENDALL, John Wilkerson (father of Joseph Morgan Kendall), a Representative from Kentucky; born in Morgan County, Ky., June 26, 1834; attended the common schools and Owingsville Academy; studied law; was admitted to the bar in 1854 and commenced practice in West Liberty, Ky.; prosecuting attorney of Morgan County 1854–1858; during the Civil War served as first lieutenant and adjutant of the Tenth Kentucky Confederate Cavalry; member of the State house of representatives 1867–1871; Commonwealth attorney for the thirteenth judicial district 1872–1878; elected as a Democrat to the Fifty-second Congress and served from March 4, 1891, until his death in Washington, D. C., on March 7, 1892; interment in Barber Cemetery, West Liberty, Morgan County, Ky.

KENDALL, Jonas (father of Joseph Gowing Kendall), a Representative from Massachusetts; born in Leominster, Worcester County, Mass., October 27, 1757; pursued an academic course; engaged in the manufacture of paper in Leominster, Mass., in 1796; member of the State house of representatives in 1800, 1801, 1803–1807, and 1821; served in the State senate 1808–1811; member of the school board in 1803, 1811, and 1814; member of the executive council in 1822; presidential elector on the Federalist ticket in 1816; elected as a Federalist to the Sixteenth Congress (March 4, 1819–March 3, 1821); unsuccessful candidate for reelection in 1820 to the Seventeenth Congress; resumed the manufacture of paper; died in Leominster, Mass., October 22, 1844; interment in Evergreen Cemetery.

KENDALL, Joseph Gowing (son of Jonas Kendall), a Representative from Massachusetts; born in Leominster, Worcester County, Mass., October 27, 1788; pursued classical studies; was graduated from Harvard University in 1810 and taught there from 1812 to 1817; studied law; was admitted to the bar in 1818 and practiced in Leominster; elected to the State senate in 1824 and served four years; elected to the Twenty-first and Twenty-second Congresses (March 4, 1829–March 3, 1833); was not a candidate for renomination in 1832; appointed clerk of the courts of Worcester County in 1833 and served until his death; moved to Worcester, Mass., in 1833 and died there October 2, 1847; interment in Evergreen Cemetery, Leominster, Mass.

KENDALL, Joseph Morgan (son of John Wilkerson Kendall), a Representative from Kentucky; born in West Liberty, Morgan County, Ky., May 12, 1863; received his early education from private tutors and in the public schools; attended the State College of Kentucky and the University of Michigan at Ann

Arbor; was examined by the court of appeals of Kentucky and admitted to the practice of law before he was of age; settled in Prestonsburg, Ky.; clerk in the Forty-ninth and Fiftieth Congresses; elected as a Democrat to the Fifty-second Congress to fill the vacancy caused by the death of his father, John W. Kendall, and served from April 21, 1892, to March 3, 1893; declined to be a candidate for renomination in 1892 on account of ill health; presented credentials as a Member-elect to the Fifty-fourth Congress and served from March 4, 1895, to February 18, 1897, when he was succeeded by Nathan T. Hopkins, who contested his election; resumed the practice of law in West Liberty, Ky.; delegate to all Democratic State conventions 1884–1933; also engaged in agricultural pursuits near Boonsboro, Clark County, Ky.; died in West Liberty, Ky., November 5, 1933; interment in Barber Cemetery.

KENDALL, Nathan Edward, a Representative from Iowa; born on a farm near Greenville, Lucas County, Iowa, March 17, 1868; attended the rural schools; studied law; was admitted to the bar in 1887 and commenced practice in Albia, Monroe County, Iowa, in 1889; city attorney 1890–1892; prosecuting attorney of Monroe County, Iowa, 1893–1897; member of the State house of representatives 1899–1909 and served as speaker in 1909; elected as a Republican to the Sixty-first and Sixty-second Congresses (March 4, 1909–March 3, 1913); was not a candidate for renomination in 1912 to the Sixty-third Congress; resumed the practice of law in Albia, Iowa; moved to Des Moines, Iowa, in 1921; Governor of Iowa 1921–1925; retired from public life and active business pursuits and resided in Des Moines, Iowa, until his death on November 5, 1936; remains were cremated and the ashes interred on the lawn of "Kendall Place," his former home in Albia, Iowa.

KENDALL, Samuel Austin, a Representative from Pennsylvania; born in Greenville Township, Somerset County, Pa., November 1, 1859; attended the public schools and was a student for some time at Valparaiso, Ind., and at Mount Union College, Alliance, Ohio; commenced teaching school at the age of seventeen and continued in that profession for fourteen years, the last five years of which he served as superintendent of the public schools of Jefferson, Iowa; returned to Somerset County, Pa., in 1890 and engaged in the lumber business and the mining of coal; vice president of the Kendall Lumber Co. of Pittsburgh and president of the Preston Railroad Co., a connection of the Baltimore & Ohio Railroad; member of the State house of representatives 1899–1903; elected as a Republican to the Sixty-sixth and to the six succeeding Congresses and served from March 4, 1919, until his death; had been unsuccessful for reelection in 1932 to the Seventy-third Congress; died in the House Office Building, Washington, D. C., January 8, 1933; interment in Hochstetler Cemetery, Greenville Township, Somerset County, Pa.

KENDRICK, John Benjamin, a Senator from Wyoming; born near Jacksonville, Cherokee County, Tex., September 6, 1857; attended the public schools; moved to Wyoming in 1879 and settled on a ranch near Sheridan; became engaged in the raising of cattle and sheep in Wyoming and Montana; member of the State senate 1910–1914; delegate to the Democratic National Convention at Baltimore in 1912 and at St. Louis in 1916; was a drafted and unsuccessful minority candidate for election to the United States Senate in 1913; Governor of Wyoming from 1915 until February 24, 1917, when he resigned, having been elected Senator; elected as a Democrat to the United States Senate in 1916; reelected in 1922 and 1928 and served from March 4, 1917, until his death at Sheridan, Wyo., November 3, 1933; interment in Mount Hope Cemetery.

KENNA, John Edward, a Representative and a Senator from West Virginia; born near St. Albans, Kanawha County, Va. (now West Virginia), April 10, 1848; moved with his mother to Missouri in 1856; received a limited schooling; during the Civil War enlisted in the Confederate Army in 1864; was wounded in that service in 1864 and was surrendered in Shreveport, La., in 1865; attended St. Vincent's College, Wheeling, W. Va.; studied law; was admitted to the bar in 1870 and commenced practice in Charleston, W. Va.; prosecuting attorney for Kanawha County 1872–1877; elected as a Democrat to the Forty-fifth, Forty-sixth, and Forty-seventh Congresses (March 4, 1877–March 3, 1883); had been reelected to the Forty-eighth Congress in 1882 but resigned to take effect March 4, 1883, having been elected Senator; elected to the United States Senate in 1883; reelected in 1889 and served from March 4, 1883, until his death in Washington, D. C., January 11, 1893; funeral services were held in the Chamber of the United States Senate; interment in Mount Olivet Cemetery, Charleston, W. Va.

KENNEDY, Ambrose, a Representative from Rhode Island; born in Blackstone, Worcester County, Mass., on December 1, 1875; attended the Blackstone public schools and St. Hyacinthe's College, Province of Quebec, Canada; was graduated from Holy Cross College, Worcester, Mass., in 1897; principal of the Blackstone High School 1898–1904 and superintendent of schools 1906–1908; studied law; was graduated from the Boston University Law School in 1906; was admitted to the bar the same year and commenced practice in Woonsocket, R. I.; aide-de-camp on the personal staff of Gov. Aram J. Pothier with the rank of colonel 1909–1913; member of the State house of representatives 1911–1913, serving as speaker in 1912; elected as a Republican to the Sixty-third and to the four succeeding Congresses (March 4, 1913–March 3, 1923); was not a candidate for renomination in 1922; resumed the practice of law; author; is a resident of Woonsocket, R. I.

KENNEDY, Ambrose Jerome, a Representative from Maryland; born in Baltimore Md., January 6, 1893; attended parochial schools, and Calvert Hall College and Polytechnic Institute in Baltimore, Md.; employed as a clerk for an insurance company 1909–1924; engaged in the brokerage and insurance business in 1924; unsuccessful candidate for election to the State house of representatives in 1918; member of the city council 1922–1926; served in the State senate in 1928 and 1929; delegate to the Democratic National Conventions in 1928 and 1932; appointed parole commissioner of Maryland in 1929 and served until elected to Congress; elected as a Democrat to the Seventy-second Congress to fill the vacancy caused by the death of J. Charles Linthicum and on the same day was elected to the Seventy-third Congress; reelected to the Seventy-fourth, Seventy-fifth, and Seventy-sixth Congresses and served from November 8, 1932, to January 3, 1941; unsuccessful candidate for renomination in 1940; resumed the brokerage and insurance business in Baltimore, Md.; member of the State Unemployment Compensation Board from June 1943 to September 1945; died in Baltimore, Md., August 29, 1950; interment in the New Cathedral Cemetery.

KENNEDY, Andrew (cousin of Case Broderick), a Representative from Indiana; born in Dayton, Ohio, July 24, 1810; moved with his parents to a farm on the Indian reserve near Lafayette, Ind.; soon afterward moved to Connersville, Ind.; became a blacksmith's apprentice; attended the common schools; studied law; was admitted to the bar in 1833 and commenced practice in Connersville; moved to Muncie (then Muncytown), Ind., in 1834 and continued the practice of law; member of the State house of representatives in 1835; served in the State senate in 1838; elected as a Democrat to the Twenty-seventh,

Twenty-eighth, and Twenty-ninth Congresses (March 4, 1841–March 3, 1847); Democratic caucus nominee for United States Senator in 1847; was stricken with smallpox on the eve of the legislative joint convention and died in Indianapolis, Ind., December 31, 1847; interment in Greenlawn Cemetery; reinterment in Beech Grove Cemetery, Muncie, Ind.

KENNEDY, Anthony (brother of John Pendleton Kennedy), a Senator from Maryland; born in Baltimore, Md., December 21, 1810; was sent by his parents to Charles Town, Va. (now West Virginia), in 1821, where he attended the Jefferson Academy; studied law and also engaged in agricultural pursuits; member of the Virginia House of Delegates 1839–1843; magistrate on the bench of the Jefferson County Court in Virginia for ten years; unsuccessful Whig candidate for election in 1844 to the Twenty-ninth Congress; declined the offer of President Fillmore as consul to Habana, Cuba, in 1850; returned to Baltimore, Md., in 1851; member of the Maryland House of Delegates in 1856; elected as a Unionist to the United States Senate and served from March 4, 1857, to March 3, 1863; delegate to the State constitutional convention which framed a new State constitution in 1867; retired from active political life and resided on his farm near Ellicott City, Howard County, Md.; died in Annapolis, Md., July 4, 1892; interment in Greenmount Cemetery, Baltimore, Md.

KENNEDY, Charles Augustus, a Representative from Iowa; born in Montrose, Lee County, Iowa, March 24, 1869; completed preparatory studies; interested in horticultural pursuits and later engaged in business as a nurseryman; mayor of Montrose 1890–1895; member of the State house of representatives 1903–1905; elected as a Republican to the Sixtieth and to the six succeeding Congresses (March 4, 1907–March 3, 1921); was not a candidate for renomination in 1920; engaged in banking until his retirement; died in Montrose, Iowa, January 10, 1951; interment in Montrose Cemetery.

KENNEDY, James, a Representative from Ohio; born in Lowellville, Mahoning County, Ohio, September 3, 1853; prepared for college at Poland Union Seminary, Ohio, and was graduated from Westminster College, New Wilmington, Pa., in 1876; studied law; was admitted to the bar in March 1879 and commenced practice in Youngstown, Ohio; member of the city council April 1886 to November 1888; chairman of the Republican State convention at Steubenville, Ohio, in 1894; elected as a Republican to the Fifty-eighth and to the three succeeding Congresses (March 4, 1903–March 3, 1911); unsuccessful candidate for reelection in 1910 to the Sixty-second Congress; resumed the practice of his profession in Youngstown, Ohio; affiliated with the Democratic party in 1916; unsuccessful Democratic candidate for election in 1926 to the Seventieth Congress; died in Youngstown, Ohio, November 9, 1928; interment in Riverside Cemetery, Poland, Ohio.

KENNEDY, John Fitzgerald (grandson of John Francis Fitzgerald), a Representative and a Senator from Massachusetts and a President of the United States; born in Brookline, Suffolk County, Mass., May 29, 1917; attended Choate School, Wallingford, Conn.; the London School of Economics at London, England, in 1935 and 1936, and Stanford University; was graduated from Harvard University, Cambridge, Mass., in 1940; during World War II served as a lieutenant in the United States Navy from September 1941 to April 1945; awarded the Navy and Marine Corps Medal and the Purple Heart; author; engaged as correspondent for a news service and covered the San Francisco Conference, the British elections in 1945, and the Potsdam meeting in 1945; elected as a Democrat to the Eightieth, Eighty-

first, and Eighty-second Congresses (January 3, 1947–January 3, 1953); did not seek renomination in 1952; elected to the United States Senate in 1952 for the term commencing January 3, 1953; reelected in 1958 for term ending January 3, 1965; nominated for the office of President of the United States by the Democratic Party at the convention in Los Angeles in 1960; elected President of the United States November 8, 1960, and inaugurated January 20, 1961, for the term ending January 20, 1965; resigned from the United States Senate December 22, 1960.

KENNEDY, John Lauderdale, a Representative from Nebraska; born in Ayrshire, Scotland, October 27, 1854; attended the public schools of Scotland; immigrated to the United States and settled in La Salle County, Ill., in 1874; engaged in agricultural pursuits; attended Knox College, Galesburg, Ill., in 1879 and was graduated from the law department of the University of Iowa at Iowa City in 1882; commenced the practice of law in Omaha, Nebr., in 1882; presidential elector on the Republican ticket of McKinley and Roosevelt in 1900; elected as a Republican to the Fifty-ninth Congress (March 4, 1905–March 3, 1907); unsuccessful candidate for reelection in 1906 to the Sixtieth Congress; resumed the practice of law in Omaha, Nebr.; member and chairman pro tempore of the board of fire and police commissioners for the city of Omaha in 1907 and 1908; chairman of the Republican State committee in 1911 and 1912; unsuccessful candidate for election to the United States Senate in 1916; Federal fuel administrator for Nebraska from October 1917 to March 1919; president of the United States National Bank 1920–1925; president of the Omaha Chamber of Commerce in 1924 and 1925; retired from active pursuits in January 1933 and moved to Pacific Palisades, Calif., where he died August 30, 1946; interment in Forestlawn Cemetery, Glendale, Calif.

KENNEDY, John Pendleton (brother of Anthony Kennedy), a Representative from Maryland; born in Baltimore, Md., October 25, 1795; attended private schools, and was graduated from Baltimore Academy in 1812; volunteered and served in the War of 1812, taking part in the Battles of Bladensburg and North Point; studied law; was admitted to the bar in 1816 and commenced practice in Baltimore, Md.; also engaged in literary pursuits and was a novelist of distinction; member of the State house of delegates 1821–1823; appointed secretary of the legation in Chile January 27, 1823, but did not proceed to his post, resigning June 23, 1823; unsuccessful candidate for election to the Twenty-fifth Congress; subsequently elected as a Whig to the same Congress to fill the vacancy caused by the death of Isaac McKim and served from April 25, 1838, to March 3, 1839; unsuccessful candidate for reelection in 1838 to the Twenty-sixth Congress; presidential elector on the Whig ticket of Harrison and Tyler in 1840; elected to the Twenty-seventh and Twenty-eighth Congresses (March 4, 1841–March 3, 1845); unsuccessful candidate for reelection in 1844 to the Twenty-ninth Congress; again a member of the State house of delegates, in 1846, and served as speaker; Secretary of the Navy in the Cabinet of President Fillmore from July 22, 1852, to March 7, 1853; resumed literary pursuits; served as vice president of the Maryland Historical Society and as chairman of the board of trustees of Peabody Academy of Baltimore; died August 18, 1870, at Newport, R. I., while on a visit; interment in Greenmount Cemetery, Baltimore, Md.

KENNEDY, Martin John, a Representative from New York; born in New York City, N. Y., August 29, 1892; attended the public schools; was graduated from Columbia University in New York City in 1909, and from the College of the City of New York in 1914; engaged in the real-estate and insurance business in 1916; chairman of the New York City School Board 1918–1924; member of the State senate 1924–1930; during the

First World War served in the Army Intelligence 1915–1918; elected as a Democrat to the Seventy-first Congress to fill the vacancy caused by the resignation of John F. Carew; reelected to the Seventy-second and to the six succeeding Congresses and served from March 11, 1930, to January 3, 1945; unsuccessful for renomination in 1944; resumed the real estate and insurance business; died in New York City, N. Y., October 27, 1955; interment in Calvary Cemetery, Maspeth, Long Island, N. Y.

KENNEDY, Michael Joseph, a Representative from New York; born in New York City, N. Y., October 25, 1897; attended the Sacred Heart Parochial School, New York, N. Y.; hotel clerk 1914–1921; clerk of the New York City Board of Elections 1921–1923; served as marshal of the city of New York 1923–1938; became engaged in the insurance business in 1939; elected as a Democrat to the Seventy-sixth and Seventy-seventh Congresses (January 3, 1939–January 3, 1943); was not a candidate for renomination in 1942; resumed the insurance business in New York City; was killed in an airplane accident at the Washington (D. C.) National Airport on November 1, 1949; interment in Gate of Heaven Cemetery, Hawthorne, N. Y.

KENNEDY, Robert Patterson, a Representative from Ohio; born in Bellefontaine, Logan County, Ohio, January 23, 1840; attended the public schools; during the Civil War served in the Union Army; commissioned second lieutenant in the Twenty-third Regiment, Ohio Volunteer Infantry, June 11, 1861; captain and assistant adjutant general October 7, 1862; major and assistant adjutant general November 16, 1864; resigned April 8, 1865; recommissioned colonel of the One Hundred and Ninety-sixth Regiment, Ohio Volunteer Infantry, April 14, 1865; brevetted lieutenant colonel of Volunteers March 13, 1865, "for gallant and meritorious services during the campaign in West Virginia and in the Shenandoah Valley"; brigadier general of Volunteers March 13, 1865, "for distinguished gallantry during the war"; mustered out September 11, 1865; returned to Bellefontaine, Ohio; studied law; was admitted to the bar in 1866 and commenced practice in Bellefontaine; appointed by President Hayes collector of internal revenue for the fourth district of Ohio and served from 1878 to 1883; Lieutenant Governor of Ohio 1885–1887; elected as a Republican to the Fiftieth and Fifty-first Congresses (March 4, 1887–March 3, 1891); was not a candidate for renomination in 1890; appointed by President McKinley in 1899 a member of the Insular Commission, which was directed to investigate and report upon conditions existing in Cuba and Puerto Rico and served as its president; resumed the practice of his profession in Bellefontaine, Ohio; died in Columbus, Ohio, May 6, 1918; interment in Bellefontaine Cemetery.

KENNEDY, William, a Representative from North Carolina; born near Washington, N. C., July 31, 1768; was graduated from the University of Pennsylvania at Philadelphia in 1782; studied law; was admitted to the bar; elected as a Federalist to the Eighth Congress (March 4, 1803–March 3, 1805); elected to the Eleventh Congress (March 4, 1809–March 3, 1811); unsuccessful candidate for reelection to the Twelfth Congress but was subsequently elected to the same Congress to fill the vacancy caused by the death of Thomas Blount; reelected to the Thirteenth Congress and served from January 30, 1813, to March 3, 1815; died in Washington, Beaufort County, N. C., on October 11, 1834; interment in Kennedy Cemetery, near Washington, N. C.

KENNEDY, William, a Representative from Connecticut; born in Naugatuck, New Haven County, Conn., December 19, 1854; attended the public schools; studied law; was admitted to the bar in 1879 and commenced practice at Naugatuck, Conn.; member of the State senate 1899–1901; delegate to the Democratic National Conventions in 1896, 1900, 1908, and 1912; member of the Board of Education of Naugatuck 1901–1918; attorney for the town and borough of Naugatuck 1893–1918; elected as a Democrat to the Sixty-third Congress (March 4, 1913–March 3, 1915); was an unsuccessful candidate for reelection in 1914; resumed the practice of his profession; died in Naugatuck, Conn., on June 19, 1918; interment in St. James' Cemetery.

KENNETT, Luther Martin, a Representative from Missouri; born in Falmouth, Pendleton County, Ky., March 15, 1807; attended private schools; deputy county clerk of Pendleton County in 1822 and 1823 and of Campbell County, Ky., in 1824; moved to St. Louis, Mo., in 1825; employed in a mercantile establishment; later engaged in lead mining and the manufacture of shot in Jefferson and St. Francis Counties, Mo.; returned to St. Louis in 1842; city alderman 1843–1846; declined to be a candidate for reelection; spent several years in Europe on account of ill health, returning to St. Louis in 1849; vice president of the Pacific Railroad Co.; mayor of St. Louis 1850–1853; president of the St. Louis & Iron Mountain Railroad in 1853; elected by the American Party to the Thirty-fourth Congress (March 4, 1855–March 3, 1857); unsuccessful candidate for reelection; retired to his country home near St. Louis, Mo.; went to Europe in 1867, where he remained until his death in Paris, France, April 12, 1873; interment in Bellefontaine Cemetery, St. Louis, Mo.

KENNEY, Edward Aloysius, a Representative from New Jersey; born in Clinton, Worcester County, Mass., August 11, 1884; attended the public schools; was graduated from Clinton High School in 1902, from Williams College, Williamstown, Mass., in 1906, and from the law department of New York University at New York City in 1908; was admitted to the New York State bar in 1908 and commenced practice in New York City; moved to Cliffside Park, Bergen County, N. J., in 1916; admitted to the New Jersey State bar in 1917 and practiced in New Jersey and New York; during the First World War served as a member of the legal advisory draft board of New Jersey in 1917; judge of recorders court, Cliffside Park, 1919–1923; unsuccessful candidate for mayor of Cliffside Park as an Independent in 1921, as a Republican in 1923, and as a Democrat in 1927; chairman of the Cliffside Park Housing Commission in 1922 and 1923; member of the Republican county committee in 1925 and 1926; elected as a Democrat to the Seventy-third, Seventy-fourth, and Seventy-fifth Congresses and served from March 4, 1933, until his death in Washington, D. C., January 27, 1938; interment in St. John's Cemetery, Clinton, Mass.

KENNEY, Richard Rolland, a Senator from Delaware; born in Laurel, Sussex County, Del., September 9, 1856; attended the public schools; and was graduated from Laurel Academy, Delaware, in June 1874; attended Hobart College, Geneva, N. Y.; studied law; was admitted to the bar in 1881 and commenced practice in Dover, Del.; State librarian 1879–1881; captain in the National Guard 1880–1889; adjutant general of the State 1887–1891; member of the Democratic State committee 1890–1917; delegate to the Democratic National Conventions in 1892, 1900, and 1904; member of the Democratic National Committee 1896–1908; elected on January 19, 1897, as a Democrat to the United States Senate for the term commencing March 4, 1895, to fill the vacancy caused by failure of the legislature to elect and served until March 3, 1901; unsuccessful candidate for reelection; resumed the practice of law in Dover, Del.; during the First World War entered the Judge Advocate General's Department on July 12, 1917; assigned as judge advocate of the Thirty-eighth Division in December 1917 at Camp Shelby, Miss.; entrained with his division for France on September 10, 1918; member of the board of contract adjustment in Paris from December 1, 1918, to May 1919; assistant counsel for the director of sales in Washington, D. C., until July 20, 1920, when, on his own application, he was discharged, and resumed the practice of law in Dover; elected counsel to the State house of representatives in 1921; elected prosecuting attorney by the levy court of Kent County in 1921, serving four years; appointed by the Governor a member of the State board of supplies in 1921, serving two years; member and secretary of the State public lands commission 1913–1925 and reappointed in April 1925 for four years; died in Dover, Del., August 14, 1931; interment in Christ Churchyard.

KENNON, William, Sr. (cousin of William Kennon, Jr.), a Representative from Ohio; born in Uniontown, Fayette County, Pa., May 14, 1793; moved with his parents to Belmont County, Ohio, in 1804; attended the common schools and Franklin College, New Athens, Ohio; studied law; was admitted to the bar in 1824 and commenced practice in St. Clairsville, Ohio; elected as a Democrat to the Twenty-first and Twenty-second Congresses (March 4, 1829–March 3, 1833); unsuccessful candidate for reelection in 1832 to the Twenty-third Congress; elected to the Twenty-fourth Congress (March 4, 1835–March 3, 1837); unsuccessful candidate for reelection in 1836 to the Twenty-fifth Congress; president judge of the court of common pleas 1840–1847; delegate to the second State constitutional convention in 1850; appointed and subsequently elected to fill the unexpired term of William B. Caldwell as judge of the Ohio Supreme Court in 1854; resigned in 1856 and resumed the practice of law in St. Clairsville, Ohio; became affiliated with the Republican Party at the outbreak of the Civil War; died in St. Clairsville, Belmont County, Ohio, November 2, 1881; interment in Methodist Cemetery.

KENNON, William, Jr. (cousin of William Kennon, Sr.), a Representative from Ohio; born in Carrickfergus, Ireland, June 12, 1802; immigrated to the United States in 1816 with his parents, who settled near Barnesville, Belmont County, Ohio; attended the common schools; was graduated from Franklin College, New Athens, Ohio, in 1826; studied law; was admitted to the bar in 1830 and commenced practice in St. Clairsville, Ohio; prosecuting attorney of Belmont County 1837–1841; elected as a Democrat to the Thirtieth Congress (March 4, 1847–March 3, 1849); was not a candidate for renomination; resumed the practice of law; judge of the court of common pleas of the fifteenth judicial district from 1865 to July 1, 1867, when he resigned; died in St. Clairsville, Ohio, October 19, 1867; interment in Union Cemetery.

KENT, Everett, a Representative from Pennsylvania; born in East Bangor, Northampton County, Pa., November 15, 1888; attended the public schools in Lansford, East Bangor, Nazareth, and Bangor, Pa.; engaged as a machinist and as a newspaper reporter; taught school; principal of Roosevelt School, Bangor, Pa.; was graduated from the law department of the University of Pennsylvania at Philadelphia in 1911; was admitted to the bar the same year and commenced practice in Bangor; counsel for several municipalities; attorney for the board of prison inspectors of Northampton County 1912–1915; solicitor of Northampton County 1920–1923; elected as a Democrat to the Sixty-eighth Congress (March 4, 1923–March 3, 1925); unsuccessful candidate for reelection in 1924 to the Sixty-ninth Congress; elected to the Seventieth Congress (March 4, 1927–March 3, 1929); unsuccessful candidate for reelection in 1928 to the

Seventy-first Congress; delegate to the Democratic National Conventions in 1936, 1940, 1944, 1948, 1952, and 1956; solicitor for the county controller of Northampton County, Pa., 1933–1943; resumed the practice of his profession in Bangor, Pa.

KENT, Joseph, a Representative and a Senator from Maryland; born in Calvert County, Md., January 14, 1779; received a liberal schooling; studied medicine; was admitted to practice in Lower Marlborough, Calvert County, in 1799; settled near Bladensburg, Md., about 1807; continued the practice of medicine and also engaged in agricultural pursuits; served in the State militia as surgeon's mate, surgeon major, lieutenant colonel, and colonel; elected as a Federalist to the Twelfth and Thirteenth Congresses (March 4, 1811–March 3, 1815); presidential elector on the Democratic ticket of Monroe and Tompkins in 1816; elected as a Democrat to the Sixteenth and to the three succeeding Congresses and served from March 4, 1819, to January 6, 1826, when he resigned, having been elected Governor of the State; Governor of Maryland 1826–1829; vice president of the National Republican convention at Baltimore in 1831 which nominated Henry Clay for President; elected as a National Republican to the United States Senate and served from March 4, 1833, until his death at his home, "Rose Mount," near Bladensburg, Md., November 24, 1837.

KENT, Moss, a Representative from New York; born in Rensselaer County, N. Y., April 3, 1766; completed preparatory studies; studied law; was admitted to the bar and practiced; appointed first judge of Jefferson County about 1795; moved to Cooperstown, N. Y.; member of the State senate 1799–1803; served in the State assembly in 1807 and 1810; appointed judge of Jefferson County, February 26, 1810; elected as a Federalist to the Thirteenth and Fourteenth Congresses (March 4, 1813–March 3, 1817); resumed the practice of law; died in Plattsburgh, N. Y., May 30, 1838; interment in Riverside Cemetery.

KENT, William, a Representative from California; born in Chicago, Ill., March 29, 1864; moved to California in 1871 with his parents, who settled in Marin County; attended private schools in California and Hopkins Grammar School, New Haven, Conn., 1881–1883; was graduated from Yale University in 1887; returned to Chicago, Ill., in 1887 and engaged in the real estate and livestock business; member of the city council 1895–1897; president of the Municipal Voters' League of Chicago in 1899 and 1900; returned to Marin County, Calif., in 1907; elected as a Progressive Republican to the Sixty-second Congress; reelected as an Independent to the Sixty-third and Sixty-fourth Congresses and served from March 4, 1911, to March 3, 1917; was not a candidate for renomination in 1916; appointed a member of the United States Tariff Commission March 21, 1917, and served until his resignation March 31, 1920; writer on political subjects and natural science; died in Kentfield, Calif., March 13, 1928; remains were cremated in Oakland, Calif., and the ashes returned to the family.

KENYON, William Scheuneman, a Representative from New York; born in Catskill, Greene County, N. Y., December 13, 1820; attended a private academy in Catskill, and the Kinderhook Academy; was graduated from Rutgers College, New Brunswick, N. J., in 1842; studied law in Kingston, N. Y.; was admitted to the bar in Albany, N. Y. in 1846 and commenced practice in Kingston; one of the incorporators of the Ulster County Savings Bank and served as trustee for forty-four years; elected as a Republican to the Thirty-sixth Congress (March 4, 1859–March 3, 1861); was not a candidate for renomination in 1860; resumed the practice of law; delegate to the

Republican National Convention at Philadelphia in 1872 and at Cincinnati in 1876; judge of Ulster County 1883–1889; chairman of the Republican county committee many years; died in Kingston, Ulster County, N. Y., February 10, 1896; interment in Wiltwyck Rural Cemetery.

KENYON, William Squire, a Senator from Iowa; born in Elyria, Lorain County, Ohio, June 10, 1869; attended the public schools; was graduated from Grinnell (Iowa) College, and from Iowa State University Law School at Iowa City in 1891; was admitted to the bar in 1891 and commenced practice in Fort Dodge, Iowa; prosecuting attorney for Webster County 1892–1896; district judge of the eleventh judicial district of Iowa 1900–1902; appointed district attorney for the Illinois Central Railroad in 1904 and general attorney in 1907; assistant to the Attorney General of the United States from March 1910 to April 1911, when he resigned, having been elected Senator; elected as a Republican to the United States Senate to fill the vacancy caused by the death of Jonathan P. Dolliver; reelected in 1912 and 1918 and served from April 12, 1911, to February 24, 1922, when he resigned; on January 31, 1922, was appointed judge of the United States Circuit Court of Appeals, Eighth Circuit, by President Harding and served from February 25, 1922, until his death; declined the appointment as Secretary of the Navy in President Coolidge's Cabinet in 1924; appointed by President Hoover in 1929 as a member of the National Commission on Law Observance and Enforcement, better known as the Wickersham Commission; died at his summer home at Sebasco Estates, Maine, September 9, 1933; interment in Oakland Cemetery, Fort Dodge, Iowa.

KEOGH, Eugene James, a Representative from New York; born in Brooklyn, N. Y., August 30, 1907; attended the public schools and Commercial High School, Brooklyn, N. Y.; was graduated from the school of commerce of New York University at New York City in 1927 and from the school of law of Fordham University, New York, N. Y., in 1930; teacher in New York City public schools in 1927 and 1928; clerk with New York City Board of Transportation 1928–1930; law clerk in 1930 and 1931; was admitted to the bar in 1932 and commenced practice in New York City; member of the New York State Assembly in 1936; elected as a Democrat to the Seventy-fifth and to the eleven succeeding Congresses (January 3, 1937–January 3, 1961). *Reelected to the Eighty-seventh Congress.*

KERN, Frederick John, a Representative from Illinois; born on a farm near Millstadt, St. Clair County, Ill., September 2, 1864; attended the public schools of Millstadt and Illinois State Normal University at Normal, Ill.; employed as a coal miner; taught in the public schools for five years; engaged in the newspaper business and became editor of the East St. Louis Gazette, and in 1891 became owner of the Belleville daily and semiweekly News-Democrat; chief enrolling clerk of the State senate in 1892; unsuccessful candidate for election in 1898 to the Fifty-sixth Congress; elected as a Democrat to the Fifty-seventh Congress (March 4, 1901–March 3, 1903); unsuccessful candidate for reelection in 1902 to the Fifty-eighth Congress; resumed his newspaper pursuits in Belleville, Ill.; mayor of Belleville 1902–1912; delegate to the Democratic National Conventions in 1904, 1908, and 1912; president of the State board of administration 1913–1919; died in Belleville, Ill., November 9, 1931; interment in Walnut Hill Cemetery.

KERN, John Worth, a Senator from Indiana; born in Alto, Howard County, Ind., December 20, 1849; attended the common schools and the normal college at Kokomo, Ind.; was graduated from the law department of the University of Michigan at Ann Arbor in 1869; was admitted to the bar the same year and commenced practice in Kokomo; unsuccessful candidate for election to the State house of representatives in 1870; city attorney of Kokomo 1871–1884; moved to Indianapolis in 1885 and continued the practice of law; member of the American Bar Association; reporter of the Indiana Supreme Court 1885–1889; member of the State senate 1893–1897; special assistant United States district attorney in 1893 and 1894; city solicitor of Indianapolis 1897–1901; unsuccessful Democratic candidate for Governor in 1900 and 1904; unsuccessful candidate for Vice President of the United States on the Democratic ticket with William Jennings Bryan for President in 1908; elected as a Democrat to the United States Senate and served from March 4, 1911, to March 3, 1917; unsuccessful candidate for reelection in 1916; died in Asheville, N. C., August 17, 1917; interment on the Kern estate near Hollins, Va.; reinterment in Crown Hill Cemetery, Indianapolis, Ind., in 1929.

KERNAN, Francis, a Representative and a Senator from New York; born in Wayne, Schuyler County, N. Y., January 14, 1816; attended public schools; was graduated from Georgetown College, District of Columbia, in 1836; studied law in Utica, N. Y.; was admitted to the bar in July 1840 and practiced in Utica; reporter of the court of appeals of New York 1854–1857; member of the State assembly in 1861; elected as a Democrat to the Thirty-eighth Congress (March 4, 1863–March 3, 1865); unsuccessful candidate for reelection in 1864 to the Thirty-ninth Congress; member of the State constitutional convention in 1867 and 1868; unsuccessful Democratic and Liberal-Republican candidate for Governor of New York in 1872; elected as a Democrat to the United States Senate and served from March 4, 1875, to March 3, 1881; unsuccessful candidate for reelection in 1880; member of the board of regents of the University of the State of New York 1870–1892; died in Utica, Oneida County, N. Y., September 7, 1892; interment in St. Agnes Cemetery.

KERR, Daniel, a Representative from Iowa; born near Dalry, Ayrshire, Scotland, June 18, 1836; immigrated to the United States with his parents, who settled in Madison County, Ill., in 1841; attended the common schools; was graduated from McKendree College in 1858; studied law; was admitted to the bar in 1862 and commenced practice in Edwardsville, Madison County, Ill.; during the Civil War enlisted in the Union Army August 12, 1862; promoted to second lieutenant, Company G, One Hundred and Seventeenth Regiment, Illinois Volunteer Infantry, in 1863 and to first lieutenant in 1864; member of the house of representatives of Illinois in 1868; moved to Grundy Center, Iowa, in 1870 and continued the practice of law; school director in 1875; elected mayor of Grundy Center in 1877; member of the State house of representatives in 1883; presidential elector on the Republican ticket of Blaine and Logan in 1884; elected as a Republican to the Fiftieth and Fifty-first Congresses (March 4, 1887–March 3, 1891); was not a candidate for renomination in 1890; delegate to the Republican National Convention at Chicago in 1888 which nominated Harrison and Morton and at St. Louis in 1896 which nominated McKinley and Hobart; resumed the practice of his profession; unsuccessful Democratic candidate for election in 1902 to the Fifty-eighth Congress; moved to Pasadena, Calif., in 1909 and resided there until 1916, when he returned to Grundy Center, Iowa, where he died October 8, 1916; interment in Rose Hill Cemetery.

KERR, James, a Representative from Pennsylvania; born in Reedsville, Mifflin County, Pa., October 2, 1851; resided in Blair County until 1864; moved to Clearfield in 1867; pursued an academic course; justice of the peace in 1878; prothonotary for Clearfield County in 1880 and 1883; engaged in the mining and shipping of bituminous coal and the cutting and transportation of lumber; elected as a Democrat to the Fifty-first Congress (March 4, 1889–March 3, 1891); unsuccessful candidate for renomination in 1890; during the Fifty-second and Fifty-third Congresses was appointed Clerk of the United States House of Representatives and served from March 4, 1891, to March 3, 1895; resumed business interests; died in New York City October 31, 1908; interment in Hillcrest Cemetery, Clearfield, Pa.

KERR, John (father of John Kerr, Jr., cousin of Bartlett Yancey, and granduncle of John Hosea Kerr), a Representative from Virginia; born near Yanceyville, Caswell County, N. C., August 4, 1782; attended the common schools; studied theology; was licensed as a Baptist minister in 1802; located in Halifax County, Va., in 1805; elected as a Democrat to the Thirteenth Congress (March 4, 1813–March 3, 1815); unsuccessful candidate for reelection to the Fourteenth Congress but was subsequently elected to fill the vacancy in the Fourteenth Congress caused by the death of Matthew Clay and served from October 30, 1815, to March 3, 1817; was not a candidate for renomination in 1816; resumed the ministry and was pastor of the Baptist churches of Arbor and Mary Creek, Va.; moved to Richmond, Va., in March 1825 and was pastor of the First Baptist Church; resigned in 1832; settled upon a farm near Danville, Pittsylvania County, Va., in 1836 and died there September 29, 1842; interment in Baptist Cemetery, Yanceyville, Caswell County, N. C.

KERR, John, Jr. (son of John Kerr), a Representative from North Carolina; born near Danville, Pittsylvania County, Va., February 10, 1811; completed academic studies in Richmond, Va.; studied law; was admitted to the bar and commenced practice in Yanceyville, N. C.; trustee of Wake Forest College, North Carolina 1844–1856 and of the University of North Carolina at Chapel Hill 1846–1868; unsuccessful Whig candidate for Governor in 1852; elected as a Whig to the Thirty-third Congress (March 4, 1853–March 3, 1855); unsuccessful candidate for reelection in 1854 to the Thirty-fourth Congress; member of the State house of representatives in 1858 and 1860; judge of the supreme court of North Carolina during the Civil War; judge of the superior court 1874–1879; died in Reidsville, N. C., September 5, 1879; interment in the City Cemetery, Yanceyville, N. C.

KERR, John Bozman (son of John Leeds Kerr), a Representative from Maryland; born in Easton, Talbot County, Md., March 5, 1809; attended the common schools and Easton (Md.) Academy; was graduated from Harvard University in 1830; studied law; was admitted to the bar and commenced practice in Easton, Md., in 1833; member of the State house of delegates 1836–1838; deputy attorney general for Talbot County 1845–1848; elected as a Whig to the Thirty-first Congress (March 4, 1849–March 3, 1851); was not a candidate for renomination in 1850; appointed by President Fillmore Chargé d'Affaires to Nicaragua March 7, 1851, and served until July 27, 1853; resumed the practice of law in Baltimore and St. Michaels, Md., in 1854; appointed one of the solicitors in the Court of Claims, Washington, D. C., and served from February 8, 1864, to June 25, 1868, when the position was abolished; solicitor in the office of the Sixth Auditor of the Treasury Department from November 6, 1869, until his death in Washington, D. C., January 27, 1878; interment in the family burial ground at "Bellville," near Oxford Neck, Talbot County, Md.

KERR, John Hosea (grandnephew of John Kerr), a Representative from North Carolina; born in Yanceyville, Caswell County, N. C., December 31, 1873; attended the local school and Bingham's Military School of North Carolina; was graduated from Wake Forest (N. C.) College in 1895; studied law; was admitted to the bar in 1895 and commenced practice in Warren-

ton, N. C.; mayor of Warrenton, N. C., in 1897 and 1898; solicitor for the third district of North Carolina 1906–1916; judge of the superior court 1916–1923; trustee of the University of North Carolina; delegate to the Democratic National Conventions in 1932 and 1940; chairman, United States delegation to the Inter-American Travel Congress in Mexico City in 1941; elected as a Democrat to the Sixty-eighth Congress to fill the vacancy caused by the death of Claude Kitchin; reelected to the Sixty-ninth and to the thirteen succeeding Congresses and served from November 6, 1923, to January 3, 1953; unsuccessful candidate for renomination in 1952; retired from political activities; died in Warrenton, N. C., June 21, 1958; interment in Fairview Cemetery.

KERR, John Leeds (father of John Bozman Kerr), a Representative and a Senator from Maryland; born at Greenbury Point, near Annapolis, Md., January 15, 1780; was graduated from St. John's College, Annapolis, Md., in 1799; studied law; was admitted to the bar at Annapolis in 1801 and commenced practice in Easton; deputy State's attorney for Talbot County 1806–1810; commanded a company of militia in the War of 1812; member of the electoral college which elected the State senate in 1816; appointed agent of the State of Maryland in 1817 to prosecute claims against the Federal Government growing out of the War of 1812; elected as a Whig to the Nineteenth and Twentieth Congresses (March 4, 1825–March 3, 1829); unsuccessful candidate for reelection in 1828 to the Twenty-first Congress; elected to the Twenty-second Congress (March 4, 1831–March 3, 1833); presidential elector on the Whig ticket of Harrison and Tyler in 1840; elected to the United States Senate to fill the vacancy caused by the death of John S. Spence and served from January 5, 1841, to March 3, 1843; died in Easton, Talbot County, Md., February 21, 1844; interment in the Bozman family cemetery at "Bellville," near Oxford Neck, Md.

KERR, Joseph, a Senator from Ohio; born in Kerrtown (now Chambersburg), Franklin County, Pa., in 1765; was privately tutored; moved to Ohio in 1792; employed by contractors furnishing supplies to troops in the Ohio Valley; held first in-lot and out-lot in Chillicothe in 1796; surveyor; justice of the peace at Manchester, Adams County, in 1797; appointed as a judge of the first quarter session court of Adams County, Northwest Territory, in 1797; surveyor and land agent during the opening of the western country; elected clerk of the board of commissioners of Adams County; moved to Chillicothe in 1801, where he owned and farmed an extensive tract of land on the Scioto River, which he lost after eighteen years of litigation to a Virginian, John Watts, who had bought a prior claim; deputy surveyor of the Virginia military lands in Ohio; became a leading industrialist, shipping produce by a fleet of keelboats, flatboats, and schooners to New Orleans for export; elected to the Ohio Senate from Ross County in 1804 and again in 1810, and to the Ohio House of Representatives in 1808, 1816, 1818, and 1819; appointed by President Jefferson on April 14, 1806, as one of the commissioners to survey the road from Cumberland, Md., to the Ohio River; adjutant general of Ohio in 1809 and 1810; appointed by General Harrison as a brigadier general of Ohio Volunteers during the War of 1812; operated a hotel, slaughter house, salting establishment, cooperage, boat building works, and general merchandise business; supplied provisions to the Army of the Northwest during the War of 1812; elected as a Democrat to the United States Senate to fill the vacancy caused by the resignation of Thomas Worthington and served from December 10, 1814, to March 3, 1815; was not a candidate for reelection; returned to Chillicothe, Ohio, and was proprietor of an inn 1815–1826; lost his extensive farm and was forced into bankruptcy; in 1826 moved to Tennessee, where he engaged in agricultural pursuits near Memphis until 1828, when he moved to Louisiana and purchased a homestead near Lake Providence, Carroll (now East Carroll) Parish; also purchased a plantation near Bunches Bend, La., and was engaged as a planter until his death at his homestead near Providence, August 22, 1837; interment in the family burying ground on the homestead located near the Mississippi River, whose changed course has destroyed the graves and the homestead.

KERR, Josiah Leeds, a Representative from Maryland; born in Vienna, Dorchester County, Md., January 10, 1861; attended the public schools in Vienna and Vienna Academy; taught school in Kennebec County; moved to Crisfield, Md., in 1880 and entered the employ of a lumber company as clerk; moved to Cambridge, Md., in 1885; elected school examiner in August 1898 and served two years; elected as a Republican to the Fifty-sixth Congress to fill the vacancy caused by the resignation of John Walter Smith and served from November 6, 1900, to March 3, 1901; was not a candidate for renomination in 1900; returned to Cambridge, Md., and became a traveling salesman; died in Cambridge, Md., September 27, 1920; interment in Christ Episcopal Church Cemetery.

KERR, Michael Crawford, a Representative from Indiana; born in Titusville, Crawford County, Pa., March 15, 1827; attended the common schools and Erie Academy; was graduated from the law department of Louisville (Ky.) University in 1851; was admitted to the bar and commenced practice in New Albany, Ind., in 1852; city attorney in 1854; prosecuting attorney of Floyd County in 1855; member of the State house of representatives in 1856 and 1857; reporter of the supreme court of Indiana 1862–1865; elected as a Democrat to the Thirty-ninth and to the three succeeding Congresses (March 4, 1865–March 3, 1873); unsuccessful candidate for reelection in 1872 to the Forty-third Congress; elected to the Forty-fourth Congress and served from March 4, 1875, until his death; elected Speaker of the House for the Forty-fourth Congress on December 6, 1875, and served until his death; died at Rockbridge Alum Springs, Rockbridge County, Va., on August 19, 1876; interment in Fairview Cemetery, New Albany, Ind.

KERR, Robert Samuel, a Senator from Oklahoma; born in Ada (Indian Territory), Okla., September 11, 1896; student at East Central Normal School, Ada, Okla., Oklahoma Baptist University at Shawnee in 1911 and 1912, and Oklahoma University at Norman in 1915 and 1916; during the First World War served as a second lieutenant with the First Field Artillery, United States Army, 1917–1919, with nine months of overseas duty; captain and later major in Oklahoma National Guard 1921–1929; was admitted to the Oklahoma bar in 1922 and commenced the practice of law in Ada, Okla.; drilling contractor and oil producer since 1926; chairman of the board of Kerr-McGee Oil Industries, Inc.; special justice, Oklahoma Supreme Court, in 1931; president, Oklahoma County Juvenile Council in 1935 and 1936; member, Unofficial Pardon and Parole Board 1935–1938; Governor of Oklahoma from January 1943 to January 1947; chairman, Southern Governors Conference in 1945 and 1946; Democratic national committeeman 1940–1948; delegate to the Democratic National Conventions 1940–1960; elected as a Democrat to the United States Senate in 1948 and again in 1954 and served from January 3, 1949, to January 3, 1961. *Reelected in 1960 for the term ending January 3, 1967.*

KERR, Winfield Scott, a Representative from Ohio; born in Monroe, Richland County, Ohio, June 23, 1852; attended the common schools of his native city; was graduated from the law department of the University of Michigan at Ann Arbor in 1879; was admitted to the bar the same year and commenced practice in Mansfield, Ohio; member of the State senate 1888–1892; elected as a Republican to the Fifty-fourth, Fifty-fifth, and Fifty-sixth Congresses (March 4, 1895–March 3, 1901); unsuccessful candidate for renomination in 1900; resumed the practice of his profession in Mansfield, Richland County, Ohio, and died there September 11, 1917; interment in Mansfield Cemetery.

KERRIGAN, James, a Representative from New York; born in New York City December 25, 1828; completed preparatory studies and attended Fordham College; served in Company D, First Regiment, New York Volunteer Infantry, during the Mexican War, after which he accompanied the Walker filibustering expedition to Nicaragua as a captain and served for a brief period as alcalde of the Nicaraguan capital; returned to New York City and was elected alderman of the sixth ward; also served as clerk of the Tombs police court; upon the outbreak of the Civil War organized and was commissioned colonel of the Twenty-fifth Regiment, New York Volunteer Infantry, in the Union Army and served from May 19, 1861, until February 21, 1862; elected as a Democrat to the Thirty-seventh Congress (March 4, 1861–March 3, 1863); became an enthusiastic Irish Nationalist and when the invasion of Canada was planned in 1866 led a company across the border; in 1867 commanded the vessel *Erin's Hope,* which landed arms and ammunition on the Irish coast; accompanied an expedition to Alaska in 1899; returned in bad health and died in Brooklyn, N. Y., on November 1, 1899; interment in St. Raymond's Cemetery.

KERSHAW, John, a Representative from South Carolina; born in Camden, Kershaw County, S. C., September 12, 1765; attended Rushworth School and Oxford College, England; studied law; was admitted to the bar and commenced practice in Camden, S. C.; engaged in planting and wheat milling; tobacco inspector in 1789; member of the constitutional convention in 1790; judge of the county court of Kershaw when first established in 1791; member of the State house of representatives in 1792 and 1800; mayor of Camden in 1798, 1801, 1811, and 1822; justice of quorum from Kershaw County in 1806; captain of the First South Carolina Light Dragoons; acted as escort, with a troop of Light Horse, to President Washington on his visit to Camden in 1791; elected as a Democrat to the Thirteenth Congress (March 4, 1813–March 3, 1815); unsuccessful candidate for reelection in 1814 to the Fourteenth Congress; engaged in the settling of his father's estates and planting; died in Camden, S. C., August 4, 1829; interment in the Kershaw family burial ground.

KERSTEN, Charles J., a Representative from Wisconsin; born in Chicago, Ill., May 26, 1902; was graduated from Marquette University College of Law, Milwaukee, Wis., in 1925 and was admitted to the bar the same year; traveled and studied in Europe and the Near East in 1925 and 1926; commenced the practice of law in Milwaukee, Wis., in 1928; first assistant district attorney of Milwaukee County 1937–1943; elected as a Republican to the Eightieth Congress (January 3, 1947–January 3, 1949); unsuccessful candidate for reelection in 1948 to the Eighty-first Congress; elected to the Eighty-second and Eighty-third Congresses (January 3, 1951–January 3, 1955); unsuccessful candidate for reelection in 1954 to the Eighty-fourth Congress; resumed the practice of law; is a resident of Milwaukee, Wis.

KETCHAM, John Clark, a Representative from Michigan; born in Toledo, Ohio, January 1, 1873; moved with his parents to Maple Grove, near Nashville, Mich., the same year; attended the common schools of Barry County and high school at Nashville; was graduated from Hastings High School in 1892; taught in rural and high schools from 1890 to 1899; county commissioner of schools for Barry County 1899–1907; chairman of the Republican county committee 1902–1908; postmaster of Hastings 1907–1914; master of the Michigan State Grange 1912–1920; lecturer of the National Grange 1917–1921; elected as a Republican to the Sixty-seventh and to the five succeeding Congresses (March 4, 1921–March 3, 1933); unsuccessful candidate for reelection in 1932 to the Seventy-third Congress; president of the National Bank of Hastings 1933–1937; State commissioner of insurance 1935–1937; counsel for the Michigan Chain Store Bureau 1938–1941; died in Hastings, Mich., December 4, 1941; interment in Riverside Cemetery.

KETCHAM, John Henry, a Representative from New York; born in Dover Plains, Dutchess County, N. Y., December 21, 1832; pursued an academic course and was graduated from Suffield Academy at Suffield, Conn.; became interested in agricultural pursuits; supervisor in 1854 and 1855; member of the State assembly in 1856 and 1857; State senator in 1860 and 1861; during the Civil War entered the Union Army as colonel of the One Hundred and Fiftieth Regiment, New York Volunteer Infantry, October 11, 1862; brevetted brigadier general December 6, 1864; brigadier general April 1, 1865; brevetted major general of Volunteers March 13, 1865, "for gallant and meritorious services during the war"; resigned December 2, 1865; elected as a Republican to the Thirty-ninth and to the three succeeding Congresses (March 4, 1865–March 3, 1873); unsuccessful candidate for reelection in 1872 to the Forty-third Congress; delegate to several Republican State conventions; delegate to the Republican National Convention at Cincinnati in 1876 and at St. Louis in 1896; Commissioner of the District of Columbia from July 3, 1874, until June 30, 1877, when he resigned; elected as a Republican to the Forty-fifth and to the seven succeeding Congresses (March 4, 1877–March 3, 1893); declined to be a candidate for renomination; elected as a Republican to the Fifty-fifth and to the four succeeding Congresses and served from March 4, 1897, until his death in New York City November 4, 1906; interment in Valley View Cemetery, Dover Plains, N. Y.

KETCHUM, Winthrop Welles, a Representative from Pennsylvania; born in Wilkes-Barre, Pa., on June 29, 1820; pursued classical studies; instructor in Wyoming Seminary, Kingston, Pa., 1844–1847 and in Girard College, Pennsylvania, in 1848 and 1849; studied law; was admitted to the bar January 8, 1850, and practiced; prothonotary of Luzerne County 1855–1857; member of the State house of representatives in 1858; served in the State senate 1859–1861; delegate to the Republican National Conventions in 1860 and 1864; unsuccessful candidate for election in 1864 to the Thirty-ninth Congress; solicitor of the United States Court of Claims 1864–1866; presidential elector on the Republican ticket of Grant and Colfax in 1868; elected as a Republican to the Forty-fourth Congress and served from March 4, 1875, until July 19, 1876, when he resigned; judge of the United States Court for the Western District of Pennsylvania and served until his death in Pittsburgh, Pa., December 6, 1879; interment in Hollenback Cemetery, Wilkes-Barre, Pa.

KETTNER, William, a Representative from California; born in Ann Arbor, Mich., November 20, 1864; moved with his parents to Minnesota in 1873 and settled in St. Paul; attended the public schools; moved to California in 1884 and lived for several years at Julian, Santa Ana, and Visalia, where he engaged in mining, the hotel business, newspaper work, and the insurance business; member of the California National Guard in 1888; city councilman of Visalia, Calif., in 1900; moved to San Diego, Calif., in 1907 and engaged in insurance work, real-estate business, and banking; elected as a Democrat to the Sixty-third and to the three succeeding Congresses (March 4, 1913–March 3, 1921); was not a candidate for reelection in 1920 to the Sixty-seventh Congress; delegate to the Democratic National Conventions in 1916 and 1924; resumed the real estate and insurance businesses; died in San Diego, Calif., November 11, 1930; interment in Greenwood Memorial Park Cemetery.

KEY, David McKendree, a Senator from Tennessee; born near Greeneville, Greene County, Tenn., January 27, 1824; attended the common schools; was graduated from Hiawassee College in 1850; studied law; was admitted to the bar at Madisonville, Monroe County, Tenn., in 1850 and commenced practice in Kingston; moved to Chattanooga in 1853; presidential elector on the Democratic ticket of Buchanan and Breckinridge in 1856 and on the Breckinridge and Lane ticket in 1860; during the Civil War enlisted in the Confederate Army and was promoted to lieutenant colonel of the Forty-third Tennessee Infantry; member of the State constitutional convention in 1870; chancellor of the third chancery division 1870–1875; unsuccessful Democratic candidate for election to the Forty-third Congress; appointed as a Democrat to the United States Senate to fill the vacancy caused by the death of Andrew Johnson and served from August 18, 1875, to January 19, 1877; unsuccessful candidate for election to fill the vacancy in 1876; Postmaster General in the Cabinet of President Hayes from March 12, 1877, to June 1, 1880, when he resigned; appointed by President Hayes United States judge for the eastern and middle districts of Tennessee May 19, 1880; retired January 26, 1894; died in Chattanooga, Tenn., February 3, 1900; interment in Forest Hill Cemetery.

KEY, John Alexander, a Representative from Ohio; born in Marion, Marion County, Ohio, December 30, 1871; attended the public schools; learned the printer's trade; city letter carrier 1897–1903; recorder of Marion County 1903–1908; secretary to Representative Carl C. Anderson, of Ohio, 1908–1912; elected as a Democrat to the Sixty-third, Sixty-fourth, and Sixty-fifth Congresses (March 4, 1913–March 3, 1919); unsuccessful candidate for reelection in 1918 to the Sixty-sixth Congress; engaged in the petroleum industry; inspector of Federal prisons from 1934 until his retirement in 1941; died in Marion, Ohio, March 4, 1954; interment in Marion Cemetery.

KEY, Philip (cousin of Philip Barton Key and great-grandfather of Barnes Compton), a Representative from Maryland; born probably on his father's estate near Leonardtown, St. Marys County, Md. in 1750; pursued an academic course in England; returned to Maryland and engaged in farming; studied law; was admitted to the bar and practiced; served in the Maryland House of Delegates in 1773; member of the committee of correspondence, St. Marys County, in 1774; again a member of the house of delegates 1779–1790; elected to the Second Congress (March 4, 1791–March 3, 1793); member of the State house of delegates in 1795 and 1796 and served as speaker; declined an appointment in the Cabinet of President Monroe and also the office of Governor of Maryland when the latter position was appointive; died in St. Marys County, Md., January 4, 1820; interment probably in the churchyard at Chaptico, Md.

KEY, Philip Barton (cousin of Philip Key), a Representative from Maryland; born near Charlestown, Cecil County, Md., April 12, 1757; pursued an academic course; served in the British Army during the Revolutionary War; taken prisoner in Florida and went to England; released on parole; returned to Maryland in 1785; studied law; was admitted to the bar in 1787 and practiced law in Leonardtown, Md.; moved to Annapolis in 1790; member of the State house of delegates 1794–1799; in the fall of 1806 purchased one thousand acres of land in Montgomery County, located on what is now know as the Brookeville and Washington road, near what is now the village of Norbeck, and became interested in agricultural pursuits; elected as a Federalist to the Tenth, Eleventh, and Twelfth Congresses (March 4, 1807–March 3, 1813); died in Georgetown, D. C., July 28, 1815; interment on his estate "Woodley," in Georgetown, D. C.; reinterment in Oak Hill Cemetery, Washington, D. C.

KEYES, Elias, a Representative from Vermont; born in Ashford, Windham County, Conn., April 14, 1758; attended the common schools; studied law; moved to Stockbridge, Vt., in 1785; served in the State house of representatives 1793–1796, 1798–1802, 1818, 1820, and 1823–1825; member of the Governor's council 1803–1813 and 1815–1817; member of the State constitutional convention in 1814; assistant judge of the Windsor County Court 1803–1814 and judge 1815–1818; elected as a Republican to the Seventeenth Congress (March 4, 1821–March 3, 1823); died in Stockbridge, Vt., July 9, 1844; interment in Maplewood Cemetery.

KEYES, Henry Wilder, a Senator from New Hampshire; born in Newbury, Orange County, Vt., May 23, 1863; attended the public schools, Nichols Latin School, Boston, Mass., Adams Academy, Quincy, Mass., and New Hampshire College and Dartmouth College, Hanover, N. H.; was graduated from Harvard University in 1887; engaged in agricultural pursuits; member of the State house of representatives 1891–1895 and 1915–1917; member of the State senate 1903–1905; treasurer of the State license commission 1903–1915; chairman of the State excise commission 1915–1917; Governor of New Hampshire 1917–1919; president of the Woodsville (N. H.) National Bank; elected as a Republican to the United States Senate in 1918; reelected in 1924 and 1930 and served from March 4, 1919, to January 3, 1937; was not a candidate for renomination in 1936; died in North Haverhill, N. H., on June 19, 1938; interment in Oxbow Cemetery, Newbury, Vt.

KIDDER, David, a Representative from Maine; born in Dresden, Lincoln County, Maine, December 8, 1787; pursued classical studies with private tutors; studied law; was admitted to the bar and commenced practice in Bloomfield; moved to Skowhegan, Maine, in 1817 and thence to Norridgewock in 1821; prosecuting attorney of Somerset County 1811–1823; elected as a Whig to the Eighteenth and Nineteenth Congresses (March 4, 1823–March 3, 1827); was not a candidate for renomination in 1826; returned to Skowhegan in 1827 and resumed the practice of law; member of the State house of representatives in 1829; died in Skowhegan, Maine, November 1, 1860; interment in Bloomfield Cemetery.

KIDDER, Jefferson Parish, a Delegate from the Territory of Dakota; born in Braintree, Orange County, Vt., June 4, 1815; attended the common schools and was graduated from the Norwich Military Academy, Northfield, Vt.; engaged in agricultural pursuits and teaching; studied law at Montpelier; was admitted to the bar in 1839 and practiced at Braintree and West Randolph; member of the State constitutional convention in 1843; State's attorney 1843–1847; member of the State senate in 1847 and 1848; Lieutenant Governor of Vermont in 1853 and 1854; delegate to the Democratic National Convention at Cincinnati in 1856; moved to St. Paul, Minn., in 1857; affiliated with the Republican Party in 1860; member of the house of representatives of Minnesota in 1863 and 1864; moved to Vermillion, Dak., having been appointed by President Lincoln as associate justice of

the supreme court of Dakota Territory February 23, 1865; reappointed by President Grant April 6, 1869; again appointed March 18, 1873, and served until February 24, 1875, when he resigned, having been elected to Congress; elected as a Republican to the Forty-fourth and Forty-fifth Congresses (March 4, 1875–March 3, 1879); unsuccessful candidate for renomination in 1878; appointed justice of the supreme court of Dakota Territory by President Hayes on April 2, 1879; reappointed by President Arthur on April 27, 1883, and served until his death; died in St. Paul, Minn., October 2, 1883; interment in Oakland Cemetery.

KIDWELL, Zedekiah, a Representative from Virginia; born in Fairfax, Fairfax County, Va., January 4, 1814; received a practical English education; studied medicine; moved with his father to Clarksburg, Va. (now West Virginia), in 1834; taught school and also clerked in a store; resumed the study of medicine; was graduated from Jefferson Medical College, Philadelphia, Pa., in 1839, and practiced in Fairfax County, Va., 1839–1849; moved to Fairmont, Va. (now West Virginia); member of the State house of delegates 1842–1845; studied law; was admitted to the bar in 1849; delegate to the State constitutional convention in 1849; again a member of the State house of delegates in 1849, 1850, and 1852; presidential elector on the Democratic ticket of Pierce and King in 1852; elected as a Democrat to the Thirty-third and Thirty-fourth Congresses (March 4, 1853–March 3, 1857); was not a candidate for reelection in 1856; resumed the practice of medicine; member of the West Virginia Board of Public Works 1857–1860; died in Fairmont, W. Va., April 27, 1872; interment in Fairmont Cemetery.

KIEFER, Andrew Robert, a Representative from Minnesota; born at Marienborn, Duchy of Hesse-Darmstadt, near the city of Mainz, on the Rhine, Germany, May 25, 1832; attended school in Mainz; immigrated to the United States in 1849 and settled in St. Paul, Minn., in 1855; inspector and collector of the wharf in 1857; engaged in mercantile pursuits; enrolling clerk of the State house of representatives in 1859 and 1860; during the Civil War entered the Union Army as captain of the Second Regiment, Minnesota Volunteer Infantry, on July 8, 1861, and served until July 18, 1863, when he was compelled to resign on account of ill health; commissioned by Governor Swift colonel of the Thirty-first Regiment of State militia in 1863; member of the State house of representatives in 1864; was engaged in the wholesale mercantile business 1865–1878 and in 1880 became interested in real estate; clerk of the district courts of Ramsey County 1878–1883; unsuccessful Republican candidate for mayor of St. Paul in 1890; elected as a Republican to the Fifty-third and Fifty-fourth Congresses (March 4, 1893–March 3, 1897); was not a candidate for reelection in 1896; mayor of St. Paul, Minn., in 1898; at the time of his death was the Republican candidate for city controller; died in St. Paul, Ramsey County, Minn., May 1, 1904; interment in Oakland Cemetery.

KIEFNER, Charles Edward, a Representative from Missouri; born in Perryville, Perry County, Mo., November 25, 1869; attended the public schools; engaged in the retail lumber business and also in road construction; mayor of Perryville 1900–1902; member of the State house of representatives 1902–1908; delegate to the Republican National Convention at Chicago in 1912, which nominated William H. Taft for the Presidency; president of the Southeast Missouri Lumbermen's Association 1918–1927; served on the staff of Gov. Arthur M. Hyde 1920–1924; elected as a Republican to the Sixty-ninth Congress (March 4, 1925–March 3, 1927); unsuccessful candidate for reelection in 1926 to the Seventieth Congress; elected to the Seventy-first Congress (March 4, 1929–March 3, 1931); unsuccessful candidate for reelection in 1930 to the Seventy-second Congress; resumed the lumber and banking business in Perryville, Mo., until his death on December 13, 1942; interment in Home Cemetery.

KIESS, Edgar Raymond, a Representative from Pennsylvania; born in Warrensville, Lycoming County, Pa., August 26, 1875; attended the public schools; was graduated from Lycoming County Normal School, Muncy, Pa., in 1892; taught in the public schools of Lycoming County for two years; engaged in the newspaper publishing business in Hughesville in 1894; became interested in the development of Eagles Mere, Sullivan County, Pa., as a summer resort in 1898; member of the State house of representatives 1904–1910; engaged in business in Williamsport in 1910; served as a trustee of Pennsylvania State College 1912–1930; appointed by Gov. M. G. Brumbaugh as a member of the Public Service Commission of Pennsylvania in 1915 but declined the appointment; elected as a Republican to the Sixty-third and to the eight succeeding Congresses and served from March 4, 1913, until his death at his summer home at Eagles Mere, Pa., July 20, 1930; interment Wildwood Cemetery, Williamsport, Pa.

KILBOURNE, James, a Representative from Ohio; born in New Britain, Conn., October 19, 1770; pursued classical studies; studied theology and entered the Episcopal ministry; one of the founders of the Scioto company to trade in Ohio and the Northwest in 1801; founded Worthington, Ohio, in 1803; appointed United States surveyor of public lands in 1805 and laid out the present city of Sandusky; appointed by President Madison a member of the commission to ascertain the western boundary of the Virginia military reservation between the Little Miami and Scioto Rivers July 1, 1812; president of Worthington College; colonel of a frontier regiment during the War of 1812; elected as a Democrat to the Thirteenth and Fourteenth Congresses (March 4, 1813–March 3, 1817); member of the State house of representatives in 1823, 1824, 1838, and 1839; president of the convention of 1839 to lay the cornerstone of the State capitol in Columbus and of the Whig State convention in 1840; died in Worthington, Ohio, April 9, 1850; interment in St. John's Episcopal Church Burying Ground.

KILBURN, Clarence Evans, a Representative from New York; born in Malone, Franklin County, N. Y., April 13, 1893; attended the public schools and was graduated from Cornell University, Ithaca, N. Y., in 1916; during the First World War served as a captain in the Twenty-sixth Infantry, First Division, in 1917 and 1918; engaged in banking; president of the People's Trust Co. of Malone since 1930; elected as a Republican to the Seventy-sixth Congress to fill the vacancy caused by the death of Wallace E. Pierce; reelected to the Seventy-seventh and to the nine succeeding Congresses and served from February 13, 1940, to January 3, 1961. *Reelected to the Eighty-seventh Congress.*

KILDAY, Paul Joseph, a Representative from Texas; born in Sabinal, Uvalde County, Tex., March 29, 1900; moved with his parents to San Antonio, Tex., in 1904; attended the public and parochial schools and St. Mary's College, San Antonio, Tex.; employed as a clerk, United States Air Force, Washington, D. C., 1918–1921 and as a law clerk, United States Shipping Board Emergency Fleet Corporation, in 1921 and 1922; was graduated from the law department of Georgetown University, Washington, D. C., in 1922; was admitted to the bar the same year and commenced practice in San Antonio, Tex.; served as first assistant district attorney of Bexar County, Tex., 1935–1938; elected as a Democrat to the Seventy-sixth and to the eleven succeeding Congresses and served from January 3, 1939, until his resignation September 24, 1961, having been appointed a judge of the Court of Military Appeals for a term of fifteen years expiring May 1, 1976; is a resident of San Antonio, Tex.

KILGORE, Constantine Buckley, a Representative from Texas; born in Newnan, Coweta County, Ga., February 20, 1835; moved with his parents to Rusk County, Tex., in 1846; received a common-school and academic training; studied law; during the Civil War entered the Confederate Army as a private and by 1862 had attained the rank of adjutant general of Ector's brigade, Army of the Tennessee; wounded at Chickamauga; captured and confined as a prisoner in Fort Delaware during 1864; was admitted to the bar and practiced in Rusk County, Tex.; elected justice of the peace in 1869; member of the State constitutional convention in 1875; presidential elector on the Democratic ticket of Hancock and English in 1880; elected to the State senate in 1884 for a term of four years; was chosen president of that body in 1885 for two years; resigned from the State senate in 1886, having been elected to Congress; elected as a Democrat to the Fiftieth and to the three succeeding Congresses (March 4, 1887–March 3, 1895); appointed by President Cleveland United States judge for the southern district of Indian Territory March 20, 1895, and served until his death in Ardmore, Indian Territory (now Oklahoma), September 23, 1897; interment in White Rose Cemetery, Wills Point, Tex.

KILGORE, Daniel, a Representative from Ohio; born at Kings Creek, Va. (now West Virginia), in 1793; received a liberal schooling; moved to Cadiz, Ohio; member of the State senate 1828–1832; elected as a Democrat to the Twenty-third Congress to fill the vacancy caused by the resignation of Humphrey H. Leavitt; reelected to the Twenty-fourth and Twenty-fifth Congresses and served from December 1, 1834, until July 4, 1838, when he resigned; died in New York City December 12, 1851.

KILGORE, David, a Representative from Indiana; born in Harrison County, Ky., April 3, 1804; moved with his father to Franklin County, Ind., in 1819; attended the common schools; studied law; was admitted to the bar in 1830 and commenced practice in Yorktown, Ind.; member of the State house of representatives 1833–1836, 1838, 1839, and 1855, and served as speaker in 1855; president judge of the Yorktown circuit 1839–1846; delegate to the State constitutional convention in 1850; elected as a Republican to the Thirty-fifth and Thirty-sixth Congresses (March 4, 1857–March 3, 1861); delegate to the Union National Convention which met in Philadelphia August 14, 1866; died near Yorktown, Delaware County, Ind., January 22, 1879; interment in Mount Pleasant Cemetery, near Yorktown, Ind.

KILGORE, Harley Martin, a Senator from West Virginia; born in Brown, Harrison County, W. Va., January 11, 1893; attended the public schools; graduated from the law department of West Virginia University at Morgantown in 1914 and was admitted to the bar the same year; taught school in Hancock, W. Va., in 1914 and 1915; organized the first high school in Raleigh County, W. Va., in 1915, serving as its principal for one year; commenced the practice of law in Beckley, W. Va., in 1916; during the First World War served in the Infantry of the United States Army from May 15, 1917, until discharged as a captain on March 13, 1920; joined the West Virginia National Guard in 1921 and retired as a colonel in 1953; served as judge of the criminal court of Raleigh County, W. Va., from January 1, 1933, until elected to the United States Senate; delegate to the Democratic National Conventions in 1944, 1948, and 1952; elected as a Democrat to the United States Senate in 1940; reelected in 1946 and again in 1952, and served from January 3, 1941, until his death in the naval hospital at Bethesda, Md., February 28, 1956; interment in Arlington National Cemetery, Fort Myer, Va.

KILGORE, Joe Madison, a Representative from Texas; born in Brown County, near Brownwood, Tex., December 10, 1918; attended the public schools of Rising Star, Tex.; moved with his family to Mission, Hidalgo County, Tex., in 1929; attended the public schools and graduated from high school in Mission, Tex.; attended Westmoreland College (now Trinity University), San Antonio, Tex., in 1935 and 1936; graduated from the law school of the University of Texas at Austin in 1945 after interrupting education to enlist in the United States Air Force in July 1941 and served as a combat pilot in the Mediterranean Theater of Operations; participated in raids on Tobruck, Bengazi, Greece, and Crete in support of the British Eighth Army; commanded the second American air raid on Naples, Italy, in December 1942; separated from the service as a lieutenant colonel in 1946; awarded the Silver Star, Distinguished Flying Cross, Air Medal with two Oak Leaf Clusters, two unit citations, and four personal citations; was admitted to the bar in 1946 and commenced the practice of law in Edinburg, Tex.; member of the State house of representatives 1947–1954; delegate to the Democratic National Convention in 1956; elected as a Democrat to the Eighty-fourth, Eighty-fifth, and Eighty-sixth Congresses (January 3, 1955–January 3, 1961). *Reelected to the Eighty-seventh Congress.*

KILLE, Joseph, a Representative from New Jersey; born near Bridgeport, Gloucester County, N. J., April 12, 1790; pursued academic studies; located in Salem; sheriff of Salem County 1822–1829; clerk of Salem County 1829–1839; member of the State house of assembly in 1856; elected as a Democrat to the Twenty-sixth Congress (March 4, 1839–March 3, 1841); died in Salem, N. J., March 1, 1865; interment in St. John's Episcopal Cemetery.

KILLINGER, John Weinland, a Representative from Pennsylvania; born in Annville, Lebanon County, Pa., September 18, 1824; attended the public schools of Annville and the Lebanon Academy, Lebanon, Pa.; was graduated from the Mercersburg Preparatory School, Mercersburg, Pa., and from the Franklin and Marshall College, Lancaster, Pa., in 1843; studied law in Lancaster; was admitted to the bar in 1846 and practiced in Lebanon County 1846–1886; prosecuting attorney for Lebanon County in 1848 and 1849; member of the State house of representatives in 1850 and 1851; served in the State senate 1854–1857; delegate to the Republican National Convention at Philadelphia in 1856; elected as a Republican to the Thirty-sixth and Thirty-seventh Congresses (March 4, 1859–March 3, 1863); was not a candidate for renomination in 1862; assessor of internal revenue 1864–1866; elected to the Forty-second and Forty-third Congresses (March 4, 1871–March 3, 1875); was not a candidate for renomination in 1874; resumed the practice of law; again elected to the Forty-fifth and Forty-sixth Congresses (March 4, 1877–March 3, 1881); was not a candidate for renomination in 1880; solicitor for the Philadelphia & Reading Railroad Co.; died in Lebanon, Pa., June 30, 1896; interment in Mount Lebanon Cemetery.

KIMBALL, Alanson Mellen, a Representative from Wisconsin; born in Buxton, York County, Maine, March 12, 1827; pursued academic studies; moved to Wisconsin in 1852 and engaged in agricultural and mercantile pursuits; served in the State senate in 1863 and 1864; elected as a Republican to the Forty-fourth Congress (March 4, 1875–March 3, 1877); was an unsuccessful candidate for election in 1876 to the Forty-fifth Congress; engaged in the lumbering business; delegate to the Republican National Convention at Chicago in 1884; died in Pine River, Waushara County, Wis., May 26, 1913; interment in Pine River Cemetery.

KIMBALL, Henry Mahlon, a Representative from Michigan; born in Orland, Steuben County, Ind., August 27, 1878; attended the common and high schools of Orland; was graduated from Hillsdale (Mich.) College; served as principal of Orland High School; attended the literary and law departments of the University of Michigan at Ann Arbor, graduating in law in 1904; commenced practice in Orland, Ind.; moved to Rosebud, Nev., in 1907 and continued the practice of law; employed as a traveling auditor in 1908 for a firm in San Francisco, Calif.; moved to Portland, Oreg., in 1909 and to Kalamazoo, Mich., in 1917, where he continued the practice of law; served as president of the Kalamazoo Bar Association in 1928 and 1929; elected as a Republican to the Seventy-fourth Congress and served from January 3, 1935, until his death in Kalamazoo, Mich., October 19, 1935; remains were cremated in White Chapel Memorial Park, Detroit, Mich., and the ashes buried in Green Lawn Cemetery, Orland, Ind.

KIMBALL, William Preston, a Representative from Kentucky; born near East Hickman, Fayette County, Ky., November 4, 1857; attended the public schools of Fayette County, the private schools of Professors Lyle and Nesbit, and the University of Kentucky (now Transylvania University) in Lexington; member of the State house of representatives in 1883 and 1884; city clerk in 1889 and 1890; studied law; was admitted to the bar in 1891 and commenced practice in Lexington; city attorney of Lexington from October 1891 to January 1, 1901; prosecuting attorney of Fayette County from January 1, 1901, to March 4, 1907, when he resigned, having been elected to Congress; elected as a Democrat to the Sixtieth Congress (March 4, 1907–March 3, 1909); unsuccessful candidate for renomination in 1908; resumed the practice of law in Lexington; died in Lexington, Ky., February 24, 1926; interment in Lexington Cemetery.

KIMMEL, William, a Representative from Maryland; born in Baltimore, Md., August 15, 1812; attended St. Mary's and Baltimore Colleges; studied law; was admitted to the bar and commenced practice in Baltimore, Md.; interested in agricultural and business pursuits; State director of the Baltimore & Ohio Railroad Co.; director in the Union Railroad Co. and in the Western Maryland extension; member of the State Democratic committee 1862–1866; delegate to the Democratic National Convention at Chicago in 1864; unsuccessful candidate for election in 1864 to the Thirty-ninth Congress; member of the State senate 1866–1871; a director of the Canton Co. of Baltimore 1869–1873; solicitor and land agent of the company in 1871 and 1872; elected as a Democrat to the Forty-fifth and Forty-sixth Congresses (March 4, 1877–March 3, 1881); resumed the practice of his profession in Baltimore, Md., and died there December 28, 1886; interment in Loudon Park Cemetery.

KINCAID, John, a Representative from Kentucky; born near Danville, Mercer County, Ky., February 15, 1791; attended the public schools; studied law; was admitted to the bar and commenced practice in Stanford, Ky.; Commonwealth attorney; member of the State house of representatives in 1819; elected as a Democrat to the Twenty-first Congress (March 4, 1829–March 3, 1831); again a member of the State house of representatives in 1836 and 1837; circuit judge in 1836 and 1837; presidential elector on the Democratic ticket of Polk and Dallas in 1844; resumed the practice of law and also engaged in agricultural pursuits; moved to Gallatin, Tenn., in 1870 and died there on February 7, 1873; interment in Bellview Cemetery, Danville, Ky.

KINCHELOE, David Hayes, a Representative from Kentucky; born near Sacramento, McLean County, Ky., April 9, 1877; attended the public schools, and was graduated from Bowling Green College, Kentucky, in 1898; studied law; was admitted to the bar in 1899 and commenced practice in Calhoun, Ky.; prosecuting attorney of McLean County 1902–1906; moved to Madisonville in 1906 and continued the practice of law; presidential elector on the Democratic ticket of Wilson and Marshall in 1912; elected as a Democrat to the Sixty-fourth and to the seven succeeding Congresses and served from March 4, 1915, until his resignation on October 5, 1930, having been appointed judge of the United States Customs Court, in which capacity he served until April 30, 1948, when he retired; died in Washington, D. C., April 16, 1950; interment in Odd Fellows Cemetery, Madisonville, Ky.

KINDEL, George John, a Representative from Colorado; born in Cincinnati, Ohio, March 2, 1855; attended the public schools and St. Augustine's School in Cincinnati; apprenticed as an upholsterer and mattress maker in 1871; moved to Denver, Colo., in 1877 and engaged in the upholstery and mattress business and later in the bedding and furniture business; member of the board of supervisors of the city and county of Denver 1910–1914; author of "Kindel's A B C on Freight Rates"; elected as a Democrat to the Sixty-third Congress (March 4, 1913–March 3, 1915); did not seek renomination in 1914, having become a candidate for the nomination of Senator; unsuccessful Independent candidate for election to the United States Senate in 1914; resumed his former business pursuits; also wrote newspaper squibs on freight rates, in Denver, Colo.; was in an automobile accident near Hillrose, Colo., which resulted in his death; died in a hospital in Brush, Colo., on February 28, 1930; interment in Fairmount Cemetery, Denver, Colo.

KINDRED, John Joseph, a Representative from New York; born near Courtland, Southampton County, Va., July 15, 1864; attended the local schools, Randolph-Macon College, Ashland, Va., and the University of Virginia at Charlottesville; taught school in Virginia in 1886 and 1887; was graduated from the Hospital College of Medicine, Louisville, Ky., in 1889 and commenced the practice of his profession in New York City, N. Y., the same year; was graduated in mental diseases from the University of Edinburgh, Scotland, in 1892; served as extra assistant physician in the Royal Asylum, Morningside, Edinburgh, Scotland, in 1892; established a mental-disease hospital in Stamford, Conn., in 1893; also established the River Crest Sanitarium for Mental Diseases at Astoria, Borough of Queens, New York City, N. Y., in 1896 and the Farm Colony Sanitarium, Bellemead, N. J., in 1909, of which he was the proprietor; was graduated in law in 1919 and admitted to the bar in 1926; elected as a Democrat to the Sixty-second Congress (March 4, 1911–March 3, 1913); was not a candidate for renomination in 1912; became interested in agricultural pursuits and in the construction of houses; elected to the Sixty-seventh and to the three succeeding Congresses (March 4, 1921–March 3, 1929); was not a candidate for renomination in 1928; resumed his medical profession as a physician-alienist in New York City 1930–1937 and also served as professor of medical jurisprudence at John B. Stetson University, De Land, Fla., during the years 1933 to 1937; died October 23, 1937, at Astoria, N. Y.; interment in Poughkeepsie Rural Cemetery, Poughkeepsie, N. Y.

KING, Adam, a Representative from Pennsylvania; born in York, Pa., in 1790; pursued academic studies; studied medicine in the University of Pennsylvania at Philadelphia and commenced practice in York; edited and published the York Gazette 1818–1835; clerk of the courts of York County 1818–1826; elected as a Democrat to the Twentieth, Twenty-first, and Twenty-second Congresses (March 4, 1827–March 3, 1833); unsuccessful candidate for reelection in 1832 to the Twenty-third Congress; resumed the practice of medicine; died in York, York County, Pa., May 6, 1835; interment in Prospect Hill Cemetery.

KING, Andrew, a Representative from Missouri; born in Greenbrier County, Va. (now West Virginia), March 20, 1812; attended the common schools; studied law; was admitted to the bar and commenced practice in St. Charles, Mo.; member of the State senate in 1846; served in the State house of delegates in 1858; judge of the circuit court for the nineteenth judicial district of Missouri 1859–1864; elected as a Democrat to the Forty-second Congress (March 4, 1871–March 3, 1873); was not a candidate for renomination in 1872; resumed the practice of law; died in Jefferson City, Mo., November 18, 1895; interment in Oak Grove Cemetery, St. Charles, Mo.

KING, Austin Augustus, a Representative from Missouri; born in Sullivan County, Tenn., September 21, 1802; attended the public schools; studied law; was admitted to the bar in 1822 and commenced practice in Jackson, Tenn.; moved to Columbia, Mo., in 1830 and continued the practice of law; served as a colonel in the Black Hawk War; member of the State house of representatives in 1834 and 1836; moved to Richmond, Mo., in 1837, having been appointed circuit judge of the fifth circuit, and served until 1848; Governor of Missouri 1848–1853; resumed the practice of law in Richmond, Mo.; delegate to the Democratic National Conventions at Charleston and at Baltimore in 1860; again circuit judge from 1862 until 1863, when he resigned; elected as a Union Democrat to the Thirty-eighth Congress (March 4, 1863–March 3, 1865); unsuccessful candidate for reelection in 1864 to the Thirty-ninth Congress; resumed the practice of law; died in St. Louis, Mo., April 22, 1870; interment in Richmond Cemetery, Richmond, Ray County, Mo.

KING, Cecil Rhodes, a Representative from California; born in Fort Niagara, N. Y., January 13, 1898; moved to Los Angeles, Calif., in 1908 and attended the public schools; during the First World War served as a private in the United States Army in 1917 and 1918; engaged in business in southern California 1919–1942; member of the California assembly 1932–1942; elected as a Democrat to the Seventy-seventh Congress to fill the vacancy caused by the death of Lee E. Geyer; reelected to the Seventy-eighth and to the eight succeeding Congresses and served from August 25, 1942, to January 3, 1961. *Reelected to the Eighty-seventh Congress.*

KING, Cyrus (half brother of Rufus King), a Representative from Massachusetts; born in Scarboro, Maine (then a district of Massachusetts), on September 6, 1772; attended Phillips Academy, Andover, Mass., and was graduated from Columbia College, New York City, in 1794; studied law; served as private secretary to Rufus King when he was United States Minister to England in 1796; completed law studies in Biddeford, Maine; was admitted to the bar in 1797 and commenced practice in Saco, Maine; served as major general of the Sixth Division, Massachusetts Militia; one of the founders of Thornton Academy, Saco, Maine; elected as a Federalist to the Thirteenth and Fourteenth Congresses (March 4, 1813–March 3, 1817); returned to Saco, York County, Maine, where he died on April 25, 1817; interment in Laurel Hill Cemetery.

KING, Daniel Putnam, a Representative from Massachusetts; born in Danvers, Mass., January 8, 1801; pursued classical studies, and was graduated from Harvard University in 1823; studied law, but did not practice; engaged in agricultural pursuits; member of the State house of representatives in 1836 and 1837; served in the State senate 1838–1841, and was its president in 1840; again a member of the State house of representatives in 1843 and 1844 and served as speaker in the latter year; elected as a Whig to the Twenty-eighth and to the three succeeding Congresses and served from March 4, 1843, until his death in South Danvers, Mass., July 25, 1850; interment in King Cemetery, Peabody, Mass.

KING, David Sjodahl (son of William H. King), a Representative from Utah; born in Salt Lake City, Utah, June 20, 1917; attended the public schools in Washington, D. C.; graduated from the University of Utah at Salt Lake City in 1937; served as a missionary for the Church of Jesus Christ of Latter-day Saints in Great Britain 1937–1939; graduated from Georgetown University School of Law, Washington, D. C., in 1942; was admitted to the bar in 1942; served as law clerk to Justice Harold M. Stephens of the United States Court of Appeals for the District of Columbia in 1943; returned to Salt Lake City, Utah, in 1943; counsel for the Utah State Tax Commission 1944–1946; private practice of law in Salt Lake City since 1945; taught commercial law at Henager Business College 1946–1958; elected as a Democrat to the Eighty-sixth Congress (January 3, 1959–January 3, 1961).   *Reelected to the Eighty-seventh Congress.*

KING, Edward John, a Representative from Illinois; born in Springfield, Mass., July 1, 1867; moved to Illinois with his parents, who settled in Galesburg, Knox County, in 1880; attended the public schools, the Galesburg (Ill.) High School, and Knox College at Galesburg, Ill., studied law; was admitted to the bar in 1893 and commenced practice in Galesburg, Ill.; city attorney in 1893 and 1894; member of the State house of representatives 1907–1914; elected as a Republican to the Sixty-fourth and to the six succeeding Congresses and served from March 4, 1915, until his death; had been reelected to the Seventy-first Congress; died in Washington, D. C., February 17, 1929; interment in Hope Abbey Mausoleum, Hope Cemetery, Galesburg, Ill.

KING, George Gordon, a Representative from Rhode Island; born in Newport, R. I., June 9, 1807; pursued classical studies in Newport and in Phillips Academy, Andover, Mass.; was graduated from Brown University, Providence, R. I., in 1825; attended the Litchfield (Conn.) Law School; was admitted to the bar in 1827 and practiced in Providence and Newport; member and speaker of the State house of representatives in 1845 and 1846; presidential elector on the Whig ticket of Taylor and Fillmore in 1848; elected as a Whig to the Thirty-first and Thirty-second Congresses (March 4, 1849–March 3, 1853); unsuccessful candidate for reelection; died in Newport, R. I., on July 17, 1870; interment in Island Cemetery.

KING, Henry (brother of Thomas Butler King and uncle of John Floyd King), a Representative from Pennsylvania; born in Palmer, Hampden County, Mass., July 6, 1790; pursued classical studies; studied law in New London, Conn., and Wilkes-Barre, Pa.; was admitted to the bar in 1815 and commenced practice in Allentown, Lehigh County, Pa.; member of the State senate 1826–1828 and 1830–1832; elected as a Democrat to the Twenty-second and Twenty-third Congresses (March 4, 1831–March 3, 1835); was not a candidate for renomination in 1834 to the Twenty-fourth Congress; resumed the practice of law; died in Allentown, Pa., July 13, 1861; interment in Union Cemetery.

KING, James Gore (son of Rufus King and brother of John Alsop King), a Representative from New Jersey; born in New York City May 8, 1791; pursued classical studies in England and France; returned to United States; was graduated from Harvard University in 1810; studied law at the Litchfield Law School; served in the War of 1812 as assistant adjutant general of New York Militia; engaged in mercantile pursuits in New York City in 1815 and in banking in Liverpool, England,

in 1818; returned to New York City in 1824 and engaged in banking, with residence in Weehawken, N. J.; president of the Erie Railroad in 1835; member of New York Chamber of Commerce 1817–1853 and its vice president 1841–1845 and president 1845–1848; elected as a Whig to the Thirty-first Congress (March 4, 1849–March 3, 1851); declined to be a candidate for renomination in 1850; resumed the banking business; died at his country place, "Highwood," near Weehawken, N. J., October 3, 1853; interment in the churchyard of Grace Church, Jamaica, N. Y.

KING, John, a Representative from New York; born in what is now Canaan, Columbia County, N. Y., in 1775; attended the common schools; supervisor of the town of Canaan 1806–1808; sheriff of Columbia County, N. Y., 1811–1813 and 1815–1819; supervisor of the town of New Lebanon (formerly a part of the town of Canaan) 1819–1823, 1826, and 1829; member of the State assembly in 1824; elected as a Democrat to the Twenty-second Congress (March 4, 1831–March 3, 1833); died in New Lebanon, Columbia County, N. Y., September 1, 1836; interment in the Cemetery of Evergreens.

KING, John Alsop (son of Rufus King and brother of James Gore King), a Representative from New York; born in New York City January 3, 1788; attended Harrow School, England, and also studied in Paris; returned to New York City; studied law; was admitted to the bar; served in the War of 1812 as lieutenant of Cavalry; engaged in farming near Jamaica, N. Y.; member of the State assembly 1819–1821; served in the State senate from 1823 until his resignation in 1825; appointed secretary of the legation at London in 1825; Chargé d'Affaires June 15 to August 5, 1826; again elected to the State assembly in 1832, 1838, and 1840; delegate to the Whig National Convention at Harrisburg, Pa., in 1839; elected as a Whig to the Thirty-first Congress (March 4, 1849–March 3, 1851); resumed the practice of law; delegate to the Whig National Convention at Baltimore in 1852; Governor of New York in 1857 and 1858; delegate to the first Republican National Convention at Philadelphia in 1856; one of the founders of the Queens County Agricultural Society and served several years as its president; also one of the founders of the New York State Agricultural Society and served as its president; presidential elector on the Republican ticket of Lincoln and Hamlin in 1860; member of the peace convention of 1861 held in Washington, D. C., in an effort to devise means to prevent the impending war; died in Jamaica, Long Island, N. Y., July 7, 1867; interment in Grace Church Cemetery.

KING, John Floyd (son of Thomas Butler King and nephew of Henry King), a Representative from Louisiana; born on St. Simons Island, off the coast of Georgia, April 20, 1842; attended the Russell School, New Haven, Conn., Bartlett's College Hill School, Poughkeepsie, N. Y., the Military Institute of Georgia, and the University of Virginia at Charlottesville; enlisted in the Confederate Army and served in the Army of Virginia throughout the Civil War, attaining the rank of colonel of Artillery; moved to Louisiana and engaged in planting; studied law; was admitted to the bar in 1872 and commenced practice in Vidalia, La.; appointed brigadier general of State troops; elected inspector of levees and president of the board of school directors of his district and also a trustee of the University of the South; elected as a Democrat to the Forty-sixth and to the three succeeding Congresses (March 4, 1879–March 3, 1887); unsuccessful candidate for renomination in 1886; engaged in mining operations, with residence in Washington, D. C.; Assistant Register of the United States Treasury from May 19, 1914, until his death in Washington, D. C., May 8, 1915; interment in Arlington National Cemetery, Fort Myer, Va.

KING, John Pendleton, a Senator from Georgia; born in Glasgow, Barren County, Ky., April 3, 1799; moved in infancy with his parents to Bedford County, Tenn., and thence to Augusta, Ga., in 1815; was graduated from Richmond Academy, Augusta, Ga.; studied law; was admitted to the bar in 1819 and practiced in Augusta; pursued legal studies in Europe 1822–1824; returned and continued the practice of law in Augusta, Ga., until 1829; member of the State constitutional conventions in 1830 and 1833; appointed judge of the court of common pleas in 1831; elected as a Democrat to the United States Senate to fill the vacancy caused by the resignation of George M. Troup; reelected in 1834 and served from November 21, 1833, until November 1, 1837, when he resigned; president of the Georgia Railroad & Banking Co. 1841–1878; member of the State constitutional convention in 1865; died in Summerville, Chattooga County, Ga., March 19, 1888; interment in St. Paul's Churchyard, Augusta, Ga.

KING, Karl Clarence, a Representative from Pennsylvania; born in Plevna, Reno County, Kans., January 26, 1897; attended high school in Bucklin, Kans., Kansas State Teachers College at Emporia, Columbia University, New York City, N. Y., and Wharton School of Business at Philadelphia, Pa.; during the First World War served in the United States Navy; newspaper reporter in Kansas City, New York, and Philadelphia; engaged in farming and the farm supply business at Morrisville, Pa., in 1922; elected as a Republican to the Eighty-second Congress to fill the vacancy caused by the death of Albert C. Vaughn; reelected to the Eighty-third and Eighty-fourth Congresses and served from November 6, 1951, to January 3, 1957; was not a candidate for renomination in 1956; resides on his farm near Morrisville, Pa.

KING, Perkins, a Representative from New York; born in New Marlboro, Mass., January 12, 1784; pursued an academic course; studied law; was admitted to the bar; moved to Greenville, N. Y., in 1802, where he commenced the practice of law; town clerk in 1815; member of the State assembly in 1827; elected as a Democrat to the Twenty-first Congress (March 4, 1829–March 3, 1831); county judge of Greene County 1838–1847; retired from public life and resumed the practice of law; died in Freehold, Greene County, N. Y., November 29, 1875; interment in Snyder Cemetery.

KING, Preston, a Representative and a Senator from New York; born in Ogdensburg, N. Y., October 14, 1806; pursued classical studies, and was graduated from Union College in 1827; studied law; was admitted to the bar and commenced practice in St. Lawrence County, N. Y.; established the St. Lawrence Republican in 1830; postmaster of Ogdensburg 1831–1834; member of the State assembly 1835–1838; elected as a Democrat to the Twenty-eighth and Twenty-ninth Congresses (March 4, 1843–March 3, 1847); elected to the Thirty-first and Thirty-second Congresses (March 4, 1849–March 3, 1853); elected as a Republican to the United States Senate and served from March 4, 1857, to March 3, 1863; resumed the practice of law; delegate to the Republican National Convention at Baltimore in 1864; presidential elector on the Republican ticket of Lincoln and Johnson in 1864; appointed collector of the port of New York August 15, 1865; drowned from a ferryboat in New York Harbor, N. Y., on November 12, 1865; interment in the City Cemetery, Ogdensburg, N. Y.

KING, Rufus (half brother of Cyrus King and father of John Alsop King and James Gore King), a Delegate from Massachusetts and a Senator from New York; born in Scarboro, Maine (then a district of Massachusetts), March 24, 1755; attended Dummer Academy, Byfield, near Newburyport, Mass., and was graduated from Harvard College in 1777; served in the Revolutionary War; became aide to General Sullivan in his expedition to Rhode Island; studied law in Newburyport; was admitted to the bar and commenced practice in 1780; member of the Massachusetts House of Representatives in 1782; Member of the Continental Congress from Massachusetts 1784–1787; delegate to the Federal constitutional convention at Philadelphia in 1787 and to the State convention in 1788 which ratified the same; moved to New York City in 1788; member of the New York Assembly in 1789 and 1790; elected as a Federalist from New York to the United States Senate in 1789; reelected in 1795 and served from July 16, 1789, until May 23, 1796, when he resigned; United States Minister to Great Britain from May 20, 1796, to May 18, 1803; unsuccessful Federalist candidate for Vice President of the United States in 1804; again elected to the United States Senate in 1813; reelected in 1819 and served from March 4, 1813, to March 3, 1825; unsuccessful Federalist candidate for Governor of New York in 1815 and for President of the United States in 1816; again United States Minister to Great Britain from May 5, 1825, to June 16, 1826; died in Jamaica, Long Island, N. Y., April 29, 1827; interment in the churchyard of Grace Church.

KING, Rufus H., a Representative from New York; born in Rensselaerville, Albany County, N. Y., January 20, 1820; completed preparatory studies and was graduated from Wesleyan University, Lima, N. Y.; studied law; was admitted to the bar in 1843 and commenced practice in Catskill, N. Y.; elected as a Whig to the Thirty-fourth Congress (March 4, 1855–March 3, 1857); was not a candidate for renomination in 1856; resumed the practice of law; president of the Catskill National Bank 1865–1867; on the consolidation of that bank with the Tanners' National Bank continued on the board of directors; presidential elector on the Republican ticket of Lincoln and Hamlin in 1860; delegate to the Republican National Convention at Chicago in 1868 which nominated Grant and Colfax and in 1880 which nominated Garfield and Arthur; died in Catskill, Greene County, N. Y., September 13, 1890; interment in Village Cemetery.

KING, Samuel Wilder, a Delegate from the Territory of Hawaii; born in Honolulu, Island of Oahu, Hawaii, December 17, 1886; attended St. Louis School at Honolulu and Honolulu High School; was graduated from the United States Naval Academy, Annapolis, Md., in 1910; served in the United States Navy from 1910 until 1924, when he resigned with the rank of lieutenant commander; engaged in the real estate and insurance business in Honolulu in 1925; member of the board of supervisors of the city and county of Honolulu 1932–1934; elected as a Republican a Delegate to the Seventy-fourth and to the three succeeding Congresses (January 3, 1935–January 3, 1943); was renominated in 1942, but withdrew to accept a commission as lieutenant commander in the United States Naval Reserve; was promoted to commander and later to captain and served in the central Pacific area from January 4, 1943, to February 21, 1946; was awarded the Legion of Merit Medal; delegate to the Republican National Conventions in 1936, 1940, 1948, and 1952; member of Governor's Emergency Housing Committee in 1946; member of Hawaii Statehood Commission in 1947 and chairman from 1949 to 1953; president of constitutional convention in 1950; chairman of Hawaiian Homes Commission in 1952; appointed Governor of Hawaii by President Eisenhower and served from February 28, 1953, until his resignation July 31, 1957; died in Honolulu, Hawaii, March 24, 1959; interment in National Memorial Cemetery of the Pacific at Punchbowl, Honolulu, Hawaii.

KING, Thomas Butler (brother of Henry King and father of John Floyd King), a Representative from Georgia; born in Palmer, Hampden County, Mass., August 27, 1800; received private instructions and also attended Westfield Academy; read law with his brother at Allentown, Pa.; was admitted to the bar in Philadelphia in 1822 and commenced practice in Waynesville, Ga., in 1823; settled on "Retreat" plantation, St. Simons Island, Ga., in 1826 and became the owner of several other plantations, engaging extensively in agricultural pursuits; also interested in canal and railroad projects; member of the State senate in 1832, 1834, 1835, and 1837; delegate to the State constitutional convention in 1833 and to the State Whig conventions in 1835 and 1843; unsuccessful candidate for election in 1836 to the Twenty-fifth Congress; elected as a Whig to the Twenty-sixth and Twenty-seventh Congresses (March 4, 1839–March 3, 1843); unsuccessful candidate for reelection in 1842 to the Twenty-eighth Congress; delegate to the Whig National Convention at Baltimore in 1844; elected to the Twenty-ninth, Thirtieth, and Thirty-first Congresses and served from March 4, 1845, until his resignation in 1850; appointed by President Fillmore as collector of the port of San Francisco, Calif., October 14, 1850, and served until October 1, 1852, when he resigned; returned to St. Simons Island, Ga.; again a member of the State senate in 1859; delegate to the Democratic National Convention at Baltimore in 1860; appointed a commissioner of Georgia in 1861 to visit Europe in the interest of trade, and was a commissioner of the Confederacy in Europe 1861–1863; died in Waresboro, Ware County, Ga., May 10, 1864; interment in the churchyard of Christ Church, Frederica, St. Simons Island, Ga.

KING, William Henry (father of David S. King), a Representative and a Senator from Utah; born in Fillmore, Millard County, Utah, June 3, 1863; attended the public schools, Brigham Young University, Provo, Utah, and the University of Utah at Salt Lake City; church missionary in Great Britain 1880–1883; returned to his home in Utah and was elected to various offices in the city of Fillmore and in Millard County; member of the Territorial legislature two terms; was graduated from the law department of the University of Michigan at Ann Arbor; was admitted to the bar in 1890 and commenced practice in Utah; member of the Territorial council in 1891 and served as president; associate justice of the Utah Supreme Court from 1894 until 1896, when Utah was admitted as a State into the Union; elected as a Democrat to the Fifty-fifth Congress (March 4, 1897–March 3, 1899); was not a candidate for renomination in 1898; elected to the Fifty-sixth Congress to fill the vacancy caused by the unseating of Brigham H. Roberts and served from April 2, 1900, to March 3, 1901; unsuccessful candidate for reelection in 1900 to the Fifty-seventh Congress and for election in 1902 to the Fifty-eighth Congress; elected as a Democrat to the United States Senate in 1916; reelected in 1922, 1928, and 1934 and served from March 4, 1917, to January 3, 1941; unsuccessful candidate for renomination in 1940; engaged in the practice of law in Washington, D. C., until April 11, 1947; returned to Salt Lake City, Utah, where he resided until his death there on November 27, 1949; interment in Salt Lake City Cemetery.

KING, William Rufus de Vane, a Representative from North Carolina, a Senator from Alabama, and a Vice President of the United States; born in Sampson County, N. C., April 7, 1786; attended private schools; was graduated from the University of North Carolina at Chapel Hill in 1803; studied law; was admitted to the bar in 1806 and commenced practice in Clinton, N. C.; member of the State house of commons 1807–1809; city solicitor of Wilmington, N. C., in 1810; elected as a Democrat to the Twelfth, Thirteenth, and Fourteenth Congresses and served from March 4, 1811, until November 4, 1816, when he resigned; secretary of the legation at Naples and later at St. Petersburg; returned to the United States in 1818 and located in Cahaba, Ala.; delegate to the convention which organized the State government; upon the admission of Alabama as a State into the Union was elected as a Democrat to the United States Senate; reelected in 1822, 1828, 1834, and 1841, and served from December 14, 1819, until April 15, 1844, when he resigned; moved to Selma, Ala., in 1826 and became a planter; Minister to France 1844–1846; appointed and subsequently elected to the United States Senate to fill the vacancy caused by the resignation of Arthur P. Bagby and served from July 1, 1848, until his resignation on December 20, 1852; was elected President pro tempore of the Senate on many occasions; elected Vice President of the United States in 1852 and took the oath of office March 4, 1853, in Habana, Cuba, where he had gone for his health, which was a privilege extended by special act of Congress; returned to his plantation, "King's Bend," Alabama, and died there April 18, 1853; interment in a vault on his plantation; reinterment in City Cemetery, Selma, Dallas County, Ala.

KING, William Smith, a Representative from Minnesota; born in Malone, Franklin County, N. Y., December 16, 1828; attended the common schools; engaged in agricultural pursuits; moved to Otsego County, N. Y., in 1846 and engaged as a solicitor for mutual insurance companies; editor of the Free Democrat in Cooperstown, N. Y., in 1852; moved to Minneapolis, Minn., in 1858; engaged in journalism and agricultural pursuits; postmaster of the National House of Representatives 1861–1865 and 1867–1873; surveyor general of logs and lumber in the Second Congressional District of Minnesota in 1874; elected as a Republican to the Forty-fourth Congress (March 4, 1875–March 3, 1877); was not a candidate for renomination in 1876 to the Forty-fifth Congress; was engaged in cattle raising near Minneapolis; died in Minneapolis, Hennepin County, Minn., on February 24, 1900; interment in Lakewood Cemetery.

KINGSBURY, William Wallace, a Delegate from the Territory of Minnesota; born in Towanda, Bradford County, Pa., June 4, 1828; attended the academies at Towanda and Athens; clerked in a store; became a surveyor; moved to Endion, Minn., in 1852; member of the Territorial house of representatives in 1857; delegate to the State constitutional convention in 1857; elected as a Democrat to the Thirty-fifth Congress and served from March 4, 1857, to May 11, 1858, when a portion of the Territory was admitted as a State into the Union; was not a candidate for renomination in 1858; returned to Towanda, Pa., in 1865 and engaged in the real estate and insurance business; engaged as a commission merchant in Baltimore, Md., for three years; moved to Tarpon Springs, Pinellas County, Fla., in 1887; engaged in real estate and mercantile pursuits until his death there on April 17, 1892; interment in Cydia Cemetery.

KINKAID, Moses Pierce, a Representative from Nebraska; born near Morgantown, Monongalia County, W. Va., January 24, 1856; attended the public schools; was graduated from the law department of the University of Michigan at Ann Arbor in 1876; was admitted to the bar and practiced in Henry County, Ill., from 1876 until 1880 and in Pierre, S. Dak., in 1880 and 1881; moved to O'Neill, Nebr., and continued the practice of law; member of the State senate in 1883; district judge 1887–1900; unsuccessful candidate for election in 1902 to the Fifty-seventh Congress; elected as a Republican to the Fifty-eighth and to the nine succeeding Congresses and served from March 4, 1903, until his death in Washington, D. C., July 6, 1922; interment in Prospect Hill Cemetery, O'Neill, Holt County, Nebr.

KINKEAD, Eugene Francis, a Representative from New Jersey; born while his parents were on a visit abroad, in Buttevant, County Cork, Ireland, March 27, 1876; attended parochial schools in Jersey City, N. J., and was graduated from Seton Hall, South Orange, N. J., in 1895; president of the Jersey Railway Advertising Co. and the Orange Publishing Co.; president of the board of aldermen of Jersey City, N. J., in 1898; elected as a Democrat to the Sixty-first, Sixty-second, and Sixty-third Congresses and served from March 4, 1909, until February 4, 1915, when he resigned; sheriff of Hudson County, N. J., 1915–1917; was instrumental in settling the Standard Oil strike in Bayonne, N. J., in 1915, in which 9,300 men were involved; commissioned major of the military intelligence division of the American forces during the First World War and stationed at the War College, Washington, D. C.; chairman of the executive committee of Colonial Trust Co., New York City, N. Y., 1929–1960; died in South Orange, N. J., September 6, 1960; interment in Gate of Heaven Cemetery, Hanover, N. J.

KINLOCH, Francis, a Delegate from South Carolina; born in Charleston, S. C., March 7, 1755; educated by private tutors; went to England in 1768 and entered Eton College, from which institution he graduated in 1774; studied law at Lincoln's Inn, London, which he entered in 1774 and was admitted to the bar in that city; traveled on the Continent and studied in Paris and Geneva with a view to a diplomatic career 1774–1777; returned to the United States and served as volunteer, lieutenant, and captain in the Revolutionary War 1778–1781; engaged in the Battle of Beaufort and in the defense of Charleston; member of the staffs of General Moultrie, General Huger, and Governor Rutledge; wounded in the attack on Savannah in 1779; served in the State house of representatives in 1779 and 1786–1788; Member of the Continental Congress in 1780 and 1781; was an extensive rice planter at "Kensington," Georgetown District, S. C.; delegate to the State convention which ratified the Federal Constitution May 23, 1788; elected warden of the city of Charleston and justice of the peace and quorum in 1789; member of the State legislative council in 1789 and of the State constitutional convention in 1790; traveled in Europe in 1790 and 1802–1806; engaged in literary pursuits; died in Charleston, S. C., February 8, 1826; interment in St. Michael's Church Cemetery.

KINNARD, George L., a Representative from Indiana; born in Pennsylvania in 1803; moved with his widowed mother to Tennessee and completed preparatory studies; moved to Indianapolis, Ind., in 1823; studied law; was admitted to the bar and practiced in Marion County, Ind.; assessor for Marion County in 1826 and 1827; member of the State house of representatives 1827–1830; county surveyor 1831–1835; State auditor for several years; colonel of the State militia; elected as a Democrat to the Twenty-third and Twenty-fourth Congresses and served from March 4, 1833, until his death from injuries received in an explosion on the steamer *Flora* on the Ohio River November 26, 1836; interment probably in Presbyterian Burying Ground (now Washington Park), Cincinnati, Ohio.

KINNEY, John Fitch, a Delegate from the Territory of Utah; born in New Haven, Oswego County, N. Y., April 2, 1816; completed preparatory studies; studied law; was admitted to the bar in 1837 and commenced practice in Marysville, Ohio; moved to Mount Vernon, Ohio, in 1839 and thence to Lee County, Iowa, in 1844; secretary of the State council in 1845 and 1846; prosecuting attorney of Lee County in 1846 and 1847; judge of the supreme court of Iowa from 1847 until January 1854, when he resigned; appointed by President Pierce chief justice of the supreme court of the Territory of Utah and served from January 1854 to 1857; moved to Nebraska City, Nebr., in 1857 and

practiced law until 1860; again appointed by President Buchanan chief justice of the Territory of Utah June 26, 1860, and served until March 1863, with residence in Salt Lake City; elected as a Democrat to the Thirty-eighth Congress (March 4, 1863–March 3, 1865); was not a candidate for renomination in 1864; returned to Nebraska City, Nebr., and resumed the practice of law; appointed by President Johnson as a commissioner in February 1867 to visit the Sioux Indians and inquire into the Fort Phil Kearney massacre of December 1866; appointed by President Arthur as agent of the Yankton Sioux Indians in Dakota June 27, 1884; confirmed December 11, 1884, and served until January 1, 1889, when he resigned; resumed the practice of law in Nebraska City, Nebr.; moved to San Diego, Calif., in 1889; died in Salt Lake City, Utah, August 16, 1902; interment in Mount Hope Cemetery, San Diego, Calif.

KINSELLA, Thomas, a Representative from New York; born in County Wexford, Ireland, December 31, 1832; immigrated to the United States and settled in New York City; attended the common schools; moved to Cambridge, N. Y., in 1851 and learned the printer's trade; compositor on and contributor to the Cambridge Post; moved to Brooklyn in 1858; became editor of the Brooklyn Daily Eagle September 7, 1861; postmaster of Brooklyn in 1866; member of the city water commission and board of education; elected as a Democrat to the Forty-second Congress (March 4, 1871–March 3, 1873); was not a candidate for renomination in 1872; established the Brooklyn Sunday Sun in 1874, afterward combined with the Daily Eagle, which he edited until his death in Brooklyn, N. Y., February 11, 1884; interment in Holy Cross Cemetery.

KINSEY, Charles, a Representative from New Jersey; born in Baltimore, Md., in 1773; attended the common schools; in early life engaged in the manufacture of paper; moved to Bloomfield Township, Essex County, N. J., and continued the industry; moved to Paterson, N. J., in 1802 and later to New Prospect (now Waldwick), Bergen County, N. J., continuing in the paper industry; member of the State general assembly in 1812, 1813, 1819, and 1826; served in the State council in 1814; elected to the Fifteenth Congress (March 4, 1817–March 3, 1819); elected to the Sixteenth Congress to fill the vacancy caused by the resignation of John Condit and served from February 2, 1820, to March 3, 1821; member of the first board of fire wardens of the town of Paterson in 1821; moved to New Prospect, near Hohokus, Bergen County, N. J., and carried on the manufacture of paper; judge of the court of common pleas and of the orphans' court of Bergen County 1830–1845; died in New Prospect, N. J., June 25, 1849; interment in Union Cemetery, near New Prospect.

KINSEY, James, a Delegate from New Jersey; born in Philadelphia, Pa., March 22, 1731; attended the common schools; studied law; was admitted to the New Jersey bar in 1753 and practiced in the courts of Pennsylvania and New Jersey, with residence in Burlington County, N. J.; member of the State general assembly 1772–1775; member of the committee of correspondence for Burlington County in 1774 and 1775; Member of the Continental Congress from July 23, 1774, until his resignation effective November 22, 1775; appointed chief justice of the supreme court of New Jersey on November 20, 1789, and served until his death in Burlington, N. J., January 4, 1803; interment in St. Mary's Churchyard.

KINSEY, William Medcalf, a Representative from Missouri; born in Mount Pleasant, Jefferson County, Ohio, October 28, 1846; attended Hopedale Academy, Harrison County, Ohio, and Monmouth College, Illinois; became a resident of Muscatine County, Iowa, in 1863; studied law in the University of Iowa at

Iowa City in 1871; was admitted to the bar in 1872 and commenced practice in Muscatine County, Iowa, the same year; moved to St. Louis, Mo., in 1875 and engaged in the practice of law; elected as a Republican to the Fifty-first Congress (March 4, 1889–March 3, 1891); unsuccessful candidate for reelection in 1890 to the Fifty-second Congress; resumed the practice of law in St. Louis, Mo.; judge of the circuit court of the city of St. Louis 1904–1917; during the First World War was chairman of the draft examining board in Carondelet; voluntarily retired and resumed the practice of his profession; died in St. Louis, Mo., June 20, 1931; interment in Sunset Hill Burial Park, St. Louis County, Mo.

KINSLEY, Martin, a Representative from Massachusetts; born in Bridgewater, Mass., June 2, 1754; was graduated from Harvard College in 1778; studied medicine; purveyor of supplies in the Revolutionary Army; member of the State house of representatives in 1787, 1788, 1790–1792, 1794–1796, 1801–1804, and 1806; treasurer of Hardwick, Mass., 1787–1792; moved to Hampden in 1797; representative of Hampden in the general court 1801–1804 and 1806; member of the executive council in 1810 and 1811; judge of the court of common pleas in 1811; judge of the probate court; served in the State senate in 1814; elected to the Sixteenth Congress (March 4, 1819–March 3, 1821); unsuccessful candidate for reelection in 1820 to the Seventeenth Congress; died in Roxbury, Mass., June 20, 1835.

KINZER, John Roland, a Representative from Pennsylvania; born on a farm near Terre Hill in East Earl Township, Lancaster County, Pa., March 28, 1874; attended the public schools; was graduated from Franklin and Marshall College, Lancaster, Pa., in 1896; studied law; was admitted to the bar in 1900 and commenced practice in Lancaster, Pa.; served as county solicitor of Lancaster County 1912–1923; delegate to the Republican National Convention at Kansas City in 1928; elected as a Republican to the Seventy-first Congress to fill the vacancy caused by the death of William W. Griest; reelected to the Seventy-second and to the seven succeeding Congresses and served from January 28, 1930, to January 3, 1947; was not a candidate for renomination in 1946; resumed the practice of law; died in Lancaster, Pa., July 25, 1955; interment in Woodward Hill Cemetery.

KIPP, George Washington, a Representative from Pennsylvania; born in Green Township, Pike County, Pa., March 28, 1847; attended the public schools; engaged in the lumber business for thirty-five years; county commissioner of Wayne County, Pa., in 1880; elected as a Democrat to the Sixtieth Congress (March 4, 1907–March 3, 1909); was not a candidate for renomination in 1908, being an unsuccessful candidate for State treasurer; resumed his former business pursuits; elected to the Sixty-second Congress and served from March 4, 1911, until his death, before Congress assembled, on the west coast of Vancouver Island, British Columbia, July 24, 1911; interment in Oak Hill Cemetery, Towanda, Bradford County, Pa.

KIRBY, William Fosgate, a Senator from Arkansas; born near Texarkana, Miller County, Ark., November 16, 1867; attended the common schools; studied law at Cumberland University, Lebanon, Tenn., and was graduated in 1885; was admitted to the bar in 1885 and commenced practice in Texarkana, Ark.; member of the State house of representatives in 1893 and 1897; served in the State senate 1899–1901; author of "Kirby's Digest of the Statutes of Arkansas" in 1904; moved to Little Rock in 1907; attorney general of Arkansas 1907–1909; elected associate justice of the supreme court of Arkansas in 1910 and served until November 15, 1916, when he resigned, having been elected as a Democrat to the United States Senate to fill the vacancy

caused by the death of James P. Clarke and served from November 8, 1916, to March 3, 1921; unsuccessful candidate for renomination in 1920 and again in 1932; resumed the practice of his profession; again elected an associate justice of the supreme court of Arkansas in 1926 and served until his death in Little Rock, Ark., July 26, 1934; interment in State Line Cemetery, Texarkana, Ark.

KIRK, Andrew Jackson, a Representative from Kentucky; born near Warfield, Martin County, Ky., on March 19, 1866; attended the common schools; was graduated from the law department of Valparaiso (Ind.) University in 1890; was admitted to the bar the same year and commenced practice in Inez, Ky.; county attorney of Martin County 1894–1898; Commonwealth attorney for the twenty-fourth judicial district of Kentucky 1898–1904; circuit judge of the same district 1904–1916; resumed the practice of law in Jenkins, Letcher County, and in Paintsville, Johnson County, Ky., in 1918; elected as a Republican to the Sixty-ninth Congress to fill the vacancy caused by the resignation of John W. Langley and served from February 13, 1926, to March 3, 1927; unsuccessful candidate for renomination in 1926; resumed the practice of law in Paintsville, Ky.; Republican candidate for nomination as circuit judge at the time of his death in Paintsville, Ky., May 25, 1933; interment in Kirk Cemetery near Inez, Ky.

KIRKLAND, Joseph, a Representative from New York; born in Newent Society, in the present town of Lisbon (then part of Norwich), Conn., January 18, 1770; was graduated from Yale College in 1790; studied law; was admitted to the bar in 1794 and commenced practice in New Hartford, Oneida County, N. Y.; member of the State assembly in 1804 and 1805; moved to Utica, N. Y., in 1813; district attorney for the fifth district of New York 1813–1816; again served in the State assembly in 1818, 1820, 1821, and 1825; elected to the Seventeenth Congress (March 4, 1821–March 3, 1823); resumed the practice of law; mayor of Utica 1832–1836; died in Utica, Oneida County, N. Y., January 26, 1844; interment in Forest Hill Cemetery.

KIRKPATRICK, Littleton, a Representative from New Jersey; born in New Brunswick, N. J., October 19, 1797; was graduated from Princeton College in 1815; studied law in Washington, D. C.; was admitted to the bar in 1821 and commenced practice in New Brunswick, N. J.; master in court chancery in 1824; surrogate of Middlesex County 1831–1836; mayor of New Brunswick in 1841 and 1842; trustee of Rutgers College 1841–1859; elected as a Democrat to the Twenty-eighth Congress (March 4, 1843–March 3, 1845); died in Saratoga Springs, N. Y., August 15, 1859; interment in Presbyterian Cemetery, New Brunswick, Middlesex County, N. J.; reinterment in Van Liew Cemetery in 1921.

KIRKPATRICK, Sanford, a Representative from Iowa; born near London, Madison County, Ohio, February 11, 1842; moved to Iowa in 1849 with his parents, who settled on a farm in Highland Township, Wapello County; attended the common schools 1854–1858; during the Civil War entered the Union Army as a private in the Second Iowa Infantry and served four years and four months; participated in the principal battles of the South and West and was promoted to first lieutenant; engaged in agricultural pursuits; moved to Ottumwa, Iowa, in 1876 and engaged in mercantile pursuits until 1887; deputy recorder of Wapello County 1876–1880; member of the Ottumwa City Council 1884–1887; representative of the Internal Revenue Service 1887–1913 and traveled extensively, being assigned to the examination of banks and other corporations; elected as a Democrat to the Sixty-third Congress (March 4, 1913–March 3,

1915); unsuccessful candidate for reelection in 1914 to the Sixty-fourth Congress; moved to Greensboro, N. C., in 1916 and engaged in agricultural pursuits; died in Greensboro, N. C., February 13, 1932; interment in Forest Lawn Cemetery.

KIRKPATRICK, Snyder Solomon, a Representative from Kansas; born near Mulkey, Franklin County, Ill., February 21, 1848; attended the common schools; during the Civil War served in the One Hundred and Thirty-sixth Regiment, Illinois Volunteer Cavalry, in 1864; engaged in mercantile pursuits in 1865; entered the law school at Ann Arbor, Mich., in 1867; returned to Illinois; admitted to the bar by the supreme court of Illinois June 30, 1868, and commenced practice at Cairo; moved to Kansas in 1873 and settled in Fredonia; engaged in the practice of law; elected prosecuting attorney of Wilson County in 1880; member of the State senate 1889–1893; unsuccessful candidate for election in 1892 to the Fifty-third Congress; elected as a Republican to the Fifty-fourth Congress (March 4, 1895–March 3, 1897); unsuccessful candidate for reelection to the Fifty-fifth Congress and for election to the Fifty-sixth and Fifty-seventh Congresses; member of the State house of representatives 1903–1905; died in Fredonia, Wilson County, Kans., April 5, 1909; interment in Fredonia Cemetery.

KIRKPATRICK, William, a Representative from New York; born in Amwell, Hunterdon County, near Zion, N. J., November 7, 1769; was graduated from Princeton College in 1788; studied medicine at the University of Pennsylvania and commenced practice in Whitestown, Oneida County, N. Y., in 1795; moved to Salina (now a part of Syracuse), Onondaga County, N. Y., in 1806 and continued the practice of medicine; subsequently became superintendent of the Onondaga Salt Springs; elected as a Democrat to the Tenth Congress (March 4, 1807–March 3, 1809); again superintendent of the Onondaga Salt Springs 1810–1831; died in Salina, N. Y., September 2, 1832; interment in Oakwood Cemetery, Syracuse, N. Y.

KIRKPATRICK, William Huntington (son of William Sebring Kirkpatrick), a Representative from Pennsylvania; born in Easton, Northampton County, Pa., October 2, 1885; attended the public schools; was graduated from Lafayette College, Easton, Pa., in 1905 and attended the law department of the University of Pennsylvania in 1905 and 1906; was admitted to the bar and commenced the practice of law in Easton, Pa., in 1908; served in the First World War as major and lieutenant colonel, judge advocate, and was a member of the board of review of courts-martial, United States Army; elected as a Republican to the Sixty-seventh Congress (March 4, 1921–March 3, 1923); unsuccessful candidate for reelection to the Sixty-eighth Congress in 1922; resumed the practice of law; appointed on March 3, 1927, judge of the United States District Court for the Eastern District of Pennsylvania, in which capacity he is now serving; resides in Easton, Pa.

KIRKPATRICK, William Sebring (father of William Huntington Kirkpatrick), a Representative from Pennsylvania; born in Easton, Northampton County, Pa., April 21, 1844; attended the public schools, and Lafayette College, Easton, Pa.; studied law; was admitted to the bar October 2, 1865, and commenced practice in Easton; solicitor of Easton 1866–1874; teacher in the Easton public schools in 1868 and 1869; appointed president judge of the third judicial district in 1874; member of the faculty of Lafayette College 1875–1877 and member of the board of trustees 1890–1932; presided temporarily over the Republican State convention in 1882; delegate to the Republican National Convention at Chicago in 1884, which nominated Blaine and Logan; attorney general of Pennsylvania 1887–1891; lecturer on municipal law at Lafayette College, also serving as trustee; unsuccessful candidate for election in 1894 to the Fifty-fourth Congress; elected as a Republican to the Fifty-fifth Congress (March 4, 1897–March 3, 1899); unsuccessful candidate for reelection in 1898 to the Fifty-sixth Congress; resumed the practice of law; died in Easton, Pa., November 3, 1932; interment in Easton Cemetery.

KIRKWOOD, Samuel Jordan, a Senator from Iowa; born in Harford County, Md., December 20, 1813; attended country schools and the academy of John McLeod in Washington, D. C.; clerk in a drug store for three years; taught school in the wintertime; moved to Mansfield, Richmond County, Ohio, in 1835 and continued teaching until 1840; studied law; was admitted to the bar in 1843 and commenced practice in Mansfield; prosecuting attorney of Richland County 1845–1849; member of the State constitutional convention in 1850 and 1851; moved to Coralville, Johnson County, Iowa, in 1855 and engaged in the milling business; member of the State senate 1856–1859; Governor of Iowa 1860–1864; appointed by President Lincoln as Minister to Denmark March 7, 1863, but declined the appointment; elected as a Republican to the United States Senate to fill the vacancy caused by the resignation of James Harlan and served from January 13, 1866, to March 3, 1867; resumed the practice of law and also served as president of the Iowa & Southwestern Railroad Co.; again Governor of Iowa from January 1876 until February 1877, when he resigned to become United States Senator, serving from March 4, 1877, to March 7, 1881, when he resigned to accept a Cabinet portfolio; Secretary of the Interior in the Cabinet of President Garfield from March 5, 1881, until April 6, 1882, when, upon the death of President Garfield, he resigned; unsuccessful candidate for election in 1886 to the Fiftieth Congress; resumed the practice of his profession; became president of the Iowa City National Bank; died in Iowa City, Johnson County, Iowa, September 1, 1894; interment in Oakland Cemetery.

KIRTLAND, Dorrance, a Representative from New York; born in Coxsackie, Greene County, N. Y., July 28, 1770; was graduated from Yale College in 1789; studied law; was admitted to the bar and commenced practice in Coxsackie; surrogate of Greene County 1808–1838; elected to the Fifteenth Congress (March 4, 1817–March 3, 1819); judge of the court of common pleas of Greene County 1828–1838; died in Coxsackie, N. Y., May 23, 1840; interment in Old Coxsackie Cemetery.

KIRWAN, Michael Joseph, a Representative from Ohio; born in Wilkes-Barre, Luzerne County, Pa., December 2, 1886; attended the public and high schools of his native city; moved to Youngstown, Mahoning County, Ohio, in 1907; during the First World War served overseas as a sergeant in the Three Hundred and Forty-eighth Machine Gun Company with the Sixty-fourth Artillery, United States Army, 1917–1919; engaged in the mercantile business 1930–1936; member of the Youngstown City Council 1932–1936; elected as a Democrat to the Seventy-fifth and to the eleven succeeding Congresses (January 3, 1937–January 3, 1961). *Reelected to the Eighty-seventh Congress.*

KISSEL, John, a Representative from New York; born in Brooklyn, N. Y., July 31, 1864; attended public and private schools; served as clerk in the Brooklyn Navy Yard; learned the printing trade and published the Kings County Republican 1889–1914; became a member of the Republican State committee in 1886; clerk to the board of supervisors in 1894 and 1895; engaged in the brewery business; presidential elector on the Republican ticket of McKinley and Roosevelt in 1900; member of

State senate in 1909 and 1910; organized and for fifteen years conducted at his own expense the first free labor bureau in this country, which was subsequently merged into the National Employment Agency; elected as a Republican to the Sixty-seventh Congress (March 4, 1921–March 3, 1923); unsuccessful candidate for reelection in 1922 to the Sixty-eighth Congress; general tax consultant with offices in Brooklyn, N. Y.; employed as an attendant at the Empire State Building in 1932; died in Brooklyn, N. Y., October 3, 1938; interment in the Lutheran Cemetery, Queens, Long Island, N. Y.

KITCHELL, Aaron, a Representative and a Senator from New Jersey; born in Hanover, N. J., July 10, 1744; attended the common schools; became a blacksmith; elected as a Democrat to the Second Congress (March 4, 1791–March 3, 1793); elected to the Third Congress to fill the vacancy caused by the death of Abraham Clark; reelected to the Fourth Congress and served from January 29, 1795, to March 3, 1797; resumed his former business activities; again elected to the Sixth Congress (March 4, 1799–March 3, 1801); elected to the United States Senate and served from March 4, 1805, to March 12, 1809, when he resigned; member of the State general assembly in 1781, 1782, 1784, 1786–1790, 1793, 1794, 1797, 1801–1804, and 1809; presidential elector on the Democratic ticket of Monroe and Tompkins in 1816; died in Hanover, Morris County, N. J., on June 25, 1820; interment in the churchyard of the Presbyterian Church.

KITCHEN, Bethuel Middleton, a Representative from West Virginia; born in Ganotown, Berkeley County, Va. (now West Virginia), March 21, 1812; attended the common schools; engaged in agricultural pursuits and stock raising; member of the Virginia House of Delegates in 1861 and 1862; served in the West Virginia State Senate in 1864 and 1865; presented credentials as a Member-elect to the Thirty-eighth Congress but was not permitted to qualify because the votes cast included those from Berkeley County, which was not mentioned in the act of Congress admitting West Virginia, and hence the assent of Congress had not yet been given, and the county was still a part of Virginia; Lewis McKenzie contested the election, but inasmuch as the voting was confined to less than half the district neither claimant was admitted; elected as a Republican to the Fortieth Congress (March 4, 1867–March 3, 1869); was not a candidate for renomination in 1868; resumed his former pursuits; president of the Agricultural and Mechanical Association of Berkeley, Jefferson, and Morgan Counties 1869–1875; master of West Virginia State Grange 1873–1879; again a member of the West Virginia State Senate in 1878 and 1879; president of the county court of Berkeley County, W. Va., 1880–1895; died in Shanghai, Berkeley County, W. Va., December 15, 1895; interment in the Presbyterian Churchyard.

KITCHENS, Wade Hampton, a Representative from Arkansas; born on a farm near Falcon, Nevada County, Ark., December 26, 1878; attended the common schools, Southern Academy, and the University of Arkansas at Fayetteville; was graduated from the law department of Cumberland University at Lebanon, Tenn., in 1900; in 1898 served as a sergeant in Company I, First Arkansas Regiment, during the Spanish American War and as a private in Company E, Twentieth and Second United States Infantry, 1900–1902 during the Philippine Insurrection; was admitted to the bar in 1900 and practiced at Manila and at Lingayen, P. I., 1902–1909; returned to the United States in 1909, located in Magnolia, Ark., and continued the practice of law; delegate to the Democratic State conventions at Little Rock, Ark., in 1910 and 1912; during the First World War enlisted in the United States Army on May 18, 1917; commissioned captain

of Infantry on August 5, 1917, and served overseas; member of the State house of representatives 1929–1933; elected as a Democrat to the Seventy-fifth and Seventy-sixth Congresses (January 3, 1937–January 3, 1941); unsuccessful candidate for renomination in 1940; resumed the practice of law in Magnolia, Ark., where he now resides.

KITCHIN, Alvin Paul (nephew of Claude Kitchin and William Walton Kitchin and grandson of William Hodges Kitchin), a Representative from North Carolina; born in Scotland Neck, Halifax County, N. C., September 13, 1908; educated in the public schools; attended Oak Ridge Military Institute 1923–1925; graduated from Wake Forest Law School in 1930; was admitted to the bar in 1930 and commenced the practice of law in Scotland Neck, N. C.; with Federal Bureau of Investigation, Washington, D. C., from January 1933 to August 1945; resumed the practice of law in Wadesboro, N. C.; elected as a Democrat to the Eighty-fifth and Eighty-sixth Congresses (January 3, 1957–January 3, 1961). *Reelected to the Eighty-seventh Congress.*

KITCHIN, Claude (son of William Hodges Kitchin, brother of William Walton Kitchin, and uncle of A. Paul Kitchin), a Representative from North Carolina; born near Scotland Neck, Halifax County, N. C., March 24, 1869; attended the common schools and was graduated from Wake Forest College, North Carolina, in 1888; studied law; was admitted to the bar in 1890 and practiced in Scotland Neck; elected as a Democrat to the Fifty-seventh and to the eleven succeeding Congresses and served from March 4, 1901, until his death; majority leader in the Sixty-fourth and Sixty-fifth Congresses; died in Wilson, N. C., May 31, 1923; interment in the Baptist Cemetery, Scotland Neck, N. C.

KITCHIN, William Hodges (father of Claude Kitchin and William Walton Kitchin, and grandfather of A. Paul Kitchin), a Representative from North Carolina; born in Lauderdale County, Ala., December 22, 1837; moved with his parents to North Carolina in 1841; attended Emory and Henry College, Emory, Va.; left college in April 1861 to enlist in the Confederate Army; was promoted to the rank of captain in 1863 and served throughout the Civil War; studied law; was admitted to the bar in 1869 and practiced in Scotland Neck, N. C.; elected as a Democrat to the Forty-sixth Congress (March 4, 1879–March 3, 1881); unsuccessful candidate for reelection in 1880 to the Forty-seventh Congress; died in Scotland Neck, Halifax County, N. C., February 2, 1901; interment in the Baptist Cemetery.

KITCHIN, William Walton (son of William Hodges Kitchin, brother of Claude Kitchin, and uncle of A. Paul Kitchin), a Representative from North Carolina; born near Scotland Neck, Halifax County, N. C., October 9, 1866; attended private schools and Vine Hill Academy; was graduated from Wake Forest College, North Carolina, in 1884; edited the Scotland Neck Democrat in 1885; studied law in Scotland Neck and in the University of North Carolina at Chapel Hill; was admitted to the bar in 1887 and commenced practice in Roxboro, N. C., in 1889; chairman of the county executive committee in 1890; nominee of his party for the State senate in 1892; elected as a Democrat to the Fifty-fifth and to the five succeeding Congresses and served from March 4, 1897, until January 11, 1909, when he resigned; Governor of North Carolina 1909–1913; resumed the practice of law in Raleigh, N. C.; died in Scotland Neck, N. C., November 9, 1924; interment in the Baptist Cemetery.

KITTERA, John Wilkes (father of Thomas Kittera), a Representative from Pennsylvania; born near Blue Ball, East Earl Township, Lancaster County, Pa., in November 1752; was graduated from Princeton College in 1776; studied law; was admitted to the bar in 1782 and commenced practice in Lancaster, Pa.; elected as a Federalist to the Second and to the four succeeding Congresses (March 4, 1791–March 3, 1801); appointed by President Jefferson as United States attorney for the eastern district of Pennsylvania March 4, 1801, and served until his death in Lancaster, Pa., on June 6, 1801; interment in the Presbyterian Cemetery.

KITTERA, Thomas (son of John Wilkes Kittera), a Representative from Pennsylvania; born in Lancaster, Pa., March 21, 1789; was graduated from the University of Pennsylvania at Philadelphia in 1805; studied law; was admitted to the bar in 1808 and commenced practice in Philadelphia; deputy attorney general of Pennsylvania in 1817 and 1818; deputy attorney general of Philadelphia 1824–1826; member of the select council and its president 1824–1826; elected as a Federalist to the Nineteenth Congress to fill the vacancy caused by the resignation of Joseph Hemphill and served from October 10, 1826, to March 3, 1827; at the same election was an unsuccessful candidate for election to the Twentieth Congress; died in Philadelphia, Pa., on June 16, 1839; interment in St. Paul's Protestant Episcopal Church Cemetery.

KITTREDGE, Alfred Beard, a Senator from South Dakota; born in Nelson, Cheshire County, N. H., March 28, 1861; attended the public schools; was graduated from the academic department of Yale College in 1882 and from the law department of that institution in 1885; was admitted to the bar in 1885 and commenced practice in Sioux Falls, S. Dak.; chairman of the Minnehaha County Republican committee in 1887; served in the State senate 1889–1891; member of the Republican National Committee 1892–1896; appointed and subsequently elected as a Republican to the United States Senate to fill the vacancy caused by the death of James H. Kyle; reelected in 1903 and served from July 11, 1901, to March 3, 1909; unsuccessful candidate for the Republican nomination for Senator in the primary election of 1908; engaged in the practice of his profession at Sioux Falls, S. Dak., until his death at Hot Springs, Ark., May 4, 1911, to which resort he had gone for his health; interment in Conant Cemetery, East Jaffrey, Cheshire County, N. H.

KITTREDGE, George Washington, a Representative from New Hampshire; born in Epping, N. H., January 31, 1805; received a liberal schooling; attended the medical department of Harvard University in Cambridge, Mass., and engaged in the practice of medicine in Newmarket, N. H., in 1835; member of the State house of representatives in 1835, 1847, 1848, and 1852, and served as speaker in the last-named year; a director of the Boston & Maine Railroad Co. 1836–1856; president of the Newmarket Savings Bank for forty years; elected as an anti-Nebraska Democrat to the Thirty-third Congress (March 4, 1853–March 3, 1855); unsuccessful candidate for reelection in 1854 to the Thirty-fourth Congress and for election in 1856 to the Thirty-fifth Congress; resumed the practice of medicine; died in Newmarket, N. H., March 6, 1881; interment in Forest Hills Cemetery near Boston, Mass.

KLEBERG, Richard Mifflin, Sr. (nephew of Rudolph Kleberg), a Representative from Texas; born on a ranch near Kingsville, Kleberg County, Tex., November 18, 1887; attended the public schools; was graduated from Corpus Christi (Tex.) High School in 1905 and from the University of Texas at Austin in 1911; studied law; was admitted to the bar in 1909; employed as foreman of the King Ranch, Kingsville, Tex., in 1911, and was active in its management from 1913 to 1924; also engaged in banking; president of the board of Texas College of Arts and

Industry 1929–1931; elected as a Democrat to the Seventy-second Congress to fill the vacancy caused by the death of Harry M. Wurzbach; reelected to the Seventy-third and to the five succeeding Congresses and served from November 24, 1931, to January 3, 1945; unsuccessful candidate for renomination in 1944; resumed ranching activities; member of the State Game and Fish Commission 1951–1955; chairman of the board of the King Ranch Corp., Kingsville, Tex., at time of death; died while on a visit in Hot Springs, Ark., May 8, 1955; interment in Chamberlain Burial Park, Kingsville, Tex.

KLEBERG, Rudolph (uncle of Richard Mifflin Kleberg, Sr.), a Representative from Texas; born in Cat Spring, Austin County, Tex., on June 26, 1847; instructed by private tutors; was graduated from Concrete College, De Witt County, in 1868; enlisted in Tom Green's brigade of Calvalry in the Confederate Army in the spring of 1864 and served until the close of the Civil War; studied law in San Antonio, Tex.; was admitted to the bar in 1872 and commenced practice in Cuero, Tex.; established the Cuero Star in 1873; prosecuting attorney of De Witt County 1876–1890; member of the State senate 1882–1886; appointed United States attorney for the western district of Texas in 1885; elected as a Democrat to the Fifty-fourth Congress to fill the vacancy caused by the death of William H. Crain; reelected to the Fifty-fifth, Fifty-sixth, and Fifty-seventh Congresses and served from April 7, 1896, to March 3, 1903; was not a candidate for renomination in 1902; resumed the practice of law; moved to Austin, Tex., in 1905; appointed official reporter for the court of criminal appeals February 24, 1905, and served until his death in Austin, December 28, 1924; interment in Oakwood Cemetery.

KLECZKA, John Casimir, a Representative from Wisconsin; born in Milwaukee, Wis., on May 6, 1885; attended the parochial schools; was graduated from Marquette University, Milwaukee, Wis., in 1905; took postgraduate courses at Catholic University at Washington, D. C., and at the University of Wisconsin at Madison; studied law; was admitted to the bar in 1909 and commenced practice in Milwaukee; served in the State senate 1909–1911; delegate to the Republican National Convention in 1912; commissioner of the circuit court of Milwaukee County 1914–1918; major judge advocate in the United States Army Reserves after the First World War; elected as a Republican to the Sixty-sixth and Sixty-seventh Congresses (March 4, 1919–March 3, 1923); did not seek renomination in 1922 but returned to the practice of law; in 1924 was awarded the Cross of the Order of Restored Poland; elected circuit court judge in 1930 and served until his retirement due to ill health in 1953; appointed a conciliation judge and court commissioner by the circuit judges in 1957 and served until his death; died in Milwaukee, Wis., April 21, 1959; interment in St. Adalbert's Cemetery.

KLEIN, Arthur George, a Representative from New York; born in New York, N. Y., August 8, 1904; attended the public schools and Washington Square College of New York University at New York City; was graduated from the law department of New York University in 1926; was admitted to the bar in 1927 and commenced practice in New York, N. Y.; connected with the Securities and Exchange Commission in Washington, D. C., and New York, N. Y., 1935–1941; elected as a Democrat to the Seventy-seventh Congress to fill the vacancy caused by the death of M. Michael Edelstein; reelected to the Seventy-eighth Congress and served from July 29, 1941, to January 3, 1945; was not a candidate for renomination in 1944; elected to the Seventy-ninth Congress to fill the vacancy caused by the resignation of Samuel Dickstein; reelected in 1946 to the Eightieth and to the four succeeding Congresses and served from February

19, 1946, until his resignation December 31, 1956; elected to the New York State Supreme Court for the term commencing January 1, 1957, and ending January 1970; is a resident of New York City, N. Y.

KLEINER, John Jay, a Representative from Indiana; born in West Hanover, Dauphin County, Pa., February 8, 1845; moved to Medina County, Ohio, in 1850 with his parents, who settled near Wadsworth; attended the public schools and assisted his father in agricultural pursuits; during the Civil War enlisted on June 20, 1863, in Company G, Eighty-sixth Regiment, Ohio Volunteer Infantry, and served until February 10, 1864; returned to Wadsworth, Ohio, where he resided until 1867; moved to Evansville, Ind., in 1867; taught in the Evansville Business College and edited the Saturday Argus of that city; member of the city council of Evansville in 1873; engaged in the manufacture and sale of lumber; mayor of Evansville 1874–1880; elected as a Democrat to the Forty-eighth and Forty-ninth Congresses (March 4, 1883–March 3, 1887); unsuccessful candidate for reelection; engaged in the real-estate business and stock raising at Pierre, S. Dak., in 1887; moved to Washington, D. C., in 1890 and engaged in the real-estate business until his death in Takoma Park, Md., April 8, 1911; interment in Rock Creek Cemetery, Washington, D. C.

KLEPPER, Frank B., a Representative from Missouri; born in St. John, Putnam County, Mo., June 22, 1864; moved with his parents to Mirabile, Caldwell County, Mo., where he remained for ten years; attended the common schools; moved to Clinton County, Mo., and engaged in agricultural pursuits; attended Baker University, Baldwin City, Kans.; engaged in teaching for two years; was graduated from the law department of the University of Missouri at Columbia in 1898; was admitted to the bar the same year, and commenced practice in Polo, Caldwell County, Mo.; prosecuting attorney of Caldwell County 1900–1905; elected as a Republican to the Fifty-ninth Congress (March 4, 1905–March 3, 1907); unsuccessful candidate for reelection; moved to Cameron, Clinton County, Mo., in 1907 and continued the practice of law; also engaged in banking; prosecuting attorney of Clinton County 1916–1920; again engaged in the practice of law in Cameron, Mo., until his death in that city on August 4, 1933; interment in Evergreen Cemetery.

KLINE, Ardolph Loges, a Representative from New York; born near Newton, Sussex County, N. J., February 21, 1858; attended public schools in Newton, N. J., and Phillips Academy, Andover, Mass.; moved to New York City in 1873 and entered the employ of W. C. Peet & Co.; joined the New York National Guard as a private in 1876; served as lieutenant colonel of the Fourteenth Regiment, New York Volunteers, during the Spanish-American War; commissioned colonel of the Fourteenth Regiment, New York National Guard, January 24, 1901; brevetted brigadier general May 23, 1901; served on the board of aldermen of New York City 1904–1907; appointed assistant appraiser of merchandise for the port of New York by President Roosevelt on January 1, 1908, and served until July 1, 1911, when he resigned; again a member of the board of aldermen in 1912 and 1913; vice chairman of the board of aldermen in 1912 and acting mayor of New York City that year; was president of the board of aldermen in 1913; upon the death of Mayor William J. Gaynor became mayor of New York City for the unexpired term and served from September 10, 1913, to January 1, 1914; again elected a member of the board of aldermen for the term 1914–1915, but resigned on January 6, 1914; commissioner of taxes and assessments 1914–1917; elected as a Republican to the Sixty-seventh Congress (March 4, 1921–March 3, 1923); unsuccessful candidate for reelection in 1922 to the Sixty-eighth Congress; served as New

York manager of the sea service bureau of the United States Shipping Board from May 4, 1923, until his death in Brooklyn, N. Y., October 13, 1930; interment in Holy Cross Cemetery.

KLINE, Isaac Clinton, a Representative from Pennsylvania; born in Mount Pleasant, Westmoreland County, Pa., August 18, 1858; attended the public schools, the State normal school, Bloomsburg, Pa., and Bucknell Academy, Lewisburg, Pa.; was graduated from Lafayette College, Easton, Pa., in 1893; taught school five years before entering college; studied law; was admitted to the bar in 1894 and commenced practice in Sunbury; unsuccessful candidate for election in 1912 to the Sixty-third Congress; elected as a Republican to the Sixty-seventh Congress (March 4, 1921–March 3, 1923); unsuccessful candidate for reelection in 1922 to the Sixty-eighth Congress; resumed the practice of his profession in Sunbury, Pa.; died in De Land, Fla., December 2, 1947; interment in Pomfret Manor, Sunbury, Pa.

KLINE, Marcus Charles Lawrence, a Representative from Pennsylvania; born in Emaus, Salisbury Township, Lehigh County, Pa., March 26, 1855; attended the common schools in the borough of Emaus, Pa., and was graduated from Muhlenberg College, Allentown, Pa., June 26, 1874; studied law; was admitted to the bar in 1876 and commenced practice in Allentown; city solicitor of Allentown in 1877; district attorney for Lehigh County 1887–1890; chairman of the Democratic county committee of Lehigh County 1895–1899; president Lehigh Valley Trust Co. 1899–1906; elected as a Democrat to the Fifty-eighth and Fifty-ninth Congresses (March 4, 1903–March 3, 1907); was not a candidate for renomination in 1906; resumed the practice of his profession and also engaged in banking; president Allentown Trust Co. 1907–1911; delegate to the Democratic National Convention at Denver in 1908; died in Allentown, Lehigh County, Pa., March 10, 1911; interment in Fairview Cemetery.

KLINGENSMITH, John, Jr., a Representative from Pennsylvania; born in Westmoreland County, Pa., in 1785; was a resident of Stewartsville; elected sheriff of Westmoreland County in 1828; elected as a Democrat to the Twenty-fourth and Twenty-fifth Congresses (March 4, 1835–March 3, 1839); secretary of the land office of Pennsylvania 1839–1842.

KLOEB, Frank Le Blond (grandson of Francis C. Le Blond), a Representative from Ohio; born in Celina, Mercer County, Ohio, June 16, 1890; attended the parochial and public schools, Ohio State University at Columbus, and the University of Wisconsin at Madison; during the First World War enlisted as a seaman in the United States Navy, advanced to quartermaster, third class, and then to ensign, and served from September 1917 to March 1919; was graduated from the College of Law of Ohio State University in 1917; was admitted to the bar the same year and commenced practice in Celina, Ohio, in April 1919; served as prosecuting attorney of Mercer County, Ohio, 1921–1924; elected as a Democrat to the Seventy-third, Seventy-fourth, and Seventy-fifth Congresses and served from March 4, 1933, to August 19, 1937, when he resigned, having been appointed United States district judge for the northern district of Ohio, western division, in which capacity he is now serving; is a resident of Toledo, Ohio.

KLOTZ, Robert, a Representative from Pennsylvania; born in Northampton (now Carbon) County, Pa., on October 27, 1819; attended the country schools; first register and recorder of Carbon County in 1843; during the war with Mexico served in the Second Pennsylvania Volunteers as a private, lieutenant, and adjutant in 1846 and 1847; member of the State house of representatives in 1848 and was reelected in 1849; moved to Pawnee, Kans., in 1855; member of the Topeka constitutional convention in 1855 and served as the first secretary of state under the constitution adopted; brigadier general under Governor Robinson; returned to Mauch Chunk, Pa., in 1857; treasurer of Carbon County in 1859; during the Civil War enlisted in the Union Army in 1861; was chosen colonel of the Nineteenth Pennsylvania Emergency Militia in 1862; trustee of Lehigh University, Bethlehem, Pa., 1874–1882; elected as a Democrat to the Forty-sixth and Forty-seventh Congresses (March 4, 1879–March 3, 1883); director and agent of the Laflin-Rand Powder Co., New York City, N. Y.; died in Mauch Chunk, Pa., on May 1, 1895; interment in City Cemetery.

KLUCZYNSKI, John Carl, a Representative from Illinois; born in Chicago, Cook County, Ill., February 15, 1896; attended the public and parochial schools; during the First World War served overseas as a corporal with the Eighth Field Artillery in 1918 and 1919; engaged in the catering business in Chicago, Ill., since 1920; member of the State house of representatives 1933–1948; elected to the State senate in 1948 and served until December 1949, having become a candidate for Congress; elected as a Democrat to the Eighty-second and to the four succeeding Congresses (January 3, 1951–January 3, 1961). *Reelected to the Eighty-seventh Congress.*

KLUTTZ, Theodore Franklin, a Representative from North Carolina; born in Salisbury, Rowan County, N. C., October 4, 1848; attended the common schools; was a druggist; studied law; was admitted to the bar in 1881 and commenced practice in Salisbury, N. C.; was presiding justice of the inferior court of Rowan County from 1884 to 1886, when he resigned; delegate to the Democratic National Convention at Chicago in 1896; presidential elector on the Democratic ticket of Hancock and English in 1880 and on the ticket of Bryan and Sewall in 1896; elected as a Democrat to the Fifty-sixth, Fifty-seventh, and Fifty-eighth Congresses (March 4, 1899–March 3, 1905); declined to be a candidate for renomination in 1904 to the Fifty-ninth Congress; engaged in the practice of his profession in Salisbury, N. C., until his death on November 18, 1918; interment in Chestnut Hill Cemetery.

KNAPP, Anthony Lausett (brother of Robert McCarty Knapp), a Representative from Illinois; born in Middletown, Orange County, N. Y., June 14, 1828; moved with his parents to Illinois in 1839 and settled in Jerseyville; completed preparatory studies; studied law; was admitted to the bar and commenced practice in Jerseyville; member of the State senate 1859–1861; elected as a Democrat to the Thirty-seventh Congress to fill the vacancy caused by the resignation of John A. McClernand; reelected to the Thirty-eighth Congress and served from December 12, 1861, to March 3, 1865; was not a candidate for renomination in 1864; moved to Chicago in 1865 and to Springfield, Ill., in 1867 and continued the practice of law; died in Springfield, Ill., May 24, 1881; interment in Springfield Cemetery; reinterment in Oak Ridge Cemetery.

KNAPP, Charles (father of Charles Junius Knapp), a Representative from New York; born in Colchester, Delaware County, N. Y., October 8, 1797; educated at home and later attended the common schools; engaged in agricultural pursuits; taught school in Delaware County; engaged in mercantile pursuits in 1825; member of the State assembly in 1841; moved to Deposit, Delaware County, N. Y., in 1848 and organized a bank in 1854 and subsequently became its president; elected as a Republican to the Forty-first Congress (March 4, 1869–March 3, 1871); was not a candidate for renomination in 1870; resumed banking; died in Deposit, N. Y., on May 14, 1880; interment in Laurel Bank Cemetery.

KNAPP, Charles Junius (son of Charles Knapp), a Representative from New York; born in Pepacton, Delaware County, N. Y., June 30, 1845; moved with his parents to Deposit, Delaware County, in 1848; was graduated from Hamilton College, Clinton, N. Y., in 1866; became engaged in banking with his father at Deposit, N. Y., in 1866; president of the board of education for many years; served on the board of supervisors of Delaware County in 1885 and 1886; member of the State assembly 1886–1888; elected as a Republican to the Fifty-first Congress (March 4, 1889–March 3, 1891); declined to be a candidate for renomination in 1890; moved to Binghamton, N. Y., and again engaged in banking; died in that city June 1, 1916; interment in Laurel Bank Cemetery, Deposit, N. Y.

KNAPP, Charles Luman, a Representative from New York; born on a farm near Harrisburg, Lewis County, N. Y., July 4, 1847; attended the rural schools, Lowville (N. Y.) Academy, and Irving Institute, Tarrytown, N. Y.; was graduated from Rutgers College, New Brunswick, N. J., in 1869; studied law; was admitted to the bar in 1873 and commenced practice in Lowville, N. Y.; served in the State senate 1886 and 1887; appointed by President Harrison as consul general at Montreal in 1889 and served until September 1893, when he returned to Lowville and resumed the practice of law; also engaged in banking; elected as a Republican to the Fifty-seventh Congress to fill the vacancy caused by the death of Albert D. Shaw; reelected to the Fifty-eighth and to the three succeeding Congresses and served from November 5, 1901, to March 3, 1911; declined to be a candidate for renomination in 1910; resumed the practice of law in Lowville, N. Y.; served as trustee of the Lowville Free Library Association and of Lowville Academy; died in Lowville, N. Y., January 3, 1929; interment in the Rural Cemetery.

KNAPP, Chauncey Langdon, a Representative from Massachusetts; born in Berlin, Vt., February 26, 1809; completed preparatory studies; learned the art of printing and engaged in newspaper work in Montpelier; for a number of years was coproprietor and editor of the State Journal; secretary of state of Vermont 1836–1849; moved to Massachusetts and located in Lowell; editor of the Lowell News and other papers; secretary of the State senate in 1851; elected by the American Party to the Thirty-fourth Congress and as a Republican to the Thirty-fifth Congress (March 4, 1855–March 3, 1859); editor of the Lowell Daily Citizen 1859–1882; died in Lowell, Mass., May 31, 1898; interment in Lowell Cemetery.

KNAPP, Robert McCarty (brother of Anthony Lausett Knapp), a Representative from Illinois; born in New York City April 21, 1831; moved with his parents to Jerseyville, Ill., in 1839; attended the common schools and the Kentucky Military Institute in Frankfort, Ky.; studied law; was admitted to the bar in 1855 and commenced practice in Jerseyville; member of the State house of representatives in 1867; mayor of Jerseyville 1871–1876; elected as a Democrat to the Forty-third Congress (March 4, 1873–March 3, 1875); unsuccessful candidate for reelection in 1874; elected to the Forty-fifth Congress (March 4, 1877–March 3, 1879); again an unsuccessful candidate for reelection in 1878; resumed the practice of law; died in Jerseyville, Jersey County, Ill., June 24, 1889; interment in Oak Grove Cemetery.

KNICKERBOCKER, Herman, a Representative from New York; born in Albany, N. Y., July 27, 1779; completed preparatory studies; studied law; was admitted to the bar in 1803 and commenced practice in Albany, N. Y.; moved to Schaghticoke, near Albany, and became known as "the Prince of Schaghticoke" on account of his hospitality and liberality; elected as a Federalist to the Eleventh Congress (March 4, 1809–March 3, 1811); was not a candidate for reelection in 1810; served in the State assembly in 1816; judge of Rensselaer County; died in Williamsburg (now a part of New York City), N. Y., January 30, 1855; interment in the Knickerbocker family cemetery, Schaghticoke, Rensselaer County, N. Y.

KNIFFIN, Frank Charles, a Representative from Ohio; born on a farm near Stryker, Williams County, Ohio, April 26, 1894; attended the public schools; studied law at Stryker, Ohio; was admitted to the bar in 1919 and commenced practice in Napoleon, Ohio; unsuccessful candidate for election in 1922 to the Sixty-eighth Congress, in 1924 to the Sixty-ninth Congress, in 1926 to the Seventieth Congress, and in 1928 to the Seventy-first Congress; elected as a Democrat to the Seventy-second and to the three succeeding Congresses (March 4, 1931–January 3, 1939); unsuccessful candidate for reelection in 1938 to the Seventy-sixth Congress; resumed the practice of law; referee in bankruptcy, northern district of Ohio, western division, since 1939; is a resident of Napoleon, Henry County, Ohio.

KNIGHT, Charles Landon, a Representative from Ohio; born near Milledgeville, Baldwin County, Ga., June 18, 1867; attended the public schools; graduated from Vanderbilt University, Nashville, Tenn., in 1889 and from Columbia University Law School, New York City, in 1890; was admitted to the bar in 1892 and commenced practice at Bluefield, W. Va.; studied in political and social institutions in Europe 1891–1893; member of the staff of the Philadelphia Times 1896–1900; editor and publisher of the Beacon Journal, Akron, Ohio, 1900–1933; also engaged in stock farming; delegate to the Republican National Convention at Chicago in 1916; during the First World War served as a member of the district exemption board in 1917; elected as a Republican to the Sixty-seventh Congress (March 4, 1921–March 3, 1923); unsuccessful candidate for the Republican nomination for Governor in 1922; delegate to the Republican National Convention at Cleveland in 1924; resumed his newspaper interests; died in Akron, Ohio, September 26, 1933; interment in Roselawn Cemetery.

KNIGHT, Jonathan, a Representative from Pennsylvania; born in Bucks County, Pa., November 22, 1787; moved with his parents to East Bethlehem, Washington County, Pa., in 1801; attended the common schools; became a civil engineer; appointed by the State in 1816 to make and report on a map of Washington County; elected county commissioner and served three years; assisted in the preliminary surveys of the Chesapeake & Ohio Canal and the national road between Cumberland, Md., and Wheeling, Va. (now West Virginia); member of the State house of representatives 1822–1828; entered the service of the Baltimore & Ohio Railroad Co. and visited England to pursue further studies in engineering; upon his return in 1830 was appointed chief engineer of that company and served until 1842; engaged in agricultural pursuits; secretary of the first agricultural society organized in Washington County; elected as a Whig to the Thirty-fourth Congress (March 4, 1855–March 3, 1857); unsuccessful candidate for reelection in 1856 to the Thirty-fifth Congress and for election in 1858 to the Thirty-sixth Congress; resumed agricultural pursuits near East Bethlehem, Pa.; died November 22, 1858; interment in West Land Cemetery, near West Brownsville, Washington County, Pa.

KNIGHT, Nehemiah (father of Nehemiah Rice Knight), a Representative from Rhode Island; born in "Knightsville," Cranston (now a part of Providence), R. I., March 23, 1746; attended the common schools; engaged in agricultural pursuits; town clerk 1773–1800; elected to the general assembly of Rhode Island and Providence Plantations in 1783 and again in 1787;

sheriff of Providence County in 1787; elected as an Anti-Federalist to the Eighth, Ninth, and Tenth Congresses and served from March 4, 1803, until his death in Cranston, R. I., June 13, 1808; interment in a small cemetery on Cranston Street and Phoenix Avenue in a locality known as "Knightsville," Providence, R. I.

KNIGHT, Nehemiah Rice (son of Nehemiah Knight), a Senator from Rhode Island; born in Cranston, R. I., December 31, 1780; attended the common schools; member of the State house of representatives in 1802; moved to Providence and was clerk of the court of common pleas 1805–1811; clerk of the circuit court 1812–1817; collector of customs the same period; Anti-Federalist Governor of Rhode Island 1817–1821; president of the Roger Williams Bank 1817–1854; elected to the United States Senate to fill the vacancy caused by the death of James Burrill, Jr.; reelected in 1823, 1829, and again in 1835, the last time as a Democrat, and served from January 9, 1821, to March 3, 1841; retired from public life; delegate to the State constitutional convention in 1843; died in Providence, R. I., April 18, 1854; interment in Grace Church Cemetery.

KNOPF, Philip, a Representative from Illinois; born near Long Grove, Lake County, Ill., November 18, 1847; attended the public schools; during the Civil War enlisted in Company I, One Hundred and Forty-seventh Regiment, Illinois Volunteer Infantry, and served until the regiment was mustered out in Savannah, Ga.; moved to Chicago in 1866 and attended Bryant and Stratton's College for one year; engaged in the teaming business until 1884, when he was appointed chief deputy coroner and served eight years; member of the State senate 1886–1894; clerk of Cook County 1894–1902; delegate to the Republican National Convention at St. Louis in 1896; member of the State central committee; elected as a Republican to the Fifty-eighth, Fifty-ninth, and Sixtieth Congresses (March 4, 1903–March 3, 1909); retired from public life; died in Chicago, Ill., August 14, 1920; interment in Rosehill Cemetery.

KNOTT, James Proctor, a Representative from Kentucky; born in Raywick, near Lebanon, Marion County, Ky., on August 29, 1830; attended the public schools; studied law; moved to Memphis, Mo., in May 1850; was admitted to the bar in 1851 and commenced practice in Memphis, Mo.; member of the Missouri House of Representatives in 1857 and resigned in August 1859; attorney general of Missouri in 1859 and 1860; returned to Kentucky and commenced the practice of law in Lebanon in 1863; elected as a Democrat to the Fortieth and Forty-first Congresses (March 4, 1867–March 3, 1871); was not a candidate for renomination in 1870; again elected to the Forty-fourth and to the three succeeding Congresses (March 4, 1875–March 3, 1883); declined to be a candidate for renomination in 1882; one of the managers appointed by the House of Representatives in 1876 to conduct the impeachment proceedings against William W. Belknap, ex-Secretary of War; Governor of Kentucky 1883–1887; delegate to the State constitutional convention in 1891; professor of civics and economics, Centre College, Danville, Ky., 1892–1894, and dean of its law school 1894–1901; died in Lebanon, Ky., June 18, 1911; interment in Ryder Cemetery.

KNOWLAND, Joseph Russell (father of William Fife Knowland), a Representative from California; born in Alameda, Alameda County, Calif., August 5, 1873; attended public and private schools and the University of the Pacific (later College of the Pacific), Stockton, Calif.; engaged in the wholesale lumber and shipping business; director of the American Trust Co.; member of the State assembly 1898–1902; served in the State senate from 1902 until 1904, when he resigned, having been elected as a Republican to the Fifty-eighth Congress to fill the vacancy caused by the resignation of Victor H. Metcalf; reelected to the Fifty-ninth and to the four succeeding Congresses and served from November 8, 1904, to March 3, 1915; unsuccessful candidate for election to the United States Senate in 1914; president and publisher of the Oakland (Calif.) Tribune; chairman of the California State Park Commission 1936–1960; chairman of California Centennial Commission in 1950; is a resident of Piedmont, Calif.

KNOWLAND, William Fife (son of Joseph Russell Knowland), a Senator from California; born in Alameda, Alameda County, Calif., June 26, 1908; attended the public schools and was graduated from the University of California at Berkeley in 1929; engaged in the newspaper publishing business in Oakland, Calif., in 1933; member of the California State Assembly 1933–1935; served in the State senate 1935–1939; Republican National committeeman from California 1938–1942 and chairman of the executive committee 1940–1942; served in World War II as an enlisted man and officer, in England, Belgium, and Germany, and was still serving overseas when appointed as a Republican to the United States Senate on August 14, 1945, to fill the vacancy caused by the death of Hiram W. Johnson and served from August 26, 1945, to January 3, 1947; elected on November 5, 1946, to fill this vacancy and also for the term ending January 3, 1953; reelected in 1952 for the term ending January 3, 1959; was not a candidate for renomination in 1958 but was unsuccessful for election as Governor of California; newspaper publisher; is a resident of Piedmont, Calif.

KNOWLES, Freeman Tulley, a Representative from South Dakota; born in Harmony, Somerset County, Maine, October 10, 1846; attended Bloomfield Academy, Skowhegan, Maine; during the Civil War enlisted in the Sixteenth Maine Regiment June 16, 1862; served three years and nineteen days in the Army of the Potomac; captured at the Battle of Reams Station August 18, 1864, and kept a prisoner in Libby, Belle Island, and Salisbury, N. C., until the close of the war; moved to Denison, Iowa; studied law; was admitted to the bar in April 1869 and commenced practice in Denison; moved to Nebraska in 1886 and began the publication of the Ceresco Times; moved to the Black Hills in 1888 and began the publication of the Meade County Times at Tilfor; moved to Deadwood and began the publication of the Evening Independent; elected as a Populist to the Fifty-fifth Congress (March 4, 1897–March 3, 1899); continued the newspaper publishing business in Deadwood, Lawrence County, S. Dak., until his death there on June 1, 1910; interment in Mount Moriah Cemetery.

KNOWLTON, Ebenezer, a Representative from Maine; born in Pittsfield, N. H., December 6, 1815; moved with his parents to South Montville, Maine, in 1825; attended the common schools; studied theology and entered the ministry; member of the State house of representatives 1844–1850 and served as speaker in 1846; elected as a Republican to the Thirty-fourth Congress (March 4, 1855–March 3, 1857); resumed his ministerial duties; died in South Montville, Maine, September 10, 1874; interment in the City Cemetery.

KNOX, James, a Representative from Illinois; born in Canajoharie, N. Y., July 4, 1807; attended Hamilton College, Clinton, N. Y., and was graduated from Yale College in 1830; studied law; was admitted to the bar in 1833 and commenced practice in Utica, N. Y.; moved to Illinois in 1836 and settled in Knoxville, Knox County; continued the practice of law; also engaged in agricultural pursuits; delegate to the State constitutional convention in 1847; elected as a Whig to the

Thirty-third and Thirty-fourth Congresses (March 4, 1853–March 3, 1857); continued the practice of law until his death in Knoxville, Ill., October 8, 1876; interment in City Cemetery.

KNOX, Philander Chase, a Senator from Pennsylvania; born in Brownsville, Fayette County, Pa., May 6, 1853; attended the University of West Virginia at Morgantown, and was graduated from Mount Union College, Alliance, Ohio, in 1872; studied law; was admitted to the bar in 1875 and commenced practice in Pittsburgh, Pa.; assistant United States district attorney for the western district of Pennsylvania in 1876; president of the Pennsylvania Bar Association in 1897; appointed Attorney General of the United States in the Cabinet of President McKinley April 5, 1901, and entered upon his duties April 9, 1901; reappointed by President Theodore Roosevelt December 16, 1901, and served until June 30, 1904, when he resigned, having been appointed as a Republican to the United States Senate to fill the vacancy caused by the death of Matthew S. Quay; subsequently elected to fill the unexpired term and for the full term in 1905 and served from June 10, 1904, until March 4, 1909, when he resigned to enter the Cabinet; appointed Secretary of State of the United States by President Taft March 5, 1909, and served until March 5, 1913; again elected to the United States Senate and served from March 4, 1917, until his death in Washington, D. C., October 12, 1921; interment in Washington Memorial Cemetery, Valley Forge, Pa.

KNOX, Samuel, a Representative from Missouri; born in Blandford, Mass., on March 21, 1815; attended the common schools; was graduated from Williams College, Williamstown, Mass., in 1836 and from the law department of Harvard University in 1838; moved to St. Louis, Mo., in 1838; was admitted to the bar and practiced; city counselor in 1845; successfully contested as a Republican the election of Francis P. Blair, Jr., to the Thirty-eighth Congress and served from June 10, 1864, to March 3, 1865; unsuccessful for reelection in 1864 to the Thirty-ninth Congress; resumed the practice of law in St. Louis, Mo.; returned to Blandford, Mass., where he died March 7, 1905; interment in Peabody Cemetery, Springfield, Mass.

KNOX, Victor Alfred, a Representative from Michigan; born on a farm in Chippewa County, Mich., January 13, 1899; attended the public schools; engaged in farming until 1943; treasurer of Soo Township in 1923 and 1924; county supervisor 1925–1931; member of the State legislature 1937–1952, serving as speaker pro tempore and Republican floor leader 1943–1946 and as speaker 1947–1952; manager of the Chippewa County Farm Bureau 1943–1946; engaged in the retail plumbing and heating business in Sault Ste. Marie, Mich., in 1946; served on the Council of State Government, State Planning Commission, State Crime Commission, and Soo Locks Centennial Commission; elected as a Republican to the Eighty-third and to the three succeeding Congresses (January 3, 1953–January 3, 1961). *Reelected to the Eighty-seventh Congress.*

KNOX, William Shadrach, a Representative from Massachusetts; born in Killingly, Conn., September 10, 1843; moved with his parents to Lawrence, Mass., in 1852; attended the public schools and Amherst (Mass.) College; studied law; was admitted to the bar in 1866 and commenced practice in Lawrence; member of the State house of representatives in 1874 and 1875; city solicitor of Lawrence in 1875, 1876, and 1887–1890; elected as a Republican to the Fifty-fourth and to the three succeeding Congresses (March 4, 1895–March 3, 1903); was not a candidate for renomination; president of the Arlington National Bank of Lawrence; died in Lawrence, Mass., September 21, 1914; interment in Bellevue Cemetery.

KNUTSON, Coya Gjesdal, a Representative from Minnesota; born in Edmore, Ramsey County, N. Dak., August 22, 1912; attended the public schools of Edmore; graduated from Concordia College, Moorhead, Minn., in 1934; postgraduate work at State Teachers College in Moorhead and Julliard School of Music, New York City, N. Y.; taught high school in Penn, N. Dak., and Plummer and Oklee, Minn., 1941-1943; member of Red Lake County Welfare Board 1948-1950; delegate to the Democratic National Convention in 1952 and 1956; served in the State house of representatives 1951-1954; member of the Youth Study Commission in 1953 and 1954; elected as a Democrat-Farmer-Labor to the Eighty-fourth and Eighty-fifth Congresses (January 3, 1955-January 3, 1959); unsuccessful candidate for reelection in 1958 to the Eighty-sixth Congress and for election in 1960 to the Eighty-seventh Congress; writes articles for farm magazines and interested in children's television programs; is a resident of Oklee, Minn.

KNUTSON, Harold, a Representative from Minnesota; was born in Skien, Norway, October 20, 1880; immigrated to the United States in 1886 with his parents, who settled in Chicago, Ill., and later moved to a farm near Clear Lake, Sherburne County, Minn.; attended the common and agricultural schools; apprenticed as a printer; published the Royalton Banner at Royalton, the Foley Independent at Foley, and the Wadena Pioneer Journal at Wadena; delegate to the Republican State conventions in 1902, 1904, and 1910, and to the Republican National Convention at Philadelphia in 1940; associate editor of the St. Cloud Daily Journal-Press in 1910 and 1911; president of the Northern Minnesota Editorial Association in 1910 and 1911; elected as a Republican to the Sixty-fifth and to the fifteen succeeding Congresses (March 4, 1917-January 3, 1949); unsuccessful candidate for reelection in 1948 to the Eighty-first Congress; again became active in the publishing of the Wadena Pioneer Journal until his death; died in Wadena, Minn., August 21, 1953; interment in North Star Cemetery, St. Cloud, Minn.

KOCIALKOWSKI, Leo Paul, a Representative from Illinois; born in Chicago, Ill., August 16, 1882; orphaned at an early age, he was forced to work for a living and an education; educated in private schools, which he supplemented by a business course; worked in various capacities in several business houses in Chicago; engaged in tax appraisal and delinquent tax supervision in Cook County, Ill., 1916-1932; delegate to the Democratic National Convention at Houston in 1928; elected as a Democrat to the Seventy-third and to the four succeeding Congresses (March 4, 1933-January 3, 1943); unsuccessful candidate for renomination in 1942; member of the Civil Service Commission of Cook County, Ill., 1945-1949; retired from public and political activities; died in Chicago, Ill., September 27, 1958; interment in St. Adelbert Cemetery.

KONIG, George, a Representative from Maryland; born near North Point, Baltimore County, Md., January 26, 1865; moved in infancy with his parents to Baltimore, Md.; was self-educated; worked as a ship calker for ten years; superintendent and general manager of the Baltimore Pulverizing Co. 1894-1913; member of the city council of Baltimore 1903-1911; elected as a Democrat to the Sixty-second and Sixty-third Congresses and served from March 4, 1911, until his death in Baltimore, Md., May 31, 1913; interment in Baltimore Cemetery.

KONOP, Thomas Frank, a Representative from Wisconsin; born in Franklin, Wis., August 17, 1879; educated at Two Rivers High School, Oshkosh State Normal School, and Northern Illinois College of Law; was graduated from the law department of the University of Nebraska at Lincoln in 1904; was admitted to the bar in 1904 and commenced practice in Kewaunee, Wis.; district attorney of Kewaunee County 1905-1911; moved to Green Bay, Wis., and practiced law 1915-1917; elected as a Democrat to the Sixty-second, Sixty-third, and Sixty-fourth Congresses (March 4, 1911-March 3, 1917); unsuccessful candidate for reelection; resumed the practice of law in Madison, Wis.; member of the Wisconsin State Industrial Commission 1917-1922; member of State board of vocational education 1917-1922; moved to Milwaukee, Wis., and continued the practice of law in 1922 and 1923; dean of the College of Law of the University of Notre Dame 1923-1941, and dean emeritus and professor of law until his retirement in 1950; resides in South Bend, Ind.

KOONTZ, William Henry, a Representative from Pennsylvania; born in Somerset, Somerset County, Pa., July 15, 1830; completed preparatory studies; studied law; was admitted to the bar in 1851 and commenced practice in Somerset; district attorney for Somerset County 1853-1856; delegate to the Republican National Convention at Chicago in 1860; prothonotary and clerk of the county court 1861-1868; successfully contested as a Republican the election of Alexander H. Coffroth to the Thirty-ninth Congress; reelected to the Fortieth Congress and served from July 18, 1866, to March 3, 1869; was not a candidate for renomination in 1868; resumed the practice of law at Somerset, Pa.; counsel for the Baltimore & Ohio Railroad Co.; member of the State house of representatives 1899-1902; died in Somerset, Pa., July 4, 1911; interment in Union Cemetery.

KOPP, Arthur William, a Representative from Wisconsin; born in Big Patch, Grant County, Wis., February 28, 1874; attended the common schools of Grant County; was graduated from the State normal school at Platteville, Wis., in 1895; taught school for three years; was graduated from the law department of the University of Wisconsin at Madison in 1900; was admitted to the bar the same year and commenced practice in Platteville, Grant County; member of the board of aldermen of that city 1903-1904; city attorney in 1903 and 1904; district attorney of Grant County 1904-1908; elected as a Republican to the Sixty-first and Sixty-second Congresses (March 4, 1909-March 3, 1913); was not a candidate for reelection to the Sixty-third Congress; resumed the practice of law; elected circuit judge of the fifth judicial district of Wisconsin in 1942 and served until his retirement January 1, 1955; acting as a reserve circuit judge and as a consultant to a law firm; is a resident of Platteville, Wis.

KOPP, William Frederick, a Representative from Iowa; born near Dodgeville, Des Moines County, Iowa, June 20, 1869; attended the common schools; was graduated from Iowa Wesleyan College at Mount Pleasant in 1892 and from the law department of the University of Iowa at Iowa City in 1894; was admitted to the bar in 1894 and commenced practice in Mount Pleasant, Iowa; prosecuting attorney of Henry County 1895-1899; postmaster of Mount Pleasant 1906-1914; member of the board of trustees of Iowa Wesleyan College 1908-1938; member of the State house of representatives 1915-1917; elected as a Republican to the Sixty-seventh and to the five succeeding Congresses (March 4, 1921-March 3, 1933); unsuccessful candidate for reelection in 1932 to the Seventy-third Congress; engaged in the practice of law at Mount Pleasant, Iowa, until his death there on August 24, 1938; interment in Forest Home Cemetery.

KOPPLEMANN, Herman Paul, a Representative from Connecticut; born in Odessa, Russia, May 1, 1880; immigrated to the United States in 1882 with his parents, who settled in Hartford, Conn.; attended the grade and high schools; engaged as publishers' agent for newspapers and magazines in 1894; member of the Hartford City Council 1904-1912, serving as president in 1911; member of the State house of representatives in 1913 and 1914; served in the State senate 1917–1920; elected as a Democrat to the Seventy-third, Seventy-fourth, and Seventy-fifth Congresses (March 4, 1933–January 3, 1939); unsuccessful candidate for reelection in 1938 to the Seventy-sixth Congress; elected to the Seventy-seventh Congress (January 3, 1941–January 3, 1943); unsuccessful candidate for reelection in 1942 to the Seventy-eighth Congress; elected to the Seventy-ninth Congress (January 3, 1945–January 3, 1947); unsuccessful candidate for reelection in 1946 to the Eightieth Congress; former chairman of State Water Commission and Metropolitan District Commission; died in Hartford, Conn., August 11, 1957; interment in Emanuel Cemetery, Wethersfield, Conn.

KORBLY, Charles Alexander, a Representative from Indiana; born in Madison, Jefferson County, Ind., March 24, 1871; attended the parochial schools of Madison and St. Joseph's College, near Effingham, Ill.; reporter and editor of the Madison Herald; studied law; was admitted to the bar in 1892 and commenced practice in Madison, Ind.; moved to Indianapolis, Ind., in 1895 and continued the practice of law; elected as a Democrat to the Sixty-first, Sixty-second, and Sixty-third Congresses (March 4, 1909–March 3, 1915); unsuccessful candidate for reelection in 1914 to the Sixty-fourth Congress; served as receiver general of insolvent national banks in Washington, D. C., 1915–1917; member of the legal staff of the Alien Property Custodian in 1918; served with the War Labor Board until it dissolved in 1919 and with the Shipping Board until 1922; resumed the practice of law in Washington, D. C., in 1922; also engaged in literary pursuits; died in Washington, D. C., July 26, 1937; interment in Mount Olivet Cemetery.

KORELL, Franklin Frederick, a Representative from Oregon; born in Portland, Oreg., July 23, 1889; attended the public schools and Bishop Scott Academy, Portland, Oreg.; was graduated from the law department of the University of Oregon at Eugene in 1910; attended Yale Law School at New Haven, Conn., in 1911 and 1912; was admitted to the bar in 1910 and commenced practice in Portland, Oreg.; during the First World War served as a first lieutenant and captain in the Twelfth Regiment Infantry, Eighth Division, later being transferred to the Eighty-second Regiment Infantry, Sixteenth Division, and served from August 1917 until March 1919; after the war resumed the practice of law in Portland, Oreg.; member of the State house of representatives 1923–1925; elected as a Republican to the Seventieth Congress to fill the vacancy caused by the death of Maurice E. Crumpacker; reelected to the Seventy-first Congress and served from October 18, 1927, to March 3, 1931; unsuccessful candidate for reelection in 1930 to the Seventy-second Congress; served as special assistant to the general counsel of the United States Treasury Department 1931–1943 and in the chief counsel's office of the Bureau of Internal Revenue 1943–1959; resides in Alexandria, Va.

KOWALSKI, Frank, a Representative from Connecticut; born in Meriden, New Haven County, Conn., October 18, 1907; attended the grade and high schools in Meriden, Conn.; graduated from the United States Military Academy in 1930, Massachusetts Institute of Technology in 1937, and studied international relations at Columbia University in 1945 and 1946; in 1925 joined the United States Army as an enlisted man and served continuously 1925–1958, with service in the European Theater; director of program for the disarmament of Germany in 1944; helped the Japanese cabinet organize its defenses as acting chief of the American Advisory Group in post-World War II days; in 1954 organized and was the first commandant of the United States Army Command Management School at

Fort Belvoir, Va., and served until his retirement from the service as a colonel July 31, 1958; writer and inventor; elected as a Democrat to the Eighty-sixth Congress (January 3, 1959–January 3, 1961). *Reelected to the Eighty-seventh Congress.*

KRAMER, Charles, a Representative from California; born in Paducah, McCracken County, Ky., April 18, 1879; moved to Chicago during his infancy; attended the public and parochial schools, Illinois College of Law, and De Paul University, Chicago, Ill.; was admitted to the bar in 1904 and began practice in Chicago, Ill.; director of a dress manufacturing concern; moved to Los Angeles, Calif., in 1920 and engaged in the practice of his chosen profession; elected as a Democrat to the Seventy-third and to the four succeeding Congresses (March 4, 1933–January 3, 1943); unsuccessful candidate for the Democratic nomination of mayor of Los Angeles, Calif., in 1941; unsuccessful candidate for reelection in 1942 to the Seventy-eighth Congress; died in Los Angeles, Calif., January 20, 1943; entombed in the mausoleum at Calvary Cemetery.

KRAUS, Milton, a Representative from Indiana; born in Kokomo, Howard County, Ind., June 26, 1866; attended the common and high schools; was graduated from the law department of the University of Michigan at Ann Arbor in 1886; was admitted to the bar in 1887 and commenced practice in Peru, Ind.; became identified with the industrial interests of the community; organized a company of volunteers for the Spanish-American War; presidential elector on the Republican ticket of Taft and Sherman in 1908; elected as a Republican to the Sixty-fifth, Sixty-sixth, and Sixty-seventh Congresses (March 4, 1917–March 3, 1923); unsuccessful candidate for reelection in 1922 to the Sixty-eighth Congress; resumed manufacturing activities; died in Wabash, Ind., November 18, 1942; interment in Mount Hope Cemetery, Peru, Ind.

KREBS, Jacob, a Representative from Pennsylvania; born in Orwigsburg, Schuylkill County, Pa., March 13, 1782; attended the public schools; engaged in agricultural pursuits; elected as a Democrat to the Nineteenth Congress to fill the vacancy caused by the death of Henry Wilson and served from December 4, 1826, to March 3, 1827; resumed agricultural pursuits; died in Orwigsburg, Pa., September 26, 1847; interment in the Lutheran Cemetery.

KREIDER, Aaron Shenk, a Representative from Pennsylvania; born on a farm in South Annville Township, Lebanon County, Pa., June 26, 1863; attended the public schools and Lebanon Valley College, Annville, Pa., and was graduated from Allentown Business College in 1880; moved to Fulton, Mo., in 1880 and engaged in agricultural pursuits and later was employed as a clerk in a store; returned to Pennsylvania and engaged in mercantile pursuits in Campbelltown in 1884 and in Roseland in 1885; established the town of Lawn in Lebanon County, Pa., in 1886; also engaged in agricultural pursuits and in the grain and coal business; moved to Palmyra, Pa., in 1893 and shortly thereafter to Annville, Pa., and became interested in shoe manufacturing and in banking; commissioner and chairman of the Board of Commissioners of Annville 1909–1912; delegate to the Republican State convention in 1910; served as president of the National Association of Shoe Manufacturers of the United States 1913–1916; elected as a Republican to the Sixty-third and to the four succeeding Congresses (March 4, 1913–March 3, 1923); unsuccessful candidate for reelection in 1922; president of the board of trustees of Lebanon Valley College, Annville, Pa.; resumed his former manufacturing pursuits in Annville, Pa., until his death there on May 19, 1929; interment in Mount Annville Cemetery.

KREMER, George, a Representative from Pennsylvania; born in Middletown, Dauphin County, Pa., November 21, 1775; received a limited schooling; studied law; was admitted to the bar and commenced practice in Lewisburg, Pa.; member of the State house of representatives in 1812 and 1813; elected to the Eighteenth, Nineteenth, and Twentieth Congresses (March 3, 1823–March 3, 1829); died in Middleburg, Snyder County (then a part of Union County), Pa., September 11, 1854; interment in the private burial ground on the family estate near Middleburg, Pa.

KRIBBS, George Frederic, a Representative from Pennsylvania; born on a farm in Clarion County, Pa., November 8, 1846; attended the common schools and the Emlenton Academy, and was graduated from Muhlenberg College, Allentown, Pa., in 1873; studied law; was admitted to the bar in 1875 and commenced practice in Clarion, Pa.; mayor in 1876, and again in 1889; edited the Clarion Democrat 1877–1889; elected as a Democrat to the Fifty-second and Fifty-third Congresses (March 4, 1891–March 3, 1895); unsuccessful candidate for renomination in 1894; resumed the practice of law in Clarion; served as mayor; president of the board of directors of the Clarion State Normal School; moved to Osceola County, Fla., in 1896 and engaged in orange culture; located in Kissimmee, Fla., in 1907 and re-engaged in the practice of law; prosecuting attorney of Osceola County in 1908; judge of the county court in 1909 and 1910; resigned and resumed the practice of law in Kissimmee, Fla., until 1926 when he retired from active pursuits; died in Kissimmee, Fla., September 8, 1938; interment in Rose Hill Cemetery.

KRONMILLER, John, a Representative from Maryland; born in Baltimore, Md., on December 6, 1858; attended private and public schools; engaged in the mercantile business and also became a manufacturer of ivory goods in Baltimore, Md.; served in the city council 1905–1907; elected as a Republican to the Sixty-first Congress (March 4, 1909–March 3, 1911); was not a candidate for renomination in 1910; served as a voluntary member of the board of visitors to the Baltimore city jail 1908–1912; director of the Maryland General Hospital in 1913 and 1914; resumed his former manufacturing pursuits; member of the board of supervisors of election for the city of Baltimore from December 29, 1914, to May 1, 1916; died in Baltimore, Md., June 19, 1928; interment in Loudon Park Cemetery.

KRUEGER, Otto, a Representative from North Dakota; born of German parents in the Volinia district of southwest Russia, September 7, 1890; attended grade and high school in Russian and German schools; immigrated to the United States in June 1910 and settled in Fessenden, N. Dak.; furthered his education through grade and high schools and two years of business school in Fargo, N. Dak., and Great Falls, Mont.; during the First World War served as a private in the Infantry from April 1918 to May 1919, with overseas service in the Ninety-first Division in the St. Mihiel, Meuse-Argonne, and Flanders sectors; county auditor of Wells County, N. Dak., 1920–1940; State treasurer in 1945; State insurance commissioner 1946–1951; budget director in 1951 and 1952; clerk of Fessenden school district 1922–1940; State treasurer of the Republican Party 1948–1952; elected as a Republican to the Eighty-third, Eighty-fourth, and Eighty-fifth Congresses (January 3, 1953–January 3, 1959); was not a candidate for renomination in 1958; engaged in accounting and farm operations; is a resident of Lodi, Calif.

KRUSE, Edward H., Jr., a Representative from Indiana; born in Fort Wayne, Allen County, Ind., October 22, 1918; attended the public schools; was graduated from the University of Indiana at Bloomington and from the Indiana University Law School in Indianapolis in January 1942; also attended Butler University at Indianapolis in 1941; was admitted to the bar in 1942; enlisted in the United States Naval Reserve in January 1942; commissioned an ensign in October 1942 and a lieutenant in May 1945; volunteered for P. T. boat duty and saw active service at Guadalcanal, New Georgia-Munda, Bougainville, and Rabaul; instructor in Officers Training School at Notre Dame University from November 1944 until discharged in December 1945; received the Secretary of the Navy Commendation Ribbon and Bronze Star; associated with the legal staff of Medical Protective Co., Fort Wayne, Ind., from December 1945 to April 1947; commenced the private practice of law in 1947 in Fort Wayne, Ind.; elected as a Democrat to the Eighty-first Congress (January 3, 1949–January 3, 1951); unsuccessful candidate for reelection in 1950 to the Eighty-second Congress; judge of Allen County Superior Court No. 2, Fort Wayne, Ind., in 1952; trust officer of Lincoln National Bank, Fort Wayne, Ind., and First National Bank, Miami, Fla., since 1952; member of an actuarial and pension consulting firm in Miami, Fla., since 1956; resides in Miami, Fla.

KUCHEL, Thomas Henry, a Senator from California; born in Anaheim, Orange County, Calif., August 15, 1910; attended the public schools; graduated from the University of Southern California in 1932 and from the law school of the same university in 1935; was admitted to the bar the same year and began practice in Anaheim, Calif.; member of the State assembly 1936–1939; chairman of the Republican State Central Committee in 1940; member of the State senate 1940–1945, and while serving as State senator volunteered and was called to active duty in the United States Naval Reserve as a lieutenant (jg), serving until 1945, when released to inactive duty as a lieutenant; State controller from February 11, 1946, to January 2, 1953; appointed and subsequently elected as a Republican to the United States Senate to fill the vacancy caused by the resignation of Richard M. Nixon and served from January 2, 1953, to January 3, 1957; reelected in 1956 for the term ending January 3, 1963.

KUHNS, Joseph Henry, a Representative from Pennsylvania; born near Greensburg, Pa., in September 1800; attended the public schools and Greensburg Academy; was graduated from Washington (later Washington and Jefferson) College, Washington, Pa., in 1820; studied law; was admitted to the bar in 1823 and commenced practice in Greensburg; elected as a Whig to the Thirty-second Congress (March 4, 1851–March 3, 1853); unsuccessful candidate for reelection in 1852 to the Thirty-third Congress; resumed the practice of law in Greensburg, Pa.; abandoned the actual practice of law in 1877 and lived in retirement until his death in Greensburg, Pa., November 16, 1883; interment in St. Clair Cemetery.

KULP, Monroe Henry, a Representative from Pennsylvania; born in Barto, Berks County, Pa., October 23, 1858; attended the public schools of Shamokin, the State Normal College, Lebanon, Ohio, and was graduated from Eastman Business College, Poughkeepsie, N. Y.; engaged in the lumber, brick, and ice business in Shamokin, Pa.; elected as a Republican to the Fifty-fourth and Fifty-fifth Congresses (March 4, 1895–March 3, 1899); unsuccessful candidate for renomination in 1898; delegate to the Republican National Convention at Philadelphia in 1900 which nominated William McKinley for President for a second term; devoted himself to the lumber business and to many other interests; died in Shamokin, Northumberland County, Pa., on October 19, 1911; interment in the City Cemetery.

KUNKEL, Jacob Michael, a Representative from Maryland; born in Frederick, Frederick County, Md., July 13, 1822; attended the Frederick Academy for Boys and was graduated from the University of Virginia at Charlottesville in 1843; studied law; was admitted to the bar and commenced practice in Frederick in 1846; served in the State senate 1850–1856; elected as a Democrat to the Thirty-fifth and Thirty-sixth Congresses (March 4, 1857–March 3, 1861); resumed the practice of law in his native city; delegate to the Loyalist convention in Philadelphia in 1866; died in Frederick, Md., April 7, 1870.

KUNKEL, John Christian (grandfather of John Crain Kunkel), a Representative from Pennsylvania; born in Harrisburg, Pa., September 18, 1816; attended the common schools of Gettysburg, Pa., and was graduated from Jefferson College, Canonsburg, Pa. (later Washington and Jefferson College, Washington, Pa.), in 1839; studied law at the Carlisle Law School; was admitted to the Dauphin County bar in 1842 and commenced practice in Harrisburg; served in the State house of representatives in 1844, 1845, and again in 1850; member of the State senate 1851–1853 and served as speaker in 1852 and 1853; elected as a Whig to the Thirty-fourth and Thirty-fifth Congresses (March 4, 1855–March 3, 1859); was not a candidate for renomination in 1858; retired from public life and resumed the practice of his profession; died in Harrisburg, Dauphin County, Pa., October 14, 1870; interment in Harrisburg Cemetery.

KUNKEL, John Crain (grandson of John Christian Kunkel, great-grandson of John Sergeant, and great-great-grandson of Jonathan Dickinson Sergeant and Robert Whitehill), a Representative from Pennsylvania; born in Harrisburg, July 21, 1898; attended Harrisburg (Pa.) Academy and Phillips Academy, Andover, Mass.; was graduated from Yale University, New Haven, Conn., in 1916 and from the law department of Harvard University, Cambridge, Mass., in 1926; during the First World War served in the Students' Army Training Corps; was admitted to the bar in Oklahoma and Pennsylvania in 1926; engaged in banking and agricultural pursuits; elected as a Republican to the Seventy-sixth and to the five succeeding Congresses (January 3, 1939–January 3, 1951); was not a candidate for renomination in 1950 but was an unsuccessful candidate for the nomination for United States Senator; county commissioner of Dauphin County, Pa., 1952–1956; elected to the Eighty-seventh Congress on May 16, 1961, to fill the vacancy caused by the death of Walter M. Mumma.

KUNZ, Stanley Henry, a Representative from Illinois; born in Nanticoke, Luzerne County, Pa., September 26, 1864; attended the public schools, St. Ignatius College, and Metropolitan Business College, all in Chicago, Ill.; member of the State house of representatives 1888–1890; served in the State senate 1902–1906; member of the Chicago City Council 1891–1921; member of the Democratic county central committee of Cook County 1891–1925; engaged in the breeding of thoroughbreds and racing horses in Palatine, Cook County, Ill., 1910–1933; delegate to the Democratic National Conventions in 1912, 1916, and 1924; elected as a Democrat to the Sixty-seventh and to the four succeeding Congresses (March 4, 1921–March 3, 1931); successfully contested the election of Peter C. Granata to the Seventy-second Congress and served from April 5, 1932, to March 3, 1933; unsuccessful candidate for renomination in 1932; retired from active political and business life and lived in Chicago, Ill., until his death there on April 23, 1946; interment in St. Adalbert's Cemetery.

KURTZ, Jacob Banks, a Representative from Pennsylvania; born in Delaware Township, Juniata County, Pa., October 31, 1867; attended the public schools; was graduated from Dickinson College, Carlisle, Pa., and from Dickinson Law School in 1893; was admitted to the bar and commenced practice in Altoona, Pa.; district attorney of Blair County 1905–1912; chairman of the committee of public safety and council of national defense for Blair County during the First World War; elected as a Republican to the Sixty-eighth and to the five succeeding Congresses (March 4, 1923–January 3, 1935); unsuccessful candidate for reelection in 1934 to the Seventy-fourth Congress; resumed the practice of law; delegate to the Republican National Conventions in 1936, 1940, and 1948; city solicitor of Altoona, Pa., 1944–1946; died in Altoona, Pa., September 18, 1960; interment in Alto Reste Burial Park.

KURTZ, William Henry, a Representative from Pennsylvania; born in York, Pa., January 31, 1804; attended the common schools and the York County Academy at York, Pa.; studied law; was admitted to the bar on January 7, 1828, and commenced practice in York, Pa.; prosecuting attorney of York County; elected as a Democrat to the Thirty-second and Thirty-third Congresses (March 4, 1851–March 3, 1855); resumed the practice of law; died in York, Pa., June 24, 1868; interment in Prospect Hill Cemetery.

KÜSTERMANN, Gustav, a Representative from Wisconsin; born in Detmold, Germany, May 24, 1850; attended the academy of his native city (Gymnasium Leopoldinum) and was graduated in 1864; employed in a wholesale dry-goods establishment in Hamburg, Germany, until 1868, when he immigrated to the United States and settled in Green Bay, Brown County, Wis.; engaged in mercantile pursuits; held various public offices; postmaster of Green Bay 1892–1896; member of the State board of control and its president 1904–1907; elected as a Republican to the Sixtieth and Sixty-first Congresses (March 4, 1907–March 3, 1911); unsuccessful candidate for reelection in 1910 to the Sixty-second Congress; engaged in literary work in Green Bay, Wis., and died there December 25, 1919; interment in Woodlawn Cemetery.

KUYKENDALL, Andrew Jackson, a Representative from Illinois; born in Gallatin County, Ill., March 3, 1815; completed preparatory studies; studied law; was admitted to the bar in 1840 and commenced practice in Vienna, Ill.; member of the State house of representatives 1842–1862; during the Civil War served one year in the Union Army as major in the Thirty-first Regiment, Illinois Volunteers; elected as a Republican to the Thirty-ninth Congress (March 4, 1865–March 3, 1867); resumed the practice of law in Vienna, Ill.; county and probate judge of Johnson County 1873–1881; member of the State senate 1878–1882; retired from public life and engaged in agricultural pursuits; died in Vienna, Johnson County, Ill., May 11, 1891; interment in the Fraternal Cemetery,

KVALE, Ole Juulson (father of Paul John Kvale), a Representative from Minnesota; born near Decorah, Winnesheik County, Iowa, February 6, 1869; attended the rural schools; was graduated from Luther College, Decorah, Iowa, in 1890, from Luther Theological Seminary, Minneapolis, Minn., in 1893, and from the University of Chicago in 1914; was ordained to the ministry in 1894 and served in Orfordville, Wis., from 1894 to 1917, and in Benson, Swift County, Minn., from 1917 until elected to Congress; unsuccessful candidate as an Independent Republican for election in 1920 to the Sixty-seventh Congress; elected as an Independent Republican to the Sixty-eighth Congress and on the Farmer-Labor ticket to the Sixty-ninth, Seventieth, and Seventy-first Congresses and served from March 4, 1923, until his death at his summer cottage near Otter Tail Lake, Minn., on September 11, 1929; interment in Benson Cemetery, Benson, Minn.

KVALE, Paul John (son of Ole Juulson Kvale), a Representative from Minnesota; born in Orfordville, Rock County, Wis., March 27, 1896; moved to Benson, Minn., with his parents in 1917; attended the Orfordville schools and the University of Illinois at Chicago; was graduated from Luther College, Decorah, Iowa, in 1917; served in the United States Army during the First World War as a sergeant in a machine-gun corps, from September 7, 1917, to August 4, 1919; student at the University of Minnesota at Minneapolis in 1919 and 1920; returned to Benson, Minn., and engaged as editor of the Swift County News in 1920 and 1921; staff editor of the Minneapolis (Minn.) Tribune in 1921; served as secretary to his father, Congressman Ole J. Kvale 1922–1929; elected as a Farmer-Laborite to the Seventy-first Congress to fill the vacancy caused by the death of his father; reelected to the Seventy-second and to the three succeeding Congresses and served from October 16, 1929, to January 3, 1939; unsuccessful candidate for reelection in 1938 to the Seventy-sixth Congress; retired and was a patient in a veterans' hospital in Minneapolis, Minn., until his death there June 14, 1960; interment in Protestant Cemetery, Benson, Minn.

KYL, John Henry, a Representative from Iowa; born in Wisner, Cumming County, Nebr., May 9, 1919; graduated from Wayne (Nebr.) Prep High School in 1937, Nebraska State Teachers College in 1940, and from the University of Nebraska in school administration in 1947; taught in the public schools of Nebraska and in Nebraska State Teachers College at Wayne 1940–1950; joined his brother in the retail clothing business in Bloomfield, Iowa, in 1953; evening newscaster for station KTVO in Ottumwa, Iowa, 1957–1960; unsuccessful candidate for election in 1958 to the Eighty-sixth Congress; elected as a Republican to the Eighty-sixth Congress to fill the vacancy caused by the death of Steven V. Carter and served from December 15, 1959, to January 3, 1961. *Reelected to the Eighty-seventh Congress.*

KYLE, James Henderson, a Senator from South Dakota; born near Xenia, Greene County, Ohio, on February 24, 1854; attended the public schools and was graduated from the high school of Urbana, Ill.; completed a course of civil engineering in the University of Illinois at Urbana in 1871; was graduated from Oberlin (Ohio) College in 1878; prepared for admission to the bar, but entered the Western Theological Seminary, Allegheny, Pa., and was graduated in 1882; pastor of Congregational churches in Echo and Salt Lake City, Utah, 1882–1885; moved to Ipswich and later to Aberdeen, S. Dak.; elected to the State senate on the Independent ticket in 1890; elected as an Independent to the United States Senate in 1891; reelected in 1897 and served from March 4, 1891, until his death; chairman of the United States Industrial Commission 1898–1901; died in Aberdeen, Brown County, S. Dak., July 1, 1901; interment in Riverside Cemetery.

KYLE, John Curtis, a Representative from Mississippi; born near Sardis, Panola County, Miss., July 17, 1851; attended Bethel College, Tennessee, and was graduated from the Cumberland University Law School in 1874; was admitted to the bar in 1874 and commenced practice in Sardis; mayor of Sardis 1879–1881; member of the State senate 1881–1885; member of the Mississippi Railroad Commission 1886–1890; chairman of the Democratic State executive committee in 1888; elected as a Democrat to the Fifty-second, Fifty-third, and Fifty-fourth Congresses (March 4, 1891–March 3, 1897); was not a candidate for renomination in 1896; resumed the practice of law and also engaged in banking in Sardis; retired from active business pursuits in 1912; died in Sardis, Miss., July 6, 1913; interment in Rosehill Cemetery.

KYLE, Thomas Barton, a Representative from Ohio; born in Troy, Miami County, Ohio, March 10, 1856; attended the public schools and Dartmouth College, Hanover, N. H.; studied law; was admitted to the bar in 1884 and commenced practice in Troy; elected prosecuting attorney of Miami County in 1890; president of the board of education of Troy; mayor of Troy; elected as a Republican to the Fifty-seventh and Fifty-eighth Congresses (March 4, 1901–March 3, 1905); was an unsuccessful candidate for renomination in 1904; resumed the practice of his profession in Troy, Ohio, where he died on August 13, 1915; interment in Riverside Cemetery.

L

LA BRANCHE, Alcée Louis, a Representative from Louisiana; born near New Orleans, La., in 1806; attended the Université de Sorreze, France; engaged in planting; member of the State house of representatives 1831–1833 and was chosen speaker of the house January 7, 1833; Chargé d'Affaires to Texas from 1837 to 1840, when he resigned; elected as a Democrat to the Twenty-eighth Congress (March 4, 1843–March 3, 1845); naval officer at the port of New Orleans in 1847; died at Hot Springs, Va., August 17, 1861; interment in Red Church Cemetery, St. Charles Parish; reinterment in Metairie Cemetery, New Orleans, La.

LACEY, Edward Samuel, a Representative from Michigan; born in Chili, Monroe County, N. Y., November 26, 1835; moved with his parents to Branch County, Mich., in October 1842, and to Eaton County in March 1843; attended the public schools and Olivet College; engaged in various business pursuits and in banking; a resident of Kalamazoo, Mich., 1853–1857; moved to Charlotte, Mich., and was register of deeds for Eaton County 1860–1864; mayor of Charlotte in 1871; trustee of the Michigan Asylum for the Insane 1874–1880; delegate to the Republican National Convention at Cincinnati in 1876; elected as a Republican to the Forty-seventh and Forty-eighth Congresses (March 4, 1881–March 3, 1885); declined to be a candidate for reelection in 1884; chairman of the Republican State central committee 1882–1884; commissioned by President Harrison to be Comptroller of the Currency April 17, 1889; reappointed December 16, 1889, and served until 1892, when he resigned; moved to Chicago, Ill., and again engaged in banking; died in Evanston, Ill., October 2, 1916; interment in Maple Hill Cemetery, Charlotte, Mich.

LACEY, John Fletcher, a Representative from Iowa; born in New Martinsville, Va. (now West Virginia), May 30, 1841; moved to Iowa in 1855 with his parents, who settled in Oskaloosa; attended the common schools and pursued classical studies; engaged in agricultural pursuits; learned the trades of bricklaying and plastering; during the Civil War enlisted in Company H, Third Regiment, Iowa Volunteer Infantry, in May 1861 and afterward served in Company D, Thirty-third Regiment, Iowa Volunteer Infantry, as sergeant major, and as lieutenant in Company C of that regiment; promoted to assistant adjutant general on the staff of Brig. Gen. Samuel A. Rice, and after that officer was killed in battle was assigned to duty on the staff of Maj. Gen. Frederick Steele; studied law; was admitted to the bar in 1865 and commenced practice in Oskaloosa, Iowa; member of the House of Representatives of Iowa in 1870; elected city councilman in 1880; served one term as city solicitor; temporary chairman of the Republican State convention in 1898; served on the city council 1880–1883; elected as a Republican to the Fifty-first Congress (March 4, 1889–March 3, 1891); unsuccessful candidate for reelection; elected to the Fifty-third and to the six succeeding Congresses (March 4, 1893–March 3, 1907); was an unsuccessful candidate for reelection; resumed the practice of law; died in Oskaloosa, Iowa, September 29, 1913; interment in Forest Cemetery.

LACOCK, Abner, a Representative and a Senator from Pennsylvania; born near Alexandria, Va., July 9, 1770; moved with his parents to Washington County, Pa., as a youth; pursued academic studies; moved to Beaver (then in Allegheny County) in 1796; justice of the peace in 1796; member of the State house of representatives in 1801; associate judge of the Beaver County Court in 1803 but resigned after one year; again a member of the State house of representatives 1804–1808; member of the Pennsylvania Militia and served as brigadier general in 1807; served in the State senate 1808–1810; elected as a Democrat to the Twelfth and Thirteenth Congresses and served from March 4, 1811, until his resignation March 3, 1813, at the close of the Twelfth Congress, having been elected Senator; elected to the United States Senate and served from March 4, 1813, to March 3, 1819; appointed a State commissioner to survey routes for canals and railways in Pennsylvania April 11, 1825, and superintended construction of the Pittsburgh-Johnstown Canal; appointed to survey and construct the Pennsylvania & Ohio Canal in 1836; died near Freedom, Pa., April 12, 1837; interment in Lacock Cemetery, Rochester, Pa.

LADD, Edwin Freemont, a Senator from North Dakota; born in Starks, Somerset County, Maine, December 13, 1859; attended the public schools, Somerset Academy, Athens, Maine, and was graduated from the University of Maine at Orono in 1884; chemist of the New York State Experiment Station, Geneva, N. Y., 1884–1890; dean of the school of chemistry and pharmacy and professor of chemistry at the North Dakota Agricultural College, Fargo, N. Dak.; chief chemist of the North Dakota Agricultural Experiment Station 1890–1916; editor of the North Dakota Farmer at Lisbon 1899–1904; president of the North Dakota Agricultural College 1916–1921; food commissioner of North Dakota 1902–1921; elected as a Nonpartisan Republican to the United States Senate in 1920 and served from March 4, 1921, until his death in Johns Hopkins Hospital, Baltimore, Md., June 22, 1925; interment in Glenwood Cemetery, Washington, D. C.

LADD, George Washington, a Representative from Maine; born in Augusta, Kennebec County, Maine, September 28, 1818; attended the common schools and Kents Hill Seminary; engaged in the drug business in Bangor, Maine; later engaged in the lumber, commission, and wholesale grocery business in Bangor; was also interested in railroad development; delegate to numerous national political conventions; elected on the Democratic and Greenback ticket to the Forty-sixth and Forty-seventh Congresses (March 4, 1879–March 3, 1883); unsuccessful candidate for reelection in 1882 to the Forty-eighth Congress; died in Bangor, Penobscot County, Maine, January 30, 1892; interment in Mount Hope Cemetery.

LA DOW, George Augustus, a Representative from Oregon; born near Syracuse, Cayuga County, N. Y., March 18, 1826; moved to McHenry County, Ill.; attended the common schools; studied law; was admitted to the bar in 1850 and commenced practice in Waupaca, Wis.; district attorney of Waupaca County 1860–1862; moved to Minnesota in 1862 and settled in Wilton, Waseca (now Beltrami) County, and continued the practice of law; member of the Minnesota House of Representatives in 1868 and 1869; moved to Oregon in 1869, settled in Pendleton, and again engaged in the practice of law; member of the Oregon House of Representatives 1872–1874; elected as a Democrat to the Forty-fourth Congress and served from March 4, 1875, until his death in Pendleton, Oreg., May 1, 1875, prior to the convening of Congress and without having qualified; interment in Pioneer Park Cemetery.

LAFEAN, Daniel Franklin, a Representative from Pennsylvania; born in York, York County, Pa., on February 7, 1861; attended the public schools; engaged in candy manufacturing and in banking in York; a director of the Gettysburg College and trustee of the Gettysburg Seminary, Gettysburg, Pa.; elected as a Republican to the Fifty-eighth and to the four succeeding Congresses (March 4, 1903–March 3, 1913); unsuccessful candidate for reelection in 1912 to the Sixty-third Congress; elected to the Sixty-fourth Congress (March 4, 1915–March 3, 1917); was not a candidate for renomination in 1916; appointed commissioner of banking of the State of Pennsylvania in 1917; again engaged in manufacturing pursuits; died in Philadelphia, Pa., April 18, 1922; interment in Prospect Hill Cemetery, York, Pa.

LAFFERTY, Abraham Walter, a Representative from Oregon; born near Farber, Audrain County, Mo., June 10, 1875; attended the public schools; studied law at the University of Missouri at Columbia in 1895 and 1896; was admitted to the bar the latter year and commenced practice in Montgomery City, Mo.; prosecuting attorney of Montgomery County, Mo., 1902–1904; appointed special agent of the United States General Land Office and moved to Portland, Oreg., March 1, 1905; resigned October 1, 1906, and engaged in the practice of law in Portland; elected as a Progressive Republican to the Sixty-second and Sixty-third Congresses (March 4, 1911–March 3, 1915); resumed the practice of law in Portland; during the First World War served as major at the San Francisco training camp; moved to New York City in 1919 and continued the practice of law there until 1933, when he moved to "Riversdale," an early American residence at Riverdale, Md.; returned to Portland, Oreg., and was unsuccessful in 1954 for nomination as a candidate for election to the Eighty-fourth Congress; is a resident of Portland, Oreg.

LAFFOON, Polk, a Representative from Kentucky; born near Madisonville, Hopkins County, Ky., October 24, 1844; attended the common schools; during the Civil War entered the Confederate Army as a member of the Eighth Infantry; captured at Fort Donelson February 16, 1862, and exchanged at Vicksburg in September 1862; member of Morgan's command during the remainder of his service; captured at Cheshire, Ohio, during the raid into that State and confined in the Pennsylvania Penitentiary as a prisoner of war; at the close of the war engaged in teaching for two years; studied law; was admitted to the bar in 1867 and practiced in Madisonville, Ky.; prosecuting attorney of Hopkins County; elected as a Democrat to the Forty-ninth and Fiftieth Congresses (March 4, 1885–March 3, 1889); was not a candidate for renomination in 1888; resumed the practice of law; died in Madisonville, Ky., October 22, 1906; interment in the Odd Fellows Cemetery.

LAFLIN, Addison Henry, a Representative from New York; born in Lee, Berkshire County, Mass., October 24, 1823; attended the common schools; was graduated from Williams College, Williamstown, Mass., in 1843; went to Herkimer County, N. Y., in 1849 and became interested in paper making; member of the State senate in 1858 and 1859; elected as a Republican to the Thirty-ninth, Fortieth, and Forty-first Congresses (March 4, 1865–March 3, 1871); was not a candidate for renomination; delegate to the Republican State convention in 1867; appointed by President Grant to be naval officer at the port of New York April 3, 1871, and served until 1877, when he resigned; died in Pittsfield, Mass., September 24, 1878; interment in Oakwood Cemetery, Syracuse, N. Y.

LA FOLLETTE, Charles Marion (great-grandson of William Heilman), a Representative from Indiana; born in New Albany, Floyd County, Ind., February 27, 1898; moved with his parents to Evansville, Ind., in 1901; attended the public schools and entered Wabash College at Crawfordsville, Ind., in September 1916; during the First World War enlisted in the United States Army and served with the One Hundred and Fifty-first Infantry, Thirty-eighth Division, 1917–1919, with four months overseas; attended Wabash College until June 1921; studied law at Vanderbilt University, Nashville, Tenn., in 1921 and also in law offices in Dayton, Ohio, and Evansville, Ind.; was admitted to the bar in 1925 and commenced practice in Evansville, Ind.; member of the State house of representatives 1927–1929; elected as a Republican to the Seventy-eighth and Seventy-ninth Congresses (January 3, 1943–January 3, 1947); was not a candidate for renomination in 1946, but was an unsuccessful candidate for the Republican nomination for United States Senator; deputy chief of counsel for war crimes, Nuremberg, Germany, from January 4, 1947, to December 15, 1947; director of the Office of Military Government for Wurttemberg-Baden, Germany, from December 15, 1947, to January 16, 1949; returned to the United States; appointed a director of Americans for Democratic Action on July 1, 1949; is a resident of Evansville, Ind.

LA FOLLETTE, Robert Marion, a Representative and a Senator from Wisconsin; born in Primrose, Dane County, Wis., June 14, 1855; was graduated from the University of Wisconsin at Madison in 1879; studied law; was admitted to the bar in 1880 and commenced practice in Madison, Wis.; district attorney of Dane County 1880–1884; elected as a Republican to the Forty-ninth, Fiftieth, and Fifty-first Congresses (March 4, 1885–March 3, 1891); unsuccessful candidate for reelection in 1890 to the Fifty-second Congress; resumed the practice of law in Madison, Wis.; delegate to the Republican National Convention at St. Louis in 1896; delegate at large to the Republican National Conventions at Chicago in 1904 and 1912; elected Governor of Wisconsin in 1900; reelected in 1902 and 1904 and served from January 1, 1901, until his resignation on January 1, 1906, having previously been elected Senator; elected as a Republican to the United States Senate on January 25, 1905, for the term beginning March 4, 1905, but did not assume these duties until later, preferring to continue as Governor; reelected in 1911, 1917, and 1923 and served from January 2, 1906, until his death; unsuccessful candidate for President of the United States in 1924 on the ticket nominated at Cleveland by the conference for progressive political action; died in Washington, D. C., June 18, 1925; interment in Forest Hill Cemetery, Madison, Wis.

LA FOLLETTE, Robert Marion, Jr. (son of the preceding), a Senator from Wisconsin; born in Madison, Wis., February 6, 1895; attended the public schools of Madison, and was graduated from Western High School, Washington, D. C., in 1913; attended the University of Wisconsin at Madison 1913–1916; private secretary to his father 1919–1925; chairman of the Republican State central committee 1920–1924; vice chairman of the Progressive National Executive Committee during the presidential campaign of Robert M. La Follette and Burton K. Wheeler in 1924; elected as a Republican (Progressive) to the United States Senate on September 29, 1925, to fill the vacancy caused by the death of his father, Robert M. La Follette; reelected in 1928, and as a Progressive in 1934 and 1940, and served from September 30, 1925, to January 3, 1947; unsuccessful candidate for the Republican nomination for United States Senator in 1946; president of a publishing company at Madison, Wis., and a broadcasting company at Milwaukee, Wis.; author and economic-research consultant at Washington, D. C.; died in Washington, D. C., February 24, 1953; interment in Forest Hill Cemetery, Madison, Wis.

LA FOLLETTE, William Leroy, a Representative from Washington; born in Thorntown, near Shammondale, Boone County, Ind., November 30, 1860; attended the graded schools in Thorntown, Ind., and at the same time clerked in a store and was employed at the jewelry trade; attended Indiana Central Normal College in Thorntown; moved to the Territory of Washington in 1876 and located in the Willamette Valley in Oregon; the following year he went on horseback to Spokane Valley, Washington, and then moved to the Palouse country in 1877; engaged in agricultural pursuits, stock raising, and fruit growing in Whitman County, and was also extensively engaged as an orchardist at Wawawai, Wash.; disposed of his fruit interests in 1908 and moved to Pullman, Wash.; member of the State house of representatives 1899–1901; member of the World's Fair Commission and had charge of the Washington State building at the Chicago Exposition in 1893; elected as a Republican to the Sixty-second and to the three succeeding Congresses (March 4, 1911–March 3, 1919); unsuccessful candidate for renomination in 1918; resided in Spokane, Wash., 1920–1923, and Princess Anne, Md., 1924 and 1925; moved to Colfax, Wash., in 1927; resumed his former business activities; died in Colfax, Wash., December 20, 1934; interment in Colfax Cemetery.

LAFORE, John Armand, Jr., a Representative from Pennsylvania; born in Bala, Montgomery County, Pa., May 25, 1905; attended the Montgomery County schools; student at Swarthmore College in 1923 and 1925 and the University of Pennsylvania in 1925 and 1926; president of the Central City Chevrolet Co. in Philadelphia 1932 to 1957; former comptroller of Montgomery County, Pa., and former chairman of the Lower Merion Township Committee; during World War II served as a lieutenant commander in the United States Navy 1942–1945; member of the State house of representatives 1950–1957; elected as a Republican to the Eighty-fifth Congress to fill the vacancy caused by the resignation of Samuel K. McConnell, Jr.; reelected to the Eighty-sixth Congress and served from November 5, 1957, to January 3, 1961; unsuccessful candidate for renomination in 1960; president of Kellett Air Craft Corp., Willow Grove, Pa.; is a resident of Haverford, Pa.

LAGAN, Matthew Diamond, a Representative from Louisiana; born in Maghera, Londonderry, Ireland, June 20, 1829; attended the common schools; immigrated to the United States and settled in New Orleans, La., December 28, 1843; engaged in manufacturing and mercantile pursuits; during the Civil War fitted out many vessels for the use of the Confederate States and later enlisted as a volunteer in the Confederate Navy; elected to the New Orleans Common Council in 1867; member of the State constitutional convention in 1879; again elected to the city council in 1882 and served as president and acting mayor during the term; elected as a Democrat to the Fiftieth Congress (March 4, 1887–March 3, 1889); declined a renomination for election to the Fifty-first Congress; elected to the Fifty-second Congress (March 4, 1891–March 3, 1893); died in New Orleans, La., April 8, 1901; interment in Metairie Cemetery.

LA GUARDIA, Fiorello Henry, a Representative from New York; born in New York City, N. Y., December 11, 1882; moved to Arizona; attended the public schools and high school at Prescott, Ariz.; returned to New York; was graduated from the New York University Law School in 1910; was admitted to the bar the same year and commenced practice in New York City; served in the American Consular Service in Budapest, Hungary, and in Trieste, Austria, 1901–1904; American consular agent at Fiume, Hungary, 1904–1906; interpreter in the Immigration Service at Ellis Island 1907–1910; deputy attorney general of the State of New York 1915–1917; elected as a Republican to the Sixty-fifth and Sixty-sixth Congresses and served from March 4, 1917, until December 31, 1919, when he resigned; during the First World War absented himself from the House and on August 15, 1917, was commissioned a first lieutenant in the Army Air Service; promoted to the rank of captain and later to that of major; commanded the United States air forces on the Italian-Austrian front and was awarded the Italian War Cross; president of the board of aldermen of New York City in 1920 and 1921; elected as a Republican to the Sixty-eighth Congress, as a Socialist to the Sixty-ninth Congress, and as a Republican Progressive to the Seventieth, Seventy-first, and Seventy-second Congresses (March 4, 1923–March 3, 1933); unsuccessful candidate for reelection in 1932 to the Seventy-third Congress; served as mayor of New York City 1934–1945; United States delegate to the Interparliamentary Conference at Berlin, Germany, in 1928, and at London, England, in 1930; president of the United States Conference of Mayors 1936–1945; United States Director of Office of Civilian Defense from May 1941 to February 1942; chairman of the United States section of the Permanent Joint Board on Defense (United States and Canada) 1940–1946; American delegate to the International Civil Aviation Conference at Chicago, Ill., in 1944; special United States Ambassador to Brazil in 1946; director general of the United Nations Relief and Rehabilitation Administration in 1946; died in New York City, N. Y., September 20, 1947; interment in Woodlawn Cemetery in the Bronx.

LAHM, Samuel, a Representative from Ohio; born in Leitersburg, Washington County, Md., April 22, 1812; completed preparatory studies; taught school; attended Washington College, Pennsylvania; studied law; was admitted to the bar in 1836 and commenced practice in Canton, Ohio; master of chancery 1837–1841; prosecuting attorney of Stark County 1841–1845; member of the State senate in 1842; delegate to the Democratic National Convention at Baltimore in 1844 which nominated Polk and Dallas; brigadier general of militia; unsuccessful candidate for election in 1844 to the Twenty-ninth Congress; elected as a Democrat to the Thirtieth Congress (March 4, 1847–March 3, 1849); engaged in agricultural pursuits and sheep raising; died in Canton, Ohio, June 16, 1876; interment in West Lawn Cemetery.

LAIDLAW, William Grant, a Representative from New York; born near Jedburgh, the county town of Roxburghshire, Scotland, January 1, 1840; immigrated to the United States in 1852 with his parents, who settled in Franklinville, Cattaraugus County, N. Y.; attended the common schools and Ten Broek Free Academy at Franklinville; studied law; was admitted to the bar in 1866 and practiced; served two years in the United States Navy during the Civil War; school commissioner of the first district of Cattaraugus County 1867–1870; moved to Ellicottville, N. Y., in 1870; assessor of internal revenue of the thirty-first collection district of New York 1871–1877; district attorney of Cattaraugus County 1877–1883; elected as a Republican to the Fiftieth and Fifty-first Congresses (March 4, 1887–March 3, 1891); resumed the practice of his profession in Ellicottville, Cattaraugus County, N. Y., and died there on August 19, 1908; interment in Sunset Hill Cemetery.

LAIRD, James, a Representative from Nebraska; born in Fowlerville, Livingston County, N. Y., June 20, 1849; in early childhood moved with his parents to Michigan, who settled in Hillsdale County; attended Adrian College; during the Civil War served with the Sixteenth Regiment, Michigan Volunteer Infantry, in the Army of the Potomac from 1862 until 1865, when he was honorably discharged; was graduated from the law department of the University of Michigan at Ann Arbor in 1871;

was admitted to the bar and engaged in practice in Hastings, Nebr., in 1872; member of the Nebraska constitutional convention in 1875; presidential elector on the Republican ticket of Garfield and Arthur in 1880; elected as a Republican to the Forty-eighth and to the three succeeding Congresses and served from March 4, 1883, until his death in Hastings, Adams County, Nebr., August 17, 1889; interment in Parkview Cemetery.

LAIRD, Melvin Robert, a Representative from Wisconsin; born in Marshfield, Wood County, Wis., September 1, 1922; attended the public schools; was graduated from Carleton College, Northfield, Minn., in 1942; secretary-treasurer of a lumber company; during World War II enlisted in the United States Navy in May 1942 and served on the destroyer *Maddox* in Task Force Fifty-eight and Pacific Third Fleet; awarded the Purple Heart, Asiatic-Pacific Ribbon with five battle stars, Philippine Liberation Medal with one battle star, American Theater Ribbon, and Japanese Occupation Ribbon; member of the State senate 1946–1952; delegate to the Republican National Conventions in 1948, 1952, 1956, and 1960; elected as a Republican to the Eighty-third and to the three succeeding Congresses (January 3, 1953–January 3, 1961). *Reelected to the Eighty-seventh Congress.*

LAIRD, William Robert, 3d, a Senator from West Virginia; born in Keswick, Shasta County, Calif., June 2, 1916; educated int he public schools; graduated from Greenbrier Military School, Kings College, Bristol, Tenn., and from West Virginia University in 1944; during World War II served in the United States Navy; was admitted to the bar in 1944 and commenced the practice of law in West Virginia; member of West Virginia Board of Education in 1955; member of the board of directors of Merchants National Bank, Montgomery, W. Va., and the Upper Kanawha Valley Development Association; member of board of trustees of Laird Foundation, Montgomery, W. Va.; appointed State tax commissioner August 1, 1955, and served until his resignation in 1956, having been appointed as a Democrat to the United States Senate to fill the vacancy caused by the death of Harley M. Kilgore and served from March 13, 1956, to November 6, 1956; was not a candidate for election to fill the vacancy; resides in Fayetteville, W. Va.

LAKE, William Augustus, a Representative from Mississippi; born near Cambridge, Dorchester County, Md., January 6, 1808; pursued classical studies, and was graduated from Jefferson College, Pennsylvania, in 1827; member of the Maryland House of Delegates in 1831; moved to Vicksburg, Miss.; studied law; was admitted to the bar in 1834 and commenced practice in Vicksburg, Miss.; member of the State senate in 1848; elected as a Whig to the Thirty-fourth Congress (March 4, 1855–March 3, 1857); unsuccessful candidate for reelection in 1856 to the Thirty-fifth Congress; served in the State house of representatives 1859–1861; resumed the practice of law; was a candidate for the Confederate Congress in 1861 and, during the canvass was killed in a duel by his opponent, Colonel Chambers, of Mississippi, October 15, 1861, at Hopefield, Ark., opposite Memphis, Tenn.; interment in the City Cemetery, Vicksburg, Miss.

LAMAR, Henry Graybill, a Representative from Georgia; born in Clinton, Jones County, Ga., July 10, 1798; pursued an academic course; studied law; was admitted to the bar and commenced practice in Macon, Ga.; judge of the State superior court; member of the State house of representatives; elected as a Democrat to the Twenty-first Congress to fill the vacancy caused by the resignation of George R. Gilmer; reelected to the Twenty-second Congress and served from December 7, 1829, to

March 3, 1833; unsuccessful candidate for reelection in 1832 to the Twenty-third Congress; unsuccessful candidate for Governor in 1857; associate justice of the State supreme court; died in Macon, Ga., September 10, 1861; interment in Rose Hill Cemetery.

LAMAR, James Robert, a Representative from Missouri; born at Edgar Springs, Phelps County, Mo., March 28, 1866; attended the common schools and Licking (Mo.) Academy; taught school in Phelps and Texas Counties; was principal of Licking Academy in 1889; studied law; was admitted to the bar in Texas County in 1889 and practiced; prosecuting attorney of Texas County 1890–1894; chairman of the Democratic congressional committee of the Thirteenth District of Missouri 1894–1896; presidential elector on the Democratic ticket of Bryan and Sewall in 1896; engaged in the practice of law in Houston, Texas County, Mo.; elected as a Democrat to the Fifty-eighth Congress (March 4, 1903–March 3, 1905); unsuccessful candidate for reelection in 1904 to the Fifty-ninth Congress; elected to the Sixtieth Congress (March 4, 1907–March 3, 1909); unsuccessful candidate for reelection in 1908 to the Sixty-first Congress; resumed the practice of law in Houston, Mo.; president of the Missouri Bar Association in 1920; died in St. Louis, Mo., where he had gone for medical treatment on August 11, 1923; interment in Houston Cemetery, Houston, Mo.

LAMAR, John Basil, a Representative from Georgia; born in Milledgeville, Baldwin County, Ga., on November 5, 1812; attended Dr. Beman's school at Mount Zion, Ga., and Franklin College (now University of Georgia) at Athens in 1827; moved to a plantation near Macon, Bibb County, Ga., in 1830 and engaged in agricultural pursuits; member of the State house of representatives in 1837 and 1838; elected as a Democrat to the Twenty-eighth Congress and served from March 4 until July 29, 1843, when he resigned; resumed the management of his plantations which extended throughout central and southwest Georgia and into Florida; trustee of the University of Georgia 1855–1858; delegate to the State convention which adopted the secession ordinance in 1861; during the Civil War served in the Confederate Army as an aide on the staff of Gen. Howell Cobb; was mortally wounded in the battle at Cramptons Gap, Md., and died the following day, September 15, 1862; interment in Rose Hill Cemetery, Macon, Ga.

LAMAR, Lucius Quintus Cincinnatus (uncle of William Bailey Lamar and cousin of Absalom Harris Chappell), a Representative and a Senator from Mississippi; born near Eatonton, Putnam County, Ga., September 17, 1825; attended the Scottsboro School near Milledgeville, Ga., and the Georgia Conference Manual Labor School 1835–1838; moved to Oxford, Miss.; was graduated from Emory College, Oxford, Ga., in 1845; studied law in Macon; was admitted to the bar in 1847; returned to Oxford, Miss., in 1849 and served one year as professor of mathematics in the University of Mississippi at Oxford; moved to Covington, Ga., in 1852 and practiced law; member of the State house of representatives 1853; returned to Lafayette County, Miss., in 1855; elected as a Democrat to the Thirty-fifth and Thirty-sixth Congresses and served from March 4, 1857, until his retirement in December 1860 to become a member of the secession convention of Mississippi January 9, 1861; during the Civil War served in the Confederate Army as lieutenant colonel and colonel of the Eighteenth Mississippi Regiment; entered the diplomatic service of the Confederacy and was sent on a special mission to Russia, France, and England in 1863; member of the State constitutional conventions in 1865, 1868, 1875, 1877, and 1881; professor of political economy and social science in the University of Mississippi in 1866; professor of law in 1867; elected to

the Forty-third and Forty-fourth Congresses (March 4, 1873–March 3, 1877); did not seek renomination in 1876, having been elected Senator; delegate to the Democratic National Convention at Cincinnati in 1880; elected to the United States Senate in 1877; reelected in 1883 and served from March 4, 1877, until March 6, 1885, when he resigned; Secretary of the Interior in the Cabinet of President Cleveland from March 6, 1885, until his resignation on January 10, 1888; appointed by President Cleveland to be Associate Justice of the United States Supreme Court; confirmed January 16, 1888; took his seat two days later and served until his death in Vineville, Ga., January 23, 1893; interment in Riverside Cemetery, Macon, Ga.; reinterment in St. Peter's Cemetery, Oxford, Miss., in 1894.

LAMAR, William Bailey (nephew of Lucius Quintus Cincinnatus Lamar), a Representative from Florida; born near Monticello, Jefferson County, Fla., June 12, 1853; attended Jefferson Academy at Monticello and the University of Georgia, Athens, Ga., where he resided from 1866 until 1873; returned to Florida in the latter year; was graduated from the Lebanon Law School, Lebanon, Tenn., in 1875; was admitted to the bar; commenced practice in Tupelo, Miss.; admitted to practice law in the courts of Florida in 1876; clerk of the circuit court of Jefferson County, Fla., January 1877 to January 1881; judge of the county court of Jefferson County 1883–1886; member of the State house of representatives in 1887 and was chosen speaker, but declined; attorney general of Florida 1889–1903; elected as a Democrat to the Fifty-eighth, Fifty-ninth, and Sixtieth Congresses (March 4, 1903–March 3, 1909); did not seek renomination; unsuccessful candidate for the nomination for United States Senator in 1908; national commissioner to the Panama-Pacific International Exposition at San Francisco in 1915; retired from public and business life; moved to Washington, D. C., in 1916; died at his winter home in Thomasville, Thomas County, Ga., September 26, 1928; interment in Oconee Hill Cemetery, Athens, Ga.

LAMB, Alfred William, a Representative from Missouri; born in Stamford, Delaware County, N. Y., March 18, 1824; moved with his parents to Ralls County, Mo., in 1836; attended Doctor Ely's school in Ely, Mo.; studied law; was admitted to the bar and commenced practice in Hannibal, Mo.; elected as a Democrat to the Thirty-third Congress (March 4, 1853–March 3, 1855); declined to be a candidate for renomination in 1854; resumed the practice of law; died in Hannibal, Marion County, Mo., April 29, 1888; interment in Riverside Cemetery.

LAMB, John, a Representative from Virginia; born in Sussex County, Va., June 12, 1840; attended a private school; during the Civil War enlisted in the Confederate Army in Company D, Third Virginia Cavalry; commanded his company three years; engaged in mercantile pursuits; served as sheriff, treasurer, and surveyor of Charles City County; elected as a Democrat to the Fifty-fifth and to the seven succeeding Congresses (March 4, 1897–March 3, 1913); unsuccessful candidate for reelection; superintendent of Battle Abbey, a Confederate memorial institute in Richmond, Va., where he died on November 21, 1924; interment in Hollywood Cemetery.

LAMB, John Edward, a Representative from Indiana; born in Terre Haute, Ind., December 26, 1852; attended the common schools and was graduated from the Terre Haute High School; studied law; was admitted to the bar in 1873 and commenced practice in Terre Haute; prosecuting attorney of the fourteenth judicial circuit 1875–1880; presidential elector on the Democratic ticket of Hancock and English in 1880; elected as a Democrat to the Forty-eighth Congress (March 4, 1883–March 3, 1885); resumed the practice of law in Terre Haute; appointed United States district attorney for Indiana July 10, 1885, and served until August 16, 1886; delegate to the Democratic National Conventions in 1892, 1896, 1904, 1908, and 1912; died in Terre Haute, Ind., August 23, 1914; interment in Calvary Cemetery.

LAMBERT, John, a Representative and a Senator from New Jersey; born in Lambertville, N. J., February 24, 1746; pursued an academic course; engaged in agricultural pursuits; member of the State general assembly 1780–1785 and in 1788; member of the State council 1790–1804 and served as vice president from 1801 to 1804; Acting Governor 1802 and 1803; elected as a Democrat to the Ninth and Tenth Congresses (March 4, 1805–March 3, 1809); elected to the United States Senate and served from March 4, 1809, to March 3, 1815; owned and managed a plantation; died near Lambertville, N. J., February 4, 1823; interment in Barber's Burying Ground, Delaware Township, Hunterdon County, N. J.

LAMBERTSON, William Purnell, a Representative from Kansas; born in Fairview, Brown County, Kans., March 23, 1880; attended the public schools, Ottawa (Kans.) University, and the law school of the University of Chicago, Chicago, Ill.; engaged in agricultural pursuits; member of the State house of representatives 1909–1911 and 1919–1921, serving as speaker pro tempore in 1911 and as speaker in 1919; served in the State senate 1913–1915; chairman of Kansas State Efficiency and Economy Commission in 1917; member of Kansas State Board of Administration 1923–1925; unsuccessful candidate for nomination for Governor in 1922 and for Congress in 1924 and 1926; elected as a Republican to the Seventy-first and to the seven succeeding Congresses (March 4, 1929–January 3, 1945); unsuccessful candidate for renomination in 1944; returned to his farm near Fairview, Kans.; was defeated for the Republican nomination to Congress in 1946; mayor of Fairview from April 1949 until he resigned in December 1952; chairman, Board of County Commissioners of Brown County, Kans., 1953–1956; died in Fairview, Kans., October 26, 1957; interment in Sabetha Cemetery, Sabetha, Kans.

LAMBETH, John Walter, a Representative from North Carolina; born in Thomasville, Davidson County, N. C., January 10, 1896; attended the public schools; was graduated from Trinity College (now Duke University), Durham, N. C., in 1916, and later attended Harvard University, Cambridge, Mass.; during the First World War entered the Army on January 15, 1918, serving overseas as a sergeant in the Service of Supplies and was discharged July 26, 1919; engaged in the manufacture of furniture 1919–1930; also interested in banking; member of the State senate in 1921; mayor of Thomasville, N. C., 1925–1929; elected as a Democrat to the Seventy-second and to the three succeeding Congresses (March 4, 1931–January 3, 1939); was not a candidate for renomination in 1938; retired; died in Washington, D. C., January 12, 1961; interment in City Cemetery, Thomasville, N. C.

LAMISON, Charles Nelson, a Representative from Ohio; born in Columbia County, Pa., in 1826; moved with his father to Dalton, Wayne County, Ohio, in 1836; privately instructed in elementary branches; studied law; was admitted to the bar in 1848 and commenced practice in Dalton, Wayne County, Ohio; moved to Lima, Ohio, in 1852 and resumed the practice of law; elected prosecuting attorney of Allen County in 1853; defeated in 1855; again elected in 1857; during the Civil War enlisted in the Union Army and was elected captain of Company F, Twentieth Regiment, Ohio Volunteer Infantry, and served in Virginia; assisted in raising the Eighty-first Regiment, Ohio Volunteer

Infantry, of which he was commissioned major; resumed the practice of law in Lima, Ohio; presidential elector on the Democratic ticket of McClellan and Johnson in 1864; unsuccessful candidate for election in 1866 to the Fortieth Congress; elected as a Democrat to the Forty-second and Forty-third Congresses (March 4, 1871–March 3, 1875); was not a candidate for renomination in 1874; appointed attorney for the Ohio Central Railroad Co. of West Virginia in 1881; also served as attorney for the Mobile & Birmingham Railroad Co. and the Memphis, Arkansas & Kansas Railroad Co.; was appointed United States land commissioner in 1892, with headquarters at Dodge City, Kans.; died in Topeka, Kans., on April 24, 1896; interment in Woodlawn Cemetery, Lima, Ohio.

LAMNECK, Arthur Philip, a Representative from Ohio; born in Port Washington, Tuscarawas County, Ohio, March 12, 1880; attended the public schools and was graduated from the Port Washington High School in 1897; engaged in sheet metal business at Columbus, Ohio, 1907 to 1929; delegate to the Democratic National Convention at New York City in 1924; member of the Columbus (Ohio) City Council 1913–1921; elected as a Democrat to the Seventy-second and to the three succeeding Congresses (March 4, 1931–January 3, 1939); unsuccessful candidate for reelection in 1938 to the Seventy-sixth Congress and for election in 1940 to the Seventy-seventh Congress; unsuccessful candidate for nomination for mayor of Columbus, Ohio, in 1943; engaged in the wholesale coal business from 1939 until his death at Columbus, Ohio, April 23, 1944; interment in Port Washington Cemetery, Port Washington, Ohio.

LAMPERT, Florian, a Representative from Wisconsin; born in West Bend, Washington County, Wis., July 8, 1863; attended the public schools; moved with his widowed mother to Oshkosh, Winnebago County, in 1875; engaged in the retail shoe business; city comptroller of Oshkosh from April 1893 to December 1896, when he resigned to take the position of sheriff of Winnebago County; sheriff in 1897 and 1898; resumed mercantile pursuits; commissioner of Oshkosh from May 1914 to November 1918, when he resigned, having been elected to Congress; elected as a Republican to the Sixty-fifth Congress to fill the vacancy caused by the death of James H. Davidson, and on the same day was elected to the Sixty-sixth Congress; reelected to the Sixty-seventh and to the four succeeding Congresses and served from November 5, 1918, until his death in a hospital at Chicago Heights, Ill., July 18, 1930; interment in Riverside Cemetery, Oshkosh, Wis.

LAMPORT, William Henry, a Representative from New York; born in Brunswick, N. Y., May 27, 1811; moved with his parents to Gorham, Ontario County, in 1826; attended the public schools; engaged in agricultural pursuits; supervisor of Gorham in 1848 and 1849; sheriff of Ontario County 1850–1853; member of the State assembly in 1854; moved to Canandaigua in 1864; president of the village of Canandaigua in 1866 and 1867; elected as a Republican to the Forty-second and Forty-third Congresses (March 4, 1871–March 3, 1875); was not a candidate for renomination in 1874; retired to Canandaigua, N. Y., where he died July 21, 1891; interment in the West Avenue Cemetery.

LANCASTER, Columbia, a Delegate from the Territory of Washington; born in New Milford, Litchfield County, Conn., August 26, 1803; moved with his family to Canfield, Ohio, in 1817; attended the common schools; moved to Detroit, Mich., in 1824; studied law; was admitted to the bar in 1830 and commenced practice in Centerville, Mich.; appointed prosecuting attorney of Michigan Territory by Governor Cass; member of the Territorial legislature in 1837; crossed the Plains in 1847 and settled in the Willamette Valley, Oreg.; associate justice of the supreme court under the provisional government; took up his residence near the mouth of the Lewis River, Oreg. (now State of Washington); unsuccessful candidate for Delegate to the Thirty-first Congress from Oregon before the separation of the Territories of Washington and Oregon; member of the Territorial council of Oregon 1850–1852; when the Territory of Washington was admitted to representation was elected as a Democrat to the Thirty-third Congress and served from April 12, 1854, until March 3, 1855; unsuccessful candidate for renomination; regent of the University of Washington at Seattle in 1862; connected with the Puget Sound & Columbia River Railroad project in 1862; died in Vancouver, Wash., September 15, 1893; interment in the City Cemetery.

LANDERS, Franklin, a Representative from Indiana; born near the village of Landersdale, Morgan County, Ind., March 22, 1825; worked on a farm in the summertime and during the winter attended school; at the age of twenty-one engaged in teaching school; was associated with his brother in mercantile pursuits at Waverly, Ind.; laid out the town of Brooklyn, Ind., where he engaged in mercantile pursuits and stock raising; member of the State senate 1860–1864; moved to Indianapolis in 1865 and engaged in the dry-goods business; in 1873 became the head of a pork-packing house; elected as a Democrat to the Forty-fourth Congress (March 4, 1875–March 3, 1877); unsuccessful candidate for reelection in 1876 and for election as Governor of Indiana in 1880; engaged in the management of his farming lands; died in Indianapolis, Ind., September 10, 1901; interment in Crown Hill Cemetery.

LANDERS, George Marcellus, a Representative from Connecticut; born in Lenox, Mass., February 22, 1813; attended the public schools; moved to New Britain, Conn., in 1830 and engaged in the manufacture of hardware; member of the State house of representatives in 1851, 1867, and 1874; served in the State senate in 1853, 1869, and 1873; State bank commissioner in 1874; elected as a Democrat to the Forty-fourth and Forty-fifth Congresses (March 4, 1875–March 3, 1879); retired from active business pursuits; died in New Britain, Conn., March 27, 1895; interment in Fairview Cemetery.

LANDES, Silas Zephaniah, a Representative from Illinois; born in Augusta County, Va., May 15, 1842; attended the public schools; studied law; was admitted to the bar by the supreme court of Illinois in August 1863 and commenced practice in Mount Carmel, Ill.; prosecuting attorney of Wabash County 1872–1884; elected as a Democrat to the Forty-ninth and Fiftieth Congresses (March 4, 1885–March 3, 1889); declined to be a candidate for renomination in 1888; resumed the practice of law in Mount Carmel; elected circuit judge of the fourth judicial circuit of Illinois June 1, 1891, and served six years; resumed the practice of law; died in Mount Carmel, Ill., May 23, 1910; interment in Rose Hill Cemetery.

LANDIS, Charles Beary (brother of Frederick Landis), a Representative from Indiana; born in Millville, Butler County, Ohio, July 9, 1858; attended the public schools of Logansport, Ind., and was graduated from Wabash College, Crawfordsville, Ind., in 1883; editor of the Logansport Journal 1883–1887 and at the time of his nomination for Congress was editor of the Delphi (Ind.) Journal; president of the Indiana Republican Editorial Association in 1894 and 1895; elected as a Republican to the Fifty-fifth and to the five succeeding Congresses (March 4, 1897–March 3, 1909); unsuccessful candidate for reelection; resumed newspaper work in Delphi, Ind.; died in Asheville, N. C., where he had gone because of impaired health, April 24, 1922; interment in Mount Hope Cemetery, Logansport, Ind.

LANDIS, Frederick (brother of Charles Beary Landis), a Representative from Indiana; born at Sevenmile, Butler County, Ohio, August 18, 1872; moved with his parents to Logansport, Ind., in 1875; attended the public schools; was graduated from the law department of the University of Michigan at Ann Arbor in 1895; was admitted to the bar the same year and commenced practice at Logansport, Ind.; elected as a Republican to the Fifty-eighth and Fifty-ninth Congresses (March 4, 1903–March 3, 1907); unsuccessful candidate for reelection in 1906 to the Sixtieth Congress; returned to Logansport and engaged in writing and lecturing; one of the organizers of the Progressive Party in 1912 and temporary chairman of its first State convention in Indiana; delegate to the National Progressive Convention at Chicago in 1912; unsuccessful candidate for Governor on the Progressive ticket in 1912; unsuccessful candidate for the nomination for Governor on the Republican ticket in 1928; author and lecturer; elected to the Seventy-fourth Congress on November 6, 1934, but died in a hospital in Logansport, Ind., November 15, 1934, before Congress had convened; interment in Mount Hope Cemetery.

LANDIS, Gerald Wayne, a Representative from Indiana; born in Bloomfield, Greene County, Ind., February 23, 1895; attended the public schools of Linton, Ind.; served as a lieutenant in the Infantry of the United States Army in 1918 and 1919; was graduated from Indiana University at Bloomington in 1923 and received master's degree in 1938; business and law instructor and athletic director of the high schools at Linton, Ind., 1923–1938; elected as a Republican to the Seventy-sixth and to the four succeeding Congresses (January 3, 1939–January 3, 1949); unsuccessful candidate for reelection in 1948 to the Eighty-first Congress; delegate to the Republican National Convention at Chicago in 1944; assistant to the Administrator, Commodity Stabilization Service, Department of Agriculture, from April 1954 to January 1961; retired; resides in Washington, D. C.

LANDRUM, John Morgan, a Representative from Louisiana; born in Edgefield District, S. C., July 3, 1815; pursued classical studies, and was graduated from South Carolina College (now the University of South Carolina) at Columbia in 1842; taught school for several years; studied law; was admitted to the bar in 1844 and commenced the practice of law in Shreveport, La.; mayor of Shreveport in 1848 and 1849; elected as a Democrat to the Thirty-sixth Congress (March 4, 1859–March 3, 1861); was not a candidate for renomination in 1860 to the Thirty-seventh Congress; continued the practice of his profession until his death in Shreveport, Caddo Parish, La., October 18, 1861; interment in Oakland Cemetery.

LANDRUM, Phillip Mitchell, a Representative from Georgia; born in Martin, Stephens County, Ga., September 10, 1909; attended the public schools and Mercer University, Macon, Ga.; graduated from Piedmont College, Demorest, Ga., in 1939 and from the Atlanta Law School in 1941; superintendent of Nelson (Ga.) High School 1937–1941; was admitted to the bar in 1941 and commenced the practice of law in Canton, Ga.; was an unsuccessful candidate for nomination to the Seventy-eighth Congress in 1942; during World War II enlisted as a private in the United States Air Force on October 2, 1942; served in Europe and was discharged on June 1, 1945, as a first lieutenant; assistant attorney general of State of Georgia in 1946 and 1947; executive secretary to the Governor of Georgia in 1947 and 1948; practiced law in Jasper, Ga., since 1949; elected as a Democrat to the Eighty-third and to the three succeeding Congresses (January 3, 1953–January 3, 1961). *Reelected to the Eighty-seventh Congress.*

LANDRY, Joseph Aristide, a Representative from Louisiana; born near Donaldsonville, Ascension Parish, La., July 10, 1817; attended school in Cape Girardeau, Mo.; member of the State house of representatives in 1840; elected as a Whig to the Thirty-second Congress (March 4, 1851–March 3, 1853); president of police jury of Ascension Parish in 1861; before the Civil War was first sergeant in the Chasseurs de l'Ascension, and later attached to Company B of the Cannoneers of Donaldsonville, but the company was disbanded before being called into Confederate service; died near Donaldsonville, La., March 9, 1881; interment in Donaldsonville Catholic Cemetery.

LANDY, James, a Representative from Pennsylvania; born in Northern Liberties District, Philadelphia, Pa., October 13, 1813; attended the public schools; studied law, but abandoned the same and engaged in mercantile pursuits; member of the board of school commissioners in 1845; elected as a Democrat to the Thirty-fifth Congress (March 4, 1857–March 3, 1859); unsuccessful candidate for reelection; elected chief commissioner of highways in 1862; died in Philadelphia, Pa., July 25, 1875; interment in Monument Cemetery.

LANE, Amos (father of James Henry Lane), a Representative from Indiana; born near Aurora, N. Y., March 1, 1778; attended the public schools; studied law; was admitted to the bar and commenced practice at Lawrenceburg, Ind., in 1808; moved to Burlington, Boone County, Ky., and practiced law; returned to Lawrenceburg, Ind., in 1814 and continued the practice of his profession; elected a member of the first State house of representatives in 1816; reelected in 1817; elected as a Democrat to the Twenty-third and Twenty-fourth Congresses (March 4, 1833–March 3, 1837); unsuccessful candidate for reelection in 1836 to the Twenty-fifth Congress; resumed the practice of law; again a member of the State house of representatives in 1839 and served as speaker; died in Lawrenceburg, Ind., September 2, 1849; interment in the Lawrenceburg Cemetery; reinterment in Greendale Cemetery.

LANE, Edward, a Representative from Illinois; born in Cleveland, Ohio, March 27, 1842; moved to Illinois in May 1858 with his parents, who settled in Hillsboro, Montgomery County; attended the common schools and was graduated from Hillsboro Academy; taught school for several years; studied law; was admitted to the bar in February 1865 and commenced practice in Hillsboro, Ill.; city attorney of Hillsboro three years; elected judge of the Montgomery County Court in November 1869 and served until 1873; elected as a Democrat to the Fiftieth and to the three succeeding Congresses (March 4, 1887–March 3, 1895); unsuccessful candidate for reelection in 1894 to the Fifty-fourth Congress; resumed the practice of law in Hillsboro, Ill., where he died October 30, 1912; interment in Oak Grove Cemetery.

LANE, Harry (grandson of Joseph Lane and nephew of La Fayette Lane), a Senator from Oregon; born in Corvallis, Benton County, Oreg., August 28, 1855; attended the public schools, and was graduated from Willamette University, Salem, Oreg., in 1876; received the medical degree from the same university in 1878; took postgraduate work in the College of Physicians and Surgeons of New York City; commenced the practice of medicine in San Francisco, Calif.; returned to Oregon and settled in Portland, where he resumed the practice of medicine; superintendent of the Oregon State Insane Asylum 1887–1891; mayor of Portland 1905–1909; elected as a Democrat to the United States Senate and served from March 4, 1913, until his death in San Francisco, Calif., May 23, 1917; interment in Lone Fir Cemetery, Portland, Oreg.

LANE, Henry Smith, a Representative and a Senator from Indiana; born near Sharpsburg, Bath County, Ky., February 24, 1811; received a classical education from private tutors; studied law; was admitted to the bar in Mount Sterling, Ky., in 1832 and commenced practice at Crawfordsville, Ind., in 1834; served in the State senate in 1837; member of the State house of representatives 1838 and 1839; elected as a Whig to the Twenty-sixth Congress to fill the vacancy caused by the resignation of Tilghman A. Howard; reelected to the Twenty-seventh Congress and served from August 3, 1840, to March 3, 1843; served in the Mexican War as lieutenant of his company; when the First Indiana Regiment was organized he was made a major; afterward became a lieutenant colonel of Volunteers; abandoned the profession of law and engaged in the banking business at Crawfordsville, Ind., in 1854; permanent chairman of the first Republican National Convention at Philadelphia in 1856; delegate to the Republican National Conventions at Chicago in 1860 and 1868 and at Philadelphia in 1872; elected Governor of Indiana in 1860; was inaugurated January 14, 1861, and served four or five days, when he resigned; elected as a Republican to the United States Senate and served from March 4, 1861, to March 3, 1867; served as special Indian commissioner from 1869 to 1871; commissioner for improvement of the Mississippi River in 1872; died in Crawfordsville, Ind., June 18, 1881; interment in Oak Hill Cemetery.

LANE, James Henry (son of Amos Lane), a Representative from Indiana and a Senator from Kansas; born in Lawrenceburg, Ind., June 22, 1814; attended the public schools; studied law; was admitted to the bar in 1840 and commenced practice in Lawrenceburg; member of the city council; served in the Mexican War; colonel of the Third Indiana Volunteers June 25, 1846; mustered out June 25, 1847; recommissioned colonel of the Fifth Indiana Infantry October 22, 1847; mustered out July 28, 1848; Lieutenant Governor of Indiana in 1849; elected as a Democrat to the Thirty-third Congress (March 4, 1853–March 3, 1855); moved to the Territory of Kansas in 1855; member of the Topeka constitutional convention; elected to the United States Senate by the legislature that convened under the Topeka constitution in 1856, but the election was not recognized by the United States Senate; president of the Leavenworth constitutional convention in 1857; elected as a Republican to the United States Senate in 1861; reelected in 1865 and served from April 4, 1861, until his death; appointed brigadier general of Volunteers for service in the Civil War December 18, 1861, but the appointment was canceled March 21, 1862; died near Fort Leavenworth, Kans., July 11, 1866; interment in the City Cemetery, Lawrence, Kans.

LANE, Joseph (father of La Fayette Lane and grandfather of Harry Lane), a Delegate and a Senator from Oregon; born in Buncombe County, N. C., December 14, 1801; moved with his parents to Henderson, Ky., in 1810; attended the common schools; moved to Vanderburg County, Ind., in 1821; member of the State house of representatives in 1822, 1823, 1831–1833, 1838, and 1839; served in the State senate 1844–1846; during the Mexican War was commissioned as colonel of the Second Indiana Volunteer Regiment on June 25, 1846; promoted to brigadier general on July 1, 1846, and brevetted major general October 9, 1847, "for gallant and meritorious conduct in the Battle of Huamantla, Mexico"; honorably discharged July 20, 1848; appointed by President Polk Governor of the Territory of Oregon and served from March 3, 1849, to June 18, 1850, when he resigned; elected as a Democrat a Delegate to the Thirty-second and to the three succeeding Congresses and served from March 4, 1851, until February 14, 1859, when the Territory became a State; during the interim between the sessions of the

Thirty-second and Thirty-third Congresses was appointed Governor of the Territory by President Pierce and served from May 16 to 19, 1853, when he again resigned; upon the admission of Oregon as a State into the Union was elected to the United States Senate and served from February 14, 1859, to March 3, 1861; did not seek reelection in 1860, having become a candidate for Vice President; nominated for Vice President of the United States on the Democratic ticket of Breckinridge and Lane in 1860; died in Roseburg, Oreg., April 19, 1881; interment in the Masonic Cemetery.

LANE, Joseph Reed, a Representative from Iowa; born in Davenport, Scott County, Iowa, May 6, 1858; attended the public schools; was graduated from Knox College, Galesburg, Ill., in 1878 and from the law department of the State University of Iowa at Iowa City in 1880; was admitted to the bar in the latter year and commenced practice in Davenport, Iowa; served as regent of the State University of Iowa; member of the city council 1884–1889; elected as a Republican to the Fifty-sixth Congress (March 4, 1899–March 3, 1901); was not a candidate for renomination in 1900; resumed the practice of law in Davenport, Iowa; delegate to the Republican National Convention at Chicago in 1908; died in Davenport, Iowa, on May 1, 1931; interment in Oakdale Cemetery.

LANE, La Fayette (son of Joseph Lane and uncle of Harry Lane), a Representative from Oregon; born near Evansville, Vanderburg County, Ind., November 12, 1842; attended the public schools at Washington, D. C., and at Stamford, Conn.; studied law; was admitted to the bar and commenced practice in Roseburg, Oreg.; member of the State house of representatives in 1864; code commissioner in 1874; elected as a Democrat to the Forty-fourth Congress to fill the vacancy caused by the death of George A. La Dow and served from October 25, 1875, to March 3, 1877; unsuccessful candidate for reelection in 1876 to the Forty-fifth Congress; resumed the practice of law; died in Roseburg, Oreg., on November 23, 1896; interment in the Catholic Cemetery.

LANE, Thomas Joseph, a Representative from Massachusetts; born in Lawrence, Essex County, Mass., July 6, 1898; attended the public schools; during the First World War served as an enlisted man in the United States Army; was graduated from Suffolk Law School, Boston, Mass., in 1925; was admitted to the bar in 1926 and commenced practice in Lawrence, Mass.; member of the State house of representatives 1927–1938; served in the State senate from 1939 until his resignation in 1941; elected as a Democrat to the Seventy-seventh Congress to fill the vacancy caused by the death of Lawrence J. Connery; reelected to the Seventy-eighth and the eight succeeding Congresses and served from December 30, 1941, to January 3, 1961. *Reelected to the Eighty-seventh Congress.*

LANGDON, Chauncey, a Representative from Vermont; born in Farmington, Conn., November 8, 1763; pursued classical studies, and was graduated from Yale College, New Haven, Conn., in 1787; studied law at Litchfield, Conn.; was admitted to the bar in 1787 and commenced practice in Castleton, Vt.; moved to "The Grants" in 1788; settled in Winsdor, Vt., later returning to Castleton, Vt.; register of probate 1792–1797; judge of probate in 1798 and 1799; State councilor in 1808; member of the State house of representatives in 1813, 1814, 1817, 1819, 1820, and 1822; trustee of Middlebury (Vt.) College 1811–1830; elected as a Federalist to the Fourteenth Congress (March 4, 1815–March 3, 1817); was not a candidate for renomination to the Fifteenth Congress; again elected as State councilor and served from 1823 until his death in Castleton, Vt., July 23, 1830; interment in the Congregational Cemetery.

LANGDON, John (brother of Woodbury Langdon), a Delegate and a Senator from New Hampshire; born in Portsmouth, N. H., June 25, 1741; attended the school of Major Hale in Portsmouth; engaged in mercantile pursuits; prominent in pre-Revolutionary affairs and during the war; a representative in the general court; Member of the Continental Congress in 1775 and 1776; resigned in June 1776 to become Navy agent and superintended the construction of several ships of war; served several terms as speaker of the State house of representatives and during the session of 1777 staked his fortune to equip Gen. John Stark's brigade; participated in the Battle of Bennington and commanded a company at Saratoga and in Rhode Island; again a Member of the Continental Congress in 1783; President of New Hampshire in 1785; delegate to the Federal Constitutional Convention in 1787; Governor of New Hampshire in 1788, 1805, and 1809–1811; elected as a Democrat to the United States Senate and served from March 4, 1789, to March 3, 1801; elected the first President pro tempore of the Senate on April 6, 1789, in order that the Senate might organize to count the electoral vote for President and Vice President of the United States; declined to accept the portfolio of Secretary of the Navy in the Cabinet of President Madison in 1811 and the Democratic nomination as a candidate for Vice President in 1812; died in Portsmouth, N. H., September 18, 1819; interment in the Langdon tomb in the North Cemetery.

LANGDON, Woodbury (brother of John Langdon), a Delegate from New Hampshire; born in Portsmouth, N. H., in 1739; attended the public schools; engaged in mercantile pursuits; prominent in pre-Revolutionary affairs and throughout the war; served in the State house of representatives in 1778 and 1779; Member of the Continental Congress in 1779 and 1780; member of the State executive council 1781–1784; judge of the State superior court in 1782 and again from 1786 to January 1791, when he resigned; appointed in December 1790 by President Washington a commissioner to settle Revolutionary War claims; died in Portsmouth, N. H., January 13, 1805; interment in the North Cemetery.

LANGEN, Odin, a Representative from Minnesota; born in Minneapolis, Minn., January 5, 1913; attended the public schools and graduated from Kennedy (Minn.) High School in 1931; attended Dunwoody Institute, Minneapolis, Minn., in 1933 and 1934; engaged in farming in Kittson County, near Kennedy, Minn.; associated with Production Marketing Administration in Kittson County, Minn., 1935–1950; member of Kennedy (Minn.) School Board, serving as president, 1948–1950, South Red River Town Board 1947–1950, and the State house of representatives 1950–1958, serving as Republican leader in 1957 and 1958; elected as a Republican to the Eighty-sixth Congress (January 3, 1959–January 3, 1961). *Reelected to the Eighty-seventh Congress.*

LANGER, William, a Senator from North Dakota; born on a farm in Everest Township, near Casselton, Cass County, N. Dak., September 30, 1886; attended a rural school and later Casselton High School; graduated from the law department of the University of North Dakota at Grand Forks in 1906 and from Columbia University, New York, N. Y., in 1910; was admitted to the bar in 1911 and began practice in Mandan, N. Dak.; State's attorney of Morton County, N. Dak., 1914–1916; moved to Bismarck, N. Dak., in 1916 and continued the practice of law; attorney general of North Dakota 1916–1920; legal adviser for Council of Defense during the First World War; unsuccessful candidate for Governor in 1920; elected Governor in 1932 and served from January 1933 to July 17, 1934, when he was removed by the supreme court of North Dakota; again

Governor from 1937 to 1939; unsuccessful candidate for the Republican nomination for United States Senator in 1938 and also for election to the United States Senate as an Independent candidate; elected as a Republican to the United States Senate in 1940; reelected in 1946, 1952, and again in 1958, and served from January 3, 1941, until his death in Washington, D. C., November 8, 1959; interment in St. Leo's Catholic Cemetery, Casselton, N. Dak.

LANGHAM, Jonathan Nicholas, a Representative from Pennsylvania; born near Hillsdale, Indiana County, Pa., August 4, 1861; attended the common schools; taught school; was graduated from the State normal school at Indiana, Pa., in 1882; studied law; was admitted to the Indiana County bar in December 1888 and commenced practice in Indiana, Pa.; postmaster of Indiana, Pa., from May 21, 1892, to April 25, 1893; assistant United States attorney for the western district of Pennsylvania 1898–1904; chief clerk and corporation deputy in the auditor general's department of Pennsylvania 1904–1909; elected as a Republican to the Sixty-first, Sixty-second, and Sixty-third Congresses (March 4, 1909–March 3, 1915); was not a candidate for renomination in 1914; elected in 1915 judge of the court of common pleas for the fortieth judicial district of Pennsylvania for a term of ten years; reelected in 1925 and served until his retirement in January 1936; died in Indiana, Pa., May 21, 1945; interment in Oakland Cemetery.

LANGLEY, John Wesley (husband of Katherine Gudger Langley), a Representative from Kentucky; born in Floyd County, Ky., January 14, 1868; attended the common schools; taught school for three years; attended the law department of the National, Georgetown, and Columbian (now George Washington) Universities in Washington, D. C., for an aggregate period of eight years; examiner in the Pension Office and a member of the Board of Pension Appeals; law clerk in the General Land Office; disbursing and appointment clerk of the Census Office 1899–1907; served in the State house of representatives 1886–1890 and was the caucus nominee of his party, who were in the minority, for speaker of the house; delegate to three Republican National Conventions; elected as a Republican to the Sixtieth and to the nine succeeding Congresses and served from March 4, 1907, until January 11, 1926, when he resigned; resumed the practice of law in Pikeville, Ky., where he died on January 17, 1932; interment in the Langley Cemetery at Middle Creek, Ky.

LANGLEY, Katherine Gudger (wife of John Wesley Langley and daughter of James Madison Gudger, Jr.), a Representative from Kentucky; born near Marshall in Madison County, N. C., February 14, 1888; attended the common schools; was graduated from the Woman's College, Richmond, Va.; attended Emerson College of Oratory, Boston, Mass.; taught expression at the Virginia Institute at Bristol, Tenn.; moved to Pikeville, Ky., in 1905; vice chairman of the Republican State Central Committee of Kentucky 1920–1922; served as the first chairman of the Kentucky Woman's Republican State Committee in 1920; alternate delegate to the Republican National Convention in 1920 and delegate in 1924; chairman of the Pike County Red Cross Society during the First World War; elected as a Republican to the Seventieth and Seventy-first Congresses (March 4, 1927–March 3, 1931); unsuccessful candidate for reelection in 1930 to the Seventy-second Congress; railroad commissioner, third Kentucky district, 1939–1942; died in Pikeville, Ky., on August 15, 1948; interment in Johnson Memorial Cemetery.

LANGSTON, John Mercer, a Representative from Virginia; born in Louisa, Louisa County, Va., December 14, 1829; was of the Negro race; attended the common schools in Ohio; was

graduated from the literary department of Oberlin College in 1849 and from the theological department in 1852; studied law in Elyria, Ohio; was admitted to the bar in 1854 and commenced practice in Oberlin, Ohio; took an active part in recruiting colored troops during the Civil War, especially for the Fifty-fourth and Fifty-fifth Massachusetts and Fifth Ohio Regiments; member of the council of Oberlin 1865–1867; member of the city board of education in 1867 and 1868; appointed inspector general of the Bureau of Freedmen, Refugees, and Abandoned Lands in 1868; moved to Washington, D. C., and practiced law; dean of the law department of Howard University 1869–1876; appointed and commissioned by President Grant a member of the Board of Health of the District of Columbia in 1871; appointed by President Hayes Minister Resident and consul general to Haiti and Chargé d'Affaires to Santo Domingo; elected vice president and acting president of Howard University in 1872; delegate to the Republican National Convention at Cincinnati in 1876; returned to Virginia, having been elected president of the Virginia Normal and Collegiate Institute, Petersburg, Va., in 1885; delegate to the Republican State convention in 1890; successfully contested as a Republican the election of Edward C. Venable to the Fifty-first Congress and served from September 23, 1890, to March 3, 1891; unsuccessful candidate for reelection in 1890 to the Fifty-second Congress; died in Washington, D. C., on November 15, 1897; interment in Woodlawn Cemetery.

LANGWORTHY, Edward, a Delegate from Georgia; born in Savannah, Ga., in 1738; attended a school kept in connection with the Bethesda Orphan House, of which he was an inmate, and later became an instructor in the institution; assisted in organizing the Georgia Council of Safety and became secretary of the council December 11, 1775; Member of the Continental Congress 1777–1779; signer of the Articles of Confederation; moved to Baltimore, Md., in 1785; engaged in newspaper work until 1787; teacher of the classics in Baltimore Academy 1787–1791; moved to Elkton, Md., about 1791, where he was engaged in writing a history of Georgia; returned to Baltimore in 1795; clerk of customs from that time until his death in Baltimore, Md., November 2, 1802.

LANHAM, Fritz Garland (son of Samuel Willis Tucker Lanham), a Representative from Texas; born in Weatherford, Tex., January 3, 1880; attended the public schools of Washington, D. C., and was graduated from Weatherford College, Weatherford, Tex., in 1897; attended Vanderbilt University in 1897 and 1898, and was graduated from the University of Texas at Austin in 1900, subsequently taking a law course in the same institution; was admitted to the bar in 1909 and commenced practice in Weatherford, Tex.; moved to Fort Worth, Tex., in 1917; elected as a Democrat to the Sixty-sixth Congress to fill the vacancy caused by the resignation of James C. Wilson; reelected to the Sixty-seventh and to the twelve succeeding Congresses and served from April 19, 1919, to January 3, 1947; was not a candidate for renomination in 1946; engaged as an adviser on legislation in Washington, D. C.; is a legal resident of Fort Worth, Tex.

LANHAM, Henderson Lovelace, a Representative from Georgia; born in Rome, Floyd County, Ga., September 14, 1888; attended the public schools of Rome, Ga., and the Piedmont Institute at Rockmart, Ga.; was graduated from the University of Georgia at Athens in 1910, from the law department of the same university in 1911, and from the Harvard University Graduate School, Cambridge, Mass., in 1912; was admitted to the bar in 1911 and commenced practice in Rome, Ga.; chairman of the board of education of Rome, Ga., in 1918 and 1919; member of the State house of representatives 1929–1933 and 1937–1940; solicitor general of Rome judicial circuit 1941–1946; elected as a Democrat to the Eightieth and to the five succeeding Congresses and served from January 3, 1947, until his death due to a train collision with his automobile at a crossing in Rome, Ga., November 10, 1957; interment in Myrtle Hill Cemetery.

LANHAM, Samuel Willis Tucker (father of Fritz Garland Lanham), a Representative from Texas; born in Spartanburg District, near Woodruff, S. C., on July 4, 1846; attended the common schools; entered the Confederate Army when a boy; moved to Texas in 1866 and settled at Boston, near Clarksville, Red River County; taught school for one year; moved to Weatherford in 1867 and continued teaching; studied law; was admitted to the bar in 1869 and engaged in practice in Weatherford, Tex.; district attorney 1871–1876; presidential elector on the Democratic ticket of Hancock and English in 1880; elected as a Democrat to the Forty-eighth and to the four succeeding Congresses (March 4, 1883–March 3, 1893); was not a candidate for renomination in 1892; elected to the Fifty-fifth, Fifty-sixth, and Fifty-seventh Congresses and served from March 4, 1897, until his resignation on January 15, 1903, having been elected Governor; Governor of Texas 1903–1907; died in Weatherford, Tex., July 29, 1908; interment in Greenwood Cemetery.

LANING, Jay Ford, a Representative from Ohio; born in New London, Huron County, Ohio, May 15, 1853; attended the public schools, the Savannah (Ohio) Academy, and Baldwin University, Berea, Ohio; studied law; was admitted to the bar in May 1875 and commenced practice in New London; justice of the peace 1875–1881; member of the village council in 1876; moved to Norwalk, Ohio, in January 1882; practiced law until 1885 and then engaged in the publishing business; member of the city council 1887–1889; member of the State senate 1893–1897; delegate to the Republican National Conventions in 1904 and 1908; elected as a Republican to the Sixtieth Congress (March 4, 1907–March 3, 1909); renominated in 1908, but withdrew and resumed the publishing business in Norwalk, Ohio; devoted his time and interest to the allied fields of writing, editing, and publishing lawbooks and school textbooks; thirty different works have been copyrighted in his name and are now collected in the Ohioanna Library; died in Norwalk, Ohio, on September 1, 1941; interment in Woodlawn Cemetery.

LANKFORD, Menalcus, a Representative from Virginia; born on the Bowers plantation near Franklin, Southampton County, Va., on March 14, 1883; attended public and private schools and the Norfolk High School; was graduated from the University of Richmond at Richmond in 1904, and from the law department of the University of Virginia at Charlottesville in 1906; was admitted to the bar the same year and commenced practice in Norfolk, Va.; during the First World War served as an ensign in the aviation service of the United States Navy; unsuccessful candidate for election in 1920 to the Sixty-seventh Congress and in 1924 to the Sixty-ninth Congress; elected as a Republican to the Seventy-first and Seventy-second Congresses (March 4, 1929–March 3, 1933); unsuccessful candidate for reelection in 1932 to the Seventy-third Congress; delegate to the Republican National Conventions in 1932 and 1936; appointed referee in bankruptcy in 1933 of the Norfolk division, United States District Court, Eastern District of Virginia, and served until his death in Norfolk, Va., December 27, 1937; interment in Forest Lawn Cemetery.

LANKFORD, Richard Estep, a Representative from Maryland; born in Wilmington, New Castle County, Del., July 22, 1914; moved to Annapolis from Baltimore in 1940; attended the public schools in Baltimore, Md., and Alexandria, Va.; graduated from the University of Virginia in 1937 and from the law school of the University of Maryland in 1940; was admitted to the bar in 1940 and commenced the practice of law in Annapolis, Md.; engaged in active management of tobacco and cattle farms; commissioned an ensign in the United States Naval Reserve in July 1942; served two and one-half years in the European Theater of Operations and released to inactive duty as a lieutenant in February 1946; appointed in 1948 to fill an unexpired term in the Maryland House of Delegates; elected in 1950 and served until 1954; unsuccessful Democratic candidate for election to the Eighty-third Congress in 1952; member of Maryland Legislative Council in 1953; member of the advisory board of Anne Arundel General Hospital; elected as a Democrat to the Eighty-fourth, Eighty-fifth, and Eighty-sixth Congresses (January 3, 1955–January 3, 1961). *Reelected to the Eighty-seventh Congress.*

LANKFORD, William Chester, a Representative from Georgia; born in Camp Creek Community, Clinch County, Ga., December 7, 1877; attended the public schools in Clinch County and Abbeville, Ga.; taught school for several years in his native county; was graduated from Jasper Normal Institute, Jasper, Fla., in 1897, from the Georgia Normal College and Business Institute, Abbeville, Ga., in 1900, and from the law department of the University of Georgia at Athens in 1901; moved to Douglas, Ga., in 1901 and commenced the practice of law; mayor of Douglas in 1906; member of the board of education of Douglas 1907–1918; judge of the city court from January 1, 1908, until May 1, 1916, when he resigned to seek the Democratic nomination for Congress, but was an unsuccessful candidate; elected as a Democrat to the Sixty-sixth and to the six succeeding Congresses (March 4, 1919–March 3, 1933); unsuccessful candidate for renomination in 1932; resumed the practice of law; with General Accounting Office in Washington, D. C., from January 1935 to October 1942, when he retired; is a resident of Washington, D. C.

LANMAN, James, a Senator from Connecticut; born in Norwich, Conn., June 14, 1767; pursued classical studies, and was graduated from Yale College in 1788; studied law; was admitted to the bar in 1791 and commenced practice in Norwich; State's attorney for New London County 1814–1819; member of the State house of representatives in 1817; delegate to the State constitutional convention in 1818; served in the State senate in 1819 and again in 1832; elected as a Democrat to the United States Senate and served from March 4, 1819, to March 3, 1825; presented credentials as a Senator-designate to fill the vacancy in the term beginning March 4, 1825, but was not permitted to qualify; judge of the State superior and supreme courts 1826–1829; mayor of Norwich 1831–1834; again a member of the State house of representatives in 1833; died in Norwich, Conn., August 7, 1841; interment in the City Cemetery.

LANNING, William Mershon, a Representative from New Jersey; born in Ewingville, Mercer County, N. J., January 1, 1849; was graduated from the Lawrenceville School in 1866; employed as a teacher in the public schools of Mercer County and in the Trenton Academy 1866–1880; studied law; was admitted to the bar in 1880 and commenced practice in Trenton, N. J.; counselor in 1883; elected city solicitor for Trenton in 1884; appointed judge of the city district court in 1887 and served until 1891, when legislated out of office; member of a commission to frame township laws and of the constitutional commission of 1894; president of the Mechanics' National Bank of Trenton in 1899; elected as a Republican to the Fifty-eighth Congress and served from March 4, 1903, to June 6, 1904, when he resigned to accept an appointment as United States district judge for New Jersey; served in that capacity until

May 18, 1909, when he was appointed United States circuit judge for the third circuit, which position he held until his death in Trenton, N. J., February 16, 1912; interment in the Presbyterian Cemetery, Ewing, near Trenton, N. J.

LANSING, Frederick, a Representative from New York; born in Manheim, Herkimer County, N. Y., February 16, 1838; attended the Little Falls Academy, New York; studied law; was admitted to the bar in 1859 and practiced in Watertown, N. Y.; served during the Civil War in the Eighth New York Cavalry; acting adjutant of that regiment from June 23 to October 11, 1863; wounded in the Battle of Bristoe Station, Va., in 1863 and the next year was discharged on account of wounds; member of the State senate 1881–1885; elected as a Republican to the Fifty-first Congress (March 4, 1889–March 3, 1891); retired from public life on account of ill health; died in Watertown, N. Y., January 31, 1894; interment in Brookside Cemetery.

LANSING, Gerrit Yates (nephew of John Lansing, Jr.), a Representative from New York; born in Albany, N. Y., August 4, 1783; pursued classical studies, and was graduated from Union College in 1800; studied law; was admitted to the bar in 1804 and commenced practice in Albany; clerk of the State assembly in 1807; judge of the court of probates 1816–1823; elected regent of the University of the State of New York in 1829 and served until his death; was appointed chancellor of the board on October 31, 1842; elected as a Jackson Democrat to the Twenty-second, Twenty-third, and Twenty-fourth Congresses (March 4, 1831–March 3, 1837); was not a candidate for reelection in 1836; president of the Albany Savings Bank 1854–1862; president of the Albany Insurance Co. 1859–1862; died in Albany, Albany County, N. Y., January 3, 1862; interment in the Albany Rural Cemetery.

LANSING, John, Jr. (uncle of Gerrit Yates Lansing), a Delegate from New York; born in Albany, N. Y., January 30, 1754; studied law in Albany and in New York City; was admitted to the bar in 1775; secretary to General Schuyler 1776 and 1777; engaged in the practice of law in Albany in 1778; member of the State assembly 1780–1786 and served as speaker in 1786; Member of the Continental Congress 1784 and 1785; delegate to the Federal Constitutional Convention in 1787; withdrew from the latter July 10, 1787, on the ground that his credentials gave him no power to assist in the framing of a Federal constitution but only to amend the Articles of Confederation; delegate to the State convention in June 1788 to ratify the Federal Constitution; again a member and speaker of the State assembly in 1789; member of the commission to settle the New York-Vermont boundary line in 1790; justice of the supreme court of New York 1790–1798 and chief justice 1798–1801; chancellor 1801–1814; unanimously nominated by the Anti-Federalists for Governor of New York in 1804, but declined; commissioner to determine the claims of the city and county of New York to certain lands in Vermont in 1817; regent of the University of the State of New York 1817–1829; presidential elector in 1824; mysteriously disappeared after leaving his hotel to post a letter at one of the docks in New York City, December 12, 1829.

LANSING, William Esselstyne, a Representative from New York; born in Perryville, Madison County, N. Y., December 29, 1821; attended the common schools; was graduated from Cazenovia Seminary in 1841; studied law in Utica, N. Y.; was admitted to the bar in 1845 and commenced practice in Chittenango; district attorney of Madison County 1850–1853; president of the village of Chittenango 1853–1855; county clerk 1855–1858; elected as a Republican to the Thirty-seventh Congress (March 4,

1861–March 3, 1863); was not a candidate for renomination in 1862; elected to the Forty-second and Forty-third Congresses (March 4, 1871–March 3, 1875); was not a candidate for renomination; resumed the practice of law in Syracuse, N. Y., in 1876 and died there July 29, 1883; interment in Oakwood Cemetery, Chittenango, N. Y.

LANTAFF, William Courtland, a Representative from Florida; born in Buffalo, Erie County, N. Y., July 31, 1913; moved to Jacksonville, Fla., in 1921 and to Miami, Fla., in 1929; graduated from high school in 1930; graduated from the University of Florida in 1935 and from its law school in 1936; was admitted to the bar in 1936 and commenced the practice of law in Miami, Fla.; assistant city judge of Miami Beach in 1939 and 1940; inducted into the Federal service with Florida National Guard as a first lieutenant on January 6, 1941, serving as executive officer for the Military Intelligence Division, War Department General Staff; was discharged as a lieutenant colonel on November 15, 1945; again on active duty from September 15 to December 15, 1950; assistant chief of staff, G–2, Fifty-first Infantry Division, Florida National Guard, since 1945; lieutenant colonel, G–2, General Staff, Department of the Army, since 1950 and promoted to colonel in 1953; member of the State house of representatives 1947–1950; elected as a Democrat to the Eighty-second and Eighty-third Congresses (January 3, 1951–January 3, 1955); was not a candidate for renomination in 1954; delegate to Democratic National Conventions in 1956 and 1960; resumed law practice; resides in Miami Springs, Fla.

LANZETTA, James Joseph, a Representative from New York; born in New York City, N. Y., December 21, 1894; attended the public schools; was graduated from the Stuyvesant High School, New York City, in 1913, from Columbia University, School of Engineering, New York City, in 1917, and from the law school of Fordham University, New York City, in 1924; served in the United States Army during the First World War as a private in Company C, Three Hundred and Second Engineers, and as a sergeant, first class, in the First Air Service Mechanics Regiment, serving overseas from February 1918 to July 1919; engineer and salesman in New York City 1919–1922; assistant supervisor, Department of Markets, 1922–1925; was admitted to the bar in 1925 and commenced the practice of law in New York City; member of the New York City Board of Aldermen from January 1932 to March 1933, when he resigned, having been elected to Congress; elected as a Democrat to the Seventy-third Congress (March 4, 1933–January 3, 1935); unsuccessful candidate for reelection in 1934 to the Seventy-fourth Congress; elected to the Seventy-fifth Congress (January 3, 1937–January 3, 1939); unsuccessful candidate for reelection in 1938 to the Seventy-sixth Congress and for election in 1940 to the Seventy-seventh Congress; resumed the practice of law; alternate to the Democratic National Convention in 1940 and the Democratic State conventions in 1942 and 1946; appointed city magistrate of New York City July 2, 1947, and served until May 26, 1948, when he was appointed a justice of the Domestic Relations Court of New York City, in which capacity he served until his death; died in New York City, N. Y., October 27, 1956; interment in Woodlawn Cemetery, New York City (the Bronx), N. Y.

LAPHAM, Elbridge Gerry, a Representative and a Senator from New York; born in Farmington, N. Y., October 18, 1814; attended the public schools and the Canandaigua Academy; studied civil engineering; studied law; was admitted to the bar in 1844 and practiced in Canandaigua, N. Y.; member of the constitutional convention of New York in 1867; elected as a Republican to the Forty-fourth and to the three succeeding Congresses and served from March 4, 1875, until his resignation

July 29, 1881, having been elected Senator; one of the managers appointed by the House of Representatives in 1876 to conduct the impeachment proceedings against ex-Secretary of War William W. Belknap; elected to the United States Senate on July 22, 1881, to fill the vacancy caused by the resignation of Roscoe Conkling and served from August 2, 1881, to March 3, 1885; was not a candidate for reelection; resumed the practice of law in Canandaigua, N. Y.; died at "Glen Gerry," on Canandaigua Lake, N. Y., January 8, 1890; interment in Woodlawn Cemetery, Canandaigua, N. Y.

LAPHAM, Oscar, a Representative from Rhode Island; born in Burrillville, Providence County, R. I., June 29, 1837; attended the seminary in Scituate, Mass., the academy in Pembroke, N. H., the University Grammar School, Providence, R. I., and was graduated from Brown University, Providence, R. I., in 1864; member of the board of trustees and of the advisory and executive committee of that university; studied law; was admitted to the bar in 1867 and practiced in Providence, R. I.; served in the Civil War as first lieutenant, adjutant, and captain in the Twelfth Rhode Island Volunteers; aide-de-camp on brigade staff; served in the Army of the Potomac and the Department of the Ohio in Kentucky; captain of the university cadets of Brown University and colonel of United Train of Artillery, an ancient military organization, under special charter; member of the State senate in 1887 and 1888; member and treasurer of the Democratic State central committee 1887–1891; unsuccessful candidate for election to the Forty-eighth, Fiftieth, and Fifty-first Congresses; elected as a Democrat to the Fifty-second and Fifty-third Congresses (March 4, 1891–March 3, 1895); unsuccessful candidate for reelection in 1894 to the Fifty-fourth Congress; resumed the practice of law in Providence, R. I., and died there March 29, 1926; interment in Swan Point Cemetery.

LAPORTE, John, a Representative from Pennsylvania; born in Asylum, Asylum Township, Bradford County, Pa., on November 4, 1798; attended the common schools; county auditor of Bradford County in 1827 and 1828; member of the State house of representatives 1828–1832 and served as speaker in 1831 and 1832; elected to the Twenty-third and Twenty-fourth Congresses (March 4, 1833–March 3, 1837); was not a candidate for renomination in 1836; associate judge of Bradford County 1837–1845; interested in the development of the North Branch Canal; surveyor general of Pennsylvania 1845–1851; engaged in banking at Towanda, Pa., 1850–1862; died in Philadelphia, Pa., August 22, 1862; interment in the family cemetery at Asylum, near Towanda, Pa.

LARCADE, Henry Dominique, Jr., a Representative from Louisiana; born in Opelousas, St. Landry Parish, La., July 12, 1890; attended the public and parochial schools, Opelousas High School, Academy Immaculate Conception, and Opelousas Institute; during the First World War served as a private in the Three Hundred and Forty-eighth Infantry, Eighty-seventh Division, at Camp Pike, Ark., later obtaining a commission as second lieutenant, Quartermaster Corps, Officers' Reserve Corps; engaged in the banking business as clerk, teller, cashier, and trust officer, also the general insurance business; member of the St. Landry Parish School Board 1913–1928; member of the State senate 1928–1932; assistant clerk of the State senate 1932–1936; served in the State house of representatives 1936–1940; elected as a Democrat to the Seventy-eighth and to the four succeeding Congresses (January 3, 1943–January 3, 1953); was not a candidate for renomination in 1952; member of the State senate 1956–1960; engaged in banking business; is a resident of Opelousas, La.

LARNED, Simon, a Representative from Massachusetts; born in Thompson, Conn., August 3, 1753; attended the common schools; sheriff of Berkshire County; served in the Revolutionary War with rank as captain in Colonel Shepherd's regiment; engaged in mercantile pursuits in Pittsfield, Mass., in 1784; was a representative in the general court in 1791; county treasurer 1792–1812; served as colonel of the Ninth United States Infantry in the War of 1812 and was engaged in action at Plattsburg, along the Mohawk River; elected to the Eighth Congress to fill the vacancy caused by the resignation of Thomson J. Skinner and served from November 5, 1804, to March 3, 1805; president of the Berkshire Bank; died in Pittsfield, Mass., on November 16, 1817; interment in the Pittsfield Cemetery.

LARRABEE, Charles Hathaway, a Representative from Wisconsin; born in Rome, N. Y., November 9, 1820; moved with his father to Ohio; attended Granville College; studied engineering and law; was admitted to the bar in 1841 and commenced practice in Pontotoc, Miss.; moved to Chicago, Ill., in 1844 and continued the practice of law; city attorney in 1846 and 1847; moved to Horicon, Wis., in 1847 and practiced law; delegate to the State constitutional convention in 1847; judge of the third judicial circuit and of the State supreme court 1848–1858; resigned; elected as a Democrat to the Thirty-sixth Congress (March 4, 1859–March 3, 1861); unsuccessful candidate for reelection in 1860 to the Thirty-seventh Congress; during the Civil War served in the Union Army from April 17, 1861, until his resignation in September 1863 and was promoted from lieutenant to colonel; moved to California in 1864 and practiced law in San Bernardino and also in Salem, Oreg., and Seattle, Wash.; was seriously injured in a railroad accident at Tehachapi, Calif., which resulted in his death in Los Angeles, Calif., on January 20, 1883; interment in the Masonic Cemetery, San Francisco, Calif.

LARRABEE, William Henry, a Representative from Indiana; born on a farm near Crawfordsville, Montgomery County, Ind., February 21, 1870; attended the public schools, Indiana Central Normal School at Danville, and Indiana State Normal School at Terre Haute; taught in public schools at New Palestine, Ind., 1889–1895; was graduated from the Indiana School of Medicine at Indianapolis in 1898; commenced practice of medicine and surgery in New Palestine, Ind., in 1898; secretary of Hancock County Board of Health in 1917 and 1918; served on the city council of New Palestine, Ind., 1916–1920; member of the State house of representatives 1923–1925; elected as a Democrat to the Seventy-second and to the five succeeding Congresses (March 4, 1931–January 3, 1943); unsuccessful candidate for reelection in 1942 to the Seventy-eighth Congress; resumed the practice of medicine and surgery; died in New Palestine, Ind., November 16, 1960; interment in New Palestine Cemetery.

LARRAZOLO, Octaviano Ambrosio, a Senator from New Mexico; born in Allende, State of Chihuahua, Mexico, December 7, 1859; came to the United States in November 1870 under the protection of the Right Reverend J. B. Salpointe, bishop of Arizona and subsequently archbishop of Santa Fe, N. Mex.; attended St. Michael's College at Santa Fe in 1875 and 1876; taught in the public schools at San Elizario, El Paso County, Tex., 1878–1884; appointed clerk of the United States District and Circuit Courts for the Western District of Texas at El Paso, Tex., in 1885; elected clerk of the district court at El Paso in 1886 and 1888; studied law; was admitted to the bar in 1888; elected district attorney for the western district of Texas in 1890 and reelected in 1892; moved to Las Vegas, N. Mex., in January 1895 and resumed the practice of law; unsuccessful Democratic candidate for election as a Delegate to Congress in 1890, 1900, and 1908, unsuccessfully contesting the election of William H. Andrews in 1908; affiliated with the Republican Party in 1910; elected as a Republican Governor of New Mexico in 1918; served in the New Mexico House of Representatives in 1927 and 1928; elected as a Republican to the United States Senate to fill the vacancy caused by the death of Andrieus A. Jones and served from December 7, 1928, to March 3, 1929; was not a candidate for the full term; resumed the practice of law; died in Albuquerque, N. Mex., April 7, 1930; interment in Santa Barbara Cemetery.

LARRINAGA, Tulio, a Resident Commissioner from Puerto Rico; born in Trujillo Alto, P. R., January 15, 1847; attended the Seminario Consiliar of San Ildefonso at San Juan, P. R.; studied civil engineering in the Polytechnic Institute, Troy, N. Y., and was graduated from the University of Pennsylvania at Philadelphia in 1871; practiced his profession for some time in the United States, taking part in the preparation of the topographical map of Kings County (Brooklyn), and engaged in the technical department of Badger & Co. in the construction of the Grand Central Depot in New York City; returned to Puerto Rico in 1872 and was appointed architect for the city of San Juan; built the first railroad in Puerto Rico in 1880 and introduced American rolling stock on the island; was for ten years chief engineer of the provincial works; in 1898 was appointed assistant secretary of the interior under the autonomic government and in 1900 was sent by his party as a delegate to Washington; member of the house of delegates for the district of Arecibo in 1902; elected as a Unionist Resident Commissioner to the United States in 1904; reelected in 1906 and 1908 and served from March 4, 1905, until March 3, 1911; delegate from the United States to the Third Pan American Congress at Rio de Janeiro in 1906; member of the executive council of Puerto Rico in 1911; resumed the practice of his profession as a civil engineer in San Juan, P. R., and died there on April 28, 1917; interment in the Municipal Cemetery at Santurce.

LARSEN, William Washington, a Representative from Georgia; born in Hagan, Tattnall (now Evans) County, Ga., August 12, 1871; attended the common schools, Bryan Institute, Lanier, Ga., South Georgia Military Academy, Thomasville, Ga., and the literary department of the University of Georgia at Athens; left college and engaged in teaching in 1895; studied law; was admitted to the bar in 1897 and commenced practice in Swainsboro, Ga., the same year; served as a second lieutenant in the Swainsboro Guards, Company C, National Guard of Georgia, 1900–1904; prosecuting attorney for the city court of Swainsboro, with jurisdiction over Emanuel County and parts of what are now Jenkins, Toombs, Candler, and Treutlen Counties, 1899–1905; member of the council and mayor pro tempore of the city of Swainsboro 1905–1909; member of the board of trustees of the State normal school at Athens, Ga., 1912–1927; delegate to the Democratic State conventions in 1902, 1906, and 1912; secretary of the executive department of the State of Georgia 1910–1912; moved to Dublin, Ga., in January 1912; resumed the practice of law and also engaged in agricultural pursuits; judge of the superior courts of Dublin circuit in 1914 and 1915; elected as a Democrat to the Sixty-fifth and to the seven succeeding Congresses (March 4, 1917–March 3, 1933); was not a candidate for renomination in 1932; member of the board of trustees of the University of Georgia 1927–1938; appointed regional manager for the Farm Credit Administration with headquarters in Columbia, S. C., in 1933 and served until his resignation in 1936; appointed a member of the Georgia Unemployment Insurance Commission in 1937 and served until his death in Dublin, Ga., January 5, 1938; interment in Northview Cemetery.

LARSON, Oscar John, a Representative from Minnesota; born in Uleaborg, Finland, May 20, 1871; immigrated in 1876 to the United States with his parents, who settled in Calumet, Mich.; attended the public schools; was graduated from the Northern Indiana Normal School (now Valparaiso University) in 1891 and from the law department of the University of Michigan at Ann Arbor in 1894; was admitted to the bar and commenced practice in Calumet, Mich., in 1894; prosecuting attorney for Houghton County 1899–1904; moved to Duluth, Minn., in 1907 and continued the practice of law; elected as a Republican to the Sixty-seventh and Sixty-eighth Congresses (March 4, 1921–March 3, 1925); was not a candidate for reelection in 1924; resumed the practice of law; died in Duluth, Minn., August 1, 1957; interment in Forest Hill Cemetery.

LA SÉRE, Emile, a Representative from Louisiana; born on the island of Santo Domingo in 1802; moved with his parents to New Orleans, La., about 1805; completed preparatory studies; employed as a clerk in a mercantile establishment at Jackson, La., and later in Mexico for several years; elected sheriff of the parish of New Orleans in 1840 and served several years; elected as a Democrat to the Twenty-ninth Congress to fill the vacancy caused by the resignation of John Slidell; reelected to the Thirtieth and Thirty-first Congresses and served from January 29, 1846, to March 3, 1851; during the Civil War served in the Confederate Army as major in the Tenth Louisiana Regiment and afterward as chief quartermaster of the Trans-Mississippi Department; chairman of the Democratic State central committee for more than fifteen years; president of the Tehuantepec Railroad Co. in Mexico; died in New Orleans, La., August 14, 1882; interment in Metairie Cemetery.

LASH, Israel George, a Representative from North Carolina; born in Bethania, Forsyth County, N. C., August 18, 1810; attended the common schools and the local academy in his native city; engaged in mercantile pursuits and subsequently became a cigar manufacturer; also engaged in banking in Salem, N. C.; delegate to the State convention in 1868 which decided that North Carolina should reenter the Union; upon the readmission of the State of North Carolina to representation was elected as a Republican to the Fortieth Congress; reelected to the Forty-first Congress and served from July 20, 1868, to March 4, 1871; was not a candidate for renomination in 1870; again engaged in banking in Salem (now Winston-Salem), N. C., until his death there on April 1, 1878; interment in the Moravian Cemetery, Bethania, N. C.

LASSITER, Francis Rives (great-nephew of Francis Everod Rives), a Representative from Virginia; born in Petersburg, Dinwiddie County, Va., February 18, 1866; attended McCabe's University School at Petersburg, and was graduated from the law department of the University of Virginia at Charlottesville in 1886; was admitted to the bar in 1887 and commenced practice in Boston, Mass.; returned to Petersburg, Va., in 1888 and continued the practice of law; city attorney of Petersburg 1888–1893; appointed by President Cleveland to be United States attorney for the eastern district of Virginia in 1893 and served until 1896, when he resigned; captain of Company G, Fourth Regiment, Virginia State Militia; appointed supervisor of the Twelfth Census for the Fourth Congressional District of Virginia in 1899; elected as a Democrat to the Fifty-sixth Congress to fill the vacancy caused by the death of Sydney P. Epes; reelected to the Fifty-seventh Congress and served from April 19, 1900, to March 3, 1903; elected to the Sixtieth and Sixty-first Congresses and served from March 4, 1907, until his death in Petersburg, Va., October 31, 1909; interment in Blanford Cemetery.

LATHAM, George Robert, a Representative from West Virginia; born near Haymarket, Prince William County, Va., March 9, 1832; attended the common schools; studied law; was admitted to the bar in 1859 and commenced practice in Grafton, Va. (now West Virginia); delegate to the convention at Wheeling for the formation of West Virginia; during the Civil War served in the Union Army as captain of Company B, Second Regiment, Virginia Volunteer Infantry, and later colonel of Volunteers; nominated as a brevet brigadier general; elected as a Republican to the Thirty-ninth Congress (March 4, 1865–March 3, 1867); was not a candidate for renomination in 1866; United States consul at Melbourne, Australia, 1867–1870; school superintendent of Upshur County, W. Va., 1875–1877; supervisor of census for the first census division of West Virginia; engaged in agricultural pursuits; died in Buckhannon, W. Va., December 16, 1917; interment in the Heavner Cemetery.

LATHAM, Henry Jepson, a Representative from New York; born in Brooklyn, N. Y., on December 10, 1908; attended the public schools, Richmond Hill High School, St. John's College, Brooklyn, N. Y., and was graduated from the Brooklyn Law School of St. Lawrence University in 1931; was admitted to the bar in 1932 and commenced practice in Jamaica, N. Y.; unsuccessful Republican candidate for the State senate in 1938; elected to the New York House of Assembly in 1941 and served until commissioned a lieutenant (jg) in the United States Navy in 1942; subsequently promoted to lieutenant and saw service in both the European and Pacific theaters of war; was on active duty in the Pacific when elected as a Republican to the Seventy-ninth Congress; reelected to the Eightieth and to the five succeeding Congresses and served from January 3, 1945, until his resignation December 31, 1958; elected in 1958 a justice of the supreme court of the State of New York for the term ending December 31, 1972; is a resident of Jamaica (Queens Village), N. Y.

LATHAM, Louis Charles, a Representative from North Carolina; born in Plymouth, Washington County, N. C., September 11, 1840; attended private schools, and was graduated from the University of North Carolina at Chapel Hill in 1859; later attended the Harvard Law School; entered the Confederate Army in 1861; was commissioned captain and afterward major of the First Regiment of North Carolina State troops, and served throughout the Civil War; immediately after the war resumed the study of law; was admitted to the bar in 1868 and commenced practice in Plymouth, N. C.; member of the State house of commons in 1864; served in the State senate in 1870; elected as a Democrat to the Forty-seventh Congress (March 4, 1881–March 3, 1883); unsuccessful candidate for renomination in 1882; elected to the Fiftieth Congress (March 4, 1887–March 3, 1889); unsuccessful candidate for reelection in 1888 to the Fifty-first Congress; resumed the practice of law in Greenville, N. C.; died at Johns Hopkins University Hospital, Baltimore, Md., October 16, 1895; interment in the City Cemetery, Greenville, N. C.

LATHAM, Milton Slocum, a Representative and a Senator from California; born in Columbus, Ohio, May 23, 1827; pursued classical studies, and was graduated from Jefferson College, Pennsylvania, in 1846; moved to Russell County, Ala.; taught school; studied law; was admitted to the bar in 1848 and commenced practice in Sacramento, Calif.; circuit court clerk for Russell County 1848–1850; moved to San Francisco, Calif., in 1850; clerk of the recorder's court in 1850; district attorney for the Sacramento district in 1851; elected as a Democrat to the Thirty-third Congress (March 4, 1853–March

3, 1855); declined to be a candidate for renomination in 1854; collector of the port of San Francisco 1855–1857; elected Governor of California in 1859 and was inaugurated January 9, 1860; served in this capacity until January 11, 1860, when he resigned, effective January 14, 1860, having been elected Senator; elected on January 11, 1860, to the United States Senate to fill the vacancy caused by the death of David C. Broderick; took his seat March 5, 1860, and served until March 3, 1863; engaged in the practice of law in San Francisco, Calif.; manager at San Francisco of the London & San Francisco Bank (Ltd.) 1865–1878; moved to New York City in 1879, where he died March 4, 1882; interment in Lone Mountain Cemetery, San Francisco, Calif.

LATHROP, Samuel, a Representative from Massachusetts; born in West Springfield, Hampden County, Mass., on May 1, 1772; pursued classical studies, and was graduated from Yale College in 1792; studied law; was admitted to the bar and commenced practice in West Springfield; clerk and treasurer 1796–1798; town moderator for eight years; elected as a Republican to the Sixteenth and to the three succeeding Congresses (March 4, 1819–March 3, 1827); resumed the practice of law and devoted considerable time to agricultural pursuits; member of the State senate in 1829 and 1830 and served as its president; died in West Springfield, Mass., July 11, 1846; interment in the Park Street Cemetery.

LATHROP, William, a Representative from Illinois; born near Le Roy, Genesee County, N. Y., April 17, 1825; attended the public schools and an academy at Brockport, N. Y.; studied law in Attica, N. Y.; moved to Knoxville, Ill., and was admitted to the bar in 1850; settled in Rockford, Ill., in 1851 and practiced his profession; city clerk and city attorney of Rockford in 1852; member of the State house of representatives in 1856 and 1857; elected as a Republican to the Forty-fifth Congress (March 4, 1877–March 3, 1879); resumed the practice of law in Rockford, Ill., where he died November 19, 1907; interment in Greenwood Cemetery.

LATIMER, Asbury Churchwell, a Representative and a Senator from South Carolina; born near Lowndesville, Abbeville County, S. C., July 31, 1851; attended the common schools; engaged in agricultural pursuits; moved to Belton, Anderson County, S. C., in 1880 and devoted his time to farming; chairman of the Democratic county committee 1890–1892; elected as a Democrat to the Fifty-third and to the four succeeding Congresses (March 4, 1893–March 3, 1903); did not seek renomination in 1902, having become a candidate for Senator; elected to the United States Senate and served from March 4, 1903, until his death; during his service in the Senate was appointed by Vice President Fairbanks in 1907 a member of the United States Immigration Commission; died in Washington, D. C., February 20, 1908; interment in Belton Cemetery, Belton, S. C.

LATIMER, Henry, a Representative and a Senator from Delaware; born in Newport, Del., on April 24, 1752; pursued classical studies; studied medicine in Philadelphia, Pa.; was graduated from the University of Pennsylvania at Philadelphia in 1773 and from the Edinburgh (Scotland) Medical College in 1775; returned to the United States and practiced his profession in Wilmington, Del.; served as a surgeon in the Revolutionary War, attached to the "flying squadron"; member of the State house of representatives in 1787, 1788, and 1790, serving as speaker in 1790; successfully contested the election of John Patton to the Third Congress and served from February 14, 1794, until February 7, 1795, when he resigned; elected to the United States Senate to fill the vacancy caused by the resignation of George Read; reelected, and served from February 7, 1795, until February 28, 1801, when he resigned; died in Philadelphia, Pa., December 19, 1819; interment in the Presbyterian Cemetery, Wilmington, Del.

LATTA, Delbert Leroy, a Representative from Ohio; born in Weston, Wood County, Ohio, March 5, 1920; attended the public schools in North Baltimore, Ohio; graduated from McComb (Ohio) High School in 1938, Ohio Northern University in 1940, and from the law school of the same university in 1943; served in the United States Army, Thirty-seventh Division, 1938–1941, and in the United States Marine Corps in 1942 and 1943; was admitted to the bar and commenced the practice of law in Bowling Green, Ohio, in 1945; member of the State senate 1953–1958; elected as a Republican to the Eighty-sixth Congress (January 3, 1959–January 3, 1961). *Reelected to the Eighty-seventh Congress.*

LATTA, James Polk, a Representative from Nebraska; born near Ashland, Ashland County, Ohio, October 31, 1844; moved with his parents to Jackson County, Iowa, in 1846; attended the district schools and worked on a farm; moved to the Territory of Nebraska in 1863; taught school in Tekamah, Nebr.; engaged in agricultural pursuits and stock raising in Burt County; became interested in banking at Tekamah in 1887; member of the State house of representatives in 1887; organized the First National Bank of Tekamah in 1890 and served as its president until his death; member of the State senate in 1907; elected as a Democrat to the Sixty-first and Sixty-second Congresses and served from March 4, 1909, until his death in the Mayo Hospital at Rochester, Minn., September 11, 1911; interment in Tekamah Cemetery, Tekamah, Nebr.

LATTIMORE, William, a Delegate from Mississippi Territory; born in Norfolk, Va., February 9, 1774; attended the common schools; studied medicine; moved to Natchez, Miss., and practiced his profession; on the formation of Mississippi Territory in 1798 took an active part in the organization of a government; elected as a Delegate to the Eighth and Ninth Congresses (March 4, 1803–March 3, 1807); elected to the Thirteenth and Fourteenth Congresses (March 4, 1813–March 3, 1817); delegate to the first State constitutional convention of Mississippi in 1817; appointed a censor of the medical profession under the constitution and code; one of the commissioners to select the site for the seat of the new State government; died in Natchez, Miss., April 3, 1843.

LAURANCE, John, a Delegate, a Representative, and a Senator from New York; born in Cornwall, England, in 1750; immigrated to the United States and settled in New York City in 1767; pursued academic studies; studied law; was admitted to the bar in 1772 and practiced in New York City; served in the Revolution as a commissioned officer in the First New York Regiment and became aide-de-camp to General Washington in October 1777; presided as judge advocate general at the trial of Maj. John André; regent of the University of the State of New York November 26, 1784; trustee of Columbia College 1784–1810; Member of the Continental Congress 1785–1787; member of the State senate in 1789; elected to the First and Second Congresses (March 4, 1789–March 3, 1793); appointed by President Washington to be United States judge of the district of New York May 5, 1794, and served until November 8, 1796, when he resigned, having been elected Senator; elected to the United States Senate to fill the vacancy caused by the resignation of Rufus King and served from November 9, 1796, until August 1800, when he resigned; elected President pro tempore of the Senate December 6, 1798; died in New York City November 11, 1810; interment in the First Presbyterian Churchyard, Fifth Avenue and Twelfth Street.

LAURENS, Henry, a Delegate from South Carolina; born in Charleston, S. C., March 6, 1724; received his early education in Charleston; went to England in 1744 to acquire a business education; upon his return to the United States in 1747 engaged in mercantile pursuits; served as lieutenant colonel in a campaign against the Cherokee Indians 1757–1761; member of the commons house of assembly in 1757 and reelected to every session, with one exception, until the Revolution; declined appointment to King's Council in Carolina in 1764 and 1768; member of the American Philosophical Society, Philadelphia, Pa., 1772–1792; was in Europe from 1771 until December 11, 1774, where he placed his sons in school; returned to Charleston, S. C., in the latter year; member of the First Provincial Congress January 9, 1775; President of the Provincial Congress in June 1775; also president of the general committee and of the first council of safety in 1775; member of the Second Provincial Congress from November 1775 to March 1776 and president of the second council of safety in 1775 and 1776; Vice President of South Carolina from March 1776 to June 27, 1777; elected as a Delegate to the Continental Congress January 10, 1777, and served as its President from November 1, 1777, to December 9, 1778; elected Minister to Holland by the Continental Congress on October 21, 1779, and sailed for his post early in 1780; was captured on the voyage and held a prisoner in the Tower of London for fifteen months; released on December 31, 1781, in exchange for Lord Cornwallis; appointed one of the peace commissioners and signed the preliminary treaty of Paris on November 30, 1782; returned to the United States on August 3, 1784, and retired to his plantation, "Mepkin," on the Cooper River, near Charleston, S. C.; subsequently elected to the Continental Congress, to the State legislature, and in 1787 to the Federal Constitutional Convention, all of which offices he declined; continued as a planter until his death at "Mepkin," near Charleston, S. C., December 8, 1792; the remains were cremated (the first white cremation on record in America) and his ashes interred on his estate, "Mepkin."

LAUSCHE, Frank John, a Senator from Ohio; born in Cleveland, Cuyahoga County, Ohio, November 14, 1895; attended Central Institute Prep School in 1915 and 1916; during the First World War served as a second lieutenant in the United States Army; graduated from John Marshall School of Law in 1920; was admitted to the bar the same year and commenced the practice of law in Cleveland, Ohio; judge of Municipal Court 1932–1937; judge of Common Pleas Court 1937–1941; mayor of Cleveland 1941–1944; Governor of Ohio in 1945 and 1946 and again from 1949 until his resignation effective noon January 3, 1957; elected as a Democrat to the United States Senate in 1956 for the term commencing January 3, 1957, and ending January 3, 1963.

LAW, Charles Blakeslee, a Representative from New York; born in Hannibal, Oswego County, N. Y., February 5, 1872; attended the public schools; was graduated from Colgate Academy, Hamilton, N. Y., in 1891, and from Amherst College, Amherst, Mass., in 1895; studied law in Rome, N. Y., and at Cornell Law School, Itahaca, N. Y.; was admitted to the bar in Rochester, N. Y., in 1897; moved to Brooklyn, N. Y., in 1898 and commenced the practice of law; elected as a Republican to the Fifty-ninth, Sixtieth, and Sixty-first Congresses (March 4, 1905–March 3, 1911); unsuccessful candidate for reelection in 1910; resumed the practice of law in the Borough of Brooklyn, New York City; sheriff of Kings County 1912 and 1913; justice of the municipal court of the city of New York from January

1, 1916, to January 1, 1926; again resumed the practice of law in Brooklyn, N. Y., and also engaged in banking; died while swimming at his summer home on Kattskill Bay, near Lake George, N. Y., on September 15, 1929; interment in Maple Grove Cemetery, Jordan, Onondaga County, N. Y.

LAW, John (son of Lyman Law and grandson of Richard Law and Amasa Learned), a Representative from Indiana; born in New London, Conn., October 28, 1796; pursued classical studies, and was graduated from Yale College in 1814; studied law; was admitted to the bar in 1817 and commenced practice in Vincennes, Ind.; prosecuting attorney 1818–1820; member of the State house of representatives in 1824 and 1825; again prosecuting attorney 1825–1828; judge of the seventh judicial circuit 1830 and 1831; receiver of the land office at Vincennes 1838–1842; again served as judge from 1844 to 1850, when he resigned; moved to Evansville, Ind., in 1851; invested in large tracts of land; was an author; appointed by President Pierce judge of the court of land claims and served from 1855 to 1857; elected as a Democrat to the Thirty-seventh and Thirty-eighth Congresses (March 4, 1861–March 3, 1865); was not a candidate for renomination in 1864; resumed the practice of law; died in Evansville, Ind., on October 7, 1873; interment in Greenlawn Cemetery, Vincennes, Ind.

LAW, Lyman (son of Richard Law and father of John Law), a Representative from Connecticut; born in New London, Conn., August 19, 1770; pursued classical studies, and was graduated from Yale College in 1791; studied law; was admitted to the bar in 1793 and commenced practice in New London; member of the State house of representatives in 1801, 1802, 1806, 1809, 1810, 1819, and 1826, and served as speaker in 1806, 1809, and 1810; elected as a Federalist to the Twelfth, Thirteenth, and Fourteenth Congresses (March 4, 1811–March 3, 1817); resumed the practice of his profession; died in New London, New London County, Conn., February 3, 1842; interment in the "Second Burial Ground"; reinterment in Cedar Grove Cemetery in 1851.

LAW, Richard (father of Lyman Law and grandfather of John Law), a Delegate from Connecticut; born in Milford, Conn., March 7, 1733; pursued classical studies, and was graduated from Yale College in 1751; studied law; was admitted to the bar in January 1755 and practiced in Milford, Conn., 1755–1757 and thereafter in New London; member of the general assembly in 1765; member of the Connecticut Council of Safety in May 1776; chief judge of the county court and of the superior court in 1784; member of the Governor's council 1776–1786; Member of the Continental Congress in 1778 and again in 1783 and 1784; mayor of New London 1784–1806; judge of the supreme court of Connecticut 1784–1789 and was appointed chief justice of the superior court in May 1786; appointed by President Washington United States district judge for Connecticut on September 24, 1789, and served until his death in New London, New London County, Conn., January 26, 1806; interment in Cedar Grove Cemetery.

LAWLER, Frank, a Representative from Illinois; born in Rochester, N. Y., June 25, 1842; attended the public schools; moved with his parents to Chicago, Ill., in 1854; news agent on a railroad for several years and also a brakeman; learned the trade of shipbuilder; was active in organizing trade and labor unions and served as president of the Ship Carpenters and Calkers' Association; employed in the Chicago post office as a letter carrier 1869–1877; member of the city council 1876–1885; engaged in business as a liquor merchant in 1878; elected as a Democrat to the Forty-ninth, Fiftieth, and Fifty-first Congresses (March 4,

1885–March 3, 1891); unsuccessful candidate for sheriff of Cook County in 1891; unsuccessful candidate for election in 1895 to the Fifty-fourth Congress; elected a member of the board of aldermen in 1896 and served until his death in Chicago, Ill., January 17, 1896; interment in Calvary Cemetery.

LAWLER, Joab, a Representative from Alabama; born in Union County, N. C., June 12, 1796; moved with his father to Tennessee and thence, in 1815, to Mississippi Territory; attended the public schools; studied theology and was licensed to preach; moved to Mardisville, Ala., in 1820 and pursued his ministerial duties; member of the State house of representatives 1826–1831; served in the State senate 1831 and 1832; receiver of public moneys for the Coosa land district 1832–1835; treasurer of the University of Alabama at Tuscaloosa 1833–1836; elected as a Whig to the Twenty-fourth and Twenty-fifth Congresses and served from March 4, 1835, until his death in Washington, D. C., on May 8, 1838; interment in the Congressional Cemetery.

LAWRENCE, Abbott, a Representative from Massachusetts; born in Groton, Mass., December 16, 1792; attended Groton Academy; became a merchant and importer in Boston; member of the Boston Common Council in 1831; elected as a Whig to the Twenty-fourth Congress (March 4, 1835–March 3, 1837); was not a candidate for renomination in 1836; elected to the Twenty-sixth Congress and served from March 4, 1839, to September 18, 1840, when he resigned; appointed a commissioner in 1842 to settle the northeastern boundary dispute between Canada and the United States; delegate to the Whig National Convention at Baltimore in 1844; declined the offer of a Cabinet position tendered by President Taylor; temporarily appointed by President Taylor to be United States Minister to Great Britain August 20, 1849; reappointed January 4, 1850; confirmed June 24, 1850, and served until October 1852, when he resigned and resumed his former business pursuits in Boston; founded the Lawrence Scientific School in Harvard University, Cambridge, Mass.; died in Boston, Mass., on August 18, 1855; interment in Mount Auburn Cemetery, Cambridge, Mass.

LAWRENCE, Cornelius Van Wyck (cousin of Effingham Lawrence), a Representative from New York; born in Flushing, N. Y., February 28, 1791; attended the common schools; moved to New York City in 1812 and engaged in mercantile pursuits; elected as a Jackson Democrat to the Twenty-third Congress and served from March 4, 1833, to May 14, 1834, when he resigned; mayor of New York City 1834–1837; presidential elector on the Democratic ticket of Van Buren and Johnson in 1836; director in several banks and trust companies; collector of customs at the port of New York 1845–1849; died in Flushing, N. Y., on February 20, 1861; interment in the family burying ground at Bayside, N. Y.

LAWRENCE, Effingham (cousin of Cornelius Van Wyck Lawrence), a Representative from Louisiana; born in Bayside, near Flushing, Long Island, N. Y., March 2, 1820; attended schools in Bayside and Flushing; moved to Louisiana about 1843; engaged in planting and the refining of sugar; member of the State house of representatives; successfully contested as a Democrat the election of Jacob Hale Sypher to the Forty-third Congress and took his seat on March 3, 1875, the last day of the session; resumed agricultural pursuits; died on Magnolia plantation, Plaquemines Parish, La., December 9, 1878; interment in Greenwood Cemetery, New Orleans, La.

LAWRENCE, George Pelton, a Representative from Massachusetts; born in Adams, Berkshire County, Mass., May 19,

1859; was graduated from Drury Academy in 1876 and from Amherst (Mass.) College in 1880; studied law at the Columbia Law School; was admitted to the bar in 1883 and commenced practice in North Adams, Mass.; appointed judge of the district of northern Berkshire in 1885; resigned in 1894 upon being elected to the Massachusetts Senate; served in the State senate 1895–1897 and was its president in 1896 and 1897; elected as a Republican to the Fifty-fifth Congress to fill the vacancy caused by the death of Ashley B. Wright; reelected to the Fifty-sixth and to the six succeeding Congresses and served from November 2, 1897, to March 3, 1913; was not a candidate for renomination in 1912; member of the Massachusetts Public Service Commission from July 1 to September 17, 1913; died in New York City on November 21, 1917; interment in Hillside Cemetery, North Adams, Mass.

LAWRENCE, George Van Eman (son of Joseph Lawrence), a Representative from Pennsylvania; born in Washington County, Pa., November 13, 1818; attended the common schools and Washington College (now Washington and Jefferson College), Washington, Pa.; engaged in agricultural pursuits; member of the State house of representatives in 1844, 1847, 1858, and 1859; served in the State senate 1849–1851 and 1861–1863; presided over the senate in 1863; elected as a Whig to the Thirty-ninth and Fortieth Congresses (March 4, 1865–March 3, 1869); was not a candidate for renomination in 1868; delegate to the State constitutional convention in 1872; member of the State senate under the new constitution in 1875, 1876, and 1878; elected as a Republican to the Forty-eighth Congress (March 4, 1883–March 3, 1885); was not a candidate for renomination in 1884; again served in the State house of representatives 1893–1896; died in Monongahela, Washington County, Pa., October 2, 1904; interment in the City Cemetery.

LAWRENCE, Henry Franklin, a Representative from Missouri; born near Greensburg, Decatur County, Ind., January 31, 1868; attended the public schools, the local high school, and Stanberry (Mo.) Normal School; moved to Cameron, Clinton County, Mo., and engaged in banking; clerk of Daviess County 1907–1911; mayor of Cameron 1914–1918; elected as a Republican to the Sixty-seventh Congress (March 4, 1921–March 3, 1923); unsuccessful candidate for reelection in 1922 to the Sixty-eighth Congress; delegate to the Republican National Convention at Cleveland in 1924; employed with the State finance department of Missouri; died in Cameron, Mo., January 12, 1950; interment in Graceland Cemetery.

LAWRENCE, John Watson, a Representative from New York; born in Flushing, N. Y., in August 1800; attended the local schools; engaged as a mercantile clerk; president of the village of Flushing 1835–1845; member of the State assembly in 1840 and 1841; was extensively interested in banking; elected as a Democrat to the Twenty-ninth Congress (March 4, 1845–March 3, 1847); declined to be a candidate for renomination in 1846 and also declined the Democratic nomination for Lieutenant Governor of New York; resumed banking pursuits; trustee of the village of Flushing 1860–1875; died in Flushing, N. Y., December 20, 1888; interment in Flushing Cemetery.

LAWRENCE, Joseph (father of George Van Eman Lawrence), a Representative from Pennsylvania; born near Hunterstown, Adams County, Pa., in 1786; moved with his widowed mother to a farm in Washington County in 1789; attended the common schools; engaged in agricultural pursuits; member of the State house of representatives 1818–1824 and served as speaker 1820–1822; elected to the Nineteenth and Twentieth Congresses (March 4, 1825–March 3, 1829); unsuccessful candidate for reelection in 1828 to the Twenty-first Congress; again a member of the State house of representatives 1834–1836; State treasurer in 1837; unsuccessful candidate for election in 1838 to the Twenty-sixth Congress; elected as a Whig to the Twenty-seventh Congress and served from March 4, 1841, until his death in Washington, D. C., April 17, 1842; interment in the Congressional Cemetery.

LAWRENCE, Samuel (brother of William Thomas Lawrence), a Representative from New York; born in Newtown (now a part of New York City), Queens County, N. Y., May 23, 1773; attended the common schools; studied law; was admitted to the bar in 1794 and commenced practice in New York City; clerk to the attorney general of the State of New York; appointed judge of marine court (later city court); member of the State assembly in 1808, 1817, and 1818; county clerk of New York County from February 19, 1811, to February 21, 1812; moved to Cayuta Lake, township of Cayuta, Chemung (now Schuyler) County, in 1814; Democratic presidential elector and secretary of the electoral college in 1816; again a member of the State assembly in 1820 and 1821; elected to the Eighteenth Congress (March 4, 1823–March 3, 1825); died at Cayuta Lake near Cayutaville, N. Y., October 20, 1837; interment in the family cemetery at that place.

LAWRENCE, Sidney, a Representative from New York; born in Weybridge, Addison County, Vt., December 31, 1801; moved with his parents to Moira, Franklin County, N. Y., in early childhood; attended the common schools; studied law; was admitted to the bar and commenced practice in Moira, N. Y.; was justice of the peace for more than half a century; served as supervisor and as assessor; surrogate of Franklin County 1837–1843; served in the State senate in 1843 and 1844; member of the State assembly in 1846; elected as a Democrat to the Thirtieth Congress (March 4, 1847–March 3, 1849); was not a candidate for renomination in 1848; resumed the practice of law; also engaged in the real-estate business and in banking; died in Moira, N. Y., May 9, 1892; interment in Moira Cemetery.

LAWRENCE, William, a Representative from Ohio; born in Washington (now Old Washington), Guernsey County, Ohio, September 2, 1814; pursued classical studies, and was graduated from Jefferson College, Canonsburg, Pa., in 1835; engaged in agricultural pursuits; member of the State house of representatives in 1843; presidential elector on the Democratic ticket of Cass and Butler in 1848; delegate to the State constitutional convention in 1851; served in the State senate in 1856 and 1857; elected as a Democrat to the Thirty-fifth Congress (March 4, 1857–March 3, 1859); declined to be a candidate for renomination in 1858; engaged in mercantile pursuits in Old Washington; again a member of the State senate in 1867, 1885, and 1886; member of the board of directors of the Ohio Penitentiary and served as president of the board; died in Old Washington, Guernsey County, Ohio, September 8, 1895; interment in the Washington Cemetery.

LAWRENCE, William, a Representative from Ohio; born in Mount Pleasant, Ohio, June 26, 1819; attended the common schools and Tidball's Academy, near Knoxville, Tenn.; worked on a farm in the summers; taught school in Pennsville and McConnelsville, Ohio; was graduated from Franklin College, New Athens, Ohio, in 1838 and from the Cincinnati Law School in 1840; was admitted to the bar in 1840 and practiced in Zanesville, Ohio, and later in McConnelsville; moved to Bellefontaine in 1841 and continued the practice of law; studied medicine 1841–1843; commissioner of bankruptcy for Logan

County in 1842; prosecuting attorney of Logan County in 1845; editor of the Logan Gazette 1845–1847; member of the State house of representatives in 1846 and 1847; served in the State senate 1847–1854; supreme court reporter in 1851; judge of the court of common pleas and of the district court from 1857 to 1864, when he resigned; one of the editors of the Western Law Monthly 1859–1862; during the Civil War entered the Union Army in 1862 as colonel of the Eighty-fourth Regiment, Ohio Volunteer Infantry; appointed United States district judge of Florida in 1863 but declined to accept the office; elected as a Republican to the Thirty-ninth, Fortieth, and Forty-first Congresses (March 4, 1865–March 3, 1871); unsuccessful candidate for reelection in 1870 to the Forty-second Congress; organized the Bellefontaine National Bank in 1871, of which he was president; elected to the Forty-third and Forty-fourth Congresses (March 4, 1873–March 3, 1877); unsuccessful candidate for renomination in 1876; First Comptroller of the United States Treasury 1880–1885; elected president of the National Wool Growers' Association in 1891; died in Kenton, Ohio, May 8, 1899; interment in Bellefontaine Cemetery, Bellefontaine, Ohio.

LAWRENCE, William Thomas (brother of Samuel Lawrence), a Representative from New York; born in New York City May 7, 1788; attended the common schools; engaged in mercantile pursuits; during the War of 1812 served in the Fourth Regiment, New York State Artillery; moved to Cayuga County in 1823 and engaged in farming; justice of the peace in 1838; elected to the Thirtieth Congress (March 4, 1847–March 3, 1849); died at his country home near Cayutaville, N. Y., October 25, 1859; interment in the family cemetery on the Shore Road, in the Borough of Queens, New York City.

LAWS, Gilbert Lafayette, a Representative from Nebraska; born near Olney, Richland County, Ill., March 11, 1838; moved with his parents to Iowa County, Wis., in 1845; attended the common schools, Haskell University, Mazomanie, Wis., and Milton College, Milton, Wis.; taught school; during the Civil War enlisted in the Fifth Regiment, Wisconsin Volunteer Infantry; was wounded in the Battle of Williamsburg, Virginia, May 5, 1862; returned to Wisconsin and settled in Richland County; county clerk in 1862 and twice reelected; engaged in the publication of a newspaper; member of the city council in 1868 and 1869; mayor of Richland Center in 1869; chairman of the county board of supervisors in 1869 and 1870; postmaster from 1866 to 1876, when he resigned and moved to Orleans, Nebr.; appointed register of the United States land office at McCook, Nebr., in 1883 and served until November 1, 1886; elected secretary of state of Nebraska in 1886 and 1888; elected as a Republican to the Fifty-first Congress to fill the vacancy caused by the death of James Laird and served from December 2, 1889, to March 3, 1891; was not a candidate for renomination in 1890; moved to Enid, Okla., and engaged in the real-estate business; returned to Nebraska in 1895 and settled in Lincoln; secretary of the State board of transportation 1896–1900; died in Lincoln, Nebr., April 25, 1907; interment in Wyuka Cemetery.

LAWSON, John Daniel, a Representative from New York; born in Montgomery, Orange County, N. Y., February 18, 1816; attended the public schools; moved to New York City and was employed as a clerk in a dry-goods store; later, in 1843, engaged in mercantile pursuits and the importation of dry goods; delegate to every Republican State, county, and district convention for thirty years; delegate to every Republican National Convention from 1868 to 1892; elected as a Republican to the Forty-third Congress (March 4, 1873–March 3, 1875);

unsuccessful candidate for reelection; withdrew from public life and resumed his former business pursuits; died in New York City January 24, 1896; interment in Greenwood Cemetery.

LAWSON, John William, a Representative from Virginia; born in James City County, Va., September 13, 1837; attended the schools of Williamsburg, William and Mary College, Williamsburg, Va., and the University of Virginia at Charlottesville; studied medicine; was graduated from the University of the City of New York March 4, 1861; returned to Virginia, and during the Civil War enlisted in the Thirty-second Regiment of Virginia Infantry, Confederate Army; served in the peninsular campaign; participated in the Battle of Williamsburg and in the series of battles beginning with Seven Pines; entered the Medical Department; assistant surgeon in charge of Artillery battalion; promoted to surgeon March 10, 1864, and served until the surrender at Appomattox April 9, 1865; settled in Isle of Wight County, Va., December 1865; practiced medicine for ten years, when he engaged in agricultural pursuits; member of the State house of delegates 1869–1873; served in the State senate 1874–1877; again a member of the State house of delegates in 1883 and 1884; elected as a Democrat to the Fifty-second Congress (March 4, 1891–March 3, 1893); was not a candidate for renomination in 1892; resumed farming; delegate to the State constitutional convention in 1901 and 1902; died in Smithfield, Va., on February 21, 1905; interment in Ivy Hill Cemetery.

LAWSON, Thomas Graves, a Representative from Georgia; born near Eatonton, Putnam County, Ga., on May 2, 1835; attended private schools, and was graduated from Mercer University, Macon, Ga., in 1855; studied law; was admitted to the bar in 1857 and commenced practice in Eatonton, Ga.; during the Civil War served two years in the Confederate Army; member of the State house of representatives 1861–1866, 1889, and 1890; delegate to the State constitutional convention in 1877; member of the board of trustees of Mercer University and the Eatonton Male and Female Academy; judge of the superior courts of Ocmulgee circuit 1879–1887; engaged in agricultural pursuits near Eatonton, Ga., 1888–1891; elected as a Democrat to the Fifty-second, Fifty-third, and Fifty-fourth Congresses (March 4, 1891–March 3, 1897); unsuccessful candidate for renomination in 1896; resumed agricultural pursuits in Putnam County, Ga.; died in Eatonton, Ga., April 16, 1912; interment in Pine Grove Cemetery.

LAWYER, Thomas, a Representative from New York; born in Schoharie, N. Y., October 14, 1785; studied law; was admitted to the bar and practiced in Schoharie County; member of the State house of representatives in 1816; brigadier general of State militia; elected to the Fifteenth Congress (March 4, 1817–March 3, 1819); district attorney of Schoharie County 1822–1831; presidential elector in 1824; again a member of the State house of representatives in 1846; died in Lawyersville, Schoharie County, N. Y., May 21, 1868.

LAY, Alfred Morrison, a Representative from Missouri; born in Lewis County, Mo., May 20, 1836; moved with his parents to Benton County in 1842; attended private schools, and was graduated from Bethany College, Virginia (now in West Virginia), in 1856; studied law; was admitted to the bar in 1857 and commenced practice in Jefferson City, Mo.; appointed United States district attorney for the western district of Missouri by President Buchanan and served until his resignation in 1861; enlisted as a private in the Missouri State Guard and was subsequently promoted to the rank of major; returned to Missouri when the command disbanded; served as captain of ordnance, Confederate Army; was captured, confined in the military prison at Alton, Ill., and exchanged at Aikens Landing, Va.; again appointed captain and assigned to the Tenth Missouri Cavalry; made quartermaster for the regiment and assistant quartermaster for the brigade and served until the close of the Civil War; resumed the practice of law in Jefferson City, Mo.; member of the State constitutional convention in 1875; elected as a Democrat to the Forty-sixth Congress and served from March 4, 1879, until his death in Washington, D. C., on December 8, 1879; interment in Woodlawn Cemetery, Jefferson City, Mo.

LAY, George Washington, a Representative from New York; born in Catskill, N. Y., July 26, 1798; pursued classical studies, and was graduated from Hamilton College at Clinton, N. Y., in 1817; studied law; was admitted to the bar and commenced practice in Batavia, N. Y., in 1820; treasurer of Genesee County, N. Y., 1825–1831; elected as a Whig to the Twenty-third and Twenty-fourth Congresses (March 4, 1833–March 3, 1837); member of the State assembly in 1840; Chargé d'Affaires to Sweden from May 12, 1842, to October 29, 1845; died in Batavia, Genesee County, N. Y., October 21, 1860; interment in Batavia Cemetery.

LAYTON, Caleb Rodney, a Representative from Delaware; born on the Long farm near Frankford, Sussex County, Del., September 8, 1851; attended the public schools and Georgetown Academy; was graduated from Amherst (Mass.) College in 1873 and from the medical department of the University of Pennsylvania at Philadelphia in 1876 and began the practice of medicine in Georgetown, Del.; secretary of the Republican county committee 1876–1888; chairman of the Union Republican county committee 1896–1901; delegate to the Republican National Conventions in 1896, 1900, and 1904; editor of the Union Republican 1897–1905; secretary of state of Delaware 1901–1905; appointed auditor for the State Department and other departments in Washington, D. C., and served from 1906 to 1910; member of the Progressive State committee 1912–1918; elected as a Republican to the Sixty-sixth and Sixty-seventh Congresses (March 4, 1919–March 3, 1923); unsuccessful candidate for reelection in 1922 to the Sixty-eighth Congress; resumed the practice of medicine in Georgetown, Sussex County, Del., until his death there on November 11, 1930; interment in St. Paul's Churchyard.

LAYTON, Fernando Coello, a Representative from Ohio; born near St. Johns, Auglaize County, Ohio, April 11, 1847; attended the public schools and Wittenberg College, Springfield, Ohio; studied law; was admitted to the bar in 1869 and practiced in Wapakoneta, Ohio; county school examiner; prosecuting attorney of Auglaize County 1875–1878; served as captain of Company G, Ohio National Guard, 1878–1883; elected as a Democrat to the Fifty-second, Fifty-third, and Fifty-fourth Congresses (March 4, 1891–March 3, 1897); was not a candidate for renomination in 1896; resumed the practice of his profession in Wapakoneta, Ohio; elected judge of the court of common pleas in 1908; reelected in 1914 and in 1920, and served until his resignation on June 9, 1926; died in Wapakoneta, Auglaize County, Ohio, on June 22, 1926; interment in Greenlawn Cemetery.

LAZARO, Ladislas, a Representative from Louisiana; born near Ville Platte, Evangeline (then St. Landry) Parish, La., June 5, 1872; attended public and private schools and Holy Cross College, New Orleans, La.; was graduated from Louisville (Ky.) Medical College in 1894 and practiced his profession in Washington, La., until 1913; became interested in agricultural pursuits;

president of the parish school board for four years; served in the State senate 1908–1912; elected as a Democrat to the Sixty-third and to the seven succeeding Congresses and served from March 4, 1913, until his death in Washington, D. C., March 30, 1927; interment in the Old City Cemetery, Ville Platte, La.

LAZEAR, Jesse, a Representative from Pennsylvania; born in Rich Hill Township, Greene County, Pa., December 12, 1804; received a limited schooling; taught school; engaged in mercantile pursuits; recorder for Greene County 1829–1832; bank cashier of the Farmers & Drovers' Bank, Waynesburg, Pa., 1835–1867; elected as a Democrat to the Thirty-seventh and Thirty-eighth Congresses (March 4, 1861–March 3, 1865); was not a candidate for renomination in 1864; delegate to the Union National Convention at Philadelphia in 1866; withdrew from political life and retired to his country home, "Windsor Mill Farm," in Baltimore County, Md., in 1867; president of the Baltimore & Powhatan Railroad Co. 1871–1874; died at his country home, "Windsor Mill Farm," September 2, 1877; interment in Green Mount Cemetery, Waynesburg, Pa.

LEA, Clarence Frederick, a Representative from California; born near Highland Springs, Lake County, Calif., July 11, 1874; attended the common schools, Lakeport Academy, and Leland Stanford Junior University, California; was graduated from the law department of the University of Denver, Denver, Colo., in 1898; was admitted to the bar the same year and commenced practice in Santa Rosa; district attorney of Sonoma County 1907–1917; president of the District Attorney's Association of California in 1916 and 1917; elected as a Democrat to the Sixty-fifth Congress and reelected as a candidate of the Democratic and Republican Parties to the Sixty-sixth and to the fourteen succeeding Congresses (March 4, 1917–January 3, 1949); was not a candidate for renomination in 1948; engaged in public relations work in Washington, D. C., 1949–1954; is a resident of Santa Rosa, Calif.

LEA, Luke (brother of Pryor Lea), a Representative from Tennessee; born in Surry County, N. C., January 21, 1783; moved to Tennessee in 1790 with his parents, who settled in Hawkins County; attended the common schools; clerk in the State house of representatives 1804–1806; commanded a regiment under General Jackson in the Creek and Seminole Wars in 1818; located at Campbells Station, Tenn., and held several minor offices; elected as a Union Democrat to the Twenty-third and Twenty-fourth Congresses (March 4, 1833–March 3, 1837); secretary of state of Tennessee 1837–1839; appointed by President Taylor to be Commissioner of Indian Affairs on June 14, 1850, to take effect July 1, 1850, and was confirmed by the Senate, but declined to accept; appointed by President Fillmore as Indian agent at Fort Leavenworth, Kans., September 23, 1850, and served until his death near Fort Leavenworth, Kans., June 17, 1851; interment in Westport Cemetery (now abandoned), Kansas City, Mo.

LEA, Luke (great-grandson of the preceding), a Senator from Tennessee; born in Nashville, Tenn., April 12, 1879; attended the public schools; was graduated from the University of the South, Sewanee, Tenn., in 1899 and from the law department of Columbia University, New York City, in 1903; was admitted to the bar in 1903 and commenced practice at Nashville; editor and publisher of the Nashville Tennessean in 1907; elected as a Democrat to the United States Senate January 23, 1911, and served from March 4, 1911, to March 3, 1917; unsuccessful candidate for renomination in 1916; during the First World War organized the First Tennessee Field Artillery on April 6, 1917, and was in command as lieutenant colonel until October 18, 1917, when he was promoted to colonel of the regiment; participated in engagements in the Toul sector on September 11, St. Mihiel offensive on September 12 and 16, Meuse-Argonne September 26 to October 8, and in the Woere sector October 11 to November 8, 1918; honorably discharged April 12, 1919; awarded the Distinguished Service Medal; returned to Nashville and resumed newspaper interests; appointed to the United States Senate in 1929 to fill the vacancy caused by the death of Lawrence D. Tyson, but declined the appointment; died in Nashville, Tenn., on November 18, 1945; interment in Mount Olivet Cemetery, Nashville, Tenn.

LEA, Pryor (brother of Luke Lea), a Representative from Tennessee; born in Knox County, Tenn., August 31, 1794; completed preparatory studies; was graduated from Greeneville College; studied law; was admitted to the bar in 1817 and commenced the practice of his profession in Knoxville, Tenn.; served in the Creek War in 1813; United States attorney for Tennessee in 1824; elected as a Jackson Democrat to the Twentieth and Twenty-first Congresses (March 4, 1827–March 3, 1831); unsuccessful candidate for reelection in 1830 to the Twenty-second Congress; moved to Jackson, Miss., in 1836 and to Goliad, Goliad County, Tex., in 1846; engaged in railroad building and management; member of the State People's Convention which met at Austin, Tex., in January 1861 and passed the ordinance of secession; died in Goliad, Tex., September 14, 1879; interment in Oak Hill Cemetery.

LEACH, De Witt Clinton, a Representative from Michigan; born in Clarence, Erie County, N. Y., November 23, 1822; moved with his parents to Genesee County, Mich., in early youth; attended the common schools; taught school; located in Lansing, Mich., in 1841; editor of the Michigan State Republican several years; member of the State house of representatives in 1849 and 1850; delegate to the State constitutional convention in 1850; was present at the formation of the Republican Party "under the oaks" at Jackson, Mich., July 6, 1854; State librarian 1855–1857; elected as a Republican to the Thirty-fifth and Thirty-sixth Congresses (March 4, 1857–March 3, 1861); was not a candidate for renomination in 1860; Indian agent for Michigan, by appointment of President Lincoln, 1861–1865; moved to Traverse City, Mich., in 1865, and engaged in journalism, which was his occupation until he retired from active business; published the Grand Traverse Herald for nine years; delegate to the State constitutional convention in 1867; moved to Springfield, Mo., in 1875, where he published the Patriot Advertiser; returned to Traverse City, Mich., in 1882 and published the Northwest Farmer; retired from active business pursuits in 1902 and returned to Springfield, Mo., where he died on December 21, 1909; interment in Maple Park Cemetery.

LEACH, James Madison, a Representative from North Carolina; born at the family homestead, "Lansdowne," Randolph County, N. C., January 17, 1815; attended the common schools and Caldwell Institute, Greensboro, N. C.; was graduated from the United States Military Academy, West Point, N. Y., in 1838; studied law; was admitted to the bar in 1842 and commenced practice in Lexington, N. C.; member of the State house of commons 1848–1858; presidential elector on the American Party ticket of Fillmore and Donelson in 1856; elected as a Whig to the Thirty-sixth Congress (March 4, 1859–March 3, 1861); captain and lieutenant colonel in the Confederate Army during the Civil War; member of the Confederate States Congress in 1864 and 1865; member of the State senate in 1865, 1866, and again in 1879; elected as a Conservative to the Forty-second and Forty-third Congresses (March 4, 1871–March 3, 1875); declined to be a candidate for renomination in 1874; died in Lexington, N. C., June 1, 1891; interment in Hopewell Cemetery, near Trinity, Randolph County, N. C.

LEACH, Robert Milton, a Representative from Massachusetts; born in Franklin, Merrimack County, N. H., April 2, 1879; attended the public schools, Phillips Academy, Andover, Mass., and Dartmouth College, Hanover, N. H.; moved to Taunton, Mass., in 1900 and engaged in the chain-store furniture business in New England; treasurer of Glenwood Range Co.; director of the Bristol County Trust Co.; trustee of the Taunton Savings Bank; treasurer of the Morton Hospital; commissioned as captain in the Ordnance Division of the United States Army during the First World War; elected as a Republican to the Sixty-eighth Congress to fill the vacancy caused by the death of William S. Greene and served from November 4, 1924, to March 3, 1925; was not a candidate for renomination in 1924; resumed his former business activities in Taunton, Mass.; died in Eustis, Fla., February 18, 1952; interment in Franklin Cemetery, Franklin, N. H.

LEADBETTER, Daniel Parkhurst, a Representative from Ohio; born in Pittsfield, Berkshire County, Mass., September 10, 1797; attended the common schools; moved to Ohio in 1816 and settled in Steubenville, Jefferson County, where he studied law; was admitted to the bar in 1821 and commenced practice in Steubenville; commissioned captain of the Second Company, Third Regiment, Sixth Division, Ohio Militia, in 1821; moved to Millersburg, Holmes County, in 1828 and continued the practice of law; commissioned quartermaster of the Fourth Division of the Ohio Militia in 1831; county recorder 1831–1836; elected as a Jackson Democrat to the Twenty-fifth and Twenty-sixth Congresses (March 4, 1837–March 3, 1841); was not a candidate for renomination in 1840; resumed the practice of his profession; also engaged in agricultural pursuits and stock raising; member of the State constitutional convention in 1851; served as a captain in the Civil War in 1862; died in Millersburg, Ohio, on February 26, 1870; interment in Oak Hill Cemetery.

LEAHY, Edward Laurence, a Senator from Rhode Island; born in Bristol, R. I., February 9, 1886; attended the public schools; student at Brown University in 1904 and 1905; graduated from the law school of Georgetown University, Washington, D. C., in 1908; was admitted to the Rhode Island bar in 1908 and commenced the practice of law in Bristol, R. I.; judge of probate court, Bristol, R. I., 1910–1939; member of the State house of representatives 1911–1913; in 1913 was elected to the Bristol school committee and also served as master of chancery in the superior court; during the First World War served as a first lieutenant, Judge Advocate General's Department, United States Army; administrator of State taxes 1919–1948; director of department of revenue and regulation in 1939; director of finance, member of State sinking fund commission, and State retirement board, 1942–1946; adviser to the department of finance in 1948 and 1949; appointed as a Democrat to the United States Senate to fill the vacancy caused by the resignation of J. Howard McGrath and served from August 24, 1949, to December 18, 1950, a successor having been elected and qualified; was not a candidate for election to the vacancy; United States judge for the district of Rhode Island from January 1951 until his death in Bristol, R. I., July 22, 1953; interment in North Cemetery.

LEAKE, Eugene Walter, a Representative from New Jersey; born in Jersey City, N. J., July 13, 1877; attended the public schools and Phillips Academy, Andover, Mass.; graduated from New York Law School in 1898; was admitted to the New Jersey bar in 1898 and commenced practice in Jersey City, N. J.; was admitted to the New York bar in 1908 and practiced in New York City, N. Y.; elected as a Democrat to the Sixtieth Congress (March 4, 1907–March 3, 1909); was not a candidate for renomination in 1908; general counsel for the Adams Express Co., 1927–1932; in 1931 was elected chairman of the board of directors of the American Railway Express Co.; director of Loew's, Inc., and chairman of the retirement plan committee; died in New York City, N. Y., August 23, 1959; interment in Cedar Lawn Cemetery, Paterson, N. J.

LEAKE, Shelton Farrar, a Representative from Virginia; born near Hillsboro, Albemarle County, Va., November 30, 1812; completed preparatory studies; taught school; studied law; was admitted to the bar in 1835 and commenced practice in Charlottesville, Va.; member of the State house of delegates in 1842 and 1843; elected as a Democrat to the Twenty-ninth Congress (March 4, 1845–March 3, 1847); resumed the practice of law; presidential elector on the Democratic ticket of Cass and Butler in 1848; elected Lieutenant Governor of Virginia in 1851; elected to the Thirty-sixth Congress (March 4, 1859–March 3, 1861); again resumed the practice of law; died in Charlottesville, Va., on March 4, 1884; interment in Maplewood Cemetery.

LEAKE, Walter, a Senator from Mississippi; born in Albemarle County, Va., May 25, 1762; served in the Revolutionary War; studied law; was admitted to the bar and practiced; appointed by President Jefferson one of the United States judges for Mississippi Territory on March 2, 1807; moved to Hinds County, Miss., and engaged in the practice of law; upon the admission of Mississippi as a State into the Union was elected as a Democrat to the United States Senate and served from December 10, 1817, to May 15, 1820, when he resigned; appointed United States marshal for the district of Mississippi March 1, 1820; Governor of Mississippi 1821–1825; died in Mount Salus, Hinds County, Miss., November 17, 1825.

LEARNED, Amasa (grandfather of John Law), a Representative from Connecticut; born in Killingly, Conn., November 15, 1750; prepared for college by a private tutor; was graduated from Yale College in 1772; taught in the Union School, New London; studied theology; received a license from the Windham Association on October 10, 1773, and preached for a short time; commenced the study of law in 1778; member of the State house of representatives in 1779; moved to New London; member of the State house of representatives 1785–1791; member of the convention which ratified the Constitution of the United States in 1788; elected to the upper house of assistants in 1791; elected to the Second and Third Congresses (March 4, 1791–March 3, 1795); engaged in land speculations; delegate to the State constitutional convention in 1818; died in New London, New London County, Conn., May 4, 1825; interment in Cedar Grove Cemetery.

LEARY, Cornelius Lawrence Ludlow, a Representative from Maryland; born in Baltimore, Md., October 22, 1813; attended the public schools; was graduated from St. Mary's College, Baltimore, in 1833; moved to Louisville, Ky.; returned to Baltimore in 1837; Whig member of the State house of delegates in 1838 and 1839; studied law; was admitted to the bar in 1840 and commenced practice in Baltimore; presidential elector on the American Party ticket of Fillmore and Donelson in 1856; elected as a Unionist to the Thirty-seventh Congress (March 4, 1861–March 3, 1863); resumed the practice of law in Baltimore, Md., and died there March 21, 1893; interment in Lorraine Cemetery.

LEATHERWOOD, Elmer O., a Representative from Utah; born on a farm near Waverly, Pike County, Ohio, September 4, 1872; attended the public schools; moved to Emporia, Kans., in 1888; was graduated from the Kansas State Normal School at Emporia, Kans., in 1894; engaged in public school work 1894–1898; studied law; was admitted to the bar at Hiawatha, Brown County, Kans., in 1898; was graduated from the law department of the University of Wisconsin at Madison in 1901 and was admitted to practice; moved to Salt Lake City, Utah, the same year and continued the practice of his profession; district attorney for the third judicial district of Utah 1908–1916; delegate to the Republican National Convention in 1924; served as president of the Western Powder Co., Leary & Warren Stockyards, Hellgate Mining & Milling Co., and the Olympus Mining & Milling Co.; elected as a Republican to the Sixty-seventh and to the four succeeding Congresses and served from March 4, 1921, until his death in Washington, D. C., on December 24, 1929; interment in Mount Olivet Cemetery, Salt Lake City, Utah.

LEAVENWORTH, Elias Warner, a Representative from New York; born in Canaan, N. Y., December 20, 1803; moved with his parents to Great Barrington, Mass., in 1806; attended the Hudson Academy, and was graduated from Yale College in 1824; studied law in Great Barrington and in the Litchfield (Conn.) Law School 1825–1827; was admitted to the bar in 1827 and practiced in Syracuse, N. Y., until 1850, when he abandoned the practice of law because of ill health; passed through the various grades and was appointed brigadier general of militia in 1836; president of Syracuse village 1839–1841, 1846, and 1847; mayor of the town in 1849, 1850, 1859, and 1860; member of the State assembly in 1850 and 1857; secretary of state of New York in 1854 and 1855; president of the Republican State convention in 1860; commissioner for the United States under the convention with New Granada in Washington, D. C., in 1861 and 1862; appointed president of the board of commissioners to locate the State asylum for the blind and a trustee of the State asylum for the insane in 1865; member of the New York and New Jersey Boundary Line Commission in 1875; elected as a Republican to the Forty-fourth Congress (March 4, 1875–March 3, 1877); declined to be a candidate for renomination in 1876; resumed business activities in Syracuse, N. Y., and died there November 25, 1887; interment in Oakwood Cemetery.

LEAVITT, Humphrey Howe, a Representative from Ohio; born in Suffield, Conn., June 18, 1796; moved to the Northwest Territory in 1800 with his parents, who settled in what became Trumbull County, Ohio; completed preparatory studies; attended an academy in western Pennsylvania; taught school; clerked in a store; studied law; was admitted to the bar in 1816 and commenced practice in Cadiz, Ohio; moved to Steubenville in 1819; prosecuting attorney of Jefferson County 1823–1829; member of the State house of representatives in 1825 and 1826; served in the State senate in 1827 and 1828; clerk of the common pleas and supreme court of Jefferson County in 1828; elected as a Jackson Democrat to the Twenty-first Congress to fill the vacancy caused by the resignation of John M. Goodenow; reelected to the Twenty-second and Twenty-third Congresses and served from December 6, 1830, until July 10, 1834, when he resigned to accept a judicial position; appointed by President Jackson to be United States judge of the district court for the district of Ohio on June 30, 1834, and served until March 31, 1871, when he resigned; moved to Cincinnati, Ohio, in 1855, when the State was divided into two Federal districts; returned to Springfield in 1871; engaged in literary pursuits; was a member of the World's Convention on Prison Reform in London in 1872; died in Springfield, Ohio, March 15, 1873; interment in Spring Grove Cemetery.

LEAVITT, Scott, a Representative from Montana; born in Elk Rapids, Antrim County, Mich., June 16, 1879; moved with his father to Bellaire, Mich., in 1881; attended the public schools; while in high school enlisted in the Thirty-third Regiment, Michigan Volunteer Infantry, during the Spanish-American War, and served in the campaign at Santiago, Cuba; attended the University of Michigan at Ann Arbor; moved to Oregon in 1901 and took up a homestead in the Coast Range Mountains near Falls City; school principal in Falls City, North Yamhill, Dayton, and Lakeview, Oreg., 1901–1907; entered the Forest Service as a ranger at Fremont National Forest in Oregon in 1907; acting supervisor of the Superior National Forest in Minnesota in 1909; supervisor of the Lewis and Clark National Forest in Montana 1910–1913; supervisor of the Jefferson National Forest in Montana 1913–1917; director of the United States Employment Service and of the Public Service Reserve of Montana during the First World War; elected as a Republican to the Sixty-eighth and to the four succeeding Congresses (March 4, 1923–March 3, 1933); unsuccessful candidate for reelection in 1932 to the Seventy-third Congress and for election in 1934 to the United States Senate; delegate to the Republican National Convention at Chicago in 1932; again became connected with the Forest Service at Milwaukee, Wis., in 1935; commander-in-chief of the United Spanish War Veterans 1936–1937; retired from the Forest Service in 1941 and moved to Newberg, Oreg.; member of Newberg Park Board 1953–; is a resident of Newberg, Oreg.

LEAVY, Charles Henry, a Representative from Washington; born on a farm near York, York County, Pa., February 16, 1884; moved to Kansas City, Mo., with his parents in 1887; attended the public schools of Missouri, the Warrensburg (Mo.) Normal School, the Bellingham (Wash.) Normal School, and the Kansas City (Mo.) School of Law; taught school near Independence, Mo., 1903–1906, and at Everson, Touchet, Kahlotus, and Connell, Wash., 1906–1913; studied law; was admitted to the bar in 1912 and commenced practice in Newport, Pend Oreille County, Wash.; prosecuting attorney of Pend Oreille County, Wash., 1915–1918; moved to Spokane, Wash., in 1918; special assistant United States district attorney for eastern Washington 1918–1921; prosecuting attorney of Spokane County, Wash., 1922–1926; member of the Central Valley High School Board 1923–1927; presidential elector on the Democratic ticket of Davis and Bryan in 1924; served as judge of the superior court of the State of Washington 1926–1936; elected as a Democrat to the Seventy-fifth, Seventy-sixth, and Seventy-seventh Congresses and served from January 3, 1937, until his resignation on August 1, 1942, having been appointed United States district judge of the western district of Washington and served until his retirement September 1, 1952; died in Tacoma, Wash., September 25, 1952; interment in Mountain View Memorial Park, Tacoma, Wash.

LE BLOND, Francis Celeste (grandfather of Frank Le Blond Kloeb), a Representative from Ohio; born in Bellville, Ohio, February 14, 1821; pursued an academic course; studied law; was admitted to the bar in 1844 and commenced practice in Celina, Ohio; member of the State house of representatives 1851–1855; served as speaker of the house in 1854 and 1855; elected as a Democrat to the Thirty-eighth and Thirty-ninth Congresses (March 4, 1863–March 3, 1867); declined to be a candidate for renomination in 1866; resumed the practice of law and also engaged in business; died in Celina, Ohio, November 9, 1902; interment in North Grove Cemetery.

LECOMPTE, Joseph, a Representative from Kentucky; born in Woodford County, near the town of Georgetown, Scott County, Ky., December 15, 1797; moved to Henry County with his parents, who settled in Lecomptes Bottom on the Kentucky River; attended the common schools; engaged in agricultural pursuits; during the War of 1812 served with the Kentucky Riflemen in the Battle of New Orleans; member of the State house of representatives in 1819, 1822, 1838, 1839, and 1844; served as a major in the State militia; elected as a Democrat to the Nineteenth and to the

three succeeding Congresses (March 4, 1825–March 3, 1833); was not a candidate for renomination in 1832; resumed agricultural pursuits; member of the State constitutional convention in 1850; died in Henry County April 25, 1851; interment in the private cemetery on the old family place in Lecomptes Bottom, on the Kentucky River, Henry County, Ky.

LE COMPTE, Karl Miles, a Representative from Iowa; born in Corydon, Wayne County, Iowa, May 25, 1887; attended the public schools and was graduated from the State University of Iowa at Iowa City in 1909; became owner and publisher of the Corydon Times-Republican in 1910; during the First World War served as a private in the medical detachment of United States General Hospital No. 26 in 1918; member of the State senate 1917–1921; elected as a Republican to the Seventy-sixth and to the nine succeeding Congresses (January 3, 1939–January 3, 1959); was not a candidate for renomination in 1958; newspaper publisher; resides in Corydon, Iowa.

LEE, Arthur (brother of Francis Lightfoot Lee and Richard Henry Lee), a Delegate from Virginia; born at "Stratford," in Westmoreland County, Va., December 20, 1740; attended Eton College, England; studied medicine at the University of Edinburgh, Scotland, and was graduated in 1765; after traveling in Europe returned to the United States and commenced the practice of medicine in Williamsburg, Va.; again went to London in 1766 and studied law at Temple Bar 1766–1770; was admitted to the bar and practiced in London 1770–1776; commissioned as agent of Massachusetts in England and France in 1770; appointed correspondent of Congress in London in 1775; commissioner to France in 1776 and to Spain in 1777; returned to Virginia in 1780; member of the State house of delegates 1781–1783, 1785, and 1786; Member of the Continental Congress 1781–1784; member of the Treasury board 1785–1789; died in Urbana, Middlesex County, Va., on December 12, 1792; interment in Lansdowne Garden, in the rear of "Lansdowne," his home, at Urbana, Va.

LEE, Blair, a Senator from Maryland; born at Silver Spring, Montgomery County, Md., August 9, 1857; attended the common schools; was graduated from Princeton College in 1880 and from the law department of Columbian (now George Washington) University, Washington, D. C., in 1882; was admitted to the bar of the District of Columbia and of Montgomery County, Md., in 1883 and commenced practice in Maryland; delegate to eight Democratic National Conventions; unsuccessful candidate for election to the Fifty-fifth Congress in 1896; elected a member of the State senate in 1905; reelected in 1909; unsuccessful candidate for the Democratic nomination for Governor of Maryland in 1911; elected as a Democrat to the United States Senate on November 4, 1913, to fill the vacancy caused by the death of Isidor Rayner; credentials were presented on December 5, 1913, but he did not qualify until January 28, 1914, and served until March 3, 1917; resumed the practice of law; died in Norwood, Md., December 25, 1944; interment in Rock Creek Cemetery, Washington, D. C.

LEE, Francis Lightfoot (brother of Arthur Lee and Richard Henry Lee), a Delegate from Virginia; born at "Stratford," Westmoreland County, Va., October 14, 1734; pursued classical studies under private teachers; member of the house of burgesses 1758–1775; signed the Westmoreland declaration against the stamp act; Member of the Continental Congress 1775–1780; member of the State house of delegates in 1780 and 1781; one of the signers of the Declaration of Independence; served in the Virginia State Senate 1778–1782; died at his home, "Menoken," in Richmond County, Va., January 11, 1797; interment in the family burying ground at Mount Airy, Richmond County, Va.

LEE, Frank Hood, a Representative from Missouri; born on a farm near De Sota, Johnson County, Kans., March 29, 1873; moved to Missouri with his parents, who settled near Virgil City, Vernon County, in 1876; attended the public schools of Virgil City, Mo.; employed as newsboy, bootblack, livery stable worker, and salesman before studying law; served as justice of the peace in 1894; was admitted to the bar in 1904 and commenced practice in Joplin, Mo.; member of the State house of representatives 1915–1918; unsuccessful candidate for election in 1922 to the Sixty-eighth Congress and in 1930 to the Seventy-second Congress; elected as a Democrat to the Seventy-third Congress (March 4, 1933–January 3, 1935); unsuccessful candidate for reelection in 1934 to the Seventy-fourth Congress; resumed the practice of law until his retirement; formerly owned and operated the Southwestern, a Jasper County newspaper, and the Jefferson Hotel; died in Joplin, Mo., November 20, 1952; interment in Ozark Memorial Park.

LEE, Gideon, a Representative from New York; born in Amherst, Mass., April 27, 1778; attended the common schools; learned the trade of shoemaker and engaged in that business in Worthington, Mass.; moved to New York City and thence to Georgia, where he engaged in the mercantile business until 1807; returned to New York City in 1807 and engaged in the leather business; member of the State assembly in 1822; member of the board of aldermen 1828–1830; mayor of New York City in 1833; declined to be a candidate for reelection; elected as a Jackson Democrat to the Twenty-fourth Congress to fill the vacancy caused by the resignation of Campbell P. White and served from November 4, 1835, to March 3, 1837; was not a candidate for renomination in 1836; retired from active business in 1836; moved to Geneva, N. Y.; presidential elector on the Democratic ticket of Van Buren and Johnson in 1840; died in Geneva, N. Y., August 21, 1841; interment in the Washington Street Cemetery.

LEE, Gordon, a Representative from Georgia; born near Ringgold, Catoosa County, Ga., May 29, 1859; attended the common schools; was graduated from Emory College, Oxford, Ga., in 1880; engaged in agricultural pursuits and in manufacturing at Chickamauga, Ga.; member of the State house of representatives in 1894 and 1895; served in the State senate 1902–1904; appointed by Governor Atkinson a member of the State memorial board; elected as a Democrat to the Fifty-ninth and to the ten succeeding Congresses (March 4, 1905–March 3, 1927); was not a candidate for renomination in 1926; member of the National Forest Reservation Commission created by the act of March 1, 1911; delegate to the Democratic National Convention at New York City in 1924; resumed agricultural pursuits; died at Chickamauga, Ga., November 7, 1927; interment in Chickamauga Cemetery.

LEE, Henry (brother of Richard Bland Lee and grandfather of William Henry Fitzhugh Lee), a Delegate and a Representative from Virginia; born at "Leesylvania," in Prince William County, Va., January 29, 1756; pursued classical studies, and was graduated from Princeton College in 1773; served in the Revolutionary War; commissioned captain of a company of Virginia Dragoons June 18, 1776, that became attached to and part of the First Continental Dragoons March 31, 1777; by a special act of Congress, April 7, 1778, in recognition of his brave and distinguished services, was promoted to a major commandant and authorized to augment his corps by the enlistment of two troops of Horse; by the act of September 24, 1779, was given the thanks of Congress "for remarkable prudence, address, and bravery displayed in the attack on the enemy's fort and works at Paulus Hook," and in terms approved his humanity and granted him a gold medal; his battalion was designated "Lee's partisan corps" by act of October 21, 1780; lieutenant colonel

November 6, 1780, and served until the close of the war; commissioned major general, United States Army, July 19, 1798; honorably discharged June 15, 1800; became universally known as "Light Horse Harry"; Member of the Continental Congress 1785–1788; advocated the adoption of the Federal Constitution in the Virginia convention of 1788; Governor of Virginia 1791–1794; commanded the United States forces in the Whisky Insurrection in 1794; elected as a Federalist to the Sixth Congress (March 4, 1799–March 3, 1801); at the request of Congress pronounced the eulogy upon President Washington before both branches of Congress, in which Washington is characterized as the man "first in war, first in peace, and first in the hearts of his countrymen"; died on Cumberland Island, Ga., March 25, 1818; interment at Dungeness, Ga.; reinterment in the Lee Mausoleum at Lexington, Va., May 30, 1913.

LEE, John (son of Thomas Sim Lee), a Representative from Maryland; born at "Needwood," near Frederick, Frederick County, Md., January 30, 1788; was educated by private tutors and at Harvard University; in early life a member of the Federalist Party; studied law, but did not practice; engaged in the management of his estate "Needwood"; elected as a Democrat to the Eighteenth Congress (March 4, 1823–March 3, 1825); chairman of the committee of the National House of Representatives appointed to escort the Marquis de Lafayette from Frederick City to Washington in 1825; member of the house of delegates; served in the State senate; one of the proponents of the Chesapeake & Ohio Canal and of the Baltimore & Ohio Railroad; resumed management of his estate; died while on a visit to his son in New York City May 17, 1871; interment in New Cathedral Cemetery, formerly called "Bonnie Brae," Baltimore, Md.

LEE, Joshua, a Representative from New York; born in Hudson, N. Y., in 1783; studied medicine and was licensed to practice in 1804; commissioned in 1811 by Gov. Daniel D. Tompkins as surgeon of Col. Avery Smith's regiment of Infantry and served in that capacity during the War of 1812, being present at the Battle of Queenstown; supervisor of the town of Benton, Yates County, in 1815; member of the State assembly in 1817 and again in 1833; elected as a Democrat to the Twenty-fourth Congress (March 4, 1835–March 3, 1837); resumed the practice of his profession; unsuccessful for election to the United States Senate in 1839; died in Penn Yan, N. Y., December 29, 1842; interment in Lake View Cemetery.

LEE, Joshua Bryan, a Representative and a Senator from Oklahoma; born in Childersburg, Talladega County, Ala., January 23, 1892; moved with his parents to Pauls Valley, Okla. (then Indian Territory), and then to Kiowa County, near Hobart in 1901; attended the public schools of Hobart and Rocky, Okla., and the Oklahoma Baptist University at Shawnee; teacher in the public schools of Rocky, Okla., 1912–1914; coach of athletics and teacher of public speaking at the Oklahoma Baptist University in 1915 and 1916; was graduated from the University of Oklahoma at Norman in 1917; instructor of public speaking at the University of Oklahoma in 1917 and 1918; during the First World War served overseas as a private in the One Hundred and Thirty-fifth Infantry, Thirty-fourth Division, in 1918 and 1919; head of the public speaking department of the University of Oklahoma 1919–1934; author and lecturer; owns and operates a ranch in western Oklahoma; elected as a Democrat to the Seventy-fourth Congress (January 3, 1935–January 3, 1937); was not a candidate for renomination in 1936; elected to the United States Senate for the term commencing January 3, 1937, and ending January 3, 1943; unsuccessful for reelection in 1942; member of the Civil Aeronautics Board from February 8, 1943, to December 31, 1955; is a resident of Norman, Okla.

LEE, Moses Lindley, a Representative from New York; born in Minisink, N. Y., May 29, 1805; pursued classical studies; was graduated from Union College in 1827 and from the College of Physicians and Surgeons of Western New York in 1830; practiced medicine in Fulton, Oswego County, N. Y.; postmaster at Fulton 1840–1844; member of the State house of representatives in 1847 and 1848; served in the State senate in 1855; elected as a Republican to the Thirty-sixth Congress (March 4, 1859–March 3, 1861); resumed the practice of medicine in Fulton, N. Y.; returning from a visit in the South became seriously ill at Petersburg, Va., and died there on May 19, 1876; interment in Mount Adnah Cemetery, Fulton, N. Y.

LEE, Richard Bland (brother of Henry Lee), a Representative from Virginia; born at "Leesylvania," in Prince William County, Va., January 20, 1761; pursued English and classical studies in private schools; attended William and Mary College, Williamsburg, Va.; member of the State house of delegates 1784–1788; elected to the First, Second, and Third Congresses (March 4, 1789–March 3, 1795); unsuccessful candidate for reelection in 1794 to the Fourth Congress; again a member of the State house of delegates 1796 and 1799–1806; moved to Washington, D. C., about 1815; appointed by President Madison in 1816 commissioner to adjudicate claims arising out of the loss or destruction of property during the War of 1812; appointed by President Monroe in 1819 judge of the Orphans' Court of the District of Columbia and served until his death in Washington, D. C., on March 12, 1827; interment in the Congressional Cemetery.

LEE, Richard Henry (brother of Arthur Lee and Francis Lightfoot Lee), a Delegate and a Senator from Virginia; born at "Stratford," in Westmoreland County, Va., January 20, 1732; after a course of private instruction attended Wakefield Academy, England; returned in 1751; justice of the peace for Westmoreland County in 1757; member of the house of burgesses 1758–1775; Member of the Continental Congress 1774–1780; a signer of the Declaration of Independence; brought forward the resolution, in accord with instructions given in the Virginia convention of May 17, 1776, declaring "that these united Colonies are, and of right ought to be, free and independent States," etc.; author of the first national Thanksgiving Day proclamation issued by Congress at York, Pa., October 31, 1777, after the capture of Burgoyne's army at Saratoga, N. Y.; member of the State house of delegates in 1777, 1780, and 1785; served as colonel of the Westmoreland Militia in engagement with the British at Stratford Landing on April 9, 1781; again a Member of the Continental Congress 1784–1787 and served as President of the Congress in 1784; member of the Virginia convention which ratified the Federal Constitution June 26, 1788; elected to the United States Senate and served from March 4, 1789, until his resignation October 8, 1792; retired from public life; died at his home, "Chantilly," Westmoreland County, Va., June 19, 1794; interment in the old family burying ground at "Mount Pleasant," near Hague, Westmoreland County, Va.

LEE, Robert Emmett, a Representative from Pennsylvania; born in Pottsville, Schuykill County, Pa., October 12, 1868; attended the common schools; apprenticed to the blacksmith's trade; engaged in mercantile pursuits in Pottsville; county treasurer in 1905; unsuccessful candidate for election in 1908 to the Sixty-first Congress; elected as a Democrat to the Sixty-second and Sixty-third Congresses (March 4, 1911–March 3, 1915); unsuccessful candidate for reelection in 1914 to the Sixty-fourth Congress; resumed his former business activities in Pottsville; unsuccessful candidate for election in 1916 to the Sixty-fifth Congress; elected as a delegate to the Democratic National Convention at St. Louis in 1916, but declined; died in Pottsville, Pa., November 19, 1916; interment in St. Patrick's Cemetery.

LEE, Robert Quincy, a Representative from Texas; born near Coldwater, Tate County, Miss., January 12, 1869; attended the public schools and the Fort Worth (Tex.) High School; moved with his father to Fort Worth, Tex., in 1886, and to Caddo, Stephens County, Tex., in 1891; engaged in the general merchandise business; moved to Cisco, Eastland County, Tex., in 1913 and engaged in ranching, agricultural pursuits, and banking; founder and builder in 1919 of the Cisco & Northeastern Railroad Co., and served as its president 1919–1927; president of the West Texas Chamber of Commerce in 1926 and 1927; elected as a Democrat to the Seventy-first Congress and served from March 4, 1929, until his death in Washington, D. C., April 18, 1930; interment in Oakwood Cemetery, Cisco, Tex.

LEE, Silas, a Representative from Massachusetts; born in Concord, Mass., July 3, 1760; pursued classical studies, and was graduated from Harvard University in 1784; studied law; and was admitted to the bar; member of the State house of representatives in 1793, 1797, and 1798; elected as a Federalist to the Sixth and Seventh Congresses and served from March 4, 1799, until August 20, 1801, when he resigned; appointed by President Jefferson to be United States attorney for the district of Maine January 6, 1802, and served until his death; justice of the peace and of the quorum in 1803; probate judge 1805–1814; chief judge of the common pleas court in 1810; died in Wiscasset, Maine, March 1, 1814; interment in Evergreen Cemetery.

LEE, Thomas, a Representative from New Jersey; born in Philadelphia, Pa., November 28, 1780; resided in Chester Valley, Pa., during his earlier years and attended the common schools; moved to Leesburg, Cumberland County, N. J., about 1798 and to Port Elizabeth in 1805; became a merchant, shipbuilder, and landowner; judge of the court of common pleas 1813–1815; member of the State general assembly in 1814 and 1815; postmaster of Port Elizabeth 1818–1833 and 1846–1849; elected as a Democrat to the Twenty-third and Twenty-fourth Congresses (March 4, 1833–March 3, 1837); founder of Port Elizabeth Library and Academy; died in Port Elizabeth, N. J., on November 2, 1856; interment in the Methodist Episcopal Churchyard.

LEE, Thomas Sim (father of John Lee), a Delegate from Maryland; born near Upper Marlboro, Prince Georges County, Md., October 29, 1745; completed preparatory studies; held several local offices; member of the provincial council in 1777; Governor of Maryland 1779–1783; Member of the Continental Congress in 1783 and 1784; member of the house of delegates in 1787; declined to serve in the convention which drafted the Constitution of the United States, but consented to serve in the State convention for the ratification of the Federal Constitution in 1788; presidential elector on the Federalist ticket of Washington and Adams in 1792; again Governor of Maryland 1792–1794; effected the organization of the State militia while he was Governor and took an active part in the suppression of the Whisky Insurrection in western Pennsylvania and Maryland; appointed to the State senate in 1794, but declined to serve; again elected Governor, but declined in 1798; retired from public life and engaged in the management of his estate, "Needwood," in Frederick County, Md., until his death, October 9, 1819; interment in a private cemetery at Melwood, Prince Georges County, Md.; reinterment in the Roman Catholic Cemetery, near Upper Marlboro, Md., April 17, 1888.

LEE, Warren Isbell, a Representative from New York; born in Bartlett, Oneida County, N. Y., February 5, 1876; attended the public schools; was graduated from Colgate Academy, Hamilton, N. Y., in 1894, from Hamilton College, Clinton, N. Y., in 1899, and from the New York Law School, New York City, in 1901; was admitted to the bar in 1901 and commenced practice in New York City; member of the State assembly 1906–1910 and in 1920; assistant district attorney of Brooklyn 1912–1914; first deputy comptroller of New York State 1914–1917; one of the counsel to the Public Service Commission of New York 1917–1919; delegate to the Republican State conventions in 1920, 1922, 1924, and 1927; trustee of Hamilton College 1917–1921; elected as a Republican to the Sixty-seventh Congress (March 4, 1921–March 3, 1923); unsuccessful candidate for reelection in 1922 to the Sixty-eighth Congress; resumed the practice of law; former director of Flatbush National Bank; died in Brooklyn, N. Y., December 25, 1955; interment in Greenwood Cemetery.

LEE, William Henry Fitzhugh (grandson of Henry Lee), a Representative from Virginia; born in the "Lee Mansion," (now situated in the area comprising Arlington National Cemetery at Fort Myer), Arlington, Va., May 31, 1837; attended private school and Harvard University; appointed second lieutenant in the Sixth Regiment, United States Infantry, and accompanied his regiment 1858 in the expedition to Utah; resigned in 1859; returned to Virginia and took charge of his estates near White House, New Kent County, in 1859; during the Civil War he raised a company of Cavalry in 1861 and joined the Confederate service; was promoted successively from captain to major general of Cavalry; was wounded at Brandy Station in June 1863; captured in Hanover County and taken to Fortress Monroe; transferred to United States prison at Fort Lafayette in 1863, where he was confined until March 1864, when he was transferred to Fortress Monroe and exchanged; returned to his command and served throughout the campaign of 1864 until the surrender of the Confederate Army at Appomattox; returned to his plantation; moved to Ravensworth, near Burke Station, Va., in 1874 and engaged in agricultural pursuits; member of the State senate 1875–1878 and served as presiding officer; served as president of the State agricultural society; elected as a Democrat to the Fiftieth, Fifty-first, and Fifty-second Congresses and served from March 4, 1887, until his death in Ravensworth, Va., on October 15, 1891; interment in the family burying ground at Ravensworth; reinterment in the Lee Mausoleum at Lexington, Va., in September 1922.

LEECH, James Russell, a Representative from Pennsylvania; born in Ebensburg, Cambria County, Pa., November 19, 1888; educated in the public and high schools and the Mercersburg (Pa.) Academy; was graduated from Washington and Jefferson College, Washington, Pa., in 1911, and from the law department of the University of Pennsylvania at Philadelphia in 1915; was admitted to the bar in 1915 and commenced practice in Ebensburg, Pa.; during the First World War was appointed as a second lieutenant on November 27, 1917, and served with the Seventh Ammunition Train; transferred to the Fourth Battalion, One Hundred and Fifty-third Depot Brigade, Fifteenth Company, and was honorably discharged on January 20, 1919; elected as a Republican to the Seventieth, Seventy-first, and Seventy-second Congresses and served from March 4, 1927, until his resignation on January 29, 1932, having been appointed a member of the United States Board of Tax Appeals (now Tax Court of the United States) to fill a vacancy; was reappointed in 1934 and again in 1946, and served on this court until his death in Chevy Chase, Md., on February 5, 1952; interment in Lloyd Cemetery, Ebensburg, Pa.

LEEDOM, John Peter, a Representative from Ohio; born in Adams County, Ohio, December 20, 1847; attended the common schools; was graduated from Smith's Mercantile College, Portsmouth, Ohio, in 1863; taught in the public schools of Portsmouth; engaged in agricultural pursuits; elected clerk of the court of common pleas of Adams County in 1874 and reelected in 1877; member of the Democratic State central committee in 1879; elected as a Democrat to the Forty-seventh Congress (March 4, 1881–March 3, 1883); unsuccessful candidate for reelection in 1882 to the Forty-eighth Congress; Sergeant at Arms of the House of Representatives 1884–1890; died in Toledo, Ohio, March 18, 1895; interment in the Odd Fellows Cemetery, Manchester, Ohio.

LEET, Isaac, a Representative from Pennsylvania; born near Washington, Pa., in 1801; pursued preparatory studies, and was graduated from Washington College (now Washington and Jefferson College), Washington, Pa., in 1822; studied law; was admitted to the bar in 1826 and commenced practice in Washington, Pa.; treasurer of Washington County 1826–1830; deputy attorney general of Washington County 1830–1834; member of the State senate 1834–1838; elected as a Democrat to the Twenty-sixth Congress (March 4, 1839–March 3, 1841); unsuccessful candidate for reelection in 1840 to the Twenty-seventh Congress; died in Washington, Pa., June 10, 1844; interment in the old Cooke private graveyard near Washington, Pa.

LE FEVER, Jacob (father of Frank Jacob Le Fevre), a Representative from New York; born in New Paltz, Ulster County, N. Y., April 20, 1830; attended New Paltz Academy and Amenia Seminary; supervisor of the town in 1861 and 1862; member of the State assembly 1863–1865 and again in 1867; delegate to many Republican State conventions; delegate to the Republican National Convention at Chicago in 1888; elected as a Republican to the Fifty-third and Fifty-fourth Congresses (March 4, 1893–March 3, 1897); was not a candidate for renomination in 1896 to the Fifty-fifth Congress; president of the Huguenot National Bank until his death in New Paltz, N. Y., on February 4, 1905; interment in New Paltz Rural Cemetery.

LEFEVER, Joseph, a Representative from Pennsylvania; born in Strasburg Township, near Paradise, Lancaster County, Pa., April 3, 1760; attended the common schools; engaged in agricultural pursuits; elected as a Democrat to the Twelfth Congress (March 4, 1811–March 3, 1813); resumed his agricultural pursuits; died in Paradise Township, Lancaster County, Pa., October 17, 1826; interment in Carpenter's Graveyard.

LE FEVRE, Benjamin, a Representative from Ohio; born near Maplewood, Shelby County, Ohio, on October 8, 1838; attended Miami University, Oxford, Ohio, in 1858 and 1859; studied law in Sidney, Ohio; during the Civil War enlisted in the Union Army in 1861 and served until the close of the war; mustered out as major of the Fiftieth Ohio Infantry and brevetted brigadier general; member of the State house of representatives in 1865; nominated in 1866 for secretary of state by the Democrats of Ohio; appointed United States consul at Batavia, Java, March 14, 1867, but declined; United States consul at Nuremberg, Bavaria, 1867–1869; elected as a Democrat to the Forty-sixth and to the three succeeding Congresses (March 4, 1879–March 3, 1887); was not a candidate for renomination in 1886; mail contract agent for Erie Railway Co.; retired from political activities and engaged in agricultural pursuits in Salem Township, Shelby County, Ohio; died in Atlantic City, N. J., on March 7, 1922; interment in Glenn Cemetery, Salem Township, Shelby County, Ohio.

LE FEVRE, Frank Jacob (son of Jacob Le Fever), a Representative from New York; born in New Paltz, Ulster County, N. Y., November 30, 1874; attended the public schools and the New Paltz Normal School; became engaged in banking; member of the State senate in 1902; appointed superintendent of the New York State building at St. Louis, Mo., during the holding of the Louisiana Purchase Exposition; elected as a Republican to the Fifty-ninth Congress (March 4, 1905–March 3, 1907); unsuccessful candidate for renomination in 1906; president of the Huguenot National Bank at New Paltz, N. Y., since 1905; delegate to many State and county conventions; member of the home defense committee of Ulster County during the First World War; engaged in banking and fruit growing; died in Atlantic City, N. J., April 29, 1941; interment in Moravian Cemetery, Richmond, Staten Island, N. Y.

LE FEVRE, Jay, a Representative from New York; born in New Paltz, Ulster County, N. Y., September 6, 1893; was graduated from the Lawrenceville (N. J.) Preparatory School and attended Dartmouth College at Hanover, N. H.; during the First World War served as a second lieutenant in the Reserve Officers Training Corps, Field Artillery, at Camp Taylor, Ark., in 1918; associated with his father in the coal, lumber, feed, and fuel-oil business in New Paltz, N. Y., 1916–1946; also engaged in the banking business; trustee of the village of New Paltz; delegate to the Republican State conventions in 1942 and 1946; Republican committeeman of New Paltz 1930–1946; elected as a Republican to the Seventy-eighth and to the three succeeding Congresses (January 3, 1943–January 3, 1951); was not a candidate for renomination in 1950; resumed his merchandising interests; member of the New York State Bridge Authority 1951–1955; is a resident of New Paltz, N. Y.

LEFFERTS, John, a Representative from New York; born in Brooklyn, N. Y., December 17, 1785; attended the public schools; elected as a Democrat to the Thirteenth Congress (March 4, 1813–March 3, 1815); delegate to the State constitutional convention of 1821; member of the State senate 1820–1825; died in Brooklyn, N. Y., September 18, 1829; interment in Greenwood Cemetery.

LEFFLER, Isaac (brother of Shepherd Leffler), a Representative from Virginia; born on his grandfather's plantation, "Sylvia's Plain," Washington County, Pa., near Wheeling, Va. (now West Virginia), November 7, 1788; attended the public schools and was graduated from Jefferson College, Canonsburg, Pa.; studied law; was admitted to the bar and commenced practice in Wheeling, Va.; member of the State house of delegates 1817–1819, 1823–1827, 1832, and 1833; member of the State board of public works in 1827; elected to the Twentieth Congress (March 4, 1827–March 3, 1829); unsuccessful candidate for reelection in 1828 to the Twenty-first Congress; moved to that portion of Michigan Territory that is now Des Moines County, Iowa, in 1835; admitted to the Des Moines County bar April 15, 1835, and practiced; chief justice of the first judicial tribunal of Des Moines County April 11, 1836; after the creation of Wisconsin Territory April 20, 1836, represented Des Moines County in the first legislature of the new Territory in 1836 and 1837 and served as speaker in 1837; unsuccessful Whig candidate for election in 1837 to the Twenty-fifth Congress; trustee of the university at Belmont, Iowa, in 1838; member of the house of representatives of the Territory of Iowa in 1841; appointed by President Tyler United States marshal for the district of Iowa December 18, 1843; confirmed January 16, 1844, and served until removed by President Polk December 29, 1845; resumed the practice of law in Burlington, Iowa; declined the appointment of register of the land office at Stillwater in 1849; appointed by President Fillmore receiver of public moneys for the Chariton land district of Iowa August 30, 1852, and served until removed by President Pierce on March 29, 1853; died in Chariton, Lucas County, Iowa, March 8, 1866; interment in Aspen Grove Cemetery, Burlington, Iowa.

LEFFLER, Shepherd (brother of Isaac Leffler), a Representative from Iowa; born on his grandfather's plantation, "Sylvia's Plain," Washington County, Pa., near Wheeling, Va. (now West Virginia), April 24, 1811; attended private schools, and was graduated from Washington College, Washington, Pa., and from the law department of Jefferson College, Canonsburg, Pa., in 1833; was admitted to the bar and commenced practice in Wheeling; moved to Burlington, Iowa (then a part of Michigan Territory), in 1835; member of the Territorial house of representatives in 1839 and 1841; served in the Territorial council 1841–1843 and in 1845; member of the constitutional conventions in 1844 and 1846; permanent president during the first convention; upon the admission of Iowa as a State into the Union was elected as a Democrat to the Twenty-ninth Congress in 1846; reelected to the Thirtieth and Thirty-first Congresses and served from December 28, 1846, to March 3, 1851; engaged in the practice of his profession and in agricultural pursuits in Burlington; unsuccessful candidate for election in 1856 to the Thirty-fifth Congress; unsuccessful Democratic candidate for Governor of Iowa in 1875; retired from active political life; died at his home, "Flint Hills," near Burlington, Des Moines County, Iowa, September 7, 1879; interment in Aspen Grove Cemetery.

LEFTWICH, Jabez, a Representative from Virginia; born in Bedford County near Liberty (now Bedford), Va., September 22, 1765; attended the rural schools; member of the State house of delegates 1801–1809; inspector general with the rank of colonel on the staff of his brother, Gen. Joel Leftwich, during the War of 1812; elected to the Seventeenth and Eighteenth Congresses (March 4, 1821–March 3, 1825); unsuccessful candidate for reelection in 1824 to the Nineteenth Congress; moved to Madison County, Ala., in 1825; engaged in agricultural and mercantile pursuits; member of the Alabama House of Representatives; died near Huntsville, Ala., June 22, 1855; interment in Maple Hill Cemetery.

LEFTWICH, John William, a Representative from Tennessee; born in Liberty (now Bedford), Bedford County, Va., September 7, 1826; attended the public schools; studied medicine and was graduated from the Philadelphia Medical College in 1850; moved to Memphis, Tenn., and engaged in mercantile pursuits; upon the readmission of the State of Tennessee to representation was elected as a Democrat to the Thirty-ninth Congress and served from July 24, 1866, to March 3, 1867; unsuccessful candidate for reelection; delegate to the Democratic National Convention at New York in 1868; mayor of Memphis in 1869 and 1870; contested the election of William J. Smith to the Forty-first Congress, but, while on his way to Washington to prosecute the contest, died in Lynchburg, Va., March 6, 1870; interment in Elmwood Cemetery, Memphis, Tenn.

LEGARDA Y TUASON, Benito, a Resident Commissioner from the Philippine Islands; born in Manila, Philippine Islands, September 27, 1853; attended the Jesuits' College and St. Tomas University of Manila; member of Aguinaldo's cabinet at Malolos and vice president of the Filipino Congress; resigned these positions to return to Manila in December 1898; appointed a member of the Philippine Commission February 1, 1901, and served until elected a Resident Commissioner; elected as a Resident Commissioner to the United States in 1907; reelected in 1909 and served from

November 22, 1907, to March 3, 1913; after his term in Congress was not a candidate for renomination in 1912; went to France; died at Evian-les-Bains, France, August 27, 1915; interment in Cementerio del Norte, Manila, Philippine Islands.

LEGARÉ, George Swinton, a Representative from South Carolina; born in Rockville, Charleston County, S. C., November 11, 1869; moved to Charleston in boyhood and engaged in the dairy business to earn the money with which to pay for his education; was graduated from Porter Academy, Charleston, S. C., in 1889 and attended the law department of the University of South Carolina at Columbia for two years; was graduated from Georgetown University Law School, Washington, D. C., in 1893; was admitted to the bar the same year and commenced practice in Charleston, S. C.; corporation counsel 1898–1903; elected as a Democrat to the Fifty-eighth and to the four succeeding Congresses and served from March 4, 1903, until his death, before the close of the Sixty-second Congress; had been reelected to the Sixty-third Congress; died in Charleston, S. C., January 31, 1913; interment in Magnolia Cemetery.

LEGARÉ, Hugh Swinton, a Representative from South Carolina; born in Charleston, S. C., January 2, 1797; attended Charleston College and the school of Rev. Moses Waddell at Abbeville; was graduated from the College of South Carolina (now University of South Carolina) at Columbia in 1814; studied law 1814–1817; pursued further studies in Paris and Edinburgh in 1818 and 1819; admitted to the bar in 1822 and commenced practice in Charleston, S. C.; member of the State house of representatives 1820–1822 and 1824–1830; one of the founders and editor of the Southern Review 1828–1832; attorney general of South Carolina 1830–1832; Chargé d'Affaires to Brussels 1832–1836; elected as a Union Democrat to the Twenty-fifth Congress (March 4, 1837–March 3, 1839); unsuccessful candidate for reelection; resumed the practice of law in Charleston; Attorney General of the United States in the Cabinet of President Tyler from September 13, 1841, until his death; also filled the office of Secretary of State ad interim from May 8, 1843, up to the time of his death, in Boston, Mass., June 20, 1843; interment in Mount Auburn Cemetery, Cambridge, Mass.; reinterment in Magnolia Cemetery, Charleston, S. C.

LEHLBACH, Frederick Reimold (nephew of Herman Lehlbach), a Representative from New Jersey; born in New York City January 31, 1876; moved with his parents to Newark, N. J., in 1884; attended the public schools; was graduated from Yale University in 1897; attended the New York Law School; was admitted to the bar in February 1899 and commenced practice in Newark, N. J.; member of the Newark Board of Education 1900–1903; member of the State house of assembly 1903–1905; clerk of the State board of equalization of taxes from April 3, 1905, until his resignation on April 14, 1908; appointed assistant prosecutor of Essex County on April 15, 1908, and served until April 6, 1913, when he resigned to resume the practice of law; elected as a Republican to the Sixty-fourth and to the ten succeeding Congresses (March 4, 1915–January 3, 1937); unsuccessful candidate for reelection in 1936 to the Seventy-fifth Congress; continued the practice of law in Washington, D. C., until his death there on August 4, 1937; interment in Fairmount Cemetery, Newark, N. J.

LEHLBACH, Herman (uncle of Frederick Reimold Lehlbach), a Representative from New Jersey; born in Heilig-Kreuz-Steinach, Baden, Germany, July 3, 1845; immigrated to the United States in 1851 with his parents, who settled in Newark, N. J.; attended the public schools and became a civil engineer; member of the State house of assembly 1884–1886; elected as a Republican to the Forty-ninth, Fiftieth, and Fifty-first Con-

gresses (March 4, 1885–March 3, 1891); was not a candidate for renomination in 1890; resumed the practice of his profession as a civil engineer in Newark; sheriff of Essex County, N. J., 1893–1896; died in Newark, N. J., on January 11, 1904; interment Fairmount Cemetery.

LEHMAN, Herbert Henry, a Senator from New York; born in New York City, N. Y., March 28, 1878; attended Sachs Collegiate Institute in New York City; was graduated from Williams College, Williamstown, Mass., in 1899; employed by the J. Spencer Turner Co., textile manufacturers, and became vice president and treasurer in 1906; in 1908 became partner in Lehman Bros., investment bankers in New York City; during the First World War was commissioned a captain in the United States Army in August 1917 and later attained the rank of colonel on the General Staff, serving as assistant director of purchase, storage, and traffic, War Department, until April 1919; awarded the Distinguished Service Medal; Lieutenant Governor of New York 1929–1932; Governor 1933–1942; Director of Foreign Relief and Rehabilitation Operations in the State Department, Washington, D. C., in 1943; Director General of the United Nations Relief and Rehabilitation Administration 1943–1946; unsuccessful candidate for election to the United States Senate in 1946; member of Public Advisory Board of the Economic Cooperation Administration in 1948; delegate to all Democratic National Conventions from 1928 to 1956; elected as a Democrat to the United States Senate to fill the vacancy caused by the resignation of Robert F. Wagner and served from November 9, 1949, to January 3, 1951; reelected in 1950 for the term ending January 3, 1957; was not a candidate for renomination in 1956; is a resident of New York City, N. Y.

LEHMAN, William Eckart, a Representative from Pennsylvania; born in Philadelphia, Pa., August 21, 1821; pursued preparatory studies; was graduated from the University of Pennsylvania at Philadelphia in 1841; studied law; was admitted to the bar in 1844 and commenced practice in Philadelphia; appointed post-office examiner for Pennsylvania and New York by President Polk; elected as a Democrat to the Thirty-seventh Congress (March 4, 1861–March 3, 1863); unsuccessful candidate for renomination in 1862; United States provost marshal of the first district of Pennsylvania with the rank of captain from April 25, 1863, to June 15, 1865; having an ample income, he did not engage in any business or professional activities; died in Atlantic City, N. J., July 19, 1895; interment in St. Peter's Episcopal Church Cemetery, Philadelphia, Pa.

LEHR, John Camillus, a Representative from Michigan; born in Monroe, Monroe County, Mich., November 18, 1878; attended St. Mary's private school and Monroe High School, graduating from the latter in 1897; was graduated from the law department of the University of Michigan at Ann Arbor in 1900; was admitted to the bar the same year and commenced practice in Monroe, Mich.; moved to Port Huron, Mich., in 1905 and continued the practice of law; returned to Monroe in 1916; served as city attorney 1918–1922 and 1928–1930; member of the board of education of Monroe 1926–1936, and served as vice president 1930–1936; elected as a Democrat to the Seventy-third Congress (March 4, 1933–January 3, 1935); unsuccessful candidate for reelection in 1934 to the Seventy-fourth Congress; member of Monroe Port Commission 1936–1942; delegate to the Democratic National Convention at Philadelphia in 1936; appointed on July 2, 1936, by President Franklin D. Roosevelt, United States attorney for the eastern district of Michigan and served until September 2, 1947, when he resigned to devote his time as head of a fraternal beneficiary association in Detroit, Mich.; died in Monroe, Mich., February 17, 1958; interment in St. Joseph Cemetery.

LEIB, Michael, a Representative and a Senator from Pennsylvania; born in Philadelphia, Pa., January 8, 1760; attended the common schools; was graduated from the medical department of the University of Pennsylvania at Philadelphia and commenced practice in Philadelphia, Pa.; commissioned surgeon of Eyre's battalion of Philadelphia Militia August 10, 1780, and served throughout the Revolutionary War; resumed the practice of medicine; member of the Pennsylvania Prison Society in 1789; member of the committee of correspondence in 1793; member of the State house of representatives in 1797 and 1798; elected as a Democrat to the Sixth and to the three succeeding Congresses and served from March 4, 1799, until February 14, 1806, when he resigned; brigadier general of the Second Brigade of Philadelphia Militia in 1807; member of the committee of correspondence on the *Chesapeake* affair July 1, 1807; presidential elector on the Democratic ticket of Madison and Clinton in 1808; elected as a Democrat to the United States Senate in 1808 for the term beginning March 4, 1809; subsequently elected to fill the vacancy in the term ending March 3, 1809, caused by the resignation of Samuel Maclay and served from January 9, 1809, to February 14, 1814, when he resigned, having been appointed postmaster of Philadelphia on that day; served in this capacity until January 4, 1815; again served as a member of the State house of representatives in 1817 and 1818; appointed as a prothonotary of the United States district court at Philadelphia and served from November 15, 1822, until his death in Philadelphia, Pa., on December 22, 1822; interment in St. John's Lutheran Churchyard, Northern Liberties, Philadelphia, Pa.

LEIB, Owen D., a Representative from Pennsylvania; born in that State; pursued classical studies; studied medicine and commenced practice in Catawissa, Pa.; elected as a Democrat to the Twenty-ninth Congress (March 4, 1845–March 3, 1847); died in Catawissa, Pa., June 17, 1848.

LEIDY, Paul, a Representative from Pennsylvania; born in Hemlock Township, Columbia County, Pa., November 13, 1813; attended the common schools; apprenticed as a tailor; taught school in Danville, Pa., for several years; studied law; was admitted to the bar in 1837 and commenced practice in Danville; district attorney of Montour County 1852–1857; elected as a Democrat to the Thirty-fifth Congress to fill the vacancy caused by the death of John G. Montgomery and served from December 7, 1857, to March 3, 1859; unsuccessful candidate for reelection in 1858 to the Thirty-sixth Congress; died in Danville, Pa., September 11, 1877; interment in the Odd Fellows Cemetery.

LEIGH, Benjamin Watkins, a Senator from Virginia; born in Chesterfield County, Va., on June 18, 1781; studied under private tutors; was graduated from William and Mary College, Williamsburg, Va., in 1802; studied law; was admitted to the bar and commenced practice in Petersburg, Va.; served in the War of 1812; member of the State house of delegates 1811–1813; moved to Richmond, Va., in 1813; prepared the revised code of 1810; delegate to the State constitutional convention of 1829 and 1830; again a member of the State house of delegates in 1830 and 1831; official reporter of the State court of appeals 1829–1841; elected as a Whig to the United States Senate to fill the vacancy in the term ending March 3, 1835, caused by the resignation of William C. Rives; reelected in 1835 and served from February 26, 1834, to July 4, 1836, when he resigned; resumed the practice of law; died in Richmond, Va., February 2, 1849; interment in Shockoe Cemetery.

LEIGHTY, Jacob D., a Representative from Indiana; born near Greensburg, Westmoreland County, Pa., November 15, 1839; in 1844 moved with his parents to De Kalb County, Ind.,

where they settled on a farm at Spencerville, near Fort Wayne; attended the public schools; taught in district schools; spent two years at a commercial school at Fort Wayne and then entered Wittenberg College, Springfield, Ohio; on July 1, 1861, after two years in college, he left to enlist in the Union Army during the Civil War; became a member of Company E, Eleventh Indiana Volunteer Zouave Infantry, a regiment being raised by Col. Lew Wallace (later General Wallace); was promoted to second and subsequently first lieutenant; severely wounded at Champion Hills, Miss., April 16, 1863; returned to service after a short furlough, but, on account of his physical condition, resigned in 1864; engaged in farming and general merchandising with his father until 1875, when, upon the completion of the Baltimore & Ohio Railroad into Chicago, he established the town of St. Joe, Ind., and, together with others in the neighborhood, contributed to the erection of a grain elevator and other facilities for handling the products of the neighborhood; established a sawmill, handle factory, creamery, and bank, in addition to conducting a general supply store and lumber yard at St. Joe; was interested in the founding of a plant for manufacturing buggy and carriage bodies at Auburn, Ind.; during this period of development of the community was generally engaged in buying practically everything that was produced and bringing in and selling everything needed but not produced at home; during most of his time was also interested in farming; member of the State house of representatives 1886–1888; elected as a Republican to the Fifty-fourth Congress (March 4, 1895–March 3, 1897); unsuccessful candidate for reelection in 1896 to the Fifty-fifth Congress; United States pension agent at Indianapolis 1897–1901; retired from active business pursuits in 1901; died at St. Joe, De Kalb County, Ind., on October 18, 1912; interment in Riverview Cemetery.

LEIPER, George Gray, a Representative from Pennsylvania; born in Philadelphia, Pa., February 3, 1786; attended the common schools; was graduated from the University of Pennsylvania at Philadelphia in 1803; moved to "Lapidea," Delaware County, Pa., in 1810 and engaged in logging; also operated bark mills and stone quarries; served as first lieutenant of the Delaware County Fencibles in 1814 and was called into active service near Brandywine Creek; member of the State house of representatives in 1822 and 1823; elected as a Democrat to the Twenty-first Congress (March 4, 1829–March 3, 1831); was not a candidate for renomination in 1830; resumed the management of his quarry properties; appointed associate judge of the courts of Delaware County on February 25, 1843; reappointed on February 16, 1848, and served until December 1, 1851, when the office became elective; died at his home, "Lapidea," on Crum Creek, Delaware County, Pa., November 18, 1868; interment in the Ridley Presbyterian Church Cemetery, Ridley Township, Delaware County, Pa.

LEISENRING, John, a Representative from Pennsylvania; born in Ashton (now Lansford), Carbon County, Pa., June 3, 1853; attended the public schools, Schwartz's Academy, Bethlehem, Pa., and academies in Merchantville and Princeton, N. J.; became a civil and mining engineer and was identified with coal, iron, and lumber industries; also interested in banking; moved from Mauch Chunk, Pa., to Upper Lehigh, Pa., in 1885; member of the State house of representatives in 1894 and 1895; elected as a Republican to the Fifty-fourth Congress (March 4, 1895–March 3, 1897); declined to be a candidate for reelection in 1896 to the Fifty-fifth Congress; delegate to the Republican State convention in 1896; resumed his former business pursuits and served as president of the Upper Lehigh Coal Co.; died at the University Hospital in Philadelphia, Pa., January 19, 1901; interment in the City Cemetery at Mauch Chunk, Pa.

LEITER, Benjamin Franklin, a Representative from Ohio; born in Leitersburg, Md., October 13, 1813; received a limited schooling; taught school in Maryland 1830–1834; moved to Ohio and taught school 1834–1842; studied law; was admitted to the bar in 1842 and commenced practice in Canton, Stark County, Ohio; justice of the peace; mayor for ten years; member of the State house of representatives in 1848 and 1849 and served as speaker in the latter year; elected as a Republican to the Thirty-fourth and Thirty-fifth Congresses (March 4, 1855–March 3, 1859); died in Canton, Ohio, June 17, 1866; interment in West Lawn Cemetery.

LEMKE, William, a Representative from North Dakota; born in Albany, Stearns County, Minn., August 13, 1878; attended the public schools; was graduated from the University of North Dakota at Grand Forks in 1902 and Yale University, New Haven, Conn., in 1905; studied law at the University of North Dakota and Georgetown University, Washington, D. C.; was admitted to the bar in 1905 and commenced practice at Fargo, N. Dak.; member of the national executive committee of the National Nonpartisan League 1917–1921; chairman of the Republican State committee 1916–1920; attorney general of North Dakota in 1921 and 1922; Union Party candidate for President in 1936; elected as a Nonpartisan on the Republican ticket to the Seventy-third and to the three succeeding Congresses (March 4, 1933–January 3, 1941); renominated as a Republican in 1940; later withdrew and was an unsuccessful Independent candidate for election to the United States Senate; resumed the practice of law; elected as a Republican to the Seventy-eighth and to the three succeeding Congresses and served from January 3, 1943, until his death in Fargo, N. Dak., May 30, 1950; interment in Riverside Cemetery.

LE MOYNE, John Valcoulon, a Representative from Illinois; born in Washington, Washington County, Pa., November 17, 1828; attended the common schools; was graduated from Washington and Jefferson College, Washington, Pa., in 1847; studied law; was admitted to the bar in Pittsburgh, Pa., in 1852; moved to Chicago the same year and commenced practice; unsuccessful candidate of the Liberal Party for election in 1872 to the Forty-third Congress; successfully contested as a Democrat the election of Charles B. Farwell to the Forty-fourth Congress and served from May 6, 1876, to March 3, 1877; unsuccessful candidate for reelection in 1876 to the Forty-fifth Congress; resumed the practice of law in Chicago, Ill.; retired from public life in 1887 and moved to Baltimore, Md., where he resided until his death on July 27, 1918; interment in Washington Cemetery, Washington, Pa.

LENAHAN, John Thomas, a Representative from Pennsylvania; born in Jenkins Township, Luzerne County, Pa., November 15, 1852; attended private schools; was graduated from Villanova (Pa.) College in 1870; studied law at the University of Pennsylvania, Philadelphia, Pa.; was admitted to the bar in 1873 and commenced practice in Wilkes-Barre, Pa.; delegate to the Democratic National Conventions in 1892 and 1896; elected as a Democrat to the Sixtieth Congress (March 4, 1907–March 3, 1909); was not a candidate for renomination in 1908; resumed the practice of law; died in Wilkes-Barre, Pa., April 28, 1920; interment in St. Mary's Cemetery.

L'ENGLE, Claude, a Representative from Florida; born in Jacksonville, Fla., October 19, 1868; attended the public schools and the Duval High School; engaged in mercantile pursuits; became editor and publisher of Dixie, a weekly newspaper; elected as a Democrat to the Sixty-third Congress (March 4, 1913–March 3, 1915); unsuccessful candidate for renomination in 1914 to the Sixty-fourth Congress; again engaged in jour-

nalism; died in Jacksonville, Duval County, Fla., November 6, 1919; interment in Evergreen Cemetery.

LENNON, Alton Asa, a Senator and a Representative from North Carolina; born in Wilmington, New Hanover County, N. C., August 17, 1906; attended the public schools; was graduated from the New Hanover High School, Wilmington, N. C., in 1925 and from Wake Forest College in 1929; studied law; was admitted to the bar in 1929 and began practice in Wilmington, N. C.; served as judge, New Hanover County Recorder's Court, 1934–1942; member of the State senate two terms 1947–1951; appointed as a Democrat to the United States Senate to fill the vacancy caused by the death of Willis Smith and served from July 10, 1953, to November 28, 1954; was an unsuccessful candidate for the nomination in 1954 to fill the vacancy; resumed law practice; elected as a Democrat to the Eighty-fifth and Eighty-sixth Congresses (January 3, 1957–January 3, 1961). *Reelected to the Eighty-seventh Congress.*

LENROOT, Irvine Luther, a Representative and a Senator from Wisconsin; born in Superior, Wis., January 31, 1869; attended the common schools; became a court reporter; studied law; was admitted to the bar in 1897 and commenced practice in Superior, Wis.; delegate to the Republican State conventions in 1900, 1902, and 1904; member of the State assembly 1901–1907 and served as speaker 1903–1907; elected as a Republican to the Sixty-first and to the four succeeding Congresses and served from March 4, 1909, until April 17, 1918, when he resigned, having been elected Senator; elected to the United States Senate on April 2, 1918, to fill the vacancy caused by the death of Paul O. Husting; reelected in 1920 and served from April 18, 1918, to March 3, 1927; unsuccessful candidate for renomination in 1926; resumed the practice of law in Washington, D. C.; appointed judge of the United States Court of Customs and Patent Appeals by President Hoover, May 17, 1929, and served until his resignation April 30, 1944; died in Washington, D. C., January 26, 1949; interment in Greenwood Cemetery, Superior, Wis.

LENT, James, a Representative from New York; born in Newtown, Long Island (now a part of the Borough of Queens), N. Y., in 1782; engaged in mercantile pursuits in New York City; judge of Queens County and served from February 5, 1823, to March 4, 1829; elected as a Jackson Democrat to the Twenty-first and Twenty-second Congresses and served from March 4, 1829, until his death in Washington, D. C., February 22, 1833; interment in the Congressional Cemetery; reinterment in the Presbyterian Cemetery, Newtown, Long Island, N. Y.

LENTZ, John Jacob, a Representative from Ohio; born near St. Clairsville, Belmont County, Ohio, January 27, 1856; attended the common schools and the St. Clairsville High School; taught school for four years; was graduated from the National Normal University, Lebanon, Ohio, in 1877; attended the University of Wooster in 1877 and 1878; was graduated from the University of Michigan at Ann Arbor in 1882 and from the law department of Columbia University, New York City, in 1883; was admitted to the bar in Columbus, Ohio, in October 1883 and practiced; founder of the American Insurance Union in 1894 and its president continuously until his death; trustee of Ohio University at Athens; elected as a Democrat to the Fifty-fifth and Fifty-sixth Congresses (March 4, 1897–March 3, 1901); unsuccessful candidate for reelection in 1900 to the Fifty-seventh Congress; delegate to the Democratic National Convention at Denver in 1908 and seconded the nominations of Bryan and Kern; participated in campaigns in many States in support of the eighteenth and nineteenth amendments to the Constitution; one of the founders and continuously a member of the board of governors of "Mooseheart"; member Moose War Relief Commission to visit the war front during the First World War; councilor representing American Fraternal Congress in the Chamber of Commerce of the United States; author of several books; retired from his law practice in 1915 and engaged in the insurance business; died in Columbus, Ohio, on July 27, 1931; interment in Green Lawn Cemetery.

LEONARD, Fred Churchill, a Representative from Pennsylvania; born in Elmer, Potter County, Pa., February 16, 1856; attended the public schools, the State normal school at Mansfield, Pa., and Williston Seminary, Easthampton, Mass.; was graduated from Yale College in 1883; studied law in Wellsboro, Pa.; was admitted to the bar in 1885; moved to Elmira, N. Y., and thence, in 1887, to Coudersport, Potter County, Pa., and practiced law; elected as a Republican to the Fifty-fourth Congress (March 4, 1895–March 3, 1897); unsuccessful candidate for renomination in 1896; resumed the practice of law in Coudersport, Pa.; served as United States marshal for the western district of Pennsylvania from January 15, 1898, until May 6, 1901, when he was transferred to the middle district and served until July 2, 1906; engaged in banking; died in Coudersport, Pa., December 5, 1921; interment in Eulalia Cemetery.

LEONARD, George, a Representative from Massachusetts; born in Norton, Mass., July 4, 1729; was graduated from Harvard College in 1748; register of probate 1749–1783; studied law; was admitted to the bar and commenced practice at Norton in 1750; member of the provincial assembly 1764–1766; executive councilor 1770–1775; judge of the probate court 1784–1790; judge of the common pleas court 1785–1798 and chief justice 1798–1804; elected to the First Congress (March 4, 1789–March 3, 1791); member of the State senate in 1792 and 1793; elected to the Fourth Congress (March 4, 1795–March 3, 1797); served in the State house of representatives in 1801 and 1802; died in Raynham, Mass., July 26, 1819; interment in the local cemetery at Norton, Mass.

LEONARD, John Edwards (grandnephew of John Edwards of Pennsylvania), a Representative from Louisiana; born in Fairville, Chester County, Pa., September 22, 1845; attended the public schools; was graduated from Phillips Exeter Academy, Exeter, N. H., in 1863 and from Harvard University, Cambridge, Mass., in 1867; studied law in Germany; returned to the United States and was admitted to the bar in Louisiana in 1870 and commenced practice at Monroe, Ouachita Parish; district attorney of the thirteenth judicial district of Louisiana in 1871 and 1872; elected associate justice of the State supreme court in 1876; resumed the practice of his profession in Monroe, La.; elected as a Republican to the Forty-fifth Congress and served from March 4, 1877, until his death in Habana, Cuba, March 15, 1878; interment in the Friends' (Hicksite) Cemetery of the Middletown Meeting House, Middletown Township, Delaware County, Pa.

LEONARD, Moses Gage, a Representative from New York; born in Stafford, Conn., July 10, 1809; attended the public schools; moved to New York City; city alderman and judge of the city court 1840–1842; elected as a Democrat to the Twenty-eighth Congress (March 4, 1843–March 3, 1845); unsuccessful candidate for reelection in 1844 to the Twenty-ninth Congress; almshouse commissioner in 1846; founder, director, secretary, and treasurer of the Knickerbocker Ice Co.; president of the Washington Ice Co.; commissioner of immigration at the port of New York; moved to San Francisco, Calif.; member of the city council of San Francisco in 1850; returned to New York and served as provost marshal in the Tenth Congressional District of New York during the Civil War; died in

Brooklyn, N. Y., on March 20, 1899; interment in Oak Hill Cemetery, Nyack, N. Y.

LEONARD, Stephen Banks, a Representative from New York; born in New York City April 15, 1793; attended the public schools; moved with his parents to Owego, N. Y., and learned the printer's trade; engaged in newspaper work in Albany, N. Y.; moved to New York City and subsequently returned to Owego; publisher and editor of the Owego Gazette 1814–1835; trustee of the village of Owego; supervisor and commissioner of excise; trustee of Owego Academy for many years; established the first stage route from Owego to Bath in 1816; postmaster of Owego 1816–1820; elected as a Democrat to the Twenty-fourth Congress (March 4, 1835–March 3, 1837); elected to the Twenty-sixth Congress (March 4, 1839–March 3, 1841); declined to be a candidate for reelection in 1840 to the Twenty-seventh Congress; engaged in mercantile and agricultural pursuits; supervisor of Owego 1854–1856; deputy United States marshal 1857–1861; died in Owego, Tioga County, N. Y., May 8, 1876; interment in the Presbyterian Church Burying Ground.

LESHER, John Vandling, a Representative from Pennsylvania; born on a farm on Blue Hill, Union Township, Union County, Pa., July 27, 1866; attended the rural schools in his native county and the State Normal School at Bloomsburg; taught school for several years in Union and Snyder Counties; was graduated from Bucknell University, Lewisburg, Pa., in 1897; enlisted in Company K, National Guard of Pennsylvania, in 1898, and when it was transferred to the Twelfth Regiment served as a first lieutenant; promoted to quartermaster with rank of captain, serving until 1902; studied law; was admitted to the bar in 1900 and commenced practice in Sunbury, Northumberland County, Pa.; served as assistant district attorney of Northumberland County, Pa.; also engaged in banking and real-estate development; elected as a Democrat to the Sixty-third and to the three succeeding Congresses (March 4, 1913–March 3, 1921); unsuccessful candidate for reelection in 1920 to the Sixty-seventh Congress; resumed the practice of law in Sunbury, Pa.; died in a hospital at Danville, Pa., May 3, 1932; interment in Riverview Cemetery, Northumberland, Pa.

LESINSKI, John, a Representative from Michigan; born in Erie, Pa., January 3, 1885; and three months later moved with his parents to Detroit, Mich.; attended St. Albertus School, St. Cyril and Methodeusz Seminary, Orchard Lake, Mich., and Detroit Business University, Detroit, Mich.; engaged extensively in the building and real-estate business in Detroit; established lumber and supply companies in Hamtramck and Dearborn areas of Detroit; president of the Polish Citizens' Committee of Detroit 1919–1932; State commissioner in charge of the sale of Polish bonds in 1920; awarded the Polonia Restituta by the Polish Government; delegate to the Democratic National Conventions at Philadelphia in 1936 and at Chicago in 1940 and 1944; delegate to the Democratic State conventions in 1936, 1940, and 1944; elected as a Democrat to the Seventy-third and to the eight succeeding Congresses and served from March 4, 1933, until his death in Dearborn, Mich., May 27, 1950; interment in Mount Olivet Cemetery, Detroit, Mich.

LESINSKI, John, Jr. (son of the preceding), a Representative from Michigan; born in Detroit, Wayne County, Mich., December 28, 1914; at the age of eleven years moved with his parents to Dearborn, Mich.; attended the parochial schools, St. Cyril and Methodeusz Seminary, Orchard Lake, Mich., and graduated from Fordson High School, Dearborn, Mich.; at the age of eighteen years enlisted in the United States Navy as an apprentice seaman and served from 1933 to 1937; was called to active duty again in February 1941 and served until October 1945; was wounded when the Japanese bombed the escort carrier *St. Lo;* awarded the Purple Heart Medal, Good Conduct Medal, and the Navy and Marine Corps Medal; vice president, Hamtramck Lumber Co., 1939–1943 and 1951–1954; president, Dearborn Lumber Co.; elected as a Democrat to the Eighty-second and to the four succeeding Congresses (January 3, 1951–January 3, 1961). *Reelected to the Eighty-seventh Congress.*

LESSLER, Montague, a Representative from New York; born in New York City January 1, 1869; attended the public schools; was graduated from the College of the City of New York in 1889 and later from the Columbia Law School; was admitted to the bar in 1891 and commenced the practice of his profession in New York City; elected as a Republican to the Fifty-seventh Congress to fill the vacancy caused by the resignation of Nicholas Muller and served from January 7, 1902, to March 3, 1903; unsuccessful candidate for reelection in 1902 to the Fifty-eighth Congress; resumed the practice of law in New York City until his death there on February 17, 1938; remains were cremated.

LESTER, Posey Green, a Representative from Virginia; born near the town of Floyd, Floyd County, Va., March 12, 1850; attended the common schools and the Jacksonville graded school at Floyd; engaged in teaching in Floyd County, Va.; ordained a minister in the primitive or old-school Baptist Church in 1876; resided in Floyd, Va., and traveled and preached in twenty-one of the States of the Union and in Ontario, Canada; became associate editor of Zion's Landmark, a church paper published at Wilson, N. C., in 1883, and editor in chief in 1920; elected as a Democrat to the Fifty-first and Fifty-second Congresses (March 4, 1889–March 3, 1893); was not a candidate for renomination in 1892; resumed his ministerial duties at Floyd, Va., until 1921, when he moved to Roanoke, Va., and served as pastor of the Primitive Baptist Church until his death in that city on February 9, 1929; interment in Evergreen Cemetery.

LESTER, Rufus Ezekiel, a Representative from Georgia; born near Waynesboro, Burke County, Ga., December 12, 1837; was graduated from Mercer University, Macon, Ga., in 1857; studied law; was admitted to the bar in Savannah, Ga., and commenced practice in 1859; entered the military service of the Confederate Army in 1861 and served throughout the Civil War; resumed the practice of law in Savannah; member of the State senate 1870–1879 and served as president of that body during the last three years; mayor of Savannah 1883–1889; elected as a Democrat to the Fifty-first and to the eight succeeding Congresses and served from March 4, 1889, until his death in Washington, D. C., on June 16, 1906; interment in Bonaventure Cemetery, Savannah, Ga.

LETCHER, John, a Representative from Virginia; born in Lexington, Rockbridge County, Va., March 29, 1813; attended private rural schools and Randolph-Macon College; was graduated from Washington Academy (now Washington and Lee University), Lexington, Va., in 1833; studied law; was admitted to the bar and commenced practice in Lexington, Va., in 1839; editor of the Valley Star from 1840 to 1850; presidential elector on the Democratic ticket of Cass and Butler in 1848; delegate to the State constitutional convention in 1850; elected as a Democrat to the Thirty-second and to the three succeeding Congresses (March 4, 1851–March 3, 1859); was not a candidate for renomination in 1858, having become a candidate for Governor; Governor of Virginia 1860–1864; prominent in the organi-

zation of the peace convention that met in Washington, D. C., February 8, 1861, in an effort to devise means to prevent the impending war; discouraged secession, but was active in sustaining the ordinance passed by Virginia April 17, 1861; after the war and the expiration of his term as Governor resumed the practice of law in Lexington; member of the State house of delegates 1875–1877; member of the board of visitors of the Virginia Military Institute 1866–1880 and served as president of the board for ten years; again resumed the practice of law in Lexington, Va., where he died on January 26, 1884; interment in the Presbyterian Cemetery.

LETCHER, Robert Perkins, a Representative from Kentucky; born in Goochland County, Va., February 10, 1788; pursued an academic course; studied law; was admitted to the bar and commenced practice in Lancaster, Ky.; member of the State house of representatives 1813–1815, 1817, and 1836–1838 and served as speaker in the latter year; elected as a Clay Democrat to the Eighteenth and Nineteenth Congresses and as a Whig to the Twentieth, Twenty-first, and Twenty-second Congresses (March 4, 1823–March 3, 1833); contested the election of Thomas P. Moore to the Twenty-third Congress, but the House did not seat either and declared a new election necessary; subsequently elected to fill the foregoing vacancy and served from August 6, 1834, to March 3, 1835; was not a candidate for renomination in 1834; presidential elector on the Whig ticket of Harrison and Granger in 1836; Governor of Kentucky 1840–1844; appointed Envoy Extraordinary and Minister Plenipotentiary to Mexico and served from August 9, 1849, to August 3, 1852; unsuccessful candidate for election in 1852 to the Thirty-third Congress; resumed the practice of his profession; died in Frankfort, Ky., January 24, 1861; interment in the State Cemetery.

LETTS, Fred Dickinson (cousin of Lester Jesse Dickinson), a Representative from Iowa; born near Ainsworth, Washington County, Iowa, April 26, 1875; attended the common schools of Washington County; was graduated from Parsons College, Fairfield, Iowa, in 1897 and from the law department of the University of Iowa at Iowa City in 1899; was admitted to the bar in 1899 and commenced practice in Davenport, Iowa; appointed judge of the seventh judicial district of Iowa on March 25, 1911, and served until December 31, 1912; elected to the same position in 1914, and served until his resignation on February 28, 1925, having been elected to Congress; elected as a Republican to the Sixty-ninth, Seventieth, and Seventy-first Congresses (March 4, 1925–March 3, 1931); unsuccessful for reelection in 1930 to the Seventy-second Congress; appointed by President Hoover an associate justice of the Supreme Court of the District of Columbia (now United States District Court for the District of Columbia) May 5, 1931, and served until his retirement May 31, 1961; resides in Washington, D. C.

LEVER, Asbury Francis, a Representative from South Carolina; born near Springhill, Lexington County, S. C., January 5, 1875; attended the country schools; was graduated from Newberry (S. C.) College in 1895; taught school for two years; private secretary to Representative J. William Stokes 1897–1901; was graduated from the law department of Georgetown University, Washington, D. C., in 1899; was admitted to the bar in South Carolina the same year but did not practice; delegate to the Democratic State conventions in 1896 and 1900; member of the State house of representatives 1900 and 1901 but resigned in the latter year, having been elected to Congress; elected as a Democrat to the Fifty-seventh Congress to fill the vacancy caused by the death of J. William Stokes; reelected to the Fifty-eighth and to the eight succeeding Congresses and served from November 5, 1901, until August 1, 1919, when he resigned to become a member of the Federal Farm Loan Board, in which capacity he served until 1922; member of the boards of trustees of Clemson (S. C.) College and Newberry (S. C.) College; elected president of the the First Carolinas Joint Stock Land Bank at Columbia, S. C., in 1922; field representative of Federal Farm Board, after which he served as director of the public relations administration of the Farm Credit Administration until his death on April 28, 1940, at "Seven Oaks," near Charleston, S. C.; interment in College Hill Cemetery, on campus of Clemson Agricultural College, Clemson, S. C.

LEVERING, Robert Woodrow (son-in-law of Usher L. Burdick and brother-in-law of Quentin N. Burdick), a Representative from Ohio; born on a farm in Knox County near Fredericktown, Ohio, October 3, 1914; attended Pinkley (one-room) School and Fredericktown High School; graduated from Denison University, Granville, Ohio, in 1936 and from George Washington University Law School, Washington, D. C., in 1940; assistant law librarian of Congress, Washington, D. C., 1937–1941; was admitted to the bar in 1941; with the United States War Department in the Philippines in defense program at the time of Pearl Harbor; in response to call of Gen. Douglas MacArthur, served as a civilian volunteer in defense of Bataan; spent three and one-half years in Japanese prisoner of war camps; major in the Army Reserve; commenced the practice of law in Mount Vernon, Ohio, in 1946; assistant to Ohio attorney general in 1949 and 1950; operates a farm in Knox County near Fredericktown, Ohio; unsuccessful Democratic candidate for election to Congress in 1948, 1950, 1954, and in 1956; elected as a Democrat to the Eighty-sixth Congress (January 3, 1959–January 3, 1961); unsuccessful candidate for reelection in 1960 to the Eighty-seventh Congress; is a resident of Fredericktown, Ohio.

LEVIN, Lewis Charles, a Representative from Pennsylvania; born in Charleston, S. C., November 10, 1808; was graduated from South Carolina College (now the University of South Carolina) at Columbia; moved to Woodville, Miss., about 1828 and taught school; studied law; was admitted to the bar and practiced in several States; settled in Philadelphia, Pa., in 1838; one of the founders of the American Party in 1842; editor of the Philadelphia Daily Sun; elected as a candidate of the American Party to the Twenty-ninth, Thirtieth, and Thirty-first Congresses (March 4, 1845–March 3, 1851); unsuccessful candidate for reelection in 1850 to the Thirty-second Congress; resumed the practice of law; died in Philadelphia, Pa., March 14, 1860; interment in Laurel Hill Cemetery.

LEVY, David, a Delegate and a Senator from Florida. (*See* YULEE, David Levy.)

LEVY, Jefferson Monroe, a Representative from New York; born in New York City April 16, 1852; attended public and private schools; was graduated from the New York University Law School in 1873; was admitted to the bar and practiced in New York City; from his uncle, Commodore Uriah P. Levy, he inherited "Monticello" (formerly the estate of Thomas Jefferson), which at the time of his death was bequeathed to his sister, Mrs. A. L. Mayhoff, and later purchased by the Thomas Jefferson Memorial Association; elected as a Democrat to the Fifty-sixth Congress (March 4, 1899–March 3, 1901); was not a candidate for renomination in 1900; resumed the practice of law in New York City; elected to the Sixty-second and Sixty-third Congresses (March 4, 1911–March 3, 1915); was not a candidate for renomination in 1914; resumed the practice of his profession in New York City and died there March 6, 1924; interment in Cypress Hills Cemetery.

LEVY, William Mallory, a Representative from Louisiana; born in Isle of Wight, Va., October 31, 1827; completed preparatory studies; was graduated from William and Mary College, Williamsburg, Va., in 1844; served in the Mexican War as second lieutenant in Company F, First Regiment, Virginia Volunteers; studied law; was admitted to the bar in 1851 and commenced practice in Norfolk, Va.; moved to Natchitoches, La., in 1852 and continued the practice of law; member of the State house of representatives 1859–1861; presidential elector on the Democratic ticket of Douglas and Johnson in 1860; served in the Confederate Army during the Civil War; commissioned captain of Company A, Second Louisiana Infantry, May 11, 1861; subsequently served as a major in the Adjutant General's Department; elected as a Democrat to the Forty-fourth Congress (March 4, 1875–March 3, 1877); unsuccessful candidate for renomination in 1876; member of the State constitutional convention in 1879; appointed associate justice of the State supreme court in 1879 and served until his death in Saratoga, N. Y., August 14, 1882; interment in the American Cemetery, Natchitoches, La.

LEWIS, Abner, a Representative from New York; born in Panama, Chautauqua County, N. Y.; attended the public schools; member of the State assembly in 1838 and 1839; elected as a Whig to the Twenty-ninth Congress (March 4, 1845–March 3, 1847); county judge 1847–1852.

LEWIS, Barbour, a Representative from Tennessee; born in Alburg, Vt., January 5, 1818; attended the common schools; was graduated from Illinois College, Jacksonville, Ill., in 1846; taught school in Mobile, Ala.; was graduated from the law department of Harvard University; was admitted to the bar and practiced; delegate to the Republican National Convention at Chicago in 1860; during the Civil War enlisted in the Union Army August 1, 1861, and served as captain of Company G, First Missouri Volunteers; appointed by the military authorities judge of the civil commission court at Memphis, Tenn., in 1863; discharged from the service November 15, 1864; president of the commissioners of Shelby County, Tenn., 1867–1869; elected as a Republican to the Forty-third Congress (March 4, 1873–March 3, 1875); unsuccessful candidate for reelection in 1874 to the Forty-fourth Congress; resumed the practice of law in Memphis, Tenn.; moved to St. Louis, Mo., in 1878; appointed to the United States land office at Salt Lake City, Utah; resigned this position in 1879 and moved to Whitman County, Territory of Washington, where he engaged in agricultural pursuits and stock raising; died in Colfax, Wash., July 15, 1893; interment in Colfax Cemetery.

LEWIS, Burwell Boykin, a Representative from Alabama; born in Montgomery, Ala., July 7, 1838; moved with his parents to Mobile, Ala.; after the death of his parents lived with an uncle in Montevallo, Shelby County, Ala.; attended a private school; was graduated from the University of Alabama at Tuscaloosa in 1857; studied law in Selma, Ala.; was admitted to the bar in 1859 and commenced practice in Montevallo; during the Civil War served in the Confederate Army and attained the rank of captain of the Second Alabama Cavalry; presidential elector on the Democratic ticket of Seymour and Blair in 1868; member of the State house of representatives 1870–1872; moved to Tuscaloosa, Ala., in 1872 and engaged in the iron and coal business; elected as a Democrat to the Forty-fourth Congress (March 4, 1875–March 3, 1877); unsuccessful candidate for reelection in 1876 to the Forty-fifth Congress; elected to the Forty-sixth Congress and served from March 4, 1879, to October 1, 1880, when he resigned to accept the presidency of the University of Alabama; served in this capacity until his death in Tuscaloosa, Ala., on October 11, 1885; interment in Evergreen Cemetery.

LEWIS, Charles Swearinger, a Representative from Virginia; born in Clarksburg, Va. (now West Virginia), February 26, 1821; attended local schools and Ohio University at Athens; was graduated from Augusta (Ky.) College in 1844; studied law; was admitted to the bar in 1846 and commenced practice in Clarksburg, Va.; member of the State house of delegates 1849–1852; elected as a Democrat to the Thirty-third Congress to fill the vacancy caused by the death of John F. Snodgrass and served from December 4, 1854, to March 3, 1855; unsuccessful candidate for reelection in 1856 to the Thirty-fourth Congress; resumed the practice of law in Clarksburg; delegate to the State constitutional convention in 1861; served in the West Virginia House of Representatives in 1871; was State superintendent of free schools and adjutant general of the State of West Virginia from 1871 to 1873, when he resigned upon his election as judge of the second judicial circuit and served until his death in Clarksburg, W. Va., January 22, 1878; interment in the Odd Fellows Cemetery.

LEWIS, Clarke, a Representative from Mississippi; born in Huntsville, Madison County, Ala., November 8, 1840; moved with his mother to Noxubee County, Miss., in 1844; attended the district schools and Somerville Institute; engaged in teaching for several years; entered the Confederate Army in February 1861 and served until the close of the Civil War; resumed teaching in 1865; employed as a clerk in a store in 1866 and 1867; engaged in mercantile and agricultural pursuits 1867–1879; member of the State house of representatives in 1878; elected as a Democrat to the Fifty-first and Fifty-second Congresses (March 4, 1889–March 3, 1893); resumed agricultural pursuits; died near Macon, Miss., March 13, 1896; interment in the Odd Fellows Cemetery, Macon, Miss.

LEWIS, David John, a Representative from Maryland; born in Nuttals Bank, Center County, near Osceola Mills, Clearfield County, Pa., May 1, 1869; self-educated; worked in the coal mines 1878–1892; while so employed studied law and Latin; was admitted to the bar in 1892 and commenced practice in Cumberland, Md.; member of the State senate 1902–1906; unsuccessful Democratic candidate for election to the Sixty-first Congress in 1908; elected as a Democrat to the Sixty-second, Sixty-third, and Sixty-fourth Congresses (March 4, 1911–March 3, 1917); was not a candidate for renomination in 1916, but was an unsuccessful Democratic candidate for election to the United States Senate; member of the United States Tariff Commission from April 1917 to March 1925; unsuccessful candidate for the Democratic nomination for United States Senator in 1922; resumed the practice of law in Cumberland, Md.; again elected to the Seventy-second and to the three succeeding Congresses (March 4, 1931–January 3, 1939); was not a candidate for renomination in 1938, but was an unsuccessful candidate for the Democratic nomination for United States Senator; member of the National Mediation Board 1939–1943; retired from public activities in February 1943; died in Cumberland, Md., August 12, 1952; interment in Hillcrest Cemetery.

LEWIS, Dixon Hall, a Representative and a Senator from Alabama; born on Bothwick plantation, Dinwiddie County, Va., August 10, 1802; moved to Hancock County, Ga., with his parents in 1806; was graduated from Mount Zion Academy and from South Carolina College at Columbia in 1822; moved to Autauga County, Ala., the same year; was admitted to the bar in 1823 and commenced the practice of law in Montgomery, Ala.; member of the State house of representatives 1825–1827; elected as a State Rights Democrat to the Twenty-first and to the seven succeeding Congresses and served from March 4, 1829, to April 22, 1844, when he resigned, having been appointed Senator; appointed and subsequently elected as a Democrat to the United States Senate to fill the vacancy caused by the resignation of William R. King; reelected in 1847 and served from April 22, 1844, until his death in New York City October 25, 1848; interment in Greenwood Cemetery, Brooklyn, N. Y.

LEWIS, Earl Ramage, a Representative from Ohio; born in Lamira, Belmont County, Ohio, February 22, 1887; attended the public and high schools; was graduated from Muskingum College, New Concord, Ohio, in 1911, and from the law department of Western Reserve University, Cleveland, Ohio, in 1914; admitted to the bar the same year and commenced practice in St. Clairsville, Ohio; member of the State senate in 1927, 1928, and 1931–1934, serving as president pro tempore in 1931 and 1932 and as Republican floor leader 1931–1934; chairman of the Republican State campaign committee for Ohio in 1930; member of the Interstate Commission on Conflicting Taxation of the American Legislators Association 1931–1935; elected as a Republican to the Seventy-sixth Congress (January 3, 1939–January 3, 1941); unsuccessful candidate for reelection in 1940 to the Seventy-seventh Congress; resumed the practice of law; again elected to the Seventy-eighth, Seventy-ninth, and Eightieth Congresses (January 3, 1943–January 3, 1949); unsuccessful candidate for reelection in 1948 to the Eighty-first Congress; resumed the practice of law; trustee of Muskingum College; died in Wheeling, W. Va., February 1, 1956; interment in Union Cemetery, St. Clairsville, Ohio.

LEWIS, Edward Taylor, a Representative from Louisiana; born in Opelousas, St. Landry Parish, October 26, 1834; received his early education from private tutors; later attended Wesleyan University, Delaware, Ohio; studied law; was admitted to the bar in 1859 and commenced practice in Opelousas, La.; enlisted as a private in an Infantry regiment of the Confederate Army and served throughout the Civil War, attaining the rank of captain of Cavalry; member of the State house of representatives in 1865; elected as a Democrat to the Forty-eighth Congress on February 15, 1883, to fill the vacancy caused by the death of Representative-elect Andrew S. Herron and served from March 4, 1883, to March 3, 1885; unsuccessful candidate for renomination in 1884; served as judge for the fifth judicial district from 1887 to 1892; again a member of the State house of representatives 1886–1888; served as judge of the court of appeals, third circuit of Louisiana, 1894–1896; judge of the sixteenth judicial district 1900–1908; resumed the practice of law; died in Opelousas, La., April 26, 1927; interment in Myrtle Grove Cemetery.

LEWIS, Elijah Banks, a Representative from Georgia; born in Coney, Dooly County, Ga., March 27, 1854; attended the common schools of Dooly and Macon Counties, Spalding Seminary, Spalding, Ga., and a business school in Macon, Ga.; moved to Montezuma, Macon County, Ga., in 1871 and engaged in banking and mercantile pursuits; member of the State senate in 1894 and 1895; elected as a Democrat to the Fifty-fifth and to the five succeeding Congresses (March 4, 1897–March 3, 1909); unsuccessful candidate for renomination in 1908 to the Sixty-first Congress; engaged in his former business activities until his death in Montezuma, Ga., on December 10, 1920; interment in Felton Cemetery.

LEWIS, Francis, a Delegate from New York; born in Llandaff, Wales, in March 1713; attended Westminster School, London; entered the countinghouse of a London merchant; immigrated to the United States in 1735 and established mercantile houses in New York and Philadelphia; secured a contract to clothe the British Army in America in 1753; participated in the French and Indian War as an aide to General Mercer; was captured in Oswego, N. Y., and taken as a prisoner to France; on his return the colonial government gave him 5,000 acres of land in recognition of his services; delegate in the Stamp Act Congress that met in New York City in 1765; retired from business in 1765 and located in Whitestone, Long Island, N. Y.; Member of the Continental Congress 1774–1779; was a signer of the Declaration of Independence; delegate to the provincial convention in 1775; member of the Committee of One Hundred in 1775; served in the Provincial Congress in 1776 and 1777; commissioner of the board of admiralty in 1779; died in New York City on December 30, 1803.

LEWIS, Fred Ewing, a Representative from Pennsylvania; born in Allentown, Lehigh County, Pa., February 8, 1865; attended the public schools, the Collegiate and Commercial Institute, New Haven, Conn., and Muhlenberg College, Allentown, Pa., studied law; was admitted to the bar in 1888 and commenced practice of his profession in Allentown, Pa.; mayor of Allentown in 1896 and 1902; organized and was president of the Merchants' National Bank and was president of the Dime Savings & Trust Co. in Allentown; elected as a Republican to the Sixty-third Congress (March 4, 1913–March 3, 1915); resumed the practice of his profession and also engaged in banking; again mayor of Allentown, Pa., 1932–1936; continued the practice of law; author; died in Allentown, Pa., June 27, 1949; interment in Union-West End Cemetery.

LEWIS, James Hamilton, a Representative from Washington and a Senator from Illinois; born in Danville, Pittsylvania County, Va., May 18, 1863; moved with his parents to Augusta, Ga., in 1866; attended Houghton College in that city and the University of Virginia at Charlottesville; studied law in Savannah, Ga., at the Ohio Northern University, Ada, Ohio, and at the Baylor University, Waco, Tex.; was admitted to the bar in 1882; moved to the Territory of Washington in 1885 and commenced the practice of law in Seattle; attached to the Joint High Commission on Canadian and Alaskan Boundaries at London in 1889 and 1890 for presentation of Pacific Northwest claims; member of the Washington Territorial Senate; unsuccessful candidate for Governor in 1892; unsuccessful candidate for the Democratic nomination for Vice President in 1896 and 1900; elected as a Democrat to the Fifty-fifth Congress (March 4, 1897–March 3, 1899); unsuccessful candidate in 1898 for reelection as a Fusionist; served during the Spanish-American War as inspector general with rank of colonel on the staff of General Brooke in Cuba and Gen. Frederick D. Grant in Puerto Rico; United States commissioner to regulate customs laws between Canada and the Northwest United States in 1899; unsuccessful Democratic candidate for United States Senator in 1899; moved to Chicago, Ill. in 1903 and resumed the practice of law; corporation counsel for Chicago, Ill., 1905–1907; unsuccessful candidate for Governor in 1908; elected as a Democrat to the United States Senate and served from March 26, 1913, to March 3, 1919; unsuccessful candidate for reelection in 1918; commissioner representing the United States Senate at London to execute treaty laws for safety at sea in 1914; did special war work in France in 1918 and was knighted by the King of Belgium and the King of Greece; unsuccessful Democratic candidate for Governor of Illinois in 1920; attendant attaché at the international conferences at Genoa (Italy) in 1921, Lausanne (Switzerland) in 1922, and Geneva in 1925, before the League of Nations on American claims; again elected to the United States Senate in 1930; reelected in 1936 and served from March 4, 1931, until his death in Washington, D. C., April 9, 1939; funeral services were held in the Chamber of the United States Senate; interment in the Abbey Mausoleum, adjoining Arlington National Cemetery, Fort Myer, Va.

LEWIS, John Francis, a Senator from Virginia; born in Lynnwood, Rockingham County, Va., March 1, 1818; attended the "old field" school; engaged in agricultural pursuits; delegate to the State secession convention in 1861 and refused to sign the ordinance of secession; elected Lieutenant Governor on the True Republican ticket in 1869; upon the readmission of the State of Virginia to representation was elected as a Republican to the United States Senate and served from January 26, 1870, to March 3, 1875; was not a candidate for reelection; appointed by President Hayes United States marshal for the western district of Virginia on April 11, 1878, and served until March 1, 1882, when he resigned; again elected Lieutenant Governor on the Readjuster ticket in 1881; resumed agricultural pursuits; died in Lynnwood, Va., September 2, 1895; interment in the family burial ground.

LEWIS, John Henry, a Representative from Illinois; born near Ithaca, Tompkins County, N. Y., July 21, 1830; moved to Illinois in 1836 with his parents, who settled on a farm in Fulton County, near Ellisville; attended the rural schools; moved to Knox County, Ill., in 1847 and engaged in agricultural pursuits near Knoxville; studied law; was admitted to the bar in 1860 and commenced practice in Knoxville, Ill.; clerk of the circuit court of Knox County 1860–1864; member of the State house of representatives in 1874 and 1875; elected as a Republican to the Forty-seventh Congress (March 4, 1881–March 3, 1883); unsuccessful candidate for reelection in 1882 to the Forty-eighth Congress; retired from political affairs and resumed the practice of law; discontinued the practice of his profession about 1900, and lived in retirement in Knoxville, Ill., where he died on January 6, 1929; interment in Knoxville Cemetery.

LEWIS, John William, a Representative from Kentucky; born near Greensburg, Green County, Ky., October 14, 1841; attended the common schools; was graduated from Centre College, Danville, Ky., in 1862; studied law; was admitted to the bar in 1863 and practiced in Greensburg, Ky.; moved to Springfield, Ky., January 1, 1869; temporary chairman of the Republican State convention April 10, 1880; delegate to the Republican National Conventions in 1880, 1884, and 1888; delegate to the State constitutional convention of Kentucky in 1890 and was unseated upon a contest; member of the Republican State central committee of Kentucky 1878–1891 and chairman in the State campaign of 1887; served as special judge in the circuit courts of Marion, Taylor, and other counties; elected as a Republican to the Fifty-fourth Congress (March 4, 1895–March 3, 1897); unsuccessful candidate for reelection in 1896 to the Fifty-fifth Congress; delegate to the Republican National Convention at Chicago in 1904 which nominated Theodore Roosevelt for President; chairman of the congressional convention of his district in 1904 and 1908; resumed the practice of his profession in Springfield, Ky.; died in Fort Worth, Tex., December 20, 1913; interment in Lebanon Cemetery, Lebanon, Marion County, Ky.

LEWIS, Joseph, Jr., a Representative from Virginia; born in that State in 1772; member of the State house of delegates 1799–1803; elected as a Federalist to the Eighth and to the six succeeding Congresses (March 4, 1803–March 3, 1817); again a member of the State house of delegates in 1817 and 1818; died in Clifton, Va., March 30, 1834.

LEWIS, Joseph Horace, a Representative from Kentucky; born near Glasgow, Barren County, Ky., October 29, 1824; attended the common schools; was graduated from Centre College, Danville, Ky., in 1843; studied law; was admitted to the bar in 1845 and commenced practice in Glasgow, Ky.; member of the State house of representatives 1850–1855; unsuccessful candidate for election in 1860 to the Thirty-seventh Congress; during the Civil War commanded the Sixth Kentucky Regiment in the Confederate Army, the Second Brigade and the First Brigade in Bates' division; returned to Glasgow at the close of the Civil War and resumed the practice of law; again a member of the State house of representatives in 1869 and 1870; elected as a Democrat to the Forty-first Congress to fill the vacancy caused by the resignation of Jacob S. Golladay; reelected to the Forty-second Congress and served from May 10, 1870, to March 3, 1873; was not a candidate for renomination in 1872; resumed the practice of his profession; elected judge of the Kentucky Court of Appeals in 1874; reelected to subsequent terms and served until 1898; moved to a farm in Scott County, near Georgetown, where he died on July 6, 1904; interment in Glasgow Cemetery.

LEWIS, Lawrence, a Representative from Colorado; born in St. Louis, Mo., June 22, 1879; attended the public schools in Evanston, Ill., Cambridge, Mass., and Pueblo, Colo., and the University of Colorado at Boulder; was graduated from Harvard University, Cambridge, Mass., in 1901; engaged in newspaper and magazine work in Pueblo and Denver, Colo., 1901–1906; assistant instructor in English, Harvard University, 1906–1909; was graduated from the law department of Harvard University in 1909; was admitted to the bar the same year and commenced practice in Denver, Colo.; member of Colorado Civil Service Commission 1917–1918; private in the Seventeenth Observation Battery, Field Artillery, Central Officers' Training School, October to December 1918; unsuccessful candidate for election in 1930 to the Seventy-second Congress; elected as a Democrat to the Seventy-third and five succeeding Congresses and served from March 4, 1933, until his death; one of the managers appointed by the House of Representatives in 1933 to conduct the impeachment proceedings against Harold Louderback, judge of the United States District Court for the Northern District of California; died in Washington, D. C., on December 9, 1943; interment in Spring Grove Cemetery, Cincinnati, Ohio.

LEWIS, Robert Jacob, a Representative from Pennsylvania; born in Dover, Dover Township, York County, Pa., December 30, 1864; attended the public schools of York, and was graduated from the high school in 1883; taught in the public schools until September 1889; was graduated from the law department of Yale University in 1891; was admitted to the New Haven (Conn.) bar June 1891 and to the bar of York County, Pa., August 3, 1891, and commenced practice in York, Pa.; elected school controller of York in 1893 and reelected in 1897 and 1903; elected city solicitor in 1895; unsuccessful candidate for election in 1898 to the Fifty-sixth Congress; elected as a Republican to the Fifty-seventh Congress (March 4, 1901–March 3, 1903); declined to be a candidate for renomination in 1902; resumed the practice of his profession; died in Camden, Ark., July 24, 1933; remains were cremated and the ashes placed in the Iris Columbarium Mausoleum, St. Louis, Mo.

LEWIS, Thomas, a Representative from Virginia; born in Augusta County, Va.; attended the common schools; presented credentials as a Representative-elect to the Eighth Congress and served from March 4, 1803, until March 5, 1804, when he was succeeded by Andrew Moore, who contested his election; by formal action of the House of Representatives counsel for the claimants in this case were heard at the bar of the House.

LEWIS, William, a Representative from Kentucky; born in Cutshin, Leslie County, Ky., September 22, 1868; was raised on a farm and attended the common schools of Leslie and Perry Counties and the Laurel County Seminary, London, Ky.; studied law at the University of Kentucky at Lexington and at the University of Michigan at Ann Arbor; sheriff of Leslie County in 1891 and 1892; superintendent of schools of Leslie County 1894–1898; member of State house of representatives in 1900 and 1901; Commonwealth attorney 1904–1909; circuit judge of the twenty-seventh judicial district of Kentucky 1909–1922 and 1928–1934; entered the private practice of law; elected as a Republican to the Eightieth Congress to fill the vacancy caused by the death of John Marshall Robsion and served from April 24, 1948, to January 3, 1949; was not a candidate for renomination in 1948 to the Eighty-first Congress; died in London, Laurel County, Ky., August 8, 1959; interment in A. R. Dyche Memorial Park.

LEWIS, William J., a Representative from Virginia; born in Augusta County, Va., July 4, 1766; attended the common schools; member of the State house of delegates; elected as a Democrat to the Fifteenth Congress (March 4, 1817–March 3, 1819); died at "Mount Athos" plantation, near Lynchburg, Campbell County, Va., November 1, 1828; interment in a vault blasted out of a solid rock at the summit of "Mount Athos," Virginia.

L'HOMMEDIEU, Ezra, a Delegate from New York; born in Southold, Long Island, N. Y., August 30, 1734; was graduated from Yale College in 1754; studied law; was admitted to the bar and practiced in Southold, N. Y.; delegate to the Provincial Congress 1775–1777; member of the State assembly 1777–1783; Member of the Continental Congress 1779–1783, 1787, and 1788; served in the State senate 1784–1792 and 1794–1809; member of the State constitutional convention in 1801; clerk of Suffolk County from January 1784 to March 1810 and from March 1811 until his death; regent of the University of the State of New York 1787–1811; was a Federalist and a follower of John Jay; died in Southold, N. Y., September 27, 1811; interment in the Presbyterian Cemetery.

LIBBEY, Harry, a Representative from Virginia; born in Wakefield, Carroll County, N. H., November 22, 1843; attended the common schools; moved to Virginia and settled in Hampton in 1863; engaged in mercantile pursuits; appointed one of the presiding justices of Elizabeth City County, Va., in 1869; elected as a Republican to the Forty-eighth and Forty-ninth Congresses (March 4, 1883–March 3, 1887); engaged in the oyster industry; served as chairman of the Republican county committee; appointed postmaster of Hampton, Va., January 18, 1907, and served until his death in Hampton, Elizabeth City County, Va., on September 30, 1913; interment in St. John's Cemetery.

LIBONATI, Roland Victor, a Representative from Illinois; born in Chicago, Ill., December 29, 1900; graduated from Lewis Institute in 1918; during the First World War served as a lieutenant in the United States Army; graduated from the University of Michigan in 1921 and from the University of Michigan and Northwestern University Law School in 1924; was admitted to the bar in 1924 and commenced law practice in Chicago, Ill.; State representative in the Fifty-seventh, Fifty-eighth, and Sixty-second State general assemblies and State senator 1942–1958, serving as Democratic whip 1944–1957 and as minority leader from August 1957; founder and owner of American Boys' Camp for indigent children at Coloma, Wis.; elected as a Democrat to the Eighty-fifth Congress to fill the vacancy caused by the death of James B. Bowler; reelected to the Eighty-sixth Congress and served from December 31, 1957, to January 3, 1961. *Reelected to the Eighty-seventh Congress.*

31671 O–61—77

LICHTENWALNER, Norton Lewis, a Representative from Pennsylvania; born in Allentown, Lehigh County, Pa., June 1, 1889; educated in the public schools, graduating from Allentown High School in 1905 and Bethlehem Preparatory School in 1906; attended Lehigh University, Bethlehem, Pa.; moved to New York City in 1908 and was employed in a banking institution; returned to Allentown, Pa., in 1915 and engaged in the retail furniture business until 1922, then in the retailing of automobiles until 1933; during the First World War enlisted as a seaman in the United States Naval Reserve; elected as a Democrat to the Seventy-second Congress (March 4, 1931–March 3, 1933); unsuccessful candidate for reelection in 1932 to the Seventy-third Congress; State director for the Pennsylvania National Emergency Council 1935–1941; State director of Office of Government Reports in 1941 and 1942; engaged in the investment securities business; in 1949 was elected to the Allentown City Council for one term and in 1955 elected treasurer of Lehigh County for one term; died in Allentown, Pa., May 3, 1960; interment in Fairview Cemetery.

LICHTENWALTER, Franklin Herbert, a Representative from Pennsylvania; born in Palmerton, Carbon County, Pa., on March 28, 1910; attended the public schools of Palmerton and Upper Saucon Township; was graduated from Allentown High School in 1929; engaged in general insurance business 1933–; member of the State house of representatives 1938–1947, serving as majority leader 1943–1946 and as speaker in 1947; elected as a Republican to the Eightieth Congress to fill the vacancy caused by the death of Charles L. Gerlach; reelected to the Eighty-first Congress and served from September 9, 1947, to January 3, 1951; was not a candidate for renomination in 1950; resumed the insurance business; vice president of Pennsylvania Electric Association, Harrisburg, Pa.; is a resident of Center Valley, Pa.

LIEB, Charles, a Representative from Indiana; born in Flehingen, Germany, May 20, 1852; immigrated to the United States in 1868 and settled in Rockport, Ind.; attended the public schools, the Rockport Collegiate Institute, and Bryant and Stratton's Business College, Louisville, Ky.; employed as a bookkeeper and expert accountant; member of the Rockport City Council 1879–1884; engaged in the lumber business and as a contractor in 1882; postmaster of Rockport 1893–1897; member of the State house of representatives 1907–1913; elected as a Democrat to the Sixty-third and Sixty-fourth Congresses (March 4, 1913–March 3, 1917); was not a candidate for renomination in 1916; delegate to the Democratic National Convention at St. Louis in 1916; chairman of the county council of defense during the First World War; director of the War Savings stamp and Liberty Loan drives; served as president and director of the Farmers' Bank, Rockport, Ind.; also engaged in agricultural pursuits; died in Rockport, Ind., September 1, 1928; interment in Sun Set Hill Cemetery.

LIEBEL, Michael, Jr., a Representative from Pennsylvania; born in Erie, Pa., December 12, 1870; attended the public schools of Erie; was graduated from Canisius College, Buffalo, N. Y.; accountant in the office of the New York, Chicago & St. Louis Railroad at Buffalo for five years; returned to Erie, Pa., and engaged in the hardware business, and later organized and was secretary-treasurer of a brewery company; in 1911 organized and became president of the Vulcan Rubber Co.; mayor of Erie, Pa., 1906–1911; delegate to the Democratic National Conventions in 1908, 1912, 1916, 1920, and 1924; elected as a Democrat to the Sixty-fourth Congress (March 4, 1915–March 3, 1917); was not a candidate for renomination in 1916; resumed his former business activities; died in Philadelphia, Pa., August 8, 1927; interment in Trinity Cemetery, Erie, Pa.

LIGON, Robert Fulwood, a Representative from Alabama; born in Watkinsville, Oconee County, Ga., December 16, 1823; attended the country schools of his native county, the academy near Watkinsville, and the University of Georgia at Athens; moved to Athens, Ga., and later, in 1844, to Tuskegee, Ala.; studied law; was admitted to the bar in 1845 and commenced practice in Tuskegee; served in the Mexican War as a captain in the First Alabama Battalion; member of the State house of representatives in 1849 and 1850; served in the State senate 1861–1864; during the Civil War served in the Confederate Army as captain of Company F, Twelfth Regiment, Alabama Infantry, Rhodes' division; resumed the practice of law; unsuccessful candidate for Governor in 1872; Lieutenant Governor of Alabama in 1874; elected as a Democrat to the Forty-fifth Congress (March 4, 1877–March 3, 1879); unsuccessful candidate for renomination in 1878; continued the practice of law until 1884, when he retired from active practice and moved to Montgomery; engaged in banking and as a planter; served forty years as president of the board of trustees of the Alabama Female College; also a trustee of the Alabama Polytechnic Institute at Auburn for many years; died in Montgomery, Ala., October 11, 1901; interment in Oakwood Cemetery.

LIGON, Thomas Watkins, a Representative from Maryland; born near Farmville, Prince Edward County, Va., May 10, 1810; attended Hampden-Sidney College and the University of Virginia at Charlottesville in 1830 and 1831; studied law at Yale College; was admitted to the bar in 1833 and practiced in Baltimore 1835–1853 and in other places in Maryland; member of the State house of delegates in 1843; elected as a Democrat to the Twenty-ninth and Thirtieth Congresses (March 4, 1845–March 3, 1849); resumed the practice of law; Governor of Maryland 1854–1858; retired from public life to "Chatham," his country place, near Ellicott City, Howard County, Md., where he died January 12, 1881; interment in St. John's Cemetery, Ellicott City, Md.

LILLEY, George Leavens, a Representative from Connecticut; born in Oxford, Worcester County, Mass., August 3, 1859; attended the common schools of Oxford, the Worcester High School, and Worcester Technical Institute, Worcester, Mass.; moved to Waterbury, Conn., in 1881 and engaged in mercantile pursuits and the real-estate business; served in the State house of representatives 1901–1903; elected as a Republican to the Fifty-eighth, Fifty-ninth, and Sixtieth Congresses and served from March 4, 1903, to January 5, 1909; did not seek renomination in 1908, having become a candidate for Governor; by resolution of the House of January 20, 1909, the seat was declared to have been vacated on January 6, 1909, for the reason that incumbent had entered upon the duties of the office of Governor of Connecticut the preceding day; Governor of Connecticut from January 5, 1909, until his death in Hartford, Conn., April 21, 1909; interment in Riverside Cemetery, Waterbury, Conn.

LILLEY, Mial Eben, a Representative from Pennsylvania; born in Canton, Bradford County, Pa., May 30, 1850; attended public and private schools; worked as a blacksmith several years; studied law in Canton; was admitted to the bar in 1880 and commenced practice in Towanda, Bradford County, Pa.; for several years was chairman of the Republican committee of Bradford County; unsuccessful candidate for prothonotary of Bradford County in 1890; elected prothonotary in 1893 and reelected in 1896; appointed assistant United States district attorney for the middle district of Pennsylvania in 1903; elected as a Republican to the Fifty-ninth Congress (March 4, 1905–March 3, 1907); unsuccessful candidate for reelection in 1906 to the Sixtieth Congress; engaged in the practice of his profession until his death in Towanda, Pa., February 28, 1915; interment in Oak Hill Cemetery.

LILLY, Samuel, a Representative from New Jersey; born in Geneva, N. Y., October 28, 1815; moved to Lambertville, N. J., in 1829; attended Rev. P. O. Studdiford's classical school; was graduated from the medical department of the University of Pennsylvania March 31, 1837, and commenced practice in Lambertville, N. J.; first mayor of Lambertville 1849–1852; elected as a Democrat to the Thirty-third Congress (March 4, 1853–March 3, 1855); director of the Board of Freeholders of Hunterdon County for eight years; brigadier general of the State militia; appointed by President Buchanan as consul general of the United States to British India, with residence in Calcutta, January 3, 1861, and served until July 4, 1862, when he resigned; judge of the court of common pleas of Hunterdon County, N. J., 1868–1873; one of the members of the board of managers of the New Jersey Insane Asylum in 1871; judge of the court of errors and appeals and also a member of the State board of pardons from 1873 until his death in Lambertville, Hunterdon County, N. J., April 3, 1880; interment in Mount Hope Cemetery.

LILLY, Thomas Jefferson, a Representative from West Virginia; born in Dunns, Mercer County, W. Va., June 3, 1878; attended the rural schools of his county; taught school and also engaged in agricultural pursuits; justice of the peace 1902–1906; was graduated from the law department of McKinley University, Chicago, Ill., in 1911; was admitted to the bar the same year and commenced the practice of law in Hinton, Summers County, W. Va.; divorce commissioner of Summers County 1914–1922; State commissioner of accounts 1914–1927; elected as a Democrat to the Sixty-eighth Congress (March 4, 1923–March 3, 1925); unsuccessful candidate for reelection in 1924 to the Sixty-ninth Congress; resumed the practice of law and was also interested in agricultural pursuits; died in Sweet Springs, W. Va., April 2, 1956; interment in Restwood Memorial Cemetery, Hinton, W. Va.

LILLY, William, a Representative from Pennsylvania; born in Penn Yan, Yates County, N. Y., June 3, 1821; moved to Carbon County, Pa., in 1838; elected colonel of one of the militia regiments of the Lehigh Valley and subsequently brigadier general; member of the State house of representatives in 1850 and 1851; was a Democrat in politics until 1862, when he affiliated with the Republican Party; delegate to six Republican National Conventions; member of every important Republican State convention; delegate at large to the convention to revise the constitution of Pennsylvania in 1872 and 1873; engaged in the mining of anthracite coal; life member of the Academy of Natural Sciences of Philadelphia; member of the Society of American Mining Engineers; elected as a Republican to the Fifty-third Congress and served from March 4, 1893, until his death in Mauch Chunk, Pa., December 1, 1893; interment in the City Cemetery.

LINCOLN, Abraham, a Representative from Illinois and a President of the United States; born in Hardin County, Ky., February 12, 1809; moved with his parents to a heavily timbered tract of land on Little Pigeon Creek, Ind., in 1816; attended a log-cabin school at short intervals and was self-instructed in elementary branches; at the age of nineteen was intrusted with a cargo of farm products, which he took to New Orleans and sold; moved with his father to a forest location in Macon County, Ill., in 1830 and a little later to an unbroken prairie farm in Coles County, Ill.; hired himself to a Sangamon County trader named Denton Offutt, whom he assisted in the construction of a flatboat for trading upon the rivers and also in maintaining a general store in New Salem, Menard County, Ill.; read the principles of law and works on surveying; during the Black Hawk War he volunteered in a company of Sangamon County Rifles organized in Richland, Ill., April 21, 1832; was elected its captain and served until May 27 following, when the company was mustered out of

service; reenlisted as a private and served until mustered out June 16, 1832; returned to New Salem, Ill., and was unsuccessful as a candidate for the State house of representatives; entered business as a general merchant in New Salem, but met reverses that were generally attributed to his partner; applied himself to the study of law; postmaster of New Salem 1833–1836; deputy county surveyor 1834–1836; elected a member of the State house of representatives in 1834, 1836, 1838, and 1840; declined to be a candidate for renomination; was admitted to the bar in 1836; moved to Springfield, Ill., in 1837 and engaged in the practice of law; elected as a Whig to the Thirtieth Congress (March 4, 1847–March 3, 1849); did not seek a renomination in 1848; an unsuccessful applicant for Commissioner of the General Land Office under President Taylor; tendered the Governorship of Oregon Territory, but declined; unsuccessful Whig candidate for election to the United States Senate before the legislature of 1855; chosen by the Republican Party to oppose Stephen A. Douglas for the United States Senate in 1858 and the debate between the candidates made memorable the campaign in which Douglas was final victor; elected as the first Republican President of the United States and was inaugurated March 4, 1861; unanimously renominated in the convention of June 8, 1864, and was inaugurated for a second term March 4, 1865; was shot by J. Wilkes Booth while attending Ford's Theater in the city of Washington, D. C., on the night of April 14, 1865, and died the following day; interment in Oak Ridge Cemetery, Springfield, Ill.

LINCOLN, Enoch (son of Levi Lincoln and brother of Levi Lincoln), a Representative from Massachusetts and from Maine; born in Worcester, Mass., December 28, 1788; was graduated from Harvard University in 1807; studied law; was admitted to the bar and commenced the practice of his profession in Salem, Mass., in 1811; United States district attorney 1815–1818; moved to Paris, Maine (then a district of Massachusetts), in 1819 and continued the practice of law; elected to the Fifteenth Congress to fill the vacancy caused by the resignation of Albion K. Parris; reelected to the Sixteenth Congress and served from November 4, 1818, to March 3, 1821; upon the admission of Maine as a State was elected to the Seventeenth, Eighteenth, and Nineteenth Congresses and served from March 4, 1821, until his resignation in 1826; Governor of Maine from 1827 until his death; had declined to be a candidate for renomination; died in Augusta, Kennebec County, Maine, on October 8, 1829; interment in a mausoleum in the State Park.

LINCOLN, Levi (father of Enoch Lincoln and Levi Lincoln), a Representative from Massachusetts; born in Hingham, Mass., May 15, 1749; attended the common schools; was graduated from Harvard College in 1772; studied law in Newburyport and Northampton, Mass.; joined the Minutemen in Cambridge at the outbreak of the Revolution; moved to Worcester, Mass.; was admitted to the bar and commenced practice in 1775; member of the committee of public safety; clerk of the court and judge of probate for Worcester County 1775–1781; was specially designated to prosecute the claims of the Commonwealth to the numerous estates of loyalists in 1779; delegate to the State constitutional convention in 1779; elected a Member of the Continental Congress in 1781, but declined to serve; member of the State house of representatives in 1796; served in the State senate in 1797 and 1798; elected as a Democrat to the Seventh Congress; subsequently elected to the Sixth Congress to fill the vacancy caused by the resignation of Dwight Foster and served from December 15, 1800, to March 5, 1801, when he resigned; appointed Attorney General of the United States in the Cabinet of President Jefferson and served from March 5, 1801, to December 31, 1804, and as Acting Secretary of State from March 5 to May 2, 1801; member of the Governor's council of Massachusetts in 1806; Lieutenant Governor of Massachusetts in 1807 and 1808; became Governor upon the death of Governor Sullivan and served in this capacity from December 10, 1808, to May 1, 1809; appointed Associate Justice of the Supreme Court of the United States by President Madison, but declined to accept by reason of failing eyesight; again a member of the Governor's council in 1810 and 1811; died in Worcester, Worcester County, Mass., April 14, 1820; interment in the Rural Cemetery.

LINCOLN, Levi (son of the preceding and brother of Enoch Lincoln), a Representative from Massachusetts; born in Worcester, Mass., October 25, 1782; attended Leicester Academy, Leicester, Mass., and was graduated from Harvard University in 1802; studied law; was admitted to the bar and commenced the practice of his profession at Worcester in 1805; served in the State senate in 1812 and 1813; member of the State house of representatives 1814–1822 and served as speaker in 1822; delegate to the State constitutional convention in 1820; elected Lieutenant Governor of Massachusetts in 1823; appointed associate justice of the State supreme court in 1824; Governor of Massachusetts 1825–1834; declined reelection; elected as a Whig to the Twenty-third Congress to fill the vacancy caused by the resignation of John Davis; reelected to the Twenty-fourth and to the three succeeding Congresses and served from February 17, 1834, to March 16, 1841, when he resigned; collector of the port of Boston, by appointment of President Harrison, 1841–1843; served in the State senate in 1844 and 1845 and was president of that body in the latter year; presidential elector on the Whig ticket of Taylor and Fillmore in 1848; first mayor of Worcester in 1848; presidential elector on the Republican ticket of Lincoln and Johnson in 1864; died in Worcester, Worcester County, Mass., May 29, 1868; interment in the Rural Cemetery.

LINCOLN, William Slosson, a Representative from New York; born in Berkshire (now Newark Valley), Tioga County, N. Y., August 13, 1813; attended the common schools; studied law; was admitted to the bar; engaged in mercantile pursuits and subsequently in the manufacture of leather; postmaster of Newark Valley from September 20, 1838, to February 24, 1841, and from December 19, 1844, to September 19, 1866; served as supervisor in 1841, 1844, 1865, and 1866; justice of the peace in 1852 and 1855; elected as a Republican to the Fortieth Congress (March 4, 1867–March 3, 1869); was not a candidate for reelection; engaged in the practice of law in Washington, D. C., until his death on April 21, 1893; interment in Oak Hill Cemetery.

LIND, James Francis, a Representative from Pennsylvania; born in York, Pa., October 17, 1900; attended the public schools in York, leaving high school to enlist in the United States Army in 1917; served overseas with the Third Infantry Division and was discharged as a first sergeant in 1920; completed formal education at Penn State Extension (night) School; cost accountant, York Ice Machinery Corp., 1922–1941; active in Organized Reserve and Pennsylvania National Guard 1931–1941; during World War II entered the service as a captain in January 1941; served with the Twenty-eighth, Eighty-ninth, and Sixty-sixth Infantry Divisions; promoted to major in 1942 and lieutenant colonel in 1944; separated from the service in February 1946; in charge of contact office of Veterans Administration of York County in 1946 and 1947; chief clerk to York County Board of Commissioners in 1948; elected as a Democrat to the Eighty-first and Eighty-second Congresses (January 3, 1949–January 3, 1953); unsuccessful candidate for reelection in 1952 to the Eighty-third Congress; went on active duty with the United States Army in 1953 as special assistant to the controller in the office of Quartermaster General, Washington, D. C.; controller of York County, Pa., 1954–; is a resident of York, Pa.

LIND, John, a Representative from Minnesota; born in Kanna, Sweden, March 25, 1854; immigrated to the United States in 1867 with his parents, who settled in Goodhue County, Minn.; moved to Sibley County in 1872; attended the public schools and the University of Minnesota at Minneapolis; taught school; studied law; was admitted to the bar in 1877 and commenced practice in New Ulm, Minn.; receiver of the United States land office at Tracy 1881–1885; elected as a Republican to the Fiftieth, Fifty-first, and Fifty-second Congresses (March 4, 1887–March 3, 1893); declined to be a candidate for renomination in 1892; unsuccessful candidate for Governor of Minnesota in 1896; during the Spanish-American War was mustered into the service on May 5, 1898, as first lieutenant and quartermaster in the Twelfth Regiment, Minnesota Volunteer Infantry; was honorably discharged with his regiment November 5, 1898; Democratic Governor of Minnesota 1898–1900; unsuccessful candidate for reelection; elected as a Democrat to the Fifty-eighth Congress (March 4, 1903–March 3, 1905); declined to be a candidate for renomination in 1904; resumed the practice of law in Minneapolis, Minn.; president of the board of regents of the University of Minnesota; was appointed by President Wilson as his personal representative to investigate the affairs of the United States Government in Mexico August 3, 1913; practiced law in Minneapolis, Minn., until his death in that city September 18, 1930; remains were cremated and the ashes interred in Lakewood Cemetery.

LINDBERGH, Charles Augustus, a Representative from Minnesota; born in Stockholm, Sweden, January 20, 1859; immigrated to the United States in 1860 with his parents, who settled on a farm near Melrose, Stearns County, Minn.; attended the common schools, Grove Lake (Minn.) Academy, and the St. Cloud (Minn.) Normal School; was graduated from the law department of the University of Michigan at Ann Arbor in 1883; was admitted to the bar the same year and commenced practice in Little Falls, Minn.; also engaged in agricultural pursuits; prosecuting attorney of Morrison County 1891–1893; elected as a Republican to the Sixtieth and to the four succeeding Congresses (March 4, 1907–March 3, 1917); did not seek renomination in 1916, having become a candidate for Senator; resumed the practice of law in Little Falls, Minn.; unsuccessful candidate for election to the United States Senate on the Non-Partisan League ticket in 1916; unsuccessful candidate for Governor of Minnesota as a Progressive Republican, with Non-Partisan League indorsement, in 1918; was a candidate for the nomination for Governor on the Farmer-Labor ticket in 1924, but his death occurred before the primary election was held; died in the city hospital at Crookston, Minn., May 24, 1924; remains were cremated and the ashes deposited in the columbarium in Lakewood Cemetery, Minneapolis, Minn.

LINDLEY, James Johnson, a Representative from Missouri; born in Mansfield, Richland County, Ohio, January 1, 1822; moved with his parents to Cynthiana, Ky., in 1836; attended Woodville College, Ohio; moved to St. Louis, Mo., in 1843; studied law; was admitted to the bar in 1846 and commenced practice in Monticello, Mo.; elected circuit attorney in 1848 and 1852; elected as a Whig to the Thirty-third and Thirty-fourth Congresses (March 4, 1853–March 3, 1857); was not a candidate for reelection in 1856; moved to Davenport, Iowa, in 1858 and continued the practice of law; commissioned to investigate the condition of Iowa troops serving in the Civil War; after the war practiced his profession in Chicago until 1868, when he moved to St. Louis, Mo.; judge of the circuit court of the eighth judicial district of Missouri 1871–1883; moved to Kansas City, Mo.; retired from business activities; died at the home of a son in Nevada, Mo., April 18, 1891; interment in Elmwood Cemetery, Kansas City, Mo.

LINDQUIST, Francis Oscar, a Representative from Michigan; born in Marinette, Marinette County, Wis., September 27, 1869; attended the common schools; moved to Greenville, Mich., in 1904 and engaged in the mail-order clothing and manufacturing business; moved to Grand Rapids, Mich., in 1915 and became president of the Canada Mills Co., of New York and Michigan; elected as a Republican to the Sixty-third Congress (March 4, 1913–March 3, 1915); was not a candidate for renomination in 1914; resumed the mail-order business in Grand Rapids; after the First World War returned to Greenville, Mich., and supervised a correspondence-school course for sales people; unsuccessful candidate for election in 1922 to the Sixty-eighth Congress; in an effort to regain his health went to Blodget Memorial Hospital, Grand Rapids, Mich., where he died on September 25, 1924; interment in Forest Rose Cemetery, Greenville, Montcalm County, Mich.

LINDSAY, George Henry (father of George Washington Lindsay), a Representative from New York; born in New York City January 7, 1837; moved with his parents to Brooklyn, N. Y., in 1843; attended the public schools; engaged in the real estate and investment business; member of the State assembly 1882–1886; coroner of Kings County 1886–1892; appointed assistant tax commissioner in 1898; delegate to various national and State conventions; elected as a Democrat to the Fifty-seventh and to the five succeeding Congresses (March 4, 1901–March 3, 1913); declined to be a candidate for renomination in 1912; lived in retirement until his death in Brooklyn N. Y., May 25, 1916; interment in Evergreen Cemetery.

LINDSAY, George Washington (son of George Henry Lindsay), a Representative from New York; born in Brooklyn, N. Y., March 28, 1865; attended the public schools; deputy coroner of Kings County 1886–1892; engaged in the real-estate business; member of the Democratic State committee and served as leader of the assembly district from 1919 to 1934; appointed as a confidential investigator in the State insurance department in 1914 and served until 1920; elected to the State assembly in 1920; declined to be a candidate for renomination; deputy tenement-house commissioner for Brooklyn and Queens County 1921–1923; elected as a Democrat to the Sixty-eighth and to the five succeeding Congresses (March 4, 1923–January 3, 1935); unsuccessful candidate for renomination in 1934; resumed the real-estate business; died in Brooklyn, N. Y., on March 15, 1938; interment in Evergreen Cemetery.

LINDSAY, John Vliet, a Representative from New York; born in New York City, N. Y., November 24, 1921; graduated from the Buckley School in New York City in 1935, St. Paul's School, Concord, N. H., in 1940, Yale University in 1944, and from the law school of the same university in 1948; joined the United States Navy in May 1943; officer aboard destroyer U. S. S. *Swanson* (DD 443), participating in landings on Sicily, Seventh Fleet landings at Biak, Hollandia, and Admiralty Islands; with Carrier Task Group 38.4 during Philippine invasion; discharged as a lieutenant in March 1946; awarded five battle stars; was admitted to the bar in 1949 and began the practice of law in New York City, N. Y.; executive assistant to the United States Attorney General from January 1955 to January 1957; delegate to the Republican National Convention in 1960; elected as a Republican to the Eighty-sixth Congress (January 3, 1959–January 3, 1961). *Reelected to the Eighty-seventh Congress.*

LINDSAY, William, a Senator from Kentucky; born near Lexington, Rockbridge County, Va., September 4, 1835; attended the common schools; settled in Clinton, Hickman County, Ky., in November 1854; studied law; was admitted to the bar and commenced the practice of his profession in Clinton in 1858; during the Civil War served in the Confederate Army from July 1861 until May 1865 and was captain in the Second Tennessee Infantry; paroled as a prisoner of war at Columbus, Miss., May 16, 1865; resumed the practice of his profession in Clinton, Ky.; member of the State senate in 1867; judge of the Kentucky Court of Appeals 1870–1878; chief justice of the court 1876–1878; resumed the practice of his profession in Frankfort, Ky.; served in the Virginia State Senate in 1889; served as United States Commissioner to the World's Columbian Exposition, held at Chicago, Ill., from its organization until February 20, 1893; was appointed a member of the Interstate Commerce Commission in January 1892 but declined to accept the position; elected as a Democrat to the United States Senate to fill the vacancy caused by the resignation of John G. Carlisle; reelected in January 1894 and served from February 15, 1893, until March 3, 1901; was not a candidate for renomination in 1900; moved to New York City and resumed the practice of his profession; appointed United States Commissioner to the Louisiana Purchase Exposition at St. Louis in March 1901; died in Frankfort, Franklin County, Ky., October 15, 1909; interment in the State Cemetery.

LINDSEY, Stephen Decatur, a Representative from Maine; born in Norridgewock, Somerset County, Maine, March 3, 1828; attended the common schools and Broomfield Academy; studied law; was admitted to the bar and commenced practice in Norridgewock in 1853; clerk of the judicial courts in Somerset County 1857–1860; member of the State house of representatives in 1856; served in the State senate 1868–1870 and was president of that body in 1869; delegate to the Republican National Conventions in 1860 and 1868; member of the executive council of Maine in 1874; elected as Republican to the Forty-fifth, Forty-sixth, and Forty-seventh Congresses (March 4, 1877–March 3, 1883); was not a candidate for renomination in 1882 to the Forty-eighth Congress; resumed the practice of his profession; died in Norridgewock, Somerset County, Maine, on April 26, 1884; interment in River View Cemetery.

LINDSLEY, James Girard, a Representative from New York; born in Orange, N. J., March 19, 1819; attended the public schools, Ransom's Military Academy, and Pierson's Orange Classical School; moved to New York and was a trustee of the village of Rondout, N. Y., 1859–1864; president of the village of Rondout in 1852 and 1867–1869; elected supervisor of Kingston, N. Y., in March 1872 and in April of the same year was elected the first mayor of Kingston, to which office he was reelected for six consecutive years; elected as a Republican to the Forty-ninth Congress (March 4, 1885–March 3, 1887); was not a candidate for reelection in 1886; general manager of the Newark Lime & Cement Manufacturing Co., Kingston, N. Y.; organizer and president of the Kingston Water Co.; died in Kingston, Ulster County, N. Y., on December 4, 1898; interment in Montrepose Cemetery, Rondout, N. Y.

LINDSLEY, William Dell, a Representative from Ohio; born in New Haven, Conn., December 25, 1812; attended the common schools; moved to Buffalo, N. Y., in 1832 and soon after to Erie County, Ohio, settling near Sandusky; engaged in agricultural pursuits; served as captain in the Ohio Militia from 1840 to 1843 and as brigadier general in 1843; elected as a Democrat to the Thirty-third Congress (March 4, 1853–March 3, 1855); unsuccessful candidate for reelection in 1854 to the Thirty-fourth Congress; resumed agricultural pursuits; died in Perkins Township, Erie County, Ohio, March 11, 1890; interment in Oakland Cemetery, Sandusky, Ohio.

LINEBERGER, Walter Franklin, a Representative from California; born near Whiteville, Hardeman County, Tenn., July 20, 1883; attended the public schools, the Agricultural and Mechanical College of Texas, and the Rensselaer Polytechnic Institute, Troy, N. Y.; engaged in mining and agriculture in Mexico; moved to Long Beach, Calif., in 1911 and engaged in banking and agriculture; president of the Guarantee Bond & Mortgage Co. (Inc.); served fifteen months in France with the engineering units of the First, Thirty-second, and Fortieth Combat Divisions during the First World War; elected as a Republican to the Sixty-seventh Congress to fill the vacancy caused by the death of Representative-elect Charles F. Van de Water; reelected to the Sixty-eighth and Sixty-ninth Congresses and served from March 4, 1921, to March 3, 1927; did not seek renomination, having become a candidate for Senator; unsuccessful candidate for the Republican nomination as United States Senator in 1926; retired from political activities; died at Santa Barbara, Calif., October 9, 1943; interment in Santa Barbara Cemetery.

LINEHAN, Neil Joseph, a Representative from Illinois; born in Chicago, Ill., September 23, 1895; attended the public schools; was graduated from John L. Marsh School in 1913; engaged in electrical business since 1919; during the First World War served in France with the Three Hundred and Fortieth Infantry, Eighty-fifth Division, United States Army; president of the Linehan Electrical Co., Chicago, Ill., 1942–1955; elected as a Democrat to the Eighty-first Congress (January 3, 1949–January 3, 1951); unsuccessful candidate for reelection in 1950 to the Eighty-second Congress and for election in 1952 to the Eighty-third Congress; Director of Price Stabilization, Chicago district, 1951; resumed electrical engineering business; is a resident of Chicago, Ill.

LINK, William Walter, a Representative from Illinois; born in Swiec, Poland, February 12, 1884; immigrated to the United States in 1897 with his parents, who settled in Chicago, Ill.; attended the parochial and public schools; was graduated from Medill High School in Chicago, Ill., and attended the department of engineering of Lewis Institute, Chicago, Ill.; engaged in the enameling business at Chicago, Ill., 1912–1932; also interested in banking; president of the Board of Local Improvements, Chicago, Ill., 1933–1936; general secretary of the Polish-American Democratic Organization of Illinois since 1932; chief clerk of the superior court of Cook County in 1942 and 1943; vice president of the Board of Civil Service Commissioners of Cook County, Ill., in 1943 and 1944; elected as a Democrat to the Seventy-ninth Congress (January 3, 1945–January 3, 1947); unsuccessful candidate for reelection in 1946 to the Eightieth Congress; resumed the banking business as a director of the Manufacturers' National Bank of Chicago; also interested in sociological work; died in Chicago, Ill., September 23, 1950; interment in St. Adelbert's Cemetery.

LINN, Archibald Ladley, a Representative from New York; born in New York City on October 15, 1802; was a member of the class of 1820 at Union College, Schenectady, N. Y.; studied law; was admitted to the bar and commenced practice in Schenectady; county judge of Schenectady County from January 17, 1840, to February 9, 1845; elected as a Whig to the Twenty-seventh Congress (March 4, 1841–March 3, 1843); member of the State assembly in 1844; died in Schenectady, N. Y., October 10, 1857.

LINN, James, a Representative from New Jersey; born in Bedminster Township, Somerset County, N. J., in 1749; pursued preparatory studies, and was graduated from Princeton College in 1769; studied law; was admitted to the bar in 1772 and commenced practice in Trenton, N. J.; returned to Somerset County, N. J.; judge of the court of common pleas; member of the Provincial Congress of New Jersey in 1776; during the Revolutionary War served as captain in the Somerset County Militia in 1776; first major 1776–1781; member of the State council in 1777; returned to Trenton; served in the State general assembly in 1790 and 1791; again a member of the State council 1793–1797; elected as a Democrat to the Sixth Congress (March 4, 1799–March 3, 1801); was not a candidate for renomination in 1800 to the Seventh Congress; was appointed by President Jefferson to be supervisor of the revenue and served from 1801 to 1809; served as secretary of state of New Jersey 1809–1820; died in Trenton, Mercer County, N. J., on January 5, 1821; interment in the Lamington Presbyterian Church Cemetery, Somerset County, N. J.

LINN, John, a Representative from New Jersey; born near Johnsonburg, Hardwick Township, Warren County, N. J., December 3, 1763; moved with his father to Sussex County, N. J.; attended the common schools; entered the Revolutionary Army as a private in the First Regiment, Captain Manning's company; promoted to sergeant; member of the State general assembly 1801–1804; judge of the court of common pleas 1805–1821; sheriff of Sussex County in 1812; elected to the Fifteenth and Sixteenth Congresses and served from March 4, 1817, until his death in Washington, D. C., January 5, 1821; interment in North Hardyston Cemetery, near Franklin Furnace, Sussex County, N. J.

LINN, Lewis Fields, a Senator from Missouri; born near Louisville, Ky., November 5, 1796; was left an orphan when eleven years of age; received an academic education; studied medicine in Louisville; served in the War of 1812 as surgeon in Col. Henry Dodge's Mounted Rifle Volunteers; completed his medical studies at Philadelphia, Pa.; was admitted to practice and located at Ste. Genevieve, Territory of Missouri, in 1815; served in the State senate in 1827; appointed on the French Land Claims Commission in Missouri in 1832; appointed and subsequently elected as a Democrat to the United States Senate to fill the vacancy caused by the death of Alexander Buckner; reelected in 1836 and again in 1842 and served from October 25, 1833, until his death in Ste. Genevieve, Mo., on October 3, 1843; interment in the Protestant Cemetery.

LINNEY, Romulus Zachariah, a Representative from North Carolina; born in Rutherford County, N. C., December 26, 1841; attended the common schools, York's Collegiate Institute, and Doctor Millen's School in Taylorsville, N. C.; during the Civil War served in the Confederate Army until the Battle of Chancellorsville, when he was severely wounded; returned to Taylorsville and joined a class in Doctor Millen's School; engaged in agricultural pursuits; studied law; was admitted to the bar by the supreme court in 1868 and commenced practice in Taylorsville; elected to the State senate in 1870, 1873, and 1882; elected as a Republican to the Fifty-fourth, Fifty-fifth, and Fifty-sixth Congresses (March 4, 1895–March 3, 1901); died in Taylorsville, Alexander County, N. C., April 15, 1910; interment in Taylorsville Cemetery.

LINTHICUM, John Charles, a Representative from Maryland; born near Baltimore, in the locality now known as Linthicum Heights, Anne Arundel County, Md., November 26, 1867; attended the public schools of that county and Baltimore; was graduated from the State normal school in Baltimore in 1886; principal of Braddock School, Frederick County, in 1887, and taught in the schools of Anne Arundel County; studied history and political science at Johns Hopkins University in Baltimore; was graduated from the law department of the University of Maryland at Baltimore in 1890; was admitted to the bar and commenced practice in Baltimore in 1890; member of the State house of delegates in 1904 and 1905; served in the State senate 1906–1909; unsuccessful candidate for mayor of Baltimore in 1907; presidential elector on the Democratic ticket of Bryan and Kern in 1908; judge advocate general on the staff of Gov. Austin L. Crothers 1908–1912; elected as a Democrat to the Sixty-second and to the ten succeeding Congresses and served from March 4, 1911, until his death; had been renominated to the Seventy-third Congress at the time of his death; delegate to the Democratic National Convention at New York City in 1924 which nominated Davis and Bryan; died in Baltimore, Md., October 5, 1932; interment in Druid Ridge Cemetery.

LINTON, William Seelye, a Representative from Michigan; born in St. Clair, St. Clair County, Mich., February 4, 1856; moved with his parents to Saginaw, Mich., in 1859; attended the public schools; engaged as clerk in a store at Farwell, Mich.; became engaged in various activities connected with the lumber industry at Wells (now Alger); member of the board of supervisors of Bay County two terms; returned to Saginaw in 1878 and engaged in the lumber business with his father and also was connected with other business enterprises; member of the East Saginaw common council in 1884 and 1885; member of the State house of representatives in 1887 and 1888; unsuccessful candidate for Lieutenant Governor on the Republican ticket in 1890; president of the Saginaw Water Board; elected mayor of Saginaw in 1892; elected as a Republican to the Fifty-third and Fifty-fourth Congresses (March 4, 1893–March 3, 1897); appointed postmaster of Saginaw, Mich., by President McKinley on March 22, 1898, and recommissioned three times and served until 1914; president of the Saginaw Board of Trade 1905–1911 and 1913–1917; unsuccessful candidate for the Republican nomination for Governor of Michigan in 1913; appointed in 1919 a member of the Michigan State Board of Tax Commissioners and was named secretary a few weeks before his death in the Sparrow Memorial Hospital, Lansing, Mich., on November 22, 1927; interment in Forest Lawn Cemetery, Saginaw, Mich.

LIPPITT, Henry Frederick, a Senator from Rhode Island; born in Providence, R. I., October 12, 1856; attended private schools; was graduated from Brown University, Providence, R. I., in 1878; entered the cotton manufacturing business, in connection with which he held various positions from day operative to general manager; director of a bank and of several mill insurance companies; vice president of the People's Savings Bank of Providence; served on the staff of Gov. Royal C. Taft with the rank of colonel in 1888 and 1889; served as president of the New England Cotton Manufacturers' Association in 1889; elected as a Republican to the United States Senate and served from March 4, 1911, to March 3, 1917; unsuccessful candidate for reelection in 1916; again became actively engaged in the textile industry; died in Providence, R. I., December 28, 1933; interment in Swan Point Cemetery.

LIPSCOMB, Glenard Paul, a Representative from California; born in Jackson, Mich., August 19, 1915, and moved to Los Angeles, Calif., with his parents in 1920; attended the Los Angeles public schools, the University of Southern California, and Woodbury College; engaged in public accountancy since 1940; during World War II served in the Finance Corps, United States Army; elected a member of the State assembly in 1947, and reelected in 1948, 1950, and 1952; delegate to the Republican National Convention in 1956; elected as a Republican to the

Eighty-third Congress to fill the vacancy caused by the resignation of Norris Poulson; reelected to the Eighty-fourth, Eighty-fifth, and Eighty-sixth Congresses, and served from November 10, 1953, to January 3, 1961. *Reelected to the Eighty-seventh Congress.*

LISLE, Marcus Claiborne, a Representative from Kentucky; born near Winchester, Clark County, Ky., September 23, 1862; attended the common schools of his native county and the University of Kentucky at Lexington; was graduated from the law department of Columbia College (now Columbia University), New York City; was admitted to the bar and commenced the practice of his profession in Winchester, Ky., in 1887; served as county judge of Clark County, Ky., in 1890; elected as a Democrat to the Fifty-third Congress and served from March 4, 1893, until his death in Winchester, Ky., July 7, 1894; interment in Winchester Cemetery.

LITCHFIELD, Elisha, a Representative from New York; born in Canterbury, Windham County, Conn., July 12, 1785; attended the common schools; learned the carpenter's trade; moved to Onondaga County, N. Y., and settled in Delphi (now Delphi Falls) in 1812; major in the War of 1812; served as justice of the peace and supervisor of Onondaga County; appointed postmaster of Delphi November 28, 1817, and served until June 25, 1821; engaged in mercantile pursuits; member of the State assembly in 1819, 1831–1833, 1844, and 1848, and served as speaker of that body in the latter year; elected as a Democrat to the Seventeenth and Eighteenth Congresses (March 4, 1821–March 3, 1825); was not a candidate for renomination in 1824 to the Nineteenth Congress and withdrew from public life and active business pursuits; moved to Cazenovia, Madison County, N. Y., in 1838 and died there August 4, 1859; interment in the City Cemetery, Delphi Falls, N. Y.

LITTAUER, Lucius Nathan, a Representative from New York; born in Gloversville, Fulton County, N. Y., January 20, 1859; moved with his parents to New York City in 1865; attended the Charlier Institute, New York City; was graduated from Harvard University, Cambridge, Mass., in 1878; engaged in the manufacture of gloves in Gloversville; officer and director of many commercial and financial institutions; elected as a Republican to the Fifty-fifth and to the four succeeding Congresses (March 4, 1897–March 3, 1907); was not a candidate for reelection in 1906 to the Sixtieth Congress; delegate to all Republican State conventions from 1897 to 1912; resumed the glove-manufacturing business; delegate to the Republican National Conventions in 1900, 1904, 1908, and 1928; regent of the University of the State of New York 1912–1914; retired in 1927 and devoted his energies to education, medical research, and philanthropic work; died at his country home near New Rochelle, N. Y., on March 2, 1944; interment in the Jewish Cemetery, New Rochelle, N. Y.

LITTLE, Chauncey Bundy, a Representative from Kansas; born in Olathe, Johnson County, Kans., February 10, 1877; attended the graded and high schools and the Kansas State College at Manhattan; was graduated from the law department of the University of Kansas at Lawrence in 1898; was admitted to the bar the same year and commenced practice in Olathe; city attorney of Olathe 1901–1906; county attorney of Johnson County, Kans., 1909–1913; elected as a Democrat to the Sixty-ninth Congress (March 4, 1925–March 3, 1927); unsuccessful candidate for reelection in 1926 to the Seventieth Congress; resumed the practice of law; unsuccessful candidate for Governor of Kansas in 1928; died in Olathe, Kans., September 29, 1952; interment in Olathe Cemetery.

LITTLE, Edward Campbell, a Representative from Kansas; born in Newark, Licking County, Ohio, December 14, 1858; moved to Kansas in 1866 with his parents, who settled in Olathe; attended the public schools of Abilene, Kans., and was graduated from the University of Kansas at Lawrence in 1883; connected with the Santa Fe Railroad for several years; studied law; was admitted to the bar in 1886 and commenced practice in Lawrence, Kans.; chairman of the Republican State convention in 1888; city attorney of Ness City in 1889; prosecuting attorney of Dickinson County 1890–1892; delegate at large to the Republican National Convention at Minneapolis in 1892 which nominated Benjamin Harrison for a second term; United States diplomatic agent and consul general with rank of Minister Resident to Egypt in 1892 and 1893; upon leaving this position he was awarded the Grand Cordon of the Medjidieh by the Sultan of Turkey; private secretary to Gov. John W. Leedy in 1896 and 1897; unsuccessful candidate for election to the United States Senate in 1897; lieutenant colonel of the Twentieth Regiment, Kansas Volunteers, during the Spanish-American War in 1898 and 1899; with that regiment he went to the Philippine Islands and participated in the Battles of Caloocan, the Rio Tulijuan, Malinta, Polo, Meycauayan, Marilao, Bocaue, Bigoa, Guiguinto, Malolos, and San Fernando; commanded the regiment in several engagements, including that of Guiguinto; received Congressional Medal of Honor as well as the Spanish War and Philippine Campaign Medals for services in the Philippines; settled in Kansas City, Kans., in 1908; elected as a Republican to the Sixty-fifth and to the three succeeding Congresses and served from March 4, 1917, until his death in Washington, D. C., June 27, 1924; interment in the City Cemetery, Abilene, Kans.

LITTLE, Edward Preble, a Representative from Massachusetts; born in Marshfield, Plymouth County, Mass., November 7, 1791; attended the public schools; at the age of nine (in 1800) he was on the U. S. frigate *Boston* with his father, Capt. George Little, at the suggestion of President Adams, who gave him a commission as midshipman; engaged in agricultural pursuits; member of the State house of representatives 1829–1834 and 1835–1838; elected as a Democrat to the Thirty-second Congress to fill the vacancy caused by the death of Orin Fowler and served from December 13, 1852, to March 3, 1853; was not a candidate for renomination to the Thirty-third Congress; served as collector of customs at the port of Plymouth, Mass., 1853–1857; resumed agricultural pursuits; died in Lynn, Mass., on February 6, 1875; interment in the Congregational Church Cemetery, Marshfield Hills, Mass.

LITTLE, John, a Representative from Ohio; born near Grape Grove, Ross Township, Greene County, Ohio, April 25, 1837; attended the common schools; was graduated from Antioch College, Yellow Springs, Ohio, in 1862; studied law; was admitted to the bar in 1865 and commenced practice in Xenia, Ohio; mayor of Xenia 1864–1866; prosecuting attorney of Greene County 1866–1870; member of the State house of representatives 1869–1873; attorney general of Ohio 1873–1877; elected as a Republican to the Forty-ninth Congress (March 4, 1885–March 3, 1887); resumed the practice of law; appointed by President Harrison a member of the United States and Venezuela Claims Commission in 1889 and was its chairman; member of the Ohio State Board of Arbitration; trustee of Antioch College 1880–1900; died in Xenia, Ohio, on October 18, 1900; interment in Woodland Cemetery.

LITTLE, John Sebastian, a Representative from Arkansas; born at Jenny Lind, Sebastian County, Ark., March 15, 1853; attended the common schools and Cane Hill College, Arkansas; studied law; was admitted to the bar in 1874 and commenced practice in Greenwood, Ark.; elected district attorney in 1877, and reelected for four successive terms; member of the State house of representatives in 1884; elected circuit judge in 1886 for a term of four years; chosen chairman of the State judicial convention in 1893; elected as a Democrat to the Fifty-third Congress to fill the vacancy caused by the resignation of Clifton R. Breckinridge; reelected to the Fifty-fourth and to the five succeeding Congresses and served from December 3, 1894, until January 14, 1907, when he resigned, having been elected Governor of Arkansas; after being sworn in as Governor in January 1907, he suffered a physical and mental break-down, from which he did not recover; died in Little Rock, Pulaski County, Ark., October 29, 1916; interment in City Cemetery, Greenwood, Ark.

LITTLE, Joseph James, a Representative from New York; born in Bristol, England, June 5, 1841; immigrated to the United States in 1846 with his parents, who settled in Morris, Otsego County, N. Y.; attended the common schools; apprenticed to the local printer and entered a New York book-printing office to complete his trade; during the Civil War served in the Union Army 1862–1864 as corporal, first sergeant, and first lieutenant; established a printing business in 1867 at New York City; member of the board of education and of the New York World's Fair Committee; elected as a Democrat to the Fifty-second Congress to fill the vacancy caused by the resignation of Roswell P. Flower and served from November 3, 1891, to March 3, 1893; was not a candidate for renomination in 1892 to the Fifty-third Congress; served as commissioner of education and president of the board of education of New York City; engaged in the printing and publishing business until his death in New York City on February 11, 1913; interment in Kensico Cemetery, Kensico, Westchester County, N. Y.

LITTLE, Peter, a Representative from Maryland; born in Petersburg, Huntingdon County, Pa., December 11, 1775; attended the common schools; became a watchmaker; moved to Freedom, Baltimore County, Md., and engaged in agricultural pursuits; member of the State house of delegates in 1806 and 1807; elected as a Democrat to the Twelfth Congress (March 4, 1811–March 3, 1813); was not a candidate for renomination in 1812; during the War of 1812 was commissioned colonel of the Thirty-eighth Maryland Infantry and served from May 19, 1813, to June 15, 1815; elected to the Fourteenth Congress to fill the vacancy caused by the resignation of William Pinkney; reelected to the six succeeding Congresses and served from September 2, 1816, to March 3, 1829; declined to be a candidate for renomination; judge of the orphans' court of Baltimore County; died in Freedom, Baltimore County, Md., February 5, 1830; interment in Freedom Methodist Episcopal Cemetery, near Eldersburg, Carroll County, Md.

LITTLEFIELD, Charles Edgar, a Representative from Maine; born in Lebanon, York County, Maine, June 21, 1851; attended the common schools and Foxcroft Academy; studied law; was admitted to the bar in 1876 and practiced in Rockland, Maine; member of the State house of representatives 1885–1887 and served as speaker the last year; attorney general of the State 1889–1893; delegate to the Republican National Conventions in 1892 and 1896; elected as a Republican to the Fifty-sixth Congress to fill the vacancy caused by the death of Nelson Dingley, Jr.; reelected to the four succeeding Congresses and served from June 19, 1899, until his resignation, effective September 30, 1908; moved to New York City and engaged in the practice of law until his death there on May 2, 1915; interment in Achorn Cemetery, Rockland, Knox County, Maine.

LITTLEFIELD, Nathaniel Swett, a Representative from Maine; born in Wells, York County, Maine, September 20, 1804; attended the common schools; studied law; was admitted to the bar in 1827 and commenced practice in Bridgton, Maine; postmaster of Bridgton, Maine, 1827–1841; filled important town offices, chiefly as selectman; active in civic affairs; secretary of the State senate in 1831 and 1832; member of the State senate 1837–1839 and president of the senate in 1838; elected as a Democrat to the Twenty-seventh Congress (March 4, 1841–March 3, 1843); elected as a Cass Democrat to the Thirty-first Congress (March 4, 1849–March 3, 1851); was not a candidate for renomination in 1850 to the Thirty-second Congress; was a member of the State house of representatives in 1854; delegate to the Union convention at Philadelphia, Pa., in 1866; died in Bridgton, Cumberland County, Maine, August 15, 1882; interment in the High Street Cemetery.

LITTLEJOHN, De Witt Clinton, a Representative from New York; born in Bridgewater, Oneida County, N. Y., February 7, 1818; pursued an academic course; engaged in mercantile pursuits and in the manufacture of flour at Oswego, N. Y.; mayor of the city in 1849 and 1850; member of the State assembly 1853–1855, 1857, 1859–1861, 1866, 1867, 1870, and 1871, and served as speaker 1859–1861, 1866, 1867, 1870, and 1871; during the Civil War served as colonel of the One Hundred and Tenth New York Volunteer Infantry; resigned February 3, 1863; elected as a Republican to the Thirty-eighth Congress (March 4, 1863–March 3, 1865); was not a candidate for renomination in 1864; brevetted brigadier general of Volunteers March 13, 1865, "for valuable services during the war"; again a member of the State assembly in 1884; died in Oswego, Oswego County, N. Y., October 27, 1892; interment in Riverside Cemetery.

LITTLEPAGE, Adam Brown, a Representative from West Virginia; born near Charleston, Kanawha County, Va. (now West Virginia), April 14, 1859; attended the common schools; studied law; was admitted to the bar and commenced practice in Newport, Ind., in 1882; moved to Charleston, W. Va., in 1884 and continued the practice of law; general counsel in West Virginia for the United Mine Workers' Association; member of the State senate 1906–1910; elected as a Democrat to the Sixty-second Congress (March 4, 1911–March 3, 1913); unsuccessful candidate for reelection in 1912 to the Sixty-third Congress; elected to the Sixty-fourth and Sixty-fifth Congresses (March 4, 1915–March 3, 1919); unsuccessful candidate for reelection in 1918 to the Sixty-sixth Congress; resumed the practice of law; died in Charleston, W. Va., June 29, 1921; interment in Spring Hill Cemetery.

LITTLETON, Martin Wiley, a Representative from New York; born near Kingston, Roane County, Tenn., January 12, 1872; moved to Texas in 1881 with his parents, who settled in Dallas; attended the common schools; studied law; was admitted to the bar in 1891 and commenced practice in Dallas, Tex.; prosecuting attorney of Dallas County 1893–1896; moved to New York City in 1896 and continued the practice of his profession; district attorney of Kings County, N. Y., 1900–1904; delegate to the Democratic National Convention at St. Louis in 1904; president of the Borough of Brooklyn in 1904 and 1905; elected as a Democrat to the Sixty-second Congress (March 4, 1911–March 3, 1913); was not a candidate for reelection in 1912 to the Sixty-third Congress; resumed the practice of law, and resided in New York City and Mineola, Nassau County, Long Island; died at Mineola, N. Y., on December 19, 1934; interment in the Littleton family mausoleum, Woodlawn Cemetery, New York City, N. Y.

LIVELY, Robert Maclin, a Representative from Texas; born in Fayetteville, Washington County, Ark., on January 6, 1855; moved to Texas in 1864 with his parents, who settled in Smith County; attended private schools in eastern Texas; studied law; was admitted to the bar in 1876 and commenced practice in Kaufman, Kaufman County, Tex.; moved to Canton, Van Zandt County, and continued the practice of law; prosecuting attorney of Van Zandt County 1882–1884; elected as a Democrat to the Sixty-first Congress to fill the vacancy caused by the resignation of J. Gordon Russell and served from July 23, 1910, to March 3, 1911; declined to be a candidate for renomination in 1910; judge of Van Zandt County, Tex., 1916–1918; died in Canton, Tex., January 15, 1929; interment in Canton Cemetery.

LIVERMORE, Arthur (son of Samuel Livermore and brother of Edward St. Loe Livermore), a Representative from New Hampshire; born in Londonderry, Rockingham County, N. H., July 29, 1766; received classical instruction from his parents; studied law; was admitted to the bar and commenced practice in Concord in 1792; moved to Chester, N. H., the following year; member of the State house of representatives in 1794 and 1795; solicitor for Rockingham County 1796–1798; moved to Holderness, N. H., in 1798; associate justice of the superior court 1798–1809 and chief justice 1809–1813; presidential elector on the Federalist ticket in 1800; associate justice of the State supreme court 1813–1816; elected as a Democrat to the Fifteenth and Sixteenth Congresses (March 4, 1817–March 3, 1821); unsuccessful candidate for reelection in 1822 to the Seventeenth Congress; served in the State senate in 1821 and 1822; judge of probate for Grafton County in 1822 and 1823; elected to the Eighteenth Congress (March 4, 1823–March 3, 1825); was not a candidate for renomination in 1824; chief justice of the court of common pleas 1825–1832; moved to Campton in 1827; trustee of Holmes Plymouth Academy 1808–1826; died in Campton, N. H., July 1, 1853; interment in Trinity Churchyard, Holderness, N. H.

LIVERMORE, Edward St. Loe (son of Samuel Livermore and brother of Arthur Livermore), a Representative from Massachusetts; born in Portsmouth, N. H., April 5, 1762; pursued classical studies; studied law; was admitted to the bar and commenced practice in Concord, N. H., in 1783 and later practiced in Portsmouth, N. H.; United States district attorney 1789–1797; State solicitor for Rockingham County 1791–1793; associate justice of the State supreme court 1797–1799; naval officer for the port of Portsmouth 1799–1802; moved to Newburyport, Mass., in 1802; elected as a Federalist to the Tenth and Eleventh Congresses (March 4, 1807–March 3, 1811); was not a candidate for renomination in 1810; resumed the practice of law; moved to Boston, Mass., in 1811, thence to Zanesville, Ohio, in 1815; returned to Boston, and then moved to Tewksbury, Middlesex County, Mass., where he lived in retirement until his death there on September 15, 1832; interment in the Granary Burying Ground, Boston, Mass.

LIVERMORE, Samuel (father of Arthur Livermore and Edward St. Loe Livermore), a Delegate, a Representative, and a Senator from New Hampshire; born in Waltham, Middlesex County, Mass., May 14, 1732; attended Waltham schools, and was graduated from Nassau Hall (now Princeton University) in 1752; studied law; was admitted to the bar in 1756 and commenced practice in Waltham, Mass.; moved to Portsmouth, N. H., in 1758 and later to Londonderry; member of the general court from Londonderry 1768–1770; moved to Holderness in 1775; State's attorney for three years; elected a Member of the Continental Congress in 1780 and served until June 21, 1782, when he resigned; again served as a Member of the Continental Congress in 1785; chief justice of the State supreme court 1782–1789; member of the State constitutional convention in 1788; elected to the First and Second Congresses (March 4, 1789–March 3, 1793); president of the State constitutional convention in 1791; elected to the United States Senate in 1792; reelected in 1798 and served from March 4, 1793, until his resignation effective June 12, 1801; died in Holderness, Grafton County, N. H., May 18, 1803; interment in Trinity Churchyard.

LIVERNASH, Edward James (subsequently Edward James de Nivernais), a Representative from California; born in Lower Calveritas, a California mining camp, near San Andreas, February 14, 1866; attended the common schools of California; became a printer at the age of fifteen, and a year later founded a country newspaper at Cloverdale, Calif.; studied law in preparation for journalism; was admitted to the bar in 1887; joined the staff of the San Francisco Examiner in 1891 and held various editorial posts; was sent by the Klondike miners in 1897 as commissioner to the Dominion of Canada to urge a modification of onerous laws; elected as the candidate of the Union Labor Party, and endorsed by the Democratic Party, to the Fifty-eighth Congress (March 4, 1903–March 3, 1905); became the editor of the Denver News in 1906; resided in France from 1909 to 1912, when he returned to the United States and settled near Belmont, Calif.; engaged in study and literary pursuits; after his congressional service he resumed the French form of the family name de Nivernais, by decree of court; died in a hospital at Agnew. Calif., June 1, 1938; remains were cremated at Cypress Lawn Cemetery, Colma, Calif.

LIVINGSTON, Edward (brother of Robert R. Livingston and nephew of Philip Livingston and William Livingston), a Representative from New York and a Representative and a Senator from Louisiana; born in Clermont, Livingston Manor, N. Y., May 26, 1764; was graduated from Princeton College in 1781; studied law in Albany, N. Y.; was admitted to the bar in 1785 and commenced practice in New York City; elected as a Democrat from New York to the Fourth, Fifth, and Sixth Congresses (March 4, 1795–March 3, 1801); United States district attorney from March 27, 1801, to July 25, 1803; mayor of New York City 1801–1803; moved to New Orleans, La., in 1804; engaged in the practice of law and in the real-estate business; author of a legal code for Louisiana; served at the Battle of New Orleans on the staff of General Jackson in 1815; member of the State house of representatives in 1820; elected as a Democrat from Louisiana to the Eighteenth, Nineteenth, and Twentieth Congresses (March 4, 1823–March 3, 1829); elected to the United States Senate and served from March 4, 1829, until May 24, 1831, when he resigned, having been appointed to the Cabinet; Secretary of State in the Cabinet of President Andrew Jackson from May 24, 1831, to May 29, 1833; Minister Plenipotentiary to France from May 29, 1833, to April 28, 1835; inherited from his sister "Montgomery Place" on the Hudson River, Barrytown, Dutchess County, N. Y., and died there May 23, 1836; interment in the family vault at Clermont, N. Y.

LIVINGSTON, Henry Walter (son of Walter Livingston and grandson of Philip Livingston), a Representative from New York; born in Linlithgo, Columbia County, N. Y., in 1768; was graduated from Yale College in 1786; studied law; was admitted to the bar and commenced practice in New York City; private secretary to Gouverneur Morris, American Minister Plenipotentiary to Paris, France, 1792–1794; judge of the court of common pleas of Columbia County, N. Y.; member of the State assembly in 1802 and again in 1810; elected to the Eighth and Ninth Congresses (March 4, 1803–March 3, 1807); died in Livingston Manor, Linlithgo, N. Y., December 22, 1810.

LIVINGSTON, Leonidas Felix, a Representative from Georgia; born near Covington, Newton County, Ga., April 3, 1832; attended the common schools; engaged in agricultural pursuits; entered the Confederate Army as a private in August 1861 and served throughout the Civil War; resumed agricultural pursuits in Newton County, Ga.; member of the State house of representatives in 1876, 1877, and 1879–1881; served in the State senate in 1882 and 1883; vice president of the Georgia State Agricultural Society for eleven years and president four years; president of the Georgia State Alliance for three years; elected as a Democrat to the Fifty-second and to the nine succeeding Congresses (March 4, 1891–March 3, 1911); unsuccessful candidate for renomination in 1910; again engaged in agricultural pursuits in Newton County; died in Washington, D. C., February 11, 1912; interment in Bethany Church Cemetery, near Covington, Ga.

LIVINGSTON, Philip (brother of William Livingston, uncle of Edward Livingston and Robert R. Livingston, and father of Walter Livingston), a Delegate from New York; born in Albany, N. Y., January 15, 1716; was graduated from Yale College in 1737; engaged in the mercantile business in New York City; member of the board of aldermen 1754–1762; member of the provincial house of representatives 1763–1769 and served as speaker in 1768; member of the New York Committee of Correspondence; delegate to the Stamp Act Congress in October 1765; register in chancery in 1768 and 1769; Member of the Continental Congress from 1774 until his death; a signer of the Declaration of Independence; president of the New York Provincial Convention in 1775; member of the State assembly in 1776; served in the State senate in 1777; prominent in commercial and educational societies; died while attending the sixth session of the Continental Congress in York, Pa., June 12, 1778; interment in a tomb in Prospect Hill Cemetery, York, York County, Pa.

LIVINGSTON, Robert Le Roy, a Representative from New York; born in Claverack, Columbia County, N. Y.; was graduated from Princeton College in 1784; was commissioned first lieutenant in the Twelfth United States Infantry on January 14, 1799, and honorably discharged on June 15, 1800; elected as a Federalist to the Eleventh and Twelfth Congresses and served from March 4, 1809, until May 6, 1812, when he resigned; participated in the War of 1812 and was commissioned lieutenant colonel of the Twenty-third Infantry on May 29, 1812, and served until February 1, 1813, when he resigned.

LIVINGSTON, Robert R. (brother of Edward Livingston and nephew of Philip Livingston and William Livingston), a Delegate from New York; born in New York City November 27, 1746; was graduated from King's College (now Columbia University), New York City, in 1765; studied law; was admitted to the bar in 1773 and commenced practice in New York City; city recorder 1773–1775; member of the provincial convention of 1775; Member of the Continental Congress 1775–1777 and 1779–1781; one of the committee of five appointed to draw up the Declaration of Independence but returned to duties in the provincial assembly before it was signed; delegate to the State constitutional convention in April 1777; Secretary of Foreign Affairs from August 1781 to August 1783; chancellor of New York State 1777–1801 and administered the oath of office to President Washington April 30, 1789; unsuccessful candidate for Governor of New York in 1798; Minister Plenipotentiary to France 1801–1804; prominent in local affairs; assisted Robert Fulton and was his partner in constructing the first steamboat; died in Clermont, N. Y., February 26, 1813; interment on his estate, "Clermont," near Clermont, N. Y.

LIVINGSTON, Walter (son of Philip Livingston and father of Henry Walter Livingston), a Delegate from New York; born

November 27, 1740; delegate to the provincial convention held in New York in April and May 1775; member of the First Provincial Congress from May to November 1775; judge of Albany County in 1774 and 1775; served as commissary of stores and provisions for the department of New York from July 17, 1775, until September 7, 1776, when he resigned; deputy commissary general of the northern department in 1775 and 1776; member of the State assembly 1777–1779 and served as speaker in 1778; member of the New York and Massachusetts Boundary Commission in 1784; a member of the board of regents of the University of the State of New York 1784–1787; Member of the Continental Congress in 1784 and 1785; appointed Commissioner of the United States Treasury in 1785; died in New York City on May 14, 1797.

LIVINGSTON, William (brother of Philip Livingston and uncle of Edward Livingston and Robert R. Livingston), a Delegate from New Jersey; born in Albany, N. Y., November 30, 1723; was graduated from Yale College in 1741; studied law; was admitted to the bar in 1748 and commenced practice in New York; established and edited the Independent Reflector in 1752; a commissioner to adjust the boundary lines between New York and Massachusetts in 1754 and New York and New Jersey in 1764; member of the provincial assembly from Livingston Manor 1759–1761; moved to Elizabethtown (now Elizabeth), N. J., in 1772; Member of the Continental Congress from July 23, 1774, to June 22, 1776; commissioned a brigadier general of the New Jersey Militia on October 28, 1775, and served until August 31, 1776, having been elected Governor; served consecutively as Governor of New Jersey from August 31, 1776, until his death; appointed one of the commissioners to superintendent the construction of Federal buildings in 1785, but declined, as he did the appointment to be Minister to The Hague tendered June 23, 1785; delegate to the Federal Constitutional Convention in Philadelphia in 1787 and one of the signers of the Constitution; died in Elizabeth, Union County, N. J., July 25, 1790; interment in the family vault in Trinity Churchyard, New York City.

LLOYD, Edward, a Delegate from Maryland; born at "Wye House," Talbot County, Md., December 15, 1744; completed preparatory studies; member of the lower house in the General Assembly of Maryland 1771–1774; member of the committee of safety for the Eastern Shore in 1775 and of the provincial convention in 1776; served on the executive council 1777–1779; member of the State house of delegates in 1780; served in the State senate in 1781, 1786, and 1791; Member of the Continental Congress 1783–1784; member of the State constitutional convention which ratified the Federal Constitution April 28, 1788; died at "Wye House," July 8, 1796; interment in the family burying ground at "Wye House."

LLOYD, Edward (son of the preceding), a Representative and a Senator from Maryland; born at "Wye House," Talbot County, Md., July 22, 1779; educated by private tutors; member of the State house of delegates 1800–1805; elected as a Democrat to the Ninth Congress to fill the vacancy caused by the resignation of Joseph H. Nicholson; reelected to the Tenth Congress and served from December 3, 1806, to March 3, 1809; Governor of Maryland 1809–1811; commissioned lieutenant colonel of the Ninth Regiment of Maryland Militia; served in the State senate from 1811 until his resignation in January 1815; Democratic presidential elector in 1812; elected to the United States Senate on December 21, 1819, for the term beginning March 4, 1819; reelected in 1825 and served until his resignation on January 14, 1826; member and president of the State senate 1826–1831; died in Annapolis, Anne Arundel County, Md., June 2, 1834; interment in the family burying ground at "Wye House," Talbot County, Md.

LLOYD, James, a Senator from Maryland; born at "Farley," near Chestertown, Kent County, Md., in 1745; pursued classical studies; studied law; was admitted to the bar and practiced; commissioned second lieutenant in the Kent County Militia on September 11, 1776, and served during the Revolutionary War; general in the War of 1812; elected as a Democrat to the United States Senate to fill the vacancy caused by the resignation of John Henry and served from December 11, 1797, until December 1, 1800, when he resigned; engaged in the practice of law; died at "Ratclift Manor," near Easton, Talbot County, Md., in 1820; interment at "Clover," the estate of his daughter, in Queen Annes County, Md.

LLOYD, James, a Senator from Massachusetts; born in Boston, Mass., in December 1769; attended the Boston Latin School, and was graduated from Harvard University in 1787; became a merchant and was interested in foreign trade; member of the State house of representatives in 1800 and 1801; served in the State senate in 1804; elected as a Federalist to the United States Senate to fill the vacancy caused by the resignation of John Quincy Adams; reelected, and served from June 9, 1808, until May 1, 1813, when he resigned; again elected to the United States Senate to fill the vacancy caused by the resignation of Harrison Gray Otis; reelected, and served from June 5, 1822, until May 23, 1826, when he resigned; retired from public life, and moved to Philadelphia, Pa., in 1826; died in New York City April 5, 1831; interment in Kings' Chapel Burying Ground, Boston, Mass.

LLOYD, James Tilghman, a Representative from Missouri; born in Canton, Lewis County, Mo., August 28, 1857; attended the public schools; was graduated from Christian University (now Culver-Stockton College), Canton, Mo., in 1878; taught school; deputy sheriff of Lewis County 1879–1881; deputy circuit clerk and recorder 1880–1882; studied law; was admitted to the bar in 1882 and commenced practice in Monticello, Lewis County, Mo.; moved to Shelbyville, Mo., in 1885 and continued the practice of law; prosecuting attorney of Shelby County 1889–1893; elected as a Democrat to the Fifty-fifth Congress to fill the vacancy caused by the death of Richard P. Giles; reelected to the Fifty-sixth and to the eight succeeding Congresses and served from June 1, 1897, to March 3, 1917; was not a candidate for renomination in 1916; delegate to the Democratic National Convention at Denver in 1908; chairman of the Democratic congressional committee 1908–1912; settled in Washington, D. C., in 1917 and practiced law until 1925; president of the board of education in 1924 and 1925; president of the chamber of commerce in 1925; returned to Missouri in 1925 and engaged in the practice of his profession in Canton; member of the board of curators of Culver-Stockton College; died in a nursing home at Quincy, Ill., where he was confined as the result of an automobile accident, on April 3, 1944; interment in Forest Grove Cemetery, Canton, Mo.

LLOYD, Wesley, a Representative from Washington; born at Arvonia, Osage County, Kans., on July 24, 1883, attended the public schools, Baker University, Baldwin, Kans., and Washburn College, Topeka, Kans.; engaged in newspaper work in Kansas City and Topeka; graduated from the Kansas City Law School in 1906; was admitted to the bar the same year; moved to Tacoma, Wash., in 1906, and engaged in newspaper work until 1908 when he commenced the practice of law in Tacoma; served as a corporal in the Washington National Guard 1918–1920; was elected as a Democrat to the Seventy-third and Seventy-fourth Congresses and served from March 4, 1933, until his death in Washington, D. C., January 10, 1936; interment in Tacoma Cemetery, Tacoma, Wash.

LOAN, Benjamin Franklin, a Representative from Missouri; born in Hardinsburg, Breckinridge County, Ky., October 4, 1819; pursued an academic course; studied law in Kentucky; moved to St. Joseph, Mo., in 1838; was admitted to the bar in 1840 and practiced in St. Joseph; served in the Union Army during the Civil War; commissioned brigadier general of Missouri State Militia in the service of the United States November 27, 1861; honorably discharged June 8, 1863; declined an appointment to the supreme court of Missouri in 1863; elected as an Emancipationist to the Thirty-eighth and Thirty-ninth Congresses and as a Radical to the Fortieth Congress (March 4, 1863–March 3, 1869); unsuccessful candidate for reelection in 1868 to the Forty-first Congress; appointed by President Grant a visitor to the United States Military Academy in 1869; declined the missions to Venezuela and Brazil, the governorship of New Mexico, and judgeships in the Territories; resumed the practice of law in St. Joseph, Mo.; delegate to the Republican National Convention at Cincinnati in 1876; unsuccessful candidate for election in 1876 to the Forty-fifth Congress; died in St. Joseph, Mo., March 30, 1881; interment in Mount Mora Cemetery.

LOBECK, Charles Otto, a Representative from Nebraska; born in Andover, Henry County, Ill., April 6, 1852; attended the public schools, the high school in Geneseo, Ill., the German Wallace College, Berea, Ohio, and the Dyhrenfurth Commercial College, Chicago, Ill.; moved to Dayton, Iowa, in 1869 and was employed as a clerk in a general store; commercial traveler in Iowa and Nebraska 1875–1892; engaged in the hardware business in Omaha 1892–1895; elected as a Republican to the State senate in 1892; member of the city council of Omaha 1897–1903, during which time he was engaged in the real estate and insurance business; affiliated with the Democratic Party in 1896; presidential elector on the Democratic ticket of Bryan and Stevenson in 1900; served as city controller from 1903 until his resignation in 1911, having been elected to Congress; elected as a Democrat to the Sixty-second and to the three succeeding Congresses (March 4, 1911–March 3, 1919); unsuccessful candidate for reelection in 1918 to the Sixty-sixth Congress; again engaged in the real estate and insurance business; died in Omaha, Nebr., January 30, 1920; interment in Prospect Hill Cemetery.

LOCHER, Cyrus, a Senator from Ohio; born on a farm in Riley Township, Putnam County, Ohio, March 8, 1878; attended the country schools and the township high school; was graduated from Ohio Wesleyan University, Delaware, Ohio, in 1903; taught in the country schools and was superintendent of schools at Woodsfield, Ohio, in 1904 and 1905; studied law at the University of Michigan at Ann Arbor and was graduated from the law school of Western Reserve University at Cleveland, Ohio, in 1906; was admitted to the bar in 1906 and commenced the practice of law in Cleveland in 1907; appointed assistant city solicitor of Cleveland in 1908 and served until 1910; member of the faculty of Western Reserve University in 1911 and 1912; was elected prosecuting attorney of Cuyahoga County in 1912, reelected in 1914, and served until 1916; served in Gov. Vic Donahey's cabinet as State director of commerce 1923–1928; appointed as a Democrat to the United States Senate to fill the vacancy caused by the death of Frank B. Willis and served from April 5, 1928, to December 14, 1928, when a duly elected successor qualified; was an unsuccessful candidate for the nomination in 1928 to fill this vacancy; continued the practice of law in Cleveland, Ohio, until his death there on August 17, 1929; interment in Ebenezer Cemetery, Bluffton, Ohio.

LOCKE, Francis (nephew of Matthew Locke), a Senator from North Carolina; born in Rowan County, N. C., October 31, 1776; attended Zion-Parnassus Academy and the University of North Carolina at Chapel Hill; studied law; was admitted to the bar and practiced; elected judge of the superior court of North Carolina in 1803 and served until 1814, when he resigned; presidential elector on the Democratic ticket of Madison and Clinton in 1808; elected to the United States Senate in 1814 to fill the vacancy caused by the resignation of David Stone, but resigned December 5, 1815, without having qualified; died in Rowan County, N. C., on January 8, 1823; interment in the Thyatira Churchyard, near Salisbury, N. C.

LOCKE, John, a Representative from Massachusetts; born in Hopkinton, Middlesex County, Mass., February 14, 1764; his boyhood schooling consisted of sixteen weeks; worked on a farm until 22 years of age; attended Andover Academy and Dartmouth College, Hanover, N. H.; taught school; was graduated from Harvard University in 1792; studied law; was admitted to the bar and commenced practice in Ashby in 1796; member of the State house of representatives in 1804, 1805, 1813, and 1823; delegate to the State constitutional convention in 1820; elected to the Eighteenth, Nineteenth, and Twentieth Congresses (March 4, 1823–March 3, 1829); declined to be a candidate for renomination in 1828; member of the State senate in 1830 and of the State executive council in 1831; resumed the practice of his profession; moved to Lowell, Mass., in 1837 and to Boston in 1849; died in Boston, Mass., March 29, 1855; interment in Lowell Cemetery, Lowell, Middlesex County, Mass.

LOCKE, Matthew (uncle of Francis Locke, and great-great-great-grandfather of Effiegene (Locke) Wingo), a Representative from North Carolina; born in the north of Ireland in 1730; immigrated to the United States and located in Rowan County, N. C.; engaged in transportation by wagon; treasury commissioner of the colony of North Carolina in 1771; elected a member of the safety committee of Rowan County on August 8, 1774, and of the committee of secrecy, intelligence, and observation of Rowan County on September 23, 1774; member of the Provincial Congress at Hillsboro, N. C., and Johnston Court House in 1775; served as paymaster of troops in the Salisbury District in 1775; member of the Colonial Congress at Halifax in 1776; delegate to the State constitutional convention in 1776; member of the State house of commons 1777–1781; brigadier general of North Carolina troops during the Revolutionary War; served in the State senate in 1781 and 1782; again a member of the State house of commons 1783–1792; delegate to the State constitutional convention in 1789 called to ratify the Federal Constitution and voted against ratification; elected as a Democrat to the Third, Fourth, and Fifth Congresses (March 4, 1793–March 3, 1799); unsuccessful candidate for reelection in 1798 to the Sixth Congress; engaged as a planter and was an extensive landowner; died in Salisbury, Rowan County, N. C., September 7, 1801; interment in the Thyatira Churchyard, near Salisbury, N. C.

LOCKHART, James, a Representative from Indiana; born in Auburn, Cayuga County, N. Y., February 13, 1806; attended the public schools; moved to Ithaca, N. Y., about 1826 and operated a woolen mill; moved to Indiana in 1832; studied law; was admitted to the bar in 1832 and commenced practice in Evansville, Ind., in 1834; city clerk in 1836 and 1837; prosecuting attorney of Vanderburg County 1841–1845; judge of the fourth judicial district from 1846 until 1851, when he resigned; delegate to the State constitutional convention in 1850; elected as a Democrat to the Thirty-second Congress (March 4, 1851–March 3, 1853); was not a candidate for reelection in 1852 to the Thirty-third Congress; resumed the practice of his profession in Evansville; appointed by President Pierce superintendent of construction of the marine hospital at Evansville in 1853; elected to the Thirty-fifth Congress and served from March 4, 1857, until his death in Evansville, Ind., on September 7, 1857; interment in Oak Hill Cemetery.

LOCKHART, James Alexander, a Representative from North Carolina; born in Anson County, N. C., June 2, 1850; attended the common schools; was graduated from Trinity College, Durham, N. C., in June 1873; studied law in Charlotte, N. C.; was admitted to the bar in 1874; settled in Wadesboro, N. C., where he practiced his profession; mayor of Wadesboro in 1875; member of the State house of representatives in 1878; served in the State senate in 1880; presented credentials as a Democratic Member-elect to the Fifty-fourth Congress and served from March 4, 1895, to June 5, 1896, when he was succeeded by Charles H. Martin, who contested his election; resumed the practice of his profession in Wadesboro, N. C.; died in Charlotte, N. C., on December 24, 1905; interment in Eastview Cemetery, Wadesboro, N. C.

LOCKWOOD, Daniel Newton, a Representative from New York; born in Hamburg, Erie County, N. Y., June 1, 1844; attended common schools; was graduated from Union College, Schenectady, N. Y., in 1865; studied law; was admitted to the bar in 1866 and practiced in Buffalo, N. Y.; district attorney of Erie County 1874–1877; elected as a Democrat to the Forty-fifth Congress (March 4, 1877–March 3, 1879); delegate to the Democratic National Convention at Cincinnati in 1880 and at Chicago in 1884 and 1896; United States attorney for the northern district of New York from October 1886 until June 1889 when he resigned; elected to the Fifty-second and Fifty-third Congresses (March 4, 1891–March 3, 1895); was not a candidate for reelection in 1894 to the Fifty-fourth Congress but was an unsuccessful candidate for Lieutenant Governor of New York; resumed the practice of his profession in Buffalo, N. Y.; general manager from New York at the Pan American Exposition in 1901; appointed in 1903 by Governor Benjamin B. Odell a member of the State lunacy commission, which office he held until his death in Buffalo, N. Y., June 1, 1906; interment in Forest Lawn Cemetery.

LODGE, Henry Cabot (great-grandson of George Cabot), a Representative and a Senator from Massachusetts; born in Boston, Mass., May 12, 1850; attended a private school, and was graduated from Harvard University in 1871; editor of the North American Review 1873–1876; was graduated from the Harvard Law School in 1875 and was admitted to the bar in 1876; lecturer on American history at Harvard University 1876–1879; editor of the International Review 1879–1881; lecturer at Lowell Institute, Boston, Mass., in 1880; member of the State house of representatives in 1880 and 1881; author of many historical, biographical, and political works; unsuccessful candidate for election in 1884 to the Forty-ninth Congress; elected as a Republican to the Fiftieth, Fifty-first, and Fifty-second Congresses and served from March 4, 1887, until March 3, 1893, when he resigned; had been reelected to the Fifty-third Congress, but was later elected to the United States Senate in 1893; reelected in 1899, 1905, 1911, 1916, and 1922, and served from March 4, 1893, until his death; delegate to the Republican National Conventions in 1884, 1888, 1892, 1896, 1900, 1904, 1908, 1916, 1920, and 1924, serving as chairman in 1900, 1908, and 1920, and as chairman of the committee on resolutions in 1904 and 1916; Regent of the Smithsonian Institution; appointed by President Roosevelt a member of the Alaskan Boundary Tribunal in 1903; member of the United States Immigration Commission 1907–1910; overseer of Harvard University from 1911 until his death; president of the Harvard Alumni in 1914; president of the Massachusetts Historical Society in 1915;

elected majority leader of the Senate in August 1918 and served until his death; represented the United States as a member of the Conference on Limitation of Armament in 1921; died in Cambridge, Mass., on November 9, 1924; interment in Mount Auburn Cemetery.

LODGE, Henry Cabot, Jr. (grandson of the preceding, brother of John Davis Lodge, and nephew of Augustus P. Gardner), a Senator from Massachusetts; born in Nahant, Essex County, Mass., on July 5, 1902; was graduated from Middlesex School, Concord, Mass., in 1920 and from Harvard University, Cambridge, Mass., in 1924; engaged in newspaper work 1924–1931; served as representative to the General Court of Massachusetts 1933–1936; delegate at large to the Republican National Convention at Philadelphia in 1940; elected as a Republican to the United States Senate in 1936 and again in 1942, and served from January 3, 1937, until his resignation on February 3, 1944, to go on active duty during World War II in the United States Army; an active member of the Army's Organized Reserve since 1925, and had reached the grade of captain, Armored Force, when on August 1, 1941, went on extended active duty; in the spring of 1942, the War Department sent a series of tank detachments to engage in actual combat in Libya as part of the British Eighth Army, after which they returned, as planned, to the United States so that their experience might be used as a nucleus for training new units; was sent to Libya as a member of the first of these detachments and saw service in May and June during the operations near El Adem as well as in the retreat from Tobruk to El Alamein; performed regular troop duty and acted as an observer, making reports of his findings to the War Department and Armored Force Headquarters on his return; Secretary of War Stimson in July 1942 denied his request for further field service, stating that "at this critical juncture, skilled legislators who fully comprehend the requirements of the military service are as important to the Army as soldiers in combat"; resigned from the Senate February 3, 1944, in order again to go on combat duty in the Army, being the first United States Senator since the Civil War to leave the Senate in order to go to war; served in the Mediterranean and European theaters; awarded the Legion of Merit Medal, Bronze Star Medal, French Legion d'Honneur, Croix de Guerre with Palm, and European-African-Middle Eastern Campaign Ribbon with five bronze stars and one bronze arrowhead; active duty ended on December 2, 1945; again elected to the United States Senate in 1946 and served from January 3, 1947, to January 3, 1953; unsuccessful candidate for reelection in 1952; United States representative to the United Nations from February 1953 until his resignation September 3, 1960; Republican nominee for Vice President of the United States in 1960; is a resident of Beverly, Mass.

LODGE, John Davis (grandson of Henry Cabot Lodge, brother of Henry Cabot Lodge, Jr., and nephew of Augustus P. Gardner), a Representative from Connecticut; born in Washington, D. C., October 20, 1903; attended the Evans School, Mesa, Ariz., the Middlesex School, Concord, Mass., and Ecole de Droit, Paris, France; was graduated from Harvard College, Cambridge, Mass., in 1925 and from the Harvard Law School in 1929; was admitted to the New York bar in 1932 and commenced practice in New York, N. Y.; affiliated with the motion-picture industry and the theater 1933–1942; during World War II served with the United States Navy as a lieutenant and lieutenant commander for three and a half years, August 1942 to January 1946, of which time more than twenty months were spent overseas as liaison officer between the French and American fleets; was decorated with the rank of Chevalier in the French Legion of Honor and with the Croix de Guerre with Palm by General de Gaulle; engaged in research work in economics; elected as a Republican to the Eightieth and Eighty-first Congresses (January 3, 1947–January 3, 1951); was not a candidate for renomination in 1950; Governor of Connecticut from January 1951 to January 1955; unsuccessful for reelection as Governor in 1954; United States Ambassador to Spain from January 1955 until January 1961; is a resident of Westport, Conn.

LOFLAND, James Rush, a Representative from Delaware; born in Milford, Del., November 2, 1823; received a classical education and was graduated from Delaware College (now the University of Delaware) at Newark in 1845; studied law; was admitted to the bar in 1848 and commenced practice in Milford; secretary of the State senate in 1849; member of the State constitutional convention in 1853; secretary of state of Delaware 1855–1859; paymaster in the United States Army 1863–1867; delegate to the Republican National Convention at Philadelphia in 1872 which nominated Grant and Wilson; elected as a Republican to the Forty-third Congress (March 4, 1873–March 3, 1875); unsuccessful candidate for reelection in 1874 to the Forty-fourth Congress; resumed the practice of law; died in Milford, Kent County, Del., on February 10, 1894; interment in the Odd Fellows Cemetery.

LOFT, George William, a Representative from New York; born in New York City February 6, 1865; attended the public schools; engaged in the manufacture of candy from early boyhood; director in several corporations; presidential elector on the Democratic ticket of Wilson and Marshall in 1912 and the ticket of Davis and Bryan in 1924; elected as a Democrat to the Sixty-third Congress to fill the vacancy caused by the death of Timothy D. Sullivan; reelected in 1914 to the Sixty-fourth Congress and served from November 4, 1913, to March 3, 1917; was not a candidate for renomination in 1916; resumed the candy manufacturing business until 1929, when he founded the South Shore Trust Co. in Rockville Centre, Nassau County, N. Y., and served as president until his death; also interested in other financial institutions; died in Baldwin, Nassau County, N. Y., November 6, 1943; interment in St. Raymond's Cemetery, Westchester, New York City, N. Y.

LOFTIN, Scott Marion, a Senator from Florida; born in Montgomery, Montgomery County, Ala., September 14, 1878; moved to Pensacola, Fla., with his parents in 1887; attended the public schools and Washington and Lee University at Lexington, Va.; studied law; was admitted to the bar in 1899 and commenced practice in Pensacola, Fla.; member of the State house of representatives 1903–1905; prosecuting attorney of Escambia County 1904–1917; moved to Jacksonville, Fla., in 1917 to continue the practice of law; president of the University of Florida Endowment Corporation in 1925; member of the United States Law Review Advisory Board 1925–1935; member of the Washington Crime Conference in 1935; member of the Attorney General's Advisory Committee on Crime in 1934; member of the committee to assist the United States Supreme Court in revision of rules of practice in Federal courts 1935–1953; receiver of Florida East Coast Railway 1931–1941, and general counsel and trustee 1941–1953; appointed as a Democrat to the United States Senate to fill the vacancy caused by the death of Park Trammell and served from May 26 to November 3, 1936, when a successor was elected; was not a candidate for election to fill the vacancy; resumed the practice of law in Jacksonville, Fla., until his death in Highlands, N. C., September 22, 1953, where he had been vacationing; interment in Oaklawn Cemetery, Jacksonville, Fla.

LOGAN, George, a Senator from Pennsylvania; born at Stenton, Philadelphia County, Pa., September 9, 1753; at the age of nine he was sent to England, where he attended school; was graduated in medicine from the University of Edinburgh, Scotland, in 1779; devoted himself to scientific farming; member of the State house of representatives; went to France in 1798 to treat unofficially for a better understanding between the two Governments, which action was subsequently responsible for the passage of the so-called Logan Act; appointed and subsequently elected as a Democrat to the United States Senate to fill the vacancy caused by the resignation of John Peter G. Muhlenberg and served from July 13, 1801, to March 3, 1807; declined to be a candidate for reelection; went to England in 1810 on a private diplomatic mission as an emissary of peace, but was not successful; published several agricultural pamphlets; died at Stenton, near Philadelphia, Pa., April 9, 1821; interment in the Logan Graveyard in Stenton Park, Philadelphia, Pa.

LOGAN, Henry, a Representative from Pennsylvania; born near Dillsburg, Monaghan Township, York County, Pa., on April 14, 1784; attended the common schools; engaged in agricultural pursuits; volunteered for the defense of Baltimore in 1814; captain in the Nineteenth Regiment, Second Brigade, Fifth Division, Pennsylvania Militia, and was commissioned lieutenant colonel August 1, 1814; member of the State house of representatives in 1818 and 1819; served in the State senate 1828–1831; elected as a Democrat to the Twenty-fourth and Twenty-fifth Congresses (March 4, 1835–March 3, 1839); was not a candidate for renomination; resumed farming; member of the Board of Commissioners of York County in 1840; served as county auditor; died on the Logania plantation in Monaghan Township, near Dillsburg, Pa., December 26, 1866; interment in the Presbyterian Church Cemetery, Dillsburg, Pa.

LOGAN, John Alexander, a Representative and a Senator from Illinois; born in Murphysboro, Jackson County, Ill., on February 9, 1826; attended the common schools and was graduated from the University of Louisville; served in the war with Mexico; second lieutenant in the First Illinois Infantry May 10, 1847; honorably mustered out October 16, 1848; returned to Illinois; clerk of the Jackson County Court in 1849; studied law and was graduated from the law department of the University of Louisville in 1851; was admitted to the bar in 1852 and practiced; member of the Illinois House of Representatives in 1852, 1853, 1856, and 1857; prosecuting attorney for the third judicial district of Illinois 1853–1857; presidential elector on the Democratic ticket of Buchanan and Breckinridge in 1856; elected as a Democrat to the Thirty-sixth and Thirty-seventh Congresses and served from March 4, 1859, until April 2, 1862, when he resigned and entered the Union Army; during the Civil War was commissioned colonel of the Thirty-first Illinois Infantry September 18, 1861; brigadier general of Volunteers March 21, 1862; major general of Volunteers November 29, 1862, and served until August 17, 1865; appointed Minister to Mexico in 1865, but declined; elected as a Republican to the Fortieth, Forty-first, and Forty-second Congresses and served from March 4, 1867, until his resignation on March 3, 1871, at the end of the Forty-first Congress, having been elected Senator; one of the managers appointed by the House of Representatives in 1868 to conduct the impeachment proceedings against Andrew Johnson, President of the United States; elected to the United States Senate and served from March 4, 1871, to March 3, 1877; resumed the practice of law in Chicago; again elected to the United States Senate in 1879; reelected, and served from March 4, 1879, until his death; was the Republican nominee for Vice President on the ticket with James G. Blaine in 1884; died in Washington, D. C., December 26, 1886; interment in a tomb in the National Cemetery, Soldiers' Home, Washington, D. C.

LOGAN, Marvel Mills, a Senator from Kentucky; born on a farm near Brownsville, Edmonson County, Ky., January 7, 1875; educated in the public and private schools at Leitchfield and Brownsville, Ky.; taught school for two years and also conducted a training school for teachers; studied law; was admitted to the bar in 1896 and commenced practice in Brownsville, Ky.; served as chairman of the Edmonson County Democratic executive committee 1896–1912; served as chairman of the board of trustees of Brownsville; served as county attorney of Edmonson County in 1902 and 1903; assistant attorney general of Kentucky 1912–1915; served as attorney general of Kentucky 1915–1917; chairman of the State Democratic convention in 1916; chairman of the Kentucky Tax Commission in 1917 and 1918; moved to Louisville, Ky., in 1918 and to Bowling Green, Ky., in 1922 and continued the practice of law; member of the State board of education, the State board of sinking fund commissioners, and the State board of printing commissioners; served as a justice of the court of appeals of Kentucky 1926–1930 and as chief justice in 1931; elected as a Democrat to the United States Denate in 1930; reelected in 1936 and served from March 4, 1931, until his death; appointed a member of Board of Regents, Smithsonian Institution in 1933; died in Washington, D. C., October 3, 1939, interment in the Logan family cemetery near Brownsville, Ky.

LOGAN, William, a Senator from Kentucky; born within the fort at Harrodsburg, Mercer County, Ky., December 8, 1776; spent his early childhood in the fort at St. Asaphs, receiving private instruction from his parents and tutors; moved with his parents to Shelby County, Ky., about 1798; studied law; was admitted to the bar and practiced; delegate to the State constitutional convention in 1799; served as a commissioner of the Kentucky River Co. in 1820; member of the State house of representatives 1803–1806 and in 1808 and served as speaker two terms; judge of the court of appeals 1808–1812; presidential elector in 1808, 1812, and 1816; elected as a Democrat to the United States Senate and served from March 4, 1819, to May 28, 1820, when he resigned to become a gubernatorial candidate; unsuccessful candidate for Governor in 1820; died at his residence in Shelby County on August 8, 1822; interment in the Logan family burial ground near Shelbyville, Ky.

LOGAN, William Turner, a Representative from South Carolina; born in Summerville, Dorchester County, S. C., June 21, 1874; attended the public schools, and was graduated from the College of Charleston, South Carolina, in 1895; studied law at the University of Virginia, Charlottesville, Va.; was admitted to the bar in 1895 and commenced practice in Charleston, Charleston County, S. C.; member of the State house of representatives 1900-1904; corporation counsel of Charleston 1914–1918; chairman of the Democratic executive committee of Charleston County 1916–1918; chairman of the city Democratic executive committee 1918–1922 and reelected in 1922; elected as a Democrat to the Sixty-seventh and Sixty-eighth Congresses (March 4, 1921–March 3, 1925); unsuccessful candidate for renomination in 1924; continued the practice of his profession in Charleston, S. C., until his death in that city on September 15, 1941; interment in Magnolia Cemetery.

LOGUE, James Washington, a Representative from Pennsylvania; born in Philadelphia, Pa., February 22, 1863; attended the public schools and was graduated from La Salle College, Philadelphia, Pa.; studied law; was admitted to the bar in 1888 and commenced the practice of his profession in Philadelphia; elected as a Democrat to the Sixty-third Congress (March 4, 1913–March 3, 1915); unsuccessful candidate for reelection in 1914 to the Sixty-fourth Congress; unsuccessful candidate for Lieutenant Governor of Pennsylvania in 1918; resumed the practice of law in Philadelphia; member of the speakers' bureau of the Council of National Defense during the First World War; secretary of the board of inspectors of the Eastern Penitentiary in 1923; died in Philadelphia, Pa., August 27, 1925; interment in Holy Sepulchre Cemetery.

LONDON, Meyer, a Representative from New York; born in Kalvaria, Russia, December 29, 1871; attended a primary school and also received private instruction, principally in languages; immigrated to the United States October 1, 1891, and settled in New York City; admitted to citizenship in the United States in 1896; studied law; was admitted to the bar in 1896 and practiced in New York City; active in the Socialist and labor movements for more than thirty years; leader of the garment workers' strike in New York City in 1910; elected as a Socialist to the Sixty-fourth and Sixty-fifth Congresses (March 4, 1915–March 3, 1919); unsuccessful candidate for reelection in 1918 to the Sixty-sixth Congress; elected to the Sixty-seventh Congress (March 4, 1921–March 3, 1923); unsuccessful candidate for reelection in 1922 to the Sixty-eighth Congress; engaged in the practice of law until his death in New York City on June 6, 1926, as the result of an automobile accident; interment in "Writers' Lane," a plot in Mount Carmel Cemetery especially set aside for Jewish people who had attained prominence in New York City.

LONERGAN, Augustine, a Representative and a Senator from Connecticut; born in Thompson, Windham County, Conn., May 20, 1874; attended the public schools of Rockville and Bridgeport; was graduated from the law department of Yale University, New Haven, Conn., in 1902; was admitted to the bar in 1901 and commenced practice in Hartford, Conn.; member of the American and State Bar Associations; member of the city planning commission 1910–1912; assistant corporation counsel of Hartford 1910–1912; elected as a Democrat to the Sixty-third Congress (March 4, 1913–March 3, 1915); unsuccessful candidate for reelection in 1914 to the Sixty-fourth Congress; chairman of the Democratic State conventions in 1918 and 1934; delegate to the Democratic National Convention at San Francisco in 1920; elected to the Sixty-fifth and Sixty-sixth Congresses (March 4, 1917–March 3, 1921); was not a candidate for renomination in 1920, having become a candidate for United States Senator; unsuccessful candidate for election to the United States Senate in 1920 and again in 1928; resumed the practice of law in Hartford, Conn.; elected to the Seventy-second Congress (March 4, 1931–March 3, 1933); was not a candidate for renomination in 1932, having become a candidate for United States Senator; elected to the United States Senate in 1932 and served from March 4, 1933, to January 3, 1939; unsuccessful candidate for reelection in 1938; engaged in the practice of law in Washington, D. C., until his death there on October 18, 1947; interment in Mount St. Benedict's Cemetery, Hartford, Conn.

LONG, Alexander, a Representative from Ohio; born in Greenville, Mercer County, Pa., December 24, 1816; received an academic training; studied law; was admitted to the bar and commenced practice in Cincinnati, Ohio; member of the State house of representatives in 1848 and 1849; elected as a Democrat to the Thirty-eighth Congress (March 4, 1863–March 3, 1865); unsuccessful candidate for reelection in 1864 to the Thirty-ninth Congress; resumed the practice of law in Cincinnati, Ohio; delegate to the Democratic National Conventions in 1864, 1868, 1872, and 1876; died in Cincinnati, Ohio, November 28, 1886; interment in Spring Grove Cemetery.

LONG, Chester Isaiah, a Representative and a Senator from Kansas; born in Greenwood Township, near Millerstown, Perry

County, Pa., October 12, 1860; moved with his parents to Daviess County, Mo., in 1865 and to Paola, Kans., in 1879; attended the country schools and was graduated from the normal school at Paola, Kans.; taught school for several years; studied law; was admitted to the bar March 4, 1885, and commenced practice in Medicine Lodge, Kans.; member of the State senate 1889–1893; unsuccessful candidate for election in 1892 to the Fifty-third Congress; elected as a Republican to the Fifty-fourth Congress (March 4, 1895–March 3, 1897); unsuccessful candidate for reelection in 1896 to the Fifty-fifth Congress; elected to the Fifty-sixth, Fifty-seventh, and Fifty-eighth Congresses and served from March 4, 1899, until his resignation, effective March 4, 1903, before the commencement of the Fifty-eighth Congress, to become Senator; elected to the United States Senate and served from March 4, 1903, to March 3, 1909; unsuccessful candidate for renomination in 1908; moved to Wichita in 1911 and continued the practice of law; chairman of the commission to revise the general statutes of Kansas 1921–1923; moved to Washington, D. C., in 1926 and continued the practice of law; died in Washington, D. C., July 1, 1934; interment in Old Mission Cemetery, Wichita, Kans.

LONG, Edward Henry Carroll, a Representative from Maryland; born in Princess Anne, Somerset County, Md., September 28, 1808; attended the common schools and was graduated from Yale College in 1828; studied law; was admitted to the bar in 1830 and commenced practice in Princess Anne, Somerset County; also engaged in agricultural pursuits; member of the State house of delegates 1833–1835, 1839, 1844, and 1861; served in the State senate in 1860; elected as a Whig to the Twenty-ninth Congress (March 4, 1845–March 3, 1847); was not a candidate for renomination in 1846; resumed the practice of his profession and also engaged in agricultural pursuits; was an unsuccessful candidate for election to the United States Senate in 1860; died in Princess Anne, Somerset County, Md., on October 16, 1865; interment in the family burying ground on his farm, "Catalpa," near Princess Anne, Md.

LONG, Edward Vaughn, a Senator from Missouri; born in Lincoln County, near Whiteside, Mo., July 18, 1908; attended the public schools of Lincoln County, Culver-Stockton College, and the University of Missouri; was admitted to the bar in 1936 and commenced the practice of law in Bowling Green, Mo.; prosecuting attorney of Pike County 1937–1941; city attorney of Bowling Green, Mo., 1941–1945; member of the State senate 1945–1955, serving as majority floor leader in the Sixty-fifth General Assembly in 1952 and president pro tempore in the Sixty-eighth General Assembly in 1955; elected Lieutenant Governor of Missouri in 1956 for a four-year term beginning in January 1957 and served until his resignation September 23, 1960; appointed as a Democrat to the United States Senate September 23, 1960, and elected November 8, 1960, to fill the vacancy caused by the death of Thomas C. Hennings, Jr., in the term ending January 3, 1963.

LONG, George Shannon (brother of Huey Pierce Long, brother-in-law of Rose McConnell Long, and uncle of Russell Billiu Long), a Representative from Louisiana; born in a log cabin on a small farm in Tunica, West Feliciana Parish, seven miles from Winnfield, La., September 11, 1883; when five years of age moved with his parents to Winnfield, Winn Parish, La.; attended the public schools and Mount Lebanon College (now Louisiana College) 1897–1899; taught school in Winn and Grant Parishes; studied dentistry in Atlanta, Ga., Louisville, Ky., and New Orleans, La.; practiced dentistry in Oklahoma 1904–1935; during the First World War was in Officers' Training School at Waco, Tex., when peace was declared; studied law; was admitted

to the Oklahoma bar in 1923; member of Oklahoma State House of Representatives 1920–1922; practiced dentistry in Monroe, La., 1935–1940, and Pineville, La., 1948–1950; superintendent of Louisiana Colony and Training School 1948–1950; institutional inspector 1950–1952; delegate to the Democratic National Convention in 1948; unsuccessful for the Democratic nomination for Congress in 1948 and 1950; founder and director of the Dr. George S. Long Corp.; elected as a Democrat to the Eighty-third, Eighty-fourth, and Eighty-fifth Congresses and served from January 3, 1953 until his death in the naval hospital at Bethesda, Md., March 22, 1958; interment in Greenwood Memorial Park, Pineville, La.

LONG, Huey Pierce (husband of Rose McConnell Long, father of Russell B. Long, and brother of George S. Long), a Senator from Louisiana; born on a farm near Winnfield, Winn Parish, La., August 30, 1893; attended the public schools at Winnfield and Oklahoma University at Norman, Okla.; was engaged as a book peddler, auctioneer, and salesman; moved to Memphis, Tenn., in 1912 and served as sales manager for a local concern; studied law at Tulane University, New Orleans, La.; was admitted to the bar in 1915 and commenced practice in Winnfield; elected railroad commissioner (later called public service commission) in 1918, when he moved to Shreveport, La., serving until 1928, and was commission chairman 1924–1928; unsuccessful candidate for the Democratic nomination for Governor of Louisiana in 1924; Democratic National committeeman 1928–1935; elected Governor of Louisiana in 1928 and served from May 21, 1928, until his resignation effective January 25, 1932, having previously been elected Senator; elected as a Democrat to the United States Senate in 1930 for the term commencing March 4, 1931, but did not assume these duties until January 25, 1932, preferring to continue as Governor, and served until his death; chairman of the Democratic State central committee in 1934 and 1935; died in Baton Rouge, La., September 10, 1935, from the effect of a gunshot wound received in the State Capitol Building on September 8, 1935; interment in the Capitol Grounds at Baton Rouge, La.

LONG, Jefferson Franklin, a Representative from Georgia; born near Knoxville, Crawford County, Ga., March 3, 1836; was of the Negro race; educated himself; became a merchant tailor in Macon, Ga.; elected as a Republican to the Forty-first Congress to fill the vacancy caused by the House declaring Samuel F. Gove not entitled to the seat and served from December 22, 1870, to March 3, 1871; was not a candidate for renomination in 1870; delegate to the Republican National Convention at Chicago in 1880 which nominated Garfield and Arthur; resumed business in Macon, Ga., and died there February 5, 1900; interment in Lynwood Cemetery.

LONG, John, a Representative from North Carolina; born in Loudoun County, Va., February 26, 1785; moved with his parents to North Carolina, who settled at Longs Mill (now Liberty), Randolph County; attended private and public schools; engaged in agricultural pursuits in Randolph County, N. C.; served in the State house of representatives in 1811 and 1812; member of the State senate in 1814 and 1815; elected as a Whig to the Seventeenth and to the three succeeding Congresses (March 4, 1821–March 3, 1829); unsuccessful candidate for reelection in 1828 to the Twenty-first Congress; resumed his agricultural pursuits; died at Longs Mill (now Liberty), Randolph County, N. C., August 11, 1857; interment in Richland Graveyard.

LONG, John Benjamin, a Representative from Texas; born in Douglass, Nacogdoches County, Tex., September 8, 1843; moved with his parents to Rusk, Tex., in 1846; educated in private schools; during the Civil War served in the Confederate Army in Company C, Third Texas Cavalry; was twice severely wounded; studied law; was admitted to the bar but never practiced; became a planter; elected as a Democrat to the Fifty-second Congress (March 4, 1891–March 3, 1893); unsuccessful candidate for renomination in 1892; engaged in the newspaper business in Rusk, Tex., 1886–1905; member of the State house of representatives in 1913 and 1914; died in Rusk, Cherokee County, Tex., April 27, 1924; interment in Cedar Hill Cemetery.

LONG, John Davis, a Representative from Massachusetts; born in Buckfield, Oxford County, Maine, October 27, 1838; attended the common schools at Buckfield and Hebron Academy, Maine; was graduated from the academic department of Harvard University in 1857; taught school in Westford Academy, Massachusetts; studied law at Harvard Law School and in private offices; was admitted to the bar in 1861 and commenced practice in Buckfield, Maine; moved to Boston, Mass., in 1863 and continued the practice of law, and in 1869 moved to Hingham, Mass.; member of the State house of representatives 1875–1878 and served the last three years as speaker of the house; Lieutenant Governor of Massachusetts in 1879; Governor of Massachusetts 1880–1882; elected as a Republican to the Forty-eighth, Forty-ninth, and Fiftieth Congresses (March 4, 1883–March 3, 1889); declined to be a candidate for renomination in 1888; continued the practice of his profession in Boston; appointed Secretary of the Navy in the Cabinet of President McKinley and served from March 5, 1897, until May 1, 1902, when he resigned; resumed the practice of law in Boston, with residence in Hingham, Mass.; president of overseers of Harvard University and of the Authors' Club of Boston; died in Hingham, Mass., August 28, 1915; interment in Hingham Cemetery.

LONG, Lewis Marshall, a Representative from Illinois; born in Gardner, Grundy County, Ill., June 22, 1883; attended the public schools of Aurora, Ill., the Plano (Ill.) High School, and the University of Illinois at Urbana; was graduated from the John Marshall Law School, Chicago, Ill., in 1929; was employed as a telegraph operator and station agent at Plano, Ill., and Sandwich, Ill., 1904–1930; was admitted to the bar in 1930 and commenced practice in Sandwich, Ill.; member of the board of aldermen 1922–1926; served as mayor of Sandwich in 1935 and 1936; member of the board of education 1932–1936; elected as a Democrat to the Seventy-fifth Congress (January 3, 1937–January 3, 1939); unsuccessful candidate for renomination in 1938 and for election in 1940 to the Seventy-seventh Congress; resumed the practice of law; served as chief examiner of the Division of Motor Carriers of the State of Illinois from November 1, 1939, to July 1, 1941, when he resigned to engage in motor carrier practice in addition to law practice; member of the National War Labor Board, Region VI, Chicago, Ill., from February 1943 to February 1947; died in Sandwich, Ill., September 9, 1957; interment in Oak Ridge Cemetery.

LONG, Oren Ethelbirt, a Senator from Hawaii; born in Altoona, Wilson County, Kans., March 4, 1889; attended the public schools; graduated from Johnson College, Kimberlin Heights, Tenn., in 1912, University of Michigan in 1916, and Columbia University in 1922; teacher of history, Johnson Academy, Kimberlin Heights, Tenn., 1912–1914, and principal 1914–1917; social settlement worker, Hilo, Hawaii, in 1917 and 1918; educational director, Army Y. M. C. A., Fort Shafter, Hawaii, in 1918 and 1919; vice principal of McKinley High School, Honolulu, Hawaii, in 1919 and 1920; personnel officer, Kohala Sugar Co., in 1920 and 1921; principal, Church Farm School, Glen Loch, Pa., 1922–1924, and Kauai High School, Hawaii, in 1924 and 1925; deputy superintendent of public

instruction for Hawaii 1925–1934, and superintendent of public instruction, Territory of Hawaii, 1934–1946; during World War II served as a lieutenant, Headquarters Staff, Hawaii Defense Volunteers; director, Department of Public Welfare in 1946; chairman, Advisory Committee on Education for Trust Territories in 1946; secretary of Territory of Hawaii 1946–1951; Governor of Territory of Hawaii 1951–1953; member and vice chairman, Hawaii Statehood Commission, 1954–1956; senator, Territory of Hawaii, 1956–1959; elected as a Democrat to the United States Senate on July 28, 1959, and upon the admission of Hawaii as a State into the Union on August 21, 1959, in the classification of Senators from that State, drew the four-year term beginning on that day and ending January 3, 1963.

LONG, Pierse, a Delegate from New Hampshire; born in Portsmouth, N. H., in 1739; completed preparatory studies; engaged in the shipping business; delegate to the Provincial Congress of New Hampshire in 1775; served in the Revolutionary War as colonel of the First New Hampshire Regiment and participated in the engagements at Ticonderoga and points on Lakes George and Champlain; was present at the surrender of General Burgoyne at Saratoga; brevetted a brigadier general; Member of the Continental Congress 1784–1786; State councilor 1786–1789; delegate to the State constitutional convention which ratified the Federal Constitution June 21, 1788; appointed by President Washington customs collector for the port of Portsmouth, N. H., in January 1789, but owing to ill health was unable to assume the duties of the office; died in Portsmouth, N. H., on April 13, 1789; interment in the Proprietors' Burying Ground.

LONG, Rose McConnell (widow of Huey Pierce Long, mother of Russell B. Long, and sister-in-law of George S. Long), a Senator from Louisiana; born in Greensburg, Decatur County, Ind., April 8, 1892; moved with her parents to Shreveport, La., in 1901; attended the public schools of Shreveport; appointed and subsequently elected as a Democrat to the United States Senate to fill the vacancy caused by the death of her husband, Huey P. Long, and served from January 31, 1936, to January 3, 1937; was not a candidate for reelection in 1936 for the full term; retired from public life and is a resident of Shreveport, La.

LONG, Russell Billiu (son of Huey Pierce Long and Rose McConnell Long, and nephew of George S. Long), a Senator from Louisiana; born in Shreveport, Caddo Parish, La., November 3, 1918; attended the public schools of Shreveport, Baton Rouge, and New Orleans, La.; was graduated from Louisiana State University at Baton Rouge in 1941 and from its law school in 1942; was admitted to the bar in 1942 and commenced practice in Baton Rouge, La., in 1946; during World War II served in the United States Naval Reserve from June 1942 until discharged as a lieutenant in December 1945 with service in North Africa, Sicily, Italy, and southern France; elected as a Democrat to the United States Senate on November 2, 1948, to fill the vacancy in the term ending January 3, 1951, caused by the death of John H. Overton and took his seat December 31, 1948; reelected in 1950 and again in 1956 for the term ending January 3, 1963.

LONGFELLOW, Stephen, a Representative from Maine; born in Gorham, Cumberland County, Maine (then a district of Massachusetts), June 23, 1775; was graduated from Harvard University in 1798; studied law; was admitted to the bar in 1801 and commenced practice in Portland, Maine; member of the general court of Massachusetts in 1814 and 1815; belonged to the Federalist Party and was a delegate to the Hartford convention in 1814 and 1815; Federalist presidential elector in 1816 and voted for King and Howard; elected to the Eighteenth

Congress (March 4, 1823–March 3, 1825); was not a candidate for renomination in 1824; resumed the practice of his profession; member of the State house of representatives in 1826; overseer of Bowdoin College, Brunswick, Maine, 1811–1817; a trustee of Bowdoin College 1817–1836; president of the Maine Historical Society in 1834; died in Portland, Maine, August 2, 1849; interment in the Western Cemetery.

LONGNECKER, Henry Clay, a Representative from Pennsylvania; born in Allen Township, Cumberland County, Pa., April 17, 1820; was graduated from the Norwich Military Academy of Vermont and from Lafayette College, Easton, Pa.; studied law; was admitted to the bar and practiced in Easton, Pa.; served during the Mexican War as first lieutenant, captain, and adjutant in all principal engagements under General Scott; was wounded at the Battle of Chapultepec September 13, 1847; returned to Pennsylvania; district attorney of Lehigh County 1848–1850; elected as a Republican to the Thirty-sixth Congress (March 4, 1859–March 3, 1861); during the Civil War participated in organizing Pennsylvania troops and served in the Union Army as colonel of the Ninth Regiment, Pennsylvania Volunteers; resumed the practice of his profession in Allentown, Pa., in 1865; associate judge of Lehigh County in 1867; died in Allentown, Lehigh County, Pa., September 16, 1871; interment in Fairview Cemetery.

LONGWORTH, Nicholas (nephew of Bellamy Storer), a Representative from Ohio; born in Cincinnati, Ohio, November 5, 1869; attended the Franklin School in Cincinnati, and was graduated from Harvard University in 1891; spent one year at Harvard Law School, and was graduated from the Cincinnati Law School in 1894; was admitted to the bar in 1894 and commenced practice in Cincinnati, Ohio; member of the board of education of Cincinnati in 1898; member of the State house of representatives in 1899 and 1900; served in the State senate 1901–1903; elected as a Republican to the Fifty-eighth and to the four succeeding Congresses (March 4, 1903–March 3, 1913); unsuccessful candidate for reelection in 1912 to the Sixty-third Congress; elected to the Sixty-fourth and to the eight succeeding Congresses and served from March 4, 1915, until his death; Republican majority floor leader during the Sixty-eighth Congress; Speaker of the House of Representatives during the Sixty-ninth, Seventieth, and Seventy-first Congresses; died in Aiken, S. C., while on a visit, April 9, 1931; interment in Spring Grove Cemetery, Cincinnati, Ohio.

LONGYEAR, John Wesley, a Representative from Michigan; born in Shandaken, Ulster County, N. Y., October 22, 1820; pursued classical studies in the Lima (N. Y.) Academy; taught school for several years; moved to Mason, Ingham County, Mich., in 1844 and taught school; studied law; was admitted to the Ingham County bar in 1846; moved to Lansing, Mich., in 1847 and engaged in the practice of law; elected as a Republican to the Thirty-eighth and Thirty-ninth Congresses (March 4, 1863–March 3, 1867); was not a candidate for renomination in 1866; delegate to the Loyalist Convention at Philadelphia, Pa., in 1866 and to the Michigan State constitutional convention in 1867; appointed by President Grant judge of the United States District Court for the Eastern District of Michigan February 7, 1870; moved to Detroit in 1871, where he died March 11, 1875; interment in Mount Hope Cemetery, Lansing, Mich.

LOOFBOUROW, Frederick Charles, a Representative from Utah; born in Atlantic, Cass County, Iowa, February 8, 1874; was educated in the common schools of Iowa; moved with his parents to Utah in 1889; was graduated from the Ogden Military Academy, Ogden, Utah, in 1892, and from the law department

of the University of California at Berkeley in 1896; was admitted to the bar the same year and commenced practice in Salt Lake City, Utah; district attorney of the third judicial district of Utah 1905–1911, and district judge 1911–1916; resumed the practice of law; elected as a Republican to the Seventy-first Congress to fill the vacancy caused by the death of Elmer O. Leatherwood and on the same day was elected to the Seventy-second Congress and served from November 4, 1930, to March 3, 1933; unsuccessful candidate for reelection in 1932 to the Seventy-third Congress and for election in 1934 to the Seventy-fourth Congress; resumed the practice of law in Salt Lake City, Utah, until his retirement; died in Salt Lake City, Utah, July 8, 1949; remains were cremated and the ashes scattered.

LOOMIS, Andrew Williams, a Representative from Ohio; born in Lebanon, Conn., June 27, 1797; was graduated in law from Union College, Schenectady, N. Y., in 1819; was admitted to the bar; moved to Canton, Ohio, and practiced; moved to New Lisbon (now Lisbon), Ohio; delegate to the National-Republican State convention at Columbus in 1827 and 1828; elected as a Whig to the Twenty-fifth Congress and served from March 4, 1837, until October 20, 1837, when he resigned; moved to Pittsburgh, Pa., in 1839 and resumed the practice of his profession; presidential elector on the Whig ticket of Taylor and Fillmore in 1848; member of the peace convention of 1861 held in Washington, D. C., in an effort to devise means to prevent the impending war; moved to Cleveland, Ohio, about 1868; died while on a visit to Cumberland, Md., August 24, 1873; interment in Allegheny Cemetery, Pittsburgh, Pa.

LOOMIS, Arphaxed, a Representative from New York; born in Winsted, Conn., April 9, 1798; moved to New York in 1801 with his parents, who settled upon a farm in the town of Salisbury, Herkimer County; attended the common schools and Fairfield Academy, Fairfield, N. Y.; studied law; was admitted to the bar at Albany in 1822 and commenced practice at Sackets Harbor, N. Y., the same year; returned to Salisbury in 1825; later in that year moved to Little Falls, N. Y., and continued the practice of his profession; surrogate of Herkimer County 1828–1836; commissioner to investigate the government and discipline of the State prisons in 1834; county judge of Herkimer County 1835–1840; elected as a Democrat to the Twenty-fifth Congress (March 4, 1837–March 3, 1839); was not a candidate for renomination in 1838; member of the State assembly in 1841 and 1842; member of the State constitutional convention in 1846; member of the commission to revise, abridge, and simplify pleadings and proceedings in civil actions in 1847; again a member of the State assembly in 1853 and 1854; delegate to the Democratic State conventions in 1861 and 1863; died at Little Falls, N. Y., September 15, 1885; interment in the Church Street Cemetery.

LOOMIS, Dwight, a Representative from Connecticut; born in Columbia, Tolland County, Conn., July 27, 1821; attended the common schools and academies in Monson and Amherst, Mass.; taught school; was graduated from the law department of Yale University in 1847; admitted to the bar the same year and commenced practice at Rockville, Conn.; member of the State house of representatives in 1851; delegate to the Republican National Convention at Philadelphia in 1856; member of the State senate 1857–1859; elected as a Republican to the Thirty-sixth and Thirty-seventh Congresses (March 4, 1859–March 3, 1863); was not a candidate for renomination in 1862; judge of the superior court of the State 1864–1875; justice of the supreme court of the State 1875–1891; moved to Hartford, Conn., in 1892; State referee from 1892 until his death in a train accident near Waterbury, Conn., September 17, 1903; interment in Grove Hill Cemetery, Rockville, Conn.

LORD, Bert, a Representative from New York; born in the town of Sanford, Broome County, N. Y., December 4, 1869; attended the public schools and the Afton (N. Y.) Union School and Academy; engaged in the mercantile business at Afton, N. Y., from 1893 to 1918, when he entered the lumber business and operated sawmills; served as supervisor of the town of Afton 1905–1915; member of the New York Assembly 1915–1922 and 1924–1929; served as commissioner of motor vehicles of the State of New York 1921–1923; member of the State senate 1929–1935; elected as a Republican to the Seventy-fourth, Seventy-fifth, and Seventy-sixth Congresses and served from January 3, 1935, until his death in Washington, D. C., May 24, 1939; interment in Glenwood Cemetery, Afton, N. Y.

LORD, Frederick William, a Representative from New York; born in Lyme, New London County, Conn., December 11, 1800; attended Lyme Academy, and was graduated from Yale College in 1821; professor of mathematics in Washington College, Chestertown, Md., for two years; in charge of an academy at Baltimore, Md., for three years; studied medicine in Baltimore and was graduated in medicine from Yale College in 1828; commenced the practice of medicine in Sag Harbor, N. Y., continuing in his profession there for fifteen years; delegate to the Whig National Convention at Harrisburg, Pa., in 1840; moved to Greenport, Long Island, N. Y., in 1846 and engaged in agricultural pursuits and the cultivation of fruit and ornamental trees; elected as a Whig to the Thirtieth Congress (March 4, 1847–March 3, 1849); resumed his former pursuits in Greenport; unsuccessful candidate for election in 1854 to the Thirty-fourth Congress and in 1856 to the Thirty-fifth Congress; elected a delegate to the Republican National Convention at Chicago in 1860, but on his way to attend the convention was taken ill on the steamer *Massachusetts,* and died in New York City May 24, 1860; interment in East Hampton Cemetery, East Hampton, Suffolk County, N. Y.

LORD, Henry William, a Representative from Michigan; born in Northampton, Mass., March 8, 1821; pursued an academic course; studied law, but did not practice; moved to Detroit, Mich., in 1839; four years later went to Pontiac, Mich., and engaged in agricultural and mercantile pursuits; returned to Detroit, Mich.; appointed by President Lincoln United States consul to Manchester, England, in 1861 and served until his resignation in 1867; served on the State board of corrections and charities 1871–1882; presidential elector on the Republican ticket of Hayes and Wheeler in 1876; elected as a Republican to the Forty-seventh Congress (March 4, 1881–March 3, 1883); unsuccessful candidate for reelection in 1882 to the Forty-eighth Congress; appointed by President Arthur register of the United States land office at Creelsburg, N. Dak., on August 1, 1883, continuing in that capacity after the office was transferred to Devils Lake, N. Dak., on January 17, 1884, and served until April 18, 1888; was killed in a railroad accident near Butte, Mont., January 25, 1891; interment in Elmwood Cemetery, Detroit, Mich.

LORD, Scott, a Representative from New York; born in Nelson, Madison County, N. Y., December 11, 1820; attended the common schools and the local academies at Morrisville and Geneseo; studied law; was admitted to the bar in 1842 and commenced practice in Mount Morris, Livingston County, N. Y.; moved to Geneseo, the county seat, in 1847; judge of Livingston County 1847–1856; resumed the practice of law; moved to Utica, Oneida County, N. Y., in 1872 and continued the practice of his profession; elected as a Democrat to the Forty-fourth Congress (March 4, 1875–March 3, 1877); one of the managers appointed by the House of Representatives in 1876 to conduct the im-peachment proceedings against William W. Belknap, ex-Secretary of War; unsuccessful candidate for reelection in 1876 to the Forty-fifth Congress; moved to New York City in 1877 and again engaged in the practice of law; died in Morris Plains, Morris County, N. J., September 10, 1885; interment in Temple Hill Cemetery, Geneseo, N. Y.

LORE, Charles Brown, a Representative from Delaware; born in Odessa, New Castle County, Del., March 16, 1831; attended the public schools and Middletown Academy, Delaware; was graduated from Dickinson College, Carlisle, Pa., in June 1852; studied law; was admitted to the bar of New Castle County, Del., in 1861 and practiced; clerk of the State house of representatives in 1857; during the Civil War served as commissioner of the draft for New Castle County, Del., in 1862; attorney general of Delaware 1869–1874; presidential elector on the Democratic ticket of Hancock and English in 1880; elected as a Democrat to the Forty-eighth and Forty-ninth Congresses (March 4, 1883–March 3, 1887); was not a candidate for renomination; presidential elector on the Democratic ticket of Cleveland and Stevenson in 1892; appointed chief justice of the supreme court of Delaware in 1893; reappointed in 1897 for a term of twelve years but retired in 1909; member of the code commission in 1909 and 1910; died in Wilmington, Del., March 6, 1911; remains were cremated and the ashes deposited in the Methodist Church Cemetery.

LORIMER, William, a Representative and a Senator from Illinois; born in Manchester, England, April 27, 1861; immigrated to the United States in 1866 with his parents, who settled in Michigan; moved to Chicago, Ill., in 1870; self-educated; apprenticed to the trade of sign painter at the age of ten; worked in the packing houses and for a street railroad company; engaged in the real-estate business, and later as a builder and brick manufacturer; delegate to the Republican National Convention at Minneapolis in 1892; elected as a Republican to the Fifty-fourth, Fifty-fifth, and Fifty-sixth Congresses (March 4, 1895–March 3, 1901); unsuccessful candidate for reelection in 1900 to the Fifty-seventh Congress; elected to the Fifty-eighth and to the three succeeding Congresses and served from March 4, 1903, until his resignation, effective June 17, 1909, having been elected Senator; presented credentials as a Senator-elect to the United States Senate for the term commencing March 4, 1909, and served from June 18, 1909, until July 13, 1912, when the Senate adopted a resolution declaring "that corrupt methods and practices were employed in his election, and that the election, therefore, was invalid"; resumed his former pursuits and was president of La Salle Street Trust & Savings Bank 1910–1915; subsequently engaged in the lumber business; died in Chicago, Ill., September 13, 1934; interment in Calvary Cemetery.

LORING, George Bailey, a Representative from Massachusetts; born in North Andover, Essex County, Mass., November 8, 1817; attended Franklin Academy at Andover; taught school; was graduated from the academic department of Harvard University in 1838 and from the medical department in 1842; practiced medicine for a short time in North Andover; surgeon of the marine hospital at Chelsea, Mass., 1843–1850; surgeon of the Seventh Regiment, Massachusetts Volunteer Militia, 1842–1844; appointed commissioner to revise the United States marine hospital system in 1849; moved to Salem, Mass., in 1851; appointed postmaster of Salem on May 4, 1853, and served until his successor was appointed on February 16, 1858; member of the State house of representatives in 1866 and 1867; chairman of the Massachusetts State Republican committee 1869–1876; served in the State senate 1873–1876 and was also president of that body; delegate to the Republican National Conventions in

1868, 1872, and 1876; appointed United States centennial commissioner for the State of Massachusetts in 1872; elected as a Republican to the Forty-fifth and Forty-sixth Congresses (March 4, 1877–March 3, 1881); unsuccessful candidate for renomination in 1880; United States Commissioner of Agriculture 1881–1885; appointed United States Minister to Portugal, in 1889 and served until his resignation in 1890; died in Salem, Mass., on September 13, 1891; interment in Harmony Grove Cemetery.

LOSER, Joseph Carlton, a Representative from Tennessee; born in Nashville, Davidson County, Tenn., October 1, 1892; educated in the public schools and the Y. M. C. A. Law School; member of Tennessee National Guard in 1910; secretary to the mayor of Nashville 1917–1920; graduated from Cumberland University, Lebanon, Tenn., in 1923; was admitted to the bar in 1922 and commenced the practice of law in Nashville, Tenn., in 1923; assistant city attorney of Nashville 1923–1929; assistant district attorney general of the tenth judicial circuit 1929–1934 and district attorney 1934–1956; delegate to the Democratic National Conventions in 1944, 1952, and 1960; member of the United States Coast Guard Reserve in 1944; presidential elector in 1956; secretary of Democratic Executive Committee of Tennessee 1954–1958; elected as a Democrat to the Eighty-fifth and Eighty-sixth Congresses (January 3, 1957–January 3, 1961). *Reelected to the Eighty-seventh Congress.*

LOUD, Eugene Francis, a Representative from California; born in Abington, Plymouth County, Mass., March 12, 1847; went to sea and afterward settled in California; during the Civil War enlisted in a California Cavalry battalion in 1862, which formed a part of the Second Regiment, Massachusetts Volunteer Cavalry; served with the Army of the Potomac and with Sheridan in the Shenandoah Valley until the close of the war; returned to California; engaged in mining and as clerk for fifteen years; studied law; clerk in the customs service at San Francisco, Calif.; member of the State assembly in 1884; cashier of the city and county of San Francisco; elected as a Republican to the Fifty-second and to the five succeeding Congresses (March 4, 1891–March 3, 1903); unsuccessful candidate for reelection in 1902 to the Fifty-eighth Congress; retired from public life and active business pursuits; died in San Francisco, Calif., December 19, 1908; remains were cremated and the ashes interred in the Odd Fellows Cemetery.

LOUD, George Alvin, a Representative from Michigan; born in Bracebridge, Ohio, June 18, 1852; moved with his parents to Massachusetts in 1856 and to Au Sable, Mich., in 1866; attended the English High School, Boston, Mass., and Professor Patterson's School at Detroit, Mich.; was graduated from the Ann Arbor High School in 1869; vice president and general manager of the Au Sable & Northwestern Railroad; for four years was a colonel on the staff of Governor Pingree; paymaster on the U. S. revenue cutter *McCulloch* when it participated in the Battle of Manila Bay during the Spanish-American War; elected as a Republican to the Fifty-eighth and to the four succeeding Congresses (March 4, 1903–March 3, 1913); unsuccessful candidate for reelection; elected to the Sixty-fourth Congress (March 4, 1915–March 3, 1917); unsuccessful candidate for renomination; engaged in the lumber business at Au Sable, Mich.; killed in an automobile accident at Myrtle Point, Mich., November 13, 1925; interment in Au Sable Cemetery, Oscoda, Mich.

LOUDENSLAGER, Henry Clay, a Representative from New Jersey; born in Mauricetown, Cumberland County, N. J., May 22, 1852; moved with his parents to Paulsboro, N. J., in 1856; attended the common schools; engaged in the produce commission business in Philadelphia, Pa., 1872–1882; county clerk of Gloucester County, N. J., 1882–1892; elected as a Republican to the Fifty-third and to the nine succeeding Congresses and served from March 4, 1893, until his death in Paulsboro, Gloucester County, N. J., August 12, 1911; interment in Eglington Cemetery, Clarksboro, N. J.

LOUGHRIDGE, William, a Representative from Iowa; born in Youngstown, Mahoning County, Ohio, July 11, 1827; attended the common schools: studied law; was admitted to the bar in 1849 and commenced practice in Mansfield, Ohio; moved to Iowa in 1852 and settled in Oskaloosa, Mahaska County; member of the State senate 1857–1860; judge of the sixth judicial circuit of Iowa 1861–1867; elected as a Republican to the Fortieth and Forty-first Congresses (March 4, 1867–March 3, 1871); elected to the Forty-third Congress (March 4, 1873–March 3, 1875); died near Reading, Pa., September 26, 1889; interment in Forest Cemetery, Oskaloosa, Iowa.

LOUNSBERY, William, a Representative from New York; born at Stone Ridge, Ulster County, N. Y., December 25, 1831; was graduated from Rutgers College, New Brunswick, N. J., in 1851; attended the law department of the New York University in Albany, N. Y.; was admitted to the bar in 1853 and engaged in practice; during the Civil War was commissary of the Twentieth Regiment, New York Militia, with the rank of first lieutenant, during its three months' service; member of the State assembly in 1868; mayor of Kingston 1878–1880; elected as a Democrat to the Forty-sixth Congress (March 4, 1879–March 3, 1881); died in Kingston, N. Y., November 8, 1905; interment in the Wiltwyck Rural Cemetery.

LOUTTIT, James Alexander, a Representative from California; born in New Orleans, La., October 16, 1848; moved with his parents to California in 1849, who settled in Calaveras County; attended private and public schools and the State normal school at Sacramento; studied law; was admitted to the bar in 1869; settled in Stockton, Calif., in 1871 and practiced law; prosecuting attorney of Stockton 1871–1879; elected as a Republican to the Forty-ninth Congress (March 4, 1885–March 3, 1887); was not a candidate for renomination in 1886; resumed the practice of law in Stockton, Calif.; died in Pacific Grove, Monterey County, Calif., July 26, 1906; interment in the Stockton Rural Cemetery, Stockton, Calif.

LOVE, Francis Johnson, a Representative from West Virginia; born in Cadiz, Harrison County, Ohio, on January 23, 1901; attended the public schools and was graduated from Cadiz High School in 1919 and from Bethany College at Bethany, W. Va., in 1924; principal of Warwood High School in Wheeling, W. Va., 1926–1929; was graduated from the West Virginia University Law School at Morgantown in 1932; was admitted to the bar the same year and commenced practice in Wheeling, W. Va.; elected as a Republican to the Eightieth Congress (January 3, 1947–January 3, 1949); unsuccessful candidate for reelection in 1948 to the Eighty-first Congress; resumed the general practice of law; is a resident of Wheeling, W. Va.

LOVE, James, a Representative from Kentucky; born in Nelson County, Ky., May 12, 1795; attended the common schools in Bardstown, Ky.; volunteered at the age of eighteen and served during the War of 1812; studied law; was admitted to the bar and commenced practice in Barboursville, Knox County, Ky.; member of the State house of representatives 1819–1831; elected to the Twenty-third Congress (March 4, 1833–March 3, 1835); declined a renomination to the Twenty-fourth Congress; moved to Texas in 1837 and settled in Galveston; represented Galveston in the convention which framed the constitution of 1846 and was the first judge of the Galveston district; resigned to become clerk of the United States court and served until the opening of the Civil War; after war was declared he enlisted and served for two years with the Terry Rangers; after the war was elected first judge of the Galveston and Harris County Criminal Court, but was removed by the military commander; died in Galveston, Tex., June 12, 1874; interment in Trinity Church Cemetery.

LOVE, John, a Representative from Virginia; pursued an academic course; studied law; was admitted to the bar in 1801 and commenced practice in Alexandria, Va.; member of the State house of delegates 1805–1807; elected as a Democrat to the Tenth and Eleventh Congresses (March 4, 1807–March 3, 1811); served in the State senate 1816–1820; resumed the practice of law; died in Alexandria, Va., August 17, 1822.

LOVE, Peter Early, a Representative from Georgia; born near Dublin, Laurens County, Ga., July 7, 1818; was graduated from Franklin College (now a part of the University of Georgia), Athens, Ga., in 1829 and from the Philadelphia College of Medicine in 1838; practiced medicine while studying law; was admitted to the bar in 1839 and commenced practice in Thomasville, Thomas County, Ga.; solicitor general of the southern district of Georgia in 1843; member of the State senate in 1849; elected judge of the State superior court for the southern circuit in 1853; elected as a Democrat to the Thirty-sixth Congress and served from March 4, 1859, until his retirement on January 23, 1861; resumed the practice of law in Thomasville, Ga.; member of the State house of representatives in 1861; died in Thomasville, Ga., November 8, 1866; interment in the Old Cemetery.

LOVE, Thomas Cutting, a Representative from New York; born in Cambridge, N. Y., November 30, 1789; attended the common schools; served as a Volunteer in the War of 1812; wounded and taken prisoner at the Battle of Fort Erie on September 17, 1814; taken to Quebec and kept imprisoned until the close of the war; studied law; was admitted to the bar and practiced; moved to Batavia, N. Y., and later to Buffalo; judge of Erie County in 1828 and 1829; district attorney 1829–1835 and surrogate 1841–1845; elected as a Whig to the Twenty-fourth Congress (March 4, 1835–March 3, 1837); declined to be a candidate for renomination in 1836; resumed the practice of law until 1847 when he retired from active practice; died in Buffalo, N. Y., September 17, 1853; interment in Forest Lawn Cemetery.

LOVE, William Carter, a Representative from North Carolina; born near Norfolk, Va., in 1784; moved to Chapel Hill, N. C.; was tutored at home; attended the University of North Carolina at Chapel Hill 1802–1804; studied law; was admitted to the bar and commenced practice in Salisbury, N. C., in 1806; elected as a Democrat to the Fourteenth Congress (March 4, 1815–March 3, 1817); resumed the practice of law in Salisbury, Rowan County, N. C., where he died in 1835; interment in a private cemetery in Salisbury.

LOVE, William Franklin, a Representative from Mississippi; born near Liberty, Amite County, Miss., March 29, 1850; attended the common schools and the University of Mississippi at Oxford; engaged in agricultural pursuits; member of the State house of representatives 1878–1882 and 1884–1888; served in the State senate 1889–1896; delegate to the State constitutional convention in 1890; elected as a Democrat to the Fifty-fifth Congress and served from March 4, 1897, until his death in Gloster, Amite County, Miss., October 16, 1898; interment in Gloster Cemetery.

LOVEJOY, Owen (cousin of Nathan Allen Farwell), a Representative from Illinois; born in Albion, Maine, on January 6, 1811; attended the common schools and was graduated from Bowdoin College, Brunswick, Maine, in 1832; studied law but never practiced; studied theology; moved to Alton, Madison County, Ill., in 1836; ordained pastor of the Congregational Church in Princeton, Ill., 1839–1856; member of the State house of representatives in 1854; elected as a Republican to the Thirty-fifth and to the three succeeding Congresses and served from March 4, 1857, until his death in Brooklyn, N. Y., March 25, 1864; interment in Oakland Cemetery, Princeton, Ill.

LOVELL, James, a Delegate from Massachusetts; born in Boston, Mass., October 31, 1737; attended the public schools; was graduated from the Boston Latin School in 1752 and from Harvard College in 1756; completed a postgraduate course at the latter institution in 1759; taught in the Boston Latin School 1757–1775 and was also master of the North Grammar (now the Eliot) School; imprisoned by General Howe during the Revolutionary War and conveyed to Halifax in 1775; Member of the Continental Congress 1776–1782; receiver of continental taxes 1784–1788; collector of customs at Boston, Mass., in 1788 and 1789; appointed naval officer of the port of Boston and Charlestown and served from August 3, 1789, until his death in Windham, Maine, July 14, 1814.

LOVERING, Henry Bacon, a Representative from Massachusetts; born in Portsmouth, N. H., April 8, 1841; attended the public schools of Lynn, Mass., and was graduated from Phillips Exeter Academy, Exeter, N. H.; during the Civil War enlisted in 1862 in the Eighth Regiment, Massachusetts Volunteer Infantry, and served out his term; reenlisted in the Third Massachusetts Cavalry; lost a leg at the Battle of Winchester; member of the State house of representatives in 1872 and 1874; city assessor in 1879 and 1880; mayor of Lynn in 1881 and 1882; elected as a Democrat to the Forty-eighth and Forty-ninth Congresses (March 4, 1883–March 3, 1887); unsuccessful candidate for reelection in 1886 to the Fiftieth Congress; unsuccessful Democratic candidate for Governor in 1887; United States marshal for Massachusetts 1888–1891; warden of the State prison 1891–1893; United States pension agent at Boston 1894–1898; sealer of weights and measures for the city of Boston, Mass., 1902–1905; superintendent of the Chardon Street Soldiers' Home at Boston 1905–1907; retired from active business pursuits; moved to Wakefield, Mass., in 1907, where he died on April 5, 1911; interment in Pine Grove Cemetery, Lynn, Essex County, Mass.

LOVERING, William Croad, a Representative from Massachusetts; born in Woonsocket, R. I., February 25, 1835; moved with his parents to Taunton, Mass., in 1837; attended the Cambridge High School and the Hopkins Classical School, Cambridge, Mass.; left school in 1859 for employment in his father's mill; during the Civil War served as quartermaster of Engineers in the Second Massachusetts Brigade, consisting of the Second and Third Regiments; retired from the service an invalid in 1863; traveled in Europe for a year; engaged in cotton manufacturing in Taunton; first president of the Taunton Street Railway; president of the American Liability Insurance Co.; interested in several other business enterprises; president of the New England Cotton Manufacturers' Association for two years; member of the State senate in 1874 and 1875; delegate to the Republican National Convention at Chicago in 1880; presided at the Republican State convention in 1892; elected as a Republican to the Fifty-fifth and to the six succeeding Congresses and served from March 4, 1897, until his death in Washington, D. C., February 4, 1910; interment in Mount Pleasant Cemetery, Taunton, Mass.

LOVETT, John, a Representative from New York; born in Newent Society, in the present township of Lisbon, Conn., February 20, 1761; was graduated from Yale College in 1782; moved to Albany, N. Y., and thence to Fort Miller, N. Y., where he was employed as general agent and land steward; moved to Lansingburg, N. Y.; member of the State assembly in 1800 and 1801; returned to Albany and served as clerk of the common council until the outbreak of the War of 1812; military secretary to Gen. Stephen Van Rensselaer at the northwestern frontier; was wounded at the Battle of Queenstown in October 1812; returned to Albany; county clerk of Albany County from March 3, 1813, to March 31, 1815; elected as a Federalist to the Thirteenth and Fourteenth Congresses (March 4, 1813–March 3, 1817); was not a candidate for renomination in 1816; began the settlement of Perrysburg, Ohio; died at Fort Meigs, Ohio, August 12, 1818.

LOVETTE, Oscar Byrd, a Representative from Tennessee; born in Greeneville, Greene County, Tenn., December 20, 1871; attended the common schools of Greene County and the Parrottsville (Tenn.) High School; was graduated from Tusculum (Tenn.) College in 1893; member of the State house of representatives 1895–1897; studied law at Vanderbilt University, Nashville, Tenn.; was admitted to the bar in 1896 and commenced practice in Greeneville, Tenn.; also engaged in banking, serving as president of a local bank 1912–1918; served as attorney general of the first judicial circuit of Tennessee 1918–1926; trustee of Tusculum College; during the First World War served as chairman of the Greene County War Savings campaign; elected as a Republican to the Seventy-second Congress (March 4, 1931–March 3, 1933); unsuccessful candidate for renomination and for reelection as an Independent candidate in 1932; continued the practice of law in Greeneville, Tenn., until his death there on July 6, 1934; interment in Oak Grove Cemetery.

LOVRE, Harold Orrin, a Representative from South Dakota; born in Toronto, Deuel County, S. Dak., January 30, 1904; attended the public schools of Toronto, S. Dak., and St. Olaf College, Northfield, Minn.; graduated from the University of South Dakota at Vermillion in 1927; was admitted to the bar in 1927 and practiced law in Hayti, Hamlin County, S. Dak., 1927–1944, and in Watertown, Codington County, S. Dak., 1944–1949; State's attorney for Hamlin County, S. Dak., 1929–1932, 1937–1940, and in 1944 was nominated but resigned; president of the State Board of Agriculture in 1939 and 1940; chairman of the South Dakota Republican Committee in 1947 and 1948; member of the State senate 1941–1944; elected as a Republican to the Eighty-first and to the three succeeding Congresses (January 3, 1949–January 3, 1957); unsuccessful candidate for reelection in 1956 to the Eighty-fifth Congress; alternate to the Republican National Convention in 1956; engaged in the private practice of law in Washington, D. C.

LOW, Frederick Ferdinand, a Representative from California; born in Frankfort (now Winterport), Waldo County, Maine, June 30, 1828; attended the common schools and Hampden Academy; moved to California, where he engaged in the shipping business in San Francisco in 1849; moved to Marysville, Calif., in 1854 and engaged in banking until 1861; presented credentials as a Republican Member-elect to the Thirty-seventh Congress but was not permitted to take his seat; subsequently qualified under authority of a special act of Congress and served from June 3, 1862, to March 3, 1863; was not a candidate for renomination in 1862; appointed collector of the port of San Francisco in 1863; later in that year was elected Governor of California and served until 1867; United States Minister to China 1869–1874; engaged in banking in San Francisco; died in San Francisco, Calif., July 21, 1894; interment in Laurel Hill Cemetery.

LOW, Isaac, a Delegate from New York; born at Raritan Landing, near New Brunswick, N. J., April 13, 1735; active in pre-Revolutionary affairs; moved to New York City and engaged in mercantile pursuits; delegate to the Stamp Act Congress in 1765; Member of the Continental Congress in 1774 and 1775; delegate to the Provincial Congress in 1775; was opposed to armed conflict with Great Britain and after the Declaration of Independence abandoned the patriot cause; was accused of treason and arrested in 1776; one of the founders and president of the New York Chamber of Commerce 1775–1783; his property was confiscated in 1779 by the American authorities, and in 1783 he moved to England, where he died in Cowes, Isle of Wight, July 25, 1791.

LOW, Philip Burrill, a Representative from New York; born in Chelsea, Suffolk County, Mass., May 6, 1836; attended the public schools and was graduated from high school; during the Civil War volunteered and was appointed acting ensign in the United States Navy and served in the North Atlantic Squadron during 1862 and 1863; resigned and engaged in commercial pursuits in Boston, Mass., until 1865, when he moved to New York City; identified with the shipping and maritime interests; elected as a Republican to the Fifty-fourth and Fifty-fifth Congresses (March 4, 1895–March 3, 1899); unsuccessful candidate for reelection in 1898 to the Fifty-sixth Congress; continued his activities in maritime pursuits in New York City until his death there on August 23, 1912; interment in Woodlawn Cemetery.

LOWDEN, Frank Orren, a Representative from Illinois; born in Sunrise, Chisago County, Minn., January 26, 1861; moved with his parents to Point Pleasant, Hardin County, Iowa, in 1868; attended the public schools of Iowa; was graduated from the Iowa State University at Iowa City in 1885 and the Union College of Law, Chicago, Ill., in 1887; was admitted to the bar in 1887 and commenced practice in Chicago; lieutenant colonel of the First Regiment Infantry, Illinois National Guard, 1898–1903; professor of law at Northwestern University, Chicago, Ill., in 1899; delegate to the Republican National Conventions in 1900 and 1904; moved to Oregon, Ill., in 1903; member of the Republican National Committee from Illinois 1904–1912 and was a member of the executive committee during the campaigns of 1904 and 1908, assigned to western headquarters in Chicago, Ill.; elected as a Republican to the Fifty-ninth Congress to fill the vacancy caused by the death of Robert R. Hitt; reelected to the Sixtieth and Sixty-first Congresses and served from November 6, 1906, to March 3, 1911; declined to be a candidate for renomination in 1910; Governor of Illinois 1917–1921; nominated as the Republican candidate for Vice President of the United States in 1924 but declined; died March 20, 1943, in Tucson, Ariz., where he had gone for his health; interment in Graceland Cemetery, Chicago, Ill.

LOWE, David Perley, a Representative from Kansas; born near Utica, Oneida County, N. Y., August 22, 1823; moved to Ohio; attended the common schools; was graduated from the Cincinnati Law College in 1851; was admitted to the bar and commenced practice in Cincinnati, Ohio; moved to Mound City, Kans., in 1861 and continued the practice of law; member of the State senate in 1863 and 1864; judge of the sixth judicial district 1867–1871; moved to Fort Scott in 1870; elected as a Republican to the Forty-second and Forty-third Congresses (March 4, 1871–March 3, 1875); declined to be a candidate for renomination in 1874; appointed chief justice of Utah Territory by President Grant in 1875; returned to Kansas and settled in Fort Scott, Bourbon County; again elected judge of the sixth judicial district of Kansas in 1879 and served until his death in Fort Scott, Kans., April 10, 1882; interment in Evergreen Cemetery.

LOWE, William Manning, a Representative from Alabama; born in Huntsville, Madison County, Ala., on June 12, 1842; attended the Wesleyan University, Florence, Ala., and the University of Virginia at Charlottesville; during the Civil War served in the Confederate Army as private, lieutenant, captain, and lieutenant colonel; studied law; was admitted to the bar and commenced practice in Huntsville, Ala.; solicitor of the fifth judicial circuit 1865–1867; member of the State house of representatives in 1870; delegate to the State constitutional convention in 1875; elected as a Greenback Democrat to the Forty-sixth Congress (March 4, 1879–March 3, 1881); successfully contested the election of Joseph Wheeler to the Forty-seventh Congress and served from June 3, 1882, until his death in "The Grove," Huntsville, Ala., October 12, 1882; interment in Maple Hill Cemetery.

LOWELL, John, a Delegate from Massachusetts; born in Newburyport, Mass., June 17, 1743; was graduated from Harvard College in 1760; studied law; was admitted to the bar in 1762 and commenced practice in Newburyport, Mass.; an officer in the militia in 1776; moved to Boston, Mass., in 1777; member of the State house of representatives 1778 and 1780–1782; delegate to the State constitutional convention in 1780; Member of the Continental Congress in 1782 and 1783; served in the State senate in 1784 and 1785; commissioner on the New York and Massachusetts boundary line in 1784; judge of the court of appeals 1784–1789, of the United States district court 1789–1801, and of the United States Circuit Court for Massachusetts, Rhode Island, and Connecticut in 1801 and 1802; died in Roxbury, Mass., May 6, 1802.

LOWELL, Joshua Adams, a Representative from Maine; born in Thomaston, Maine, March 20, 1801; attended the common schools; taught school; studied law; was admitted to the bar and commenced practice in East Machias, Maine, in 1826; member of the State house of representatives in 1832, 1833, 1835, and 1837; elected as a Democrat to the Twenty-sixth and Twenty-seventh Congresses (March 4, 1839–March 3, 1843); was not a candidate for renomination in 1842; resumed the practice of law; presidential elector on the Democratic ticket of Polk and Dallas in 1844; died in East Machias, Maine, March 13, 1874; interment in the Village Cemetery.

LOWER, Christian, a Representative from Pennsylvania; born in Tulpehocken Township, Berks County, Pa., January 7, 1740; attended school; worked as a blacksmith and was later proprietor of an iron foundry; colonel of associated battalions in 1775 and sublieutenant in 1780; county commissioner of Berks County 1777–1779; member of the State house of representatives 1783–1785, 1793, 1794, and 1796; served in the State senate 1797–1804; elected as a Democrat to the Ninth Congress and served from March 4, 1805, until his death at his home in Tulpehocken Township, Pa., on December 19, 1806; interment in Tulpehocken Church Burial Ground.

LOWNDES, Lloyd, Jr., a Representative from Maryland; born in Clarksburg, Harrison County, Va. (now West Virginia), February 21, 1845; attended the common schools; was graduated from Allegheny College, Meadville, Pa., in 1865 and from the law department of the University of Pennsylvania at Philadelphia in 1867; was admitted to the bar and commenced practice in Cumberland, Md.; elected as a Republican to the Forty-third Congress (March 4, 1873–March 3, 1875); unsuccessful candidate for reelection in 1874 to the Forty-fourth Congress; engaged in banking; Governor of Maryland 1895–1899; unsuccessful candidate for reelection in 1898; died in Cumberland, Md., January 8, 1905; interment in Rose Hill Cemetery.

LOWNDES, Thomas (brother of William Lowndes), a Representative from South Carolina; born in Charleston, S. C., January 22, 1766; educated at home and in grammar schools of Charleston; studied law; was admitted to the bar in 1789 and commenced practice in Charleston; member of the State house of representatives 1796–1800; elected as a Federalist to the Seventh and Eighth Congresses (March 4, 1801–March 3, 1805); unsuccessful candidate for reelection in 1804 to the Ninth Congress; unsuccessful candidate in 1808 for election to the Eleventh Congress; devoted himself to the management of his estate, with a residence on his Oaklands plantation and also in Charleston, S. C.; died in Charleston, S. C., on July 8, 1843; interment in St. Paul's Churchyard.

LOWNDES, William (brother of Thomas Lowndes), a Representative from South Carolina; born on "Horseshoe" plantation, near Jacksonborough, St. Bartholomew's parish, South Carolina, February 11, 1782; pursued classical studies in England and at home; studied law; was admitted to the bar in 1804 and commenced practice in Charleston, S. C.; also engaged in agricultural pursuits; member of the State house of representatives 1806–1810; captain of militia in 1807; elected as a Democrat to the Twelfth and to the five succeeding Congresses and served from March 4, 1811, until May 8, 1822, when he resigned; nominated by the General Assembly of South Carolina for the office of President of the United States in 1821; declined Cabinet positions and foreign missions from Presidents Madison and Monroe; died at sea while en route to England October 27, 1822; remains were buried at sea.

LOWREY, Bill Green, a Representative from Mississippi; born in Kossuth, Alcorn County, Miss., May 25, 1862; attended the public schools and Blue Mountain Academy, Blue Mountain, Miss.; was graduated from Mississippi College at Clinton in 1887; was a student at Tulane University, New Orleans, La., in 1888 and 1889; professor of English in Blue Mountain College, Blue Mountain, Miss., 1889–1898; president of the college 1898–1911; president of the Amarillo (Tex.) Military Academy 1911–1916; field secretary for Hillman College and Mississippi College at Clinton and Blue Mountain College at Blue Mountain, all Baptist colleges in Mississippi, 1916–1920; vice president of Blue Mountain College in 1920 and 1921; served as president of the board of trustees of Mississippi Heights Academy; was a member of the board of trustees of the Baptist Memorial Hospital at Memphis, Tenn.; elected as a Democrat to the Sixty-seventh and to the three succeeding Congresses (March 4, 1921–March 3, 1929); was an unsuccessful candidate for renomination in 1928 to the Seventy-first Congress; served as clerk of the United States Court for the Northern District of Mississippi 1929–1935; retired to private life; died in Olive Branch, De Soto County, Miss., September 2, 1947; interment in Blocker Cemetery.

LOWRIE, Walter, a Senator from Pennsylvania; born in Edinburgh, Scotland, December 10, 1784; immigrated to the United States in 1791 with his parents, who settled in Butler County, Pa.; pursued classical studies; taught school for several years and then became engaged in surveying and agricultural pursuits; member of the State house of representatives in 1811 and 1812; served in the State senate 1813–1819; elected as a Democrat to the United States Senate and served from March 4, 1819, to March 3, 1825; was not a candidate for reelection in 1824; Secretary of the United States Senate from December 12, 1825, to December 11, 1836; secretary of the Presbyterian Board of Foreign Missions from 1836 until his death in New York City December 14, 1868; interment in the crypt of the First Presbyterian Church.

LOWRY, Robert, a Representative from Indiana; born in Killeleigh, County Down, Ireland, April 2, 1824; immigrated to the United States and settled in Rochester, N. Y.; educated in private schools and had partial academic course; librarian of Rochester Athenaeum and Young Men's Association; studied law; moved to Fort Wayne, Ind., in 1843; city recorder in 1844 and 1845; was admitted to the bar in 1846 and commenced practice in Goshen, Ind.; auditor of Elkhart County in 1852; circuit judge in 1852; president of the Democratic State convention; delegate to the Democratic National Conventions at Baltimore in 1860 and 1872; served as circuit judge from 1864 until January 1875, when he resigned; judge of the superior court in 1877 and 1878; elected the first president of the Indiana State Bar Association in July 1879; elected as a Democrat to the Forty-eighth and Forty-ninth Congresses (March 4, 1883–March 3, 1887); unsuccessful candidate for reelection in 1886 to the Fiftieth Congress; resumed the practice of law; died in Fort Wayne, Allen County, Ind., January 27, 1904; interment in Linderwood Cemetery.

LOYALL, George, a Representative from Virginia; born in Norfolk, Va., May 29, 1789; was graduated from William and Mary College, Williamsburg, Va., in 1808; studied law but did not practice; visited England in 1815; member of the State house of delegates 1818–1827; delegate to the State constitutional convention in 1829; successfully contested the election of Thomas Newton to the Twenty-first Congress and served from March 9, 1830, to March 3, 1831; elected as a Democrat to the Twenty-third and Twenty-fourth Congresses (March 4, 1833–March 3, 1837); Navy agent at Norfolk, Va., 1837–1861, with the exception of two years; died in Norfolk, Va., February 24, 1868; interment in Elmwood Cemetery.

LOZIER, Ralph Fulton, a Representative from Missouri; born near Hardin, Ray County, Mo., January 28, 1866; attended the public schools; was graduated from the Carrollton (Mo.) High School in 1883; engaged in teaching for several years; studied law; was admitted to the bar in 1886 and commenced practice in Carrollton; also interested in agricultural pursuits and the raising of livestock; served as city attorney of Carrollton, Mo., 1915–1944; for many years was member of the board of trustees of William Woods College for Girls at Fulton, Mo.; delegate to the Democratic National Convention at Houston in 1928 and to many Democratic State conventions; elected as a Democrat to the Sixty-eighth and to the five succeeding Congresses (March 4, 1923–January 3, 1935); unsuccessful candidate for renomination in 1934; judge of the circuit court, seventh judicial circuit of Missouri, in 1936; resumed the practice of law, with offices in Carrollton, Mo., and Washington, D. C., and also engaged in agricultural pursuits in Carroll County, Mo.; died in St. Luke's Hospital, Kansas City, Mo., May 28, 1945; interment in Oak Hill Cemetery, Carrollton, Mo.

LUCAS, Edward (brother of William Lucas), a Representative from Virginia; born near Shepherdstown, Jefferson County, Va. (now West Virginia), October 20, 1780; attended the common schools; was graduated from Dickinson College, Carlisle, Pa., in 1809; served in the War of 1812 as first lieutenant and acting captain; studied law; was admitted to the bar and practiced in Shepherdstown until 1818; engaged in mercantile pursuits; member of the State house of delegates 1819–1822, 1830, and 1831; elected as a Democrat to the Twenty-third and Twenty-fourth Congresses (March 4, 1833–March 3, 1837); was not a candidate for renomination in 1836; resumed mercantile pursuits; served as military storekeeper of ordnance at the Harpers Ferry Armory from May 12, 1847, until his death at Harpers Ferry, Va. (now West Virginia), March 4, 1858; interment in the Harper Cemetery.

LUCAS, John Baptiste Charles, a Representative from Pennsylvania; born in Pont-Audemer, Normandy, France, August 14, 1758; attended the Honfleur and Paris Law Schools, and was graduated from the law department of the University of Caen in 1782; practiced law in France until 1784; immigrated to the United States, settled near Pittsburgh, Pa., and engaged in agricultural pursuits; member of the State house of representatives 1792–1798; judge of the common pleas court in 1794; elected as a Democrat to the Eighth and Ninth Congresses and served from March 4, 1803, until his resignation in 1805, before the assembling of the Ninth Congress; moved to St. Louis, La. (now Missouri), having been appointed district judge for the northern district of Louisiana (which became Missouri Territory in 1812), and served from 1805 until 1820, when he resigned; also served as commissioner of land claims of northern Louisiana 1805–1812; resumed agricultural pursuits; died near St. Louis, Mo., August 17, 1842; interment in Calvary Cemetery.

LUCAS, Scott Wike, a Representative and a Senator from Illinois; born on a farm near Chandlerville, Cass County, Ill., February 19, 1892; attended the public schools and was graduated from the law department of Illinois Wesleyan University at Bloomington in 1914; was admitted to the bar in 1915 and commenced practice at Havana, Ill.; during the First World War served as an enlisted man and later as a lieutenant in the United States Army; State's attorney of Mason County 1920–1925; delegate to the Democratic National Conventions in 1932, 1940, 1944, 1952, 1956, and 1960; chairman of State Tax Commission 1933–1935; elected as a Democrat to the Seventy-fourth and Seventy-fifth Congresses (January 3, 1935–January 3, 1939); did not seek renomination, having become a candidate for Senator; elected to the United States Senate in 1938 and reelected in 1944 and served from January 3, 1939, to January 3, 1951; unsuccessful candidate for reelection in 1950; engaged in the practice of law in Springfield, Ill., and Washington, D. C., where he now resides.

LUCAS, William (brother of Edward Lucas), a Representative from Virginia; born at "Cold Spring," near Shepherdstown, Jefferson County, Va. (now West Virginia), November 30, 1800; attended the village schools; was graduated from the Tucker Law School, Winchester, Va., in 1825; was admitted to the bar the same year and commenced practice in Shepherdstown; moved to Charles Town, Va. (now West Virginia), in 1830 and continued the practice of law; also engaged in horticultural pursuits; member of the Virginia House of Delegates in 1838 and 1839; elected as a Democrat to the Twenty-sixth Congress (March 4, 1839–March 3, 1841); unsuccessful candidate for reelection in 1840 to the Twenty-seventh Congress; elected to the Twenty-eighth Congress (March 4, 1843–March 3, 1845); unsuccessful candidate for renomination in 1844; resumed the practice of law and horticultural pursuits; delegate to the Virginia constitutional convention in 1850 and 1851; died at his home, "Rion Hall," in Jefferson County, W. Va., August 29, 1877; interment in the Zion Episcopal Churchyard, Charles Town, W. Va.

LUCAS, William Vincent, a Representative from South Dakota; born near Delphi, Carroll County, Ind., July 3, 1835; attended the common schools; moved to Bremer County, Iowa, in 1856 and engaged in agricultural pursuits; during the Civil War enlisted in the Union Army in the Fourteenth Regiment, Iowa Volunteer Infantry; promoted to captain in 1863; treasurer of Bremer County 1866–1872; editor of the Waverly Republican 1872–1876; editor of the Cerro Gordo Republican, Mason City, Iowa, 1876–1883; presidential elector on the Republican ticket of Hayes and Wheeler in 1876; chief clerk of the Iowa House of Representatives 1878–1880; mayor of

Mason City, Iowa, in 1879 and 1880; State auditor in 1881 and 1882; declined nomination for reelection; moved to Chamberlain, S. Dak., in 1883 and again engaged in agricultural pursuits; treasurer of Brule County 1888–1890; moved to Hot Springs, S. Dak., in 1890; appointed commandant of the South Dakota Soldiers' Home at Hot Springs in 1890; elected as a Republican to the Fifty-third Congress (March 4, 1893–March 3, 1895); unsuccessful candidate for renomination in 1894; delegate to the Republican National Convention at St. Louis in 1896 and to the Republican State convention at Huron, S. Dak., the same year; again appointed commandant of the South Dakota Soldiers' Home in 1896 and served one year; returned to Chamberlain, S. Dak., in 1897; register of the United States land office 1897–1901; again appointed commandant of the South Dakota Soldiers' Home in 1901 and served until his resignation in 1904; moved to Santa Cruz, Santa Cruz County, Calif., in 1904 and died there on November 10, 1921; interment in Oakwood Cemetery.

LUCAS, Wingate Hezekiah, a Representative from Texas; born in Grapevine, Tarrant County, Tex., May 1, 1908; attended the public schools, the North Texas Teachers College at Denton, the Oklahoma Agricultural and Mechanical College at Stillwater, and the Texas University at Austin; studied law; was admitted to the bar in 1938 and commenced practice in Grapevine, Tex.; during World War II served as an enlisted man in the United States Army from 1943 to 1945 with overseas service in the European theater of operations; resumed the practice of law; elected as a Democrat to the Eightieth and to the three succeeding Congresses (January 3, 1947–January 3, 1955); unsuccessful candidate for renomination in 1954; engaged in the practice of law in Fort Worth, Tex., specializing in labor relations; moved to New York City to become government relations consultant to the General Electric Co.; resides in Greenwich, Conn.

LUCE, Clare Boothe (stepdaughter of Albert E. Austin), a Representative from Connecticut; born in New York City, N. Y., April 10, 1903; was graduated from St. Mary's School at Garden City, Long Island, N. Y., and from Miss Mason's School at Tarrytown, N. Y., in 1919; writer, associate editor, and managing editor of Vanity Fair, 1929–1934; administrative representative of the public to the National Recovery Administration Code Authority for the legitimate theater and motion pictures in 1934; author, playwright, journalist, foreign correspondent, and lecturer; elected as a Republican to the Seventy-eighth and Seventy-ninth Congresses (January 3, 1943–January 3, 1947); was not a candidate for renomination in 1946; engaged in writing; United States Ambassador to Italy from March 2, 1953, to January 4, 1957; confirmed as United States Ambassador to Brazil April 28, 1959, but resigned three days later on May 1, 1959; is a resident of Ridgefield, Conn.

LUCE, Robert, a Representative from Massachusetts; born in Auburn, Androscoggin County, Maine, December 2, 1862; attended the public schools of Auburn and Lewiston, Maine, and Somerville, Mass., and was graduated from Harvard University, Cambridge, Mass., in 1882; taught in the Waltham (Mass.) High School for a year; engaged in journalism, founding and serving as president of the Luce's Press Clipping Bureau in Boston and New York in 1888; Republican member of the State house of representatives in 1899 and 1901–1908; studied law and was admitted to the bar in Boston in 1908, but did not engage in extensive practice; president of the Republican State convention in 1910; chairman of the commission on cost of living in 1910, 1916, and 1917; Lieutenant Governor of Massachusetts in 1912; member of the Massachusetts Teachers Retirement Board 1914–1919; delegate to the State constitutional convention 1917–1919; president of the Republican Club of Massachusetts in 1918; Regent of the Smithsonian Institution 1929–1931; author, notably on the subject of political science; elected as a Republican to the Sixty-sixth and the seven succeeding Congresses (March 4, 1919–January 3, 1935); unsuccessful candidate for reelection in 1934 to the Seventy-fourth Congress; elected to the Seventy-fifth and Seventy-sixth Congresses (January 3, 1937–January 3, 1941); unsuccessful candidate for reelection in 1940 to the Seventy-seventh Congress; resumed his former business pursuits; died in Waltham, Mass., April 7, 1946; the remains were cremated and the ashes interred in Mount Auburn Cemetery, Cambridge, Mass.

LUCKEY, Henry Carl, a Representative from Nebraska; born near East St. Louis, St. Clair County, Ill., November 22, 1868; moved to Nebraska with his parents, who settled on a farm near Columbus in Platte County in 1873; attended the public schools and the Lutheran parochial school in Columbus, Nebr.; was graduated from the University of Nebraska at Lincoln in 1912; pursued a postgraduate course at Columbia University, New York, N. Y., in 1914 and 1915; engaged in agricultural pursuits near Columbus, Nebr., 1894–1900; moved to Lincoln, Nebr., in 1900; was admitted to the bar in 1912, but did not practice; engaged in the real-estate business and in the construction of homes 1917–1927; member of the board of trustees of Midland College, Fremont, Nebr., 1919–1925; elected as a Democrat to the Seventy-fourth and Seventy-fifth Congresses (January 3, 1935–January 3, 1939); unsuccessful candidate for reelection in 1938 to the Seventy-sixth Congress and for election in 1940 to the Seventy-seventh Congress; resumed the real-estate business and also engaged in agricultural pursuits until 1946, when he retired and moved to Richmond, Calif.; died in El Cerrito, Calif., December 31, 1956; interment in Sunset View Cemetery.

LUCKING, Alfred, a Representative from Michigan; born in Ingersoll, Ontario, Canada, December 18, 1856; moved with his parents to Ypsilanti, Mich., in 1858; attended the public schools, the Ypsilanti High School, and the Michigan State Normal College at Ypsilanti; was graduated from the law department of the University of Michigan at Ann Arbor in 1878; was admitted to the bar the same year and practiced in Jackson, Mich.; moved to Detroit, Mich., in 1880 and continued the practice of law; declined the appointment of park and boulevard commissioner of Detroit, Mich., in 1896; temporary chairman of the Democratic State convention in 1900 and was both temporary and permanent chairman of the State conventions in 1902, 1908, and 1924; permanent chairman in 1928; elected as a Democrat to the Fifty-eighth Congress (March 4, 1903–March 3, 1905); unsuccessful candidate for reelection in 1904 to the Fifty-ninth Congress; resumed the practice of his profession in Detroit, Mich.; unsuccessful candidate for election to the United States Senate in 1912; general counsel for the Ford Motor Co. and the Henry Ford interests from 1914 to 1923; president of the Detroit-Vancouver Timber Co.; delegate at large to the Democratic National Convention at New York City in 1924 which nominated Davis and Bryan; died in Detroit, Mich., on December 1, 1929; interment in Woodlawn Cemetery.

LUDLOW, Louis Leon, a Representative from Indiana; born on a farm near Connersville, Fayette County, Ind., June 24, 1873; attended the grade and high schools; moved to Indianapolis, Ind., in 1892 and became a reporter and later a political writer; Washington correspondent for Indiana and Ohio newspapers and member of the Congressional Press Galleries 1901–1929; author; elected as a Democrat to the Seventy-first and to the nine succeeding Congresses (March 4, 1929–January 3,

1949); election to the Seventy-first Congress was unsuccessfully contested by Ralph E. Updike; was not a candidate for renomination in 1948 to the Eighty-first Congress; author of a proposed amendment to the Constitution for a referendum on war, applicable except in the case of attack or invasion of a country in the Western Hemisphere by a non-American country; resumed work as a newspaper correspondent until his death in Washington, D. C., November 28, 1950; interment in Rock Creek Cemetery.

LUECKE, John Frederick, a Representative from Michigan; born in Escanaba, Delta County, Mich., July 4, 1889; attended the public elementary schools; employed as a commercial and railroad telegrapher and station agent; served as a private in Company A, Signal Corps, United States Army, with the Punitive Expeditionary Force in Mexico in 1916 and 1917; during the First World War served as a sergeant, first class, in Company B, Second Field Signal Battalion, American Expeditionary Forces, 1917–1919; commissioned a second lieutenant, Reserve Corps, while in Germany; engaged as a mill worker in a paper mill in Escanaba, Mich., 1923–1936; member of the Escanaba City Council 1934–1936; county supervisor of Delta County, Mich., 1934–1936; served in the State senate in 1935 and 1936; elected as a Democrat to the Seventy-fifth Congress (January 3, 1937–January 3, 1939); unsuccessful candidate for reelection in 1938 to the Seventy-sixth Congress; in 1939 was appointed commissioner of conciliation for the United States Department of Labor for upper Michigan and northern Wisconsin; died in Escanaba, Mich., March 21, 1952; interment in Lakeview Cemetery.

LUFKIN, Willfred Weymouth, a Representative from Massachusetts; born in Essex, Essex County, Mass., March 10, 1879; attended the public schools; newspaper correspondent; private secretary to Congressman Augustus P. Gardner 1902–1917; member and chairman of the Essex School Board 1901–1906; member of the State constitutional convention 1917–1919; elected as a Republican to the Sixty-fifth Congress to fill the vacancy caused by the resignation of Augustus P. Gardner; reelected to the Sixty-sixth and Sixty-seventh Congresses and served from November 6, 1917, to June 30, 1921, when he resigned to accept a Treasury position; appointed by President Warren G. Harding to be collector of customs at the port of Boston July 1, 1921, and served until his retirement in 1933; again elected a member of the Essex School Board in 1922, 1925, and 1928; moderator of the town meeting in 1925; died in Essex, Mass., March 28, 1934; interment in Essex Cemetery.

LUHRING, Oscar Raymond, a Representative from Indiana; born in Haubstadt, Gibson County, Ind., February 11, 1879; attended the public schools; was graduated in law from the University of Virginia at Charlottesville in 1900; was admitted to the bar the same year and commenced practice in Evansville, Vanderburg County, Ind.; member of the State house of representatives in 1903 and 1904; deputy prosecuting attorney for the first judicial circuit 1904–1908; prosecuting attorney of the same circuit 1908–1912; elected as a Republican to the Sixty-sixth and Sixty-seventh Congresses (March 4, 1919–March 3, 1923); unsuccessful candidate for reelection in 1922 to the Sixty-eighth Congress; special assistant to the Secretary of Labor 1923–1925; appointed by President Coolidge to be Assistant Attorney General of the United States on September 9, 1925; appointed by President Hoover as an associate justice of the supreme court for the District of Columbia (now United States District Court) on July 3, 1930, and served until his death in Washington, D. C., August 20, 1944; interment in the Abbey Mausoleum, adjoining Arlington National Cemetery, Fort Myer, Va.

LUMPKIN, Alva Moore, a Senator from South Carolina; born in Milledgeville, Baldwin County, Ga., on November 13, 1886; moved with his parents to Columbia, S. C., in 1898; attended the public schools of Milledgeville, Ga., and Columbia, S. C.; was graduated from the law department of the University of South Carolina at Columbia in 1908; was admitted to the bar the same year and commenced the practice of law in Columbia, S. C.; served as assistant clerk of the State senate 1906–1908; member of the State house of representatives 1911–1913; appointed a member of the Conciliation Commission for Advancement of Peace between the United States and Uruguay in 1914; served as acting assistant attorney general of South Carolina in 1918; member of the State board of pardons in 1922 and 1923; appointed acting associate justice of the State supreme court in 1926 and 1934; served as Federal judge of the United States District Court for the Eastern and Western Districts of South Carolina from May 22, 1939, until his resignation on July 21, 1941; appointed on July 17, 1941, as a Democrat to the United States Senate to fill the vacancy caused by the resignation of James F. Byrnes and served from July 22, 1941, until his death in Washington, D. C., August 1, 1941; interment in Elmwood Cemetery, Columbia, S. C.

LUMPKIN, John Henry (nephew of Wilson Lumpkin), a Representative from Georgia; born in Lexington, Oglethorpe County, Ga., June 13, 1812; attended rural schools and Franklin College (now the University of Georgia) at Athens and Yale College in 1831 and 1832; appointed private secretary to his uncle, Wilson Lumpkin, Governor of Georgia; studied law; was admitted to the bar in 1834 and commenced practice in Rome, Ga.; member of the State house of representatives in 1835; solicitor general of the Cherokee circuit in 1838; unsuccessful candidate for election in 1840 to the Twenty-seventh Congress; elected as a Democrat to the Twenty-eighth, Twenty-ninth, and Thirtieth Congresses (March 4, 1843–March 3, 1849); judge of the superior court, Rome circuit, 1850–1853; elected to the Thirty-fourth Congress (March 4, 1855–March 3, 1857); was not a candidate for renomination in 1856 to the Thirty-fifth Congress; resumed the practice of law in Rome, Ga.; was an unsuccessful candidate for Governor of Georgia in 1857; served as a delegate to the Democratic National Convention at Charleston, S. C., in 1860; died in Rome, Ga., July 10, 1860; interment in Oak Hill Cemetery.

LUMPKIN, Wilson (uncle of John Henry Lumpkin and grandfather of Middleton Pope Barrow), a Representative and a Senator from Georgia; born near Dan River, Pittsylvania County, Va., January 14, 1783; moved in 1784 to Oglethorpe (then a part of Wilkes), County, Ga., with his parents, who settled near Point Peter, and subsequently at Lexington, Ga.; attended the common schools and was graduated from the University of Georgia, Athens, Ga.; served as trustee of the University of Georgia until his death; studied law; was admitted to the bar and commenced practice in Athens, Ga.; member of the State house of representatives 1808–1812; served in the State senate; elected as a Democrat to the Fourteenth Congress (March 4, 1815–March 3, 1817); elected to the Twentieth, Twenty-first, and Twenty-second Congresses and served from March 4, 1827, until his resignation in 1831 before the convening of the Twenty-second Congress; one of the commissioners on the Georgia-Florida boundary line; Governor of Georgia 1831–1835; appointed commissioner under the Cherokee treaty in 1835; elected to the United States Senate to fill the vacancy caused by the resignation of John P. King and served from November 22, 1837, to March 3, 1841; member of the State board of public works; died in Athens, Ga., December 28, 1870; interment in Oconee Cemetery.

LUNA, Tranquilino, a Delegate from the Territory of New Mexico; born in Los Lunas, Valencia County, N. Mex., February 25, 1849; attended the public schools and was graduated from the University of Missouri at Columbia; engaged extensively in stock raising; delegate to the Republican National Conventions in 1880 and 1888; elected as a Republican to the Forty-seventh Congress (March 4, 1881–March 3, 1883); presented credentials as a Delegate-elect to the Forty-eighth Congress and served from March 4, 1883, until March 5, 1884, when he was succeeded by Francisco A. Manzanares, who contested his election; sheriff of Valencia County 1888–1892; died in Peralta, Valencia County, N. Mex., November 20, 1892; interment in Los Lunas Cemetery, Los Lunas, N. Mex.

LUNDEEN, Ernest, a Representative and a Senator from Minnesota; born near Beresford, Union County, S. Dak., August 4, 1878; attended the common schools; was graduated from the high school of Dayton, Iowa, in 1895 and from Carleton College, Northfield, Minn., in 1901; studied law at the University of Minnesota at Minneapolis; was admitted to the bar in 1906 and commenced practice at Minneapolis, Minn.; served in Company B, Twelfth Minnesota Volunteers, during the Spanish-American War; member of the State house of representatives 1910–1914; delegate to the Republican National Conventions in 1912 and 1916; elected as a Republican to the Sixty-fifth Congress (March 4, 1917–March 3, 1919); unsuccessful candidate for renomination in 1918; resumed the practice of law; was a candidate for nomination and election to Congress on numerous occasions; elected as a Farmer-Laborite to the Seventy-third and Seventy-fourth Congresses (March 4, 1933–January 3, 1937); elected on the Farmer-Labor ticket to the United States Senate in 1936 and served from January 3, 1937, until his death in an airplane crash near Lovettsville, Va., on August 31, 1940; interment in Little Arlington National Cemetery, Minneapolis, Minn.

LUNDIN, Frederick, a Representative from Illinois; born in the parish of Vestra Tollstad, Hastholmen, Sweden, May 18, 1868; immigrated to the United States and settled in Chicago, Ill., in 1880; completed academic studies; president of Lundin & Co., manufacturing chemists; member of the State senate 1894–1898; elected as a Republican to the Sixty-first Congress (March 4, 1909–March 3, 1911); unsuccessful candidate for reelection in 1910 to the Sixty-second Congress; resumed manufacturing interests until retirement in 1916; died in Beverly Hills, Calif., August 20, 1947; interment in Forest Home Cemetery, Forest Park, Ill.

LUNN, George Richard, a Representative from New York; born near Lenox, Taylor County, Iowa, June 23, 1873; attended the public schools at Lenox and Des Moines, Iowa; was graduated from Bellevue College, Bellevue, Nebr., in 1897; during the Spanish-American War served as corporal in Company I, Third Nebraska Regiment; pursued postgraduate work in Princeton, New York, and Columbia Universities; was graduated from Union Theological Seminary, New York City, in 1901; became associate pastor of Lafayette Avenue Presbyterian Church in Brooklyn the same year; moved to Schenectady, N. Y., in 1904 and became pastor of the First Dutch Reformed Church; in 1909 organized the Independent People's Church, which was united with the First Congregational Church of which he was pastor until 1914; served as mayor of Schenectady in 1912, 1913, 1916, and 1917; elected as a Democrat to the Sixty-fifth Congress (March 4, 1917–March 3, 1919); unsuccessful candidate for reelection in 1918 to the Sixty-sixth Congress; mayor of Schenectady in 1920 and served until January 1, 1923, when he resigned; delegate to the Democratic National Conventions in 1920, 1924, 1928, 1932, and 1936; Lieutenant Governor of New York in 1923 and 1924; appointed

public service commissioner of the State of New York in 1925, and served in that capacity until 1942 when he resigned due to ill health; died in Rancho Santa Fe, Calif., November 27, 1948; interment in Forest Lawn Cemetery, Los Angeles, Calif.

LUSK, Georgia Lee, a Representative from New Mexico; born in Carlsbad, Eddy County, N. Mex., May 12, 1893; attended the public schools, Highlands University, Las Vegas, N. Mex., and the Colorado State Teachers College at Greeley; was graduated from New Mexico State Teachers College at Silver City in 1914; school teacher; manager of family ranch 1919–1943; county school superintendent of Lea County 1925–1929; State superintendent of public instruction 1931–1935 and 1943–1947; rural school supervisor in Guadalupe County in 1941 and 1942; delegate to the Democratic National Conventions in 1928 and 1948; elected as a Democrat to the Eightieth Congress (January 3, 1947–January 3, 1949); unsuccessful candidate for renomination in 1948; member of the War Claims Commission from September 1949 to December 1953; again State superintendent of public instruction for New Mexico 1955–1960; retired; is a resident of Santa Fe, N. Mex.

LUSK, Hall Stoner, a Senator from Oregon; born in Washington, D. C., September 21, 1883; attended Georgetown Preparatory School 1897–1900; graduated from Georgetown University in 1904 and from Georgetown Law School in 1907; secretary to Chief Justice Shepard of the Court of Appeals for the District of Columbia 1906–1909; admitted to the District of Columbia bar in 1907 and to the Oregon bar in 1910 and commenced the practice of law in Portland, Oreg., the same year; assistant United States district attorney of Oregon 1918–1920; unsuccessful for election to the Oregon Legislature in 1922; circuit judge of Multnomah County, Oreg., 1930–1937; appointed and subsequently elected to the Oregon Supreme Court and was reelected in 1956 for a six-year term and served from July 21, 1937, until his resignation on March 15, 1960; appointed as a Democrat to the United States Senate to fill the vacancy caused by the death of Richard L. Neuberger and served from March 16, 1960, to November 8, 1960; was not a candidate for election to a full term; returned to Oregon Supreme Court as a justice pro tempore January 1, 1961; is a resident of Salem, Oreg.

LUTTRELL, John King, a Representative from California; born near Knoxville, Knox County, Tenn., June 27, 1831; attended the common schools; moved with his parents to a farm in Alabama in 1844; joined a volunteer company for service in the Mexican War, but was rejected on account of age; moved to Missouri in 1845 with his parents, who settled on a farm near St. Joseph; employed with a surveying crew on the St. Joseph & Hannibal Railroad; engaged in teaching for one term; employed as a clerk in a mercantile establishment in St. Joseph, Mo.; moved to California in 1852 and engaged in mining; settled in Yolo County and engaged in agricultural pursuits; moved to Prairie City (later Folsom) in 1853 and continued farming and also engaged in teaming; moved to El Dorado County in 1854 and engaged in mining, thence to Watsonville, Santa Cruz County, and engaged in agricultural pursuits, thence to Alameda County, where he continued farming; studied law; was admitted to the bar and commenced practice in Oakland in 1856; justice of the peace in Brooklyn (now a part of Oakland) in 1856 and 1857; moved to Siskiyou County in 1858 and purchased a ranch near Fort Jones; engaged in agricultural pursuits, mining, and the practice of law; sergeant at arms of the State assembly in 1865 and 1866; member of the State house of representatives in 1871 and 1872; elected as a Democrat to the Forty-third, Forty-fourth, and Forty-fifth Congresses (March 4, 1873–March 3,

1879); declined to be a candidate for reelection; resumed the practice of law, farming, and mining; member of the board of State prison directors 1887–1889; appointed United States Commissioner of Fisheries and special agent of the United States Treasury for Alaska in 1893; died in Sitka, Alaska, on October 4, 1893; interment in Fort Jones Cemetery, Fort Jones, Siskiyou County, Calif.

LYBRAND, Archibald, a Representative from Ohio; born in Tarlton, Pickaway County, Ohio, May 23, 1840; moved to Delaware, Ohio, in 1857; attended the common schools and the Ohio Wesleyan University at Delaware; during the Civil War enlisted in the Union Army April 26, 1861, and served in Company I, Fourth Regiment, Ohio Volunteer Infantry; transferred to Company E, Seventy-third Regiment, Ohio Volunteer Infantry, and promoted to first lieutenant; commissioned captain; remained in service three years; returned to Delaware, Ohio; mayor of Delaware in 1869; studied law; was admitted to the bar in 1871; landowner and engaged in agricultural and mercantile pursuits; postmaster of Delaware 1881–1885; elected as a Republican to the Fifty-fifth and Fifty-sixth Congresses (March 4, 1897–March 3, 1901); unsuccessful candidate for renomination in 1900; resumed business activities in Delaware, Ohio; died in Daytona, Fla., February 7, 1910; interment in Oak Grove Cemetery, Delaware, Ohio.

LYLE, Aaron, a Representative from Pennsylvania; born in Mount Bethel, Northampton County, Pa., November 17, 1759; attended the common schools; engaged in agricultural pursuits; served in the Revolutionary War; member of the State house of representatives 1797–1801; served in the State senate 1802–1804; commissioner of Washington County, Pa., 1806–1809; elected as a Democrat to the Eleventh and to the three succeeding Congresses (March 4, 1809–March 3, 1817); resumed agricultural pursuits; trustee of Jefferson (later Washington and Jefferson) College, Washington, Pa., 1802–1822; died at Cross Creek, Washington County, Pa., September 24, 1825; interment in the Old Cemetery.

LYLE, John Emmett, Jr., a Representative from Texas; born in Boyd, Wise County, Tex., September 4, 1910; attended the public schools, Wichita Falls High School, the Junior College at Wichita Falls, the University of Texas at Austin, and the Houston (Tex.) Law School; was admitted to the bar in 1934 and commenced practice in Corpus Christi, Tex.; served in the State house of representatives from January 1941 until his resignation in 1942, when he enlisted in the United States Army; served as an operations officer in the Five Hundred and Thirty-sixth Antiaircraft Battalion in the European theater until October 1944; elected as a Democrat to the Seventy-ninth and to the four succeeding Congresses (January 3, 1945–January 3, 1955); was not a candidate for renomination in 1954 to the Eighty-fourth Congress; resumed the practice of law; is a resident of Corpus Christi, Tex.

LYMAN, Joseph, a Representative from Iowa; born in Lyons, Ionia County, Mich., September 13, 1840; attended the common schools in Ohio; moved to Big Grove, Iowa, in 1857; attended Iowa College, Grinnell, Iowa; during the Civil War enlisted in the Union Army in 1861 and served in Company E, Fourth Regiment, Iowa Volunteer Cavalry; adjutant of the Twenty-ninth Regiment, Iowa Volunteer Infantry, from October 19, 1862, to February 21, 1865, and major of the same regiment from February 21, 1865, to August 10, 1865; studied law; was admitted to the bar in 1866 and commenced practice in Council Bluffs, Iowa; deputy collector of internal revenue of the fifth district of Iowa 1867–1870; judge of the circuit

court in 1884; elected as a Republican to the Forty-ninth and Fiftieth Congresses (March 4, 1885–March 3, 1889); declined to be a candidate for renomination in 1888; resumed the practice of law; died in Council Bluffs, Iowa, July 9, 1890; interment in Fairview Cemetery.

LYMAN, Joseph Stebbins, a Representative from New York; born in Northfield, Franklin County, Mass., February 14, 1785; attended the common schools; was graduated from Dartmouth College, Hanover, N. H., in 1806; studied law; was admitted to the bar and commenced practice in Cooperstown, N. Y.; elected to the Sixteenth Congress (March 4, 1819–March 3, 1821); was not a candidate for renomination in 1821; died in Cooperstown, Otsego County, N. Y., March 21, 1821; interment in Greenfield, Franklin County, Mass.

LYMAN, Samuel, a Representative from Massachusetts; born in Goshen, Conn., January 25, 1749; attended Goshen Academy; was graduated from Yale College in 1770; taught school; studied law in Litchfield, Conn.; was admitted to the bar in 1773 and commenced practice in Hartford, Conn.; moved to Springfield, Mass., in 1784; member of the State house of representatives 1786–1788; served in the State senate 1790–1793; justice of the court of common pleas of Hampshire County 1791–1800; elected to the Fourth, Fifth, and Sixth Congresses and served from March 4, 1795, until November 6, 1800, when he resigned; died in Springfield, Mass., June 5, 1802; interment in Goshen, Conn.

LYMAN, Theodore, a Representative from Massachusetts; born in Waltham, Mass., August 23, 1833; was educated by private tutors; studied in Europe 1847–1849; was graduated from Harvard University in 1855 and from the Lawrence Scientific School of Harvard University in 1858; served during the Civil War as lieutenant colonel and volunteer aide-de-camp on the staff of Major General Meade from September 2, 1863, to April 20, 1865; member of the American Academy of Arts and Sciences and of the National Academy of Sciences; trustee of the Peabody Education Fund; one of the State fishery commissioners 1865–1882; overseer of Harvard University 1868–1880; elected as an Independent to the Forty-eighth Congress (March 4, 1883–March 3, 1885); retired on account of ill health; died in Nahant, Mass., September 9, 1897; interment in Mount Auburn Cemetery, Cambridge, Mass.

LYMAN, William, a Representative from Massachusetts; born in Northampton, Mass., December 7, 1755; was graduated from Yale College in 1776; during Shays' Rebellion was aide to General Shepard, with rank of major; served in the Revolutionary War; member of the State house of representatives in 1787; served in the State senate in 1789; elected as a Democrat to the Third and Fourth Congresses (March 4, 1793–March 3, 1797); brigadier general of State militia 1796–1800; United States consul at London, England, from 1805 until his death; died in Cheltenham, Gloucestershire, England, on September 2, 1811; interment in the cathedral at Gloucester, England, and later a monument was erected to his memory in the Old Cemetery, Northampton, Mass.

LYNCH, John, a Representative from Maine; born in Portland, Maine, February 18, 1825; attended the public schools; was graduated from the Portland High School in 1842; engaged in mercantile pursuits; manager of the Portland Daily Press in 1862; member of the State house of representatives 1862–1864; elected as a Republican to the Thirty-ninth and to the three succeeding Congresses (March 4, 1865–March 3, 1873); moved to Washington, D. C., and established the Washington Daily

Union in 1877; engaged in the manufacture of bricks and drain pipes in Washington, D. C.; died while on a visit in Portland, Cumberland County, Maine, on July 21, 1892; interment in Evergreen Cemetery.

LYNCH, John, a Representative from Pennsylvania; born in Providence, R. I., November 1, 1843; moved to Pennsylvania in 1856 with his parents, who settled in Wilkes-Barre; attended the public schools and Wyoming Seminary, Kingston, Pa.; worked on a farm and in the coal mines; taught school; studied law; was admitted to the bar November 1, 1868, and commenced practice in Wilkes-Barre, Pa.; elected as a Democrat to the Fiftieth Congress (March 4, 1887–March 3, 1889); unsuccessful candidate for reelection in 1888 to the Fifty-first Congress; resumed the practice of law in Wilkes-Barre; judge of the court of common pleas 1892–1910; died in Atlantic City, N. J., August 17, 1910; interment in St. Mary's Cemetery, Wilkes-Barre, Luzerne County, Pa.

LYNCH, John Roy, a Representative from Mississippi; born near Vidalia, Concordia Parish, La., September 10, 1847; was of the Negro race; after his father's death moved with his mother to Natchez, Miss., in 1863, where they were held as slaves; after emancipation engaged in photography and obtained a fair education by attending evening school; appointed by Governor Ames as a justice of the peace in 1869; member of the State house of representatives 1869–1873 and served the last term as speaker; delegate to the Republican National Conventions in 1872, 1884, 1888, 1892, and 1900; elected as a Republican to the Forty-third and Forty-fourth Congresses (March 4, 1873–March 3, 1877); unsuccessful candidate for reelection in 1876 to the Forty-fifth Congress; successfully contested the election of James R. Chalmers to the Forty-seventh Congress and served from April 29, 1882, to March 3, 1883; unsuccessful candidate for reelection in 1882 to the Forty-eighth Congress; returned to his plantation in Adams County, Miss., and engaged in agricultural pursuits; chairman of the Republican State executive committee 1881–1889; member of the Republican National Committee for the State of Mississippi 1884–1889; temporary chairman of the Republican National Convention at Chicago in 1884; Fourth Auditor of the Treasury for the Navy Department under President Harrison 1889–1893; studied law; was admitted to the Mississippi bar in 1896; returned to Washington, D. C., in 1897, where he practiced his profession until 1898, when he was appointed a major and additional paymaster of Volunteers during the Spanish-American War by President William McKinley; was appointed by President McKinley as a paymaster in the Regular Army with the rank of captain in 1901; was promoted to major in 1906; retired from the Regular Army in 1911; moved to Chicago, Ill., in 1912 and continued the practice of his profession until his death in that city on November 2, 1939; interment in Arlington National Cemetery, Fort Myer, Va.

LYNCH, Thomas, a Representative from Wisconsin; born in Granville, Milwaukee County, Wis., November 21, 1844; attended the common schools; moved to Chilton, Calumet County, in 1864; engaged in agricultural pursuits; taught school; held various local offices; member of the State assembly in 1873 and 1883; was graduated from the law department of the Wisconsin University at Madison in 1875; was admitted to the bar in the same year and commenced practice in Chilton, Wis.; district attorney 1878–1882; moved to Antigo, Langlade County, Wis., in 1883; mayor of Antigo in 1885 and 1888; elected as a Democrat to the Fifty-second and Fifty-third Congresses (March 4, 1891–March 3, 1895); died in Antigo, Wis., May 4, 1898; interment in St. John's Cemetery.

LYNCH, Thomas, Sr., a Delegate from South Carolina; born in St. James' Parish, Berkeley County, S. C., in 1727; attended the common schools; engaged in planting, with extensive rice plantations on the Santee River and elsewhere; served in the commons house of assembly 1751–1757, 1761–1763, 1765, 1768, and 1772; delegate to the Colonial Congress in 1765; member of the general committee 1769–1774; delegate to the First and Second Provincial Congresses in 1775 and 1776; member of the first State general assembly in 1776; Member of the Continental Congress 1774–1776; reelected in 1776, but was unable to sign the Declaration of Independence because of illness; died in Annapolis, Anne Arundel County, Md., in December 1776 while en route to his home; interment in St. Anne's Churchyard, Annapolis, Md.

LYNCH, Thomas, Jr. (son of the preceding), a Delegate from South Carolina; born in Prince George's Parish, Winyah, S. C., August 5, 1749; educated at Eton and Cambridge, England, and studied law at the Middle Temple in London, 1764–1772; returned to America in 1772; became a planter on the North Santee River; member of the First and Second Provincial Congresses of South Carolina 1774–1776; member of the constitutional committee in 1776; member of the State general assembly in 1776; served as a captain in the First South Carolina Regiment, subsequently of the Continental Line, in the Revolutionary War from June 1775 until his election as a Delegate to the Continental Congress on February 1, 1776, in place of John Rutledge, not then in attendance, and served in 1776 and 1777; signer of the Declaration of Independence; did not seek reelection to the Continental Congress owing to ill health; embarked on an ocean voyage to France in 1779 and was lost at sea in that year.

LYNCH, Walter Aloysius, a Representative from New York, born in New York, N. Y., July 7, 1894; attended St. Jerome's Parochial School and Fordham Preparatory School; was graduated from Fordham University, New York, N. Y., in 1915 and from the law department of the same university in 1918; was admitted to the bar the same year and commenced practice in New York, N. Y.; served as a magistrate of New York City in 1930; delegate to the New York State constitutional convention in 1938; elected as a Democrat to the Seventy-sixth Congress to fill the vacancy caused by the death of Edward W. Curley; reelected to the Seventy-seventh and to the four succeeding Congresses and served from February 20, 1940, to January 3, 1951; had been renominated in 1950 to the Eighty-second Congress but withdrew and was an unsuccessful candidate for election as Governor of New York; elected to the New York Supreme Court in 1954 and served from January 1955 until his death; died in Belle Harbor (Queens), Long Island, N. Y., September 10, 1957; interment in Gate of Heaven Cemetery, Hawthorne, N. Y.

LYNDE, William Pitt, a Representative from Wisconsin; born in Sherburne, Chenango County, N. Y., December 16, 1817; attended Hamilton Academy and Hamilton College, and was graduated from Yale College in 1838; attended the law department of the New York University for a year and was graduated from the Harvard Law School in 1841; was admitted to the bar in New York in 1841; moved to Wisconsin the same year and settled in Milwaukee; attorney general of Wisconsin in 1844; United States district attorney for Wisconsin in 1845; upon the admission of Wisconsin as a State into the Union was elected as a Democrat to the Thirtieth Congress and served from June 5, 1848, to March 3, 1849; unsuccessful candidate for reelection in 1848 to the Thirty-first Congress; unsuccessful candidate for election as associate justice of the State supreme court in 1849; elected mayor of Milwaukee in 1860; member of the State assembly in 1866; served in the State senate 1869 and 1870; elected to the Forty-fourth and Forty-fifth Congresses (March 4, 1875–March 3, 1879); one of the managers appointed by the House of Representatives in 1876 to conduct the impeachment proceedings against William W. Belknap, Secretary of War in President Grant's Cabinet; was not a candidate for renomination in 1878; withdrew from political life; died in Milwaukee, Wis., December 18, 1885; interment in Forest Home Cemetery.

LYON, Asa, a Representative from Vermont; born in Pomfret, Conn., December 31, 1763; attended the common schools; was graduated from Dartmouth College, Hanover, N. H., in 1790; divinity student with the Rev. Charles Backus at Somers, Conn.; ordained pastor of the Congregational Church in Sunderland, Mass., in 1792; moved to South Hero, Vt., in 1794; studied law; member of the State house of representatives from South Hero 1799–1802, 1804–1806, and 1808, and was a member of the State executive council in 1808; pastor of South Hero 1802–1840; chief judge of Grand Isle County Courts 1805–1809, 1813, and 1814; member of the State house of representatives from Grand Isle 1810–1814; elected as a Federalist to the Fourteenth Congress (March 4, 1815–March 3, 1817); died in South Hero, Grand Isle County, Vt., April 4, 1841; interment in Grand Isle Cemetery, town of Grand Isle, Vt.

LYON, Caleb, a Representative from New York; born in Greig, N. Y., December 7, 1822; attended the common school in Lyonsdale and the schools in Montreal, Canada; was graduated from Norwich University, Northfield, Vt., in 1841; widely known as an extensive traveler and student of foreign countries and customs; became a noted lecturer, poet, author, and writer; appointed United States consul to Shanghai, China, in 1847, but intrusted the office to a deputy and moved to California, where he was chosen a secretary of the California constitutional convention; was the designer of the State seal adopted in 1849; returned to Lyonsdale, N. Y., and was elected to the State assembly in 1850; resigned after opposing Erie Canal improvement; served in the State senate in 1851; active in State and local improvements and free schools; elected as an Independent to the Thirty-third Congress (March 4, 1853–March 3, 1855); moved to Staten Island, N. Y.; appointed the first Governor of the Territory of Idaho 1864–1866; successfully negotiated the treaty for lands with the Shoshone Indians; returned to his home, "Lyonsmere," in Rossville, Staten Island, N. Y., where he died September 8, 1875; interment in Greenwood Cemetery, New York City.

LYON, Chittenden (son of Matthew Lyon), a Representative from Kentucky; born in Fair Haven, Vt., February 22, 1787; attended the common schools; in 1801 moved to Kentucky with his parents, who settled in Caldwell County; engaged in mercantile pursuits in Eddyville, Caldwell County, Ky., and had large agricultural interests; member of the State house of representatives 1822–1824; served in the State senate 1827–1835; elected as a Democrat to the Twentieth and to the three succeeding Congresses (March 4, 1827–March 3, 1835); was not a candidate for reelection in 1835 to the Twenty-fourth Congress; continued his business activities until his death; Lyon County, which was separated from Caldwell County in 1854, was named in his honor; died in Eddyville, Ky., November 23, 1842; interment in Eddyville Cemetery.

LYON, Francis Strother, a Representative from Alabama; born near Danbury, Stokes County, N. C., February 25, 1800; attended the common schools; moved to St. Stephens (an Indian agency), Ala., in 1817; employed in the bank at St. Stephens and in the office of the clerk of the county court; studied law; was

admitted to the bar in 1821 and commenced practice in Demopolis; secretary of the State senate 1822–1830; member of the State senate in 1833; unsuccessful candidate for president of the senate in 1833; reelected to the State senate in 1834 and served as president of that body; elected as a Whig to the Twenty-fourth and Twenty-fifth Congresses (March 4, 1835–March 3, 1839); was not a candidate for renomination; resumed the practice of law and also engaged in agriculture; in 1845, when the State banks were placed in liquidation, he was selected as one of three commissioners to adjust all claims and was afterward chosen sole commissioner until the final settlement in 1853; chairman of the Democratic State convention in 1860; delegate to the Democratic National Convention at Charleston in 1860, when the southern delegates withdrew, he among them; member of the State house of representatives in 1861; elected to the Provisional Confederate Congress but declined to serve; elected to the First and Second Confederate Congresses and served from 1862 until the close of the Civil War; delegate to the State constitutional convention in 1875 and made the draft of the constitution adopted by the convention; again elected to the State senate in 1876; died in Demopolis, Ala., December 31, 1882; interment in the Old Glover Vault.

LYON, Homer Le Grand, a Representative from North Carolina; born in Elizabethtown, Bladen County, N. C., March 1, 1879; attended the public schools, the Davis Military School, Winston, N. C., and the law department of the University of North Carolina at Chapel Hill; was admitted to the bar in 1900 and commenced practice in Whiteville, Columbus County, N. C.; delegate to every Democratic State convention from 1901 to 1921; delegate to the Democratic National Conventions in 1904 and 1940; solicitor of the eighth judicial district of North Carolina 1913–1920; elected as a Democrat to the Sixty-seventh and to the three succeeding Congresses (March 4, 1921–March 3, 1929); was not a candidate for renomination in 1928; resumed the practice of law in Whiteville, N. C., until his retirement in 1950; died in Whiteville, N. C., May 31, 1956; interment in Memorial Cemetery.

LYON, Lucius, a Delegate, a Senator, and a Representative from Michigan; born in Shelburne, Chittenden County, Vt., February 26, 1800; attended the common schools; moved to Bronson, Mich., in 1821; became a land surveyor; elected as a Democrat a Delegate to the Twenty-third Congress (March 4, 1833–March 3, 1835); served as a member of the convention which framed the State constitution in 1835; upon the admission of Michigan as a State into the Union was elected as a Democrat to the United States Senate and served from January 26, 1837, to March 3, 1839; was not a candidate for reelection; moved to Grand Rapids, Mich., in 1839; member of the board of regents of the University of Michigan 1837–1839; appointed Indian commissioner at La Pointe, Wis., in 1839; elected as a Representative to the Twenty-eighth Congress (March 4, 1843–March 3, 1845); declined to be a candidate for renomination in 1844; appointed by President James K. Polk in 1845 surveyor general for Ohio, Indiana, and Michigan, moving the office from Cincinnati to Detroit for his convenience; served in this capacity until 1850; delegate to the Democratic National Convention at Baltimore in 1848 which nominated Lewis Cass, of Michigan, for President and W. O. Butler, of Kentucky, for Vice President; died in Detroit, Mich., September 24, 1851; interment in Elmwood Cemetery.

LYON, Matthew (father of Chittenden Lyon and great-grandfather of William Peters Hepburn), a Representative from Vermont and from Kentucky; born near Dublin, County Wicklow, Ireland, July 14, 1746; attended school in Dublin; began to learn the trade of printer in 1763; immigrated to the United

States in 1765; was landed as a redemptioner and worked on a farm in Woodbury, Conn., where he continued his education; moved to Wallingford, Vt. (then known as the New Hampshire Grants), in 1774 and organized a company of militia; assisted in the capture of Fort Ticonderoga; served as-adjutant in Colonel Warner's regiment in Canada in 1775; commissioned second lieutenant in the regiment known as the Green Mountain Boys in July 1776; commissioned a paymaster with the rank of captain in 1776; acted as guide to General St. Clair on the march to Fort Edward in 1777; moved to Arlington, Vt., in 1777; resigned from the Army in 1778; member of the State house of representatives 1779–1783; founded the town of Fair Haven, Vt., in 1783; was a member of the State house of representatives for ten years during the period 1783–1796; built and operated various kinds of mills, including one for the manufacture of paper from wood pulp; established a printing office in 1793 and published the Farmers' Library, afterward the Fair Haven Gazette; unsuccessful Anti-Federalist candidate for election to the Second and Third Congresses; unsuccessfully contested the election of Israel Smith to the Fourth Congress; elected to the Fifth and Sixth Congresses (March 4, 1797–March 3, 1801); was not a candidate for renomination in 1800; moved to Kentucky in 1801 and settled in Caldwell (now Lyon) County; member of the House of Representatives of Kentucky in 1802; elected to the Eighth and to the three succeeding Congresses (March 4, 1803–March 3, 1811); unsuccessful candidate for reelection in 1810 to the Twelfth Congress; contracted with the Government to build gunboats for the War of 1812; was appointed United States factor to the Cherokee Nation in Arkansas Territory in 1820; unsuccessfully contested the election of James W. Bates as a Delegate from Arkansas Territory to the Seventeenth Congress; died in Spadra Bluff, Ark., August 1, 1822; interment in Spadra Bluff Cemetery; reinterment in Eddyville Cemetery, Eddyville, Caldwell (now Lyon) County, Ky., in 1833.

LYTLE, Robert Todd (nephew of John Rowan), a Representative from Ohio; born in Williamsburg, Clermont County, Ohio, May 19, 1804; attended the common schools and Cincinnati College; studied law in Louisville, Ky.; was admitted to the bar in that city in 1824 and commenced the practice of his profession in Cincinnati, Ohio; elected county prosecuting attorney; member of the State house of representatives in 1828 and 1829; elected as a Jackson Democrat to the Twenty-third Congress and served from March 4, 1833, until March 10, 1834, when he`resigned; reelected to fill the vacancy caused by his own resignation and served from December 27, 1834, to March 3, 1835; unsuccessful candidate for reelection in 1834 to the Twenty-fourth Congress; resumed the practice of law; surveyor general of public lands in the Northwest Territory in 1836; major general of Ohio Militia in 1838; died in New Orleans, La., December 22, 1839; interment in Spring Grove Cemetery, Cincinnati, Ohio.

M

MAAS, Melvin Joseph, a Representative from Minnesota; born in Duluth, Minn., May 14, 1898; moved with his parents to St. Paul, Minn., in 1898; educated in the public schools; was graduated from St. Thomas College at St. Paul in 1919; attended the University of Minnesota at Minneapolis; employed by a surety company as a salesman in 1921 and as a district supervisor of the bond department 1924–1926; engaged in the general insurance business in 1926; during the First World War served in the aviation branch of the Marine Corps in 1918 and 1919; officer in the Marine Corps Reserve in 1925 and retired with rank of major general August 1, 1952; elected as a Republican to the Seventieth, Seventy-first, and Seventy-second

Congresses (March 4, 1927–March 3, 1933); unsuccessful candidate for renomination in 1932; received the Carnegie Silver Medal for disarming a maniac in the United States House of Representatives in December 1932; elected to the Seventy-fourth and to the four succeeding Congresses (January 3, 1935–January 3, 1945); unsuccessful candidate for reelection in 1944 to the Seventy-ninth Congress; during World War II served in the South Pacific as a colonel in the United States Marine Corps 1942–1945, while still a Member of Congress; received the Silver Star, Purple Heart, and Legion of Merit Medals; special adviser to the House Naval Affairs Committee in 1946; assistant to the chairman of the board of the Sperry Corporation, New York, N. Y., 1947–1951; vice president of Maas-Keefe Co., St. Paul, Minn.; chairman of President's Committee on Employment of the Physically Handicapped 1954–; chairman of Committee for the Handicapped, People-to-People Program, 1956–; resides in Chevy Chase, Md.

MacCRATE, John, a Representative from New York; born in Dumbarton, Scotland, March 29, 1885; immigrated with his mother to the United States in 1893 and settled in Greenpoint, Brooklyn, N. Y., where his father had provided a home; attended the public schools and the Commercial High School in Brooklyn; was graduated from the law department of New York University in 1906; was admitted to the bar the same year and commenced practice in New York City; delegate to the Republican National Conventions in 1916 and 1920; was nominated in the primaries by both the Republican and Democratic Parties and was elected as a Republican to the Sixty-sixth Congress and served from March 4, 1919, to December 30, 1920, when he resigned; elected justice of the supreme court of the State of New York in 1920; reelected in 1934 and 1948 and served in the appellate division of the supreme court until December 31, 1955, when he reached age limit; official referee, New York State Supreme Court, in 1956, 1957, and to June 1958; is a resident of Brooklyn, N. Y.

MacDONALD, John Lewis, a Representative from Minnesota; born in Glasgow, Scotland, February 22, 1838; immigrated to Nova Scotia, Canada, with his parents, who later, in 1847, settled in Pittsburgh, Pa.; moved to Minnesota in 1855 and settled in Scott County; studied law; was admitted to the bar in 1859 and commenced practice at Belle Plain, Minn.; judge of the probate court of Scott County in 1860 and 1861; during the Civil War was commissioned to enlist and muster volunteers for the Union Army; prosecuting attorney of Scott County in 1863 and 1864; county superintendent of schools in 1865 and 1866; member of the State house of representatives in 1869 and 1870; served in the State senate in 1871 and 1873–1876; unsuccessful Democratic candidate for attorney general in 1872; mayor of Shakopee in 1876; elected judge of the eighth judicial district of Minnesota in 1876 for a term of seven years and reelected without opposition in 1883; resigned in the fall of 1886, having been elected to Congress; elected as a Democrat to the Fiftieth Congress (March 4, 1887–March 3, 1889); unsuccessful candidate for reelection in 1888 to the Fifty-first Congress; engaged in the practice of his profession in St. Paul, Minn.; moved to Kansas City, Mo., in 1898 and continued the practice of law until his death from injuries received in a streetcar accident July 13, 1903; interment in St. Mary's Cemetery, Kansas City, Mo.

MACDONALD, Moses, a Representative from Maine; born in Limerick, Maine, April 8, 1815; received an academic education; studied law; was admitted to the bar in 1837 and commenced practice in Biddeford, Maine, in 1837; member of the State house of representatives in 1841, 1842, and 1845; served as speaker in 1845; served in the State senate in 1847; State treasurer 1847–1850; elected as a Democrat to the Thirty-second and Thirty-third Congresses (March 4, 1851–March 3, 1855); appointed collector of customs at Portland, Maine, by President Buchanan in 1857 and served until 1861; died in Saco, Maine, on October 18, 1869; interment in Laurel Hill Cemetery.

MACDONALD, Torbert Hart, a Representative from Massachusetts; born in Boston, Suffolk County, Mass., June 6, 1917; attended Malden public schools, Medford High School, and Phillips Academy, Andover, Mass.; was graduated from Harvard University, Cambridge, Mass., in 1940 and from its law school in 1946; during World War II served in the United States Navy as a P. T. boat commander in the Southwest Pacific 1942–1944; wounded in action; awarded Silver Star Combat Award and Presidential Citation; was admitted to the bar in 1946 and commenced the practice of law in Boston, Mass.; member of the National Labor Relations Board for New England area 1948–1952; delegate to the Democratic National Convention in 1960; elected as a Democrat to the Eighty-fourth, Eighty-fifth, and Eighty-sixth Congresses (January 3, 1955–January 3, 1961). *Reelected to the Eighty-seventh Congress.*

MacDONALD, William Josiah, a Representative from Michigan; born in Potosi, Grant County, Wis., November 17, 1873; attended the common schools, and was graduated from the high school at Fairmont, Minn.; attended the University of Minnesota at Minneapolis and Georgetown Law School, Washington, D. C.; was admitted to the bar and commenced practice at Calumet, Mich., in 1895; prosecuting attorney for Keweenaw County, Mich., 1898–1904; prosecuting attorney for Houghton County, Mich., 1906–1912; successfully contested as a Progressive the election of H. Olin Young to the Sixty-third Congress and served from August 26, 1913, to March 3, 1915; unsuccessful candidate for reelection in 1914 to the Sixty-fourth Congress and for election in 1916 to the Sixty-fifth Congress; resumed the practice of law in Springfield, Ill., in 1917; moved to East St. Louis, Ill., in 1922 and engaged in the practice of his profession; died in Chicago, Ill., March 29, 1946; interment in Graceland Cemetery, Chicago, Ill.

MacDOUGALL, Clinton Dugald, a Representative from New York; born near Glasgow, Scotland, June 14, 1839; immigrated to Canada in 1842 with his parents, who later settled in Auburn, N. Y.; pursued an academic course; studied law; engaged in banking 1856–1869; served in the Union Army during the Civil War; commissioned captain in the Seventy-fifth Regiment, New York Volunteer Infantry, September 16, 1861; lieutenant colonel of the One Hundred and Eleventh Regiment, New York Volunteer Infantry, August 20, 1862; colonel January 3, 1863; brevetted brigadier general of Volunteers February 25, 1865; honorably mustered out June 4, 1865; appointed postmaster of Auburn, N. Y., in 1869; elected as a Republican to the Forty-third and Forty-fourth Congresses (March 4, 1873–March 3, 1877); unsuccessful candidate for renomination in 1876; served as United States marshal of the northern judicial district of New York 1877–1885 and 1901–1910; died in Paris, France, May 24, 1914; interment in Arlington National Cemetery, Fort Myer, Va.

MACE, Daniel, a Representative from Indiana; born in Pickaway County, Ohio, September 5, 1811; attended the public schools; studied law; was admitted to the bar in 1835 and practiced in LaFayette, Ind.; member of the State house of representatives in 1836; clerk of the State house of representatives in 1837; United States attorney for Indiana 1849–1853; elected as a Democrat to the Thirty-second and Thirty-third Congresses (March 4, 1851–March 3, 1855); reelected as a Republican to the Thirty-fourth Congress (March 4, 1855–March 3, 1857); resumed

the practice of law; postmaster of LaFayette from September 22, 1866, until his death in LaFayette, July 26, 1867; interment in Greenbush Cemetery.

MacGREGOR, Clarence, a Representative from New York; born in Newark, Wayne County, N. Y., September 16, 1872; attended the public schools in Gloversville, Auburn, and Buffalo, N. Y., and was graduated from Hartwick Seminary, Otsego County, N. Y., in 1893; took a special course at the University of Rochester, Rochester, N. Y., in 1894 and 1895; was admitted to the bar in 1897 and commenced the practice of his profession in Buffalo, N. Y.; member of the State assembly 1908–1912; elected as a Republican to the Sixty-sixth and to the four succeeding Congresses and served from March 4, 1919, until his resignation on December 31, 1928, having been elected as a justice of the supreme court of the State of New York, and serving until his retirement on December 31, 1942; appointed official referee of the supreme court of the State of New York on January 7, 1943, and served until his death in Buffalo, N. Y., February 18, 1952; interment in Forest Lawn Cemetery.

MACHEN, Willis Benson, a Senator from Kentucky; born in Caldwell (now Lyon) County, Ky., April 10, 1810; attended the common schools and Cumberland College, Princeton, Ky.; engaged in agricultural pursuits near Eddyville; delegate to the State constitutional convention in 1849; served in the State senate in 1854; member of the State house of representatives in 1856 and 1860; elected to the First and Second Confederate Congresses; appointed as a Democrat to the United States Senate to fill the vacancy caused by the death of Garrett Davis and served from September 27, 1872, to March 3, 1873; resumed agricultural interests; died in Hopkinsville, Ky., September 29, 1893; interment in Riverview Cemetery, Eddyville, Lyon County, Ky.

MACHIR, James, a Representative from Virginia; born in that State; member of the State house of delegates 1793–1796; elected to the Fifth Congress (March 4, 1797–March 3, 1799); again a member of the State house of delegates 1811–1813 and 1818–1821; died June 25, 1827.

MACHROWICZ, Thaddeus Michael, a Representative from Michigan; born in Gostyn, Poland, August 21, 1899; immigrated to the United States with his parents in 1902 and settled in Chicago, Ill., later moving to Milwaukee, Wis.; naturalized in 1910; attended the parochial school in Milwaukee, Wis., Alliance College, Cambridge Springs, Pa., 1912–1916, and University of Chicago in 1917; during the First World War served as a lieutenant in the Polish Army of American Volunteers in Canada, France, and Poland, 1917–1920; served with the American Advisory Commission to Polish Government in 1920 and 1921; also acted as war correspondent with Floyd Gibbons in Poland 1919–1921; attended De Paul University in 1921 and graduated from the Detroit College of Law in 1924; was admitted to the Michigan bar in 1924 and commenced practice in Detroit; city attorney of Hamtramck, Mich., 1934–1936; legal director, Michigan Public Utilities Commission, in 1938 and 1939; municipal judge in Hamtramck, Mich., 1942–1950; public member of War Labor Board during World War II; elected as a Democrat to the Eighty-second and to the five succeeding Congresses and served from January 3, 1951, to September 18, 1961, when he resigned, having been appointed a judge of the United States District Court for the eastern district of Michigan; is a resident of Hamtramck, Mich.

MACIEJEWSKI, Anton Frank, a Representative from Illinois; born in Anderson, Grimes County, Tex., January 3, 1893; attended the public schools of Cicero, Ill., and Lewis Institute,

Chicago, Ill.; became engaged in the wholesale and retail coal business in Cicero, Ill., in 1916; assistant agent in charge of relief of Cook County, Ill., 1925–1928; member of the Democratic State and National Committees; delegate to the Democratic National Convention at Houston, Tex., in 1928; supervisor and treasurer of Cicero, Ill., 1932–1939; elected as a Democrat to the Seventy-sixth and Seventy-seventh Congresses and served from January 3, 1939, until his resignation on December 8, 1942; was not a candidate for renomination in 1942; resumed the wholesale and retail coal business; also engaged in the construction of defense housing; elected to the board of trustees of the sanitary district of Chicago in December 1942 and served until his death; died in Chicago, Ill., September 25, 1949; interment in Resurrection Cemetery, Justice, Ill.

MacINTYRE, Archibald Thompson, a Representative from Georgia; born near Marion, Twiggs County, Ga., October 27, 1822; moved with his parents to Thomas County, Ga., in 1826; attended the common schools and was graduated from Thomasville Academy; studied law in Monticello, Fla., and Macon, Ga.; was admitted to the bar in 1843 and commenced the practice of law at Thomasville; member of the State house of representatives in 1849; during the Civil War served as colonel of the Eleventh Infantry, Georgia Guards, in the Confederate Army; delegate to the State constitutional convention in 1865; elected as a Democrat to the Forty-second Congress (March 4, 1871–March 3, 1873); was not a candidate for renomination in 1872; resumed the practice of law in Thomasville, Ga.; member of the board of trustees of the University of Georgia and Georgia State Sanitarium; died in Thomasville on January 1, 1900; interment in Laurel Hill Cemetery.

MACIORA, Lucien John, a Representative from Connecticut; born in New Britain, Hartford County, Conn., August 17, 1902; attended the grade and high schools; engaged in the grocery business 1920–1928; member of the New Britain Common Council 1926–1934; engaged in the furniture and undertaking business 1928–1939; member of the board of directors of Peoples Savings Bank, New Britain, Conn., 1935–; served in the State house of representatives 1931–1937; chairman of the New Britain Police Board 1934–1940; delegate to the Democratic State convention at New Britain in 1938; engaged in the insurance business in 1939; elected as a Democrat to the Seventy-seventh Congress (January 3, 1941–January 3, 1943); unsuccessful candidate for reelection in 1942 to the Seventy-eighth Congress; resumed the insurance business; collector of taxes for the city of New Britain 1950–; is a resident of New Britain, Conn.

MACK, Peter Francis, Jr., a Representative from Illinois; born in Carlinville, Macoupin County, Ill., November 1, 1916; attended the public schools and Blackburn College in Carlinville, Ill., and St. Louis (Mo.) University; took special courses in aviation at Springfield (Ill.) Junior College and St. Louis (Mo.) University; engaged in the automotive sales and service business in Carlinville, Ill.; qualified in jet-type aircraft; licensed commercial pilot with flight instructor and instrument flight ratings in single- and multi-engine airplanes; enlisted in United States Navy in 1942 and served four years in naval air force during World War II; Naval Reserve officer with rank of commander; sponsor of Mack Educational Tours for handicapped and dependent school children; pilot of single-engine "Friendship Flame" on round-the-world solo flight in 1951; was awarded the 1952 air trophy for achievement in general aviation by the Washington Air Derby Association, Certificate of Merit in the Naval Air Reserve, Citation of Achievement by the Aero Club of Washington, Citation of Recognition by the American Legion, and selected as Flying Farmer of the Year; elected as a Democrat to

the Eighty-first and to the five succeeding Congresses (January 3, 1949–January 3, 1961). *Reelected to the Eighty-seventh Congress.*

MACK, Russell Vernon, a Representative from Washington; born in Hillman, Montmorency County, Mich., June 13, 1891; moved with his parents to Aberdeen, Grays Harbor County, Wash., in 1895; attended the public schools, Stanford University of California in 1913 and 1914, and the University of Washington at Seattle in 1914 and 1915; joined the Aberdeen (Wash.) Daily World in 1913 as a cub reporter and was business manager 1920–1934; during the First World War served as a corporal in the Thirty-ninth Field Artillery, Thirteenth Division; owner and publisher of the Hoquiam Daily Washingtonian 1934–1950; elected as a Republican to the Eightieth Congress to fill the vacancy caused by the death of Fred B. Norman; reelected to the Eighty-first and to the five succeeding Congresses and served from June 7, 1947, until his death on the floor of the United States House of Representatives, Washington, D. C., March 28, 1960; interment in Fern Hill Cemetery, Aberdeen, Wash.

MACKEY, Edmund William McGregor, a Representative from South Carolina; born in Charleston, S. C., March 8, 1846; pursued classical studies; appointed assistant assessor of internal revenue in South Carolina September 8, 1865; delegate to the State constitutional convention in 1867; studied law; was admitted to the bar in 1868 and practiced; took a prominent part in the work of reconstruction during the period following the Civil War; sheriff of Charleston County 1868–1872; elected an alderman of the city of Charleston in 1868, 1873, and 1875; editor and proprietor of the Charleston Republican 1871 and 1872; member of the State house of representatives in 1873; presented credentials as an Independent Republican Member-elect to the Forty-fourth Congress and served from March 4, 1875, to July 19, 1876, when the seat was declared vacant; again a member of the State house of representatives in 1877 and served as speaker; delegate to the Republican National Convention at Philadelphia in 1872 which nominated Grant and Wilson and at Chicago in 1880 which nominated Garfield and Arthur; assistant United States attorney for South Carolina 1878–1881; unsuccessfully contested as a Republican the election of Michael P. O'Connor to the Forty-sixth Congress; successfully contested the election of Michael P. O'Connor to the Forty-seventh Congress, succeeding Samuel Dibble, who presented credentials as a Member-elect to fill the vacancy thought to exist upon the death of Mr. O'Connor, which occurred while the contest was pending; reelected to the Forty-eighth Congress and served from May 31, 1882, until his death in Washington, D. C., on January 27, 1884; interment in Glenwood Cemetery.

MACKEY, Levi Augustus, a Representative from Pennsylvania; born in Whitedeer Township, Union County, Pa., November 25, 1819; moved with his parents in 1829 to Milton, Pa.; received an academic education and was graduated from Union College, Schenectady, N. Y., in 1837; studied law in Dickinson College, Carlisle, Pa.; was admitted to the bar in 1840 and practiced law in Lock Haven, Pa., from 1841 until 1855; engaged in banking and was elected president of the Lock Haven Bank in 1855; delegate to the Whig National Convention at Baltimore in 1852 and to the Democratic National Convention at Baltimore in 1872; unsuccessful candidate for election in 1868 to the Forty-first Congress; mayor of Lock Haven, Pa., in 1870; served as president of the Bald Eagle Valley Railroad Co. and of several other corporations; member of the board of trustees of the normal school at Lock Haven, Pa., from 1870 until the time of his death; elected as a Democrat to the Forty-fourth and Forty-fifth Congresses (March 4, 1875–March 3, 1879); resumed his former business pursuits; died in Lock Haven, Pa., February 8, 1889; interment in Highland Cemetery.

MacKINNON, George Edward, a Representative from Minnesota; born in St. Paul, Ramsey County, Minn., April 22, 1906; attended the public schools and the University of Colorado at Boulder; was graduated from the law school of the University of Minnesota at Minneapolis in 1929; was admitted to the bar the same year and commenced practice in Minneapolis, Minn.; served in the State house of representatives 1935–1942; during World War II served in the United States Navy 1942–1946; elected as a Republican to the Eightieth Congress (January 3, 1947–January 3, 1949); unsuccessful candidate for reelection in 1948 to the Eighty-first Congress; resumed the general practice of law; appointed United States attorney for the district of Minnesota on March 23, 1953, reappointed June 26, 1957, and served until his resignation June 6, 1958; unsuccessful candidate for Governor of Minnesota in 1958; in private practice of law December 1958 to March 1960; special assistant to United States Attorney General January 1960 to February 1961; general counsel and vice president, Investors Mutual, Inc., Minneapolis, Minn., March 1961–; resides in Minneapolis, Minn.

MacLAFFERTY, James Henry, a Representative from California; born in San Diego, Calif., February 27, 1871; moved with his parents to Oakland, Calif., in 1874, to Eugene, Oreg., in 1880, to Astoria, Oreg., in 1883, and to Tacoma, Wash., in 1884; attended the public schools; entered the lumber business in Tacoma and continued the same in Seattle until 1889; engaged in the wholesale paper business at Chicago in 1899; returned to the Pacific coast in 1900 and settled in Oakland, Calif.; engaged as a traveling salesman between cities from Vancouver, British Columbia, to San Diego, Calif.; engaged extensively in wholesale paper business, also in the automobile insurance business; elected as a Republican to the Sixty-seventh Congress to fill the vacancy caused by the death of John A. Elston; reelected to the Sixty-eighth Congress and served from November 7, 1922, to March 3, 1925; unsuccessful candidate for reelection in 1924 to the Sixty-ninth Congress; assistant to Secretary of Commerce from March 24, 1925, until August 31, 1927; resumed business activities in Oakland, Calif.; served as vice president of the Pacific American Steamship Association and of the Shipowners' Association of the Pacific Coast; died in Oakland, Calif., June 9, 1937, and the remains were cremated.

MACLAY, Samuel (brother of William Maclay and father of William Plunkett Maclay), a Representative and a Senator from Pennsylvania; born in Lurgan Township, Franklin County, Pa., June 17, 1741; completed preparatory studies; engaged in agricultural pursuits and surveying; served in the Revolutionary War; associate judge of Franklin County 1792–1795; elected to the Fourth Congress (March 4, 1795–March 3, 1797); member of the State senate 1797–1803 and served as speaker from December 2, 1801, until his resignation March 16, 1803; elected to the United States Senate and served from March 4, 1803, until his resignation, January 4, 1809; retired, and died in Buffalo Township, Union County, Pa., October 5, 1811; interment in Driesbach Church Cemetery.

MACLAY, William (brother of Samuel Maclay), a Senator from Pennsylvania; born in New Garden, Pa., July 20, 1737; pursued classical studies; served as a lieutenant in Gen. John Forbes' expedition to Fort Duquesne in 1758, and in other expeditions against the French and Indians; studied law; was

admitted to the bar in 1760; became a surveyor in the employ of the Penn family April 28, 1760; prothonotary and clerk of the courts of Northumberland County in 1772; served in the Continental Army as a commissary in the Revolutionary War; member of the Provincial Assembly in 1781; Indian commissioner, judge of the court of common pleas, and member of the executive council; elected as a Democrat to the United States Senate and served from March 4, 1789, to March 3, 1791; retired to his farm in Dauphin, Pa.; member of the State house of representatives in 1795; presidential elector in 1796; county judge 1801–1803; again a member of the State house of representatives in 1803 and 1804; died in Harrisburg, Dauphin County, Pa., April 16, 1804; interment in Old Paxtang Church Cemetery.

MACLAY, William, a Representative from Pennsylvania; born in Lurgan Township, Franklin County, Pa., March 22, 1765; attended the country schools; studied law; was admitted to the bar in 1800 and commenced the practice of his profession at Chambersburg, Franklin County, Pa.; county commissioner in 1805 and 1806; was a member of the State house of representatives in 1807 and 1808; associate judge for the Cumberland district in 1809; elected to the Fourteenth and Fifteenth Congresses (March 4, 1815–March 3, 1819); retired from public life; died in Lurgan, Franklin County, Pa., January 4, 1825; interment in Middle Springs Cemetery.

MACLAY, William Brown, a Representative from New York; born in New York City March 20, 1812; received private instruction; was graduated from the College of the City of New York in 1836; associate editor of the New York Quarterly Review in 1836; taught Latin; studied law; was admitted to the bar in 1839 and commenced the practice of his profession in New York City; member of the State assembly 1840–1842; elected as a Democrat to the Twenty-eighth, Twenty-ninth, and Thirtieth Congresses (March 4, 1843–March 3, 1849); unsuccessful candidate for reelection in 1848 to the Thirty-first Congress; elected to the Thirty-fifth and Thirty-sixth Congresses (March 4, 1857–March 3, 1861); was not a candidate for reelection in 1860 to the Thirty-seventh Congress; withdrew from public life; died in New York City February 19, 1882; interment in Greenwood Cemetery, Brooklyn Borough, N. Y.

MACLAY, William Plunkett (son of Samuel Maclay), a Representative from Pennsylvania; born in Northumberland County, near Lewisburg, Union County, Pa., August 23, 1774; attended the common schools; prothonotary of Mifflin County 1808–1814; member of the State house of representatives; elected as a Democrat to the Fourteenth Congress to fill the vacancy caused by the resignation of Thomas Burnside; reelected to the Fifteenth and Sixteenth Congresses and served from October 8, 1816, until March 3, 1821; was not a candidate for renomination in 1820; member of the State convention to alter and amend the constitution at Harrisburg, Pa., in 1837; engaged as a surveyor and in agricultural pursuits; died in Milroy, Mifflin County, Pa., September 2, 1842; interment in Milroy Presbyterian Cemetery.

MACON, Nathaniel (uncle of Willis Alston and Micajah Thomas Hawkins, and great-grandfather of Charles Henry Martin), a Representative and a Senator from North Carolina; born near Warrenton, Warren County, N. C., December 17, 1757; pursued classical studies and attended Princeton College; served in the Revolutionary War; member of the State senate 1780–1782, 1784, and 1785; moved to a plantation on the Roanoke River; elected as a Democrat to the Second and to the twelve succeeding Congresses and served from March 4, 1791, until December 13, 1815, when he resigned, having been elected Senator; served as Speaker of the House of Representatives 1801–1807; elected to the United States Senate on December 5, 1815, to fill the vacancy caused by the resignation of Francis Locke; reelected in 1819 and 1825 and served from December 13, 1815, until his resignation on November 14, 1828; elected President pro tempore of the Senate May 20, 1826, January 2, 1827, and March 2, 1827; received twenty-four electoral votes for Vice President in 1825; president of the State constitutional convention in 1835; presidential elector on the Democratic ticket of Van Buren and Johnson in 1836; died near Macon, Warren County, N. C., June 29, 1837; interment in the private grounds of his home at Bucks Creek, Warren County, N. C.

MACON, Robert Bruce, a Representative from Arkansas; born near Trenton, Phillips County, Ark., July 6, 1859; was left an orphan at the age of nine; attended the public schools, and studied at home; engaged in agricultural pursuits; studied law; was admitted to the bar in 1891 and commenced practice in Helena, Ark.; member of the State house of representatives 1883–1887; clerk of the circuit court 1892–1896; prosecuting attorney for the first judicial district 1898–1902; elected as a Democrat to the Fifty-eighth and to the four succeeding Congresses (March 4, 1903–March 3, 1913); unsuccessful candidate for renomination; continued the practice of law in Helena, Ark., until he retired in 1917; died in Marvell, Ark., October 9, 1925; interment in Elmwood Cemetery, Memphis, Tenn.

MACY, John B., a Representative from Wisconsin; born in Nantucket, Mass., March 25, 1799; received a liberal education; moved to New York City in 1826 and later in that year to Buffalo, N. Y.; resided in Cincinnati, Ohio, 1842–1845; one of the founders of Toledo, Ohio, and one of the proprietors of the Rock River Valley Railroad; moved to Fond du Lac, Wis., in 1845 and engaged in the real-estate business; moved with his family to the town of Empire, near de Nevew Lake, Wis., in 1850; elected as a Democrat to the Thirty-third Congress (March 4, 1853–March 3, 1855); unsuccessful for reelection in 1854 to the Thirty-fourth Congress; resumed his former business pursuits; lost his life in the burning of the steamer *Niagara* about one mile from Port Washington on Lake Michigan on September 24, 1856; his body was never recovered.

MACY, William Kingsland, a Representative from New York; born in New York City, November 21, 1889; was graduated from Groton (Mass.) School in 1908 and from Harvard University, Cambridge, Mass., in 1912; engaged in wholesaling and importing 1912–1915; during the First World War served as a dollar-a-year man for the United States Food Administration and War Trade Board 1917–1919; president of Union Pacific Tea Co., 1919–1922; member of a stock brokerage firm 1922–1938; banker and publisher; chairman of the Suffolk County Republican Committee 1926–1951; chairman of the New York State Republican Committee 1930–1934; delegate to the Republican National Conventions in 1928, 1932, 1940, 1944, and 1948, and to the Republican State Conventions 1928–1946; was active in the investigation of the New York State Banking Department in 1929 and also in promoting the Seabury inquiry into the affairs of New York City in 1931 and 1932; Regent of the State of New York 1941–1953; member of the State senate in 1946; elected as a Republican to the Eightieth and Eighty-first Congresses (January 3, 1947–January 3, 1951); was defeated for reelection in 1950 to the Eighty-second Congress; chairman of the board of Suffolk Consolidated Press Co., Inc., and of Suffolk Broadcasting Corp.; died in Islip, N. Y., July 15, 1961, and the remains placed in a receiving vault at Oakwood Cemetery.

MADDEN, Martin Barnaby, a Representative from Illinois; born in Darlington, England, March 20, 1855; immigrated to the United States with his parents, who settled in Chicago, Ill., in 1860; attended the public schools in Chicago, and was graduated from Bryant and Stratton Business College in 1873; was also graduated from an engineering trade school as an engineer; president of the Quarry Owners' Association of the United States 1885–1889; vice president and director of the Builders and Traders' Exchange of Chicago in 1886 and 1887; member of the Chicago City Council 1889–1897; served as presiding officer of that body 1891–1893 and chairman of the finance committee for seven years; chairman of the Republican committee of Chicago 1890–1896; president of the Western Stone Co. 1890–1915; director of the Metropolitan Trust & Savings Bank of Chicago 1895–1910; delegate to every Republican National Convention from 1896 to 1924, serving as a member of the resolutions committee in practically every convention and as a member of the committee in the 1900 convention wrote the plank which committed the United States to the construction of the Panama Canal; president of the Illinois Manufacturers' Association in 1901 and 1902; unsuccessful candidate for election in 1902 to the Fifty-eighth Congress; organized the first military training camp west of the Allegheny Mountains at Fort Sheridan, Ill., in 1915, recruiting the men and serving as a private in Company A; elected as a Republican to the Fifty-ninth and to the eleven succeeding Congresses and served from March 4, 1905, until his death; had been nominated for reelection to the Seventy-first Congress; died in the room of the Committee on Appropriations of the House of Representatives, Capitol Building, Washington, D. C., April 27, 1928; interment in Fairview Cemetery, near Hinsdale, Du Page County, Ill.

MADDEN, Ray John, a Representative from Indiana; born in Waseca, Waseca County, Minn., February 25, 1892; attended the public schools and Sacred Heart Academy in his native city; was graduated from the law department of Creighton University, Omaha, Nebr., in 1913; was admitted to the bar the same year and commenced practice in Omaha, Nebr.; elected municipal judge of Omaha, Nebr., in 1916, resigning during the First World War to serve in the United States Navy; engaged in the practice of law in Gary, Ind.; city comptroller of Gary 1935–1938; treasurer of Lake County, Ind., 1938–1942; elected as a Democrat to the Seventy-eighth and to the eight succeeding Congresses (January 3, 1943–January 3, 1961). *Reelected to the Eighty-seventh Congress.*

MADDOX, John W., a Representative from Georgia; born on a farm near Gore, Chattooga County, Ga., June 3, 1848; attended the common schools; during the Civil War enlisted in the Confederate Army in Company E, Sixth Georgia Cavalry, in 1863 and served until the end of the war; attended school in Summerville and Bethel Church; engaged in agricultural pursuits and in railroad construction work in 1871; deputy sheriff of Chattooga County; studied law; was admitted to the bar in 1877 and commenced practice in Summerville, Ga.; mayor of Summerville in 1877; county commissioner 1878–1880; member of the State house of representatives 1880–1884; served in the State senate 1884–1886; elected judge of the superior court, Rome circuit, in 1886, and was reelected in 1890, resigning the office September 1, 1892; moved to Rome, Ga., in 1890; elected as a Democrat to the Fifty-third and to the five succeeding Congresses (March 4, 1893–March 3, 1905); was not a candidate for renomination in 1904; resumed the practice of law; mayor of Rome in 1906 and 1907; appointed judge of the Superior Court of Georgia in 1908; elected in 1910 and served until his resignation on February 1, 1912, having become president of the State Mutual Life Insurance Co.; also engaged in the practice of law; died in Rome, Ga., September 27, 1922; interment in Myrtle Hill Cemetery.

MADISON, Edmond Haggard, a Representative from Kansas; born in Plymouth, Hancock County, Ill., December 18, 1865; attended the common schools; taught school; moved to Wichita, Kans., in 1885; studied law; was admitted to the bar in 1888 and commenced the practice of his profession in Dodge City, Kans.; prosecuting attorney of Ford County, Kans., 1889–1893; appointed judge of the thirty-first judicial district of Kansas on January 1, 1900, and served until September 17, 1906, when he resigned to become a candidate for Congress; elected as a Republican to the Sixtieth, Sixty-first, and Sixty-second Congresses and served from March 4, 1907, until his death in Dodge City, Ford County, Kans., September 18, 1911; interment in Maple Grove Cemetery.

MADISON, James, a Delegate and a Representative from Virginia and a President of the United States; born in Port Conway, King George County, Va., March 16, 1751; studied under private tutors, and was graduated from Princeton College in 1771; studied law at Princeton College one year; returned to Virginia and continued the study of law; was admitted to the bar; member of the committee of safety from Orange County in 1774; delegate in the Williamsburg (Va.) convention of May 1776; member of the First General Assembly of Virginia in 1776, and was unanimously elected a member of the executive council in 1778; Member of the Continental Congress 1780–1783 and 1786–1788; prominent delegate in the Federal Constitutional Convention at Philadelphia, Pa., in 1787; elected as a Democrat to the First and to the three succeeding Congresses (March 4, 1789–March 3, 1797); declined the mission to France, tendered by President Washington in 1794 and also the position of Secretary of State, tendered the same year; again a member of the Virginia Assembly from Orange County in 1799; presidential elector on the Democratic ticket in 1800 and voted for Jefferson and Burr; appointed by President Jefferson as Secretary of State March 5, 1801; entered upon the duties of that office May 2, 1801, and served until March 4, 1809; elected as a Democrat President of the United States; reelected and served from March 4, 1809, to March 3, 1817; retired to his estate, "Montpelier," Orange County, Va.; delegate in the Virginia constitutional convention of 1829; rector of the University of Virginia at Charlottesville and visitor to the College of William and Mary, Williamsburg, Va.; died in the Montpelier mansion, Orange County, Va., June 28, 1836; interment in the private cemetery on the grounds at "Montpelier."

MAFFETT, James Thompson, a Representative from Pennsylvania; born in Clarion Township, Clarion County, Pa., February 2, 1837; attended the common schools, Rimersburg Academy, and Jefferson College, Canonsburg, Pa.; taught school in Missouri for one year, and then, in 1859, moved to California, where he taught school in Amador County and began the study of law; returned to Pennsylvania in 1870 and continued the study of law; was admitted to the bar in Brookville, Pa., in 1872 and commenced the practice of his profession in Clarion, Pa.; presidential elector on the Republican ticket of Garfield and Arthur in 1880; unsuccessful candidate for the Republican nomination for Congress in 1884; elected as a Republican to the Fiftieth Congress (March 4, 1887–March 3, 1889); was not a candidate for renomination in 1888; resumed the practice of his profession; died in Clarion, Pa., on December 19, 1912; interment in Clarion Cemetery.

MAGEE, Clare, a Representative from Missouri; born on a farm in Putnam County near Livonia, Mo., March 31, 1899; graduate of Unionville (Mo.) High School; student in Kirksville State Teachers College in 1916; during the First World War served in the United States Navy as a seaman first-class and small-arms instructor; homesteaded in Big Horn Basin, Wyo., and worked as a laborer for the United States Reclamation Service at Deaver, Wyo., in 1920 and 1921; was graduated from the University of Missouri at Columbia in 1922; was admitted to the bar in 1922 and commenced the practice of law in Unionville, Putnam County, Mo.; has owned and operated farm where he was born since 1932; postmaster of Unionville, Mo., 1935–1941; served as a private in the Field Artillery, United States Army, in 1942 and as a captain in the Army Air Corps 1942–1944; elected as a Democrat to the Eighty-first and Eighty-second Congresses (January 3, 1949–January 3, 1953); was not a candidate for renomination in 1952; resumed the practice of law; is a resident of Unionville, Mo.

MAGEE, James McDevitt, a Representative from Pennsylvania; born in Evergreen, near Pittsburgh, Pa., April 5, 1877; attended the common schools; was graduated from Yale University in 1899 and from the law department of the University of Pennsylvania at Philadelphia in 1902; was admitted to the bar in 1903 and commenced practice at Pittsburgh, Pa.; was commissioned a first lieutenant in the Air Service during the First World War; promoted to captain and served until January 1919; later commissioned a lieutenant colonel in the Reserve; during his entire period of service was attached to the executive office of the Department of Military Aeronautics; elected as a Republican to the Sixty-eighth and Sixty-ninth Congresses (March 4, 1923–March 3, 1927); unsuccessful candidate for renomination in 1926; president, board of trustees, Elizabeth Steel Magee Hospital, Pittsburgh, Pa.; chairman, Pennsylvania Securities Commission, Harrisburg, Pa., 1931–1935; continued the practice of law in Pittsburgh, Pa., until his death there on April 16, 1949; interment in Calvary Cemetery.

MAGEE, John, a Representative from New York; born in Easton, Northumberland County, Pa., September 3, 1794; attended the common schools; served in the War of 1812; moved to Bath, Steuben County, N. Y., in 1812; elected constable in 1818 and served until 1820; appointed sheriff of Steuben County in 1821 and elected to that office in 1822; elected as a Democrat to the Twentieth and Twenty-first Congresses (March 4, 1827–March 3, 1831); was not a candidate for renomination in 1830; tendered an appointment in the Cabinet of President Jackson, which he declined; delegate to the State constitutional convention in 1867; devoted the remaining years of his life to banking, railroading, and was also interested in mining; died at Watkins, Schuyler County, N. Y., April 5, 1868; interment in Glenwood Cemetery.

MAGEE, John Alexander, a Representative from Pennsylvania; born in Landisburg, Perry County, Pa., October 14, 1827; attended the common schools and was graduated from New Bloomfield Academy; engaged in the printing business and for a number of years published the Perry County Democrat; member of the State house of representatives in 1863; delegate to the Democratic National Convention at New York City in 1868, at St. Louis in 1876, and at Chicago in 1896; elected as a Democrat to the Forty-third Congress (March 4, 1873–March 3, 1875); was an unsuccessful candidate for renomination in 1874 to the Forty-fourth Congress; resumed his former business pursuits; died in New Bloomfield, Perry County, Pa., November 18, 1903; interment in Bloomfield Cemetery.

MAGEE, Walter Warren, a Representative from New York; born in Groveland, Livingston County, N. Y., May 23, 1861; attended the common schools and Geneseo State Normal School; was graduated from Phillips Exeter Academy, Exeter, N. H., in 1885 and from Harvard University in 1889; studied law; was admitted to the bar in 1891 and commenced practice in Syracuse, N. Y.; served as a member of the board of supervisors of Onondaga County in 1892 and 1893; corporation counsel of Syracuse 1904–1914; elected as a Republican to the Sixty-fourth and to the six succeeding Congresses and served from March 4, 1915, until his death in Syracuse, N. Y., May 25, 1927; interment in Oakwood Cemetery.

MAGINNIS, Martin, a Delegate from the Territory of Montana; born near Pultneyville, Wayne County, N. Y., October 27, 1841; moved with his parents to Minnesota in 1852; pursued an academic course; attended Hamline University, but left to take charge of a Democratic newspaper; during the Civil War enlisted as a private in the First Regiment, Minnesota Volunteer Infantry, April 18, 1861; was made a second lieutenant after the first Battle of Bull Run; promoted to first lieutenant in September 1862 and to captain in July 1863; served with his regiment in all the campaigns and nearly all the battles of the Army of the Potomac until September 1864, then appointed major of the Eleventh Minnesota Volunteers and ordered to join the Army of the Cumberland, where he served under the command of General Thomas until mustered out with his regiment in July 1865; moved to Helena, Mont., in 1866; engaged in mining and subsequently in publishing and editing the Helena Daily Gazette; elected as a Democrat to the Forty-third and to the five succeeding Congresses (March 4, 1873–March 3, 1885); unsuccessful Democratic candidate for election in 1890 to the Fifty-first Congress; presented credentials on May 25, 1900, as a Senator-designate to fill the vacancy caused by the resignation of William A. Clark, but was not seated; State commissioner of mineral land 1890–1893; president of the board of managers of the Montana Soldiers' Home 1906–1919; died in Los Angeles, Calif., March 27, 1919; interment in Resurrection Cemetery, Helena, Mont.

MAGNER, Thomas Francis (uncle of John Francis Carew), a Representative from New York; born in Brooklyn, N. Y., March 8, 1860; attended the public schools; was graduated from St. Xavier College in 1880 and from Columbia University, New York City, in 1882; taught in a public school in Brooklyn; studied law; was admitted to the bar in 1883 and commenced practice in Brooklyn, N. Y., the same year; member of the State assembly in 1888; elected as a Democrat to the Fifty-first, Fifty-second, and Fifty-third Congresses (March 4, 1889–March 3, 1895); declined to be a candidate for renomination in 1894; resumed the practice of law; corporation counsel of the Borough of Brooklyn 1913–1917; continued the practice of his profession in Brooklyn, N. Y., until his death there on December 22, 1945; interment in Holy Cross Cemetery.

MAGNUSON, Donald Hammer, a Representative from Washington; born on a farm near Freeman, Spokane County, Wash., March 7, 1911; attended the public schools and Spokane University 1926–1928; was graduated from the University of Washington at Seattle in 1931; worked way through university as a service-station attendant and as a janitor; after graduation worked as a harvester and then as a riveter in an aircraft factory; newspaper reporter for the Daily Olympian and Seattle Times 1934–1952; elected as a Democrat to the Eighty-third and to the three succeeding Congresses (January 3, 1953–January 3, 1961). *Reelected to the Eighty-seventh Congress.*

MAGNUSON, Warren Grant, a Representative and a Senator from Washington; born in Moorhead, Clay County, Minn., April 12, 1905; attended the public schools, the University of North Dakota at Grand Forks, and North Dakota State College; was graduated from the law school of the University of Washington at Seattle in 1929; was admitted to the bar the same year and commenced practice in Seattle, Wash.; secretary of the Seattle Municipal League in 1930 and 1931; served as special prosecuting attorney of King County, Wash., in 1931; member of the State house of representatives in 1933 and 1934; delegate to the State constitutional convention in 1933; member of the United States Naval Reserve, with rank of lieutenant commander; United States district attorney in 1934 and prosecuting attorney of King County, Wash., 1934–1936; elected as a Democrat to the Seventy-fifth and to the three succeeding Congresses and served from January 3, 1937, until his resignation on December 13, 1944; appointed to the United States Senate to fill the vacancy caused by the resignation of Homer T. Bone, and served from December 14, 1944, to January 3, 1945; elected in 1944 for the term commencing January 3, 1945; reelected in 1950 and again in 1956 for the term ending January 3, 1963.

MAGOON, Henry Sterling, a Representative from Wisconsin; born in Monticello, Lafayette County, Wis., January 31, 1832; attended the Rock River Seminary, Mount Morris, Ill., and was graduated from the Western Military College, Drennon, Ky., in 1853; studied law in the Montrose Law School, Frankfort, Ky.; was admitted to the bar in 1857 and commenced practice in Shullsburg, Wis.; professor of ancient languages in Nashville (Tenn.) University 1855–1857; returned to Wisconsin and practiced law at Darlington, Lafayette County; elected district attorney in 1858; member of the State senate in 1871 and 1872; elected as a Republican to the Forty-fourth Congress (March 4, 1875–March 3, 1877); was not a candidate for renomination in 1876; resumed the practice of law in Milwaukee, Wis.; regent of the University of Wisconsin at Madison one term; first native of Wisconsin to serve in the State senate or in the National House of Representatives; died while on a visit to his summer home in Darlington, Wis., March 3, 1889; interment in Union Grove Cemetery.

MAGRADY, Frederick William, a Representative from Pennsylvania; born near Pottsville, Schuylkill County, Pa., November 24, 1863; attended the public schools in Mount Carmel Township and was graduated from the State Normal School (now Bloomsburg State Teachers' College) at Bloomsburg, Pa., in 1890; taught school thirteen years in Mount Carmel Borough; engaged in the coal business for a short time at Gauley, W. Va.; was graduated from Dickinson School of Law, Carlisle, Pa., in 1909; was admitted to the bar the same year and commenced practice in Mount Carmel, Pa.; director and solicitor of the First National Bank of Mount Carmel; president and solicitor of the Shamokin-Mount Carmel Transit Co., and of the Ashland & Shamokin Auto Bus Co., Inc.; director of the Mount Carmel Water Co.; during the First World War served as a public speaker for war activities and as director of the four-minute men in the Mount Carmel area; elected as a Republican to the Sixty-ninth and to the three succeeding Congresses (March 4, 1925–March 3, 1933); unsuccessful candidate for renomination in 1932; resumed the practice of law; legal adviser for the Selective Service System, local board No. 5, of Northumberland County, Pa., during World War II; adviser to registrants of local board No. 116, Selective Service System, Shamokin, Pa.; died in Danville, Pa., August 27, 1954; interment in Mount Carmel Cemetery, Mount Carmel, Pa.

MAGRUDER, Allan Bowie, a Senator from Louisiana; born in Kentucky in 1775; attended the common schools; pursued an academic course; studied law; was admitted to the bar in 1796 and practiced in Lexington, Ky.; moved to Louisiana and practiced his profession; member of the State house of representatives; elected as a Democrat to the United States Senate and served from September 3, 1812, to March 3, 1813; resumed the practice of law; died in Opelousas, St. Landry Parish, La., April 16, 1822.

MAGRUDER, Patrick, a Representative from Maryland; born at "Locust Grove," near Rockville, Montgomery County Md., in 1768; attended Princeton College a short time; studied law; was admitted to the bar and practiced; elected to the Ninth Congress (March 4, 1805–March 3, 1807); Clerk of the House of Representatives from March 4, 1807, until his resignation on January 18, 1815; Librarian of Congress from 1807 until January 18, 1815, when he resigned; died in Petersburg, Va., on December 24, 1819; interment in the family burying ground on the ancestral estate, "Sweden," near Petersburg, Dinwiddie County, Va.

MAGUIRE, James George, a Representative from California; born in Boston, Mass., February 22, 1853; moved with his parents to California in April 1854; attended the public schools of Watsonville, Santa Cruz County, Calif., and the private academy of Joseph K. Fallon in Watsonville; member of the State assembly 1875–1877; studied law; was admitted to the bar by the supreme court of California in January 1878 and commenced practice in San Francisco, Calif.; judge of the superior court of the city and county of San Francisco 1882–1888; elected as a Democrat to the Fifty-third, Fifty-fourth, and Fifty-fifth Congresses (March 4, 1893–March 3, 1899); did not seek renomination, having become a candidate for Governor; unsuccessful Democratic candidate for Governor of California in 1898; resumed the practice of law in San Francisco, Calif., and died in that city June 20, 1920; interment in Greenlawn Cemetery.

MAGUIRE, John Arthur, a Representative from Nebraska; born near Elizabeth, Jo Daviess County, Ill., November 29, 1870; moved to Dakota Territory in 1882 with his parents, who settled near Plankinton, Aurora County (now in South Dakota); attended the district school, and was graduated from the Plankinton High School in 1889; taught in the district and city schools; attended the Agricultural College of South Dakota at Brookings 1890–1893; was graduated from the Iowa State College of Agriculture at Ames in 1893 and from the law department of the University of Nebraska at Lincoln in 1899; deputy treasurer of Lancaster County 1899–1901; was admitted to the bar in 1899 and commenced practice in Lincoln, Nebr., in 1902; delegate to the Democratic National Convention at St. Louis in 1904; secretary to the Democratic State committee in 1905; elected as a Democrat to the Sixty-first, Sixty-second, and Sixty-third Congresses (March 4, 1909–March 3, 1915); unsuccessful candidate for reelection in 1914; resumed the practice of law in Lincoln, Nebr.; appointed a municipal judge on January 1, 1938, to fill an unexpired term; died in Lincoln, Nebr., on July 1, 1939; interment in Calvary Cemetery.

MAHAN, Bryan Francis, a Representative from Connecticut; born in New London, New London County, Conn., May 1, 1856; attended the public schools and was graduated from the Robert Bartlett High School; learned the trade of plumber; studied law at the Albany (N. Y.) Law School, from which he graduated in 1880; was admitted to the bar in 1881 and commenced practice in New London; member of the State house of representatives in 1882 and 1883; member of the board of school visitors 1885–1887, and served as secretary; unsuccessful Democratic candidate for election as town clerk in 1878 and as secretary of state of Connecticut in 1886, although receiving a plurality of votes in the latter election; unsuccessful candidate for election as judge of probate in 1888; appointed prosecuting attorney in 1891, but resigned in 1892; one of the organizers of the City of Richmond Steamboat Co. in 1893 and served as president; postmaster of New London from October 30, 1894, to December 20, 1898; served as mayor 1904–1906 and 1910–1913; member of the State senate in 1910 and 1911; delegate to the Democratic National Conventions in 1904, 1908, 1912, and 1916; elected as a Democrat to the Sixty-third Congress (March 4, 1913–March 3, 1915); unsuccessful candidate for reelection in 1914 to the Sixty-fourth Congress; again appointed postmaster of New London, Conn., March 23, 1915, and served until his death there on November 16, 1923; interment in St. Mary's Cemetery.

MAHANY, Rowland Blennerhassett, a Representative from New York; born in Buffalo, N. Y., September 28, 1864; attended the public schools, Hobart College, Geneva, N. Y., and Union College, Schenectady, N. Y.; was graduated from Harvard University in 1888; studied law in Buffalo, N. Y.; associate editor of the Buffalo Express in 1888; instructor in Buffalo High School in 1889 and 1890; declined the appointment as secretary of the legation to Chile in 1890; appointed Envoy Extraordinary and Minister Plenipotentiary to Ecuador on February 24, 1892, and served until his resignation on June 12, 1893; unsuccessful candidate for election in 1892 to the Fifty-third Congress; returned to Ecuador in 1893 and concluded the Santos Convention, negotiations for which had remained unsettled for nearly nineteen years; elected as a Republican to the Fifty-fourth and Fifty-fifth Congresses (March 4, 1895–March 3, 1899); unsuccessful candidate for reelection in 1898; was admitted to the bar in 1899 and engaged in the practice of law in Buffalo, N. Y.; harbor commissioner of Buffalo 1899–1906; editor of the Buffalo Enquirer in 1910 and 1911; commissioner of conciliation, Labor Department, in 1914 and 1915; assistant to the Secretary of Labor in 1918 and 1919; member of the Foreign Trades Relation Committee of the State Department in 1919; appointed by President Wilson as one of the ten Federal umpires for the War Labor Board in 1919; member of the United States Housing Corporation in 1919; appointed representative of the United States to the International Commission on Immigration and Emigration at Geneva, Switzerland, in 1920; solicitor and Acting Secretary of Labor in 1920 and 1921; resumed the practice of law in Washington, D. C., retaining his residence in Buffalo, N. Y.; delegate to the Democratic National Conventions in 1924 and 1928; died in Washington, D. C., May 2, 1937; interment in the Congressional Cemetery.

MAHER, James Paul, a Representative from New York; born in Brooklyn, N. Y., November 3, 1865; was graduated from St. Patrick's Academy, Brooklyn, N. Y.; apprenticed to the hatter's trade; moved to Danbury, Conn., in 1887 and was employed as a journeyman hatter; treasurer of the United Hatters of North America in 1897; returned to Brooklyn in 1902; unsuccessful candidate for election in 1908 to the Sixty-first Congress; elected as a Democrat to the Sixty-second and to the four succeeding Congresses (March 4, 1911–March 3, 1921); unsuccessful candidate for reelection in 1920 to the Sixty-seventh Congress; engaged in the real-estate business in Brooklyn, N. Y.; moved to Keansburg, Monmouth County, N. J., and continued in the real-estate business; elected mayor of Keansburg, N. J., in 1926; retired from public life and political activities in 1930; died in Keansburg, N. J., on July 31, 1946; interment in St. Joseph's Cemetery, Keyport, N. J.

MAHON, Gabriel Heyward, Jr., a Representative from South Carolina; born in Williamston, Anderson County, S. C., November 11, 1889; moved with his parents to Greenville, S. C., in 1898; attended the public schools and the Citadel, a military college, Charleston, S. C.; employed as a clerk in a retail store 1900–1907 and as a traveling salesman 1907–1911; engaged in the retail clothing business in 1911; during the First World War served as a captain and later as a major of the First Battalion of the One Hundred and Eighteenth Infantry, Thirtieth Division, American Expeditionary Forces; severely wounded in action and was discharged on April 3, 1920; awarded the Order of the Purple Heart and the Silver Star medal "for distinguished service"; trustee of Greenville Woman's College, Greenville, S. C., 1921–1936; elected as a Democrat to the Seventy-fourth Congress to fill the vacancy caused by the death of John J. McSwain and on the same day was elected to the Seventy-fifth Congress and served from November 3, 1936, to January 3, 1939; unsuccessful candidate for renomination in 1938; resumed his former business pursuits; is a resident of Greenville, S. C.

MAHON, George Herman, a Representative from Texas; born in the village of Mahon, near Homer, Claiborne Parish, La., September 22, 1900; moved to Texas in 1908 with his family, who settled on a farm near Loraine, Mitchell County; attended the public schools; was graduated from the high school at Loraine, Tex., in 1918, from Simmons University, Abilene, Tex., in 1924, and from the law department of the University of Texas at Austin in 1925; also attended the University of Minnesota at Minneapolis; was admitted to the bar in 1925 and commenced practice in Colorado (now Colorado City), Tex.; served as county attorney of Mitchell County, Tex., in 1926; district attorney of the thirty-second judicial district of Texas 1927–1933; elected as a Democrat to the Seventy-fourth and to the twelve succeeding Congresses (January 3, 1935–January 3, 1961). *Reelected to the Eighty-seventh Congress.*

MAHON, Thaddeus Maclay, a Representative from Pennsylvania; born in Green Village, Franklin County, Pa., May 21, 1840; pursued an academic course; during the Civil War enlisted as a private in Company A, One Hundred and Twenty-sixth Regiment, Pennsylvania Volunteers, in August 1862; after a term of service in this regiment reenlisted as a veteran in January 1864 in the Twenty-first Regiment, Pennsylvania Volunteer Cavalry, and served until September 1865; participated in many of the engagements with the Army of the Potomac, Fifth Corps; was seriously wounded at Boydton Plank Road, Virginia, on November 4, 1864; studied law; was admitted to the bar in 1871 and commenced practice in southern Pennsylvania; member of the State house of representatives 1870–1872; president of Baltimore & Cumberland Valley Railroad; member of the commission having charge of the soldiers' orphan schools of Pennsylvania; unsuccessful candidate for election in 1876 to the Forty-fourth Congress; elected as a Republican to the Fifty-third and to the six succeeding Congresses (March 4, 1893–March 3, 1907); was not a candidate for renomination in 1906; engaged in business in Chambersburg, Franklin County, Pa.; died in Scotland, Franklin County, Pa., May 31, 1916; interment in Cedar Grove Cemetery, Chambersburg, Pa.

MAHONE, William, a Senator from Virginia; born in Southampton County, Va., December 1, 1826; was graduated from the Virginia Military Institute at Lexington in 1847; taught two years at the Rappahannock Military Academy; became a civil engineer and constructor of the Norfolk & Petersburg Railroad; participated in the Civil War and took part in the capture of Norfolk Navy Yard; raised and commanded the Sixth Virginia Regiment; was engaged in most of the battles of the Peninsular campaign, those on the Rappahannock, and those around Petersburg; was commissioned brigadier general and major general in 1864 and afterward commanded a corps in Hill's division; at the close of the Civil War returned to railroad engineering, and later became president of a trunk line from Norfolk into Tennessee; served in the State senate 1863–1865; elected to the United States Senate as a Readjuster and served from March 4, 1881, until March 3, 1887; unsuccessful candidate for reelection in 1887; died in Washington, D. C., October 8, 1895; interment in Blandford Cemetery, Petersburg, Dinwiddie County, Va.

MAHONEY, Peter Paul, a Representative from New York; born in New York City June 25, 1848; educated in the common schools of New York City; engaged in the dry-goods business for several years; moved to Brooklyn, N. Y., and engaged in the sale of liquor; elected as a Democrat to the Forty-ninth and Fiftieth Congresses (March 4, 1885–March 3, 1889); was not a candidate in 1888 for reelection to the Fifty-first Congress; became ill while attending the inauguration ceremonies of President Benjamin Harrison March 4, 1889, and died in Washington, D. C., March 27, 1889; interment in Calvary Cemetery, Long Island City, Queens County, N. Y.

MAHONEY, William Frank, a Representative from Illinois; born in Chicago, Ill., February 22, 1856; educated in the public schools of Chicago; engaged in mercantile pursuits in 1876; served as alderman in the Chicago City Council from 1884 to 1887 and again from 1890 to 1896; elected as a Democrat to the Fifty-seventh and Fifty-eighth Congresses and served from March 4, 1901, until his death in Chicago, Ill., December 27, 1904; interment in Calvary Cemetery, Evanston, Cook County, Ill.

MAILLIARD, William Somers, a Representative from California; born in Belvedere, Marin County, Calif., June 10, 1917; attended elementary and secondary schools in the San Francisco Bay area, and the Taft School, Watertown, Conn., 1933–1935; was graduated from Yale University in 1939; engaged in the banking business with American Trust Co., San Francisco, Calif., in 1940 and 1941; was in London, England, on September 1, 1939, three days before England declared war on Germany, and volunteered and served as assistant naval attaché in the United States Embassy in London in 1939 and 1940; with Bureau of Naval Personnel, Washington, D. C., in 1941 and 1942; attended the Naval War College in 1942; was assigned to duty on staff of Seventh Amphibious Force as flag lieutenant and aide to Vice Adm. D. E. Barbey in 1943 and released to inactive duty in March 1946 as a lieutenant commander; was awarded the Silver Star, Legion of Merit, and Bronze Star; promoted to commander in 1950 and to captain in 1958 in the Naval Reserve; resumed banking career in 1946 and 1947; assistant to the director of California Youth Authority in 1947 and 1948; unsuccessful Republican candidate for Congress in 1948; secretary to Governor Earl Warren 1948–1951; executive assistant to the director of the California Academy of Sciences in 1951 and 1952; elected as a Republican to the Eighty-third and to the three succeeding Congresses (January 3, 1953–January 3, 1961). *Reelected to the Eighty-seventh Congress.*

MAIN, Verner Wright, a Representative from Michigan; born in Ashley, Delaware County, Ohio, December 16, 1885; attended the public schools; was graduated from Marion (Ohio) High School, from Hillsdale (Mich.) College in 1907, and from the law department of the University of Michigan at Ann Arbor in 1914; principal of the high schools at Hudson, Mich., in 1908 and 1909 and at Niles, Mich., 1909–1912; was admitted to the bar in 1914 and commenced the practice of law in Battle Creek, Mich.; during the First World War volunteered for military service with the Field Artillery and was in training at the officers' training camp at Louisville, Ky., when the armistice was signed; assistant prosecuting attorney of Calhoun County in 1926; served in the State house of representatives 1927–1929; member of the Battle Creek School Board 1929–1932; elected as a Republican to the Seventy-fourth Congress to fill the vacancy caused by the death of Henry M. Kimball and served from December 17, 1935, to January 3, 1937; unsuccessful candidate for renomination in 1936; resumed the practice of law and is a resident of Battle Creek, Mich.

MAISH, Levi, a Representative from Pennsylvania; born in Conewago Township, York County, Pa., November 22, 1837; attended the common schools and the York County Academy; taught school in Manchester Township and in York; during the Civil War recruited a company for the Union Army in 1862, and with it joined the One Hundred and Thirtieth Regiment, Pennsylvania Volunteer Infantry; was promoted to lieutenant colonel; wounded at the Battle of Antietam; promoted to colonel after the Battle of Fredericksburg; again wounded while leading his regiment at the Battle of Chancellorsville; mustered out with his regiment at the expiration of its term of service May 21, 1863; attended lectures in the law department of the University of Pennsylvania at Philadelphia, and was admitted to the bar in 1864; member of the State house of representatives in 1867 and 1868; appointed by the legislature in 1872 one of a commission to reexamine and reaudit the accounts of certain public officers of York County; elected as a Democrat to the Forty-fourth and Forty-fifth Congresses (March 4, 1875–March 3, 1879); was an unsuccessful candidate for reelection in 1878 to the Forty-sixth Congress; elected to the Fiftieth and Fifty-first Congresses (March 4, 1887–March 3, 1891); was an unsuccessful candidate for reelection in 1890 to the Fifty-second Congress; engaged in the practice of law in Washington, D. C., until his death there on February 26, 1899; interment in Arlington National Cemetery, Fort Myer, Va.

MAJOR, James Earl, a Representative from Illinois; born in Donellson, Montgomery County, Ill., January 5, 1887; attended the common and high schools of his native city; was graduated from Brown's Business College in 1907 and from the Illinois College of Law at Chicago in 1909; was admitted to the bar in 1910 and commenced the practice of law in Hillsboro, Ill.; prosecuting attorney of Montgomery County 1912–1920; elected as a Democrat to the Sixty-eighth Congress (March 4, 1923–March 3, 1925); unsuccessful candidate for reelection in 1924 to the Sixty-ninth Congress; resumed the practice of the legal profession in Hillsboro, Ill.; elected to the Seventieth Congress (March 4, 1927–March 3, 1929); unsuccessful candidate for reelection in 1928 to the Seventy-first Congress; elected to the Seventy-second and Seventy-third Congresses and served from March 4, 1931, until his resignation, effective October 6, 1933, having been appointed to the bench; appointed as a judge of the United States District Court for the Southern District of Illinois and served until March 23, 1937, when he was appointed as a judge of the United States Circuit Court of Appeals for the Seventh Circuit, in which capacity he served until March 23, 1956, when he voluntarily retired; served as chief judge of the court from November 17, 1948, until September 1, 1954; one of the managers appointed by the House of Representatives in 1933 to conduct the impeachment proceedings against Harold Louderback, judge of the United States District Court for the Northern District of California; is a resident of Hillsboro, Ill.

MAJOR, Samuel Collier, a Representative from Missouri; born in Fayette, Howard County, Mo., July 2, 1869; attended the public schools and Central College at Fayette; was graduated from St. James Military Academy, Macon, Mo., in 1888; studied law; was admitted to the bar in 1890 and commenced practice in Fayette, Mo.; appointed prosecuting attorney of Howard County in 1892, and later was elected to the office for two terms; served in the State senate 1907–1911; unsuccessful candidate for election in 1916 to the Sixty-fifth Congress; elected as a Democrat to the Sixty-sixth Congress (March 4, 1919–March 3, 1921); unsuccessful candidate for reelection in 1920 to the Sixty-seventh Congress; resumed the practice of law in Fayette, Mo.; elected to the Sixty-eighth, Sixty-ninth, and Seventieth Congresses (March 4, 1923–March 3, 1929); unsuccessful candidate for reelection in 1928 to the Seventy-first Congress; elected to the Seventy-second Congress and served from March 4, 1931, until his death in Fayette, Mo., July 28, 1931; interment in Fayette City Cemetery.

MAJORS, Thomas Jefferson, a Representative from Nebraska; born in Libertyville, Jefferson County, Iowa, June 25, 1841; attended the common and select schools of Libertyville and the Nebraska State Normal School; moved to Peru, Nebr., in 1860 and engaged in mercantile pursuits; entered the Union Army in June 1861 as first lieutenant of Company C, First Regiment, Nebraska Volunteer Infantry, and served successively as captain, major, and lieutenant colonel of that regiment; mustered out June 15, 1866; member of the last Territorial council of Nebraska in 1866; member of the first State senate 1867–1869; appointed assessor of internal revenue for the district of Nebraska in 1869, which office he held until the offices of collector and assessor were merged into one; elected as a Republican to the Forty-fifth Congress as a contingent (or additional) Member but did not present his credentials; subsequently elected to the Forty-fifth Congress to fill the vacancy caused by the death of Frank Welch and served from November 5, 1878, until March 3, 1879; was reelected a contingent (or additional) Member to the Forty-sixth and Forty-seventh Congresses, but the House, on February 24, 1883, disallowed Nebraska's claim to an additional Member and refused to seat him; a director of the Citizens' State Bank of Peru; Lieutenant-Governor of Nebraska 1890–1894; unsuccessful candidate for Governor in 1894; member of the State board of education and served as its president; died in Peru, Nebr., on July 11, 1932; interment in Mount Vernon Cemetery.

MALBONE, Francis, a Representative and a Senator from Rhode Island; born in Newport, R. I., March 20, 1759; received a limited schooling; engaged as a merchant in Newport; colonel of the Newport Artillery 1792–1809; elected as a Federalist to the Third and Fourth Congresses (March 4, 1793–March 3, 1797); was not a candidate for renomination; resumed his former pursuits; member of the State house of representatives in 1807 and 1808; elected to the United States Senate and served from March 4, 1809, until his death on the steps of the Capitol in Washington, D. C., June 4, 1809; interment in the Congressional Cemetery, Washington, D. C.

MALBY, George Roland, a Representative from New York; born in Canton, St. Lawrence County, N. Y., September 16, 1857; attended Canton Union School and St. Lawrence University, Canton, N. Y.; studied law; was admitted to the bar in 1881 and commenced the practice of law in Ogdensburg, St. Lawrence County, N. Y.; justice of the peace of Oswegatchie; member of the State assembly in 1890–1895; elected leader of his party in that body in 1893 and served as speaker in 1894;

served in the State senate 1895–1907; elected as a Republican to the Sixtieth, Sixty-first, and Sixty-second Congresses and served from March 4, 1907, until his death in New York City July 5, 1912; interment in Ogdensburg Cemetery, Ogdensburg, N. Y.

MALLARY, Rollin Carolas, a Representative from Vermont; born in Cheshire, New Haven County, Conn., May 27, 1784; was graduated from Middlebury (Vt.) College in 1805; moved to Poultney, Rutland County, Vt.; studied law; was admitted to the bar and commenced practice in Castleton, Vt., in 1807; elected trustee of the Rutland County Grammar School in 1807; secretary to the Governor and council in 1807, 1809–1812, and 1815–1819; State's attorney for Rutland County 1811–1813, 1815, and 1816; moved to Poultney in 1818; successfully contested the election of Orsamus C. Merrill to the Sixteenth Congress; reelected to the Seventeenth and to the five succeeding Congresses and served from January 13, 1820, until his death in Baltimore, Md., April 16, 1831; interment in East Poultney Cemetery, East Poultney, Vt.

MALLORY, Francis, a Representative from Virginia; born at "Poplars," near Hampton, Elizabeth City County, Va., on December 12, 1807; attended the common schools and Hampton Academy; appointed midshipman in the United States Navy in 1822 and resigned in 1828; studied law but abandoned it for the study of medicine; was graduated from the medical department of the University of Pennsylvania at Philadelphia in 1831 and practiced in Norfolk, Va.; abandoned the practice of medicine and devoted himself to agricultural pursuits in Elizabeth City County, Va.; elected as a Whig to the Twenty-fifth Congress (March 4, 1837–March 3, 1839); unsuccessful candidate for reelection in 1838 to the Twenty-sixth Congress; subsequently elected to the Twenty-sixth Congress to fill the vacancy caused by the resignation of Joel Holleman; reelected to the Twenty-seventh Congress and served from December 28, 1840, to March 3, 1843; was not a candidate for renomination in 1842; resumed agricultural pursuits; delegate to the Southern Commercial Convention at Richmond, Va., in 1838; appointed by President Fillmore as Navy agent at Norfolk on November 1, 1850, and served in this capacity until 1853, when he resigned; member of the State house of delegates 1853–1855, 1857, and 1858; member of the Common Council of Norfolk for several years; president of the Norfolk & Petersburg Railroad Co. 1853–1859; died in Norfolk, Va., March 26, 1860; interment in Elmwood Cemetery.

MALLORY, Meredith, a Representative from New York; born in Connecticut; attended the common schools; served as supervisor of the town of Benton, Yates County, N. Y., in 1820; moved to Hammondsport, Steuben County, N. Y.; owned and operated a mill for grinding wheat and plaster, and also operated a sawmill; held several local offices; member of the State assembly in 1835; served as justice of the peace in 1838; elected as a Democrat to the Twenty-sixth Congress (March 4, 1839–March 3, 1841).

MALLORY, Robert, a Representative from Kentucky; born at Madison Court House, Madison County, Va., November 15, 1815; attended private schools, and was graduated from the University of Virginia at Charlottesville in 1827; engaged in agricultural pursuits in La Grange, Ky.; studied law; was admitted to the bar in 1837 and commenced practice in New Castle, Ky.; elected as a Union Democrat to the Thirty-sixth, Thirty-seventh, and Thirty-eighth Congresses (March 4, 1859–March 3, 1865); unsuccessful candidate for reelection in 1864 to the Thirty-ninth Congress; delegate to the Union National Convention at Phila-

delphia in 1866; one of the vice presidents of the Centennial Exhibition at Philadelphia in 1876; resumed agricultural pursuits; died near La Grange, Ky., August 11, 1885; interment in the family cemetery at Spring Hill, Oldham County, Ky.

MALLORY, Rufus, a Representative from Oregon; born in Coventry, Chenango County, N. Y., January 10, 1831; attended the common schools and the Alfred (N. Y.) University; moved to New London, Iowa, and taught school 1855–1858; moved to Roseburg, Oreg., in 1858 and continued teaching; studied law; was admitted to the bar in 1860 and commenced practice in Salem, Oreg.; district attorney of the first judicial district in 1860 and of the third district 1862–1866; member of the State house of representatives in 1862; elected as a Union Republican to the Fortieth Congress (March 4, 1867–March 3, 1869); was not a candidate for renomination in 1868; delegate to the Republican National Conventions at Chicago in 1868 which nominated Grant and Colfax and 1888 which nominated Harrison and Morton; resumed the practice of law in Salem; member of the State house of representatives in 1872 and served as speaker; United States district attorney 1874–1882; commissioned as special agent of the United States Government at Singapore, British Malaya; returned to Portland, Oreg., and resumed the practice of law in 1883; died in Portland, Multnomah County, Oreg., April 30, 1914; remains were cremated and the ashes deposited in the vaults of the Portland Cremation Association.

MALLORY, Stephen Russell, a Senator from Florida; born in Trinidad, West Indies, in 1812; immigrated to the United States with his parents, who settled in Key West, Fla., in 1820; attended schools in Mobile, Ala., and Nazareth, Pa.; appointed by President Jackson customs inspector at Key West in 1833; studied law; was admitted to the bar in 1840 and practiced in Key West until 1858; county judge of Monroe County 1837–1845; appointed collector of the port of Key West in 1845; served in the Seminole War; elected as a Democrat to the United States Senate in 1851; reelected in 1857 and served from March 4, 1851, until his retirement on January 21, 1861; served as Secretary of the Navy of the Confederacy; at the close of the Civil War went to Lagrange, Troup County, Ga.; moved to Pensacola, Fla., in March 1866 and engaged in the practice of his profession; died in Pensacola, Fla., November 9, 1873; interment in St. Michael's Cemetery.

MALLORY, Stephen Russell (son of the preceding), a Representative and a Senator from Florida; born in Columbia, Richland County, S. C., November 2, 1848; during the Civil War entered the Confederate Army in Virginia in the fall of 1864; appointed midshipman in the Confederate Navy in the spring of 1865 and served until the end of the war; was graduated from Georgetown College, Washington, D. C., in 1869, where he then served as instructor in Latin and Greek until July 1871; studied law; was admitted to the bar by the supreme court of Louisiana in 1872 and commenced practice in New Orleans; moved to Pensacola, Fla., in 1874 and continued the practice of law; member of the State house of representatives in 1876; served in the State senate in 1880 and reelected in 1884; elected as a Democrat to the Fifty-second and Fifty-third Congresses (March 4, 1891–March 3, 1895); was not a candidate for renomination in 1894; elected to the United States Senate on May 14, 1897, for the term commencing March 4, 1897; appointed in 1903 and subsequently elected for the term commencing March 4, 1903, and served from May 15, 1897, until his death in Pensacola, Fla., December 23, 1907; interment in St. Michael's Cemetery.

MALONE, George Wilson, a Senator from Nevada; born in Fredonia, Wilson County, Kans., August 7, 1890; attended the public schools; was graduated from the University of Nevada at Reno in 1917; engaged as a civil and hydraulic engineer at Reno, Nev., in 1914; during the First World War enlisted as a private in the Field Artillery; promoted to sergeant while with the Fortieth Division and later became a lieutenant and regimental intelligence officer, serving in England and France 1917–1919; State engineer of Nevada from 1927 until his resignation in 1935 to resume general engineering; special consultant to the United States Senate Military Affairs subcommittee on strategic and critical minerals and materials and for examination of military establishments during World War II; elected as a Republican to the United States Senate in 1946 for the term commencing January 3, 1947; reelected in 1952 for the term ending January 3, 1959; unsuccessful candidate for reelection in 1958 and for election to the United States House of Representatives in 1960; consultant engineer in Washington, D. C., until his death there May 19, 1961; interment in Arlington National Cemetery, Fort Myer, Va.

MALONEY, Francis Thomas, a Representative and a Senator from Connecticut; born in Meriden, New Haven County, Conn., March 31, 1894; attended the public and parochial schools in his native city; was a newspaper reporter in Meriden, Conn., 1914–1921; during the First World War enlisted in the United States Navy as a seaman first class, on December 4, 1917, and served until honorably discharged on December 6, 1918; engaged in the real-estate and insurance business in 1921; mayor of Meriden, Conn., 1929–1933; elected as a Democrat to the Seventy-third Congress (March 4, 1933–January 3, 1935); did not seek renomination, having become a candidate for Senator; elected to the United States Senate in 1934; reelected in 1940 and served from January 3, 1935, until his death in Meriden, Conn., on January 16, 1945; interment in Sacred Heart Cemetery.

MALONEY, Franklin John, a Representative from Pennsylvania; born in Philadelphia, Pa., March 29, 1899; attended the public schools and graduated from Temple University Law School in 1922; was admitted to the bar in 1923 and practiced in Philadelphia, Pa.; unsuccessful Republican candidate for election to the Seventy-ninth Congress in 1944; elected as a Republican to the Eightieth Congress (January 3, 1947–January 3, 1949); unsuccessful for reelection in 1948 to the Eighty-first Congress; resumed the practice of law; died in Philadelphia, Pa., September 15, 1958; interment in West Laurel Hill Cemetery.

MALONEY, Paul Herbert, a Representative from Louisiana; born in New Orleans, La., February 14, 1876; attended the public school and Mrs. Ashe's Private School, Pass Christian, Miss.; employed as an office boy in 1893 for a drayage company, advancing to president in 1916; also engaged in a linen supply company, a trucking and storage company, and an automobile distributing company; member of the Louisiana National Guard 1895–1898; served in the State house of representatives 1914–1916; member of the New Orleans Levee Board 1917–1920, serving as president in 1919 and 1920; member of the commission council of New Orleans; commissioner of public utilities 1920–1925; delegate to the Democratic National Conventions in 1924, 1928, 1932, and 1936; elected as a Democrat to the Seventy-second and to the four succeeding Congresses and served from March 4, 1931, until December 15, 1940, when he resigned to become collector of internal revenue for the New Orleans district, and served from December 16, 1940, to July 31, 1942; administrator, United States Savings Bonds, State of Louisiana, in 1941 and 1942; unsuccessful candidate for renomination in 1940; again elected to the Seventy-eighth and Seventy-ninth Congresses (January 3, 1943–January 3, 1947); was not a candidate for renomination in 1946; engaged in the trucking and storage business; is a resident of New Orleans.

MALONEY, Robert Sarsfield, a Representative from Massachusetts; born in Lawrence, Essex County, Mass., February 3, 1881; attended the public schools; learned the printer's trade; fraternal delegate of the American Federation of Labor to the Canadian Trades and Labor Congress, Winnipeg, Manitoba, in 1907; New England organizer for the International Typographical Union 1908–1912; member of the board of aldermen in 1909 and served as president; director of the Department of Public Health and Charities of Lawrence in 1912 and 1915–1920; engaged in commercial printing in 1913 and 1914; member of the city council 1916–1920 and served as president; elected as a Republican to the Sixty-seventh Congress (March 4, 1921–March 3, 1923); was not a candidate for renomination in 1922; again served as director of the Department of Public Health and Charities, from 1924 until 1928; published a weekly newspaper and, later, engaged in the restaurant business until his death in Lawrence, Mass., November 8, 1934; interment in Immaculate Conception Cemetery.

MANAHAN, James, a Representative from Minnesota; born near Chatfield, Fillmore County, Minn., on March 12, 1866; attended the country schools, and was graduated from Winona (Minn.) Normal School in 1886; taught school for two years at Graceville, Minn.; attended the law department of the University of Wisconsin at Madison, and was graduated from the law department of the University of Minnesota at Minneapolis in 1889; was admitted to the bar the same year and commenced practice in St. Paul, Minn.; moved to Lincoln, Lancaster County, Nebr., in 1895 and continued the practice of his profession; moved to Minneapolis, Minn., in 1905 and practiced law until 1912; elected as a Republican to the Sixty-third Congress (March 4, 1913–March 3, 1915); was not a candidate for renomination in 1914; resumed the practice of law; died in St. Paul, Minn., January 8, 1932; interment in Calvary Cemetery.

MANASCO, Carter, a Representative from Alabama; born in Townley, Walker County, Ala., January 3, 1902; attended the public schools and Howard College, Birmingham, Ala.; was graduated from the law department of the University of Alabama at Tuscaloosa in 1927; was admitted to the bar the same year and began practice in Jasper, Ala.; member of the State house of representatives 1930–1933; served as secretary to Speaker William B. Bankhead 1933–1940; elected as a Democrat to the Seventy-seventh Congress to fill the vacancy caused by the resignation of Walter W. Bankhead; reelected to the Seventy-eighth, Seventy-ninth, and Eightieth Congresses and served from June 24, 1941, to January 3, 1949; unsuccessful candidate for renomination in 1948; resumed the practice of law and engaged in public relations work; resides in Falls Church, Va.

MANDERSON, Charles Frederick, a Senator from Nebraska; born in Philadelphia, Pa., February 9, 1837; attended the schools and academies of his native city; moved to Canton, Ohio, in 1856; studied law; was admitted to the bar in 1859 and commenced practice in Canton; city solicitor of Canton in 1860; during the Civil War entered the Army as first lieutenant of Company A, Nineteenth Regiment, Ohio Volunteer Infantry, in April 1861; participated in the campaign under General McClellan in West Virginia in the summer of 1861 and afterward in the campaigns of the Army of the Cumberland; rose through the grades of captain, major, lieutenant colonel, and colonel of the Nineteenth Regiment, Ohio Volunteer Infantry; was in command of the regiment from the date of the Battle of Shiloh; resigned in April 1865; brevetted brigadier general of Volunteers, United States Army, in March 1865, "for gallant, long-continued, and meritorious services"; resumed the practice of law in Canton, Ohio; twice elected attorney of Stark

County, and served until November 1869, when he moved to Omaha, Nebr., and continued the practice of law; city attorney of Omaha for six years; elected by both political parties a member of the State constitutional conventions in 1871 and in 1874; elected as a Republican to the United States Senate; reelected in 1888 and served from March 4, 1883, to March 3, 1895; elected President pro tempore of the Senate and served from March 2, 1891, until he resigned the position March 22, 1893; voluntarily retired from public life; appointed general solicitor of the Burlington system of railroads west of the Missouri River; vice president of the American Bar Association in 1899 and president in 1900; died on board the steamship *Cedric* in the harbor of Liverpool, England, September 28, 1911; interment in Forest Lawn Cemetery, Omaha, Nebr.

MANGUM, Willie Person, a Representative and a Senator from North Carolina; born near Red Mountain (now Rougemont), Orange (now Durham) County, N. C., May 10, 1792; attended the Fayetteville and Raleigh Academies, and was graduated from the University of North Carolina at Chapel Hill in 1815; studied law; was admitted to the bar in 1817 and commenced practice in Red Mountain, N. C.; member of the State house of representatives in 1818; twice elected a superior court judge; elected to the Eighteenth and Nineteenth Congresses and served from March 4, 1823, until March 18, 1826, when he resigned; elected to the United States Senate and served from March 4, 1831, until his resignation on November 26, 1836; received the eleven electoral votes of South Carolina for President of the United States in 1837; again elected, as a Whig, to the United States Senate to fill the vacancy caused by the resignation of Bedford Brown; reelected in 1841 and in 1847, and served from November 25, 1840, to March 3, 1853; President pro tempore of the Senate from May 31, 1842, until March 4, 1845; continued the practice of law until his death in Red Mountain, N. C., September 7, 1861; interment in the family burial ground at his home, "Walnut Hall," near Red Mountain, N. C.

MANKIN, Helen Douglas, a Representative from Georgia; born in Atlanta, Fulton County, Ga., on September 11, 1896; attended public and private schools; was graduated from Rockford (Ill.) College in 1917 and from Atlanta (Ga.) Law School in 1920; was admitted to the bar in 1920 and commenced practice in Atlanta, Ga.; during the First World War was an ambulance driver in a unit attached to the French Army in 1918 and 1919, receiving two citations; member of the general assembly of Georgia 1937–1946; elected as a Democrat to the Seventy-ninth Congress to fill the vacancy caused by the resignation of Robert Ramspeck and served from February 12, 1946, to January 3, 1947; unsuccessful candidate for renomination in 1946; had her name written in by voters in the general election but was defeated; unsuccessfully contested election of James C. Davis to the Eightieth Congress; resumed the practice of law in Atlanta, Ga., and resided in Stonewall, Ga.; died as the result of an automobile accident near College Park, Ga., July 25, 1956; remains were cremated.

MANLOVE, Joe Jonathan, a Representative from Missouri; born on a farm near Carthage, Jasper County, Mo., October 1, 1876; attended the public schools and was graduated from Presbyterian Academy at Mount Vernon, Mo.; studied law; was admitted to the bar in 1897 and commenced practice in Mount Vernon, Lawrence County, Mo.; also engaged in agricultural pursuits, in the livestock business, and in the general development of southwest Missouri; executive secretary of the Ozark Playgrounds Association 1920–1922; unsuccessful Republican candidate for election in 1914 to the Sixty-fourth Congress and

in 1916 to the Sixty-fifth Congress; elected as a Republican to the Sixty-eighth and to the four succeeding Congresses (March 4, 1923–March 3, 1933); unsuccessful candidate for reelection in 1932 to the Seventy-third Congress; unsuccessful for the Republican nomination for Congress in 1934; resumed the practice of law and also engaged in the real-estate business in Joplin, Mo.; in 1943 was elected one of the delegates to write a new constitution for the State of Missouri and served as a member of the constitutional convention; died in Joplin, Mo., January 31, 1956; interment in Mount Hope Cemetery near Joplin, Mo.

MANN, Abijah, Jr., a Representative from New York; born in Fairfield, Herkimer County, N. Y., September 24, 1793; attended the common schools; engaged in mercantile pursuits; justice of the peace; appointed by President Jackson postmaster of Fairfield and served from May 28, 1830, to January 16, 1833; member of the State assembly 1828–1830 and in 1838; elected as a Democrat to the Twenty-third and Twenty-fourth Congresses (March 4, 1833–March 3, 1837); moved to New York City; unsuccessful candidate for attorney general of New York in 1855; delegate to the Republican State convention in 1856; unsuccessful candidate for State senator in 1857; died in Auburn, N. Y., September 6, 1868.

MANN, Edward Coke, a Representative from South Carolina; born in Lowndesville, Abbeville County, S. C., November 21, 1880; attended the common schools, and was graduated from The Citadel, Charleston, S. C., in 1901; taught school one year and was connected with a tobacco company for four years; was graduated from the law department of the University of South Carolina at Columbia in 1906 and commenced practice in St. Matthews, Calhoun County, S. C.; solicitor of the first circuit of South Carolina 1916–1919; elected as a Democrat to the Sixty-sixth Congress to fill the vacancy caused by the resignation of Asbury Francis Lever and served from October 7, 1919, to March 3, 1921; unsuccessful for renomination in 1920; practiced law in Orangeburg, S. C.; appointed master in equity for Orangeburg County in November 1923; reappointed in November 1927 and served until his death; was accidently killed November 11, 1931, near Rowesville, S. C., while on a hunting trip; interment in Sunnyside Cemetery, Orangeburg, S. C.

MANN, Horace, a Representative from Massachusetts; born in Franklin, Norfolk County, Mass., May 4, 1796; attended the public schools and prepared for college under a private teacher; was graduated from Brown University, Providence, R. I., in 1819; tutored there 1819–1821; studied law in Litchfield, Conn.; was admitted to the bar and commenced practice in Dedham, Mass., in 1823; member of the State house of representatives 1827–1833; moved to Boston in 1833; commissioner for the revision of the Massachusetts statutes in 1835; member of the State senate 1833–1837 and served as president 1835–1837; secretary of the State board of education 1837–1848 and in this position reorganized the public-school system; elected as a Whig to the Thirtieth Congress to fill the vacancy caused by the death of John Quincy Adams; reelected to the Thirty-first Congress and as a Free-Soiler to the Thirty-second Congress and served from April 3, 1848, to March 3, 1853; declined to be a candidate for renomination in 1852; declined the nomination for Governor in 1852 to accept the position of president of Antioch College, Yellow Springs, Ohio, and served in that position from 1852 until his death at Yellow Springs, Ohio, August 2, 1859; interment in North Burial Ground, Providence, R. I.

MANN, James, a Representative from Louisiana; born in Gorham, Cumberland County, Maine, June 22, 1822; member of the Maine House of Representatives in 1849 and 1850; served in the State senate 1851–1853; treasurer of Cumberland County in 1862 and 1863; customhouse officer in Portland, Maine; during the Civil War served in the Union Army as paymaster with rank of major; Treasury agent for Louisiana in 1867 and 1868, and resided in New Orleans; upon the readmission of the State of Louisiana to representation was elected as a Democrat to the Fortieth Congress and served from July 18, 1868, until his death in New Orleans, La., August 26, 1868; interment in Eastern Cemetery, Gorham, Maine.

MANN, James Robert, a Representative from Illinois; born near Bloomington, McLean County, Ill., on October 20, 1856; attended the public schools; was graduated from the University of Illinois at Urbana in 1876 and from the Union College of Law, Chicago, Ill., in 1881; was admitted to the bar in 1881 and commenced practice at Chicago, Ill.; member of the Oakland Board of Education in Chicago in 1887; attorney for Hyde Park and the South Park commissioners of Chicago; secretary of the citizens' association which secured the adoption of Jackson Park as the site for the World's Fair; master in chancery of the superior court of Cook County; member of the city council of Chicago 1892–1896; proponent of the low-level sewer system for Chicago; chairman of the Illinois State Republican convention in 1894, and chairman of the Republican county conventions at Chicago in 1895 and 1902; elected as a Republican to the Fifty-fifth and to the thirteen succeeding Congresses and served from March 4, 1897, until his death before the close of the Sixty-seventh Congress; minority floor leader from the Sixty-second to the Sixty-fifth Congress; died in Washington, D. C., on November 30, 1922; interment in Oakwood Cemetery, Chicago, Ill.

MANN, Job, a Representative from Pennsylvania; born in Bethel Township, Bedford (now Fulton) County, Pa., March 31, 1795; attended the common schools and the Bedford Academy; clerk to the board of county commissioners in 1816; was register, recorder, and clerk of Bedford County 1818–1835; elected as a Democrat to the Twenty-fourth Congress (March 4, 1835–March 3, 1837); unsuccessful candidate for reelection in 1836 to the Twenty-fifth Congress; studied law; was admitted to the bar in 1839 and commenced practice in Bedford, Pa.; State treasurer of Pennsylvania 1842–1848; member of the State house of representatives; again elected to the Thirtieth and Thirty-first Congresses (March 4, 1847–March 3, 1851); was not a candidate for renomination in 1850; resumed the practice of law; died in Bedford, Pa., October 8, 1873; interment in Bedford Cemetery.

MANN, Joel Keith, a Representative from Pennsylvania; born in Cheltenham Township, Montgomery County, Pa., August 1, 1780; attended the common schools; engaged in agricultural pursuits; member of the State house of representatives 1817–1820; served in the State senate 1824–1829; elected as a Democrat to the Twenty-second and Twenty-third Congresses (March 4, 1831–March 3, 1835); resumed agricultural pursuits; died in Jenkintown, Montgomery County, Pa., August 28, 1857; interment in the Presbyterian Cemetery, Abington, Montgomery County, Pa.

MANNING, James, a Delegate from Rhode Island; born in Elizabethtown (now Elizabeth), N. J., October 22, 1738; attended Hopewell Academy, and was graduated from the College of New Jersey (now Princeton University) in 1762; studied theology and entered the Baptist ministry in 1763; moved to Warren, R. I., in 1764, and was one of the founders and first president of Rhode Island College (now Brown University); moved to Providence with the college in May 1770; served as pastor of the First Baptist Church of Providence from July 1771, until his resignation in

April 1791; also resigned the college presidency the same year; Member of the Continental Congress in 1785 and 1786; died in Providence, R. I., July 29, 1791; interment in North Burial Ground.

MANNING, John, Jr., a Representative from North Carolina; born in Edenton, Chowan County, N. C., July 30, 1830; attended Edenton Academy, the Norfolk Military Academy, and was graduated from the University of North Carolina at Chapel Hill in 1850; studied law; was admitted to the bar in 1853 and commenced practice in Pittsboro, Chatham County, N. C.; delegate to the constitutional convention in 1861; enlisted in the Chatham Rifles in 1861; was made first lieutenant, later becoming adjutant of the Fifteenth Regiment, North Carolina Volunteers, and served throughout the Civil War; elected as a Democrat to the Forty-first Congress to fill the vacancy caused by the resignation of John T. Deweese and served from December 7, 1870, to March 3, 1871; was not a candidate for reelection in 1870; member of the State constitutional convention in 1875; member of the State house of representatives in 1881; commissioner to codify the laws of the State in 1881; professor of law in the University of North Carolina and member of the board of trustees of that institution 1881–1899; died in Chapel Hill, N. C., February 12, 1899; interment in Episcopal Churchyard, Pittsboro, N. C.

MANNING, Richard Irvine, a Representative from South Carolina; born near Sumter, Sumter District, S. C., May 1, 1789; attended private schools, and was graduated from South Carolina College at Columbia in 1811; served as captain of Volunteers in the War of 1812; engaged in agricultural pursuits; member of the State house of representatives 1820–1822; served in the State senate 1822–1824; Governor of South Carolina 1824–1826; unsuccessful candidate for election in 1826 to the Twentieth Congress; elected as a Democrat to the Twenty-third Congress to fill the vacancy caused by the death of James Blair; reelected to the Twenty-fourth Congress and served from December 8, 1834, until his death in Philadelphia, Pa., May 1, 1836; interment in Trinity Churchyard, Columbia, Richland County, S. C.

MANNING, Vannoy Hartrog, a Representative from Mississippi; born near Raleigh, Wake County, N. C., July 26, 1839; moved with his parents to Mississippi in 1841; attended Horn Lake Male Academy, De Soto County, Miss., and the University of Nashville, Tennessee; moved to Arkansas in 1860; studied law; was admitted to the bar in 1861 and commenced practice in Hamburg, Ark.; during the Civil War served in the Confederate Army as a captain and subsequently as colonel of the Third Arkansas Infantry and Second Arkansas Battalion; captured at the Battle of the Wilderness and held as a prisoner of war until August 1865; after the war resumed the practice of law in Holly Springs, Miss.; elected as a Democrat to the Forty-fifth, Forty-sixth, and Forty-seventh Congresses (March 4, 1877–March 3, 1883); presented credentials as a Member-elect to the Forty-eighth Congress but did not qualify, and on June 25, 1884, the seat was awarded to James R. Chalmers, who contested his election; resumed the practice of law in Washington, D. C., in 1883; died in Branchville, Prince Georges County, Md., November 3, 1892; interment in Glenwood Cemetery, Washington, D. C.

MANSFIELD, Joseph Jefferson, a Representative from Texas; born in Wayne, Wayne County, Va. (now West Virginia), February 9, 1861; attended the public schools; moved to Alleyton, Tex., in 1881; employed as a farm and nursery laborer and later as a baggage-master and freight clerk with the Southern Pacific

Railway; studied law; was admitted to the bar in 1886 and commenced practice at Eagle Lake, Tex.; also established the first newspaper in that city; organized two companies of the National Guard of Texas in 1886; received commissions successively as second lieutenant, first lieutenant, and captain, and was appointed adjutant of the Fourth Texas Regiment with the rank of captain; prosecuting attorney of Eagle Lake, Tex., in 1888; mayor in 1889; prosecuting attorney of Colorado County 1892–1896; ex officio county superintendent of schools 1896–1910; judge of Colorado County 1896–1916; elected as a Democrat to the Sixty-fifth and to the fifteen succeeding Congresses and served from March 4, 1917, until his death in the naval hospital at Bethesda, Md., July 12, 1947; interment in Masonic Cemetery, Eagle Lake, Tex.

MANSFIELD, Michael Joseph (Mike), a Representative and a Senator from Montana; born in New York, N. Y., March 16, 1903; moved with his parents to Great Falls, Cascade County, Mont., in 1906; attended the public schools and the Montana School of Mines at Butte in 1927 and 1928; was graduated from Montana State University at Missoula in 1934; also attended the University of California at Berkeley in 1936 and 1937; served as a seaman in the United States Navy during the First World War, as a private in the United States Army in 1919 and 1920, and as a private first class in the United States Marine Corps 1920–1922; worked as a miner and mining engineer in Butte, Mont., 1922–1930; was professor of history and political science at the Montana State University 1933–1942; elected as a Democrat to the Seventy-eighth and to the four succeeding Congresses (January 3, 1943–January 3, 1953); was not a candidate for renomination in 1952; elected to the United States Senate in 1952 for the term commencing January 3, 1953; reelected in 1958 for the term ending January 3, 1965.

MANSON, Mahlon Dickerson, a Representative from Indiana; born in Piqua, Ohio, February 20, 1820; attended the common schools; moved to Montgomery County, Ind., and taught school for a year; studied medicine at the Ohio Medical College at Cincinnati; served as captain of Volunteers in the Mexican War October 8, 1847–July 28, 1848; member of the State house of representatives 1851 and 1852; engaged in the retail drug business at Crawfordsville; served in the Civil War; commissioned captain of the Tenth Regiment, Indiana Volunteer Infantry, April 17, 1861; major, April 25, 1861; colonel, May 10, 1861; honorably mustered out August 6, 1861; recommissioned colonel of the same regiment September 18, 1861; brigadier general of Volunteers March 24, 1862; resigned December 21, 1864; unsuccessful Democratic candidate for Lieutenant Governor of Indiana in 1864; elected as a Democrat to the Forty-second Congress (March 4, 1871–March 3, 1873); unsuccessful candidate for reelection in 1872 to the Forty-third Congress; elected auditor of Indiana in 1878; elected Lieutenant Governor in 1884; appointed collector of internal revenue of the seventh district of Indiana August 11, 1886, and resigned November 5, 1889; died in Crawfordsville, Montgomery County, Ind., on February 4, 1895; interment in Oak Hill Cemetero.

MANSUR, Charles Harley, a Representative from Missouri; born in Philadelphia, Pa., March 6, 1835; attended Lawrence Academy, Groton, Mass.; studied law; and was admitted to the bar in Richmond, Mo., August 30, 1856; moved to Chillicothe, Mo., in 1856 and practiced law; member of the board of education of Chillicothe for eight years; member of the Democratic State central committee 1864–1868; delegate to the Democratic National Convention at New York City in 1868; prosecuting attorney of Livingston County 1875–1879; joint nominee of the Democrats and Liberal Republicans for Congress in 1872, and

again the nominee of the Democrats in the same district in 1880; delegate at large to the Democratic National Convention at Chicago in 1884; elected as a Democrat to the Fiftieth, Fifty-first, and Fifty-second Congresses (March 4, 1887–March 3, 1893); unsuccessful candidate for renomination in 1892; appointed by President Cleveland as second Comptroller of the Treasury on May 29, 1893, and served until September 30, 1894; Assistant Comptroller from October 1, 1894, until his death in Washington, D. C., April 16, 1895; interment in Sunny Slope Cemetery, Richmond, Ray County, Mo.

MANTLE, Lee, a Senator from Montana; born in Birmingham, England, December 13, 1851; immigrated to the United States with his mother, who settled at Salt Lake City, Utah, in 1864; attended a village school for a few months; moved to Idaho Territory in 1870; became a telegraph operator for the Western Union Telegraph Co.; stage agent and telegraph operator at Pleasant Valley, old Overland Stage Line, until 1877; moved to Butte, Mont., in 1877 and became agent of the Wells-Fargo Express Co.; established the Inter Mountain, a daily Republican newspaper, in 1881; served as alderman the same year; member of the Territorial house of representatives in 1882, 1884, and 1888, and served as speaker the last-named year; delegate to the Republican National Convention at Chicago in 1884 and at St. Louis in 1896; mayor of Butte in 1892; many times chairman of local and State conventions; appointed to the United States Senate to fill the vacancy in the term commencing March 4, 1893, caused by the failure of the legislature to elect, but was not seated; elected as a Republican to fill the vacancy and served from January 16, 1895, to March 3, 1899; unsuccessful candidate for renomination in 1899; organized and became chairman of the Silver Republican Party of Montana in 1896, but returned to the Republican Party in 1900; resumed his occupation as manager and part of the time editor of the Inter Mountain until 1901; engaged in the real-estate and mining business in Butte, Mont.; moved to Los Angeles, Calif., in 1921; discontinued active business in 1926; died in Los Angeles, Calif., November 18, 1934; interment in Mount Moriah Cemetery, Butte, Mont.

MANZANARES, Francisco Antonio, a Delegate from the Territory of New Mexico; born in Abiquiu, N. Mex., January 25, 1843; early training was in Spanish; commenced the study of the English language, and attended St. Louis (Mo.) University in 1863 and 1864; engaged in mercantile pursuits at Las Vegas in 1866; successfully contested as a Democrat the election of Tranquilino Luna to the Forty-eighth Congress and served from March 5, 1884, to March 3, 1885; was not a candidate for reelection in 1884; engaged in the wholesale grocery business; member of the board of county commissioners in 1896 and 1897; died in Las Vegas, N. Mex., September 17, 1904; interment in Calvary Cemetery.

MAPES, Carl Edgar, a Representative from Michigan; born on a farm near Kalamo, Eaton County, Mich., December 26, 1874; attended the common schools; was graduated from Olivet (Mich.) College in 1896 and from the law department of the University of Michigan at Ann Arbor in 1899; was admitted to the bar and commenced the practice of law in Grand Rapids, Mich., in 1899; assistant prosecuting attorney of Kent County, Mich., 1900–1904; member of the State house of representatives 1905–1907; unsuccessful candidate for renomination in 1907; member of the State senate 1909–1913; elected as a Republican to the Sixty-third and to the thirteen succeeding Congresses and served from March 4, 1913, until his death; member of the House subcommittee to take testimony in New Orleans, La., on a bill to conserve oil production, and died in that city on December 12, 1939; interment in Oak Hill Cemetery, Grand Rapids, Mich.

MARABLE, John Hartwell, a Representative from Tennessee; born near Lawrenceville, Brunswick County, Va., November 18, 1786; pursued an academic course; studied medicine in Philadelphia, Pa., and practiced; moved to Yellow Creek, Tenn., and engaged in the practice of medicine; member of the State senate in 1817 and 1818; elected as a National-Republican to the Nineteenth and Twentieth Congresses (March 4, 1825–March 3, 1829); unsuccessful candidate for reelection to the Twenty-first Congress; resumed the practice of medicine; died in Montgomery County, Tenn., April 11, 1844; interment in Marable Cemetery, near Clarksville, Tenn.

MARCANTONIO, Vito, a Representative from New York; born in New York City, N. Y., December 10, 1902; attended the grade and high schools; was graduated from the law department of New York University at New York City in 1925; was admitted to the bar in June 1926 and commenced practice in New York City; served as assistant United States district attorney in 1930 and 1931; elected as a Republican to the Seventy-fourth Congress (January 3, 1935–January 3, 1937;) unsuccessful candidate for reelection in 1936 to the Seventy-fifth Congress; resumed the practice of law; elected as an American Laborite to the Seventy-sixth and to the five succeeding Congresses (January 3, 1939–January 3, 1951); unsuccessful candidate for reelection in 1950 to the Eighty-second Congress; unsuccessful American-Labor Party candidate for mayor of New York City in 1949; practiced law in Washington, D. C., and later in New York City, N. Y., until his death; died in New York City, N. Y., August 9, 1954; interment in Woodlawn Cemetery, New York City (Bronx), N. Y.

MARCHAND, Albert Gallatin (son of David Marchand), a Representative from Pennsylvania; born near Greensburg, Westmoreland County, Pa., February 27, 1811; attended the common schools; studied law; was admitted to the bar in 1833 and commenced practice in Greensburg; elected as a Democrat to the Twenty-sixth and Twenty-seventh Congresses (March 4, 1839–March 3, 1843); declined to be a candidate for renomination in 1842 to the Twenty-eighth Congress; resumed the practice of law; died in Greensburg, Pa., February 5, 1848; interment in Greensburg Cemetery.

MARCHAND, David (father of Albert Gallatin Marchand), a Representative from Pennsylvania; born near Irwin, Westmoreland County, Pa., December 10, 1776; attended private schools; studied medicine and practiced in Westmoreland County; major general of the Thirteenth Division of the State militia 1812–1814; elected to the Fifteenth and Sixteenth Congresses (March 4, 1817–March 3, 1821); elected prothonotary of Westmoreland County in 1821; resumed the practice of medicine; died in Greensburg, Westmoreland County, Pa., March 11, 1832; interment in Greensburg Cemetery.

MARCHANT, Henry, a Delegate from Rhode Island; born at Marthas Vineyard, Mass., April 9, 1741; attended school in Newport, R. I., where his father had moved, and was graduated from Philadelphia College (now the University of Pennsylvania) at Philadelphia in 1762; studied law; was admitted to the bar about 1767 and commenced practice in Newport, R. I.; attorney general of Rhode Island 1771–1777; prominent in ante-Revolutionary affairs; Member of the Continental Congress 1777–1780, 1783, and 1784, and was one of the signers of the Articles of Confederation; delegate to the Rhode Island State Convention in 1789 for the adoption of the Federal Constitution; served as United States district judge for the district of Rhode Island 1790–1796; died in Newport, R. I., on August 30, 1796; interment in the Common Burial Ground.

MARCY, Daniel, a Representative from New Hampshire; born in Portsmouth, N. H., November 7, 1809; attended the common schools; followed the sea and later engaged in shipbuilding; member of the State house of representatives 1854–1857; served in the State senate in 1857 and 1858; unsuccessful candidate for election to the Thirty-sixth Congress in 1858, and to the Thirty-seventh Congress in 1860; elected as a Democrat to the Thirty-eighth Congress (March 4, 1863–March 3, 1865); unsuccessful candidate for reelection in 1864 to the Thirty-ninth Congress; again served in the State senate in 1871 and 1872; died in Portsmouth, N. H., November 3, 1893; interment in Proprietors' Burying Ground.

MARCY, William Learned, a Senator from New York; born in Southbridge, Mass., December 12, 1786; attended the common schools and Leicester Academy; was graduated from Brown University, Providence, R. I., in 1808; taught school in Newport, R. I.; studied law; was admitted to the bar in 1811 and commenced practice in Troy, N. Y.; served in the War of 1812; recorder of Troy 1816–1818; editor of the Troy Budget; adjutant general of New York in 1821; State comptroller 1823–1829; associate justice of the State supreme court 1829–1831; elected as a Jackson Democrat to the United States Senate and served from March 4, 1831, until his resignation on January 1, 1833, to become Governor; Governor of New York 1833–1839; unsuccessful candidate for reelection; commissioner on Mexican claims 1839–1842; presiding officer of the Democratic State convention in Syracuse, N. Y., in 1843; appointed Secretary of War in the Cabinet of President Polk and served from March 5, 1845, to March 3, 1849; resumed the practice of law; appointed Secretary of State in the Cabinet of President Pierce and served from March 7, 1853, to March 4, 1857; died in Ballston Spa, N. Y., July 4, 1857; interment in the Rural Cemetery, Albany, N. Y.

MARDIS, Samuel Wright, a Representative from Alabama; born in Fayetteville, Tenn., June 12, 1800; received an academic training; attended an "old field" school; studied law; was admitted to the bar and commenced practice in Montevallo, Ala., in 1823; member of the State house of representatives 1823–1825, 1828, and 1830; elected as a Democrat to the Twenty-second and Twenty-third Congresses (March 4, 1831–March 3, 1835); moved to Mardisville, Talladega County, Ala., in 1835 and continued the practice of his profession until his death in Talladega, Talladega County, Ala., November 14, 1836; interment in Oak Hill Cemetery.

MARION, Robert, a Representative from South Carolina; born in Berkeley District, S. C.; pursued an academic course, and was graduated from the University of the State of Pennsylvania (now the University of Pennsylvania) at Philadelphia in 1784; elected to the Ninth, Tenth, and Eleventh Congresses and served from March 4, 1805, until his resignation on December 4, 1810.

MARKELL, Henry (son of Jacob Markell), a Representative from New York; born in Stone Arabia, Montgomery County, N. Y., February 7, 1792; attended the common schools; studied law; was admitted to the bar and practiced; elected as a Democrat to the Nineteenth and Twentieth Congresses (March 4, 1825–March 3, 1829); died in Palatine, N. Y., on August 30, 1831; interment in the cemetery at St. Johnsville, Montgomery County, N. Y.

MARKELL, Jacob (father of Henry Markell), a Representative from New York; born in Schenectady County, N. Y., May 8, 1770; attended the common schools; moved to Manheim in 1790 and engaged in agricultural pursuits; justice of the peace; supervisor of the town of Manheim 1797–1819 and 1824–

1829; served as judge of the court of common pleas of Montgomery County; elected as a Federalist to the Thirteenth Congress (March 4, 1813–March 3, 1815); member of the State assembly from Herkimer County in 1820; died in Manheim, Herkimer County, N. Y., November 26, 1852; interment in Snells Bush Cemetery, Manheim, N. Y.

MARKHAM, Henry Harrison, a Representative from California; born in Wilmington, Essex County, N. Y., November 16, 1840; attended the common schools of his home town and Wheeler's Academy, Vermont; moved to Wisconsin in 1861; during the Civil War enlisted in the Union Army as a private in Company G, Thirty-second Regiment, Wisconsin Volunteer Infantry; promoted to second lieutenant; was wounded at the Battle of Whippy Swamp on February 3, 1865, from the effects of which he never entirely recovered; honorably discharged June 12, 1865; returned to Wisconsin and settled in Milwaukee; studied law; was admitted to the bar in 1867 and practiced in Milwaukee before the State and United States courts; moved to Pasadena, Los Angeles County, Calif., in 1879 and continued the practice of his profession; was also interested in gold and silver mining; elected as a Republican to the Forty-ninth Congress (March 4, 1885–March 3, 1887); declined to be a candidate for renomination in 1886; appointed a member of the Board of Managers of the National Home for Disabled Volunteer Soldiers on March 16, 1889, but resigned to become Governor of California 1891–1895; was again appointed a member of the Board of Managers of the National Home for Disabled Volunteer Soldiers in 1904 and served until his death in Pasadena, Calif., October 9, 1923; interment in Mountain View Cemetery.

MARKLEY, Philip Swenk, a Representative from Pennsylvania; born in Skippack, near Norristown, Montgomery County, Pa., July 2, 1789; pursued an academic course; located in Norristown; studied law; was admitted to the bar in 1810 and commenced practice in Norristown, Pa.; deputy State's attorney for Pennsylvania 1819 and 1820; member of the State senate 1820–1823; elected as a Democrat to the Eighteenth and Nineteenth Congresses (March 4, 1823–March 3, 1827); unsuccessful candidate for reelection in 1826 to the Twentieth Congress; resumed the practice of law; appointed naval officer of Philadelphia by President Jackson; attorney general of Pennsylvania in 1829; died in Norristown, Pa., September 12, 1834; interment in St. John's Episcopal Church Cemetery.

MARKS, William, a Senator from Pennsylvania; born near "Fogg's Manor," Chester County, Pa., October 13, 1778; moved with his father to Allegheny County in early childhood and settled on the Steubenville Pike at a place later called Remington; received a limited schooling; learned the trade of tanner; studied law; was admitted to the bar and commenced practice in Pittsburgh, Pa.; held several local offices; coroner of Allegheny County; member of the State house of representatives 1810–1819 and served as speaker during the last six years; commanded the Pennsylvania State Militia in 1814; served in the State senate 1820–1825; elected as a Democrat to the United States Senate and served from March 4, 1825, to March 3, 1831; unsuccessful candidate for reelection; resumed the practice of law in Pittsburgh; moved to Beaver, Pa., in 1850 and retired to private life; died in Beaver, Beaver County, Pa., April 10, 1858; interment in the McCreery lot in the old cemetery on Buffalo Street.

MARLAND, Ernest Whitworth, a Representative from Oklahoma; born in Pittsburgh, Pa., May 8, 1874; attended the grade and high schools, and a private school at Rugby, Tenn.; was graduated from the law department of the University of Michigan at Ann Arbor in 1893; was admitted to the bar in 1895 and commenced practice in Pittsburgh, Pa.; abandoned the practice of law, was employed as an oil and lease buyer in Pennsylvania, Ohio, and West Virginia, and engaged in the production, refining, and marketing of oil at Congo, W. Va., from 1900 to 1907 and at Ponca City, Okla., in 1908; became an independent oil producer and royalty owner in 1928; elected as a Democrat to the Seventy-third Congress (March 4, 1933–January 31, 1935); was not a candidate for renomination in 1934, having received the Democratic nomination for Governor; elected Governor of Oklahoma in 1934 for the four-year term commencing January 14, 1935; unsuccessful candidate for the Democratic nomination for United States Senator in 1936; resumed his former business pursuits; erected the statue of the Pioneer Woman at Ponca City, Okla.; unsuccessful candidate for nomination in 1940 to the Seventy-seventh Congress; died in Ponca City, Okla., October 4, 1941; interment in Odd Fellows Cemetery.

MARQUETTE, Turner Mastin, a Representative from Nebraska; born near Springfield, Clark County, Ohio, July 19, 1831; attended the common schools, the Springfield High School, and Wittenberg College, Springfield, Ohio, and was graduated from Ohio University at Athens in 1855; moved to Plattsmouth, Nebr., in 1856; studied law; was admitted to the bar and commenced practice in Plattsmouth, Nebr., in 1859; member of the Territorial assembly 1857–1859; served in the Territorial council in 1860 and 1861; upon the admission of Nebraska as a State into the Union was elected as a Republican to the Thirty-ninth Congress and served two days only, March 2 and 3, 1867; had also been elected as a Delegate from the Territory of Nebraska to the Fortieth Congress, but the admission of the State voided the election; resumed the practice of law in Plattsmouth; moved to Lincoln, Nebr., in 1874; general attorney for the Chicago, Burlington & Quincy Railroad from 1869 until his death; died in Tampa, Hillsborough County, Fla., December 22, 1894; interment in Wyuka Cemetery, Lincoln, Nebr.

MARR, Alem, a Representative from Pennsylvania; born in Upper Mount Bethel, Northampton County, Pa., June 18, 1787; moved to Northumberland County in 1795 with his parents, who settled near Milton, Pa.; attended the common schools, and was graduated from Princeton College in 1807; studied law; was admitted to the bar in 1813 and commenced practice in Danville, Montour County, Pa.; elected as a Democrat to the Twenty-first Congress (March 4, 1829–March 3, 1831); was not a candidate for renomination; at the close of the term in Congress he retired from the practice of law and moved to his farm near Milton, Northumberland County, where he died March 29, 1843; interment in Milton Cemetery.

MARR, George Washington Lent, a Representative from Tennessee; born near Marrs Hill, Henry County, Va., May 25, 1779; attended rural schools and the University of North Carolina at Chapel Hill; attorney general for west Tennessee 1807–1809; attorney general of the fifth district 1809–1813; served in the Creek War and was wounded; elected to the Fifteenth Congress (March 4, 1817–March 3, 1819); unsuccessful candidate for renomination in 1818; engaged in planting; was one of the largest landowners in west Tennessee; moved from Clarksville to Obion County in 1821; member of the Tennessee State Constitutional Convention in 1834; affiliated with the Whig Party after its formation; died at his residence on Island No. 10 (since washed away), in the Mississippi River, near New Madrid, New Madrid County, Mo., on September 5, 1856; interment in Troy Cemetery, Troy, Tenn.

MARSALIS, John Henry, a Representative from Colorado; born in McComb, Pike County, Miss., May 9, 1904; attended the public schools of McComb, Miss.; moved with his parents to Colorado Springs, Colo., in 1922 and graduated from high school in 1923; student at the University of Mississippi in 1925 and 1926; graduated from the University of Colorado Law School in 1934; was admitted to the bar March 14, 1935, and commenced the practice of law in Pueblo, Colo.; investigator in district attorney's office in Pueblo in 1935 and 1936; entered the United States Army May 11, 1942, and assigned to the Weather Squadron, United States Air Force, and was serving as senior weather observer when discharged on June 16, 1945; elected district attorney, tenth judicial district of Colorado, in 1944 and took oath of office while on furlough January 9, 1945; assumed duties upon release from Army and served until December 1948; elected as a Democrat to the Eighty-first Congress (January 3, 1949–January 3, 1951); unsuccessful candidate for reelection in 1950 to the Eighty-second Congress and for election in 1952 to the Eighty-third Congress; appointed city attorney December 15, 1952; elected district judge, tenth judicial district of Colorado, in November 1954 and took the oath of office January 11, 1955; reelected in 1958 for a six-year term; is a resident of Pueblo, Colo.

MARSH, Benjamin Franklin, a Representative from Illinois; born in Wythe Township, Hancock County, Ill., in 1839; attended private schools and Jubilee College; studied law; was admitted to the bar in 1860 and practiced in Warsaw, Hancock County, Ill.; during the Civil War enlisted as a private in the Sixteenth Regiment, Illinois Volunteer Infantry; recruited a company of Cavalry, was commissioned captain, and assigned to the Second Regiment, Illinois Volunteer Cavalry; commissioned Colonel and served until January 1866; returned to Warsaw, Ill., and engaged in the practice of law until 1877; Republican candidate for member of the State constitutional convention in 1869; elected as a Republican to the Forty-fifth, Forty-sixth, and Forty-seventh Congresses (March 4, 1877–March 3, 1883); unsuccessful candidate for reelection in 1882 to the Forty-eighth Congress; engaged in agricultural pursuits and stock raising in Hancock County; appointed in 1889 State railroad and warehouse commissioner, and served four years; delegate to the Republican National Convention at Chicago in 1888 which nominated Benjamin Harrison, of Indiana, for President and Levi P. Morton, of New York, for Vice President; elected to the Fifty-third and to the three succeeding Congresses (March 4, 1893–March 3, 1901); unsuccessful candidate in 1900 for reelection to the Fifty-seventh Congress; elected to the Fifty-eighth and Fifty-ninth Congresses and served from March 4, 1903, until his death in Warsaw, Ill., June 2, 1905; interment in Oakland Cemetery.

MARSH, Charles (father of George Perkins Marsh), a Representative from Vermont; born in Lebanon, New London County, Conn., July 10, 1765; moved with his parents to Hartford, Conn., in 1773; educated under private tutors, and was graduated from Dartmouth College, Hanover, N. H., in 1786; studied law in the law school of Judge Reeves at Litchfield, Conn.; was admitted to the bar in 1788 and commenced the practice of law in Woodstock, Windsor County, Vt., the same year; appointed by President Washington United States district attorney for Vermont and served from 1797 to 1801; elected as a Federalist to the Fourteenth Congress (March 4, 1815–March 3, 1817); founder of the American Colonization Society while in Washington; resumed the practice of law in Woodstock, Windsor County, Vt.; trustee of Dartmouth College 1809–1849; died in Woodstock, Vt., on January 11, 1849; interment in River Street Cemetery.

MARSH, George Perkins (son of Charles Marsh), a Representative from Vermont; born in Woodstock, Windsor County, Vt., March 15, 1801; was graduated from Dartmouth College, Hanover, N. H., in 1820; studied law; was admitted to the bar in 1825 and commenced practice in Burlington, Vt.; was an authority on languages; member of the Governor's council in 1835; elected as a Whig to the Twenty-eighth and to the three succeeding Congresses and served from March 4, 1843, until his resignation in 1849, having been appointed by President Taylor as Minister Resident to Turkey, in which office he served from May 29, 1849, to December 19, 1853; charged with a special mission to Greece in 1852; fish commissioner of Vermont in 1857 and railroad commissioner 1857–1859; appointed by President Lincoln as Envoy Extraordinary and Minister Plenipotentiary to Italy on March 20, 1861, and served until his death in Vallombrosa, Italy, July 24, 1882; interment in English Cemetery, Rome, Italy.

MARSHALL, Alexander Keith, a Representative from Kentucky; born at Buck Pond, near Versailles, Woodford County, Ky., on February 11, 1808; completed preparatory studies; settled in Nicholasville, Ky.; was graduated from the medical department of the University of Pennsylvania at Philadelphia in 1844; engaged in the practice of medicine at Nicholasville; member of the State constitutional convention held in Frankfort in 1849; elected by the American Party to the Thirty-fourth Congress (March 4, 1855–March 3, 1857); moved to Missouri, but returned to Kentucky and settled in Fayette County; engaged in agricultural pursuits; died near East Hickman, Ky., April 28, 1884; interment in Lexington Cemetery, Lexington, Ky.

MARSHALL, Alfred, a Representative from Maine; born in New Hampshire about 1797; member of the State house of representatives in 1827, 1828, 1834, and 1835; served as a general in the State militia; elected as a Democrat to the Twenty-seventh Congress (March 4, 1841–March 3, 1843); collector at Belfast, Maine, 1846–1849; engaged in mercantile pursuits and the hotel business; died in China, Kennebec County, Maine, October 2, 1868; interment in Village Cemetery.

MARSHALL, Edward Chauncey, a Representative from California; born in Woodford County, Ky., June 29, 1821; attended Centre College, Danville, Ky., and was graduated from Transylvania University, Lexington, Ky.; attended Washington College (now Washington and Lee University) during the session of 1832–1833; studied law and was admitted to the bar; moved to San Francisco and later to Sonora, Calif.; practiced law; served in the Mexican War; elected as a Democrat to the Thirty-second Congress (March 4, 1851–March 3, 1853); was renominated in 1852, but withdrew before the election; settled in Marysville, Calif., and again engaged in the practice of law; unsuccessful candidate for election to the United States Senate in 1856; moved to Kentucky and devoted himself to legal pursuits for twenty-one years; returned to San Francisco in 1877 and continued the practice of law; attorney general of California 1883–1886; died in San Francisco, Calif., July 9, 1893; interment in Mountain View Cemetery, Oakland, Calif.

MARSHALL, Fred, a Representative from Minnesota; born in Union Grove Township, near Grove City, Meeker County, Minn., March 13, 1906; graduated from Paynesville (Minn.) High School; actively engaged in farming and operating the family farm; member of the Minnesota Agriculture Administration Committee 1937–1941; State director of the Farm Security Administration (later the Farmers Home Administration) 1941–1948; elected as a Democrat to the Eighty-first and to the five succeeding Congresses (January 3, 1949–January 3, 1961). *Reelected to the Eighty-seventh Congress.*

MARSHALL, George Alexander, a Representative from Ohio; born near Sidney, Shelby County, Ohio, September 14, 1851; attended the public schools of Shelby County, and later the Ohio Wesleyan University, Delaware, Ohio; studied law; was admitted to the bar in 1876 and commenced practice in Sidney, Ohio; prosecuting attorney of Shelby County for eight years, being elected in 1878, 1880, and 1883; elected as a Democrat to the Fifty-fifth Congress (March 4, 1897–March 3, 1899); was not a candidate for reelection in 1898; died in Sidney, Ohio, April 21, 1899; interment in Presbyterian Cemetery, Hardin, Shelby County, Ohio.

MARSHALL, Humphrey (father of Thomas Alexander Marshall and cousin of John Marshall), a Senator from Kentucky; born in Orlean, Fauquier County, Va., in 1760; pursued classical studies under the direction of his wife; became a surveyor; captain in the Virginia Cavalry in the Revolutionary War; moved to Kentucky in 1780; studied law; was admitted to the bar and commenced practice in Fayette County; delegate to the Danville convention in 1787 to consider the separation of Kentucky from Virginia, which he opposed; delegate to the Virginia convention which ratified the Constitution of the United States; member of the Kentucky House of Representatives in 1793, 1807, 1808, and 1823; elected as a Federalist to the United States Senate and served from March 4, 1795, to March 3, 1801; engaged in literary pursuits and was the author of the first history of Kentucky, published in 1812 and enlarged in 1824; engaged in agricultural pursuits; died near Frankfort, Franklin County, Ky., July 1, 1841; interment on his farm, "Glen Willis," Leestown, Ky.

MARSHALL, Humphrey (grandson of the preceding), a Representative from Kentucky; born in Frankfort, Franklin County, Ky., January 13, 1812; pursued academic studies; was graduated from the United States Military Academy at West Point in 1832; resigned from the Army April 30, 1833; studied law; was admitted to the bar in 1833 and practiced in Frankfort in 1833 and 1834 and in Louisville 1834–1846; served in the State militia; colonel of Volunteers in the Mexican War; engaged in agricultural pursuits in Henry County, Ky.; elected as a Whig to the Thirty-first and Thirty-second Congresses and served from March 4, 1849, until his resignation on August 4, 1852; Minister to China 1852–1854; elected on the American Party ticket to the Thirty-fourth and Thirty-fifth Congresses (March 4, 1855–March 3, 1859); renominated by acclamation, but declined; during the Civil War served as a brigadier general in the Confederate Army; moved to Richmond, Va., and continued the practice of law; elected to the Confederate Congress; after the surrender of General Lee moved to New Orleans, La.; civil disabilities were removed by President Johnson December 18, 1867; returned to Louisville and resumed the practice of law; died in Louisville, Ky., March 28, 1872; interment in the State Cemetery, Frankfort, Ky.

MARSHALL, James William, a Representative from Virginia; born near Staunton, Augusta County, Va., March 31, 1844; attended the country schools of his native county; during the Civil War served in the Confederate Army as a private for four years; was graduated from Roanoke College, Salem, Va., in 1870; studied law and was admitted to the bar; Commonwealth attorney for Craig County 1870–1875; served in the State senate 1875–1878; member of the State house of delegates in 1883 and 1884; elected Commonwealth attorney for Craig County in 1884 and served four years; presidential elector on the Democratic ticket of Cleveland and Thurman in 1888; again served in the State senate in 1891 and 1892; elected as a Democrat to the Fifty-third Congress (March 4, 1893–March 3,

1895); unsuccessful candidate for renomination in 1894; resumed the practice of his profession in Newcastle; elected a delegate to the State constitutional convention of 1901; died in Newcastle, Craig County, Va., November 27, 1911; interment in West View Cemetery.

MARSHALL, John (uncle of Thomas Francis Marshall and cousin of Humphrey Marshall), a Representative from Virginia; born in Germantown, Fauquier County, Va., September 24, 1755; received elementary instruction from his parents, and pursued more advanced studies under a private tutor, James Thompson, and in the classical academy of the Messrs. Campbell in Westmoreland County, Va.; at the age of eighteen began the study of law, but at the outbreak of the Revolutionary War joined a company of State militia that subsequently became part of the Eleventh Regiment of Virginia Troops; was lieutenant of a company, and promoted to captain in May 1777; participated in a number of the more important engagements from 1775 to 1779; was ordered to Virginia in 1779 to take charge of the militia then being organized; studied law at William and Mary College, Williamsburg, Va.; was admitted to the bar on August 28, 1780; returned to the command of his company, then at the Army's headquarters, and to Virginia later in the year, where he joined the forces of Baron von Steuben for the defense of the State; resigned his commission in 1781 and engaged in the practice of law in Fauquier County; delegate in the Virginia House of Burgesses in 1780; settled in Richmond and practiced law; member of the executive council 1782–1795; again a member of the house of burgesses 1782–1788; delegate to the State constitutional convention for the ratification of the Federal Constitution that met in Richmond June 2, 1788; declined the Cabinet position of Attorney General and also a foreign mission tendered by President Washington; one of the special commissioners to France in 1797 and 1798 to demand redress and reparation for hostile actions of that country; resumed the practice of law in Virginia; declined the appointment of Associate Justice of the Supreme Court of the United States tendered by President Adams September 26, 1798; elected to the Sixth Congress and served from March 4, 1799, to June 7, 1800, when he resigned; was appointed Secretary of War by President Adams May 7, 1800, but the appointment was not considered, and on May 12, 1800, was appointed Secretary of State; entered upon his new duties June 6, 1800, and although appointed Chief Justice of the United States January 20, 1801, and notwithstanding he took the oath of office as Chief Justice February 4, 1801, continued to serve in the Cabinet until March 4, 1801; member of the Virginia convention of 1829; continued as Chief Justice until his death in Philadelphia, Pa., July 6, 1835; interment in the "New Burying Ground" on Shockoe Hill, Richmond, Va.

MARSHALL, Leroy Tate, a Representative from Ohio; born on a farm near Bellbrook, Greene County, Ohio, November 8, 1883; attended the public schools of Greene County; teacher in the public schools of Greene County, Ohio, 1903–1907; was graduated from Cedarville (Ohio) College in 1909; moved to Xenia, Ohio, and served as clerk of courts, Greene County, 1909–1913; studied law; was admitted to the Ohio bar in 1911 and commenced the practicing of law in Xenia, Ohio; served as chairman of the Greene County Republican county committee 1920–1932; member of the Ohio State Senate 1925–1928; elected as a Republican to the Seventy-third and Seventy-fourth Congresses (March 4, 1933–January 3, 1937); unsuccessful candidate for reelection in 1936 to the Seventy-fifth Congress; returned to Xenia, Ohio, and continued the practice of law until his death there on November 22, 1950; interment in Woodland Cemetery.

MARSHALL, Lycurgus Luther, a Representative from Ohio; born in Bucyrus, Crawford County, Ohio, July 9, 1888; attended the public schools; was graduated from Ohio Wesleyan University, Delaware, Ohio, in 1909 and from the law department of Western Reserve University, Cleveland, Ohio, in 1915; was admitted to the bar in 1915 and commenced practice in Cleveland, Ohio; member of the State house of representatives in 1921 and 1922; served in the State senate 1923–1935; member of the Euclid (Ohio) School Board for eight years; elected as a Republican to the Seventy-sixth Congress (January 3, 1939–January 3, 1941); unsuccessful candidate for reelection in 1940 to the Seventy-seventh Congress; resumed the practice of law; died in Aurora, Ohio, January 12, 1958; interment in Lake View Cemetery, Cleveland, Ohio.

MARSHALL, Samuel Scott, a Representative from Illinois; born near Shawneetown, Gallatin County, Ill., March 12, 1821; attended public and private schools in McLeansboro, Ill., and Cumberland College, Kentucky; studied law; was admitted to the bar in 1845 and commenced practice in McLeansboro, Ill.; member of the State house of representatives in 1846 and 1847; State's attorney for the third judicial circuit of Illinois in 1847 and 1848; circuit court judge 1851–1854 and 1861–1864; delegate to the Democratic National Conventions in 1860, 1864, and 1880; delegate to the Union National Convention at Philadelphia in 1866; elected as a Democrat to the Thirty-fourth and Thirty-fifth Congresses (March 4, 1855–March 3, 1859); was the candidate of his party, who were in the minority, for United States Senator in 1861; elected to the Thirty-ninth and to the four succeeding Congresses (March 4, 1865–March 3, 1875), and was the candidate of his party for Speaker of the House in 1867; unsuccessful candidate for reelection in 1874 to the Forty-fourth Congress; president of the board of managers of Hamilton College 1875–1880; died in McLeansboro, Hamilton County, Ill., July 26, 1890; interment in Odd Fellows Cemetery.

MARSHALL, Thomas Alexander (son of Humphrey Marshall), a Representative from Kentuky; born near Versailles, Woodford County, Ky., January 15, 1794; pursued preparatory studies; was graduated from Yale College in 1815; studied law; was admitted to the bar and commenced practice in Frankfort in 1817; moved to Paris, Ky., in 1819; member of the State house of representatives in 1827 and 1828; elected as a Whig to the Twenty-second and Twenty-third Congresses (March 4, 1831–March 3, 1835); unsuccessful candidate for reelection in 1834 to the Twenty-fourth Congress; judge of the State court of appeals 1835–1856; professor in the law department of Transylvania College, Lexington, Ky., 1836–1849; moved to Louisville in 1859; member of the State house of representatives in 1863; chief justice of the court of appeals in 1866 and 1867; died in Louisville, Ky., April 17, 1871; interment in Lexington Cemetery, Lexington, Ky.

MARSHALL, Thomas Francis (nephew of John Marshall), a Representative from Kentucky; born in Frankfort, Franklin County, Ky., June 7, 1801; pursued classical studies in Virginia; studied law; was admitted to the bar and commenced practice in Versailles, Ky., in 1828; member of the State house of representatives 1832–1836, 1838, 1839, and 1854; moved to Louisville in 1833; unsuccessful candidate for election in 1836 to the Twenty-fifth Congress; elected to the Twenty-seventh Congress (March 4, 1841–March 3, 1843); unsuccessful candidate for reelection in 1842 to the Twenty-eighth Congress; served in the Mexican War as captain of Volunteers; moved to Chicago, Ill., in 1856; returned to Kentucky and engaged in the practice of law until his death near Versailles, Ky., September 22, 1864; interment in State Cemetery, Frankfort, Ky.

MARSHALL, Thomas Frank, a Representative from North Dakota; born in Hannibal, Marion County, Mo., March 7, 1854; attended the common schools and the State normal school at Platteville, Grant County, Wis.; left school in 1873 two months before graduation, but received his diploma forty years later; became a surveyor; moved to Yankton, Dak. (now South Dakota), in 1873 and engaged in mercantile pursuits; moved to Columbia, Dak. (now North Dakota), in 1882 and engaged in banking; moved in 1886 to Oakes, Dak., where he engaged in banking and surveying; mayor 1888–1892; member of the State senate 1896–1900; delegate to the Republican National Convention at Minneapolis in 1892; elected as a Republican to the Fifty-seventh and to the three succeeding Congresses (March 4, 1901–March 3, 1909); was not a candidate for renomination in 1908, having become a candidate for the United States Senate, in which he was unsuccessful; again engaged in banking; died at his summer home in Detroit (now Detroit Lakes), Becker County, Minn., August 20, 1921; interment in Oakesview Cemetery, Oakes, Dickey County, N. Dak.

MARSHALL, Thomas Riley, a Vice President of the United States; born in North Manchester, Wabash County, Ind., March 14, 1854; attended the common schools, and was graduated from Wabash College, Crawfordsville, Ind., in 1873; studied law; was admitted to the bar in 1875 and commenced practice in Columbia City, Ind.; Governor of Indiana 1909–1913; choice of the Indiana delegation for the Democratic nomination for President of the United States in 1912; elected, as a Democrat, Vice President of the United States on the ticket with Woodrow Wilson and qualified on March 4, 1913; reelected in 1916 and served until March 3, 1921; resumed the practice of law and literary work in Indianapolis, Ind.; member of the Federal Coal Commission in 1922 and 1923; died in Washington, D. C., June 1, 1925; interment in Crown Hill Cemetery, Indianapolis, Ind.

MARSTON, Gilman, a Representative and a Senator from New Hampshire; born in Oxford, N. H., August 20, 1811; was graduated from Dartmouth College, Hanover, N. H., in 1837 and from the law department of Harvard University in 1840; was admitted to the bar and commenced practice in Exeter, Rockingham County, N. H., in 1841; member of the State house of representatives 1845–1849; delegate to the State constitutional convention of 1850; elected as a Republican to the Thirty-sixth and Thirty-seventh Congresses (March 4, 1859–March 3, 1863); served in the Union Army during the Civil War; commissioned colonel of the Tenth Regiment, New Hampshire Volunteer Infantry, June 10, 1861; brigadier general of Volunteers November 29, 1862; resigned his commission April 20, 1865; elected to the Thirty-ninth Congress (March 4, 1865–March 3, 1867); declined the Governorship of Idaho Territory in 1870; again a member of the State house of representatives 1872, 1873, and 1876–1878; unsuccessful candidate for election in 1876 to the Forty-fifth Congress; delegate to the State constitutional convention of 1876; appointed to the United States Senate on March 4, 1889, to fill the vacancy in the term commencing on that date and served until June 18, 1889, when a successor was elected; died in Exeter, N. H., July 3, 1890; interment in Exeter Cemetery.

MARTIN, Alexander, a Senator from North Carolina; born on a farm in Amwell Township, Hunterdon County, N. J., in 1740; attended the common schools and Newark College; was graduated from the College of New Jersey (now Princeton University) in 1756; moved to Virginia and, later, to Guilford (then a part of Rowan) County, N. C.; studied law; was admitted to the bar and commenced practice in Guilford County, N. C., in 1772; member of the colonial assembly in 1774 and 1775; appointed lieutenant colonel of the Second North Carolina Regiment in the Continental Army on September 1, 1775; was promoted to the rank of colonel on April 10, 1776, and was present at the Battles of Brandywine and Germantown; resigned November 22, 1777; member of the State senate 1779–1782 and 1785–1788 and served as speaker 1780–1782; Acting Governor of North Carolina in 1781 and 1782 and Governor 1782–1784 and 1789–1792; delegate to the State convention for the adoption of the Federal Constitution in 1787; trustee of the University of North Carolina 1790–1807 and served as president of the board in 1792 and 1793; elected to the United States Senate and served from March 4, 1793, to March 3, 1799; died on his plantation, "Danbury," on the Dan River, Rockingham County, near Crawford (now Danbury), Stokes County, N. C., November 10, 1807; interment on his estate.

MARTIN, Augustus Newton, a Representative from Indiana; born near Whitestown, Butler County, Pa., March 23, 1847; attended the common schools and Witherspoon Institute, Butler, Pa., and was graduated from Eastman College, Poughkeepsie, N. Y., in February 1867; during the Civil War enlisted July 3, 1863, in Company I, Fifty-eighth Regiment, Pennsylvania Volunteer Militia, which assisted in the capture of Gen. John Morgan's command; enlisted again February 22, 1865, in Company E, Seventy-eighth Regiment, Pennsylvania Volunteer Infantry, and served until discharged for disability August 30, 1865; taught school; studied law in Bluffton, Wells County, Ind., in 1869; was admitted to the bar in 1870 and practiced; member of the State house of representatives in 1875; elected reporter of the Supreme Court of Indiana in 1876 and served four years; unsuccessful candidate for reelection in 1880; resided in Austin, Tex., 1881–1883; returned to Bluffton, Ind., in 1883; elected as a Democrat to the Fifty-first, Fifty-second, and Fifty-third Congresses (March 4, 1889–March 3, 1895); unsuccessful candidate for reelection to the Fifty-fourth Congress; engaged in the practice of law in Bluffton, Ind., until his death at the Soldiers' Home Hospital, Marion, Ind., July 11, 1901; interment in Fairview Cemetery, Bluffton, Ind.

MARTIN, Barclay (uncle of Lewis Tillman), a Representative from Tennessee; born in Edgefield District, S. C., December 17, 1802; moved to Bourbon County, Ky., with his parents in 1804 and to Bedford County, Tenn., in 1806; pursued an academic course; moved to Columbia, Maury County, Tenn.; studied law; was admitted to the bar and practiced; member of the State house of representatives in 1839 and 1840; served in the State senate 1841–1843; elected as a Democrat to the Twenty-ninth Congress (March 4, 1845–March 3, 1847); resumed the practice of his profession; again served in the State house of representatives 1847–1849 and 1851–1853; member of the board of trustees of the Columbia Athenaeum from 1852 until his death; died in Columbia, Tenn., November 8, 1890; interment in Zion Cemetery

MARTIN, Benjamin Franklin, a Representative from West Virginia; born near Farmington, Marion County, Va. (now West Virginia), October 2, 1828; was graduated from Allegheny College, Meadville, Pa., in June 1854; taught school in Fairmont, Marion County; studied law; was admitted to the bar and commenced practice in March 1856; moved to Pruntytown in 1856; member of the constitutional convention of West Virginia in 1872; delegate to the Democratic National Convention at Baltimore in 1872; elected as a Democrat to the Forty-fifth and Forty-sixth Congresses (March 4, 1877–March 3, 1881); unsuccessful candidate for renomination in 1880; presidential elector on the Democratic ticket of Cleveland and Hendricks in 1884; delegate at large to the Democratic National Convention at St. Louis in 1888; resumed the practice of law in Grafton, Taylor County, W. Va., and died there January 20, 1895; interment in Woodlawn Cemetery, Fairmont, W. Va.

MARTIN, Charles, a Representative from Illinois; born near Ogdensburg, St. Lawrence County, N. Y., May 20, 1856; moved with his parents to Chicago, Ill., in 1860; attended the public schools; engaged in business as a sewer contractor and later as a coal dealer; served as alderman in the city council 1894–1903, 1905–1907, and 1910–1913, and again elected in 1915; elected as a Democrat to the Sixty-fifth Congress and served from March 4, 1917, until his death in Chicago, Ill., October 28, 1917; interment in Mount Olivet Cemetery.

MARTIN, Charles Drake, a Representative from Ohio; born in Mount Vernon, Knox County, Ohio, August 5, 1829; attended the public schools and Kenyon College, Gambier, Ohio; studied law; was admitted to the bar in 1850 and commenced practice in Lancaster, Fairfield County, Ohio; elected as a Democrat to the Thirty-sixth Congress (March 4, 1859–March 3, 1861); unsuccessful candidate for reelection in 1860 to the Thirty-seventh Congress; resumed the practice of law; member of the supreme court commission 1883–1886; continued the practice of law in Lancaster, Ohio, until his death there August 27, 1911; interment in Forest Rose Cemetery.

MARTIN, Charles Henry (great-grandson of Nathaniel Macon), a Representative from North Carolina; born near Youngsville, Franklin County, N. C., August 28, 1848; attended the common schools and the preparatory department of Wake Forest (N. C.) College; was graduated from Wake Forest College in 1872 and from the University of Virginia at Charlottesville in 1875; studied in the Southern Baptist Theological Seminary, Louisville, Ky.; principal of the high schools at Badin and Lumberton, N. C.; professor of Latin in the female college at Murfreesboro, N. C., and later taught in Wake Forest College; studied law; was admitted to the bar in 1879 and commenced practice in Louisburg, Franklin County, N. C.; moved to Raleigh, N. C., and continued the practice of law; ordained as a Baptist minister in 1887; successfully contested as a Populist the election of James A. Lockhart to the Fifty-fourth Congress; reelected to the Fifty-fifth Congress and served from June 5, 1896, to March 3, 1899; did not seek renomination in 1898; resumed his ministerial duties and had charge of a Baptist church at Polkton, N. C.; died in Polkton, N. C., April 19, 1931; interment in Williams Cemetery.

MARTIN, Charles Henry, a Representative from Oregon; born on a farm near Albion, Edwards County, Ill., October 1, 1863; attended the public schools of Carmi, Ill., and Ewing (Ill.) College; was graduated from the United States Military Academy at West Point, N. Y., in 1887; served in the United States Army and saw active service with combat troops in the Spanish-American War, Philippine Insurrection, Boxer campaign in China, and was a division commander in the First World War; awarded the Distinguished Service Medal and two citations for bravery in action; assistant chief of staff, United States Army, 1922–1924; commanded the Panama Canal Department 1925–1927; retired from the Army as a major general on October 1, 1927, and established his residence in Portland, Oreg.; elected as a Democrat to the Seventy-second and Seventy-third Congresses (March 4, 1931–January 3, 1935); was not a candidate for renomination in 1934, having received the Democratic nomination for Governor; elected Governor of Oregon and served from January 14, 1935, to January 9, 1939; retired from public life and resided in Portland, Oreg., until his death there on September 22, 1946; interment in Riverview Cemetery.

MARTIN, Eben Wever, a Representative from South Dakota; born in Maquoketa, Jackson County, Iowa, April 12, 1855; attended the public schools, and was graduated from Cornell

College, Mount Vernon, Iowa, in 1879; attended the law department of the University of Michigan at Ann Arbor in 1879 and 1880 and was president of his class; was admitted to the bar in 1880 and commenced the practice of law in Deadwood, Dak. (now South Dakota); member of the Territorial House of Representatives of Dakota in 1884 and 1885; served as president of the board of education of the city of Deadwood 1886–1900; elected as a Republican to the Fifty-seventh, Fifty-eighth, and Fifty-ninth Congresses (March 4, 1901–March 3, 1907); did not seek the renomination in 1906, having become a candidate for the United States Senate; unsuccessful candidate for the United States Senate in 1906; elected to the Sixtieth Congress to fill the vacancy caused by the death of William H. Parker; reelected to the Sixty-first, Sixty-second, and Sixty-third Congresses and served from November 3, 1908, until March 3, 1915; was not a candidate for renomination in 1914 to the Sixty-fourth Congress; resumed the practice of law in Hot Springs, S. Dak., until his death in that city on May 22, 1932; interment in Evergreen Cemetery.

MARTIN, Edward, a Senator from Pennsylvania; born at Ten Mile, Washington Township, Greene County, Pa., September 18, 1879; attended the public schools; was graduated from Waynesburg College, Waynesburg, Pa., in 1901; studied law; was admitted to the bar in 1905 and commenced practice in Waynesburg, Pa.; enlisted in the Pennsylvania National Guard May 9, 1898, and served in the Spanish-American War, on the Mexican Border, and in the First and Second World Wars, in all grades from private to major general, being placed on the inactive list April 1, 1942; was awarded the Distinguished Service Cross with Oak Leaf Cluster and the Purple Heart with Oak Leaf Cluster; burgess of East Waynesburg 1902–1905; solicitor of Greene County 1908–1910 and 1916–1920; auditor general of Pennsylvania 1925–1929; president of Auditors', Controllers' and Treasurers' Association of the United States in 1932; chairman of the Republican State Committee 1928–1934; State treasurer 1929–1933; adjutant general of Pennsylvania 1939–1943; president of the National Guard Association of the United States in 1940; Governor of Pennsylvania 1943–1946; had varied business interests, including fire insurance, oil and gas, and banking; author and editor of "The History of the Twenty-eighth Division"; chairman of the executive committee of the Governors' Conferences in 1945 and 1946; president of the Council of State Governments in 1946; delegate to the Republican National Conventions in 1932, 1936, 1940, 1944, 1948, 1952, 1956, and 1960; elected as a Republican to the United States Senate in 1946 for the term commencing January 3, 1947; reelected in 1952 for the term ending January 3, 1959; was not a candidate for renomination in 1958; retired; is a resident of Washington, Pa.

MARTIN, Edward Livingston, a Representative from Delaware; born in Seaford, Sussex County, Del., March 29, 1837; attended private schools, Newark Academy, Bolmar's Academy, West Chester, Pa., and Delaware College, Newark, Del.; was graduated from the University of Virginia at Charlottesville in 1859; served as clerk of the State senate 1863–1865; delegate to the Democratic National Conventions in 1864, 1872, 1876, 1880, and 1884; studied law at the University of Virginia in 1866; was admitted to the bar the same year and practiced in Dover, Del., until 1867; returned to Seaford and engaged in agricultural and horticultural pursuits; served as director of the Delaware Board of Agriculture, president of the Peninsula Horticultural Society, and lecturer of the Delaware State Grange; commissioner to settle disputed boundary line between the States of Delaware and New Jersey 1873–1875; elected as a Democrat to the Forty-sixth and Forty-seventh Congresses (March 4, 1879–March 3, 1883); was not a candi-

date for renomination in 1882 to the Forty-eighth Congress; resumed horticultural and agricultural pursuits; twice an unsuccessful candidate for election to the United States Senate; died in Seaford, Del., January 22, 1897; interment in St. Luke's Episcopal Churchyard.

MARTIN, Elbert Sevier (brother of John Preston Martin), a Representative from Virginia; born near Jonesville, Lee County, Va., about 1829; attended the public schools, and Emory and Henry College, Emory, Va., 1845–1848; engaged in mercantile pursuits in Jonesville, Va.; elected on the American Party ticket to the Thirty-sixth Congress (March 4, 1859–March 3, 1861); unsuccessful candidate for reelection in 1860 to the Thirty-seventh Congress; served in the Confederate Army during the Civil War as captain of a company of volunteers formed in Jonesville, Va.; moved to Dallas, Tex., in 1870 and became interested in the newspaper publishing business; died in Dallas, Tex., September 3, 1876.

MARTIN, Frederick Stanley, a Representative from New York; born in Rutland County, Vt., April 25, 1794; because of the death of his father, left his mother's home at the age of seven and resided with relatives; went to New Hartford, N. Y., in 1804 and remained for six years; attended the local schools; moved to Whitehall, Vt., in 1810 and became employed in a mercantile establishment; in 1812 became a steward on a Government vessel plying on Lake Champlain; in 1815 shipped from Newport, R. I., on board a merchantman as a common sailor; settled in Olean, Cattaraugus County, N. Y., in the spring of 1818, ran a hotel, and also carried on a lumber business; in 1831 entered the mercantile business in which he engaged for twenty years; member of the board of supervisors of Olean in 1830, 1831, 1836, and 1838; appointed by Governor Clinton as a major in the Two Hundred and Twenty-sixth Regiment, New York State Militia, in 1826, in which capacity he served until 1830, when he was promoted to lieutenant colonel, which rank he held until 1833, when he resigned; appointed by President Jackson as postmaster at Olean, N. Y., December 23, 1830, and served until November 14, 1839; appointed judge of the county courts in January 1840 by Governor Seward and served for five years; was actively interested in the construction of the Genesee Valley Canal; member of the New York State Senate 1847–1849; served in the State assembly in 1850 and 1851; elected as a Whig to the Thirty-second Congress (March 4, 1851–March 3, 1853); renewed his former business pursuits; died in Olean, N. Y., June 28, 1865; interment in Oak Lawn Cemetery; reinterment on April 29, 1896, in Mount View Cemetery.

MARTIN, George Brown (grandson of John Preston Martin), a Senator from Kentucky; born in Prestonsburg, Floyd County, Ky., August 18, 1876; moved with his parents to Catlettsburg, Boyd County, Ky., in 1877; attended the public schools and was graduated from Centre University, Richmond (now at Danville), Ky., in 1895; studied law; was admitted to the bar in 1900 and commenced practice in Catlettsburg, Ky., the same year; general counsel and director of the Big Sandy & Kentucky River Railway Co.; vice president, Ohio Valley Electric Railway Co.; director, Kentucky-Farmers Bank of Catlettsburg; county judge of Boyd County in 1904; member of the Council of National Defense for Kentucky in 1917; appointed major in the Judge Advocate General's Department of the United States Army, but did not serve, having been appointed Senator; appointed as a Democrat to the United States Senate to fill the vacancy caused by the death of Ollie M. James and served from September 7, 1918, to March 3, 1919; was not a candidate for election to the full term; resumed the practice of law in Catlettsburg, Ky., where he died November 12, 1945; interment in Catlettsburg Cemetery.

MARTIN, James Stewart, a Representative from Illinois; born in Estillville (now Gate City), Scott County, Va., August 19, 1826; attended the common schools and Emory and Henry College, Emory, Va.; moved to Salem, Marion County, Ill., in 1846; served during the Mexican War in Company C, First Regiment of Illinois Volunteers; studied law; was admitted to the bar in 1861 and commenced practice in Salem, Ill.; clerk of Marion County Court; during the Civil War served in the Union Army; commissioned colonel of the One Hundred and Eleventh Regiment, Illinois Volunteer Infantry, September 18, 1862; brevetted brigadier general of Volunteers February 26, 1865; honorably mustered out June 7, 1865; judge of Marion County Court; appointed by President Grant as United States pension agent April 13, 1869; elected as a Republican to the Forty-third Congress (March 4, 1873–March 3, 1875); unsuccessful candidate for reelection; commissioner of the Southern Illinois Penitentiary at Menard in 1879; died in Salem, Ill., November 20, 1907; interment in East Lawn Cemetery.

MARTIN, John, a Senator from Kansas; born near Hartsville, Wilson County, Tenn., November 12, 1833; attended the common schools; clerked in stores and in the post office; moved to Tecumseh, Shawnee County, Kans., in 1855; elected assistant clerk of the first house of representatives in the Territory in 1855; county clerk and register of deeds 1855–1857; studied law; was admitted to the bar in 1856 and commenced practice in Tecumseh; justice of the peace in 1857; county attorney of Shawnee County 1858–1860; postmaster of Tecumseh in 1858 and 1859; deputy United States attorney 1859–1861; reporter of the State supreme court in 1860; moved to Topeka and practiced law in 1861; served in the State house of representatives 1871–1875; delegate to the Democratic National Convention at Baltimore in 1872; chairman of Kansas Democratic State executive committee in 1872; unsuccessful Democratic candidate for Governor in 1876; unsuccessful candidate for election to the United States Senate in 1877; appointed and subsequently elected district judge and served from 1883 to 1885; unsuccessful candidate for election to the Fiftieth Congress; unsuccessful candidate for Governor in 1888; elected as a Democrat to the United States Senate on January 25, 1893, to fill the vacancy caused by the death of Preston B. Plumb and served from March 4, 1893, to March 3, 1895; clerk of the Supreme Court of Kansas 1897–1899; died in Topeka, Kans., September 3, 1913; interment in Topeka Cemetery.

MARTIN, John Andrew, a Representative from Colorado; born in Cincinnati, Ohio, April 10, 1868; moved with his parents to Fulton, Mo., in 1872; attended the public schools of Mexico and Fulton, Mo.; moved with his parents to Kansas in 1884 and worked on a farm; moved to Colorado in 1887; employed on railroad construction work and as a locomotive fireman 1887–1894; member of the city council of La Junta in 1895 and 1896, and published the La Junta Times during the same period; studied law; was admitted to the bar in 1896 and commenced practice in Pueblo, Colo., in 1897; member of the State house of representatives in 1901 and 1902; city attorney in 1905 and 1906; elected as a Democrat to the Sixty-first and Sixty-second Congresses (March 4, 1909–March 3, 1913); declined to be a candidate for reelection in 1912; resumed the practice of law; again city attorney in 1916 and 1917; during the First World War recruited a volunteer battalion, in which he enlisted as a private and was commissioned a major on the mustering in of the battalion, serving as commanding officer of the One Hundred and Fifteenth Supply Train, Fortieth Division; resumed the practice of law in Pueblo, Colo.; elected to the Seventy-third and to the three succeeding Congresses and served from March 4, 1933, until his death in Washington, D. C., December 23, 1939; interment in Mountain View Cemetery, Pueblo, Colo.

MARTIN, John Cunningham, a Representative from Illinois; born in Salem, Marion County, Ill., April 29, 1880; attended the public schools and Illinois College, Jacksonville, Ill.; became engaged in banking in 1907; director of the Federal Reserve Bank of St. Louis 1922–1932; president of the Salem National Bank 1933–1952; served as State treasurer of Illinois 1933–1935 and 1937–1939; member of the Illinois Tax Commission and served as chairman in 1935 and 1936; chairman of the Illinois Emergency Relief Commission 1935–1938; elected as a Democrat to the Seventy-sixth Congress (January 3, 1939–January 3, 1941); was not a candidate for renomination in 1940; resumed his banking interests; died while on a business trip in Long Beach, Calif., January 27, 1952; interment in East Lawn Cemetery, Salem, Ill.

MARTIN, John Mason (son of Joshua Lanier Martin), a Representative from Alabama; born in Athens, Limestone County, Ala., January 20, 1837; attended the common schools, the high school in Green Springs, Ala., and the University of Alabama at Tuscaloosa; was graduated from Centre College, Danville, Ky., in 1856; studied law; was admitted to the bar in 1858 and commenced practice in Tuscaloosa, Ala.; member of the State senate 1871–1876 and served as president pro tempore 1873–1876; professor of equity jurisprudence in the University of Alabama 1875–1886; elected as a Democrat to the Forty-ninth Congress (March 4, 1885–March 3, 1887); unsuccessful candidate for reelection in 1886 to the Fiftieth Congress; resumed the practice of law in Birmingham, Ala.; died in Bowling Green, Warren County, Ky., June 16, 1898; interment in Greenwood Cemetery, Tuscaloosa, Ala.

MARTIN, John Preston (brother of Elbert Sevier Martin and grandfather of George Brown Martin), a Representative from Kentucky; born near Jonesville, Lee County, Va., October 11, 1811; pursued an academic course; moved to Prestonsburg, Floyd County, Ky., in 1828; member of the State house of representatives 1841–1843; elected as a Democrat to the Twenty-ninth Congress (March 4, 1845–March 3, 1847); was not a candidate for renomination in 1846; member of the State senate 1855–1859; delegate to the Democratic National Convention at Cincinnati in 1856; died in Prestonsburg, Ky., December 23, 1862; interment in May Cemetery.

MARTIN, Joseph John, a Representative from North Carolina; born in Williamston, Martin County, N. C., November 21, 1833; attended Williamston Academy; studied law; was admitted to the bar in 1859 and practiced; prosecuting attorney of Martin County, N. C.; elected solicitor for the second judicial district of North Carolina in 1868; reelected in 1874, and served in this capacity until his nomination for Congress in 1878, when he resigned; delegate to the Republican National Convention at Cincinnati in 1876; presented credentials as a Republican Member-elect to the Forty-sixth Congress and served from March 4, 1879, until January 29, 1881, when he was succeeded by Jesse J. Yeates, who contested the election; resumed the practice of law in Tarboro, Edgecombe County, N. C.; postmaster of Tarboro from 1897 until his death in that city on December 18, 1900; interment in Williamston Cemetery, Williamston, N. C.

MARTIN, Joseph William, Jr., a Representative from Massachusetts; born in North Attleboro, Bristol County, Mass., November 3, 1884; attended the public schools, and was graduated from North Attleboro High School in 1902; reporter on the Attleboro Sun and Providence Journal 1902–1908; publisher of the Evening Chronicle at North Attleboro since 1908 and also publisher of the Franklin (Mass.) Sentinel; member of the State house of representatives 1912–1914; served in the State senate 1914–1917; chairman of the Massachusetts Street

Railway Investigating Commission in 1917; chairman of the Massachusetts legislative campaign committee in 1917; presidential elector on the Republican ticket of Harding and Coolidge in 1920; executive secretary of the Republican State committee 1922–1925; delegate to the Republican National Conventions in 1916, 1936, 1940, 1948, 1952, and 1956; permanent chairman of the Republican National Conventions in 1940, 1944, 1948, 1952, 1956, and 1960; member of the Republican National Committee, serving as chairman 1940–1942; elected as a Republican to the Sixty-ninth and to the seventeen succeeding Congresses (March 4, 1925–January 3, 1961); minority leader in the Seventy-sixth, Seventy-seventh, Seventy-eighth, Seventy-ninth, Eighty-first, Eighty-second, Eighty-fourth, and Eighty-fifth Congresses; Speaker of the House in the Eightieth and Eighty-third Congresses. *Reelected to the Eighty-seventh Congress.*

MARTIN, Joshua Lanier (father of John Mason Martin), a Representative from Alabama; born in Blount County, Tenn., December 5, 1799; attended the country schools; taught school; studied law in Maryville, Tenn.; moved to Russellville, Franklin County, Ala., in 1819 and continued the study of law; was admitted to the bar and practiced in Athens, Limestone County, Ala.; member of the State house of representatives 1822–1828; served as State solicitor 1827–1831; judge of the circuit court in 1834; chancellor of middle Alabama in 1841; elected as a Democrat to the Twenty-fourth and Twenty-fifth Congresses (March 4, 1835–March 3, 1839); was not a candidate for renomination in 1838 to the Twenty-sixth Congress; Governor of Alabama 1845–1847; resumed the practice of law in Tuscaloosa, Ala.; again a member of the State house of representatives in 1853; died in Tuscaloosa, Tuscaloosa County, Ala., on November 2, 1856; interment in Evergreen Cemetery.

MARTIN, Lewis J., a Representative from New Jersey; born near Deckertown, Sussex County, N. J., on February 22, 1844; attended the common schools; studied law; was admitted to the bar in 1867 and commenced practice in Branchville, N. J.; chief clerk in the office of the county clerk of Sussex County in 1868 and 1869; county clerk of Sussex County in 1869; member of the State house of assembly 1879–1881; judge of Sussex County Court 1881–1896; served as attorney to the board of freeholders of Sussex County from 1896 to 1911, when he was appointed county judge by Governor Wilson and served until his death; member of the town committee 1896–1907; member of the State senate 1898–1903; elected as a Democrat to the Sixty-third Congress and served from March 4, 1913, until his death in Washington, D. C., on May 5, 1913; interment in Newton Cemetery, Newton, N. J.

MARTIN, Luther, a Delegate from Maryland; born in New Brunswick, Middlesex County, N. J., February 9, 1744; was graduated from Princeton College in 1766; taught school in Queenstown, Md., 1766–1771; studied law; was admitted to the bar in Williamsburg, Va., September 1, 1771, and commenced practice in Accomac County, Va.; member of the Annapolis convention of 1774; attorney general of Maryland 1778–1805; counsel for Judge Samuel Chase in 1804 in the latter's impeachment and for Aaron Burr in his trial for treason; Member of the Continental Congress in 1784 and 1785; member of the Federal Constitutional Convention in 1787; chief justice of the court of oyer and terminer in 1814; again attorney general of Maryland 1818–1820; having suffered a stroke of paralysis, the Maryland Legislature passed an act requiring every lawyer in the State to pay an annual license tax of $5 to be turned over to trustees for his use; passed his last years with Aaron Burr in New York City, where he died on July 10, 1826; interment in Trinity Cemetery.

MARTIN, Morgan Lewis (cousin of James Duane Doty), a Delegate from the Territory of Wisconsin; born in Martinsburg, Lewis County, N. Y., March 31, 1805; attended the common schools, and was graduated from Hamilton College, Clinton, N. Y., in 1824; studied law; was admitted to the bar and commenced practice in Detroit, Mich.; moved to Green Bay, Wis., in 1827 (then a part of Michigan Territory); member of the Michigan Territorial Legislature 1831–1835; member of the Wisconsin Territorial Legislature 1838–1844 and served as president in 1842 and 1843; elected as a Democrat to the Twenty-ninth Congress (March 4, 1845–March 3, 1847); president of the second State constitutional convention in 1847 and 1848; again elected to the State assembly in 1855; member of the State senate in 1858 and 1859; during the Civil War served in the Union Army as paymaster with the rank of major 1861–1865; Indian agent 1866–1869; unsuccessful candidate for election in 1866 to the Fortieth Congress; resumed the practice of his profession; elected judge of Brown County in 1875, in which capacity he served until his death at Green Bay, Brown County, Wis., December 10, 1887; interment in Woodlawn Cemetery.

MARTIN, Robert Nicols, a Representative from Maryland; born in Cambridge, Dorchester County, Md., January 14, 1798; attended the public schools: studied law; was admitted to the bar and practiced at Princess Anne, Md., 1819–1827; elected as a Democrat to the Nineteenth Congress (March 4, 1825–March 3, 1827); settled in Baltimore and resumed the practice of law; appointed by Governor Pratt chief justice of the western judicial district in 1845, in which capacity he served until the office was vacated by the constitution of 1851; again engaged in the practice of his profession in Baltimore; judge of the superior court of Baltimore 1859–1867; professor of international law in the University of Maryland at Baltimore 1867–1870; died while on a visit for his health at Saratoga Springs, N. Y., July 20, 1870; interment in Christ Protestant Episcopal Church Cemetery, Cambridge, Md.

MARTIN, Thomas Ellsworth, a Representative and a Senator from Iowa; born in Melrose, Monroe County, Iowa, January 18, 1893; attended the public schools; was graduated from the State University of Iowa at Iowa City in 1916 and from its law college in 1927; awarded a fellowship by Columbia University, New York, N. Y., and was graduated in 1928; sales analyst and accountant for a rubber company in Akron, Ohio, and Dallas, Tex., in 1916 and 1917; during the First World War served as a first lieutenant with the Thirty-fifth Infantry, United States Army, 1917–1919; continued work in the rubber industry in Oklahoma City, Okla., and St. Louis, Mo., 1919–1921; assistant professor of military science and tactics, University of Iowa, 1921–1923; accountant in Iowa City, Iowa, 1923–1927; admitted to the bar in 1927 and commenced practice in Iowa City; city attorney for Iowa City 1933–1935; mayor of Iowa City 1935–1937; elected as a Republican to the Seventy-sixth and to the seven succeeding Congresses (January 3, 1939–January 3, 1955); was not a candidate for renomination in 1954; elected to the United States Senate in 1954 for the term commencing January 3, 1955, and ending January 3, 1961; was not a candidate for renomination in 1960; is a resident of Iowa City, Iowa.

MARTIN, Thomas Staples, a Senator from Virginia; born in Scottsville, Albemarle County, Va., July 29, 1847; attended the Virginia Military Institute at Lexington from March 1, 1864, to April 9, 1865, and the University of Virginia at Charlottesville from October 1, 1865, to June 29, 1866, and from October 1, 1866, to June 29, 1867; though not a regularly enlisted soldier during the Civil War, part of the time during which he was enrolled as a cadet in the Virginia Military Institute was spent in the military service of the Confederacy with the battalion of cadets from the institute; studied law; was admitted to the bar in 1869 and practiced in Albemarle County; member of the board of visitors of the Miller Manual Labor School of Albemarle County; member of the board of visitors of the University of Virginia; elected as a Democrat to the United States Senate in 1893; reelected in 1899, 1905, 1911, and 1918, and served from March 4, 1895, until his death in Charlottesville, Va., November 12, 1919; interment in the University of Virginia Cemetery.

MARTIN, Whitmell Pugh, a Representative from Louisiana; born near Napoleonville, Assumption Parish, La., August 12, 1867; attended the public schools and was privately tutored; was graduated from the Louisiana State University, Baton Rouge, La., in 1888; professor of chemistry at the Kentucky Military Institute in 1889 and 1890; chemist for the Sugar Land Refinery, Texas, in 1890 and 1891; studied law at the University of Virginia, Charlottesville, Va., in 1891 and 1892; was admitted to the bar in 1892 and commenced practice in Napoleonville, La.; moved to Thibodaux, La., the same year and continued the practice of law; superintendent of schools for the parish of Lafourche, La., 1894–1900; district attorney of the twentieth district 1900–1906 and judge of the same district 1906–1914; elected as a Progressive to the Sixty-fourth and Sixty-fifth Congresses, and as a Democrat to the Sixty-sixth and to the five succeeding Congresses, and served from March 4, 1915, until his death in Washington, D. C., April 6, 1929; interment in St. John's Episcopal Cemetery, Thibodaux, La.

MARTIN, William Dickinson, a Representative from South Carolina; born in Martintown, Edgefield District, S. C., October 20, 1789; pursued an academic course; studied law at Edgefield and attended the Litchfield Law School; was admitted to the bar in 1811 and commenced practice in Edgefield, S. C., the same year; moved to Coosawhatchie, Beaufort County, in 1813; member of the State house of representatives for St. Luke's Parish 1816–1818; clerk of the State senate 1818–1826; elected as a Democrat to the Twentieth and Twenty-first Congresses (March 4, 1827–March 3, 1831); judge of the circuit courts of law and appeal 1831–1833; moved to Columbia, S. C., where he resided until his death; died in Charleston, S. C., November 17, 1833; interment in the churchyard cemetery of St. Michael's Church.

MARTIN, William Harrison, a Representative from Texas; born near Eufaula, Barbour County, Ala., May 23, 1823; attended the common schools; studied law in Troy, Ala., and was admitted to the bar; moved to Texas in 1850 and engaged in the practice of law; member of the State senate 1853–1857; during the Civil War raised a company for the Confederate Army in 1861 and was mustered into the Fourth Texas Regiment; assigned to Lee's army and participated in all the battles of that army until its surrender in April 1865; returned to Texas and engaged in the practice of law at Athens; elected district attorney in 1872; elected as a Democrat to the Fiftieth Congress to fill the vacancy caused by the resignation of John H. Reagan; reelected to the Fifty-first Congress and served from November 4, 1887, to March 3, 1891; resumed the practice of law in Athens, Tex.; died at his home near Hillsboro, Tex., February 3, 1898; interment in Hillsboro Cemetery.

MARTINDALE, Henry Clinton, a Representative from New York; born in Berkshire County, Mass., on May 6, 1780; was graduated from Williams College, Williamstown, Mass., in 1800; studied law; was admitted to the bar and practiced at Sandy Hill, Washington County, N. Y., 1801–1860; surrogate of Washington County 1816–1819; district attorney 1821–1828; elected as a Whig to the Eighteenth and to the three succeeding

Congresses (March 4, 1823–March 3, 1831); elected to the Twenty-third Congress (March 4, 1833–March 3, 1835); appointed by Governor Seward as canal appraiser 1840–1843; died at Sandy Hill, N. Y., April 22, 1860; interment in Kingsbury Cemetery, Kingsbury, N. Y.

MARTINE, James Edgar, a Senator from New Jersey; born in New York City August 25, 1850; moved with his parents to Plainfield, N. J., in 1857; attended the public schools; engaged in agricultural pursuits, the real-estate business, and in building; member of the Plainfield Common Council; unsuccessful candidate for election as mayor of Plainfield; unsuccessful candidate in 1906 for election to the Sixtieth Congress; elected as a Democrat to the United States Senate and served from March 4, 1911, to March 3, 1917; unsuccessful candidate for reelection in 1916; resumed agricultural pursuits; died, while on a visit to recover his health, in Miami, Fla., February 26, 1925; interment in Hillside Cemetery, Plainfield, N. J.

MARVIN, Dudley, a Representative from New York; born in Lyme, New London County, Conn., May 9, 1786; attended Colchester (Conn.) Academy; moved to Canandaigua, N. Y., in 1807 and studied law; was admitted to the bar in 1811 and commenced practice in Erie, Pa.; returned to Canandaigua, N. Y., the same year and continued the practice of law; lieutenant in the State militia in 1812; promoted successively to colonel, brigadier general, and major general; elected as an Adams Democrat to the Eighteenth, Nineteenth, and Twentieth Congresses (March 4, 1823–March 3, 1829); devoted his time to developing various mechanical improvements, which he patented; moved to New York City in 1835 and to Ripley, Chautauqua County, N. Y. in 1843, and continued the practice of law; elected as a Whig to the Thirtieth Congress (March 4, 1847–March 3, 1849); resumed practice of law in Ripley, N. Y., where he died June 25, 1856; interment in East Ripley Cemetery.

MARVIN, Francis, a Representative from New York; born in New York City March 8, 1828; attended the public schools in Port Jervis, Orange County; entered upon a commercial career and engaged in the promotion, construction, and operation of railroads, water-supply companies, bridges, manufacture of illuminating gas, and in banking; postmaster of Port Jervis in 1851; justice of the peace in the town of Deerpark in 1852; one of the founders of the Minisink Valley Historical Society and later served as president; employed as bookkeeper in a bank in 1856; unsuccessful candidate of the Republican Party for member of the assembly in 1864 and for the State senate in 1881; was president of the village of Port Jervis in 1865; elected as a Republican to the Fifty-third Congress (March 4, 1893–March 3, 1895); declined to be a candidate for renomination in 1894 and devoted his time to the management of his several business enterprises; died in Port Jervis, N. Y., August 14, 1905; interment in Laurel Grove Cemetery.

MARVIN, James Madison, a Representative from New York; born in Ballston, Saratoga County, N. Y., February 27, 1809; attended the common schools; moved to Saratoga Springs, N. Y., and engaged in the hotel business in Saratoga Springs and Albany, N. Y.; Whig member of the State assembly in 1845; member of the board of supervisors of Saratoga County and served as chairman of the board in 1845, 1857, 1862, and 1874; elected as a Unionist to the Thirty-eighth, Thirty-ninth, and Fortieth Congresses (March 4, 1863–March 3, 1869); was not a candidate for renomination; president of the First National Bank of Saratoga Springs, N. Y.; director of the New York Central Railroad; died at Saratoga Springs, N. Y., April 25, 1901; interment in Greenridge Cemetery.

MARVIN, **Richard Pratt,** a Representative from New York; born in Fairfield, Herkimer County, N. Y., December 23, 1803; moved with his parents to Dryden, N. Y., in 1809; attended the public schools; studied law; was admitted to the bar in 1829 and commenced practice in Jamestown, Chautauqua County, N. Y.; member of the State assembly in 1836 and 1837; elected as a Whig to the Twenty-fifth and Twenty-sixth Congresses (March 4, 1837–March 3, 1841); was not a candidate for renomination in 1840; delegate to the State constitutional convention in 1846; judge of the eighth judicial district 1847–1871; resumed the practice of law in Jamestown, N. Y., and died there January 11, 1892; interment in Lakeview Cemetery.

MASON, **Armistead Thomson** (son of Stevens Thomson Mason), a Senator from Virginia; born at the home of his maternal grandparents, the Armisteads, in Louisa County, Va., August 4, 1787; was graduated from William and Mary College, Williamsburg, Va., in 1807; engaged in agricultural pursuits; colonel of Virginia Volunteers in the War of 1812 and subsequently brigadier general of Virginia Militia; elected as a Democrat to the United States Senate to fill the vacancy caused by the resignation of William B. Giles and served from January 3, 1816, to March 3, 1817; moved to Loudoun County, Va.; unsuccessful candidate for election in 1816 to the Fifteenth Congress against Charles Fenton Mercer in a campaign of much bitterness, which gave rise to several duels, and later resulted in his being killed in a duel with his brother-in-law, John Mason McCarty, at Bladensburg, Md., near Washington, D. C., February 6, 1819; interment in the churchyard of the Episcopal Church at Leesburg, Loudoun County, Va.

MASON, **Harry Howland,** a Representative from Illinois; born on a farm in McLean County, near Farmer City, De Witt County, Ill., December 16, 1873; moved to Delavan, Tazewell County, with his parents and attended the public schools; engaged in newspaper work; moved to Pawnee, Sangamon County, Ill., in 1903 and engaged in the newspaper publishing business; secretary to Congressman J. Earl Major 1930–1933; treasurer of Sangamon County in 1933 and 1934; elected as a Democrat to the Seventy-fourth Congress (January 3, 1935–January 3, 1937); was not a candidate for renomination in 1936; resumed the newspaper publishing business in Pawnee, Ill.; died March 10, 1946, in a hospital in Springfield, Ill., where he had gone for medical treatment; interment in Prairie Rest Cemetery, Delavan, Ill.

MASON, **James Brown,** a Representative from Rhode Island; born in Thompson, Windham County, Conn., in January 1775; pursued classical studies; was graduated from Brown University, Providence, R. I., in 1791; studied medicine and was admitted to practice; moved to Charleston, S. C., and practiced 1795–1798; returned to Providence, R. I., and engaged in mercantile pursuits 1798–1819; member of the State house of representatives 1804–1814 and served as speaker from February 1812 to May 1814; elected as a Federalist to the Fourteenth and Fifteenth Congresses (March 4, 1815–March 3, 1819); was not a candidate for renomination in 1818 to the Sixteenth Congress; served as a trustee of Brown University 1804–1819; died in Providence, R. I., August 31, 1819; interment in North Burial Ground.

MASON, **James Murray,** a Representative and a Senator from Virginia; born on Analostan Island, Fairfax County, Va. (now District of Columbia), November 3, 1798; studied under a private tutor and at an academy at Georgetown, D. C.; was graduated from the University of Pennsylvania at Philadelphia in 1818 and from the law department of William and Mary College at Williamsburg in 1820; was admitted to the bar and practiced in Winchester, Va., in 1820 and 1821; delegate to the Virginia constitutional convention in 1829; member of the State house of delegates 1826–1832; presidential elector on the Democratic ticket of Jackson and Van Buren in 1832; elected as a Jackson Democrat to the Twenty-fifth Congress (March 4, 1837–March 3, 1839); elected to the United States Senate to fill the vacancy caused by the death of Isaac S. Pennybacker; reelected in 1850 and 1856 and served from January 21, 1847, until March 28, 1861, when he withdrew; Delegate from Virginia to the Provisional Congress of the Confederacy; appointed commissioner of the Confederacy to Great Britain and France and while on his way to his post was taken from the British mail steamer *Trent* November 8, 1861, and confined in Fort Warren, Boston Harbor; released on the order of Secretary Seward January 2, 1862; proceeded to London and represented the Confederacy until its downfall in April 1865; resided in Canada after the close of the war until 1868, when he returned to Virginia; died near the city of Alexandria, Va., April 28, 1871; interment in St. Paul's Cemetery, Alexandria, Va.

MASON, **Jeremiah,** a Senator from New Hampshire; born in Lebanon, New London County, Conn., April 27, 1768; was graduated from Yale College in 1788; studied law; moved to Vermont and was admitted to the bar in 1791; moved to New Hampshire and practiced in Westmoreland 1791–1794, in Walpole 1794–1797, and in Portsmouth 1798–1832; attorney general of New Hampshire 1802–1805; elected as a Federalist to the United States Senate to fill the vacancy in the term beginning March 4, 1813, and served from June 10, 1813, until June 16, 1817, when he resigned; member of the State house of representatives in 1820, 1821, and 1824; president of the Portsmouth branch of the United States Bank 1825–1829; moved to Boston, Mass., in 1832; abandoned the practice of law in 1838, but continued as chamber counsel up to the time of his death in Boston, Mass., October 14, 1848; interment in Mount Auburn Cemetery, Cambridge, Mass.

MASON, **John Calvin,** a Representative from Kentucky; born near Mount Sterling, Montgomery County, Ky., August 4, 1802; attended country and city schools in Montgomery County and Mount Sterling Law School in Lexington, Ky.; was graduated from Transylvania University, Lexington, Ky., in 1823; was admitted to the bar and practiced in Mount Sterling; engaged extensively in the manufacture of iron; member of the State house of representatives in 1839, 1844, and 1848; served in the war with Mexico in 1846 and 1847 in Ben McCollough's company of Texas Rangers, Worth's division, under General Taylor; wounded in the Battle of Monterey; sent to Washington, D. C., with dispatches to President Polk; on March 9, 1847, was appointed by President Polk "quartermaster with the rank of major in the service of the United States for gallantry on the field"; moved to Owingsville, Bath County, Ky., in 1847; elected as a Jackson Democrat to the Thirty-first and Thirty-second Congresses (March 4, 1849–March 3, 1853); was not a candidate for renomination in 1852; elected to the Thirty-fifth Congress (March 4, 1857–March 3, 1859); was not a candidate for renomination in 1858; delegate to the Democratic National Convention at Charleston, S. C., in 1860; presidential elector on the Democratic ticket of Douglas and Johnson in 1860; during the Civil War served with Texas State troops from Brenham, Tex. ("Graybeards" in service of the Confederate States of America), in 1863; died in August 1865 near New Orleans on board a steamer on the Mississippi River en route from Texas to Kentucky; interment in the State Cemetery, Frankfort, Ky.

MASON, John Thomson, a Representative from Maryland; born at "Montpelier," near Hagerstown, Washington County, Md., May 9, 1815; educated by a private tutor and was graduated from Princeton College in 1836; studied law; was admitted to the bar and commenced practice in Hagerstown, Md., in 1838; member of the State house of representatives in 1838 and 1839; elected as a Democrat to the Twenty-seventh Congress (March 4, 1841–March 3, 1843); judge of the court of appeals 1851–1857; collector of customs at Baltimore 1857–1861; moved to Annapolis, Md., where he died March 28, 1873; interment in Rose Hill Cemetery, Hagerstown, Md.

MASON, John Young, a Representative from Virginia; born near Hicksford (now Emporia), Greensville County, Va., April 18, 1799; was graduated from the University of North Carolina at Chapel Hill in 1816; studied law; was admitted to the bar in 1819 and commenced practice in Hicksford, Va.; member of the State house of delegates 1823–1827; served in the State senate 1827–1831; elected as a Democrat to the Twenty-second, Twenty-third, and Twenty-fourth Congresses and served from March 4, 1831, until his resignation January 11, 1837; appointed United States district judge for the eastern district of Virginia in 1837; delegate to the State constitutional conventions of 1829 and 1850; appointed Secretary of the Navy in the Cabinet of President John Tyler and served from March 14, 1844, to March 10, 1845, and again in the Cabinet of President James K. Polk from September 9, 1846, to March 7, 1849; Attorney General of the United States from March 11, 1845, to September 9, 1846; resumed the practice of law in Richmond, Va., 1849–1854; appointed United States Minister Plenipotentiary to France on January 22, 1854, and served until his death, in Paris, France, on October 3, 1859; his remains were conveyed to the United States and interred in Hollywood Cemetery, Richmond, Va.

MASON, Jonathan, a Senator and a Representative from Massachusetts; born in Boston, Mass., August 30, 1752; completed preparatory studies in the Boston Latin School, and was graduated from Princeton College in 1774; studied law; was admitted to the bar in 1777 and commenced practice in Boston; member of the State house of representatives 1786–1796; member of the executive council in 1797 and 1798; served in the State senate in 1799 and 1800; elected as a Federalist to the United States Senate to fill the vacancy caused by the resignation of Benjamin Goodhue and served from November 14, 1800, to March 3, 1803; resumed the practice of law; elected as a Federalist to the Fifteenth and Sixteenth Congresses and served from March 4, 1817, until his resignation on May 15, 1820; again engaged in the practice of his profession in Boston, Mass., where he died November 1, 1831; interment in Mount Auburn Cemetery, Cambridge, Mass.

MASON, Joseph, a Representative from New York; born in Plattsburg, Clinton County, N. Y., March 30, 1828; moved with his parents to Hamilton, Madison County, N. Y., in 1840; attended Hamilton Academy and Madison College (later Colgate University), Hamilton, N. Y.; studied law; was admitted to the bar in 1849 and practiced in Hamilton, N. Y.; elected justice of the peace in 1849 and served in that capacity until 1904; elected county judge and surrogate of Madison County for the term commencing January 1, 1864, and served four years; collector of internal revenue 1871–1876; served as city attorney for many years; elected as a Republican to the Forty-sixth and Forty-seventh Congresses (March 4, 1879–March 3, 1883); was not a candidate for renomination in 1882; resumed the practice of law in Hamilton, N. Y., and died there May 31, 1914; interment in Woodlawn Cemetery.

MASON, Moses, Jr., a Representative from Maine; born in Dublin, Cheshire County, N. H., June 2, 1789; moved with his parents to Bethel, Oxford County, Maine, in 1799; attended the common schools; studied medicine; and commenced practice in Bethel in 1813; appointed first postmaster of Bethel April 1, 1815, serving until December 27, 1833; justice of the peace 1821–1866; county commissioner 1831–1834; elected as a Democrat to the Twenty-third and Twenty-fourth Congresses (March 4, 1833–March 3, 1837); executive councilor 1843–1845; trustee of the State insane hospital in 1844; selectman of Bethel for fourteen years; president of Gould's Academy 1854–1856; died in Bethel, Maine, June 25, 1866; interment in Woodlawn Cemetery.

MASON, Noah Morgan, a Representative from Illinois; born in Glamorganshire, Wales, July 19, 1882; immigrated to the United States in 1888 with his parents, who settled in La Salle, Ill.; attended the public schools and Dixon (Ill.) College; was graduated from the Illinois State Normal University at Normal; teacher and principal of schools at Oglesby, Ill., 1902–1905 and was superintendent of schools 1908–1936; city commissioner of Oglesby 1918–1926; member of the Illinois State Normal School Board 1926–1930; served in the State senate 1930–1936; elected as a Republican to the Seventy-fifth and to the eleven succeeding Congresses (January 3, 1937–January 3, 1961). *Reelected to the Eighty-seventh Congress.*

MASON, Samson, a Representative from Ohio; born in Fort Ann, Washington County, N. Y., July 24, 1793; attended the common schools in Onondaga, N. Y.; studied law; was admitted to the bar and practiced in Springfield, Ohio; prosecuting attorney of Clark County in 1822; member of the State senate 1829–1831; president judge of the court of common pleas in 1834; elected as a Whig to the Twenty-fourth and to the three succeeding Congresses (March 4, 1835–March 3, 1843); was not a candidate for renomination; member of the State house of representatives in 1845 and 1846; United States attorney for Ohio 1850–1853; delegate to the Ohio constitutional convention in 1850; served in the State senate 1862–1864; served from captain to major general in the State militia; died in Springfield, Ohio, February 1, 1869; interment in Ferncliff Cemetery.

MASON, Stevens Thomson (father of Armistead Thomson Mason), a Senator from Virginia; born in "Chappawamsic," Stafford County, Va., December 29, 1760; attended William and Mary College, Williamsburg, Va.; studied law; was admitted to the bar and commenced practice in Dumfries, Prince William County, Va.; served in the Revolutionary Army as an aide to General Washington at Yorktown; brigadier general in the Virginia Militia; member of the State house of delegates in 1783 and 1794; served in the State senate 1787–1790; delegate to the State constitutional convention in 1788; elected as a Democrat to the United States Senate to fill the vacancy caused by the resignation of James Monroe; reelected in 1797 and again in 1803, and served from November 18, 1794, until his death in Philadelphia, Pa., May 10, 1803; interment in the family burying ground at "Raspberry Plain" in Loudoun County, Va.

MASON, William, a Representative from New York; born in Lebanon, New London County, Conn., September 10, 1786; studied medicine and surgery in Vermont and practiced in Preston, N. Y.; surgeon of the Chenango County Company, New York Volunteers, in 1812; clerk of Chenango County in 1820–1821; member of the State assembly in 1821 and 1822; elected as a Democrat to the Twenty-fourth Congress (March 4, 1835–March 3, 1837); presidential elector on the Democratic ticket of Polk and Dallas in 1844; died in Norwich, N. Y., January 13, 1860; interment in Mount Hope Cemetery.

MASON, William Ernest (father of Winnifred Sprague Mason Huck), a Representative and a Senator from Illinois; born in Franklinville, Cattaragus County, N. Y., July 7, 1850; moved with his parents to Bentonsport, Van Buren County, Iowa, in 1858; attended the Bentonsport Academy and Birmingham College 1863–1865; taught school in Bentonsport 1866–1868 and in Des Moines, Iowa, 1868–1870; studied law; moved to Chicago, Ill., in 1872; was admitted to the bar and commenced practice; member of the State house of representatives in 1879; served in the State senate 1882–1885; elected as a Republican to the Fiftieth and Fifty-first Congresses (March 4, 1887–March 3, 1891); unsuccessful candidate for reelection in 1890 to the Fifty-second Congress; resumed the practice of law in Chicago; elected to the United States Senate and served from March 4, 1897, to March 3, 1903; again resumed the practice of law in Chicago; elected to the Sixty-fifth, Sixty-sixth, and Sixty-seventh Congresses and served from March 4, 1917, until his death in Washington, D. C., on June 16, 1921; interment in Oakwood Cemetery, Waukegan, Ill.

MASSEY, William Alexander, a Senator from Nevada; born in Oakfield, Trumbull County, Ohio, October 7, 1856; moved with his parents to Edgar County, Ill., in 1865; attended the common schools, Union Christian College, Merom, Ind., and the Indiana Asbury (now De Pauw) University, Greencastle, Ind.; studied law; was admitted to the bar in 1877 and commenced practice in Sullivan, Ind.; moved to San Diego, Calif., in 1886; moved to Nevada in 1887, where he prospected and mined, subsequently taking up the practice of law in Elko, Nev.; member of the State house of representatives 1892–1894; district attorney 1894–1896; justice of the State supreme court from 1896 to 1902, when he resigned; moved to Reno, Nev., and resumed the practice of law; appointed as a Republican to the United States Senate to fill the vacancy caused by the death of George S. Nixon and served from July 1, 1912, to January 29, 1913, when a successor was elected; resumed the practice of law in Reno, Nev.; died on a train near Litchfield, Nev., while en route from Reno to Susanville, Calif., March 5, 1914; interment in Mountain View Cemetery, Reno, Nev.

MASSEY, Zachary David, a Representative from Tennessee; born near Marshall, Madison County, N. C., November 14, 1864; attended the public schools; taught in the public schools of Marshall 1882–1886; studied medicine in the Louisville (Ky.) Medical College and commenced the practice of his profession in Wears Valley, Tenn., in 1889; moved to Sevierville, Sevier County, in 1890; during the Spanish-American War served as an assistant surgeon; postmaster of Sevierville 1899–1904; member of the State senate 1904–1906; elected as a Republican to the Sixty-first Congress to fill the vacancy caused by the death of Walter P. Brownlow and served from November 8, 1910, to March 3, 1911; was not a candidate for renomination in 1910; resumed the practice of medicine and also engaged in the real-estate business; died in Sevierville, Tenn., July 13, 1923; interment in Shiloh Cemetery.

MASSINGALE, Samuel Chapman, a Representative from Oklahoma; born in Quitman, Clarke County, Miss., August 2, 1870; attended the public schools and the University of Mississippi at Oxford; moved to Fort Worth, Tex., in 1887 and was employed for a short time as a section hand; studied law; was admitted to the bar in 1895 and commenced practice in Cordell, Washita County, Okla., in 1900; during the Spanish-American War served as a private in Company D, Second Texas Infantry; member of the Oklahoma Territorial Council in 1902; unsuccessful candidate for election in 1906 to the Sixtieth Congress; elected as a Democrat to the Seventy-fourth and to the three

succeeding Congresses and served from January 3, 1935, until his death in Washington, D. C., January 17, 1941; interment in Lawnview Cemetery, Cordell, Okla.

MASTERS, Josiah, a Representative from New York; born in Woodbury, Litchfield County, Conn., November 22, 1763; was graduated from Yale College in 1783; studied law; was admitted to the bar and commenced practice in Schaghticoke, Rensselaer County, N. Y.; member of the State assembly in 1792, 1800, and 1801; served as supervisor of Schaghticoke in 1796; justice of the peace in Rensselaer County 1801–1805; trustee of Lansingburgh Academy; school commissioner of Schaghticoke; elected as a Democrat to the Ninth and Tenth Congresses (March 4, 1805–March 3, 1809); founder of the Schaghticoke Powder Co.; judge of the court of common pleas of Rensselaer County 1808–1822; died in Fairfield, Conn., June 30, 1822; interment in the Masters Cemetery, near Schaghticoke, N. Y.

MATHEWS, Frank Asbury, Jr., a Representative from New Jersey; born in Philadelphia, Pa., August 3, 1890; attended the public schools of Palmyra, N. J.; during the First World War served in the Ordnance Department, United States Army, September 1917 to May 1919, with nineteen months' service overseas; was graduated from Temple University Law School, Philadelphia, Pa.; in 1920; was admitted to the bar in 1919 and commenced practice in Camden, N. J.; judge of the district court of the first judicial district of Burlington County, N. J., 1929–1933; assistant counsel for the State Highway Department of New Jersey 1933–1944; deputy attorney general of New Jersey in 1944 and 1945; during World War II was inducted into service September 16, 1940, serving as division judge advocate of the Forty-fourth Division until relieved from active duty on October 15, 1940; elected as a Republican to the Seventy-ninth Congress to fill the vacancy caused by the resignation of D. Lane Powers; reelected in 1946 to the Eightieth Congress and served from November 6, 1945, to January 3, 1949; was not a candidate for renomination in 1948; again appointed deputy attorney general of New Jersey and served from 1949 to 1953; chief condemnation counsel, New Jersey Highway Authority in 1953; resumed the practice of law; is a resident of Riverton (Cinnaminson Township), N. J.

MATHEWS, George, a Representative from Georgia; born in Augusta County, Va., August 30, 1739; commanded a volunteer company against the Indians in 1757 and in the Battle of Point Pleasant October 10, 1774; colonel of the Ninth Virginia Regiment in the Revolutionary War; fought at Brandywine and Germantown, where he was wounded and captured; was exchanged in December 1781 and joined General Greene's army as colonel of the Third Virginia Regiment; engaged in farming in Oglethorpe County, Ga., in 1785; Governor of Georgia in 1787 and 1793–1796; elected to the First Congress (March 4, 1789–March 3, 1791); brigadier general in the expedition for the capture of West Florida in 1811; died in Augusta, Ga., August 30, 1812; interment in St. Paul's Churchyard.

MATHEWS, George Arthur, a Delegate from the Territory of Dakota; born in Potsdam, St. Lawrence County, N. Y., June 4, 1852; attended the common schools, Upper Iowa University, Fayette, Iowa, in 1874, and the law department of the University of Iowa at Iowa City in 1878; was admitted to the bar in 1878 and commenced practice in Corning, Iowa; moved to Brookings, Dakota Territory (now South Dakota), in 1879 and continued the practice of law; prosecuting attorney of the fifth judicial circuit for the Territory of Dakota in 1884; member of the Territorial council and served as its president in 1887; elected as a Republican a Delegate to the Fifty-first Congress and served from March 4, 1889, to November 2, 1889, when the Territory was admitted into the Union as the States of North Dakota and South Dakota; mayor of the city of Brookings, S. Dak., 1897–1903; resumed the practice of law at Brookings, S. Dak.; retired from active practice and moved to Los Angeles, Calif., in 1910, where he died on April 19, 1941; the remains were cremated and the ashes deposited in Greenwood Cemetery, Brookings, S. Dak.

MATHEWS, James, a Representative from Ohio; born in Liberty, Trumbull County, Ohio, June 4, 1805; attended the common schools; studied law; was admitted to the bar in 1830 and commenced practice in Coshocton, Ohio; member of the State house of representatives 1832–1837; served in the State senate in 1838 and 1839; elected as a Democrat to the Twenty-seventh and Twenty-eighth Congresses (March 4, 1841–March 3, 1845); was not a candidate for renomination in 1844; moved to Knoxville, Marion County, Iowa, in 1855; prosecuting attorney of Marion County, Iowa, 1857–1859; during the Civil War was appointed provost marshal of his district in 1861 and served until the close of the war; postmaster of Knoxville 1869–1870; resigned to take the chair of pomology at the Iowa State College at Ames and served four years; died in Knoxville, Iowa, March 30, 1887; interment in Graceland Cemetery.

MATHEWS, John, a Delegate from South Carolina; born in Charleston, S. C., in 1744; commissioned ensign on September 20, 1760, and lieutenant November 16, 1760, in the South Carolina Provincial Regiment in the Cherokee expedition; passed the Middle Temple, London, England, as a barrister in 1764; returned to South Carolina and was elected to the commons house of assembly in 1772; appointed by the convention of 1774 a member of the "general committee of ninety-nine"; member of the First and Second Provincial Congresses of South Carolina in 1775 and 1776; associate judge of the circuit court of the State in 1776; during the Revolutionary War served as a captain in the Colleton County regiment; member of the State house of representatives 1776–1780 and served as speaker in 1777 and 1778; Member of the Continental Congress 1778–1782; Governor of South Carolina in 1782 and 1783; elected judge of the court of chancery in March 1784; again elected to the State house of representatives in November 1784; elected judge of the court of equity in 1791 and served until 1797, when he resigned; died in Charleston, S. C., November 17, 1802.

MATHEWS, Vincent, a Representative from New York; born at "Matthew's Field," near Newburgh, Orange County, N. Y., June 29, 1766; pursued an academic course in Noah Webster's School, Goshen, N. Y., and at the academy at Hackensack, N. J.; studied law in New York City; was admitted to the bar in 1790 and commenced practice in Elmira, N. Y.; member of the State assembly in 1794; served in the State senate in 1796, 1797, and 1809; bounty land claims commissioner in 1798; served as Cavalry commander and brigadier general in the State militia; elected as a Federalist to the Eleventh Congress (March 4, 1809–March 3, 1811); district attorney for the seventh district of New York 1813–1815; moved to Bath and thence to Rochester in 1821; again a member of the State assembly in 1826; district attorney of Monroe County in 1831; resumed the practice of law in Rochester, N. Y., where he died August 23, 1846; interment in Mount Hope Cemetery.

MATHEWSON, Elisha, a Senator from Rhode Island; born in Scituate, R. I., April 18, 1767; pursued an academic course; justice of the peace of Scituate, R. I.; engaged in agricultural pursuits; member of the State house of representatives from May to October 1821 and served as speaker during that period; member of the State senate from May to October 1822; elected as a

Democrat to the United States Senate to fill the vacancy caused by the resignation of James Fenner and served from October 26, 1807, to March 3, 1811; resumed agricultural pursuits; died in Scituate, R. I., October 14, 1853; interment on his farm at the north end of Moswansicut Lake, Scituate, R. I.

MATHIOT, Joshua, a Representative from Ohio; born in Connellsville, Fayette County, Pa., April 4, 1800; moved to Newark, Licking County, Ohio, about 1830; studied law; was admitted to the bar and practiced in Newark; prosecuting attorney 1832–1836; mayor of Newark in 1834; elected as a Whig to the Twenty-seventh Congress (March 4, 1841–March 3, 1843); grand worthy patriarch of the Sons of Temperance in Ohio, and while attending a temperance convention at Sandusky contracted cholera, from which he died in Newark, Ohio, July 30, 1849; interment in Cedar Hill Cemetery.

MATLACK, James, a Representative from New Jersey; born in Woodbury, Gloucester County, N. J., January 11, 1775; attended the common schools; large landowner; interested in various business enterprises; justice of the peace in 1803, 1808, 1813, 1816, and 1820; surrogate in 1815; chairman of the township committee; judge of the court of common pleas of Gloucester County 1806–1817; member of the board of freeholders 1812–1815, 1819–1821, and 1828; member of the State senate in 1817 and 1818; elected to the Seventeenth and Eighteenth Congresses (March 4, 1821–March 3, 1825); was not a candidate for renomination in 1824; affiliated with the Whig Party when it was formed; resumed business interests; died in Woodbury, N. J., January 16, 1840; interment in Eglington Cemetery, Clarksboro, N. J.

MATLACK, Timothy, a Delegate from Pennsylvania; born in Haddonfield, Camden County, N. J., in 1730; attended Quaker schools in Haddonfield and Philadelphia; engaged in mercantile pursuits in Philadelphia; was in command of a battalion of "Associators" during the Revolution and took part in the Battle of Princeton; member of the provincial conference held in Carpenter's Hall, Philadelphia, June 18, 1775; delegate to the convention of July 15, 1776, and appointed secretary of state; member of the committee of safety in 1776; in 1777 was appointed keeper of the great seal; member of the board of trustees of the University of Pennsylvania in 1779; Member of the Continental Congress in 1780 and 1781; moved to Lancaster, Pa.; master of the rolls of Pennsylvania 1800–1809; moved to Philadelphia and was prothonotary of the district court for several years; member of the board of aldermen 1813–1818; died at Holmesburg, near Philadelphia, Pa., April 14, 1829; interment in the Free Quaker Burial Ground, Philadelphia, Pa.; reinterment in 1905 in Fatlands, on the Schuylkill River, opposite Valley Forge, Pa.

MATSON, Aaron, a Representative from New Hampshire; born in Plymouth, Mass., in 1770; moved to Cheshire County, N. H.; judge of probate of Cheshire County; member of the State house of representatives 1806–1808, 1810–1814, 1817, and 1818; member of the executive council 1819–1821; elected to the Seventeenth and Eighteenth Congresses (March 4, 1821–March 3, 1825); again a member of the State house of representatives in 1827 and 1828; died in Newport, Orleans County, Vt., July 18, 1855.

MATSON, Courtland Cushing, a Representative from Indiana; born in Brookville, Franklin County, Ind., April 25, 1841; was graduated from Indiana Asbury (later De Pauw) University in 1862; during the Civil War enlisted as a private in the Sixteenth Regiment, Indiana Volunteers; after one year's service entered the Sixth Regiment, Indiana Volunteer Cavalry (Seventy-first Volunteers), and served until October 1865, and was subsequently promoted to the rank of colonel; studied law; was admitted to the bar and commenced practice in Greencastle, Putnam County, Ind.; was three times elected prosecuting attorney of the county; chairman of the Democratic State central committee in 1878; elected as a Democrat to the Forty-seventh and to the three succeeding Congresses (March 4, 1881–March 3, 1889); was not a candidate for renomination; unsuccessful Democratic candidate for Governor of Indiana in 1888; resumed the practice of law in Greencastle, Ind.; member of the board of tax commissioners 1909–1913; retired from public life and active business; died in Chicago, Ill., September 4, 1915; interment in Forest Hill Cemetery, Greencastle, Ind.

MATTESON, Orsamus Benajah, a Representative from New York; born in Verona, Oneida County, N. Y., August 28, 1805; attended the common schools; studied law in Utica, N. Y.; was admitted to the bar in 1830 and commenced practice in Utica; city attorney of Utica in 1834 and 1836; State supreme court commissioner; unsuccessful candidate for election in 1846 to the Thirtieth Congress; elected as a Whig to the Thirty-first Congress (March 4, 1849–March 3, 1851); unsuccessful candidate for reelection in 1850 to the Thirty-second Congress; elected to the Thirty-third and Thirty-fourth Congresses and served from March 4, 1853, until his resignation on February 27, 1857; elected to the Thirty-fifth Congress (March 4, 1857–March 3, 1859); interested in a scheme for the construction of the St. Mary's Ship Canal; engaged in lumbering and iron manufacturing and in the acquisition of large tracts of land; died in Utica, N. Y., December 22, 1889; interment in Forest Hill Cemetery.

MATTHEWS, Charles, a Representative from Pennsylvania; born in New Castle, Lawrence County, Pa., October 15, 1856; attended the public schools until fourteen years of age; later employed in rolling mills as a roll turner and attended night school; delegate to the Republican State convention in 1886; member of the city council 1887–1893; sheriff of Lawrence County 1897–1900; engaged in manufacturing and banking; elected as a Republican to the Sixty-second Congress (March 4, 1911–March 3, 1913); unsuccessful candidate for reelection in 1912 to the Sixty-third Congress; again engaged in banking; delegate to the Republican National Convention at Chicago in 1916; appointed county commissioner of Lawrence County, Pa., on November 26, 1924, and served until January 2, 1928; died in New Castle, Pa., December 12, 1932; interment in Graceland Cemetery.

MATTHEWS, Donald Ray (Billy), a Representative from Florida; born in Micanopy, Alachua County, Fla., October 3, 1907; attended the public schools of Hawthorne, Fla.; graduated from the University of Florida at Gainesville in 1929; taught school in Leesburg, Fla., and in Orlando, Fla., 1929–1935; high-school principal in Newberry, Fla., in 1935 and 1936; member of the State house of representatives in 1935; member of the administrative staff of the University of Florida 1936–1952; during World War II served in the United States Army 1942–1946 and was discharged as a captain of Infantry; assistant State 4–H agent in the summers of 1928–1938; elected as a Democrat to the Eighty-third and to the three succeeding Congresses (January 3, 1953–January 3, 1961). *Reelected to the Eighty-seventh Congress.*

MATTHEWS, Nelson Edwin, a Representative from Ohio; born in Ottawa, Putnam County, Ohio, April 14, 1852; attended the public schools; engaged in banking, mercantile, and manufacturing pursuits in Ottawa; delegate to the Republican National Convention at Chicago in 1908; delegate to the fourth

State constitutional convention in 1912; elected as a Republican to the Sixty-fourth Congress (March 4, 1915–March 3, 1917); unsuccessful candidate for reelection in 1916 to the Sixty-fifth Congress; retired from active pursuits; died in Maumee, Lucas County, Ohio, on October 13, 1917; interment in Fort Meigs Cemetery, Perrysburg, Wood County, Ohio.

MATTHEWS, Stanley (uncle of Henry Watterson), a Senator from Ohio; born in Cincinnati, Ohio, July 21, 1824; attended the public schools and Woodward High School; was graduated from Kenyon College, Gambier, Ohio, in 1840; studied law; was admitted to the bar in 1842 and commenced practice in Maury County, Tenn., the same year; returned to Cincinnati in 1844; appointed assistant prosecuting attorney of Hamilton County in 1845; editor of the Cincinnati Herald 1846–1849; clerk of the State house of representatives 1848–1850; judge of the court of common pleas of Hamilton County 1850–1852; member of the State senate in 1856 and 1857; appointed by President Buchanan as United States district attorney for southern Ohio in 1858 and served until his resignation in March 1861; during the Civil War served as lieutenant colonel of the Twenty-third Regiment, Ohio Volunteers; was promoted to colonel of the Fifty-seventh Regiment, Ohio Volunteers, in October 1861; resigned in the spring of 1863; resumed the practice of law in Cincinnati; judge of the Cincinnati superior court from 1863 until his resignation in July 1864; Republican presidential elector in 1864 and 1868; unsuccessful candidate for election in 1876 to the Forty-fifth Congress; was counsel before the electoral commission in 1877; elected as a Republican to the United States Senate to fill the vacancy caused by the resignation of John Sherman and served from March 21, 1877, to March 3, 1879; was not a candidate for renomination in 1878; appointed by President Hayes as Associate Justice of the United States Supreme Court on January 26, 1881, but was not confirmed; was renominated by President Garfield March 14, 1881, and confirmed by the Senate May 12, 1881, and served until his death in Washington, D. C., March 22, 1889; interment in Spring Grove Cemetery, Cincinnati, Ohio.

MATTHEWS, William, a Representative from Maryland; born in Cecil County, Md., April 26, 1755; judge of Cecil County Court in 1778, 1780, and 1782–1786; member of the State general assembly 1786–1789; presidential elector in 1788, when Washington was unanimously elected President; elected to the Fifth Congress (March 4, 1797–March 3, 1799).

MATTOCKS, John, a Representative from Vermont; born in Hartford, Conn., March 4, 1777; moved with his parents to Tinmouth, Vt., in 1778; pursued an academic course; studied law in Middlebury and Fairfield; was admitted to the bar in 1797 and commenced practice in Danville; moved to Peacham, Caledonia County, Vt.; member of the State house of representatives in 1807, 1815, 1816, 1823, and 1824; brigadier general of militia in the War of 1812; elected to the Seventeenth Congress (March 4, 1821–March 3, 1823); elected to the Nineteenth Congress (March 4, 1825–March 3, 1827); judge of the State supreme court in 1833 and 1834; declined to be a candidate for renomination; delegate to the State constitutional convention in 1836; elected as a Whig to the Twenty-seventh Congress (March 4, 1841–March 3, 1843); Governor of Vermont in 1843 and 1844; died in Peacham, Vt., August 14, 1847; interment in Peacham Cemetery.

MATTOON, Ebenezer, a Representative from Massachusetts; born in North Amherst, Hampshire County, Mass., on August 19, 1755; attended the common schools and received private instruction; was graduated from Dartmouth College, Hanover, N. H., in 1776; served in the Revolutionary Army and attained the rank of major; taught school and also engaged in agricultural pursuits; member of the State house of representatives in 1781 and 1794; justice of the peace 1782–1796; presidential elector in 1792, 1796, 1820, and 1828; served in the State senate in 1795 and 1796; served from the rank of captain to that of major general of the Fourth Division, State militia; appointed sheriff of Hampshire County in 1796 and served twenty years; elected as a Federalist to the Sixth Congress to fill the vacancy caused by the resignation of Samuel Lyman; reelected to the Seventh Congress and served from February 2, 1801, to March 3, 1803; again a member of the State house of representatives in 1812; major general of Massachusetts Militia 1799–1816; adjutant general of the State militia 1816–1818; became totally blind in 1818 and retired from active public life; delegate to the State constitutional convention in 1820; died in Amherst, Mass., September 11, 1843; interment in West Cemetery.

MAURICE, James, a Representative from New York; born in New York City November 7, 1814; attended Broad Street Academy; became clerk in a law office at the age of twelve years; studied law; was admitted to the bar in 1835 and practiced in Maspeth, Queens County, N. Y.; appointed master in chancery by Governor Bouck in 1843; member of the State assembly in 1850; delegate to the Democratic State conventions in 1851, 1853, and 1856; elected as a Democrat to the Thirty-third Congress (March 4, 1853–March 3, 1855); was not a candidate for renomination in 1854; resumed the practice of law; declined the nomination as justice of the State supreme court in 1865; elected as a Republican to the State assembly in 1866; retired from public life; died in Maspeth, N. Y., August 4, 1884; interment in Mount Olivet Cemetery.

MAURY, Abram Poindexter (cousin of Fontaine Maury Maverick), a Representative from Tennessee; born near Franklin, Williamson County, Tenn., December 26, 1801; completed preparatory studies and was editor of a newspaper in St. Louis, Mo., at the age of sixteen; entered the United States Military Academy, West Point, N. Y., in 1820, but left the following year to study law and edit a newspaper in Nashville, Tenn.; purchased and cultivated the family homestead in Williamson County; member of the State house of representatives in 1831, 1832, 1843, and 1844; was admitted to the bar in 1839 and practiced in Williamson County; elected as a Whig to the Twenty-fourth and Twenty-fifth Congresses (March 4, 1835–March 3, 1839); was not a candidate for renomination in 1838; resumed the practice of law in Williamson County; also engaged in literary pursuits and lecturing; served in the State senate in 1845 and 1846; died near Franklin, Tenn., July 22, 1848; interment in the family cemetery at his home near Franklin, Tenn.

MAVERICK, Fontaine Maury (cousin of Abram P. Maury, nephew of James L. Slayden, and cousin of John W. Fishburne), a Representative from Texas; born in San Antonio, Tex., October 23, 1895; attended the common schools of Texas, Virginia Military Institute at Lexington, and the University of Texas at Austin; studied law; was admitted to the bar in 1916 and commenced practice in San Antonio, Tex.; during the First World War served as a first lieutenant in the One Hundred and Fifty-seventh Infantry, Fortieth Division, and was overseas with the Twenty-eighth Infantry, First Division; was wounded in action and discharged on February 7, 1919; was awarded the Silver Star and the Purple Heart Medal; engaged in the lumber, building-material, housing, and mortgage businesses 1925–1930; collector of taxes of Bexar County, Tex., 1929–1931; delegate to several Democratic State conventions and to the Democratic National Conventions in 1928 and 1940; elected as a Democrat to

the Seventy-fourth and Seventy-fifth Congresses (January 3, 1935–January 3, 1939); unsuccessful candidate for renomination in 1938; mayor of San Antonio 1939–1941; divisional director and later vice chairman of the War Production Board and chairman of the Smaller War Plants Corporation, Washington, D. C., 1941–1946; resumed the practice of law; died in San Antonio, Tex., June 7, 1954; interment in San Jose Burial Park, San Antonio, Tex.

MAXEY, Samuel Bell, a Senator from Texas; born in Tomkinsville, Monroe County, Ky., March 30, 1825; attended the common schools, and was graduated from the United States Military Academy, West Point, N. Y., in 1846; served in the Mexican War until September 17, 1849, when he resigned and returned to Kentucky; studied law; was admitted to the bar in 1850 and commenced practice in Albany, Ky.; served as clerk of the county and circuit courts and as master in chancery 1852–1856; moved to Paris, Tex., in 1857 and practiced his profession; district attorney of Lamar County, Tex., in 1858 and 1859; elected to the State senate in 1861, but declined; during the Civil War raised the Ninth Regiment, Texas Infantry, of which he was colonel, for the Confederate Army; was promoted to the rank of brigadier general in 1862 and major general in 1864; commanded the Indian Territory military district 1863–1865 and was also superintendent of Indian affairs; remained in the service until the surrender of the trans-Mississippi department May 26, 1865; resumed the practice of his profession in Paris, Tex.; commissioned as judge of the eighth district of Texas April 18, 1873, but declined the position; elected as a Democrat to the United States Senate in 1875; reelected in 1881 and served from March 4, 1875, to March 3, 1887; was an unsuccessful candidate for reelection in 1887; continued the practice of law in Paris, Tex., until his death at Eureka Springs, Ark., August 16, 1895; interment in Evergreen Cemetery, Paris, Tex.

MAXWELL, Augustus Emmett (grandfather of Emmett Wilson), a Representative from Florida; born in Elberton, Elbert County, Ga., September 21, 1820; attended private school; was graduated from the University of Virginia at Charlottesville in 1841; studied law; was admitted to the Alabama bar in 1843 and practiced in Eutaw, Ala., 1843–1845; moved to Tallahassee, Fla., in 1845; attorney general of Florida in 1846 and 1847; member of the State house of representatives in 1847; secretary of state in 1848; served in the State senate in 1849 and 1850; elected as a Democrat to the Thirty-third and Thirty-fourth Congresses (March 4, 1853–March 3, 1857; was not a candidate for renomination in 1856 to the Thirty-fifth Congress; United States Navy agent at Pensacola 1857–1861; served in the Senate of the Confederate States 1862–1865; judge of the State supreme court in 1865 and 1866; elected president of the Pensacola & Montgomery Railroad in 1866; judge of the circuit court of Florida 1877–1885; member of the State constitutional convention of 1885; chief justice and later associate justice of the State supreme court 1887–1891; died in Chipley, Washington County, Fla., on May 5, 1903; interment in St. John's Cemetery, Pensacola, Fla.

MAXWELL, George Clifford (father of John Patterson Bryan Maxwell), a Representative from New Jersey; born in Sussex County, N. J., on May 31, 1771; was graduated from Princeton College in 1792; studied law; was admitted to the bar in 1797 and practiced in Hunterdon County, N. J.; elected to the Twelfth Congress (March 4, 1811–March 3, 1813); resumed the practice of law in Flemington, N. J., where he died March 16, 1816; interment in Pleasant Ridge Cemetery, Raritan Township, Hunterdon County, N. J.

MAXWELL, John Patterson Bryan (son of George Clifford Maxwell and uncle of George Maxwell Robeson), a Representative from New Jersey; born in Flemington, Hunterdon County, N. J., September 3, 1804; was graduated from Princeton College in 1823; studied law; was admitted to the bar in 1827 and commenced practice in Newark, N. J.; moved to Belvidere, Warren County, N. J.; for a while was editor of the Belvidere Apollo; elected as a Whig to the Twenty-fifth Congress (March 4, 1837–March 3, 1839); presented credentials as a Member-elect to the Twenty-sixth Congress, but the House declined to seat him; elected to the Twenty-seventh Congress (March 4, 1841–March 3, 1843); trustee of Princeton College 1842–1845; died in Belvidere, Warren County, N. J., November 14, 1845; interment in Belvidere Cemetery.

MAXWELL, Lewis, a Representative from Virginia; born in Chester County, Pa., April 17, 1790; moved with his mother to Virginia about 1800; completed a preparatory course; studied law; was admitted to the bar and commenced practice in Weston, Va. (now West Virginia); member of the State house of delegates 1821–1824; elected as a National-Republican to the Twentieth, Twenty-first, and Twenty-second Congresses (March 4, 1827–March 3, 1833); was not a candidate for renomination in 1832; resumed the practice of law and was also engaged as a surveyor and land patentee; died in West Union, Doddridge County, Va. (now West Virginia), February 13, 1862; interment in Odd Fellows Cemetery.

MAXWELL, Samuel, a Representative from Nebraska; born in Lodi (then a suburb of Syracuse), N. Y., May 20, 1825; attended the common schools; moved with his family to Michigan in 1844; taught school and also engaged in agricultural pursuits; studied law; moved to Nebraska in 1856, settled in Cass County, and engaged in agricultural pursuits; returned to Michigan, completed his law studies, and was admitted to the bar in 1859; returned to Nebraska the same year and commenced the practice of law at Plattsmouth; delegate to the first Republican Territorial convention; member of the Territorial house of representatives in 1859, 1860, 1864, and 1865; delegate to the Territorial constitutional conventions in 1864 and 1866 and to the State constitutional convention in 1875; member of the first State house of representatives in 1866; appointed by the Governor a member of the board of commissioners to select capitol building plans and university lands in 1867; elected associate justice of the State supreme court in 1872; reelected in 1875, 1881, and again in 1887; elected as a Fusionist to the Fifty-fifth Congress (March 4, 1897–March 3, 1899); resumed the practice of law in Fremont, Dodge County, Nebr., where he died February 11, 1901; interment in Pleasant Hill Cemetery, Plattsmouth, Nebr.

MAXWELL, Thomas, a Representative from New York; born at Tioga Point (now Athens), Bradford County, Pa., February 16, 1792; moved to Elmira (then Newtown Point), N. Y., in 1796; received a good education; appointed quartermaster of a regiment of Cavalry attached to the brigade of Gen. Vincent Matthews during the War of 1812, but the organization was never called into active service; clerk of Tioga County, N. Y., 1819–1829; elected as a Democrat to the Twenty-first Congress (March 4, 1829–March 3, 1831); engaged in the prosecution of pension claims; studied law and was admitted to practice in the court of common pleas of old Tioga County, N. Y., in 1832; editor of the Elmira Gazette 1834–1836; postmaster of Elmira 1834–1839; deputy clerk of Chemung County in 1836; treasurer of Chemung County 1836–1843; a vice president of the New York & Erie Railroad Co. in 1841; commissioner of loans of United States deposit and of State funds in

1843; moved to Geneva, N. Y., about 1845, upon his appointment as deputy clerk of the State supreme court; died in Elmira, Chemung County, N. Y., November 4, 1864; interment in Woodlawn Cemetery.

MAY, Andrew Jackson, a Representative from Kentucky; born on Beaver Creek, near Langley, Floyd County, Ky., June 24, 1875; attended the public schools; taught in the schools of Floyd and Magoffin Counties, Ky., for five years; was graduated from Southern Normal University Law School, Huntingdon, Tenn. (later Union College, Jackson, Tenn.), in 1898; was admitted to the bar the same year and commenced practice in Prestonsburg, Ky.; county attorney of Floyd County 1901–1909; special judge of the circuit court of Johnson and Martin Counties in 1925 and 1926; also engaged in agricultural pursuits, coal mining, and banking; elected to the Seventy-second and to the seven succeeding Congresses (March 4, 1931–January 3, 1947); unsuccessful candidate for reelection in 1946 to the Eightieth Congress; resumed the practice of law; died in Prestonsburg, Ky., September 6, 1959; interment in Mayo Cemetery.

MAY, Catherine Dean (Barnes), a Representative from Washington; born in Yakima, Wash., May 18, 1914; attended the grade schools in Yakima; graduated from Yakima High School in 1932, Yakima Valley Junior College in 1934, University of Washington in 1936 and with five-year degree in education in 1937; studied speech at the University of Southern California in 1939; teacher of English in Chehalis (Wash.) High School 1937–1940; women's editor and news broadcaster, station KMO, Tacoma, Wash., in 1940 and 1941; writer and special events broadcaster, station KOMO–KJR, Seattle, Wash., in 1941 and 1942; head of radio department, Strang & Prosser Advertising Agency, Seattle, Wash., in 1942 and 1943; head of radio and motion picture department, Federal Insurance Co., Seattle, Wash., in 1943 and 1944; writer and assistant commentator, National Broadcasting Co., New York, N. Y., 1944–1946; women's editor, station KIT, Yakima, Wash., 1948–1957; member of Washington State Legislature 1952–1958; office manager and medical secretary, Yakima Medical Center, in 1957 and 1958; vice chairman of Governor's State-wide Committee on Educational Television in 1955 and 1956; member of Governor's Safety Council 1953–1956; legislative representative for Yakima unit of Association for Retarded Children 1953–1958; member of Washington Association for Retarded Children 1953–1960; elected as a Republican to the Eighty-sixth Congress (January 3, 1959–January 3, 1961). *Reelected to the Eighty-seventh Congress.*

MAY, Edwin Hyland, Jr., a Representative from Connecticut; born in Hartford, Conn., May 28, 1924; educated in the public schools and graduated from Wethersfield (Conn.) High School in 1942; attended Wesleyan University, Middletown, Conn., but interrupted education to enlist in November 1942 in the United States Army Air Corps and served until October 1945 as a second lieutenant, instructor, and P–38 fighter pilot in the Fourth Air Force; returned to Wesleyan University and graduated in 1948; president of May, Potter & Murphy, Inc., an insurance firm in Hartford, Conn., 1956–; elected as a Republican to the Eighty-fifth Congress (January 3, 1957–January 3, 1959); unsuccessful candidate for reelection in 1958 to the Eighty-sixth Congress; Republican State Chairman 1958–; is a resident of Wethersfield, Conn.

MAY, Henry, a Representative from Maryland; born in Washington, D. C., February 13, 1816; pursued an academic course; attended Columbian College (later George Washington University), Washington, D. C.; studied law; was admitted to the bar in 1840 and practiced; sent by President Pierce to Mexico to investigate the celebrated Galpin frauds based on pretended claims under our treaty of peace with Mexico; moved to Baltimore, Md., in 1850; elected as a Democrat to the Thirty-third Congress (March 4, 1853–March 3, 1855); unsuccessful candidate for reelection in 1854 to the Thirty-fourth Congress; elected to the Thirty-seventh Congress (March 4, 1861–March 3, 1863); died in Baltimore, Md., September 25, 1866; interment in Cathedral Cemetery.

MAY, Mitchell, a Representative from New York; born in Brooklyn, N. Y., July 10, 1870; attended the public schools and Brooklyn Polytechnic Institute; was graduated from the law department of Columbia University, New York City, in 1892; was admitted to the bar in 1893 and commenced practice in Brooklyn; elected as a Democrat to the Fifty-sixth Congress (March 4, 1899–March 3, 1901); was not a candidate for renomination in 1900 to the Fifty-seventh Congress; member of the New York City Board of Education 1906–1910; assistant district attorney of Kings County in 1910 and 1911; secretary of state of New York in 1913 and 1914; county judge of Kings County 1916–1921; justice of the State supreme court from January 1, 1922, to December 31, 1940, when he retired because of age limitation; resumed the practice of law; died in Brooklyn, N. Y., March 24, 1961; interment in Valhalla Cemetery, Staten Island, N. Y.

MAY, William L., a Representative from Illinois; born in Kentucky about 1793; attended the common schools; moved to Edwardsville, Madison County, Ill., and afterward to Jacksonville, Ill.; appointed justice of the peace in Madison County on December 10, 1817; captain of militia in 1822; elected justice of the peace in Morgan County August 6, 1827, and resigned August 29, 1829; member of the State house of representatives in 1828; moved to Springfield, having been appointed by President Jackson as receiver of public moneys for the United States Land Office in that city; studied law; was admitted to the bar and practiced; also operated a ferry across the Illinois River at Peoria and organized the Peoria Bridge Co., which in 1849 erected the first bridge at that point; elected as a Democrat to the Twenty-third Congress to fill the vacancy caused by the resignation of Joseph Duncan; reelected to the Twenty-fourth and Twenty-fifth Congresses and served from December 1, 1834, to March 3, 1839; was not a candidate for renomination in 1838 to the Twenty-sixth Congress; moved to Peoria, Ill., and continued the practice of law; mayor of Springfield, Ill., in May 1841; went to California during the gold rush; died in Sacramento, Calif., September 29, 1849.

MAYALL, Samuel, a Representative from Maine; born in North Gray, Cumberland County, Maine, June 21, 1816; attended the public schools and was tutored privately at home; moved to Gray, Maine; member of the State house of representatives in 1845, 1847, and 1848; served in the State senate in 1847 and 1848; declined the Democratic nomination as a candidate for Rep esentative to the Thirty-second Congress; elected as a Democrat to the Thirty-third Congress (March 4, 1853–March 3, 1855); owing to business and family cares was not a candidate for renomination in 1854; delegate to the Republican National Convention at Philadelphia in 1856; moved to St. Paul, Minn., in 1857; became a large landowner; commissioned as a captain at the beginning of the Civil War; was wounded twice and taken prisoner several times; resigned in 1863, but Secretary of War Stanton refused to accept his resignation, and he served one more year; devoted his time to looking after his large business interests; died in St. Paul, Minn., September 17, 1892; interment in Oakland Cemetery.

MAYBANK, Burnet Rhett, a Senator from South Carolina; born in Charleston, S. C., March 7, 1899; attended the public and high schools; was graduated from Porter Military Academy, Charleston, S. C., and from the College of Charleston, South Carolina; during the First World War served as a seaman and naval air cadet in the United States Naval Reserve 1918–1921; engaged in the cotton export business 1920–1938; alderman of Charleston, S. C., 1927–1931, serving as mayor pro tempore in 1930; mayor of Charleston 1931–1938; member of the South Carolina State Advisory Board of the Federal Administration of Public Works in 1933 and 1934; chairman of the South Carolina Public Service Authority 1934–1939; member of the Board of Bank Control in 1933 and 1934; Governor of South Carolina 1939–1941; was elected to the United States Senate in 1941 to fill the vacancy caused by the resignation of James F. Byrnes; reelected in 1942 and again in 1948, and served from November 5, 1941, until his death; had been renominated in the Democratic primary election July 13, 1954, for a third full term; member of the American Battle Monuments Commission 1947–1954; died at his summer home in Flat Rock, N. C., September 1, 1954; interment in Magnolia Cemetery, Charleston, S. C.

MAYBURY, William Cotter, a Representative from Michigan; born in Detroit, Mich., November 20, 1848; attended the public schools; was graduated from the academic department of the University of Michigan at Ann Arbor in 1870 and from the law department in 1871; was admitted to the bar in the latter year and commenced practice in Detroit; city attorney of Detroit 1876–1880; lecturer on medical jurisprudence in the Michigan College of Medicine at Detroit in 1881 and 1882; elected as a Democrat to the Forty-eighth and Forty-ninth Congresses (March 4, 1883–March 3, 1887); was not a candidate for reelection in 1886; resumed the practice of law in Detroit; mayor of Detroit 1897–1905; unsuccessful candidate for Governor in 1900; died in Detroit, Wayne County, Mich., May 6, 1909; interment in Elmwood Cemetery.

MAYFIELD, Earle Bradford, a Senator from Texas; born in Overton, Rusk County, Tex., April 12, 1881; attended the public schools in eastern Texas; was graduated from Southwestern University, Georgetown, Tex., in 1900; studied law at the University of Texas at Austin in 1900 and 1901; was admitted to the bar in 1907 and commenced practice in Meridian, Tex.; also engaged in agricultural pursuits and in the wholesale grocery business; served in the State senate 1907–1913; member of the State railroad commission 1913–1923; delegate to the Democratic State conventions 1912–1948 and to the Democratic National Convention at New York in 1924; elected as a Democrat to the United States Senate and served from March 4, 1923, to March 3, 1929; unsuccessful candidate for renomination in 1928; resumed the practice of law in Tyler, Tex., until retiring in 1952; is a resident of Tyler, Tex.

MAYHAM, Stephen Lorenzo, a Representative from New York; born in Blenheim, N. Y., October 8, 1826; pursued an academic course; studied law in Ithaca, N. Y.; was admitted to the bar and commenced practice in 1848; superintendent of schools in Schoharie County, N. Y., 1852–1857, and supervisor 1857–1860; district attorney of Schoharie County 1859–1862; member of the State assembly in 1863; elected as a Democrat to the Forty-first Congress (March 4, 1869–March 3, 1871); elected to the Forty-fifth Congress (March 4, 1877–March 3, 1879); judge of Schoharie County 1883–1887; delegate to the Democratic National Conventions at Chicago in 1884 and 1892; judge of the supreme court of New York and afterward presiding justice 1886–1896; died in Schoharie, N. Y., March 3, 1908; interment in St. Paul's Lutheran Cemetery.

MAYNARD, Harry Lee, a Representative from Virginia; born in Portsmouth, Va., June 8, 1861; attended the common schools of Norfolk County; was graduated from the Virginia Agricultural and Mechanical College at Blacksburg in 1880; engaged in the real-estate business and the promotion of public utilities; member of the State house of delegates in 1889 and 1890; served in the State senate 1893–1901; elected as a Democrat to the Fifty-seventh and to the four succeeding Congresses (March 4, 1901–March 3, 1911); unsuccessful candidate for renomination in 1910; moved to New York City and engaged in the insurance and real-estate business; his health having failed, he entered a hospital at Fort Totten, N. Y., where he died October 23, 1922; interment in Oak Grove Cemetery, Portsmouth, Va.

MAYNARD, Horace, a Representative from Tennessee; born in Westboro, Worcester County, Mass., August 30, 1814; attended the common schools of Westboro and the Millbury (Mass.) Academy, where he afterward taught, and was graduated from Amherst (Mass.) College in 1838; instructor and professor of mathematics in the University of East Tennessee 1839–1844; studied law; was admitted to the bar in 1844 and commenced practice in Knoxville, Tenn.; presidential elector on the Whig ticket of Scott and Graham in 1852 and on the Republican ticket of Lincoln and Johnson in 1864; elected by the American Party to the Thirty-fifth, Thirty-sixth, and Thirty-seventh Congresses (March 4, 1857–March 3, 1863); attorney general of Tennessee 1863–1865; delegate to the Southern Loyalist Convention at Philadelphia in 1866; upon the readmission of the State of Tennessee to representation was elected as a Republican to the Thirty-ninth and to the four succeeding Congresses and served from July 24, 1866, to March 3, 1875; was not a candidate for renomination in 1874; unsuccessful Republican candidate for Governor of Tennessee in 1874; Minister to Turkey from March 9, 1875, until May 1880; appointed Postmaster General in the Cabinet of President Hayes and served from June 2, 1880, to March 5, 1881; died in Knoxville, Tenn., May 3, 1882; interment in Old Gray Cemetery.

MAYNARD, John, a Representative from New York; born in Whitestone, N. Y.; was graduated from Union College, Schenectady, N. Y., in 1810; studied law; was admitted to the bar and commenced practice at Seneca Falls, N. Y.; clerk of Seneca County in 1821 and 1822; member of the State assembly in 1822; elected to the Twentieth Congress (March 4, 1827–March 3, 1829); district attorney of Seneca County in 1836 and 1837; elected as a Whig to the Twenty-seventh Congress (March 4, 1841–March 3, 1843); member of the State senate 1838–1841; moved to Auburn, N. Y.; served as judge of the State supreme court, seventh district, from June 7, 1847, until his death in Auburn, N. Y., March 24, 1850.

MAYO, Robert Murphy, a Representative from Virginia; born in Hague, Westmoreland County, Va., April 28, 1836; attended private schools and William and Mary College, Williamsburg, Va.; was graduated from Virginia Military Institute at Lexington in 1858; was instructor in mathematics at Mount Pleasant Military Academy, Sing Sing (now Ossining), N. Y., and later at Virginia Military Institute; studied law at Lexington Law School (now Washington and Lee University) in 1858 and 1859; served throughout the Civil War in the Confederate Army, first as major and later as colonel of the Forty-seventh Regiment of Virginia; was admitted to the bar and commenced practice in Hague, Va., in 1865; member of the State house of delegates in 1881, 1882, and 1885–1888; presented credentials as a Readjuster Member-elect to the Forty-eighth Congress and served from March 4, 1883, to March 20, 1884, when he was succeeded by George T. Garrison, who contested the election; unsuccessful candidate for reelection; resumed the practice of law; died in Hague, Va., March 29, 1896; interment in Yeocomico Cemetery, Tucker Hill, Westmoreland County, Va.

MAYRANT, William, a Representative from South Carolina; born in that State; elected to the Fourteenth Congress and served from March 4, 1815, until October 21, 1816, when he resigned; unsuccessful candidate for reelection.

MAYS, Dannite Hill, a Representative from Florida; born near Madison, Madison County, Fla., April 28, 1852; attended the county schools, the public schools of Savannah, Ga., and Washington and Lee University, Lexington, Va.; moved to Monticello, Fla., and engaged in agricultural pursuits, developing large plantations in Madison, Jefferson, and Leon Counties, Fla.; delegate to the Democratic State convention at St. Augustine in 1888; member of the State house of representatives in 1891, 1895, and 1897, serving as speaker in 1897; unsuccessful candidate for Governor in 1900 and 1904; elected as a Democrat to the Sixty-first and Sixty-second Congresses (March 4, 1909–March 3, 1913); unsuccessful candidate for renomination in 1912; returned to Monticello, Fla., and resumed agricultural pursuits in Jefferson, Madison, and Leon Counties, Fla.; died in Monticello, Fla., May 9, 1930; interment in Roseland Cemetery.

MAYS, James Henry, a Representative from Utah; born in Morristown, Hamblen County, Tenn., June 29, 1868; attended the district schools; moved to Kansas in 1883 with his parents, who settled in Galena, Kans.; worked in the mines and as a lumberman; attended the Kansas State Normal School; from 1893 to 1902 engaged in the life insurance business at Chicago, Ill., Dubuque, Iowa, and Salt Lake City, Utah; was graduated from the law department of the University of Michigan at Ann Arbor in 1895; was admitted to the bar and commenced practice in Ann Arbor, Mich.; moved to Indianapolis, Ind., in 1896 and to Utah in 1902; organized several industrial organizations; elected as a Democrat to the Sixty-fourth, Sixty-fifth, and Sixty-sixth Congresses (March 4, 1915–March 3, 1921); was not a candidate for reelection in 1920; retired to his stock ranch near Wendell, Idaho, and died there on April 19, 1926; interment in Gooding Cemetery, Gooding, Idaho.

McADOO, William, a Representative from New Jersey; born near Ramelton, County Donegal, Ireland, October 25, 1853; immigrated to the United States with his parents, who settled in Jersey City, N. J., in 1865; attended the common schools; studied law; was admitted to the bar in 1874 and commenced practice in Jersey City, N. J.; employed as a newspaper reporter 1870–1875; member of the State house of assembly in 1882; elected as a Democrat to the Forty-eighth and to the three succeeding Congresses (March 4, 1883–March 3, 1891); unsuccessful candidate for renomination in 1890; moved to New York City in 1892 and resumed the practice of law; appointed by President Grover Cleveland as Assistant Secretary of the Navy and served from March 20, 1893, to April 18, 1897, when he resigned; police commissioner of New York City in 1904 and 1905; again resumed the practice of law and also engaged in literary pursuits; appointed by Mayor Gaynor as chief magistrate of the city magistrates' courts, first division, city of New York, July 1, 1910, in which capacity he served until his death in New York City, N. Y., June 7, 1930; interment in Woodlawn Cemetery.

McADOO, William Gibbs, a Senator from California; born on a farm near Marietta, Cobb County, Ga., October 31, 1863; attended the rural schools, and the University of Tennessee at Knoxville; appointed deputy clerk of the United States Circuit Court for the Southern Division, Eastern District of Tennessee, in 1882; studied law; admitted to the bar in 1885 and commenced practice in Chattanooga, Tenn.; moved to New York City in 1892 and continued the practice of law; developed the system of rapid-transit tunnels under the Hudson River between New York City and New Jersey and from 1902 to 1913 was president of the company which constructed and operated them; delegate to the Democratic National Conventions in 1912, 1932, and 1936; vice chairman of the Democratic National Committee in 1912; served as Secretary of the Treasury in the Cabinet of President Wilson from March 6, 1913, until his resignation on December 16, 1918; during the First World War served as director general of railways from December 28, 1917, until he resigned on January 10, 1919; resumed the practice of law in New York City in 1919; was the leading candidate for nomination for President of the United States for many ballots at the Democratic National Convention in San Francisco in 1920, and at the convention in New York City in 1924 led on more than 100 ballots for nomination for President; moved to Los Angeles, Calif., in 1922 and continued the practice of law; also engaged as an author; member of the Democratic National Committee 1932–1940; elected as a Democrat to the United States Senate and served from March 4, 1933, to November 8, 1938, when he resigned; unsuccessful candidate for renomination in 1938; returned to Los Angeles, Calif., and served as chairman of the board of directors of a steamship line; died while on a visit in Washington, D. C., February 1, 1941; interment in Arlington National Cemetery, Fort Myer, Va.

McALEER, William, a Representative from Pennsylvania; born in County Tyrone, Ireland, January 6, 1838; immigrated to the United States with his parents, who settled in Philadelphia, Pa., in 1851; attended public and private schools; in 1861 became a partner with his father and brothers in the firm of John McAleer & Sons, flour merchants; member of the common council 1871–1873; president of the first district charity organization; president of the Friendly Sons of St. Patrick, organized for the relief of immigrants; member of the board of guardians of the poor 1873–1898, and served as vice president and later as president of the board; member of the commercial exchange and served successively as director, vice president, and president of the same; director of the chamber of commerce in 1880; member of the State senate 1886–1890; elected as a Democrat to the Fifty-second and Fifty-third Congresses (March 4, 1891–March 3, 1895); unsuccessful candidate for renomination in 1894; elected to the Fifty-fifth and Fifty-sixth Congresses (March 4, 1897–March 3, 1901); unsuccessful candidate for reelection in 1900 to the Fifty-seventh Congress; resumed business activities in Philadelphia, Pa.; died in Germantown, Philadelphia, Pa., April 19, 1912; interment in Holy Sepulchre Cemetery.

McALLISTER, Archibald (grandson of John Andre Hanna), a Representative from Pennsylvania; born at Fort Hunter, near Rockville, Dauphin County, Pa., October 12, 1813; attended the common schools and Dickinson College, Carlisle, Pa.; moved to Blair County, Pa., in 1842 and engaged in manufacturing charcoal iron at Springfield Furnace; elected as a Democrat to the Thirty-eighth Congress (March 4, 1863–March 3, 1865); was not a candidate for renomination in 1864; resumed the manufacture of iron at Springfield Furnace (now Royer); died in Royer, Blair County, Pa., July 18, 1883; interment in Mountain Cemetery.

McANDREWS, James, a Representative from Illinois; born in Woonsocket, Providence County, R. I., October 22, 1862; attended the common schools; moved to Chicago, Ill., and engaged in business; served as building commissioner of Chicago;

elected as a Democrat to the Fifty-seventh and Fifty-eighth Congresses (March 4, 1901–March 3, 1905); elected to the Sixty-third and to the three succeeding Congresses (March 4, 1913–March 3, 1921); unsuccessful candidate for reelection in 1920 to the Sixty-seventh Congress; resumed his business activities; unsuccessful candidate for election in 1932 to the Seventy-third Congress; elected to the Seventy-fourth, Seventy-fifth, and Seventy-sixth Congresses (January 3, 1935–January 3, 1941); was an unsuccessful candidate for reelection in 1940 to the Seventy-seventh Congress; died in Chicago, Ill., August 31, 1942; interment in Calvary Cemetery, Evanston, Ill.

McARDLE, Joseph A., a Representative from Pennsylvania; born in Muncie, Delaware County, Ind., June 29, 1903; moved to Pittsburgh, Pa., with his parents in 1905; attended the parochial schools; engaged in the insurance and bonding business; served in the State house of representatives 1936–1938; elected as a Democrat to the Seventy-sixth and Seventy-seventh Congresses and served from January 3, 1939, until his resignation on January 5, 1942, to become a member of the city council of Pittsburgh, Pa., in which capacity he is now serving; is a resident of Pittsburgh, Pa.

McARTHUR, Clifton Nesmith (grandson of James Willis Nesmith), a Representative from Oregon; born in The Dalles, Wasco County, Oreg., June 10, 1879; attended the public schools at Rickreall, Oreg., and the Bishop Scott Academy, Portland, Oreg.; was graduated from the University of Oregon at Eugene in 1901; reporter on the Morning Oregonian 1901–1903; engaged in agricultural pursuits near Rickreall, Oreg., 1903–1906; studied law; was admitted to the bar in 1906 and commenced practice in Portland; secretary of the Republican State central committee in 1908; secretary to Gov. Frank W. Benson 1908–1911; member of the State house of representatives 1909–1913 and served as speaker two sessions; elected as a Republican to the Sixty-fourth and to the three succeeding Congresses (March 4, 1915–March 3, 1923); unsuccessful candidate for reelection in 1922 to the Sixty-eighth Congress; resumed the practice of his profession and his former business activities in Portland, Oreg., where he died December 9, 1923; remains were cremated and the ashes deposited in the vaults of the Portland Cremation Association.

McARTHUR, Duncan, a Representative from Ohio; born in Dutchess County, N. Y., June 14, 1772; moved with his father to western Pennsylvania in 1780; received a limited education; served in the Indian campaign in 1790 under General Harmer; participated in the Battle of Captina in 1792; moved to Maysville, Ky., in 1793 and was employed in the salt works; settled in Ross County, Ohio, in 1796; acted as a spy among the Indians; surveyed the town of Chillicothe, Ohio; member of the State house of representatives in 1804; helped to organize the Militia and was commissioned colonel in 1805 and major general in 1808; served in the State senate 1805–1814 and was speaker in 1809 and 1810; raised a regiment of Volunteers during the War of 1812 and was commissioned colonel; elected as a Democrat to the Thirteenth Congress, but never qualified, resigning on April 5, 1813; commissioned brigadier general of Volunteers in March 1813; commanded Fort Meigs and successfully invaded Canada; Indian treaty commissioner in 1816; member of the State house of representatives in 1817 and 1818 and served as speaker; served in the State senate 1821–1823; elected as an advocate of the United States Bank to the Eighteenth Congress (March 4, 1823–March 3, 1825); declined to be a candidate for renomination in 1824; again a member of the State house of representatives in 1826; again served in the State senate in 1829 and 1830; Governor of Ohio

1830–1832; unsuccessful candidate for election in 1834 to the Twenty-third Congress; retired from political life and active business pursuits; died in Chillicothe, Ohio, on April 29, 1839; interment in Grandview Cemetery.

McBRIDE, George Wycliffe (brother of John Rogers McBride), a Senator from Oregon; born near Lafayette, Yamhill County, Oreg., March 13, 1854; attended the public schools, the preparatory department of Willamette University, Salem, Oreg., and Christian College, Monmouth, Oreg., for two years; studied law and was admitted to the bar, but never practiced; engaged in mercantile pursuits; member of the State house of representatives in 1882 and served as speaker; secretary of state of Oregon in 1886 and 1895; elected as a Republican to the United States Senate on February 23, 1895, and served from March 4, 1895, to March 3, 1901; unsuccessful candidate for renomination in 1900; appointed a United States commissioner to the St. Louis Exposition in 1904; engaged as an agent of the Western Pacific Railroad in California; died in Portland, Oreg., June 18, 1911; remains were cremated and the ashes interred in Masonic Cemetery, St. Helens, Oreg.

McBRIDE, John Rogers (brother of George Wycliffe McBride), a Representative from Oregon; born near St. Louis, in Franklin County, Mo., August 22, 1832; attended the country schools in Missouri and Oregon; moved to Oregon in 1851 with his parents, who settled near Lafayette, in Yamhill County; superintendent of schools in 1854; studied law; was admitted to the bar in 1855 and commenced practice in Lafayette; delegate to the State constitutional convention in 1857; member of the State senate 1860–1862; elected as a Republican to the Thirty-eighth Congress (March 4, 1863–March 3, 1865); unsuccessful candidate for renomination in 1864; appointed by President Lincoln in 1865 to be chief justice of Idaho Territory; appointed by President Grant in 1869 to be superintendent of the United States assay office at Boise, Idaho; practiced law in Boise, Idaho, and Salt Lake City, Utah; moved to Spokane, Wash., and continued the practice of his profession; member of the Republican National Committee 1880–1892; died in Spokane, Wash., July 20, 1904; interment in Germany Hill Cemetery, St. Helens, Oreg.

McBRYDE, Archibald, a Representative from North Carolina born in Wigtownshire, Scotland, September 28, 1766; immigrated at an early age with his parents, who settled in Carbonton, Moore County, N. C.; studied under private teachers; studied law; was admitted to the bar and practiced; also engaged in agricultural pursuits; served as clerk of the superior court of Moore County 1792–1816; elected as a Democrat to the Eleventh and Twelfth Congresses (March 4, 1809–March 3, 1813); member of the State senate in 1813 and 1814; resumed the practice of his profession; died in Carbonton, N. C., February 15, 1816; interment in Farrar Cemetery.

McCALL, John Ethridge, a Representative from Tennessee; born in Clarksburg, Carroll County, Tenn., August 14, 1859; attended public and private schools, and was graduated from the University of Tennessee at Knoxville in 1881; studied law in Huntingdon, Tenn.; was admitted to the bar in 1882 and commenced practice in Huntingdon; edited the Tennessee Republican in 1882; settled in Lexington, Tenn., in December 1883 and continued the practice of law; unsuccessful candidate for district attorney in 1886; member of the State house of representatives in 1887 and 1889; delegate to the Republican National Convention at Chicago in 1888; appointed assistant United States district attorney for western Tennessee in 1890, which office he resigned in 1891; unsuccessful candidate for

nomination as Governor before the Republican State convention in 1892; elected as a Republican to the Fifty-fourth Congress (March 4, 1895–March 3, 1897); unsuccessful candidate for reelection in 1896 to the Fifty-fifth Congress; delegate to the Republican National Convention at Philadelphia in 1900; unsuccessful Republican candidate for Governor of Tennessee in 1900; collector of internal revenue for the fifth district of Tennessee 1902–1905; appointed United States district judge for the western district of Tennessee on January 17, 1905, and served until his death in Huntingdon, Tenn., August 8, 1920; interment in Forest Hill Cemetery, Memphis, Tenn.

McCALL, Samuel Walker, a Representative from Massachusetts; born in East Providence, Bedford County, Pa., February 28, 1851; spent his early life in Illinois; attended the Mount Carroll (Ill.) Seminary; was graduated from New Hampton (N. H.) Academy in 1870 and from Dartmouth College, Hanover, N. H., in 1874; studied law; was admitted to the bar in 1875 and practiced in Worcester, Mass., and later in Boston, Mass.; editor of the Boston Daily Advertiser; member of the Massachusetts House of Representatives in 1888, 1889, and 1892; delegate to the Republican National Conventions in 1888, 1900, and 1916; elected as a Republican to the Fifty-third and to the nine succeeding Congresses (March 4, 1893–March 3, 1913); was not a candidate for renomination in 1912; resumed the practice of law in Boston; Governor of Massachusetts 1916–1918; engaged in literary pursuits; died in Winchester, Mass., November 4, 1923; interment in Wildwood Cemetery.

McCANDLESS, Lincoln Loy, a Delegate from the Territory of Hawaii; born in Indiana, Indiana County, Pa., September 18, 1859; moved to Volcano, Wood County, W. Va., with his parents in 1867; attended the public schools in Volcano, W. Va.; engaged in the oil and mining business in West Virginia and in Leadville, Colo.; moved to Hawaii in 1882, settled in Honolulu, and engaged in the drilling of artesian wells; also engaged in cattle ranching in 1887; served in the legislature of the Republic of Hawaii as a representative 1898–1900 and in the legislature of the Territory of Hawaii as a senator 1902–1906; unsuccessful candidate for election as a Delegate to the United States Congress on numerous occasions; elected as a Democrat a Delegate to the Seventy-third Congress (March 4, 1933–January 3, 1935); unsuccessful candidate for reelection in 1934 to the Seventy-fourth Congress; resumed his former business pursuits in Honolulu, Hawaii; also engaged in the building of roads and sewers and in the operation of his large plantations; died in Honolulu, Hawaii, October 5, 1940; the remains were cremated and interred in Nuuanu Cemetery.

McCARRAN, Patrick Anthony (Pat), a Senator from Nevada; born in Reno, Nev., August 8, 1876; attended the public schools and was graduated from the University of Nevada at Reno in 1901; engaged in farming and in stock raising; member of the State legislature in 1903; represented Nevada in an irrigation congress in 1903; studied law; was admitted to the bar in 1905 and practiced in Tonopah and Goldfield, Nev.; district attorney of Nye County, Nev., 1907–1909; resumed the practice of law in Reno, Nev., in 1909; associate justice of the supreme court of Nevada 1913–1917 and chief justice in 1917 and 1918; member of Nevada Board of Pardons 1913–1919; member of Nevada State Board of Parole Commissioners 1913–1918; chairman of the Nevada State Board of Bar Examiners 1919–1932; elected as a Democrat to the United States Senate in 1932; reelected in 1938, 1944, and again in 1950 and served from March 4, 1933, until his death in Hawthorne, Nev., September 28, 1954; interment in Mountain View Cemetery, Reno, Nev.

McCARTHY, Dennis, a Representative from New York; born in Salina, N. Y., March 19, 1814; pursued an academic course; attended Valley Academy, Salina, N. Y.; engaged in the manufacture of salt; member of the State assembly in 1846; mayor of Syracuse, N. Y., in 1853; elected as a Republican to the Fortieth and Forty-first Congresses (March 4, 1867–March 3, 1871); unsuccessful candidate for reelection in 1870 to the Forty-second Congress; resumed his former business pursuits; served in the State senate 1876–1885, and was president pro tempore of that body in 1885; served as Lieutenant Governor of New York from January 6, 1885, to January 1, 1886; died in Syracuse, N. Y., February 14, 1886; interment in Oakwood Cemetery.

McCARTHY, Eugene Joseph, a Representative and a Senator from Minnesota; born in Watkins, Meeker County, Minn., March 29, 1916; attended elementary and high schools in Watkins, Minn.; graduated from St. John's University, Collegeville, Minn., in 1935, and from the University of Minnesota at Minneapolis in 1939; taught in the public high schools of Minnesota and North Dakota 1935–1940; professor of economics and education at St. John's University 1940–1943; civilian technical assistant in the Military Intelligence Division of the War Department in 1944; instructor in sociology and economics at St. Thomas College, St. Paul, Minn., 1946–1949; delegate to the Democratic National Convention in 1952; elected as a Democrat to the Eighty-first and to the four succeeding Congresses (January 3, 1949–January 3, 1959); was not a candidate for renomination in 1958; elected as a Democrat to the United States Senate in 1958 for the term beginning January 3, 1959, and ending January 3, 1965.

McCARTHY, John Henry, a Representative from New York; born in New York City November 16, 1850; attended De La Salle Institute, Christian Brothers, and St. Francis Xavier College; engaged in mercantile pursuits; studied law; was admitted to the bar in 1873 and commenced practice in New York City; member of the State assembly in 1880 and 1881; civil justice for the fifth judicial district in the city of New York 1882–1888; elected as a Democrat to the Fifty-first Congress and served from March 4, 1889, until his resignation on January 14, 1891, to accept a judicial position; appointed on January 11, 1891, by Gov. David B. Hill justice of the city court of New York City to fill a vacancy; elected and reelected to the same office and served from 1891 until his death in New York City February 5, 1908; interment in Calvary Cemetery, Long Island City, N. Y.

McCARTHY, John Jay, a Representative from Nebraska; born in Stoughton, Dane County, Wis., July 19, 1857; attended the common schools and Albion (Wis.) Academy; moved to David City, Nebr., in 1879 and thence to Dixon County in 1882; studied law; was admitted to the bar in 1884 and commenced practice in Emerson, Nebr.; elected prosecuting attorney of Dixon County in 1890, 1892, and 1894; elected as a member of the State house of representatives in 1898 and 1900; elected as a Republican to the Fifty-eighth and Fifty-ninth Congresses (March 4, 1903–March 3, 1907); unsuccessful candidate for renomination in 1906; delegate to the Republican National Convention at Chicago in 1912; continued the practice of his profession in Ponca, Nebr., until his death there on March 30, 1943; interment in Ponca Cemetery.

McCARTHY, Joseph Raymond, a Senator from Wisconsin; born in Grand Chute, Outagamie County, Wis., November 14, 1908; attended the Underhill country school; worked on a farm and later started his own chicken farm; at the age of nineteen moved to Manawa and enrolled in Little Wolf High School while working in a grocery store and ushering at a theater in the evenings, completing a four-year course in one year; in 1930 entered Marquette University at Milwaukee, Wis., to study engineering but later transferred to the law department and graduated in 1935; was admitted to the bar the same year and commenced practice in Waupaca; in 1936 moved to Shawano, Wis., and continued the practice of his chosen profession; elected circuit judge of the tenth judicial circuit of Wisconsin in 1939 and while serving in this capacity enlisted in 1942 as a private in the United States Marine Corps; was later commissioned a lieutenant, serving thirty months on active duty with nineteen months in the South Pacific area; unsuccessful candidate for United States Senator in 1944 while in military service; reelected circuit judge of Wisconsin in 1945 while still in the Marine Corps; elected as a Republican to the United States Senate in 1946; reelected in 1952 and served from January 3, 1947, until his death in the naval hospital at Bethesda, Md., May 2, 1957; funeral services were held in the Chamber of the United States Senate; interment in St. Mary's Cemetery, Appleton, Wis.

McCARTHY, Kathryn O'Loughlin, a Representative from Kansas. (*See* O'LOUGHLIN, Kathryn Ellen.)

McCARTY, Andrew Zimmerman, a Representative from New York; born in Rhinebeck, Dutchess County, N. Y., July 14, 1808; studied law; was admitted to the bar in 1831 and commenced practice in Pulaski, Oswego County, N. Y.; county clerk of Oswego County 1840–1843; member of the State assembly in 1846 and 1847; elected as a Whig to the Thirty-fourth Congress (March 4, 1855–March 3, 1857); resumed the practice of his profession in Pulaski; register of bankruptcy 1875–1879; died in Pulaski, Oswego County, N. Y., April 23, 1879; interment in Pulaski Cemetery.

McCARTY, Johnathan, a Representative from Indiana; born in Culpeper County, Va., August 3, 1795; attended the public schools; moved to Indiana in 1803 with his father, who settled in Franklin County; engaged in mercantile pursuits; member of the State house of representatives in 1818; moved to Connersville, Fayette County, Ind.; clerk of the county court 1819–1827; elected as a Whig to the Twenty-second, Twenty-third, and Twenty-fourth Congresses (March 4, 1831–March 3, 1837); unsuccessful candidate for reelection in 1836 to the Twenty-fifth Congress; presidential elector on the Whig ticket of Harrison and Tyler in 1840; moved to Keokuk, Iowa, where he died March 30, 1852; interment in Oakland Cemetery.

McCARTY, Richard, a Representative from New York; born in Coeymans, Albany County, N. Y., February 19, 1780; attended the common schools; county clerk of Greene County 1811–1813; flour inspector of the State of New York; elected as a Democrat to the Seventeenth Congress (March 4, 1821–March 3, 1823); president of the Lafayette Bank in New York City; was one of the committee appointed to receive General Lafayette when he visited the United States in 1824 and 1825; died in New York City May 18, 1844; interment in Adams Cemetery, Coxsackie, Greene County, N. Y.

McCARTY, William Mason, a Representative from Virginia; born at "Cedar Grove," Fairfax County, Va., about 1789; received his early education from private tutors; attended William and Mary College, Williamsburg, Va., in 1813 and 1814; studied law; was admitted to the bar and commenced practice in Virginia; member of the State senate in 1823; moved to Florida and was prominently identified with the administration of the newly acquired territory; member of the commission to select the site for the capitol in 1824; appointed by President John Quincy Adams as secretary of the Territory of Florida to fill the vacancy caused by the resignation of George Walton in 1826; served as Governor of the Territory for a short time in 1827; returned to Virginia in 1830 and settled in Loudoun County; resumed the practice of his profession; again a member of the State senate 1830–1839; elected as a Whig to the Twenty-sixth Congress to fill the vacancy caused by the resignation of Charles F. Mercer and served from January 25, 1840, to March 3, 1841; disposed of his ancestral estate, "Cedar Grove," and moved to Richmond, Va., in 1852; died in Richmond, Va., December 20, 1863; interment in Shockoe Hill Cemetery.

McCAUSLEN, William Cochran, a Representative from Ohio; born near Steubenville, Jefferson County, Ohio, in 1796; attended the public schools; studied law; was admitted to the bar and practiced in Steubenville; was a law partner of Secretary of War Stanton; member of the State house of representatives in 1829, 1830, 1832, and 1833; owned and edited a Democratic newspaper in Steubenville; elected as a Democrat to the Twenty-eighth Congress (March 4, 1843–March 3, 1845); commissioned August 31, 1846, during the Mexican War as a captain and commissary of subsistence of the Third Regiment, Ohio Infantry; honorably discharged June 24, 1847; died in Steubenville, Jefferson County, Ohio, March 13, 1863; interment in Union Cemetery.

McCLAMMY, Charles Washington, a Representative from North Carolina; born at Scotts Hill, Pender County, N. C., May 29, 1839; pursued an academic course, and was graduated from the University of North Carolina at Chapel Hill in 1859; engaged in teaching 1859–1861; entered the Confederate Army in 1861; by successive promotions became major in the Third North Carolina Cavalry Regiment and served throughout the Civil War; engaged in agricultural pursuits at Scotts Hill; member of the State house of representatives in 1866; served in the State senate in 1871; presidential elector on the Democratic ticket of Cleveland and Hendricks in 1884; elected as a Democrat to the Fiftieth and Fifty-first Congresses (March 4, 1887–March 3, 1891); resumed agricultural pursuits; unsuccessful candidate for reelection in 1890 to the Fifty-second Congress; died at Scotts Hill, N. C., February 26, 1896; interment in the family cemetery.

McCLEAN, Moses, a Representative from Pennsylvania; born in Gettysburg, Pa., June 17, 1804; pursued an academic course; studied law; was admitted to the bar in 1825 and commenced practice in Gettysburg, Pa.; elected as a Democrat to the Twenty-ninth Congress (March 4, 1845–March 3, 1847); resumed the practice of law in Gettysburg, Pa.; member of the State house of representatives in 1855; continued the practice of law until his death in Gettysburg, Pa., September 30, 1870; interment in Evergreen Cemetery.

McCLEARY, James Thompson, a Representative from Minnesota; born in Ingersoll, Ontario, Canada, February 5, 1853; was educated at Ingersoll High School and McGill University, Montreal, Canada; engaged as superintendent of the Pierce County (Wis.) schools until 1881 when he resigned; moved to Minnesota and became State institute conductor of Minnesota and professor of civil government and history in the normal school in Mankato, Minn.; continued in this position until June 1892, when he became a candidate for Congress; president of the Minnesota Educational Association in 1891; elected as a Republican to the Fifty-third and to the six succeeding Congresses (March 4, 1893–March 3, 1907); unsuccessful candidate for reelection in 1906 to the Sixtieth Congress; appointed Second Assistant Postmaster General during Theodore Roosevelt's administration and served from March 29, 1907, until his resignation on September

15, 1908; secretary of the American Iron and Steel Institute in New York City 1911–1920; moved to Maiden Rock, Pierce County, Wis., and engaged in farming; thence to Mill Valley, Calif., and engaged in literary pursuits; returned to Maiden Rock, Wis., in 1924; died in La Crosse, Wis., December 17, 1924; interment in Lakewood Cemetery, Maiden Rock, Wis.

McCLEERY, James, a Representative from Louisiana; born in Mecca Township, Trumbull County, Ohio, December 2, 1837; attended Oberlin (Ohio) College in 1859 and 1860; served in the Union Army during the Civil War; commissioned second lieutenant of Company A, Forty-first Regiment, Ohio Volunteer Infantry, in 1861, first lieutenant in 1862, captain in 1863, and major in 1865; lost his right arm at the Battle of Shiloh; was wounded at Stone River December 31, 1862; entered the Regular Army as captain in the Forty-fifth Infantry in 1866 and subsequently received the brevets of major and brigadier general of Volunteers; retired December 15, 1870, and settled in St. Marys Parish, La.; purchased a plantation; practiced law and was connected with the Freedmen's Bureau in North Carolina and Louisiana; moved to Shreveport, La.; appointed superintendent of public education for the fourth division, comprising ten parishes; elected as a Republican to the Forty-second Congress and served from March 4, 1871, until his death while on a visit in New York City November 5, 1871; interment in the Christian Church Cemetery, Cortland, Ohio.

McCLELLAN, Abraham, a Representative from Tennessee; born at "White Top," on Beaver Creek, Sullivan County, Tenn., October 4, 1789; attended the common schools and was graduated from Washington (Tenn.) College; engaged in agricultural pursuits; member of the State house of representatives 1823–1825, 1827–1829; served in the State senate 1829–1833; member of the convention to revise the State constitution in 1834; member of the Second Regiment, Second Brigade, Tennessee Mounted Volunteer Militia, in 1836 and 1837 during the Seminole War; elected as a Democrat to the Twenty-fifth, Twenty-sixth, and Twenty-seventh Congresses (March 4, 1837–March 3, 1843); resumed agricultural pursuits; died at his home, "White Top," in Sullivan County, Tenn., May 3, 1866; interment in Weavers Cemetery, near Bristol, Tenn.

McCLELLAN, Charles A. O., a Representative from Indiana; born in Ashland, Ashe County, Ohio, May 25, 1835; moved to Auburn, Ind., in 1856; attended the public schools; studied law in Auburn and Waterloo, Ind.; was admitted to the bar in 1863 and commenced practice in Waterloo; became engaged in banking in 1868; appointed judge of the fortieth judicial circuit of Indiana by Governor Williams in 1879, and served for two years; elected as a Democrat to the Fifty-first and Fifty-second Congresses (March 4, 1889–March 3, 1893); was not a candidate for renomination in 1892; again engaged in banking and the practice of law; died in Auburn, Ind., January 31, 1898; interment in Waterloo Cemetery, Waterloo, Ind.

McCLELLAN, George, a Representative from New York; born in Schodack, Rensselaer County, N. Y., October 10, 1856; attended the public schools and the local academies at Spencertown and Chatham, N. Y.; was graduated from the Albany Law School in 1880; was admitted to the bar and commenced practice in Chatham, N. Y.; police justice for two terms; president of the Columbia County Agriculture Society for ten years; served as postmaster of Chatham; surrogate of Columbia County 1907–1913; elected as a Democrat to the Sixty-third Congress (March 4, 1913–March 3, 1915); unsuccessful candidate for reelection in 1914 to the Sixty-fourth Congress; delegate to the Democratic National Convention at San Francisco in 1920; resumed the practice of his profession in Chatham, N. Y.; moved to Kinderhook, Columbia County, and died there February 20, 1927; interment in Nassau Cemetery at Nassau, Rensselaer County, N. Y.

McCLELLAN, George Brinton, a Representative from New York; born November 23, 1865, in Dresden, Saxony, where his parents were visiting; attended St. John's School, Sing Sing (now Ossining), N. Y.; was graduated from Princeton College in 1886; worked as a reporter and in editorial positions on several New York newspapers; studied law; was admitted to the bar in 1892 and commenced practice in New York City; treasurer of the New York and Brooklyn Bridge 1889–1893; president of the Board of Aldermen of New York City in 1893 and 1894; delegate to all Democratic National, State, and city conventions between 1890 and 1903; elected as a Democrat to the Fifty-fourth and to the four succeeding Congresses and served from March 4, 1895, to December 21, 1903, when he resigned, having been elected mayor of New York City; served as mayor from 1903 to 1910; university lecturer on public affairs 1908–1912; elected professor of economic history at Princeton University in 1912; an incorporator, trustee, and vice president of the American Academy in Rome; during the First World War entered the military service as major in the Ordnance Department in May 1917 and was honorably discharged in May 1919 as lieutenant colonel; served in the United States and overseas; commissioned colonel in the Ordnance Officers' Reserve Corps; resumed his position of professor of economic history in Princeton University; resided in Washington, D. C., until his death on November 30, 1940; interment in Arlington National Cemetery, Fort Myer, Va.

McCLELLAN, John Little, a Representative and a Senator from Arkansas; born in Sheridan, Grant County, Ark., February 25, 1896; attended the public schools; was admitted to the bar in 1913 and commenced practice in Sheridan, Ark.; during the First World War served in the United States Army as a first lieutenant in the Aviation Section of the Signal Corps from August 1917 to February 1919; moved to Malvern, Ark., in 1919 and continued the practice of law; prosecuting attorney of the seventh judicial district of Arkansas 1927–1930; elected as a Democrat to the Seventy-fourth and Seventy-fifth Congresses (January 3, 1935–January 3, 1939); did not seek renomination in 1938, but was an unsuccessful candidate for the Democratic nomination for United States Senator; resumed the practice of law in Camden, Ark.; elected to the United States Senate in 1942, 1948, and again in 1954, and served from January 3, 1943, to January 3, 1961. *Reelected in 1960 for the term ending January 3, 1967.*

McCLELLAN, Robert, a Representative from New York; born in Livingston, N. Y., October 2, 1806; was graduated from Williams College, Williamstown, Mass., in 1825; studied law; was admitted to the bar and practiced his profession in Middleburg, N. Y., 1828–1843; elected as a Democrat to the Twenty-fifth Congress (March 4, 1837–March 3, 1839); elected to the Twenty-seventh Congress (March 4, 1841–March 3, 1843); died in Greenpoint, Brooklyn, N. Y., June 28, 1860; interment in Greenwood Cemetery.

McCLELLAND, Robert, a Representative from Michigan; born in Greencastle, Franklin County, Pa., August 1, 1807; was graduated from Dickinson College, Carlisle, Pa., in 1829; engaged in teaching; studied law; was admitted to the bar in Chambersburg, Pa., in 1832; moved to Pittsburgh, Pa., and thence, in February 1833 to Monroe, Mich., and engaged in the practice of law; delegate to the convention called to frame a constitution for the proposed State of Michigan in 1835 and to the State constitutional conventions in 1850 and 1867; declined the office of first bank commissioner of the State and subsequently that

of attorney general of Michigan; member of the board of regents of the University of Michigan at Ann Arbor in 1837 and 1850; member of the State house of representatives in 1837, 1839, and 1843, in the latter year being chosen speaker; mayor of Monroe in 1841; elected as a Democrat to the Twenty-eighth, Twenty-ninth, and Thirtieth Congresses (March 4, 1843–March 3, 1849); was not a candidate for renomination in 1848; delegate to the Democratic National Conventions in 1848, 1852, and 1868; delegate to the Democratic State convention in 1850; Governor of Michigan 1851–1853; resigned to accept appointment as Secretary of the Interior in the Cabinet of President Pierce March 7, 1853, and served until March 6, 1857; resumed the practice of law in Detroit, Mich., where he died August 30, 1880; interment in Elmwood Cemetery.

McCLELLAND, William, a Representative from Pennsylvania; born in Mount Jackson, Lawrence County, Pa., March 2, 1842; attended Westminster College, New Wilmington, Pa.; served in the Civil War four years; attended Allegheny College; studied law; was admitted to the bar and commenced practice at Mount Jackson in 1870; elected as a Democrat to the Forty-second Congress (March 4, 1871–March 3, 1873); unsuccessful candidate for reelection in 1872 to the Forty-third Congress; resumed the practice of his profession; died in Harrisburg, Pa., February 7, 1892; interment in Allegheny Cemetery, Pittsburgh, Pa.

McCLENACHAN, Blair, a Representative from Pennsylvania; born in Ireland; immigrated to the United States at an early age and settled in Philadelphia, Pa.; engaged in mercantile pursuits and in banking and shipping; one of the founders of and served with the First Troop of Philadelphia Cavalry during the Revolutionary War; in 1780 he subscribed a large sum of money to help the American forces and aided the Continental Congress with money and credit; member of the State house of representatives 1790–1795; elected to the Fifth Congress (March 4, 1797–March 3, 1799); died in Philadelphia, Pa., May 8, 1812; interment in a vault in St. Paul's Cemetery.

McCLENE, James, a Delegate from Pennsylvania; born in New London, Pa., October 11, 1730; moved to Antrim Township, Cumberland (now Franklin) County, in 1754; delegate to the State constitutional convention of 1776 to form a constitution for Pennsylvania; member of the State house of representatives in 1776 and 1777; member of the supreme executive council in 1778 and 1779; Member of the Continental Congress in 1779 and 1780; delegate to the State constitutional convention in 1789 and 1790; again a member of the State house of representatives in 1790, 1791, 1793, and 1794; died in Antrim Township, Pa., March 13, 1806.

McCLERNAND, John Alexander, a Representative from Illinois; born in Breckinridge County, Ky., on May 30, 1812; moved with his parents to Shawneetown, Ill., in 1813; attended the village schools; engaged in agricultural pursuits; studied law; was admitted to the bar in 1832; served in the Black Hawk War; engaged as a trader on the Ohio and Mississippi Rivers in 1833 and 1834; established the Shawneetown Democrat in 1835 and in the same year commenced the practice of law; member of the State house of representatives in 1836, 1840, 1842, and 1843; presidential elector on the Democratic ticket of Van Buren and Johnson in 1840 and of Pierce and King in 1852; elected as a Democrat to the Twenty-eighth and to the three succeeding Congresses (March 4, 1843–March 3, 1851); declined to be a candidate for renomination in 1850; moved to Jacksonville, Ill., in 1851 and to Springfield in 1856; elected to the Thirty-sixth Congress to fill the vacancy caused by the death of Thomas L.

Harris; reelected to the Thirty-seventh Congress and served from November 8, 1859, until October 28, 1861, when he resigned to accept a commission as brigadier general of Volunteers for service in the Civil War; returned to Illinois to raise troops for the Union Army; was promoted to major general in 1862; participated in numerous battles and was in command at the capture of the Arkansas Post; resigned his commission on November 30, 1864; elected circuit judge of the Sangamon District of Illinois in 1870 and served until 1873; resumed the practice of law; presided over the Democratic National Convention at St. Louis in 1876; appointed by President Cleveland as a member of the Utah Commission; died in Springfield, Ill., September 20, 1900; interment in Oak Ridge Cemetery.

McCLINTIC, James Vernon, a Representative from Oklahoma; born near Bremond, Robertson County, Tex., September 8, 1878; moved with his parents to Groesbeck, Limestone County, Tex., in 1880; attended the public schools, and Add-Ran University (now Texas Christian University), Fort Worth, Tex.; accepted a position with a wholesale dry-goods company at St. Louis, Mo., in 1901; traveling salesman in 1902; moved to Oklahoma Territory and engaged in mercantile pursuits at Snyder; homesteaded a farm in Texas County; city clerk of Snyder, Kiowa County, Okla., in 1908; clerk of Kiowa County in 1909; member of the State house of representatives in 1911; served in the State senate in 1913 and 1914; studied law at Georgetown University, Washington, D. C.; was admitted to the bar in 1928 and licensed to practice in all the courts of Oklahoma; elected as a Democrat to the Sixty-fourth and to the nine succeeding Congresses (March 4, 1915–January 3, 1935); unsuccessful candidate for renomination in 1934; executive assistant to the Governor of Oklahoma 1935–1940; unsuccessful candidate for nomination in 1941 to fill a vacancy in the Seventy-seventh Congress; administrative assistant in the District of Columbia Department of Vehicles and Traffic in 1940 and 1941; special assistant to the Secretary of the Interior 1941–1944; member of the Readjustment Division of the War Department in 1944 and 1945; resumed the practice of law; died April 22, 1948, on a train in the vicinity of Chicago, Ill., while returning from the Mayo Clinic to his home in Washington, D. C.; interment in Rose Hill Cemetery, Oklahoma City, Okla.

McCLINTOCK, Charles Blaine, a Representative from Ohio; born in Paint Township, Wayne County, Ohio, near Beach City, Stark County, May 25, 1886; educated in the elementary and high schools of Beach City; attended Wooster (Ohio) University, and was graduated from the law school of Western Reserve University, Cleveland, Ohio, in 1912; was admitted to the bar the same year and commenced law practice in Canton, Ohio; assistant prosecuting attorney of Stark County 1919–1923 and prosecuting attorney 1923–1927; elected as a Republican to the Seventy-first and Seventy-second Congresses (March 4, 1929–March 3, 1933); was an unsuccessful candidate for reelection in 1932 to the Seventy-third Congress and for election in 1934 to the Seventy-fourth Congress; resumed the practice of law; elected in 1946 as a judge of the court of appeals from the fifth appellate district of Ohio; reelected in 1952 and again in 1958 for a six-year term; is a resident of Canton, Ohio.

McCLOSKEY, Augustus, a Representative from Texas; born in San Antonio, Bexar County, Tex., September 23, 1878; attended Atascosa (Tex.) School, St. Joseph's Academy, San Antonio, Tex., and St. Mary's College, San Antonio, Tex.; employed as a stenographer 1903–1907; studied law; was admitted to the bar in 1907 and commenced practice in San Antonio, Tex.; judge of Bexar County 1920–1928; president of the High-

way Club of Texas in 1926 and 1927; delegate to the Democratic National Convention at Houston, Tex., in 1928; presented credentials as a Democratic Member-elect to the Seventy-first Congress and served from March 4, 1929, to February 10, 1930, when he was succeeded by Harry M. Wurzbach, who successfully contested his election; was not a candidate for renomination in 1930; resumed the practice of law; judge of the corporation court of San Antonio, Tex., from January 1943 to July 1947; practiced law until his death in San Antonio, Tex., July 21, 1950; interment in San Fernando Cemetery.

McCLURE, Addison S., a Representative from Ohio; born in Wooster, Wayne County, Ohio, October 10, 1839; pursued an academic course in Jefferson College, Canonsburg, Pa.; studied law; was admitted to the bar in 1861 and commenced practice in Wooster; entered the Army as a private in April 1861; was elected captain of Company H, Sixteenth Regiment, Ohio Volunteer Infantry, in October of the same year; discharged on expiration of service in the fall of 1864; recorder of Wayne County in 1867; appointed postmaster of Wooster in 1867 and reappointed in 1872 and 1876; delegate to the Republican National Convention at Chicago in 1868 and at Cincinnati in 1876; elected as a Republican to the Forty-seventh Congress (March 4, 1881–March 3, 1883); unsuccessful candidate for reelection in 1882 to the Forty-eighth Congress; elected to the Fifty-fourth Congress (March 4, 1895–March 3, 1897); was an unsuccessful candidate for reelection in 1896 to the Fifty-fifth Congress; resumed the practice of law; died in Wooster, Ohio, April 17, 1903; interment in Wooster Cemetery.

McCLURE, Charles, a Representative from Pennsylvania; born on Willow Grove farm, near Carlisle, Pa., in 1804; was graduated from Dickinson College, Carlisle, Pa., in 1824; studied law; was admitted to the bar in 1826 and practiced; member of the State house of representatives in 1835; elected as a Democrat to the Twenty-fifth Congress (March 4, 1837–March 3, 1839); elected to the Twenty-sixth Congress to fill the vacancy caused by the death of William S. Ramsey and served from December 7, 1840, to March 3, 1841; served as secretary of state of Pennsylvania 1843–1845, and was active in promoting the public-school system of Pennsylvania; died in Allegheny, Pa., on January 10, 1846; interment in Allegheny Cemetery, Pittsburgh, Pa.

McCLURG, Joseph Washington, a Representative from Missouri; born near Lebanon, St. Louis County, Mo., February 22, 1818; attended Xenia (Ohio) Academy and Oxford (Ohio) College; taught school in Louisiana and Mississippi in 1835 and 1836; moved to Texas in 1839; studied law and was admitted to practice at Columbus, Tex.; clerk of the circuit court in 1840; returned to Missouri in 1841 and engaged in mercantile pursuits; served during the Civil War as colonel of Cavalry in the Union Army; member of the State convention 1861–1863; elected as an Emancipationist to the Thirty-eighth Congress; reelected as a Radical to the Thirty-ninth and Fortieth Congresses and served from March 4, 1865, until his resignation in 1868, having been elected Governor; elected as a Republican Governor of Missouri and served from January 31, 1869, to January 31, 1871; unsuccessful candidate for reelection; resumed mercantile pursuits at Linn Creek, Mo., and also engaged in steamboating and lead mining; register of the land office at Springfield, Mo., in 1889; died in London, Mo., on December 2, 1900; interment in Lebanon Cemetery.

McCOID, Moses Ayers, a Representative from Iowa; born near Bellefontaine, Logan County, Ohio, November 5, 1840; attended the public schools, Fairfield University, and Washington (now Washington and Jefferson) College, Washington, Pa.; studied law in Fairfield, Iowa; was admitted to the bar in 1861 and commenced practice in Fairfield; during the Civil War enlisted as a private in Company E, Second Regiment, Iowa Volunteer Infantry, May 6, 1861; was commissioned a second lieutenant; acting adjutant of the regiment during the advance on Corinth and in the spring of 1862; resumed the practice of law in Fairfield; district attorney of the sixth judicial district of Iowa in 1867 and 1871; member of the State senate 1872–1879; elected as a Republican to the Forty-sixth, Forty-seventh, and Forty-eighth Congresses (March 4, 1879–March 3, 1885); unsuccessful candidate for renomination in 1884; again resumed the practice of law; died in Fairfield, Iowa, May 19, 1904; interment in Evergreen Cemetery.

McCOMAS, Louis Emory, a Representative and a Senator from Maryland; born near Hagerstown, Washington County, Md., October 28, 1846; attended St. James College, Maryland; was graduated from Dickinson College, Carlisle, Pa., in 1866; studied law; was admitted to the bar in 1868 and practiced in Hagerstown, Md., until 1892; professor of international law in the law school of Georgetown University, Washington, D. C.; unsuccessful Republican candidate for election in 1876 to the Forty-fifth Congress; elected as a Republican to the Forty-eighth and the three succeeding Congresses (March 4, 1883–March 3, 1891); unsuccessful candidate for reelection in 1890 to the Fifty-second Congress; delegate at large to the Republican National Convention at Minneapolis in 1892 and at Philadelphia in 1900; during the presidential campaign of 1892 was secretary of the Republican National Committee; on November 17, 1892, was appointed by President Harrison an associate justice of the supreme court of the District of Columbia, which office he held until elected Senator; elected as a Republican to the United States Senate and served from March 4, 1899, until March 3, 1905; was the caucus nominee of his party, who were in the minority, for Senator in 1905; appointed by President Theodore Roosevelt as a justice of the Court of Appeals of the District of Columbia on July 1, 1905, and served until his death; died in Washington, D. C., November 10, 1907; interment in Rose Hill Cemetery, Hagerstown, Washington County, Md.

McCOMAS, William, a Representative from Virginia; born near Pearisburg, Giles County, Va., in 1795; attended private schools and Emory and Henry College, Emory, Va.; engaged in agricultural pursuits and in the practice of law; also was a Methodist minister; member of the State senate 1830–1833; elected as a Whig to the Twenty-third and Twenty-fourth Congresses (March 4, 1833–March 3, 1837); resumed his former activities; unsuccessful candidate for election in 1848 to the Thirty-first Congress; delegate to the State secession convention in 1861 and voted against the ordinance; judge of the United States district court during the Civil War; died on his farm near Barboursville, Va. (now West Virginia), June 3, 1865; interment in the family cemetery.

McCOMB, Eleazer, a Delegate from Delaware; served in the Revolutionary War as captain of militia; appointed privy councilor in 1779; Member of the Continental Congress in 1783 and 1784; appointed as one of the commissioners to confer on the subject of the Chesapeake and Delaware Canal in 1786; auditor of accounts of the State of Delaware 1787–1793; moved from Dover to Wilmington about 1792; engaged in commercial pursuits and shipping in Wilmington; director of the Bank of Delaware in 1795; died at Wilmington, New Castle County, Del., in December 1798.

McCONNELL, Felix Grundy, a Representative from Alabama; born in Nashville, Tenn., April 1, 1809; moved with his parents to Fayetteville, Lincoln County, Tenn., in 1811; received a limited education and became a saddler; moved to Talladega, Talladega County, Ala., in 1834; studied law; was admitted to the bar in 1836 and commenced practice in Talladega, Ala.; member of the State house of representatives in 1838; served in the State senate 1839–1843; elected as a Democrat to the Twenty-eighth and Twenty-ninth Congresses and served from March 4, 1843, until his death in Washington, D. C., September 10, 1846; interment in the Congressional Cemetery.

McCONNELL, Samuel Kerns, Jr., a Representative from Pennsylvania; born in Eddystone, Delaware County, Pa., April 6, 1901; attended the grade schools at Easton and Philadelphia, Pa., and was graduated from the University of Pennsylvania at Philadelphia in 1923; engaged in the investment banking business in 1926; member of the board of trustees of the Norristown State Hospital 1939–1944, serving as president 1940–1944; served as township commissioner of Lower Merion Township 1941–1944; elected as a Republican to the Seventy-eighth Congress to fill the vacancy caused by the death of J. William Ditter; reelected to the Seventy-ninth and to the six succeeding Congresses and served from January 18, 1944, until his resignation September 1, 1957, to become executive director of United Cerebral Palsy Associations, Inc.; is a resident of Wynnewood, Pa.

McCONNELL, William John, a Senator from Idaho; born in Commerce, Oakland County, Mich., September 18, 1839; pursued an academic course; moved to California in 1860 and engaged in mining, in the cattle business, merchandising, and banking; resided in Oregon in 1862 and 1863 and taught school in Yamhill County; moved to Idaho in 1863; deputy United States marshal 1865–1867; returned to Oregon and was engaged in the cattle business five years; member of the Oregon State Senate in 1882 and served as president; delegate to the Republican National Convention at Chicago in 1884; returned to Idaho in 1886; member of the constitutional convention of Idaho in 1890; upon the admission of Idaho as a State into the Union was elected as a Republican to the United States Senate and served from December 18, 1890, to March 3, 1891; was not a candidate for renomination; Governor of Idaho 1892–1896; appointed Indian inspector by President McKinley on July 8, 1897, and served until July 5, 1901; appointed by President Taft an inspector in the Immigration Service on August 3, 1909, with station at Moscow, Latah County, Idaho, and served until his death in that city on March 30, 1925; interment in Moscow Cemetery.

McCOOK, Anson George, a Representative from New York; born in Steubenville, Jefferson County, Ohio, October 10, 1835; attended the common schools of Lisbon (then New Lisbon), Ohio; employed as a drug clerk in Pittsburgh, Pa., 1850–1852; returned to Ohio and taught school in a small country place near Lisbon; crossed the Plains to California in 1854 and engaged in mining in that State and also in Nevada; returned East in 1859, and at the outbreak of the Civil War was engaged in the study of law; organized a company of Infantry in Steubenville; entered the Union Army as captain of the Second Regiment, Ohio Volunteer Infantry, April 17, 1861; honorably mustered out July 31, 1861; on the reorganization of the regiment was commissioned major August 6, 1861; lieutenant colonel January 1, 1863; colonel January 20, 1863; brevetted brigadier general of Volunteers March 13, 1865, "for meritorious services"; honorably discharged October 21, 1865; returned to Steubenville and was admitted to the bar in 1866; appointed assessor of internal revenue for the seventeenth Ohio district in November 1865; moved to New York City in May 1873, and was admitted to the bar of that State in 1875; founded the Law Journal, and became president of the New York Law Publishing Co., which position he held until his death; elected as a Republican to the Forty-fifth, Forty-sixth, and Forty-seventh Congresses (March 4, 1877–March 3, 1883); unsuccessful candidate for renomination in 1882; Secretary of the United States Senate 1883–1893; appointed by Mayor William L. Strong city chamberlain of the city of New York and served from 1895 to 1898; died in New York City December 30, 1917; interment in Union Cemetery, Steubenville, Ohio.

McCORD, Andrew, a Representative from New York; born at what is now Stony Ford, Wallkill Township, Orange County, N. Y., about 1754; attended the common schools and Newburgh Academy; delegate to the convention at New Paltz, N. Y., November 7, 1775, to choose deputies to the Second Provincial Congress; quartermaster in Ulster County Militia January 31, 1787; served as captain of Ulster County Militia, and resigned April 10, 1798; member of the State assembly in 1795, 1796, 1798, 1800, 1802, and 1807, and served as speaker in 1807; elected to the Eighth Congress (March 4, 1803–March 3, 1805); engaged in agricultural pursuits; died at Stony Ford, Orange County, N. Y., in 1808; interment in the family burying ground on his farm near Stony Ford.

McCORD, James Nance, a Representative from Tennessee; born in Unionville, Bedford County, Tenn., March 17, 1879; attended the public schools and also had private instructors; employed as a clerk in a hardware store in 1894; engaged in selling books and stationery at Lewisburg, Tenn., 1897–1900; traveling salesman 1900–1910; editor and publisher of the Marshall Gazette, Lewisburg, Tenn., since 1910; mayor of Lewisburg, Tenn., 1916–1942; auctioneer 1920–1943; member of the Marshall County Court 1915–1942; presidential elector for the State at large on the Roosevelt and Garner ticket in 1932; elected as a Democrat to the Seventy-eighth Congress (January 3, 1943– January 3, 1945); was not a candidate for renomination in 1944; elected Governor of Tennessee in 1944; reelected in 1946 for the term ending in January 1949; resumed the publishing business; member of State constitutional convention in 1953; Commissioner of Conservation, State of Tennessee, 1953–1958; delegate at large to the National Democratic Conventions in 1940 and 1956; is a resident of Lewisburg, Tenn.

McCORD, Myron Hawley, a Representative from Wisconsin; born in Ceres, McKean County, Pa., November 26, 1840; attended Richburg Academy, New York; moved to Wisconsin in 1854 and settled in Shawano, Shawano County; moved to Merrill in 1875; became a publisher, lumberman, and farmer; published a newspaper 1868–1883; served in the State senate in 1873 and 1874; member of the State assembly in 1881; delegate to the Republican National Convention at Cincinnati in 1876; register of the United States land office at Wausau, Wis., from February 26, 1884, to June 24, 1885; elected as a Republican to the Fifty-first Congress (March 4, 1889–March 3, 1891); unsuccessful candidate for reelection in 1890 to the Fifty-second Congress and for election in 1892 to the Fifty-third Congress; returned to Merrill, Wis., and engaged in agricultural pursuits and lumbering; appointed by President McKinley as Governor of Arizona Territory in 1897; resigned in 1898 and organized the Territorial Regiment for the Spanish-American War; appointed United States marshal for the district of Arizona May 1, 1902, and served until July 1, 1905; later appointed collector of customs for the port of Nogales, Ariz.; died in Phoenix, Ariz., on April 27, 1908; interment in Merrill Cemetery, Merrill, Lincoln County, Wis.

McCORKLE, Joseph Walker, a Representative from California; born in Piqua, Ohio, June 24, 1819; attended the common schools and Kenyon College, Gambier, Ohio; studied law; was admitted to the bar about 1842 and commenced practice in Dayton, Ohio; postmaster of Dayton 1845–1849; moved to San Francisco, Calif., in 1849; unsuccessful candidate for judge of the eighth judicial district in 1850; member of the State assembly 1850–1852; elected as a Democrat to the Thirty-second Congress (March 4, 1851–March 3, 1853); unsuccessful candidate for renomination in 1852; moved to Marysville, Calif.; appointed judge of the ninth judicial district in 1853 and served in that capacity until 1857; unsuccessful candidate for election to the United States Senate in 1855; resumed the practice of his profession in San Francisco, Calif.; moved to Virginia City, Nev., in 1860 and continued the practice of law; moved to Washington, D. C., in 1870 and practiced before the Mexican Claims Commission; died in Branchville, Md., March 18, 1884; interment in Forest Hill Cemetery, Piqua, Ohio.

McCORKLE, Paul Grier, a Representative from South Carolina; born in Yorkville (now York), York County, S. C., December 19, 1863; attended the public schools of his native city and Kings Mountain Military School, York, S. C.; employed as a clerk in York, S. C.; became an expert cotton buyer and grader and in that capacity was employed in Lancaster, S. C., and then in Chester, S. C., where he lost his eyesight in an accident; returned to York, S. C., and engaged in business as a cotton broker and export classifier; elected as a Democrat to the Sixty-fourth Congress to fill the vacancy caused by the death of David E. Finley and served from February 24, 1917, to March 3, 1917; was not a candidate for renomination in 1916; engaged in the cotton brokerage business in York, S. C.; coroner of York County, S. C., from 1920 until his death; died while on a visit at Knoxville, Tenn., on June 2, 1934; interment in Rose Hill Cemetery, York, S. C.

McCORMACK, John William, a Representative from Massachusetts; born in Boston, Suffolk County, Mass., December 21, 1891; attended the public school; studied law in a private law office; was admitted to the bar in 1913 and began practice in Boston, Mass.; member of the State constitutional convention in 1917 and 1918; during the First World War served in the United States Army in 1917 and 1918; served in the State house of representatives 1920–1922; member of the State senate 1923–1926, serving as Democratic floor leader in 1925 and 1926; delegate to all Democratic State conventions since 1920; delegate to the Democratic National Conventions in 1932, 1940, 1944, and 1948; elected as a Democrat to the Seventieth Congress to fill the vacancy caused by the death of James A. Gallivan and on the same day was elected to the Seventy-first Congress; reelected to the Seventy-second and to the fourteen succeeding Congresses and served from November 6, 1928, to January 3, 1961; majority floor leader from September 16, 1940, to January 3, 1947; from January 3, 1949, to January 3, 1953; and from January 3, 1955, to January 3, 1961; minority whip from January 3, 1947, to January 3, 1949, and from January 3, 1953, to January 3, 1955. *Reelected to the Eighty-seventh Congress.*

McCORMICK, Henry Clay, a Representative from Pennsylvania; born in Washington Township, Lycoming County, Pa., June 30, 1844; attended the common schools and Dickinson Seminary, Williamsport, Pa.; studied law; was admitted to the bar in 1866, and practiced in Williamsport, Pa.; elected as a Republican to the Fiftieth and Fifty-first Congresses (March 4, 1887–March 3, 1891); delegate to the Republican National Convention at Minneapolis in 1892 which nominated Benjamin Harrison, of Indiana, for a second term; elected president of the

Williamsport & North Branch Railroad January 1, 1892; attorney general of Pennsylvania 1895–1899; resumed the practice of law; died in Williamsport, Lycoming County, Pa., May 26, 1902; interment in Wildwood Cemetery.

McCORMICK, James Robinson, a Representative from Missouri; born near Irondale, Washington County, Mo., on August 1, 1824; attended the public schools in Washington County, Mo; received private instruction and entered Transylvania University, Lexington, Ky., as a medical student; was graduated from the Memphis (Tenn.) Medical College in 1849 and commenced practice in Wayne County, Mo.; moved to Perry County in 1850 and continued the practice of his profession; delegate to the State constitutional convention in 1861; during the Civil War served as a surgeon in the Sixth Regiment, Missouri Volunteer Infantry, Union Army; served in the State senate in 1862, but resigned on account of duties in the Army; brigadier general of militia in 1863; after the war located in Arcadia, Mo., and resumed the practice of medicine; again served in the State senate in 1866, but resigned the following year; elected as a Democrat to the Fortieth Congress to fill the vacancy caused by the death of Thomas E. Noel; reelected to the Forty-first and Forty-second Congresses and served from December 17, 1867, to March 3, 1873; was not a candidate for reelection in 1872; moved to Farmington, Mo., in 1874; practiced medicine and engaged in the drug business; died in Farmington, St. Francois County, Mo., May 19, 1897; interment in Masonic Cemetery.

McCORMICK, John Watts, a Representative from Ohio; born near Gallipolis, Gallia County, Ohio, December 20, 1831; attended the common schools, the Ohio Wesleyan University at Delaware, and the Ohio University at Athens; engaged in agricultural pursuits and stock raising; taught school, and later became a Methodist minister; delegate to the Ohio constitutional convention in 1873; elected as a Republican to the Forty-eighth Congress (March 4, 1883–March 3, 1885); unsuccessful candidate for reelection in 1884 to the Forty-ninth Congress; trustee of Rio Grande College 1883–1885; resumed agricultural pursuits; died in Gallipolis, Ohio, June 25, 1917; interment in Mount Zion Cemetery near Gallipolis, Ohio.

McCORMICK, (Joseph) Medill (husband of Ruth Hanna McCormick), a Representative and a Senator from Illinois; born in Chicago, Ill., May 16, 1877; attended the public schools of Chicago and a preparatory school at Groton, Mass.; was graduated from Yale University in 1900; engaged in newspaper work as reporter, publisher, and owner of the Chicago Daily Tribune, and later purchased an interest in the Cleveland Leader and Cleveland News; war correspondent in the Philippine Islands in 1901; vice chairman of the national campaign committee of the Progressive Republican movement from 1912 to 1914; chairman of the Republican State convention in 1916; delegate to the Republican National Convention at Chicago in 1916 which nominated Charles E. Hughes, of New York, and Charles W. Fairbanks, of Indiana; member of the State house of representatives in 1912; reelected in 1914; elected as a Republican to the Sixty-fifth Congress (March 4, 1917–March 3, 1919); elected to the United States Senate and served from March 4, 1919, until his death; unsuccessful candidate for renomination in 1924; died in Washington, D. C., on February 25, 1925; interment in Middlecreek Cemetery, near Byron, Ogle County, Ill.

McCORMICK, Nelson B., a Representative from Kansas; born near Waynesburg, Greene County, Pa., November 20, 1847; attended the common schools; moved to Marion County, Iowa, in 1867, where he engaged in farming and stock raising until his removal to Phillips County, Kans., where he settled upon a homestead in 1877; studied law; was admitted to the bar in 1882 and commenced practice in Phillipsburg, Kans.; deputy prosecuting attorney of Phillips County 1886–1888; prosecuting attorney 1890–1894; declined to be a candidate for renomination; elected as a Populist to the Fifty-fifth Congress (March 4, 1897–March 3, 1899); unsuccessful candidate for reelection in 1898 to the Fifty-sixth Congress; resumed the practice of law in Phillipsburg, Kans.; delegate to the Democratic State conventions in 1904 and 1908; prosecuting attorney of Phillips County 1910–1914; died in Phillipsburg, Kans., April 10, 1914; interment in Fairview Cemetery.

McCORMICK, Richard Cunningham, a Delegate from the Territory of Arizona and a Representative from New York; born in New York City May 23, 1832; attended the common schools; entered business in Wall Street in 1852; at Sevastopol as newspaper correspondent during the Crimean War in 1854 and 1855; editor, Young Men's Magazine, New York, 1857–1859; with Army of the Potomac during the Civil War as correspondent of the New York Evening Post and New York Commercial Advertiser in 1861 and 1862; first chief clerk, Department of Agriculture, in 1862; appointed by President Lincoln secretary of Arizona Territory in 1863 and by President Johnson governor of the Territory in 1866; established the Prescott Arizona Miner in 1864 and the Tucson Arizona Citizen in 1870; elected as a Unionist as Delegate from the Territory of Arizona to the Forty-first, Forty-second, and Forty-third Congresses (March 4, 1869–March 3, 1875); was not a candidate for renomination in 1874; delegate to the Republican National Conventions in 1872, 1876, and 1880; returned to New York; United States commissioner to the Centennial Exposition at Philadelphia in 1876; First Assistant Secretary of the Treasury in 1877; commissioner general to the Paris Exposition in 1878; decorated Commander, Legion of Honor, by the President of France in 1878; declined appointments as Minister to Brazil in 1877 and as Minister to Mexico in 1879; elected as a Republican from New York to the Fifty-fourth Congress (March 4, 1895–March 3, 1897); was not a candidate for renomination in 1896; president, board of managers, State Normal School, Jamaica, N. Y.; died in Jamaica, Queens County, N. Y., June 2, 1901; interment in Grace Churchyard.

McCORMICK, Ruth Hanna (daughter of Marcus Alonzo Hanna, wife of Joseph Medill McCormick, and of Albert Gallatin Simms), a Representative from Illinois; born in Cleveland, Ohio, March 27, 1880; attended Hathaway Brown School in Cleveland, Dobbs Ferry (N. Y.) School, and Miss Porter's School in Farmington, Conn.; owned and operated a dairy and breeding farm near Byron, Ill.; publisher and president of the Rockford Consolidated Newspapers (Inc.), Rockford, Ill.; chairman of the first woman's executive committee of the Republican National Committee, and an associate member of the national committee 1919–1924, in the latter year becoming the first elected national committeewoman from Illinois and served until 1928; active worker for the suffrage amendment from 1913 until the Constitution was amended; elected as a Republican to the Seventy-first Congress (March 4, 1929–March 3, 1931); was not a candidate for renomination in 1930, having received the Republican nomination for United States Senator, in which election she was unsuccessful; resumed her newspaper interests; married Albert Gallatin Simms, of New Mexico, who was also a Member of the Seventy-first Congress; and resided in Albuquerque, N. Mex.; died in Chicago, Ill., on December 31, 1944; interment in Fairview Cemetery, Albuquerque, N. Mex.

McCORMICK, Washington Jay, a Representative from Montana; born in Missoula, Missoula County, Mont., January 4, 1884; attended the public schools, the State University of

Montana at Missoula, and the University of Notre Dame, Indiana; was graduated from Harvard University in 1906 and from the law department of Columbia University, New York City, in 1910; was admitted to the New York bar the same year; returned to Missoula, Mont.; was admitted to the Montana bar in 1911 and engaged in the practice of law; member of the State house of representatives 1918–1920; elected as a Republican to the Sixty-seventh Congress (March 4, 1921–March 3, 1923); unsuccessful candidate for reelection in 1922 to the Sixty-eighth Congress; continued the practice of law until his retirement, when he devoted his time to writing; resided in Bitter Root Valley, near Stevensville, Mont., until his death in Missoula, Mont., March 7, 1949; interment in Missoula Cemetery.

McCOWEN, Edward Oscar, a Representative from Ohio; born in Bloom Township, Scioto County, Ohio, June 29, 1877; attended the public schools of South Webster, Ohio; was graduated from Ohio Northern University at Ada in 1908, Ohio State University at Columbus in 1917, and from the Graduate School of the University of Cincinnati, Cincinnati, Ohio, in 1939; when in his teens he was a newsboy, worked in coal mines, in a brickyard, as a farm hand, and as a store clerk; began teaching at the age of seventeen and was successively a high-school teacher, principal, and superintendent; superintendent of the Scioto County public schools 1914–1942; precinct committeeman and delegate to the Ohio Republican State conventions in 1935 and 1946; trustee of Rio Grande (Ohio) College; elected as a Republican to the Seventy-eighth, Seventy-ninth, and Eightieth Congresses (January 3, 1943–January 3, 1949); unsuccessful candidate for reelection in 1948 to the Eighty-first Congress; returned to Wheelersburg, Ohio, and continued his activity in politics until his death there November 4, 1953; interment in South Webster Cemetery, South Webster, Ohio.

McCOY, Robert, a Representative from Pennsylvania; born in Carlisle, Pa.; attended the common schools; prothonotary of Cumberland County; brigadier general of militia; State canal commissioner; elected to the Twenty-second Congress to fill the vacancy caused by the death of William Ramsey and served from November 22, 1831, to March 3, 1833; died in Wheeling, Va. (now West Virginia), June 7, 1849.

McCOY, Walter Irving, a Representative from New Jersey; born in Troy, Rensselaer County, N. Y., December 8, 1859; attended the public schools, Troy Academy, Phillips Exeter Academy, Exeter, N. H., and Princeton College, the latter for two years; was graduated from Harvard University in 1882 and from the law department of that institution in 1886; was admitted to the bar the same year and commenced practice in New York City; trustee of the village of South Orange, N. J., 1893–1895, 1901–1905, and in 1910; delegate to the Democratic National Convention at St. Louis in 1904 which nominated the presidential ticket of Parker and Davis and at Denver in 1908 which nominated Bryan and Kern; vice president of the Essex County (N. J.) Democratic committee; elected as a Democrat to the Sixty-second and Sixty-third Congresses and served from March 4, 1911, until October 3, 1914, when he resigned; appointed by President Wilson on October 5, 1914, as an associate justice, and on May 31, 1918, as chief justice, of the supreme court of the District of Columbia and served until his retirement on December 8, 1929; resided in Washington, D. C., until 1932, when he moved to Cambridge, Mass., where he died on July 17, 1933; interment in Troy Cemetery, Troy, N. Y.

McCOY, William, a Representative from Virginia; born near Warrenton, Fauquier County, Va.; member of the State house of delegates 1798–1804; delegate to the State constitutional con-

vention in 1829 and 1830; elected as a Democrat to the Twelfth and to the ten succeeding Congresses (March 4, 1811–March 3, 1833); died in Charlottesville, Va., in 1864; interment in the University of Virginia Cemetery.

McCRACKEN, Robert McDowell, a Representative from Idaho; born in Vincennes, Knox County, Ind., March 15, 1874; moved to Carmi, Ill., in 1880; attended the public schools; went West in 1891 and settled in Blackfoot, Bingham County, Idaho; taught school in Blackfoot until 1897; employed as a clerk in the United States Surveyor General's office in Boise, Idaho, 1897–1902; studied law; was admitted to the bar in 1902 and commenced practice in Blackfoot; chief clerk of the State house of representatives in 1903; prosecuting attorney of Bingham County 1904–1906; elected a member of the State house of representatives from Bingham County in 1906 for a two-year term; moved to Boise in 1907 and continued the practice of law; elected to the State house of representatives from Ada County in 1908 for a two-year term; elected as a Republican to the Sixty-fourth Congress (March 4, 1915–March 3, 1917); unsuccessful candidate for renomination; during the First World War was commissioned a captain in the Chemical Warfare Service; resumed the practice of his profession in Boise, Ada County, Idaho; was seeking the Republican nomination for election to Congress and while campaigning was in an automobile accident, which resulted in his death, in Emmett, Idaho, May 16, 1934; interment in Blackfoot Cemetery, Blackfoot, Idaho.

McCRARY, George Washington, a Representative from Iowa; born near Evansville, Vanderburg County, Ind., August 29, 1835; moved to the Territory of Iowa in 1836 with his parents, who settled in Van Buren County; attended the public schools; studied law; was admitted to the bar in 1856 and commenced practice in Keokuk, Iowa; member of the State house of representatives in 1857; served in the State senate in 1861–1865; elected as a Republican to the Forty-first and to the three succeeding Congresses (March 4, 1869–March 3, 1877); was not a candidate for renomination in 1876; Secretary of War in the Cabinet of President Hayes from March 12, 1877, to December 11, 1879, when he resigned; served as United States judge of the eighth judicial circuit 1880–1884; moved to Kansas City, Mo.; became general counsel for the Atchison, Topeka & Santa Fe Railroad Co. in 1884; died at the home of his daughter in St. Joseph, Mo., June 23, 1890; interment in Oakland Cemetery, Keokuk, Iowa.

McCRATE, John Dennis, a Representative from Maine; born in Wiscasset, Maine, October 1, 1802; was graduated from Bowdoin College, Brunswick, Maine, in 1819; studied law; was admitted to the bar and practiced in Damariscotta, Maine, 1823–1835 and in Wiscasset 1835–1850; member of the State house of representatives 1831–1835; customs collector 1836–1841; elected as a Democrat to the Twenty-ninth Congress (March 4, 1845–March 3, 1847); resumed the practice of law in Wiscasset, Maine; moved to Boston, Mass., and continued the practice of his profession until 1852 when he moved to Sutton, Mass., and engaged in agricultural pursuits; died in Sutton, Worcester County, Mass., on September 11, 1879; interment in Ancient Cemetery, Wiscasset, Lincoln County, Maine.

McCREARY, George Deardorff, a Representative from Pennsylvania; born at York Springs, Adams County, Pa., on September 28, 1846; moved with his parents to Philadelphia in 1864; attended public and private schools; entered the University of Pennsylvania at Philadelphia in 1864 and remained until 1867, when he left to take a position with a coal company of which his father was president; began an independent business career in

1870; elected treasurer of the city and county of Philadelphia in November 1891, and during his term of office, from 1892 to 1895, reorganized the finances of the city; elected as a Republican to the Fifty-eighth and to the four succeeding Congresses and served from March 4, 1903, to March 3, 1913; was not a candidate for renomination in 1912; engaged in banking; died in Philadelphia, Pa., July 26, 1915; interment in Laurel Hill Cemetery.

McCREARY, James Bennett, a Representative and a Senator from Kentucky; born in Richmond, Madison County, Ky., July 8, 1838; attended the common schools; was graduated from Centre College, Danville, Ky., in 1857 and from the law department of Cumberland University at Lebanon, Tenn., in 1859; was admitted to the bar in the latter year and commenced practice in Richmond, Ky.; entered the Confederate Army as a private in 1862 and attained the rank of lieutenant colonel of the Eleventh Kentucky Cavalry before the close of the Civil War; delegate to the Democratic National Convention at New York City in 1868 which nominated Horatio Seymour, of New York, for President and Francis P. Blair, Jr., of Missouri, for Vice President; declined the nomination for presidential elector on the Democratic ticket of Seymour and Blair in 1868; member of the State house of representatives 1869–1873; served as speaker in 1871 and 1873; Governor of Kentucky 1875–1879; appointed by President Benjamin Harrison a delegate to the International Monetary Conference held in Brussels, Belgium, in 1892; elected as a Democrat to the Forty-ninth and to the five succeeding Congresses (March 4, 1885–March 3, 1897); unsuccessful candidate for renomination in 1896; resumed the practice of law; chairman of the State Democratic committee in the campaign of 1900; delegate to the Democratic National Conventions in 1900, 1904, 1908, and 1912; elected as a Democrat to the United States Senate in 1902 and served from March 4, 1903, to March 3, 1909; unsuccessful candidate for reelection in 1908; again Governor of Kentucky 1912–1916; unsuccessful candidate for election to the United States Senate in 1914; resumed the practice of his profession; died in Richmond, Ky., October 8, 1918; interment in Richmond Cemetery.

McCREARY, John, a Representative from South Carolina; born near Fishing Creek, about eighteen miles from Chester, S. C., in 1761; received his schooling from private tutors; became a surveyor; also engaged in agricultural pursuits; served in the Revolutionary War; member of the State house of representatives and the State senate; sheriff of Chester District (now Chester County); elected to the Sixteenth Congress (March 4, 1819–March 3, 1821); resumed agricultural pursuits and surveying; died on his plantation in South Carolina November 4, 1833; interment in the Richardson Church Cemetery, Chester County, S. C.

McCREDIE, William Wallace, a Representative from Washington; born in Montrose, Susquehanna County, Pa., April 27, 1862; moved to Iowa with his parents, who settled on a farm near Manchester, Delaware County; attended the common schools; was graduated from Cornell College, Mount Vernon, Iowa, in 1885; taught school at Parkersburg, Iowa, 1885–1889; attended the law school of the University of Iowa at Iowa City in 1889 and 1890; moved to Portland, Oreg., in 1890 and completed the study of law; was admitted to the bar the same year and commenced practice in Vancouver, Wash.; prosecuting attorney of Clarke County, Wash., 1894–1896; judge of the superior court at Vancouver, Wash., 1904–1909; became part owner of the Portland baseball club in 1904; elected as a Republican to the Sixty-first Congress to fill the vacancy caused by the death of Francis W. Cushman and served from November 2, 1909, to March 3, 1911; unsuccessful candidate for renomination

in 1910 to the Sixty-second Congress; resumed his interest in the Portland club of the Pacific Coast Baseball League, serving as president until 1921, when he retired; continued the practice of law in Portland, Oreg., until his death in that city on May 10, 1935; interment in Lincoln Memorial Cemetery.

McCREERY, Thomas Clay, a Senator from Kentucky; born near Owensboro, Daviess County, Ky., on December 12, 1816; attended the common schools, and was graduated from Centre College, Danville, Ky., in 1837; studied law; was admitted to the bar and commenced practice in Frankfort, Franklin County, Ky., and practiced his profession for about two years; returned to his home near Owensboro and engaged in literary pursuits; unsuccessful candidate for election in 1842 to the Twenty-eighth Congress and again in 1844 to the Twenty-ninth Congress; presidential elector on the Democratic tickets of Pierce and King in 1852, of Buchanan and Breckinridge in 1856, and of Breckinridge and Lane in 1860; elected as a Democrat to the United States Senate to fill the vacancy caused by the resignation of James Guthrie and served from February 19, 1868, to March 3, 1871; unsuccessful candidate for reelection; again elected to the United States Senate and served from March 4, 1873, to March 3, 1879; declined to be a candidate for reelection; retired from public life and lived on his farm in Daviess County; moved to Owensboro, Ky., where he died July 10, 1890; interment in Elmwood Cemetery.

McCREERY, William, a Representative from Maryland; born in the Province of Ulster, Ireland, in 1750; received a limited education; immigrated to the United States in his youth and located in Maryland; engaged in agricultural pursuits; elected to the Eighth, Ninth, and Tenth Congresses (March 4, 1803–March 3, 1809); resumed agricultural pursuits; member of the State senate from September 1811 until his death at his country home, "Clover Hill," near Reisterstown, Baltimore County, Md., March 8, 1814.

McCREERY, William, a Representative from Pennsylvania; born in Omagh, County Tyrone, Ireland, May 17, 1786; immigrated to the United States in 1791 with his parents, who settled near Fairfield, Westmoreland County, Pa.; attended private school; moved to Paris, Washington County, Pa., in 1812 and engaged in agricultural pursuits; member of the State house of representatives 1824–1827; constructor of the Pennsylvania State Canal and of the State highway 1826–1831; elected as a Democrat to the Twenty-first Congress (March 4, 1829–March 3, 1831); unsuccessful candidate for reelection in 1830 to the Twenty-second Congress; served as collector of internal revenue at Pittsburgh 1831–1833; again a member of the State house of representatives 1833–1836; superintendent of the Pennsylvania State Canal in 1835, residing in Allegheny City, Allegheny County, Pa.; acting president of the Pennsylvania Board of Canal Appraisers at the time of his death; died in Fairfield, Pa., on September 27, 1841; interment in Up-the-Valley United Presbyterian Church Cemetery.

McCULLOCH, George, a Representative from Pennsylvania; born in Maysville, Mason County, Ky., February 22, 1792; upon the death of his parents was sent to Cumberland County, Pa., where he was reared by relatives; ironmaster, with extensive iron interests in Center County; member of the State senate in 1835 and 1836; one of the proprietors of Hannah Furnace 1836–1850; elected as a Democrat to the Twenty-sixth Congress to fill the vacancy caused by the death of William W. Potter and served from November 20, 1839, to March 3, 1841; unsuccessful candidate for election in 1842 to the Twenty-eighth Congress; retired from political life and active business pursuits with residence in

Lewistown, Mifflin County, Pa.; died at the home of his daughter in Port Royal, Juniata County, Pa., April 6, 1861; interment in Church Hill Cemetery, southwest of Port Royal, Pa.

McCULLOCH, John, a Representative from Pennsylvania; born in McCulloch Mills, Pa., November 15, 1806; attended the common schools, and was graduated from Jefferson College, Canonsburg, Pa., in 1825; studied medicine and was graduated from the medical department of the University of Pennsylvania in 1829; commenced practice in Green Tree, Huntingdon County, Pa.; moved to Petersburg in 1830, where he engaged in the practice of his profession until 1852; elected as a Whig to the Thirty-third Congress (March 4, 1853–March 3, 1855); was not a candidate for renomination in 1854; resumed the practice of medicine in Huntingdon, Pa.; affiliated with the Republican Party upon its formation in 1856; member of the State constitutional convention in 1874; died in Huntingdon, Pa., May 15, 1879; interment in Riverside Cemetery.

McCULLOCH, Philip Doddridge, Jr., a Representative from Arkansas; born in Murfreesboro, Rutherford County, Tenn., June 23, 1851; moved with his parents to Trenton, Gibson County, Tenn.; attended private schools and Andrew College in that city; studied law; was admitted to the bar in 1872 and commenced practice in Trenton; moved to Marianna, Ark., in February 1874 and continued the practice of law; elected prosecuting attorney for the first judicial district in 1878; reelected for three successive terms and served until 1884; chairman of the Democratic central committee of Lee County, Ark., 1875–1893; elected mayor of Marianna, Ark., in 1875, but declined to serve; member of the board of education; presidential elector on the Democratic ticket of Cleveland and Thurman in 1888; delegate to the Democratic State convention in 1890; elected as a Democrat to the Fifty-third and to the four succeeding Congresses (March 4, 1893–March 3, 1903); declined to be a candidate for renomination; resumed the practice of law in Marianna, Ark.; died in Marianna November 26, 1928; interment in Cedar Heights Cemetery.

McCULLOCH, Roscoe Conkling, a Representative and a Senator from Ohio; born near Millersburg, Holmes County, Ohio, November 27, 1880; attended the public schools, Canton High School, the University of Wooster at Wooster, Ohio, Ohio State University Law School at Columbus, and Western Reserve University Law School, Cleveland, Ohio; was admitted to the bar in 1903 and commenced practice in Canton, Ohio; assistant prosecuting attorney of Stark County 1905–1907; unsuccessful Republican candidate for election in 1912 to the Sixty-third Congress; elected as a Republican to the Sixty-fourth, Sixty-fifth, and Sixty-sixth Congresses (March 4, 1915–March 3, 1921); was not a candidate for renomination in 1920; unsuccessful candidate for the Republican nomination for Governor of Ohio in 1920; special Assistant Attorney General of the United States 1922–1925; appointed to the United States Senate to fill the vacancy caused by the death of Theodore E. Burton and served from November 5, 1929, until November 30, 1930, when a duly elected successor qualified; was unsuccessful for election to fill the vacancy; resumed the practice of law in Columbus, Ohio; died in West Palm Beach, Fla., March 17, 1958; interment in Hillcrest Cemetery.

McCULLOCH, William Moore, a Representative from Ohio; born near Holmesville, Holmes County, Ohio, November 24, 1901; attended the public schools, College of Wooster, Wooster, Ohio; was graduated from the college of law of Ohio State University at Columbus in 1925; was admitted to the bar the same year and commenced practice in Piqua, Ohio; member of the State house of representatives 1933–1944, serving as minority leader 1936–1939 and as speaker 1939–1944; during World War II

served in the Military Government Forces from December 26, 1943, to October 12, 1945; elected as a Republican to the Eightieth Congress to fill the vacancy caused by the resignation of Robert F. Jones; reelected to the Eighty-first and to the five succeeding Congresses and served from November 4, 1947, to January 3, 1961. *Reelected to the Eighty-seventh Congress.*

McCULLOGH, Welty, a Representative from Pennsylvania; born in Greensburg, Westmoreland County, Pa., October 10, 1847; attended the common schools, and Washington and Jefferson College, Washington, Pa.; served as second clerk under Capt. W. B. Coulter, provost marshal of twenty-first district of Pennsylvania, during the Civil War; graduated from Princeton College in June 1870; studied law; was admitted to the bar in 1872 and commenced practice in Greensburg; assistant solicitor for the Baltimore & Ohio Railroad; elected as a Republican to the Fiftieth Congress (March 4, 1887–March 3, 1889); unsuccessful candidate for renomination in 1888; continued the practice of law until his death in Greensburg, Pa., August 31, 1889; interment in the new St. Clair Cemetery.

McCULLOUGH, Hiram, a Representative from Maryland; born near Elkton, Cecil County, Md., September 26, 1813; pursued an academic course at Elkton Academy; studied law; was admitted to the bar in 1837 and practiced in Elkton; served in the State senate 1845–1851; unsuccessful candidate in 1850 for election to the Thirty-second Congress; in 1850 appointed one of the codifiers of the laws of Maryland; elected as a Democrat to the Thirty-ninth and Fortieth Congresses (March 4, 1865–March 3, 1869); resumed the practice of law and was for many years counsel for the Philadelphia, Wilmington & Baltimore Railroad; delegate to the Democratic National Convention at Chicago in 1864 and at New York in 1868; member of the State house of delegates in 1880 and 1881 and served as speaker in 1880; died in Elkton, Md., March 4, 1885; interment in Presbyterian Cemetery.

McCULLOUGH, Thomas Grubb, a Representative from Pennsylvania; born in Greencastle, Franklin County, Pa., April 20, 1785; attended the common schools; studied law; was admitted to the Franklin County bar April 8, 1806; served in the War of 1812 as a private and later as quartermaster; elected to the Sixteenth Congress to fill the vacancy caused by the resignation of David Fullerton and served from October 17, 1820, to March 4, 1821; served in the State house of representatives 1831–1835; first president of the Cumberland Valley Railroad Co.; managed and edited the Franklin Repository; was president of the Bank of Chambersburg at the time of his death; died in Chambersburg, Pa., September 10, 1848.

McCUMBER, Porter James, a Senator from North Dakota; born in Crete, Will County, Ill., February 3, 1858; moved with his parents to Rochester, Minn., the same year; attended the common schools; taught school for a few years; was graduated from the law department of the University of Michigan at Ann Arbor in 1880; was admitted to the bar and commenced practice at Lisbon, Dak. (now North Dakota), in 1881; moved to Wahpeton, Dak., in 1882 and continued the practice of law; served as State's attorney of Richland County 1883–1885; member of the Territorial house of representatives in 1885 and served in the Territorial senate in 1887; elected as a Republican to the United States Senate in 1899; reelected in 1905, 1911, and 1916 and served from March 4, 1899, to March 3, 1923; unsuccessful candidate for renomination; resumed the practice of law in Washington, D. C.; appointed by President Coolidge on June 8, 1925, as a member of the International Joint Commission created by treaty to pass upon all cases involving the use of the boundary waters between the United States and Canada, in which capacity he served until his death in Washington, D. C., May 18, 1933; interment in the Abbey Mausoleum, adjoining Arlington National Cemetery, Fort Myer, Va.

McDANIEL, William, a Representative from Missouri; member of the State senate in 1838 and 1840; elected president of the bank in Palmyra, Marion County, Mo., on December 9, 1840; elected as a Democrat to the Twenty-ninth Congress to fill the vacancy caused by the resignation of Sterling Price and served from December 7, 1846, to March 3, 1847; was operating an agency for the location of land claims at Palmyra on June 10, 1847; died about 1854.

McDANNOLD, John James, a Representative from Illinois; born in Mount Sterling, Brown County, Ill., August 29, 1851; attended the common schools and a private school in Quincy; was graduated from the law department of the University of Iowa at Iowa City in June 1874; was admitted to the bar of Illinois in September 1874 and commenced practice in Mount Sterling; appointed master in chancery for Brown County in October 1885; elected county judge of Brown County in 1886; reelected in November 1890 and served until October 2, 1892, when he resigned, having been nominated for Congress; elected as a Democrat to the Fifty-third Congress (March 4, 1893–March 3, 1895); was not a candidate for renomination in 1894; moved to Chicago, Ill., in 1895 and resumed the practice of law; died in Chicago, Ill., February 3, 1904; interment in City Cemetery, Mount Sterling, Ill.

McDEARMON, James Calvin, a Representative from Tennessee; born in New Canton, Buckingham County, Va., June 13, 1844; moved with his parents to Gibson County, Tenn., in 1846; attended Andrew College, Trenton, Tenn., 1858–1861; during the Civil War entered the Confederate Army in April 1862 and served throughout the war in Cheatham's division, Army of the Tennessee; was wounded slightly at Murfreesboro and severely at Franklin; surrendered at Greensboro, N. C., with Johnston's army April 26, 1865; studied law; was admitted to the bar in 1867 and commenced practice in Trenton, Tenn.; elected as a Democrat to the Fifty-third and Fifty-fourth Congresses (March 4, 1893–March 3, 1897); unsuccessful candidate for renomination in 1896; resumed the practice of his profession; died in Trenton, Gibson County, Tenn., July 19, 1902; interment in Oakwood Cemetery.

McDERMOTT, Allan Langdon, a Representative from New Jersey; born in South Boston, Mass., March 30, 1854; attended the common schools; was graduated from the law department of New York University; was admitted to the bar in the November term in 1877 and commenced practice in Jersey City, N. J.; corporation attorney of Jersey City 1879–1883; member of the State house of assembly in 1880 and 1881; district court judge 1883–1886; president of the Jersey City Board of Finance and Taxation 1883–1886; member of the State board of taxation 1884–1886; chairman of the New Jersey State Democratic committee 1885–1895; member of the commission to revise the constitution of New Jersey in 1894; candidate of the Democratic legislative caucus for United States Senator in 1895 and 1902; delegate at large to the Democratic National Convention at Chicago in 1896; member of the State senate in 1899 and 1900; elected as a Democrat to the Fifty-sixth Congress to fill the vacancy caused by the death of William B. Daly; reelected to the Fifty-seventh, Fifty-eighth, and Fifty-ninth Congresses and served from December 3, 1900, to March 3, 1907; was not a candidate for renomination in 1906; died in Jersey City, N. J., October 26, 1908; interment in Hoboken Cemetery, North Bergen, N. J.

McDERMOTT, James Thomas, a Representative from Illinois; born in Grand Rapids, Mich., February 13, 1872; attended the graded schools and St. Andrew's Cathedral School at Grand Rapids; moved with his parents in 1884 to Detroit, Mich., where he was taught telegraphy; employed in this occupation until 1889, when he moved to Chicago, Ill.; engaged in the retail tobacco business; elected as a Democrat to the Sixtieth and to the three succeeding Congresses and served from March 4, 1907, until July 21, 1914, when he resigned; delegate to the Democratic National Convention at Baltimore in 1912 which nominated Woodrow Wilson for President; again elected to the Sixty-fourth Congress (March 4, 1915–March 3, 1917); declined to be a candidate for renomination in 1916; resumed his former business pursuits; died in Chicago, Ill., on February 7, 1938; interment in All Saints Cemetery.

McDILL, Alexander Stuart, a Representative from Wisconsin; born near Meadville, Crawford County, Pa., on March 18, 1822; attended Allegheny College; was graduated from Cleveland Medical College in 1848 and practiced medicine in Crawford County, Pa., 1848–1856; moved to Plover, Portage County, Wis., in 1856; member of the State assembly in 1862; member of the board of managers of the Wisconsin State Hospital for the Insane 1862–1868; served in the State senate in 1863 and 1864; presidential elector on the Republican ticket of Lincoln and Johnson in 1864; medical superintendent of the Wisconsin State Hospital for the Insane 1868–1873 and in 1875; elected as a Republican to the Forty-third Congress (March 4, 1873–March 3, 1875); unsuccessful candidate for reelection to the Forty-fourth Congress; died near Madison, Wis., November 12, 1875; interment in Forest Hill Cemetery, Madison, Wis.

McDILL, James Wilson, a Representative and a Senator from Iowa; born in Monroe, Butler County, Ohio, March 4, 1834; attended the common schools, Hanover College, and Salem Academy; was graduated from Miami University, Oxford, Ohio, in 1853; studied law in Columbus, Ohio, and was admitted to the bar in 1856; moved to Afton, Iowa, and commenced practice; elected superintendent of Union County, Iowa, in 1859; elected county judge of Union County in 1860; clerk in the office of the Third Auditor of the Treasury, Washington, D. C., from 1862 to 1865, when he resigned and returned to Iowa; circuit judge of the second district, third judicial circuit of Iowa, in 1868; appointed in 1870 and then elected district judge of the third judicial circuit of Iowa in 1871 and served until elected to Congress; elected as a Republican to the Forty-third and Forty-fourth Congresses (March 4, 1873–March 3, 1877); declined to be a candidate for renomination in 1876; resumed the practice of law in Afton, Iowa; member of the Board of Railroad Commissioners of the State of Iowa 1878–1881; appointed and subsequently elected as a Republican to the United States Senate to fill the vacancy caused by the resignation of Samuel J. Kirkwood and served from March 8, 1881, until March 3, 1883; was not a candidate for reelection; appointed by President Harrison a member of the Interstate Commerce Commission and served from January 13, 1892, until his death in Creston, Iowa, February 28, 1894; interment in Graceland Cemetery.

McDONALD, Alexander, a Senator from Arkansas; born near Lock Haven, Clinton County, Pa., April 10, 1832; attended Dickinson Seminary, Williamsport, Pa., and Lewisburg University, Lewisburg, Pa.; moved to Kansas in 1857 and engaged in general business; served in the Union Army during the Civil War; became interested in banking in Arkansas in 1863 and finally settled in Little Rock; member of the State constitutional convention; upon the readmission of the State of Arkansas to representation was elected as a Republican to the United States Senate and served from June 22, 1868, to March 3, 1871; unsuccessful candidate for reelection in 1870 to the United States Senate; commissioned by President Arthur to examine into the conditions of two divisions of the Northern Pacific Railroad in 1885; delegate to the Republican National Convention at Chicago in 1888 which nominated Benjamin Harrison, of Indiana, for President; engaged in development of railroads; moved to New York City in 1900; died in Norwood Park, St. Lawrence County, N. Y., December 13, 1903; interment in Highland Cemetery, Lock Haven, Pa.

McDONALD, Edward Francis, a Representative from New Jersey; born in Ireland September 21, 1844; immigrated to the United States when six years of age with his parents, who settled in Newark, N. J.; attended the public schools; during the Civil War enlisted in Company I, Seventh Regiment, New Jersey Volunteer Infantry, in 1861 and served under McClellan and Hooker in the Peninsular Campaign and the Seven Days' Battles, acting as sergeant in command of his company in the latter engagements; was honorably discharged in 1862; learned the machinist trade and became a skilled mechanic; moved to Harrison, N. J., in 1874; member of the State house of assembly in 1874; director at large of the Board of Chosen Freeholders of Hudson County in 1877; reelected in 1879 and served four years; nominated presidential elector by the Democratic State convention in 1884, but declined to accept the position; presented credentials as a member-elect to the State senate in 1890 and served throughout the session until the last day, when he was unseated, but was restored to the seat in the following session; largely interested in real-estate business; treaurer of Harrison, Hudson County, N. J., in 1881; elected as a Democrat to the Fifty-second Congress and served from March 4, 1891, until his death in Harrison, N. J., November 5, 1892; interment in Holy Sepulchre Cemetery, Newark, N. J.

McDONALD, John, a Representative from Maryland; born in Dingle, County Kerry, Ireland, May 24, 1837; attended the schools of Ireland; immigrated to the United States and enlisted in the United States Army at Boston, Mass., in 1857; joined his regiment in Arizona; participated in several Indian campaigns in that Territory and in California; served in the Cavalry Corps of the Army of the Potomac throughout the Civil War; after the war was ordered to the West, where he again took part in several campaigns against hostile Indians; retired as a captain of Cavalry July 1, 1868, for disabilities incurred in the line of service; settled in Maryland; elected as a Republican to the Maryland House of Delegates in 1881; elected as a Republican to the Fifty-fifth Congress (March 4, 1897–March 3, 1899); engaged in agricultural pursuits near Potomac, Montgomery County, Md.; died in Rockville, Md., January 30, 1917; interment in Union Cemetery.

McDONALD, Joseph Ewing, a Representative and a Senator from Indiana; born in Butler County, Ohio, August 29, 1819; moved with his mother to Montgomery County, Ind., in 1826; apprenticed to the saddler's trade when twelve years of age in La Fayette, Ind.; attended Asbury (now De Pauw) University, Greencastle, Ind., and Wabash College, Crawfordsville, Ind., but did not graduate; studied law in La Fayette, Ind.; was admitted to the bar before the supreme court of Indiana in 1843 and practiced; prosecuting attorney 1843–1847; moved to Crawfordsville, Ind., in 1847, where he practiced law until 1859; elected as a Democrat to the Thirty-first Congress (March 4, 1849–March 3, 1851); was not a candidate for renomination in 1850; elected attorney general of Indiana in 1856 and reelected in 1858; moved to Indianapolis in 1859; unsuccessful Democratic candidate for Governor of Indiana in 1864; elected to the United States Senate and served from

March 4, 1875, to March 3, 1881; was the caucus nominee of his party, who were in the minority, for reelection; died in Indianapolis, Ind., June 21, 1891; interment in Crown Hill Cemetery.

McDONOUGH, Gordon Leo, a Representative from California; born in Buffalo, Erie County, N. Y., January 2, 1895; moved with his parents to Emporium, Cameron County, Pa., in 1898; attended the public schools; was graduated from the high school at Emporium, Pa.; engaged as an industrial chemist at Emporium, Pa., 1915–1918; moved to Los Angeles, Calif., and resumed his former occupation 1918–1933; member of the Los Angeles County Board of Supervisors 1933–1944, serving as chairman for one year; elected as a Republican to the Seventy-ninth and to the seven succeeding Congresses (January 3, 1945–January 3, 1961). *Reelected to the Eighty-seventh Congress.*

McDOUGALL, Alexander, a Delegate from New York; born in the Parish of Kildalton, on the island of Islay, Scotland, in 1731; immigrated to the United States in 1740, with his parents, who settled in New York; commanded two privateers during the war with France in 1756; at the conclusion of peace engaged in mercantile pursuits; was an ardent patriot and was imprisoned as the author of Revolutionary pamphlets; member of the provincial convention in April 1775; served in the Revolutionary War; commissioned colonel of the First New York Infantry June 30, 1775; promoted to brigadier general, Continental Army, August 9, 1776; and major general October 20, 1777, and served until the close of the war; Member of the Continental Congress in 1781, 1782, 1784, and 1785; declined to accept the appointment of Minister of Marine in 1782; member of the State senate from 1783 until his death; first president of the New York Society of the Cincinnati; first president of the Bank of New York; died in New York City June 9, 1786; interment in the family vault in the First Presbyterian Church, New York City.

McDOUGALL, James Alexander, a Representative and a Senator from California; born in Bethlehem, N. Y., November 19, 1817; attended the Albany public schools; studied law; was admitted to the bar and commenced practice in Cook County, Ill., in 1837; attorney general of Illinois 1842–1846; made explorations of the southwestern part of the United States; finally settled in San Francisco; attorney general of California from October 7, 1850, until he resigned December 30, 1851; elected as a Democrat to the Thirty-third Congress (March 4, 1853–March 3, 1855); was not a candidate for renomination in 1854; elected to the United States Senate and served from March 4, 1861, to March 3, 1867; was not a candidate for reelection; delegate to the Democratic National Convention at Chicago in 1864 and to the Union National Convention at Philadelphia in 1866; died in Albany, N. Y., September 3, 1867; interment in Lone Mountain (later Calvary) Cemetery, San Francisco, Calif.

McDOWELL, Alexander, a Representative from Pennsylvania; born in Franklin, Venango County, Pa., March 4, 1845; attended the common schools; learned the printing trade; studied law but never practiced; during the Civil War served in the Union Army in the One Hundred and Twenty-first Regiment of Pennsylvania Volunteers; mustered out at the close of the war as brevet major; editor and publisher of the Venango Citizen until 1870, when he moved to Sharon and engaged in banking; treasurer and director of the School Board of Sharon 1880–1913; treasurer of the borough of Sharon 1880–1909; elected as a Republican to the Fifty-third Congress (March 4, 1893–March 3, 1895); was not a candidate for renomination in 1894; elected Clerk of the National House of Representatives on March 4, 1895, and served in that capacity until March 3, 1911; delegate to the Republican National Conventions at Philadelphia in 1900 and at Chicago in 1904 and 1908; resumed banking interests; died in Sharon, Mercer County, Pa., September 30, 1913; interment in Oakwood Cemetery.

McDOWELL, Harris Brown, Jr., a Representative from Delaware; born on a farm near Middletown, New Castle County, Del., February 10, 1906; attended the public schools of Middletown, Wilmington (Del.) High School, and the Y. M. C. A. schools; graduated from Beacom Business College, Wilmington, Del.; engaged in farming, also in the insurance and real-estate business; member of the State Board of Agriculture 1937–1940; served in the State house of representatives 1940–1942; director of Interstate Milk Producers Cooperative and member of Delaware Farm Bureau 1941–1948; member of the State senate 1942–1946; secretary of state of the State of Delaware 1949–1953; member of New Castle County Zoning Commission in 1953 and 1954; delegate to the Democratic National Conventions in 1944, 1948, 1952, 1956, and 1960; elected as a Democrat to the Eighty-fourth Congress (January 3, 1955–January 3, 1957); was an unsuccessful candidate for reelection in 1956 to the Eighty-fifth Congress; elected to the Eighty-sixth Congress (January 3, 1959–January 3, 1961).   *Reelected to the Eighty-seventh Congress.*

McDOWELL, James, a Representative from Virginia; born at "Cherry Grove," near Rockbridge County, Va., October 13, 1796; attended a classical school at Greenville, Va., a private school at Brownsburg, Washington College (now Washington and Lee University), Lexington, Va., and Yale College; was graduated from Princeton College in 1817; studied law; was admitted to the bar but did not practice; member of the State house of delegates 1830–1835 and again in 1838; Governor of Virginia 1842–1846; elected as a Democrat to the Twenty-ninth Congress to fill the vacancy caused by the death of William Taylor; reelected to the Thirtieth and Thirty-first Congresses and served from March 6, 1846, to March 3, 1851; died on his estate "Colalts" near Lexington, Va., August 24, 1851; interment in Presbyterian Cemetery.

McDOWELL, James Foster, a Representative from Indiana; born in Mifflin County, Pa., December 3, 1825; moved with his parents to Ohio in 1835; attended the public schools; worked in a printing office; studied law; was admitted to the bar in 1846 and practiced; prosecuting attorney of Darke County, Ohio, in 1848; moved to Marion, Ind., in 1851 and engaged in the practice of law; established the Marion Journal in 1851; Democratic presidential elector in 1852 and 1860; elected as a Democrat to the Thirty-eighth Congress (March 4, 1863–March 3, 1865); unsuccessful candidate for reelection in 1864 to the Thirty-ninth Congress; delegate to the Democratic National Convention at St. Louis in 1876; engaged in the practice of law in Marion, Ind., until his death in that city April 18, 1887; interment in Odd Fellows Cemetery.

McDOWELL, John Anderson, a Representative from Ohio; born in Killbuck, Holmes County, Ohio, September 25, 1853; attended the common schools, the Millersburg High School, and Lebanon (Ohio) Normal College; was graduated from the Mount Union College, Alliance, Ohio, in 1887; taught winter terms of rural schools 1870–1877; principal of Millersburg High School 1877–1879; superintendent of Millersburg schools 1879–1896; county school examiner for twenty years; instructor in teachers' institutes in several counties in Ohio; instructor in the summer school of the College of Wooster, Ohio, 1896–1917 and in the summer school of Ashland (Ohio) College in 1918; elected as a Democrat to the Fifty-fifth and Fifty-sixth Congresses (March 4, 1897–March 3, 1901); unsuccessful candidate for renomination in 1900; superintendent of public instruction

of the Ashland city schools 1908–1927; trustee of the State normal college at Kent, Ohio, 1911–1922; president of Northeastern Ohio Teachers' Association in 1921 and of Ohio State Teachers' Association in 1926; member of the Ohio Sesquicentennial Commission; also interested in agricultural pursuits; died in Cleveland, Ohio, October 2, 1927; interment in Oak Hill Cemetery, Millersburg, Ohio.

McDOWELL, John Ralph, a Representative from Pennsylvania; born in Pitcairn, Allegheny County, Pa., November 6, 1902; attended the public and high schools; was graduated from Randolph-Macon Military Academy, Front Royal, Va., in 1923; employed as a reporter on the Pitcairn Express in 1923 and worked on various newspapers until 1929; magistrate of Pitcairn 1925–1928; became editor of the Wilkinsburg Gazette in 1929 and president of the Wilkinsburg Gazette Publishing Co., in 1933; alternate delegate to the Republican National Convention at Cleveland in 1936; elected as a Republican to the Seventy-sixth Congress (January 3, 1939–January 3, 1941); unsuccessful candidate for reelection in 1940 to the Seventy-eighth Congress and for election in 1942 to the Seventy-eighth Congress; elected in 1946 to the Eightieth Congress (January 3, 1947–January 3, 1949); unsuccessful for reelection in 1948 to the Eighty-first Congress; resumed the publishing business; died in Wilkinsburg, Pa., December 11, 1957; interment in Woodlawn Cemetery.

McDOWELL, Joseph (father of Joseph Jefferson McDowell and cousin of Joseph McDowell (P G)), a Representative from North Carolina; born in Winchester, Va., February 15, 1756; moved to North Carolina with his parents in 1758; attended the common schools and Washington College (now Washington and Lee University), Lexington, Va.; served against the Indians on the frontier and later took an active part in the Revolution, attaining the rank of colonel before the close of the war; engaged in planting; delegate to the State constitutional convention which ratified the Constitution of the United States in 1789; member of the State house of commons in 1791 and 1792; unsuccessful candidate for election in 1794 to the Fourth Congress; elected to the Fifth Congress (March 4, 1797–March 3, 1799); was not a candidate for renomination in 1798; moved to Kentucky in 1800, but returned to North Carolina in 1801; died at his brother's home at Quaker Meadows, near Morganton, Burke County, N. C., February 5, 1801; interment in Quaker Meadow Cemetery, on his father's plantation, near Morganton, N. C.

McDOWELL, Joseph (P G) (cousin of Joseph McDowell), a Representative from North Carolina; born at "Pleasant Gardens," near Morganton, Burke (now McDowell) County, N. C., February 25, 1758; attended schools at Winchester, Va.; served in the Revolutionary Army; was commissioned a major and served in the Battle of Kings Mountain; was subsequently general of militia; studied law; was admitted to the bar in 1791 and practiced in Burke, Rowan, and Rutherford Counties, N. C.; member of the State house of commons 1785–1792; elected to the Third Congress (March 4, 1793–March 3, 1795); renominated but declined to be a candidate for reelection in 1794 to the Fourth Congress; resumed the practice of law and engaged in agricultural pursuits; member of the commission appointed to settle the boundary line between North Carolina and Tennessee in 1796; died on his estate, "Pleasant Gardens," near Morganton, N. C., March 7, 1799; interment at Round Hill on his estate.

McDOWELL, Joseph Jefferson (son of Joseph McDowell), a Representative from Ohio; born in Burke (now McDowell) County, N. C., November 13, 1800; moved to Kentucky with his mother in 1805 and to Augusta County, Va., in 1817; pursued preparatory studies; engaged in agricultural pursuits; moved to

Highland County, Ohio, in 1824 and continued agricultural pursuits; moved to Hillsboro, Highland County, in 1829 and engaged in mercantile pursuits; member of the State house of representatives in 1832; served in the State senate in 1833; appointed brigadier general of the State militia in 1834; studied law; was admitted to the bar in 1835 and commenced the practice of his profession in Hillsboro, Ohio; unsuccessful candidate for election in 1840 to the Twenty-seventh Congress; elected as a Democrat to the Twenty-eighth and Twenty-ninth Congresses (March 4, 1843–March 3, 1847); resumed the practice of law and also engaged in agricultural pursuits; died in Hillsboro, Ohio, January 17, 1877; interment in Hillsboro Cemetery.

McDUFFIE, George, a Representative and a Senator from South Carolina; born in Columbia County, Ga., August 10, 1790; was graduated from South Carolina College (now the University of South Carolina) at Columbia in 1813; studied law; was admitted to the bar in 1814 and commenced practice in Pendleton, Anderson County, S. C.; member of the State house of representatives 1818–1820; elected as a Democrat to the Seventeenth and to the six succeeding Congresses and served from March 4, 1821, until his resignation in 1834; one of the managers appointed by the House of Representatives in 1830 to conduct the impeachment proceedings against James H. Peck, United States judge for the district of Missouri; Governor of South Carolina 1834–1836; president of the board of trustees of South Carolina College; elected to the United States Senate to fill the vacancy caused by the resignation of William C. Preston; reelected, and served from December 23, 1842, until August 17, 1846, when he resigned; died at Cherry Hill, Sumter District, S. C., March 11, 1851.

McDUFFIE, John, a Representative from Alabama; born in River Ridge, Monroe County, Ala., September 25, 1883; educated by private tutors and attended Southern University, Greensboro, Ala.; was graduated from Alabama Polytechnic Institute at Auburn in 1904 and from the law department of the University of Alabama at Tuscaloosa in 1908; member of the State house of representatives 1907–1911; was admitted to the bar in 1908 and commenced practice in Monroeville, Ala.; prosecuting attorney for the first judicial circuit of Alabama 1911–1919; elected as a Democrat to the Sixty-sixth and to the eight succeeding Congresses and served from March 4, 1919, until his resignation, effective March 2, 1935, having been appointed a judge in the United States district court, and served until his death in Mobile, Ala., November 1, 1950; interment in Pine Crest Cemetery.

McDUFFIE, John Van, a Representative from Alabama; born in Addison, Steuben County, N. Y., May 16, 1841; attended the common schools; moved with his parents to Bureau County, Ill., in 1855; attended Luther College, Decorah, Iowa; enlisted in Company B, Second Regiment, Iowa Volunteer Cavalry, in July 1861 and served during the entire Civil War, leaving the Army in Selma, Ala.; settled in Lowndes County, Ala., and became a planter; studied law; was admitted to the bar and commenced practice in Hayneville, Ala.; elected judge of probate in 1868; reelected in 1874 and served until 1880; elected a member of the State constitutional convention in 1875, but did not serve; delegate to the Republican National Convention at Philadelphia in 1872 and at Cincinnati in 1876; unsuccessful Republican candidate for election in 1886 to the Fiftieth Congress; successfully contested the election of Louis W. Turpin to the Fifty-first Congress and served from June 4, 1890, until March 3, 1891; unsuccessfully contested the election of Louis W. Turpin to the Fifty-second Congress; engaged in mercantile pursuits and continued as a planter; died in Hayneville, Lowndes County, Ala., November 18, 1896; interment in Pines Cemetery.

McENERY, Samuel Douglas, a Senator from Louisiana; born in Monroe, Ouachita Parish, La., May 28, 1837; attended the public schools, Spring Hill (Ala.) College, the United States Naval Academy at Annapolis, Md., and the University of Virginia at Charlottesville; was graduated from the State and National Law School, Poughkeepsie, N. Y., in 1859; at the beginning of the Civil War entered the Confederate Army as a member of a volunteer company called the Pelican Greys, and in 1862 was commissioned a lieutenant under General Magruder in Virginia; was later placed in charge of a camp of instruction at Trenton, La.; was admitted to the bar at Monroe, La., in 1866 and commenced the practice of his profession; elected as a Democrat Lieutenant Governor of Louisiana in 1879; upon the death of Gov. L. A. Wiltz in October 1881, was his successor as executive of the State; elected Governor of Louisiana in 1884; unsuccessful candidate for reelection in 1888; appointed associate justice of the supreme court of Louisiana in 1888 for a term of twelve years and served until March 4, 1897, when he resigned, having been elected Senator; unsuccessful candidate for Governor of Louisiana in 1892; elected as a Democrat to the United States Senate in 1896; reelected in 1902 and again in 1908, and served from March 4, 1897, until his death in New Orleans, La., June 28, 1910; interment in Metairie Cemetery.

McETTRICK, Michael Joseph, a Representative from Massachusetts; born in Roxbury, Norfolk County, Mass., June 22, 1848; was graduated from the Washington Grammar and the Roxbury Latin Schools; became a journalist; assistant assessor of Boston in 1884; member of the State house of representatives 1885–1891, and chairman of the Democratic members of the house; served in the State senate in 1892; elected as a Democrat to the Fifty-third Congress (March 4, 1893–March 3, 1895); was an unsuccessful candidate for renomination in 1894 to the Fifty-fourth Congress; again a member of the State house of representatives in 1906, 1907, and 1913; served in the State senate in 1908; engaged in the real-estate business in Boston, Mass., until his death there on December 31, 1921; interment in Calvary Cemetery.

McEWAN, Thomas, Jr., a Representative from New Jersey; born in Paterson, N. J., February 26, 1854; attended the public schools; became a civil engineer; delegate to and secretary of every Republican convention of New Jersey and Hudson County 1877–1896; secretary of the Hudson County Republican general committee 1878–1893; attended the law department of Columbia University; was admitted to the bar about 1885 and commenced practice in New York City and Jersey City, N. J.; assessor of the fourth district, Jersey City, in 1886 and 1887; secretary to Dr. Morgan Dix, rector of Trinity Church, New York City, 1886–1906; tax assessor of Jersey City in 1887 and 1888; secretary and one of the governors of the Union League Club of Hudson County from the time of its formation until 1896; United States commissioner and chief supervisor of elections for the district of New Jersey from August 1892 to October 1893; delegate to the Republican National Convention at Minneapolis in 1892 which nominated Harrison and Reid, and at St. Louis in 1896 which nominated McKinley and Hobart; member of the State house of assembly in 1893 and 1894 and served as Republican leader in 1894; elected as a Republican to the Fifty-fourth and Fifty-fifth Congresses (March 4, 1895–March 3, 1899); was not a candidate for renomination in 1898; resumed the practice of law and also engaged in banking; president of the Highland Trust Co., West Hoboken, N. J., from 1904 until July 1, 1924, when he retired; controller of Jersey City 1906 and 1907; died in Jersey City, N. J., September 11, 1926; interment in Flower Hill Cemetery, North Bergen, N. J.

McFADDEN, Louis Thomas, a Representative from Pennsylvania; born in Granville Center, Troy Township, Bradford County, Pa., July 25, 1876; attended the public schools; worked on a farm during his boyhood; was graduated from Warner's Commercial College, Elmira, N. Y.; at the age of sixteen entered the employ of the First National Bank, Canton, Pa.; in 1899 was elected cashier, and became its president on January 11, 1916, serving until 1925; served as treasurer of the Pennsylvania Bankers' Association in 1906 and 1907 and as president in 1914 and 1915; appointed in 1914 by the agricultural societies of the State of Pennsylvania as a trustee of Pennsylvania State College; elected as a Republican to the Sixty-fourth and to the nine succeeding Congresses (March 4, 1915–January 3, 1935); unsuccessful candidate for reelection in 1934 to the Seventy-fourth Congress and for nomination in 1936 to the Seventy-fifth Congress; died October 1, 1936, while on a visit in New York City, N. Y.; interment in East Canton Cemetery, Canton, Pa.

McFADDEN, Obadiah Benton, a Delegate from the Territory of Washington; born in West Middletown, Washington County, Pa., November 18, 1815; attended the public schools and McKeever Academy, West Middletown, Pa.; studied law; was admitted to the bar in 1843 and commenced practice; member of the State house of representatives in 1843; elected prothonotary of Washington County; appointed associate justice of the supreme court of the Territory of Oregon in 1853 and of the Territory of Washington in 1854 and served as chief justice of the latter from 1858 to 1861; member of the legislative council and chosen its president in 1861; resumed the practice of law in Olympia, Wash., and also engaged in agricultural pursuits; elected as a Democrat to the Forty-third Congress (March 4, 1873–March 3, 1875); was not a candidate for renomination in 1874; died in Olympia, Wash., June 25, 1875; interment in the Masonic Cemetery.

McFALL, John Joseph, a Representative from California; born in Buffalo, Erie County, N. Y., February 20, 1918; attended the public schools of Manteca, Calif., and graduated from Modesto (Calif.) Junior College in 1936, from the University of California in 1938, and from the law school of the same university in 1941; admitted to the bar in 1941 and employed as an attorney in Oakland, Calif., in 1941 and 1942; in World War II served as staff sergeant in Security Intelligence Corps 1942–1946; engaged in the practice of law in Manteca, Calif., in 1946; elected city councilman and mayor of Manteca in 1948, resigning in 1950; member of California Assembly 1951–1956; delegate to all State Democratic Conventions 1948–1958; elected as a Democrat to the Eighty-fifth and Eighty-sixth Congresses (January 3, 1957–January 3, 1961). *Reelected to the Eighty-seventh Congress.*

McFARLAN, Duncan, a Representative from North Carolina; born at Laurel Hill, Scotland County, N. C.; attended the common schools; engaged in agricultural pursuits; member of the State house of commons in 1792; served in the State senate in 1793, 1795, 1800, and 1807–1809; unsuccessful candidate for election in 1802 to the Eighth Congress; elected to the Ninth Congress (March 4, 1805–March 3, 1807); engaged in mercantile and agricultural pursuits; died at Laurel Hill, N. C., September 7, 1816; interment in Laurel Hill Cemetery.

McFARLAND, Ernest William, a Senator from Arizona; born on a farm near Earlsboro, Pottawatomie County, Okla., October 9, 1894; attended the rural schools and Earlsboro and Seminole High Schools; was graduated from East Central State Teachers' College, Ada, Okla., and from the University of Oklahoma at Norman; during the First World War served in the United States Navy; after the war moved to Phoenix, Ariz., and was employed as a clerk in a bank; was graduated from the law department of Stanford (Calif.) University; was admitted to the bar in 1920 and commenced practice in Casa Grande, Pinal County, Ariz.; assistant attorney general of Arizona in 1923 and 1924, and county attorney of Pinal County 1925–1930; moved to Florence, Ariz., in 1925; judge of the superior court of Pinal County 1936–1940; elected as a Democrat to the United States Senate in 1940; reelected in 1946 and served from January 3, 1941, to January 3, 1953; unsuccessful candidate for reelection in 1952; elected Governor of Arizona in 1954; reelected in 1956 and served from January 1955 to January 1959; unsuccessful candidate for election to the United States Senate in 1958; lawyer; is a resident of Phoenix, Ariz.

McFARLAND, William, a Representative from Tennessee; born at Springvale Farm, near Morristown, Jefferson (now Hamblen) County, Tenn., September 15, 1821; attended the common schools and Tusculum College, Greene County, Tenn.; studied law; was admitted to the bar in 1861 and engaged in the practice of law in 1865 in Dandridge, Morristown, and Greeneville; held several local judicial offices; appointed judge of the county court in 1870; elected as a Democrat to the Forty-fourth Congress (March 4, 1875–March 3, 1877); unsuccessful candidate for reelection in 1876 to the Forty-fifth Congress; again resumed the practice of his profession; mayor of Morristown four years; member of the board of education; died in Morristown, Tenn., April 12, 1900; interment in City Cemetery.

McFARLANE, William Doddridge, a Representative from Texas; born in Greenwood, Sebastian County, Ark., July 17, 1894; attended the public schools and the University of Arkansas at Fayetteville 1909–1914; engaged in the mercantile business in Greenwood Ark., 1914–1918; during the First World War served as a private during training, was commissioned a second lieutenant in August 1918, and served until honorably discharged on December 13, 1918; returned to the University of Arkansas in 1919 and was graduated therefrom the same year; graduated from Kent Law School, Chicago, Ill., in 1921; was admitted to the bar the same year and commenced practice in Graham, Young County, Tex.; member of the State house of representatives 1923–1927; served in the State senate 1927–1931; delegate to several Democratic State conventions; elected as a Democrat to the Seventy-third, Seventy-fourth, and Seventy-fifth Congresses (March 4, 1933–January 3, 1939); unsuccessful candidate for renomination in 1938; resumed the practice of law; special assistant to the attorney general at Texarkana, Tex., 1941–1944; director of the Surplus Property Smaller War Plants Corporation, Washington, D. C., from December 1944 to January 1946; special assistant to the Attorney General in Washington, D. C., January 1946 to July 1, 1951; unsuccessful candidate in 1951 to fill a vacancy in the Eighty-second Congress; with Lands Division, Justice Department, since December 1, 1951; resides in Washington, D. C.

McGANN, Lawrence Edward, a Representative from Illinois; born in Galway, Ireland, February 2, 1852; immigrated to the United States in 1855 with his mother, who settled in Milford, Mass.; attended the public schools; moved to Chicago, Ill. with his mother in 1865 and worked at the boot and shoe trade until 1879; employed as a clerk in the service of the city until 1885; appointed superintendent of streets January 1, 1885, and served until his resignation in May 1891; elected as a Democrat to the Fifty-second and Fifty-third Congresses (March 4, 1891–March 3, 1895); presented credentials as a Member-elect to the Fifty-fourth Congress and served from March 4, 1895, until December 2, 1895, when he was succeeded by Hugh R. Belknap, who contested his election; served as president of the

Chicago General Railways in 1896 and 1897; commissioner of public works of Chicago 1898–1901; city controller 1901–1907; again commissioner of public works 1911–1915; retired from active business pursuits in 1916 and resided in Oak Park, Ill., until his death in that city on July 22, 1928; interment in Mount Olivet Cemetery, Chicago, Ill.

McGARVEY, Robert Neill, a Representative from Pennsylvania; born in Philadelphia, Pa., August 14, 1888; attended the public and parochial schools and the University of Pennsylvania Business College; engaged as a telegrapher and as manager of a news bureau; became an investment broker in 1922; elected as a Republican to the Eightieth Congress (January 3, 1947–January 3, 1949); unsuccessful candidate for reelection in 1948 to the Eighty-first Congress; returned to the investment brokerage business; died in Philadelphia, Pa., June 28, 1952; interment in Holy Cross Cemetery, Yeadon, Delaware County, Pa.

McGAUGHEY, Edward Wilson, a Representative from Indiana; born near Greencastle, Putnam County, Ind., January 16, 1817; attended the public schools; deputy clerk of Putnam County; studied law; was admitted to the bar in 1835 and commenced practice in Greencastle. Ind.; member of the State house of representatives in 1839 and 1840; served in the State senate for the session December 5, 1842, to February 13, 1843; resigned before the beginning of the next session; unsuccessful candidate for election to the Twenty-eighth Congress; elected as a Whig to the Twenty-ninth Congress (March 4, 1845–March 3, 1847); unsuccessful candidate for reelection in 1846 to the Thirtieth Congress; moved to Rockville, Parke County, Ind., in 1846 and resumed the practice of law; elected to the Thirty-first Congress (March 4, 1849–March 3, 1851); unsuccessful candidate for reelection in 1850 to the Thirty-second Congress; nominated by President Taylor as Governor of Minnesota Territory in 1849, but the Senate failed to confirm the nomination; moved to California in 1852; died in San Francisco, Calif., August 6, 1852; interment in Yerba Buena Cemetery.

McGAVIN, Charles, a Representative from Illinois; born in Riverton, Sangamon County, Ill., January 10, 1874; attended the common schools in Springfield and the high school in Mount Olive, Ill.; studied law; was admitted to the bar in 1897 and practiced two years in Springfield; moved to Chicago in 1899 and resumed the practice of law; assistant city attorney of Chicago in 1903 and 1904; elected as a Republican to the Fifty-ninth and Sixtieth Congresses (March 4, 1905–March 3, 1909); was not a candidate for renomination in 1908; resumed the practice of law in Chicago; moved to Los Angeles in 1912 and practiced law until 1915, when he returned to Chicago; delegate to the Republican National Convention at Chicago in 1920; died in Chicago, Ill., December 17, 1940; interment in Mount Auburn Cemetery, Berwyn, Ill.

McGEE, Gale William, a Senator from Wyoming; born in Lincoln, Lancaster County, Nebr., March 17, 1915; graduated from Norfolk (Nebr.) High School in 1932, Nebraska State Teachers College at Wayne in 1936, University of Colorado at Boulder in 1939, and University of Chicago in 1947; professor of American History at Crofton (Nebr.) High School in 1936 and 1937, Kearney (Nebr.) High School 1937–1940, Nebraska Wesleyan University 1940–1943, Iowa State College of Agricultural and Mechanical Arts in 1943 and 1944, University of Notre Dame in 1944 and 1945, University of Chicago in 1945 and 1946, and University of Wyoming 1946–1958; legislative assistant to Senator Joseph C. O'Mahoney of Wyoming in 1955 and 1956; elected as a Democrat to the United States Senate for the term commencing January 3, 1959, and ending January 3, 1965.

McGEHEE, Daniel Rayford, a Representative from Mississippi; born in Little Springs, Miss., September 10, 1883; attended the public schools; was graduated from Mississippi College at Clinton in 1903 and from the law department of the University of Mississippi at Oxford in 1909; was admitted to the bar in 1909 and commenced practice at Meadville, Miss.; also engaged in agricultural pursuits and banking; member of the State senate 1924–1928; served in the State house of representatives 1928–1932; again a member of the State senate 1932–1934; elected as a Democrat to the Seventy-fourth and to the five succeeding Congresses (January 3, 1935–January 3, 1947); unsuccessful candidate for renomination in 1946 to the Eightieth Congress; resumed the practice of law, agricultural pursuits, and banking, and is a resident of Meadville, Miss.

McGILL, George, a Senator from Kansas; born on a farm near Russell, Lucas County, Iowa, February 12, 1879; moved to Kansas with his parents, who settled on a farm near Dundee, Barton County, in 1884; attended the common schools; was graduated from Central Normal College, Great Bend, Kans., in 1900; studied law; was admitted to the bar in 1902 and commenced practice in Hoisington, Kans.; moved to Wichita, Sedgwick County, Kans., in 1904 and continued the practice of law; deputy county attorney of Sedgwick County, Kans., 1907–1911 and county attorney 1911–1915; delegate to the Democratic State conventions in 1924, 1928, and 1944; serving as chairman in 1924; delegate to the Democratic National Conventions in 1928, 1936, and 1944; elected as a Democrat to the United States Senate in 1930 to fill the vacancy caused by the resignation of Charles Curtis; reelected in 1932 and served from December 1, 1930, to January 3, 1939; unsuccessful candidate for reelection in 1938 and for election in 1942, 1948, and 1954; member of the United States Tariff Commission from August 7, 1944, until his resignation on June 16, 1954; resumed the practice of law in Wichita, Kans., where he now resides.

McGILLICUDDY, Daniel John, a Representative from Maine; born in Lewiston, Maine, August 27, 1859; attended the common schools, and was graduated from Bowdoin College, Brunswick, Maine, in 1881; studied law; was admitted to the bar in 1883 and commenced practice in Lewiston, Maine; member of the State house of representatives in 1884 and 1885; mayor of Lewiston in 1887, 1890, and 1902; delegate at large from Maine to the Democratic National Conventions in 1892, 1904, 1912, and 1920; unsuccessful candidate for election in 1906 to the Sixtieth Congress and in 1908 to the Sixty-first Congress; elected as a Democrat to the Sixty-second, Sixty-third, and Sixty-fourth Congresses (March 4, 1911–March 3, 1917); unsuccessful candidate for reelection in 1916 to the Sixty-fifth Congress and for election in 1918 to the Sixty-sixth Congress; member of the Democratic National Committee 1917–1932; continued the practice of law in Lewiston, Maine, until his death in that city on July 30, 1936; interment in Mount Hope Cemetery.

McGINLEY, Donald Francis, a Representative from Nebraska; born on a ranch in Keith County, near Keystone, Nebr., June 30, 1920; attended the public schools in Keystone, Nebr.; graduated from Ogallala (Nebr.) High School in 1938 and from Notre Dame University in 1942; during World War II enlisted in the United States Army Air Corps in 1942 and served until discharged in 1945, with twenty months in England as a cryptographer with a B–24 group of the Eighth Air Force; reporter and copy reader on the Denver Register in 1945 and 1946; graduated from Georgetown University, Washington, D. C., in 1949; was admitted to the bar and commenced the practice of law in Ogallala, Nebr., in 1950; Arthur County attorney 1951–1955; member of the Nebraska Legislature 1955–1959; elected as a Democrat to the Eighty-sixth Congress (January 3, 1959–January 3, 1961); unsuccessful candidate for reelection in 1960 to the Eighty-seventh Congress; resides in Ogallala, Nebr.

McGLENNON, Cornelius Augustine, a Representative from New Jersey; born in East Newark, N. J., December 10, 1878; attended Holy Cross School, Harrison, N. J., and St. Francis Xavier's High School in New York City; was graduated from Seton Hall College, South Orange, N. J., in 1899; public and high-school principal 1901–1926; studied law at the New Jersey Law School, Newark, N. J.; was admitted to the bar in 1916 and commenced practice in East Newark, N. J.; member of the State senate in 1917 and 1918, serving as Democratic floor leader in 1918; mayor of East Newark 1907–1919; elected as a Democrat to the Sixty-sixth Congress (March 4, 1919–March 3, 1921); unsuccessful candidate for reelection in 1920 to the Sixty-seventh Congress; resumed the practice of his profession in East Newark, N. J.; delegate to the Democratic National Convention at San Francisco in 1920; appointed judge of the court of errors and appeals in 1924 and served until his death; also supervising principal at Harrison, N. J., 1926–1931; died in Newark, N. J., June 13, 1931; interment in Holy Sepulchre Cemetery, East Orange, N. J.

McGLINCHEY, Herbert Joseph, a Representative from Pennsylvania; born in Philadelphia, Pa., November 7, 1904; attended the public and parochial schools; engaged as a manufacturers' agent in Philadelphia, Pa.; supervisor of labor and industry for the eastern district of Pennsylvania 1935–1937; president of the Board of Mercantile Appraisers, Philadelphia, Pa., 1937–1944; member of the Philadelphia Democratic county committee since 1933; elected as a Democrat to the Seventy-ninth Congress (January 3, 1945–January 3, 1947); was an unsuccessful candidate for reelection in 1946 to the Eightieth Congress, for election in 1948 to the Eighty-first Congress, and for election in 1956 to the Eighty-fifth Congress; resumed his occupation as a manufacturers' agent; member of Tax Equalization Board 1957–; is a resident of Philadelphia, Pa.

McGOVERN, George Stanley, a Representative from South Dakota; born in Avon, Bon Homme County, S. Dak., July 19, 1922; attended the public schools of Mitchell, S. Dak., and Dakota Wesleyan University 1940–1942; enlisted in the United States Army Air Force in June 1942, flew thirty-five combat missions as a pilot of B–24 bombers in the European Theater, and was discharged from the service in July 1945; awarded Distinguished Flying Cross and Air Medal with three Oak Leaf Clusters; returned to Dakota Wesleyan University and graduated in 1946; held teaching assistantship and fellowship at Northwestern University, Evanston, Ill., 1948–1950; professor of history and government at Dakota Wesleyan University 1950–1953; executive secretary of South Dakota Democratic Party 1953–1956; member of Advisory Committee on Political Organization of Democratic National Committee 1954–1956; elected as a Democrat to the Eighty-fifth and Eighty-sixth Congresses (January 3, 1957–January 3, 1961); was not a candidate for renomination in 1960, but was unsuccessful for election to the United States Senate; appointed special assistant to the President January 20, 1961, as director of the Food for Peace Program; is a resident of Mitchell, S. Dak.

McGOWAN, Jonas Hartzell, a Representative from Michigan; born in the township of Smithtown, Columbiana (now Mahoning) County, Ohio, April 2, 1837; attended a seminary in Alliance, Ohio; moved with his parents to Orland, Steuben County, Ind., in 1854; was graduated from the University of Michigan at Ann Arbor in 1861; taught in the city schools of Coldwater, Mich.,

for one year; during the Civil War enlisted as a private in the Fifth Regiment, Michigan Volunteer Cavalry; afterward promoted to captain; raised a company for the Ninth Regiment, Michigan Volunteer Cavalry, and went into active service with that regiment in the spring of 1863; by reason of injuries received in a cavalry charge was disabled, and resigned his commission in February 1864, and returned to Coldwater, Mich.; studied law; was admitted to the bar in 1867 and commenced practice; prosecuting attorney of Branch County 1868–1872; member of the State senate; served as regent of the University of Michigan for seven years; elected as a Republican to the Forty-fifth and Forty-sixth Congresses (March 4, 1877–March 3, 1881); declined to be a candidate for renomination in 1880 to the Forty-seventh Congress; resumed the practice of his profession in Washington, D. C., where he died on July 5, 1909; interment in Oak Grove Cemetery, Coldwater, Mich.

McGRANERY, James Patrick, a Representative from Pennsylvania; born in Philadelphia, Pa., July 8, 1895; attended the parochial schools and Maher Preparatory School, Philadelphia, Pa.; during the First World War served as observation pilot in the United States Air Force and as adjutant in the One Hundred and Eleventh Infantry 1917–1919; was graduated from the law department of Temple University, Philadelphia, Pa., in 1928; was admitted to the bar the same year and commenced practice in Philadelphia, Pa.; admitted to practice before the United States Supreme Court in 1939; member of the Democratic State committee 1928–1932; unsuccessful candidate for election as district attorney of Philadelphia in 1931 and for election to the Seventy-fourth Congress in 1934; served as chairman of the Registration Commission of the city of Philadelphia in 1935; elected as a Democrat to the Seventy-fifth and to the three succeeding Congresses and served from January 3, 1937, until his resignation on November 17, 1943, to become the assistant to the Attorney General at Washington, D. C., and served until October 9, 1946, at which time he was sworn in as a United States district judge for the eastern district of Pennsylvania, in which capacity he served until May 26, 1952, when he resigned to accept an appointment as Attorney General of the United States, which office he held from May 27, 1952, until January 20, 1953; returned to the general practice of law in Washington, D. C., in 1954, where he now resides.

McGRATH, Christopher Columbus, a Representative from New York; born in New York City, N. Y., May 15, 1902; attended parochial schools; was graduated from Clason Military Academy, Bronx, N. Y., in 1921 and from Fordham University School of Law, New York, N. Y., in 1924; was admitted to the bar in 1927 and commenced the practice of law in New York City; member of the State assembly 1928–1935; elected judge of the Municipal Court of New York City in 1935, reelected in 1945 for ten-year term, and served until his resignation on December 31, 1948, having been elected to Congress; elected as a Democrat to the Eighty-first and Eighty-second Congresses (January 3, 1949–January 3, 1953); was not a candidate for renomination in 1952; elected surrogate judge of Bronx County in 1952 for a fourteen-year term; member of faculty of Fordham University School of Law; is a resident of New York City, N. Y.

McGRATH, James Howard, a Senator from Rhode Island; born in Woonsocket, Providence County, R. I., November 28, 1903; attended the parochial schools; was graduated from La Salle Academy, Providence, R. I., in 1922, from Providence (R. I.) College in 1926, and from the law department of Boston University, Boston, Mass., in 1929; was admitted to the bar the same year and commenced practice in Providence; city solicitor of Central Falls, R. I., 1930–1934; engaged in the real estate and insurance business and was also interested in banking; member and vice chairman of the Democratic State Committee of Rhode Island 1928–1930 and chairman 1930–1934; delegate to the Democratic National Conventions in 1932, 1936, 1944, 1948, 1952, 1956, and 1960; chairman of the Democratic National Committee 1947–1949; United States district attorney for Rhode Island from 1934 until his resignation in 1940, having been elected Governor; elected Governor of Rhode Island in 1940, 1942, and 1944 and served until his resignation in October 1945, having been appointed solicitor general of the United States and served until his resignation in October 1946 to become a candidate for United States Senator; elected as a Democrat in 1946 to the United States Senate for the term commencing January 3, 1947, and served until his resignation on August 23, 1949, having been appointed Attorney General of the United States, taking the oath of office August 24, 1949; resigned April 3, 1952; resumed the practice of law in Washington, D. C., and Providence, R. I.; unsuccessful candidate for the nomination as United States Senator in 1960; is a resident of Providence, R. I.

McGRATH, John Joseph, a Representative from California; born in Limerick, Ireland, July 23, 1872; attended the national schools and Christian Brothers College in Cork; immigrated to the United States when seventeen and located in Chicago, Ill.; studied law for two years; engaged as a salesman for two years and as a sales manager for eighteen years; naturalized July 25, 1896; postmaster of San Mateo, Calif., 1916–1925; justice of the peace of San Mateo County 1928–1932; president of Tri-City Chamber of Commerce for four years; elected as a Democrat to the Seventy-third, Seventy-fourth, and Seventy-fifth Congresses (March 4, 1933–January 3, 1939); unsuccessful candidate for reelection in 1938 to the Seventy-sixth Congress; commissioner of immigration and naturalization for San Francisco, Calif., in 1939 and 1940; retired; died in San Mateo, Calif., August 25, 1951; interment in St. John's Cemetery.

McGREGOR, J. Harry, a Representative from Ohio; born on a farm near Unionport, Jefferson County, Ohio, September 30, 1896; attended the public schools, West Lafayette (Ohio) College, and Oberlin (Ohio) College; during the First World War served as a sergeant with the One Hundred and Seventy-sixth Field Artillery, United States Army, in 1917 and 1918; engaged in the lumber and general contracting business at West Lafayette, Ohio, 1918–1945; member of the school board of West Lafayette, Ohio, for eight years; member of the State house of representatives 1935–1940, serving as minority whip 1937–1939 and as majority leader and speaker pro tempore in 1939 and 1940; elected as a Republican to the Seventy-sixth Congress to fill the vacancy caused by the death of William A. Ashbrook; reelected to the Seventy-seventh and to the eight succeeding Congresses and served from February 27, 1940, until his death; had been renominated to the Eighty-sixth Congress; died in Coshocton, Ohio, October 7, 1958; interment in Fairfield Cemetery, West Lafayette, Ohio.

McGREW, James Clark, a Representative from West Virginia; born near Brandonville, Monongalia County, Va. (now West Virginia), September 14, 1813; attended the common schools; engaged in mercantile pursuits and banking; delegate to the Virginia secession convention in 1861 and voted against disunion; mayor of Kingwood, Preston County, Va. (now West Virginia), 1863–1865; member of the West Virginia House of Delegates 1863–1865; managing director of the West Virginia Insane Hospital for four years; elected as a Republican to the Forty-first and Forty-second Congresses (March 4, 1869–March 3, 1873); declined to be a candidate for renomination in 1872; again mayor of Kingwood in 1879 and 1880; resumed banking

in Kingwood, W. Va., from 1886 until his death; last survivor of the Virginia secession convention; died in Kingwood, W. Va., September 18, 1910; interment in Maplewood Cemetery.

McGROARTY, John Steven, a Representative from California; born near Wilkes-Barre in Foster Township, Luzerne County, Pa., August 20, 1862; attended the public schools and Harry Hillman Academy, Wilkes-Barre, Pa.; treasurer of Luzerne County, Pa., 1890–1893; studied law; was admitted to the bar in 1894 and commenced practice in Wilkes-Barre; moved to Montana and was employed in an executive position with the Anaconda Copper Mining Co. at Butte and Anaconda 1896–1901; moved to Los Angeles, Calif., in 1901 and engaged in journalism; Knight of St. Gregory, conferred by Pope Pius XI in 1930; Knight Commander of Isabella the Catholic, conferred by King Alfonso XIII of Spain in 1932 and confirmed in 1933 by the Spanish Republic; elected poet laureate of California by the State legislature in 1933; author of numerous books and dramas; elected as a Democrat to the Seventy-fourth and Seventy-fifth Congresses (January 3, 1935–January 3, 1939); was not a candidate for renomination in 1938; resumed the profession of journalism in Tujunga, Los Angeles County, Calif.; unsuccessful candidate for the Democratic nomination for secretary of state of California in 1938; died in Los Angeles, Calif., August 7, 1944; interment in Calvary Cemetery.

McGUGIN, Harold Clement, a Representative from Kansas; born on a farm near Liberty, Montgomery County, Kans., November 22, 1893; attended the public schools of Liberty, Kans.; moved to Coffeyville, Kans., in 1908; was graduated from the high school at Coffeyville in 1912, and from the law department of Washburn College, Topeka, Kans., in 1915, and took a postgraduate course in English law at the Inns of Court, London, England, in 1919; was admitted to the bar in 1915 and commenced practice in Coffeyville, Kans.; during the First World War served as a second lieutenant, Adjutant General's Department, at Brest, France; member of the State house of representatives 1927–1929; city attorney of Coffeyville in 1929; elected as a Republican to the Seventy-second and Seventy-third Congresses (March 4, 1931–January 3, 1935); unsuccessful candidate for reelection in 1934 to the Seventy-fourth Congress and for election in 1936 to the Seventy-fifth Congress; resumed the practice of law; during the Second World War enlisted in the United States Army in 1942, advancing from captain to lieutenant colonel, and served in France, where he contacted an incurable disease; died in the Army and Navy General Hospital at Hot Springs, Ark., March 7, 1946; interment in Restlawn Cemetery, Coffeyville, Kans.

McGUIRE, Bird Segle (cousin of William Neville), a Delegate and a Representative from Oklahoma; born in Belleville, St. Clair County, Ill., October 13, 1865; moved to Randolph County, Mo., in 1867 with his parents, who settled on a farm attended the common schools; moved to Chautauqua County, Kans., in the spring of 1881, and then to Indian Territory; engaged in the cattle business; attended the State normal school at Emporia, Kans.; taught school several terms; later attended the law department of the University of Kansas at Lawrence; was admitted to the bar in 1889 and commenced practice in Chautauqua, Kans.; prosecuting attorney of Chautauqua County, Kans., 1890–1894; moved to Pawnee County, Okla., in 1894 and practiced law in Pawnee; appointed assistant United States attorney for Oklahoma Territory in 1897, in which capacity he served until after his nomination for Congress; elected as a Republican a Delegate to the Fifty-eighth and Fifty-ninth Congresses and served from March 4, 1903, to March 3, 1907; elected as a Representative to the Sixtieth and to the three succeeding Congresses and served from November 16, 1907, when Oklahoma was admitted as a State into the Union, until March 3, 1915; was not a candidate for renomination in 1914 to the Sixty-fourth Congress; resumed the practice of his profession in Tulsa, Okla.; also owned and operated a large ranch near Bartlesville, Okla.; died in Tulsa, Okla., November 9, 1930; interment in Memorial Park Cemetery.

McGUIRE, John Andrew, a Representative from Connecticut; born in Wallingford, New Haven County, Conn., February 28, 1906; attended the public schools; student at Lyman Hall, Wallingford, Conn., in 1924 and graduated from Dartmouth College, Hanover, N. H., in 1928; employed as a bank clerk 1928–1934; town clerk of Wallingford from January 1, 1934, to December 31, 1949; Democratic State Chairman in 1946; engaged in general insurance business in Wallingford, Conn., in 1935; elected as a Democrat to the Eighty-first and Eighty-second Congresses (January 3, 1949–January 3, 1953); unsuccessful candidate for reelection in 1952 to the Eighty-third Congress; resumed insurance, real-estate, and travel business; member of Connecticut State Legislature 1961–; resides in Wallingford, Conn.

McHATTON, Robert Lytle, a Representative from Kentucky; born in Fayette County, Va. (now Kentucky), November 17, 1788; attended the common schools; engaged in agricultural pursuits; member of the State house of representatives 1814–1816; served as major of the Seventy-seventh Regiment of State militia in 1816; elected as a Jackson Democrat to the Nineteenth Congress to fill the vacancy caused by the death of James Johnson; reelected to the Twentieth Congress and served from December 7, 1826, to March 3, 1829; resumed agricultural pursuits; died in Marion County, Ind., May 20, 1835; interment in the Old Cemetery, Georgetown, Ky.

McHENRY, Henry Davis (son of John Hardin McHenry), a Representative from Kentucky; born in Hartford, Ohio County, Ky., February 27, 1826; attended the public schools at Hartford, and was graduated from the law department of Transylvania University, Lexington, Ky., in 1845; was admitted to the bar in 1845 and commenced practice in Hartford; member of the State house of representatives 1851–1853 and 1865–1867; served in the State senate 1861–1865; member of the Democratic National Committee from 1872 until his death; elected as a Democrat to the Forty-second Congress (March 4, 1871–March 3, 1873); resumed the practice of his profession in Hartford; delegate to the State constitutional convention in 1890; died in Hartford, Ky., December 17, 1890; interment in Oakwood Cemetery.

McHENRY, James, a Delegate from Maryland; born in Ballymena, County Antrim, Ireland, November 16, 1753; pursued classical studies; immigrated to the United States about 1771 and settled in Philadelphia, Pa.; attended Newark Academy in Delaware; studied medicine under Dr. Benjamin Rush, Philadelphia, Pa.; during the Revolution was appointed assistant surgeon in 1776 and later surgeon in the Fifth Pennsylvania Battalion; secretary to General Washington 1778–1780; appointed in 1780 on the staff of General Lafayette and served in that capacity until the end of the war; member of the State senate 1781–1786; Member of the Continental Congress 1783–1786; delegate to the Federal Constitutional Convention in Philadelphia in 1787; appointed Secretary of War in the Cabinet of President Washington and served from January 29, 1796, to May 13, 1800; retired from public life and active pursuits and resided at "Fayetteville," his country estate, near Baltimore, Md., until his death on May 3, 1816; interment in Westminster (Presbyterian) Churchyard, Baltimore, Md.

McHENRY, John Geiser, a Representative from Pennsylvania; born in Benton Township, Columbia County, Pa., April 26, 1868; attended the public schools and Orangeville Academy; banker and manufacturer, and also engaged in agricultural pursuits; organizer of the Grange national banks throughout Pennsylvania; elected as a Democrat to the Sixtieth, Sixty-first, and Sixty-second Congresses and served from March 4, 1907, until his death in Benton, Pa., December 27, 1912; interment in Benton Cemetery.

McHENRY, John Hardin (father of Henry Davis McHenry), a Representative from Kentucky; born near Springfield, Washington County, Ky., October 13, 1797; was tutored privately; studied law; was admitted to the bar in 1818 and commenced practice in Leitchfield, Ky.; appointed postmaster of Leitchfield October 8, 1819; major of the Eighty-seventh Regiment, Kentucky Militia, in 1821; appointed Commonwealth attorney by Governor Adair in 1822; moved to Hartford, Ky., in 1823; appointed Commonwealth attorney by Governor Metcalfe in 1831 and again by Governor Moorehead in 1837; commissioned colonel in the State militia in 1837; member of the State house of representatives from Ohio County in 1840; unsuccessful Whig candidate for election in 1840 to the Twenty-seventh Congress; appointed on the board of the Transylvania University in 1843; elected as a Whig to the Twenty-ninth Congress (March 4, 1845–March 3, 1847); was nominated for reelection in 1846, but withdrew his name on the eve of election; resumed the practice of law; member of the State constitutional convention in 1849 and served as chairman; moved to Owensboro, Ky., in 1854; judge of the circuit court of several counties in 1854; died in Owensboro, Ky., on November 1, 1871; interment in Elmwood Cemetery

McILVAINE, Abraham Robinson, a Representative from Pennsylvania; born in Ridley, Delaware County, Pa., August 14, 1804; attended the common schools; engaged in agricultural pursuits in Chester County, Pa.; member of the State house of representatives in 1836 and 1837; presidential elector on the Whig ticket of Harrison and Tyler in 1840; elected as a Whig to the Twenty-eighth, Twenty-ninth, and Thirtieth Congresses (March 4, 1843–March 3, 1849); unsuccessful candidate for renomination in 1848; resumed agricultural interests and also engaged in the iron business; died on his estate, "Springton Farms" in Chester County, Pa., August 22, 1863; interment in Caln Orthodox Quaker Meeting Burial Ground in the Chester Valley, near Downingtown; reinterment in Northwood Cemetery, Downingtown, Pa.

McILVAINE, Joseph, a Senator from New Jersey; born in Bristol, Bucks County, Pa., October 2, 1769; pursued an academic course; studied law; was admitted to the bar of the supreme court of New Jersey in 1790 and commenced practice in Burlington, N. J., in 1791; clerk of Burlington County 1796–1800; clerk of the county court 1800–1823; United States attorney for New Jersey 1801–1820; appointed judge of the superior court of New Jersey in 1818, but declined; elected as a Democrat to the United States Senate to fill the vacancy caused by the resignation of Samuel L. Southard and served from November 12, 1823, until his death in Burlington, N. J., August 19, 1826; interment in St. Mary's Cemetery.

McINDOE, Walter Duncan, a Representative from Wisconsin; born in Dumbartonshire, Scotland, March 30, 1819; immigrated to the United States in 1834; engaged in business in New York, Charleston, and St. Louis; finally settled in Wisconsin in 1845 and engaged in the lumber business; member of the State assembly in 1850, 1854, and 1855; unsuccessful candidate for gubernatorial nomination in 1857; provost marshal of Wisconsin during the

Civil War; presidential elector on the Republican tickets of Frémont and Dayton in 1856, of Lincoln and Hamlin in 1860, and of Grant and Wilson in 1872; elected as a Republican to the Thirty-seventh Congress to fill the vacancy caused by the death of Luther Hanchett; reelected to the Thirty-eighth and Thirty-ninth Congresses and served from January 26, 1863, to March 3, 1867; declined to be a candidate for renomination in 1866; resumed his former interests in the lumber business; died in Wausau, Marathon County, Wis., on August 22, 1872; interment in Pine Grove Cemetery.

McINTIRE, Clifford Guy, a Representative from Maine; born in Perham, Aroostock County, Maine, May 4, 1908; attended the public schools of Perham and Washburn (Maine) High School; was graduated from the University of Maine College of Agriculture at Orono in 1930; engaged in farming at Perham in 1930; appraiser, supervisor, and regional manager for Farm Credit Administration, Springfield, Mass., 1933–1947; assistant general manager of Maine Potato Growers, Inc., at Presque Isle 1947–1951; elected as a Republican to the Eighty-second Congress to fill the vacancy caused by the death of Frank Fellows; reelected to the Eighty-third and to the three succeeding Congresses and served from October 22, 1951, to January 3, 1961. *Reelected to the Eighty-seventh Congress.*

McINTIRE, Rufus, a Representative from Maine; born in York, York County, Maine, December 19, 1784; attended the common schools; was graduated from Dartmouth College, Hanover, N. H., in 1809; studied law; was admitted to the bar and commenced practice in Parsonfield, Maine, in 1812; served in the War of 1812; member of the State house of representatives in 1820; prosecuting attorney of York County 1820–1843; member of the boundary commission in 1820 to settle the northern and northeastern boundaries of Maine; elected as a Jackson Democrat to the Twentieth Congress to fill the vacancy caused by the death of William Burleigh; reelected to the Twenty-first, Twenty-second, and Twenty-third Congresses and served from September 10, 1827, to March 3, 1835; State land agent in 1839 and 1840; appointed by President Polk United States marshal for Maine in 1845, and served as surveyor of customs of the port of Portland, Maine, from April 13, 1853, to April 1, 1857; died in Parsonfield, Maine, April 28, 1866; interment in Middleroad Cemetery.

McINTIRE, William Watson, a Representative from Maryland; born in Chambersburg, Franklin County, Pa., June 30, 1850; moved with his parents to Washington County, Md.; attended public and private schools; learned the trade of machinist; moved in July 1872 to Baltimore; received an appointment in the United States Railway Mail Service in 1874; remained in this service until 1885, when he resigned; attended Hagerstown (Md.) Academy; was graduated from the law department of the University of Maryland at Baltimore and was admitted to the bar in Baltimore, Md.; elected as a Republican to the city council of Baltimore in 1887 and 1888; in the campaign of 1895 was treasurer of the Maryland Republican State and city committees; general agent of the United States Life Insurance Co. 1905–1912; elected as a Republican to the Fifty-fifth Congress (March 4, 1897–March 3, 1899); unsuccessful candidate for reelection in 1898 to the Fifty-sixth Congress; member of Baltimore Sewerage Commission in 1911 and 1912; died on a boat in the Middle River, in Baltimore County, Md., March 30, 1912; interment in Loudon Park Cemetery, Baltimore, Md.

McINTOSH, Lachlan, a Delegate from Georgia; born near Raits, in Badenoch, Scotland, March 17, 1725; immigrated with his parents to Georgia in 1736 and established the settlement of New Inverness; acquired an education and became a surveyor;

delegate to the Provincial Congress at Savannah in 1775; entered the military service of Georgia and later served in the Continental Army and rose to the rank of brigadier general; fought a duel on May 16, 1777, with Button Gwinett, fatally wounding his opponent; elected a Delegate to the Continental Congress in 1784; died in Savannah, Ga., February 20, 1806.

McINTOSH, Robert John, a Representative from Michigan; born in Port Huron, Saint Clair County, Mich., September 16, 1922; attended public schools and Michigan State University 1940–1942; graduated from University of Michigan Law School in 1948; was admitted to the bar in 1948 and commenced the practice of law in Port Huron, Mich.; in World War II served in the United States Air Force 1942–1945 and was assigned to the Eighth Air Force in England as a fighter pilot; assistant prosecuting attorney, Saint Clair County, 1949–1951; postmaster at Port Huron, Mich., from October 1, 1953, to February 4, 1955; elected as a Republican to the Eighty-fifth Congress (January 3, 1957–January 3, 1959); unsuccessful candidate for reelection in 1958 to the Eighty-sixth Congress and for election in 1960 to the Eighty-seventh Congress; engaged in the practice of law; is a resident of Port Huron, Mich.

McINTYRE, John Joseph, a Representative from Wyoming; born on a farm in Dewey County, Okla., December 17, 1904; attended the grade schools at Ramona, Okla.; was graduated from the high school at Tulsa, Okla., and from the law department of the University of Colorado at Boulder in 1928; was admitted to the bar in 1929 and commenced practice in Glenrock, Wyo.; moved to Douglas, Converse County, Wyo., in 1931 and continued the practice of law; served as county and prosecuting attorney of Converse County 1933–1936; special attorney for the Department of Justice at Washington, D. C., 1936–1938; associate attorney in the solicitor's office, Department of Agriculture, Washington, D. C., in 1938; member of the Wyoming National Guard, with rank of captain, 1935–1941; elected as a Democrat to the Seventy-seventh Congress (January 3, 1941–January 3, 1943); unsuccessful candidate for reelection in 1942 to the Seventy-eighth Congress; deputy attorney general of Wyoming in 1943 and 1944; during World War II served as a staff sergeant, Headquarters Battery, Six Hundred and Sixtieth Field Artillery, from February 9, 1944, to August 22, 1945; decorated with the French Croix de Guerre; State auditor for Wyoming in 1946; unsuccessful candidate for election in 1946 to the Eightieth Congress; Democratic nominee for Governor in 1950; elected in 1960 as a justice of the Wyoming Supreme Court for a four-year term; resides in Casper, Wyo.

McJUNKIN, Ebenezer, a Representative from Pennsylvania; born at Center Top, Butler County, Pa., March 28, 1819; attended the common schools; was graduated from Jefferson College, Canonsburg, Pa., in 1841; studied law; was admitted to the bar in 1843, and commenced practice in Butler, Butler County, Pa.; deputy attorney general for Butler County in 1850; delegate to the Republican National Convention at Chicago in 1860; served during the Civil War as first lieutenant of militia; presidential elector on the Republican ticket of Lincoln and Johnson in 1864; elected as a Republican to the Forty-second and Forty-third Congresses and served from March 4, 1871, until he resigned January 1, 1875; president judge of the seventeenth judicial district of Pennsylvania 1875–1885; resumed the practice of his profession until 1900, when he retired; died in Butler, Pa., November 10, 1907; interment in North Cemetery.

McKAIG, William McMahon, a Representative from Maryland; born in Cumberland, Allegany County, Md., July 29, 1845; attended the Carroll School and the Allegany County

Academy; studied law; was admitted to the Allegany bar in 1868; moved to Colorado Territory in 1873, where he lived an outdoor life to regain his health, and afterward visited Utah, California, Mexico, and Central and South America; returned to Maryland; appointed city attorney of Cumberland in 1876; member of the State house of delegates in 1877; served in the State senate in 1887; mayor of Cumberland in 1890; elected as a Democrat to the Fifty-second and Fifty-third Congresses (March 4, 1891–March 3, 1895); was not a candidate for renomination in 1894; resumed the practice of his profession; died in Cumberland, Md., June 6, 1907; interment in Rose Hill Cemetery.

McKAY, James Iver, a Representative from North Carolina; born near Elizabethtown, Bladen County, N. C., in 1793; pursued classical studies; studied law; was admitted to the bar and practiced; appointed United States attorney for the district of North Carolina on March 6, 1817; served in the State senate 1815–1819, 1822, 1826, and 1830; elected as a Democrat to the Twenty-second and to the eight succeeding Congresses (March 4, 1831–March 3, 1849); died in Goldsboro, Wayne County, N. C., September 4, 1853.

McKEAN, James Bedell (nephew of Samuel McKean), a Representative from New York; born in Bennington, Vt., August 5, 1821; moved to New York; pursued an academic course; taught in the district schools for several terms and was one of the professors in Jonesville Academy for some time; superintendent of the common schools in Half Moon in 1842; elected colonel of the One Hundred and Forty-fourth Regiment, New York Militia, in 1844; studied law; was admitted to the bar in 1849 and commenced practice in Ballston Spa, N. Y.; moved to Saratoga Springs in 1851; county judge of Saratoga County 1854–1858; elected as a Republican to the Thirty-sixth and Thirty-seventh Congresses (March 4, 1859–March 3, 1863); during the Civil War organized the Seventy-seventh Regiment, New York Volunteers, in 1861 and served as colonel of the regiment until July 27, 1863, when he resigned his commission; appointed treaty commissioner to Honduras in 1865; declined the appointment of consul to Santo Domingo; appointed chief justice of the supreme court of Utah Territory by President Grant in 1870 and served until 1875; died in Salt Lake City, Utah, January 5, 1879; interment in Mount Olivet Cemetery.

McKEAN, Samuel (uncle of James Bedell McKean), a Representative and a Senator from Pennsylvania; born in Kishocaquillas Valley in Bradford County, Pa., April 7, 1787; attended the common schools; moved to Maryland and lived with an uncle until the latter's death; returned to Bradford County and engaged in mercantile pursuits in Burlington; member of the board of commissioners for Bradford County in 1814; member of the State house of representatives 1815–1819; secretary of state under Governor Wolf; served in the State militia as major general; elected as a Democrat to the Eighteenth, Nineteenth, and Twentieth Congresses (March 4, 1823–March 3, 1829); member of the State senate in 1829 and 1830; presidential elector on the Democratic ticket in 1832 and voted for Jackson and Wilkins in 1832; elected to the United States Senate and served from March 4, 1833, to March 3, 1839; died in West Burlington, Bradford County, Pa., December 14, 1841; interment in the Old Church Cemetery in the eastern part of West Burlington Township.

McKEAN, Thomas, a Delegate from Delaware; born in New London, Chester County, Pa., March 19, 1734; was privately taught; engaged as clerk to the prothonotary of the court of common pleas for two years; deputy prothonotary and register for the probate of wills for New Castle County, studying law at the same time; was admitted to the bar in 1755 and commenced practice in New Castle, Del.; appointed deputy attorney general for Sussex County in 1756 and served until 1758 when he resigned; went to England and resumed the study of law at the Middle Temple in London; member of the Delaware House of Assembly 1762–1775 and served as speaker in 1772; appointed one of the three trustees of the loan office for New Castle County in 1764 and served until 1776; member of the Stamp-Act Congress in 1765; delegate from Delaware to the General Congress in New York City in 1765; appointed by the Governor sole notary for the lower counties of Delaware July 10, 1765; in the same year received the commission of a justice of the peace, of the court of common pleas and quarter sessions, and of the orphans' court for New Castle County; appointed collector of the port of New Castle in 1771; Member of the Continental Congress 1774–1783 and served as President of Congress in 1781; a signer of the Declaration of Independence; member of the State house of representatives in 1776 and 1777 and served as speaker in the latter year; President of the State of Delaware in 1777; chief justice of Pennsylvania 1777–1799; served in the Revolutionary War; member of the convention of Pennsylvania which ratified the Constitution of the United States December 12, 1787; delegate to the State constitutional convention in 1789; Governor of Pennsylvania 1799–1808; retired from public life; died in Philadelphia, Pa., June 24, 1817; interment in Laurel Hill Cemetery.

McKEE, George Colin, a Representative from Mississippi; born in Joliet, Ill., October 2, 1837; attended Knox College and Lombard College, both at Galesburg, Ill.; studied law; was admitted to the bar in 1858 and commenced practice in Centralia, Ill.; city attorney of Centralia 1858–1861; served throughout the Civil War with distinction from private in the Eleventh Regiment, Illinois Volunteer Infantry, to brigadier general of Volunteers; resumed the practice of law in Vicksburg, Miss., and engaged in planting in Hinds County; appointed register in bankruptcy in 1867; member of the State constitutional convention in 1868; elected as a Republican to the Fortieth Congress, but his credentials were never presented to the House; elected as a Republican to the Forty-first, Forty-second, and Forty-third Congresses (March 4, 1869–March 3, 1875); was appointed postmaster of Jackson, Miss., and served from June 28, 1881, to November 12, 1885; resumed the practice of his profession; receiver of public moneys from 1889 until his death in Jackson, Miss., on November 17, 1890; interment in Greenwood Cemetery.

McKEE, John, a Representative from Alabama; born in Augusta (now Rockbridge) County, Va., in 1771; attended Liberty Hall Academy (now Washington and Lee University), Lexington, Va.; United States agent for the Choctaw Indians in East Mississippi 1802–1816; was largely influential in causing the Choctaws and Chickasaws to side with the Government against the Creeks and marched with a large force of friendly Indians to destroy the Creek town, at the Falls of Tuscaloosa, Ala.; appointed an officer in the land office at Tuscaloosa March 9, 1821, and was one of the first settlers of Tuscaloosa County; member of the commission to settle the boundary line between the States of Kentucky and Tennessee; elected to the Eighteenth, Nineteenth, and Twentieth Congresses (March 4, 1823–March 3, 1829); was not a candidate for renomination in 1828 to the Twenty-first Congress; was one of the commissioners in 1829 who negotiated the treaty of Dancing Rabbit, by which a large tract of land west of the Tombigbee River was acquired from the Choctaw Indians; died at his home, "Hill of Howth," near Boligee, Green County, Ala., August 12, 1832; interment in Bethsalem Cemetery, Boligee, Ala.

McKEE, Samuel, a Representative from Kentucky; born near Lexington, Augusta (now Rockbridge) County, Va., October 13, 1774; was graduated from Liberty Hall Academy (now Washington and Lee University), Lexington, Va., in 1794; studied law; was admitted to the bar in 1800 and commenced practice in Somerset, Pulaski County, Ky.; served as surveyor of Pulaski County; moved to Lancaster, Garrard County, Ky., in 1807 and continued the practice of law; member of the State house of representatives 1802–1808; elected as a Democrat to the Eleventh and to the three succeeding Congresses (March 4, 1809–March 3, 1817); served in the War of 1812 on the staff of General Harrison; after the war resumed the practice of his profession in Lancaster; appointed by President Monroe a member of the commission to clear the Ohio and Mississippi Rivers of obstructions and served until his death at the residence of Mr. Flourney in Hickman County, Ky., on October 16, 1826; interment in Frankfort Cemetery, Frankfort, Ky.

McKEE, Samuel, a Representative from Kentucky; born near Mount Sterling, Montgomery County, Ky., November 5, 1833; attended the common schools; was graduated from Miami University, Oxford, Ohio, in 1857, and the Cincinnati Law School in 1858; was admitted to the bar and commenced practice in Mount Sterling, Ky., in 1858; served in the Federal Army during the Civil War as a captain in the Fourteenth Regiment, Kentucky Volunteer Cavalry; elected as a Republican to the Thirty-ninth Congress (March 4, 1865–March 3, 1867); successfully contested the election of John D. Young to the Fortieth Congress and served from June 22, 1868, to March 3, 1869; was not a candidate for renomination in 1868; delegate to the Southern Loyalist Convention at Philadelphia in 1866; pension agent in Louisville, Ky., 1869–1871; resumed the practice of law; died in Louisville, Ky., December 11, 1898; interment in Cave Hill Cemetery.

McKEIGHAN, William Arthur, a Representative from Nebraska; born in Millville, Cumberland County, N. J., January 19, 1842; moved with his parents to Fulton County, Ill., in 1848; attended the common schools; during the Civil War enlisted in the Eleventh Regiment, Illinois Volunteer Cavalry, in September 1861; at the close of the war located on a farm near Pontiac, Ill., and engaged in agricultural pursuits; moved to Nebraska in 1880 and resumed agricultural pursuits near Red Cloud; took an active interest in organizing the Farmers' Alliance; probate judge of Webster County 1885–1887; unsuccessful candidate in 1888 for election to the Fifty-first Congress; elected as a Democrat to the Fifty-second and as an Independent to the Fifty-third Congresses (March 4, 1891–March 3, 1895); unsuccessful candidate in 1894 for reelection to the Fifty-fourth Congress; died in Hastings, Adams County, Nebr., December 15, 1895; interment in Red Cloud Cemetery, Red Cloud, Webster County, Nebr.

McKELLAR, Kenneth Douglas, a Representative and a Senator from Tennessee; born in Richmond, Dallas County, Ala., January 29, 1869; received private instruction from his parents and his sister; was graduated from the academic department of the University of Alabama at Tuscaloosa in 1891 and from its law department in 1892; moved to Tennessee in 1892 and settled in Memphis; was admitted to the bar the same year and commenced the practice of law; presidential elector on the Democratic ticket of Parker and Davis in 1904; delegate to the Democratic National Convention at Denver in 1908; elected as a Democrat to the Sixty-second Congress to fill the vacancy caused by the death of George W. Gordon; reelected to the Sixty-third and Sixty-fourth Congresses and served from November 9, 1911, to March 3, 1917; did not seek renomination, having become a candidate for Senator; elected to the United States Senate in 1916; reelected in 1922, 1928, 1934, 1940, and 1946, and served

from March 4, 1917, to January 3, 1953; unsuccessful candidate for renomination in 1952; president pro tempore of the Senate January 1945–January 1947 and January 1949–January 1953; retired; died in Memphis, Tenn., October 25, 1957; interment in Elmwood Cemetery.

McKENNA, Joseph, a Representative from California; born in Philadelphia, Pa., August 10, 1843; moved with his parents to Benicia, Calif., in January 1855; attended the public schools, and was graduated from the law department of Benicia Collegiate Institute in 1865; was admitted to the bar in 1865 and commenced practice in Benicia, Calif.; moved to Fairfield, Solano County, in 1866 and continued the practice of law for eight years; district attorney of Solano County 1866–1868; member of the State house of representatives in 1875 and 1876; unsuccessful Republican candidate in 1876 for election to the Forty-fifth Congress and in 1878 to the Forty-sixth Congress; elected as a Republican to the Forty-ninth and to the three succeeding Congresses and served from March 4, 1885, to March 28, 1892, when he resigned; appointed by President Harrison as United States circuit judge for the ninth judicial circuit February 11, 1892, and was confirmed March 17, 1892; served five years and resigned; appointed Attorney General of the United States in the Cabinet of President McKinley and served from March 7, 1897, to January 25, 1898, when he resigned, having been appointed by President McKinley as an Associate Justice of the United States Supreme Court January 26, 1898, to succeed Justice Stephen K. Field, retired, and served from January 26, 1898, to January 25, 1925, when he resigned; died in Washington, D. C., November 21, 1926; interment in Mount Olivet Cemetery.

McKENNAN, Thomas McKean Thompson, a Representative from Pennsylvania; born in New Castle, New Castle County, Del., March 31, 1794; moved to Washington, Pa.; attended the public schools; was graduated from Washington (now Washington and Jefferson) College, Washington, Pa., in 1810; studied law; was admitted to the bar in 1814 and commenced practice in Washington, Pa.; deputy attorney general in 1815 and 1816; elected as a Whig to the Twenty-second and to the three succeeding Congresses (March 4, 1831–March 3, 1839); presidential elector on the Whig ticket of Harrison and Tyler in 1840; again elected to the Twenty-seventh Congress to fill the vacancy caused by the death of Joseph Lawrence and served from May 30, 1842, to March 3, 1843; president of the Pennsylvania Electoral College in 1848; appointed Secretary of the Interior in the Cabinet of President Fillmore and served from August 15 to September 12, 1850; resigned and became president of the Hempfield Railroad, now the Baltimore & Ohio Railroad; died in Reading, Pa., July 9, 1852; interment in the Washington Cemetery, Washington, Pa.

McKENNEY, William Robertson, a Representative from Virginia; born in Petersburg, Dinwiddie County, Va., December 2, 1851; attended McCabe's University School at Petersburg and the University of Virginia at Charlottesville; taught school; graduated from the law school of the University of Virginia in June 1876; was admitted to the bar and practiced in Petersburg, Va.; elected president of the city council of Petersburg in 1888 and served six years; presidential elector on the Democratic ticket of Cleveland and Thurman in 1888; delegate to the Democratic National Convention in 1892; member of the Democratic State executive committee; presented credentials as a Democratic Member-elect to the Fifty-fourth Congress and served from March 4, 1895, to May 2, 1896, when he was succeeded by Robert T. Thorp, who successfully contested his election; resumed the practice of law in Petersburg, Va., and died there January 3, 1916; interment in Blandford Cemetery.

McKENTY, Jacob Kerlin, a Representative from Pennsylvania; born in Douglassville, Amity Township, Berks County, Pa., January 19, 1827; was graduated from Yale College in 1848 and from the law department of that college in 1851; was admitted to the bar in 1851 and commenced practice in Reading, Pa.; prosecuting attorney of Berks County 1856–1858; elected as a Democrat to the Thirty-sixth Congress to fill the vacancy caused by the death of John Schwartz and served from December 3, 1860, to March 3, 1861; was not a candidate in 1860 to succeed himself in the Thirty-seventh Congress; unsuccessful candidate for nomination in 1862 and 1864; resumed the practice of his profession in Reading, Pa.; died in Douglassville, Berks County, Pa., January 3, 1866; interment in St. Gabriel's Episcopal Church Cemetery.

McKENZIE, Charles Edgar, a Representative from Louisiana; born in Pelican, De Soto Parish, La., October 3, 1896; attended the public schools of Monroe, La., and Louisiana State University at Baton Rouge; volunteered for service on the Mexican border in 1916 with the Louisiana National Guard; during the First World War was mustered into the Federal service on April 1, 1917, as a sergeant in the First Louisiana Infantry; commissioned a second lieutenant in the One Hundred and Fifty-sixth Infantry, serving overseas in the Thirty-ninth and Eighty-ninth Divisions from June 1918 to September 1919; engaged in oil drilling and as an oil operator at Wichita Falls and Burkburnett, Tex., 1919–1921; returned to Monroe, La., in 1921, and engaged in the oil, gas, finance-brokerage, trucking, and insurance businesses; also agricultural pursuits; served as executive assistant director in the Louisiana Department of Highways 1940–1942; director of planning, housing, and aeronautics in the Louisiana Department of Public Works in 1942 and 1943; elected as a Democrat to the Seventy-eighth and Seventy-ninth Congresses (January 3, 1943–January 3, 1947); unsuccessful candidate for renomination in 1946; resumed supervision of his business enterprises; died in Monroe, La., June 7, 1956; interment in Riverview Cemetery.

McKENZIE, James Andrew (uncle of John McKenzie Moss), a Representative from Kentucky; born in Bennettstown, Christian County, Ky., August 1, 1840; attended the common schools of Christian County and Centre College, Danville, Ky.; studied law; was admitted to the bar in 1861 and commenced practice in Hopkinsville, Ky.; also engaged in agricultural pursuits; during the Civil War served as a private in the Confederate Army; member of the State house of representatives 1867–1871; presidential elector on the Democratic ticket of Greeley and Brown in 1872; elected as a Democrat to the Forty-fifth, Forty-sixth, and Forty-seventh Congresses (March 4, 1877–March 3, 1883); unsuccessful candidate for renomination in 1882; secretary of state of Kentucky under Gov. J. Proctor Knott 1884–1888; commissioner from Kentucky to the World's Columbian Exposition at Chicago, Ill., in 1893; appointed Envoy Extraordinary and Minister Plenipotentiary to Peru by President Cleveland in 1893; resigned and settled on his farm near Long View, Ky.; died at Oak Grove, Christian County, Ky., on June 25, 1904; interment in Fairview Cemetery, Bowling Green, Ky.

McKENZIE, John Charles, a Representative from Illinois; born on a farm near Elizabeth, Woodbine Township, Jo Daviess County, Ill., February 18, 1860; attended the common schools, and the normal school at Valparaiso, Ind.; taught school in Jo Daviess County for six years; engaged in the grain, flour, and feed business; studied law; was admitted to the bar in 1890 and commenced the practice of his profession in Elizabeth, Ill.; director of the Elizabeth Exchange Bank; member of the State house of representatives 1892–1896; member of Illinois Claims

Commission 1896–1900; served in the State senate from 1900 until his resignation on May 11, 1911, and was president pro tempore 1903–1905; elected as a Republican to the Sixty-second and to the six succeeding Congresses (March 4, 1911–March 3, 1925); was not a candidate for renomination in 1924; appointed on March 26, 1925, a member of the commission to report the most practical method of utilizing the nitrate plant at Muscle Shoals, Ala., and served until November 14, 1925, when the commission submitted its conclusions to President Coolidge; resumed the practice of his profession in Elizabeth, Ill., until his death in that city on September 17, 1941; interment in Elizabeth Cemetery.

McKENZIE, Lewis, a Representative from Virginia; born in Alexandria, Va., October 7, 1810; pursued an academic course; prominently engaged in shipping and mercantile pursuits; member of the city council 1855–1859, 1863–1866, and 1868–1870; mayor of Alexandria 1861–1863; elected as a Unionist to the Thirty-seventh Congress to fill the vacancy caused by the unseating of Charles H. Upton and served from February 16, 1863, to March 3, 1863; upon the readmission of the State of Virginia to representation was elected as a Union Conservative to the Forty-first Congress and served from January 31, 1870, to March 3, 1871; president of the Washington & Ohio Railroad Co.; appointed postmaster of Alexandria, Va., in 1878; again a member of the city council 1887–1891; died in Alexandria, Va., June 28, 1895; interment in Presbyterian Cemetery.

McKEON, John, a Representative from New York; born in Albany, N. Y., March 29, 1808; attended private schools, and was graduated from the law department of Columbia College (later Columbia University), New York City, in 1828; was admitted to the bar the same year and practiced in New York City; a member of the State assembly 1832–1834; elected as a Democrat to the Twenty-fourth Congress (March 4, 1835–March 3, 1837); unsuccessful candidate for reelection in 1836 to the Twenty-fifth Congress; elected to the Twenty-seventh Congress (March 4, 1841–March 3, 1843); unsuccessful candidate for reelection in 1842 to the Twenty-eighth Congress; district attorney for New York County 1846–1850; appointed by President Pierce as United States district attorney for the southern district of New York and served from July 10, 1854, to January 7, 1858; again district attorney for New York County from November 1881 until his death; died in New York City November 22, 1883; interment in family vault under St. Patrick's Cathedral on Mott Street.

McKEOUGH, Raymond Stephen, a Representative from Illinois; born in Chicago, Ill., April 29, 1888; attended public and parochial schools; was graduated from De La Salle Institute, Chicago, Ill., in 1905; worked in stock commission houses of the Union Stock Yards, Chicago, Ill., 1905–1909; employed in clerical work with a railroad 1909–1925; engaged in the investment securities business 1925–1929 and in the brokerage business 1929–1934; alternate delegate to the Democratic National Convention in 1932 and delegate to the Democratic National Convention in 1940; elected as a Democrat to the Seventy-fourth and to the three succeeding Congresses (January 3, 1935–January 3, 1943); was not a candidate for renomination in 1942, but was an unsuccessful candidate for election to the United States Senate; regional administrator of the Office of Price Administration, Chicago, Ill., from February 5, 1943, to January 15, 1944; appointed a member of the United States Maritime Commission on October 11, 1945, effective September 26, 1945, and served until 1950; Commissioner, International Claims Commission of the United States 1951–1953; associated with Great American Oil Co., Chicago, in 1956; appointed administrative assistant to the State's attorney, criminal division, Chicago, Ill., December 3, 1956, and resigned December 3, 1960; engaged in general insurance business since April 1961; is a resident of Chicago, Ill.

McKEOWN, Thomas Deitz, a Representative from Oklahoma; born in Blackstock, Chester County, S. C., June 4, 1878; attended the common schools, studied under a private tutor, and attended lectures at Cornell University, Ithaca, N. Y., in 1898; was admitted to the bar in 1899 and began practice in Malvern, Ark.; moved to Ada, Indian Territory (now Oklahoma), in 1901 and resumed the practice of law; appointed a member of the first State bar commission and elected president in 1909; judge of the seventh district of Oklahoma 1910–1914; presiding judge of the fifth division of the supreme court commission in 1915 and 1916; elected as a Democrat to the Sixty-fifth and Sixty-sixth Congresses (March 4, 1917–March 3, 1921); unsuccessful candidate for reelection in 1920 to the Sixty-seventh Congress; elected to the Sixty-eighth and to the five succeeding Congresses (March 4, 1923–January 3, 1935); unsuccessful candidate for renomination in 1934; moved to Chicago, Ill., and resumed the practice of law in 1935 and 1936; returned to Ada, Okla., in 1937 and engaged in farming and oil production; delegate to the Democratic State convention in 1942; county attorney of Pontotoc County, Okla., from April 1, 1946, to January 1, 1947; appointed county judge in 1947 and elected in 1948 and again in 1950 and served until his death in Ada, Okla., October 22, 1951; interment in Rosedale Cemetery.

McKIBBIN, Joseph Chambers, a Representative from California; born in Chambersburg, Franklin County, Pa., May 14, 1824; received a common-school education and attended Princeton College 1840–1842; moved to California and settled in Sierra County in 1849; studied law; was admitted to the bar in July 1852 and practiced in Downieville; member of the State senate in 1852 and 1853; elected as a Democrat to the Thirty-fifth Congress (March 4, 1857–March 3, 1859); unsuccessful candidate for reelection in 1858 to the Thirty-sixth Congress; during the Civil War enlisted in the Union Army in 1861 and was one of the first six Cavalry officers appointed by President Lincoln; served as a colonel and aide-de-camp on the staffs of Major General Halleck and Major General Thomas; settled in Washington, D. C., after the Civil War, as a general contractor; purchased the property at Marshall Hall, Charles County, Md., in 1883; died at Marshall Hall, Md., near Washington, D. C., July 1, 1896; interment in Arlington National Cemetery, Fort Myer, Va.

McKIM, Alexander (uncle of Isaac McKim), a Representative from Maryland; born in Brandywine, Del., January 10, 1748; pursued an academic course; moved to Baltimore, Md.; member of the house of delegates in 1778; served in the Revolutionary War as a member of the Baltimore Independent Cadets and of the First Baltimore Cavalry; fought under Lafayette in the Virginia campaign of 1791; member of the State senate 1806–1810; elected as a Democrat to the Eleventh, Twelfth, and Thirteenth Congresses (March 4, 1809–March 3, 1815); engaged in mercantile pursuits; justice of court of quarter sessions; presiding judge of the Baltimore County Orphans' Court at the time of his death in Baltimore, Md., January 18, 1832; interment in Greenmount Cemetery.

McKIM, Isaac (nephew of Alexander McKim), a Representative from Maryland; born in Baltimore, Md., July 21, 1775; attended the public schools; engaged in mercantile pursuits; served in the War of 1812 as aide-de-camp to Gen. Samuel

Smith; member of the State senate from December 4, 1821, until January 8, 1823, when he resigned; elected as a Democrat to the Seventeenth Congress to fill the vacancy caused by the resignation of Samuel Smith; elected to the Eighteenth Congress to fill the vacancy caused by the resignation of Representative-elect Samuel Smith and served from January 4, 1823, to March 3, 1825; a director of the Baltimore & Ohio Railroad Co. from 1827 until 1831; again elected to the Twenty-third, Twenty-fourth, and Twenty-fifth Congresses and served from March 4, 1833, until his death in Baltimore, Md., on April 1, 1838; interment in the burying ground of St. Paul's Church.

McKINIRY, Richard Francis, a Representative from New York; born in New York City March 23, 1878; attended the public schools; was graduated from the College of St. Francis Xavier, New York City, and from the New York Law School; was admitted to the bar in 1899 and commenced the practice of his profession in New York City; assistant district attorney of Bronx County 1914–1917; secretary of the State supreme court, first district, 1917–1919; elected as a Democrat to the Sixty-sixth Congress (March 4, 1919–March 3, 1921); unsuccessful candidate for reelection in 1920 to the Sixty-seventh Congress; appointed a magistrate of New York City on January 1, 1923, and served until August 15, 1943, when he retired due to ill health; died in Yonkers, N. Y., May 30, 1950; interment in Calvary Cemetery, Long Island City, N. Y.

McKINLAY, Duncan E., a Representative from California; born in Orillia, Ontario, Canada, October 6, 1862; attended the common schools; later learned the trade of carriage painting and worked in Flint, Mich., and San Francisco, Sacramento, and Santa Rosa, Calif.; studied law; was admitted to the bar by the supreme court of California in 1892 and commenced practice in Santa Rosa, Calif.; presidential elector on the Republican ticket of McKinley and Hobart in 1896; second assistant United States attorney at San Francisco 1901–1904; first assistant United States attorney 1904–1907; elected as a Republican to the Fifty-ninth, Sixtieth, and Sixty-first Congresses (March 4, 1905–March 3, 1911); unsuccessful candidate for reelection in 1910 to the Sixty-second Congress; appointed by President Taft as United States surveyor of customs for the port of San Francisco, Calif., in 1910; died in Berkeley, Calif., December 30, 1914; interment in Sunset Cemetery.

McKINLEY, John, a Senator and a Representative from Alabama; born in Culpeper County, Va., May 1, 1780; moved to Kentucky; studied law; was admitted to the bar and commenced the practice of his profession in Louisville, Ky.; moved to Huntsville, Madison County, Ala.; member of the State house of representatives; elected as a Jackson Democrat to the United States Senate to fill the vacancy caused by the death of Henry Chambers and served from November 27, 1826, to March 3, 1831; moved to Florence, Lauderdale County, Ala.; elected to the Twenty-third Congress (March 4, 1833–March 3, 1835); again elected to the United States Senate for the term beginning March 4, 1837, and resigned April 22, 1837, before qualifying; appointed by President Van Buren as an Associate Justice of the United States Supreme Court April 22, 1837, and served until his death in Louisville, Ky., July 19, 1852; interment in Cave Hill Cemetery.

McKINLEY, William, a Representative from Virginia; born in that State; completed preparatory studies; member of the State house of delegates from Ohio County, Va. (now West Virginia), 1798–1804, 1806, and 1807; elected as a Democrat to the Eleventh Congress to fill the vacancy caused by the resignation of John G. Jackson and served from December 21, 1810, to March 3, 1811; again a member of the State house of delegates in 1820, 1821, and 1824–1826.

McKINLEY, William, Jr., a Representative from Ohio and a President of the United States; born in Niles, Ohio, January 29, 1843; attended the public schools, Poland Academy, and Allegheny College; taught school; during the Civil War enlisted in the Union Army on June 23, 1861, as a private soldier in the Twenty-third Regiment, Ohio Volunteer Infantry, and was mustered out as captain and brevet major of the same regiment in September 1865; studied law; was admitted to the bar in 1867 and commenced practice in Canton, Ohio; prosecuting attorney of Stark County, Ohio, 1869–1871; elected as a Republican to the Forty-fifth, Forty-sixth, and Forty-seventh Congresses (March 4, 1877–March 3, 1883); presented credentials as a Member-elect to the Forty-eighth Congress and served from March 4, 1883, until May 27, 1884, when he was succeeded by Jonathan H. Wallace, who successfully contested his election; again elected to the Forty-ninth, Fiftieth, and Fifty-first Congresses (March 4, 1885–March 3, 1891); unsuccessful candidate for reelection in 1890 to the Fifty-second Congress; delegate to the Republican National Conventions in 1884, 1888, and 1892; elected Governor of Ohio in 1891 and was inaugurated on January 11, 1892; reelected in 1893, and served until January 13, 1896; elected President of the United States in 1896; reelected in 1900 and served from March 4, 1897, until his death; was shot on September 6, 1901, by an anarchist, Leon Czolgosz, while attending the Pan American Exposition in Buffalo, N. Y., and died in that city on September 14, 1901; interment in the McKinley Monument, Canton, Ohio.

McKINLEY, William Brown, a Representative and a Senator from Illinois; born in Petersburg, Menard County, Ill., September 5, 1856; attended the common schools and the University of Illinois at Urbana; employed as a drug clerk in Springfield, Ill.; engaged in banking in Champaign, Ill., and also in the building and operation of public utilities; traveled extensively in foreign countries and made a number of trips around the world; trustee of the University of Illinois 1902–1905; delegate to the Republican National Convention at Chicago in 1908; elected as a Republican to the Fifty-ninth and to the three succeeding Congresses (March 4, 1905–March 3, 1913); was an unsuccessful candidate for reelection in 1912 to the Sixty-third Congress; again elected to the Sixty-fourth, Sixty-fifth, and Sixty-sixth Congresses (March 4, 1915–March 3, 1921); was not a candidate for reelection, having become a candidate for Senator; elected to the United States Senate in 1920 and served from March 4, 1921, until his death; unsuccessful candidate for renomination in 1926; died in a hospital in Martinsville, Morgan County, Ind., on December 7, 1926; interment in Mount Hope Cemetery, Champaign, Ill.

McKINNEY, James, a Representative from Illinois; born in Oquawka, Henderson County, Ill., April 14, 1852; attended the public schools, and was graduated from Monmouth (Ill.) College in 1874; president of the Aledo (Ill.) Bank 1892–1907; member of the Republican State central committee 1894–1906; delegate to the Republican State convention in 1896 and 1900; appointed by Governor Yates in 1901 a member of the State railroad and warehouse commission, but resigned in 1902; president of the Aledo Board of Education in 1902 and 1903; elected as a Republican to the Fifty-ninth Congress to fill the vacancy caused by the death of Benjamin F. Marsh; reelected to the Sixtieth, Sixty-first, and Sixty-second Congresses and served from November 7, 1905, to March 3, 1913; declined renomination in 1912; president of the

Illinois State Bankers' Association in 1908 and 1909; engaged in the real-estate loan business in Aledo, Ill., until his death in that city on September 29, 1934; interment in Aledo Cemetery.

McKINNEY, John Franklin, a Representative from Ohio; born near Piqua, Miami County, Ohio, April 12, 1827; attended the country and private schools, the Piqua Academy, and the Ohio Wesleyan College, Delaware, Ohio; studied law; was admitted to the bar in 1850 and commenced practice in Piqua; delegate to all the Democratic National Conventions from 1850 to 1888; elected as a Democrat to the Thirty-eighth Congress (March 4, 1863–March 3, 1865); unsuccessful candidate in 1864 for reelection to the Thirty-ninth Congress; again elected to the Forty-second Congress (March 4, 1871–March 3, 1873); was not a candidate for renomination in 1872; resumed the practice of law; chairman of the Democratic State executive committee in 1879 and 1880; died in Piqua, Ohio, June 13, 1903; interment in Forest Hill Cemetery.

McKINNEY, Luther Franklin, a Representative from New Hampshire; born in Newark, Licking County, Ohio, April 25, 1841; attended common and private schools; taught school; during the Civil War enlisted in Company D, First Regiment, Ohio Volunteer Cavalry, August 5, 1861, and served until February 1863, when he was discharged with the rank of sergeant for disabilities resulting from typhoid fever; moved to Iowa in 1865, where he engaged in agricultural pursuits and also taught school until 1867; was graduated from St. Lawrence University, Canton, N. Y., June 30, 1870; moved to Bridgton, Maine, in 1871, where he was ordained a pastor of the Universalist Church; moved to Newfields, N. H., in 1873, and subsequently, in 1875, to Manchester, N. H., pursuing his ministerial duties in both places; unsuccessful candidate for election in 1884 to the Forty-ninth Congress; elected as a Democrat to the Fiftieth Congress (March 4, 1887–March 3, 1889); unsuccessful candidate for reelection in 1888 to the Fifty-first Congress; elected to the Fifty-second Congress (March 4, 1891–March 3, 1893); was not a candidate for renomination in 1892; unsuccessful candidate for Governor of New Hampshire in 1892; United States Minister to Colombia, South America, 1893–1897; returned to Bridgton, Maine, and engaged in the furniture business; member of the State house of representatives in 1907 and 1908; again pastor of the Universalist Church at Bridgton, Cumberland County, Maine, and served in that capacity until his death there on July 30, 1922; interment in Forest Hill Cemetery.

McKINNON, Clinton Dotson, a Representative from California; born in Dallas, Tex., February 5, 1906; moved with his parents to Caldwell, Sumner County, Kans., in 1909, to San Diego, Calif., in 1918, and attended the Lincoln Grammar School; moved to Palo Alto, Calif., in 1920, and graduated from high school; attended Stanford University in 1924; served as a postal clerk at Barstow, Calif., in 1925 and 1926; returned to college in 1926 and graduated from the University of Redlands, Redlands, Calif., in 1930; took postgraduate work at the University of Geneva in Switzerland in 1930; reporter, editor, and advertising manager of newspapers in Brawley, San Bernardino, Los Angeles, and North Hollywood, Calif., 1931–1935; president and general manager of Valley News Corporation, North Hollywood, Calif., 1935–1943; purchased the San Diego Progress-Journal and in March 1944 converted it into the San Diego Daily Journal; established a radio station in San Diego, Calif., in 1946; sold both the paper and radio station in order to campaign for Congress; elected as a Democrat to the Eighty-first and Eighty-second Congresses (January 3, 1949–January 3, 1953); was not a candidate for renomination in 1952, but was an unsuccessful candidate for the Democratic nomination for United States Senator; editor and publisher of several newspapers; president and general manager of broadcasting companies in Tucson, Ariz., and Albuquerque, N. Mex.; is a resident of San Diego, Calif.

McKISSOCK, Thomas, a Representative from New York; born in Montgomery, Orange County, N. Y., April 17, 1790; studied medicine and law; was admitted to the bar and commenced practice in Newburgh, N. Y.; appointed a puisne justice of the State supreme court in 1847; elected as a Whig to the Thirty-first Congress (March 4, 1849–March 3, 1851); unsuccessful candidate for reelection in 1850 to the Thirty-second Congress; died in St. Andrews, Orange County, N. Y., June 26, 1866; interment in Oldtown Cemetery, Newburgh, N. Y.

McKNIGHT, Robert, a Representative from Pennsylvania; born in Pittsburgh, Pa., January 20, 1820; attended the common schools and a private school at Xenia, Ohio; was graduated from Princeton College in 1839; studied law; was admitted to the bar in 1842 and commenced practice in Pittsburgh; city councilman 1847–1849; elected as a Republican to the Thirty-sixth and Thirty-seventh Congresses (March 4, 1859–March 3, 1863); resumed the practice of his profession; died in Pittsburgh, Pa., October 25, 1885; interment in Allegheny Cemetery.

McLACHLAN, James, a Representative from California; born in Argyllshire, Scotland, August 1, 1852; immigrated to the United States in 1855 with his parents, who settled in Tompkins County, N. Y.; reared on a farm and attended the public schools; taught in the public schools, and while engaged in that work prepared himself for college; elected school commissioner of Tompkins County, N. Y., in 1877; was graduated from Hamilton College, Clinton, N. Y., in 1878; studied law; was admitted to practice before the supreme court of New York in 1880; practiced in Ithaca, N. Y., 1881–1888; moved to Pasadena, Calif., in 1888, and there continued the practice of law; district attorney of Los Angeles County 1890–1892; elected as a Republican to the Fifty-fourth Congress (March 4, 1895–March 3, 1897); unsuccessful candidate for reelection in 1896 to the Fifty-fifth Congress; elected to the Fifty-seventh and to the four succeeding Congresses (March 4, 1901–March 3, 1911); unsuccessful candidate for reelection in 1910 to the Sixty-second Congress; resumed the practice of his profession in Los Angeles, Calif.; served as a member of the National Monetary Commission in 1911 and 1912; died in Los Angeles, Calif., November 21, 1940; interment in Forest Lawn Memorial Park, Glendale, Calif.

McLAIN, Frank Alexander, a Representative from Mississippi; born near Gloster, Amite County, Miss., January 29, 1852; attended the public schools, and was graduated from the University of Mississippi at Oxford in 1874; studied law; was admitted to the bar and commenced practice in Liberty, Miss., in 1880; member of the State house of representatives 1881–1883; district attorney for the judicial district from 1883 until January 1, 1896, when he resigned; resumed the practice of law in Gloster, Miss.; member of the State constitutional convention in 1890; elected as a Democrat to the Fifty-fifth Congress to fill the vacancy caused by the death of William F. Love; reelected to the Fifty-sixth and to the four succeeding Congresses and served from December 12, 1898, to March 3, 1909; State supreme court commissioner 1910–1912; died in Gloster, Miss., October 10, 1920; interment in the City Cemetery.

McLANAHAN, James Xavier (grandson of Andrew Gregg), a Representative from Pennsylvania; born near Greencastle, Franklin County, Pa., in 1809; was graduated from Dickinson College, Carlisle, Pa., in 1827; studied law; was admitted to the bar in 1837 and commenced practice in Chambersburg, Pa.; member of the State senate 1842–1844; elected as a Democrat to the Thirty-first and Thirty-second Congresses (March 4, 1849–March 3, 1853); was not a candidate for renomination in 1852; resumed the practice of law; died in New York City December 16, 1861; interment in First Presbyterian Church Cemetery.

McLANE, Louis (father of Robert Milligan McLane), a Representative and a Senator from Delaware; born in Smyrna, Del., May 28, 1786; attended private schools; entered the United States Navy in 1798 as a midshipman on the U. S. S. *Philadelphia* and served one year; attended Delaware College at Newark; studied law; was admitted to the bar and commenced practice in Smyrna in 1807; served in the War of 1812; elected as a Federalist to the Fifteenth and to the four succeeding Congresses (March 4, 1817–March 3, 1827); reelected to the Twentieth Congress, but resigned, having been elected a Senator; elected to the United States Senate and served from March 4, 1827, until April 16, 1829, when he resigned; appointed by President Jackson as Envoy Extraordinary and Minister Plenipotentiary to England and served from April 18, 1829, to July 6, 1831; appointed Secretary of the Treasury in the Cabinet of President Jackson and served from August 8, 1831, to May 29, 1833; appointed Secretary of State in the second administration of President Jackson and served from May 29, 1833, to June 2, 1834; again Minister to England from June 16, 1845, to August 18, 1846; delegate to the Maryland constitutional convention in 1850; president of the Baltimore & Ohio Railroad Co. 1837–1847; died in Baltimore, Md., October 7, 1857; interment in Greenmount Cemetery.

McLANE, Patrick, a Representative from Pennsylvania; born in County Mayo, Ireland, March 14, 1875; immigrated to the United States in 1882 with his parents, who settled in Scranton, Pa.; attended the public schools; worked in the coal mines of Scranton, Pa., for thirteen years; during the Spanish-American War served in the Eleventh Regiment, United States Army, in 1898 and 1899; became a locomotive engineer; member of the Scranton School Board 1904–1911; delegate to the Democratic State convention in 1905; member of the Democratic State committee in 1914; presented credentials as a Democratic Member-elect to the Sixty-sixth Congress and served from March 4, 1919, to February 25, 1921, when he was succeeded by John R. Farr, who contested the election; unsuccessful candidate for election in 1922 to the Sixty-seventh Congress and in 1924 to the Sixty-eighth Congress; employed as a locomotive engineer until his death in Scranton, Pa., November 13, 1946; interment in Cathedral Cemetery.

McLANE, Robert Milligan (son of Louis McLane), a Representative from Maryland; born in Wilmington, Del., June 23, 1815; attended private schools in Wilmington, St. Mary's College in Baltimore, and the College Bourbon in Paris; appointed a cadet in the United States Military Academy at West Point by President Jackson in 1833; was graduated in July 1837 and commissioned second lieutenant of Artillery; served with his regiment during the Seminole War in 1837 and 1838; transferred to the Corps of Topographical Engineers in 1838, then newly reorganized, and served until he resigned from the Army in 1843; studied law; was admitted to the bar in 1843 and commenced practice in Baltimore, Md.; member of the State house of delegates in 1845; elected as a Democrat to the Thirtieth and Thirty-first Congresses (March 4, 1847–March 3, 1851); was not a candidate for renomination in 1850; presidential elector on the Democratic ticket of Pierce and King in 1852; appointed commissioner to China in 1853, with the powers of a Minister Plenipotentiary, and at the same time accredited to Japan, Siam, Korea, and Cochin China; delegate to the Democratic National Convention at Cincinnati in 1856; appointed Envoy Extraordinary and Minister Plenipotentiary to the Republic of Mexico March 7, 1859, and served until December 22, 1860; delegate to the Democratic National Convention at St. Louis in 1876; member of the State Senate of Maryland in 1877; elected as a Democrat to the Forty-sixth and Forty-seventh Congresses (March 4, 1879–March 3, 1883); elected Governor of Maryland in 1883, and resigned in 1885; appointed by President Cleveland as United States Minister Plenipotentiary to France March 23, 1885, and served four years; died in Paris, France, April 16, 1898; interment in Greenmount Cemetery, Baltimore, Md.

McLAUGHLIN, Charles Francis, a Representative from Nebraska; born in Lincoln, Lancaster County, Nebr., June 19, 1887; attended the public schools; was graduated from the University of Nebraska at Lincoln in 1908 and from the law department of Columbia University, New York, N. Y., in 1910; was admitted to the bar in 1910 and commenced practice in Omaha, Nebr; special master in chancery in Federal Court 1916–1918; during the First World War served from November 27, 1917, as captain of the Three Hundred and Forty-seventh Field Artillery, Ninety-first Division, American Expeditionary Forces, until his discharge April 30, 1919; accepted appointment June 11, 1919, as a major in the Officers' Reserve Corps, from which he resigned March 1, 1921; delegate to the Nebraska State constitutional convention in 1920; elected as a Democrat to the Seventy-fourth and to the three succeeding Congresses (January 3, 1935–January 3, 1943); unsuccessful candidate for reelection in 1942 to the Seventy-eighth Congress; member of the American-Mexican Claims Commission, Washington, D. C., from April 5, 1943, to April 5, 1947; member of the Indian Claims Commission from April 5, 1947, until November 14, 1949, when he retired to accept an appointment to the bench; took the oath of office November 15, 1949, as a United States district judge for the District of Columbia, in which capacity he is now serving; is a legal resident of Omaha, Nebr.

McLAUGHLIN, James Campbell, a Representative from Michigan; born in Beardstown, Cass County, Ill., January 26, 1858; moved to Muskegon, Mich., in 1864; attended the grade and high schools of Muskegon; was graduated from the literary department of the University of Michigan at Ann Arbor in 1879 and from its law department in 1883; was admitted to the bar and commenced practice at Muskegon, Mich., in 1883; prosecuting attorney of Muskegon County 1887–1901; in 1901 was appointed by the Governor of Michigan as a member of the board of State tax commissioners and State board of assessors, in the latter capacity taking part in the first assessment of railroad property of the State for taxation, and served until 1906; elected as a Republican to the Sixtieth and to the twelve succeeding Congresses and served from March 4, 1907, until his death; unsuccessful candidate for reelection in 1932 to the Seventy-third Congress; died in Marion, Va., November 29, 1932, while en route to Washington, D. C.; interment in Evergreen Cemetery, Muskegon, Mich.

McLAUGHLIN, Joseph, a Representative from Pennsylvania; born in Burt, County Donegal, Ireland, June 9, 1867; immigrated to the United States and settled in Philadelphia in 1889; employed as a mechanic in the Baldwin Locomotive Works, advancing through successive grades until he became shop superintendent of his department; interested in various business enterprises; elected as a Republican to the Sixty-fifth Congress (March 4, 1917–March 3, 1919); unsuccessful candidate for renomination in 1918; elected to the Sixty-seventh Congress (March 4, 1921–March 3, 1923); the State having been redistricted, was not a candidate for renomination in 1922; retired from active business pursuits; died in Philadelphia, Pa., November 21, 1926; interment in Holy Cross Cemetery, Yeadon, Delaware County, Pa.

McLAUGHLIN, Melvin Orlando, a Representative from Nebraska; born in Osceola, Clarke County, Iowa, August 8, 1876; moved with his parents to Nebraska in 1884; attended the common schools and was graduated from the College View (Nebr.) High School; subsequently pursued his studies at the Lincoln (Nebr.) Normal University and the Nebraska State Normal School at Peru; taught school near Lincoln 1895–1900; was a student at the Iowa Christian College at Oskaloosa, Iowa, Omaha (Nebr.) University, and the Union Biblical Seminary, Dayton, Ohio; served in the ministry of the United Brethren Church, Omaha, Nebr., 1900–1913; moved to York, Nebr., in 1913; president of York College 1913–1918; was elected as a Republican to the Sixty-sixth and to the three succeeding Congresses (March 4, 1919–March 3, 1927); unsuccessful candidate for reelection in 1926 to the Seventieth Congress; engaged in mining and investments; died in York, York County, Nebr., on June 18, 1928; interment in Greenwood Cemetery.

McLAURIN, Anselm Joseph, a Senator from Mississippi; born in Brandon, Rankin County, Miss., March 26, 1848; moved with his parents to Smith County; attended the common schools and Summerville Institute; during the Civil War enlisted in the Confederate Army in 1864 and served as captain; again attended the Summerville Institute 1865–1867; studied law; was admitted to the bar in 1868 and began practice in Raleigh, Miss.; district attorney in 1871; member of the State house of representatives in 1879; presidential elector for the State at large on the Democratic ticket of Cleveland and Thurman in 1888; delegate to the State constitutional convention in 1890; elected as a Democrat to the United States Senate to fill the vacancy caused by the resignation of Edward C. Walthall and served from February 7, 1894, to March 3, 1895; Governor of Mississippi 1895–1900; again elected in 1900 to the United States Senate; reelected in 1906 and served from March 4, 1901, until his death; appointed a member of the United States Immigration Commission on February 25, 1908, and was holding that position when he died in Brandon, Miss., December 22, 1909; interment in Brandon Cemetery.

McLAURIN, John Lowndes, a Representative and a Senator from South Carolina; born in Red Bluff, Marlboro County, S. C., May 9, 1860; attended schools at Bennettsville, S. C., and Englewood, N. J., Bethel Military Academy, near Warrenton, Va., and Swarthmore (Pa.) College; was graduated from the Carolina Military Institute; studied law in the University of Virginia at Charlottesville; was admitted to the bar in 1883 and practiced in Bennettsville, Marlboro County, S. C.; member of the State house of representatives in 1890; attorney general of the State 1891–1897; elected as a Democrat to the Fifty-second Congress to fill the vacancy caused by the death of Eli T. Stackhouse; reelected to the Fifty-third, Fifty-fourth, and Fifty-fifth Congresses and served from December 5, 1892, until May 31, 1897, when he resigned; appointed and subsequently elected to the United States Senate to fill the vacancy caused by the death of Joseph H. Earle and served from June 1, 1897, to March 3, 1903; was not a candidate for reelection; moved to New York City and resumed the practice of law; returned to Bennettsville, S. C., and engaged in agricultural pursuits; member of the State senate in 1914 and 1915; author of the State warehouse system for storing and financing cotton; served as State warehouse commissioner from 1915 until his resignation in 1917; died at his estate near Bennettsville, S. C., July 29, 1934; interment in McCall Cemetery.

McLEAN, Alney, a Representative from Kentucky; born in Burke County, N. C., June 10, 1779; pursued preparatory studies; moved to Kentucky; appointed surveyor of Muhlenberg County in 1799 and elected one of the trustees of Greenville on its formation; studied law; was admitted to the bar and commenced practice in Greenville, Muhlenberg County, Ky., about 1805; member of the State house of representatives in 1812 and 1813; served as a captain in the War of 1812; elected to the Fourteenth Congress (March 4, 1815–March 3, 1817); elected to the Sixteenth Congress (March 4, 1819–March 3, 1821); served as judge of the fourteenth district of Kentucky from 1821 until his death; presidential elector on the Clay ticket in 1824 and on the National-Republican ticket of Clay and Sergeant in 1832; died near Greenville, Muhlenberg County, Ky., December 30, 1841; interment in Old Caney Station Cemetery, near Greenville, Ky.

McLEAN, Donald Holman, a Representative from New Jersey; born in Paterson, Passaic County, N. J., March 18, 1884; attended the public schools; was graduated from the law department of George Washington University, Washington, D. C., in 1906; served as a page in the United States Senate 1897–1902; secretary to Senator John Kean 1902–1911; admitted to the bar in 1909 and commenced practice in Elizabeth, N. J.; special master in chancery of New Jersey; supreme court commissioner of New Jersey; assistant prosecutor of the pleas of Union County, N. J., 1918–1923; elected as a Republican to the Seventy-third and to the five succeeding Congresses (March 4, 1933–January 3, 1945); was not a candidate for renomination in 1944; served as prosecutor of the pleas of Union County, N. J., from June 24, 1944, to April 18, 1946, when he was appointed judge of the New Jersey Court of Errors and Appeals; became judge of New Jersey Superior Court under reorganization of New Jersey judiciary in September 1948; reappointed in April 1952; retired March 18, 1954, under age requirement and returned to law practice; is a resident of Elizabeth (Hillside Township), N. J.

McLEAN, Finis Ewing, a Representative from Kentucky; born near Russellville, Logan County, Ky., February 19, 1806; attended the country schools and Lebanon Academy in Logan County; studied law; was admitted to the bar and commenced practice in Elkton, Ky., in 1827; also engaged in agricultural pursuits; member of the State house of representatives in 1837; presidential elector on the Whig ticket of Taylor and Fillmore in 1848; elected as a Whig to the Thirty-first Congress (March 4, 1849–March 3, 1851); resumed the practice of law and also engaged in agricultural pursuits; moved to Andrew County, Mo., in 1860 and engaged in farming until 1865; moved to Greencastle, Ind., in 1865, in which city he died April 12, 1881; interment in Forest Hill Cemetery.

McLEAN, George Payne, a Senator from Connecticut; born in Simsbury, Hartford County, Conn., October 7, 1857; attended the common schools, and the high school in Hartford, Conn.; studied law; was admitted to the bar in 1881 and commenced practice in Hartford, Conn.; member of the State house of representatives in 1883 and 1884; member of the commission to revise the Connecticut statutes in 1885; served in the State senate in 1886; United States district attorney for Connecticut 1892–1896; resumed the practice of law in Hartford; Governor of Connecticut in 1901 and 1902; elected as a Republican to the United States Senate in 1911; reelected in 1916 and again in 1922 and served from March 4, 1911, to March 3, 1929, when he voluntarily

retired, having declined to be a candidate for reelection in 1928; resumed the practice of law in Hartford, Conn.; died in Simsbury, Conn., June 6, 1932; interment in Simsbury Cemetery.

McLEAN, James Henry, a Representative from Missouri; born in Ayrshire, Scotland, August 13, 1829; reared in Nova Scotia, Canada; immigrated to the United States in 1842 and settled in Philadelphia, Pa.; employed as a clerk in a drug store; moved to St. Louis, Mo., in 1849, and in the following year to New Orleans, La., to take charge of financial operations of the Lopez expedition to Cuba; returned to St. Louis in 1851; studied medicine and surgery; was graduated from the St. Louis (Mo.) Medical College in 1863 and practiced in St. Louis; elected as a Republican to the Forty-seventh Congress to fill the vacancy caused by the death of Thomas Allen and served from December 15, 1882, to March 3, 1883; died in Dansville, Livingston County, N. Y., August 12, 1886; interment in Bellefontaine Cemetery, St. Louis, Mo.

McLEAN, John (brother of William McLean), a Representative from Ohio; born in Morris County, N. J., March 11, 1785; moved with his parents to Morgantown, Va., in 1789, to Nicholasville, Ky., in 1790, to Maysville, Ky., in 1793, and to Lebanon, Ohio, in 1797; attended the common schools and studied under private tutors; studied law; was admitted to the bar in 1807 and commenced practice in Lebanon, Ohio; founded the Western Star, a weekly newspaper; elected as a War Democrat to the Thirteenth and Fourteenth Congresses and served from March 4, 1813, until his resignation in 1816; associate judge of the State supreme court 1816–1822; appointed by President Monroe as Commissioner of the United States General Land Office in 1822; appointed Postmaster General in the Cabinet of President Monroe; reappointed by President John Quincy Adams and served from December 9, 1823, until March 7, 1829, when he resigned; declined Cabinet portfolios as Secretary of War and Secretary of the Navy in the administration of President Jackson; engaged in literary pursuits; Associate Justice of the Supreme Court of the United States from March 7, 1829, until his death in Cincinnati, Ohio, April 4, 1861; interment in Spring Grove Cemetery.

McLEAN, John (uncle of James David Walker), a Representative and a Senator from Illinois; born near Guilford Court House (now Greensboro), Guilford County, N. C., February 4, 1791; moved with his parents to Logan County, Ky., in 1795; pursued an academic course; moved to Illinois Territory in 1815; studied law; was admitted to the bar and commenced practice in Shawneetown, Gallatin County, Ill.; upon the admission of Illinois as a State into the Union was elected as a Democrat to the Fifteenth Congress and served from December 3, 1818, to March 3, 1819; unsuccessful candidate for reelection in 1818 to the Sixteenth Congress and for election in 1820 and 1822 to the Seventeenth and Eighteenth Congresses, respectively; member of the State house of representatives in 1820, 1826, and 1828, and served as speaker; elected to the United States Senate to fill the vacancy caused by the resignation of Ninian Edwards and served from November 23, 1824, to March 3, 1825; was not a candidate for reelection; resumed the practice of law; again elected to the United States Senate and served from March 4, 1829, until his death in Shawneetown, Ill., October 14, 1830; interment in Westwood Cemetery, near Shawneetown, Ill.

McLEAN, Samuel, a Delegate from the Territory of Montana; born at Summit Hill, Carbon County, Pa., August 7, 1826; attended the select schools of Wyoming Valley, Pa., and Lafayette College, Easton, Pa.; studied law; was admitted to the bar in 1849 and commenced practice in Mauch Chunk, Pa.; prosecuting attorney of Carbon County, Pa., 1855–1860;

attorney general of the provisional Territory of Jefferson (afterward Colorado) in 1860; moved to Bannock, Mont., in 1862; when the Territory of Montana was formed was elected as a Democrat to the Thirty-eighth and Thirty-ninth Congresses and served from January 6, 1865, to March 3, 1867; was not a candidate for renomination in 1866; president of McLean Silver Mining Co. in 1870; moved to Virginia and settled on a plantation near Burkeville in 1870; died in Burkeville, Nottoway County, Va., July 16, 1877; interment in the churchyard of the Presbyterian Church.

McLEAN, William (brother of John McLean), a Representative from Ohio; born in Mason County, Ky., August 10, 1794; moved with his parents to a farm in Warren County, Ohio, in 1799; attended the common schools; studied law; was admitted to the bar in 1814 and commenced practice in Cincinnati, Ohio; moved to Piqua, Miami County, Ohio, in 1820; receiver of public moneys in Piqua, Ohio; through his efforts a subsidy of 500,000 acres of land was procured for building the Ohio Canal from Cincinnati to Cleveland; elected to the Eighteenth, Nineteenth, and Twentieth Congresses (March 4, 1823–March 3, 1829); returned to Cincinnati, Ohio; engaged in mercantile pursuits and the practice of his profession in Cincinnati; also interested in agricultural pursuits; died in Cincinnati October 12, 1839; interment in the Catharine Street Burying Ground; reinterment in Spring Grove Cemetery April 2, 1863.

McLEAN, William Pinkney, a Representative from Texas; born in Copiah County, Miss., August 9, 1836; moved with his mother to Marshall, Tex., in 1839; attended private schools until seventeen years of age, and was graduated from the law department of the University of North Carolina at Chapel Hill in 1857; was admitted to the bar in 1857 and commenced the practice of his profession at Jefferson, Marion County, Tex.; member of the State house of representatives in 1861; resigned to enter the Confederate Army as a private; was promoted to captain and then major, and served throughout the Civil War; again a member of the State house of representatives in 1869; elected as a Democrat to the Forty-third Congress (March 4, 1873–March 3, 1875); was not a candidate for renomination in 1874; resumed the practice of law in Mount Pleasant, Titus County, Tex.; member of the State constitutional convention in 1875; elected judge of the fifth judicial district in 1884; declined to be a candidate for reelection; appointed by Governor Hogg a member of the first State railroad commission in 1891; resigned, and moved to Fort Worth, Tarrant County, Tex., in 1893; resumed the practice of his profession; died in Fort Worth on March 13, 1925; interment in Mount Olivet Cemetery.

McLEMORE, Atkins Jefferson (Jeff), a Representative from Texas; born on a farm near Spring Hill, Maury County, Tenn., March 13, 1857; educated in the rural schools and by private tutors; moved to Texas in 1878; employed as a cowboy, printer, and newspaper reporter, and later as a miner in Colorado and Mexico; returned to Texas and settled in San Antonio and engaged principally in newspaper work; moved to Corpus Christi, Tex., in 1889, to Austin in 1895, and to Houston in 1911, where he engaged in the newspaper publishing business; member of the Texas House of Representatives of 1892–1896; member of the board of aldermen of Austin, Tex., 1896–1898; secretary of the Democratic State executive committee 1900–1904; elected as a Democrat to the Sixty-fourth and Sixty-fifth Congresses (March 4, 1915–March 3, 1919); was an unsuccessful candidate for reelection in 1918 to the Sixty-sixth Congress; resumed the newspaper publishing business in Hebronville, Jim Hogg County, Tex., and resided in Laredo, Tex.; was an unsuccessful

candidate for election to the United States Senate in 1928; died in Laredo, Tex., March 4, 1929; interment in Oakwood Cemetery, Austin, Tex.

McLENE, Jeremiah, a Representative from Ohio; born in Cumberland County, Pa., in 1767; attended the common schools; served in the Revolutionary War as major general of militia; moved to Ohio and settled in Chillicothe, Ross County; member of the State house of representatives in 1807 and 1808; secretary of state of Ohio 1808–1831; moved to Columbus, Ohio, in 1816; elected as a Democrat to the Twenty-third and Twenty-fourth Congresses (March 4, 1833–March 3, 1837); unsuccessful for reelection in 1836 to the Twenty-fifth Congress; died in Washington D. C., March 19, 1837; interment in Congressional Cemetery.

McLEOD, Clarence John, a Representative from Michigan; born in Detroit, Wayne County, Mich., July 3, 1895; attended the public schools; was graduated from Detroit Central High School and from the Detroit College of Law in 1918; during the First World War served as a private in the aviation section at the ground school, Cornell University, Ithaca, N. Y., from March 1, 1918, until his discharge July 17, 1918; again served as sergeant in the Intelligence Division, from September 10, 1918, until his discharge April 24, 1919; accepted appointment May 12, 1919, as second lieutenant in the Officers' Reserve Corps, and successively as captain, major, and lieutenant colonel; was admitted to the bar in 1919 and commenced practice in Detroit, Mich.; elected as a Republican to the Sixty-sixth Congress to fill the vacancy caused by the death of Charles A. Nichols and served from November 2, 1920, to March 3, 1921; was not a candidate for election to the Sixty-seventh Congress; elected to the Sixty-eighth and to the six succeeding Congresses (March 4, 1923–January 3, 1937); unsuccessful candidate for reelection in 1936 to the Seventy-fifth Congress; defeated for the Republican nomination for Governor in 1934 and for mayor of Detroit in 1937; elected to the Seventy-sixth Congress (January 3, 1939–January 3, 1941); unsuccessful candidate for reelection in 1940 to the Seventy-seventh Congress, for election in 1942 to the Seventy-eighth Congress, and in 1944 to the Seventy-ninth Congress; unsuccessful candidate for the Republican nomination to the Eightieth Congress in 1946; unsuccessful candidate in 1950 to to the Eighty-second Congress and in 1952 to the Eighty-third Congress; practiced law; consultant to Administrator of Federal Civil Defense Administration; died in Detroit, Mich., May 15, 1959; interment in Mount Olivet Cemetery.

McMAHON, Gregory, a Representative from New York; born in New York, N. Y., March 19, 1915; attended a parochial school; was graduated from St. John's Prep School, Brooklyn, N. Y., in 1933 and from St. John's University, Brooklyn, N. Y., in 1938; also attended St. John's Law School 1939–1941; certified public accountant since 1939; taught at St. John's College 1939–1942; during World War II served in the United States Navy as an ensign from December 1941 to October 1945; was in the Pacific area for eighteen months, participating in thirty-two engagements or supporting operations, and was awarded eleven battle stars; elected as a Republican to the Eightieth Congress (January 3, 1947–January 3, 1949); unsuccessful candidate for reelection in 1948 to the Eighty-first Congress; accountant and tax consultant; is a resident of Ozone Park, N. Y.

McMAHON, James O'Brien, a Senator from Connecticut; born in Norwalk, Fairfield County, Conn., October 6, 1903; attended the public schools; was graduated from Fordham University, New York, N. Y., in 1924 and from the law school of Yale University, New Haven, Conn., in 1927; was admitted to the bar the same year and commenced practice in Norwalk, Conn.;

city judge of Norwalk, Conn., in 1933, but resigned to become special assistant to the Attorney General of the United States 1933–1935; Assistant Attorney General of the United States in charge of the Department of Justice Criminal Division 1935–1939; resumed the practice of his profession in Washington, D. C., and Norwalk, Conn.; elected as a Democrat to the United States Senate in 1944; reelected in 1950 and served from January 3, 1945, until his death in Washington, D. C., July 28, 1952; interment in St. Mary's Cemetery, Norwalk, Conn.

McMAHON, John A. (nephew of Clement Laird Vallandigham), a Representative from Ohio; born in Frederick County, Md., February 19, 1833; pursued academic studies; attended St. Xavier's College, Cincinnati, and was graduated in 1849; studied law; was admitted to the bar in 1854 and commenced practice in Dayton, Ohio; delegate to the Democratic National Convention at Baltimore in 1872 and at St. Louis in 1904; elected as a Democrat to the Forty-fourth, Forty-fifth, and Forty-sixth Congresses (March 4, 1875–March 3, 1881); one of the managers appointed by the House of Representatives in 1876 to conduct the impeachment proceedings against William W. Belknap, Secretary of War; unsuccessful candidate for reelection in 1880 to the Forty-seventh Congress; resumed the practice of his profession in Dayton, Montgomery County, Ohio; served as president of the Ohio State Bar Association in 1886; unsuccessful candidate for election to the United States Senate in 1889; died in Dayton, Ohio, March 8, 1923; interment in Woodland Cemetery.

McMANUS, William, a Representative from New York; born in Brunswick, Rensselaer County, N. Y., in 1780; received an academic education; studied law; was admitted to the bar in 1817 and commenced practice in Troy, Rensselaer County, N. Y.; surrogate of Rensselaer County 1815–1818; district attorney 1818–1821; elected to the Nineteenth Congress (March 4, 1825–March 3, 1827); resumed the practice of law; moved to Texas in 1833; returned to Brunswick, N. Y., the following year, where he died January 18, 1835.

McMASTER, William Henry, a Senator from South Dakota; born in Ticonic, Monona County, Iowa, May 10, 1877; attended the public schools at Sioux City, Iowa; was graduated from Sioux City High School in 1895 and from Beloit (Wis.) College in 1899; moved to Yankton, Yankton County, S. Dak., in 1901 and engaged in banking; member of the State house of representatives in 1911 and 1912; served in the State senate 1913–1916; Lieutenant Governor of South Dakota 1917–1920 and Governor 1921–1924; elected as a Republican to the United States Senate and served from March 4, 1925, to March 3, 1931; unsuccessful candidate for reelection in 1930; moved to Dixon, Ill., in 1933 and is now engaged in the banking business.

McMILLAN, Alexander, a Representative from North Carolina; member of the State senate 1810–1812; elected to the Fifteenth Congress and served from March 4, 1817, until his death in that year.

McMILLAN, Clara Gooding (widow of Thomas S. McMillan), a Representative from South Carolina; born in Brunson, Hampton County, S. C., August 17, 1894; attended the public schools, Confederate Home College, Charleston, S. C., and Flora MacDonald College, Red Springs, N. C.; elected as a Democrat to the Seventy-sixth Congress to fill the vacancy caused by the death of her husband, Thomas S. McMillan, and served from November 7, 1939, to January 3, 1941; was not a candidate for nomination in 1940; appointed information liaison officer for the Department of State, Washington, D. C., on January 1, 1946, and served until July 31, 1957; is a resident of Ulmers, S. C.

McMILLAN, James, a Senator from Michigan; born in Hamilton, Ontario, May 12, 1838; educated in the public schools of Hamilton; moved to Detroit, Mich., in 1855, where he entered upon a business career; purchasing agent of the Detroit & Milwaukee Railroad; an organizer of the Michigan Car Co. in 1863; built the Duluth, South Shore & Atlantic Railroad and was its president; largely interested in shipbuilding and lake transportation companies; member of the Republican State central committee in 1876, and on the death of Zachariah Chandler was made chairman; again in 1886 and 1890 elected chairman of the committee; for three years was president of the Detroit Board of Park Commissioners and for four years a member of the Detroit Board of Estimates; presidential elector on the Republican ticket of Blaine and Logan in 1884; elected as a Republican to the United States Senate in 1889; reelected in 1895 and 1901, and served from March 3, 1889, until his death in Manchester, Essex County, Mass., August 10, 1902; interment in Elmwood Cemetery, Detroit, Mich.

McMILLAN, John Lanneau, a Representative from South Carolina; born on a farm near Mullins, Marion County, S. C., April 12, 1898; attended the public schools, the University of North Carolina at Chapel Hill, and the law school of the University of South Carolina at Columbia; during the First World War served in the United States Navy from August 2, 1918, to December 17, 1918; moved to Florence, S. C.; served as secretary to Congressman Allard H. Gasque from December 1, 1923, until elected to Congress; elected as a Democrat to the Seventy-sixth and to the ten succeeding Congresses (January 3, 1939–January 3, 1961). *Reelected to the Eighty-seventh Congress.*

McMILLAN, Samuel, a Representative from New York; born in County Down, town of Drumore, Ireland, August 6, 1850; immigrated to the United States with his parents, who settled in New York City and later moved to Niles, Trumbull County, Ohio; attended the common schools; returned to New York City and took up the trade of carpenter; attended night school as a student of architecture; engaged in banking; was also vice president of the Ryan-Parker Construction Company, contractors for the Manhattan Bridge over the East River from New York City to Brooklyn; served as a member of the board of examiners of the building department, city of New York, for twelve years, and park commissioner and president of the board for three years under Mayor Strong's administration; elected as a Republican to the Sixtieth Congress (March 4, 1907–March 3, 1909); was not a candidate for renomination in 1908 to the Sixty-first Congress; engaged in banking; died in New York City on May 6, 1924; interment in Woodlawn Cemetery.

McMILLAN, Samuel James Renwick, a Senator from Minnesota; born in Brownsville, Fayette County, Pa., February 22, 1826; completed preparatory studies; was graduated from Duquesne College, Pittsburgh, Pa., in 1846; studied law; was admitted to the bar in 1849 and commenced practice in Pittsburgh, Pa.; moved to St. Paul, Minn., in 1852, then to Stillwater, Minn., in 1854, and engaged in the practice of law in both cities; returned to St. Paul in 1856; judge of the first judicial district 1858–1864; served as second lieutenant of the Stillwater Frontier Guards during the Indian war of 1862; appointed and subsequently elected associate justice of the State supreme court in 1864 for a term of seven years; reelected in 1871 and served until his resignation in 1874; appointed in 1874 and subsequently elected chief justice of the State supreme court and served until March 10, 1875, when he resigned; elected as a Republican to the United States Senate in 1875; reelected in 1881 and served from March 4, 1875, to March 3,

1887; was not a candidate for renomination in 1886; engaged in the practice of law until his death in St. Paul, Minn., October 3, 1897; interment in Oakland Cemetery.

McMILLAN, Thomas Sanders (husband of Clara Gooding McMillan), a Representative from South Carolina; born near Ulmers, Allendale County (formerly part of Barnwell County), S. C., November 27, 1888; attended the common schools near Ulmers, and was graduated from Orangeburg (S. C.) Collegiate Institute in 1907; taught school at Perry, Aiken County, S. C., in 1907 and 1908; won a competitive scholarship from Barnwell County to the University of South Carolina at Columbia in 1908 and was graduated from that institution in 1912; returned to the university in the fall of 1912 and completed the law course in 1913; was admitted to the bar in 1913 and commenced the practice of law in Charleston, S. C.; also interested in agricultural pursuits; member of the State house of representatives 1917–1924, serving as speaker pro tempore in 1921 and 1922 and as speaker in 1923 and 1924; was not a candidate for renomination in 1924; elected as a Democrat to the Sixty-ninth and to the seven succeeding Congresses and served from March 4, 1925, until his death; member of the executive committee of the Interparliamentary Union 1937–1939, serving as delegate to the convention held in Oslo, Norway, in 1939; died in Charleston, S. C., September 29, 1939; interment in Magnolia Cemetery.

McMILLAN, William, a Delegate from the Territory Northwest of the River Ohio; born near Abingdon, Washington County, Va., March 2, 1764; was graduated from William and Mary College, Williamsburg, Va.; studied law; moved to Fort Washington (now Cincinnati, Ohio) in 1787; was admitted to the bar in 1788 and commenced practice in Cincinnati; first justice of the court of general quarter sessions in 1790; member of the Territorial house of representatives in 1799 and 1800; elected to the Sixth Congress to fill the vacancy caused by the resignation of William H. Harrison and served from November 24, 1800, to March 3, 1801; declined renomination in 1800; after admission of Ohio into the Union in 1803 was appointed United States district attorney for Ohio, but owing to declining health did not assume the duties; died in Cincinnati, Ohio, in May 1804; interment in Spring Grove Cemetery.

McMILLEN, Rolla Coral, a Representative from Illinois; born near Monticello, Piatt County, Ill., October 5, 1880; attended the public schools of Monticello, Ill., and the University of Illinois at Chicago; was graduated from the University of Michigan Law School at Ann Arbor in 1906; was admitted to the bar the same year and commenced practice in Decatur, Ill.; delegate to the Republican National Convention at Philadelphia in 1940; member of State housing board 1940–1944; elected as a Republican to the Seventy-eighth Congress to fill the vacancy caused by the death of William H. Wheat; reelected to the Seventy-ninth, Eightieth, and Eighty-first Congresses, and served from June 13, 1944, to January 3, 1951; was not a candidate for renomination in 1950; died in Evanston, Ill., May 6, 1961; interment in Greenwood Cemetery, Decatur, Ill.

McMILLIN, Benton, a Representative from Tennessee; born in Monroe County, Ky., September 11, 1845; attended Philomath Academy, Tennessee, and the University of Kentucky at Lexington; studied law; was admitted to the bar and commenced practice in Celina, Clay County, Tenn., in 1871; member of the State house of representatives in 1874; commissioned by the Governor to treat with the State of Kentucky for the purchase of territory in 1875; presidential elector on the Democratic ticket of Tilden and Hendricks in 1876; commissioned by the Governor as a special judge of the circuit court in 1877; elected

as a Democrat to the Forty-sixth and to the nine succeeding Congresses and served from March 4, 1879, until his resignation on January 6, 1899, to become Governor; elected Governor of Tennessee in 1898, reelected in 1900, and served until 1903; engaged in the insurance business in Nashville, Tenn.; appointed Envoy Extraordinary and Minister Plenipotentiary to Peru July 2, 1913, and served until September 22, 1919; represented the United States at Guatemala in the same capacity from September 23, 1919, to January 5, 1922; resumed the insurance business in Nashville, Tenn., where he died on January 8, 1933; interment in Mount Olivet Cemetery.

McMORRAN, Henry Gordon, a Representative from Michigan; born in Port Huron, Mich., June 11, 1844; attended the Crawford Private School; engaged in the wholesale grocery business in 1865 and also in the milling, grain, and elevator business; member of the board of aldermen in 1867; city treasurer of Port Huron in 1875; general manager of the Port Huron & Northwestern Railway 1878–1889; member of the State canal commission; elected as a Republican to the Fifty-eighth and to the four succeeding Congresses (March 4, 1903–March 3, 1913); was not a candidate for renomination in 1912; engaged in numerous business enterprises at Port Huron, Mich.; organized the Great Lakes Foundry Co., serving as its president; director of the First National Bank & Trust Co.; died in Port Huron, Mich., July 19, 1929; interment in Lakeside Cemetery.

McMULLEN, Chester Bartow, a Representative from Florida; born in Largo, Pinellas County, Fla., December 6, 1902; attended the public schools of Largo, Fla.; was graduated from the college of law at the University of Florida in 1924; was admitted to the bar in 1924 and commenced the practice of law in Clearwater, Fla.; prosecuting attorney of Pinellas County, Fla., in 1927 and 1928; elected State attorney for the sixth judicial circuit of Florida in 1930 and served until elected to Congress in 1950; director of the First National Bank of Clearwater; elected as a Democrat to the Eighty-second Congress (January 3, 1951–January 3, 1953); was not a candidate for renomination in 1952; died in Clearwater, Fla., November 3, 1953; interment in Sylvan Abbey, Clearwater, Fla.

McMULLEN, Fayette, a Representative from Virginia; born in Estellville (now Gate City), Scott County, Va., May 18, 1805; attended private schools; State driver and teamster; member of the State senate 1839–1849; elected as a Democrat to the Thirty-first and to the three succeeding Congresses (March 4, 1849–March 3, 1857); delegate to the Democratic National Convention at Baltimore in 1852 and at Cincinnati in 1856; Governor of Washington Territory 1857–1861; elected as a Representative from Virginia to the Second Confederate Congress and served to the end of the Confederacy; engaged in agricultural pursuits and banking; was killed by a train in Wytheville, Va., November 8, 1880; interment in Round Hill Cemetery, Marion, Va.

McMURRAY, Howard Johnstone, a Representative from Wisconsin; born in Harvey County, near Mount Hope, Kans., March 3, 1901; attended the public schools, Berea Academy at Berea, Ky., and high school at Madison, Wis.; was graduated from the University of Wisconsin at Madison in 1936; engaged in the life insurance business 1923–1928; executive with air transport companies 1928–1935; teacher of political science at the University of Wisconsin 1936–1942; elected as a Democrat to the Seventy-eighth Congress (January 3, 1943–January 3, 1945); was not a candidate for renomination in 1944, but was an unsuccessful Democratic candidate for election to the United States Senate in 1944 and again in 1946; lecturer in political science at the University of Wisconsin in 1945 and 1946; professor of political science and chairman curriculum in applied politics and economics at Occidental College, Los Angeles, Calif., 1947–1949; professor of government, University of New Mexico, from 1949 until his death in Albuquerque, N. Mex., August 14, 1961; interment in Fairview Park Cemetery.

McNAGNY, William Forgy, a Representative from Indiana; born in Talmadge, Summit County, Ohio, April 19, 1850; moved in early life to Whitley County, Ind.; attended the public schools and the Springfield Academy, South Whitley, Ind.; taught school; worked on his father's farm for six years; station agent for the Pennsylvania Railroad Co. at Larwill, Ind., 1868–1875; studied law; was admitted to the bar in 1875 and commenced practice in Columbia City, Whitley County, Ind.; elected as a Democrat to the Fifty-third Congress (March 4, 1893–March 3, 1895); unsuccessful candidate for reelection in 1894 to the Fifty-fourth Congress; resumed the practice of law in Columbia City, Ind., and died there August 24, 1923; interment in Masonic Cemetery.

McNAIR, John, a Representative from Pennsylvania; born in Bucks County, Pa., June 8, 1800; received an academic education; taught school; principal of Loller Academy, Hatboro, Pa., in 1825; established a school for boys in the village of Abington; clerk of the courts of Montgomery County 1845–1848; became a resident of Norristown, Pa.; elected as a Democrat to the Thirty-second and Thirty-third Congresses (March 4, 1851–March 3, 1855); settled on a plantation in Prince William County, near Gainesville, Va.; died at Evansport, near Aquia Creek, Va., August 12, 1861.

McNAMARA, Patrick Vincent, a Senator from Michigan; born in North Weymouth, Mass., October 4, 1894; attended the public schools in Weymouth and Fore River Apprentice School in Quincy, Mass.; moved to Detroit, Mich., in 1921; engaged in the construction industry 1921–1955; Director, Detroit area of Office of Price Administration, Rent Division, 1942–1945; vice president of Stanley-Carter Co., Detroit, Mich., 1946–1954; member of the Detroit City Council in 1946 and 1947, and the Detroit Board of Education 1949–1955; elected as a Democrat to the United States Senate in 1954 for the term commencing January 3, 1955, and ending January 3, 1961. *Reelected in 1960 for the term ending January 3, 1967.*

McNARY, Charles Linza, a Senator from Oregon; born on a farm near Salem, Marion County, Oreg., June 12, 1874; attended the public schools and Leland Stanford Junior University, California; studied law; was admitted to the bar in 1898 and commenced practice in Salem, Oreg.; deputy district attorney of the third judicial district 1906–1913; dean of the law department of Willamette University, Salem, Oreg., 1908–1913; associate justice of the State supreme court 1913–1915; chairman of the Republican State central committee in 1916 and 1917; appointed as a Republican to the United States Senate to fill the vacancy in the term ending March 3, 1919, caused by the death of Harry Lane and served from May 29, 1917, until November 5, 1918, when Frederick W. Mulkey was elected to fill this vacancy; again appointed to the United States Senate, on December 12, 1918, to become effective December 18, 1918, to fill the vacancy in the same term caused by the resignation of Frederick W. Mulkey, having been previously elected for the term beginning March 4, 1919; reelected in 1924, 1930, 1936, and again in 1942, and served from December 18, 1918, until his death; unsuccessful candidate for Vice President of the United States on the Republican ticket with Wendell Willkie for President in 1940; elected minority leader in March 1933, in which capacity he was serving when he died at Fort Lauderdale, Fla., February 25, 1944; interment in Odd Fellows Cemetery, Salem, Oreg.

McNARY, William Sarsfield, a Representative from Massachusetts; born in Abington, Plymouth County, Mass., March 29, 1863; attended the public schools of Abington and graduated from the Boston English High School; engaged in newspaper work; reporter and managing editor of the Boston Commercial Bulletin 1880–1892; also engaged in the retail and wholesale furniture business; member of the Boston City Council in 1887 and 1888; member of the State house of representatives in 1889 and 1890; served in the State senate in 1891 and 1892; water commissioner of Boston in 1893 and 1894; again a member of the State house of representatives 1900–1902; engaged in the insurance business and a dealer in real estate; delegate to the Democratic National Convention at Kansas City in 1900 and at St. Louis in 1904; elected as a Democrat to the Fifty-eighth and Fifty-ninth Congresses (March 4, 1903–March 3, 1907); was not a candidate for renomination in 1906; continued his former business pursuits in Boston, Mass., until his death in that city on June 26, 1930; interment in St. Joseph's Cemetery, West Roxbury, Mass.

McNEELY, Thompson Ware, a Representative from Illinois; born in Jacksonville, Morgan County, Ill., October 5, 1835; attended the public schools and Jubilee College, Peoria, Ill.; was graduated from Lombard College, Galesburg, Ill., in 1856 and from the law department of the University of Louisville, Kentucky, in 1857; was admitted to the bar in 1857 and commenced practice in Petersburg, Menard County, Ill.; member of the Illinois constitutional convention in 1862; elected as a Democrat to the Forty-first and Forty-second Congresses (March 4, 1869–March 3, 1873); did not seek renomination in 1872; delegate to the Democratic National Conventions in 1872, 1892, and 1896; presidential elector on the Democratic ticket of Cleveland and Stevenson in 1892 and of Bryan and Sewall in 1896; resumed the practice of law in Petersburg, Ill.; master in chancery for Menard County from 1910 until his death in Petersburg, Ill., July 23, 1921; interment in Rosehill Cemetery.

McNEILL, Archibald, a Representative from North Carolina; born in Moore County, N. C.; member of the State house of commons in 1808 and 1809; served in the State senate 1811–1813, 1820, and 1821; elected to the Seventeenth Congress (March 4, 1821–March 3, 1823); elected to the Nineteenth Congress (March 4, 1825–March 3, 1827); moved to Texas in 1836; in 1849 raised and was chosen captain of about one hundred men who started for California, where gold had been discovered; struck by a sandstorm while crossing a desert (in what is now part of Arizona), he and most of the men were killed; his remains were never recovered.

McNULTA, John, a Representative from Illinois; born in New York City November 9, 1837; pursued an academic course; visited the West Indies and Europe; moved to Attica, Fountain County, Ind., in 1853 and to Bloomington, Ill., in 1859; engaged in the manufacture of cigars; studied law; during the Civil War served in the Union Army; captain of the First Regiment, Illinois Volunteer Cavalry, July 3, 1861; honorably mustered out July 14, 1862; recommissioned lieutenant colonel of the Ninety-fourth Regiment, Illinois Volunteer Infantry, August 20, 1862; colonel June 21, 1863; brevetted brigadier general of Volunteers March 13, 1865, "for gallant and meritorious services in the siege and reduction of Spanish Fort, Ala."; mustered out July 17, 1865; was admitted to the bar in 1865 and commenced the practice of law in Bloomington, Ill.; member of the State senate 1869–1873; elected as a Republican to the Forty-third Congress (March 4, 1873–March 3, 1875); unsuccessful candidate for reelection in 1874 to the Forty-fourth Congress; resumed the practice of law; died in Washington, D. C., February 22, 1900; interment in Evergreen Cemetery, Bloomington, Ill.

McNULTY, Frank Joseph, a Representative from New Jersey; born in Londonderry, Ireland, August 10, 1872; immigrated to the United States in 1876 with his parents, who settled in New York City; attended the public schools of New York City; vice president of the International Brotherhood of Electrical Workers in 1901; elected president of the same organization in 1903, and served until 1918, when he resigned; president emeritus and chairman of the international board of directors of that organization; member of the commission to study municipal and public ownership of public utilities in England, Ireland, and Scotland by the National Civic Federation; during the First World War served as vice chairman of the Railway Board of Adjustment No. 2; resigned to visit France and Italy on an important commission at the request of the Government; deputy director of public safety of Newark 1917–1921; elected as a Democrat to the Sixty-eighth Congress (March 4, 1923–March 3, 1925); unsuccessful candidate for reelection in 1924 to the Sixty-ninth Congress; resumed his former business activities; died in Newark, N. J., May 26, 1926; interment in Holy Sepulchre Cemetery, East Orange, N. J.

McPHERSON, Edward, a Representative from Pennsylvania; born in Gettysburg, Pa., July 31, 1830; attended the common schools; was graduated from Pennsylvania College in 1848; studied law; edited the Harrisburg American in 1851, the Independent Whig, Lancaster, Pa., 1851–1854, and the Daily Times, Pittsburgh, Pa., in 1855; elected as a Republican to the Thirty-sixth and Thirty-seventh Congresses (March 4, 1859–March 3, 1863); unsuccessful candidate for reelection in 1862 to the Thirty-eighth Congress; appointed Deputy Commissioner of Internal Revenue in 1863; Clerk of the National House of Representatives from December 8, 1863, to December 5, 1875; permanent president of the Republican National Convention at Cincinnati in 1876; Director of the United States Bureau of Engraving and Printing in 1877 and 1878; editor of the Philadelphia Press 1877–1880; again served as Clerk of the House of Representatives from December 1881 to December 1883 and from December 1889 to December 1891; editor and proprietor of a paper in Gettysburg, Pa., 1880–1895; editor of the New York Tribune Almanac 1877–1895; American editor of the Almanach de Gotha; died in Gettysburg, Pa., December 14, 1895; interment in Evergreen Cemetery.

McPHERSON, Isaac Vanbert, a Representative from Missouri; born near Rome, Douglas County, Mo., March 8, 1868; moved to Bradleyville, Taney County, Mo., with his parents; attended the graded schools, Springfield (Mo.) High School, and Marionville (Mo.) College; studied law; was admitted to the bar in 1889 and commenced practice in Mount Vernon, Lawrence County, Mo.; prosecuting attorney of Lawrence County in 1901 and 1902; member of the State house of representatives in 1903 and 1904; appointed postmaster at Aurora, Lawrence County, Mo., in 1905 and served until 1912; continued the practice of law in Aurora, Mo.; elected as a Republican to the Sixty-sixth and Sixty-seventh Congresses (March 4, 1919–March 3, 1923); unsuccessful candidate for renomination in 1922; appointed as assistant counsel in the legal department of the United States Shipping Board Emergency Fleet Corporation in 1923 and served in that capacity until his death in Aurora, Mo., October 31, 1931; interment in Maple Park Cemetery.

McPHERSON, John Rhoderic, a Senator from New Jersey; born in York, Livingston County, N. Y., May 9, 1833; attended the common schools and pursued an academic course; moved to Jersey City, N. J., in 1859; engaged in agricultural pursuits and was also a dealer in livestock; member of the board of aldermen of Jersey City 1864–1870 and served as president of the board for three years; member of the State senate 1871–1873; presidential elector on the Democratic ticket of Tilden and Hendricks in 1876; elected as a Democrat to the United States Senate in 1877; reelected in 1883 and 1889, and served from March 4, 1877, to March 3, 1895; delegate to the Democratic National Conventions in 1884, 1888, and 1892, in each of which Grover Cleveland received the nomination for President; died in Jersey City, N. J., October 8, 1897; interment in Oak Hill Cemetery, Washington, D. C.

McPHERSON, Smith, a Representative from Iowa; born near Mooresville, Morgan County, Ind., February 14, 1848; attended the common schools and Mooresville Academy; was graduated from the law department of the University of Iowa at Iowa City in June 1870; was admitted to the bar the same year and commenced practice in Red Oak, Montgomery County, Iowa; State's attorney in 1872; attorney general of Iowa 1881–1885; resumed the practice of law; elected as a Republican to the Fifty-sixth Congress and served from March 4, 1899, until his resignation on June 6, 1900, to accept the appointment of United States district judge for the southern district of Iowa; served until his death in Red Oak, Iowa, January 17, 1915; interment in Evergreen Cemetery.

McQUEEN, John, a Representative from South Carolina; born in Queensdale, near the town of Maxton, Robeson County, N. C., February 9, 1804; completed preparatory studies under private tutors, and was graduated from the University of North Carolina at Chapel Hill; studied law; was admitted to the bar in 1828 and commenced practice in Bennettsville, S. C.; served in the State militia 1833–1837; unsuccessful candidate for election in 1844 to the Twenty-ninth Congress; elected as a Democrat to the Thirtieth and Thirty-first Congresses to fill the vacancies caused by the death of Alexander D. Sims; reelected to the Thirty-second and to the four succeeding Congresses, and served from February 12, 1849, until his retirement on December 21, 1860; Representative from South Carolina in the First Confederate Congress; died at Society Hill, S. C., August 30, 1867; interment in Episcopal Cemetery, Society Hill, S. C.

McRAE, John Jones, a Senator and a Representative from Mississippi; born in Sneedsboro (now McFarlan), N. C., January 10, 1815; moved with his parents to Winchester, Wayne County, Miss., in 1817; pursued an academic course; was graduated from Miami University, Oxford, Ohio, in 1834; studied law in Pearlington, Miss.; was admitted to the bar and practiced; founded the Eastern Clarion at Paulding, Miss.; member of the State house of representatives 1848–1850, serving as speaker in 1850; appointed as a Democrat to the United States Senate to fill the vacancy caused by the resignation of Jefferson Davis and served from December 1, 1851, to March 17, 1852, when a successor was elected and qualified; Governor of Mississippi 1854–1858; elected as a State Rights Democrat to the Thirty-fifth Congress to fill the vacancy caused by the death of John A. Quitman; reelected to the Thirty-sixth Congress and served from December 7, 1858, until he withdrew on January 12, 1861, with the entire delegation; Representative from Mississippi in the Confederate Congress 1862–1864; went to British Honduras in May 1868, and died at Belize May 31, 1868; interment at Belize, British Honduras.

McRAE, Thomas Chipman (cousin of Thomas Banks Cabaniss), a Representative from Arkansas; born in Mount Holly, Union County, Ark., December 21, 1851; attended private schools in Shady Grove, Columbia County, in Mount Holly, Union County, and in Falcon, Nevada County, Ark.; was graduated from Soule Business College, New Orleans, La., in 1869, and from the law school of Washington and Lee University, Lexington, Va., in 1872; was admitted to the bar in 1873 and commenced practice in Rosston, Nevada County, Ark.; appointed election commissioner in 1874; member of the State house of representatives in 1877, in which year the county seat was changed, when he moved from Rosston to Prescott; presidential elector on the Democratic ticket of Hancock and English in 1880; chairman of the Democratic State conventions of 1884 and 1902; delegate to the Democratic National Convention at Chicago in 1884; elected as a Democrat to the Forty-ninth Congress to fill the vacancy caused by the resignation of James K. Jones; reelected to the Fiftieth and to the seven succeeding Congresses and served from December 7, 1885, to March 3, 1903; voluntarily retired; resumed the practice of law and also engaged in banking in Prescott, Ark.; president of the Arkansas Bankers' Association in 1909 and 1910; chairman of the committee that prepared the Arkansas bank law; president of the Arkansas Bar Association in 1917 and 1918; member of the Arkansas constitutional convention in 1918; Governor of Arkansas from January 14, 1921, to January 14, 1925; elected life member Arkansas Democratic State convention in 1926; resumed the practice of law and engaged in banking until his death in Prescott, Ark., on June 2, 1929; interment in De Ann Cemetery.

McREYNOLDS, Samuel Davis, a Representative from Tennessee; born on a farm near Pikeville, Bledsoe County, Tenn., April 16, 1872; attended the rural schools, People's College, Pikeville, Tenn., and Cumberland University, Lebanon, Tenn.; studied law; was admitted to the bar in 1893 and commenced practice at Pikeville; served as assistant district attorney of the sixth judicial circuit of Tennessee in 1894 and 1896; moved to Chattanooga in 1896 and continued the practice of law; appointed judge of the criminal court for the sixth circuit of Tennessee on April 16, 1903; subsequently elected and twice reelected to the same office and served until February 1, 1923, when he resigned, having been elected to Congress; elected as a Democrat to the Sixty-eighth and to the eight succeeding Congresses and served from March 4, 1923, until his death; delegate to the International Monetary and Economic Conference at London, England, in 1933; died in Washington, D. C., July 11, 1939; interment in Forest Hill Cemetery, Chattanooga, Tenn.

McROBERTS, Samuel, a Senator from Illinois; born near Maeystown, Monroe County, Ill. (then a portion of the Territory Northwest of the River Ohio), April 12, 1799; educated by private tutors; was graduated from the law department of Transylvania University, Lexington, Ky.; was admitted to the bar in 1821 and commenced practice in Monroe County, Ill.; clerk of the circuit court of Monroe County 1819–1821; elected by the legislature one of the five circuit judges of the State and served from 1824 to 1827; member of the State senate 1828–1830; appointed United States district attorney by President Jackson in 1830 and served until 1832, when he resigned; appointed by President Van Buren receiver of the land office at Danville in 1832; appointed Solicitor of the General Land Office at Washington in 1839 and served in that capacity until his resignation in 1841; elected as a Democrat to the United States Senate and served from March 4, 1841, until his death in Cincinnati, Ohio, March 27, 1843; interment in the Moore Cemetery, Waterloo, Monroe County, Ill.

McRUER, Donald Campbell, a Representative from California; born in Bangor, Maine, March 10, 1826; pursued an academic course; moved to San Francisco, Calif., in 1851 and engaged in the business of a commission merchant in San Francisco; member of the board of education of San Francisco in 1859 and 1860; was a leader in commercial, educational, and political life; during the Civil War was a member of the United States Sanitary Commission; elected as a Republican to the Thirty-ninth Congress (March 4, 1865–March 3, 1867); was not

a candidate for renomination in 1866; traveled in Europe for two years; returned to San Francisco and served as harbor commissioner for four years; retired, except serving for many years on the board of directors of the Security Savings Bank of San Francisco; died in St. Helena, Calif., January 29, 1898; interment in St. Helena Public Cemetery.

McSHANE, John Albert, a Representative from Nebraska; born in New Lexington, Perry County, Ohio, August 25, 1850; attended the common schools; moved to Wyoming Territory in 1871, and later, in 1874, to Omaha, Nebr., but retained his interests in Wyoming until 1883, when he merged his individual cattle interests in the Bay State Live Stock Co.; director in the First National Bank of Omaha; member of the State house of representatives 1880–1882; served in the State senate 1882–1886; elected as a Democrat to the Fiftieth Congress (March 4, 1887–March 3, 1889); resumed former business activities; died in Omaha, Nebr., on November 10, 1923; interment in Holy Sepulchre Cemetery.

McSHERRY, James, a Representative from Pennsylvania; born in Littlestown, Adams County, Pa., July 29, 1776; attended the Lancaster (Pa.) Academy; engaged in mercantile pursuits; member of the State house of representatives 1807–1812; served in the State senate in 1813; during the War of 1812 served in the defense of the city of Baltimore; delegate to the State constitutional convention of 1837 and 1838; elected to the Seventeenth Congress (March 4, 1821–March 3, 1823); unsuccessful candidate for reelection in 1822 to the Eighteenth Congress; again a member of the State house of representatives 1824–1830, 1834, and 1835; resumed mercantile pursuits; died in Littlestown, Pa., February 3, 1849; interment in St. Aloysius' Catholic Cemetery.

McSWAIN, John Jackson, a Representative from South Carolina; born on a farm near Cross Hill, Laurens County, S. C., May 1, 1875; attended the public schools; was graduated from Wofford College Fitting School in 1893 and from the University of South Carolina at Columbia in 1897; taught school in Marlboro, Abbeville, and Anderson Counties; studied law; was admitted to the bar in 1901 and commenced practice in Greenville, S. C.; referee in bankruptcy 1912–1917; entered the officers' training camp at Fort Oglethorpe, Ga., May 12, 1917, and served in the First World War as captain of Company A, One Hundred and Fifty-fourth Infantry, until March 6, 1919, when he was honorably discharged; resumed the practice of law in Greenville, S. C.; elected as a Democrat to the Sixty-seventh and to the seven succeeding Congresses and served from March 4, 1921, until his death; declined to be a candidate for renomination in 1936; died in Columbia, S. C., while returning from a visit at Fort Moultrie, S. C., on August 6, 1936; interment in Springwood Cemetery, Greenville, S. C.

McSWEEN, Harold Barnett, a Representative from Louisiana; born in Alexandria, Rapides Parish, La., July 19, 1926; attended the public schools in Alexandria; during World War II served in the United States Merchant Marine, United States Naval Reserve, 1944–1946; graduated from Louisiana State University in 1950; was admitted to the bar in 1950 and commenced the practice of law in Alexandria, La.; member of Rapides Parish School Board in 1955 and 1956 and Louisiana State Board of Education in 1957 and 1958; elected as a Democrat to the Eighty-sixth Congress (January 3, 1959–January 3, 1961). *Reelected to the Eighty-seventh Congress.*

McSWEENEY, John, a Representative from Ohio; born in Wooster, Wayne County, Ohio, December 19, 1890; attended the public schools and was graduated from Wooster University in 1912; employed in the engineering corps of the Pennsylvania Railroad Co. in 1912 and 1913; taught at Wooster High School 1913–1917; served overseas during the First World War from May 10, 1917, to August 11, 1919, and was promoted to captain and aide-de-camp to General Farnsworth on August 16, 1918; awarded the Purple Heart Medal and received the Croix de Guerre from the Government of France; studied law at the Inns of Court, London, England; returned to the United States in 1919 and resumed teaching at Wooster High School; member of the Wooster City Council 1919–1921 and served as president; unsuccessful candidate for election in 1922 to the Sixty-seventh Congress; was admitted to the bar in 1925 and commenced practice in Wooster; elected as a Democrat to the Sixty-eighth, Sixty-ninth, and Seventieth Congresses (March 4, 1923–March 3, 1929); unsuccessful candidate for reelection in 1928 to the Seventy-first Congress; resumed the practice of law in Wooster; State director of public welfare 1931–1935; elected to the Seventy-fifth Congress (January 3, 1937–January 3, 1939); unsuccessful candidate for reelection in 1938 to the Seventy-sixth Congress; unsuccessful Democratic candidate for election to the United States Senate in 1940 and for election as Governor of Ohio in 1942; during World War II served as a lieutenant colonel with the Military Government in Italy 1943–1946, receiving the Legion of Merit, the Italian Red Cross Medal, the Order of Malta, the Order of Saint George, and a medal from the Pope; resumed the practice of law; elected to the Eighty-first Congress (January 3, 1949–January 3, 1951); unsuccessful candidate for reelection in 1950 to the Eighty-second Congress, for election in 1952 to the Eighty-third Congress, and in 1956 to the Eighty-fifth Congress; former member of the Price Stabilization Board; is a resident of Wooster, Ohio.

McVEAN, Charles, a Representative from New York; born near Johnstown, N. Y., in 1802; pursued an academic course; studied law; was admitted to the bar and commenced practice in Johnstown; editor of a newspaper in Canajoharie 1827–1831; elected as a Democrat to the Twenty-third Congress (March 4, 1833–March 3, 1835); was not a candidate for renomination in 1834; district attorney of Montgomery County 1836–1839; moved to New York City in 1839; resumed the practice of his profession; appointed surrogate of New York County January 24, 1844, and served until 1848; appointed United States attorney for the southern district of New York September 1, 1848; died in New York City, December 22, 1848; interment in St. Andrew's Cemetery.

McVEY, William Estus, a Representative from Illinois; born on a farm near Lee's Creek, Clinton County, Ohio, December 13, 1885; attended the public schools; was graduated from Ohio University in 1916 and from the University of Chicago in 1919; division superintendent in the Bureau of Education, Philippine Islands, 1908–1914; director of extension, University of Ohio, 1916–1919; superintendent of Thornton Township High School and Junior College, Harvey, Ill., 1919–1947; lecturer at the University of Pennsylvania, summer of 1928, and Emory University, summer of 1929; president of North Central Association of Colleges and Secondary Schools in 1943 and 1944; professor of education at De Paul University 1948–1950; member of board of directors Ingalls Memorial Hospital, Harvey, Ill.; president, Harvey Memorial Y. M. C. A.; author of several books and magazine articles; elected assessor of Thornton Township in 1949; elected as a Republican to the Eighty-second and to the three succeeding Congresses and served from January 3, 1951, until his death; had been renominated to the Eighty-sixth Congress; died in Washington, D. C., August 10, 1958; interment in Linwood Cemetery, Galesburg, Ill.

McWILLIAMS, John Dacher, a Representative from Connecticut; born in Norwich, New London County, Conn., July 23, 1891; attended the public schools and Norwich Free Academy; was graduated from Mercersburg (Pa.) Academy in 1910; associated with the building industry in Norwich, Conn., after graduation; during the First World War served as a private in the Twentieth Engineers, United States Army, with overseas service, from March 26, 1918, until discharged on July 1, 1919; after his discharge from the Army resumed the building business; selectman of the town of Norwich, Conn., 1935–1942; elected as a Republican to the Seventy-eighth Congress (January 3, 1943–January 3, 1945); was an unsuccessful candidate for reelection in 1944 to the Seventy-ninth Congress; was employed at the electric boat division of General Dynamics Corporation, Groton, Conn.; presently employed by the city of Norwich and is a resident of Norwich, Conn.

McWILLIE, William, a Representative from Mississippi; born in Kershaw District, S. C., November 17, 1795; served in the War of 1812 as adjutant in his father's regiment; was graduated from South Carolina College in 1817; studied law; was admitted to the bar in 1818 and commenced practice in Camden, S. C.; president of the Camden Bank in 1836; member of the State senate 1836–1840; moved to Madison County, Miss., in September 1845 and engaged in planting; elected as a Democrat to the Thirty-first Congress (March 4, 1849–March 3, 1851); unsuccessful candidate for reelection in 1850 to the Thirty-second Congress; Governor of Mississippi 1858–1860; active in the support of the Confederacy; died on his estate "Kirkwood," Madison County, Miss., March 3, 1869; interment in St. Philip's Churchyard.

MEACHAM, James, a Representative from Vermont; born in Rutland, Rutland County, Vt., August 16, 1810; was graduated from Middlebury (Vt.) College in 1832; taught in the seminary at Castleton, Vt., and in the local academy at St. Albans, Vt.; attended Andover (Vt.) Theological Seminary, where he studied for the ministry and was ordained as a Congregational minister in 1838, assuming his duties as pastor in New Haven, Vt., and served from 1839 to 1846; tutor and professor at Middlebury College 1846–1850; elected as a Whig to the Thirty-first Congress to fill the vacancy caused by the resignation of George P. Marsh; reelected to the Thirty-second, Thirty-third, and Thirty-fourth Congresses and served from December 3, 1849, until his death in Rutland, Vt., August 23, 1856; interment in West Cemetery, Middlebury, Vt.

MEAD, Cowles, a Representative from Georgia; born in Virginia October 18, 1776; moved to Georgia at an early age; received a good English education; studied law; was admitted to the bar and practiced; presented credentials as a Member-elect to the Ninth Congress and served from March 4, 1805, to December 24, 1805, when he was succeeded by Thomas Spalding, who contested his election; appointed secretary of Mississippi Territory by President Jefferson in March 1806 and served until 1807; Acting Governor from June 1806 to January 1807 during the absence of Gov. Robert Williams; resumed the practice of law; member of the Mississippi House of Representatives in 1807; unsuccessful candidate for election in 1812 to the Thirteenth Congress; delegate to the first constitutional convention of Mississippi in 1817; unsuccessful candidate for election in 1818 to the Sixteenth Congress; served in the State senate in 1821; again a member of the State house of representatives in 1822 and 1823; unsuccessful candidate for election as Governor of Mississippi in 1825; died on his plantation, "Greenwood," near Clinton, Jefferson County, Miss., May 17, 1844; interment on his estate.

MEAD, James Michael, a Representative and a Senator from New York; born in Mount Morris, Livingston County, N. Y., December 27, 1885; moved to Buffalo, N. Y., with his parents in 1890; attended the grammar, technical, and evening schools of Buffalo, N. Y.; employed on the Erie Railroad as a switchman in 1913; served on the board of supervisors of Erie County in 1914; member of the State assembly 1915–1918; elected as a Democrat to the Sixty-sixth and to the nine succeeding Congresses and served from March 4, 1919, until his resignation on December 2, 1938; was not a candidate for renomination in 1938, having become a candidate for Senator; elected to the United States Senate to fill the vacancy caused by the death of Royal C. Copeland; reelected in 1940 and served from December, 3, 1938, to January 3, 1947; was not a candidate for renomination in 1946; unsuccessful for the gubernatorial nomination in 1942 and for election as Governor in 1946; appointed as a member of the Federal Trade Commission and served from November 16, 1949, to September 25, 1955; director of Washington office of Department of Commerce, State of New York, from October 1955 to September 1956; resides in Clermont, Fla.

MEADE, Edwin Ruthven, a Representative from New York; born in Norwich, Chenango County, N. Y., July 6, 1836; pursued an academic course; studied law; was admitted to the bar in 1858 and commenced practice in Norwich, N. Y.; moved to New York City in 1872 and continued the practice of law; elected as a Democrat to the Forty-fourth Congress (March 4, 1875–March 3, 1877); was not a candidate for reelection in 1876; resumed the practice of his profession; died in New York City November 28, 1889; interment in Greene Cemetery, Greene, Chenango County, N. Y.

MEADE, Hugh Allen, a Representative from Maryland; born in Netcong, Morris County, N. J., April 4, 1907; attended the public schools; moved to Baltimore, Md., in 1923; was graduated from Loyola High School, Baltimore, Md., in 1925, from Loyola College, Baltimore, Md., in 1929, and from the University of Maryland Law School in 1932; was admitted to the bar in 1933 and commenced practice in Baltimore, Md.; secretary to Gov. Albert C. Ritchie in 1934; member of the State house of delegates 1934–1936; supervisor of assessments of the city of Baltimore 1936–1938; assistant attorney general of Maryland 1938–1946; during World War II served in the United States Navy as a lieutenant in 1944 and 1945; resigned from the attorney general's office in 1946 to enter the private practice of law; elected as a Democrat to the Eightieth Congress (January 3, 1947–January 3, 1949); unsuccessful candidate for renomination in 1948; appointed general counsel of the Merchant Marine and Fisheries Committee of the United States House of Representatives in January 1949 and served until his death in Washington, D. C., July 8, 1949; interment in the New Cathedral Cemetery, Baltimore, Md.

MEADE, Richard Kidder, a Representative from Virginia; born near Lawrenceville, Brunswick County, Va., July 29, 1803; pursued an academic course; studied law; was admitted to the bar and commenced practice in Petersburg, Dinwiddie County, Va.; served in the State senate 1835–1838; elected as a Democrat to the Thirtieth Congress to fill the vacancy caused by the death of George C. Drumgoole; reelected to the Thirty-first and Thirty-second Congresses and served from August 5, 1847, to March 3, 1853; declined the appointment of Chargé d'Affaires to Sardinia tendered by President Pierce in 1853; appointed by President Buchanan as Minister to Brazil and served from July 27, 1857, to July 9, 1861; returned to Virginia and devoted himself to the cause of the Confederacy; died in Petersburg, Va., April 20, 1862; interment in Old Blandford Cemetery.

MEADE, Wendell Howes, a Representative from Kentucky; born in Paintsville, Johnson County, Ky., January 18, 1912; attended the grade schools; was graduated from high school at Kentucky Military Institute at Lyndon, Ky., in 1929; attended Western State Teachers College, Bowling Green, Ky., 1930–1933; engaged in the banking business 1933 to 1936; graduated from the University of Louisville Law School, Louisville, Ky., in 1939; was admitted to the bar the same year and commenced practice in Paintsville, Ky.; during World War II served as a lieutenant in the United States Navy from November 1943 until January 1946, with twenty months' service in the South Pacific; resumed the practice of law; elected as a Republican to the Eightieth Congress (January 3, 1947–January 3, 1949); was an unsuccessful candidate for reelection in 1948 to the Eighty-first Congress; was an unsuccessful candidate for the Republican gubernatorial nomination in 1951; zone operations commissioner, Federal Housing Administration, 1957–1961; employed with a building contractor in Phoenix, Ariz.; is a resident of Paintsville, Ky.

MEADER, George, a Representative from Michigan; born in Benton Harbor, Berrien County, Mich., September 13, 1907; attended the public schools of various cities in Michigan; student at Ohio Wesleyan University 1923–1925; was graduated from the University of Michigan in 1927 and from the University of Michigan Law School in 1931; was admitted to the bar in 1932 and commenced the practice of law in Ann Arbor, Mich.; prosecuting attorney of Washtenaw County, Mich., 1941–1943; assistant counsel, United States Senate special committee investigating the national defense program, from July 1, 1943, to October 1, 1945, and chief counsel from October 1, 1945, to July 15, 1947; practiced law 1948–1950; chief counsel, United States Senate Banking and Currency subcommittee investigating the Reconstruction Finance Corporation in 1950; elected as a Republican to the Eighty-second and to the four succeeding Congresses (January 3, 1951–January 3, 1961). *Reelected to the Eighty-seventh Congress.*

MEANS, Rice William, a Senator from Colorado; born in St. Joseph, Mo., November 16, 1877; moved with his parents to Yuma County, Colo., in 1887; settled in Denver in 1889; attended the public schools and Sacred Heart College, Denver, Colo.; served in the Spanish-American War with the First Regiment, Colorado Volunteer Infantry, in 1898 and 1899; commanded a company of scouts in the Philippine campaign in 1899; was graduated from the law department of the University of Michigan at Ann Arbor in 1901; was admitted to the bar in 1901 and commenced practice in Denver; county judge of Adams County 1902–1904; unsuccessful candidate for election in 1908 to the Sixty-first Congress; served during the First World War as lieutenant colonel and commandant of the Fortieth Division School of Arms; commander in chief of the Army of the Philippines in 1913 and of the Veterans of Foreign Wars in 1914; unsuccessful candidate for election to the United States Senate in 1920; manager of safety for the city and county of Denver from June 1 to September 1, 1923, when he resigned; attorney for the city and county of Denver from September 1, 1923, to November 4, 1924; elected as a Republican to the United States Senate on November 4, 1924, to fill the vacancy caused by the death of Samuel D. Nicholson and served from December 1, 1924, to March 3, 1927; was an unsuccessful candidate for renomination in 1926; was awarded the Distinguished Service Cross in 1925 for bravery during the Philippine Insurrection; served as commander in chief of the United Spanish War Veterans in 1926 and 1927; served as president of the National Tribune Corporation and publisher of the National Tribune and Stars and Stripes at Washington, D. C., from December 1, 1927, to July 4, 1937, when he retired; died in Denver, Colo., January 30, 1949; interment in Fairmount Cemetery.

MEBANE, Alexander, a Representative from North Carolina; born in Hawfields, N. C., November 26, 1744; attended the common schools of Orange County; delegate to the Provincial Congress of North Carolina in 1776; justice of the peace in 1776 and sheriff of Orange County in 1777; auditor of the Hillsboro district in 1783 and 1784; member of the Hillsboro convention in 1788 and of the Fayetteville convention in 1789; member of the State house of commons 1787–1792; elected to the Third Congress (March 1793–March 3, 1795); died at Hawfields, Orange County, N. C., July 5, 1795.

MEDILL, William, a Representative from Ohio; born in New Castle County, Del., in 1802; completed preparatory studies, and was graduated from Newark (Del.) Academy (later Delaware College) in 1825; studied law; was admitted to the bar and commenced practice in Lancaster, Fairfield County, Ohio, in 1830; member of the State house of representatives 1835–1838 and served as speaker in 1836 and 1837; elected as a Democrat to the Twenty-sixth and Twenty-seventh Congresses (March 4, 1839–March 3, 1843); unsuccessful candidate for reelection to the Twenty-eighth Congress; Second Assistant Postmaster General in 1845; Commissioner of Indian Affairs 1845–1850; president of the State constitutional convention in 1850; Lieutenant Governor of Ohio in 1852 and 1853 and became Acting Governor on July 13, 1853, when Gov. Reuben Wood resigned; elected Governor the same year and served in 1854 and 1855; unsuccessful candidate for reelection as Governor; First Comptroller of the United States Treasury 1857–1861; died in Lancaster, Ohio, on September 2, 1865; interment in Elmwood Cemetery.

MEECH, Ezra, a Representative from Vermont; born in New London, Conn., July 26, 1773; moved to Hinesburg, Vt., in 1785; attended the common schools; engaged in the fur trade in the Northwest and in ship-timber contracts in Canada; moved to Shelburne, Vt., and engaged in agricultural pursuits and stock raising; member of the State house of representatives 1805–1807; elected as a Democrat to the Sixteenth Congress (March 4, 1810–March 3, 1821); delegate to the State constitutional conventions in 1822 and 1826; chief justice of Chittenden County Court in 1822 and 1823; elected to the Nineteenth Congress (March 4, 1825–March 3, 1827); unsuccessful Democratic candidate for Governor of Vermont in 1830, 1831, 1832, and 1833; presidential elector on the Whig ticket of Harrison and Tyler in 1840; resumed agricultural pursuits; died in Shelburne, Chittenden County, Vt., on September 23, 1856; interment in Shelburne Cemetery.

MEEKER, Jacob Edwin, a Representative from Missouri; born near Attica, Fountain County, Ind., October 7, 1878; attended the public schools; was graduated from Union Christian College, Merom, Ind., in 1900, and from Oberlin (Ohio) Theological Seminary in 1904; while a student at Union Christian College he became pastor of a rural church in Vermilion County, Ill.; was ordained as a minister in 1901 and assumed his duties in Vermilion County, Ill.; missionary at Eldon, Mo., for the Congregational Church in 1904; moved to St. Louis, Mo., in 1906 to take charge of the Compton Hill Congregational Church; resigned in 1912; studied law at Benton College of Law and was admitted to the bar in 1914; elected as a Republican to the Sixty-fourth and Sixty-fifth Congresses and served from March 4, 1915, until his death in St. Louis, Mo., October 16, 1918; interment in Union Cemetery, Attica, Ind.

MEEKISON, David, a Representative from Ohio; born in Dundee, Scotland, November 14, 1849; immigrated to the United States in 1855 with his parents, who settled in Napoleon, Ohio; attended the common schools; apprenticed to the printer's trade; served with the Artillery in the United States Army 1866–1869; returned to Napoleon and studied law; was appointed city clerk in 1872; was admitted to the bar in 1873 and commenced practice in Napoleon, Ohio; prosecuting attorney of Henry County 1873–1879; probate judge 1881–1888; delegate to the Democratic National Convention at Chicago in 1884 which nominated Cleveland and Hendricks; engaged in banking; established the Meekison Bank at Napoleon, Ohio, in 1886; mayor of Napoleon 1890–1897; elected as a Democrat to the Fifty-fifth and Fifty-sixth Congresses (March 4, 1897–March 3, 1901); was not a candidate for renomination in 1900; resumed the practice of his profession; also engaged in banking; died in Napoleon, Henry County, Ohio, February 12, 1915; interment in Glenwood Cemetery.

MEEKS, James Andrew, a Representative from Illinois; born in New Matamoras, Washington County, Ohio, March 7, 1864; moved to Illinois with his parents, who settled on a farm near Danville, Vermilion County, in 1865; attended the public schools, Westfield (Ill.) College, and Illinois College at Jacksonville; studied law; was admitted to the bar in 1890 and commenced practice in Danville, Ill.; master in chancery of the circuit court 1903–1915; corporation counsel of Danville 1925–1931; delegate to the Democratic National Conventions in 1920, 1924, 1928, and 1932; elected as a Democrat to the Seventy-third, Seventy-fourth, and Seventy-fifth Congresses (March 4, 1933–January 3, 1939); unsuccessful candidate for reelection in 1938 to the Seventy-sixth Congress and for election in 1940 to the Seventy-seventh Congress; resumed the practice of law and also engaged in banking until his death in Danville, Ill., November 10, 1946; interment in Spring Hill Cemetery.

MEIGS, Henry, a Representative from New York; born in New Haven, Conn., October 28, 1782; attended the common schools; was graduated from Yale College in 1799; studied law; was admitted to the bar and commenced practice in New York City; served in the War of 1812 with the rank of adjutant; member of the State assembly in 1818; elected as a Democrat to the Sixteenth Congress (March 4, 1819–March 3, 1821); served as president of the board of aldermen of New York City in 1832 and 1833; judge of one of the city courts and afterward clerk of the court of general sessions; elected recording secretary of the American Institute in 1845, and retained this position in connection with the secretaryship of the Farmers' Club until his death; died in New York City on May 20, 1861; interment in St. Ann's Churchyard, Perth Amboy, N. J.

MEIGS, Return Jonathan, Jr., a Senator from Ohio; born in Middletown, Conn., November 16, 1764; was graduated from Yale College in 1785; studied law; was admitted to the bar and commenced practice in Marietta, Washington County, Ohio (then known as the Northwest Territory), in 1788; participated in the Indian fighting of that period; Territorial judge in 1802 and 1803; chief justice of the Ohio Supreme Court in 1803 and 1804; brevetted colonel in the United States Army and commanded in the St. Charles district in Louisiana 1804–1806; judge of the supreme court of Louisiana in 1805 and 1806; judge of the United States District Court for the Territory of Michigan in 1807 and 1808; returned to Ohio and was elected as a Democrat to the United States Senate to fill the vacancy caused by the resignation of John Smith; reelected in 1809 and served from December 12, 1808, to May 1, 1810, when he resigned; Governor of Ohio 1810–1814; Postmaster General in the Cabinet of President Madison and President Monroe and served from March 17, 1814, to June 26, 1823; died in Marietta, Ohio, March 29, 1825; interment in Mound Cemetery.

MEIKLEJOHN, George de Rue, a Representative from Nebraska; born in Weyauwega, Waupaca County, Wis., on August 26, 1857; attended the State normal school in Oshkosh, Wis.; principal of the high schools in Weyauwega, Wis., and Liscomb, Iowa; was graduated from the law department of Michigan University at Ann Arbor in 1880; was admitted to the bar and commenced practice in Fullerton, Nance County, Nebr., the same year; prosecuting attorney for Nance County 1881–1884; member of the State senate 1884–1888 and served as its president 1886–1888; chairman of the Republican State convention of 1887; chairman of the Republican State central committee in 1887 and 1888; decorated by King Oscar of Sweden in 1889 a Knight of the Royal Order of the Sword; Lieutenant Governor of Nebraska 1889–1891; elected as a Republican to the Fifty-third and Fifty-fourth Congresses (March 4, 1893–March 3, 1897); was not a candidate for renomination in 1896; appointed by President McKinley as Assistant Secretary of War April 14, 1897, and served until March 1901, when he resigned; unsuccessful candidate for election to the United States Senate in 1901; resumed the practice of law in Omaha, Nebr.; moved to Los Angeles, Calif., in 1918 and continued the practice of his profession; also interested in mining; died in Los Angeles, Calif., April 19, 1929; interment in Forest Lawn Cemetery, Glendale, Calif.

MELLEN, Prentiss, a Senator from Massachusetts; born in Sterling, Worcester County, Mass., on October 11, 1764; was graduated from Harvard University in 1784; studied law; was admitted to the bar in 1786 and commenced practice in Sterling, Mass.; practiced in Bridgewater, Mass., 1789–1791, in Dover, N. H., in 1791 and 1792, in Biddeford, Maine (until 1820 a district of Massachusetts) 1792–1806, and in Portland, Maine, 1806–1840; member of the executive council in 1808, 1809, and 1817; presidential elector in 1817 and voted for King and Howard; trustee of Bowdoin College, Brunswick, Maine, 1817–1836; elected to the United States Senate to fill the vacancy caused by the resignation of Eli P. Ashmun and served from June 5, 1818, to May 15, 1820, when he resigned; upon the admission of the State of Maine into the Union in 1820 became chief justice of the supreme court of that State and served until his resignation in 1834; member and chairman of the commission to revise and codify the public statutes of Maine in 1838; died in Portland, Maine, December 31, 1840; interment in Western Cemetery.

MELLISH, David Batcheller, a Representative from New York; born in Oxford, Worcester County, Mass., January 2, 1831; attended the public schools; became a printer in Worcester; taught school in Massachusetts, Maryland, and Pennsylvania; proofreader in New York City; reporter on the New York Tribune; stenographer to the police board of New York City for ten years; appointed assistant appraiser of merchandise for the port of New York in 1871; elected as a Republican to the Forty-third Congress and served from March 4, 1873, until his death in Washington, D. C., on May 23, 1874; interment in Hillside Cemetery, Auburn, Mass.

MENEFEE, Richard Hickman, a Representative from Kentucky; born in Owingsville, Bath County, Ky., December 4, 1809; attended the public schools and was graduated from Transylvania University, Lexington, Ky.; taught school for several years; studied law; was admitted to the bar in 1830 and commenced practice in Mount Sterling, Ky.; appointed as Commonwealth attorney in 1832; member of the State house of representatives in 1836 and 1837; elected as a Whig to the Twenty-fifth Congress (March 4, 1837–March 3, 1839); voluntarily retired from public life, resuming the practice of law in Lexington; presidential elector on the Whig ticket of Harrison and Tyler in 1840; died in Frankfort, Franklin County, Ky., February 21, 1841; interment in a private cemetery in Fayette County, Ky.; reinterred in Cave Hill Cemetery, Louisville, Ky., October 28, 1893.

MENGES, Franklin, a Representative from Pennsylvania; born at Menges Mills, York County, Pa., October 26, 1858; attended the public schools in North Codorus Township, York County, Pa., and Baugher Academy Preparatory School, Hanover, Pa.; was graduated from Gettysburg (Pa.) College in 1886; instructor in chemistry and physics at that college 1886–1896; head of the science department of York High School 1897–1903; lecturer at farmers' institutes in Pennsylvania and other States 1898–1918; represented the Pennsylvania State Agriculture Department at the Louisiana Purchase Exposition at the World's Fair in 1904; made a soil survey of the State of Pennsylvania, giving the geological origin and crop adaptation of the soils of the State; author of numerous articles on scientific agriculture; elected as a Republican to the Sixty-ninth, Seventieth, and Seventy-first Congresses (March 4, 1925–March 3, 1931); unsuccessful candidate for reelection in 1930 to the Seventy-second Congress; engaged in agricultural pursuits on his farm near York, Pa., until his retirement in 1947; moved to Arlington, Va., where he died May 12, 1956; interment in Evergreen Cemetery, Gettysburg, Pa.

MENZIES, John William, a Representative from Kentucky; born in Bryants Station, Bourbon County, Ky., April 12, 1819; attended the common schools, and was graduated from the University of Virginia at Charlottesville in 1840; studied law; was admitted to the bar and commenced practice in Covington, Ky., in 1841; member of the State house of representatives in 1848 and 1855; elected as a Unionist to the Thirty-seventh Congress (March 4, 1861–March 3, 1863); resumed the practice of law in Covington; delegate to the Democratic National Convention at Chicago in 1864; judge of the chancery court 1873–1893; again resumed the practice of law; died in Falmouth, Pendleton County, Ky., on October 3, 1897; interment in Linden Grove Cemetery, Covington, Ky.

MERCER, Charles Fenton (cousin of Robert Selden Garnett), a Representative from Virginia; born in Fredericksburg, Va., June 16, 1778; was graduated from Princeton College in 1797; took a postgraduate course in the same college and received his degree in 1800; offered commissions as lieutenant and captain of Cavalry in the United States Army in 1798 and 1800, but declined; studied law; was admitted to the bar in 1802 and commenced practice in Aldie, Loudoun County, Va.; member of the State house of delegates 1810–1817; during the War of 1812 was appointed lieutenant colonel of a Virginia regiment and then major in command at Norfolk, Va.; inspector general in 1814; aide-de-camp to Governor Barbour and brigadier general in command of the Second Virginia Brigade; projector and first president of the Chesapeake & Ohio Canal Co. 1828–1833; delegate to the State constitutional convention in 1829; elected as a Democrat to the Fifteenth and to the eleven succeeding Congresses and served from March 4, 1817, to December 26, 1839, when he resigned; was one of the originators of the plan for establishing the Free State of Liberia; vice president of the Virginia Colonization Society in 1836; vice president of the National Society of Agriculture in 1842; retired from public service and spent the remainder of his life in travel and study; died in Howard, near Alexandria, Va., May 4, 1858; interment in Union Cemetery, Leesburg, Loudoun County, Va.

MERCER, David Henry, a Representative from Nebraska; born in Benton County, Iowa, July 9, 1857; moved with his parents to Adams County, Ill., in 1858; at the close of the Civil War moved with his parents to Brownville, Nebr., where he attended the public schools, and was graduated from the University of Nebraska at Lincoln in 1880; was graduated from the law department of Michigan University at Ann Arbor in 1882; was admitted to the bar and commenced practice in Brownville, Nebr.; served one term as city clerk and police judge; moved to Omaha in 1885, and for several years was chairman of the Republican city and county committees; secretary of the Republican State central committee in 1896; elected secretary of the Republican National Congressional Committee in 1896; chairman of the Republican State Central Committee of Nebraska in 1897 and 1898; elected as a Republican to the Fifty-third and to the four succeeding Congresses (March 4, 1893–March 3, 1903); unsuccessful candidate for reelection in 1902 to the Fifty-eighth Congress; settled in Washington, D. C., and resumed the practice of law; died in Omaha, Nebr., January 10, 1919; interment in Forest Lawn Cemetery.

MERCER, James (brother of John Francis Mercer), a Delegate from Virginia; born at "Marlborough," Stafford County, Va., February 26, 1736; received private schooling at home; was graduated from William and Mary College, Williamsburg, Va.; served as a captain in the French and Indian War; commander of Fort Loudoun, Winchester, Va., in 1756; studied law and was admitted to the bar; active in pre-Revolutionary affairs; member of the Virginia House of Burgesses 1762–1776; member of the Virginia conventions of 1774, 1775, and 1776; member of the committee of public safety in 1775 and 1776; member of the State constitutional convention in May 1776; Member of the Continental Congress in 1779 and 1780; served as a judge of the General Court of Virginia 1779–1789; trustee and president of the Fredericksburg Academy 1786–1790; judge of the first Virginia Court of Appeals from 1789 until his death; died in Richmond, Va., on October 31, 1793; interment in St. John's Church Cemetery.

MERCER, John Francis (brother of James Mercer), a Delegate from Virginia and a Representative from Maryland; born at "Marlborough," Stafford County, Va., on May 17, 1759; after receiving his education at home from private teachers was graduated from William and Mary College, Williamsburg, Va., in 1775; studied law; was admitted to the bar and commenced practice in Williamsburg, Va., in 1781; during the Revolutionary War served as lieutenant in the Third Virginia Regiment; wounded at the Battle of Brandywine; promoted to captain in 1777, and was aide-de-camp to Gen. Charles Lee in 1778 and 1779; lieutenant colonel of Virginia Cavalry; Delegate from Virginia to the Continental Congress 1782–1785; moved to West River, Anne Arundel County, Md.; delegate from Maryland to the Federal convention which met at Annapolis in 1787 to consider the needs of the Nation; delegate to the State convention which ratified the Federal Constitution in 1788; member of the State house of delegates in 1788, 1789, 1791, and 1792; elected as a Democrat to the Second Congress to fill the vacancy caused by the resignation of William Pinkney; reelected to the Third Congress and served from February 5, 1792, until his resignation April 13, 1794; again a member of the State house of delegates in 1800 and 1803–1806; Governor of Maryland 1801–1803; retired to his estate "Cedar Park," West River, Md.; died in Philadelphia, Pa., August 30, 1821; remains deposited in a vault at St. Peter's Church, Philadelphia, Pa.; subsequently interred in a private cemetery at "Cedar Park," West River, Anne Arundel County, Md.

MERCUR, Ulysses, a Representative from Pennsylvania; born in Towanda, Bradford County, Pa., August 12, 1818; pursued classical studies; was graduated from Jefferson College, Canonsburg, Pa., in 1842; studied law; was admitted to the bar and commenced practice in Towanda in 1843; delegate to the Republican National Convention at Philadelphia in 1856 which nominated Frémont and Dayton; presidential elector on the Republican ticket of Lincoln and Hamlin in 1860; president judge of the thirteenth judicial district of Pennsylvania from 1861 until March 4, 1865, when he resigned; elected as a Republican to the Thirty-ninth and to the three succeeding Congresses and served from March 4, 1865, until December 2, 1872, when he resigned to accept a judicial position; associate justice of the supreme court of Pennsylvania 1872–1883; appointed chief justice in 1883 and served until his death in Wallingford, Pa., June 6, 1887; interment in Oak Hill Cemetery, Towanda, Pa.

MEREDITH, Elisha Edward, a Representative from Virginia; born in Sumter County, Ala., December 26, 1848; attended Hampden-Sidney College, Virginia; studied law; was admitted to the bar in 1869 and commenced practice in Prince William County; prosecuting attorney for Prince William County 1876–1883; member of the State senate 1883–1887; presidential elector on the Democratic ticket of Cleveland and Thurman in 1888; elected as a Democrat to the Fifty-second Congress to fill the vacancy caused by the death of William H. F. Lee; reelected to the Fifty-third and Fifty-fourth Congresses and served from December 9, 1891, to March 3, 1897; resumed the practice of his profession; died in Manassas, Prince William County, Va., on July 29, 1900; interment in Manassas Cemetery.

MEREDITH, Samuel, a Delegate from Pennsylvania; born in Philadelphia, Pa., in 1741; attended Doctor Allison's Academy in Philadelphia; engaged in mercantile pursuits; active in ante-Revolutionary affairs; served in the Revolutionary War as major and lieutenant colonel of the Third Battalion of Associators in 1776; promoted brigadier general of Pennsylvania Militia April 5, 1777, "for gallant services in the Battles of Brandywine and Germantown"; resigned in 1778; twice a member of the Pennsylvania Colonial Assembly; Member of the Continental Congress in 1787 and 1788; appointed surveyor of the port of Philadelphia August 1, 1789; was the first United States Treasurer, appointed under the Constitution, and served from September 11, 1789, until his resignation December 1, 1801; retired to his country home, "Belmont Manor," near Pleasant Mount, Wayne County, Pa., where he died February 10, 1817; interment in the family cemetery on his estate.

MERIWETHER, David (father of James Meriwether), a Representative from Georgia; born at Clover Field, near Charlottesville, Albemarle County, Va., April 10, 1755; completed preparatory studies; during the Revolutionary War was a lieutenant and served in New Jersey, and afterward with Virginia troops at the last siege of Savannah, Ga.; settled in Wilkes County, Ga., in 1785; commissioned brigadier general of State militia September 21, 1797; member of the State house of representatives and served as speaker 1797–1800; elected as a Democrat to the Seventh Congress to fill the vacancy caused by the resignation of Benjamin Taliaferro; reelected to the Eighth and Ninth Congresses and served from December 6, 1802, to March 3, 1807; was not a candidate for reelection and retired to his plantation near Athens, Ga.; appointed a commissioner to the Creek Indians in 1804 and repeatedly reappointed to treat with other tribes; presidential elector on the Democratic ticket of Monroe and Tompkins in 1816 and 1820; died near Athens, Ga., November 16, 1822; interment in the private burial ground on his plantation.

MERIWETHER, David, a Senator from Kentucky; born in Louisa County, Va., October 30, 1800; moved with his parents to Jefferson County, Ky., in 1803; attended the common schools; engaged in fur trading in 1818 near what is now Council Bluffs, Iowa; later engaged in agricultural pursuits in Jefferson County, Ky.; studied law; was admitted to the bar and commenced practice; member of the State house of representatives 1832–1845; unsuccessful candidate for election in 1846 to the Thirtieth Congress; delegate to the State constitutional convention in 1849; secretary of state of Kentucky in 1851; appointed as a Democrat to the United States Senate to fill the vacancy caused by the death of Henry Clay and served from July 6, to August 31, 1852, when a successor was elected; was not a candidate for renomination in 1852; appointed by President Franklin Pierce as Governor of the Territory of New Mexico May 6, 1853, and served until January 5, 1855; member of the Kentucky House of Representatives 1858–1885 and served as speaker in 1859; retired to his plantation near Louisville, Ky., where he died April 4, 1893; interment in Cave Hill Cemetery.

MERIWETHER, James (son of David Meriwether and uncle of James A. Meriwether), a Representative from Georgia; born near Washington, Wilkes County, Ga., in 1789; attended the common schools; was graduated from the University of Georgia at Athens in 1807; instructor in the university for a year; studied law; was admitted to the bar and practiced for a short period, later engaging in agricultural pursuits; served under General Floyd in the war against the Creek Indians in 1813; United States commissioner to the Cherokee Indians; trustee of the University of Georgia 1816–1831; member of the State house of representatives 1821–1823; elected to the Nineteenth Congress (March 4, 1825–March 3, 1827); was not a candidate for renomination in 1826; resumed agricultural pursuits; died while on a trip to the West, near Memphis, Tenn., in 1854; interment in the family burying ground on the plantation in Clarke County, near Athens, Ga.

MERIWETHER, James A. (nephew of James Meriwether), a Representative from Georgia; born near Washington, Wilkes County, Ga., on September 20, 1806; completed preparatory studies; was graduated from the University of Georgia at Athens in 1826; studied law; was admitted to the bar and commenced practice in Eatonton, Putnam County, Ga.; engaged in agricultural pursuits; member of the State house of representatives 1831–1836 and 1838; delegate to the State internal improvement convention at Eatonton, Ga., in 1839; judge of the superior court for the Eatonton (Ocmulgee) district 1845–1849; elected as a Whig to the Twenty-seventh Congress (March 4, 1841–March 3, 1843); member of the State house of representatives in 1843, 1851, and 1852, serving as speaker; died in Eatonton, Ga., April 18, 1852; interment in the Union Cemetery.

MERRIAM, Clinton Levi, a Representative from New York; born in Leyden, N. Y., March 25, 1824; attended the common schools and Copenhagen Academy, Copenhagen, N. Y.; engaged in mercantile pursuits in Utica, N. Y.; moved to New York City in 1847 and became an importer; engaged in banking in 1860; returned to Leyden in 1864; elected as a Republican to the Forty-second and Forty-third Congresses (March 4, 1871–March 3, 1875); retired from active business pursuits and lived in retirement on his estate, "Homewood," Locust Grove, N. Y.; died while on a vist in Washington, D. C., February 18, 1900; interment in Leyden Hill Cemetery, Port Leyden, N. Y.

MERRICK, William Duhurst (father of William Matthew Merrick), a Senator from Maryland; born in Annapolis, Md., October 25, 1793; completed preparatory studies and was graduated from Georgetown University, Washington, D. C.; held several local offices; served in the War of 1812; returned to his home in Charles County, Md.; register of wills of Charles County 1825–1832; studied law; was admitted to the bar and commenced practice in Port Tobacco, Md.; member of the State house of delegates 1832–1838; elected as a Whig to the United States Senate to fill the vacancy caused by the death of Joseph Kent; reelected in 1839 and served from January 4, 1838, to March 3, 1845; member of the State constitutional convention in 1850; again a member of the State house of delegates and served from January 1856 until his death in Washington, D. C., February 5, 1857; interment in Mount Olivet Cemetery.

MERRICK, William Matthew (son of William Duhurst Merrick), a Representative from Maryland; born near Faulkner, Charles County, Md., September 1, 1818; was graduated from Georgetown University, Washington, D. C., in 1831; studied law in the University of Virginia at Charlottesville; was admitted to the bar in Baltimore in 1839 and commenced practice in Frederick, Md., in 1844; deputy attorney general for Frederick County 1845–1850; moved to Washington, D. C., in 1854; associate justice of the United States Circuit Court for the District of Columbia 1854–1863; resumed the practice of law in Maryland; professor of law in Columbian College (now George Washington University), Washington, D. C., in 1866 and 1867; delegate to the State constitutional convention of 1867; member of the State house of delegates in 1870; elected as a Democrat to the Forty-second Congress (March 4, 1871–March 3, 1873); unsuccessful candidate for reelection in 1872 to the Forty-third Congress; resumed the practice of law; associate judge of the supreme court of the District of Columbia by appointment of President Cleveland 1885–1889; died in Washington, D. C., February 4, 1889; interment in Mount Olivet Cemetery.

MERRILL, D. Bailey, a Representative from Indiana; born in Hymera, Sullivan County, Ind., November 22, 1912; attended the public schools; was graduated from Indiana State Teachers College, Terre Haute, Ind., in 1933; taught high school in Hymera, Ind., 1933–1935; studied law at Indiana University Law School, Bloomington, Ind., graduating in 1937; was admitted to the bar in 1937 and began practice in Terre Haute, Ind.; moved to Evansville, Ind., in 1939 and continued law practice; in 1942 volunteered as a private in the Field Artillery and served overseas with the Two Hundred and Ninety-first Field Artillery Observation Battalion, participating in the Battle of the Bulge, the Rhineland Campaign, the Central European Campaign, and in the Army of Occupation; was released from active duty as a captain in March 1946; resumed the practice of law; elected as a Republican to the Eighty-third Congress (January 3, 1953–January 3, 1955); was an unsuccessful candidate for reelection in 1954 to the Eighty-fourth Congress and for election in 1956 to the Eighty-fifth Congress; resumed law practice; is a resident of Evansville, Ind.

MERRILL, Orsamus Cook, a Representative from Vermont; born in Farmington, Conn., June 18, 1775; completed preparatory studies; moved to Bennington, Vt., in 1791; studied law; was admitted to the bar in 1804; served in the War of 1812; commissioned major of the Eleventh Regiment, United States Infantry, March 3, 1813; lieutenant colonel of the Twenty-sixth Infantry, September 4, 1814; transferred back to the Eleventh Infantry as lieutenant colonel September 26, 1814; honorably discharged June 15, 1815; register of probate in 1815; clerk of the courts in 1816; elected as a Democrat to the Fifteenth

Congress (March 4, 1817–March 3, 1819); presented credentials as a Member-elect to the Sixteenth Congress and served from March 4, 1819, until January 12, 1820, when he was succeeded by Rollin C. Mallary, who contested his election; delegate to the State constitutional convention in 1822; served in the State house of representatives in 1822; judge of the probate court in 1822 and 1823; State's attorney 1823–1825; member of the State executive council 1824–1827; member of the State senate in 1836; again judge of probate court 1841–1847; postmaster of Bennington, Bennington County, Vt., several years; resumed the practice of law at Bennington, where he died April 12, 1865; interment in the Old Cemetery on Bennington Hill.

MERRIMAN, Truman Adams, a Representative from New York; born in Auburn, N. Y., September 5, 1839; attended the Auburn Academy, and was graduated from Hobart College, Geneva, N. Y., in 1861; during the Civil War entered the Union Army in September 1861 as captain of a company which he had raised and which was attached to the Ninety-second Regiment, New York Volunteer Infantry; was mustered out as a lieutenant colonel in December 1864; studied law and was admitted to the bar in 1867; moved to New York City and entered the profession of journalism in 1871; president of the New York Press Club in 1882, 1883, and 1884; elected as a Democrat to the Forty-ninth and Fiftieth Congresses (March 4, 1885–March 3, 1889); was not a candidate for renomination in 1888, died in New York City April 16, 1892; interment in Fort Hill Cemetery, Auburn, N. Y.

MERRIMON, Augustus Summerfield, a Senator from North Carolina; born at "Cherryfields," near Asheville, Buncombe County, N. C., September 15, 1830; received his early education from private schools and tutors; studied law; was admitted to the bar in 1852 and commenced practice in Asheville, N. C.; prosecuting attorney of Buncombe and other counties in western North Carolina; member of the State house of commons in 1860 and 1861; entered the Confederate Army upon the outbreak of the Civil War and was captain on the staff of Col. William Johnston; resigned in the fall of 1861; solicitor for the eighth judicial district of North Carolina 1861–1865; judge of the superior court in 1866 and 1867; resigned; settled in Raleigh, N. C., in 1867 and resumed the practice of law; declined to be a candidate for Governor of North Carolina in 1868; chairman of the Democratic State central committee in 1868; unsuccessful candidate for associate justice of the State supreme court in 1868; unsuccessful candidate for Governor of North Carolina in 1872; elected as a Democrat to the United States Senate and served from March 4, 1873, to March 3, 1879; was not a candidate for renomination in 1878; resumed the practice of his profession at Raleigh, N. C.; associate judge of the supreme court of North Carolina 1883–1889; served as chief justice of the court from 1889 until his death in Raleigh, N. C., November 14, 1892; interment in Oakwood Cemetery.

MERRITT, Edwin Albert, a Representative from New York; born in Pierrepont, St. Lawrence County, N. Y., July 25, 1860; attended the common schools; was graduated from Potsdam Normal School in 1879 and from Yale College in 1884; deputy consul general in London in 1885; connected with various business enterprises in Potsdam; member of the board of supervisors 1896–1903; studied law; was admitted to the bar in 1902 and commenced practice in Potsdam, N. Y.; member of the State assembly 1902–1912, minority leader from 1908, and served as speaker in 1912; elected as a Republican to the Sixty-second Congress to fill the vacancy caused by the death of George R. Malby; reelected to the Sixty-third and Sixty-fourth Congresses and served from November 5, 1912, until his death, before the

close of the Sixty-third Congress; died in Potsdam, St. Lawrence County, N. Y., December 4, 1914; interment in the family cemetery plot, Pierrepont, N. Y.

MERRITT, Matthew Joseph, a Representative from New York; born in New York, N. Y., April 2, 1895; attended the public and high schools; during the First World War served in 1918 as a sergeant in Company C, Three Hundred and Twenty-seventh Battalion, Tank Corps; engaged in the real estate and insurance business in New York City 1926–1933; served with the New York loan agency of the Reconstruction Finance Corporation in 1933 and 1934; elected as a Democrat to the Seventy-fourth and to the four succeeding Congresses (January 3, 1935–January 3, 1945); was not a candidate for renomination in 1944; engaged in the real estate and insurance business in New York City; died at Malba, Queens County, N. Y., September 29, 1946; interment in Mount St. Mary's Cemetery, Whitestone, N. Y.

MERRITT, Samuel Augustus, a Delegate from the Territory of Idaho; born in Staunton, Augusta County, Va., August 15, 1827; attended the Staunton Military Academy, and was graduated from Washington College (now Washington and Lee University), Lexington, Va., in 1848; moved to Mariposa County, Calif., in 1849; county clerk and public administrator of Mariposa County in 1850; member of the State house of representatives in 1851 and 1852; studied law; was admitted to the bar in 1852 and commenced practice; served in the State senate 1857–1862; moved to the Territory of Idaho in 1862; elected as a Democrat to the Forty-second Congress (March 4, 1871–March 3, 1873); was an unsuccessful candidate for renomination in 1872 to the Forty-third Congress; moved to Salt Lake City, Utah, in 1873 and engaged in mining operations and the practice of law; city attorney 1888–1890; member of the Democratic National Committee in 1892; chief justice of the supreme court of the Territory of Utah 1894–1896; died in Salt Lake City on September 8, 1910; interment in Salt Lake City Cemetery.

MERRITT, Schuyler, a Representative from Connecticut; born in New York City, N. Y., December 16, 1853; moved with his parents to Stamford, Conn., in 1855; prepared for college at private schools in that city; was graduated from Yale College, New Haven, Conn., in 1873, and from Columbia Law School, New York City, N. Y., in 1876; interested in the manufacture of locks and keys and also engaged in banking 1877–1917; member of the Connecticut constitutional convention in 1904; member of the State board of education 1910–1916; delegate to the Republican National Convention at Chicago in 1916; elected as a Republican to the Sixty-fifth Congress to fill the vacancy caused by the death of Ebenezer J. Hill; reelected to the Sixty-sixth and to the five succeeding Congresses and served from November 6, 1917, to March 3, 1931; unsuccessful candidate for reelection in 1930 to the Seventy-second Congress; again elected to the Seventy-third and Seventy-fourth Congresses (March 4, 1933–January 3, 1937); unsuccessful candidate for reelection in 1936 to the Seventy-fifth Congress; continued his interests in the Yale & Towne Manufacturing Co. and the First Stamford National Bank; died in Stamford, Conn., April 1, 1953; interment in Woodland Cemetery.

MERROW, Chester Earl, a Representative from New Hampshire; born in Center Ossipee, Carroll County, N. H., November 15, 1906; attended the public schools and Brewster Free Academy 1921–1925; was graduated from Colby College, Waterville, Maine, in 1929 and from Teachers College (summers), Columbia University, New York, N. Y., in 1937; instructor of general science, physics, chemistry, and biology at Kents Hill (Maine) School in 1929 and 1930 and at Montpelier (Vt.) Seminary 1930–1937; assistant headmaster of Montpelier Seminary 1935–1938; instructor of political science and history at Vermont Junior College, Montpelier, Vt., in 1937 and 1938; member of the New Hampshire House of Representatives in 1939 and 1940; radio news commentator and lecturer on national and international affairs; delegate to international conference on education and cultural relations of the United Nations held in London in 1945; congressional adviser to the first conference of the United Nations Educational, Scientific, and Cultural Organization held in Paris in 1946; member of the United States delegation to the United Nations Education, Scientific, and Cultural Organization 1946–1949; elected as a Republican to the Seventy-eighth and to the eight succeeding Congresses (January 3, 1943–January 3, 1961). *Reelected to the Eighty-seventh Congress.*

MERWIN, Orange, a Representative from Connecticut; born in Merryall, near New Milford, Litchfied County, Conn., April 7, 1777; attended the common schools; engaged in agricultural pursuits; member of the State house of representatives 1815–1820; delegate to the State constitutional convention in 1818; served in the State senate 1821–1825; member of the committee of twenty-four to draft the State constitution; elected to the Nineteenth and Twentieth Congresses (March 4, 1825–March 3, 1829); was not a candidate for renomination in 1828; resumed agricultural pursuits; was an unsuccessful candidate for Lieutenant Governor of Connecticut in 1831; died in New Milford, Conn., September 4, 1853; interment in Center Cemetery.

MESICK, William Smith, a Representative from Michigan; born in Newark, Wayne County, N. Y., August 26, 1856; attended the common schools, Kalamazoo (Mich.) Business College, and was graduated from the law department of the University of Michigan at Ann Arbor in 1881; was admitted to the bar in 1881 and commenced the practice of his profession in Mancelona, Mich.; prosecuting attorney of Antrim County, Mich., for one term; elected as a Republican to the Fifty-fifth and Fifty-sixth Congresses (March 4, 1897–March 3, 1901); unsuccessful candidate for renomination in 1900; resumed the practice of his profession in Mancelona and subsequently moved to Petoskey, Emmet County, Mich., and continued practice; died in Petoskey, Mich., on December 1, 1942; interment in Greenwood Cemetery.

METCALF, Arunah, a Representative from New York; was born August 15, 1771; attended the common schools; moved from Connecticut to New York and settled in Otsego (now Cooperstown), in 1802; elected as a Democrat to the Twelfth Congress (March 4, 1811–March 3, 1813); member of the State assembly 1814–1816; president of the Otsego County Agricultural Society in 1818; unsuccessful candidate for election to the State senate in 1819; again a member of the New York State Assembly in 1828; died in Cooperstown, Otsego County, N. Y., August 15, 1848.

METCALF, Jesse Houghton, a Senator from Rhode Island; born in Providence, R. I., November 16, 1860; educated in private schools of Providence; studied textile manufacturing in Yorkshire, England; engaged in textile manufacturing; member of the State house of representatives 1889–1891 and 1907; member of the Providence Common Council 1888–1892; chairman of the Metropolitan Park Commission of Rhode Island 1909–1924; member of the penal and charitable board 1917–1923; president of the Rhode Island Hospital; trustee of the Rhode Island School of Design at Providence; member of the board of trustees of Brown University, Providence, R. I.; Republican National committeeman 1935–1940; elected as a Republican to the United States Senate on November 4, 1924, to fill the vacancy caused by the death of LeBaron B. Colt; on the same day was also elected for the term commencing March 4, 1925; reelected in 1930 and served from November 5, 1924, to January 3, 1937; unsuccessful candidate for reelection in 1936; died in Providence, R. I., October 9, 1942; interment in Swan Point Cemetery.

METCALF, Lee, a Representative and a Senator from Montana; born in Stevensville, Ravalli County, Mont., January 28, 1911; attended the public schools; graduated from Stanford (Calif.) University in 1936 and received his law degree from Montana State University Law School; was admitted to the Montana bar in 1936 and commenced the practice of law; member of the State house of representatives in 1937; assistant attorney general of Montana 1937–1941; in January 1942 resumed the practice of law in Hamilton, Mont.; in December 1942 enlisted in the Army and was assigned to the Six Hundred and Seventh Tank Destroyer Battalion; attended officers' training school and was commissioned; went overseas in 1944 and participated in the Normandy invasion as a staff officer of the Fifth Corps; also served in the Seventh Corps and with the First Army; during the Battle of the Bulge was assigned to the Ninth Infantry Division and finished out the war as an officer of the Sixtieth Infantry Regiment; after V–E Day was concerned with displaced persons, their camps, feeding, and repatriation; helped in drafting ordinances for the first free local elections in Germany and supervised the free elections in Bavaria; discharged from the Army as a first lieutenant in April 1946; associate justice of the Montana Supreme Court 1946–1952; delegate to State Democratic Conventions in 1936, 1940, 1952–1958; delegate to the Democratic National Convention in 1956; elected as a Democrat to the Eighty-third and to the three succeeding Congresses (January 3, 1953–January 3, 1961); was not a candidate for renomination in 1960. *Elected to the United States Senate for the term commencing January 3, 1961, and ending January 3, 1967.*

METCALF, Victor Howard, a Representative from California; born in Utica, Oneida County, N. Y., October 10, 1853; attended the public schools of Utica, and was graduated from the Utica Free Academy in 1871, from Russell's Military Academy, New Haven, Conn., in 1872, and from the law department of Yale College in 1876; was admitted to the Connecticut bar in June 1876 and to the New York bar in 1877, and commenced practice in Utica, N. Y., in 1877; moved to Oakland, Alameda County, Calif., in 1879 and continued the practice of law; elected as a Republican to the Fifty-sixth, Fifty-seventh, and Fifty-eighth Congresses and served from March 4, 1899, until his resignation July 1, 1904, to accept a Cabinet portfolio; appointed Secretary of Commerce and Labor by President Theodore Roosevelt and served from July 1, 1904, to December 16, 1906, when he resigned; appointed by President Theodore Roosevelt Secretary of the Navy December 17, 1906, and served until December 1, 1908, when he resigned; returned to Oakland, Calif., engaged in banking for several years, and then resumed the practice of law; retired from active pursuits; died in Oakland, Calif., February 20, 1936; interment in Mountain View Cemetery.

METCALFE, Henry Bleecker, a Representative from New York; born in Albany, N. Y., January 20, 1805; moved to New York City in 1811 and to Richmond County in 1816; studied law; was admitted to the bar and commenced practice in New York City in 1826; prosecuting attorney of Richmond County 1826–1832; elected county judge in 1840 and served until 1841 when he resigned; again county judge 1847–1875; elected as a Democrat to the Forty-fourth Congress (March 4, 1875–March 3, 1877); died in Richmond, Staten Island, N. Y., February 7, 1881; interment in the Moravian Cemetery, New Dorp, Staten Island, N. Y.

METCALFE, Lyne Shackelford, a Representative from Missouri; born in Madisonville, Hopkins County, Ky., April 21, 1822; attended the common schools, Shurtleff College, Alton, Ill., and Illinois College, Jacksonville, Ill.; engaged in mercantile pursuits in Alton, Ill., in 1844; member of the board of aldermen of Alton; elected mayor of Alton; during the Civil War served in the Union Army as assistant quartermaster with rank of captain and later promoted to colonel; moved to St. Louis, Mo., in 1863; engaged in manufacturing; served in the city council of St. Louis; elected as a Republican to the Forty-fifth Congress (March 4, 1877–March 3, 1879); unsuccessful candidate for reelection in 1878 to the Forty-sixth Congress; died in Kirkwood, St. Louis County, Mo., January 31, 1906; interment in Alton Cemetery, Alton, Madison County, Ill.

METCALFE, Thomas, a Representative and a Senator from Kentucky; born in Fauquier County, Va., March 20, 1780; moved with his parents to Fayette County, Ky.; attended the common schools; learned the mason's trade; served as captain in the War of 1812; member of the State house of representatives 1812–1816; elected as a Democrat to the Sixteenth and to the four succeeding Congresses and served from March 4, 1819, until his resignation June 1, 1828; Governor of Kentucky 1829–1833; member of the State senate in 1834; president of the board of internal improvements in 1840; appointed and subsequently elected to the United States Senate to fill the vacancy caused by the resignation of John J. Crittenden and served from June 23, 1848, to March 3, 1849; engaged in agricultural pursuits; died near Carlisle, Nicholas County, Ky., August 18, 1855; interment in the family burial ground at "Forest Retreat," in Nicholas County, Ky.

METZ, Herman August, a Representative from New York; born in New York City October 19, 1867; attended private and public schools; manufacturer and importer of dyestuffs, chemicals, and pharmaceuticals, with plants in Brooklyn, N. Y., Newark, N. J., and Worcester, Mass.; member of the board of education of Brooklyn and the city of New York; comptroller of the city of New York 1906–1910; member of the commission appointed by Governor Hughes to draft the New York City charter in 1907 and 1908 and of the charter commission appointed by Governor Miller in 1922; commissioner of the State board of charities; was the nominee of Kings County for Governor in 1912, but withdrew in favor of William Sulzer after the second ballot; first lieutenant, captain, lieutenant colonel, and brigadier general of the Fourteenth Infantry, New York National Guard; elected as a Democrat to the Sixty-third Congress (March 4, 1913–March 3, 1915); was not a candidate for renomination in 1914; resumed former business activities; delegate to the Democratic National Conventions in 1904, 1908, and 1920; during the First World War was ordnance officer, with the rank of lieutenant colonel, in the Twenty-seventh Division; colonel in the ordnance department of the Officers' Reserve Corps; unsuccessful candidate for election in 1922 to the Sixty-eighth Congress; died in a hospital in New Rochelle, N. Y., May 17, 1934; interment in Kensico Cemetery, Westchester, N. Y.

MEYER, Adolph, a Representative from Louisiana; born in Natchez, Adams County, Miss., October 19, 1842; attended the common schools; matriculated at the University of Virginia at Charlottesville, but before graduation enlisted in the Confederate Army in 1862; served until the close of the Civil War on the staff of Brig. Gen. John S. Williams, of Kentucky, and attained the rank of assistant adjutant general; returned to Natchez and engaged extensively in the cultivation of cotton, sugar cane, and rice; also engaged in banking in the city of New Orleans; elected colonel of the First Regiment of the Louisiana State National Guard in 1879; appointed by Governor Wiltz brigadier general of the First Brigade, embracing all the uniformed militia in the State, in 1881; elected as a Democrat to the Fifty-second and to the eight succeeding Congresses and served from March 4, 1891, until his death in New Orleans, La., March 8, 1908; interment in Metairie Cemetery.

MEYER, Herbert Alton, a Representative from Kansas; born in Chillicothe, Ross County, Ohio, August 30, 1886; attended the grade schools, Washington, D. C., the Staunton Military Academy, Staunton, Va., 1900–1904, the George Washington University, Washington, D. C., 1905–1908, and was graduated from National University Law School, Washington, D. C., in 1910; was admitted to the bar in 1910; during the First World War served as a captain in the United States Army Air Corps; served as assistant to the Secretary of the Interior 1915–1917; executive of an oil marketing company 1919–1937; in 1940 became publisher of the Independence (Kans.) Daily Reporter; elected as a Republican to the Eightieth and Eighty-first Congresses and had won renomination for a third term; served from January 3, 1947, until his death in the naval hospital at Bethesda, Md., October 2, 1950; interment in Mount Hope Cemetery, Independence, Kans.

MEYER, John Ambrose, a Representative from Maryland; born in Baltimore, Md., May 15, 1899; attended the grade schools and Loyola High School; during the First World War enlisted as a private in the Students' Army Training Corps at Georgetown University, Washington, D. C., and served until honorably discharged from the United States Army; was graduated from Loyola College, Baltimore, Md., in 1921 and from the law department of the University of Maryland at Baltimore in 1922; was admitted to the bar in 1921 and commenced practice in Baltimore; associate judge of the traffic court of Baltimore 1929–1935; special assistant city solicitor in 1939 and 1940; elected as a Democrat to the Seventy-seventh Congress (January 3, 1941–January 3, 1943); was an unsuccessful candidate for renomination in 1942 to the Seventy-eighth Congress; served as district rent attorney for the Office of Price Administration during World War II; engaged in the general practice of law in Baltimore, Md., where he now resides.

MEYER, William Henry, a Representative from Vermont; born in Philadelphia, Pa., December 29, 1914; attended the public schools of Philadelphia; graduated from Pennsylvania State University in 1936; worked as a timber cruiser, State and Federal forester, Civilian Conservation Corps technician and supervisor in West Virginia, Maryland, Wisconsin, and New Jersey, 1936–1940; moved to a farm in Bennington County, Vt., in 1945; with Soil Conservation Service in Vermont in 1949 and 1950; in 1951 entered private practice as a consulting forester and became executive director of the Vermont Forest and Farmland Foundation; chairman of Vermont Forest Festival Committee and Vermont Land Use Conference; delegate to the State Democratic Convention in 1956; elected as a Democrat to the Eighty-sixth Congress (January 3, 1959–January 3, 1961); unsuccessful candidate for reelection in 1960 to the Eighty-seventh Congress; appointed as a consultant, Technical Review Staff, Department of the Interior, in May 1961; is a resident of West Rupert, Vt.

MEYERS, Benjamin Franklin, a Representative from Pennsylvania; born near New Centerville, Somerset County, Pa., July 6, 1833; attended Somerset Academy, and Jefferson College, Canonsburg (now Washington and Jefferson College, Washington), Pa.; studied law; was admitted to the bar and commenced practice in 1855; member of the State house of representatives in 1864; delegate to the Democratic National Conventions of 1864, 1880, 1884, 1888, and 1902; editor of the Bedford Gazette and in 1868 of the Harrisburg Daily Patriot; elected as a Democrat to the Forty-second Congress (March 4, 1871–March 3, 1873); unsuccessful candidate for reelection in 1872 to the Forty-third Congress; postmaster of Harrisburg, Pa., by appointment of President Cleveland, 1886–1891; publisher of the Daily Star Independent, Harrisburg, Pa.; engaged in public utilities; died in Harrisburg, Pa., August 11, 1918; interment in Harrisburg Cemetery.

MICHAELSON, Magne Alfred, a Representative from Illinois; born in Kristiansand, Norway, on September 7, 1878; immigrated to the United States with his parents, who settled in Chicago, Ill., in October 1885; attended the public schools, and was graduated from Chicago Normal School in 1898; taught in the public schools of Chicago 1898–1914; member of the common council of Chicago 1915–1918; delegate to the State constitutional convention in 1920; chairman of the board of directors of the Madison and Kedzie State Bank of Chicago 1924–1927; elected as a Republican to the Sixty-seventh and to the four succeeding Congresses (March 4, 1921–March 3, 1931); unsuccessful candidate for renomination in 1930; retired from active business pursuits and political activities; died in Chicago, Ill., October 26, 1949; interment in Mount Olivet Cemetery.

MICHALEK, Anthony, a Representative from Illinois; born in Radvanov, Bohemia, January 16, 1878; immigrated to the United States with his parents, who settled in Chicago, Ill., in 1878; attended the common schools; became engaged as bookkeeper; was the first man of Bohemian blood in America elected to the National House of Representatives; elected as a Republican to the Fifty-ninth Congress (March 4, 1905–March 3, 1907); unsuccessful candidate for reelection in 1906 to the Sixtieth Congress and for election in 1908 to the Sixty-first Congress; president and manager of the musical conservatory, Chicago, Ill.; died in Chicago, Ill., December 21, 1916; interment in St. Adalbert's Cemetery.

MICHEL, Robert Henry, a Representative from Illinois; born in Peoria, Ill., March 2, 1923; attended the public schools; during World War II served with the Thirty-ninth Infantry Regiment as a combat infantryman in England, France, Belgium, and Germany from February 10, 1943, to January 26, 1946; was wounded by machine-gun fire; awarded the Bronze Star, the Purple Heart, and four battle stars; was graduated from Bradley University, Peoria, Ill., in 1948, majoring in business administration and economics; administrative assistant to Representative Harold Velde 1949–1956; elected as a Republican to the Eighty-fifth and Eighty-sixth Congresses (January 3, 1957–January 3, 1961). *Reelected to the Eighty-seventh Congress.*

MICHENER, Earl Cory, a Representative from Michigan; born near Attica, Seneca County, Ohio, November 30, 1876; moved with his parents to Adrian, Mich., in 1889; attended the public schools of Adrian; during the Spanish-American War served as a private in Company B, Thirty-first Regiment, Michigan Volunteer Infantry, from April 26, 1898, to May 17, 1899; studied law at the University of Michigan at Ann Arbor in 1901 and 1902 and was graduated from the law department of Columbian University (now George Washington University) Washington, D. C., in 1903; was admitted to the bar the same year and commenced practice in Adrian, Mich.; assistant prosecuting attorney for Lenawee County, Mich., 1907–1910;

prosecuting attorney 1911–1914; elected as a Republican to the Sixty-sixth and to the six succeeding Congresses (March 4, 1919–March 3, 1933); one of the managers appointed by the House of Representatives in 1926 to conduct the impeachment proceedings against George W. English, judge of the United States District Court for the Eastern District of Illinois; unsuccessful candidate for reelection in 1932 to the Seventy-third Congress; elected to the Seventy-fourth and to the seven succeeding Congresses (January 3, 1935–January 3, 1951); was not a candidate for renomination in 1950; maintained law offices in Adrian, Mich., until his death there July 4, 1957; interment in Oakwood Cemetery.

MICKEY, J. Ross, a Representative from Illinois; born on a farm in Eldorado Township, McDonough County, Ill., January 5, 1856; attended the public schools and Lincoln (Ill.) College; taught in the public schools of Macomb, McDonough County, Ill., for a number of years; studied law; was admitted to the bar in 1889 and practiced in Macomb, Ill., until 1898; elected judge of McDonough County in 1898 for a term of four years, but resigned February 22, 1901, having been elected to Congress; elected as a Democrat to the Fifty-seventh Congress (March 4, 1901–March 3, 1903); declined to be a candidate for renomination in 1902; resumed the practice of law in Macomb, Ill.; served as president of the Mystic Workers of the World 1908–1918 and as a director from 1918 until his death; died in Excelsior Springs, Mo., on March 20, 1928; interment in Oakwood Cemetery, Macomb, Ill.

MIDDLESWARTH, Ner, a Representative from Pennsylvania; born in Glasgow, Scotland, December 12, 1783; immigrated to the United States in 1792 with his parents, who settled in New Jersey; moved to Beavertown, Pa., the same year; had a very limited education; served as a captain in the War of 1812; member of the State house of representatives 1815–1841 and served as speaker two terms; served in the State senate 1853–1855; elected as a Whig to the Thirty-third Congress (March 4, 1853–March 3, 1855); was not a candidate for renomination in 1854; engaged in agricultural pursuits; president of the Beaver Furnace Co. in Snyder County; associate judge of Snyder County in 1858; died in Beavertown, Snyder County, Pa., June 2, 1865; interment in Union Cemetery.

MIDDLETON, Arthur (son of Henry Middleton), a Delegate from South Carolina; born at "Middleton Place," his father's estate, on the Ashley River, near Charleston, Berkeley County, S. C., June 26, 1742; received his early education from private tutors and schools in Charleston; attended school at Hackney, Westminster School, and St. John's College, Cambridge University, in England; studied law at the Temple in London, but did not practice; returned to South Carolina in 1763 and engaged in planting; justice of the peace of Berkeley County in 1765; member of the provincial house of commons 1765–1768; traveled extensively in Europe 1768–1771; again a member of the provincial house of commons 1772–1775; delegate to the provincial convention in 1774 and 1775; again justice of the peace 1776–1786; member of the council of safety in 1775 and 1776; delegate to the provincial congress which formed a State constitution in 1776; served in the Revolutionary War; held a prisoner by the British from May 1780 to July 1781 when he was exchanged and returned to South Carolina; Member of the Continental Congress 1776–1778 and 1781–1783; a signer of the Declaration of Independence; elected Governor of South Carolina in 1778, but declined; member of the State house of representatives 1778–1780, 1785, and 1786; served in the State senate in 1781 and 1782; member of the privy council in 1782; member of the board of trustees of Charleston College; died at

"The Oaks," near Charleston, S. C., January 1, 1787; interment in the family mausoleum at "Middleton Place," near Charleston, S. C.

MIDDLETON, George, a Representative from New Jersey; born in Philadelphia, Pa., October 14, 1800; moved to Burlington, N. J.; attended the public schools; became a tanner; moved to Allentown, Monmouth County, N. J.; held several local offices; member of the State general assembly in 1858 and 1859; elected as a Democrat to the Thirty-eighth Congress (March 4, 1863–March 3, 1865); unsuccessful candidate for reelection in 1864 to the Thirty-ninth Congress; resumed the business of tanning; died in Allentown, N. J., December 31, 1888; interment in Crosswicks Community Cemetery, Crosswicks, Burlington County, N. J.

MIDDLETON, Henry (father of Arthur Middleton), a Delegate from South Carolina; born at "The Oaks," near Charleston, S. C., in 1717; educated at home and in England; justice of the peace and quorum 1742–1780; member of the provincial house of commons 1742–1755 and served as speaker 1745–1747, 1754, and 1755; commissioned officer of horse of the provincial forces in 1743; commissioner of Indian affairs in 1755, of the church act, of free schools, and internal improvements; member of the King's Provincial Council from 1755 until his resignation in September 1770; member of the provincial convention in 1774; Member of the Continental Congress from 1774 until 1776, when he resigned; served as president of that body from October 22, 1774, to May 10, 1775; member of the council of safety in 1775 and 1776; member of the Provincial Congress of South Carolina in 1775 and 1776, and as its Delegate in Congress received the thanks of that body for his services in the cause of liberty; member of the committee to prepare a form of government in 1776; member of the legislative council under the transition government 1776–1778; member of the State senate 1778–1780; large landowner and planter in Berkeley, Colleton, and Granville Counties, residing at his estates, "The Oaks" and "Middleton Place;" died in Charleston, Charleston County, S. C., June 13, 1784; interment behind the chancel of the Church of St. James Parish, Berkeley County, S. C.

MIDDLETON, Henry (son of Arthur Middleton and grandson of the preceding), a Representative from South Carolina; born in London, England, September 28, 1770; his parents, then traveling in Europe, returned a year later to South Carolina; pursued classical studies with tutors at his father's estate, "Middleton Place," near Charleston, S. C., with a year in England; returned to America after his father's death in 1787; later returned to England and resided at Clifton, Gloucestershire, until his return to Charleston in 1800; engaged in planting in South Carolina; member of the State house of representatives 1802–1810; elected to the State senate 1810; elected Governor of South Carolina in December 1810 and served until December 1812; elected as a Democrat to the Fourteenth and Fifteenth Congresses (March 4, 1815–March 3, 1819); unsuccessful candidate for renomination in 1818; Minister to Russia from April 6, 1820, to August 3, 1830; leader of the Union Party of South Carolina and vice president of the Union Convention in 1833; retired to private life; died in Charleston, S. C., June 14, 1846; interment in the family mausoleum at "Middleton Place," near Charleston, S. C.

MIERS, Robert Walter, a Representative from Indiana; born near Greensburg, Decatur County, Ind., January 27, 1848; attended the common schools; was graduated from the academic department of Indiana University at Bloomington in 1870 and from its law department in 1871; was admitted to the bar in April 1872 and commenced practice in Bloomington, Ind.; prosecuting attorney for the tenth judicial circuit of Indiana 1875–1879; member of the State house of representatives in 1879; member of the board of trustees of Indiana University 1879–1897; appointed judge of the tenth judicial circuit of Indiana in 1883, elected in 1884 and again in 1890, and served until September 1896, when he resigned to become a candidate for Congress; unsuccessful Democratic nominee for secretary of state in 1886 and in 1888; elected as a Democrat to the Fifty-fifth and to the three succeeding Congresses (March 4, 1897–March 3, 1905); unsuccessful candidate for reelection in 1904 to the Fifty-ninth Congress; resumed the practice of law; again elected judge of the tenth circuit of Indiana on November 3, 1914, and served until November 22, 1920; continued the practice of law in Bloomington, Ind., until 1928, when he discontinued active practice and lived in retirement; died while on a visit in Martinsville, Ind., February 20, 1930; interment in Rosehill Cemetery, Bloomington, Ind.

MIFFLIN, Thomas, a Delegate from Pennsylvania; born in Philadelphia, Pa., January 10, 1744; was graduated from the University of Pennsylvania at Philadelphia in 1760; member of the American Philosophical Society 1765–1799; member of the colonial legislature 1772–1774; Member of the Continental Congress 1774–1776 and 1782–1784, and was its President in 1783; assisted in organizing troops and in training them for service in the Continental Army; major and chief aide-de-camp to General Washington July 4, 1775; major and Quartermaster General of the Continental Army August 14, 1775; colonel December 22, 1775; brigadier general May 16, 1776; major general February 19, 1777; resigned as Quartermaster General November 7, 1777, but continued in the performance of that duty to December 8, 1777; member of board of war November 7, 1777; resigned as major general February 25, 1779; trustee of the University of Pennsylvania 1778–1791; in January 1780 appointed a member of a special board to consider general expenses and was given the thanks of Congress for the "wise and salutary plans recommended"; served as speaker of the State house of representatives 1785–1788; delegate to the Federal Constitutional Convention in 1787; president of the supreme executive council of Pennsylvania October 1788 to October 1790; president of the State constitutional convention in 1790; Governor of Pennsylvania 1790–1799; again a member of the State house of representatives in 1799 and 1800; died in Lancaster, Pa., January 19, 1800; interment in the front yard of Trinity Lutheran Church.

MILES, Frederick, a Representative from Connecticut; born in Goshen, Litchfield County, Conn., on December 19, 1815; attended the common schools and pursued an academic course; engaged in mercantile pursuits in Goshen until 1857; moved to Twinlakes and later, in 1858, to Salisbury and engaged in the manufacture of iron; member of the State senate from 1877 until February 1879, when he resigned; elected as a Republican to the Forty-sixth and Forty-seventh Congresses (March 4, 1879–March 3, 1883); declined a nomination for reelection; again elected to the Fifty-first Congress (March 4, 1889–March 3, 1891); unsuccessful candidate for reelection in 1890 to the Fifty-second Congress; resumed business activities; died near Salisbury, Litchfield County, Conn., November 20, 1896; interment in Salisbury Cemetery.

MILES, John Esten, a Representative from New Mexico; born in Murfreesboro, Rutherford County, Tenn., July 28, 1884; attended the grade schools of Rutherford County, Tenn.; in 1902 began farming in Fannin County, Tex., and in 1905 moved to Granite, Okla.; in 1906 moved to New Mexico and homesteaded on a farm near Endee, Quay County; purchased a general store in Endee, N. Mex., in 1918; member of the school board 1918–1921; postmaster of Endee 1917–1920; moved to Tucumcari in 1920 and served as county assessor of Quay County 1920–1924; secretary of the State Tax Commission 1925–1927; in 1927 acquired an interest in and was associate editor of the New Mexico Democrat and the Las Vegas Independent; in 1920 organized and operated the New Mexico Taxpayer's Service; again secretary of the State Tax Commission 1931–1934; chief of the field division of the Bureau of Internal Revenue, Albuquerque, N. Mex., in 1934; delegate to all Democratic National Conventions since 1936; Governor of New Mexico 1939–1942; chairman, New Mexico Public Service Commission 1943–1945; Commissioner of Public Lands 1945–1948; elected as a Democrat to the Eighty-first Congress (January 3, 1949–January 3, 1951); was not a candidate for renomination in 1950, but was the unsuccessful Democratic candidate for Governor; president of New Mexico School Book Depository; appointed director of enforcement, Office of Price Stabilization, Denver, Colo., in April 1951 and resigned June 30, 1952; appointed chairman of Public Service Commission in January 1959, in which capacity he is still serving; is a resident of Santa Fe, N. Mex.

MILES, Joshua Weldon, a Representative from Maryland; born on his father's farm on the Great Annamessex River, near the village of Marion, Somerset County, Md., December 9, 1858; attended private schools and Marion (Md.) Academy; was graduated from Western Maryland College, Westminster, Md., in 1878; attended the law department of Maryland University; was admitted to the bar in July 1880 and commenced practice in Princess Anne, Md.; State's attorney of Somerset County 1883–1887; unsuccessful candidate for reelection; elected as a Democrat to the Fifty-fourth Congress (March 4, 1895–March 3, 1897); unsuccessful candidate for reelection in 1896 to the Fifty-fifth Congress; resumed the practice of law in Princess Anne, Md.; also interested in banking, serving as president of the Bank of Somerset from 1900 until his death; delegate at large to the Democratic National Conventions of 1900, 1912, 1920, and 1924; trustee of Western Maryland College for thirty years; collector of internal revenue for the district of Maryland 1914–1921; resumed the practice of law; died while on a visit for medical treatment in a Baltimore, Md., hospital on March 4, 1929; interment in Manokin Cemetery, Princess Anne, Md.

MILES, William Porcher, a Representative from South Carolina; born in Charleston, S. C., July 4, 1822; attended Wellington School in Charleston, and was graduated from Charleston College in 1842; studied law; was admitted to the bar and commenced practice in Charleston; mayor of Charleston 1855–1857; elected as a Democrat to the Thirty-fifth and Thirty-sixth Congresses and served from March 4, 1857, until his retirement in December 1860; member of the Confederate Provisional Congress in Montgomery, Ala., in February 1861; Member of the Confederate Congress from February 1862 to March 1864; colonel on the staff of General Beauregard; president of the University of South Carolina at Columbia 1880–1882; died in Burnside, La., on May 11, 1899; interment in Union Cemetery, Union, Monroe County, W. Va.

MILLARD, Charles Dunsmore, a Representative from New York; born in Tarrytown, Westchester County, N. Y., December 1, 1873; attended the public schools, Phillips Academy, Andover, Mass., and Brown University, Providence, R. I., and was graduated from New York Law School, New York City, in 1897; was admitted to the bar in 1898 and commenced practice in Westchester County, N. Y.; member of the Westchester County Board of Supervisors 1907–1931, and chairman

in 1916, 1917, 1927, and 1928; member of the Republican State committee 1920–1937; delegate to many of the Republican State conventions; elected as a Republican to the Seventy-second and to the three succeeding Congresses and served from March 4, 1931, to September 29, 1937, when he resigned, having been elected surrogate of Westchester County, N. Y., in which capacity he served until his retirement in 1943; died in New York City, N. Y., December 11, 1944; interment in Sleepy Hollow Cemetery, North Tarrytown, N. Y.

MILLARD, Joseph Hopkins, a Senator from Nebraska; born in Hamilton, Province of Ontario, Canada, April 20, 1836, while his parents, natives of the United States, were temporarily residing in that country; moved to Iowa with his parents, who settled near Sabula, Jackson County; attended the district school; clerked in a store; moved to Omaha, Nebr., in 1856 and engaged in the land business; moved to Montana in 1864 and, through the assistance of an Iowa capitalist, opened a bank in Virginia City; returned to Omaha in 1866 and became a director of the Omaha National Bank; served as its president and cashier 1867–1919; one of the incorporators of the Omaha & Northwestern Railroad Company in 1869; elected treasurer of the State school for the deaf and dumb in 1869; served as mayor of Omaha in 1871; for fifteen years was a director of the Union Pacific Railroad Company, six years of which he served in the capacity of a Government director; elected as a Republican to the United States Senate and served from March 4, 1901, to March 3, 1907; was not a candidate for reelection in 1906; resumed the banking business in Omaha, Nebr., and died there on January 13, 1922; interment in Prospect Hill Cemetery.

MILLARD, Stephen Columbus, a Representative from New York; born in Stamford, Bennington County, Vt., January 14, 1841; attended Powers Institute, and was graduated from Williams College, Williamstown, Mass., in 1865; attended Harvard Law School; was admitted to the bar of the State of New York in May 1867 and commenced practice in Binghamton; chairman of the Republican county committee 1872–1879; elected as a Republican to the Forty-eighth and Forty-ninth Congresses (March 4, 1883–March 3, 1887); was not a candidate for renomination in 1886; resumed the practice of law in Binghamton, N. Y., where he died June 21, 1914; interment in Spring Forest Cemetery.

MILLEDGE, John, a Representative and a Senator from Georgia; born in Savannah, Ga., in 1757; was tutored privately; studied law; was admitted to the bar and commenced practice in Savannah, Ga.; served in the Revolutionary War, and was one of the patriots who rifled the powder magazine in Savannah, and thus furnished powder that was subsequently used by Continental soldiers at the Battle of Bunker Hill; attorney general of Georgia in 1780; member of the State house of representatives in 1782; elected to the Second Congress to fill the vacancy caused by the House declaring the seat of Anthony Wayne vacant, and served from November 22, 1792, to March 3, 1793; subsequently elected to the Fourth and Fifth Congresses (March 4, 1795–March 3, 1799); again elected to the Seventh Congress and served from March 4, 1801, until his resignation in May 1802; Governor of Georgia 1802–1806; elected to the United States Senate to fill the vacancy caused by the death of James Jackson; reelected in 1806 and served from June 19, 1806, until November 14, 1809, when he resigned; elected President pro tempore of the Senate January 30, 1809; died on his plantation near Augusta, Ga., February 9, 1818; interment in Summerville Cemetery.

MILLEN, John, a Representative from Georgia; born in Savannah, Ga., in 1804; completed preparatory studies; studied law; was admitted to the bar and practiced in Savannah many years; member of the State house of representatives in 1828, 1834, 1835, 1839, and 1840; elected as a Democrat to the Twenty-eighth Congress and served from March 4, 1843, until his death in Savannah, Ga., October 15, 1843; interment in Laurel Grove Cemetery.

MILLER, Arthur Lewis, a Representative from Nebraska; born on a farm near Plainview, Pierce County, Nebr., May 24, 1892; attended the public schools; was graduated from the high school at Plainview, Nebr., in 1911 and from Loyola Medical School, Chicago, Ill., in 1918; taught in a rural school at Plainview, Nebr., 1911–1913; member of the United States Medical Reserve Corps 1917–1919; practiced medicine and surgery in Kimball, Nebr., 1919–1942 and also engaged in agricultural pursuits; mayor of Kimball in 1933 and 1934; member of the Nebraska Legislature 1937–1941; a fellow of the American College of Surgeons; unsuccessful candidate for the Republican gubernatorial nomination in 1940; State health director in 1941 and 1942; elected as a Republican to the Seventy-eighth and to the seven succeeding Congresses (January 3, 1943–January 3, 1959); unsuccessful candidate for reelection in 1958 to the Eighty-sixth Congress; director, Office of Saline Water, Department of the Interior, Washington, D. C., from February 1959 to January 1961; resides in Chevy Chase, Md.

MILLER, Bert Henry, a Senator from Idaho; born in St. George, Washington County, Utah, December 15, 1879; was graduated from Brigham Young University, Provo, Utah, in 1901 and from Cumberland University Law School, Lebanon, Tenn., in 1902; was admitted to the bar and commenced practice of law in St. Anthony, Idaho, in 1903; prosecuting attorney of Fremont County, Idaho, 1912–1914; was an unsuccessful Democratic candidate for Congress in 1914; elected attorney general of Idaho in 1932 and reelected in 1934; unsuccessful candidate for the Democratic gubernatorial nomination in 1936; served for two months in 1938 as Idaho's labor commissioner; unsuccessful Democratic candidate for election in 1938 to the Seventy-sixth Congress; attorney in the Wage and Hour Division, Department of Labor, at Seattle, Wash., in 1939 and 1940; again attorney general of Idaho 1940–1944; elected a justice of the State supreme court in 1944 for a six-year term; elected as a Democrat to the United States Senate in 1948 for the term commencing January 3, 1949, and served until his death in Washington, D. C., October 8, 1949; interment in Morris Hill Cemetery, Boise, Idaho.

MILLER, Clarence Benjamin, a Representative from Minnesota; born in Pine Island, Goodhue County, Minn., March 13, 1872; attended the country school, high school, and the Minneapolis (Minn.) Academy; was graduated from the academic department of the University of Minnesota at Minneapolis in 1895 and from the law department of the same institution in 1900; superintendent of the public schools of Rushford, Minn., 1895–1898; was admitted to the bar in 1900 and commenced the practice of law in Duluth, Minn.; member of the State house of representatives in 1907; elected as a Republican to the Sixty-first and to the four succeeding Congresses (March 4, 1909–March 3, 1919); unsuccessful candidate for reelection in 1918; member of the congressional investigating committee to the Philippine Islands in 1915; special investigator for the War Department to the western front in France in 1917; elected assistant secretary of the Republican National Committee in 1919 and was chosen its secretary in 1920; engaged in the practice of law in Washington, D. C.; died in a hospital at St. Paul, Minn., January 10, 1922; interment in Pine Island Cemetery, Pine Island, Minn.

MILLER, Clement Woodnutt (nephew of Thomas W. Miller), a Representative from California; born in Wilmington, New Castle County, Del., October 28, 1916; graduated from Lawrenceville (N. J.) School, from Williams College, Williamstown, Mass., in 1940, and from Cornell University School of Industrial and Labor Relations in 1946; during World War II enlisted in the United States Army in 1940; served as a private in the Two Hundred and Fifty-eighth Field Artillery Regiment and was discharged in 1945 as a captain in the One Hundred and Fourth Infantry Division, with service in Holland and Germany; awarded the Bronze Star and twice recommended for the Legion of Merit; veterans service officer in Nevada in 1946 and 1947; employment service, State of Nevada, in 1947; field examiner and hearing officer of the National Labor Relations Board for Northern California 1948–1953; landscape consultant since 1954; unsuccessful Democratic candidate for election in 1956 to the Eighty-fifth Congress; elected as a Democrat to the Eighty-sixth Congress (January 3, 1959–January 3, 1961). *Reelected to the Eighty-seventh Congress.*

MILLER, Daniel Fry, a Representative from Iowa; born in Cumberland, Allegany County, Md., October 4, 1814; moved with his parents to Wayne County, Ohio, in 1816; attended the public schools; taught for several years; engaged in newspaper work in Wooster, Ohio; moved to Pittsburgh, Pa., in 1830; employed as a clerk in stores; studied law; was admitted to the bar in 1839 and commenced practice in Fort Madison, Iowa; member of the Territorial house of representatives in 1840; contested the election of William H. Thompson to the Thirty-first Congress, but the House decided that neither was entitled to the seat; subsequently elected as a Whig to fill this vacancy and served from December 20, 1850, to March 3, 1851; resumed the practice of law; presidential elector on the Republican ticket of Frémont and Dayton in 1856; mayor of Fort Madison in 1859; moved to Keokuk, Iowa, and continued the practice of law; unsuccessful candidate for election as judge of the supreme court in 1860; elected mayor of Keokuk, Iowa, in 1873; member of the State house of representatives in 1894; retired from active practice in 1895 and moved to Omaha, Nebr., where he died December 9, 1895; interment in St. Peter's Cemetery, Keokuk, Lee County, Iowa.

MILLER, Daniel H., a Representative from Pennsylvania; born in Philadelphia, Pa.; elected as a Jackson Democrat to the Eighteenth and to the three succeeding Congresses (March 4, 1823–March 3, 1831); died in Philadelphia, Pa., in 1846.

MILLER, Edward Edwin, a Representative from Illinois; born in Creston, Union County, Iowa, July 22, 1880; attended the common schools; moved to East St. Louis, St. Clair County, Ill., in 1892; engaged in the real estate and insurance business in 1900; served as private secretary to Congressman William A. Rodenberg; delegate to the Republican National Convention at Chicago in 1912; State treasurer of Illinois 1921–1923; elected as a Republican to the Sixty-eighth Congress (March 4, 1923–March 3, 1925); declined to be a candidate for renomination in 1924; engaged in the real estate and insurance business until 1942; director of transportation, American Red Cross, at St. Louis, Mo., from 1942 until his death; died at St. Louis, Mo., August 1, 1946; interment in St. Clair Memorial Park Cemetery, East St. Louis, Ill.

MILLER, Edward Tylor, a Representative from Maryland; born in Woodside, Montgomery County, Md., February 1, 1895; attended Sidwell Friends School, Washington, D. C.; was graduated from Yale University, New Haven, Conn., in 1916; during the First World War served in the United States Army as commanding officer of Company C, Three Hundred and Twentieth Infantry, Eightieth Division, from May 14, 1917, to August 8, 1919, participating in the Somme, St. Mihiel, and Meuse-Argonne engagements; studied law at George Washington University, Washington, D. C.; was admitted to the bar in 1920 and commenced practice in Easton, Md.; referee in bankruptcy 1923–1941; police and juvenile judge for Talbot County, Md., 1934–1938; during World War II served as a colonel in the Infantry, United States Army, 1942–1946, in North Africa, India, and China; elected as a Republican to the Eightieth and to the five succeeding Congresses (January 3, 1947–January 3, 1959); unsuccessful candidate for reelection in 1958 to the Eighty-sixth Congress and for election in 1960 to the Eighty-seventh Congress; vice chairman, United States Delegation to Second United Nations Conference on the Law of the Sea at Geneva, Switzerland, in 1960; resumed the practice of law; is a resident of Easton, Md.

MILLER, George Funston, a Representative from Pennsylvania; born in Chillisquaque Township, Northumberland County, Pa., on September 5, 1809; attended Kirkpatrick's Academy in Milton, Pa.; taught school; studied law; was admitted to the bar of Union County May 15, 1833, and commenced practice in Lewisburg; member of the board of curators of the university at Lewisburg (now Bucknell University) 1846–1882; scribe of curators 1847–1851; secretary of the board of trustees of Bucknell University 1848–1864; elected as a Republican to the Thirty-ninth and Fortieth Congresses (March 4, 1865–March 3, 1869); resumed the practice of law; was interested in the formation of the Lewisburg, Centre & Spruce Creek Railroad and was its first president; a director of the Northumberland Bank and a director of the Lewisburg National Bank; died in Lewisburg, Union County, Pa., October 21, 1885; interment in Lewisburg Cemetery.

MILLER, George Paul, a Representative from California; born in San Francisco, Calif., January 15, 1891; attended public and private schools; was graduated from St. Mary's (Calif.) College in 1912; engaged as a civil engineer 1912–1917; during the First World War graduated from the School of Fire for Field Artillery, Fort Sill, Okla., and served as a lieutenant in the Thirty-sixth and Three Hundred and Forty-sixth Field Artillery 1917–1919; member of the staff, United States Veterans Bureau, United States Government, 1921–1925; resumed activities as a civil engineer; also coowner of the Mack Travel Service of San Francisco since 1928; member of the California State Assembly 1937–1941; was executive secretary to the California Division of Fish and Game 1942–1944; elected as a Democrat to the Seventy-ninth and to the seven succeeding Congresses (January 3, 1945–January 3, 1961). *Reelected to the Eighty-seventh Congress.*

MILLER, Homer Virgil Milton, a Senator from Georgia; born in Pendleton District, S. C., April 29, 1814; moved with his parents to Rabun County, Ga., in 1820; attended the common schools, and was graduated from the Medical College of South Carolina in 1835; continued medical studies in Paris and commenced practice in Cassville, Ga., in 1838; unsuccessful Whig candidate for election to the Twenty-ninth Congress in 1844; served during the Civil War in the Confederate Army as surgeon in the Eighth Georgia Infantry and subsequently as brigade and division surgeon in Virginia, with General Beauregard at Charleston, S. C., and as medical director, surgeon of posts, and inspector of hospitals in Georgia; resumed the practice of medicine in Rome, Ga.; member of the State reconstruction convention in 1867; member of the faculty of the Atlanta Medical College; upon the readmission of Georgia to representation was elected as a Democrat to the United States Senate on July 28, 1868; qualified on February 24, 1871, and served until March 3, 1871; trustee of the University of Georgia at

Athens; died in Atlanta, Fulton County, Ga., May 31, 1896; interment in Myrtle Hill Cemetery, Rome, Ga.

MILLER, Howard Shultz, a Representative from Kansas; born in Somerset County, Pa., February 27, 1879; moved with his family in 1882 to Morrill, Kans.; attended the public schools of Brown County, and Sabetha (Kans.) High School; taught school 1894–1899; graduated from the University of Nebraska College of Law in 1900; was admitted to the bar in 1901 and began law practice in Kansas; engaged in agricultural pursuits and as a lawyer 1901–1952; elected as a Democrat to the Eighty-third Congress (January 3, 1953–January 3, 1955); unsuccessful candidate for reelection in 1954 to the Eighty-fourth Congress and for election in 1956 to the Eighty-fifth Congress; resumed farming operations; is a resident of Hiawatha, Kans.

MILLER, Jacob Welsh, a Senator from New Jersey; born in German Valley, Morris County, N. J., August 29, 1800; attended the public schools; studied law; was admitted to the bar in 1823 and practiced in Morristown, N. J.; elected to the State general assembly in 1832; served in the State council 1838–1840; elected as a Whig to the United States Senate in 1840; reelected in 1846 and served from March 4, 1841, to March 3, 1853; died in Morristown, N. J., September 30, 1862; interment in St. Peter's Parish Churchyard.

MILLER, James Francis, a Representative from Texas; born in Winnsboro, Fairfield District, S. C., August 1, 1830; moved with his parents to Texas in 1842; attended the common schools and Reutersville College; studied law; was admitted to the bar in 1857 and commenced practice in Gonzales, Tex.; enlisted as a private in Company I, Eighth Texas Cavalry, better known as "Terry's Texas Rangers," and served throughout the Civil War; resumed the practice of law in Gonzales, Tex.; engaged in banking and stock raising; elected as a Democrat to the Forty-eighth and Forty-ninth Congresses (March 4, 1883–March 3, 1887); declined renomination; resumed former pursuits; elected as first president of the Texas Bankers' Association in 1885; died in Gonzales, Tex., on July 3, 1902; interment in Masonic Cemetery.

MILLER, James Monroe, a Representative from Kansas; born at Three Springs, Huntingdon County, Pa., May 6, 1852; attended the district school and was graduated from Dickinson Seminary, Williamsport, Pa., in 1875; moved to Skiddy, Morris County, Kans., in 1875; superintendent of schools in Council Grove, Kans., for two terms, and while holding this position studied law; was admitted to the bar in 1879 and commenced practice in Council Grove, Kans.; elected prosecuting attorney of Morris County, Kans., in 1880 and again in 1884 and 1886; presidential elector on the Republican ticket of Blaine and Logan in 1884, and was selected as the messenger to carry the electoral vote of the State to Washington, D. C.; member of the State house of representatives in 1894 and 1895; elected as a Republican to the Fifty-sixth and to the five succeeding Congresses (March 4, 1899–March 3, 1911); unsuccessful candidate for renomination in 1910; resumed the practice of law in Council Grove, Morris County, Kans., and died there January 20, 1926; interment in Greenwood Cemetery.

MILLER, Jesse (father of William Henry Miller), a Representative from Pennsylvania; born near Landisburg, Perry County, Pa., in 1800; attended the common schools; first clerk to county commissioner of Perry County 1820–1823; sheriff of Perry County 1823–1826; member of the State house of representatives from 1826 until February 7, 1828, when he resigned; served in the State senate 1828–1832; elected as a Democrat to the Twenty-third and Twenty-fourth Congresses and served from March 4, 1833, until his resignation on October 30, 1836; First Auditor of the Treasury Department, by appointment of President Jackson, 1836–1842; canal commissioner of Pennsylvania in 1844 and 1845; secretary of state of Pennsylvania 1845–1848; died in Harrisburg, Pa., August 20, 1850; interment in Harrisburg Cemetery.

MILLER, John, a Representative from New York; born in Amenia, Dutchess County, N. Y., November 10, 1774; attended the district school one year and a private classical school in Kent, Conn., for a like period; studied medicine in the University of Pennsylvania at Philadelphia and commenced practice in Washington County, N. Y., in 1798; moved to Fabius, Onondaga County (now Truxton, Cortland County), N. Y., in 1801; coroner of Cortland County in 1802; postmaster of Truxton 1805–1825; organized the Cortland County Medical Society, and in 1808 was its first vice president; justice of the peace 1812–1821; member of the State assembly in 1817, 1820, and 1845; judge of the county court 1817–1820; elected to the Nineteenth Congress (March 4, 1825–March 3, 1827); delegate to the State constitutional convention in 1846; died in Truxton, Cortland County, N. Y., March 31, 1862; interment in the City Cemetery.

MILLER, John, a Representative from Missouri; born near Martinsburg, Berkeley County, Va. (now West Virginia), November 25, 1781; attended the common schools; moved to Steubenville, Ohio, about 1803 and published the Western Herald and Steubenville Gazette; served in the War of 1812 as lieutenant colonel of the Seventeenth United States Infantry and as colonel in command of the Nineteenth Infantry; resigned his Army commission February 10, 1818; was appointed register of the land office at Franklin, Howard County, Mo., which position he held for eight years; elected Governor of Missouri to fill the vacancy caused by the death of Governor Bates; reelected, and served from 1825 to 1832; elected as a Van Buren Democrat to the Twenty-fifth, Twenty-sixth, and Twenty-seventh Congresses (March 4, 1837–March 3, 1843); declined to be a candidate for renomination in 1842, and retired to his residence near Florissant, Mo., where he died March 18, 1846; interment in Col. John O'Fallon's private vault on the O'Fallon farm; reinterment in Bellefontaine Cemetery, St. Louis, Mo.

MILLER, John Elvis, a Representative and a Senator from Arkansas; born in Aid, Stoddard County, Mo., May 15, 1888; attended the public schools, Southeast Missouri State Teachers College at Cape Girardeau, and Valparaiso (Ind.) University; was graduated from the law department of the University of Kentucky at Lexington in 1912; was admitted to the bar the same year and commenced practice in Searcy, White County, Ark.; also engaged in banking; delegate to the State constitutional convention in 1918; served as prosecuting attorney, first judicial circuit of Arkansas, 1919–1922; elected as a Democrat to the Seventy-second and to the three succeeding Congresses and served from March 4, 1931, to November 14, 1937, when he resigned to become Senator; elected to the United States Senate to fill the vacancy caused by the death of Joseph T. Robinson for the term ending January 3, 1943, and served from November 15, 1937, until his resignation effective March 31, 1941, having been appointed United States district judge for the western district of Arkansas, in which capacity he is now serving; is a legal resident of Fort Smith, Sebastian County, Ark.

MILLER, John Franklin, a Senator from California; born in South Bend, St. Joseph County, Ind., November 21, 1831; pursued an academic course; studied law and was graduated from the New York State Law School in 1852; was admitted to the bar and commenced practice in South Bend, Ind.; moved to California, where he practiced for a short time, and then returned to South Bend; member of the Indiana State Senate in 1860; resigned to enter the Union Army during the Civil War; commissioned colonel of the Twenty-ninth Regiment, Indiana Volunteer Infantry, August 27, 1861; brigadier general of Volunteers January 5, 1864; brevetted major general March 13, 1865, "for gallant and meritorious services at Nashville, Tenn."; resigned September 25, 1865; returned to California; collector of the port of San Francisco four years; declined a reappointment; Republican candidate for presidential elector in 1872, 1876, and 1880; delegate to the second State constitutional convention of 1878 and 1879; elected as a Republican to the United States Senate and served from March 4, 1881, until his death in Washington, D. C., March 8, 1886; interment in Laurel Hill Cemetery, San Francisco, Calif.; reinterment in Arlington National Cemetery, Fort Myer, Va., May 5, 1913.

MILLER, John Franklin (nephew of the preceding), a Representative from Washington; born on a farm near South Bend, St. Joseph County, Ind., June 9, 1862; attended the public schools; was graduated from the law department of Valparaiso (Ind.) University in 1887 and was admitted to the bar the same year; moved to Seattle, Wash., in 1888 and commenced the practice of law; prosecuting attorney of King County 1890–1894; deputy prosecuting attorney 1905–1908; mayor of Seattle 1908–1910; elected as a Republican to the Sixty-fifth and to the six succeeding Congresses (March 4, 1917–March 3, 1931); unsuccessful candidate for renomination in 1930; was a member of the congressional delegation which, with the Secretary of War, visited the American forces in France and Germany in 1919; resumed the practice of law; died in Seattle, Wash., May 28, 1936; interment in Acacia Mausoleum.

MILLER, John Gaines, a Representative from Missouri; born in Danville, Ky., November 29, 1812; attended the common schools and was graduated from Centre College, Danville, Ky.; studied law, and was admitted to the bar in 1834; moved to Boonville, Mo., in 1835; served as a member of the State house of representatives in 1840; elected as a Whig to the Thirty-second, Thirty-third, and Thirty-fourth Congresses and served from March 4, 1851, until his death near Marshall, Saline County, Mo., May 11, 1856; interment in Mount Olive Cemetery, near Marshall, Mo.

MILLER, John Krepps, a Representative from Ohio; born in Mount Vernon, Knox County, Ohio, May 25, 1819; attended the public schools; was graduated from Jefferson College, Canonsburg, Pa., in 1838; studied law; was admitted to the bar in 1841 and commenced practice in Mount Vernon, Ohio; delegate to the Democratic National Convention at Baltimore in 1844 which nominated James K. Polk for President; elected as a Democrat to the Thirtieth and Thirty-first Congresses (March 4, 1847–March 3, 1851); declined the chief justiceship of Washington Territory in 1853 tendered by President Pierce; died in Mount Vernon, Ohio, on August 11, 1863; interment in Mound View Cemetery.

MILLER, Joseph, a Representative from Ohio; born in Virginia September 9, 1819; attended the common schools; moved to Ohio and settled in Chillicothe; was graduated from Miami University, Oxford, Ohio, in 1839; studied law; was admitted to the bar in 1841 and commenced practice in Chillicothe, Ohio; prosecuting attorney of Ross County, Ohio, 1844–1848; member of the State house of representatives in 1856; elected as a Democrat to the Thirty-fifth Congress (March 4, 1857–

March 3, 1859); unsuccessful candidate for reelection in 1858 to the Thirty-sixth Congress; appointed United States judge for Nebraska Territory March 5, 1859; died in Cincinnati, Ohio, on May 27, 1862; interment in Grandview Cemetery, Chillicothe, Ohio.

MILLER, Killian, a Representative from New York; born in Claverack, Columbia County, N. Y., July 30, 1785; pursued an academic course; studied law; was admitted to the bar and commenced practice in Livingston, N. Y., in 1806; member of the State assembly in 1825 and 1828; moved to Hudson, N. Y., in 1833 and continued the practice of law; clerk of Columbia County 1837–1840; elected as a Whig to the Thirty-fourth Congress (March 4, 1855–March 3, 1857); resumed the practice of his profession; died in Hudson, Columbia County, N. Y., January 9, 1859; interment in Hudson City Cemetery.

MILLER, Louis Ebenezer, a Representative from Missouri; born in Willisburg, Washington County, Ky., April 30, 1899; attended the grade schools of Washington County, Ky., Springfield (Ky.) High School, and St. Mary's College, St. Marys, Kans.; during the First World War served as a private; was graduated from the law department of St. Louis University, St. Louis, Mo., in 1921; was admitted to the bar the same year and commenced practice in St. Louis, Mo.; member of the Republican city central committee of St. Louis 1936–1942; member of the advisory council of the Republican National Committee in 1943; delegate to the Republican National Convention at Philadelphia in 1940; elected as a Republican to the Seventy-eighth Congress (January 3, 1943–January 3, 1945); unsuccessful candidate for reelection in 1944 to the Seventy-ninth Congress; resumed the practice of law and is a resident of St. Louis, Mo.

MILLER, Lucas Miltiades, a Representative from Wisconsin; born in Livadia, Greece, September 15, 1824; was left an orphan at the age of four, when he was adopted by J. P. Miller, an American who served as a colonel in the Greek Army during the Greek revolution; accompanied his foster father upon his return to the United States and settled in Montpelier, Vt., in 1828; attended the common schools; studied law; was admitted to the bar in 1845 and commenced practice in Oshkosh, Winnebago County, Wis., in 1846; also engaged in agricultural pursuits; served as colonel of militia in the Mexican War; member of the State assembly in 1853; served as commissioner of the Wisconsin Board of Public Works; served ten years as chairman of the Winnebago County Board of Supervisors; elected as a Democrat to the Fifty-second Congress (March 4, 1891–March 3, 1893); unsuccessful candidate for renomination in 1892; retired from active pursuits; died in Oshkosh, Winnebago County, Wis., December 4, 1902; interment in Riverside Cemetery.

MILLER, Morris Smith (father of Rutger Bleecker Miller), a Representative from New York; born in New York City July 31, 1779; was graduated from Union College, Schenectady, N. Y., in 1798; studied law and was admitted to the bar; served as private secretary to Governor Jay, and subsequently, in 1806, commenced the practice of his profession in Utica, N. Y.; president of the village of Utica in 1808; judge of the court of common pleas of Oneida County from 1810 until his death; elected as a Federalist to the Thirteenth Congress (March 4, 1813–March 3, 1815); represented the United States Government at the negotiation of a treaty between the Seneca Indians and the proprietors of the Seneca Reservation at Buffalo, N. Y., in July 1819; died in Utica, N. Y., November 16, 1824; interment in Rural Cemetery, Albany, N. Y.

MILLER, Nathan, a Delegate from Rhode Island; born in Warren, R. I., March 20, 1743; attended a private school; merchant and shipbuilder; deputy to the general assembly 1772–1774, 1780, 1782, 1783, and 1790; prominent in pre-Revolutionary movements; advanced through various grades until he was made brigadier general of the Rhode Island Militia for Newport and Bristol Counties and held this office from 1772 to 1778; deputy in the Rhode Island State Assembly for six years; Member of the Continental Congress and served from July 14 to November 3, 1786; reelected, but did not take his seat; member of the State constitutional convention in 1790; died in Warren, Bristol County, R. I., May 20, 1790; interment in Kickamuet Cemetery.

MILLER, Orrin Larrabee, a Representative from Kansas; born in Newburg, Penobscot County, Maine, January 11, 1856; attended the common schools and was graduated from the Maine Central Institute at Pittsfield; studied law; was admitted to the bar in 1880 and commenced practice in Bangor, Maine; moved to Kansas City, Kans., in 1880 and engaged in the practice of law; appointed and subsequently elected district judge for the twenty-ninth judicial district of Kansas in 1887, and served until 1891, when he resigned to resume the practice of law; counsel for many years for several large railroad corporations; elected as a Republican to the Fifty-fourth Congress (March 4, 1895–March 3, 1897); declined to be a candidate for renomination in 1896; continued the practice of law in Kansas City, Kans., until his death there on September 11, 1926; interment in Woodlawn Cemetery.

MILLER, Pleasant Moorman, a Representative from Tennessee; born in Lynchburg, Campbell County, Va.; moved to Rogersville, Hawkins County, Tenn., in 1796, and thence to Knoxville, Knox County, Tenn., in 1800; one of the commissioners for the government of Knoxville in 1801 and 1802; elected to the Eleventh Congress (March 4, 1809–March 3, 1811); moved to west Tennessee about 1824, and was chancellor of that division in 1836 and 1837; died in 1849; interment in Trenton, Gibson County, Tenn.

MILLER, Rutger Bleecker (son of Morris Smith Miller), a Representative from New York; born in Lowville, Lewis County, N. Y., July 28, 1805; attended the common schools in Utica, the Catholic College, Montreal, Canada, and Yale College; was graduated from the Litchfield Law School in 1824; was admitted to the bar and practiced in Utica, N. Y., 1829–1831; manager of the Utica Wilberforce Society 1829; interested in banking and railroads 1832–1833; trustee of the village of Utica 1829–1831; member of the first board of aldermen of the city of Utica; member of the State assembly in 1832; clerk of the United States district court in 1833 and 1834; elected as a Democrat to the Twenty-fourth Congress to fill the vacancy caused by the resignation of Samuel Beardsley and served from November 9, 1836, to March 3, 1837; engaged in the erection of buildings and in railroad construction, and subsequently in the management of his farm in Boonville, Oneida County; died in Utica, Oneida County, N. Y., November 12, 1877; interment in Forest Hill Cemetery.

MILLER, Samuel Franklin, a Representative from New York; born in Franklin, Delaware County, N. Y., May 27, 1827; was graduated from the Delaware Literary Institute and Hamilton College, Clinton, N. Y., in 1852; studied law and was admitted to the bar in 1853, but did not engage in extensive practice; engaged in farming and lumbering; member of the State assembly in 1854; served as a colonel in the State militia; elected as a Republican to the Thirty-eighth Congress (March

4, 1863–March 3, 1865); member of the State constitutional convention in 1867; district collector of internal revenue 1869–1873; member of the State board of charities 1869–1877; elected to the Forty-fourth Congress (March 4, 1875–March 3, 1877); continued agricultural pursuits and lumbering; died in Franklin, N. Y., on March 16, 1892; interment in Ouleout Valley Cemetery.

MILLER, Samuel Henry, a Representative from Pennsylvania; born at Coolspring, near Mercer, Mercer County, Pa., April 19, 1840; attended the common schools, and was graduated from Westminster College, New Wilmington, Pa., in 1860; taught school during the winter of 1860–1861 in Madison County, Ky.; during the Civil War served in the Fifty-fifth Regiment, Pennsylvania Militia; edited and published the Mercer (Pa.) Dispatch 1861–1870; studied law; was admitted to the bar and commenced practice in Mercer in 1871; elected as a Republican to the Forty-seventh and Forty-eighth Congresses (March 4, 1881–March 3, 1885); declined to be a candidate for renomination in 1884; resumed the practice of law in Mercer; president judge of the several courts of Mercer County, Pa., 1894–1904; resumed the practice of law; elected to the Sixty-fourth Congress (March 4, 1915–March 3, 1917); declined to be a candidate for renomination in 1916; resumed the practice of his profession; died in Mercer, Pa., September 4, 1918; interment in Mercer Cemetery.

MILLER, Smith, a Representative from Indiana; born near Charlotte, N. C., May 30, 1804; moved to Gibson County, Ind., with his parents who settled in Patoka in 1813; received a limited schooling; engaged in agricultural pursuits; member of the State house of representatives 1835–1839 and in 1846; served in the State senate 1841–1844 and 1847–1850; delegate to the State constitutional convention in 1850; elected as a Democrat to the Thirty-third and Thirty-fourth Congresses (March 4, 1853–March 3, 1857); resumed agricultural pursuits; delegate to the Democratic National Convention at Charleston, S. C., in 1860; died near Patoka, Ind., March 21, 1872; interment in Robb Cemetery.

MILLER, Stephen Decatur, a Representative and a Senator from South Carolina; born in Waxhaw settlement, Lancaster District, S. C., May 8, 1787; studied under a private tutor; was graduated from South Carolina College at Columbia in 1808; studied law; was admitted to the bar and commenced practice in Sumterville in 1811; elected as a Democrat to the Fourteenth Congress to fill the vacancy caused by the resignation of William Mayrant; reelected to the Fifteenth Congress and served from January 2, 1817, to March 3, 1819; resumed the practice of his profession; member of the State senate 1822–1828; Governor of South Carolina 1828–1830; elected as a Nullifier to the United States Senate and served from March 4, 1831, until March 2, 1833, when he resigned on account of ill health; delegate to the South Carolina nullification conventions in 1830 and 1832; engaged in cotton planting in Mississippi in 1835; died in Raymond, Hinds County, Miss., March 8, 1838.

MILLER, Thomas Byron, a Representative from Pennsylvania; born in Plymouth, Luzerne County, Pa., August 11, 1896; attended the public schools and Hillman Academy; was graduated from the law school of Dickinson College, Carlisle, Pa.; was admitted to the bar and commenced practice in Wilkes-Barre, Pa.; during the First World War served as a second lieutenant in the Sixteenth Field Artillery from February 25, 1918, until his discharge as a first lieutenant on September 23, 1919; elected as a Republican to the Seventy-seventh Congress to fill the vacancy caused by the resignation of J. Harold Flannery; reelected to the

Seventy-eighth Congress and served from May 9, 1942, to January 3, 1945; unsuccessful candidate for reelection in 1944 to the Seventy-ninth Congress; resumed the practice of law in Washington, D. C.; is a resident of Wilkes-Barre, Pa.

MILLER, Thomas Ezekiel, a Representative from South Carolina; born in Ferrebeville, Beaufort County, S. C., June 17, 1849; was of the Negro race; moved with his parents to Charleston, S. C., in 1851; attended the public schools in Charleston, S. C., and in Hudson, N. Y.; employed as a newsboy on a railroad; was graduated from Lincoln University, Chester County, Pa., in 1872; moved to Grahamville, S. C., and served as school commissioner of Beaufort County in 1872; member of the State house of representatives in 1874, 1876, and 1878; studied law; was admitted to the bar in 1875 and practiced law in Beaufort, S. C.; member of the State executive committee 1878–1880; served in the State senate in 1880; successfully contested as a Republican the election of William Elliott to the Fifty-first Congress and served from September 24, 1890, to March 3, 1891; unsuccessful candidate for reelection in 1890 to the Fifty-second Congress; again a member of the State house of representatives in 1894; member of the State constitutional convention in 1895; president of the State colored college in Orangeburg, S. C., from 1896 until 1911, when he resigned; retired from active pursuits in 1911 and lived in Charleston, S. C., until 1923, when he moved to Philadelphia, Pa.; in 1934 returned to Charleston, S. C., where he resided until his death there on April 8, 1938; interment in Brotherhood Cemetery.

MILLER, Thomas Woodnutt (uncle of Clement W. Miller), a Representative from Delaware; born in Wilmington, Del., June 26, 1886; attended the Hotchkiss School; was graduated from Yale University, New Haven, Conn., in 1908; interested in mining in Nevada since early youth; employed as a steel roller by the Bethlehem Steel Co., in 1908 and 1909; secretary to Representative William H. Heald of Delaware 1910–1912, and during this period studied law in Washington, D. C.; secretary of state of Delaware 1913–1915; elected as a Republican to the Sixty-fourth Congress (March 4, 1915–March 3, 1917); unsuccessful candidate for reelection in 1916 to the Sixth-fifth Congress; attended Plattsburg training camp in 1915; during the First World War enlisted in July 1917 as a private in the Infantry of the United States Army; promoted to lieutenant colonel and served in France with the Seventy-ninth Division until discharged in September 1919; cited in divisional orders "for gallantry in action" and by the commanding general of the American Expeditionary Forces "for especially meritorious conduct"; awarded the Order of the Purple Heart; a founder and incorporator of the American Legion and vice chairman of the Paris caucus in March 1919; State departmental commander of Delaware 1932–1933 and of Nevada 1943–1944, and member of the national executive committee from Delaware 1919–1928 and from Nevada since 1946; appointed by President Harding as a member of the special committee investigating methods of rehabilitation and hospitalization of ex-servicemen in 1921; Alien Property Custodian 1921–1925; member of the American Battle Monuments Commission 1923–1926; founder Nevada State park system and chairman of the Nevada State Park Commission in 1935 and 1936, and 1953–1959; member of the Nevada Council of Defense 1942–1959; staff field representative of the United States Veterans' Employment Service, 1945–1957, when he retired; is a resident of Reno, Nev.

MILLER, Ward MacLaughlin, a Representative from Ohio; born in Portsmouth, Ohio, November 29, 1902; graduate of Portsmouth High School, Ohio State University in 1923, and Harvard University in 1931; assistant to the late Irving Babbitt

(Harvard University) 1929–1931; on editorial staff, Bookman Magazine, 1931–1933; engaged in real-estate business in 1939; president, Portsmouth Real Estate Board for five terms; trustee, Ohio Association of Real Estate Boards 1957–1960; vice president, Scioto County Historical Society 1959 and 1960; elected a member of the first Ohio Board of Education November 6, 1955, for a six-year term; member of the Royal Institute of Philosophy, Great Britian; elected as a Republican to the Eighty-sixth Congress in 1960 to fill the vacancy caused by the death of James G. Polk and served from November 8, 1960, to January 3, 1961; was not a candidate for the Eighty-seventh Congress; is a resident of Beechwood Heights, Portsmouth, Ohio.

MILLER, Warner, a Representative and a Senator from New York; born in Hannibal, Oswego County, N. Y., August 12, 1838; attended the common schools and Charlottesville Academy; was graduated from Union College, Schenectady, N. Y., in 1860; professor of Latin and Greek in the Fort Edward Collegiate Institute; during the Civil War enlisted as a private in the Fifth Regiment, New York Volunteer Cavalry, in 1861; served in the Shenandoah Valley; promoted to the rank of sergeant major and lieutenant; taken prisoner at the Battle of Winchester; exchanged and honorably discharged; delegate to the Republican National Convention at Philadelphia in 1872; member of the State assembly in 1874 and 1875; chairman of the Republican county committee for ten years; delegate to all Republican county and State conventions for more than forty years; engaged in agricultural pursuits; founder of the wood-pulp business and president of the American Paper & Pulp Association; interested in various other business enterprises; vice president of the Union League Club; member of the Herkimer County Historical Society; trustee of Herkimer Free Library; elected as a Republican to the Forty-sixth and Forty-seventh Congresses and served from March 4, 1879, until his resignation July 26, 1881; elected in 1881 to the United States Senate to fill the vacancy caused by the resignation of Thomas C. Platt and served from July 27, 1881, to March 3, 1887; unsuccessful candidate for reelection to the United States Senate in 1887; unsuccessful candidate for Governor of New York in 1888; delegate to all Republican National Conventions from 1884 to 1896; chairman of the Special Tax Commission of the State of New York in 1906; retired and resided in Herkimer, N. Y.; died in New York City, March 21, 1918; interment in Oak Hill Cemetery, Herkimer, N. Y.

MILLER, Warren, a Representative from West Virginia; born at Apple Grove, Meigs County, Ohio, April 2, 1847; moved about 1850 to that portion of Virginia which later became West Virginia and settled in Millwood, Jackson County; attended the common schools, and was graduated from the Ohio University at Athens; taught school; studied law; was admitted to the bar and commenced practice in Ripley, Jackson County, W. Va., in 1871; mayor of Ripley in 1871; assistant prosecuting attorney of Jackson County 1878–1880; prosecuting attorney 1881–1890; delegate to the Republican National Convention at Chicago in 1884 which nominated Blaine and Logan; member of the State house of representatives in 1890 and 1891; unsuccessful candidate for judge of the State supreme court in 1892; elected as a Republican to the Fifty-fourth and Fifty-fifth Congresses (March 4, 1895–March 3, 1899); was not a candidate for renomination in 1898; resumed the practice of law and also engaged in agricultural pursuits; appointed judge of the fifth judicial circuit of West Virginia; elected in 1902, and served from 1900 until his resignation in 1903; judge of the State supreme court of appeals in 1903 and 1904; member of the State senate 1914–1918; member of the draft appeal board, southern district of West Virginia, in 1917 and 1918; died in Ripley, W. Va., on December 29, 1920; interment in Cottageville Cemetery, Cottageville, W. Va.

MILLER, William Edward, a Representative from New York; born in Lockport, Niagara County, N. Y., March 22, 1914; attended the parochial schools and Lockport High School; was graduated from Notre Dame University, South Bend, Ind., in 1935, and from Albany Law School of Union University in 1938; was admitted to the bar in 1938 and commenced the practice of law in Lockport, N. Y.; appointed United States Commissioner for the Western District of New York in January 1940, and served until entering the United States Army July 1, 1942; after basic training with the Seventy-sixth Infantry Division at Fort George G. Meade, Md., was assigned to the Military Intelligence Branch; attended the Officers Candidate School and in May 1945 was commissioned a first lieutenant and assigned to the War Criminals Branch at Washington, D. C., until August 1945; assistant prosecutor of Nazi war criminals at Nürnburg, Germany, in 1945 and 1946; was discharged in March 1946; appointed assistant district attorney of Niagara County in March 1946; appointed district attorney on January 1, 1948, and elected district attorney in November 1948; chairman of National Republican Congressional Committee in 1960 and Republican National Committee in 1961; elected as a Republican to the Eighty-second and to the four succeeding Congresses (January 3, 1951–January 3, 1961). *Reelected to the Eighty-seventh Congress.*

MILLER, William Henry (son of Jesse Miller), a Representative from Pennsylvania; born in Landisburg, Perry County, Pa., February 28, 1829; attended the public schools in Landisburg, Pa., and a private school in Harrisburg, Pa.; was graduated from Franklin and Marshall College, Lancaster, Pa., in 1846; studied law; was admitted to the bar the same year and practiced in Harrisburg, Pa., and later in New Bloomfield in 1849; returned to Harrisburg in 1854; clerk of the State supreme court 1854–1863; clerk of the State senate in 1858 and 1859; elected as a Democrat to the Thirty-eighth Congress (March 4, 1863–March 3, 1865); unsuccessful candidate for reelection in 1864 to the Thirty-ninth Congress; resumed the practice of law and also engaged in journalism; died in Harrisburg, Pa., September 12, 1870; interment in Harrisburg Cemetery.

MILLER, William Jennings, a Representative from Connecticut; born in North Andover, Essex County, Mass., March 12, 1899; attended the public schools; was graduated from Cannon's Commercial College, Lawrence, Mass., in 1917; during the First World War enlisted August 5, 1917, as a private in the United States Army and served in the Air Service in the Eightieth and One Thousand One Hundred and Fourth Aero Squadrons; later commissioned a second lieutenant; injured in an airplane crash in France in 1918, resulting in the loss of both legs; discharged April 26, 1919; patient in United States veterans' hospitals 1919–1931; moved to Wethersfield, Conn., in 1926; engaged in the insurance business in 1931; elected as a Republican to the Seventy-sixth Congress (January 3, 1939–January 3, 1941); unsuccessful candidate for reelection in 1940 to the Seventy-seventh Congress; elected to the Seventy-eighth Congress (January 3, 1943–January 3, 1945); unsuccessful candidate for reelection in 1944 to the Seventy-ninth Congress; elected in 1946 to the Eightieth Congress (January 3, 1947–January 3, 1949); unsuccessful candidate for reelection in 1948 to the Eighty-first Congress; resumed the general insurance business; died in Wethersfield, Conn., November 22, 1950; interment in Jordan Cemetery, Waterford, Conn.

MILLER, William Starr, a Representative from New York; born in Wintonbury (now Bloomfield), Conn., August 22, 1793; completed preparatory studies; member of the Board of Aldermen of New York City in 1845; elected to the Twenty-ninth Congress (March 4, 1845–March 3, 1847); unsuccessful candidate for reelection in 1846 to the Thirtieth Congress; died in New York City November 9, 1854; interment in Greenwood Cemetery, Brooklyn, N. Y.

MILLIGAN, Jacob Le Roy, a Representative from Missouri; born in Richmond, Ray County, Mo., March 9, 1889; attended the public schools and the law department of the University of Missouri at Columbia 1910–1914; was admitted to the bar in 1913 and commenced practice in Richmond, Mo., in 1914; during the First World War enlisted in the Sixth Regiment, Missouri Infantry, on April 8, 1917; served as captain of Company G, One Hundred and Fortieth Infantry Regiment, Thirty-fifth Division, from August 4. 1917, to May 15, 1919; embarked for France April 23, 1918; received two citations, the Purple Heart and Silver Star; returned April 28, 1919; elected as a Democrat to the Sixty-sixth Congress to fill the vacancy caused by the resignation of Joshua W. Alexander and served from February 14, 1920, to March 3, 1921; unsuccessful candidate for reelection in 1920 to the Sixty-seventh Congress; delegate to the Democratic National Convention at Houston in 1928; elected to the Sixty-eighth and to the five succeeding Congresses (March 4, 1923–January 3, 1935); was not a candidate for renomination in 1934, but was an unsuccessful candidate for nomination for United States Senator; resumed the practice of law; president of Kansas City Police Board from May 3, 1949, to April 27, 1950; died in Kansas City, Mo., March 9, 1951; interment in Fairview Cemetery, Liberty, Clay County, Mo.

MILLIGAN, John Jones, a Representative from Delaware; born at Bohemia Manor, Cecil County, Md., December 10, 1795; attended Wilmington Academy and St. Mary's College, Baltimore, Md., and was graduated from Princeton College, Princeton, N. J., in 1814; studied law; was admitted to the bar and commenced practice in New Castle County, Del., in 1818; elected as a Whig to the Twenty-second and to the three succeeding Congresses (March 4, 1831–March 3, 1839); unsuccessful candidate for reelection in 1838 to the Twenty-sixth Congress; appointed judge of the State superior court on September 19, 1839, and served until September 16, 1864, when he resigned; died in Philadelphia, Pa., April 20, 1875; interment in Wilmington and Brandywine Cemetery, Wilmington, Del.

MILLIKEN, Charles William, a Representative from Kentucky; born near Murray, Calloway County, Ky., August 15, 1827; moved with his parents to Simpson County, Ky., in 1829 and settled near Franklin; pursued preparatory studies, and was graduated from Wirt College, Sumner County, Tenn., in 1849; studied law; was admitted to the bar in 1850 and commenced practice in Franklin, Ky.; prosecuting attorney of Simpson County 1857–1862; Commonwealth attorney of the fourth judicial district of Kentucky from 1867 until his resignation on February 24, 1872; elected as a Democrat to the Forty-third and Forty-fourth Congresses (March 4, 1873–March 3, 1877); declined to be a candidate for reelection in 1876 to the Forty-fifth Congress; resumed the practice of law; referee in bankruptcy for the Bowling Green (Ky.) district and served from September 28, 1907, until his death in Franklin, Simpson County, Ky., October 16, 1915; interment in Greenlawn Cemetery.

MILLIKEN, Seth Llewellyn, a Representative from Maine; born in Montville, Waldo County, Maine, December 12, 1831; attended the common schools and Waterville College; was graduated from Union College, Schenectady, N. Y., in 1856; member of the State house of representatives in 1857 and 1858; moved to Belfast, Maine; clerk of the supreme judicial court 1859–1871; studied law; was admitted to the bar in 1871, but did not practice; delegate to the Republican National Convention at Cincin-

nati in 1876 and at Chicago in 1884; presidential elector on the Republican ticket of Hayes and Wheeler in 1876; elected as a Republican to the Forty-eighth and to the seven succeeding Congresses and served from March 4, 1883, until his death in Washington, D. C., April 18, 1897; interment in Grove Cemetery, Belfast, Waldo County, Maine.

MILLIKEN, William H., Jr., a Representative from Pennsylvania; born in Philadelphia, Pa.; resident of Sharon Hill, Delaware County, Pa., since 1906; attended Sharon Hill public schools; graduated from Drexel Institute, Philadelphia, Pa.; worked as a construction foreman; sales executive for the Whitehall Cement Manufacturing Co., Philadelphia, Pa.; member of the State house of representatives; clerk of courts of Delaware County, Pa.; appointed burgess of Sharon Hill, Pa., to fill unexpired term September 14, 1948, elected in 1949, reelected in 1953 and 1957 and served until elected to Congress; elected as a Republican to the Eighty-sixth Congress (January 3, 1959–January 3, 1961). *Reelected to the Eighty-seventh Congress.*

MILLIKIN, Eugene Donald, a Senator from Colorado; born in Hamilton, Butler County, Ohio, February 12, 1891; attended the public schools; was graduated from the law school of the University of Colorado at Boulder in 1913; was admitted to the bar the same year and commenced practice in Salt Lake City, Utah; executive secretary to Gov. George A. Carlson of Colorado 1915–1917; during the First World War enlisted as a private in the Colorado National Guard in 1917; served in the United States with the Thirty-fourth Division and in France with the Forty-second and Seventh Divisions and the Fourth Corps, and in the Army of Occupation in Germany with the Sixth Division; was commissioned captain and major of Infantry and lieutenant colonel of Engineers; graduated from General Staff College, Langres, France; received the Pershing citation for distinguished and meritorious service; resumed the practice of law in Denver, Colo; president of Kinney-Coastal Oil Co.; appointed and subsequently elected as a Republican to the United States Senate to fill the vacancy in the term ending January 3, 1945, caused by the death of Alva B. Adams; reelected in 1944 and again in 1950 and served from December 20, 1941, to January 3, 1957; was not a candidate for renomination in 1956; died in Denver, Colo., July 26, 1958; interment in Fairmount Cemetery.

MILLINGTON, Charles Stephen, a Representative from New York; born in Norway, Herkimer County, N. Y., March 13, 1855; attended the district schools of Poland, the Fairfield Academy, and Hungerford Collegiate Institute; entered the employ of the Hungerford National Bank, Adams, N. Y.; organized and became cashier of the Bank of Poland; moved to Herkimer, N. Y., in 1894 and continued in the banking business; delegate to the Republican National Convention at Chicago in 1908; elected as a Republican to the Sixty-first Congress (March 4, 1909–March 3, 1911); unsuccessful candidate for reelection in 1910 to the Sixty-second Congress; resumed business activities in Herkimer, N. Y.; appointed by President Taft as assistant treasurer of the United States in charge of the subtreasury at New York May 12, 1911, and served until his death in Herkimer, N. Y., October 25, 1913; interment in Pine Grove Cemetery, Poland, Herkimer County, N. Y.

MILLS, Daniel Webster, a Representative from Illinois; born near Waynesville, Warren County, Ohio, February 25, 1838; attended the common schools of Rayesville and the Waynesville High School; moved to Corwin, Ohio, in 1859 and engaged in the mercantile, grain-shipping, and pork-packing businesses; during the Civil War served in the Union Army as captain of Company D, One Hundred and Eightieth Regiment, Ohio Volunteers, until the close of the war; moved to Chicago, Ill.; engaged in lake shipping 1866–1869, and later in the real-estate business; served as warden of the Cook County Hospital 1877–1881; member of the board of aldermen of Chicago 1889–1893; elected as a Republican to the Fifty-fifth Congress (March 4, 1897–March 3, 1899); unsuccessful candidate for reelection in 1898 to the Fifty-sixth Congress; resumed the real-estate business; died in Chicago, Ill., on December 16, 1904; interment in Graceland Cemetery.

MILLS, Elijah Hunt, a Representative and a Senator from Massachusetts; born in Chesterfield, Mass., December 1, 1776; educated by private tutors, and was graduated from Williams College, Williamstown, Mass., in 1797; studied law; was admitted to the bar and commenced practice in Northampton; member of the State senate in 1811; district attorney for Hampshire County; elected as a Federalist to the Fourteenth and Fifteenth Congresses (March 4, 1815–March 3, 1819); elected to the United States Senate to fill the vacancy caused by the resignation of Prentiss Mellen; reelected and served from June 12, 1820, to March 3, 1827; was not a candidate for reelection and retired from public life on account of ill health; died in Northampton, Hampshire County, Mass., on May 5, 1829; interment in Bridge Street Cemetery.

MILLS, Newt Virgus, a Representative from Louisiana; born in Calhoun, Ouachita Parish, La., September 27, 1899; attended the public schools of his native city, Louisiana Polytechnic Institute at Ruston, Louisiana State University at Baton Rouge, Louisiana State Normal College at Natchitoches, and Spencer Business College, New Orleans, La.; also studied law; taught school at Mer Rouge, La., 1921–1932; supervisor of public accounts of Louisiana 1933–1936; also engaged in agricultural pursuits, cattle raising, real estate, and oil; colonel on the staff of the Governor in 1936; elected as a Democrat to the Seventy-fifth, Seventy-sixth, and Seventy-seventh Congresses (January 3, 1937–January 3, 1943); unsuccessful candidate for renomination in 1942; resumed his former pursuits and also engaged in the building supply business; is a resident of Monroe, La.

MILLS, Ogden Livingston, a Representative from New York; born in Newport, R. I., August 23, 1884; attended the public schools; was graduated from the academic department of Harvard University in 1904 and from the law department of that institution in 1907; admitted to the New York bar in 1908 and commenced practice in New York City; unsuccessful Republican candidate for election in 1912 to the Sixty-third Congress; delegate to the Republican National Conventions at Chicago in 1912, 1916, and 1920; member of the State senate from 1914 until 1917, when he resigned to enlist in the United States Army, and served with the rank of captain until the close of the First World War; president of the New York State Tax Association; interested in various business enterprises; elected as a Republican to the Sixty-seventh, Sixty-eighth, and Sixty-ninth Congresses (March 4, 1921–March 3, 1927); was not a candidate for renomination in 1926; unsuccessful candidate for election as Governor of New York in 1926; appointed by President Coolidge Undersecretary of the Treasury on February 1, 1927, and served from March 4, 1927, until February 11, 1932; appointed by President Hoover as Secretary of the Treasury on February 12, 1932, and served until March 3, 1933; engaged as an author and lecturer; died in New York City, N. Y., October 11, 1937; interment in St. James Churchyard, Staatsburg, N. Y.

MILLS, Roger Quarles, a Representative and a Senator from Texas; born in Todd County, Ky., March 30, 1832; attended the common schools; moved to Texas in 1849; studied law; was admitted to the bar in 1852 and commenced practice in Corsicana, Tex.; member of the State house of representatives in 1859 and 1860; enlisted in the Confederate Army, and served throughout the Civil War, attaining the rank of colonel of the Tenth Regiment, Texas Infantry; was wounded in the engagements at Missionary Ridge and Atlanta; elected as a Democrat to the Forty-third and to the nine succeeding Congresses and served from March 4, 1873, until his resignation on March 28, 1892, having been elected Senator; unsuccessful candidate for Speaker in the Fifty-second Congress; elected to the United States Senate to fill the vacancy caused by the resignation of John H. Reagan; reelected in 1893 and served from March 29, 1892, to March 3, 1899; was not a candidate for reelection; died in Corsicana, Tex., September 2, 1911; interment in Oakwood Cemetery.

MILLS, Wilbur Daigh, a Representative from Arkansas; born in Kensett, White County, Ark., May 24, 1909; attended the public schools; was graduated from Hendrix College, Conway, Ark., in 1930 and from the law department of Harvard University, Cambridge, Mass., in 1933; was admitted to the bar the same year and commenced practice in Searcy, Ark.; served as county and probate judge of White County, Ark., 1934–1938; elected as a Democrat to the Seventy-sixth and to the ten succeeding Congresses (January 3, 1939–January 3, 1961). *Reelected to the Eighty-seventh Congress.*

MILLSON, John Singleton, a Representative from Virginia; born in Norfolk, Va., October 1, 1808; pursued an academic course; studied law; was admitted to the bar in 1829 and commenced practice in Norfolk; presidential elector on the Democratic ticket of Polk and Dallas in 1844 and of Cass and Butler in 1848; elected as a Democrat to the Thirty-first and to the five succeeding Congresses (March 4, 1849–March 3, 1861); resumed the practice of law; died in Norfolk, Va., March 1, 1874; interment in Cedar Grove Cemetery.

MILLSPAUGH, Frank Crenshaw, a Representative from Missouri; born in Shawneetown, Gallatin County, Ill., January 14, 1872; attended the public schools; entered the grain commission business in New Orleans, La., in 1891; moved to Chicago in 1892 and to St. Louis, Mo., in 1894 and continued in the grain business; moved to Canton, Mo., in 1896 and resumed the grain-shipping business; engaged in banking 1900–1921; delegate to the Republican State convention at St. Louis, Mo., in 1912; mayor of Canton, Mo., 1915–1919; elected as a Republican to the Sixty-seventh Congress and served from March 4, 1921, to December 5, 1922, when he resigned; unsuccessful candidate in 1922 for reelection to the Sixty-eighth Congress; State commissioner of finance in 1923 and 1924; moved to Jefferson City, Mo., in 1925 and engaged in the real-estate business until 1929, when he entered the brokerage business; elected county judge of Jasper County, Mo., in 1942; reelected in 1944 and 1946 and served until his death in Joplin, Mo., July 8, 1947; interment in Forest Grove Cemetery, Canton, Mo.

MILLWARD, William, a Representative from Pennsylvania; born in the old district of Northern Liberties, Philadelphia, Pa., June 30, 1822; attended the public schools; engaged in the manufacture of leather; elected as a Whig to the Thirty-fourth Congress (March 4, 1855–March 3, 1857); unsuccessful as the Union candidate for reelection in 1856; elected to the Thirty-sixth Congress (March 4, 1859–March 3, 1861); United States marshal for the eastern district of Pennsylvania 1861–1865; appointed Director of the United States Mint in September 1866 but, as his appointment was not confirmed by the Senate, served for six months only; died in Kirkwood, New Castle County, Del., November 28, 1871; interment in Laurel Hill Cemetery, Philadelphia, Pa.

MILNES, Alfred, a Representative from Michigan; born in Bradford, Yorkshire, England, May 28, 1844; immigrated to the United States in 1854 with his parents, who settled in Newton, Jasper County, Iowa; moved to Coldwater, Branch County, Mich., in 1860; attended the common schools of Salt Lake City, Utah, and Newton, Iowa, and the high school of Coldwater, Mich.; enlisted as a private in Company C, Seventeenth Regiment, Michigan Volunteer Infantry, the "Old Stonewall Regiment," June 30, 1862, and served throughout the Civil War; participated with his regiment in every battle and skirmish in which it took part, from South Mountain, Md., in 1862 to Lee's surrender at Appomattox in April 1865; engaged in mercantile pursuits; member of the board of aldermen of Coldwater in 1876 and 1877; mayor in 1885 and 1886; member of the State senate 1888–1890; Lieutenant Governor of Michigan in 1894, and presided over the State senate until his resignation June 1, 1895, when he became a candidate for Congress; elected as a Republican to the Fifty-fourth Congress to fill the vacancy caused by the resignation of Julius C. Burrows and served from December 2, 1895, to March 3, 1897; unsuccessful candidate for reelection in 1896 to the Fifty-fifth Congress; appointed postmaster of Coldwater in 1898 and served until 1902; delegate to the Michigan constitutional convention of 1907 and 1908; member of the board of managers of the Michigan Soldiers' Home 1902–1916; engaged in the real estate and insurance business in Coldwater, Mich., until his death there on January 15, 1916; interment in Oak Grove Cemetery.

MILNES, William, Jr., a Representative from Virginia; born in Yorkshire, England, December 8, 1827; immigrated to the United States in 1829 with his parents, who settled in Pottsville, Pa.; attended the public schools; learned the machinist's trade; engaged in mining and shipping coal; moved to Virginia in 1865 and settled in Shenandoah; engaged in the iron business; member of the State house of delegates in 1870 and 1871; upon the readmission of Virginia to representation was elected as a Conservative to the Forty-first Congress and served from January 27, 1870, to March 3, 1871; resumed the iron business; died in Shenandoah, Va., August 14, 1889; interment in the family plot in Old Cemetery.

MILNOR, James, a Representative from Pennsylvania; born in Philadelphia, Pa., June 20, 1773; attended the Philadelphia Grammar School and also the University of Pennsylvania at Philadelphia, but did not graduate; studied law; was admitted to the bar in 1794 and commenced practice in Norristown, Pa.; moved to Philadelphia in 1797 and continued the practice of his profession; member of the Philadelphia Common Council in 1800; member of the select council 1805–1810 and served as president in 1808 and 1809; elected as a Federalist to the Twelfth Congress (March 4, 1811–March 3, 1813); studied theology and was ordained as a minister of the Protestant Episcopal Church; in 1814 was appointed assistant minister of St. Peter's Church in Philadelphia and in 1816 rector of St. George's Church in New York City, in which capacity he served until his death in New York City April 8, 1844; interment in Greenwood Cemetery, Brooklyn, N. Y.

MILNOR, William, a Representative from Pennsylvania; born in Philadelphia, Pa., June 26, 1769; pursued an academic course; engaged in mercantile pursuits in Philadelphia; elected as a Federalist to the Tenth and Eleventh Congresses (March 4, 1807–March 3, 1811); elected to the Fourteenth Congress

(March 4, 1815–March 3, 1817); again elected to the Seventeenth Congress and served from March 4, 1821, until his resignation on May 8, 1822; elected mayor of Philadelphia October 20, 1829, and served one year; died in Burlington, Burlington County, N. J., December 13, 1848; interment in St. Mary's Churchyard.

MILTON, John Gerald, a Senator from New Jersey; born in Jersey City, N. J., January 21, 1881; attended the public schools and was graduated from Jersey City High School in 1898; studied law; was admitted to the bar in 1903 and commenced practice in Jersey City, N. J.; appointed as a Democrat to the United States Senate to fill the vacancy caused by the resignation of A. Harry Moore and served from January 18, 1938, to November 8, 1938, when a successor was elected; was not a candidate to fill the vacancy; resumed the practice of law and is a resident of Jersey City, N. J.

MILTON, William Hall, a Senator from Florida; born near Marianna, Jackson County, Fla., March 2, 1864; attended the public schools of Jackson County, Marianna Academy, and the Agricultural and Mechanical College, Auburn, Ala.; city clerk and treasurer of Marianna 1885–1893; delegate to the Democratic State conventions in 1888, 1892, 1896, and 1900; served in the State house of representatives 1889–1891; studied law and was admitted to the bar in 1890; court commissioner 1890–1894; engaged in banking at Marianna 1890–1918; presidential elector on the Democratic ticket of Cleveland and Stevenson in 1892; United States surveyor general of Florida 1894–1897; president of the board of managers of the State reform school at Marianna 1897–1902; mayor of Marianna in 1898 and 1899; unsuccessful candidate for Governor of Florida in 1900 and 1912; appointed as a Democrat to the United States Senate March 27, 1908, to fill the vacancy caused by the deaths of Stephen R. Mallory and William James Bryan and served from March 27, 1908, to March 3, 1909; was not a candidate for reelection in 1908; resumed the practice of law and also engaged in the real estate and insurance business at Marianna, Fla., for more than 40 years; delegate to the Democratic National Convention at Denver in 1908 and at Baltimore in 1912; member of the city council in 1916 and 1917; appointed United States commissioner for the northern district of Florida in 1923, reappointed in 1927, and served until his death; district member of the State board of social welfare 1937–1942; died in Marianna, Fla., January 4, 1942; interment in St. Luke's Episcopal Cemetery

MINAHAN, Daniel Francis, a Representative from New Jersey; born in Springfield, Ohio, August 8, 1877; attended Stevens Institute Preparatory School and Seton Hall College, South Orange, N. J.; superintendent of work for his father, who was a contractor; mayor of Orange, N. J., from May 1914 until August 1919, when he resigned; elected as a Democrat to the Sixty-sixth Congress (March 4, 1919–March 3, 1921); unsuccessful candidate for reelection in 1920 to the Sixty-seventh Congress; again elected to the Sixty-eighth Congress (March 4, 1923–March 3, 1925); unsuccessful candidate for reelection in 1924 to the Sixty-ninth Congress and for election in 1930 to the Seventy-second Congress; delegate to the Democratic National Convention at Houston, Tex., in 1928; engaged in land development and resided in East Orange, N. J., until his death on April 29, 1947; interment in St. John's Cemetery, Orange, N. J.

MINER, Ahiman Louis, a Representative from Vermont; born in Middletown, Rutland County, Vt., September 23, 1804; attended the common schools and Castleton Academy; studied law in Poultney and Rutland, Vt.; was admitted to the bar in 1832 and practiced in Wallingford 1833–1836; moved to Manchester, Bennington County, Vt., in 1836 and continued the practice of law; clerk of the State house of representatives in 1836 and 1837; member of the State house of representatives in 1838, 1839, 1846, and 1854; served in the State senate in 1840; State's attorney for Bennington County in 1843 and 1844; register of probate for seven years; judge of probate 1846–1849; justice of the peace 1846–1886; elected as a Whig to the Thirty-second Congress (March 4, 1851–March 3, 1853); declined to be a candidate for renomination in 1852; resumed the practice of law; died in Manchester, Vt., July 19, 1886; interment in Dellwood Cemetery.

MINER, Charles, a Representative from Pennsylvania; born in Norwich, Conn., February 1, 1780; attended the public schools of Norwich; moved in 1797 to his father's lands in Wyoming Valley, Pa., and to Wilkes-Barre, Pa., in 1802; became publisher of the Luzerne County Federalist; elected as a Federalist a member of the State house of representatives and served in 1807 and 1808; moved to West Chester, Pa., in 1816; elected to the Nineteenth and Twentieth Congresses (March 4, 1825–March 3, 1829); was not a candidate for renomination in 1828; editor and publisher of the Village Record 1829–1832; returned to Wilkes-Barre in 1834; retired to private life, owing to great deafness; he spent much time in writing a history of Wyoming County and helping direct the mining of the large fields of anthracite coal in the Wyoming Valley; died in Wilkes-Barre, Pa., on October 26, 1865; interment in Hollenback Cemetery, Wilkes-Barre, Pa.

MINER, Henry Clay, a Representative from New York; born in New York City March 23, 1842; attended the public schools and the American Institute of Physicians and Surgeons in New York City; engaged in the drug business; in 1864 became interested in the theatrical business and eventually owned five metropolitan theaters in New York City and Newark, N. J.; president of a lithographing company and also publisher of the American Dramatic Directory; for many years president of the Actors' Fund Association; elected as a Democrat to the Fifty-fourth Congress (March 4, 1895–March 3, 1897); was not a candidate for renomination in 1896; resumed his theatrical and other business pursuits; died in New York City February 22, 1900; interment in Greenwood Cemetery, Brooklyn, N. Y.

MINER, Phineas, a Representative from Connecticut; born in Winchester, Litchfield County, Conn., November 27, 1777; completed preparatory studies; studied law; was admitted to the bar in 1797 and commenced practice in Winchester; elected justice of the peace in 1809; member of the State house of representatives in 1809, 1811, 1813, 1814, and 1816; moved to Litchfield, Conn., in 1816; again a member of the State house of representatives in 1823, 1827, and 1829; served in the State senate in 1830 and 1831; elected as a Whig to the Twenty-third Congress to fill the vacancy caused by the resignation of Jabez W. Huntington and served from December 1, 1834, to March 3, 1835; resumed the practice of law; served in the State house of representatives in 1835; elected judge of the probate court for Litchfield district in 1838; died in Litchfield, Conn., September 15, 1839; interment in the East Burying Ground.

MINOR, Edward Sloman, a Representative from Wisconsin; born at Point Peninsula, Jefferson County, N. Y., December 13, 1840; moved to Wisconsin in 1845 with his parents, who settled in Greenfield, Milwaukee County, and subsequently in the city of Milwaukee; attended the common schools; went with his parents to a farm in Sheboygan County in 1852 and engaged in agricultural pursuits; completed a common-school education; during the Civil War enlisted as a private in Company G,

Second Regiment, Wisconsin Volunteer Cavalry, in 1861; participated in all the expeditions, raids, and battles in which the regiment was engaged until the close of the war; mustered out as first lieutenant in November 1865; engaged in the hardware business in Sturgeon Bay, Wis., 1865–1884; member of the Wisconsin Assembly in 1877, 1881, and 1882; served in the State senate 1883–1886 and as president pro tempore of the senate during the last term; superintendent of the Sturgeon Bay and Lake Michigan Ship Canal 1884–1891; member of the Wisconsin Fish Commission for four years; mayor of Sturgeon Bay in 1894; elected as a Republican to the Fifty-fourth and to the five succeeding Congresses (March 4, 1895–March 3, 1907); unsuccessful candidate for renomination in 1906; engaged in horticulture; postmaster of Sturgeon Bay 1911–1915; again mayor of Sturgeon Bay in 1918; died at Sturgeon Bay, Wis., July 26, 1924; interment in Bayside Cemetery.

MINSHALL, William Edwin, Jr., a Representative from Ohio; born in East Cleveland, Cuyahoga County, Ohio, October 24, 1911; attended the public schools of East Cleveland, the University School, Shaker Heights, Ohio, and the University of Virginia at Charlottesville; was graduated from the Cleveland Law School in 1940; was admitted to the bar the same year and commenced the practice of law in Cleveland, Ohio; member of the State house of representatives in 1939 and 1940; during World War II enlisted in December 1940 as a private in the Army of the United States and served in the European Theater, G–2 section, Headquarters III Corps, and was discharged as a lieutenant colonel in March 1946; awarded Bronze Star and four battle stars; special assistant attorney general of Ohio 1948–1952; general counsel, Maritime Administration, Washington, D. C., in 1953 and 1954; elected as a Republican to the Eighty-fourth, Eighty-fifth, and Eighty-sixth Congresses (January 3, 1955–January 3, 1961). *Reelected to the Eighty-seventh Congress.*

MINTON, Sherman, a Senator from Indiana; born in Georgetown, Floyd County, Ind., October 20, 1890; attended the graded schools; was graduated from New Albany (Ind.) High School in 1910, from the law department of Indiana University at Bloomington in 1915, and from Yale University, New Haven, Conn., in 1916; was admitted to the bar in 1915 and commenced practice in New Albany, Ind.; during the First World War served as a captain in the Motor Transport Corps from November 27, 1917, to August 1, 1919, serving overseas one year; captain in the Infantry section, Officers' Reserve Corps, 1919–1943; moved to Miami, Fla., in 1925 and continued the practice of law; returned to New Albany, Ind., in 1928 and resumed the practice of law; public counselor of Indiana from March 1, 1933, to July 31, 1934; delegate to the Democratic National Conventions in 1936 and 1940; elected as a Democrat to the United States Senate and served from January 3, 1935, to January 3, 1941; unsuccessful candidate for reelection in 1940; served as administrative assistant in the Executive Office of the President in 1941; judge of the circuit court of appeals for the seventh circuit 1941–1949; appointed by President Harry S. Truman as an Associate Justice of the United States Supreme Court, taking the oath of office October 12, 1949, and served until October 15, 1956, when he resigned due to ill health; is a resident of New Albany, Ind.

MITCHEL, Charles Burton, a Senator from Arkansas; born in Gallatin, Gallatin County, Tenn., September 19, 1815; attended the common schools; was graduated from the University of Nashville, Tennessee, in 1833 and from the Jefferson Medical College, Philadelphia, Pa., in 1836; moved to Washington, Hempstead County, Ark., and pursued the practice of medicine for twenty-five years; served in the State house of representatives in 1848; receiver of public moneys 1853–1856; unsuccessful candidate for election in 1860 to the Thirty-seventh Congress; elected as a Democrat to the United States Senate and served from March 4, 1861, until July 11, 1861, when he withdrew; elected to the Confederate Senate at the first session of the State legislature and served until his death in Little Rock, Ark., September 20, 1864; interment in Presbyterian Cemetery, Washington, Ark.

MITCHELL, Alexander (father of John Lendrum Mitchell), a Representative from Wisconsin; born in Ellon, Aberdeenshire, Scotland, October 18, 1817; attended the parish schools and completed a commercial course; studied law; became a banking-house clerk; immigrated to the United States in 1839 and settled in Milwaukee, Wis.; engaged in banking; first member of the Milwaukee Debt Commission; president of the Chicago, Milwaukee & St. Paul Railroad Co. 1864–1887; unsuccessful candidate for election in 1868 to the Forty-first Congress; elected as a Democrat to the Forty-second and Forty-third Congresses (March 4, 1871–March 3, 1875); declined to be a candidate for renomination in 1874; nominated in 1877 for Governor, but declined to be a candidate; resumed banking interests; died while on a visit in New York City April 19, 1887; interment in Forest Home Cemetery, Milwaukee, Wis.

MITCHELL, Alexander Clark, a Representative from Kansas; born in Cincinnati, Ohio, October 11, 1860; moved to Kansas in 1867 with his parents, who settled in Douglas County, near Lawrence; attended the public schools, and was graduated from the law department of the University of Kansas at Lawrence in 1889; was admitted to the bar the same year and commenced practice in Lawrence, Kans.; prosecuting attorney of Douglas County 1894–1898; member of the Kansas University board of regents 1904–1910; member of the State board of law examiners 1907–1910; member of the State house of representatives 1907–1911; elected as a Republican to the Sixty-second Congress and served from March 4, 1911, until his death in Lawrence, Kans., July 7, 1911; interment in Oak Hill Cemetery.

MITCHELL, Anderson, a Representative from North Carolina; born on a farm near Milton, Caswell County, N. C., June 13, 1800; attended Bingham's School, Orange County, N. C., and was graduated from the University of North Carolina at Chapel Hill in 1821; studied law; was admitted to the bar and commenced practice in Morganton, Burke County, N. C., in 1830; moved to Jefferson, Ashe County, N. C., in 1831; clerk of the superior court of Ashe County; moved to Wilkesboro, Wilkes County, N. C., in 1835, and resumed the practice of law; elected as a Whig to the Twenty-seventh Congress to fill the vacancy caused by the death of Lewis Williams and served from April 27, 1842, to March 3, 1843; unsuccessful candidate for reelection in 1842 to the Twenty-eighth Congress; member of the State house of commons 1852–1854; elected to the State senate in 1860; delegate to the State convention of May 20, 1861, that passed the ordinance of secession, and voted against secession; was appointed judge of the superior court by Provisional Governor Holden in September 1865, subsequently elected and reelected, and served until June 30, 1875, when he resigned; died in Statesville, N. C., December 24, 1876; interment in the Presbyterian Cemetery.

MITCHELL, Arthur Wergs, a Representative from Illinois; born on a farm near Lafayette, Chambers County, Ala., December 22, 1883; is of the Negro race; attended the public schools, Tuskegee Institute at Tuskegee Institute, Ala.; Columbia University, New York, N. Y., and Harvard University, Cambridge, Mass.; taught school in the rural schools of Alabama for many years; founder and president of the Armstrong Agricultural School, West Butler, Ala.; studied law; was admitted to the bar in 1927 and commenced practice in Washington, D. C.; moved to Chicago in 1929 and continued the practice of law; also engaged in the real-estate business; alternate delegate to the Democratic National Convention in 1936, delegate at large in 1940, and was the first of his race to address a national convention; elected as a Democrat to the Seventy-fourth and to the three succeeding Congresses (January 3, 1935–January 3, 1943); was not a candidate for renomination in 1942; resumed the practice of law; also engaged in inter-racial work, public lecturing, and farming near Petersburg, Va., where he now resides.

MITCHELL, Charles F., a Representative from New York; born in New York City about 1808; attended the public schools; moved to Lockport, N. Y., in 1829; appointed one of the firemen of the village May 21, 1829; engaged in the milling business in 1835; elected as a Whig to the Twenty-fifth and Twenty-sixth Congresses (March 4, 1837–March 3, 1841); engaged in milling in the West.

MITCHELL, Charles Le Moyne, a Representative from Connecticut; born in New Haven, Conn., August 6, 1844; was graduated from Cheshire Academy in 1863; traveled in Europe, Asia, and Africa; returned to New Haven, Conn., and engaged in the manufacture of silver-plated ware and brass; member of the State house of representatives in 1877; elected as a Democrat to the Forty-eighth and Forty-ninth Congresses (March 4, 1883–March 3, 1887); was not a candidate for renomination in 1886; moved to New York City in 1886; but retained his former business interests in Connecticut; died in New York City March 1, 1890; interment in Evergreen Cemetery, New Haven, Conn.

MITCHELL, Edward Archibald, a Representative from Indiana; born in Binghamton, Broome County, N. Y., December 2, 1910; attended the grade and high schools and had three years of college training at the American Institute and Columbia University, New York City; moved to Evansville, Ind., in September 1937; engaged as a warehouseman and later as district manager for a large food distributor 1934–1937; in 1937 purchased a half interest in a food marketing and brokerage company and served as president; during World War II served in the United States Navy from November 1942 until his discharge as a lieutenant commander in January 1946, having been commanding officer of underwater demolition teams in the Pacific Theater for two years; awarded the Silver Star Medal at Okinawa; elected as a Republican to the Eightieth Congress (January 3, 1947–January 3, 1949); unsuccessful candidate for reelection in 1948 to the Eighty-first Congress; resumed his former business pursuits; is a resident of Evansville, Ind.

MITCHELL, George Edward, a Representative from Maryland; born at Head of Elk (now Elkton), Cecil County, Md., March 3, 1781; completed preparatory studies, and was graduated from the medical department of the University of Pennsylvania at Philadelphia June 5, 1805; practiced medicine in Elkton, Md., 1806–1812; member of the State house of delegates in 1808; member of the executive council of Maryland and served as president 1809–1812; served in the War of 1812; commissioned major of the Third Maryland Artillery May 1, 1812; lieutenant colonel March 3, 1813; transferred to Artillery Corps May 12, 1814, and to the Third Artillery June 1, 1814; brevetted colonel May 5, 1814, for gallant conduct in repelling attack of British forces at Fort Oswego, N. Y.; resigned June 1, 1821; elected as a Democrat to the Eighteenth and Nineteenth Congresses (March 4, 1823–March 3, 1827); was not a candidate for renomination in 1826; unsuccessful candidate for the governorship in 1829; elected to the Twenty-first and Twenty-second Congresses and served from December 7, 1829, until his death in Washington, D. C., June 28, 1832; interment in the Congressional Cemetery.

MITCHELL, Harlan Erwin, a Representative from Georgia; born in Dalton, Whitfield County, Ga., August 17, 1924; attended the public schools in Dalton, Ga., and The Citadel, Charleston, S. C.; during World War II served as a first lieutenant in the United States Army Air Corps 1943–1946 and again in the United States Air Force in 1951 and 1952; received Air Medal with two stars and Pacific Ribbon with two battle stars; graduated from the University of Georgia in 1948; was admitted to the bar April 17, 1948, and commenced the practice of law in Dalton, Ga.; solicitor general, Cherokee Judicial Circuit, from January 1, 1953, to December 31, 1956; judge, Superior Court, Cherokee Judicial Circuit, from January 1, 1957, to January 8, 1958; elected as a Democrat to the Eighty-fifth Congress to fill the vacancy caused by the death of Henderson L. Lanham; reelected to the Eighty-sixth Congress and served from January 8, 1958, to January 3, 1961; was not a candidate for renomination in 1960; is a resident of Dalton, Ga.

MITCHELL, Henry, a Representative from New York; born in Woodbury, Litchfield County, Conn., in 1784; pursued classical studies under private tutors and was graduated from the medical department of Yale College in 1804; engaged in the practice of medicine in Norwich, Chenango County, N. Y.; member of the State assembly in 1827; elected as a Jackson Democrat to the Twenty-third Congress (March 4, 1833–March 3, 1835); resumed the practice of medicine; died in Norwich, Chenango County, N. Y., January 12, 1856; interment in Mount Hope Cemetery.

MITCHELL, Hugh Burnton, a Senator and a Representative from Washington; born in Great Falls, Cascade County, Mont., March 22, 1907; attended the public schools at Great Falls, Wash., and Dartmouth College, Hanover, N. H., 1926–1929; engaged in editorial work on a newspaper in Everett, Wash., 1931–1933; served as executive assistant to Monrad C. Wallgren during his services in the United States House of Representatives and the United States Senate 1933–1945; appointed to the United States Senate to fill the vacancy caused by the resignation of Monrad C. Wallgren and served from January 10, 1945, until his resignation on December 25, 1946; unsuccessful Democratic candidate for election to the United States Senate in 1946; engaged in economic research and public relations; elected to the Eighty-first and Eighty-second Congresses (January 3, 1949–January 3, 1953); was not a candidate for renomination in 1952 but was unsuccessful for election as Governor of Washington; was unsuccessful candidate for election in 1954 to the Eighty-fourth Congress and in 1958 to the Eighty-sixth Congress; engaged in the transportation business; is a resident of Seattle, Wash.

MITCHELL, James Coffield, a Representative from Tennessee; born in Staunton, Augusta County, Va., in March 1786; attended the common schools; studied law; was admitted to the bar and practiced; moved to Tennessee and settled in Rhea County; solicitor general of the second district of Tennessee 1813–1817; moved to Athens, McMinn County, in 1817; elected to the Nineteenth and Twentieth Congresses (March 4, 1825–March 3, 1829); unsuccessful candidate for reelection; judge of the eleventh circuit 1830–1836; moved to Hinds County, Miss., and settled near Jackson about 1837, engaging in agricultural pursuits; unsuccessful candidate on the Whig ticket for Governor of Mississippi and for the State house of representatives; author of Mitchell's Justice; died near Jackson, Miss., August 7, 1843.

MITCHELL, James S., a Representative from Pennsylvania; born near Rossville, Warrington Township, York County, Pa., in 1784; attended the common schools; member of the State house of representatives 1812–1814; elected as a Democrat to the Seventeenth, Eighteenth, and Nineteenth Congresses (March 4, 1821–March 3, 1827); moved to Jefferson County, Ohio, in 1827, and later to Belleville, St. Clair County, Ill., where he died in 1844; interment at Dillsburg, Pa.

MITCHELL, John, a Representative from Pennsylvania; born near Newport, Perry County, Pa., March 8, 1781; attended the common schools; moved to Bellefonte, Centre County, in 1800 and was employed as a clerk in the ironworks; elected sheriff of Centre County in 1818; engineer and surveyor; laid out the Centre and Kishacoquillas Turnpike in 1821; constructed many of the turnpikes in middle and northern Pennsylvania; member of the State house of representatives in 1822 and 1823; elected as a Democrat to the Nineteenth and Twentieth Congresses (March 4, 1825–March 3, 1829); surveyed proposed canal routes between the Susquehanna and Potomac Rivers in 1826; engineer on the Erie extension in 1827; canal commissioner in 1829; presidential elector on the Democratic ticket of Van Buren and Johnson in 1836; moved to Bridgewater, Pa., in 1842; engaged in civil engineering and iron manufacturing; member of the canal survey commission from 1845 until his death in Bridgewater, Pa., August 3, 1849; interment in Old Beaver Cemetery.

MITCHELL, John Hipple, a Senator from Oregon; born in Washington County, Pa., June 22, 1835; moved with his parents to Butler County, Pa., in 1837; attended public and private schools and Witherspoon Institute; studied law; was admitted to the bar in 1856 and practiced; moved to San Luis Obispo, Calif., and thence to San Francisco, where he continued the practice of law; moved to Portland, Oreg., in 1860; corporation attorney of Portland in 1861; member of the State senate 1862–1866 and served the last two years as its president; commissioned by the Governor of Oregon in 1865 lieutenant colonel in the State militia; unsuccessful candidate for election to the United States Senate in 1866; professor of medical jurisprudence in Willamette University, Salem, Oreg., in 1867; elected as a Republican to the United States Senate and served from March 4, 1873, to March 3, 1879; unsuccessful candidate for election to the United States Senate in 1882; elected to the United States Senate on November 18, 1885, for the term beginning March 4, 1885; reelected in 1891 and served until March 3, 1897; unsuccessful candidate for reelection; resumed the practice of law; again elected to the United States Senate and served from March 4, 1901, until his death in Portland, Oreg., December 8, 1905; interment in Riverview Cemetery.

MITCHELL, John Inscho, a Representative and a Senator from Pennsylvania; born in Tioga Township, Tioga County, Pa., July 28, 1838; attended the common schools and received private instruction; attended the University of Lewisburg (later Bucknell University), Pennsylvania, 1857–1859, but did not graduate; taught school 1859–1861; during the Civil War served in the Union Army as a lieutenant and captain in the One Hundred and Thirty-sixth Regiment, Pennsylvania Volunteer Infantry; studied law; was admitted to the bar in 1864 and practiced in Tioga County; district attorney of Tioga County 1868–1871; edited the Tioga County Agitator in 1870; member of the State house of representatives 1872–1876; elected as a Republican to the Forty-fifth and Forty-sixth Congresses (March 4, 1877–March 3, 1881); elected to the United States Senate and served from March 4, 1881, to March 3, 1887; president judge of the court of common pleas of the fourth Pennsylvania district 1888–1899; judge of the superior court of Pennsylvania and served one session; died in Wellsboro, Tioga County, Pa., August 20, 1907; interment in Wellsboro Cemetery.

MITCHELL, John Joseph, a Representative from Massachusetts; born in Marlboro, Middlesex County, Mass., May 9, 1873; attended the public schools, Boston College, and the Albany Law School; was admitted to the bar in 1901 and commenced practice in Marlboro; member of the State house of representatives 1903–1906; served in the State senate in 1907 and 1908; elected as a Democrat to the Sixty-first Congress to fill the vacancy caused by the death of Charles Q. Tirrell and served from November 8, 1910, to March 3, 1911; unsuccessful candidate for reelection in 1910 to the Sixty-second Congress; elected to the Sixty-third Congress to fill the vacancy caused by the resignation of John W. Weeks and served from April 15, 1913, to March 3, 1915; unsuccessful candidate for reelection in 1914 to the Sixty-fourth Congress; served as United States marshal for Massachusetts during the First World War; collector of internal revenue for the district of Massachusetts 1919–1921; engaged in the practice of his profession in Boston, Suffolk County, Mass., until his death on September 13, 1925; interment in Immaculate Conception Cemetery, Marlboro, Mass.

MITCHELL, John Lendrum (son of Alexander Mitchell), a Representative and a Senator from Wisconsin; born in Milwaukee, Wis., October 19, 1842; attended the common schools at Milwaukee, and the military academy at Hampton, Conn.; studied in Dresden and Munich, Germany, and Geneva, Switzerland, for the next six years; returned to the United States in 1860; served in the Civil War in the Twenty-fourth Regiment, Wisconsin Volunteer Infantry; first lieutenant and later chief of ordnance on the staff of Gen. Absalom Bayard; resigned in 1864; engaged in agricultural pursuits near Milwaukee; member of the State senate in 1872, 1873, 1875, and 1876; chairman of the county Democratic central committee; Wisconsin member of the Democratic National Committee in 1888; president of the Milwaukee Public School Board in 1884 and 1885; member of the board of managers of the National Home for Disabled Volunteer Soldiers 1886–1892; president of the Milwaukee Gas Co. 1890–1892; elected as a Democrat to the Fifty-second and Fifty-third Congresses and served from March 4, 1891, until his resignation on March 3, 1893, before the beginning of the Congress, having been elected Senator; elected to the United States Senate and served from March 4, 1893, to March 3, 1899; was not a candidate for renomination in 1898; went to Europe in 1899, and studied at Grenoble University, Grenoble, France; returned to the United States in 1902; president of the Wisconsin State Agricultural Society and of numerous banking institutions; trustee, director, and patron of numerous public institutions, including the Layton Art Gallery, Milwaukee College, and the city hospital; died in Milwaukee, Wis., June 29, 1904; interment in Forest Home Cemetery.

MITCHELL, John Murray, a Representative from New York; born in New York City March 18, 1858; attended Leggett's School at New York, N. Y.; was graduated from Columbia College, New York City, in 1877 and from the law department of that college in 1879; was admitted to the bar in 1879 and practiced in New York City; successfully contested as a Republican the election of James J. Walsh to the Fifty-fourth Congress; reelected to the Fifty-fifth Congress and served from June 2, 1896, to March 3, 1899; unsuccessful candidate for reelection in 1898 to the Fifty-sixth Congress; resumed the practice of law; died in Tuxedo Park, Orange County, N. Y., May 31, 1905; interment in Greenwood Cemetery, Brooklyn, N. Y.

MITCHELL, John Ridley, a Representative from Tennessee; born in Livingston, Overton County, Tenn., September 26, 1877; attended the public schools; was graduated from Peabody College of Teachers, Nashville, Tenn., in 1896; private secretary to Representative C. E. Snodgrass 1899–1903; was graduated from

the law department of Cumberland University, Lebanon, Tenn., in 1904; was admitted to the bar the same year and commenced practice in Crossville, Tenn.; presidential elector on the Democratic ticket of Parker and Davis in 1904; member of the State Democratic executive committee 1910–1914; assistant attorney general of the fifth circuit of Tennessee 1908–1918 and attorney general of the same circuit 1918–1925; served as judge of the fifth circuit 1925–1931; moved to Cookeville, Tenn., in 1931; elected as a Democrat to the Seventy-second and to the three succeeding Congresses (March 4, 1931–January 3, 1939); was not a candidate for renomination in 1938, but was unsuccessful for the Democratic nomination for United States Senator; resumed the practice of law; attorney in the office of Alien Property Custodian from January 1943 to September 1945; special assistant to Attorney General in the Antitrust Division, Department of Justice, Washington, D. C., 1945–1951; is a resident of Crossville, Tenn.

MITCHELL, Nahum, a Representative from Massachusetts; born in East Bridgewater, Plymouth County, Mass., February 12, 1769; attended the local school; was graduated from Harvard University in 1789; studied law in Plymouth, Mass.; was admitted to the bar and commenced practice in East Bridgewater, Mass.; member of the State house of representatives 1798–1802; elected as a Federalist to the Eighth Congress (March 4, 1803–March 3, 1805); was not a candidate for renomination; again a member of the State house of representatives in 1809 and 1812; judge of the common pleas court 1811–1821 and chief justice 1819–1821; served in the State senate in 1813 and 1814; member of the State treasurer of Massachusetts 1822–1827; librarian in 1835 and 1836 and treasurer 1839–1845 of the Massachusetts Historical Society; died in Plymouth, Mass., August 1, 1853; interment in Old Central Street Cemetery, East Bridgewater, Mass.

MITCHELL, Nathaniel, a Delegate from Delaware; born near Laurel, Sussex County, Del., in 1753; engaged in agricultural pursuits; during the Revolutionary War became an adjutant in Colonel Dogworth's battalion of militia, afterward was with Colonel Patterson's battalion of the flying camp, and still later with Colonel Grayson's Continental regiment; in April 1779 he was transferred to Colonel Gist's regiment and subsequently was brigade major and inspector to Gen. Peter Muhlenberg; Member of the Continental Congress 1786–1788; prothonotary of Sussex County 1788–1805; Federalist presidential elector in 1800 and voted for Adams and Pinckney; Governor of Delaware 1805–1808; member of the State house of representatives in 1808; served in the State senate 1810–1812; died in Laurel, Del., February 21, 1814; interment in Broad Creek Episcopal Graveyard, near Laurel, Del.

MITCHELL, Robert, a Representative from Ohio; born in Westmoreland County, Pa., in 1778; attended the common schools; studied medicine; moved to Ohio in 1807 and practiced in Zanesville; clerk to the commissioners of Muskingum County in 1811 and 1812; county collector in 1812 and 1813; served in the War of 1812 as a member of Capt. John De Vault's company; member of the State house of representatives in 1815 and 1816; judge of the court of common pleas in 1818; brigadier general of the State militia in 1822; elected as a Democrat to the Twenty-third Congress (March 4, 1833–March 3, 1835); unsuccessful candidate for reelection in 1834 to the Twenty-fourth Congress; resumed the practice of medicine in Zanesville, Ohio, where he died November 13, 1848; interment in Greenwood Cemetery.

MITCHELL, Stephen Mix, a Delegate and a Senator from Connecticut; born in Wethersfield, Hartford County, Conn., December 9, 1743; pursued academic studies; was graduated from Yale College in 1763; served as tutor in Yale College 1766–1769; studied law; was admitted to the bar in 1770 and commenced practice in Newton, Conn.; returned to Wethersfield in 1772 and continued the practice of law for seven years; member of the Connecticut General Assembly 1778–1784; judge of the Hartford County Court 1779–1795; associate justice of the county court of Hartford County 1779–1790 and was presiding judge of the court 1790–1793; Member of the Continental Congress 1783–1788; member of the State convention which ratified the Constitution of the United States in 1788; elected as a Federalist to the United States Senate to fill the vacancy caused by the death of Roger Sherman and served from December 2, 1793, to March 3, 1795; was not a candidate for renomination in 1794; judge of the State supreme court 1795–1807 and its chief justice 1807–1814; presidential elector on the Federalist ticket of Adams and Pinckney in 1800; member of the State constitutional convention in 1818; resumed the practice of law; died in Wethersfield, Conn., September 30, 1835; interment in Wethersfield Cemetery.

MITCHELL, Thomas Rothmaler, a Representative from South Carolina; born in Georgetown, Georgetown County, S. C., in May 1783; was graduated from Harvard University in 1802; studied law; was admitted to the bar in 1808 and commenced practice in Georgetown, S. C.; elected to the Seventeenth Congress (March 4, 1821–March 3, 1823); unsuccessful candidate for reelection in 1822 to the Eighteenth Congress; elected to the Nineteenth and Twentieth Congresses (March 4, 1825–March 3, 1829); unsuccessful candidate for reelection in 1828 to the Twenty-first Congress; elected to the Twenty-second Congress (March 4, 1831–March 3, 1833); unsuccessful candidate for reelection in 1832 to the Twenty-third Congress; died in Georgetown, S. C., November 2, 1837.

MITCHELL, William, a Representative from Indiana; born in Root, Montgomery County, N. Y., January 19, 1807; attended the public schools; studied law; was admitted to the bar in 1836; moved to Kendallville, Noble County, Ind., and commenced the practice of law; appointed first postmaster of Kendallville December 7, 1836, and served until a successor was appointed March 7, 1846; member of the State house of representatives in 1841; justice of the peace; elected as a Republican to the Thirty-seventh Congress (March 4, 1861–March 3, 1863); unsuccessful candidate for reelection in 1862 to the Thirty-eighth Congress; engaged in the cotton business; died while on a business trip in Macon, Ga., September 11, 1865; interment in Lake View Cemetery, Kendallville, Ind.

MITCHILL, Samuel Latham, a Representative and a Senator from New York; born in Hempstead, Nassau County, N. Y., August 20, 1764; pursued classical studies; studied medicine and was graduated from the University of Edinburgh, Scotland, in 1786; studied law and was admitted to the bar; commissioner to purchase the lands of the Iroquois Indians in western New York in 1788; member of the State assembly in 1791 and 1798; professor of chemistry and natural history in Columbia College in 1792; one of the founders of the State Society for the Promotion of Agriculture in 1793; editor of the quarterly, New York Medical Repository, 1797–1813; elected as a Democrat to the Seventh, Eighth, and Ninth Congresses and served from March 4, 1801, until his resignation November 22, 1804, before the close of the Eighth Congress, having been elected Senator; one of the managers appointed by the House of Representatives in 1804 to conduct the impeachment proceedings against John Pickering, judge of the United States District Court of New Hampshire; elected to the United States Senate on November 9, 1804, to fill the vacancy caused by the resignation of John

Armstrong, but did not qualify immediately, retaining his seat in the House, and served in the Senate from November 23, 1804, to March 3, 1809; elected to the Eleventh Congress to fill the vacancy caused by the resignation of William Denning; reelected to the Twelfth Congress and served from December 4, 1810, to March 3, 1813; surgeon general of the State militia in 1818; founder and president of the Lyceum of Natural History of New York City 1817–1823; professor of natural history in the New York College of Physicians and Surgeons 1808–1820 and of botany and materia medica 1820–1826; vice president of Rutgers Medical School 1826–1830; died in New York City September 7, 1831; interment in Greenwood Cemetery, Brooklyn, N. Y.

MOBLEY, William Carlton, a Representative from Georgia; born near Hillsboro, Jones County, Ga., December 7, 1906; attended the common schools; was graduated from the law department of Mercer University, Macon, Ga., in 1928; was admitted to the bar in 1928 and commenced practice in Forsyth, Ga.; served as secretary to Congressman Samuel Rutherford 1929–1932; elected as a Democrat to the Seventy-second Congress to fill the vacancy caused by the death of Samuel Rutherford and served from March 2, 1932, to March 3, 1933; was not a candidate for nomination in 1932; secretary in the executive department of the State of Georgia 1934–1937; assistant attorney general of Georgia 1941–1943; during World War II served as a lieutenant commander in the United States Navy 1943–1946; resumed the practice of law in Macon, Ga.; associate justice, supreme court of Georgia, from June 1, 1954, to December 1, 1960; reelected in 1960 for the term ending December 31, 1966; is a resident of Atlanta, Ga.

MOELLER, Walter Henry, a Representative from Ohio; born on a farm in Hancock County, near Indianapolis, Ind., March 15, 1910; attended local elementary and high schools; graduated from Concordia College and Seminary, Springfield, Ill., in 1935, Defiance (Ohio) College in 1951 and Indiana University in 1953; worked way through college by operating small campus print shop and as a machinist helper at the Big Four Railroad shops; Lutheran Church minister, Decatur, Ind., 1936–1942, and Van Wert and Lancaster, Ohio, 1942–1956; instructor in English composition, German, and sociology at Giffen Junior College, Van Wert, Ohio, 1942–1952; delegate to North Atlantic Treaty Organization Congress in London in 1959; farm owner; elected as a Democrat to the Eighty-sixth Congress (January 3, 1959–January 3, 1961). *Reelected to the Eighty-seventh Congress.*

MOFFATT, Seth Crittenden, a Representative from Michigan; born in Battle Creek, Calhoun County, Mich., August 10, 1841; attended the common schools; was graduated from the law department of the University of Michigan at Ann Arbor in 1863; was admitted to the bar and commenced practice in Traverse City, Mich.; prosecuting attorney for Grand Traverse and Leelanaw Counties for ten years; member of the State senate in 1871 and 1872; member of the constitutional commission in 1873; register of the United States Land Office at Traverse City 1874–1878; member of the State house of representatives in 1881 and 1882, and served as speaker in both terms; delegate to the Republican National Convention at Chicago in 1884 which nominated Blaine and Logan; elected as a Republican to the Forty-ninth and Fiftieth Congresses and served from March 4, 1885, until his death in Washington, D. C., December 22, 1887; interment in Oakwood Cemetery, Traverse City, Grand Traverse County, Mich.

MOFFET, John, a Representative from Pennsylvania; born in County Antrim, Ireland, April 5, 1831; immigrated to the United States with his parents, who settled in Philadelphia, Pa.;

attended the public schools in Philadelphia, Pa.; studied medicine in the University of Pennsylvania at Philadelphia, and became an apothecary in 1853; also engaged in the practice of medicine; presented credentials as a Democratic Member-elect to the Forty-first Congress and served from March 4 to April 9, 1869, when he was succeeded by Leonard Myers, who contested his election; delegate to several Democratic National Conventions; resumed the practice of pharmacy and medicine in Philadelphia, Pa., where he died June 19, 1884; interment in Laurel Hill Cemetery.

MOFFITT, Hosea, a Representative from New York; born in Stephentown, Rensselaer County, N. Y., November 17, 1757; during the Revolutionary War served as ensign and later as lieutenant in the Fourth (Second Rensselaerwyck Battalion) Regiment, Albany County Militia, under the command of Col. Killian Van Rensselaer; justice of the peace in 1791; town clerk in 1791 and 1797; member of the State assembly in 1794, 1795, and 1801; appointed brigadier general of militia March 22, 1806; supervisor of the town of Stephentown 1806–1809; sheriff of Rensselaer County 1810–1811; elected as a Federalist to the Thirteenth and Fourteenth Congresses (March 4, 1813–March 3, 1817); member of the board of managers of the Rensselaer County Bible Society in 1815; died in Stephentown, N. Y., August 31, 1825; interment in Old Presbyterian Cemetery on "Presbyterian Hill," at Garfield, in the town of Stephentown, N. Y.

MOFFITT, John Henry, a Representative from New York; born near Chazy, Clinton County, N. Y., January 8, 1843; attended the district school and Plattsburg (N. Y.) Academy; during the Civil War enlisted as a private in Company C, Sixteenth Regiment, New York Volunteers, April 27, 1861; severely wounded at the Battle of Gaines Mills, Va., June 27, 1862; awarded the Congressional Medal of Honor; mustered out of the service with his regiment May 18, 1863; was graduated from Fort Edward (N. Y.) Collegiate Institute in 1864-deputy collector of customs at Rouses Point, N. Y., 1866–1872; engaged in the manufacture of charcoal bloom iron at Moffitsville, Clinton County, and at Belmont, Franklin (now Allegany) County, 1872–1891; elected supervisor of Saranac, Clinton County, in 1877; elected as a Republican to the Fiftieth and Fifty-first Congresses (March 4, 1887–March 3, 1891); was not a candidate for renomination in 1890; manager of the Syracuse Street Railway Co. 1891–1899; superintendent of the city water department 1900–1902; cashier of the Plattsburg National Bank 1902–1904, and from 1904 until his death was president of the Plattsburg National Bank & Trust Co.; served as chairman of the Republican committee of Clinton County; delegate to several Republican State conventions and to the Republican National Convention at Chicago in 1912; died in Plattsburg, Clinton County, N. Y., August 14, 1926; interment in Mount Carmel Cemetery.

MOLLOHAN, Robert Homer, a Representative from West Virginia; born in Grantsville, Calhoun County, W. Va., September 18, 1909; attended the public schools, Glenville College, and Shepherd College 1929–1931; deputy collector of internal revenue at Parkersburg, W. Va., in 1933 and chief of miscellaneous tax division and cashier 1935–1938; district manager of Works Progress Administration in 1939; State director for the Census Bureau in 1940; superintendent of State Industrial School for Boys 1941–1948; clerk of the United States Senate District of Columbia Committee in 1949 and 1950; United States marshal for the northern district of West Virginia in 1950; again served as clerk of the Senate District of Columbia Committee 1950–1952; elected as a Democrat to the Eighty-third and Eighty-

fourth Congresses (January 3, 1953–January 3, 1957); was not a candidate for renomination in 1956 but was an unsuccessful candidate for Governor; unsuccessful candidate in 1958 for election to the Eighty-sixth Congress; engaged in general insurance business; is a resident of Fairmont, W. Va.

MOLONY, Richard Sheppard, a Representative from Illinois; born in Northfield, N. H., June 28, 1811; studied medicine; was graduated from Dartmouth Medical School, Hanover, N. H., in 1838 and commenced the practice of his profession in Belvidere, Boone County, Ill., delegate to the Democratic National Convention at Baltimore in 1852; elected as a Democrat to the Thirty-second Congress (March 4, 1851–March 3, 1853); was not a candidate for renomination in 1852; moved to Humboldt, Nebr., and engaged in agricultural pursuits 1866–1891; in 1882 declined the Democratic nomination for United States Senator from Nebraska on account of ill health; again a delegate to the Democratic National Convention at Chicago in 1884; died in Humboldt, Nebr., December 14, 1891; interment in Belvidere Cemetery, Belvidere, Ill.

MONAGAN, John Stephen, a Representative from Connecticut; born in Waterbury, New Haven County, Conn., December 23, 1911; attended Driggs, St. Mary's, and Crosby high schools in Waterbury; graduated from Dartmouth College in 1933 and from Harvard Law School in 1937; was admitted to the Connecticut bar in 1938 and commenced the practice of law in Waterbury, Conn., the same year; president of the Waterbury Board of Aldermen 1940–1943; mayor of Waterbury 1943–1948; member of the board of directors of Waterbury Savings Bank; delegate to the Democratic National Conventions in 1944 and 1948; elected as a Democrat to the Eighty-sixth Congress (January 3, 1959–January 3, 1961). *Reelected to the Eighty-seventh Congress.*

MONAGHAN, Joseph Patrick, a Representative from Montana; born in Butte, Mont., March 26, 1906; attended public and parochial schools; graduated from Mount St. Charles (Carroll College), Helena, Mont., in 1928; member of the State house of representatives 1929–1931; studied law at Montana State University at Missoula; was admitted to the bar in 1931 and commenced practice in Butte, Mont.; unsuccessful candidate for election in 1930 to the Seventy-second Congress; elected as a Democrat to the Seventy-third and Seventy-fourth Congresses (March 4, 1933–January 3, 1937); did not seek renomination in 1936, but was unsuccessful both as a candidate for the Democratic nomination for United States Senator and for election as an Independent candidate for the same office; resumed the practice of law and is a resident of Butte, Mont.

MONAHAN, James Gideon, a Representative from Wisconsin; born at Willow Springs, near Darlington, Lafayette County, Wis., January 12, 1855; attended the common schools, and was graduated from the Darlington High School in 1875; taught school; studied law; was admitted to the bar in 1878 and commenced practice in Mineral Point, Wis.; returned to Darlington in 1880; district attorney of Lafayette County 1880–1884; purchased an interest in and became editor of the Darlington Republican Journal in 1883; sole owner and publisher 1885–1919; delegate to the Republican National Convention at Chicago in 1888; collector of internal revenue for the second Wisconsin district 1900–1908; elected as a Republican to the Sixty-sixth Congress (March 4, 1919–March 3, 1921); unsuccessful candidate for renomination in 1920 to the Sixty-seventh Congress; retired from public life and active business pursuits; died in Dubuque, Iowa, December 5, 1923; interment in Union Grove Cemetery, Darlington, Wis.

MONAST, Louis, a Representative from Rhode Island; born in Marieville de Monior, Iberville, Province of Quebec, Canada, July 1, 1863; in the spring of 1865 immigrated to the United States with his father, who settled in Pawtucket, R. I.; attended parochial and night schools; employed in the textile mills from 1872 to 1882 and as a bricklayer, plasterer, and carpenter from 1882 to 1892; engaged in building construction and in the real-estate business in 1892, and also operated several bakeries; member of the State house of representatives 1909–1911; delegate to the Republican National Convention at Cleveland in 1924; unsuccessful candidate for election in 1924 to the Sixty-ninth Congress; elected as a Republican to the Seventieth Congress (March 4, 1927–March 3, 1929); unsuccessful candidate for reelection in 1928 to the Seventy-first Congress; resumed the real-estate business; died in Pawtucket, R. I., April 16, 1936; interment in Notre Dame Cemetery.

MONDELL, Franklin Wheeler, a Representative from Wyoming; born in St. Louis, Mo., November 6, 1860; his parents having died before he reached his seventh year, he went to live with friends in Dickinson County, Iowa, until he was eighteen years of age; attended the common schools and also received instruction in the higher branches from a private teacher; engaged in mercantile pursuits, mining, and railway construction in various Western States and Territories; settled in Wyoming in 1887 and engaged in the development of coal mines and oil property in the vicinity of Newcastle and Cambria; took an active part in the establishment and building of the town of Newcastle, Wyo., and the development of the Cambria, Wyo., mines; elected mayor of Newcastle in 1888 and served until 1895; member of the first State senate in 1890 and served as president of the second senate in 1892; delegate to the Republican National Conventions in 1892, 1900, 1904, 1908, and 1912; elected as a Republican to the Fifty-fourth Congress (March 4, 1895–March 3, 1897); unsuccessful candidate for reelection in 1896 to the Fifty-fifth Congress; appointed assistant commissioner of the General Land Office on November 15, 1897, and served until March 3, 1899; elected to the Fifty-sixth and to the eleven succeeding Congresses (March 4, 1899–March 3, 1923); did not seek renomination in 1922, having become a candidate for Senator; majority floor leader in the Sixty-sixth and Sixty-seventh Congresses; unsuccessful candidate for United States Senator in 1922; declined the offer of President Harding to appoint him Ambassador to Japan or Governor of Puerto Rico; appointed a director of the War Finance Corporation in 1923 and served until his resignation in July 1925; studied law; was admitted to the bar in 1924 and commenced practice in Washington, D. C.; delegate to the Republican National Convention at Cleveland in 1924, serving as chairman, and delivered the address notifying President Coolidge of his nomination; died in Washington, D. C., August 6, 1939; interment in Cedar Hill Cemetery.

MONELL, Robert, a Representative from New York; born in Columbia County, N. Y., in 1786; pursued classical studies; studied law; was admitted to the bar in 1809 and commenced practice at Binghamton, N. Y.; moved to Greene, Chenango County, in 1811 and continued the practice of his profession; member of the State assembly in 1814 and 1815; elected as a Democrat to the Sixteenth Congress (March 4, 1819–March 3, 1821); again a member of the State assembly in 1825, 1826, and 1828; district attorney of Chenango County in 1827; elected to the Twenty-first Congress, and served from March 4, 1829, until February 21, 1831, when he resigned; circuit judge of the sixth circuit 1831–1845; clerk of the State supreme court in 1846; resumed the practice of law; died in Greene, Chenango County, N. Y., November 29, 1860; interment in Hornby Cemetery.

MONEY, Hernando De Soto, a Representative and a Senator from Mississippi; born at Zeiglersville, Homes County, Miss., August 26, 1839; moved in early childhood to Carrollton, Carroll County, Miss.; received his early education in the public schools and from a private teacher; was graduated from the law department of the University of Mississippi at Oxford; was admitted to the bar and commenced practice in Carrollton about 1860; during the Civil War served in the Confederate Army until forced to resign September 26, 1864, on account of defective eyesight; engaged in planting in Leflore County; returned to Carrollton and edited the Conservative; moved to Winona, Montgomery County, Miss., and edited the Winona Advance; mayor of Winona in 1873 and 1874; elected as a Democrat to the Forty-fourth and to the four succeeding Congresses (March 4, 1875–March 3, 1885); declined to be a candidate for renomination in 1884; engaged in the practice of law in Washington, D. C., until 1891, when he returned to Carrollton, Miss.; delegate to many Democratic National Conventions; elected to the Fifty-third and Fifty-fourth Congresses (March 4, 1893–March 3, 1897); elected to the United States Senate for the term commencing March 4, 1899; during the interim was appointed and subsequently elected to the United States Senate to fill the vacancy caused by the death of James Z. George; reelected in 1906 and served from October 8, 1897, to March 3, 1911; declined to be a candidate for reelection; returned to his home near Biloxi, Harrison County, Miss., and died there September 18, 1912; interment in the family vault at Carrollton, Carroll County, Miss.

MONKIEWICZ, Boleslaus Joseph, a Representative from Connecticut; born in Syracuse, N. Y., August 8, 1898; moved with his parents to New Britain, Conn., in 1899; attended the public schools and was graduated from New Britain (Conn.) High School in 1917; served as an apprentice seaman in the United States Navy (Columbia University Naval Unit), October 3, 1918, to December 17, 1918; was graduated from the law department of Fordham University, New York, N. Y., in 1921; was admitted to the bar in 1923 and commenced practice in New Britain, Conn.; also engaged in banking; clerk of the New Britain, Conn., city and police court from July 1932 to August 1933; prosecuting attorney, police court, 1937–1939; elected as a Republican to the Seventy-sixth Congress (January 3, 1939–January 3, 1941); unsuccessful candidate for reelection in 1940 to the Seventy-seventh Congress; elected to the Seventy-eighth Congress (January 3, 1943–January 3, 1945); unsuccessful candidate for reelection in 1944 to the Seventy-ninth Congress; resumed the practice of law and also was unemployment compensation commissioner of Connecticut; member of the United States Board of Parole at Washington, D. C., 1947–1953; resumed the practice of law in New Britain, Conn., and resides in Kensington, Conn.

MONROE, James (nephew of Joseph Jones), a Delegate and a Senator from Virginia and a President of the United States; born in Westmoreland County, Va., April 28, 1758; pursued classical studies; attended William and Mary College, Williamsburg, Va., in 1776 and left to enter the Continental Army in the Revolutionary War; appointed a lieutenant in the Third Virginia Regiment and participated in numerous engagements; severely wounded in the Battle of Harlem Heights; volunteer aide with rank of major on the staff of General Stirling; military commissioner for Virginia in 1780 with rank of lieutenant colonel and visited the southern army under General DeKalb; member of the State assembly in 1782; Member of the Continental Congress 1783–1786; resumed the study of law; was admitted to the bar and engaged in practice in Fredericksburg, Va.; again a member of the State assembly in 1786; delegate to the State convention to consider the Federal Constitution in 1788; elected to the United States Senate to fill the vacancy caused by the death of William Grayson; reelected in 1791 and served from November 9, 1790, until his resignation May 27, 1794; appointed by President Washington as Minister Plenipotentiary to France and served from May 28, 1794, to December 30, 1796; Governor of Virginia 1799–1802; appointed by President Jefferson as Minister Plenipotentiary to France January 11, 1803, and served from January 12 to July 12, 1803; Minister Plenipotentiary to England 1803–1807 and during this period headed a diplomatic mission to Spain; returned home in 1808; again elected member of the State assembly in 1810 and 1811; again Governor of Virginia in 1811; appointed Secretary of State in the Cabinet of President Madison and served from November 25, 1811, to March 3, 1817; elected and reelected President of the United States and served from March 4, 1817, to March 3, 1825; retired to his farm in Loudoun County, Va.; member and president of the Virginia Constitutional Convention of 1829; moved to New York City in 1831, and died there July 4, 1831; interment in Marble Cemetery on Second Street, New York City; reinterred in Hollywood Cemetery, Richmond, Va., July 4, 1858.

MONROE, James (nephew of the preceding), a Representative from New York; born in Albemarle County, Va., September 10, 1799; was graduated from the United States Military Academy, West Point, N. Y., in 1815 and assigned to the Artillery Corps; served in the war with Algiers, under Commodore Decatur's command in the same year, in which he was wounded; served as aide to Gen. Winfield Scott 1817–1822; commissioned a second lieutenant in the Fourth Artillery in 1821 and served on garrison and commissary duty until 1832, when he was again appointed General Scott's aide on the Black Hawk expedition, but did not reach the seat of war, owing to illness; resigned his commission September 30, 1832; moved to New York City in 1832; assistant alderman of New York City in 1832; alderman 1833–1835 and served as president of the board in 1834; declined the appointment as aide to Gov. William L. Marcy in 1836; elected as a Whig to the Twenty-sixth Congress (March 4, 1839–March 3, 1841); unsuccessful candidate for reelection in 1840 to the Twenty-seventh Congress; contested the election of David S. Jackson to the Thirtieth Congress in 1847, but the House decided that neither was entitled to the seat; declined a renomination for the vacancy thus created; member of the State senate 1852–1855; retired from public life; moved to Orange, N. J., where he died September 7, 1870; interment in Trinity Cemetery, One Hundred and Fifty-fifth Street and Broadway, New York City, N. Y.

MONROE, James, a Representative from Ohio; born in Plainfield, Windham County, Conn., July 18, 1821; attended the common schools and Plainfield Academy; was graduated from Oberlin (Ohio) College in 1846; pursued a postgraduate course in theology; professor in Oberlin College 1849–1862; member of the State House of Representatives of Ohio 1856–1859; served in the State senate 1860–1862; chosen president pro tempore in 1861 and 1862; resigned his seat in the senate in October 1862 to accept the position of United States consul to Rio de Janeiro and served from 1863 to 1869; served for several months in 1869 as Chargé d'Affaires ad interim to Brazil; elected as a Republican to the Forty-second and to the four succeeding Congresses (March 4, 1871–March 3, 1881); was not a candidate for renomination; professor in Oberlin College 1883–1896; died in Oberlin, Ohio, July 6, 1898; interment in Westwood Cemetery.

MONRONEY, Almer Stillwell Mike, a Representative and a Senator from Oklahoma; born in Oklahoma City, Okla., March 2, 1902; attended the public schools and was graduated from the University of Oklahoma at Norman in 1924; reporter and political writer for the Oklahoma News 1924–1928; in 1928 became president of a retail furniture store; elected as a Democrat to the Seventy-sixth and to the five succeeding Congresses (January 3, 1939–January 3, 1951); was not a candidate for renomination in 1950; winner of Collier's Award for Distinguished Congressional Service in 1945; elected to the United States Senate in 1950 for the term commencing January 3, 1951, and reelected in 1956 for the term ending January 3, 1963.

MONTAGUE, Andrew Jackson, a Representative from Virginia; born near Lynchburg, Campbell County, Va., October 3, 1862; attended public and private schools; was graduated from Richmond (Va.) College in 1882 and from the law department of the University of Virginia at Charlottesville in 1885; was admitted to the bar in 1885 and commenced practice in Danville, Va., on October 1 of the same year; appointed by President Cleveland as United States attorney for the western district of Virginia in 1893 and served until 1898; attorney general of Virginia 1898–1902; Governor of Virginia 1902–1906; delegate at large to the Democratic National Convention at St. Louis in 1904; unsuccessful candidate for nomination as United States Senator in 1905; American delegate to the Third Conference of American Republics at Rio de Janeiro in 1906; dean of Richmond College Law School 1906–1909; resumed the practice of law in Richmond in 1909; delegate to the Third International Conference on Maritime Law at Brussels in 1909 and 1910; trustee of Carnegie Institute, Washington, D. C., and Carnegie Endowment for International Peace in 1910, being vice president of the endowment, member of the executive committee 1911–1935, assistant treasurer 1917–1923, and treasurer 1923–1929; elected as a Democrat to the Sixty-third and to the twelve succeeding Congresses and served from March 4, 1913, until his death; president of the American Society for Judicial Settlement of International Disputes in 1917; president of the American Peace Society 1920–1924; one of the managers appointed by the House of Representatives in 1926 to conduct the impeachment proceedings against George W. English, judge of the United States District Court for the Eastern District of Illinois; president of the American group of the Interparliamentary Union 1930–1935 and participated in its sessions at Stockholm, Vienna, Copenhagen, Berne, Washington, Paris, and Berlin; member of the council and executive committee of the American Institute of Law; died at his country home in Urbanna, Middlesex County, Va., January 24, 1937; interment in Christ Church Episcopal Cemetery, near Urbanna, Va.

MONTET, Numa Francois, a Representative from Louisiana; born in Thibodaux, La Fourche Parish, La., September 17, 1892; attended the common schools and Louisiana State Normal College at Natchitoches; was graduated from the law department of Tulane University, New Orleans, La., in 1913; was admitted to the bar the same year and commenced practice in Franklin, La.; served as secretary-treasurer of the city of Thibodaux in 1914 and as city attorney in 1915; member of the State house of representatives 1916–1920; unsuccessful candidate for attorney general of Louisiana in 1924; delegate to the Democratic National Conventions in 1924 and 1932; acting prosecuting attorney for the twentieth judicial district of Louisiana in 1925; general counsel for State highway commission in 1928 and 1929; elected as a Democrat to the Seventy-first Congress to fill the vacancy caused by the death of Whitmell P. Martin; reelected to the Seventy-second, Seventy-third, and Seventy-fourth Congresses and served from August 6, 1929, to January 3, 1937; unsuccessful candidate for renomination in 1936; resumed the practice of law in Thibodaux, La., where he now resides.

MONTGOMERY, Alexander Brooks, a Representative from Kentucky; born near Tip Top, Hardin County, Ky., December 11, 1837; attended the common and private schools; was graduated from Georgetown (Ky.) College in 1859 and from the Louisville Law School in 1861; engaged in agricultural pursuits in Hardin County, Ky., 1861-1870; was admitted to the bar and commenced the practice of law in Elizabethtown, Hardin County, Ky., in 1870; county judge of Hardin County, Ky., 1870-1874; member of the State senate 1877-1881; elected as a Democrat to the Fiftieth and to the three succeeding Congresses (March 4, 1887-March 3, 1895); unsuccessful candidate for reelection to the Fifty-fourth Congress; member of the Dawes Indian Commission, appointed under act of Congress to treat with the Five Civilized Tribes, 1895-1898; resumed the practice of law at Elizabethtown, Ky., where he died December 27, 1910; interment in City Cemetery.

MONTGOMERY, Daniel, Jr., a Representative from Pennsylvania; born in Londonderry, Chester County, Pa., October 30, 1765; moved to Danville, Pa.; chief promoter of turnpike roads in the section around Danville; elected as a member of the State house of representatives in 1800; lieutenant colonel of the Eighty-first Pennsylvania Militia in 1805; appointed major general of the Ninth Division of Militia on July 27, 1809; elected as a Democrat to the Tenth Congress (March 4, 1807-March 3, 1809); appointed canal commissioner in 1828; died in Danville, Montour County, Pa., December 30, 1831.

MONTGOMERY, John, a Delegate from Pennsylvania; elected as a Delegate to the Continental Congress November 12, 1782, and took his seat December 18, 1782; reelected a Delegate and took his seat May 8, 1783; again elected to the Continental Congress and served in the 1784 session.

MONTGOMERY, John, a Representative from Maryland; born in Carlisle, Cumberland County, Pa., in 1764; pursued classical studies; studied law; was admitted to the bar in 1791 and commenced practice in Harford County, Md.; member of the State house of delegates 1793-1798; State's attorney 1793-1796; elected as a Democrat to the Tenth, Eleventh, and Twelfth Congresses and served from March 4, 1807, until April 29, 1811, when he resigned; moved to Baltimore, Md., in 1811; appointed attorney general of Maryland on April 29, 1811, and served until February 11, 1818; appointed captain of the Baltimore Union Artillery on March 25, 1814, and took part in the Battle of North Point; again a member of the State house of delegates in 1819; mayor of Baltimore 1820-1826; died in Baltimore, Md., July 17, 1828; interment in the cemetery of the Methodist Episcopal Church (now abandoned) at Bel Air, Harford County, Md.

MONTGOMERY, John Gallagher, a Representative from Pennsylvania; born in Northumberland, Northumberland County, Pa., June 27, 1805; studied under a private tutor; was graduated from Washington (now Washington and Jefferson) College, Washington, Pa., in 1824; studied law; was admitted to the bar in 1827 and commenced practice in Danville, Montour County, Pa.; member of the State house of representatives in 1855; elected as a Democrat to the Thirty-fifth Congress and served from March 4, 1857, until his death, which occurred before the assembling of Congress, in Danville, Pa., April 24, 1857, presumably from the effects of poison secretly placed in food served at a banquet in Washington, D. C., during the inauguration of President Buchanan; interment in Episcopal Cemetery.

MONTGOMERY, Joseph, a Delegate from Pennsylvania; born in Paxtang, Dauphin County, Pa., September 23, 1733; pursued classical studies, and was graduated from Princeton College in 1755; studied for the ministry; licensed to preach by the presbytery of Philadelphia in 1759 and ordained as a minister in 1761; held several pastorates 1761-1777; commissioned a chaplain in Col. Smallwood's Maryland Regiment of the Continental Army and served from 1777 until 1780; delegate to the general assembly of Pennsylvania 1780-1782; Member of the Continental Congress 1780-1782; recorder of deeds and register of wills for Dauphin County 1785-1794; justice of the court of common pleas 1786-1794; died in Harrisburg, Pa., on October 14, 1794; interment in the Lutheran Church Cemetery.

MONTGOMERY, Samuel James, a Representative from Oklahoma; born in Buffalo, Ky., December 1, 1896; moved to Oklahoma in 1902 with his parents, who settled in Bartlesville; attended the public schools; studied law at the University of Oklahoma at Norman; was admitted to the bar in 1919 and commenced practice in Bartlesville; during the First World War enlisted as a private in the Sixth Regiment, United States Marine Corps, on July 18, 1917, at Parris Island, S. C., and served in the Second Division, American Expeditionary Forces, until May 19, 1919, when he was honorably discharged at Quantico, Va.; was wounded three times and cited in general orders for "gallantry in action," and received the Croix de Guerre from the Republic of France; elected as a Republican to the Sixty-ninth Congress (March 4, 1925-March 3, 1927); unsuccessful candidate for reelection in 1926 to the Seventieth Congress; practiced law in Tulsa and later in Oklahoma City; died in Oklahoma City, Okla., June 4, 1957; interment in Memorial Park Cemetery, Bartlesville, Okla.

MONTGOMERY, Thomas, a Representative from Kentucky; born in what is now Nelson County, Va., in 1779; received a thorough English training; studied law; was admitted to the bar and commenced practice in Stanford, Lincoln County, Ky.; judge of the circuit court of Lincoln County; member of the State house of representatives in 1811; elected as a Democrat to the Thirteenth Congress (March 4, 1813-March 3, 1815); unsuccessful candidate for reelection to the Fourteenth Congress; again elected to the Sixteenth Congress to fill the vacancy caused by the resignation of Tunstall Quarles; reelected to the Seventeenth Congress and served from August 1, 1820, to March 3, 1823; died in Stanford, Ky., April 2, 1828.

MONTGOMERY, William, a Delegate and a Representative from Pennsylvania; born in Londonderry Township, Chester County, Pa., August 3, 1736; served in the Revolutionary War as colonel of the Fourth Battalion of Chester County Militia; after the Battle of Long Island his regiment became known as the Flying Camp; delegate to the provincial conventions of 1775 and 1776; moved to Northumberland County in 1776; elected in 1779 to the State assembly from Northumberland County and several times reelected; sent to Wyoming, Pa., in 1783 to settle boundary disputes which threatened the peace and safety of the community; in 1784 was elected a Delegate to the Continental Congress and served until February 7, 1785, when he resigned to accept appointment as judge of Northumberland and Luzerne Counties in 1785; appointed deputy surveyor of Chester County on April 18, 1787; member of the first Pennsylvania State Senate in 1790; appointed justice of the peace for Northumberland County in 1791; elected to the Third Congress (March 4, 1793-March 3, 1795); commissioned major general of Pennsylvania Militia in 1793 and served for fourteen years; associate judge of Northumberland County 1801-1813; upon the establishment of a post office at Danville, he was made its first postmaster and served from April 1, 1801, to April 1, 1803; elected presidential elector on the Democratic ticket of Madison and Clinton in 1808; died in Danville, Montour County, Pa., May 1, 1816.

MONTGOMERY, William, a Representative from North Carolina; born in Guilford County, N. C., December 29, 1789; studied medicine and practiced his profession in Albrights, Orange County, N. C.; member of the State senate 1824–1827 and 1829–1834; elected as a Democrat to the Twenty-fourth, Twenty-fifth, and Twenty-sixth Congresses (March 4, 1835–March 3, 1841); declined to be a candidate for renomination in 1840; died in Albrights, N. C., November 27, 1844.

MONTGOMERY, William, a Representative from Pennsylvania; born in Canton Township, Washington County, Pa., April 11, 1818; pursued classical studies, and was graduated from Washington (now Washington and Jefferson) College, Washington, Pa., in 1839; studied law; was admitted to the bar in 1841 and commenced practice in Washington, Pa.; district attorney in 1845; unsuccessful candidate for election in 1854 to the Thirty-fourth Congress; elected as a Democrat to the Thirty-fifth and Thirty-sixth Congresses (March 4, 1857–March 3, 1861); was not a candidate for renomination in 1860; resumed the practice of law; unsuccessful candidate for election in 1866 to the Fortieth Congress; died in Washington, Pa., April 28, 1870; interment in Washington Cemetery.

MONTOYA, Joseph Manuel, a Representative from New Mexico; born in Penablanca, Sandoval County, N. Mex., September 24, 1915; student at Regis College, Denver, Colo., in 1931, 1933, and 1934; graduated from Georgetown University Law School, Washington, D. C., in 1938; was admitted to the bar in 1939 and commenced the practice of law in Santa Fe, N. Mex.; elected to the State house of representatives in 1936 while still in law school; reelected in 1938 and was majority floor leader in 1939 and 1940; member of State senate 1940–1946 and served as majority whip; Lieutenant Governor 1947–1951; again State senator in 1953 and 1954; Lieutenant Governor from 1955 until elected to Congress; elected as a Democrat to the Eighty-fifth Congress to fill the vacancy caused by the death of Antonio M. Fernandez; reelected to the Eighty-sixth Congress and served from April 9, 1957, to January 3, 1961. *Reelected to the Eighty-seventh Congress.*

MONTOYA, Nestor, a Representative from New Mexico; born in Old Albuquerque, Bernalillo County, N. Mex., April 14, 1862; attended the common schools, and was graduated from St. Michael's College, Santa Fe, N. Mex., in 1881; began newspaper work in 1889; owned and edited the Spanish paper called "La Bandera Americana" (The American Flag); member of the Territorial house of representatives 1892–1903 and served as speaker in the latter year; member of the Territorial senate in 1905 and 1906; president of the State press association 1908–1923; delegate to the convention that drafted and adopted the State constitution of New Mexico in 1910; regent of the University of New Mexico 1916–1919; member of the Council of National Defense 1917–1919; chairman of the Bernalillo County draft board during the first World War; clerk of Bernalillo County in 1919 and 1920; elected as a Republican to the Sixty-seventh Congress and served from March 4, 1921, until his death in Washington, D. C., January 13, 1923; interment in Santa Barbara Cemetery, Albuquerque, N. Mex.

MOODY, Arthur Edson Blair, a Senator from Michigan; born in New Haven, Conn., February 13, 1902; attended the public schools in Providence, R. I.; was graduated from Brown University, Providence, R. I., in 1922; instructor in history, Moses Brown Preparatory School, Providence, R. I., in 1922 and 1923; sports writer and reporter Detroit (Mich.) News 1923–1933, and Washington, D. C., correspondent and columnist 1933–1951; correspondent for Barren's Financial Weekly 1934–1948 and also wrote extensively for the North American Newspaper Alliance and the Bell Syndicate; combat war correspondent in 1944, covering the war on Anzio Beachhead, Cassino, and other sections of Italy, Africa, the British Isles, the Middle East, and Iran; moderated a radio and television program "Meet Your Congress" 1946–1952; foreign correspondent in 1947 and 1948; appointed as a Democrat to the United States Senate to fill the vacancy caused by the death of Arthur H. Vandenberg, and served from April 23, 1951, to November 4, 1952; unsuccessful candidate for election to fill the vacancy and also for election to the full term; president and chairman of the board of the Michigan Rotary Press, Inc., of Detroit; partner in the Independent Newspaper Co. of Detroit, and chairman of the board of the Leader Newspaper, Inc., Plymouth, Mich.; died in Ann Arbor, Mich., while campaigning for the Democratic nomination for United States Senator, July 20, 1954; interment in Woodlawn Cemetery, Detroit, Mich.

MOODY, Gideon Curtis, a Senator from South Dakota; born in Cortland, Cortland County, N. Y., October 16, 1832; attended the common schools and pursued an academic course; studied law in Syracuse, N. Y.; moved to Indiana in 1852 and was admitted to the bar in 1853; appointed prosecuting attorney for Floyd County in 1854; member of the House of Representatives of Indiana in 1861; during the Civil War entered the Union Army as captain in the Ninth Regiment, Indiana Volunteer Infantry, in April 1861 and served as captain, lieutenant colonel, and colonel; appointed in August 1861 captain in the Nineteenth Regiment, United States Infantry, and served until his resignation in March 1864; moved to the Territory of Dakota in May 1864; member of the house of representatives of the Territory of Dakota 1867–1868, 1868–1869, and 1874–1875, and served as speaker in 1868–1869 and 1874–1875; delegate to the Republican National Conventions at Chicago in 1868 and 1888; appointed associate justice of the supreme court of the Territory of Dakota in September 1878 and served until April 1, 1883; member of the constitutional conventions of South Dakota in 1883 and 1885; upon the admission of South Dakota as a State into the Union was elected as a Republican to the United States Senate and served from November 2, 1889, to March 3, 1891; unsuccessful candidate for reelection; died in Los Angeles, Calif., March 17, 1904; interment in Rosedale Cemetery.

MOODY, James Montraville, a Representative from North Carolina; born near what is now Robbinsville, Graham (then Cherokee) County, N. C., February 12, 1858; moved with his parents to Haywood County; attended the common schools and Waynesville Academy, also Candler College, Buncombe County, N. C.; studied law; was admitted to the bar in 1881 and commenced practice in Waynesville, Haywood County, N. C.; delegate to the Republican State conventions in 1888, 1892, 1896, and 1900; prosecuting attorney of the twelfth judicial district of North Carolina 1886–1900; member of the State senate 1894–1896; delegate to the Republican National Convention at St. Louis in 1896 and at Philadelphia in 1900; during the Spanish-American War served as major and chief commissary of United States Volunteers on the staff of Maj. Gen. J. Warren Keifer; elected as a Republican to the Fifty-seventh Congress and served from March 4, 1901, until his death in Waynesville, N. C., February 5, 1903; interment in Green Hill Cemetery.

MOODY, Malcolm Adelbert, a Representative from Oregon; born in Linn County, near the present town of Brownsville, Oreg., November 30, 1854; moved with his parents to Illinois the next year and to The Dalles, Wasco County, Oreg., in 1862; attended the public schools and the University of California at Berkeley; engaged in mercantile pursuits at The Dalles, Oreg.; cashier of The Dalles National Bank; member of the city council 1885–1889; elected mayor of The Dalles in 1889 and served two terms; member of the Republican State central and congressional committees from 1888 to 1898; elected as a Republican to the Fifty-sixth and Fifty-seventh Congresses (March 4, 1899–March 3, 1903); was not a candidate for renomination in 1902 to the Fifty-eighth Congress; resumed the mercantile business at The Dalles, Oreg.; died in Portland, Oreg., on March 19, 1925; interment in Odd Fellows Cemetery, The Dalles, Oreg.

MOODY, William Henry, a Representative from Massachusetts; born in Newbury, Mass., December 23, 1853; was graduated from Phillips Academy, Andover, Mass., in 1872 and from Harvard University in 1876; studied law; was admitted to the bar in 1878 and practiced in Haverhill, Mass.; city solicitor 1888–1890; district attorney for the eastern district of Massachusetts 1890–1895; elected as a Republican to the Fifty-fourth Congress to fill the vacancy caused by the death of William Cogswell; reelected to the Fifty-fifth, Fifty-sixth, and Fifty-seventh Congresses and served from November 5, 1895, until his resignation May 1, 1902; appointed Secretary of the Navy in the Cabinet of President Theodore Roosevelt and served from May 1, 1902, until July 1, 1904; Attorney General of the United States July 1, 1904, to December 12, 1906; appointed by President Theodore Roosevelt as an Associate Justice of the Supreme Court of the United States December 3, 1906, and served from December 16, 1906, until his retirement by special act of Congress approved June 23, 1910, on account of ill health; died in Haverhill, Mass., July 2, 1917; interment in Byfield Cemetery, Georgetown, Mass.

MOON, John Austin, a Representative from Tennessee; born near Charlottesville, Albemarle County, Va., April 22, 1855; moved with his parents to Bristol, Va., in 1857 and then to Chattanooga, Tenn., in 1870; attended private and public schools and King College, Bristol, Tenn.; studied law; was admitted to the bar in March 1874 and commenced practice in Chattanooga, Tenn.; city attorney of Chattanooga in 1881 and 1882; member of the State Democratic executive committee in 1888; was commissioned in May 1889 as special circuit judge, twice reappointed, and held the office until January 3, 1891; appointed regular judge for the fourth circuit and served until August 1892; elected circuit judge in 1892; reelected in 1894 for a term of eight years but resigned when elected to Congress; elected as a Democrat to the Fifty-fifth and to the eleven succeeding Congresses (March 4, 1897–March 3, 1921); delegate to the Democratic National Convention at Kansas City in 1900; was renominated for Congress in 1921, but before election was taken ill and died in Chattanooga, Tenn., June 26, 1921; interment in Forest Hill Cemetery.

MOON, John Wesley, a Representative from Michigan; born near Ypsilanti, Wayne County, Mich., January 18, 1836; attended the common schools; moved to northern Michigan in 1854 and engaged in the lumber business; settled in Muskegon, Muskegon County, Mich., in 1856 and engaged in the manufacture of lumber and in banking; held the offices of supervisor, township treasurer, and president of the village; elected to the State senate in 1884 and reelected in 1886; elected president of the Muskegon Savings Bank in 1887; member of the board of education of Muskegon in 1891; elected as a Republican to the Fifty-third Congress (March 4, 1893–March 3, 1895); was not a candidate for renomination in 1894; resumed former business activities; died in Muskegon, Mich., April 5, 1898; interment in Evergreen Cemetery.

MOON, Reuben Osborne, a Representative from Pennsylvania; born in Jobstown, Burlington County, N. J., July 22, 1847; attended the common schools, and was graduated from the National School of Oratory, in Philadelphia, in 1874; professor in the National School of Oratory; engaged in lecturing; studied law; was admitted to the bar in 1884 and commenced practice in Philadelphia; one of the founders and president of the Columbia Club; a member of the Lawyers' Club and of the Historical Society of Pennsylvania; elected as a Republican to the Fifty-eighth Congress to fill the vacancy caused by the death of Robert H. Foerderer; reelected to the Fifty-ninth and to the three succeeding Congresses and served from November 2, 1903, to March 3, 1913; unsuccessful candidate for renomination in 1912; continued the practice of law until his death in Philadelphia, Pa., on October 25, 1919; interment in West Laurel Hill Cemetery.

MOONEY, Charles Anthony, a Representative from Ohio; born in St. Marys, Auglaize County, Ohio, January 5, 1879; attended the public and Jesuit schools; was graduated from St. Marys High School in 1895; engaged in the life insurance business at St. Marys; moved to Cleveland, Ohio, in 1910 and continued the life insurance business; member of the State senate 1915–1919; elected as a Democrat to the Sixty-sixth Congress (March 4, 1919–March 3, 1921); unsuccessful candidate for reelection in 1920 to the Sixty-seventh Congress; delegate to the Democratic National Conventions in 1920, 1924, and 1928; elected to the Sixty-eighth and to the four succeeding Congresses and served from March 4, 1923, until his death in Cleveland, Ohio, on May 29, 1931; interment in Gethsemane Cemetery, St. Marys, Ohio.

MOONEY, William Crittenden, a Representative from Ohio; born in Beallsville, Monroe County, Ohio, June 15, 1855; attended the public schools and Ohio Wesleyan College at Delaware; engaged in banking and filled various positions, including that of president of the Monroe Bank of Woodsfield, Ohio; was a director of many manufacturing, insurance, and oil companies; elected as a Republican to the Sixty-fourth Congress (March 4, 1915–March 3, 1917); unsuccessful candidate for reelection in 1916 to the Sixty-fifth Congress; again engaged in banking; died in New York City, while on a visit to regain his health, July 24, 1918; interment in Oaklawn Cemetery, Woodsfield, Monroe County, Ohio.

MOOR, Wyman Bradbury Seavy, a Senator from Maine; born in Waterville, Kennebec County, Maine, November 11, 1811; attended the town school; prepared for college at China Academy, and was graduated from Waterville College; taught school for one year in St. Stephen's, New Brunswick, and then returned to his native town to study law; attended Dane Law School, Cambridge, Mass.; was admitted to the bar in 1835 and commenced practice in Waterville, Maine; member of the State house of representatives in 1839; attorney general of Maine 1844–1848; moved to Bangor, Maine, in 1847 and continued the practice of his profession; appointed as a Democrat to the United States Senate to fill the vacancy caused by the death of John Fairfield and served from January 5, 1848, to June 7, 1848, when a successor was elected; was one of the victims who was taken ill from the effects of poison secretly placed in food served at a banquet in Washington, D. C., in March 1857 during the inauguration of President Buchanan; resumed the practice of law in Bangor; returned to Waterville, Maine, in 1852 and continued his law practice; superintendent of the construction of a railroad from Waterville to Bangor; appointed by President Buchanan as consul general to the British North American Provinces and served from 1859 to 1861; returned to Waterville in 1861 and resumed the practice of law; purchased an estate near Lynchburg, Va., in 1868 and engaged in the operation of an iron furnace; died in Lynchburg, Va., March 10, 1869; interment in Pine Grove Cemetery, Waterville, Maine.

MOORE, Allen Francis, a Representative from Illinois; was born in St. Charles, Kane County, Ill., September 30, 1869; moved to Piatt County in 1870 with his parents, who settled in Monticello; attended the common schools; was graduated from the Monticello High School in 1886 and from Lombard College, Galesburg, Knox County, Ill., in 1889; engaged in the manufacture of proprietary medicines and later in banking; trustee of the University of Illinois 1908–1914; elected as a Republican to the Sixty-seventh and Sixty-eighth Congresses (March 4, 1921–March 3, 1925); declined to be a candidate for reelection in 1924 to the Sixty-ninth Congress; member of the Republican National Committee in 1925; resumed his former business pursuits in Monticello, Ill.; moved to San Antonio, Tex., in 1939 and engaged in oil development until his death there August 18, 1945; interment in Monticello Cemetery, Monticello, Ill.

MOORE, Andrew (father of Samuel McDowell Moore), a Representative and a Senator from Virginia; born at "Cannicello," near Fairfield, Rockbridge (formerly Augusta) County, Va., in 1752; attended Augusta Academy (now Washington and Lee University), Lexington, Va.; studied law; was admitted to the bar in 1774 and practiced; served in the Revolutionary War; lieutenant under General Gates at the Battle of Saratoga and was present at the surrender of Burgoyne; resigned in 1779 with the rank of captain and was commissioned brigadier general of Virginia Militia; major general in 1808; member of the State house of delegates 1780–1783 and 1785–1788; delegate to the Virginia convention that ratified the Federal Constitution in 1788; elected to the First and to the three succeeding Congresses (March 4, 1789–March 3, 1797); served in the State senate in 1800 and 1801; successfully contested the election of Thomas Lewis to the Eighth Congress and served from March 5 to August 11, 1804, when he was appointed to the United States Senate to fill the vacancy in the term beginning March 4, 1799, caused by the resignation of Wilson C. Nicholas; while holding the office of Senator-designate was elected on December 4, 1804, to fill the vacancy in the term beginning March 4, 1803, caused by the resignation of Abraham B. Venable and served successively in the two classes from August 11, 1804, until March 3, 1809; resumed the practice of law; again a member of the State house of delegates in 1799 and 1800; died in Lexington, Va., April 14, 1821; interment in Lexington Cemetery.

MOORE, Arch Alfred, Jr., a Representative from West Virginia; born in Moundsville, Marshall County, W. Va., April 16, 1923; educated in the public schools of Marshall County and studied at Lafayette College, Easton, Pa., in 1943; graduated from West Virginia University in 1948 and from its law school in 1951; admitted to the bar the same year and commenced the practice of law in Moundsville, W. Va.; in World War II served from May 15, 1943, to April 1, 1946, as a sergeant with the Three Hundred and Twenty-fifth Infantry Regiment with one year and a half in the European Theater; awarded the Purple Heart Medal; member of the State house of delegates 1953–1955; elected as a Republican to the Eighty-fifth and Eighty-sixth Congresses (January 3, 1957–January 3, 1961). *Reelected to the Eighty-seventh Congress.*

MOORE, Arthur Harry, a Senator from New Jersey; born in Jersey City, N. J., July 3, 1879; attended the public schools and Cooper Union College, New York City, N. Y.; was graduated from the New Jersey Law School at Newark in 1924; was admitted

to the bar in 1922 and commenced practice in Jersey City, N. J.; served on the faculty of John Marshall College of Law, Jersey City, N. J., in 1928 and on the faculty of the New Jersey Law School 1930–1935; secretary to the mayor of Jersey City 1908–1911; city collector 1911–1913; commissioner of Jersey City 1913–1925; Governor of New Jersey 1926–1928, 1932–1934, and 1938–1940; the A. Harry Moore School for Crippled Children was built and named by Jersey City in recognition for his services for physically handicapped children; elected as a Democrat to the United States Senate and served from January 3, 1935, to January 17, 1938, when he resigned, having been elected Governor of New Jersey for the third time; after his term as Governor resumed the practice of law in Jersey City, N. J.; died from a heart attack while driving his car along State Highway 29 in Branchburg Township, Somerset County, N. J., November 18, 1952; interment in New York Bay Cemetery, Jersey City, N. J.

MOORE, Charles Ellis, a Representative from Ohio; born near Middlebourne, Guernsey County, Ohio, on January 3, 1884; attended the common schools and Mount Union College, Alliance, Ohio; taught school in Oxford Township, Ohio; was graduated from Muskingum College, New Concord, Ohio, in 1907 and from the law department of Ohio State University at Columbus in 1910; was admitted to the bar in 1910 and commenced practice in Cambridge, Guernsey County, Ohio; prosecuting attorney of Guernsey County 1914–1918; elected as a Republican to the Sixty-sixth and to the six succeeding Congresses (March 4, 1919–March 3, 1933); unsuccessful candidate for reelection in 1932 to the Seventy-third Congress; one of the managers appointed by the House of Representatives in 1926 to conduct the impeachment proceedings against George W. English, judge of the United States District Court for the Eastern District of Illinois; resumed the practice of law in Cambridge, Ohio; also engaged in the banking business; died in Cambridge, Guernsey County, Ohio, April 2, 1941; interment in Northwood Cemetery.

MOORE, Edward Hall, a Senator from Oklahoma; born on a farm near Maryville, Nodaway County, Mo., November 19, 1871; attended the public schools and Chillicothe (Mo.) Normal School; taught school in Nodaway, Atchinson, and Jackson Counties, Mo.; was graduated from the Kansas City School of Law in 1900; was admitted to the bar in 1901 and began practice in Maryville, Mo.; moved shortly thereafter to Okmulgee, Indian Territory, Okla., and practiced law until 1919; oil producer, farmer, and cattle raiser 1919–1942; elected as a Republican to the United States Senate in 1942 for the term commencing January 3, 1943, and ending January 3, 1949; was not a candidate for renomination in 1948; retired from public life and political activities; died in Tulsa, Okla., September 2, 1950; interment in Okmulgee Cemetery, Okmulgee, Okla.

MOORE, Eliakim Hastings, a Representative from Ohio; born in Boylston, Worcester County, Mass., June 19, 1812; moved with his parents to Marietta and thence to Athens County, Ohio, in 1817; attended the common schools; educated himself at night as a civil engineer; county surveyor 1836–1846; auditor for Athens County 1846–1860; collector of internal revenue for the Marietta-Athens district of Ohio 1862–1866; organized the First National Bank of Athens in 1863 and was connected therewith as president and director until about 1895; elected as a Republican to the Forty-first Congress (March 4, 1869–March 3, 1871); was not a candidate for renomination in 1870; engaged in railroad enterprises in Athens, Athens County, Ohio; trustee of Ohio University at Athens; died in Athens April 4, 1900; interment in West Union Street Cemetery.

MOORE, Ely, a Representative from New York; born near Belvidere, Warren County, N. J., July 4, 1798; attended the public schools; moved to New York City; studied medicine, but did not engage in extensive practice; became a printer and subsequently became editor of the National Trades Union, a labor paper in New York City; elected as a Democrat to the Twenty-fourth and Twenty-fifth Congresses (March 4, 1835–March 3, 1839); political editor of the New York Evening Post in 1838 and 1839; president of the board of trade and surveyor of the port of New York City 1839–1845; appointed by President Polk United States marshal for the southern district of New York in 1845; became owner and editor of the Warren Journal of Belvidere, N. J.; declined the appointment as Minister to England, and was tendered the appointment of Governor of the Territory of Kansas in 1852, but declined; appointed agent for the Miami and other tribes of Indians in Kansas in 1853; appointed register of the United States land office in Lecompton, Kans., in 1855 and served until 1860; died in Lecompton, Douglas County, Kans., January 27, 1861; interment on his farm near Lecompton.

MOORE, Gabriel, a Representative and a Senator from Alabama; born in Stokes County, N. C., in 1785; pursued an academic course and was graduated from the University of North Carolina at Chapel Hill in 1810; studied law; was admitted to the bar in 1810 and commenced practice in Huntsville, Ala.; member of the Territorial house of representatives and served as speaker in 1817; delegate to the State constitutional convention in 1819; member of the State senate in 1821 and served as president; elected to the Seventeenth and to the three succeeding Congresses (March 4, 1821–March 3, 1829); was not a candidate for renomination in 1828; Governor of Alabama 1829–1831; elected to the United States Senate and served from March 4, 1831, to March 3, 1837; unsuccessful candidate for election in 1836 to the Twenty-fifth Congress; moved to Caddo, Tex., in 1843, where he died June 9, 1845.

MOORE, Heman Allen, a Representative from Ohio; born in Plainfield, Washington County, Vt., August 27, 1809; pursued an academic course; studied law in Rochester, N. Y.; was admitted to the bar and commenced practice in Columbus, Ohio; elected as a Democrat to the Twenty-eighth Congress and served from March 4, 1843, until his death in Columbus, Ohio, April 3, 1844; interment in Green Lawn Cemetery.

MOORE, Henry Dunning, a Representative from Pennsylvania; born in Goshen, Orange County, N. Y., April 13, 1817; moved with his parents to New York City in 1828; attended the public schools; engaged in the tailoring business; moved to Philadelphia, Pa., in 1844 and engaged in the mahogany and marble business; elected as a Whig to the Thirty-first and Thirty-second Congresses (March 4, 1849–March 3, 1853); was not a candidate for reelection in 1852; unsuccessful candidate for mayor of Philadelphia in 1856; elected State treasurer during Governor Curtin's administration and served 1861–1863, 1864–1865; appointed collector of the port of Philadelphia, Pa., on March 30, 1869, and served until March 26, 1871, when he resigned; traveled in Europe and resided in St. Petersburg, Russia, 1870–1877; became associated with and managed the silver mines known as "The Daisy" in Big Evens Gulch near Leadville, Colo., from 1885 until his death there on August 11, 1887; interment in Monument Cemetery, Philadelphia, Pa.

MOORE, Horace Ladd, a Representative from Kansas; born in Mantua, Portage County, Ohio, February 25, 1837; attended the common schools and the Western Reserve Eclectic Institute, Hiram, Ohio; moved to Lawrence, Douglas County, Kans., in 1858; studied law and one month after his admission to the bar enlisted in the Union Army in the Second Regiment, Kansas Volunteer Infantry, on May 14, 1861, and served continuously until June 30, 1865, when he was mustered out of the service as lieutenant colonel of the Fourth Regiment, Arkansas Volunteer Cavalry; as major of the Eighteenth and colonel of the Nineteenth Regiments of Kansas Cavalry served against the Indians on the Plains in 1867 and 1868; again engaged in the practice of law and later, from 1886 to 1892, engaged in the wholesale grocery business in Trinidad, Colo.; treasurer of Douglas County, Kans., in 1886 and 1887; successfully contested as a Democrat the election of Edward H. Funston to the Fifty-third Congress and served from August 2, 1894, until March 3, 1895; unsuccessful candidate for reelection in 1894 to the Fifty-fourth Congress; vice president of a national bank in Lawrence, Kans., until his death on May 1, 1914; interment in Oak Hill Cemetery.

MOORE, Jesse Hale, a Representative from Illinois; born near Lebanon, St. Clair County, Ill., April 22, 1817; was graduated from McKendree College, Lebanon, Ill., in 1842; taught school in Nashville, Ill., 1842–1844; and at Georgetown, Ill., 1844–1848; studied for the ministry, and was ordained a Methodist minister in 1849; served in the Union Army during the Civil War; colonel of the One Hundred and Fifteenth Regiment, Illinois Volunteer Infantry, September 13, 1862; brevetted brigadier general of Volunteers May 15, 1865, "for meritorious services"; honorably mustered out June 11, 1865; presiding elder of the Decatur district of the Illinois conference in 1868 and resided in Decatur, Ill.; elected as a Republican to the Forty-first and Forty-second Congresses (March 4, 1869–March 3, 1873); unsuccessful candidate for renomination in 1872 to the Forty-third Congress; United States pension agent, Springfield, Ill., 1873–1877; served as pastor of Mechanicsburg (Ill.) Methodist Church; was appointed by President Arthur as United States consul at Callao, Peru, October 27, 1881, and served until his death there on July 11, 1883; interment in Callao, Peru; reinterment in Greenwood Cemetery, Decatur, Ill.

MOORE, John, a Representative from Louisiana; born in Berkeley County, Va. (now West Virginia), in 1788; pursued an academic course; moved to Franklin, La.; member of the State house of representatives 1825–1834; elected as a Whig to the Twenty-sixth Congress to fill the vacancy caused by the resignation of Rice Garland; reelected to the Twenty-seventh Congress and served from December 17, 1840, to March 3, 1843; moved to New Iberia, La.; elected to the Thirty-second Congress (March 4, 1851–March 3, 1853); presidential elector on the Whig ticket of Taylor and Fillmore in 1848; delegate to the State secession convention in 1861; died in Franklin, La., June 17, 1867; interment on his estate, "The Shadows," near New Iberia, Iberia Parish, La.

MOORE, John Matthew, a Representative from Texas; born on a farm near Richmond, Fort Bend County, Tex., November 18, 1862; attended the common schools and the Agricultural and Mechanical College, College Station, Tex.; engaged in mercantile pursuits, banking, stock raising, and farming; member of the State house of representatives 1896–1898; declined to be a candidate for renomination; delegate to the Democratic National Convention at Kansas City in 1900 and at St. Louis in 1916; elected as a Democrat to the Fifty-ninth Congress to fill the vacancy caused by the death of John M. Pinckney; reelected to the Sixtieth, Sixty-first, and Sixty-second Congresses and served from June 6, 1905, to March 3, 1913; was not a candidate for renomination in 1912; continued agricultural pursuits and stock raising near Richmond, Fort Bend County, Tex., until his death February 3, 1940; interment in Morton Cemetery.

MOORE, John William, a Representative from Kentucky; born in Morgantown, Butler County, Ky., June 9, 1877; attended the public schools, and completed a commercial course at Bryant and Stratton College at Louisville in 1897; became a clerk with the Morgantown Deposit Bank in 1898; engaged in the timber business 1899–1919; cashier for the Morgantown Deposit Bank 1920–1925; elected as a Democrat to the Sixty-ninth Congress to fill the vacancy caused by the death of Robert Y. Thomas, Jr.; reelected to the Seventieth Congress and served from November 3, 1925, to March 3, 1929; was an unsuccessful candidate for reelection in 1928 to the Seventy-first Congress, but was subsequently elected to the Seventy-first Congress to fill the vacancy caused by the death of Charles W. Roark; reelected to the Seventy-second Congress and served from June 1, 1929, to March 3, 1933; was not a candidate for renomination in 1932; resumed his former business pursuits; employed in the Federal Housing Administration at Washington, D. C., as an assistant comptroller 1935–1941; died in Washington, D. C., December 11, 1941; interment in Morgantown Cemetery, Morgantown, Ky.

MOORE, Joseph Hampton, a Representative from Pennsylvania; born in Woodbury, Gloucester County, N. J., March 8, 1864; attended the common schools; studied law; reporter on the Philadelphia Public Ledger and the Court Combination 1881–1894; chief clerk to the city treasurer of Philadelphia 1894–1897; secretary to the mayor in 1900; president of the Allied Republican Clubs of Philadelphia, of the Pennsylvania State League, and of the National League of Republican Clubs 1900–1906; city treasurer 1901–1903; appointed by President Theodore Roosevelt as the first Chief of the Bureau of Manufactures, Department of Commerce and Labor, in January 1905, but resigned after six months' service to become president of a Philadelphia trust company; president of the Atlantic Deeper Waterways Association 1907–1947; elected as a Republican to the Fifty-ninth Congress to fill the vacancy caused by the death of George A. Castor; reelected to the Sixtieth and to the six succeeding Congresses and served from November 6, 1906, to January 4, 1920, when he resigned to become mayor of Philadelphia; delegate to the Republican National Convention at Chicago in 1920; mayor of Philadelphia, Pa., 1920–1923; appointed by the State Department as a delegate to the International Navigation Congress at Cairo, Egypt, in 1926; again elected mayor of Philadelphia 1932–1935; died in Philadelphia, Pa., May 2, 1950; interment in West Laurel Hill Cemetery.

MOORE, Laban Theodore, a Representative from Kentucky; born in Wayne County, Va. (now West Virginia), near Louisa, Ky., January 13, 1829; attended Marshall Academy in Virginia and was graduated from Marietta College in Ohio; attended Transylvania Law College at Lexington; was admitted to the bar in 1849 and commenced practice in Louisa, Ky.; unsuccessful candidate for election 1857 to the State house of representatives; elected as a National American to the Thirty-sixth Congress (March 4, 1859–March 3, 1861); was not a candidate for renomination in 1860; during the Civil War raised and enlisted the Fourteenth Regiment, Kentucky Volunteer Infantry, of which he was elected colonel November 19, 1861, and resigned January 1, 1862; moved to Catlettsburg, where he resumed the practice of law; became a Democrat after the war; member of the State senate in 1881; member of the State constitutional convention in 1890 and 1891; died in Catlettsburg, Boyd County, Ky., November 9, 1892; interment in Ashland Cemetery, Ashland, Ky.

MOORE, Littleton Wilde, a Representative from Texas; born in Marion County, Ala., March 25, 1835; moved with his parents to Mississippi in 1836; was graduated from the University of Mississippi at Oxford in 1855; studied law and was admitted to the bar in 1857; moved to Texas in 1857 and commenced practice in Bastrop; served as captain in the Confederate Army throughout the Civil War; elected to the State constitutional convention in 1875; district judge 1876–1885; elected as a Democrat to the Fiftieth, Fifty-first, and Fifty-second Congresses (March 4, 1887–March 3, 1893); resumed the practice of his profession; appointed judge of the twenty-second judicial district in 1901 and served until his death in Lagrange, Fayette County, Tex., October 29, 1911; interment in the City Cemetery.

MOORE, Nicholas Ruxton, a Representative from Maryland; born near Baltimore Town, Baltimore County, Md., July 21, 1756; attended the common schools; member of Gist's Baltimore Independent Cadets, the first military company organized in Maryland for the Revolution; served throughout the greater part of the Revolutionary War, attaining the rank of captain; took an active part in the suppression of the Whisky Insurrection in 1794; member of the State house of delegates in 1801 and 1802; elected as a Democrat to the Eighth and to the three succeeding Congresses (March 4, 1803–March 3, 1811); unsuccessful candidate for reelection to the Twelfth Congress; appointed lieutenant colonel commandant of the sixth regimental cavalry district of Maryland on February 20, 1812; elected to the Thirteenth and Fourteenth Congresses and served from March 4, 1813, until his resignation in 1815 before the convening of the Fourteenth Congress; died in Baltimore, Md., October 7, 1816; interment in a private cemetery near Ruxton, Baltimore County, Md.

MOORE, Orren Cheney, a Representative from New Hampshire; born in New Hampton, Belknap County, N. H., August 10, 1839; attended the public schools; learned the trade of printer and became a journalist; member of the State house of representatives in 1863, 1864, 1875, 1876, and 1878; established the Nashua Daily Telegraph in 1869; member of the State tax commission in 1878; served in the State senate 1879–1881; again a member of the State house of representatives in 1887; chairman of the State railroad commission 1884–1888; elected as a Republican to the Fifty-first Congress (March 4, 1889–March 3, 1891); unsuccessful candidate for reelection in 1890 to the Fifty-second Congress; resumed former pursuits as editor and publisher; died in Nashua, Hillsborough County, N. H., on May 12, 1893; interment in the Woodlawn Cemetery.

MOORE, Oscar Fitzalleh, a Representative from Ohio; born in Lagrange, Jefferson County, Ohio, January 27, 1817; attended the public schools and Wellsburg Academy, and was graduated from Washington (now Washington and Jefferson) College, Washington, Pa., in 1836; studied law; was admitted to the bar in 1838 and commenced practice in Portsmouth, Ohio, in 1839; member of the State house of representatives in 1850 and 1851; member of the State senate in 1852 and 1853; elected as a Republican to the Thirty-fourth Congress (March 4, 1855–March 3, 1857); unsuccessful candidate for reelection in 1856 to the Thirty-fifth Congress; served as lieutenant colonel and later as colonel of the Thirty-third Regiment, Ohio Volunteer Infantry, during the Civil War; resumed the practice of his profession in Portsmouth, Ohio; died at Waverly, Ohio, June 24, 1885; interment in Greenlawn Cemetery, Portsmouth, Ohio.

MOORE, Paul John, a Representative from New Jersey; born in Newark, N. J., August 5, 1868; attended the public and parochial schools and St. Benedict's College, at Newark, N. J.; entered the fire department as fireman November 1, 1892, and was promoted to lieutenant August 10, 1899, to captain May 1,

1901, to battalion chief March 15, 1907, to deputy chief December 27, 1911, and to chief engineer in 1912; served until his retirement on August 1, 1924, when he engaged as a fire-fighting-equipment salesman; member of the International Association of Fire Engineers 1912–1924 and of the New Jersey State Fire Chiefs' Association 1912–1938; elected as a Democrat to the Seventieth Congress (March 4, 1927–March 3, 1929); unsuccessful candidate for reelection in 1928 to the Seventy-first Congress and for election in 1930 to the Seventy-second Congress; served as chairman of the Essex County Democratic committee in 1928 and 1929; again engaged as a fire-fighting-equipment salesman in Newark, N. J., until 1931, when he moved to Maplewood, N. J., and retired from active pursuits; died in Newark, N. J., January 10, 1938; interment in Holy Sepulchre Cemetery, East Orange, N. J.

MOORE, Robert (grandfather of Michael Daniel Harter), a Representative from Pennsylvania; born on a farm near Washington, Washington County, Pa., March 30, 1778; pursued an academic course; attended Washington (now Washington and Jefferson) College, Washington, Pa.; studied law; was admitted to the bar in 1802 and commenced practice in Beaver, Beaver County, Pa.; treasurer of Beaver County 1805–1811; served in the Pennsylvania State Militia in the War of 1812; elected to the Fifteenth and Sixteenth Congresses (March 4, 1817–March 3, 1821); was not a candidate for renomination; resumed the practice of law; member of the State house of representatives in 1830 and 1831; died in Beaver, Pa., January 14, 1831; interment in Beaver Cemetery.

MOORE, Robert Lee, a Representative from Georgia; born near Scarboro, Screven County, Ga., November 27, 1867; attended the common schools, Scarboro Academy, Georgia Military College, Milledgeville, Ga., and Moore's Business University, Atlanta, Ga.; was graduated from the law department of the University of Georgia at Athens in 1890; was admitted to the bar and commenced practice in Statesboro, Ga., the same year; mayor of Statesboro in 1906 and 1907; solicitor general of the middle judicial circuit 1913–1916; elected as a Democrat to the Sixty-eighth Congress (March 4, 1923–March 3, 1925); unsuccessful candidate for renomination in 1924; continued the practice of law in Statesboro, Ga., until his death there on January 14, 1940; interment in the City Cemetery.

MOORE, Robert Walton, a Representative from Virginia; born in Fairfax, Fairfax County, Va., February 6, 1859; attended the Episcopal High School near Alexandria, Va., and the University of Virginia at Charlottesville; studied law; was admitted to the bar in 1880 and practiced in Virginia and Washington, D. C.; member of the Virginia State Senate 1887–1890; presidential elector on the Democratic ticket of Cleveland and Stevenson in 1892; member of the State constitutional convention in 1901 and 1902; president of the Virginia State Bar Association in 1911; member of the board of visitors to William and Mary College and the University of Virginia; from 1907 until the First World War was special counsel for carriers of the South in cases before the Interstate Commerce Commission, the Commerce Court, and the United States Supreme Court; assistant general counsel of the United States Railroad Administration in 1918 and 1919; elected as a Democrat to the Sixty-sixth Congress to fill the vacancy caused by the resignation of Charles C. Carlin; reelected to the Sixty-seventh and to the four succeeding Congresses and served from May 27, 1919, to March 3, 1931; was not a candidate for renomination in 1930; appointed a member of the Board of Regents of the Smithsonian Institution December 7, 1922; member of the George Washington Bicentennial Commission; served as chairman of the Fredericksburg Battlefield Park Commission and as vice president of the Washington National Monument Association; appointed as Assistant Secretary of State by President Franklin D. Roosevelt September 19, 1933, was made counselor in 1937, and served until his death in Fairfax, Va., February 8, 1941; interment in Fairfax Cemetery.

MOORE, Samuel, a Representative from Pennsylvania; born in Deerfield (now Deerfield Street), Cumberland County, N. J., February 8, 1774; pursued an academic course, and was graduated from the University of Pennsylvania at Philadelphia in 1791; instructor in the university 1792–1794; studied medicine and practiced in Dublin, Bucks County, Pa., and later at Greenwich, N. J.; spent several years in trading to the East Indies; returned to Bucks County, Pa., and in 1808 purchased and operated grist and oil mills at Bridge Point (now Edison) near Doylestown; later erected and operated a sawmill and woolen factory; elected as a Democrat to the Fifteenth Congress to fill the vacancy caused by the resignation of Samuel D. Ingham; reelected to the Sixteenth and Seventeenth Congresses and served from October 13, 1818, until his resignation May 20, 1822; appointed by President Monroe as Director of the United States Mint on July 15, 1824, and served until 1835; moved to Philadelphia, Pa.; became interested in the mining and marketing of coal and served as president of the Hazleton Coal Co. until his death in Philadelphia, Pa., February 18, 1861; interment in Woodland Cemetery.

MOORE, Samuel McDowell (son of Andrew Moore), a Representative from Virginia; born in Philadelphia, Pa., on February 9, 1796; attended the public schools and Washington College (now Washington and Lee University), Lexington, Va., where he settled after leaving college; member of the State house of delegates 1825–1833; member of the Virginia constitutional convention of 1829; elected as a Whig to the Twenty-third Congress (March 4, 1833–March 3, 1835); unsuccessful candidate for reelection in 1834 to the Twenty-fourth Congress; again a member of the house of delegates in 1836 and 1837; served in the State senate 1845–1847; delegate to the secession convention in 1861; during the Civil War served in the Confederate Army; resumed the practice of his profession; died in Lexington, Rockbridge County, Va., on September 17, 1875; interment in Lexington Cemetery.

MOORE, Sydenham, a Representative from Alabama; born in Rutherford County, Tenn., May 25, 1817; pursued classical studies; attended the University of Alabama at Tuscaloosa 1833–1836; studied law; was admitted to the bar and commenced practice in Greensboro, Ala.; judge of Greene County Court 1840–1846 and 1848–1850; judge of the circuit court in 1857; served in the war with Mexico as captain in Colonel Coffey's regiment of Alabama Infantry from June 1846 to June 1847; elected brigadier general of Alabama Militia; elected as a Democrat to the Thirty-fifth and Thirty-sixth Congresses and served from March 4, 1857, until January 21, 1861, when he withdrew; during the Civil War served as colonel of the Eleventh Alabama Regiment in the Confederate Army; died in Richmond, Va., from wounds received in the Battle of Seven Pines, Virginia, May 31, 1862; interment in the City Cemetery, Greensboro, Hale County, Ala.

MOORE, Thomas, a Representative from South Carolina; born in Spartanburg District, S. C., in 1759; served in the Revolutionary War, taking part in the Battle of Cowpens at the age of sixteen; brigadier general in the War of 1812; engaged in planting; was one of the founders of the first high school in Spartanburg

District; elected to the Seventh and to the five succeeding Congresses (March 4, 1801–March 3, 1813); elected to the Fourteenth Congress (March 4, 1815–March 3, 1817); resumed his agricultural pursuits; died near Moores Station, Spartanburg County, S. C., on July 11, 1822; interment in Moore's Burying Ground.

MOORE, Thomas Love, a Representative from Virginia; born near Charles Town, Jefferson County, Va. (now West Virginia); pursued an academic course; studied law and practiced; elected to the Sixteenth Congress to fill the vacancy caused by the resignation of George F. Strother; reelected to the Seventeenth Congress and served from November 13, 1820, to March 3, 1823; resumed the practice of law at Warrenton, Va.; made the principal speech upon the visit of General Lafayette to Warrenton on August 23, 1825, ex-President Monroe being among those present; died in Warrenton, Fauquier County, Va., in 1862; interment in Warrenton Cemetery.

MOORE, Thomas Patrick, a Representative from Kentucky; born in Charlotte County, Va., in 1797; attended the common schools; moved with his parents to Harrodsburg, Mercer County, Ky.; attended Transylvania University, Lexington, Ky.; served in the War of 1812; captain in the Twelfth Virginia Infantry March 12, 1812; major in the Eighteenth Infantry September 20, 1813; honorably discharged June 15, 1815; member of the State house of representatives in 1819 and 1820; elected as a Democrat to the Eighteenth, Nineteenth, and Twentieth Congresses (March 4, 1823–March 3, 1829); appointed by President Jackson as Minister Plenipotentiary to New Grenada March 13, 1829, and served until April 16, 1833; returned to Kentucky; presented credentials as a Member-elect to the Twenty-third Congress, but the election was contested by Robert P. Letcher and the House declared a new election necessary; appointed lieutenant colonel of the Third United States Dragoons in the war with Mexico and served from March 3, 1847, to July 31, 1848; delegate to the Kentucky constitutional convention in 1849 and 1850; died in Harrodsburg, Ky., July 21, 1853.

MOORE, William, a Representative from New Jersey; born in Norristown, Montgomery County, Pa., December 25, 1810; attended private schools for a short time; became engaged in mercantile pursuits and later in ironworks; moved to New Jersey in 1845 and settled in Weymouth; engaged in the iron business; also became interested in the building and sailing of vessels and in the development of banks and other financial institutions; judge of the court of common pleas for Atlantic County 1855–1865; was one of the founders of the Republican Party and a delegate to the Republican National Convention held at Philadelphia in 1856; moved to Mays Landing, N. J., in 1865 and engaged in the shipbuilding business, in banking, and in the iron industry; elected as a Republican to the Fortieth and Forty-first Congresses (March 4, 1867–March 3, 1871); unsuccessful candidate for renomination in 1870; resumed his former business pursuits; served in the State senate 1872–1875; died at Mays Landing, N. J., April 26, 1878; interment in Union Cemetery.

MOORE, William Robert, a Representative from Tennessee; born in Huntsville, Ala., March 28, 1830; moved with his mother to Beech Grove, Tenn., while an infant, and when six years old the family settled in Fosterville, Rutherford County; attended the district schools; at the age of fifteen became a clerk in a dry-goods store in Beech Grove and later in Nashville, Tenn.; engaged in the wholesale dry-goods business in New York City as a salesman 1856–1859; moved to Memphis, Tenn., in 1859 and organized a large wholesale dry-goods store; elected as a Republican to the Forty-seventh Congress (March 4, 1881–March 3,

1883); declined to accept a renomination in 1882; resumed his business activities; declined to accept the Republican nomination for Governor of Tennessee in 1890; died in Memphis, Tenn., June 12, 1909; interment in Forest Hill Cemetery.

MOORE, William Sutton, a Representative from Pennsylvania; born near Amity, Amwell Township, Washington County, Pa., November 18, 1822; attended the rural schools, and was graduated from Washington (now Washington and Jefferson) College, Washington, Pa., in 1847; studied law; was admitted to the bar in November 1848 and commenced practice in Washington, Pa.; prothonotary of Washington County 1854–1857; delegate to the Republican National Convention at Philadelphia in 1856; also engaged in the newspaper business as editor and part owner of the Reporter in 1857; treasurer of Washington County 1863–1866; elected as a Republican to the Forty-third Congress (March 4, 1873–March 3, 1875); was not a candidate for renomination in 1874; retired from active business pursuits in 1875 due to failing health; died in Washington, Pa., December 30, 1877; interment in Washington Cemetery.

MOORES, Merrill, a Representative from Indiana; born in Indianapolis, Ind., April 21, 1856; attended the public schools, Butler University, Indianapolis, Ind., and Willamette University, Salem, Oreg.; was graduated from Yale University in 1878 and from the Central Law School of Indiana (now Indiana Law School) at Indianapolis in 1880; was admitted to the bar in 1880 and commenced practice in Indianapolis, Ind.; chairman of the Marion County Republican committee 1892–1896; assistant attorney general of Indiana 1894–1903; president of the Indiana State Bar Association and of the Indianapolis Bar Association in 1908; Indiana commissioner of the National Conference on Uniform State Laws 1909–1925; member of the executive council of the Interparliamentary Union in 1919; elected as a Republican to the Sixty-fourth and to the four succeeding Congresses (March 4, 1915–March 3, 1925); unsuccessful candidate for renomination in 1924 and for nomination in 1926; resumed the practice of law in Indianapolis, Ind.; served as vice president of the American Systems and Audit Co.; died October 21, 1929, in Indianapolis, Ind., from the result of an automobile accident; interment in Crown Hill Cemetery.

MOORHEAD, James Kennedy, a Representative from Pennsylvania; born in Halifax, Dauphin County, Pa., September 7, 1806; attended the common schools; served an apprenticeship at the tanner's trade, after which he became a canal contractor; superintendent and supervisor on the Juniata Canal in 1828; projected and established the first passenger packet line on the Pennsylvania Canal in 1835; appointed adjutant general of Pennsylvania in 1838; constructed the Monongahela Navigation Canal and was president of the company twenty-one years; president of the Atlantic & Ohio Telegraph Co., which later became the Western Union Telegraph Co.; elected as a Republican to the Thirty-sixth and to the four succeeding Congresses (March 4, 1859–March 3, 1869); declined to be a candidate for renomination in 1868; resumed his former business activities; delegate to the Republican National Convention at Chicago in 1868; was an unsuccessful candidate for election to the United States Senate in 1880; president of the chamber of commerce of Pittsburgh from 1877 until his death; member of the board of trustees of Allegheny Cemetery; died in Pittsburgh, Pa., March 6, 1884; interment in Allegheny Cemetery.

MOORHEAD, William Singer, a Representative from Pennsylvania; born in Pittsburgh, Allegheny County, Pa., April 8, 1923; attended Shady Side Academy; graduated from Phillips

Andover Academy in 1941 and from Yale University in 1944; during World War II served in the United States Navy from 1943 until discharged as a lieutenant (jg) in 1946 with service in the Pacific Theater; graduated from Harvard Law School in 1949; was admitted to the bar in 1949 and commenced the practice of law in Pittsburgh, Pa.; assistant city solicitor of Pittsburgh 1954–1957; member of Allegheny County Housing Authority 1956–1958 and Pittsburgh Art Commission in 1958; member of the board of trustees of Pittsburgh Tuberculosis League, Pittsburgh Child Guidance Center, Shadyside Hospital, and Western Pennsylvania Conservancy; elected as a Democrat to the Eighty-sixth Congress (January 3, 1959–January 3, 1961). *Reelected to the Eighty-seventh Congress.*

MOORMAN, Henry DeHaven, a Representative from Kentucky; born on a farm near Glen Dean, Breckinridge County, Ky., June 9, 1880; attended the public schools; studied law; was admitted to the bar in 1900 and commenced practice in Hardinsburg; also engaged in agricultural pursuits and in banking; county judge of Breckinridge County 1905–1909 and Commonwealth attorney of the ninth judicial district 1914–1927; served in the Spanish-American War as a private in Company C, First Regiment, Kentucky Volunteer Infantry, with service in Puerto Rico; during the First World War enlisted in the United States Army on January 14, 1918, and was assigned to Headquarters Company, Tenth Field Artillery; promoted to corporal and assigned to duty with the Judge Advocate General, Headquarters, Service of Supply, and was discharged April 1, 1919; elected as a Democrat to the Seventieth Congress (March 4, 1927–March 3, 1929); unsuccessful candidate for reelection in 1928 to the Seventy-first Congress; resumed his former professional and business pursuits in Hardinsburg, Ky.; died while on a visit in Hot Springs, Ark., February 3, 1939; interment in Ivy Hill Cemetery, Hardinsburg, Ky.

MORAN, Edward Carleton, Jr., a Representative from Maine; born in Rockland, Knox County, Maine, December 29, 1894; attended the public schools and was graduated from Bowdoin College, Brunswick, Maine, in 1917; during the First World War served from July 25, 1917, to March 14, 1919, in the Regular Army as a first lieutenant in Battery A, Seventy-third Artillery, Coast Artillery Corps, with service overseas; became engaged in the insurance business in Rockland, Maine, in 1919; delegate to the Democratic State conventions 1922–1936 and to the Democratic National Conventions in 1924 and 1932; unsuccessful candidate for Governor of Maine in 1928 and 1930; elected as a Democrat to the Seventy-third and Seventy-fourth Congresses (March 4, 1933–January 3, 1937); was not a candidate for renomination in 1936; member of the United States Maritime Commission from April 17, 1937, to August 1, 1940; State director of the Office of Price Administration from April 12 to December 23, 1942; Second Assistant Secretary of Labor, Washington, D. C., from July 1 to November 22, 1945; chairman of the Rockland (Maine) City Council in 1946 and 1947; resumed the general insurance business and is a resident of Rockland, Maine.

MORANO, Albert Paul, a Representative from Connecticut; born in Paterson, Passaic County, N. J., January 18, 1908; moved to Greenwich, Conn., in 1912; attended the public schools of Greenwich, Conn.; started working at an early age; member of Greenwich Board of Tax Review 1933–1935; chairman of Chickahominy Town Meeting District 1935–1937; secretary to Representative Albert E. Austin in 1939 and 1940; engaged in the real-estate and insurance business in Greenwich, Conn., in 1942; secretary to Representative Clare Boothe Luce 1943–1947; State unemployment compensation commissioner 1947–1950,

serving as chairman of the commission in 1949 and 1950; elected as a Republican to the Eighty-second and to the three succeeding Congresses (January 3, 1951–January 3, 1959); unsuccessful candidate for reelection in 1958 to the Eighty-sixth Congress; special assistant to the president of Conetta Tool & Die Co., Inc., Stamford, Conn., since March 1959; resides at Indian Harbor, Greenwich, Conn.

MOREHEAD, Charles Slaughter, a Representative from Kentucky; born near Bardstown, Nelson County, Ky., July 7, 1802; attended the public schools and Transylvania University, Lexington, Ky.; studied law; was admitted to the bar and commenced practice in Christian County, Ky.; was also a planter, having plantations in Mississippi and Louisiana; member of the State house of representatives in 1828 and 1829; moved to Frankfort, Ky.; attorney general of Kentucky 1830–1835; again a member of the State house of representatives 1838–1842 and 1844, and served as speaker in 1841, 1842, and 1844; elected as a Whig to the Thirtieth and Thirty-first Congresses (March 4, 1847–March 3, 1851); resumed the practice of law and the management of his plantations; presidential elector on the Whig ticket of Scott and Graham in 1852; again a member of the State house of representatives in 1853; elected Governor on the American Party ticket and served from 1855 to 1859; moved to Louisville in 1859 and continued the practice of his profession; member of the peace convention of 1861 held in Washington, D. C., in an effort to devise means to prevent the impending war; arrested by the Federal authorities on the charge of disloyalty in September 1861 and confined in Fort Lafayette, New York Harbor, until January 1862; traveled in Europe until the close of the war, when he settled in Greenville, Miss.; died on one of his plantations near Greenville, Miss., December 21, 1868; interment in Frankfort Cemetery, Frankfort, Ky.

MOREHEAD, James Turner, a Senator from Kentucky; born near Shepherdsville, Bullitt County, Ky., May 24, 1797; attended public school at Russellville, Ky., and Transylvania University, Lexington, Ky.; studied law; was admitted to the bar in 1818 and commenced practice in Bowling Green, Ky.; member of the State house of representatives 1827–1830; elected Lieutenant Governor of Kentucky in 1831 and served from 1832 until the death of Governor Breathitt, on February 21, 1834, when he became Governor and served until 1836; again a member of the State house of representatives in 1837; president of the State board of internal improvements 1838–1841; elected as a Whig to the United States Senate and served from March 4, 1841, to March 3, 1847; continued the practice of his profession in Covington, Kenton County, Ky., until his death in that city on December 28, 1854; interment in the State lot of Frankfort Cemetery, Frankfort, Ky.

MOREHEAD, James Turner, a Representative from North Carolina; born in Rockingham County, N. C., January 11, 1799; attended the common schools; was graduated from the University of North Carolina at Chapel Hill in 1819; studied law; was admitted to the bar and commenced practice in Greensboro, N. C.; commissioner of Greensboro in 1832, 1834, and 1835; served as a member of the North Carolina State Senate in 1835, 1836, 1838, 1840, and 1842; trustee of the University of North Carolina 1836–1868; elected as a Whig to the Thirty-second Congress (March 4, 1851–March 3, 1853); declined to be a candidate for renomination in 1852 to the Thirty-third Congress; resumed the practice of his profession; also engaged in agricultural pursuits and operated an iron works; died in Greensboro, Guilford County, N. C., on May 5, 1875; interment in the Presbyterian Cemetery.

MOREHEAD, John Henry, a Representative from Nebraska; born on a farm near Columbia, Lucas County, Iowa, December 3, 1861; attended the public schools, and a business college in Shenandoah, Iowa; moved to Nebraska in 1884 and settled in Richardson County; taught in a country school; engaged in agricultural pursuits and in the mercantile and banking business at Barada, Nebr.; moved to Falls City, Nebr., in 1895; treasurer of Richardson County 1896–1899; mayor of Falls City in 1900; member of the State senate 1910–1912, serving as president pro tempore; upon the death of the Lieutenant Governor he succeeded to that office, as provided by the State constitution; Governor of Nebraska 1913–1917; unsuccessful candidate for election to the United States Senate in 1918 and for Governor of Nebraska in 1920; elected as a Democrat to the Sixty-eighth and to the five succeeding Congresses (March 4, 1923–January 3, 1935); was not a candidate for renomination in 1934; resumed agricultural pursuits and also engaged in the real-estate business; delegate to the Democratic National Convention at Chicago in 1940; died in a hospital at St. Joseph, Mo., May 31, 1942; interment in Steele Cemetery, Falls City, Nebr.

MOREHEAD, John Motley, a Representative from North Carolina; born in Charlotte, Mecklenburg County, N. C., July 20, 1866; attended the public schools and the Bingham Military School of North Carolina at Mebane; was graduated from the University of North Carolina at Chapel Hill in 1886; also completed a business course in Bryant and Stratton College, Baltimore, Md.; collecting teller of the Charlotte National Bank, of Charlotte, N. C.; buyer and dealer in leaf tobacco at Durham, N. C.; interested in manufacturing and agricultural pursuits; elected as a Republican to the Sixty-first Congress (March 4, 1909–March 3, 1911); declined to be a candidate for renomination in 1910; chairman of the Republican State committee 1910–1916; member of the Republican National Committee from 1916 until 1922, when he resigned; became extensively engaged in the manufacture of woolen goods and other commodities; discontinued active business pursuits and lived in retirement until his death in Charlotte, N. C., December 13, 1923; interment in Elmwood Cemetery.

MOREY, Frank, a Representative from Louisiana; born in Boston, Mass., July 11, 1840; attended the public schools; moved to Illinois in 1857; studied law; entered the Union Army in 1861 in the Thirty-third Regiment, Illinois Volunteer Infantry, and served until the close of the Civil War, principally on staff duty, with the rank of captain; settled in Louisiana in 1866 and engaged in cotton planting and the insurance business; member of the State house of representatives in 1868 and 1869; appointed a commissioner to revise the statutes and codes of the State; commissioner to the Vienna Exposition in 1873; elected as a Republican to the Forty-first, Forty-second, and Forty-third Congresses; presented credentials as a Member-elect to the Forty-fourth Congress and served from March 4, 1869, to June 8, 1876, when he was succeeded by William B. Spencer, who contested the election; moved to Washington, D. C., and died there September 22, 1889; interment in the Congressional Cemetery.

MOREY, Henry Lee, a Representative from Ohio; born in Milford Township, near Collinsville, Butler County, Ohio, April 8, 1841; attended the common schools and Miami University, Oxford, Ohio; served in the Civil War, and was successively promoted to second lieutenant, first lieutenant, and captain; was graduated from the Indianapolis Law School in 1867; was admitted to the bar and commenced practice in Hamilton, Ohio; city solicitor of Hamilton 1871–1875; prosecuting attorney of Butler County, Ohio, in 1873; unsuccessful candidate for election

to the State senate in 1875; elected as a Republican to the Forty-seventh Congress (March 4, 1881–March 3, 1883); presented credentials as a Member-elect to the Forty-eighth Congress and served from March 4, 1883, to June 20, 1884, when he was succeeded by James E. Campbell, who contested the election; delegate to the Republican National Convention at Chicago in 1884; elected to the Fifty-first Congress (March 4, 1889–March 3, 1891); unsuccessful candidate for reelection in 1890 to the Fifty-second Congress; resumed the practice of law; died in Hamilton, Butler County, Ohio, December 29, 1902; interment in Greenwood Cemetery.

MORGAN, Charles Henry, a Representative from Missouri; born in Cuba, Allegany County, N. Y., July 5, 1842; moved to Wisconsin in 1845 with his parents, who settled in Pewaukee; attended the common schools and the Fond du Lac (Wis.) High School; during the Civil War served in the Union Army four years and three months as a private, noncommissioned officer, second and first lieutenant, and captain in the First Regiment and Twenty-first Regiment, Wisconsin Volunteer Infantry; was graduated from the Albany (N. Y.) Law School; was admitted to the bar and commenced practice in Lamar, Barton County, Mo., in 1868; prosecuting attorney of Barton County, Mo., four years; member of the Missouri House of Representatives 1872–1874; elected as a Democrat to the Forty-fourth and Forty-fifth Congresses (March 4, 1875–March 3, 1879); unsuccessful candidate for reelection in 1878 to the Forty-sixth Congress; elected to the Forty-eighth Congress (March 4, 1883–March 3, 1885); unsuccessful candidate for reelection in 1884 to the Forty-ninth Congress; delegate to the Democratic National Convention at Cincinnati in 1880; presidential elector at large on the Democratic ticket of Cleveland and Thurman in 1888; elected to the Fifty-third Congress (March 4, 1893–March 3, 1895); unsuccessful candidate for renomination in 1894; served in the war with Spain as lieutenant colonel of the Fifth Missouri Volunteer Infantry; moved to Joplin, Mo., in 1907 and engaged in mining; elected as a Republican to the Sixty-first Congress (March 4, 1909–March 3, 1911); unsuccessful candidate for reelection in 1910 to the Sixty-second Congress; died in Joplin, Mo., January 4, 1912; interment in Mount Hope Cemetery.

MORGAN, Christopher (brother of Edwin Barbour Morgan and nephew of Noyes Barber), a Representative from New York; born in Aurora, N. Y., June 4, 1808; pursued classical studies, and was graduated from Yale College in 1830; studied law; was admitted to the bar and commenced practice in Aurora, Cayuga County, N. Y.; elected as a Whig to the Twenty-sixth and Twenty-seventh Congresses (March 4, 1839–March 3, 1843); unsuccessful candidate for reelection in 1842 to the Twenty-eighth Congress; moved to Auburn, N. Y., in 1843 and continued the practice of his profession; secretary of state of New York 1847–1851; superintendent of the New York public schools 1848–1852; served as mayor of Auburn in 1860 and 1862; trustee of the State lunatic asylum in Utica, N. Y.; died in Auburn, N. Y., April 3, 1877; interment in Fort Hill Cemetery.

MORGAN, Daniel, a Representative from Virginia; born near Junction, Hunterdon County, N. J., in 1736; moved to Charles Town, Va. (now West Virginia), in 1754; served with the Colonial forces during the French and Indian War; during the Revolution was commissioned captain of a company of Virginia riflemen in July 1775; was taken prisoner at Quebec December 31, 1775; became colonel of the Eleventh Virginia Regiment November 12, 1776 (designated the Seventh Virginia Regiment September 14, 1778); brigadier general in the Continental Army October 30, 1780; given thanks of Congress and a gold medal (resolution of March 9, 1781) "for fortitude and good conduct of himself and officers and men under his command in the action at the Cowpens, S. C., January 17, 1781"; at the close of the war retired to his estate, known as "Saratoga," near Winchester, Va.; commanded the Virginia Militia ordered out by President Washington in 1794 to suppress the Whisky Insurrection in Pennsylvania; was an unsuccessful Federalist candidate for election to the Fourth Congress; elected to the Fifth Congress (March 4, 1797–March 3, 1799); declined to be a candidate for renomination in 1798 on account of ill health; died in Winchester, Va., on July 6, 1802; interment in Mount Hebron Cemetery.

MORGAN, Dick Thompson, a Representative from Oklahoma; born at Prairie Creek, Vigo County, Ind., December 6, 1853; attended the country schools and the Prairie Creek High School; was graduated from Union Christian College, Merom, Ind., in 1876, and later was professor of mathematics in that college; was graduated from the Central Law School, Indianapolis, Ind., in 1880; was admitted to the bar the same year and commenced practice in Terre Haute, Ind.; member of the State house of representatives in 1880 and 1881; appointed register of the United States land office at Woodward, Okla., by President Roosevelt in 1904 and served until May 1, 1908; elected as a Republican to the Sixty-first and to the five succeeding Congresses and served from March 3, 1909, until his death in Danville, Ill., July 4, 1920; interment in Rose Hill Cemetery, Oklahoma City, Okla.

MORGAN, Edwin Barbour (brother of Christopher Morgan and nephew of Noyes Barber), a Representative from New York; born in Aurora, Cayuga County, N. Y., May 2, 1806; attended the common schools; engaged in mercantile pursuits and banking in Aurora; elected as a Republican to the Thirty-third, Thirty-fourth, and Thirty-fifth Congresses (March 4, 1853–March 3, 1859); was not a candidate for renomination in 1858; one of the founders and the first president of the Wells-Fargo Express Co. and a director of the American Express Co. up to the time of his death; trustee of Cornell University, Ithaca, N. Y., 1865–1874; charter trustee of Wells College, Aurora, N. Y., 1868–1881, and served as president of the board 1878–1881; member of the board of trustees of Auburn Theological Seminary 1870–1881; died in Aurora, N. Y., on October 13, 1881; interment in Oak Glen Cemetery.

MORGAN, Edwin Dennison (cousin of Morgan Gardner Bulkeley), a Senator from New York; born in Washington, Mass., February 8, 1811; moved with his parents to Windsor County, Conn., in 1822; attended the public schools and Bacon Academy, Colchester, Conn.; moved to Hartford, Conn., in 1828 and engaged in mercantile pursuits; member of the city council of Hartford in 1832; moved to New York City in 1836 and engaged in the wholesale grocery business; alderman of New York City in 1849; member of the State senate 1850–1855; State commissioner of immigration 1855–1858; vice president of the Republican National Convention at Philadelphia in 1856, and delegate to the convention at Chicago in 1860; chairman of the Republican National Committee 1856–1864; Governor of New York 1859–1862; chairman of the Union congressional committee in 1864; during the Civil War served as major general of Volunteers in the Union Army from September 28, 1861, to January 1, 1863, serving as commander of the Department of New York; elected as a Union Republican to the United States Senate and served from March 4, 1863, to March 3, 1869; was the caucus nominee of his party, who were in the minority, in 1869; chairman of the Republican National Committee in 1872; unsuccessful candidate for elec-

tion to the United States Senate in 1875; unsuccessful candidate for Governor in 1876; declined the office of Secretary of the Treasury in the Cabinet of President Arthur in 1881; died in New York City February 14, 1883; interment in Cedar Hill Cemetery, Hartford, Conn.

MORGAN, George Washington, a Representative from Ohio; born in Washington, Pa., September 20, 1820; attended Washington (now Washington and Jefferson) College, Washington, Pa., until 1836; enlisted in a company commanded by his brother and assisted Texas in gaining her independence; attained the rank of captain; returned to the United States; was a cadet in the United States Military Academy, West Point, N. Y., 1841–1843; studied law; was admitted to the bar and commenced practice in Mount Vernon, Ohio, in 1843; served in the Mexican War; commissioned colonel of the Second Regiment, Ohio Volunteer Infantry, June 23, 1846, and colonel of the Fifteenth Regiment, United States Infantry, April 9, 1847; brevetted brigadier general August 20, 1847, "for gallant and meritorious conduct at the Battles of Contreras and Churubusco, Mexico"; honorably discharged August 7, 1848; appointed consul at Marseille, France, in 1855; appointed Minister Resident at Lisbon, Portugal, in 1858; served in the Civil War; commissioned a brigadier general of Volunteers November 12, 1861, and had command of the Seventh Division of the Army of the Ohio; was with General Sherman at Vicksburg; assigned to the Thirteenth Army Corps; was in command at the taking of Fort Hindman, Ark.; resigned June 8, 1863, on account of ill health; unsuccessful candidate for election as Governor of Ohio in 1865; presented credentials as a Democratic Member-elect to the Fortieth Congress and served from March 4, 1867, until June 3, 1868, when he was succeeded by Columbus Delano, who contested the election; elected to the Forty-first and Forty-second Congresses (March 4, 1869–March 3, 1873); unsuccessful candidate for reelection in 1872 to the Forty-third Congress; delegate to the Democratic National Convention at St. Louis in 1876; died at Fortress Monroe, Va., July 26, 1893; interment in Mound View Cemetery, Mount Vernon, Knox County, Ohio.

MORGAN, James, a Representative from New Jersey; born in Amboy, N. J., on December 29, 1756; attended the public schools; served as an officer in the New Jersey Line during the Revolutionary War; representative in the general assembly in Philadelphia, Pa., 1794–1799; elected as a Federalist to the Twelfth Congress (March 4, 1811–March 3, 1813); engaged in agricultural pursuits; became major general of militia; died in South Amboy, Middlesex County, N. J., November 11, 1822; interment in the Morgan private cemetery, Morgan, N. J.

MORGAN, James Bright, a Representative from Mississippi; born near Fayetteville, Lincoln County, Tenn., March 14, 1833; moved with his parents to De Soto County, Miss., in 1840 and settled in Hernando; received an academic education; studied law; was admitted to the bar in 1857 and commenced practice in Hernando, Miss.; elected probate judge of De Soto County and served from 1857 until 1861, when he resigned; during the Civil War enlisted in the Confederate Army as a private; was promoted to the rank of captain, and in the organization of the Twenty-ninth Mississippi Infantry was elected a major; later became lieutenant colonel and colonel, and served until the close of the war; resumed the practice of law; again elected probate judge of De Soto County; member of the State senate 1876–1878; delegate to all State conventions 1876–1890; chancellor of the third chancery district 1878–1882; elected as a Democrat to the Forty-ninth, Fiftieth, and Fifty-first Congresses (March 4, 1885–March 3, 1891); resumed the practice of law; died near Horn Lake, Miss., June 18, 1892; interment in Baptist Cemetery, Hernando, Miss.

MORGAN, John Jordan (father-in-law of John Adams Dix), a Representative from New York; born in Queens County, N. Y., in 1770; attended the public schools; member of the State assembly in 1819; elected as a Democrat to the Seventeenth and Eighteenth Congresses (March 4, 1821–March 3, 1825); elected to the Twenty-third Congress to fill the vacancy caused by the resignation of Cornelius W. Lawrence and served from December 1, 1834, to March 3, 1835; again a member of the State assembly in 1836 and 1840; died in Port Chester, Westchester County, N. Y., on July 29, 1849; interment in Trinity Churchyard, New York City, N. Y.

MORGAN, John Tyler, a Senator from Alabama; born in Athens, McMinn County, Tenn., June 20, 1824; moved with his parents to Alabama in 1833 and settled in Calhoun County; pursued academic studies; studied law; was admitted to the bar in 1845 and commenced practice in Talladega, Ala.; moved to Dallas County, Ala., in 1855 and resumed the practice of law in Selma and Cahaba; presidential elector on the Democratic ticket of Breckenridge and Lane in 1860; delegate from Dallas County in the State convention of 1861 which passed the ordinance of secession; during the Civil War enlisted in the Confederate Army as a private in Company I, Cahaba Rifles, in May 1861, and when that company was assigned to the Fifth Alabama Regiment, under Col. Robert E. Rhodes, was elected major and later lieutenant colonel of that regiment; commissioned in 1862 as colonel and raised the Fifty-first Alabama Cavalry; appointed brigadier general in 1863 and assigned to a brigade in Virginia, but resigned to join his regiment, whose colonel had been killed in battle; appointed brigadier general and assigned to an Alabama brigade, which included his regiment; after the war resumed the practice of law in Selma, Ala.; presidential elector on the Democratic ticket of Tilden and Hendricks in 1876; elected as a Democrat to the United States Senate in 1876; reelected in 1882, 1888, 1894, 1900, and 1906, and served from March 4, 1877, until his death in Washington, D. C., June 11, 1907; interment in Live Oak Cemetery, Selma, Dallas County, Ala.

MORGAN, Lewis Lovering, a Representative from Louisiana; born in Mandeville, St. Tammany Parish, La., March 2, 1876; attended the public schools and St. Eugene's College, St. Tammany Parish, La.; was graduated from the law department of Tulane University, New Orleans, La., in 1899; was admitted to the bar and commenced practice in Covington, La., in 1902; member of the State house of representatives in 1908; resigned to become district attorney and served from 1908 to 1912; delegate to the Democratic National Conventions in 1912, 1928, and 1936; delegate to the Democratic State conventions in 1912, 1916, 1920, and 1924; elected as a Democrat to the Sixty-second Congress to fill the vacancy caused by the death of Robert C. Wickliffe; reelected to the Sixty-third and Sixty-fourth Congresses and served from November 5, 1912, to March 4, 1917; was not a candidate for renomination in 1916; resumed the practice of law in New Orleans and Covington; unsuccessful candidate for the Democratic gubernatorial nomination in 1944; died in New Orleans, La., June 10, 1950; interment in Covington Cemetery, Covington, La.

MORGAN, Stephen, a Representative from Ohio; born in Jackson County, Ohio, January 25, 1854; attended the common schools, Central College, Worthington, Ohio, and the Normal University, Lebanon, Ohio; taught in the public schools of Jackson County for a number of years; school examiner for nine years and principal of Oak Hill Academy for fifteen years; elected as a Republican to the Fifty-sixth, Fifty-seventh, and Fifty-eighth Congresses (March 4, 1899–March 3, 1905); unsuccessful candidate for reelection in 1904 to the Fifty-ninth Congress; moved to Columbus, Ohio, and retired from public life; died at Magnetic Springs, Union County, Ohio, February 9, 1928; interment in Horeb Cemetery, near Oak Hill, Jackson County, Ohio.

MORGAN, Thomas Ellsworth, a Representative from Pennsylvania; born in Ellsworth, Washington County, Pa., October 13, 1906; attended the public schools of Washington County and East Bethlehem Township High School, Fredericktown, Pa.; was graduated from Waynesburg (Pa.) College in 1930, Detroit (Mich.) College of Medicine and Surgery in 1933, and Wayne University, Detroit, Mich., in 1934; served an internship at Grace Hospital, Detroit, Mich.; practiced medicine and surgery at Fredericktown, Pa., since 1935; elected as a Democrat to the Seventy-ninth and to the seven succeeding Congresses (January 3, 1945–January 3, 1961). *Reelected to the Eighty-seventh Congress.*

MORGAN, William Mitchell, a Representative from Ohio; born in Brownsville, Licking County, Ohio, August 1, 1870; attended the public schools; pursued various occupations until 1898, when he moved to Newark, Ohio; employed as a laborer and later as a musician; studied literature and science; engaged in agriculture, merchandizing, and in the wool-buying business; also active in organized labor movements, serving as president of the Newark (Ohio) Musicians' Union; elected as a Republican to the Sixty-seventh and to the four succeeding Congresses (March 4, 1921–March 3, 1931); unsuccessful candidate for reelection in 1930 to the Seventy-second Congress and for election in 1932 to the Seventy-third Congress; resumed his former business pursuits; president of the Ohio State Federation of Labor in 1935, resigning the same year to become a member of the State industrial commission, in which he served until his death in Columbus, Ohio, on September 17, 1935; interment in Cedar Hill Cemetery, Newark, Ohio.

MORGAN, William Stephen, a Representative from Virginia; born in Monongalia County, Va. (now West Virginia), September 7, 1801; attended the public schools and was reared on a farm; engaged in agricultural pursuits at White Day, Va.; unsuccessful candidate for election in 1832 to the Twenty-third Congress; elected as a Democrat to the Twenty-fourth and Twenty-fifth Congresses (March 4, 1835–March 3, 1839); declined to be a candidate for renomination in 1838; employed as a clerk in the House of Representatives in 1840; transferred as a clerk to the legislature of Virginia; member of the State house of delegates 1841–1844; presidential elector on the Democratic ticket of Polk and Dallas in 1844; appointed a clerk in the Treasury Department and served from August 3, 1845, until June 30, 1861; employed in the Smithsonian Institution 1861–1863; moved to Rivesville, W. Va.; died September 3, 1878, while on a visit to Washington, D. C.; interment in the Congressional Cemetery.

MORIN, John Mary, a Representative from Pennsylvania; born in Philadelphia, Pa., April 18, 1868; moved with his parents to Pittsburgh, Pa.; attended the common schools; began work in a glass factory in 1882; employed in steel mills until 1885; moved to Missoula, Mont., in 1889 and engaged in mercantile pursuits, during which time he took a night course at Haskins' Business College at Missoula and was graduated in 1892; returned to Pittsburgh, Allegheny County, Pa.; engaged in the hotel business; a director of the Washington Trust Co. since 1910; member of the Pittsburgh Common Council 1904–1906; delegate to the Republican State conventions 1905–1912; director of public safety in Pittsburgh 1909–1913; elected as a Republican to the Sixty-third and to the seven succeeding Congresses (March 4, 1913–March 3, 1929); unsuccessful candidate for renomination in 1928; appointed a commissioner of United States

Employees Compensation Commission in Washington, D. C., and served from 1928 until his death; died in Marine Hospital, Baltimore, Md., March 3, 1942; interment in Calvary Cemetery, Pittsburgh, Pa.

MORITZ, Theodore Leo, a Representative from Pennsylvania; born in Toledo, Lucas County, Ohio, February 10, 1892; attended the parochial schools; graduated from the University of Dayton, Dayton, Ohio, in 1913 and from the law department of the University of Duquesne, Pittsburgh, Pa., in 1923; engaged as a teacher in parochial schools in Dayton, Ohio, 1910–1913, in Cleveland, Ohio, 1913–1916, and in Duquesne University Prep School, Pittsburgh, Pa., 1918–1923; was admitted to the bar in 1924 and commenced practice in Pittsburgh, Pa., in 1925; secretary to the mayor of Pittsburgh 1933–1935; elected as a Democrat to the Seventy-fourth Congress (January 3, 1935–January 3, 1937); did not seek renomination as a Democrat, but was an unsuccessful candidate for nomination as a Republican in 1936 and for reelection as an Independent candidate to the Seventy-fifth Congress; resumed the practice of law and is a resident of Pittsburgh, Pa.

MORPHIS, Joseph Lewis, a Representative from Mississippi; born near Pocahontas, McNairy County, Tenn., April 17, 1831; pursued elementary studies; engaged in planting; member of the State house of representatives in 1859; entered the Confederate Army as captain in August 1861 and served until the close of the Civil War; moved with his family to Pontotoc, Miss., in 1863; member of the State constitutional convention in 1865; member of the State house of representatives 1866–1868; upon the readmission of the State of Mississippi to representation was elected as a Republican to the Forty-first and Forty-second Congresses and served from February 23, 1870, to March 3, 1873; unsuccessful candidate for renomination in 1872; appointed by President Hayes as United States marshal of the northern district of Mississippi and served from 1877 to 1885; licensed as an Indian trader on the Osage Reservation in 1890 and engaged in that occupation until 1901; discontinued active pursuits and lived in retirement until his death in Cleveland, Pawnee County, Okla., July 29, 1913; interment in Woodland Cemetery.

MORRELL, Daniel Johnson, a Representative from Pennsylvania; born in North Berwick, York County, Maine, August 8, 1821; attended the public schools; moved to Philadelphia, Pa., in 1836; entered a counting room as clerk and afterward engaged in mercantile pursuits; moved to Johnstown, Pa., in 1855 and became general manager of the Cambria Iron Co.; also served as president of the local gas and water company 1860–1884 and president of the First National Bank of Johnstown 1863–1884; president of the city council many years; elected as a Republican to the Fortieth and Forty-first Congresses (March 4, 1867–March 3, 1871); unsuccessful candidate for reelection in 1870 to the Forty-second Congress; commissioner to the Paris Exposition of 1878; again engaged in banking; died in Johnstown, Cambria County, Pa., August 20, 1885; interment in Grandview Cemetery.

MORRELL, Edward de Veaux, a Representative from Pennsylvania; born in Newport, R. I., August 7, 1863; attended private schools, and was graduated from the University of Pennsylvania at Philadelphia in 1885; studied law; was admitted to the bar in 1887 and commenced practice in Philadelphia; member of the select council of Philadelphia 1891–1894; active in the National Guard of Pennsylvania; colonel of the Third Regiment; afterward commissioned brigadier general and commanded the First Brigade; elected as a Republican to the Fifty-sixth Congress to fill the vacancy caused by the death of Alfred C. Harmer; reelected to the Fifty-seventh, Fifty-eighth, and Fifty-ninth Congresses and served from November 6, 1900, to March 3, 1907; was not a candidate for renomination in 1906; built several macadamized roads at his own expense; established the first telephone line north of Frankford, Pa., and built an electric-light plant in that section; member of the board of education of Philadelphia 1912–1916; a resident of Torresdale, Philadelphia, Pa.; went to Colorado Springs, Colo., for his health, and died there September 1, 1917; interment in the family crypt at Eden Hall, Torresdale, Philadelphia, Pa.

MORRIL, David Lawrence, a Senator from New Hampshire; born in Epping, N. H., June 10, 1772; taught by his grandfather and later attended Phillips Exeter Academy, Exeter, N. H.; studied medicine and engaged in practice in Epsom, N. H., 1793–1800; studied theology; was ordained; pastor of the Presbyterian Church of Goffstown in 1802 and served until 1811; resumed the practice of medicine in 1807 and continued until 1830; member of the State house of representatives 1808–1817 and served as speaker in 1816; elected as an Adams Democrat to the United States Senate and served from March 4, 1817, to March 3, 1823; was not a candidate for renomination; member and president of the State senate in 1823 and 1824; Governor of New Hampshire 1824–1827; moved to Concord in 1831; edited the New Hampshire Observer 1831–1833; died in Concord, N. H., January 28, 1849; interment in Old North Cemetery.

MORRILL, Anson Peaslee (brother of Lot Myrick Morrill), a Representative from Maine; born in Belgrade, Maine, June 10, 1803; attended the district schools; appointed postmaster at Dearborn, Kennebec County, Maine, and served from November 1, 1825, to June 3, 1841; engaged in mercantile pursuits in 1824; moved to Madison, and thence to Readfield, Maine, in 1844, where he took charge of a wool mill, which he ultimately purchased; member of the State house of representatives in 1833; sheriff of Somerset County in 1839; land agent 1850–1853; there being no choice in the popular election, he was appointed by the legislature the first Republican Governor of Maine in 1855; delegate to the Republican National Convention at Philadelphia in 1856; elected as a Republican to the Thirty-seventh Congress (March 4, 1861–March 3, 1863); was not a candidate for renomination in 1862; resumed his manufacturing pursuits; moved to Augusta, Maine, in 1879; member of the State house of representatives in 1880; president of the Maine Central Railroad in 1866 and vice president 1873–1887; died in Augusta, Maine, July 4, 1887; interment in Forest Grove Cemetery.

MORRILL, Edmund Needham, a Representative from Kansas; born in Westbrook, Cumberland County, Maine, February 12, 1834; attended school in his native town, and was graduated from Westbrook Seminary in 1855; superintendent of the Westbrook schools in 1856 and 1857; moved to Kansas in 1857 and settled in Brown County, where he erected a sawmill; member of the Territorial legislature in 1857 and 1858; enlisted on October 5, 1861, in the Union Army during the Civil War and served in the Seventh Regiment, Kansas Volunteer Cavalry; promoted to sergeant October 10, 1861; appointed captain and commissary of subsistence in August 1862; mustered out as major in October 1865; clerk of the district court of Brown County, Kans., 1866–1870; county clerk 1866–1873; founded the Morrill & Janes Bank, the first bank in Brown County, in 1871, and was its president from 1887 until his death; president of the First National Bank of Leavenworth, Kans., for seven years; member of the State senate 1872–1874 and 1876–1880, and served as president pro tempore in 1877;

founded the Morrill Free Public Library at Hiawatha, Kans., in 1882; elected as a Republican to the Forty-eighth and to the three succeeding Congresses (March 4, 1883–March 3, 1891); was not a candidate for renomination in 1890; resumed banking; founded the Hiawatha Academy, Hiawatha, Kans., in 1889; local manager of the soldiers' home at Leavenworth, Kans., in 1890; Governor of Kansas 1895–1897; unsuccessful candidate for reelection as Governor; died in San Antonio, Tex., March 14, 1909; interment in Mount Hope Cemetery, Hiawatha, Brown County, Kans.

MORRILL, Justin Smith, a Representative and a Senator from Vermont; born in Strafford, Orange County, Vt., April 14, 1810; attended the common schools and Thetford and Randolph Academies; a merchant's clerk in Strafford 1825–1828 and in Portland, Maine, 1828–1831; merchant in Strafford 1831–1848; engaged in agriculture and horticulture 1848–1855; elected as a Whig to the Thirty-fourth and to the five succeeding Congresses (March 4, 1855–March 3, 1867), when he became Senator; author of the Tariff Act of 1861 and of the land-grant bill, which passed both Houses of Congress and was vetoed by President Buchanan, but which became a law in 1862; elected as a Union Republican to the United States Senate in 1866; reelected in 1872, 1878, 1884, 1890, and again in 1896, and served from March 4, 1867, until his death; his service in the House and Senate combined covered a period of forty-three years nine months and twenty-four days; Regent of the Smithsonian Institution 1883–1898; trustee of the University of Vermont 1865–1898; died in Washington, D. C., December 28, 1898; interment in the City Cemetery, Strafford, Vt.

MORRILL, Lot Myrick (brother of Anson Peaslee Morrill), a Senator from Maine; born in Belgrade, Maine, May 3, 1813; attended the district schools and Waterville (now Colby) College, Maine; studied law; was admitted to the bar in 1837 and commenced practice in Readfield; moved to Augusta in 1841; member of the State senate in 1854 and 1856 and presided over the senate the last year; Governor of Maine 1858–1860; elected as a Republican to the United States Senate to fill the vacancy caused by the resignation of Hannibal Hamlin; reelected in 1863 and served from January 17, 1861, to March 3, 1869; member of the peace convention of 1861 held in Washington, D. C., in an effort to devise means to prevent the impending war; resumed the practice of law in Augusta; appointed and subsequently elected to the United States Senate to fill the vacancy caused by the death of William Pitt Fessenden; reelected in 1871 and served from October 30, 1869, until his resignation on July 7, 1876; Secretary of the Treasury of the United States in the Cabinets of Presidents Grant and Hayes and served from July 7, 1876, to March 8, 1877; appointed by President Hayes collector of customs in Portland, Maine, March 13, 1877; died in Augusta, Maine, on January 10, 1883; interment in Forest Grove Cemetery.

MORRILL, Samuel Plummer, a Representative from Maine; born in Chesterville, Franklin County, Maine, February 11, 1816; attended the common schools and Farmington Academy, Farmington, Maine; studied theology; was ordained a minister and held pastorates in Farmington 1848–1853; elected in 1857 for a five-year term as register of deeds for Franklin County and was reelected to the same office in 1862; elected as a Republican to the Forty-first Congress (March 4, 1869–March 3, 1871); unsuccessful candidate for renomination in 1870; resumed his ministerial duties in East Dixfield 1877–1879; moved to Vienna in 1885; retired from the ministry in 1886; died in Chesterville, Franklin County, Maine, August 4, 1892; interment in Chesterville Hill Cemetery.

MORRIS, Cadwalader, a Delegate from Pennsylvania; born in Philadelphia, Pa., February 19, 1741; attended the rural school; engaged in commercial pursuits and in the management of his estate; resided for a time in the West Indies; during the Revolutionary War was a member of the Philadelphia Troop of Light Horse; assisted in the establishment and served as an inspector of the Bank of Pennsylvania in 1780; one of the founders and a director of the Bank of North America in 1781; Member of the Continental Congress in 1783 and 1784; was elected for another term, but declined; after the war operated an iron furnace in Birdsborough, Pa., but subsequently engaged in mercantile pursuits in Philadelphia; member of the Democratic Society of Philadelphia organized to show sympathy with the French Revolution; died in Philadelphia January 25, 1795.

MORRIS, Calvary, a Representative from Ohio; born in Charleston, Kanawha County, Va. (now West Virginia), January 15, 1798; attended the common schools; moved to Ohio in 1819 and settled in Athens; sheriff of Athens County 1823–1827; member of the State house of representatives 1827–1829; member of the State senate 1829–1835; again a member of the State house of representatives in 1835 and 1836; elected as a Whig to the Twenty-fifth, Twenty-sixth, and Twenty-seventh Congresses (March 4, 1837–March 3, 1843); was not a candidate for renomination in 1842; engaged in wool growing; moved to Cincinnati, Ohio, in 1847; engaged in mercantile pursuits; returned to Athens, and in 1854 was elected probate judge of Athens County; died in Athens, Ohio, on October 13, 1871; interment in Athens Cemetery.

MORRIS, Daniel, a Representative from New York; born in Fayette, Seneca County, N. Y., January 4, 1812; attended the public schools and the Canandaigua Academy in Ontario County, N. Y.; studied law; was admitted to the bar in 1845 and commenced practice in Penn Yan, Yates County, N. Y.; district attorney of Yates County, N. Y., 1847–1850; member of the State assembly in 1859; elected as a Republican to the Thirty-eighth and Thirty-ninth Congresses (March 4, 1863–March 3, 1867); was not a candidate for reelection in 1866; resumed the practice of law; died in Penn Yan, N. Y., April 22, 1889; interment in Lake View Cemetery.

MORRIS, Edward Joy, a Representative from Pennsylvania; born in Philadelphia, Pa., July 16, 1815; attended the common schools and the University of Pennsylvania at Philadelphia; was graduated from Harvard University in 1836; studied law; was admitted to the bar in 1842 and practiced in Philadelphia; member of the State house of representatives 1841–1843; elected as a Whig to the Twenty-eighth Congress (March 4, 1843–March 3, 1845); unsuccessful candidate for reelection in 1844 to the Twenty-ninth Congress; Chargé d'Affaires to Naples from January 20, 1850, to August 26, 1853; member of the board of directors of Girard College, Philadelphia; again a member of the State house of representatives in 1856; elected to the Thirty-fifth, Thirty-sixth, and Thirty-seventh Congresses and served from March 4, 1857, until June 8, 1861, when he resigned; appointed Minister Resident to Turkey and served from June 8, 1861, to October 25, 1870; died in Philadelphia, Pa., December 31, 1881; interment in Laurel Hill Cemetery.

MORRIS, Gouverneur (half brother of Lewis Morris and uncle of Lewis Robert Morris), a Delegate and a Senator from New York; born in Morrisania (now a part of New York City), N. Y., January 31, 1752; instructed by private tutors; was graduated from Kings College (now Columbia University), New York, in 1768; studied law; was admitted to the colonial bar in 1771 and commenced practice in New York City; member of the New York Provincial Congress 1775–1777; signer of the Articles of Confederation in 1775; lieutenant colonel in the State militia in 1776; member of the committee to prepare a form of government for the State of New York in August 1776; member of the committee to design the great seal of the State of New York in April 1777; member of the first State council of safety in May 1777; member of the first State assembly in 1777 and 1778; Member of the Continental Congress in 1777 and 1778; appointed assistant minister of finance in 1781 and served four years; member of the convention that framed the Constitution of the United States in 1787; commissioner to England in 1789; Minister Plenipotentiary to France from January 12, 1792, to August 15, 1794; returned to the United States in 1798; elected as a Federalist to the United States Senate to fill the vacancy caused by the resignation of James Watson and served from April 3, 1800, to March 3, 1803; returned to New York City; chairman of the Erie Canal Commission 1810–1813; author on legal and political subjects; died in Morrisania, N. Y., November 6, 1816; interment in St. Anne's Episcopal Churchyard, Bronx, N. Y.

MORRIS, Isaac Newton (son of Thomas Morris and brother of Jonathan David Morris), a Representative from Illinois; born in Bethel, Ohio, January 22, 1812; attended Miami University, Oxford, Ohio; studied law; was admitted to the bar in 1835 and commenced practice in Warsaw, Ill., in 1836; moved to Quincy, Ill., in 1838 and continued the practice of law; appointed secretary of state of Illinois in 1840, but declined; president of the Illinois & Michigan Canal Co. in 1841; member of the State house of representatives 1846–1848; promoted the construction of the Northern Cross Railroad, undertaken by the State of Illinois; elected as a Democrat to the Thirty-fifth and Thirty-sixth Congresses (March 4, 1857–March 3, 1861); was not a candidate for renomination in 1860; appointed by President Grant commissioner for the Union Pacific Railroad in 1869; died in Quincy, Adams County, Ill., October 29, 1879; interment in Woodland Cemetery.

MORRIS, James Remley (son of Joseph Morris), a Representative from Ohio; born in Rogersville, Greene County, Pa., January 10, 1819; attended the public schools; moved with his parents to Waynesburg, Ohio, in 1829; moved to Woodsfield the next year; served two years' apprenticeship at the printing trade in 1833 and 1834; studied under private tutor until 1839; studied law; was admitted to the bar in 1843 and commenced practice at Woodsfield; engaged in taking the census of Monroe County; appointed county treasurer to fill the unexpired term of his father, who had been elected to Congress; editor and manager of the Spirit of Democracy 1844–1848; member of the first State house of representatives in 1848; member of the Ohio State Board of Equalization in 1859; elected as a Democrat to the Thirty-seventh and Thirty-eighth Congresses (March 4, 1861–March 3, 1865); unsuccessful candidate for reelection in 1864 to the Thirty-ninth Congress; resumed the practice of his profession at Woodsfield; judge of the probate court 1872–1877; postmaster 1886–1889; died in Woodsfield, Monroe County, Ohio, December 24, 1899; interment in Morris Cemetery, near Woodsfield.

MORRIS, Jonathan David (son of Thomas Morris and brother of Isaac Newton Morris), a Representative from Ohio; born in Columbia, Hamilton County, Ohio, October 8, 1804; attended the public schools; studied law; was admitted to the bar and commenced practice in Batavia, Ohio; clerk of the courts of Clermont County; elected as a Democrat to the Thirtieth Congress to fill the vacancy caused by the death of Thomas L. Hamer; reelected to the Thirty-first Congress and

served from March 4, 1847, to March 3, 1851; died in Connersville, Fayette County, Ind., May 16, 1875; interment in Citizens Cemetery, Batavia, Ohio.

MORRIS, Joseph (father of James Remley Morris), a Representative from Ohio; born in Greene County, Pa., October 16, 1795; attended the public schools; sheriff of Greene County in 1824; moved to Woodsfield, Monroe County, Ohio, in 1829 and engaged in mercantile pursuits; member of the State house of representatives in 1833 and 1834; treasurer of Monroe County; elected as a Democrat to the Twenty-eighth and Twenty-ninth Congresses (March 4, 1843–March 3, 1847); was not a candidate for renomination in 1846; resumed business interests; died in Woodsfield, Ohio, October 23, 1854; interment in Morris Cemetery, near Woodsfield.

MORRIS, Joseph Watkins, a Representative from Kentucky; born in Sulphur, Henry County, Ky., on February 26, 1879; moved to New Castle, Ky., with his father in 1889; attended the public schools and was graduated from the New Castle High School in 1899; engaged in mercantile pursuits at New Castle; secretary to Representative J. Campbell Cantrill 1909–1923; delegate to every Democratic State convention since 1904; chairman of the Democratic State campaign committee in 1923; elected as a Democrat to the Sixty-eighth Congress to fill the vacancy caused by the death of J. Campbell Cantrill and served from November 30, 1923, to March 3, 1925; was not a candidate for renomination in 1924; State revenue agent for Kentucky 1925–1927; manager of a bus terminal in Louisville, Ky., from 1929 until his death; died in Louisville, Ky., December 21, 1937; interment in Odd Fellows Cemetery, Carrollton, Ky.

MORRIS, Lewis (half brother of Gouverneur Morris and uncle of Lewis Robert Morris), a Delegate from New York; born in Morrisania (now a part of New York City), N. Y., April 8, 1726; instructed by private tutors, and was graduated from Yale College in 1746; engaged in agricultural pursuits; appointed by the Crown a judge of the Court of Admiralty in 1760 and resigned in 1774; again appointed by the provincial congress in 1776, but declined; elected to the Colonial Assembly of New York in 1769, but was declared disqualified for non-residence; delegate to the provincial convention of the colony in April 1775; Member of the Continental Congress 1775–1777, and was a signer of the Declaration of Independence; deputy to the State provincial congress in 1776 and 1777; county judge of Westchester County in 1777; member of the committee on detection of conspiracies in 1777; served in the State senate 1777–1781 and 1784–1788, and was a member of the council of appointment in 1786; member of the first board of regents of the University of New York and served from 1784 until his death; delegate to the State convention which adopted the Federal Constitution in 1788; Federalist presidential elector and voted for the Adams and Pinckney ticket in 1796; died in Morrisania, N. Y., January 22, 1798; interment in St. Anne's Episcopal Churchyard, Bronx, N. Y.

MORRIS, Lewis Robert (nephew of Gouverneur Morris and Lewis Morris), a Representative from Vermont; born in Scarsdale, N. Y., November 2, 1760; attended the common schools; moved to Springfield, Vt.; secretary of foreign affairs 1781–1783; member of the Springfield meeting-house committee in 1785; tax collector in 1786 and 1787; clerk of Windsor County Court 1789–1796 and judge of the same court until 1801; clerk of the State house of representatives in 1790 and 1791; member of the commission which presented Vermont's plea for statehood to the United States Congress in 1791; member of the convention to ratify the Federal Constitution; secretary of the constitutional convention in Windsor in 1793; brigadier general in the State militia in 1793; major general of the First Division 1795–1817; member of the State house of representatives 1795–1797 and 1803–1808, and served as speaker; elected as a Federalist to the Fifth, Sixth, and Seventh Congresses (March 4, 1797–March 3, 1803); in the contest between Jefferson and Burr for the Presidency, which was decided by the House of Representatives, he withheld his vote on the thirty-sixth ballot, thus giving Jefferson the vote of Vermont and making possible his election; retired, being a large landowner; died in Springfield, Vt., December 29, 1825; interment in Forest Hill Cemetery, Charlestown, Sullivan County, N. H.

MORRIS, Mathias, a Representative from Pennsylvania; born in Hilltown, Bucks County, Pa., September 12, 1787; attended the common schools in Newtown and Doylestown, Pa.; studied law; was admitted to the bar in 1809 and commenced practice in Newtown; deputy attorney general in 1819; member of the State senate 1828–1833; elected as a Whig to the Twenty-fourth and Twenty-fifth Congresses (March 4, 1835–March 3, 1839); unsuccessful candidate for reelection in 1838 to the Twenty-sixth Congress; died in Doylestown, Bucks County, Pa., November 9, 1839; interment in Hilltown Baptist Church Cemetery, near Fricks, Pa.

MORRIS, Robert (father of Thomas Morris), a Delegate and a Senator from Pennsylvania; born in Liverpool, England, January 20, 1734; immigrated to the United States in 1747 and settled in Oxford, Md.; attended the public schools; became a merchant in Philadelphia in 1748; signed the nonimportation agreement of 1765; Member of the Continental Congress 1776–1778; signer of the Declaration of Independence; settled upon the Manheim estate; member of the State assembly 1778–1780; superintendent of finance 1781–1784; established the Bank of North America; member of the State house of representatives 1785–1787; delegate to the Constitutional Convention of 1787; elected to the United States Senate and served from March 4, 1789, to March 3, 1795; declined to be a candidate for renomination; declined the position of Secretary of the Treasury in the Cabinet of President Washington; became financially involved by unsuccessful land speculations, which caused him to be imprisoned for debt from February 16, 1798, to August 26, 1801; died in Philadelphia, Pa., May 8, 1806; interment in the family vault of William White in the churchyard of Christ Church.

MORRIS, Robert Page Walter, a Representative from Minnesota; born in Lynchburg, Campbell County, Va., June 30, 1853; attended a private school and William and Mary College, Williamsburg, Va.; was graduated from the Virginia Military Institute, Lexington, Va., in 1872; assistant professor of mathematics, Virginia Military Institute, in 1872 and 1873; professor of mathematics in the Texas Military Institute in 1873; moved to Austin, Tex.; professor of applied mathematics in the Agricultural and Mechanical College of Texas in 1876; settled near Bryan, Tex.; studied law; was admitted to the bar and commenced practice in Lynchburg, Va., in 1880; unsuccessful candidate for election in 1884 to the Forty-ninth Congress; moved to Duluth, Minn., in 1886; elected municipal judge of Duluth in February 1889; elected city attorney of Duluth in March 1894; appointed district judge of the eleventh judicial district of Minnesota in August 1895; resigned in 1896; elected as a Republican to the Fifty-fifth, Fifty-sixth, and Fifty-seventh Congresses (March 4, 1897–March 3, 1903); declined to be a candidate for renomination; United States district judge for the district of Minnesota 1903–1923; retired from public life in 1923 and moved to Pasadena, Los Angeles County, Calif.; died in Rochester, Olmsted County, Minn., December 16, 1924; interment in Forest Hill Cemetery, Duluth, Minn.

MORRIS, Samuel Wells, a Representative from Pennsylvania; born in Philadelphia, Pa., September 1, 1786; pursued an academic course at Princeton College; studied law; was admitted to the bar and commenced practice in Wellsboro, Tioga County, Pa.; judge of the district court; first treasurer of Wellsboro County; postmaster of Wellsboro from July 1, 1808, to April 1, 1813; member of the State house of representatives; elected as a Democrat to the Twenty-fifth and Twenty-sixth Congresses (March 4, 1837–March 3, 1841); was not a candidate for reelection in 1840 to the Twenty-seventh Congress; died in Wellsboro, Tioga County, Pa., May 25, 1847.

MORRIS, Thomas (son of Robert Morris), a Representative from New York; born in Philadelphia, Pa., February 26, 1771; attended school in Geneva, Switzerland, 1781–1786 and the University of Leipsic, Germany, 1786–1788; returned to Philadelphia; studied law; was admitted to the bar and commenced practice in Canandaigua, N. Y.; member of the State assembly 1794–1796; elected to the Seventh Congress (March 4, 1801–March 3, 1803); was not a candidate for renomination; resumed the practice of law in New York City in 1803; appointed United States marshal for the southern district of New York in 1816, 1820, 1825, and 1829; died in New York City March 12, 1849.

MORRIS, Thomas (father of Isaac Newton Morris and Jonathan David Morris), a Senator from Ohio; born in Berks County, Pa., January 3, 1776; attended the common schools; enlisted as a ranger and fought against the Indians in 1793; moved to Columbia, Ohio (now a part of Cincinnati), in 1795 and clerked in a store; moved to Williamsburg, Ohio, in 1800; studied law; was admitted to the bar in 1804 and commenced practice in Bethel, Ohio; member of the State house of representatives from Clermont County 1806–1808, 1810, 1820, and 1821; served in the State senate 1813–1815, 1821–1823, 1825–1829, and 1831–1833; elected as a Democrat to the United States Senate and served from March 4, 1833, to March 3, 1839; was not a candidate for renomination; engaged in agricultural pursuits; nominated for Vice President of the United States on the Liberty ticket with James Gillespie Birney in 1844; died at his home near Bethel, Clermont County, Ohio, December 7, 1844; interment in First Bethel Cemetery.

MORRIS, Thomas Gayle, a Representative from New Mexico; born in Eastland County, Tex., August 20, 1919; moved to New Mexico; during World War II served as an enlisted man in the United States Navy from November 12, 1937, to March 22, 1944; engaged in farming and ranching in Quay County, N. Mex.; graduated from the University of New Mexico in 1948; member of the State house of representatives 1953–1958; chairman of the New Mexico Interstate Streams Commission; member of New Mexico Farm and Livestock Bureau, National Reclamation Association, and New Mexico Cattle Growers Association; elected as a Democrat to the Eighty-sixth Congress (January 3, 1959–January 3, 1961). *Reelected to the Eighty-seventh Congress.*

MORRIS, Toby, a Representative from Oklahoma; born in Granbury, Hood County, Tex., February 28, 1899; moved to what was then Comanche County, Okla., in 1906 and to Walters, Cotton County, Okla., in 1913; attended the public schools, leaving high school in his senior year, during the First World War, to enlist in the United States Army; served successively as private, corporal, and sergeant with the One Hundred and Tenth Combat Engineers, attached to the Thirty-fifth Division, from October 1917 to May 1919; studied law in his father's law office and at home; was admitted to the bar in 1920; court clerk of Cotton County, Okla., 1921–1925 and prosecuting attorney 1925–1929; engaged in the private practice of law in Walters,

Okla., since 1929; district judge of the twenty-first judicial district of Oklahoma from 1937 to 1946; elected as a Democrat to the Eightieth, Eighty-first, and Eighty-second Congresses (January 3, 1947–January 3, 1953); was an unsuccessful candidate for renomination in 1952; district judge of the fifth judicial district of Oklahoma from January 1955 to December 1956; elected to the Eighty-fifth and Eighty-sixth Congresses (January 3, 1957–January 3, 1961); unsuccessful candidate for renomination in 1960; is a resident of Lawton, Okla.

MORRISON, Cameron A., a Senator and a Representative from North Carolina; born near Rockingham, Richmond County, N. C., October 5, 1869; attended private schools at Ellerbe Springs and at Rockingham, N. C.; studied law; was admitted to the bar in 1892 and commenced practice in Rockingham, N. C.; mayor of Rockingham in 1893; presidential elector at large in 1916; moved to Charlotte, N. C., and continued the practice of law; Governor of North Carolina 1921–1925; member of the Democratic National Committee in 1928; appointed as a Democrat to the United States Senate to fill the vacancy caused by the death of Lee S. Overman and served from December 13, 1930, until December 4, 1932, when a duly elected successor qualified; was an unsuccessful candidate for election to fill the vacancy; resumed the practice of law; elected to the Seventy-eighth Congress (January 3, 1943–January 3, 1945); was not a candidate for renomination in 1944, but was an unsuccessful candidate for the nomination for United States Senator; again resumed the practice of his profession in Charlotte, N. C.; died in Quebec, Canada, on August 20, 1953; interment in Elmwood Cemetery, Charlotte, N. C.

MORRISON, George Washington, a Representative from New Hampshire; born in Fairlee, Orange County, Vt., October 16, 1809; attended the common schools and Thetford (Vt.) Academy; engaged in teaching; studied law; was admitted to the bar in 1835 and commenced practice in Manchester in 1836; member of the State house of representatives in 1840 and 1841; solicitor of Hillsborough County 1845–1849; served in the State senate in 1849 and 1850; elected as a Democrat to the Thirty-first Congress to fill the vacancy caused by the resignation of James Wilson and served from October 8, 1850, to March 3, 1851; unsuccessful candidate for reelection in 1850 to the Thirty-second Congress; elected to the Thirty-third Congress (March 4, 1853–March 3, 1855); unsuccessful candidate for reelection in 1854 to the Thirty-fourth Congress; continued the practice of law until 1872, when he retired; died in Manchester, Hillsborough County, N. H., December 21, 1888; interment in Valley Cemetery.

MORRISON, James Hobson, a Representative from Louisiana; born in Hammond, Tangipahoa Parish, La., December 8, 1908; attended the public schools; was graduated from the law department of Tulane University at New Orleans, La., in 1935; was admitted to the bar in 1934 and commenced practice in Hammond, La.; unsuccessful candidate for Governor in 1939 and again in 1944; elected as a Democrat to the Seventy-eighth and to the eight succeeding Congresses (January 3, 1943–January 3, 1961). *Reelected to the Eighty-seventh Congress.*

MORRISON, James Lowery Donaldson, a Representative from Illinois; born in Kaskaskia, Ill., April 12, 1816; appointed midshipman in the Navy in 1832 and served until December 31, 1839, when he resigned; studied law; was admitted to the bar and commenced practice in Belleville, Ill.; member of the State house of representatives in 1844; raised a company and served in the Mexican War as lieutenant colonel of Bissell's regiment of Illinois Volunteers from July 1, 1846, to July 1,

1847; was presented a sword by the Illinois Legislature for services at Buena Vista; member of the State senate in 1848; unsuccessful Whig candidate for Lieutenant Governor in 1852; elected as a Democrat to the Thirty-fourth Congress to fill the vacancy caused by the resignation of Lyman Trumbull and served from November 4, 1856, to March 3, 1857; at the same election was not the nominee for the Thirty-fifth Congress; was an unsuccessful candidate for the Democratic nomination for Governor of Illinois in 1860; died in St. Louis, Mo., on August 14, 1888; interment in Calvary Cemetery.

MORRISON, John Alexander, a Representative from Pennsylvania; born in Colerain, Lancaster County, Pa., January 31, 1814; attended the public schools; studied medicine; was graduated from the Jefferson Medical College at Philadelphia, Pa., in 1837 and commenced practice in Cochranville, Pa.; elected as a Democrat to the Thirty-second Congress (March 4, 1851–March 3, 1853); inspector and appraiser of imports of drugs at the port of Philadelphia, Pa., 1853–1861; resumed the practice of medicine in Cochranville, Pa., 1861–1865; engaged in agricultural and mercantile pursuits; again resumed the practice of medicine in Cochranville, Pa., and died there July 25, 1904; interment in Fagg's Manor Presbyterian Church Cemetery, Londonderry Township, Chester County, Pa.

MORRISON, Martin Andrew, a Representative from Indiana; born in Frankfort, Clinton County, Ind., April 15, 1862; attended the public schools; was graduated from Butler College, Irvington, Ind., in June 1883 and from the law department of the University of Virginia at Charlottesville in 1886; was admitted to the bar the same year and commenced practice in Frankfort, Ind.; county attorney of Clinton County in 1905 and 1906; member of the board of education 1907–1909; elected as a Democrat to the Sixty-first and to the three succeeding Congresses (March 4, 1909–March 3, 1917); was not a candidate for renomination in 1916; resumed the practice of law; president of the United States Civil Service Commission from March 1919 to July 1921; became a member of the legal staff of the chief counsel of the Federal Trade Commission at Washington, D. C., on December 10, 1925, and served until his retirement on April 30, 1942, maintaining his residence in Washington, D. C.; died in Abingdon, Va., July 9, 1944, while on a vacation; interment in Bunnell Cemetery, Frankfort, Ind.

MORRISON, William Ralls, a Representative from Illinois; born on a farm at Prairie du Long, near the present town of Waterloo, Monroe County, Ill., September 14, 1825; attended the common schools and McKendree College, Lebanon, Ill.; served in the war with Mexico; went to California with the gold seekers in 1849, but returned to Illinois in 1851; studied law; was admitted to the bar in 1855 and commenced practice in Waterloo, Ill.; clerk of the circuit court of Monroe County, Ill., 1852–1854; member of the State house of representatives 1854–1860, 1870, and 1871, and served as speaker in 1859 and 1860; organized and was colonel of the Forty-ninth Regiment, Illinois Volunteer Infantry, during the Civil War; was severely wounded in the siege of Fort Donelson; while in command of his regiment in the field was elected as a Democrat to the Thirty-eighth Congress (March 4, 1863–March 3, 1865); unsuccessful candidate in 1864 and 1866 for reelection to the Thirty-ninth and Fortieth Congresses; continued the practice of law in Waterloo, Ill.; elected to the Forty-third and to the six succeeding Congresses (March 4, 1873–March 3, 1887); unsuccessful candidate for reelection in 1886 to the Fiftieth Congress; delegate to the Democratic National Conventions in 1856, 1868, 1884, and 1888; also a delegate to the Union National Convention at Philadelphia in 1866; appointed in 1887 by President Cleveland a member of the Interstate Commerce Commission; reappointed by President Harrison on January 5, 1892, and served from March 22, 1887, to December 31, 1897; was chairman of the commission from March 19, 1892, to the end of his term; resumed the practice of law in Waterloo, Monroe County, Ill., and died there September 29, 1909; interment in Waterloo Cemetery.

MORRISSEY, John, a Representative from New York; born in County Tipperary, Ireland, February 12, 1831; immigrated to the United States in 1833 with his parents, who settled in South Troy, N. Y.; attended the public schools; moved to New York City in 1848 and worked as a molder; moved to California in 1851; returned to New York and became a proprietor of gambling houses in New York and Saratoga; was the champion heavyweight boxer of the world in 1858; purchased the controlling interest in the Saratoga race course in 1863; elected as a Democrat to the Fortieth and Forty-first Congresses (March 4, 1867–March 3, 1871); was not a candidate for renomination in 1870; resumed his former business pursuits; elected to the State senate in 1875; reelected in 1877 and served until his death in Saratoga Springs, N. Y., May 1, 1878; interment in St. Peter's Cemetery, Troy, N. Y.

MORROW, Dwight Whitney, a Senator from New Jersey; born in Huntington, Cabell County, W. Va., January 11, 1873; moved with his parents to Allegheny (now a part of Pittsburgh), Pa., in 1875; attended the public schools; worked in the office of the county treasurer 1887–1891; entered Amherst College and was graduated in 1895; studied law at Columbia University; was admitted to the bar in 1899 and engaged in practice in New York City; moved to Englewood, N. J., in 1903; engaged in banking in 1914 and served as director of many industrial and financial corporations; during the First World War was a director of the National War Savings Committee for the State of New Jersey; served abroad as advisor to the Allied Maritime Transport Council, as a member of the Military Board of Allied Supply, and as chief civilian aid to General Pershing at Chaumont; was awarded the Distinguished Service Medal "for exceptionally meritorious and distinguished services," and was also decorated by France, Italy, and Greece; chairman of the New Jersey Prison Inquiry Commission in 1917 and 1918 and of the New Jersey State Board of Institutions and Agencies 1918–1920; chairman of the Aircraft Board created by President Coolidge in 1925; appointed Ambassador to Mexico by President Coolidge and served from September 21, 1927, until September 30, 1930, when he resigned; delegate to the Sixth Pan American Conference held at Habana in 1928 and to the London Naval Conference in 1930; elected as a Republican to the United States Senate in 1930 to fill the vacancy in the term ending March 3, 1931, caused by the resignation of Walter E. Edge, and at the same time was elected for the term commencing March 4, 1931, and served from December 3, 1930, until his death in Englewood, N. J., on October 5, 1931; interment in Brookside Cemetery.

MORROW, Jeremiah, a Representative and a Senator from Ohio; born near Gettysburg, Pa., October 6, 1771; attended the public schools; moved to that part of the Northwest Territory which is now the State of Ohio in 1795; engaged in agricultural pursuits; member of the Territorial house of representatives in 1801 and 1802; delegate to the State constitutional convention in 1802; member of the State senate in 1803; upon the admission of Ohio as a State into the Union was elected as a Democrat to the Eighth and to the four succeeding Congresses and served from October 17, 1803, to March 3, 1813; did not seek renom-

ination in 1812, having become a candidate for Senator; elected to the United States Senate and served from March 4, 1813, to March 3, 1819; was not a candidate for reelection; presidential elector on the Monroe and Tompkins ticket in 1820; State canal commissioner in 1822; Governor of Ohio 1822–1826; again a member of the State senate in 1827; served in the State house of representatives in 1829 and 1835; elected as a Whig to the Twenty-sixth Congress to fill the vacancy caused by the resignation of Thomas Corwin and on the same day was elected to the Twenty-seventh Congress and served from October 13, 1840, to March 3, 1843; declined to be a candidate for renomination in 1842; resumed agricultural pursuits; died at Twenty-mile Stand, near Lebanon, Warren County, Ohio, March 22, 1852; interment in Union Cemetery, on the Montgomery Pike, near his home, in Warren County, Ohio.

MORROW, John, a Representative from Virginia; elected to the Ninth and Tenth Congresses (March 4, 1805–March 3, 1809).

MORROW, John, a Representative from New Mexico; born near Darlington, Lafayette County, Wis., on April 19, 1865; attended the public schools and the normal university; taught school in Wisconsin, Iowa, Nebraska, and New Mexico; superintendent of public schools of Colfax County, N. Mex., 1892–1896; studied law; was admitted to the bar in 1895 and commenced practice in Raton, N. Mex.; member of the Territorial house of representatives in 1897 and 1898; city attorney of Raton in 1900 and 1901; president of the board of education 1903–1923; delegate to the Democratic National Convention at Denver in 1908; regent of New Mexico Normal University, Las Vegas, N. Mex., in 1921 and 1922; elected as a Democrat to the Sixty-eighth, Sixty-ninth, and Seventieth Congresses (March 4, 1923–March 3, 1929); unsuccessful candidate for reelection in 1928 to the Seventy-first Congress; engaged in banking, had extensive ranch and livestock holdings, and was a large owner of real estate in Raton; died in a hospital in Santa Fe, N. Mex., on February 25, 1935; interment in the Fairmont Cemetery, Raton, N. Mex.

MORROW, William W., a Representative from California; born near Milton, Wayne County, Ind., July 15, 1843; moved with his parents to Adams County, Ill., in 1845; attended the common schools and received private instruction; moved to Santa Rosa, Calif., in 1859; taught school; explored mining regions; during the Civil War went East in 1862 to join the Union Army and served in the National Rifles of the District of Columbia; while in the Army of the Potomac was appointed special agent of the Treasury Department in January 1865 and was detailed to California; remained there and was employed during the next four years in confidential positions under the Secretary of the Treasury; studied law; was admitted to the bar in 1869 and commenced practice in San Francisco; assistant United States attorney for California 1870–1874; assisted in organizing the San Francisco Bar Association in 1872 and served as its president in 1892 and 1893; chairman of the Republican State central committee of California 1879–1882; attorney for the State board of harbor commissioners 1880–1883; also special United States attorney before the French and American Claims Commission 1881–1883, and before the Alabama Claims Commission 1882–1885; delegate to the Republican National Convention at Chicago in 1884; elected as a Republican to the Forty-ninth, Fiftieth, and Fifty-first Congresses (March 4, 1885–March 3, 1891); was not a candidate for renomination in 1890; United States district judge for the northern district of California 1891–1897; United States circuit judge of the ninth judicial circuit 1897–1922; retired from the bench on January 1, 1923; was one of the incorporators of the American Red Cross; resided in San Francisco, San Francisco County, Calif., until his death in that city on July 24, 1929; interment in Cypress Lawn Cemetery, Colma, Calif.

MORSE, Elijah Adams, a Representative from Massachusetts; born in South Bend, St. Joseph County, Ind., May 25, 1841; moved to Massachusetts with his parents, who settled in Boston in 1852; attended the public schools, the Boylston School in Boston, and Onondaga Academy, New York; enlisted in the Union Army in the Fourth Regiment, Massachusetts Volunteers, during the Civil War; served three months under General Butler in Virginia and one year under General Banks in Louisiana; promoted to corporal; taken prisoner at the capture of Brashear City, La.; manufacturer of stove polish in Canton, Mass.; member of the State house of representatives in 1876; unsuccessful Prohibition Party candidate for Lieutenant Governor in 1877; served in the State senate in 1886 and 1887; member of the Governor's council in 1888; elected as a Republican to the Fifty-first and to the three succeeding Congresses (March 4, 1889–March 3, 1897); was not a candidate for renomination in 1896; resumed manufacturing activities; died in Canton, Norfolk County, Mass., June 5, 1898; interment in Canton Cemetery.

MORSE, Elmer Addison, a Representative from Wisconsin; born in Franksville, Racine County, Wis., on May 11, 1870; attended the common schools of Racine County; was graduated from Ripon College, Wisconsin, in 1893; elected county superintendent of schools of Racine County in 1893 and reelected in 1895; attended the law school of the University of Wisconsin at Madison; was admitted to the bar in 1900 and commenced practice in Antigo, Wis.; city attorney of Antigo 1900–1906; also engaged in the insurance and real-estate business from 1900 until his death; elected as a Republican to the Sixtieth, Sixty-first, and Sixty-second Congresses (March 4, 1907–March 3, 1913); unsuccessful candidate for reelection in 1912 to the Sixty-third Congress; resumed the practice of law at Antigo, Wis.; delegate to the Republican State conventions in 1934 and 1940; secretary to the Selective Service Board during World War II; died at Rochester, Minn., on October 4, 1945; interment in Elmwood Cemetery, Antigo, Wis.

MORSE, Freeman Harlow, a Representative from Maine; born in Bath, Maine, February 19, 1807; attended private schools and the academy in Bath; engaged in business as a carver of figureheads for ships; member of the State house of representatives 1840–1844; elected as a Whig to the Twenty-eighth Congress (March 4, 1843–March 3, 1845); mayor of Bath, Maine, in 1849, 1850, and again in 1855; again served in the State house of representatives in 1853 and 1856; elected as a Republican to the Thirty-fifth and Thirty-sixth Congresses (March 4, 1857–March 3, 1861); was not a candidate for renomination in 1860; delegate to the peace convention held in Washington, D. C., in 1861, in an effort to devise means to prevent the impending war; appointed by President Lincoln as United States consul at London March 22, 1861, and consul general April 16, 1869, and served until July 1870; resided in England after his retirement from office; died in Surbiton, Surrey, England, February 5, 1891; interment in the parish churchyard of St. Mary's, Long Ditton, Surrey County, England.

MORSE, Isaac Edward, a Representative from Louisiana; born in Attakapas, La., May 22, 1809; attended school in Elizabethtown, N. J., and the Norwich (Vt.) Military Academy, and was graduated from Harvard University in 1829; studied law; was admitted to the bar and practiced in New Orleans, La., and St. Martinville, La., 1835–1842; member of the State senate 1842–1844; elected as a Democrat to the Twenty-

eighth Congress to fill the vacancy caused by the death of Peter E. Bossier; reelected to the Twenty-ninth, Thirtieth, and Thirty-first Congresses and served from December 2, 1844, to March 3, 1851; was an unsuccessful candidate for reelection in 1850 to the Thirty-second Congress; delegate to the Democratic National Convention at Baltimore in 1848; attorney general of Louisiana 1853–1855; appointed by President Pierce on December 2, 1856, one of two special commissioners to New Granada to negotiate concerning the transit of citizens, officers, soldiers, and seamen of the United States across the Isthmus of Panama; died in New Orleans, La., February 11, 1866; interment in Washington Cemetery.

MORSE, Leopold, a Representative from Massachusetts; born in Wachenheim, Rhenish Palatinate, Bavaria, August 15, 1831; attended the common schools in Wachenheim; immigrated to the United States in 1849 and resided for about a year in Sandwich, N. H.; moved to Boston, Mass., and worked in a clothing store, which he later purchased and operated until his death; delegate to the Democratic National Convention at St. Louis in 1876 and at Cincinnati in 1880; unsuccessful Democratic candidate in 1870 and 1872 for election to the Forty-second and Forty-third Congresses; elected to the Forty-fifth and to the three succeeding Congresses (March 4, 1877–March 3, 1885); declined to accept a renomination in 1884; elected president of the Post Publishing Co. in 1884; elected to the Fiftieth Congress (March 4, 1887–March 3, 1889); was not a candidate for renomination in 1888; resumed business activities; died in Boston, Mass., December 15, 1892; interment in Mount Auburn Cemetery, Cambridge, Mass.

MORSE, Oliver Andrew, a Representative from New York; born in Cherry Valley, Otsego County, N. Y., March 26, 1815; pursued classical studies, and was graduated from Hamilton College, Clinton, N. Y., in 1833; studied law; was admitted to the bar and commenced practice in Cherry Valley, N. Y.; elected as a Republican to the Thirty-fifth Congress (March 4, 1857–March 3, 1859); was not a candidate for renomination in 1858; writer and translator; died in New York City April 20, 1870; interment in Cherry Valley Cemetery, Cherry Valley, Otsego County, N. Y.

MORSE, Wayne Lyman, a Senator from Oregon; born near Madison, Dane County, Wis., October 20, 1900; attended the public schools; was graduated from the University of Wisconsin at Madison in 1923, from the law department of the University of Minnesota at Minneapolis in 1928, and from Columbia University, New York, N. Y., in 1932; completed a four-year advanced military training course at the University of Wisconsin at Madison (1919–1923) and held a reserve commission as second lieutenant, Field Artillery, United States Army, 1923–1929; taught argumentation at the Universities of Wisconsin and Minnesota; assistant professor of law at the University of Oregon at Eugene in 1929, associate professor in 1930, and dean and professor of law 1931–1944; member of the Oregon Crime Commission; administrative director, United States Attorney General's Survey of Release Procedures, 1936–1939; Pacific Coast arbitrator for the United States Department of Labor (maritime industry) 1938–1942, and also served in other capacities for the Labor Department; chairman of the President's Railway Emergency Board in 1941; alternate public member of the National Defense Mediation Board in 1941; public member of the National War Labor Board 1942–1944; elected as a Republican to the United States Senate in 1944 for the term commencing January 3, 1945; reelected in 1950 for the term ending January 3, 1957; elected as a Democrat in 1956 for the term ending January 3, 1963.

MORTON, Jackson (brother of Jeremiah Morton), a Senator from Florida; born near Fredericksburg, Spotsylvania County, Va., August 10, 1794; attended the common schools, and was graduated from Washington College (now Washington and Lee University), Lexington, Va., in 1814, and from William and Mary College, Williamsburg, Va., in 1815; moved to Pensacola, Fla., in 1820 and engaged in the lumber business; member of the Florida Legislative Council in 1836 and 1837; president of the council in 1837; delegate to the constitutional convention of Florida in 1838; Navy agent at Pensacola 1841–1845; presidential elector on the Whig ticket of Taylor and Fillmore in 1848; elected as a Whig to the United States Senate and served from March 4, 1849, to March 3, 1855; was not a candidate for reelection to the Thirty-fifth Congress; again became engaged in the lumber business; deputy to the Provisional Congress of the Confederate States in Montgomery, Ala., in February 1861; Member of the Confederate Congress 1862–1865; died at his country home, "Mortonia," near Milton, Santa Rosa County, Fla., November 20, 1874; interment in the private cemetery at "Mortonia."

MORTON, Jeremiah (brother of Jackson Morton), a Representative from Virginia; born in Fredericksburg, Spotsylvania County, Va., September 3, 1799; attended a private school and Washington College (now Washington and Lee University), Lexington, Va., in 1814 and 1815; was graduated from William and Mary College, Williamsburg, Va., in 1819; studied law; was admitted to the bar and practiced at Raccoon Ford, Va.; on account of illness abandoned the practice of law and engaged in agricultural pursuits; elected as a Whig to the Thirty-first Congress (March 4, 1849–March 3, 1851); unsuccessful candidate for reelection in 1850 to the Thirty-second Congress; resumed agricultural pursuits; member of the State secession convention in 1861; trustee of the Theological Seminary of Virginia at Alexandria; died at "Lessland," Orange County, Va., November 28, 1878; interment in the private cemetery at his old home, "Morton Hall," Orange County, Va.

MORTON, John, a Delegate from Pennsylvania; born near the old Morris Ferry (now the Darby Creek Bridge), Ridley Township, Delaware County, Pa., in 1724; attended the common school for about three months, and received some tutoring in surveying; a land surveyor for many years; became justice of the peace in 1757; member of the colonial general assembly 1756–1766 and 1769–1775 and served as speaker 1771–1775; member of the Colonial (Stamp Act) Congress in 1765; high sheriff 1766–1770; appointed as a judge in 1770, serving as president judge of the court of general sessions and common pleas of the county, and in April 1774 was appointed an associate justice of the supreme court of appeals of Pennsylvania; member of the Continental Congress 1774–1777; cast the deciding vote of the Pennsylvania delegation on the adoption of the Declaration of Independence, and was a signer thereof; died in Ridley Park, Delaware County, Pa., in April 1777; interment in St. Paul's Churchyard, Chester, Pa.

MORTON, Levi Parsons, a Representative from New York and a Vice President of the United States; born in Shoreham, Addison County, Vt., May 16, 1824; attended the public schools and Shoreham Academy; clerk in a general store in Enfield, Mass., 1838–1840; taught school in Boscawen, N. H., in 1840 and 1841; engaged in mercantile pursuits in Hanover, N. H., in 1845; moved to Boston in 1850; entered the dry-goods business in New York City in 1854; engaged in banking in New York City in 1863; unsuccessful candidate for election in 1876 to the Forty-fifth Congress; was appointed by President Hayes honorary commissioner to the Paris Exhibition of 1878; elected as a Republican to the Forty-sixth and Forty-seventh Congresses and served from March 4, 1879, until his resignation, effective March 21, 1881; United States Minister to France from August 5, 1881, to May 14, 1885; elected Vice President of the United States on the Republican ticket of Harrison and Morton and served from March 4, 1889, to March 3, 1893; Governor of New York 1895–1897; was an investor in real estate; died in Rhinebeck, Dutchess County, N. Y., on May 16, 1920; interment in the Rhinebeck Cemetery.

MORTON, Marcus, a Representative from Massachusetts; born in Freetown, Mass., December 19, 1784; pursued classical studies, and was graduated from Brown University, Providence, R. I., in 1804; studied law; was admitted to the bar and commenced the practice of his profession in Taunton, Mass.; clerk of the State senate in 1811; elected as a Democrat to the Fifteenth and Sixteenth Congresses (March 4, 1817–March 3, 1821); unsuccessful candidate for reelection to the Seventeenth Congress; executive councilor in 1823; elected Lieutenant Governor in 1823; judge of the supreme court 1825–1840; Governor of Massachusetts in 1840, 1841, 1843, and 1844; appointed by President Polk collector of customs in Boston and served from 1845 to 1849; delegate to the State constitutional convention in 1853; member of the State house of representatives in 1858; died in Taunton, Bristol County, Mass., February 6, 1864; interment in Mount Pleasant Cemetery.

MORTON, Oliver Hazard Perry Throck, a Senator from Indiana; born in Saulsbury, Wayne County, Ind., August 4, 1823; attended a private school in Springfield, Ohio; apprenticed to a hatter and worked at the trade four years; pursued a course of study at the Wayne County Seminary, Centerville, Ind., for one year, and was graduated from Miami University, Oxford, Ohio, in 1845; studied law; was admitted to the bar in 1847 and commenced practice in Centerville, Ind.; elected judge of the sixth judicial circuit of Indiana in 1852; unsuccessful Republican candidate for Governor in 1856; elected Lieutenant Governor in 1860 and upon the election of Gov. Henry S. Lane to the United States Senate became Governor of Indiana in 1861; elected Governor in 1864; elected as a Union Republican to the United States Senate in 1867; reelected in 1872 and served from March 4, 1867, until his death; was appointed a member of the Electoral Commission created by act of Congress approved January 29, 1877, to decide the contests in various States in the presidential election of 1876; died in Indianapolis, Ind., November 1, 1877; interment in Crown Hill Cemetery.

MORTON, Thruston Ballard, a Representative and a Senator from Kentucky; born in Louisville, Jefferson County, Ky., August 19, 1907; attended the public schools and Woodberry Forest School, Orange, Va.; was graduated from Yale University, New Haven, Conn., in 1929; engaged in the grain and milling business since 1931; during World War II served as a lieutenant commander in the United States Naval Reserve from August 15, 1941, to December 1, 1946; former director of the Louisville Board of Trade; director of Louisville Goodwill Industries, Frontier Nursing Service, and Lincoln Institute; also interested in banking; elected as a Republican to the Eightieth, Eighty-first, and Eighty-second Congresses (January 3, 1947–January 3, 1953); was not a candidate for renomination in 1952 to the Eighty-third Congress; was appointed Assistant Secretary of State for Congressional Relations by Dwight D. Eisenhower on January 29, 1953, and served until his resignation on February 29, 1956; elected to the United States Senate in 1956 for the term commencing January 3, 1957, and ending January 3, 1963; served as chairman of the Republican National Committee from April 11, 1959, to June 2, 1961.

MOSELEY, Jonathan Ogden, a Representative from Connecticut; born in East Haddam, Conn., April 9, 1762; attended the common schools; was graduated from Yale College in 1780; studied law; was admitted to the bar and commenced practice in East Haddam, Conn.; member of the State house of representatives 1794–1804; justice of the peace of East Haddam, Conn., 1794–1817; State's attorney of Middlesex County 1801–1805; colonel of the Twenty-fourth Regiment, Connecticut Militia, in 1802; elected as a Federalist to the Ninth and to the seven succeeding Congresses (March 4, 1805–March 3, 1821); moved to Saginaw, Mich., and continued the practice of law until his death on September 9, 1838.

MOSELEY, William Abbott, a Representative from New York; born in Whitesboro, Oneida County, N. Y., October 20, 1798; was graduated from Yale College in 1816; studied medicine and practiced; studied law; was admitted to the bar and practiced in Buffalo, N. Y.; member of the State assembly in 1835; served in the State senate 1838–1841; elected as a Whig to the Twenty-eighth and Twenty-ninth Congresses (March 4, 1843–March 3, 1847); resumed the practice of law; died in New York City on November 19, 1873; interment in Forest Lawn Cemetery, Buffalo, N. Y.

MOSER, Guy Louis, a Representative from Pennsylvania; born on a farm in Amity Township, Berks County, Pa., January 23, 1886; attended the rural schools, and Keystone State Teachers' College, Kutztown, Pa.; engaged in painting and paperhanging 1898–1904; taught school in Amity Township, Berks County, Pa., in 1903 and 1904; railway postal clerk 1904–1914; post office inspector 1914–1926; engaged in investment banking in Philadelphia, Pa., 1926–1931 and later in agricultural pursuits; unsuccessful candidate for the Democratic nomination for Congress in 1932 and 1934; elected as a Democrat to the Seventy-fifth, Seventy-sixth, and Seventy-seventh Congresses (January 3, 1937–January 3, 1943); unsuccessful candidate for renomination in 1942 and for the Democratic nomination in 1944, 1948, and in 1950; resumed agricultural pursuits and also engaged in public speaking; died in Reading, Pa., May 9, 1961; interment in Amityville Church Cemetery, Athol, Pa.

MOSES, Charles Leavell, a Representative from Georgia; born near Turin, Coweta County, Ga., May 2, 1856; attended the country schools, and was graduated from Mercer University, Macon, Ga., in 1876; engaged in teaching and agricultural pursuits; for several years principal of the Newnan Academy for Boys; after 1886 devoted his time exclusively to agricultural interests; member of the Farmers' Alliance; elected as a Democrat to the Fifty-second, Fifty-third, and Fifty-fourth Congresses (March 4, 1891–March 3, 1897); unsuccessful candidate for renomination in 1896; resumed agricultural pursuits in Turin, Ga.; delegate to several Democratic State and National conventions; returned to his farm near Turin, Ga., and resumed agricultural pursuits; member of the State house of representatives 1900–1904; discontinued active pursuits and moved to Atlanta, Ga., where he died October 10, 1910; interment in Oak Hill Cemetery.

MOSES, George Higgins, a Senator from New Hampshire; born in Lubec, Washington County, Maine, February 9, 1869; attended the public schools of Eastport, Maine, and Franklin, N. H.; was graduated from Phillips Exeter Academy, Exeter, N. H., in 1887 and from Dartmouth College, Hanover, N. H., in 1890; private secretary to Gov. David H. Goodell 1889–1891 and to Gov. John McLane in 1905, during the sessions of the Portsmouth Peace Conference between Russia and Japan; secretary

to the chairman of the Republican State committee in 1890; member and secretary of the New Hampshire Forestry Commission 1893–1907; member of the board of education of Concord 1902, 1903, 1906–1909, and 1913–1916; United States Minister to Greece and Montenegro 1909–1912; editor of the Concord Evening Monitor 1892–1918; delegate at large to the Republican National Conventions at Chicago in 1908 and 1916; elected as a Republican to the United States Senate on November 5, 1918, to fill the vacancy caused by the death of Jacob H. Gallinger; reelected in 1920, and again in 1926, and served from November 6, 1918, to March 3, 1933; served as President pro tempore of the Senate from March 6, 1925, to March 3, 1933; unsuccessful candidate for reelection to the United States Senate in 1932; unsuccessful candidate for the Republican nomination for United States Senator in 1936; engaged in literary work in Concord, N. H., and Washington, D. C.; died in Concord, N. H., December 20, 1944; interment in Franklin Cemetery, Franklin, N. H.

MOSES, John, a Senator from North Dakota; born in Strand, Norway, June 12, 1885; attended the public and high schools and was graduated from Junior College, Oslo, Norway; immigrated to the United States in 1905 and settled in Benson, Swift County, Minn.; worked as laborer, farm hand, clerk, and freight-claim investigator; secretary of the State Teachers College, Valley City, N. Dak., 1911–1913; was graduated from the law school of the University of North Dakota at Grand Forks in 1915; was admitted to the bar in 1915 and practiced law in Hope and Hebron, N. Dak., before moving to Hazen, N. Dak., in 1917; also engaged in agricultural pursuits and banking; served as State's attorney of Mercer County, N. Dak., 1919–1923 and 1927–1933; unsuccessful candidate for Governor in 1936; elected Governor in 1938 and reelected in 1940 and 1942; elected as a Democrat to the United States Senate in 1944 and served from January 3, 1945, until his death on March 3, 1945, at Rochester, Minn., where he had gone for an operation; interment in St. Mary's Cemetery, Bismarck, N. Dak.

MOSGROVE, James, a Representative from Pennsylvania; born in Kittanning, Armstrong County, Pa., June 14, 1821; attended the common schools; engaged in the iron business; unsuccessful candidate in 1878 on the Greenback ticket for election to the Forty-sixth Congress; elected as the Democratic and Greenback candidate to the Forty-seventh Congress (March 4, 1881–March 3, 1883); declined to be a candidate for renomination in 1882; also declined to be a candidate for the Democratic nomination for Governor; engaged in banking and was president of the First National Bank from 1882 until his death in Kittanning, Armstrong County, Pa., on November 27, 1900; interment in Kittanning Cemetery.

MOSIER, Harold Gerard, a Representative from Ohio; born in Cincinnati, Hamilton County, Ohio, July 24, 1889; attended the public and high schools of his native city; was graduated from Dartmouth College, Hanover, N. H., in 1912 and from the law department of Harvard University, Cambridge, Mass., in 1915; was admitted to the bar in 1916 and commenced practice in Cleveland, Ohio; member of the State senate 1932–1934; Lieutenant Governor of Ohio 1934–1936; elected as a Democrat to the Seventy-fifth Congress (January 3, 1937–January 3, 1939); unsuccessful candidate for renomination in 1938; resumed the practice of law in Cleveland, Ohio, Baltimore, Md., and Washington, D. C., where he now resides.

MOSS, Frank Edward, a Senator from Utah; born in Holladay (Salt Lake City), Salt Lake County, Utah, September 23, 1911; attended the public schools and Granite High School; graduated from the University of Utah in 1933 and from George Washington University Law School, Washington, D. C., in 1937; was admitted to the bar in 1937; attorney for the Securities and Exchange Commission, Washington, D. C., 1937–1939; during World War II served as judge advocate in the European Theater with the Air Corps 1942–1945; colonel in the United States Air Force Reserve; elected Salt Lake City judge in 1940, reelected in 1945 and served until 1950 when he resigned; elected Salt Lake County attorney in 1950, reelected in 1954 and served until 1959; delegate to all State Democratic Conventions from 1950 to 1958; delegate to the Democratic National Conventions in 1952, 1956, and 1960; elected as a Democrat to the United States Senate for the term commencing January 3, 1959, and ending January 3, 1965.

MOSS, Hunter Holmes, Jr., a Representative from West Virginia; born in Parkersburg, Wood County, W. Va., May 26, 1874; attended the public schools; in early youth was employed in a bank; was graduated from the law department of West Virginia University at Morgantown in 1896; was admitted to the bar and commenced practice in Parkersburg, W. Va., in 1896; prosecuting attorney of Wood County, W. Va., 1900–1904; judge of the fourth circuit court of West Virginia 1904–1912; elected as a Republican to the Sixty-third and Sixty-fourth Congresses and served from March 4, 1913, until his death in Atlantic City, N. J., July 15, 1916; interment in Odd Fellows Cemetery, Parkersburg, W. Va.

MOSS, John Emerson, Jr., a Representative from California; born in Hiawatha, Carbon County, Utah, April 13, 1913; moved to Sacramento, Calif., with his parents in 1923; attended the public schools and Sacramento Junior College 1931–1933; engaged in sales, credit executive, and retail business 1938–1943; member of California Democratic State Central Committee since 1938; director of California Young Democrats in 1938; secretary of the Sacramento County Democratic Committee in 1939; national committeeman of California Young Democrats 1942–1944; during World War II served in the United States Navy 1943–1945; engaged in the real-estate business since 1945; member of the State assembly and served as assistant Democratic floor leader at the 1949–1952 sessions; elected as a Democrat to the Eighty-third and to the three succeeding Congresses (January 3, 1953–January 3, 1961). *Reelected to the Eighty-seventh Congress.*

MOSS, John McKenzie (nephew of James Andrew McKenzie), a Representative from Kentucky; born on a farm near Bennettstown, Christian County, Ky., January 3, 1868; attended the common and private schools; employed in the Railway Mail Service 1888–1891; studied law at Kent Law School in Chicago; was admitted to the bar in 1893 and practiced in Bowling Green, Warren County, Ky., and adjoining counties; successfully contested as a Republican the election of John S. Rhea to the Fifty-seventh Congress and served from March 25, 1902, to March 3, 1903; unsuccessful candidate for reelection in 1902 to the Fifty-eighth Congress; resumed the practice of law in Bowling Green; elected judge of the eighth judicial district of Kentucky in 1909; reelected in 1915 and served until 1921, when he resigned; appointed assistant general counsel for the Alien Property Custodian on July 13, 1921, and served until January 1, 1922, when he was made general counsel; resigned on February 6, 1922, to become Deputy Commissioner of Internal Revenue in charge of estate and capital tax, in which capacity he served until his resignation March 2, 1923; appointed on March 3, 1923, Assistant Secretary of the Treasury and served until July 13, 1926, when he resigned; assumed the duties of associate judge of the Court of Claims on July 14,

1926, and served until his death in Washington, D. C., June 11, 1929; interment in La Fayette Cemetery, Bennettstown, near Hopkinsville, Christian County, Ky.

MOSS, Ralph Wilbur, a Representative from Indiana; born in Center Point, Clay County, Ind., April 21, 1862; educated in the common schools of the township and attended Purdue University, West Lafayette, Ind., for two years; taught school in Sugar Ridge Township; principal of the graded schools in Harmony, Ind.; subsequently became engaged in agricultural pursuits; member of the State senate 1905–1909; elected as a Democrat to the Sixty-first and to the three succeeding Congresses (March 4, 1909–March 3, 1917); unsuccessful candidate for reelection in 1916 to the Sixty-fifth Congress and for election in 1918 to the Sixty-sixth Congress; retired to his farm near Ashboro, Clay County, Ind., where he died on April 26, 1919; interment in Moss Cemetery, near his home.

MOTT, Gordon Newell, a Delegate from the Territory of Nevada; born in Zanesville, Ohio, on October 21, 1812; completed preparatory studies; studied law; was admitted to the bar and commenced practice in Zanesville in 1836; moved to Texas during its struggle for independence and served nine months as a volunteer; returned to Ohio and resumed the practice of law; moved to California in 1849; judge of Sutter County in 1850; district judge 1851–1854; moved to Nevada in 1861; appointed by President Lincoln associate justice of the supreme court of Nevada Territory on March 27, 1861, and served until his resignation in 1863, having been elected to Congress; elected as a Republican to the Thirty-eighth Congress and served from March 4, 1863, to October 31, 1864, when the Territory of Nevada became a State; was not a candidate for Representative from the new State in 1864; died in San Francisco, San Francisco County, Calif., April 27, 1887; interment in Laurel Hill Cemetery.

MOTT, James, a Representative from New Jersey; born near Middletown, Monmouth County, N. J., January 18, 1739; educated by private teachers; engaged in agricultural pursuits; captain in the Second Regiment of Monmouth County Militia in 1775; member of the State house of assembly 1776–1779; State treasurer 1783–1799; elected as a Democrat to the Seventh and Eighth Congresses (March 4, 1801–March 3, 1805); presidential elector on the Democratic ticket of Madison and Clinton in 1808; died on his farm near Middletown, N. J., on October 18, 1823; interment in Middletown Baptist Churchyard.

MOTT, James Wheaton, a Representative from Oregon; born near New Washington, Clearfield County, Pa., November 12, 1883; moved with his parents to Salem, Oreg., in 1890; attended the public schools, the University of Oregon at Eugene, and Stanford University, Stanford University, Calif.; was graduated from Columbia University, New York, N. Y., in 1909; engaged as a newspaper reporter in New York City, N. Y., San Francisco, Calif., and Salem, Oreg., 1909–1917; was graduated from the law department of Willamette University, Salem, Oreg., in 1917; was admitted to the bar in the same year and commenced practice in Astoria, Oreg.; during the First World War served as a seaman first class in the United States Navy; city attorney of Astoria, Oreg., 1920–1922; member of the State house of representatives 1922–1928 and 1930–1932; moved to Salem, Oreg., in 1929; corporation commissioner of Oregon 1931–1932; elected as a Republican to the Seventy-third and to the six succeeding Congresses and served from March 4, 1933, until his death in the naval hospital at Bethesda, Md., on November 12, 1945; interment in Mount Crest Abbey Mausoleum, Salem, Oreg.

MOTT, Luther Wright, a Representative from New York; born in Oswego, Oswego County, N. Y., November 30, 1874; attended the public schools, and was graduated from Harvard University in 1896; engaged in banking in Oswego; appointed State superintendent of banks in 1907, but resigned after five days' service; delegate to the Republican National Convention at Chicago in 1908; president of the New York State Bankers' Association in 1910 and 1911; elected as a Republican to the Sixty-second and to the six succeeding Congresses and served from March 4, 1911, until his death in Oswego, N. Y., July 10, 1923; interment in Riverside Cemetery.

MOTT, Richard, a Representative from Ohio; born in Mamaroneck, Westchester County, N. Y., July 21, 1804; attended the Quaker Seminary in Dutchess County, N. Y.; engaged in banking in New York City; moved to Toledo, Ohio, in 1836 and engaged in the real-estate business and other enterprises; mayor of Toledo in 1845 and 1846; elected as a Republican to the Thirty-fourth and Thirty-fifth Congresses (March 4, 1855–March 3, 1859); was not a candidate for renomination in 1858; returned to Toledo, Ohio, and engaged in banking and the real-estate business; served as chairman of the citizens' military committee during the Civil War; died in Toledo, Ohio, January 22, 1888; interment in Mount Hope Cemetery, Rochester, Monroe County, N. Y.

MOTTE, Isaac, a Delegate from South Carolina; born in Charleston, S. C., December 8, 1738; appointed ensign in His Majesty's Sixtieth Royal American Regiment, December 19, 1756, and promoted to lieutenant April 15, 1759; served in Canada in the French and Indian War in 1756; resigned and returned to Charleston in 1766; member of the house of commons in 1772; delegate to the provincial congresses of 1774, 1775, and 1776; during the Revolution was commissioned lieutenant colonel of the Second South Carolina (Continental) Regiment June 17, 1775; was active in the defense of Fort Moultrie, and was promoted to the rank of colonel September 16, 1776; resigned on election to the privy council in 1779; elected to the assembly from Charleston in 1779; Member of the Continental Congress 1780–1782; delegate to the State convention that ratified the Federal Constitution on May 23, 1788; appointed naval officer for the port of Charleston by General Washington; died in Charleston, S. C., May 8, 1795; interment in St. Philip's Churchyard.

MOULDER, Morgan Moore, a Representative from Missouri; born in Linn Creek, Camden County, Mo., August 31, 1904; attended the public schools of Linn Creek and Lebanon, Mo., and the University of Missouri at Columbia; was graduated from Cumberland University, Lebanon, Tenn., in 1927; was admitted to the bar in 1928 and commenced the practice of law in Linn Creek, Mo.; elected prosecuting attorney of Camden County, Mo., in 1928; reelected for three succeeding terms and served until 1938, when he returned to the private practice of law; special assistant to the United States attorney for the western district of Missouri 1943–1946; appointed by the Governor in April 1947 to serve as a judge of the circuit court in the eighteenth judicial circuit and served until December 31, 1948; elected as a Democrat to the Eighty-first and to the five succeeding Congresses (January 3, 1949–January 3, 1961). *Reelected to the Eighty-seventh Congress.*

MOULTON, Mace, a Representative from New Hampshire; born in Concord, N. H., May 2, 1796; attended the public schools; sheriff of Hillsborough County in 1845; elected as a Democrat to the Twenty-ninth Congress (March 4, 1845–March 3, 1847); State councilor in 1848 and 1849; engaged in banking; died in Manchester, Hillsborough County, N. H., May 5, 1867; interment in Valley Cemetery.

MOULTON, Samuel Wheeler, a Representative from Illinois; born in Wenham, Essex County, Mass., January 20, 1821; attended the public schools; moved to Kentucky, where he taught school for several years, thence to Mississippi where he continued to teach; moved to Illinois in 1845 and settled in Oakland, Coles County; studied law; was admitted to the bar in 1847 and commenced practice in Sullivan, Ill.; moved to Shelbyville in 1849 and continued the practice of law; member of the State house of representatives 1852–1859; presidential elector on the Democratic ticket of Buchanan and Breckinridge in 1856; president of the board of education of the State of Illinois 1859–1876; unsuccessful candidate for election in 1862 to the Thirty-eighth Congress; elected as a Democrat to the Thirty-ninth Congress (March 4, 1865–March 3, 1867); elected to the Forty-seventh and Forty-eighth Congresses (March 4, 1881–March 3, 1885); was not a candidate for renomination in 1884; resumed the practice of law in Shelbyville; affiliated with the Republican Party after 1896; died in Shelbyville, Shelby County, Ill., June 3, 1905; interment in Glenwood Cemetery.

MOUSER, Grant Earl, a Representative from Ohio; born in Larue, Marion County, Ohio, September 11, 1868; attended the Larue Union Schools and Ada University, Ada, Ohio; was graduated from the Cincinnati Law School in 1890; was admitted to the bar the same year and commenced practice in Marion, Ohio; prosecuting attorney of Marion County 1893–1896; delegate to many State conventions; elected as a Republican to the Fifty-ninth and Sixtieth Congresses (March 4, 1905–March 3, 1909); unsuccessful candidate for reelection in 1908 to the Sixty-first Congress; delegate to the Republican National Convention at Chicago in 1908; resumed the practice of law in Marion; judge of the court of common pleas of Marion County 1916–1925; resumed the practice of law until 1935 when he retired; died in Marion, Ohio, May 6, 1949; interment in Marion Cemetery.

MOUSER, Grant Earl, Jr. (son of the preceding), a Representative from Ohio; born in Marion, Marion County, Ohio, February 20, 1895; attended the public schools and Ohio Wesleyan University at Delaware in 1913 and 1914; was graduated from the law college of Ohio State University at Columbus in 1917 and was admitted to the bar the same year; during the First World War was graduated from the Army Medical School at Washington, D. C., in 1918, and served in the United States Army as a second lieutenant in the Medical Corps with the Western Reserve University College Ambulance Unit; commenced the practice of law in Marion, Ohio, in 1920; city solicitor of Marion 1924–1927, resigning to become special counsel in the State attorney's office, and served in this capacity until 1929; also served as attorney for the State highway department in 1927 and 1928; elected as a Republican to the Seventy-first and Seventy-second Congresses (March 4, 1929–March 3, 1933); unsuccessful candidate for reelection in 1932 to the Seventy-third Congress and for election in 1936 to the Seventy-fifth Congress; continued the practice of law until his death in Marion, Ohio, December 21, 1943; interment in Marion Cemetery.

MOUTON, Alexander, a Senator from Louisiana; born in Attakapas district, in what is now Lafayette Parish, La., November 19, 1804; pursued classical studies and was graduated from Georgetown College, District of Columbia; studied law; was admitted to the bar in 1825 and commenced practice in Lafayette Parish, La.; member of the State house of representatives 1827–1832 and served as speaker during the sessions of 1831 and 1832; unsuccessful candidate for election in 1830 to the Twenty-second Congress; again a member of the State house of representatives in 1836; elected as a Democrat to the United States

Senate to fill the vacancy caused by the resignation of Alexander Porter and served from January 12, 1837, until his resignation on March 1, 1842; Governor of Louisiana 1842–1846; president of the Southwestern Railroad Convention which met in New Orleans in January 1852; president of the vigilance committee of Lafayette Parish in 1858; delegate to the Democratic National Convention in 1860; president of the State secession convention in 1861; died near Vermillionville (now Lafayette), La., on February 12, 1885; interment in St. John's Cemetery.

MOUTON, Robert Louis, a Representative from Louisiana; born in Duchamp, St. Martin Parish, La., October 20, 1892; moved with his parents to Lafayette, La., where he attended the public schools; was graduated from Southwestern Louisiana Institute, Lafayette, La.; employed as a clerk in a bank in 1911 and 1912; member of the faculty of St. Charles College, Grand Coteau, La., 1912–1914; engaged in the insurance business and also operated a night school at Lafayette, La., in 1915 and 1916; served as aide to the general receiver of customs on the island of Haiti, West Indies, in 1916 and as collector of customs at Gonaives, Haiti, from March 1917 to April 1919; during the First World War enlisted in the United States Marine Corps; served as an interpreter and intelligence officer attached to the first squadron of the first marine aviation outfit overseas from May 1918 to January 1919; returned to Lafayette and engaged in horticultural pursuits; mayor of Lafayette 1919–1927 and 1931–1935; postmaster from May 1929 until his resignation in November 1930; member of the United States Marine Corps Reserve, with rank of captain; delegate to the Democratic National Convention at Philadelphia in 1936; elected as a Democrat to the Seventy-fifth and Seventy-sixth Congresses (January 3, 1937–January 3, 1941); unsuccessful candidate for renomination in 1940; resumed his horticultural and real-estate interests; died in New Orleans, La., November 26, 1956; interment in St. John's Catholic Cemetery, Lafayette, La.

MOWRY, Daniel, Jr., a Delegate from Rhode Island; born in Smithfield, Providence County, R. I., August 17, 1729; received a limited schooling and learned the cooper's trade; town clerk of Smithfield 1760–1780; member of the general assembly 1766–1776; judge of the court of common pleas 1776–1781; took an active part in pre-Revolutionary movements; Member of the Continental Congress 1780–1782; declined to be a candidate for renomination; engaged in agricultural pursuits until his death in the town of Smithfield, near Woonsocket, Providence County, R. I., July 6, 1806; interment in the family cemetery in North Smithfield, R. I.

MOXLEY, William James, a Representative from Illinois; born in County Cork, Ireland, May 22, 1851; as an infant immigrated with his parents to the United States and settled in Chicago, Ill.; attended the common schools; engaged in the manufacture of oleomargarine in 1881 and, later, in banking; member of the Republican State central committee; member of the executive board of the Cook County central committee; colonel on the staff of Gov. Richard Yates 1900–1904; presidential elector on the Republican ticket of McKinley and Roosevelt in 1900 and of Roosevelt and Fairbanks in 1904; was selected as the messenger to deliver the electoral vote of Illinois in 1900; elected as a Republican to the Sixty-first Congress to fill the vacancy caused by the resignation of William Lorimer and served from November 23, 1909, to March 3, 1911; unsuccessful candidate for reelection in 1910 to the Sixty-second Congress; continued his former business activities in Chicago, Ill., until his retirement; died at his summer home on Delavan Lake, near Delavan, Wis., August 4, 1938; interment in Calvary Cemetery, Chicago, Ill.

MOYNIHAN, Patrick Henry, a Representative from Illinois; born in Chicago, Cook County, Ill., September 25, 1869; attended the public schools and St. Patrick's High School at Chicago, Ill.; engaged in the publishing and printing business and also in the coal business; member of the city council of Chicago 1901–1909; member of the Illinois State Commerce Commission 1921–1929, serving as chairman in 1928 and 1929; elected as a Republican to the Seventy-third Congress (March 4, 1933–January 3, 1935); unsuccessful candidate for reelection in 1934 to the Seventy-fourth Congress, for election in 1936 to the Seventy-fifth Congress, and in 1940 to the Seventy-seventh Congress; continued his former business activities in Chicago, Ill., until his death on May 20, 1946; interment in Mount Olivet Cemetery.

MOZLEY, Norman Adolphus, a Representative from Missouri; born on a farm in Johnson County, Ill., December 11, 1865; attended the common schools; moved to Stoddard County, Mo., in 1887 and taught school; studied law; was admitted to the bar in 1891 and practiced in Bloomfield, Stoddard County, Mo.; elected as a Republican to the Fifty-fourth Congress (March 4, 1895–March 3, 1897); was not a candidate for renomination in 1896; resumed the practice of law in Bloomfield, Mo.; commissioner of the State supreme court 1919–1921; moved to Poplar Bluff, Mo., and continued the practice of his profession; delegate to the State constitutional convention of 1921 and 1922; died in Bloomfield, Mo., May 9, 1922; interment in Bloomfield Cemetery.

MRUK, Joseph, a Representative from New York; born in Buffalo, N. Y., November 6, 1903; engaged in the jewelry business in Buffalo, N. Y., in 1928; served as district councilman to the Buffalo Common Council 1937–1941; was elected councilman at large in 1941 and served until December 22, 1942, when he resigned; elected as a Republican to the Seventy-eighth Congress (January 3, 1943–January 3, 1945); unsuccessful candidate for renomination in 1944; resumed the retail jewelry business and is a resident of Buffalo, N. Y.

MUDD, Sydney Emanuel, a Representative from Maryland; born at "Gallant Green," Charles County, Md., February 12, 1858; attended Georgetown University, Washington, D. C., and was graduated from St. John's College, Annapolis, Md., in 1878; studied law privately and also attended the law department of the University of Virginia at Charlottesville; was admitted to the bar in 1880 and practiced; member of the State house of delegates in 1879 and 1881; presidential elector on the Republican ticket of Garfield and Arthur in 1880; successfully contested as a Republican the election of Barnes Compton to the Fifty-first Congress and served from March 20, 1890, to March 3, 1891; unsuccessful candidate for reelection in 1890 to the Fifty-second Congress; elected to the State house of delegates in 1895 and served as speaker; moved to La Plata in 1896; delegate to the Republican National Convention in 1896; elected to the Fifty-fifth and to the six succeeding Congresses (March 4, 1897–March 3, 1911); died in Philadelphia, Pa., October 21, 1911; interment in St. Ignatius' Catholic Church Cemetery, Chapel Point, near La Plata, Charles County, Md.

MUDD, Sydney Emanuel (son of the preceding), a Representative from Maryland; born at "Gallant Green," Charles County, Md., June 20, 1885; attended the public schools of Charles County and the District of Columbia; moved with his parents to La Plata, Md., in 1896; was graduated from the academic department of Georgetown University, Washington, D. C., in 1906 and from the law department in 1909; unsuccessful candidate for election to the Maryland House of Delegates in 1909; was admitted to the bar in 1910; professor of criminal law at Georgetown University Law School in 1910; appointed assistant district attorney of the District of Columbia in February 1911 and resigned in March 1912; unsuccessful candidate for nomination in 1912 for election to the Sixty-third Congress; reappointed assistant district attorney in July 1912 and resigned in March 1914, to become a candidate for Congress; elected as a Republican to the Sixty-fourth and to the four succeeding Congresses and served from March 4, 1915, until his death in Baltimore, Md., October 11, 1924; interment in St. Ignatius' Catholic Church Cemetery, Chapel Point, near La Plata, Charles County, Md.

MUHLENBERG, Francis Swaine (son of John Peter Gabriel Muhlenberg and nephew of Frederick Augustus Conrad Muhlenberg), a Representative from Ohio; born in Philadelphia, Pa., April 22, 1795; attended the public schools of Philadelphia and Dickinson College, Carlisle, Pa.; studied law; was admitted to the bar in 1816 and commenced practice in Reading, Pa.; private secretary to Governor Hiester 1820–1823; moved to Pickaway County, Ohio; member of the State house of representatives in 1827; elected as a National-Republican to the Twentieth Congress to fill the vacancy caused by the resignation of William Creighton, Jr., and served from December 19, 1828, to March 3, 1829; engaged in the real-estate business in Ohio and Kentucky; died in Pickaway County, Ohio, on December 17, 1831; interment in Protestant Cemetery, Circleville, Pickaway County, Ohio.

MUHLENBERG, Frederick Augustus (great-great-grandson of Frederick Augustus Conrad Muhlenberg, great-great-grand-nephew of John Peter Gabriel Muhlenberg, and the sixth Muhlenberg to serve in Congress), a Representative from Pennsylvania; born in Reading, Berks County, Pa., September 25, 1887; attended the public schools; graduated from Gettysburg (Pa.) College in 1908 and from the University of Pennsylvania at Philadelphia in 1912; during the First World War served as captain of the Three Hundred and Fourteenth Infantry from September 1917 to March 1919, engaging in the Meuse-Argonne and St. Mihiel offensives; awarded the Distinguished Service Cross, Purple Heart with Palm, Legion d'Honneur, and the Croix de Guerre; engaged as an architect at Reading, Pa., since 1920; city councilman of Reading, Pa., 1934–1938; Republican county chairman in 1935 and 1936; during World War II served as a lieutenant colonel and later as a colonel in the Corps of Engineers, United States Army, from December 1940 to March 1946; awarded the Legion of Merit; elected as a Republican to the Eightieth Congress (January 3, 1947–January 3, 1949); unsuccessful candidate for reelection in 1948 to the Eighty-first Congress; resumed the practice of architecture in Reading, Pa.; chairman, State Art Commission 1952– and the County Planning Commission 1958–; is a resident of Wernersville, Pa.

MUHLENBERG, Frederick Augustus Conrad (brother of John Peter Gabriel Muhlenberg, uncle of Francis Swaine Muhlenberg and of Henry Augustus Philip Muhlenberg, and great-great-grandfather of Frederick Augustus Muhlenberg), a Delegate and a Representative from Pennsylvania; born in Trappe, Pa., January 1, 1750; pursued an academic course; attended the University of Halle, Germany; studied theology and was ordained by the ministerium of Pennsylvania a minister of the Lutheran Church October 25, 1770; preached in Stouchsburg and Lebanon, Pa., 1770–1774, and in New York City 1774–1776; when the British entered New York he felt obliged to leave, and returned to Trappe, Pa.; moved to New Hanover, Pa., and was pastor of Lutheran congregations there and in Oley and New Goshenhoppen until August 1779; Member of the Continental Congress

in 1779 and 1780; served in the State house of representatives 1780–1783 and was elected speaker November 3, 1780; delegate to and president of the State constitutional convention in 1787 called to ratify the Federal Constitution; elected to the First and to the three succeeding Congresses (March 4, 1789–March 3, 1797); served as Speaker during the First and Third Congresses; was not a candidate for renomination in 1796; president of the council of censors of Pennsylvania; appointed receiver general of the Pennsylvania Land Office on January 8, 1800, and served until his death in Lancaster, Pa., June 5, 1801; interment in Woodward Hill Cemetery.

MUHLENBERG, Henry Augustus (son of Henry Augustus Philip Muhlenberg and grandson of Joseph Hiester), a Representative from Pennsylvania; born in Reading, Pa., July 21, 1823; pursued classical studies; was graduated from Dickinson College, Carlisle, Pa., in 1841; studied law; was admitted to the bar in 1844 and commenced practice in Reading, Pa.; member of the State senate 1849–1852; elected as a Democrat to the Thirty-third Congress and served from March 4, 1853, until his death in Washington, D. C., January 9, 1854; interment in Charles Evans Cemetery, Reading, Pa.

MUHLENBERG, Henry Augustus Philip (father of Henry Augustus Muhlenberg and nephew of John Peter Gabriel Muhlenberg and of Frederick Augustus Conrad Muhlenberg), a Representative from Pennsylvania; born in Lancaster, Pa., May 13, 1782; pursued classical studies; studied theology and was ordained to the Lutheran ministry by the ministerium of Pennsylvania in 1802; pastor of Trinity Church, Reading, Pa., from April 1803 to June 1829; resigned on account of ill health; elected as a Jackson Democrat to the Twenty-first and to the four succeeding Congresses and served from March 4, 1829, until his resignation February 9, 1838; unsuccessful Democratic candidate for Governor in 1835 and 1837; offered by President Van Buren in 1837 the position of Secretary of the Navy and that of Minister to Russia, both of which he declined; Minister to Austria from February 8, 1838, to September 18, 1840; was nominated as the Democratic candidate for Governor of Pennsylvania in 1844, but died in Reading, Pa., August 11, 1844, before the election; interment in Charles Evans Cemetery.

MUHLENBERG, John Peter Gabriel (father of Francis Swaine Muhlenberg, brother of Frederick Augustus Conrad Muhlenberg, and uncle of Henry Augustus Philip Muhlenberg, and great-great-granduncle of Frederick Augustus Muhlenberg), a Representative and a Senator from Pennsylvania; born in Trappe, Pa., October 1, 1746; pursued classical studies; attended the Academy of Philadelphia (later the University of Pennsylvania) 1760–1763; studied in the University of Halle, Germany, 1763–1766, and served in a German regiment of dragoons; returned to Philadelphia, Pa., in 1766; studied theology and was ordained by the ministerium of Pennsylvania in 1768; was a pastor of Lutheran churches in New Germantown and Bedminster, N. J.; moved to Woodstock, Va., and on a visit to England was ordained a priest in the Episcopal Church April 23, 1772, by the Bishop of London; member of the Virginia House of Burgesses in 1774; chairman of the committee of safety for Dunmore County, Va.; entered the Revolutionary Army as colonel of the Eighth Virginia (German) Regiment; commissioned brigadier general of the Continental Army February 21, 1777, and served until the close of the war; brevetted major general September 30, 1783; returned to Pennsylvania and settled in Montgomery County; elected a member of the supreme executive council of Pennsylvania in 1784 and served as vice president 1785–1787; elected to the First Congress (March 4, 1789–March 3, 1791); elected to the Third Congress (March 4, 1793–March 3, 1795);

presidential elector in 1796; elected to the Sixth Congress (March 4, 1799–March 3, 1801); elected as a Democrat to the United States Senate and served from March 4, 1801, until his resignation on June 30, 1801; appointed by President Jefferson supervisor of revenue for Pennsylvania in 1801 and collector of customs at Philadelphia in 1802, in which latter capacity he served until his death in Providence, Montgomery County, Pa., October 1, 1807; interment in the Augustus Lutheran Church Cemetery, Trappe, Pa.

MULDOWNEY, Michael Joseph, a Representative from Pennsylvania; born in Philadelphia, Pa., on August 10, 1889; moved with his parents to Pittsburgh, Pa., in 1894; attended the public schools; was graduated from Duquesne University, Pittsburgh, Pa., in 1908; member of the State house of representatives 1925–1929; served in the city council of Pittsburgh 1930–1933; elected as a Republican to the Seventy-third Congress (March 4, 1933–January 3, 1935); unsuccessful candidate for reelection in 1934 to the Seventy-fourth Congress; member of the State board of mercantile appraisers 1935–1937; appointed State unemployment compensation referee in 1940 and served in that capacity until his death in Pittsburgh, Pa., on March 30, 1947; interment in Calvary Cemetery.

MULDROW, Henry Lowndes, a Representative from Mississippi; born near Tibbes Station, Clay County, Miss., February 8, 1837; was graduated from the literary department of the University of Mississippi at Oxford in 1857 and from the law department of the same university in 1858; was admitted to the bar in 1859 and commenced practice in Starkville, Miss.; entered the Confederate Army as a private in 1861 and before the close of the Civil War attained the rank of colonel of Cavalry; district attorney for the sixth judicial district of Mississippi 1869–1871; member of the State house of representatives in 1875; trustee of the University of Mississippi 1876–1898; elected as a Democrat to the Forty-fifth and to the three succeeding Congresses (March 4, 1877–March 3, 1885); First Assistant Secretary of the Interior during the first administration of President Cleveland; resigned in 1889 and resumed the practice of law in Starkville, Miss.; delegate to the State constitutional convention in 1890; appointed chancellor of the first district of Mississippi in September 1899 and served until 1905; died in Starkville, Oktibbeha County, Miss., March 1, 1905; interment in Odd Fellows Cemetery.

MULKEY, Frederick William (nephew of Joseph Norton Dolph), a Senator from Oregon; born in Portland, Oreg., January 6, 1874; attended the public schools; was graduated from the University of Oregon at Eugene in 1896 and from the New York Law School of New York City in 1899; was admitted to the Oregon bar and commenced the practice of law at Portland, Oreg.; member of the Portland City Council 1900–1902, and served as its president in 1901; served as chairman of the Oregon State Tax Commission in 1905 and 1906; elected as a Republican to the United States Senate to fill the vacancy caused by the death of John H. Mitchell and served from January 23, 1907, until March 3, 1907; was not a candidate for reelection in 1907; resumed the practice of law in Portland, Oreg.; chairman of the public docks commission, Portland, Oreg., 1911–1916; elected to the United States Senate to fill the vacancy caused by the death of Harry Lane and served from November 6, 1918, until his resignation, effective December 17, 1918; resumed the practice of his profession in Portland, Oreg.; served as chairman of the Multnomah County Tax Supervising and Conservation Commission from 1921 to 1924; died in Portland, Multnomah County, on May 5, 1924; interment in Riverview Cemetery.

MULKEY, William Oscar, a Representative from Alabama; born in Brundidge, Pike County, Ala., July 27, 1871; attended the public schools, and was graduated from State Normal College, Troy, Ala., in 1892; studied law; was admitted to the bar in 1893 and commenced practice in Troy, Geneva County, Ala., in 1894; member of the State constitutional convention in 1901; served in the State house of representatives in 1911; elected as a Democrat to the Sixty-third Congress to fill the vacancy caused by the resignation of Henry D. Clayton and served from June 29, 1914, to March 3, 1915; was not a candidate for renomination in 1914; resumed the practice of law; died in Geneva, Ala., June 30, 1943; interment in Geneva Cemetery.

MULLER, Nicholas, a Representative from New York; born in the Grand Duchy of Luxemburg November 15, 1836; attended the common schools in the city of Metz and afterward the Luxemburg Athenaeum; immigrated to the United States with his parents, who settled in New York City; employed as a railroad ticket agent for over twenty years; one of the promoters and original directors of the Germania Bank, New York City; served in the State assembly in 1875 and 1876; member of the State central committee in 1875; elected as a Democrat to the Forty-fifth and Forty-sixth Congresses (March 4, 1877–March 3, 1881); unsuccessful candidate for reelection in 1880 to the Forty-seventh Congress; elected to the Forty-eighth and Forty-ninth Congresses (March 4, 1883–March 3, 1887); was not a candidate for renomination in 1886; appointed president of the city police board in 1888; subsequently served as president of the excise board and as quarantine commissioner; elected to the Fifty-sixth and Fifty-seventh Congresses and served from March 4, 1899, until his resignation, on December 1, 1902; unsuccessful candidate for president of Richmond Borough in 1901; appointed as tax commissioner in 1904; withdrew from political life and active business pursuits in 1909; died in New Brighton, Richmond Borough, New York City, December 12, 1917; interment in Greenwood Cemetery, Brooklyn, N. Y.

MULLIN, Joseph, a Representative from New York; born in Dromore, County Down, Ireland, August 6, 1811; immigrated to the United States in 1820 with his parents, who settled in Watertown, Jefferson County, N. Y.; attended the public schools; worked in a printing office; attended Union Academy, Belleville, N. Y., and was graduated from Union College, Schenectady, N. Y., in 1833; principal of Union Academy and subsequently taught in the Watertown Academy; studied law; was admitted to the bar in 1837; appointed examiner of chancery, supreme court commissioner, and commissioner in bankruptcy in 1841; prosecuting attorney of Jefferson County 1843–1849; elected as a Republican to the Thirtieth Congress (March 4, 1847–March 3, 1849); president of the village of Watertown in 1853 and 1854; associate justice of the supreme court 1857–1881 and also served as presiding justice; died at Saratoga Springs, N. Y., May 17, 1882; interment in Brookside Cemetery, Watertown, N. Y.

MULLINS, James, a Representative from Tennessee; born in Bedford County, Tenn., September 15, 1807; completed preparatory studies; apprenticed to the millwright's trade; colonel of the State militia in 1831; sheriff of Bedford County 1840–1846; compelled to flee from his home in 1862 on account of his loyalty to the Union; during the Civil War served in the Union Army 1862–1864; member of the State house of representatives and served as speaker in 1865; elected as a Republican to the Fortieth Congress (March 4, 1867–March 3, 1869); died in Shelbyville, Bedford County, Tenn., June 26, 1873; interment in the Arnold Graveyard, a private cemetery, about nine miles northeast of Shelbyville.

MULTER, Abraham Jacob, a Representative from New York; born in New York, N. Y., December 24, 1900; attended the public schools of Coney Island, N. Y., Boys' High School, Brooklyn, N. Y., and evening classes at City College of New York; was graduated from Brooklyn Law School in 1921; was admitted to the bar in 1923 and commenced practice in New York, N. Y.; special assistant attorney general of New York State in election matters for ten years; delegate to all Democratic State conventions since 1936; elected as a Democrat to the Eightieth Congress to fill the vacancy caused by the resignation of Leo F. Rayfiel; reelected to the Eighty-first and to the five succeeding Congresses and served from November 4, 1947, to January 3, 1961. *Reelected to the Eighty-seventh Congress.*

MUMFORD, George, a Representative from North Carolina; born in Rowan County, N. C.; attended the common schools; member of the State house of commons in 1810 and 1811; elected as a Democrat to the Fifteenth Congress and served from March 4, 1817, until his death in Washington, D. C., December 31, 1818; interment in the Congressional Cemetery.

MUMFORD, Gurdon Saltonstall, a Representative from New York; born in New London, Conn., January 29, 1764; attended the common schools; private secretary to Benjamin Franklin during the latter part of his official residence in Paris; returned with Mr. Franklin to America in 1785 and settled in New York City; became associated with his brothers in the commission business in 1791; elected as a Federalist to the Ninth Congress to fill the vacancy caused by the resignation of Representative-elect Daniel D. Tompkins; reelected to the Tenth and Eleventh Congresses and served from March 4, 1805, to March 3, 1811; presidential elector in 1812 and voted for Clinton and Ingersoll; elected director of the Bank of New York the same year; opened a broker's office in Wall Street in 1813 and was one of the founders of the New York Exchange; died in New York City April 30, 1831; interment in Old Collegiate Dutch Church Cemetery.

MUMMA, Walter Mann, a Representative from Pennsylvania; born in Steelton, Dauphin County, Pa., November 20, 1890; attended the public schools of Steelton; graduated from Pennsylvania State Forestry Academy, Mont Alto, Pa., in 1911; employed with the State Forestry Department 1911–1916; with sales department, Lehigh Portland Cement Co., Allentown, Pa., 1916–1921; organizer, president, and manager of the Pennsylvania Supply Co. of Harrisburg, Pa., 1921–1947, and vice president 1947–1951; register of wills, Dauphin County, Pa., 1940–1944; reemployment director, Selective Service Board, Harrisburg, Pa., 1941–1944; elected as a Republican to the Eighty-second and to the five succeeding Congresses and served from January 3, 1951, until his death in the naval hospital, Bethesda, Md., February 25, 1961; interment in East Harrisburg Cemetery, Harrisburg, Pa.

MUNDT, Karl Earl, a Representative and a Senator from South Dakota; born in Humboldt, Minnehaha County, S. Dak., June 3, 1900; attended the public schools of Humboldt, Pierre, and Madison, S. Dak.; was graduated from Carleton College, Northfield, Minn., in 1923 and from Columbia University, New York, N. Y., in 1927; teacher of speech and social science in Bryant (S. Dak.) High School in 1923 and 1924; superintendent of schools in Bryant, S. Dak., 1924–1927; speech and social science teacher in General Beadle State Teachers College, Madison, S. Dak., 1927–1936; also engaged in the real estate and insurance business and in agricultural pursuits; member of the State Game and Fish Commission 1931–1937; also engaged in literary pursuits; elected as a Republican to the Seventy-sixth and to the four succeeding Congresses and served from January 3, 1939, until his resignation on December 30, 1948, having been appointed to the United States Senate to fill the vacancy caused by the death of Harlan J. Bushfield and the resignation of Vera C. Bushfield and served from December 31, 1948, to January 3, 1949; did not seek renomination to the Eighty-first Congress; elected as a Republican to the United States Senate in 1948 and again in 1954 and served from January 3, 1949, to January 3, 1961. *Reelected in 1960 for the term ending January 3, 1967.*

MUNGEN, William, a Representative from Ohio; born in Baltimore, Md., May 12, 1821; moved with his parents to Ohio in 1830; attended the common schools; taught school; editor and publisher of the Findlay Democratic Courier; auditor of Hancock County, Ohio, 1846–1850; member of the State senate in 1851 and 1852; studied law; was admitted to the bar in 1853 and commenced practice in Findlay, Hancock County, Ohio; delegate to the Democratic National Convention at Cincinnati in 1856; during the Civil War entered the Union Army on December 5, 1861, as lieutenant colonel of the Fifty-seventh Regiment, Ohio Volunteer Infantry; commissioned colonel December 16, 1861, and served until April 24, 1863, when he was honorably discharged, upon tender of his resignation, on account of ill health; elected as a Democrat to the Fortieth and Forty-first Congresses (March 4, 1867–March 3, 1871); was not a candidate for renomination in 1870; resumed the practice of law; died in Findlay, Ohio, September 9, 1887; interment in Maple Grove Cemetery.

MURCH, Thompson Henry, a Representative from Maine; born in Hampden, Penobscot County, Maine, March 29, 1838; attended the common schools; passed his early life at sea; learned the stonecutter's trade and engaged in that occupation for eighteen years; became editor and publisher of the Granite Cutters' International Journal in 1877; secretary of the Granite Cutters' International Association of America in 1877 and 1878; elected as a Greenback Labor Reformer to the Forty-sixth and Forty-seventh Congresses (March 4, 1879–March 3, 1883); unsuccessful candidate for reelection in 1882 to the Forty-eighth Congress; engaged in mercantile pursuits; died in Danvers, Mass., December 15, 1886; interment in Hampden Cemetery, Hampden, Maine.

MURDOCK, John Robert, a Representative from Arizona; born in Homestead near Lewistown, Lewis County, Mo., April 20, 1885; attended the public schools; was graduated from State Teachers' College, Kirksville, Mo., in 1912 and from the State University of Iowa at Iowa City in 1925; took graduate work at the University of Arizona at Tucson and at the University of California at Berkeley; taught elementary school in Missouri 1904–1908; served as principal of the high school at Lewistown, Mo., 1908–1910 and at Ridgeway, Mo., 1912–1914; instructor in the Normal School at Tempe, Ariz., 1914–1932; dean of the Arizona State Teachers' College at Tempe 1933–1937; author of textbooks on history and government; elected as a Democrat to the Seventy-fifth and to the seven succeeding Congresses (January 3, 1937–January 3, 1953); was an unsuccessful candidate for reelection in 1952 to the Eighty-third Congress; retired and resides in Washington, D. C.

MURDOCK, Orrice Abram, Jr. (Abe), a Representative and a Senator from Utah; born in Austin, Lander County, Nev., July 18, 1893; moved with his parents to Beaver, Beaver County, Utah, in 1898; attended the public schools, Murdock Academy, Beaver, Utah, and the University of Utah at Salt Lake City; studied law; was admitted to the bar in 1922 and commenced practice in Beaver, Utah; member of the Beaver (Utah) City

Council in 1920 and 1921; county attorney of Beaver County, Utah, in 1923, 1924, 1927, 1928, 1931, and 1932; city attorney of Beaver 1926–1933; unsuccessful Democratic candidate for district attorney for the fifth Utah district in 1928; elected as a Democrat to the Seventy-third and to the three succeeding Congresses (March 4, 1933–January 3, 1941); was not a candidate for renomination in 1940, having become a candidate for United States Senator; elected to the United States Senate in 1940 and served from January 3, 1941, to January 3, 1947; unsuccessful candidate for reelection in 1946; resumed the practice of law and engaged in agricultural pursuits and livestock raising; member of the National Labor Relations Board from December 16, 1947, to December 16, 1957; retired and resides in Washington, D. C.

MURDOCK, Victor, a Representative from Kansas; born in Burlingame, Osage County, Kans., March 18, 1871; moved with his parents to Wichita in 1872; attended the common schools and Lewis Academy at Wichita; served as a reporter on the Wichita Eagle; moved to Chicago in 1891 and was employed as a newspaper reporter on the Chicago Inter-Ocean; returned to Wichita; managing editor of the Daily Eagle 1894–1903; clerk of the central division, southern department, Kansas Appellate Court 1895–1897; elected as a Republican to the Fifty-eighth Congress to fill the vacancy caused by the resignation of Chester I. Long; reelected to the Fifty-ninth and to the four succeeding Congresses and served from May 26, 1903, to March 3, 1915; was not a candidate for renomination in 1914; chairman of the National Committee of the Progressive Party in 1915 and 1916; war correspondent in 1916; member of the Federal Trade Commission from September 4, 1917, to January 31, 1924, when he resigned; chairman of the Commission in 1919, 1920, 1922, and 1923; appointed a member of the United States Meat Commission in April 1918; editor of the Wichita Eagle until his death in Wichita, Kans., July 8, 1945; interment in Old Mission Mausoleum.

MURFREE, William Hardy (uncle of David W. Dickinson), a Representative from North Carolina; born in Hertford County, N. C., October 2, 1781; was graduated from the University of North Carolina at Chapel Hill in 1801; studied law; was admitted to the bar and commenced practice in Edenton, N. C.; also interested in agricultural pursuits; member of the State house of representatives in 1805 and 1812; presidential elector on the Democratic ticket of Madison and Gerry in 1812; elected as a Democrat to the Thirteenth and Fourteenth Congresses (March 4, 1813–March 3, 1817); moved from Murfreesboro, N. C., to his estate in Williamson County, Tenn., in 1823 and died there on January 19, 1827; interment in Murfree Cemetery, northwest of Franklin, Williamson County, Tenn.

MURPHEY, Charles, a Representative from Georgia; born near Anderson, Anderson County, S. C., May 9, 1799; attended the country schools; studied law; was admitted to the bar in 1825 and commenced practice in Decatur, Ga.; clerk of the superior court of De Kalb County, Ga., 1825–1827; member of the State house of representatives 1839–1841; served in the State senate in 1842, 1845, 1849–1850, 1855–1856; elected as a Democrat to the Thirty-second Congress (March 4, 1851–March 3, 1853); resumed the practice of law; delegate to the Democratic National Convention at Baltimore in 1860; died in Decatur, Ga., January 16, 1861; interment in Decatur City Cemetery.

MURPHY, Arthur Phillips, a Representative from Missouri; born in Hancock, Pulaski County, Mo., December 10, 1870; attended the public schools of Pulaski County and the School of Mines and Metallurgy at Rolla, Phelps County, Mo.; became a telegraph operator; studied law; was admitted to the bar March 4, 1894, and commenced practice in Rolla, Mo.;

unsuccessful candidate for election as prosecuting attorney of Pulaski County in 1898; attorney for the Creek Nation of Indians 1902–1904; elected as a Republican to the Fifty-ninth Congress (March 4, 1905–March 3, 1907); unsuccessful candidate for reelection in 1906 to the Sixtieth Congress; elected to the Sixty-first Congress (March 4, 1909–March 3, 1911); unsuccessful candidate for reelection in 1910 to the Sixty-second Congress; resumed the practice of law; died in Rolla, Mo., February 1, 1914; interment in Rolla Cemetery.

MURPHY, Benjamin Franklin, a Representative from Ohio; born in Steubenville, Jefferson County, Ohio, December 24, 1867; attended the public schools; learned the glassworker's trade; later engaged in the retail shoe business, in banking, and in the real-estate business; vice president of the Peoples National Bank; president of the Steubenville Chamber of Commerce and of the Chamber of Commerce of the Upper Ohio Valley; during the First World War served with the Young Men's Christian Association, stationed at Camp Sheridan, Montgomery, Ala., in 1917 and 1918; elected as a Republican to the Sixty-sixth and to the six succeeding Congresses (March 4, 1919–March 3, 1933); unsuccessful candidate for reelection in 1932 to the Seventy-third Congress and for election in 1934 to the Seventy-fourth Congress; retired from active business pursuits and resided in Washington, D. C.; died in Takoma Park, Md., March 6, 1938; interment in Union Cemetery, Steubenville, Ohio.

MURPHY, Edward, Jr., a Senator from New York; born in Troy, Rensselaer County, N. Y., December 15, 1836; attended the common schools; was graduated from St. John's College, Fordham, N. Y., in 1857; engaged in the brewing business; city alderman 1864–1866; mayor of Troy 1875–1883; delegate to the Democratic National Conventions in 1876, 1880, 1884, 1888, 1892, and 1896; chairman of the Democratic State committee of New York in 1887, and reelected four times; elected as a Democrat to the United States Senate and served from March 4, 1893, to March 3, 1899; was the nominee of his party, who were in the minority, for reelection; resumed his former business activities and was also president of the Troy Gas Co. and vice president of the Manufacturers' National Bank of Troy; died in Elberon, Monmouth County, N. J., August 3, 1911; interment in St. Mary's Cemetery, Troy, N. Y.

MURPHY, Everett Jerome, a Representative from Illinois; born in Nashville, Washington County, Ill., July 24, 1852; moved with his parents to Sparta, Randolph County, Ill.; attended the public and high schools; city clerk of Sparta in 1877, but resigned in 1878 and moved to Chester, the county seat, to accept the appointment of deputy clerk of the circuit court; sheriff of Randolph County; member of the State house of representatives 1886–1888; warden of the Southern Illinois Penitentiary at Menard, Ill., in 1889; moved to East St. Louis in 1892; elected as a Republican to the Fifty-fourth Congress (March 4, 1895–March 3, 1897); unsuccessful candidate for reelection in 1896 to the Fifty-fifth Congress; member of the State board of pardons 1897–1899; warden of the State penitentiary at Joliet, Ill., 1899–1913; engaged in banking at Joliet, Ill., reappointed warden of the penitentiary on July 1, 1917, and served until his death in Joliet, Ill., April 10, 1922; interment in Elmherst Cemetery.

MURPHY, Henry Cruse, a Representative from New York; born in Brooklyn, N. Y., July 5, 1810; was graduated from Columbia College in New York City in 1830; studied law; was admitted to the bar in 1833 and commenced practice in Brooklyn, N. Y.; prosecuting attorney for Kings County in 1841 and 1842; edited the Brooklyn Daily Eagle; mayor of Brooklyn,

N. Y., in 1842 and 1843; delegate to the State constitutional convention in 1846; elected as a Democrat to the Twenty-eighth Congress (March 4, 1843–March 3, 1845); unsuccessful candidate for reelection in 1844 to the Twenty-ninth Congress; elected to the Thirtieth Congress (March 4, 1847–March 3, 1849); unsuccessful candidate for renomination in 1848; unsuccessful presidential candidate at the Democratic National Convention at Baltimore in 1852; appointed Minister Resident to the Netherlands June 1, 1857, and served until June 8, 1861; member of the State senate 1861–1873; delegate to the State constitutional convention of 1867 and 1868; owner and editor of the Brooklyn Daily Eagle; died in Brooklyn, N. Y., December 1, 1882; interment in Greenwood Cemetery.

MURPHY, James Joseph, a Representative from New York; born in Brooklyn, Kings County, N. Y., November 3, 1898; educated in the public schools of Staten Island, N. Y.; served as a noncommissioned officer with the First New York Cavalry on the Mexican border in 1916; during the First World War served as a sergeant with the One Hundred and Fourth Machine Gun Battalion, Twenty-seventh Division, with service in France and Belgium, 1918–1920; engaged in the import and export shipping business in New York City since 1920; elected as a Democrat to the Eighty-first and Eighty-second Congresses (January 3, 1949–January 3, 1953); unsuccessful candidate for reelection in 1952 to the Eighty-third Congress; city councilman of Staten Island 1954–1958; freight and shipping broker; resides at Grymes Hill, Staten Island, N. Y.

MURPHY, James William, a Representative from Wisconsin; born in Platteville, Grant County, Wis., April 17, 1858; attended the public schools, and was graduated from the State normal school at Platteville in 1873; taught school in Grant and Lafayette Counties for five years; studied law and was admitted to the bar in 1879; was graduated from the law department of the University of Michigan at Ann Arbor in 1880 and commenced the practice of his profession in Platteville, Wis., the same year; district attorney of Grant County 1887–1891; mayor of Platteville 1904–1906; elected as a Democrat to the Sixtieth Congress (March 4, 1907–March 3, 1909); unsuccessful candidate for reelection in 1908 to the Sixty-first Congress; resumed the practice of law; also engaged in lead and zinc mining; unsuccessful candidate for election in 1920 to the Sixty-seventh Congress; during the First World War was a member of the local council of defense and of the legal advisory board; died in Rochester, Minn., July 11, 1927; interment in Calvary (Catholic) Cemetery, Platteville, Wis.

MURPHY, Jeremiah Henry, a Representative from Iowa; born in Lowell, Mass., February 19, 1835; moved with his parents to Fond du Lac County, Wis., in 1849, and to Iowa County, Iowa, in 1852; attended the Boston public schools and Appleton (Wis.) University; was graduated from the University of Iowa at Iowa City in 1857; studied law; was admitted to the bar in 1858 and commenced practice in Marengo, Iowa; elected alderman in 1860; delegate to the Democratic National Convention at Chicago in 1864 and at New York City in 1868; moved to Davenport in 1867 and continued the practice of law; elected mayor of Davenport in 1873 and again in 1878; member of the State senate 1874–1878; was an unsuccessful candidate for election in 1876 to the Forty-fifth Congress; presidential elector on the Democratic ticket of Hancock and English in 1880; elected as a Democrat to the Forty-eighth and Forty-ninth Congresses (March 4, 1883–March 3, 1887); was an unsuccessful candidate for renomination in 1886; lived in retirement in Washington, D. C., until his death in that city on December 11, 1893; interment in St. Marguerite's Cemetery, Davenport, Iowa.

MURPHY, John, a Representative from Alabama; born in Columbia, Robeson County, N. C., in 1786; was graduated from South Carolina College (now the University of South Carolina) at Columbia in 1808; served as clerk of the State senate 1810–1817; moved to Alabama in 1818; delegate to the State constitutional convention in 1819; studied law and was admitted to the bar; member of the State senate in 1822; Governor of Alabama 1825–1829; unsuccessful candidate for election to the Twenty-second Congress; elected as a Democrat to the Twenty-third Congress (March 4, 1833–March 3, 1835); unsuccessful candidate for election to the Twenty-sixth Congress; died near Gosport, Clarke County, Ala., September 21, 1841; interment on his plantation near Gosport, Ala.

MURPHY, John William, a Representative from Pennsylvania; born in Avoca, Luzerne County, Pa., April 26, 1902; attended the public schools; was graduated from the Wharton School of the University of Pennsylvania at Philadelphia in 1926 and from the law department of the same university in 1929; was admitted to the bar in 1929 and commenced practice in Scranton, Pa., assistant district attorney of Lackawanna County 1934–1941; elected as a Democrat to the Seventy-eighth and Seventy-ninth Congresses and served from January 3, 1943, until his resignation on July 17, 1946, to become judge of the United States District Court for the middle district of Pennsylvania; became chief judge in June 1955, in which capacity he is now serving; is a resident of Scranton, Pa.

MURPHY, Nathan Oakes, a Delegate from the Territory of Arizona; born in Jefferson, Lincoln County, Maine, October 14, 1849; attended the public schools; taught school in Wisconsin; upon becoming of age went to the western frontier and finally settled in Prescott, Ariz., in April 1883 where he engaged in mining and the real-estate business; secretary to the Governor of Arizona Territory in 1885; appointed secretary of Arizona Territory March 21, 1889; delegate to the Republican National Convention at Minneapolis in 1892; Governor of Arizona Territory 1892–1894; elected as a Republican to the Fifty-fourth Congress (March 4, 1895–March 3, 1897); was not a candidate for renomination in 1896; again Governor of Arizona Territory and served from 1898 to 1902, when he resigned; unsuccessful Republican candidate for election in 1900 to the Fifty-seventh Congress; died in Coronado, San Diego County, Calif., August 22, 1908; interment in the Masonic Cemetery, San Diego, Calif.

MURPHY, Richard Louis, a Senator from Iowa; born in Dubuque, Dubuque County, Iowa, November 6, 1875; attended the graded and high schools of his native city; employed as a reporter for the Galena (Ill.) Gazette 1890–1892; returned to Dubuque, Iowa, in 1892 and was successively a reporter, city editor, and editor 1892–1914; member of the Dubuque County Library Board 1909–1914; served as collector of internal revenue for Iowa 1913–1920; engaged as an income tax counselor from 1920 until 1931, when he retired from active pursuits; delegate to the Democratic National Convention at San Francisco in 1920; elected as a Democrat to the United States Senate and served from March 4, 1933, until his death in an automobile accident near Chippewa Falls, Wis., July 16, 1936; interment in Mount Olivet Cemetery, Key West (a suburb of Dubuque), Iowa.

MURPHY, William Thomas, a Representative from Illinois; born in Chicago, Cook County, Ill., August 7, 1899; attended Yale and Harvard elementary schools and Calumet High School in Chicago; graduated from Loyola University School of Law in 1926; was admitted to the bar in 1927 and commenced the practice of law in Chicago, Ill.; during the First World War served in the United States Army; alderman of the seventeenth ward, city of Chicago, 1935–1959; chairman, Committee on Labor-Management, 1940–1947; chairman, Committee on Planning, 1947–1955; member of Chicago Planning Commission 1947–1959; chairman, Committee on Planning and Housing, 1955–1959; licensed professional engineer; registered land surveyor; delegate to the Democratic National Conventions in 1944, 1948, 1952, and 1956; elected as a Democrat to the Eighty-sixth Congress (January 3, 1959–January 3, 1961). *Reelected to the Eighty-seventh Congress.*

MURRAY, Ambrose Spencer (brother of William Murray), a Representative from New York; born in Wallkill, Ulster County, N. Y., November 27, 1807; attended the common schools; employed as a clerk in a mercantile establishment in Middletown, N. Y., 1824–1831; moved to Goshen, Orange County, N. Y., and engaged in banking; treasurer of Orange County 1851–1854; elected as a Republican to the Thirty-fourth and Thirty-fifth Congresses (March 4, 1855–March 3, 1859); resumed banking in Goshen, N. Y.; delegate to the Republican National Convention at Chicago in 1860; interested in various other business enterprises; died in Goshen, N. Y., November 8, 1885; interment in St. James' Cemetery.

MURRAY, George Washington, a Representative from South Carolina; born near Rembert, Sumter County, S. C., September 22, 1853; was of the Negro race; attended the public schools and the University of South Carolina at Columbia; taught school for fifteen years; inspector of customs at the port of Charleston, S. C., 1890–1892; elected as a Republican to the Fifty-third Congress (March 4, 1893–March 3, 1895); successfully contested the election of William Elliott to the Fifty-fourth Congress and served from June 4, 1896, to March 3, 1897; engaged in the real-estate business; moved to Chicago, Ill., in 1905 and engaged in literary pursuits and lecturing; delegate to several Republican National Conventions; died in Chicago, Ill., April 21, 1926; interment in Lincoln Cemetery.

MURRAY, James Cunningham, a Representative from Illinois; born in Chicago, Cook County, Ill., May 16, 1917; attended the parochial schools, De Paul University College of Commerce, and Quigley Preparatory Seminary; graduated from De Paul University Law School, Chicago, Ill., in 1940; was admitted to the bar in 1940; employed in leases and contracts division of the Illinois Bell Telephone Co., 1940–1942; during World War II served in the United States Army Air Force from May 1942 until discharged as a sergeant in October 1945; assistant attorney general of Illinois 1945–1951; regional enforcement director for the Office of Price Stabilization 1951–1953; assistant States attorney for Cook County, Ill., in 1953 and 1954; elected as a Democrat to the Eighty-fourth Congress (January 3, 1955–January 3, 1957); unsuccessful candidate for reelection in 1956 to the Eighty-fifth Congress; engaged in the private practice of law; elected alderman, eighteenth ward, city of Chicago, in February 1959 for four-year term; is a resident of Chicago, Ill.

MURRAY, James Edward, a Senator from Montana; born on a farm near St. Thomas, Ontario, Canada, May 3, 1876; attended the public schools of Canada; was graduated from St. Jerome's College, Berlin, Canada, in 1895 and from the law department of New York University at New York City in 1900; came to the United States in 1897 and was naturalized in 1900; admitted to the bar in 1901 and commenced practice in Butte, Mont.; also engaged in banking; county attorney of Silver Bow County, Mont., 1906–1908; chairman of the State advisory board of the Public Works Administration in 1933 and 1934; delegate to the Democratic National Conventions in 1920, 1932, 1936, 1940, 1944, and 1948; elected as a Democrat to the United

States Senate to fill the vacancy caused by the death of Thomas J. Walsh; reelected in 1936, 1942, 1948, and again in 1954, and served from November 7, 1934, to January 3, 1961; was not a candidate for renomination in 1960; died in Butte, Mont., March 23, 1961; interment in Holy Cross Cemetery.

MURRAY, John (cousin of Thomas Murray, Jr.), a Representative from Pennsylvania; born near Potts Grove, East Chillisquaque Township, Northumberland County, Pa., in 1768; attended private schools; engaged in agricultural pursuits; member of the State house of representatives 1807–1810; elected to the Fifteenth Congress to fill the vacancy caused by the resignation of David Scott; reelected to the Sixteenth Congress and served from October 14, 1817, to March 3, 1821; resumed agricultural pursuits; died in East Chillisquaque Township, Northumberland County, Pa., March 7, 1834; interment in Chillisquaque Cemetery, near Potts Grove, Pa.

MURRAY, John L., a Representative from Kentucky; born in the State of Pennsylvania, January 25, 1806; studied law and was admitted to the bar; moved to Kentucky and held several local offices; served three terms in the Kentucky House of Representatives 1830–1835; elected as a Democrat to the 25th Congress (March 4, 1837–March 3, 1839); died in Wadesboro, Calloway County, Ky., January 31, 1842; interment in Irvin Cemetery.

MURRAY, Reid Fred, a Representative from Wisconsin; born in Ogdensburg, Waupaca County, Wis., October 16, 1887; attended the public schools and Manawa High School; was graduated from the College of Agriculture of the University of Wisconsin at Madison in 1916; served as agricultural agent for railroads in St. Paul, Minn., 1914–1917, for Winnebago County, Wis., 1917–1919, and for the First National Bank, Oshkosh, Wis., 1919–1922; professor of animal husbandry, at the College of Agriculture, University of Wisconsin, 1922–1927; owner and manager of the Waupaca Cattle Credit Co.; engaged in agricultural pursuits and in the buying and selling of cattle and farms, Waupaca, Wis., 1927–1939; elected as a Republican to the Seventy-sixth and to the six succeeding Congresses and served from January 3, 1939, until his death in the naval hospital at Bethesda, Md., April 29, 1952; interment in Park Cemetery, one mile north of Ogdensburg, Wis.

MURRAY, Robert Maynard, a Representative from Ohio; born in Concord, Lake County, Ohio, November 28, 1841; attended the common schools of Willoughby, Lake County, Ohio, and Oberlin, Ohio; studied law; was admitted to the bar but did not practice; cashier of the First National Bank in Painesville, Ohio; mayor of Painesville, Ohio, 1877–1879; moved to Piqua, Ohio, in 1879; engaged in the manufacture of handles for agricultural implements; elected as a Democrat to the Forty-eighth Congress (March 4, 1883–March 3, 1885); unsuccessful candidate for reelection in 1884 to the Forty-ninth Congress; resumed his former business pursuits; moved to Cleveland in 1892 and engaged in the storage business; died in Cleveland, Ohio, August 2, 1913; interment in Evergreen Cemetery, Painesville, Ohio.

MURRAY, Thomas, Jr. (cousin of John Murray), a Representative from Pennsylvania; born near Potts Grove, East Chillisquaque Township, Northumberland County, Pa., in 1770; attended private schools; engaged in agricultural pursuits; member of the State house of representatives in 1813; served in the State senate in 1814; elected as a Democrat to the Seventeenth Congress to fill the vacancy caused by the resignation of William Cox Ellis and served from October 9, 1821, to March

3, 1823; declined to be a candidate for renomination in 1822 to the Eighteenth Congress; died in East Chillisquaque Township, Northumberland County, Pa., August 26, 1823; interment in Chillisquaque Cemetery, near Potts Grove, Pa.

MURRAY, Thomas Jefferson, a Representative from Tennessee; born in Jackson, Madison County, Tenn., August 1, 1894; attended the public and high schools; was graduated from Union University at Jackson, Tenn., in 1914 and from the law department of Cumberland University at Lebanon, Tenn., in 1917; taught high school in Pinson and Alamo, Tenn., 1914–1916; during the First World War served overseas in the United States Army as a private in the Ordnance Department, Fifth Army Corps, in 1918 and 1919; was admitted to the bar in 1917 and commenced practice in Jackson, Tenn., in 1919; district attorney general for the twelfth judicial circuit of Tennessee from 1922 until his resignation in 1933 to become associated with the office of the Solicitor of the Post Office Department at Washington, D. C., and served from 1933 to 1942; chairman of the Democratic Executive Committee of Madison County, Tenn., 1924–1933; member of the State Democratic Executive Committee of Tennessee in 1923 and 1924; delegate to the Democratic National Conventions in 1928, 1932, and 1936; elected as a Democrat to the Seventy-eighth and to the eight succeeding Congresses (January 3, 1943–January 3, 1961). *Reelected to the Eighty-seventh Congress.*

MURRAY, William (brother of Ambrose Spencer Murray), a Representative from New York; born near Middletown, Orange County, N. Y., October 1, 1803; attended the common schools; employed as a clerk in mercantile establishments in Middletown, N. Y., and later in New York City; subsequently engaged in mercantile pursuits; moved to Goshen, Orange County, N. Y., in 1841; elected as a Democrat to the Thirty-second and Thirty-third Congresses (March 4, 1851–March 3, 1855); engaged in agricultural pursuits; was instrumental in the organization of the Republican Party in 1856 and was afterward affiliated therewith; president of the Goshen Bank from 1857 until his death in Goshen, N. Y., August 25, 1875; interment in St. James' Cemetery.

MURRAY, William Francis, a Representative from Massachusetts; born in Boston, Mass., September 7, 1881; attended the public schools and the Boston Latin School; was graduated from Harvard University in 1904 and from Harvard Law School in 1906; practiced law in Boston; served during the Spanish-American War as a corporal in the United States Volunteer Signal Corps; member of Boston Common Council in 1904 and 1905; member of the State house of representatives in 1907 and 1908; member of the Governor's council in 1910; elected as a Democrat to the Sixty-second and Sixty-third Congresses and served from March 4, 1911, until September 28, 1914, when he resigned, having been appointed postmaster; postmaster of Boston from October 1, 1914, until his death in that city on September 21, 1918; interment in Holyhood Cemetery, Chestnut Hill, Mass.

MURRAY, William Henry, a Representative from Oklahoma; born near Collinsville, Grayson County, Tex., November 21, 1869; attended the public schools and was graduated from College Hill Institute, Springtown, Tex.; editor of newspapers in Dallas, Tex., in 1893 and in Corsicana, Tex., in 1894 and 1895; studied law; was admitted to the bar in 1895 and commenced practice in Fort Worth, Tex.; engaged in teaching in Limestone and Navarro Counties, Tex., 1886–1890; moved to Tishomingo, Johnston County, Indian Territory (now Oklahoma) in 1898; legal adviser to the Governor of the Chickasaw Nation

1898–1901; engaged in ranching near Tishomingo, Okla.; member of the Choctaw-Chickasaw Coal Commission in 1903; chairman of the Oklahoma Code Commission in 1903; vice president of the Sequoyah constitutional convention in 1905; member of the Oklahoma constitutional convention in 1906 and served as president; chairman of the first Democratic State convention held in Oklahoma in 1907; member of the State house of representatives 1907–1909 and served as speaker in the first legislative session; delegate to the Democratic National Conventions in 1908, 1912, 1916, and 1932; elected as a Democrat to the Sixty-third and Sixty-fourth Congresses (March 4, 1913–March 3, 1917); unsuccessful candidate for renomination in 1916; moved to South America and became engaged in colonizing southeast Bolivia 1924–1929; returned to Oklahoma in 1929; Governor of Oklahoma from January 12, 1931, to January 14, 1935; unsuccessful for the Democratic gubernatorial nomination in 1910, 1918, and 1938; attempted by petition to enter the 1938 general election as an Independent candidate for the United States Senate but the State supreme court ruled that the petition was filed too late; unsuccessful Democratic candidate for nomination for United States Senator in 1942; retired to his farm near Tishomingo, Okla.; author of several books; died in Oklahoma City, Okla., October 15, 1956; interment in Tishomingo Cemetery, Tishomingo, Okla.

MURRAY, William Vans, a Representative from Maryland; born in Cambridge, Dorchester County, Md., February 9, 1760; completed preparatory studies; studied law at the Temple in London, which he entered April 28, 1784, and studied three years; returned to the United States; was admitted to the bar and commenced practice in Cambridge, Md., in 1791; member of the State house of delegates in 1791; elected as a Federalist to the Second, Third, and Fourth Congresses (March 4, 1791–March 3, 1797); Minister Resident to the Netherlands from March 2, 1797, to September 2, 1801; while holding this post was appointed by President Adams in 1799 a member of a diplomatic mission to France with satisfactory results; died on his estate in Dorchester County, near Cambridge, Md., December 11, 1803; interment in the Christ Protestant Episcopal Church Cemetery, Cambridge, Md.

MUSKIE, Edmund Sixtus, a Senator from Maine; born in Rumford, Oxford County, Maine, March 28, 1914; attended the public schools and graduated from Rumford High School in 1932, Bates College, Lewiston, Maine, in 1936, and Cornell University Law School, Ithaca, N. Y., in 1939; was admitted to the Massachusetts bar in 1939 and Maine bar in 1940; commenced the practice of law in Waterville, Maine, in 1940; during World War II enlisted in the United States Naval Reserve, V–7, on March 26, 1942; served in the Atlantic and Asiatic-Pacific Theaters; released to inactive duty as a lieutenant on December 18, 1945; awarded three battle stars; member and secretary of Waterville Board of Zoning Adjustment 1948–1955; appointed district director for Maine Office of Price Stabilization on January 29, 1951, and served until July 1952; city solicitor of Waterville in 1954; member of State house of representatives during the ninety-third, ninety-fourth, and ninety-fifth legislatures, 1947–1951, and was Democratic floor leader during the ninety-fourth and ninety-fifth legislatures, 1949–1951; Governor of Maine 1955–1959; delegate to the Democratic National Conventions in 1956 and 1960; elected as a Democrat to the United States Senate for the term commencing January 3, 1959, and ending January 3, 1965.

MUSSELWHITE, Harry Webster, a Representative from Michigan; born on a farm near Coldwater, Branch County, Mich., May 23, 1868; attended the district school and the high school in Coldwater, Mich.; apprenticed, and later employed, as a printer in Coldwater, Mich., 1886–1888; moved to Detroit, Mich., in 1888 and was employed as a newspaper reporter 1888–1905; served as city editor and sports writer of the Grand Rapids Herald 1905–1914; moved to Manistee, Mich., in 1915 and engaged in the newspaper publishing business, being owner, editor, and publisher of the Manistee Daily News-Advocate 1915–1928; supervisor of census for the ninth Michigan district in 1920 and for the fourth Michigan district in 1930; member and vice chairman of the Michigan Hospital Commission 1927–1932; elected as a Democrat to the Seventy-third Congress (March 4, 1933–January 3, 1935); unsuccessful candidate for reelection in 1934 to the Seventy-fourth Congress; engaged in the management of newspaper properties until his retirement; died in San Lorenzo, Calif., December 14, 1955; interment in Cypress Lawn Cemetery, Colma, Calif.

MUTCHLER, Howard (son of William Mutchler), a Representative from Pennsylvania; born in Easton, Northampton County, Pa., February 12, 1859; attended the public schools of his native city and Phillips Academy, Andover, Mass.; studied law with his father at Easton, but before qualifying for admission to the bar became editor and publisher of the Daily Express and the Northampton Democrat at Easton; elected as a Democrat to the Fifty-third Congress to fill the vacancy caused by the death of his father, William Mutchler, and served from August 7, 1893, to March 3, 1895; was not a candidate for renomination in 1894 to the Fifty-fourth Congress; elected to the Fifty-seventh Congress (March 4, 1901–March 3, 1903); was not a candidate for renomination to the Fifty-eighth Congress; resumed newspaper activities; died in Easton, Pa., on January 4, 1916; interment in Easton Cemetery.

MUTCHLER, William (father of Howard Mutchler), a Representative from Pennsylvania; born in Palmer Township, Northampton County, Pa., December 21, 1831; attended the public schools, and Vandeveer's Academy, Easton, Pa.; studied law; was admitted to the bar and commenced practice at Easton, Northampton County, Pa.; sheriff of Northampton County 1854–1860; prothonotary of Northampton County 1861–1867; adjutant of the Thirty-eighth Pennsylvania Volunteers in 1863; appointed assessor of internal revenue in March 1867 and served until May 1869; chairman of the Democratic State committee of Pennsylvania in 1869 and 1870; delegate to the Democratic National Conventions from 1876 until his death; elected as a Democrat to the Forty-fourth Congress (March 4, 1875–March 3, 1877); was not a candidate for renomination in 1876; elected to the Forty-seventh and Forty-eighth Congresses (March 4, 1881–March 3, 1885); was not a candidate for renomination in 1884; again elected to the Fifty-first, Fifty-second, and Fifty-third Congresses, and served from March 4, 1889, until his death in Easton, Northampton County, Pa., June 23, 1893; interment in Easton Cemetery.

MYERS, Amos, a Representative from Pennsylvania; born in Petersburg, Lancaster County, Pa., April 23, 1824; attended a private school near Clarion, Pa., and was graduated from Meadville College in 1843; studied law; was admitted to the bar in 1846 and commenced practice in Clarion, Clarion County, Pa.; held several local offices; was appointed district attorney of Clarion County in 1847; elected as a Republican to the Thirty-eighth Congress (March 4, 1863–March 3, 1865); resumed the practice of law in Clarion; moved to Kentucky, was ordained to the Baptist ministry, and preached in Kentucky, Pennsylvania, and New York; died in East Carleton (now Kent), Orleans County, N. Y., on October 18, 1893; interment in Crown Hill Cemetery, Indianapolis, Ind.

MYERS, Francis John, a Representative and a Senator from Pennsylvania; born in Philadelphia, Pa., December 18, 1901; attended the public schools; was graduated from St. Joseph's High School in 1919, from St. Joseph's College in 1923, and from the law department of Temple University, Philadelphia, Pa., in 1927; instructor in St. Joseph's High School, Philadelphia, Pa., 1923–1927; was admitted to the bar in 1927 and commenced practice in Philadelphia, Pa.; secretary to the district attorney of Philadelphia 1929–1931; attorney for the Home Owners' Loan Corporation in 1934 and 1935; deputy attorney general of Pennsylvania in 1937; elected as a Democrat to the Seventy-sixth, Seventy-seventh, and Seventy-eighth Congresses (January 3, 1939–January 3, 1945); was not a candidate for renomination in 1944, having received the Democratic nomination for Senator; elected to the United States Senate in 1944 and served from January 3, 1945, to January 3, 1951; was an unsuccessful candidate for reelection in 1950; delegate to the Democratic National Convention in Philadelphia in 1948; resumed the practice of law; at time of death was chairman of Philadelphia Redevelopment Authority and a member of the General State Authority and the Greater Philadelphia Movement; died in Philadelphia, Pa., July 5, 1956; interment in Holy Sepulchre Cemetery.

MYERS, Henry Lee, a Senator from Montana; born near Boonville, Cooper County, Mo., October 9, 1862; attended private schools, Cooper Institute, and Boonville (Mo.) Academy; studied law; was admitted to the bar in 1884 and commenced practice in Boonville, Mo.; moved to Hamilton, Ravalli County, Mont., in 1893; delegate to the State Democratic conventions in 1894, 1898, and 1900; prosecuting attorney of Ravalli County 1895–1899; member of the State senate 1899–1903; district judge of the fourth judicial district of Montana 1907–1911; elected as a Democrat to the United States Senate in 1911; reelected in 1916 and served from March 4, 1911, until March 3, 1923; declined to be a candidate for renomination in 1922; delegate to the Democratic National Convention at Baltimore in 1912; moved to Billings, Mont., in 1923 and continued the practice of his profession; appointed associate justice of the supreme court of Montana by Gov. John E. Erickson on January 5, 1927, to fill a vacancy; resumed the private practice of law in January 1929; died in Billings, Mont., November 11, 1943; interment in Riverview Cemetery, Hamilton, Mont.

MYERS, Leonard, a Representative from Pennsylvania; born in Attleboro (now Langhorne), Bucks County, Pa., on November 13, 1827; attended private academic schools and the University of Pennsylvania at Philadelphia; studied law; was admitted to the bar in 1848 and practiced in Philadelphia, Pa.; held local offices; major of the Ninth Regiment, Pennsylvania Militia, during the emergency service of September 1862; elected as a Republican to the Thirty-eighth, Thirty-ninth, and Fortieth Congresses (March 4, 1863–March 3, 1869); successfully contested the election of John Moffet to the Forty-first Congress; reelected to the Forty-second and Forty-third Congresses and served from April 9, 1869, to March 3, 1875; unsuccessful candidate for reelection in 1874; presidential elector on the Republican ticket of McKinley and Hobart in 1896; resumed the practice of law; died in Philadelphia, Pa., February 11, 1905; interment in De Benneville family cemetery.

MYERS, William Ralph, a Representative from Indiana; born near Wilmington, Clinton County, Ohio, June 12, 1836; moved with his parents to Anderson, Madison County, Ind., in October 1836; attended the common schools; learned the painter's trade, at which he worked in summer, teaching in the local schools in winter; surveyor of Madison County 1858–1860; during the Civil War enlisted as a private in Company

G, Forty-seventh Regiment, Indiana Volunteer Infantry; was promoted to orderly sergeant, second lieutenant, first lieutenant, and captain, and served four years and three months; after returning from the Army taught school; superintendent of the public schools of Anderson, Ind., in 1868 and 1869; member of the school board of Anderson 1871–1879; studied law; was admitted to the bar in 1871 and commenced practice in Anderson; elected as a Democrat to the Forty-sixth Congress (March 4, 1879–March 3, 1881); unsuccessful candidate for reelection in 1880 to the Forty-seventh Congress; secretary of state of Indiana 1882–1886; purchased the Anderson Democrat in 1886 and was its editor; unsuccessful Democratic candidate for Governor; again secretary of state 1892–1894; resumed the practice of law and also engaged in lecturing; retired from active business pursuits in 1905; at the time of his death was commander of the Loyal Legion of Indiana; died in Anderson, Ind., April 18, 1907; interment in East Maplewood Cemetery.

N

NABERS, Benjamin Duke, a Representative from Mississippi; born in Franklin, Williamson County, Tenn., November 7, 1812; attended the common schools; moved to Hickory Flat, Miss.; engaged as a commission merchant; held several local offices; elected as a Unionist to the Thirty-second Congress (March 4, 1851–March 3, 1853); unsuccessful Unionist candidate for reelection in 1852 to the Thirty-third Congress; moved to Memphis, Tenn.; studied law; was admitted to the bar in 1860 and commenced practice in Memphis, Tenn.; presidential elector on the Constitutional-Union ticket of Bell and Everett in 1860; returned to Mississippi and settled at Holly Springs, Marshall County, in 1860; chancery clerk 1870–1874; member of the governing board of the State penitentiary at Jackson, Miss., for two years; died at Holly Spring, Miss., September 6, 1878; interment in Hill Crest Cemetery.

NAPHEN, Henry Francis, a Representative from Massachusetts; born in Ireland August 14, 1852; immigrated to the United States with his parents, who settled in Lowell, Mass.; was educated by private tutors and also attended the public schools; was graduated from Harvard University in 1878; attended the Boston University Law School; was admitted to the bar in 1880 and commenced practice in Boston; member of the school committee of Boston 1882–1885; member of the State senate in 1885 and 1886; appointed bail commissioner by the justices of the superior court; elected as a Democrat to the Fifty-sixth and Fifty-seventh Congresses (March 4, 1899–March 3, 1903); was not a candidate for renomination in 1902; died in Boston, Mass., June 8, 1905; interment in Calvary Cemetery.

NAREY, Harry Elsworth, a Representative from Iowa; born in Spirit Lake, Dickinson County, Iowa, May 15, 1885; attended the public schools and Grinnell College, Grinnell, Iowa; was graduated from the State University of Iowa at Iowa City in 1907; was admitted to the bar the same year and commenced practice in Spirit Lake, Iowa; county attorney of Dickinson County, Iowa, 1914–1920 and 1943–1945; city attorney of Spirit Lake, Iowa, 1918–1943; delegate to the Republican State conventions since 1916; chairman of the Dickinson County Republican Central Committee 1918–1943; elected as a Republican to the Seventy-seventh Congress to fill the vacancy caused by the resignation of Vincent F. Harrington and served from November 3, 1942, to January 3, 1943; was not a candidate for reelection in 1942 to the Seventy-eighth Congress; resumed the practice of law; appointed judge of the fourteenth judicial dis-

trict of Iowa in 1944 and served until his resignation in 1959; reentered the private practice of law in Spirit Lake, Iowa, where he now resides.

NASH, Abner, a Delegate from North Carolina; born at Templeton Manor, on the Appomattox River, near Farmville, Prince Edward County, Va., August 8, 1740; attended the rural schools in Virginia; moved to Halifax, N. C., and subsequently to New Bern, N. C.; studied law; was admitted to the bar and commenced practice in Halifax, N. C.; member of the State house of commons in 1777, 1778, and 1782, serving as speaker in 1777; member of the State senate in 1779 and 1780 and was president of that body in 1779; Governor of North Carolina in 1780 and 1781; Member of the Continental Congress from 1782 until his death in New York City on December 2, 1786, while attending a session of Congress; interment in St. Paul's Churchyard; reinterment in the family burial ground at "Pembroke," near New Bern, N. C.

NASH, Charles Edmund, a Representative from Louisiana; born in Opelousas, St. Landry Parish, La., May 23, 1844; was of the Negro race; attended the common schools; was a bricklayer by trade; during the Civil War enlisted in 1863 as a private in the Eighty-second Regiment, United States Volunteers, and was promoted to the rank of sergeant major; lost a leg at Fort Blakely and was honorably discharged; appointed night inspector of customs in 1865; elected as a Republican to the Forty-fourth Congress (March 4, 1875–March 3, 1877); unsuccessful candidate for reelection in 1876 to the Forty-fifth Congress; postmaster at Washington, St. Landry Parish, La., from February 15, 1882, until May 1, 1882; died in New Orleans, La., June 21, 1913; interment in St. Louis Cemetery No. 3.

NATCHER, William Huston, a Representative from Kentucky; born in Bowling Green, Warren County, Ky., September 11, 1909; attended the public schools and received high school education at Ogden Preparatory Department of Ogden College, Bowling Green, Ky.; graduated from Western Kentucky State College, Bowling Green, Ky., in 1930 and from Ohio State University, Columbus, Ohio, in 1933; was admitted to the bar in 1934 and commenced practice of law in Bowling Green, Ky.; Federal conciliation commissioner for the western district of Kentucky in 1936 and 1937; county attorney of Warren County 1938–1950; past president of the Young Democratic Clubs of Kentucky 1941–1946; during World War II served in the United States Navy 1942–1945; commonwealth attorney for the eighth judicial district of Kentucky 1951–1953; elected as a Democrat to the Eighty-third Congress to fill the vacancy caused by the death of Garrett L. Withers; reelected to the Eighty-fourth, Eighty-fifth, and Eighty-sixth Congresses and served from August 1, 1953, to January 3, 1961. *Reelected to the Eighty-seventh Congress.*

NAUDAIN, Arnold, a Senator from Delaware; born near Dover, Del., January 6, 1790; completed preparatory studies; was graduated from Princeton College in 1806 and from the medical department of the University of Pennsylvania at Philadelphia in 1810 and commenced the practice of medicine in Dover, Del.; surgeon general of the Delaware Militia in the War of 1812; member of the State house of representatives 1823–1827, serving as speaker in 1826; unsuccessful candidate for Governor of Delaware in 1832; elected to the United States Senate to fill the vacancy caused by the resignation of Louis McLane; reelected in 1832 and served from January 13, 1830, until his resignation on June 16, 1836; resumed the practice of medicine in Wilmington, Del.; served in the State senate 1836–1839; collector of the port of Wilmington, Del., 1841–1845; moved to Philadelphia, Pa., in

1845 and practiced his profession; died in Odessa, New Castle County, Del., January 4, 1872; interment in the Old Drawyer's Presbyterian Churchyard.

NAYLOR, Charles, a Representative from Pennsylvania; born in Philadelphia County, Pa., October 6, 1806; completed preparatory studies; studied law; was admitted to the bar in 1828 and commenced practice in Philadelphia, Pa.; held several local offices; unsuccessful candidate for election in 1836 to the Twenty-fifth Congress; subsequently elected as a Whig to the Twenty-fifth Congress to fill the vacancy caused by the death of Francis J. Harper; reelected to the Twenty-sixth Congress and served from June 29, 1837, to March 3, 1841; declined to be a candidate for renomination in 1840; resumed the practice of law; during the Mexican War raised a company of volunteers known as the Philadelphia Rangers and served as captain; after the war settled in Pittsburgh, Pa., and continued the practice of law; returned to Philadelphia and practiced law until his death there on December 24, 1872; interment in South Laurel Hill Cemetery.

NEAL, Henry Safford, a Representative from Ohio; born in Gallipolis, Gallia County, Ohio, August 25, 1828; attended the common schools; was graduated from Marietta (Ohio) College in 1847; studied law; was admitted to the bar in 1851 and commenced practice in Ironton, Ohio; prosecuting attorney of Lawrence County about 1851; member of the State senate 1861–1863; appointed consul to Lisbon, Portugal, in 1869; by the resignation of the Minister Resident became Chargé d'Affaires in December 1869 and served until July 1870, when he resigned and returned to Ohio; delegate to the Ohio constitutional convention in 1873; elected as a Republican to the Forty-fifth, Forty-sixth, and Forty-seventh Congresses (March 4, 1877–March 3, 1883); was not a candidate for renomination in 1882; resumed the practice of his profession at Ironton, Ohio; appointed Solicitor of the Treasury by President Arthur and served from July 3, 1884, to April 13, 1885, when a successor was appointed by President Cleveland; again resumed the practice of law; died in Ironton, Ohio, July 13, 1906; interment in Woodland Cemetery.

NEAL, John Randolph, a Representative from Tennessee; born near Clinton, Anderson County, Tenn., November 26, 1836; attended the common schools and Hiwassee College, Monroe County, Tenn.; was graduated from Emory and Henry College, Emory, Va., in 1858; studied law; was admitted to the bar in 1859 and commenced practice in Athens, Tenn.; during the Civil War enlisted in the Confederate Army and was elected captain of a Cavalry troop, which afterward became a part of the Sixteenth Battalion, Tennessee Cavalry, and was subsequently promoted to lieutenant colonel of the battalion; taught school for several years; settled at Rhea Springs, Tenn., and continued the practice of law; member of the State house of representatives in 1874; served in the State senate in 1878 and 1879 and as presiding officer in 1879; presidential elector on the Democratic ticket of Hancock and English in 1880; elected as a Democrat to the Forty-ninth and Fiftieth Congresses (March 4, 1885–March 3, 1889); declined to be a candidate for renomination in 1888 on account of ill health; died at Rhea Springs, Rhea County, Tenn., March 26, 1889; interment in the W. F. Brown family cemetery, Post Oak Springs, Tenn.

NEAL, Lawrence Talbot, a Representative from Ohio; born in Parkersburg, Va. (now West Virginia), September 22, 1844; pursued classical studies; moved to Chillicothe, Ohio, in 1864; studied law; was admitted to the bar in 1866 and commenced practice in Chillicothe, Ross County, Ohio, in 1867; city solicitor in 1867 and 1868; member of the State house of representatives in 1867 and 1868; declined to be a candidate for reelection; elected prosecut-

ing attorney of Ross County, Ohio, in 1870 and resigned in October 1872 to become a candidate for Congress; elected as a Democrat to the Forty-third and Forty-fourth Congresses (March 4, 1873–March 3, 1877); unsuccessful candidate for reelection in 1876 to the Forty-fifth Congress and for election in 1878 to the Forty-sixth Congress; unsuccessful candidate for election to the State senate in 1887; resumed the practice of law; delegate to the Democratic National Conventions in 1888 and 1892; was defeated by William McKinley for Governor of Ohio in 1893; died in Chillicothe, Ohio, November 2, 1905; interment in Grand View Cemetery.

NEAL, William Elmer, a Representative from West Virginia; born on a farm near Proctorville, Lawrence County, Ohio, October 14, 1875; attended the public schools; graduated from Proctorville High School in 1894; taught school in Ohio and Kentucky for six years; graduated from National Normal University, Lebanon, Ohio, in 1900 and received medical degree from the University of Cincinnati in 1906; commenced the general practice of medicine in Huntington, W. Va., in 1907; served as mayor of Huntington 1925–1928; member of Huntington Park Board 1931–1952, and West Virginia Public Health Council 1936–1940; member of West Virginia House of Delegates in 1951 and 1952; elected as a Republican to the Eighty-third Congress (January 3, 1953–January 3, 1955); unsuccessful candidate for reelection in 1954 to the Eighty-fourth Congress; served as medical consultant to Foreign Operations Administration in Afghanistan from February 17, 1955, to June 20, 1955; elected to the Eighty-fifth Congress (January 3, 1957–January 3, 1959); unsuccessful candidate for reelection in 1958 to the Eighty-sixth Congress; died in Huntington, W. Va., November 12, 1959; interment in Spring Hill Cemetery.

NEALE, Raphael, a Representative from Maryland; born in St. Marys County, Md., and resided in Leonardtown; received a limited education; elected to the Sixteenth, Seventeenth, and Eighteenth Congresses (March 4, 1819–March 3, 1825); died in Leonardtown, Md., October 19, 1833.

NEECE, William Henry, a Representative from Illinois; born near Springfield, Sangamon County (later part of Logan County), Ill., February 26, 1831; moved with his parents to McDonough County; attended the common schools; taught school; studied law; was admitted to the bar in 1858 and commenced practice in Macomb, Ill.; member of the city council in 1861; member of the State house of representatives in 1864 and 1870; member of the State constitutional convention of 1869 and 1870; served in the State senate 1878–1882; elected as a Democrat to the Forty-eighth and Forty-ninth Congresses (March 4, 1883–March 3, 1887); unsuccessful candidate for reelection in 1886 to the Fiftieth Congress; resumed the practice of his profession and also interested in stock raising; died in Chicago, Ill., January 3, 1909; interment in Oakwood Cemetery, Macomb, Ill.

NEEDHAM, James Carson, a Representative from California; born in a covered wagon at Carson City, Nev., September 17, 1864; arrived with his parents at Mayfield, Santa Clara, Calif., October 1, 1864; attended the public schools; was graduated from the University of the Pacific at San Jose in 1886 and from the law department of the University of Michigan at Ann Arbor in 1889; clerk in The Adjutant General's Office of the War Department in Washington, D. C., from September 1, 1887, until September 1, 1888, when he resigned to complete his law course; was admitted to the bar in 1889 and commenced practice in Modesto, Stanislaus County, Calif.; unsuccessful candidate for election to the State senate in 1890;

elected as a Republican to the Fifty-sixth and to the six succeeding Congresses (March 4, 1899–March 3, 1913); unsuccessful candidate in 1912 for reelection to the Sixty-third Congress; resumed the practice of law in San Diego, Calif., 1913–1916, when he returned to Modesto, Calif., and continued his profession; appointed judge of the superior court of California January 1, 1919; elected to the same office in 1920 to fill an unexpired term; reelected in 1922 and again in 1926, and served until January 1, 1935; died in Modesto, Calif., July 11, 1942; interment in the Masonic Cemetery.

NEELEY, George Arthur, a Representative from Kansas; born in Detroit, Pike County, Ill., August 1, 1879; attended the public schools; moved to Ingram, Indian Territory (now Wellston, Okla.), in 1893 and engaged in agricultural pursuits; taught school and worked his way through the high-school course; attended the Southwestern Baptist University, Jackson, Tenn., and was graduated in law from the University of Kansas at Lawrence in 1904; was admitted to the bar and commenced practice in Wellston, Okla.; continued the practice of law in Chandler 1905–1908 and in Hutchinson, Reno County, Kans., 1908–1919; unsuccessful candidate for election in 1910 to the Sixty-first Congress; elected as a Democrat to the Sixty-second Congress to fill the vacancy caused by the death of Edmond H. Madison; reelected to the Sixty-third Congress and served from November 11, 1912, to March 3, 1915; did not seek renomination in 1914, having become a candidate for Senator; unsuccessful candidate for election to the United States Senate in 1914; resumed the practice of his chosen profession in Hutchinson, Kans., where he died on January 1, 1919; interment in Oak Park Cemetery, Chandler, Okla.

NEELY, Matthew Mansfield, a Representative and a Senator from West Virginia; born in Grove, Doddridge County, W. Va., November 9, 1874; attended the public schools and Salem College at Salem, W. Va.; served as a private in Company D, First West Virginia Volunteer Infantry, during the Spanish-American War; was graduated from the military and literary departments of the University of West Virginia at Morgantown in 1901 and from the law department of the same university in 1902; was admitted to the bar in 1902 and commenced practice in Fairmont, Marion County; mayor of Fairmont 1908–1910; clerk of the State house of delegates 1911–1913; was elected as a Democrat to the Sixty-third Congress to fill the vacancy caused by the resignation of John W. Davis; reelected to the Sixty-fourth, Sixty-fifth, and Sixty-sixth Congresses and served from October 14, 1913, to March 3, 1921; unsuccessful candidate for reelection in 1920 to the Sixty-seventh Congress; elected in 1922 as a Democrat to the United States Senate and served from March 4, 1923, to March 3, 1929; unsuccessful candidate for reelection in 1928; elected to the United States Senate in 1930; reelected in 1936 and served from March 4, 1931, until his resignation on January 12, 1941, having been elected Governor of West Virginia, serving until January 15, 1945; unsuccessful candidate for election in 1942 to the United States Senate; elected to the Seventy-ninth Congress (January 3, 1945–January 3, 1947); unsuccessful candidate for reelection in 1946 to the Eightieth Congress; elected to the United States Senate in 1948; reelected in 1954 and served from January 3, 1949, until his death in the naval hospital, Bethesda, Md., January 18, 1958; interment in Woodlawn Cemetery, Fairmont, W. Va.

NEGLEY, James Scott, a Representative from Pennsylvania; born in East Liberty, Allegheny County, Pa., December 22, 1826; attended the village schools and was graduated from the Western University of Pennsylvania at Allegheny in 1846; served in the Mexican War in the Duquesne Grays, First Regi-

ment, Pennsylvania Volunteers; during the Civil War entered the Union Army as brigadier general April 19, 1861; commanded a division in Patterson's command for three months' service; took part in the Battle of Falling Waters; organized and equipped a brigade of Infantry and Artillery for the West and joined General Sherman in October 1861; participated in the Buell campaign in Tennessee; defended Nashville in 1862 and received special commendation for this service; promoted to major general for distinguished service and gallantry on the field at the Battle of Stone River; commanded a division and took a prominent part in the campaigns of Tullahoma, Chattanooga, Alabama, and Georgia; member of the board of managers of the National Home for Disabled Volunteer Soldiers 1874–1878 and 1882–1888; elected as a Republican to the Forty-first, Forty-second, and Forty-third Congresses (March 4, 1869–March 3, 1875); unsuccessful candidate for reelection in 1874 to the Forty-fourth Congress; elected to the Forty-ninth Congress (March 4, 1885–March 3, 1887); unsuccessful candidate for reelection in 1886 to the Fiftieth Congress; engaged in railroading; died in Plainfield, Union County, N. J. August 7, 1901; interment in Allegheny Cemetery, Pittsburgh, Pa.

NEILL, Robert, a Representative from Arkansas; born near Desha, Independence County, Ark., on November 12, 1838; attended the common schools; took a course in land surveying under a tutor in Ohio in 1859; elected county surveyor of his native county in August 1860; during the Civil War entered the Confederate Army in May 1861 and served as a private in Company K, First Regiment, Arkansas Mounted Riflemen, Gen. Benjamin McCulloch's Brigade, Army of the West; promoted to first lieutenant in 1862 and to captain in 1863; clerk of the circuit court of Independence County 1866–1868; read law; was admitted to the bar in 1868 and commenced practice in Batesville in 1872; lieutenant colonel of Arkansas State Guards 1874–1877; brigadier general of State militia 1877–1882; delegate to the Democratic National Convention at St. Louis in 1888 and vice president of the convention for Arkansas; elected as a Democrat to the Fifty-third and Fifty-fourth Congresses (March 4, 1893–March 3, 1897); unsuccessful candidate for renomination in 1896; resumed the practice of law; served one year as chairman of the Arkansas Railroad Commission, having been appointed in 1899 by Governor Jones; died in Batesville, Independence County, Ark., February 16, 1907; interment in Oak Lawn Cemetery.

NEILSON, John, a Delegate from New Jersey; born at Raritan Landing, near New Brunswick, N. J., March 11, 1745; completed preparatory studies; attended the University of Pennsylvania at Philadelphia in 1758; engaged in mercantile pursuits in New Brunswick 1769–1775; member of the Revolutionary Army as captain of New Jersey Militia in 1775; appointed colonel of the Second Regiment, Middlesex County (N. J.) Militia, in 1776; brigadier general of militia in 1777; deputy quartermaster general for New Jersey 1780–1783; elected as a Member of the Continental Congress November 6, 1778, and declined December 12, 1778; trustee of Rutgers College at New Brunswick, N. J., from 1782 until his death; delegate to the State constitutional convention which ratified the Federal Constitution in 1790; member of the State general assembly in 1800 and 1801; engaged as a shipping merchant; General Lafayette presented him with a sword in 1824; died in New Brunswick, N. J., March 3, 1833; interment in Van Liew Cemetery, on the Cranberry Turnpike.

NELSEN, Ancher, a Representative from Minnesota; born on a farm in Renville County, near Buffalo Lake, Minn., October 11, 1904; attended grade school and graduated from high school in

Brownton, Minn., in 1923; served on District No. 75 School Board 1926–1935 and on the Lynn Township Board 1929–1935; operates a farm in McLeod County, near Hutchinson, Minn.; member of the State senate from McLeod County 1935–1949; delegate to the Republican National Conventions in 1948 and 1952; Lieutenant Governor of Minnesota in 1953; national administrator of the Rural Electrification Administration program 1953–1956; elected as a Republican to the Eighty-sixth Congress (January 3, 1959–January 3, 1961). *Reelected to the Eighty-seventh Congress.*

NELSON, Adolphus Peter, a Representative from Wisconsin; born in Holmes City, near Alexandria, Douglas County, Minn., March 28, 1872; attended the public schools, and was graduated from Hamline University, St. Paul, Minn., in 1897; moved to Grantsburg, Burnett County, Wis., in 1897; engaged in banking; regent of the University of Wisconsin 1906–1919 and president of the board of regents 1916–1920; president of the local school board 1910–1916; mayor of Grantsburg 1914–1916; vice president of the board of trustees of Hamline University 1914–1918; elected as a Republican to the Sixty-fifth Congress to fill the vacancy caused by the resignation of Irvine L. Lenroot; reelected to the Sixty-sixth and Sixty-seventh Congresses and served from November 5, 1918, to March 3, 1923; unsuccessful candidate for renomination in 1922; again engaged in banking in Grantsburg, Wis., until his death in that city August 21, 1927; interment in Riverside Cemetery.

NELSON, Arthur Emanuel, a Senator from Minnesota; born in Browns Valley, Traverse County, Minn., May 10, 1892; attended the public schools, Macalester College, St. Paul, Minn., 1910–1912, and St. Paul College of Law 1912–1915; was admitted to the Minnesota bar in 1915 and the Illinois bar in 1939; commenced practice in St. Paul, Minn.; during the First World War enlisted as a private, Heavy Artillery, and served from August 1918 to November 1918; corporation counsel of St. Paul, Minn., 1920–1922; mayor of St. Paul 1922–1926; unsuccessful for election to the United States Senate in 1928; elected as a Republican to the United States Senate on November 3, 1942, to fill the vacancy caused by the death of Ernest Lundeen and served from November 18, 1942, to January 3, 1943; was not a candidate for election to the full term; practiced law in St. Paul, Minn., and Chicago, Ill.; died in Chicago, Ill., April 11, 1955; interment in Oakland Cemetery, St. Paul, Minn.

NELSON, Charles Pembroke (son of John E. Nelson), a Representative from Maine; born in Waterville, Kennebec County, Maine, July 2, 1907; graduated from Cony High School, Augusta, Maine, in 1924, Colby College, Waterville, Maine, in 1928, and from Harvard Law School, Cambridge, Mass., in 1931; was admitted to the Maine bar in 1931; secretary to his father, Representative John E. Nelson, in 1931 and 1932; engaged in the general practice of law in Augusta, Maine, in 1932; city solicitor of Augusta 1934–1942; delegate to the Republican National Convention in 1936; chief, State Arson Division, in 1941 and 1942; entered the military service in 1942 as a second lieutenant in the United States Army Air Corps and served until discharged in 1946 as a lieutenant colonel with two years of service in the European Theater of Operations; member of the National Guard and Reserves; member of the State board of bar examiners 1946–1948; mayor of Augusta in 1947 and 1948; elected as a Republican to the Eighty-first and to the three succeeding Congresses (January 3, 1949–January 3, 1957); was not a candidate for renomination in 1956; teacher at University of Florida at Gainesville 1957–1959; chief trial attorney, State highway commission, 1959; moderator, town of West Bath, 1960; is a resident of West Bath, Maine.

NELSON, Homer Augustus, a Representative from New York; born in Poughkeepsie, Dutchess County, N. Y., August 31, 1829; completed preparatory studies; studied law; was admitted to the bar and commenced practice in Poughkeepsie, N. Y.; judge of Dutchess County 1855–1862; colonel of the One Hundred and Fifty-ninth Regiment, New York Volunteer Infantry, during the Civil War; resigned in 1863; elected as a Democrat to the Thirty-eighth Congress (March 4, 1863–March 3, 1865); unsuccessful candidate for reelection in 1864 to the Thirty-ninth Congress; delegate to the State constitutional convention in 1867; secretary of state of New York 1867–1870; member of the State senate in 1882 and 1883; appointed a member of the commission to report a revision of the judiciary article of the State constitution in 1890; died in Poughkeepsie, N. Y., April 25, 1891; interment in the Poughkeepsie Rural Cemetery.

NELSON, Hugh (son of Thomas Nelson, Jr.), a Representative from Virginia; born in Yorktown, York County, Va., September 30, 1768; completed preparatory studies; was graduated from William and Mary College, Williamsburg, Va., in 1780; served in the State senate 1786–1791; member of the State house of delegates in 1793 and served as speaker; judge of the general court; presidential elector on the Democratic ticket of Madison and Clinton in 1808; elected to the Twelfth and to the five succeeding Congresses and served from March 4, 1811, until his resignation on January 14, 1823, having received an appointment in the diplomatic service; appointed by President James Monroe United States Minister to Spain on January 15 1823, and served until November 23, 1824; died at his home, "Belvoir," Albemarle County, Va., March 18, 1836; interment in Belvoir Cemetery, Cismont, Albemarle County, Va.

NELSON, Jeremiah, a Representative from Massachusetts; born in Rowley, Essex County, Mass., September 14, 1769; completed preparatory studies; was graduated from Dartmouth College, Hanover, N. H., in 1790; engaged in the mercantile business in Newburyport, Essex County, Mass.; member of the general court of Massachusetts in 1803 and 1804; elected as a Federalist to the Ninth Congress (March 4, 1805–March 3, 1807); was not a candidate for renomination in 1806 to the Tenth Congress; chairman board of selectmen of Newburyport in 1811; elected to the Fourteenth and to the four succeeding Congresses (March 4, 1815–March 3, 1825); was not a candidate for renomination in 1824 to the Nineteenth Congress; president of the Newburyport Mutual Fire Insurance Co. in 1829; again elected to the Twenty-second Congress (March 4, 1831–March 3, 1833); declined to be a candidate for renomination in 1832; engaged in the shipping business; died in Newburyport, Mass., October 2, 1838; interment in Oak Hill Cemetery.

NELSON, John (son of Roger Nelson), a Representative from Maryland; born in Frederick, Frederick County, Md., June 1, 1794; was graduated from William and Mary College, Williamsburg, Va., in 1811; studied law; was admitted to the bar in 1813 and commenced practice in Frederick, Md.; held several local offices; elected as a Democrat to the Seventeenth Congress (March 4, 1821–March 3, 1823); was not a candidate for reelection in 1822 to the Eighteenth Congress; appointed by President Jackson United States Chargé d'Affaires to the Two Sicilies on October 24, 1831, and served until October 15, 1832; Attorney General of the United States and Secretary of State ad interim in the Cabinet of President Tyler 1843–1845; died in Baltimore, Md., January 18, 1860; interment in Greenmount Cemetery.

NELSON, John Edward (father of Charles Pembroke Nelson), a Representative from Maine; born in China, Kennebec County,

Maine, July 12, 1874; attended the common and high schools of Waterville, Maine; was graduated from Friends School, Providence, R. I., in 1894, from Colby College, Waterville, Maine, in 1898, and from the law department of the University of Maine at Orono in 1904; was admitted to the bar in 1904 and commenced practice in Waterville, Maine; moved to Augusta, Maine, in 1913 and continued the practice of his chosen profession; elected as a Republican to the Sixth-seventh Congress to fill the vacancy caused by the resignation of John A. Peters; reelected to the Sixty-eighth and to the four succeeding Congresses and served from March 27, 1922, to March 3, 1933; unsuccessful candidate for reelection in 1932 to the Seventy-third Congress trustee of Colby College 1926–1931; also served as trustee of Monmouth (Maine) Academy; practiced law until his retirement in 1946; died in Augusta, Maine, April 11, 1955; interment in Pine Grove Cemetery, Waterville, Maine.

NELSON, John Mandt, a Representative from Wisconsin; born in Burke, Dane County, Wis., October 10, 1870; attended the public schools and was graduated from the University of Wisconsin at Madison in 1892; superintendent of schools in Dane County in 1892 and 1894; bookkeeper in the office of the secretary of state 1894–1897; editor of The State, published in Madison, Wis., in 1897 and 1898; correspondent in the State treasury 1898–1902; was graduated from the law department of the University of Wisconsin in 1896, and pursued a postgraduate course 1901–1903; elected as a Republican to the Fifty-ninth Congress to fill the vacancy caused by the death of Henry C. Adams; reelected to the Sixtieth and to the five succeeding Congresses and served from September 4, 1906, to March 3, 1919; unsuccessful candidate for renomination in 1918; elected to the Sixty-seventh and to the five succeeding Congresses (March 4, 1921–March 3, 1933); was an unsuccessful candidate for renomination in 1932 to the Seventy-third Congress; retired from business and political activities; died in Madison, Wis., January 29, 1955; interment in Forest Hill Cemetery.

NELSON, Knute, a Representative and a Senator from Minnesota; born in Voss, Norway, February 2, 1843; immigrated to the United States in July 1849 with his mother, who settled in Chicago, Ill.; moved to Dane County, Wis., in 1850; attended the common schools and Albion Academy, Albion, Wis., three years; served as a private and noncommissioned officer in the Fourth Regiment, Wisconsin Volunteer Infantry, during the Civil War; wounded and taken prisoner at Port Hudson, La., June 14, 1863; at the close of the war he returned to Albion College and completed the course; studied law; was admitted to the bar in 1867 and commenced practice in Cambridge, Wis.; member of the Wisconsin Assembly in 1868 and 1869; moved to Alexandria, Douglas County, Minn., in 1871; county attorney 1872–1874; member of the State senate 1875–1878; presidential elector on the Republican ticket of Garfield and Arthur in 1880; member of the board of regents of the University of Minnesota from February 1, 1882, to January 1, 1893; elected as a Republican to the Forty-eighth, Forty-ninth, and Fiftieth Congresses (March 4, 1883–March 3, 1889); was not a candidate for renomination in 1888; elected Governor of Minnesota in 1892; reelected in 1894 and served from January 4, 1893, until January 31, 1895, when he resigned, preparatory to becoming Senator; elected to the United States Senate in 1895; reelected in 1901, 1907, 1913, and 1918, and served from March 4, 1895, until his death; upon his eightieth birthday was the recipient of congratulatory messages from the King of Norway, the President of the Norwegian Congress, and President Warren G. Harding, and in the Senate addresses of felicitation were delivered; died on a train near Timonium, Md., April 28, 1923, while en route to his home; interment in Kinkead Cemetery, Alexandria, Minn.

NELSON, Roger (father of John Nelson), a Representative from Maryland; born on "Point of Rocks" plantation, near Frederick, Md., in 1759; completed preparatory studies; attended William and Mary College, Williamsburg, Va.; served in the Revolutionary Army; wounded at the Battle of Camden and attained the rank of brigadier general; studied law; was admitted to the bar about 1785 and practiced in Taneytown and Frederick; held several local offices; member of the State house of delegates in 1795, 1801, and 1802; served in the State senate from November 1803 to November 1804; elected as a Democrat to the Eighth Congress to fill the vacancy caused by the death of Daniel Hiester; reelected to the Ninth, Tenth, and Eleventh Congresses and served from November 6, 1804, until his resignation May 14, 1810; one of the managers appointed by the House of Representatives in 1804 to conduct the impeachment proceedings against Samuel Chase, Associate Justice of the Supreme Court of the United States; elected associate justice of the fifth (later sixth) judicial circuit of Maryland in 1810; died in Frederick, Md., June 7, 1815; interment in Mount Olivet Cemetery.

NELSON, Thomas, Jr. (father of Hugh Nelson), a Delegate from Virginia; born in Yorktown, Va., on December 26, 1738; attended private schools, and was graduated from the Trinity College, Cambridge, England, in 1761; elected a member of the house of burgesses while on his way home from England; member of the House of Burgesses of Virginia in 1774; member of the first provincial convention in Williamsburg in 1774; Member of the Continental Congress 1775–1777; a signer of the Declaration of Independence; appointed commander of the Virginia State forces in 1777 and served in this capacity until 1781 when he resigned on account of ill health as a result of his service in the field in the campaign against Cornwallis; was publicly thanked by Washington and by Congress for his services; again elected a Member of the Continental Congress in 1779 and 1780; Governor of Virginia in 1781; retired to his son's estate, "Mont Air," Hanover County, Va., and died there on January 4, 1789; interment in the Nelson Cemetery, Yorktown, Va.

NELSON, Thomas Amos Rogers, a Representative from Tennessee; born in Kingston, Roane County, Tenn., March 19, 1812; completed preparatory studies, and was graduated from East Tennessee College in 1828; studied law; was admitted to the bar in 1832 and commenced practice in Washington County, Tenn.; served two terms as attorney general of the first judicial circuit; presidential elector on the Whig ticket of Clay and Frelinghuysen in 1844 and of Taylor and Fillmore in 1848; appointed commissioner (diplomatic) to China March 6, 1851, and resigned July 2, 1851; elected as a Unionist to the Thirty-sixth Congress (March 4, 1859–March 3, 1861); reelected to the Thirty-seventh Congress, and while en route to Washington to take his seat, during the Civil War, was arrested by Confederate scouts, conveyed to Richmond as a prisoner, paroled, and allowed to return to his home; upon the advent of the Union Army into East Tennessee in 1863 he moved to Knoxville; delegate to the Union National Convention at Philadelphia in 1866 and to the Democratic National Convention at New York in 1868; one of the counsel who defended President Andrew Johnson in his impeachment trial in 1868; elected judge of the State supreme court in 1870 and served until his resignation in 1871; died in Knoxville, Tenn., August 24, 1873; interment in Gray Cemetery.

NELSON, Thomas Maduit, a Representative from Virginia; born in Oak Hill, Mecklenburg County, Va., September 27, 1782; attended the common schools; commissioned a captain in the Tenth Infantry Regiment and subsequently a major in the Thirtieth and Eighteenth Infantry Regiments in the War of 1812; after the war was reduced to the grade of captain, and resigned his commission May 15, 1815; elected as a Democrat to the Fourteenth Congress to fill the vacancy caused by the death of Thomas Gholson, Jr.; reelected to the Fifteenth Congress and served from December 4, 1816, to March 3, 1819; was not a candidate for renomination in 1818; died near Columbus, Muscogee County, Ga., November 10, 1853; interment in Linwood Cemetery.

NELSON, William, a Representative from New York; born in Hyde Park, Dutchess County, N. Y., June 29, 1784; attended the common schools and was graduated from Poughkeepsie Academy; studied law; was admitted to the bar and commenced practice in Peekskill, Westchester County, N. Y., in 1807; for thirty years served as district attorney for Putnam, Rockland, and Westchester Counties; member of the State assembly in 1820 and 1821; served in the State senate 1824–1827; judge of the court for the correction of errors 1824–1827; elected as a Whig to the Thirtieth and Thirty-first Congresses (March 4, 1847– March 3, 1851); resumed the practice of his profession; died in Peekskill, N. Y., October 3, 1869; interment in Hillside Cemetery.

NELSON, William Lester, a Representative from Missouri; born on a farm near Bunceton, Cooper County, Mo., August 4, 1875; attended the country schools in his native county, Hooper Institute, William Jewell College at Liberty, Mo., and the Missouri College of Agriculture at Columbia; taught school for five years; subsequently entered the newspaper business at Bunceton, Mo.; member of the State house of representatives 1901–1903 and 1905–1907; moved to Columbia, Boone County, Mo., to become assistant secretary of the State board of agriculture and served from 1908 to 1918; member of the editorial staff of the Iowa Homestead and other Pierce publications 1921–1924; also engaged in agricultural pursuits; author of various agricultural publications; elected as a Democrat to the Sixty-sixth Congress (March 4, 1919–March 3, 1921); unsuccessful candidate for reelection in 1920 to the Sixty-seventh Congress; resumed journalistic pursuits in Columbia, Mo.; elected to the Sixty-ninth and to the three succeeding Congresses (March 4, 1925–March 3, 1933); unsuccessful candidate for renomination in 1932; elected to the Seventy-fourth and to the three succeeding Congresses (January 3, 1935–January 3, 1943); unsuccessful candidate for reelection in 1942 to the Seventy-eighth Congress; served as assistant to War Food Administrator Marvin Jones in 1943; returned to Columbia, Mo., and became active in rural life and wrote numerous pamphlets on farming; died in Columbia, Mo., December 31, 1946; interment in Columbia Cemetery.

NES, Henry, a Representative from Pennsylvania; born in York, Pa., May 20, 1799; completed preparatory studies and was graduated from Princeton College; studied medicine and practiced in York, Pa.; elected as an Independent to the Twenty-eighth Congress (March 4, 1843–March 3, 1845); elected to the Thirtieth and Thirty-first Congresses and served from March 4, 1847, until his death in York, Pa., September 10, 1850; interment in Prospect Hill Cemetery.

NESBIT, Walter, a Representative from Illinois; born in Belleville, St. Clair County, Ill., on May 1, 1878; attended the grade and night schools; employed as a coal miner 1892–1912; held various offices in the United Mine Workers of America, serving as subdistrict secretary 1912–1915, as traveling auditor 1915–1917, and as secretary-treasurer of district No. 12 1917– 1933; elected as a Democrat to the Seventy-third Congress (March 4, 1933–January 3, 1935); unsuccessful candidate for renomination in 1934; owned and operated the Club Congress in Belleville, Ill.; unsuccessful candidate for sheriff of St. Clair County, Ill., in 1938; died in Belleville, Ill., December 6, 1938; interment in Green Mount Cemetery.

NESBITT, Wilson, a Representative from South Carolina; resided in Spartanburg, Spartanburg County, S. C.; attended the common schools and was a student at South Carolina College (now the University of South Carolina) at Columbia in 1805 and 1806; engaged in agricultural pursuits and conducted an iron foundry; justice of quorum of Spartanburg County in 1810; member of the State house of representatives 1810–1814; elected as a Democrat to the Fifteenth Congress (March 4, 1817–March 3, 1819); moved to Alabama; died in Montgomery, Ala., May 13, 1861; interment in Oakwood Cemetery.

NESMITH, James Willis (cousin of Joseph Gardner Wilson and grandfather of Clifton Nesmith McArthur), a Senator and a Representative from Oregon; born in New Brunswick, Canada, while his parents were on a visit from their home in Washington County, Maine, July 23, 1820; moved with his father to Claremont, N. H., about 1828; received a limited schooling; moved to Cincinnati, Ohio, in 1838, and to Oregon City, Oreg., in 1843; studied law; was admitted to the bar but never practiced extensively; engaged in agricultural pursuits and stock raising; elected judge of the provisional government of Oregon in 1845; captain in 1848 and 1853 in expeditions against hostile Indians; United States marshal for Oregon from 1853 to 1855, when he resigned; colonel of Oregon Volunteer Troops in the Indian wars; appointed superintendent of Indian affairs for Oregon and Washington Territories in 1857; elected as a Democrat to the United States Senate and served from March 4, 1861, to March 3, 1867; unsuccessful candidate for reelection; appointed Minister to Austria, but his nomination was not confirmed; served as road supervisor of Polk County in 1868; elected to the Forty-third Congress to fill the vacancy caused by the death of Joseph G. Wilson and served from December 1, 1873, to March 3, 1875; did not seek renomination in 1874 to the Forty-fourth Congress; died in Rickreall, Oreg., June 17, 1885; interment in Polk County, Oreg., on the south bank of Rickreall Creek.

NEUBERGER, Maurine Brown (widow of Richard L. Neuberger), a Senator from Oregon; born in Cloverdale, Tillamook County, Oreg., January 9, 1907; attended the public schools, Oregon College of Education at Monmouth 1922–1924, the University of Oregon in 1928 and 1929, and the University of California at Los Angeles in 1936 and 1937; teacher in Oregon public schools 1932–1944; member of the State house of representatives 1951–1955; writer and photographer; member, board of directors, American Association for the United Nations; elected as a Democrat to the United States Senate to fill the vacancy caused by the death of her husband, Richard L. Neuberger, and served from November 9, 1960, to January 3, 1961. *Also elected in 1960 for the term commencing January 3, 1961, and ending January 3, 1967.*

NEUBERGER, Richard Lewis (husband of Maurine B. Neuberger), a Senator from Oregon; born in Multnomah County, near Portland, Oreg., December 26, 1912; attended the public schools of Portland, Oreg.; graduated from the University of Oregon at Eugene in 1935; author; correspondent for the New York Times 1939–1954; served in the State house of representatives in 1941 and 1942; during World War II was commissioned a lieutenant and later a captain in the United States Army and served from July 15, 1942, to August 12, 1945; aide-de-camp to Gen. James A. O'Connor during the construction of the Alaska Military Highway; in 1945 served as military aide to the American delegation at the United Nations Conference in San Francisco, Calif.; member of the State senate 1949–1954; elected as a Democrat to the United States Senate and served from January 3, 1955, until his death in Portland, Oreg., March 9, 1960; interment in Beth Israel Cemetery.

NEVILLE, Joseph, a Representative from Virginia; born in 1730; burgess for Hampshire County 1773–1776; member of the conventions of December 1, 1775, and May 6, 1776; served in the Continental Army during the Revolutionary War; member of the State house of delegates in 1777, 1780, and 1781; in 1782 was engaged with Col. Alexander McLean, of Pennsylvania, in settling by survey the long-standing dispute over the boundary line between the States of Pennsylvania and Maryland; elected to the Third Congress (March 4, 1793–March 3, 1795); was not a candidate for reelection in 1794; died in Hardy County, Va., March 4, 1819.

NEVILLE, William (cousin of Bird Segle McGuire), a Representative from Nebraska; born in Nashville, Washington County, Ill., December 29, 1843; moved with his parents to Chester, Randolph County, in 1851; attended the public schools and McKendree College, Lebanon, Ill.; during the Civil War served in the Union Army as second sergeant in Company H, One Hundred and Forty-second Regiment, Illinois Volunteer Infantry; studied law; was admitted to the bar in Chester, Ill., in 1874 and practiced; member of the Illinois House of Representatives in 1872; moved to Nebraska in May 1874; member of the Nebraska House of Representatives in 1876; moved to North Platte, Nebr., in April 1877 and continued the practice of law; unsuccessful candidate for election in 1884 to the Forty-ninth Congress; judge of the thirteenth judicial district 1891–1895; elected as a Populist to the Fifty-sixth Congress to fill the vacancy caused by the death of William L. Greene; reelected to the Fifty-seventh Congress and served from December 4, 1899, to March 3, 1903; was not a candidate for renomination in 1902; resumed the practice of law; moved to Douglas, Ariz., in 1903 and resumed the practice of his profession; member of the Arizona House of Representatives in 1905; died in Douglas, Ariz., April 5, 1909; interment in North Platte Cemetery, North Platte, Nebr.

NEVIN, Robert Murphy, a Representative from Ohio; born in Danville, Highland County, Ohio, May 5, 1850; attended the public schools in Hillsboro, Ohio; was graduated from the Ohio Wesleyan University, Delaware, Ohio, in June 1868; moved to Dayton, Ohio, in 1868; studied law; was admitted to the bar in 1871 and commenced law practice in Dayton; counsel for the New York Central Railroad 1882–1912; prosecuting attorney of Montgomery County 1887–1890; delegate to the Republican National Convention at Minneapolis in 1892; elected as a Republican to the Fifty-seventh, Fifty-eighth, and Fifty-ninth Congresses (March 4, 1901–March 3, 1907); declined renomination in 1906; resumed the practice of law; died in Dayton, Ohio, December 17, 1912; interment in Woodland Cemetery.

NEW, Anthony, a Representative from Virginia and from Kentucky; born in Gloucester County, Va., in 1747; completed preparatory studies; studied law; was admitted to the bar and practiced; colonel in the Revolutionary Army; elected as a Democrat from Virginia to the Third and to the five succeeding Congresses (March 4, 1793–March 3, 1805); moved to Kentucky and settled in Elkton; elected as a Democrat from Kentucky to the Twelfth Congress (March 4, 1811–March 3, 1813); elected to the Fifteenth Congress (March 4, 1817–March 3, 1819); elected to the Seventeenth Congress (March 4, 1821–March 3, 1823); engaged in agricultural pursuits; died on his estate, "Dunheath," near Elkton, Todd County, Ky., March 2, 1833; interment in the family burying ground on his estate.

NEW, Harry Stewart, a Senator from Indiana; born in Indianapolis, Ind., December 31, 1858; attended the public schools and Butler University, Indianapolis, Ind.; served with the Indianapolis Journal as reporter, editor, part owner, and publisher 1878–1903; member of the State senate 1896–1900; delegate to the Republican National Conventions in 1896, 1912, 1920, and 1924; member of the Republican National Committee 1900–1912 and served as chairman in 1907 and 1908; captain and assistant adjutant general in the Third Brigade, Second Division, Seventh Army Corps, during the Spanish-American War; engaged in the stone quarrying and construction business in 1903; elected as a Republican to the United States Senate and served from March 4, 1917, to March 3, 1923; unsuccessful candidate for renomination in 1922; appointed Postmaster General in the Cabinet of President Harding on February 27, 1923; reappointed by President Coolidge in 1925 and served from March 5, 1923, to March 4, 1929; retired from active business pursuits and resided in Washington, D. C.; served as United States Commissioner, Century of Progress Exposition, Chicago, Ill., in 1933; died in Baltimore, Md., where he had gone for medical treatment on May 9, 1937; interment in the Crown Hill Cemetery, Indianapolis, Ind.

NEW, Jeptha Dudley, a Representative from Indiana; born in Vernon, Jennings County, Ind., November 28, 1830; was graduated from Vernon (Ind.) Academy and Bethany (W. Va.) College; studied law; was admitted to the bar in 1851 and practiced in Vernon, Ind., until 1864; mayor of Vernon 1852–1854; prosecuting attorney of Jennings County, Ind., 1860–1864; judge of the district court of common pleas 1864–1868; resumed the practice of law in Vernon; elected as a Democrat to the Forty-fourth Congress (March 4, 1875–March 3, 1877); declined to be a candidate for reelection in 1876 to the Forty-fifth Congress; elected to the Forty-sixth Congress (March 4, 1879–March 3, 1881); was not a candidate for reelection in 1880; judge of the sixth judicial circuit of Indiana 1882–1888; appellate judge in 1891; was nominated by the Democratic Party as a candidate for judge of the supreme court of Indiana in 1892, but died before the election in Vernon, Ind., July 9, 1892; interment in Vernon Cemetery.

NEWBERRY, John Stoughton (father of Truman Handy Newberry), a Representative from Michigan; born in Waterville, Oneida County, N. Y., November 18, 1826; moved with his parents to Michigan when a child, residing successively in Detroit, Ann Arbor, and Romeo; completed preparatory studies in Romeo Academy; was graduated from Michigan University at Ann Arbor in 1847; spent two years in civil engineering on railroads; studied law in Detroit and was admitted to the bar in 1853; made the admiralty law of the western lakes and rivers a specialty for seventeen years and published the first volume of admiralty reports of decisions of cases arising on those waters; established the Michigan Car Co. of Detroit in 1862; later established the Detroit Car Wheel Co.; appointed the first provost marshal for the State of Michigan by President Lincoln in 1862 with the rank of captain of Cavalry; resigned in 1864; engaged in several large manufacturing enterprises in 1864; traveled through the West Indies in 1865 and toured Europe in 1871; declined political honors of every kind previous to his election as a Republican to the Forty-sixth Congress (March 4, 1879–March 3, 1881); declined to be a candidate for renomination in 1880; died in Detroit, Mich., January 2, 1887; interment in Elmwood Cemetery.

NEWBERRY, Truman Handy (son of John Stoughton Newberry), a Senator from Michigan; born in Detroit, Mich., November 5, 1864; attended public and private schools; was graduated from Yale College in 1885; superintendent of construction, paymaster, and general freight and passenger agent of the Detroit, Bay City & Alpena Railway 1885–1887; president and treasurer of the Detroit Steel & Spring Co. 1887–1901; engaged in various other manufacturing activities; organizer of the Michigan State Naval Brigade, serving as landsman in 1895; lieutenant and navigator in 1897 and 1898; commissioned lieutenant (junior grade) in the United States Navy in May 1898 and served on the U. S. S. *Yosemite* in the Spanish-American War; colonel and aide-de-camp to the Governor of Michigan in 1899; Assistant Secretary of the Navy 1905–1908; Secretary of the Navy in the Cabinet of President Roosevelt from December 1, 1908, to March 6, 1909; lieutenant commander United States Navy Fleet Reserve June 6, 1917, and assistant to the commandant third naval district of New York until January 9, 1919; elected as a Republican to the United States Senate and served from March 4, 1919, until his resignation on November 18, 1922; engaged in manufacturing; died in Grosse Pointe, Mich., October 3, 1945; interment in Elmwood Cemetery, Detroit, Mich.

NEWBERRY, Walter Cass, a Representative from Illinois; born in Sangerfield, Oneida County, N. Y., December 23, 1835; pursued an academic course; engaged in mercantile pursuits in Chicago and Detroit; enlisted in the Union Army during the Civil War as a private in the Eighty-first Regiment, New York Volunteers; promoted to lieutenant in 1861, captain in 1862, major of the Twenty-fourth Regiment, New York Cavalry, in 1863, lieutenant colonel and colonel in 1864, and was brevetted brigadier general March 31, 1865, "for gallant and meritorious services at Dinwiddie Court House," where he was severely wounded; moved to Petersburg, Va., in 1865; mayor of Petersburg in 1869 and 1870, resigning in the latter year; moved to Richmond, Va., in 1870; superintendent of public property for the State for four years; moved to Chicago, Ill., in 1876; postmaster of Chicago in 1888 and 1889; elected as a Democrat to the Fifty-second Congress (March 4, 1891–March 3, 1893); was not a candidate for renomination in 1892; retired from active business pursuits; died in Chicago, Ill., July 20, 1912; interment in Graceland Cemetery.

NEWBOLD, Thomas, a Representative from New Jersey; born in Springfield Township, Burlington County, N. J., August 2, 1760; engaged in agricultural pursuits; at one time was sole owner of League Island, at Philadelphia, Pa.; member of the State general assembly in 1797; was a presidential elector in 1804, casting his vote for Thomas Jefferson; engaged in banking; elected as a Democrat to the Tenth, Eleventh, and Twelfth Congresses (March 4, 1807–March 3, 1813); unsuccessful candidate for reelection in 1812 to the Thirteenth Congress; again a member of the State general assembly 1820–1822; died in Springfield Township, Burlington County, N. J., December 18, 1823; interment in the Old Upper Springfield Friends Burying Ground.

NEWCOMB, Carman Adam, a Representative from Missouri; born in Mercer, Mercer County, Pa., July 1, 1830; completed preparatory studies; moved to Kentucky, and later to Shreveport, La., where he studied law and was admitted to the bar; moved to West Union, Iowa, in 1854 and commenced the practice of law; judge of the circuit court of Fayette County, Iowa, 1855–1860; during the Civil War served as captain of Company F, Third Regiment, Iowa Volunteer Infantry, from June 18, 1861, until his discharge on account of illness April 8, 1862; moved to Vineland, Jefferson County, Mo., and resumed the practice of law; member of the State house of representatives in 1865 and 1866; elected as a Republican to the Fortieth Congress (March 4, 1867–March 3, 1869); was not a candidate for renomination in 1868; United States marshal for the eastern district of Missouri 1869–1875; census enumerator of St. Louis, Mo., in 1870; again resumed the practice of his profession;

died in St. Louis, Mo., April 6, 1902; the remains were cremated at the Missouri Crematory in St. Louis, Mo., and the ashes deposited in the columbarium.

NEWELL, William Augustus, a Representative from New Jersey; born while his parents were on a visit in Franklin, Ohio, September 5, 1817; attended the common schools of New Brunswick, N. J.; was graduated from Rutgers College, New Brunswick, N. J., in 1836 and from the medical department of the University of Pennsylvania at Philadelphia in 1839; commenced practice in Allentown, N. J.; elected as a Whig to the Thirtieth and Thirty-first Congresses (March 4, 1847–March 3, 1851); was not a candidate for renomination in 1850; Governor of New Jersey 1857–1860; surgeon to superintend the drafting of Monmouth County Militia in 1862; delegate to the Republican National Convention at Baltimore in 1864; elected as a Republican to the Thirty-ninth Congress (March 4, 1865–March 3, 1867); unsuccessful candidate for reelection in 1866 to the Fortieth Congress; resumed the practice of medicine in Allentown; unsuccessful candidate for Governor of New Jersey in 1877; Territorial Governor of Washington 1880–1884; United States Indian inspector from August 14, 1884, to June 26, 1885; died in Allentown, N. J., August 8, 1901; interment in the Presbyterian Cemetery.

NEWHALL, Judson Lincoln, a Representative from Kentucky; born in Hunterstown (later changed to Louise), Province of Quebec, Canada, March 26, 1870; moved to Covington, Ky., with his parents in 1874; attended the public schools and was graduated from Martin's Academy, Covington, Ky., in 1886; attended the law department of Indiana University at Bloomington 1896–1898, and took special academic courses at the University of Cincinnati 1924–1926; employed in the United States Internal Revenue Service as a storekeeper-gauger from 1899 until his resignation in 1905 to engage in musical work; served as director of music in the Covington public schools 1913–1917; during the First World War served as a secretary in the Y. M. C. A. welfare service; after the war resumed his position with the Covington schools; elected as a Republican to the Seventy-first Congress (March 4, 1929–March 3, 1931); unsuccessful candidate for reelection in 1930 to the Seventy-second Congress and for election in 1934 to the Seventy-fourth Congress; engaged in the oil and gasoline business; died in Park Hills, Covington, Ky., July 23, 1952; interment in Forest Lawn Cemetery, Erlanger, Ky.

NEWHARD, Peter, a Representative from Pennsylvania; born in Allentown, Pa., July 26, 1783; completed preparatory studies and attended a private school in Allentown; opened the first hardware store in Allentown in 1812; street commissioner of the borough of Allentown in 1812; coroner of Lehigh County in 1816 and 1817; elected to the State house of representatives in October 1817; reelected in 1818, 1819, 1824, 1825, and 1829, the term then being one year; chairman of the town council in 1824 and again in 1837; elected as a Democrat to the Twenty-sixth and Twenty-seventh Congresses (March 4, 1839–March 3, 1843); was not a candidate for renomination in 1842; burgess in 1843 and trustee of Allentown Academy in 1822, 1826, and 1843; died in Allentown, Lehigh County, Pa., February 19, 1860; interment in the City Cemetery.

NEWLANDS, Francis Griffith, a Representative and a Senator from Nevada; born in Natchez, Adams County, Miss., August 28, 1848; moved to Illinois in 1848 with his parents, who settled in Quincy; privately tutored; attended the Chicago High School, Yale College, and the Columbian College Law School (now George Washington University), Washington,

D. C., but prior to graduation was admitted to the bar in 1869; moved to San Francisco in 1870 and practiced law; moved to Nevada in 1888 and continued the practice of law in Carson City; moved to Reno, Nev., the following year and continued to practice his profession; engaged actively in the agitation of the silver question and was for years vice chairman of the national silver committee; elected as a Democrat to the Fifty-third and to the four succeeding Congresses (March 4, 1893–March 3, 1903); did not seek renomination in 1902, having become a candidate for Senator; elected to the United States Senate in 1903; reelected in 1909 and again in 1914 and served from March 4, 1903, until his death in Washington, D. C., December 24, 1917; interment in Oak Hill Cemetery.

NEWMAN, Alexander, a Representative from Virginia; born near Orange, Va., on October 5, 1804; pursued an academic course; held several local offices; member of the State house of delegates 1836–1838; served in the State senate 1841–1846; postmaster of Wheeling, Va. (now West Virginia), from April 2, 1846, to March 2, 1849, when he resigned; elected as a Democrat to the Thirty-first Congress and served from March 4, 1849, until his death, before the assembling of Congress, while on a visit to Pittsburgh, Pa., September 8, 1849; interment in the Old First Street Cemetery, Moundsville, W. Va.

NEWNAN, Daniel, a Representative from Georgia; born in Salisbury, Rowan County, N. C., about 1780; completed preparatory studies; attended the University of North Carolina at Chapel Hill in 1796 and 1797; commissioned ensign and second lieutenant in the Fourth United States Infantry March 3, 1799; promoted to first lieutenant the following November and resigned January 1, 1801; engaged in planting; commanded the Georgia Volunteers in the Creek War 1812–1814; major general of the third division of State militia in 1817; superintendent of the State penitentiary 1823–1825; secretary of State of Georgia 1825–1827; the city of Newnan, Ga., was named for him in 1828; elected as a State Rights Democrat to the Twenty-second Congress (March 4, 1831–March 3, 1833); unsuccessful for reelection in 1832 to the Twenty-third Congress; died near Rossville, Ga., January 16, 1851; interment in Newnan Springs (Ga.) Churchyard, then located in an open field, but later an improved cemetery.

NEWSHAM, Joseph Parkinson, a Representative from Louisiana; born in Preston, Lancashire, England, on May 24, 1837; received an academic education; immigrated to the United States with his parents, who settled in Monroe County, Ill., in 1839; employed in a mercantile establishment for two years; studied law; was admitted to the bar in 1860 and commenced practice in Edwardsville, Ill.; served during the Civil War in the Union Army on the staffs of General Frémont and General Smith; adjutant of the Thirty-second Regiment, Missouri Volunteer Infantry; was wounded at the Battles of Chickasaw Bayou and Vicksburg; resigned on account of disabilities incurred in action July 4, 1864; moved to Donaldsonville, La., in 1864; clerk of the fourth judicial district court of the parish of Ascension; was admitted to the Louisiana bar in 1865 and practiced law in Donaldsonville, La.; moved to St. Francisville, La., in 1867; member of the constitutional convention in 1867 and 1868; upon the readmission of the State of Louisiana to representation was elected as a Republican to the Fortieth Congress and served from July 18, 1868, to March 3, 1869; established the Feliciana Republican in 1869; successfully contested the election of Michael Ryan to the Forty-first Congress and served from May 23, 1870, until March 3, 1871; was not a candidate for renomination in 1870; planter and merchant in St. Francisville, La., until 1913, when he retired; died in St. Francisville, West Feliciana Parish, La., October 22, 1919; interment in Grace Church Cemetery.

NEWSOME, John Parks, a Representative from Alabama; born in Memphis, Shelby County, Tenn., February 13, 1893; attended the public schools of Thompsons Station, Tenn., and Battle Ground Academy, Franklin, Tenn.; stock clerk for wholesale hardware company in 1912; engaged as salesman 1913–1920; president and treasurer of an electrical company since 1920; during the First World War was commissioned a first lieutenant on November 27, 1917; later promoted to captain of Infantry, Fifth Division, and served until April 29, 1919, with overseas service; chairman of Appeals Board No. 2, State of Alabama, Selective Service System in 1942 and 1943; elected as a Democrat to the Seventy-eighth Congress (January 3, 1943–January 3, 1945); unsuccessful candidate for renomination in 1944; president of Associated Industries of Alabama 1953–1955; died in Birmingham, Ala., November 10, 1961.

NEWTON, Cherubusco, a Representative from Louisiana; born in Greensburg, St. Helena Parish, La., May 15, 1848; attended private schools in Bastrop, La., and the Louisiana State University, then at Alexandria, La.; taught school; studied law; was admitted to the bar in 1870 and commenced practice in Bastrop, La.; member of the State senate 1879–1883; declined a judgeship in 1885; elected as a Democrat to the Fiftieth Congress (March 4, 1887–March 3, 1889); unsuccessful candidate for renomination in 1888: delegate to the Democratic National Convention at St. Louis in 1888; resumed the practice of law in Bastrop, La., for several years, and then moved to Monroe, Ouachita Parish, La., where he continued the practice of law until his death on May 26, 1910; interment in the New Cemetery, Bastrop, La.

NEWTON, Cleveland Alexander, a Representative from Missouri; born in Wright County, Mo., September 3, 1873; attended the common schools and Drury College at Springfield, Mo.; was graduated from the law department of the University of Missouri at Columbia in 1902; was admitted to the bar and commenced practice in Hartville, Mo., the same year; member of the State house of representatives 1902–1906; assistant United States attorney for the western district of Missouri from 1905 to 1907, when he resigned to become assistant attorney United States circuit court at St. Louis; resigned this office in 1911 to become special assistant to the Attorney General of the United States, which office he resigned in 1912 to resume the practice of law in St. Louis, Mo.; elected as a Republican to the Sixty-sixth and to the three succeeding Congresses (March 4, 1919–March 3, 1927); was not a candidate for renomination in 1926 to the Seventieth Congress; unsuccessful candidate for election in 1934 to the Seventy-fourth Congress; again resumed the practice of law in St. Louis, Mo., and Washington, D. C.; served as general counsel of the Mississippi Valley Association 1928–1943; died in Washington, D. C., on September 17, 1945; interment in Valhalla Mausoleum, St. Louis, Mo.

NEWTON, Eben, a Representative from Ohio; born in Goshen, Conn., October 16, 1795; attended the common schools; moved to Portage County, Ohio, in 1814 and engaged in agricultural pursuits; studied law; was admitted to the bar in 1823 and commenced practice in Canfield, Mahoning County, Ohio; member of the State senate 1842–1851; president judge of the court of common pleas 1844–1851; elected as a Whig to the Thirty-second Congress (March 4, 1851–March 3, 1853); was an unsuccessful candidate for reelection in 1852 to the Thirty-third Congress; served as president of the Ashtabula & New Lisbon Railroad 1856–1859; again served in the State senate 1862–1864; resumed the practice of law and also engaged in agricultural pursuits; died in Canfield, Ohio, on November 6, 1885; interment in Canfield Village Cemetery.

NEWTON, Thomas, Jr., a Representative from Virginia; born in Norfolk, Va., November 21, 1768; completed preparatory studies; studied law; was admitted to the Virginia bar and commenced practice in Norfolk; member of the Virginia State House of Delegates 1796–1799; elected as a Democrat to the Seventh and to the thirteen succeeding Congresses (March 4, 1801–March 3, 1829); one of the managers appointed by the House of Representatives in 1804 to conduct the impeachment proceedings against John Pickering, judge of the United States District Court for New Hampshire; presented credentials as a Member-elect to the Twenty-first Congress and served from March 4, 1829, until March 9, 1830, when he was succeeded by George Loyall, who successfully contested the election; elected to the Twenty-second Congress (March 4, 1831–March 3, 1833); was not a candidate for reelection in 1832 to the Twenty-third Congress; died in Norfolk, Va., on August 5, 1847; interment in St. Paul's Churchyard.

NEWTON, Thomas Willoughby, a Representative from Arkansas; born in Alexandria, Va., January 18, 1804; attended the local schools; moved to Arkansas in 1820 and settled in Little Rock; clerk of the court of Pulaski County 1825–1829; moved to Shelby County, Ky.; returned to Little Rock in 1837 and became cashier in a bank; member of the State senate 1844–1848; elected as a Whig to the Twenth-ninth Congress to fill the vacancy caused by the resignation of Archibald Yell and served from February 6 to March 3, 1847; was not a candidate for renomination in 1846 to the Thirtieth Congress; died in New York City on September 22, 1853; interment in Mount Holly Cemetery, Little Rock, Ark.

NEWTON, Walter Hughes, a Representative from Minnesota; born in Minneapolis, Hennepin County, Minn., October 10, 1880; attended the public schools and was graduated from the law department of the University of Minnesota at Minneapolis in 1905; was admitted to the bar the same year and commenced practice in Minneapolis, Minn.; first assistant prosecuting attorney of Hennepin County 1914–1918; elected as a Republican to the Sixty-sixth and to the five succeeding Congresses and served from March 4, 1919, until his resignation on June 30, 1929, having been appointed secretary to President Hoover, serving in that capacity until March 3, 1933; appointed on January 14, 1924, Regent of the Smithsonian Institution; reappointed in 1925, 1927, and 1929; appointed a member of the Federal Home Loan Bank Board by President Franklin D. Roosevelt in 1933 and served until 1934 when he resumed the practice of law in Minneapolis, Minn.; also engaged as an author; unsuccessful candidate for election in 1936 to the Seventy-fifth Congress; appointed Federal referee in bankruptcy in 1938 and served until his death in Minneapolis, Minn., August 10, 1941; interment in Lakewood Cemetery.

NEWTON, Willoughby, a Representative from Virginia; born at "Lee Hall," near Hague, Westmoreland County, Va., December 2, 1802; received a liberal education from private tutors and attended William and Mary College, Williamsburg, Va.; studied law; was admitted to the bar and commenced the practice of his profession in Westmoreland County, Va.; member of the State house of delegates 1826–1832; elected as a Whig to the Twenty-eighth Congress (March 4, 1843–March 3, 1845); unsuccessful candidate for reelection in 1844 to the Twenty-ninth Congress; resumed the practice of his profession in Westmoreland County and also engaged in agricultural pursuits; president of the Virginia Agricultural Society in 1852; again a member of the State house of delegates 1861–1863; died at "Linden," Westmoreland County, Va., on May 23, 1874; interment in a private cemetery on the family estate.

NIBLACK, Silas Leslie (cousin of William Ellis Niblack), a Representative from Florida; born in Camden County, Ga., March 17, 1825; attended the common schools; studied law; was admitted to the bar about 1851 and commenced practice in Lake City, Columbia County, Fla.; judge of the probate court of Columbia County; successfully contested as a Democrat the election of Josiah T. Walls to the Forty-second Congress and served from January 29 to March 3, 1873; unsuccessful candidate for reelection in 1872 to the Forty-third Congress; member of the State senate in 1879; carried on extensive farming operations and engaged in the practice of law in Lake City, Columbia County, Fla., until his death on February 13, 1883; interment in the Old Cathey Cemetery.

NIBLACK, William Ellis (cousin of Silas Leslie Niblack), a Representative from Indiana; born in Dubois County, Ind., May 19, 1822; attended the country schools and the Indiana University at Bloomington; studied law; was admitted to the bar in 1843 and commenced practice in Vincennes, Ind.; surveyor of Dubois County; member of the State house of representatives in 1849 and 1850; served in the State senate 1850–1853; judge of the circuit court of the third judicial district from January 1854 until October 1859, when he resigned; moved to Vincennes, Ind., in 1855; elected as a Democrat to the Thirty-fifth Congress to fill the vacancy caused by the death of James Lockhart; reelected to the Thirty-sixth Congress and served from December 7, 1857, to March 3, 1861; was not a candidate for renomination in 1860; again a member of the State house of representatives in 1862 and 1863; delegate to the Democratic National Conventions in 1864, 1868, and 1876; elected to the Thirty-ninth and to the four succeeding Congresses (March 4, 1865–March 3, 1875); was not a candidate for renomination in 1874; resumed the practice of law; judge of the supreme court of Indiana 1877–1889; moved to Indianapolis in 1889 and retired from public life; died in Indianapolis, Ind., May 7, 1893; interment in Crown Hill Cemetery.

NICHOLAS, John (brother of Wilson Cary Nicholas and uncle of Robert Carter Nicholas), a Representative from Virginia; born in Williamsburg, Va., about 1757; attended the common schools; was graduated from William and Mary College, Williamsburg, Va.; studied law; was admitted to the bar and practiced in his native county; elected as a Democrat to the Third and to the three succeeding Congresses (March 4, 1793–March 3, 1801); moved to Geneva, Ontario County, N. Y.; member of the New York State Senate 1806–1809; judge of the court of common pleas 1806–1819; engaged in agricultural pursuits; died in Geneva, Ontario County, N. Y., December 31, 1819; interment in Glenwood Cemetery.

NICHOLAS, Robert Carter (nephew of John Nicholas and Wilson Cary Nicholas), a Senator from Louisiana; born in Hanover, Hanover County, Va., in 1793; served in the War of 1812 as captain and major; attended William and Mary College, Williamsburg, Va., in 1816 and 1817; moved to Louisiana and became a sugar planter in Terrebonne Parish in 1820; elected as a Democrat to the United States Senate to fill the vacancy caused by the resignation of Senator-elect Charles E. A. Gayarre and served from January 13, 1836, to March 3, 1841; secretary of state of Louisiana from March 24, 1843, until February 7, 1846, when he resigned; died in Terrebonne Parish, La., on December 24, 1857; interment in the Burthe vault, St. Louis Cemetery, New Orleans, La.

NICHOLAS, Wilson Cary (brother of John Nicholas and uncle of Robert Carter Nicholas), a Senator and a Representative from Virginia; born in Williamsburg, Va., January 31,

1761; was graduated from William and Mary College, Williamsburg, Va.; served in the Revolutionary Army and commanded Washington's Life Guard until it disbanded in 1783; member of the State house of delegates 1784–1788; delegate to the State constitutional convention which ratified the Federal Constitution in 1788; again a member of the State house of delegates in 1789 and 1794–1800; elected as a Democrat to the United States Senate to fill the vacancy caused by the death of Henry Tazewell and served from December 5, 1799, until May 22, 1804, when he resigned; collector of the port of Norfolk 1804–1807; elected to the Tenth and Eleventh Congresses and served from March 4, 1807, until his resignation November 27, 1809; Governor of Virginia 1814–1817; died at "Tufton," near Charlottesville, Va., October 10, 1820; interment in the Jefferson burying ground at "Monticello," near Charlottesville.

NICHOLLS, John Calhoun, a Representative from Georgia; born in Clinton, Jones County, Ga., April 25, 1834; attended private schools and was graduated from William and Mary College, Williamsburg, Va., in 1855; studied law; was admitted to the bar in 1855 and practiced in Clinch and Ware Counties, Ga.; also engaged as a planter; during the Civil War served in the Confederate Army as captain, Company I, Fourth Regiment, Georgia Cavalry; member of the State constitutional convention in 1865; delegate to the Democratic National Convention at Cincinnati in 1866; presidential elector on the Democratic ticket of Seymour and Blair in 1868; served in the State senate 1870–1875; delegate to the Democratic National Convention at St. Louis in 1876; elected as a Democrat to the Forty-sixth Congress (March 4, 1879–March 3, 1881); unsuccessful candidate for renomination in 1880; elected to the Forty-eighth Congress (March 4, 1883–March 3, 1885); unsuccessful candidate for renomination in 1884; resumed the practice of law in Blackshear, Pierce County, Ga., where he died December 25, 1893; interment in Blackshear Cemetery.

NICHOLLS, Samuel Jones, a Representative from South Carolina; born in Spartanburg, Spartanburg County, S. C., May 7, 1885; attended Bingham Military Institute, Asheville, N. C., Wofford College, Spartanburg, S. C., Virginia Polytechnic Institute, Blacksburg, Va., and the law department of the University of Chicago; was admitted to the bar in 1906 and commenced practice in Spartanburg; city attorney of Spartanburg and prosecuting attorney of Spartanburg County since 1907; member of the State house of representatives 1906–1908; served by special appointment as circuit judge and as associate justice of the supreme court of South Carolina; organized and was captain for three years of Company I, First Regiment, South Carolina National Guard Infantry; elected as a Democrat to the Sixty-fourth Congress to fill the vacancy caused by the resignation of Joseph T. Johnson; reelected to the Sixty-fifth and Sixty-sixth Congresses and served from September 14, 1915, to March 3, 1921; declined to be a candidate for renomination in 1920; resumed the practice of law in Spartanburg, S. C., until his death there on November 23, 1937; interment in West Oakwood Cemetery.

NICHOLLS, Thomas David, a Representative from Pennsylvania; born in Wilkes-Barre, Luzerne County, Pa., September 16, 1870; moved to Nanticoke, Pa., with his parents; attended the public schools; began work as a breaker boy when nine years of age; at the age of twelve secured work inside the mines, continuing at various occupations therein until 1900; studied mining by correspondence; passed a State examination in 1897, received a mine foreman's certificate of competency, and was appointed superintendent of mines; district president of District No. 1, United Mine Workers of America, from 1899 to 1909, resigning

on account of ill health; elected as an Independent Democrat to the Sixtieth and Sixty-first Congresses (March 4, 1907–March 3, 1911); was not a candidate for renomination in 1910; moved to a farm in Somerset County, Md., near Princess Anne, in 1911 and engaged in the raising of poultry; died in Princess Anne, Md., January 19, 1931; interment in Antioch Methodist Episcopal Cemetery.

NICHOLS, Charles Archibald, a Representative from Michigan; born in Boyne City, Charlevoix County, Mich., August 25, 1876; attended the public schools; engaged in newspaper work as reporter and criminal investigator and was associated with the Detroit Journal and the Detroit News from 1898 to 1905; secretary of the police department of the city of Detroit 1905–1908; city clerk 1908–1912; elected as a Republican to the Sixty-fourth, Sixty-fifth, and Sixty-sixth Congresses and served from March 4, 1915, until his death in Washington, D. C., April 25, 1920; interment in Grand Lawn Cemetery, Detroit, Mich

NICHOLS, John, a Representative from North Carolina; born near Eagle Rock, Wake County, N. C., November 14, 1834; attended the common schools; learned the printing trade, serving six years; at the age of twenty-one attended Lovejoy Academy, Raleigh, N. C., for one year; engaged in the book and job printing business and newspaper publishing; principal of the North Carolina Institute for the Deaf and Dumb and the Blind 1873–1877; revenue-stamp agent in Durham, N. C., 1879–1881; postmaster of Raleigh, N. C., 1881–1885; secretary and treasurer of the State fair association; elected as an Independent to the Fiftieth Congress (March 4, 1887–March 3, 1889); unsuccessful candidate for reelection in 1888 to the Fifty-first Congress; during President Harrison's administration was appointed chief of the division of mail and files, Treasury Department, July 22, 1889; transferred as private secretary to the Assistant Secretary of the Treasury April 1, 1893, and resigned June 30, 1893; returned to Raleigh, N. C., and served in the office of the collector of internal revenue from November 26 to December 17, 1893; appointed United States commissioner for the eastern district of North Carolina on July 1, 1897, and served until his death in Raleigh, N. C., September 22, 1917; interment in Oakwood Cemetery.

NICHOLS, John Conover (Jack), a Representative from Oklahoma; born in Joplin, Mo., August 31, 1896; attended the public schools in Joplin, Mo., and Colorado Springs, Colo., and the teachers college at Emporia, Kans.; studied law in the office of his brother in Eufaula, Okla.; was admitted to the bar in 1926 and commenced practice in Eufaula, Okla.; during the First World War served in the Nineteenth Infantry, United States Army, 1917–1919; elected as a Democrat to the Seventy-fourth and to the four succeeding Congresses and served from January 3, 1935, until his resignation on July 3, 1943, to become vice president of Transcontinental & Western Air, Inc., in which capacity he served until his death in an airplane crash at Asmara, Eritrea, November 7, 1945; interment in the United States military cemetery in Asmara, Eritrea; reinterment in Greenwood Cemetery, Eufaula, Okla.

NICHOLS, Matthias H., a Representative from Ohio; born in Sharptown, Salem County, N. J., October 3, 1824; attended the common schools; learned the trade of a printer; moved to Ohio in 1842 and settled in Lima; studied law; was admitted to the bar in 1849 and commenced practice in Lima, Ohio; elected prosecuting attorney for Allen County in 1851, but resigned the following year to campaign for Congress; elected as a Whig to the Thirty-third Congress and as a Republican to the Thirty-fourth and Thirty-fifth Congresses (March 4,

1853–March 3, 1859); unsuccessful candidate for reelection in 1858 to the Thirty-sixth Congress; resumed the practice of his profession; died in Cincinnati, Hamilton County, Ohio, September 15, 1862; interment in the Old Cemetery, Lima, Ohio; reinterment in Woodlawn Cemetery.

NICHOLSON, Alfred Osborn Pope, a Senator from Tennessee; born near Franklin, Williamson County, Tenn., August 31, 1808; attended the rural schools; was graduated from the University of North Carolina at Chapel Hill in 1827; studied law; was admitted to the bar in 1831 and commenced practice in Columbia, Tenn.; edited the Western Mercury in Columbia 1832–1835; member of the State house of representatives 1833–1839; appointed as a Democrat to the United States Senate to fill the vacancy caused by the death of Felix Grundy and served from December 25, 1840, to February 7, 1842, when his appointment expired, the legislature having adjourned without electing a successor; member of the State senate 1843–1845; moved to Nashville, Tenn., and edited the Nashville Union 1844–1846; a director and subsequently president of the Bank of Tennessee in 1846 and 1847; returned to Columbia, Tenn., in 1850 and served as chancellor of the middle division for one year; declined an appointment to the Cabinet of President Pierce in 1853; edited the Washington Union 1853–1856; again elected to the United States Senate and served from March 4, 1859, until March 3, 1861, when he retired, and was subsequently formally expelled by resolution of July 11, 1861; chief justice of the supreme court of Tennessee 1870–1876; died in Columbia, Maury County, Tenn., March 23, 1876; interment in Rose Hill Cemetery.

NICHOLSON, Donald William, a Representative from Massachusetts; born in Wareham, Plymouth County, Mass., August 11, 1888; attended the public schools and took college extension courses; engaged as a salesman; during the First World War served in the United States Army 1917–1919, with overseas service; selectman, assessor, and overseer of the poor, Town of Wareham, Mass., 1920–1925; delegate to all Republican State conventions 1924–1947; served in the State house of representatives in 1925 and 1926; member of the State senate 1926–1947, serving as president in 1946 and 1947; elected as a Republican to the Eightieth Congress to fill the vacancy caused by the death of Charles L. Gifford; reelected to the Eighty-first and to the four succeeding Congresses and served from November 18, 1947, to January 3, 1959; was not a candidate for renomination in 1958 to the Eighty-sixth Congress; retired; is a resident of Wareham, Mass.

NICHOLSON, John, a Representative from New York; born in Herkimer, N. Y., in 1765; received a limited education; studied law; was admitted to the bar and practiced; held various local offices; elected as a Democrat to the Eleventh Congress (March 4, 1809–March 3, 1811); died in Herkimer, N. Y., January 20, 1820.

NICHOLSON, John Anthony, a Representative from Delaware; born in Laurel, Sussex County, Del., November 17, 1827; completed preparatory studies and was graduated from Dickinson College, Carlisle, Pa., in 1847; superintendent of free schools for Kent County in 1851; studied law in Dover, Del.; was admitted to the bar in 1850 and commenced practice in Dover; brigadier general of militia in Kent County in 1861; elected as a Democrat to the Thirty-ninth and Fortieth Congresses (March 4, 1865–March 3, 1869); was not a candidate for renomination in 1868; resumed the practice of his profession; died in Dover, Kent County, Del., November 4, 1906; interment in the Presbyterian Church Cemetery.

NICHOLSON, Joseph Hopper, a Representative from Maryland; born in Chestertown, Kent County, Md., May 15, 1770; completed preparatory studies; studied law; was admitted to the bar and practiced; member of the State house of delegates 1796–1798; elected as a Democrat to the Sixth and to the three succeeding Congresses and served from March 4, 1799, until his resignation on March 1, 1806; one of the managers appointed by the House of Representatives in January 1804 to conduct the impeachment proceedings against John Pickering, judge of the United States District Court for New Hampshire, and in December of the same year against Samuel Chase, Associate Justice of the Supreme Court of the United States; declined the appointment as collector of the port of Baltimore in 1805; participated in the defense of Fort McHenry during the War of 1812; served as chief justice of the sixth judicial district of Maryland and was associate justice of the court of appeals from March 26, 1806, until his death at his home in Baltimore County, Md., March 4, 1817; interment in the family cemetery on the Lloyd estate, known as "Wye House," near Easton, Talbot County, Md.

NICHOLSON, Samuel Danford, a Senator from Colorado; born in Springfield, Prince Edward Island, Canada, February 22, 1859; attended the public schools; moved to Michigan, then to Nebraska, and later, in 1881, to Leadville, Colo.; became interested in mining, advancing from miner to foreman, superintendent, manager, and president; discovered the zinc ore which bears his name, "Nicholsoiti"; mayor of Leadville 1893–1897; moved to Denver in 1902; during the First World War served as State chairman of the Liberty and Victory loan campaigns; member of the United States Fuel Administration; elected as a Republican to the United States Senate and served from March 4, 1921, until his death in Denver, Colo., March 24, 1923; interment in Fairmount Cemetery.

NICOLL, Henry, a Representative from New York; born in New York City October 23, 1812; was graduated from Columbia College, New York City, in 1830; studied law; was admitted to the bar in 1835 and commenced practice in New York City; delegate to the State constitutional convention in 1847; elected as a Democrat to the Thirtieth Congress (March 4, 1847–March 3, 1849); resumed the practice of law; died in New York City on November 28, 1879; interment in the family burying ground, Mastic, Long Island, N. Y.

NIEDRINGHAUS, Frederick Gottlieb (uncle of Henry Frederick Niedringhaus), a Representative from Missouri; born in Luebbecke, Westphalia, North Germany, on October 21, 1837; attended the common schools; learned the glazing, painting, and tinning trades; immigrated to the United States in November 1855 and settled in St. Louis, Mo.; began the stamping of tinware in 1862; invented what is called "granite ironware" in 1874 and established an extensive business, now merged in the National Enameling & Stamping Co.; became interested in various other business enterprises in St. Louis; elected as a Republican to the Fifty-first Congress (March 4, 1889–March 3, 1891); was not a candidate for renomination in 1890; resumed his former business pursuits; died in St. Louis, Mo., November 25, 1922; interment in Bellefontaine Cemetery.

NIEDRINGHAUS, Henry Frederick (nephew of Frederick Gottlieb Niedringhaus), a Representative from Missouri; born in St. Louis, Mo., December 15, 1864; attended the public schools, Central Wesleyan College, Warrenton, Mo., and Smith Academy, a branch of Washington University, St. Louis, Mo.; engaged in manufacturing pursuits, serving as general manager of the National Enameling & Stamping Co. in Granite City, Ill.; chairman of the board of governors of Shriners' Hospital for Crippled Children, St. Louis, Mo., 1924–1941; elected as a Republican to the Seventieth, Seventy-first, and Seventy-second Congresses (March 4, 1927–March 3, 1933); unsuccessful candidate for reelection in 1932 to the Seventy-third Congress; retired from active business pursuits and resided in St. Louis, Mo., until his death in that city August 3, 1941; interment in Bellefontaine Cemetery.

NILES, Jason, a Representative from Mississippi; born in Burlington, Vt., December 19, 1814; attended the common schools, and was graduated from the University of Vermont at Burlington in 1837; taught school in Ohio and Tennessee for a number of years; studied law; was admitted to the bar in 1851 and commenced practice in Kosciusko, Attala County, Miss.; delegate to the State constitutional conventions in 1851, 1865, and 1868; member of the State house of representatives in 1870; circuit judge for the thirteenth judicial district in 1871 and 1872; elected as a Republican to the Forty-third Congress (March 4, 1873–March 3, 1875); unsuccessful candidate for reelection in 1874 to the Forty-fourth Congress; editor of the Kosciusko Chronicle 1876-1880; resumed the practice of his profession; died in Kosciusko, Miss., July 7, 1894; interment in the City Cemetery.

NILES, John Milton, a Senator from Connecticut; born in Windsor, Hartford County, Conn., August 20, 1787; completed preparatory studies; studied law; was admitted to the bar in 1817 and commenced practice in Hartford, Conn.; established the Hartford Times in 1817 and was connected with it as editor or contributor until he became a Republican in the early fifties; associate judge of Hartford County Court 1821–1826; member of the State house of representatives in 1826; postmaster of Hartford 1829–1836; appointed as a Democrat to the United States Senate to fill the vacancy caused by the death of Nathan Smith; subsequently elected and served from December 21, 1835, to March 3, 1839; was not a candidate for renomination in 1838; unsuccessful candidate for Governor of Connecticut in 1839 and 1840; Postmaster General in the Cabinet of President Martin Van Buren in 1840 and 1841; again elected to the United States Senate and served from March 4, 1843, to March 3, 1849; was not a candidate for reelection; was the author of many books; died in Hartford, Conn., May 31, 1856; interment in Old North Cemetery.

NILES, Nathaniel, a Representative from Vermont; born in South Kingston, R. I., April 3, 1741; attended Harvard College, and was graduated from Princeton College in 1766; studied law and medicine; taught in New York City; studied theology and preached in Norwich and Torrington, Conn.; invented a process for making wire and erected mills in Norwich; after the Revolution moved to West Fairlee, Orange County, Vt.; member of the State house of representatives in 1784 and served as speaker; judge of the supreme court 1784–1788; member of the council in 1785 and 1787; delegate to the State constitutional convention of 1791; upon the admission of Vermont as a State into the Union was elected to the Second Congress; reelected to the Third Congress and served from October 17, 1791, to March 3, 1795; again a member of the State house of representatives 1800–1803 and 1812–1815; member of the Governor's council 1803–1809; presidential elector on the Jefferson ticket in 1804 and on the Madison ticket in 1813; delegate to the State constitutional convention of 1814; discontinued active pursuits and retired to his home in West Fairlee in 1815; died in Fairlee, Vt., October 31, 1828; interment in West Fairlee Center Cemetery.

NIMTZ, F. Jay, a Representative from Indiana; born in South Bend, Saint Joseph County, Ind., December 1, 1915;

attended the public schools; graduated from Indiana University in 1938 and from the same university law school in 1940; admitted to the bar in 1940 and commenced the practice of law in South Bend, Ind.; enlisted in the United States Army as a private June 13, 1941, and served until February 14, 1947, attaining the rank of lieutenant colonel, with overseas service in England, France, and Germany; served fourteen months as assistant executive officer, Office of United States Chief of Counsel for Prosecution of Axis Criminality; decorated with Legion of Merit and Bronze Star, French Legion of Honor, Polish Polonia Restituta and Golden Cross of Merit, Czechoslovakian Medal for Military Merit and Order of the White Lion, Norwegian Order of St. Olaf, and United Kingdom Order of the British Empire; member of board of directors, Saint Joseph County Department of Public Welfare; elected as a Republican to the Eighty-fifth Congress (January 3, 1957–January 3, 1959); unsuccessful candidate for reelection in 1958 to the Eighty-sixth Congress and for election in 1960 to the Eighty-seventh Congress; is a resident of South Bend, Ind.

NISBET, Eugenius Aristides (cousin of Mark Anthony Cooper), a Representative from Georgia; born near Union Point, Greene County, Ga., December 7, 1803; completed preparatory studies; attended the Powellton Academy, Hancock County, Ga., 1815–1817 and the University of South Carolina at Columbia 1817–1819; was graduated from the University of Georgia at Athens in 1821; was admitted to the bar by a special act of the legislature before he was twenty-one and commenced the practice of law in Madison, Morgan County, Ga., in 1824; member of the State house of representatives 1827–1830; served in the State senate 1830–1837; moved to Macon, Ga., in 1837 and resumed the practice of law; unsuccessful Whig candidate for election in 1836 to the Twenty-fifth Congress; elected as a Whig to the Twenty-sixth and Twenty-seventh Congresses and served from March 4, 1839, until October 12, 1841, when he resigned; associate judge of the supreme court of Georgia 1845–1853; supported James Buchanan for President in 1856 and Stephen A. Douglas in 1860; member of the secession convention of Georgia in January 1861 and was the author of the ordinance of secession; writer and lecturer; died in Macon, Bibb County, Ga., March 18, 1871; interment in Rose Hill Cemetery.

NIVEN, Archibald Campbell, a Representative from New York; born in Newburgh, Orange County, N. Y., December 8, 1803; completed preparatory studies; surrogate of Sullivan County 1828–1840; adjutant general of New York in 1844; elected as a Democrat to the Twenty-ninth Congress (March 4, 1845–March 3, 1847); district attorney of Sullivan County 1847–1850; member of the State senate in 1864 and 1865; died in Monticello, Sullivan County, N. Y., February 21, 1882; interment in Rock Ridge Cemetery.

NIX, Robert Nelson Cornelius, Sr., a Representative from Pennsylvania; born in Orangeburg, S. C., August 9, 1905; is of the Negro race; graduated from Townsend Harris Hall High School, New York City, N. Y., Lincoln University, Chester County, Pa., and from University of Pennsylvania Law School at Philadelphia in 1924; was admitted to the bar in 1925 and commenced the practice of law in Philadelphia, Pa.; special deputy attorney general of the Pennsylvania State Department of Revenue, and special assistant deputy attorney general of the Commonwealth of Pennsylvania 1934–1938; delegate to the Democratic National Convention in 1956; elected as a Democrat to the Eighty-fifth Congress to fill the vacancy caused by the resignation of Earl Chudoff; reelected to the Eighty-sixth Congress and served from May 20, 1958, to January 3, 1961. *Reelected to the Eighty-seventh Congress.*

NIXON, George Stuart, a Senator from Nevada; born in Placer County, Calif., on April 2, 1860; attended the public schools; at the age of nineteen entered the employ of a railroad company and studied telegraphy; was transferred in 1881 to Nevada, where he served three years as a telegraph operator; in 1884 accepted a clerical position in a bank in Reno; organized and became cashier of a bank at Winnemucca, Nev.; built an opera house in Reno and a theater in Winnemucca; engaged in banking and agricultural pursuits; also largely interested in mining and stock raising; member of the State house of representatives in 1891; elected January 25, 1905, as a Republican to the United States Senate; reelected in 1911 and served from March 4, 1905, until his death in Washington, D. C., June 5, 1912; interment in Masonic Cemetery, Reno, Nev.

NIXON, John Thompson, a Representative from New Jersey; born in Fairton, Cumberland County, N. J., on August 31, 1820; attended private schools and was graduated from Princeton College in 1841; studied law; was admitted to the bar in 1845 and commenced practice in Bridgeton, N. J.; member of the State house of assembly 1848–1850 and served as speaker in the latter year; elected as a Republican to the Thirty-sixth and Thirty-seventh Congresses (March 4, 1859–March 3, 1863); was not a candidate for renomination in 1862; resumed the practice of law in Bridgeton, N. J., 1863–1870; appointed United States judge for the district of New Jersey on April 28, 1870, and served until his death at his summer home in Stockbridge, Berkshire County, Mass., September 28, 1889; interment in the City Cemetery, Bridgeton, N. J.

NIXON, Richard Milhous, a Representative and a Senator from California and a Vice President of the United States; born in Yorba Linda, Orange County, Calif., January 9, 1913; attended the public schools; graduated from Whittier (Calif.) College in 1934 and Duke University Law School, Durham, N. C., in 1937; was admitted to the bar the same year and commenced practice in Whittier, Calif.; trustee of Whittier College since 1939; attorney in Office of Emergency Management, Washington, D. C., January 1942 to August 1942; during World War II served as a lieutenant commander in the United States Navy from August 1942 to January 1946; elected as a Republican to the Eightieth and Eighty-first Congresses and served from January 3, 1947, until his resignation November 30, 1950; appointed to the United States Senate to fill the vacancy caused by the resignation of Sheridan Downey and served from December 1, 1950, to January 3, 1951; elected to the United States Senate in 1950 for the term commencing January 3, 1951, and ending January 3, 1957; nominated for the office of Vice President of the United States by the Republican Party at the convention in Chicago in 1952; elected Vice President of the United States on November 4, 1952, for the term beginning January 20, 1953; resigned from the United States Senate January 1, 1953; reelected Vice President of the United States November 6, 1956, and served until January 20, 1961; Republican nominee for President of the United States in 1960; resumed the practice of law and resides in Los Angeles, Calif.

NOBLE, David Addison, a Representative from Michigan; born in Williamstown, Berkshire County, Mass., November 9, 1802; attended a private school in Plainfield, Mass., and was graduated from Williams College, Williamstown, Mass., in 1825; studied law in Albany and New York City; was admitted to the bar in 1831 and commenced practice in New York City; moved to Monroe, Mich., in 1831 and continued the practice of law; city recorder of Monroe in 1838, 1839, and 1844–1850; mayor in 1852; served two terms as alderman; member of the State house of representatives in 1847 and 1848; prosecuting

attorney and probate judge of Monroe County; elected as a Democrat to the Thirty-third Congress (March 4, 1853–March 3, 1855); unsuccessful candidate for reelection in 1854 to the Thirty-fourth Congress; appointed manager of the Louisville, New Albany & Chicago Railroad in 1858 and served four years; delegate to the Democratic National Convention at Chicago in 1864 which nominated the presidential ticket of McClellan and Pendleton; died in Monroe, Monroe County, Mich., October 13, 1876; interment in Woodlawn Cemetery.

NOBLE, James, a Senator from Indiana; born near Berryville, Clarke County, Va., December 16, 1785; moved with his parents to Campbell County, Ky., in 1795; studied law; was admitted to the bar and practiced; moved to Brookville, Franklin County, Ind., in 1811; member of the convention to draft the constitution of the State in 1816; member of the first State house of representatives in 1816 which elected him to the United States Senate; reelected in 1821 and again in 1827 and served from December 11, 1816, until his death in Washington, D. C., on February 26, 1831; interment in the Congressional Cemetery.

NOBLE, Warren Perry, a Representative from Ohio; born near Berwick, Luzerne County, Pa., June 14, 1820; moved to Ohio; attended the common schools; taught school; was graduated from Wadsworth Academy, Wadsworth, Ohio, in 1840; studied law; was admitted to the bar in 1843 and commenced practice in Tiffin, Ohio; member of the State house of representatives 1846–1850; prosecuting attorney of Seneca County 1851–1854; elected as a Democrat to the Thirty-seventh and Thirty-eighth Congresses (March 4, 1861–March 3, 1865); unsuccessful candidate for reelection to the Thirty-ninth Congress; resumed the practice of law in Tiffin, Ohio, and died there July 9, 1903; interment in Green Lawn Cemetery.

NOBLE, William Henry, a Representative from New York; born in New Milford, Litchfield County, Conn., September 22, 1788; moved to Ballston Spa, then to Cato, N. Y., and later to Rochester, N. Y.; received a limited education; was a tanner by trade and later a farmer; member of the New York State Assembly 1828–1830; identified politically with the "Bucktail" wing, so called, and with the Democratic supporters of the administrations of Presidents Jackson and Van Buren; elected as a Democrat to the Twenty-fifth Congress (March 4, 1837–March 3, 1839); unsuccessful candidate for reelection in 1838 to the Twenty-sixth Congress; inspector of Auburn Prison 1843–1845; died in Rochester, N. Y., February 5, 1850.

NODAR, Robert Joseph, Jr., a Representative from New York; born in Brooklyn, N. Y., March 23, 1916; attended the public schools of New York City and was graduated from Newtown High School, Elmhurst, N. Y., in 1935; engaged as a clerk in the Manufacturers Trust Co. in New York City 1935–1939 and with the Crucible Steel Corp. of America 1940–1942; during World War II served in the United States Army Air Force, with service in the South Pacific, from March 18, 1942, until discharged as a master sergeant on January 6, 1946; elected as a Republican to the Eightieth Congress (January 3, 1947–January 3, 1949); unsuccessful candidate for reelection in 1948 to the Eighty-first Congress; engaged as a position clerk with Solomon Brothers & Hutzzer, New York City, N. Y.; is a resident of Maspeth, N. Y.

NOELL, John William (father of Thomas Estes Noell), a Representative from Missouri; born in Bedford County, Va., February 22, 1816; attended the rural schools; at the age of seventeen moved to Missouri with his parents, who settled near

Perryville; engaged in milling and storekeeping; studied law; was admitted to the bar in 1843 and commenced practice in Perryville, Mo.; clerk of the circuit court for Perry County 1841–1850; member of the State senate 1851–1855; elected as a Democrat to the Thirty-sixth, Thirty-seventh, and Thirty-eighth Congresses and served from March 4, 1859, until his death in Washington, D. C., March 14, 1863; interment in St. Mary's Cemetery, Perryville, Mo.

NOELL, Thomas Estes (son of John William Noell), a Representative from Missouri; born in Perryville, Perry County, Mo., April 3, 1839; attended the public schools; studied law; was admitted to the bar in 1858 and commenced practice in Perryville, Mo., the same year; during the Civil War was appointed a military commissioner in 1861; served as major in the State militia from July 1861 to April 1862; appointed captain unassigned in Company C, Nineteenth Infantry, United States Army, and served from April 1, 1862, until his resignation on February 20, 1865, to take his seat in the National House of Representatives; elected as a Radical to the Thirty-ninth and Fortieth Congresses and served from March 4, 1865, until his death in St.Louis, Mo., on October 3, 1867; interment in St. Mary's Cemetery, Perryville, Mo.

NOLAN, John Ignatius (husband of Mae Ella Nolan), a Representative from California; born in San Francisco, Calif., January 14, 1874; attended the public schools; was an iron molder; member of the board of supervisors of the city and county of San Francisco in 1911; secretary of the San Francisco Labor Council in 1912; elected as a Republican to the Sixty-third and to the four succeeding Congresses and served from March 4, 1913, until his death; had been reelected in 1922 to the Sixty-eighth Congress; died in San Francisco, Calif., November 18, 1922; interment in Holy Cross Cemetery.

NOLAN, Mae Ella (widow of John Ignatius Nolan), a Representative from California; born in San Francisco, Calif., September 20, 1886; attended the public schools and St. Vincent's Convent of San Francisco; elected as a Republican to the Sixty-seventh and to the Sixty-eighth Congresses to fill the vacancies caused by the death of her husband, John Ignatius Nolan, who had been reelected in 1922, and served from January 23, 1923, to March 3, 1925; was not a candidate for renomination in 1924; is a resident of San Francisco, Calif.

NOLAN, Michael Nicholas, a Representative from New York; born in County Carlow, Ireland, May 4, 1833; immigrated to the United States at the age of ten years; attended the public schools in Albany; studied law but did not complete the course; went to California during the gold rush; was employed on the street railway system of San Francisco and soon became manager; returned to Albany, N. Y., and engaged in business as a brewer; director of the National Savings Bank of Albany; fire commissioner of Albany 1869–1878; elected mayor of Albany and served from May 1878 to June 24, 1883, when he resigned; elected as a Democrat to the Forty-seventh Congress (March 4, 1881–March 3, 1883); did not seek renomination in 1882, having been reelected mayor; continued his business activities; died in Albany, N. Y., May 31, 1905; interment in St. Agnes' Cemetery.

NOLAN, William Ignatius, a Representative from Minnesota; born in St. Paul, Minn., May 14, 1874; moved with his parents to Minneapolis, Minn., in 1877; educated in the public schools of Minneapolis; member of the Minnesota National Guard 1891–1896; engaged as a lecturer and humorist in 1894 and later as a Chautauqua lecturer; member of the State house of representatives 1903–1907, 1911–1913, and 1917–1923, serving as speaker

1919–1923; Lieutenant Governor of the State 1925–1929; chairman of the Minnesota Reforestation Commission in 1927; elected as a Republican to the Seventy-first Congress to fill the vacancy caused by the resignation of Walter H. Newton; reelected to the Seventy-second Congress and served from June 17, 1929, to March 3, 1933; unsuccessful candidate for reelection in 1932 to the Seventy-third Congress and unsuccessful candidate for nomination in 1934, 1936, and 1938; resumed his profession as a lecturer; elected State railroad and warehouse commissioner in 1942 and served until his death August 3, 1943, at Winona (Minn.) General Hospital, while on a visit; interment in Lakewood Cemetery, Minneapolis, Minn.

NOLAND, James E., a Representative from Indiana; born in La Grange, Lewis County, Mo., April 22, 1920; with his parents moved to Indiana; attended the public schools of Spencer and Bloomington, Ind.; graduated from Indiana University in 1942 and from Harvard Graduate School of Business Administration in 1943; during World War II was commissioned a second lieutenant in June 1943 in the Army Transportation Corps and assigned to the New Orleans Port of Embarkation and served until discharged as a captain on May 26, 1946; awarded the Army Commendation Ribbon; unsuccessful Democratic candidate for election in 1946 to the Eightieth Congress; graduated from Indiana University Law School in 1948; was admitted to the bar and commenced the practice of law; president of Kirkwood Hotel Corp., Indianapolis, Ind.; elected as a Democrat to the Eighty-first Congress (January 3, 1949–January 3, 1951); unsuccessful candidate for reelection in 1950 to the Eighty-second Congress; resumed the practice of law in Indianapolis, Ind.

NOONAN, Edward Thomas, a Representative from Illinois; born in Macomb, McDonough County, Ill., October 23, 1861; studied law in Chicago and was admitted to the bar in 1882; after admission to the bar was graduated from the University of Michigan at Ann Arbor in 1883 and commenced practice; member of the State senate 1890–1894; colonel on the staff of Governor Altgeld 1893–1897; attorney for the Board of West Chicago Park Commissioners 1893–1898; unsuccessful candidate for election to Congress in 1894 and 1896; elected as a Democrat to the Fifty-sixth Congress (March 4, 1899–March 3, 1901); was not a candidate for renomination in 1900; resumed the practice of law in Chicago, Ill., until his death in that city on December 19, 1923; interment in St. Paul's Catholic Cemetery, Macomb, Ill.

NOONAN, George Henry, a Representative from Texas; born in Newark, N. J., August 20, 1828; received a liberal education; studied law; was admitted to the bar and practiced; moved to Texas in 1852 and settled in Castroville, Medina County; resumed the practice of law; elected judge of the eighteenth judicial district of Texas in 1862 and served until 1894 when he resigned; elected as a Republican to the Fifty-fourth Congress (March 4, 1895–March 3, 1897); unsuccessful candidate for reelection in 1896 to the Fifty-fifth Congress; resumed the practice of law in San Antonio, Tex., and died there on August 17, 1907; interment in St. Mary's Cemetery.

NORBECK, Peter, a Senator from South Dakota; born near Vermillion, Clay County, Dakota (now South Dakota), August 27, 1870; attended the public schools and the University of South Dakota at Vermillion; moved to Bloomington, Charles Mix County, S. Dak., in 1886 and to Redfield, Spink County, S. Dak., in 1900; engaged in agricultural pursuits and in 1895 also engaged as a contractor and driller of deep water, oil, and gas wells; member of the State senate 1909–1915; served as Lieutenant Governor in 1915 and 1916 and as Governor of South Dakota

1917–1921; delegate to all the Republican National Conventions from 1916 to 1932; was instrumental in the establishment of the Rushmore National Monument and was a member of the Rushmore Commission from its inception; elected as a Republican to the United States Senate in 1920; reelected in 1926 and again in 1932 and served from March 4, 1921, until his death in Redfield, S. Dak., December 20, 1936; interment in Bloomington Church Cemetery, near Platte, S. Dak.

NORBLAD, Albin Walter, Jr., a Representative from Oregon; born in Escanaba, Delta County, Mich., September 12, 1908, and moved with his parents to Astoria, Oreg., the same year; attended the public schools of Astoria and the New Mexico Military Academy at Roswell; was graduated from the University of Oregon at Eugene in 1932 and also took graduate work at the Harvard Law School, Cambridge, Mass.; was admitted to the bar in 1932 and commenced practice in Astoria, Clatsop County, Oreg.; member of the State house of representatives 1935–1937; member of the board of trustees of Linfield College; delegate to the Republican National Convention at Philadelphia in 1940; during World War II served as combat intelligence officer, Ninth Air Force, 1942–1945; awarded Air Medal; elected as a Republican to the Seventy-ninth Congress to fill the vacancy caused by the death of James W. Mott; reelected to the Eightieth and to the six succeeding Congresses and served from January 11, 1946, to January 3, 1961. *Reelected to the Eighty-seventh Congress.*

NORCROSS, Amasa, a Representative from Massachusetts; born in Rindge, Cheshire County, N. H., January 26, 1824; attended the common schools and Appleton Academy, New Ipswich, N. H.; studied law; was admitted to the bar in 1847 and commenced practice in Worcester, Mass.; member of the Massachusetts House of Representatives in 1858, 1859, and again in 1862; assessor of internal revenue from August 1862 until May 1873, when the office was abolished; mayor of the city of Fitchburg, Mass., in 1873 and 1874; served in the State senate in 1874; elected as a Republican to the Forty-fifth, Forty-sixth, and Forty-seventh Congresses (March 4, 1877–March 3, 1883); was not a candidate for renomination in 1882; resumed the practice of law; died in Paris, France, April 2, 1898, while on a visit to his daughter; interment in Laurel Hill Cemetery, Fitchburg, Worcester County, Mass.

NORMAN, Fred Barthold, a Representative from Washington; born on a farm near Martinsville, Clark County, Ill., March 21, 1882; attended the public schools and was graduated from Martinsville (Ill.) High School; moved to Lebam, Pacific County, Wash., in 1901; worked on farms, in logging camps, sawmills, shingle mills, and shipyards 1901–1922; engaged in the wholesale and retail tobacco and candy business since 1922; member of the city council of Raymond, Wash., 1916–1918; served in the State house of representatives in 1919 and 1920; member of the State senate 1925–1935; elected as a Republican to the Seventy-eighth Congress (January 3, 1943–January 3, 1945); unsuccessful candidate for reelection in 1944 to the Seventy-ninth Congress; elected in 1946 to the Eightieth Congress and served from January 3, 1947, until his death in Washington, D. C., on April 18, 1947; interment in Fern Hill Cemetery, Menlo, Wash.

NORRELL, William Frank (husband of Catherine D. Norrell), a Representative from Arkansas; born in Milo, Ashley County, Ark., August 29, 1896; attended the public schools, the Arkansas Agricultural and Mechanical College of Monticello, the College of the Ozarks, Clarksville, Ark., and the University of Arkansas Law School at Little Rock; during the First World War served in the Quartermaster Corps of the United States Army; was admitted to the bar in 1920 and commenced practice in Monticello, Ark.; member of the State senate 1930–1938, serving as president for four years; elected as a Democrat to the Seventy-sixth and to the eleven succeeding Congresses and served from January 3, 1939, until his death in Washington, D. C., February 15, 1961; interment in Oakland Cemetery, Monticello, Ark.

NORRIS, Benjamin White, a Representative from Alabama; born in Monmouth, Maine, January 22, 1819; prepared for college at Monmouth Academy, and was graduated from Waterville (now Colby) College, Maine, in 1843; in early life a Democrat; taught one term in Kents Hill Seminary; engaged in the grocery business in Skowhegan, Maine; delegate to the Free-Soil Convention at Buffalo in 1848; went to California in 1849, remaining one year, then returned to Skowhegan, and studied law; was admitted to the bar of Somerset County in January 1852 and commenced practice there; land agent for the State of Maine 1860–1863; commissioner for Maine of the Soldiers' National Cemetery at Gettysburg in 1863; delegate to the Republican National Convention at Baltimore in 1864 which nominated Lincoln and Johnson; during the Civil War served as paymaster in the Union Army in 1864 and 1865; appointed major and additional paymaster in the Bureau of Freedmen and Abandoned Lands, serving from May 1 to August 2, 1865, at Mobile, Ala.; resided on a plantation in Elmore County and in Wetumpka, Ala., until 1872; member of the constitutional convention of Alabama in 1868; upon the readmission of Alabama to representation was elected as a Republican to the Fortieth Congress and served from July 21, 1868, to March 3, 1869; unsuccessful candidate for election in 1870 to the Forty-second Congress; died in Montgomery, Ala., January 26, 1873; interment in South Cemetery, Skowhegan, Somerset County, Maine.

NORRIS, George William, a Representative and a Senator from Nebraska; born on a farm near Clyde, Sandusky County, Ohio, on July 11, 1861; attended the district schools, Baldwin University, Berea, Ohio, and the Northern Indiana Normal School at Valparaiso; taught school while studying law; was graduated from the law department of Valparaiso (Ind.) University in 1883 and was admitted to the bar the same year; continued teaching until he moved to Beaver City, Furnas County, Nebr., in 1885 and engaged in the practice of law; county attorney of Furnas County for three terms; declined to be a candidate for further nomination; district judge of the fourteenth district 1895–1902; moved to McCook, Red Willow County, Nebr., in 1899; elected as a Republican to the Fifty-eighth and to the four succeeding Congresses (March 4, 1903–March 3, 1913); did not seek renomination in 1912, having become a candidate for Senator; one of the managers appointed by the House of Representatives in 1912 to conduct the impeachment proceedings against Robert W. Archbald, judge of the United States Commerce Court; elected as a Republican to the United States Senate in 1912; reelected in 1918, 1924, and 1930, and as an Independent Republican in 1936, and served from March 4, 1913, to January 3, 1943; unsuccessful candidate for reelection in 1942; retired from public life; died in McCook, Nebr., September 2, 1944; interment in Memorial Park Cemetery.

NORRIS, Moses, Jr., a Representative and a Senator from New Hampshire; born in Pittsfield, N. H., November 8, 1799; attended the public schools and the Pittsfield Academy, and was graduated from Dartmouth College, Hanover, N. H., in 1828; studied law; was admitted to the bar in 1832 and commenced practice in Barnstead; returned to Pittsfield in 1834; served in the State house of representatives 1837–1840 and 1842; member of the State council in 1841 and 1842; elected as a Democrat to the Twenty-eighth and Twenty-ninth Congresses (March 4,

1843–March 3, 1847); again a member of the State house of representatives in 1847 and 1848, and served as speaker; elected to the United States Senate and served from March 4, 1849, until his death in Washington, D. C., January 11, 1855; interment in Floral Park Cemetery, Pittsfield, N. H.

NORTH, Solomon Taylor, a Representative from Pennsylvania; born in Jefferson County, Pa., May 24, 1853; attended the public schools; taught school six years and served as a school director for twenty years; lumber merchant, farmer, and banker; member of the National Guard of Pennsylvania; delegate to the Republican State convention in 1898; director of the Punxsutawney National Bank; member of the board of education; member of the State house of representatives 1905–1907, 1911, and 1913; elected as a Republican to the Sixty-fourth Congress (March 4, 1915–March 3, 1917); unsuccessful candidate for renomination in 1916; died near Punxsutawney, Jefferson County, Pa., October 19, 1917; interment in Circle Hill Cemetery.

NORTH, William, a Senator from New York; born in Fort Frederick, Pemaquid, Maine, in 1755; attended the common schools; moved with his mother to Boston, Mass.; entered the Revolutionary Army in 1775 and was a member of Arnold's Canadian expedition and was later aide-de-camp to Major General Baron von Steuben; after the war settled in Duanesburg, N. Y.; appointed as a Federalist to the United States Senate to fill the vacancy caused by the resignation of John S. Hobart and served from May 5, 1798, to August 17, 1798, when a successor was elected and qualified; appointed adjutant general of the Army with the rank of brigadier general and served from 1798 to 1800; member and speaker of the State assembly in 1810; died in Duanesburg, Schenectady County, N. Y., on January 3, 1836; interment in the crypt under Christ Episcopal Church.

NORTHWAY, Stephen Asa, a Representative from Ohio; born in Christian Hollow, Onondaga County, N. Y., June 19, 1833; moved with his parents in 1840 to the township of Orwell, Ashtabula County, Ohio; attended the district school, Kingsville Academy, and Orwell Academy; taught school; studied law; was admitted to the bar in 1859 and commenced practice in Jefferson, Ashtabula County, Ohio; prosecuting attorney of Ashtabula County 1861–1865; member of the State house of representatives in 1865 and 1866; resumed the practice of law; elected as a Republican to the Fifty-third, Fifty-fourth, and Fifty-fifth Congresses and served from March 4, 1893, until his death in Jefferson, Ashtabula County, Ohio, on September 8, 1898; interment in Oakdale Cemetery.

NORTON, Daniel Sheldon, a Senator from Minnesota; born in Mount Vernon, Knox County, Ohio, on April 12, 1829; pursued classical studies and was graduated from Kenyon College, Gambier, Ohio; served in the Mexican War; after the war returned to Ohio; studied law; was admitted to the bar and commenced practice in Mount Vernon in 1852; moved to St. Paul, Minn., in 1855, and thence to Winona, Minn., in 1856, where he continued the practice of his profession; member of the State house of representatives 1857–1860; served in the State senate 1861–1864; elected as a Union Conservative to the United States Senate and served from March 4, 1865, until his death in Washington, D. C., July 13, 1870; interment in Greenmount Cemetery, Baltimore, Md.

NORTON, Ebenezer Foote, a Representative from New York; born in Goshen, Litchfield County, Conn., November 7, 1774; completed preparatory studies; studied law; was admitted to the bar and practiced; moved to Buffalo, N. Y., in 1815; attorney for the Niagara Bank; held several local offices; was one of the nine leading citizens of Buffalo who formed the original Buffalo Harbor Co. in 1819 and petitioned the legislature for a State loan to be used for harbor improvement; elected as a Democrat to the Twenty-first Congress (March 4, 1829–March 3, 1831); unsuccessful for reelection in 1830 to the Twenty-second Congress; resumed his law practice; died in Buffalo, N. Y., May 11, 1851.

NORTON, Elijah Hise, a Representative from Missouri; was born in Russellville, Logan County, Ky., November 24, 1821; attended the public schools and Centre College, Danville, Ky.; was graduated from the law department of Transylvania University, Lexington, Ky., in 1842; was admitted to the bar and commenced practice in Platte City, Mo., in 1845; county attorney in 1850; judge of the circuit court of Missouri 1852–1860; elected as a Democrat to the Thirty-seventh Congress (March 4, 1861–March 3, 1863); unsuccessful candidate for reelection in 1862 to the Thirty-eighth Congress; delegate to the State constitutional convention in 1875; appointed and subsequently elected as judge of the State supreme court, serving from 1876 to 1879; resumed the practice of law and the care of his estate; died in Platte City, Platte County, Mo., August 5, 1914; interment in Platte City Cemetery.

NORTON, James, a Representative from South Carolina; born near Mullins, Marion County, S. C., October 8, 1843; pursued an academic course; left school in 1861 to enter the Confederate Army; served throughout the Civil War in the Army of Northern Virginia; more than once wounded, a minié ball at one time passing through his body and right lung; after the war reentered school, but did not finish the regular course; teacher in the public schools 1866–1870; engaged in agricultural pursuits and merchandising; elected county school commissioner in 1870 and reelected in 1872; member of the State house of representatives in 1886, 1887, 1890, and 1891; assistant comptroller general of the State of South Carolina 1890–1894; comptroller general of the State from 1894 until 1897, when he resigned; elected as a Democrat to the Fifty-fifth Congress to fill the vacancy caused by the resignation of John L. McLaurin; reelected to the Fifty-sixth Congress and served from December 6, 1897, to March 3, 1901; was not a candidate for reelection in 1900 to the Fifty-seventh Congress; resumed agricultural pursuits and also engaged in the real-estate business; again a member of the State house of representatives in 1907; died in Mullins, S. C., October 14, 1920; interment in Miller's Churchyard.

NORTON, James Albert, a Representative from Ohio; born in Bettsville, Seneca County, Ohio, November 11, 1843; attended the district schools and was graduated from the Tiffin High School; during the Civil War enlisted in the Union Army in August 1862; sergeant of Company K, One Hundred and First Regiment, Ohio Volunteer Infantry; promoted to first lieutenant and adjutant of the One Hundred and Twenty-third Regiment, United States Colored Infantry, in 1864; mustered out of the service in 1865; studied medicine and commenced practice in Iowa in 1867; continued in that profession until 1879; studied law and was admitted to the bar in 1874; member of the State house of representative 1873–1879, serving as speaker in 1877 and 1878; chairman of the State Democratic committee 1887–1892; county auditor 1885–1892; commissioner of railroads and telegraphs from 1889 to 1895, when he resigned to accept a position in the legal department of the Baltimore & Ohio Railroad Co.; elected as a Democrat to the Fifty-fifth, Fifty-sixth, and Fifty-seventh Congresses (March 4, 1897–March 3, 1903); unsuccessful candidate for reelection in 1902 to the Fifty-eighth Congress; resumed legal service with the Baltimore & Ohio Railroad Co.; died in Tiffin, Ohio, July 24, 1912; interment in a mausoleum in Green Lawn Cemetery.

NORTON, Jesse Olds, a Representative from Illinois; born in Bennington, Bennington County, Vt., December 25, 1812; was graduated from Williams College, Williamstown, Mass., in 1835; moved to Illinois; studied law; was admitted to the bar in 1840 and began practice in Joliet, Ill.; member of the State constitutional convention in 1847; member of the State house of representatives in 1851 and 1852; elected as a Republican to the Thirty-third and Thirty-fourth Congresses (March 4, 1853–March 3, 1857); was not a candidate for renomination in 1856; judge of the eleventh judicial district of Illinois 1857–1862; elected to the Thirty-eighth Congress (March 4, 1863–March 3, 1865); was not a candidate for renomination in 1864; delegate to the Union National Convention at Philadelphia in 1866; resumed the practice of his profession; died in Chicago, Ill., August 3, 1875; interment in Oakwood Cemetery, Joliet, Ill.

NORTON, John Nathaniel, a Representative from Nebraska; born on a farm near Stromsburg, Polk County, Nebr., May 12, 1878; attended the public schools and Bryant Normal University, Stromsburg, Nebr.; was graduated from the Nebraska Wesleyan University at Lincoln in 1901 and from the University of Nebraska at Lincoln in 1903; served as clerk and recorder of Polk County 1906–1909; mayor of Osceola, Nebr., in 1908 and 1909; moved to a farm near Polk, Nebr., and engaged in agricultural pursuits 1910–1922; member of the Nebraska House of Representatives 1911–1918; member of the State constitutional convention in 1919 and 1920; Democratic nominee for Governor of Nebraska in 1924; engaged as a Chautauqua and Lyceum lecturer 1922–1927; elected as a Democrat to the Seventieth Congress (March 4, 1927–March 3, 1929); unsuccessful candidate for reelection in 1928 to the Seventy-first Congress; elected to the Seventy-second Congress (March 4, 1931–March 3, 1933); unsuccessful candidate for renomination in 1932; representative and adviser in Agricultural Adjustment Administration from June 1933 to December 1936; member of the Nebraska Unicameral Legislature in 1937 and 1938; special adviser in the Federal Crop Insurance Corporation at Washington, D. C., 1939–1948; died in Washington, D. C., October 5, 1960; interment in Swede Plain Cemetery, Polk County, Nebr.

NORTON, Mary Teresa, a Representative from New Jersey; born in Jersey City, N. J., March 7, 1875; attended parochial schools and the Jersey City High School; was graduated from Packard Business College, New York, N. Y., in 1896; president of the Queen's Daughters' Day Nursery Association of Jersey City 1916–1927; appointed to represent Hudson County on the State Democratic committee in 1920; elected a member of that committee in 1921 and served as vice chairman 1921–1931 and as chairman 1932–1935; also served as vice chairman of the Hudson County Democratic Committee; elected county freeholder in 1922; delegate at large to the Democratic National Conventions in 1924, 1928, 1932, 1936, 1940, 1944, and 1948; delegate to International Labor Conference at Paris, France, in 1945; elected as a Democrat to the Sixty-ninth and to the twelve succeeding Congresses (March 4, 1925–January 3, 1951); was not a candidate for renomination in 1950; consultant, Women's Advisory Committee on Defense Manpower, Department of Labor, 1951 and 1952; died in Greenwich, Conn., August 2, 1959; interment in Holy Name Cemetery, Jersey City, N. J.

NORTON, Miner Gibbs, a Representative from Ohio; born in Andover, Ashtabula County, Ohio, May 11, 1857; attended the public schools, the National Normal University, Lebanon, Ohio, and Baldwin-Wallace College, Berea, Ohio; was graduated from Mount Union College, Alliance, Ohio, in 1878 and from the law department of Yale College in 1880; was admitted to the bar in the latter year and commenced practice in Cleveland, Ohio; director of law of Cleveland, Ohio, 1895–1899; chairman of the Republican State executive committee in the early nineties; United States appraiser for the northern district of Ohio 1905–1909; elected as a Republican to the Sixty-seventh Congress (March 4, 1921–March 3, 1923); unsuccessful candidate for reelection in 1922 to the Sixty-eighth Congress; resumed the practice of law in Cleveland; appointed by President Coolidge collector of customs at Cleveland on February 7, 1925, and served until his death in Cleveland, Ohio, September 7, 1926; interment in Oakdale Cemetery, Jefferson, Ashtabula County, Ohio.

NORTON, Nelson Ira, a Representative from New York; born near Salamanca, in Great Valley, Cattaraugus County, N. Y., March 30, 1820; received a limited education; engaged in agricultural pursuits; county supervisor of Cattaraugus County 1860 and 1865–1867; justice of the peace 1852–1870; member of the State assembly in 1861 and 1862; presidential elector on the Republican ticket of Grant and Wilson in 1872; elected as a Republican to the Forty-fourth Congress to fill the vacancy caused by the death of Augustus F. Allen and served from December 6, 1875, to March 3, 1877; resumed agricultural pursuits; died in Hinsdale, Cattaraugus County, N. Y., October 28, 1887; interment in Maplehurst Cemetery.

NORTON, Patrick Daniel, a Representative from North Dakota; born in Ishpeming, Marquette County, Mich., May 17, 1876; moved with his parents to Ramsey County, Dak., in 1883; attended the public schools; was graduated from the University of North Dakota at Grand Forks in 1897; studied law at the University of North Dakota; was admitted to the bar in 1903 and commenced practice at Devils Lake, N. Dak.; superintendent of the schools of Ramsey County 1905–1907; chief clerk of the State house of representatives in 1907 and 1908; moved to Hettinger, Adams County, in 1907; prosecuting attorney of Adams County 1907–1911; secretary of state of North Dakota 1911–1913; elected as a Republican to the Sixty-third, Sixty-fourth, and Sixty-fifth Congresses (March 4, 1913–March 3, 1919); unsuccessful candidate for renomination in 1918; moved to Mandan, N. Dak., in 1919 and engaged in farming, livestock raising, banking, and the practice of law; national bank receiver at Brookings, S. Dak., 1924–1927; moved to Minot, N. Dak., in 1927; delegate to the Republican National Convention in 1928; delegate to Republican State conventions 1920–1940; died in Minot, N. Dak., October 14, 1953; interment in Rosehill Cemetery.

NORTON, Richard Henry, a Representative from Missouri; born in Troy, Lincoln County, Mo., November 6, 1849; attended the common schools and the St. Louis (Mo.) University, where he took a classical course; was graduated from the law department of Washington University, St. Louis, Mo., in 1870; was admitted to the bar and commenced practice in Troy, Mo.; elected as a Democrat to the Fifty-first and Fifty-second Congresses (March 4, 1889–March 3, 1893); unsuccessful candidate for reelection in 1892 to the Fifty-third Congress; resumed the practice of law and also engaged in agricultural pursuits; died in a hospital in St. Louis, Mo., March 15, 1918; interment in City Cemetery, Troy, Mo.

NORVELL, John, a Senator from Michigan; born in Danville, Va. (now Kentucky), December 21, 1789; attended the common schools; learned the trade of printer; edited a paper in Hagerstown, Md.; studied law; was admitted to the bar in 1814 and commenced practice in Baltimore, Md.; enlisted as a private in the War of 1812; edited an Anti-Federalist paper in Philadelphia 1816–1832; moved to Michigan Territory; appointed postmaster of Detroit April 11, 1831, and served until June 18, 1836, when a successor was appointed; delegate to the State constitutional convention at Detroit in 1837; upon the admission of Michigan as a State into the Union was elected as a Democrat to the United States Senate and served from January 26, 1837, to March 3, 1841; was not a candidate for reelection; resumed the practice of law in Detroit; member of the State senate in 1841; member of the State house of representatives in 1842; United States district attorney of Michigan 1846–1849; died in Detroit, Mich., April 24, 1850; interment in Elmwood Cemetery.

NORWOOD, Thomas Manson, a Senator and a Representative from Georgia; born in Talbot County, Ga., April 26, 1830; pursued an academic course; was graduated from Emory College, Oxford, Ga., in 1850; studied law; was admitted to the bar in 1852 and commenced practice in Savannah, Ga.; member of the State house of representatives in 1861 and 1862; presidential elector on the Democratic ticket of Seymour and Blair in 1868; elected as a Democrat to the United States Senate and served from November 14, 1871, to March 3, 1877; resumed the practice of law in Savannah, Ga.; elected as a Representative to the Forty-ninth and Fiftieth Congresses (March 4, 1885–March 3, 1889); again resumed the practice of law; appointed judge of the city court of Savannah in 1896 and served twelve years; retired to his country home, "Hancock Hall," near Savannah, Ga., and died there June 19, 1913, interment in Laurel Grove Cemetery, Savannah, Ga.

NOTT, Abraham, a Representative from South Carolina; born in Saybrook, Middlesex County, Conn., February 5, 1768; educated in early life by a private teacher; was graduated from Yale College in 1787; moved in 1788 to McIntosh County, Ga., where he was employed as a private tutor for one year; moved to Camden, S. C., in 1789; studied law; was admitted to the bar in 1791 and commenced practice in Union, S. C.; held several local offices; elected as a Federalist to the Sixth Congress (March 4, 1799–March 3, 1801); resumed the practice of his profession at Columbia, S. C., in 1804; elected a member of the board of trustees of South Carolina University in 1805; intendant of Columbia in 1807; elected judge of the circuit court in 1810 and served until his death; president of the court of appeals in 1824; died in Fairfield, S. C., June 19, 1830; interment in the First Presbyterian Churchyard, Columbia, S. C.

NOURSE, Amos, a Senator from Maine; born in Bolton, Worcester County, Mass., December 17, 1794; pursued a preparatory course and was graduated from Harvard University in 1812; postmaster at Hallowell, Maine, 1822–1841; moved to Bath, Maine, in 1841; collector of customs at Bath in 1845 and 1846; studied medicine and commenced practice in Bath; medical lecturer and professor of obstetrics at Bowdoin College, Brunswick, Maine, 1846–1854; elected to the United States Senate to fill the vacancy caused by the resignation of Hannibal Hamlin and served from January 16 to March 3, 1857; judge of probate of Sagadohoc County; died in Bath, Maine, April 7, 1877; interment in Hallowell Cemetery, Hallowell, Maine.

NOYES, John, a Representative from Vermont; born in Atkinson, Rockingham County, N. H., April 2, 1764; attended private schools, and was graduated from Dartmouth College, Hanover, N. H., in 1795; tutor at Chesterfield (N. H.) Academy 1795–1797 and at Dartmouth College 1797–1799, having among his pupils Daniel Webster at the latter institution; studied theology; moved to Brattleboro, Vt., in 1800 and engaged in mercantile pursuits; member of the State house of representatives 1808–1810 and in 1812; moved to Dummesston in 1812 and resumed his mercantile pursuits; held several local offices in

Vermont; elected as a Federalist to the Fourteenth Congress (March 4, 1815–March 3, 1817); resumed mercantile pursuits until 1819, when he retired from active life and settled on a farm near Putney, where he died October 26, 1841; interment in Maple Grove Cemetery, Putney, Vt.

NOYES, Joseph Cobham, a Representative from Maine; born in Portland, Maine, September 22, 1798; attended the common schools; moved to Eastport, Maine, in 1819; ship chandler and shipper of merchandise in Eastport; member of the State house of representatives in 1833; elected as a Whig to the Twenty-fifth Congress (March 4, 1837–March 3, 1839); unsuccessful candidate for reelection in 1838 to the Twenty-sixth Congress; collector of customs for the district of Passamaquoddy, Maine, 1841–1843; moved to Portland and engaged in the flour and commission business; treasurer of the Portland Co. (locomotive works) in 1859; one of the founders of the Portland Savings Bank in 1852 and served as treasurer from 1859 until his death in Portland, Cumberland County, Maine, July 28, 1868; interment in Evergreen Cemetery.

NUCKOLLS, Stephen Friel, a Delegate from the Territory of Wyoming; born in Grayson County, Va., August 16, 1825; completed preparatory studies; moved to Linden, Atchison County, Mo., in 1846; engaged in mercantile pursuits 1847–1853; moved to the Territory of Nebraska in 1854 and founded Nebraska City; held several local offices; established the Platte Valley Bank in 1855; served in the Nebraska Territorial Legislature in 1859; moved to the Territory of Colorado in 1860 and engaged in banking and mining; moved to New York City in 1864; moved to the Territory of Dakota in 1867 and settled in Cheyenne; engaged in mercantile pursuits; upon the organization of the Territory of Wyoming was elected in 1869 as a Democrat to the Forty-first Congress and served from December 6, 1869, to March 3, 1871; was an unsuccessful candidate for reelection in 1870 to the Forty-second Congress; resumed his mercantile pursuits; served as a member of the second legislative council of Wyoming in 1871 and served as presiding officer; delegate to the Democratic National Convention at Baltimore in 1872 which nominated Horace Greeley and B. Gratz Brown and at St. Louis in 1876 which nominated Samuel J. Tilden and Thomas A. Hendricks; moved to Salt Lake City, Utah, in July 1872 and engaged in milling; died in Salt Lake City, February 14, 1879; interment in Mount Olivet Cemetery.

NUCKOLLS, William Thompson, a Representative from South Carolina; born near Hancockville, Union (now Cherokee) County, S. C., February 23, 1801; was graduated from South Carolina College (now the University of South Carolina) at Columbia in 1820; studied law; was admitted to the bar in 1823 and commenced practice in Spartanburg, S. C.; elected to the Twentieth, Twenty-first, and Twenty-second Congresses (March 4, 1827–March 3, 1833); died on his plantation near Hancockville, S. C., on September 27, 1855; interment in Whig Hill Cemetery.

NUGEN, Robert Hunter, a Representative from Ohio; born near Hallidays Cove, Washington County, Pa., on July 16, 1809; moved to Ohio in 1811 with his parents, who settled in Columbiana County; received a limited education; moved to Tuscarawas County in 1828; engaged in agricultural pursuits; contractor; held several local offices; delegate to the Democratic National Convention at Charleston in 1860; elected as a Democrat to the Thirty-seventh Congress (March 4, 1861–March 3, 1863); superintendent of the Ohio Canal until his death in Newcomerstown, Tuscarawas County, Ohio, February 28, 1872; interment in Newcomerstown Cemetery.

NUGENT, John Frost, a Senator from Idaho; born in La Grande, Union County, Oreg., June 28, 1868; attended the public schools; studied law; was admitted to the bar in 1898 and commenced practice in Silver City, Idaho; prosecuting attorney of Owyhee County, Idaho, 1899–1906; chairman of the Democratic State central committee 1908–1912; appointed and subsequently elected as a Democrat to the United States Senate to fill the vacancy caused by the death of James H. Brady and served from January 22, 1918, until his resignation, effective January 14, 1921; unsuccessful candidate for reelection in 1920 to the United States Senate; appointed by President Wilson a member of the Federal Trade Commission in 1920 and served from January 15, 1921, to September 25, 1927; delegate to the Democratic National Convention at San Francisco in 1920; unsuccessful candidate for election in 1926 to the United States Senate; resumed the practice of his profession in Washington, D. C.; died in Silver Spring, Md., September 18, 1931; interment in Cedar Hill Cemetery, Washington, D. C.

NUNN, David Alexander, a Representative from Tennessee; born near Brownsville, Haywood County, Tenn., July 26, 1833; attended private schools and the West Tennessee College at Jackson, Tenn.; studied law; graduated from Cumberland University, Lebanon, Tenn., in 1853; was admitted to the bar and commenced practice in Brownsville; presidential elector on the Constitutional Union ticket of Bell and Everett in 1860 and on the Republican ticket of Lincoln and Johnson in 1864; member of the State house of representatives in 1866 and 1867; elected as a Republican to the Fortieth Congress (March 4, 1867–March 3, 1869); unsuccessful Independent Republican candidate for reelection in 1868 to the Forty-first Congress; appointed by President Grant as Minister Resident to Ecuador April 21, 1869; resigned November 2, 1869; elected to the Forty-third Congress (March 4, 1873–March 3, 1875); unsuccessful candidate for reelection in 1874 to the Forty-fourth Congress; secretary of state of Tennessee 1881–1885; appointed by President McKinley collector of internal revenue at Nashville, Tenn., July 20, 1897, and served until his resignation January 17, 1902; retired to private life; died in Brownsville, Tenn., September 11, 1918; interment in Oakwood Cemetery.

NUTE, Alonzo, a Representative from New Hampshire; born in Milton, Strafford County, N. H., February 12, 1826; attended the common schools; moved to Natick, Mass., in 1842; returned to New Hampshire in 1848 and engaged in the manufacture of boots and shoes in Farmington; in the spring of 1861, during the Civil War, entered the Union Army in the Sixth Regiment, New Hampshire Volunteer Infantry, and served on the staffs of Generals Griffin and Rush Hawkins until incapacitated for duty; member of the New Hampshire House of Representatives in 1866; served in the State senate in 1867 and 1868; delegate to the Republican National Convention at Cincinnati in 1876 which nominated Hayes and Wheeler; elected as a Republican to the Fifty-first Congress (March 4, 1889–March 3, 1891); was not a candidate for renomination in 1890; died in Farmington, Strafford County, N. H., December 24, 1892; interment in Pine Grove Cemetery.

NUTTING, Newton Wright, a Representative from New York; born in West Monroe, Oswego County, N. Y., October 22, 1840; pursued an academic course; studied law; was admitted to the bar and practiced in Oswego, N. Y.; member of the school committee of Oswego County from January 1, 1864, to January 1, 1867; district attorney of Oswego County from January 1, 1869, to January 1, 1872; county judge of Oswego County from January 1, 1878, until March 4, 1883, when he resigned; elected as a Republican to the Forty-eighth Con-

gress (March 4, 1883–March 3, 1885); resumed the practice of law in Oswego; elected to the Fiftieth and Fifty-first Congresses and served from March 4, 1887, until his death in Oswego, N. Y., October 15, 1889; interment in Riverside Cemetery.

NYE, Frank Mellen, a Representative from Minnesota; born in Shirley, Piscataquis County, Maine, March 7, 1852; moved to Wisconsin with his parents, who settled on a farm near River Falls, Pierce County, in 1855; attended the common schools and the local academy in River Falls, Wis.; taught school for several years and then studied law; was admitted to the bar in 1878 and commenced practice in Hudson, Wis.; district attorney of Polk County, Wis., 1879–1884; member of the Wisconsin House of Representatives in 1884 and 1885; moved to Minnesota in 1886, settled in Minneapolis, and continued the practice of law; assistant prosecuting attorney of Hennepin County; prosecuting attorney 1893–1897; elected as a Republican to the Sixtieth, Sixty-first, and Sixty-second Congresses (March 4, 1907–March 3, 1913); declined to be a candidate for renomination in 1912; resumed the practice of his profession in Minneapolis, Minn.; elected in 1920 judge of the district court of Hennepin County for a six-year term; reelected in 1926 and served until his retirement in 1932; died in Minneapolis, Minn., November 29, 1935; interment in Greenwood Cemetery, River Falls, Wis.

NYE, Gerald Prentice, a Senator from North Dakota; born in Hortonville, Outagamie County, Wis., December 19, 1892; attended the public schools and was graduated from the Wittenberg (Wis.) High School in 1911; engaged in newspaper work in Hortonville, Wis., 1911–1914 and in Creston, Iowa, in 1914 and 1915; moved to Fryburg, N. Dak., in 1915 and was publisher of the Billings County Pioneer; moved to Cooperstown, N. Dak., in 1919 and became editor and publisher of the Griggs County Sentinel-Courier; unsuccessful candidate in 1924 for election to the Sixty-ninth Congress; appointed and subsequently elected as a Republican to the United States Senate to fill the vacancy caused by the death of Edwin F. Ladd; reelected in 1926, 1932, and again in 1938 and served from November 14, 1925, to January 3, 1945; unsuccessful candidate for reelection in 1944; president of Records Engineering, Inc., Washington, D. C., 1937–1959; special assistant for elderly housing, Federal Housing Administration, since April 1960; resides in Chevy Chase, Md.

NYE, James Warren, a Senator from Nevada; born in De Ruyter, Madison County, N. Y., June 10, 1815; attended the common schools; was educated in Cortland Academy, Homer, N. Y.; studied law in Troy, N. Y.; was admitted to the bar and practiced in Madison County, N. Y.; district attorney in 1839; served as judge of Madison County 1840–1848; unsuccessful candidate for election on the Anti-Slavery ticket in 1846 to the Thirtieth Congress; moved to Syracuse, N. Y., in 1848 and practiced law until 1857; was the first president of the Metropolitan Board of Police, New York City, 1857–1860; appointed by President Lincoln in 1861 Governor of Washoe (Nevada) Territory and served until elected Senator; upon the admission of Nevada as a State into the Union in 1864 was elected as a Republican to the United States Senate; reelected in 1867 and served from December 16, 1864, to March 3, 1873; died in White Plains, Westchester County, N. Y., December 25, 1876; interment in Woodlawn Cemetery, New York City, N. Y.

O

OAKEY, Peter Davis, a Representative from Connecticut; born in East Millstone, Somerset County, N. J., February 25, 1861; attended the public schools and the high school of Millstone, N. J.; moved to Hartford, Conn., in 1886 and engaged in mercantile pursuits; member of the city council 1891–1894; city alderman in 1894 and 1895; collector of city taxes of Hartford in 1894 and 1895; member of the Connecticut National Guard 1895–1901; city assessor 1900–1915; elected as a Republican to the Sixty-fourth Congress (March 4, 1915–March 3, 1917); unsuccessful candidate for reelection in 1916 to the Sixty-fifth Congress; retired from public life and active business pursuits; died in New Haven, Conn., November 18, 1920; interment in Cedar Hill Cemetery, Hartford, Conn.

OAKLEY, Thomas Jackson, a Representative from New York; born near Poughkeepsie, Dutchess County, N. Y., November 10, 1783; was graduated from Yale College in 1801; studied law; was admitted to the bar in 1804 and commenced practice in Poughkeepsie, N. Y.; surrogate of Dutchess County in 1810 and 1811; elected as a Federalist to the Thirteenth Congress (March 4, 1813–March 3, 1815); member of the State assembly in 1816 and 1818–1820; attorney general of New York in 1819; elected as a Clinton Democrat to the Twentieth Congress and served from March 4, 1827, until May 9, 1828, when he resigned to go on the bench; judge of the superior court of New York City 1828–1847; appointed chief justice in October 1847 and served until his death in New York City May 11, 1857; interment in Trinity Churchyard.

OAKMAN, Charles Gibb, a Representative from Michigan; born in Detroit, Wayne County, Mich., September 4, 1903; attended the public schools and Wayne State University; graduated from the University of Michigan at Ann Arbor in 1926; engaged in the real-estate and transportation business 1927–1940; member of the Wayne County Board of Supervisors 1941–1952; served as executive secretary to the mayor of Detroit in 1941 and 1942; city controller 1942–1945; served four terms as city councilman 1947–1952; secretary of the Detroit-Wayne Joint Building Authority 1948–1954; elected as a Republican to the Eighty-third Congress (January 3, 1953–January 3, 1955); was an unsuccessful candidate for reelection in 1954 to the Eighty-fourth Congress; general manager of the Detroit-Wayne Joint Building Authority since 1955; is a resident of Detroit, Mich.

OATES, William Calvin, a Representative from Alabama; born at Oates Cross Roads, near Troy, Pike County, Ala., November 30, 1835; pursued elementary studies at home and attended an academy at Lawrenceville, Ala.; studied law; was admitted to the bar in 1858 and practiced in Abbeville, Ala., from 1859 to 1861; during the Civil War entered the Confederate Army as captain of Company G, Fifteenth Regiment, Alabama Infantry, in July 1861; appointed colonel in the Provisional Army of the Confederacy May 1, 1863, for valor and skill displayed on the field and assigned to the command of his old regiment; the Forty-eighth Alabama Regiment was also placed under his command; wounded four times slightly and twice severely, losing his right arm in the siege of Richmond; resumed the practice of law in Abbeville in 1865; delegate to the Democratic National Convention at New York City in 1868; member of the State house of representatives 1870–1872; unsuccessful candidate for the nomination for Governor in 1872; member of the State constitutional convention in 1875; elected as a Democrat to the Forty-seventh and to the six succeeding Congresses and served from March 4, 1881, until November 5, 1894, when he resigned, having been elected Governor; Governor of Alabama 1894–1896; brigadier general of Volunteers in the Spanish-American War and stationed at Camp Meade, Pa.; resigned and resumed the practice of law; died in Montgomery, Ala., September 9, 1910; interment in Oakwood Cemetery.

O'BRIEN, Charles Francis Xavier, a Representative from New Jersey; born in Jersey City, N. J., March 7, 1879; attended the public schools, St. Aloysius Academy, and St. Peter's College, Jersey City, N. J.; was graduated from Fordham University, New York City; studied law at the New York Law School; was admitted to the bar and commenced practice in Jersey City, N. J.; judge of the second criminal court; director of public safety of Jersey City 1917–1921; delegate to the Democratic National Convention at San Francisco in 1920; elected as a Democrat to the Sixty-seventh and Sixty-eighth Congresses (March 4, 1921–March 3, 1925); voluntarily retired to accept the position of registrar of records of Hudson County, N. J., 1926–1936; was serving in the city law department at the time of his death in Jersey City, N. J., November 14, 1940; interment in Holy Name Cemetery.

O'BRIEN, George Donoghue, a Representative from Michigan; born in Detroit, Mich., January 1, 1900; attended the public and parochial schools; was graduated from the University of Detroit, Detroit, Mich., in 1921 and from the law school of the same university in 1924; was admitted to the bar in 1924 and commenced practice in Detroit, Mich.; during the First World War served as a private and was assigned to the Students' Training Corps; elected as a Democrat to the Seventy-fifth Congress (January 3, 1937–January 3, 1939); unsuccessful candidate for reelection in 1938 to the Seventy-sixth Congress; elected to the Seventy-seventh, Seventy-eighth, and Seventy-ninth Congresses (January 3, 1941–January 3, 1947); unsuccessful candidate for reelection in 1946 to the Eightieth Congress; delegate to the Democratic National Convention at Chicago in 1944; elected to the Eighty-first, Eighty-second, and Eighty-third Congresses (January 3, 1949–January 3, 1955); unsuccessful candidate for renomination in 1954; assistant corporation counsel of the District of Columbia, assigned to Civil Proceedings Division from July 11, 1955, until his death; died in Washington, D. C., October 25, 1957; interment in Mount Olivet Cemetery, Detroit, Mich.

O'BRIEN, James, a Representative from New York; born in County Kings, Ireland, March 13, 1841; attended the common schools; immigrated to the United States in 1861 and settled in New York City; alderman of the city of New York in 1864 and 1866; sheriff of the city and county of New York in 1867; served in the State senate in 1872 and 1873; unsuccessful candidate for mayor of the city of New York in 1873; unsuccessful candidate for election in 1874 to the Forty-fourth Congress; elected as an Anti-Tammany Democrat to the Forty-sixth Congress (March 4, 1879–March 3, 1881); unsuccessful candidate for renomination in 1880; engaged as a broker until his death in New York City March 5, 1907; interment in Calvary Cemetery, Long Island, N. Y.

O'BRIEN, James Henry, a Representative from New York; born in Jamaica, Long Island, N. Y., July 15, 1860; attended the public schools and was graduated from Browne's Business College, Brooklyn, N. Y.; commenced work as a machinist and became an engineer; established a scale and overhead tramway business in New York City; member of the State senate in 1911 and 1912; delegate to the Democratic National Conventions in 1908, 1912, and 1916; elected as a Democrat to the Sixty-third Congress (March 4, 1913–March 3, 1915); unsuccessful candidate for reelection in 1914 to the Sixty-fourth Congress; resumed his former manufacturing pursuits; died in Brooklyn, N. Y., September 2, 1924; interment in Holy Cross Cemetery.

O'BRIEN, Jeremiah, a Representative from Maine; born in Machias, Washington County, Maine, on January 21, 1778;

attended the common schools; engaged in lumber manufacturing and in shipping; member of the State senate 1821–1824; elected as a Democrat to the Eighteenth, Nineteenth, and Twentieth Congresses (March 4, 1823–March 3, 1829); unsuccessful candidate for reelection in 1828 to the Twenty-first Congress; member of the State house of representatives 1832–1834; resumed his former lumber manufacturing and shipping business; died in Boston, Mass., May 30, 1858; interment in O'Brien Cemetery, Machias, Maine.

O'BRIEN, Joseph John, a Representative from New York; born in Rochester, Monroe County, N. Y., October 9, 1897; attended the public schools, SS. Peter and Paul's Catholic School, and the Cathedral High School, Rochester, N. Y., St. Jerome's College, Berlin (now Kitchener), Ontario, and McGill University, Montreal, Canada; during the First World War served as a master at arms in the United States Navy 1917–1919; chief construction inspector, New York Central Railroad, 1919–1938; professional football player 1919–1925; professional heavyweight wrestler 1919–1926; treasurer of East Rochester, N. Y., 1932–1935, and assessor 1935–1938; elected as a Republican to the Seventy-sixth, Seventy-seventh, and Seventy-eighth Congresses (January 3, 1939–January 3, 1945); unsuccessful candidate for reelection in 1944 to the Seventy-ninth Congress; district administrator for New York State Compensation Board from June 1, 1945, until his death; was also executive vice president of the General Sheet Signal Co., of Rochester, N. Y.; died in Rochester, N. Y., January 23, 1953; interment in Holy Sepulchre Cemetery.

O'BRIEN, Leo William, a Representative from New York; born in Buffalo, Erie County, N. Y., September 21, 1900; graduated from the Niagara (N. Y.) University in 1922; engaged in the newspaper field 1922–1952 as a reporter and also as radio and television commentator; member of the Albany Port District Commission 1935–1952; elected as a Democrat to the Eighty-second Congress to fill the vacancy caused by the death of William T. Byrne; reelected to the Eighty-third and to the three succeeding Congresses and served from April 1, 1952, to January 3, 1961. *Reelected to the Eighty-seventh Congress.*

O'BRIEN, Thomas Joseph, a Representative from Illinois; born in Chicago, Ill., April 30, 1878; attended the grade and high schools and took advance courses in business law and accounting; engaged as a public accountant in 1918; member of the State house of representatives 1907–1910 and 1929–1932; served as State bank examiner 1913–1924; elected as a Democrat to the Seventy-third, Seventy-fourth, and Seventy-fifth Congresses (March 4, 1933–January 3, 1939); did not seek renomination in 1938, having become a candidate for sheriff of Cook County, Ill.; sheriff of Cook County, Ill., 1939–1942; elected to the Seventy-eighth and to the eight succeeding Congresses (January 3, 1943–January 3, 1961). *Reelected to the Eighty-seventh Congress.*

O'BRIEN, William James, a Representative from Maryland; born in Baltimore, Md., May 28, 1836; attended the common schools and pursued classical studies in the old St. Mary's College, Baltimore; studied law; was admitted to the bar in 1858 and commenced practice in Baltimore; elected as a Democrat to the Forty-third and Forty-fourth Congresses (March 4, 1873–March 3, 1877); was not a candidate for renomination in 1876; resumed the practice of law in Baltimore; appointed in 1901 and elected in 1903 judge of the orphans' court of Baltimore and served in that capacity until his death in Baltimore, Md., November 13, 1905; interment in Bonnie Brae Cemetery.

O'BRIEN, William Smith, a Representative from West Virginia; born in Audra, near Philippi, Barbour County, Va. (now West Virginia), January 8, 1862; attended the common schools, the Weston (W. Va.) Academy, and the University of West Virginia at Morgantown; worked on farms, in brick yards, and on public works; also taught school and was engaged as an editor; was graduated from the law school of the West Virginia University at Morgantown in 1891; was admitted to the bar the same year and commenced practice in Buckhannon, Upshur County, W. Va., in 1892; served as a captain in the West Virginia National Guard in 1894 and 1895; served as judge of the twelfth judicial circuit of West Virginia 1913–1919; elected as a Democrat to the Seventieth Congress (March 4, 1927–March 3, 1929); unsuccessful candidate for reelection in 1928 to the Seventy-first Congress; resumed the practice of law; elected secretary of state of West Virginia in 1932, 1936, 1940, and again in 1944, in which capacity he served until his death in Buckhannon, W. Va., on August 10, 1948; interment in Heavner Cemetery.

O'BRYEN, William, a Delegate from Georgia; treasurer of Georgia in 1778; nominated for commissioner of the Continental Loan Office by Georgia delegation in 1785; elected as a Delegate to the Continental Congress in 1789.

OCAMPO, Pablo, a Resident Commissioner from the Philippine Islands; born in Manila, Philippine Islands, January 25, 1853; attended San Juan de Letran College, and was graduated from Santo Tomas University in 1882; studied law; was admitted to the bar in 1882 and practiced in Manila; prosecuting attorney of the district of Tondo 1883 and 1884; secretary of the Royal Court of Manila under the Spanish regime 1885–1887; relator of the supreme court of the Philippine Islands in 1887 and 1888; counsel to the Economic Association of the Philippines 1888–1890; secretary of the Bar Association of Manila; was a representative of the Provinces of Principe, Infanta, Lepanto, and Bontoc in the Filipino Government in Malolos and was elected secretary of the Filipino Parliament; professor of law in the University of Malolos in 1898; declined appointment to the supreme court; editor of La Patria at Manila, in 1899 and 1900; editor of the Faro Juridico y Consultor de los Jueces de Paz, the first law publication in the Philippine Islands, in 1907 and 1908; appointed by the Government of the Filipino Republic as its representative in Manila; elected as a Resident Commissioner to the United States and served from November 22, 1907, to November 22, 1909; one of the delegates of the American Congress to the Interparliamentary Congress of Nations held in the Reichstag at Berlin, Germany, in 1908; representative from Manila in the Second Philippine Legislature; member of the first independence mission to the United States; adviser and counsel of Gen. Emilio Aguinaldo from the time of his connection with the revolutionary government until 1925; died in Manila, Philippine Islands, February 5, 1925; interment in La Loma Catholic Cemetery.

OCHILTREE, Thomas Peck, a Representative from Texas; born in Nacogdoches, Nacogdoches County, Tex., October 26, 1837; attended the public schools; volunteered in 1854 as a private in Capt. John G. Walker's company of Texas Rangers in the campaign against the Apache and Comanche Indians in 1854 and 1855; admitted to the bar by special act of the Texas Legislature in 1857; clerk of the State house of representatives 1856–1859; secretary of the State Democratic convention in 1859; editor of the Jeffersonian in 1860 and 1861; delegate to the Democratic National Conventions at Charleston, S. C., and Baltimore, Md., in 1860; during the Civil War enlisted in the Confederate Army in the First Texas Regiment and was promoted successively to lieutenant, captain, and major; served on the staffs of Generals Longstreet, Taylor, Green, and Maxey; editor of the Houston Daily Telegraph 1866 and 1867; appointed commissioner of immigration for Texas in Europe 1870–1873; appointed United States marshal for the eastern district of Texas by President Grant January 8, 1874; elected as an Independent to the Forty-eighth Congress (March 4, 1883–March 3, 1885); moved to New York City, N. Y., and retired from public and political activities; died at Hot Springs, Bath County, Va., on November 25, 1902; interment in Greenwood Cemetery, Brooklyn, N. Y.; reinterment in Mount Hope Cemetery, Westchester County, N. Y., November 8, 1903.

O'CONNELL, David Joseph, a Representative from New York; born in New York City December 25, 1868; attended the public schools; employed in the publishing business in New York City, later becoming sales manager for Funk & Wagnalls; an organizer and first secretary of the Twenty-eighth Ward Board of Trade and the Allied Board of Trade, Brooklyn, N. Y.; president of the Booksellers' League of New York; delegate to the Democratic National Convention at San Francisco in 1920; elected as a Democrat to the Sixty-sixth Congress (March 4, 1919–March 3, 1921); unsuccessful candidate for reelection in 1920 to the Sixty-seventh Congress; elected to the Sixty-eighth and to the three succeeding Congresses and served from March 4, 1923, until his death; had been reelected in 1930 to the Seventy-second Congress; died in New York City, N. Y., December 29, 1930; interment in St. John's Cemetery, Middle Village, Brooklyn, N. Y.

O'CONNELL, Jeremiah Edward, a Representative from Rhode Island; born in Wakefield, Middlesex County, Mass., July 8, 1883; attended the public schools; was graduated from Boston University at Boston in 1906 and from the law school of the same university in 1908; was admitted to the bar in 1907 and commenced practice in Boston, Mass.; moved to Providence, R. I., in 1908 and continued the practice of law; member of the city council 1913–1919; member of the board of aldermen 1919–1921; elected as a Democrat to the Sixty-eighth and Sixty-ninth Congresses (March 4, 1923–March 3, 1927); unsuccessful candidate for reelection in 1926 to the Seventieth Congress; elected to the Seventy-first Congress and served from March 4, 1929, until his resignation on May 9, 1930, having been appointed an associate justice of the Rhode Island Superior Court, serving until January 10, 1935, when he was appointed presiding justice and served until his resignation in 1948; elected as an associate justice of the Rhode Island Supreme Court and served until his resignation on January 18, 1956; is a resident of Cranston, R. I.

O'CONNELL, Jerry Joseph, a Representative from Montana; born in Butte, Silver Bow County, Mont., June 14, 1909; attended the parochial schools and Butte Central High School; was graduated from Carroll College (formerly Mount St. Charles College), Helena, Mont., in 1931, and from Georgetown University, Washington, D. C., in 1934; studied law and was admitted to the bar in 1934; served in the State house of representatives 1931–1934; member of the Montana Public Service Commission 1934–1936; delegate to the Democratic State conventions 1930–1940; elected as a Democrat to the Seventy-fifth Congress (January 3, 1937–January 3, 1939); unsuccessful candidate for reelection in 1938 to the Seventy-sixth Congress and for election in 1940 to the Seventy-seventh Congress; newspaper editor and publisher in Hamilton, Mont., 1939–1941; commenced the practice of law in Butte, Mont., in 1940; delegate to the Democratic National Convention at Chicago in 1944; moved to Seattle, Wash., in June 1944; executive secretary of the Washington State Democratic

Central Committee from December 1944 to January 1947, for the Roosevelt Democrats in 1947, and for the Washington State Progressive Party in 1948 and 1949; returned to Montana in 1950 and practiced law in Great Falls until his death there January 16, 1956; interment in Great Falls Mausoleum.

O'CONNELL, John Matthew, a Representative from Rhode Island; born in Westerly, Washington County, R. I., August 10, 1872; attended the public schools; taught in the local schools 1892–1902; was graduated from the Philadelphia (Pa.) Dental College (now a branch of Temple University) in 1905 and commenced practice in Westerly, R. I., the same year; during the First World War served for sixteen months with Headquarters Sanitary Train, Twelfth Division, and later as major in the United States Dental Reserve; member of the State house of representatives 1929–1932; elected as a Democrat to the Seventy-third, Seventy-fourth, and Seventy-fifth Congresses (March 4, 1933–January 3, 1939); was not a candidate for renomination in 1938; retired from public life because of ill health and died in Westerly, R. I., December 6, 1941; interment in St. Sebastian Cemetery.

O'CONNELL, Joseph Francis, a Representative from Massachusetts; born in Boston, Mass., December 7, 1872; attended the Mather School of Boston and prepared for college at St. Mary's Parochial School; was graduated from Boston College in 1893 and from the law department of Harvard University in 1896; was admitted to the Suffolk bar in 1897 and commenced practice in Boston; elected as a Democrat to the Sixtieth and Sixty-first Congresses (March 4, 1907–March 3, 1911); unsuccessful candidate for renomination in 1910; resumed the practice of law in Boston, Mass.; delegate to the Democratic National Convention at Baltimore in 1912 and at San Francisco in 1920; member of the Massachusetts constitutional convention 1918–1920; appointed member of the National Conference on Uniform State Laws by Gov. David I. Walsh September 2, 1914; reappointed by each succeeding Governor until his death; member of the State commission to revise the charter of the city of Boston in 1923; professor of law and vice president of the board of trustees of Suffolk Law School, Boston, Mass.; unsuccessful candidate for nomination to the United States Senate in 1930 and for mayor of Boston in 1933; trustee of the George Robert White Fund for creating health centers; died in Boston, Mass., December 10, 1942; interment in St. Joseph's Cemetery, West Roxbury, Mass.

O'CONNOR, Charles, a Representative from Oklahoma; born on a farm near Edina, Knox County, Mo., October 26, 1878; attended the rural schools; was graduated from the State Teachers' College, Greeley, Colo., in 1901 and from the law department of the University of Colorado at Boulder in 1904; was admitted to the bar the same year and commenced practice in Boulder, Colo.; served as first assistant attorney general of Colorado 1911–1913; city attorney of Boulder 1917–1918; moved to Tulsa, Okla., in 1919 and continued the practice of his profession; elected as a Republican to the Seventy-first Congress (March 4, 1929–March 3, 1931); unsuccessful candidate for reelection in 1930 to the Seventy-second Congress; resumed the practice of law in Tulsa, Okla.; moved to Boulder, Colo., in 1936 on account of failing health and died in Denver, Colo., November 15, 1940; interment in Green Mountain Cemetery, Boulder, Colo.

O'CONNOR, James, a Representative from Louisiana; born in New Orleans, La., April 4, 1870; attended the public schools, and was graduated from the law department of Tulane University, New Orleans, La., in 1900; member of the State constitutional conventions in 1898 and 1913; served in the State house of representatives 1900–1912; assistant city attorney of Orleans

Parish from 1918 until his resignation in 1919, having been elected to the United States House of Representatives; elected as a Democrat to the Sixty-sixth Congress to fill the vacancy caused by the death of Albert Estopinal; reelected to the Sixty-seventh and to the four succeeding Congresses and served from June 5, 1919, to March 3, 1931; unsuccessful candidate for renomination in 1930; resumed the practice of law; served on the State attorney general's staff in New Orleans; died in Covington, La., January 7, 1941; interment in Metairie Cemetery, New Orleans.

O'CONNOR, James Francis, a Representative from Montana; born on a farm near California Junction, Iowa, May 7, 1878; attended the grade schools and normal school in Iowa; was graduated from the law department of the University of Nebraska at Lincoln in 1904; was admitted to the bar and commenced practice in Livingston, Mont., in 1905; also engaged in stock raising, ranching, and banking; judge of the sixth judicial district of Montana in 1912; member of the State house of representatives 1917–1918 and served as speaker; special counsel for the Federal Trade Commission in Washington, D. C., in 1918; member of Park County High School Board for a number of years; elected as a Democrat to the Seventy-fifth and to the four succeeding Congresses and served from January 3, 1937, until his death in Washington, D. C., on January 15, 1945; interment in Mount Calvary Cemetery, Livingston, Mont.

O'CONNOR, John Joseph, a Representative from New York; born in Raynham, near Taunton, Bristol County, Mass., on November 23, 1885; attended the public schools; was graduated from Brown University, Providence, R. I., in 1908, and from the law department of Harvard University, Cambridge, Mass., in 1911; was admitted to the Massachusetts bar in 1910; moved to New York City, N. Y., in 1911; was admitted to the New York bar in 1912 and commenced the practice of law; secretary to the Democratic members of the New York State constitutional convention in 1915; member of the State assembly 1920–1923; legislative secretary for the Child Welfare Commission in 1921 and 1922; vice chairman of the legislative committee on the exploitation of immigrants in 1922 and 1923; member of the legislative committee on the revision of the corporation laws of New York in 1922 and 1923; delegate to all New York State and county conventions from 1919 to 1938; delegate at large to the Democratic National Convention at Philadelphia in 1936; elected as a Democrat to the Sixty-eighth Congress to fill the vacancy caused by the death of W. Bourke Cockran; reelected to the Sixty-ninth and to the six succeeding Congresses and served from November 6, 1923, to January 3, 1939; unsuccessful candidate for the Democratic nomination in 1938, but received the Republican nomination and was unsuccessful for reelection to the Seventy-sixth Congress; engaged in the practice of law in New York City, N. Y., and Washington, D. C., until his death in Washington, D. C., January 26, 1960; interment in Gate of Heaven Cemetery, Silver Spring, Md.

O'CONNOR, Michael Patrick, a Representative from South Carolina; born in Beaufort, Beaufort County, S. C., September 29, 1831; attended the public schools and was graduated from St. John's College, Fordham, N. Y., in 1850; studied law; was admitted to the bar in 1854 and commenced practice in Charleston, S. C.; member of the State house of representatives 1858–1866; served in the Civil War as a lieutenant in the Lafayette Artillery; delegate to the Democratic National Convention at Baltimore in 1872 and at St. Louis in 1876; unsuccessful candidate for election in 1874 to the Forty-fourth and in 1876 to the Forty-fifth Congresses; elected as a Democrat to the Forty-sixth Congress (March 4, 1879–March 3, 1881); received credentials as a Member-elect to the Forty-seventh Con-

gress, but died, pending a contest by Edmund W. M. Mackey (which subsequently resulted successfully for the contestant), in Charleston, Charleston County, S. C., April 26, 1881; interment in St. Lawrence Cemetery.

O'CONOR, Herbert Romulus, a Senator from Maryland; born in Baltimore, Md., on November 17, 1896; attended the parochial schools; was graduated from Loyola College, Baltimore, Md., in 1917 and from the law department of the University of Maryland in 1920; during the First World War served in the United States Naval Reserve; was admitted to the bar in 1919 and commenced practice in Baltimore, Md.; member of the staff of the Baltimore Sun and Evening Sun in 1920; assistant State's attorney 1920–1922; appointed people's counsel to the Public Service Commission January 1, 1923; State's attorney 1923–1934; attorney general 1935–1939; Governor of Maryland 1939–1946; chairman of Governors' Conference, Asheville, N. C., in 1942; chairman of Interstate Commission on Potomac River Basin 1943–1945; president and national chairman of Council of State Governments in 1943; national chairman Interstate Committee on Postwar Reconstruction and Development 1943–1946; director of Fidelity-Baltimore National Bank & Trust Co., and of Arundel Corp.; member senior advisory council of McCormick & Co.; elected as a Democrat to the United States Senate and served from January 3, 1947, to January 3, 1953; was not a candidate for renomination in 1952; continued the practice of law in Baltimore, Md., and Washington, D. C., until his death in Baltimore, Md., March 4, 1960; interment in New Cathedral Cemetery.

O'DANIEL, Wilbert Lee, a Senator from Texas; born in Malta, Morgan County, Ohio, March 11, 1890; reared on a cattle ranch near Arlington, Kans.; attended the grade and high schools, Arlington, Kans., and business college, Hutchinson, Kans.; engaged in the flour milling and merchandising business, Fort Worth, Tex., 1909–1938; elected Governor of Texas in 1938; reelected in 1940, and served until August 3, 1941, when he resigned, having been elected as a Democrat to the United States Senate to fill the vacancy caused by the death of Morris Sheppard and served from August 4, 1941, to January 3, 1943; reelected in 1942 for the term ending January 3, 1949; was not a candidate for renomination in 1948; unsuccessful candidate for the gubernatorial nomination in 1956; owns and operates several life insurance companies in Texas; is a resident of Dallas, Tex.

O'DAY, Caroline Love Goodwin, a Representative from New York; born in Perry, Houston County, Ga., June 22, 1875; attended private schools and was graduated from Lucy Cobb Institute, Athens, Ga.; studied art in Paris, Munich, and Holland; served as president of Rye (N. Y.) School Board; vice chairman of New York Democratic State committee 1916–1920; associate chairman 1923–1942; delegate to the Democratic National Conventions in 1924, 1928, 1932, and 1936; commissioner, State board of social welfare, 1923–1934; elected as a Democrat to the Seventy-fourth and to the three succeeding Congresses (January 3, 1935–January 3, 1943); was not a candidate for renomination in 1942; died in Rye, N. Y., January 4, 1943; interment in Kensico Cemetery, Valhalla, N. Y.

ODDIE, Tasker Lowndes, a Senator from Nevada; born in Brooklyn, Kings County, N. Y., October 24, 1870; reared in East Orange, N. J.; attended the public schools; while engaged in active business in New York attended night law school for three years; was graduated from the law department of New York University at New York City in 1895; was admitted to the bar the same year, but did not engage in extensive practice; moved to Nevada in 1898 and settled in Austin; became interested in mining, agricultural pursuits, and in livestock raising; developed the principal gold and silver mining properties in the Tonopah and Goldfield districts; district attorney for Nye County in 1901 and 1902; member of the State senate 1903–1906; resumed his former business pursuits; Governor of Nevada 1911–1915; elected as a Republican to the United States Senate in 1920; reelected in 1926 and served from March 4, 1921, to March 3, 1933; unsuccessful candidate for reelection in 1932; engaged in mining; died in San Francisco, Calif., February 17, 1950; interment in Lone Mountain Cemetery, Carson City, Nev.

ODELL, Benjamin Baker, Jr., a Representative from New York; born in Newburgh, Orange County, N. Y., January 14, 1854; attended the public schools, Newburgh Academy, Bethany (W. Va.) College, and Columbia College, New York City; entered upon a commercial career; for ten years represented the seventeenth district on the Republican State committee and was chairman of the executive committee; elected as a Republican to the Fifty-fourth and Fifty-fifth Congresses (March 4, 1895–March 3, 1899); president of the Orange County Traction Co. and the Central Hudson Steamboat Co.; elected Governor of New York in 1900 and reelected in 1902; president of the chamber of commerce of Newburgh, N. Y.; died in Newburgh, N. Y., on May 9, 1926; interment in Woodlawn Cemetery, New Windsor, Orange County, N. Y.

ODELL, Moses Fowler, a Representative from New York; born in Tarrytown, Westchester County, N. Y., February 24, 1818; completed preparatory studies; appointed entry clerk in the New York customhouse in 1845, and after securing several promotions became public appraiser; elected as a Democrat to the Thirty-seventh and Thirty-eighth Congresses (March 4, 1861–March 3, 1865); appointed Navy agent at the city of New York in 1865 and served until his death in Brooklyn, N. Y., June 13, 1866; interment in Greenwood Cemetery.

ODELL, Nathaniel Holmes, a Representative from New York; born in Greenburgh, near Tarrytown, Westchester County, N. Y., October 10, 1828; attended private schools; engaged in the steamboat business on the North River; served in the State assembly 1857–1861; established the First National Bank at Tarrytown and served as cashier from 1862 to 1864; elected county treasurer of Westchester County in 1866; reelected in 1869 and again in 1872; elected as a Democrat to the Forty-fourth Congress (March 4, 1875–March 3, 1877); was not a candidate for renomination in 1876; engaged in the real-estate business; postmaster of Tarrytown 1887–1892 and 1894–1898; died in Tarrytown, N. Y., October 30, 1904; interment in Sleepy Hollow Cemetery.

O'DONNELL, James, a Representative from Michigan; born in Norwalk, Fairfield County, Conn., March 25, 1840; moved to Michigan with his parents, who settled in Jackson in 1848; pursued preparatory studies and learned the printing trade; during the Civil War enlisted as a private in the First Regiment, Michigan Volunteer Infantry, and served two years; participated in the first Battle of Bull Run; recorder of the city of Jackson 1863–1866; established the Jackson Daily Citizen in 1865; presidential elector on the Republican ticket of Grant and Wilson in 1872; mayor of Jackson in 1876 and 1877; appointed in 1878 aide-de-camp on the staff of Governor Crosswell, with the rank of colonel; elected as a Republican to the Forty-ninth and to the three succeeding Congresses (March 4, 1885–March 3, 1893); unsuccessful candidate for reelection in 1892 to the Fifty-third Congress; returned to Jackson, Mich., and devoted his time to the publication of the Jackson Daily Citizen; disposed of his paper and retired in 1910; known as the originator

of the rural free delivery system of America; father of the beet-sugar industry of Michigan; died in Jackson, Jackson County, Mich., March 17, 1915; interment in Mount Evergreen Cemetery.

O'FERRALL, Charles Triplett, a Representative from Virginia; born in Brucetown, Frederick County, Va., October 21, 1840; attended the common schools; appointed clerk pro tempore of the circuit court of Morgan County, Va., in 1855; elected clerk in 1857; enlisted in the Confederate Cavalry as a private in May 1861; passed through all the grades from sergeant to colonel and at the close of the Civil War was in command of all the Confederate Cavalry in the Shenandoah Valley; was graduated from the law department of Washington College, Lexington, Va., in 1869; was admitted to the bar and commenced practice in Harrisonburg, Va.; member of the State house of delegates 1871–1873; unsuccessful candidate for election in 1872 to the Forty-third Congress; judge of the county court of Rockingham County 1874–1880; Democratic State canvasser 1880–1883; successfully contested as a Democrat the election of John Paul to the Forty-eighth Congress; reelected to the Forty-ninth and to the four succeeding Congresses and served from May 5, 1884, until December 28, 1893, when he resigned, having been elected Governor; Governor of the State of Virginia 1894–1898; resumed the practice of law and also engaged in writing reminiscences of the Civil War; died in Richmond, Va., September 22, 1905; interment in Hollywood Cemetery.

OGDEN, Aaron, a Senator from New Jersey; born in Elizabeth (formerly Elizabethtown), N. J., December 3, 1756; was graduated from Princeton College in 1773; tutor in Barber's Grammar School 1773–1775; served in the Revolutionary Army as a lieutenant, captain, and brigade major; appointed colonel of the Fifteenth Regiment and served during the war with France in 1799; studied law; was admitted to the bar in 1784 and commenced practice in Elizabeth; presidential elector in 1796; clerk of Essex County 1785–1803; elected as a Federalist to the United States Senate to fill the vacancy caused by the resignation of James Schureman and served from February 28, 1801, to March 3, 1803; was a candidate for reelection in 1802, but at a joint meeting of the legislature the choice resulted in a tie vote and the legislature for that session adjourned in deadlock; elected trustee of Princeton College in 1803 and served until his death; Governor of New Jersey in 1812; nominated by President Madison major general of the Army in 1812, but declined the appointment; became engaged in steamboat navigation in 1813; moved to Jersey City in 1829 and continued the practice of law; appointed on March 23, 1830, collector of customs and served until his death in Jersey City, N. J., April 19, 1839; interment in the First Presbyterian Church Burial Ground, Elizabeth, N. J.

OGDEN, Charles Franklin, a Representative from Kentucky; born in Charlestown, Clark County, Ind.; attended the public schools and the Jeffersonville (Ind.) High School; was graduated from the University of Louisville Law School in 1896; was admitted to the bar and commenced practice in Louisville, Ky., in 1897; member of the State house of representatives in 1898 and 1899; was an officer of the old Louisville Legion; served in the Spanish-American War as captain of Company H, Eighth Regiment, United States Volunteer Infantry; unsuccessful candidate for county attorney in 1901 and for State senator in 1902; elected as a Republican to the Sixty-sixth and Sixty-seventh Congresses (March 4, 1919–March 3, 1923); was not a candidate for renomination in 1922; resumed the practice of law in Louisville, Ky., where he died on April 10, 1933; interment in Resthaven Cemetery.

OGDEN, David A., a Representative from New York; born in Morristown, Morris County, N. J., January 10, 1770; attended King's College (now Columbia University), New York City; studied law; was admitted to the bar in November 1791 and began practice in Newark, N. J.; became counselor at law in New Jersey in 1796; moved to Hamilton (now Waddington), St. Lawrence County, N. Y., and continued the practice of law; associate judge of the court of common pleas of St. Lawrence County, N. Y., 1811–1815; member of the State assembly in 1814 and 1815; elected as a Federalist to the Fifteenth Congress (March 4, 1817–March 3, 1819); unsuccessful candidate for reelection in 1818 to the Sixteenth Congress; first judge of the court of common pleas 1820–1824 and 1825–1829; one of the commissioners to settle the boundary between Canada and the United States; died in Montreal, Canada, June 9, 1829; interment in Brookside Cemetery, Waddington, St. Lawrence County, N. Y.

OGDEN, Henry Warren, a Representative from Louisiana; born in Abingdon, Washington County, Va., October 21, 1842; moved with his parents to Warrensburg, Mo., in 1851; attended the common schools; entered the Confederate Army and served throughout the Civil War; first lieutenant of Company D, Sixteenth Regiment, Missouri Infantry, and afterward on the staff of Brigadier General Lewis, Second Brigade, Parsons' division, Missouri Infantry; paroled at Shreveport on June 8, 1865; remained in Louisiana and engaged in agricultural pursuits; member of the State constitutional convention in 1879; served in the State house of representatives 1880–1888 and was speaker of the house from 1884 to 1888; elected as a Democrat to the Fifty-third Congress to fill the vacancy caused by the resignation of Newton C. Blanchard; reelected to the Fifty-fourth and Fifty-fifth Congresses and served from May 12, 1894, to March 3, 1899; resumed agricultural pursuits; died in Benton, Bossier Parish, La., on July 23, 1905; interment in Cottage Grove Cemetery.

OGLE, Alexander (father of Charles Ogle and grandfather of Andrew Jackson Ogle), a Representative from Pennsylvania; born in Frederick, Frederick County, Md., August 10, 1766; completed preparatory studies; moved to Somerset, Pa., in 1795; member of the State house of representatives in 1803, 1804, 1807, 1808, and 1811; served as major general in the State militia; prothonotary, recorder of deeds, and clerk of courts 1812–1817; elected as a Democrat to the Fifteenth Congress (March 4, 1817– March 3, 1819); was not a candidate for renomination in 1818; again a member of the State house of representatives 1819–1823; served in the State senate in 1827 and 1828; died in Somerset, Pa., October 14, 1832; interment in Union Cemetery.

OGLE, Andrew Jackson (grandson of Alexander Ogle), a Representative from Pennsylvania; born in Somerset, Somerset County, Pa., March 25, 1822; completed preparatory studies; attended Jefferson College, Canonsburg, Pa.; studied law; was admitted to the bar in 1843 and commenced practice in Somerset, Pa.; prothonotary of Somerset County in 1845; elected as a Whig to the Thirty-first Congress (March 4, 1849–March 3, 1851); unsuccessful candidate for reelection in 1850 to the Thirty-second Congress; appointed United States Chargé d'Affaires to Denmark January 22, 1852, but did not assume his duties at that post; died in Somerset, Pa., October 14, 1852; interment in Union Cemetery.

OGLE, Charles (son of Alexander Ogle), a Representative from Pennsylvania; born in Somerset, Somerset County, Pa., in 1798; completed preparatory studies; studied law; was admitted to the bar in 1822 and commenced practice in Somerset; elected as a Whig to the Twenty-fifth, Twenty-sixth, and Twenty-seventh Congresses and served from March 4, 1837, until his death in Somerset, Pa., May 10, 1841; interment in Union Cemetery.

OGLESBY, Richard James (cousin of Woodson Ratcliffe Oglesby), a Senator from Illinois; born in Floydsburg, Oldham County, Ky., July 25, 1824; moved with his parents to Decatur, Ill., in 1836; received a limited schooling; studied law; was admitted to the bar in 1845 and commenced practice in Decatur; during the Mexican War served as first lieutenant of Company C, Fourth Illinois Regiment; spent two years mining in California; returned to Decatur, Ill., and resumed the practice of law; unsuccessful candidate for election in 1858 to the Thirty-sixth Congress; elected to the State senate in 1860 and served during one session, when he resigned to enter the Union Army during the Civil War; served as colonel of the Eighth Regiment, Illinois Volunteer Infantry, April 25, 1861; brigadier general of Volunteers March 21, 1862; major general November 29, 1862; resigned May 26, 1864; Governor of Illinois 1865–1869; again elected Governor in 1872 and served from January 13, 1873, until his resignation on January 23, 1873, having been elected Senator; elected as a Republican to the United States Senate and served from March 4, 1873, to March 3, 1879; declined to be a candidate for reelection; again Governor of Illinois 1885–1889; retired to his farm, near "Oglehurst," Elkhart, Ill., where he died April 24, 1899; interment in Elkhart Cemetery.

OGLESBY, Woodson Ratcliffe (cousin of Richard James Oglesby), a Representative from New York; born near Shelbyville, Shelby County, Ky., February 9, 1867; attended the public schools, Kentucky Wesleyan College (then at Millersburg), and the Illinois Wesleyan University at Bloomington; studied law; was admitted to the bar in 1890 and commenced practice in New York City; served during the Spanish-American War as a private in Company C, Seventy-first Regiment, New York National Guard; member of the State assembly in 1906; delegate to the Democratic National Convention at Baltimore in 1912; elected as a Democrat to the Sixty-third and Sixty-fourth Congresses (March 4, 1913–March 3, 1917); unsuccessful candidate for reelection in 1916 to the Sixty-fifth Congress; resumed the practice of law in New York City until his retirement in 1928 and resided in Yonkers, N. Y., and Quincy, Fla.; died in Quincy, Fla., April 30, 1955; interment in Eastern Cemetery, Quitman, Ga.

O'GORMAN, James Aloysius, a Senator from New York; born in New York City on May 5, 1860; attended the public schools and the College of the City of New York; was graduated from the law department of New York University in 1882; was admitted to the bar the same year and commenced practice in New York City; justice of the New York District Court 1893–1900; elected justice of the New York State Supreme Court for the term 1900–1914 and served until March 31, 1911, when he resigned, having been elected Senator; elected as a Democrat to the United States Senate and served from March 4, 1911, to March 3, 1917; was not a candidate for renomination in 1916; president of the New York County Lawyers' Association; trustee of New York University 1920–1927 and of the College of New Rochelle; resumed the practice of law in New York City; official referee of the New York Supreme Court from 1934 until his death in New York City May 17, 1943; interment in Calvary Cemetery, Long Island City, N. Y.

O'GRADY, James Mary Early, a Representative from New York; born in Rochester, N. Y., March 31, 1863; attended the public schools; was graduated from the University of Rochester, New York, in 1885; studied law; was admitted to the bar in 1885 and commenced practice in Rochester, N. Y.; member of the board of education of Rochester 1887–1892, serving as president in 1891 and 1892; member of the State assembly from 1893 to 1898, serving as speaker in 1897 and 1898; elected as a Republican to the Fifty-sixth Congress (March 4, 1899–March 3, 1901); was not a candidate for renomination in 1900; continued the practice of his profession in Rochester, N. Y., until his death in that city on November 3, 1928; interment in Holy Sepulchre Cemetery.

O'HAIR, Frank Trimble, a Representative from Illinois; born near Paris, Edgar County, Ill., March 12, 1870; attended the common schools and was graduated from the law department of De Pauw University, Greencastle, Ind., in 1893; was admitted to the bar the same year and commenced practice in Paris, Ill.; elected as a Democrat to the Sixty-third Congress (March 4, 1913–March 3, 1915); unsuccessful candidate for reelection in 1914 to the Sixty-fourth Congress; resumed the practice of his profession in Paris, Ill., until his death there August 3, 1932; interment in Edgar Cemetery.

O'HARA, Barratt, a Representative from Illinois; born in Saint Joseph, Berrien County, Mich., April 28, 1882; attended the public schools of Berrien Springs and Benton Harbor, Mich.; went to Nicaragua with his father and attended school at San Juan del Norte; at the age of fifteen years enlisted during the Spanish-American War and served as a corporal in Company I, Thirty-third Michigan Volunteer Infantry, at the siege of Santiago; after two years returned to Benton Harbor, Mich., and graduated from high school; reporter, Benton Harbor Evening News, 1900; attended Missouri University in 1901 and 1902 and Northwestern University in 1909 and 1910; graduated from Chicago-Kent College of Law in 1912; sporting editor of St. Louis, Mo., Chronicle in 1902; sporting editor of Chicago American 1903–1905; cable editor of Chicago Chronicle in 1906; Sunday editor of Chicago Examiner 1907–1910; editor Chicago Magazine and Sunday Telegram 1910–1912; Lieutenant Governor of Illinois 1913–1917; chairman of Illinois Senate vice and wage investigations 1913–1915; was admitted to the bar in 1912 and commenced the practice of law in Chicago, Ill.; unsuccessful Democratic candidate for the United States Senate in 1915; during the First World War served as a major with the Eightieth and Twelfth Infantry Divisions and later as divisional judge advocate of the Fifteenth Division; president of the Arizona Film Co., with studios in Hollywood, Calif., in 1916 and 1917; unsuccessful candidate for Governor in 1920, and for Congressman-at-large in 1936 to the Seventy-fifth Congress; radio commentator over station WCFL in Chicago 1933–1935; elected as a Democrat to the Eighty-first Congress (January 3, 1949–January 3, 1951); unsuccessful candidate for reelection in 1950 to the Eighty-second Congress; elected to the Eighty-third and to the three succeeding Congresses (January 3, 1953–January 3, 1961). *Reelected to the Eighty-seventh Congress.*

O'HARA, James Edward, a Representative from North Carolina; born in New York City February 26, 1844; was of the Negro race; pursued an academic course; studied law in North Carolina and at Howard University, Washington, D. C.; engrossing clerk in the constitutional convention of North Carolina in 1868, also in the State house of representatives in 1868 and 1869; chairman of the board of commissioners for Halifax County 1872–1876; was admitted to the bar in 1873 and practiced; member of the State constitutional convention in 1875; unsuccessfully contested the election of William H. Kitchin to the Forty-sixth Congress; elected as a Republican to the Forty-eighth and Forty-ninth Congresses (March 4, 1883–March 3, 1887); unsuccessful candidate for reelection in 1886 to the Fiftieth Congress; resumed the practice of law in New Bern, Craven County, N. C., and died there September 15, 1905; interment in Greenwood Cemetery.

O'HARA, James Grant, a Representative from Michigan; born in Washington, D. C., November 8, 1925; moved with his parents to Detroit, Mich., in 1939; graduated from University of Detroit High School in 1943; during World War II served as an enlisted man in the United States Army with Company B, Five Hundred and Eleventh Parachute Infantry Regiment, Eleventh Airborne Division, seeing action in the Pacific Theater of Operations; graduated from the University of Michigan in 1954 and from the law department of the same university in 1955; was admitted to the bar in 1955 and commenced the practice of law in Detroit, Macomb County, Mich.; delegate to the Democratic National Convention in 1960; elected as a Democrat to the Eighty-sixth Congress (January 3, 1959–January 3, 1961). *Reelected to the Eighty-seventh Congress.*

O'HARA, Joseph Patrick, a Representative from Minnesota; born in Tipton, Cedar County, Iowa, January 23, 1895; attended the public schools and graduated from Spirit Lake, Iowa, High School; during the First World War was commissioned a second lieutenant of Infantry in the Officers' Reserve Corps and later promoted to captain in the Quartermaster Corps, and served from May 13, 1917, to August 15, 1919, with overseas service; commissioned a major of Infantry in the Reserve Corps; attended Inns of Court, London, England, and was graduated from the law department of Notre Dame University, South Bend, Ind., in 1920; was admitted to the bar in 1921 and commenced practice in Blencoe, Minn.; served as attorney for various villages, cities, towns, and school districts, and as county attorney of McLeod County 1934–1938; elected as a Republican to the Seventy-seventh and to the eight succeeding Congress (January 3, 1941–January 3, 1959); was not a candidate for renomination in 1958; practicing law in Washington, D. C., where he now resides.

OHLIGER, Lewis Philip, a Representative from Ohio; born in Rheinpfalz, Bavaria, Germany, January 3, 1843; immigrated to the United States in October 1854 with his parents; settled in Canton, Ohio, in 1857; attended the public schools; moved to Wooster, Ohio, and engaged in the wholesale drug and grocery business; county treasurer 1875–1879; presidential elector on the Democratic ticket of Cleveland and Hendricks in 1884; postmaster of Wooster from February 1885 until February 1890; trustee of the Wooster & Lodi Railway; delegate to the Democratic National Convention at Chicago in 1892; elected as a Democrat to the Fifty-second Congress to fill the vacancy caused by the death of John G. Warwick and served from December 5, 1892, to March 3, 1893; unsuccessful for renomination in 1892; internal-revenue collector of the Cleveland district by appointment of President Grover Cleveland 1893–1898; resumed his former business pursuits; died in San Diego, Calif., January 9, 1923; interment in Wooster Cemetery, Wooster, Ohio.

O'KONSKI, Alvin Edward, a Representative from Wisconsin; born on a farm near Kewaunee, Kewaunee County, Wis., May 26, 1904; attended the public schools and the University of Iowa at Iowa City; was graduated from State Teachers College, Oshkosh, Wis., in 1927, and from the University of Wisconsin at Madison in 1932; instructor in high schools at Omro and Oconto, Wis., 1926–1929; member of the faculty of Oregon State College at Corvallis 1929–1931, and at the University of Detroit, Detroit, Mich., 1936–1938; superintendent of schools, Pulaski, Wis., 1932–1935; dean of a junior college, Coleraine, Minn., in 1936; educator, journalist, and lecturer; editor and publisher, Hurley, Wis., 1940–1942; elected as a Republican to the Seventy-eighth and to the eight succeeding Congresses (January 3, 1943–January 3, 1961); unsuccessful candidate for the senatorial nomination in 1957 to fill a vacancy. *Reelected to the Eighty-seventh Congress.*

OLCOTT, Jacob Van Vechten, a Representative from New York; born in New York City May 17, 1856; attended the public schools and the College of the City of New York; was graduated from the Columbia College Law School at New York City in May 1877; was admitted to the bar May 17, 1877, and commenced the practice of law in New York City in 1881; member of the Civil Service Commission of New York City 1895–1897; trustee and vice president of St. Luke's Hospital, New York City; elected as a Republican to the Fifty-ninth, Sixtieth, and Sixty-first Congresses (March 4, 1905–March 3, 1911); was not a candidate for renomination in 1910; continued the practice of law in New York City until his death June 1, 1940; interment in Greenwood Cemetery, Brooklyn, N. Y.

OLCOTT, Simeon, a Senator from New Hampshire; born in Bolton, Tolland County, Conn., October 1, 1735; was graduated from Yale College in 1761; studied law; was admitted to the bar and commenced practice in Charlestown, N. H.; selectman 1769–1771; judge of probate for Cheshire County in 1773; representative in the general assembly of the Province in 1772 and 1773; appointed chief justice of the court of common pleas in 1784, judge of the superior court in 1790, and chief judge of the court in 1795; elected as a Federalist to the United States Senate to fill the vacancy caused by the resignation of Samuel Livermore and served from June 17, 1801, to March 3, 1805; died in Charlestown, N. H., February 22, 1815; interment in Forest Hill Cemetery.

OLDFIELD, Pearl Peden (widow of William Allan Oldfield), a Representative from Arkansas; born in Cotton Plant, Woodruff County, Ark., on December 2, 1876; educated in the public schools and at Arkansas College, Batesville, Ark.; elected January 9, 1929, as a Democrat to fill the vacancy in both the Seventieth and Seventy-first Congresses caused by the death of her husband William A. Oldfield, who had been reelected in 1928, and served from January 9, 1929, to March 3, 1931; was not a candidate for renomination in 1930; is now a resident of Washington, D. C.

OLDFIELD, William Allan (husband of Pearl Peden Oldfield), a Representative from Arkansas; born in Franklin, Izard County, Ark., February 4, 1874; attended the public schools, and was graduated from Arkansas College at Batesville in 1896; taught school; enlisted in 1898 as a private in Company M, Second Regiment, Arkansas Infantry, during the war with Spain; was promoted to first sergeant of the same company and later to first lieutenant, and was mustered out with that rank in March 1899; studied law; was admitted to the bar in 1900 and commenced practice in Batesville, Ark.; prosecuting attorney of Independence County 1902–1906; unsuccessful candidate for election in 1906 to the Sixtieth Congress; elected as a Democrat to the Sixty-first and to the nine succeeding Congresses and served from March 4, 1909, until his death; had been reelected to the Seventy-first Congress; died in Washington, D. C., November 19, 1928; interment in Oak Lawn Cemetery, Batesville, Ark.

OLDS, Edson Baldwin, a Representative from Ohio; born in Marlboro, Windham County, Vt., June 3, 1802; completed preparatory studies; moved to Ohio about 1820; taught school; was graduated from the medical department of the University of Pennsylvania at Philadelphia in 1824; commenced the practice of medicine in Kingston in 1824; moved to Circleville, Ohio, in 1828 and continued practice until 1837, when he engaged in the general produce business and mercantile pursuits; member of the State house of representatives in 1842, 1843, 1845, and 1846; served in the State senate 1846–1848 and was its presiding officer in 1846 and 1847; elected as a Democrat to the Thirty-first,

Thirty-second, and Thirty-third Congresses (March 4, 1849–March 3, 1855); unsuccessful candidate for reelection in 1854 to the Thirty-fourth Congress; moved to Lancaster, Ohio, in 1857; was arrested for disloyalty and imprisoned in Fort Lafayette in 1862; while in prison was again elected a member of the State house of representatives; after his release from prison served in the above capacity from 1862 to 1866; resumed mercantile pursuits; died in Lancaster, Ohio, January 24, 1869; interment in Forest Cemetery at Circleville, Ohio.

O'LEARY, Denis, a Representative from New York; born in Manhasset, Queens County, N. Y., January 22, 1863; attended the public schools; taught in the public schools; was graduated from the law school of the University of the City of New York (now New York University) in 1890; was admitted to the bar the same year and commenced practice in New York City; assistant corporation counsel of New York City in 1905 and 1906; commissioner of public works of Queens Borough in 1911 and 1912; elected as a Democrat to the Sixty-third Congress and served from March 4, 1913, until December 31, 1914, when he resigned; district attorney of Queens County 1915–1921; resumed the practice of law until 1929 when he retired; died in Douglaston, Queens County, N. Y., September 27, 1943; interment in Mount St. Mary's Cemetery, Flushing, N. Y.

O'LEARY, James Aloysius, a Representative from New York; born in New Brighton, Staten Island, N. Y., April 23, 1889; attended St. Peter's Academy, Augustinian Academy, and Westerleigh Collegiate Institute, all Staten Island institutions; studied law while engaged in the real estate and insurance business; became associated with the North Shore Ice Co. in 1917 and served as general manager and vice president 1920–1934; also an official in numerous other Staten Island enterprises; unsuccessful candidate for the nomination of State senator in 1930; elected as a Democrat to the Seventy-fourth and to the four succeeding Congresses and served from January 3, 1935, until his death at West Brighton, Staten Island, N. Y., March 16, 1944; interment in St. Peter's Cemetery.

OLIN, Abram Baldwin (son of Gideon Olin), a Representative from New York; born in Shaftsbury, Bennington County, Vt., September 21, 1808; attended the common schools, and was graduated from Williams College, Williamstown, Mass., in 1835; studied law; was admitted to the bar in 1838 and commenced practice in Troy, N. Y.; recorder of the city of Troy 1844–1852; elected as a Republican to the Thirty-fifth, Thirty-sixth, and Thirty-seventh Congresses (March 4, 1857–March 3, 1863); appointed by President Lincoln an associate justice of the supreme court of the District of Columbia and served from March 11, 1863, until he voluntarily retired January 13, 1879; died near Sligo, Montgomery County, Md., July 7, 1879; interment in the Danforth family lot adjacent to West Lawn Cemetery, Williamstown, Berkshire County, Mass.

OLIN, Gideon (father of Abram Baldwin Olin and uncle of Henry Olin), a Representative from Vermont; born in East Greenwich, Kent County, R. I., November 2, 1743; received a limited schooling; engaged in agricultural pursuits; moved to Vermont and settled in Shaftsbury in 1776; delegate to the Windsor convention in 1777; member of the State house of representatives in 1778, 1780–1793, and in 1799, serving as speaker 1788–1793; during the Revolutionary War served as a major in the Second Regiment under Colonel Herrick in 1778 and afterward under Lieutenant Colonel Walbridge; assistant judge of Bennington County Court 1781–1798 and chief judge 1807–1811; delegate to the State constitutional convention in 1791; member of the Governor's council 1793–1798; elected as a Democrat to the

Eighth and Ninth Congresses (March 4, 1803–March 3, 1807); resumed agricultural pursuits; died in Shaftsbury, Bennington County, Vt., January 21, 1823; interment at Shaftsbury Center.

OLIN, Henry (nephew of Gideon Olin), a Representative from Vermont; born in Shaftsbury, Bennington County, Vt., May 7, 1768; attended the common schools; studied law; was admitted to the bar and practiced; moved to Leicester, Vt., in 1788; member of the State house of representatives 1799–1804, 1806–1815, 1817–1819, and 1822–1824; delegate to the State constitutional conventions in 1814, 1822, and 1828; associate judge and afterwards chief judge of the Addison County Court 1801–1824; member of the executive council in 1820 and 1821; elected as a Jeffersonian Democrat to the Eighteenth Congress to fill the vacancy caused by the death of Charles Rich and served from December 13, 1824, to March 3, 1825; Lieutenant Governor of Vermont 1827–1830; died in Salisbury, Addison County, Vt., August 16, 1837; interment in Brookside Cemetery, Leicester, Vt.

OLIVER, Andrew, a Representative from New York; born in Springfield, N. Y., January 16, 1815; was graduated from Union College, Schenectady, N. Y., in 1835; studied law; was admitted to the bar and commenced practice in Penn Yan, Yates County, N. Y., in 1838; judge of the court of common pleas 1843–1847; judge of the surrogate and county courts in 1846; elected as a Democrat to the Thirty-third and Thirty-fourth Congresses (March 4, 1853–March 3, 1857); unsuccessful candidate on the American Party ticket for reelection in 1856 to the Thirty-fifth Congress; engaged in agricultural pursuits and also in the practice of law; again served as county judge and surrogate 1872–1877; died in Penn Yan, N. Y., March 6, 1889; interment in Lake View Cemetery.

OLIVER, Daniel Charles, a Representative from New York; born in New York City October 6, 1865; attended the public schools and graduated from the College of the City of New York; served twenty years as a member of the school board and devoted much time to the advancement of popular education; importer of dry goods since 1894; member of the Commercial Travelers' Association; member of the State assembly in 1914 and 1915; elected as a Democrat to the Sixty-fifth Congress (March 4, 1917–March 3, 1919); did not seek renomination in 1918 to the Sixty-sixth Congress; resumed his former business pursuits in New York City, where he died March 26, 1924; interment in Calvary Cemetery, Long Island City, N. Y.

OLIVER, Frank, a Representative from New York; born in New York City October 2, 1883; attended the public schools and the Morris High School, Borough of the Bronx; was graduated from Fordham University at New York City in 1905; studied law at the New York Law School; was admitted to the bar in 1908 and commenced practice in New York City; appointed on December 1, 1908, chief of the bureau of licenses for New York City and served until April 16, 1911, when he resigned to become secretary to United States Senator James A. O'Gorman, of New York, in which capacity he served until his resignation on January 3, 1916; was appointed chief clerk to the magistrates' courts of New York City and served from January 3, 1916, until December 31, 1919; appointed assistant district attorney for Bronx County on January 1, 1920, and served until February 28, 1923, when he resigned, having been elected to Congress; elected as a Democrat to the Sixty-eighth and to the five succeeding Congresses and served from March 4, 1923, until his resignation on June 18, 1934; appointed on June 19, 1934, justice of the court of special sessions, in which capacity he is now serving; resides in New York City, N. Y.

OLIVER, George Tener, a Senator from Pennsylvania; born January 26, 1848, in Donoughmore, County Tyrone, Ireland, during a visit abroad of his parents, who at that time were residents of Pittsburgh, Pa.; attended the common schools, and was graduated from Bethany (W. Va.) College in 1868; studied law; was admitted to the bar of Allegheny County, Pa., in 1871 and practiced for over ten years in Pittsburgh, Pa.; retired from his profession in 1881 and engaged in steel manufacturing until 1901, when he disposed of his interests; engaged in the newspaper business in 1900 and became publisher of the Pittsburgh Gazette-Times and Pittsburgh Chronicle-Telegraph; president of the Pittsburgh Central Board of Education 1881–1884; presidential elector on the Republican ticket of Blaine and Logan in 1884; delegate to the Republican National Conventions at Chicago in 1904 and 1916; declined the appointment as United States Senator tendered by Governor Pennypacker in 1904 to fill the vacancy caused by the death of Matthew S. Quay; elected as a Republican to the United States Senate in 1909 to fill the vacancy caused by the resignation of Philander C. Knox; reelected in 1911 and served from March 17, 1909, to March 3, 1917; declined to be a candidate for reelection; retired from public life and resided in Pittsburgh, Pa., until his death there January 22, 1919; interment in Allegheny Cemetery.

OLIVER, James Churchill, a Representative from Maine; born in South Portland, Cumberland County, Maine, August 6, 1895; attended the public schools and was graduated from Bowdoin College, Brunswick, Maine, in 1917; during the First World War enlisted on June 4, 1917, attended the Plattsburg Barracks Training Camp, and was commissioned a captain on November 27, 1917; was promoted to major of Infantry on October 9, 1918, and transferred to the Inspector General's Department until honorably discharged on July 22, 1919; engaged in the general insurance business in Portland, Maine, 1930–1937; member of the board of aldermen of South Portland, Maine, in 1932 and 1933; elected as a Republican to the Seventy-fifth, Seventy-sixth, and Seventy-seventh Congresses (January 3, 1937–January 3, 1943); unsuccessful candidate for renomination in 1942; during World War II served as lieutenant commander in the United States Coast Guard from January 26, 1943, to April 23, 1946; in 1946 engaged in the real-estate and insurance business in Maine and California; unsuccessful Democratic candidate for Governor in 1952; unsuccessful Democratic candidate for Congress in 1954 and 1956; unsuccessfully contested the election of Robert Hale to the Eighty-fifth Congress in 1956; elected as a Democrat to the Eighty-sixth Congress (January 3, 1959–January 3, 1961); unsuccessful candidate for reelection in 1960 to the Eighty-seventh Congress; real-estate developer; is a resident of Cape Elizabeth, Maine.

OLIVER, Mordecai, a Representative from Missouri; born in Anderson County, Ky., October 22, 1819; attended the common schools; studied law; was admitted to the bar in 1842 and commenced practice in Richmond, Mo.; prosecuting attorney for the fifth judicial circuit in 1848; elected as a Whig to the Thirty-third and Thirty-fourth Congresses (March 4, 1853–March 3, 1857); elected as a Unionist secretary of state of Missouri in 1861; resumed the practice of law in St. Louis, Mo.; judge of the criminal court 1889–1893; moved to Springfield, Greene County, Mo., where he died April 25, 1898; interment in Hazelwood Cemetery.

OLIVER, Samuel Addison, a Representative from Iowa; born near Washington, Washington County, Pa., on July 21, 1833; attended the common schools and West Alexandria Academy; was graduated from Washington (Pa.) College in 1851; moved to Arkansas, where he taught school; returned to Pennsylvania and engaged in agricultural pursuits; studied law; was admitted to the bar in 1857 and commenced practice in Onawa, Monona County, Iowa, in 1858; county supervisor in 1861; served as provost marshal during the Civil War; member of the State house of representatives in 1863 and 1864; delegate to the Republican National Convention at Baltimore in 1864; served in the State senate 1865–1867; judge of the fourth judicial circuit 1868–1875; elected as a Republican to the Forty-fourth and Forty-fifth Congresses (March 4, 1875–March 3, 1879); declined to be a candidate for renomination in 1878; mayor of Onawa several times; again engaged in agricultural pursuits; died in Onawa, Monona County, Iowa, July 7, 1912; interment in Onawa Cemetery.

OLIVER, William Bacon (cousin of Sydney Parham Epes), a Representative from Alabama; born in Eutaw, Greene County, Ala., May 23, 1867; attended the common schools of his native city; was graduated from the Verner College Preparatory School at Tuscaloosa in 1883, the academic department of the University of Alabama at Tuscaloosa in 1887, and from its law department in 1889; took a special course at the law school of the University of Virginia at Charlottesville in 1889; was admitted to the bar in 1889 and commenced practice in Tuscaloosa, Ala.; appointed solicitor for the sixth judicial circuit of Alabama in 1898 and served until his resignation in 1909; dean of the law school of the University of Alabama from 1909 until 1913, when he resigned; chairman of the Democratic central committee of Tuscaloosa County for a number of years; delegate to the Democratic National Convention at New York City in 1924; elected as a Democrat to the Sixty-fourth and to the ten succeeding Congresses (March 4, 1915–January 3, 1937); was not a candidate for renomination in 1936; served as special assistant to the Attorney General at Washington, D. C., from July 22, 1939, to May 1, 1944, when he retired from political and public affairs; died while on a visit in New Orleans, La., May 27, 1948; interment in Eutaw Cemetery, Eutaw, Ala.

OLIVER, William Morrison, a Representative from New York; born in Londonderry, N. H., October 15, 1792; received a limited schooling; moved to Cherry Valley, Otsego County, and thence to Penn Yan, Yates County, N. Y.; studied law; was admitted to the bar about 1812 and commenced practice in Penn Yan; first judge of the court of common pleas for Yates County 1823–1828; member of the State senate 1827–1830; Lieutenant Governor in 1830; again judge of the court of common pleas 1838–1845; elected as a Democrat to the Twenty-seventh Congress (March 4, 1841–March 3, 1843); clerk of the supreme court of New York about 1844; president of the Yates County Bank from the issuance of its charter until 1857; died in Penn Yan, N. Y., July 21, 1863; interment in Lake View Cemetery.

OLMSTED, Marlin Edgar, a Representative from Pennsylvania; born near Ulysses, Ulysses Township, Potter County, Pa., May 21, 1847; attended the common schools and Coudersport (Pa.) Academy; assistant corporation clerk and promoted to corporation clerk in charge of collection of taxes from corporations under Pennsylvania's revenue system; studied law; was admitted to the bar November 25, 1878, and commenced practice in Harrisburg; elected to represent Dauphin County in the proposed constitutional convention in 1891; elected as a Republican to the Fifty-fifth and to the seven succeeding Congresses (March 4, 1897–March 3, 1913); one of the managers appointed by the House of Representatives in 1905 to conduct the impeachment proceedings against Charles Swayne, judge of the United States District Court for the Northern District of Florida; was not a candidate for renomination in 1912 to the Sixty-third Congress; resumed the practice of his profession in Harrisburg, Pa.; died in New York City on July 19, 1913; interment in the Harrisburg Cemetery.

OLNEY, Richard, a Representative from Massachusetts; born in Milton, Stafford County, N. H., January 5, 1871; attended the public schools and Leicester Academy; was graduated from Brown University, Providence, R. I., in 1892; wool merchant; member of the State house of representatives in 1902; chairman of selectmen of Leicester in 1902 and 1903; unsuccessful candidate for Lieutenant Governor in 1903; member of the Massachusetts Minimum Wage Commission in 1911; delegate to the Democratic National Convention at Baltimore in 1912; elected as a Democrat to the Sixty-fourth, Sixty-fifth, and Sixty-sixth Congresses (March 4, 1915–March 3, 1921); unsuccessful candidate for reelection in 1920 to the Sixty-seventh Congress; appointed a member of the World War Foreign Debt Commission in February 1923 and reappointed by President Coolidge in 1925; chairman of the State parole board 1932–1937; chairman of the State Commission of the Necessaries of Life from 1938 until his death at Boston, Mass., on January 15, 1939; interment in Cherry Valley Cemetery, Leicester, Mass.

O'LOUGHLIN, Kathryn Ellen (after election was married to Daniel M. McCarthy and thereupon served under the name of Kathryn O'Loughlin McCarthy), a Representative from Kansas; born near Hays, Ellis County, Kans., April 24, 1894; attended the rural schools; was graduated from the Hays (Kans.) High School in 1913, from the State Teachers College, Hays, Kans., in 1917, and from the law school of the University of Chicago, Chicago, Ill., in 1920; was admitted to the bar in 1921 and commenced practice in Chicago, Ill.; returned to Kansas in 1928 and continued the practice of law in Hays; delegate to the State Democratic conventions in 1930, 1931, 1932, 1934, and 1936, and to the Democratic National Conventions in 1940 and 1944; member of the State house of representatives in 1931 and 1932; elected as a Democrat to the Seventy-third Congress (March 4, 1933–January 3, 1935); was an unsuccessful candidate for reelection in 1934 to the Seventy-fourth Congress; resumed the practice of law; also owned and operated a large ranch and was part owner of the Chevrolet & Oldsmobile Agency at Hays and Ellis, Kans.; died in Hays, Kans., January 16, 1952; interment in St. Joseph's Cemetery.

OLPP, Archibald Ernest, a Representative from New Jersey; born in South Bethlehem, Northampton County, Pa., May 12, 1882; attended the public schools; was graduated from the Moravian School, Bethlehem, Pa., in 1899, Lehigh University, Bethlehem, Pa., in 1903, and from the medical department of the University of Pennsylvania at Philadelphia in 1908; instructor in chemistry at Lehigh University in 1903 and 1904; instructor in biological chemistry at the College of Physicians and Surgeons (Columbia University), New York City, in 1908 and 1909; began the practice of medicine in West Hoboken, N. J., in 1909; served as town physician 1912–1914; surgeon at North Hudson Hospital, Weehawken, N. J., 1910–1920; police surgeon and physician to public schools, Secaucus, N. J., 1916–1924; served as first lieutenant in the United States Medical Corps during the First World War; elected as a Republican to the Sixty-seventh Congress (March 4, 1921–March 3, 1923); was an unsuccessful candidate for reelection in 1922 to the Sixty-eighth Congress; resumed his medical profession; died in Cliffside Park, N. J., July 26, 1949; interment in Brookside Cemetery, Englewood, N. J.

O'MAHONEY, Joseph Christopher, a Senator from Wyoming; born in Chelsea, Suffolk County, Mass., November 5, 1884; moved to Lawrence, Mass., with his parents in 1892 and to Cambridge, Mass., in 1898; attended the parochial and public schools and Columbia University, New York, N. Y.; moved to Boulder, Colo., in 1908 and engaged as a reporter on the Boulder

Herald; moved to Cheyenne, Wyo., in 1916 and served as city editor of the Cheyenne State Leader; executive secretary to Senator John B. Kendrick at Washington, D. C., 1917–1920; was graduated from the Georgetown University Law School, Washington, D. C., in 1920; was admitted to the bar in 1920 and commenced practice in Cheyenne, Wyo., and Washington, D. C.; delegate to the Democratic State conventions 1924–1932 and to the Democratic National Conventions 1924–1948; member of conference on uniform State laws in 1925 and 1926; city attorney of Cheyenne, Wyo., 1929–1931; served as a Democratic National committeeman 1929–1934; appointed First Assistant Postmaster General on March 6, 1933, and served until December 31, 1933; appointed as a Democrat to the United States Senate to fill the vacancy caused by the death of John B. Kendrick, and on November 6, 1934, was elected to fill this vacancy and also for the term commencing January 3, 1935; reelected in 1940 and again in 1946, and served from January 1, 1934, to January 3, 1953; unsuccessful for reelection in 1952; elected on November 2, 1954, to fill the vacancy caused by the death of Lester C. Hunt, and also elected for the full term commencing January 3, 1955, and served from November 29, 1954, to January 3, 1961; was not a candidate for renomination in 1960; resumed the practice of law in Washington, D. C., and Cheyenne, Wyo.; is a resident of Cheyenne, Wyo.

O'MALLEY, Matthew Vincent, a Representative from New York; born in Brooklyn, N. Y., June 26, 1878; attended the Parochial School of the Assumption and the grade and high schools of Brooklyn; secretary to the health officer of Brooklyn from 1894 to 1898; engaged in the real estate, insurance, and bonding business in 1899 and continued therein throughout the remainder of his life; secretary of the Citizens Publishing Co., of Brooklyn 1925–1931; elected as a Democrat to the Seventy-second Congress to fill the vacancy caused by the death of John F. Quayle and served from March 4, 1931, until his death, before the convening of Congress, in Brooklyn, N. Y., May 26, 1931; interment in Holy Cross Cemetery.

O'MALLEY, Thomas David Patrick, a Representative from Wisconsin; born in Milwaukee, Wis., March 24, 1903; attended the parochial schools; was graduated from Loyola Academy in 1920, after which he attended Loyola College, and the Y. M. C. A. College of Liberal Arts, Chicago, Ill.; engaged as a salesman, advertising writer, and as an author; delegate to the National Conference on Street and Highway Safety, Washington, D. C., in 1930; delegate to the Democratic National Convention at Chicago in 1932; unsuccessful candidate for election in 1928 to the Seventy-first Congress and in 1930 to the Seventy-second Congress; elected as a Democrat to the Seventy-third, Seventy-fourth, and Seventy-fifth Congresses (March 4, 1933–January 3, 1939); unsuccessful candidate for reelection in 1938 to the Seventy-sixth Congress; member of the Democratic national congressional committee 1933–1939; resumed advertising and public relations work; regional director of Wage and Hour and Public Contracts Division, United States Department of Labor, Chicago, Ill., 1939–1956; engaged in public relations and management counseling; is a resident of Milwaukee, Wis.

O'NEAL, Emmet, a Representative from Kentucky; born in Louisville, Jefferson County, Ky., on April 14, 1887; attended the public schools; was graduated from Centre College, Danville, Ky., in 1907, from Yale University, New Haven, Conn., in 1908, and from the law department of the University of Louisville, Louisville, Ky., in 1910; was admitted to the bar in 1910 and commenced practice in Louisville; during the First World War served overseas in the United States Army as an enlisted man in the Fifth Field Artillery in the First Division,

and as an officer in the One Hundred and Third Field Artillery in the Twenty-sixth Division 1917–1919; resumed the practice of law in Louisville; also engaged in banking; elected as a Democrat to the Seventy-fourth and to the five succeeding Congresses (January 3, 1935–January 3, 1947); unsuccessful candidate for reelection in 1946 to the Eightieth Congress; Ambassador to the Philippines from June 20, 1947, to January 20, 1949; resumed the practice of law in Washington, D. C.; member and later chairman of the Corregidor-Bataan Memorial Commission 1953–; resides in Washington, D. C.

O'NEALL, John Henry, a Representative from Indiana; born in Newberry, Newberry County, S. C., October 30, 1838; was left an orphan when eight years of age and was reared by his grandfather, who resided in Daviess County, Ind.; attended country schools, and was graduated from Indiana University at Bloomington in 1862; was graduated from the law department of the University of Michigan at Ann Arbor in 1864; was admitted to the bar the same year and commenced practice in Terre Haute; moved to Washington, Ind., in a few months and continued the practice of law; represented Daviess County in the State legislature in 1866; appointed prosecuting attorney for the eleventh judicial circuit in 1873; elected to the office in 1874, but resigned before his term was completed; elected as a Democrat to the Fiftieth and Fifty-first Congresses (March 4, 1887–March 3, 1891); was not a candidate for renomination in 1890; resumed the practice of law in Washington, Ind.; school trustee of Washington for fifteen years; delegate to the Democratic National Convention at Chicago in 1896 which nominated Bryan and Sewall; city attorney of Washington 1899–1907; organized the Federal Trust Co. in 1899 and was its president until 1902, when it was made a national bank; died in Washington, Daviess County, Ind., July 15, 1907; interment in St. John's Cemetery.

O'NEIL, Joseph Henry, a Representative from Massachusetts; born in Fall River, Bristol County, Mass., March 23, 1853; moved with his parents to Boston in 1854; attended the common schools; graduated from Quincy Grammar School, Boston; ten years at the carpenter's trade; member of the Boston school committee 1874–1877; member of the State house of representatives 1878–1882 and in 1884; member of the board of directors for public institutions from 1880 to 1886 and was chairman of the board the last eighteen months; city clerk of Boston in 1887 and 1888; elected as a Democrat to the Fifty-first, Fifty-second, and Fifty-third Congresses (March 4, 1889–March 3, 1895); unsuccessful candidate for renomination in 1894; assistant treasurer of the United States at Boston by appointment of President Cleveland 1895–1899; organized the Federal Trust Co., of Boston, in 1899 and served as its president until 1922, when it merged into the Federal National Bank, and then served as chairman of the board of directors until his death; member of the board of sinking fund commissioners 1899–1909; trustee of St. Elizabeth's Hospital, Boston, 1910–1935, and of Massachusetts General Hospital, Boston, 1912–1935; presidential elector on the Democratic ticket of Wilson and Marshall in 1912; delegate to the Democratic National Convention at St. Louis in 1916 which nominated Wilson and Marshall for a second term; died in Boston, Mass., February 19, 1935; interment in Holyhood Cemetery, Brookline, Mass.

O'NEILL, Charles, a Representative from Pennsylvania; born in Philadelphia, Pa., March 21, 1821; was graduated from Dickinson College, Carlisle, Pa., in 1840; studied law; was admitted to the bar in 1843 and commenced practice in Philadelphia; member of the State house of representatives 1850–1852 and in 1860; served in the State senate in 1853; elected as a Republican to the Thirty-eighth and to the three succeeding Congresses (March 4, 1863–March 3, 1871); unsuccessful candidate for reelection in 1870 to the Forty-second Congress; elected to the Forty-third and to the ten succeeding Congresses and served from March 4, 1873, until his death in Philadelphia, Pa., on November 25, 1893; interment in West Laurel Hill Cemetery, Montgomery County, Pa.

O'NEILL, Edward Leo, a Representative from New Jersey; born in Newark, N. J., July 10, 1903; attended the parochial schools; during the First World War served in the United States Navy 1919–1923; became engaged in the real-estate business in Newark, N. J.; unsuccessful candidate for election in 1934 to the Seventy-fourth Congress; elected as a Democrat to the Seventy-fifth Congress (January 3, 1937–January 3, 1939); unsuccessful candidate for reelection in 1938 to the Seventy-sixth Congress; lieutenant in the United States Naval Reserve in 1939 and 1940; during World War II served as a captain in the Quartermaster Corps, United States Army, in 1942 and 1943; commissioner of the Essex County Board of Taxation 1940–1945; realtor and mortgage broker in Newark, N. J., until his death December 12, 1948; interment in Holy Sepulchre Cemetery, East Orange, N. J.

O'NEILL, Harry Patrick, a Representative from Pennsylvania; born in Dunmore, Lackawanna County, Pa., February 10, 1889; left school at the age of ten and went to work as a slate picker in the O. S. Johnson Colliery, Dunmore, Pa.; worked evenings as an apprentice barber until the age of sixteen and at the age of eighteen purchased his employer's business; also engaged as an insurance broker; served in the Pennsylvania House of Representatives 1929–1948; elected as a Democrat to the Eighty-first and Eighty-second Congresses (January 3, 1949–January 3, 1953); unsuccessful candidate for reelection in 1952 to the Eighty-third Congress; died in Scranton, Pa., June 24, 1953; interment in Cathedral Cemetery.

O'NEILL, John, a Representative from Ohio; born in Philadelphia, Pa., December 17, 1822; attended the common schools at Frederick, Md., and Georgetown College, Washington, D. C.; was graduated from Mount St. Mary's College, Emmitsburg, Md., and from the law department of Georgetown College, Washington, D. C., in 1841; was admitted to the bar in 1842; moved to Zanesville, Muskingum County, Ohio, in 1844 and commenced the practice of law; prosecuting attorney of Muskingum County in 1845; held various county offices; elected as a Democrat to the Thirty-eighth Congress (March 4, 1863–March 3, 1865); resumed the practice of his profession; member of the State senate 1883–1885; practiced law until his death in Zanesville, Ohio, May 25, 1905; interment in St. Thomas' Cemetery.

O'NEILL, John Joseph, a Representative from Missouri; born in St. Louis, Mo., June 25, 1846; attended the common schools; studied law; was admitted to the bar in 1870 and commenced practice in St. Louis; engaged in the manufacture of gold pens; member of the State house of representatives 1872–1878; member of the municipal assembly 1879–1881; elected as a Democrat to the Forty-eighth, Forty-ninth, and Fiftieth Congresses (March 4, 1883–March 3, 1889); unsuccessful candidate for reelection in 1888 to the Fifty-first Congress; elected to the Fifty-second Congress (March 4, 1891–March 3, 1893); successfully contested the election of Charles F. Joy to the Fifty-third Congress and served from April 3, 1894, to March 3, 1895; was not a candidate for renomination in 1894; resumed the practice of law; died in St. Louis, Mo., February 19, 1898; interment in Calvary Cemetery.

O'NEILL, Thomas Phillip, Jr., a Representative from Massachusetts; born in Cambridge, Middlesex County, Mass., December 9, 1912; attended the parochial schools; was graduated from St. John's High School in 1931 and from Boston College in 1936; engaged in the insurance and real-estate business in Cambridge, Mass., since 1938; member of the State house of representatives 1936–1952, serving as minority leader in 1947 and 1948 and as speaker 1949–1952; member of Democratic State Committee 1942–1952; member of Cambridge School Committee in 1946 and 1947; elected as a Democrat to the Eighty-third and to the three succeeding Congresses (January 3, 1953–January 3, 1961). *Reelected to the Eighty-seventh Congress.*

O'REILLY, Daniel, a Representative from New York; born in Limerick, Ireland, June 3, 1838; pursued an academic course; immigrated to the United States in July 1856 with his parents, who settled in Brooklyn, N. Y.; member of the Brooklyn Board of Aldermen 1873–1875, 1878, and 1879; president pro tempore of the board of aldermen and acting mayor of the city; elected as an Independent Democrat to the Forty-sixth Congress (March 4, 1879–March 3, 1881); unsuccessful candidate for reelection in 1880 to the Forty-seventh Congress; studied law; was admitted to the bar in 1888 and commenced practice in Brooklyn, N. Y.; in charge of the transfer tax department of Kings County from 1898 until his death; died in Bayville, Long Island, N. Y., September 23, 1911; interment in Holy Cross Cemetery, Flatbush, Brooklyn, N. Y.

ORMSBY, Stephen, a Representative from Kentucky; born in County Sligo, Ireland, in 1759; immigrated to the United States when a boy and settled in Philadelphia, Pa.; pursued classical studies; studied law; was admitted to the bar in 1786 and commenced the practice of his profession in Danville, Ky.; deputy attorney general of Jefferson County in 1787; served in the early Indian wars, and as a brigadier general under Gen. Josiah Harmar in the campaign of 1790; judge of the district court of Jefferson County in 1791; presidential elector in 1796; judge of the circuit court 1802–1810; elected as a Democrat to the Twelfth Congress (March 4, 1811–March 3, 1813); unsuccessful candidate for reelection to the Thirteenth Congress; elected to the Thirteenth Congress to fill the vacancy caused by the death of Representative-elect John Simpson; reelected to the Fourteenth Congress and served from April 20, 1813, to March 3, 1817; unsuccessful candidate for reelection to the Fifteenth Congress; appointed first president of the branch of the United States Bank at Louisville, Ky., in 1817; retired to private life; died near Louisville, Ky., in 1844; interment in the Ormsby Burial Ground (later the property of the Kentucky Military Institute) at Lyndon, near Louisville, Ky.

ORR, Alexander Dalrymple (nephew of William Grayson and cousin of William John Grayson), a Representative from Kentucky; born in Alexandria, Loudoun County, Va., November 6, 1761; attended the local schools; about 1782 moved to Bourbon County, Ky. (then a part of Virginia), thence to a plantation on the Ohio River below Maysville, Mason County, Ky., and engaged in agricultural pursuits; member of the Virginia House of Delegates in 1790; elected to the State senate in 1792 and served until his election to Congress; upon the admission of Kentucky as a State into the Union was elected to the Second, Third, and Fourth Congresses and served from November 8, 1792, to March 3, 1797; resumed agricultural pursuits in Mason County near Maysville; died in Paris, Bourbon County, Ky., June 21, 1835; interment in Paris Cemetery.

ORR, Benjamin, a Representative from Massachusetts; born in Bedford, N. H., December 1, 1772; his early education was self-obtained; apprenticed as a carpenter; attended Fryeburg (N. H.) Academy; taught school at Concord and New Milford, N. H.; graduated from Dartmouth College, Hanover, N. H., in 1798; studied law; was admitted to the bar in 1801 and commenced the practice of law in Brunswick, Maine (then a part of Massachusetts); moved to Topsham, Maine, the same year and continued the practice of law; overseer of Bowdoin College, Brunswick, Maine, and served as trustee from 1814 to 1828 and as treasurer in 1815 and 1816; elected as a Federalist to the Fifteenth Congress (March 4, 1817–March 3, 1819); was not a candidate for renomination in 1818; resumed the practice of law in Topsham, Maine; returned to Brunswick, Maine, in 1822 and continued the practice of law; died in Brunswick, Cumberland County, Maine, on September 3, 1828; interment in Pine Grove Cemetery.

ORR, Jackson, a Representative from Iowa; born at Washington Court House, Fayette County, Ohio, September 21, 1832; moved with his parents to Benton, Elkhart County, Ind., in 1836; attended the common schools and Indiana University at Bloomington; moved to Jefferson, Greene County, Iowa, in 1856; served during the Civil War in the Union Army as captain of Company H, Tenth Regiment, Iowa Volunteer Infantry, 1861–1863; engaged in mercantile pursuits in Boone, Iowa; member of the State house of representatives in 1868; elected as a Republican to the Forty-second and Forty-third Congresses (March 4, 1871–March 3, 1875); was not a candidate for renomination in 1874; moved to Silverton, San Juan County, Colo., in 1875; elected county judge and served for three years; moved to Denver, Colo., and engaged in the practice of his profession and also in the real-estate business; president of the Denver Fire and Police Board in 1893 and 1894; died in Denver, Colo., March 15, 1926; interment in Fairmount Cemetery.

ORR, James Lawrence, a Representative from South Carolina; born in Craytonville, Anderson County, S. C., May 12, 1822; attended the public schools, and was graduated from the University of Virginia at Charlottesville in 1842; studied law; was admitted to the bar and commenced practice in Anderson, S. C., in 1843; engaged in newspaper work; member of the State house of representatives 1844–1848; elected as a Democrat to the Thirty-first and to the four succeeding Congresses (March 4, 1849–March 3, 1859); Speaker of the House in the Thirty-fifth Congress; was not a candidate for renomination in 1858; resumed the practice of law at Craytonville; member of the southern rights convention held in Charleston, S. C., in 1851; delegate to the Democratic National Convention at Charleston in 1860; member of the secession convention in 1860; one of three commissioners sent to Washington, D. C., to treat with the Federal Government for the surrender of the forts in Charleston Harbor; Member of the Confederate Senate in 1861; served in the Confederate Army during the Civil War; special commissioner sent to President Johnson to negotiate the establishment of provisional government for the State of South Carolina in 1865; member of the State constitutional convention in 1865; elected Governor of South Carolina as a Republican in 1866; president of the State convention held at Columbia in July 1866; delegate to the Union National Convention at Philadelphia in August 1866; judge of the eighth judicial circuit 1868–1870; member of the Republican State convention at Columbia in August 1872; delegate to the Republican National Convention at Philadelphia in 1872; appointed by President Grant as Minister to Russia in December 1872; died in St. Petersburg, Russia, May 5, 1873; interment in the Presbyterian Cemetery, Anderson, S. C.

ORR, Robert, Jr., a Representative from Pennsylvania; born near Hannastown, Westmoreland County, Pa., March 5, 1786; attended the public schools; at an early age moved with his parents to Armstrong County; later moved to Kittanning; deputy sheriff of Armstrong County in 1805; studied surveying

and was appointed deputy district surveyor; served in the War of 1812 and received promotions until he attained the rank of colonel; member of the State house of representatives 1817–1820; served in the State senate 1821–1826; elected as a Democrat to the Nineteenth Congress to fill the vacancy caused by the resignation of James Allison, Jr.; reelected to the Twentieth Congress and served from October 11, 1825, to March 3, 1829; retained his interest in military affairs, acquiring the rank and title of general; became a large landowner, and leased and sold as he had opportunities; resided in Orrsville a short time in 1845, and later in Allegheny City 1848–1852; returned to Kittanning, Armstrong County, Pa., and died there May 22, 1876; interment in Kittanning Cemetery.

ORTH, Godlove Stein, a Representative from Indiana; born in Lebanon, Pa., on April 22, 1817; attended the Gettysburg College, Pennsylvania; studied law; was admitted to the bar in 1839 and commenced practice in LaFayette, Ind.; member of the State senate 1843–1848 and served one year as president; presidential elector on the Whig ticket of Taylor and Fillmore in 1848; delegate to the peace convention held in Washington, D. C., in 1861 in an effort to devise means to prevent the impending war; served as captain of a company of Volunteers during the Civil War; elected as a Republican to the Thirty-eighth and to the three succeeding Congresses (March 4, 1863–March 3, 1871); was not a candidate for reelection in 1870 to the Forty-second Congress; elected to the Forty-third Congress (March 4, 1873–March 3, 1875); was not a candidate for renomination in 1874; declined appointment as Minister to Brazil tendered by President Grant; appointed Envoy Extraordinary and Minister Plenipotentiary to Austria-Hungary March 9, 1875, and served until May 23, 1876, when he resigned; elected as a Republican to the Forty-sixth and Forty-seventh Congresses and served from March 4, 1879, until his death in LaFayette, Tippecanoe County, Ind., December 16, 1882; interment in Springvale Cemetery.

OSBORN, Thomas Ward, a Senator from Florida; born in Scotch Plains, Union County, N. J., March 9, 1836; moved to New York in 1842 with his parents, who settled in North Wilna; attended the common schools, and was graduated from Madison (now Colgate) University, Hamilton, N. Y., in 1860; studied law and was admitted to the bar in 1861; during the Civil War entered the Union Army in 1861 as lieutenant and became captain of Battery D, First Regiment, New York Light Artillery; subsequently promoted to major; attained the rank of colonel in 1865; appointed assistant commissioner of the Bureau of Refugees and Freedmen for Florida in 1865 and 1866; settled in Tallahassee, Fla., and commenced the practice of law; appointed register in bankruptcy in 1867; member of the State constitutional convention in 1868 and drew up the constitution which was adopted; moved to Pensacola, Fla.; member of the State senate; upon the readmission of Florida to representation was elected as a Republican to the United States Senate and served from June 25, 1868, to March 3, 1873; was not a candidate for reelection; served as United States commissioner at the Centennial Exposition in Philadelphia, Pa., in 1876; moved to New York City and resumed the practice of law; also engaged in literary pursuits; died in New York City December 18, 1898; interment in Hillside Cemetery, North Adams, Berkshire County, Mass.

OSBORNE, Edwin Sylvanus, a Representative from Pennsylvania; born in Bethany, Wayne County, Pa., August 7, 1839; attended the public schools and the University of Northern Pennsylvania at Bethany; was graduated from the New York State and National Law School at Albany, N. Y., in 1860; was admitted to the bar and practiced law in Wilkes-Barre, Pa.;

during the Civil War entered the Union Army August 30, 1862, as captain of Company F, One Hundred and Forty-ninth Regiment, Pennsylvania Volunteer Infantry; was promoted to major of that regiment on February 25, 1865, and served until honorably discharged on July 25, 1865; appointed brevet major of Volunteers, to rank from March 13, 1865, "for gallant and meritorious services during the war"; appointed by Governor Geary as major general of the National Guard, Third Division, of Pennsylvania in 1870; served as commander of the Department of Pennsylvania, Grand Army of the Republic, in 1883; elected as a Republican to the Forty-ninth, Fiftieth, and Fifty-first Congresses (March 4, 1885–March 3, 1891); was not a candidate for renomination in 1890; delegate to the Republican National Convention at Chicago in 1888; resumed the practice of law in Wilkes-Barre, Pa.; moved to Washington, D. C., in 1898 and lived in retirement until his death on January 1, 1900; interment in Arlington National Cemetery, Fort Myer, Va.

OSBORNE, Henry, a Delegate from Georgia; elected as a Delegate to the Continental Congress in 1786; chief justice of Georgia March 1787–January 1789; judge of the superior court in the western district 1789–1791.

OSBORNE, Henry Zenas, a Representative from California; born in New Lebanon, Columbia County, N. Y., October 4, 1848; attended the public schools; served in the One Hundred and Ninety-second Regiment, New York Volunteer Infantry, during the Civil War; engaged in newspaper work as printer, reporter, editor, and publisher, with residences in New York City, Cincinnati, Memphis, New Orleans, Austin, Bodie, and Los Angeles; receiver of public moneys at Bodie, Calif., 1878–1884; collector of customs in Los Angeles 1890–1894; United States marshal, southern district of California, 1898–1906; delegate to the Republican National Convention at Chicago in 1888; commissioner of the board of public works, Los Angeles, in 1914 and 1915; elected as a Republican to the Sixty-fifth, Sixty-sixth, and Sixty-seventh Congresses and served from March 4, 1917, until his death; had been reelected to the Sixty-eighth Congress; died in Los Angeles, Los Angeles County, Calif., February 8, 1923; interment in Rosedale Cemetery.

OSBORNE, John Eugene, a Representative from Wyoming; born in Westport, Essex County, N. Y., June 19, 1858; attended the common schools and was graduated from the high school at Westport; studied medicine and was graduated from the University of Vermont at Burlington in 1880; moved to Rawlins, Wyo., and engaged in the practice of medicine; later engaged in raising livestock on the open range; member of the Wyoming Territorial Legislature 1883–1885; served as chairman of the Territorial penitentiary building commission in 1888, and as mayor of the city of Rawlins the same year; Governor of Wyoming 1893–1895; was renominated but declined; chairman of the Wyoming delegation to the Democratic National Convention at Chicago in 1896; elected as a Democrat to the Fifty-fifth Congress (March 4, 1897–March 3, 1899); declined to be a candidate for renomination in 1898; member of the Democratic National Committee 1900–1920; First Assistant Secretary of State 1913–1917; engaged in banking and stock raising; died in Rawlins, Wyo., on April 24, 1943; interment in Cedar Hill Cemetery, Princeton, Ky.

OSBORNE, Thomas Burr, a Representative from Connecticut; born in Weston (now Easton), Conn., July 8, 1798; was graduated from Yale College in 1817; studied law; was admitted to the bar in 1820 and commenced practice in Fairfield, Conn.; clerk of the county and superior courts 1826–1839; member of the State house of representatives in 1836; elected as a Whig to the Twenty-sixth and Twenty-seventh Congresses (March 4, 1839–March 3, 1843); served in the State senate in 1844, and the same year was appointed judge of the Fairfield County Court, which office he held for several years; again a member of the State house of representatives in 1850; judge of probate for Fairfield district in 1851; moved to New Haven in 1854; professor in Yale Law School from 1855 until 1865, when he resigned and retired from public life; died in New Haven, Conn., on September 2, 1869; interment in Evergreen Cemetery.

OSGOOD, Gayton Pickman, a Representative from Massachusetts; born in Salem, Mass., July 4, 1797; was graduated from Harvard University in 1815; studied law; was admitted to the bar and commenced practice in Salem; moved to North Andover in 1819; member of the State house of representatives 1829–1831; elected as a Democrat to the Twenty-third Congress (March 4, 1833–March 3, 1835); unsuccessful candidate for renomination in 1834; retired from public life and engaged in agricultural pursuits; died in Andover, Essex County, Mass., June 26, 1861; interment in the Old North Parish Burying Ground, North Andover, Mass.

OSGOOD, Samuel, a Delegate from Massachusetts; born in Andover, Essex County, Mass., February 3, 1748; was graduated from Harvard College in 1770; studied theology; engaged in mercantile pursuits; delegate to the Essex County convention in 1774; member of the Provincial Congress; entered the Revolutionary Army as captain and left the service as colonel and assistant quartermaster; Member of the Continental Congress 1780–1784; member of the State house of representatives in 1784; first commissioner of the United States Treasury 1785–1789; Postmaster General in the Cabinet of President Washington 1789–1791; moved to New York City; member of the State assembly 1800–1803; supervisor of New York State in 1801; appointed naval officer at the port of New York May 10, 1803, and served until his death, August 12, 1813; interment in the Brick Presbyterian Church, Nassau and Beekman Streets (now Fifth Avenue and Thirty-seventh Street), New York City.

O'SHAUNESSY, George Francis, a Representative from Rhode Island; born in Galway, Ireland, May 1, 1868; immigrated to the United States in 1872 with his parents, who settled in New York; attended St. Theresa's School, De La Salle Institute, and Columbia College Law School, New York City; was admitted to the bar in 1889 and practiced in New York City until 1907; deputy attorney general of New York in 1904 and 1905; assistant corporation counsel of New York City in 1906; resigned and moved to Providence, R. I., in 1907; was admitted to the Rhode Island bar the same year and practiced in Providence; member of the State house of representatives in 1910; elected as a Democrat to the Sixty-second and to the three succeeding Congresses (March 4, 1911–March 3, 1919); did not seek renomination in 1918, having become a candidate for Senator; unsuccessful candidate for election in 1918 to the United States Senate; appointed collector of internal revenue for Rhode Island October 1, 1919, and served until July 31, 1921; resumed the practice of law; died in Providence, R. I., November 28, 1934; interment in St. Francis Cemetery, Pawtucket, R. I.

OSIAS, Camilo, a Resident Commissioner from the Philippine Islands; born in Balaoan, La Union, Philippine Islands, March 23, 1889; attended school in Balaoan, Vigan (Ilocos Sur), San Fernando (La Union), and continued in America, being appointed government student to the United States in 1905; was graduated from the Western Illinois State Teachers College at Macomb in 1908; attended the University of Chicago, Chicago, Ill., in 1906 and 1907; was graduated from Columbia University in New York City, N. Y., and from the Teachers College of New York

City in 1910; returned to the Philippine Islands and taught in the San Fernando High School in 1910; supervising teacher, Bacnotan, San Juan, and San Fernando 1910–1914; first Filipino superintendent of schools in 1915 and 1916, being assigned to Bataan and later to Mindoro; assistant chief of the academic division bureau of education in 1916; superintendent of schools of Tayabas in 1917; assistant director of education 1917–1921; secretary-treasurer and first vice president of the Philippine Amateur Athletic Federation 1918–1929; member of the first Philippine mission to the United States in 1919 and 1920; professorial lecturer at the University of the Philippines 1919–1921; president of the National University 1921–1936; awarded the Columbia University medal for meritorious public service especially in the field of education in 1929; author of eight readers used in the Philippine schools and also other books; elected a member of the Philippine Senate in 1925; elected as a Nationalist a Resident Commissioner to the United States in 1928; reelected in 1931 and served from March 4, 1929, until January 3, 1935, when his term expired in accordance with the new Philippine Commonwealth Government; unsuccessful candidate for election to the Philippine Senate in 1934; member of the Constitutional Convention in 1934; member of the first National Assembly in 1935; member of the Economic Mission to the United States in 1939; chairman of Educational Mission 1938–1941; chairman of National Council of Education in 1941; director of publicity and propaganda until January 1942; chairman of National Cooperative Administration in 1941; subsequently assistant commissioner of the Department of Education, Health, and Public Welfare, then Minister of Education of the Republic of the Philippines until 1945; chancellor of Osias Colleges; writer; elected to the Philippine Senate in 1947 for the term expiring in 1953; Philippine representative to the Interparliamentary Union in Rome and to the International Trade Conference in Genoa in 1948; unsuccessful candidate for the Nationalist party nomination for President of the Philippines in 1953; unsuccessful candidate for the Philippine Senate in 1955; is a resident of Manndaluyong, Rizal, Philippines.

OSMER, James H., a Representative from Pennsylvania; born in Tenterdon (near London), England, January 23, 1832; when an infant his parents immigrated to the United States and settled near Bellefonte, Centre County, Pa.; attended private schools, Bellefonte Academy, Centre County, Pa., Mount Pleasant College, Westmoreland County, Pa., and Pennsylvania and Dickinson Seminary, Williamsport, Pa.; studied law at Elmira, N. Y.; was admitted to the bar of the supreme court of New York at Cortland in 1858 and practiced at Horseheads, near Elmira, until 1865, when he moved to Franklin, Pa., where he was admitted to the bar and practiced; delegate to the Republican National Convention at Cincinnati in 1876; delegate to several State conventions; elected as a Republican to the Forty-sixth Congress (March 4, 1879–March 3, 1881); was not a candidate for renomination in 1880; continued the practice of his profession in Franklin, Venango County, Pa., until his death, October 3, 1912; interment in Franklin Cemetery.

OSMERS, Frank Charles, Jr., a Representative from New Jersey; born in Leonia, Bergen County, N. J., December 30, 1907; attended the public schools and Williams College, Williamstown, Mass.; engaged in the jewelry business; gem expert and appraiser; member of the Haworth, N. J., Borough Council 1930–1934; mayor of Haworth, N. J., in 1935 and 1936; member of the State house of assembly 1935–1937; elected as a Republican to the Seventy-sixth and Seventy-seventh Congresses (January 3, 1939–January 3, 1943); while a member of the Seventy-seventh Congress enlisted during World War II as a private and was graduated from the Infantry School at Fort Benning, Ga., as

a second lieutenant; placed on inactive list by Presidential directive and finished his term in Congress; was not a candidate for renomination in 1942; during World War II went on active duty as a second lieutenant in the Seventy-seventh Infantry Division on January 4, 1943, transferred to the Twenty-fourth Corps and served in the Philippine and Okinawa invasions and Korean occupation, and was discharged on February 22, 1946; major in Officers' Reserve Corps; resumed his former business pursuits; also interested in real estate, insurance, and publishing businesses; elected as a Republican to the Eighty-second Congress to fill the vacancy caused by the resignation of Harry L. Towe; reelected to the Eighty-third and to the three succeeding Congresses and served from November 6, 1951, to January 3, 1961. *Reelected to the Eighty-seventh Congress.*

OSTERTAG, Harold Charles, a Representative from New York; born in Attica, Wyoming County, N. Y., June 22, 1896; attended the public schools; was graduated from Chamberlain Military Institute at Perry, N. Y., in 1915; during the First World War enlisted in the Seventy-fourth Infantry, Twenty-seventh Division, and served in France with the Fifty-fifth Pioneer Infantry; employed with the New York Central Railroad 1917–1950, advancing to assistant to the vice president, traffic department; member of the State assembly 1932–1950; member of board of managers of the Council of State Governments 1935–1950; delegate to the Republican State Conventions 1930–1958; delegate to the Republican National Conventions in 1952, 1956, and 1960; elected as a Republican to the Eighty-second and to the four succeeding Congresses (January 3, 1951–January 3, 1961). *Reelected to the Eighty-seventh Congress.*

O'SULLIVAN, Eugene Daniel, a Representative from Nebraska; born on a cattle ranch near Kent, Reno County, Kans., May 31, 1883; attended the public schools of Kent, Kans.; was graduated from Christian Brothers College, St. Joseph, Mo., in 1903; attended St. Benedict's College, Atchison, Kans., in 1904 and 1905; graduated from Creighton University Law School, Omaha, Nebr., in 1910; was admitted to the bar in 1910 and commenced the practice of law in Omaha, Nebr.; unsuccessful Democratic candidate for the gubernatorial nomination in 1934; was unsuccessful as a write-in candidate for election to the United States Senate in 1934; delegate to the Democratic National Conventions in 1924, 1928, 1932, 1940, and 1944; elected as a Democrat to the Eighty-first Congress (January 3, 1949–January 3, 1951); unsuccessful candidate for reelection in 1950 to the Eighty-second Congress; resumed the practice of law; is a resident of Omaha, Nebr.

O'SULLIVAN, Patrick Brett, a Representative from Connecticut; born in Derby, New Haven County, Conn., August 11, 1887; attended the public schools; was graduated from the Derby High School in 1904, from Yale University in 1908, from Georgetown University, Washington, D. C., in 1909, and from Yale Law School in 1913; was admitted to the bar in 1913 and commenced practice in Derby; corporation counsel of Derby 1914–1917; delegate to the Democratic National Convention at St. Louis in 1916; member of the State senate and its minority leader in 1917; in 1918, during the First World War, resigned from the State senate to enlist in the United States Navy; served on the U. S. S. *North Dakota* as ensign; elected as a Democrat to the Sixty-eighth Congress (March 4, 1923–March 3, 1925); unsuccessful candidate for reelection in 1924 to the Sixty-ninth Congress; resumed the practice of law; associate professor of law at the Yale Law School; judge of the Connecticut Superior Court 1931–1950, associate justice of Connecticut Supreme Court 1950–1957, and chief justice in 1957; is a resident of Orange, Conn.

OTERO, Mariano Sabino (nephew of Miguel Antonio Otero), a Delegate from the Territory of New Mexico; born in Peralta, Valencia County, N. Mex., August 29, 1844; attended private and parochial schools and St. Louis University, Missouri; engaged in commercial pursuits and stock raising, and subsequently became a banker; probate judge of Bernalillo County 1871–1879; nominated by the Democratic State convention as a candidate for Delegate to the Forty-fourth Congress, but declined; elected as a Republican to the Forty-sixth Congress (March 4, 1879–March 3, 1881); declined to be a candidate for renomination in 1880; engaged in his former business pursuits; commissioner of Bernalillo County 1884–1886; unsuccessful candidate for election in 1888 to the Fifty-first Congress and in 1890 to the Fifty-second Congress; moved to Albuquerque, N. Mex., in 1889; interested in the manufacture of sulphur and engaged in banking; died in Albuquerque, Bernalillo County, N. Mex., February 1, 1904; interment in Santa Barbara Cemetery.

OTERO, Miguel Antonio (uncle of Mariano Sabino Otero), a Delegate from the Territory of New Mexico; born in Valencia, N. Mex., June 21, 1829; attended private and parochial schools and St. Louis University, Missouri; was graduated from Pingree's College, Fishkill, N. Y., and later became a member of the faculty; returned to St. Louis, Mo.; studied law; was admitted to the bar in 1851 and commenced practice in Albuquerque, N. Mex., in 1852; declined the appointment as United States district attorney tendered by President Pierce; member of the Territorial house of representatives 1852–1854; attorney general for the Territory of New Mexico in 1854; successfully contested as a Democrat the election of José M. Gallegos to the Thirty-fourth Congress and served from July 23, 1856, to March 3, 1857; reelected to the Thirty-fifth and Thirty-sixth Congresses (March 4, 1857–March 3, 1861); was not a candidate for renomination in 1860; delegate to the Democratic National Convention at Charleston, S. C., in 1860; declined the appointment as Minister to Spain tendered by President Lincoln in 1861; appointed by President Lincoln as secretary of the Territory of New Mexico and Acting Governor in 1861, and served for one year; engaged in mercantile pursuits at Westport Landing (now Kansas City), Mo., 1861–1864, and at several other places in the West until 1877; interested in the construction of railroads, serving as a director and vice president; also engaged in banking; unsuccessful candidate for election in 1880 to the Forty-seventh Congress; died in Las Vegas, N. Mex., May 30, 1882; interment in Riverside Cemetery, Denver, Colo.

OTEY, Peter Johnston, a Representative from Virginia; was born in Lynchburg, Campbell County, Va., December 22, 1840; attended private schools in Lynchburg; was graduated from the Virginia Military Institute at Lexington in 1859; while a cadet he participated in the defense of Virginia in the John Brown raid; engaged in civil engineering; joined the Confederate Army in 1861 and served throughout the Civil War; organized and built the Lynchburg & Durham Railroad and was president of the company; engaged in banking and was general manager of the Rivermont Land Co.; elected as a Democrat to the Fifty-fourth and to the three succeeding Congresses and served from March 4, 1895, until his death; delegate to the Democratic National Convention at Chicago in 1896; died in Lynchburg, Va., May 4, 1902; interment in the Presbyterian Cemetery.

OTIS, Harrison Gray (son of Samuel Allyne Otis), a Representative and a Senator from Massachusetts; born in Boston, Mass., on October 8, 1765; was graduated from Harvard University in 1783; studied law; was admitted to the bar in 1786 and commenced practice in Boston; member of the State house of representatives in 1796; appointed by President Wash-

ington district attorney for the district of Massachusetts on May 26, 1796, and served until December 21, 1796; elected as a Federalist to the Fifth and Sixth Congresses (March 4, 1797–March 3, 1801); was not a candidate for renomination in 1800; appointed United States district attorney for Massachusetts by President John Adams February 18, 1801, and served until January 6, 1802; member and speaker of the State house of representatives 1802–1804; served in the State senate 1805–1816, and was its president in 1805 and 1808–1810; overseer of Harvard University 1810–1823; delegate to the Hartford convention in 1814; judge of the court of common pleas 1814–1818; elected to the United States Senate and served from March 4, 1817, to May 30, 1822, when he resigned; unsuccessful candidate for Governor of Massachusetts in 1823; fellow of Harvard University 1823–1825; mayor of Boston 1829–1832; retired from public life; died in Boston, Mass., October 28, 1848; interment in Mount Auburn Cemetery, Cambridge, Mass.

OTIS, John, a Representative from Maine; born in Leeds, Maine, August 3, 1801; attended the common schools, and was graduated from Bowdoin College, Brunswick, Maine, in 1823; studed law; was admitted to the bar and commenced practice in Hallowell, Maine, in 1826; member of the State house of representatives in 1841; appointed a member of the Northeastern Boundary Commission in 1842; served in the State senate in 1842; again a member of the State house of representatives in 1846 and 1847; elected as a Whig to the Thirty-first Congress (March 4, 1849–March 3, 1851); retired from public life on account of ill health; died in Hallowell, Kennebec County, Maine, October 17, 1856; interment in Hallowell Cemetery.

OTIS, John Grant, a Representative from Kansas; born near Danby, Rutland County, Vt., February 10, 1838; pursued an academic course at Burr Seminary, Manchester, Vt.; attended Williams College, Williamstown, Mass., and the law department of Harvard University; was admitted to the bar of Rutland County, Vt., in 1859; moved to Topeka, Kans., in May 1859 and commenced the practice of law; assisted in recruiting the first colored regiment of Kansas in 1862; a member of the Second Regiment, Volunteer Infantry, at the time of Price's raid; paymaster general of the Governor's military staff from February 1863 to 1865, with rank of colonel; mustered out in 1865; engaged in agricultural pursuits and in the dairy business near Topeka; was State agent of the Grange 1873–1875; State lecturer for the Grange 1889–1891; elected as the People's Party candidate to the Fifty-second Congress (March 4, 1891–March 3, 1893); unsuccessful candidate for renomination in 1892; engaged in his former business pursuits until his death in Topeka, Kans., February 22, 1916; interment in Topeka Cemetery.

OTIS, Norton Prentiss, a Representative from New York; born in Halifax, Windham County, Vt., March 18, 1840; attended public schools of Halifax, Vt., and Albany, Hudson, and Yonkers, N. Y.; in early youth entered in business with his father and engaged in the manufacture of elevators for nearly fifty years; mayor of Yonkers, N. Y., 1880–1882; member of the State assembly in 1884; president of the New York State Commission to the World's Exposition at Paris, France, in 1900; president of St. John's Riverside Hospital of Yonkers; unsuccessful candidate for election in 1900 to the Fifty-seventh Congress; elected as a Republican to the Fifty-eighth Congress and served from March 4, 1903, until his death at Hudson Terrace, Westchester County, N. Y., February 20, 1905; interment in Oakland Cemetery.

OTIS, Samuel Allyne (father of Harrison Gray Otis), a Delegate from Massachusetts; born in Barnstable, Barnstable County, Mass., November 24, 1740; was graduated from Harvard College in 1759; engaged in mercantile pursuits in Boston; member of the State house of representatives in 1776; member of the Board of War in 1776; collector of clothing for the Continental Army in 1777; member of the Massachusetts constitutional convention which framed the constitution of that State; again a member of the State house of representatives 1784–1787 and elected speaker of the house in 1784; Member of the Continental Congress in 1787 and 1788; elected Secretary of the United States Senate on April 8, 1789, and served until his death in Washington, D. C., April 22, 1814; interment in Congressional Cemetery.

OTJEN, Theobald, a Representative from Wisconsin; born in West China, St. Clair County, Mich., on October 27, 1851; attended the Marine City (Mich.) Academy and a private school in Detroit; employed as foreman in the rolling mill of the Milwaukee Iron Co. in Milwaukee 1870–1872; was graduated from the law department of the University of Michigan at Ann Arbor March 25, 1875; admitted to the bar at Ann Arbor in 1875 and commenced practice in Detroit, Mich.; moved to Milwaukee, Wis., in 1883; member of the common council of Milwaukee 1887–1894; trustee of the Milwaukee Public Library 1887–1891; trustee of the public museum 1891–1894; unsuccessful candidate for comptroller of the city in April 1892; unsuccessful candidate for election in 1892 to the Fifty-third Congress and in 1893 to the same Congress to fill the vacancy caused by the resignation of John L. Mitchell; elected as a Republican to the Fifty-fourth and to the five succeeding Congresses (March 4, 1895–March 3, 1907); unsuccessful candidate for renomination in 1906; resumed the practice of law in Milwaukee, Wis., chairman of the local draft board during the First World War; died in Milwaukee, Wis., April 11, 1924; interment in Forest Home Cemetery.

O'TOOLE, Donald Lawrence, a Representative from New York; born in Brooklyn, N. Y., August 1, 1902; attended the public and parochial schools; was graduated from St. James Academy, Brooklyn, N. Y., in 1916 and from the law department of Fordham University, New York, N. Y., in 1925; postgraduate student at Columbia University and New York University, New York, N. Y.; was admitted to the bar in 1927 and commenced practice in New York City; member of the board of aldermen 1934–1936; elected as a Democrat to the Seventy-fifth and to the seven succeeding Congresses (January 3, 1937–January 3, 1953); unsuccessful candidate for reelection in 1952 to the Eighty-third Congress and for election in 1954 to the Eighty-fourth Congress; resumed the practice of law; executive director of New York State Department of Commerce and Industry January 1955–1957, and commissioner of the department from August 1, 1958, to April 29, 1959; retired; is a resident of Brooklyn, N. Y.

OURY, Granville Henderson, a Delegate from the Territory of Arizona; born in Abingdon, Washington County, Va., March 12, 1825; moved with his parents to Bowling Green, Mo., in 1836; pursued academic studies; studied law; was admitted to the bar in 1848 at Bowling Green, Mo.; moved to San Antonio, Tex., the same year, and in 1849 moved to Marysville, Calif., and engaged in mining; went to Tucson, Ariz., in 1856 and began the practice of law; was chosen captain of a party sent from Tucson to the relief of the Crabbe Expedition besieged at Caborca, Sonora, Mex., in 1857; presided as judge of the district court for Arizona and New Mexico at Mesilla, N. Mex.; elected delegate from Arizona to the Confederate Congress and took his seat January 21, 1862; resigned in 1862 to serve as captain, Herbert's Battalion, Arizona Cavalry, Confederate Army; colonel on the staff of General Sibley in Texas and Louisiana 1862–1864; took oath of allegiance October 8, 1865, at Fort Mason, Ariz., and then resumed the practice of law at Tucson; elected to the Territorial house of representatives in 1866;

appointed Territorial attorney general in 1869; moved to Phoenix in 1871; appointed district attorney of Maricopa County and served from 1871 to 1873; again elected to the Territorial house of representatives in 1873 and 1875, serving as speaker in 1866 and 1873; unsuccessful candidate for election in 1878 to the Forty-sixth Congress; appointed district attorney of Pinal County in 1879; elected as a Democrat to the Forty-seventh and Forty-eighth Congresses (March 4, 1881–March 3, 1885); was not a candidate for renomination in 1884; delegate to the Democratic National Convention in 1884 which nominated Cleveland and Hendricks; returned to Florence, Ariz., in 1885 and resumed the practice of law; district attorney for Pinal County in 1889 and 1890; died in Tucson, Ariz., January 11, 1891; interment in the Masonic Cemetery, Florence, Ariz.

OUTHWAITE, Joseph Hodson, a Representative from Ohio; born in Cleveland, Ohio, December 5, 1841; attended the public schools of Zanesville, Ohio; taught in the high school of that city 1862–1864; principal of a grammar school in Columbus, Ohio, 1864–1867; studied law while teaching; was admitted to the bar in 1866 and practiced from 1867 to 1871 at Osceola, Mo.; prosecuting attorney of Franklin County, Ohio, 1874–1878; trustee of the county children's home 1879–1883; trustee of the sinking fund of the city of Columbus in 1883; reappointed in 1884 for a term of five years; elected as a Democrat to the Forty-ninth and to the four succeeding Congresses (March 4, 1885–March 3, 1895); appointed a member of the commission to codify the laws of the United States; civilian member of the Board of Ordnance and Fortification 1895–1899; member of the board of trustees of Ohio State University at Columbus from December 1896 to January 1898; dean of the law school of Ohio State University from 1904 until his death in Columbus, Ohio, December 9, 1907; interment in Greenlawn Cemetery.

OUTLAND, George Elmer, a Representative from California; born in Santa Paula, Ventura County, Calif., October 8, 1906; attended the public schools; was graduated from Whittier (Calif.) College in 1928, from Harvard University, Cambridge, Mass., in 1929, and from Yale University, New Haven, Conn., in 1937; also attended the University of Southern California at Los Angeles; served as assistant director of boys' work, Hale House, Boston, Mass., 1928–1930; director of boys' work, Denison House, Boston, Mass., 1929–1933, and of Neighborhood House, Los Angeles, Calif., in 1933 and 1934; supervisor of boys' welfare for Federal Transient Service of Southern California in 1934 and 1935; director of New Haven (Conn.) Community College in 1935 and 1936; instructor at Yale University 1935–1937; served on the faculty of Santa Barbara (Calif.) State College 1937–1942; elected as a Democrat to the Seventy-eighth and Seventy-ninth Congresses (January 3, 1943–January 3, 1947); unsuccessful candidate for reelection in 1946 to the Eightieth Congress; engaged in teaching at the San Francisco (Calif.) State College, and is a resident of San Francisco, Calif.

OUTLAW, David (cousin of George Outlaw), a Representative from North Carolina; born near Windsor, Bertie County, N. C., September 14, 1806; attended the private schools and academies of Bertie County; was graduated from the University of North Carolina at Chapel Hill in 1824; studied law; was admitted to the bar in 1825 and commenced practice in Windsor, N. C.; member of the State house of representatives 1831–1834, 1854, and 1858; delegate to the State constitutional convention at Raleigh in 1835; solicitor of the first judicial district 1836–1844; delegate to the Whig National Convention at Baltimore in 1844; colonel of the Bertie County Regiment of State militia; elected as a Whig to the Thirtieth, Thirty-first, and Thirty-second Congresses (March 4, 1847–March 3, 1853); unsuccessful candidate for reelection in 1852 to the Thirty-third Congress; resumed the practice of law in Windsor, Bertie County, N. C.; served in the State senate in 1860 and 1866; died in Windsor, N. C., October 22, 1868; interment in the Episcopal Cemetery.

OUTLAW, George (cousin of David Outlaw), a Representative from North Carolina; born near Windsor, Bertie County, N. C.; educated by private teachers and in the common schools; engaged in agricultural and mercantile pursuits; member of the State house of commons 1796–1797; served in the State senate in 1802, 1806–1808, 1810–1814, 1817, 1821, and 1822, and served as speaker in 1812, 1813, and 1814; elected as a Jefferson Democrat to the Eighteenth Congress to fill the vacancy caused by the resignation of Hutchins G. Burton and served from January 19, 1825, to March 3, 1825; was not a candidate for reelection to the Nineteenth Congress; resumed agricultural and mercantile pursuits; died in Windsor, Bertie County, N. C., August 15, 1825; interment in the family cemetery.

OVERMAN, Lee Slater, a Senator from North Carolina; born in Salisbury, Rowan County, January 3, 1854; attended private schools, and was graduated from Trinity College (now Duke University), Durham, N. C., in 1874; taught school two years; private secretary to Gov. Zebulon B. Vance in 1877 and 1878 and private secretary to Gov. Thomas J. Jarvis in 1879; studied law; was admitted to the bar in 1878 and began practice in Salisbury, N. C., in 1880; member of the State house of representatives in 1883, 1885, 1887, 1893, and 1899, and served as speaker in 1893; choice of the Democratic caucus for speaker in 1887, but defeated by one vote; president of the North Carolina Railroad Co. in 1894; unsuccessful Democratic candidate for United States Senator in 1895; president of the Democratic State conventions in 1900 and 1911; president of the Salisbury Savings Bank; member of the board of trustees of the University of North Carolina for ten years; presidential elector on the Democratic ticket of Bryan and Stevenson in 1900; member of the board of trustees of Duke University; elected as a Democrat to the United States Senate in 1903; reelected in 1909, 1914, 1920, and again in 1926, and served from March 4, 1903, until his death in Washington, D. C., December 12, 1930; funeral services were held in the Chamber of the United States Senate; interment in Chestnut Hill Cemetery, Salisbury, N. C.

OVERMYER, Arthur Warren, a Representative from Ohio; born near Lindsey, Sandusky County, Ohio, on May 31, 1879; attended the public schools and also Lima Lutheran College; taught school; was graduated from the Ohio Northern University Law School at Ada in 1902; was admitted to the bar in 1902 and commenced practice in Fremont, Ohio; clerk of the Fremont Board of Health 1907–1910; city solicitor 1910–1914; elected as a Democrat to the Sixty-fourth and Sixty-fifth Congresses (March 4, 1915–March 3, 1919); unsuccessful candidate for reelection in 1918 to the Sixty-sixth Congress; appointed judge of the court of common pleas by Gov. A. V. Donahey April 10, 1926, and elected to that position in November of the same year; reelected in 1930 and served until his resignation on December 1, 1934, having been appointed by Gov. George White to a vacancy in the Ohio Sixth District Court of Appeals; elected in 1936 for a six-year term; in 1942 was chosen as chief justice of the nine courts of appeals of Ohio; retired from the courts on February 8, 1943; resumed the private practice of law in Fremont, Ohio, until his retirement in 1951; died in North Royalton, Ohio, March 8, 1952; interment in Four-Mile House Cemetery, near Fremont, Ohio.

OVERSTREET, James, a Representative from South Carolina; born near Barnwell Court House, Barnwell District, S. C., February 11, 1773; attended the common schools; studied law; was admitted to the bar in 1798 and commenced practice in Barnwell District; held several local offices; elected to the Sixteenth and Seventeenth Congresses and served from March 4, 1819, until his death May 24, 1822, at China Grove, Rowan County, N. C., while en route to his home from Washington, D. C.; interment in Savitz Cemetery at Mount Zion Reformed Church, China Grove, N. C.

OVERSTREET, James Whetstone, a Representative from Georgia; born on a farm near Sylvania, Screven County, Ga., August 28, 1866; attended the rural schools and Sylvania High School; was graduated from Mercer (Ga.) University in 1888; studied law in Augusta; was admitted to the bar in 1892 and commenced practice in Sylvania, Ga.; member of the State house of representatives in 1898 and 1899; member of the Democratic executive committee in 1905 and 1906; appointed judge of the city court of Sylvania in December 1902 and served until October 1, 1906, when he resigned; elected as a Democrat to the Fifty-ninth Congress to fill the vacancy caused by the death of Rufus E. Lester and served from October 3, 1906, to March 4, 1907; resumed the practice of law in Sylvania; delegate to the Democratic National Convention at Baltimore in 1912; elected to the Sixty-fifth, Sixty-sixth, and Sixty-seventh Congresses (March 4, 1917–March 3, 1923); unsuccessful candidate for renomination in 1922; resumed the practice of law in Sylvania, Ga., where he died December 4, 1938; interment in Sylvania Cemetery.

OVERSTREET, Jesse, a Representative from Indiana; born in Franklin, Johnson County, Ind., December 14, 1859; attended the schools of his native city; was graduated from the Franklin High School in 1877 and from Franklin College in 1882; studied law; was admitted to the bar in 1886 and commenced practice in Franklin; member of the Republican State central committee of Indiana in 1892; elected as a Republican to the Fifty-fourth and to the six succeeding Congresses (March 4, 1895–March 3, 1909); unsuccessful candidate for reelection in 1908 to the Sixty-first Congress; resumed the practice of his profession; died in Indianapolis, Ind., May 27, 1910; interment in the Columbus City Cemetery, Columbus, Ind.

OVERTON, Edward, Jr., a Representative from Pennsylvania; born in Towanda, Bradford County, Pa., February 4, 1836; attended Susquehanna Collegiate Institute, Towanda, Pa., and was graduated from Princeton College in 1856; studied law; was admitted to the bar in 1858 and commenced practice in Towanda, Pa.; solicitor of Bradford County in 1861; during the Civil War entered the Union Army in September 1861 as a major in the Fiftieth Regiment, Pennsylvania Volunteer Infantry; promoted to lieutenant colonel in 1863 and from that time commanded the regiment until mustered out in October 1864; served as register in bankruptcy 1867–1876; elected as a Republican to the Forty-fifth and Forty-sixth Congresses (March 4, 1877–March 3, 1881); unsuccessful candidate for renomination in 1880; resumed the practice of law; president of the Citizens' National Bank of Towanda from 1897 until his death in Towanda, Pa., September 18, 1903; interment in Oak Hill Cemetery.

OVERTON, John Holmes (uncle of Overton Brooks), a Representative and a Senator from Louisiana; born in Marksville, Avoyelles Parish, La., September 17, 1875; attended the public schools; was graduated from the Louisiana State University at Baton Rouge in 1895 and from the law department of Tulane University, New Orleans, La., in 1897; was admitted to the bar in 1898 and commenced practice in Alexandria, La.; member of the board of supervisors of Louisiana State University; elected as a Democrat to the Seventy-second Congress to fill the vacancy caused by the death of James B. Aswell and served from May 12, 1931, to March 3, 1933; did not seek renomination in 1932, having become a candidate for Senator; elected to the United States Senate in 1932; reelected in 1938, and again in 1944, and served from March 4, 1933, until his death in the naval hospital at Bethesda, Md., on May 14, 1948; interment in Mount Olivet Cemetery, Pineville, La.

OVERTON, Walter Hampden, a Representative from Louisiana; born near Louisa Court House, Va., in 1788; moved in infancy with his father to North Carolina, and thence to Tennessee in 1801; attended the common schools; entered the Army May 3, 1808, as first lieutenant in the Seventh Infantry; promoted to the rank of captain December 3, 1810, and to major in the Third Rifles February 21, 1814; transferred to the Artillery Corps May 17, 1815; brevetted lieutenant colonel December 23, 1814, "for gallant conduct at the Battle of New Orleans," where he commanded Forts Jackson and St. Phillip below New Orleans; resigned October 31, 1815; commissioned major general of militia by the Louisiana Legislature; settled near Alexandria, Rapides Parish, La.; member of courthouse building commission in 1820 and 1821; member of the commission on navigation of Bayou Rapides in 1824; engaged in planting; elected as a Democrat to the Twenty-first Congress (March 4, 1829–March 3, 1831); was not a candidate for renomination in 1830 to the Twenty-second Congress; returned to his plantation near Alexandria, Rapides Parish, La.; died near Alexandria December 24, 1845; interment in McNutt Hill Cemetery.

OWEN, Allen Ferdinand, a Representative from Georgia; born on a plantation near the Yadkin River, Wilkes County, N. C., October 9, 1816; moved to Talbotton, Talbot County, Ga.; studied under private teachers; was graduated from Franklin College, Athens, Ga., from Yale College in 1837, and from the Dane Law School of Harvard University in 1839; was admitted to the bar at Boston in 1839 and commenced practice in Talbotton, Ga., in 1840; member of the State house of representatives 1843–1847; clerk of the State house of representatives in 1848; delegate to the Whig National Convention at Philadelphia in 1848; elected as a Whig to the Thirty-first Congress (March 4, 1849–March 3, 1851); later became affiliated with the Democratic Party; consul at Habana, Cuba, from May to December 1851; resumed the practice of law in Talbotton, Ga.; died in Upatoi, Muscogee County, Ga., April 7, 1865, while on a visit with relatives; interment in Oak Hill Cemetery, Talbotton, Ga.

OWEN, Emmett Marshall, a Representative from Georgia; born on a farm near Hollonville, Pike County, Ga., October 19, 1877; attended the Hollonville grammar school; was graduated from Gordon Institute, Barnesville, Ga., in 1898 and from the law department of the University of Georgia at Athens in 1900; taught school in Butts County, Ga., in 1901 and 1902; was admitted to the bar in 1902 and commenced practice in Zebulon, Ga.; also operated a large peach farm; member of the State house of representatives 1902–1906; mayor of Zebulon 1905–1907; served as solicitor of the Pike County Court 1906–1909, as solicitor of the city court of Zebulon, Ga., 1909–1912, as solicitor general for the Flint judicial circuit 1913–1923, and as solicitor general for the Griffin judicial circuit 1923–1933; elected as a Democrat to the Seventy-third and to the three succeeding Congresses and served from March 4, 1933, until his death in Washington, D. C., on June 21, 1939; interment in East View Cemetery, Zebulon, Ga.

OWEN, George Washington, a Representative from Alabama; born in Brunswick County, Va., on October 20, 1796; moved with his parents to Tennessee; attended the common schools and was graduated from the University of Nashville, Tennessee; studied law; was admitted to the bar in 1816 and

commenced practice in Claiborne, Ala.; unsuccessful candidate for election in 1821 to the Seventeenth Congress; member of the State house of representatives 1819–1821 and served as speaker in 1821; elected to the Eighteenth, Nineteenth, and Twentieth Congresses (March 4, 1823–March 3, 1829); appointed collector of the port of Mobile by President Jackson and served from April 20, 1828, to July 20, 1836; elected mayor of Mobile in 1836 and held the position until his death, which occurred on his plantation near Mobile, Ala., August 18, 1837; interment in the Old Church Street Cemetery, Mobile, Ala.

OWEN, James, a Representative from North Carolina; born near Wilmington, Bladen County, N. C., on December 7, 1784; educated at Bingham's Academy, Pittsboro, N. C.; engaged in agricultural pursuits; member of the State house of commons 1808–1811; served as president of the Wilmington & Raleigh Railroad Co.; elected as a Democrat to the Fifteenth Congress (March 4, 1817–March 3, 1819); died in Wilmington, N. C., September 4, 1865; interment in Oakdale Cemetery.

OWEN, Robert Dale, a Representative from Indiana; born in Glasgow, Scotland, November 9, 1800; studied under private teachers and attended the Emanuel von Fellenberg School at Hofwyl, near Berne, Switzerland, 1820–1823; immigrated to the United States in 1825 with his parents, who settled in Posey County, Ind.; aided his father in the establishment of the social community of New Harmony, Ind., and on the failure of that project he returned to Europe for further study; returned to the United States in 1827 and became a citizen; was the founder and editor of the Free Enquirer, published in New York, 1828–1832; returned to New Harmony in 1832; member of the State house of representatives 1835–1838; unsuccessful candidate for election in 1838 to the Twenty-sixth Congress and in 1840 to the Twenty-seventh Congress; elected as a Democrat to the Twenty-eighth and Twenty-ninth Congresses (March 4, 1843–March 3, 1847); unsuccessful candidate for reelection in 1846 to the Thirtieth Congress; member of the State constitutional convention in 1850; member of the State house of representatives in 1851; appointed by President Franklin Pierce as Chargé d'Affaires to the Two Sicilies May 24, 1853, and Minister Resident June 29, 1854, serving until September 20, 1858; devoted the remainder of his life to writing on social problems; died at his summer home "Cosy Cove," at Crosbyside, on Lake George, N. Y., June 24, 1877; interment in the Village Cemetery at Lake George, Warren County, N. Y.

OWEN, Robert Latham, a Senator from Oklahoma; born in Lynchburg, Campbell County, Va., February 3, 1856; attended private schools in Lynchburg, Va., and Baltimore, Md.; was graduated from Washington and Lee University, Lexington, Va., in 1877; studied law; was admitted to the bar in 1880 and commenced practice in Tahlequah, Indian Territory (now the State of Oklahoma); moved to Salina, Okla., in September 1879; member of the Democratic National Committee 1892–1896; organized the First National Bank of Muskogee in 1890 and was its president for ten years; delegate to the Democratic National Conventions in 1892, 1896, and 1924; vice chairman of the Democratic campaign committee in Oklahoma in 1906; upon the admission of Oklahoma as a State into the Union was elected as a Democrat to the United States Senate for the term ending March 3, 1913; reelected in 1912, and again in 1918, and served from December 11, 1907, to March 3, 1925; declined to be a candidate for renomination in 1924 and retired from public service; resumed the practice of law in Washington, D. C.; organized and served as chairman of the National Popular Government League from 1913 until his death in Washington, D. C., July 19, 1947; interment in Spring Hill Cemetery, Lynchburg, Va.

OWEN, Ruth Bryan (later Mrs. Borge Rohde; daughter of William Jennings Bryan), a Representative from Florida; born in Jacksonville, Morgan County, Ill., October 2, 1885; moved to Lincoln, Nebr., with her parents in 1887; educated in the public schools; attended Monticello Seminary, Godfrey, Ill., and the University of Nebraska at Lincoln; spent three years in Jamaica, West Indies, 1910–1912, and three years in London, England, 1912–1915; member of the executive committee of the American Women's War Relief Fund in London, England, which financed and operated the American Women's War Hospital at Paignton, Devonshire, in 1914 and 1915; served as war nurse in the Voluntary Aid Detachment in the Egypt-Palestine campaign 1915–1918; returned to the United States in 1919 and settled in Miami, Fla.; Lyceum and Chautauqua lecturer 1918–1928; author; vice president of the board of regents of the University of Miami 1925–1928, and member of the faculty 1926–1928; elected as a Democrat to the Seventy-first and Seventy-second Congresses (March 4, 1929–March 3, 1933); unsuccessful candidate for renomination in 1932; delegate to the Interparliamentary Union at London in 1930; appointed Minister to Denmark by President Franklin D. Roosevelt on April 13, 1933, and served until her resignation on August 30, 1936; special assistant in the Division of Public Liaison of the Department of State at the San Francisco Conference in 1945; member of the Advisory Board of the Federal Reformatory for Women 1938–1954; member of the board of trustees of the Starr Commonwealth for Boys 1941–1954; engaged in literary work and lecturing and resided in Ossining, N. Y.; died while on a visit in Copenhagen, Denmark, July 26, 1954; remains were cremated and the ashes buried in Ordrup Cemetery, near Copenhagen, Denmark.

OWEN, William Dale, a Representative from Indiana; born in Bloomington, Ind., on September 6, 1846; attended Indiana University at Bloomington in 1865 and entered upon the study of law; relinquished law for the ministry; pastor of the Logansport (Ind.) Christian Church until 1878; presidential elector on the Republican ticket of Garfield and Arthur in 1880; elected as a Republican to the Forty-ninth, Fiftieth, and Fifty-first Congresses (March 4, 1885–March 3, 1891); unsuccessful candidate for reelection in 1890 to the Fifty-second Congress; elected secretary of state of Indiana and served from January 16, 1895, to January 15, 1899; engaged in real-estate speculation and interested in rubber plantations in Mexico; in 1906 went to Europe, where he died.

OWENS, George Welshman, a Representative from Georgia; born in Savannah, Ga., August 29, 1786; attended school in Harrow, England, and was graduated from the University of Cambridge; studied law in the office of Mr. Chitty in London; returned to Savannah, Ga.; was admitted to the bar and practiced; elected as a Unionist to the Twenty-fourth and Twenty-fifth Congresses (March 4, 1835–March 3, 1839); resumed the practice of law; died in Savannah, Ga., March 2, 1856; interment in Laurel Grove Cemetery.

OWENS, James W., a Representative from Ohio; born in Springfield Township, Franklin County, Ind., October 24, 1837; pursued academic studies; was graduated from Miami University, Oxford, Ohio, in 1862; during the Civil War enlisted in the Union Army as a private in the Twentieth Regiment, Ohio Volunteer Infantry, for three months' service; reenlisted and was made first lieutenant of Company A, Eighty-sixth Regiment, Ohio Volunteer Infantry, and on the reorganization of that regiment was made captain of Company K; attended the law department of the University of Michigan at Ann Arbor in 1864 and 1865; was admitted to the bar in 1865 and commenced practice in Newark, Licking County, Ohio; elected

prosecuting attorney of Licking County in 1867 and reelected in 1869; elected to the State senate in 1875; reelected in 1877, and served as president of that body; member of the board of trustees of Miami University 1878–1896; elected as a Democrat to the Fifty-first and Fifty-second Congresses (March 4, 1889–March 3, 1893); was not a candidate for renomination in 1892; resumed the practice of his profession; died in Newark, Licking County, Ohio, on March 30, 1900; interment in Cedar Hill Cemetery.

OWENS, Thomas Leonard, a Representative from Illinois; born in Chicago, Cook County, Ill., December 21, 1897; attended the parochial schools, Northwestern University, Chicago, Ill., and De Paul University, Chicago, Ill.; was graduated from Loyola University Law School, Chicago, Ill., in 1926; was admitted to the bar in 1927 and commenced practice in Chicago, Ill.; during the First World War served in the Students' Army Training Corps at Loyola University in 1918; elected as a Republican to the Eightieth Congress and served from January 3, 1947, until his death in the naval hospital, Bethesda, Md., June 7, 1948; interment in All Saints' Cemetery, Chicago, Ill.

OWENS, William Claiborne, a Representative from Kentucky; born near Georgetown, Scott County, Ky., October 17, 1849; attended the common schools, also Kentucky Wesleyan College, Millersburg Ky., Transylvania University, Lexington, Ky., and was graduated from Columbia Law College, New York City, in 1872; was admitted to the bar in the same year and commenced practice in Georgetown, Ky.; prosecuting attorney for Scott County from 1874 to 1877, when he resigned; member of the State house of representatives 1877–1887 and served as speaker in 1882 and 1883; presidential elector on the Democratic ticket of Hancock and English in 1880; delegate to the Democratic National Convention at Chicago in 1892; elected as a Democrat to the Fifty-fourth Congress (March 4, 1895–March 3, 1897); was not a candidate for renomination in 1896; became affiliated with the Republican Party in 1896; major in the Second Regiment, Kentucky Volunteers, during the Spanish-American War in 1898; moved to Louisville, Ky., in 1900 and resumed the practice of law; died in Louisville, Ky., November 18, 1925; interment in Georgetown Cemetery, Georgetown, Ky.

OWSLEY, Bryan Young, a Representative from Kentucky; born near Crab Orchard, Lincoln County, Ky., August 19, 1798; attended the common schools of Lincoln County; studied law and was admitted to the bar; moved to Jamestown, Ky.; clerk of the circuit court in 1827; presidential elector on the Whig ticket of Harrison and Tyler in 1840; elected as a Whig to the Twenty-seventh Congress (March 4, 1841–March 3, 1843); unsuccessful candidate for reelection in 1842 to the Twenty-eighth Congress; register of the United States land office, with residence in Frankfort, 1845–1849; died in Frankfort, Franklin County, Ky., on October 27, 1849.

P

PACA, William, a Delegate from Maryland; born at "Wye Hall," near Abingdon, Queen Anne (now Harford) County, Md., October 31, 1740; was graduated from Philadelphia College in 1759; studied law in Annapolis, Md., and in the Middle Temple, London, England; was admitted to the bar in 1764; returned home and commenced the practice of his profession at Annapolis in 1764; member of the provincial assembly 1771–1774; Member of the Continental Congress 1774–1779; a signer of the Declaration of Independence; served in the State senate 1777–1779; chief judge of the superior court of Maryland 1778–1780; chief justice of the court of appeals in prize and admiralty cases 1780–1782; Governor of Maryland from November 1782 to November 1785; was influential in establishing Washington College in Chestertown, Md., in 1786; delegate to the State convention in 1788 which ratified the Federal Constitution; appointed by President Washington as judge of the United States Court for Maryland and served from 1789 until his death at "Wye Hall," Queen Anne County, Md., October 23, 1799; interment in the family burial ground, Queen Anne County, Md.

PACE, Stephen, a Representative from Georgia; born in Terrell County, Ga., near Dawson, March 9, 1891; attended the public schools and Georgia School of Technology at Atlanta; was graduated from the law department of the University of Georgia at Athens in 1914; was admitted to the bar the same year and commenced practice in Americus, Ga.; also engaged in agricultural pursuits; served in the State house of representatives 1917–1920; was a member of the State senate in 1923 and 1924; elected as a Democrat to the Seventy-fifth and to the six succeeding Congresses (January 3, 1937–January 3, 1951); did not seek renomination in 1950; resumed the practice of law in Americus, Ga., where he now resides.

PACHECO, Romualdo, a Representative from California; born in Santa Barbara, Calif., October 31, 1831; was instructed by private tutors; engaged in nautical pursuits and subsequently in agriculture; member of the State senate in 1851 and again in 1861; member of the State assembly 1853–1855 and 1868–1870; county judge 1855–1859; State treasurer 1863–1866; Lieutenant Governor 1871–1875, and became Governor when Governor Booth was elected to the United States Senate in 1875; presented credentials as a Republican Member-elect to the Forty-fifth Congress and served from March 4, 1877, to February 7, 1878, when he was succeeded by Peter D. Wigginton, who contested his election; elected as a Republican to the Forty-sixth and Forty-seventh Congresses (March 4, 1879–March 3, 1883); appointed Envoy Extraordinary and Minister Plenipotentiary to the Central American States December 11, 1890, to Honduras and Guatemala July 1, 1891, and served to June 21, 1893; discontinued active pursuits in 1893 and lived in retirement until his death in Oakland, Calif., January 23, 1899; interment in Mountain View Cemetery.

PACKARD, Jasper, a Representative from Indiana; born in Austintown, Mahoning County, Ohio, February 1, 1832; moved with his parents to Indiana in 1835; attended the public schools, and was graduated from the University of Michigan at Ann Arbor in 1855; taught school; settled in La Porte, Ind.; studied law and was admitted to the bar in 1861; during the Civil War enlisted in the Union Army as a private in the Forty-eighth Regiment, Indiana Volunteer Infantry, October 24, 1861; promoted to first lieutenant January 1, 1862; captain September 12, 1862; lieutenant colonel of the One Hundred and Twenty-eighth Regiment, Indiana Volunteer Infantry, March 17, 1864; colonel June 26, 1865; brevetted brigadier general March 13, 1865, "for meritorious services"; mustered out April 10, 1866; auditor of La Porte County from November 15, 1866, to March 1, 1869, when he resigned; elected as a Republican to the Forty-first, Forty-second, and Forty-third Congresses (March 4, 1869–March 3, 1875); was not a candidate for renomination in 1874; engaged in newspaper pursuits; appointed July 1, 1899, commandant of the State soldiers' home at LaFayette, Ind., and died there December 13, 1899; interment in the Soldiers' Home Cemetery.

PACKER, Asa, a Representative from Pennsylvania; born in Mystic, New London County, Conn., December 29, 1805; attended the district schools; moved to Springfield, Pa., in 1820; learned the trade of carpenter; moved to Mauch Chunk, Pa., in 1833; engaged in mercantile pursuits, and established a boat yard for the construction of canal boats; became interested in the production of coal and also in railroads; member of the State house of representatives in 1842 and 1843; associate judge of Carbon County in 1843 and 1844; built the Lehigh Valley Railroad in 1852 and was president of the company at the time of his death; elected as a Democrat to the Thirty-third and Thirty-fourth Congresses (March 4, 1853–March 3, 1857); declined to be a candidate for renomination in 1856; resumed his former business interests; founded Lehigh University, Bethlehem, Pa.; delegate to the Democratic National Convention at New York City in 1868; died in Philadelphia, Pa., on May 17, 1879; interment in the Mauch Chunk Cemetery, Mauch Creek, Pa.

PACKER, Horace Billings, a Representative from Pennsylvania; born in Wellsboro, Tioga County, Pa., on October 11, 1851; attended the common schools, the Wellsboro Academy, and Alfred (N. Y.) University; studied law; was admitted to the bar of Tioga County in 1873 and commenced practice in Wellsboro; also engaged in the real-estate business; district attorney of Tioga County 1875–1879; elected to the State house of representatives in 1884 and reelected in 1886; member of the State senate 1888–1892; served many years as a member of the borough council; presided over the Republican State conventions of 1893 and 1894; elected as a Republican to the Fifty-fifth and Fifty-sixth Congresses (March 4, 1897–March 3, 1901); was not a candidate for renomination in 1900; resumed the practice of law in Wellsboro, Pa.; also engaged in the real-estate, banking, and lumber businesses; presidential elector on the Republican ticket of Hughes and Fairbanks in 1916; delegate to the Republican National Convention at Cleveland in 1924; died in Wellsboro, Pa., April 13, 1940; interment in Wellsboro Cemetery.

PACKER, John Black, a Representative from Pennsylvania; born in Sunbury, Northumberland County, Pa., March 21, 1824; received private instructions and later attended Sunbury (Pa.) Academy; member of the corps of engineers employed by the State in the survey and construction of public improvements 1839–1842; studied law; was admitted to the bar on August 6, 1844, and commenced the practice of his profession in Sunbury; also engaged in banking; deputy attorney general 1845–1847; served in the State house of representatives in 1850 and 1851; one of the organizers of the Susquehanna Railroad Co., in 1851; elected as a Republican to the Forty-first and to the three succeeding Congresses (March 4, 1869–March 3, 1877); declined to be a candidate for renomination in 1876; declined the appointment as Postmaster General in the Cabinet of President Grant in 1874; resumed the practice of law in Sunbury, Pa.; also resumed his banking activities; died in Sunbury, Pa., July 7, 1891; interment in Pomfret Manor Cemetery.

PADDOCK, Algernon Sidney, a Senator from Nebraska; born at Glens Falls, Warren County, N. Y., November 9, 1830; attended the public schools, Glens Falls Academy, and Union College, Schenectady, N. Y., until his senior year; taught school and studied law; moved to Omaha, Nebr., in 1857; was admitted to the bar in 1857 and commenced practice in Omaha; unsuccessful candidate for the Territorial house of representatives in 1858; delegate to the first Territorial convention in 1859; engaged in editorial work on the Omaha Republican in 1858 and 1859; delegate to the Republican National Convention at Chicago in 1860 and at Baltimore in 1864; appointed secretary of the Territory of Nebraska in 1861, which office he held until the Territory was admitted as a State into the Union in 1867; performed the duties of Acting Governor part of this time; unsuccessful candidate for election in 1866 to the Fortieth Congress; unsuccessful Republican candidate for United States Senator in 1867; declined to accept the position of Governor of the Territory of Wyoming in 1868; moved to Beatrice, Gage County, Nebr., in 1872 and engaged in manufacturing and agricultural pursuits; elected as a Republican to the United States Senate and served from March 4, 1875, to March 3, 1881; unsuccessful candidate for reelection; member of the Federal commission having jurisdiction over elections in the Territory of Utah, from June 1882 until October 1, 1886, when he resigned; again elected to the United States Senate and served from March 4, 1887, to March 3, 1893; engaged in the brokerage business; died in Beatrice, Nebr., October 17, 1897; interment in Prospect Hill Cemetery, Omaha, Nebr.

PADDOCK, George Arthur, a Representative from Illinois; born in Winnetka, Cook County, Ill., March 24, 1885; attended the public schools; was graduated from Chicago (Ill.) Manual Training School in 1902 and from the University of Virginia at Charlottesville in 1906; studied law at the University of Virginia; was admitted to the bar in 1907 and commenced practice in Chicago, Ill.; attended Plattsburg Training Camp in 1916 and the officers' training camp at Fort Sheridan in 1917; during the First World War served as a captain and later as a major of the Three Hundred and Forty-second Infantry, Eighty-sixth Division, 1917–1919; resumed the practice of law at Chicago, Ill.; investment banker since 1921; served as alderman of Evanston, Ill., 1931–1937 and as park commissioner 1929–1931, 1937, and 1938; delegate to the Republican State convention in 1936; member of the Soldiers' and Sailors' Service Commission of Illinois; member and treasurer of Cook County Republican central committee 1938–1942; elected as a Republican to the Seventy-seventh Congress (January 3, 1941–January 3, 1943); unsuccessful candidate for renomination in 1942; resumed investment banking and is a resident of Evanston, Ill.

PADGETT, Lemuel Phillips, a Representative from Tennessee; born in Columbia, Maury County, Tenn., November 28, 1855; attended private schools in the county, and was graduated from Erskine College, Due West, S. C., in 1876; began the study of law in September 1876; was admitted to the bar in March 1877 and commenced practice in Columbia, Tenn., in January 1879; presidential elector on the Democratic ticket of Cleveland and Hendricks in 1884; member of the State senate in 1898; elected as a Democrat to the Fifty-seventh and to the ten succeeding Congresses and served from March 4, 1901, until his death in Washington, D. C., August 2, 1922; interment in Rose Hill Cemetery, Columbia, Tenn.

PAGÁN, Bolívar, a Resident Commissioner from Puerto Rico; born in Guayanilla, P. R., May 16, 1897; attended the public schools of Adjuntas, P. R., and Ponce (P. R.) High School; was graduated from the law department of the University of Puerto Rico at Río Piedras in 1921; was admitted to the bar the same year and commenced practice in San Juan, P. R.; judge of Fajardo, P. R., in 1922; member of the insular board of elections 1923–1951; unsuccessful candidate for election to the Puerto Rican House of Representatives in 1924; city treasurer of San Juan, P. R., 1925–1929; unsuccessful candidate for election to the Puerto Rican Senate in 1928; associate commissioner of the Public Service Commission of Puerto Rico 1930–1933; member of the Puerto Rican Senate 1933–1939 and served as president pro tempore and majority floor leader; city manager of San Juan, P. R., in 1936 and 1937; member of the American Group of the Interparliamentary Union; also engaged as writer and editor; appointed by Governor Leahy as a Coalitionist a Resident

Commissioner to the United States on December 26, 1939, to fill the vacancy caused by the death of Santiago Iglesias for the term ending January 3, 1941; elected in 1940 for the term ending January 3, 1945; was not a candidate for renomination in 1944; again elected a member of the senate of Puerto Rico for terms 1945–1949 and 1949–1953; practiced law in San Juan, P. R., until his death there February 9, 1961; interment in Puerto Rico Memorial Cemetery, Carolina, P. R.

PAGE, Carroll Smalley, a Senator from Vermont; born in Westfield, Orleans County, Vt., January 10, 1843; attended the common schools, People's Academy, Morrisville, Vt., and Lamoille Central Academy, Hyde Park, Lamoille County, Vt.; dealer in raw calfskins at Hyde Park, Vt.; president of the Lamoille County Savings Bank & Trust Co. and of the Lamoille County National Bank, both of Hyde Park, Vt.; director of the Swanton Savings Bank & Trust Co. of Swanton, Vt., and of several other corporations; member of the State house of representatives 1869–1872; served in the State senate 1874–1876; secretary of the Republican State committee 1872–1890 and served as chairman 1886–1890; delegate to the Republican National Conventions at Chicago in 1880 and 1912; register of probate court 1880–1891; savings-bank examiner 1884–1888; Governor of Vermont 1890–1892; elected as a Republican to the United States Senate in 1908 to fill the vacancy caused by the death of Redfield Proctor; reelected in 1910 and 1916 and served from October 21, 1908, to March 3, 1923; was not a candidate for reelection in 1922; resided in Hyde Park, Vt., until his death on December 3, 1925; interment in Hyde Park Cemetery.

PAGE, Charles Harrison, a Representative from Rhode Island; born in Gloucester, Providence County, R. I., July 19, 1843; attended the public schools; during the Civil War enlisted in the Union Army as a private at the age of nineteen in Company A, Twelfth Regiment, Rhode Island Volunteer Infantry, and was mustered out July 29, 1863; resumed studies in the Illinois State Normal School at Bloomington and at Southern Illinois College at Carbondale; returned to Rhode Island in 1869 and taught school in Scituate until the spring of 1870, when he entered the law department of the University of Albany, New York; was graduated in 1871; was admitted to the bar the same year and commenced practice in Scituate, and in Providence, R. I., in 1872; member of the State house of representatives in 1872 and 1873; served in the State Senate in 1874, 1875, 1884, 1885, and 1890; unsuccessful candidate for election in 1876 to the Forty-fifth Congress; candidate for attorney general in 1879; delegate to the Democratic National Conventions in 1880, 1884, and 1888; contested as a Democrat the election of William A. Pirce to the Forty-ninth Congress, but the seat was declared vacant; subsequently elected at a special election to fill the vacancy thus caused and served from February 21 to March 3, 1887; elected to the Fifty-second Congress (March 4, 1891–March 3, 1893); reelected to the Fifty-third Congress at a special election (no candidate receiving a majority at the regular election), and served from April 5, 1893, to March 3, 1895; was not a candidate for renomination in 1894; resumed the practice of law until his death in Providence, R. I., July 21, 1912; interment in Swan Point Cemetery.

PAGE, Henry, a Representative from Maryland; born in Princess Anne, Somerset County, Md., June 28, 1841; received preparatory instruction at the school of Anthony Bolivar, West Chester, Pa.; attended the University of Virginia at Charlottesville; studied law; was admitted to the bar in 1864 and commenced practice in Princess Anne, Somerset County, Md.; member of the constitutional convention in 1867; State's attorney for Somerset County 1870–1884; presidential elector on the Democratic ticket of Cleveland and Thurman in 1888; elected as a Democrat to the Fifty-second Congress and served from March 4, 1891, until September 3, 1892, when he resigned to become a judge of the Maryland Court of Appeals; appointed chief judge of the first judicial district of Maryland in August 1892; elected to the position in November 1893 for a term of fifteen years; died in Princess Anne, Md., January 7, 1913; interment in Manokin Presbyterian Church Cemetery.

PAGE, Horace Francis, a Representative from California; born near Medina, Orleans County, N. Y., October 20, 1833; attended the public schools and Millville Academy; taught school in La Porte County, Ind., until 1854, when he moved to California and engaged in the sawmill business near Colfax; moved to Placerville and engaged in the livery-stable business; became engaged in mining and as a mail contractor and stage proprietor; studied law; was admitted to the bar and commenced practice in California; unsuccessful Republican candidate for the State senate in 1869; major in the California Militia; elected as a Republican to the Forty-third and to the four succeeding Congresses (March 4, 1873–March 3, 1883); unsuccessful candidate for reelection in 1882 to the Forty-eighth Congress; delegate to the Republican National Convention at Chicago in 1884; resumed the practice of law in Washington, D. C.; died in San Francisco, Calif., August 23, 1890; interment in Mountain View Cemetery, Oakland, Calif.

PAGE, John (brother of Mann Page), a Representative from Virginia; born at "Rosewell," Gloucester County, Va., April 17, 1744; was graduated from William and Mary College, Williamsburg, Va., in 1763; served under Washington in an expedition against the French and Indians; delegate to the State constitutional convention in 1776; Lieutenant Governor of Virginia when the Revolution started; raised a regiment of militia from Gloucester County; colonel in the Revolutionary Army; member of the State house of delegates 1781–1783 and 1785–1788; elected as a Democrat to the First and to the three succeeding Congresses (March 4, 1789–March 3, 1797); again a member of the State house of delegates in 1797, 1798, 1800, and 1801; presidential elector in 1800; Governor of Virginia 1802–1805; appointed United States commissioner of loans for Virginia and held office until his death in Richmond, Va., October 11, 1808; interment in St. John's Churchyard.

PAGE, John, a Senator from New Hampshire; born in Haverhill, Grafton County, N. H., May 21, 1787; attended the public schools; engaged in agricultural pursuits; served as lieutenant in the War of 1812; assistant United States tax assessor in 1813, and assessor in 1815; member of the State house of representatives 1818–1820 and again in 1835; register of deeds for Grafton County in 1827 and 1829–1835; selectman of Haverhill for fourteen terms; served as town clerk; member of Governor's council in 1836 and 1838; elected as a Democrat to the United States Senate to fill the vacancy caused by the resignation of Isaac Hill and served from June 8, 1836, to March 3, 1837; unsuccessful candidate for reelection; resumed agricultural pursuits; Governor of New Hampshire 1840–1842; died in Haverhill, N. H., September 8, 1865; interment in Ladd Street Cemetery.

PAGE, Mann (brother of John Page, of Virginia), a Delegate from Virginia; born at "Rosewell," Gloucester County, Va., in 1749; studied under a private teacher, and was graduated from the College of William and Mary, Williamsburg, Va.; studied law; was admitted to the bar and practiced; managed a large estate; member of the State house of burgesses; moved to Spotsylvania County; Member of the Continental Congress in

1777; died on his estate, "Mansfield," near Fredericksburg, Spotsylvania County, Va., in 1781; interment near Fredericksburg.

PAGE, Robert, a Representative from Virginia; born at "North End," Gloucester (now Mathews) County, Va., February 4, 1765; received a liberal education from tutors at home; attended the College of William and Mary, Williamsburg, Va., which he left to join the Revolutionary Army, serving as a captain; studied law; was admitted to the bar and practiced in Frederick (now Clarke) and adjacent counties; planter; member of the council of state; member of the State house of delegates in 1795; elected as a Federalist to the Sixth Congress (March 4, 1799–March 3, 1801); resumed former activities; died at "Janeville," Clarke County, Va., December 8, 1840; interment in Old Chapel Cemetery near Millwood, Clarke (then Frederick) County, Va.

PAGE, Robert Newton, a Representative from North Carolina; born in Cary, Wake County, N. C., October 26, 1859; attended the Cary High School and Bingham Military School, Mebane, N. C.; moved to Aberdeen, Moore County, N. C., in 1880 and engaged in the lumber business near Aberdeen until 1900; mayor of Aberdeen 1890–1898; treasurer of the Aberdeen & Asheboro Railroad Co. 1894–1902; moved to Biscoe, Montgomery County, N. C., in 1897; member of the State house of representatives in 1901 and 1902; elected as a Democrat to the Fifty-eighth and to the six succeeding Congresses (March 4, 1903–March 3, 1917); was not a candidate for renomination in 1916; returned to Aberdeen in 1920; engaged in banking, and was president of the Page Trust Co.; died in Aberdeen, N. C., October 3, 1933; interment in Old Bethesda Cemetery.

PAGE, Sherman, a Representative from New York; born in Cheshire, Conn., May 9, 1779; attended the common schools; taught school in Coventry, N. Y., in 1799; studied law; was admitted to the bar in 1805 and commenced practice in Unadilla, Otsego County, N. Y.; member of the State assembly in 1827; judge of the court of common pleas in Otsego County; elected as a Jackson Democrat to the Twenty-third and Twenty-fourth Congresses (March 4, 1833–March 3, 1837); died in Unadilla, N. Y., September 27, 1853; interment in St. Matthew's Cemetery.

PAIGE, Calvin DeWitt, a Representative from Massachusetts; born in Southbridge, Worcester County, Mass., May 20, 1848; attended the public schools and was graduated from the high school; president of the Central Cotton Mills Co., the Southbridge Savings Bank, and the Edwards Co.; served as selectman of Southbridge; member of the State house of representatives in 1878 and 1879; delegate to the Republican National Convention at Chicago in 1884; member of the Governor's council in 1906 and 1907; elected as a Republican to the Sixty-third Congress to fill the vacancy caused by the death of William H. Wilder; reelected to the Sixty-fourth and to the four succeeding Congresses and served from November 26, 1913, to March 3, 1925; voluntarily withdrew from public life, and engaged in banking in Southbridge, Mass., until his death there on April 24, 1930; interment in Oak Ridge Cemetery.

PAIGE, David Raymond, a Representative from Ohio; born in Madison, Lake County, Ohio, April 8, 1844; attended the public schools and Western Reserve Academy (a preparatory school), Hudson, Ohio; was graduated from Union College, Schenectady, N. Y., in 1865; engaged in the hardware business in Akron, Ohio; treasurer of Summit County 1875–1879; elected as a Democrat to the Forty-eighth Congress (March 4, 1883–March 3, 1885); engaged in the contracting business; died in New York City June 30, 1901; interment in Evergreen Cemetery, Painesville, Lake County, Ohio.

PAINE, Elijah, a Senator from Vermont; born in Brooklyn, Conn., January 21, 1757; attended the public schools; served in the Revolutionary War; was graduated from Harvard University in 1781; studied law; was admitted to the bar and commenced practice in Windsor, Vt.; practiced law and cultivated a farm; began a settlement at Williamstown; established a cloth factory and a saw and grist mill; secretary of the constitutional convention in 1786; member of the State house of representatives 1787–1791; judge of the State supreme court 1791–1795; elected as a Federalist to the United States Senate; reelected in 1800 and served from March 4, 1795, to September 1, 1801, when he resigned; United States judge of the district of Vermont from 1801 until his death in Williamstown, Orange County, Vt., April 28, 1842; interment in Old Williamstown Cemetery.

PAINE, Ephraim, a delegate from New York; was born in Canterbury, Conn., August 19, 1730; moved with his parents to Nine Partners, N. Y.; pursued preparatory studies; studied medicine and practiced in Amenia, Dutchess County, N. Y.; delegate to the Provincial Congress in 1775; county judge 1778–1781; member of the council of appointment in 1780; supervisor of Amenia in 1782 and 1783; served in the State senate 1780–1784; Member of the Continental Congress in 1784 and 1785; died in Amenia, N. Y., August 10, 1785; interment in Red Meeting House Cemetery, near Amenia.

PAINE, Halbert Eleazer, a Representative from Wisconsin; born in Chardon, Geauga County, Ohio, February 4, 1826; attended the common schools; was graduated from the Western Reserve College, Hudson, Ohio, in 1845; taught school for a season in Mississippi; studied law; was admitted to the bar in 1848 and commenced practice in Cleveland, Ohio; moved to Milwaukee, Wis., in 1857 and continued the practice of law; during the Civil War entered the Union Army in May 1861 as colonel of the Fourth Regiment, Wisconsin Volunteers; promoted to the rank of brigadier general on March 13, 1863, and in the following June lost a leg at Port Hudson; brevetted major general on March 13, 1865, and resigned on May 15, 1865; elected as a Republican to the Thirty-ninth, Fortieth, and Forty-first Congresses (March 4, 1865–March 3, 1871); was not a candidate for renomination in 1870; continued the practice of law in Washington, D. C.; through his efforts the taking of meteorological observations in the interior was inaugurated; appointed Commissioner of Patents by President Grant and served from November 1, 1878, to May 7, 1880; author of "Paine on Contested Elections," a work which is recognized as a legal authority on that phase of constitutional law, and one which was used in the Hayes-Tilden contest; died in Washington, D. C., April 14, 1905; interment in Arlington National Cemetery, Fort Myer, Va.

PAINE, Robert Treat, a Delegate from Massachusetts; born in Boston, Mass., March 11, 1731; attended the Boston Public Latin School, and was graduated from Harvard College in 1749; studied theology; was chaplain of troops on the northern frontier in 1755; studied law; was admitted to the bar in 1757 and commenced practice in Boston; moved to Taunton in 1761; delegate to the State convention at Boston in 1768; member of the colonial house of representatives in 1773; delegate to the Provincial Congress in 1774 and 1775; Member of the Continental Congress 1774–1778; a signer of the Declaration of Independence; member of the State house of representatives in 1777; attorney general of Massachusetts 1777–1790; member of the Governor's council in 1779 and 1780; delegate to the constitutional convention in 1779; moved to Boston in 1781; judge of the Massachusetts Supreme Court 1790–1804; died in Boston, Mass., May 12, 1814; interment in Granary Burying Ground.

PAINE, Robert Treat, a Representative from North Carolina; born in Edenton, Chowan County, N. C., February 18, 1812; attended private schools and was graduated from Washington (now Trinity) College, Hartford, Conn.; studied law; was admitted to the bar and practiced; held several local offices; owned and operated shipyards and engaged in the shipping business; member of the State house of commons in 1838, 1840, 1844, 1846, and 1848; served as colonel of a North Carolina regiment during the Mexican War; War Governor of Monterey, Mexico, in 1846; member of the Mexican Claims Commission after the war; elected by the American Party to the Thirty-fourth Congress (March 4, 1855–March 3, 1857); moved to Austin County, Tex., in 1860 and engaged in agricultural pursuits; died in Galveston, Tex., February 8, 1872; interment in Brenham Cemetery, Brenham, Tex.

PAINE, William Wiseham, a Representative from Georgia; born in Richmond, Va., on October 10, 1817; moved with his parents to Milledgeville, Baldwin County, Ga., in 1827; attended school in Mount Zion, Ga.; served in the Seminole Indian War in 1836; studied law in Washington, Wilkes County, Ga., and was admitted to the bar in 1838; moved to Telfair, Ga., in 1840 and commenced the practice of law; member of the State constitutional convention in 1850; served as private secretary to Gov. Howell Cobb in 1851 and 1852; served in the State senate 1857–1860; entered the Confederate Army and served as captain in the First Georgia Regiment throughout the Civil War; moved to Savannah, Ga., at the close of the Civil War and continued the practice of law; elected as a Democrat to the Forty-first Congress to fill the vacancy caused by the House declaring Joseph W. Clift not entitled to the seat, and served from December 22, 1870, to March 3, 1871; member of the State house of representatives 1877–1879; curator of the Georgia Historical Society; died in Savannah, Ga., August 5, 1882; interment in Bonaventure Cemetery.

PALEN, Rufus, a Representative from New York; born in Palenville, Greene County, N. Y., February 25, 1807; moved with his parents to Fallsburg, where he received a limited schooling; engaged in the manufacture of leather; held several local offices; elected as a Whig to the Twenty-sixth Congress (March 4, 1839–March 3, 1841); died in New York City April 26, 1844; interment in the Old Cemetery, Palenville, N. Y.

PALFREY, John Gorham, a Representative from Massachusetts; born in Boston, Mass., May 2, 1796; completed preparatory studies in Phillips Exeter Academy, Exeter, N. H., and was graduated from Harvard University in 1815; studied theology and was ordained minister of Brattle Square Unitarian Church, Boston, June 17, 1818; editor of the North American Review 1835–1843; member of the State house of representatives in 1842 and 1843; secretary of state of Massachusetts 1844–1848; elected as a Whig to the Thirtieth Congress (March 4, 1847–March 3, 1849); unsuccessful candidate on the Free-Soil ticket for reelection in 1848 to the Thirty-first Congress; postmaster of Boston 1861–1867; devoted himself to literary pursuits; died in Cambridge, Mass., April 26, 1881; interment in Mount Auburn Cemetery.

PALMER, Alexander Mitchell, a Representative from Pennsylvania; born near White Haven, Luzerne County, Pa., May 4, 1872; attended the public schools and prepared for college at the Moravian Parochial School, Bethlehem, Pa.; was graduated from Swarthmore (Pa.) College in 1891; appointed official stenographer of the forty-third judicial district of Pennsylvania in 1892; studied law; was admitted to the bar in 1893 and practiced in Stroudsburg, Pa.; director of various banks and public-service corporations; member of the Democratic State executive committee of Pennsylvania; elected as a Democrat to the Sixty-first, Sixty-second, and Sixty-third Congresses (March 4, 1909–March 3, 1915); was not a candidate for renomination in 1914; delegate to the Democratic National Convention at Baltimore in 1912 and at St. Louis in 1916; member of the Democratic National Committee 1912–1920; appointed Alien Property Custodian October 22, 1917, by President Wilson, and served until March 4, 1919, when he resigned to become Attorney General of the United States, in which capacity he served from March 5, 1919, until March 4, 1921; engaged in the practice of law in Washington, D. C., and Stroudsburg, Pa.; died in Washington, D. C., May 11, 1936; interment in Laurelwood Cemetery, Stroudsburg, Pa.

PALMER, Beriah, a Representative from New York; born in Bristol County, Mass., in 1740; attended the common schools; moved to Cornwall, Orange County, N. Y., in 1769; studied law; was admitted to the bar and practiced in New York; engaged in surveying and farming near Burnt Hills; moved to Ballston Spa, Saratoga County, N. Y., in 1774; served in the Twelfth Regiment of the New York Militia during the Revolutionary War; served as assessor in 1779; commissioner of roads, district of Ballston, in 1780, 1783, and 1784; served as postmaster in 1784; member of the committee of safety of Albany County; supervisor of Saratoga County in 1790, 1791, and 1799; moderator of the first board of supervisors of Saratoga County in 1791; appointed judge of the court of common pleas in 1791; member of the State assembly in 1792–1795; delegate to the State constitutional convention in 1801; elected to the Eighth Congress (March 4, 1803–March 3, 1805); surrogate of Saratoga County 1808–1812; died in Ballston Spa, N. Y., May 20, 1812; interment in the Village Cemetery.

PALMER, Cyrus Maffet, a Representative from Pennsylvania; born in Pottsville, Schuylkill County, Pa., February 12, 1887; educated in the public and high schools of Pottsville, and attended the University of Pennsylvania at Philadelphia, Pa., in 1907; studied law; was admitted to the bar in 1911 and commenced practice in Pottsville, Pa.; served in the State house of representatives 1916–1920; district attorney of Schuylkill County, Pa., 1920–1927; elected as a Republican to the Seventieth Congress (March 4, 1927–March 3, 1929); unsuccessful candidate for renomination in 1928; resumed the practice of law; alternate delegate to the Republican National Convention at Philadelphia in 1940; elected judge of the common pleas court of Schuylkill County, twenty-first judicial district of Pennsylvania, in 1931; reelected in 1941 and again in 1951; became president judge of the court January 1, 1940, and served until his death in Pottsville, Pa., August 16, 1959; interment in Charles Baber Cemetery.

PALMER, Francis Wayland (Frank), a Representative from Iowa; born in Manchester, Dearborn County, Ind., October 11, 1827; moved with his parents to Jamestown, N. Y., in boyhood; learned the printing trade on the Jamestown Journal in 1841; joint owner and subsequently sole proprietor of the Jamestown Journal 1848–1858; member of the State assembly in 1853 and again in 1854; moved to Dubuque, Iowa, in 1858, and became editor and one of the proprietors of the Dubuque Times; State printer of Iowa 1861–1869; settled in Des Moines in 1861 and was publisher and owner of the Iowa State Register; elected as a Republican to the Forty-first and Forty-second Congresses (March 4, 1869–March 3, 1873); was not a candidate for renomination in 1872; moved to Chicago, Ill., in 1873, purchased an interest in the Inter-Ocean and became its editor in chief; delegate to the Republican National Convention at Cincinnati

in 1876; postmaster of Chicago by appointment of President Hayes from February 26, 1877, to May 5, 1885; Public Printer of the United States from May 7, 1889, to May 2, 1894, and again from March 31, 1897, until September 8, 1905, when he was removed; died in Chicago, Ill., December 3, 1907; interment in Graceland Cemetery.

PALMER, George William (nephew of John Palmer and cousin of William Elisha Haynes), a Representative from New York; born in Hoosick, Rensselaer County, N. Y., January 13, 1818; attended the common schools, the Schodack Academy, Schodack, N. Y., and Yale College; studied law; was admitted to the bar about 1840 and commenced practice in Plattsburgh, N. Y.; surrogate of Clinton County, N. Y.; elected as a Republican to the Thirty-fifth and Thirty-sixth Congresses (March 4, 1857–March 3, 1861); was not a candidate for renomination in 1860; delegate to the Republican National Convention at Baltimore in 1864; appointed United States consul to Crete by President Lincoln; United States judge on the International Court for Suppression of Slave Trade on the West Coast of Africa from 1866 to 1870, when he resigned; member of the State assembly in 1884 and 1885; engaged in iron manufacturing at Clinton, N. Y.; died in Plattsburgh, N. Y.; March 2, 1916; interment in Riverside Cemetery.

PALMER, Henry Wilber, a Representative from Pennsylvania; born in Clifford, Susquehanna County, Pa., July 10, 1839; attended Wyoming Seminary, Kingston, Pa., Fort Edward Institute, Fort Edward, N. Y., and the National Law School, Poughkeepsie, N. Y.; was graduated from the last-named institution in 1860; was admitted to the bar in Peekskill, N. Y., the same year and in Wilkes-Barre, Pa., in 1861; prothonotary's clerk in 1861; during the Civil War served in the pay department of the Union Army at New Orleans in 1862 and 1863; member of the constitutional convention of Pennsylvania in 1872 and 1873; attorney general of the State 1879–1883; elected as a Republican to the Fifty-seventh, Fifty-eighth, and Fifty-ninth Congresses (March 4, 1901–March 3, 1907); one of the managers appointed by the House of Representatives in 1905 to conduct the impeachment proceedings against Charles Swayne, judge of the United States Court for the Northern District of Florida; elected to the Sixty-first Congress (March 4, 1909–March 3, 1911); practiced law until his death in Wilkes-Barre, Pa., February 15, 1913; interment in Hollenback Cemetery.

PALMER, John (uncle of George William Palmer), a Representative from New York; born in Hoosick, Rensselaer County, N. Y., January 29, 1785; completed preparatory studies; graduated from Williams College, Williamstown, Mass.; studied law; was admitted to the bar and commenced practice in Plattsburg, N. Y., in 1810; served as paymaster in the Eighth Regiment, New York Militia, in 1812; elected as a Democrat to the Fifteenth Congress (March 4, 1817–March 3, 1819); district attorney 1818–1832; member of the State assembly in 1832; judge of Clinton County from 1832 until 1837, when he resigned, having been elected to Congress; elected to the Twenty-fifth Congress (March 4, 1837–March 3, 1839); was not a candidate for renomination; retired from public and business life; died in St. Bartholomew, French West Indies, December 8, 1840; interment in St. Bartholomew Cemetery.

PALMER, John McAuley, a Senator from Illinois; born at Eagle Creek, Scott County, Ky., September 13, 1817; moved with his father to Christian County, Ky., in 1819 and then to Madison County, Ill., in 1831; attended the common schools of Kentucky and Illinois; in 1835 entered Alton (later Shurtleff) College, where he remained a year; taught school and studied law 1835–1838; was admitted to the bar in December 1839 and practiced in Carlinville, Ill., 1839–1861; was probate judge of Macoupin County in 1843 and 1847; member of the State constitutional convention in 1847; county judge 1849–1852; member of the State senate 1852–1854; resigned in 1854; became an independent candidate; was reelected in 1855 and again resigned in 1856; delegate to the Republican National Convention at Philadelphia in 1856; presidential elector on the Republican ticket of Lincoln and Hamlin in 1860; member of the peace convention of 1861 held in Washington, D. C., in an effort to devise means to prevent the impending war; during the Civil War was appointed colonel of the Fourteenth Regiment, Illinois Volunteer Infantry, May 25, 1861; brigadier general of Volunteers December 20, 1861; major general November 29, 1862; mustered out September 1, 1866; settled in Springfield, Ill., in 1867; Republican Governor of Illinois 1869–1873; supported Horace Greeley for President in 1872 and Samuel J. Tilden in 1876; delegate to the Democratic National Convention at Chicago in 1884; elected as a Democrat to the United States Senate and served from March 4, 1891, to March 3, 1897; was not a candidate for reelection in 1896; resumed the practice of law; unsuccessful candidate for President as a Gold Democrat in 1896; died in Springfield, Ill., September 25, 1900; interment in Carlinville City Cemetery, Carlinville, Ill.

PALMER, John William, a Representative from Missouri; born on a farm near Macks Creek, Camden County, Mo., August 20, 1866; attended the local schools; taught school in Hickory County, Mo.; engaged in the drug business at Cross Timbers, Hickory County, Mo., in 1888 and in the general merchandise business at Climax Springs, Camden County, Mo., 1891–1909; attended the University Medical College at Kansas City, Mo., in 1894 and 1895; practiced medicine in Climax Springs 1895–1908; completed the required course from the law school of Lincoln-Jefferson University, Hammond, Ind., in 1896; was admitted to the bar in 1897 and commenced the practice of law in Climax Springs, Mo.; served as representative in the Fortieth and Forty-first General Assemblies of Missouri 1898–1902; moved to Linn Creek, Mo., in 1909; prosecuting attorney of Camden County 1909–1915; moved to Sedalia, Mo., in 1915 and continued the practice of law; unsuccessful candidate for State senator in 1904; elected as a Republican to the Seventy-first Congress (March 4, 1929–March 3, 1931); unsuccessful candidate for reelection in 1930 to the Seventy-second Congress, for election in 1931 to fill a vacancy in the Seventy-second Congress, and for election in 1932 to the Seventy-third Congress; resumed the practice of law; died in Sedalia, Mo., November 3, 1958; interment in Crown Hill Cemetery.

PALMER, Thomas Witherell, a Senator from Michigan; born in Detroit, Mich., January 25, 1830; attended the public schools and Thompson's Academy in Palmer (now St. Clair), Mich., and the University of Michigan at Ann Arbor; engaged in lumbering and agricultural pursuits; served on the Board of Estimates of Detroit in 1873; member of the State senate in 1879 and 1880; elected as a Republican to the United States Senate and served from March 4, 1883, to March 3, 1889; was not a candidate for reelection; appointed United States Minister to Spain in 1889 by President Harrison and served for two years; president of the National Commission of the World's Columbian Exposition at Chicago 1890–1893; retired to his Wayne County farm near Detroit, Mich.; died in Detroit, Mich., June 1, 1913; interment in Elmwood Cemetery.

PALMER, William Adams, a Senator from Vermont; born in Hebron, Conn., September 12, 1781; completed preparatory studies; moved to Chelsea, Vt., in 1802; studied law in Hebron

and Chelsea; was admitted to the bar and commenced practice in St. Johnsbury, Vt., in 1805; moved to Danville, Vt., in 1807; served as clerk of the Caledonia County Court 1807–1815; member of the State house of representatives in 1811, 1812, and 1818; judge of probate of Caledonia County 1811–1817; judge of the State supreme court 1816–1818; elected as a Democrat to the United States Senate to fill the vacancy caused by the resignation of James Fisk; reelected in 1819 and served from October 20, 1818, to March 3, 1825; was not a candidate for renomination in 1824; engaged in agricultural pursuits; again a member of the State house of representatives in 1825, 1826, and 1829; assistant judge of Caledonia County 1826–1828; delegate to the State constitutional conventions in 1828, 1836, and 1850; Governor of Vermont 1831–1835; died in Danville, Caledonia County, Vt., December 3, 1860; interment in Green Cemetery.

PALMISANO, Vincent Luke, a Representative from Maryland; born in Termini Imerse, Italy, August 5, 1882; immigrated to the United States with his parents, who settled in Baltimore, Md., in 1887; attended parochial schools and studied law at the University of Maryland at Baltimore; was admitted to the bar in 1909 and commenced practice in Baltimore, Md.; member of the State house of delegates in 1914 and 1915; member of the city council 1915–1923; member of the Democratic State central committee of Baltimore 1923–1927; police examiner of Baltimore, Md., 1925–1927; elected as a Democrat to the Seventieth and to the five succeeding Congresses (March 4, 1927–January 3, 1939); unsuccessful for renomination in 1938; resumed the practice of law; served on the Baltimore Zoning Board until his resignation in 1952; disappeared from his home on January 12, 1953, and his body was recovered from the Baltimore Harbor on March 5, 1953; interment in New Cathedral Cemetery, Baltimore, Md.

PANTIN, Santiago Iglesias, a Resident Commissioner from Puerto Rico. (*See* IGLESIAS, Santiago.)

PAREDES, Quintin, a Resident Commissioner from the Commonwealth of the Philippines; born in Bangued, Abra Province, Philippine Islands, September 9, 1884; attended the primary and seminary schools; was graduated from the law school of Manila in 1907; was admitted to the bar the same year and commenced practice in Manila; appointed fourth prosecuting attorney on July 9, 1908, first prosecuting attorney on November 1, 1913, and served until March 1, 1917; served on the faculty and became dean of the law school (Escuela de Derecho) of Manila 1913–1917; served as solicitor general in 1917 and 1918, as attorney general 1918–1920, and as secretary of justice in 1920 and 1921; member of the first parliamentary mission to the United States in 1919; resumed the practice of law at Manila, Philippine Islands, in 1921; elected a member of the Philippine House of Representatives in 1925, 1928, 1931, and 1934, serving as speaker 1929–1931 and again in 1934; member of the Philippine Assembly in 1935; appointed as a Nationalist on December 21, 1935, the first Resident Commissioner under the Tydings-McDuffie law creating the Philippine Commonwealth Government, and served from February 14, 1936, until his resignation on September 29, 1938; resumed the practice of law; again elected a member of the Philippine Assembly in 1938; member of the Philippine Senate 1941–1945; served as a member of the Philippine House of Representatives 1946–1949; member of the Philippine Senate in 1950; reelected in 1955 for the term ending in November 1961; is a resident of Bangued, Abra Province, Philippines.

PARK, Frank, a Representative from Georgia; born in Tuskegee, Macon County, Ala., March 3, 1864; attended the common schools and the University of Georgia at Athens; engaged in teaching 1882–1885; railway civil engineer 1885–1889; was graduated from the old Atlanta Medical College in 1891; studied law; was admitted to the bar in 1891 and commenced practice in Atlanta, Ga.; chairman of the Democratic executive committee of Worth County, Ga., 1891–1902; judge of the county court 1898–1903; chairman of the Democratic congressional committee for the second district of Georgia 1902–1904; judge of the city court of Sylvester, Ga., 1903–1908; judge of the Albany judicial circuit 1908–1913; chairman of the board of trustees of the State Agricultural and Mechanical School, Tifton, Ga., 1911–1915; elected as a Democrat to the Sixty-third Congress to fill the vacancy caused by the death of Seaborn A. Roddenbery; reelected to the Sixty-fourth and to the four succeeding Congresses and served from November 5, 1913, to March 3, 1925; unsuccessful candidate for renomination in 1924; resumed the practice of law; died at Fort Lauderdale, Fla., November 20, 1925; interment in White Springs Cemetery, White Springs, Fla.

PARKE, Benjamin, a Delegate from the Territory of Indiana; born in New Jersey on September 22, 1777; received a limited schooling; moved to Lexington, Ky., in 1797; studied law and was admitted to the bar; moved to Vincennes, Territory of Indiana, in 1799 and practiced; attorney general of the Territory 1804–1808; member of the Territorial house of representatives in 1805; when the Territory was formed, was elected as a Democrat the first Delegate to the Ninth and Tenth Congresses and served from December 12, 1805, until March 1, 1808, when he resigned; served on the staff of Gov. William Harrison; Territorial judge 1808–1817; judge of the United States District Court for Indiana 1817–1835; was the first president of the Indiana Historical Society, serving in that capacity at the time of his death; died in Salem, Washington County, Ind., July 12, 1835; interment in Crown Hill Cemetery.

PARKER, Abraham X., a Representative from New York; born in Granville, Addison County, Vt., November 14, 1831; attended the St. Lawrence Academy and the Albany (N. Y.) Law School; was admitted to the bar in Albany, N. Y., in 1854 and in 1856 commenced practice in Potsdam, N. Y.; member of the State assembly in 1863 and 1864; postmaster of Potsdam in 1865 and 1866; president of the village of Potsdam; served in the State senate 1868–1871; presidential elector on the Republican ticket of Hayes and Wheeler in 1876; secretary of the State normal school at Potsdam; elected as a Republican to the Forty-seventh and to the three succeeding Congresses (March 4, 1881–March 3, 1889); was not a candidate for renomination in 1888; appointed by President Cleveland a member of the first labor investigation commission; delegate to the Republican National Convention at Minneapolis in 1892; First Assistant Attorney General from September 8, 1890, to March 4, 1893; returned to Potsdam, N. Y., and resumed the practice of law; president of the Thomas S. Clarkson Memorial School of Technology; died in Potsdam, St. Lawrence County, N. Y., on August 9, 1909; interment in Bayside Cemetery.

PARKER, Amasa Junius, a Representative from New York; born in Sharon, Litchfield County, Conn., June 2, 1807; moved with his parents to Hudson, N. Y., in 1816; taught by private tutors, and in 1825, having passed an examination on the entire college course at Union College, Schenectady, N. Y., was graduated from that institution; principal of Hudson (N. Y.) Academy 1823–1827; studied law; was admitted to the bar in 1828 and commenced practice in Delhi, N. Y.; member of the State assembly in 1833 and 1834; regent of the State university 1835–1844; elected as a Democrat to the Twenty-fifth Congress (March 4, 1837–March 3, 1839); declined to be a candidate for renomination in 1838; resumed the practice of law; vice chancellor and circuit judge 1844–1847; moved to Albany, N. Y., in

1844; judge of the supreme court for the third district 1847–1855; unsuccessful candidate for reelection; unsuccessful candidate for Governor of New York in 1856 and 1858; one of the founders of the Albany (N. Y.) Law School in 1851; declined the position of United States attorney for the district of New York in 1859; tendered the Russian mission the same year, but declined that proffer also; delegate to the State constitutional convention of 1867 and 1868; died in Albany, N. Y., May 13, 1890; interment in the Albany Rural Cemetery.

PARKER, Andrew, a Representative from Pennsylvania; born in Cumberland County, Pa., May 21, 1805; attended the common schools; was graduated from Dickinson College, Carlisle, Pa., in 1824; studied law in Carlisle; was admitted to the bar in 1826 and commenced practice in Lewistown, Pa.; appointed deputy attorney general of Mifflin County; moved to Mifflintown in 1831, where he practiced law; elected as a Democrat to the Thirty-second Congress (March 4, 1851–March 3, 1853); continued the practice of law in Mifflintown, Juniata County, Pa., until his death there on January 15, 1864; interment in the Presbyterian Cemetery.

PARKER, Homer Cling, a Representative from Georgia; born in Baxley, Appling County, Ga., September 25, 1885; attended the public schools; was graduated from Statesboro (Ga.) High School in 1904 and from the law department of Mercer University, Macon, Ga., in 1908; was admitted to the bar the same year and commenced practice in Statesboro, Bulloch County, Ga.; served as solicitor of the city court 1914–1917; served in the United States Army during the First World War as a cadet, First Officers' Training Camp, May 15 to August 15, 1917; captain of Infantry, August 15, 1917, to May 20, 1919; major and judge advocate, May 20, 1919, to September 16, 1920; captain, Judge Advocate General's Department, September 16, 1920, to December 7, 1922; resumed the practice of law in Statesboro in 1923; served as mayor 1924–1927; appointed adjutant general of Georgia on June 28, 1927, and served until June 27, 1931; member of the Georgia National Guard and served as brigadier general, Adjutant General's Department, from July 12, 1927, to May 31, 1931; unsuccessful candidate for nomination as comptroller general of Georgia in 1930; elected as a Democrat to the Seventy-second Congress to fill the vacancy caused by the death of Charles G. Edwards; reelected to the Seventy-third Congress and served from September 10, 1931, to January 3, 1935; unsuccessful candidate for renomination in 1934; resumed the practice of law in Statesboro, Ga.; was appointed comptroller general of Georgia on June 16, 1936, and served until January 13, 1937; elected comptroller general of Georgia in 1940, in which capacity he served until his death in Atlanta, Ga., on June 22, 1946; interment in East Side Cemetery, Statesboro, Ga.

PARKER, Hosea Washington, a Representative from New Hampshire; born in Lempster, Sullivan County, N. H., May 30, 1833; pursued classical studies; attended Tufts College, Medford, Mass., and was graduated from the Green Mountain Liberal Institute, South Woodstock, Vt.; studied law; was admitted to the bar in 1859 and commenced practice in Lempster, N. H.; member of the State house of representatives in 1859 and 1860; moved to Claremont, N. H., in 1860; delegate to the Democratic National Convention at New York City in 1868; elected as a Democrat to the Forty-second and Forty-third Congresses (March 4, 1871–March 3, 1875); unsuccessful candidate for reelection in 1874 to the Forty-fourth Congress; resumed the practice of his profession; again a delegate to the Democratic National Conventions in 1880, 1884, and 1888; member of the State constitutional convention in 1918; died in Claremont, Sullivan County, N. H., August 21, 1922; interment in Mountain View Cemetery.

PARKER, Isaac, a Representative from Massachusetts; born in Boston, Mass., June 17, 1768; attended the common schools, and was graduated from Harvard University in 1786; studied law; was admitted to the bar and commenced practice in Castine, Maine (until 1820 a part of Massachusetts); held several local offices; moved to Portland, Maine, and continued the practice of law; elected to the Fifth Congress (March 4, 1797–March 3, 1799); appointed United States marshal for Maine district on March 5, 1799, and served until December 21, 1803; moved to Boston, Mass., having been appointed by Governor Strong an associate justice of the supreme court of Massachusetts on January 28, 1806, and presided as chief justice from August 24, 1814, until his death; professor of law in Harvard University 1815–1827; served as president of the State constitutional convention in 1820; served as a trustee of Bowdoin College for eleven years and as an overseer of Harvard University for twenty years; died in Boston, Mass., July 26, 1830; interment in Copps Hill Cemetery.

PARKER, Isaac Charles, a Representative from Missouri; born near Barnesville, Belmont County, Ohio, October 15, 1838; completed preparatory studies; attended Barnesville Academy; studied law and was admitted to the bar in 1859; moved to Missouri in 1859 and began practice in St. Joseph; during the Civil War was a corporal in Company A, Sixty-first Missouri Emergency Regiment; city attorney for St. Joseph, Mo., 1862–1864; elected circuit attorney in 1864 and resigned in 1867; elected circuit judge in 1868, but resigned in 1870 to become a candidate for Congress; elected as a Republican to the Forty-second and Forty-third Congresses (March 4, 1871–March 3, 1875); was the caucus nominee of his party, which was in the minority, for United States Senator in 1874; appointed chief justice of Utah Territory, but declined; appointed judge of the United States District Court for Western Arkansas March 19, 1875, and served until his death in Fort Smith, Sebastian County, Ark., November 17, 1896; interment in the National Cemetery, Fort Smith, Ark.

PARKER, James, a Representative from Massachusetts; born in Boston, Mass., in 1768; completed preparatory studies; studied medicine and began practice in Gardiner, Maine (then a part of Massachusetts); member of the Massachusetts Senate in 1811 and 1812; elected as a Democrat to the Thirteenth Congress (March 4, 1813–March 3, 1815); elected to the Sixteenth Congress (March 4, 1819–March 3, 1821); resumed the practice of medicine; died in Gardiner, Kennebec County, Maine, November 9, 1837; interment in Oak Grove Cemetery.

PARKER, James (grandfather of Richard Wayne Parker), a Representative from New Jersey; born in Bethlehem, N. J. (his father's temporary residence), March 3, 1776; moved to Perth Amboy, N. J., after the Revolution; was graduated from Columbia College, New York City, in 1793; engaged in the management and settlement of large landed properties left by his father, also as a land surveyor and as a lawyer, although never admitted to the bar; member of the State general assembly 1806–1810, 1812, 1813, 1815, 1816, 1818, and 1827; mayor of Perth Amboy in 1815 and again in 1850; presidential elector on the Democratic ticket of Jackson and Calhoun in 1824; collector of customs at Perth Amboy, N. J., 1829–1833; elected as a Democrat to the Twenty-third and Twenty-fourth Congresses (March 4, 1833–March 3, 1837); resumed his former activities; registrar of the board of proprietors of East Jersey; member of the different boundary commissions to obtain a settlement of the boundary question between the States of New York and New Jersey; delegate to the State constitutional convention in 1844; died in Perth Amboy, N. J., April 1, 1868; interment in St. Peter's Churchyard.

PARKER, James Southworth, a Representative from New York; born in Great Barrington, Berkshire County, Mass., on June 3, 1867; attended the public and high schools, and was graduated from Cornell University, Ithaca, N. Y., in 1887; taught at St. Paul's School, Concord, N. H., in 1887; moved to Salem, Washington County, N. Y., in 1888 and taught at St. Paul's School at Salem; engaged in agricultural pursuits in 1888; also interested in breeding harness racing horses; member of the State assembly in 1904, 1905, and 1908–1912; elected as a Republican to the Sixty-third and to the ten succeeding Congresses and served from March 4, 1913, until his death in Washington, D. C., December 19, 1933; interment in Evergreen Cemetery, Salem, N. Y.

PARKER, John, a Delegate from South Carolina; born in Charleston, S. C., June 24, 1759; attended school in Charleston, S. C., and later in England; was graduated from the Middle Temple, London, England; returned to South Carolina; was admitted to the bar in 1785 and commenced practice in Charleston, S. C.; also engaged in the cultivation of rice on his plantation near there; Member of the Continental Congress 1786–1788; resided at Charleston and also on his estates, "Hayes" and "Cedar Grove," and engaged in their cultivation; was also employed as executor in the management of large rice estates; died near Charleston, S. C., April 20, 1832; interment in the family burying ground on the "Hayes" estate in St. James' Parish, Goose Creek, near Charleston, S. C.

PARKER, John Mason, a Representative from New York; born in Granville, N. Y., June 14, 1805; attended Granville Academy, and was graduated from Middlebury College, Vermont, in 1828; studied law; was admitted to the bar and commenced practice in Owego, N. Y., in 1833; elected as a Whig to the Thirty-fourth and Thirty-fifth Congresses (March 4, 1855–March 3, 1859); was not a candidate for renomination in 1858; justice of the supreme court of New York 1859–1873, and sat as a justice of the general term of the third department 1867–1873; member of the court of appeals; died in Owego, N. Y., December 16, 1873; interment in Evergreen Cemetery.

PARKER, Josiah, a Representative from Virginia; born in "Macclesfield," Isle of Wight County, Va., May 11, 1751; pursued preparatory studies; member of the committee of safety in 1775 and of the Virginia convention that held sessions in March, July, and December of that year; enlisted in the Revolutionary War and was commissioned major in the Fifth Virginia Regiment February 13, 1776; lieutenant colonel July 28, 1777, and colonel April 1, 1778; served under Gen. Charles Lee in Virginia until the fall of 1776, when he was transferred to Washington's army; rendered distinguished service at the Battles of Trenton, Princeton, and the Brandywine; resigned from the Army July 12, 1778; member of the Virginia House of Delegates in 1780 and 1781; naval officer at Portsmouth, Va., in 1786; unsuccessful candidate for delegate to the Virginia convention in 1788; elected to the First and to the five succeeding Congresses (March 4, 1789–March 3, 1801); engaged in agricultural pursuits; died in Macclesfield, Va., March 18, 1810; interment in the private burial ground on his estate, "Macclesfield," in Isle of Wight County, Va.

PARKER, Nahum, a Senator from New Hampshire; born in Shrewsbury, Mass., March 4, 1760; during the Revolutionary War served in the Continental Army under General Gates and in the battles that resulted in the capture of Burgoyne's forces at Saratoga in 1777; settled in Fitzwilliam, Cheshire County, N. H., in 1786; member of the board of selectmen 1790–1794; clerk and town treasurer 1792–1815; served in the State house of representatives 1794–1804, 1806, and 1807; member of the Governor's council in 1804 and 1805; elected to the United States Senate and served from March 4, 1807, to June 1, 1810, when he resigned; justice of the court of common pleas for Cheshire and Sullivan Counties 1807–1813; an associate justice of the western circuit 1813–1816; judge of the court of sessions, Cheshire County, in 1821 and of the court of common pleas, Hillsborough County, in 1822; member of the State senate and its president in 1828; died in Fitzwilliam, N. H., November 12, 1839; interment in the Town Cemetery.

PARKER, Richard, a Representative from Virginia; born in Richmond, Va., on December 22, 1810; completed preparatory studies; studied law; was admitted to the bar and commenced practice in Berryville, Clarke County, Va.; held several local offices; elected as a Democrat to the Thirty-first Congress (March 4, 1849–March 3, 1851); elected judge of the thirteenth judicial circuit of Virginia on January 15, 1851, and served until 1869; pronounced the sentence of death on John Brown, who was captured at Harpers Ferry, Jefferson County, Va. (now West Virginia), after his unsuccessful attempt to raise an insurrection in 1859; resumed the practice of his profession in Winchester, Frederick County, Va., and died there November 10, 1893; interment in Mount Hebron Cemetery.

PARKER, Richard Elliott, a Senator from Virginia; born at Rock Spring, Westmoreland County, Va., December 27, 1783; attended the public schools, and was graduated from Washington College (now Washington and Lee University), Lexington, Va., in 1803; studied law; was admitted to the bar in 1804 and practiced in Westmoreland County; member of the State house of delegates 1807–1809; served as colonel of the Thirty-fifth Virginia Regiment 1812–1814; returned to practice in Westmoreland County; for many years judge of the general court and circuit court of Virginia; elected as a Democrat to the United States Senate to fill the vacancy caused by the resignation of Benjamin W. Leigh and served from December 12, 1836, to March 13, 1837, when he resigned; elected by the legislature of Virginia one of the judges of the court of appeals to fill the vacancy caused by the death of Dabney Carr; declined the position of Attorney General tendered by President Van Buren in 1840; died on his estate, "The Retreat," near Snickersville (now Bluemont, Loudoun County), Va., September 6, 1840; interment in the family cemetery near Warsaw, Richmond County, Va.

PARKER, Richard Wayne (grandson of James Parker), a Representative from New Jersey; born in Morristown, Morris County, N. J., August 6, 1848; was graduated from Princeton College in 1867 and from the law school of Columbia College in 1869; was admitted to the bar of New Jersey in 1870 and commenced practice in Newark; member of the State house of assembly in 1885 and 1886; unsuccessful Republican candidate for election to the Fifty-third Congress; elected as a Republican to the Fifty-fourth and to the seven succeeding Congresses (March 4, 1895–March 3, 1911); unsuccessful candidate for reelection in 1910 to the Sixty-second Congress; resumed the practice of law in Newark, N. J.; elected to the Sixty-third Congress to fill the vacancy caused by the resignation of Walter I. McCoy; reelected to the Sixty-fourth and Sixty-fifth Congresses and served from December 1, 1914, to March 3, 1919; unsuccessful candidate for reelection in 1918 to the Sixty-sixth Congress; delegate to the Republican National Convention at Chicago in 1916, which nominated Hughes and Fairbanks; again elected to the Sixty-seventh Congress (March 4, 1921–March 3, 1923); unsuccessful candidate for reelection in 1922 to the Sixty-eighth Congress; died in Paris, France, on November 28, 1923; interment in St. Peter's Churchyard, Perth Amboy, N. J.

PARKER, Samuel Wilson, a Representative from Indiana; born near Watertown, Jefferson County, N. Y., September 9, 1805; pursued academic studies; was graduated from Miami University, Oxford, Ohio, in 1828; studied law; was admitted to the bar in 1831 and commenced practice in Connersville, Fayette County, Ind.; served as prosecuting attorney of Fayette County from December 10, 1836, to December 10, 1838; member of the State house of representatives in 1839 and 1843; served in the State senate 1841–1843; unsuccessful candidate for election in 1849 to the Thirty-first Congress; elected as a Whig to the Thirty-second and Thirty-third Congresses (March 4, 1851–March 3, 1855); did not seek renomination in 1855; died near Sackets Harbor, N. Y., February 1, 1859; interment in the private cemetery on the Old Elm farm, near Sackets Harbor.

PARKER, Severn Eyre, a Representative from Virginia; born near Eastville, Northampton County, Va., July 19, 1787; attended the common schools; studied law; was admitted to the bar and practiced; member of the State house of delegates 1809–1821; appointed deputy clerk of Northampton County March 8, 1813; captain of a rifle company in 1814; served in the State senate 1817–1820; elected to the Sixteenth Congress (March 4, 1819–March 3, 1821); again a member of the State house of delegates in 1828, 1829, and 1834–1836; died in Northampton County, Va., October 21, 1836; interment in the private cemetery on Kendall Grove farm, near Eastville, Va.

PARKER, William Henry, a Representative from South Dakota; born in Keene, Cheshire County, N. H., May 5, 1847; during the Civil War served in the Union Army from June 24, 1861, to October 16, 1866; resigned from the Army while stationed at Fort Kearney, Nebr.; was graduated from the law department of Columbian College (now George Washington University), Washington, D. C., in 1868 and was admitted to the bar of the supreme court of the District of Columbia the same year; appointed collector of internal revenue of Colorado Territory by President Grant June 24, 1874; resigned in July 1876 upon his appointment as assistant United States attorney of Colorado Territory; subsequently appointed United States attorney of Colorado; moved to Deadwood, Territory of Dakota (now South Dakota), in July 1877 and practiced law; member of the constitutional convention of the proposed State of South Dakota June 30, 1885; elected a member of the State house of representatives in 1889; prosecuting attorney of Lawrence County 1903–1907; elected to the Sixtieth Congress and served from March 4, 1907, until his death in Deadwood, Lawrence County, S. Dak., on June 26, 1908; interment in Arlington National Cemetery, Fort Myer, Va.

PARKS, Gorham, a Representative from Maine; born in Westfield, Mass., May 27, 1794; attended the common schools, and was graduated from Harvard College, Cambridge, Mass., in 1813; studied law; was admitted to the bar in 1819 and practiced; moved to Bangor, Maine, in 1823 and continued the practice of law; elected as a Democrat to the Twenty-third and Twenty-fourth Congresses (March 4, 1833–March 3, 1837); United States marshal for the district of Maine 1838–1841; United States attorney for the district of Maine in 1843 and resigned in 1845 to enter the consular service; United States consul at Rio de Janeiro, Brazil, which position he held until 1849; died in Bay Ridge, Kings County, N. Y., November 23, 1877; interment in Greenwood Cemetery, Brooklyn, N. Y.

PARKS, Tilman Bacon, a Representative from Arkansas; born near Lewisville, Lafayette County, Ark., May 14, 1872; attended the common schools, the University of Texas at Austin, and the University of Virginia at Charlottesville; studied law;

was admitted to the bar in 1900 and commenced practice in Lewisville, Ark.; member of the State house of representatives in 1901, 1903, and 1909; presidential elector at large on the Democratic ticket of Parker and Davis in 1904, being selected as the messenger to deliver the electoral vote of the State of Arkansas; temporary chairman of the Democratic State convention in 1910; prosecuting attorney of the eighth judicial circuit of Arkansas 1914–1918; in 1915 moved to Hope, Hempstead County, Ark., where he engaged in the practice of law; elected as a Democrat to the Sixty-seventh and to the seven succeeding Congresses (March 4, 1921–January 3, 1937); was not a candidate for renomination in 1936; continued the practice of law until his retirement; died in Washington, D. C., February 12, 1950; interment in the Congressional Cemetery.

PARMENTER, William, a Representative from Massachusetts; born in Boston, Mass., March 30, 1789; attended the public schools and the Boston Latin School; member of the State house of representatives in 1829; served in the State senate in 1836; selectman of Cambridge in 1836; one of the pioneers in the glass industry in East Cambridge and was manager and agent of the New England Crown Glass Co. 1824–1836; was president of the Middlesex Bank and filled other positions of trust; elected as a Democrat to the Twenty-fifth and to the three succeeding Congresses (March 4, 1837–March 3, 1845); naval officer at the port of Boston 1845–1849; died in East Cambridge, Mass., February 25, 1866; interment in Cambridge Cemetery.

PARRAN, Thomas, a Representative from Maryland; born near St. Leonard, Calvert County, Md., February 12, 1860; attended the public schools and Charlotte Hall (Md.) Academy; member of the State house of delegates 1884–1888; served as chief deputy collector for the Bureau of Internal Revenue, Baltimore district, 1889–1893; engaged in farming at St. Leonard, Md., in 1890; served in the State senate 1892–1894; assistant enrolling clerk 1895–1897; index clerk of the House of Representatives of the United States 1897–1901; clerk of the court of appeals of Maryland 1901–1907; delegate to the Republican National Conventions in 1888, 1904, and 1908; elected as a Republican to the Sixty-second Congress (March 4, 1911–March 3, 1913); unsuccessful candidate for reelection in 1912 to the Sixty-third Congress; member of the Maryland Road Commission 1913–1916; Immigration Commissioner in 1917 and 1918; resumed farming interests; member of the board of directors of the County Trust Co., in Prince Frederick, Md.; died in St. Leonard, Md., March 29, 1955; interment in Christ Church Cemetery, Port Republic, Md.

PARRETT, William Fletcher, a Representative from Indiana; born near Blairsville, Posey County, Ind., August 10, 1825; attended the public schools and the Indiana Asbury (now De Pauw) University at Greencastle; studied law; was admitted to the bar and practiced in Evansville, Ind., until 1852; moved to Oregon, where he practiced law for two and a half years; returned to Evansville in 1854, and moved to Boonville, Warrick County, Ind., in 1855; presidential elector on the Democratic ticket of Buchanan and Breckinridge in 1856; member of the State house of representatives in 1858 and served during the general and special sessions; appointed and subsequently elected judge of the fifteenth circuit and served from 1859 to 1865; returned to Evansville; reelected circuit judge and served from 1865 to 1871; appointed judge of the first circuit and elected in 1873, 1879, and 1884; resigned in December 1888; elected as a Democrat to the Fifty-first and Fifty-second Congresses (March 4, 1889–March 3, 1893); was not a candidate for renomination in 1892; resumed the practice of law until his death in Evansville, Ind., June 30, 1895; interment in Oak Hill Cemetery.

PARRIS, Albion Keith (cousin of Virgil Delphini Parris), a Representative from Massachusetts and a Senator from Maine; born in Hebron, Maine (at that time a part of Massachusetts), January 19, 1788; was graduated from Dartmouth College, Hanover, N. H., in 1806; studied law; was admitted to the bar and commenced practice in Paris, Maine, in 1809; prosecuting attorney of Oxford County in 1811; member of the Massachusetts House of Representatives in 1813; served in the State senate in 1814; elected as a Democrat from the State of Massachusetts to the Fourteenth and Fifteenth Congresses and served from March 4, 1815, to February 3, 1818, when he resigned; judge of the District Court of the United States for the District of Maine 1818–1820; delegate to the Maine constitutional convention in 1819; judge of probate for Cumberland County, Maine, in 1820 and 1821; Governor of Maine 1822–1827; elected to the United States Senate from Maine and served from March 4, 1827, to August 26, 1828, when he resigned; judge of the supreme court of Maine 1828–1836; Second Comptroller of the United States Treasury 1836–1850; mayor of Portland, Maine, in 1852; was not a candidate for reelection; unsuccessful candidate for Governor in 1854; died in Portland, Maine, February 22, 1857; interment in Western Cemetery.

PARRIS, Virgil Delphini (cousin of Albion Keith Parris), a Representative from Maine; born in Buckfield, Maine, February 18, 1807; attended the common schools, Hebron Academy, Hebron, Maine, and Colby College, Waterville, Maine; was graduated from Union College, Schenectady, N. Y., in 1827; studied law; was admitted to the bar in 1830 and commenced practice in Buckfield, Maine; assistant secretary of the Maine Senate in 1831; member of the State house of representatives 1832–1837; elected as a State Rights Democrat to the Twenty-fifth Congress to fill the vacancy caused by the death of Timothy J. Carter; reelected to the Twenty-sixth Congress and served from May 29, 1838, to March 3, 1841; unsuccessful candidate for renomination in 1840; member of the State senate in 1842 and 1843, part of the time serving as president pro tempore and as Acting Governor of the State; United States marshal for the district of Maine 1844–1848; special mail agent for New England in 1853; appointed naval storekeeper at Kittery Navy Yard in 1856; delegate to the Democratic National Conventions at Baltimore in 1852 and 1872; died in Paris, Oxford County, Maine, June 13, 1874; interment in the Rawson family knoll in the Old Cemetery.

PARRISH, Isaac, a Representative from Ohio; born near St. Clairsville, Belmont County, Ohio, in March 1804; resided in Cambridge, Guernsey County; studied law; was admitted to the bar and practiced; prosecuting attorney of Guernsey County in 1833; member of the State house of representatives in 1837; elected as a Democrat to the Twenty-sixth Congress (March 4, 1839–March 3, 1841); unsuccessful candidate for reelection in 1840 to the Twenty-seventh Congress; elected to the Twenty-ninth Congress (March 4, 1845–March 3, 1847); was not a candidate for renomination in 1846; resumed the practice of law and his former business pursuits in Sharon; also interested in the real-estate business and engaged in freighting by steamboat on the Mississippi River; established the Harrison County Flag, published at Calhoun; died in Parrish City, Iowa, August 9, 1860; interment in Calhoun Cemetery, Calhoun, Harrison County, Iowa.

PARRISH, Lucian Walton, a Representative from Texas; born in Sister Grove, near Van Alstyne, Grayson County, Tex., January 10, 1878; moved with his parents to Clay County in 1887 and settled near Joy, Tex.; attended the public schools of Joy and Bowie, Tex., and the North Texas State Normal College at Denton, Tex.; taught school for two years; was graduated from the law department of the University of Texas at Austin in 1909; was admitted to the bar the same year and commenced practice in Henrietta, Tex.; elected as a Democrat to the Sixty-sixth and Sixty-seventh Congresses and served from March 4, 1919, until his death in Wichita Falls, Wichita County, Tex., March 27, 1922; interment in Hope Cemetery, Henrietta, Tex.

PARROTT, John Fabyan, a Representative and a Senator from New Hampshire; born in Portsmouth, N. H., August 8, 1767; attended the common schools; member of the State house of representatives 1809–1814; held various local offices; unsuccessful war candidate for election in 1812 to the Thirteenth Congress; elected as a Democrat to the Fifteenth Congress (March 4, 1817–March 3, 1819); elected to the United States Senate and served from March 4, 1819, to March 3, 1825; postmaster of Portsmouth, N. H., in 1826; served in the State senate in 1830 and 1831; died in Greenland, Rockingham County, N. H., July 9, 1836; interment in the family burying ground on the Parrott estate.

PARROTT, Marcus Junius, a Delegate from Kansas; born in Hamburg, Aiken County, S. C., October 27, 1828; attended the common schools, and was graduated from Dickinson College, Carlisle, Pa., in 1849; studied law at Cambridge University; was admitted to the bar and commenced practice in Dayton, Ohio; member of the State house of representatives in 1853 and 1854; moved to Leavenworth, Kans., in 1855; court reporter of the first session of the Territorial supreme court in 1855; delegate to the State constitutional convention in 1855; elected as a Republican to the Thirty-fifth and Thirty-sixth Congresses and served from March 4, 1857, to January 29, 1861, when the Territory of Kansas was admitted as a State into the Union; unsuccessful candidate for election on the Independent ticket to the Thirty-eighth Congress and on the Democratic ticket to the Forty-third Congress; engaged in agricultural pursuits near Leavenworth, Kans.; died in Dayton, Ohio, October 4, 1879; interment in Woodland Cemetery.

PARSONS, Claude VanCleve, a Representative from Illinois; born on a farm near McCormick, Pope County, Ill., October 7, 1895; attended the public schools; taught in the rural schools of Pope County, Ill., 1914–1922; was graduated from Southern Illinois State Normal School at Carbondale in 1923; moved to Golconda, Pope County, Ill., in 1922 to become county superintendent of schools, in which capacity he served until 1930; was also engaged as an editor and newspaper publisher from 1924 to 1930; elected on November 4, 1930, as a Democrat to the Seventy-first Congress to fill the vacancy caused by the resignation of Thomas S. Williams and on the same day was elected to the Seventy-second Congress; reelected to the Seventy-third and to the three succeeding Congresses and served from November 4, 1930, to January 3, 1941; unsuccessful candidate for reelection in 1940 to the Seventy-seventh Congress; appointed first assistant administrator of the United States Housing Authority February 14, 1941, and served until his death in Washington, D. C., May 23, 1941; interment in Zion Church Cemetery, near Ozark, Ill.

PARSONS, Edward Young, a Representative from Kentucky; born in Middletown, Jefferson County, Ky., December 12, 1842; attended the public schools at Louisville until twelve years of age; studied one year in the St. Louis High School; returned to Louisville and was graduated from the municipal university in 1861, where he taught school for three years; was graduated from the Louisville Law School in 1865; was admitted to the bar and commenced practice in Henderson, Ky.; moved to Louisville, Ky., in 1865 and continued the practice of law;

elected as a Democrat to the Forty-fourth Congress and served from March 4, 1875, until his death in Washington, D. C., July 8, 1876; interment in Cave Hill Cemetery, Louisville, Ky.

PARSONS, Herbert, a Representative from New York; born in New York City October 28, 1869; attended private schools in New York City, St. Paul's School, Concord, N. H., Yale University, the University of Berlin, Germany, the Harvard Law School, and was graduated from Yale University in 1890; was admitted to the bar in 1894 and commenced practice in New York City; member of the board of aldermen of New York City 1900–1904; elected as a Republican to the Fifty-ninth, Sixtieth, and Sixty-first Congresses (March 4, 1905–March 3, 1911); unsuccessful candidate for reelection in 1910 to the Sixty-second Congress; resumed the practice of law in New York City; delegate to all Republican New York State conventions 1904–1920; delegate to the Republican National Conventions at Chicago in 1908, 1912, 1916, and 1920; served on the general staff of the American Expeditionary Forces during the First World War; died in Pittsfield, Mass., September 16, 1925; interment in Lenox Cemetery, Lenox, Mass.

PARSONS, Richard Chappel, a Representative from Ohio; born in New London, Conn., October 10, 1826; pursued classical studies; moved to Norwalk, Ohio, in 1845; studied law; was admitted to the bar in 1851 and commenced practice at Cleveland; member of the city council in 1852 and 1853 and served as president in 1853; member of the State house of representatives 1858–1861 and served one term as speaker; declined to accept the appointment as Minister to Chile tendered by President Lincoln in 1861; appointed consul to Rio de Janeiro, Brazil, on March 27, 1862, but resigned, effective October 1, 1862; collector of internal revenue at Cleveland 1862–1866; marshal of the Supreme Court of the United States 1867–1872; declined to accept the offices of Governor of the Territory of Montana and Assistant Secretary of the Treasury; elected as a Republican to the Forty-third Congress (March 4, 1873–March 3, 1875); unsuccessful Republican candidate for reelection to the Forty-fourth Congress; resumed the practice of law in Cleveland, Ohio; editor and part owner of the Cleveland Daily Herald in 1877; died in Cleveland, Ohio, January 9, 1899; interment in Lake View Cemetery.

PARTRIDGE, Donald Barrows, a Representative from Maine; born in Norway, Oxford County, Maine, June 7, 1891; attended the common and high schools of his local community and was graduated from Bates College, Lewiston, Maine, in 1914; principal of the high school, at Canton, Maine, 1914–1917; was elected clerk of the supreme judicial court for Oxford County in 1918 and served from 1919 to 1931; studied law; was admitted to the bar in 1924 and commenced practice in Norway, Maine, the same year; served as town clerk 1924–1931; member of the board of education of Norway 1926–1931; served as chairman of the Oxford County Republican committee for six years; elected as a Republican to the Seventy-second Congress (March 4, 1931–March 3, 1933); was not a candidate for renomination in 1932; resumed the practice of law in Norway, Maine; member of the Maine Industrial Accident Commission; died in Portland, Maine, June 5, 1946, while on a business trip; interment in Norway Pine Grove Cemetery, South Paris, Maine.

PARTRIDGE, Frank Charles, a Senator from Vermont; born in East Middlebury, Vt., May 7, 1861; attended the district and high schools of East Middlebury, and was graduated from Amherst (Mass.) College in 1882 and from the Columbia University Law School at New York City in 1884; was admitted to the bar in 1885 and commenced practice in Rutland, Vt.;

moved to Proctor, Vt., in 1886 and engaged in the marble industry; also interested in and served as president of other business corporations; served as town clerk 1887–1889; member of the school committee in 1888 and 1889; was private secretary to the Secretary of War in 1889 and 1890; solicitor of the Department of State 1890–1893; United States Minister to Venezuela in 1893 and 1894; consul general at Tangier, Morocco, in 1897 and 1898; rewrote the consular regulations in 1898; member of the Vermont State Senate 1898–1900; appointed umpire of the British-Venezuela Claims Commission and the Netherlands-Venezuela Claims Commission in 1903, but was unable to serve; member of the executive council of the American Society of International Law 1906–1923; chairman of the commission to propose amendments to the Vermont Constitution in 1909; member of the Vermont committee of public safety 1917–1919; delegate of the United States to the Fifth Pan-American Conference at Santiago, Chile, in 1923; member of the New England Council 1925–1927; president of the Vermont Flood Credit Corporation, which was organized after the great flood in 1927; appointed as a Republican to the United States Senate to fill the vacancy caused by the death of Frank L. Greene and served from December 23, 1930, to March 31, 1931, when a successor was elected; unsuccessful candidate for the nomination to fill this vacancy; resumed his former activities in the marble industry; died in Proctor, Vt., March 2, 1943; interment in Proctor Cemetery.

PARTRIDGE, George, a Delegate and a Representative from Massachusetts; born in Duxbury, Mass., February 8, 1740; was graduated from Harvard College in 1762; taught school in Kingston, Mass.; studied theology; delegate to the Provincial Congress in 1774 and 1775; member of the State house of representatives 1775–1779; sheriff of Plymouth County 1777–1812; Member of the Continental Congress 1779–1782 and 1783–1785; member of the State house of representatives in 1788; elected to the First Congress and served from March 4, 1789, to August 14, 1790, when he resigned; endowed Partridge Seminary in Duxbury; died in Duxbury, Plymouth County, Mass., on July 7, 1828; interment in Mayflower Cemetery.

PARTRIDGE, Samuel, a Representative from New York; born in Norwich, Windsor County, Vt., November 29, 1790; received a limited schooling; during the War of 1812 enlisted as a private in the Vermont Militia; later appointed a captain of Engineers in the Regular Army, and won honorable distinction in the Battle of Lundy's Lane; served two terms as high sheriff of Windsor County; moved to New York and engaged in mercantile pursuits at Cold Spring on the Hudson in 1820; moved to Chemung County, N. Y., in 1830 and bought considerable land near the city of Elmira; moved to Elmira in 1837 and again engaged in mercantile pursuits; elected as a Democrat to the Twenty-seventh Congress (March 4, 1841–March 3, 1843); engaged in agricultural pursuits and the real-estate business; died in Elmira, Chemung County, N. Y., March 30, 1883; interment in Second Street Cemetery.

PASCHAL, Thomas Moore, a Representative from Texas; born in Alexandria, Rapides Parish, La., December 15, 1845; moved with his parents to San Antonio, Tex., in 1846; educated in private schools; attended St. Mary's College, San Antonio, Tex.; was graduated from Centre College, Danville, Ky., in 1866; studied law; was admitted to the bar in 1867 and commenced practice in San Antonio; city attorney in 1867; United States commissioner for the western district of Texas 1867–1869; judge of the district criminal court for San Antonio in 1870 and 1871; moved to Castroville, Tex., in 1870; district attorney of the twenty-fourth district 1871–1875; moved to Brackett, King

County, in 1873; elected judge of the thirty-eighth judicial district in 1876; reelected in 1880 and 1884, and served until 1892; appointed by Governor Coke as extradition agent between the United States and Mexico in 1876 and reappointed by Governor Roberts in 1880; returned to Castroville in 1885; elected as a Democrat to the Fifty-third Congress (March 4, 1893–March 3, 1895); unsuccessful candidate for renomination in 1894; resumed the practice of law in San Antonio, Tex.; delegate to the Democratic National Convention at Chicago in 1896; died in New York City January 28, 1919; interment in Mission Burial Park, San Antonio, Tex.

PASCO, Samuel, a Senator from Florida; born in London, England, June 28, 1834; immigrated to the United States with his father, who settled in Charlestown, Mass., in 1844; was graduated from the Charlestown High School in 1854 and from Harvard University in 1858; moved to Florida in January 1859 and was principal of Waukeenah Academy, near Monticello, 1850–1861; during the Civil War entered the Confederate Army as a private in the Third Florida Volunteers in July 1861; wounded and captured at Missionary Ridge, and remained in prison until March 1865, when paroled; returned to Florida in 1865 and was again principal of Waukeenah Academy in 1865 and 1866; clerk of the circuit court of Jefferson County 1866–1868; studied law; was admitted to the bar in 1868 and commenced practice in Monticello, Fla.; elected a member of the State Democratic committee in 1872 and served as chairman 1876–1878; presidential elector on the Democratic ticket of Hancock and English in 1880; president of the State constitutional convention in 1885; member of the State house of representatives in 1886 and 1887 and served as speaker in the latter year; elected as a Democrat to the United States Senate to fill the vacancy in the term beginning March 4, 1887; was appointed in 1893 and subsequently elected; again appointed in 1899 and served from May 19, 1887, to April 19, 1899, when a successor was elected; unsuccessful candidate for reelection in 1899; member of the Isthmian Canal Commission 1899–1905; retired and resided in Monticello; died in Tampa, Fla., March 13, 1917; interment in Roseland Cemetery, Monticello, Fla.

PASSMAN, Otto Ernest, a Representative from Louisiana; born on a farm near Franklinton, Washington Parish, La., June 27, 1900; attended the Pine Ridge grade school; was graduated from Baton Rouge (La.) High School and from the Commercial Business College at Bogalousa, La.; in 1929 engaged in the manufacture of commercial refrigerators, and as a distributor of hotel and restaurant supplies and electrical appliances at Monroe, La.; during World War II was commissioned a lieutenant in the United States Navy and served from October 11, 1942, until his discharge as lieutenant commander on September 5, 1944; resumed the mercantile business; delegate to the Democratic National Convention in 1948; elected as a Democrat to the Eightieth and to the six succeeding Congresses (January 3, 1947–January 3, 1961). *Reelected to the Eighty-seventh Congress.*

PASTORE, John Orlando, a Senator from Rhode Island; born in Providence, R. I., March 17, 1907; attended the public schools; was graduated from the law school of Northeastern University, Boston, Mass., in 1931; was admitted to the bar in 1932 and commenced the practice of law at Providence, R. I.; member of the State house of representatives 1935–1937; assistant attorney general of Rhode Island in 1937 and 1938; member Providence Charter Revision Commission in 1939 and 1940; again assistant attorney general 1940–1944; delegate to all Democratic National and State Conventions since 1944; elected Lieutenant Governor of Rhode Island in 1944 and assumed the office of Governor on October 6, 1945; elected Governor in 1946, reelected in 1948, and resigned December 18, 1950, having been elected Senator; elected as a Democrat to the United States Senate to fill the vacancy caused by the resignation of J. Howard McGrath and served from December 19, 1950, to January 3, 1953; reelected in 1952 and again in 1958 for the term ending January 3, 1965.

PATERSON, John, a Representative from New York; born in New Britain, Hartford County, Conn., in 1744; attended the common schools; completed preparatory studies, and was graduated from Yale College in 1762; studied law; was admitted to the bar and practiced in New Britain and Lenox, Mass.; member of the Berkshire convention of 1774 and of the general court that became the first Provincial Congress in 1774; raised a regiment and participated in the Revolutionary War; colonel of the regiment from April to December 1775; colonel of the Fifteenth Continental Infantry January 1, 1776; brigadier general February 21, 1777, and served until the close of the war; brevetted major general September 30, 1783; after the war returned to Lenox, Mass., and was commander of the Massachusetts troops in putting down Shays' Rebellion; moved to Lisle, Broome County, N. Y., in 1790; member of the State assembly in 1792 and 1793; county judge of Broome County in 1798 and 1806; member of the committee to revise the constitution of the State of New York in 1801; elected to the Eighth Congress (March 4, 1803–March 3, 1805); from 1805 until his death he devoted himself to farming; died in Lisle, N. Y. (now Whitneys Point), July 19, 1808; interment in Lenox Cemetery.

PATERSON, William, a Delegate and a Senator from New Jersey; born in Antrim, Ireland, December 24, 1745; immigrated to the United States in 1747 with his parents, who settled in New Castle, Pa.; moved with them to New London and to other places in Connecticut; moved to Trenton and to Princeton, N. J., in 1750; attended private schools; was graduated from Princeton College in 1763; studied law; was admitted to the bar in 1768 and commenced practice in New Bromly, N. J., in 1769; delegate and secretary to the Provincial Congress in 1775 and 1776; member of the State senate in 1776 and 1777; delegate to the State constitutional convention in 1776; attorney general of New Jersey from September 4, 1776, to June 13, 1783, when he resigned; moved to Raritan, N. J., in 1779; elected as a Delegate to the Continental Congress November 23, 1780, but declined June 12, 1781, owing to his duties as attorney general; moved to New Brunswick, N. J., in 1783; delegate to the Federal Constitutional Convention in Philadelphia in 1787 and one of the signers of the Constitution; again elected as a Delegate to the Continential Congress October 31, 1787, but declined November 6, 1787; elected as a Federalist to the United States Senate and served from March 4, 1789, to November 13, 1790, when he resigned, having been elected Governor of New Jersey; reelected as Governor and served from October 30, 1790, to March 30, 1793, when he resigned to become an Associate Justice of the Supreme Court of the United States and served from March 30, 1793, until his death in Albany, N. Y., September 9, 1806; interment in the Van Rensselaer Manor House vault, near Albany, N. Y.

PATMAN, Wright, a Representative from Texas; born on a farm near Hughes Springs, Cass County, Tex., August 6, 1893; attended the public schools; was graduated from Hughes Springs (Tex.) High School in 1912 and from the law department of Cumberland University, Lebanon, Tenn., in 1916; engaged in agricultural pursuits in Texas in 1913 and 1914; was admitted to the bar in 1916 and commenced practice in Hughes Springs, Tex.; assistant county attorney of Cass County, Tex., in 1916 and 1917; during the First World War served as a private and later

as a machine-gun officer in the United States Army 1917–1919; member of the State house of representatives 1921–1924; district attorney of the fifth judicial district of Texas 1924–1929; elected as a Democrat to the Seventy-first and to the fifteen succeeding Congresses (March 4, 1929–January 3, 1961). *Reelected to the Eighty-seventh Congress.*

PATRICK, Luther, a Representative from Alabama; born near Decatur, Morgan County, Ala., January 23, 1894; attended the public schools, Louisiana State University at Baton Rouge, and Purdue University, Lafayette, Ind.; in 1918 was graduated from the law department of the University of Alabama at Tuscaloosa; during the First World War served as a private, assigned to the Army training detachment and to the Central Officers' Training School, from June 14, 1918, to December 4, 1918; was admitted to the bar in 1919 and commenced practice in Fairfield, Ala.; city attorney of Fairfield 1920–1922; author of many poems and books; began career of radio commentator in 1925 with stations WAPI and WBRC; assistant attorney general of Alabama 1927–1929; assistant United States district attorney of the northern Alabama district in 1933 and 1934; elected as a Democrat to the Seventy-fifth, Seventy-sixth, and Seventy-seventh Congresses (January 3, 1937–January 3, 1943); unsuccessful candidate for renomination in 1942; served as a consultant to the War Production Board in 1943 and 1944; elected to the Seventy-ninth Congress (January 3, 1945–January 3, 1947); unsuccessful candidate for renomination in 1946; resumed law practice in Birmingham, Ala.; delegate to the Democratic National Convention in 1956; died in Birmingham, Ala., May 26, 1957; interment in Elmwood Cemetery.

PATTEN, Harold Ambrose, a Representative from Arizona; born in Husted, El Paso County, Colo., October 6, 1907; moved to Tucson, Pima County, Ariz., in 1916; graduated from Tucson High School in 1925 and from the University of Arizona in 1930; coach and teacher of physical education in Tucson High School in 1931 and 1932; director of recreation for city of Tucson and city schools 1933–1939; State director of recreation in 1939 and 1940; entered military service with the Seventh Cavalry Regiment as a first lieutenant in August 1940; transferred to the Air Corps in 1941 and was trained as a combat observer; spent thirty-one months on foreign service in Africa and Italy and was discharged as a major on November 21, 1945; awarded the European-African-Middle Eastern Theater Service Medal, American Defense Medal, American Theater Service Medal, Air Medal, ten battle stars, one invasion arrowhead (U. S.), and Wings-Aviation Francaise d'Afrique; retired July 1, 1960, as lieutenant colonel, Air Force Reserve; assistant manager, Phoenix agency of Mutual Life Insurance Co. of New York, 1946–1948; elected as a Democrat to the Eighty-first, Eighty-second, and Eighty-third Congresses (January 3, 1949–January 3, 1955); was not a candidate for renomination in 1954; engaged in the insurance business with Mutual Life Insurance Co. of New York; member Arizona Development Board 1959–; defeated for the Democratic nomination in 1961 to fill a vacancy in the Eighty-seventh Congress; is a resident of Tucson, Ariz.

PATTEN, John, a Delegate and a Representative from Delaware; born in Kent County, Del., April 26, 1746; attended the common schools; engaged in agricultural pursuits; entered the Revolutionary Army as a lieutenant; was promoted to the rank of major and served in all the battles from Long Island to Camden; Member of the Continental Congress in 1785 and 1786; presented credentials as a Member-elect to the Third Congress and served from March 4, 1793, to February 14, 1794, when he was succeeded by Henry Latimer, who contested his election; elected to the Fourth Congress (March 4, 1795–March 3, 1797); was not a candidate for renomination; engaged in farming until his death at "Tynhead Court," near Dover, Del., December 26, 1800; interment in the Presbyterian Churchyard.

PATTEN, Thomas Gedney, a Representative from New York; born in New York City September 12, 1861; attended Mount Pleasant Academy, Ossining, N. Y., Columbia College, New York City, 1877–1879, and Columbia Law School 1880–1882; engaged in the shipping business and subsequently operated a fleet of tugboats in New York Harbor; served as president of the New York & Long Branch Steamboat Co.; elected as a Democrat to the Sixty-second, Sixty-third, and Sixty-fourth Congresses (March 4, 1911–March 3, 1917); unsuccessful candidate for reelection in 1916 to the Sixty-fifth Congress; postmaster of New York City 1917–1921; moved to Hollywood, Calif., in 1922 and served on the staff of the Motion Picture Producers and Distributors of America, Inc., until 1924 when he retired from active business pursuits; died in Hollywood, Calif., February 23, 1939; interment in Forest Lawn Memorial Park, Los Angeles, Calif.

PATTERSON, David Trotter, a Senator from Tennessee; born at Cedar Creek, near Greeneville, Greene County, Tenn., February 28, 1818; attended the common schools and Greeneville College for two years; studied law; was admitted to the bar in 1841 and commenced practice in Greeneville, Tenn.; engaged in manufacturing; judge of the first circuit court of Tennessee 1854–1863; upon the readmission of the State of Tennessee to representation was elected as a Democrat to the United States Senate and served from July 24, 1866, to March 3, 1869; was not a candidate for reelection; engaged in the management of his extensive agricultural interests; died in Afton, near Greeneville, Tenn., November 3, 1891; interment in the Andrew Johnson National Cemetery, Greeneville, Tenn.

PATTERSON, Edward White, a Representative from Kansas; born in Pittsburg, Crawford County, Kans., October 4, 1895; attended the public schools; during the First World War served as a sergeant in the Thirty-fifth Division, American Expeditionary Forces, from May 1917 to March 1919; after the war attended the University of Chicago at Chicago, Ill.; was graduated from the law department of the University of Kansas at Lawrence in 1922; was admitted to the bar the same year and commenced practice in Pittsburg, Kans.; prosecuting attorney of Crawford County, Kans., 1926–1928; elected as a Democrat to the Seventy-fourth and Seventy-fifth Congresses (January 3, 1935–January 3, 1939); unsuccessful candidate for reelection in 1938 to the Seventy-sixth Congress; resumed the practice of law in Pittsburg, Kans., until his death in Weir, Kans., March 6, 1940; interment in Highland Park Cemetery, Pittsburg, Kans.

PATTERSON, Ellis Ellwood, a Representative from California; born in Yuba City, Sutter County, Calif., November 28, 1897; attended the public schools; was graduated from the University of California at Berkeley in 1921; during the First World War served as a seaman in the United States Navy in 1917 and 1918; taught school in Colusa County, Calif., 1922–1924; district superintendent of schools of South Monterey County, Calif., 1923–1932; studied law at Stanford University and at the University of California 1931–1936; was admitted to the bar in 1937 and commenced practice in Sacramento and Los Angeles, Calif.; member of the State assembly 1932–1938; Lieutenant Governor 1938–1942; elected as a Democrat to the Seventy-ninth Congress (January 3, 1945–January 3, 1947); did not seek renomination in 1946, but was an unsuccessful candidate for nomination for United States Senator; unsuccessful candidate for election in 1948 to the Eighty-first Congress; resumed the practice of law and is a resident of Los Angeles, Calif.

PATTERSON, Francis Ford, Jr., a Representative from New Jersey; born in Newark, N. J., July 30, 1867; moved with his parents to Woodbury, N. J., in 1874; attended the public schools; employed in a newspaper office at the age of thirteen; moved to Camden, N. J., in 1882; connected with the Camden Courier 1883–1890; New Jersey editor of the Philadelphia Record 1890–1894; owner and publisher of the Camden Post-Telegram 1894–1923; president of the West Jersey Trust Co. 1916–1925; director of the West Jersey Title Co. 1920–1925; member of the State house of assembly in 1900; county clerk of Camden County 1900–1920; delegate to the Republican National Convention at Chicago in 1920; elected as a Republican to the Sixty-sixth Congress to fill the vacancy caused by the death of William J. Browning; reelected to the Sixty-seventh, Sixty-eighth, and Sixty-ninth Congresses and served from November 2, 1920, to March 3, 1927; unsuccessful candidate for renomination in 1926; engaged in banking, serving as president of the West Jersey Parkside Trust Co., of Camden, N. J., until his death; died in Merchantville, N. J., on November 30, 1935; interment in Colestown Cemetery, located between Merchantville and Moorestown, N. J.

PATTERSON, George Robert, a Representative from Pennsylvania; born in Lewistown, Mifflin County, Pa., November 9, 1863; attended the public schools and Lewistown (Pa.) Academy; engaged in mercantile pursuits in 1880; moved to Ashland, Schuylkill County, in 1886 and engaged in the wholesale grain and feed business; frequent delegate to local and State conventions; delegate to the Republican National Convention at Philadelphia in 1900 and at Chicago in 1904; elected as a Republican to the Fifty-seventh, Fifty-eighth, and Fifty-ninth Congresses and served from March 4, 1901, until his death in Washington, D. C., March 21, 1906; interment in Citizens' Cemetery, Ashland, Pa.

PATTERSON, George Washington (brother of William Patterson), a Representative from New York; born in Londonderry, Rockingham County, N. H., November 11, 1799; completed preparatory studies, and was graduated from Pinkerton Academy; moved to New York and settled in Genesee County in 1818; engaged in the manufacture of fanning mills; settled in Leicester, N. Y., in 1825 and engaged in agricultural pursuits and the manufacture of farming implements; commissioner of highways of Leicester; justice of the peace; member of the State assembly 1832, 1833, and 1835–1840, and served as speaker in 1839 and 1840; basin commissioner at Albany in 1839 and 1840; moved to Westfield, N. Y., in 1841 to take charge of the Chautauqua land office; delegate to the State constitutional convention in 1846; elected Lieutenant Governor of New York in 1848; chairman of the harbor commission at New York 1855–1857; quarantine commissioner of the port of New York in 1859; supervisor and president of the board of education for many years; delegate to the Republican National Convention at Philadelphia in 1856 and at Chicago in 1860; elected as a Republican to the Forty-fifth Congress (March 4, 1877–March 3, 1879); was not a candidate for renomination in 1878; died in Westfield, Chautauqua County, N. Y., October 15, 1879; interment in Westfield Cemetery.

PATTERSON, Gilbert Brown, a Representative from North Carolina; born near Maxton, Robeson County, N. C., May 29, 1863; attended Shoe Heel Academy, Shoe Heel (now Maxton), N. C., and the Lurinburg (N. C.) High School; was graduated from the University of North Carolina at Chapel Hill in 1886; studied law; was admitted to the bar in 1890 and commenced practice in Maxton, N. C.; member of the State house of representatives 1899–1901; elected as a Democrat to the Fifty-eighth and Fifty-ninth Congresses (March 4, 1903–March 3, 1907); resumed the practice of law; died in Maxton, N. C., January 26, 1922; interment in Maxton Cemetery.

PATTERSON, James O'Hanlon, a Representative from South Carolina; born in Barnwell, Barnwell County, S. C., June 25, 1857; attended private schools in Barnwell, S. C., and Augusta, Ga.; studied law; was admitted to the bar in 1886 and commenced practice in Barnwell, S. C.; probate judge of Barnwell County 1888–1892; member of the State house of representatives 1898–1904; elected as a Democrat to the Fifty-ninth, Sixtieth, and Sixty-first Congresses (March 4, 1905–March 3, 1911); resumed the practice of his profession in Barnwell, S. C., where he died on October 25, 1911; interment in the Episcopal Cemetery.

PATTERSON, James Thomas, a Representative from Connecticut; born in Naugatuck, New Haven County, Conn., on October 20, 1908; attended the public schools; was graduated from Peekskill (N. Y.) Military Academy in 1929, from Georgetown University, Washington, D. C., in 1933, from the University of Miami, Coral Gables, Fla., in 1934, and from National University Law School, Washington, D. C., in 1939; while attending school worked for the Connecticut highway department as a laborer 1924–1933, in the mill room of a rubber company in 1934, for the United States Department of Labor 1934–1937, for the Social Security Board in 1937 and 1938, and for the United States Treasury 1938–1940; during World War II served with the United States Marine Corps from September 1941 until discharged as a major in July 1946, with overseas service in the African and European theaters and in India, Burma, and China; elected as a Republican to the Eightieth and to the five succeeding Congresses (January 3, 1947–January 3, 1959); unsuccessful candidate for reelection in 1958 to the Eighty-sixth Congress and for election in 1960 to the Eighty-seventh Congress; is a resident of Naugatuck, Conn.

PATTERSON, James Willis, a Representative and a Senator from New Hampshire; born in Henniker, N. H., July 2, 1823; pursued classical studies; was graduated from Dartmouth College, Hanover, N. H., in 1848; teacher in the academy at Woodstock, Conn., for two years; attended the Theological Seminary at New Haven, Conn.; professor in Dartmouth College 1854–1865; member of the State house of representatives in 1862; elected as a Republican to the Thirty-eighth and Thirty-ninth Congresses (March 4, 1863–March 3, 1867); elected to the United States Senate and served from March 4, 1867, to March 3, 1873; Regent of the Smithsonian Institution; again a member of the State house of representatives in 1877 and 1878; State superintendent of public instruction 1885–1893; president of American Institute of Instruction; died in Hanover, N. H., on May 4, 1893; interment in Dartmouth Cemetery.

PATTERSON, John (half brother of Thomas Patterson), a Representative from Ohio; born in Little Britain Township, Lancaster County, Pa., February 10, 1771; moved with his parents to Pattersons Mills, Cross Creek Township, Washington County, Pa., in 1778; attended the common schools; moved to St. Clairsville, Belmont County, Ohio; engaged in mercantile pursuits; first mayor of St. Clairsville in 1807 and 1808; member of the State house of representatives in 1807 and 1808; served in the State senate 1815–1818; associate judge of the court of common pleas of Belmont County from February 1810 to February 1815; elected as a Democrat to the Eighteenth Congress (March 4, 1823–March 3, 1825); engaged in the hardware business and in agricultural pursuits; died in St. Clairsville, Ohio, February 7, 1848; interment in Union Cemetery.

PATTERSON, John James, a Senator from South Carolina; born in Waterloo, Juniata County, Pa., August 8, 1830; attended the common schools, and was graduated from Jefferson College, Canonsburg, Pa., in 1848; engaged in newspaper work; publisher of the Juniata Sentinel in 1852 and became editor and part owner of the Harrisburg Telegraph in 1853; engaged in banking; member of the State house of representatives 1854–1856; delegate to the Republican National Convention at Philadelphia in 1856 and at Chicago in 1860; during the Civil War served in the Union Army as a captain in the Fifteenth United States Volunteer Infantry; unsuccessful candidate for election in 1862 to the Thirty-eighth Congress; engaged in banking 1863–1869; moved to Columbia, S. C., in 1869 and engaged in railroad construction; elected as a Republican to the United States Senate and served from March 4, 1873, to March 3, 1879; was not a candidate for reelection to the Senate; resided in Washington, D. C., and engaged in various financial enterprises; moved to Mifflintown, Juniata County, Pa., in 1886; engaged in the construction of electric railways and electric lighting plants; died in Mifflintown, Pa., September 28, 1912; interment in Westminster Presbyterian Cemetery.

PATTERSON, Josiah (father of Malcolm Rice Patterson), a Representative from Tennessee; born in Morgan County, Ala., April 14, 1837; attended the common schools and Somerville (Ala.) Academy; studied law; was admitted to the bar and commenced the practice of law in Morgan County in 1859; during the Civil War entered the Confederate Army in September 1861; commissioned a first lieutenant in the First Regiment of Alabama Cavalry in 1862; promoted to the rank of captain, then to colonel, and subsequently assigned to the command of the Fifth Regiment of Alabama Cavalry; commanded a brigade of Cavalry during the last year of the war; surrendered the Fifth Regiment of Alabama Cavalry May 19, 1865; resumed the practice of law; settled in Florence, Lauderdale County, Ala., in January 1867; moved to Memphis, Tenn., in March 1872 and continued the practice of his profession; member of the State house of representatives in 1882; presidential elector on the Democratic ticket of Cleveland and Thurman in 1888; elected as a Democrat to the Fifty-second, Fifty-third, and Fifty-fourth Congresses (March 4, 1891–March 3, 1897); unsuccessful candidate for reelection in 1896 to the Fifty-fifth Congress as a Gold Democrat; again resumed the practice of his profession; died in Memphis, Shelby County, Tenn., February 10, 1904; interment in Forest Hill Cemetery.

PATTERSON, LaFayette Lee, a Representative from Alabama; born near Delta, Clay County, Ala., August 23, 1888; attended the rural schools; engaged in agricultural pursuits and taught in the rural schools; was graduated from Jacksonville (Ala.) State Teachers' College in 1922, from Birmingham-Southern College, Birmingham, Ala., in 1924, and from Leland Stanford University, California, in 1927; superintendent of education of Tallapoosa County, Ala., 1924–1926; elected as a Democrat to the Seventieth Congress to fill the vacancy caused by the resignation of William B. Bowling; reelected to the to the Seventy-first and Seventy-second Congresses and served from November 6, 1928, to March 3, 1933; unsuccessful candidate for renomination in 1932; moved to Gadsden, Etowah County, Ala., in 1931; field representative for the Agricultural Adjustment Administration 1933–1943; special assistant to the War Food Administration in 1943–1945; special adviser to the Secretary of Agriculture 1945–1947; liaison officer for the Democratic National Committee in 1948; assistant professor of history at Jacksonville (Ala.) State College and faculty director for college citizenship forum 1948–1951; delegate at large to the Democratic National Convention in 1952; moved to Raleigh,

N. C., in 1952 and engaged in the travel business as president of Patterson Travel Service, Inc., 1957–; author and world traveler; resides in Raleigh, N. C.

PATTERSON, Malcolm Rice (son of Josiah Patterson), a Representative from Tennessee; born in Somerville, Morgan County, Ala., June 7, 1861; attended the common schools; moved to Memphis, Tenn., with his parents in 1872; was graduated from the Christian Brothers' College, Memphis, Tenn., and subsequently took a special literary course at Vanderbilt University, Nashville, Tenn.; studied law; was admitted to the bar in 1883 and commenced practice in Memphis, Tenn.; elected district attorney of Shelby County in 1894 for a term of eight years but resigned on September 10, 1900, having been nominated as a candidate for Congress; elected as a Democrat to the Fifty-seventh, Fifty-eighth, and Fifty-ninth Congresses and served from March 4, 1901, to November 5, 1906, when he resigned, having been elected Governor; elected Governor of Tennessee for two terms 1906–1910; resumed the practice of his profession in Memphis, Tenn.; unsuccessful candidate for election to the United States Senate in 1915; appointed in 1923 and subsequently elected judge of the first circuit court of Shelby County, Tenn., serving until his retirement September 1, 1934; unsuccessful candidate for nomination for Governor in 1932; died while on a visit to Sarasota, Fla., on March 8, 1935; interment in Forest Hill Cemetery, Memphis, Tenn.

PATTERSON, Roscoe Conkling, a Representative and a Senator from Missouri; born in Springfield, Greene County, Mo., September 15, 1876; attended public and private schools, Drury College, Springfield, Mo., and the University of Missouri at Columbia; was graduated from the law department of Washington University, St. Louis, Mo., in 1897; was admitted to the bar the same year and commenced practice in Springfield, Mo.; was prosecuting attorney of Greene County, Mo., 1903–1907; member of the Republican State committee 1912–1920; chairman of the Republican State conventions in 1918 and 1920; elected as a Republican to the Sixty-seventh Congress (March 4, 1921–March 3, 1923); unsuccessful candidate for reelection in 1922 to the Sixty-eighth Congress; resumed the practice of law in Springfield, Mo.; presidential elector on the Republican ticket of Coolidge and Dawes in 1924; moved to Kansas City, Mo., in 1925; appointed United States district attorney for the western district of Missouri December 21, 1925, and served until his resignation March 4, 1929; elected as a Republican to the United States Senate and served from March 4, 1929, to January 3, 1935; unsuccessful candidate for reelection in 1934; delegate to the Republican National Convention in 1932; resumed the practice of law in Springfield, Mo.; member of the Missouri Appellate Judicial Commission for a term of six years, ending January 1952; died in Springfield, Mo., October 22, 1954; interment in Maple Park Cemetery, southeast of the city.

PATTERSON, Thomas (half brother of John Patterson), a Representative from Pennsylvania; born in Little Britain Township, Lancaster County, Pa., October 1, 1764; moved with his parents to Pattersons Mills, Cross Creek Township, Washington County, Pa., in 1778; completed preparatory studies; engaged in agricultural pursuits; also operated a flour mill; served as a major general of militia in the War of 1812; presidential elector on the Democratic ticket of Monroe and Tompkins in 1816; elected as a Democrat to the Fifteenth and to the three succeeding Congresses (March 4, 1817–March 3, 1825); did not seek renomination in 1824; resumed former business pursuits; died in Cross Creek Township, near Pattersons Mills, Washington County, Pa., on November 16, 1841; interment in West Middletown Cemetery, West Middletown, Pa.

PATTERSON, Thomas J., a Representative from New York; born in that State about 1808; attended the public schools; elected as a Whig to the Twenty-eighth Congress (March 4, 1843–March 3, 1845); engaged as a land agent in Rochester, Monroe County, N. Y.

PATTERSON, Thomas MacDonald, a Delegate, a Representative, and a Senator from Colorado; born in County Carlow, Ireland, November 4, 1839; immigrated to the United States with his parents, who settled in New York City in 1849; attended the public schools; moved with his parents to Crawfordsville, Ind., in 1853; worked in a printing office for three years and as a watchmaker and jeweler for five years; during the Civil War enlisted in the Eleventh Regiment, Indiana Volunteer Infantry, in 1861; attended the Indiana Asbury (now De Pauw) University, Greencastle, Ind., in 1862 and Wabash College, Crawfordsville, Ind., in 1863; studied law; was admitted to the bar in 1867 and commenced practice in Crawfordsville, Ind.; moved to Denver, Colo., in December 1872 and continued the practice of law; city attorney in 1873 and 1874; elected as a Democrat a Delegate to the Forty-fourth Congress and served from March 4, 1875, to August 1, 1876, when the Territory became a State; successfully contested the election of James B. Belford to the Forty-fifth Congress and served from December 13, 1877, to March 3, 1879; was not a candidate for renomination in 1878; resumed the practice of law in Denver; member of the Democratic National Committee 1874–1880; delegate to the Democratic National Conventions in 1876, 1880, 1888, and 1892, and to the Populist National Convention in 1895; purchased the Rocky Mountain News in 1890 and later the Denver Times; elected to the United States Senate and served from March 4, 1901, to March 3, 1907; was not a candidate for reelection; resumed newspaper activities in Denver, Colo., and died there July 23, 1916; interment in Fairmount Cemetery.

PATTERSON, Walter, a Representative from New York; born in Columbia County, N. Y.; completed preparatory studies; member of the State assembly in 1818; served as supervisor of the town of Ancram 1821–1823; elected to the Seventeenth Congress (March 4, 1821–March 3, 1823); moved to Livingston, Columbia County, N. Y.; supervisor for the town of Livingston 1826–1828; associate justice of the Columbia County Court and served from 1828 to 1830.

PATTERSON, William (brother of George Washington Patterson and uncle of Augustus Frank), a Representative from New York; born in Londonderry, Rockingham County, N. H., June 4, 1789; attended the common schools; moved to Rensselaerville, Albany County, N. Y., in 1815, and in the following year to Lyons, Wayne County; engaged in the manufacture and sale of fanning mills; moved to a farm near Warsaw, N. Y., in 1822 and engaged in agricultural pursuits; settled in Warsaw, N. Y., in 1837; held several local offices; elected as a Whig to the Twenty-fifth Congress and served from March 4, 1837, until his death in Warsaw, Wyoming County, N. Y., August 14, 1838; interment in Warsaw Town Cemetery.

PATTERSON, William, a Representative from Ohio; born in Maryland in 1790; moved to Mansfield, Ohio; completed preparatory studies; studied law; was admitted to the bar and practiced; held several local offices; associate judge of the court of common pleas in 1820 and 1827; elected as a Democrat to the Twenty-third and Twenty-fourth Congresses (March 4, 1833–March 3, 1837); died in Van Wert, Van Wert County, Ohio, on August 17, 1868; interment in Mansfield Cemetery, Mansfield, Ohio.

PATTISON, John M., a Representative from Ohio; born near Owensville, Clermont County, Ohio, June 13, 1847; during the Civil War entered the Union Army in 1864; was graduated from the Ohio Wesleyan University, Delaware, Ohio, in 1869; studied law; was admitted to the bar in 1872 and commenced practice in Cincinnati, Ohio; member of the State house of representatives in 1873; attorney for the committee of safety of Cincinnati 1874–1876; vice president and manager of the Union Central Life Insurance Co. of Cincinnati in 1881 and became president in 1891; member of the State senate in 1890; elected as a Democrat to the Fifty-second Congress (March 4, 1891–March 3, 1893); unsuccessful candidate for reelection; elected Governor of Ohio and served from January 8, 1906, until his death in Milford, Clermont County, Ohio, June 18, 1906; interment in Greenlawn Cemetery.

PATTON, Charles Emory (son of John Patton and brother of John Patton, Jr.), a Representative from Pennsylvania; born in Curwensville, Clearfield County, Pa., July 5, 1859; attended the common schools and was graduated from Dickinson Seminary, Williamsport, Pa., in 1878; engaged in the lumber business; owned and operated the Curwensville Electric Co., and then engaged in the construction contracting business; also largely interested in agricultural pursuits; director of the Curwensville National Bank; member of the school board, serving as president; member of the city council, and served as burgess; elected to the Sixty-second and Sixty-third Congresses (March 4, 1911–March 3, 1915); was not a candidate for renomination in 1914; appointed secretary of agriculture for the State of Pennsylvania October 15, 1915, and served in this capacity until January 22, 1920; retired from active public pursuits and moved to a farm near West Grove, Chester County, Pa., and resumed his interest in agricultural pursuits; died on his estate, the "Maples," near West Grove, Pa., December 15, 1937; interment in Oak Hill Cemetery, Curwensville, Pa.

PATTON, David Henry, a Representative from Indiana; born in Flemingsburg, Fleming County, Ky., November 26, 1837; attended the Collegiate Institute, Waveland, Ind.; enlisted in the Thirty-eighth Indiana Regiment in 1861 and served to the end of the Civil War; was mustered out in July 1865, after having attained the rank of colonel; was graduated from the Chicago Medical College in 1867 and practiced medicine in Remington, Jasper County, Ind.; pension examiner at Remington 1886–1890; delegate to the Democratic National Convention at Chicago in 1892 and at Kansas City in 1900; elected as a Democrat to the Fifty-second Congress (March 4, 1891–March 3, 1893); was not a candidate for renomination in 1892; moved to Woodward, Woodward County, Indian Territory (now Oklahoma), in 1893; appointed receiver of public lands for Oklahoma in 1893, and later resumed the practice of medicine; member of the district board of health of Woodward, Okla.; appointed pension examiner at Woodward; died in Otterbein, Benton County, Ind., on January 17, 1914; interment in Remington Cemetery, Remington, Ind.

PATTON, John (father of Charles Emory Patton and John Patton Jr., and uncle of William Irvin Swoope), a Representative from Pennsylvania; born in Covington, Tioga County, Pa., January 6, 1823; moved to Curwensville, Clearfield County, Pa., in 1828; attended the public schools; engaged in mercantile pursuits and in lumbering 1844–1860; organized the First National Bank of Curwensville in 1864 and was elected its president; organized the Curwensville Bank, which succeeded the First National Bank, and was elected its president; delegate to the Whig National Convention at Baltimore in 1852 and to the Republican National Convention at Chicago in 1860; elected as a Republican to the Thirty-seventh Congress (March 4, 1861–March 3, 1863); declined to be a candidate for renomination in 1862; presidential elector on the Republican ticket of Lincoln and Johnson in 1864; elected to the Fiftieth Congress (March 4, 1887–March 3, 1889); was not a candidate for renomination in 1888; resumed banking; died in Philadelphia, Pa., where he had gone for medical treatment, on December 23, 1897; interment in Oak Hill Cemetery, Curwensville, Pa.

PATTON, John, Jr. (son of the preceding and brother of Charles Emory Patton), a Senator from Michigan; born in Curwensville, Clearfield County, Pa., October 30, 1850; prepared for college at Phillips Academy, Andover, Mass.; was graduated from Yale College in 1875 and from the law department of Columbia College, New York City, in 1877; moved to Grand Rapids, Mich., in 1878; was admitted to the bar the same year and commenced the practice of law; member of the Republican State committee 1884–1886; president of the State League of Republican Clubs; appointed to the United States Senate to fill the vacancy caused by the death of Francis B. Stockbridge and served from May 5, 1894, to January 14, 1895, when a successor was elected and qualified; unsuccessful candidate for election in 1895 for above vacancy; vice president of the People's Savings Bank of Grand Rapids; member and later president of the Board of Library Commissioners of Grand Rapids from September 1903 until his death in that city on May 24, 1907; interment in Oak Hill Cemetery.

PATTON, John Denniston, a Representative from Pennsylvania; born in Indiana, Indiana County, Pa., November 28, 1829; attended the public schools; worked in a tannery for several years; engaged in mercantile pursuits in Indiana, Pa.; elected as a Democrat to the Forty-eighth Congress (March 4, 1883–March 3, 1885); declined to be a candidate for renomination in 1884; retired from public life; died in Indiana, Pa., February 22, 1904; interment in Oakland Cemetery.

PATTON, John Mercer, a Representative from Virginia; born in Fredericksburg, Va., August 10, 1797; attended Princeton College, and was graduated from the medical department of the University of Pennsylvania at Philadelphia in 1818, but never practiced; studied law; was admitted to the bar and commenced practice in Fredericksburg, Va.; elected as a Democrat to the Twenty-first Congress to fill the vacancy caused by the resignation of Philip P. Barbour; reelected to the Twenty-second and to the three succeeding Congresses and served from November 25, 1830, to April 7, 1838, when he resigned; senior councilor of Virginia and became Acting Governor of Virginia upon the resignation of Governor Gilmore in 1841; moved to Richmond, Va., and resumed the practice of law; died in Richmond, Va., October 29, 1858; interment in Shockee Cemetery.

PATTON, Nat, a Representative from Texas; born on a farm near Tadmor, Houston County, Tex., February 26, 1884; attended the rural schools and Sam Houston Normal School, Huntsville, Tex.; taught in the rural and high schools 1899–1918; also engaged in agricultural pursuits at Belott, Houston County, Tex., in 1915 and 1916; member of the State house of representatives in 1912 and 1913; attended the law department of the University of Texas at Austin; was admitted to the bar in 1918 and commenced practice in Crockett, Houston County, Tex.; served as county judge of Houston County, Tex., 1918–1922; member of the State senate 1929–1934; delegate to the Democratic State convention at Beaumont in 1924 and at Forth Worth in 1935; during the First World War enlisted in the United States Army on November 1, 1918, but was never sworn in due to the armistice being signed; was commissioned a first lieutenant in the Intelligence Department but did not report for duty; elected as a Democrat to the Seventy-fourth and to the four succeeding Congresses (January 3, 1935–January 3, 1945); unsuccessful candidate for renomination in 1944; resumed the practice of law; died in Crockett, Tex., July 27, 1957; interment in Evergreen Memorial Park.

PAUL, John, a Representative from Virginia; born in Rockingham County, Va., June 30, 1839; attended the common schools and Roanoke College, Salem, Va.; during the Civil War entered the Confederate Army; became a captain in the First Virginia Cavalry; wounded at Brandy Station; was captured at the Battle of the Wilderness and imprisoned in Fort Delaware until the end of the war; studied law in the University of Virginia at Charlottesville and was graduated in 1867; was admitted to the bar in 1867 and commenced practice in Harrisonburg, Va.; Commonwealth attorney of Rockingham County 1870–1877; served in the State senate 1877–1880; unsuccessful candidate for election in 1878 to the Forty-sixth Congress; elected as a Readjuster to the Forty-seventh Congress (March 4, 1881–March 3, 1883); presented credentials as a Member-elect to the Forty-eighth Congress and served from March 4, 1883, until September 5, 1883, when he resigned, having been appointed to a judicial position; the election subsequently was successfully contested by Charles T. O'Farrall; appointed judge of the United States District Court for the Western District of Virginia by President Arthur and served from September 5, 1883, until his death in Harrisonburg, Va., November 1, 1901; interment in Woodbine Cemetery.

PAUL, John (son of the preceding), a Representative from Virginia; born in Harrisonburg, Rockingham County, Va., December 9, 1883; attended private and public schools; was graduated from Virginia Military Institute at Lexington in 1903 and was an instructor in that institution in 1903 and 1904; was graduated from the law department of the University of Virginia at Charlottesville in 1906; was admitted to the bar and commenced practice in Harrisonburg, Va., in 1907; member of the State senate 1911–1915; entered the United States Army in May 1917; commissioned captain of Field Artillery and served throughout the First World War with the Three Hundred and Thirteenth Field Artillery of the One Hundred and Fifty-fifth Field Artillery Brigade, being in the American Expeditionary Forces from May 1918 to May 1919; again served in the State senate, 1919–1922; city attorney of Harrisonburg 1919–1923; successfully contested as a Republican the election of Thomas W. Harrison to the Sixty-seventh Congress and served from December 15, 1922, to March 3, 1923; unsuccessful candidate for reelection in 1922 to the Sixty-eighth Congress; special assistant to the Attorney General of the United States in 1923 and 1924; delegate to the Republican National Conventions in 1912, 1916, 1920, and 1924; resumed the private practice of law in 1924; United States district attorney for the western district of Virginia 1929–1932; appointed United States district judge for the western district of Virginia in 1932 and served until his retirement in 1959; is a resident of Rockingham County (Dayton), Va.

PAULDING, William, Jr., a Representative from New York; born in Philipsburgh (now Tarrytown), N. Y., March 7, 1770; completed preparatory studies; studied law; was admitted to the bar and commenced practice in New York City; elected as a Democrat to the Twelfth Congress (March 4, 1811–March 3, 1813); brigadier general of militia; served in the War of 1812; delegate to the State constitutional convention in 1821; adjutant general of the State of New York; mayor of New York City 1824–1826; died in Tarrytown, Westchester County, N. Y., February 11, 1854; interment in Old Dutch Burying Ground at Sleepy Hollow, Tarrytown.

PAWLING, Levi, a Representative from Pennsylvania; born in Fatland, near Norristown, Pa., July 25, 1773; attended the common schools and was graduated from the University of Pennsylvania at Philadelphia; moved to Norristown, Montgomery County, Pa., in November 1795; studied law; was admitted to the bar in 1795 and practiced in Norristown and Philadelphia; trustee of lands belonging to the University of Pennsylvania; appointed chairman of the commission to raise funds relative to lock navigation on the Schuylkill River in 1816; elected as a Democrat to the Fifteenth Congress (March 4, 1817–March 3, 1819); elected burgess of Norristown in 1818; president of the board of directors of the Bank of Montgomery County; died in Norristown, Pa., September 7, 1845; interment in St. John's Protestant Episcopal Cemetery.

PAYNE, Frederick George, a Senator from Maine; born in Lewiston, Androscoggin County, Maine, July 24, 1900; attended the public schools of Lewiston, Maine, and the Bentley School of Accounting and Finance, Boston, Mass.; during early school days worked as a newsboy, usher and doorman in a theater, and as a reporter for a weekly newspaper; engaged in automobile and farm machinery sales and theater auditing and managing 1925–1935; industrial consultant 1936–1940; mayor of Augusta, Maine, 1935–1941; Maine commissioner of finance and director of budget 1940–1942; during World War II entered the United States Air Force in April 1942 as a captain and served until inactivated to the Reserves in October 1945 as a lieutenant colonel; business manager, Waldoboro Garage Co., 1945–1949; Governor of Maine 1949–1953; elected as a Republican to the United States Senate in 1952 for the term commencing January 3, 1953, and ending January 3, 1959; unsuccessful candidate for reelection in 1958; trustee of Bentley School of Accounting and Finance; industrial consultant and district manager of Walsh Engineers, Inc.; is a resident of Waldoboro, Maine.

PAYNE, Henry B. (grandfather of Frances P. Bolton), a Representative and a Senator from Ohio; born in Hamilton, Madison County, N. Y., November 30, 1810; was graduated from Hamilton College, Clinton, N. Y., in 1832; studied law; was admitted to the bar and practiced in Cleveland, Ohio, 1834–1846; city clerk in 1836; presidential elector on the Democratic ticket of Cass and Butler in 1848; member of the State senate 1849–1851; unsuccessful Democratic candidate for election to the United States Senate in 1851 and for Governor of Ohio in 1857; delegate to the Democratic National Conventions in 1856, 1860, and 1872; elected as a Democrat to the Forty-fourth Congress (March 4, 1875–March 3, 1877); unsuccessful candidate for reelection in 1876 to the Forty-fifth Congress; appointed a member of the Electoral Commission created by act of Congress approved January 29, 1877, to decide the contests in various States in the presidential election of 1876; unsuccessful candidate for the Democratic presidential nomination in 1880 and again in 1884; elected to the United States Senate and served from March 4, 1885, to March 3, 1891; died in Cleveland, Cuyahoga County, Ohio, September 9, 1896; interment in Lake View Cemetery.

PAYNE, Sereno Elisha, a Representative from New York; born in Hamilton, Madison County, N. Y., June 26, 1843; attended the Auburn (N. Y.) Academy and was graduated from the University of Rochester, N. Y., in 1864; studied law; was admitted to the bar in 1866 and practiced in Auburn, N. Y.; city clerk of Auburn in 1867 and 1868; supervisor in 1871 and 1872; district attorney of Cayuga County 1873–1879; president of the board of education of Auburn 1879–1882; appointed a member of the American-British Joint High Commission in January 1899; elected as a Republican to the Forty-eighth and Forty-ninth Congresses (March 4, 1883–March 3, 1887); elected to the Fifty-first Congress to fill the vacancy caused by the death of Newton W. Nutting; reelected to the Fifty-second and to the eleven succeeding Congresses and served from March 4, 1889, until his death; had been reelected to the Sixty-fourth Congress; died in Washington, D. C., December 10, 1914; interment in Fort Hill Cemetery, Auburn, N. Y.

PAYNE, William Winter, a Representative from Alabama; born at "Granville," near Warrenton, Fauquier County, Va., January 2, 1807; completed preparatory studies; studied law but never practiced; moved to Franklin County, Ala., in 1825 and engaged in planting; member of the State house of representatives in 1831; moved to Sumter County, Ala.; again a member of the State house of representatives 1834–1838 and in 1840; unsuccessful candidate for the State senate in 1839; elected as a Democrat to the Twenty-seventh, Twenty-eighth, and Twenty-ninth Congresses (March 4, 1841–March 3, 1847); unsuccessful candidate for reelection in 1846 to the Thirtieth Congress; returned to Virginia in 1847 and engaged in planting near Warrenton; chairman of the Democratic State convention at Richmond in 1859; died in Warrenton, Va., September 2, 1874; interment in the City Cemetery.

PAYNTER, Lemuel, a Representative from Pennsylvania; born in Lewes, Sussex County, Del., in 1788; attended the common schools; moved to Philadelphia, Pa.; served in the War of 1812 and became major and lieutenant colonel of the Ninety-third Regiment, Pennsylvania Militia; member of the board of commissioners of the Southwark district for many years and also served as president of the board; member of the guardians of the poor and also school director; elected a member of the State senate in 1833; elected as a Democrat to the Twenty-fifth and Twenty-sixth Congresses (March 4, 1837–March 3, 1841); was not a candidate for renomination in 1840; retired from public life on account of ill health but again served as a member of the board of commissioners of the Southwark district; died in Philadelphia, Pa., August 1, 1863; interment in Union Sixth Street Cemetery.

PAYNTER, Thomas Hanson, a Representative and a Senator from Kentucky; born on a farm near Vanceburg, Lewis County, Ky., December 9, 1851; attended the common schools, Rand's Academy in Lewis County, Ky., and Centre College, Danville, Ky.; studied law; was admitted to the bar in 1872 and commenced practice in Greenup, Ky.; prosecuting attorney of Greenup County by appointment 1876–1878 and by election 1878–1882; resumed the practice of law in Greenup; elected as a Democrat to the Fifty-first, Fifty-second, and Fifty-third Congresses and served from March 4, 1889, until his resignation, effective January 5, 1895, having been elected to the judiciary; judge of the court of appeals of Kentucky from January 1895 until August 1906, when he resigned, having been elected Senator; elected as a Democrat to the United States Senate and served from March 4, 1907, to March 3, 1913; was not a candidate for reelection in 1912; moved to Frankfort, Ky., in 1913 and continued the practice of law; also interested in agricultural pursuits; died in Frankfort, Ky., March 8, 1921; interment in the State Cemetery.

PAYSON, Lewis Edwin, a Representative from Illinois; born in Providence, R. I., September 17, 1840; moved with his parents to Illinois in 1852; attended the common schools and Lombard University, Galesburg, Ill.; studied law; was admitted to the bar and commenced practice in Ottawa, Ill., in 1862; moved to Pontiac, Livingston County, Ill., in January 1865 and continued the practice of law; judge of the county court 1869–1873; elected as a Republican to the Forty-seventh and to the four succeeding Congresses (March 4, 1881–March 3, 1891); resumed the practice of law; died in Washington, D. C., October 4, 1909; interment in Rock Creek Cemetery.

PEABODY, Nathaniel, a Delegate from New Hampshire; born in Topsfield, Essex County, Mass., March 1, 1741; tutored by his father; studied medicine; commenced practice in Plaistow, N. H., in 1761; moved to Atkinson, N. H., in 1770; resigned a royal commission to enter the Revolutionary Army; served at the capture of Fort William and Mary, New Castle, N. H.; elected a member of the committee of safety January 10, 1776, and was its chairman; member of the State house of representatives 1776–1779, 1781–1785, 1787–1790, and 1793–1796, serving as speaker in 1793; adjutant general of the New Hampshire Militia July 19, 1777, and commanded a brigade in Rhode Island in 1779; Member of the Continental Congress in 1779 and 1780; delegate to the State constitutional conventions of 1782 and 1783; again elected a Member of the Continental Congress in 1786 but did not take his seat; member of the State senate in 1785, 1786, and 1790–1793; chosen from the house in 1784 and from the senate in 1785 to serve as councilor; major general of militia 1793–1798; because of pecuniary embarrassment was confined within the limits of a debtor's prison for about twenty years; died in Exeter, Rockingham County, N. H., on June 27, 1823; interment probably in the Old Cemetery.

PEACE, Roger Craft, a Senator from South Carolina; born in Greenville, Greenville County, S. C., May 19, 1899; attended the public schools and was graduated from Furman University, Greenville, S. C., in 1919; reporter in Greenville, S. C., 1914–1919; sports editor in 1919 and 1920; editor 1920–1924; business manager 1924–1934; publisher since 1934; during the First World War entered the R. O. T. C. at Plattsburg, N. Y., and served as an instructor in the United States Army at Camp Perry in 1918; colonel on the staff of Governor Blackwood 1930–1934; trustee of Furman University 1938–1948; appointed as a Democrat to the United States Senate to fill the vacancy caused by the death of Alva M. Lumpkin, who had been appointed to fill the vacancy caused by the resignation of James F. Byrnes, and served from August 5, 1941, until November 4, 1941; was not a candidate for election to the vacancy; resumed former pursuits; is a resident of Greenville, S. C.

PEARCE, Charles Edward, a Representative from Missouri; born in Whitesboro, Oneida County, N. Y., May 29, 1842; attended Fairfield Seminary, and was graduated from Union College, Schenectady, N. Y., in 1863; during the Civil War enlisted in the Union Army; commissioned captain of Battery D, Sixteenth Regiment, New York Heavy Artillery, in 1863; promoted to the rank of major in June 1864; appointed to the staff of Maj. Gen. A. H. Terry after the capture of Fort Fisher; on the occupation of Wilmington was detailed as provost marshal general of the eastern district of North Carolina; resigned from the Army in the fall of 1865; settled in St. Louis, Mo., in 1866; studied law; was admitted to the bar in 1867 and commenced practice in St. Louis, Mo.; also interested in the manufacture of bagging, rope, and twine; organized and commanded the First Regiment of the Missouri National Guard in 1877; delegate to the Republican National Convention at Chicago in 1888, which nominated Benjamin Harrison for President and Levi P. Morton for Vice President; appointed chairman of the commission to treat with the Sioux Indians of the Northwest in 1891; elected as a Republican to the Fifty-fifth and Fifty-sixth Congresses (March 4, 1897–March 3, 1901); declined to be a candidate for renomination in 1900; died in St. Louis, Mo., on January 30, 1902; interment in Fort Hill Cemetery, Auburn, N. Y.

PEARCE, Dutee Jerauld, a Representative from Rhode Island; born on the island of Prudence, R. I., April 3, 1789; was graduated from Brown University, Providence, R. I., in 1808; studied law; was admitted to the bar and commenced practice in Newport, R. I.; held various local offices; attorney general of Rhode Island 1819–1825; presidential elector on the Democratic ticket of Monroe and Tompkins in 1820; United States district attorney in 1824 and 1825; member of the State house of representatives; elected as a Democrat to the Nineteenth and to the five succeeding Congresses (March 4, 1825–March 3, 1837); unsuccessful candidate for reelection in 1836 to the Twenty-fifth Congress; died in Newport, R. I., May 9, 1849; interment in the Common Burial Ground.

PEARCE, James Alfred, a Representative and a Senator from Maryland; born in Alexandria, Va., December 8, 1804; was graduated from Princeton College in 1822; studied law; was admitted to the bar and commenced practice in Cambridge, Dorchester County, Md., in 1824; moved to Louisiana in 1825 and engaged in planting; returned to Maryland and settled in Kent County in 1828; resumed the practice of law in Chestertown; served in the State house of delegates in 1831; elected as a Whig to the Twenty-fourth and Twenty-fifth Congresses (March 4, 1835–March 3, 1839); unsuccessful candidate for reelection in 1838 to the Twenty-sixth Congress; elected to the Twenty-seventh Congress (March 4, 1841–March 3, 1843); elected as a Whig to the United States Senate in 1843; reelected in 1849, 1855, and 1861, the last time as a Democrat, and served from March 4, 1843, until his death in Chestertown, Md., on December 20, 1862; interment in New Chester Cemetery.

PEARCE, John Jamison, a Representative from Pennsylvania; born in Wilkes-Barre, Pa., February 28, 1826; completed preparatory studies; was ordained a minister in the Methodist Episcopal Church when eighteen years of age; joined the Baltimore Conference and served as pastor at Warriors Mark, Jersey Shore, and Lock Haven, Pa.; elected as a Whig to the Thirty-fourth Congress (March 4, 1855–March 3, 1857); declined to be a candidate for reelection in 1856 to the Thirty-fifth Congress; renewed his connections with the Wyoming general and other conferences and served in various localities until he retired to Lock Haven in 1888; moved to Conneaut, Ashtabula County, Ohio, where he died May 26, 1912; interment in Highland Cemetery, Lock Haven, Pa.

PEARRE, George Alexander, a Representative from Maryland; born in Cumberland, Md., July 16, 1860; attended private schools, Allegany County Academy at Cumberland, St. James College near Hagerstown, Md., and Princeton College; was graduated from the West Virginia University at Morgantown in 1880 and from the law department of Maryland University at Baltimore in 1882; was admitted to the bar in 1882 and commenced practice in Cumberland, Md., in 1887; member of the Maryland National Guard and served as adjutant and lieutenant colonel 1887–1892; member of the State senate 1890–1892; prosecuting attorney of Allegany County 1895–1899; elected as a Republican to the Fifty-sixth and to the five succeeding Congresses (March 4, 1899–March 3, 1911); declined to be a candidate for reelection in 1910 to the Sixty-second Congress; engaged in the practice of his profession until his death in Cumberland, Md., on September 19, 1923; interment in Rose Hill Cemetery.

PEARSON, Albert Jackson, a Representative from Ohio; born in Centerville, Belmont County, Ohio, May 20, 1846; at an early age moved with his parents to Beallsville, Monroe County, Ohio; attended the common schools and the normal school at Lebanon, Ohio; served as a private in Company I, One Hundred and Eighty-sixth Regiment, Ohio Volunteer Infantry, during the Civil War; studied law; was admitted to the bar in 1868 and commenced practice in Woodsfield, Ohio; prosecuting attorney of Monroe County 1871–1877; member of the State senate in 1881 and 1882; probate judge of Monroe County 1884–1890; elected as a Democrat to the Fifty-second and Fifty-third Congresses (March 4, 1891–March 3, 1895); was not a candidate for reelection in 1894 to the Fifty-fourth Congress; resumed the practice of his profession; died in Woodsfield, Monroe County, Ohio, on May 15, 1905; interment in Woodsfield Cemetery.

PEARSON, Herron Carney, a Representative from Tennessee; born in Taylor, Williamson County, Tex., July 31, 1890; moved to Jackson, Tenn., in 1891; attended the public and high schools; was graduated from Union University, Jackson, Tenn., in 1910 and from the law department of Cumberland University, Lebanon, Tenn., in 1912; was admitted to the bar the same year and commenced practice in Jackson, Tenn.; presidential elector in 1912 on the Democratic ticket of Wilson and Marshall; served as municipal judge of the city of Jackson, Tenn., in 1915; city attorney of Jackson, Tenn., 1920–1923; elected as a Democrat to the Seventy-fourth and to the three succeeding Congresses (January 3, 1935–January 3, 1943); was not a candidate for renomination in 1942; resumed the practice of law; died in Jackson, Tenn., April 24, 1953; interment in Hollywood Cemetery.

PEARSON, John James, a Representative from Pennsylvania; born near Darby, Delaware County, Pa., October 25, 1800; moved with his parents to Mercer, Pa., in 1805; attended private schools and a grammar boarding school; studied law; was admitted to the bar in August 1822 and commenced practice in Mercer County; elected as a Whig to the Twenty-fourth Congress to fill the vacancy caused by the resignation of John Banks and served from December 5, 1836, to March 3, 1837; was not a candidate for renomination in 1836; resumed the practice of law; member of State senate 1838–1842; appointed president judge of Dauphin and Lebanon Counties, Pa., April 7, 1849, and served until January 1, 1882; died in Harrisburg, Pa., May 30, 1888; interment in Mount Kalmia Cemetery.

PEARSON, Joseph, a Representative from North Carolina; born in Rowan County, N. C., in 1776; completed preparatory studies; studied law; was admitted to the bar and commenced practice in Salisbury, N. C.; member of the State house of commons; elected as a Federalist to the Eleventh, Twelfth, and Thirteenth Congresses (March 4, 1809–March 3, 1815); while in Congress fought a duel with John George Jackson, of Virginia, and on the second fire wounded his opponent in the hip; died in Salisbury, N. C., October 27, 1834.

PEARSON, Richmond, a Representative from North Carolina; born at "Richmond Hill," Yadkin County, N. C., January 26, 1852, attended Horner's School, Oxford, N. C., and was graduated from Princeton College in 1872; studied law; was admitted to the bar in 1874; in the same year was appointed United States consul to Verviers and Liege, Belgium; resigned in 1877; member of the State house of representatives 1884–1886; elected as a Republican to the Fifty-fourth and Fifty-fifth Congresses (March 4, 1895–March 3, 1899); successfully contested the election of William T. Crawford to the Fifty-sixth Congress and served from May 10, 1900, to March 3, 1901; appointed by President Theodore Roosevelt as United States consul to Genoa, Italy, December 11, 1901, as Envoy Extraordinary and Minister

Plenipotentiary to Persia in 1902, and as Minister to Greece and Montenegro in 1907; resigned from the diplomatic service in 1909; retired; died at "Richmond Hill," Asheville, N. C., September 12, 1923; interment in Riverside Cemetery.

PEASE, Henry Roberts, a Senator from Mississippi; born in Winsted, Litchfield County, Conn., February 19, 1835; received a normal-school training; engaged in teaching 1848–1859; studied law; was admitted to the bar in 1859 and commenced practice in Washington, D. C.; during the Civil War entered the Union Army as a private in 1862 and attained the rank of captain; superintendent of education of Louisiana while that State was under military rule; appointed superintendent of education of freedmen in Mississippi in 1867; elected State superintendent of education of Mississippi in 1869; elected as a Republican to the United States Senate to fill the vacancy caused by the resignation of Adelbert Ames, and served from February 3, 1874, to March 3, 1875; was not a candidate for reelection; postmaster of Vicksburg, Miss., from March 3, 1875, to November 6, 1875; established and edited the Mississippi Educational Journal; moved to Dakota in 1881 and settled in Watertown; receiver of the United States land cffice at Watertown 1881–1885; member of the State senate in 1904; died in Watertown, S. Dak., January 2, 1907; interment in Mount Hope Cemetery.

PEASLEE, Charles Hazen, a Representative from New Hampshire; born in Gilmanton, N. H., on February 6, 1804; attended Gilmanton Academy, and was graduated from Dartmouth College, Hanover, N. H., in 1824; studied law; was admitted to the bar in 1828 and commenced practice in Concord, N. H.; member of the State house of representatives 1833–1837; adjutant general of the State militia 1839–1847; elected as a Democrat to the Thirtieth, Thirty-first, and Thirty-second Congresses (March 4, 1847–March 3, 1853); was not a candidate for renomination in 1852; collector of the port of Boston by appointment of President Pierce 1853–1857; moved to Portsmouth, N. H., in 1860; died while on a visit to St. Paul, Minn., on September 18, 1866; interment in Harmony Grove Cemetery, Portsmouth, N. H.

PEAVEY, Hubert Haskell, a Representative from Wisconsin, born in Adams, Mower County, Minn., on January 12, 1881; moved with his parents to Redwood Falls, Minn., in 1886; attended the public schools, the high school at Redwood Falls, and Pillsbury Academy, Owatonna, Minn.; pursued various activities in Nebraska, Kansas, and Oklahoma from 1900 until 1904, when he moved to South Dakota and engaged in the real-estate business and in the development of the town sites of Carlyle, Cresbard, and Lowry; moved to Washburn, Bayfield County, Wis., in 1909 and continued the real-estate business; served as alderman in 1911 and as mayor of Washburn in 1912 and 1920–1922; member of the State assembly 1913–1915; became editor and publisher of the Washburn News in 1915; during the First World War recruited Company D, Sixth Infantry, Wisconsin National Guard, and served as captain; reported for duty July 15, 1917, and commanded the company until October 15, 1917, when it became Company D, Thirty-second Division, which he also commanded; served until honorably discharged on October 29, 1918; resumed his former newspaper activities in Washburn, Wis.; unsuccessful candidate for the Republican nomination in 1920 to the Sixty-seventh Congress; elected as a Republican to the Sixty-eighth and to the five succeeding Congresses (March 4, 1923–January 3, 1935); unsuccessful candidate for reelection in 1934 to the Seventy-fourth Congress; again engaged in the real-estate business and also operated a fur ranch; died in Washburn, Wis., November 21, 1937; interment in Woodland Cemetery.

PECK, Erasmus Darwin, a Representative from Ohio; born in Stafford, Conn., September 16, 1808; attended the common schools of Munson, Mass., and was graduated from the medical department of Yale College in 1829; moved to Portage County, Ohio, in 1830 and practiced medicine; moved to Perrysburg, Wood County, Ohio, in 1834 and continued the practice of his profession; member of the State house of representatives 1856–1859; elected as a Republican to the Forty-first Congress to fill the vacancy caused by the death of Truman H. Hoag; reelected to the Forty-second Congress and served from April 23, 1870, to March 3, 1873; did not seek renomination in 1872; practiced medicine in Perrysburg, Ohio, until his death there December 25, 1876; interment in Fort Meigs Cemetery.

PECK, George Washington, a Representative from Michigan; born in New York City June 4, 1818; pursued classical studies; attended Yale College; studied law in New York City; moved to Michigan in 1839 and settled in Brighton, Livingston County; was admitted to the bar in 1842 and commenced practice in Brighton the same year; member of the State house of representatives in 1846 and 1847 and served as speaker the last term; moved to Lansing, Mich., when the State capital was located there in 1847; was the first postmaster of Lansing; secretary of state of Michigan in 1848 and 1849; editor and proprietor of the Lansing Journal; State printer 1852–1855; elected as a Democrat to the Thirty-fourth Congress (March 4, 1855–March 3, 1857); unsuccessful for reelection in 1856 to the Thirty-fifth Congress; mayor of Lansing in 1864; moved to East Saginaw, Mich., and engaged in the practice of law 1864–1873; moved to St. Louis, Mo., in 1873, to Hot Springs, Ark., in 1880, and to Bismarck, Mo., in 1882; died in Saginaw, Mich., June 30, 1905; interment in Brady Hill Cemetery.

PECK, Jared Valentine, a Representative from New York; born in Port Chester, Westchester County, N. Y., September 21, 1816; attended the common schools; engaged in the lumber, brick, hardware, and building-material business; auditor for the town of Rye in 1844 and 1845; member of the State assembly in 1848; elected as a Democrat to the Thirty-third Congress (March 4, 1853–March 3, 1855); was not a candidate for renomination in 1854; resumed his former business pursuits; presidential elector on the Republican ticket of Frémont and Dayton in 1856; appointed warden of the port of New York by Governor Morgan in 1859, with residence in New York City, and served until 1865; one of the founders of the Union League Club; returned to Westchester County and settled in Rye; member of the town board of auditors; donated the Brundage Building in Port Chester for use as a public library; died at "The Cedars," in Rye, Westchester County, N. Y., December 25, 1891; interment in Greenwood Union Cemetery.

PECK, Lucius Benedict, a Representative from Vermont; born in Waterbury, Vt., November 17, 1802; pursued classical studies and attended the United States Military Academy, West Point, N. Y., for one year; studied law; was admitted to the bar and commenced practice in Barre, Washington County, Vt., in 1825; member of the State house of representatives in 1831; moved to Montpelier, Vt., in 1832, where he practiced his profession; elected as a Democrat to the Thirtieth and Thirty-first Congresses (March 4, 1847–March 3, 1851); did not seek renomination in 1850, having become a gubernatorial candidate; unsuccessful candidate for Governor of Vermont in 1850; resumed the practice of law; United States district attorney for Vermont by appointment of President Pierce 1853–1857; president of the Vermont & Canada Railroad from 1859 until his death in Lowell, Mass., December 28, 1866; interment in Green Mount Cemetery, Montpelier, Vt.

PECK, Luther Christopher, a Representative from New York; born in Connecticut in January 1800; completed preparatory studies; studied law; was admitted to the bar and practiced; moved to Allegheny County, Pa., and later to Pike, Wyoming County, N. Y., and continued the practice of law; held various local offices; elected as a Whig to the Twenty-fifth and Twenty-sixth Congresses (March 4, 1837–March 3, 1841); affiliated with the Republican Party after it was formed; resumed the practice of his profession at Pike, N. Y.; moved to Nunda, N. Y., and continued the practice of law; died in Nunda, Livingston County, N. Y., February 5, 1876; interment in Oakwood Cemetery.

PECKHAM, Rufus Wheeler, a Representative from New York; was born in Rensselaerville, Albany County, N. Y., on December 20, 1809; completed preparatory studies; was graduated from Union College at Schenectady, N. Y., in 1827; studied law; was admitted to the bar in 1830 and commenced practice in Albany, N. Y.; district attorney of Albany County 1838–1841; elected as a Democrat to the Thirty-third Congress (March 4, 1853–March 3, 1855); resumed the practice of law; justice of the supreme court for the third judicial district and served from 1861 to 1869; associate judge of the court of appeals from May 17, 1870, until his death; lost at sea November 22, 1873, in a collision between two steamers in mid-ocean.

PEDDIE, Thomas Baldwin, a Representative from New Jersey; born in Edinburgh, Scotland, February 11, 1808; attended elementary schools; immigrated to the United States in 1833 and settled in Newark, N. J.; engaged in the manufacture of traveling bags and trunks; member of the State house of assembly in 1864 and 1865; mayor of Newark 1866–1869; served as president of the Newark Board of Trade in 1873; elected as a Republican to the Forty-fifth Congress (March 4, 1877–March 3, 1879); declined to be a candidate in 1878 for renomination; resumed his former manufacturing pursuits; vice president of the Essex County National Bank and president of the Security Savings Bank of Newark; died in Newark, N. J., February 16, 1889; interment in Mount Pleasant Cemetery.

PEDEN, Preston Elmer, a Representative from Oklahoma; born in Duke, Jackson County, Okla., June 28, 1914; moved to Altus, Okla., in 1920; attended the public schools; was graduated from Altus (Okla.) High School in 1932, from the University of Oklahoma at Norman in 1936, and from the law school of the same university in 1939; was admitted to the bar in 1939 and commenced practice in Altus, Okla.; attorney for the State insurance fund of the State of Oklahoma 1939–1942; during World War II enlisted in June 1942 as a private in the United States Army; promoted through the ranks to captain, being discharged May 5, 1946; while serving overseas sent a notification and declaration for the office of Congressman to the election board and subsequently received the nomination; elected as a Democrat to the Eightieth Congress (January 3, 1947–January 3, 1949); was an unsuccessful candidate for renomination in 1948; staff member of the Public Lands Committee of the United States House of Representatives in May 1949; appointed Alaskan regional counsel, Bureau of Land Management, Department of the Interior, in 1950; counsel to House Committee on Interior and Insular Affairs 1950–1952; operated own farm and served as manager of estate of Gordon Strong, Dickerson, Md., February 1953–September 1954; in September 1954 became director of governmental affairs of the Chicago Association of Commerce and Industry; is a resident of La Grange, Ill.

PEEK, Harmanus, a Representative from New York; born in Albany, N. Y., June 24, 1782; completed preparatory studies; was graduated from Union College, Schenectady, N. Y., in 1804;

studied law; was admitted to the bar and commenced practice in Schenectady; member of the State assembly in 1816 and 1817; elected to the Sixteenth Congress (March 4, 1819–March 3, 1821); was not a candidate for reelection; died in Schenectady, N. Y., September 27, 1838; interment in Dutch Church Cemetery; reinterred in Vale Cemetery.

PEEL, Samuel West, a Representative from Arkansas; born near Batesville, Independence County, Ark., September 13, 1831; attended the common schools; clerk of the circuit court of Carroll County, Ark., 1858–1860; during the Civil War entered the Confederate service in 1861 as a private; elected major of the Third Regiment, Arkansas Infantry, and later colonel of the Fourth Regiment, Arkansas Infantry; studied law; was admitted to the bar and commenced the practice of his profession in Carrollton, Ark., in 1865; moved to Bentonville, Benton County, in 1867 and continued the practice of law; prosecuting attorney of the fourth judicial circuit of Arkansas 1873–1876; elected as a Democrat to the Forty-eighth and to the four succeeding Congresses (March 4, 1883–March 3, 1893); unsuccessful candidate for renomination in 1892; resumed the practice of law in Bentonville, Ark., and before the Court of Claims at Washington, D. C., until 1915; retired from active business and public life; died in Bentonville, Ark., December 18, 1924; interment in Bentonville Cemetery.

PEELLE, Stanton Judkins, a Representative from Indiana; born near Richmond, Wayne County, Ind., February 11, 1843; attended the common schools and Winchester Seminary; during the Civil War enlisted in Company G, Eighth Regiment, Indiana Volunteers, August 5, 1861; promoted to a second lieutenancy in Company K, Fifty-seventh Regiment, Indiana Volunteers, December 10, 1862, and served until near the close of the war; studied law; was admitted to the bar in 1866 and commenced practice in Winchester, Ind.; moved to Indianapolis in 1869; deputy district attorney of Marion County in 1872 and 1873; member of the State house of representatives 1877–1879; elected as a Republican to the Forty-seventh Congress (March 4, 1881–March 3, 1883); presented credentials as a Member-elect to the Forty-eighth Congress and served from March 4, 1883, to May 22, 1884, when he was succeeded by William E. English, who contested his election; delegate to the Republican National Convention at Minneapolis in 1892; served on the board of control of the Indiana Reform School for Boys 1890–1892; appointed judge of the United States Court of Claims in 1892 and served until January 1, 1906, when he was advanced to chief justice and served until February 11, 1913, when he resigned; professor of law at George Washington University (D. C.) 1901–1911; member of the board of trustees of Howard University, Washington, D. C., 1906–1925; president of the board of the Washington College of Law 1910–1925; member of the board of directors of the Garfield Memorial Hospital 1910–1925; retired and resided in Washington, D. C., until his death there September 4, 1928; interment in Rock Creek Cemetery.

PEERY, George Campbell, a Representative from Virginia; born in Cedar Bluff, Tazewell County, Va., October 28, 1873; attended the common schools, and was graduated from Emory and Henry College, Emory, Va., in 1894; principal of Tazewell High School 1894–1896; was graduated from the law department of Washington and Lee University, Lexington, Va., in 1897; was admitted to the bar the same year and commenced practice in Tazewell, Va.; presidential elector at large on the Democratic ticket of Wilson and Marshall in 1916; delegate to the Democratic National Conventions in 1920 and 1924; local food administrator for Tazewell County during the First World War; elected as a Democrat to the Sixty-eighth, Sixty-ninth, and

Seventieth Congresses (March 4, 1923–March 3, 1929); was not a candidate for renomination in 1928; resumed the practice of law and also engaged in the raising of livestock; temporary chairman of the Democratic State convention in 1928; member of the Virginia State Corporation Commission 1929–1933; served as Governor 1934–1938; member of the board of trustees of Washington and Lee University and of Hollins College; died in Richlands, Va., October 14, 1952; interment in Maplewood Cemetery, Tazewell, Va.

PEERY, William, a Delegate from Delaware; settled with his father's family near Lewes, Del.; engaged in agricultural pursuits; during the Revolutionary War he raised and equipped an independent company at his own expense and was commissioned its captain April 13, 1777; member of the State house of representatives in 1782, 1784, 1787, 1793, and 1794; studied law; was admitted to the bar in 1785 and commenced practice in Sussex County; Member of the Continental Congress in 1785 and 1786; treasurer of Sussex County 1785–1796; appointed a member of a commission to purchase land and build thereon a courthouse and prison for Sussex County in 1791; died at Cool Spring, Sussex County, Del., December 17, 1800; interment in the churchyard of the Cool Spring Presbyterian Church.

PEFFER, William Alfred, a Senator from Kansas; born in Cumberland County, Pa., September 10, 1831; attended the public schools, and commenced teaching at the age of fifteen; moved to San Francisco, Calif., in 1850; thence to St. Joseph County, Ind., in 1853, and engaged in agricultural pursuits; moved to Morgan County, Mo., in September 1859 and continued agricultural pursuits; then moved to Warren County, Ill., in February 1862; during the Civil War enlisted in the Union Army as a private in Company F, Eighty-third Regiment, Illinois Volunteer Infantry; was promoted to second lieutenant in March 1863; served as regimental quartermaster and adjutant, post adjutant, judge advocate of the military commission, and department quartermaster in the engineering department at Nashville; mustered out of the service June 26, 1865; studied law while in the Army; was admitted to the bar in 1865 and commenced practice in Clarksville, Tenn.; moved to Fredonia, Kans., in 1870 and continued the practice of law; purchased the Fredonia Journal and changed the name to the Wilson County Courier in 1870; member of the State senate 1874–1876; moved to Coffeyville, Montgomery County; established and edited the Coffeyville Journal in 1875 and also practiced law; presidential elector on the Republican ticket of Garfield and Arthur in 1880; editor of the Kansas Farmer at Topeka in 1881; elected as a Populist to the United States Senate and served from March 4, 1891, to March 3, 1897; unsuccessful candidate for reelection to the United States Senate; unsuccessful candidate for Governor of Kansas in 1898; engaged in literary pursuits and in statistical compilation for Congress in Washington, D. C.; died in Grenola, Kans., October 7, 1912; interment in Topeka Cemetery, Topeka, Kans.

PEGRAM, John, a Representative from Virginia; born at "Bonneville," in Dinwiddie County, Va., November 16, 1773; attended the common schools; held various local offices; member of the State house of delegates 1797–1801; served in the State senate 1804–1808; major general of the State militia in the War of 1812; again a member of the State house of delegates 1813–1815; elected to the Fifteenth Congress to fill the vacancy caused by the death of Peterson Goodwyn and served from April 21, 1818, to March 3, 1819; appointed United States marshal for the eastern district of Virginia on April 23, 1821; lost his life during the burning of a boat on the Ohio River April 8, 1831, his body never being recovered.

PEIRCE, Joseph, a Representative from New Hampshire; born in Portsmouth, N. H., on June 25, 1748; attended school in Portsmouth; served during the Revolutionary War in Col. Pierce Long's regiment in 1775 and 1776; was a member of the State house of representatives in 1788, 1789, 1792–1795, 1800, and 1801; town clerk 1789–1794; was elected to the Seventh Congress and served from March 4, 1801, until his resignation in 1802; engaged in agricultural pursuits; died in Alton, N. H., September 12, 1812.

PEIRCE, Robert Bruce Fraser, a Representative from Indiana; born in Laurel, Franklin County, Ind., February 17, 1843; attended the public schools and also educated by private tutors served in the Civil War as second lieutenant of Company H, One Hundred and Thirty-fifth Regiment, Indiana Volunteers; was graduated from Wabash College, Crawfordsville, Ind., in 1866; studied law at Shelbyville, Ind.; was admitted to the bar in 1866 and commenced practice in Crawfordsville in 1867; elected prosecuting attorney of Montgomery County in 1868 and reelected in 1870 and 1872; elected as a Republican to the Forty-seventh Congress (March 4, 1881–March 3, 1883); unsuccessful candidate for reelection in 1882 to the Forty-eighth Congress; resumed the practice of law; appointed receiver for the Toledo, St. Louis & Western Railway (Clover Leaf route); died in Indianapolis, Ind., December 5, 1898; interment in Oak Hill Cemetery, Crawfordsville, Ind.

PELHAM, Charles, a Representative from Alabama; born in Person County, N. C., March 12, 1835; moved with his parents to Alabama in 1838; attended the common schools; studied law; was admitted to the bar and commenced practice in Talladega, Ala., in 1858; entered the Confederate Army in 1862 and served during the Civil War as first lieutenant of Company C, Fifty-first Regiment, Alabama Infantry; judge of the tenth judicial circuit of Alabama 1868–1873; elected as a Republican to the Forty-third Congress (March 4, 1873–March 3, 1875); was not a candidate for renomination in 1874; resumed the practice of law in Washington, D. C.; late in life was appointed a clerk in the Treasury Department; moved to Poulan, Worth County, Ga., in 1907; died in Poulan, Ga., January 18, 1908; interment in the Presbyterian Cemetery.

PELL, Herbert Claiborne, Jr. (great-grandson of John Francis Hamtramck Claiborne, great-great-grandnephew of William Charles Cole Claiborne and Nathaniel Herbert Claiborne, and father of Claiborne de Borda Pell), a Representative from New York; born in New York City, February 16, 1884; attended Pomfret (Conn.) School, Harvard University, Cambridge, Mass., and Columbia University, New York City; member of the Progressive committee of Orange County, N. Y., 1912–1914; elected as a Democrat to the Sixty-sixth Congress (March 4, 1919–March 3, 1921); unsuccessful candidate for reelection in 1920 to the Sixty-seventh Congress; chairman of the Democratic State committee 1921–1926; delegate to the Democratic National Convention at New York in 1924, which nominated Davis and Bryan; occasional lecturer at Columbia University, Harvard University, and other institutions of learning; decorated Officier d'Instruction Publique by the French Government for educational work; also received the Grand Cross of the Order of Christ, Portugal, and, for his work on the War Crimes Commission, the White Lion of Czechoslovakia and the grade of Officer of the Legion of Honor of France; author; member of the Institute of Coimbra University and of the Athenaeum of London; vice chairman of the Democratic National Campaign Committee in 1936; appointed from Rhode Island as Minister to Portugal from May 27, 1937, until February 11, 1941, when he was appointed Minister to Hungary, serving in that capacity until his resignation on November 30, 1942, after he had received the Hungarian declaration of war; United States representative on the War Crimes Commission from August 1943 to January 1945; died in Munich, Germany, July 17, 1961; remains cremated and the ashes scattered off Beaver Tail Light, Jamestown, R. I.

PELL, Philip, a Delegate from New York; born in Pelham Manor, N. Y., July 7, 1753; was graduated from King's College (now Columbia University), New York City, in 1770; studied law; was admitted to the bar and practiced in New York City and Westchester County; lieutenant, New York Volunteers, in 1776; deputy judge advocate, Continental Army, in 1777; member of the State assembly 1779–1781; Judge Advocate General, United States Army, 1781–1783; member of General Washington's staff at the evacuation of the city of New York in 1783; again a member of the State assembly 1784–1786; regent of the University of the State of New York 1784–1787; surrogate of Westchester County from March 13, 1787, to October 31, 1800; appointed a Delegate to the Continental Congress by Gov. George Clinton on January 13, 1788, and served until March 3, 1789; engaged in the practice of his profession; died in Pelham Manor, N. Y., May 1, 1811; interment in St. Paul's Churchyard, Eastchester (now in the Bronx), N. Y.

PELLY, Thomas Minor, a Representative from Washington; born in Seattle, King County, Wash., August 22, 1902; attended the public schools, the University School, Victoria, B. C., and the Hoosac School, Hoosick, N. Y.; was first employed by a real-estate office, then engaged in the banking business, first as a messenger and through promotions to assistant trust officer, Seattle National Bank, 1921–1930; vice president of Lowman & Hanford Co., a printing and stationery company, in 1930, and president and general manager 1937–1955; director of Seattle Trust Co., Olympia State Bank & Trust Co., and Northern Life Insurance Co. of Seattle; elected as a Republican to the Eighty-third and to the three succeeding Congresses (January 3, 1953–January 3, 1961). *Reelected to the Eighty-seventh Congress.*

PELTON, Guy Ray, a Representative from New York; born near Great Barrington, Berkshire County, Mass., August 3, 1824; attended the common schools and the Connecticut Literary Institute, Suffield, Conn.; taught school; studied law; was admitted to the bar and commenced practice in New York City in 1851; held various local offices; elected as a Whig to the Thirty-fourth Congress (March 4, 1855–March 3, 1857); unsuccessful candidate for reelection in 1856 to the Thirty-fifth Congress; resumed the practice of law in Great Barrington; died while on a tour in an attempt to climb Mary's Mountain in the Yellowstone National Park, Wyo., July 24, 1890; interment in Mahaiwe Cemetery, Great Barrington, Mass.

PENCE, Lafayette, a Representative from Colorado; born in Columbus, Bartholomew County, Ind., December 23, 1857; attended the common schools; was graduated from Hanover (Ind.) College in 1877; studied law; was admitted to the bar in 1878 and practiced in Columbus, Ind., until September 1879, when he moved to Winfield, Kans.; moved to Rico, Dolores County, Colo., in 1881 and continued the practice of law until 1884; member of the State house of representatives in 1885; settled in Denver in 1885 and continued the practice of law; prosecuting attorney for Arapahoe County in 1887 and 1888; elected as the candidate of the Populists and Silver Democrats to the Fifty-third Congress (March 4, 1893–March 3, 1895); unsuccessful candidate for reelection in 1894 to the Fifty-fourth Congress; moved to New York City and engaged in railroad work; returned to Denver and from there moved to San Francisco, Calif., and subsequently to Washington, D. C., and continued the practice

of law; also engaged in hydraulic mining in Breckenridge, Colo., and Portland, Oreg.; died in Washington, D. C., October 22, 1923; interment in Garland Brook Cemetery, Columbus, Ind.

PENDLETON, Edmund (uncle of Nathaniel Pendleton and John Penn), a Delegate from Virginia; born in Caroline County, Va., September 9, 1721; completed preparatory studies; clerk, Caroline County Court, in 1740; studied law; was admitted to the bar in 1741 and practiced; justice of the peace in 1751; member of the Virginia House of Burgesses 1752–1774; member of the committee of correspondence in 1773 and of the colonial convention in 1774; Member of the Continental Congress in 1774 and 1775; president of the committee of safety in 1775; governor of the embryo colony 1774–1776; member of the State house of delegates in 1776 and 1777; judge of the general court and the court of chancery in 1777; presiding judge of the court of appeals in 1779; member and president of the Virginia constitutional convention in 1788; died in Richmond, Va., October 23, 1803; interment at Edmundsbury, eight miles southeast of Bowling Green, Va.; in 1907 was reinterred in Bruton Parish Church Cemetery, Williamsburg, Va.

PENDLETON, Edmund Henry, a Representative from New York; born in Savannah, Ga., in 1788; received a liberal schooling; studied law; was admitted to the bar and practiced for several years in Hyde Park, Dutchess County, N. Y.; county judge of Dutchess County 1830–1840; was elected as a Whig to the Twenty-second Congress (March 4, 1831–March 3, 1833); died in New York City February 25, 1862; interment in St. James' Churchyard, Hyde Park, N. Y.

PENDLETON, George Cassety, a Representative from Texas; born near Viola, Warren County, Tenn., April 23, 1845; attended the country schools and the Hannah High School; moved with his parents to Ellis County, Tex., in 1857; settled in Belton, Tex., and engaged in mercantile and agricultural pursuits; during the Civil War entered the Confederate service as a private in Captain Forrest's Company, Watson's Regiment, Parson's Brigade, Texas Cavalry; at the close of the war attended Waxahachie Academy in Ellis County, Tex.; employed as a commercial traveler for twelve years; engaged in mercantile and agricultural pursuits; delegate to every Democratic State convention from 1876 to 1910; member of the State house of representatives 1882–1888 and served as speaker in 1886; Lieutenant Governor of Texas 1890–1892; delegate to the Democratic National Convention at Chicago in 1896; elected as a Democrat to the Fifty-third and Fifty-fourth Congresses (March 4, 1893–March 3, 1897); declined to be a candidate for renomination in 1896; engaged in banking in Temple, Bell County, Tex.; studied law; was admitted to the bar in 1900 and practiced in Temple until his death there on January 19, 1913; interment in City Cemetery.

PENDLETON, George Hunt (son of Nathanael Greene Pendleton), a Representative and a Senator from Ohio; born in Cincinnati, Ohio, July 19, 1825; pursued an academic course in the schools of Cincinnati and attended Heidelberg University, Germany; studied law; was admitted to the bar in 1847 and commenced practice in Cincinnati; member of the State senate 1854–1856; unsuccessful candidate for election in 1854 to the Thirty-fourth Congress; elected as a Democrat to the Thirty-fifth and to the three succeeding Congresses (March 4, 1857–March 3, 1865); unsuccessful candidate for reelection in 1864 to the Thirty-ninth Congress; one of the managers appointed by the House of Representatives in 1862 to conduct the impeachment proceedings against West H. Humphreys, United States judge for the several districts of Tennessee; Democratic candidate for Vice President on the ticket headed by George B.

McClellan in 1864; unsuccessful candidate for election in 1866 to the Fortieth Congress; delegate to the Loyalist Convention at Philadelphia in 1866; unsuccessful Democratic candidate for Governor of Ohio in 1869; president of the Kentucky Central Railroad 1869–1879; elected as a Democrat to the United States Senate and served from March 4, 1879, to March 3, 1885; unsuccessful candidate for renomination; appointed Envoy Extraordinary and Minister Plenipotentiary to Germany on March 23, 1885, and served until his death in Brussels, Belgium, November 24, 1889; interment in Spring Grove Cemetery, Cincinnati, Ohio.

PENDLETON, James Monroe, a Representative from Rhode Island; born in North Stonington, New London County, Conn., January 10, 1822; attended school in North Stonington and Suffield, Conn.; moved to Westerly, R. I., and engaged in mercantile pursuits and later in the insurance business and banking; served in the State senate 1862–1865; delegate to the Republican National Convention at Chicago in 1868; presidential elector on the Republican ticket of Grant and Colfax in 1868; elected as a Republican to the Forty-second and Forty-third Congresses (March 4, 1871–March 3, 1875); unsuccessful for reelection in 1874 to the Forty-fourth Congress; member of the State house of representatives 1879–1884; chairman of the State board of charities and corrections 1884–1889; died in Westerly, R. I., February 16, 1889; interment in River Bend Cemetery.

PENDLETON, John Overton, a Representative from West Virginia; born in Wellsburg, Brooke County, Va. (now West Virginia), July 4, 1851; moved with his parents to Wheeling, Va. (now West Virginia), in 1851; attended Aspen Hill Academy, Louisa County, Va., 1865–1869, and Bethany College, West Virginia, 1869–1871; studied law; was admitted to the bar and commenced practice in Wheeling, W. Va., in 1874; unsuccessful Democratic candidate for State senator in 1886; presented credentials as a Democratic Member-elect to the Fifty-first Congress and served from March 4, 1889, to February 26, 1890, when he was succeeded by George W. Atkinson, who contested the election; elected as a Democrat to the Fifty-second and Fifty-third Congresses (March 4, 1891–March 3, 1895); unsuccessful candidate for renomination in 1894; resumed the practice of law in Wheeling, W. Va., and died there December 24, 1916; interment in Greenwood Cemetery.

PENDLETON, John Strother, a Representative from Virginia; born near Culpeper, Culpeper County, Va., March 1, 1802; pursued preparatory studies; studied law; was admitted to the bar in 1824 and practiced in Culpeper County; member of the State house of delegates 1830–1833 and 1836–1839; Chargé d'Affaires to Chile 1841–1844; elected as a Whig to the Twenty-ninth and Thirtieth Congresses (March 4, 1845–March 3, 1849); Chargé d'Affaires to the Argentine Confederation 1851–1854; empowered jointly with Robert C. Schenck, American Minister to Brazil, April 27, 1852, to negotiate a treaty of commerce with Paraguay and Uruguay; engaged in farming; died near Culpeper, Va., November 19, 1868; interment in the family burying ground, "Redwood," Culpeper, Va.

PENDLETON, Nathanael Greene (father of George Hunt Pendleton), a Representative from Ohio; born in Savannah, Ga., August 25, 1793, moved to New York City with his parents; was graduated from Columbia College at New York City in 1813; studied law; was admitted to the bar; served in the War of 1812, moved to Cincinnati, Ohio, in 1818 and practiced law; member of the State senate 1825–1829; elected as a Whig to the Twenty-seventh Congress (March 4, 1841–March 3, 1843); did not seek renomination in 1842; died in Cincinnati, Ohio, June 16, 1861; interment in Spring Grove Cemetery.

PENDLETON, Nathaniel (nephew of Edmund Pendleton and cousin of John Penn), a Delegate from Georgia; born in New Kent County, Va., in 1756; entered the Revolutionary Army at the age of 19 years; aide-de-camp to Gen. Nathaniel Greene in the campaigns in the Southern States and was thanked by Congress for gallant conduct at the battle of Eutaw Springs, N. C., September 8, 1781; at the close of the war settled in Georgia and studied law, ultimately becoming a district judge; elected a member of the convention which framed the Constitution of the United States in 1787; appointed to a Federal judgeship in Georgia in 1789 and served until 1796 when he resigned; Delegate to the Continental Congress in 1789; moved to New York City, N. Y., in 1796 and practiced law; died in Hyde Park, N. Y., October 20, 1821.

PENINGTON, John Brown, a Representative from Delaware; born near New Castle, Del., December 20, 1825; pursued an academic course in New Castle and Newark, Del., and was graduated from Jefferson College, Canonsburg, Pa.; engaged in teaching in the State of Indiana for several years; returned to Delaware; studied law; was admitted to the bar in 1857 and commenced practice in Dover, Del.; member of the State house of representatives in 1857; clerk of the State house of representatives in 1859, 1863, and 1871; delegate to the Democratic National Conventions at Charleston and Baltimore in 1860; appointed United States attorney for the district of Delaware in 1868 by President Johnson and served until 1872; appointed attorney general of the State by Governor Ponder in 1874 and served until 1878; elected as a Democrat to the Fiftieth and Fifty-first Congresses (March 4, 1887–March 3, 1891); was not a candidate for renomination in 1890; resumed the practice of law at Dover, Del., where he died June 1, 1902; interment in the Presbyterian Cemetery.

PENN, Alexander Gordon, a Representative from Louisiana; born near Stella, Patrick County, Va., May 10, 1799; moved with his parents to Lexington, Ky.; completed preparatory studies and attended Henry and Emory College, Marion, Va.; moved to the parish of St. Tammany, La., in 1821 and engaged in planting near Covington; served in the State house of representatives; postmaster of New Orleans from December 19, 1843, to April 18, 1849; delegate to the Democratic National Conventions in 1844, 1852, 1856, and 1860; elected as a Democrat to the Thirty-first Congress to fill the vacancy caused by the death of John H. Harmanson; reelected to the Thirty-second Congress and served from December 30, 1850, to March 3, 1853; returned to St. Tammany Parish and engaged in planting and the operation of a lumber mill near Covington; at the conclusion of the Civil War returned to Washington, D. C., where he died May 7, 1866; interment in Glenwood Cemetery.

PENN, John (nephew of Edmund Pendleton and cousin of Nathaniel Pendleton), a Delegate from North Carolina; born near Port Royal, Caroline County, Va., May 17, 1741; was educated under private tutors; studied law; was admitted to the bar in 1762 and commenced practice in Bowling Green, Caroline County, Va.; moved to Granville County, N. C., in 1774; elected to the Provincial Congress which met in Hillsboro, N. C., in August 1775; Member of the Continental Congress 1775–1780; a signer of the Declaration of Independence; one of the three representatives from North Carolina to ratify the Articles of Confederation on behalf of the State; member of board of war in North Carolina in 1780; receiver of taxes for North Carolina in 1784; resumed the practice of law; died near Williamsboro, Granville County, N. C., September 14, 1788; interment on his estate in Granville County, N. C.; reinterment at Guilford Battle Grounds, near Greensboro, N. C., in 1894.

PENNIMAN, Ebenezer Jenckes, a Representative from Michigan; born in Lansingburgh, Rensselaer County, N. Y., January 11, 1804; attended the common schools; apprenticed as a printer; moved to New York City in 1822 and to Orwell, Addison County, Vt., where he engaged in business as a dry-goods merchant; moved to Plymouth, Mich., in 1840 and again engaged as a dry-goods merchant; supervisor of Plymouth Township, Wayne County; member of the board to locate the State reform school in 1849; elected as a Whig and Free-Soiler to the Thirty-second Congress (March 4, 1851–March 3, 1853); was not a candidate for renomination in 1852; resumed mercantile pursuits until 1871 when he engaged in banking and served as president of the First National Bank of Plymouth; member of the convention that met under the oaks at Jackson, Mich., July 6, 1854, at the organization of the Republican Party in Michigan; died in Plymouth, Mich., April 12, 1890; interment in Riverside Cemetery.

PENNINGTON, Alexander Cumming McWhorter (cousin of William Pennington), a Representative from New Jersey; born in Newark, N. J., July 2, 1810; completed preparatory studies; attended the United States Military Academy, West Point, N. Y., 1826–1828; studied law; was admitted to the bar in 1833 and commenced practice in Newark; member of the State general assembly in 1837 and 1838; alderman of Newark 1837–1840; elected as a Whig to the Thirty-third and Thirty-fourth Congresses (March 4, 1853–March 3, 1857); moved to New York City, where he died January 25, 1867; interment in Mount Pleasant Cemetery, Newark, N. J.

PENNINGTON, William (cousin of Alexander Cumming Mc-Whorter Pennington), a Representative from New Jersey; born in Newark, N. J., May 4, 1796; completed preparatory studies; was graduated from Princeton College in 1813; clerk of the United States district court 1815–1826; studied law; was admitted to the bar and commenced practice in Newark in 1820; member of the State general assembly in 1828; served as sergeant at law in 1834; Governor of New Jersey from 1837 to 1843; appointed Governor of Minnesota Territory by President Fillmore but declined to accept; elected as a Whig to the Thirty-sixth Congress (March 4, 1859–March 3, 1861) and served as Speaker; unsuccessful Republican candidate for reelection in 1860 to the Thirty-seventh Congress; died in Newark, N. J., February 16, 1862; interment in Mount Pleasant Cemetery.

PENNYBACKER, Isaac Samuels (cousin of Green Berry Samuels), a Representative and a Senator from Virginia; born at Pine Forge, near Newmarket, Shenandoah County, Va., September 3, 1805; attended the "old field" school and the Winchester Law School; was admitted to the bar and commenced practice in Harrisonburg, Rockingham County, Va.; elected as a Democrat to the Twenty-fifth Congress (March 4, 1837–March 3, 1839); judge of the United States District Court for the Western District of Virginia by appointment of President Van Buren 1839–1845; declined the office of United States Attorney General offered him by President Van Buren and subsequently that of justice of the supreme court of Virginia; elected to the United States Senate to fill the vacancy in the term beginning March 4, 1845, caused by the failure of the legislature to elect and served from December 3, 1845, until his death; member of the Board of Regents of the Smithsonian Institution from August 10, 1846; died in Washington, D. C., January 12, 1847; interment in Woodbine Cemetery, Harrisonburg, Va.

PENROSE, Boies, a Senator from Pennsylvania; born in Philadelphia, Pa., November 1, 1860; attended the public schools and was prepared for college by private tutors; graduated from Harvard University in 1881; studied law; was admitted to the bar in 1883 and commenced practice in Philadelphia; served in the State house of representatives 1884–1886; member of the State senate from 1886 until January 27, 1897, when he resigned, having been elected United States Senator; president pro tempore of the State senate 1889–1891; elected as a Republican to the United States Senate in 1897; reelected in 1903, 1909, 1914, and 1920, and served from March 4, 1897, until his death; delegate to the Republican National Conventions in 1900, 1904, and 1908; chairman of the Republican State committee 1903–1905; elected a member of the Republican National Committee in 1904 and reelected in 1908; died in Washington, D. C., December 31, 1921; interment in Laurel Hill Cemetery, Philadelphia, Pa.

PEPPER, Claude Denson, a Senator from Florida; born on a farm near Dudleyville, Chambers County, Ala., September 8, 1900; attended the public schools of Camp Hill, Ala.; taught school in Dothan, Ala., and worked in a steel mill in Ensley, Ala., before attending college; served in Students Army Training Corps, University of Alabama, in 1918; was graduated from the University of Alabama at Tuscaloosa in 1921 and from law department of Harvard University, Cambridge, Mass., in 1924; taught law in the University of Arkansas in 1924 and 1925; was admitted to the bar in 1925 and commenced practice in Perry, Fla.; member of the State house of representatives in 1929 and 1930; moved to Tallahassee, Fla., in 1930 and continued the practice of law; served on the State board of public welfare in 1931 and 1932; member of the State board of law examiners in 1933; delegate to the Interparliamentary Union at The Hague in 1938 and at Dublin in 1950; delegate to the Democratic National Conventions in 1940, 1944, 1948, 1952, 1956, and 1960; elected as a Democrat to the United States Senate to fill the vacancy caused by the death of Duncan U. Fletcher; reelected in 1938 and again in 1944 and served from November 4, 1936, to January 3, 1951; unsuccessful candidate for renomination in 1950 and for nomination in 1958; engaged in the practice of law at Miami Beach, Coral Gables, and Tallahassee, Fla., and in Washington, D. C.; is a resident of Tallahassee, Fla.

PEPPER, George Wharton, a Senator from Pennsylvania; born in Philadelphia, Pa., March 16, 1867; prepared privately for college; was graduated from the literary department of the University of Pennsylvania at Philadelphia in 1887 and from the law department in 1889; was admitted to the bar in 1889 and commenced practice in Philadelphia, Pa.; Algernon Sydney Biddle professor of law in the University of Pennsylvania 1894–1910 and trustee of the university since 1911; participated in the movement for national preparedness in 1914; Lyman Beecher lecturer at Yale University in 1915; member of the Provisional Training Regiment at Plattsburgh in 1915 and 1916 and chairman of the Pennsylvania Council of National Defense 1917–1919; member of the commission on constitutional revision in Pennsylvania in 1920 and 1921; appointed as a Republican and subsequently elected to the United States Senate to fill the vacancy caused by the death of Boies Penrose and served from January 9, 1922, to March 3, 1927; unsuccessful candidate for renomination in 1926; Republican national committeeman 1922–1928; delegate to the Republican National Convention in 1924 at Cleveland, Ohio, which nominated the presidential ticket of Coolidge and Dawes; resumed the practice of law in Philadelphia, Pa.; died in Devon, Pa., May 24, 1961; interment in Old St. David's Churchyard Cemetery, Wayne, Pa.

PEPPER, Irvin St. Clair, a Representative from Iowa; born in Davis County, Iowa, June 10, 1876; attended the public schools; was graduated from Southern Iowa Normal School at

Bloomfield in 1897; principal of the Atalissa High School and of the Washington School at Muscatine; secretary for Congressman Martin J. Wade of Iowa 1903–1905; graduated from the law department of George Washington University, Washington, D. C., in 1905; was admitted to the bar the same year and commenced practice in Muscatine, Iowa; served as prosecuting attorney of Muscatine County 1906–1910; elected as a Democrat to the Sixty-second and Sixty-third Congresses and served from March 4, 1911, until his death in Clinton County, Iowa, December 22, 1913; interment in Shaul Cemetery, near Ottumwa, Wapello County, Iowa.

PERCE, Legrand Winfield, a Representative from Mississippi; born in Buffalo, N. Y., June 19, 1836; completed preparatory studies; attended Wesleyan College, Lima, N. Y., and was graduated from the Albany (N. Y.) Law School in 1857; was admitted to the bar the same year and commenced practice in Buffalo, N. Y.; enlisted in the Union Army in April 1861, at the outbreak of the Civil War; was commissioned a second lieutenant in the Sixth Regiment, Michigan Volunteer Infantry, in August 1861; promoted to the rank of captain in June 1862; brevetted major for gallant and meritorious services at Port Hudson in May 1863; appointed captain in the United States Volunteers in August 1863 and was brevetted lieutenant colonel and colonel in 1865; settled in Natchez, Miss.; appointed register in bankruptcy in June 1867; upon readmission of the State of Mississippi to representation was elected as a Republican to the Forty-first Congress; reelected to the Forty-second Congress and served from February 23, 1870, to March 3, 1873; was not a candidate for reelection in 1872; engaged in the practice of law and also in the real-estate business at Chicago, Ill., where he died March 16, 1911; interment in Rose Hill Cemetery.

PERCY, Le Roy, a Senator from Mississippi; born near Greenville, Washington County, Miss., on November 9, 1860; attended the public schools; was graduated from the University of the South, Sewanee, Tenn., in 1879 and from the law department of the University of Virginia at Charlottesville in 1881; was admitted to the bar in 1881 and commenced practice in Greenville, Miss.; also interested in agricultural pursuits; elected as a Democrat to the United States Senate to fill the vacancy caused by the death of Anselm J. McLaurin and served from February 23, 1910, to March 3, 1913; was an unsuccessful candidate for renomination in 1912; appointed on March 16, 1910, a member of the United States Joint Immigration Commission and served until December 1910; delegate to several Democratic State conventions; resumed the practice of law in Greenville, Miss.; also supervised his extensive land acreage holdings; appointed a director of the Federal Reserve Board branch at St. Louis, Mo., in August 1914 and served until his death on December 24, 1929, in Memphis, Tenn., while en route to his home in Mississippi; interment in Greenville Cemetery, Greenville, Miss.

PEREA, Francisco (cousin of Pedro Perea), a Delegate from the Territory of New Mexico; born in Los Padillas, N. Mex. (then in the Republic of Mexico), January 9, 1830; attended select schools in Bernalillo County and at Santa Fe 1836–1839; enrolled at the Jesuit College, St. Louis, Mo., 1843–1845, traveling the old Santa Fe Trail from New Mexico to Missouri, and received collegiate training at the Bank Street Academy in New York City 1847–1849; from 1850 to 1864 was engaged in stock raising and commercial pursuits and in carrying merchandise by mule train from St. Louis and Independence, Mo., to points in Mexico; moved large numbers of sheep to California during the gold rush and again in 1860; member of the Territorial council in

1858, 1866, and 1884; during the Civil War served as lieutenant colonel of Perea's Battalion in 1861 and 1862; participated in the Battle of Glorietta, March 27 and 28, 1862; delegate to the Republican National Convention in 1864; was in Ford's Theater the night of President Lincoln's assassination; elected as a Republican to the Thirty-eighth Congress (March 4, 1863–March 3, 1865); unsuccessful candidate for renomination in 1864; moved from Bernalillo County to Jemez Springs, Sandoval County, N. Mex., in 1881; proprietor of the springs and a hotel; postmaster of Jemez Springs 1894–1905; moved to Albuquerque, N. Mex., in 1906 and died there May 21, 1913; interment in Fairview Cemetery.

PEREA, Pedro (cousin of Francisco Perea), a Delegate from the Territory of New Mexico; born in Bernalillo, Sandoval County, N. Mex., April 22, 1852; attended St. Michael's College, Santa Fe, N. Mex., Georgetown University, Washington, D. C., and was graduated from the St. Louis University, St. Louis, Mo., in 1871; principally engaged in agricultural pursuits and sheep raising; president of the First National Bank of Santa Fe 1890–1894; member of the council of the New Mexico Legislature in 1889, 1891, and 1895; delegate to the Republican National Convention at St. Louis in 1896, which nominated the presidential ticket of McKinley and Hobart; elected as a Republican to the Fifty-sixth Congress (March 4, 1899–March 3, 1901); was not a candidate for renomination in 1901; engaged in banking and also interested in stock raising; appointed Territorial insurance commissioner in 1906 and served until his death in Bernalillo, N. Mex., January 11, 1906; interment in Bernalillo Cemetery.

PERHAM, Sidney, a Representative from Maine; born in Woodstock, Maine, on March 27, 1819; attended the common schools; engaged in agricultural pursuits; member of the State house of representatives in 1854 and served as speaker; presidential elector on the Republican ticket of Frémont and Dayton in 1856; clerk of the courts of Oxford County, Maine, 1859–1863; elected as a Republican to the Thirty-eighth, Thirty-ninth, and Fortieth Congresses (March 4, 1863–March 3, 1869); was not a candidate for renomination in 1868; Governor of Maine 1871–1874; president of the board of trustees of Westbrook Seminary, Deering, Maine, 1865–1880 and of the Maine Industrial School at Hallowell 1873–1898; secretary of state of Maine in 1875 to fill a vacancy; served as appraiser in the customhouse at Portland, Maine, 1877–1885; member of the board of trustees of the Universalist General Convention for twenty-seven years and served as president of the board part of the time; died in Washington, D. C., April 10, 1907; interment in Lakeside Cemetery, Bryant Pond, Oxford County, Maine.

PERKINS, Bishop, a Representative from New York; born in Becket, Berkshire County, Mass., September 5, 1787; attended private school at East Granville, Mass., and was graduated from Williams College, Williamstown, Mass., in 1807; studied law; was admitted to the bar in 1812 and commenced practice in Lisbon, N. Y.; subsequently moved to Ogdensburg, St. Lawrence County, N. Y., and continued the practice of law; clerk of the board of supervisors of St. Lawrence County 1820–1852; appointed district attorney of St. Lawrence County February 24, 1821, and served until May 21, 1840; member of the State constitutional convention in 1846; member of the State assembly in 1846, 1847, and again in 1849; elected as a Democrat to the Thirty-third Congress (March 4, 1853–March 3, 1855); was not a candidate for renomination in 1854; returned to Ogdensburg, N. Y., and continued the practice of his profession until his death there November 20, 1866; interment in Ogdensburg Cemetery.

PERKINS, Bishop Walden, a Representative and a Senator from Kansas; born in Rochester, Lorain County, Ohio, October 18, 1841; attended the common schools and Knox College, Galesburg, Ill.; prospected through California and New Mexico 1860–1862; served four years in the Union Army during the Civil War as sergeant of the Eighty-third Regiment, Illinois Volunteer Infantry, and as adjutant and captain in the Sixteenth Regiment, United States Colored Infantry; studied law in Ottawa, Ill.; was admitted to the bar in 1867, and commenced the practice of law in Princeton, Ind.; moved to Oswego, Labette County, Kans., and continued practice; local county attorney for the Missouri, Kansas & Texas Railroad for two years; prosecuting attorney of Labette County in 1869; judge of the probate court of Labette County 1870–1882; became editor of the Oswego Register in 1873; elected as a Republican to the Forty-eighth and to the three succeeding Congresses (March 4, 1883–March 3, 1891); unsuccessful candidate for reelection in 1890 to the Fifty-second Congress; appointed to the United States Senate to fill the vacancy caused by the death of Preston B. Plumb and served from January 1, 1892, to March 3, 1893, when a successor was elected and qualified; resumed the practice of his profession in Washington, D. C., and died there June 20, 1894; interment in Rock Creek Cemetery.

PERKINS, Carl Dewey, a Representative from Kentucky; born in Hindman, Knott County, Ky., October 15, 1912; attended the Knott County grade schools, Hindman High School, and Caney Junior College; was graduated from Jefferson School of Law, Louisville, Ky., in 1935; was admitted to the bar in 1935 and commenced the practice of law in Hindman, Ky.; in 1939 served an unexpired term as commonwealth attorney from the thirty-first judicial district; member of Kentucky General Assembly from the ninety-ninth district in 1940; elected Knott County attorney in 1941, reelected in 1945, and resigned January 1, 1948, to become counsel for Department of Highways, Frankfort, Ky.; during World War II enlisted in the United States Army and saw service in the European Theater, participating in battles of northern France, the Ardennes, the Rhineland, and central Europe; elected as a Democrat to the Eighty-first and to the five succeeding Congresses (January 3, 1949–January 3, 1961). *Reelected to the Eighty-seventh Congress.*

PERKINS, Elias, a Representative from Connecticut; born in Newent Society (now Lisbon), Conn., April 5, 1767; was graduated from Yale College in 1786; studied law; was admitted to the bar and commenced practice in New London, New London County, Conn.; member of the State house of representatives 1795–8100, 1814, and 1815 and served as speaker in 1798 and 1815; was assistant judge of the New London County Court in 1799 and chief justice of the same court 1807–1825; elected as a Federalist to the Seventh Congress (March 4, 1801–March 3, 1803); resumed the practice of law; member of the State senate 1817–1822; mayor of New London 1829–1832; died in New London, Conn., September 27, 1845; interment in Cedar Grove Cemetery.

PERKINS, George Clement, a Senator from California; born in Kennebunk Port, York County, Maine, August 23, 1839; had limited educational advantages; at the age of twelve went to sea as a cabin boy; followed the sea for several years; shipped before the mast on a sailing vessel bound for San Francisco, Calif., in 1855; engaged in mercantile pursuits in Oroville, Calif.; subsequently engaged in banking, milling, mining, farming, whale fishing, and in operating steamships on the coasts of California, Oregon, Washington, British Columbia, Alaska, and Mexico; elected to the State senate in 1869 and served for eight years; president of the chamber of commerce of San Francisco and of the San Francisco Art Association; director of the California Academy of Sciences and other public institutions; elected Governor of California in 1879 and served until January 1883; appointed in 1893 and subsequently elected as a Republican to the United States Senate to fill the vacancy caused by the death of Leland Stanford; reelected in 1897, 1903, and 1909 and served from July 26, 1893, to March 3, 1915; on account of ill health was not a candidate for reelection; returned to his home in Oakland, Calif., and lived in retirement until his death there on February 26, 1923; interment in Mountain View Cemetery.

PERKINS, George Douglas, a Representative from Iowa; born in Holly, Orleans County, N. Y., February 29, 1840; attended the common schools; moved to Wisconsin and learned the printer's trade in Baraboo, Sauk County; moved to Iowa, established the Gazette in Cedar Falls in 1860, and continued that publication until 1866; during the Civil War enlisted as a private in Company B, Thirty-first Regiment, Iowa Volunteer Infantry, August 12, 1862, and served until honorably discharged at Jefferson Barracks, Mo., January 12, 1863; went to Chicago, Ill., and was engaged as agent of the Northwestern Associated Press until 1869; moved to Sioux City, Iowa, in 1869 and became editor of the Journal; member of the State senate 1874–1876; commissioner of immigration for the State of Iowa 1880–1882; appointed United States marshal for the northern district of Iowa by President Arthur on January 29, 1883, and was removed by President Cleveland in 1885; elected as a Republican to the Fifty-second and to the three succeeding Congresses (March 4, 1891–March 3, 1899); unsuccessful candidate for renomination in 1898; resumed his journalistic activities at Sioux City, Iowa; delegate to the Republican National Conventions in 1876, 1880, 1888, 1908, and 1912; unsuccessful candidate for Governor of Iowa in 1904; editor and publisher of the Sioux City Journal; died in Sioux City, Woodbury County, Iowa, February 3, 1914; interment in Floyd Cemetery.

PERKINS, James Breck, a Representative from New York; born at St. Croix Falls, Polk County, Wis., November 4, 1847; moved with his parents to Rochester, N. Y., in 1856; attended the public schools; was graduated from the University of Rochester (New York) in 1867; studied law; was admitted to the bar in 1868 and commenced practice in Rochester; city attorney 1874–1880; lived in Paris, France, from 1890 to 1895, and engaged in the study of European literature and in historical research; author of several historical works; returned to Rochester in 1895; served in the State assembly 1898–1900; elected as a Republican to the Fifty-seventh and to the four succeeding Congresses and served from March 4, 1901, until his death; one of the managers appointed by the House of Representatives in 1905 to conduct the impeachment proceedings against Charles Swayne, judge of the United States District Court for the Northern District of Florida; died in Washington, D. C., March 11, 1910; interment in Mount Hope Cemetery, Rochester, N. Y.

PERKINS, Jared, a Representative from New Hampshire; born in Unity, Sullivan County, N. H., January 5, 1793; attended the common schools of Unity and Claremont; studied theology; was ordained as a minister in 1824 and served for thirty years; State councilor 1846–1848; served in the State house of representatives in 1850; elected as a Whig to the Thirty-second Congress (March 4, 1851–March 3, 1853); unsuccessful candidate for reelection in 1852 to the Thirty-third Congress; nominated for Governor of New Hampshire in 1854 but died before the election; appointed justice of the peace in 1854 and served until his death in Nashua, N. H., October 15, 1854; interment in West Unity Cemetery, Unity, N. H.

PERKINS, John, Jr., a Representative from Louisiana; born in Natchez, Miss., July 1, 1819; received his early education from private tutors; was graduated from Yale College in 1840 and from the law department of Harvard University in 1842; was admitted to the bar in 1843 and commenced practice in New Orleans, La.; engaged in cotton planting; traveled in Europe for several years; appointed judge of the circuit court for the district comprising Tensas and Madison Parishes in 1851; elected as a Democrat to the Thirty-third Congress (March 4, 1853–March 3, 1855); was not a candidate for renomination in 1854; chairman of the State secession convention in 1861; served in the Confederate Senate 1862-1865; traveled extensively in Mexico and Europe; returned to the United States in 1878 and spent the remaining years of his life in Louisiana and Canada; died in Baltimore, Md., November 28, 1885; interment in Natchez Cemetery, Natchez, Miss.

PERKINS, Randolph, a Representative from New Jersey; born in Dunellen, Middlesex County, N. J., November 30, 1871; moved to Jersey City N. J., with his parents in 1879; attended the grade and high schools, and Cooper Union School, New York City; studied law; was admitted to the bar in 1893 and commenced practice in Jersey City, N. J.; moved to Westfield, N. J., in 1902, to Woodcliff Lake, N. J., in 1909, and continued the practice of law; mayor of Westfield, Union County, 1903–1905; member of the State assembly from 1905 to 1911, serving as speaker in 1907; chairman of the Bergen County Republican committee 1911–1916; elected as a Republican to the Sixty-seventh and to the seven succeeding Congresses and served from March 4, 1921, until his death; was renominated for election to the Seventy-fifth Congress at the time of his death; one of the managers appointed by the House of Representatives in 1933 to conduct the impeachment proceedings against Harold Louderback, judge of the United States District Court for the Northern District of California, and again in 1936 to conduct the impeachment proceedings against Halsted L. Ritter, judge of the United States District Court for the Southern District of Florida; died in Washington, D. C., May 25, 1936; interment in Fairview Cemetery, West New Brighton, Staten Island, N. Y.

PERKY, Kirtland Irving, a Senator from Idaho; born in Smithville, Wayne County, Ohio, February 8, 1867; attended the public schools and was graduated from Ohio Northern University at Ada in 1888; studied law at the University of Iowa, Iowa City; was admitted to the bar in 1890 and commenced practice in Wahoo, Saunders County, Nebr.; moved to Albion, Idaho, in 1894; district judge of the fourth judicial district of the State of Idaho in 1901; moved to Boise, Idaho, and continued the practice of law; appointed as a Democrat to the United States Senate to fill the vacancy caused by the death of Weldon B. Heyburn and served from November 18, 1912, to February 5, 1913, when a successor was elected and qualified; resumed the practice of law in Boise; delegate to the Democratic National Convention at St. Louis in 1916, which nominated Woodrow Wilson for the Presidency for a second term; moved to Los Angeles, Calif., in 1923 and continued the practice of law until his death there on January 9, 1939; interment in Forest Lawn Cemetery, Glendale, Calif.

PERLMAN, Nathan David, a Representative from New York; born in Poland August 2, 1887; immigrated to the United States in 1891 with his mother, who settled in New York City; attended the public schools and the College of the City of New York; was graduated from New York University Law School in 1907; was admitted to the bar in 1909 and commenced practice in New York City; special deputy attorney general of the State of New York 1912–1914; member of the State assembly 1915–1917; elected as a Republican to the Sixty-sixth Congress to fill the vacancy caused by the resignation of Fiorello H. LaGuardia; reelected to the Sixty-seventh, Sixty-eighth, and Sixty-ninth Congresses and served from November 2, 1920, to March 3, 1927; unsuccessful candidate for reelection in 1926 to the Seventieth Congress; resumed the practice of law; delegate to the New York State Convention to repeal prohibition; magistrate of the city of New York May 1, 1935, to September 1, 1936; appointed justice of the court of special sessions of the city of New York November 26, 1936; reappointed July 1, 1945, and served until his death in New York City, N. Y., June 29, 1952; interment in Mount Hebron Cemetery, Queens County, N. Y.

PERRILL, Augustus Leonard, a Representative from Ohio; born near Moorefield, Hardy County, Va. (now West Virginia), January 20, 1807; in 1816 moved to Ohio with his parents, who settled in Madison Township near Lithopolis, Pickaway County; attended the local schools; taught school near Circleville, Ohio, and then engaged in agricultural pursuits; appointed deputy sheriff in January 1833; elected sheriff in 1834 and served until 1837; member of the State house of representatives 1839–1841; elected as a Democrat to the Twenty-ninth Congress (March 4, 1845–March 3, 1847); unsuccessful candidate for reelection in 1846 to the Thirtieth Congress; resumed agricultural pursuits near Circleville, Ohio; member of the State senate 1858–1863; again served in the State house of representatives 1865–1867; died on his farm near Circleville, Pickaway County, Ohio, June 2, 1882; interment in Forest Cemetery, Circleville, Ohio.

PERRY, Aaron Fyfe, a Representative from Ohio; born in Leicester, Vt., January 1, 1815; attended the public schools and Yale Law School; was admitted to the bar of Connecticut in 1838; moved to Columbus, Ohio, where he was admitted to the bar in 1840 and commenced practice; member of the State house of representatives in 1847 and 1848; moved to Cincinnati, Ohio, in 1854 and continued the practice of law; declined appointment as Associate Justice of the United States Supreme Court in 1861 tendered by President Lincoln; delegate to the Republican National Convention at Baltimore in 1864, which nominated Abraham Lincoln for a second term; elected as a Republican to the Forty-second Congress and served from March 4, 1871, until his resignation in 1872; resumed the practice of his profession and also engaged in literary pursuits; appointed chief counsel for the Government in the Crédit Mobilier case in 1873; appointed a member of the board of sinking-fund trustees of Cincinnati in 1877 and was president of the board from 1884 to 1892, when he resigned; elected a member of the third class of the Military Order of the Loyal Legion of the United States in 1889 for distinguished civilian services; died in Cincinnati, Ohio, March 11, 1893; interment in Spring Grove Cemetery.

PERRY, Eli, a Representative from New York; born in Cambridge, Washington County, N. Y., December 25, 1799; attended the common schools; engaged in business in Albany, N. Y., in 1827 and continued until 1852; member of the Board of Aldermen of Albany for two years; served in the State assembly in 1851; mayor of Albany 1851–1853, 1856–1860, 1862–1866; elected as a Democrat to the Forty-second and Forty-third Congresses (March 4, 1871–March 3, 1875); unsuccessful candidate for reelection in 1874 to the Forty-fourth Congress; died in Albany, Albany County, N. Y., May 17, 1881; interment in Albany Rural Cemetery.

PERRY, John Jasiel, a Representative from Maine; born in Portsmouth, N. H., August 2, 1811; moved with his parents to Hebron (now Oxford), Maine, in 1812; attended the common schools and Maine Wesleyan Seminary; deputy sheriff of Oxford County; member of the State house of representatives in 1840, 1842, 1843, and 1872; studied law; was admitted to the bar in 1844 and commenced practice in Oxford; member of the State senate in 1846 and 1847; clerk of the State house of representatives in 1854; elected as a Republican to the Thirty-fourth Congress (March 4, 1855–March 3, 1857); was not a candidate for renomination in 1856; elected to the Thirty-sixth Congress (March 4, 1859–March 3, 1861); was not a candidate for renomination in 1860; member of the peace convention of 1861 held in Washington, D. C., in an effort to devise means to prevent the impending war; editor of the Oxford Democrat from 1860 to 1875 and extensively connected with newspapers, both in and out of the State, as correspondent; member of the State executive council in 1866 and 1867; moved to Portland, Cumberland County, Maine, in 1875 and engaged in the practice of his profession until his death in that city on May 2, 1897; interment in Evergreen Cemetery.

PERRY, Nehemiah, a Representative from New Jersey; born in Ridgefield, Fairfield County, Conn., March 30, 1816; educated at the Wesleyan Seminary of Ridgefield; clerked in a store in Norwalk, Conn., and New York City; moved to Newark, N. J., in 1836; engaged in the manufacture of cloth and in the clothing business; member of the State house of assembly in 1850 and 1856 and served as speaker in the latter year; member of the common council in 1852; elected as a candidate of the Constitutional-Union Party to the Thirty-seventh and Thirty-eighth Congresses (March 4, 1861–March 3, 1865); was not a candidate for renomination in 1864; resumed his former manufacturing pursuits; mayor of Newark in 1873; died in Newark, Essex County, N. J., November 1, 1881; interment in Mount Pleasant Cemetery.

PERRY, Thomas Johns, a Representative from Maryland; born in Cumberland, Md., February 17, 1807; completed preparatory studies; studied law; was admitted to the bar in 1828 and commenced practice in Cumberland, Md.; member of the State house of delegates 1834–1836; elected as a Democrat to the Twenty-ninth Congress (March 4, 1845–March 3, 1847); was not a candidate for renomination in 1846; associate judge of the sixth judicial district of Maryland 1851–1861 and 1864–1871; delegate to the State constitutional convention in 1867; died in Cumberland, Allegany County, Md., June 27, 1871; interment in Rose Hill Cemetery.

PERRY, William Hayne, a Representative from South Carolina; born in Greenville, Greenville County, S. C., June 9, 1839; attended Greenville Academy, and was graduated from Furman University at Greenville in 1857; attended South Carolina College (now the University of South Carolina) at Columbia, and was graduated from Harvard University, Cambridge, Mass., in 1859; studied law in Greenville; was admitted to the bar in 1861 and commenced practice in Greenville; served as a private and subsequently as lieutenant in the Confederate Cavalry during the Civil War; resumed the practice of law in Greenville in 1865; member of the State constitutional convention in 1865; member of the State house of representatives in 1865 and 1866; solicitor of the eighth judicial circuit of South Carolina 1868–1872; served in the State senate 1880–1884; elected as a Democrat to the Forty-ninth, Fiftieth, and Fifty-first Congresses (March 4, 1885–March 3, 1891); declined to be a candidate for renomination in 1890; resumed the practice of law; died at his home, "San Souci," near Greenville, S. C., July 7, 1902; interment in Christ Church Cemetery, Greenville, S. C.

PERSON, Seymour Howe, a Representative from Michigan; born on a farm near Howell, Howell Township, Livingston County, Mich., February 2, 1879; attended the district schools and the Howell graded and high schools; was graduated from the law department of the University of Michigan at Ann Arbor in 1901; was admitted to the bar the same year and commenced practice in Lansing, Mich.; member of the State house of representatives 1915–1921; served in the State senate 1927–1931; delegate to all State conventions for thirty years; elected as a Republican to the Seventy-second Congress (March 4, 1931–March 3, 1933); unsuccessful candidate for reelection in 1932 to the Seventy-third Congress; resumed the practice of his profession; died in Lansing, Mich., on April 7, 1957; interment in Deepdale Cemetery.

PERSONS, Henry, a Representative from Georgia; born near Smarrs, Monroe County, Ga., January 30, 1834; moved to Talbot County, Ga., in 1836; attended the Talbotton schools; was graduated from the University of Georgia at Athens in 1855; served as captain of Cavalry in the Third Georgia regiment of the Confederate Army during the Civil War; engaged in agricultural pursuits in Talbot County, Ga.; elected as a Democrat to the Forty-sixth Congress (March 4, 1879–March 3, 1881); unsuccessful candidate for renomination in 1880; returned to Geneva, Ga.; studied law; was admitted to the bar in 1885 and commenced practice in Talbotton, Ga.; ordinary of Talbot County 1898–1910; trustee of the University of Georgia 1894–1910; died in Talbotton, Ga., June 17, 1910; interment in Rose Hill Cemetery.

PESQUERA, José Lorenzo, a Resident Commissioner from Puerto Rico; born in Bayamon, P. R., August 10, 1882; was graduated from Provincial Institute of Puerto Rico in 1897; attended the Keystone State Normal School, Kutztown, Pa., in 1901 and 1902; was graduated from the law department of West Virginia University at Morgantown in 1904; was admitted to the bar the same year and commenced practice in Puerto Rico; also engaged in agricultural pursuits and dairying; member of the Puerto Rico House of Representatives 1917–1920; director and president of the Agricultural Association of Puerto Rico; appointed as a Nonpartisan a Resident Commissioner to the United States to fill the vacancy caused by the resignation of Felix Cordova Davila and served from April 15, 1932, until March 3, 1933; was not a candidate for election in 1932; returned to his law practice and agricultural interests; died in Bayamon, P. R., July 25, 1950; interment in Municipal Cemetery.

PETER, George, a Representative from Maryland; born in Georgetown, Md. (now the District of Columbia), September 28, 1779; pursued classical studies and was graduated from Georgetown College; at the age of fifteen joined the Maryland troops in the campaign against the Whisky Insurrectionists in 1794, but at the request of his parents, was sent home; entered the Army as second lieutenant in the Ninth Infantry in July 1799; transferred to the Artillery and in May 1808 organized and commanded the first light battery of artillery in the country; resigned June 11, 1809; engaged in agricultural pursuits; served as a major of Volunteers in the War of 1812; elected as a Democrat to the Fourteenth Congress to fill the vacancy caused by the resignation of Alexander C. Hanson; reelected to the Fifteenth Congress and served from October 7, 1816, to March 3, 1819; served in the State house of delegates 1819–1823; elected to the Nineteenth Congress (March 4, 1825–March 3, 1827); unsuccessful candidate for reelection in 1826 to the Twentieth Congress; resumed agricultural activities; commissioner of public works of Maryland in 1855; retired to his plantation; died near Darnestown, Montgomery County, Md., June 22, 1861; interment in Oak Hill Cemetery, Georgetown, D. C.

PETERS, Andrew James, a Representative from Massachusetts; born in West Roxbury, Mass., April 3, 1872; attended Hopkinson's and St. Paul's Schools; was graduated from Harvard University in 1895 and from the Harvard Law School in 1898; was admitted to the bar in 1897 and commenced practice in Boston, Mass.; member of the State house of representatives in 1902; served in the State senate in 1904 and 1905; served five years in the Massachusetts Militia; elected as a Democrat to the Sixtieth and to the three succeeding Congresses and served from March 4, 1907, until his resignation, effective August 15, 1914; appointed Assistant Secretary of the Treasury and served from August 17, 1914, to March 15, 1917; mayor of Boston 1918–1922; resumed the practice of law; president of the Boston Chamber of Commerce 1926–1928; died in Jamaica Plain, Mass., June 26, 1938; interment in Forest Hills Cemetery.

PETERS, John Andrew, a Representative from Maine; born in Ellsworth, Hancock County, Maine, October 9, 1822; attended Gorham Academy, and was graduated from Yale College, New Haven, Conn., in 1842; studied law; was admitted to the bar in 1844 and commenced practice in Bangor, Maine, in 1844; member of the State senate in 1862 and 1863; served in the State house of representatives in 1864; attorney general of the State 1864–1866; elected as a Republican to the Fortieth, Forty-first, and Forty-second Congresses (March 4, 1867–March 3, 1873); declined to be a candidate for renomination in 1872; judge of the supreme judicial court of Maine 1873–1883 and served as chief justice from 1883 until January 1, 1900, when he resigned; died in Bangor, Penobscot County, Maine, April 2, 1904; interment in Mount Hope Cemetery.

PETERS, John Andrew (nephew of the preceding), a Representative from Maine; born in Ellsworth, Hancock County, Maine, August 13, 1864; attended the common schools; was graduated from Bowdoin College, Brunswick, Maine, in 1885; studied law; was admitted to the bar and commenced practice in Ellsworth in 1887; judge of the municipal court of Ellsworth 1896–1908; member of the State house of representatives in 1909, 1911, and 1913, serving as speaker in 1913; elected as a Republican to the Sixty-third Congress to fill the vacancy caused by the death of Forrest Goodwin; reelected to the Sixty-fourth and to the three succeeding Congresses and served from September 8, 1913, until his resignation January 2, 1922, to become judge of the United States District Court for Maine, in which capacity he served until his resignation in 1947; delegate at large to the Republican National Convention at Chicago in 1916; former vice president of the board of trustees of Bowdoin College; died in Ellsworth, Maine, August 22, 1953; interment in Woodbine Cemetery.

PETERS, Mason Summers, a Representative from Kansas; born near Kearney, Clay County, Mo., September 3, 1844; attended the William Jewell College, Liberty, Mo.; taught in the grammar schools of Clay County, Mo., 1867–1870; clerk of the court of Clinton County, Mo., 1870–1874; studied law; was admitted to the bar in 1875 and commenced practice in Plattsburg, Mo.; moved to Wyandotte County, Kans., in 1886; organized the Union Live Stock Commission Co. in 1895; elected as a Democrat-Populist to the Fifty-fifth Congress (March 4, 1897–March 3, 1899); was unsuccessful for reelection in 1898 to the Fifty-sixth Congress; resumed his business and professional pursuits in Kansas City, Kans.; died in Kansas City, Mo., February 14, 1914; interment in Forest Hill Cemetery.

PETERS, Richard, Jr., a Delegate from Pennsylvania; born near Philadelphia, Pa., June 22, 1743; was graduated from the University of Pennsylvania at Philadelphia in 1761; studied law; was admitted to the bar and commenced practice in Philadelphia; register of the admiralty from 1771 until the Revolution; entered the Revolutionary Army and served as captain in 1771; served as secretary of the Continental Board of War from June 13, 1776, to June 8, 1781; Member of the Continental Congress in 1782 and 1783; member of the State assembly 1787–1790 and served as speaker; served in the State senate in 1791 and was speaker; judge of the district court of Pennsylvania 1792–1828; died in Philadelphia, Pa., August 22, 1828; interment in St. Peter's Churchyard.

PETERS, Samuel Ritter, a Representative from Kansas; born in Walnut Township, near Circleville, Pickaway County, Ohio, August 16, 1842; attended the common schools and the Ohio Wesleyan University at Delaware; during the Civil War enlisted in the Union Army as a private in Company E, Seventy-third Regiment, Ohio Volunteer Infantry, in October 1861 and was mustered out in June 1865, having held successively the ranks of sergeant, second lieutenant, first lieutenant, and captain; served as adjutant; was graduated in law from the University of Michigan at Ann Arbor in 1867; was admitted to the bar the same year and commenced practice in Memphis, Mo.; editor of the Memphis Reveille 1868–1873; delegate to the Republican National Convention at Philadelphia in 1872; mayor of Memphis in 1873; moved to Marion, Kans., in 1873 and resumed the practice of law; elected a member of the State senate in 1874 and served until his resignation in March 1875; appointed and subsequently elected judge of the ninth judicial district and served from 1875 until 1883, when he resigned; moved to Newton, Harvey County, Kans., in 1876; elected as a Republican to the Forty-eighth and to the three succeeding Congresses (March 4, 1883–March 3, 1891); was not a candidate for renomination in 1890; resumed the practice of law in Newton; member of the board of managers of the State reformatory 1895–1899; postmaster of Newton 1898–1910; editor of the Newton Daily Kansas-Republican in 1899; died in Newton, Kans., April 21, 1910; interment in Greenwood Cemetery.

PETERSEN, Andrew Nicholas, a Representative from New York; born near Thisted, Denmark, March 10, 1870; immigrated to the United States in 1873 with his parents, who settled in Boston, Mass.; moved to New York City in 1879; attended the public schools; learned the patternmaker's trade; president of the Brooklyn Foundry Co. 1900–1952; elected as a Republican to the Sixty-seventh Congress (March 4, 1921–March 3, 1923); unsuccessful candidate for reelection in 1922 to the Sixty-eighth Congress; resumed manufacturing pursuits in Brooklyn, N. Y.; died in East Rockaway, N. Y., September 28, 1952; interment in Cypress Hills Abbey, Brooklyn, N. Y.

PETERSON, Hugh, a Representative from Georgia; born on a farm near Ailey, Montgomery County, Ga., August 21, 1898; attended the public schools, Brewton Parker Institute, Mount Vernon-Ailey, Ga., and the University of Georgia at Athens; studied law; was admitted to the bar in 1921 and commenced practice in Mount Vernon, Ga.; also engaged in agricultural pursuits and editorial work; served as mayor of Ailey, Ga., in 1922; member of the State house of representatives 1923–1931; served in the State senate in 1931 and 1932; elected as a Democrat to the Seventy-fourth and to the five succeeding Congresses (January 3, 1935–January 3, 1947); unsuccessful for renomination in 1946; practiced law in Ailey, Ga.; died in Sylva, N. C., October 3, 1961; interment in the Peterson family cemetery, Ailey, Ga.

PETERSON, James Hardin, a Representative from Florida; born in Batesburg, Lexington County, S. C., February 11,

1894; moved to Lakeland, Fla., in 1903; attended the public schools; was graduated from the law department of the University of Florida at Gainesville in 1914; was admitted to the bar in 1914; law clerk in United States General Land Office in 1914; commenced the practice of law in Lakeland, Fla., in 1915; city attorney of Lakeland, Fla., in 1916, 1917, and 1919–1932, of Frostproof, Fla., 1918–1929, of Lake Wales, Fla., 1920–1930, and of Eagle Lake, Fla., 1923–1933; during the First World War served as a chief yeoman in the United States Navy 1917–1919; prosecuting attorney and county solicitor of Polk County, Fla., 1921–1932; special counsel for the State department of agriculture 1930–1932; elected as a Democrat to the Seventy-third and to the eight succeeding Congresses (March 4, 1933–January 3, 1951); was not a candidate for renomination in 1950; resumed the practice of law in Lakeland, Fla.; special counsel for the Territorial Government of Guam; chairman of Commission on Federal Application of Laws to Guam; chairman, board of directors, First State Bank of Lakeland; member, board of trustees of Monteverde School; is a resident of Lakeland, Fla.

PETERSON, John Barney (cousin of Horatio Clifford Claypool and Harold Kile Claypool), a Representative from Indiana; born near Lowell, Lake County, Ind., July 4, 1850; attended the public schools; studied law; was admitted to the bar in 1870 and commenced practice in Crown Point, Lake County, Ind.; prosecuting attorney of the thirty-first judicial circuit 1880–1884; elected as a Democrat to the Sixty-third Congress (March 4, 1913–March 3, 1915); unsuccessful candidate for reelection in 1914 to the Sixty-fourth Congress; resumed the practice of law in Crown Point, Ind.; also engaged in banking and served as president of the Commercial Bank, Crown Point, Ind., and of the First Calumet Trust & Savings Bank of East Chicago, Ind., until 1939, when he retired; died in Crown Point, Ind., July 16, 1944; interment in Maplewood Cemetery.

PETRIE, George, a Representative from New York; born at Little Falls, Herkimer County, N. Y., September 8, 1793; attended the common schools; elected as a Republican to the Thirtieth Congress (March 4, 1847–March 3, 1849); employed in the Post Office Department, Washington, D. C., from January 1, 1869, until August 31, 1875, when he resigned; died at Little Falls, N. Y., May 8, 1879; interment in Church Street Cemetery.

PETRIKIN, David, a Representative from Pennsylvania; born in Bellefonte, Centre County, Pa., December 1, 1788; completed preparatory studies; studied medicine and was admitted to practice; moved to Danville (then in Columbia County), Pa., and engaged in the practice of medicine; during the War of 1812 served as a surgeon with the Second Regiment of the Pennsylvania Riflemen; after the war returned to Danville, Pa., and continued the practice of medicine; also erected and operated a woolen mill; elected prothonotary of Columbia County March 15, 1821; member of the State house of representatives; served as postmaster of Danville from February 1, 1834, to March 21, 1837; elected as a Democrat to the Twenty-fifth and Twenty-sixth Congresses (March 4, 1837–March 3, 1841); died in Catawissa, Columbia County, Pa., March 1, 1847; interment in Petrikin Cemetery, Danville, Pa., which was later converted into a memorial park.

PETTENGILL, Samuel Barrett (nephew of William Horace Clagett), a Representative from Indiana; born in Portland, Oreg., January 19, 1886; in 1892 moved to Vermont with his father (mother being deceased), who settled on a farm in Grafton, Windham County; attended the common schools; was

graduated from Vermont Academy at Saxtons River in 1904, from Middlebury College, Middlebury, Vt., in 1908, and from the law department of Yale University, New Haven, Conn., in 1911; was admitted to the bar in 1912 and commenced practice in South Bend, Ind.; member of the board of education of South Bend 1926–1928; elected as a Democrat to the Seventy-second and to the three succeeding Congresses (March 4, 1931–January 3, 1939); was not a candidate for renomination in 1938; trustee, Middleburg College 1936–1939; author; resumed the practice of law; newspaper columnist 1939–1948; vice president and general counsel of the Transportation Association of America 1943–1945; national radio commentator 1946–1948; attorney for the Pure Oil Co., Chicago, Ill., 1949–1956; consultant, the Coe Foundation, 1956–; resides in Grafton, Vt.

PETTIBONE, Augustus Herman, a Representative from Tennessee; born in Bedford, Cuyahoga County, Ohio, January 21, 1835; was graduated from Hiram College, Ohio, and from the University of Michigan at Ann Arbor in 1859; studied law; was admitted to the bar in 1860 and commenced practice in La Crosse, Wis.; during the Civil War enlisted in the Union Army as a private in 1861; promoted to second lieutenant, captain, and major in the Twentieth Regiment, Wisconsin Volunteer Infantry; continued the practice of law in Greenville in 1865; alderman of Greeneville 1866–1868; presidential elector on the Republican ticket of Grant and Colfax in 1868; attorney general for the first judicial circuit of Tennessee in 1869 and 1870; appointed assistant United States district attorney for the eastern district of Tennessee December 27, 1871, and served until 1880; presidential elector on the Republican ticket of Hayes and Wheeler in 1876; unsuccessful candidate for election in 1878 to the Forty-sixth Congress; delegate to the Republican National Convention at Chicago in 1880, which nominated Garfield and Arthur; elected as a Republican to the Forty-seventh, Forty-eighth, and Forty-ninth Congresses (March 4, 1881–March 3, 1887); was not a candidate for renomination in 1886; resumed the practice of law; member of the State house of representatives 1896–1898; appointed special agent of the General Land Office and served from July 17, 1899, to January 31, 1905, when he resigned; died in Nashville, Tenn., November 26, 1918; interment in Nashville National Cemetery, Madison, Davidson County, Tenn.

PETTIGREW, Ebenezer, a Representative from North Carolina; born near Plymouth, Tyrrell County, N. C., March 10, 1783; studied under tutors at home and later attended the University of North Carolina at Chapel Hill; engaged in planting; member of the State senate in 1809 and 1810; elected as a Whig to the Twenty-fourth Congress (March 4, 1835–March 3, 1837); resumed agricultural pursuits; died at Magnolia plantation on Lake Scuppernong, Tyrrell County, N. C., July 8, 1848; interment in the family cemetery.

PETTIGREW, Richard Franklin, a Delegate from the Territory of Dakota and a Senator from South Dakota; born in Ludlow, Windsor County, Vt., July 23, 1848; moved with his parents to Dane County, Wis., in 1854 and shortly thereafter to Evansville, Rock County, Wis.; attended the public schools and Evansville Academy; entered Beloit College, Beloit, Wis., in 1864; spent one year teaching school and studying law in Iowa; entered the law department of the University of Wisconsin at Madison in 1867; went to Dakota in July 1869 in the employ of a United States deputy surveyor; settled in Sioux Falls; was admitted to the bar about 1871; practiced law and engaged in Government surveying and the real-estate business until 1875; member of the Territorial house of representatives in 1872; served in the Territorial council in 1877 and 1879; elected as a

Republican a Delegate to the Forty-seventh Congress (March 4, 1881–March 3, 1883); unsuccessful candidate for reelection in 1882 to the Forty-eighth Congress; again a member of the Territorial council in 1885; upon the admission of South Dakota as a State into the Union was elected as a Republican to the United States Senate in 1889; reelected in 1895 and served from November 2, 1889, to March 3, 1901; unsuccessful Republican candidate for reelection in 1900; delegate to the Republican National Convention at St. Louis in 1896, but left the convention and supported Bryan for President; engaged in the practice of law in New York City; moved to Sioux Falls, Minnehaha County, S. Dak., and was active in politics and business until his death in that city October 5, 1926; interment in Woodlawn Cemetery.

PETTIS, Solomon Newton, a Representative from Pennsylvania; born in Lenox, Ashtabula County, Ohio, October 10, 1827; completed preparatory studies; studied law; was admitted to the bar in 1848 and commenced practice in Meadville, Crawford County, Pa.; associate justice of the Territory of Colorado in 1861 and 1862; returned to Meadville, Pa., and continued the practice of his profession; elected as a Republican to the Fortieth Congress to fill the vacancy caused by the death of Darwin A. Finney and served from December 7, 1868, to March 3, 1869; unsuccessful candidate for reelection in 1868 to the Forty-first Congress; resumed the practice of law in Meadville; appointed Minister to Bolivia September 4, 1878, and served until November 1, 1879; again engaged in the practice of law until his death in Meadville, Pa., September 18, 1900; interment in Greendale Cemetery.

PETTIS, Spencer Darwin, a Representative from Missouri; born in Culpeper County, Va., in 1802; completed preparatory studies; studied law; was admitted to the bar about 1824 and commenced practice in Fayette, Howard County, Mo.; held various local offices; appointed secretary of state on July 22, 1826, and served until December 31, 1828, when he resigned; elected as a Democrat to the Twenty-first and Twenty-second Congresses and served from March 4, 1829, until his death; during the campaign of 1830 his feeling regarding the United States bank issue precipitated a quarrel and subsequently a duel with Maj. Thomas Biddle, in which both fell mortally wounded; Mr. Pettis died the next day, August 28, 1831, in St. Louis; interment in the Old City Cemetery, St. Louis, Mo.

PETTIT, Charles, a Delegate from Pennsylvania; born near Amwell, Hunterdon County, N. J., in 1736; received a thorough English training; studied law; was admitted to the bar in 1770 but did not commence practice until 1773; deputy secretary of the Province of New Jersey 1769–1778; clerk of the council; clerk of the supreme court and of the pleas court; surrogate and keeper and register of the records of the Province of New Jersey; appointed aide-de-camp to Gov. William Franklin March 8, 1771; secretary of state of New Jersey and aide to Governor Livingston October 8, 1776; assistant adjutant general on the staff of Gen. Nathanael Greene in the Revolutionary Army from 1778 until his resignation in 1781; declined the promotion to quartermaster general; became an importing merchant in Philadelphia; member of the State house of representatives in 1783 and 1784; Member of the Continental Congress from 1785 to 1787; died in Philadelphia, Pa., September 4, 1806.

PETTIT, John, a Representative and a Senator from Indiana; born in Sackets Harbor, N. Y., June 24, 1807; completed preparatory studies; studied law and was admitted to the bar in 1831; moved to LaFayette, Tippecanoe County, Ind., where he commenced practice in 1838; member of the State house of representatives in 1838 and 1839; United States district attorney

1839–1843; elected as a Democrat to the Twenty-eighth, Twenty-ninth, and Thirtieth Congresses (March 4, 1843–March 3, 1849); unsuccessful candidate for renomination in 1848; delegate to the State constitutional convention in 1850; presidential elector on the Democratic ticket of Pierce and King in 1852; elected to the United States Senate to fill the vacancy caused by the death of James Whitcomb and served from January 11, 1853, to March 3, 1855; unsuccessful candidate for reelection in 1854; chief justice of the United States courts in the Territory of Kansas 1859–1861; judge of the supreme court of Indiana 1870–1877; died in LaFayette, Ind., January 17, 1877; interment in Greenbush Cemetery.

PETTIT, John Upfold, a Representative from Indiana; born in Fabius, Onondaga County, N. Y., September 11, 1820; received an academic education; attended Hamilton College, Clinton, N. Y., and was graduated from Union College, Schenectady, N. Y., in 1839; studied law; was admitted to the bar in 1841 and commenced practice in Wabash, Wabash County, Ind.; American consul to Maranham, Brazil, 1850–1853; elected as a Republican to the Thirty-fourth, Thirty-fifth, and Thirty-sixth Congresses (March 4, 1855–March 3, 1861); member of the State house of representatives in 1865 and served as speaker; judge of the twenty-seventh judicial district of Indiana 1872–1880; died in Wabash, Ind., March 21, 1881; interment in Falls Cemetery.

PETTUS, Edmund Winston, a Senator from Alabama; born in Limestone County, Ala., July 6, 1821; attended the common schools of Alabama and Clinton College in Smith County, Tenn.; studied law; was admitted to the bar in 1842 and commenced practice in Gainesville, Ala.; elected solicitor for the seventh circuit in 1844; served as a lieutenant in the Mexican War; resigned the office of solicitor in 1849 and went with a party of his neighbors on horseback to California; elected judge of the seventh circuit after his return to Alabama in 1855 but resigned in 1858 and moved to Dallas County; resumed the practice of law; served as envoy from Alabama to Mississippi during the formation of the Southern Confederacy; entered the Confederate Army as major in the Twentieth Alabama Infantry in 1861 and soon afterward was made lieutenant colonel of that regiment; was made a brigadier general of Infantry in October 1863 and served until the close of the Civil War; returned to Selma, Ala., and practiced law; delegate to the Democratic National Conventions from 1876 to 1896; elected as a Democrat to the United States Senate for the term commencing March 4, 1897; reelected in 1903 and served from March 4, 1897, until his death at Hot Springs, Madison County, N. C., July 27, 1907; interment in Live Oak Cemetery, Selma, Ala.

PEYSER, Theodore Albert, a Representative from New York; born in Charleston, W. Va., February 18, 1873; attended the public schools; engaged in various occupations until 1893, when he moved to Cincinnati, Ohio, and became employed as a traveling salesman, in which capacity he served until 1900; moved to New York City, N. Y., in 1900 and engaged in the life-insurance business; elected as a Democrat to the Seventy-third, Seventy-fourth, and Seventy-fifth Congresses and served from March 4, 1933, until his death in New York City, N. Y., August 8, 1937; interment in United Cemetery, Cincinnati, Ohio.

PEYTON, Balie (brother of Joseph Hopkins Peyton), a Representative from Tennessee; born near Gallatin, Tenn., November 26, 1803; completed preparatory studies; studied law; was admitted to the bar and commenced practice in Gallatin in 1824; elected as a Whig to the Twenty-third and Twenty-fourth Congresses (March 4, 1833–March 3, 1837); resumed the practice of law; tendered the portfolio of Secretary of War in the Cabinet of President Tyler but declined; moved to New Orleans in 1841, having been appointed United States attorney for the eastern district of Louisiana, which position he held for four years; served as aide-de-camp on the staff of Gen. W. J. Worth during the Mexican War; and was voted a sword by the Legislature of Louisiana for gallantry; appointed as Minister to Chile by President Taylor and served from August 9, 1849, to September 14, 1853, when he resigned; President Pierce tendered him the same mission but, preferring private life, he declined; moved to San Francisco, Calif., in 1853 and continued the practice of law; prosecuting attorney of San Francisco 1853–1859; returned to Gallatin, Tenn., in 1859 and resumed the practice of law; presidential elector on the Constitutional-Union ticket of Bell and Everett in 1860; unsuccessful candidate for election in 1866 to the Fortieth Congress; member of the State senate in 1869 and 1870; resumed the practice of law; died on his farm near Gallatin, Sumner County, Tenn., August 18, 1878; interment in the family burying ground on his estate.

PEYTON, Joseph Hopkins (brother of Balie Peyton), a Representative from Tennessee; born near Gallatin, Sumner County, Tenn., May 20, 1808; completed preparatory studies and was graduated from college in 1837; studied medicine and practiced; held various local offices; member of the State senate of Tennessee in 1840; elected as a Whig to the Twenty-eighth and Twenty-ninth Congresses and served from March 4, 1843, until his death near Gallatin, Tenn., November 11, 1845; interment in the family burying ground near Gallatin, Sumner County, Tenn.

PEYTON, Samuel Oldham, a Representative from Kentucky; born in Bullitt County, Ky., January 8, 1804; completed preparatory studies; was graduated from the medical department of Transylvania University, Lexington, Ky., in 1827 and began practice in Hartford, Ohio County, Ky.; member of the State house of representatives in 1835; elected as a Democrat to the Thirtieth Congress (March 4, 1847–March 3, 1849); unsuccessful candidate for reelection in 1848 to the Thirty-first Congress; elected to the Thirty-fifth and Thirty-sixth Congresses (March 4, 1857–March 3, 1861); unsuccessful candidate for renomination in 1860; resumed the practice of medicine; died in Hartford, Ky., January 4, 1870; interment in Oakwood Cemetery.

PFEIFER, Joseph Lawrence, a Representative from New York; born in Brooklyn, Kings County, N. Y., February 6, 1892; attended St. Nicholas Parochial School, St. Leonard's Academy, and St. Francis College, Brooklyn, N. Y.; was graduated from Long Island (N. Y.) Medical College in 1914; was licensed to practice the same year; interned in St. Catherine's Hospital, Brooklyn, N. Y., in 1914 and 1915; connected with numerous hospitals as attending surgeon and assistant surgeon; lecturer and author on surgical topics; during the First World War served on the medical advisory board, instructing medical officers going overseas; elected as a Democrat to the Seventy-fourth and to the seven succeeding Congresses (January 3, 1935–January 3, 1951); unsuccessful candidate for renomination in 1950; resumed the practice of medicine; is a resident of Brooklyn, N. Y.

PFEIFFER, William Louis, a Representative from New York; born in Buffalo, Erie County, N. Y., May 29, 1907; attended public schools and graduated from Tech High School; chief aide to New York State Republican Congressional Committee in 1938; member of New York State journal clerk's staff in 1939 and 1940; secretary of Erie County New York Republican Committee in 1941 and 1942; county personnel officer of Erie County Board of Supervisors in 1942 and 1943; executive assistant to New York State comptroller 1943–1946; deputy comptroller of

New York State 1946–1948; elected as a Republican to the Eighty-first Congress (January 3, 1949–January 3, 1951); was not a candidate for renomination in 1950; chairman of New York State Republican Committee 1949–1953; delegate to the Republican National Convention in 1952; engaged in the investment mortgage business in New York City, N. Y.; industrialist and banker; resides in Old Westbury, N. Y.

PFOST, Gracie Bowers, a Representative from Idaho; born in Harrison, Boone County, Ark., March 12, 1906; moved with her parents to a farm in the Boise Valley, Idaho, in 1911; attended the public schools and graduated from Link's Business University, Boise, Idaho, in 1929; chemist for milk products company for two years; deputy county clerk, auditor, and recorder of Canyon County, Idaho, 1929–1939; treasurer of Canyon County 1941–1951; engaged in the real-estate business in Nampa, Idaho, in 1951 and 1952; delegate to the Democratic National Conventions in 1944, 1948, 1952, 1956, and 1960; unsuccessful Democratic candidate for Congress in 1950; elected as a Democrat to the Eighty-third and to the three succeeding Congresses (January 3, 1953–January 3, 1961). *Reelected to the Eighty-seventh Congress.*

PHEIFFER, William Townsend, a Representative from New York; born in Purcell, Indian Territory (now Oklahoma), July 15, 1898; attended the public schools of Purcell, Ardmore, and Oklahoma City, Okla., and the University of Southern California at Los Angeles; during the First World War served as a private in the Cavalry, United States Army, in 1918; was graduated from the law department of the University of Oklahoma at Norman in 1919; was admitted to the bar the same year and practiced law in Sayre, Okla., 1923–1926; moved to Amarillo, Tex., in 1926 and continued the practice of law until 1939, when he moved to New York City, N. Y.; delegate to the Republican National Convention at Chicago in 1932 and to the Republican State conventions in 1936 and 1942; elected as a Republican to the Seventy-seventh Congress (January 3, 1941–January 3, 1943); unsuccessful candidate for reelection in 1942 to the Seventy-eighth Congress; during World War II entered the United States Army as a captain of Cavalry and served from March 12, 1943, to April 22, 1944; received the Army Award of Merit; appointed counsel for the Petroleum Administration for War, Washington, D. C., on August 1, 1944, and served until February 8, 1945, when he resumed the private practice of law; executive assistant to the chairman of the Republican National Committee 1945–1948; United States Ambassador to Dominican Republic 1953–1957; is a resident of New York, N. Y.

PHELAN, James, a Representative from Tennessee; born in Aberdeen, Monroe County, Miss., December 7, 1856; moved with his father to Memphis, Tenn., in 1867; attended private schools and the Kentucky Military Institute near Frankfort in 1871; entered the University of Leipsic, Saxony, in 1874 and was graduated in February 1878; returned to Memphis; studied law; was admitted to the bar and commenced practice in 1881; elected as a Democrat to the Fiftieth and Fifty-first Congresses and served from March 4, 1887, until his death in Nassau, Bahama Islands, on January 30, 1891; interment in Elmwood Cemetery, Memphis, Tenn.

PHELAN, James Duval, a Senator from California; born in San Francisco, Calif., April 20, 1861; was graduated from St. Ignatius University, San Francisco, in 1881; studied law at the University of California at Berkeley; engaged in banking; mayor of San Francisco 1897–1902; president of Relief and Red Cross Funds after the San Francisco earthquake disaster in 1906; delegate to the Democratic National Conventions in 1900 and 1924;

elected as a Democrat to the United States Senate and served from March 4, 1915, to March 3, 1921; unsuccessful candidate for reelection in 1920; traveled extensively in 1921 and 1922; chairman of the board of directors of the United Bank & Trust Co. at San Francisco; died at his country estate "Villa Montalvo," Saratoga, Santa Clara County, Calif.; interment in the family mausoleum in Holy Cross Cemetery, San Mateo County, near San Francisco, Calif.

PHELAN, Michael Francis, a Representative from Massachusetts; born in Lynn, Essex County, Mass., October 22, 1875; attended the public schools; was graduated from Lynn Classical High School, from the academic department of Harvard University in 1897, and from the law department of the same university in 1900; was admitted to the bar in 1900 and commenced practice in Lynn; member of the State house of representatives in 1905 and 1906; elected as a Democrat to the Sixty-third and to the three succeeding Congresses (March 4, 1913–March 3, 1921); unsuccessful candidate for reelection in 1920 to the Sixty-seventh Congress; practiced law in Lynn and Boston, Mass., and Washington, D. C.; member of the Merrimac Valley Sewage Commission in 1937; appointed a member of the Massachusetts Labor Relations Board in 1937 and served until his death in Boston, Mass., October 12, 1941; interment in St. Mary's Cemetery, Lynn, Mass.

PHELPS, Charles Edward, a Representative from Maryland; born in Guilford, Windham County, Vt., May 1, 1833; moved with his parents to New Jersey in 1837 and to Maryland in 1841; pursued classical studies in St. Timothy's Hall, near Catonsville, Md., and was graduated from Princeton College in 1852; attended the law department of Harvard University; was admitted to the bar and commenced practice in Baltimore, Md., in 1855; elected a member of the city council in 1860; during the Civil War entered the Union Army August 20, 1862, as lieutenant colonel of the Seventh Regiment, Maryland Volunteers; was promoted to colonel April 13, 1864; honorably discharged September 9, 1864; brevetted brigadier general March 13, 1865, "for gallant and meritorious services"; awarded the Congressional Medal of Honor March 30, 1898, "for, when the division and brigade commanders were wounded in the assault at Laurel Hill, May 8, 1864, he succeeded to the command and led the brigade with distinguished gallantry and was wounded within a few feet of the enemy's works and taken prisoner"; elected as a Union War candidate to the Thirty-ninth Congress and as a Union Conservative to the Fortieth Congress (March 4, 1865–March 3, 1869); resumed the practice of law in Baltimore, Md.; served as commissioner of public schools; judge on the supreme bench of the city of Baltimore 1882–1908; member of the law faculty of the University of Maryland 1884–1907; died in Walbrook, Baltimore, Md., December 27, 1908; interment in Woodlawn Cemetery, Baltimore, Md.

PHELPS, Darwin, a Representative from Pennsylvania; born in East Granby, Conn., April 17, 1807; was left an orphan at an early age and went to live with his grandparents in Portage, Ohio, where he completed preparatory studies; attended Western University, Pittsburgh, Pa.; studied law in Pittsburgh, Pa.; was admitted to the bar and commenced practice in Kittanning, Pa., in 1835; member of the board of trustees of Kittanning Academy; member of the town council in 1841 and 1848; burgess in 1844, 1845, 1849, 1852, 1855, 1858, 1859, and 1861; presidential elector on the Whig ticket of Scott and Graham in 1852; unsuccessful Republican candidate for auditor general in 1856; delegate to the Republican National Convention at Chicago in 1860; major of the Twenty-second Regiment, Pennsylvania Volunteer Militia, in 1862; member of the State house of repre-

sentatives in 1865; elected as a Republican to the Forty-first Congress (March 4, 1869–March 3, 1871); was not a candidate for renomination in 1870; died in Kittanning, Armstrong County, Pa., on December 14, 1879; interment in Kittanning Cemetery.

PHELPS, Elisha (father of John Smith Phelps), a Representative from Connecticut; born in Simsbury, Hartford County, Conn., November 16, 1779; was graduated from Yale College in 1800 and from Litchfield (Conn.) Law School; was admitted to the bar in 1803 and began practice in Simsbury; member of the State house of representatives in 1807, 1812, and 1814–1818; elected as a Democrat to the Sixteenth Congress (March 4, 1819–March 3, 1821); again a member of the State house of representatives in 1821 and served as speaker; served in the State senate 1822–1824; elected to the Nineteenth and Twentieth Congresses (March 4, 1825–March 3, 1829); declined to be a candidate for renomination in 1828; State comptroller 1831–1837; again a member of the State house of representatives in 1829 and 1835 and served as speaker in 1829; appointed a commissioner to revise and codify the State laws in 1835; died in Simsbury, Conn., April 6, 1847; interment in Hop Meadow Cemetery.

PHELPS, James (son of Lancelot Phelps), a Representative from Connecticut; born in Colebrook, Litchfield County, Conn., January 12, 1822; attended the public schools, the Episcopal Academy, Cheshire, Conn., Trinity College, Hartford, Conn., and the law department of Yale College; was admitted to the bar in 1845 and commenced practice in Essex, Conn.; member of the State house of representatives in 1853, 1854, and 1856; served in the State senate in 1858 and 1859; judge of the superior court of Connecticut 1863–1873; judge of the supreme court of errors of the State from 1873 until his resignation in 1875, having been elected to Congress; elected as a Democrat to the Forty-fourth and to the three succeeding Congresses (March 4, 1875–March 3, 1883); declined to be a candidate for renomination in 1882; resumed the practice of law; again judge of the superior court 1885–1892; resumed the practice of his profession and also engaged in banking; delegate to several State conventions; died in Essex, Middlesex County, Conn., January 15, 1900; interment in River View Cemetery.

PHELPS, John Smith (son of Elisha Phelps), a Representative from Missouri; born in Simsbury, Hartford County, Conn., December 22, 1814; attended the common schools and was graduated from Trinity College, Hartford, Conn., in 1832; studied law; was admitted to the bar in 1835 and commenced practice in Simsbury; moved to Springfield, Greene County, Mo., in 1837; member of the State house of representatives in 1840; elected as a Democrat to the Twenty-ninth and to the eight succeeding Congresses (March 4, 1845–March 3, 1863); was not a candidate for renomination in 1862; during the Civil War enlisted as a private in Captain Coleman's Company of Missouri Infantry; promoted to lieutenant colonel October 2, 1861, and to colonel December 19, 1861; mustered out May 13, 1862; appointed by President Lincoln in July 1862 as Military Governor of Arkansas; resumed the practice of his profession in Springfield; unsuccessful Democratic candidate in 1868 for Governor of Missouri; Governor of Missouri 1877–1881; resumed the practice of his profession; died in St. Louis, Mo., November 20, 1886; interment in Hazelwood Cemetery, Springfield, Mo.

PHELPS, Lancelot (father of James Phelps), a Representative from Connecticut; born in Windsor, Conn., November 9, 1784; moved with his father to Colebrook, Conn., in 1794; attended the common schools; studied medicine and commenced practice in Colebrook, Litchfield County, Conn.; also engaged in agricultural and mercantile pursuits in Hitchcockville (now Riverton), Conn.; returned to Colebrook; held various local offices; member of the State house of representatives in 1817, 1819–1821, 1824, 1827, 1828, and 1830; elected as a Democrat to the Twenty-fourth and Twenty-fifth Congresses (March 4, 1835–March 3, 1839); died in Colebrook, Conn., September 1, 1866; interment in Center Cemetery, Winsted, Conn.

PHELPS, Oliver, a Representative from New York; born in Poquonock, Hartford County, Conn., October 21, 1749; completed preparatory studies; engaged in mercantile pursuits in Granville, Mass., in 1770; during the Revolution was deputy commissary in the Continental Army and served until the end of the war; settled in Suffield, Mass.; member of the State house of representatives 1778–1780; member of the constitutional convention in 1779 and 1780; served in the State senate in 1785; member of the Governor's council in 1786; assisted in the organization of the Phelps & Gorham syndicate in 1788 and acted as the representative of that company in the exploration of the Genesee country in western New York and in negotiations for the title to the land; first judge of Ontario County, N. Y., 1789–1793; moved to Canandaigua, N. Y., in 1802; elected as a Democrat to the Eighth Congress (March 4, 1803–March 3, 1805); died in Canandaigua, N. Y., February 21, 1809; interment in West Avenue Cemetery.

PHELPS, Samuel Shethar, a Senator from Vermont; born in Litchfield, Conn., May 13, 1793; was graduated from Yale College in 1811; studied law; was admitted to the bar and commenced practice in Middlebury, Addison County, Vt., in 1812; served in the War of 1812 as paymaster; member of the Vermont State House of Representatives 1821–1832; judge of the supreme court of Vermont 1832–1838; served in the Vermont State Senate in 1838 and 1839; elected as a Whig to the United States Senate; reelected in 1845 and served from March 4, 1839, to March 3, 1851; was appointed to the United States Senate to fill the vacancy caused by the death of William Upham and served from January 17, 1853, until March 16, 1854, when the Senate decided that he could not hold his seat by appointment; died in Middlebury, Addison County, Vt., on March 25, 1855; interment in West Cemetery.

PHELPS, Timothy Guy, a Representative from California; born in Chenango County, N. Y., December 20, 1824; completed preparatory studies; moved to New York City and engaged in mercantile pursuits; returned to Chenango County and began the study of law but discontinued it; moved to San Francisco, Calif., in December 1849; engaged in mining in Tuolumne County; his health becoming impaired, he returned to San Francisco and resumed mercantile pursuits; engaged in the real-estate business in 1853; unsuccessful candidate for the State assembly in 1854; member of the State assembly from 1855 to 1857; served in the State senate 1858–1861; unsuccessful candidate for Governor in 1861; elected as a Republican to the Thirty-seventh Congress (March 4, 1861–March 3, 1863); was not a candidate for renomination in 1862; resumed the real-estate business until 1870; collector of customs at the port of San Francisco 1870–1872 and 1890–1893; engaged in agricultural pursuits; unsuccessful Republican candidate for Governor in 1875; moved to San Mateo County; regent of the University of California at Berkeley from December 6, 1880, until his death; chairman of the board of regents of Lick Observatory for nineteen years; died near San Carlos, San Mateo County, Calif., June 11, 1899; interment in Cypress Lawn Memorial Park Cemetery, Lawndale, San Mateo County, Calif.

PHELPS, William Wallace, a Representative from Minnesota; born in Oakland County, Mich., June 1, 1826; attended the country schools; was graduated from the University of Michigan at Ann Arbor in 1846; studied law; was admitted to the bar in 1848 and commenced practice; register of the United States land office at Red Wing, Goodhue County, Minn.; upon the admission of Minnesota as a State into the Union was elected as a Democrat to the Thirty-fifth Congress and served from May 11, 1858, to March 3, 1859; resumed the practice of his profession in Red Wing, Minn.; died in Spring Lake, Ottawa County, Mich., August 3, 1873; interment in Oakwood Cemetery, Red Wing, Minn.

PHELPS, William Walter, a Representative from New Jersey; born in New York City August 24, 1839; attended private schools near Bridgeport, Conn., and Mount Washington Institute, New York; was graduated from Yale College in 1860 and from the law department of Columbia College, New York City, in 1863; was admitted to the bar and commenced practice in New York City; retired from the practice of law in 1868; declined a judgeship offered by Governor Fenton of New York; engaged in banking in New York City, with residence in Englewood, N. J.; also served as a director of numerous railroads; elected to the Forty-third Congress (March 4, 1873–March 3, 1875); unsuccessful candidate for reelection in 1874 to the Forty-fourth Congress; delegate to the Republican National Conventions in 1880 and 1884; Envoy Extraordinary and Minister Plenipotentiary to Austria in 1881; relinquished the position in 1882; elected as a Republican to the Forty-eighth, Forty-ninth, and Fiftieth Congresses (March 4, 1883–March 3, 1889); declined to be a candidate for renomination in 1888; appointed by President Harrison one of the commissioners to represent the United States at the International Congress on the Samoan Question, which met in Berlin in 1889; appointed Envoy Extraordinary and Minister Plenipotentiary to Germany in 1889 and served until 1893; appointed a special judge of the court of errors and appeals of the State of New Jersey in 1893; died in Englewood, Bergen County, N. J., June 17, 1894; interment in the City Cemetery, Simsbury, Conn.

PHILBIN, Philip Joseph, a Representative from Massachusetts; born in Clinton, Worcester County, Mass., May 29, 1898; attended the public and high schools; during the First World War served as a seaman in the United States Navy 1917–1919; was graduated from Harvard University, Cambridge, Mass., in 1920 and from Columbia University Law School, New York, N. Y., in 1924; was admitted to the bar the same year and commenced practice in Boston, Mass., and later in Clinton, Mass.; also engaged in the realty and fuel businesses and in agricultural pursuits; secretary, campaign manager, and personal representative at intervals for Senator David I. Walsh 1921–1940; special counsel for the United States Senate Committee on Education and Labor 1934–1936; referee in the United States Department of Labor in 1936 and 1937; member of the advisory board of the Massachusetts Unemployment Compensation Commission 1937–1940; in 1935 became chairman of the town of Clinton Finance Committee; elected as a Democrat to the Seventy-eighth and to the eight succeeding Congresses (January 3, 1943–January 3, 1961). *Reelected to the Eighty-seventh Congress.*

PHILIPS, John Finis, a Representative from Missouri; born in Thralls Prairie, Boone County, Mo., December 31, 1834; attended the common schools, the University of Missouri at Columbia, and was graduated from Centre College, Danville, Ky., in 1855; studied law; was admitted to the bar in 1857 and commenced practice in Georgetown, Pettis County, Mo.; member of the State constitutional convention in 1861; during the Civil War was commissioned colonel in 1862 and commanded the Seventh Regiment, Missouri Volunteer Cavalry; served until the close of the war and was commended for gallantry by Gov. Williard B. Hall; resumed the practice of his profession at Sedalia, Mo.; served as mayor; delegate to the Democratic National Convention at New York City in 1868; unsuccessful candidate for election in 1868 to the Forty-first Congress; elected as a Democrat to the Forty-fourth Congress (March 4, 1875–March 3, 1877); elected to the Forty-sixth Congress to fill the vacancy caused by the death of Alfred M. Lay and served from January 10, 1880, to March 3, 1881; unsuccessful candidate for reelection in 1880 to the Forty-seventh Congress; moved to Kansas City, Mo., in 1881 and resumed the practice of law; commissioner of the Missouri Supreme Court 1883–1885; judge of the Kansas City Court of Appeals 1885–1888; appointed United States judge of the western district of Missouri by President Cleveland in 1888 and served until 1910, when he retired from public life; died at Hot Springs Ark., while on a visit, March 13, 1919; interment in Mount Washington Cemetery, Kansas City, Mo.

PHILLIPS, Alfred Noroton, a Representative from Connecticut; born in Darien, Fairfield County, Conn., April 23, 1894; attended the public schools, Betts Academy, Stamford, Conn., and Hotchkiss School, Lakeville, Conn.; was graduated from Yale University, New Haven, Conn., in 1917; enlisted as a private in the Tenth Field Artillery, Connecticut National Guard, in 1916; during the First World War served as a first lieutenant in the Field Artillery, United States Army, in 1917 and 1918, with overseas service; moved to Stamford, Conn., in 1918; served as major in the Connecticut National Guard Reserve 1928–1933; employed with the Charles H. Phillips Chemical Co. from early youth until 1923, and as publisher of a newspaper in Darien, Conn., since 1922; mayor of Stamford in 1923 and 1924, in 1927 and 1928, and 1935 and 1936; commander of the American Legion of Connecticut in 1919; delegate to many Democratic State and National conventions; member of the Democratic State Central Committee; elected as a Democrat to the Seventy-fifth Congress (January 3, 1937–January 3, 1939); unsuccessful candidate for reelection in 1938 to the Seventy-sixth Congress; resumed his publishing business in Darien, Conn., and the management of his dairy farm in Cecilton, Md.; during World War II was commissioned as a captain, Military Police, Army of the United States, and served from July 17, 1942, to August 16, 1944, with service in North Africa; resumed his former pursuits and is a resident of Darien, Conn.

PHILLIPS, Dayton Edward, a Representative from Tennessee; born in Shell Creek, Carter County, Tenn., March 29, 1910; raised on a farm; attended the country school, and Cloudland High School, Roan Mountain, Tenn., Milligan (Tenn.) College 1929–1931, and the University of Tennessee at Knoxville 1932–1934; taught school in Carter County, Tenn., in 1931 and 1932; was graduated from the National University Law School, Washington, D. C., in 1936; was admitted to the bar in 1935 and commenced practice in Elizabethton, Tenn.; attorney for Carter County 1938–1942; district attorney general, first judicial circuit of Tennessee, 1942–1947; during World War II served as an enlisted man in the United States Army, with overseas service in the European Theater of Operations, 1943–1945; elected as a Republican to the Eightieth and Eighty-first Congresses (January 3, 1947–January 3, 1951); unsuccessful candidate for renomination in 1950; resumed the practice of law; chancellor of the First Chancery Court of Tennessee 1952–; is a resident of Elizabethton, Tenn.

PHILLIPS, Fremont Orestes, a Representative from Ohio; born in Lafayette, Medina County, Ohio, March 16, 1856; attended the public schools; moved to Medina, Ohio, in 1873;

attended Medina High School, Medina Normal School, and Kenyon College, Gambier, Ohio; studied law; was admitted to the bar in 1880 and commenced practice in Medina, Ohio; justice of the peace; mayor of Medina 1886–1890; served as probate judge of Medina County 1892–1897; elected as a Republican to the Fifty-sixth Congress (March 4, 1899–March 3, 1901); unsuccessful candidate for renomination in 1900; resumed the practice of law in Medina, Ohio; chairman of the Medina County Republican Central Committee 1916–1934; again elected probate judge of Medina County in 1924; reelected in 1928 and served until 1932; died in Medina, Ohio, February 21, 1936; interment in Spring Grove Cemetery.

PHILLIPS, Henry Myer, a Representative from Pennsylvania; born in Philadelphia, Pa., June 30, 1811; attended the Philadelphia schools and Franklin Institute; studied law; was admitted to the bar in 1832 and commenced practice in Philadelphia; clerk of the court of common pleas of Philadelphia; elected as a Democrat to the Thirty-fifth Congress (March 4, 1857–March 3, 1859); unsuccessful candidate for reelection in 1858 to the Thirty-sixth Congress; resumed the practice of law in Philadelphia; trustee of Jefferson Medical College in 1862; appointed a member of the Board of Fairmount Park Commissioners in 1867 and elected its president in 1881; member of the Board of City Trusts in 1869, vice president of the board 1870–1878, and president 1878–1882; director of the Academy of Music in 1870 and its president in 1872, resigning in 1884; member of the commission to supervise the erection of the municipal buildings in Philadelphia in 1870, resigning in 1871; director of the Pennsylvania Railroad Co. in 1874; died in Philadelphia, Pa., August 28, 1884; interment in Mount Sinai Cemetery, Frankford (Philadelphia), Pa.

PHILLIPS, John, a Representative from Pennsylvania; was born in Chester County, Pa.; received a limited schooling; elected as a Federalist to the Seventeenth Congress (March 4, 1821–March 3, 1823).

PHILLIPS, John, a Representative from California; born in Wilkes-Barre, Luzerne County, Pa., September 11, 1887; moved to St. David, Pa., in 1891; attended the public schools; was graduated from Haverford (Pa.) College in 1910; during the First World War served in the Adjutant General's Office and in Ordnance 1917–1919; moved to California in 1924; business analyst, organizer, and rancher; member of the city council of Banning, Calif., 1930–1932; served in the State assembly 1932–1936; member of the State senate 1936–1942; member of the United States delegation to the XIth World's Dairy Congress in Berlin in 1937; elected as a Republican to the Seventy-eighth and to the six succeeding Congresses (January 3, 1943–January 3, 1957); was not a candidate for renomination in 1956; delegate to Republican National Conventions in 1944, 1948, 1952, 1956, and 1960; member of the American Battle Monuments Commission 1952–; engaged as a public relations counselor; is a resident of Banning, Calif.

PHILLIPS, Philip, a Representative from Alabama; born in Charleston, S. C., December 13, 1807; pursued classical studies; studied law; was admitted to the bar and commenced practice in Charleston, S. C., December 14, 1828; member of the State constitutional convention in 1832; member of the State house of representatives in 1833 and 1834; moved to Mobile, Ala., and continued the practice of law; member of the State house of representatives in 1844 and 1851; delegate to the Democratic National Convention at Baltimore in 1852; elected as a Democrat to the Thirty-third Congress (March 4, 1853–March 3, 1855); declined to be a candidate for renomination in 1854 to the Thirty-fourth Congress; resumed the practice of law in Washington, D. C., and died there on January 14, 1884; interment in Laurel Hill Cemetery, Savannah, Ga.

PHILLIPS, Stephen Clarendon, a Representative from Massachusetts; born in Salem, Mass., November 4, 1801; was graduated from Harvard University in 1819; engaged in mercantile pursuits in Salem; member of the State house of representatives 1824–1829; served in the State senate in 1830; elected as a Whig to the Twenty-third Congress to fill the vacancy caused by the resignation of Rufus Choate; elected to the Twenty-fourth and Twenty-fifth Congresses and served from December 1, 1834, to September 28, 1838, when he resigned; mayor of Salem 1838–1842; defeated as the Free-Soil candidate for Governor in 1848 and 1849; engaged in the lumber business in Canada; perished in the burning of the steamer *Montreal* on the St. Lawrence River June 26, 1857, and the remains were never recovered.

PHILLIPS, Thomas Wharton (father of Thomas Wharton Phillips, Jr.), a Representative from Pennsylvania; born near Mount Jackson in that section of Beaver County now included in Lawrence County, Pa., February 23, 1835; attended the common schools and was also privately instructed; engaged in the production of oil; president of the Producers' Protective Association 1887–1890; president of the Citizens' National Bank of New Castle; member of the board of trustees of Bethany College, West Virginia, and of Hiram College, Ohio; elected as a Republican to the Fifty-third and Fifty-fourth Congresses (March 4, 1893–March 3, 1897); did not seek renomination in 1896; resumed his former pursuits; appointed a member of the United States Industrial Commission by President McKinley and served until its dissolution; delegate to the Republican National Convention in 1908; died in New Castle, Pa., July 21, 1912; interment in Oak Park Cemetery, New Castle, Pa.

PHILLIPS, Thomas Wharton, Jr. (son of the preceding), a Representative from Pennsylvania; born in New Castle, Lawrence County, Pa., November 21, 1874; attended the common schools; was graduated from Phillips Academy, Andover, Mass., in 1894 and from the Sheffield Scientific School, Yale University, in 1897; engaged in the petroleum, natural-gas, and coal businesses; delegate to the Republican National Convention at Chicago in 1916; elected as a Republican to the Sixty-eighth and Sixty-ninth Congresses (March 4, 1923–March 3, 1927); did not seek renomination for Congress in 1926; was an unsuccessful candidate for the Republican nomination for Governor in 1926, 1930, and 1934; resumed his former occupation and was president of the Phillips Gas and Oil Co.; also a director of the Butler Consolidated Coal Co., and the Pennsylvania Investment and Real Estate Corp., of Butler; died at Phillips Hall, Penn Township, Butler County, Pa., January 2, 1956; interment in North Cemetery, Butler, Pa.

PHILLIPS, William Addison, a Representative from Kansas; born in Paisley, Scotland, January 14, 1824; attended the common schools of Paisley; immigrated to the United States in 1838 with his parents, who settled in Randolph County, Ill.; engaged in agricultural pursuits; employed as a newspaper correspondent 1845–1862; studied law; was admitted to the bar in 1855 and commenced practice in Lawrence, Kans.; first justice of the supreme court under the Leavenworth constitution; founded the city of Salina, Kans., in 1858; during the Civil War raised some of the first troops in Kansas in 1861; was afterward commissioned colonel and served as commander of the famous Cherokee Indian Regiment; prosecuting attorney of Cherokee County in 1865; served in the State house of representatives in 1865; attorney for the Cherokee Indians at Washington, D. C.; elected as a Republican to the Forty-third, Forty-fourth, and Forty-fifth Congresses (March 4, 1873–March 3, 1879); unsuccessful candidate for renomination in 1878; president of the Kansas Historical Society and engaged in literary pursuits; unsuccessful candidate for election in 1890 to the Fifty-second Congress; died at Fort Gibson, Muskogee County, Indian Territory (now Oklahoma), November 30, 1893; interment in Gypsum Hill Cemetery, Salina, Kans.

PHILSON, Robert, a Representative from Pennsylvania; born in County Tyrone, Ireland, in 1759; immigrated to the United States and settled in Berlin, Pa., in 1785; received a limited schooling; engaged in agricultural pursuits; held various town and county offices; served as associate judge of Somerset County for twenty years; commissioned brigadier general of the Second Brigade, Tenth Division, Pennsylvania Militia, May 9, 1800; during the War of 1812 served as brigadier general of the Second Brigade, Twelfth Division, Pennsylvania Volunteers; elected to the Sixteenth Congress (March 4, 1819–March 3, 1821); retired from public life and active pursuits; died in Berlin, Pa., July 25, 1831; interment in Reformed Church Cemetery.

PHIPPS, Lawrence Cowle, a Senator from Colorado; born in Amwell Township, Washington County, Pa., August 30, 1862; moved with his parents to Pittsburgh, Pa., in 1867; attended the common schools and was graduated from Pittsburgh High School in 1879; entered the employ of the Carnegie Steel Co., advancing to the position of first vice president; retired from active participation in the steel business upon the absorption of the company by the United States Steel Corp. on April 1, 1901; moved to Denver, Colo., and engaged in the investment business; donor of the Agnes Memorial Sanatorium in Denver; president of the Colorado Taxpayers' Protective League in 1913; chairman of the mountain division in the Red Cross campaign in 1917; member of the Colorado council of defense in 1917; delegate to the Republican National Conventions in 1920, 1924, 1928, and 1936; elected as a Republican to the United States Senate in 1918; reelected in 1924, and served from March 4, 1919, to March 3, 1931; was not a candidate for reelection in 1930; engaged in railroad and electric power investments; died in Santa Monica, Calif., March 1, 1958; interment in Fairmount Mausoleum, Denver, Colo.

PHISTER, Elijah Conner, a Representative from Kentucky; born in Maysville, Mason County, Ky., October 8, 1822; attended the Seminary of Rand and Richardson, Maysville, Ky., and was graduated from Augusta College, Kentucky, in August 1840; studied law; was admitted to the bar and commenced practice in 1844; mayor of Maysville in 1848; circuit judge 1856–1862; member of the State house of representatives 1867–1871; appointed one of the commissioners to revise the State statutes in 1872 but declined; elected as a Democrat to the Forty-sixth and Forty-seventh Congresses (March 4, 1879–March 3, 1883); resumed the practice of law; died in Maysville, Ky., May 16, 1887; interment in the City Cemetery.

PHOENIX, Jonas Phillips, a Representative from New York; born in Morristown, Morris County, N. J., January 14, 1788; received a limited schooling; became a merchant in New York City; alderman of the first ward in 1840, 1842, and 1847; presidential elector on the Whig ticket of Harrison and Tyler in 1840; appointed a commissioner of the Croton Aqueduct Works in 1842; elected as a Whig to the Twenty-eighth Congress (March 4, 1843–March 3, 1845); declined to be a candidate for renomination in 1844; unsuccessful candidate for election in 1846 to the Thirtieth Congress; chairman of the Whig

General Committee in 1846 and 1847; member of the State assembly in 1848; elected to the Thirty-first Congress (March 4, 1849–March 3, 1851); renominated in 1850 but declined to be a candidate; died in New York City May 4, 1859; interment in the Presbyterian Cemetery, Morristown, N. J.

PICKENS, Andrew (grandfather of Francis Wilkinson Pickens), a Representative from South Carolina; born in Paxton, Bucks County, Pa., September 13, 1739; attended the common schools; moved with his parents to the Waxhaw settlement in South Carolina in 1752; served in the provincial militia in the campaign against the Cherokee Indians in 1760; entered the Revolutionary Army as captain of militia and attained the rank of brigadier general; at the head of a partisan corps he participated in many engagements and received a sword from Congress for his conduct at the Battle of Cowpens; commanded an expedition against the Cherokee Indians in 1782; member of the State house of representatives 1781–1794; one of the commissioners named to settle the boundary line between South Carolina and Georgia in 1787; member of the State constitutional convention in 1790; elected as a Democrat to the Third Congress (March 4, 1793–March 3, 1795); appointed major general of militia in 1795; unsuccessful candidate for election to the United States Senate in 1797; member of the State house of representatives 1800–1812; declined the nomination for Governor in 1812; died in Tomassee, Pendleton District, S. C., August 11, 1817; interment in Old Stone Churchyard, near Pendleton, S. C.

PICKENS, Francis Wilkinson (grandson of Andrew Pickens), a Representative from South Carolina; born on a plantation on the Toogoodoo River, St. Pauls Parish, Colleton District, S. C., April 7, 1805; completed preparatory studies; attended Franklin College, Athens, Ga., and was graduated from South Carolina College (now the University of South Carolina) at Columbia; studied law; was admitted to the bar and commenced practice in Edgefield District in 1829; engaged in planting; member of the State house of representatives 1832–1834; elected as a Nullifier Democrat to the Twenty-third Congress to fill the vacancy caused by the resignation of George McDuffie; reelected to the Twenty-fourth and to the three succeeding Congresses and served from December 8, 1834, to March 3, 1843; member of the State senate 1844–1846; member of the Nashville southern convention in 1850; delegate to the Democratic National Convention at Cincinnati in 1856; Minister to Russia 1858–1860; Governor of South Carolina 1860–1862; died in Edgefield, Edgefield County, S. C., January 25, 1869; interment in Edgefield Cemetery.

PICKENS, Israel, a Representative from North Carolina and a Senator from Alabama; born near Concord, Mecklenburg (now Cabarrus) County, N. C., January 30, 1780; moved to Burke County, N. C.; received instruction from private teachers and was graduated from Jefferson College, Canonsburg, Pa., in 1802; studied law; was admitted to the bar and practiced; member of the State senate in 1809; elected as a Democrat from North Carolina to the Twelfth, Thirteenth, and Fourteenth Congresses (March 4, 1811–March 3, 1817); register of the land office of Mississippi Territory (which included the present State of Alabama) 1817–1821; Governor of Alabama 1821–1825; appointed to the United States Senate from Alabama to fill the vacancy caused by the death of Henry Chambers and served from February 17, 1826, to November 27, 1826, when a successor was elected; was not a candidate for election to the vacancy; declined an appointment as judge of the United States Court for the District of Alabama in 1826; died near Matanzas, Cuba, on April 24, 1827; interment in the family cemetery near Greensboro, Hale County, Ala.

PICKERING, Timothy, a Senator and a Representative from Massachusetts; born in Salem, Mass., July 17, 1745; attended the grammar school and was graduated from Harvard College in 1763; clerk in the office of register of deeds; studied law; was admitted to the bar in 1768 and commenced practice in Salem; selectman and assessor 1772–1777; member of Committee on State of Rights of Colonists in 1773; member of Committee of Correspondence and Safety in 1774 and 1775; town clerk 1774–1776; elected register of deeds in 1775 and resigned in 1777 to enter the Army; appointed in 1775 a judge of the court of common pleas for Essex County and judge of the provincial maritime court; elected to the State legislature in 1776; entered the Revolutionary Army as colonel; appointed adjutant general May 24, 1777; elected on November 7, 1777, by the Continental Congress as a member of Board of War; became Quartermaster General of the Army (vice General Greene) on August 5, 1780; moved to Philadelphia in 1785 and to Wyoming County, Pa., in 1787; member of the State constitutional convention 1789–1790; appointed Postmaster General in the Cabinet of President Washington August 12, 1791, as Secretary of War January 2, 1795, and as Secretary of State December 10, 1795, holding the latter position until May 10, 1800; returned to Massachusetts in 1802; unsuccessful candidate for election in 1802 to the Eighth Congress; appointed chief justice of court of common pleas and general sessions of the peace in 1802; elected to the United States Senate to fill the vacancy caused by the resignation of Dwight Foster; reelected and served from March 4, 1803, to March 3, 1811; unsuccessful candidate for reelection in 1811; member of the executive council of Massachusetts in 1812; elected as a Federalist to the Thirteenth and Fourteenth Congresses (March 4, 1813–March 3, 1817); declined to be a candidate for renomination; returned to his farm near Wenham, Mass.; returned to Salem in 1820; unsuccessful candidate for election to the Seventeenth Congress; member and chairman of the Salem School Committee in 1821; died in Salem, Essex County, Mass., January 29, 1829; interment in Broad Street Cemetery.

PICKETT, Charles Edgar, a Representative from Iowa; born near Bonaparte, Van Buren County, Iowa, January 14, 1866; attended the common schools; was graduated from Iowa State University at Iowa City in 1888 and from its law department in 1890; was admitted to the bar in 1890 and commenced practice in Waterloo, Iowa; vice president of the Pioneer National Bank; regent of the State University of Iowa 1896–1909; elected as a Republican to the Sixty-first and Sixty-second Congresses (March 4, 1909–March 3, 1913); unsuccessful candidate for reelection in 1912 to the Sixty-third Congress; resumed the practice of law in Waterloo, Iowa; chairman of the Republican State conventions in 1899 and 1916; delegate at large to the Republican National Convention at Chicago in 1920; unsuccessful candidate for the Republican nomination for United States Senator in 1926; died in Waterloo, Iowa, July 20, 1930; interment in Elmwood Cemetery.

PICKETT, Thomas Augustus (Tom), a Representative from Texas; born in Travis, Falls County, Tex., August 14, 1906; attended the public schools of Palestine, Tex., and the University of Texas at Austin; studied law; was admitted to the bar in 1929 and commenced practice in Palestine, Tex.; county attorney of Anderson County 1931–1935; district attorney of the third judicial district of Texas 1935–1945; elected as a Democrat to the Seventy-ninth and to the three succeeding Congresses and served from January 3, 1945, until his resignation June 30, 1952; vice president of the National Coal Association from July 1, 1952, to March 31, 1961; vice president of the Association of American Railroads April 1, 1961–, with offices in Washington, D. C.; resides in Alexandria, Va.

PICKLER, John Alfred, a Representative from South Dakota; born near Salem, Washington County, Ind., January 24, 1844; moved with his father to Davis County, Iowa; attended the district school; during the Civil War entered the Union Army and served in the Third Regiment, Iowa Volunteer Cavalry; was mustered out as captain in that regiment; subsequently served six months as major in the One Hundred and Thirty-eighth Regiment, Iowa Volunteer Cavalry; was graduated from the University of Iowa at Iowa City in 1870; attended the Chicago University Law School in 1871 and was graduated from the Ann Arbor (Mich.) Law School in 1872; was admitted to the bar and commenced practice in Kirksville, Mo.; elected district attorney of Adair County, Mo., in 1872; moved to Muscatine, Iowa, in 1874; presidential elector on the Republican ticket of Garfield and Arthur in 1880; member of the State legislature 1881–1883; moved to the Territory of Dakota in 1883; elected to the Dakota Legislature in 1884; upon the admission of South Dakota as a State into the Union was elected as a Republican to the Fifty-first and to the three succeeding Congresses and served from November 2, 1889, to March 3, 1897; was not a candidate for renomination in 1896; resumed the practice of his profession; also engaged in the real-estate business; died in Faulkton, Faulk County, S. Dak., on June 13, 1910; interment in Faulkton Cemetery.

PICKMAN, Benjamin, Jr., a Representative from Massachusetts; born in Salem, Mass., September 30, 1763; was graduated from Harvard University in 1784; studied law in Newburyport, Mass., and was admitted to the bar, but soon relinquished the practice of law and engaged in commercial pursuits; member of the State house of representatives 1797–1802, 1812, and 1813; served in the State senate in 1803; member of the executive council of the State in 1805, 1808, 1813, 1814, and 1819–1821; drafted the answers of the house to the Governor's speeches in several sessions; elected to the Eleventh Congress (March 4, 1809–March 3, 1811); was not a candidate for renomination in 1810; member of the convention to revise the constitution of the State of Massachusetts in 1820; overseer of Harvard University 1810–1818; president of the board of directors of the Theological School at Cambridge and prominently identified with many religious and educational societies; died in Salem, Essex County, Mass., August 16, 1843; interment in Broad Street Cemetery.

PIDCOCK, James Nelson (cousin of Alvah Augustus Clark), a Representative from New Jersey; born in Whitehouse, Hunterdon County, N. J., February 8, 1836; attended the district schools and Lebanon Grammar School, Lebanon, N. J.; engaged in civil engineering 1850–1857; engaged in agricultural pursuits and was also a dealer in livestock after 1857; member of the State senate from Hunterdon County, N. J., 1877–1880; delegate to the Democratic National Convention at Chicago in 1884 and at St. Louis in 1888; elected as a Democrat to the Forty-ninth and Fiftieth Congresses (March 4, 1885–March 3, 1889); was not a candidate for renomination in 1888; again resumed his agricultural pursuits; built the Georgia Northern Railroad in southern Georgia, where he owned large timber tracts; served as president of the board of managers of the New Jersey State Hospital for the Insane 1891–1896; was an orchardist in New Jersey; died at Whitehouse Station, N. J., on December 17, 1899; interment in Elmwood Cemetery, Lebanon, Hunterdon County, N. J.

PIERCE, Charles Wilson, a Representative from Alabama; born in Benton, Yates County, N. Y., October 7, 1823; completed preparatory studies; moved with his father to Sandusky, Ohio, in 1829, and from there to Huntsville, Ohio, in 1847; moved to Havana, Ill., in 1855; during the Civil War enlisted in Company B, Eighty-fifth Regiment, Illinois Volunteer Infantry, and was elected first lieutenant; appointed quartermaster June 14, 1864; commissioned major in 1865; settled in Demopolis, Ala.; held various public offices; upon the readmission of Alabama to representation was elected as a Democrat to the Fortieth Congress and served from July 21, 1868, to March 3, 1869; declined to be a candidate for renomination; moved to Nebraska in 1872; member of the Nebraska State constitutional convention in 1875; elected to the State senate in 1877 and reelected in 1880; resigned in 1881 to become register of the United States land office, which position he held until May 1886; returned to his farm and devoted his attention to agricultural pursuits and stock raising; died in Hastings, Fla., February 18, 1907; interment in the family plot on the home farm near Waverly, Lancaster County, Nebr.

PIERCE, Franklin, a Representative and a Senator from New Hampshire and a President of the United States; born in Hillsboro, N. H., November 23, 1804; attended the academies of Hancock and Francestown, N. H.; prepared for college at Exeter and was graduated from Bowdoin College, Brunswick, Maine, in 1824; studied law; was admitted to the bar and commenced practice in Hillsboro in 1827; member of the State house of representatives 1829–1833 and served as speaker in 1832 and 1833; elected as a Democrat to the Twenty-third and Twenty-fourth Congresses (March 4, 1833–March 3, 1837); elected to the United States Senate and served from March 4, 1837, to February 28, 1842, when he resigned; resumed the practice of law in Concord; declined the appointment as Attorney General of the United States tendered by President Polk; served in the Mexican War as colonel; commissioned brigadier general in March 1847 and remained in Mexico until the close of the war; member of the New Hampshire State constitutional convention in 1850 and served as its president; elected President of the United States on the Democratic ticket of Pierce and King and served from March 4, 1853, to March 3, 1857; resumed the practice of his profession; died in Concord, N. H., October 8, 1869; interment in Minat Inclosure Cemetery.

PIERCE, Gilbert Ashville, a Senator from North Dakota; born in East Otto, Cattaraugus County, N. Y., January 11, 1839; attended the public schools; moved to Indiana in 1854 and settled near Valparaiso; attended the University of Chicago Law School two years; during the Civil War enlisted in Company H, Ninth Regiment, Indiana Volunteer Infantry, in 1861 and was elected second lieutenant of the company; appointed captain and assistant quartermaster by President Lincoln; promoted to lieutenant colonel and chief quartermaster in 1864; appointed colonel and inspector and special commissioner of the War Department in 1865; was brevetted major and lieutenant colonel United States Volunteers in 1865 "for faithful and meritorious services during the Civil War"; was admitted to the bar and commenced practice in Valparaiso, Porter County, Ind., in 1865; member of the State house of representatives in 1868; assistant financial clerk of the United States Senate 1869–1871; resigned to accept an editorial position on the Chicago Inter-Ocean, serving as associate editor and managing editor for twelve years; became associated with the Chicago News in 1883; appointed Governor of Dakota Territory in July 1884 and served until November 1886, when he resigned; upon the admission of North Dakota as a State into the Union was elected as a Republican to the United States Senate and served from November 21, 1889, to March 3, 1891; unsuccessful candidate for reelection; moved to Minneapolis, Minn.; purchased the Minneapolis Tribune and became its editor in chief in 1891; appointed Minister to Portugal January 6, 1893, but resigned April 26, 1893; retired from active business pursuits; died in Chicago, Ill., February 15, 1901; interment in Adams Cemetery, near Valparaiso, Ind.

PIERCE, Henry Lillie, a Representative from Massachusetts; born in Stoughton, Norfolk County, Mass., August 23, 1825; pursued classical studies; attended the State normal school at Bridgewater, Mass.; engaged in manufacturing; member of the State house of representatives 1860–1862 and in 1866; member of the Boston Board of Aldermen in 1870 and 1871; mayor of Boston in 1873; elected as a Republican to the Forty-third Congress to fill the vacancy caused by the death of William Whiting; reelected to the Forty-fourth Congress and served from December 1, 1873, to March 3, 1877; declined to be a candidate for renomination; again mayor of Boston in 1878; died in Boston, Mass., December 17, 1896; interment in Dorchester Burying Ground, Dorchester, Mass.

PIERCE, Ray Vaughn, a Representative from New York; born in Stark, Herkimer County, N. Y., August 6, 1840; attended public and private schools; was graduated from the Eclectic Medical College, Cincinnati, Ohio, in 1862; practiced medicine in Titusville, Pa., 1862–1866; moved to Buffalo, N. Y., in 1867; engaged in the manufacture and sale of proprietary medicines and established the Invalids' Hotel and Surgical Institute; member of the State senate 1877–1879; elected as a Republican to the Forty-sixth Congress and served from March 4, 1879, to September 18, 1880, when he resigned; was publisher of the Medical Adviser and also a manufacturer; died on St. Vincents Island, Fla., February 4, 1914; interment in Forest Lawn Cemetery, Buffalo, N. Y.

PIERCE, Rice Alexander, a Representative from Tennessee; born in Dresden, Weakley County, Tenn., July 3, 1848; attended the common schools in Tennessee; during the Civil War served in the Confederate States Army with the Eighth Tennessee Cavalry; after the war attended school in London, Canada; studied law in Halifax, N. C.; was admitted to the bar of the supreme court in Raleigh, N. C., in 1868 and commenced practice in Union City, Obion County, Tenn., in 1869; served as mayor in 1872; elected district attorney general of the twelfth judicial circuit in 1874; reelected in 1878 and served until 1883; elected as a Democrat to the Forty-eighth Congress (March 4, 1883–March 3, 1885); unsuccessful candidate for renomination in 1884; elected to the Fifty-first and Fifty-second Congresses (March 4, 1889–March 3, 1893); unsuccessful candidate for reelection in 1892 to the Fifty-third Congress; elected to the Fifty-fifth and to the three succeeding Congresses (March 4, 1897–March 3, 1905); unsuccessful candidate for reelection in 1904 to the Fifty-ninth Congress; resumed the practice of law in Union City, Tenn.; chairman of the Democratic State campaign committee in 1929; died in Union City, Tenn., July 12, 1936; interment in the City Cemetery.

PIERCE, Wallace Edgar, a Representative from New York; born in the town of Black Brook, Clinton County, N. Y., December 9, 1881; attended the rural schools; was graduated from Plattsburg (N. Y.) State Normal School in 1903; taught school in Clinton County, N. Y., and, later, in Ogdensburg (N. Y.) High School; served as secretary to Congressman George R. Malby 1909–1912 and to Congressman Edwin A. Merritt 1912–1914; studied law; was admitted to the bar in 1913 and commenced practice in Plattsburg, N. Y., in 1914; member of the State assembly 1916–1920; served as president of the board of visitors of the Plattsburg State Normal School 1926–1940; chairman of the Clinton County Republican committee 1926–1940; member of the New York State Republican executive

committee 1934–1940; elected as a Republican to the Seventy-sixth Congress and served from January 3, 1939, until his death in Washington, D. C., January 3, 1940; interment in Riverside Cemetery, Plattsburg, N. Y.

PIERCE, Walter Marcus, a Representative from Oregon; born on a farm near Morris, Grundy County, Ill., May 30, 1861; attended the common schools, Morris (Ill.) Academy, and the University of Michigan at Ann Arbor; taught school in Grundy County, Ill., 1877–1880, and in Franklin County, Kans., in 1881; moved to Oregon and taught school in Milton and Weston, Umatilla County, 1883–1890; superintendent of schools of Umatilla County, Oreg., 1886–1890; county clerk of Umatilla County 1890–1894; was graduated from the law department of Northwestern University, Evanston, Ill., in 1896; was admitted to the bar and practiced in Pendleton, Oreg., 1895–1907; engaged in banking and in the power and light business 1898–1907; operated stock and wheat farms 1907–1937; served in the Oregon Senate 1903–1907 and 1917–1921; Governor of Oregon 1923–1927; member of the board of regents of Oregon State College 1905–1927; delegate to all Democratic State conventions from 1890 to 1908; delegate to the Democratic National Conventions in 1920, 1932, and 1936; Democratic National committeeman from Oregon 1932–1936; elected as a Democrat to the Seventy-third and to the four succeeding Congresses (March 4, 1933–January 3, 1943); unsuccessful candidate for reelection in 1943 to the Seventy-eighth Congress; retired and lived near Salem, Oreg., with farming interests in Union County, Oreg.; died at his home in Eola Hills, west of Salem, Oreg., March 27, 1954; remains were cremated and the ashes deposited in Mount Crest Abbey Mausoleum, Salem, Oreg.

PIERCE, William, a Delegate from Georgia; born in that State in 1740; completed preparatory studies; served in the Continental Army during the Revolutionary War as aide-de-camp to Gen. Nathanael Greene; complimented by Congress and presented with a sword for his meritorious conduct at the Battle of Eutaw Springs; engaged in mercantile pursuits in Savannah, Ga.; member of the State house of representatives in 1786; member of the Continental Congress in 1787; delegate from Georgia to the convention at Philadelphia in 1787 which framed the Federal Constitution; was an original member and vice president of the Society of the Cincinnati; trustee of Chatham County Academy at the time of his death; died in Savannah, Ga., December 10, 1789.

PIERSON, Isaac, a Representative from New Jersey; born in Orange, Essex County, N. J., August 15, 1770; attended private schools; was graduated from Princeton College in 1789; studied medicine; was graduated from the College of Physicians and Surgeons, New York City, and commenced practice in Orange, N. J.; elected assessor of Orange April 13, 1807, and served one year; president of the Medical Society of New Jersey in 1827; sheriff of Essex County 1807–1809; elected as a Whig to the Twentieth and Twenty-first Congresses (March 4, 1827–March 3, 1831); unsuccessful candidate for reelection in 1830 to the Twenty-second Congress; died in Orange, N. J., September 22, 1833; interment in Old Burying Ground; reinterment in Rosedale Cemetery in 1840.

PIERSON, Jeremiah Halsey, a Representative from New York; born in Newark, N. J., September 13, 1766; moved with his parents to Richmond, Mass., in 1772; attended the public schools of Richmond and Stockbridge, Mass., and completed preparatory studies; studied law; was admitted to the bar and practiced in Massachusetts; moved to New York in 1795 and settled in Ramapo; practiced law and engaged in mercantile pursuits; built a dam on the Ramapo River to create power; engaged in the manufacture of files and wood screws; justice of the peace 1800–1811; associate justice of the court of common pleas in 1808; largely instrumental in securing the construction of the Erie Railroad; elected as a Federalist to the Seventeenth Congress (March 4, 1821–March 3, 1823); was not a candidate for renomination in 1822; resumed his former business pursuits; delegate to the National-Republican Convention at Baltimore in 1831 that nominated Henry Clay for President; died in Ramapo, Rockland County, N. Y., December 12, 1855; interment in Ramapo Cemetery.

PIERSON, Job, a Representative from New York; born in East Hampton, Suffolk County, N. Y., September 23, 1791; attended the common schools; was graduated from Williams College in 1811; studied law in Salem and Schaghticoke; was admitted to the bar in 1815 and commenced practice in Rensselaer County; district attorney 1824–1833; elected as a Democrat to the Twenty-second and Twenty-third Congresses (March 4, 1831–March 3, 1835); unsuccessful candidate for reelection in 1834 to the Twenty-fourth Congress; resumed the practice of law; surrogate of Rensselaer County 1835–1840; delegate to the Democratic National Conventions in 1848, 1852, and 1856; died in Troy, N. Y., April 9, 1860; interment in Oakwood Cemetery.

PIGOTT, James Protus, a Representative from Connecticut; born in New Haven, Conn., September 11, 1852; attended the common schools, and was graduated from Yale College in 1878 and from the law school of the same institution in 1880; was admitted to the bar in 1880 and commenced practice in New Haven, Conn.; served as city clerk of New Haven 1881–1884; member of the State house of representatives in 1885 and 1886; delegate to the Democratic National Conventions in 1888 and 1900; elected as a Democrat to the Fifty-third Congress (March 4, 1893–March 3, 1895); unsuccessful candidate for reelection to the Fifty-fourth Congress; resumed the practice of law; died in New Haven, Conn., July 1, 1919; interment in St. Lawrence Cemetery.

PIKE, Austin Franklin, a Representative and a Senator from New Hampshire; born in Hebron, N. H., October 16, 1819; pursued an academic course; studied law; was admitted to the bar of Merrimack County in July 1845; member of the State house of representatives 1850–1852, 1865, and 1866 and served as speaker during the last two years; delegate to the Republican National Convention at Philadelphia in 1856; member of the State senate in 1857 and 1858, serving as president the last year; served as chairman of the Republican State Committee 1858–1860; elected as a Republican to the Forty-third Congress (March 4, 1873–March 3, 1875); unsuccessful candidate for reelection in 1874 to the Forty-fourth Congress; elected as a Republican to the United States Senate and served from March 4, 1883, until his death in Franklin, Merrimack County, N. H., October 8, 1886; interment in Franklin Cemetery.

PIKE, Frederick Augustus, a Representative from Maine; born in Calais, Maine, December 9, 1816; attended the common schools and the Washington Academy, East Machias, Maine; was graduated from Bowdoin College, Brunswick, Maine, in 1837; studied law; was admitted to the bar and commenced practice in Calais, Washington County, in 1840; mayor of Calais in 1852 and 1853; member of the State house of representatives 1858–1860 and served as speaker in 1860; elected as a Republican to the Thirty-seventh and to the three succeeding Congresses (March 4, 1861–March 3, 1869); unsuccessful candidate for renomination in 1868; resumed the practice of law; again a member of the State house of representatives in 1870 and 1871;

unsuccessful candidate for election in 1872 to the Forty-third Congress; died in Calais, Maine, December 2, 1886; interment in Calais Cemetery.

PIKE, James, a Representative from New Hampshire; born in Salisbury, Essex County, Mass., November 10, 1818; pursued classical studies; studied theology at the Wesleyan University, Connecticut, 1837–1839; served as a minister from 1841 to 1854; moved to Pembroke, N. H., in 1854; elected as the candidate of the American Party to the Thirty-fourth and Thirty-fifth Congresses (March 4, 1855–March 3, 1859); was not a candidate for renomination in 1858; during the Civil War served as colonel of the Sixteenth Regiment, New Hampshire Volunteer Infantry, from November 1, 1862, to August 20, 1863; unsuccessful candidate for Governor of New Hampshire in 1871; resumed preaching and became presiding elder of the Dover district; discontinued active duties in 1886 and lived in retirement until his death in Newfields, Rockingham County, N. H., July 26, 1895; interment in Locust Cemetery.

PILCHER, John Leonard, a Representative from Georgia; born on a farm in Thomas County, Ga., August 27, 1898; attended the public schools; engaged in agricultural pursuits for thirty-five years; also operated general mercantile business, cotton gin, warehouses, fertilizer manufacturing plant, and sirup canning plant; former mayor and councilman of Meigs, Ga.; member of the board of education and a county commissioner; member of the State house of representatives; member of the State senate 1940–1944; State purchasing agent in 1948 and 1949; elected as a Democrat to the Eighty-third Congress to fill the vacancy caused by the death of E. E. Cox; reelected to the Eighty-fourth Eighty-fifth, and Eighty-sixth Congresses and served from February 4, 1953, to January 3, 1961. *Reelected to the Eighty-seventh Congress.*

PILE, William Anderson, a Representative from Missouri; born near Indianapolis, Ind., February 11, 1829; completed preparatory studies; studied theology and became a minister in the Methodist Episcopal Church and a member of the Missouri conference; during the Civil War entered the Union Army; commissioned chaplain of the First Regiment, Missouri Light Artillery, June 12, 1861; lieutenant colonel of the Thirty-third Regiment, Missouri Infantry, September 5, 1862; colonel December 23, 1862; brigadier general of Volunteers December 26, 1863; brevetted major general April 9, 1865, "for gallant and meritorious services in the siege and capture of Fort Blakeley, Ala."; mustered out August 24, 1865; elected as a Republican to the Fortieth Congress (March 4, 1867–March 3, 1869); unsuccessful for reelection in 1868 to the Forty-first Congress; Governor of New Mexico in 1869 and 1870; Minister Resident to Venezuela from 1871 to 1874, when he resigned; died in Monrovia, Calif., July 7, 1889; interment in Live Oak Cemetery.

PILES, Samuel Henry, a Senator from Washington; born near Smithland, Livingston County, Ky., December 28, 1858; attended private schools in Smithland, Ky.; studied law; was admitted to the bar and commenced practice in Snohomish, Territory of Washington, in 1883; moved to Spokane, Wash., in 1886 and later in the same year to Seattle, where he engaged in the practice of law; assistant prosecuting attorney for the third judicial district of the Territory of Washington 1887–1889; city attorney of Seattle in 1888 and 1889; had attended almost every Republican State convention since the State was admitted into the Union; general counsel of the Pacific Coast Co. 1895–1905; elected as a Republican to the United States Senate and served from March 4, 1905, to March 3, 1911; was not a candidate for renomination in 1910; resumed the practice of law in Seattle, Wash.; appointed by President Harding as Envoy Extraordinary and Minister Plenipotentiary to Colombia on May 22, 1922, and served until 1928; retired from active pursuits and moved to Los Angeles, Calif., where he died March 11, 1940; interment in Lakeview Cemetery, Seattle, Wash.

PILLION, John Raymond, a Representative from New York; born in Conneaut, Ashtabula County, Ohio, August 10, 1904; moved to Lackawanna, N. Y., in 1907; attended the public schools of Lackawanna, South Park High School at Buffalo, and Cornell School of Engineering; graduated from Cornell University in 1927; was admitted to the bar in 1928 and commenced practice of law in Lackawanna, N. Y., in 1929; served as city court judge 1932–1936; corporation counsel and tax attorney, city of Lackawanna, 1936–1941; president and treasurer of Bison Storage & Warehouse Corp., Buffalo, N. Y., 1945–1953; operator of a fruit and vegetable farm in Niagara County since 1935; member of the State assembly 1941–1950; elected as a Republican to the Eighty-third and to the three succeeding Congresses (January 3, 1953–January 3, 1961). *Reelected to the Eighty-seventh Congress.*

PILSBURY, Timothy, a Representative from Texas; born in Newburyport, Mass., April 12, 1789; attended the common schools; employed in a store for about two years; became a sailor and during the War of 1812 commanded the privateer *Yankee*; engaged in shipping; settled in Eastport, Maine; member of the Maine House of Representatives in 1825 and 1826; member of the executive council 1827–1836; unsuccessful candidate for election in 1836 to the Twenty-fifth Congress; moved to Ohio, thence to New Orleans, La., and later to Brazoria, Tex.; member of the house of representatives of the Republic of Texas in 1840 and 1841 and served in the senate of that Republic in 1842; chief justice of the county court; judge of probate for Brazoria County; again a member of the Texas Senate in 1845; upon the admission of Texas as a State into the Union was elected as a Calhoun Democrat to the Twenty-ninth and Thirtieth Congresses and served from March 30, 1846, to March 3, 1849; unsuccessful candidate for reelection in 1848 to the Thirty-first Congress; died in Henderson, Rusk County, Tex., November 23, 1858; interment in the City Cemetery.

PINCKNEY, Charles (father of Henry Laurens Pinckney), a Delegate, a Senator, and a Representative from South Carolina; born in Charles Town (now Charleston), S. C., October 26, 1757; pursued classical studies; studied law at the Middle Temple, London, England; was admitted to the bar and commenced practice in 1779; member of the State house of representatives 1779–1784, 1786–1789, 1792–1796, 1805, 1806, and 1810–1814; taken prisoner by the British in 1780; Member of the Continental Congress in 1777, 1778, and 1784–1787; member of the United States Constitutional Convention in 1787; member of the State constitutional conventions in 1788 and 1790 and served as president; Governor of South Carolina 1789–1792 and 1796–1798; received President Washington on his visit to Charleston in 1791; elected to the State house of representatives in 1798 and qualified on December 6, 1798, when his term as Governor expired; was elected on the same day as a Democrat to the United States Senate to fill the vacancy caused by the resignation of John Hunter and also for the full term expiring March 3, 1805, and served from December 6, 1798, until his resignation in 1801; Minister to Spain from June 6, 1801, to November 22, 1804; again served as Governor of South Carolina 1806–1808; elected as a Democrat to the Sixteenth Congress (March 4, 1819–March 3, 1821); resumed the practice of law and also engaged in agricultural pursuits; died in Charleston, S. C., October 29, 1824; interment in St. Philip's Churchyard.

PINCKNEY, Henry Laurens (son of Charles Pinckney), a Representative from South Carolina; born in Charleston, S. C., September 24, 1794; attended private schools; was graduated from South Carolina College (now the University of South Carolina) at Columbia in 1812; studied law; was admitted to the bar and commenced practice in Charleston; member of the State house of representatives 1816–1832; founded the Charleston Mercury in 1819 and was its sole editor for fifteen years; published many orations, addresses, and memoirs; intendant of Charleston 1830–1832; elected as a Democrat to the Twenty-third and Twenty-fourth Congresses (March 4, 1833–March 3, 1837); was not a candidate for renomination in 1836; mayor of Charleston 1837–1840; collector of the port of Charleston in 1841 and 1842; tax collector of St. Philip's and St. Michael's parishes 1845–1863; died in Charleston, S. C., February 3, 1863; interment in the Circular Congregational Church Burying Ground.

PINCKNEY, John McPherson, a Representative from Texas; born in Grimes County, Tex., near the town of Hempstead, Waller County, May 4, 1845; attended the public schools and was privately instructed; enlisted as a private in the Confederate Army and served in Company D, Fourth Texas Brigade, until the close of the Civil War, attaining the rank of first lieutenant; studied law; was admitted to the bar in 1875 and commenced practice in Hempstead, Tex.; district attorney for the twenty-third judicial district of Texas 1890–1900; voluntarily retired; county judge of Waller County 1900–1903; elected as a Democrat to the Fifty-eighth Congress to fill the vacancy caused by the resignation of Thomas H. Ball; reelected to the Fifty-ninth Congress and served from November 17, 1903, until April 24, 1905, when he was assaulted and killed at Hempstead, Tex.; interment in the City Cemetery at Hempstead.

PINCKNEY, Thomas, a Representative from South Carolina; born in Charleston, S. C., October 23, 1750; attended Westminster School, Oxford, England, and was graduated from Oxford University, England; also attended the French Military College, Caen, France, for one year; studied law at the Inner Temple, London; was admitted to the bar in 1774 and commenced practice in Charleston, S. C.; captain of Engineers, First Regiment, Continental Army, in 1775; major in the Florida campaign in 1778; served under Gen. Benjamin Lincoln in 1778 and 1779 and with Count d'Estaing in 1779; served in the defense of Charleston; was wounded and captured at the Battle of Camden and held as a prisoner of war for one year; Governor of South Carolina 1787–1789; presided over the State convention which ratified the Federal Constitution in 1788; member of the State house of representatives in 1791; United States Minister to Great Britain from January 12, 1792, to July 28, 1796; also Envoy Extraordinary to Spain from November 24, 1794, to November 1795 and negotiated the treaty settling the boundary between the United States and East and West Florida and between the United States and Louisiana, securing the freedom of the Mississippi River for navigation to its mouth; elected as a Federalist to the Fifth Congress to fill the vacancy caused by the resignation of William L. Smith; reelected to the Sixth Congress and served from November 23, 1797, to March 3, 1801; one of the managers appointed by the House of Representatives in 1798 to conduct the impeachment proceedings against William Blount, a Senator from Tennessee; resumed the practice of law and also engaged in agricultural pursuits; appointed major general in the War of 1812 and served throughout the war; president general of the Society of the Cincinnati 1825–1828; died in Charleston, S. C., November 2, 1828; interment in St. Philip's Churchyard.

PINDALL, James, a Representative from Virginia; born in Monongalia County, Va. (now West Virginia), about 1783;

attended the common schools; studied law; was admitted to the bar in 1803 and practiced in Morgantown; moved to Clarksburg and continued the practice of his profession; held various local offices; served in the State senate 1808–1812; was colonel of militia; elected as a Federalist to the Fifteenth and Sixteenth Congresses and served from March 4, 1817, until his resignation on July 26, 1820; died in Clarksburg, Harrison County, Va. (now West Virginia), November 22, 1825; interment in what was known as the Daniel Davisson burial ground located on the south side of what is now Main Street in Clarksburg, W. Va.

PINDAR, John Sigsbee, a Representative from New York; born in Sharon, Schoharie County, N. Y., November 18, 1835; attended the common schools and Richmondville Seminary; studied law; was admitted to the bar in 1865; president of the village of Cobleskill 1882–1884; chairman of the Democratic county committee for ten years; elected as a Democrat to the Forty-ninth Congress (March 4, 1885–March 3, 1887); delegate to the Democratic National Convention at St. Louis in 1888; resumed the practice of law in Cobleskill, N. Y.; unsuccessful candidate in 1888 for election to the Fifty-first Congress; subsequently elected to the Fifty-first Congress to fill the vacancy caused by the death of David Wilber and served from November 4, 1890, to March 3, 1891; resumed the practice of law; died in Cobleskill, Schoharie County, N. Y., June 30, 1907; interment in Cobleskill Cemetery.

PINE, William Bliss, a Senator from Oklahoma; born in Bluffs, Scott County, Ill., December 30, 1877; attended the public schools; taught school three years; employed as a salesman of harvesters in several Central States; moved to Chanute, Kans., and was employed in the oil producing business, moving to Oklahoma in 1904 and continuing in the oil industry; in 1909 located in Okmulgee, Okla., where he eventually became extensively engaged in the production of oil and as a manufacturer; elected as a Republican to the United States Senate and served from March 4, 1925, to March 3, 1931; unsuccessful candidate for reelection in 1930; resumed his former business pursuits; unsuccessful candidate for Governor in 1934; died in Okmulgee, Okla., August 25, 1942; was the Republican nominee for the United States Senate at the time of his death; interment in Okmulgee Cemetery.

PIÑERO, Jesús T., a Resident Commissioner from Puerto Rico; born in Carolina, P. R., April 16, 1897; attended the grade schools, Colegio Janer (a private school), Baltimore, Md., and the School of Engineering at the University of Pennsylvania at Philadelphia; was graduated from the College of Liberal Arts, University of Puerto Rico at Rio Piedras, in 1914; engaged in agricultural pursuits and in the sugarcane and dairy industries 1920–1944; member and president of the municipal assembly at Carolina, P. R., 1928–1932; member of the Puerto Rico House of Representatives 1940–1944; delegate to the Popular Democratic Convention at San Juan, P. R., in 1940; elected as a Popular Democrat a Resident Commissioner to the United States and served from January 3, 1945, until his resignation on September 2, 1946, having been appointed Governor of Puerto Rico, serving until December 1948; died in Loiza, P. R., November 19, 1952; interment in Carolina Cemetery, Carolina, P. R.

PINKNEY, William, a Representative and a Senator from Maryland; born in Annapolis, Md., March 17, 1764; pursued classical studies; studied medicine but did not practice; studied law; was admitted to the bar in 1786 and commenced practice in Harford County, Md.; member of the State constitutional convention in 1788; served in the State house of delegates 1789–1792; elected to the Second Congress and served from March 4, 1791, to November of that year, when he resigned, the question of ineligibility having been raised on account of nonresidence; member of the executive council of Maryland 1792–1795; again a member of the State house of delegates in 1795; one of the commissioners at London under Jay's treaty 1796–1804; attorney general of Maryland in 1805; Joint Minister to Great Britain with James Monroe in 1806 and 1807 and Minister Plenipotentiary 1807–1811; returned to Baltimore, Md., in 1811; served in the State senate; appointed Attorney General of the United States in the Cabinet of President Madison and served from December 11, 1811, to February 10, 1814; wounded at the Battle of Bladensburg, Md., August 24, 1814; elected to the Fourteenth Congress and served from March 4, 1815, to April 18, 1816, when he resigned; appointed by President Madison as Minister Plenipotentiary to Russia with a special mission to Naples and served from 1816 to 1818; elected to the United States Senate to fill the vacancy caused by the death of Alexander Contee Hanson and served from December 21, 1819, until his death in Washington, D. C., February 25, 1822; interment in Congressional Cemetery.

PIPER, William, a Representative from Pennsylvania; born at Bloody Run (now Everett), Bedford County, Pa., January 1, 1774; commanded a regiment during the War of 1812; adjutant general of Pennsylvania after the war; elected to the Twelfth, Thirteenth, and Fourteenth Congresses (March 4, 1811–March 3, 1817); died in Hopewell Township, near Everett, Pa., in 1852; interment in the Piper Cemetery on his farm in Hopewell Township.

PIPER, William Adam, a Representative from California; born in Franklin County, Pa., May 21, 1826; attended the common schools; moved to St. Louis, Mo.; during the Mexican War served in Company A, Eighth Missouri Light Artillery, from June 8, 1846, to June 24, 1847; moved to California in 1848, and in 1849 settled in San Francisco, where he engaged in mercantile pursuits; elected as a Democrat to the Forty-fourth Congress (March 4, 1875–March 3, 1877); unsuccessful candidate for reelection in 1876 to the Forty-fifth Congress; continued business activities; died in San Francisco, Calif., August 5, 1899; interment in Odd Fellows Cemetery.

PIRCE, William Almy, a Representative from Rhode Island; born in Hope, Providence County, R. I., February 29, 1824; attended the common schools and Smithville Seminary (now Lapham Institute); taught school; manager of the store and countingroom of his father's cotton mill in Simmons Upper Village, R. I., for ten years; engaged in the manufacture of cotton goods 1854–1863; served in the State senate in 1855; member of the State house of representatives in 1858 and 1862; assessor of internal revenue for the second district of Rhode Island 1862–1873; appointed paymaster with rank of major in the State militia in 1863; again a member of the State house of representatives 1879–1881; again served in the State senate in 1882; chairman of the Rhode Island delegation to the Republican National Convention at Chicago in 1880; member of the Republican National Committee in 1880 and 1884; presented credentials as a Republican Member-elect to the Forty-ninth Congress and served from March 4, 1885, to January 25, 1887, when the seat was declared vacant on account of irregularities in the election; justice of the peace and assessor of taxes in Johnston, R. I.; died in Johnston, R. I., March 5, 1891; interment in Swan Point Cemetery, Providence, R. I.

PIRNIE, Alexander, a Representative from New York; born in Pulaski, Oswego County, N. Y., April 16, 1903; graduated from Pulaski Academy in 1920, Cornell University in 1924, and from

Cornell Law School in 1926; was admitted to the bar in 1926 and commenced the practice of law in Utica, N. Y.; in 1924 was commissioned a second lieutenant, Infantry, Officers Reserve Corps, and was promoted to first lieutenant in 1928; during World War II volunteered for active duty on December 4, 1942; successively promoted to lieutenant colonel in the Judge Advocate General's Corps; served one year in Washington, D. C., as executive officer of the claims division and one and one-half years in the European Theater; Theater Director of Foreign Claims Commissions; separated from the service February 14, 1946; colonel in the Judge Advocate General's Corps Reserve; elected as a Republican to the Eighty-sixth Congress (January 3, 1959– January 3, 1961). *Reelected to the Eighty-seventh Congress.*

PITCHER, Nathaniel, a Representative from New York; born in Litchfield, Conn., in 1777; received a limited schooling; moved to Sandy Hill, N. Y.; supervisor 1804–1810; member of the State assembly in 1806 and 1815–1817; assessor of Kingsbury in 1812; surrogate of Washington County in 1812 and 1813; town clerk of Kingsbury in 1813 and 1814 and justice of the peace; studied law; was admitted to the bar and practiced; delegate to the State constitutional convention in 1821; Lieutenant Governor of New York in 1826 and Acting Governor upon the death of Governor Clinton 1827–1829; elected as a Democrat to the Sixteenth and Seventeenth Congresses (March 4, 1819–March 3, 1823); elected to the Twenty-second Congress (March 4, 1831–March 3, 1833); died in Sandy Hill (now Hudson Falls), Washington County, N. Y., May 25, 1836; interment in Wright Cemetery.

PITKIN, Timothy, a Representative from Connecticut; born in Farmington, Conn., on January 21, 1766; received private instruction and was graduated from Yale College in 1785; taught in the academy at Plainfield, Conn., for one year; studied law; was admitted to the bar in 1788 and commenced practice in Farmington; member of the State house of representatives in 1790, 1792, and 1794–1805, serving as clerk of the house 1800–1802 and as speaker 1803–1805; elected as a Federalist to the Ninth Congress to fill in part the vacancies caused by the resignations of Calvin Goddard and Roger Griswold; reelected to the Tenth and to the five succeeding Congresses and served from September 16, 1805, to March 3, 1819; was not a candidate for renomination in 1818; delegate to the convention which framed the new State constitution in 1818; resumed the practice of law and engaged in literary work; again a member of the State house of representatives 1819–1830; retired from his profession and all public business; died in New Haven, Conn., December 18, 1847; interment in Grove Street Cemetery.

PITMAN, Charles Wesley, a Representative from Pennsylvania; born in New Jersey; attended the common schools; was graduated from Dickinson College, Carlisle, Pa., in 1838; moved to Pottsville, Pa., the same year and conducted a school for boys, known as the Pottsville Academy; elected as a Whig to the Thirty-first Congress (March 4, 1849–March 3, 1851); later became affiliated with the Republican Party; engaged extensively in the lumber business; elected sheriff of Schuylkill County in 1870 and served from January 1871 until his death in Pottsville, Schuylkill County, Pa., June 8, 1871; interment in Presbyterian Cemetery.

PITNEY, Mahlon, a Representative from New Jersey; born in Morristown, Morris County, N. J., February 5, 1858; attended the public schools; was graduated from Princeton College in 1879; studied law; was admitted to the bar in June 1882 and practiced in Dover and Morristown, Morris County, N. J., 1882– 1889; elected as a Republican to the Fifty-fourth and Fifty-

fifth Congresses and served from March 4, 1895, to January 10, 1899, when he resigned; member of the State senate 1899–1901 and its president in 1901; associate justice of the supreme court of New Jersey 1901–1908; chancellor of New Jersey from 1908 to 1912, when he resigned; appointed by President Taft as an Associate Justice of the Supreme Court of the United States February 19, 1912, and took the oath of office March 18, 1912; served until December 31, 1922, when he resigned; died in Washington, D. C., December 9, 1924; interment in Evergreen Cemetery, Morristown, N. J.

PITTENGER, William Alvin, a Representative from Minnesota; born on a farm near Crawfordsville, Montgomery County, Ind., December 29, 1885; attended rural schools; was graduated from Wabash College, Crawfordsville, Ind., in 1909, and from Harvard Law School, Cambridge, Mass., in 1912; was admitted to the bar in 1912 and commenced practice in Duluth, Minn.; member of the State house of representatives 1917–1920; elected as a Republican to the Seventy-first and Seventy-second Congresses (March 4, 1929–March 3, 1933); unsuccessful candidate for reelection in 1932 to the Seventy-third Congress; resumed the practice of law in Duluth, Minn.; elected to the Seventy-fourth Congress (January 3, 1935–January 3, 1937); unsuccessful candidate for reelection in 1936 to the Seventy-fifth Congress; elected to the Seventy-sixth and to the three succeeding Congresses (January 3, 1939–January 3, 1947); unsuccessful candidate for reelection in 1946 to the Eightieth Congress; resumed the practice of law; died in Duluth, Minn., November 26, 1951; interment in Forest Hill Cemetery.

PITTMAN, Key, a Senator from Nevada; born in Vicksburg, Warren County, Miss., September 19, 1872; educated by private tutors and at the Southwestern Presbyterian University, Clarksville, Tenn.; studied law; was admitted to the bar in 1892 and commenced practice in Seattle, Wash.; joined in the gold rush to Klondike, Alaska, in 1897 and worked as a miner until 1901; practiced law in Alaska and assisted in forming the "consent" government for Nome; first prosecuting attorney of Nome, in 1899; moved to Tonopah, Nev., in 1902 and continued the practice of law; appointed to represent the State of Nevada at the St. Louis Exposition, the Lewis and Clark Exposition, and the irrigation congress; unsuccessful Democratic candidate for election to the United States Senate in 1910; elected as a Democrat to the United States Senate in 1913 to fill the vacancy caused by the death of George S. Nixon; reelected in 1916, 1922, 1928, and 1934 and served from January 29, 1913, until his death; had been reelected in 1940 for the term beginning January 3, 1941; elected president pro tempore of the United States Senate on March 9, 1933, reelected January 3, 1935, and served until his death in Reno, Nev., November 10, 1940; interment in a crypt in Mountain View Cemetery.

PLAISTED, Harris Merrill, a Representative from Maine; born in Jefferson, Coos County, N. H., November 2, 1828; attended the common schools, and was graduated from Waterville (Maine) College in 1853 and from the Albany (N. Y.) Law School in 1856; was admitted to the bar and commenced practice in Bangor, Maine, in 1856; during the Civil War served in the Union Army and was commissioned lieutenant colonel of the Eleventh Regiment, Maine Infantry, October 30, 1861, and colonel May 12, 1862; brevetted brigadier general of Volunteers February 21, 1865, and major general March 13, 1865, "for gallant and meritorious service during the war"; honorably discharged March 25, 1865; member of the State house of representatives in 1867 and 1868; delegate to the Republican National Convention at Chicago in 1868; attorney general of Maine 1873–1875; elected as a Republican to the Forty-fourth

Congress to fill the vacancy caused by the death of Samuel F. Hersey and served from September 13, 1875, to March 3, 1877; was not a candidate for renomination in 1876; author of "Digest of Maine Reports from 1820 to 1880"; Governor of Maine 1881–1883; editor and publisher of the New Age, Augusta, from 1883 until his death in Bangor, Maine, January 31, 1898; interment in Mount Hope Cemetery.

PLANT, David, a Representative from Connecticut; born in Stratford, Conn., March 29, 1783; attended the Episcopal Academy, Cheshire, Conn.; was graduated from Yale College in 1804; studied law in the Litchfield (Conn.) Law School; was admitted to the bar in 1804 and commenced practice in Stratford; judge of the probate court of Fairfield County; member of the State house of representatives 1817–1820 and served as speaker; served in the State senate in 1821 and 1822; Lieutenant Governor of Connecticut 1823–1827; elected as a National-Republican to the Twentieth Congress (March 4, 1827–March 3, 1829); did not seek renomination in 1828; resumed the practice of law; died in Stratford, Conn., October 18, 1851; interment in the Congregational Burying Ground.

PLANTS, Tobias Avery, a Representative from Ohio; born at Sewickley, Beaver County, Pa., March 17, 1811; apprenticed to a saddler at the age of twelve; received a limited common school education, studying at night to prepare for admission to Beaver College, Meadville, Pa., which he attended a short time; taught school, and while teaching studied law with Edwin M. Stanton in the office of Judge David Powell at Steubenville, Ohio; was admitted to the bar and commenced practice in Athens, Ohio, in 1846, but soon moved to Pomeroy; member of the State house of representatives 1858–1861; owner and publisher of the Pomeroy Weekly Telegraph about 1860; elected as a Republican to the Thirty-ninth and Fortieth Congresses (March 4, 1865–March 3, 1869); was not a candidate for renomination in 1868; judge of the court of common pleas in Meigs County from 1873 to 1875, when he resigned to resume the practice of law; president of the First City Bank of Pomeroy from 1878 until his death in Pomeroy, Meigs County, Ohio, June 19, 1887; interment in Beech Grove Cemetery.

PLATER, George (father of Thomas Plater), a Delegate from Maryland; born in Sotterly, near Leonardtown, St. Marys County, Md., November 8, 1735; was graduated from William and Mary College, Williamsburg, Va., in 1753; studied law; was admitted to the bar and commenced practice in Annapolis, Md.; member of the Maryland Assembly in 1758; naval officer at Patuxent 1767–1771; judge of the provincial court 1771–1773; member of the council in 1773 and 1774; represented St. Marys County in the Annapolis conventions of 1776; Member of the Continental Congress 1778–1781; president of the State constitutional convention in 1788 which ratified the Federal Constitution; presidential elector in 1789; elected Governor of Maryland in 1791; died before the expiration of his term, in Annapolis, Md., February 10, 1792; interment in the garden of "Sotterly," his home, near Leonardtown, Md.

PLATER, Thomas (son of George Plater), a Representative from Maryland; born in Annapolis, Md., May 9, 1769; attended William and Mary College, Williamsburg, Va.; studied law; was admitted to the bar and practiced; served as lieutenant colonel in the State militia in 1794 for duty during the Whisky Insurrection; held several local offices; elected to the Seventh and Eighth Congresses (March 4, 1801–March 3, 1805); resumed the practice of law and resided at "Greenwood," on heights overlooking Georgetown, Md. (now District of Columbia); moved to Poolesville, Md., where he died May 1, 1830.

PLATT, Edmund, a Representative from New York; born in Poughkeepsie, N. Y., February 2, 1865; attended a private school and Riverview Academy; was graduated from Eastman Business College, Poughkeepsie, N. Y.; learned the printer's trade; was graduated from Harvard University in 1888; taught school and studied law; moved to Wisconsin and edited the Superior (Wis.) Evening Telegram in 1890 and 1891; returned to Poughkeepsie in 1891 and engaged in editing and publishing the Poughkeepsie Eagle; author of "History of Poughkeepsie"; member of the board of water commissioners of Poughkeepsie, N. Y.; elected as a Republican to the Sixty-third and to the three succeeding Congresses and served from March 4, 1913, to June 7, 1920, when he resigned to accept appointment by President Wilson to the Federal Reserve Board; became vice governor of the board in August 1920 and served until 1930 when he resigned; returned to Poughkeepsie, N. Y., and engaged in an extensive banking business; died in Chazy, Clinton County, N. Y., while on a visit, August 7, 1939; interment in the Poughkeepsie Rural Cemetery, Poughkeepsie, N. Y.

PLATT, James Henry, Jr., a Representative from Virginia; born in St. John's, Canada, July 13, 1837; moved to Burlington, Vt.; attended the common schools; completed preparatory studies and was graduated from the medical department of the University of Vermont at Burlington in 1859; during the Civil War entered the Union Army as first sergeant of the Third Regiment, Vermont Volunteer Infantry; served as captain and lieutenant colonel; declined assignment to duty as chief quartermaster of the Sixth Corps; settled in Petersburg, Va., April 6, 1865; member of the State constitutional convention in 1867; member of the city council in 1867 and 1868; moved to Norfolk, Va.; upon the readmission of the State of Virginia to representation was elected as a Republican to the Forty-first, Forty-second, and Forty-third Congresses and served from January 26, 1870, to March 3, 1875; unsuccessful candidate for reelection in 1874 to the Forty-fourth Congress; moved to New York in 1876 and engaged in the manufacture of oil products; moved to Colorado in 1887 and settled in Denver; engaged in the insurance business, paper manufacturing, and in mining; was drowned in Green Lake, near Georgetown, Colo., August 13, 1894; interment in Fairmont Cemetery, Denver, Colo.

PLATT, Jonas (son of Zephaniah Platt), a Representative from New York; born in Poughkeepsie, N. Y., June 30, 1769; attended a French academy at Montreal, Canada; studied law; was admitted to the bar in 1790 and practiced in Poughkeepsie; county clerk of Herkimer County 1791–1798 and of Oneida County 1798–1802; member of the State assembly in 1796; elected as a Federalist to the Sixth Congress (March 4, 1799–March 3, 1801); resumed the practice of law; general of Cavalry in the State militia; was an unsuccessful candidate for Governor in 1810; member of the State senate 1810–1813; member of the council of appointment in 1813; served as associate justice of the supreme court of New York 1814–1821; delegate to the New York Constitutional Convention in 1821; resumed the practice of law; died in Peru, Clinton County, N. Y., February 22, 1834; interment in Riverside Cemetery, Plattsburg, N. Y.

PLATT, Orville Hitchcock, a Senator from Connecticut; born in Washington, Litchfield County, Conn., July 19, 1827; attended the common schools and was graduated from the Gunnery Academy, Washington, Conn.; studied law in Litchfield, Conn.; was admitted to the bar in 1850 and commenced practice in Towanda, Pa.; moved to Meriden, Conn., in 1850 and continued the practice of his profession; clerk of the State senate in 1855 and 1856; secretary of state of Connecticut in 1857; served in the State senate in 1861 and 1862; member of the State house of representatives in 1864 and 1869 and served as speaker in the latter year; State's attorney for New Haven County 1877–1879; elected as a Republican to the United States Senate in 1879; reelected in 1885, 1891, 1897, and 1903 and served from March 4, 1879, until his death in Washington, Conn., April 21, 1905; interment in Washington Cemetery on the Green.

PLATT, Thomas Collier, a Representative and a Senator from New York; born in Owego, Tioga County, N. Y., July 15, 1833; was prepared for college in the Owego Academy and attended Yale College in 1849 and 1850; in 1852 engaged in business as a druggist and continued for twenty years; was president of the Tioga National Bank at its organization, and was greatly interested in the lumbering business in Michigan; clerk of Tioga County 1859–1861; elected as a Republican to the Forty-third and Forty-fourth Congresses (March 4, 1873–March 3, 1877); elected to the United States Senate January 18, 1881, and served from March 4, 1881, to May 16, 1881, when he resigned with his colleague, Roscoe Conkling, on account of a disagreement with President Garfield over Federal appointments in New York; unsuccessful candidate for election to the United States Senate to succeed himself; secretary and director of the United States Express Co. in 1879 and elected president of the company in 1880; member and president of the Board of Quarantine Commissioners of New York 1880–1888; delegate to the Republican National Conventions in 1876, 1880, 1884, 1888, 1892, 1896, 1900, and 1904; member of the Republican National Committee; elected to the United States Senate in 1896; reelected in 1903 and served from March 4, 1897, to March 3, 1909; died in New York City March 6, 1910; interment in Owego Cemetery, Owego, N. Y.

PLATT, Zephaniah (father of Jonas Platt), a Delegate from New York; born in Huntington, Long Island, Suffolk County, N. Y., May 27, 1735; received a thorough English education; studied law; was admitted to the bar and commenced practice in Poughkeepsie, N. Y.; Member of the Provincial Congress 1775–1777; member of the council of safety in 1777; served in the State senate 1777–1783; Member of the Continental Congress 1784–1786; member of the council of appointment in 1778 and 1781; county judge of Dutchess County 1781–1795; founded the town of Plattsburg in 1784; delegate to the State constitutional convention in 1788; moved to Plattsburg, N. Y., in 1798 and continued the practice of law; regent of the State university from 1791 until his death; one of the projectors of the Erie Canal; died in Plattsburg, N. Y., September 12, 1807; interment in Riverside Cemetery.

PLAUCHÉ, Vance, a Representative from Louisiana; born in Plaucheville, Avoyelles Parish, La., August 25, 1897; attended private and public schools; was graduated from the law department of Loyola University, New Orleans, La., in 1918; during the First World War served overseas as a private, first class, in Base Hospital 102, in 1918 and 1919; was admitted to the bar in 1918 and commenced practice in Lake Charles, La.; city attorney of Lake Charles, La., 1928–1932; district counsel for the Home Owners' Loan Corporation 1933–1935; served as secretary of the State Civil Service Commission in 1940; delegate to the Democratic State Convention at Baton Rouge, La., in 1940; elected as a Democrat to the Seventy-seventh Congress (January 3, 1941–January 3, 1943); was not a candidate for renomination in 1942; engaged in the practice of law in Lake Charles, La.

PLEASANTS, James, a Representative and a Senator from Virginia; born at "Cold Comfort," in Powhatan County, Va., October 24, 1769; pursued classical studies and was graduated from William and Mary College, Williamsburg, Va.; studied law; was admitted to the bar and commenced practice in Amelia County in 1791; member of the State house of delegates 1797–1802; elected as a Democrat to the Twelfth and to the four succeeding Congresses and served from March 4, 1811, to December 14, 1819, when he resigned, having been elected Senator December 10; elected to the United States Senate to fill the vacancy caused by the resignation of John W. Eppes and served from December 14, 1819, to December 15, 1822, when he resigned; Governor of Virginia 1822–1825; delegate to the State constitutional convention in 1829 and 1830; retired and lived on his estate, "Contention," near Goochland, Goochland County, Va., where he died on November 9, 1836; interment on his estate.

PLOESER, Walter Christian, a Representative from Missouri; born in St. Louis, Mo., January 7, 1907; attended the public schools of St. Louis, Mo., Casper and Lusk, Wyo., and the City College of Law and Finance, St. Louis, Mo.; engaged in the insurance business in St. Louis, Mo., 1922–; founder, president, and director of Ploeser, Watts & Co. 1933–; organizer and chairman of the board of Marine Underwriters Corp. 1935–; president of Grant, Ploeser & Associates, Inc., national and international public relations firm; founded the Insurance Institute of Missouri in 1938, president 1938–1940; and the Young Republican Federation of Missouri; served in the State house of representatives in 1931 and 1932; elected as a Republican to the Seventy-seventh and to the three succeeding Congresses (January 3, 1941–January 3, 1949); unsuccessful candidate for reelection in 1948 to the Eighty-first Congress; resumed the insurance business; director of First National Bank of Clayton, Mo.; appointed by President Eisenhower as Ambassador to Paraguay and served from August 5, 1957, to October 27, 1959; is a resident of Manchester, Mo.

PLOWMAN, Thomas Scales, a Representative from Alabama; born in Talladega, Talladega County, Ala., June 8, 1843; attended the common schools; during the Civil War joined the Confederate Army in May 1862 as a member of Company F, Fifty-first Alabama Cavalry, and was engaged in all the battles of his regiment from Murfreesboro to Atlanta, being severely wounded at the latter place July 22, 1864; engaged in agricultural and mercantile pursuits in Talladega, Ala.; elected mayor in 1872 and served three terms; delegate to the Democratic National Convention at St. Louis in 1888; for a number of years president of the First National Bank of Talladega; presented credentials as a Democratic Member-elect to the Fifty-fifth Congress and served from March 4, 1897, to February 9, 1898, when he was succeeded by William F. Aldrich, who contested his election; member and chairman of the Talladega County Jury Commission in 1910 and 1911; member of the State senate in 1912; first president of the Bankhead Highway; died in Talladega, Ala., July 26, 1919; interment in Oak Hill Cemetery.

PLUMB, Preston B., a Senator from Kansas; born in Delaware County, Ohio, October 12, 1837; attended the common schools; learned the trade of printing and afterward purchased and edited the Xenia News; moved to Lawrence, Kans., in 1856; was one of five who organized and laid out the town of Emporia, where he established the Kansas News in 1857; secretary of the Free-State convention in 1857; member of the Leavenworth constitutional convention in 1859; studied law; was admitted to the bar in 1861; elected to the State house of representatives in 1862; reporter for the supreme court; during the Civil War entered the Union Army in August 1862 as second lieutenant in the Eleventh Regiment, Kansas Infantry, and served successively as captain, major, and lieutenant colonel; again a member of the State house of representatives in 1867 and 1868 and served as speaker in the latter year; prosecuting attorney of Lyon County; president of the Emporia National Bank in 1873; elected as a Republican to the United States Senate in 1877; reelected in 1883 and 1888 (at the latter election by unanimous vote) and served from March 4, 1877, until his death in Washington, D. C., December 20, 1891; interment in Maplewood Cemetery, Emporia, Lyon County, Kans.

PLUMB, Ralph, a Representative from Illinois; born in Busti, Chautauqua County, N. Y., March 29, 1816; attended the common schools; engaged in mercantile pursuits; moved to Ohio; member of the State house of representatives in 1855; studied law; was admitted to the bar in 1857 and commenced practice in Oberlin, Lorain County, Ohio; during the Civil War served in the Union Army as captain and quartermaster of Volunteers 1861–1865; was brevetted lieutenant colonel; moved to Illinois in 1866 and settled in Streator; engaged in the mining of coal and the building of railroads; mayor of Streator, Ill., 1882–1885; elected as a Republican to the Forty-ninth and Fiftieth Congresses (March 4, 1885–March 3, 1889); engaged in banking until his death in Streator, Ill., April 8, 1903; interment in Riverview Cemetery.

PLUMER, Arnold, a Representative from Pennsylvania; born near Cooperstown, Venango County, Pa., June 6, 1801; was privately tutored at home; completed preparatory studies; sheriff of Venango County in 1823; prothonotary of the county in 1829 and clerk of the courts and recorder 1830–1836; elected as a Democrat to the Twenty-fifth Congress (March 4, 1837–March 3, 1839); appointed marshal of the western district of Pennsylvania by President Van Buren on May 20, 1839, and served until May 6, 1841; elected to the Twenty-seventh Congress (March 4, 1841–March 3, 1843); again appointed United States marshal for the western district of Pennsylvania December 14, 1847, and served until April 3, 1848, when he resigned; State treasurer of Pennsylvania in 1848; engaged in mining and banking enterprises; declined appointment as Postmaster General in the Cabinet of President Buchanan; died in Franklin, Venango County, Pa., on April 28, 1869; interment in Franklin Cemetery.

PLUMER, George, a Representative from Pennsylvania; born near Pittsburgh, Pa., December 5, 1762; received a limited schooling; member of the State house of representatives 1812–1815 and again in 1817; elected as a Democrat to the Seventeenth, Eighteenth, and Nineteenth Congresses (March 4, 1821–March 3, 1827); declined to be a candidate for renomination; engaged in agricultural pursuits; died near West Newton, Westmoreland County, Pa., June 8, 1843; interment in Old Sewickley Presbyterian Church Cemetery.

PLUMER, William (father of William Plumer, Jr.), a Senator from New Hampshire; born in Newburyport, Mass., June 25, 1759; moved with his parents to Epping, N. H., in 1768; completed preparatory studies; studied law; was admitted to the bar in 1787 and commenced practice in Epping, N. H.; held various local offices; member of the State house of representatives 1788–1791 and 1797–1800 and served as speaker in 1791 and 1797; member of the State constitutional convention in 1791 and 1792; elected as a Federalist to the United States Senate to fill the vacancy caused by the resignation of James Sheafe and served from June 17, 1802, to March 3, 1807; was not a candidate for reelection; affiliated with the Democratic

Party; member of the State senate in 1810 and 1811 and chosen president of that body in both years; Governor of New Hampshire in 1812, 1813, and 1816–1819; presidential elector on the Democratic ticket of Monroe and Tompkins in 1820; retired from public life and engaged in literary pursuits; author of the letters of "Cincinnatus"; one of the founders and the first president of the New Hampshire Historical Society; died in Epping, Rockingham County, N. H., December 22, 1850; interment in the family burial ground on his estate near Epping, N. H.

PLUMER, William, Jr. (son of William Plumer), a Representative from New Hampshire; born in Epping, Rockingham County, N. H., February 9, 1789; attended Phillips Exeter Academy, Exeter, N. H., and was graduated from Harvard University in 1809; studied law; was admitted to the bar in 1812 and commenced practice in Epping, N. H.; engaged in political and historical investigations; United States commissioner of loans in 1816 and 1817; member of the State house of representatives in 1818; elected as a Democrat to the Sixteenth, Seventeenth, and Eighteenth Congresses (March 4, 1819–March 3, 1825); member of the State senate in 1827 and 1828; engaged in literary pursuits; author of a biography of his father, William Plumer; member of the State constitutional convention in 1850; died in Epping, N. H., September 18, 1854; interment in the family burial ground on his father's estate near Epping, N. H.

PLUMLEY, Charles Albert (son of Frank Plumley), a Representative from Vermont; born in Northfield, Washington County. Vt., April 14, 1875; attended the public schools; was graduated from Norwich University, Northfield, Vt., in 1896; assistant secretary of the State senate in 1894; principal and superintendent of the Northfield graded and high schools 1896–1900; assistant clerk and clerk of the State house of representatives 1900–1910; captain in the Vermont National Guard in 1901; colonel in the Officers' Reserve Corps; studied law; was admitted to the bar in 1903 and commenced practice in Northfield, Vt.; secretary of the French-Venezuela Mixed Commission in 1906; member of the State house of representatives 1912–1915, serving as speaker; commissioner of taxes for the State of Vermont 1912–1919; general counsel and tax attorney for a rubber company in Akron, Ohio, in 1919 and 1920; president of Norwich University 1920–1934; reading clerk of the Republican National Conventions of 1936 and 1940; also engaged in banking; elected as a Republican to the Seventy-third Congress to fill the vacancy caused by the resignation of Ernest W. Gibson; reelected to the Seventy-fourth and to the seven succeeding Congresses and served from January 16, 1934, to January 3, 1951; was not a candidate for renomination in 1950; resumed the practice of law; is a resident of Northfield, Vt.

PLUMLEY, Frank (father of Charles Albert Plumley), a Representative from Vermont; born in Eden, Lamoille County, Vt., December 17, 1844; attended the public schools and People's Academy; taught school near Morrisville, Vt.; studied law in Morrisville and in the University of Michigan at Ann Arbor; was admitted to the bar in Lamoille County, Vt., in May 1869 and commenced practice in Northfield; State's attorney of Washington County 1876–1880; elected to the State house of representatives in 1882; chairman of the Republican State convention in 1886; delegate to the Republican National Convention at Chicago in 1888; United States district attorney for the district of Vermont 1889–1894; served in the State senate in 1894; member of the Vermont Court of Claims 1902–1904 and chief justice 1904–1908; appointed by President Theodore Roosevelt in 1903 as umpire of the mixed commissions of Great Britain and Venezuela, and Holland and Venezuela, sitting in Caracas, Venezuela; was later selected by France and by Venezuela as umpire in the French-Venezuela mixed commission. which sat in Northfield, Vt., in 1905; trustee of Norwich University, Northfield, Vt.; elected as a Republican to the Sixty-first, Sixty-second, and Sixty-third Congresses (March 4, 1909–March 3, 1915); declined to be a candidate for renomination in 1914; resumed the practice of law in Northfield, Washington County, Vt.; was one of the four delegates from the Congress of the United States to the Interparliamentary Union of the World at Geneva, Switzerland, in 1912; died in Northfield, Vt., April 30, 1924; interment in Mount Hope Cemetery.

PLUMMER, Franklin E., a Representative from Mississippi; born in Massachusetts; completed preparatory studies; moved to Mississippi and taught school in Copiah County, Miss.; studied law; was admitted to the bar and commenced practice in Westville, Miss.; held various local offices; member of the State house of representatives; founded the town of Pittsburg (now part of Grenada); elected to the Twenty-second and Twenty-third Congresses (March 4, 1831–March 3, 1835); unsuccessful candidate for the United States Senate; died in Jackson, Miss., September 24, 1847.

POAGE, William Robert, a Representative from Texas; born in Waco, McLennan County, Tex., December 28, 1899; in 1901 moved to Throckmorton County, Tex., with his parents, who settled near Woodson; attended the rural schools of Throckmorton County, Tex.; during the First World War served as an apprentice seaman in the United States Navy; attended the University of Texas at Austin and the University of Colorado at Boulder; was graduated from Baylor University, Waco, Tex., in 1921; engaged in agricultural pursuits 1920–1922; instructor in geology at Baylor University 1922–1924; was graduated from the law department of Baylor University in 1924; was admitted to the bar the same year and commenced practice in Waco, Tex.; instructor in law at Baylor University 1924–1928; member of the State house of representatives 1925–1929; served in the State senate 1931–1937; elected as a Democrat to the Seventy-fifth and to the eleven succeeding Congresses (January 3, 1937–January 3, 1961). *Reelected to the Eighty-seventh Congress.*

POEHLER, Henry, a Representative from Minnesota; born in Hiddeson, Lippe-Detmold, Germany, August 22, 1833; attended his father's academy; immigrated to the United States in April 1848 and settled in Burlington, Iowa, where he attended the public schools; moved to St. Paul, Minn., in 1853 and to Henderson, Sibley County, Minn., in 1854; engaged in general merchandising and as a grain merchant; appointed postmaster at Henderson, Minn., February 25, 1856, and served until April 12, 1861; served in the State house of representatives in 1857, 1858, and 1865; county commissioner of Sibley County and chairman of the board from January 1865 to January 1868; member of the State senate in 1872 and 1873 and again in 1876 and 1877; elected as a Democrat to the Forty-sixth Congress (March 4, 1879–March 3, 1881); unsuccessful candidate for reelection in 1880 to the Forty-seventh Congress; unsuccessful candidate for treasurer of Minnesota; served as mayor of Henderson for several terms; moved to Minneapolis in 1889 and engaged in the general merchandise and grain business; moved to Los Angeles, Calif., in 1895; died in Henderson, Minn., while on a visit to his sister, on July 18, 1912; interment in Maj. James R. Browne's Cemetery.

POFF, Richard Harding, a Representative from Virginia; born in Radford, Montgomery County, Va., October 19, 1923; moved with his parents to Christiansburg, Va., in 1927; attended the public schools; undergraduate work at Roanoke College, Salem, Va.; during World War II volunteered for service in the United

States Air Force in February 1943 as a cadet and was commissioned in June 1944; as the pilot of a B–24 bomber, with the Eighth Air Force in England, flew thirty-five successful missions over Europe; was awarded the Distinguished Flying Cross and his combat unit received a special Presidential citation; was inactivated from the service as a first lieutenant in August 1945; entered the law school of the University of Virginia at Charlottesville and graduated in 1948, having passed the Virginia bar examination in June 1947; began practice in Radford, Va., in 1948; elected as a Republican to the Eighty-third and to the three succeeding Congresses (January 3, 1953–January 3, 1961). *Reelected to the Eighty-seventh Congress.*

POINDEXTER, George, a Delegate, a Representative, and a Senator from Mississippi; born in Louisa County, Va., in 1779; completed preparatory studies; studied law; was admitted to the bar in 1800 and commenced practice in Richmond, Va.; moved to the Territory of Mississippi in 1802 and practiced law in Natchez; attorney general of the Territory under Governor Claiborne; member of the Territorial general assembly in 1805; elected as a Delegate from Mississippi Territory to the Tenth, Eleventh, and Twelfth Congresses (March 4, 1807–March 3, 1813); appointed United States district judge for the Territory March 3, 1813, and served until March 6, 1817; served in the War of 1812; upon the admission of Mississippi as a State into the Union was elected to the Fifteenth Congress and served from December 10, 1817, to March 3, 1819; Governor of Mississippi 1819–1821; unsuccessful candidate for election in 1820 to the Seventeenth Congress and in 1822 to the Eighteenth Congress; appointed to the United States Senate to fill the vacancy caused by the death of Robert H. Adams; subsequently elected, and served from October 15, 1830, to March 3, 1835; unsuccessful candidate for reelection; moved to Kentucky and resumed the practice of his profession in Lexington; returned to Jackson, Miss., and continued the practice of law until his death on September 5, 1855; interment in Jackson Cemetery.

POINDEXTER, Miles, a Representative and a Senator from Washington; born in Memphis, Tenn., April 22, 1868; attended the Fancy Hill Academy, Rockbridge County, Va., and the academic and law departments of Washington and Lee University, Lexington, Va., graduating in law from that university in June 1891; settled in Walla Walla, Wash., October 10, 1891; was admitted to the bar and began the practice of law; prosecuting attorney of Walla Walla County in 1892; moved to Spokane, Wash., in 1897 and continued the practice of law; assistant prosecuting attorney for Spokane County 1898–1904; judge of the superior court 1904–1908; elected as a Republican to the Sixty-first Congress (March 4, 1909–March 3, 1911); elected to the United States Senate in 1910; reelected in 1916 and served from March 4, 1911, to March 3, 1923; unsuccessful candidate for reelection in 1922; appointed by President Harding as Ambassador to Peru on February 19, 1923, and served until his resignation on March 21, 1928, when he retired to private life; returned to his home, "Elk Cliff," Greenlee, Rockbridge County, Va., where he died September 21, 1946; interment in the Presbyterian Cemetery, Lexington, Va.

POINSETT, Joel Roberts, a Representative from South Carolina; born in Charleston, S. C., March 2, 1779; spent his early childhood in England; returned to America in 1788; attended private school at Greenfield Hill, Conn., and later in Wandsworth, near London, England; studied medicine at the University of Edinburgh, Scotland, and attended the military school in Woolwich, England; returned to Charleston, S. C., in 1800; studied law for a few months; traveled extensively in Europe from 1801 to 1809, returning to the United States for short intervals; sent to South America by President Madison in 1809 to investigate the prospects of the revolutionists there in their struggle for independence from Spain; returned to Charleston, S. C., in 1816; member of the State house of representatives 1816–1820; served as president of the board of public works; declined the offer of commissioner to South America by President Monroe; elected as a Democrat to the Seventeenth, Eighteenth, and Nineteenth Congresses and served from March 4, 1821, to March 7, 1825, when he resigned to enter the diplomatic service; Minister to Mexico 1825–1829; Secretary of War in the Cabinet of President Van Buren 1837–1841; died near what is now Statesburg, Sumter County, S. C., December 12, 1851; interment in the Church of the Holy Cross (Episcopal) Cemetery.

POLAND, Luke Potter, a Senator and a Representative from Vermont; born in Westford, Vt., November 1, 1815; attended the common schools and Jericho Academy; studied law; was admitted to the bar in December 1836 and practiced in Waterville, Vt.; register of probate in 1839 and 1840; member of the State constitutional convention in 1843; prosecuting attorney of Lamoille County in 1844 and 1845; judge of the supreme court of Vermont 1848–1860; became chief justice in 1860 and served until November 1865, when he resigned; appointed and subsequently elected as a Republican to the United States Senate to fill the vacancy caused by the death of Jacob Collamer and served from November 21, 1865, to March 3, 1867; elected to the Fortieth and to the three succeeding Congresses (March 4, 1867–March 3, 1875); unsuccessful candidate for reelection to the Forty-fourth Congress; member of the Vermont House of Representatives in 1878; trustee of the University of Vermont at Burlington and of the State Agricultural College; president of the First National Bank of St. Johnsbury for twenty years; elected as a Republican to the Forty-eighth Congress (March 4, 1883–March 3, 1885); was not a candidate for renomination; died at his country home near Waterville, Lamoille County, Vt., July 2, 1887; interment in Mount Pleasant Cemetery, St. Johnsbury, Vt.

POLK, Albert Fawcett, a Representative from Delaware; born in Frederica, Kent County, Del., October 11, 1869; attended public and private schools; was graduated from Delaware College (now the University of Delaware), Newark, Del., in 1889; studied law; was admitted to the bar in 1892 and began practice in Georgetown, Del.; secretary of the Bar Association of Sussex County, Del., 1898–1921; attorney for the Delaware State Senate in 1899; chairman of the Democratic county committee of Sussex County 1902–1908, 1915, and 1916; also a member of the Democratic State committee during the same periods; delegate to many Democratic State conventions; one of the legislative attorneys in 1905; member of the Georgetown Board of Education 1905–1912; member and secretary of the Board of Law Examiners of Sussex County 1914–1921; elected as a Democrat to the Sixty-fifth Congress (March 4, 1917–March 3, 1919); was an unsuccessful candidate for reelection in 1918 to the Sixty-sixth Congress; resumed the practice of law; moved to Wilmington, Del., in 1921 and continued the practice of his profession; appointed United States Commissioner for the district of Delaware in 1929 and served until his retirement in 1951; died in Wilmington, Del., on February 14, 1955; interment in Union Cemetery, Georgetown, Del.

POLK, James Gould, a Representative from Ohio; born on a farm in Penn Township, Highland County, Ohio, October 6, 1896; attended elementary school in Highland, Ohio; graduated from New Vienna (Ohio) High School in 1915; during the First World War, while attending the Agricultural College of Ohio State University was inducted into the military service on September 5, 1918, and sent to Camp Sherman, Ohio; was dis-

charged on September 19, 1918, due to a physical disability; graduated from Ohio State University in 1919; principal of New Vienna (Ohio) High School 1919–1920; superintendent of schools, New Vienna, 1920–1922; engaged in farming; graduated from Wittenberg College, Springfield, Ohio, in 1923; principal of Hillsboro (Ohio) High School 1923–1928; elected as a Democrat to the Seventy-second and to the four succeeding Congresses (March 4, 1931–January 3, 1941); was not a candidate for renomination in 1940; special assistant in the Department of Agriculture, Washington, D. C., from October 1942 to May 1946; elected as a Democrat to the Eighty-first and to the five succeeding Congresses and served from January 3, 1949, until his death in Washington, D. C., April 28, 1959; interment in Highland Cemetery, Highland, Ohio.

POLK, James Knox (brother of William Hawkins Polk), a Representative from Tennessee and a President of the United States; born near Little Sugar Creek, Mecklenburg County, N. C., November 2, 1795; moved to Tennessee in 1806 with his parents, who settled in what later became Maury County; attended the common schools and was tutored privately; was graduated from the University of North Carolina at Chapel Hill in 1818; studied law; was admitted to the bar in 1820 and commenced practice in Columbia, Tenn.; chief clerk of the State senate 1821–1823; member of the State house of representatives 1823–1825; elected as a Democrat to the Nineteenth and to the six succeeding Congresses (March 4, 1825–March 3, 1839); did not seek renomination in 1838 having become a candidate for Governor; served as Speaker during the sessions of the Twenty-fourth and Twenty-fifth Congresses; Governor of Tennessee 1839–1841; elected President of the United States in 1844 on the Democratic ticket with George M. Dallas as Vice President; was inaugurated on March 4, 1845, and served until March 3, 1849; declined to be a candidate for renomination; died in Nashville, Tenn., June 15, 1849; interment within the grounds of the State capitol.

POLK, Rufus King, a Representative from Pennsylvania; born in Columbia, Maury County, Tenn., August 23, 1866; attended Webb's Academy, Culleoka, Tenn.; was graduated from Lehigh University, South Bethlehem, Pa., in 1887 and then took a postgraduate course in mining engineering; settled in Danville, Montour County, Pa., and was employed as a chemist; held supervisory positions with several steel companies and ultimately became engaged in the manufacture of structural iron; served as first lieutenant of Company F, Twelfth Regiment, Pennsylvania Volunteer Infantry, in the war with Spain; delegate to the Democratic National Convention at Kansas City in 1900; elected as a Democrat to the Fifty-sixth and Fifty-seventh Congresses and served from March 4, 1899, until his death in Philadelphia, Pa., where he had gone to transact some business matters, March 5, 1902; interment in Fairview Cemetery, Danville, Pa.

POLK, Trusten, a Senator from Missouri; born near Bridgeville, Sussex County, Del., May 29, 1811; attended the common schools; was graduated from Yale College in 1831; studied law; was admitted to the bar in 1835 and commenced practice in St. Louis, Mo.; delegate to the Missouri State constitutional convention in 1845; presidential elector on the Democratic ticket of Cass and Butler in 1848; inaugurated as Governor of Missouri in January 1857 but soon afterward resigned; elected as a Democrat to the United States Senate and served from March 4, 1857, to January 10, 1862, when he was expelled for disloyalty; during the Civil War served as colonel in the Confederate Army; judge in the military courts of the department of Mississippi in 1864 and 1865; resumed the practice of law in St. Louis, Mo., and died there April 16, 1876; interment in Bellefontaine Cemetery.

POLK, William Hawkins (brother of James Knox Polk), a Representative from Tennessee; born in Maury County, Tenn., May 24, 1815; attended the city schools, Columbia, Tenn., and the University of North Carolina at Chapel Hill in 1832 and 1833; was graduated from the University of Tennessee at Knoxville; studied law; was admitted to the bar in 1839 and commenced practice in Columbia, Tenn.; member of the State house of representatives 1842–1845; Minister to the Kingdom of Naples and served from March 13, 1845, to August 31, 1847; served as major of the Third Dragoons in the Mexican War in 1847 and 1848; elected as a Democrat to the Thirty-second Congress (March 4, 1851–March 3, 1853); resumed the practice of law; died in Nashville, Tenn., December 16, 1862; interment in Greenwood Cemetery, Columbia, Tenn.

POLLARD, Ernest Mark, a Representative from Nebraska; born in Nehawka, Cass County, Nebr., April 15, 1869; attended the district school in Nehawka and was graduated from Nebraska State University at Lincoln in 1893; engaged in agricultural pursuits near Nehawka, Nebr., making a specialty of apple growing; member of the State house of representatives 1896–1899; president of the Nebraska Republican League in 1900; elected as a Republican to the Fifty-ninth Congress to fill the vacancy caused by the resignation of Elmer J. Burkett; reelected to the Sixtieth Congress and served from July 18, 1905, to March 3, 1909; unsuccessful candidate for reelection in 1908 to the Sixty-first Congress; delegate to the Republican National Convention at Chicago in 1912; member of the State constitutional convention in 1920 and 1921; resumed agricultural pursuits; moved to Lincoln, Nebr., in 1929; appointed secretary of the State department of welfare and labor by Governor Weaver in January 1929 and served until January 1931; died in Lincoln, Nebr., on September 24, 1939; interment in Mount Pleasant Cemetery, Nehawka, Nebr.

POLLARD, Henry Moses, a Representative from Missouri; born in Plymouth, Windsor County, Vt., June 14, 1836; attended the common schools; was graduated from Dartmouth College, Hanover, N. H., in 1857; moved to Milwaukee, Wis., where he studied law; was admitted to the bar in 1861; returned to Vermont and served during the Civil War in the Union Army as major in the Eighth Regiment, Vermont Volunteers; moved to Chillicothe, Mo., in 1865 and commenced the practice of law; mayor in 1874; county attorney in 1876; elected as a Republican to the Forty-fifth Congress (March 4, 1877–March 3, 1879); unsuccessful candidate for reelection to the Forty-sixth Congress; moved to St. Louis, Mo., in 1879 and continued the practice of law in that city until his death on February 24, 1904; interment in Edgewood Cemetery, Chillicothe, Mo.

POLLOCK, James, a Representative from Pennsylvania; born in Milton, Pa., September 11, 1810; attended the Kirkpatrick Private School at Milton; was graduated from Princeton College in 1831; studied law; was admitted to the bar in Northumberland County, Pa., in 1833 and practiced in Milton, Pa.; appointed deputy attorney general for Northumberland County in 1836; judge of the court of common pleas; elected as a Whig to the Twenty-eighth Congress to fill the vacancy caused by the death of Henry Frick; reelected to the Twenty-ninth and Thirtieth Congresses and served from April 5, 1844, to March 4, 1849; was not a candidate for renomination in 1848; appointed president judge of the eighth judicial district on January 15, 1851, and served until the adoption of the amendment to the constitution making the judgeship an elective office; Governor of Pennsylvania 1855–1858; declined a renomination; member of the peace convention of 1861 held in Washington, D. C., in an effort to devise means to prevent the impending war; Director of the Mint in Philadelphia 1861–1866 and 1869–1873; was the originator of the motto "In God we trust" for all coins of the United States large enough to contain the same; naval officer at Philadelphia in 1879; appointed chief supervisor of election in 1886; died in Lock Haven, Clinton County, Pa., April 19, 1890; interment in Milton Cemetery, Milton, Pa.

POLLOCK, William Pegues, a Senator from South Carolina; born near Cheraw, Chesterfield County, S. C., December 9, 1870; attended private and public schools and the University of South Carolina at Columbia; was graduated from the law department of that university in 1891; served as clerk of the Committee on the District of Columbia in the House of Representatives 1891–1893; was admitted to the bar in 1893 and commenced practice in Cheraw, S. C.; also engaged in agricultural pursuits; member of the State house of representatives 1894–1898; delegate to most State and county conventions from Chesterfield County 1894–1922; presidential elector on the Democratic ticket of Bryan and Stevenson in 1900; again elected to the State house of representatives in 1902, 1904, and 1906; unsuccessful candidate for election to the Sixty-second Congress; delegate to the Democratic National Convention at St. Louis in 1916; chairman of the Democratic State convention in 1918; elected to the United States Senate to fill the vacancy caused by the death of Benjamin R. Tillman and served from November 6, 1918, to March 3, 1919; resumed the practice of law in Cheraw, S. C., and died there June 2, 1922; interment in St. David's Cemetery.

POLSLEY, Daniel Haymond, a Representative from West Virginia; born at Palatine, near Fairmont, Va. (now West Virginia), November 28, 1803; attended the country schools; completed preparatory studies; studied law; was admitted to the bar in 1827 and commenced practice in Wellsburg, Brooke County, Va. (now West Virginia); edited the Western Transcript 1833–1845; moved to Mason County in 1845 and engaged in agricultural pursuits and practiced law; member of the Wheeling loyal conventions of May 13 and June 11, 1861; chosen Lieutenant Governor of the "restored government" of the State of Virginia in 1861; judge of the seventh judicial district of West Virginia 1863–1866; elected as a Republican to the Fortieth Congress (March 4, 1867–March 3, 1869); was not a candidate for renomination in 1868; resumed the practice of his profession; died in Point Pleasant, Mason County, W. Va., October 14, 1877; interment in Lone Oak Cemetery.

POMERENE, Atlee, a Senator from Ohio; born in Berlin, Holmes County, Ohio, December 6, 1863; attended the common schools and Vermillion Institute, Hayesville, Ohio; was graduated from Princeton College in 1884 and from the Cincinnati Law School in 1886; was admitted to the bar in 1886 and commenced practice in Canton, Ohio; city solicitor 1887–1891; prosecuting attorney of Stark County 1897–1900; member of the Ohio Honorary Tax Commission in 1906; unsuccessful candidate for the Democratic nomination for Governor in 1908; chairman of the Democratic State conventions in 1910 and 1918; elected Lieutenant Governor of Ohio in 1910 and served from January 9 until April 4, 1911, when he resigned to assume the duties of United States Senator; elected as a Democrat to the United States Senate in 1911; reelected in 1916 and served from March 4, 1911, to March 3, 1923; unsuccessful candidate in 1922 for reelection and again in 1926 for election; moved to Cleveland, Ohio, in 1923 and resumed the practice of law; appointed by President Harding in March 1923 as a delegate representing the United States at the Fifth Pan American Congress, which met at Santiago, Chile; appointed by President Coolidge in February 1924 as special counsel for the United States to prosecute the

Teapot Dome oil fraud cases; unsuccessful candidate for the Democratic nomination for President of the United States in 1928; appointed chairman of the Reconstruction Finance Corporation by President Hoover and served from August 1, 1932, to March 4, 1933; resumed the practice of law in Cleveland, Ohio; died in Cleveland, Ohio, November 12, 1937; interment in West Lawn Cemetery, Canton, Ohio.

POMEROY, Charles, a Representative from Iowa; born in Meriden, New Haven County, Conn., September 3, 1825; received an academic education; studied law and practiced; moved to Iowa in 1855 and engaged in agricultural pursuits; presidential elector on the Republican ticket of Lincoln and Hamlin in 1860; served as receiver of the United States land office at Fort Dodge, Iowa, from September 11, 1861, until March 3, 1869, when he resigned; elected as a Republican to the Forty-first Congress (March 4, 1869–March 3, 1871); unsuccessful candidate for renomination in 1870; was a claim agent until his death in Washington, D. C., February 11, 1891; interment in Oak Hill Cemetery.

POMEROY, Samuel Clarke, a Senator from Kansas; born in Southampton, Mass., January 3, 1816; attended Amherst College, Massachusetts, 1836–1838; moved to New York City in 1838; returned to Southampton, Mass., in 1842; held various local offices; member of the State house of representatives in 1852 and 1853; organizer and financial agent of the New England Emigrant Aid Co.; moved to Kansas in 1854 and settled in Lawrence; moved to Atchison, Kans.; served as mayor of Atchison from March 1858 to May 1859; member of the free State convention at Lawrence in 1859; president of the relief committee during the famine in Kansas in 1860 and 1861; delegate to the Republican National Convention at Philadelphia in 1856 and at Chicago in 1860; upon the admission of Kansas as a State into the Union was elected as a Republican to the United States Senate; reelected in 1867 and served from April 4, 1861, to March 3, 1873; unsuccessful candidate for reelection in 1872; resided in Washington, D. C., for several years; died in Whitinsville, Worcester County, Mass., August 27, 1891; interment in Forest Hills Cemetery, Boston, Mass.

POMEROY, Theodore Medad, a Representative from New York; born in Cayuga, N. Y., December 31, 1824; attended the common schools and Munroe Collegiate Institute, Ellridge, N. Y.; was graduated from Hamilton College, Clinton, N. Y., in 1842; studied law; was admitted to the bar in 1846 and commenced practice in Auburn, N. Y.; district attorney of Cayuga County 1850–1856; member of the State assembly in 1857; delegate to the Republican National Conventions in 1860 and 1876, and served as temporary chairman of the latter convention; elected as a Republican to the Thirty-seventh and to the three succeeding Congresses (March 4, 1861–March 3, 1869); declined to be a candidate renomination in 1868; during the Fortieth Congress was elected Speaker of the House on the last day of the session, March 3, 1869, serving one day only; first vice president and general counsel of the American Express Co. in 1868; engaged in banking in Auburn, N. Y., after 1870; mayor of Auburn in 1875 and 1876; member of the State senate in 1878 and 1879; died in Auburn, N. Y., March 23, 1905; interment in Fort Hill Cemetery.

POND, Benjamin, a Representative from New York; born in Stockbridge, Mass., in 1768; attended the common schools; moved to Poultney, Vt., and thence to that part of the town of Crown Point (later Schroon) now comprised in the town of North Hudson, N. Y., in 1800; engaged in agricultural pursuits; justice of the peace and supervisor in 1804; judge of the court of common pleas of Essex County in 1808, with residence in Schroon; member of the State assembly 1808–1810; elected as a Democrat to the Twelfth Congress (March 4, 1811–March 3, 1813); served in the War of 1812 and participated in the siege and Battle of Plattsburg in September 1814 as a volunteer in Capt. Russell Walker's company of the Thirty-seventh Regiment, New York Militia; elected to the Fourteenth Congress but died of disease, incurred through exposure at the siege of Plattsburg, in Schroon, N. Y., October 6, 1814, before the beginning of the congressional term; interment in Pine Ridge Cemetery, North Hudson, Essex County, N. Y.; reinterment in Riverside Cemetery, Elizabethtown, Essex County, N. Y., September 3, 1923.

POOL, John (uncle of Walter Freshwater Pool), a Senator from North Carolina; born near Elizabeth City, Pasquotank County, N. C., June 16, 1826; attended the common schools, and was graduated from the University of North Carolina at Chapel Hill in 1847; studied law; was admitted to the bar in 1847 and practiced in Elizabeth City, N. C., 1847–1856; also engaged in agricultural pursuits; member of the State senate in 1856, 1858, 1864, and 1865; unsuccessful Whig candidate for Governor in 1860; delegate to the State constitutional convention in 1865; presented credentials dated December 29, 1865, as a Senator-elect to the United States Senate on February 8, 1866, but was not permitted to take his seat because the State had not been readmitted to representation; upon the readmission of North Carolina was again elected to the United States Senate and served from July 4, 1868, to March 3, 1873; was not a candidate for reelection; resumed the practice of law in Washington, D. C., where he died August 16, 1884; interment in Oak Hill Cemetery.

POOL, Walter Freshwater (nephew of John Pool), a Representative from North Carolina; born at "Elm Grove," near Elizabeth City, Pasquotank County, N. C., October 10, 1850; attended the public school conducted by his family and the University of North Carolina at Chapel Hill; moved with his parents to Elizabeth City, N. C., in 1870; studied law; was admitted to the bar in 1873 and commenced practice in Elizabeth City; elected as a Republican to the Forty-eighth Congress and served from March 4, 1883, until his death in Elizabeth City, N. C., on August 25, 1883, before the assembling of Congress; interment in the Pool Cemetery, near Elizabeth City, N. C.

POOLE, Theodore Lewis, a Representative from New York; born in Jordan, Onondaga County, N. Y., April 10, 1840; moved with his parents to Syracuse, N. Y., in 1842; attended the common schools; during the Civil War enlisted as quartermaster sergeant in the One Hundred and Twenty-second Regiment, New York Volunteers, in July 1862; wounded in the Battle of Cold Harbor, Virginia, June 1, 1864; discharged as captain and brevet major July 3, 1865; county clerk of Onondaga County 1868–1870; United States pension agent for the western district of New York 1879–1888; commander of the Department of New York, Grand Army of the Republic, in 1892; connected with various manufacturing industries and corporations; director of the Bank of Syracuse; elected as a Republican to the Fifty-fourth Congress (March 4, 1895–March 3, 1897); unsuccessful candidate for reelection in 1896 to the Fifty-fifth Congress; appointed United States marshal of New York in 1899 and served until his death in Syracuse, N. Y., December 23, 1900; interment in Oakwood Cemetery.

POPE, James Pinckney, a Senator from Idaho; born on a farm near Jonesboro, Jackson Parish, La., March 31, 1884; attended the common schools; was graduated from Louisiana Polytechnic Institute, Ruston, La., in 1906 and from the law department of the University of Chicago, Chicago, Ill., in 1909; was admitted to the bar in 1909 and commenced practice in Boise, Idaho; deputy collector of internal revenue in 1916; served as city attorney of Boise in 1916 and 1917; assistant attorney general of Idaho in 1918 and 1919; member of the board of education of Boise 1924–1929; served as mayor of Boise from April 1929 until February 15, 1933, when he resigned, having been elected to Congress; delegate to every Idaho Democratic State convention from 1914 to 1930; delegate to the Democratic National Conventions in 1924, 1928, 1932, and 1936; chairman of the Democratic State central committee 1920–1922; elected as a Democrat to the United States Senate and served from March 4, 1933, to January 3, 1939; unsuccessful candidate for renomination in 1938; appointed a director of the Tennessee Valley Authority by President Franklin D. Roosevelt on January 12, 1939, and served until his resignation May 18, 1951; associated with law firm in Knoxville, Tenn.; member of board of directors, Federal Savings & Loan Association, Knoxville, Tenn., where he now resides.

POPE, John, a Senator and a Representative from Kentucky; born in Prince William County, Va., in 1770; completed preparatory studies; studied law; moved to Springfield, Ky.; was admitted to the bar and practiced in Washington, Shelby, and Fayette Counties; presidential elector on the Democratic ticket of Jefferson and Burr in 1800; member of the State house of representatives in 1802, 1806, and 1807; elected as a Democrat to the United States Senate and served from March 4, 1807, to March 3, 1813; President pro tempore of that body on February 23, 1811; member of the State senate 1825–1829; Territorial Governor of Arkansas 1829–1835; resumed the practice of law in Springfield, Ky.; elected as a Democrat to the Twenty-fifth, Twenty-sixth, and Twenty-seventh Congresses (March 4, 1837–March 3, 1843); unsuccessful candidate for reelection in 1842 to the Twenty-eighth Congress; died in Springfield, Washington County, Ky., on July 12, 1845; interment in the cemetery at Springfield, Ky.

POPE, Nathaniel, a Delegate from Illinois Territory; born in Louisville, Ky., January 5, 1784; attended Transylvania University, Lexington, Ky.; studied law; was admitted to the bar; settled in Ste. Genevieve, Mo., in 1804, where he commenced the practice of his profession; moved to Springfield, Ill.; appointed secretary of Illinois Territory by President Madison in 1809; reappointed in 1813 and served from March 7, 1809, until his resignation in 1816 to become Delegate; elected on September 5, 1816, a Delegate to Congress for a term of two years (Fourteenth and Fifteenth Congresses); appointed register of the land office at Edwardsville, Ill., on November 30, 1818, and served until March 3, 1819; appointed United States judge for the district of Illinois on March 3, 1819, and served in that capacity until his death; unsuccessful candidate for election to the United States Senate in 1824; died in St. Louis, Mo., January 22, 1850; interment in the Colonel O'Fallon Burying Ground, on the Bellefontaine Road.

POPE, Patrick Hamilton, a Representative from Kentucky; born in Louisville, Ky., March 17, 1806; attended the common schools and was graduated from St. Joseph College, Bardstown, Ky.; studied law; was admitted to the bar in 1827 and commenced practice in Louisville; declined the position of secretary of state tendered by Gov. John Breathitt in 1832; elected as a Democrat to the Twenty-third Congress (March 4, 1833–March 3, 1835); unsuccessful candidate for reelection in 1834; elected a member of the State house of representatives in 1836; resumed the practice of law; died in Louisville, Ky., May 4, 1841; interment in Cave Hill Cemetery.

POPPLETON, Earley Franklin, a Representative from Ohio; born in Belleville, Richland County, Ohio, September 29, 1834; pursued classical studies; educated at the Ohio Wesleyan University at Delaware; studied law; was admitted to the bar and commenced law practice in Elyria, Ohio; moved to Delaware, Ohio, in 1861 and continued the practice of his profession; presidential elector on the Democratic ticket of Seymour and Blair in 1868; member of the State senate in 1870; elected as a Democrat to the Forty-fourth Congress (March 4, 1875–March 3, 1877); unsuccessful candidate for reelection; resumed the practice of law; died in Delaware, Ohio, May 6, 1899; interment in Oak Grove Cemetery.

PORTER, Albert Gallatin, a Representative from Indiana; born in Lawrenceburg, Dearborn County, Ind., April 20, 1824; attended the public schools and the preparatory department of Hanover (Ind.) College, and was graduated from Indiana Asbury University (now De Pauw University), Greencastle, Ind., in 1843; studied law; was admitted to the bar in 1845 and commenced practice in Indianapolis; city attorney 1851–1853; reporter of the Indiana Supreme Court 1853–1857; member of the city council 1857–1859; elected as a Republican to the Thirty-sixth and Thirty-seventh Congresses (March 4, 1859–March 3, 1863); declined to be a candidate for renomination in 1862; resumed the practice of law; appointed First Comptroller of the Treasury March 5, 1878, and served until 1880; Governor of Indiana 1881–1885; delegate to the Republican National Convention at Chicago in 1888; United States Minister to Italy 1889–1892; died in Indianapolis, Ind., May 3, 1897; interment in Crown Hill Cemetery.

PORTER, Alexander, a Senator from Louisiana; born near Armagh, County Tyrone, Ireland, in 1786; immigrated to the United States in 1801 with an uncle, who settled in Nashville, Tenn.; received a limited schooling; studied law; was admitted to the bar and commenced practice in Attakapas, La.; moved to St. Martinville, La., in 1810; delegate to the convention which framed the first State constitution in 1812; judge of the State supreme court 1821–1833; elected as a Whig to the United States Senate to fill the vacancy caused by the death of Josiah S. Johnson and served from December 19, 1833, until January 5, 1837, when he resigned; continued the practice of law in Attakapas; again elected to the United States Senate for the term beginning March 4, 1843, but did not qualify or take his seat; died in Attakapas, La., January 13, 1844; interment on Oakland plantation in Franklin, La.

PORTER, Augustus Seymour (nephew of Peter Buell Porter), a Senator from Michigan; born in Canandaigua, N. Y., January 18, 1798; attended Canandaigua Academy, Canandaigua, N. Y.; was graduated from Union College, Schenectady, N. Y., in 1818; studied law; was admitted to the bar and commenced practice in Detroit, Mich.; recorder of Detroit in 1830; mayor of that city in 1838; elected as a Whig to the United States Senate on January 20, 1840, for the term beginning March 4, 1839, and served until March 3, 1845; was not a candidate for renomination; moved to his father's residence in Niagara Falls, N. Y., in 1848; delegate to the Union National Convention at Philadelphia in 1866; died at Niagara Falls, N. Y., September 18, 1872; interment in Oakwood Cemetery.

PORTER, Charles Howell, a Representative from Virginia; born in Cairo, Greene County, N. Y., June 21, 1833; completed preparatory studies; was graduated from the law university at Albany, N. Y., in 1853; was admitted to the bar in 1854 and commenced practice in Ashland, Greene County, N. Y.; during the Civil War entered the Union Army in 1861 as a member of the First Regiment, New York Mounted Rifles; was in Fortress Monroe, Va., during the battle between the *Monitor* and the *Merrimac*; settled in Norfolk, Va.; served as city attorney for one year; Commonwealth attorney 1863–1867; moved to Richmond, Va., in 1867; member of the constitutional convention of Virginia in 1867 and 1868; upon the readmission of Virginia to representation was elected as a Republican to the Forty-first and Forty-second Congresses and served from January 26, 1870, to March 3, 1873; declined to be a candidate for renomination in 1872; engaged in the practice of law in New York City and Beacon, N. Y.; died in Cairo, N. Y., July 9, 1897; interment in Cairo Cemetery.

PORTER, Charles Orlando, a Representative from Oregon; born in Klamath Falls, Klamath County, Oreg., April 4, 1919; moved to Eugene, Lane County, Oreg., in 1923 and attended the public schools; graduated from Harvard College in 1941 and from Harvard Law School in 1947; during World War II served with the United States Air Force from private to first lieutenant 1941–1945, with overseas service in England, France, Belgium, Luxembourg, Germany, and Czechoslovakia; awarded three battle stars and a distinguished unit citation; major in the Air Force Reserve; law clerk in the United States Court of Appeals in San Francisco in 1947 and 1948; was admitted to the bar in 1948; assistant to the director, American Bar Association's Survey of the Legal Profession, Boston, Mass., 1948–1951; practiced law in Eugene, Oreg., 1951–1956; elected as a Democrat to the Eighty-fifth and Eighty-sixth Congresses (January 3, 1957–January 3, 1961); was an unsuccessful candidate for reelection in 1960 to the Eighty-seventh Congress; is a resident of Eugene, Oreg.

PORTER, Gilchrist, a Representative from Missouri; born in Windsor, near Fredericksburg, Va., November 1, 1817; received a limited schooling; studied law; was admitted to the bar and commenced practice in Bowling Green, Mo.; elected as a Whig to the Thirty-second Congress (March 4, 1851–March 3, 1853); unsuccessful candidate for reelection in 1852 to the Thirty-third Congress; elected to the Thirty-fourth Congress (March 4, 1855–March 3, 1857); circuit judge 1866–1880; resumed the practice of law; died in Hannibal, Marion County, Mo., November 1, 1894; interment in Riverside Cemetery.

PORTER, Henry Kirke, a Representative from Pennsylvania; born in Concord, N. H., November 24, 1840; attended public and private schools, and was prepared for college at the New London Academy, New London, N. H.; was graduated from Brown University, Providence, R. I., in 1860; one of the founders of the Young Men's Christian Association in 1860; pursued professional studies in Newton Theological Seminary, Newton Center, Mass., and in Rochester Theological Seminary, Rochester, N. Y., 1861–1866; during the Civil War enlisted in the Forty-fifth Regiment, Massachusetts Volunteer Militia, in 1862 and was mustered out of service in July 1863; served on the United States Christian Commission in 1863; engaged with his father in the manufacture of light locomotives at Pittsburgh, Pa., in May 1866 and became president of the company; president of the Pittsburgh Y. M. C. A. 1868–1887; vice president of the Pittsburgh Chamber of Commerce 1892–1906; elected to the Fifty-eighth Congress (March 4, 1903–March 3, 1905); unsuccessful candidate for reelection to the Fifty-ninth Congress in 1904; member of the board of trustees and president of the board of directors of the Western Pennsylvania Institute for the Blind in 1904; resumed the manufacture of locomotives; member of the International Committee of the Y. M. C. A. 1875–1921; trustee of the Carnegie Institute 1890–1921; trustee

of the Crozier Theological Seminary 1871–1921; member of the Board of Fellows of Brown University from 1899 until his death in Washington, D. C., April 10, 1921; interment in Allegheny Cemetery, Pittsburgh, Pa.

PORTER, James, a Representative from New York; born in Williamstown, Mass., April 18, 1787; was graduated from Williams College, Williamstown, Mass., in 1810; studied law; was admitted to the bar and commenced practice in Skaneateles, N. Y.; member of the State assembly in 1814 and 1815; elected as a Democrat to the Fifteenth Congress (March 4, 1817–March 3, 1819); was not a candidate for renomination; resumed the practice of law; surrogate of Onondaga County 1822–1824; moved to Albany, N. Y., and served as register of the court of chancery until his death there February 7, 1839; interment in Greenwood Cemetery, Brooklyn, N. Y.

PORTER, John, a Representative from Pennsylvania; born in that State; received a limited schooling; elected to the Ninth Congress to fill the vacancy caused by the resignation of Michael Leib; reelected to the Tenth and Eleventh Congresses and served from December 8, 1806, to March 4, 1811.

PORTER, Peter Augustus (grandson of Peter Buell Porter), a Representative from New York; born at Niagara Falls, N. Y., October 10, 1853; taught by private teachers; attended St. Paul's Schools, Concord, N. H., 1865–1871 and was graduated from Yale College in 1874; engaged in banking and was an extensive landowner; president of the village of Niagara Falls, N. Y., in 1878; member of the State assembly in 1886 and 1887; nominated by Independent Republicans, endorsed by the Democrats and Independence League, and elected to the Sixtieth Congress (March 4, 1907–March 3, 1909); declined to be a candidate for renomination; engaged in the study and writing of history of the Niagara frontier; died in Buffalo, N. Y., December 15, 1925; interment in Oakwood Cemetery, Niagara Falls, N. Y.

PORTER, Peter Buell (grandfather of Peter Augustus Porter and uncle of Augustus Seymour Porter), a Representative from New York; born in Salisbury, Conn., August 4, 1773; was graduated from Yale College in 1791; studied law in Litchfield, Conn.; was admitted to the bar and commenced practice in Canandaigua, N. Y., in 1793; clerk of Ontario County 1797–1804; member of the State assembly in 1802 and again in 1828; moved to Buffalo, N. Y., in the fall of 1809; elected as a Democrat to the Eleventh and Twelfth Congresses (March 4, 1809–March 3, 1813); declined to be a candidate for renomination; appointed a canal commissioner in 1811; served in the War of 1812; major general of New York Volunteers 1812–1815; presented a gold medal under joint resolution of Congress dated November 3, 1814, "for gallantry and good conduct in the several conflicts of Chippewa, Niagara, and Erie"; elected to the Fourteenth Congress and served from March 4, 1815, to January 23, 1816, when he resigned; secretary of state of New York in 1815 and 1816; unsuccessful candidate for Governor of the State of New York in 1817; regent of the University of the State of New York 1824–1830; appointed Secretary of War in the Cabinet of President John Quincy Adams and served from June 21, 1828, to March 9, 1829; moved to Niagara Falls in 1836; presidential elector on the Whig ticket which nominated Harrison and Tyler in 1840; died at Niagara Falls, Niagara County, N. Y., March 20, 1844; interment in Oakwood Cemetery.

PORTER, Stephen Geyer, a Representative from Pennsylvania; born near Salem, Columbiana County, Ohio, May 18, 1869; moved to Pennsylvania with his parents, who settled in Allegheny (now Pittsburgh), Pa., in 1877; attended the common schools and Allegheny High School; studied medicine for two years, after which he studied law; was admitted to the bar in December 1893 and commenced practice in Pittsburgh; city solicitor of Allegheny 1903–1906; chairman of the Republican State convention in 1912; elected as a Republican to the Sixty-second and to the nine succeeding Congresses and served from March 4, 1911, until his death; unsuccessful candidate for mayor of Pittsburgh in 1913; appointed in 1921 to represent the House of Representatives on the advisory committee to the Washington conference on armament limitations; represented the United States at the centennial of Brazil's independence, in 1922; member and chairman of the American delegation to the Second International Conference on Opium, at Geneva in 1923 and 1924; chairman of the Foreign Service Buildings Commission 1926–1930; died in Pittsburgh, Pa., on June 27, 1930; interment in Highwood Cemetery.

PORTER, Timothy H., a Representative from New York; born in New Haven, Conn.; completed preparatory studies; moved to New York and settled in Cattaraugus County; member of the State assembly in 1816 and 1817; county judge of Cattaraugus County 1817–1820; studied law; was admitted to the bar of Tioga and Cattaraugus Counties in 1819 and commenced practice in Olean, N. Y.; first judge of the court of common pleas in 1819; district attorney for Cattaraugus County in 1819, 1820, and 1824; served in the State senate in 1823; presidential elector in 1824; elected to the Nineteenth Congress (March 4, 1825–March 3, 1827); resumed the practice of law in Olean, N. Y.; again a member of the State senate 1828–1831 and of the State assembly in 1838 and 1840; died in Olean Township, near the city of Olean, N. Y., about 1840; interment in Mount View Cemetery, Olean, N. Y.

POSEY, Francis Blackburn, a Representative from Indiana; born in Petersburg, Pike County, Ind., April 28, 1848; attended the public schools, Blythewood Academy, and Indiana Asbury (now De Pauw) University, Greencastle, Ind.; was graduated from the law department of the Indiana University at Bloomington in 1869; was admitted to the bar the same year and commenced practice in Petersburg, Ind.; presidential elector on the Republican ticket of Garfield and Arthur in 1880; delegate to the Republican National Convention at Chicago in 1884; unsuccessful Republican candidate for election in 1888 to the Fifty-first Congress; was subsequently elected to the Fiftieth Congress to fill the vacancy caused by the resignation of Alvin P. Hovey and served from January 29, 1889, to March 3, 1889; resumed the practice of law in Evansville, Ind.; surveyor of the port of Evansville 1903–1913; died in Rockport, Spencer County, Ind., on October 31, 1915; interment in Walnut Hills Cemetery, Petersburg, Ind.

POSEY, Thomas, a Senator from Louisiana; born in Fairfax County, Va., July 9, 1750; received a limited schooling; moved to the western frontier of Virginia in 1769; served in the French and Indian wars; member of the Virginia committee of correspondence; at the outbreak of the Revolutionary War was appointed captain in a Virginia regiment and served under Washington, Morgan, and Gates in New Jersey and New York 1776–1778; promoted to the rank of major in 1778 and the following year was made colonel; commanded a battalion under General Wayne in 1779 and was one of the first to enter the enemy's works at Stony Point; was at the surrender of Yorktown in 1781; held various county and militia offices; appointed brigadier general in 1793; moved to Kentucky in 1794; served in the State senate and was its presiding officer in 1805 and 1806; Lieutenant Governor of Kentucky for four years; major general of Kentucky levies after 1809; moved to Attakapas, La.; appointed to the

United States Senate to fill the vacancy caused by the resignation of John N. Destréhan and served from October 8, 1812, to February 4, 1813; unsuccessful candidate for election to fill the vacancy; Governor of Indiana Territory 1813–1816; appointed Indian agent in 1816, and held the position until his death in Shawneetown, Ill., on March 19, 1818; interment in Westwood Cemetery.

POST, George Adams, a Representative from Pennsylvania; born in Cuba, Allegany County, N. Y., September 1, 1854; pursued an academic course at Oswego Academy; moved to Susquehanna Depot, Pa.; secretary of the motive power department of the Erie Railway; elected burgess in February 1877 and served one year; candidate for presidential elector on the Democratic ticket in 1880; studied law; was admitted to the bar in 1881 and commenced practice in Montrose, Pa.; one of the owners and editors of the Montrose Democrat 1883–1889; elected as a Democrat to the Forty-eighth Congress (March 4, 1883–March 3, 1885); delegate to the Democratic National Convention at Chicago in 1884; chairman of the Democratic State convention in 1885; moved to New York City in 1889; engaged as a writer for the New York World; engaged in the manufacture of railway equipment in 1892 and served as vice president and later president of the Standard Coupler Co.; president of the George A. Post Co.; founder and president of the Railway Business Association; chairman of the railroad committee of the United States Chamber of Commerce; died in Somerville, Somerset County, N. J., on October 31, 1925; interment in Evergreen Cemetery, Oswego, N. Y.

POST, James Douglass, a Representative from Ohio; born near Milledgeville, Fayette County, Ohio, November 25, 1863; attended the common schools and was graduated from the National Normal University, Lebanon, Ohio, in 1882; engaged in teaching for five years; studied law; was admitted to the bar in 1887 and commenced practice at Washington Court House, Fayette County, Ohio; elected as a Democrat to the Sixty-second and Sixty-third Congresses (March 4, 1911–March 3, 1915); was not a candidate for renomination in 1914; resumed the practice of law at Washington Court House, Ohio, and died there April 1, 1921; interment in Washington Cemetery.

POST, Jotham, Jr., a Representative from New York; born near Westbury, Nassau County, N. Y., April 4, 1771; was graduated from Columbia College, New York City, in 1792; studied medicine but did not practice; engaged in the drug-importing business in New York City; member of the board of aldermen; served in the State assembly 1795 and 1805–1808; director of the New York Hospital 1798–1802; elected as a Federalist to the Thirteenth Congress (March 4, 1813–March 3 1815); died in New York City, N. Y., May 15, 1817.

POST, Morton Everel, a Delegate from the Territory of Wyoming; born in West Henrietta (near Rochester), Monroe County, N. Y., December 25, 1840; pursued an academic course in the Albion and Medina Academies, New York; moved to Denver, Colo., in 1860 and engaged in the freighting business between the Missouri River and Denver; engaged in mining in Alder Gulch, Mont., in 1864; delegate to the Democratic National Convention at Chicago in 1864; moved in 1867 to that portion of Dakota which is now Wyoming; county commissioner of Laramie County 1870–1876; member of the Territorial legislative council 1878–1880; engaged in banking and stock raising near Cheyenne, Wyo.; elected as a Democrat to the Forty-seventh and Forty-eighth Congresses (March 4, 1881–March 3, 1885); declined to be a candidate for renomination in 1884; resumed banking and stock raising; moved to California in 1895 and engaged in farming and fruit growing near Cucamonga; also engaged in fruit raising at Alhambra, Calif., in 1914; retired from active pursuits in 1916 and resided in Los Angeles, Calif., until 1928 when he moved to Alhambra, Calif.; died in Alhambra, Calif., March 19, 1933; interment in Inglewood Park Cemetery, Inglewood, Calif.

POST, Philip Sidney, a Representative from Illinois; born in Florida, Orange County, N. Y., March 19, 1833; pursued classical studies and was graduated from Union College, Schenectady, N. Y., in 1855; entered the Poughkeepsie Law School; was admitted to the bar in Illinois in 1856; during the Civil War entered the Union Army; commissioned second lieutenant in the Fifty-ninth Regiment, Illinois Infantry, on July 17, 1861; first lieutenant and adjutant July 21, 1861; major January 17, 1862; colonel March 20, 1862; brevetted brigadier general of Volunteers December 16, 1864, "for gallant and distinguished services in the Battle of Nashville, Tennessee"; honorably mustered out December 8, 1865; awarded a Congressional Medal of Honor March 8, 1893, "for having with his brigade attacked a strong position at Nashville, Tenn., December 15 and 16, 1864, under a terrible fire of grape, canister, and musketry, where he was struck down by a grapeshot"; appointed consul to Vienna in 1866; promoted consul general to Austria-Hungary in 1874; resigned in 1879; commander of the department of Illinois, Grand Army of the Republic, in 1886; elected as a Republican to the Fiftieth and to the four succeeding Congresses and served from March 4, 1887, until his death, before the close of the Fifty-third Congress, in Washington, D. C., on January 6, 1895; interment in Hope Cemetery, Galesburg, Ill.

POSTON, Charles Debrille, a Delegate from the Territory of Arizona; born near Elizabethtown, Hardin County, Ky., April 20, 1825; attended the public schools; clerk in the county clerk's office; clerk of the supreme court at Nashville, Tenn.; moved to California in 1850 and settled in San Francisco; clerk in the customhouse at San Francisco 1850–1853; moved to Arizona in 1854 and became interested in silver mining; appointed by President Lincoln superintendent of Indian affairs in 1863 and was civilian aide to General Heintzelman the same year; when Arizona Territory was formed was elected as a Republican to the Thirty-eighth Congress and served from December 5, 1864, to March 3, 1865; unsuccessful candidate for reelection in 1864 to the Thirty-ninth Congress; studied law; was admitted to the bar in 1867 and commenced the practice of his profession in Washington, D. C.; appointed by President Hayes register of the United States land office at Florence, Ariz., in 1878; consular agent at El Paso, Tex., in 1890; died in Phoenix, Ariz., June 24, 1902; interment in Arizona Cemetery; reinterment under a rock cairn erected by the State of Arizona at the summit of Poston Butte, overlooking the town of Florence, Ariz., April 26, 1925.

POTTER, Allen, a Representative from Michigan; born in Galloway, Saratoga County, N. Y., October 2, 1818; attended the common schools; moved to Adrian, Mich., in 1830 and to Jonesville, Mich., in 1838; learned the trade of tinsmith; moved to Kalamazoo, Mich., in 1845 and engaged in the retail hardware business until 1858, when he engaged in banking and in the manufacture of gas; member of the State house of representatives in 1857; president of the village council in 1859, 1863, 1870, and again in 1872; elected a member of the board of education in 1867, 1869, and 1871, serving as president in 1869; member of the board of water commissioners in 1872; unsuccessful Liberal candidate for election in 1872 to the Forty-third Congress; elected as an Independent candidate to the Forty-fourth Con-

gress (March 4, 1875–March 3, 1877); was not a candidate for reelection in 1876; resumed banking activities; also financially interested in railroads and Colorado mining enterprises; member of the sewer commission 1880–1883; elected as the first mayor of Kalamazoo, in 1884; treasurer of the State asylum for the insane; died in Kalamazoo, Mich., May 8, 1885; interment in the City Cemetery.

POTTER, Charles Edward, a Representative and a Senator from Michigan; born in Lapeer, Mich., October 30, 1916; attended the public schools; was graduated from Eastern Michigan University, Ypsilanti, Mich., in 1938; administrator of Bureau of Social Aid, Cheboygan County, Mich., 1938–1942; in May 1942 enlisted as a private in the United States Army with combat service in the European Theater of Operations; seriously wounded for the third time at Colmar, France, January 31, 1945, resulting in the loss of lower limbs; discharged from the service as a major July 10, 1946; engaged as vocational rehabilitation representative for the Retraining and Reemployment Administration until his resignation in June 1947; elected as a Republican to the Eightieth Congress to fill the vacancy caused by the death of Frederick V. Bradley; reelected to the Eighty-first and Eighty-second Congresses and served from August 26, 1947, until his resignation November 4, 1952; elected to the United States Senate in 1952 to fill the vacancy caused by the death of Arthur H. Vandenberg and served from November 5, 1952, to January 3, 1953; also elected in 1952 for the term commencing January 3, 1953, and ending January 3, 1959; unsuccessful candidate for reelection in 1958; engaged as an industrial consultant; executive vice president of Swesnik, Blum & Potter Securities Corporation; resides in Kenwood, Md.

POTTER, Clarkson Nott, a Representative from New York; born in Schenectady, N. Y., April 25, 1825; completed preparatory studies, and was graduated from Union College, Schenectady, N. Y., in 1842 and from Rensselaer Polytechnic Institute as a civil engineer in 1843; served as a surveyor in Wisconsin in 1843; studied law; was admitted to the bar in 1846 and commenced practice in New York City in 1847; elected as a Democrat to the Forty-first, Forty-second, and Forty-third Congresses (March 4, 1869–March 3, 1875); declined to be a candidate for renomination in 1874; elected to the Forty-fifth Congress (March 4, 1877–March 3, 1879); declined to be a candidate for renomination in 1878; president of the Democratic State conventions in 1875 and 1877; delegate to the Democratic National Conventions in 1872 and 1876; unsuccessful candidate for Lieutenant Governor in 1879; trustee of Union College 1863–1882; president of the American Bar Association in 1881 and 1882; died in New York City on January 23, 1882; interment probably in the Vale Cemetery, Schenectady, N. Y.

POTTER, Elisha Reynolds, a Representative from Rhode Island; born in Little Rest (now Kingston), R. I., November 5, 1764; learned the blacksmith's trade and also engaged in agricultural pursuits; served as a private in the Revolutionary War; attended Plainfield Academy; studied law; was admitted to the bar about 1789 and commenced practice in South Kingstown Township, R. I.; member of the State house of representatives 1793–1796 and served as speaker in 1795 and 1796; elected as a Federalist to the Fourth and Fifth Congresses to fill the vacancies caused by the resignation of Benjamin Bourn and served from November 15, 1796, until his resignation in 1797; again a member of the State house of representatives 1798–1808 and speaker in 1802 and 1806–1808; elected to the Eleventh, Twelfth, and Thirteenth Congresses (March 4, 1809–March 3, 1815); from 1816 to 1835 was a member of the State house of representatives except the year 1818, when he was an unsuccessful candidate for Governor of Rhode Island; died in South Kingston, R. I., September 26, 1835; interment in the family burial ground at Kingston, R. I.

POTTER, Elisha Reynolds (son of the preceding), a Representative from Rhode Island; born in Little Rest (now Kingston), R. I., June 20, 1811; attended the Kingston Academy and was graduated from Harvard University in 1830; studied law; was admitted to the bar in 1832 and practiced in South Kingstown Township, R. I.; adjutant general of the State 1833–1837; member of the State house of representatives 1838–1840; elected as a Whig to the Twenty-eighth Congress (March 4, 1843–March 3, 1845); unsuccessful candidate for reelection in 1844 to the Twenty-ninth Congress; served in the State senate 1847–1852 and 1861–1863; State commissioner of public schools from 1849 to 1854, when he resigned; associate justice of the Rhode Island Supreme Court from March 16, 1868, until his death in Kingston, Washington County, R. I., April 10, 1882; interment in the family burial ground.

POTTER, Emery Davis, a Representative from Ohio; born in Providence, R. I., October 7, 1804; attended the district school and the academy in Herkimer County, N. Y.; studied law in Cooperstown, N. Y.; was admitted to the New York State bar at Utica in 1833 and commenced practice in Cooperstown, N. Y.; moved to Toledo, Ohio, in 1834 and continued the practice of law; judge of the circuit court for the northern counties of Ohio; president judge of the court of common pleas from 1834 to 1843, when he resigned; elected as a Democrat to the Twenty-eighth Congress (March 4, 1843–March 3, 1845); was not a candidate for renomination; mayor of Toledo 1846–1848; member of the State house of representatives 1848–1850; elected to the Thirty-first Congress (March 4, 1849–March 3, 1851); was not a candidate for renomination; resumed the practice of law in Toledo; declined the appointment of judge of the Territory of Utah in 1858; city solicitor of Toledo in 1861 and 1862; member of the board of education in 1864 and 1865; member of the State senate 1874–1876 and served as president; retired from active practice in 1880; died in Toledo, Ohio, February 12, 1896; interment in Forest Cemetery.

POTTER, John Fox, a Representative from Wisconsin; born in Augusta, Maine, May 11, 1817; attended the common schools and Phillips Exeter Academy, Exeter, N. H.; studied law; was admitted to the bar in 1837 and commenced practice in East Troy, Wis.; judge of Walworth County 1842–1846; member of the State assembly in 1856; delegate to the Whig National Conventions at Baltimore in 1852 and 1856 and to the Republican National Convention at Chicago in 1860 and at Baltimore in 1864; elected as a Republican to the Thirty-fifth, Thirty-sixth, and Thirty-seventh Congresses (March 4, 1857–March 3, 1863); unsuccessful candidate for reelection in 1862 to the Thirty-eighth Congress; consul general of the United States to the British Provinces in North America from 1863 to 1866, residing in Montreal, Canada; practiced law in East Troy, Wis., and died there May 18, 1899; interment in Oak Ridge Cemetery.

POTTER, Orlando Brunson, a Representative from New York; born in Charlemont, Franklin County, Mass., March 10, 1823; attended the district school, Williams College, Williamstown, Mass., and the Dane Law School, Cambridge, Mass.; studied law; was admitted to the bar in 1848 and commenced practice in Boston, Mass.; engaged in manufacturing; moved to New York in 1853 and engaged in agricultural pursuits; unsuccessful for election in 1878 to the Forty-sixth Congress; elected as a Union Democrat to the Forty-eighth Congress (March 4, 1883–March 3, 1885); declined to be a candi-

date for renomination in 1884; member of the Rapid Transit Commission of New York City 1890–1894; died in New York City, N. Y., January 2, 1894; interment in Greenwood Cemetery.

POTTER, Robert, a Representative from North Carolina; born in Granville County, near Williamsboro, N. C., about 1800; attended the common schools; midshipman in the United States Navy 1815–1821; studied law; was admitted to the bar and practiced in Halifax, Halifax County, N. C.; member of the State house of commons in 1826 and 1828; moved to Oxford, Granville County, N. C., in 1827 and continued the practice of law; elected as a Jacksonian Democrat to the Twenty-first and Twenty-second Congresses and served from March 4, 1829, until his resignation in November 1831; again a member of the State house of commons, in 1834; moved to Harrison County, Tex., in 1835 and settled on a farm overlooking Lake Soda, near Marshall; member of the convention that declared the independence of Texas March 2, 1836; during the Texas Revolution was Secretary of the Navy in the cabinet of the Provincial President, David G. Burnett; fought in the Battle of San Jacinto, and refused to sign the treaty with Santa Ana after his capture; represented the Red River District in the Texas Congress 1837–1841; participated in the Regulator-Moderator War in east Texas as a leader of the Harrison County Moderators; his home being surrounded by the Regulators on March 2, 1841, he ran to the edge of Lake Soda and dived in, his body sinking to the bottom riddled with bullets; interred at "Potter's Point," a bluff near his home; reinterred in the Texas State Cemetery, at Austin, in 1931.

POTTER, Samuel John, a Senator from Rhode Island; born in South Kingston Township, R. I., June 29, 1753; completed preparatory studies; studied law; was admitted to the bar and practiced; elected Deputy Governor of Rhode Island, as the position of Lieutenant Governor was known at that time, and served for thirteen years, 1790–1803; presidential elector in 1792 and cast his vote for George Washington for President and John Adams for Vice President and again in 1796 and cast his vote for John Adams for President and Thomas Jefferson for Vice President; elected to the United States Senate and served from March 4, 1803, until his death in Washington, D. C., October 14, 1804; interment in the family burial ground, Kingston (formerly Little Rest), Washington County, R. I.

POTTER, William Wilson, a Representative from Pennsylvania; born at Potters Mills, Pa., December 18, 1792; completed preparatory studies in Bellefonte, Centre County, Pa., and was graduated from Dickinson College, Carlisle, Pa.; studied law; was admitted to the bar in 1814 and practiced his profession; elected as a Democrat to the Twenty-fifth and Twenty-sixth Congresses and served from March 4, 1837, until his death, before the assembling of the Twenty-sixth Congress, in Bellefonte, Pa., on October 28, 1839; interment in Union Cemetery, Bellefonte, Pa.

POTTLE, Emory Bemsley, a Representative from New York; born in Naples, Ontario County, N. Y., July 4, 1815; pursued classical studies at Penn Yan (N. Y.) Academy; studied law; was admitted to the bar at New York City in 1838 and commenced practice in Springfield, Clark County, Ohio; returned to Naples, N. Y., and continued the practice of law; member of the State assembly in 1847; elected as a Republican to the Thirty-fifth and Thirty-sixth Congresses (March 4, 1857–March 3, 1861); again resumed the practice of his profession; appointed by President Lincoln a member of the commission which prepared a bill providing for a tariff on wool; died in Naples, N. Y., April 18, 1891; interment in Rose Ridge Cemetery.

POTTS, David, Jr., a Representative from Pennsylvania; born at Warwick Furnace, about eight miles from Pottstown, Chester County, Pa., November 27, 1794; completed preparatory studies in Pottstown; became an ironmaster; owner and manager of Warwick Furnace; member of the State house of representatives 1824–1826; elected as a Whig to the Twenty-second and to the three succeeding Congresses (March 4, 1831–March 3, 1839); was not a candidate for renomination in 1838; resumed his former business pursuits; died at Warwick Furnace (now Warwick), Chester County, Pa., June 1, 1863; interment in Coventry Cemetery, near Warwick.

POTTS, David Matthew, a Representative from New York; born in New York, N. Y., March 12, 1906; attended the public schools and the College of the City of New York 1927–1929; was graduated from Brooklyn Law School of St. Lawrence University in 1932; was admitted to the New York bar in 1933 and commenced practice in New York City; counsel to the New York Senate Committee on Affairs of the City of New York during the 1945 session; elected as a Republican to the Eightieth Congress (January 3, 1947–January 3, 1949); unsuccessful candidate for reelection in 1948 to the Eighty-first Congress; resumed the practice of law; appointed surrogate of Bronx County by Governor Dewey and served from November 1951 to January 1953; special referee, Appellate Division, First Department, Supreme Court of State of New York, in June 1953; resides in New York, N. Y.

POTTS, Richard, a Delegate and a Senator from Maryland; born in Upper Marlboro, Md., July 19, 1753; moved with his father to the Barbados Islands in 1757; returned to Maryland and settled in Annapolis in 1761; studied law; commenced practice in Frederick County, Md., in 1775; clerk to the committee of observation for Frederick County in 1776; clerk of the county court in 1777 and 1778; served as aide to Gov. Thomas Johnson in the Flying Camp in 1777; member of the Maryland House of Delegates in 1779 and 1780; Member of the Continental Congress in 1781 and 1782; prosecuting attorney for Frederick, Montgomery, and Washington Counties in 1784; again served in the house of delegates in 1787 and 1788; declined the nomination for State senator in 1787; sat in the Maryland convention which ratified the Constitution of the United States in 1788; appointed by President Washington United States attorney for Maryland and served from 1789 to 1791; chief judge of the fifth judicial circuit of the State 1791–1793; presidential elector in 1792 and cast his vote for George Washington for President and John Adams for Vice President; elected as a Federalist to the United States Senate to fill the vacancy caused by the resignation of Charles Carroll of Carrollton and served from January 10, 1793, to October 24, 1796, when he resigned; again appointed chief judge of the fifth judicial circuit 1796–1801; associate justice of the Maryland Court of Appeals 1801–1804; resumed the practice of his profession; died in Frederick, Md., November 26, 1808; interment in All Saints' Parish Cemetery; reinterment in Mount Olivet Cemetery.

POU, Edward William (cousin of James Paul Buchanan), a Representative from North Carolina; born in Tuskegee, Macon County, Ala., September 9, 1863; moved to North Carolina with his parents, who settled in Smithfield in 1867; received private instructions and attended the common schools and the University of North Carolina at Chapel Hill; studied law; was admitted to the bar in 1885 and practiced in Smithfield, Johnston County, N. C.; chairman of the Democratic executive committee of Johnston County in 1886; presidential elector on the Democratic ticket of Cleveland and Thurman in 1888 and was selected as the messenger to deliver the electoral vote of the State of North Carolina; solicitor of the fourth judicial district of North Carolina 1890–1901; unsuccessful candidate for election in 1896 to the Fifty-fifth Congress; elected as a Democrat to the Fifty-seventh and to the sixteen succeeding Congresses and served from March 4, 1901, until his death; his service covered a period of thirty-three years and twenty-nine days; delegate to the Democratic National Convention at St. Louis in 1916, which nominated Woodrow Wilson for a second term; died in Washington, D. C., April 1, 1934; funeral services were held in the Chamber of the United States House of Representatives; interment in Riverside Cemetery, Smithfield, N. C.

POULSON, Norris, a Representative from California; born and reared on a ranch near Haines, Baker County, Oreg., July 23, 1895; attended the public schools, Oregon State College at Corvallis, and Southwestern University, Los Angeles, Calif., 1923–1925; moved to Los Angeles, Calif., in 1923; certified public accountant since 1933; member of the California assembly 1938–1942; elected as a Republican to the Seventy-eighth Congress (January 3, 1943–January 3, 1945); unsuccessful candidate for reelection in 1944 to the Seventy-ninth Congress; elected in 1946 to the Eightieth and to the three succeeding Congresses and served from January 3, 1947, until his resignation on June 11, 1953; elected mayor of Los Angeles, Calif., in 1953 and again in 1957 and served from June 1953 to June 1961; unsuccessful for reelection as mayor in 1961; is a resident of Los Angeles, Calif.

POUND, Thaddeus Coleman, a Representative from Wisconsin; born in Elk, Warren County, Pa., December 6, 1833; moved with his parents to Monroe County, N. Y., in 1838; later moved to Rochester, N. Y.; attended the common schools, Milton (Wis.) Academy, and Rushford Academy, Allegany County, N. Y.; moved to Rock County, Wis., in May 1856; engaged in the manufacture of lumber; president of the Union Lumbering Co. and of the Chippewa Falls & Western Railway Co.; member of the State assembly in 1864, 1866, 1867, and 1869, and served the last year as speaker pro tempore; Lieutenant Governor of Wisconsin in 1870 and 1871; delegate to the Republican National Convention at Philadelphia in 1872 which nominated Ulysses S. Grant for a second term; elected as a Republican to the Forty-fifth, Forty-sixth, and Forty-seventh Congresses (March 4, 1877–March 3, 1883); was not a candidate for renomination in 1882 to the Forty-eighth Congress; president of the Chippewa Spring Water Co.; died in a hospital in Chicago, Ill., on November 21, 1914; interment in Forest Hill Cemetery, Chippewa Falls, Wis.

POWELL, Adam Clayton, Jr., a Representative from New York; born in New Haven, Conn., November 29, 1908; is of the Negro race; attended the public schools of New York City; was graduated from Colgate University, Hamilton, N. Y., in 1930, from Columbia University, New York, N. Y., in 1932, and from the theological department of Shaw University, Raleigh, N. C., in 1934; studied four months in Europe, North Africa, and Asia Minor; was ordained to the ministry and officiated in New York, N. Y., since 1931; member of the New York City Council in 1941; publisher and editor of a newspaper in New York City 1941–1945; instructor at Columbia University Extension School, Department of Religious Education, 1932–1940; editorial writer for a New York daily newspaper in 1934; cofounder of the National Negro Congress; member of the Consumer Division, State of New York, Office of Price Administration, 1942–1944; member of the Manhattan Civilian Defense 1942–1945; elected as a Democrat to the Seventy-ninth and to the seven succeeding Congresses (January 3, 1945–January 3, 1961). *Reelected to the Eighty-seventh Congress.*

POWELL, Alfred H., a Representative from Virginia; born in Loudoun County, Va., March 6, 1781; was graduated from Princeton College; studied law; was admitted to the bar and commenced the practice of his profession in Winchester, Va., in 1800; member of the State senate 1812–1819; elected to the Nineteenth Congress (March 4, 1825–March 3, 1827); delegate to the State constitutional convention in 1830; died in Loudoun County, Va., in 1831.

POWELL, Cuthbert (son of Levin Powell), a Representative from Virginia; born in Alexandria, Va., March 4, 1775; completed preparatory studies; studied law; was admitted to the bar and practiced in Alexandria; mayor of Alexandria; moved to Loudoun County; engaged in agricultural pursuits; held various local offices; served in the State senate 1815–1819; member of the State house of delegates in 1828 and 1829; elected as a Whig to the Twenty-seventh Congress (March 4, 1841–March 3, 1843); died in "Llangollen," Loudoun County, Va., May 8, 1849; interment in the private cemetery on his estate, "Llangollen," in Loudoun County, Va.

POWELL, Joseph, a Representative from Pennsylvania; born in Towanda, Bradford County, Pa., June 23, 1828; completed preparatory studies; engaged in mercantile pursuits; president of the First National Bank of Towanda 1870–1889; elected as a Democrat to the Forty-fourth Congress (March 4, 1875–March 3, 1877); unsuccessful candidate for reelection in 1876 to the Forty-fifth Congress; appointed special deputy collector of the port of Philadelphia in 1885 and served four years; sheriff of Bradford County 1889–1893; died in Towanda, Pa., April 24, 1904; interment in Oak Hill Cemetery.

POWELL, Lazarus Whitehead, a Senator from Kentucky; born near Henderson, Henderson County, Ky., October 6, 1812; attended the common schools; was graduated from St. Joseph College, Bardstown, Ky., in 1833; studied law; was admitted to the bar and commenced practice at Henderson in 1835; member of the State house of representatives in 1836; presidential elector on the Democratic ticket of James K. Polk and George M. Dallas in 1844; Governor of Kentucky 1851–1855; elected as a Democrat to the United States Senate and served from March 4, 1859, to March 3, 1865; resumed the practice of his profession; delegate to the Union National Convention at Philadelphia in 1866; died near Henderson, Ky., July 3, 1867; interment in Fernwood Cemetery.

POWELL, Levin (father of Cuthbert Powell), a Representative from Virginia; born near Manassas, Prince William County, Va., in 1737; studied in private schools; deputy sheriff of Prince William County; moved to Loudoun County in 1763; engaged in mercantile pursuits; served as major in the Revolutionary Army in 1775; appointed lieutenant colonel of the Sixteenth Regiment of the Continental Line in 1777; resigned on account of ill health in 1778; member of the State house of delegates in 1779; was delegate to the Virginia State Convention which ratified the Federal Constitution in 1788; again a member of the State house of delegates in 1787, 1788, 1791, and 1792; as presidential elector was the only one from Virginia to vote for John Adams for President in 1796; elected as a Federalist to the Sixth Congress (March 4, 1799–March 3, 1801); helped to build a turnpike from Alexandria, Va., to the upper country; died in Bedford, Bedford County, Pa., on August 23, 1810; interment in Old Presbyterian Graveyard.

POWELL, Paulus, a Representative from Virginia; born in Amherst County, Va., in 1809; attended private schools and Amherst College, Amherst, Va.; held various local offices; mem-

ber of the State house of delegates 1843–1849, 1863, and 1864; elected as a Democrat to the Thirty-first and to the four succeeding Congresses (March 4, 1849–March 3, 1859); unsuccessful candidate for reelection in 1858 to the Thirty-sixth Congress; died in Amherst, Amherst County, Va., June 10, 1874; interment in the private burying ground of his brother-in-law on the estate, "Kenmore," near Amherst, Va.

POWELL, Samuel, a Representative from Tennessee; born in Norristown, Montgomery County, Pa., July 10, 1776; attended the common schools and Philadelphia (Pa.) College; studied law; was admitted to the bar in Norristown, Pa., prior to 1800; moved to Blountville, Sullivan County, Tenn., in 1800; established the first law school in Tennessee at his home; moved to Rogersville Hawkins County, Tenn., in 1805 and practiced law; member of the superior court of law and equity 1807–1809; judge of the first circuit court of Tennessee in 1812 and 1813; elected to the Fourteenth Congress (March 4, 1815–March 3, 1817); was not a candidate for renomination in 1816; resumed the practice of law; again judge of the first circuit court 1819–1841; died in Rogersville, Tenn., August 2, 1841; interment in the Old Presbyterian Cemetery.

POWER, Thomas Charles, a Senator from Montana; born near Dubuque, Dubuque County, Iowa, May 22, 1839; attended the common schools and took a three years' course in civil engineering in Sinsiniwa College, Wisconsin; practiced engineering and taught school three years; employed on a survey in Dakota in 1860; engaged in trade on the Missouri River 1861–1867; president of a line of steamers; moved to Fort Benton, Mont.; settled in Helena in 1876; engaged in mercantile pursuits and in banking; member of the first constitutional convention of Montana in 1883; delegate to the Republican National Convention at Chicago in 1888; unsuccessful candidate for Governor of Montana in 1889; upon the admission of Montana as a State into the Union was elected as a Republican to the United States Senate and served from January 2, 1890, to March 3, 1895; was not a candidate for renomination; engaged in banking, stock raising, and mercantile pursuits; died in Helena, Mont., February 16, 1923; interment in Resurrection Cemetery.

POWERS, Caleb, a Representative from Kentucky; born near Williamsburg, Whitley County, Ky., February 1, 1869; attended the public schools, Union College, Barbourville, Ky., the University of Kentucky at Lexington, and Centre College, Danville, Ky.; was graduated from Valparaiso University, Valparaiso, Ind.; attended West Point Military Academy in 1890 and 1891; studied law; was admitted to the bar in 1894 and commenced practice at Barbourville, Ky.; superintendent of public schools for Knox County 1894–1899; elected secretary of state of Kentucky in 1899 but was unseated after a contest; convicted of complicity in the assassination of Gov. William Goebel in 1900 and sentenced to prison; was pardoned in 1908; author of "My Own Story" in 1905; elected as a Republican to the Sixty-second and to the three succeeding Congresses (March 4, 1911–March 3, 1919); was not a candidate for renomination in 1918; delegate to the Republican National Convention at Chicago in 1912; moved to Washington, D. C., and served as assistant counsel for the United States Shipping Board from 1921 until his death; died in a hospital at Baltimore, Md., July 25, 1932; interment in City Cemetery, Barbourville, Ky.

POWERS, David Lane, a Representative from New Jersey; born in Philadelphia, Pa., July 29, 1896; attended the public schools, and was graduated from Pennsylvania Military College at Chester in 1915; during the First World War was commissioned a second lieutenant on August 15, 1917; promoted to first lieutenant and served as battalion adjutant in the Eight Hundred and Seventh Pioneer Infantry, with overseas service, and was discharged on April 4, 1919; moved to Trenton, N. J., in 1919 and engaged in the building business; member of the State house of assembly 1928–1930; elected as a Republican to the Seventy-third and to the six succeeding Congresses and served from March 4, 1933, until his resignation on August 30, 1945, to become a member of the Public Utilities Commission of New Jersey; is a resident of Trenton, N. J.

POWERS, Gershom, a Representative from New York; born in Croydon, Sullivan County, N. H., July 11, 1789; attended the common schools and was largely self-taught; taught school in the town of Sempronius, Cayuga County, N. Y., while attending the local law school, from which he graduated in 1810; was admitted to the bar the same year and commenced practice in Auburn, Cayuga County, N. Y.; appointed superintendent of Auburn prison in 1820; first judge of the court of common pleas of Cayuga County 1823–1828; elected as a Jackson Democrat to the Twenty-first Congress (March 4, 1829–March 3, 1831); declined to be a candidate for renomination in 1830; appointed inspector of Auburn prison on April 2, 1830, and served until his death; died in Auburn, N. Y., June 25, 1831; interment in North Street Cemetery.

POWERS, Horace Henry, a Representative from Vermont; born in Morristown, Lamoille County, Vt., May 29, 1835; attended Peoples Academy; was graduated from the University of Vermont at Burlington in 1855; studied law; was admitted to the bar in 1858 and practiced in Hyde Park, Vt., 1859–1862; member of the State house of representatives in 1858; prosecuting attorney of Lamoille County in 1861 and 1862; member of the council of censors in 1869; member of the State constitutional convention in 1870; served in the State senate in 1872 and 1873; again a member of the State house of representatives in 1874 and served as speaker; judge of the supreme court of Vermont from December 1874 to December 1890; trustee of the University of Vermont from 1883 until his death; delegate to the Republican National Convention at Minneapolis in 1892 which nominated Harrison and Reid; elected as a Republican to the Fifty-second and to the four succeeding Congresses (March 4, 1891–March 3, 1901); unsuccessful candidate for renomination in 1900; resumed the practice of law in Morrisville, Vt.; died in Morrisville, Vt., December 8, 1913; interment in Pleasant View Cemetery.

POWERS, Llewellyn, a Representative from Maine; born in Pittsfield, Somerset County, Maine, October 14, 1836; attended the common schools of Pittsfield and St. Albans Academy; was graduated from the Colburn Classical Institute; attended Colby University, Waterville, Maine, and was graduated from the law department of Union University, Albany, N. Y., in 1860; was admitted to the bar in Albany, N. Y., and Somerset, Maine, in 1860 and commenced practice in Houlton, Maine, in January 1861; prosecuting attorney for Aroostook County 1864–1871; collector of customs for the district of Aroostook 1868–1872; member of the State house of representatives 1873–1876, 1883, 1892, and 1895 and served as speaker during the last term; elected as a Republican to the Forty-fifth Congress (March 4, 1877–March 3, 1879); unsuccessful candidate for reelection in 1878 to the Forty-sixth Congress; Governor of Maine 1896–1900; elected as a Republican to the Fifty-seventh Congress to fill the vacancy caused by the resignation of Charles A. Boutelle; reelected to the Fifty-eighth, Fifty-ninth, and Sixtieth Congresses and served from April 8, 1901, until his death in Houlton, Maine, July 28, 1908; interment in West Pittsfield Cemetery, near Pittsfield, Maine.

POWERS, Samuel Leland, a Representative from Massachusetts; born in Cornish, N. H., October 26, 1848; prepared for college at Kimball Union Academy, Meriden, N. H., and was graduated from Dartmouth College, Hanover, N. H., in 1874; studied law in the law school of the University of the City of New York, and also in Worcester, Mass.; was admitted to the bar in 1875 and commenced practice in Boston, Mass., in 1876; moved to Newton, Mass., in 1882; member of the Newton City Council 1883–1887, serving as president in 1885 and 1886; elected as a Republican to the Fifty-seventh and Fifty-eighth Congresses (March 4, 1901–March 3, 1905); declined to be a candidate for renomination in 1904; one of the managers appointed by the House of Representatives in 1905 to conduct the impeachment proceedings against Charles Swayne, judge of the United States District Court for the Northern District of Florida; resumed the practice of law in Boston and resided in Newton, Mass.; also engaged as an author; trustee of Dartmouth College 1905–1915; member of the Massachusetts Board of Education in 1915–1919; member of the Massachusetts constitutional convention in 1918 and 1919; served in the State militia for ten years; trustee of the board of public control for the operation of the Boston Elevated Railway 1918–1928, serving as chairman 1923–1928; died in Newton, Mass., on November 30, 1929; interment in Newton Cemetery, Newton Center, Mass.

POYDRAS, Julien de Lallande, a Delegate from the Territory of Orleans; born in Nantes, France, April 3, 1740; completed preparatory studies; served in the French Navy in his youth; was captured by the British in 1760 and taken to England; escaped on board a West Indian merchantman to San Domingo, whence he immigrated to New Orleans, La., in 1768; wrote the first poetical work printed in Louisiana in 1779; president of the first legislative council of the Territory of Orleans; founded the Female Orphan Asylum in New Orleans; elected to the Eleventh Congress (March 4, 1809–March 3, 1811); president of the first State constitutional convention; presidential elector in 1812 and cast his vote for James Madison for President and Elbridge Gerry for Vice President; founded and endowed the Poydras Asylum; died in Pointe Coupee, La., June 14, 1824; interment in Old St. Francis Cemetery; reinterment in the grounds of the Poydras High School, New Roads, La.

PRACHT, Charles Frederick, a Representative from Pennsylvania; born in Pitman, Schuylkill County, Pa., October 20, 1880; attended the public schools; associated in the toy novelty and notions business 1897–1914; children's agent and investigator in the county commissioner's office 1915–1929; served in the department of accounts under the clerk of quarters sessions in 1930 and 1931; personal property assessor in the board of revision department 1932–1942; member of the Republican executive ward committee since 1904, serving as chairman for twenty-five consecutive years; elected as a Republican to the Seventy-eighth Congress (January 3, 1943–January 3, 1945); unsuccessful candidate for reelection in 1944 to the Seventy-ninth Congress; retired from public and political activities; died in Philadelphia, Pa., December 22, 1950; interment in Lawnview Cemetery (Rockledge), Philadelphia, Pa.

PRALL, Anning Smith, a Representative from New York; born in Port Richmond, Staten Island, N. Y., September 17, 1870; attended the public schools and New York University; employed as a clerk in a New York City newspaper office; was in charge of a real-estate department of a bank 1908–1918; served as clerk of the first district municipal court; appointed a member of the New York City Board of Education January 1, 1918, and served until December 31, 1921, and three times elected its president; commissioner of taxes and assessment in 1922 and 1923; delegate to the Democratic National Convention at New York City in 1924; elected as a Democrat to the Sixty-eighth Congress to fill the vacancy caused by the death of Daniel J. Riordan; reelected to the Sixty-ninth and to the four succeeding Congresses and served from November 6, 1923, to January 3, 1935; was not a candidate for renomination in 1934; served as a member and chairman of the Federal Communications Commission from January 15, 1935, until his death at his summer home in Boothbay Harbor, Maine, July 23, 1937; interment in Moravian Cemetery, New Dorp, Staten Island, N. Y.

PRATT, Charles Clarence, a Representative from Pennsylvania; born in New Milford, Susquehanna County, Pa., April 23, 1854; attended the rural schools in his community, Sedgwick Institute, Great Barrington, Mass., and was graduated from the State normal school at Bloomsburg, Pa.; became engaged in the lumber and oil businesses at New Milford in 1879; served as assessor, school director, and justice of the peace; colonel on the respective staffs of Governors Stone, Pennypacker, and Tener 1899–1907; elected as a Republican to the Sixty-first Congress (March 4, 1909–March 3, 1911); unsuccessful candidate for reelection in 1910 to the Sixty-second Congress; resumed his former business pursuits, residing in Binghamton, N. Y., during the winters and in New Milford, Pa., during the summers; died in Binghamton, N. Y., January 27, 1916; interment in New Milford Cemetery, New Milford, Pa.

PRATT, Daniel Darwin, a Senator from Indiana; born in Palermo, Maine, October 26, 1813; moved to New York with his parents, who settled in Fenner, Madison County; attended the public schools and Cazenovia Seminary; was graduated from Hamilton College, Clinton, N. Y., in 1831; moved to Indiana in 1832 and taught school; settled in Indianapolis in 1834 and was employed in the office of the secretary of state; studied law; was admitted to the bar and commenced practice in Logansport, Ind., in 1836; member of the State house of representatives in 1851 and 1853; secretary of the Republican National Convention at Chicago in 1860; elected in 1868 as a Republican to the Forty-first Congress but resigned January 27, 1869, before the beginning of the congressional term, having been elected to the United States Senate and served from March 4, 1869, to March 3, 1875; appointed by President Grant as Commissioner of Internal Revenue and served from May 15, 1875, to August 1, 1876; died in Logansport, Cass County, Ind., June 17, 1877; interment in Mount Hope Cemetery.

PRATT, Eliza Jane, a Representative from North Carolina; born in Morven, Anson County, N. C., March 5, 1902; attended the public schools of Morven and Raeford, N. C., and Queens College at Charlotte, N. C.; newspaper editor at Troy, N. C., in 1923 and 1924; served as secretary to Members of Congress from the Eighth Congressional District of North Carolina 1924–1946; elected as a Democrat to the Seventy-ninth Congress to fill the vacancy caused by the death of William O. Burgin and served from May 25, 1946, to January 3, 1947; was not a candidate for renomination in 1946; employed with the Office of Alien Property, Washington, D. C., from May 27, 1947, until February 2, 1951; with Department of Agriculture from February 5, 1951, to April 12, 1954; with Library of Congress from April 13, 1954, to December 7, 1956; secretary to Representative Kitchin of North Carolina since 1957; is a resident of Lexington, N. C.

PRATT, Harcourt Joseph, a Representative from New York; born in Highland, Ulster County, N. Y., October 23, 1866; attended the public schools and Claverack Academy at Clav-

erack, N. Y.; engaged in the lumber and coal business; also interested in banking; member of the Board of Supervisors of Ulster County 1895–1897; member of the State assembly in 1897; director of the First National Bank of Highland since 1900 and of the Kingston Trust Co. since 1921; was president of the Board of Education of Highland, N. Y., 1908–1926; elected as a Republican to the Sixty-ninth and to the three succeeding Congresses (March 4, 1925–March 3, 1933); was not a candidate for renomination in 1932; resumed his former business interests; died from injuries received in an automobile accident near Highland, N. Y., May 21, 1934; interment in Highland Cemetery.

PRATT, Harry Hayt, a Representative from New York; born in Corning, Steuben County, N. Y., November 11, 1864; attended Corning Union School and was graduated from Corning Free Academy in 1882; associate editor of the Corning Weekly Journal 1882–1891 and of the Corning Daily Journal 1891–1906; editor of the same and manager of the Corning Journal Publishing Co. 1906–1919; supervisor of Corning in 1898 and 1899; delegate to the Republican State conventions in 1908 and 1910; postmaster of Corning from September 8, 1905, to January 27, 1914; elected as a Republican to the Sixty-fourth and Sixty-fifth Congresses (March 4, 1915–March 3, 1919); unsuccessful candidate for renomination in 1918; engaged in publicity work for the United States Department of Labor and the War Risk Insurance Bureau 1919–1921; public relations counselor for the Erie Railroad Co. 1923–1928, and managing editor of the Erie Railroad Magazine; director of the Corning Free Library and the Chamber of Commerce; died in Corning, N. Y., November 13, 1932; interment in Hope Cemetery.

PRATT, Henry Otis, a Representative from Iowa; born in Foxcroft, Piscataquis County, Maine, February 11, 1838; attended the common schools and Foxcroft Academy; was graduated from the law department of Harvard University; moved to Charles City, Iowa, in 1862 and taught school; was admitted to the bar in Mason City, Iowa, in 1862; during the Civil War enlisted in the Union Army in August 1862 and served in Company B, Thirty-second Regiment, Iowa Volunteer Infantry, until March 1863, when he was discharged at Fort Pillow, Tenn.; commenced the practice of law in Charles City, Iowa, in 1864; county superintendent of public schools of Floyd County in 1868 and 1869; member of the State house of representatives 1870–1872; elected as a Republican to the Forty-third and Forty-fourth Congresses (March 4, 1873–March 3, 1877); was not a candidate for renomination in 1876; president of the Republican State convention at Des Moines, Iowa, in 1877; studied for the ministry; was ordained and entered the ministry of the Methodist Episcopal Church in October 1877 and continued his ministerial duties until retired on account of age in October 1918; died in Cedar Rapids, Iowa, May 22, 1931; interment in Oak Hill Cemetery.

PRATT, James Timothy, a Representative from Connecticut; born in Cromwell, Conn., December 14, 1802; attended the common schools; engaged in mercantile and agricultural pursuits in Hartford, Conn.; enlisted in the "Horse Guard" in 1820; mayor 1826–1829; elected major of the First Regiment of Cavalry in 1834; colonel in 1836; brigadier general 1837–1839; major general 1839–1846; adjutant general in 1846; retired from mercantile pursuits and settled in Rocky Hill, Conn.; member of the State house of representatives in 1847, 1848, and 1850; served in the State senate in 1852; again a member of the State house of representatives in 1857 and 1862; elected as a Democrat to the Thirty-third Congress (March 4, 1853– March 3, 1855); unsuccessful candidate for reelection in 1854 to the Thirty-fourth Congress; unsuccessful candidate for election as Governor in 1858 and 1859; member of the peace convention of 1861 held in Washington, D. C., in an effort to devise means to prevent the impending war; again a member of the State house of representatives in 1870 and 1871; engaged in agricultural pursuits; died in Wethersfield, Hartford County, Conn., April 11, 1887; interment in Indian Hill Cemetery, Middletown, Conn.

PRATT, Joseph Marmaduke, a Representative from Pennsylvania; born in Paterson, Passaic County, N. J., September 4, 1891; moved with his parents to Philadelphia, Pa., in 1892; attended the public schools and business colleges; was graduated from Temple University, Philadelphia, Pa., in 1919; engaged in the manufacture of industrial and marine products; member of the Republican city committee of Philadelphia 1937–1946; elected as a Republican to the Seventy-eighth Congress to fill the vacancy caused by the resignation of James P. McGranery and served from January 18, 1944, to January 3, 1945; unsuccessful candidate for reelection in 1944 to the Seventy-ninth Congress; resumed his former business pursuits in Philadelphia, Pa.; received the Republican nomination for State senator in the second senatorial district of Pennsylvania in 1946; died in Washington, D. C., on July 19, 1946, while on a business trip; interment in Arlington Cemetery, Upper Darby, Pa.

PRATT, Le Gage, a Representative from New Jersey; born in Sterling, Worcester County, Mass., December 14, 1852; educated in the common schools; in 1869 entered upon a commercial career in Boston; subsequently moved with his parents to Chicago, Ill.; engaged in newspaper work in Chicago 1884–1886; was employed for several years in the life-insurance business in Texas; was subsequently transferred to Illinois and continued in this business; in 1895 was appointed State agent for a large life-insurance company with headquarters in St. Paul, Minn., and the following year was appointed general superintendent of agencies at the home office; in 1897 tendered his resignation and moved to East Orange, N. J., and in 1903 accepted a similar position with a large insurance company at Newark, N. J., being elected vice president, which office he held until elected to Congress; elected as a Democrat to the Sixtieth Congress (March 4, 1907–March 3, 1909); unsuccessful candidate for reelection in 1908 to the Sixty-first Congress; resumed the insurance business and became connected with the Puritan Life Insurance Co., of Providence, R. I.; died in Newark, N. J., March 9, 1911; interment in Fairmount Cemetery.

PRATT, Ruth Sears Baker, a Representative from New York; born in Ware, Mass., August 24, 1877; attended private schools and Wellesley (Mass.) College; moved to Greenwich, Conn., in 1894 and to New York City, N. Y., in 1904; presidential elector in 1920; member of the board of aldermen of New York City in 1925, being the first woman to serve; reelected in 1927 and served until March 1, 1929; member of the Republican National Committee 1929–1943; delegate to the Republican National Conventions in 1924, 1932, 1936, 1940, and an alternate in 1944; delegate to the Republican State conventions in 1922, 1924, 1926, 1928, 1930, 1936, and 1938; served as president of the Woman's National Republican Club 1943–1946; trustee of Wellesley College since 1934; elected as a Republican to the Seventy-first and Seventy-second Congresses (March 4, 1929–March 3, 1933); unsuccessful candidate for reelection in 1932 to the Seventy-third Congress; is a resident of New York City, N. Y.

PRATT, Thomas George, a Senator from Maryland; born in Georgetown, Md. (now a part of Washington, D. C.), February 18, 1804; completed preparatory studies and attended the Georgetown University, Washington, D. C., and Princeton College; studied law; was admitted to the bar and commenced practice in Upper Marlboro, Md., in 1823; member of the State house of delegates 1832–1835; Whig presidential elector in 1836 and cast his vote for William H. Harrison for President and John Tyler for Vice President; appointed president of the executive council in 1836; served in the State senate 1838–1843; Governor of Maryland 1845–1848; moved to Annapolis, Md., in 1848 and resumed the practice of law; elected as a Whig to the United States Senate in 1849 to fill the vacancy caused by the resignation of Reverdy Johnson; reelected in 1851 and served from January 12, 1850, to March 3, 1857; delegate to the Democratic National Convention at Chicago in 1864; moved to Baltimore, Md., in 1864 and again resumed the practice of his profession; delegate to the Philadelphia Union Convention in 1866; unsuccessful candidate for election to the United States Senate in 1867; died in Baltimore, Md., November 9, 1869; interment in St. Anne's Cemetery, Annapolis, Md.

PRATT, Zadock, a Representative from New York; born in Stephentown, N. Y., October 30, 1790; moved with his parents to Windham (later Jewett), Greene County, in 1802; received a limited schooling; engaged in tanning leather in Greene County, where he established a town called Prattsville; member of the State militia 1819–1823; justice of the peace in 1824; supervisor of the town of Windham in 1827; member of the State senate in 1830; presidential elector on the Democratic ticket of Van Buren and Johnson in 1836; elected as a Democrat to the Twenty-fifth Congress (March 4, 1837–March 3, 1839); elected to the Twenty-eighth Congress (March 4, 1843–March 3, 1845); resumed his former business activities; also engaged in banking and agricultural pursuits near Prattsville, Greene County, N. Y.; presidential elector on the Democratic ticket of Pierce and King in 1852; delegate to the Democratic National Convention at Baltimore in 1852; retired from active business pursuits in 1860; died in Bergen, N. J., on April 6, 1871; interment in the City Cemetery, Prattsville, N. Y.

PRAY, Charles Nelson, a Representative from Montana; born in Potsdam, St. Lawrence County, N. Y., April 6, 1868; attended the public schools in Salisbury and Middlebury, Vt.; graduate of the Middlebury High School; attended Middlebury (Vt.) College 1886–1888 and was graduated from the Chicago College of Law; was admitted to the bar in 1892 and commenced practice at Fort Benton, Mont.; served as assistant prosecuting attorney of Chouteau County in 1897 and 1898; elected prosecuting attorney in 1898 and reelected in 1900, 1902, and 1904; elected as a Republican to the Sixtieth, Sixty-first, and Sixty-second Congresses (March 4, 1907–March 3, 1913); unsuccessful candidate for reelection in 1912 to the Sixty-third Congress; resumed the practice of law in Great Falls, Cascade County, Mont., January 1, 1914; unsuccessful candidate for election to the United States Senate in 1916; appointed judge of the United States District Court of Montana on January 21, 1924, in which capacity he served until his retirement in 1957; is a resident of Great Falls, Mont.

PRENTISS, John Holmes (brother of Samuel Prentiss), a Representative from New York; born in Worcester, Mass., April 17, 1784; attended local and private schools; foreman of the New York Evening Post in 1808; moved to Cooperstown, Otsego County, N. Y., in October 1808; established the Freeman's Journal in the same year and served as editor; appointed colonel of militia by Governor Clinton and served as division inspector on the staff of the commander in chief; postmaster of Cooperstown from April 24, 1833, to February 17, 1837; vice president of the Democratic State convention at Albany; elected as a Democrat to the Twenty-fifth and Twenty-sixth Congresses (March 4, 1837–March 3, 1841); was not a candidate for renomination in 1840; resumed his former newspaper pursuits; also served as president of the Bank of Cooperstown; retired from active business pursuits in 1849 and resided in Cooperstown, N. Y., until his death in that city on June 26, 1861; interment in Lakewood Cemetery.

PRENTISS, Samuel (brother of John Holmes Prentiss), a Senator from Vermont; born in Stonington, Conn., March 31, 1782; moved to Northfield, Mass.; completed preparatory studies and was instructed in the classics by a private tutor; studied law in Northfield and in Brattleboro, Vt.; was admitted to the bar in 1802 and practiced in Montpelier 1803–1822; member of the State house of representatives in 1824 and 1825; associate justice of the supreme court of Vermont; elected chief justice of the State supreme court in 1829; elected in 1831 as a Whig to the United States Senate; reelected in 1837 and served from March 4, 1831, to April 11, 1842, when he resigned to accept a judicial assignment; originator and successful advocate of the law to suppress dueling in the District of Columbia; appointed judge of the United States District Court of Vermont in 1842, and served in this capacity until his death in Montpelier, Vt., January 15, 1857; interment in Green Mount Cemetery.

PRENTISS, Sergeant Smith, a Representative from Mississippi; born in Portland, Cumberland County, Maine, September 30, 1808; attended Gorham (Maine) Academy and was graduated from Bowdoin College, Brunswick, Maine, in 1826; studied law in Gorham, Maine, and in Cincinnati, Ohio; moved to Natchez, Adams County, Miss.; was admitted to the bar in 1829 and commenced practice in Vicksburg, Miss.; member of the State house of representatives in 1835; contested the election of John F. H. Claiborne to the Twenty-fifth Congress and the election was set aside by the House; subsequently elected to fill the vacancy caused by this action and served from May 30, 1838, to March 3, 1839; was not a candidate for renomination in 1838; resumed the practice of law at Vicksburg; moved to New Orleans, La., in 1845 and resumed the practice of law; died at "Longwood," near Natchez, Miss., July 1, 1850; interment in the private burying ground at "Longwood."

PRESCOTT, Cyrus Dan, a Representative from New York; born in New Hartford, Oneida County, N. Y., August 15, 1836; pursued an academic course and was graduated from Utica Free Academy; studied law in Utica and in Rome, N. Y.; was admitted to the bar in 1859 and commenced practice in Rome in 1860; moved to New York City in 1867 and was employed as a financial clerk in a wholesale house; returned to Rome, N. Y., in 1868 and continued the practice of law; member of the Board of Aldermen of Rome 1874–1876; served in the State assembly in 1878; elected as a Republican to the Forty-sixth and Forty-seventh Congresses (March 4, 1879–March 3, 1883); was not a candidate for renomination in 1882; resumed the practice of law in Rome, N. Y.; attorney for the New York Central Railroad Co. for over thirty years; died in Rome, Oneida County, N. Y., October 23, 1902; interment in Sauquoit Valley Cemetery, near Clayville, Oneida County, N. Y.

PRESTON, Francis (father of William Campbell Preston and uncle of William Ballard Preston and William Preston), a Representative from Virginia; born in Greenfield, Botetourt County, Va., August 2, 1765; was graduated from the College of William and Mary, Williamsburg, Va., in 1783; studied law; was admitted to the bar and practiced in Montgomery and Washington Counties; member of the State house of delegates in 1788 and 1789; elected to the Third and Fourth Congresses

(March 4, 1793–March 3, 1797); declined to be a candidate for renomination; settled in Abingdon, Va., and resumed the practice of law; again a member of the State house of delegates 1812–1814; colonel of Volunteers in the War of 1812; served in the State senate 1816–1820; died at the home of his brother, William C. Preston, in Columbia, S. C., May 26, 1836; interment in Aspinvale Cemetery, near Seven Mile Ford, Va.

PRESTON, Jacob Alexander, a Representative from Maryland; born in Bel Air, Harford County, Md., March 12, 1796; attended the common schools; was graduated from the medical department of the University of Maryland at Baltimore in 1816; practiced his profession in Harford, Baltimore, and Cecil Counties; also engaged in agricultural pursuits; served with a Maryland regiment as lieutenant in the War of 1812; elected as a Whig to the Twenty-eighth Congress (March 4, 1843–March 3, 1845); was not a candidate for renomination in 1844; resumed the practice of medicine and also engaged in agricultural pursuits; died in Perryman, Harford County, Md., on August 2, 1868; interment in St. George's Churchyard, Spesutia Island, Md.

PRESTON, Prince Hulon, Jr., a Representative from Georgia; born in Monroe, Walton County, Ga., July 5, 1908; attended the public schools of Statesboro, Ga.; was graduated from the law department of the University of Georgia at Athens in 1930; was admitted to the bar the same year and commenced practice in Statesboro, Ga.; member of the State house of representatives 1935–1938; during World War II enlisted in September 1942 as a private in the United States Army; was promoted through the ranks to captain, being discharged October 13, 1945; elected judge of the city court of Statesboro in 1946 but did not serve, having been elected to Congress; elected as a Democrat to the Eightieth and to the six succeeding Congresses (January 3, 1947–January 3, 1961); unsuccessful candidate for renomination in 1960; died in Savannah, Ga., February 8, 1961; interment in Eastside Cemetery, Statesboro, Ga.

PRESTON, William (nephew of Francis Preston), a Representative from Kentucky; born near Louisville, Ky., October 16, 1816; pursued preparatory studies and was graduated from St. Joseph's College, Kentucky; attended Yale College in 1835; was graduated from the law department of Harvard University in 1838; was admitted to the bar and commenced practice in Louisville, Ky., in 1839; served as lieutenant colonel of the Fourth Kentucky Volunteers in the war with Mexico 1846–1848; delegate to the State constitutional convention in 1849; member of the State house of representatives in 1850; served in the State senate 1851–1853; presidential elector on the Whig ticket of Scott and Graham in 1852; elected as a Whig to the Thirty-second Congress to fill the vacancy caused by the resignation of Humphrey Marshall; reelected to the Thirty-third Congress and served from December 6, 1852, to March 3, 1855; unsuccessful candidate for reelection in 1854 to the Thirty-fourth Congress; Envoy Extraordinary and Minister Plenipotentiary to Spain 1858–1861; during the Civil War served in the Confederate Army and attained the rank of major general; appointed Envoy Extraordinary and Minister Plenipotentiary from the Confederacy to Maximilian, Emperor of Mexico, in 1864; again a member of the State house of representatives in 1868 and 1869; died in Louisville, Ky., September 21, 1887; interment in Cave Hill Cemetery.

PRESTON, William Ballard (nephew of Francis Preston), a Representative from Virginia; born in Smithfield, Va., November 25, 1805; was graduated from William and Mary College, Williamsburg, Va., in 1823; studied law and was graduated from the

University of Virginia at Charlottesville; was admitted to the bar and commenced practice in 1826; member of the State house of delegates 1830–1832; served in the State senate 1840–1844; again a member of the State house of delegates in 1844 and 1845; elected as a Whig to the Thirtieth Congress (March 4, 1847–March 3, 1849); appointed Secretary of the Navy in the Cabinet of President Taylor and served from March 8, 1849, to July 22, 1850; delegate to the State constitutional convention in 1861; served in the Confederate States Congress; died in Smithfield, Va., on November 16, 1862; interment probably in the cemetery of the Old Brick Church, near Smithfield, Isle of Wight County, Va.

PRESTON, William Campbell (son of Francis Preston), a Senator from South Carolina; born in Philadelphia, Pa., on December 27, 1794; studied under private tutors; attended Washington College (later Washington and Lee University), Lexington, Va., and was graduated from South Carolina College (later the University of South Carolina) at Columbia in 1812; traveled and studied in Europe for several years; studied law at the University of Edinburgh, Scotland; returned to the United States in 1819; was admitted to the bar in Virginia in 1820 and practiced; moved to Columbia, S. C., in 1822; unsuccessful candidate for election in 1828 to the Twenty-second Congress; member of the State house of representatives 1828–1834; elected as a Calhoun Nullifier to the United States Senate to fill the vacancy caused by the resignation of Stephen D. Miller; reelected in 1837 and served from November 26, 1833, until his resignation on November 29, 1842; resumed the practice of law in Columbia, S. C.; president of South Carolina College from 1845 until 1851, when he resigned on account of ill health; trustee of the same college 1851–1857; founded the Columbia Atheneum; presented his library, containing nearly 3,000 volumes, to the institution and served as president of the board of directors; died in Columbia, S. C., on May 22, 1860; interment in the Trinity Episcopal Churchyard, Columbia, S. C.

PRICE, Andrew, a Representative from Louisiana; born on Chatsworth plantation, near Franklin, St. Mary Parish, La., April 2, 1854; attended various private schools; was graduated from the law department of Cumberland University, Lebanon, Tenn., in 1875 and from the law department of Washington University, St. Louis, Mo., in 1877; was admitted to the bar and practiced in St. Louis until 1880, when he returned to Louisiana and engaged in sugar planting; was a delegate to the Democratic National Convention at St. Louis in 1888 which nominated Cleveland and Thurman; elected as a Democrat to the Fifty-first Congress to fill the vacancy caused by the death of his father-in-law, Hon. Edward J. Gay; reelected to the Fifty-second, Fifty-third, and Fifty-fourth Congresses and served from December 2, 1889, to March 3, 1897; resumed his former pursuits; died at Acadia plantation, Lafourche Parish, La., on February 5, 1909; interment in Mount Olivet Cemetery, Nashville, Davidson County, Tenn.

PRICE, Charles Melvin, a Representative from Illinois; born in East St. Louis, St. Clair County, Ill., January 1, 1905; attended the parochial schools, St. Louis (Mo.) University High School, and St. Louis (Mo.) University; sports editor 1925–1927 and newspaper correspondent 1927–1933; member of the St. Clair County Board of Supervisors 1929–1931; secretary to Congressman Edwin M. Schaefer 1933–1943; enlisted in the United States Army in October 1943 and served in the Quartermaster Corps at Camp Lee, Va., until elected to Congress in 1944; elected as a Democrat to the Seventy-ninth and to the seven succeeding Congresses (January 3, 1945–January 3, 1961). *Reelected to the Eighty-seventh Congress.*

PRICE, Emory Hilliard, a Representative from Florida; born in Bostwick, Putnam County, Fla., December 3, 1899; attended the public schools of Duval County, Fla.; was graduated from Jacksonville (Fla.) Law College in 1936; was admitted to the bar the same year and commenced practice in Jacksonville, Fla.; member of the city council of Jacksonville, Fla., 1929–1932; supervisor of registration of Duval County, Fla., 1932–1942; elected as a Democrat to the Seventy-eighth, Seventy-ninth, and Eightieth Congresses (January 3, 1943–January 3, 1949); unsuccessful candidate for renomination in 1948; resumed the practice of law; is a resident of Jacksonville, Fla.

PRICE, Hiram, a Representative from Iowa; born in Washington County, Pa., January 10, 1814; attended the common schools; was engaged in agricultural pursuits on his father's farm for several years; employed as a bookkeeper for a large commission house near Pittsburgh, Pa., and equipped himself for mercantile life; moved to Davenport, Iowa, in 1844 and engaged in the mercantile business; served as collector, treasurer, and recorder of Scott County, Iowa; was president of the State Bank of Iowa 1859–1866 and became president of the First National Bank of Davenport in 1873; during the early days of the Civil War was appointed by Governor Kirkwood as paymaster general of the Iowa troops, to whom he advanced large sums of money; elected as a Republican to the Thirty-eighth, Thirty-ninth, and Fortieth Congresses (March 4, 1863–March 3, 1869); declined to be a candidate for renomination in 1868; made an extended tour to Europe in 1869; president of the Davenport & St. Paul Railroad Co.; elected to the Forty-fifth and Forty-sixth Congresses (March 4, 1877–March 3, 1881); declined to accept a renomination in 1880; appointed chief clerk for the Indian Office on April 13, 1881; appointed United States Commissioner of Indian Affairs during the administration of President Garfield and served from May 6, 1881, to March 27, 1885; lived in retirement in Washington, D. C., until his death in that city on May 30, 1901; interment in Oakdale Cemetery, Davenport, Iowa.

PRICE, Hugh Hiram (son of William Thompson Price), a Representative from Wisconsin; born at Black River Falls, Jackson County, Wis., December 2, 1859; attended the grade and high schools, and the University of Wisconsin at Madison; engaged in milling and in the lumber business; member of the city council in 1885 and 1886, and of the Jackson County Board of Wisconsin in 1885 and 1886; secretary of the Jackson County Agricultural Society in 1885; elected as a Republican to the Forty-ninth Congress to fill the vacancy caused by the death of his father, William T. Price, and served from January 18 to March 3, 1887; resumed his former business pursuits; member of the State senate of Wisconsin in 1889; moved to Silver City, N. Mex., in 1894 and engaged in silver mining; moved to Phoenix, Ariz., and served as surveyor general of Arizona Territory for two years; owing to ill health moved to Denver, Colo., and lived in retirement until his death on December 25, 1904; interment in Fairmont Cemetery.

PRICE, Jesse Dashiell, a Representative from Maryland; born in Whitehaven, Somerset (later Wicomico) County, Md., August 15, 1863; attended the public schools; engaged in mercantile and manufacturing enterprises and in banking; member of the city council of Salisbury in 1903; treasurer of Wicomico County 1903–1907; member of the State senate 1908–1916 and served as president of the senate and ex officio Lieutenant Governor 1912–1916, when he resigned to enter Congress; elected as a Democrat to the Sixty-third Congress to fill the vacancy caused by the resignation of J. Harry Covington; reelected to the Sixty-fourth and Sixty-fifth Congresses and served from November 3, 1914, to March 3, 1919; unsuccessful candidate for reelection in 1918 to the Sixty-sixth Congress; resumed his former business pursuits; member of the Maryland State tax commission 1923–1935; died at Ocean City, Md., May 14, 1939; interment in Parsons Cemetery, Salisbury, Md.

PRICE, Rodman McCamley, a Representative from New Jersey; born in Newton, Sussex County, N. J., May 5, 1816; attended the public schools of New York City and the Lawrenceville (N. J.) Academy; pursued classical studies in Princeton College, but did not graduate; studied law; was admitted to the bar; appointed purser in the Navy in 1840 and was stationed in San Francisco; during the Mexican War served as an officer of the Navy on the steam frigates *Fulton* and *Missouri* and on the sloop of war *Cyane* with Commodore Sloat's squadron on the west coast of Mexico; prefect and alcalde of Monterey in 1846 and the first American to exercise judicial functions in California; naval agent 1848–1850; delegate to the first constitutional convention of California; returned to New Jersey; elected as a Democrat to the Thirty-second Congress (March 4, 1851–March 3, 1853); unsuccessful candidate for reelection in 1852 to the Thirty-third Congress; Governor of New Jersey 1854–1857; father of the public-school system of New Jersey; established a ferry from Weehawken to New York; engaged in the quarrying business and in the reclamation of lands along the Hackensack River; delegate to the peace convention held at Washington, D. C., in 1861 in an effort to devise means to prevent the impending war; died in Oakland, Bergen County, N. J., June 7, 1894; interment in Reformed Cemetery, Mahwah, N. J.

PRICE, Samuel, a Senator from West Virginia; born in Fauquier County, Va., July 28, 1805; moved with his parents to Preston County in 1815; received a preparatory training; studied law; was admitted to the bar in 1832 and commenced the practice of his profession in Nicholas and Braxton Counties; county clerk of Nicholas County in 1830; prosecuting attorney in 1833; member of the State house of delegates 1834–1836; moved to Wheeling, Va. (now West Virginia), in 1836 and to Lewisburg, Greenbrier County, in 1838; prosecuting attorney for Braxton County 1836–1850; again a member of the State house of delegates 1847–1850 and in 1852; delegate to the constitutional conventions in 1850, 1851, and 1861; elected Lieutenant Governor of Virginia in 1863 and served until the close of the Civil War; delegate to the constitutional convention of West Virginia in 1872 and was its president; appointed to the United States Senate to fill the vacancy caused by the death of Allen T. Caperton and served from August 26, 1876, to January 26, 1877, when a successor was elected; unsuccessful candidate in 1876 for election to fill the vacancy; died in Lewisburg, Greenbrier County, W. Va., on February 25, 1884; interment in the Stuart Burying Ground at Stuart Manor, near Lewisburg, W. Va.

PRICE, Sterling, a Representative from Missouri; was born near Farmville, Prince Edward County, Va., on September 20, 1809; completed preparatory studies and attended Hampden-Sidney College, Virginia; studied law; was admitted to the bar and practiced; moved to Fayette and later to Keytesville, Mo.; member of the State house of representatives 1840–1844 and served as speaker; elected as a Democrat to the Twenty-ninth Congress and served from March 4, 1845, to August 12, 1846, when he resigned to participate in the Mexican War; appointed colonel of the Second Regiment, Missouri Infantry, August 12, 1846; promoted to brigadier general of Volunteers July 20, 1847, and was honorably discharged November 25, 1848; returned to Missouri and engaged in agricultural pursuits on the Bowling Green prairie; Governor of Missouri 1853–1857; State bank commissioner 1857–1861; during the Civil War served in the Confederate Army as a major general and took part in many

engagements; after the war went to Mexico but later returned to Missouri; died in St. Louis, Mo., September 29, 1867; interment in Bellefontaine Cemetery.

PRICE, Thomas Lawson, a Representative from Missouri; born near Danville, Va., on January 19, 1809; attended the country schools; moved to Missouri in 1831 and settled in Jefferson City; conducted stage lines and engaged in manufacturing and mercantile pursuits; first mayor of Jefferson City 1839–1842; unsuccessful candidate for the State senate in 1845; commissioned brevet major general of the Sixth Division of Missouri Militia in 1847; elected Lieutenant Governor in 1849; member of the State house of representatives 1860–1862; was one of the incorporators of the Capital City Bank and president of the Jefferson Land Co.; actively engaged in the promotion of various railway lines; brigadier general of Volunteers in 1861 and 1862; elected as a Democrat to the Thirty-seventh Congress to fill the vacancy caused by the expulsion of John W. Reid and served from January 21, 1862, to March 3, 1863; unsuccessful candidate for reelection in 1862 to the Thirty-eighth Congress; delegate to the Democratic National Convention at Chicago in 1864 and at New York City in 1868; died in Jefferson City, Mo., July 15, 1870; interment in a private cemetery; reinterment in Riverview Cemetery, Jefferson City, Mo., in 1912.

PRICE, William Pierce, a Representative from Georgia; born in Dahlonega, Lumpkin County, Ga., January 29, 1835; attended the common schools; was apprenticed to the printer's trade; moved to Greenville, S. C., in 1851; attended Furman University, Greenville, S. C., but left before graduating to take charge of the editorial department of the Southern Enterprise, a Greenville newspaper; studied law; was admitted to the bar in 1856 and commenced practice in Greenville, S. C.; during the Civil War served in the Confederate Army as orderly sergeant in Kershaw's Second South Carolina Regiment; was in the Battle of Bull Run, and was wounded at Lewinsville, Va.; served on the staff of General Preston until the close of the war; member of the South Carolina House of Representatives 1864–1866; moved to Dahlonega, Ga., in 1866; member of the Georgia House of Representatives 1868–1870; elected as a Democrat to the Forty-first Congress to fill the vacancy caused by failure to elect; reelected to the Forty-second Congress and served from December 22, 1870, to March 3, 1873; was not a candidate for renomination in 1872; again a member of the State house of representatives 1877–1879, of the State senate in 1880 and 1881, and of the State house of representatives in 1894 and 1895; delegate to the Democratic National Convention at Cincinnati in 1880; resumed the practice of law; president of the board of trustees of North Georgia Agricultural College 1870–1908; died in Dahlonega, Ga., November 4, 1908; interment in Hill Crest Cemetery.

PRICE, William Thompson (father of Hugh Hiram Price), a Representative from Wisconsin; born in Huntingdon County, Pa., June 17, 1824; attended the common schools; was a clerk in a store in Hollidaysburg, Pa., and also studied law; moved to Mount Pleasant, Iowa, in 1845, and in the following autumn moved to Black River Falls, Wis.; engaged in lumbering and agricultural pursuits; deputy sheriff of Crawford County in 1849; member of the Wisconsin State assembly in 1851 and again in 1882; was admitted to the bar in 1852 and engaged in the practice of law; in 1854 moved to La Crosse, Wis., and operated a stage line between La Crosse and Black River Falls; moved to Black River Falls and continued the practice of law until 1857; judge of Jackson County in 1854 and 1859; under sheriff of Crawford County in 1855; county treasurer in 1856 and 1857; served in the State senate in 1857, 1870, and 1878–1881, and was president of the Senate in 1879; collector of internal revenue 1863–1865; presidential elector on the Republican ticket of Grant and Colfax in 1868; elected as a Republican to the Forty-eighth and Forty-ninth Congresses and served from March 4, 1883, until his death at Black River Falls, Jackson County, Wis., December 6, 1886; interment in Riverside Cemetery.

PRIDEMORE, Auburn Lorenzo, a Representative from Virginia; born in Scott County, Va., June 27, 1837; received a limited education; completed preparatory studies; during the Civil War raised a company of volunteer infantry for the Confederate Army and served as its captain until June 1862; promoted to major, lieutenant colonel of Infantry, and to colonel of Cavalry; commanded the Sixty-fourth Virginia Cavalry until the close of the war; was elected a member of the State house of delegates in 1865 but the war prevented him from taking his seat; studied law; was admitted to the bar in 1867 and commenced practice in Jonesville; member of the State senate 1871–1875; elected as a Democrat to the Forty-fifth Congress (March 4, 1877–March 3, 1879); continued the practice of law in Jonesville, Lee County, Va., until his death there on May 17, 1900; interment in Hill Cemetery.

PRIEST, James Percy, a Representative from Tennessee; born in Carters Creek, Maury County, Tenn., April 1, 1900; attended the public schools of Maury County, Tenn., Central High School, Columbia, Tenn., State Teachers' College, Murfreesboro, Tenn., George Peabody College for Teachers, Nashville, Tenn., and the University of Tennessee at Knoxville; taught school in Culleoka, Tenn., 1920–1926; member of the editorial staff of the Nashville Tennessean 1926–1940; elected as a Democrat to the Seventy-seventh and to the seven succeeding Congresses and had been renominated in the 1956 primary election; served from January 3, 1941, until his death in Nashville, Tenn., October 12, 1956; interment in Woodlawn Memorial Park.

PRINCE, Charles Henry, a Representative from Georgia; born in Buckfield, Oxford County, Maine, May 9, 1837; attended local schools; engaged in mercantile pursuits; appointed postmaster in 1861; during the Civil War was captain of Company C, Twenty-third Regiment, Maine Volunteer Infantry, from September 10, 1862, to July 15, 1863; settled in Augusta, Ga., in 1866 and was cashier of a bank; State superintendent of education; delegate to the State constitutional convention; upon the readmission of Georgia to representation was elected as a Republican to the Fortieth Congress and served from July 25, 1868, to March 3, 1869; presented credentials as a Member-elect to the Forty-first Congress but was not permitted to qualify; postmaster of Augusta 1870–1882; delegate to the Republican National Conventions in 1872, 1876, and 1880; returned to Buckfield, Oxford County, Maine, in 1882 and engaged in mercantile pursuits; also engaged in the insurance business and in the manufacture of brushes; member of the Maine State Senate in 1901; died in Buckfield, Maine, April 3, 1912; interment in Buckfield Village Cemetery.

PRINCE, George Washington, a Representative from Illinois; born in Tazewell County, Ill., March 4, 1854; attended the public schools; was graduated from Knox College, Galesburg, Ill., in 1878; studied law; was admitted to the bar in 1880 and commenced practice in Galesburg, Knox County, Ill.; city attorney of Galesburg 1881–1883; chairman of the Republican county central committee of Knox County in 1884; member of the State house of representatives in 1888; reelected in 1890; unsuccessful candidate for attorney general of Illinois on the Republican ticket in 1892; elected as a Republican to the Fifty-fourth Congress to fill the vacancy caused by the death of Philip Sidney Post; reelected to the Fifty-fifth and to the seven succeeding Congresses

and served from December 2, 1895, to March 3, 1913; unsuccessful candidate for reelection in 1912 to the Sixty-third Congress; moved to Los Angeles, Calif., in 1913 and continued the practice of law; retired from active business pursuits in 1917 and resided in Los Angeles, Calif., until his death in that city on September 26, 1939; interment in Inglewood Park Cemetery, Inglewood, Calif.

PRINCE, Oliver Hillhouse, a Senator from Georgia; born in Montville, Conn., in 1787; completed preparatory studies; moved to Georgia in 1796 with his parents, who settled in Washington, Wilkes County; engaged in newspaper work, studying law at the same time; was admitted to the bar in 1806 and commenced practice in Macon, Ga.; one of the five commissioners who laid out the town of Macon in 1824; member of the State senate in 1824; elected to the United States Senate to fill the vacancy caused by the resignation of Thomas W. Cobb and served from November 7, 1828, to March 3, 1829; returned to Macon, Ga.; author and editor; presided over the first railroad convention in Georgia and was one of the first stockholders and directors of the Georgia Railroad Co.; abandoned the practice of law to become editor of the Georgia Journal in 1830; retired to Athens, Ga., in 1835; perished in the wreck of the packet ship *Home* near Ocracoke Inlet, N. C., October 9, 1837, and the remains were never recovered.

PRINCE, William, a Representative from Indiana; born in Ireland in 1772; immigrated to the United States and settled in Indiana; studied law; served in the State senate in 1816; delegate to the State constitutional convention in 1816; served as captain in the Battle of Tippecanoe; member of the State house of representatives in 1821 and 1822; was elected to the Eighteenth Congress and served from March 4, 1823, until his death near Princeton, Gibson County, Ind., September 8, 1824; interment in the Old Cemetery, near Princeton, Ind.

PRINDLE, Elizur H., a Representative from New York; born in Newtown, Conn., May 6, 1829; completed preparatory studies; attended the local academy at Homer, N. Y.; studied law; was admitted to the bar in 1854 and practiced; moved to New York and practiced law in Norwich, Chenango County; was district attorney of Chenango County, N. Y., 1859–1863; member of the State assembly in 1863; member of the State constitutional convention in 1867 and 1868; elected as a Republican to the Forty-second Congress (March 4, 1871–March 3, 1873); resumed the practice of law; died in Norwich, Chenango County, N. Y., October 7, 1890; interment in Mount Hope Cemetery.

PRINGEY, Joseph Colburn, a Representative from Oklahoma; born in Somerset, Somerset County, Pa., May 22, 1858; attended the common schools; moved to Missouri in 1870; attended a business college in Sedalia, Mo.; moved to Chandler, Lincoln County, Okla., in 1891; engaged in agricultural pursuits and in the loan and insurance business; member of the Territorial senate in 1893; member of the board of regents of the University of Oklahoma at Norman in 1893 and 1894; delegate to the Republican National Convention at Philadelphia in 1900 which nominated McKinley and Roosevelt; county clerk of Lincoln County, Okla., 1912–1920; elected as a Republican to the Sixty-seventh Congress (March 4, 1921–March 3, 1923); unsuccessful candidate for reelection in 1922 to the Sixty-eighth Congress; acting postmaster of Chandler, Okla., in 1923 and 1924; resumed agricultural pursuits; died in Chandler, Okla., on February 11, 1935; interment in Oak Park Cemetery.

PRINGLE, Benjamin, a Representative from New York; born in Richfield Springs, Otsego County, N. Y., November 9,

1807; completed preparatory studies; studied law; was admitted to the bar in 1830 and practiced for a number of years; president of a bank in Batavia, Genesee County, N. Y.; judge of the Genesee County Court 1841–1846; elected as a Whig to the Thirty-third and Thirty-fourth Congresses (March 4, 1853–March 3, 1857); unsuccessful candidate for reelection in 1856 to the Thirty-fifth Congress; member of the State assembly in 1863; appointed by President Lincoln in 1863 judge of the court of arbitration in Cape Town, Africa, under the treaty with Great Britain of April 7, 1862, for the suppression of the African slave trade; appointed a member of the board of trustees of the State Institution for the Blind in 1873; died in Hastings, Dakota County, Minn., June 7, 1887; interment in the Old Cemetery, Batavia, N. Y.

PRITCHARD, George Moore (son of Jeter Connelly Pritchard), a Representative from North Carolina; born near Mars Hill in Madison County, N. C., January 4, 1886; attended the public schools of Marshall, N. C., and Washington, D. C., Emerson Institute, Washington, D. C., the University of North Carolina at Chapel Hill, and the law department of the University of South Carolina at Columbia; was admitted to the bar in 1908 and commenced practice in Greenville, S. C.; moved to Marshall, N. C., in 1910 and continued the practice of law; member of the North Carolina State House of Representatives in 1916 and 1917; elected trustee of the University of North Carolina in 1917; solicitor of the nineteenth judicial district 1919–1922; moved to Asheville, N. C., in 1919 and continued the practice of law; chairman of the Buncombe County Republican committee in 1928; elected as a Republican to the Seventy-first Congress (March 4, 1929–March 3, 1931); was not a candidate for renomination to the Seventy-second Congress, but was an unsuccessful candidate for election to the United States Senate in 1930; resumed the practice of law in Asheville and Marshall, N. C.; delegate to the Republican National Convention at Chicago in 1932; served one term as a member of the board of trustees of the University of North Carolina; was an unsuccessful candidate for Governor of North Carolina in 1948; died in Asheville, N. C., April 24, 1955; interment in Pritchard Cemetery, Marshall, N. C.

PRITCHARD, Jeter Connelly (father of George Moore Pritchard), a Senator from North Carolina; born in Jonesboro, Washington County, Tenn., July 12, 1857; attended Martins Creek Academy; apprenticed to the printer's trade in the Jonesboro Tribune-Herald office; moved to Bakersville, Mitchell County, N. C., in 1873; joint editor and owner of the Roan Mountain Republican until 1887, when he moved to Marshall, Madison County; presidential elector on the Republican ticket of Garfield and Arthur in 1880; member of the State house of representatives in 1884, 1886, and 1890; studied law; was admitted to the bar in 1887 and commenced practice in Marshall, N. C.; unsuccessful candidate for Lieutenant Governor in 1888; Republican caucus nominee for United States Senator in 1892; delegate to the Republican National Convention at Minneapolis in 1892 which nominated Benjamin Harrison for President; president of the North Carolina Protective Tariff League in 1891; unsuccessful candidate for election in 1892 to the Fifty-third Congress; elected as a Republican to the United States Senate to fill the vacancy caused by the death of Zebulon B. Vance; reelected in 1897 and served from January 23, 1895, to March 3, 1903; justice of the supreme court of the District of Columbia from March 30, 1903, to June 1, 1904; appointed judge of the United States Circuit Court of Appeals, Fourth Judicial Circuit, and served from June 1, 1904, until his death in Asheville, N. C., on April 10, 1921; interment in Riverside Cemetery.

PROCTOR, Redfield, a Senator from Vermont; born in Proctorsville, Windsor County, Vt., June 1, 1831; was graduated from Dartmouth College, Hanover, N. H., in 1851 and from the Albany Law School in 1859; was admitted to the bar and practiced in Boston, Mass., in 1860 and 1861; during the Civil War enlisted in the Third Regiment, Vermont Volunteers, in 1861; was appointed quartermaster, with the rank of lieutenant; served on the staff of Gen. William F. Smith as brigade and division quartermaster; promoted major in the Fifth Regiment and colonel of the Fifteenth; was mustered out in 1863; returned to Vermont, engaged in the practice of law, and became interested in the development of the marble industry; member of the State house of representatives in 1867 and 1868; served in the State senate and as president pro tempore in 1874 and 1875; Lieutenant Governor of the State 1876–1878; Governor of Vermont 1878–1880; delegate to the Republican National Conventions in 1884, 1888, and 1896; again a member of the State house of representatives in 1888; appointed Secretary of War in the Cabinet of President Harrison in March 1889; resigned from the Cabinet in November 1891 to become Senator; appointed in 1891 and subsequently elected as a Republican to the United States Senate to fill the vacancy caused by the resignation of George F. Edmunds; reelected in 1892, 1898, and 1904 and served from November 2, 1891, until his death in Washington, D. C., on March 4, 1908; interment in the City Cemetery, Proctor, Rutland County, Vt.

PROFFIT, George H., a Representative from Indiana; born in New Orleans, La., September 7, 1807; completed preparatory studies; moved to Petersburg, Pike County, Ind., in 1828; engaged in mercantile pursuits in Petersburg and Portersville, Ind.; studied law; was admitted to the bar and commenced practice in Petersburg, Ind.; member of the State house of representatives in 1831, 1832, and 1836–1838; elected as a Whig to the Twenty-sixth and Twenty-seventh Congresses (March 4, 1839–March 3, 1843); was not a candidate for renomination in 1842; appointed by President Tyler as Envoy Extraordinary and Minister Plenipotentiary to Brazil and served from June 7, 1843, to August 10, 1844, when he returned home, the Senate having refused to confirm his appointment; died in Louisville, Ky., September 7, 1847; interment in Walnut Hills Cemetery, Petersburg, Ind.

PROKOP, Stanley A., a Representative from Pennsylvania; born in Throop, Lackawanna County, Pa.; graduated from Villanova (Pa.) University; elected as a Democrat to the Eighty-sixth Congress (January 3, 1959–January 3, 1961); unsuccessful candidate for reelection in 1960 to the Eighty-seventh Congress; is a resident of Lake Ariel, Pa.

PROSSER, William Farrand, a Representative from Tennessee; born in Williamsport, Lycoming County, Pa., on March 16, 1834; received a limited schooling; taught school; studied law but never practiced; moved to California in 1854; engaged in mining; returned to Pennsylvania in 1861; during the Civil War entered the Union Army November 30, 1861, as quartermaster sergeant of Captain Palmer's independent company, Pennsylvania Cavalry (Anderson troop); quartermaster sergeant of the Fifteenth Regiment, Pennsylvania Cavalry, and promoted to acting first lieutenant; transferred to the Second Regiment, Tennessee Cavalry, and served as adjutant during its organization; commissioned major in March 1863, lieutenant colonel in March 1864, and colonel in June 1865; after the war settled on a farm near Nashville, Tenn.; elected to the State house of representatives in 1867 and served as speaker pro tempore in 1869; elected as a Republican to the Forty-first Congress (March 4, 1869–March 3, 1871); unsuccessful candidate for reelection in 1870 to the Forty-second Congress; postmaster of Nashville

1872–1875; a director of the Tennessee, Edgefield & Kentucky Railroad; appointed in 1872 as one of the State commissioners to the Centennial Exposition at Philadelphia in 1876 and sent on a special mission in 1873 to vist the Vienna Congress and assist in arranging participation of European countries in the exposition at Philadelphia; published the Nashville Republican for several years; appointed by President Hayes in 1879 as special agent of the Interior Department for Oregon, Washington, and Idaho and moved to Washington in the same year; delegate to the first State constitutional convention of Washington; chairman of the State harbor line commission; mayor of North Yakima; city treasurer of Seattle 1908–1910; died in Seattle, Wash., September 23, 1911; interment in Lakeview Cemetery.

PROUTY, Solomon Francis, a Representative from Iowa; born in Delaware, Ohio, January 17, 1854; moved with his father to Marion County, Iowa, in 1855; attended the public schools, Central University, Pella, Iowa, 1870–1873, Simpson College, Indianola, Iowa, 1873–1875, and was graduated from Central University in 1877; professor at Central University 1878–1882; member of the State house of representatives in 1880 and 1881; studied law; was admitted to the bar in 1882 and commenced practice in Pella, Marion County, Iowa; moved to Des Moines, Iowa, in 1891 and engaged in the practice of law; judge of the district court in 1899; unsuccessful candidate for election to Congress in 1902, 1904, and 1908; elected as a Republican to the Sixty-second and Sixty-third Congresses (March 4, 1911–March 3, 1915); was not a candidate for renomination in 1914; resumed the practice of his profession; trustee of the Central University of Iowa; retired in 1923; died in Des Moines, Polk County, Iowa, July 16, 1927; interment in Glendale Cemetery.

PROUTY, Winston Lewis, a Representative and a Senator from Vermont; born in Newport, Orleans County, Vt., September 1, 1906; attended the public schools of Newport, Bordentown (N. J.) Military Institute, and Lafayette College, Easton, Pa.; mayor of Newport 1938–1941; member of the State house of representatives in 1941, 1945, and 1947, serving as speaker in 1947; chairman of Vermont State Water Conservation Board 1948–1950; officer and director of family-owned lumber and building material enterprises; director of the National Bank of Newport; elected as a Republican to the Eighty-second and to the three succeeding Congresses (January 3, 1951–January 3, 1959); was not a candidate for renomination in 1958; elected to the United States Senate in 1958 for the term commencing January 3, 1959, and ending January 3, 1965.

PROXMIRE, William, a Senator from Wisconsin; born in Lake Forest, Lake County, Ill., November 11, 1915; attended the public schools of Lake Forest, Ill., and the Hill School, Pottstown, Pa.; graduated from Yale University in 1938, from Harvard Business School in 1940, and from Harvard Graduate School of Arts and Sciences in 1948; during World War II served in the Military Intelligence Service 1941–1946, retiring with rank of first lieutenant; member of the State assembly in 1951 and 1952; worked for J. P. Morgan & Co., New York, N. Y., in 1940 and 1941; unsuccessful Democratic candidate for Governor of Wisconsin in 1952, 1954, and 1956; president of Artcraft Press, Waterloo, Wis., 1954–1957; delegate to the Democratic National Conventions in 1956 and 1960; elected as a Democrat to the United States Senate to fill the vacancy caused by the death of Joseph R. McCarthy and served from August 28, 1957, to January 3, 1959; reelected in 1958 for the term ending January 3, 1965.

PRUYN, John Van Schaick Lansing, a Representative from New York; born in Albany, N. Y., June 22, 1811; pursued classical studies and was graduated from the Albany Academy in 1826; studied law; was admitted to the bar and commenced practice in Albany in 1832; held several local offices; appointed a regent of the University of the State of New York in 1844; unsuccessful candidate for election to the Thirty-fourth Congress in 1854; member of the State senate in 1861; elected as a Democrat to the Thirty-eighth Congress to fill the vacancy caused by the resignation of Erastus Corning and served from December 7, 1863, to March 3, 1865; elected to the Fortieth Congress (March 4, 1867–March 3, 1869); was not a candidate for renomination in 1864 and 1868; resumed the practice of law at Albany, N. Y.; chancellor of the University of the State of New York from 1868 until his death in Clifton Springs, Ontario County, N. Y., November 21, 1877; interment in Albany Rural Cemetery, Albany, N. Y.

PRYOR, Luke, a Senator and a Representative from Alabama; born in Huntsville, Madison County, Ala., July 5, 1820; moved with his parents to Limestone County in 1824; pursued academic studies; studied law; was admitted to the bar in 1841 and commenced practice in Athens, Ala.; also engaged in agricultural pursuits; member of the State house of representatives in 1855 and 1856; appointed to the United States Senate to fill the vacancy caused by the death of George S. Houston and served from January 7 to November 23, 1880, when a successor was elected; elected as a Democrat to the Forty-eighth Congress (March 4, 1883–March 3, 1885); declined to be a candidate for reelection in 1884; retired to his farm near Athens, Ala., where he died August 5, 1900; interment in the City Cemetery.

PRYOR, Roger Atkinson, a Representative from Virginia; born near Petersburg, Dinwiddie County, Va., July 19, 1828; was graduated from Hampden-Sidney College, Virginia, in 1845 and from the University of Virginia at Charlottesville in 1848; studied law; was admitted to the bar in 1849 and practiced a short time in Petersburg, but abandoned law on account of ill health; engaged on the editorial staff of the Washington Union in 1852 and the Richmond Enquirer in 1854; appointed special United States Minister to Greece in 1854; returned and established The South in 1857; associated himself with the staff of the Washington States; elected as a Democrat to the Thirty-sixth Congress to fill the vacancy caused by the death of William O. Goode and served from December 7, 1859, to March 3, 1861; during the Civil War served in the Confederate Army as a colonel in 1861 and brigadier general in 1863; later resigned his commission and reenlisted as a private soldier; member of the Virginia Confederate House of Representatives; captured by the Union troops in November 1864 and confined in Fort Lafayette, but soon afterward was released; moved to New York City and practiced law 1866–1890; delegate to the Democratic National Convention at St. Louis in 1876; judge of the court of common pleas of New York 1890–1894; justice of the New York Supreme Court 1894–1899; retired upon reaching the age limit; appointed official referee by the appellate division of the supreme court April 10, 1912, and served until his death in New York City March 14, 1919; interment in Princeton Cemetery, Princeton, N. J.

PUCINSKI, Roman Conrad, a Representative from Illinois; born in Buffalo, Erie County, N. Y., May 13, 1919; attended the public schools in Chicago, Ill., Northwestern University 1938–1941, and John Marshall Law School 1945–1949; staff reporter and writer for the Chicago Sun-Times 1939–1959; on November 1, 1940, enlisted as a private in the One Hundred and Sixth Cavalry; served with the Twentieth Global (Superfort) Air Force; led his bomber group on the first B–29 bombing raid over Tokyo in 1944; flew forty-eight missions over Japan; separated from the service as a captain on December 1, 1945; awarded the Distinguished Flying Cross and Air Medal with

Clusters; served as chief investigator for a select committee of Congress investigating the mass murder by the Communists of fifteen thousand Polish army officers in World War II; elected as a Democrat to the Eighty-sixth Congress (January 3, 1959– January 3, 1961). *Reelected to the Eighty-seventh Congress.*

PUGH, George Ellis, a Senator from Ohio; born in Cincinnati, Ohio, November 28, 1822; attended private schools; was graduated from Miami University at Oxford, Ohio, in 1840; studied law; was admitted to the bar in 1843 and commenced practice the same year in Cincinnati, Ohio; served in the Mexican War as captain of the Fourth Regiment, Ohio Volunteer Infantry; returned to Cincinnati and resumed the practice of law; member of the State house of representatives 1848–1850; city solicitor in 1850; State attorney general 1852–1854; elected as a Democrat to the United States Senate and served from March 4, 1855, to March 3, 1861; unsuccessful candidate for reelection; resumed the practice of law in Cincinnati; delegate to the Democratic National Convention at Baltimore in 1860; unsuccessful Democratic candidate for election in 1863 as Lieutenant Governor and for election in 1864 to the Thirty-ninth Congress; delegate to the State constitutional convention in 1873 but withdrew from its deliberations; retired from public life; died in Cincinnati, Ohio, July 19, 1876; interment in Spring Grove Cemetery.

PUGH, James Lawrence, a Representative and a Senator from Alabama; born in Burke County, Ga., December 12, 1820; moved with his parents to Alabama in 1824; pursued an academic course in Alabama and Georgia; studied law; was admitted to the bar in 1841 and commenced practice in Eufaula, Ala.; also engaged in agricultural pursuits; Democratic presidential elector in 1848, 1856, and 1876; elected to the Thirty-sixth Congress and served from March 4, 1859, to January 21, 1861, when he withdrew; during the Civil War joined the Eufaula Rifles, First Alabama Regiment, as a private; elected to the Confederate Congress in 1861 and reelected in 1863; after the war resumed the practice of law; president of the Democratic State convention in 1874; member of the convention that framed the State constitution in 1875; presidential elector on the Democratic ticket of Tilden and Hendricks in 1876; elected as a Democrat to the United States Senate to fill the vacancy caused by the death of George S. Houston; reelected, and served from November 24, 1880, to March 3, 1897; was not a candidate for reelection; retired from active business and resided in Washington, D. C., until his death there on March 9, 1907; interment in the Fairview Cemetery, Eufaula, Barbour County, Ala.

PUGH, John, a Representative from Pennsylvania; born in Hilltown Township, Bucks County, Pa., June 2, 1761; attended the common schools; served in the Revolutionary Army as a private, ensign, and captain; engaged in agricultural and mercantile pursuits; justice of the peace; member of the State house of representatives 1800–1804; elected as a Democrat to the Ninth and Tenth Congresses (March 4, 1805–March 3, 1809); unsuccessful candidate for reelection in 1808 to the Eleventh Congress; register of wills and recorder of deeds of Bucks County 1810–1821; retired from public life; died in Doylestown, Bucks County, Pa., on July 13, 1842; interment in the Presbyterian Churchyard.

PUGH, John Howard, a Representative from New Jersey; born in Unionville, Chester County, Pa., June 23, 1827; attended the common schools and the Friends' School, Westtown, Pa.; taught school in Marietta, Pa., in 1847; was graduated from the medical department of the University of Pennsylvania

at Philadelphia in 1852; began the practice of his profession in Bristol, Pa., in 1852; moved to Burlington, Burlington County, N. J., in 1854 and continued the practice of medicine; during the Civil War served as a physician without compensation at the United States general hospital in Beverly, N. J.; president of the Mechanics' National Bank of Burlington for thirty-six years; elected as a Republican to the Forty-fifth Congress (March 4, 1877–March 3, 1879); unsuccessful candidate for reelection in 1878 to the Forty-sixth Congress; resumed the practice of medicine; member of the State board of education; served as president of the Burlington Library Association; died in Burlington, N. J., April 30, 1905; interment in St. Mary's Churchyard.

PUGH, Samuel Johnson, a Representative from Kentucky; born in Greenup County, Ky., January 28, 1850; moved with his parents to Lewis County in 1852; attended Chandler's Select School, Rand's Academy, and Centre College, Danville, Ky.; studied law; was admitted to the bar and commenced practice in Vanceburg, Lewis County, Ky.; city attorney in 1872 and 1873; master commissioner of the circuit court 1874– 1880; county attorney 1878–1886; county judge 1886–1890; delegate to the State constitutional convention in 1890 and 1891; member of the State senate in 1893 and 1894; elected as a Republican to the Fifty-fourth, Fifty-fifth, and Fifty-sixth Congresses (March 4, 1895–March 3, 1901); resumed the practice of law in Vanceburg, Ky., and died there April 17, 1922; interment in Greenlawn Cemetery.

PUGSLEY, Cornelius Amory, a Representative from New York; born in Peekskill, Westchester County, N. Y., July 17, 1850; attended the public schools and was instructed in higher education by a private tutor; clerk and assistant postmaster 1867–1870; engaged in the banking business in 1870; member of the chamber of commerce, New York City; president of the board of trustees of the Field Library at Peekskill; president of the board of trustees of the Peekskill Military Academy; elected as a Democrat to the Fifty-seventh Congress (March 4, 1901– March 3, 1903); unsuccessful candidate for reelection in 1902 to the Fifty-eighth Congress; resumed banking in Peekskill; president general of the Sons of the American Revolution in 1906 and 1907; president of the American Flag Association; delegate to the National Democratic Convention at Denver in 1908; president of the New York State Bankers' Association in 1913; president of the Westchester County National Bank, Peekskill, N. Y.; member of the Westchester County Park Commission; died in Peekskill, N. Y., on September 10, 1936; interment in Raymond Hill Cemetery, Carmel, N. Y.

PUGSLEY, Jacob Joseph, a Representative from Ohio; born in Dutchess County, N. Y., January 25, 1838; moved to Ohio with his parents in 1839; was graduated from Miami University, Oxford, Ohio; studied law; was admitted to the bar and commenced practice in Dayton, Ohio; moved to Hillsboro and continued the practice of law; member of the State house of representatives 1880–1883; served in the State senate in 1886 and 1887; elected as a Republican to the Fiftieth and Fifty-first Congresses (March 4, 1887–March 3, 1891); was not a candidate for renomination in 1890; trustee of the Boys' Industrial School, Lancaster, Ohio, for fifteen years; retired from public life and resided in Hillsboro, Highland County, Ohio, where he died February 5, 1920; interment in Hillsboro Cemetery.

PUJO, Arsène Paulin, a Representative from Louisiana; born near Lake Charles, Calcasieu Parish, La., December 16, 1861; attended public and private schools; studied law; was admitted to the bar in 1886 and commenced practice in Lake Charles,

La.; delegate to the State constitutional convention in 1898; elected as a Democrat to the Fifty-eighth and to the four succeeding Congresses (March 4, 1903–March 3, 1913); was not a candidate for renomination in 1912; resumed the practice of law in Lake Charles, La.; during the First World War served as chairman of the district board for the western district of Louisiana under the selective service act of 1917; died in New Orleans, La., December 31, 1939, while on a visit for medical treatment; interment in Orange Grove Cemetery, Lake Charles, La.

PULITZER, Joseph, a Representative from New York; born in Makdo, near Budapest, Hungary, April 10, 1847; received his early training from a private tutor; immigrated to the United States in 1864; during the Civil War enlisted as a private in the Union Army at the age of seventeen in the First Regiment, New York (Lincoln) Cavalry, in Kingston, N. Y., September 30, 1864; mustered out in Alexandria, Va., June 5, 1865; resumed civil life in St. Louis, Mo.; studied law and was admitted to practice by the supreme court of Missouri; entered journalism in 1867 as a reporter on the St. Louis Westliche Post and became managing editor and part proprietor; elected to the Missouri Legislature in 1869; delegate to the Reform Republican Convention at Cincinnati in 1872 that nominated Horace Greeley for the Presidency; member of the State constitutional convention in 1874; founded the St. Louis Post-Dispatch December 10, 1878, by purchasing the Dispatch and uniting it with the Evening Post, and continued to own and publish it until his death; delegate to the Democratic National Convention at Cincinnati in 1880 which nominated Hancock and English; moved to New York City in the spring of 1883 and bought the New York World; elected as a Democrat to the Forty-ninth Congress and served from March 4, 1885, until April 10, 1886, when he resigned; died aboard his yacht in the harbor of Charleston, S. C., October 29, 1911; interment in Woodlawn Cemetery, New York City.

PURCELL, William Edward, a Senator from North Dakota; born in Flemington, Hunterdon County, N. J., August 3, 1856; attended the common schools; studied law; was admitted to the bar of New Jersey in 1880 and commenced practice in Flemington, N. J.; moved to Wahpeton, Territory of Dakota, in 1881 and continued the practice of law; was appointed by President Cleveland as United States attorney for the Territory of Dakota, April 5, 1888; resigned in May 1889, having been elected a member of the constitutional convention for the new State of North Dakota; was a member of the joint committee appointed by the constitutional convention of North Dakota to divide the property and adjust the indebtedness between the States of North Dakota and South Dakota; district attorney of Richland County, N. Dak., from October 1889 to January 1, 1891; member of the State senate 1907–1909; appointed as a Democrat to the United States Senate to fill the vacancy caused by the death of Martin N. Johnson and the resignation of Fountain L. Thompson and served from February 1, 1910, to February 1, 1911, when a successor was elected and qualified; unsuccessful candidate for reelection; continued the practice of law until his death; delegate to the Democratic National Conventions in 1912 and 1916; appointed chairman of the Food Conservation Commission in 1917; died in Wahpeton, Richland County, N. Dak., November 23, 1928; interment in Calvary Cemetery.

PURDY, Smith Meade, a Representative from New York; born in North Norwich, Chenango County, N. Y., July 31, 1796; attended the common schools; studied law; was admitted to the bar and commenced practice at Sherburne, N. Y., in 1819; moved to Norwich, N. Y., in 1827 and continued the practice of law; appointed judge of the court of common pleas and surrogate of Chenango County in 1833 and served until his resignation in 1837; elected as a Democrat to the Twenty-eighth Congress (March 4, 1843–March 3, 1845); was not a candidate for renomination in 1844; declined the appointment of Attorney General in the Cabinet of President Polk in 1844; resumed the practice of law; elected judge and surrogate of Chenango County in 1847 and served until 1851; declined a renomination owing to poor health and retired from active pursuits; died in Norwich, N. Y., March 30, 1870; interment in Mount Hope Cemetery.

PURMAN, William James, a Representative from Florida; born in Millheim, Centre County, Pa., April 11, 1840; attended the common schools and completed his studies at Aaronsburg Academy, Centre County, Pa.; taught school; studied law at Lock Haven, Pa.; during the Civil War entered the Union Army as a private and served on special duty at the War Department until transferred to Florida in 1865; was admitted to the bar in 1868 and commenced practice in Tallahassee, Fla.; member of the State constitutional convention in 1868; served in the State senate 1869–1872; appointed by the Governor and confirmed by the State senate as secretary of state in 1869, but declined; also later declined appointment as judge of Jackson County; chairman of the Florida Commission in 1869 for entering into negotiations for transfer of West Florida to the State of Alabama, which transfer was not ratified by Alabama; assessor of United States internal revenue for the district of Florida 1870–1872; chairman of the Republican State committee 1870–1872; member of the Republican National Committee 1876–1880; elected as a Republican to the Forty-third Congress and served from March 4, 1873, to January 25, 1875, when he resigned; member of the State house of representatives for one session and resigned when elected to Congress; elected to the Forty-fourth Congress (March 4, 1875–March 3, 1877); unsuccessful candidate for reelection in 1876 to the Forty-fifth Congress; returned in 1878 to Millheim, Pa., and engaged in agricultural pursuits; moved to Boston, Mass., in 1883; discontinued active pursuits and moved to Washington, D. C., where he lived in retirement until his death on August 14, 1928; the remains were cremated and the ashes deposited in a vault at Glenwood Cemetery.

PURNELL, Fred Sampson, a Representative from Indiana; born on a farm near Veedersburg, Fountain County, Ind., October 25, 1882; attended the common schools and the high school at Veedersburg; was graduated from the law department of Indiana University at Bloomington in 1904; was admitted to the bar the same year and commenced practice in Attica, Fountain County, Ind.; city attorney of Attica 1910–1914; resumed the practice of his profession; unsuccessful candidate for election in 1914 to the Sixty-fourth Congress; elected as a Republican to the Sixty-fifth and to the seven succeeding Congresses (March 4, 1917–March 3, 1933); unsuccessful candidate for reelection in 1932 to the Seventy-third Congress and for election in 1934 to the Seventy-fourth Congress; resumed the practice of law in Attica, Ind.; moved to Washington, D. C., in April 1939 and served as an attorney in the General Accounting Office until his resignation on October 1, 1939; died in Washington, D. C., October 21, 1939; interment in Rockfield Cemetery, near Veedersburg, Ind.

PURTELL, William Arthur, a Senator from Connecticut; born in Hartford, Conn., May 6, 1897; attended the public and parochial schools; was a newsboy at the age of eight, then grocery errand boy at the age of ten, and janitor of an apartment house at the age of thirteen; left school at the age of fifteen and worked as a waterboy on a construction job, as a file clerk in an insurance office, and later as a car checker in a freight yard; during the First World War enlisted in the United States

Army in 1918 and served with radio section of the Signal Corps with overseas service, and was discharged as a corporal in 1919; engaged as a salesman 1919–1929; in 1929 with others organized the Holo–Krome Screw Corp. and became its president, treasurer, and general manager; in 1936 was named president, treasurer, and general manager of Billings & Spencer, another industrial concern; also was director in many other business enterprises; unsuccessful candidate for the Republican nomination for Governor in 1950; appointed as a Republican to the United States Senate to fill the vacancy caused by the death of Brien McMahon and served from August 29, 1952, to November 4, 1952, when a successor was duly elected; was not a candidate for election to the vacancy; elected to the United States Senate November 4, 1952, for the full term commencing January 3, 1953, and ending January 3, 1959; was an unsuccessful candidate for reelection in 1958; resumed manufacturing interests; is a resident of West Hartford, Conn.

PURVIANCE, Samuel Anderson, a Representative from Pennsylvania; born in Butler, Pa., January 10, 1809; after receiving a preliminary education, entered college and pursued a partial course and then applied himself to the study of law; was admitted to the bar in 1827 and commenced practice in Butler, Pa.; moved to Warren County and was prosecuting attorney for two years; returned to Butler, where he continued the practice of law; delegate to the State constitutional convention of 1837 and 1838; member of the State house of representatives in 1838 and 1839; delegate to the Whig National Convention at Baltimore in 1844 and to the Republican National Convention at Philadelphia in 1856; presidential elector on the Whig ticket of Taylor and Fillmore in 1848 and on the Scott and Graham ticket in 1852; elected as a Whig to the Thirty-fourth and Thirty-fifth Congresses (March 4, 1855–March 3, 1859); unsuccessful candidate for renomination in 1858; moved to Pittsburgh in 1859 and continued the practice of law; delegate to the Republican National Conventions in 1860, 1864, and 1868; served as attorney general of Pennsylvania in 1861; resumed the practice of his profession in Pittsburgh until 1876, when he retired; member of the National Executive Committee of the Republican Party 1864–1868; member of the State constitutional convention of 1872; unsuccessful candidate for election in 1874 to the Forty-fourth Congress; died in Allegheny (now a part of Pittsburgh), Pa., February 14, 1882; interment in Highwood (formerly Bellevue) Cemetery.

PURVIANCE, Samuel Dinsmore, a Representative from North Carolina; born on Masonboro Sound at Castle Fin House, near Wilmington, New Hanover County, N. C., January 7, 1774; attended a private school; studied law; was admitted to the bar and practiced at Fayetteville, N. C.; also owned and operated a large plantation; member of the State house of commons in 1798 and 1799; member of the State senate from Cumberland County in 1801; trustee of Fayetteville Academy in 1803; elected as a Federalist to the Eighth Congress (March 4, 1803–March 3, 1805); continued the practice of law in Fayetteville; died on the Red River about 1806, while on an exploring expedition into the West.

PURYEAR, Richard Clauselle, a Representative from North Carolina; born in Mecklenburg County, Va., February 9, 1801; moved with his parents to Surry County, N. C.; pursued classical studies; engaged in planting near Huntsville, N. C.; colonel of militia; magistrate of Surry County; served in the State house of commons in 1838, 1844, 1846, and in 1852; member of the State senate; elected as a Whig to the Thirty-third and Thirty-fourth Congresses (March 4, 1853–March 3, 1857); unsuccessful candidate for reelection in 1856 to the Thirty-fifth Congress; was a delegate to the Confederate Provisional Congress which assembled at Richmond in 1861; delegate to the peace congress held in Philadelphia after the Civil War; resumed agricultural pursuits; died on his plantation, "Shallow Ford," in Yadkin County, N. C., July 30, 1867; interment in the family burial ground.

PUSEY, William Henry Mills, a Representative from Iowa; born in Washington County, Pa., on July 29, 1826; attended Washington and Jefferson College, Pennsylvania, and was graduated in 1847; studied law and was admitted to the bar but did not engage in extensive practice; moved to Iowa and engaged in banking; member of the State senate 1858–1862; elected as a Democrat to the Forty-eighth Congress (March 4, 1883–March 3, 1885); unsuccessful candidate for reelection in 1884 to the Forty-ninth Congress; resumed banking activities; died in Council Bluffs, Pottawattamie County, Iowa, November 15, 1900; interment in Walnut Hill Cemetery.

PUTNAM, Harvey, a Representative from New York; born in Brattleboro, Vt., January 5, 1793; attended the common schools; studied law; was admitted to the bar in 1816 and commenced practice in Attica, N. Y., in 1817; held several local offices; elected as a Whig to the Twenty-fifth Congress to fill the vacancy caused by the death of William Patterson and served from November 7, 1838, to March 3, 1839; appointed surrogate of Genessee County in 1840, which office he held until the division of the county, when he was appointed surrogate of Wyoming County, serving until 1842; member of the State senate 1843–1846; elected as a Whig to the Thirtieth and Thirty-first Congresses (March 4, 1847–March 3, 1851); was not a candidate for renomination in 1850; resumed the practice of law; died in Attica, Wyoming County, N. Y., September 20, 1855; interment in Forest Hill Cemetery.

PYLE, Gladys, a Senator from South Dakota; born in Huron, Beadle County, S. Dak., October 4, 1890; attended the public schools; was graduated from Huron (S. Dak.) College in 1911; taught in the public high schools at Miller, Wessington, and Huron, S. Dak., 1912–1918; member of the State house of representatives 1923–1926; served as secretary of state of South Dakota 1927–1931; served as a member of the State securities commission 1931–1933; became engaged in the life insurance business in 1933; elected as a Republican to the United States Senate to fill the vacancy caused by the death of Peter Norbeck and served from November 9, 1938, to January 3, 1939; was not a candidate for election in 1938 to the full term; resumed the life insurance business and also engaged in farm management; delegate to the Republican National Convention at Philadelphia in 1940; member of the South Dakota Board of Charities and Corrections from July 1941 to March 1955; agent for Northwestern Mutual Life Insurance Co. 1950–; is a resident of Huron, S. Dak.

Q

QUACKENBUSH, John Adam, a Representative from New York; born in Schaghticoke, Rensselaer County, N. Y., October 15, 1828; attended the district schools and the local academy in Stillwater, N. Y.; engaged in agricultural pursuits and was also interested in the lumber business; supervisor of Schaghticoke 1860–1862; chairman of the Board of Supervisors of Rensselaer County in 1862; member of the State assembly in 1862; sheriff of Rensselaer County 1873–1876; elected as a Republican to the Fifty-first and Fifty-second Congresses (March 4, 1889–March 3, 1893); was an unsuccessful candidate for reelection in 1892 to the Fifty-third Congress; resumed agricultural pursuits; died in Schaghticoke, N. Y., May 11, 1908; interment in the City Cemetery.

QUARLES, James Minor, a Representative from Tennessee; born near Louisa Court House, Louisa County, Va., February 8, 1823; attended the common schools; in 1833 moved to Kentucky with his father who settled in Christian County; completed preparatory studies; studied law; was admitted to the bar in 1845 and commenced practice in Clarksville, Tenn.; elected attorney general for the tenth judicial circuit in 1853 and served until 1859, when he resigned, having been elected to Congress; elected as a Whig to the Thirty-sixth Congress (March 4, 1859–March 3, 1861); resumed the practice of law; during the Civil War served in the Confederate Army in the brigade of his brother, Brig. Gen. W. A. Quarles, until the close of the war; moved to Nashville, Tenn., in 1872 and continued the practice of law; elected judge of the criminal court in 1878 and served until 1882, when he resigned; resumed the practice of law; died in Nashville, Tenn., March 3, 1901; interment in Mount Olivet Cemetery.

QUARLES, Joseph Very, a Senator from Wisconsin; born in Kenosha (then Southport), Kenosha County, Wis., December 16, 1843; attended the common schools and was graduated from the Kenosha High School; entered the University of Michigan at Ann Arbor in 1862, during the Civil War served in the Union Army in the Thirty-ninth Regiment, Wisconsin Volunteers, in 1864 and was mustered out as first lieutenant of Company C; returned to the University of Michigan and was graduated from the literary department in 1866 and from the law department in 1867; was admitted to the bar in 1868 and commenced practice in Kenosha; district attorney for Kenosha County 1870–1876; mayor of Kenosha in 1876; member of the State assembly in 1879; served in the State senate 1880–1882; moved to Racine, Wis., and six years later made Milwaukee his home; elected as a Republican to the United States Senate and served from March 4, 1899, to March 3, 1905; was not a candidate for reelection in 1905; appointed United States district judge for the eastern district of Wisconsin by President Theodore Roosevelt on March 6, 1905, and served until his death in Milwaukee, Wis., October 7, 1911; interment in the City Cemetery, Kenosha, Wis.

QUARLES, Julian Minor, a Representative from Virginia; born near Ruther Glen, Caroline County, Va., September 25, 1848; attended the primary schools in Caroline and Augusta Counties and Pine Hill and Aspen Hill Academies, Louisa County, Va.; taught school three years and then attended the University of Virginia at Charlottesville; studied law; was admitted to the bar and commenced practice in Staunton, Augusta County, Va., in September 1874; judge of the county court of Augusta County, Va., from January 1880 to June 1883, when he resigned; moved to Minneapolis, Minn., and practiced his profession for two years; returned to Staunton, Va., and continued the practice of law; elected as a Democrat to the Fifty-sixth Congress (March 4, 1899–March 3, 1901); was not a candidate for renomination in 1900; member of the State constitutional convention in 1901; resumed the practice of law in Staunton, Va., until 1924 when he retired from active business pursuits; died in Staunton, Va., November 18, 1929; interment in Thornrose Cemetery.

QUARLES, Tunstall, a Representative from Kentucky; born in King William County, Va., about 1770; attended the local schools; moved with his parents to Woodford County, Ky., about 1790; studied law; was admitted to the bar and practiced; member of the State house of representatives in 1796; moved

to Somerset, Pulaski County, Ky.; member of the State house of representatives in 1811 and 1812; during the War of 1812, at his own expense, armed and equipped a company of the Second Regiment, Kentucky Militia, which he commanded; appointed circuit judge by the Governor; elected as a Democrat to the Fifteenth and Sixteenth Congresses and served from March 4, 1817, until his resignation effective June 15, 1820; appointed receiver of public moneys for the Cape Girardeau land district, with offices at Jackson, Mo., and served from May 1821 to July 1824; returned to Somerset, Ky., and engaged in agricultural pursuits and the practice of law; member and speaker of the State house of representatives in 1828; presidential elector on the Democratic ticket of Jackson and Calhoun in 1829; served in the State senate in 1840; died in Somerset, Ky., January 7, 1855; interment in the old Baptist Cemetery.

QUAY, Matthew Stanley, a Senator from Pennsylvania; born in Dillsburg, York County, Pa., on September 30, 1833; attended Beaver and Indiana Academies and was graduated from Jefferson College, Canonsburg, Pa., in 1850; studied law; was admitted to the bar in 1854 and commenced practice in Beaver, Pa.; elected prothonotary of Beaver County in 1856; reelected in 1859 and served until 1860; lieutenant in the Tenth Pennsylvania Reserves; colonel of the One Hundred and Thirty-fourth Regiment, Pennsylvania Volunteers; lieutenant colonel and assistant commissary general; military State agent at Washington; private secretary to Gov. Andrew G. Curtin; major and chief of transportation and telegraphs; military secretary to Governor Curtin from 1861 to 1865; member of the State house of representatives 1865–1867; owned and edited the Beaver Radical 1867–1872; secretary of the Commonwealth 1872–1878 and 1879–1882; recorder of the city of Philadelphia and chairman of the Republican State committee in 1878 and 1879; delegate to the Republican National Conventions 1872, 1876, 1880, 1888, and 1892; State treasurer 1885–1887; elected in 1887 as a Republican to the United States Senate; reelected in 1893 and served from March 4, 1887, to March 3, 1899; member and chairman of the Republican National Committee in 1888; unsuccessful candidate for reelection to the United States Senate in 1899 caused by a deadlock existing throughout the session of the legislature; appointed by Gov. William A. Stone to the United States Senate to fill the vacancy in the term commencing March 4, 1899, occasioned by the failure of the legislature to elect, but by resolution of the Senate of April 24, 1900, was declared not entitled to the seat; elected in 1901 to fill the existing vacancy, and served from January 16, 1901, until his death in Beaver, Pa., May 28, 1904; interment in Beaver Cemetery.

QUAYLE, John Francis, a Representative from New York; born in Brooklyn, N. Y., on December 1, 1868; attended the public schools, St. James Academy, and St. Francis College, in Brooklyn; engaged in the retail butcher business; also became engaged in building construction in 1902; served as deputy collector of internal revenue for the first district of New York from November 12, 1914, until February 19, 1919, when he resigned to enter upon his duties as deputy city clerk of Brooklyn Borough, in which capacity he served from March 1919 to February 1923, when he resigned, having been elected to Congress; elected as a Democrat to the Sixty-eighth and to the three succeeding Congresses and served from March 4, 1923, until his death; had been reelected to the Seventy-second Congress; died in Brooklyn, N. Y., November 27, 1930; interment in St. John's Cemetery.

QUEZON, Manuel Luis, a Resident Commissioner from the Philippine Islands; born in Baler, Province of Tayabas, Philippine Islands, August 19, 1878; attended the public schools and the

College of San Juan de Letran, Manila; studied law at the University of Santo Tomas; was admitted to the bar in April 1903; major in the Philippine Army and detailed to General Aguinaldo's staff; later served as chief of staff to the general commanding the department of central Luzon; under the American Government held the office of prosecuting attorney for the Province of Mindoro and was subsequently transferred to the Province of Tayabas; elected Provincial Governor of Tayabas and served from 1906 to 1907, when he resigned; delegate to the first Philippine Assembly and was the floor leader of his party in 1907 and 1908; elected by the Nationalist Party a Resident Commissioner to the United States in 1909; reelected in 1912 and served from November 23, 1909, to October 15, 1916, when he resigned; member and president of the Philippine Senate 1916–1935; elected President of the Philippine Islands on September 17, 1935, and served from the inauguration of the Commonwealth of the Philippines on November 15, 1935, until his death; escaped from Luzon in the Philippine Islands on February 20, 1942, in a United States submarine after the Philippines had fallen to the Japanese; died in Saranac Lake, N. Y., on August 1, 1944; remains interred temporarily in a mausoleum at Arlington (Va.) National Cemetery; subsequently the remains were removed to the Philippines and interred in Cemeterio del Norte, Manila, Philippines.

QUIE, Albert Harold, a Representative from Minnesota; born on a farm in Wheeling Township, Rice County, near Dennison, Minn., September 18, 1923; attended the grade schools in Nerstrand and high school in Northfield; graduated from St. Olaf College, Northfield, Minn., in 1950; during World War II served as a pilot in the United States Navy 1943–1945; owner and operator of a two-hundred-and-forty-acre dairy farm; member, District 43 School Board 1949–1952; supervisor, Rice County Soil Conservation District 1950–1954; delegate and presiding officer at Republican State Convention in 1956 and alternate delegate to Republican National Convention in 1956; served in the State senate 1955–1958; elected as a Republican to the Eighty-fifth Congress to fill the vacancy caused by the death of August H. Andresen; reelected to the Eighty-sixth Congress and served from February 18, 1958, to January 3, 1961. *Reelected to the Eighty-seventh Congress.*

QUIGG, Lemuel Ely, a Representative from New York; born near Chestertown, Kent County, Md., on February 12, 1863; attended the public schools of Wilmington, Del.; moved to New York City in 1880 and engaged in journalism; editor of the Flushing (N. Y.) Times in 1883 and 1884; member of the editorial staff of the New York Tribune 1884–1894; editor in chief of the New York Press in 1895; elected as a Republican to the Fifty-third Congress to fill the vacancy caused by the resignation of John R. Fellows; reelected to the Fifty-fourth and Fifty-fifth Congresses and served from January 30, 1894, to March 3, 1899; unsuccessful candidate for reelection in 1898 to the Fifty-sixth Congress; chairman of the Republican State conventions in 1896 and 1902; delegate to the Republican National Convention in 1896, 1900, and 1904; president of the Republican county committee 1896–1900; studied law; was admitted to the bar in 1903; delegate to the State constitutional convention in 1915; engaged in the practice of law in New York City until his death there July 1, 1919; interment in Flushing Cemetery, Flushing, Queens County, N. Y.

QUIGLEY, James Michael, a Representative from Pennsylvania; born in Mount Carmel, Northumberland County, Pa., March 30, 1918; attended the public schools of Mount Carmel; was graduated from Villanova College in 1939 and from Dickinson School of Law, Carlisle, Pa., in 1942; was admitted to the bar in 1942 and commenced the practice of law in Harrisburg, Pa.; during World War II served in the United States Navy 1943–1946, eighteen months of which were spent on a destroyer in the Pacific Theater; engaged in the Philippine and Okinawa campaigns, and after V–J Day served with the occupation forces in Korea and Japan; resumed law practice in Harrisburg, Pa.; unsuccessful Democratic candidate for election to the Eighty-second Congress in 1950; elected as a Democrat to the Eighty-fourth Congress (January 3, 1955–January 3, 1957); unsuccessful candidate in 1956 for reelection to the Eighty-fifth Congress; in 1957 became administrative assistant to Senator Joseph S. Clark of Pennsylvania; elected to the Eighty-sixth Congress (January 3, 1959–January 3, 1961); unsuccessful candidate for reelection in 1960 to the Eighty-seventh Congress; appointed Assistant Secretary of Health, Education, and Welfare for Federal and State matters on February 24, 1961; is a resident of Camp Hill, Pa.

QUIN, Percy Edwards, a Representative from Mississippi; born near Liberty, Amite County, Miss., October 30, 1872; attended the public schools; was graduated from Gillsburg Collegiate Institute, Amite County, Miss., in 1890 and from Mississippi College, Clinton, Miss., in 1893; taught school in McComb City, Pike County, Miss., in 1893 and 1894; studied law; was admitted to the bar in 1894 and commenced practice in McComb City; city attorney in 1895; delegate to the Democratic State conventions in 1899 and 1912; member of the State house of representatives 1900–1902; unsuccessful candidate for election in 1910 to the Sixty-second Congress; elected as a Democrat to the Sixty-third and to the nine succeeding Congresses and served from March 4, 1913, until his death in Washington, D. C., on February 4, 1932; interment in the City Cemetery of Natchez, Miss.

QUINCY, Josiah, a Representative from Massachusetts; born in Boston, Mass., February 4, 1772; attended Phillips Academy, Andover, Mass., and was graduated from Harvard University in 1790; studied law; was admitted to the bar in 1793 and commenced the practice of his profession in Boston; unsuccessful candidate for election to the Seventh and Eighth Congresses, served in the State senate in 1804 and 1805; elected as a Federalist to the Ninth and to the three succeeding Congresses (March 4, 1805–March 3, 1813); was not a candidate for renomination in 1812 to the Thirteenth Congress; again served in the State senate 1813–1820; member of the State house of representatives in 1821 and 1822, serving the last year as speaker; delegate to the Massachusetts State Constitutional Convention in 1820; judge of the Boston municipal court in 1822; mayor of Boston 1823–1829; during his administration the Faneuil Hall Market was established and the erection of the Bunker Hill Monument was begun; president of Harvard University from 1829 to 1845; died in Quincy, Norfolk County, Mass., on July 1, 1864; interment in Mount Auburn Cemetery, Cambridge, Middlesex County, Mass.

QUINN, James Leland, a Representative from Pennsylvania; born in Emlenton, Venango County, Pa., September 8, 1875; moved to Braddock, Allegheny County, Pa., with his parents in 1880 and attended St. Thomas School; employed as a newspaper reporter 1891–1896; became owner and publisher of the Braddock (Pa.) Journal in 1896; member of the State house of representatives 1933–1935; elected as a Democrat to the Seventy-fourth and Seventy-fifth Congresses (January 3, 1935–January 3, 1939); unsuccessful candidate for reelection in 1938 to the Seventy-sixth Congress; resumed the newspaper publishing business; died in Braddock, Pa., November 12, 1960; interment in Braddock Catholic Cemetery.

QUINN, John, a Representative from New York; born in County Tipperary, Ireland, August 9, 1839; attended Clonmel College, Tipperary; immigrated to the United States in 1866 and settled in New York City, N. Y.; engaged in the real-estate and building business; president of the West Side Electric Light & Power Company and was one of the founders and a director of the Homestead Bank of New York; served as a member of the New York State Assembly in 1882; member of the board of aldermen 1885–1887; delegate to the Democratic National Convention at Chicago in 1884 and at St. Louis in 1888; elected as a Democrat to the Fifty-first Congress (March 4, 1889–March 3, 1891); died in New York City on February 23, 1903; interment in Calvary Cemetery, Long Island City, N. Y.

QUINN, Peter Anthony, a Representative from New York; born in New York City, N. Y., May 10, 1904; attended the St. Brigid's and St. Raymond's School; was graduated from Manhattan Preparatory School in 1922, Manhattan College in New York City in 1926, and from the law department of Fordham University in New York City in 1929; was admitted to the bar in 1931 and commenced practice in New York City; member of the New York State Assembly 1936–1944; elected as a Democrat to the Seventy-ninth Congress (January 3, 1945–January 3, 1947); was an unsuccessful candidate for reelection in 1946 to the Eightieth Congress; resumed the practice of law until January 1, 1949, when he became a justice of the municipal court of New York City; in 1955 was elected a justice and in 1957 a chief justice of the city court of New York City, serving until 1960, then elected justice of the supreme court of the State of New York for a fourteen-year term; is a resident of New York City.

QUINN, Terence John, a Representative from New York; born in Albany, Albany County, N. Y., October 16, 1836; educated at a private school and the Boys' Academy in his native city; early in life entered the brewery business with his father and subsequently became senior member of the firm; at the outbreak of the Civil War was second lieutenant in Company B, Twenty-fifth Regiment, New York State Militia Volunteers, which was ordered to the defense of Washington, D. C., in April 1861 and assigned to duty at Arlington Heights; was credited with having captured the first prisoner taken during the war; member of the common council of Albany 1869–1872; elected a member of the State assembly in 1873; elected as a Democrat to the Forty-fifth Congress and served from March 4, 1877, until his death in Albany, N. Y., June 18, 1878; interment in St. Agnes' Cemetery.

QUINN, Thomas Vincent, a Representative from New York; born in Long Island City, Queens County, N. Y., March 16, 1903; attended the grade and high schools of Queens County, N. Y.; graduated from Fordham University Law School in 1924; was admitted to the bar in 1924 and commenced the practice of law in New York City in June 1925; assistant district attorney of Queens County from September 1931 to August 1934; assistant United States attorney, eastern district of New York, 1934–1947; Assistant Attorney General of the United States from July 21, 1947, until his resignation August 10, 1948, to pursue congressional campaign; elected as a Democrat to the Eighty-first and Eighty-second Congresses and served from January 3, 1949, until his resignation December 30, 1951, to become district attorney of Queens County, N. Y., and served until December 31, 1955; unsuccessful for the Democratic nomination for district attorney of Queens County in 1955; appointed a city magistrate in 1957 for a ten-year term ending December 31, 1967; is a resident of Jackson Heights, N. Y.

QUITMAN, John Anthony, a Representative from Mississippi; born in Rhinebeck, Dutchess County, N. Y., September 1, 1799; pursued classical studies and was graduated from Hartwick Seminary in 1816; instructor in Mount Airy College, Pennsylvania, in 1818; studied law; was admitted to the bar; moved to Chillicothe, Ohio, in 1820, and thence to Natchez, Miss., in 1821, where he practiced law; member of the State house of representatives in 1826 and 1827; chancellor of the State from 1828 until 1835, when he resigned; member of the State constitutional convention in 1832; served in the State senate in 1835 and 1836 and was made its president; Acting Governor of Mississippi in 1835 and 1836; judge of the high court of errors and appeals in 1838; during the Mexican War was appointed a brigadier general of Volunteers July 1, 1846; commissioned a major general in the Regular Army April 14, 1847, and honorably discharged July 20, 1848; presidential elector on the Democratic ticket of Cass and Butler in 1848; Governor of Mississippi in 1850 and 1851; elected as a Democrat to the Thirty-fourth and Thirty-fifth Congresses and served from March 4, 1855, until his death on his plantation, "Monmouth," near Natchez, Miss., July 17, 1858, presumably from poison secretly placed in food served at a banquet in Washington, D. C., during the inauguration of President Buchanan; interment in the Natchez City Cemetery.

R

RABAUT, Louis Charles, a Representative from Michigan; born in Detroit, Mich., December 5, 1886; attended parochial schools; was graduated from Detroit (Mich.) College in 1909, and from the Detroit College of Law in 1912; was admitted to the bar in 1912 and commenced practice in Detroit; also engaged in the building business; delegate to the Democratic National Conventions in 1936 and 1940; delegate to the Interparliamentary Union at Oslo, Norway, in 1939; elected as a Democrat to the Seventy-fourth and to the five succeeding Congresses (January 3, 1935–January 3, 1947); unsuccessful for reelection in 1946; elected to the Eighty-first and to the six succeeding Congresses and served from January 3, 1949, until his death in Hamtramck, Mich., November 12, 1961.

RABIN, Benjamin J., a Representative from New York; born in Rochester, Monroe County, N. Y., June 3, 1896; attended the public schools of his native city, and New York University until May 30, 1917, when he enlisted in the United States Navy as a seaman; was subsequently commissioned as an ensign and served until January 1919; discharged as an ensign from the Naval Reserve in May 1921; reentered New York University and was graduated from the law department in 1919; was admitted to the bar the same year and commenced practice in New York City; counsel to the New York State joint legislative committee investigating guaranteed mortgages in 1934 and 1935; counsel to the Mortgage Commission of the State of New York 1935–1937 and served as chairman 1937–1939; elected as a Democrat to the Seventy-ninth and Eightieth Congresses and served from January 3, 1945, until his resignation effective midnight December 31, 1947, having been elected a justice of the New York State Supreme Court and took the oath of office on January 5, 1948, and designated by the Governor as associate justice of appellate division in January 1955 for the term ending December 31, 1961; resides in New York City, N. Y.

RADCLIFFE, Amos Henry, a Representative from New Jersey; born in Paterson, N. J., January 16, 1870; attended the public schools of Paterson; was graduated from the Paterson High School and from the New York Trade School; blacksmith and ornamental and structural iron worker; sergeant in the National Guard of New Jersey 1888–1893; in 1896 became associated with his father's firm and in 1907 was made secretary of James Radcliffe & Sons Co., a structural iron manufacturing company; member of the State house of assembly 1907–1912; delegate to the Republican State conventions in 1910, 1911, and 1912; sheriff of Passaic County 1912–1915; fish and game commissioner 1914–1919; mayor of Paterson 1916–1919; elected as a Republican to the Sixty-sixth and Sixty-seventh Congresses (March 4, 1919–March 3, 1923); was an unsuccessful candidate for reelection in 1922 to the Sixty-eighth Congress; resumed active interests in Radcliffe & Sons Company and was treasurer at the time of his death; founder and a former president of the Franklin Trust Company, of Paterson, and served as chairman of the board; in 1925 became a member of the Board of Standards and Appeals, Paterson, N. J.; died in Baleville, N. J., on December 29, 1950; interment in Cedar Lawn Cemetery, Paterson, N. J.

RADCLIFFE, George L., a Senator from Maryland; born on a farm at Lloyds, near Cambridge, Dorchester County, Md., August 22, 1877; attended the public schools; was graduated from Cambridge (Md.) Seminary in 1893, from Johns Hopkins University, Baltimore, Md., in 1897, and from the law department of the University of Maryland in Baltimore in 1903; principal of the Cambridge (Md.) Seminary in 1900 and 1901; teacher in the Baltimore City College in 1901 and 1902; was admitted to the bar in 1903 and commenced practice in Baltimore; also interested in banking and farming; member of the Liquor License Commission, Baltimore, 1916–1919; member of the Maryland State Council of Defense during the First World War; secretary of state of Maryland in 1919 and 1920; regional adviser of the Public Works Administration for Maryland, Delaware, Virginia, West Virginia, North Carolina, Tennessee, Kentucky, and the District of Columbia in 1933 and 1934; delegate to the Democratic State conventions in 1936, 1940, and 1944; elected as a Democrat to the United States Senate in 1934; reelected in 1940 and served from January 3, 1935, to January 3, 1947; was an unsuccessful candidate for renomination in 1946; resumed banking and farming interests; president of Maryland Historical Society; trustee of Harry S. Truman Library; is a resident of Baltimore, Md.

RADFORD, William, a Representative from New York; born in Poughkeepsie, Dutchess County, N. Y., June 24, 1814; received a limited schooling; moved to New York City in 1829 and engaged in mercantile pursuits; elected as a Democrat to the Thirty-eighth and Thirty-ninth Congresses (March 4, 1863–March 3, 1867); unsuccessful candidate for reelection in 1866 to the Fortieth Congress; resumed his former business pursuits; died in Yonkers, Westchester County, N. Y., January 18, 1870; interment in the Old Presbyterian Cemetery, Westfield, Union County, N. J.

RADWAN, Edmund Patrick, a Representative from New York; born in Buffalo, Erie County, N. Y., September 22, 1911; attended the public schools; graduated from the University of Buffalo Law School in 1934; athletic coach of East High School, Buffalo, N. Y., 1929–1934; was admitted to the bar in 1935 and commenced the practice of law in Buffalo, N. Y.; village attorney of Sloan, N. Y., 1938–1940; during World War II served as a corporal in the United States Army 1943–1945; member of the State senate from 1945 to December 31, 1950; elected as a Republican to the Eighty-second and to the three succeeding Congresses (January 3, 1951–January 3, 1959); was not a candidate for renomination in 1958; died in Buffalo, N. Y., September 7, 1959; interment in St. Stanislaus Cemetery.

RAGON, Heartsill, a Representative from Arkansas; born in Dublin, Logan County, Ark., March 20, 1885; attended the common schools, the Clarksville High School, the College of the Ozarks, Clarksville, Ark., and the University of Arkansas at Fayetteville; was graduated from the law department of Washington and Lee University, Lexington, Va.; was admitted to the bar in 1908 and commenced practice in Clarksville, Ark.; member of the State house of representatives 1911–1913; district attorney 1916–1920; secretary of the Democratic State convention in 1918; chairman of the Democratic State convention in 1920; delegate to the Democratic National Convention at San Francisco in 1920; elected as a Democrat to the Sixty-eighth and to the five succeeding Congresses and served from March 4, 1923, until his resignation effective June 16, 1933, having been appointed judge of the United States District Court for the Western District of Arkansas on May 12, 1933, in which capacity he served until his death in Fort Smith, Ark., September 15, 1940; interment in Forest Park Cemetery.

RAGSDALE, James Willard, a Representative from South Carolina; born in Timmonsville, Florence County, S. C., December 14, 1872; attended the public schools; employed in a railroad office at Wilmington, N. C., for several years; attended the University of South Carolina at Columbia; studied law; was admitted to the bar in 1898 and commenced practice in Florence, Florence County, S. C.; engaged in agricultural pursuits and banking; trustee of the South Carolina Industrial School; member of the State house of representatives 1898–1900; member of the State senate 1902–1904; unsuccessful candidate for attorney general of South Carolina and for election in 1910 to the Sixty-second Congress; elected as a Democrat to the Sixty-third and to the three succeeding Congresses and served from March 4, 1913, until his death in Washington, D. C., July 23, 1919; interment in Mount Hope Cemetery, Florence, S. C.

RAINES, John, a Representative from New York; born in Canandaigua, Ontario County, N. Y., May 6, 1840; attended the public schools; taught school; studied law and was graduated from the Albany (N. Y.) Law School in 1861; was admitted to the bar the same year and commenced practice in Geneva, N. Y.; during the Civil War organized and was captain of Company G, Eighty-fifth Regiment, New York Volunteer Infantry, in 1861 and served in the Armies of the Potomac and North Carolina until July 1863; member of the State assembly 1881–1883 and in 1885; member of the State senate 1886–1889; president of the board of education of Canandaigua 1887–1909; delegate to the Republican National Convention at Chicago in 1888; elected as a Republican to the Fifty-first and Fifty-second Congresses (March 4, 1889–March 3, 1893); was not a candidate for renomination in 1892; elected to the State senate in 1894 to fill an unexpired term; reelected and served continuously until his death; was president of the State senate after 1904; died in Canandaigua, N. Y., December 16, 1909; interment in Woodlawn Cemetery.

RAINEY, Henry Thomas, a Representative from Illinois; born in Carrollton, Greene County, Ill., on August 20, 1860; attended the public schools and Knox Academy and Knox College, Galesburg, Ill.; was graduated from Amherst (Mass.) College in 1883 and from the Union College of Law, Chicago, Ill., in 1885; was admitted to the bar in 1885 and commenced practice in Carrollton, Ill.; master in chancery for Greene County, Ill., from 1887 to 1895, when he resigned; elected as a Democrat to the Fifty-eighth and to the eight succeeding Congresses (March 4, 1903–March 3, 1921); unsuccessfully contested the election of Guy L. Shaw to the Sixty-seventh Congress;

engaged in agricultural pursuits; elected to the Sixty-eighth and to the five succeeding Congresses and served from March 4, 1923, until his death; elected Speaker of the House of Representatives on March 9, 1933, and served until his death in a hospital in St. Louis, Mo., on August 19, 1934; interment in the Carrollton Cemetery, Carrollton, Ill.

RAINEY, John William, a Representative from Illinois; born in Chicago, Ill., December 21, 1880; attended the public schools of his native city, De La Salle Institute, and the Kent College of Law; was admitted to the bar in 1910 and commenced the practice of law in Chicago; assistant judge of the probate court of Cook County 1910–1912; clerk of the circuit court 1912–1916; elected as a Democrat to the Sixty-fifth Congress to fill the vacancy caused by the death of Charles Martin; reelected to the Sixty-sixth, Sixty-seventh, and Sixty-eighth Congresses and served from April 2, 1918, until his death in Chicago, Ill., on May 4, 1923; interment in Calvary Cemetery.

RAINEY, Joseph Hayne, a Representative from South Carolina; born in Georgetown, Georgetown County, S. C., June 21, 1832; was of the Negro race; received a limited schooling; followed the trade of barber until 1862, when upon being forced to work on the Confederate fortifications in Charleston, S. C., he escaped to the West Indies and remained there until the close of the war; delegate to the State constitutional convention in 1868; member of the State senate in 1870 but resigned; elected as a Republican to the Forty-first Congress to fill the vacancy caused by the action of the House of Representatives in declaring the seat of B. Franklin Whittemore vacant and was the first Negro to be elected to the National House of Representatives; reelected to the Forty-second and to the three succeeding Congresses and served from December 12, 1870, to March 3, 1879; appointed internal-revenue agent of South Carolina on May 22, 1879, and served until July 15, 1881, when he resigned; engaged in banking and the brokerage business in Washington, D. C.; retired from all business activities in 1886, returned to Georgetown, S. C., and died there August 2, 1887; interment in the Baptist Cemetery.

RAINEY, Lilius Bratton, a Representative from Alabama; born in Dadeville, Tallapoosa County, Ala., July 27, 1876; attended the common schools; moved to Fort Payne, De Kalb County, Ala.; was graduated from the Alabama Polytechnic Institute, Auburn, Ala., in 1899 and from the law department of the University of Alabama at Tuscaloosa in 1902; was admitted to the bar in the latter year and commenced practice in Gadsden, Ala.; elected a captain in the Alabama National Guard in 1903; reelected and commissioned in 1906, but resigned the command in 1907; city solicitor of Gadsden 1911–1917; elected as a Democrat to the Sixty-sixth Congress to fill the vacancy caused by the death of John L. Burnett; reelected to the Sixty-seventh Congress and served from September 30, 1919, to March 3, 1923; declined to be a candidate for renomination in 1922; trustee of the State department of archives and history, Montgomery, Ala.; resumed the practice of law in Gadsden, Ala., until his death there September 27, 1959; interment in Glenwood Cemetery, Fort Payne, Ala.

RAINS, Albert M., a Representative from Alabama; born in Groveoak, De Kalb County, Ala., March 11, 1902; attended the public schools, Snead Seminary, Boaz, Ala., State Teachers College, Jacksonville, Ala., and the University of Alabama at Tuscaloosa; studied law; was admitted to the bar in 1928 and commenced practice in Gadsden, Ala.; deputy solicitor for Etowah County, Ala., 1930–1935; city attorney for the city of Gadsden, Ala., 1935–1944; served as a member of the State

house of representatives 1942–1944; elected as a Democrat to the Seventy-ninth and to the seven succeeding Congresses (January 3, 1945–January 3, 1961). *Reelected to the Eighty-seventh Congress.*

RAKER, John Edward, a Representative from California; born near Knoxville, Knox County, Ill., February 22, 1863; moved with his parents to Lassen County, Calif., in 1873; attended the public schools and the State normal school at San Jose 1882–1884; studied law; was admitted to the bar in 1885 and commenced practice in Susanville; moved to Alturas December 6, 1886; district attorney of Modoc County 1895–1899; judge of the superior court of Modoc County from January 5, 1903, to December 19, 1910, when he resigned; chairman of the Democratic State central committee 1908–1910; delegate to the Democratic National Convention at Denver in 1908; elected as a Democrat to the Sixty-second and to the seven succeeding Congresses and served from March 4, 1911, until his death in Washington, D. C., January 22, 1926; interment in Susanville Cemetery, Susanville, Calif.

RALSTON, Samuel Moffett, a Senator from Indiana; born near Cumberland, Tuscarawas County, Ohio, on December 1, 1857; attended the public schools; moved with his parents to Owen County, Ind., in 1865; taught school for several years; was graduated from the Central Normal College, Danville, Ind., in 1884; studied law; was admitted to the bar January 1, 1886, and began practice in Lebanon, Ind.; presidential elector on the Democratic ticket of Cleveland and Thurman in 1888 and of Cleveland and Stevenson in 1892; president of the Lebanon School Board 1908–1911; Governor of Indiana 1913–1917; resumed the practice of law in Indianapolis; elected as a Democrat to the United States Senate and served from March 4, 1923, until his death near Indianapolis, Ind., October 14, 1925; interment in Oak Hill Cemetery, Lebanon, Ind.

RAMEY, Frank Marion, a Representative from Illinois; born in Hillsboro, Montgomery County, Ill., September 23, 1881; attended the public schools and was graduated from Hillsboro High School in 1900; also attended Eastern Illinois Normal School at Charleston, Ill.; taught school in Hillsboro, Ill., 1902–1905; studied law; was admitted to the bar of Illinois in December 1907 and commenced practice in Hillsboro; served as city attorney of Hillsboro 1907–1911; State's attorney of Montgomery County, Ill., 1920–1928; elected as a Republican to the Seventy-first Congress (March 4, 1929–March 3, 1931); was not a candidate for renomination in 1930; served as assistant district attorney 1931–1934; unsuccessful candidate for election in 1934 to the Seventy-fourth Congress, in 1936 to the Seventy-fifth Congress, and in 1938 to the Seventy-sixth Congress; resumed the practice of law; was appointed an examiner for the Illinois Commerce Commission in 1942 and served until his death; died in Hillsboro, Ill., March 27, 1942; interment in Oak Grove Cemetery.

RAMEY, Homer Alonzo, a Representative from Ohio; born on a farm near Sparta, South Bloomfield Township, Morrow County, Ohio, March 2, 1891; attended the grade and high schools; was graduated from Park College, Parkville, Mo., in 1913 and from the law school of Ohio Northern University at Ada in 1916; was admitted to the bar in 1917 and commenced practice in Put-in-Bay, Ohio; member of the State house of representatives 1920–1924; served in the State senate in 1925 and 1926; judge of the municipal court of Toledo, Ohio, 1926–1943; unsuccessful candidate for election in 1938 to the Seventy-sixth Congress; elected as a Republican to the Seventy-eighth, Seventy-ninth, and Eightieth Congresses (January 3, 1943–

January 3, 1949); unsuccessful candidate for reelection in 1948 to the Eighty-first Congress and for election in 1950 to the Eighty-second Congress; appointed in 1949 and subsequently elected judge of the municipal court of Toledo and served in that capacity until his death in Toledo, Ohio, April 13, 1960; interment in Ottawa Hills Memorial Park.

RAMSAY, David (brother of Nathaniel Ramsay), a Delegate from South Carolina; born in Dunmore, Lancaster County, Pa., April 2, 1749; attended the common schools, and was graduated from the College of New Jersey (now Princeton University) in 1765; was graduated from the medical department of the University of Pennsylvania at Philadelphia in 1773 and began practice in Cecil County, Md.; settled in Charleston, S. C., in 1773; member of the State house of representatives 1776–1783; served in the Revolutionary Army as surgeon of the Charleston Battalion of Artillery, State militia; captured at the fall of Charleston in May 1780 and imprisoned at St. Augustine, Fla., for eleven months; Member of the Continental Congress 1782–1786 and served as President pro tempore during the last term; unsuccessfully contested the election of William L. Smith to the First Congress (the first contested-election case); State historian and author of several historical works; member of the State senate of South Carolina and served as president of that body for seven years; shot by a maniac on May 6, 1815, in Charleston, Charleston County, S. C., and died in that city May 8, 1815.

RAMSAY, Nathaniel (brother of David Ramsay), a Delegate from Maryland; born in Lancaster County, Pa., May 1, 1741; was graduated from the College of New Jersey (now Princeton University) in 1767; a signer of the declaration of freemen of Maryland; delegate to the Maryland convention of 1775; appointed captain in Smallwood's Maryland Regiment January 14, 1776; joined the Continental Army in July 1776 and was promoted to lieutenant colonel of the Third Regiment, Maryland Line, December 10, 1776; was with the Army at Valley Forge during the winter of 1777–1778; was wounded and taken prisoner while checking the advance of the British during the retreat of Gen. Charles Lee at the Battle of Monmouth June 28, 1778, and while in command of a regiment; he obtained an exchange December 14, 1780; retired from the Army January 1, 1781; practiced law in Cecil County, Md., 1781–1783 and in Baltimore 1783–1790; Member of the Continental Congress 1785–1787; appointed United States marshal for Maryland by President Washington and served from 1790 to 1798; naval officer of the port of Baltimore 1794–1817; died in Baltimore, Md., October 23, 1817; interment in the burial ground of the First Presbyterian Church.

RAMSAY, Robert Lincoln, a Representative from West Virginia; born in Durham, England, March 24, 1877; immigrated to the United States in 1881 with his parents, who settled in New Cumberland, Hancock County, W. Va.; attended the public schools and was graduated from the law department of the West Virginia University at Morgantown in 1901; was admitted to the bar in 1901 and commenced practice in New Cumberland; moved to Wellsburg, Brooks County, W. Va., in 1905 and continued the practice of law; city attorney of Follansbee, Brooks County, 1905–1930; prosecuting attorney of Brooks County 1908–1912 and 1916–1920; member of the board of governors for West Virginia University 1927–1930; elected as a Democrat to the Seventy-third, Seventy-fourth, and Seventy-fifth Congresses (March 4, 1933–January 3, 1939); was an unsuccessful candidate for reelection in 1938 to the Seventy-sixth Congress; resumed the practice of law in Wellsburg, W. Va.; elected to the Seventy-seventh Congress (January 3, 1941–January 3, 1943); was an unsuccessful candidate for reelection in 1942 to the

Seventy-eighth Congress; special assistant to the United States Attorney General 1943–1945; assistant attorney general of West Virginia 1945–1948; elected to the Eighty-first and Eighty-second Congresses (January 3, 1949–January 3, 1953); unsuccessful candidate for renomination in 1952; resumed the practice of law and was assistant prosecuting attorney 1952–1956; died in Wheeling, W. Va., November 14, 1956; interment in Oak Grove Cemetery, Follansbee, W. Va.

RAMSEY, Alexander, a Representative from Pennsylvania and a Senator from Minnesota; born near Harrisburg, Pa., September 8, 1815; attended the common schools and Lafayette College, Easton, Pa.; studied law; was admitted to the bar in 1839 and commenced practice in Harrisburg; secretary to the electoral college of Pennsylvania in 1840; clerk of the State house of representatives in 1841; elected from Pennsylvania as a Whig to the Twenty-eighth and Twenty-ninth Congresses (March 4, 1843–March 3, 1847); declined a renomination in 1846; appointed by President Taylor as Territorial Governor of Minnesota April 2, 1849, and served until 1853; mayor of St. Paul in 1855; unsuccessful candidate for election as Governor of Minnesota in 1857; Governor of Minnesota 1860–1863; elected in 1863 as a Republican to the United States Senate; reelected in 1869 and served from March 4, 1863, to March 3, 1875; appointed Secretary of War in the Cabinet of President Hayes and served from 1879 to 1881; appointed chairman of the Edmunds Commission, dealing with the question of Mormonism in Utah, in 1882 and served until 1886, when he resigned; president of the Minnesota Historical Society 1849–1863 and 1891–1903; delegate to the centennial celebration of the adoption of the Federal Constitution in 1887; died in St. Paul, Ramsey County, Minn., April 22, 1903; interment in Oakland Cemetery.

RAMSEY, John Rathbone, a Representative from New Jersey; born in Wyckoff, Bergen County, N. J., April 25, 1862; attended the public schools and a private school in Parkersburg, W. Va., where he lived from 1872 to 1879; studied law in Hackensack, N. J.; was admitted to the bar in 1883 and commenced practice in Hackensack, N. J.; county clerk of Bergen County 1895–1910; delegate to the Republican National Convention at Chicago in 1908; president of the Hackensack Brick Co. 1909–1933; director of several banks; elected as a Republican to the Sixty-fifth and Sixty-sixth Congresses (March 4, 1917–March 3, 1921); was an unsuccessful candidate for renomination in 1920; resumed the manufacture of brick; died in Hackensack, N. J., April 10, 1933; interment in Hackensack Cemetery.

RAMSEY, Robert, a Representative from Pennsylvania; born in Warminster Township, Bucks County, Pa., February 15, 1780; attended the public schools of Hartsville; member of the State house of representatives 1825–1831; elected as a Whig to the Twenty-third Congress (March 4, 1833–March 3, 1835); was not a candidate for reelection in 1834 to the Twenty-fourth Congress; elected to the Twenty-seventh Congress (March 4, 1841–March 3, 1843); was not a candidate for reelection; engaged in agricultural pursuits; died in Warwick, Bucks County, Pa., December 12, 1849; interment in Neshaminy Cemetery.

RAMSEY, William, a Representative from Pennsylvania; born at Sterretts Gap, Cumberland County, Pa., September 7, 1779; attended the public schools; appointed surveyor for Cumberland County in 1803; clerk of the orphans' court of Cumberland County; studied law; was admitted to the bar and commenced practice in Carlisle, Pa.; elected as a Democrat to the Twentieth, Twenty-first, and Twenty-second Congresses and served from March 4, 1827, until his death in Carlisle, Pa., September 29, 1831; interment in Ashland Cemetery.

RAMSEY, William Sterrett, a Representative from Pennsylvania; born in Carlisle, Cumberland County, Pa.; June 12, 1810; pursued classical studies in the United States and Europe; attaché of the American Legation in London; elected as a Democrat to the Twenty-sixth Congress and served from March 4, 1839, until his death before the commencement of the Twenty-seventh Congress, to which he had been reelected; died in Baltimore, Md., October 17, 1840; interment in Ashland Cemetery, Carlisle, Pa.

RAMSEYER, Christian William, a Representative from Iowa; born near Collinsville, Butler County, Ohio, March 13, 1875; moved to Davis County, Iowa, in 1887 and settled near Pulaski; attended the public schools; was graduated from the Southern Iowa Normal School in 1897 and from the Iowa State Teachers College, Cedar Falls, Iowa, in 1902; taught school for nine years; was principal and later superintendent of the Bloomfield High School; was graduated from the law department of the University of Iowa at Iowa City in 1906; was admitted to the bar the same year and commenced the practice of law in Bloomfield, Iowa; prosecuting attorney of Davis County 1911–1915; elected as a Republican to the Sixty-fourth and to the eight succeeding Congresses (March 4, 1915–March 3, 1933); unsuccessful candidate for renomination in 1932 to the Seventy-third Congress; served as commissioner for the United States Court of Claims, Washington, D. C., from 1933 until his death in Washington, D. C., on November 1, 1943; interment in Odd Fellows Cemetery, Bloomfield, Iowa.

RAMSPECK, Robert C. Word, a Representative from Georgia; born in Decatur, De Kalb County, Ga., September 5, 1890; attended the public schools and the Donald Fraser School at Decatur, Ga.; deputy clerk of the superior court of Georgia 1907–1911; chief clerk of the post office in the United States House of Representatives in 1911; secretary to Congressman William Schley Howard in 1912; deputy United States marshal for the northern district of Georgia 1914–1916; chief deputy United States marshal 1917–1919; engaged in the insurance and real-estate business 1919–1921; was graduated from the Atlanta (Ga.) Law School in 1920; was admitted to the bar in 1920; engaged in the newspaper business in 1922; solicitor for the city court of Decatur, Ga., 1923–1927; city attorney of Decatur 1927–1929; member of the State house of representatives in 1929; elected as a Democrat to the Seventy-first Congress to fill the vacancy caused by the death of Leslie J. Steele; reelected to the Seventy-second and to the seven succeeding Congresses and served from October 2, 1929, until his resignation on December 31, 1945, to become executive vice president of the Air Transport Association; Democratic whip 1942–1945; chairman of the United States Civil Service Commission from March 7, 1951, until his resignation on December 31, 1952; vice president of Eastern Air Lines, Washington, D. C., January 1, 1953–; resides in Kensington, Md.

RANDALL, Alexander, a Representative from Maryland; born in Annapolis, Md., on January 3, 1803; educated under private tutors; was graduated from St. John's College, Annapolis, in 1822; studied law; was admitted to the bar and commenced practice in Annapolis, Md., in 1824; elected as a Whig to the Twenty-seventh Congress (March 4, 1841–March 3, 1843); declined to be a candidate for renomination in 1842; resumed the practice of law and also engaged in banking at Annapolis; auditor of the high court of chancery of Maryland 1844–1848; delegate to the State constitutional convention in 1850; attorney general of Maryland from 1864 to 1868; died in Annapolis, Anne Arundel County, Md., November 21, 1881; interment in St. Anne's Cemetery.

RANDALL, Benjamin, a Representative from Maine; born in Topsham, Maine (then a district of Massachusetts), November 14, 1789; pursued an academic course; was graduated from Bowdoin College, Brunswick, Maine, in 1809; studied law; was admitted to the bar in 1812 and commenced practice in Bath, Maine; served in the State militia in Colonel Reed's regiment stationed at Coxes Head in September 1814; member of the Maine Senate in 1833, 1835, and 1838; elected as a Whig to the Twenty-sixth and Twenty-seventh Congresses (March 4, 1839–March 3, 1843); resumed the practice of law; appointed collector of customs for the port of Bath in 1849 and served until his death in Bath, Sagadahoc County, Maine, October 11, 1859; interment in Maple Grove Cemetery.

RANDALL, Charles Hiram, a Representative from California; born in Auburn, Nemaha County, Nebr., July 23, 1865; attended the public schools; published newspapers at Kimball and Harrisburg, Nebr., 1885–1892; railway mail clerk 1892–1904; moved to Los Angeles, Calif., in 1904; engaged in newspaper work as editor and publisher; member of the Municipal Park Commission of Los Angeles in 1909 and 1910; member of the State assembly in 1911 and 1912; elected as the nominee of the Prohibition and Democratic Parties to the Sixty-fourth Congress; reelected as the nominee of the Prohibition, Democratic, Republican, and Progressive Parties to the Sixty-fifth and Sixty-sixth Congresses and served from March 4, 1915, to March 3, 1921; unsuccessful candidate for reelection in 1920 to the Sixty-seventh Congress; resumed work for the advancement of the national and international prohibition movement; member of the city council of Los Angeles, Calif., from July 1, 1925, to July 1, 1933; unsuccessful candidate for election in 1934 to the Seventy-fourth Congress; retired from public and political activities; died in Los Angeles, Calif., February 18, 1951; interment in Forest Lawn Memorial Park, Glendale, Calif.

RANDALL, Charles Sturtevant, a Representative from Massachusetts; born in New Bedford, Bristol County, Mass., February 20, 1824; attended a private school, the Friends Academy, New Bedford, and also studied in France; joined the gold rush to California in 1849 but returned two years later to engage in the commission and shipping business, from which he retired in 1872; served in the State senate in 1883 and 1884; elected as a Republican to the Fifty-first, Fifty-second, and Fifty-third Congresses (March 4, 1889–March 3, 1895); unsuccessful candidate for renomination in 1894; retired from his former business pursuits; died in New Bedford, Mass., August 17, 1904; interment in the Rural Cemetery.

RANDALL, Clifford Ellsworth, a Representative from Wisconsin; born in Troy Center, Walworth County, Wis., December 25, 1876; attended the public schools; was graduated from the public high school of East Troy, Wis., in 1894 and from the Whitewater Normal School in 1901; taught school at Lake Beulah, Troy Center, and Rochester, Wis.; was graduated from the law department of the University of Wisconsin at Madison in 1906; was admitted to the bar the same year and commenced the practice of law in Kenosha, Wis.; judge of the municipal court 1909–1917; elected as a Republican to the Sixty-sixth Congress (March 4, 1919–March 3, 1921); unsuccessful candidate for renomination in 1920; resumed the practice of law in Kenosha, Wis.; elected city attorney in 1921 and served until 1930; continued the practice of law in Kenosha, Wis., until his death there on October 16, 1934; interment in Green Ridge Cemetery.

RANDALL, Samuel Jackson, a Representative from Pennsylvania; born in Philadelphia, Pa., October 10, 1828; attended the common schools and the University Academy in Philadelphia; engaged in mercantile pursuits; member of the common council of Philadelphia 1852–1855; member of the State senate in 1858 and 1859; during the Civil War served as a member of the First Troop of Philadelphia in 1861 and was in the Union Army three months of that year and again as captain in 1863; was promoted to provost marshal at Gettysburg; elected as a Democrat to the Thirty-eighth and to the thirteen succeeding Congresses and served from March 4, 1863, until his death; Speaker of the House during the last session of the Forty-fourth and also during the Forty-fifth and Forty-sixth Congresses; died in Washington, D. C., April 13, 1890; interment in Laurel Hill Cemetery, Philadelphia, Pa.

RANDALL, William Harrison, a Representative from Kentucky; born near Richmond, Madison County, Ky., July 15, 1812; completed preparatory studies; studied law; was admitted to the bar and commenced practice in London, Laurel County, Ky., in 1835; clerk of the circuit court and county court of Laurel County 1836–1844; elected as a Republican to the Thirty-eighth and Thirty-ninth Congresses (March 4, 1863–March 3, 1867); district judge of the fifteenth Kentucky district 1870–1880; died in London, Ky., August 1, 1881; interment in the family cemetery at London, Ky.

RANDALL, William Joseph, a Representative from Missouri; born in Independence, Jackson County, Mo., July 16, 1909; graduated from William Chrisman High School in 1927, Junior College of Kansas City, Mo., in 1929, University of Missouri in 1931, and Kansas City School of Law, University of Kansas City, in 1933; was admitted to the bar in 1936 and commenced the practice of law in Independence, Mo.; during World War II served from March 1943 in the United States Army as a sergeant in an amphibious unit in the Southwest Pacific and the Philippines until discharged in December 1945; elected as judge of the Jackson County Court in 1946, reelected to six additional terms, and served until March 1959; delegate to Democratic National Convention in 1956; elected as a Democrat to the Eighty-sixth Congress to fill the vacancy caused by the death of George H. Christopher and served from March 3, 1959, to January 3, 1961. *Reelected to the Eighty-seventh Congress.*

RANDELL, Choice Boswell (nephew of Lucius Jeremiah Gartrell), a Representative from Texas; born near Spring Place, Murray County, Ga., January 1, 1857; attended public and private schools and the North Georgia Agricultural College at Dahlonega; studied law; was admitted to the bar in 1878 and commenced practice in Denison, Grayson County, Tex., in January 1879; moved to Sherman, Tex., in 1882 and continued the practice of law; elected as a Democrat to the Fifty-seventh and to the five succeeding Congresses (March 4, 1901–March 3, 1913); unsuccessful candidate for nomination to the United States Senate in 1912; resumed the practice of law; died in Sherman, Tex., October 19, 1945; interment in West Hill Cemetery.

RANDOLPH, Edmund Jennings (nephew of Peyton Randolph), a Delegate from Virginia; born in Williamsburg, Va., August 10, 1753; was graduated from William and Mary College, Williamsburg, Va.; studied law; was admitted to the bar and commenced practice in Williamsburg; served in the Revolutionary Army and was aide-de-camp to General Washington; attorney general of Virginia in 1776; Member of the Continental Congress 1779–1782; elected Governor of Virginia in 1786 but resigned in 1788 to serve in the State house of delegates in order that he might participate in the codification of the laws of Virginia in 1788 and 1789; member of the convention that framed the Federal Constitution; was appointed the first Attorney General of the United States, in the Cabinet of President Washington, on September 26, 1789; transferred to the State Department as Secretary of State on January 2, 1794, and served until August 19, 1795, when he was requested to resign following charges (subsequently found to be false) preferred by Minister Fauchet of France; was the principal counsel for Aaron Burr when the latter was tried for treason; died in Clarke County, Va., September 12, 1813; interment in the Old Chapel Cemetery, Millwood, Va.

RANDOLPH, James Fitz (father of Theodore Fitz Randolph), a Representative from New Jersey; born in Middlesex County, N. J., June 26, 1791; received a limited schooling; learned the printing trade; edited the New Brunswick Fredonian 1812–1842; United States collector of internal revenue 1815–1846; clerk of the court of common pleas; member of the State house of assembly in 1823 and 1824; elected to the Twentieth Congress to fill the vacancy caused by the death of George Holcombe; reelected to the Twenty-first and Twenty-second Congresses and served from December 1, 1827, to March 3, 1833; president of a bank in New Brunswick, N. J.; died in Easton, Pa., January 25, 1872; interment in Easton Cemetery.

RANDOLPH, James Henry, a Representative from Tennessee; born near Dandridge, Jefferson County, Tenn., October 18, 1825; attended New Market Academy and was graduated from Holston College, New Market, Tenn.; studied law; was admitted to the bar in 1850 and commenced practice in Dandridge, Tenn.; member of the State house of representatives in 1857, 1858, 1860, and 1861; served in the State senate in 1865; elected judge of the second judicial circuit of Tennessee in 1869; reelected after the constitutional convention in 1870; elected as a Republican to the Forty-fifth Congress (March 4, 1877–March 3, 1879); engaged in agricultural pursuits and milling; died in Newport, Cocke County, Tenn., August 22, 1900; interment in Union Cemetery.

RANDOLPH, Jennings, a Representative and a Senator from West Virginia; born in Salem, Harrison County, W. Va., March 8, 1902; attended the public schools; was graduated from the Salem (W. Va.) Academy in 1920 and Salem (W. Va.) College in 1924; engaged in newspaper work in Clarksburg, W. Va., in 1924; associate editor of West Virginia Review at Charleston in 1925; head of the department of public speaking and journalism at Davis and Elkins College at Elkins, W. Va., 1926–1932; trustee of Salem College and Davis and Elkins College; unsuccessful candidate for election in 1930 to the Seventy-second Congress; elected as a Democrat to the Seventy-third and to the six succeeding Congresses (March 4, 1933–January 3, 1947); unsuccessful candidate for reelection in 1946 to the Eightieth Congress; professor of public speaking at Southeastern University, Washington, D. C., 1935–1953, and dean of School of Business Administration 1952–1958; assistant to president and director of public relations, Capital Airlines, Washington, D. C., February 1947–April 1958; delegate to the Democratic National Conventions in 1948, 1952, 1956, and 1960; elected as a Democrat to the United States Senate to fill the vacancy caused by the death of Matthew M. Neely and served from November 5, 1958, to January 3, 1961. *Reelected in 1960 for the term ending January 3, 1967.*

RANDOLPH, John, a Representative and a Senator from Virginia; born in Cawsons, Prince George County, Va., June 2, 1773; studied under private tutors; attended Walker Maury's School at Burlington, Orange County, Va., the grammar schools of the College of William and Mary at Williamsburg, Va., the College of New Jersey (now Princeton University) in 1787 and 1788, and Columbia College, New York City in 1788 and 1789; studied law in Philadelphia, Pa., but never practiced; elected as a State Rights Democrat to the Sixth and to the six succeeding Congresses (March 4, 1799–March 3, 1813); one of the managers appointed by the House of Representatives in January 1804 to conduct the impeachment proceedings against John Pickering, judge of the United States District Court for New Hampshire, and in December of the same year against Samuel Chase, Associate Justice of the Supreme Court of the United States; unsuccessful anti-Madison candidate for election in 1812 to the Thirteenth Congress; elected to the Fourteenth Congress (March 4, 1815–March 3, 1817); unsuccessful candidate for reelection in 1816 to the Fifteenth Congress; elected to the Sixteenth and to the three succeeding Congresses and served from March 4, 1819, until his resignation, effective December 26, 1825; appointed to the United States Senate December 8, 1825, to fill the vacancy in the term beginning March 4, 1821, caused by the resignation of James Barbour and served from December 26, 1825, to March 3, 1827; participated in a harmless duel with Henry Clay on April 8, 1826; unsuccessful candidate for reelection to the Senate in 1827, elected to the Twentieth Congress (March 4, 1827–March 3, 1829); was not a candidate for reelection to the Twenty-first Congress; member of the Virginia constitutional convention at Richmond in 1829; appointed United States Minister to Russia by President Jackson and served from May 26 to September 19, 1830, when he resigned; elected to the Twenty-third Congress and served from March 4, 1833, until his death in Philadelphia, Pa., May 24, 1833; interment at his residence, "Roanoke," in Charlotte County, Va.; reinterment at "Hollywood," Richmond, Va.

RANDOLPH, Joseph Fitz, a Representative from New Jersey; born in New York City March 14, 1803; in early childhood moved with his parents to Piscataway, Middlesex County, N. J.; educated by private tutors and in private schools; prepared for the class of 1825 in Rutgers College, New Brunswick, N. J., but did not enter; studied law; was admitted to the bar in 1825 and commenced practice in Freehold, N. J.; prosecuting attorney for Monmouth County about 1836; elected as a Whig to the Twenty-fifth, Twenty-sixth, and Twenty-seventh Congresses (March 4, 1837–March 3, 1843); was not a candidate for renomination in 1842; moved to New Brunswick in 1843 and resumed the practice of law; delegate to the State constitutional convention in 1844; member of the committee appointed by the Governor in 1844 to revise the statutes of New Jersey; moved to Trenton in 1845; associate justice of the State supreme court 1845–1852; member of the peace convention held in Washington, D. C., in 1861 in an effort to prevent the impending war; moved to Jersey City in 1864; presidential elector on the Democratic ticket of Seymour and Blair in 1868; died in Jersey City, N. J., on March 20, 1873; interment in Easton Cemetery, Easton, Pa.

RANDOLPH, Peyton (uncle of Edmund Jennings Randolph), a Delegate from Virginia; born at Tazewell Hall, Williamsburg, Va., in September 1721; received his early education under private tutors; was graduated from William and Mary College, Williamsburg, Va.; studied law at the Inner Temple, London, England, and was appointed King's attorney for Virginia in 1748; member of the Virginia House of Burgesses 1764–1774 and served as speaker in 1766; chairman of the committee of correspondence in 1773; president of the Virginia conventions of 1774 and 1775; Member of the Continental Congress in Philadelphia, Pa., September 5, 1774, and elected its President but resigned October 22, 1774, to attend the State legislature; reelected to the Continental Congress, which met in Philadelphia in 1775, but was forced to resign on account of ill health; died in Philadelphia, Pa., October 22, 1775; interment beneath the chapel of the College of William and Mary, Williamsburg, Va.

RANDOLPH, Theodore Fitz (son of James Fitz Randolph), a Senator from New Jersey; born in Mansfield, Tioga County, Pa., June 24, 1826; attended the common schools of New Brunswick, N. J., engaged in mercantile pursuits; moved to Vicksburg, Miss., and engaged in business in 1840; returned to New Jersey and settled in Jersey City in 1852; became interested in mining and the transportation of ores and was president of the Morris & Essex Railroad; member of the State house of assembly in 1859; member of the State senate in 1862 and 1863; Governor of New Jersey 1869–1872; elected as a Democrat to the United States Senate and served from March 4, 1875, to March 3, 1881; died in Morristown, Morris County, N. J., November 7, 1883; interment in Woodlawn Cemetery.

RANDOLPH, Thomas Mann, a Representative from Virginia; born at "Tuckahoe," in Goochland County, Va., October 1, 1768; received his early education from private teachers; attended William and Mary College, Williamsburg, Va., and the University of Edinburgh, Scotland, 1785–1788; served in the State senate in 1793 and 1794; was elected as a Democrat to the Eighth and Ninth Congresses (March 4, 1803–March 3, 1807); colonel of the Twentieth Infantry during the War of 1812; member of the State house of delegates in 1819, 1820, and 1823–1825; Governor of Virginia 1819–1822; died at "Monticello," the ancestral home of Thomas Jefferson, his father-in-law, on June 20, 1828; interment in the family burial ground.

RANEY, John Henry, a Representative from Missouri; born in Gravelton, Wayne County, Mo., September 28, 1849; attended Union School, Des Arc, Mo., and Woods School, Virginia Settlement, Mo.; judge of the county court of Wayne County 1880–1882; studied law; was admitted to the bar in 1881 and commenced practice at Greenville, Mo.; also engaged in agricultural pursuits and as a stock raiser; prosecuting attorney of Wayne County 1882–1888; unsuccessful candidate for election in 1888 to the State house of representatives; delegate to all Republican State conventions 1884–1927; delegate to the Republican National Convention at Minneapolis in 1892; one of the board of regents of the State normal school, Cape Girardeau, Mo., 1893–1895; elected as a Republican to the Fifty-fourth Congress (March 4, 1895–March 3, 1897); unsuccessful candidate for reelection in 1896 to the Fifty-fifth Congress; resumed the practice of law in Piedmont, Mo.; unsuccessful candidate for circuit judge of the twenty-first judicial district in 1898; again prosecuting attorney of Wayne County in 1921 and 1922; died near Patterson, Wayne County, Mo., January 23, 1928; interment in the Masonic Cemetery, Piedmont, Mo.

RANKIN, Christopher, a Representative from Mississippi; born in Washington County, Pa., in 1788; completed preparatory studies at Canonsburg, Pa., moved to Georgia; taught a village school and studied law at the same time; was admitted to the bar in 1809 and commenced practice in Liberty, Amite County, Miss.; member of the Territorial legislature in 1813; moved to Natchez, Miss., in 1816 and practiced law; member of the State constitutional convention in 1817; unsuccessful candidate for United States Senator in 1817; held several local offices; elected as a Democrat to the Sixteenth and to the three succeeding Congresses and served from March 4, 1819, until his death in Washington, D. C., March 14, 1826; interment in the Congressional Cemetery.

RANKIN, Jeannette, a Representative from Montana; born near Missoula, Missoula County, Mont., June 11, 1880; attended the public schools, and was graduated from the University of Montana at Missoula in 1902; student at the School of Philanthropy, New York, N. Y., in 1908 and 1909; social worker in

Seattle, Wash., in 1909; engaged in promoting the cause of woman suffrage in the State of Washington in 1910, in California in 1911, and in Montana 1912–1914; visited New Zealand in 1915 and worked as a seamstress in order to gain personal knowledge of social conditions; elected as a Republican to the Sixty-fifth Congress (March 4, 1917–March 3, 1919); was the first woman to be elected to the National House of Representatives; did not seek renomination in 1918, having become a candidate for the Republican nomination for Senator, but was unsuccessful; was also an unsuccessful candidate on an independent ticket for election to the United States Senate; engaged in social work; elected to the Seventy-seventh Congress (January 3, 1941–January 3, 1943); was not a candidate for renomination in 1942; resumed lecturing and ranching, and is a resident of Helena (Avalanch Ranch), Mont.

RANKIN, John Elliott, a Representative from Mississippi; born near Bolanda, Itawamba County, Miss., March 29, 1882; attended the common and high schools; was graduated from the law department of the University of Mississippi at Oxford in 1910; was admitted to the bar the same year and commenced practice in West Point, Clay County, Miss.; moved to Tupelo, Miss., the following November and continued the practice of law; prosecuting attorney of Lee County 1911–1915; also engaged as a lecturer and newspaper writer; served in the United States Army during the First World War; delegate to the Democratic National Conventions in 1932, 1936, and 1940; coauthor of bill to create the Tennessee Valley Authority; elected as a Democrat to the Sixty-seventh and to the fifteen succeeding Congresses (March 4, 1921–January 3, 1953); unsuccessful candidate for renomination in 1952; was an unsuccessful candidate for the Democratic nomination for United States Senator in 1946; resumed the practice of law; also interested in farming and real estate; died in Tupelo, Miss., November 26, 1960; interment in Greenwood Cemetery, West Point, Miss.

RANKIN, Joseph, a Representative from Wisconsin; born in Passaic, N. J., September 25, 1833; pursued an academic course; moved to Mishicott, Manitowoc County, Wis., in 1854 and engaged in mercantile pursuits; member of the county board in 1859; member of the State assembly in 1860; during the Civil War enlisted in the Union Army in 1862 and was chosen captain of Company D, Twenty-sixth Regiment, Wisconsin Volunteer Infantry; after the war settled in Manitowoc, Wis.; city clerk of Manitowoc 1866–1871; again a member of the State assembly 1871–1874; served in the State senate 1877–1882; elected as a Democrat to the Forty-eighth and Forty-ninth Congresses and served from March 4, 1883, until his death in Washington, D. C., January 24, 1886; interment in Evergreen Cemetery, Manitowoc, Wis.

RANNEY, Ambrose Arnold, a Representative from Massachusetts; born in Townshend, Windham County, Vt., April 17, 1821; was graduated from Dartmouth College, Hanover, N. H., in 1844; studied law in Woodstock, Vt.; was admitted to the bar in 1848 and commenced practice in Boston, Mass.; corporation counsel for the city 1855–1857; member of the State house of representatives in 1857, 1863, and 1864; elected as a Republican to the Forty-seventh, Forty-eighth, and Forty-ninth Congresses (March 4, 1881–March 3, 1887); unsuccessful candidate for reelection in 1886 to the Fiftieth Congress; resumed the practice of law; died in Boston, Mass., March 5, 1899; interment in Forest Hill Cemetery.

RANSDELL, Joseph Eugene, a Representative and a Senator from Louisiana; born in Alexandria, Rapides Parish, La., October 7, 1858; attended the public schools and was graduated from

Union College, Schenectady, N. Y., in 1882; studied law; was admitted to the bar in 1883 and practiced at Lake Providence, La., 1883–1889; district attorney for the eighth judicial district of Louisiana 1884–1896; interested in cotton planting and pecan groves since 1899; member of the levee board, fifth levee district, 1896–1899; member of the State constitutional convention in 1898; elected as a Democrat to the Fifty-sixth Congress to fill the vacancy caused by the death of Samuel T. Baird; reelected to the Fifty-seventh and to the five succeeding Congresses and served from August 29, 1899, to March 3, 1913; was not a candidate for renomination in 1912, having become a candidate for the United States Senate; elected to the United States Senate in 1912, reelected in 1918 and 1924, and served from March 4, 1913, to March 3, 1931; unsuccessful candidate for renomination in 1930; in 1920 founded Ransdell, Inc., a printing firm in Washington, D. C., and served as a director until 1931 when he returned to Lake Providence, La.; engaged in the real-estate business, cotton planting, and pecan growing; member of the board of supervisors, Louisiana State University and Agricultural College at Baton Rouge, 1940–1944; died in Lake Providence, La., July 27, 1954; interment in Lake Providence Cemetery.

RANSIER, Alonzo Jacob, a Representative from South Carolina; born in Charleston, S. C., January 3, 1834; was of the Negro race; received a limited schooling; employed as shipping clerk in 1850; member of a convention of the Friends of Equal Rights at Charleston in 1865 and was deputed to present the memorial there framed to Congress; member of the State constitutional convention in 1868 and 1869; presidential elector on the Republican ticket of Grant and Colfax in 1868; Lieutenant Governor of South Carolina in 1870; president of the Southern States Convention at Columbia in 1871; delegate to the Republican National Convention at Philadelphia in 1872; elected as a Republican to the Forty-third Congress (March 4, 1873–March 3, 1875); United States internal-revenue collector for the second district of South Carolina in 1875 and 1876; died in Charleston, S. C., on August 17, 1882; interment in Unity Friendship Cemetery.

RANSLEY, Harry Clay, a Representative from Pennsylvania; born in Philadelphia, Pa., February 5, 1863; attended the public and private schools; engaged in mercantile pursuits; served in the State house of representatives 1891–1894; member of the Select Council of Philadelphia for sixteen years and president for eight years; delegate to the Republican National Convention at Chicago in 1912 which nominated Taft and Sherman; sheriff of Philadelphia County 1916–1920; chairman of the Republican city committee 1916–1919; elected as a Republican to the Sixty-sixth Congress to fill the vacancy caused by the resignation of J. Hampton Moore; reelected to the Sixty-seventh and to the seven succeeding Congresses and served from November 2, 1920, to January 3, 1937; unsuccessful candidate for reelection in 1936 to the Seventy-fifth Congress; resumed his interest in mercantile pursuits until his death in Philadelphia, Pa., November 7, 1941; interment in West Laurel Hill Cemetery.

RANSOM, Matt Whitaker (cousin of Wharton Jackson Green), a Senator from North Carolina; born in Warren County, N. C., October 8, 1826; attended the common schools, and was graduated from the University of North Carolina at Chapel Hill in 1847; studied law; was admitted to the bar and commenced practice in Warrenton N. C.; was a presidential elector on the Whig ticket of Scott and Graham in 1852; elected attorney general of North Carolina the same year and served until 1855, when he resigned; member of the State house of commons 1858–1860; peace commissioner to the Provisional Congress at Montgomery, Ala., in 1861; entered the Confederate Army as a private and served throughout the Civil War, attaining the rank of major general; moved to Weldon, N. C., in 1866; elected as a Democrat to the United States Senate in 1872 to fill the vacancy in the term commencing March 4, 1871; reelected in 1876, 1883, and 1889 and served from January 30, 1872, to March 3, 1895; unsuccessful candidate for reelection; United States Minister to Mexico 1895–1897; delegate to the Democratic National Convention at St. Louis in 1876 and at Chicago in 1896; engaged in agricultural pursuits; died near Garysburg, Northampton County, N. C., on October 8, 1904; interment in the private burying ground on his estate, "Verona," near Weldon, Halifax County, N. C.

RANTOUL, Robert, Jr., a Senator and a Representative from Massachusetts; born in Beverly, Mass., August 13, 1805; attended the common schools, and Phillips Andover Academy, Andover, Mass.; was graduated from Harvard University in 1826; studied law; was admitted to the bar in 1829 and commenced practice in Salem; moved to South Reading in 1830 and continued the practice of law; moved to Gloucester in 1832; member of the State house of representatives in 1834–1838; member of the commission to revise the laws of Massachusetts; member of the board of education in 1837; moved to Boston in 1839; served as United States district attorney for Massachusetts from 1845 to 1849, when he resigned; elected as a Democrat to the United States Senate to fill the vacancy caused by the resignation of Daniel Webster and served from February 1 to March 3, 1851; elected as a Democrat to the Thirty-second Congress and served from March 4, 1851, until his death in Washington, D. C., on August 7, 1852; interment in Central Cemetery, Beverly, Mass.

RAPIER, James Thomas, a Representative from Alabama; born in Florence, Lauderdale County, Ala., November 13, 1837; was of the Negro race; educated by private tutors in Alabama and studied in Canada; studied law and was admitted to the bar; taught school; returned to the South and traveled as a correspondent for a northern newspaper; became a cotton planter in Alabama in 1865; appointed a notary public by the Governor of Alabama in 1866; member of the first Republican convention held in Alabama and was one of the committee that framed the platform; member of the State constitutional convention at Montgomery in 1867; unsuccessful candidate for secretary of state in 1870; appointed assessor of internal revenue in 1871; appointed State commissioner to the Vienna Exposition by the Governor of Alabama in 1873; commissioner on the part of the United States to the World's Fair in Paris; elected as a Republican to the Forty-third Congress (March 4, 1873–March 3, 1875); unsuccessful candidate for reelection in 1874 to the Forty-fourth Congress; appointed collector of internal revenue for the second district of Alabama on August 8, 1878, and served until his death in Montgomery, Ala., May 31, 1883; interment in Calvary Cemetery, St. Louis, Mo.

RARIDEN, James, a Representative from Indiana; born near Cynthiana, Harrison County, Ky., February 14, 1795; received a limited schooling; moved to Brookville, Ind., and thence to Salisbury; deputy clerk of court; studied law; was admitted to the bar in 1818 and began practice in Centerville, Ind., in 1820; prosecuting attorney 1822–1825; served in the State senate in 1823; member of the State house of representatives in 1829, 1830, 1832, and 1833; elected as a Whig to the Twenty-fifth and Twenty-sixth Congresses (March 4, 1837–March 3, 1841); moved to Cambridge City, Ind., in 1846; delegate to the State constitutional convention in 1850; died in Cambridge City, Wayne County, Ind., October 20, 1856; interment in Riverside Cemetery.

RATHBONE, Henry Riggs (grandson of Ira Harris), a Representative from Illinois; born in Washington, D. C., February 12, 1870; was graduated from Phillips Academy, Andover, Mass., in 1887, from Yale University in 1892, and from the law department of the University of Wisconsin at Madison in 1894; was admitted to the bar in 1895 and commenced practice in Chicago, Ill.; member of the American, Illinois State, and Chicago Bar Associations; delegate to the Republican National Convention in 1916; elected as a Republican to the Sixty-eighth, Sixty-ninth, and Seventieth Congresses and served from March 4, 1923, until his death; nominated for reelection in 1928; died at Chicago, Ill., on July 15, 1928; interment in Rosehill Cemetery.

RATHBUN, George Oscar, a Representative from New York; born in Scipioville, near Auburn, N. Y., in 1803; attended the Auburn schools and was graduated from Hamilton College; studied law; was admitted to the bar and commenced practice in Auburn; member of the State assembly; elected as a Democrat to the Twenty-eighth and Twenty-ninth Congresses (March 4, 1843–March 3, 1847); resumed the practice of his profession; died in Auburn, Cayuga County, N. Y., January 5, 1870; interment in Fort Hill Cemetery.

RAUCH, George Washington, a Representative from Indiana; born on a farm near Warren in Salamonie Township, Huntington County, Ind., February 22, 1876; attended the common schools and Valparaiso (Ind.) Normal School (now Valparaiso University); was graduated from the Northern Indiana Law School at Valparaiso in 1902; was admitted to the bar the same year and commenced the practice of law in Marion, Grant County, Ind.; elected as a Democrat to the Sixtieth and to the four succeeding Congresses (March 4, 1907–March 3, 1917); unsuccessful candidate for reelection in 1916 to the Sixty-fifth Congress; resumed the practice of his profession in Marion, Ind., served on the board of directors of the Motor Securities Corporation and as president and treasurer of the Davis Records Co.; appointed a Federal bank receiver for banks in Swayzee, Sheridan, and Marion, Ind., serving from 1930 to 1939; member of the city school board 1927–1933; died in Marion, Ind., November 4, 1940; interment in Masonic Cemetery, Warren, Ind.

RAUM, Green Berry, a Representative from Illinois; born in Golconda, Pope County, Ill., December 3, 1829; attended the common schools; studied law; was admitted to the bar in 1853 and practiced in Golconda 1853–1856; moved to Kansas in 1856 and practiced his profession for two years; returned to Illinois and settled in Harrisburg; during the Civil War served in the Union Army as major in the Fifty-sixth Regiment, Illinois Volunteer Infantry, and attained the rank of brigadier general; resigned his commission May 6, 1865, and engaged in railroad building; elected as a Republican to the Fortieth Congress (March 4, 1867–March 3, 1869); unsuccessful candidate for reelection in 1868 to the Forty-first Congress; United States Commissioner of Internal Revenue 1876–1883; United States Commissioner of Pensions 1889–1893; engaged in the practice of law in Chicago, Ill., until his death there on December 18, 1909; interment in Arlington National Cemetery, Fort Myer, Va.

RAWLINS, Joseph Lafayette, a Delegate from the Territory of Utah and a Senator from Utah; born at Mill Creek, Salt Lake County, Utah, March 28, 1850; attended the common schools and the University of Utah, Salt Lake City; pursued a classical course at Indiana University, Bloomington, Ind.; professor in the University of Deseret, Salt Lake City, Utah, 1873–1875; studied law; was admitted to the bar in 1875 and commenced practice in Salt Lake City, Utah; elected as a Democrat to the Fifty-third Congress (March 4, 1893–March 3, 1895); unsuccessful candidate for reelection in 1894 to the Fifty-fourth Congress; delegate to the Democratic National Conventions in 1896 and 1900; elected to the United States Senate and served from March 4, 1897, to March 3, 1903; unsuccessful candidate for renomination; continued the practice of law; withdrew from public life and active business in 1921; died in Salt Lake City, Utah, May 24, 1926; interment in Salt Lake City Cemetery.

RAWLS, Morgan, a Representative from Georgia; born near Statesboro, Bulloch County, Ga., June 29, 1829; attended the common schools and pursued an academic course; engaged in agricultural pursuits; moved to Guyton, Ga., in 1856; unsuccessful Union candidate for delegate to the convention of 1860, which passed the ordinance of secession; during the Civil War enlisted in the Confederate Army as a captain of Infantry; elected colonel of the Fifty-fourth Regiment, Georgia Infantry, in 1863; wounded July 22, 1864, in the battles around Atlanta, Ga.; member of the State house of representatives 1863–1865, 1868–1872, 1886–1889, and 1896–1904; member of the State reconstruction convention in 1865; presented credentials as a Democratic Member-elect to the Forty-third Congress and served from March 4, 1873, to March 24, 1874, when he was succeeded by Andrew Sloan, who contested his election; served in the office of the Clerk of the National House of Representatives 1874–1882 and 1891–1895; engaged in agricultural pursuits; died in Guyton, Effingham County, Ga., October 18, 1906; interment in Guyton Cemetery.

RAWSON, Charles Augustus, a Senator from Iowa; born in Des Moines, Iowa, May 29, 1867; attended the public schools and Grinnell (Iowa) College; engaged in banking and the insurance business and also in the manufacture of clay products; chairman of the Republican State central committee 1912–1924; delegate to all Republican State conventions from 1912 to 1926; member of the board of trustees of Grinnell College; State chairman of the war work council of the Young Men's Christian Association and served overseas with that organization during the First World War; delegate to the Republican National Convention at Chicago in 1920; appointed as a Republican to the United States Senate to fill the vacancy caused by the resignation of William S. Kenyon and served from February 24 to December 1, 1922, when a successor was elected and qualified; was not a candidate for election to fill this vacancy; member of the Republican National Committee 1924–1932; resumed the manufacture of clay products; also interested in banking.; died in Des Moines, Iowa, September 2, 1936; interment in Woodland Cemetery.

RAY, George Washington, a Representative from New York; born in Otselic, Chenango County, N. Y., February 3, 1844; attended the common schools and Norwich Academy; private in Company B, Ninetieth New York Volunteers, and brigade clerk, First Brigade, First Division, Nineteenth Army Corps, during the Civil War; discharged at the close of the war; studied law, and was admitted to the bar in November 1867; chairman of the Republican county committee of Chenango County; member of the Republican State committee in 1880; elected as a Republican to the Forty-eighth Congress (March 4, 1883–March 3, 1885); member of the board of education of Norwich Academy and Union Free School; elected to the Fifty-second and to the five succeeding Congresses and served from March 4, 1891, to September 11, 1902, when he resigned to accept the United States judgeship for the northern district of New York, in which capacity he served until his death in Norwich, Chenango County, N. Y., January 10, 1925; interment in Mount Hope Cemetery.

RAY, John Henry, a Representative from New York; born in Mankato, Blue Earth County, Minn., September 27, 1886; attended the public schools; was graduated from the University of Minnesota in 1908 and from Harvard Law School in 1911; was admitted to the Minnesota bar in 1912 and commenced practice in Minneapolis, Minn.; assistant trust officer of Wells Dickey Trust Co. in 1918 and 1919; served as a first lieutenant in Judge Advocate General's Department 1918–1919; assistant to special representative of Secretary of War Newton D. Baker in 1919, concerned with United States war claims with Allies; was decorated with the Order of the Crown of Italy in 1920; member and vice president of State Teachers College Board 1921–1923; moved to Dongan Hills, N. Y., and became associated with the American Telephone & Telegraph Co., 1923–1951; resumed the practice of law in New York City; elected as a Republican to the Eighty-third and to the three succeeding Congresses (January 3, 1953–January 3, 1961). *Reelected to the Eighty-seventh Congress.*

RAY, Joseph Warren, a Representative from Pennsylvania born near Nineveh, Morris Township, Greene County, Pa., May 25, 1849; attended the common schools and was graduated from Waynesburg (Pa.) College in 1874; studied law; was admitted to the bar in 1876 and commenced practice in Waynesburg, Greene County, Pa.; elected as a Republican to the Fifty-first Congress (March 4, 1889–March 3, 1891); unsuccessful candidate for renomination in 1890; resumed the practice of law in Waynesburg, Pa.; trustee of Waynesburg College from 1902 until his death; elected president judge of the thirteenth judicial district of Pennsylvania in 1915 and served until 1926; declined to be a candidate for reelection; again resumed the practice of law in Waynesburg, Pa., where he died September 15, 1928; interment in Greenmont Cemetery.

RAY, Ossian, a Representative from New Hampshire; born in Hinesburg, Chittenden County, Vt., December 13, 1835; moved to Irasburg, Vt., in early childhood; attended the common schools and an academy in Derby, Vt.; studied law in Irasburg and in Lancaster, N. H., to which latter place he moved in 1854; was admitted to the bar in 1857 and practiced in Essex and Coos Counties; solicitor for Coos County 1862–1872; member of the State house of representatives in 1868 and 1869; delegate to the Republican National Convention at Philadelphia in 1872; United States attorney for the district of New Hampshire from February 22, 1879, to December 23, 1880, when he resigned; elected as a Republican to the Forty-sixth Congress to fill the vacancy caused by the death of Evarts W. Farr; reelected to the Forty-seventh and Forty-eighth Congresses and served from January 8, 1881, to March 3, 1885; did not seek renomination in 1884; died in Lancaster, N. H., January 28, 1892; interment in the Summer Street Cemetery.

RAY, William Henry, a Representative from Illinois; born in Amenia, Dutchess County, N. Y., December 14, 1812; moved to Oneida County, N. Y., in 1813 with his parents who settled in Utica; attended the common schools; moved to Rushville, Ill., in 1834; engaged in mercantile pursuits; also interested in banking; member of the first State board of equalization 1867–1869; elected as a Republican to the Forty-third Congress (March 4, 1873–March 3, 1875); resumed his former business pursuits in Rushville, Schuyler County, Ill., and died there January 25, 1881; interment in Rushville Cemetery.

RAYBURN, Sam, a Representative from Texas; born near Kingston, Roane County, Tenn., January 6, 1882; moved to Fannin County, Tex., in 1887 with his parents who settled near Windom; attended the rural schools and was graduated from the East Texas Normal College, Commerce, Tex., in 1903; studied law at the University of Texas at Austin; was admitted to the bar in 1908 and commenced practice in Bonham, Fannin

County, Tex.; member of the State house of representatives 1907–1913, and served as speaker during the last two years; elected as a Democrat to the Sixty-third and to the twenty-four succeeding Congresses and served March 4, 1913, until his death; majority leader in the Seventy-fifth and Seventy-sixth Congresses; minority leader in the Eightieth and Eighty-third Congresses; elected Speaker September 16, 1940, to fill the vacancy caused by the death of Speaker William B. Bankhead; reelected Speaker in the Seventy-seventh, Seventy-eighth, Seventy-ninth, Eighty-first, Eighty-second, Eighty-fourth, Eighty-fifth, Eighty-sixth, and Eighty-seventh Congresses; died in Bonham, Tex., November 16, 1961.

RAYFIEL, Leo Frederick, a Representative from New York; born in New York City, N. Y., March 22, 1888; attended the grade and high schools; was graduated from the New York University Law School in 1908; was admitted to the bar in 1918 and commenced practice in Brooklyn, N. Y.; member of the New York State Assembly 1939–1944; elected as a Democrat to the Seventy-ninth and Eightieth Congresses and served from January 3, 1945, until his resignation on September 13, 1947, having been appointed a judge of the United States District Court for the Eastern District of New York, in which capacity he is now serving; is a resident of Brooklyn, N. Y.

RAYMOND, Henry Jarvis, a Representative from New York; born in Lima, Livingston County, N. Y., January 24, 1820; attended the common schools; was graduated from the University of Vermont at Burlington in 1840; moved to New York City and studied law; engaged in journalism; was connected with the New York Tribune 1841–1848, with the Courier and Enquirer 1848–1850, and with Harper's Magazine in 1850; member of the State assembly in 1850 and 1851 and served as speaker in the latter year; established the New York Times in 1851; delegate to the Whig National Convention at Baltimore in 1852; Lieutenant Governor of New York in 1854; declined a renomination; delegate to the Republican National Convention at Chicago in 1860; again a member of the State assembly in 1862 and served as speaker; elected as a Republican to the Thirty-ninth Congress (March 4, 1865–March 3, 1867); unsuccessful candidate for renomination in 1866; retired from public life and resumed newspaper activities with the New York Times; died in New York City June 18, 1869; interment in Greenwood Cemetery, Brooklyn, N. Y.

RAYMOND, John Baldwin, a Delegate from the Territory of Dakota; born in Lockport, Niagara County, N. Y., December 5, 1844; moved with his parents to Tazewell County, Ill., in 1853; attended the public schools and the Poughkeepsie (N. Y.) Business College in 1865 and 1866; during the Civil War enlisted as a private in the Thirty-first Regiment, Illinois Infantry, in 1861; promoted to captain of Company E of that regiment after the siege of Vicksburg in 1863; served throughout the war and settled in Mississippi; published the Mississippi Pilot at Jackson, Miss., during the reconstruction of that State and until 1877; assistant State treasurer 1873–1875 appointed United States marshal of Dakota Territory in 1877, with headquarters at Yankton, later at Fargo, and served until 1882; declined a reappointment; elected as a Republican to the Forty-eighth Congress (March 4, 1883–March 3, 1885); unsuccessful candidate for renomination in 1884; engaged in wheat raising; died in Fargo, Dak. (now North Dakota), January 3, 1886; interment in the public vault in Rock Creek Cemetery, Washington, D. C.

RAYNER, Isidor, a Representative and a Senator from Maryland; born in Baltimore, Md., April 11, 1850; attended private schools and the University of Maryland at Baltimore; was graduated from the University of Virginia at Charlottesville in 1869; in the latter institution he took the academic course in 1865–1868 and the law course in 1869; upon his return to Baltimore was admitted to the bar in 1871; member of the State house of delegates 1878–1884; served in the State senate 1884–1886; resigned, and was elected as a Democrat to the Fiftieth Congress (March 4, 1887–March 3, 1889); unsuccessful candidate for reelection in 1888 to the Fifty-first Congress; elected to the Fifty-second and Fifty-third Congresses (March 4, 1891–March 3, 1895); declined to be a candidate for renomination in 1894; attorney general of Maryland 1899–1903; elected in 1905 to the United States Senate; reelected in 1911 and served from March 4, 1905, until his death; delegate to the Democratic National Convention at Baltimore in 1912; died in Washington, D. C., November 25, 1912; interment in Rock Creek Cemetery.

RAYNER, Kenneth, a Representative from North Carolina; born in Bertie County, N. C., June 20, 1808; attended Tarborough Academy; studied law; was admitted to the bar in 1829; moved to Hertford County and practiced; member of the State constitutional convention in 1835; member of the State house of commons in 1835, 1836, 1846, 1848, and 1850; elected as a Whig to the Twenty-sixth, Twenty-seventh, and Twenty-eighth Congresses (March 4, 1839–March 3, 1845); was not a candidate for renomination in 1844; presidential elector on the Whig ticket of Taylor and Fillmore in 1848; member of the State senate in 1854; appointed by President Grant as court commissioner of *Alabama* claims at its organization and served until its dissolution; Solicitor of the United States Treasury 1877–1884; died in Washington, D. C., March 4, 1884; interment in the Old City Cemetery, Raleigh, N. C.

REA, David, a Representative from Missouri; born near New Marion, Ripley County, Ind., January 19, 1831; attended the common schools; moved to Missouri with his parents, who settled in Andrew County in 1842; engaged in agricultural pursuits near Rosendale; taught school in the country 1849–1854; studied law; was admitted to the bar in 1862 and commenced practice in Savannah, Mo., in 1863; during the Civil War enlisted in the Union Army and served successively as first lieutenant, captain, quartermaster, and lieutenant colonel; resumed the practice of his profession in Savannah; member of the board of education; elected as a Democrat to the Forty-fourth and Forty-fifth Congresses (March 4, 1875–March 3, 1879); was an unsuccessful candidate for reelection in 1878 to the Forty-sixth Congress; retired from public life and engaged in the practice of law in Savannah, Mo., until his death in that city on June 13, 1901; interment in the City Cemetery.

REA, John, a Representative from Pennsylvania; born at "Rea's Mansion," near Chambersburg, Pa., January 27, 1755; completed preparatory studies; served as lieutenant and captain with the Cumberland County (Pa.) Militia during the Revolutionary War; commissioned the first coroner of Franklin County, Pa., on October 20, 1784; member of the State house of representatives in 1785, 1786, 1789, 1790, 1792, 1793, 1801, and 1802; county auditor in 1793 and 1794; elected as a Democrat to the Eighth and to the three succeeding Congresses (March 4, 1803–March 3, 1811); was an unsuccessful candidate for reelection in 1810 to the Twelfth Congress; served in the War of 1812 as major general of the Eleventh Division of Militia; elected to the Thirteenth Congress to fill the vacancy caused by the death of Robert Whitehill and served from May 11, 1813, to March 3, 1815; member of the State senate in 1823 and 1824, when he resigned; died in Chambersburg, Franklin County, Pa., February 26, 1829; interment in Rocky Spring Churchyard, near Chambersburg, Pa.

READ, Almon Heath, a Representative from Pennsylvania; born in Shelburne, Chittenden County, Vt., June 12, 1790; was graduated from Williams College, Williamstown, Mass., in 1811; county clerk 1815–1820; studied law; was admitted to the bar in 1816 and commenced practice in Montrose, Susquehanna County, Pa.; member of the State house of representatives 1827–1832; served in the State senate 1833–1837; State treasurer in 1840; elected as a Democrat to the Twenty-seventh Congress to fill the vacancy caused by the death of Davis Dimock, Jr.; reelected to the Twenty-eighth Congress and served from March 18, 1842, until his death in Montrose, Pa., June 3, 1844; interment in Montrose Cemetery.

READ, George, a Delegate and a Senator from Delaware; born near North East, Cecil County, Md., September 18, 1733; completed preparatory studies; studied law; was admitted to the bar and began practice in New Castle, Del., in 1752; attorney general for lower Delaware in 1763; Member of the Continental Congress 1774–1777; a signer of the Declaration of Independence; president of the State constitutional convention in 1776; vice president of the State under this constitution; delegate from Delaware to the Federal Constitutional Convention; member of the State house of representatives in 1779 and 1780; judge of the United States Court of Appeals in admiralty cases in 1782; elected to the United States Senate and served from March 4, 1789, to September 18, 1793, when he resigned, having been appointed chief justice of Delaware; served until his death in New Castle, Del., September 21, 1798; interment in Immanuel Churchyard.

READ, Jacob, a Delegate and a Senator from South Carolina; born on the Hobcaw plantation, in Christ Church Parish, near Charleston, S. C., in 1751; completed preparatory studies; studied law in England 1773–1775; joined other Americans in London in 1774 in a petition against the Boston port bill; returned to the United States and served as colonel in the Revolutionary Army and in other military and civil capacities; sent as a prisoner to St. Augustine in 1785; member of the State house of representatives in 1781, 1782, and 1789–1794 and served as speaker 1789–1794; member of the State legislative council in 1783 and 1784 and justice of quorum; Member of the Continental Congress 1783–1785; elected as a Federalist to the United States Senate and served from March 4, 1795, to March 3, 1801; was admitted to the bar in Charleston, S. C., in 1799 and began practice there; judge of the United States Court for the District of South Carolina from March 3, 1801, until his death; brigadier general, Seventh Brigade, South Carolina State troops, 1810–1816; died in Charleston, S. C., July 17, 1816; interment in the family cemetery on the Hobcaw plantation, in Christ Church Parish, near Charleston, S. C.

READ, Nathan, a Representative from Massachusetts; born in Warren, Mass., July 2, 1759; attended the common schools and was graduated from Harvard University in 1781; taught school in Beverly and Salem and was elected a tutor in Harvard University, where he continued until 1787; opened an apothecary store in Salem; interested in an iron factory at Danvers, Mass.; elected as a Federalist to the Sixth Congress to fill the vacancy caused by the resignation of Samuel Sewall; reelected to the Seventh Congress and served from November 25, 1800, to March 3, 1803; was not a candidate for renomination in 1802; judge of the court of common pleas of Essex County in 1803; moved to Belfast, Maine, in 1807; judge of the county court of Hancock County in 1807; instrumental in establishing Belfast Academy and served as trustee for forty years; died near Belfast, Waldo County, Maine, January 20, 1849; interment in Grove Cemetery, Belfast, Maine.

READ, William Brown, a Representative from Kentucky; born in Hardin County, near Hodgenville, Ky., December 14, 1817; completed preparatory studies; studied law; was admitted to the bar and commenced practice in Hodgenville, Ky., in 1849; member of the State senate 1857–1865; unsuccessful candidate for election as Lieutenant Governor of Kentucky in 1863; delegate to the Democratic National Conventions at Charleston and Baltimore in 1860 and at Chicago in 1864; member of the State house of representatives 1867–1869; elected as a Democrat to the Forty-second and Forty-third Congresses (March 4, 1871–March 3, 1875); unsuccessful candidate for renomination in 1874; resumed the practice of his profession; died in Hodgenville, Ky., August 5, 1880; interment in Red Hill Cemetery.

READE, Edwin Godwin, a Representative from North Carolina; born on a farm in Person County, N. C., November 13, 1812; completed preparatory studies; engaged in agricultural pursuits; studied law; was admitted to the bar in 1835 and commenced practice in Roxboro, Person County, N. C.; elected as the candidate of the American Party to the Thirty-fourth Congress (March 4, 1855–March 3, 1857); declined to be a candidate for renomination in 1856; served in the Confederate Senate in 1863 by appointment of Governor Vance; president of the reconstruction convention which met in Raleigh in 1865; associate justice of the supreme court of North Carolina 1868–1879; engaged in banking in Raleigh, N. C., and died there October 18, 1894; interment in Oakwood Cemetery.

READING, John Roberts, a Representative from Pennsylvania; born in Somerton, Philadelphia County, Pa., November 1, 1826; completed preparatory studies; was graduated from the Jefferson Medical College, Philadelphia, Pa., in 1847 and began practice in Somerton, Pa.; later graduated from Hahnemann College, Philadelphia, Pa., and practiced homeopathy; presented credentials as a Democratic Member-elect to the Forty-first Congress and served from March 4, 1869, to April 13, 1870, when he was succeeded by Caleb N. Taylor, who contested his election; unsuccessful Democratic candidate for election in 1870 to the Forty-second Congress; died in Philadelphia, Pa., February 14, 1886; interment in the William Penn Cemetery, Somerton, Pa.

READY, Charles (uncle of William T. Haskell), a Representative from Tennessee; born in Readyville, Rutherford (now Cannon) County, Tenn., December 22, 1802; attended the common schools and was graduated from Greeneville (Tenn.) College; studied law; was admitted to the bar in 1825 and commenced practice in Murfreesboro, Tenn.; member of the State house of representatives in 1835; elected as a Whig to the Thirty-third, Thirty-fourth, and Thirty-fifth Congresses (March 4, 1853–March 3, 1859); unsuccessful candidate for reelection in 1858 to the Thirty-sixth Congress; resumed the practice of law; died in Murfreesboro, Rutherford County, Tenn., June 4, 1878; interment in Evergreen Cemetery.

REAGAN, John Henninger, a Representative and a Senator from Texas; born in Sevierville, Sevier County, Tenn., October 8, 1818; attended the common schools, Nancy Academy, Boyds Creek Academy, and Maryville Academy, Maryville, Tenn.; joined the Army and participated in campaigns against the Cherokee Indians; deputy surveyor of the public lands 1839–1843; studied law; was admitted to the bar in 1846 and practiced in Buffalo and Palestine, Tex.; member of the State house of representatives 1847–1849; judge of the district court from 1852 to 1857, when he resigned; elected as a Democrat to the Thirty-fifth and Thirty-sixth Congresses (March 4, 1857–March

3, 1861); elected to the secession convention of Texas in 1861; deputy to the Provisional Congress of the Confederacy; appointed Postmaster General of the Confederacy March 6, 1861; reappointed in 1862 and occupied the position until the close of the war; also appointed Acting Secretary of the Treasury of the Confederacy for a short time preceding the close of the war; member of the State constitutional convention in 1875; elected as a Democrat to the Forty-fourth and to the five succeeding Congresses (March 4, 1875–March 3, 1887); had been reelected to the Fiftieth Congress but resigned March 4, 1887, to become Senator; elected to the United States Senate and served from March 4, 1887, until June 10, 1891, when he resigned; returned to Texas and was appointed a member of the railroad commission of the State and served as chairman 1897–1903; died in Palestine, Anderson County, Tex., March 6, 1905; interment in East Hill Cemetery.

REAMES, Alfred Evan, a Senator from Oregon; born in Jacksonville, Jackson County, Oreg., February 5, 1870; attended the public schools, the University of the Pacific, San Jose, Calif., and the University of Oregon at Eugene; was graduated from the law department of Washington and Lee University, Lexington, Va., in 1893; was admitted to the bar the same year and commenced practice in Eugene, Oreg., the same year; later practiced law in Portland, Oreg., in 1894 and 1895, in Medford, Jackson County, Oreg., in 1895 and 1896, and in Jacksonville, Oreg., 1897–1900; served as district attorney of Jackson, Josephine, Klamath, and Lake Counties, Oreg., 1900–1908; returned to Medford, Oreg., in 1908 and continued the practice of law; also engaged in mining; appointed as a Democrat to the United States Senate to fill the vacancy caused by the resignation of Frederick Steiwer and served from February 1 to November 8, 1938, when a successor was elected; was not a candidate for election in 1938 to fill the vacancy; served as chairman of the executive committee of the Democratic State central committee of Oregon 1936–1943; resumed the practice of his profession; died in Medford, Oreg., on March 4, 1943; interment in Siskiyou Memorial Park.

REAMS, Henry Frazier, a Representative from Ohio; born in Franklin, Williamson County, Tenn., January 15, 1897; attended the public schools of Tennessee; during First World War enlisted as a private in 1918 and served with the Fifty-eighth Field Artillery, United States Army, until discharged as a lieutenant in 1919; graduated from the University of Tennessee at Knoxville in 1919 and from Vanderbilt University Law School, Nashville, Tenn., in 1922; was admitted to the Tennessee bar in 1920 and commenced the practice of law in Nashville, Tenn.; moved to Toledo, Ohio, in 1922, admitted to the Ohio bar in 1923, and continued the practice of law; delegate to Democratic National Conventions in 1928, 1932, 1936, 1940, 1944, 1948, and 1956; prosecuting attorney of Lucas County, Ohio, 1933–1937; appointed by Governor as special investigator of Ohio State Penitentiary in 1935; member of Toledo Port Commission 1939–1945; director, Civilian Defense, Fifth Service Command, in 1941 and 1943; collector of internal revenue at Toledo, Ohio, 1942–1944; State director of public welfare in 1945 and 1946; president and treasurer of Community Broadcasting Co. (Station WTOL) 1937–1960; also interested in the banking business; trustee of Bowling Green State University 1948–1957; delegate to the Council of Europe at Strasbourg in 1951 and to the Interparliamentary Union Conferences in Washington, D. C., in 1953 and in Vienna, Austria, in 1954; elected as an Independent to the Eighty-second and Eighty-third Congresses (January 3, 1951–January 3, 1955); unsuccessful candidate for reelection in 1954 to the Eighty-fourth Congress; resumed the practice of law; is a resident of Toledo, Ohio.

REAVIS, Charles Frank, a Representative from Nebraska; born in Falls City, Richardson County, Nebr., September 5, 1870; attended the public schools and Northwestern University, Evanston, Ill.; studied law; was admitted to the bar in 1892 and commenced practice in Falls City; prosecuting attorney of Richardson County 1894–1896; elected as a Republican to the Sixty-fourth and to the three succeeding Congresses and served from March 4, 1915, to June 3, 1922, when he resigned; appointed in June 1922 special assistant to the Attorney General in the prosecution of so-called war fraud cases and served until June 1, 1924; moved to Lincoln, Nebr., in 1924 and continued the practice of law; died in Lincoln, Nebr., May 26, 1932; interment in Steele Cemetery, Falls City, Nebr.

REBER, John, a Representative from Pennsylvania; born in South Manheim Township, Schuylkill County, Pa., February 1, 1858; attended the public schools, and was graduated from the Eastman Business College, Poughkeepsie, N. Y., in 1875; taught school for several years and was later employed as a bookkeeper; deputy county treasurer of Schuylkill County 1882–1884; engaged in the manufacture of hosiery in Pottsville 1885–1917 and also interested in banking; elected as a Republican to the Sixty-sixth and Sixty-seventh Congresses (March 4, 1919–March 3, 1923); was not a candidate for renomination in 1922; resumed banking activities in Pottsville, Pa., and served as president of the Reber Investment Co.; died in Pottsville, Pa., on September 26, 1931; interment in the Charles Baber Cemetery.

REDDEN, Monroe Minor, a Representative from North Carolina; born in Hendersonville, Henderson County, N. C., September 24, 1901; attended the public schools; was graduated from the law school of Wake Forest College, Wake Forest, N. C., in 1923; was admitted to the bar the same year and commenced practice in Hendersonville, N. C.; chairman of Henderson County Democratic Committee 1930–1946; chairman of the State Democratic executive committee from February 1942 to August 1944; elected as a Democrat to the Eightieth, Eighty-first, and Eighty-second Congresses (January 3, 1947–January 3, 1953); was not a candidate for renomination in 1952; resumed the practice of law; president of the Southern Heritage Life Insurance Co. 1956–1959; resides in Hendersonville, N. C.

REDFIELD, William Cox, a Representative from New York; born in Albany, N. Y., June 18, 1858; moved with his parents to Pittsfield, Mass., in 1867; attended the public schools and received home instruction; employed in the Pittsfield post office and later as a traveling salesman for a paper company; went to New York City, N. Y., at the age of nineteen and was employed in the stationery and printing business; leaving this in 1883, he became connected in different capacities with the manufacture of steel and iron forgings in Brooklyn, N. Y.; interested in many other manufacturing concerns and banking and life-insurance companies; delegate to the Gold Democrats National Convention at Indianapolis in 1896; unsuccessful candidate as a Gold Democrat for election in 1896 to the Fifty-fifth Congress; commissioner of public works for Brooklyn Borough in 1902 and 1903; elected as a Democrat to the Sixty-second Congress (March 4, 1911–March 3, 1913); unsuccessful candidate for nomination as Vice President of the United States and therefore declined to be a candidate for renomination to Congress in 1912; appointed Secretary of Commerce in the Cabinet of President Wilson and served from March 4, 1913, to November 1, 1919, when he resigned; while Secretary he served on the Federal Board of Vocational Education, the Council of National Defense, and the War Trade Council; chairman of the American-Canadian Fisheries Conference; engaged in banking and the investment and insurance business in New York City and Brooklyn, N. Y.; also engaged as an author; died in New York City, N. Y., June 13, 1932; interment in the Albany Rural Cemetery, Albany, N. Y.

REDING, John Randall, a Representative from New Hampshire; born in Portsmouth, N. H., October 18, 1805; attended the common schools; was apprenticed to the printer's trade and subsequently became an editor; elected as a Democrat to the Twenty-seventh and Twenty-eighth Congresses (March 4, 1841–March 3, 1845); naval storekeeper at Portsmouth 1853–1858; mayor of Portsmouth in 1860; member of the State house of representatives 1867–1870; died in Portsmouth, N. H., October 8, 1892; interment in Haverhill Cemetery, Haverhill, N. H.

REECE, Brazilla Carroll (husband of Louise G. Reece), a Representative from Tennessee; born on a farm near Butler, Johnson County, Tenn., December 22, 1889; attended the public schools, Watauga Academy, Carson-Newman College, New York University, and the University of London; assistant secretary and instructor in the New York University in 1916 and 1917; during the First World War enlisted in May 1917 and served with the American Expeditionary Forces from October 1917 to July 1919; was at the front two hundred and ten days; commanded the Third Battalion of the One Hundred and Second Infantry Regiment, Twenty-sixth Division; cited for bravery by Marshal Petain and Generals Pershing, Hale, and Edwards; was decorated with the Distinguished Service Cross, Distinguished Service Medal, Purple Heart, and the French Croix de Guerre with Palm; director of the School of Business Administration of New York University in 1919 and 1920; elected as a Republican to the Sixty-seventh and to the four succeeding Congresses (March 4, 1921–March 3, 1931); unsuccessful candidate for reelection in 1930 to the Seventy-second Congress; elected to the Seventy-third and to the six succeeding Congresses (March 4, 1933–January 3, 1947); was not a candidate for renomination in 1946; delegate to the Republican National Conventions in 1928, 1932, 1936, 1940, 1944, and 1948; lawyer, banker, and publisher; member of the Board of Regents of the Smithsonian Institution in 1945 and 1946; chairman of the Republican National Committee 1946–1948; unsuccessful candidate for election to the United States Senate in 1948; elected to the Eighty-second and to the five succeeding Congresses and served from January 3, 1951, until his death in the naval hospital at Bethesda, Md., March 19, 1961; interment in Monte Vista Burial Park, Johnson City, Tenn.

REED, Charles Manning, a Representative from Pennsylvania; born in Erie, Erie County, Pa., April 3, 1803; attended the public schools and was graduated from Washington College, Washington, Pa.; studied law; was admitted to the bar in Philadelphia in 1824 but did not practice; engaged in business in Erie with his father, an extensive owner of vessels on the Great Lakes; appointed colonel of militia in 1831 and brigadier general at the expiration of his commission; member of the State house of representatives in 1837 and 1838; elected as a Whig to the Twenty-eighth Congress (March 4, 1843–March 3, 1845); unsuccessful candidate for reelection in 1844 to the Twenty-ninth Congress; resumed shipping on the Great Lakes; also engaged in banking, mercantile pursuits, and railroad business 1846–1849; died in Erie, Pa., December 16, 1871; interment in Erie Cemetery.

REED, Chauncey William, a Representative from Illinois; born in West Chicago, Du Page County, Ill., June 2, 1890; attended the public schools and Northwestern University, Evanston, Ill.; city treasurer of West Chicago, Ill., in 1913 and 1914; was graduated from the Webster College of Law, Chicago, Ill., in 1915; was admitted to the bar the same year and commenced practice in Naperville, Ill.; during the First World War served as a sergeant of Infantry, Eighty-sixth Division; resumed practice of law at Naperville, Ill.; served as State's attorney of Du Page County 1920–1935; chairman of Du Page County Republican central committee 1926–1934; elected as a Republican to the Seventy-fourth and to the ten succeeding Congresses, and served from January 3, 1935, until his death in the naval hospital at Bethesda, Md., February 9, 1956; interment in Glen Oak Cemetery, West Chicago, Ill.

REED, Clyde Martin, a Senator from Kansas; born near Champaign, Champaign County, Ill., October 19, 1871; moved with his family to Labette County, Kans., in 1875; attended the public schools; taught school one year; served in the Railway Mail Service 1889–1910, rising through all grades to field superintendent of divisions at Cleveland and Cincinnati, Ohio, New Orleans, La., Omaha, Nebr., and St. Paul, Minn., and superintendent, Railway Adjustment Division, Post Office Department; resigned in 1917 to manage and publish a newspaper at Parsons, Kans.; secretary to Gov. Henry J. Allen, of Kansas, in 1919; member of Kansas Industrial Court in 1920; chairman of the Kansas Public Utilities Commission 1921–1924; served as Governor of Kansas 1929–1931; practiced extensively before the Interstate Commerce Commission; elected as a Republican in 1938 to the United States Senate for the term commencing January 3, 1939; while a Member of the United States Senate was an unsuccessful candidate for the Republican gubernatorial nomination in 1942; reelected to the United States Senate in 1944 and served from January 3, 1939, until his death in Parsons, Kans., November 8, 1949; interment in Oakwood Cemetery.

REED, Daniel Alden, a Representative from New York; born in Sheridan, Chautauqua County, N. Y., September 15, 1875; attended the public schools in Sheridan and in Silver Creek, N. Y.; was graduated from Cornell University, Ithaca, N. Y., in 1898; studied law; was admitted to the bar in 1900 and practiced in Silver Creek and later in Dunkirk, N. Y.; attorney for the excise department of the State of New York 1903–1909; sent by the Government of the United States on a special mission to France in 1917 and 1918; director of the Dunkirk Trust Co.; lecturer on commercial and civic subjects; elected as a Republican to the Sixty-sixth and to the twenty succeeding Congresses and served from March 4, 1919, until his death; delegate to the Interparliamentary Union meeting in Rome, Italy, in 1948, and represented the United States at subsequent meetings in Sweden, Switzerland, and France; died in Washington, D. C., February 19, 1959; interment in Sheridan Cemetery, Sheridan, N. Y.

REED, David Aiken, a Senator from Pennsylvania; born in Pittsburgh, Pa., December 21, 1880; attended private schools; was graduated from Shadyside Academy, Pittsburgh, Pa., in 1896 and from Princeton University, Princeton, N. J., in 1900; studied law; was admitted to the bar in 1903 and practiced in Pittsburgh, Pa., 1903–1917; chairman of the Pennsylvania Industrial Accidents Commission 1912–1915; during the First World War served as major of the Three Hundred and Eleventh Field Artillery from August 15, 1917, until his discharge February 26, 1919; lieutenant colonel, Field Artillery Reserve, 1919–1922; awarded the Distinguished Service Medal; chevalier, French Legion of Honor; member of the American Battle Monuments Commission 1923–1948; resumed the practice of law in Pittsburgh in 1919; delegate to the Republican National Conventions in 1924, 1932, 1936, and 1940; appointed on August 8, 1922, and elected on November 7, 1922, to the United States Senate to fill the vacancy in the term ending March 3, 1923, caused by the death of William E. Crow, and on the same day was elected for the term commencing March 4, 1923; reelected in 1928, and served from August 8, 1922, to January 3, 1935; unsuccessful candidate for reelection in 1934; resumed the practice of law in Pittsburgh, Pa.; died in Sarasota, Fla., February 10, 1953; interment in Arlington National Cemetery, Fort Myer, Va.

REED, Edward Cambridge, a Representative from New York; born in Fitzwilliam, N. H., March 8, 1793; attended the common schools; was graduated from Dartmouth College, Hanover, N. H., in 1812; served in the War of 1812 under Governor Marcy; studied law in Troy, N. Y.; was admitted to the bar in 1816 and commenced practice in Homer, N. Y.; secretary of the board of trustees of Cortland Academy, Homer, N. Y., 1822–1870; district attorney of Cortland County 1827–1836; was admitted to the court of chancery in 1830; elected as a Democrat to the Twenty-second Congress (March 4, 1831–March 3, 1833); resumed the practice of law; associate judge of the court of common pleas of Cortland County 1836–1840; again district attorney in 1856; moved to Ithaca, N. Y., in 1875 and resumed the practice of his profession; died in Ithaca, Tompkins County, N. Y., on May 1, 1883; interment in Glenwood Cemetery, Homer, Cortland County, N. Y.

REED, Eugene Elliott, a Representative from New Hampshire; born in Manchester, N. H., April 23, 1866; attended the public schools and received instruction from private tutors; studied law; employed in the traffic department of the Boston & Maine Railroad; director and officer of numerous New England and New York corporations and engaged in construction contracting business; alderman of Manchester 1899–1903 and mayor 1903–1911; Democratic National and State committeeman for twelve years; delegate to Democratic National Conventions in 1908, 1912, 1916, and 1924; unsuccessful candidate for election in 1910 to the Sixty-second Congress; elected as a Democrat to the Sixty-third Congress (March 4, 1913–March 3, 1915); unsuccessful candidate for reelection in 1914 to the Sixty-fourth Congress; appointed by President Wilson on the Philippine Commission and served as secretary of commerce and police in 1916; negotiated the purchase and was first president under the Philippine ownership of Manila railroads; returned to the United States in 1918; unsuccessful candidate for United States Senator in 1918; engaged in the general export business in New York 1919–1922; vice president in charge of production of the United Life & Accident Insurance Co., Concord, N. H., 1922–1931; National Recovery Administration director for New Hampshire in 1933 and 1934; State director, National Emergency Council and Federal Housing Agency 1934–1939; member, New Hampshire Emergency Flood Relief and Rehabilitation Committee in 1936; member New Hampshire Disaster Relief Committee in 1938; regional director for New England, Office of Government Reports, in 1939 and 1940; died at Manchester, N. H., December 15, 1940; interment in Pine Grove Cemetery.

REED, Isaac, a Representative from Maine; born in Waldoboro, Maine, August 22, 1809; prepared for college at Bloomfield Academy, but by preference became a merchant-ship builder; also engaged in banking; town clerk of Waldoboro 1836–1838; served in the State senate in 1839, 1840, 1850, and 1863; member of the State house of representatives in 1842, 1843, and 1846; president of the town board 1843–1868; selectman 1849–1853, 1855, and 1856; member of the State board of agriculture and a trustee of the Maine Insane Hospital; unsuccessful candidate for election in 1850 to the Thirty-second Congress; subsequently elected as a Whig to the Thirty-second Congress to fill the vacancy caused by the death of Charles Andrews and served from June 25, 1852, to March 3, 1853; unsuccessful candidate for Governor of Maine in 1854 and 1855; resumed shipbuilding; State treasurer in 1856; upon the dissolution of the Whig Party

became a Democrat; again a member of the State house of representatives in 1870 and 1871; died in Waldoboro, Lincoln County, Maine, September 19, 1887; interment in Central Cemetery.

REED, James Alexander, a Senator from Missouri; born on a farm near Mansfield, Richland County, Ohio, November 9, 1861; moved with his parents to Cedar Rapids, Linn County, Iowa, in 1864; attended the public schools and Coe College, Cedar Rapids, Iowa; studied law; was admitted to the bar in 1885 and commenced practice in Cedar Rapids, Iowa; moved to Kansas City, Mo., in 1887 and continued the practice of law; counselor of Kansas City in 1897 and 1898; prosecuting attorney of Jackson County from 1898 until 1900, when he resigned; mayor of Kansas City 1900–1904; delegate to the Democratic National Conventions in 1908, 1912, 1916, 1920, and 1924; elected as a Democrat to the United States Senate in 1910; reelected in 1916 and again in 1922 and served from March 4, 1911, to March 3, 1929; was not a candidate for renomination in 1928; resumed the practice of his profession in Kansas City, Mo.; died at his summer home near Fairview, Oscoda County, Mich., September 8, 1944; interment in Mount Washington Cemetery, near Kansas City, Mo.

REED, James Byron, a Representative from Arkansas; born near Lonoke, Lonoke County, Ark., January 2, 1881; attended the rural schools of his county and Hendrix College and was graduated from the law department of the University of Arkansas at Fayetteville in 1906; was admitted to the bar in 1906 and commenced the practice of law in Lonoke, Ark.; member of the State house of representatives in 1907; prosecuting attorney of the seventeenth judicial district of Arkansas 1912–1916; presidential elector of the Democratic ticket of Cox and Roosevelt in 1920 and was selected as the messenger to deliver the electoral vote of the State of Arkansas; elected as a Democrat to the Sixty-eighth Congress to fill the vacancy caused by the death of Lewis E. Sawyer; reelected to the Sixty-ninth and Seventieth Congresses and served from October 20, 1923, to March 3, 1929; unsuccessful candidate for renomination in 1928; resumed the practice of law in Lonoke, Ark.; moved to Little Rock, Ark., in 1931 and continued the practice of law until his death there on April 27, 1935; interment in Lonoke Cemetery, Lonoke, Ark.

REED, John, a Representative from Massachusetts; born in Framingham, Mass., November 11, 1751; moved with his parents to Titicut Parish, in the northwestern part of Middleboro, Mass., in 1756; was graduated from Yale College in 1772; studied theology; was ordained as a Congregational minister in 1780; served as chaplain in the United States Navy for two years; moved to West Bridgewater, Mass., in 1780, where he became pastor of the First Congregational Society, which position he retained until his death; elected as a Federalist to the Fourth, Fifth, and Sixth Congresses (March 4, 1795–March 3, 1801); was not a candidate for renomination in 1800; again resumed his ministerial duties; died in West Bridgewater, Plymouth County, Mass., on February 17, 1831; interment in the Old Graveyard.

REED, John (son of the preceding), a Representative from Massachusetts; born in West Bridgewater, Mass., September 2, 1781; was graduated from Brown University, Providence, R. I., in 1803; tutor of languages in that institution for two years and principal of the Bridgewater (Mass.) Academy in 1806 and 1807; studied law; was admitted to the bar and commenced practice in Yarmouth, Mass.; elected as a Federalist to the Thirteenth and Fourteenth Congresses (March 4, 1813–March 3, 1817); elected as a Whig to the Seventeenth and to the nine succeeding Congresses (March 4, 1821–March 3, 1841); declined to be candidate for reelection in 1840; Lieutenant

Governor of Massachusetts 1845–1851; retired from public life; died in West Bridgewater, Plymouth County, Mass., November 25, 1860.

REED, Joseph, a Delegate from Pennsylvania; was born in Trenton, N. J., August 27, 1741; attended Philadelphia Academy; was graduated from the College of New Jersey (now Princeton University) in 1757; studied law; was admitted to the bar in 1762; was a law student in the Temple in London; returned in 1767 and commenced practice in Trenton, N. J.; took an active part in pre-Revolutionary affairs; moved to Philadelphia, Pa., in October 1770; member of the committee of correspondence in 1774; president of the Pennsylvania convention in January 1775; accompanied General Washington to Cambridge as his aide-de-camp and military secretary in July 1775; served during the campaign of 1776 as adjutant general of the Army from June 5, 1776, to January 22, 1777; Member of the Continental Congress in 1777 and 1778; president of the supreme executive council of Pennsylvania 1778–1781; aided in founding the University of Pennsylvania, of which he was a trustee 1782–1785; died in Philadelphia, Pa., March 5, 1785; interment in the Arch Street Presbyterian Church Cemetery.

REED, Joseph Rea, a Representative from Iowa; born in Ashland County, Ohio, March 12, 1835; attended the common schools and Vermillion Institution, Hayesville, Ohio, 1854–1857; moved to Adel, Dallas County, Iowa, in 1857; studied law; was admitted to the bar in 1859 and engaged in the practice of law at Adel until 1861; during the Civil War enlisted as first lieutenant in the Second Battery, Iowa Light Artillery, in July 1861, promoted to captain in October 1864, and served until June 10, 1865; resumed the practice of law in Adel; member of the State senate in 1866 and 1868; moved to Council Bluffs, Iowa, in 1869; judge of the district court 1872–1884; judge of the supreme court of the State 1884–1889; elected as a Republican to the Fifty-first Congress (March 4, 1889–March 3, 1891); unsuccessful candidate for reelection in 1890 to the Fifty-second Congress; chief justice of the court of private land claims in 1891–1904; resumed the practice of law in Council Bluffs, Pottawattamie County, Iowa, where he died on April 2, 1925; interment in Walnut Hill Cemetery.

REED, Philip, a Senator and a Representative from Maryland; born near Chestertown, Kent County, Md., in 1760; completed preparatory studies; served in the Revolutionary Army, attaining the rank of captain of Infantry; member of the State house of delegates in 1787; sheriff of Kent County 1791–1794; member of the executive council in 1805 and 1806; resigned; elected to the United States Senate in 1806 to fill the vacancy caused by the resignation of Robert Wright; reelected the same year and served from November 25, 1806, to March 3, 1813; lieutenant colonel of the Twenty-first Regiment, Maryland Militia, in the War of 1812 and lieutenant colonel commandant of the First Regiment, Maryland Militia, in 1814, when he defeated the British in the Battle of Caulk's Field; in recognition of his service was made a brigadier general of Maryland Militia; elected to the Fifteenth Congress (March 4, 1817–March 3, 1819); unsuccessful candidate for reelection in 1818 to the Sixteenth Congress; successfully contested the election of Jeremiah Cosden to the Seventeenth Congress and served from March 19, 1822, to March 3, 1823; died in Huntingtown, Kent County, Md., November 2, 1829; interment in the cemetery of Christ Church, near Chestertown, Md.

REED, Robert Rentoul, a Representative from Pennsylvania; born in Washington, Pa., March 12, 1807; completed preparatory studies; was graduated from Washington and Jefferson College, Washington, Pa., in 1824 and from the medical department of the University of Pennsylvania in 1829; began the practice of medicine in Washington, Pa.; elected as a Whig to the Thirty-first Congress (March 4, 1849–March 3, 1851); member of the State house of representatives in 1863 and 1864; died near Washington, Washington County, Pa., on December 14, 1864; interment in Washington Cemetery.

REED, Stuart Felix, a Representative from West Virginia; born near Philippi, Barbour County, W. Va., January 8, 1866; attended the common schools; taught in country schools; was graduated from the Fairmont State Normal School in 1885 and from the law department of the University of West Virginia at Morgantown in 1889; founded and edited the Athenaeum (college journal) in 1889; editor of the Telegram in Clarksburg 1890–1898; member of the State senate 1895–1899; postmaster of Clarksburg 1897–1901; president of the board of trustees of Broaddus College 1901–1908; declined appointment as consul general to Buenos Aires in 1905; member of the International Tax Conference at Louisville, Ky., in 1909; secretary of state of West Virginia 1909–1917; vice president of the West Virginia Semicentennial Commission in 1913; president of the Association of American Secretaries of State in 1915; elected as a Republican to the Sixty-fifth and to the three succeeding Congresses (March 4, 1917–March 3, 1925); declined to be a candidate for renomination in 1924; engaged in literary pursuits; resided in Washington, D. C., until his death there July 4, 1935; interment in Elkview Masonic Cemetery, Clarksburg, W. Va.

REED, Thomas Brackett, a Representative from Maine; born in Portland, Cumberland County, Maine, October 18, 1839; attended the public schools; was graduated from Bowdoin College, Brunswick, Maine, in 1860; studied law; acting assistant paymaster, United States Navy, from April 19, 1864, to November 4, 1865; was admitted to the bar in 1865 and commenced practice in Portland, Maine; member of the State house of representatives in 1868 and 1869; served in the State senate in 1870; attorney general of Maine 1870–1872; city solicitor of Portland 1874–1877; elected as a Republican to the Forty-fifth and to the eleven succeeding Congresses and served from March 4, 1877, to September 4, 1899, when he resigned; served as Speaker of the House of Representatives in the Fifty-first, Fifty-fourth, and Fifty-fifth Congresses; moved to New York City, N. Y., and engaged in the practice of his profession; died in Washington, D. C., on December 7, 1902; interment in Evergreen Cemetery, Portland, Maine.

REED, Thomas Buck, a Senator from Mississippi; born near Lexington, Ky., May 7, 1787; attended the public schools and Princeton College; studied law; was admitted to the bar and commenced practice in Lexington in 1808; moved to Natchez, Miss., in 1809; city clerk in 1811; unsuccessful candidate for Delegate to Congress in 1813; attorney general of Mississippi 1821–1826; elected to the State house of representatives in 1825 but declined to take his seat; elected as a Democrat to the United States Senate to fill the vacancy caused by the resignation of David Holmes and served from January 28, 1826, to March 3, 1827; unsuccessful candidate for reelection in 1827; again elected to the United States Senate in 1828 and served from March 4, 1829, until his death in Lexington, Ky., November 26, 1829; interment in the Old Baptist Cemetery.

REED, William, a Representative from Massachusetts; born in Marblehead, Mass., June 6, 1776; received a limited education; engaged in mercantile pursuits; elected as a Federalist to the Twelfth and Thirteenth Congresses (March 4, 1811–March 3,

1815); member of the board of the Andover Theological Seminary; trustee of Dartmouth College, Hanover, N. H.; resumed mercantile pursuits; died in Marblehead, Essex County, Mass., February 18, 1837; interment in a private burying ground on Harris Street.

REEDER, William Augustus, a Representative from Kansas; born near Shippensburg, Cumberland County, Pa., August 28, 1849; moved with his parents to Ipava, Fulton County, Ill., in 1853; attended the public schools; taught school in Illinois 1863–1871; moved to Beloit, Mitchell County, Kans., in 1871; principal of the Beloit public schools 1871–1879; moved to Logan, Phillips County, Kans., in 1880 and engaged in banking; also interested in irrigation farming 1891–1901; elected as a Republican to the Fifty-sixth and to the five succeeding Congresses (March 4, 1899–March 3, 1911); was an unsuccessful candidate for renomination in 1910; moved to Los Angeles, Calif., in 1911 and to Beverly Hills, Calif., in 1913, where he engaged in banking and in the real-estate business until 1926, when he retired from active business pursuits; died in Beverly Hills, Calif., on November 7, 1929; interment in Hollywood Cemetery, Hollywood, Calif.

REES, Edward Herbert, a Representative from Kansas; born on a farm near Emporia, Lyon County, Kans., June 3, 1886; attended the public schools and the Kansas State Teachers' College at Emporia; taught school in Lyon County, Kans., 1909–1911; clerk of the court of Lyon County, Kans., 1912–1918; studied law; was admitted to the bar in 1915 and commenced practice in Emporia, Kans.; also engaged in agricultural pursuits; member of the State house of representatives 1927–1933; served in the State senate 1933–1935; member of the Kansas Judicial Council 1933–1937; elected as a Republican to the Seventy-fifth and to the eleven succeeding Congresses (January 3, 1937–January 3, 1961); was not a candidate for renomination in 1960; is a resident of Emporia, Kans.

REES, Rollin Raymond, a Representative from Kansas; born in Camden, Preble County, Ohio, January 10, 1865; moved with his parents to Ottawa County, Kans., in 1867; attended the public schools; was graduated from the agricultural college at Manhattan, Kans., in 1885; studied law; was admitted to the bar in 1887 and commenced practice in Minneapolis, Kans.; prosecuting attorney of Ottawa County 1895–1899; member of the State house of representatives 1899–1903; judge of the thirtieth judicial district 1903–1910; resigned to become a candidate for Congress; elected as a Republican to the Sixty-second Congress (March 4, 1911–March 3, 1913); unsuccessful candidate for reelection in 1912 to the Sixty-third Congress; resumed the practice of law in Minneapolis, Ottawa County, Kans.; moved to California and engaged in banking and ranching; died in Anaheim, Calif., on May 30, 1935; interment in Fairhaven Cemetery, Orange, Calif.

REESE, David Addison, a Representative from Georgia; born in Charlotte, N. C., March 3, 1794; attended the public schools and was instructed in the classics by a private tutor; studied medicine; was graduated from the Jefferson Medical College, Philadelphia, Pa., and commenced practice in Elberton, Ga.; moved to Monticello, Ga., and continued the practice of medicine; member of the State senate in 1829, 1830, 1834, 1835, and 1836; member of the board of trustees of the University of Georgia at Athens for twenty-five years; elected as a Whig to the Thirty-third Congress (March 4, 1853–March 3, 1855); moved to Auburn, Ala., and resumed the practice of medicine; died in Auburn December 16, 1871; interment in Hopewell Cemetery, West Point, Troup County, Ga.

REESE, Seaborn, a Representative from Georgia; born in Madison, Morgan County, Ga., November 28, 1846; attended a private school for boys in Hancock County and the University of Georgia at Athens, which institution he left in his senior year, 1868; studied law; was admitted to the bar in 1871 and commenced practice in Madison, Ga.; moved to Augusta and then to Sparta; member of the General Assembly of Georgia 1872–1874; solicitor general of the northern judicial circuit 1877–1880; presidential elector on the Democratic ticket of Hancock and English in 1880; elected as a Democrat to the Forty-seventh Congress to fill the vacancy caused by the resignation of Alexander H. Stephens; reelected to the Forty-eighth and Forty-ninth Congresses and served from December 4, 1882, to March 4, 1887; judge of the northern judicial circuit 1893–1900; died in Sparta, Hancock County, Ga., March 1, 1907; interment in the Methodist Church Cemetery.

REEVES, Albert Lee, Jr., a Representative from Missouri; born in Steelville, Crawford County, Mo., on May 31, 1906; attended the public schools of Kansas City, Mo.; was graduated from William Jewell College, Liberty, Mo., in 1927; taught at Baylor University in Waco, Tex., in 1927 and 1928; student at Harvard University, Cambridge, Mass., in 1928 and 1929; was graduated from the University of Missouri Law School at Columbia in 1931; was admitted to the bar the same year and commenced practice in Kansas City, Mo.; during World War II entered on active duty in July 1942 as captain, Corps of Engineers, Missouri River Division, subsequently serving in India, Burma, and China; promoted through the ranks to lieutenant colonel and relieved from active duty April 23, 1946; resumed the practice of law; elected as a Republican to the Eightieth Congress (January 3, 1947–January 3, 1949); unsuccessful candidate for reelection in 1948 to the Eighty-first Congress; practiced law in Kansas City, Mo., and Washington, D. C.; senior vice president, Utah Construction & Mining Co., San Francisco, Calif.; is a resident of Menlo Park, Calif.

REEVES, Henry Augustus, a Representative from New York; born in Sag Harbor, N. Y., December 7, 1832; attended private schools in Sag Harbor, the Southampton Academy, the University of Michigan at Ann Arbor for three years, and was graduated from Union College, Schenectady, N. Y., in 1852; studied law; was admitted to the bar; edited the Republican Watchman in Greenport from 1858 until his death; elected as a Democrat to the Forty-first Congress (March 4, 1869–March 3, 1871); resumed newspaper interests; supervisor of Southold Town 1872–1894; member of the State assembly in 1887; member of the State commission in lunacy 1889–1897; died in Greenport, Suffolk County, N. Y., March 4, 1916; interment in Southampton Cemetery, Southampton, N. Y.

REEVES, Walter, a Representative from Illinois; born near Brownsville, Fayette County, Pa., September 25, 1848; moved with his parents to Illinois in 1856, where they settled upon a farm in La Salle County; attended the public schools; taught school; studied law; was admitted to the bar in Mount Vernon, Ill., in 1875, and commenced practice in Streator, Ill.; elected as a Republican to the Fifty-fourth and to the three succeeding Congresses (March 4, 1895–March 3, 1903); was not a candidate for renomination in 1902; unsuccessful candidate for the Republican nomination for Governor in 1900; resumed the practice of law; died in Streator, La Salle County, Ill., April 9, 1909; interment in Riverview Cemetery.

REGAN, Kenneth Mills, a Representative from Texas; born in Mount Morris, Ogle County, Ill., March 6, 1893; attended the public schools and Vincennes (Ind.) University; during the First

World War served as a flyer in the United States Army Signal Corps; in 1920 engaged in the real-estate business and as an oil operator in Pecos, Tex.; alderman of the city of Pecos; mayor of Pecos 1929–1932; member of the State senate 1933–1937; in World War II served as an intelligence officer in the Air Corps and was discharged with the rank of captain; moved to Midland, Tex., and continued oil operations; elected as a Democrat to the Eightieth Congress to fill the vacancy caused by the resignation of Robert Ewing Thomason; reelected to the Eighty-first, Eighty-second, and Eighty-third Congresses, and served from August 23, 1947, to January 3, 1955; unsuccessful candidate for renomination in 1954 to the Eighty-fourth Congress; representative of Texas railroads in Washington, D. C.; died in Santa Fe, N. Mex., on August 15, 1959; interment in Resthaven Memorial Park, Midland, Tex.

REID, Charles Chester, a Representative from Arkansas; born in Clarksville, Johnson County, Ark., June 15, 1868; attended the public schools and the University of Arkansas at Fayetteville 1883–1885; was graduated from the law department of Vanderbilt University, Nashville, Tenn., in 1887; was admitted to the bar the same year and commenced practice in Morrillton, Ark.; prosecuting attorney of Conway County 1894–1898; voluntarily retired from office in 1898 and resumed the practice of law; elected as a Democrat to the Fifty-seventh and to the four succeeding Congresses (March 4, 1901–March 3, 1911); was not a candidate for renomination in 1910 to the Sixty-second Congress; again engaged in the practice of his profession in Little Rock, Ark., where he died on May 20, 1922; interment in Oakland Cemetery.

REID, David Settle (nephew of Thomas Settle), a Representative and a Senator from North Carolina; born near Reidsville, Rockingham County, N. C., on April 19, 1813; attended the common schools; studied law; was admitted to the bar in 1833 and commenced practice in Wentworth, N. C., the following year; member of the State senate 1835–1842; elected as a Democrat to the Twenty-eighth and Twenty-ninth Congresses (March 4, 1843–March 3, 1847); was not a candidate for renomination; unsuccessful candidate for Governor in 1848; elected Governor in 1850 and 1852; elected to the United States Senate to fill a vacancy in the term commencing March 4, 1853, caused by the failure of the legislature to elect, and served from December 6, 1854, until March 3, 1859; unsuccessful candidate for reelection; delegate to the peace convention held at Washington, D. C., in 1861 in an effort to devise means to prevent the impending war; member of the State constitutional convention in 1875; practiced law at Reidsville, N. C., and died there June 19, 1891; interment in Greenview Cemetery.

REID, Frank R., a Representative from Illinois; born in Aurora, Kane County, Ill., April 18, 1879; attended the public schools, the University of Chicago, and the Chicago College of Law; was admitted to the bar in 1901 and commenced practice in Aurora, Ill.; prosecuting attorney of Kane County 1904–1908; State's attorney 1904–1908; president of the Illinois State Attorneys' Association during a part of his term as State's attorney; assistant United States attorney at Chicago 1908–1910; member of the State house of representatives in 1911 and 1912; chairman of the Kane County Republican central committee 1914–1916; secretary of the League of Illinois Municipalities in 1916 and 1917; elected as a Republican to the Sixty-eighth and to the five succeeding Congresses (March 4, 1923–January 3, 1935); was not a candidate for renomination in 1934; engaged in the general practice of law at Chicago and Aurora, Ill.; died in Aurora, Ill., on January 25, 1945; interment in Spring Lake Cemetery.

REID, James Randolph, a Delegate from Pennsylvania; born in Hamiltonban Township, York (now Adams) County, Pa., August 11, 1750; graduated from Princeton University with a bachelor of arts degree; served in the Revolutionary Army as a lieutenant and took part in the battles of Three Rivers and Ticonderoga with Anthony Wayne's Fourth Pennsylvania Regiment and later was promoted to major in "Congress' Own" Regiment; received a land grant for services during the Revolution; Member of the Continental Congress 1787–1789; died in Middlesex, Cumberland County, Pa., January 25, 1789.

REID, James Wesley, a Representative from North Carolina; born in Wentworth, Rockingham County, N. C., June 11, 1849; pursued an academic course; was graduated from Emory and Henry College, Emory, Va., in 1869 and subsequently taught in the same college; studied law; was admitted to the bar in 1873 and commenced practice in Wentworth, N. C.; treasurer of Rockingham County 1874–1884; elected as a Democrat to the Forty-eighth Congress to fill the vacancy caused by the resignation of Alfred M. Scales; reelected to the Forty-ninth Congress and served from January 28, 1885, to December 31, 1886, when he resigned; moved to Lewiston, Idaho, in 1887 and engaged in the practice of law; member of the State constitutional convention in 1889 and vice president of that body; president of the board of trustees of the Lewiston State Normal College from the foundation of that institution in 1893 until the time of his death; delegate to the Democratic National Convention at Chicago in 1896 and at Kansas City in 1900; died in Lewiston, Nez Perce County, Idaho, January 1, 1902; interment in the Masonic Cemetery.

REID, John William, a Representative from Missouri; born near Lynchburg, Bedford County, Va., June 14, 1821; attended the common schools; moved to Missouri in 1840; taught school; studied law; was admitted to the bar and commenced practice in Jefferson City, Mo., in 1844; served as captain in the Mexican War; member of the State house of representatives 1854–1856; elected as a Democrat to the Thirty-seventh Congress and served from March 4 to August 3, 1861, when he withdrew; during the Civil War served in the Confederate Army as volunteer aide to General Price; appointed a commissioner to adjust claims against the Confederate Government; settled in Kansas City, Mo.; resumed the practice of his profession and engaged in banking; died at Lees Summit, Jackson County, Mo., November 22, 1881; interment in Elmwood Cemetery, Kansas City, Mo.

REID, Robert Raymond, a Representative from Georgia; born in Prince William Parish, Beaufort District, S. C., September 8, 1789; attended South Carolina College at Columbia; moved to Augusta, Ga.; studied law; was admitted to the bar and began practice in 1810; elected judge of the superior court of Georgia in 1816 and served until he was elected to Congress; elected as a Democrat to the Fifteenth Congress to fill the vacancy caused by the resignation of John Forsyth; reelected to the Sixteenth and Seventeenth Congresses and served from February 18, 1819, to March 3, 1823; was not a candidate for renomination; judge of the middle circuit court of Georgia 1823–1825; judge of the city court of Augusta 1827–1832; Democratic presidential elector in 1828; United States judge for the district of east Florida 1832–1839; Governor of the Territory of Florida 1839–1841; president of the convention which framed a constitution for the State of Florida; died in Blackwood, near Tallahassee, Leon County, Fla., July 1, 1841.

REILLY, James Bernard, a Representative from Pennsylvania; born in Pinedale, West Brunswick Township, Schuylkill County, Pa., August 12, 1845; attended the public schools and was graduated from the Bunker Hill School, Pottsville, Pa., in 1862; studied law; was admitted to the bar in 1869 and commenced practice in Pottsville; district attorney of Schuylkill County 1871–1875; elected as a Democrat to the Forty-fourth and Forty-fifth Congresses (March 4, 1875–March 3, 1879); resumed the practice of law in Pottsville, Pa.; delegate to the Democratic National Convention at Cincinnati in 1880; unsuccessful candidate for law judge of Schuylkill County in 1881 and again in 1882; unsuccessful Democratic candidate for election in 1884 to the Forty-ninth Congress; elected to the Fifty-first, Fifty-second, and Fifty-third Congresses (March 4, 1889–March 3, 1895); unsuccessful candidate for reelection in 1894 to the Fifty-fourth Congress; United States marshal for the eastern district of Pennsylvania 1896–1900; again resumed the practice of law in Pottsville, Pa.; unsuccessful candidate for justice of the superior court in 1913; died in Pottsville, Schuylkill County, Pa., May 14, 1924; interment in St. Patrick's No. 3 Cemetery.

REILLY, John, a Representative from Pennsylvania; born in Abnerville, Indiana County, Pa., February 22, 1836; received home instruction and attended the public schools; entered the service of the Pennsylvania Railroad Co. April 10, 1854; appointed superintendent of transportation April 1, 1865; served until his resignation in 1875, having been elected to Congress; president of the Bells Gap Railroad Co. 1871–1873; president of the board of city commissioners of Altoona in 1872 and 1873; elected as a Democrat to the Forty-fourth Congress (March 4, 1875–March 3, 1877); unsuccessful candidate for reelection in 1876 to the Forty-fifth Congress; again superintendent of transportation of the Pennsylvania Railroad Co. and served from 1877 until his resignation in 1885 on account of ill health; moved to Philadelphia, Pa., in 1881; interested in various business enterprises; died in Philadelphia, Pa., April 19, 1904; interment in West Laurel Hill Cemetery.

REILLY, Michael Kieran, a Representative from Wisconsin; born in Empire, Fond du Lac County, Wis., July 15, 1869; attended the public schools; was graduated from Oshkosh Normal School in 1889, from the University of Wisconsin at Madison in 1894, and from the law department of the latter university in 1895; was admitted to the bar the same year and commenced practice in Fond du Lac, Wis.; district attorney of Fond du Lac County in 1899 and 1900; city attorney 1905–1910; delegate to the Democratic National Conventions in 1908 and 1924; elected as a Democrat to the Sixty-third and Sixty-fourth Congresses (March 4, 1913–March 3, 1917); unsuccessful candidate for reelection in 1916 to the Sixty-fifth Congress; resumed the practice of law; again elected to the Seventy-first Congress to fill the vacancy caused by the death of Florian Lampert; reelected to the Seventy-second and to the three succeeding Congresses and served from November 4, 1930, to January 3, 1939; unsuccessful candidate for reelection in 1938 to the Seventy-sixth Congress; resumed the practice of his chosen profession; died in a hospital in Neptune, N. J., October 14, 1944; interment in Woodlawn Cemetery, Woodlawn, N. Y.

REILLY, Thomas Lawrence, a Representative from Connecticut; was born in New Britain, Hartford County, Conn., September 20, 1858; attended the common schools, and was graduated from the Connecticut State Normal School in 1876; assistant town clerk of New Britain in 1876; moved with his parents to Meriden, Conn., in 1877; studied law for a year; employed as a bookkeeper for several years; engaged as a newspaper correspondent until 1886; one of the founders of the Meriden Journal in 1886 and became the city editor; member of the Meriden Board of Education 1896–1903; chairman of the town committee in 1900; mayor of Meriden 1906–1912;

elected as a Democrat to the Sixty-second and Sixty-third Congresses (March 4, 1911–March 3, 1915); unsuccessful candidate for reelection in 1914 to the Sixty-fourth Congress; employed in the Internal Revenue Service in 1916 and 1917; elected sheriff of New Haven County in 1918; reelected and served until his death in New Haven, Conn., July 6, 1924; interment in Sacred Heart Cemetery, Meriden, Conn.

REILLY, Wilson, a Representative from Pennsylvania; was born in Waynesboro, Franklin County, Pa., August 8, 1811; attended the common schools; engaged as a hatter in Waynesboro and Chambersburg, Pa.; studied law; was admitted to the bar in 1837 and commenced practice in Chambersburg, Pa.; prosecuting attorney of Franklin County 1842–1845; unsuccessful Democratic candidate for election in 1854 to the Thirty-fourth Congress; elected to the Thirty-fifth Congress (March 4, 1857–March 3, 1859); unsuccessful candidate for reelection in 1858 to the Thirty-sixth Congress; became captain of the McClure Rifles, which joined the Pennsylvania Reserve Corps at Camp Curtin, Harrisburg, Pa.; resumed the practice of law; died in Chambersburg, Franklin County, Pa., August 26, 1885; interment in Falling Spring Cemetery.

REILY, Luther, a Representative from Pennsylvania; born in Myerstown, Pa., October 17, 1794; completed preparatory studies; studied medicine and began practice in Harrisburg; held various local offices; in the War of 1812 served as a private in Capt. R. M. Crane's company of Pennsylvania Volunteers from August 3 to September 7, 1814, and as surgeon's mate in Maj. Gen. R. Watson's company from September 7 to December 5, 1814; resumed the practice of medicine; elected as a Democrat to the Twenty-fifth Congress (March 4, 1837–March 3, 1839); again resumed the practice of his profession; died in Harrisburg, Pa., on February 20, 1854; interment in Harrisburg Cemetery.

RELFE, James Hugh, a Representative from Missouri; born in Virginia October 17, 1791; moved to Washington County, Mo., about 1816 with his father, who settled in Caledonia; received a limited schooling; studied medicine and practiced in Caledonia, Mo.; appointed a member of the commission to adjust Spanish land claims to fill the vacancy occasioned by the resignation of Dr. Lewis F. Linn; member of the State house of representatives 1835–1844; served in the Black Hawk War; appointed United States marshal for the district of Missouri February 17, 1841; elected as a Democrat to the Twenty-eighth and Twenty-ninth Congresses (March 4, 1843–March 3, 1847); continued the practice of medicine in Caledonia, Washington County Mo., until his death there September 14, 1863; interment in the Methodist Cemetery.

REMANN, Frederick, a Representative from Illinois; born in Vandalia, Fayette County, Ill., May 10, 1847; attended the common schools of Vandalia and the Mifflin (Pa.) Academy; was graduated from the Iron City Business College, Pittsburgh, Pa., in April 1865; during the Civil War served as corporal in Company E, One Hundred and Forty-third Regiment, Illinois Volunteer Infantry; again attended Mifflin Academy in 1866 and 1867 and was graduated from Illinois College at Jacksonville in 1868; returned to Vandalia and engaged in mercantile pursuits; served as county supervisor of Fayette County and as alderman of Vandalia; delegate to numerous Republican State conventions; member of the State house of representatives in 1877 and 1878; elected as a Republican to the Fifty-fourth Congress and served from March 4, 1895, until his death in Vandalia, Ill., July 14, 1895, before the convening of Congress; interment in South Hill Cemetery.

RENCHER, Abraham, a Representative from North Carolina; born near Raleigh, Wake County, N. C., August 12, 1798; tutored at home and attended the common schools and Pittsboro (N. C.) Academy; was graduated from the University of North Carolina at Chapel Hill in 1822; studied law; was admitted to the bar in 1825 and commenced practice in Pittsboro, Chatham County, N. C.; elected as a Democrat to the Twenty-first and to the four succeeding Congresses (March 4, 1829–March 3, 1839); declined to be a candidate for renomination in 1838; elected to the Twenty-seventh Congress (March 4, 1841–March 3, 1843); declined to be candidate for renomination in 1842 on account of ill health; Minister to Portugal 1843–1847; presidential elector on the Democratic ticket of Pierce and King in 1852; declined the portfolio of Secretary of the Navy under President Buchanan; appointed Governor of New Mexico by President Buchanan and served from 1857 to 1861; capitalist and agriculturist; retired to his home in Pittsboro, N. C.; died in Chapel Hill, N. C., on July 6, 1883; interment in St. Bartholomew's Protestant Episcopal Churchyard, Pittsboro, N. C.

RESA, Alexander John, a Representative from Illinois; born in Chicago, Cook County, Ill., August 4, 1887; attended the public schools of Chicago, Ill., and St. Joseph's College, Kirkwood, Mo.; was graduated from the John Marshall Law School, Chicago, Ill., in 1911; was admitted to the bar the same year and commenced practice in Chicago, Ill., assistant corporation counsel of the city of Chicago, serving as head of the appeals division and public improvement division 1937–1944; member of the faculty of the John Marshall Law School 1918–1942; elected as a Democrat to the Seventy-ninth Congress (January 3, 1945–January 3, 1947); unsuccessful candidate for reelection in 1946 to the Eightieth Congress; returned to practice of law, and retired December 31, 1959; is a resident of Evanston, Ill.

REUSS, Henry Schoellkopf, a Representative from Wisconsin; born in Milwaukee, Wis., February 22, 1912; attended Milwaukee schools; was graduated from Cornell University, Ithaca, N. Y., in 1933 and from Harvard Law School, Cambridge, Mass., in 1936; was admitted to the bar in 1936 and commenced the practice of law in Milwaukee, Wis.; assistant corporation counsel for Milwaukee County in 1939 and 1940; assistant general counsel for Office of Price Administration, Washington, D. C., in 1941 and 1942; entered the United States Army as a private in January 1943; commissioned a second lieutenant in November 1943 and served with the Sixty-third and Seventy-fifth Infantry Divisions until 1945; Chief of Price Control, Office of Military Government for Germany, in 1945; awarded the Bronze Star Medal for action at Rhine Crossing and Bronze Battle Stars for Normandy, northern France, and central Germany; engaged in private law practice 1936–1955; deputy general counsel for the Marshall Plan in Paris in 1949; special prosecutor, Milwaukee County Grand Jury in 1950; lecturer at Wisconsin State College in 1950 and 1951; member of Milwaukee School Board in 1953 and 1954; personal counsel to the secretary of state for reapportionment and redistricting case in 1953; president of White Elm Nursery Co., Hartland, Wis., 1949–1953; director of Marshall & Ilsley Bank, Milwaukee, Wis., 1946–1948, and Niagara Share Corp., Buffalo, N. Y., 1947–1949; member of legal advisory committee, National Resources Board, Washington, D. C., 1948–1952; unsuccessful candidate for mayor of Milwaukee in 1960; elected as a Democrat to the Eighty-fourth, Eighty-fifth, and Eighty-sixth Congresses (January 3, 1955–January 3, 1961). *Reelected to the Eighty-seventh Congress.*

REVELS, Hiram Rhodes, a Senator from Mississippi; born in Fayetteville, Cumberland County, N. C., September 27, 1827; was of the Negro race; attended the Quaker Seminary, Union County, Ind., and Darke County (Ohio) Seminary; was graduated from Knox College, Bloomington, Ill., and was ordained a minister in the African Methodist Episcopal Church at Baltimore, Md., in 1845; lectured among his people in the States of Indiana, Illinois, Kansas, Kentucky, Tennessee, and Missouri; taught school in St. Louis, Mo.; accepted a pastorate in Baltimore, Md., in 1860; at the outbreak of the Civil War assisted in the organization of the first two colored regiments in Maryland; served in Vicksburg, Miss., as chaplain of a colored regiment in 1864; settled in Natchez, Miss., in 1866; was alderman in that city in 1868; member of the State Senate of Mississippi in 1870; upon the readmission of Mississippi to representation was elected as a Republican to the United States Senate and served from February 23, 1870, to March 3, 1871; secretary of state ad interim of Mississippi in 1873; president of the Alcorn Agricultural College, Rodney, Miss., 1876–1882; moved to Holly Springs, Marshall County, Miss., and became district superintendent in the African Methodist Episcopal Church; died in Aberdeen, Miss., January 16, 1901, while attending a church conference; interment in Hill Crest Cemetery, Holly Springs, Miss.

REVERCOMB, William Chapman, a Senator from West Virginia; born in Covington, Alleghany County, Va., July 20, 1895; attended the public schools at Covington, Va.; student Washington and Lee University, Lexington, Va., 1914–1916; graduated from law department of the University of Virginia at Charlottesville in 1919; was admitted to the bar the same year and practiced in Covington, Va., during the First World War enlisted in the United States Army and served as a corporal in Battery A, Thirty-fifth Coast Artillery, 1917–1919; moved to Charleston, W. Va., in 1922 and continued the practice of law; member of the Republican State executive committee 1932–1936; chairman of the State judicial convention of 1936; delegate to the Republican National Convention in 1944; elected as a Republican to the United States Senate in 1942 for the term commencing January 3, 1943, and ending January 3, 1949; unsuccessful candidate for reelection in 1948 and for election in 1952; elected to the United States Senate in 1956 to fill the vacancy caused by the death of Harley M. Kilgore and served from November 7, 1956, to January 3, 1959; unsuccessful candidate for reelection in 1958 and for the gubernatorial nomination in 1960; lawyer; is a resident of Charleston, W. Va.

REYBURN, John Edgar (father of William Stuart Reyburn), a Representative from Pennsylvania; born in New Carlisle, Clark County, Ohio, February 7, 1845; was instructed by a private tutor and attended Saunders Institute, West Philadelphia, Pa.; studied law, was admitted to the bar in 1870 and commenced practice in Philadelphia; member of the State house of representatives in 1871 and 1874–1876; member of the State senate 1876–1892 and served as president pro tempore during the session of 1883; elected as a Republican to the Fifty-first Congress to fill the vacancy caused by the death of William D. Kelley; reelected to the Fifty-second, Fifty-third, and Fifty-fourth Congresses and served from February 18, 1890, to March 3, 1897; unsuccessful candidate for renomination in 1896; presidential elector on the Republican ticket of Roosevelt and Fairbanks in 1904; elected to the Fifty-ninth Congress to fill the vacancy caused by the death of Robert Adams; reelected to the Sixtieth Congress and served from November 6, 1906, to March 31, 1907, when he resigned, having been elected mayor of Philadelphia, Pa.; served as mayor from April 1, 1907, to December 4, 1911; engaged in manufacturing in Philadelphia, Pa., but retained a residence in Washington, D. C., where he died on January 4, 1914; interment in Laurel Hill Cemetery, Philadelphia, Pa.

REYBURN, William Stuart (son of John Edgar Reyburn), a Representative from Pennsylvania; born in Philadelphia, Pa., December 17, 1882; attended the Hill School, Pottstown, Pa.; was graduated from Yale University in 1904 and from the law department of Georgetown University, Washington, D. C.; was admitted to the bar in 1908 and commenced practice in Washington, D. C.; member of President Taft's party which visited the Philippines, Japan, and China in 1905; served in the State house of representatives from 1909 until May 25, 1911, when he resigned; elected as a Republican to the Sixty-second Congress to fill the vacancy caused by the death of Joel Cook and served from May 23, 1911, to March 3, 1913; declined to be a candidate for renomination in 1912; resumed the practice of his profession in Washington, D. C., and subsequently retired from active business pursuits; resided in Aiken, Aiken County, S. C., and later moved to his estate "Black Hill," Old Lyme, Conn.; died in New Haven, Conn., on July 25, 1946; interment in Laurel Hill Cemetery, Philadelphia, Pa.

REYNOLDS, Edwin Ruthvin, a Representative from New York; born at Fort Ann, N. Y., February 16, 1816; pursued classical studies; was principal of Albion Academy, Orleans County, N. Y., for six years; was county superintendent 1843–1845; studied law; was admitted to the bar in 1843 and commenced practice in Albion, N. Y., in 1846; elected as a Republican to the Thirty-sixth Congress to fill the vacancy caused by the death of Silas M. Burroughs and served from December 5, 1860, to March 3, 1861; judge and surrogate of Orleans County 1864–1868; resumed the practice of law; died in Albion, N. Y., July 4, 1908; interment in Mount Albion Cemetery.

REYNOLDS, Gideon, a Representative from New York; born in Petersburg, N. Y., August 9, 1813; educated in private schools; moved with his father to Hoosick in 1836 and engaged in agricultural pursuits; member of the State assembly in 1839; sheriff of Rensselaer County, N. Y., 1843–1846; elected as a Whig to the Thirtieth and Thirty-first Congresses (March 4, 1847–March 3, 1851); was not a candidate for renomination in 1850; resumed agricultural pursuits in Rensselaer County; delegate to the first Republican National Convention at Philadelphia 1856 and to that at Chicago in 1860; member of the Republican State central committee; was appointed internal-revenue collector for the fifteenth district of New York on September 9, 1862, and served until March 31, 1865, when he resigned; member of the board of supervisors of Hoosick in 1875; died in Hoosick, Rensselaer County, N. Y., July 13, 1896; interment in the Hoosick Rural Cemetery.

REYNOLDS, James B., a Representative from Tennessee; born in County Antrim, Ireland, in 1779; attended the common schools; immigrated to the United States and settled in Clarksville, Tenn.; studied law; was admitted to the bar in 1804 and practiced; elected as a Democrat to the Fourteenth Congress (March 4, 1815–March 3, 1817); elected to the Eighteenth Congress (March 4, 1823–March 3, 1825); resumed the practice of law; died in Clarksville, Montgomery County, Tenn., June 10, 1851; interment in the City Cemetery.

REYNOLDS, John, a Representative from Illinois; born in Montgomery County, near Philadelphia, Pa., February 26, 1789; moved to Illinois in 1800 with his parents, who settled in the vicinity of Kaskaskia; pursued classical studies; studied law; was admitted to the bar and commenced practice in Cahokia, Ill., in 1812; elected a justice of the Illinois Supreme Court in 1818; unsuccessful candidate for election to the United States Senate in 1823; member of the State house of representatives 1827–1829; Governor of Illinois from December 6, 1830, to November 17, 1834, when he resigned, having been elected to Congress; in 1832 took the field as commander of the State militia in the Black Hawk War; elected as a Democrat to the Twenty-third Congress to fill the vacancy caused by the death of Charles Slade; reelected to the Twenty-fourth Congress and served from December 1, 1834, to March 3, 1837; unsuccessful candidate for reelection in 1836 to the Twenty-fifth Congress; elected to the Twenty-sixth and Twenty-seventh Congresses (March 4, 1839–March 3, 1843); again a member of the State house of representatives in 1846 and 1852 and served during the latter term as speaker; unsuccessful candidate for election to the State senate in 1848; unsuccessful candidate for State superintendent of schools in 1858; engaged in newspaper work; was the author of several books and pamphlets; died in Belleville, St. Clair County, Ill., on May 8, 1865; interment in Walnut Hill Cemetery.

REYNOLDS, John Hazard, a Representative from New York; born in Moriah, N. Y., June 21, 1819; attended the public schools in Sandy Hill (now Hudson Falls), N. Y., and Bennington, Vt.; engaged in civil engineering; was graduated from Kinderhook Academy in 1840; studied law; was admitted to the bar and began practice in Kinderhook in 1843; moved to Albany in 1851 and continued the practice of law; elected as a Republican to the Thirty-sixth Congress (March 4, 1859–March 3, 1861); was not a candidate for renomination in 1860; resumed the practice of his profession; appointed a judge of the commission of appeals of the State in 1873, which position he held until the expiration of the court by limitation July 1, 1875; died in Kinderhook, Columbia County, N. Y., September 24, 1875; interment in Kinderhook Cemetery.

REYNOLDS, John Merriman, a Representative from Pennsylvania; born near Quarryville, Lancaster County, Pa., March 5, 1848; attended the public schools; was graduated from the first Pennsylvania State Normal School in 1867 and from Columbian (now George Washington) University, Washington, D. C., in 1895; principal of public schools of Bedford, Pa., 1867–1869; studied law; was admitted to the bar February 15, 1870, and commenced practice in Bedford, Pa.; publisher of the Bedford Gazette 1872–1880; member of the State house of representatives in 1873 and 1874; prosecuting attorney of Bedford County 1875–1879; president of the board of education of Bedford 1884–1900; delegate to the Democratic National Convention at St. Louis in 1888 and at Chicago in 1892; member of the commission to select a site and build an asylum for the chronic insane at Wernersville 1891–1896; engaged in the banking business in 1893; Assistant Secretary of the Interior from April 15, 1893, to June 1, 1897; elected as a Republican to the Fifty-ninth, Sixtieth, and Sixty-first Congresses and served from March 4, 1905, to January 17, 1911, when he resigned to accept the office of Lieutenant Governor of Pennsylvania, which office he held from 1911 to 1915, performing the duties of president of the State senate and of the board of pardons; resumed the practice of law and again engaged in banking in Bedford, Pa.; member of the commission to revise the banking laws of the State of Pennsylvania 1917–1925; died in Bedford, Pa., September 14, 1933; interment in Bedford Cemetery.

REYNOLDS, Joseph, a Representative from New York; born in Easton, Washington County, N. Y., September 14, 1785; completed academic studies; moved to Virgil, N. Y., in 1809; engaged in agricultural pursuits; organized a company of riflemen for service in the War of 1812; was major, colonel, and brigadier general in the State troops; justice of the peace 1815–1837; member of the State assembly in 1818; judge of Cortland County 1821–1839; supervisor of the town of Cortlandville 1825–1835;

presidential elector on the Democratic ticket of Jackson and Van Buren in 1832; elected as a Democrat to the Twenty-fourth Congress (March 4, 1835–March 3, 1837); first president of the village of Cortland in 1864; died in Cortland, Cortland County, N. Y., September 24, 1864; interment in the Cortland Rural Cemetery.

REYNOLDS, Robert Rice, a Senator from North Carolina; born in Asheville, Buncombe County, N. C., June 18, 1884; attended the public schools, Weaverville (N. C.) College, and the University of North Carolina at Chapel Hill; studied law; was admitted to the bar in 1907 and commenced practice in Asheville, N. C.; served as prosecuting attorney of the fifteenth judicial district of North Carolina 1910–1914; unsuccessful candidate for nomination for Lieutenant Governor in 1924 and for United States Senator in 1926; presidential elector in 1928 on the ticket of Alfred E. Smith and Joseph T. Robinson; elected as a Democrat on November 8, 1932, to the United States Senate to fill the vacancy caused by the death of Lee S. Overman for the term ending March 3, 1933, and on the same day was elected for the term beginning March 4, 1933; reelected in 1938 and served from the time he qualified, December 5, 1932, to January 3, 1945; was not a candidate for renomination in 1944; practiced law in Washington, D. C.; operates a two-hundred-and-fifty-acre estate at Reynolds Mountain, near Asheville, N. C., where he now resides.

REYNOLDS, Samuel Williams, a Senator from Nebraska; born in Omaha, Douglas County, Nebr., August 11, 1890; attended the public schools of Omaha, Nebr.; was graduated from Omaha High School in 1908; engaged in the wholesale coal business in Omaha, Nebr., in 1908; served in the Air Service during the First World War in 1917 and 1918; during World War II served as a colonel in the Army Specialist Corps as director of corps activities in the Seventh Service Command with headquarters in Omaha, Nebr., in 1942 and 1943; delegate to Republican National Conventions in 1936, 1940, 1952, and 1956; appointed as a Republican to the United States Senate to fill the vacancy caused by the death of Hugh Butler and served from July 3, 1954, to November 7, 1954; was not a candidate for election to fill the vacancy; resumed wholesale coal business; resides in Omaha, Nebr.

RHEA, John, a Representative from Tennessee; born in the parish of Langhorn, County Londonderry, Ireland, in 1753; immigrated to the United States in 1769 with his parents, who settled in Philadelphia, Pa.; moved to Piney Creek, Md., in 1771 and to eastern Tennessee in 1778; completed preparatory studies and was graduated from Princeton College in 1780; member of the Patriot force in the Battle of King's Mountain in October 1780; clerk of the Sullivan County Court in the proposed State of Franklin and subsequently in North Carolina 1785–1790; member of the House of Commons of North Carolina; was a delegate to the State convention that ratified the Federal Constitution in 1789; studied law; was admitted to the bar in 1789; delegate to the constitutional convention of Tennessee in 1796; attorney general of Greene County, Tenn., in 1796; member of the State house of representatives in 1796 and 1797; elected as a Democrat to the Eighth and to the five succeeding Congresses (March 4, 1803–March 3, 1815); appointed United States commissioner to treat with the Choctaw Nation in 1816; elected to the Fifteenth, Sixteenth, and Seventeenth Congresses (March 4, 1817–March 3, 1823); actively connected with higher education in Tennessee; retired from active pursuits and resided on the Rhea plantation near Blountville, Sullivan County, Tenn., where he died May 27, 1832; interment in the Blountville Cemetery.

RHEA, John Stockdale, a Representative from Kentucky; born in Russellville, Logan County, Ky., March 9, 1855; pursued preparatory studies; attended Bethel College, Russellville, Ky., and Washington and Lee University, Lexington, Va.; studied law; was admitted to the bar and commenced practice in 1873; prosecuting attorney for Logan County in 1878 and 1882; presidential elector on the Democratic ticket of Cleveland and Hendricks in 1884 and Cleveland and Thurman in 1888; delegate to the Democratic National Conventions in 1892 and 1896; elected as the candidate of the Democratic and Populist Parties to the Fifty-fifth and Fifty-sixth Congresses (March 4, 1897–March 3, 1901); presented credentials as a Member-elect to the Fifty-seventh Congress and served from March 4, 1901, to March 25, 1902, when he was succeeded by J. McKenzie Moss, who contested his election; elected to the Fifty-eighth Congress (March 4, 1903–March 3, 1905); was not a candidate for renomination in 1904; resumed the practice of his profession in Russellville; appointed circuit court judge in 1913 and subsequently elected in 1915 and served until January 1, 1922; died in Russellville, Ky., on July 29, 1924; interment in Maple Grove Cemetery.

RHEA, William Francis, a Representative from Virginia; born on a farm near Bristol, Washington County, Va., April 20, 1858; attended rural and private schools; was graduated from King College, Bristol, Tenn., in 1878; studied law; was admitted to the bar in 1879 and commenced practice in Bristol, Va.; judge of the Washington County Court 1880–1885; member of the State senate 1885–1888; judge of the city court of Bristol; resigned in 1895 and resumed the practice of law; elected as a Democrat to the Fifty-sixth and Fifty-seventh Congresses (March 4, 1899–March 3, 1903); unsuccessful candidate for reelection in 1902 to the Fifty-eighth Congress; resumed the practice of law in Bristol, Va.; moved to Richmond, Va., when appointed a member of the State corporation commission in 1908 and served until 1925 when he resigned and retired from active political and business pursuits; died in Richmond, Va., March 23, 1931; interment in Hollywood Cemetery.

RHETT, Robert Barnwell (formerly Robert Barnwell Smith), a Representative and a Senator from South Carolina; born in Beaufort, S. C., December 24, 1800; completed preparatory studies; studied law; was admitted to the bar and commenced practice in Beaufort in 1824; elected to the State house of representatives for St. Bartholomew's Parish in 1826, 1828, 1830, and 1832; elected attorney general of South Carolina November 29, 1832; elected as a Democrat to the Twenty-fifth and to the five succeeding Congresses (March 4, 1837–March 3, 1849); at his request and by act of the General Assembly of South Carolina, his name was changed to Robert Barnwell Rhett in 1838; member of the Nashville convention in 1850; elected to the United States Senate to fill the vacancy caused by the death of John C. Calhoun and served from December 18, 1850, until his resignation effective May 7, 1852; delegate to the South Carolina secession convention in 1860; delegate to the Confederate Provisional Congress in 1861; was chairman of the committee which reported the constitution of the Confederate States; moved to St. James Parish, La., in 1867; delegate to the Democratic National Convention at New York City in 1868; died in St. James Parish, La., on September 14, 1876; interment in Magnolia Cemetery, Charleston, S. C.

RHINOCK, Joseph Lafayette, a Representative from Kentucky; born in Owenton, Owen County, Ky., January 4, 1863; moved to Covington, Ky.; attended the Covington public schools; engaged in the oil-refining business; president of the Covington Public Library Board two terms; member of the city council of Covington; mayor 1893–1900; was the organizer and first president of the Jefferson Democratic Club of Covington; elected as a Democrat to the Fifty-ninth, Sixtieth, and Sixty-first Congresses (March 4, 1905–March 3, 1911); was not a candidate for renomination in 1910; for twenty-two years was connected with theatrical enterprises in New York City, N. Y., and Cincinnati, Ohio, serving as vice president, secretary, and treasurer of the Shubert theatrical companies; director of the Shubert Theatre Corporation and a number of other theaters and film corporations; vice president of the Loew theatrical enterprises; became actively interested in horse racing and racetrack corporations; died at his home, "Bonnie Crest," New Rochelle, Westchester County, N. Y., on September 20, 1926; interment in Highland Cemetery, Covington, Ky.

RHOADS, Samuel, a Delegate from Pennsylvania; born in Philadelphia, Pa., in 1711; received a limited schooling and became a carpenter and builder; member of the city council in 1741; member of the provincial assembly 1761–1764 and 1771–1774; commissioner to a conference of western Indians and the Six Nations at Lancaster, Pa., in 1761; Member of the Continental Congress in 1774 and 1775; mayor of Philadelphia in 1774; founder and member of board of managers of the Pennsylvania Hospital 1751–1781; director of the Philadelphia Library; died in Philadelphia, Pa., April 7, 1784.

RHODES, George Milton, a Representative from Pennsylvania; born in Reading, Berks County, Pa., February 24, 1898; attended Reading public schools; during the First World War served in the United States Army; printer, Reading Eagle Co., July 1913–December 1927; business manager, Reading Labor Advocate 1927–1942; A. F. of L. labor representative; editor and manager of The New Era, 1942–1949; president of Federated Trades Council, A. F. of L. Central Labor Union 1928–1951; member of the Reading Housing Authority 1938–1948; member of the board of directors of the Community General Hospital; during World War II served on the local Rationing Board and War Manpower Committee; delegate to the Democratic National Conventions in 1952 and 1956; elected as a Democrat to the Eighty-first and to the five succeeding Congresses (January 3, 1949–January 3, 1961). *Reelected to the Eighty-seventh Congress.*

RHODES, John Jacob, a Representative from Arizona; born in Council Grove, Morris County, Kans., September 18, 1916; attended the public schools; was graduated from Kansas State College, Manhattan, Kans., in 1938 and from Harvard Law School, Cambridge, Mass., in 1941; was admitted to the Kansas bar in 1942 and the Arizona bar in 1945; commenced practice of law in Mesa, Ariz., in 1946; during World War II served in the United States Air Force from September 5, 1941, to June 28, 1946; staff judge advocate of Arizona National Guard 1947–1952; vice chairman Arizona Board of Public Welfare in 1951 and 1952; alternate delegate to Republican National Convention in 1952; elected as a Republican to the Eighty-third and to the three succeeding Congresses (January 3, 1953–January 3, 1961). *Reelected to the Eighty-seventh Congress.*

RHODES, Marion Edwards, a Representative from Missouri; born on a farm near Glen Allen, Bollinger County, Mo., January 4, 1868; attended the public schools and Will Mayfield College; was graduated from the State normal school at Cape Girardeau, Mo., in 1891 and from Stansbury College in 1893; taught school; studied law; was admitted to the bar in 1896 and commenced practice in Potosi, Washington County, Mo., in 1898; delegate to all Republican State conventions from 1896 to 1920; prosecuting attorney of Washington County 1900–1904; elected as a Republican to the Fifty-ninth Congress (March 4,

1905–March 3, 1907); was an unsuccessful candidate for reelection in 1906 to the Sixtieth Congress; mayor of Potosi in 1908 and 1909; member of the State house of representatives 1908–1910; delegate to the Republican National Convention at Chicago in 1908; member of the Missouri State Board of Law Examiners 1912–1914; elected to the Sixty-sixth and Sixty-seventh Congresses (March 4, 1919–March 3, 1923); unsuccessful candidate for reelection in 1922 to the Sixty-eighth Congress; appointed assistant to the Comptroller General of the United States at Washington, D. C., and served from April 1, 1923, until his death in that city, December 25, 1928; interment in the Masonic Cemetery, Potosi, Mo.

RIBICOFF, Abraham A., a Representative from Connecticut; born in New Britain, Hartford County, Conn., April 9, 1910; attended the public schools of New Britain; graduated from the University of Chicago Law School in 1933 and was admitted to the bar the same year; member of the Connecticut Legislature 1938–1942; judge of Hartford Police Court 1941–1943 and 1945–1947; chairman, assembly of municipal court judges for the State of Connecticut in 1941 and 1942; member of the Charter Revision Commission of the city of Hartford in 1945 and 1946; hearing examiner, Connecticut Fair Employment Practices Act 1937–1939; elected as a Democrat to the Eighty-first and Eighty-second Congresses (January 3, 1949–January 3, 1953); was not a candidate for renomination in 1952 but was unsuccessful for election to fill a vacancy in the United States Senate; delegate to Democratic National Conventions in 1952, 1956, and 1960; elected Governor of Connecticut in 1954 and reelected in 1958 and served from January 1955 until January 21, 1961, when he was sworn in as Secretary of the Department of Health, Education, and Welfare; is a resident of Hartford, Conn.

RICAUD, James Barroll, a Representative from Maryland; born in Baltimore, Md., February 11, 1808; attended the common schools, and was graduated from Washington College, Chestertown, Kent County, Md., in 1828; studied law; was admitted to the bar in 1829 and commenced practice in Chestertown; member of the State house of delegates in 1834; served in the State senate 1836–1844; presidential elector on the Whig tickets of Harrison and Tyler in 1840 and Clay and Frelinghuysen in 1844; elected as the candidate of the American Party to the Thirty-fourth and Thirty-fifth Congresses (March 4, 1855–March 3, 1859); resumed the practice of his profession; appointed associate judge of the second Maryland judicial district in 1864 by Governor Bradford and served during the May term; died in Chestertown, Md., on January 24, 1866; interment in St. Paul's Church Cemetery.

RICE, Alexander Hamilton, a Representative from Massachusetts; born in Newton Lower Falls, Mass., August 30, 1818; was graduated from Union College in 1844; engaged in the manufacture of paper at Boston; mayor of Boston in 1856 and 1857; elected as a Republican to the Thirty-sixth and to the three succeeding Congresses (March 4, 1859–March 3, 1867); was not a candidate for renomination in 1866; resumed his former business pursuits in Boston; delegate to the Philadelphia Loyalist Convention in 1866; delegate to the Republican National Convention at Chicago in 1868; Governor of Massachusetts 1876–1878; died in Boston, Mass., July 22, 1895; interment in Newton Cemetery, Newton, Mass.

RICE, Americus Vespucius, a Representative from Ohio; born in Perryville, Ashland County, Ohio, on November 18, 1835; pursued classical studies; attended Antioch College and was graduated from Union College, Schenectady, N. Y., in 1860; was a law student when he enlisted in the Union Army in 1861;

during the Civil War was commissioned as captain in the Twenty-first Ohio Infantry April 27, 1861; became captain in the Fifty-seventh Ohio Infantry September 2, 1861; promoted to lieutenant colonel February 8, 1862, to colonel May 31, 1865, and to brigadier general in 1865; mustered out January 15, 1866; manager of a private banking house in Ottawa, Ohio; delegate to the Democratic National Convention at Baltimore in 1872; elected as a Democrat to the Forty-fourth and Forty-fifth Congresses (March 4, 1875–March 3, 1879); was not a candidate for renomination in 1878; president of A. V. Rice & Co., a banking concern of Ottawa; director in various business enterprises; appointed pension agent for Ohio in 1893 and served from May 1, 1894, until the fall of 1898; moved to Washington, D. C., in 1899 and engaged in banking and various other enterprises; appointed purchasing agent of the United States Census Bureau, which position he held at the time of his death in Washington, D. C., on April 4, 1904; interment in Arlington National Cemetery, Fort Myer, Va.

RICE, Benjamin Franklin, a Senator from Arkansas; born in East Otto, Cattaraugus County, N. Y., on May 26, 1828; attended private schools; studied law; was admitted to the bar and practiced in Irvine, Estill County, Ky.; member of the State house of representatives in 1855 and 1856; presidential elector on the Republican ticket of Frémont and Dayton in 1856; moved to Minnesota in 1860; during the Civil War served in the Union Army as a captain and was promoted to judge advocate in the Minnesota Volunteers; settled in Little Rock, Ark., in 1864 and resumed the practice of law; active in organizing the Republican Party in Arkansas; appointed chairman of the committee to prepare a code of practice for the State in 1868; upon the readmission of the State of Arkansas to representation was elected as a Republican to the United States Senate and served from June 23, 1868, to March 3, 1873; resumed the practice of law in Arkansas; because of ill health moved to Colorado in 1875; moved to Washington, D. C., in 1882, where he continued the practice of law until his death; died in Tulsa, Okla., January 19, 1905; interment in Oak Hill Cemetery, Washington, D. C.

RICE, Edmund (brother of Henry Mower Rice), a Representative from Minnesota; born in Waitsfield, Vt., February 14, 1819; attended the common schools; moved to Kalamazoo, Mich., in November 1838; studied law; was admitted to the bar in 1842 and commenced practice in Kalamazoo, Mich.; register of the court of chancery in 1841; master in chancery in 1845; enlisted to serve in the Mexican War in 1847; commissioned first lieutenant of Company A, First Regiment, Michigan Volunteers; detailed as acting assistant commissary of subsistence and acting assistant quartermaster; mustered out in August 1848; moved to St. Paul, Minn., in July 1849; clerk of the State supreme court, third circuit, in 1849; member of the Territorial house of representatives in 1851; practiced law until 1856; elected commissioner of Ramsey County in 1856; president of the Minnesota & Pacific Railroad Co. 1857–1863 and of the St. Paul & Pacific Railroad 1863–1872 and trustee of the latter in 1879; president of the St. Paul & Chicago Railroad 1863–1877; served in the State senate 1864–1866 and 1874–1876; member of the State house of representatives in 1867, 1872, 1877, and 1878; elected mayor of St. Paul and served from 1881 to 1883; again elected mayor in 1885 and served until February 1887, when he resigned, having been elected to Congress; elected as a Democrat to the Fiftieth Congress (March 4, 1887–March 3, 1889); was an unsuccessful candidate for reelection in 1888 to the Fifty-first Congress; retired from public and political activities; died at White Bear Lake, Ramsey County, Minn., on July 11, 1889; interment in Oakland Cemetery, St. Paul, Minn.

RICE, Edward Young, a Representative from Illinois; born near Russellville, Logan County, Ky., February 8, 1820; pursued classical studies; studied law; was admitted to the bar in 1844; moved to Montgomery County, Ill., and commenced practice in Hillsboro, Montgomery County, Ill.; elected county recorder in 1847; member of the State house of representatives in 1849 and 1850; judge of the Montgomery County Court in 1851 and 1852; master in chancery 1853–1857; elected judge of the eighteenth circuit of Illinois in 1857 and reelected in 1861 and 1867; member of the State constitutional convention in 1869 and 1870; elected as a Democrat to the Forty-second Congress (March 4, 1871–March 3, 1873); unsuccessful candidate for renomination in 1872; resumed the practice of law in Hillsboro and Springfield, Ill.; died in Hillsboro, Ill., April 16, 1883; interment in Oak Grove Cemetery.

RICE, Henry Mower (brother of Edmund Rice), a Delegate and a Senator from Minnesota; born in Waitsfield, Vt., November 29, 1817; attended the common schools of Detroit and Kalamazoo, Mich., 1835–1839; resided in the Territories of Iowa and Wisconsin; moved to the Territory of Minnesota in 1839; post sutler for the United States Army at Fort Atkinson; engaged in the fur business; settled in St. Paul in 1848; negotiated a treaty with the Winnebago and Chippewa Indians in 1847; through his personal influence secured the consent of the objecting Sioux Indians to confirmation of the treaty of 1851 whereby all of Minnesota west of the Mississippi River and south of Ojibway County was opened to white settlers; elected as a Democrat a Delegate to the Thirty-third and Thirty-fourth Congresses (March 4, 1853–March 3, 1857); was not a candidate for renomination in 1856; upon the admission of Minnesota as a State into the Union was elected as a Democrat to the United States Senate and served from May 11, 1858, to March 3, 1863; was not a candidate for reelection in 1862; member of the board of regents of the University of Minnesota from 1851 to 1859; unsuccessful candidate for election as Governor of Minnesota in 1865; president of the State historical society; president of the board of public works; treasurer of Ramsey County 1878–1884; United States commissioner in making several Indian treaties in 1887 and 1888; died while on a visit in San Antonio, Tex., January 15, 1894; interment in Oakland Cemetery, St. Paul, Minn.

RICE, John Birchard, a Representative from Ohio; born in Fremont, Sandusky County, Ohio, June 23, 1832; attended the common schools of Lower Sandusky (now Fremont) and Oberlin College, Ohio; was graduated from the medical department of the University of Michigan at Ann Arbor in 1857; took a postgraduate course at Jefferson Medical College, Philadelphia, Pa., and at Bellevue Hospital, New York City, in 1859; lecturer on military surgery and obstetrics in the Charity Hospital Medical College and the medical department of the University of Wooster in Cleveland, Ohio; served on the medical staff during the Civil War as assistant surgeon of the Tenth and surgeon of the Seventy-second Regiment, Ohio Volunteer Infantry; also surgeon in chief of a division in the Fifteenth Army Corps and of the district of Memphis; appointed a trustee of the State hospital, Toledo, Ohio; member of the Board of Health of Fremont, Ohio; elected as a Republican to the Forty-seventh Congress (March 4, 1881–March 3, 1883); was not a candidate for renomination in 1882; engaged in the practice of medicine in Fremont, Ohio; died in Fremont, Ohio, January 14, 1893; interment in Oakwood Cemetery.

RICE, John Blake, a Representative from Illinois; born in Easton, Talbot County, Md., May 28, 1809; received a limited schooling; went on the stage in New York in 1839; moved to Chicago, Ill., in 1847 and was manager of a theater; also managed theaters in Bangor, Maine, Buffalo, N. Y., and Milwaukee, Wis.; retired from the stage in 1857 and from theatrical management in 1861; mayor of Chicago 1865–1869; elected as a Republican to the Forty-third Congress and served from March 4, 1873, until his death in Norfolk, Va., December 17, 1874; interment in Rosehill Cemetery, Chicago, Ill.

RICE, John Hovey, a Representative from Maine; born in Mount Vernon, Maine, February 5, 1816; attended the common schools; clerk in the office of the register of deeds, Augusta, Maine, 1831–1841; engaged in the mercantile business; deputy sheriff; aide-de-camp to General Bachelor in the "Aroostook War," the northeastern boundary dispute with Great Britain, in 1838; moved to Piscataquis County, Maine, in 1843; studied law; was admitted to the bar and commenced practice in Piscataquis County in 1848; prosecuting attorney for Piscataquis County 1852–1860; delegate to the first Republican National Convention at Philadelphia in 1856; elected as a Republican to the Thirty-seventh, Thirty-eighth, and Thirty-ninth Congresses (March 4, 1861–March 3, 1867); declined to be a candidate for renomination; United States collector of customs at the port of Bangor, Maine, 1861–1871; moved to Washington, D. C., where he practiced law for twelve years; thence to New York City in 1884 and practiced until 1899; moved to Chicago, Ill., in May 1899 and remained there until his death on March 14, 1911; interment in Oakwood Cemetery.

RICE, John McConnell, a Representative from Kentucky; born in Prestonsburg, Floyd County, Ky., February 19, 1831; received a limited schooling; was graduated from a Louisville law school in 1852; was admitted to the bar in 1853 and commenced practice in Pikeville, Ky.; superintendent of schools of Pike County in 1854; elected prosecuting attorney of Pike County in 1856; member of the State house of representatives in 1858; moved to Louisa, Lawrence County, Ky., in 1860; again a member of the State house of representatives in 1861; elected as a Democrat to the Forty-first and Forty-second Congresses (March 4, 1869–March 3, 1873); was not a candidate for renomination in 1872; resumed the practice of law in Louisa, Ky.; appointed judge of the Lawrence County criminal court in 1883; was elected to the same office in 1884; reelected in 1890 and served until his death in Louisa, Ky., September 18, 1895; interment in Pine Hill Cemetery.

RICE, Theron Moses, a Representative from Missouri; born in Mecca, Trumbull County, Ohio, on September 21, 1829; attended the academy in Chester, Ohio, where he remained four years; taught in the district school during the winter months; studied law; was admitted to the bar in June 1854 and practiced for about three years in Mahoning County, Ohio; moved in the spring of 1858 to California, Moniteau County, Mo.; served during the Civil War, 1861–1865, in the United States Infantry Volunteer Service from Missouri; received gradual promotions from first lieutenant to colonel; returned to Missouri in the spring of 1866 and resumed the practice of his profession in Tipton, Moniteau County, Mo.; was circuit judge 1868–1874; elected as a National Greenbacker to the Forty-seventh Congress (March 4, 1881–March 3, 1883); was not a candidate for renomination in 1882; resumed the practice of law in Boonville, Mo., until his death in that city November 7, 1895; interment in Tipton Cemetery, Tipton, Mo.

RICE, Thomas, a Representative from Massachusetts; born in Pownalborough (now Wiscasset), Maine (then a part of Massachusetts), March 30, 1768; was graduated from Harvard University in 1791; studied law; was admitted to the bar in Suffolk County, Mass., in 1794 and commenced practice in

Winslow, Maine, the following year; appointed in 1807 by the supreme judicial court of Maine one of the examiners of counselors and attorneys for Kennebec County; member of the State house of representatives in 1814; elected to the Fourteenth and Fifteenth Congresses (March 4, 1815–March 3, 1819); unsuccessful candidate for reelection in 1818 to the Sixteenth Congress; resumed the practice of law; died in Winslow, Kennebec County, Maine, August 25, 1854; interment in Pine Grove Cemetery, Waterville, Maine.

RICE, William Whitney, a Representative from Massachusetts; born in Deerfield, Franklin County, Mass., on March 7, 1826; attended Gorham Academy, Maine, and was graduated from Bowdoin College, Brunswick, Maine, in 1846; preceptor in Leicester Academy, Massachusetts, 1847–1851; studied law in Worcester; was admitted to the bar in 1854 and commenced practice in that city; appointed judge of insolvency for Worcester County in 1858; mayor of the city of Worcester in 1860; district attorney for the middle district of Massachusetts 1869–1874; member of the State house of representatives in 1875; elected as a Republican to the Forty-fifth and to the four succeeding Congresses (March 4, 1877–March 3, 1887); unsuccessful candidate for reelection in 1886 to the Fiftieth Congress; resumed the practice of law in Worcester, Mass., and died there March 1, 1896; interment in the Rural Cemetery.

RICH, Charles, a Representative from Vermont; born in Warwick, Hampshire County, Mass., on September 13, 1771; received a limited schooling; moved to Shoreham, Addison County, Vt., in 1787; member of the State house of representatives 1800–1811; was county judge for six years; elected as a Democrat to the Thirteenth Congress (March 4, 1813–March 3, 1815); elected to the Fifteenth and to the three succeeding Congresses and served from March 4, 1817, until his death in Shoreham, Vt., on October 15, 1824; interment in the family vault on his farm near Shoreham, Vt.

RICH, John Tyler, a Representative from Michigan; born in Conneautville, Crawford County, Pa., April 23, 1841; moved with his parents to Addison County, Vt., in 1846 and to Elba, Lapeer County, Mich., in 1848; attended the public schools; engaged in agricultural pursuits; member and chairman of the board of supervisors of Lapeer County 1869–1872; member of the State house of representatives 1873–1881 and served as speaker during the last two terms; delegate to the Republican State conventions in 1873, 1875, and 1878; served in the State senate from January 1, 1881, until March 21, 1881, when he resigned, having been elected to Congress; elected as a Republican to the Forty-seventh Congress to fill the vacancy caused by the resignation of Omar D. Conger and served from April 5, 1881, to March 3, 1883; unsuccessful candidate for reelection in 1882 to the Forty-eighth Congress; State railroad commissioner 1887–1891; delegate to the Republican National Conventions in 1884 and 1892; Governor of Michigan 1892–1896; United States collector of customs at Detroit from February 16, 1898, to January 30, 1906; was elected State treasurer of Michigan to fill a vacancy and served from January 23, 1908, to January 1, 1909; collector of customs at Port Huron, Mich., from December 11, 1908, to May 30, 1913; discontinued active pursuits and lived in retirement until his death, which occurred while sojourning in St. Petersburg, Fla., on March 28, 1926; interment in Mount Hope Cemetery, Lapeer, Mich.

RICH, Robert Fleming, a Representative from Pennsylvania; born in Woolrich, Clinton County, Pa., June 23, 1883; attended the public schools, Dickinson Seminary, Williamsport, Pa., and Williamsport (Pa.) Commercial College; was graduated from

Mercersburg (Pa.) Academy in 1902 and attended Dickinson College, Carlisle, Pa., 1903–1906; engaged in the woolen-mills business in 1906; also engaged in banking and became financially interested in various business and manufacturing enterprises; delegate to the Republican National Convention at Cleveland in 1924, 1952, and 1956; member of the board of trustees of Dickinson College 1912–, of Lock Haven (Pa.) Teachers College 1918–1928, of Lock Haven (Pa.) Hospital 1920–1951, and of Lycoming College 1931–; elected as a Republican to the Seventy-first Congress to fill the vacancy caused by the death of Edgar R. Kiess; reelected to the Seventy-second and to the five succeeding Congresses and served from November 4, 1930, to January 3, 1943; did not seek renomination in 1942; elected to the Seventy-ninth, Eightieth, and Eighty-first Congresses (January 3, 1945–January 3, 1951); was not a candidate for renomination in 1950; general manager and later president of the Woolrich Woolen Mills; resides in Woolrich, Pa.

RICHARD, Gabriel, a Delegate from Michigan Territory; born in La Ville de Saintes, France, October 15, 1767; pursued classical studies; studied theology in the seminary of Augers, France, and in Paris, and was ordained as a priest on October 15, 1790; immigrated to the United States in 1792 and settled in Baltimore, Md.; professor of mathematics in St. Mary's College, Maryland; sent by Bishop Carroll as a missionary to the Indians in the Northwest Territory and was stationed in what is now Kaskaskia, Ill., and later as a missionary in Detroit, Mich.; published a periodical in the French language entitled "Essais du Michigan" and some Roman Catholic books; was elected to the Eighteenth Congress (March 4, 1823–March 3, 1825); unsuccessful candidate for reelection in 1824 to the Nineteenth Congress; returned to Detroit and officiated as grand vicar; died in Detroit, Mich., September 13, 1832; interment in the cemetery of the Roman Catholic Church of St. Anne.

RICHARDS, Charles Lenmore, a Representative from Nevada; born in Austin, Lander County, Nev., October 3, 1877; attended the public schools in Nevada and Pennsylvania and was graduated from the law department of Leland Stanford Junior University, California, in 1901; studied law; was admitted to the bar and commenced practice in Tonopah, Nev., in 1901; served as district attorney of Nye County in 1903 and 1904; member of the State house of representatives in 1919; moved to Reno, Nev., in 1919; chairman of the Democratic State committee in 1922; councilor from Nevada to the United States Chamber of Commerce from March 29, 1923, to May 20, 1924; member of the American and Nevada State Bar Associations and also the bar associations of Washoe and Nye Counties; elected as a Democrat to the Sixty-eighth Congress (March 4, 1923–March 3, 1925); unsuccessful candidate for reelection in 1924 to the Sixty-ninth Congress; practiced law in Reno, Nev., until his death there on December 22, 1953; interment in Mountain View Cemetery.

RICHARDS, Jacob, a Representative from Pennsylvania; born near Chester, Delaware County, Pa., in 1773; was graduated from the University of Pennsylvania at Philadelphia in 1794; studied law; was admitted to the bar in 1795 and commenced practice in Philadelphia; elected as a Democrat to the Eighth, Ninth, and Tenth Congresses (March 4, 1803–March 3, 1809); was commissioned as colonel of militia in Delaware County, Pa.; engaged in the practice of law until his death near Chester, Pa., July 20, 1816.

RICHARDS, James Alexander Dudley, a Representative from Ohio; born in Boston, Mass., March 22, 1845; spent his early life in Boston and New York City, where he received a common-school education; moved to New Philadelphia, Tuscarawas County, Ohio, in 1861; studied law; was admitted to the bar in 1867 and commenced practice in New Philadelphia; elected as a Democrat to the Fifty-third Congress (March 4, 1893–March 3, 1895); unsuccessful candidate for reelection in 1894 to the Fifty-fourth Congress; resumed the practice of law in Washington, D. C., and subsequently returned to New Philadelphia, Ohio, and continued the practice of his profession; died in New Philadelphia, Ohio, on December 4, 1911; interment in the East Fair Street Cemetery.

RICHARDS, James Prioleau, a Representative from South Carolina; born in Liberty Hill, Kershaw County, S. C., August 31, 1894; attended the county schools and Clemson College, Clemson, S. C.; during the First World War served overseas as a private, corporal, sergeant, and second lieutenant in the Trench Mortar Battery, Headquarters Company, One Hundred and Eighteenth Regiment, Thirtieth Division, 1917–1919; was graduated from the law department of the University of South Carolina at Columbia in 1921; was admitted to the bar the same year and commenced practice in Lancaster, S. C.; judge of the probate court of Lancaster County, S. C., 1923–1933; elected as a Democrat to the Seventy-third and to the eleven succeeding Congresses (March 4, 1933–January 3, 1957); was not a candidate for renomination in 1956; delegate to the Japanese Peace Conference and United States delegate to the United Nations in 1953; special assistant to President Eisenhower from January 1957 to January 1958; president and executive director of Tobacco Institute, Inc., from 1957 until his retirement in 1961; resides in Heath Springs, S. C.

RICHARDS, John (brother of Matthias Richards), a Representative from Pennsylvania; born in New Hanover, Philadelphia County, Pa., April 18, 1753; educated under private tutors; served as magistrate during the Revolutionary War; appointed justice of the peace for Philadelphia County June 6, 1777, and served until his death; judge of the court of common pleas for Montgomery County in 1784; member of the Federal Constitutional Convention in 1787; elected to the Fourth Congress (March 4, 1795–March 3, 1797); was not a candidate for renomination in 1796; was an ironmaster and also engaged in mercantile and agricultural pursuits; member of the State senate 1801–1807; died in New Hanover, Pa., November 13, 1822; interment in Faulkner Swamp (Lutheran) Church Cemetery.

RICHARDS, John, a Representative from New York; born in Wales April 13, 1765; immigrated to the United States and settled in Johnsburg, Warren County, N. Y.; received a limited schooling; member of the State assembly from January 29, 1811, to April 8, 1811; State surveyor 1810–1812; delegate to the State constitutional convention in 1821; elected to the Eighteenth Congress (March 4, 1823–March 3, 1825); died at Lake George, Warren County, N. Y., April 18, 1850.

RICHARDS, Mark, a Representative from Vermont; born in Waterbury, Conn., July 15, 1760; received a limited schooling; enlisted during the Revolutionary War in 1776; served at Stony Point, Monmouth, Red Bank, and Valley Forge; settled in Boston after the Revolution and engaged in mercantile and mechanical pursuits; moved to Westminster, Vt., in 1796; member of the State house of representatives 1801–1805; sheriff of Windham County 1806–1810; presidential elector on the Democratic ticket of Madison and Gerry in 1812; member of the Governor's council in 1816; elected as a Democrat to the Fifteenth and Sixteenth Congresses (March 4, 1817–March 3, 1821); again a member of the State house of representatives 1824–1826, 1828, and 1832–1834; Lieutenant Governor of Vermont in 1830 and 1831; died in Westminster, Vt., August 10, 1844; interment in the Bradley tomb, Old Cemetery.

RICHARDS, Matthias (brother of John Richards), a Representative from Pennsylvania; born near Pottstown, New Hanover Township, Montgomery County, Pa., on February 26, 1758; completed preparatory studies under private tutoring; served during the Revolutionary War as a private in Col. Daniel Udree's second battalion, Berks County Militia, from August 5, 1777, until January 5, 1778, participating in the Battles of Brandywine and Germantown; major of the Fourth Battalion, Philadelphia County Militia, in 1780; appointed justice of the peace in 1788 and held this office for forty years; judge of Berks County Court in Pennsylvania 1791–1797; inspector of customs in 1801 and 1802; elected to the Tenth and Eleventh Congresses (March 4, 1807–March 3, 1811); was not a candidate for renomination in 1810; appointed collector of revenue for the ninth district of Pennsylvania in 1813; clerk of the orphans' court for Berks County in 1823; was appointed associate judge of Berks County Courts by Governor Shulze; engaged in mercantile pursuits in Reading, Pa., until his death in that city on August 4, 1830; interment in the Charles Evans Cemetery.

RICHARDSON, David Plunket, a Representative from New York; born in Macedon, Wayne County, N. Y., May 28, 1833; attended the common school and the local academy at Macedon; was graduated from Yale College in 1856; studied law in Rochester, N. Y.; was admitted to the bar in 1859, and practiced; during the Civil War entered the Union Army in 1861, and served over three years; moved to Angelica, N. Y., in 1866; elected as a Republican to the Forty-sixth and Forty-seventh Congresses (March 4, 1879–March 3, 1883); was not a candidate for reelection in 1882; resumed the practice of law in Angelica, N. Y., where he died on June 21, 1904; interment in Angelica Cemetery.

RICHARDSON, George Frederick, a Representative from Michigan; born in Jamestown, Ottawa County, Mich., July 1, 1850; attended the common schools; engaged in agricultural and mercantile pursuits; elected township clerk eight years in succession; member of the State house of representatives 1885–1887, 1891, and 1892, and served as speaker in the two last-named years; moved to Grand Rapids, Mich., in 1893; elected as a Democrat to the Fifty-third Congress (March 4, 1893–March 3, 1895); declined to be a candidate for renomination in 1894; operated a dairy farm in Grand Rapids; moved to Kennewick, Wash., in 1904 and engaged in agricultural pursuits and in the transfer, livery, and fuel business; was twice elected mayor of Kennewick and also served as chairman of the school board; moved to Ellensburg, Wash., and in 1916 engaged in agricultural pursuits; retired to private life in 1919 and made his home in Bellevue, Wash., where he died on March 1, 1923; interment in the Odd Fellows Cemetery, Ellensburg, Wash.

RICHARDSON, Harry Alden, a Senator from Delaware; born in Camden, Kent County, Del., January 1, 1853; moved with his parents to Dover, Kent County, in 1856; attended the common schools and the academy in East Greenwich, R. I.; at the age of sixteen he started to learn the trade of packer and canner in his father's establishment at Dover, Del.; upon the death of the junior member of the firm in 1876 became a partner of his father and assumed entire control in 1894; elected State senator in 1888; president of the First National Bank of Dover; also interested in public-service corporations; unsuccessful Republican candidate for Governor of Delaware in 1890; delegate to the Republican National Conventions in 1908 and 1912; elected as a Republican to the United States Senate in 1907 and served from March 4, 1907, to March 3, 1913; was not a candidate for reelection; again engaged in the manufacture of canned food products; died in Dover, Del., June 16, 1928; interment in Lakeside Cemetery.

RICHARDSON, James Daniel, a Representative from Tennessee; born in Rutherford County, Tenn., March 10, 1843; attended the country schools and Franklin College, near Nashville; during the Civil War entered the Confederate Army before graduating from college and served nearly four years, the first year as a private and the remaining three years as adjutant of the Forty-fifth Regiment, Tennessee Infantry; studied law; was admitted to the bar and commenced practice January 1, 1867, in Murfreesboro, Tenn.; member of the State house of representatives and elected speaker of the house in 1871; served in the State senate in 1873 and 1874; delegate to the Democratic National Conventions in 1876, 1896, and 1900; presided as permanent chairman at the last-named convention; chairman of the Democratic congressional committee in 1900; editor and compiler of the Government publication entitled "Messages and Papers of the Presidents"; elected as a Democrat to the Forty-ninth and to the nine succeeding Congresses (March 4, 1885–March 3, 1905); Democratic caucus nominee for Speaker in the Fifty-sixth and Fifty-seventh Congresses; voluntarily retired to devote his time to the cause of Masonry and was sovereign grand commander of Scottish Rite Masonry for the southern jurisdiction until his death in Murfreesboro, Tenn., July 24, 1914; interment in Evergreen Cemetery.

RICHARDSON, James Montgomery, a Representative from Kentucky; born in Mobile, Ala., July 1, 1858; moved to Glasgow, Ky., in early youth and resided with his uncle; attended the common schools; became editor of the Glasgow (Ky.) Times in 1878; delegate to the Democratic National Convention at Chicago in 1896; member of the State house of representatives in 1896; served as prison commissioner from 1900 to 1905, when he resigned, having been elected to Congress; elected as a Democrat to the Fifty-ninth Congress (March 4, 1905–March 3, 1907); unsuccessful candidate for reelection; resumed newspaper activities; postmaster at Glasgow from May 22, 1913, to May 9, 1922; died in Glasgow, Barren County, Ky., February 9, 1925; interment in Glasgow Cemetery.

RICHARDSON, John Peter, a Representative from South Carolina; born at Hickory Hill, S. C., April 14, 1801; was graduated from South Carolina College at Columbia in 1819; studied law; was admitted to the bar and commenced practice in Fulton, S. C.; member of the State house of representatives; judge of the circuit court; elected as a State Rights Democrat to the Twenty-fourth Congress to fill the vacancy caused by the death of Richard I. Manning; reelected to the Twenty-fifth Congress and served from December 19, 1836, to March 3, 1839; Governor of South Carolina 1840–1842; died in Fulton (later Pinewood), Sumter County, S. C., January 24, 1864.

RICHARDSON, John Smythe, a Representative from South Carolina; born on the Bloomhill plantation, near Sumter, Sumter County, S. C., February 29, 1828; pursued an academic course in Cokesbury, S. C., and was graduated from South Carolina College (now the University of South Carolina) at Columbia in 1850; studied law; was admitted to the bar in 1852 and began practice in Sumter, S. C.; during the Civil War entered the Confederate Army as a captain of Infantry, and served under Gen. Joseph Brevard Kershaw until after the first Battle of Manassas, where he was wounded; later promoted to adjutant of the Twenty-third Regiment, South Carolina Infantry, and served until the close of the war in 1865; member of the State house of representatives 1865–1867; appointed agent of the State of South Carolina in 1866 to apply for and receive the land script donated to South Carolina by Congress; delegate to the Democratic National Convention at St. Louis in 1876; elected as a Democrat to the Forty-sixth and Forty-seventh Congresses (March 4, 1879–March 3, 1883); master in equity for Sumter County 1884–1893; died at his country home, "Shadyside," near Sumter, S. C., February 24, 1894; interment in Sumter Cemetery.

RICHARDSON, Joseph, a Representative from Massachusetts; born in Billerica, Mass., February 1, 1778; attended public and private schools; was graduated from Dartmouth College, Hanover, N. H., in 1802; teacher in Charlestown 1804–1806; studied theology: was ordained a minister and assigned to the first parish of the Unitarian Church in Hingham July 2, 1806; delegate to the State constitutional convention in 1820; member of the State house of representatives in 1821 and 1822; served in the State senate in 1823, 1824, and 1826; elected to the Twentieth and Twenty-first Congresses (March 4, 1827–March 3, 1831); declined to be a candidate for renomination in 1830 to the Twenty-second Congress; retired from public life and resumed his ministerial duties; died in Hingham, Plymouth County, Mass., on September 25, 1871; interment in Old Ship Cemetery.

RICHARDSON, William, a Representative from Alabama; born in Athens, Limestone County, Ala., May 8, 1839; attended the public schools; during the Civil War served in the Confederate Army and was severely wounded at the Battle of Chickamauga; paroled in April 1865 in Marietta, Ga.; member of the Alabama House of Representatives 1865–1867; studied law; was admitted to the bar in 1867 and commenced practice in Huntsville, Ala.; judge of the probate and county courts of Madison County, Ala., 1875–1886; presidential elector on the Democratic ticket of Grover Cleveland and Allen G. Thurman in 1888; delegate to the Democratic National Convention at St. Louis in 1904; elected as a Democrat to the Fifty-sixth Congress to fill the vacancy caused by the resignation of Joseph Wheeler; reelected to the Fifty-seventh and to the six succeeding Congresses and served from August 6, 1900, until his death in Atlantic City, N. J., where he had gone for the benefit of his health, on March 31, 1914; interment in Maple Hill Cemetery, Huntsville, Ala.

RICHARDSON, William Alexander, a Representative and a Senator from Illinois; born near Lexington, Fayette County, Ky., January 16, 1811; attended college at Walnut Hill, Ky., Centre College at Danville, Ky., and Transylvania University at Lexington, Ky.; taught school; studied law; was admitted to the bar in 1831 and commenced practice in Shelbyville, Ill.; State's attorney in 1834 and 1835; member of the State house of representatives 1836–1838 and 1844–1846, and served as speaker in 1844; member of the State senate 1838–1842; presidential elector on the Democratic ticket of Polk and Dallas in 1844; during the Mexican War enlisted as a captain and was promoted to the rank of major; moved to Quincy, Ill., in 1849; elected as a Democrat to the Thirtieth Congress to fill the vacancy caused by the resignation of Stephen A. Douglas; reelected to the Thirty-first and to the three succeeding Congresses and served from December 6, 1847, to August 25, 1856, when he resigned; delegate to the Democratic National Convention at Charleston, S. C., in 1860; elected to the Thirty-seventh Congress and served from March 4, 1861, until his resignation on January 29, 1863, having previously been elected Senator; elected to the United States Senate in 1863 to fill the vacancy caused by the death of Stephen A. Douglas and served from January 30, 1863, to March 3, 1865; was not a candidate for renomination in 1864; delegate to the Democratic National Convention at New York City in 1868; engaged in newspaper work; died in Quincy, Adams County, Ill., December 27, 1875; interment in Woodland Cemetery.

RICHARDSON, William Emanuel, a Representative from Pennsylvania; born on a farm (the old Daniel Boone homestead) near Stonersville, in Exeter Township, Berks County, Pa., on September 3, 1886; moved to Bernville, Berks County, Pa., with his parents at an early age, where he attended the public schools; was graduated from Princeton University, Princeton, N. J., in 1910, and from the law department of Columbia University, New York City, N. Y., in 1913; was admitted to the bar the same year and commenced practice in Reading, Pa., in 1914; served with Section I, Ambulance Americaine, in Belgium and France in 1915, and with Squadron A, New York Cavalry, on the Mexican border in 1916; during the First World War was commissioned a second lieutenant on August 15, 1917, and served with the Eightieth Cavalry Division, United States Army, and later with the Seventh Machine Gun Battalion, Third Division, and was discharged a first lieutenant on September 15, 1919; after the war resumed the practice of law in Reading, Pa.; elected as a Democrat to the Seventy-third and Seventy-fourth Congresses (March 4, 1933–January 3, 1937); unsuccessful candidate for renomination in 1936; attended the Interparliamentary Union Conference in Budapest, Hungary, in 1936; resumed the practice of law in Reading, Pa.; died in Wyomissing, Pa., November 3, 1948; interment in Schwartzwald Cemetery, Jacksonwald, Pa.

RICHARDSON, William Merchant, a Representative from Massachusetts; born in Pelham, Hillsborough County, N. H., January 4, 1774; was graduated from Harvard University in 1797; studied law; was admitted to the bar and commenced practice in Groton, Mass., in 1804; elected as a Federalist to the Twelfth Congress to fill the vacancy caused by the resignation of Joseph B. Varnum; reelected to the Thirteenth Congress and served from November 4, 1811, to April 18, 1814, when he resigned; moved to Portsmouth, Rockingham County, N. H., in 1814; United States attorney in 1814; appointed chief justice of New Hampshire in 1816 and served until his death; died in Chester, Rockingham County, N. H., March 15, 1838; interment in the Old Cemetery.

RICHMOND, Hiram Lawton, a Representative from Pennsylvania; born in Chautauqua, Chautauqua County, N. Y., May 17, 1810; received his early education from a private instructor and in the common schools; studied medicine two years with his father; attended Allegheny College, Meadville, Pa., in 1834 and 1835 but did not graduate; studied law; was admitted to the bar in 1838 and commenced the practice of law in Meadville, Crawford County, Pa.; in early manhood was a staunch Whig but united with the Republican Party upon its organization; elected as a Republican to the Forty-third Congress (March 4, 1873–March 3, 1875); was not a candidate for renomination in 1874; member of the board of trustees of Allegheny College for many years; resumed the practice of law; died in Meadville, Pa., February 19, 1885; interment in Greendale Cemetery.

RICHMOND, James Buchanan, a Representative from Virginia; born in Turkey Cove, Lee County, Va., February 27, 1842; attended Emory and Henry College, Emory, Va.; studied law; was admitted to the bar and practiced in the circuit and county courts of Lee, Scott, and Wise Counties, Va., and in the court of appeals at Wytheville, Va.; served as orderly sergeant and promoted to captain of Company A, Fiftieth Regiment, Virginia Infantry, during the first year of the Civil War; afterward major in the Sixty-fourth Virginia Regiment for a time, and was subsequently promoted to the rank of lieutenant colonel of the same regiment; member of the State house of delegates in 1874 and 1875; was elected as a Democrat to the Forty-sixth

Congress (March 4, 1879–March 3, 1881); county judge of Scott County 1886–1892; delegate to the State constitutional convention at Richmond in 1901 and 1902; chief counsel of the South Atlantic & Ohio Railroad for a number of years; also engaged in banking; died in Baltimore, Md., April 30, 1910; interment in Estil Cemetery, Gate City, Va.

RICHMOND, Jonathan, a Representative from New York; born in Dartmouth, Mass., July 31, 1774; completed preparatory studies; moved to western New York in 1813 and settled in Aurora, Cayuga County; sheriff of Cayuga County, N. Y., from 1808 to 1812; United States internal revenue collector; was elected to the Sixteenth Congress (March 4, 1819–March 3, 1821); died in Aurora, Cayuga County, N. Y., July 28, 1853; interment in Aurora Cemetery.

RICKETTS, Edwin Darlington, a Representative from Ohio; born near Maxville, Perry County, Ohio, August 3, 1867; attended the public schools; for twelve years was a teacher and superintendent of schools; studied law; was admitted to the bar in 1899 and commenced practice in Logan, Hocking County, Ohio; elected as a Republican to the Sixty-fourth Congress (March 4, 1915–March 3, 1917); was an unsuccessful candidate for reelection in 1916 to the Sixty-fifth Congress; elected to the Sixty-sixth and Sixty-seventh Congresses (March 4, 1919–March 3, 1923); was an unsuccessful candidate for reelection in 1922 to the Sixty-eighth Congress; resumed the practice of law; delegate to the Republican National Convention at Kansas City in 1928; died in Logan, Ohio, on July 3, 1937; interment in Oak Grove Cemetery.

RIDDICK, Carl Wood, a Representative from Montana; born in Wells, Faribault County, Minn., February 25, 1872; attended the common schools; was graduated from Menominee (Mich.) High School in 1890; attended Albion (Mich.) College and Lawrence University, Appleton, Wis.; editor and publisher of the Winamac (Ind.) Republican 1899–1910; secretary of the Indiana Republican State central committee in 1906 and 1908; moved to Montana and settled on a homestead in Fergus County in 1910; engaged in wheat and cattle raising 1910–1918; county assessor of Fergus County, Mont., 1915–1918; elected as a Republican to the Sixty-sixth and Sixty-seventh Congresses (March 4, 1919–March 3, 1923); did not seek renomination in 1922, but was an unsuccessful candidate for election to the United States Senate; former president of the National Republic, a magazine published in Washington, D. C.; owned and operated a home development at Sylvan Shores on South River, Riva, Md.; retired and moved to Florida; died in Fort Lauderdale, Fla., July 9, 1960; interment in Hillcrest Memorial Cemetery, Annapolis, Md.

RIDDLE, Albert Gallatin, a Representative from Ohio; was born in Monson, Mass., May 28, 1816; moved with his parents to Newbury, in the Western Reserve of Ohio, in 1817; completed preparatory studies; studied law; was admitted to the bar in 1840 and began practice in Geauga County; prosecuting attorney of that county 1840–1846; member of the State house of representatives 1848–1850; moved to Cleveland, Ohio, in 1856; elected as a Republican to the Thirty-seventh Congress (March 4, 1861–March 3, 1863); was not a candidate for renomination in 1862; consul at Matanzas, Cuba, in 1863 and 1864; returned to Washington, D. C., and again engaged in the practice of law; was retained by the State Department to aid in the prosecution of John H. Surratt as one of the accomplices in the murder of President Lincoln; law officer of the District of Columbia 1877–1889; died in Washington, D. C., May 16, 1902; interment in Rock Creek Cemetery.

RIDDLE, George Read, a Representative and a Senator from Delaware; born in New Castle, Del., in 1817; pursued classical studies and attended Delaware College; studied civil engineering and engaged in the construction of railroads and canals; studied law; was admitted to the bar in 1848 and commenced practice in Wilmington, Del., the same year; commissioner to retrace Mason and Dixon's line in 1849; delegate to several Democratic National Conventions; served as deputy attorney general in 1849 and 1850; elected as a Democrat to the Thirty-second and Thirty-third Congresses (March 4, 1851–March 3, 1855); unsuccessful candidate for reelection in 1854 to the Thirty-fourth Congress; elected to the United States Senate to fill the vacancy caused by the resignation of James A. Bayard and served from February 2, 1864, until his death in Washington. D. C., on March 29, 1867; interment in the Wilmington and Brandywine Cemetery, Wilmington, Del.

RIDDLE, Haywood Yancey, a Representative from Tennessee; born in Van Buren, Hardeman County, Tenn., June 20, 1834; completed preparatory studies, and was graduated from Union University, Murfreesboro, Tenn., in 1854; adjunct professor of mathematics and languages at that institution for fifteen months, when he resigned to pursue the study of law; was graduated from the law department of Cumberland University, Lebanon, Tenn., in 1857 and was admitted to the bar in Ripley, Miss., the same year; moved to Smith County, Tenn., in 1858 and engaged in agricultural pursuits; during the Civil War enlisted in the Confederate Army as a private in 1861 and served throughout the war, the last year on the staffs of Brigadier Generals Wright and Mackall; moved to Lebanon, Wilson County, Tenn., in 1865 to practice law, but was employed as a deputy clerk in the chancery clerk's office for five years; appointed clerk for a term of six years in 1870 and served until December 31, 1875, when he resigned, having been elected to Congress; elected as a Democrat to the Forty-fourth Congress to fill the vacancy caused by the death of Samuel M. Fite; reelected to the Forty-fifth Congress and served from December 14, 1875, to March 3, 1879; died in Lebanon, Tenn., March 28, 1879; interment in Cedar Grove Cemetery.

RIDDLEBERGER, Harrison Holt, a Senator from Virginia; born in Edinburg, Shenandoah County, Va., October 4, 1844; attended the common schools; served three years during the Civil War in the Confederate Army as second and first lieutenant of Infantry and as captain of Cavalry; returned to Edinburg and became editor of the Tenth Legion Banner; studied law; was admitted to the bar and commenced practice in Woodstock, Va.; member of the State house of delegates 1871–1875; served as Commonwealth attorney of Shenandoah County 1876–1880; served in the State senate 1879–1882; editor of the Shenandoah Democrat and later of the Virginian at Woodstock; member of the State committee of the Conservative Party until 1875; presidential elector on the Democratic ticket of Tilden and Hendricks in 1876 and on the Readjuster ticket in 1880; elected as a Readjuster to the United States Senate in 1881 and served from March 4, 1883, to March 3, 1889; died in Woodstock, Va., January 24, 1890; interment in Cedarwood Cemetery, Edinburg, Shenandoah County, Va.

RIDER, Ira Edgar, a Representative from New York; born in Jersey City, N. J., November 17, 1868; attended the public schools and the College of the City of New York; was graduated from the St. Lawrence University, Canton, N. Y.; studied law; was admitted to the bar and commenced practice in New York City; secretary to the president of Manhattan Borough 1898–1902; elected as a Democrat to the Fifty-eighth Congress (March 4, 1903–March 3, 1905); owing to ill health was not a candidate for renomination in 1904; resumed the practice of law; died in New York City May 29, 1906; interment in Calvary Cemetery.

RIDGELY, Edwin Reed, a Representative from Kansas; born near Lancaster, Wabash County, Ill., May 9, 1844; attended district school in the winter months; during the Civil War enlisted as a private in Company C, One Hundred and Fifteenth Regiment, Illinois Volunteer Infantry, in 1862; promoted to sergeant and served until the end of the war; moved to Girard, Kans., in 1869 and engaged in general merchandising and in agricultural pursuits; left the Republican Party in 1876 because of its financial policy; lived in Ogden, Utah, from 1889 to 1893 and then returned to Kansas; elected by the People's and Democratic Parties to the Fifty-fifth and Fifty-sixth Congresses (March 4, 1897–March 3, 1901); was not a candidate for renomination in 1900; resumed agricultural pursuits in Mulberry, Crawford County, Kans.; died in Girard, Kans., April 23, 1927; interment in Girard Cemetery.

RIDGELY, Henry Moore, a Representative and a Senator from Delaware; born in Dover, Del., August 6, 1779; completed preparatory studies; studied law; was admitted to the bar in 1802 and began practice in Dover; secretary of state of Delaware 1817–1827; elected as a Federalist to the Twelfth and Thirteenth Congresses (March 4, 1811–March 3, 1815); was not a candidate for renomination in 1814; returned to Dover, Del., and resumed the practice of law; elected to the United States Senate to fill the vacancy caused by the death of Nicholas Van Dyke and served from January 12, 1827, to March 3, 1829; was not a candidate for reelection; continued the practice of law; died in Dover, Del., August 6, 1847; interment in the Episcopal Cemetery.

RIDGELY, Richard, a Delegate from Maryland; born in Queen Caroline Parish, Anne Arundel County, Md., August 3, 1755; attended St. John's College, Annapolis, Md.; assistant clerk of the council of safety in 1776, and later clerk; studied law; was admitted to the bar in 1780 and commenced practice in Baltimore; advocate in the Maryland Court of Chancery; elected a Member of the Continental Congress in 1785 and 1786 but declined to serve in the latter year; served in the State senate 1786–1791; resumed the practice of law in Baltimore; appointed judge of the county court July 30, 1811, which position he held until his death in Howard County, Md., February 25, 1824; interment on the "Dorsey Hall" estate, near Columbia, Howard County, Md.

RIDGWAY, Joseph, a Representative from Ohio; born on Staten Island, N. Y., May 6, 1783; attended the public schools; learned the trade of carpenter; moved to Cayuga County, N. Y., in 1811 and engaged in the manufacture of plows; settled in Columbus, Franklin County, Ohio, in 1822 and established an iron foundry; member of the State house of representatives 1828–1832; elected as a Whig to the Twenty-fifth, Twenty-sixth, and Twenty-seventh Congresses (March 4, 1837–March 3, 1843); unsuccessful candidate for reelection in 1842 to the Twenty-eighth Congress; member of the State board of equalization; director of the Clinton Bank for twenty years; member of the city council; died in Columbus, Ohio, February 1, 1861; interment in Green Lawn Cemetery.

RIDGWAY, Robert, a Representative from Virginia; born in Lynchburg, Amherst County, Va., April 21, 1823; pursued academic studies; attended Emory and Henry College, Emory, Va.; was graduated from the University of Virginia at Charlottesville; studied law; was admitted to the bar and commenced practice in Liberty (now Bedford), Va.; edited the Bedford Sentinel; moved to Richmond, Va., in 1853; edited the Richmond Whig until the outbreak of the Civil War, when he retired to Amherst; elected as a Whig to the Fortieth Congress, but as reconstruction measures were not completed was not permitted to qualify; elected as a Conservative to the Forty-first Congress in July 1869; took his seat January 27, 1870, and served until his death at Cool Well, Amherst County, Va., October 16, 1870; interment in the family cemetery at Amherst, Va.

RIEHLMAN, Roy Walter, a Representative from New York; born in Otisco, Onondaga County, N. Y., August 26, 1899; attended the public schools of Tully, N. Y.; was graduated from the Manlius Military Academy, Manlius, N. Y., in 1919 and the Central City Business School, Syracuse, N. Y., in 1921; operated a general store and served as postmaster of Nedrow, N. Y., 1921–1923; in 1923 became owner and operator of a bakery at Tully, N. Y.; member of Tully Board of Education 1933–1938; member of the board of supervisors of Onondaga County 1938–1943; county clerk of Onondaga County 1943–1946; member of the advisory board of the Marine Midland Trust Co., Tully, N. Y.; elected as a Republican to the Eightieth and to the six succeeding Congresses (January 3, 1947–January 3, 1961). *Reelected to the Eighty-seventh Congress.*

RIFE, John Winebrenner, a Representative from Pennsylvania; born in Middletown, Dauphin County, Pa., August 14, 1846; attended the common schools; learned the trade of tanner; during the Civil War enlisted July 15, 1864, as a private in Company D, One Hundred and Ninety-fourth Regiment, Pennsylvania Volunteer Infantry, and served until honorably discharged on November 6, 1864; member of the city council in 1871; burgess of Middletown, Pa., in 1877 and 1878; member of the State house of representatives in 1885 and 1886; president of the Middletown & Hummelstown Railroad Co.; elected as a Republican to the Fifty-first and Fifty-second Congresses (March 4, 1889–March 3, 1893); was not a candidate for renomination; died in Middletown, Pa., April 17, 1908; interment in Middletown Cemetery.

RIGGS, James Milton, a Representative from Illinois; born on a farm near Winchester, Scott County, Ill., April 17, 1839; attended the common schools and Eureka (Ill.) College in 1862 and 1863; engaged in agricultural pursuits and taught school; sheriff of Scott County from December 1, 1864, to December 1, 1866; studied law; was admitted to the bar December 28, 1867, and commenced practice in Winchester, Scott County, Ill.; secretary of the Winchester School Board 1868–1884 and served as president 1889–1892; member of the State house of representatives in 1871 and 1872; State's attorney for Scott County 1872–1876; mayor of Winchester in 1876 and 1877; was elected as a Democrat to the Forty-eighth and Forty-ninth Congresses (March 4, 1883–March 3, 1887); was not a candidate for renomination in 1886; resumed the practice of law in Winchester, Ill.; president of the State bar association in 1891; delegate to several State conventions; was elected judge of Scott County in 1922; reelected in 1926 and served until 1930 when he retired from active pursuits; died in Winchester, Ill., November 18, 1933; interment in Winchester Cemetery.

RIGGS, Jetur Rose, a Representative from New Jersey; born near Drakesville (now Ledgewood), Morris County, N. J., June 20, 1809; received an academic education; was graduated from the New York College of Physicians and Surgeons in 1837 and commenced practice in Newfoundland, N. J.; member of the State general assembly in 1836; one of the founders of the

District Medical Society of Passaic County, N. J., in 1844 and served as president 1846–1848; moved to California in 1849 and was in charge of the hospital at Sutters Fort; returned to New Jersey and settled in Paterson in 1852; member of the State senate in 1855–1858; elected as a Democrat to the Thirty-sixth Congress (March 4, 1859–March 3, 1861); was not a candidate for renomination in 1860; resumed the practice of medicine in Paterson, Passaic County, N. J., later moved to Drakesville (now Ledgewood), N. J., and died there November 5, 1869; interment in the Presbyterian Cemetery, Succasunna, Morris County, N. J.

RIGGS, Lewis, a Representative from New York; born in Norfolk, Conn., January 16, 1789; attended the common schools and schools of Latin and Greek; was apprenticed to the carpenter's trade; studied medicine in the village of Torringford, Litchfield County, Conn., and received his diploma in May 1812; also attended medical lectures given by Dr. Benjamin Rush at the University of Pennsylvania, Philadelphia, Pa., in 1812; practiced in East Winsted, Conn.; moved to Vernon, Oneida County, N. Y., in 1813 and later to Homer, N. Y., continuously practicing his profession; also engaged in business as a retail druggist and in 1828 in the sale of dry goods; served as secretary of the Cortland County Medical Society 1820–1823 and as president in 1825 and 1826; appointed postmaster of Homer by President Jackson on April 25, 1829, and served until August 7, 1839; was elected as a Democrat to the Twenty-seventh Congress (March 4, 1841–March 3, 1843); resumed the practice of medicine; also operated a flour mill; died in Homer, Cortland County, N. Y., November 6, 1870; interment in Glenwood Cemetery.

RIGNEY, Hugh McPheeters, a Representative from Illinois; born in Arthur, Moultrie County, Ill., July 31, 1873; attended the local schools and was graduated from the high school of his native city; apprenticed to the printer's trade and worked as a journeyman; editor and owner of the Arthur (Ill.) Graphic-Clarion 1900–1925; served as city treasurer 1910–1911; member of the school board 1910–1916; chairman of Moultrie County Democratic central committee 1930–1934 and reelected chairman in 1942; member of the State house of representatives 1935–1937; elected as a Democrat to the Seventy-fifth Congress (January 3, 1937–January 3, 1939); unsuccessful candidate for reelection in 1938 to the Seventy-sixth Congress; engaged in the real estate brokerage business 1939–1943; appointed to a position in the office of the secretary of state on September 15, 1943, and served until his death in Springfield, Ill., October 12, 1950; interment in Arthur Cemetery, Arthur, Ill.

RIKER, Samuel, a Representative from New York; born in Newtown, Long Island, N. Y., April 8, 1743; attended the common schools; member of the Newtown committee of correspondence in 1774; was supervisor of Suffolk County in 1783; lieutenant of Light Horse in the Revolution; member of the State assembly in 1784; elected to the Eighth Congress to fill the vacancy caused by the resignation of John Smith and served from November 5, 1804, to March 3, 1805; elected to the Tenth Congress (March 4, 1807–March 3, 1809); died in Newtown, Long Island, N. Y., May 19, 1823; interment in the Dutch Reformed Cemetery.

RILEY, John Jacob, a Representative from South Carolina; born on a farm near Orangeburg, S. C., February 1, 1895; attended the public schools in Orangeburg County and Orangeburg (S. C.) High School; was graduated from Wofford College, Spartanburg, S. C., in 1915; taught in the Orangeburg city schools 1915–1917, and at Clemson (S. C.) Agricultural and

Mechanical College in 1917 and 1918; during the First World War served in the United States Navy as a seaman, second class, and as a yeoman, third class, in 1918 and 1919; engaged in the real-estate and insurance business in Sumter, S. C., 1919–1945; secretary of a building and loan association 1923–1945; delegate to Democratic State conventions 1928–1944; elected as a Democrat to the Seventy-ninth and Eightieth Congresses (January 3, 1945–January 3, 1949); unsuccessful candidate for renomination in 1948; elected to the Eighty-second and to the four succeeding Congresses (January 3, 1951–January 3, 1961). *Reelected to the Eighty-seventh Congress.*

RINAKER, John Irving, a Representative from Illinois; born in Baltimore, Md., November 1, 1830; moved with his parents to Springfield, Ill., in December 1836; attended the Illinois College for one term and was graduated from McKendree College, Lebanon, Ill., in 1851; studied law; was admitted to the bar in 1854 and commenced practice in Carlinville, Ill.; during the Civil War raised and organized the One Hundred and Twenty-second Regiment, Illinois Volunteer Infantry, in 1862; commissioned colonel September 4, 1862; commanded a brigade in the Sixteenth Corps of the Army of the Tennessee, and was brevetted brigadier general for "gallant and meritorious services in the field" February 13, 1865; mustered out July 15, 1865; presidential elector on the Republican ticket of Grant and Wilson in 1872 and of Hayes and Wheeler in 1876; delegate to the Republican National Conventions in 1876 and 1884; chairman of the Board of Railroad and Warehouse Commissioners of Illinois 1885–1889; successfully contested as a Republican the election of Finis E. Downing to the Fifty-fourth Congress and served from June 5, 1896, to March 3, 1897; unsuccessful candidate for reelection in 1896 to the Fifty-fifth Congress; returned to Carlinville, Ill., and resumed the practice of law; died in Eustis, Lake County, Fla., January 15, 1915; interment in the City Cemetery, Carlinville, Ill.

RINGGOLD, Samuel, a Representative from Maryland; born in Chestertown, Md., January 15, 1770; received a limited schooling; moved to Washington County, Md., and settled at Fountain Rock, near Hagerstown; engaged in agricultural pursuits and became a large landowner; member of the State house of delegates in 1795; served in the State senate 1801–1806; judge of the levy court of Washington County 1806–1810 and 1822–1826; appointed a brigadier general in the Maryland Militia on July 7, 1810; elected as a Democrat to the Eleventh Congress to fill the vacancy caused by the resignation of Roger Nelson; reelected to the Twelfth and Thirteenth Congresses and served from October 15, 1810, to March 3, 1815; served in the War of 1812; elected to the Fifteenth and Sixteenth Congresses (March 4, 1817–March 3, 1821); resumed agricultural pursuits; died in Frederick, Frederick County, Md., October 18, 1829; interment in Fountain Rock Cemetery, near Hagerstown, Washington County, Md.

RIORDAN, Daniel Joseph, a Representative from New York; born in New York City July 7, 1870; attended the public schools until 1886, when he entered Manhattan College, from which he graduated in 1890; engaged in the real-estate business; elected as a Democrat to the Fifty-sixth Congress (March 4, 1899–March 3, 1901); elected a member of the State senate in 1902 and again in 1904; elected to the Fifty-ninth Congress to fill the vacancy caused by the resignation of Timothy D. Sullivan and on the same day was elected to the Sixtieth Congress; reelected to the Sixty-first and to the seven succeeding Congresses and served from November 6, 1906, until his death in Washington, D. C., April 28, 1923; interment in Calvary Cemetery, Long Island City, N. Y.

RIPLEY, Eleazar Wheelock (brother of James Wheelock Ripley), a Representative from Louisiana; born in Hanover, N. H., April 15, 1782; was graduated from Dartmouth College, Hanover, N. H., in 1800; studied law; was admitted to the bar and commenced practice in Waterville, Maine (a district of Massachusetts until 1820); was a member of the Massachusetts House of Representatives in 1807 and 1811 and served as speaker the last term; moved to Portland, Maine, in 1812; member of the Massachusetts Senate; served in the War of 1812, being commissioned lieutenant colonel of the Twenty-first Infantry March 12, 1812; colonel March 12, 1813; brigadier general April 15, 1814; brevetted major general on July 25, 1814, "for gallant conduct in the Battle of Niagara Falls, Canada"; by a resolution of Congress dated November 3, 1814, was presented a gold medal, with suitable emblems and devices in testimony of the high sense entertained by Congress of his gallantry and good conduct in the several conflicts of Chippewa, Niagara, and Erie; resigned from the Army February 1, 1820, and settled in Jackson, La., where he resumed the private practice of law; member of the State senate; elected as a Democrat to the Twenty-fourth and Twenty-fifth Congresses and served from March 4, 1835, until his death in West Feliciana Parish, La., on March 2, 1839; interment in a private cemetery at St. Francisville, La.

RIPLEY, James Wheelock (brother of Eleazar Wheelock Ripley), a Representative from Maine; born in Hanover, N. H., March 12, 1786; attended the common schools and Fryeburg (Maine) Academy; studied law; was admitted to the bar and commenced practice in Fryeburg, Maine (until 1820 a part of Massachusetts); served in the War of 1812; member of the Massachusetts House of Representatives 1814–1819; elected from Maine as a Democrat to the Nineteenth Congress to fill the vacancy caused by the resignation of Enoch Lincoln and on the same day was elected to the Twentieth Congress; reelected to the Twenty-first Congress and served from September 11, 1826, to March 12, 1830, when he resigned; resumed the practice of law; collector of customs for the district of Passamaquoddy, Maine, from December 16, 1830, until his death in Fryeburg, Oxford County, Maine, June 17, 1835; interment in the Village Cemetery.

RIPLEY, Thomas C., a Representative from New York; born in Schaghticoke, N. Y.; received a limited schooling; studied law; was admitted to the bar and practiced in Harts Falls, N. Y.; elected to the Twenty-ninth Congress to fill the vacancy caused by the death of Richard P. Herrick and served from December 7, 1846, to March 3, 1847; was not a candidate for renomination in 1846.

RISK, Charles Francis, a Representative from Rhode Island; born in Central Falls, Providence County, R. I., August 19, 1897; attended the public and high schools; worked in textile plants; during the First World War served in the United States Army as a private at Camp Meigs in 1918; was employed in the Treasury Department, Washington, D. C., 1919–1922; was graduated from the law department of Georgetown University, Washington, D. C., in 1922; was admitted to the bar in 1923 and commenced practice in Central Falls, R. I., the same year; served as probate judge of Central Falls 1929–1931, as coroner of Lincoln, R. I., in 1931 and 1932, and as judge of the eleventh district court of Rhode Island 1932–1935; served as commander of the American Legion, Department of Rhode Island, in 1933; delegate to the Republican State conventions in 1936, 1940, and 1942; elected as a Republican to the Seventy-fourth Congress to fill the vacancy caused by the resignation of Francis B. Condon and served from August 6, 1935, to January 3, 1937; unsuccessful

candidate for reelection in 1936 to the Seventy-fifth Congress; elected to the Seventy-sixth Congress (January 3, 1939–January 3, 1941); unsuccessful candidate for reelection in 1940 to the Seventy-seventh Congress; resumed the practice of law in Pawtucket, R. I.; died in Saylesville, in the township of Lincoln, R. I., December 26, 1943; interment in St. Francis Cemetery, Pawtucket, R. I.

RISLEY, Elijah, a Representative from New York; born in Connecticut on May 7, 1787; completed preparatory studies; moved to Fredonia, Chautauqua County, N. Y., in 1807; engaged in mercantile pursuits; sheriff of Chautauqua County 1825–1828; supervisor of town of Pomfret in 1835; engaged in the culture of garden seeds 1833–1853; elected as a Whig to the Thirty-first Congress (March 4, 1849–March 3, 1851); was not a candidate for renomination in 1850; major general in the State militia; died in Fredonia, Chautauqua County, N. Y., January 9, 1870; interment in the East Main Street Cemetery.

RITCHEY, Thomas, a Representative from Ohio; born in Bedford County, Pa., January 19, 1801; moved to Somerset, Ohio; attended the common schools; engaged in agricultural pursuits; treasurer of Perry County in 1835, 1837, and 1839; elected as a Democrat to the Thirtieth Congress (March 4, 1847–March 3, 1849); elected to the Thirty-third Congress (March 4, 1853–March 3, 1855); appointed Philip H. Sheridan as a cadet to the United States Military Academy, West Point, N. Y.; engaged in agricultural pursuits near Somerset, Perry County, Ohio, until his death on March 9, 1863; interment in the Zion Methodist Episcopal Cemetery, Madison Township, Perry County, Ohio.

RITCHIE, Byron Foster (son of James Monroe Ritchie), a Representative from Ohio; born in Grafton, Lorain County, Ohio, January 29, 1853; moved with his parents to Toledo, Ohio, in 1860; attended the public schools of that city and was graduated from the Toledo High School in 1870; studied law; was admitted to the bar in 1874 and commenced practice in Toledo; elected as a Democrat to the Fifty-third Congress (March 4, 1893–March 3, 1895); unsuccessful candidate for reelection in 1894 to the Fifty-fourth Congress; resumed the practice of law in Toledo, Ohio; elected judge of the court of common pleas of Lucas County, Ohio, in 1914; reelected in 1916 and again in 1922, and served until his death in Toledo, Ohio, August 22, 1928; interment in Woodlawn Cemetery.

RITCHIE, David, a Representative from Pennsylvania; born in Canonsburg, Washington County, Pa., August 19, 1812; was graduated from Jefferson College, Canonsburg, Pa., in 1829, and subsequently at Heidelberg, Germany; studied law; was admitted to the bar in 1835 and commenced practice in Pittsburgh, Pa.; elected as a Republican to the Thirty-third, Thirty-fourth, and Thirty-fifth Congresses (March 4, 1853–March 3, 1859); was appointed associate judge of the court of common pleas of Allegheny County in 1862 and served nine months; resumed the practice of his profession; died in Pittsburgh, Pa., January 24, 1867.

RITCHIE, James Monroe (father of Byron Foster Ritchie), a Representative from Ohio; born in Dunfermline, Scotland, July 28, 1829; immigrated to the United States in 1832 with his parents, who settled in St. Lawrence County, N. Y.; his early schooling was limited and he received instruction at home from his father and mother; studied law; was admitted to the bar in 1858 and commenced practice in Toledo, Ohio; delegate to the Republican National Convention at Chicago which nominated Garfield and Arthur in 1880; elected as a Republican to the Forty-seventh Congress (March 4, 1881–March 3, 1883); was not a candiate for renomination in 1882; again resumed the practice of his profession in Toledo, Ohio, and died there August 17, 1918; interment in Grafton Cemetery, Grafton, Lorain County, Ohio.

RITCHIE, John, a Representative from Maryland; born in Frederick, Frederick County, Md., August 12, 1831; completed preparatory studies at the Frederick Academy; commenced the study of medicine but abandoned it for law; attended the law department of Harvard University; was admitted to the bar and began practice in Frederick in 1854; captain of the Junior Defenders (militia) and was ordered by President Buchanan to the scene of John Brown's raid at Harpers Ferry; presidential elector on the Democratic ticket of Breckinridge and Lane in 1860; served as State's attorney for Frederick County 1867–1871; elected as a Democrat to the Forty-second Congress (March 4, 1871–March 3, 1873); unsuccessful candidate in 1872 for reelection to the Forty-third Congress; resumed the practice of law in Frederick; appointed by Governor Hamilton on March 16, 1881, chief judge of the sixth judicial circuit and associate justice of the court of appeals to fill the unexpired term of Judge Richard Bowie; elected in November 1881 to this office for a term of fifteen years and served until his death; died in Frederick, Md., October 27, 1887; interment in Mount Olivet Cemetery.

RITTER, Burwell Clark (uncle of Walter Evans), a Representative from Kentucky; born near Russellville, Barren County, Ky., January 6, 1810; received a limited schooling; member of the State house of representatives in 1842 and 1850; presidential elector on the Democratic ticket of McClellan and Pendleton in 1864; elected as a Conservative to the Thirty-ninth Congress (March 4, 1865–March 3, 1867); was not a candidate for renomination in 1866; engaged in agricultural pursuits; died in Hopkinsville, Christian County, Ky., October 1, 1880; interment in Hopewell (later known as Riverside) Cemetery, Hopkinsville, Ky.

RITTER, John, a Representative from Pennsylvania; born in Exeter, Pa., February 6, 1779; received a limited schooling; apprenticed as a printer; member of the State constitutional convention in 1836; elected as a Democrat to the Twenty-eighth and Twenty-ninth Congresses (March 4, 1843–March 3, 1847); was not a candidate for renomination in 1846; editor and publisher of the Adler, a German newspaper, at Reading; died in Reading, Berks County, Pa., November 24, 1851; interment in the Charles Evans Cemetery.

RIVERA, Luis Muñoz, a Resident Commissioner from Puerto Rico; born in Barranquitas, P. R., July 17, 1859; attended the common schools; engaged in commerce and general business; contributed poems to several newspapers; founded La Democracia, a daily newspaper, in Ponce, P. R., in 1889; was sent to Madrid in 1896 as a special representative to confer with the Liberal Party of Spain on establishing home rule in Puerto Rico; one of the founders of the Liberal Party in Puerto Rico in 1897; appointed secretary of state under the home-rule government and president of the cabinet in 1897; created and organized the insular police; resigned in 1898, when American sovereignty was declared, but his resignation not being accepted, he continued to serve until 1899; representative of his party to Washington, D. C., regarding the establishment of free-trade relations between the United States and Puerto Rico; organized the Federal Party in 1900 and on its dissolution in 1902 organized the Unionist Party; founded the Porto Rico Journal in 1900; published the Porto

Rico Herald in New York City in 1901; served in the Puerto Rico House of Delegates 1906–1910; presided over a special commission of the house of delegates which was sent to Washington, D. C., in 1909; elected as a Unionist a Resident Commissioner to the United States in 1910; reelected in 1912 and 1914 and served from March 4, 1911, until his death in San Juan, P. R., November 15, 1916; interment in San Antonio de Padua's Cemetery, Barranquitas, P. R.

RIVERS, Lucius Mendel, a Representative from South Carolina; born in Gumville, Berkeley County, S. C., September 28, 1905; attended the public schools, the College of Charleston, Charleston, S. C., and the University of South Carolina at Columbia; studied law; was admitted to the bar in 1932 and commenced practice in Charleston, S. C.; member of the State house of representatives 1933–1936; delegate to the Democratic National Convention at Philadelphia in 1936; elected as a Democrat to the Seventy-seventh and to the nine succeeding Congresses (January 3, 1941–January 3, 1961). *Reelected to the Eighty-seventh Congress.*

RIVERS, Ralph Julian, a Representative from Alaska; born in Seattle, King County, Wash., May 23, 1903; attended grammar school in Flat, Alaska, and Franklin High School, Seattle, Wash.; gold miner, Flat, Alaska, 1921–1923; graduated from the University of Washington at Seattle in 1929; was admitted to Washington State bar in 1930; practiced law in Seattle, Wash., in 1930 and 1931; was admitted to the Alaska bar in 1931 and practiced law in Fairbanks, Alaska, 1931–1933; United States district attorney, fourth judicial division, district of Alaska, from 1933 until his resignation in 1944; elected attorney general of Alaska in 1945 and served until 1949; chairman of Employment Security Commission of Alaska 1950–1952; mayor of Fairbanks 1952–1954; president, League of Alaskan Cities, in 1954; member of Alaska Territorial Senate in 1955; second vice president of Alaska constitutional convention at College, Alaska, in 1955 and 1956; United States Representative-elect under Alaska-Tennessee Plan, Washington, D. C., provisional basis, pending statehood, in 1957 and 1958; upon the admission of Alaska as a State into the Union was elected as a Democrat to the Eighty-sixth Congress (January 3, 1959–January 3, 1961). *Reelected to the Eighty-seventh Congress.*

RIVERS, Thomas, a Representative from Tennessee; born in Franklin County, Tenn., September 18, 1819; received an academic education and attended La Grange College, Alabama; studied law; was admitted to the bar in 1839 and commenced practice in Somerville, Tenn.; served for many years in the State militia, ranking as brigadier general; elected as the candidate of the American Party to the Thirty-fourth Congress (March 4, 1855–March 3, 1857); was not a candidate for renomination in 1856; continued the practice of law until his death on his plantation near Somerville, Tenn., March 18, 1863; interment in the Somerville Cemetery.

RIVES, Francis Everod, a Representative from Virginia; born in Prince George County, near Petersburg, Dinwiddie County, Va., January 14, 1792; completed preparatory studies; engaged in planting and in the building and management of railways in Virginia and North Carolina; member of the State house of delegates 1821–1831; served in the State senate 1831–1836, 1848–1851; elected as a Democrat to the Twenty-fifth and Twenty-sixth Congresses (March 4, 1837–March 3, 1841); declined to be a candidate for renomination; engaged in the development of internal improvements in Virginia; mayor of Petersburg, Va., from May 6, 1847, to May 5, 1848; died in Petersburg, Va., December 26, 1861; interment in Blandford Cemetery.

RIVES, William Cabell, a Representative and a Senator from Virginia; born at "Oak Ridge," Nelson County, Va., May 4, 1792; attended Hampden-Sidney College in Virginia and was graduated from William and Mary College, Williamsburg, Va., in 1809; studied law; was admitted to the bar about 1814 and commenced practice in Charlottesville, Albemarle County; delegate to the State constitutional convention in 1816; member of the State house of delegates 1817–1820, 1822, and 1823; moved to "Castle Hill," Albemarle County, in 1821; elected as a Democrat to the Eighteenth and to the three succeeding Congresses and served from March 4, 1823, until his resignation in 1829; Minister to France 1829–1832; elected to the United States Senate to fill the vacancy caused by the resignation of Littleton W. Tazewell and served from December 10, 1832, to February 22, 1834, when he resigned; again elected to the United States Senate to fill the vacancy caused by the resignation of John Tyler and served from March 4, 1836, to March 3, 1839; subsequently reelected as a Whig on January 18, 1841, for the term beginning March 4, 1839, and served until March 3, 1845; again Minister to France 1849–1853; member of the peace convention of 1861 held in Washington, D. C., in an effort to devise means to prevent the impending war; delegate from Virginia to the Confederate Provisional Congress in Montgomery, Ala., and Richmond, Va., in 1861; member of the house of representatives from Virginia in the Second Confederate Congress; died on his plantation, "Castle Hill," near Charlottesville, Albemarle County, Va., April 25, 1868; interment in the private burial ground on the family estate.

RIVES, Zeno John, a Representative from Illinois; born near Greenfield, Hancock County, Ind., February 22, 1874; moved with his parents to Litchfield, Montgomery County, Ill., in 1880; attended the public schools; studied law; was admitted to the bar in 1901 and commenced practice in Litchfield, Ill.; appointed city clerk in June 1903; elected as a Republican to the Fifty-ninth Congress (March 4, 1905–March 3, 1907); unsuccessful candidate for reelection in 1906 to the Sixtieth Congress; resumed the practice of law in Litchfield, Ill.; was postmaster of Litchfield 1912–1916; moved to Decatur, Macon County, Ill., in 1919, and engaged in the practice of law and also the real-estate business; died in Decatur, Ill., September 2, 1939; interment in Graceland Cemetery.

RIXEY, John Franklin, a Representative from Virginia; born in Culpeper County, Va., August 1, 1854; attended the common schools, Bethel Academy, and the University of Virginia at Charlottesville; studied law; was admitted to the bar in 1876 and commenced practice in Culpeper, Va.; Commonwealth attorney for Culpeper County, Va., 1879–1891; elected as a Democrat to the Fifty-fifth and to the four succeeding Congresses and served from March 4, 1897, until his death in Washington, D. C., February 8, 1907, before the close of the Fifty-ninth Congress; had been reelected to the Sixtieth Congress; interment in Fairview Cemetery, Culpeper, Va.

RIZLEY, Ross, a Representative from Oklahoma; born on a farm near Beaver, Okla., July 5, 1892; attended the public schools; taught in the rural schools of Beaver County, Okla., in 1909 and 1910; served as a deputy register of deeds of Beaver County, Okla., in 1911 and 1912; was graduated from the law department of the University of Kansas City, Kansas City, Mo., in 1915; was admitted to the bar the same year and commenced practice in Beaver, Okla.; elected county attorney of Beaver County in 1918 and served until 1920, when he resigned and moved to Guymon, Texas County, Okla., and resumed the practice of law; member of the Guymon Board of Education 1924–1932; city attorney of Guymon 1928–1938; member of the

State senate 1931–1934; unsuccessful candidate for election as Governor of Oklahoma in 1938; elected as a Republican to the Seventy-seventh and to the three succeeding Congresses (January 3, 1941–January 3, 1949); delegate to the Republican National Conventions in 1932, 1936, and 1948; was not a candidate for renomination in 1948 but was unsuccessful for election to the United States Senate; solicitor for the Post Office Department, Washington, D. C., from March to December 1953; Assistant Secretary of Agriculture from December 1953 until his resignation December 16, 1954; member of the Civil Aeronautics Board from February 25, 1955, until April 15, 1956, when he resigned; judge of the United States District Court for the western district of Oklahoma since 1956; is a resident of Guymon, Okla.

ROACH, Sidney Crain, a Representative from Missouri; born at Linn Creek, Camden County, Mo., on July 25, 1876; attended the public schools and the St. Louis Law School (now Washington University) in St. Louis; was admitted to the bar in 1897 and commenced practice at Linn Creek, Mo.; prosecuting attorney for Camden County 1898–1909; member of the board of directors of the National Bank of Linn Creek 1900–1924; member of the State house of representatives 1909–1913; delegate to the Republican National Convention at Chicago in 1912; elected as a Republican to the Sixty-seventh and Sixty-eighth Congresses (March 4, 1921–March 3, 1925); unsuccessful candidate for reelection in 1924 to the Sixty-ninth Congress; moved to St. Louis, Mo., December 27, 1924, and resumed the practice of law; died at Kansas City, Mo., June 29, 1934; interment in Roach Cemetery near Roach, Mo.

ROACH, William Nathaniel, a Senator from North Dakota; born in Washington, D. C., September 25, 1840; attended the public schools and Georgetown University, Washington, D. C.; clerk in the quartermaster's department during the Civil War; moved to Dakota Territory in 1879 and settled in Larimore; interested in mail contracts for several years; took up land in Dakota and engaged in agricultural pursuits; mayor of Larimore 1883–1887; member of the Territorial house of representatives in 1885; unsuccessful Democratic candidate for Governor at the first State election in 1889 and again in 1891; elected as a Democrat to the United States Senate and served from March 4, 1893, to March 3, 1899; was the caucus nominee of his party, which was in the minority, for reelection; discontinued active business pursuits and lived in retirement in Washington, D. C.; died in New York City, where he had gone for medical treatment, on September 7, 1902; interment in the Congressional Cemetery, Washington, D. C.

ROANE, John (father of John Jones Roane), a Representative from Virginia; born at "Uppowac," King William County, Va., February 9, 1766; completed preparatory studies; presidential elector on the Washington ticket; member of the State house of delegates 1788–1790 and in 1792; delegate to the State constitutional convention in 1788; elected as a Democrat to the Eleventh, Twelfth, and Thirteenth Congresses (March 4, 1809–March 3, 1815); engaged in agricultural pursuits; elected to the Twentieth and Twenty-first Congresses (March 4, 1827–March 3, 1831); elected to the Twenty-fourth Congress (March 4, 1835–March 3, 1837); died at his residence, "Uppowac," King William County, Va., November 15, 1838; interment in the old family burying ground, Rumford, Va.

ROANE, John Jones (son of John Roane), a Representative from Virginia; born in Essex County, Va., October 31, 1794; completed preparatory studies; attended Rumford Academy in King William County, Va., and Princeton College, New

Jersey, but did not graduate; engaged in agricultural pursuits; served in the War of 1812 as a private in the Fourth Regiment, Virginia Militia; member of the State house of delegates 1820–1823; elected as a Democrat to the Twenty-second Congress (March 4, 1831–March 3, 1833); clerk in the United States Patent Office 1836–1851; special agent in the Treasury Department 1855–1867; died in Washington, D. C., December 18, 1869; interment in Glenwood Cemetery.

ROANE, William Henry (grandson of Patrick Henry), a Representative and a Senator from Virginia; born in that State September 17, 1787; completed preparatory studies; member of the State house of delegates 1812–1815; elected as a Democrat to the Fourteenth Congress (March 4, 1815–March 3, 1817); was not a candidate for renomination; member of the executive council of Virginia; elected to the United States Senate to fill the vacancy caused by the resignation of Richard E. Parker and served from March 14, 1837, to March 3, 1841; unsuccessful candidate for reelection in 1841; engaged in agricultural pursuits; died in Tree Hill, near Richmond, Va., May 11, 1845; interment in the private cemetery of the Lyons family in Hanover County, Va.

ROARK, Charles Wickliffe, a Representative from Kentucky; born in Greenville, Muhlenberg County, Ky., January 22, 1887; attended the public schools and the Greenville Seminary; founder and president of the Greenville Milling Co.; served as president of the Kentucky Retail Lumbermen in 1908 and of the Tri-State Lumber Dealers' Association in 1909; elected mayor of Greenville and served from 1918 to 1922; chairman of the selective service board of Greenville during the First World War; elected as a Republican to the Seventy-first Congress and served from March 4, 1929, until his death, before the convening of Congress; died in Louisville, Ky., April 5, 1929; interment in the family lot in Evergreen Cemetery, Greenville, Ky.

ROBB, Edward, a Representative from Missouri; born in Brazeau, Perry County, Mo., March 19, 1857; attended the common schools, Brazeau (Mo.) Academy, Fruitland (Mo.) Normal Institute, and the University of Missouri at Columbia; was graduated from the law department of the University of Missouri in March 1879; was admitted to the bar in 1879 and commenced practice in Perryville; elected prosecuting attorney of Perry County in 1880 and reelected in 1882; member of the State house of representatives 1884–1886; assistant attorney general of the State 1889–1893; elected as a Democrat to the Fifty-fifth and to the three succeeding Congresses (March 4, 1897–March 3, 1905); unsuccessful candidate for reelection in 1904 to the Fifty-ninth Congress; delegate to the Democratic National Convention at Denver in 1908; resumed the practice of law until his death in Perryville, Mo., March 13, 1934; interment in Home Cemetery.

ROBBINS, Asher, a Senator from Rhode Island; born in Wethersfield, Conn., October 26, 1757; was graduated from Yale College in 1782; tutor in Rhode Island College (now Brown University) 1782–1790; studied law; was admitted to the bar in 1792 and began practice in Providence, R. I.; moved to Newport in 1795 appointed United States district attorney in 1812; member of the State assembly 1818–1825; elected as a Whig to the United States Senate in 1825 to fill the vacancy caused by the resignation of James De Wolf; reelected in 1827 and 1833 and served from October 31, 1825, to March 3, 1839; again a member of the State assembly in 1840 and 1841; postmaster of Newport, Newport County, R. I., from 1841 until his death in that city February 25, 1845; interment in Burial Ground Common.

ROBBINS, Edward Everett, a Representative from Pennsylvania; born at Robbins Station, Westmoreland County, Pa., September 27, 1860; attended the public schools, Indiana (Pa.) Normal School, and Eldersridge (Pa.) Academy; was graduated from Washington and Jefferson College, Washington, Pa., in 1881 and from the law department of Columbia College, New York City, in 1884; was admitted to the bar in 1884 and commenced practice in Greensburg, Pa.; also engaged in banking and coal-mining enterprises; member of the State senate 1888–1892; chairman of the Republican county committee in 1885; member of the Pennsylvania National Guard; served as major of Volunteers in the Spanish-American War in 1898; elected as a Republican to the Fifty-fifth Congress (March 4, 1897–March 3, 1899); was not a candidate for renomination in 1898; resumed the practice of his profession in Greensburg, Pa.; elected to the Sixty-fifth Congress and served from March 4, 1917, until his death; had been reelected to the Sixty-sixth Congress; died in Somerset, Somerset County, Pa., January 25, 1919; interment in St. Clair Cemetery, Greensburg, Pa.

ROBBINS, Gaston Ahi, a Representative from Alabama; born in Goldsboro, Wayne County, N. C., September 26, 1858; moved to Randolph County, N. C.; attended Trinity College at Durham and was graduated from the University of North Carolina at Chapel Hill in 1879; studied law; was admitted to the bar in 1880 and commenced practice in Selma, Ala.; presidential elector on the Democratic ticket of Cleveland and Hendricks in 1884; elected as a Democrat to the Fifty-third Congress (March 4, 1893–March 3, 1895); presented credentials as a Member-elect to the Fifty-fourth Congress and served from March 4, 1895, to March 13, 1896, when he was succeeded by William F. Aldrich, who contested his election; presented credentials to the Fifty-sixth Congress and served from March 4, 1899, to March 8, 1900, when he was again succeeded by William F. Aldrich, who contested his election; resumed the practice of law in New York City, where he died on February 22, 1902; interment in Oakwood Cemetery, Statesville, N. C.

ROBBINS, George Robbins, a Representative from New Jersey; born near Allentown, Monmouth County, N. J., September 24, 1808; received a good literary education; was graduated from the Jefferson Medical College at Philadelphia in 1837 and commenced the practice of medicine in Falsington, Bucks County, Pa.; moved to Hamilton Square, N. J., the same year and continued the practice of medicine; elected as a Whig to the Thirty-fourth and Thirty-fifth Congresses (March 4, 1855–March 3, 1859); was not a candidate for renomination; resumed the practice of his profession; died in Hamilton Square, N. J., February 22, 1875; interment in the Presbyterian Church Cemetery.

ROBBINS, John, a Representative from Pennsylvania; born in Bustleton (now a part of Philadelphia), near Lower Dublin, Pa., in 1808; attended the public schools; student at the Gunmere Academy in Burlington, N. J.; moved to Philadelphia in 1836 and engaged in the manufacture of steel; member of the board of commissioners of the district of Kensington and served as president several years; elected as a Democrat to the Thirty-first, Thirty-second, and Thirty-third Congresses (March 4, 1849–March 3, 1855); declined to be a candidate for renomination in 1854; unsuccessful candidate for office of mayor of Philadelphia in 1862; resumed the steel manufacturing business and held several municipal offices; elected to the Forty-fourth Congress (March 4, 1875–March 3, 1877); declined to be a candidate for renomination in 1876; member of the board of education and served as president for many years; president and director of the Kensington National Bank; died in Philadelphia, Pa., April 27, 1880; interment in Laurel Hill Cemetery.

ROBBINS, William McKendree, a Representative from North Carolina; born in the old homestead near Trinity, Randolph County, N. C., October 26, 1828; pursued classical studies; attended Old Trinity College and was graduated from Randolph-Macon College, Virginia, about 1850; studied law; was admitted to the bar in 1854 and commenced practice the same year in Eufaula, Ala.; served four years as major in the Fourth Alabama Regiment of the Confederate Army during the Civil War; member of the State senate in 1868 and 1872; elected as a Democrat to the Forty-third, Forty-fourth, and Forty-fifth Congresses (March 4, 1873–March 3, 1879); appointed by President Cleveland as the southern commissioner on the Gettysburg Battle Field Commission in 1894, which position he held until his death in Salisbury, Rowan County, N. C., on May 5, 1905; interment in Oakwood Cemetery, Statesville, N. C.

ROBERDEAU, Daniel, a Delegate from Pennsylvania; born on the island of St. Christopher, West Indies, in 1727; immigrated to the United States and settled in Philadelphia, Pa., in boyhood; completed preparatory studies; engaged in the lumber business; member of the State assembly 1756–1760; manager of the Pennsylvania Hospital 1756–1758 and 1766–1776; member of the council of safety; first brigadier general of Pennsylvania troops in 1776; Member of the Continental Congress from 1777 to 1779; moved to Alexandria, Va., in 1785; died in Winchester, Frederick County, Va., on January 5, 1795; interment in Mount Hebron Cemetery.

ROBERTS, Anthony Ellmaker (grandfather of Robert Grey Bushong), a Representative from Pennsylvania; born near Barneston Station, Chester County, Pa., on October 29, 1803; received a limited schooling; engaged in mercantile pursuits in New Holland, Lancaster County, Pa., 1816–1839; moved to Lancaster, Pa., in 1839; sheriff of Lancaster County 1839–1842; unsuccessful candidate for election in 1842 to the Twenty-eighth Congress; was appointed United States marshal for the eastern district of Pennsylvania on May 16, 1850, and served until March 29, 1853; elected as a Whig to the Thirty-fourth and Thirty-fifth Congresses (March 4, 1855–March 3, 1859); was not a candidate for renomination in 1858; was active in organization of the Republican Party in Pennsylvania; engaged in operating his real-estate holdings in Lancaster and was executor for various estates; died in Lancaster, Pa., on January 25, 1885; interment in the Lancaster Cemetery.

ROBERTS, Brigham Henry, a Representative from Utah; born in Warrington, Lancashire, England, March 13, 1857; immigrated to the United States in 1866 with his parents, who settled in Bountiful, Davis County, Utah; attended the district schools; worked as a farm hand during boyhood and later, for some years, in the mining camps of the Territory of Utah; at the age of seventeen became an apprentice in the blacksmith trade at Centerville; was graduated from Deseret University, Salt Lake City, in 1878; taught school for several years and later engaged in journalism; associate and, for a time, editor in chief of the Salt Lake Herald; member of the State constitutional convention which framed the organic law of Utah in 1894; unsuccessful Democratic candidate for election in 1895 to the Fifty-fifth Congress; presented credentials as a Democratic Member-elect to the Fifty-sixth Congress and served from March 4, 1899, to January 25, 1900, when the seat was declared vacant; author of numerous historical, biographical, and doctrinal works; served on the State board of equalization tax department in 1916 and subsequently ordained as a minister of the gospel; during the First World War served as chaplain of the One Hundred and Forty-fifth Regiment, Field Artillery; served six months in France; honorably discharged at Logan, Utah,

January 28, 1919; resumed his ministerial duties and served as president of the Eastern States Mission of the Church of Jesus Christ of Latter Day Saints in Brooklyn, N. Y.; died in Salt Lake City, Utah, September 27, 1933; interment in Centerville Ward Cemetery, Centerville, Davis County, Utah.

ROBERTS, Charles Boyle, a Representative from Maryland; born in Uniontown, Carroll County, Md., on April 19, 1842; was graduated from Calvert College, New Windsor, Md., in 1861; studied law; was admitted to the bar in 1864 and commenced practice in Westminster, Carroll County, Md.; presidential elector on the Democratic ticket of Seymour and Blair in 1868; elected as a Democrat to the Forty-fourth and Forty-fifth Congresses (March 4, 1875–March 3, 1879); elected attorney general of Maryland in 1883, serving one term; elected associate judge of the fifth judicial district in 1891; appointed chief judge of the district to fill the vacancy caused by the death of Judge Miller and in 1893 was elected for the full term of fifteen years; died in Westminster, Md., September 10, 1899; interment in the Catholic Cemetery.

ROBERTS, Edwin Ewing, a Representative from Nevada; born in Pleasant Grove, Sutter County, Calif., December 12, 1870; attended the public schools, and was graduated from the State normal school at San Jose, Calif., in 1891; taught school at Hollister, Calif., 1891–1897, and at Empire, Nev., 1897–1899; studied law; was admitted to the bar in 1899 and commenced practice in Carson City, Nev.; also engaged in the newspaper publishing business; district attorney of Ormsby County 1900–1910; elected as a Republican to the Sixty-second and to the three succeeding Congresses (March 4, 1911–March 3, 1919); did not seek renomination in 1918, having become a candidate for Senator; unsuccessful candidate for the United States Senate in 1918, delegate to the Republican National Convention at Chicago in 1912 and at Cleveland in 1924; resumed the practice of law in Reno, Nev., in 1920; elected mayor of Reno in 1923; reelected in 1927 and again in 1931 and served until his death; unsuccessful candidate for nomination as United States Senator in 1926 and for Governor in 1930; died in Reno, Nev., December 11, 1933; interment in the Odd Fellows Cemetery.

ROBERTS, Ellis Henry, a Representative from New York; born in Utica, Oneida County, N. Y., September 30, 1827; attended the common schools and the Whitestown (N. Y.) Seminary; was graduated from Yale College in 1850; principal of Utica Free Academy in 1850 and 1851; editor and proprietor of the Utica Morning Herald 1851–1889; delegate to the Republican National Conventions in 1864, 1868, and 1876; member of the State assembly in 1866; elected as a Republican to the Forty-second and Forty-third Congresses (March 4, 1871–March 3, 1875); unsuccessful candidate for reelection in 1874 to the Forty-fourth Congress; resumed his former newspaper activities in Utica, N. Y.; Assistant Treasurer of the United States 1889–1893; president of the Franklin National Bank of New York City 1893–1897; appointed Treasurer of the United States on July 1, 1897, and served until June 30, 1905, when he resigned; again engaged in banking; died in Utica, N. Y., January 8, 1918; interment in Forest Hill Cemetery.

ROBERTS, Ernest William, a Representative from Massachusetts; born in East Madison, Maine, November 22, 1858; attended the public schools in Chelsea, Mass.; was graduated from Highland Military Academy, Worcester, Mass., in 1877, and from the law school of Boston University; was admitted to the bar in 1881 and commenced practice in Boston; member of the city council of Chelsea in 1887 and 1888; member of the State house of representatives in 1894 and 1896;

served in the State senate in 1897 and 1898; elected as a Republican to the Fifty-sixth and to the eight succeeding Congresses (March 4, 1899–March 3, 1917); unsuccessful candidate for renomination in 1916; after retiring from public life practiced law in Washington, D. C., until his death on February 27, 1924; interment in Woodlawn Cemetery, Everett, Middlesex County, Mass.

ROBERTS, Jonathan, a Representative and a Senator from Pennsylvania; born near Norristown, Pa., August 16, 1771; received a limited schooling under private tutors; member of the State house of representatives in 1799 and 1800; served in the State senate in 1811 and 1812; elected as a Republican to the Twelfth and Thirteenth Congresses and served from March 4, 1811, to February 24, 1814, when he resigned, having been elected Senator; elected to the United States Senate to fill the vacancy caused by the resignation of Michael Leib; reelected in 1815 and served from February 24, 1814, to March 3, 1821; appointed collector of customs at the port of Philadelphia by President Tyler on April 14, 1841; removed by President Tyler; died on his farm, "Robertsville," King of Prussia, Montgomery County, Pa., on July 24, 1854; interment in the Roberts family cemetery near Norristown, Pa.

ROBERTS, Kenneth Allison, a Representative from Alabama; born in Piedmont, Calhoun County, Ala., November 1, 1912; attended the public schools and Howard College, Birmingham, Ala.; was graduated from the University of Alabama Law School in 1935; was admitted to the bar in 1936 and commenced the practice of law in Anniston, Ala.; abstractor, Department of Agriculture, Talladega, Ala., 1935–1937; practiced law in Talladega 1937–1942; elected to the State senate in 1942, but resigned the same year; during World War II was commissioned an ensign in the United States Navy in 1942 and served until discharged as a lieutenant in 1945 with service in both Atlantic and Pacific Theaters; president, Piedmont Development Co., 1945–1950; member of Alabama State Board of Veterans Affairs and city attorney of Piedmont, Ala., 1948–1950; elected as a Democrat to the Eighty-second and to the four succeeding Congresses (January 3, 1951–January 3, 1961). *Reelected to the Eighty-seventh Congress.*

ROBERTS, Robert Whyte, a Representative from Mississippi; born in Kent County, Del., November 28, 1784; received a liberal education; studied law; was admitted to the bar; shortly after reaching his majority moved to Tennessee, where he was elected a circuit judge; moved to Limestone County, Ala. in 1822, and to Scott County, Miss., in 1826, and settled near Hillsboro; engaged in agricultural pursuits; commenced the practice of law in Hillsboro; circuit judge of Scott County 1830–1838; member of the State house of representatives 1838–1844 and served as speaker in 1842 and 1843; elected as a Democrat to the Twenty-eighth and Twenty-ninth Congresses (March 4, 1843–March 3, 1847); resumed the practice of law; also engaged in planting; died on his plantation, "Long Avenue," near Hillsboro, Miss., January 4, 1865; interment in a private cemetery on the Roberts plantation.

ROBERTS, William Randall, a Representative from New York; born in County Cork, Ireland, February 6, 1830; immigrated to the United States in July 1849; received a limited schooling; merchant in New York City until 1869 when he retired; president of the Fenian Brotherhood in 1865 and aided in the foray into Canada the following year, for which he was arrested by the Government; elected as a Democrat to the Forty-second and Forty-third Congresses (March 4, 1871–March 3, 1875); member of the board of aldermen of New York City in 1877; unsuccessful candidate for sheriff in 1879; appointed

as Envoy Extraordinary and Minister Plenipotentiary to Chile by President Cleveland on April 2, 1885, and served until August 19, 1889; returned to the United States; died in New York City on August 9, 1897; interment in Calvary Cemetery, Long Island City, N. Y.

ROBERTSON, Alice Mary, a Representative from Oklahoma; born at Tullahassee Mission, Creek Nation, Indian Territory (now Tullahassee, Okla.), January 2, 1854; self-taught in early life under the supervision of missionary parents; attended Elmira College, Elmira, N. Y.; clerk in the Indian Office, Washington, D. C., 1873–1879; returned to Indian Territory and taught in the school at Tullahassee and later in the Carlisle Indian School, Carlisle, Pa., 1880–1882; again returned to Indian Territory and established Nuyaka Mission; engaged in teaching at Okmulgee, Okla., and had charge of a boarding school for Indian girls, which developed into Henry Kendall College (now the University of Tulsa); Government supervisor of Creek Indian schools 1900–1905; postmaster of Muskogee, Okla., 1905–1913; elected as a Republican to the Sixty-seventh Congress (March 4, 1921–March 3, 1923); was an unsuccessful candidate for reelection in 1922 to the Sixty-eighth Congress; appointed by President Harding a welfare worker at Veterans' Hospital No. 90 at Muskogee in May 1923; engaged in Indian historical work under special appointment of the Oklahoma State Historical Society; died in Muskogee, Okla., on July 1, 1931; interment in Greenhill Cemetery.

ROBERTSON, A. Willis, a Representative and a Senator from Virginia; born in Martinsburg, Berkeley County, W. Va., May 27, 1887; moved to Lynchburg, Va., with his parents in 1891; attended the public schools of Lynchburg and Rocky Mount, Va.; was graduated from the University of Richmond, Richmond, Va., in 1907, and from the law department of the same university in 1908; was admitted to the bar in 1908 and commenced practice in Buena Vista, Rockbridge County, Va.; moved to Lexington, Rockbridge County, Va., in 1919 and continued the practice of law; member of the State senate 1916–1922; during the First World War served in the United States Army with the Three Hundred and Eighteenth Infantry, Eightieth Division, as assistant camp adjutant at Camp Lee, Va., and in the Adjutant General's Office, Washington, D. C., with the rank of first lieutenant, captain, and major, from August 1917 to June 1919; served as Commonwealth's attorney for Rockbridge County 1922–1928; chairman of the State commission of game and inland fisheries 1926–1932; elected as a Democrat to the Seventy-third Congress and to the six succeeding Congresses and served from March 4, 1933, until November 5, 1946, when he resigned; was nominated to the Eightieth Congress in 1946 but withdrew, having received the nomination for United States Senator; elected in 1946 as a Democrat to the United States Senate to fill the vacancy in the term ending January 3, 1949, caused by the death of Carter Glass, and again elected in 1948 and 1954, and served from November 6, 1946, to January 3, 1961. *Reelected in 1960 for the term ending January 3, 1967.*

ROBERTSON, Charles Raymond, a Representative from North Dakota; born on a farm near Madison, Wis., on September 5, 1889; assisted his father on a grain and stock farm in Columbia County, Wis., while attending public schools at Arlington and Poynette, Wis.; was graduated from Parker College, Winnebago, Minn.; held executive positions in wholesale and retail department stores in Minneapolis, Winnebago, and Fergus Falls, Minn., and Aberdeen, S. Dak.; copartner of a shoe store in Aberdeen, S. Dak., and a department store in Redfield, S. Dak., and Mandan, N. Dak.; operated a women's wear store in Valley City, Jamestown, Wahpeton, and Bismarck, N. Dak.; delegate to the Republican National Convention at Philadelphia in 1940; member of the Republican State executive committee; elected as a Republican to the Seventy-seventh Congress (January 3, 1941–January 3, 1943); unsuccessful candidate for renomination in 1942; engaged in the retail business in Bismarck, N. Dak.; again elected to the Seventy-ninth and Eightieth Congresses (January 3, 1945–January 3, 1949); unsuccessful candidate for renomination in 1948; resumed the merchandising business in Bismarck, N. Dak., and paint manufacturing in Washington, D. C.; in 1949 was named an advisory member of the Hoover Commission on the reorganization of the Government and was serving as North Dakota chairman for the Hoover Report at the time of his death; died in Bismarck, N. Dak., February 18, 1951; interment in Lakewood Cemetery, Minneapolis, Minn.

ROBERTSON, Edward Vivian, a Senator from Wyoming; born in Cardiff, Wales, May 27, 1881; attended the grammar and high schools in Wales; served in the Third Battalion of the Welsh Regiment during the Boer War 1899–1902; engaged in mechanical and electric power engineering 1902–1912; immigrated to the United States in 1912 and settled in Park County, Wyo.; engaged in the raising of livestock and the mercantile business at Cody, Wyo., 1912–1942; vice chairman of Wyoming Republican State Central Committee in 1934 and 1935; Republican National committeeman from Wyoming 1935–1937; life trustee of Cody General Hospital; elected as a Republican to the United States Senate in 1942 for the term commencing January 3, 1943, and ending January 3, 1949; unsuccessful candidate for reelection in 1948; retired from political and public life; is a resident of Cody, Wyo.

ROBERTSON, Edward White (father of Samuel Matthews Robertson), a Representative from Louisiana; born near Nashville, Davidson County, Tenn., on June 13, 1823; moved with his parents to Iberville Parish, La., in 1825; attended the country schools and the preparatory department of Centenary College, Jackson, La.; attended Augusta College, Kentucky, in 1842; entered Nashville (Tenn.) University and commenced the study of law in 1845; served in the War with Mexico in 1846 as orderly sergeant in the Second Regiment, Louisiana Volunteers, a six months' regiment; member of the State house of representatives 1847–1849; was graduated from the law department of the University of Louisiana in 1850; was admitted to the bar the same year and practiced in Iberville and East Baton Rouge Parishes; again elected to the State house of representatives in 1853; State auditor of public accounts 1857–1862; during the Civil War entered the Confederate service in March 1862 as captain of a company which he had raised for the Twenty-seventh Regiment, Louisiana Infantry; after the war resumed the practice of law in Baton Rouge; elected as a Democrat to the Forty-fifth, Forty-sixth, and Forty-seventh Congresses (March 4, 1877–March 3, 1883); unsuccessful candidate for renomination in 1882 to the Forty-eighth Congress; elected to the Fiftieth Congress and served from March 4, 1887, until his death in Baton Rouge, East Baton Rouge Parish, La., on August 2, 1887, before the Congress assembled; interment in Magnolia Cemetery.

ROBERTSON, George, a Representative from Kentucky; born near Harrodsburg, Mercer County, Ky., November 18, 1790; pursued preparatory studies, and later attended Transylvania University, Lexington, Ky., until 1806; studied law; was admitted to the bar in 1809 and commenced practice in Lancaster, Ky.; elected to the Fifteenth, Sixteenth, and Seventeenth Congresses and served from March 4, 1817, until his resignation in 1821, before the convening of the Seventeenth Congress; member of the State house of representatives 1822–1827, serving four years as speaker; declined the appointment as Governor of Arkansas Territory tendered by President Monroe and the diplomatic posts of United States Minister to Colombia in 1824 and to Peru in 1828; secretary of state of Kentucky in 1828; appointed associate justice of the court of appeals of Kentucky in 1829 and served as chief justice from 1829 to 1834, when he resigned; resumed the practice of law in Lexington, Ky.; professor of law in Transylvania University 1834–1857; elected as a Whig a member of the State house of representatives in 1848, 1851, and 1852, and served as speaker in the two last-named years; justice of the court of appeals for the second district of Kentucky 1864–1871 and acting chief justice part of the time; died in Lexington, Ky., May 16, 1874; interment in Lexington Cemetery.

ROBERTSON, John (brother of Thomas Bolling Robertson), a Representative from Virginia; born at "Bellefield," near Petersburg, Dinwiddie County, Va., April 13, 1787; completed preparatory studies and was graduated from William and Mary College, Williamsburg, Va.; studied law; was admitted to the bar and practiced in Richmond, Va.; attorney general of Virginia; elected as a Whig to the Twenty-third Congress to fill the vacancy caused by the resignation of Andrew Stevenson; reelected to the Twenty-fourth and Twenty-fifth Congresses and served from December 8, 1834, to March 3, 1839; judge of the circuit court of chancery for Henrico County, Va., for several years; delegate to the peace convention held at Washington, D. C., in 1861 in an effort to devise means to prevent the impending war; died at "Mount Athos," near Lynchburg, Va., July 5, 1873; interment in a private cemetery at "Mount Athos."

ROBERTSON, Samuel Matthews (son of Edward White Robertson), a Representative from Louisiana; born in Plaquemine, Iberville Parish, La., January 1, 1852; attended Magruder's Collegiate Institute, Baton Rouge, La., and was graduated from the Louisiana State University in 1874; studied law; was admitted to the bar in 1874 and commenced practice in Baton Rouge, La.; elected a member of the State house of representatives in 1879; member of the faculty of the Louisiana State University and Agriculture and Mechanical College in 1880; filled the chair of natural history in that institution and the position of commandant of cadets; elected as a Democrat to the Fiftieth Congress to fill the vacancy caused by the death of his father, Edward White Robertson; reelected to the Fifty-first and to the eight succeeding Congresses and served from December 5, 1887, to March 3, 1907; unsuccessful candidate for renomination in 1906; resumed the practice of law in Baton Rouge; superintendent of the Louisiana School for the Deaf and Dumb 1908–1911; died in Baton Rouge, La., December 24, 1911; interment in Magnolia Cemetery.

ROBERTSON, Thomas Austin, a Representative from Kentucky; born in Hodgenville, Larue County, Ky., September 9, 1848; pursued preparatory studies; was graduated from Cecilian College and afterwards from the law department of the University of Louisville; was admitted to the bar in 1871 and commenced practice at Hodgenville, Ky.; county attorney of Larue County 1874–1877; member of the State house of representatives in 1877 and 1878; Commonwealth attorney of the eighteenth judicial district 1878–1883; elected as a Democrat to the Forty-eighth and Forty-ninth Congresses (March 4, 1883–March 3, 1887); unsuccessful candidate for renomination in 1886; resumed the practice of law at Elizabethtown, Hardin County, Ky., and died there July 18, 1892; interment in Red Hill Cemetery, Hodgenville, Ky.

ROBERTSON, Thomas Bolling (brother of John Robertson), a Representative from Louisiana; born at "Bellefield," near Petersburg, Dinwiddie County, Va., February 27, 1779; was graduated from William and Mary College, Williamsburg, Va.; studied law; was admitted to the bar in 1806 and commenced practice in Petersburg, Va.; moved to the Territory of Orleans in 1807; appointed by President Jefferson secretary of the Territory of Louisiana and served from 1807 to 1811; upon the admission of the Territory into the Union as the State of Louisiana, was elected as a Democrat to the Twelfth and to the three succeeding Congresses and served from April 30, 1812, to April 20, 1818, when he resigned; Governor of Louisiana from December 18, 1820, until his resignation on November 15, 1822; attorney general of Louisiana in 1822; judge of the United States Court for the District of Louisiana 1825–1827; returned to Petersburg, Va.; died at White Sulphur Springs, Va. (now West Virginia), October 5, 1828; interment in Copeland Hill Cemetery.

ROBERTSON, Thomas James, a Senator from South Carolina; born near Winnsboro, Fairfield County, S. C., August 3, 1823; completed preparatory studies and was graduated from South Carolina College (now the University of South Carolina) at Columbia in 1843; engaged in planting; member of the State constitutional convention in 1865; upon the readmission of the State of South Carolina to representation was elected as a Republican to the United States Senate; reelected in 1871 and served from July 15, 1868, to March 3, 1877; was not a candidate for reelection; retired from public life and active business on account of ill health; died in Columbia, S. C., October 13, 1897; interment in Elmwood Cemetery.

ROBERTSON, William Henry, a Representative from New York; born in Bedford, N. Y., October 10, 1823; attended the common schools and Bedford Union Academy, at Bedford; studied law; was admitted to the bar in 1847 and commenced practice at White Plains, N. Y.; member of the State assembly in 1849 and 1850; served in the State senate in 1854 and 1855; judge of Westchester County, N. Y., 1855–1867; presidential elector on the Republican ticket of Lincoln and Hamlin in 1860; draft commissioner of Westchester County during the Civil War; inspector of the Seventh Brigade New York State Militia 1860–1866; elected as a Republican to the Fortieth Congress (March 4, 1867–March 3, 1869); was not a candidate for renomination; again a member of the State senate 1872–1881 and president pro tempore 1874–1881; collector of the port of New York 1881–1885; again a member of the State senate in 1888 and 1889; died in Katonah, N. Y., December 7, 1898; interment in Union Cemetery, Bedford, N. Y.

ROBESON, Edward John, Jr., a Representative from Virginia; born in Waynesville, Haywood County, N. C., August 9, 1890; moved from Wythe County, Va., with his parents to Cartersville, Ga., in 1891; attended the public schools in Quitman, Marietta, and Sparta, Ga.; graduated from the University of Georgia at Athens in 1910; civil engineer, L. & N. Railroad, Sibley Land Co., Bay Minette, Ala., and Newport Mining Co., Ironwood, Mich., 1910–1915; employed with the Newport News (Va.) Shipbuilding & Dry Dock Co. from 1915 until his retirement April 30, 1950, as vice president and personnel manager; former director and vice president of Citizens Marine Jefferson Bank, Newport News, Va.; Chairman, board of managers, Riverside Hospital, Newport News, Va.; elected as a Democrat to the Eighty-first Congress to fill the vacancy caused by the death of Schuyler Otis Bland; reelected to the Eighty-second and to the three succeeding Congresses and served from May 2, 1950, to January 3, 1959; unsuccessful candidate for renomination in 1958; is a resident of Newport News, Va.

ROBESON, George Maxwell (nephew of George Clifford Maxwell), a Representative from New Jersey; born at Oxford Furnace, near Belvidere, Warren County, N. J., March 16, 1829; pursued an academic course and was graduated from Princeton College in 1847; studied law; was admitted to the bar in 1850 and practiced in Newark and subsequently in Camden; appointed prosecuting attorney for Camden County in 1858; was active in organizing the State troops for service in the Civil War and was commissioned brigadier general by Governor Parker; elected attorney general of New Jersey in 1867 and served until his resignation June 22, 1869; appointed Secretary of the Navy in the Cabinet of President Grant and served from June 25, 1869, to March 12, 1877; resumed the practice of law in Camden, N. J.; elected as a Republican to the Forty-sixth and Forty-seventh Congresses (March 4, 1879–March 3, 1883); unsuccessful candidate for reelection in 1882 to the Forty-eighth Congress; resumed the practice of law in Trenton, N. J., where he died September 27, 1897; interment in Belvidere Cemetery, Belvidere, N. J.

ROBIE, Reuben, a Representative from New York; born in Corinth, Orange County, Vt., July 15, 1799; attended the common schools; at the age of twenty moved to Bath, Steuben County, N. Y.; engaged in mercantile pursuits in 1822; town clerk 1825–1830; supervisor in 1831 and 1832; appointed postmaster in 1837, holding the office for four years; treasurer of Steuben County 1844–1847; elected as a Democrat to the Thirty-second Congress (March 4, 1851–March 3, 1853); was not a candidate for renomination in 1852; resumed mercantile pursuits in Bath, Steuben County, N. Y., where he died January 21, 1872; interment in Grove Cemetery.

ROBINSON, Arthur Raymond, a Senator from Indiana born in Pickerington, Fairfield County, Ohio, on March 12, '1881; attended the common schools; was graduated from the Ohio Northern University at Ada in 1901, the Indiana Law School at Indianapolis in 1910, and the University of Chicago, Chicago, Ill., in 1913; was admitted to the bar in 1910 and commenced practice in Indianapolis, Ind.; served in the State senate 1914–1918 and was the Republican floor leader during the entire period; during the First World War entered officers' training camp, Fort Benjamin Harrison, Ind., May 10, 1917; was commissioned first lieutenant of Infantry and assigned to the Three Hundred and Thirty-fourth Infantry Regiment at Camp Zachary Taylor in August 1917; promoted to the rank of captain of Infantry; sailed for France on September 1, 1918; was transferred to the Thirty-ninth Infantry in France; promoted to the rank of major of Infantry while serving in the Army of Occupation; was honorably discharged as major of Infantry at Camp Sherman, Ohio, on August 27, 1919; resumed the practice of law; appointed judge of Marion County Superior Court in May 1921, to fill the vacancy caused by the death of Judge Vincent Clifford and served until November 1922; resumed the practice of law in Indianapolis, Ind., in 1922; delegate to the Republican National Conventions in 1924 and 1932; appointed as a Republican to the United States Senate and subsequently elected on November 2, 1926, to fill the vacancy caused by the death of Samuel M. Ralston; reelected in 1928, and served from October 20, 1925, to January 3, 1935; was an unsuccessful candidate for reelection in 1934; practiced law in Indianapolis, Ind., until his death there March 17, 1961; interment in Washington Park Cemetery East.

ROBINSON, Christopher, a Representative from Rhode Island; born in Providence, R. I., on May 15, 1806; was graduated from Brown University, Providence, R. I., in 1825; studied law; was admitted to the bar in 1833 and commenced practice in Woonsocket, R. I.; attorney general of Rhode Island in 1854; elected as the candidate of the American Party to the Thirty-sixth Congress (March 4, 1859–March 3, 1861); unsuccessful candidate for reelection; Minister to Peru 1861–1866; delegate from Rhode Island to the Loyalist Convention held in Philadelphia in 1866; died in Woonsocket, R. I., October 3, 1889; interment in Oak Hill Cemetery.

ROBINSON, Edward, a Representative from Maine; born in Cushing, Maine, November 25, 1796; self-educated while engaged in seafaring; engaged in mercantile pursuits at Thomaston, Maine, in 1837; member of the State senate in 1836 and 1837; elected as a Whig to the Twenty-fifth Congress to fill the vacancy caused by the death of Jonathan Cilley and served from April 28, 1838, to March 3, 1839; presidential elector on the Whig ticket of Harrison and Tyler in 1840; engaged in mercantile pursuits, banking, and shipbuilding until his death in Thomaston, Knox County, Maine, February 19, 1857; interment in Thomaston Cemetery.

ROBINSON, George Dexter, a Representative from Massachusetts; born in Lexington, Mass., January 20, 1834; attended Lexington Academy and Hopkins Classical School, Cambridge, Mass., and was graduated from Harvard University in 1856; principal teacher at the Chicopee High School 1856–1865; studied law; was admitted to the bar in Cambridge, Mass., in 1866 and commenced practice in Chicopee, Hampden County, Mass.; member of the State house of representatives in 1874; served in the State senate in 1876; elected as a Republican to the Forty-fifth and to the three succeeding Congresses and served from March 4, 1877, to January 7, 1884, when he resigned, having been elected Governor; Governor of Massachusetts 1884–1887; resumed the practice of his profession in Springfield, Mass.; died in Chicopee, Mass., February 22, 1896; interment in Fairview Cemetery.

ROBINSON, James Carroll, a Representative from Illinois; born near Paris, Edgar County, Ill., August 19, 1823; moved to Clark County, Ill., with his parents in 1825; received a limited schooling; engaged in agricultural pursuits; served as a corporal during the Mexican War; resumed agricultural pursuits; studied law; was admitted to the bar in 1850 and commenced practice in Marshall, Clark County, Ill.; elected as a Democrat to the Thirty-sixth, Thirty-seventh, and Thirty-eighth Congresses (March 4, 1859–March 3, 1865); did not seek renomination in 1864, having become a gubernatorial candidate; unsuccessful candidate for Governor of Illinois in 1864; resumed the practice of law in Marshall; moved to Sangamon County, Ill., in 1869 and continued the practice of law in Springfield; elected to the Forty-second and Forty-third Congresses (March 4, 1871–March 3, 1875); declined to be a candidate for renomination in 1874 to the Forty-fourth Congress; resumed the practice of law; appointed a member of the Illinois Board of Livestock Commissioners in 1886; died in Springfield, Ill., November 3, 1886; interment in Oak Ridge Cemetery.

ROBINSON, James McClellan, a Representative from Indiana; born on a farm near Fort Wayne, Allen County, Ind., May 31, 1861; attended the public schools; studied law; was admitted to the bar in 1882 and commenced practice in Fort Wayne, Ind.; prosecuting attorney for the thirty-eighth judicial circuit of Indiana 1886–1890; resumed the practice of law; elected as a Democrat to the Fifty-fifth and to the three succeeding Congresses (March 4, 1897–March 3, 1905); unsuccessful candidate for reelection in 1904 to the Fifty-ninth Congress; continued the practice of law in Fort Wayne, Ind., until 1908; retired from political life and the practice of his profession; moved to Los Angeles, Calif., in 1911; died in Los Angeles, Calif., January 16, 1942; interment in Lindenwood Cemetery, Fort Wayne, Ind.

ROBINSON, James Sidney, a Representative from Ohio; born near Mansfield, Richland County, Ohio, October 14, 1827; attended the common schools; acquired the art of printing; moved to Kenton, Ohio, December 31, 1845; edited and published the Kenton Republican; chief clerk of the Ohio House of Representatives in 1856; during the Civil War enlisted in Company G, Fourth Regiment, Ohio Volunteer Infantry, April 17, 1861; first lieutenant April 18, 1861; captain May 4, 1861; appointed major of the Eighty-second Regiment, Ohio Volunteer Infantry, December 31, 1861; lieutenant colonel April 9, 1862; colonel August 29, 1862; brevetted a brigadier general December 9, 1864; brigadier general January 12, 1865; brevetted major general March 13, 1865, "for gallant and meritorious services during the war"; mustered out August 31, 1865; chairman of the Republican State executive committee of Ohio 1877–1879; appointed commissioner of railroads and telegraphs in Ohio in January 1880; elected as a Republican to the Forty-seventh and Forty-eighth Congresses and served from March 4, 1881, to January 12, 1885, when he resigned; secretary of state of Ohio 1885–1889; died in Kenton, Ohio, January 14, 1892; interment in Grove Cemetery.

ROBINSON, James Wallace, a Representative from Ohio; born in the township of Carby, near Unionville Center, Union County, Ohio, on November 26, 1826; attended the common schools and Marysville Academy; was graduated from Jefferson College, Canonsburg, Pa., in 1848 and from the Cincinnati Law School in 1851; was admitted to the bar in the latter year and commenced practice in London, Ohio; prosecuting attorney of Union County for two terms; moved to Marysville, Ohio, in 1855; member of the State house of representatives 1860–1862, and in 1864 was elected to fill an unexpired term; elected as a Republican to the Forty-third Congress (March 4, 1873–March 3, 1875); unsuccessful candidate for reelection in 1874 to the Forty-fourth Congress; resumed the practice of his profession; died in Marysville, Union County, Ohio, June 28, 1898; interment in Oakdale Cemetery.

ROBINSON, James William, a Representative from Utah; born in Coalville, Summit County, Utah, January 19, 1878; attended public schools; graduated from Brigham Young University, Provo, Utah, and from the law school of the University of Chicago, Chicago, Ill., in 1912; principal of Uinta Academy, Vernal, Utah, and of the Wasatch High School, Heber, Utah; admitted as member of the bar of the State of Utah in 1912; engaged in practice of law in Provo, Utah County, Utah, 1912–1933; during the First World War served as food administrator for Utah County; county attorney of Utah County 1918–1921; Democratic candidate for attorney general of Utah in 1924; member of the board of regents of the University of Utah 1925–1935; elected as a Democrat to the Seventy-third and to the six succeeding Congresses (March 4, 1933–January 3, 1947); unsuccessful candidate for reelection in 1946 to the Eightieth Congress; served as director of grazing in the Office of Land Management, Interior Department, Washington, D. C., from January 3, 1947, to January 31, 1949; returned to Salt Lake City, Utah, where he now resides.

ROBINSON, John Buchanan, a Representative from Pennsylvania; born in Allegheny City, Pa., May 23, 1846; studied with a private tutor at the University of Pittsburgh, and Amherst (Mass.) College; during the Civil War enlisted in the Union Army in 1864, but resigned to accept an appointment to the United States Naval Academy at Annapolis, Md., from which he was graduated in 1868, and served in the Navy until he resigned in 1875; studied law; was admitted to the bar in 1876 and commenced practice in Philadelphia, Pa.; moved to Media,

Pa., in 1878 and continued the practice of law; editor of the Delaware County Gazette in 1881 and 1882; newspaper correspondent; owner of the Media Ledger; member of the State house of representatives 1885–1887; served in the State senate in 1889; elected as a Republican to the Fifty-second, Fifty-third, and Fifty-fourth Congresses (March 4, 1891–March 3, 1897); unsuccessful candidate for reelection in 1896; president of the League of Republican Clubs of Pennsylvania 1891–1897; member of the Board of Visitors to the United States Naval Academy in 1893; delegate to the Republican National Conventions in 1892, 1896, and 1908; United States marshal for the eastern district of Pennsylvania 1900–1914; retired from political life and active business and resided in Philadelphia, Pa., where he died January 28, 1933; interment in Allegheny Cemetery, Pittsburgh, Pa.

ROBINSON, John Larne, a Representative from Indiana; born near Maysville, Mason County, Ky., May 3, 1813; attended the public schools; moved to Rush County, Ind.; engaged in the mercantile business in Milroy, Ind.; county clerk of Rush County, Ind., 1841–1845; elected as a Democrat to the Thirtieth, Thirty-first, and Thirty-second Congresses (March 4, 1847–March 3, 1853); appointed by President Pierce as United States marshal for the southern district of Indiana in 1853; reappointed by President Buchanan in 1858 and served until his death; appointed brigade inspector of the fourth military district of Indiana in 1854; trustee of Indiana University at Bloomington 1856–1859; died at Rushville, Ind., March 21, 1860; interment in East Hill Cemetery.

ROBINSON, John McCracken, a Senator from Illinois; born near Georgetown, Scott County, Ky., April 10, 1794; attended the common schools, and was graduated from Transylvania University at Lexington, Ky.; studied law; was admitted to the bar and began practice in Carmi, Ill., in 1818; judge of the State supreme court; served as general in the State militia; elected as a Democrat to the United States Senate to fill the vacancy caused by the death of John McLean; reelected in 1835 and served from December 11, 1830, to March 3, 1841; was not a candidate for reelection; elected an associate justice of the State supreme court in 1843 and served until his death two months later in Ottawa, Ill., April 25, 1843; interment in the Old Graveyard, Carmi, Ill.

ROBINSON, John Seaton, a Representative from Nebraska; born in Wheeling, W. Va., May 4, 1856; attended the public schools; studied law; was admitted to the bar by the supreme court of West Virginia in 1880; moved to Madison, Nebr., in 1884; prosecuting attorney of Madison County 1886–1888 and 1890–1892; judge of the ninth judicial district 1893–1895; elected as a Democrat to the Fifty-sixth and Fifty-seventh Congresses (March 4, 1899–March 3, 1903); was an unsuccessful candidate for reelection in 1902 to the Fifty-eighth Congress; died in Madison, Nebr., on May 25, 1903; interment in Crownhill Cemetery.

ROBINSON, Jonathan (brother of Moses Robinson), a Senator from Vermont; born in Hardwick, Mass., August 11, 1756; received a limited schooling; moved with his father to Bennington, Vt., in 1761; studied law; was admitted to the bar in 1796 and commenced practice in Bennington, Vt.; town clerk 1795–1801; member of the State house of representatives 1789–1802; judge of the Vermont Probate Court 1795–1798; chief justice of the supreme court of Vermont 1801–1807; elected to the United States Senate to fill the vacancy caused by the resignation of Israel Smith; reelected in 1809 and served from October 10, 1807, to March 3, 1815; was not a candidate for reelection in 1814; again judge of the probate court 1815–1819;

member of the State house of representatives in 1818; died in Bennington, Vt., on November 3, 1819; interment in the Old Cemetery, Old Bennington, Vt.

ROBINSON, Joseph Taylor, a Representative and a Senator from Arkansas; born on a farm near Lonoke, Lonoke County, Ark., August 26, 1872; attended the common schools, the University of Arkansas at Fayetteville, and the law department of the University of Virginia at Charlottesville; was admitted to the bar in 1895 and commenced practice in Lonoke, Ark.; member of the State general assembly in 1895; presidential elector on the Democratic ticket of Bryan and Stevenson in 1900 and was selected as the messenger to deliver the electoral vote of the State of Arkansas; elected as a Democrat to the Fifty-eighth and to the four succeeding Congresses and served from March 4, 1903, to January 14, 1913, when he resigned, having been elected Governor; Governor of Arkansas from January 16, 1913, to March 8, 1913, when he resigned, having been elected Senator on January 28, 1913; moved to Little Rock, Ark., in 1913; elected to the United States Senate in 1913; reelected in 1918, 1924, 1930, and 1936 and served from March 4, 1913, until his death; delegate to the Democratic National Conventions in 1920, 1924, 1928, 1932, and 1936, serving as chairman of the 1920, 1928, and 1936 conventions; served as Democratic minority leader of the Senate 1923–1933 and as Democratic majority leader from 1933 until his death; appointed a member of the Board of Regents, Smithsonian Institution, in 1927; unsuccessful candidate for Vice President of the United States on the Democratic ticket with Alfred E. Smith for President in 1928; died in Washington, D. C., July 14, 1937; funeral services were held in the Chamber of the United States Senate; interment in Roselawn Memorial Park near Little Rock, Ark.

ROBINSON, Leonidas Dunlap, a Representative from North Carolina; born in Gulledge Township, Anson County, N. C., April 22, 1867; attended the common schools; moved to Wadesboro in 1888; studied law; was admitted to the bar in 1889 and practiced in Wadesboro; delegate to every Democratic State convention 1888–1941; mayor of Wadesboro 1890–1893; member of the State house of representatives in 1894 and 1900; appointed solicitor of the thirteenth judicial district in 1901; elected to the same office in 1902 and served in that capacity until 1910, when he resigned; became president of the Bank of Wadesboro in 1910; delegate to the Democratic National Conventions in 1912, 1920, and 1924; elected as a Democrat to the Sixty-fifth and Sixty-sixth Congresses (March 4, 1917–March 3, 1921); declined to be a candidate for renomination; resumed banking and also engaged in agricultural pursuits; died in Wadesboro, N. C., November 7, 1941; interment in Eastview Cemetery.

ROBINSON, Milton Stapp, a Representative from Indiana; born in Versailles, Ripley County, Ind., April 20, 1832; received a limited schooling; studied law; was admitted to the bar in 1851 and began practice in Anderson, Ind.; presidential elector on the Republican ticket of Frémont and Dayton in 1856; appointed a director of the Indiana State Penitentiary at Michigan City in 1861, but resigned after a few months; during the Civil War entered the Union Army in September 1861 as lieutenant colonel of the Forty-seventh Regiment, Indiana Volunteer Infantry; promoted to colonel of the Seventy-fifth Regiment, Indiana Volunteer Infantry, October 29, 1862, and served until March 29, 1864, when he resigned; brevetted brigadier general March 13, 1865, "for gallant and meritorious services during the war"; served in the State senate 1866–1870; delegate to the Republican National Convention at Philadelphia in 1872; elected as a Republican to the Forty-fourth and Forty-fifth Congresses (March 4, 1875–March 3, 1879); was not a candidate for renomination in 1878; resumed the practice of law; appointed associate justice of the appellate court of Indiana in March 1891; subsequently appointed chief justice and served until his death in Anderson, Ind., July 28, 1892; interment in Maplewood Cemetery.

ROBINSON, Moses (brother of Jonathan Robinson), a Senator from Vermont; born in Hardwick, Mass., on March 20, 1741; pursued classical studies in Dartmouth College, Hanover, N. H.; moved to Bennington, Vt., in 1761; elected town clerk of Bennington in March 1762 and kept its records for nineteen years; studied law; was admitted to the bar by special act of the Vermont Legislature in 1777 and practiced; colonel of militia and was at the head of his regiment on Mount Independence when Ticonderoga was evacuated by St. Clair in 1777; served on the Governor's council 1778–1785; chief justice of Vermont 1778–1781, 1782–1784, and 1785–1789; sent to the Continental Congress as State agent to adjust the controversy with New York in 1782; Governor of Vermont in 1789 and 1790; upon the admission of Vermont as a State into the Union was elected as a Democrat to the United States Senate and served from October 17, 1791, to October 15, 1796, when he resigned; member of the State house of representatives in 1802; resumed the practice of his profession at Bennington, Vt., where he died on May 26, 1813; interment in the Old Bennington Cemetery.

ROBINSON, Orville, a Representative from New York; born in Richfield, Oswego County, N. Y., October 28, 1801; completed preparatory studies; studied law; was admitted to the bar in 1827 and commenced practice in Mexico, N. Y.; justice of the peace of Mexico, N. Y., in 1828; town clerk in 1829; surrogate of Oswego County 1830–1838; member of the State assembly in 1834, 1836, and 1837; district attorney of Oswego County 1841–1843; supervisor of the town of Mexico in 1843; elected as a Democrat to the Twenty-eighth Congress (March 4, 1843–March 3, 1845); moved to Oswego, N. Y., in 1847; recorder of Oswego in 1853; again a member of the State assembly in 1856 and served as speaker; collector of customs for the district of Oswego 1858–1860; died in Oswego, N. Y., December 1, 1882; interment in Riverside Cemetery.

ROBINSON, Thomas, Jr., a Representative from Delaware; born in Georgetown, Sussex County, Del., in 1800; attended the common schools and was graduated from Princeton College; studied law; was admitted to the bar in 1823 and commenced practice in Georgetown, Del.; treasurer of Sussex County in 1825; levy court commissioner in 1831 and 1832; elected as a Democrat to the Twenty-sixth Congress (March 4, 1839–March 3, 1841); died in Georgetown, Del., October 28, 1843; interment in the Old Cemetery of St. George's Chapel.

ROBINSON, Thomas John Bright, a Representative from Iowa; born in New Diggings, Lafayette County, Wis., August 12, 1868; moved with his parents to Hampton, Iowa, in 1870; attended the public schools and the Hampton High School; engaged in agricultural pursuits; president of the Citizens' National Bank of Hampton 1907–1923; member of the Hampton Board of Education and board of trustees of Cornell College, Mount Vernon, Iowa; member of the State senate 1912–1916; during the First World War was prominently identified with war activities of Franklin County; delegate to many Republican State conventions; elected as a Republican to the Sixty-eighth and to the four succeeding Congresses (March 4, 1923–March 3, 1933); unsuccessful candidate for reelection in 1932 to the Seventy-third Congress; engaged in the real-estate and investment business; died in Hampton, Iowa, January 27, 1958; interment in Hampton Cemetery.

ROBINSON, William Erigena, a Representative from New York; born in Unagh, near Cookstown, County Tyrone, Ireland, May 6, 1814; attended the classical school in Cookstown and Belfast College in 1834; immigrated to the United States and settled in New York City in November 1836; was graduated from Yale College in 1841; connected for two years with the Yale Law School; engaged in lecturing before literary associations; assistant editor of the New York Tribune in 1843 and its only Washington correspondent, writing under the name of "Richelieu"; also wrote Washington correspondence for the Richmond (Va.) Whig, the Boston Atlas, the Louisville Journal, and other papers; was admitted to the New York bar in 1854 and practiced law in New York City; appointed by President Lincoln assessor of internal revenue for the third district of New York in 1862; elected as a Democrat to the Fortieth Congress (March 4, 1867–March 3, 1869); resumed the practice of law; elected to the Forty-seventh and Forty-eighth Congresses (March 4, 1881–March 3, 1885); died in Brooklyn, N. Y., on January 23, 1892; interment in Greenwood Cemetery.

ROBISON, David Fullerton (nephew of David Fullerton), a Representative from Pennsylvania; born in Antrim Township, near Greencastle, Franklin County, Pa., May 28, 1816; attended the public schools; taught school; studied law; was admitted to the Franklin County bar in 1843 and commenced practice in Chambersburg, Pa., elected as a Whig to the Thirty-fourth Congress (March 4, 1855–March 3, 1857); was not a candidate for renomination; continued the practice of law in Chambersburg, Pa., until his death there June 24, 1859, presumably from the effects of poison secretly placed in food served at a banquet in Washington, D. C., during the inauguration of President Buchanan; interment in Cedar Hill Cemetery, Greencastle, Franklin County, Pa.

ROBISON, Howard Winfield, a Representative from New York; born in Owego, Tioga County, N. Y., October 30, 1915; attended the public schools of Owego, N. Y.; graduated from Cornell University in 1937 and from the law school of the same university in 1939; was admitted to the bar in 1939 and commenced the practice of law in Owego, N. Y.; during World War II served in the United States Army Counter Intelligence Corps 1942–1946; county attorney of Tioga County from 1946 until elected to Congress; elected as a Republican to the Eighty-fifth Congress to fill the vacancy caused by the resignation of W. Sterling Cole; reelected to the Eighty-sixth Congress and served from January 14, 1958, to January 3, 1961. *Reelected to the Eighty-seventh Congress.*

ROBSION, John Marshall, a Representative and a Senator from Kentucky; born near Berlin, Bracken County, Ky., January 2, 1873; attended the common schools, the National Northern University, Ada, Ohio, and Holbrook College, Knoxville, Tenn.; was graduated from the National Normal University, Lebanon, Ohio, and from the law department of Centre College, Danville, Ky., in 1900; taught in the public schools of Kentucky for several years, and in Union College, Barbourville, Ky.; was admitted to the bar in 1898 and commenced practice at Barbourville, Ky.; president of the First National Bank of Barbourville, Ky.; delegate to the Republican National Convention at Chicago in 1916; elected as a Republican to the Sixty-sixth and to the five succeeding Congresses and served from March 4, 1919, until January 10, 1930, when he resigned to serve as United States Senator; appointed to the Senate to fill the vacancy caused by the resignation of Frederick M. Sackett and served from January 11 to November 30, 1930, when a duly elected successor qualified; unsuccessful candidate for election to the vacancy and also for the full term in 1930; resumed the practice of law; elected to the Seventy-fourth and to the six succeeding Congresses and served from January 3, 1935, until his death in Barbourville, Ky., February 17, 1948; interment in Barbourville Cemetery.

ROBSION, John Marshall, Jr. (son of the preceding), a Representative from Kentucky; born in Barbourville, Knox County, Ky., August 28, 1904; graduated from Union College Academy, Barbourville, Ky., in 1919, attended George Washington University, Washington, D. C., Georgetown University, Washington, D. C., and National University in 1926; congressional secretary 1919–1928; was admitted to the bar in 1926; established home in Louisville, Ky., in 1928; chief of law division, United States Bureau of Pensions, 1929–1935; resigned from Government service in 1935; returned to Louisville and engaged in the practice of law; during World War II served in the United States Army 1942–1946 with overseas service in Africa, Italy, and Austria, part of the time on the staff of Gen. Mark Clark; served as special circuit judge in Kentucky by appointment of both political parties 1946–1952; general counsel of Kentucky Republicans 1938–1942; elected as a Republican to the Eighty-third, Eighty-fourth, and Eighty-fifth Congresses (January 3, 1953–January 3, 1959); unsuccessful candidate for reelection in 1958 to the Eighty-sixth Congress; unsuccessful gubernatorial candidate in 1959; trustee for the Kentucky Jockey Club and engaged in the practice of law; is a resident of Louisville, Ky.

ROCHESTER, William Beatty, a Representative from New York; born in Hagerstown, Md., January 29, 1789; attended the public schools and was graduated from Charlotte Hall, St. Marys County, Md.; was aide-de-camp to General McClure in the War of 1812; studied law; was admitted to the bar and began practice in Bath, N. Y.; moved to Angelica, N. Y.: member of the State assembly in 1816–1818; presidential elector on the Democratic ticket of Monroe and Tompkins in 1821; elected to the Seventeenth and Eighteenth Congresses and served from March 4, 1821, until his resignation in 1823; State circuit judge for the eighth circuit from April 21, 1823, until 1826, when he resigned; unsuccessful Democratic candidate for Governor in 1826; secretary to special Envoy Extraordinary and Minister Plenipotentiary, Colombia, in 1826; Chargé d'Affaires to Central America in 1827; settled in Buffalo, N. Y., in 1828; president of the branch bank of the United States at Buffalo, N. Y.; president of the Bank of Pensacola, Fla.; director of the Alabama & Florida Railroad Co. in 1837 and 1838; was lost in the wreck of the steamer *Pulaski* off the coast of North Carolina June 14, 1838.

ROCKEFELLER, Lewis Kirby, a Representative from New York; born in Schenectady, N. Y., November 25, 1875; attended the public schools; was graduated from New York State College, Albany, N. Y., in 1898; principal of grammar school at North Germantown, N. Y.; employed in finance bureau of New York State Department of Public Instruction 1898–1904; chief accountant, municipal accounts bureau, in State comptroller's office, 1905–1915; deputy State tax commissioner 1915–1921; deputy State commissioner of taxation and finance 1921–1933; engaged in accounting and auditing business in 1933; delegate to the Republican National Convention at Cleveland in 1936; elected as a Republican to the Seventy-fifth Congress to fill the vacancy caused by the death of Philip A. Goodwin; reelected to the Seventy-sixth and Seventy-seventh Congresses and served from November 2, 1937, to January 3, 1943; was not a candidate for renomination in 1942; resumed activities as an accountant and tax consultant in Chatham, N. Y.; died in Canaan, N. Y., on September 18, 1948; interment in Kinderhook Cemetery, Kinderhook, N. Y.

ROCKHILL, William, a Representative from Indiana; born in Burlington, N. J., February 10, 1793; attended the public schools; moved to Fort Wayne, Ind., in 1822; engaged in agricultural pursuits; commissioner of Allen County, Ind., in 1825 justice of the peace; member of the first city council of Fort Wayne and also city assessor; member of the State house of representatives 1834–1837; served in the State senate 1844–1847 elected as a Democrat to the Thirtieth Congress (March 4, 1847–March 3, 1849); resumed agricultural pursuits; died at Fort Wayne, Allen County, Ind., January 15, 1865; interment in Lindenwood Cemetery.

ROCKWELL, Francis Williams (son of Julius Rockwell), a Representative from Massachusetts; born in Pittsfield, Berkshire County, Mass., on May 26, 1844; attended the public schools and Edwards Place School, Stockbridge, Mass.; was graduated from Amherst (Mass.) College in 1868 and from the law department of Harvard University in 1871; commenced the practice of law in Pittsfield in 1871; appointed one of the special justices of the district court of central Berkshire in 1873, resigning in 1875; served in the State house of representatives in 1879; served in the State senate in 1881 and 1882; elected as a Republican to the Forty-eighth Congress to fill the vacancy caused by the resignation of George D. Robinson; reelected to the Forty-ninth, Fiftieth, and Fifty-first Congresses and served from January 17, 1884, to March 3, 1891; unsuccessful candidate for reelection in 1890 to the Fifty-second Congress; resumed the practice of law in Pittsfield, Mass., until 1916 when he retired from the practice of law; president of the City Savings Bank 1893–1916; delegate to the Republican National Convention at Philadelphia in 1900; member of the Greylock Reservation Commission 1898–1926; died in Pittsfield, Mass., June 26, 1929; interment in Pittsfield Cemetery.

ROCKWELL, Hosea Hunt, a Representative from New York; born in Lawrenceville, Tioga County, Pa., on May 31, 1840; attended the common schools; during the Civil War served as a private in the Twenty-third Regiment, New York Volunteers, in 1861 and 1862; studied law; was admitted to the bar in 1869 and commenced practice in Elmira, N. Y.; member of the State assembly in 1877; city attorney of Elmira; elected as a Democrat to the Fifty-second Congress (March 4, 1891–March 3, 1893); was not a candidate for renomination in 1892; delegate to the Democratic National Convention at Chicago in 1896; chairman of the Democratic State convention in 1896; resumed the practice of law in Elmira, N. Y.; died in Elmira, Chemung County, N. Y., December 18, 1918; interment in Woodlawn Cemetery.

ROCKWELL, John Arnold, a Representative from Connecticut; born in Norwich, Conn., August 27, 1803; attended the common schools; was graduated from Yale College in 1822; studied law; was admitted to the bar and practiced in Norwich; member of the State senate in 1839; judge of the county court; elected as a Whig to the Twenty-ninth and Thirtieth Congresses (March 4, 1845–March 3, 1849); unsuccessful candidate for reelection in 1848 to the Thirty-first Congress; engaged in the practice of law before the court of claims of the United States at Washington, D. C., until his death in that city on February 10, 1861; interment in Yantic Cemetery, Norwich, Conn.

ROCKWELL, Julius (father of Francis Williams Rockwell), a Representative and a Senator from Massachusetts; born in Colebrook, Conn., April 26, 1805; attended private schools; was graduated from Yale College in 1826; studied law; was admitted to the bar and commenced practice in Pittsfield, Mass., in 1830; member of the State house of representatives 1834–1838 and served three years as speaker; State bank commissioner 1838–1840; elected as a Whig to the Twenty-eighth and to the three succeeding Congresses (March 4, 1843–March 3, 1851); was not a candidate for renomination in 1850; delegate to the State constitutional convention in 1853; appointed to the United States Senate to fill the vacancy caused by the resignation of Edward Everett and served from June 3, 1854, to January 31, 1855, when a successor was elected; presidential elector on the Republican ticket of Frémont and Dayton in 1856; again a member of the State house of representatives in 1858 and served as speaker; appointed a judge of the superior court of Massachusetts in 1859 and resigned in 1886; died in Lenox, Berkshire County, Mass., May 19, 1888; interment in Lenox Cemetery.

ROCKWELL, Robert Fay, a Representative from Colorado; born in Cortland, N. Y., February 11, 1886; attended the public schools of New York State, the Hill School, Pottstown, Pa., and Princeton University, Princeton, N. J.; moved to Paonia, Colo., in 1907 and engaged in cattle raising and fruit growing; member of the State house of representatives 1916–1920; served in the State senate 1920–1924 and 1938–1941; Lieutenant Governor 1922–1924; unsuccessful candidate for Governor in 1930; member of the State board of agriculture 1932–1946; elected as a Republican to the Seventy-seventh Congress to fill the vacancy caused by the death of Edward T. Taylor; reelected to the Seventy-eighth, Seventy-ninth, and Eightieth Congresses and served from December 9, 1941, to January 3, 1949; unsuccessful candidate for reelection in 1948 to the Eighty-first Congress; resumed cattle ranching in Colorado; chairman of the board of directors of Tuttle & Rockwell Co., Hornell, N. Y., and Rockwell Co., Corning, N. Y.; died in Maher, Colo., September 29, 1950; interment in Hornell Cemetery, Hornell, N. Y.

RODDENBERY, Seaborn Anderson, a Representative from Georgia; born near Bainbridge, Decatur County, Ga., January 12, 1870; moved to Thomas County in early childhood; attended the common schools and Mercer University, Macon, Ga., for three years; occupied the chair of languages and mathematics in South Georgia College one year; member of the State house of representatives in 1892 and 1893 and declined to be a candidate for reelection; studied law; was admitted to the bar in 1894 and commenced practice in Thomasville, Thomas County, Ga.; president of the board of education of Thomas County 1895–1898; appointed judge of the county court of Thomas County in 1897 and served four years; declined reappointment; mayor of Thomasville in 1903 and 1904; member of the board of trustees of Young's Female College and of the Normal Institute; elected as a Democrat to the Sixty-first Congress to fill the vacancy caused by the death of James M. Griggs; reelected to the Sixty-second and Sixty-third Congresses and served from February 16, 1910, until his death in Thomasville, Ga., September 25, 1913; interment in Laurel Hill Cemetery.

RODENBERG, William August, a Representative from Illinois; born near Chester, Randolph County, Ill., October 30, 1865; attended the public schools; was graduated from Central Wesleyan College, Warrenton, Mo., in 1884; engaged in teaching for seven years; attended the St. Louis Law School; was admitted to the bar in 1893 and commenced practice in East St. Louis, St. Clair County, Ill.; delegate to the Republican National Conventions in 1896, 1908, 1916, and 1920; elected as a Republican to the Fifty-sixth Congress (March 4, 1899–March 3, 1901); unsuccessful candidate for reelection in 1900 to the Fifty-seventh Congress; appointed a member of the United States Civil Service Commission by President McKinley March 25, 1901, and served until April 1, 1902, when he resigned;

resumed the practice of law in East St. Louis; also financially interested in various business enterprises; elected to the Fifty-eighth and to the four succeeding Congresses (March 4, 1903–March 3, 1913); unsuccessful candidate for reelection in 1912 to the Sixty-third Congress; elected to the Sixty-fourth and to the three succeeding Congresses (March 4, 1915–March 3, 1923); voluntarily retired from public life and engaged in the practice of law in Washington, D. C.; died in Alpena, Mich., while on a visit, September 10, 1937; interment in Rock Creek Cemetery, Washington, D. C.

RODEY, Bernard Shandon, a Delegate from the Territory of New Mexico; born in County Mayo, Ireland, March 1, 1856; immigrated with his parents to Canada in 1862; attended the public schools at Sherbrooke, Province of Quebec, Canada; studied law in Boston, Mass.; moved to Albuquerque, N. Mex., in 1881; was private secretary to the general manager of the A. & P. Railroad; court stenographer of the second district of New Mexico in 1882; was admitted to the bar in 1883 and commenced practice in Albuquerque; city attorney of Albuquerque in 1887 and 1888; member of the Territorial senate in 1889; was the author of the bill creating the University of New Mexico; member of the constitutional convention of New Mexico in 1890; elected as a Republican to the Fifty-seventh and Fifty-eighth Congresses (March 4, 1901–March 3, 1905); unsuccessful candidate for reelection in 1904 to the Fifty-ninth Congress; delegate to the Republican National Convention at Chicago in 1908; judge of the Federal Court of Puerto Rico 1906–1910; United States attorney for the second division of Alaska 1910–1913; appointed on March 6, 1912, as special assistant United States attorney, western district of Washington, to assist in the prosecution of coal frauds in Alaska, and served until December 16, 1913; resumed the practice of law; died in Albuquerque, Bernalillo County, N. Mex., March 10, 1927; interment in Fairview Cemetery.

RODGERS, Robert Lewis, a Representative from Pennsylvania; born in El Dorado, Butler County, Kans., June 2, 1875; upon the death of his mother in 1878 was reared by his grandparents on a farm near Jamestown, Mercer County, Pa.; attended district school and Fredonia (Pa.) Institute; during the War with Spain enlisted in Company K, Fifteenth Regiment, Pennsylvania Volunteer Infantry; taught in the district schools; engaged in agricultural pursuits; moved to Erie, Erie County, Pa., in 1914 and engaged in the insurance, real estate, and mortgage business; elected as a Republican to the Seventy-sixth and to the three succeeding Congresses (January 3, 1939–January 3, 1947); unsuccessful candidate for renomination in 1946 to the Eightieth Congress; retired and resided in Erie, Pa., until his death there May 9, 1960; interment in Rocky Glen Cemetery, Adamsville, Pa.

RODINO, Peter Wallace, Jr., a Representative from New Jersey; born in Newark, Essex County, N. J., June 7, 1909; attended the McKinley Grammar School and Barringer High School; graduated from the University of Newark and from the New Jersey Law School in 1937; was admitted to the bar in 1938 and commenced the practice of law in Newark, N. J.; teacher, public speaking and citizenship classes, Y. M. C. A. and Federation of Clubs, Newark, N. J., 1930–1932; managing editor of the Jersey Review in 1934 and 1935; during World War II enlisted in the United States Army March 10, 1941, and served with the First Armored Division in North Africa and Italy and on military missions with the Italian Army; discharged as a captain in April 1946; awarded Bronze Star for military operations, War Cross, and Knight of Order of Crown from Italy; unsuccessful candidate in 1946 to the Eightieth Congress;

elected as a Democrat to the Eighty-first and to the five succeeding Congresses (January 3, 1949–January 3, 1961). *Reelected to the Eighty-seventh Congress.*

RODMAN, William, a Representative from Pennsylvania; born in Bensalem Township, near Bristol, Bucks County, Pa., October 7, 1757; completed preparatory studies; served in the Revolutionary War as a private and subsequently as brigade quartermaster; commanded a company during the Whisky Insurrection in 1794; justice of the peace 1791–1800; member of the State senate 1804–1808; presidential elector in 1809; elected as a Democrat to the Twelfth Congress (March 4, 1811–March 3, 1813); died at "Flushing" near Bristol, Bucks County, Pa., July 27, 1824; interment in the Episcopal Cemetery (later known as the St. James Burying Ground).

RODNEY, Caesar (brother of Thomas Rodney and cousin of George Brydges Rodney), a Delegate from Delaware; born in Dover, Del., October 7, 1728; completed preparatory studies; engaged in agricultural pursuits; high sheriff of Kent County 1755–1758; justice of the peace; judge of all lower courts; captain in the Kent County Militia in 1756; superintendent of the printing of Delaware currency in 1759; member of the State assembly 1762–1769; superintendent of the loan office in 1769; associate justice of the Delaware Supreme Court 1769–1777; Member of the Continental Congress 1774–1776; a signer of the Declaration of Independence; served in the Revolutionary Army as a brigadier general; again a Member of the Continental Congress in 1777 and 1778; reelected, but before taking his seat was elected President of Delaware, and served from 1778 to 1782; again a Member of the Continental Congress in 1782 and 1783; died in Dover, Del., June 29, 1784; interment on his farm, "Byfield," near Dover; reinterment in the Episcopal Cemetery, Dover, Del.

RODNEY, Caesar Augustus (son of Thomas Rodney and cousin of George Brydges Rodney), a Representative and a Senator from Delaware; born in Dover, Del., January 4, 1772; completed preparatory studies and was graduated from the University of Pennsylvania at Philadelphia in 1789; studied law; was admitted to the bar and began practice in Wilmington, Del., in 1793; elected as a Democrat to the Eighth Congress (March 4, 1803–March 3, 1805); was not a candidate for renomination in 1804; one of the managers appointed by the House of Representatives in January 1804 to conduct the impeachment proceedings against John Pickering, judge of the United States District Court for New Hampshire, and in December of the same year against Samuel Chase, Associate Justice of the Supreme Court of the United States; appointed Attorney General of the United States in the Cabinet of President Jefferson; was continued in the same capacity by President Madison and served from January 20, 1807 to December 5, 1811, when he resigned; served in the War of 1812; member of the Delaware Committee of Safety in 1813; member of the State senate in 1815; was sent to South America by President Monroe as one of the commissioners to investigate and report on the propriety of recognizing the independence of the Spanish-American Republics; elected as a Democrat to the Seventeenth Congress and served from March 4, 1821, to January 24, 1822, when he resigned; elected to the United States Senate and served from January 24, 1822, to January 29, 1823, when he resigned; appointed Minister Plenipotentiary to Argentina on January 27, 1823, and served until his death in Buenos Aires, June 10, 1824; interment in the English Churchyard.

RODNEY, Daniel, a Representative and a Senator from Delaware; born in Lewes, Sussex County, Del., September 10, 1764; received a limited schooling; engaged in mercantile pursuits; associate judge of the court of common pleas 1793–1806; presidential elector on the Federalist ticket of Pinckney and King in 1808; Governor of Delaware 1814–1817; elected as a Federalist to the Seventeenth Congress to fill the vacancy caused by the resignation of Caesar A. Rodney and served from October 1, 1822, to March 3, 1823; appointed to the United States Senate to fill the vacancy caused by the death of Nicholas Van Dyke and served from November 8, 1826, to January 12, 1827, when a successor was elected; died in Lewes, Del., September 2, 1846; interment in St. Peter's Churchyard.

RODNEY, George Brydges (cousin of Caesar Rodney, Caesar Augustus Rodney, and Thomas Rodney), a Representative from Delaware; born in Lewes, Del., April 2, 1803; received a liberal education and was graduated from Princeton College in 1820; register in chancery and clerk of the orphans' court of Sussex County 1826–1830; studied law; was admitted to the bar in 1828 and engaged in practice in New Castle; declined appointment as chief justice of Delaware in 1830; elected as a Whig to the Twenty-seventh and Twenty-eighth Congresses (March 4, 1841–March 3, 1845); resumed the practice of law; delegate to the peace convention held in Washington, D. C., in 1861 in an effort to prevent the impending war; died in New Castle, New Castle County, Del., June 18, 1883; interment in the Immanuel Churchyard.

RODNEY, Thomas (father of Caesar Augustus Rodney, brother of Caesar Rodney, and cousin of George Brydges Rodney), a Delegate from Delaware; born near Dover, Kent County, Del., June 4, 1744; justice of the peace in 1770 and 1784; member of the assembly to elect delegates in 1774; member of the council of safety in 1775; colonel of Delaware Militia during the Revolutionary War; chief justice of Kent County Court in 1778; register of wills in 1779; Member of the Continental Congress 1781–1783 and 1785–1787; was not a candidate for renomination in 1786; member of the State assembly in 1787 and served as speaker; superintendent of Kent County Almshouse in 1802; appointed an associate justice of the supreme court of Delaware on December 17, 1802, and served until August 1803, when he resigned, having been appointed United States judge for Mississippi Territory; died in Natchez, Miss., January 2, 1811.

ROE, Dudley George, a Representative from Maryland; born in Sudlersville, Queen Annes County, Md., March 23, 1881; attended the public schools; was graduated from Washington College, Chestertown, Md., in 1903 and from the law department of the University of Maryland at Baltimore in 1905; was admitted to the bar in 1905 and commenced practice in Baltimore, Md.; served in the State house of delegates 1907–1909; member of the State senate 1923–1935 and 1939–1943, serving as Democratic floor leader 1939–1943; delegate to the Democratic National Convention at Houston in 1928; alternate to the Democratic National Convention at Chicago in 1932; elected as a Democrat to the Seventy-ninth Congress (January 3, 1945–January 3, 1947); unsuccessful candidate for reelection in 1946 to the Eightieth Congress; farmer, banker, and grain dealer in Sudlersville, Md.; director and later president of Sudlersville Bank of Maryland; is a resident of Georgetown, Md.

ROE, James A., a Representative from New York; born in Flushing, Queens County, N. Y., July 9, 1896; attended the public and parochial schools; studied law, engineering, and accounting; was graduated from the United States School of Military Aeronautics, Cornell University, Ithaca, N. Y., in

August 1917; during the First World War enlisted on September 17, 1917, as a private in the United States Army Air Corps, was promoted to lieutenant and instructor of advanced flying, and was discharged on January 4, 1919; served as pilot-instructor at various Government flying fields until March 1919; real-estate and insurance broker; also interested in the contracting and engineering business; director of Flushing National Bank; chairman of the Democratic County Committee of Queens County 1939–1952; delegate to the Democratic National Conventions in 1940, 1948, and 1960; during World War II entered the United States Army in July 1943 with rank of major and was assigned to duty with the Corps of Engineers, and served until January 1945, when he was honorably discharged with the rank of lieutenant colonel to enter Congress; elected as a Democrat to the Seventy-ninth Congress (January 3, 1945–January 3, 1947); was not a candidate for renomination in 1946; resumed his former business pursuits, and is a resident of Flushing, N. Y.

ROGERS, Andrew Jackson, a Representative from New Jersey; born in Hamburg, Sussex County, N. J., July 1, 1828; attended the common schools; employed as clerk in a hotel and in a country store; engaged in teaching for two years; studied law; was admitted to the bar in 1852 and commenced practice in La Fayette, Sussex County, N. J.; moved to Newton, N. J., in 1857 and continued the practice of law; elected as a Democrat to the Thirty-eighth and Thirty-ninth Congresses (March 4, 1863–March 3, 1867); unsuccessful candidate for reelection in 1866 to the Fortieth Congress; moved to New York City in 1867 and became counsel for the city in important litigation; moved to Denver, Colo., in 1892; served as police commissioner of the city of Denver; returned to New York City in 1896 and died there on May 22, 1900; interment in Woodlawn Cemetery.

ROGERS, Anthony Astley Cooper, a Representative from Arkansas; born in Clarksville, Sumner County, Tenn., February 14, 1821; received a limited schooling; engaged in mercantile pursuits; moved to Arkansas in 1854; candidate of the Union supporters for delegate to the State convention in 1861; earnestly opposed secession; arrested for his loyalty, was imprisoned, and forced to give bond to answer the charge of "treason against the Confederate Government"; elected to the Thirty-eighth Congress but was not allowed to take his seat, his State not having been readmitted; moved to Chicago, Ill., in 1864 and engaged in the real-estate business; returned to Arkansas in 1868; elected as a Democrat to the Forty-first Congress (March 4, 1869–March 3, 1871); unsuccessful candidate for reelection in 1870 to the Forty-second Congress; postmaster at Pine Bluff, Ark., from January 7, 1881, to July 24, 1885; again engaged in mercantile pursuits; moved to Los Angeles, Calif., in 1888 and died there July 27, 1899; interment in Rosedale Cemetery.

ROGERS, Byron Giles, a Representative from Colorado; born in Greenville, Hunt County, Tex., August 1, 1900; moved with his parents to Oklahoma in April 1902; attended the public schools of Checotah, Okla.; during the First World War served as a private in the Infantry, United States Army; attended the University of Arkansas in 1918, the University of Oklahoma 1919–1922, and the University of Colorado 1923 and 1924; was graduated from the law school of the University of Denver in 1925, and commenced the practice of law in Las Animas, Colo.; city attorney of Las Animas 1929–1933; member of the State house of representatives 1932–1935, serving as speaker in 1933; county attorney of Bent County, Colo., in 1933; on legal staff of Agricultural Adjustment Administration and National Recovery Administration, Washington, D. C., in 1933 and 1934;

assistant United States attorney of Colorado 1934–1936, and attorney general 1936–1941; public member War Labor Board 1942–1945; Democratic presidential elector in 1948; elected as a Democrat to the Eighty-second and to the four succeeding Congresses (January 3, 1951–January 3, 1961). *Reelected to the Eighty-seventh Congress.*

ROGERS, Charles, a Representative from New York; born in Northumberland, Saratoga County, N. Y., April 30, 1800; attended Granville Academy and was graduated from Union College, Schenectady, N. Y., in 1818; studied law; was admitted to the bar but did not engage in extensive practice; served in the State assembly in 1833 and 1837; unsuccessful candidate for election to the State senate; elected as a Whig to the Twenty-eighth Congress (March 4, 1843–March 3, 1845); was not a candidate for renomination in 1844; retired from public life; affiliated with the Republican Party; died in Sandy Hill (now Hudson Falls), Washington County, N. Y., January 13, 1874; interment in Union Cemetery, near Sandy Hill.

ROGERS, Dwight Laing (father of Paul G. Rogers), a Representative from Florida; born near Reidsville, Tattnall County, Ga., August 17, 1886; attended the public schools and Locust Grove Institute at Locust Grove, Ga.; was graduated from the University of Georgia at Athens in 1909 and from the law department of Mercer University, Macon, Ga., in 1910; was admitted to the bar in 1910 and commenced practice in Ocilla, Ga.; moved to Fort Lauderdale, Fla., in 1925 and continued the practice of law; member of the State house of representatives 1930–1938, serving as speaker pro tempore in 1933; chairman of Appeal Board No. 4 of the Selective Service System 1941–1944; elected as a Democrat to the Seventy-ninth and to the four succeeding Congresses and served from January 3, 1945, until his death; had been reelected to the Eighty-fourth Congress; died in Fort Lauderdale, Fla., December 1, 1954; interment in Lauderdale Memorial Park.

ROGERS, Edith Nourse (wife of John Jacob Rogers), a Representative from Massachusetts; born in Saco, York County, Maine, in 1881; attended the common schools; was graduated from the Rogers Hall School, Lowell, Mass., and from Madame Julien's School, Paris, France; served with the American Red Cross in the care of disabled soldiers of the First World War 1917–1922; appointed a personal representative of President Harding in the care of disabled veterans in 1922, and was reappointed by President Coolidge in 1923; presidential elector on the Republican ticket of Coolidge and Dawes in 1924; president, board of trustees, Rogers Hall School, Lowell, Mass.; elected as a Republican to the Sixty-ninth Congress to fill the vacancy caused by the death of her husband, John Jacob Rogers; reelected to the Seventieth and to the sixteen succeeding Congresses and served from June 30, 1925, until her death in Boston, Mass., September 10, 1960; interment in Lowell Cemetery, Lowell, Mass.

ROGERS, Edward, a Representative from New York; born in Cornwall, Conn., on May 30, 1787; completed preparatory studies and was graduated from Williams College, Williamstown, Mass., in 1809; moved to New York State about the close of the War of 1812; was graduated from Yale College; studied law; was admitted to the bar and commenced practice in Madison, N. Y.; delegate to the State convention to revise the constitution in 1822; judge of the court of common pleas for Madison County; elected as a Democrat to the Twenty-sixth Congress (March 4, 1839–March 3, 1841); resumed the practice of law; also engaged in literary pursuits; died in Galway, Saratoga County, N. Y., May 29, 1857; interment in Madison Cemetery, Madison, N. Y.

ROGERS, George Frederick, a Representative from New York; born in Harwood, Ontario, Canada, March 19, 1887; attended the public schools in Canada and Rochester, N. Y.; immigrated to the United States in 1899 and settled in Rochester, N. Y.; food merchant in Rochester, N. Y., 1911–1943; supervisor of Monroe County, N. Y., in 1934 and 1935; served in the State senate in 1937 and 1938; member of the Genesee State Park Commission 1942–1948; elected as a Democrat to the Seventy-ninth Congress (January 3, 1945–January 3, 1947); unsuccessful candidate for reelection in 1946 to the Eightieth Congress and for election in 1948 to the Eighty-first Congress; retired from public and political activities and resided in Rochester, N. Y.; died in Coburg, Ontario, Canada, November 20, 1948; interment in Riverside Cemetery, Rochester, N. Y.

ROGERS, James, a Representative from South Carolina; born in what is now Goshen Hill Township, Union County, S. C., October 24, 1795; completed preparatory studies and was graduated from South Carolina College (now the University of South Carolina) at Columbia in 1813; studied law; was admitted to the bar and began practice in Yorkville (now York), S. C.; held various local offices; elected as a Democrat to the Twenty-fourth Congress (March 4, 1835–March 3, 1837); unsuccessful candidate for reelection in 1836 to the Twenty-fifth Congress; elected to the Twenty-sixth and Twenty-seventh Congresses (March 4, 1839–March 3, 1843); died in South Carolina on December 21, 1873; interment in what was formerly called the Irish Graveyard at Kings Creek A. R. P. Church near Newberry, S. C.

ROGERS, John, a Delegate from Maryland; born in Annapolis, Anne Arundel County, Md., in 1723; received a liberal schooling; studied law; was admitted to the bar and commenced practice; member of the committee of safety in 1774 and 1775; member of the Maryland provincial conventions in 1774, 1775, and 1776; one of the trustees of the Lower Marlboro Academy in 1775; second major of battalion, Prince Georges County; Member of the Continental Congress in 1775 and 1776; judge of the court of admiralty in 1776; member of the executive council on the organization of the State government in February 1777; presidential elector in 1788 and voted for Washington and Adams; chancellor of Maryland from March 10, 1778, until his death in Upper Marlboro, Prince Georges County, Md., September 23, 1789.

ROGERS, John, a Representative from New York; born in Caldwell, N. Y., May 9, 1813; completed preparatory studies; moved to Black Brook, Clinton County, in 1832 and engaged in the manufacture of iron; supervisor of the town of Black Brook for ten years and held other local offices; elected as a Democrat to the Forty-second Congress (March 4, 1871–March 3, 1873); resumed manufacturing activities; died at the "Rogers Place," near Fort Edward, Washington County, N. Y., May 11, 1879; interment in the family burial ground on his estate at Moreau, near Fort Henry, N. Y.

ROGERS, John Henry, a Representative from Arkansas; born near Roxobel, Bertie County, N. C., October 9, 1845; moved to Mississippi in 1852 with his parents, who settled near Madison Station; attended the common schools; during the Civil War joined the Ninth Mississippi Volunteer Regiment, Confederate service, as a private in March 1862; promoted to first lieutenant in the same regiment and served throughout the war; attended Centre College, Danville, Ky., and was graduated from the law department of the University of Mississippi at Oxford in 1868; was admitted to the bar in 1868 and commenced practice in Canton, Miss.; moved to Fort Smith, Ark., in 1869 and practiced law; elected circuit judge in 1877;

reelected in 1878 and resigned in May 1882; elected as a Democrat to the Forty-eighth and to the three succeeding Congresses (March 4, 1883–March 3, 1891); declined to be a candidate for renomination; resumed the practice of law in Fort Smith, Ark.; member of the Democratic State convention in 1892; delegate to the Democratic National Convention at Chicago in 1892; appointed United States district judge for the western district of Arkansas by President Cleveland on November 27, 1896, and served until his death in Little Rock, Pulaski County, Ark., on April 16, 1911; interment in Oak Cemetery, Fort Smith, Sebastian County, Ark.

ROGERS, John Jacob (husband of Edith Nourse Rogers), a Representative from Massachusetts; born in Lowell, Middlesex County, Mass., August 18, 1881; attended the public schools, and was graduated from Harvard University in 1904 and from the law department of that university in 1907; was admitted to the bar the same year and commenced practice in Lowell in 1908; member of the Lowell city government in 1911; school commissioner in 1912; elected as a Republican to the Sixty-third and to the six succeeding Congresses and served from March 4, 1913, until his death; during the First World War enlisted on September 12, 1918, as a private with the Twenty-ninth Training Battery, Tenth Training Battalion, Field Artillery, Fourth Central Officers' Training School, and served until honorably discharged on November 29, 1918; died in Washington, D. C., March 28, 1925; interment in Lowell Cemetery, Lowell, Mass.

ROGERS, Paul Grant (son of Dwight L. Rogers), a Representative from Florida; born in Ocilla, Irwin County, Ga., June 4, 1921; at the age of four years moved with his parents to Fort Lauderdale, Fla.; attended the public schools; was graduated from the University of Florida at Gainesville, in 1942; during World War II served in the Field Artillery, United States Army, with service in the European Theater as battalion commander from 1942 until discharged as a major in 1946; awarded the Bronze Star Medal and two battle stars; studied law at George Washington University, Washington, D. C., in 1946, and graduated from the University of Florida in 1948; was admitted to the bar in 1948 and commenced the practice of law in West Palm Beach, Fla.; elected as a Democrat to the Eighty-fourth Congress to fill the vacancy caused by the death of his father, Dwight L. Rogers; reelected to the Eighty-fifth and Eighty-sixth Congresses and served from January 11, 1955, to January 3, 1961. *Reelected to the Eighty-seventh Congress.*

ROGERS, Sion Hart, a Representative from North Carolina; born near Raleigh, Wake County, N. C., September 30, 1825; attended the common schools, and was graduated from the University of North Carolina at Chapel Hill in 1846; studied law; was admitted to the bar in 1848 and commenced practice in Raleigh; elected as a Whig to the Thirty-third Congress (March 4, 1853–March 3, 1855); declined to be a candidate for renomination in 1854; solicitor of the Raleigh district of the superior court; during the Civil War served in the Confederate Army as a lieutenant in the Fourteenth Regiment of North Carolina State Troops in 1861; was commissioned colonel of the Forty-seventh North Carolina Infantry April 8, 1862; resigned January 5, 1863, upon being elected attorney general of the State of North Carolina; served in that capacity until 1866; unsuccessful candidate for election in 1868 to the Forty-first Congress; elected as a Democrat to the Forty-second Congress (March 4, 1871–March 3, 1873); unsuccessful candidate for reelection in 1872 to the Forty-third Congress; died in Raleigh, Wake County, N. C., on August 14, 1874; interment in the City Cemetery.

ROGERS, Thomas Jones (father of William Findlay Rogers), a Representative from Pennsylvania; born in Waterford, Ireland, in 1781; immigrated to the United States in 1784 with his parents, who settled in Easton, Pa.; learned the printing trade; editor and owner of the Northampton Farmer 1805–1814; elected as a Democrat to the Fifteenth Congress to fill the vacancy caused by the resignation of John Ross; reelected to the Sixteenth, Seventeenth, and Eighteenth Congresses and served from March 3, 1818, to April 20, 1824, when he resigned; trustee of Lafayette College 1826–1832; register and recorder of deeds for Northampton County, Pa., from 1828 to 1830; served as brigadier general in the State militia; United States naval officer at the port of Philadelphia; died in New York City December 7, 1832; interment in the graveyard of the New Market Street Baptist Church, Philadelphia, Pa., reinterment in Glenwood Cemetery in 1851.

ROGERS, Walter Edward, a Representative from Texas; born in Texarkana, Miller County, Ark., July 19, 1908; attended the public schools in McKinney, Tex.; graduated from Austin College, Sherman, Tex., in 1926, and from the law school of the University of Texas at Austin in 1935; was admitted to the bar in 1935 and commenced the practice of law in 1936 in Pampa, Tex.; city attorney of Pampa 1938–1940; district attorney of the thirty-first judicial district of Texas 1943–1947; elected as a Democrat to the Eighty-second and to the four succeeding Congresses (January 3, 1951–January 3, 1961). *Reelected to the Eighty-seventh Congress.*

ROGERS, Will, a Representative from Oklahoma; born on a farm near Bessie, Oklahoma Territory (now Oklahoma), December 12, 1898; attended the public schools, and Southwestern Teachers College, Weatherford, Okla.; was graduated from Central Teachers College, Edmond, Okla., in 1926 and from the University of Oklahoma at Norman in 1930; teacher in the public schools at Bessie, Okla., 1917–1919; principal of the public schools at Bartlesville, Okla., 1919–1923; superintendent of schools at Cheyenne, Okla., 1923–1925, at Rush Springs, Okla., in 1926 and 1927, at Chattanooga, Okla., in 1927 and 1928, and at Moore, Okla., 1928–1932; elected as a Democrat to the Seventy-third and to the four succeeding Congresses (March 4, 1933–January 3, 1943); while serving as a Representative at large was an unsuccessful candidate for nomination in 1941 to fill the vacancy caused by the death of Sam C. Massingale in the Seventh District for the Seventy-seventh Congress; was not a candidate for renomination in 1942; unsuccessful candidate for the Democratic nomination of secretary of state of Oklahoma in 1943; employed by the Department of the Interior 1943–1945; assistant to the Secretary of Agriculture, Washington, D. C., in 1946 and 1947; hearing examiner, Department of Agriculture, since May 1947; resides in Arlington, Va.

ROGERS, Will, Jr., a Representative from California; born in New York City, N. Y., October 20, 1911; attended the grade and high schools at Beverly Hills, Calif., and was graduated from Stanford University, Palo Alto, Calif., in 1935; newspaper publisher; second lieutenant in the Field Artillery, Reserve Officers Training Corps 1935–1940; during World War II enlisted as a private in the United States Army in June 1942; commissioned a second lieutenant of Field Artillery in July 1942; assigned to the Eight Hundred and Ninety-ninth Tank Destroyer Battalion and served until December 1942; elected as a Democrat to the Seventy-eighth Congress and served from January 3, 1943, until his resignation May 23, 1944, to return to the United States Army, serving as a lieutenant in the Eight Hundred and Fourteenth Tank Destroyer Battalion until March 1, 1946; unsuccessful for election to the United States Senate in 1946; resumed newspaper publishing, and is a resident of Culver City, Calif.

ROGERS, William Findlay (son of Thomas Jones Rogers), a Representative from New York; born in Forks Township, near the borough of Easton, Pa., March 1, 1820; moved with his parents to Philadelphia, where he attended the common schools; returned to Easton, Pa., and entered a printing office in 1832; returned to Philadelphia in 1834 and continued working at his trade; established a paper at Honesdale, Pa., in 1840; moved to Buffalo, N. Y., in 1846; was foreman in the office of the Buffalo Daily Courier; established and managed the Buffalo Republic in 1850; member of Company D, Buffalo City Guard, in 1846; served in the Civil War as colonel of the Twenty-first Regiment, New York Volunteers; mustered out in 1863; appointed commissioner of enrollment and afterward provost marshal of the thirty-second district of New York; brevetted brigadier general, United States Volunteers, in 1865 for "faithful and meritorious services"; comptroller of the city of Buffalo in 1867 and mayor in 1869; secretary and treasurer of the park commissioners in 1871; nominated for the State senate in 1878, but declined; elected as a Democrat to the Forty-eighth Congress (March 4, 1883–March 3, 1885); was not a candidate for renomination in 1884; superintendent of the Soldiers and Sailors' Home at Bath, N. Y., from 1887 to 1897; died in Buffalo, N. Y., on December 16, 1899; interment in Forest Lawn Cemetery.

ROGERS, William Nathaniel, a Representative from New Hampshire; born in Sanbornville, Carroll County, N. H., January 10, 1892; attended the public schools, Brewster Free Academy, Wolfeboro, N. H., and Dartmouth College, Hanover, N. H.; was graduated from the law department of the University of Maine at Orono in 1916; was admitted to the bar the same year and practiced in Sanbornville and Rochester, N. H.; member of the State house of representatives in 1917, 1919, and 1921; elected as a Democrat to the Sixty-eighth Congress (March 4, 1923–March 3, 1925); unsuccessful candidate for reelection in 1924 to the Sixty-ninth Congress; resumed the practice of his profession in Concord, N. H.; moderator of the town of Wakefield, N. H., 1928–1945; elected January 5, 1932, to fill the vacancy in the Seventy-second Congress caused by the death of Fletcher Hale; reelected to the Seventy-third and Seventy-fourth Congresses and served from January 5, 1932, to January 3, 1937; was not a candidate for renomination, but was an unsuccessful candidate for election to the United States Senate in 1936; resumed the practice of law in Concord, N. H., until 1943, when he moved to Sanbornville, N. H., and continued the practice of his chosen profession until his death in Wolfeboro, N. H., September 25, 1945; interment in Lovell Lake Cemetery, Sanbornville, N. H.

ROHRBOUGH, Edward Gay, a Representative from West Virginia; born in 1874, near Buckhannon, Upshur County, W. Va.; attended the public schools and West Virginia Wesleyan College at Buckhannon; graduated from Allegheny College, Meadville, Pa., in 1900 and from Harvard University, Cambridge, Mass., in 1906; later studied at the University of Chicago; instructor at West Virginia Wesleyan College and at West Virginia University at Morgantown; taught school in Brookville, Pa., in 1900 and 1901, and at Glenville (W. Va.) State Normal School 1901–1907; vice president of Fairmont (W. Va.) State Teachers College in 1907 and 1908; president of Glenville (W. Va.) State Teachers College 1908–1942; also engaged in banking; during the First World War was chairman of the County Council of Defense and Four-Minute Men; elected as a Republican to the Seventy-eighth Congress (January 3, 1943–January 3, 1945); was an unsuccessful candidate for reelection in 1944 to the Seventy-ninth Congress; again elected in 1946 to the Eightieth Congress (January 3, 1947–January 3, 1949); unsuccessful candidate for reelection in 1948 to the Eighty-first Congress; died in Washington, D. C., December 12, 1956; interment in Stalnaker Cemetery Glenville, W. Va.

ROLLINS, Edward Henry, a Representative and a Senator from New Hampshire; born in Somersworth (Rollinsford), Strafford County, N. H., October 3, 1824; attended the common schools and the academies in Dover, N. H., and South Berwick, Maine; engaged in mercantile pursuits at Concord, N. H.; chairman of the Republican State committee of New Hampshire at its organization and for many succeeding years; member of the State house of representatives 1855–1857 and served the last two years as speaker; chairman of the New Hampshire delegation in the Republican National Convention at Chicago in 1860 which nominated Lincoln and Hamlin; elected as a Republican to the Thirty-seventh, Thirty-eighth, and Thirty-ninth Congresses (March 4, 1861–March 3, 1867); was not a candidate for renomination in 1866; secretary of the Union Pacific Railroad Co. in May 1869 and treasurer in April 1871 and resigned from both positions, having been elected United States Senator; elected as a Republican to the United States Senate and served from March 4, 1877, to March 3, 1883; unsuccessful candidate for reelection; president of the Boston, Concord & Montreal Railroad Co. 1886–1889; founder of the First National Bank of Concord, N. H., and of the banking house of E. H. Rollins & Sons, of Boston, Mass.; died on Isle of Shoals, N. H., July 31, 1889; interment in Blossom Hill Cemetery, Concord, N. H.

ROLLINS, James Sidney, a Representative from Missouri; born in Richmond, Madison County, Ky., April 19, 1812; completed preparatory studies; attended Centre College, Danville, Ky., and was graduated from the University of Indiana at Bloomington in 1830; studied law; was admitted to the bar in 1834 and commenced practice in Columbia, Mo.; served as major in the Black Hawk War; member of the State house of representatives 1838–1840, 1854, and 1867; delegate to the Whig National Convention at Baltimore in 1844; served in the State senate 1846–1848; unsuccessful Whig candidate for Governor in 1848 and 1857; elected as a Conservative to the Thirty-seventh and Thirty-eighth Congresses (March 4, 1861–March 3, 1865); resumed the practice of his profession; Whig delegate to the Philadelphia Union Convention in 1866; was styled "the father of the University of Missouri," and was for twenty years a member of its board of curators; later president of the board from 1869 to 1886, when he resigned; died in Columbia, Boone County, Mo., January 9, 1888; interment in Columbia Cemetery.

ROLPH, Thomas, a Representative from California; born in San Francisco, Calif., January 17, 1885; attended the public schools; at the age of sixteen left Mission High School and started working as an office boy for Williams-Dimond Shipping Co.; later graduated from Humboldt Evening High School; in 1912 founded the Rolph-Mills & Co., a building materials sales agency, which he headed until his death; elected as a Republican to the Seventy-seventh and Seventy-eighth Congresses (January 3, 1941–January 3, 1945); unsuccessful candidate for reelection in 1944 to the Seventy-ninth Congress; returned to his building material sales agency; died in San Francisco, Calif., May 10, 1956; interment in Cypress Lawn Memorial Park, Colma, San Mateo County, Calif.

ROMAN, James Dixon, a Representative from Maryland; born in Chester County, Pa., August 11, 1809; attended the common schools and a private school at West Nottingham (now Nottingham); moved to Cecil County, Md.; studied law in Frederick, Md.; was admitted to the bar in 1834 and commenced practice in Hagerstown, Md.; member of the State senate in

1847; elected as a Whig to the Thirtieth Congress (March 4, 1847–March 3, 1849); presidential elector on the Whig ticket of Taylor and Fillmore in 1848 and on the Democratic ticket of Buchanan and Breckinridge in 1856; again resumed the practice of law in Hagerstown; president of the Old Hagerstown Bank from 1851 until his death; member of the peace convention held in Washington, D. C., in 1861 in an effort to devise means to prevent the impending war; died near Hagerstown, Washington County, Md., January 19, 1867; interment in Rose Hill Cemetery.

ROMEIS, Jacob, a Representative from Ohio; born in Weisenbach, Bavaria, Germany, December 1, 1835; attended the village schools; immigrated in 1847 to the United States with his parents, who settled in Erie County, N. Y., and attended the public and select schools of Buffalo, N. Y.; engaged in the shipping business and railroading; moved to Toledo, Ohio, in 1856; elected to the board of aldermen of the city of Toledo in 1874; reelected in 1876 and served as president of the board in 1877; mayor of Toledo 1879–1885; elected as a Republican to the Forty-ninth and Fiftieth Congresses (March 4, 1885–March 3, 1889); unsuccessful candidate for reelection in 1888 to the Fifty-first Congress; retired from public life; engaged in fruit growing near Toledo; died in Toledo, Lucas County, Ohio, March 8, 1904; interment in Woodlawn Cemetery.

ROMERO, Trinidad, a Delegate from the Territory of New Mexico; born in Santa Fe, Santa Fe County (then a part of the Republic of Mexico), N. Mex., June 15, 1835; educated by private tutors; engaged in merchandising, freighting with ox teams from Kansas City to Santa Fe, and later in stock raising; member of the Territorial house of representatives in 1863; probate judge of San Miguel County, N. Mex., in 1869 and 1870; elected as a Republican to the Forty-fifth Congress (March 4, 1877–March 3, 1879); was not a candidate for renomination in 1878; appointed United States marshal by President Harrison and served from November 13, 1889, to May 30, 1893; engaged in mercantile pursuits and stock raising on his ranch near Wagon Mound, N. Mex.; died in Las Vegas, San Miguel County, N. Mex., August 28, 1918; interment in Calvary Cemetery.

ROMJUE, Milton Andrew, a Representative from Missouri; born in Love Lake, Macon County, Mo., December 5, 1874; attended the public schools and the Kirksville State Normal School; was graduated from the law department of the University of Missouri at Columbia in 1904; was admitted to the bar the same year and commenced practice in Macon, Macon County, Mo.; city attorney of Higbee, Randolph County, Mo., in 1904 and 1905; judge of the Macon County probate court 1907–1915; delegate to the Democratic State conventions 1920–1940; delegate to the Democratic National Convention in 1928; elected as a Democrat to the Sixty-fifth and Sixty-sixth Congresses (March 4, 1917–March 3, 1921); member of the congressional committee to meet President Wilson on his return in 1919 from the peace conference at Paris; unsuccessful candidate for reelection in 1920 to the Sixty-seventh Congress; elected to the Sixty-eighth and to the nine succeeding Congresses (March 4, 1923–January 3, 1943); unsuccessful candidate for reelection in 1942 to the Seventy-eighth Congress; resumed the practice of law and also engaged in farming and stock-raising; is a resident of Macon, Mo.

ROMULO, Carlos Peña, a Resident Commissioner from the Commonwealth of the Philippines; born in Camiling, Tarlac, Philippine Islands, January 14, 1901; attended the Camiling and Tarlac schools; was graduated from the University of the Philippines at Manila in 1918, from Columbia University at New York City, N. Y., in 1921, and from Notre Dame (Ind.) University in 1935; member of the faculty of the University of the Philippines 1923–1928; author, editor, and publisher at Manila, Philippine Islands, 1922–1941; also interested in a broadcasting corporation; secretary to Manuel L. Quezon, president of the Philippine Senate, in 1922; member of the independence missions to the United States in 1921, 1924, 1928, 1929, 1933, and 1937; member of the Board of Regents of the University of the Philippines 1929–1941; secretary of Information and Public Relations and member of the President's war cabinet in 1943 and 1944; member of the Filipino Rehabilitation Commission 1944–1946; secretary of public instruction from October 1944 to February 1945; aide-de-camp to Gen. Douglas MacArthur at Bataan, Corregidor, and Australia; received the Silver Star, Purple Heart with two Oak Leaf Clusters, and Distinguished Service Star of the Philippines; promoted to brigadier general in the Philippine Army in September 1944; appointed Resident Commissioner to the United States August 10, 1944, to fill the vacancy caused by the resignation of Joaquin M. Elizalde and served until July 4, 1946, when the office of Resident Commissioner terminated; appointed by President Roxas on July 9, 1946, as permanent delegate of the Republic of the Philippines to the United Nations, and is chief delegate of the Philippines to the Far Eastern Commission; Ambassador to the United States in 1952 and 1953 and 1955–; secretary of foreign affairs 1949–1951; president of the United Nations General Assembly in 1949 and 1950, and of United Nations Security Council in 1957; is a resident of Manila, Philippines.

ROONEY, John James, a Representative from New York; born in Brooklyn, N. Y., November 29, 1903; attended the parochial schools and St. Francis Preparatory School and College; was graduated from the law department of Fordham University, New York, N. Y., in 1925; was admitted to the bar in 1926 and commenced practice in Brooklyn, N. Y.; served as assistant district attorney in Brooklyn 1940–1944; elected as a Democrat to the Seventy-eighth Congress to fill the vacancy caused by the death of Thomas H. Cullen; reelected to the Seventy-ninth and to the seven succeeding Congresses and served from June 6, 1944, to January 3, 1961. *Reelected to the Eighty-seventh Congress.*

ROOSEVELT, Franklin Delano, Jr. (son of President Franklin D. Roosevelt and brother of James Roosevelt), a Representative from New York; born in Campobello, New Brunswick, Canada, August 17, 1914; graduated from Groton School, Harvard University in 1937, and the University of Virginia Law School at Charlottesville in 1940; was admitted to the bar in 1942; was called from the Naval Reserve on March 13, 1941, to active duty as an ensign in the United States Navy; service began on the North Atlantic, Murmansk and Caribbean runs, and then the North African invasion and the Sicilian campaign; in 1944 was commissioned captain of destroyer escort *Ulvert M. Moore*, and took part in the Philippine, Okinawa, and Iwo Jima campaigns; discharged from active duty in January 1946; awarded the Purple Heart Medal for injuries, the Silver Star for bravery in the Sicilian campaign, the Legion of Merit Combat V for sinking a Japanese submarine during the Philippine campaign, and the Secretary of Navy commendation with ribbon for action during the invasion of Africa; member of a law firm in New York City since 1946; vice president of President Truman's Committee on Civil Rights in 1947 and 1948; chairman of mayor's committee on unity in New York City in 1948 and 1949; delegate to Democratic National Conventions in 1952 and 1956; elected as a candidate of the Liberal and Four Freedoms parties to the Eighty-first Congress to fill the vacancy caused by the death of Sol Bloom; reelected as a Democrat to the Eighty-second and Eighty-third Congresses and served from May 17, 1949, to January 3,

1955; was not a candidate for renomination in 1954, but was unsuccessful for the Democratic gubernatorial nomination; unsuccessful candidate for election for attorney general of New York in 1954; resumed the practice of law in New York City; engaged in the automobile import business since 1957; resides in New York City, N. Y.

ROOSEVELT, James (son of President Franklin D. Roosevelt and brother of Franklin D. Roosevelt, Jr.), a Representative from California; born in New York City, N. Y., December 23, 1907; attended schools in New York and St. Albans School of Washington, D. C.; was graduated from Groton School in 1926 and from Harvard University, Cambridge, Mass., in 1930; began business career in 1930 as an insurance broker in Boston, Mass.; organized Roosevelt & Sargent, Inc., and served as president until January 1937; secretary to father, President Franklin D. Roosevelt, in 1937 and 1938; motion-picture industry November 1938–November 1940; went on active duty as a captain in the United States Marine Corps in November 1940; promoted to colonel April 13, 1944, and served in the Pacific Theater, including the Solomon and Gilbert Islands, the second battle at Midway Island and at Kiska in the Aleutian Islands; released from active duty in August 1945; brigadier general U.S. Marine Corps Reserve, retired; awarded the Navy Cross and Silver Star; rejoined Roosevelt & Sargent, Inc., as executive vice president and established an office in Los Angeles, Calif., in June 1946; served as chairman of the board, Roosevelt & Haines, Inc.; member of the board of trustees of American Medical Center, Denver, Colo.; was an unsuccessful Democratic candidate for Governor of California in 1950; delegate to the Democratic National Conventions in 1948 and 1952; elected as a Democrat to the Eighty-fourth, Eighty-fifth, and Eighty-sixth Congresses (January 3, 1955–January 3, 1961). *Reelected to the Eighty-seventh Congress.*

ROOSEVELT, James I. (uncle of Robert Barnwell Roosevelt), a Representative from New York; born in New York City December 14, 1795; was graduated from Columbia College, New York City, in 1815; studied law; was admitted to the bar in 1818 and commenced practice in New York City; councilman; member of the State assembly in 1835 and 1840; elected as a Democrat to the Twenty-seventh Congress (March 4, 1841–March 3, 1843); declined to be a candidate for renomination in 1842 to the Twenty-eighth Congress; studied foreign law in the courts of England, Holland, and France; justice of the supreme court of the State of New York 1851–1859; served one term as ex officio judge of the State court of appeals in 1859; appointed United States district attorney for southern New York by President Buchanan and served in 1860 and 1861; engaged in agricultural pursuits; died in New York City on April 5, 1875; interment in Greenwood Cemetery, Brooklyn, N. Y.

ROOSEVELT, Robert Barnwell (nephew of James I. Roosevelt and uncle of Theodore Roosevelt), a Representative from New York; born in New York City August 7, 1829; completed preparatory studies; studied law; was admitted to the bar in 1850 and commenced practice in New York City; fish commissioner of the State of New York 1868–1888; for several years edited the New York Citizen; elected as a Democrat to the Forty-second Congress (March 4, 1871–March 3, 1873); appointed by President Cleveland as Minister to The Hague and served from 1888 to 1890; treasurer of the Democratic National Committee in 1892; member of the Board of Aldermen of New York City; served as trustee representing the city of New York for the New York and Brooklyn Bridge from 1879 to 1882; died in Sayville, Suffolk County, N. Y., on June 14, 1906; interment in Greenwood Cemetery, Brooklyn, N. Y.

ROOSEVELT, Theodore (great-great-grandson of Archibald Bulloch and nephew of Robert Barnwell Roosevelt), a Vice President and a President of the United States; born in New York City October 27, 1858; attended the public schools; was graduated from Harvard University in 1880; studied law; traveled abroad; member of the New York State Assembly 1882–1884; delegate to the Republican National Convention at Chicago in 1884; moved to North Dakota and lived on his ranch; returned to New York City in 1886; appointed by President Harrison a member of the United States Civil Service Commission in 1889 and served until 1895, when he resigned to become president of the New York Board of Police Commissioners; resigned this position upon his appointment by President McKinley as Assistant Secretary of the Navy in April 1897 and served until 1898, when he resigned to enter the war with Spain; during the war organized the First Regiment, United States Volunteer Cavalry, popularly known as Roosevelt's Rough Riders; appointed lieutenant colonel and later colonel of this regiment; Governor of New York in 1899 and 1900; elected Vice President of the United States on the Republican ticket headed by William McKinley in 1900 and was inaugurated March 4, 1901; upon the death of President McKinley on September 14, 1901, became President of the United States and served until March 3, 1905; elected President of the United States on the Republican ticket with Charles W. Fairbanks as Vice President in 1904; was inaugurated March 4, 1905, and served until March 3, 1909; organized a scientific expedition to South Africa, outfitted by the Smithsonian Institution, to gather natural-history materials for the new United States National Museum at Washington, D. C., in 1910; special ambassador of the United States at the funeral of King Edward VII of England in 1910; unsuccessful candidate of the Progressive Party for President of the United States in 1912; headed an exploring party to South America in 1914; was again nominated as a candidate for the Presidency of the United States by the Progressive Party Convention at Chicago in 1916, but declined; engaged in literary pursuits; died at Oyster Bay, Nassau County, N. Y., January 6, 1919; interment in Young's Memorial Cemetery.

ROOT, Elihu, a Senator from New York; born in Clinton, Oneida County, N. Y., February 15, 1845; attended the common schools; was graduated from Hamilton College, Clinton, N. Y., in 1864; taught in the Rome (N. Y.) Academy in 1865; was graduated from the law school of the University of the City of New York in 1867; was admitted to the bar in the same year and commenced practice in the city of New York; appointed United States attorney for the southern district of New York by President Arthur in March 1883, and served until July 1885; delegate to the State constitutional convention in 1894; appointed Secretary of War by President McKinley August 1, 1899, and retired January 31, 1904; member of the Alaskan Boundary Tribunal which sat in London in 1903; appointed Secretary of State by President Theodore Roosevelt July 7, 1905, and served until January 26, 1909; elected as a Republican to the United States Senate and served from March 4, 1909, to March 3, 1915; declined to be a candidate for reelection; resumed the practice of law in New York City; author; chairman of the Republican National Conventions in 1904 and 1912; chairman of the Republican State conventions in 1908, 1910, 1913, 1914, 1916, 1920, and 1922; counsel for the United States in the North Atlantic fisheries arbitration at The Hague in 1910; member of the Permanent Court of Arbitration at The Hague in 1910; president of the Carnegie Endowment for International Peace 1910–1925; awarded the Nobel Peace Prize for 1912, the Roosevelt Medal for Administration of Public Office in 1924, and the Woodrow Wilson Foundation Medal and Prize in 1926; president of The Hague Tribunal of Arbitration between Great Britain, France, Spain, and Portugal, concerning church property, in

1913; served as trustee of Hamilton College and chairman of the board of trustees of Carnegie Institution of Washington, D. C.; president of the State constitutional convention in 1915; appointed by President Wilson to be Ambassador Extraordinary at the head of a special diplomatic mission from the United States to Russia in 1917; represented the United States as Commissioner Plenipotentiary to the Conference on Limitation of Armament at Washington, D. C., in 1921 and 1922; member of the Committee of International Jurists, which, on invitation of the Council of the League of Nations, reported the plan for a new Permanent Court of International Justice in 1921; president of the New York college of presidential electors in 1925; died in New York City, N. Y., February 7, 1937; interment in Hamilton College Cemetery, Clinton, N. Y.

ROOT, Erastus, a Representative from New York; born in Hebron, Conn., March 16, 1773; was graduated from Dartmouth College, Hanover, N. H., in 1793; taught school for several years; studied law; was admitted to the bar in 1796 and commenced practice in Delhi, N. Y.; member of the State assembly 1798–1802; elected as a Democrat to the Eighth Congress (March 4, 1803–March 3, 1805); resumed the practice of law; again elected to the Eleventh Congress (March 4, 1809–March 3, 1811); appointed in 1811 a member of the commission to revise and codify the laws of New York State; served in the State Senate 1812–1815; successfully contested the election of John Adams to the Fourteenth Congress and served from December 26, 1815, to March 3, 1817; again a member of the State assembly 1818–1822; member of the State constitutional convention of 1821; Lieutenant Governor of New York State 1822–1824; unsuccessful candidate for reelection in 1824; again became a member of the State assembly 1826–1828, and in 1830, and served as speaker during the terms in 1827 and 1828; again elected to the Twenty-second Congress (March 4, 1831–March 3, 1833); unsuccessful Whig candidate for election in 1838 to the Twenty-sixth Congress; major general of militia; again served in the State senate 1840–1844; delegate to the Whig State convention at Utica in 1846; died in New York City December 24, 1846; interment in the Old (High Street) Cemetery, Delhi, N. Y.

ROOT, Jesse, a Delegate from Connecticut; born in Coventry, Tolland County, Conn., December 28, 1736; was graduated from Princeton College in 1756; studied theology in Andover; was ordained as a minister and preached from 1758 to 1763; studied law; was admitted to the bar in 1763 and commenced practice in Hartford, Conn.; captain, lieutenant colonel, and adjutant general in the Revolutionary Army; Member of the Continental Congress 1778–1783; State's attorney 1785–1789; appointed a judge of the superior court in 1789 and served as chief justice from 1796 to 1807, when he resigned; member of the State house of representatives 1807–1809; author of legal reports; presidential elector in 1808; delegate to the State constitutional convention in 1818; died in Coventry, Conn., March 29, 1822; interment in Nathan Hale Cemetery, South Coventry, Tolland County, Conn.

ROOT, Joseph Mosley, a Representative from Ohio; born in Brutus, Cayuga County, N. Y., October 7, 1807; pursued classical studies; studied law in Auburn, N. Y.; moved to Ohio in 1829; was admitted to the bar in 1830 and commenced practice in Norwalk, Huron County, Ohio; elected prosecuting attorney of Huron County in 1837; member of the State senate in 1840 and 1841; elected as a Whig to the Twenty-ninth, Thirtieth, and Thirty-first Congresses (March 4, 1845–March 3, 1851); assisted in the organization of the Republican Party; presidential elector on the Republican ticket of Lincoln and Hamlin in

1860; appointed United States attorney for the northern district of Ohio in 1861; again a member of the State Senate in 1869; Democratic delegate to the State constitutional convention in 1873; unsuccessful Democratic candidate for probate judge of Erie County in 1875; died in Sandusky, Erie County, Ohio, April 7, 1879; interment in Oakland Cemetery.

ROOTS, Logan Holt, a Representative from Arkansas; born near Tamaroa, Perry County, Ill., March 26, 1841: completed preparatory studies and was graduated from the Illinois State Normal University in 1862; assisted in recruiting the Eighty-first Illinois Volunteers; served in various responsible positions in the Army until the close of the Civil War; settled in Arkansas and engaged in planting and trading; upon the readmission of Arkansas to representation was elected as a Republican to the Fortieth Congress; reelected to the Forty-first Congress and served from June 22, 1868, to March 3, 1871; unsuccessful candidate for reelection in 1870 to the Forty-second Congress; engaged in banking and served as president of the First National Bank of Little Rock, Ark., until his death in that city May 30, 1893; interment in Oaklawn Cemetery.

ROSE, John Marshall, a Representative from Pennsylvania; born in Johnstown, Cambria County, Pa., on May 18, 1856; attended the public schools; was graduated from Washington and Jefferson College, Washington, Pa., in 1880; taught school; studied law; was admitted to the bar in 1884 and commenced practice in Johnstown; member of the State house of representatives in 1889; declined reelection; elected as a Republican to the Sixty-fifth, Sixty-sixth, and Sixty-seventh Congresses (March 4, 1917–March 3, 1923); declined to be a candidate for renomination in 1922; died in Washington, D. C., April 22, 1923; interment in Grandview Cemetery, Johnstown, Pa.

ROSE, Robert Lawson (son of Robert Selden Rose and son-in-law of Nathaniel Allen), a Representative from New York; born in Geneva, N. Y., October 12, 1804; received a limited schooling; moved to Allens Hill, N. Y., and engaged in agricultural pursuits; held several local offices; elected as a Whig to the Thirtieth and Thirty-first Congresses (March 4, 1847–March 3, 1851); resumed agricultural pursuits; returned to Geneva, Ontario County, N. Y.; subsequently moved to Pleasant Grove, near Funkstown, Washington County, Md., in 1868 and engaged in the manufacture of paper until his death there March 14, 1877; interment in Rose Hill Cemetery, Hagerstown, Washington County, Md.

ROSE, Robert Selden (father of Robert Lawson Rose), a Representative from New York; born in Amherst County, Va., February 24, 1774; attended the common schools; moved to Seneca County, N. Y., in 1803 and settled at Fayette, near Geneva, N. Y.; engaged in agricultural pursuits; member of the State assembly in 1811, 1820, and 1821; member of the State constitutional convention in 1821 at Albany; elected to the Eighteenth and Nineteenth Congresses (March 4, 1823–March 3, 1827); elected to the Twenty-first Congress (March 4, 1829–March 3, 1831); later affiliated with the Whig Party; again resumed agricultural pursuits; died in Waterloo, Seneca County, N. Y., while attending a session of the circuit court, on Novmber 24, 1835; interment in the Old Pulteney Street Cemetery; reinterment in Glenwood Cemetery, Geneva, Ontario County, N. Y.

ROSECRANS, William Starke, a Representative from California; born in Kingston, Ross County, Ohio, September 6, 1819; completed preparatory studies; was appointed to the United States Military Academy at West Point in 1838 and graduated in 1842; brevetted second lieutenant, United States Corps of Engineers, July 1, 1842; second lieutenant April 3, 1843; assistant professor of engineering at the United States Military Academy 1843–1847; superintendent of repairs at Fort Adams, Mass., and in charge of various Government surveys and improvements 1847–1853; brevetted first lieutenant March 3, 1853; resigned from the Army April 1, 1854; engaged as an architect and civil engineer, with residence in Cincinnati; president of the Coal River Navigation Co., Kanawha County, Va. (now West Virginia), in 1856; organized the Preston Coal Oil Co. in 1857 and engaged in the manufacture of kerosene; during the Civil War reentered the service on June 7, 1861, as colonel of the Twenty-third Regiment, Ohio Volunteer Infantry; commissioned brigadier general, United States Army, May 16, 1861; major general, United States Volunteers, March 21, 1862; by resolution of March 3, 1863, received the thanks of Congress "for distinguished gallantry and good conduct at the Battle of Murfreesboro, Tenn."; brevetted major general, United States Army, March 13, 1865, "for gallant and distinguished services at the Battle of Stone River, Tenn."; honorably mustered out of Volunteers January 15, 1866; resigned from the United States Army March 28, 1867; moved to California and settled in Los Angeles; declined the offer of the directorship of the branch mint in 1867 and the Democratic nomination for Governor of California; United States Minister to Mexico in 1868 and 1869; again engaged in civil engineering; president of the Safety Powder Co., Los Angeles, Calif., in 1875; elected as a Democrat to the Forty-seventh and Forty-eighth Congresses (March 4, 1881–March 3, 1885); was not a candidate for renomination in 1884; regent of the State university in 1884 and 1885; Register of the Treasury 1885–1893; reappointed brigadier general on the retired list, United States Army (act of Congress, February 27, 1889), and retired March 1, 1889; died near Redondo, Los Angeles County, Calif., March 11, 1898; interment in Rosedale Cemetery, Los Angeles, Calif.; reinterment in the Arlington National Cemetery, Fort Myer, Va., May 17, 1902.

ROSENBLOOM, Benjamin Louis, a Representative from West Virginia; born in Braddock, Allegheny County, Pa., June 3, 1880; attended the public schools; was graduated from the North Braddock High School; attended the University of West Virginia at Morgantown; studied law; was admitted to the bar in 1904 and commenced practice in Wheeling, Ohio County, W. Va., in 1905; member of the State senate 1914–1918; elected as a Republican to the Sixty-seventh and Sixty-eighth Congresses (March 4, 1921–March 3, 1925); was not a candidate for renomination in 1924, having become a candidate for the United States Senate; unsuccessful candidate for the Republican nomination for United States Senator in 1924; again resumed the practice of his profession and is a resident of Wheeling, W. Va.

ROSIER, Joseph, a Senator from West Virginia; born in Wilsonburg, Harrison County, W. Va., January 24, 1870; attended the public schools; was graduated from Salem (W. Va.) College in 1895; teacher of the village school at Bristol, W. Va., in 1890; principal of the public schools of Salem, W. Va., in 1891 and 1892; superintendent of schools of Harrison County, W. Va., in 1893 and 1894; member of the faculty of Salem (W. Va.) College 1894–1896; teacher in the State normal school at Glenville, W. Va., in 1896 and 1897; member of the faculty of the State Teachers' College, Fairmont, W. Va., 1897–1900; superintendent of schools of Fairmont, W. Va., 1900–1915; president of Fairmont State College, Fairmont, W. Va., 1915–1945 and then president emeritus; during the First World War served as county food administrator in 1917 and 1918; consultant on education for the Works Progress Administration 1933–1937; appointed as a Democrat to the United States Senate to fill the vacancy caused by the resignation of Matthew M. Neely and served from January 13, 1941, to November 17, 1942, when a duly elected successor qualified; unsuccessful candidate for election to the unexpired term; resumed his former pursuits; elected to the State house of delegates in 1946 and served in the biennial session of 1947; former member of the West Virginia State Board of Education; died in Fairmont, W. Va., October 7, 1951; interment in I. O. O. F. Cemetery, Salem, W. Va.

ROSS, David, a Delegate from Maryland; born in Prince Georges County, Md., February 12, 1755; appointed by General Washington major of Grayson's additional Continental regiment January 1, 1777, and served until December 20, 1777, when he resigned; upon the death of his father devoted his time to the management of the large estate descending to the family; studied law; was admitted to the bar in 1783 and commenced the practice of his profession in Frederick County, Md.; Member of the Continental Congress 1786–1788; died in Frederick County, Md., in 1800.

ROSS, Edmund Gibson, a Senator from Kansas; born in Ashland, Ashland County, Ohio, December 7, 1826; received an academic education; learned the printing trade in Sandusky, Ohio; moved to Milwaukee, Wis., in 1849 and was connected with the Milwaukee Sentinel; moved to Topeka, Kans., in 1856; published the Topeka Tribune 1856–1858 and established the Kansas State Record in 1859; member of the State constitutional convention 1859–1861; promoter and director of the Santa Fe Railroad and suggested the name Atchison, Topeka & Santa Fe Railway; during the Civil War entered the Union Army as a private in 1862; promoted to captain of Company E, Eleventh Regiment, Kansas Volunteer Infantry, and was mustered out as major in 1865; editor of the Kansas Tribune in 1865 and 1866; appointed and subsequently elected as a Republican to the United States Senate to fill the vacancy caused by the death of James H. Lane and served from July 19, 1866, to March 3, 1871; unsuccessful candidate for reelection; affiliated with the Democratic Party; publisher of several newspapers 1871–1882 and 1890–1893; delegate to the Democratic National Convention at St. Louis in 1876; unsuccessful candidate for Governor in 1880; moved to Albuquerque, N. Mex., in 1882; appointed Governor of the Territory of New Mexico by President Cleveland in May 1885 and served four years; studied law; was admitted to the bar in 1889 and commenced practice in Albuquerque; secretary of the Bureau of Immigration 1894–1896; resumed the practice of his profession; died in Albuquerque, Bernalillo County, N. Mex., May 8, 1907; interment in Fairview Cemetery.

ROSS, George, a Delegate from Pennsylvania; born in New Castle, Del., May 10, 1730; completed preparatory studies; studied law; was admitted to the bar in 1750 and commenced practice in Lancaster, Pa.; member of the colonial assembly 1768–1776; delegate to the State convention in 1774; Member of the Continental Congress 1774–1777; a signer of the Declaration of Independence; appointed judge of the court of admiralty for Pennsylvania in April 1779 and served in that capacity until his death near Philadelphia, Pa., July 14, 1779; interment in Christ Churchyard.

ROSS, Henry Howard, a Representative from New York; born in Essex, Essex County, N. Y., May 9, 1790; instructed by private tutors; was graduated from Columbia College, New York City, in 1808; studied law; was admitted to the bar and commenced practice in Essex, N. Y.; during the War of 1812 served as second lieutenant and adjutant in the Thirty-seventh Infantry Regiment, New York State Militia, at the Battle of Boquet River, Willsboro, N. Y., and at the Battle of Plattsburg, N. Y.; subsequently rose to the rank of major general; elected as a Whig to the Nineteenth Congress (March 4, 1825–March 3, 1827); resumed the practice of law in Essex, N. Y.; county judge of Essex County in 1847 and 1848; presidential elector on the Whig ticket of Taylor and Fillmore in 1848; resumed the practice of his profession; died in Essex, N. Y., September 14, 1862; interment in a vault on his family place, "Hickory Hill," Essex, N. Y.

ROSS, James, a Senator from Pennsylvania; born near Delta, Peachbottom Township, York County, Pa., July 12, 1762; attended a classical school near Delta and later became an instructor of Latin in what is now known as Washington and Jefferson College, Washington, Pa.; studied law; was admitted to the bar in 1784 and commenced practice in Washington, Washington County, Pa.; delegate to the State constitutional convention in 1789 and 1790; elected as a Federalist to the United States Senate to fill the vacancy caused by the Senate declaring the election of Albert Gallatin void on the ground that he had not been a citizen for the number of years prescribed by the Constitution; reelected and served from April 24, 1794, to March 3, 1803; moved to Pittsburgh in 1795; unsuccessful candidate for Governor of Pennsylvania in 1799, 1801, and 1808; resumed the practice of law; died in Pittsburgh, Pa., November 27, 1847; interment in Allegheny Cemetery.

ROSS, John (father of Thomas Ross), a Representative from Pennsylvania; born in Solebury, Bucks County, Pa., February 24, 1770; studied law in West Chester, Pa.; was admitted to the bar in 1792 and engaged in practice in Easton, Pa.; member of the State house of representatives in 1800; clerk of the orphans' court and recorder 1800–1803; county register 1800–1809; burgess of Easton in 1804; elected to the Eleventh Congress (March 4, 1809–March 3, 1811); elected to the Fourteenth and Fifteenth Congresses and served from March 4, 1815, to February 24, 1818, when he resigned to become president judge of the seventh judicial district of the State; was transferred to the State supreme bench in 1830 and served until his death in Easton, Northampton County, Pa., January 31, 1834; interment in a private cemetery on the family estate, "Ross Common," Ross Township, Pa.

ROSS, Jonathan, a Senator from Vermont; born in Waterford, Caledonia County, Vt., April 30, 1826; attended the public schools and St. Johnsbury (Vt.) Academy; was graduated from Dartmouth College, Hanover, N. H., in 1851; principal of the Chelsea and Craftsbury Academies 1851–1856; studied law; was admitted to the bar in January 1856 and practiced in St. Johnsbury until 1870; State's attorney for Caledonia County in 1862 and 1863; appointed a member of the State board of education in 1866 and served until 1870; member of the State house of representatives 1865–1867; served in the State senate in 1870; judge of the supreme court of Vermont 1870–1890; chief justice of the State of Vermont 1890–1899; appointed as a Republican to the United States Senate to fill the vacancy caused by the death of Justin S. Morrill and served from January 11, 1899, to October 18, 1900, when a successor was elected; was not an active candidate for reelection in 1900, although a recipient of some votes; chairman of the board of State railroad commissioners 1900–1902; died in St. Johnsbury, Vt., February 23, 1905; interment in Mount Pleasant Cemetery.

ROSS, Lewis Winans, a Representative from Illinois; born near Seneca Falls, Seneca County, N. Y., December 8, 1812; moved to Illinois and settled in Lewistown; completed preparatory studies and attended Illinois College at Jacksonville in 1837; studied law; was admitted to the bar in 1839 and commenced practice in Lewistown, Ill.; member of the State house of representatives in 1840, 1841, 1844, and 1845; presidential elector on the Democratic ticket of Cass and Butler in 1848; member of the State constitutional conventions in 1861 and 1870; elected as a Democrat to the Thirty-eighth, Thirty-ninth, and Fortieth Congresses (March 4, 1863–March 3, 1869); was not a candidate for renomination in 1868; resumed the practice of law; died in Lewistown, Ill., October 20, 1895; interment in Oak Hill Cemetery.

ROSS, Miles, a Representative from New Jersey; born in Raritan Township, Middlesex County, N. J., April 30, 1827; received a practical English training; engaged with his father in the transportation of freight by water and in the coal business; one of the chosen freeholders of New Brunswick, N. J., 1859–1864; member of the State house of assembly in 1863 and 1864; director of several banks; member of the board of street commissioners in 1865 and 1866; mayor of New Brunswick 1867–1869; elected as a Democrat to the Forty-fourth and to the three succeeding Congresses (March 4, 1875–March 3, 1883); unsuccessful candidate for reelection in 1882 to the Forty-eighth Congress; delegate at large to the Democratic National Conventions in 1884, 1888, and 1892; engaged in the wholesale and retail coal business; died in New Brunswick, Middlesex County, N. J., on February 22, 1903; interment in Elmwood Cemetery.

ROSS, Robert Tripp, a Representative from New York; born in Washington, Beaufort County, N. C., June 4, 1903; attended the public schools; moved to New York City in 1929 and engaged as a druggist; for seventeen years associated with a large drug firm in managerial and executive positions; elected as a Republican to the Eightieth Congress (January 3, 1947–January 3, 1949); unsuccessful candidate for reelection in 1948 to the Eighty-first Congress; engaged in the manufacture of clothing and athletic equipment; unsuccessful candidate for election in 1950 to the Eighty-second Congress; subsequently elected to the Eighty-second Congress at a special election to fill the vacancy caused by the resignation of T. Vincent Quinn and served from February 19, 1952, to January 3, 1953; unsuccessful candidate for reelection in 1952 to the Eighty-third Congress; Deputy Assistant Secretary of Defense for Legislative Affairs from March 1954 to March 1956; Assistant Secretary of Defense for Legislative and Public Affairs from March 1956 to March 1957; assistant borough works commissioner, Queens, N. Y., from March 1957 to January 1958; is a resident of Jackson Heights, N. Y.

ROSS, Sobieski, a Representative from Pennsylvania; born in Coudersport, Potter County, Pa., May 16, 1828; attended the common schools and Coudersport Academy; engaged in civil engineering and the real-estate business; also interested in agricultural pursuits; appointed associate judge in 1852; elected as a Republican to the Forty-third and Forty-fourth Congresses (March 4, 1873–March 3, 1877); declined to be a candidate for renomination in 1876; resumed the real-estate business; died in Coudersport, Pa., October 24, 1877; interment in Eulalia Cemetery.

ROSS, Thomas (son of John Ross), a Representative from Pennsylvania; born in Easton, Northampton County, Pa., December 1, 1806; attended the Doylestown, Pa., schools; was graduated from Princeton College in 1823; studied law; was admitted to the bar in 1829 and commenced practice in Doylestown, Pa.; appointed deputy attorney general of the State for Bucks County in 1829; frequently a candidate of the Democratic Party and also affiliated with the Anti-Masonic Party; elected as a Democrat to the Thirty-first and Thirty-second Congresses (March 4, 1849–March 3, 1853); resumed the practice of law in Doylestown, Bucks County, Pa.; died July 7, 1865; interment in Doylestown Cemetery.

ROSS, Thomas Randolph, a Representative from Ohio; born in New Garden Township, Chester County, Pa., October 26, 1788; completed preparatory studies; studied law; was admitted to the bar and began practice in Lebanon, Warren County, Ohio, in 1810; elected as a Democrat to the Sixteenth, Seventeenth, and Eighteenth Congresses (March 4, 1819–March 3, 1825); unsuccessful candidate for reelection in 1824 to the Nineteenth Congress; resumed the practice of law in Lebanon; lost his eyesight in 1866; died on his farm near Lebanon, Ohio, June 28, 1869; interment in Lebanon Cemetery.

ROSSDALE, Albert Berger, a Representative from New York; born in New York City October 23, 1878; attended the public schools; clerk in the New York post office 1900–1910; president of the New York Federation of Post Office Clerks in 1906 and 1907 and vice president of the national organization in 1908 and 1909; member of the Hudson-Fulton Celebration Commission in 1908 and 1909; engaged in the wholesale jewelry business in 1910; elected as a Republican to the Sixty-seventh Congress (March 4, 1921–March 3, 1923); unsuccessful candidate for reelection in 1922 to the Sixty-eighth Congress and for election in 1924 to the Sixty-ninth Congress; delegate to the Republican State conventions in 1922 and 1924; delegate to the Republican National Convention at Cleveland in 1924; again engaged in the wholesale jewelry business; moved to Sandy Hook, Conn., in 1939 and to Bronxville, N. Y., in 1946, where he now resides.

ROSTENKOWSKI, Daniel David (Dan), a Representative from Illinois; born in Chicago, Ill., January 2, 1928; graduated from St. John's Military Academy in 1946 and from Loyola University in 1951; served in Korea with the United States Infantry 1946–1948; served in the State house of representatives in the Sixty-eighth general assembly in 1952; member of the State senate from the thirty-third senatorial district in the sixty-ninth and seventieth general assemblies 1954–1956; elected as a Democrat to the Eighty-sixth Congress (January 3, 1959–January 3, 1961). *Reelected to the Eighty-seventh Congress.*

ROTHERMEL, John Hoover, a Representative from Pennsylvania; born in Richmond Township, Berks County, Pa., March 7, 1856; attended the common schools and pursued an academic course at Brunner's Business College, Reading, Pa.; taught school in Blandon Township 1876–1881; served as a member of the faculty at Brunner's Scientific Academy; studied law; was admitted to the bar in 1881 and commenced practice in Reading, Pa.; assistant district attorney of Reading, Pa., 1886–1889; county solicitor of Berks County 1895–1898; unsuccessful candidate for judge of the court of common pleas in 1899; elected as a Democrat to the Sixtieth and to the three succeeding Congresses (March 4, 1907–March 3, 1915); unsuccessful candidate for reelection in 1914; resumed the practice of law; died in Reading, Pa., in August 1922; interment in the Charles Evans Cemetery.

ROTHWELL, Gideon Frank, a Representative from Missouri; born near Fulton, Callaway County, Mo., on April 24, 1836; was graduated from the University of Missouri at Columbia; studied law; was admitted to the bar in 1864 and commenced practice in Huntsville, Randolph County, Mo.; elected as a Democrat to the Forty-sixth Congress (March 4, 1879–March 3, 1881); unsuccessful candidate for renomination in 1880; resumed the practice of law in Moberly, Mo.; presidential elector on the Democratic ticket of Cleveland and Hendricks in 1884; appointed in 1889 a member of the board of curators of the University of Missouri, and served as its president 1890–1894; died in Moberly, Mo., on January 18, 1894; interment in Oakland Cemetery.

ROUSE, Arthur Blythe, a Representative from Kentucky; born in Burlington, Boone County, Ky., June 20, 1874; attended the public schools; was graduated from Hanover College, Indiana, in 1896 and from the Louisville Law School in 1900; was admitted to the bar in 1900 and commenced practice in Burlington; in 1907 became the first secretary of the Kentucky State Racing Commission and served four years; served as State revenue commissioner under Governor Ruby Laffoon; secretary to Representative Daniel Lynn Gooch and Representative Joseph L. Rhinoch; member of the Democratic State executive committee from 1903 to 1910, when he resigned, having been nominated as a candidate for Congress; elected as a Democrat to the Sixty-second and to the seven succeeding Congresses (March 4, 1911–March 3, 1927); was not a candidate for renomination in 1926; chairman of the Democratic National Congressional Committee from 1921 until he resigned in December 1924; resumed the practice of law in Erlanger, Ky.; operated five bus lines out of Erlanger and launched the first bus line (Blue Coach Line) from Cincinnati to Lexington; also operated the Dixie Traction Co. and a city bus line in Maysville, Ky.; appointed clerk of the United States District Court for the Eastern District of Kentucky on October 8, 1935, and served until his resignation due to ill health in January 1953; died in Lexington, Ky., January 25, 1956; interment in Lexington Cemetery.

ROUSH, John Edward, a Representative from Indiana; born in Barnsdall, Osage County, Okla., September 12, 1920; moved with parents to Huntington, Ind., in 1924; attended the elementary schools in Huntington; was graduated from Huntington High School in 1938 and Huntington College in 1942; during World War II served as an Infantry officer with the United States Army 1942–1946; graduated from Indiana University School of Law in 1949; was admitted to the bar in 1949 and commenced the practice of law in Huntington, Ind.; served one term in the Indiana State Legislature in 1949; in 1950 was recalled to active duty in the United States Army and served as a Counterintelligence Corps agent until separated from the service in June 1952; elected prosecuting attorney of Huntington County in 1954 for a four-year term and served until elected to Congress; vice president of the board of trustees of Huntington College 1958–1960; elected as a Democrat to the Eighty-sixth Congress (January 3, 1959–January 3, 1961). *Reelected to the Eighty-seventh Congress.*

ROUSSEAU, Lovell Harrison, a Representative from Kentucky; born near Stanford, Lincoln County, Ky., August 4, 1818; attended the common schools; studied law; was admitted to the bar in 1841 and began practice in Bloomfield, Ind.; member of the Indiana State House of Representatives in 1844 and 1845; captain in the Mexican War; served in the Indiana State Senate 1847–1849; returned to Kentucky in 1849 and resumed the practice of law in Louisville; member of the Kentucky State Senate 1860–1861; served as a colonel, brigadier general, and major general in the Union Army during the Civil War and resigned November 17, 1865; elected as a Republican to the Thirty-ninth Congress and served from March 4, 1865, to July 21, 1866, when he resigned, after having

made an assault upon Representative Grinnell, of Iowa, in the Capitol Building; was subsequently reelected to fill the vacancy caused by his own resignation and took his seat December 3, 1866, and served until March 3, 1867; appointed a brigadier general in the Regular Army with the brevet rank of major general on March 27, 1867, and assigned to duty in Alaska; on July 28, 1868, was placed in command of the Department of Louisiana and served in that capacity until his death in New Orleans, La., January 7, 1869; interment in Arlington National Cemetery, Fort Myer, Va.

ROUTZOHN, Harry Nelson, a Representative from Ohio; born in Dayton, Ohio, November 4, 1881; attended the public grade schools; served one year at the blacksmith trade; became court page in common pleas court of Montgomery County, Ohio; studied law; was admitted to the bar in 1904 and commenced practice in Dayton, Ohio; assistant county prosecutor of Montgomery County, Ohio, 1906–1909; taught law at the University of Dayton, Dayton, Ohio, 1923–1930; probate judge 1917–1929; assistant United States district attorney 1930–1932; delegate to the Republican National Conventions in 1928 and 1932; captain in the Officers' Reserve Corps 1925–1935; elected as a Republican to the Seventy-sixth Congress (January 3, 1939–January 3, 1941); was an unsuccessful candidate for reelection in 1940 to the Seventy-seventh Congress; resumed the practice of law in Dayton, Ohio; appointed Solicitor for the Department of Labor, Washington, D. C., and served from March 6, 1953, until his death in Washington, D. C., April 14, 1953; interment in Memorial Park Cemetery, Dayton, Ohio.

ROWAN, John (uncle of Robert Todd Lytle), a Representative and a Senator from Kentucky; born near York, York County, Pa., July 12, 1773; moved to Louisville, Ky.; received a thorough classical training; studied law in Lexington; was admitted to the bar in 1795 and commenced practice in Louisville; member of the second State constitutional convention held at Frankfort in 1799; secretary of state of Kentucky 1804–1806; elected as a Democrat to the Tenth Congress (March 4, 1807–March 3, 1809); member of the State house of representatives 1813–1817, 1822, and 1824; appointed judge of the court of appeals in 1819 and resigned in 1821; elected as a Democrat to the United States Senate and served from March 4, 1825, to March 3, 1831; appointed commissioner for carrying out the treaty of 1839 with the Republic of Mexico; president of the Kentucky Historical Society and served from 1838 until his death in Louisville, Ky., July 13, 1843; interment in the family burial ground at Federal Hill, near Bardstown, Nelson County, Ky.

ROWAN, Joseph, a Representative from New York; born in New York City September 8, 1870; attended the public schools; was graduated from Columbia College Law School in 1891; was admitted to the bar in 1892 and commenced the practice of law in New York City; elected as a Democrat to the Sixty-sixth Congress (March 4, 1919–March 3, 1921); was not a candidate for renomination in 1920; continued the practice of his profession in New York City until his death there on August 3, 1930; interment in Woodlawn Cemetery.

ROWAN, William A., a Representative from Illinois; born in Chicago, Cook County, Ill., November 24, 1882; was graduated from St. Patrick Grade School and St. Patrick High School and attended the University of Chicago; employed in a steel plant after graduation; associated with a daily community newspaper in Chicago, becoming city editor and editor, 1907–1927; served as alderman of the tenth ward of Chicago 1927–1942; elected as a Democrat to the Seventy-eighth and Seventy-ninth Congresses

(January 3, 1943–January 3, 1947); unsuccessful candidate for reelection in 1946 to the Eightieth Congress; appointed United States Comptroller of Customs at Chicago, Ill., on January 21, 1947, in which capacity he served until 1953; died in Chicago, Ill., May 31, 1961; interment in Holy Sepulchre Cemetery, Worth, Ill.

ROWBOTTOM, Harry Emerson, a Representative from Indiana; born in Aurora, Dearborn County, Ind., November 3, 1884; moved with his parents to Ludlow, Ky., in 1885; attended the common schools; was graduated from Ludlow High School in 1901; attended Kentucky State College at Lexington 1902–1904; salesman of lubricating oils 1904–1907; attended the Cincinnati Business College and was graduated in accountancy in 1907; engaged as an auditor in Cincinnati 1907–1910 and in Chicago 1910–1912; moved to Evansville, Ind., in 1913 and was employed as chief clerk for the Indiana Refining Co. 1913–1918; member of the Indiana State House of Representatives 1919–1923; elected as a Republican to the Sixty-ninth, Seventieth, and Seventy-first Congresses (March 4, 1925–March 3, 1931); unsuccessful for reelection in 1930 to the Seventy-second Congress; engaged as commercial agent for a truck line; died in Evansville, Ind., March 22, 1934; interment in Locust Hill Cemetery.

ROWE, Edmund (Ed), a Representative from Ohio; born in Sherodsville, Carroll County, Ohio, December 21, 1892; attended the public schools; worked in the coal mines 1905–1909, in the rubber industry 1909–1913, and at the machinist trade 1913–1916; during the First World War served as machinist mate, second class, Submarine Chaser Service, United States Navy, 1917–1919; owner of a bowling academy 1919–1929; engaged in the real-estate business in 1920 and the insurance business in 1928; organizer of the Rowe Oil & Chemical Co. in 1936; member of the city council of Akron, Ohio, 1928–1942, serving one term as president; elected as a Republican to the Seventy-eighth Congress (January 3, 1943–January 3, 1945); was an unsuccessful candidate for reelection in 1944 to the Seventy-ninth Congress and for election in 1948 to the Eighty-first Congress; member of the Ohio General Assembly 1955–1959; unsuccessful candidate for mayor of Akron in 1957; real-estate broker; is a resident of Akron, Ohio.

ROWE, Frederick William, a Representative from New York; born at Wappingers Falls, Dutchess County, N. Y., March 19, 1863; attended the common schools; was graduated from De Garmo Institute in 1882 and from Colgate University, Hamilton, N. Y., in 1887; studied law; was admitted to the bar in New York City in 1889 and practiced in Brooklyn and New York City until 1904, when he became interested in the development of real estate in Brooklyn; president of several companies, including a street railway company; director of the Dime Savings Bank of Brooklyn; member of the Brooklyn Chamber of Commerce; elected as a Republican to the Sixty-fourth, Sixty-fifth, and Sixty-sixth Congresses (March 4, 1915–March 3, 1921); was not a candidate for renomination in 1920; resumed his former business activities in New York City; died in Rockville Centre, Nassau County, N. Y., June 20, 1946; interment in Greenwood Cemetery, Brooklyn, N. Y.

ROWE, Peter, a Representative from New York; born in Crescent, Saratoga County, N. Y., March 10, 1807; completed preparatory studies and was graduated from Schenectady (N. Y.) Academy; engaged in mercantile pursuits; chief auditor of the New York Central Railroad; mayor of Schenectady 1846–1850; elected as a Democrat to the Thirty-third Congress (March 4, 1853–March 3, 1855); died in Schenectady, N. Y., April 17, 1876; interment in Vale Cemetery.

ROWELL, Jonathan Harvey, a Representative from Illinois; born in Haverhill, Grafton County, N. H., February 10, 1833; attended Rock Creek School; was graduated from Eureka College, Illinois; during the Civil War served as a company officer in the Seventeenth Regiment, Illinois Volunteer Infantry; studied law; was admitted to the bar in 1866 and commenced practice in Bloomington, Ill.; State's attorney of the eighth judicial circuit of Illinois 1868–1872; presidential elector on the Republican ticket of Garfield and Arthur in 1880; elected as a Republican to the Forty-eighth and to the three succeeding Congresses (March 4, 1883–March 3, 1891); unsuccessful candidate for reelection in 1890 to the Fifty-second Congress; resumed the practice of law; died in Bloomington, McLean County, Ill., May 15, 1908; interment in Evergreen Cemetery.

ROWLAND, Alfred, a Representative from North Carolina; born in Lumberton Robeson County, N. C., February 9, 1844; attended the common schools; during the Civil War entered the Confederate Army in May 1861 and served as a lieutenant in Company D, Eighteenth Regiment of North Carolina State Troops, until May 12, 1864; captured in the Battle of Spotsylvania Court House and imprisoned at Fort Delaware until June 1865; studied law; was admitted to the bar in 1867 and commenced practice in Lumberton; register of deeds for Robeson County in 1867; member of the State house of representatives in 1876, 1877, 1880, and 1881; presidential elector on the Democratic ticket of Cleveland and Hendricks in 1884; elected as a Democrat to the Fiftieth and Fifty-first Congresses (March 4, 1887–March 3, 1891); was not a candidate for renomination in 1890; resumed the practice of law; died in Lumberton, N. C., August 2, 1898; interment in Meadow Brook Cemetery.

ROWLAND, Charles Hedding, a Representative from Pennsylvania; born in Hancock, Washington County, Md., December 20, 1860; moved to Huntingdon County, Pa., in 1866 and to Houtzdale, Pa., in 1874; attended the public schools; when very young entered on a business career and became interested in the production of soft coal; president of the Moshannon Coal Mining Co. and of the Pittsburgh & Susquehanna Railroad Co.; trustee and director of many institutions of public service and welfare; elected as a Republican to the Sixty-fourth and Sixty-fifth Congresses (March 4, 1915–March 3, 1919); declined to be a candidate for renomination in 1918; died in Philipsburg, Centre County, Pa., on November 24, 1921; interment in the Philipsburg Cemetery.

ROY, Alphonse, a Representative from New Hampshire; born in St. Simon, Province of Quebec, Canada, October 26, 1897; moved to Manchester, N. H., in 1901; attended the parochial schools; engaged in the real-estate business; served as alderman 1925–1931; member of the State house of representatives 1925–1931; served as executive councilor of New Hampshire 1933–1937; successfully contested as a Democrat the election of Arthur B. Jenks to the Seventy-fifth Congress and served from June 9, 1938, to January 3, 1939; unsuccessful candidate for reelection in 1938 to the Seventy-sixth Congress and for election in 1940 to the Seventy-seventh Congress; appointed sealer of weights and measures of Manchester, N. H., in 1943 and served until his resignation in 1945; United States marshal for the district of New Hampshire 1945–1953; unsuccessful candidate for election in 1958 to the Eighty-sixth Congress; unsuccessful candidate for nomination for the United States Senate in 1960; resumed the real-estate business; is a resident of Manchester, N. H.

ROYCE, Homer Elihu, a Representative from Vermont; born in East Berkshire, Franklin County, Vt., June 14, 1819; attended the local academies of St. Albans and Enosburg, Vt.;

studied law; was admitted to the bar and commenced practice in East Berkshire, Vt., in 1844; member of the State house of representatives in 1846 and 1847; State prosecuting attorney in 1848; served in the State senate 1849–1851, 1861, and 1868; elected as a Republican to the Thirty-fifth and Thirty-sixth Congresses (March 4, 1857–March 3, 1861); was not a candidate for renomination in 1860; again a member of the State senate in 1861 and 1868; elected associate justice of the supreme court of Vermont in 1870; was appointed chief justice of that court in 1882, and served until 1890, when he resigned; died in St. Albans, Vt., April 24, 1891; interment in Calvary Cemetery, East Berkshire, Vt.

ROYSE, Lemuel Willard, a Representative from Indiana; born near Pierceton, Kosciusko County, Ind., January 19, 1847; attended the common schools; studied law; was admitted to the bar in 1874 and commenced practice in Warsaw, Kosciusko County, Ind.; prosecuting attorney for the thirty-third judicial circuit of Indiana in 1876; mayor of Warsaw 1885–1891; presidential elector on the Republican ticket of Blaine and Logan in 1884; member of the Republican State central committee from 1886 to 1890; delegate to the Republican National Convention at Minneapolis in 1892; elected as a Republican to the Fifty-fourth and Fifty-fifth Congresses (March 4, 1895–March 3, 1899); unsuccessful candidate for renomination in 1898; resumed the practice of law in Warsaw, Ind.; judge of the Kosciusko County Circuit Court 1904–1908; resumed the practice of his profession; reelected circuit judge and served from 1920 to 1932; again resumed the practice of law until his retirement in 1940; died in Warsaw, Ind., December 18, 1946; interment in Oakwood Cemetery.

RUBEY, Thomas Lewis, a Representative from Missouri; born in Lebanon, Laclede County, Mo., September 27, 1862; attended the common schools; was graduated from the University of Missouri at Columbia in 1885; superintendent of schools of Lebanon, Mo., 1886–1891; teacher in the Missouri School of Mines 1891–1898; member of the State house of representatives in 1891 and 1892; moved to La Plata, Macon County, Mo., in 1898 and organized a bank; served in the State senate 1901–1903; elected president of the senate in 1903 and upon the resignation of Lieut. Gov. John A. Lee in that year became Lieutenant Governor, serving in that capacity until 1905; returned to Lebanon in 1905 and engaged in banking; president of the State Bank, Lebanon, Mo., from 1914 until his death; elected as a Democrat to the Sixty-second and to the four succeeding Congresses (March 4, 1911–March 3, 1921); unsuccessful candidate for reelection in 1920 to the Sixty-seventh Congress; elected to the Sixty-eighth, Sixty-ninth, and Seventieth Congresses and served from March 4, 1923, until his death in Lebanon, Mo., on November 2, 1928; interment in Lebanon Cemetery.

RUCKER, Atterson Walden, a Representative from Colorado; born in Harrodsburg, Mercer County, Ky., April 3, 1847; moved in early youth with his parents to Missouri; attended the common schools; served four years in the Confederate Army during the Civil War; studied law; was admitted to the bar in 1868 and commenced practice in Lexington, Mo., the following year; moved to Baxter Springs, Kans., in 1873 and resumed the practice of law; moved to Leadville, Colo., in 1879 and continued the practice of his profession; was also interested in mining; judge of the court of records of Lake County in 1881 and 1882; moved to Aspen, Pitkin County, Colo., in 1885 and became largely interested in the development of mining projects; elected as a Democrat to the Sixty-first and Sixty-second Congresses (March 4, 1909–March 3, 1913);

unsuccessful candidate for renomination in 1912; returned to Colorado and settled in Denver; resumed the practice of his profession; discontinued the practice of law and devoted much of his time to agricultural pursuits; died near Mount Morrison, Jefferson County, Colo., on July 19, 1924; interment in the Littleton Cemetery, Littleton, Arapahoe County, Colo.

RUCKER, Tinsley White, a Representative from Georgia; born near Farm Hill, Elbert County, Ga., March 24, 1848; attended the public schools, Princeton College, and the Georgia Military Academy at Marietta; served in the Confederate Army from March 24, 1864, until the close of the Civil War; returned to Athens; was graduated from the law department of the University of Georgia at Athens in 1868; was admitted to the bar in 1871 and commenced practice in Athens, Clarke County, Ga.; was appointed by President Cleveland as assistant United States district attorney for the northern district of Georgia in 1893 and resided in Atlanta; returned to Athens in 1912 and continued the practice of law; elected as a Democrat to the Sixty-fourth Congress to fill the vacancy caused by the death of Samuel J. Tribble and served from January 11 to March 3, 1917; was not a candidate for renomination in 1916; engaged in the practice of law until his death in Athens, Ga., November 18, 1926; interment in Oconee Cemetery.

RUCKER, William Waller, a Representative from Missouri; born near Covington, Alleghany County, Va., February 1, 1855; moved with his parents to western Virginia in 1861; attended the common schools; moved to Chariton County, Mo., in 1873; engaged in teaching in the district schools; studied law; was admitted to the bar in 1876 and commenced practice in Keytesville, Chariton County, Mo.; prosecuting attorney of Chariton County 1886–1892; judge of the twelfth circuit 1892–1899; elected as a Democrat to the Fifty-sixth and to the eleven succeeding Congresses (March 4, 1899–March 3, 1923); unsuccessful candidate for reelection in 1922 to the Sixty-eighth Congress; resumed the practice of law in Keytesville, Mo.; also engaged in agricultural pursuits; died in Keytesville, Mo., May 30, 1936; interment in the City Cemetery.

RUDD, Stephen Andrew, a Representative from New York; born in Brooklyn, N. Y., December 11, 1874; attended the public schools and the New York Preparatory School; studied law at the Brooklyn Law School of St. Lawrence University, Brooklyn, N. Y.; was admitted to the bar in 1914 and commenced practice in Brooklyn; member of the New York City Board of Aldermen 1922–1930; elected as a Democrat to the Seventy-second Congress to fill the vacancy caused by the death of David J. O'Connell; reelected to the Seventy-third and Seventy-fourth Congresses and served from March 4, 1931, until his death in Brooklyn, N. Y., March 31, 1936; interment in Evergreen Cemetery.

RUFFIN, James Edward, a Representative from Missouri; born on a farm near Covington, Tipton County, Tenn., July 24, 1893; in 1905 moved to Missouri with his parents, who settled in Aurora, Lawrence County; attended the grade schools; was graduated from the Aurora High School in 1912 and from Drury College, Springfield, Mo., in 1916; taught school at Nickerson (Kans.) College in 1917; during the First World War was commissioned a first lieutenant on November 27, 1917; served in the Fifty-third Regiment, Pioneer Infantry, overseas with the First and Thirty-fifth Divisions, and was discharged on June 3, 1919; was graduated from the law department of Cumberland University, Lebanon, Tenn., in 1920; was admitted to the bar the same year and commenced practice in Springfield, Mo.; served as assistant city attorney 1926–1928; elected as a Democrat to the Seventy-third Congress (March 4, 1933–January 3, 1935); unsuccessful candidate for renomination in 1934; appointed special assistant to the Attorney General of the United States on May 9, 1935, assigned to the criminal division of the Department of Justice, and served until August 1953; resumed the practice of law at Springfield, Mo., where he now resides.

RUFFIN, Thomas, a Representative from North Carolina; born in Louisburg, Franklin County (formerly a part of Edgecombe County), N. C., September 9, 1820; attended the common schools; was graduated from the law department of the University of North Carolina at Chapel Hill in 1841; was admitted to the bar the same year and commenced practice in Goldsboro, N. C.; circuit attorney of the seventh judicial district of the State of Missouri 1844–1848; returned to Goldsboro, N. C., in 1850; elected as a Democrat to the Thirty-third and to the three succeeding Congresses (March 4, 1853–March 3, 1861); delegate to the Confederate Provisional Congress at Richmond in July 1861; during the Civil War served in the Confederate Army as colonel of the First North Carolina Cavalry; mortally wounded in action at Bristoe Station, near Alexandria, Va., and died while a prisoner of war at Alexandria on October 13, 1863; interment in the private cemetery on the Ruffin homestead, near Louisburg, N. C.

RUGGLES, Benjamin, a Senator from Ohio; born in Abington, Windham County, Conn., February 21, 1783; completed preparatory studies; studied law; was admitted to the bar and began practice in Marietta, Ohio, in 1807; moved to St. Clairsville, Ohio; president judge of the court of common pleas for the third judicial circuit 1810–1815; elected as a Democrat to the United States Senate in 1815; reelected in 1821 and again in 1827 and served from March 4, 1815, to March 3, 1833; was not a candidate for renomination in 1832; presidential elector on the Whig ticket of Harrison and Granger in 1836; resumed the practice of law and was also interested in agricultural pursuits; died in St. Clairsville, Belmont County, Ohio, September 2, 1857; interment in Union Cemetery.

RUGGLES, Charles Herman, a Representative from New York; born in New Milford, Conn., February 10, 1789; completed preparatory studies; studied law; was admitted to the bar and began practice in Kingston, N. Y.; member of the State assembly in 1820; elected to the Seventeenth Congress (March 4, 1821–March 3, 1823); circuit judge and vice chancellor of the second judicial district of New York 1833–1846; moved to Poughkeepsie, Dutchess County, N. Y.; member of the State constitutional convention in 1846; judge of the Dutchess County court; again elected a member of the State assembly; judge of the court of appeals 1847–1855; died in Poughkeepsie, N. Y., June 16, 1865.

RUGGLES, John, a Senator from Maine; born in Westboro, Mass., October 8, 1789; attended the common schools; was graduated from Brown University, Providence, R. I., in 1813; studied law; was admitted to the bar and commenced practice in Skowhegan, Maine, in 1815; moved to Thomaston, Maine, in 1817; member of the State house of representatives 1823–1831, and served as speaker 1825–1829 and in 1831; justice of the supreme judicial court of Maine 1831–1834; elected as a Democrat to the United States Senate to fill the vacancy caused by the resignation of Peleg Sprague, and at the same time was elected for the full term beginning March 4, 1835, and served from January 20, 1835, to March 3, 1841: was an unsuccessful candidate for reelection in 1840; framer of the bill for the reorganization of the United States Patent Office, which was enacted into law July 4, 1836; resumed the practice

of his profession in Thomaston, Knox County, Maine; also engaged as an inventor, orator, and writer; died in Thomaston, Maine, on June 20, 1874; interment in Elm Grove Cemetery.

RUGGLES, Nathaniel, a Representative from Massachusetts; born in Roxbury, Mass., November 11, 1761; pursued preparatory studies; was graduated from Harvard University in 1781; studied law; was admitted to the bar and practiced law in Roxbury, Mass.; appointed judge of the general sessions in 1807; chief justice of Massachusetts in 1808; was elected as a Federalist to the Thirteenth, Fourteenth, and Fifteenth Congresses (March 4, 1813–March 3, 1819); died in Roxbury, Mass., December 19, 1819.

RUMPLE, John Nicholas William, a Representative from Iowa; born near Fostoria, Seneca County, Ohio, March 4, 1841; attended the public schools, Western College, Iowa, and the Iowa State University; during the Civil War enlisted in Company H, Second Iowa Cavalry, in August 1861 and remained in the Army until October 1865, when mustered out as captain; studied law; was admitted to the bar in 1867 and commenced practice in Marengo, Iowa County, Iowa; member of the State senate 1873–1878; member of the board of regents of the State University of Iowa 1880–1886; curator of the State Historical Society of Iowa 1881–1885; member of the city council; mayor of Marengo, Iowa, in 1885 and 1886; attorney for the city council of Marengo 1896–1900; member of the school board; elected as a Republican to the Fifty-seventh Congress and served from March 4, 1901, until his death in Chicago, Ill., January 31, 1903; interment in the Odd Fellows Cemetery, Marengo, Iowa.

RUMSEY, Benjamin, a Delegate from Maryland; born in Bohemia Manor, Cecil County, Md., October 6, 1734; attended Princeton College; member of the Maryland convention of December 29, 1775; one of the committee to prepare instructions to the Maryland Delegates in Congress; member of the committee to raise supplies for the provincial forces; was appointed by the provincial convention colonel of the Lower Battalion of Harford County in 1776; member of the council of safety in 1776; Member of the Continental Congress 1776–1778; chief justice of the Maryland Court of Appeals from 1778 to 1805, when he resigned; died in Joppa, Hartford County, Md., March 7, 1808; interment in the Old St. John's Cemetery.

RUMSEY, David, a Representative from New York; born in Salem, Washington County, N. Y., December 25, 1810; attended school at Auburn, N. Y., and Hobart College at Geneva, N. Y.; studied law; was admitted to the bar in 1831 and commenced practice in Bath, N. Y.; surrogate of Steuben County 1840–1844; held many local offices; elected as a Whig to the Thirtieth and Thirty-first Congresses (March 4, 1847–March 3, 1851); delegate to the State constitutional convention in 1867; member of the commission to propose amendments to the State constitution in 1872; appointed in 1873 as an associate justice of the State supreme court to fill a vacancy; elected to the same office in the fall of that year; died in Bath, Steuben County, N. Y., March 12, 1883; interment in private cemetery on the Rumsey place.

RUMSEY, Edward, a Representative from Kentucky; born in Botecourt County, Va., November 5, 1796; moved when a child with his parents to Christian County, Ky.; completed preparatory studies in Hopkinsville; moved to Greenville, Ky.; studied law; was admitted to the bar and commenced practice in Greenville; held several local offices; member of the State house of representatives in 1822; presidential elector on the Whig ticket of Harrison and Granger in 1836; elected as a Whig to the Twenty-fifth Congress (March 4, 1837–March 3, 1839); again resumed the practice of his profession; died in Greenville, Muhlenberg County, Ky., on April 6, 1868; interment in the Old Caney Station Cemetery, near Greenville, Ky.

RUNK, John, a Representative from New Jersey; born in Milltown (now Idell), Hunterdon County, N. J., July 3, 1791; attended the district schools; took charge of the mills and general store on his father's property in Milltown, N. J.; member of the board of chosen freeholders from Kingwood 1825–1833; unsuccessful candidate for sheriff in 1830; high sheriff of Hunterdon County 1836–1838; presidential elector on the Whig ticket of Harrison and Tyler in 1840 and of Taylor and Fillmore in 1848; elected as a Whig to the Twenty-ninth Congress (March 4, 1845–March 3, 1847); unsuccessful candidate for reelection in 1849 to the Thirtieth Congress; unsuccessful candidate for Governor of New Jersey in 1850; moved to Lambertville, Hunterdon County, N. J., in 1854 and engaged in the milling business and mercantile pursuits; died in Lambertville, September 22, 1872; interment in Rosemont Cemetery, Rosemont, Hunterdon County, N. J.

RUPLEY, Arthur Ringwalt, a Representative from Pennsylvania; born in West Fairview, Cumberland County, Pa., November 13, 1868; attended the Harrisburg Academy and the Cumberland Valley State Normal School, Shippensburg, Pa.; was graduated from the Dickinson School of Law, Carlisle, Pa., in 1890; was admitted to the bar in 1891 and practiced; chairman of the Republican county committee 1895–1898; district attorney of Cumberland County 1895–1899; county and city solicitor 1900–1906; delegate to the Republican State convention in 1910 and to the Republican National Convention at Chicago in 1912; elected as a Progressive Republican to the Sixty-third Congress (March 4, 1913–March 3, 1915); resumed the practice of law and specialized in public-service work; died in Carlisle, Pa., on November 11, 1920; interment in Ashland Cemetery.

RUPPERT, Jacob, Jr., a Representative from New York; born in New York City, N. Y., August 5, 1867; attended the Columbia Grammar School; engaged in the brewing business with his father in 1887; served as a private in the Seventh Regiment, National Guard of New York, 1886–1889; appointed a colonel on the staff of Gov. David B. Hill, serving as aide-de-camp; subsequently served as senior aide on the staff of Gov. Roswell P. Flower 1892–1895; elected as a Democrat to the Fifty-sixth and to the three succeeding Congresses (March 4, 1899–March 3, 1907); was not a candidate for renomination in 1906; resumed his activities in the brewing business; served as president of the United States Brewers Association 1911–1914; financially interested in various business and real-estate holdings; served as president of the Astoria Silk Works; became president of the New York American League Baseball Club on December 31, 1914, in which capacity he served until his death in New York City, N. Y., January 13, 1939; interment in Kensico Cemetery, Valhalla, Westchester County, N. Y.

RUSH, Benjamin, a Delegate from Pennsylvania; born in Byberry Township, near Philadelphia, Pa., December 24, 1745; educated under private tutors and at a private school in Nottingham, Md.; was graduated from Princeton College in 1760; studied medicine in Philadelphia, Edinburgh, London, and Paris, and commenced practice in Philadelphia in August 1769; held several professorships in the Philadelphia Medical College; Member of the Continental Congress in 1776 and 1777; a signer of the Declaration of Independence; entered the Revolutionary Army as surgeon general of the Middle Department in April 1777; made physician general in July 1777; resigned in February

1778; resumed the practice of medicine; delegate to the State constitutional convention of Pennsylvania which adopted the Federal Constitution December 12, 1787; founder of the Pennsylvania Hospital in Philadelphia; president of the Philadelphia Medical Society; vice president and one of the founders of the Philadelphia Bible Society; one of the founders of Dickinson College at Carlisle, Pa.; assisted in the establishment of the Philadelphia dispensary in 1786; received from the King of Prussia in 1805 a coronation medal, from the Queen of Etruria in 1807 a gold medal, and from the Czar of Russia a diamond ring in 1811, for his contributions to medical science; author of many books and treatises; treasurer of the United States Mint at Philadelphia from 1799 until his death in that city April 19, 1813; interment in Christ Church Cemetery.

RUSK, Harry Welles, a Representative from Maryland; born in Baltimore, Md., October 17, 1852; attended private schools; was graduated from the Baltimore City College in 1866 and from the Maryland University Law School at Baltimore in 1882; was admitted to the bar in 1873 and commenced practice in Baltimore; member of the State house of delegates in 1876, 1878, and 1880; served in the State senate 1882–1884; delegate to the Democratic National Convention at Chicago in 1884; elected as a Democrat to the Forty-ninth Congress to fill the vacancy caused by the death of William H. Cole; reelected to the Fiftieth and to the four succeeding Congresses and served from November 2, 1886, to March 3, 1897; declined to be a candidate for renomination in 1896; chairman of the Democratic State central committee for Baltimore from 1898 to 1908, when he resigned; resumed the practice of law in Baltimore, Md., where he died on January 28, 1926; interment in Greenmount Cemetery.

RUSK, Jeremiah McLain, a Representative from Wisconsin; born in Malta, Morgan County, Ohio, June 17, 1830; received a limited schooling; moved to Vernon County, Wis., in 1853 and engaged in agricultural pursuits; sheriff of Viroqua, Wis., 1855–1857; coroner in 1857; member of the State assembly in 1862; served in the Civil War and became major in the Twenty-fifth Regiment, Wisconsin Volunteer Infantry, August 14, 1862; lieutenant colonel September 16, 1863; brevetted colonel and brigadier general of Volunteers March 13, 1865, "for gallant and meritorious services during the war"; mustered out June 7, 1865; bank comptroller of Wisconsin 1866–1869; elected as a Republican to the Forty-second, Forty-third, and Forty-fourth Congresses (March 4, 1871–March 3, 1877); was not a candidate for renomination in 1876; declined the appointment as United States Minister to Uruguay and Paraguay tendered by President Garfield; Governor of Wisconsin 1882–1889; appointed Secretary of Agriculture in the Cabinet of President Benjamin Harrison and served from March 5, 1889, to March 5, 1893, the last two days of the service being in the succeeding Cabinet of President Grover Cleveland; died in Viroqua, Vernon County, Wis., on November 21, 1893; interment in Viroqua Cemetery.

RUSK, Thomas Jefferson, a Senator from Texas; born in Pendleton District, S. C., December 5, 1803; completed preparatory studies; studied law; was admitted to the bar and commenced practice in Georgia; moved to Nacogdoches, Tex., in 1835; delegate to the convention which declared for the independence of Texas March 21, 1836; first Secretary of War of the new Republic; at the Battle of San Jacinto took command of the forces after General Houston was wounded and retained command until October 1836, when he resumed his duties as Secretary of War; member of the Second Congress of the Republic of Texas; chief justice of the supreme court of Texas 1838–1842; appointed brigadier general of militia of the Republic of Texas in 1843; president of the convention that confirmed the annexation of Texas to the United States in 1845; upon the admission of Texas as a State into the Union was elected as a Democrat to the United States Senate; reelected in 1851 and 1857 and served from February 21, 1846, until his death; was elected President pro tempore of the Senate on March 14, 1857, in the special session of the Senate; died in Nacogdoches, Tex., July 29, 1857; interment in Oak Grove Cemetery.

RUSS, John, a Representative from Connecticut; was born in Ipswich, Mass., on October 29, 1767; completed preparatory studies; moved to Hartford, Conn.; engaged in mercantile pursuits; elected as a Democrat to the Sixteenth and Seventeenth Congresses (March 4, 1819–March 3, 1823); was not a candidate for reelection in 1823; unsuccessful candidate for election in 1823 to the State house of representatives; elected to the State house of representatives in 1824; elected judge of the Hartford Probate Court in 1824 and served until 1830; resumed his former business pursuits; died in Hartford, Conn., June 22, 1833; interment in the Old North Cemetery.

RUSSELL, Benjamin Edward (cousin of Rienzi Melville Johnston), a Representative from Georgia; born in Monticello, Jefferson County, Fla., on October 5, 1845; moved with his parents to Decatur County, Ga., in 1854; attended the common schools; entered the Confederate Army as a drummer boy in the First Georgia Regiment; upon the disbanding of this regiment he immediately enlisted in the Eighth Florida Regiment and continued with it during the last three years of the war, with the rank of first lieutenant; captured at the Battle of Sailors Creek, Virginia, April 6, 1865, and imprisoned at Johnsons Island, Ohio, until all of the Confederate armies had surrendered; entered the printing business; editor of the Bainbridge (Ga.) Democrat; delegate to the State constitutional convention in 1877; delegate to the Democratic National Convention at Cincinnati in 1880; mayor of Bainbridge in 1881 and 1882; member of the State house of representatives in 1882 and 1883; postmaster of Bainbridge 1885–1890; elected as a Democrat to the Fifty-third and Fifty-fourth Congresses (March 4, 1893–March 3, 1897); was not a candidate for renomination in 1896; resumed the publication of the Bainbridge Democrat; died in Bainbridge, Decatur County, Ga., December 4, 1909; interment in Oak City Cemetery.

RUSSELL, Charles Addison, a Representative from Connecticut; born in Worcester, Mass., March 2, 1852; attended the public schools; was graduated from Yale College in 1873; city editor of the Worcester Press 1873–1879 and associate editor of the Worcester Spy in 1879 and 1880; moved to Killingly, Conn., in 1879 and engaged in the manufacture of woolen products; aide-de-camp on the staff of Gov. Hobart B. Bigelow in 1881; member of the State house of representatives in 1883; secretary of state of Connecticut in 1885 and 1886; was elected as a Republican to the Fiftieth and to the seven succeeding Congresses and served from March 4, 1887, until his death; was renominated as the Republican candidate for reelection in 1902 to the Fifty-eighth Congress but died before the election in Killingly, Conn., October 23, 1902; interment in the High Street Cemetery, Dayville, Killingly, Conn.

RUSSELL, Charles Hinton, a Representative from Nevada; born in Lovelock, Pershing County, Nev., December 27, 1903; attended the public schools; was graduated from Elko County High School in 1922 and the University of Nevada at Reno in 1926; taught school in 1926 and 1927; employed in a mine office in Ruth, Nev., in 1928 and 1929; editor of a newspaper since 1929; served in the State assembly 1935–1940; member of the State senate 1941–1946, resigning in 1946 to become a candidate

for Congress; served as president pro tempore of the State senate in 1943; elected as a Republican to the Eightieth Congress (January 3, 1947–January 3, 1949); unsuccessful candidate for reelection in 1948 to the Eighty-first Congress; member of the staff of the Joint Congressional Committee on Foreign Economic Cooperation in Washington, D. C., in 1949 and 1950; Governor of Nevada from January 1, 1951, to January 1, 1959; director of International Cooperation Administration mission to Paraguay since December 15, 1959; is a resident of Ely, Nev.

RUSSELL, Daniel Lindsay, a Representative from North Carolina; born on Winnabow plantation, Brunswick County, near Wilmington, N. C., on August 7, 1845; received his early education from private teachers and attended the Bingham School in Orange County, N. C.; entered the University of North Carolina at Chapel Hill, but the outbreak of the Civil War ended his university career; during the Civil War served as a captain in the Confederate Army; member of the State house of commons 1864–1866; studied law, was admitted to the bar in 1866 and commenced practice in Wilmington, N. C.; judge of the superior courts for the fourth judicial circuit 1868–1874; elected as a delegate to the State constitutional convention in 1871; member of the State house of representatives in 1876; was a delegate to the Republican National Convention at Cincinnati in 1876; presidential elector on the Republican ticket of Hayes and Wheeler in 1876; elected as a Republican to the Forty-sixth Congress (March 4, 1879–March 3, 1881); was not a candidate for renomination in 1880; Governor of North Carolina 1896–1900; resumed the practice of law and also engaged in agricultural pursuits; died on Belville plantation, near Wilmington, N. C., May 14, 1908; interment in the family burying ground, Hickory Hill, Onslow County, N. C.

RUSSELL, David Abel, a Representative from New York; born in Petersburg, N. Y., in 1780; completed preparatory studies; studied law; was admitted to the bar and commenced practice in Salem, N. Y.; appointed justice of the peace in 1807; admitted to practice as counselor in 1809; district attorney for the northern judicial district of New York in 1813; member of the State assembly in 1816, 1830, and 1833; elected as a Whig to the Twenty-fourth, Twenty-fifth, and Twenty-sixth Congresses (March 4, 1835–March 3, 1841); died in Salem, Washington County, N. Y., November 24, 1861; interment in Evergreen Cemetery.

RUSSELL, Gordon James, a Representative from Texas; born in Huntsville, Madison County, Ala., December 22, 1859; attended the common schools, the Sam Bailey Institute, Griffin, Ga., and Crawford High School, Dalton, Ga.; was graduated from the University of Georgia at Athens in 1877; taught school in Dalton, Ga.; studied law; was admitted to the bar in 1878 and commenced practice in Dalton; moved to Texas in 1879 and later, in 1884, settled in Van Zandt County; elected county judge in 1890 and at the end of one term relinquished the office to resume the practice of law in Willsport, Tex.; district attorney of the seventh judicial district 1892–1896; judge of the seventh judicial district 1896–1904; elected as a Democrat to the Fifty-seventh Congress to fill the vacancy caused by the death of Reese C. de Graffenreid; reelected to the Fifty-eighth and to the three succeeding Congresses and served from November 4, 1902, to June 14, 1910, when he resigned to become United States district judge of the eastern district of Texas, which office he held until his death in Kerrville, Kerr County, Tex., September 14, 1919; interment in Oakwood Cemetery, Tyler, Smith County, Tex.

RUSSELL, James McPherson (father of Samuel Lyon Russell), a Representative from Pennsylvania; born in York, Pa.,

November 10, 1786; moved with his parents to a farm near Gettysburg, Adams County, Pa.; attended the classical academy of James Ross in Chambersburg; studied law; was admitted to the bar of Franklin County in 1807; was admitted to the Bedford County bar in 1808 and commenced practice in Bedford, Pa.; first burgess of Bedford Borough in 1818 and 1819; member of the State constitutional convention in 1837; elected as a Whig to the Twenty-seventh Congress to fill the vacancy caused by the death of Henry Black and served from December 21, 1841, to March 3, 1843; was not a candidate for renomination in 1842; resumed the practice of law; trustee of the Bedford Academy and secretary of the Chambersburg & Bedford Turnpike Co.; died in Bedford, Pa., November 14, 1870; interment in Bedford Cemetery.

RUSSELL, Jeremiah, a Representative from New York; born in Saugerties, N. Y., January 26, 1786; received a limited schooling; engaged in mercantile pursuits, the real-estate business, and banking; served several times as supervisor; presidential elector on the Democratic ticket of Van Buren and Johnson in 1836; member of the State house of representatives in 1842; elected as a Democrat to the Twenty-eighth Congress (March 4, 1843–March 3, 1845); unsuccessful candidate for reelection in 1844 to the Twenty-ninth Congress; resumed banking; died in Saugerties, Ulster County, N. Y., September 30, 1867; interment in Mountain View Cemetery.

RUSSELL, John, a Representative from New York; born in Branford, Conn., September 7, 1772; attended the public school; moved to New York State; studied medicine and practiced a short time in Cooperstown, N. Y.; county clerk of Otsego County 1801–1804; elected to the Ninth and Tenth Congresses (March 4, 1805–March 3, 1809); presidential elector on the Clinton ticket in 1812; engaged in mercantile pursuits; died in Cooperstown, Otsego County, N. Y., August 2, 1842; interment in Christ Churchyard.

RUSSELL, John Edwards, a Representative from Massachusetts; born in Greenfield, Franklin County, Mass., January 20, 1834; was instructed by private tutors; traveled extensively in South and Central America; returned to Massachusetts and became interested in mail transportation west of the Mississippi River and in steamship lines on the Pacific coast; engaged in agricultural pursuits; elected secretary of the Massachusetts State Board of Agriculture in 1880; reelected five times; elected as a Democrat to the Fiftieth Congress (March 4, 1887–March 3, 1889); delegate to the Democratic National Convention at Chicago in 1892; unsuccessful candidate for Governor of Massachusetts in 1893 and 1894; member of the Deep Waterways Commission; died in Leicester, Worcester County, Mass., October 28, 1903; interment in Pine Grove Cemetery.

RUSSELL, Jonathan, a Representative from Massachusetts; born in Providence, R. I., February 27, 1771; was graduated from Brown University (then Rhode Island College), Providence, R. I., in 1791; studied law; was admitted to the bar, but did not practice; engaged in mercantile pursuits; appointed by President Madison to the Diplomatic Service in France in 1811; transferred to England, where he was Chargé d'Affaires when war was declared against the United States in 1812; Minister to Norway and Sweden from January 18, 1814, to October 16, 1818; one of the five commissioners that negotiated the treaty of peace at Ghent with Great Britain in 1814; returned to the United States in 1818 and settled in Mendon, Mass.; writer and orator; member of the State house of representatives in 1820; elected as a Democrat to the Seventeenth Congress (March 4, 1821–March 3, 1823); died in Milton, Norfolk County, Mass., February 16, 1832; interment in the family plot on his estate in Milton.

RUSSELL, Joseph, a Representative from New York; born in that State and resided in Warrensburg, N. Y.; received a limited schooling; sheriff of Warren County from November 1834 to November 1837; member of the State assembly in 1840; elected as a Democrat to the Twenty-ninth Congress (March 4, 1845–March 3, 1847); again elected to the Thirty-second Congress (March 4, 1851–March 3, 1853).

RUSSELL, Joseph James, a Representative from Missouri; born near Charleston, Mississippi County, Mo., August 23, 1854; attended the public schools and Charleston Academy; was admitted to the bar in 1876 and commenced practice in Charleston, Mo.; graduated from the law department of the University of Missouri at Columbia in 1880; school commissioner for Mississippi County in 1878 and 1879; prosecuting attorney 1880–1884; delegate to the Democratic National Convention at Chicago in 1884 which nominated Grover Cleveland for President; presidential elector on the Democratic ticket of Cleveland and Hendricks in 1884; member of the State house of representatives 1886–1890 and served as speaker pro tempore of the house in 1886 and as speaker in 1888; elected as a Democrat to the Sixtieth Congress (March 4, 1907–March 3, 1909); unsuccessful candidate for reelection in 1908 to the Sixty-first Congress; elected to the Sixty-second and to the three succeeding Congresses (March 4, 1911–March 3, 1919); was not a candidate for renomination; retired from public life and active business pursuits on account of ill health; died in Charleston, Mo., October 22, 1922; interment in the Odd Fellows Cemetery.

RUSSELL, Joshua Edward, a Representative from Ohio; born near Sidney, Shelby County, Ohio, on August 9, 1867; attended the common schools and Sidney High School; studied law; was admitted to the bar in 1893 and commenced practice in Sidney; member of the city board of education in 1894 and 1895; city solicitor 1895–1899; member of the State senate 1905–1908; elected as a Republican to the Sixty-fourth Congress (March 4, 1915–March 3, 1917); was an unsuccessful candidate for reelection in 1916 to the Sixty-fifth Congress; resumed the practice of law; died in Sidney, Ohio, June 21, 1953; interment in Graceland Cemetery.

RUSSELL, Leslie W., a Representative from New York; born in Canton, St. Lawrence County, N. Y., April 15, 1840; attended the common schools; studied law; was admitted to the bar in 1861 and commenced practice in Canton; delegate to the State constitutional convention of 1867; district attorney of St. Lawrence County in 1869; member of the board of regents of the University of the State of New York 1878–1891; county judge of St. Lawrence County 1877–1881; attorney general of New York 1881–1883; practiced law in New York City 1883–1891; elected to the Fifty-second Congress and served from March 4, 1891, to September 11, 1891, when he resigned, having been elected justice of the supreme court of the State of New York; resigned as justice on October 1, 1902; died in New York City on February 3, 1903; interment in Evergreen Cemetery, Canton, N. Y.

RUSSELL, Richard Brevard, a Senator from Georgia; born in Winder, Barrow County, Ga., November 2, 1897; attended the public schools; was graduated from the Seventh District Agricultural and Mechanical School, Powder Springs, Ga., in 1914, from Gordon Institute, Barnesville, Ga., in 1915, and from the law department of the University of Georgia at Athens in 1918; was admitted to the bar and commenced practice at Winder, Ga., in 1919; served with the United States Naval Reserve in 1918; member of the State house of representatives 1921–1931, serving as speaker 1927–1931; served as Governor of Georgia

1931–1933; delegate to the Democratic National Convention at Chicago in 1932; elected as a Democrat to the United States Senate to fill the vacancy caused by the death of William J. Harris, and again elected in 1936, 1942, 1948, and 1954, and served from January 12, 1933, to January 3, 1961. *Reelected in 1960 for the term ending January 3, 1967.*

RUSSELL, Richard Manning, a Representative from Massachusetts; born in Cambridge, Mass., March 3, 1891; attended the Middlesex School, Concord, Mass.; was graduated from the law department of Harvard University, Cambridge, Mass., in 1917; during the First World War served from August 15, 1917, as a second lieutenant in the Three Hundred and Third Field Artillery and as a first lieutenant and communications officer of the One Hundred and Fifty-first Field Artillery Brigade, with service in France, and was discharged on February 20, 1919; was admitted to the bar in 1919 and commenced practice in Boston, Mass.; member of the Cambridge City Council in 1926 and 1927; mayor of Cambridge 1930–1935; elected as a Democrat to the Seventy-fourth Congress (January 3, 1935–January 3, 1937); unsuccessful candidate for reelection in 1936 to the Seventy-fifth Congress, for election in 1950 to fill a vacancy in the Eighty-first Congress, and for election in 1950 to the Eighty-second Congress; resumed the practice of law in Boston, Mass.; resides in Essex, Mass.

RUSSELL, Sam Morris, a Representative from Texas; born on a farm near Stephenville, Erath County, Tex., August 9, 1889; attended the rural schools and the John Tarleton College, Stephenville, Tex.; taught school in Erath County, Tex., 1913–1918; also engaged in agricultural pursuits; during the First World War served as a private in the Forty-sixth Machine Gun Company, United States Army, in 1918 and 1919; studied law; was admitted to the bar in 1919 and commenced practice in Stephenville, Tex.; served as county attorney of Erath County, Tex., 1919–1924; district attorney of the twenty-ninth judicial district 1924–1928; served as judge of the twenty-ninth judicial district 1928–1940; elected as a Democrat to the Seventy-seventh, Seventy-eighth, and Seventy-ninth Congresses (January 3, 1941–January 3, 1947); was not a candidate for renomination in 1946; resumed the practice of law, and is a resident of Stephenville, Tex.

RUSSELL, Samuel Lyon (son of James McPherson Russell), a Representative from Pennsylvania; born in Bedford, Pa., July 30, 1816; attended the common schools and Bedford Academy; was graduated from Washington College, Pennsylvania, in 1834; studied law; was admitted to the bar in 1837 and commenced practice in Bedford; prosecuting attorney of Bedford County during the forties; elected as a Whig to the Thirty-third Congress (March 4, 1853–March 3, 1855); was not a candidate for renomination; resumed the practice of law in Bedford, Bedford County, Pa.; became a Republican upon the organization of that party in 1856; member of the State constitutional convention in 1873; member of the town council and the school board; trustee of the cemetery association; died in Bedford, Pa., September 27, 1891; interment in Bedford Cemetery.

RUSSELL, William, a Representative from Ohio; born in Ireland in 1782; immigrated to the United States and settled in West Union, Ohio; received a limited schooling; held several local offices; member of the State house of representatives in 1809, 1810, and 1811–1813; served in the State senate 1819–1821; elected as a Jackson Democrat to the Twentieth, Twenty-first, and Twenty-second Congresses (March 4, 1827–March 3, 1833); unsuccessful candidate for reelection in 1832 to the Twenty-third Congress; moved to Portsmouth, Scioto County, Ohio; was elected as a Whig to the Twenty-seventh Congress (March 4, 1841–March 3, 1843); was not a candidate for renomination in 1842; retired to his farm on Scioto Brush Creek, where he died September 28, 1845; interment in a church burying ground at Rushtown, Scioto County, Ohio, west of Portsmouth.

RUSSELL, William Augustus, a Representative from Massachusetts; born at Wells River, Orange County, Vt., April 22, 1831; pursued an academic course in Franklin, N. H.; engaged in the manufacture of paper in Exeter, N. H., in 1852; moved to Lawrence, Mass., in 1852, where he continued in that business; member of the State house of representatives in 1869; delegate to the Republican National Conventions in 1868 and 1876; elected as a Republican to the Forty-sixth, Forty-seventh, and Forty-eighth Congresses (March 4, 1879–March 3, 1885); after leaving Congress devoted his time to the manufacture of paper; died in Boston, Mass., January 10, 1899; interment in Bellevue Cemetery, Lawrence, Essex County, Mass.

RUSSELL, William Fiero, a Representative from New York; born in Saugerties, Ulster County, N. Y., January 14, 1812; completed preparatory studies; engaged in mercantile pursuits and banking; founder and president of the Saugerties Bank; served as postmaster of Saugerties from October 19, 1836, to January 25, 1841; member of the State assembly in 1851; elected as a Democrat to the Thirty-fifth Congress (March 4, 1857–March 3, 1859); appointed as naval agent for the port of New York City in 1859; resumed the banking business; died in Saugerties, N. Y., April 29, 1896; interment in Mountain View Cemetery.

RUST, Albert, a Representative from Arkansas; was born in Virginia; completed preparatory studies; studied law; was admitted to the bar and commenced practice in El Dorado, Union County, Ark.; member of the State house of representatives 1842–1848 and 1852–1854; elected as a Democrat to the Thirty-fourth Congress (March 4, 1855–March 3, 1857); unsuccessful candidate for reelection in 1856 to the Thirty-fifth Congress; elected to the Thirty-sixth Congress (March 4, 1859–March 3, 1861); brigadier general in the Confederate Army during the Civil War; resumed the practice of his profession; died in El Dorado, Ark., April 3, 1870; interment in the Old Methodist Cemetery.

RUTHERFORD, Albert Greig, a Representative from Pennsylvania; born in Watford, Ontario Province, Canada, January 3, 1879; immigrated to the United States in 1883 with his parents, who settled in Carbondale, Pa.; attended the public schools, Carbondale High School, Blair Academy, Blairstown, N. J., and Scranton-Lackawanna Business College; was graduated from the law department of the University of Pennsylvania at Philadelphia in 1904; was admitted to the bar October 10, 1904, and commenced practice in Scranton, Pa.; affiliated with the Democratic Party; served as deputy prothonotary of Lackawanna County, Pa., 1907–1914; moved to Honesdale, Wayne County, Pa., in 1918 and continued the practice of law; enlisted in the Pennsylvania National Guard in 1904; became regimental sergeant major in 1908; subsequently was commissioned a first lieutenant and later a captain; served as major and inspector from 1910 to 1916 and as major and judge advocate general in 1917; served as a lieutenant colonel of the Second Pennsylvania Reserve Militia in 1918; elected as a Republican to the Seventy-fifth, Seventy-sixth, and Seventy-seventh Congresses and served from January 3, 1937, until his death in Washington, D. C., on August 10, 1941; interment in Glen Dyberry Cemetery, Honesdale, Pa.

RUTHERFORD, J. T., a Representative from Texas; born in Hot Springs, Ark., May 30, 1920; moved to Odessa, Tex., in 1934 and attended the public schools; during World War II served as an enlisted man in the United States Marine Corps 1942–1946 with twenty-eight months overseas; awarded the Purple Heart Medal; captain in the United States Marine Corps Reserve; student at San Angelo (Tex.) College in 1946 and 1947 and Sul Ross State College, Alpine, Tex., in 1947 and 1948; attended Baylor University Law School, Waco, Tex., 1948–1950; partner in industrial electrical construction firm; served in the State house of representatives 1948–1952; member of the State senate 1952–1954; elected as a Democrat to the Eighty-fourth, Eighty-fifth, and Eighty-sixth Congresses (January 3, 1955–January 3, 1961). *Reelected to the Eighty-seventh Congress.*

RUTHERFORD, Robert, a Representative from Virginia; born in Scotland, October 20, 1728; completed preparatory studies and was educated at the Royal College of Edinburgh; immigrated to the United States and settled in Berks County, Tenn., and subsequently moved to Virginia; was high sheriff of Frederick County, Va., 1743–1744; held several local offices; delegate to the conventions in Richmond and Williamsburg, July and December 1775 and May 1776; served in the State senate 1776–1790; elected to the Third and Fourth Congresses (March 4, 1793–March 3, 1797); unsuccessful candidate for reelection in 1796 to the Fifth Congress; settled on his estate "Flowing Spring" near Charles Town, Va. (now West Virginia) and resided there until his death in October 1803; interment on "Flowing Spring" estate (later owned by the widow of John C. Burns) located about three miles northeast of Charles Town on the Charles Town-Duffield road.

RUTHERFORD, Samuel, a Representative from Georgia; born near Culloden, Crawford County, Ga., March 15, 1870; attended the public schools at Culloden and Washington and Lee University, Lexington, Va.; was graduated from the law department of the University of Georgia at Athens in 1894; was admitted to the bar the same year and commenced practice in Forsyth, Monroe County, Ga.; mayor of Forsyth for three consecutive years; member of the State house of representatives in 1896 and 1897; solicitor of the city court of Forsyth 1898–1900; interested in banking 1901–1916; served in the State senate in 1909 and 1910; resumed the practice of law and also engaged in agricultural pursuits; again a member of the State house of representatives 1921–1924; elected as a Democrat to the Sixty-ninth and to the three succeeding Congresses and served from March 4, 1925, until his death in Washington, D. C., on February 4, 1932; interment in Oakland Cemetery, Forsyth, Ga.

RUTHERFURD, John, a Senator from New Jersey; born in New York City on September 20, 1760; was graduated from Princeton College in 1779; studied law; was admitted to the bar and commenced practice in New York City in 1784; moved to a farm near Allamuchy, Warren County, N. J., in 1787; presidential elector in 1788; member of the State general assembly in 1788 and 1789; elected in 1790 as a Federalist to the United States Senate; reelected in 1796 and served from March 4, 1791, to December 5, 1798, when he resigned; president of the Board of Proprietors of East Jersey 1804–1840; appointed by the New York Legislature as commissioner to lay out the city of New York north of Fourteenth Street, and served from 1807 to 1811; moved to a large farm on the banks of the Passaic River, between Belleville and Passaic, in 1808, which he called "Edgerston"; appointed by the New Jersey Legislature as commissioner to determine the route and cost of a canal to connect the Delaware and Raritan Rivers in 1816; served as a commissioner to deter-

mine the boundary lines between the States of New Jersey and New York and New Jersey and Pennsylvania 1826–1833; delegate to the Anti-Masonic Convention at Baltimore, Md., in 1831; died at his home, "Edgerston," New Jersey, February 23, 1840; interment in the family vault in the burying ground of Christ Church, Belleville, Essex County, N. J.

RUTLEDGE, Edward (brother of John Rutledge), a Delegate from South Carolina; born in Christ Church Parish, S. C., November 23, 1749; completed preparatory studies; studied law at the Middle Temple in London; returned to South Carolina; was admitted to the bar and commenced practice in 1773; Member of the Continental Congress 1774–1777; a signer of the Declaration of Independence; was a delegate to the first provincial congress in 1775 and to the second provincial congress 1775–1776; appointed a member of the first board of war in June 1776; member of the general assembly in 1778; elected a Member of the Continental Congress in 1779 but did not take his seat; captain in the Charleston Battalion of Artillery in the Militia of South Carolina in the Revolution; taken prisoner when the British captured Charleston May 12, 1780, imprisoned at St. Augustine until July 1781, when he was exchanged; member of the State house of representatives in 1782, 1786, 1788, and 1792; member of the State constitutional convention in 1790 and was author of the act abolishing the law of primogeniture in 1791; presidential elector in 1796 and voted for Thomas Jefferson, of Virginia, and Thomas Pinckney, of South Carolina; was tendered the appointment of Associate Justice of the United States Supreme Court in 1794 by President Washington, but did not accept; elected Governor of South Carolina and served from December 6, 1798, until his death in Charleston, S. C., January 23, 1800; interment in St. Philip's Churchyard.

RUTLEDGE, John (brother of Edward Rutledge and father of John Rutledge, Jr.), a Delegate from South Carolina; born in Christ Church Parish, S. C., in 1739; pursued classical studies; studied law in Charleston and later at the Middle Temple in London; returned to Charleston, S. C., and commenced practice in 1761; elected to the provincial assembly in 1762; attorney general pro tempore in 1764 and 1765; delegate to the Stamp Act Congress at New York City in 1765 and, although the youngest member of the Congress, was made chairman of the committee that drafted the memorial and petition to the House of Lords; continued the practice of law; Member of the Continental Congress 1774–1776; served as President and commander in chief of South Carolina 1776–1778 and as Governor 1779–1782; again a Member of the Continental Congress in 1782 and 1783; appointed Minister to Holland in 1783 but declined; elected one of the State chancellors in 1784; delegate to the Constitutional Convention in 1787; member of the State convention to ratify the Federal Constitution in 1788; received the electoral vote of South Carolina for Vice President in 1789; Associate Justice of the United States Supreme Court 1789–1791; elected chief justice of South Carolina in 1790 and served until 1795, when he resigned; nominated in 1795 to be Chief Justice of the Supreme Court of the United States and presided at the August term, but the Senate on December 15, 1795, refused to confirm him; died in Charleston, S. C., July 23, 1800; interment in St. Michael's Churchyard.

RUTLEDGE, John, Jr. (son of the preceding), a Representative from South Carolina; born in Charleston, S. C., in 1766; received private instruction and also attended school in Charleston and Philadelphia; studied law with his father; was admitted to the bar about 1787 and practiced in Charleston, S. C.; also engaged as a planter; member of the State house of representatives 1788–1794 and in 1811; unsuccessful candidate for election in 1794 to the Fourth Congress; elected as a Federalist to the Fifth, Sixth, and Seventh Congresses (March 4, 1797–March 3, 1803); unsuccessful candidate for election to the Thirteenth Congress; commanded a company of the Twenty-eighth Regiment, South Carolina Militia, in 1799; promoted to major and in 1804 succeeded to the command of the regiment and served as its commander in the War of 1812; commanded the Seventh Brigade from 1816 until his death; died in Philadelphia, Pa., September 1, 1819.

RYALL, Daniel Bailey, a Representative from New Jersey; born in Trenton, N. J., January 30, 1798; completed preparatory studies at Trenton, N. J.; attended Trenton Academy; studied law; was admitted to the bar in 1820 and commenced practice in Freehold, N. J.; member of the State general assembly 1831 and 1833–1835 and served as speaker 1833–1835; elected as a Democrat to the Twenty-sixth Congress (March 4, 1839–March 3, 1841); resumed the practice of law; died in Freehold, Monmouth County, N. J., December 17, 1864; interment in Maplewood Cemetery.

RYAN, Elmer James, a Representative from Minnesota; born in Rosemount, Dakota County, Minn., May 26, 1907; attended the public schools; was graduated from the law department of the University of Minnesota at Minneapolis in 1929; was admitted to the bar the same year and commenced practice in South St. Paul, Minn.; city attorney of South St. Paul 1933–1934; delegate to the Democratic National Conventions in 1936 and 1940; elected as a Democrat to the Seventy-fourth, Seventy-fifth, and Seventy-sixth Congresses (January 3, 1935–January 3, 1941); unsuccessful candidate for reelection in 1940 to the Seventy-seventh Congress; resumed the practice of law; during World War II entered on active duty in the United States Army on June 23, 1942, as a lieutenant in the Selective Service; was promoted to captain and transferred to the Judge Advocate General's department, later promoted to major and was discharged on October 1, 1945; again resumed the practice of law in South St. Paul, Minn.; died in an automobile accident on Highway 35, five miles north of Somerset, Wis., February 1, 1958; interment in Rosemount Cemetery, Rosemount, Minn.

RYAN, James Wilfrid, a Representative from Pennsylvania; born in Norwegian Township, Schuylkill County, Pa., October 16, 1858; moved to Mahanoy City with his parents, where he attended the public schools; was graduated from the high school of Frackville, Pa.; engaged in teaching in the public schools; studied law; was admitted to the bar in 1884 and commenced practice in Pottsville, Pa.; elected district attorney in 1892 and served until January 1896; elected as a Democrat to the Fifty-sixth Congress (March 4, 1899–March 3, 1901); resumed the practice of law; died in Mahanoy City, Pa., on February 26, 1907; interment in the Holy Rosary Cemetery, Frackville, Pa.

RYAN, Thomas, a Representative from Kansas; born in Oxford, Chenango County, N. Y., November 25, 1837; moved with his parents to Bradford County, Pa.; attended Dickson Seminary in Williamsport, Pa.; studied law; was admitted to the bar in 1861; during the Civil War served in the Union Army 1862–1864; moved to Topeka, Kans., 1865; prosecuting attorney of Shawnee County 1865–1873; assistant United States attorney for Kansas 1873–1877; elected as a Republican to the Forty-fifth and to the six succeeding Congresses and served from March 4, 1877, to April 4, 1889, when he resigned; Minister to the Republic of Mexico 1889–1893; appointed First Assistant Secretary of the Interior by President McKinley in 1897, reappointed by President Theodore Roosevelt, and served in that capacity until 1907, when he was sent to Muskogee, Okla.,

as the personal resident representative of the Secretary of the Interior; died in Muskogee, Okla., April 5, 1914; interment in Topeka Cemetery, Topeka, Kans.

RYAN, Thomas Jefferson, a Representative from New York; born in New York City June 17, 1890; attended the public schools and the College of the City of New York; was graduated from the scientific school of Fordham University, New York City, in 1908 and from the law department of that institution in 1911; was admitted to the bar in 1912 and commenced practice in New York City; was wounded while serving as an aviator in France during the First World War; cited for bravery in action and decorated with the Croix de Guerre with Palm; elected as a Republican to the Sixty-seventh Congress (March 4, 1921–March 3, 1923); unsuccessful candidate for reelection in 1922 to the Sixty-eighth Congress; delegate to the State convention in 1922; resumed the practice of law; delegate to the Republican National Convention at Cleveland in 1924; special deputy attorney general of New York in 1925; served as counsel to the Alien Property Custodian 1925–1930; affiliated with the Democratic Party since 1926; resumed the practice of law in New York City; resides in Coral Gables, Fla.

RYAN, William, a Representative from New York; born in Tipperary, Ireland, March 8, 1840; immigrated to the United States with his parents, who settled in Stanwich, Conn., in 1844; attended the district schools; in the spring of 1859 went to the Rocky Mountains and engaged in prospecting, mining, and also in campaigns against the Indians until 1861, when he returned East and settled in Port Chester, Westchester County, N. Y.; engaged in agricultural pursuits and teaching and later in mercantile pursuits; supervisor of the town of Rye 1883–1885; member of the State assembly in 1891 and 1892; elected as a Democrat to the Fifty-third Congress (March 4, 1893–March 3, 1895); unsuccessful candidate for reelection in 1894 to the Fifty-fourth Congress; resumed business as a merchant in Port Chester, N. Y.; president of the Port Chester Savings Bank and president of the village of Port Chester in 1912; died in Crescent City, Fla., February 18, 1925; interment in St. Mary's Cemetery, Greenwich, Conn.

RYAN, William Henry, a Representative from New York; born in Hopkinton, Middlesex County, Mass., May 10, 1860; moved to Buffalo, N. Y., with his parents in 1866; attended the grade and high schools; engaged in the retail shoe business and later in the general insurance and bonding business; elected to the board of supervisors of Erie County in 1894; reelected in 1897, and served as chairman in 1898; elected as a Democrat to the Fifty-sixth and to the four succeeding Congresses (March 4, 1899–March 3, 1909); unsuccessful candidate for renomination in 1908; delegate to the Democratic National Conventions in 1904 and 1924; resumed the insurance and bonding business in Buffalo, N. Y., and also engaged in banking; member of the grade crossing and terminal commission 1919–1939; member of the Allegany State Park Commission 1930–1939; died in Buffalo, N. Y., November 18, 1939; interment in Mount Calvary Cemetery, at Pine Hill, near Buffalo, N. Y.

RYON, John Walker, a Representative from Pennsylvania; born in Elkland, Tioga County, Pa., March 4, 1825; attended the common schools, Millville Academy, Orleans County, N. Y., and Wellsboro Academy, Wellsboro, Pa.; studied law; was admitted to the bar in 1847 and commenced practice in Lawrenceville, Pa.; district attorney of Tioga County 1850–1856; during the Civil War assisted in the organization of Company A of the famous Bucktail Regiment; appointed by Governor Curtin paymaster with the rank of major in the reserve corps; moved to

Pottsville, Pa., and resumed the practice of law; elected as a Democrat to the Forty-sixth Congress (March 4, 1879–March 3, 1881); president of the Pennsylvania National Bank for several years; also interested in various other business enterprises; died in Pottsville, Schuylkill County, Pa., March 12, 1901; interment in St. Patrick's (No. 3) Cemetery.

RYTER, Joseph Francis, a Representative from Connecticut; born in Hartford, Conn., February 4, 1914; attended the parochial schools and St. Thomas Seminary, Bloomfield, Conn.; was graduated from Trinity College, Hartford, Conn., in 1935 and from Hartford (Conn.) College of Law in 1938; was admitted to the bar in 1938 and commenced practice in Hartford, Conn.; assistant clerk of Hartford Police Court 1939–1941, and of Hartford City Court 1941–1943; delegate to the Democratic National Convention at Chicago in 1940; president of Pulaski Federation of Democratic Clubs of Connecticut 1939–1942; elected as a Democrat to the Seventy-ninth Congress (January 3, 1945–January 3, 1947); was an unsuccessful candidate for reelection in 1946 to the Eightieth Congress; resumed the practice of his profession and is a resident of West Hartford, Conn.

S

SABATH, Adolph Joachim, a Representative from Illinois; born in Zabori, Czechoslovakia, April 4, 1866; attended the schools of his native town; immigrated to the United States in 1881 and settled in Chicago, Ill.; was graduated from the Chicago College of Law in 1891; was admitted to the bar in 1892 and commenced practice in Chicago, Ill.; ward committeeman and district leader in Chicago 1892–1944; appointed justice of the peace for the city of Chicago in 1895; police magistrate 1897–1906; member of the central and executive committees of the Democratic Party from 1909 to 1920; delegate to all the Democratic State conventions 1890–1952; delegate to all Democratic National Conventions 1896–1944; declined nomination for municipal judge; elected as a Democrat to the Sixtieth and to the twenty-three succeeding Congresses, but died before the convening of the Eighty-third Congress; served from March 4, 1907, until his death in the naval hospital at Bethesda, Md., November 6, 1952; interment in Forest Home Cemetery, Forest Park, Ill.

SABIN, Alvah, a Representative from Vermont; born in Georgia, Franklin County, Vt., October 23, 1793; attended the common schools and Burlington College; member of the State militia and served during the War of 1812; studied theology in Philadelphia; was graduated from Columbian College (now George Washington University), Washington, D. C., in 1821; was ordained a minister and preached at Cambridge, Westfield, and Underhill until 1825, when he returned to Georgia, Vt.; was pastor of the Georgia Baptist Church over forty years; member of the State house of representatives 1826–1835, 1838–1840, 1847–1849, 1851, 1861, and 1862; served in the State senate in 1841, 1843, and 1845; secretary of state of Vermont in 1841; elected as a Whig to the Thirty-third and Thirty-fourth Congresses (March 4, 1853–March 3, 1857); was not a candidate for renomination in 1856; delegate to the first Anti-Slavery National Convention; county commissioner of Franklin County in 1861 and 1862; moved to Sycamore, De Kalb County, Ill., in 1867 and continued his ministerial duties; died in Sycamore, Ill., January 22, 1885; interment in Georgia Plain Cemetery, Georgia Plain, Franklin County, Vt.

SABIN, Dwight May, a Senator from Minnesota; born near Marseilles, La Salle County, Ill., April 25, 1843; moved to Connecticut with his parents in 1857; attended the country schools and Phillips Academy, Andover, Mass.; served in the Union Army during the Civil War; employed as a clerk in Washington, D. C.; returned to Connecticut in 1864 and engaged in agricultural pursuits and also the lumber business; moved to Stillwater, Minn., in 1868; engaged in lumbering and the general manufacture of railroad cars and agricultural machinery; member of the Minnesota State Senate 1872–1875; served in the State house of representatives in 1878 and 1881; member of the Republican National Committee for Minnesota; delegate to the Republican National Conventions in 1872, 1876, 1880, and 1884; served as chairman of the Republican National Committee in 1883 and 1884; elected as a Republican to the United States Senate and served from March 4, 1883, to March 3, 1889; unsuccessful candidate for renomination in 1886; engaged in the coal, lumber, and manufacturing business; died in Chicago, Ill., on December 22, 1902; interment in Fairview Cemetery, Stillwater, Washington County, Minn.

SABINE, Lorenzo, a Representative from Massachusetts; born in New Concord (now Lisbon), N. H., February 28, 1803; moved to Boston, Mass., with his parents in 1811 and to Hampden, Maine, in 1814; completed preparatory studies; at the age of eighteen moved to Eastport, Maine, and became employed as a clerk and afterward engaged in mercantile pursuits; editor of the Eastport Sentinel; founder of the Eastport Lyceum; incorporator of Eastport Academy and Eastport Athenaeum; member of the Maine House of Representatives in 1833 and 1834; deputy collector of customs at Eastport 1841–1843; moved to Framingham, Mass., in 1848, having been appointed trial justice; elected as a Whig to the Thirty-second Congress to fill the vacancy caused by the death of Benjamin Thompson and served from December 13, 1852, to March 3, 1853; was not a candidate for the Thirty-third Congress; moved to Roxbury, Mass., having been appointed secretary of the Boston Board of Trade; also served as special agent of the United States Treasury Department; engaged in literary pursuits; died in Roxbury, Mass., April 14, 1877; interment in Hillside Cemetery, Eastport, Washington County, Maine.

SACKETT, Frederic Mosley, a Senator from Kentucky; born in Providence, R. I., December 17, 1868; attended the public schools; was graduated from Brown University at Providence in 1890 and from the law department of Harvard University in 1893; was admitted to the bar in 1893 and commenced practice in Columbus, Ohio, the same year; moved to Cincinnati, Ohio, in 1897, to Louisville, Ky., in 1898, and continued the practice of his profession until 1907; was also interested in the mining of coal and the manufacture of cement; president of the Louisville Gas Co. and of the Louisville Lighting Co. 1907–1912; member of the Board of Trade of Louisville, serving as president in 1917, 1922, and 1923; director of the Louisville Branch of the Federal Reserve Bank 1917–1924; during the First World War served as Federal food administrator for Kentucky 1917–1919; member of the Kentucky State Board of Charities and Corrections 1919–1924; elected as a Republican to the United States Senate in 1924 and served from March 4, 1925, to January 9, 1930, when he resigned, having been appointed Ambassador to Germany by President Hoover, in which capacity he served from January 9, 1930, until April 23, 1933, when he resigned; resumed his former business activities; died on May 18, 1941, while on a visit in Baltimore, Md.; interment in Cave Hill Cemetery, Louisville, Ky.

SACKETT, William Augustus, a Representative from New York; born in Aurelius, near Auburn, N. Y., November 18, 1811; attended private schools and Aurora Academy; moved to Seneca Falls, Seneca County, N. Y., in 1831; studied law;

was admitted to the bar in 1834 and commenced practice at Seneca Falls; elected as a Whig to the Thirty-first and Thirty-second Congresses (March 4, 1849–March 3, 1853); resumed the practice of law at Seneca Falls, N. Y.; moved to Saratoga Springs in 1857; register in bankruptcy during the term of the 1867 bankruptcy law; died at Saratoga Springs, N. Y., September 6, 1895; interment in Greenridge Cemetery.

SACKS, Leon, a Representative from Pennsylvania; born in Philadelphia, Pa., October 7, 1902; attended the public schools; was graduated from the Wharton School of the University of Pennsylvania at Philadelphia in 1923, and from the law department of the University of Pennsylvania in 1926; was admitted to the bar in 1926 and commenced the practice of law in Philadelphia, Pa.; appointed deputy attorney general of Pennsylvania in February 1935 and served until January 1937; elected as a member of the Democratic State committee in 1936 and served until 1942; elected as a Democrat to the Seventy-fifth, Seventy-sixth, and Seventy-seventh Congresses (January 3, 1937–January 3, 1943); was an unsuccessful candidate for reelection in 1942 to the Seventy-eighth Congress; during World War II served at Headquarters, Army Air Forces Eastern Flying Training Command, with the rank of lieutenant colonel, from January 4, 1943, to January 10, 1946; resumed the practice of his profession; member of State Veterans Commission 1951–; registration commissioner of Philadelphia 1952–; member of Military Reservations Commission 1957–; is a resident of Philadelphia, Pa.

SADLAK, Antoni Nicholas, a Representative from Connecticut; born in Rockville, Tolland County, Conn., June 13, 1908; attended the parochial school; was graduated from George Sykes Manual Training and High School in 1926 and from the Georgetown University School of Law, Washington, D. C., in 1931; special inspector for the Department of Justice from July 1941 to December 1942; assistant secretary-treasurer of the Farmers' Production Credit Association, Hartford, Conn., 1944–1946; secretary to former Representative Boleslaus Joseph Monkiewicz in 1939, 1940, 1943, and 1944, from which he resigned in March 1944 to accept a commission in the United States Naval Reserve; served in New Guinea, the Philippines, and China and was discharged as a lieutenant in April 1946; educational supervisor in the Connecticut Department of Education from July 1, 1946, to September 15, 1946; elected as a Republican to the Eightieth and to the five succeeding Congresses (January 3, 1947–January 3, 1959); unsuccessful candidate for reelection in 1958; regional assistant manager, Veterans Administration, Hartford, Conn., from March 30, 1959, to May 2, 1960; engaged in lecturing and legislative consultation; is a resident of Rockville, Conn.

SADLER, Thomas William, a Representative from Alabama; born near Russellville, Franklin County, Ala., April 17, 1831; moved with his parents to Jefferson County, Ala., in 1833; pursued an academic course; moved to Autauga County, Ala., in 1855 and engaged in mercantile pursuits; during the Civil War volunteered and served in the division of the Confederate Army commanded by Gen. Joseph Wheeler; engaged in agricultural pursuits; studied law; was admitted to the bar in 1867 and commenced practice in Prattville, Ala.; county superintendent of education 1875–1884; presidential elector on the Democratic ticket of Hancock and English in 1880; elected as a Democrat to the Forty-ninth Congress (March 4, 1885–March 3, 1887); unsuccessful candidate for renomination in 1886; resumed the practice of law; died in Prattville, Autauga County, Ala., October 29, 1896; interment in Oak Hill Cemetery.

SADOWSKI, George Gregory, a Representative from Michigan; born in Detroit, Mich., March 12, 1903; attended the Ferry School, Detroit, Mich., and high school in Foley, Ala.; was graduated from Northeastern High School, Detroit, Mich., in 1920 and from the law department of the University of Detroit, Detroit, Mich., in 1924; was admitted to the bar in 1926 and commenced practice in Detroit, Mich.; also interested in the real estate and building businesses; member of the State senate in 1931 and 1932; member of the State Democratic central committee 1930–1936; delegate to the Democratic National Conventions in 1932, 1936, 1940, 1944, and 1948; elected as a Democrat to the Seventy-third, Seventy-fourth, and Seventy-fifth Congresses (March 4, 1933–January 3, 1939); unsuccessful for renomination in 1938; elected to the Seventy-eighth and to the three succeeding Congresses (January 3, 1943–January 3, 1951); unsuccessful for renomination in 1950; owner of the Sunnybrook Golf Club, Utica, Mich., and the Rochester Golf Club, Rochester, Mich.; died in Utica, Mich., October 9, 1961; interment in Mount Olivet Cemetery, Detroit, Mich.

SAGE, Ebenezer, a Representative from New York; born in Chatham (now Portland), Conn., August 16, 1755; received his early education from a private tutor and was graduated from Yale College in 1778; studied medicine; commenced practice in Easthampton, Suffolk County, Long Island, N. Y., in 1784; moved to Sag Harbor, N. Y., about 1801; elected as a Democrat to the Eleventh, Twelfth, and Thirteenth Congresses (March 4, 1809–March 3, 1815); was not a candidate for reelection; credentials of his election to the Sixteenth Congress were presented but he did not qualify, and on January 14, 1820, James Guyon, Jr., successfully contested his election; resumed the practice of medicine at Sag Harbor, N. Y.; delegate to the State constitutional convention of 1821; died at Sag Harbor, Suffolk County, N. Y., January 20, 1834; interment in the Old Burying Ground; reinterment in Oakland Cemetery.

SAGE, Russell, a Representative from New York; born in Shenandoah, Oneida County, N. Y., August 4, 1816; moved with his parents to Durhamville in 1818; attended the public schools; engaged in mercantile pursuits in Troy, N. Y.; treasurer of Rensselaer County 1844–1851; alderman of Troy 1845–1848; delegate to the Whig National Convention at Baltimore in 1848; elected as a Whig to the Thirty-third and Thirty-fourth Congresses (March 4, 1853–March 3, 1857); was not a candidate for renomination in 1856; moved to New York City in 1863; became president and director of several railroad companies and financial institutions; died in Lawrence, Long Island, N. Y., July 22, 1906; interment in Oakwood Cemetery, Troy, N. Y.

SAILLY, Peter, a Representative from New York; born in Lorraine, France, April 20, 1754; immigrated to the United States in 1783 and settled in Plattsburg, N. Y.; engaged in mercantile pursuits and as a fur trader; also engaged in the manufacture of potash and in the shipping of lumber; associate justice of the court of common pleas 1788–1796; commissioner of highways and school commissioner in 1797 and 1798; supervisor of schools in 1799 and 1800; member of the State assembly in 1803; judge of Clinton County 1804–1806; elected as a Democrat in the Ninth Congress (March 4, 1805–March 3, 1807); declined a renomination in 1806; collector of customs at Plattsburg from 1807 until his death there March 16, 1826; interment in Riverside Cemetery.

ST. CLAIR, Arthur, a Delegate from Pennsylvania; born in Thurso, Caithness, Scotland, March 23, 1734 (old style); attended the University of Edinburgh and studied medicine under Dr. John Hunter; purchased a commission as ensign in the Sixtieth Foot, May 13, 1757, and came to America with Admiral Boscawen's fleet; served under General Amherst at the capture of Louisburg July 26, 1758, and under Gen. James Wolfe at Quebec September 30, 1758; resigned April 16, 1762; settled in Ligonier Valley, Pa., in 1764, where he erected mills; surveyor of the district of Cumberland in 1770; justice of the court of quarter sessions and of common pleas; member of the proprietary council, justice, recorder, and clerk of the orphans' court; prothonotary of Bedford and Westmoreland Counties; colonel of the Pennsylvania Militia in July 1775; colonel of the Second Pennsylvania Battalion January 3, 1776; brigadier general in the Continental Army August 9, 1776; major general February 19, 1777, and served until the close of the Revolutionary War; member of the military tribunal that tried and convicted Major André in 1780; major general and commander of the United States Army March 4, 1791, being the only soldier from Pennsylvania who attained that rank during the Revolutionary War; resigned March 5, 1792; was a member of the Pennsylvania council of censors in 1783; Member of the Continental Congress from November 2, 1785, to November 28, 1787, and its President in 1787; appointed Governor of the Northwest Territory upon its formation in 1789 and served until November 22, 1802; returned to Ligonier Valley, Pa., and engaged in the iron business; was one of the founders of the iron business in Pittsburgh, Pa.; died near his old home, "Hermitage," near Youngstown, Pa., August 31, 1818; interment in General Arthur St. Clair Cemetery, Greensburg, Pa.

ST. GEORGE, Katharine Price Collier, a Representative from New York; born in Bridgenorth, England; at the age of two came to United States with her parents, who had been living abroad, and resided in Tuxedo, Orange County, N. Y.; attended private schools; at the age of eleven returned to Europe and was educated in England, France, and Germany; returned to Tuxedo, N. Y., in 1914; member of the town board of Tuxedo Park 1926–1949; member, treasurer, vice chairman, and chairman of the Orange County Republican committee 1942–1948; delegate to the Republican National Convention at Chicago in 1944; member of the Tuxedo Park Board of Education 1926–1946, serving as president 1930–1946; elected as a Republican to the Eightieth and to the six succeeding Congresses (January 3, 1947–January 3, 1961). *Reelected to the Eighty-seventh Congress.*

ST. JOHN, Charles, a Representative from New York; born at Mount Hope, Orange County, N. Y., October 8, 1818; attended the common schools and Goshen and Newburgh (N. Y.) Academies; engaged in lumbering on the Delaware River and in mercantile pursuits and banking at Port Jervis, N. Y.; served as internal revenue collector during the Civil War and later as president of the Barrett Bridge Co.; elected as a Republican to the Forty-second and Forty-third Congresses (March 4, 1871–March 3, 1875); resumed his former business activities; presidential elector on the Republican ticket of Garfield and Arthur in 1880; died in Port Jervis, N. Y., July 6, 1891; interment in Laurel Grove Cemetery.

ST. JOHN, Daniel Bennett, a Representative from New York; born in Sharon, Conn., October 8, 1808; engaged in mercantile pursuits and the real-estate business at Monticello, N. Y., in 1831; member of the State assembly in 1840; elected as a Whig to the Thirtieth Congress (March 4, 1847–March 3, 1849); moved to Newburgh, N. Y.; delegate to the Constitutional-Union National Convention at Baltimore in 1860; unsuccessful Democratic candidate for election to the Thirty-seventh Congress in 1860; member of the State senate in 1875; delegate to the Democratic National Convention at St. Louis in 1876; chief registrar in the banking department of New York State; died in New York City February 18, 1890; interment in Woodlawn Cemetery, Newburgh, Orange County, N. Y.

ST. JOHN, Henry, a Representative from Ohio; born in Washington County, Vt., July 16, 1783; received a limited schooling; served during the War of 1812; moved to Wooster, Ohio, in 1815, to Crawford County, Ohio, in 1828, and in 1837 to Seneca County, where he engaged in agricultural pursuits, milling, and storekeeping near Tiffin, Ohio; elected as a Democrat to the Twenty-eighth and Twenty-ninth Congresses (March 4, 1843–March 3, 1847); was not a candidate for renomination; resumed agricultural pursuits; retired from public life, and resided in Tiffin, Ohio, where he died in May 1869.

ST. MARTIN, Louis, a Representative from Louisiana; born in St. Charles Parish, La., on May 17, 1820; attended St. Mary's College, Missouri, and Jefferson College, Louisiana; entered a notarial office and studied law until appointed a clerk in the post office at New Orleans; elected a member of the State house of representatives in 1840; appointed by President Polk register of the United States land office for the southeastern district of Louisiana in 1846 and served until 1849; member of the State house of representatives 1846–1850; elected as a Democrat to the Thirty-second Congress (March 4, 1851–March 3, 1853); was not a candidate for reelection in 1852; engaged in mercantile pursuits; appointed register of voters for the city of New Orleans by Gov. Robert C. Wickliffe and reappointed by Gov. Thomas O. Moore; credentials of election to the Thirty-ninth Congress were presented, but as the State had not been readmitted to representation, did not qualify; presented credentials as a Member-elect to the Forty-first Congress, but the House decided that no valid election had been held; delegate to the Democratic National Conventions in 1852, 1868, 1876, and 1880; presidential elector on the Democratic ticket of Seymour and Blair in 1868 and of Tilden and Hendricks in 1876; again engaged in mercantile pursuits; elected as a Democrat to the Forty-ninth Congress (March 4, 1885–March 3, 1887); was connected with the office of public accounts in the city hall at the time of his death; died in New Orleans, La., February 9, 1893; interment in St. Vincent de Paul Cemetery.

SALMON, Joshua S., a Representative from New Jersey; born at Mount Olive, Morris County, N. J., February 2, 1846; at an early age moved with his parents to the village of Bartley; attended the district school; taught school for two years; completed an academic course at the Charlotteville (N. Y.) Seminary and at Schooley's Mountain Seminary, New Jersey, where he afterward became an instructor; was graduated from the Albany (N. Y.) Law School in 1873; was admitted to the New York bar in 1873, to the New Jersey bar in 1875, and commenced practice in Jersey City, N. J.; moved to Boonton, Morris County, and practiced there and in Morristown, the county seat; held several county offices; member of the State house of assembly in 1877 and 1878; prosecuting attorney of Morris County 1893–1898; delegate to the Democratic National Convention at Kansas City in 1900; elected as a Democrat to the Fifty-sixth and Fifty-seventh Congresses and served from March 4, 1899, until his death in Boonton, N. J., May 6, 1902; interment in Greenwood Cemetery.

SALMON, William Charles, a Representative from Tennessee; born near Paris, Henry County, Tenn., on April 3, 1868; attended the public schools, Edgewood Normal School, Dickson College, and Valparaiso University at Valparaiso, Ind; was graduated in law from Cumberland University, Lebanon, Tenn., in 1897; was admitted to the bar the same year and commenced practice in Columbia, Maury County, Tenn.; taught in public and private schools for six years and also engaged in agricultural pursuits; served as special circuit judge of the eleventh judicial circuit of Tennessee in 1908; president of the Columbia Board of Education 1912–1922; commanded an Artillery battery during the First World War; elected as a Democrat to the Sixty-eighth Congress (March 4, 1923–March 3, 1925); died in Washington, D. C., on May 13, 1925; interment in Rose Hill Cemetery, Columbia, Tenn.

SALTONSTALL, Leverett, a Representative from Massachusetts; born in Haverhill, Mass., June 13, 1783; pursued classical studies; attended Phillips Exeter Academy, Exeter, N. H., and was graduated from Harvard University in 1802; studied law; was admitted to the bar and commenced practice in Salem in 1805; unsuccessful candidate for election in 1820 to the Seventeenth Congress from Essex south district; delegate to the State constitutional convention in 1820; member of the State house of representatives in 1813, 1814, 1816, 1822, 1829, and 1834; served in the State senate 1817–1819, 1831, and 1832, and was its president in 1831 and 1832; first mayor of Salem, Mass., 1836–1838; presidential elector on the Whig ticket of Webster and Granger in 1836; elected as a Whig to the Twenty-fifth Congress to fill the vacancy caused by the resignation of Stephen C. Phillips; reelected to the Twenty-sixth and Twenty-seventh Congresses and served from December 5, 1838, to March 3, 1843; unsuccessful candidate for reelection to the Twenty-eighth Congress; again a member of the State house of representatives in 1844; overseer of Harvard University 1835–1845; died in Salem, Essex County, Mass., May 8, 1845; interment in Harmony Grove Cemetery.

SALTONSTALL, Leverett (great-grandson of the preceding), a Senator from Massachusetts; born in Chestnut Hill, Middlesex County, Mass., September 1, 1892; attended the public schools and Noble and Greenough School, Dedham, Mass.; was graduated from Harvard University, Cambridge, Mass., in 1914 and from its law school in 1917; during the First World War served in the United States Army as a first lieutenant in the Three Hundred and First Field Artillery, Seventy-sixth Division, 1917–1919, serving five months in France; was admitted to the bar in 1919 and commenced practice in Boston, Mass.; member of the board of aldermen of Newton, Mass., 1920–1922; assistant district attorney of Middlesex County, Mass., in 1921 and 1922; member of the State house of representatives 1923–1936, serving as speaker 1929–1936; director of a community fund drive in 1938; Governor of Massachusetts 1939–1944; chairman of the National Governors' Conference in 1944; delegate to the Republican National Conventions in 1932, 1940, and 1944; elected as a Republican to the United States Senate in 1944 to fill the vacancy in the term ending January 3, 1949, caused by the resignation of Henry Cabot Lodge, Jr.; again elected in 1948 and 1954 and served from January 4, 1945, to January 3, 1961. *Reelected in 1960 for the term ending January 3, 1967.*

SAMFORD, William James, a Representative from Alabama; born in Greenville, Meriwether County, Ga., September 16, 1844; moved in early childhood with his parents to Chambers County, Ala.; attended a private school in Auburn, Ala., and the University of Georgia at Athens in 1860; during the Civil War enlisted in the Confederate Army in 1862 as a private in the Forty-sixth Alabama Regiment; promoted to first lieutenant and was in command of a company at the close of the war; studied law; was admitted to the bar in 1867 and commenced practice in Opelika, Lee County, Ala., in 1867; presidential elector on the Democratic ticket of Greeley and Brown in 1872 and of Tilden and Hendricks in 1876; delegate to the State constitutional convention in 1875; elected as a Democrat to the Forty-sixth Congress (March 4, 1879–March 3, 1881); was not a candidate for renomination in 1880; again

resumed the practice of his profession; member of the State house of representatives in 1882; served in the State senate 1884–1886 and in 1892 and was its president in 1886; Governor of Alabama in 1900 and 1901; president of the board of trustees of the University of Alabama; died in Tuscaloosa, Tuscaloosa County, Ala., June 11, 1901; interment in Rosemere Cemetery, Opelika, Ala.

SAMMONS, Thomas (grandfather of John Henry Starin), a Representative from New York; born in Shamenkop, Ulster County, N. Y., October 1, 1762; attended the rural schools; served as an officer in the Revolutionary War; engaged in agricultural pursuits; delegate to the State constitutional convention in 1801; member of the council of appointment; served as lieutenant, captain, and major in the State militia; elected as a Democrat to the Eighth and Ninth Congresses (March 4, 1803–March 3, 1807); unsuccessful Democratic candidate for reelection; elected to the Eleventh and Twelfth Congresses (March 4, 1809–March 3, 1813); resumed agricultural pursuits; died on the Sammons homestead, in Montgomery County, near Johnstown, N. Y., November 20, 1838; interment on the homestead in the Simeon Sammons Cemetery.

SAMPLE, Samuel Caldwell, a Representative from Indiana; born in Elkton, Cecil County, Md., on August 15, 1796; attended the rural school; learned the trade of carpenter and assisted his father, who was a contractor; moved with his father's family to Connersville, Ind., about 1823; studied law; was admitted to the bar in 1833 and commenced practice in South Bend, St. Joseph County, Ind.; elected prosecuting attorney in 1834; elected judge of the ninth judicial circuit in 1836 and served until 1843, when he resigned; was the first president of the First National Bank of South Bend; elected as a Whig to the Twenty-eighth Congress (March 4, 1843–March 3, 1845); unsuccessful candidate for reelection in 1844 to the Twenty-ninth Congress; resumed the practice of his profession in South Bend, Ind., and died there December 2, 1855; interment in the City Cemetery.

SAMPSON, Ezekiel Silas, a Representative from Iowa; born in Huron County, Ohio, December 6, 1831; moved to Keokuk County, Iowa, in 1843; attended the public schools, Howe's Academy in Mount Pleasant, Iowa, and Knox College, Illinois; studied law; was admitted to the bar in 1856 and commenced practice in Sigourney, Keokuk County, Iowa; prosecuting attorney 1856–1858; during the Civil War enlisted in the Union Army as captain in the Fifth Regiment, Iowa Volunteer Infantry, in 1861 and was lieutenant colonel of the same regiment when mustered out in 1864; returned to the practice of law in Sigourney, Iowa; member of the State senate in 1866; judge of the sixth district of Iowa from January 1867 to January 1875; elected as a Republican to the Forty-fourth and Forty-fifth Congresses (March 4, 1875–March 3, 1879); unsuccessful candidate for reelection in 1878 to the Forty-sixth Congress; resumed the practice of his chosen profession; died in Sigourney, Keokuk County, Iowa, October 7, 1892; interment in West Cemetery.

SAMPSON, Zabdiel, a Representative from Massachusetts; born in Plympton, Mass., August 22, 1781; pursued classical studies and was graduated from Brown University, Providence, R. I., in 1803; studied law; was admitted to the bar in 1806 and commenced practice in Plymouth; elected as a Democrat to the Fifteenth and Sixteenth Congresses and served from March 4, 1817, to July 26, 1820, when he resigned; appointed collector of customs at Plymouth, Mass., July 26, 1820, and served until his death there July 19, 1828; interment in Burial Hill Cemetery.

SAMUEL, Edmund William, a Representative from Pennsylvania; born in Blaenavon, Wales, on November 27, 1857; immigrated to the United States with his parents, who settled in Ashland, Schuylkill County, Pa., in 1859; attended the public schools; worked in a coal breaker and engaged in coal mining; learned the drug business and began the study of medicine; was graduated from the Jefferson Medical College at Philadelphia March 13, 1880, and commenced practice in Mount Carmel, Pa.; school director of Mount Carmel 1890–1894; elected as a Republican to the Fifty-ninth Congress (March 4, 1905–March 3, 1907); unsuccessful candidate for reelection in 1906 to the Sixtieth Congress and for election in 1908 to the Sixty-first Congress; resumed the practice of medicine in Mount Carmel, Pa.; president and general manager of the Shamokin-Mount Carmel Transit Co. 1908–1924; retired from active business pursuits in 1925 and moved to Brooklyn, N. Y.; died in Mount Carmel, Pa., on March 7, 1930; interment in Mount Carmel Cemetery.

SAMUELS, Green Berry (cousin of Isaac Samuels Pennybacker), a Representative from Virginia; born near Red Banks, Shenandoah County, Va., February 1, 1806; pursued classical studies; studied law; was admitted to the Pennsylvania bar in 1827 and commenced the practice of law; resided at Woodstock, Va.; elected as a Democrat to the Twenty-sixth Congress (March 4, 1839–March 3, 1841); resumed the practice of law; member of the State constitutional convention in 1850 and 1851; elected judge of the circuit court in 1850 and of the court of appeals in 1852; died in Richmond, Va., on January 5, 1859; interment in the Old Lutheran Graveyard, Woodstock, Shenandoah County, Va.

SANBORN, John Carfield, a Representative from Idaho; born in Chenoa, McLean County, Ill., September 28, 1885; attended the public schools; was graduated from Oberlin (Ohio) College in 1908 and Columbia University Law School, New York, N. Y., in 1912; engaged in agricultural pursuits; trustee of Hagerman Independent School District 1921–1924; served in the State house of representatives 1921–1929; member of the State senate 1939–1941; elected as a Republican to the Eightieth and Eighty-first Congresses (January 3, 1947–January 3, 1951); did not seek renomination to the Eighty-second Congress but was unsuccessful in 1950 and 1956 for the Republican nomination for United States Senator; resumed agricultural pursuits; president of Hagerman Farms, Inc.; member of board of directors of Idaho Farm Bureau Federation and legislative representative before the 1959 and 1961 sessions of Idaho Legislature; is a resident of Hagerman, Idaho.

SANDAGER, Harry, a Representative from Rhode Island; born in Providence, R. I., April 12, 1887; attended the public schools at Cranston, R. I., and Georgetown University, Washington, D. C.; was graduated from George Washington University, Washington, D. C., in 1922; newspaper reporter 1905–1918; secretary to Congressman Walter R. Stiness 1918–1922; returned to Providence, R. I., and served as an office executive 1922–1931; member of the State house of representatives 1928–1936; moved to Cranston, R. I., in 1931 and engaged in business as an automobile dealer; elected as a Republican to the Seventy-sixth Congress (January 3, 1939–January 3, 1941); unsuccessful candidate for reelection in 1940 to the Seventy-seventh Congress and for election in 1942 to the Seventy-eighth Congress; resumed the automobile business until his death; member of the Republican National Committee 1941–1944; Chairman of the Cranston Civilian Defense Council in 1941 and 1942; died in Cranston, R. I., December 24, 1955; interment in St. Francis Cemetery, Pawtucket, R. I.

SANDERS, Archie Dovell, a Representative from New York; born in Stafford, Genesee County, June 17, 1857; attended the common schools, Le Roy Academy, and Buffalo Central High School; in 1873 became a partner with his father in the produce business at Stafford, N. Y.; elected highway commissioner of Stafford in 1894 and supervisor in 1895; member of the State assembly in 1895 and 1896; delegate to many State conventions; delegate to the Republican National Convention at St. Louis in 1896; appointed by President McKinley as collector of internal revenue for the twenty-eighth district of New York in 1898 and served until 1913; Republican State committeeman for the Thirtieth Congressional District in 1900 and 1901; member of the State senate in 1914 and 1915; delegate to the Republican National Convention at Cleveland, Ohio, in 1924; elected as a Republican to the Sixty-fifth and to the seven succeeding Congresses (March 4, 1917–March 3, 1933); was not a candidate for renomination in 1932; retired from active business pursuits and resided in Stafford, N. Y.; was serving as chairman of the Genesee County Republican Committee at the time of his death; died July 15, 1941, while a patient in a Rochester, N. Y., hospital; interment in Stafford Rural Cemetery, Stafford, N. Y.

SANDERS, Everett, a Representative from Indiana; born near Coalmont, Clay County, Ind., March 8, 1882; attended the public schools and the Indiana State Normal School at Terre Haute; was graduated from the law department of Indiana University at Bloomington in 1907; was admitted to the bar the same year and practiced his profession in Terre Haute, Ind., until elected to Congress; elected as a Republican to the Sixty-fifth and to the three succeeding Congresses (March 4, 1917–March 3, 1925); declined to be a candidate for renomination in 1924; was director of the speakers' bureau of the Republican National Committee in 1924; appointed secretary to President Calvin Coolidge on March 4, 1925, and served until March 4, 1929; served as Republican National Chairman from 1932 to 1934; resumed the practice of law in Washington, D. C., where he died May 12, 1950; interment in Highland Lawn Cemetery, Terre Haute, Ind.

SANDERS, Jared Young, a Representative from Louisiana; born near Morgan City, St. Mary Parish, La., January 29, 1869; attended the public schools; was graduated from the law department of Tulane University, New Orleans, La., in 1893; was admitted to the bar the same year and commenced practice in New Orleans; elected as an antilottery member of the State house of representatives in 1892 and served until 1904, being elected speaker in 1900; member of the State constitutional convention in 1898; Lieutenant Governor of Louisiana 1904–1908; Governor 1908–1912; elected to the United States Senate July 6, 1910, to fill the vacancy caused by the death of Samuel D. McEnery, but did not qualify, preferring to finish term as Governor; elected as a Democrat to the Sixty-fifth and Sixty-sixth Congresses (March 4, 1917–March 3, 1921); was not a candidate for renomination in 1920; member of the State constitutional convention in 1921; resumed the practice of law; unsuccessful candidate for the Democratic nomination for United States Senator in 1920 and 1926; died in Baton Rouge, La., March 23, 1944; interment in Franklin Cemetery, Franklin, La.

SANDERS, Jared Young, Jr. (son of the preceding), a Representative from Louisiana; born in Franklin, St. Mary Parish, La., April 20, 1892; attended the public schools, Dixon Academy, Covington, La., and Washington and Lee University, Lexington, Va.; was graduated from the Louisiana State University at Baton Rouge in 1912, and from the law department of Tulane University, New Orleans, La., in 1914; was admitted to the bar in 1914 and commenced practice in Baton Rouge, La.; during the First World War served in the United States Army from May 1917 to April 1919 as captain of the Three Hundred and Forty-sixth Infantry, Eighty-seventh Division; member of the State house of representatives 1928–1932; elected to the State senate in 1932 and served until elected to Congress; elected as a Democrat to the Seventy-third Congress to fill the vacancy caused by the death of Bolivar E. Kemp; reelected to the Seventy-fourth Congress and served from May 1, 1934, to January 3, 1937; unsuccessful candidate for renomination in 1936; resumed the practice of law; delegate to the Democratic National Conventions in 1940 and 1944; elected to the Seventy-seventh Congress (January 3, 1941–January 3, 1943); was an unsuccessful candidate for renomination in 1942; resumed the practice of law; also interested in banking; died in Baton Rouge, La., November 29, 1960; interment in Roselawn Memorial Park.

SANDERS, Morgan Gurley, a Representative from Texas; born near Ben Wheeler, Van Zandt County, Tex., on July 14, 1878; attended the public schools; graduated from Alamo Institute and taught school for three years; owned and published a weekly newspaper; studied law at the University of Texas at Austin; was admitted to the bar in 1901 and commenced practice in Canton, Tex.; member of the State house of representatives 1902–1906; prosecuting attorney of Van Zandt County 1910–1914; district attorney of the seventh judicial district of Texas in 1915 and 1916; voluntarily retired and resumed the practice of law in Canton, Van Zandt County, Tex.; delegate to many Democratic State conventions; elected as a Democrat to the Sixty-seventh and to the eight succeeding Congresses (March 4, 1921–January 3, 1939); unsuccessful candidate for renomination in 1938; resumed the practice of law in Canton, Tex., until his death; died in Corsicana, Tex., January 7, 1956; interment in Hillcrest Cemetery, Canton, Tex.

SANDERS, Newell, a Senator from Tennessee; born on a farm near Bloomington, Owen County, Ind., July 12, 1850; attended the rural schools; was graduated from Indiana University at Bloomington in 1873; owned and operated a book store in Bloomington, Ind., 1873–1877; moved to Chattanooga, Tenn., in 1877 and became a manufacturer of agricultural implements; member of the school board in 1881 and 1882; served as alderman 1882–1886; president of the Chattanooga Plow Co., 1882–1901; chairman of the Republican State executive committee 1894–1912; member of the board of managers of the American Society of Mechanical Engineers 1902–1905; president of the National Association of Agricultural Implement and Vehicle Manufacturers in 1907 and 1908; member of the board of directors of the Nashville, Chattanooga & St. Louis Railway; delegate to the Republican National Conventions in 1900, 1908, 1912, 1916, 1920, and 1924; appointed as a Republican to the United States Senate to fill the vacancy caused by the death of Robert L. Taylor and served from April 11, 1912, to January 24, 1913, when a successor was elected; was the first Republican Senator from Tennessee in forty years; was not a candidate for election; continued his former manufacturing pursuits in Chattanooga until 1927, when he retired from active pursuits; died at his home on Lookout Mountain, Tenn., January 26, 1939; interment in Forest Hills Cemetery, Chattanooga, Tenn.

SANDERS, Wilbur Fiske, a Senator from Montana; born in Leon, Cattaraugus County, N. Y., May 2, 1834; attended the common schools; taught school in New York; moved to Ohio in 1854, where he continued teaching; studied law in Akron, Ohio, and was admitted to the bar in 1856; during the Civil War recruited a company of Infantry and a battery of Artillery in the summer of 1861 and in October following was commissioned a first lieutenant in the Sixty-fourth Regiment,

Ohio Infantry, of which regiment he was made adjutant; acting assistant adjutant general on the staff of Gen. James W. Forsyth; assisted in 1862 in the construction of defenses along the railroads south of Nashville; resigned and settled in that part of Idaho which later became Montana; engaged in the practice of law and also became interested in mining and stock raising; unsuccessful Republican candidate for election in 1864, 1867, 1880, and 1886 as a Delegate to Congress; delegate to the Republican National Conventions in 1868, 1872, 1876, and 1884; member of the Territorial House of Representatives of Montana 1873–1879; declined the appointment of United States attorney for Montana tendered by President Grant in 1872; upon the admission of Montana as a State into the Union was elected as a Republican to the United States Senate and served from January 1, 1890, to March 3, 1893; unsuccessful candidate for reelection; died in Helena, Mont., July 7, 1905; interment in Forestvale Cemetery.

SANDFORD, James T., a Representative from Tennessee; born in Virginia; attended the common schools; moved to Columbia, Tenn.; engaged in agricultural pursuits; elected to the Eighteenth Congress (March 4, 1823–March 3, 1825); unsuccessful candidate for reelection in 1825 to the Nineteenth Congress; contributed a part of his wealth to the establishment of Jackson College at Columbia, Tenn.

SANDFORD, Thomas, a Representative from Kentucky; born in Westmoreland County, Va., in 1762; pursued classical studies; served in the Revolutionary War; settled on the highlands back of Covington, Ky., in 1792 and engaged in agricultural pursuits; delegate to the State constitutional convention in 1799; member of the State senate 1800–1802; served in the State house of representatives in 1802; elected as a Democrat to the Eighth and Ninth Congresses (March 4, 1803–March 3, 1807); drowned in the Ohio River near Covington, Ky., on December 10, 1808; interment in Highland Cemetery, Fort Mitchell, near Covington, Kenton County, Ky.

SANDIDGE, John Milton, a Representative from Louisiana; born near Carnesville, Franklin County, Ga., January 7, 1817; moved to Louisiana and became a planter; served as colonel in the Mexican War; member of the State house of representatives 1846–1855 and served two years as speaker; delegate to the State constitutional convention in 1852; elected as a Democrat to the Thirty-fourth and Thirty-fifth Congresses (March 4, 1855–March 3, 1859); served throughout the Civil War as colonel of Bossier Cavalry; surrendered the archives of the State to the Federal authorities in the absence of Gov. Henry W. Allen; died in Bastrop, Morehouse Parish, La., on March 30, 1890; interment in Christ Church Cemetery.

SANDLIN, John Nicholas, a Representative from Louisiana; born near Minden, Webster Parish, La., on February 24, 1872; attended the public schools; studied law, was admitted to the bar in 1896, and commenced practice in Minden, La.; prosecuting attorney for the second district of Louisiana 1904–1910; judge of the second judicial district of Louisiana 1910–1920; delegate to the Democratic National Convention at St. Louis in 1916; elected as a Democrat to the Sixty-seventh and to the seven succeeding Congresses (March 4, 1921–January 3, 1937); was not a candidate for renomination in 1936, but was an unsuccessful candidate for nomination for United States Senator; engaged in the practice of law; died Minden, La.. December 25, 1957; interment in Minden Cemetery.

SANDS, Joshua, a Representative from New York; born in Cow Neck (now Sands Point), Queens County, Long Island, N. Y., October 12, 1757; received a limited schooling; served as captain in the American Army during the Revolutionary War; engaged in mercantile pursuits; member of the State senate 1792–1799; collector of customs at the port of New York in 1797; elected to the Eighth Congress (March 4, 1803–March 3, 1805); was not a candidate for renomination; president of the board of trustees of the village of Brooklyn in 1824; elected to the Nineteenth Congress (March 4, 1825–March 3, 1827); died in Brooklyn, N. Y., September 13, 1835; interment in St. Paul's Church Cemetery, Eastchester, N. Y.; reinterment in Greenwood Cemetery, Brooklyn, N. Y., in 1852.

SANFORD, John (father of Stephen Sanford), a Representative from New York; born in Roxbury, Conn., June 3, 1803; received a good education; moved to Amsterdam, N. Y., in 1821; taught school in Amsterdam and afterward in Mayfield, where he also engaged in mercantile pursuits; returned to Amsterdam and continued in commercial pursuits until 1840; elected as a Democrat to the Twenty-seventh Congress (March 4, 1841–March 3, 1843); founder of the largest firm in the carpet manufacturing industry in New York, but the factory was destroyed by fire in 1849, whereupon he retired from active business; died in Amsterdam, Montgomery County, N. Y., on October 4, 1857; interment in Green Hill Cemetery.

SANFORD, John (son of Stephen Sanford and grandson of the preceding), a Representative from New York; born in Amsterdam, Montgomery County, N. Y., January 18, 1851; attended the common schools, Amsterdam Academy, and Poughkeepsie Military Institute; was graduated from Yale College in 1872; engaged with his father in the carpet manufacturing industry in Amsterdam, N. Y.; elected as a Republican to the Fifty-first and Fifty-second Congresses (March 4, 1889–March 3, 1893); was not a candidate for renomination in 1892; resumed former business pursuits; delegate to the Republican National Convention at Minneapolis in 1892; presidential elector on the Republican ticket of McKinley and Hobart in 1896; interested in the breeding of race horses and owner of the Sanford Racing Stable; member of the New York Racing Commission; died in Saratoga, N. Y., September 26, 1939; interment in Green Hill Cemetery, Amsterdam, N. Y.

SANFORD, John W. A., a Representative from Georgia; born near Milledgeville, Baldwin County, Ga., August 28, 1798; attended the Baldwin County schools, and Yale University, New Haven, Conn.; engaged in agricultural pursuits; elected as a Union Democrat to the Twenty-fourth Congress and served from March 4, 1835, to July 25, 1835, when he resigned, before the convening of Congress, to assist in the removal of the Cherokee Indians; served in the Cherokee War in 1836 with the rank of major general; was a member of the Baldwin Blues, being discharged on surgeon's certificate of disability due to wounds; elected to the State senate in 1837, but resigned before taking his seat; served as secretary of state of Georgia 1841–1843; member of the State convention of 1850; died in Milledgeville. Ga., September 12, 1870; interment in Milledgeville Cemetery,

SANFORD, Jonah (great-grandfather of Rollin Brewster Sanford), a Representative from New York; born in Cornwall, Vt., November 30, 1790; attended the district schools; moved to Hopkinton, N. Y., in 1811; enlisted as a volunteer and participated in the battle at Plattsburg September 11, 1814; appointed justice of the peace in 1818 and served for twenty-two years; studied law; was admitted to the bar and practiced in Franklin County; supervisor of Hopkinton 1823–1826; appointed a commissioner to lay out the Port Kent Road in 1827 and subsequently a commissioner to build the road; commissioned a captain of Volunteer Cavalry in 1827; promoted to lieutenant colonel

in 1828, colonel in 1831, and brigadier general of State militia in 1832 and 1833; member of the State assembly in 1829 and 1830; elected as a Jackson Democrat to the Twenty-first Congress to fill the vacancy caused by the resignation of Silas Wright, Jr., and served from November 3, 1830, to March 3, 1831; judge of the court of common pleas 1831–1837; delegate to the convention to revise the State constitution in 1846; became a Republican upon the formation of that party in 1856; raised a regiment during the Civil War and was elected its colonel; accompanied the regiment to the banks of the James River, where his advanced age (seventy-two years) and ill health compelled him to abandon the field; died in Hopkinton, St. Lawrence County, N. Y., on December 25, 1867; interment in Hopkinton Cemetery.

SANFORD, Nathan, a Senator from New York; born in Bridgehampton, Long Island, N. Y., November 5, 1777; completed preparatory studies; studied law; was admitted to the bar in 1799 and commenced practice in New York City; United States commissioner in bankruptcy in 1802; United States attorney for the district of New York 1803–1816; member of the State assembly in 1810 and 1811 and served as speaker in the latter year; member of the State senate 1812–1815; elected as a Democrat to the United States Senate and served from March 4, 1815, to March 3, 1821; delegate to the State constitutional convention in 1821; chancellor of New York from August 1, 1823, until January 1826, when he resigned, having been elected Senator; elected to the United States Senate to fill the vacancy in the term commencing March 4, 1825, and served from January 14, 1826, to March 3, 1831; was not a candidate for reelection; resumed the practice of law in Flushing, Queens County, N. Y., and died there October 17, 1838.

SANFORD, Rollin Brewster (great-grandson of Jonah Sanford), a Representative from New York; born in Nicholville, St. Lawrence County, N. Y., May 18, 1874; attended the public schools; was graduated from the Albany (N. Y.) High School in 1893, from Tufts College, Medford, Mass., in 1897, and from the Albany Law School in 1899; was admitted to the bar in 1899 and commenced practice in Albany, N. Y.; member of the New York National Guard 1901–1906; prosecuting attorney of Albany County 1908–1914; elected as a Republican to the Sixty-fourth, Sixty-fifth, and Sixty-sixth Congresses (March 4, 1915–March 3, 1921); declined to be a candidate for reelection in 1920; resumed the practice of law; member of the New York State Board of Law Examiners 1921–1940; died in Loudonville (town of Colonie), Albany, N. Y., May 16, 1957; interment in Albany Rural Cemetery, Cemetery Avenue, Menands, Albany, N. Y.

SANFORD, Stephen (son of John Sanford born in 1803 and father of John Sanford born in 1851), a Representative from New York; born in Mayfield, Fulton County, N. Y., May 26, 1826; attended the common schools and local academy at Amsterdam, N. Y., Georgetown College, Washington, D. C., for two years, and the United States Military Academy at West Point, N. Y.; engaged in the carpet manufacturing business from 1844 until his death; elected as Republican to the Forty-first Congress (March 4, 1869–March 3, 1871); declined to be a candidate for renomination; presidential elector on the Republican ticket of Grant and Wilson in 1872; delegate to the Republican National Convention at Cincinnati in 1876; died in Amsterdam, N. Y., February 13, 1913; interment in Green Hill Cemetery.

SANTANGELO, Alfred Edward, a Representative from New York; born in the Borough of Manhattan, New York City, N. Y., June 4, 1912; attended public schools; graduated from Curtis High School in 1929, the College of the City of New York in 1935, and Columbia University School of Law in 1938; was admitted to the bar in 1939 and commenced the practice of law; assistant district attorney in 1945; New York State senator 1947–1950 and 1953–1956; elected as a Democrat to the Eighty-fifth and Eighty-sixth Congresses (January 3, 1957–January 3, 1961). *Reelected to the Eighty-seventh Congress.*

SAPP, William Fletcher (nephew of William R. Sapp), a Representative from Iowa; born in Danville, Knox County, Ohio, November 20, 1824; attended the public schools and Martinsburg Academy; studied law; was admitted to the bar in 1850 and commenced practice in Mount Vernon, Ohio; unsuccessful candidate for prosecuting attorney of Knox County in 1850; elected prosecuting attorney of Knox County in 1854 and 1856; moved to Omaha, Nebr., in 1860; appointed adjutant general of Nebraska Territory in 1861; member of the Territorial legislative council; during the Civil War entered the Union Army in 1862 as lieutenant colonel of the Second Nebraska Cavalry and served until mustered out; moved to Council Bluffs, Iowa, and resumed the practice of law; member of the State house of representatives in 1865; United States district attorney for Iowa 1869–1873; elected as a Republican to the Forty-fifth and Forty-sixth Congresses (March 4, 1877–March 3, 1881); was not a candidate for renomination in 1880; presidential elector on the Republican ticket of Blaine and Logan in 1884; resumed the practice of law; died in Council Bluffs, Iowa, November 22, 1890; interment in Mound View Cemetery, Mount Vernon, Ohio.

SAPP, William Robinson (uncle of William F. Sapp), a Representative from Ohio; born at Cadiz, Ohio, March 4, 1804; moved to Knox County, where he attended the public schools; engaged in the mercantile business in Danville; studied law; was admitted to the bar in 1833 and commenced practice at Millersburg, Holmes County, Ohio; prosecuting attorney of Holmes County; presidential elector on the Whig ticket of Clay and Frelinghuysen in 1844; moved to Mount Vernon, Knox County, in 1846; elected as a Whig to the Thirty-third and Thirty-fourth Congresses (March 4, 1853–March 3, 1857); unsuccessful candidate for reelection; assessor of internal revenue for the thirteenth district 1869–1872; collector of internal revenue from 1872 until his death in Mount Vernon, Knox County, Ohio, January 3, 1875; interment in Mound View Cemetery.

SARBACHER, George William, Jr., a Representative from Pennsylvania; born in Philadelphia, Pa., September 30, 1919; attended the public schools; was graduated from Olney High School in 1938 and from Temple University, Philadelphia, Pa., in 1942; during World War II enlisted in the United States Marine Corps and served from January 1942 to January 1947; was commissioned a lieutenant and later a captain and served overseas in the Southwest Pacific for two and a half years, participating in the invasions of Guadalcanal, Bougainville, and Guam; was awarded the Presidential Citation, Navy Unit Citation, and the Asiatic Pacific Ribbon with three battle stars; while serving on active duty was elected to Congress; elected as a Republican to the Eightieth Congress (January 3, 1947–January 3, 1949); unsuccessful candidate for reelection in 1948 to the Eighty-first Congress and for election in 1950 to the Eighty-second Congress; former director of highway safety, Commonwealth of Pennsylvania; president and member of board of directors of the National Scientific Laboratories, Inc., Washington, D. C., and NSL Electronics, Ltd., Hamilton, Ontario, Canada; resides in Chevy Chase, Md.

SARGENT, Aaron Augustus, a Representative and a Senator from California; born in Newburyport, Essex County, Mass., September 28, 1827; attended the common schools; ap-

prenticed to a cabinetmaker for a short time; learned the printer's trade; worked for several months in 1847 as a printer in Philadelphia, Pa.; moved to Washington, D. C., the same year and became secretary to a Member of Congress; moved to California in 1849 and settled in Nevada City in 1850; employed on the staff of the Nevada City Journal and later became owner of the paper; studied law; was admitted to the bar in 1854 and commenced practice in Nevada City, Calif.; district attorney for Nevada County in 1855 and 1856; member of the State senate in 1856; resumed the practice of law; delegate to the Republican National Convention at Chicago in 1860; elected as a Republican to the Thirty-seventh Congress (March 4, 1861–March 3, 1863); declined to be a candidate for renomination in 1862; elected to the Forty-first and Forty-second Congresses (March 4, 1869–March 3, 1873); was not a candidate for renomination in 1872, having become a candidate for United States Senator; elected to the United States Senate and served from March 4, 1873, to March 3, 1879; was not a candidate for reelection; engaged in the practice of law in San Francisco 1879–1882; appointed Minister to Germany in 1882 and served in that capacity until April 1884, when he resigned; declined to accept the appointment of Minister to Russia; returned to California in 1884 and resumed the practice of law; unsuccessful candidate for the Republican nomination for Senator in 1885; died in San Francisco, Calif., August 14, 1887; interment in Laurel Hill Cemetery.

SASSCER, Lansdale Ghiselin, a Representative from Maryland; born in Upper Marlboro, Prince Georges County, Md., September 30, 1893; attended the public schools, Central High School, Washington, D. C., and Tome School, Port Deposit, Md.; was graduated from Dickinson Law School, Carlisle, Pa., in 1914; was admitted to the bar the same year and commenced practice in Upper Marlboro, Md.; served during the First World War 1917–1919, being overseas for thirteen months as a first lieutenant in the Fifty-ninth Artillery and participating in the St. Mihiel and Argonne offensives; resumed the practice of law; member of the State senate 1922–1938, serving as president in 1935 and 1937; delegate to the Democratic National Conventions in 1924 and 1936; vice chairman of the committee on reorganization of the State government in 1939; elected as a Democrat to the Seventy-sixth Congress to fill the vacancy caused by the death of Stephen W. Gambrill; reelected to the Seventy-seventh and to the five succeeding Congresses and served from February 3, 1939, to January 3, 1953; was not a candidate for renomination in 1952 but was unsuccessful for the nomination for United States Senator; resumed the practice of law; is a resident of Upper Marlboro, Md.

SATTERFIELD, Dave Edward, Jr., a Representative from Virginia; born in Richmond, Va., September 11, 1894; attended the public schools; was graduated from the law department of the University of Richmond, Richmond, Va., in 1916; was admitted to the bar the same year and commenced practice in Richmond, Va.; during the First World War enlisted in the United States Navy in 1917; was transferred to the Naval Flying Corps and commissioned as a first lieutenant; lieutenant commander, United States Naval Reserve Force, 1917–1919; Commonwealth's attorney for Richmond, Va., 1922–1933; resigned to return to the private practice of law; elected as a Democrat to the Seventy-fifth Congress to fill the vacancy caused by the death of Andrew J. Montague; reelected to the Seventy-sixth and to the three succeeding Congresses and served from November 2, 1937, until his resignation on February 15, 1945, to become general counsel and executive director of the Life Insurance Association of America at New York, N. Y.; died in Richmond, Va., December 27, 1946; interment in Hollywood Cemetery.

SAUERHERING, Edward, a Representative from Wisconsin; born in Mayville, Dodge County, Wis., June 24, 1864; attended the public schools; was graduated from the Chicago College of Pharmacy in 1885; engaged in the drug business in Chicago, Ill., for three years; returned to Mayville, Wis., and continued in the same business; elected as a Republican to the Fifty-fourth and Fifty-fifth Congresses (March 4, 1895–March 3, 1899); was not a candidate for renomination in 1898 to the Fifty-sixth Congress; superintendent of the commission of public works of Mayville 1909–1918; engaged in the construction of waterworks; justice of the peace 1912–1920; died in Mayville, Wis., on March 1, 1924; interment in Graceland Cemetery.

SAULSBURY, Eli (brother of Willard Saulsbury), a Senator from Delaware; born in Mispillion Hundred, Kent County, Del., December 29, 1817; attended the common schools and Dickinson College, Carlisle, Pa.; member of the State house of representatives in 1853 and 1854; moved to Dover, Del., in 1856; studied law; was admitted to the bar in 1857 and practiced in Dover; delegate to the Democratic National Convention at Chicago in 1864; elected as a Democrat to the United States Senate in 1870; reelected in 1876 and again in 1883 and served from March 4, 1871, to March 3, 1889; unsuccessful candidate for reelection; resumed the practice of his profession; died in Dover, Kent County, Del., March 22, 1893; interment in Silver Lake Cemetery.

SAULSBURY, Willard (brother of Eli Saulsbury), a Senator from Delaware; born in Mispillion Hundred, Kent County, Del., June 2, 1820; attended the common schools, Dickinson College, Carlisle, Pa., and Delaware College (now the University of Delaware), Newark, Del.; studied law; was admitted to the bar and commenced practice in Georgetown, Del.; attorney general of Delaware 1850-1855; delegate to the Democratic National Convention at Cincinnati in 1856 and at Chicago in 1864; elected as a Democrat to the United States Senate in 1858; reelected in 1864 and served from March 4, 1859, to March 3, 1871; unsuccessful candidate for reelection; resumed the practice of law; chancellor of the State from 1874 until his death in Dover, Del., April 6, 1892; interment in Christ Episcopal Churchyard.

SAULSBURY, Willard (son of the preceding), a Senator from Delaware; born in Georgetown, Sussex County, Del., April 17, 1861; attended private schools and the University of Virginia at Charlottesville; studied law; was admitted to the bar in 1882 and commenced practice in Wilmington, Del.; president of the New Castle Bar Association and chairman of the board of censors; interested in banking and sundry business organizations; chairman of the Democratic county executive committee 1892–1900; member of the State committee 1892–1919 and served as chairman 1900–1906; member of the Democratic National Committee 1908–1920; delegate to the Democratic National Conventions in 1896, 1904, 1912, 1916, and 1920; Democratic caucus nominee for United States Senator in 1899, 1901, 1903, 1905, 1907, and 1911; elected as a Democrat to the United States Senate and served from March 4, 1913, to March 3, 1919; unsuccessful candidate for reelection in 1918; President pro tempore of the Senate from December 4, 1916, to March 3, 1919; member of the advisory committee of the Conference on Limitation of Armaments in Washington, D. C., in 1921 and 1922; member of the Pan American Conference in Santiago, Chile, in 1923; engaged in the practice of law in Wilmington, Del., and Washington, D. C., until his death in Wilmington, Del., February 20, 1927; interment in Christ Episcopal Churchyard, Dover, Del.

SAUND, Dalip Singh, a Representative from California; born in Amritsar, India, September 20, 1899; educated in boarding schools and graduated from the University of Punjab in 1919; came to the United States in 1920 to attend the University of California and graduated in 1922; became a lettuce farmer in the Imperial Valley of California 1930–1953; also distributor of chemical fertilizer in Westmorland, Calif., since 1953; became a citizen of the United States in 1949 and less than a year later was elected judge of Justice Court, Westmorland Judicial District, County of Imperial, but was denied seat, not having been a citizen one year when elected; elected judge of the same court in 1952 and served until his resignation January 1, 1957; elected as a Democrat to the Eighty-fifth and Eighty-sixth Congresses (January 3, 1957–January 3, 1961). *Reelected to the Eighty-seventh Congress.*

SAUNDERS, Alvin (grandfather of William Henry Harrison of Wyoming), a Senator from Nebraska; born in Fleming County, Ky., July 12, 1817; attended the common schools and pursued an academic course; moved with his father to Illinois in 1829 and to Mount Pleasant, Iowa (then a part of Wisconsin Territory), in 1836; postmaster of Mount Pleasant for seven years; studied law but never entered upon its practice; engaged in mercantile pursuits and banking; delegate to the State constitutional convention in 1846; served in the State senate 1854–1856 and 1858–1860; member of the first Republican convention held in Iowa, in Iowa City, on February 22, 1856; delegate to the Republican National Conventions in 1860 and 1868; one of the commissioners appointed by Congress to organize the Pacific Railroad Co.; Governor of the Territory of Nebraska 1861–1867; elected as a Republican to the United States Senate and served from March 5, 1877, to March 3, 1883; died in Omaha, Nebr., November 1, 1899; interment in Forest Lawn Cemetery.

SAUNDERS, Edward Watts, a Representative from Virginia; born near Rockymount, Franklin County, Va., October 20, 1860; received his early education under private teachers; attended Bellevue High School, Bedford County, Va., and was graduated from the University of Virginia at Charlottesville in 1882; studied law; was admitted to the bar and commenced practice in Rockymount, Va., in 1883; member of the State house of delegates 1887–1901 and served as speaker in 1899; elected judge of the Fourth Circuit Court of Virginia in 1901 and judge of the seventh circuit in 1904; elected as a Democrat to the Fifty-ninth Congress to fill the vacancy caused by the resignation of Claude A. Swanson; reelected to the Sixtieth and to the six succeeding Congresses and served from November 6, 1906, to February 29, 1920, when he resigned, having been elected judge of the State supreme court of appeals, which position he held until his death in Rockymount, Franklin County, Va., on December 16, 1921; interment in High Street Cemetery.

SAUNDERS, Romulus Mitchell, a Representative from North Carolina; born near Milton, Caswell (then Orange) County, N. C., March 3, 1791; attended the common schools and the University of North Carolina at Chapel Hill, 1809–1811; studied law; was admitted to the bar in Nashville, Tenn., in 1812 and commenced practice in Milton, N. C.; member of the State house of commons in 1815, 1817, and 1819, and served two years as speaker; trustee of the University of North Carolina 1819–1864; moved to Raleigh, N. C., in 1823; elected as a Democrat to the Seventeenth, Eighteenth, and Nineteenth Congresses (March 4, 1821–March 3, 1827); declined to be a candidate for reelection; attorney general of the State 1828–1831; judge of the superior court 1835–1840; defeated by one vote for

Governor of North Carolina in 1840 on the Democratic ticket; was elected to the Twenty-seventh and Twenty-eighth Congresses (March 4, 1841–March 3, 1845); unsuccessful candidate for reelection; Minister to Spain 1846–1849; again a member of the State house of commons 1850–1852; judge of the superior court of North Carolina 1852–1856; member of the board of commissioners to revise the laws of North Carolina; died in Raleigh, N. C., April 21, 1867; interment in Old City Cemetery.

SAUTHOFF, Harry, a Representative from Wisconsin; born in Madison, Dane County, Wis., June 3, 1879; attended the public schools; was graduated from the University of Wisconsin at Madison in 1902; taught school at Lake Geneva (Wis.) High School 1902–1905 and at Northern Illinois State Normal School at De Kalb in 1905 and 1906; was graduated from the law department of the University of Wisconsin in 1909; was admitted to the bar the same year and commenced practice in Madison, Wis.; district attorney of Dane County, Wis., 1915–1919; secretary to Gov. John J. Blaine in 1921; delegate to the International Conference on the St. Lawrence Deep Waterway between the United States and Canada, in 1921, and to the Mississippi Valley Conference on Mississippi River Improvement, in 1921; served in the State senate 1925–1929; elected as a Progressive to the Seventy-fourth and Seventy-fifth Congresses (January 3, 1935–January 3, 1939); unsuccessful candidate for reelection in 1938 to the Seventy-sixth Congress; elected to the Seventy-seventh and Seventy-eighth Congresses (January 3, 1941–January 3, 1945); was not a candidate for renomination in 1944, but was unsuccessful for election to the United States Senate on the Progressive ticket; resumed the practice of law until his retirement in 1955; is a resident of Madison, Wis.

SAVAGE, Charles Raymon, a Representative from Washington; born on a farm at La Farge, Vernon County, Wis., April 12, 1906; attended the public schools; took special courses in mechanics, building construction, business law, and salesmanship; moved to Washington State and engaged in the building construction and logging businesses; held executive positions in unions affiliated with the American Federation of Labor and the Congress of Industrial Organizations; took the short training course at Fort Lewis, Wash., known as the "soldier-for-a-day course," to study the importance of war production; member of the board of directors of the Shelton General Hospital Association; chairman of the Mason County chapter of the American Red Cross; member of the State house of representatives 1938–1944; elected as a Democrat to the Seventy-ninth Congress (January 3, 1945–January 3, 1947); unsuccessful candidate for reelection in 1946 to the Eightieth Congress and for election in 1948 to the Eighty-first Congress; continued his logging pursuits until his appointment as district manager of an insurance society, in which capacity he is now serving; is a resident of Shelton, Wash.

SAVAGE, John, a Representative from New York; born in Salem, Washington County, N. Y., February 22, 1779; attended the common schools; was graduated from Union College, Schenectady, N. Y., in 1799; studied law; was admitted to the bar in 1800 and commenced practice in Salem, N. Y.; district attorney for the fourth New York district 1806–1811 and 1812 and 1813; member of the State assembly in 1814; elected as a Democrat to the Fourteenth and Fifteenth Congresses (March 4, 1815–March 3, 1819); district attorney of Washington County 1818–1820; State comptroller 1821–1823; chief justice of the State supreme court 1823–1836; appointed Treasurer of the United States in 1828 but did not accept; presidential elector on the Democratic ticket of Polk and Dallas in 1844; died in Utica, N. Y., October 19, 1863; interment in Forest Hill Cemetery.

SAVAGE, John Houston, a Representative from Tennessee; born in McMinnville, Tenn., on October 9, 1815; attended the common schools; served as a private in the Seminole War; studied law; was admitted to the bar and commenced practice in Smithville, Tenn.; colonel of State militia; attorney general of the fourth Tennessee district 1841–1847; presidential elector on the Democratic ticket of Polk and Dallas in 1844; major of the Fourteenth United States Infantry during the Mexican War and subsequently promoted to lieutenant colonel; elected to the Thirty-first and Thirty-second Congresses (March 4, 1849–March 3, 1853); declined to be a candidate for reelection; elected to the Thirty-fourth and Thirty-fifth Congresses (March 4, 1855–March 3, 1859); colonel of the Sixteenth Regiment Tennessee Infantry, in the Confederate Army during the Civil War and was wounded at Perryville and Murfreesboro; member of the State house of representatives 1877–1879 and in 1887; died in McMinnville, Tenn., on April 5, 1904; interment in Riverside Cemetery.

SAVAGE, John Simpson, a Representative from Ohio; born in Clermont County, Ohio, October 30, 1841; attended the public schools; taught school; studied law; was admitted to the bar in 1865 and commenced practice in Wilmington, Clinton County, Ohio, the same year; elected as a Democrat to the Forty-fourth Congress (March 4, 1875–March 3, 1877); unsuccessful candidate for reelection in 1876 to the Forty-fifth Congress; resumed the practice of law; died in Wilmington, Ohio, November 24, 1884; interment in Sugar Grove Cemetery.

SAWTELLE, Cullen, a Representative from Maine; born in Norridgewock, Maine, September 25, 1805; received his early education under private tutors and was graduated from Bowdoin College, Brunswick, Maine, in 1825; studied law; was admitted to the bar in 1828 and practiced in Norridgewock until 1841; register of probate 1830–1838; member of the State senate 1842–1844; elected as a Democrat to the Twenty-ninth Congress (March 4, 1845–March 3, 1847); elected to the Thirty-first Congress (March 4, 1849–March 3, 1851); attorney and credit manager for several mercantile firms in New York City 1852–1882; died in Englewood, Bergen County, N. J., November 10, 1887; interment in Brookside Cemetery.

SAWYER, Frederick Adolphus, a Senator from South Carolina; born in Bolton, Worcester County, Mass., December 12, 1822; attended the public schools; was graduated from Harvard University in 1844; taught school in Gardiner, Maine, 1844–1847; in Wiscasset, Maine, 1847–1851; in Lowell, Mass., and Nashua, N. H., in 1852; in Wakefield, Mass., 1853–1855; and in Boston, Mass., 1855–1859; took charge of the State normal school at Charleston, S. C., in 1859; during the Civil War was given a pass for himself and his family through the lines and allowed to return to the North in 1864; returned to Charleston in February 1865 and was active in advancing reconstruction measures; appointed collector of internal revenue in the second South Carolina district May 30, 1865; upon the readmission of the State of South Carolina to representation was elected as a Republican to the United States Senate and served from July 16, 1868, to March 3, 1873; Assistant Secretary of the Treasury from March 8, 1873, to June 11, 1874; was employed in the United States Coast Survey 1874–1880; special agent of the War Department 1880–1887; conducted a preparatory school in Ithaca, N. Y., and gave private instruction to students in Cornell University; moved to Tennessee and became president of a company at Cumberland Gap to promote the sale of agricultural lands in that vicinity; died suddenly in a hotel at Shawnee, Tenn., July 31, 1891; interment in "Sawyer Heights," on the property of his land company, about one-fourth mile northeast of Scott Cemetery, near East Cumberland Gap.

SAWYER, John Gilbert, a Representative from New York; born in Brandon, Rutland County, Vt., June 5, 1825; attended the common schools and Millville (N. Y.) Academy; moved to Albion, N. Y., in 1845; superintendent of schools for Orleans County, N. Y., 1848–1851; studied law; was admitted to the bar in 1850 and commenced practice in Albion, N. Y.; justice of the peace of Barre, Orleans County, N. Y., 1851–1862; prosecuting attorney of Orleans County 1862–1865; judge and surrogate of Orleans County 1867–1883; delegate to several Republican State conventions; elected as a Republican to the Forty-ninth, Fiftieth, and Fifty-first Congresses (March 4, 1885–March 3, 1891); was not a candidate for renomination in 1890; resumed the practice of his profession in Albion, N. Y., and died there September 5, 1898; interment in Mount Albion Cemetery.

SAWYER, Lemuel, a Representative from North Carolina; born in Camden County, near Elizabeth City, N. C., in 1777; attended Flatbush Academy, Long Island, N. Y., and was graduated from the University of North Carolina at Chapel Hill in 1799; attended the University of Pennsylvania at Philadelphia for a time; studied law; was admitted to the bar in 1804 and commenced practice in Elizabeth City, N. C.; member of the State house of commons in 1800 and 1801; presidential elector on the Democratic ticket of Jefferson and Clinton in 1804; elected as a Democrat to the Tenth, Eleventh, and Twelfth Congresses (March 4, 1807–March 3, 1813); elected to the Fifteenth, Sixteenth, and Seventeenth Congresses (March 4, 1817–March 3, 1823); unsuccessful candidate for reelection in 1822 to the Eighteenth Congress; elected to the Nineteenth and Twentieth Congresses (March 4, 1825–March 3, 1829); unsuccessful candidate for reelection in 1828 to the Twenty-first Congress; department clerk in Washington, D. C., until his death in that city on January 9, 1852; interment in the family burying ground at Lambs Ferry, Camden County, about four miles from Elizabeth City, Pasquotank County, N. C.

SAWYER, Lewis Ernest, a Representative from Arkansas; born in Shelby County, Ala., June 24, 1867; moved with his parents to Lee County, Miss.; attended the public schools and was graduated from the University of Mississippi at Oxford; studied law; was admitted to the bar and commenced practice at Friars Point, Miss., in 1895; mayor of Friars Point from 1896 until he enlisted in the Spanish-American War in June 1898; served in the Philippine Islands during the war; resumed the practice of law in Iuka, Miss., in 1900; moved to Hot Springs, Ark., in 1908 and continued the practice of his profession; member of the State house of representatives in 1913 and 1915 and was its speaker in the latter year; elected as a Democrat to the Sixty-eighth Congress and served from March 4, 1923, until his death at Hot Springs, Ark., May 5, 1923; interment in Hollywood Cemetery.

SAWYER, Philetus, a Representative and a Senator from Wisconsin; born in Whiting, Rutland County, Vt., September 22, 1816; moved with his father to Crown Point, N. Y., in 1817; attended the common schools; moved to Fond du Lac County, Wis., in 1847 and engaged in the lumber business; member of the Wisconsin Assembly in 1857 and 1861; mayor of Oshkosh in 1863 and 1864; delegate to the Republican National Conventions in 1864, 1876, and 1880; elected as a Republican to the Thirty-ninth and to the four succeeding Congresses (March 4, 1865–March 3, 1875); declined to be a candidate for renomination in 1874; elected to the United States Senate in 1881; reelected in 1887 and served from March 4, 1881, to March 3, 1893; was not a candidate for reelection; resumed his former business pursuits; died in Oshkosh, Winnebago County, Wis., March 29, 1900; interment in the family vault at Riverside, Oshkosh.

SAWYER, Samuel Locke, a Representative from Missouri; born in Mount Vernon, N. H., November 27, 1813; was graduated from Dartmouth College, Hanover, N. H., in 1833; studied law; was admitted to the bar in Amherst, N. H., in 1836; moved to Lexington, Mo., in 1838 and practiced; elected circuit attorney of the sixth judicial circuit of Missouri in 1848 and reelected in 1852; delegate to the Missouri constitutional convention in 1861; delegate to the Democratic National Convention at New York City in 1868; elected judge of the twenty-fourth judicial circuit and served from 1871 until February 15, 1876, when he resigned; elected as a Democrat to the Forty-sixth Congress (March 4, 1879–March 3, 1881); did not seek renomination in 1880; practiced law and engaged in banking; died in Independence Mo., March 29, 1890; interment in Woodlawn Cemetery.

SAWYER, Samuel Tredwell, a Representative from North Carolina; born in Edenton, Chowan County, N. C., in 1800; attended Edenton Academy and the University of North Carolina at Chapel Hill; studied law; was admitted to the bar and commenced practice in Edenton; member of the State house of representatives 1829–1832; served in the State senate in 1834; elected as a Democrat to the Twenty-fifth Congress (March 4, 1837–March 3, 1839); unsuccessful candidate for reelection to the Twenty-sixth Congress; moved to Norfolk, Va., and resumed the practice of law; editor of the Norfolk Argus for several years; appointed collector of customs at Norfolk on May 16, 1853, and served until April 6, 1858; moved to Washington, D. C.; during the Civil War was appointed, September 17, 1861, commissary with the rank of major in the Confederate service and served until August 2, 1862; died in Bloomfield, Essex County, N. J., November 29, 1865.

SAWYER, William, a Representative from Ohio; born in Montgomery County, Ohio, August 5, 1803; apprenticed to a blacksmith in 1818 and worked in Dayton, Ohio, and near Grand Rapids, Mich.; moved to Miamisburg, Ohio, in 1829; member of the State house of representatives 1832–1835 and served as speaker in 1835; unsuccessful candidate for election to the Twenty-sixth and Twenty-seventh Congresses; moved to St. Marys, Ohio, in 1843; elected as a Democrat to the Twenty-ninth and Thirtieth Congresses (March 4, 1845–March 3, 1849); was not a candidate for renomination; delegate to the State constitutional convention 1850–1851; again a member of the State house of representatives in 1856; receiver of the land office of the Otter Trail district in Minnesota 1855–1861; trustee of Ohio Agricultural and Mechanical College (later Ohio State University) 1870–1874; mayor and justice of the peace of St. Marys 1870–1877; died at St. Marys, Auglaize County, Ohio, September 18, 1877; interment in Elm Grove Cemetery.

SAY, Benjamin, a Representative from Pennsylvania; born in Philadelphia, Pa., in 1756; attended the Friends schools; was graduated from the medical department of the University of Pennsylvania at Philadelphia in 1780 and practiced in that city; was also an apothecary; served in the Revolutionary War; was a fellow of the College of Physicians of Philadelphia, of which he was one of the founders in 1787, and was treasurer from 1791 to 1809; member of the Pennsylvania Prison Society and president of the Pennsylvania Humane Society; elected to the Tenth Congress to fill the vacancy caused by the resignation of Joseph Clay; reelected to the Eleventh Congress and served from November 16, 1808, until his resignation in June 1809; died in Philadelphia, Pa., April 23, 1813.

SAYERS, Joseph Draper, a Representative from Texas; born in Grenada, Grenada County, Miss., September 23, 1841; moved with his father to Bastrop, Tex., in 1851; attended

Bastrop Military Institute; entered the Confederate Army in 1861 and served throughout the Civil War, attaining the rank of major; taught school; studied law; was admitted to the bar in 1866 and commenced practice in Bastrop, Tex.; member of the State senate 1873–1879; chairman of the Democratic State executive committee 1875–1878; Lieutenant Governor of Texas in 1879 and 1880; elected as a Democrat to the Forty-ninth and to the six succeeding Congresses and served from March 4, 1885, until his resignation on January 16, 1899; Governor of Texas 1899–1903; resumed the practice of his profession in Austin, Travis County, Tex.; member of the State board of regents of the University of Texas at Austin in 1913; chairman of the State industrial accident board in 1914 and 1915; member of the State board of legal examiners 1923–1925; appointed a member of the State pardon board in 1927 and served until his death in Austin, Tex., May 15, 1929; interment in Fairview Cemetery, Bastrop, Tex.

SAYLER, Henry Benton (cousin of Milton Sayler), a Representative from Indiana; born in Montgomery County, Ohio, March 31, 1836; moved to Clinton County, Ind.; attended the common schools of the county; studied law; was admitted to the bar in 1856 and commenced practice in Eaton, Preble County, Ohio; during the Civil War served in the Union Army as lieutenant, captain, and major; elected as a Republican to the Forty-third Congress (March 4, 1873–March 3, 1875); was not a candidate for renomination in 1874; judge of the twenty-eighth judicial circuit court of Indiana 1875–1900; died in Huntington, Huntington County, Ind., June 18, 1900; interment in Mount Hope Cemetery.

SAYLER, Milton (cousin of Henry Benton Sayler), a Representative from Ohio; born in Lewisburg, Preble County, Ohio, November 4, 1831; attended the public schools; pursued classical studies and was graduated from Miami University, Oxford, Ohio, in 1852; studied law at the Cincinnati Law School; was admitted to the bar and commenced practice in Cincinnati, Ohio; member of the State house of representatives in 1862 and 1863; member of the city council of Cincinnati in 1864 and 1865; elected as a Democrat to the Forty-third, Forty-fourth, and Forty-fifth Congresses (March 4, 1873–March 3, 1879); unsuccessful candidate for reelection in 1878 to the Forty-sixth Congress; served as Speaker pro tempore of the House of Representatives on June 4, 1876; moved to New York City and resumed the practice of his profession; died in that city November 17, 1892; interment in Spring Grove Cemetery, Cincinnati, Ohio.

SAYLOR, John Phillips, a Representative from Pennsylvania; born in Conemaugh Township, Somerset County, Pa., July 23, 1908; attended the public schools in Johnstown, Pa.; was graduated from Mercersburg Academy in 1925, Franklin and Marshall College, Lancaster, Pa., in 1929, and Dickinson Law School, Carlisle, Pa., in 1933; was admitted to the bar in 1934 and commenced the practice of law in Johnstown, Pa.; elected city solicitor of Johnstown, Pa., in 1938 and served until 1940; enlisted in the United States Navy on August 6, 1943; commissioned a lieutenant (jg) in 1943; trained at Harvard Communications School, First Naval District of Boston; assigned to Office of Chief of Naval Operations at Washington, D. C.; communications officer aboard the U. S. S. *Missoula*, APA 211; participated in the invasion of Iwo Jima and Okinawa; was present in Tokyo Bay on V-J Day; discharged in January 1946; elected as a Republican to the Eighty-first Congress to fill the vacancy caused by the death of Robert L. Coffey; reelected to the Eighty-second and to the four succeeding Congresses and served from September 13, 1949, to January 3, 1961. *Reelected to the Eighty-seventh Congress.*

SCALES, Alfred Moore, a Representative from North Carolina; born in Reidsville, Rockingham County, N. C., November 26, 1827; pursued classical studies; attended the Caldwell Institute, Greensboro, N. C., and the University of North Carolina at Chapel Hill in 1845 and 1846; studied law; was admitted to the bar in 1851 and practiced in Madison, N. C.; solicitor of Rockingham County in 1853; member of the State house of commons in 1852, 1853, 1856, and 1857; elected as a Democrat to the Thirty-fifth Congress (March 4, 1857–March 3, 1859); presidential elector on the Democratic ticket of John C. Breckinridge and Joseph Lane in 1860; volunteered as a private in the Confederate Army and served throughout the Civil War, attaining the rank of brigadier general; resumed the practice of law in Greensboro, Guilford County, N. C.; member of the State house of representatives 1866–1869; elected as a Democrat to the Forty-fourth and to the four succeeding Congresses and served from March 4, 1875, to December 30, 1884, when he resigned, having been elected Governor; served as Governor of North Carolina 1884–1888; engaged in banking in Greensboro, N. C., and died there on February 9, 1892; interment in Green Hill Cemetery.

SCAMMAN, John Fairfield, a Representative from Maine; born in Wells, Maine (then a district of Massachusetts), October 24, 1786; attended the common schools; engaged in mercantile pursuits; member of the Massachusetts House of Representatives in 1817; member of the Maine House of Representatives in 1820 and 1821; collector of customs in Saco, Maine, 1829–1841; elected as a Democrat to the Twenty-ninth Congress (March 4, 1845–March 3, 1847); served in the State senate in 1855; died in Saco, York County, Maine, May 22, 1858; interment in Laurel Hill Cemetery.

SCANLON, Thomas Edward, a Representative from Pennsylvania; born in Pittsburgh, Pa., September 18, 1896; attended the public schools, Forbes School, and Duquesne University, Pittsburgh, Pa.; learned the pressman's trade and was employed on Pittsburgh newspapers 1914–1936; during the First World War served as a private, first class, in the United States Army from September 6, 1918, to May 14, 1919; delegate to the Pittsburgh Central Labor Union 1920–1940; member of the Allegheny County Board for the Assessment and Revision of Taxes 1936–1941; elected as a Democrat to the Seventy-seventh and Seventy-eighth Congresses (January 3, 1941–January 3, 1945); unsuccessful candidate for reelection in 1944 to the Seventy-ninth Congress; member of the Boards of Viewers of Allegheny County, Pa.; died in Pittsburgh, Pa., August 9, 1955; interment in North Side Catholic Cemetery.

SCARBOROUGH, Robert Bethea, a Representative from South Carolina; born in Chesterfield, Chesterfield County, S. C., October 29, 1861; attended the common schools and Mullins (S. C.) Academy; taught school; studied law; was admitted to the bar in 1884 and commenced practice in Conway, S. C.; county attorney of Horry County 1885–1893; served as clerk of the county board 1885–1890; member of the South Carolina State Senate in 1897 and 1898 and was elected president pro tempore in 1898; Lieutenant Governor of South Carolina in 1899; elected as a Democrat to the Fifty-seventh and Fifty-eighth Congresses (March 4, 1901–March 3, 1905); declined to be a candidate for renomination in 1904 to the Fifty-ninth Congress; resumed the practice of law in Conway, S. C., and was also interested in banking; during the First World War served on the eastern district exemption board; served as chairman of the board of regents of the South Carolina State Hospital; died in Conway, Horry County, S. C., on November 23, 1927; interment in Lake Side Cemetery.

SCHAEFER, Edwin Martin, a Representative from Illinois; born in Belleville, St. Clair County, Ill., May 14, 1887; attended the public schools, Western Military Academy, Alton, Ill., and the University of Illinois at Urbana; was graduated from Washington University, St. Louis, Mo., in 1910; chemical engineer with Morris & Co., packers, East St. Louis, Ill., 1913–1916, assistant general superintendent 1916–1918, and general superintendent 1919–1928; assistant recorder of deeds of St. Clair County, Ill., 1928–1930; county treasurer of St. Clair County, Ill., 1930–1932; delegate to the Democratic State conventions in 1928, 1932, and 1936; elected as a Democrat to the Seventy-third and to the four succeeding Congresses (March 4, 1933–January 3, 1943); was not a candidate for renomination in 1942; member of the board of directors of Griesedieck-Western Brewery Co., Belleville, Ill., at the time of his death; died in St. Louis, Mo., November 8, 1950; interment in Walnut Hill Cemetery, Belleville, Ill.

SCHAFER, John Charles, a Representative from Wisconsin; born in Milwaukee, Wis., May 7, 1893; attended the public schools of Wauwatosa and West Allis High School; employed in the office of the Allis-Chalmers Co.; during the First World War enlisted in the Thirteenth Engineers on May 24, 1917, and served twenty-two months in France with the French Fourth Army at Champagne and with the French Second Army at Verdun, St. Mihiel, and Meuse-Argonne and was discharged on May 14, 1919; engaged as a locomotive engineer on the Chicago & North Western Railroad; member of Wauwatosa School Board, district No. 11; member of the State assembly in 1921; elected as a Republican to the Sixty-eighth and to the four succeeding Congresses (March 4, 1923–March 3, 1933); unsuccessful candidate for reelection in 1932 to the Seventy-third Congress and for election in 1934 to the Seventy-fourth Congress and in 1936 to the Seventy-fifth Congress; elected to the Seventy-sixth Congress (January 3, 1939–January 3, 1941); unsuccessful candidate for reelection in 1940 to the Seventy-seventh Congress and for election in 1942 to the Seventy-eighth Congress; unsuccessfully contested the election of Congressman Wasielewski in the Seventy-eighth Congress; unsuccessful candidate for election in 1952 to the Eighty-third Congress, in 1954 to the Eighty-fourth Congress, and in 1957 for the senatorial nomination to fill a vacancy; engaged in the sale of automotive electrical equipment and in the insurance business; is a resident of Oak Park, Ill.

SCHALL, Thomas David, a Representative and a Senator from Minnesota; born in Reed City, Osceola County, Mich., June 4, 1878; moved with his mother to Campbell, Minn., in 1884; attended the common schools of Wheaton, Minn., Ortonville High School, and Hamline University, St. Paul, Minn.; was graduated from the University of Minnesota at Minneapolis in 1902 and from St. Paul College of Law in 1904; was admitted to the bar in 1904 and commenced practice at Minneapolis; in 1907 lost his sight by an electric shock but continued the practice of his profession; elected as a Republican to the Sixty-fourth and to the four succeeding Congresses (March 4, 1915–March 3, 1925); was not a candidate for renomination, having become a candidate for the United States Senate; elected in 1924 as a Republican to the United States Senate; reelected in 1930 and served from March 4, 1925, until his death in Washington, D. C., December 22, 1935, as the result of being struck by an automobile; interment in Lakewood Cemetery, Minneapolis, Minn.

SCHELL, Richard, a Representative from New York; born in Rhinebeck, Rhinebeck County, N. Y., May 15, 1810; completed preparatory studies; engaged in mercantile pursuits; moved to New York City in 1830 and became a wholesale dry-goods merchant; member of the State senate in 1857; elected as a Democrat to the Forty-third Congress to fill the vacancy caused by the death of David B. Mellish and served from December 7, 1874, to March 3, 1875; resumed mercantile pursuits; died in New York City, November 10, 1879; interment in the Old Dutch Cemetery, Rhinebeck, N. Y.

SCHENCK, Abraham Henry (uncle of Isaac Teller), a Representative from New York; born in Matteawan, Dutchess County, N. Y., January 22, 1775; received a thorough English education; became engaged in the manufacture of machinery and also furnished some parts for cannons built at the old West Point Foundry at Cold Spring, N. Y.; member of the State assembly 1804–1806; elected as a Democrat to the Fourteenth Congress (March 4, 1815–March 3, 1817); engaged in the manufacture of cotton goods after the passage of the non-intercourse act; died in Fishkill, Dutchess County, N. Y., June 1, 1831; interment in the Dutch Reform Churchyard, Beacon (formerly Fishkill Landing), N. Y.

SCHENCK, Ferdinand Schureman, a Representative from New Jersey; born in Millstone, Somerset County, N. J., February 11, 1790; completed preparatory studies; studied medicine at the College of Physicians and Surgeons of New York, graduating in 1814; commenced practice at Six-Mile Run (now Franklin Park), N. J.; member of the State general assembly 1829–1831; elected as a Jackson Democrat to the Twenty-third and Twenty-fourth Congresses (March 4, 1833–March 3, 1837); was not a candidate for renomination; trustee of Rutgers College, New Brunswick, N. J., 1841–1861; member of the State constitutional convention in 1844; judge of the State court of errors and appeals 1845–1857; unsuccessful Republican candidate for the State senate in 1856; continued the practice of medicine; died in Camden, N. J., May 16, 1860; interment in a private cemetery at Pleasant Plains (near Franklin Park), N. J.

SCHENCK, Paul Fornshell, a Representative from Ohio; born in Miamisburg, Montgomery County, Ohio, April 19, 1899; moved to Dayton, Ohio, in 1908 and graduated from Steele High School in 1917; two years of college training; assistant chemistry teacher in Steele High School from September 1917 to June 1919; automotive service business from July 1919 to August 1923; automotive training teacher and faculty manager of athletics at Roosevelt High School from September 1923 to January 1929; director of recreation, city of Dayton, 1929–1935; established own real-estate, mortgage loan, and insurance business in September 1935; member of the board of education 1941–1950, serving as president for seven years; vice chairman of the Dayton Safety Council in 1946 and 1947; president Dayton Real Estate Board 1947–1949; executive secretary for the Dayton Council for Defense during World War II; elected as a Republican to the Eighty-second Congress to fill the vacancy caused by the resignation of Edward F. Breen; reelected to the Eighty-third and to the three succeeding Congresses and served from November 6, 1951, to January 3, 1961. *Reelected to the Eighty-seventh Congress.*

SCHENCK, Robert Cumming, a Representative from Ohio; born in Franklin, Ohio, October 4, 1809; attended the rural schools and was graduated from Miami University, Oxford, Ohio, in 1827; became a professor in that university 1827–1829; studied law; was admitted to the bar in 1833 and commenced practice in Dayton, Ohio; member of the State house of representatives 1839–1843; elected as a Whig to the Twenty-eighth and to the three succeeding Congresses (March 4, 1843–March 3, 1851); was not a candidate for renomination; Minister to Brazil and also accredited to Uruguay, Argentine Confederation, and Paraguay, 1851–1853; during the Civil War entered the Union Army May 17, 1861, and served as brigadier general of Volunteers; promoted to major general September 18, 1862, to date from August 30, 1862; resigned his commission in the Army on December 3, 1863, to take his seat in Congress; elected as a Republican to the Thirty-eighth and to the three succeeding Congresses and served from March 4, 1863, to January 5, 1871, when he resigned to accept a position in the diplomatic service; unsuccessful candidate for reelection in 1870 to the Forty-second Congress; Minister to Great Britain from December 1870 until March 1876, when he resigned; delegate to the Philadelphia Loyalist Convention in 1866; member of the Alabama Claims Commission in 1871; resumed the practice of law in Washington, D. C., where he died March 23, 1890; interment in Woodland Cemetery, Dayton, Ohio.

SCHERER, Gordon Harry, a Representative from Ohio; born in Cincinnati, Hamilton County, Ohio, December 26, 1906; graduated from the Salmon P. Chase College of Law in 1929 and attended the University of Cincinnati; was admitted to the Ohio bar in 1929 and commenced the practice of law in Cincinnati; assistant prosecuting attorney of Hamilton County 1933–1940; director of safety in Cincinnati in 1943 and 1944; member of the city planning commission in 1945 and 1946; member of the city council 1945–1949; elected as a Republican to the Eighty-third and to the three succeeding Congresses (January 3, 1953–January 3, 1961). *Reelected to the Eighty-seventh Congress.*

SCHERMERHORN, Abraham Maus, a Representative from New York; born in Schenectady, N. Y., December 11, 1791; completed preparatory studies and was graduated from Union College, Schenectady, in 1810; studied law; was admitted to the bar in 1812; moved to Rochester, N. Y., in 1813; engaged in banking; supervisor of Rochester in 1834; mayor in 1837; member of State assembly in 1848; elected as a Whig to the Thirty-first and Thirty-second Congresses (March 4, 1849–March 3, 1853); died at Savin Rock, near New Haven, Conn., August 22, 1855; interment in Mount Hope Cemetery, Rochester, N. Y.

SCHERMERHORN, Simon Jacob, a Representative from New York; born in Rotterdam, Schenectady County, N. Y., September 25, 1827; attended the common schools; engaged in agricultural pursuits; supervisor of the town of Rotterdam in 1856; served two terms as school commissioner; member of the State assembly in 1862 and 1865; a director and trustee in local banks; presidential elector on the Democratic ticket of Cleveland and Thurman in 1888; elected as a Democrat to the Fifty-third Congress (March 4, 1893–March 3, 1895); was not a candidate for renomination in 1894; declined the appointment of Postmaster General in the Cabinet of President Cleveland in 1895; retired to his farm in Rotterdam, N. Y., and died there July 21, 1901; interment in Viewland Cemetery.

SCHIFFLER, Andrew Charles, a Representative from West Virginia; born in Wheeling, W. Va., August 10, 1889; attended the public schools; studied law in law offices in Wheeling, W. Va.; was admitted to the bar and commenced practice in Wheeling in 1913; referee in bankruptcy, northern district of West Virginia, 1918–1922; prosecuting attorney of Ohio County, W. Va., 1925–1932; chairman of the Ohio County Republican Committee 1936–1938; elected as a Republican to the Seventy-sixth Congress (January 3, 1939–January 3, 1941); unsuccessful candidate for reelection in 1940 to the Seventy-seventh Congress; elected to the Seventy-eighth Congress (January 3, 1943–January 3, 1945); unsuccessful candidate for reelection in 1944 to the Seventy-ninth Congress; resumed the practice of law and is a resident of Wheeling, W. Va.

SCHIRM, Charles Reginald, a Representative from Maryland; born in Baltimore, Md., August 12, 1864; attended the public schools; commenced, but did not complete, an apprenticeship at iron molding; attended Washington and Jefferson College, Washington, Pa.; taught school in Pennsylvania and Maryland; studied law; was admitted to the Baltimore County bar in 1896 and practiced; member of the State house of delegates 1898–1900; counsel to the board of police commissioners of the city of Baltimore in 1899 and 1900; elected as a Republican to the Fifty-seventh Congress (March 4, 1901–March 3, 1903); unsuccessful candidate for reelection in 1902 to the Fifty-eighth Congress; delegate to the Bull Moose National Convention at Chicago in 1912; continued the practice of law in Baltimore, Md., until his death there on November 2, 1918; interment in Loudon Park Cemetery.

SCHLEICHER, Gustave, a Representative from Texas; was born in Darmstadt, Germany, on November 19, 1823; attended the University of Giessen; became a civil engineer and was employed in the construction of several European railroads; immigrated to the United States in 1847 and settled in San Antonio, Tex., in 1850; member of the State house of representatives in 1853 and 1854; served in the State senate 1859–1861; elected as a Democrat to the Forty-fourth and Forty-fifth Congresses and served from March 4, 1875, until his death; had been reelected in 1878 to the Forty-sixth Congress; died in Washington, D. C., January 10, 1879; interment in the United States National Cemetery, San Antonio, Tex., where he was buried at the request of the city of San Antonio.

SCHLEY, William, a Representative from Georgia; born in Frederick, Frederick County, Md., December 15, 1786; in childhood moved with his parents to Georgia; completed preparatory studies; attended the local academies in Louisville and Augusta, Ga.; studied law; was admitted to the bar and commenced practice in Augusta, Ga., in 1812; served as judge of the superior court 1825–1828; member of the State house of representatives in 1830; elected as a Democrat to the Twenty-third and Twenty-fourth Congresses and served from March 4, 1833, to July 1, 1835, when he resigned, having been nominated for Governor; Governor of Georgia 1835–1837; president of the Georgia Medical College at Augusta; died near Augusta, Ga., November 20, 1858; interment in the family burying ground at Richmond Hill, near Augusta, Ga.

SCHNEEBELI, Gustav Adolphus, a Representative from Pennsylvania; born in Neusalz, Germany, May 23, 1853; immigrated to the United States with his parents, who settled in Bethlehem, Pa.; attended the Moravian Parochial School; later moved to Nazareth, Pa., and entered upon a mercantile career; founded the knit-goods industry of the Nazareth Waist Co.; in 1888 he established a lace manufacturing company, of which he became sole owner; elected as a Republican to the Fifty-ninth Congress (March 4, 1905–March 3, 1907); unsuccessful candidate for reelection in 1906 to the Sixtieth Congress; continued in the lace manufacturing business until his death in Nazareth, Northampton County, Pa., February 6, 1923; interment in Moravian Cemetery.

SCHNEEBELI, Herman T., a Representative from Pennsylvania; born in Lancaster, Pa., July 7, 1907; attended the public schools; graduated from Mercersburg Academy in 1926, Dartmouth College in 1930, and Amos Tuck School in 1931; commission distributor Gulf Oil Corporation and automobile dealer in Williamsport, Pa.; during World War II served as a captain Ordnance Department, 1942–1946; member of board of managers of Williamsport Hospital; elected as a Republican to the Eighty-sixth Congress to fill the vacancy caused by the death of Alvin R. Bush and served from April 26, 1960, to January 3, 1961. *Reelected to the Eighty-seventh Congress.*

SCHNEIDER, George John, a Representative from Wisconsin; born in the town of Grand Chute, Outagamie County, Wis., October 30, 1877; moved to Appleton with his parents, attended the public schools of Appleton, Wis.; learned the trade of paper making; vice president of the International Brotherhood of Paper Makers 1909–1927; member of the executive board of the Wisconsin State Federation of Labor 1921–1928; elected as a Republican (Progressive) to the Sixty-eighth and to the four succeeding Congresses (March 4, 1923–March 3, 1933); unsuccessful candidate for reelection in 1932 to the Seventy-third Congress; elected as a Progressive to the Seventy-fourth and Seventy-fifth Congresses (January 3, 1935–January 3, 1939); unsuccessful candidate for reelection in 1938 to the Seventy-sixth Congress; resumed labor activities and died in Toledo, Ohio, March 12, 1939, while attending a labor meeting; interment in Riverside Cemetery, Appleton, Wis.

SCHOEPPEL, Andrew Frank, a Senator from Kansas; born on a farm in Barton County, near Chaflin, Kans., November 23, 1894; attended the district school in Ness County and graduated from Ransom High School in 1915; student, Kansas University, in 1916 and 1917; left school during the First World War and enlisted in the Naval Air Service; following the armistice entered University of Nebraska Law School in 1919 and graduated in 1922; was admitted to the Kansas bar in February 1923 and commenced the practice of law in Ness City, Kans.; county attorney of Ness County; mayor of Ness City; appointed to and served as chairman of the Corporation Commission of the State of Kansas and served from February 1939 until his resignation in May 1942; Governor of Kansas 1943–1947; chairman of the Interstate Oil Compact Commission of the United States 1943–1945; in 1947 joined a law firm in Wichita, Kans.; elected as a Republican to the United States Senate in 1948 and again in 1954 and served from January 3, 1949, to January 3, 1961. *Reelected in 1960 for the term ending January 3, 1967.*

SCHOOLCRAFT, John Lawrence, a Representative from New York; born in Albany, N. Y., in 1804; received a limited schooling; engaged in mercantile pursuits; elected as a Whig to the Thirty-first and Thirty-second Congresses (March 4, 1849–March 3, 1853); was not a candidate for renomination in 1852; chosen president of the Commercial Bank at Albany, N. Y., and served from 1854 until his death; delegate to the Republican National Convention at Chicago in 1860; died while returning to his home from the convention at Chicago, in St. Catherines, Ontario, Canada, July 7, 1860; interment in the Rural Cemetery, Albany, N. Y.

SCHOONMAKER, Cornelius Corneliusen (grandfather of Marius Schoonmaker), a Representative from New York; born in Shawangunk (now Wallkill), Ulster County, N. Y., in June 1745; received a limited schooling; became a surveyor and engaged in agricultural pursuits; member of the committees of vigilance and safety during the Revolutionary War; served in the State assembly 1777–1790; member of the State convention for the adoption of the Federal Constitution in 1788; elected to the Second Congress (March 4, 1791–March 3, 1793); again a member of the State assembly in 1795; died in Shawangunk, N. Y., in the spring of 1796; interment in Old Shawangunk Churchyard at Bruynswick, in Shawangunk (now Wallkill), Ulster County, N. Y.

SCHOONMAKER, Marius (grandson of Cornelius Corneliusen Schoonmaker), a Representative from New York; born in Kingston, Ulster County, N. Y., April 24, 1811; attended the common schools, Kingston Academy, and was graduated from Yale College in 1830; was admitted to the bar in 1833 and commenced practice in Kingston, N. Y.; member of the State senate in 1850 and 1851; elected as a Whig to the Thirty-second Congress (March 4, 1851–March 3, 1853); declined to be a candidate for renomination in 1852; resumed the practice of law in Kingston, N. Y.; auditor of the canal department of New York State in 1854 and 1855; superintendent of the banking department 1854–1856; president of the Kingston Board of Education for nine years; president of the village of Kingston in 1866, 1869, and 1870; delegate to the State constitutional convention in 1867; president of the board of directors of Kingston; died in Kingston, N. Y., January 5, 1894; interment in Wiltwyck Rural Cemetery.

SCHUETZ, Leonard William, a Representative from Illinois; born in Posen, Germany (later Poland), November 16, 1887; in 1888 immigrated to the United States with his father, who settled in Chicago, Ill.; went to work at the age of 10; attended the public schools, Lane Technical High School, and Bryant and Stratton Business College, Chicago, Ill.; engaged as a stenographer and secretary until 1906, when he became associated with Swift & Co. in an executive capacity; organized the Schuetz Construction Co. in 1923 and served as its president and treasurer; elected as a Democrat to the Seventy-second and to the six succeeding Congresses and served from March 4, 1931, until his death in Washington, D. C., on February 13, 1944; interment in St. Adabert's Cemetery, Chicago, Ill.

SCHULTE, William Theodore, a Representative from Indiana; born in St. Bernard, Platte County, Nebr., August 19, 1890; attended the public schools of St. Bernard, Nebr.; moved with his parents to Hammond, Ind., where he attended high school and received a business training; engaged in the theatrical business until 1918; also interested in agricultural pursuits; member of the city council of Hammond, Ind., 1918–1922; resumed the theatrical business until 1932; elected as a Democrat to the Seventy-third and to the four succeeding Congresses (March 4, 1933–January 3, 1943); unsuccessful candidate for renomination in 1942 to the Seventy-eighth Congress, coordinator of field operations in the labor division of the War Production Board, Washington, D. C., 1942–1944; returned to Lake County, Ind., and engaged in agricultural pursuits, engaged in the automobile business at Michigan City, Ind., from October 1947 to March 1949; resides in Munster, Ind.

SCHUMAKER, John Godfrey, a Representative from New York; born in Claverack, Columbia County, N. Y., June 27, 1826; completed preparatory studies in the Lenox (Mass.) Academy; studied law; was admitted to the bar and commenced practice in 1847; moved to Brooklyn, N. Y., in 1853 and continued the practice of law; district attorney for Kings County 1856–1859; corporation counsel for the city of Brooklyn 1862–1864; member of the State constitutional conventions in 1862, 1867, and 1894; delegate to the Democratic National Convention at Chicago in 1864; elected as a Democrat to the Forty-first Congress (March 4, 1869–March 3, 1871); was not a candidate for renomination in 1870; elected to the Forty-third and Forty-fourth Congresses (March 4, 1873–March 3, 1877); was not a candidate for renomination in 1876 to the Forty-fifth Congress; resumed the practice of law; died in Brooklyn, N. Y., on November 23, 1905; interment in Greenwood Cemetery.

SCHUNEMAN, Martin Gerretsen, a Representative from New York; born in Catskill, Albany (now Greene) County, N. Y., February 10, 1764; educated by his father, who was one of the most learned Dutch Reformed ministers in the colony; justice of the peace of Albany County in 1792; engaged in mercantile pursuits and owned an inn at Madison; supervisor for Catskill in Albany and Greene Counties in 1797, 1799, and 1802; member of the State assembly from Ulster County 1798–1800 and from Greene County in 1803; delegate from Greene County to the State constitutional convention which decided the relative powers of the Governor and the council of appointment in 1801; elected as a Democrat to the Ninth Congress (March 4, 1805–March 3, 1807); resumed his former business pursuits; died in Catskill, N. Y., February 21, 1827; interment in the Old Cemetery, Madison (now Leeds), N. Y.

SCHUREMAN, James, a Delegate, a Representative, and a Senator from New Jersey; born in New Brunswick, N. J., February 12, 1756; attended the common schools, and was graduated from Rutgers College, New Brunswick, N. J., in 1775; engaged in mercantile pursuits; served in the Revolutionary Army; member of the State general assembly 1783–1785 and in 1788; delegate to the Provincial Congress of New Jersey in 1786; Member of the Continental Congress in 1786 and 1787; elected as a Federalist to the First Congress (March 4, 1789–March 3, 1791); president of New Brunswick in 1792; elected to the Fifth Congress (March 4, 1797–March 3, 1799); elected to the United States Senate on February 14, 1799, to fill the vacancy caused by the resignation of John Rutherfurd, but did not qualify until later, preferring to serve out his term in the House; served as Senator from March 4, 1799, to February 16, 1801, when he resigned; mayor of New Brunswick, N. J., 1801–1813; member of the State council in 1808 and 1810; elected to the Thirteenth Congress (March 4, 1813–March 3, 1815); was not a candidate for renomination in 1814; again elected mayor and served from 1821 until his death; died in New Brunswick January 22, 1824; interment in First Reformed Church Cemetery.

SCHURZ, Carl, a Senator from Missouri; born in Liblar, near Cologne, Germany, March 2, 1829; was educated at the Gymnasium of Cologne and the University of Bonn; having taken part in the revolution of 1848, he was compelled to flee from Germany; was a newspaper correspondent in Paris and later taught school in London; immigrated to the United States in 1852 and settled in Philadelphia, Pa.; moved to Watertown, Wis., in 1855; studied law; was admitted to the bar and practiced in Milwaukee, Wis.; unsuccessful candidate for Lieutenant Governor of Wisconsin; delegate to the Republican National Conventions in 1860 and 1868; appointed Minister to Spain in 1861 but soon afterward resigned; during the Civil War was appointed brigadier general of Volunteers in the Union Army; engaged in newspaper work after the war in St. Louis, Mo.; elected as a Republican to the United States Senate and served from March 4, 1869, to March 3, 1875; was not a candidate for reelection in 1874; served in the Cabinet of President Hayes as Secretary of the Interior from March 12, 1877, to March 4, 1881; editor of the New York Evening Post 1881–1884; contributor to Harper's Weekly 1892–1898; president of the National Civil Service Reform League 1892–1901; engaged in literary pursuits; died in New York City, May 14, 1906; interment in Sleepy Hollow Cemetery, Tarrytown, N. Y.

SCHUYLER, Karl Cortlandt, a Senator from Colorado; born in Colorado Springs, Colo., April 3, 1877; attended the Colorado Springs public schools; at the age of fourteen was call boy for the Colorado Midland Railroad; graduated from the law school of the University of Denver in 1898; was admitted to the bar the same year and commenced practice in Colorado Springs; in 1905 moved to Denver, Colo., where he continued the practice of law; trustee of the University of Denver and of Colorado Woman's College at Denver, Colo.; unsuccessful candidate for the Republican nomination for United States Senator in 1920; elected on November 8, 1932, as a Republican to the United States Senate to fill the vacancy caused by the death of Charles W. Waterman and served from December 7, 1932, to March 3, 1933; at the same election was an unsuccessful candidate for the full term beginning March 4, 1933; resumed the practice of law in Denver; was struck by an automobile while on a business trip in New York City and died in Lenox Hill Hospital, New York City, N. Y., July 31, 1933; interment in Fairmount Cemetery, Denver, Colo.

SCHUYLER, Philip Jeremiah (son of Philip John Schuyler), a Representative from New York; born in Albany, Albany County, N. Y., January 21, 1768; received a limited schooling under private tutors; engaged in agriculture in Dutchess County; member of the State assembly in 1798; elected to the Fifteenth Congress (March 4, 1817–March 3, 1819); was not a candidate for reelection in 1818; resumed agricultural pursuits; died in New York City February 21, 1835; interment in the family burial grounds on the Schuyler estate near Rhinebeck, Dutchess County, N. Y.; reinterment in Poughkeepsie Rural Cemetery, Poughkeepsie.

SCHUYLER, Philip John (father of Philip Jeremiah Schuyler), a Delegate and a Senator from New York; born in Albany, N. Y., November 20, 1733; attended the common schools of Albany and studied under a private tutor in New Rochelle, N. Y.; served in the British Army and was commissioned captain June 14, 1755; served under Gen. Phineas Lyman; appointed chief commissary in 1756; resigned from the British Army in 1757; in 1758 rejoined General Bradstreet as commissary with the rank of major; sent to England to settle colonial claims in 1758; returned in 1763 and engaged in the lumber business in Saratoga, N. Y.; built the first flax mill in America; commissioner to settle the boundary between New York and Massachusetts in 1764; Member of the Continental Congress 1775–1777; appointed one of the four major generals in the Continental Army in 1775, but became involved in military disputes and resigned in 1779; again a Member of the Continental Congress 1778–1781; State senator from the western New York district 1780–1784 and 1786–1790; elected as a Federalist to the United States Senate and served from March 4, 1789, to March 3, 1791; unsuccessful candidate for reelection; again a member of the State senate 1792–1797; elected to the United States Senate and served from March 4, 1797, to January 3, 1798, when he resigned on account of ill health; died in Albany, N. Y., November 18, 1804; interment in Albany Rural Cemetery.

SCHWABE, George Blaine (brother of Max Schwabe), a Representative from Oklahoma; born in Arthur, Vernon County, Mo., July 26, 1886; attended the country and town schools of Pettis County, Mo., and Sedalia (Mo.) High School; in 1910 was graduated from the law department of the University of Missouri at Columbia; was admitted to the bar the same year and commenced practice in Columbia, Mo.; moved to Nowata, Okla., in 1911 and continued the practice of law; mayor of Nowata, Okla., in 1913 and 1914; member of the Nowata Board of Education 1918–1922; member of the State house of representatives from Nowata County 1918–1922, serving as speaker in 1921 and 1922; moved to Tulsa, Okla., in 1922 and continued the practice of law; chairman of the Republican county committee of Tulsa County, Okla., 1928–1936; delegate to all Republican State conventions since 1912 and to the Republican

National Convention at Cleveland, Ohio, in 1936; elected as a Republican to the Seventy-ninth and Eightieth Congresses (January 3, 1945–January 3, 1949); unsuccessful candidate for reelection in 1948 to the Eighty-first Congress; elected to the Eighty-second Congress and served from January 3, 1951, until his death in Alexandria, Va., April 2, 1952; interment in Memorial Park Cemetery, Tulsa, Okla.

SCHWABE, Max (brother of George Blaine Schwabe), a Representative from Missouri; born on a farm near Columbia, Boone County, Mo., December 6, 1905; attended the public schools and the University of Missouri at Columbia, completing a major in political science and taking a course in law; engaged in the life insurance business in Columbia, Mo., 1926–1942; elected as a Republican to the Seventy-eighth, Seventy-ninth, and Eightieth Congresses (January 3, 1943–January 3, 1949); unsuccessful candidate for reelection in 1948 to the Eighty-first Congress; is a resident of Columbia, Mo.

SCHWARTZ, Henry Herman (Harry), a Senator from Wyoming; born on a farm near Fort Recovery, Mercer County, Ohio, May 18, 1869; educated in the public schools of Mercer County and Cincinnati, Ohio; engaged in the newspaper business at Fort Recovery, Ohio, 1892–1894 and at Sioux Falls, S. Dak., 1894–1896; studied law; was admitted to the bar in 1895 and commenced practice in Sioux Falls; member of the South Dakota House of Representatives in 1896 and 1897; chief of the field division of the United States General Land Office, at Spokane, Wash., and Helena, Mont., 1897–1907; special assistant to the Attorney General in 1907; chief of field service, General Land Office, Washington, D. C., 1907–1910; moved to Casper, Wyo., in 1915; president of the Casper Board of Education and the Natrona County High School Board 1928–1934; trustee of Memorial Hospital, Casper, Wyo., 1926–1932; member of the Wyoming State senate 1933–1935; chairman of the Democratic State committee 1932–1936; delegate to the Wyoming Democratic State conventions 1927–1935; delegate to the Democratic National Conventions in 1928 and 1932; unsuccessful candidate for election to the United States Senate in 1930; elected as a Democrat to the United States Senate in 1936 for the term commencing January 3, 1937, and ending January 3, 1943; unsuccessful candidate for reelection in 1942; appointed by President Franklin D. Roosevelt to the National Mediation Board on February 26, 1943, and served until February 1, 1947; resumed the practice of law in Casper, Wyo., until his death there April 24, 1955; interment in Highland Cemetery.

SCHWARTZ, John, a Representative from Pennsylvania; born in Sunbury, Northumberland County, Pa., October 27, 1793; received a limited schooling; at the age of ten years was apprenticed to a merchant in Reading, Pa., and became a partner at the expiration of his apprenticeship; served in the War of 1812 as a major; engaged in the manufacture of iron products; elected as a Democrat to the Thirty-sixth Congress and served from March 4, 1859, until his death in Washington, D. C., June 20, 1860; interment in Charles Evans Cemetery, Reading, Berks County, Pa.

SCHWELLENBACH, Lewis Baxter, a Senator from Washington; born in Superior, Douglas County, Wis., September 20, 1894; moved to Spokane, Wash., with his parents in 1902; attended the grade and high schools in Spokane and was graduated from the law department of the University of Washington at Seattle in 1917; assistant instructor at the University of Washington in 1916 and 1917; during the First World War served from July 26, 1918, as a private in the Twelfth Regiment, United States Infantry, until discharged as a corporal February

14, 1919; was admitted to the bar in 1919 and commenced practice in Seattle, Wash.; State commander of the American Legion in 1922; member of the board of regents of the University of Washington in 1933 and 1934, serving as president in 1933; chairman of the Democratic State convention in 1924; chairman of the King County Democratic committee 1928–1930; unsuccessful candidate for nomination for Governor in 1932; delegate to the Interparliamentary Union at The Hague in 1938; elected as a Democrat to the United States Senate and served from January 3, 1935, to December 16, 1940, when he resigned; was not a candidate for renomination in 1940, having been appointed United States district judge for the eastern district of Washington, in which capacity he served until his resignation to become Secretary of Labor; appointed Secretary of Labor by President Harry S. Truman and served from June 1, 1945, until his death in Walter Reed Hospital, Washington, D. C., June 10, 1948; interment in Washelli Cemetery, Seattle, Wash.

SCHWENGEL, Frederick Delbert, a Representative from Iowa; born on a farm near Sheffield, Franklin County, Iowa, May 28, 1907; attended the rural schools in West Fork Township and high schools in Chapin and Sheffield, Iowa; graduated from Northeast Missouri Teachers College at Kirksville in 1930, and attended Iowa University graduate school 1933–1935; athletic coach and instructor of history and political science in public schools of Shelbina and Kirksville, Mo., 1930–1937; engaged in the insurance business in Davenport, Iowa, from September 1, 1937, to December 31, 1954; served in the Missouri National Guard 1929–1936; member of the State house of representatives 1945–1954; member, Iowa Development Commission, 1949–1955; elected as a Republican to the Eighty-fourth, Eighty-fifth, and Eighty-sixth Congresses (January 3, 1955–January 3, 1961). *Reelected to the Eighty-seventh Congress.*

SCHWERT, Pius Louis, a Representative from New York; born in Angola, Erie County N. Y., November 22, 1892; attended the public schools in Angola and Lafayette High School, Buffalo, N. Y.; was graduated from Wharton School of Commerce, University of Pennsylvania, Philadelphia, Pa., in 1914; played professional baseball with the New York American League Ball Club 1914–1917; during the First World War served in the United States Navy as a yeoman, first class, and later was commissioned as an ensign; engaged in mercantile and banking pursuits in Angola; president of the Bank of Angola, N. Y., 1921–1931; member of the first salary survey committee of Erie County in 1932; moved to Buffalo, N. Y., and served as county clerk 1933–1938; elected as a Democrat to the Seventy-sixth and Seventy-seventh Congresses and served from January 3, 1939, until his death in Washington, D. C., March 11, 1941; interment in Forest Avenue Cemetery, Angola, N. Y.

SCOBLICK, James Paul, a Representative from Pennsylvania; born in Archbald, Lackawanna County, Pa., May 10, 1909; attended the public school and St. Thomas High School, Scranton, Pa.; was graduated from Fordham University, New York, N. Y., in 1930 and took postgraduate work at Columbia University, New York, N. Y.; member of the Department of Public Assistance Board of Lackawanna County, Pa.; engaged in fruit growing and processing since 1937; elected as a Republican to the Seventy-ninth Congress to fill the vacancy caused by the resignation of John W. Murphy and at the same time was elected to the Eightieth Congress and served from November 5, 1946, to January 3, 1949; unsuccessful candidate for renomination in 1948; resumed former business pursuits; is a resident of Archbald, Pa.

SCOFIELD, Glenni William, a Representative from Pennsylvania; born in Dewittville, Chautauqua County, N. Y., on

March 11, 1817; attended the common schools; learned the printing trade; returned to classical study and was graduated from Hamilton College, Clinton, N. Y., in 1840; engaged in teaching; studied law; was admitted to the bar in 1842 and commenced practice in Warren, Pa.; district attorney 1846–1848; member of the State house of representatives 1849–1851; affiliated with the Republican Party in 1856; served in the State senate 1857–1859; appointed president judge of the eighteenth judicial district of Pennsylvania in 1861; elected as a Republican to the Thirty-eighth and to the five succeeding Congresses (March 4, 1863–March 3, 1875); was not a candidate for renomination in 1874; resumed the practice of law in Warren; appointed Register of the Treasury by President Hayes and served from 1878 to 1881; associate justice of the United States Court of Claims 1881–1891; retired from active pursuits; died in Warren, Warren County, Pa., August 30, 1891; interment in Oakland Cemetery.

SCOTT, Byron Nicholson, a Representative from California; born in Council Grove, Morris County, Kans., March 21, 1903; attended the public schools; was graduated from the University of Kansas at Lawrence in 1924, from the University of Southern California at Los Angeles in 1930, and from the National University School of Law in 1949; taught school at Tucson, Ariz., 1924–1926; moved to Long Beach, Los Angeles County, Calif., in 1926 and taught school until 1934; delegate to the California Democratic State conventions 1934–1940; delegate to the Democratic National Convention at Philadelphia in 1936; elected as a Democrat to the Seventy-fourth and Seventy-fifth Congresses (January 3, 1935–January 3, 1939); unsuccessful candidate for reelection in 1938 to the Seventy-sixth Congress and for election in 1940 to the Seventy-seventh Congress; secretary of the California State Highway Commission in 1939 and 1940; engaged in the construction business in 1941 and 1942; served with the War Production Board in Washington, D. C., 1942–1945; engaged in the practice of law in Washington, D. C., where he now resides.

SCOTT, Charles Frederick, a Representative from Kansas; born near Iola, Allen County, Kans., on September 7, 1860; attended the common schools; was graduated from the University of Kansas at Lawrence in 1881; went to Colorado, New Mexico, and Arizona, and was engaged chiefly in clerical work; returned to Iola, Kans., in 1882 and edited the Iola Register; appointed regent of the university in 1891–1900; member of the State senate 1892–1896; presidential elector on the Republican ticket of McKinley and Hobart in 1896; elected as a Republican to the Fifty-seventh and to the four succeeding Congresses (March 4, 1901–March 3, 1911); unsuccessful candidate for reelection in 1910 to the Sixty-second Congress; appointed one of five delegates to the International Institute of Agriculture at Rome in 1911; director of publicity in Republican National Headquarters in Chicago in 1912; lectured on Chautauqua platform in 1913, 1915, and 1916; delegate to the Republican National Conventions in 1916 and 1932; unsuccessful candidate for nomination to the United States Senate in 1918 and again in 1928; resumed newspaper work until his death in Iola, Kans., on September 18, 1938; interment in Iola Cemetery.

SCOTT, Charles Lewis, a Representative from California; born in Richmond, Henrico County, Va., January 23, 1827; attended the public schools and Richmond Academy and was graduated from William and Mary College, Williamsburg, Va., in 1846; studied law; was admitted to the bar in 1847 and commenced practice in Richmond, Va.; moved to California in 1849 and engaged in gold mining; resumed the practice of his profession in Sonora, Calif., in 1851; member of the State assembly 1854–1856; elected as a Democrat to the Thirty-fifth

and Thirty-sixth Congresses (March 4, 1857–March 3, 1861); was not a candidate for reelection; during the Civil War served as a major in the Fourth Regiment, Alabama Volunteer Infantry, of the Confederate Army and was wounded in the Battle of Bull Run July 21, 1861; after the war engaged in agricultural pursuits in Wilcox County, Ala., and from 1869 to 1879 was engaged in journalism; was a delegate to every Democratic National Convention from the end of the Civil War to 1896; appointed by President Cleveland on August 10, 1885, Minister Resident to Venezuela and consul general at Caracas and served until his resignation, effective March 8, 1889; returned to the United States and engaged in agricultural pursuits until his death near Mount Pleasant, Monroe County, Ala., April 30, 1899; interment in the private cemetery of Mrs. Robert G. Scott at Cedar Hill, Ala.

SCOTT, David, a Representative from Pennsylvania; elected to the Fifteenth Congress but resigned in 1817, before the Congress assembled, having been appointed president and judge of the court of common pleas.

SCOTT, Frank Douglas, a Representative from Michigan; born in Alpena, Alpena County, Mich., on August 25, 1878; attended the public schools; was graduated from the law department of the University of Michigan at Ann Arbor in 1901; was admitted to the bar the same year and commenced practice in Alpena; city attorney of Alpena in 1903 and 1904; city prosecutor 1906–1910; member of the State senate 1911–1914 and served as president pro tempore in 1913 and 1914; elected as a Republican to the Sixty-fourth and to the five succeeding Congresses (March 4, 1915–March 3, 1927); unsuccessful candidate for renomination in 1926; resumed the practice of his profession in Washington, D. C.; died in Palm Beach, Fla., February 12, 1951; interment in Evergreen Cemetery, Alpena, Mich.

SCOTT, George Cromwell, a Representative from Iowa; born near East Kendall (now Morton), Monroe County, N. Y., August 8, 1864; moved to Iowa in 1880; attended the country schools and the high school at Dallas Center, Iowa; studied law; was admitted to the bar in 1887 and commenced practice in Le Mars, Iowa, in 1888; moved to Sioux City in 1901 and continued the practice of law; elected as a Republican to the Sixty-second Congress to fill the vacancy caused by the death of Elbert H. Hubbard; reelected to the Sixty-third Congress and served from November 5, 1912, to March 3, 1915; unsuccessful candidate for reelection in 1914 to the Sixty-fourth Congress; elected to the Sixty-fifth Congress (March 4, 1917–March 3, 1919); was not a candidate for renomination in 1918; resumed the practice of law in Sioux City; appointed by President Harding judge of the United States District Court for the Northern District of Iowa and served from March 4, 1922, until his retirement on November 1, 1943; died in Sioux City, Iowa, October 6, 1948; interment in Graceland Park Cemetery.

SCOTT, Gustavus (grandfather of William Lawrence Scott), a Delegate from Maryland; born at "Westwood," Prince William County, Va., in 1753; went with his brother to Scotland in 1765 and studied at King's College, Aberdeen, Scotland; entered the Middle Temple, London, England, in 1767, and completed his law studies in 1771; returned to the United States in the latter year and settled in Somerset County, Md., where he practiced law; delegate to the Annapolis convention in 1774 and 1775; member of the Association of the Freemen of Maryland; member of the first State constitutional convention in 1776; moved to Dorchester County; member of the house of delegates in 1780; Member of the Continental Congress in 1784 and 1785; resumed the practice of law; moved to

Montgomery County in 1794; one of the commissioners to superintend the erection of the public buildings in Washington, D. C., 1794–1800; died in Washington, D. C., December 25, 1800; interment on his farm in Virginia.

SCOTT, Hardie (son of John Roger Kirkpatrick Scott), a Representative from Pennsylvania; born in Cynwyd, Montgomery County, Pa., June 7, 1907; was graduated from Taft School, Watertown, Conn., in 1926, from Yale University, New Haven, Conn., in 1930, and from the University of Pennsylvania Law School at Philadelphia in 1934; was admitted to the bar in 1935 and commenced practice in Philadelphia, Pa.; elected as a Republican to the Eightieth, Eighty-first, and Eighty-second Congresses (January 3, 1947–January 3, 1953); was not a candidate for renomination in 1952; resumed the practice of law; is a resident of Chester County, Pa.

SCOTT, Harvey David, a Representative from Indiana; born near Ashtabula, Union County, Ohio, October 18, 1818; attended the public schools and the Asbury (now De Pauw) University at Greencastle, Ind.; studied law; was admitted to the bar and commenced practice in Terre Haute, Ind.; held several local offices; elected as a Republican to the Thirty-fourth Congress (March 4, 1855–March 3, 1857); resumed the practice of law; judge of the circuit court of Vigo County 1881–1884; moved to California in 1887; died in Pasadena, Calif., July 11, 1891; interment in Mountain View Cemetery.

SCOTT, Hugh Doggett, Jr., a Representative and a Senator from Pennsylvania; born in Fredericksburg, Spotsylvania County, Va., on November 11, 1900; attended public and private schools; was graduated from Randolph-Macon College, Ashland, Va., in 1919 and from the law department of the University of Virginia at Charlottesville in 1922; was admitted to the bar in 1922 and commenced practice in Philadelphia, Pa.; during the First World War enrolled in the Student Reserve Officers' Training Corps and the Students' Army Training Corps; assistant district attorney of Philadelphia, Pa., 1926–1941; member of the Governor's Commission on Reform of the Magistrates System 1938–1940; president of the Woodmere Art Gallery in 1944 and 1945; director of the Hayes Mechanics Home for Aged 1938–1943; during World War II was on active duty for two years with the United States Navy with final rank of commander, serving in the North Atlantic and Pacific areas and in the occupation of Japan; awarded the Navy Commendation Ribbon; elected as a Republican to the Seventy-seventh and Seventy-eighth Congresses (January 3, 1941–January 3, 1945); unsuccessful candidate for reelection in 1944 to the Seventy-ninth Congress; resumed the practice of law; chairman of the Republican National Committee in 1948 and 1949; elected to the Eightieth and to the five succeeding Congresses (January 3, 1947–January 3, 1959); did not seek renomination in 1958 to the Eighty-sixth Congress; elected in 1958 to the United States Senate for the term commencing January 3, 1959, and ending January 3, 1965.

SCOTT, John, a Delegate and a Representative from Missouri; born in Hanover County, Va., May 18, 1785; moved with his parents to Indiana Territory in 1802; was graduated from Princeton College in 1805; studied law; was admitted to the bar and commenced practice in Ste. Genevieve, Mo., in 1806; presented credentials as a Delegate-elect to the Fourteenth Congress from the Territory of Missouri and served from August 6, 1816, to January 13, 1817, when the election was declared illegal and the seat vacant; elected as a Delegate to the Fifteenth and Sixteenth Congresses and served from August 4, 1817, to March 3, 1821; upon the admission of Missouri as a State into the Union was elected to the Seventeenth, Eighteenth, and Nineteenth Congresses and served from August 10, 1821, to March 3, 1827; unsuccessful candidate for reelection in 1826 to the Twentieth Congress; resumed the practice of law; died in Ste. Genevieve, Ste. Genevieve County, Mo., October 1, 1861.

SCOTT, John, a Representative from Pennsylvania; born at Marsh Creek, near Gettysburg, Pa., December 25, 1784; moved to Alexandria, Pa., in 1806; engaged as tanner and shoemaker; served as major in the War of 1812; member of the State house of representatives in 1819 and 1820; elected to the Twenty-first Congress (March 4, 1829–March 3, 1831); unsuccessful candidate for reelection to the Twenty-second Congress; resumed his former business pursuits; retired from business in 1842; died in Alexandria, Huntingdon County, Pa., on September 22, 1850; interment in Alexandria Cemetery.

SCOTT, John (son of the preceding), a Senator from Pennsylvania; born in Alexandria, Huntingdon County, Pa., July 24, 1824; attended the common schools and Marshall College, Chambersburg, Pa.; studied law; was admitted to the bar in 1846 and practiced in Huntingdon, Pa., 1846–1869; prosecuting attorney 1846–1849; member of the revenue commission in 1851; member of the State house of representatives in 1862; elected as a Republican to the United States Senate and served from March 4, 1869, to March 3, 1875; was not a candidate for reelection in 1875; moved to Pittsburgh, Pa., in 1875; general counsel of the Pennsylvania Railroad 1875–1877 and general solicitor 1877–1895; died in Philadelphia, Pa., November 29, 1896; interment in Woodlands Cemetery.

SCOTT, John Guier, a Representative from Missouri; born in Philadelphia, Pa., December 26, 1819; completed preparatory studies; was graduated from Bethlehem Academy, Pennsylvania, in civil engineering; moved to Missouri in 1842; general manager of the Iron Mountain Co. at Iron Mountain; established the Irondale Iron Co. at Irondale in 1858; unsuccessful Democratic candidate for election in 1862 to the Thirty-eighth Congress; subsequently elected as a Democrat to the Thirty-eighth Congress to fill the vacancy caused by the death of John W. Noell and served from December 7, 1863, to March 3, 1865; engaged in the drug business in St. Louis; resumed mining, and built furnaces, at Scotia, Crawford County, Mo., in 1868 and at Nova Scotia a year later; returned in 1870 to St. Louis; moved to east Tennessee about 1880; died at Oliver Springs, Roane County, Tenn., May 16, 1892; interment in Bellefontaine Cemetery, St. Louis, Mo.

SCOTT, John Morin, a Delegate from New York; born in New York City in 1730; attended the common schools; was graduated from Yale College in 1746; studied law; was admitted to the bar in 1752 and commenced practice in New York City; one of the founders of the Sons of Liberty; alderman 1756–1761; member of the New York General Committee in 1775; member of the Provincial Congress 1775–1777; brigadier general in the Revolutionary War; member of the committee to draw up a constitution for the State of New York in 1776; elected associate justice of the supreme court of New York in 1777, but declined to accept the position; member of the State senate 1777–1782; secretary of state of New York 1778–1784; Member of the Continental Congress 1780–1783; died in New York City September 14, 1784; interment at the north entrance of Trinity Church.

SCOTT, John Roger Kirkpatrick (father of Hardie Scott), a Representative from Pennsylvania; born in Bloomsburg, Columbia County, Pa., July 6, 1873; moved with his parents to Wilkes-Barre, Pa., and later to Philadelphia; attended the public schools; was graduated from the Central High School of Philadelphia in 1893; attended the law school of the University of Pennsylvania at Philadelphia; was admitted to the bar in December 1895 and commenced the practice of law in Philadelphia; member of the State house of representatives in 1899 and again in 1909, 1911, and 1913; elected as a Republican to the Sixty-fourth and Sixty-fifth Congresses and served from March 4, 1915, until his resignation, effective January 5, 1919; resumed the practice of his profession; died in Philadelphia, Pa., December 9, 1945; interment in West Laurel Hills Cemetery.

SCOTT, Lon Allen, a Representative from Tennessee; born on a farm near Cypress Inn, Wayne County, Tenn., September 25, 1888; moved with his parents to Savannah, Hardin County, Tenn.; attended the public schools and Savannah (Tenn.) Institute; was graduated from the law department of Cumberland University, Lebanon Tenn., in 1915; engaged in mercantile pursuits and the real estate and lumber business; member of the State house of representatives 1913–1917 and served as minority floor leader in 1915 and 1917; represented Tennessee in the prosecution of Attorney General Estes in an impeachment proceeding before the State senate; resigned as a State representative and enlisted as a private in the United States Marine Corps during the First World War; was promoted to a lieutenancy; elected as a Republican to the Sixty-seventh Congress (March 4, 1921–March 3, 1923); unsuccessful candidate for reelection in 1922 to the Sixty-eighth Congress; resumed his former business pursuits and resided in Savannah, Tenn., until his death there on February 11, 1931; interment in Savannah Cemetery.

SCOTT, Nathan Bay, a Senator from West Virginia; born near Quaker City, Guernsey County, Ohio, December 18, 1842; attended the common schools; engaged in mining near Colorado Springs, Colo., 1859–1862; during the Civil War entered the Union Army July 20, 1863, as a corporal in Company E, Eighty-eighth Regiment, Ohio Volunteer Infantry; appointed as a sergeant April 9, 1864; promoted to regimental commissary sergeant April 28, 1865; mustered out of the service July 3, 1865; after the war engaged in the manufacture of glass in Wheeling, W. Va.; also engaged in banking; member of the city council 1881–1883 and served as president 1881–1883; served in the State senate 1883–1890; member of the Republican National Committee in 1888 serving on the executive committee a greater portion of the time; appointed Commissioner of Internal Revenue by President McKinley January 1, 1898, and served until February 28, 1899, when he resigned to become Senator; elected as a Republican to the United States Senate on January 25, 1899; reelected in 1905 and served from March 4, 1899, to March 3, 1911; unsuccessful candidate for renomination; appointed a member of the Lincoln Memorial Commission March 3, 1911, and served until the Memorial was dedicated, when the commission automatically ceased to exist; engaged in banking in Washington, D. C., until his death on January 2, 1924; remains were cremated and the ashes deposited in a mausoleum in Rock Creek Cemetery.

SCOTT, Owen, a Representative from Illinois; born on a farm in Jackson Township, Effingham County, Ill., on July 6, 1848; attended the common schools, a private school in Kinmundy, and the State normal school in Normal, Ill.; taught school; superintendent of schools for Effingham County, Ill., 1873–1881; studied law; was admitted to the bar in 1873 and commenced practice in Effingham, Ill.; engaged in newspaper work; published the Effingham Democrat; mayor of Effingham in 1882; city attorney in 1883 and 1884; moved to Bloomington, Ill., in 1884 and became proprietor and manager of the Bloomington Daily and Weekly Bulletins; deputy collector of internal revenue by

appointment of President Cleveland 1885–1889; chairman of the Illinois Democratic convention at Springfield, Ill., in 1888; elected as a Democrat to the Fifty-second Congress (March 4, 1891–March 3, 1893); unsuccessful candidate for reelection in 1892 to the Fifty-third Congress; moved to Decatur, Ill., in 1899 and managed the Decatur Herald until 1904, when he engaged in the insurance business; retired from the insurance business in 1921 to become secretary of the Masonic Grand Lodge of Illinois, which position he held until his death in Decatur, Ill., December 21, 1928; interment in Oak Ridge Cemetery, Effingham, Ill.

SCOTT, Ralph James, a Representative from North Carolina; born in Surry County, near Danbury, N. C., October 15, 1905; educated in the public schools and Pinnacle High School in Stokes County; graduated from Wake Forest College in 1930; was admitted to the bar in 1930 and commenced the practice of law in Danbury, N. C.; member of the State house of representatives in 1937; solicitor of the twenty-first judicial district of North Carolina 1938–1956; elected as a Democrat to the Eighty-fifth and Eighty-sixth Congresses (January 3, 1957–January 3, 1961). *Reelected to the Eighty-seventh Congress.*

SCOTT, Thomas, a Representative from Pennsylvania; born in Chester County, Pa., in 1739; as a child moved with his parents to Lancaster County; attended the rural schools; studied law; was admitted to the bar and practiced; moved to Westmoreland County in 1770 and settled on Dunlaps Creek, near the Monongahela River; justice of the peace in 1773; member of the first Pennsylvania Assembly in 1776; member of the supreme council in 1777; upon the formation of Washington County in 1781 was appointed prothonotary and served until March 28, 1789, when he resigned, having been elected to Congress; commissioned a justice of Washington County on November 21, 1786; member of the State convention that ratified the Federal Constitution in 1787; elected to the First Congress (March 4, 1789–March 3, 1791); declined to be a candidate for reelection in 1790; again a member of the State assembly in 1791; elected to the Third Congress (March 4, 1793–March 3, 1795); died in Washington, Pa., March 2, 1796; interment in the old graveyard on First Walnut Street; reinterment in Washington Cemetery.

SCOTT, William Kerr, a Senator from North Carolina; born in Haw River, Alamance County, N. C., April 17, 1896; attended the public schools of Hawfield, N. C.; graduated from North Carolina State College at Raleigh in 1917; during the First World War served as a private in the Field Artillery, United States Army, in 1918; farmer and dairyman; Alamance County farm agent 1920–1930; master, North Carolina State Grange 1930–1933; regional director, Farm Debt Adjustment Program of Resettlement Administration 1934–1936; North Carolina State Commissioner of Agriculture from 1937 until his resignation February 14, 1948; member of a special United States Commission to Mexico for Study of Hoof and Mouth Disease in 1947; member of National Advisory Committee of Agricultural Research and Marketing 1946–1948; Governor of North Carolina 1949–1952; elected as a Democrat to the United States Senate November 2, 1954, to fill the vacancy caused by the death of Willis Smith, and at the same time was elected to a full term beginning January 3, 1955, and served from November 29, 1954, until his death in Burlington, N. C., April 16, 1958; interment in Hawfields Presbyterian Church Cemetery near Mebane, N. C.

SCOTT, William Lawrence (grandson of Gustavus Scott), a Representative from Pennsylvania; born in Washington, D. C., July 2, 1828; attended the common schools and Hampden Academy (later Hampden-Sidney), near Fortress Monroe, Va.; page in the National House of Representatives 1840–1846;

moved to Erie, Pa., in 1846 and was employed as a shipping clerk until 1850; was subsequently engaged in shipping, coal mining, iron manufacturing, banking, and railroad construction; instrumental in extending the Chicago, Rock Island & Pacific Railway to the Missouri River in 1862; was also interested in establishing the first elevated railroad in New York City and in the construction of the New York, Philadelphia & Norfolk Railroad; stockholder in several major railroads, and was active in the development of the Canada Southern, Canadian Pacific, Denver & Rio Grande, and the Union Pacific Railroads; had extensive land holdings and was interested in the raising of purebred cattle; mayor of Erie in 1866 and again in 1871; unsuccessful candidate for election in 1866 to the Fortieth Congress and in 1876 to the Forty-fifth Congress; elected a member of the Democratic National Committee in 1876, 1880, and 1884; delegate to the Democratic National Conventions in 1876, 1880, and 1888; elected as a Democrat to the Forty-ninth and Fiftieth Congresses (March 4, 1885–March 3, 1889); was renominated in 1888 and again in 1890 but each time declined to be a candidate because of the condition of his health; withdrew from political life; director in a number of railroad companies and president of the Erie & Pittsburgh Railroad at the time of his death in Newport, R. I., September 19, 1891; interment in Erie Cemetery, Erie, Pa.

SCOVILLE, Jonathan, a Representative from New York; born in Salisbury, Litchfield County, Conn., July 14, 1830; attended various educational institutions in Massachusetts, including the scientific department of Harvard University; engaged in business in Canaan, Conn., in 1854 as an iron manufacturer and mine owner; moved to Buffalo, N. Y., in 1860 and established a car-wheel foundry, and the next year established another in Toronto, Canada; elected as a Democrat to the Forty-sixth Congress to fill the vacancy caused by the resignation of Ray V. Pierce; reelected to the Forty-seventh Congress and served from November 12, 1880, to March 3, 1883; was not a candidate for renomination in 1882; mayor of Buffalo in 1884 and 1885; died in New York City, March 4, 1891; interment in Salisbury Cemetery, Salisbury, Conn.

SCRANTON, George Whitfield (second cousin of Joseph Augustine Scranton), a Representative from Pennsylvania; born in Madison, New Haven County, Conn., May 11, 1811; attended the common schools and Lee's Academy; moved to Belvidere, N. J., in 1828 and became a teamster; subsequently engaged in mercantile pursuits, first as a clerk and later as a partner in the business; from 1835 to 1839 was interested in agricultural pursuits and in the latter year engaged in the manufacture of iron, and began experimenting with the practicability of smelting ore by means of anthracite coal in Slocum (now Scranton), Pa.; founder of the Lackawanna Iron & Coal Co. and the city of Scranton, Pa.; projected and constructed the Northumberland division of the Lackawanna Railroad; president of two railroad companies; elected as a Republican to the Thirty-sixth and Thirty-seventh Congresses and served from March 4, 1859, until his death in Scranton, Pa., March 24, 1861; interment in Dunmore Cemetery.

SCRANTON, Joseph Augustine (second cousin of George Whitfield Scranton), a Representative from Pennsylvania; born in Madison, New Haven County, Conn., July 26, 1838; moved with his parents to Pennsylvania in 1847; pursued an academic course at Phillips Academy, Andover, Mass.; attended Yale College 1857–1861; collector of internal revenue 1862–1866; founded the Scranton Daily Republican in 1867; delegate to the Republican National Convention at Philadelphia in 1872; postmaster of Scranton from March 19, 1874, to May 5, 1881;

elected as a Republican to the Forty-seventh Congress (March 4, 1881–March 3, 1883); unsuccessful candidate for reelection in 1882 to the Forty-eighth Congress; elected to the Forty-ninth Congress (March 4, 1885–March 3, 1887); unsuccessful candidate for reelection in 1886 to the Fiftieth Congress; elected to the Fifty-first Congress (March 4, 1889–March 3, 1891); unsuccessful candidate for reelection in 1890 to the Fifty-second Congress; resumed the newspaper business in Scranton; elected to the Fifty-third and Fifty-fourth Congresses (March 4, 1893–March 3, 1897); was not a candidate for renomination in 1896; resumed the publication and editorship of the Scranton Republican, a daily paper; treasurer of Lackawanna County 1901–1903; died in Scranton, Lackawanna County, Pa., October 12, 1908; interment in Forest Hill Cemetery.

SCRIVNER, Errett Power, a Representative from Kansas; born in Newton, Harvey County, Kans., March 20, 1898; attended the grade schools and was graduated from Manual Training High School, Kansas City, Mo.; during the First World War enlisted in Battery B, One Hundred and Twenty-ninth Field Artillery, in July 1917; served overseas as a private first class in the One Hundred and Thirtieth Field Artillery and the One Hundred and Thirty-seventh Infantry (Medical Detachment), Thirty-fifth Division, in 1918 and 1919; awarded the Silver Star and Purple Heart Medals; was graduated from the law department of the University of Kansas at Lawrence in 1925; was admitted to the bar the same year and commenced practice in Kansas City, Kans.; elected as a Republican to the Seventy-eighth Congress to fill the vacancy caused by the death of U. S. Guyer; reelected to the Seventy-ninth and to the six succeeding Congresses and served from September 14, 1943, to January 3, 1959; unsuccessful candidate for reelection in 1958 to the Eighty-sixth Congress; special assistant to the comptroller, Department of Defense, Washington, D. C., from January 1959 to March 1960; Deputy Assistant Secretary of Defense, Public Affairs, from March 7, 1960, to January 20, 1961; retired and is a resident of Kansas City, Kans.

SCROGGY, Thomas Edmund, a Representative from Ohio; born in Harveysburg, Warren County, Ohio, March 18, 1843; attended the public schools; engaged in manufacturing; during the Civil War enlisted in July 1861 as a private in Company H, Thirty-ninth Regiment, Ohio Volunteer Infantry, and served in that capacity and as corporal until July 4, 1864, when he was shot through the right shoulder and lung in an assault on the Confederate works at Nickajack Creek, Ga.; honorably discharged and mustered out at Camp Dennison in March 1865; in June 1865 engaged in the retail business in Xenia, Ohio; was elected justice of the peace in 1869 and served one term; studied law; was admitted to the bar September 8, 1871, and commenced practice in Xenia, Ohio; served three terms as clerk and three terms as solicitor of the city of Xenia; common pleas judge in 1898, and again elected for a term of five years beginning February 1904 from which he resigned upon his election to Congress; elected as a Republican to the Fifty-ninth Congress (March 4, 1905–March 3, 1907); was not a candidate for renomination in 1906; resumed the practice of his profession; moved to Tulsa, Okla., in 1912, where he died March 6, 1915; interment in Woodlawn Cemetery, Xenia, Ohio.

SCRUGHAM, James Graves, a Representative and a Senator from Nevada; born in Lexington, Fayette County, Ky., January 19, 1880; attended the public schools and was graduated from the engineering department of the University of Kentucky at Lexington in 1906; served in an engineering capacity successively in Cincinnati, Ohio, Chicago, Ill., and San Francisco, Calif.; professor of mechanical engineering, Engineering College,

University of Nevada, at Reno, 1903–1914 and as dean 1914–1917; commissioned as a major in the United States Army in 1917 and was promoted to the rank of lieutenant colonel in 1918; State engineer of Nevada 1917–1923; State public service commissioner 1919–1923; Governor of Nevada 1923–1927; editor and publisher of the Nevada State Journal 1927–1932: special adviser to the Secretary of the Interior on Colorado River development projects in 1927; elected as a Democrat to the Seventy-third and to the four succeeding Congresses and served from March 4, 1923, to December 7, 1942, when he resigned to become a Senator; elected to the United States Senate on November 3, 1942, to fill the vacancy caused by the death of Key Pittman for the term ending January 3, 1947, and served from December 7, 1942, until his death at the United States Naval Hospital in San Diego, Calif., June 23, 1945; interment in Mountain View Cemetery, Reno, Nev.

SCUDDER, Henry Joel (uncle of Townsend Scudder), a Representative from New York; born in Northport, Suffolk County, N. Y., on September 18, 1825; attended the district school and Huntington Academy: was graduated from Trinity College, Hartford, Conn., in 1846; studied law; was admitted to the bar in 1848 and practiced in New York City; commissioned captain in the Thirty-seventh Regiment, New York National Guard, in 1862 and served throughout the Civil War; elected as a Republican to the Forty-third Congress (March 4, 1873–March 3, 1875); declined to be a candidate for renomination in 1874; trustee of Trinity College for over twenty years; resumed the practice of law in New York City, where he died February 10, 1886; interment in the family cemetery at Northport, Suffolk County, N. Y.

SCUDDER, Hubert Baxter, a Representative from California; born in Sebastopol, Sonoma County, Calif., November 5, 1888; graduated from the public schools; supplemented school training with correspondence courses, night schools, and reading of law; served apprenticeship in house painting; superintendent of utilities for the city of Sebastopol from July 1, 1912 to November 4, 1920; during the First World War served in the United States Coast Artillery from May 1918 to December 1918; engaged in the insurance and real-estate business in November 1920; elected city councilman of Sebastopol in April 1924 and mayor in 1926; member of the California State Assembly from January 1925 to January 1940; appointed real estate commissioner of the State of California in January 1943 and resigned March 1, 1948; president of the National Association of License Law Officials from November 1947 to September 1948; elected as a Republican to the Eighty-first and to the four succeeding Congresses (January 3, 1949–January 3, 1959); was not a candidate for renomination in 1958 to the Eighty-sixth Congress; engaged in the real-estate and insurance business; resides in Sebastopol, Calif.

SCUDDER, Isaac Williamson, a Representative from New Jersey; born in Elizabethtown (now Elizabeth), N. J., in 1816; completed preparatory studies; studied law; was admitted to the bar in 1838 and commenced practice in Elizabeth, N. J.; moved to Jersey City; prosecutor of the pleas of Hudson County 1845–1855; appointed as a member of the first police commission of Jersey City, in 1866; elected director and counsel of the New Jersey Railroad & Transportation Co. May 14, 1866, and director of the United New Jersey Railroad & Canal Co. May 21, 1872; elected as a Republican to the Forty-third Congress (March 4, 1873–March 3, 1875); was not a candidate for reelection in 1874 appointed solicitor of the Pennsylvania Railroad Co. for Hudson County, N. J., June 23, 1875; died in Jersey City September 10, 1881; interment in St. John's Churchyard, Elizabeth, Union County, N. J.

SCUDDER, John Anderson, a Representative from New Jersey; born in Freehold, Monmouth County, N. J., March 22, 1759; completed preparatory studies, and was graduated from Princeton College in 1775; studied medicine and commenced practice in Monmouth County, N. J.; during the Revolutionary War served as surgeon's mate in the First Regiment of Monmouth County, in 1777; secretary of the New Jersey Medical Society in 1788 and 1789; member of the State general assembly 1801–1807; elected as a Democrat to the Eleventh Congress to fill the vacancy caused by the death of James Cox and served from October 31, 1810, to March 3, 1811; was not a candidate for renomination to the Twelfth Congress; resumed the practice of medicine; moved to Kentucky after 1810 and to Daviess County, Ind., in 1819; died in Washington, Daviess County, Ind., November 6, 1836; interment in the Old City Cemetery.

SCUDDER, Nathaniel, a Delegate from New Jersey; born at Monmouth Court House, Monmouth County, N. J., May 10, 1733; was graduated from Princeton College in 1751; studied medicine and commenced practice in Monmouth County, N. J.; member of the committee of safety; delegate to the Provincial Congress of New Jersey in 1774; member of the State general assembly, serving as speaker in 1776; lieutenant colonel of the New Jersey Militia in 1776 and colonel in 1781; Member of the Continental Congress 1777–1779; trustee of Princeton College 1778–1781; was killed October 17, 1781, at Blacks Point, near Shrewsbury, Monmouth County, N. J., while resisting an invading party of the British Army during the Revolutionary War; interment in Tennent Church Graveyard, Tennent, N. J.

SCUDDER, Townsend (nephew of Henry Joel Scudder), a Representative from New York; born in Northport, Suffolk County, N. Y., July 26, 1865; attended preparatory schools in Europe; was graduated from Columbia Law School, New York City, in 1888; was admitted to the bar in 1889 and commenced practice in New York City; corporation counsel for Queens County, N. Y., 1893–1899; elected as a Democrat to the Fifty-sixth Congress (March 4, 1899–March 3, 1901); declined to be a candidate for renomination in 1900 and resumed the practice of law; elected to the Fifty-eighth Congress (March 4, 1903–March 3, 1905); was not a candidate for renomination in 1904; justice of the State supreme court for the second judicial district 1907–1920; again resumed the practice of his profession in New York City; State park commissioner and vice president of the Long Island State Park Commission 1924–1927; appointed to the State supreme court bench by Gov. Alfred E. Smith in February 1927; subsequently nominated by the two major political parties to succeed himself for the full term of fourteen years; elected on November 8, 1927, and served until January 1, 1936, when he retired; died in Greenwich, Conn., February 22, 1960; interment in Putnam Cemetery.

SCUDDER, Tredwell, a Representative from New York; born in Islip, Suffolk County, N. Y., January 1, 1778; attended the public schools; engaged in agricultural pursuits; town supervisor of Islip in 1795, 1796, and 1804–1815; member of the State assembly in 1802, 1810, 1811, 1814, and 1815; elected to the Fifteenth Congress (March 4, 1817–March 3, 1819); was not a candidate for renomination in 1818; resumed agricultural pursuits; again served in the State assembly in 1822 and 1828; again town supervisor of Islip 1824-1833; died in Islip, N. Y., October 31, 1834; interment in that village.

SCUDDER, Zeno, a Representative from Massachusetts; born in Osterville, Barnstable County, Mass., August 18, 1807; completed preparatory studies; studied law; was admitted to the bar in 1836 and commenced practice in Falmouth, Mass.;

member of the State senate 1846–1848, serving as president; elected as a Whig to the Thirty-second and Thirty-third Congresses and served from March 4, 1851, until his resignation on March 4, 1854, because of an accident, from the effects of which he never recovered; died in Barnstable, Mass., June 26, 1857; interment in Hillside Cemetery, Osterville, Mass.

SCULL, Edward, a Representative from Pennsylvania; born in Pittsburgh, Pa., February 5, 1818; attended the common schools and pursued an academic course; studied law; was admitted to the bar in 1844; moved to Somerset, Pa., in 1846 and practiced until 1857, prothonotary and clerk of the court for three years; appointed collector of internal revenue by President Lincoln in 1863; removed by President Johnson in September 1866; delegate to the Republican National Conventions in 1864, 1876, and 1884; appointed assessor of internal revenue by President Grant in April 1869; again appointed collector, on March 22, 1873, and served until August 1883, when the district was consolidated with another; published and edited the Somerset Herald 1852–1887; elected as a Republican to the Fiftieth, Fifty-first, and Fifty-second Congresses (March 4, 1887–March 3, 1893); died in Somerset, Somerset County, Pa., July 10, 1900; interment in Union Cemetery.

SCULLY, Thomas Joseph, a Representative from New Jersey; born in South Amboy, Middlesex County, N. J., September 19, 1868; attended the public schools, and Seton Hall College, South Orange, N. J.; engaged in the towing and transportation business; member of the board of education 1893–1895; presidential elector on the Democratic ticket of Bryan and Kern in 1908; mayor of South Amboy, N. J., in 1909 and 1910; elected as a Democrat to the Sixty-second and to the four succeeding Congresses (March 4, 1911–March 3, 1921); delegate to the Democratic National Convention at Baltimore in 1912, which nominated Wilson and Marshall; again mayor of South Amboy, from 1921 until his death in that city December 14, 1921; interment in St. Mary's Cemetery.

SCURRY, Richardson, a Representative from Texas; born in Gallatin, Sumner County, Tenn., November 11, 1811; educated by private tutors; studied law; was admitted to the bar about 1830 and commenced practice in Covington, Tipton County, Tenn.; moved to Texas and settled in Clarksville, where he continued the practice of law; delegate to the State convention at Washington, Tex., which issued the Texas declaration of independence; a pioneer in the formation of State government; took an active part in the Texan War; elected as a Democrat to the Thirty-second Congress (March 4, 1851–March 3, 1853); resumed the practice of law; died in Hempstead, Waller (formerly Austin) County, Tex., April 9, 1862; interment in Hempstead Cemetery.

SEAMAN, Henry John, a Representative from New York; born in Marshland (now Greenridge), Staten Island, N. Y., April 16, 1805; engaged in agricultural pursuits; promoter of Richmond village in 1836; elected as the candidate of the American Party to the Twenty-ninth Congress (March 4, 1845–March 3, 1847); director of the Staten Island Railroad in 1851; secretary of the Plank Road Co. in 1856; constructed the bridge over Fresh Kills; died on Staten Island, N. Y., May 3, 1861; interment in Woodlawn Cemetery, New York, N. Y.

SEARING, John Alexander, a Representative from New York; born in North Hempstead, N. Y., May 14, 1805; completed preparatory studies; sheriff of Queens County, N. Y., 1843–1846; member of the State assembly in 1854; elected as a Democrat to the Thirty-fifth Congress (March 4, 1857–March

3, 1859); declined to be a candidate for renomination in 1858; died in Mineola, Nassau County, N. Y., May 6, 1876; interment in Greenfield Cemetery, Hempstead, N. Y.

SEARLE, James, a Delegate from Pennsylvania; born in New York City in 1730; completed preparatory studies; engaged in business at Madeira in 1757; moved to Philadelphia, Pa., in 1762; one of the managers of the United States lottery 1776–1778; member of the Navy board in 1778; Member of the Continental Congress 1778–1780; trustee of the University of Pennsylvania at Philadelphia 1779–1781; was commissioner to France and Holland to negotiate a loan for the State of Pennsylvania 1780–1782, but was unsuccessful; located in New York City in 1784 as agent for an importing house; returned to Pennsylvania in 1785; died in Philadelphia, Pa., on August 7, 1797; interment in St. Peter's Churchyard.

SEARS, William Joseph, a Representative from Florida; born in Smithville, Lee County, Ga., December 4, 1874; moved with his parents to Ellaville, Ga., and thence to Kissimmee, Osceola County, Fla., in January 1881; attended the public schools; was graduated from Florida State College at Lake City in 1895 and from Mercer University, Macon, Ga., in 1896; studied law; was admitted to the bar in 1905 and commenced practice in Kissimmee, Fla.; mayor of Kissimmee 1907–1911; superintendent of public instruction of Osceola County 1905–1915; elected as a Democrat to the Sixty-fourth and to the six succeeding Congresses (March 4, 1915–March 3, 1929); unsuccessful candidate for renomination in 1928; resumed the practice of his legal profession at Kissimmee, Fla.; moved to Jacksonville, Fla., and continued the practice of law; elected to the Seventy-third and Seventy-fourth Congresses (March 4, 1933–January 3, 1937); was an unsuccessful candidate for renomination in 1936; associate member of the Board of Veterans' Appeals of the Veterans' Administration in Washington, D. C., from 1937 until his retirement due to ill health in October 1942; died in Kissimmee, Fla., March 30, 1944; interment in Rose Hill Cemetery.

SEARS, Willis Gratz, a Representative from Nebraska; born in Willoughby, Lake County, Ohio, August 16, 1860; attended the common schools; moved to Nebraska in 1879 and studied law at the University of Kansas at Lawrence; was admitted to the bar in 1884 and commenced the practice of his profession in Tekamah, Burt County, Nebr.; prosecuting attorney for Burt County 1895–1901; member of the State house of representatives 1901–1904, serving as speaker in 1901; elected as judge of the fourth judicial district of Nebraska, November 6, 1903, and served until March 10, 1923, when he resigned, having been elected to Congress; elected as a Republican to the Sixty-eighth and to the three succeeding Congresses (March 4, 1923–March 3, 1931); was an unsuccessful candidate for renomination in 1930 to the Seventy-second Congress; resumed the practice of law; again elected judge of the fourth judicial district of Nebraska and served from 1932 to 1948; died in Omaha, Nebr., on June 1, 1949; interment in Tekamah Cemetery, Tekamah, Nebr.

SEATON, Frederick Andrew, a Senator from Nebraska; born in Washington, D. C., December 11, 1909; attended the public schools in Manhattan, Kans., and Kansas State College at Manhattan; president of Seaton Publishing Co., Hastings, Nebr., and publisher of Hastings Daily Tribune since 1937; also interested in several daily and weekly newspapers and operating radio and TV stations; served in the State senate 1945–1949 and as chairman of legislative council 1947–1949; secretary to Alfred M. Landon in 1936 presidential campaign; trustee of Hastings College and University of Nebraska Foundation; appointed as a

Republican to, the United States Senate to fill the vacancy caused by the death of Kenneth S. Wherry and served from December 10, 1951, to November 4, 1952; was not a candidate for election to the vacancy; appointed Assistant Secretary of Defense September 3, 1953, and took oath of office September 16, 1953, serving until February 18, 1955; administrative assistant to President Eisenhower from February 19, 1955, to June 15, 1955, then made deputy assistant, in which capacity he served until May 28, 1956; appointed Secretary of the Interior and confirmed June 6, 1956, and served until January 20, 1961; resumed the publishing business; is a resident of Hastings, Nebr.

SEAVER, Ebenezer, a Representative from Massachusetts; born in Roxbury, Mass., July 5, 1763; was graduated from Harvard University in 1784; engaged in agricultural pursuits; member of the State house of representatives 1794–1802; elected as a Democrat to the Eighth and to the four succeeding Congresses (March 4, 1803–March 3, 1813); unsuccessful candidate for reelection in 1812 to the Thirteenth Congress; member of the State constitutional convention in 1820; again a member of the State house of representatives in 1822, 1823, and 1826; died in Roxbury, Mass., March 1, 1844.

SEBASTIAN, William King, a Senator from Arkansas; born in Centerville, Hickman County, Tenn., in 1812; was graduated from Columbia College, Tennessee, about 1834; studied law; was admitted to the bar and commenced practice in Helena, Ark., in 1835; later became a cotton planter; prosecuting attorney 1835–1837; elected circuit judge in 1840 and served until 1843; associate justice of the State supreme court 1843–1845; member and president of the State senate in 1846 and 1847; presidential elector on the Democratic ticket of Polk and Dallas in 1846; appointed and subsequently elected as a Democrat to the United States Senate to fill the vacancy caused by the death of Chester Ashley; reelected in 1853 and 1859 and served from May 12, 1848, to July 11, 1861, when he was expelled; returned to Helena, Ark., where he resided during the Civil War and practiced law; did not take any part in the Confederate movements; after the Federal troops occupied Helena, Ark., he moved to Memphis, Tenn., in 1864 and resumed the practice of law; the Senate on March 3, 1877, revoked the resolution of expulsion and paid the full amount of his compensation to his children; died in Memphis, Tenn., May 20, 1865; interment five miles north of Helena, Ark., in the Dunn family burying ground.

SECCOMBE, James, a Representative from Ohio; born in Mineral City, Tuscarawas County, Ohio, February 12, 1893; moved with his parents to Canton, Ohio, in 1906; attended the public schools in Mineral City and Canton, Ohio; during the First World War served from July 17, 1917, with Headquarters Company of the One Hundred and Thirty-fourth Field Artillery, Sixty-second Brigade, Thirty-seventh Ohio Buckeye Division, with service overseas, until discharged April 10, 1919; served as an apprentice to the machinist trade and worked in various factories as machinist and foreman from 1913 to 1932; attended the Y. M. C. A. night school of automobile engineering in 1930 and 1931; member of the Canton City Council 1928–1933, serving as vice president, president, and mayor; delegate to the Republican State conventions at Canton, Ohio, in 1932, 1934, and 1936; elected mayor of Canton in 1935 and served until his resignation in December 1938; elected as a Republican to the Seventy-sixth Congress (January 3, 1939–January 3, 1941); was an unsuccessful candidate for reelection in 1940 to the Seventy-seventh Congress; served as State tax examiner, Canton, Ohio, in 1941 and 1942; clerk of Stark County Board of Elections 1942–; president of the Ohio Association of Election Officials in 1959; is a resident of Canton, Ohio.

SECREST, Robert Thompson, a Representative from Ohio; born on a farm near Senecaville, Noble County, Ohio, January 22, 1904; attended the public and high schools; was graduated from Muskingum College, New Concord, Ohio, in 1926; principal of Senecaville (Ohio) High School 1926–1930; superintendent of schools of Murray City, Ohio, in 1931 and 1932; member of the State house of representatives in 1931 and 1932; elected as a Democrat to the Seventy-third and to the four succeeding Congresses and served from March 4, 1933, until his resignation on August 3, 1942; lieutenant commander in the United States Navy and later promoted to commander and served until February 28, 1946; unsuccessful candidate for election in 1946 to the Eightieth Congress; engaged as a legal supervisor at the Library of Congress from December 15, 1946, until his resignation in June 1947; elected to the Eighty-first, Eighty-second and Eighty-third Congresses and served from January 3, 1949, until his resignation September 26, 1954; had been renominated in the primary election May 4, 1954, to the Eighty-fourth Congress; appointed a commissioner on the Federal Trade Commission and served from September 27, 1954, to September 26, 1961; is a resident of Senecaville, Ohio.

SEDDON, James Alexander, a Representative from Virginia; born in Falmouth, Va., July 13, 1815; studied under private tutors, and was graduated from the law department of the University of Virginia at Charlottesville in 1835; was admitted to the bar about 1838 and commenced practice in Richmond, Va.; elected as a Democrat to the Twenty-ninth Congress (March 4, 1845–March 3, 1847); declined to be a candidate for renomination in 1846; elected to the Thirty-first Congress (March 4, 1849–March 3, 1851); declined to be a candidate for renomination; member of the peace convention held in Washington, D. C., in 1861 in an effort to devise means to prevent the impending war; delegate from Virginia to the Provisional Confederate Congress at Richmond, Va., in July 1861; appointed Secretary of War in the Cabinet of the Confederate States on November 20, 1862; retired in January 1865; died at "Sabot Hill," Goochland County, Va., August 19, 1880; interment in Hollywood Cemetery, Richmond, Va.

SEDGWICK, Charles Baldwin, a Representative from New York; born in Pompey, Onondaga County, N. Y., March 15, 1815; attended Pompey Hill Academy, and Hamilton College, Clinton, N. Y.; studied law; was admitted to the bar in 1848 and commenced practice in Syracuse, N. Y.; elected as a Republican to the Thirty-sixth and Thirty-seventh Congresses (March 4, 1859–March 3, 1863); unsuccessful candidate for renomination in 1862; engaged for the next two years in codifying naval laws for the Navy Department at Washington, D. C.; resumed the practice of law in Syracuse, N. Y., where he died February 3, 1883; interment in Oakwood Cemetery.

SEDGWICK, Theodore, a Delegate, a Representative, and a Senator from Massachusetts; born in West Hartford, Conn., May 9, 1746; attended Yale College; studied theology and law; was admitted to the bar in 1766 and commenced practice in Great Barrington, Mass.; moved to Sheffield, Mass.; during the Revolutionary War served in the expedition against Canada in 1776; member of the State house of representatives in 1780, 1782, and 1783; served in the State senate in 1784 and 1785; Member of the Continental Congress 1785–1788; again a member of the State house of representatives, in 1787 and 1788, and served as speaker; delegate to the State convention that adopted the Federal Constitution in 1788; elected as a Federalist to the First and to the three succeeding Congresses and served from March 4, 1789, until his resignation in June 1796; elected to the United States Senate to fill the vacancy caused by the resignation of Caleb Strong and served from June 11, 1796, to March 3, 1799; elected President pro tempore of the Senate June 27, 1798; elected to the Sixth Congress (March 4, 1799–March 3, 1801) and served as Speaker; judge of the supreme court of Massachusetts 1802–1813; died in Boston, Mass., January 24, 1813; interment in the family cemetery, Stockbridge, Mass.

SEELEY, John Edward, a Representative from New York; born in Ovid, Seneca County, N. Y., August 1, 1810; attended Ovid Academy, and was graduated from Yale College in 1835; studied law; was admitted to the bar and commenced practice in Monroe, Mich.; returned to Ovid, N. Y., in 1839; supervisor of Ovid in 1842; county judge and surrogate of Seneca County, N. Y., 1851–1855; delegate to the Republican National Convention at Philadelphia in 1856, which nominated Frémont and Dayton; presidential elector on the Republican ticket of Lincoln and Hamlin in 1860 and of Lincoln and Johnson in 1864; elected as a Republican to the Forty-second Congress (March 4, 1871–March 3, 1873); resumed the practice of his profession in Ovid, N. Y., and died there March 30, 1875; interment on his farm near Ovid.

SEELY-BROWN, Horace, Jr., a Representative from Connecticut; born in Kensington, Montgomery County, Md., May 12, 1908; attended the public schools of Hoosick, N. Y.; was graduated from Hamilton College, Clinton, N. Y., in 1929; student at Yale University, New Haven, Conn., in 1929 and 1930; taught school in Hoosick, N. Y., 1930–1932 and in New Lebanon, N. Y., 1932–1934; moved to Pomfret, Conn., in 1934 and taught school until 1942; delegate to the Democratic State conventions in 1938, 1940, and 1942; during World War II served as Air Operations Officer, Carrier Aircraft Service Unit No. 2, from February 1943 to January 1946; engaged in agricultural pursuits in 1946; elected as a Republican to the Eightieth Congress (January 3, 1947–January 3, 1949); unsuccessful candidate for reelection in 1948 to the Eighty-first Congress; elected to the Eighty-second and to the three succeeding Congresses (January 3, 1951–January 3, 1959); unsuccessful candidate for reelection in 1958 to the Eighty-sixth Congress. *Elected to the Eighty-seventh Congress.*

SEELYE, Julius Hawley, a Representative from Massachusetts; born in Bethel, Fairfield County, Conn., September 14, 1824; prepared himself for college while a clerk in a store; was graduated from Amherst (Mass.) College in 1849; studied theology, and was graduated from Auburn Theological Seminary in 1852; ordained as a minister in 1853 and became pastor of the First Reformed Protestant Dutch Church, Schenectady, N. Y., 1853–1858; professor of mental and moral philosophy in Amherst College 1858–1876; accepted an invitation to deliver a course of lectures in India in 1872; elected as an Independent to the Forty-fourth Congress (March 4, 1875–March 3, 1877); declined to be a candidate for reelection; member of the commission to revise the tax laws of Massachusetts; president of Amherst College 1876–1890; died in Amherst, Mass., May 12, 1895; interment in Wildwood Cemetery.

SEERLEY, John Joseph, a Representative from Iowa; born on a farm near Toulon, Stark County, Ill., March 13, 1852; in 1854 moved to Iowa with his parents, who settled on a farm in Keokuk County; attended the common schools; was graduated from the University of Iowa at Iowa City in 1875; principal of the Iowa City High School in 1876; was graduated from the law department of the University of Iowa in 1877; was admitted to the bar in 1877 and commenced practice in Burlington, Des Moines County, Iowa; city solicitor of Burlington 1885–1890 and 1893–1895; unsuccessful Democratic candidate for election

in 1888 to the Fifty-first Congress; elected as a Democrat to the Fifty-second Congress (March 4, 1891–March 3, 1893); unsuccessful candidate for reelection in 1892 to the Fifty-third Congress; resumed the practice of law in Burlington, Iowa; also interested in banking and agricultural pursuits; delegate to the Democratic National Convention at San Francisco in 1920, which nominated James M. Cox and Franklin D. Roosevelt; died in Burlington, Iowa, on February 23, 1931; interment in Aspin Grove Cemetery.

SEGAR, Joseph Eggleston, a Representative from Virginia; born in King William County, Va., June 1, 1804; attended the common schools; studied law; was admitted to the bar and practiced; held several local offices; member of the State house of delegates 1836–1838, 1848–1852, and 1855–1861; presented credentials as a Unionist Member-elect to the Thirty-seventh Congress from an election held on October 24, 1861, but the House on February 11, 1862, decided he was not entitled to the seat; subsequently elected to the same Congress and served from March 15, 1862, to March 3, 1863; presented credentials as a Member-elect to the Thirty-eighth Congress, but was declared not entitled to the seat by resolution of May 17, 1864. presented credentials on February 17, 1865, as a United States Senator-elect to fill the vacancy in the term commencing March 4, 1863, caused by the death of Lemuel J. Bowden, but was not permitted to take his seat; presented credentials as a Member-elect to the Forty-first Congress, but was not permitted to qualify; unsuccessful Republican candidate for election in 1876 to the Forty-fifth Congress; died on the steamer *George Leary* while en route from Norfolk, Va., to Washington, D. C., April 30, 1880; interment in St. John's Cemetery, Hampton, Elizabeth City County, Va.

SEGER, George Nicholas, a Representative from New Jersey; born in New York City January 4, 1866; attended the public schools; settled in Passaic, N. J., in 1899 and engaged in the building business; member of the board of education of Passaic 1906–1911; mayor of Passaic 1911–1919; delegate to the Republican National Convention at Chicago in 1916, which nominated the presidential ticket of Hughes and Fairbanks; president of the New Jersey League of Municipalities in 1917 and 1918; city director of finance 1919–1923; member of the Council of National Defense during the First World War; elected as a Republican to the Sixty-eighth and to the eight succeeding Congresses and served from March 4, 1923, until his death in Washington, D. C., on August 26, 1940; interment in Greenwood Cemetery, Brooklyn, N. Y.

SEIBERLING, Francis, a Representative from Ohio; born in Des Moines, Iowa, September 20, 1870; moved with his parents to Wadsworth, Summit County, Ohio, in 1873; attended the public schools and Wittenberg College, Springfield, Ohio, and was graduated from the College of Wooster (Ohio) in 1892; studied law; was admitted to the bar in 1894 and commenced practice in Akron, Ohio; also interested in the manufacture of rubber and tires and served as a director in various manufacturing companies; served as a trustee of Wittenberg College; elected as a Republican to the Seventy-first and Seventy-second Congresses (March 4, 1929–March 3, 1933); unsuccessful candidate for reelection in 1932 to the Seventy-third Congress; resumed the practice of law; died in Akron, Ohio, February 1, 1945; interment in Rose Hill Cemetery.

SELBY, Thomas Jefferson, a Representative from Illinois; born in Delaware County, Ohio, December 4, 1840; attended the common schools; studied law; was admitted to the bar in 1869 and commenced the practice of his profession in 1875;

sheriff of Jersey County, Ill., 1864–1866; published the Jersey County Democrat 1866–1870; county clerk 1869–1877; mayor of Jerseyville, Ill., two terms; State attorney for Calhoun County 1888–1900; elected as a Democrat to the Fifty-seventh Congress (March 4, 1901–March 3, 1903); resumed the practice of law; State's attorney; died in Hardin, Calhoun County, Ill., March 10, 1917; interment in Hardin Cemetery.

SELDEN, Armistead Inge, Jr., a Representative from Alabama; born in Greensboro, Hale County, Ala., February 20, 1921; attended the public schools; graduated from Greensboro High School in 1938 and from the University of the South, Sewanee, Tenn., in 1942; during World War II served in the United States Navy from August 1942 until March 1946, with 31 months aboard ship, primarily in the North Atlantic, and was discharged as a lieutenant; lieutenant commander in the United States Naval Reserve; after naval service entered the University of Alabama School of Law and graduated in 1948; was admitted to the bar in 1948 and commenced practice in Greensboro, Ala.; member of the State house of representatives in 1951 and 1952; elected as a Democrat to the Eighty-third and to the three succeeding Congresses (January 3, 1953–January 3, 1961). *Reelected to the Eighty-seventh Congress.*

SELDEN, Dudley, a Representative from New York; was graduated from Union College, Schenectady, N. Y., in 1819; studied law; was admitted to the bar and commenced the practice of his profession in New York City in 1831; member of the State assembly in 1831; elected as a Democrat to the Twenty-third Congress and served from March 4, 1833, to July 1, 1834, when he resigned; died in Paris, France, November 7, 1855; interment in Greenwood Cemetery, Brooklyn, N. Y.

SELDOMRIDGE, Harry Hunter, a Representative from Colorado; born in Philadelphia, Pa., October 1, 1864; attended the public schools of Philadelphia; moved to Colorado Springs, Colo., in February 1878; was graduated from Colorado College at Colorado Springs in 1885; city editor of the Colorado Springs Gazette 1886–1888; engaged in the grain and hay business in 1888; delegate to the Democratic National Convention at Chicago in 1896; member of the State senate 1896–1904; member and president of the State charter convention at Colorado Springs in 1909; elected as a Democrat to the Sixty-third Congress (March 4, 1913–March 3, 1915); unsuccessful candidate for reelection in 1914 to the Sixty-fourth Congress; resumed his former business pursuits; receiver of the Mercantile National Bank of Pueblo 1915–1923; appointed public trustee of El Paso County, Colo., by Governor Sweet; died at Colorado Springs, El Paso County, Colo., November 2, 1927; interment in Evergreen Cemetery.

SELLS, Sam Riley, a Representative from Tennessee; born in Bristol, Sullivan County, Tenn., August 2, 1871; attended the rural schools and King College in Bristol, Tenn., 1885–1890; studied law; was admitted to the bar and commenced practice in Blountville, Tenn.; served as a private in Company F, Third Regiment, Tennessee Volunteer Infantry, during the Spanish-American War; moved to Johnson City, Tenn., and engaged in the lumber business; member of the State senate 1909–1911; elected as a Republican to the Sixty-second and to the four succeeding Congresses (March 4, 1911–March 3, 1921); unsuccessful candidate for renomination in 1920; delegate to the Republican National Conventions in Chicago in 1912 and 1916; resumed the lumber business in Johnson City, Tenn.; also engaged in the manufacture of shale brick and in numerous other business enterprises; died in Johnson City, Tenn., November 2, 1935; interment in Oak Hill Cemetery.

SELVIG, Conrad George, a Representative from Minnesota; born in Rushford, Fillmore County, Minn., October 11, 1877; attended the public schools and was graduated from Rushford High School in 1895; in the war with Spain served as a private with the Twelfth Minnesota Volunteer Infantry; taught rural and village schools; was graduated from the University of Minnesota at Minneapolis in 1907; superintendent of schools at Harmony and Glencoe, Minn., 1901–1910; delegate to the Republican State convention in 1908; was appointed director of the University of Minnesota Northwest School of Agriculture and Experiment Station, Crookston, Minn., in 1910; president of various Red River Valley farm and community development organizations; elected as a Republican to the Seventieth, Seventy-first, and Seventy-second Congresses (March 4, 1927–March 3, 1933); unsuccessful candidate for reelection in 1932 to the Seventy-third Congress; writer and lecturer; moved to Santa Monica, Calif., in 1935; vice president of the National Hearing Society and was the society's legislative chairman; died in Santa Monica, Calif., August 2, 1953; interment in Oakdale Cemetery, Crookston, Minn.

SELYE, Lewis, a Representative from New York; born in Chittenango, Madison County, N. Y., July 11, 1803; attended the common schools; learned the blacksmith trade; moved to Rochester, N. Y., in 1824 and engaged in the manufacture of iron; member of the Board of Supervisors of Monroe County several terms; elected alderman in 1841; member of the common council in 1843, 1856, and 1871; county treasurer of Monroe County 1848–1851 and 1854; elected as an Independent to the Fortieth Congress (March 4, 1867–March 3, 1869); in 1868 established the Rochester Daily Chronicle, which was merged with the Rochester Democrat and Chronicle in 1870; trustee of the Monroe County Savings Bank; died in Rochester, N. Y., January 27, 1883; interment in Mount Hope Cemetery.

SEMMES, Benedict Joseph, a Representative from Maryland; born in Charles County, Md., November 1, 1789; attended the rural schools and a medical college in Philadelphia; was graduated from Baltimore Medical School in 1811; commenced practice in Piscataway, Prince Georges County, Md., and later engaged in farming; member of the State house of delegates 1825–1828 and served as speaker; served in the State senate; elected as a Democrat to the Twenty-first and Twenty-second Congresses (March 4, 1829–March 3, 1833); again a member of the State house of delegates in 1842 and 1843; abandoned public life and lived in retirement until his death at Oak Lawn, Prince Georges County, Md., February 10, 1863.

SEMPLE, James, a Senator from Illinois; born in Green County, Ky., January 5, 1798; moved with his parents to Clinton County; received private instructions and attended the common schools; enlisted in the Army in 1814 and served under General Jackson; ensign in the Eighty-first Regiment of Kentucky Militia in 1816; moved to Edwardsville, Ill., in 1818 and to Chariton, Mo., in 1819, where he engaged in business; elected as a commissioner of the loan office; studied law in Louisville, Ky.; was admitted to the bar and commenced practice in Clinton County, Ky.; returned to Edwardsville, Ill., in 1827 and continued the practice of law; member of the State house of representatives 1828–1833, serving as speaker four years; served as a private, adjutant, and judge advocate during the Black Hawk War; attorney general of Illinois in 1833; unsuccessful candidate for election in 1836 to the United States Senate; moved to Alton, Ill., in 1837; Chargé d'Affaires to Colombia from October 14, 1837, to April 1, 1842; elected judge of the State supreme court and served in 1842 and 1843; appointed and subsequently elected as a Democrat to the United States Senate to fill the vacancy caused by the death of Samuel McRoberts and served from December 4, 1843, to March 3, 1847; was not a candidate for renomination in 1846; returned to Alton and engaged in the real-estate business; moved to Jersey County, Ill., in 1853 and founded the town of Elsah; continued in the real-estate business; also engaged in literary pursuits; died in Elsah, Ill., December 20, 1866; interment in Bellefontaine Cemetery, St. Louis, Mo.

SENER, James Beverley, a Representative from Virginia; born in Fredericksburg, Spotsylvania County, Va., May 18, 1837; attended private schools, and in 1859 was graduated from the University of Virginia at Charlottesville; was graduated in law from Washington College (now Washington and Lee University) at Lexington in 1860; was admitted to the bar the same year and commenced practice in Fredericksburg, Va.; sheriff of Fredericksburg in 1860; sergeant of the city of Fredericksburg 1863–1865; army correspondent of the Southern Associated Press with the army of Gen. Robert E. Lee; became editor of the Fredericksburg (Va.) Ledger in 1865; delegate to the Republican National Convention at Philadelphia in 1872, which nominated Grant and Wilson; elected as a Republican to the Forty-third Congress (March 4, 1873–March 3, 1875); unsuccessful candidate for reelection in 1874 to the Forty-fourth Congress; resumed the practice of his profession; served as chief justice of Wyoming Territory 1878–1882; died in Washington, D. C., on November 18, 1903; interment in Citizens Cemetery, Fredericksburg, Va.

SENEY, George Ebbert, a Representative from Ohio; born in Uniontown, Fayette County, Pa., May 29, 1832; moved with his parents to Tiffin, Seneca County, Ohio, in November 1832; attended Norwalk (Ohio) Seminary; studied law; was admitted to the bar in 1853 and practiced in Tiffin; presidential elector on the Democratic ticket of Buchanan and Breckinridge in 1856; judge of the court of common pleas in 1857; in July 1862, during the Civil War, enlisted in the One Hundred and First Regiment, Ohio Volunteer Infantry; was subsequently commissioned first lieutenant and acted as quartermaster of the regiment until near the close of the war; delegate to the Democratic National Convention at St. Louis in 1876, which nominated Samuel J. Tilden for President; elected as a Democrat to the Forty-eighth and to the three succeeding Congresses (March 4, 1883–March 3, 1891); was not a candidate for renomination in 1890; resumed the practice of his profession in Tiffin, Seneca County, Ohio, where he died June 11, 1905; interment in Greenlawn Cemetery.

SENEY, Joshua, a Delegate and a Representative from Maryland; born near Church Hill, Queen Annes County, Md., March 4, 1756; attended the common schools, and was graduated from the University of Pennsylvania at Philadelphia in 1773; studied law; was admitted to the bar and practiced; high sheriff of Queen Annes County in 1779; member of the State house of delegates 1785–1787; Member of the Continental Congress in 1787 and 1788; engaged in agricultural pursuits; elected to the First and Second Congresses and served from March 4, 1789, until his resignation May 1, 1792, to accept a judicial appointment; chief justice of the third judicial district of Maryland, composed of Baltimore, Harford, and Cecil Counties, 1792–1796; presidential elector in 1792 and supported Washington and Adams; died near Church Hill, Queen Annes County, Md., October 20, 1798; interment in a private cemetery on the Everett farm, between Church Hill and Sudlersville, Md.

SENTER, William Tandy, a Representative from Tennessee; born at Bean Station, Grainger County, Tenn., May 12, 1801; attended the common schools; held several local offices; engaged in agricultural pursuits; minister in the Methodist Episcopal Church South, Holston Conference; member of the State con-

stitutional convention which met at Nashville from May 19 to August 30, 1834; elected as a Whig to the Twenty-eighth Congress (March 4, 1843–March 3, 1845); resumed agricultural pursuits and ministerial work; died at Panther Springs, Hamblen County, Tenn., August 28, 1848; interment in Senter Memorial Church Cemetery.

SERGEANT, John (son of Jonathan Dickinson Sergeant, grandfather of John Sergeant Wise and Richard Alsop Wise, and great-grandfather of John Crain Kunkel), a Representative from Pennsylvania; born in Philadelphia, Pa., December 5, 1779; attended the common schools and the University of Pennsylvania at Philadelphia; was graduated from Princeton College in 1795; studied law; was admitted to the bar in 1799 and practiced in Philadelphia for fifty years; deputy attorney general for Philadelphia in 1800; commissioner of bankruptcy for Pennsylvania in 1801; member of the State house of representatives 1808–1810; elected as a Federalist to the Fourteenth Congress to fill the vacancy caused by the death of Jonathan Williams; reelected to the Fifteenth, Sixteenth, and Seventeenth Congresses and served from October 10, 1815, to March 3, 1823; was not a candidate for reelection; president of the Pennsylvania Board of Canal Commissioners in 1825; envoy to the Panama Congress in 1826; elected to the Twentieth Congress (March 4, 1827–March 3, 1829); unsuccessful candidate for reelection; unsuccessful National-Republican candidate for election as Vice President of the United States in 1832; president of the State constitutional convention in 1838; elected to the Twenty-fifth, Twenty-sixth, and Twenty-seventh Congresses and served from March 4, 1837, until his resignation on September 15, 1841; declined the appointment as Minister to England in 1841; died in Philadelphia, Pa., November 23, 1852; interment in Laurel Hill Cemetery.

SERGEANT, Jonathan Dickinson (father of John Sergeant), a Delegate from New Jersey; born in Newark, N. J., in 1746; moved with his parents to Princeton, N. J., in 1758; completed preparatory studies; was graduated from Princeton College in 1762 and from the University of Pennsylvania at Philadelphia in 1763; studied law; was admitted to the bar in 1767 and commenced practice in Princeton, N. J.; surrogate of Somerset County, N. J., in 1769; secretary of the State provincial convention in 1774; member of the New Jersey Provincial Congress from May 23 to October 3, 1775, and from June 10 to August 21, 1776; secretary from May 24 to May 30, 1775, treasurer from August 17 to October 3, 1775, and member of the committee of safety from August 17 to October 3, 1775; appointed on June 24, 1776, as a member of the committee that drafted the first constitution of New Jersey; Member of the Continental Congress from February 14 to June 22, 1776, when he resigned; elected clerk of the supreme court on September 4, 1776, but declined; again elected a Member of the Continental Congress on November 30, 1776, and served until his resignation on September 6, 1777, to accept the office of attorney general of Pennsylvania; moved to Philadelphia, Pa., in 1777; member of the council of safety of Pennsylvania in 1777; attorney general of Pennsylvania 1777–1780; counsel for the State in the Wyoming land controversy with Connecticut in 1782; died in Philadelphia, Pa., October 8, 1793; interment in the Presbyterian Churchyard, then located at Fourth and Pine Streets; reinterment in Laurel Hill Cemetery in 1878.

SESSINGHAUS, Gustavus, a Representative from Missouri; born in Koela, Prussia, November 8, 1838; pursued preparatory studies; immigrated to the United States and settled in St. Louis, Mo.; during the Civil War served as a private in Company A, Fifth Regiment, United States Reserve Corps, Missouri Volunteer Infantry; member of the school board 1878–1880;

successfully contested as a Republican the election of Richard G. Frost to the Forty-seventh Congress and served two days only, March 2 and 3, 1883; unsuccessful candidate for reelection in 1882 to the Forty-eighth Congress; engaged in the milling business; died in St. Louis, Mo., November 16, 1887; interment in Bellefontaine Cemetery.

SESSIONS, Walter Loomis, a Representative from New York; born in Brandon, Rutland County, Vt., October 4, 1820; as a child was brought to Chautauqua County, N. Y.; attended the common schools of the county and Westfield (N. Y.) Academy; studied law; was admitted to the bar in 1849 and commenced the practice of his profession in Panama, Chautauqua County, N. Y.; engaged in teaching; commissioner of schools for several years; member of the State assembly in 1853 and 1854; served in the State senate in 1860, 1861, 1866, and 1867; supervisor of the town of Harmony, Chautauqua County, N. Y., 1870–1872; elected as a Republican to the Forty-second and Forty-third Congresses (March 4, 1871–March 3, 1875); unsuccessful candidate for reelection in 1874 to the Forty-fourth Congress; resumed the practice of law; elected to the Forty-ninth Congress (March 4, 1885–March 3, 1887); unsuccessful candidate for renomination in 1886 and for the nomination in 1890; engaged in the practice of his profession in Jamestown and Panama, N. Y.; appointed commissioner of the State of New York to the World's Columbian Exposition at Chicago, Ill., in 1893; died in Panama, N. Y., on May 27, 1896; interment in Forest Hill Cemetery.

SETTLE, Evan Evans, a Representative from Kentucky; born in Frankfort, Ky., December 1, 1848; attended the public schools; was graduated from Louisville High School in June 1864; studied law; was admitted to the bar in 1870 and commenced practice in Owenton, Owenton County, Ky.; elected prosecuting attorney of Owenton County in 1878, 1882, and 1886; resigned in 1887; member of the State house of representatives 1887–1890; delegate to the Democratic National Convention at St. Louis in 1888, which nominated Cleveland and Thurman; elected as a Democrat to the Fifty-fifth and Fifty-sixth Congresses and served from March 3, 1897, until his death in Owenton, Ky., November 16, 1899; interment in Odd Fellows Cemetery.

SETTLE, Thomas (uncle of David Settle Reid), a Representative from North Carolina; born near Reidsville, Rockingham County, N. C., March 9, 1789; educated by private tutors; studied law; was admitted to the bar in 1812 and commenced practice in Wentworth, N. C.; member of the State house of commons in 1816; elected as a Democrat to the Fifteenth and Sixteenth Congresses (March 4, 1817–March 3, 1821); declined to be a candidate for reelection; resumed the practice of law; again a member of the State house of commons, in 1826 and 1827, and served as speaker in the last session; judge of the superior courts of North Carolina in 1832; died in Rockingham County, N. C., August 5, 1857; interment in the Settle family graveyard, near Reidsville, N. C.

SETTLE, Thomas (grandson of the preceding), a Representative from North Carolina; born near Wentworth, Rockingham County, N. C., March 10, 1865; attended the public schools and Georgetown College, District of Columbia; studied law in Greensboro, N. C.; was admitted to the bar in 1885 and commenced practice at Wentworth, N. C.; solicitor of the ninth judicial district 1886–1894; elected as a Republican to the Fifty-third and Fifty-fourth Congresses (March 4, 1893–March 3, 1897); unsuccessful candidate for reelection in 1896 to the Fifty-fifth Congress; resumed the practice of his profession in Asheville, N. C.; appointed by the Department of Justice as special attorney to the United States Court of Customs in New York City in 1909, and served in that capacity until 1910; unsuccessful candidate for Governor of North Carolina in 1912; died in Asheville, N. C., January 20, 1919; interment in Oakdale Cemetery, Wilmington, N. C.

SEVERANCE, Luther, a Representative from Maine; born in Montague, Mass., October 26, 1797; moved with his parents to Cazenovia, N. Y., in 1799; attended the common schools; learned the printer's trade in Peterboro, N. Y.; established the Kennebec Journal in Augusta, Maine, in 1825; member of the State house of representatives in 1829, 1839, 1840, 1842, and 1848; served in the State senate in 1835 and 1836; elected as a Whig to the Twenty-eighth and Twenty-ninth Congresses (March 4, 1843–March 3, 1847); vice president of the Whig National Convention at Philadelphia in 1848; United States commissioner to the Sandwich Islands 1850–1854; died in Augusta, Maine, January 25, 1855; interment in Forest Grove Cemetery.

SEVIER, Ambrose Hundley (cousin of Henry Wharton Conway), a Delegate and a Senator from Arkansas; born in Greene County, Tenn., November 10, 1801; completed preparatory studies; moved to Missouri in 1820 and to Little Rock, Ark., in 1821; clerk of the Territorial house of representatives; studied law; was admitted to the bar in 1823 and practiced; member of the Territorial house of representatives 1823–1827, serving as speaker in 1827; elected as a Whig to the Twentieth Congress to fill the vacancy caused by the death of Henry W. Conway; reelected to the Twenty-first and to the three succeeding Congresses and served from February 13, 1828, to June 15, 1836, when the Territory was admitted as a State into the Union; elected as a Democrat to the United States Senate; reelected in 1837 and 1843 and served from September 18, 1836, until his resignation on March 15, 1848; was appointed Minister to Mexico to negotiate the treaty of peace between that Republic and the United States and served from March 15 to June 4, 1848; died on his plantation near Little Rock, Pulaski County, Ark., December 31, 1848; interment in Mount Holly Cemetery, where the State erected a monument to his memory.

SEVIER, John, a Representative from North Carolina and from Tennessee; born near Harrisonburg, Rockingham County, Va., September 23, 1745; attended the common schools and the academy at Fredericksburg, Va.; moved with his brothers to Watauga County, N. C., in 1773 and settled on the Holston River, N. C. (now Tennessee); captain of Colonial Militia under Washington in Governor Dunmore's war against the Indians in 1773 and 1774; county clerk and district judge 1777–1780; received the thanks of the North Carolina Legislature for meritorious services at the Battle of Kings Mountain October 7, 1780; elected Governor of "the proclaimed" State of Franklin in March 1785 and served for three years; elected as a Democrat from North Carolina to the First Congress (March 4, 1789–March 3, 1791); appointed in 1791 as brigadier general of militia for the Washington district of the territory south of the Ohio; upon the admission of Tennessee as a State into the Union was chosen Governor and served from 1796 to 1801, and again from 1803 to 1809; appointed in 1798 as brigadier general of the Provisional Army; served one term in the State senate 1810–1811; elected from Tennessee to the Twelfth, Thirteenth, and Fourteenth Congresses and served from March 4, 1811, until his death; appointed in 1815 as one of the commissioners to determine the boundary between Georgia and the Creek territory in Alabama and served until his death, near Fort Decatur, Ala., September 24, 1815; interment at Fort Decatur, Ala.; in 1889 his remains were removed to Knoxville, Tenn., and reinterred in the yard of the county courthouse, a tall marble shaft later being erected at the grave.

SEWALL, Charles S., a Representative from Maryland; born in Queen Annes County, Md., in 1779; attended the common schools; served in the Forty-second Regiment, Maryland Militia, in the War of 1812; served in the State house of delegates; was member of the State senate; was elected to the Twenty-second Congress to fill the vacancy caused by the death of George E. Mitchell and served from October 1, 1832, to March 3, 1833; was elected to the Twenty-seventh Congress to fill the vacancy which was caused by the death of James W. Williams and served from January 2 to March 3, 1843; moved to Harford County, Md.; died at Rose Hill, Harford County, Md., on November 3, 1848.

SEWALL, Samuel, a Representative from Massachusetts; born in Boston, Mass., December 11, 1757; attended the common schools, and was graduated from Harvard College in 1776; studied law; was admitted to the bar and commenced practice in Marblehead, Mass.; member of the State house of representatives 1784 and 1788–1796; elected to the Fourth Congress to fill the vacancy caused by the resignation of Benjamin Goodhue; reelected to the Fifth and Sixth Congresses and served from December 7, 1796, until his resignation on January 10, 1800; one of the managers appointed by the House of Representatives in 1798 to conduct the impeachment proceedings against William Blount, a Senator from Tennessee; associate judge of the supreme court of Massachusetts 1801–1813 and served as chief justice in 1813 and 1814; died in Wiscasset, Maine, June 8, 1814; interment in Ancient Cemetery; reinterment in the family tomb at Marblehead, Mass.

SEWARD, James Lindsay, a Representative from Georgia; born in Dublin, Laurens County, Ga., on October 30, 1813; attended the common schools; moved with his parents to Thomas County in 1826; studied law; was admitted to the bar in 1835 and commenced practice in Thomasville, Thomas County, Ga.; member of the State house of representatives 1835–1839, 1847, 1848, 1851, and 1852; elected as a Democrat to the Thirty-third, Thirty-fourth, and Thirty-fifth Congresses (March 4, 1853–March 3, 1859); was not a candidate for renomination in 1858; resumed the practice of law and also engaged as a planter; delegate to the Democratic State conventions in 1858, 1859, and 1860; served in the State senate 1859–1865; delegate to the Democratic National Conventions at Charleston and Baltimore in 1860; member of the board of trustees of Young's Female College 1860–1886 and of the University of Georgia at Athens 1865–1886; delegate to the reconstruction constitutional convention in 1865; delegate to the Democratic Conservative Convention in 1870; delegate to the State constitutional convention in 1877; died in Thomasville, Ga., on November 21, 1886; interment in Laurel Hill Cemetery.

SEWARD, William Henry, a Senator from New York; born in Florida, Orange County, N. Y., on May 16, 1801; attended Farmers' Hall Academy in Goshen, N. Y., and Union College 1816–1819; left college and engaged in teaching in 1819 and 1820; returned to college and was graduated in 1820; studied law; was admitted to the bar and commenced practice in Auburn, N. Y., in 1823; member of the State senate 1830–1834; unsuccessful Whig candidate for Governor in 1834; Governor of New York 1838–1842; elected as a Whig to the United States Senate in 1849; reelected as a Republican in 1855 and served from March 4, 1849, to March 3, 1861; was one of the most prominent aspirants for the Republican nomination for President in 1860;

Secretary of State in the Cabinets of Presidents Lincoln and Johnson and served from March 5, 1861, to March 3, 1869; while Secretary of State concluded the convention with Great Britain for the settlement of the *Alabama* claims and the treaty with Russia for the purchase of Alaska; made a tour of the world and was received with the highest honors at all foreign courts; died in Auburn, Cayuga County, N. Y., October 16, 1872; interment in Fort Hill Cemetery.

SEWELL, William Joyce, a Senator from New Jersey; born in Castlebar, Ireland, December 6, 1835; immigrated to the United States in 1851; engaged in mercantile pursuits in Chicago, Ill.; moved to Camden, N. J., in 1860; during the Civil War was commissioned captain in the Fifth Regiment, New Jersey Volunteers, August 28, 1861, lieutenant colonel July 7, 1862, colonel January 6, 1863, and resigned July 6, 1864; recommissioned colonel of the Thirty-eighth Regiment, New Jersey Volunteer Infantry, October 1, 1864; brevetted March 13, 1865, brigadier general of Volunteers "for gallant and meritorious services in the Battle of Chancellorsville, Virginia," and major general of Volunteers "for gallant and meritorious services during the war"; honorably mustered out June 30, 1865; awarded the Congressional Medal of Honor March 25, 1896, "for having assumed command of a brigade at Chancellorsville, Va., May 3, 1863, where he rallied around his colors a mass of men from other regiments and fought those troops with great brilliancy through several hours of desperate conflict, remaining in command though wounded and inspiring them by his presence and the gallantry of his personal example"; after the war became connected with railroads in New Jersey; elected a member of the State senate from Camden County in 1872, 1875, and 1878, serving as president in 1876, 1879, and 1880; elected as a Republican to the United States Senate and served from March 4, 1881, to March 3, 1887; was the caucus nominee of his party, who were in the minority, for election to the United States Senate in 1887, 1889, and 1893; delegate to the Republican National Conventions of 1876, 1880, 1884, 1888, 1892, 1896, and 1900; was one of the national commissioners for New Jersey to the World's Columbian Exposition in Chicago in 1893; was in command of the Second Brigade of the National Guard of New Jersey; appointed a member of the Board of Managers of the National Home for Disabled Volunteer Soldiers; again elected to the United States Senate in 1895 and 1901, and served from March 4, 1895, until his death in Camden, N. J., December 27, 1901; interment in Harleigh Cemetery.

SEXTON, Leonidas, a Representative from Indiana; born in Rushville, Rush County, Ind., May 19, 1827; attended the public schools of his native county and was graduated from Jefferson College, Canonsburg, Pa., in 1847; studied law in Rushville and in 1848 and 1849 attended the Cincinnati Law School; was admitted to the Indiana bar in 1850 and commenced the practice of his profession in Rushville, Ind.; member of the State house of representatives in 1856; elected Lieutenant Governor of Indiana and served from January 1873 to January 1877; elected as a Republican to the Forty-fifth Congress (March 4, 1877–March 3, 1879); unsuccessful candidate for reelection in 1878 to the Forty-sixth Congress; died in Parsons, Labette County, Kans., July 4, 1880; interment in East Hill Cemetery, Rushville, Ind.

SEYBERT, Adam, a Representative from Pennsylvania; born in Philadelphia, Pa., May 16, 1773; attended the common schools; completed the medical course at the University of Pennsylvania at Philadelphia in 1793 and continued studies in Europe, where he attended schools in Edinburgh, Gottingen, and Paris; returned to Philadelphia and devoted himself to chemistry and mineralogy; elected as a member of the American Philosophical Society in 1797; elected as a Democrat to the Eleventh Congress to fill the vacancy caused by the resignation of Benjamin Say; reelected to the Twelfth and Thirteenth Congresses and served from October 10, 1809, to March 3, 1815; elected to the Fifteenth Congress (March 4, 1817–March 3, 1819); visited Europe 1819–1821 and again in 1824 and settled in Paris, France, where he died May 2, 1825.

SEYMOUR, David Lowrey, a Representative from New York; born in Wethersfield, Conn., December 2, 1803; pursued preparatory studies; was graduated from Yale College in 1826; tutor at Yale College 1828–1830; studied law; was admitted to the bar in 1829 and commenced the practice of his profession in Troy, N. Y.; member of the State assembly in 1836; district attorney of Rensselaer County from October 14, 1839, to October 14, 1842; master in chancery in 1839; elected as a Democrat to the Twenty-eighth Congress (March 4, 1843–March 3, 1845); unsuccessful candidate for reelection in 1844 to the Twenty-ninth Congress; elected to the Thirty-second Congress (March 4, 1851–March 3, 1853); unsuccessful candidate for reelection in 1852 to the Thirty-third Congress; resumed the practice of his profession; unsuccessful candidate in 1858 to the Thirty-sixth Congress; member of the constitutional convention of New York in 1867; died in Lanesboro, Berkshire County, Mass., on October 11, 1867; interment in Mount Ida Cemetery, Troy, N. Y.

SEYMOUR, Edward Woodruff (son of Origen Storrs Seymour), a Representative from Connecticut; born in Litchfield, Conn., August 30, 1832; attended the public schools, and was graduated from Yale College in 1853; studied law; was admitted to the bar in 1856 and practiced in Litchfield and Bridgeport, Conn.; member of the State house of representatives in 1859, 1860, 1870, and 1871; served in the State senate in 1876; elected as a Democrat to the Forty-eighth and Forty-ninth Congresses (March 4, 1883–March 3, 1887); resumed the practice of his profession; appointed as a judge of the Connecticut Supreme Court in 1889; died in Litchfield, Conn., on October 16, 1892; interment in East Cemetery.

SEYMOUR, Henry William, a Representative from Michigan; born in Brockport, Monroe County, N. Y., July 21, 1834; attended the public schools, Brockport Collegiate Institute, and Canandaigua Academy and was graduated from Williams College, Williamstown, Mass., in 1855; studied law in Albany, N. Y., taking lectures at Albany Law School; was admitted to the bar in May 1856, but never practiced; engaged in mercantile pursuits in Brockport; moved to Michigan in 1872 and settled in Sault Ste. Marie, where he engaged in the manufacture of reapers and subsequently in the manufacture of lumber and in agricultural pursuits; member of the State house of representatives 1880–1882; member of the State senate 1882–1884 and 1886–1888; elected as a Republican to the Fiftieth Congress to fill the vacancy caused by the death of Seth C. Moffatt and served from February 14, 1888, to March 3, 1889; unsuccessful candidate for renomination in 1888; retired from active business pursuits; died, while on a visit, in Washington, D. C., April 7, 1906; interment in Lakeview Cemetery, Brockport, N. Y.

SEYMOUR, Horatio (uncle of Origen Storrs Seymour), a Senator from Vermont; born in Litchfield, Conn., May 31, 1778; attended the common schools, and was graduated from Yale College in 1797; taught school in Cheshire, Conn.; pursued legal studies in Litchfield Law School; was admitted to the bar in 1800 and commenced the practice of law in Middlebury, Vt.; postmaster of Middlebury 1800–1809; member of the State executive council 1809–1814; State's attorney for Addison County 1810–1813 and 1815–1819; elected as a Clay Democrat to the United States Senate in 1821; reelected in 1827 and served from March 4, 1821, to March 3, 1833; was not a candidate for reelection; unsuccessful Whig candidate for Governor of Vermont in 1836; judge of the probate court 1847–1856; died in Middlebury, Addison County, Vt., November 21, 1857; interment in West Cemetery.

SEYMOUR, Origen Storrs (father of Edward Woodruff Seymour and nephew of Horatio Seymour), a Representative from Connecticut; born in Litchfield, Conn., February 9, 1804; attended the public schools, and was graduated from Yale College in 1824; studied law; was admitted to the bar in 1826 and commenced practice in Litchfield, Conn.; served as county clerk 1836–1844; member of the State house of representatives in 1842, 1849, and 1850, and served as speaker in 1850; elected as a Democrat to the Thirty-second and Thirty-third Congresses (March 4, 1851–March 3, 1855); judge of the superior court of Connecticut 1855–1863; unsuccessful Democratic candidate for Governor in 1864 and 1865; judge of the State supreme court in 1870, chief justice in 1873, and served until retired by age limitation in 1874; chairman of the commission to settle the boundary dispute between Connecticut and New York in 1876; again a member of the State house of representatives in 1880; died in Litchfield, Conn., August 12, 1881; interment in East Cemetery.

SEYMOUR, Thomas Hart, a Representative from Connecticut; born in Hartford, Conn., September 29, 1807; attended the public schools, and was graduated from Middletown (Conn.) Military Academy in 1829; studied law; was admitted to the bar in 1833 and commenced practice in Hartford, Conn.; editor of the Jeffersonian in 1837 and 1838; judge of probate 1836–1838; elected as a Democrat to the Twenty-eighth Congress (March 4, 1843–March 3, 1845); declined the renomination in 1844; served in the Mexican War; commissioned major in the Connecticut Infantry March 16, 1846, and in the Ninth United States Infantry April 9, 1847; lieutenant colonel of the Twelfth Infantry August 12, 1847; brevetted colonel September 13, 1847, "for gallant and meritorious conduct in the Battle of Chapultepec, Mexico"; honorably mustered out July 25, 1848; unsuccessful candidate for Governor of Connecticut in 1849; Governor of Connecticut 1850–1853; presidential elector on the Democratic ticket of Pierce and King in 1852; Minister to Russia 1853–1858; again an unsuccessful candidate for Governor in 1863; died in Hartford, Conn., September 3, 1868; interment in Cedar Hill Cemetery.

SEYMOUR, William, a Representative from New York; born in Connecticut about 1780; moved to Windsor, Broome County, N. Y., about 1793; attended the public schools; studied law; was admitted to the bar in 1806 and commenced practice in Binghamton, N. Y.; returned to Windsor in 1807; justice of the peace 1812–1828; in 1833, upon his appointment as first judge of the court of common pleas of Broome County, returned to Binghamton; elected as one of the first trustees of the village in 1834; elected as a Democrat to the Twenty-fourth Congress (March 4, 1835–March 3, 1837); again served as first judge of the court of common pleas in Broome County until 1847; resumed the practice of his profession in Binghamton, where he died December 28, 1848; interment in Binghamton Cemetery.

SHACKELFORD, John Williams, a Representative from North Carolina; born in Richlands, Onslow County, N. C., November 16, 1844; attended the common schools and Richlands (N. C.) Academy; during the Civil War entered the Confederate Army at the age of seventeen and served throughout the war, attaining the rank of lieutenant; member of the

State house of representatives 1872–1878; served in the State senate 1878–1880; was elected to preside over the convention that nominated him for Congress in 1880; elected as a Democrat to the Forty-seventh Congress, and served from March 4, 1881, until his death in Washington, D. C., January 18, 1883; interment in the Wallace Graveyard, Richlands, N. C.

SHACKLEFORD, Dorsey William, a Representative from Missouri; born near Sweet Springs, Saline County, Mo., August 27, 1853; attended the public schools and William Jewell College, Liberty, Mo.; taught school 1877–1879; studied law; was admitted to the bar in 1878 and commenced practice in Boonville, Mo.; prosecuting attorney of Cooper County, Mo., 1882–1886 and 1890–1892; judge of the fourteenth judicial circuit of Missouri from June 1, 1892, until his resignation on September 9, 1899, having been elected to Congress; elected as a Democrat to the Fifty-sixth Congress to fill the vacancy caused by the death of Richard P. Bland; reelected to the Fifty-seventh and to the eight succeeding Congresses, and served from August 29, 1899, to March 3, 1919; was an unsuccessful candidate for renomination in 1918 to the Sixty-sixth Congress; moved to Jefferson City, Mo., in 1919 and continued the practice of law; died in Jefferson City, Mo., on July 15, 1936; interment in Walnut Grove Cemetery, Boonville, Mo.

SHAFER, Jacob K., a Delegate from the Territory of Idaho; born near Broadway, Rockingham County, Va., December 26, 1823; was graduated from Washington College, Lexington, Va., in 1843; and from the law school of L. P. Thompson in Staunton, Va., in 1846; moved to Stockton, Calif., in 1849; was admitted to the bar and practiced; district attorney of the fifth judicial district of California in 1850; mayor of Stockton in 1852; judge of the San Joaquin County Court 1853–1862; moved in 1862 to what later became Idaho Territory; elected as a Democrat to the Forty-first Congress (March 4, 1869–March 3, 1871); unsuccessful candidate for renomination; resumed the practice of law; moved to Eureka, Nev., where he died November 22, 1876; interment in the Masonic Cemetery.

SHAFER, Paul Werntz, a Representative from Michigan; born in Elkhart, Ind., April 27, 1893; moved with his parents to Three Rivers, Mich., and attended the public schools; student at Ferris Institute, Big Rapids, Mich., and studied law by correspondence with the Blackstone Institute of Chicago, Ill.; reporter, editor, and publisher of newspapers in Elkhart, Ind., Battle Creek, Mich., and Bronson, Mich.; member of Indiana State Militia in 1916 and 1917; municipal judge in Battle Creek, Mich., 1929–1936; elected as a Republican to the Seventy-fifth and to the eight succeeding Congresses and served from January 3, 1937, until his death; had been renominated in the Republican primary election August 3, 1954, to the Eighty-fourth Congress; died in Walter Reed Hospital, Washington, D. C., August 17, 1954; interment in Memorial Park Cemetery, Battle Creek, Mich.

SHAFFER, Joseph Crockett, a Representative from Virginia; born near Wytheville, Wythe County, Va., January 19, 1880; attended the Wytheville public schools; was graduated from Plummer College, Wytheville, Va., in 1902 and from the law department of the University of Virginia at Charlottesville in 1904; was admitted to the bar in 1904 and commenced practice in Wytheville, Va.; served as Commonwealth attorney of Wythe County 1908–1912; assistant United States district attorney 1920–1924 and served as United States district attorney for the western district of Virginia 1924–1929; elected as a Republican to the Seventy-first Congress (March 4, 1929–March 3, 1931); unsuccessful candidate for reelection in 1930 to the Seventy-

second Congress; United States district attorney for the western district of Virginia from 1931 until his resignation in 1932; resumed the practice of law; stockholder and officer in Wythe County National Bank; delegate to the Republican National Convention in 1940; died in Abingdon, Va., October 19, 1958; interment in St. John's Church Cemetery, Wytheville, Va.

SHAFROTH, John Franklin, a Representative and a Senator from Colorado; born in Fayette, Mo., June 9, 1854; attended the common schools and was graduated from the University of Michigan at Ann Arbor in 1875; studied law; was admitted to the bar in 1876 and commenced practice in Fayette, Mo.; moved to Denver, Colo., in October 1879 and continued law practice; city attorney 1887–1891; elected as a Republican to the Fifty-fourth Congress; reelected as a Silver Republican and Democrat to the Fifty-fifth, Fifty-sixth, and Fifty-seventh Congresses; presented credentials as a Democratic Member-elect to the Fifty-eighth Congress and served from March 4, 1895, until his resignation on February 15, 1904, when he declared his conviction that Robert W. Bonynge, contestant, was duly elected; Governor of Colorado 1908–1912; elected as a Democrat to the United States Senate and served from March 4, 1913, to March 3, 1919; unsuccessful candidate for reelection; chairman of the War Minerals Relief Commission from 1919 to 1921; died in Denver, Colo., February 20, 1922; interment in Fairmount Cemetery.

SHALLENBERGER, Ashton Cokayne, a Representative from Nebraska; born in Toulon, Stark County, Ill., December 23, 1862; attended the common schools and the University of Illinois at Urbana; moved to Stromsburg, Polk County, Nebr., in 1881, to Osceola, Polk County, Nebr., in 1883, and to Alma, Harlan County, Nebr., in 1887; engaged in banking and also in stock raising; temporary chairman of the Democratic State conventions in 1897 and 1919; elected as a Democrat to the Fifty-seventh Congress (March 4, 1901–March 3, 1903); unsuccessful candidate for reelection in 1902 to the Fifty-eighth Congress; Governor of Nebraska 1908–1911; unsuccessful Democratic candidate for election in 1912 to the United States Senate; elected to the Sixty-fourth and Sixty-fifth Congresses (March 4, 1915–March 3, 1919); unsuccessful candidate for reelection in 1918 to the Sixty-sixth Congress; delegate to the Democratic National Convention at San Francisco in 1920; elected to the Sixty-eighth, Sixty-ninth, and Seventieth Congresses (March 4, 1923–March 3, 1929); unsuccessful candidate for reelection in 1928 to the Seventy-first Congress; elected to the Seventy-second and Seventy-third Congresses (March 4, 1931–January 3, 1935); was an unsuccessful candidate for renomination in 1934; resumed banking and also engaged in agricultural pursuits and the breeding of shorthorn cattle; died in Franklin, Nebr., while on a visit, February 22, 1938; interment in Alma Cemetery, Alma, Nebr.

SHALLENBERGER, William Shadrack, a Representative from Pennsylvania; born in Mount Pleasant, Westmoreland County, Pa., November 24, 1839; attended the public schools and Mount Pleasant Academy; was graduated from Lewisburg University (now Bucknell University), Lewisburg, Pa., in 1862; engaged in mercantile pursuits; during the Civil War enlisted in the Union Army in 1862 in the One Hundred and Fortieth Regiment, Pennsylvania Volunteer Infantry, and soon afterward was appointed adjutant of the regiment; wounded in the Battles of Chancellorsville, Gettysburg, and the Wilderness; mustered out of the service in October 1864 and again engaged in mercantile pursuits in Rochester, Pa.; chairman of the Beaver County Republican committee in 1872 and 1874; elected as a Republican to the Forty-fifth, Forty-sixth, and Forty-seventh

Congresses (March 4, 1877–March 3, 1883); appointed by President McKinley as Second Assistant Postmaster General and served from 1897 to 1907; retired from active business life; died in Washington, D. C., April 15, 1914; interment in Arlington National Cemetery, Fort Myer, Va.

SHANKLIN, George Sea, a Representative from Kentucky; born in Jessamine County, Ky., December 23, 1807; attended a private school at Nicholasville, Ky.; studied law; was admitted to the bar and commenced practice in Nicholasville; member of the State house of representatives in 1838 and 1844; appointed Commonwealth attorney in 1854; again a member of the State house of representatives, and served from 1861 to 1865; presidential elector on the Democratic ticket of McClellan and Pendleton in 1864; elected as a Democrat to the Thirty-ninth Congress (March 4, 1865–March 3, 1867); retired to his farm in Jessamine County, where he died April 1, 1883; interment in Lexington Cemetery, Lexington, Ky.

SHANKS, John Peter Cleaver, a Representative from Indiana; born in Martinsburg, Va. (now West Virginia), June 17, 1826; pursued an academic course; studied law; was admitted to the bar in 1848 and commenced practice in Portland, Ind., in 1849; prosecuting attorney of Jay County in 1850 and 1851; member of the State house of representatives in 1855; during the Civil War served in the Union Army; colonel and aide-de-camp to General Frémont from September 20 to November 19, 1861; colonel and aide-de-camp from March 31, 1862, to October 9, 1863; colonel of the Seventh Indiana Cavalry October 9, 1863; brevetted brigadier general of Volunteers December 8, 1864, and major general of Volunteers March 13, 1865, "for faithful and meritorious services during the war"; mustered out September 19, 1865; elected as a Republican to the Thirty-seventh Congress (March 4, 1861–March 3, 1863); unsuccessful candidate for reelection in 1862 to the Thirty-eighth Congress; elected to the Fortieth and to the three succeeding Congresses (March 4, 1867–March 3, 1875); unsuccessful candidate for renomination in 1874; resumed the practice of his profession; was again a member of the State house of representatives in 1879; died in Portland, Jay County, Ind., January 23, 1901; interment in Green Park Cemetery.

SHANLEY, James Andrew, a Representative from Connecticut; born in New Haven, Conn., April 1, 1896; attended the public schools; graduate of Battery Commander School at Fort Sill, Ark., in 1917; during the First World War served as a lieutenant in the Forty-fifth Field Artillery, United States Army, in 1917 and 1918; was graduated from Yale University, New Haven, Conn., in 1920; taught mathematics at Carlton Academy, Summit, N. J., in 1920 and 1921 and at Hill House High School, New Haven, Conn., 1921–1934; educational and athletic adviser of the New Haven Boys Club 1926–1928; graduated from the law department of Yale University in 1928; was admitted to the bar in 1928 and commenced practice in New Haven; captain in the Artillery Reserves 1923–1935; adjutant in the Connecticut National Guard 1929–1935; major on the staff of Gov. Wilbur L. Cross 1931–1935; lecturer on parliamentary government and legislation at the Catholic University of America in Washington, D. C., 1941–1945; elected as a Democrat to the Seventy-fourth and to the three succeeding Congresses (January 3, 1935–January 3, 1943); unsuccessful candidate for reelection in 1942 to the Seventy-eighth Congress; receiver for the Hartford Empire Co. from September 1942 to February 1946; resumed the practice of law; elected November 5, 1949, as judge of probate for the towns of New Haven, East Haven, North Haven, Orange, and Woodbridge, Conn., in which capacity he is still serving; is a resident of New Haven, Conn.

SHANNON, Joseph Bernard, a Representative from Missouri; born in St. Louis, Mo., March 17, 1867; attended the public schools of St. Louis and Spalding Business College, Kansas City, Mo.; moved with his parents to Girard, Kans., in early youth; upon the death of his father moved to Kansas City, Mo., in 1879; became constable in the justice court in 1890; was city market-master in 1892 and served two years; studied law; was admitted to the bar in 1905 and commenced practice in Kansas City, Mo.; chairman of the Democratic State committee in 1910; delegate to the Democratic National Conventions in 1908, 1912, 1920, 1924, 1928, 1932, and 1940; member of the Missouri constitutional convention in 1922 and 1923; elected as a Democrat to the Seventy-second and the five succeeding Congresses (March 4, 1931–January 3, 1943); was not a candidate for renomination in 1942; died in Kansas City, Mo., March 28, 1943; interment in Calvary Cemetery.

SHANNON, Richard Cutts, a Representative from New York; born in New London, Conn., February 12, 1839; was graduated from the grammar and high schools at Biddeford, Maine, and from Waterville College (now Colby College), Maine; during the Civil War enlisted in Company H, Fifth Regiment, Maine Volunteer Infantry, June 24, 1861; appointed first lieutenant October 10, 1861; aide-de-camp to General Slocum March 15, 1862; captain and assistant adjutant general of Volunteers October 2, 1862; brevetted major of Volunteers March 13, 1865, "for faithful and meritorius services during the war," and lieutenant colonel of Volunteers "for gallant and meritorious services in the Battle of Chancellorsville, Virginia"; honorably discharged February 10, 1866; appointed secretary of the United States legation at Rio de Janeiro, Brazil, in 1871, and served until March 1875, when he resigned; took charge of the Botanical Garden Railroad Co. in 1876, an American enterprise in Brazil, of which he subsequently became the vice president and general manager and finally president; returned to the United States in 1883 and was graduated from the law department of Columbia College, New York City, in 1885; was admitted to the New York bar in 1886 and commenced practice in New York City; appointed Envoy Extraordinary and Minister Plenipotentiary to Nicaragua, Salvador, and Costa Rica in 1891, and served until April 1893; elected as a Republican to the Fifty-fourth and Fifty-fifth Congresses (March 4, 1895–March 3, 1899); declined to be a candidate for renomination in 1898; resumed the practice of his profession in New York City; retired in 1903 and moved to Brockport, Monroe County, N. Y., where he died October 5, 1920; interment in Lake View Cemetery.

SHANNON, Thomas (brother of Wilson Shannon), a Representative from Ohio; born in Washington County, Pa., November 15, 1786; attended the public schools; moved to Ohio with his parents, who settled in Belmont County in 1800; engaged in agricultural pursuits; moved to Barnesville, Belmont County, Ohio, in 1812 and engaged in mercantile pursuits; during the War of 1812 served as captain of Belmont County Company in Colonel Delong's regiment; member of the Ohio House of Representatives 1819–1822, 1824, and 1825; elected as a Democrat to the Nineteenth Congress to fill the vacancy caused by the resignation of David Jennings and served from December 4, 1826, to March 3, 1827; was not a candidate for renomination in 1827; returned to Barnesville, Ohio, and became a leaf-tobacco merchant; served in the State senate 1829 and 1837–1841; died in Barnesville, Belmont County, Ohio, March 16, 1843; interment in Green Mount Cemetery.

SHANNON, Thomas Bowles, a Representative from California; born in Westmoreland County, Pa., September 21, 1827; attended the public schools; moved to Illinois in 1844 and to

California in 1849; engaged in mercantile pursuits; member of the State assembly in 1859, 1860, and 1862; elected as a Republican to the Thirty-eighth Congress (March 4, 1863–March 3, 1865); was not a candidate for renomination in 1864; appointed surveyor at the port of San Francisco August 11, 1865, and served four years; again a member of the State assembly in 1871 and 1872, and served as speaker the first year; appointed by President Grant collector of customs at San Francisco, Calif., and served from July 1, 1872, to August 10, 1880; resumed mercantile pursuits; died in San Francisco, Calif., February 21, 1897; interment in the Masonic Cemetery.

SHANNON, Wilson (brother of Thomas Shannon), a Representative from Ohio; born at Mount Olivet, Belmont County, Ohio, February 24, 1802; attended Ohio University, Athens, Ohio, 1820–1822 and Transylvania College, Lexington, Ky., in 1823; studied law; was admitted to the bar in 1830 and began practice in St. Clairsville, Ohio; unsuccessful candidate for election in 1832 to the Twenty-third Congress; prosecuting attorney for Belmont County 1833–1835; State prosecuting attorney in 1835; Governor of Ohio 1838–1840; unsuccessful candidate for Governor in 1840; again Governor of Ohio 1842–1844; unsuccessful candidate for the United States Senate in 1842; United States Minister to Mexico in 1844 and 1845; elected as a Democrat to the Thirty-third Congress (March 4, 1853–March 3, 1855); was not a candidate for renomination in 1854; Governor of Kansas Territory in 1855 and 1856; engaged in the practice of law in Lawrence, Kans., where he died August 31, 1877; interment in Oak Hill Cemetery.

SHARON, William, a Senator from Nevada; born in Smithfield, Jefferson County, Ohio, January 9, 1821; attended Athens College; moved to St. Louis, Mo.; studied law; was admitted to the bar and practiced; engaged in mercantile pursuits in Carrollton, Greene County, Ill.; moved to California in 1849 and engaged in business in Sacramento; moved to San Francisco in 1850 and was a dealer in real estate; moved to Virginia City, Storey County, Nev., in 1864 as manager of the branch of the Bank of California and became largely interested in silver mining; elected as a Republican to the United States Senate and served from March 4, 1875, to March 3, 1881; resided in San Francisco, Calif., until his death on November 13, 1885; interment in Laurel Hill Cemetery.

SHARP, Edgar Allan, a Representative from New York; born in Patchogue, Suffolk County, N. Y., June 3, 1876; attended the public and high schools; engaged as a clerk in the post office at Patchogue, N. Y., 1898–1906 and served as assistant postmaster 1906–1918; in charge of construction work for the Knights of Columbus in France and England from April 1918 to January 1920; engaged in the real estate and insurance business in Patchogue, N. Y., and as real-estate appraiser for Suffolk County 1920–1944; auctioneer 1929–1944; also interested in banking; member of the zoning and planning board of Brookhaven, N. Y., 1930–1933; supervisor of Brookhaven, N. Y., 1935–1943; elected as a Republican to the Seventy-ninth Congress (January 3, 1945–January 3, 1947); was not a candidate for renomination in 1946; resumed his former business pursuits; died in Patchogue, N. Y., November 27, 1948; interment in Holy Sepulchre Cemetery, Coram, N. Y.

SHARP, Solomon P., a Representative from Kentucky; born in Abingdon, Washington County, Va., in 1780; moved with his parents to Kentucky; pursued preparatory studies; engaged in agricultural pursuits; studied law; was admitted to the bar in 1809 and began practice in Russellville, Ky.; member of the State house of representatives 1809–1811, 1817, and

1818; entered the War of 1812 as captain of a company which he organized and later was made a colonel of militia; elected as a Democrat to the Thirteenth and Fourteenth Congresses (March 4, 1813–March 3, 1817); again a member of the State house of representatives in 1817 and 1818; resumed the practice of law; moved to Frankfort, Ky., in 1820; attorney general of Kentucky 1820–1824; again served in the State house of representatives in 1825; assassinated in Frankfort, Ky., November 7, 1825; interment in the State Cemetery.

SHARP, William Graves, a Representative from Ohio; born in Mount Gilead, Morrow County, Ohio, March 14, 1859; moved with his parents to Elyria, Ohio; was graduated from the public schools and from the law department of the University of Michigan at Ann Arbor in 1881; was admitted to the bar the same year and commenced practice in Elyria, Ohio; served as prosecuting attorney of Lorain County, Ohio, 1885–1888; also interested in the manufacture of charcoal, pig iron, and chemicals; presidential elector on the Democratic ticket of Cleveland and Stevenson in 1892; unsuccessful Democratic candidate for election in 1900 to the Fifty-seventh Congress; delegate to the Democratic National Convention at St. Louis in 1904; elected as a Democrat to the Sixty-first, Sixty-second, and Sixty-third Congresses and served from March 4, 1909, to July 23, 1914, when he resigned to become Ambassador to France, in which capacity he served until April 14, 1919; returned to Elyria, Lorain County, Ohio, and engaged in literary pursuits; died in Elyria, Ohio, November 17, 1922; interment in Ridgelawn Cemetery.

SHARPE, Peter, a Representative from New York; born in that State; completed preparatory studies; member of the Columbia County Medical Society in 1807; represented New York County as a member of the State assembly 1814–1821, and served as speaker in 1820 and 1821; delegate to the State constitutional convention in 1821; credentials of his election to the Seventeenth Congress were presented, but he did not qualify, and on December 12, 1821, Cadwallader D. Colden successfully contested his election; elected to the Eighteenth Congress (March 4, 1823–March 3, 1825); unsuccessful candidate for reelection in 1824 to the Nineteenth Congress.

SHARPE, William, a Delegate from North Carolina; born near Rock Church, Cecil County, Md., December 13, 1742; pursued classical studies; studied law; was admitted to the bar and commenced practice in Mecklenburg County, N. C. in 1763; also engaged in surveying; moved to Rowan (now Iredell) County; member of the Provincial Congress in 1775; aide to General Rutherford in the Indian campaign in 1776 and was one of four commissioners appointed by Governor Caswell to form a treaty with the Indians in 1777; delegate to the convention in Halifax in 1776 and helped to frame the first constitution of the State; Member of the Continental Congress 1779–1782; member of the State house of representatives in 1781 and 1782; died near Statesville, Iredell County, N. C., on July 1, 1818; interment in Snow Creek Graveyard.

SHARTEL, Cassius McLean, a Representative from Missouri; born in Crawford County, Pa., April 27, 1860; moved with his parents to Knox County, Mo., and resided there until 1873; moved with his parents to Chautauqua County, Kans.; attended the common schools and Kansas State Agricultural College at Manhattan; taught school; studied law; was admitted to the bar in 1881 and commenced practice in Sedan, Kans.; moved to Nevada, Mo., in 1887 and then to Neosho, Newton County, Mo., the same year and continued the practice of law; delegate to the Republican National Conventions in 1900 and 1936; elected as a Republican to the Fifty-ninth Congress

(March 4, 1905–March 3, 1907); was not a candidate for renomination in 1906; interested in farm loans; president of the Missouri constitutional convention in 1922 and 1923; died in Neosho, Mo., September 27, 1943; interment in Odd Fellows Cemetery.

SHATTUC, William Bunn, a Representative from Ohio; born in North Hector, Schuyler County, N. Y., June 11, 1841; moved to Ohio in 1852 with his parents, who settled near Sandusky; attended the public schools; during the Civil War enlisted in Company I, Second Regiment, Ohio Volunteer Cavalry, August 13, 1861, as second lieutenant; mustered out February 21, 1863, as first lieutenant; assistant and afterward general passenger agent of the Ohio & Mississippi Railway Co. 1865–1894; member of the State senate in 1895; elected as a Republican to the Fifty-fifth, Fifty-sixth and Fifty-seventh Congresses (March 4, 1897–March 3, 1903); was not a candidate for renomination in 1902; died in Madisonville, near Cincinnati, Ohio, July 13, 1911; interment in Spring Grove Cemetery, Cincinnati, Hamilton County, Ohio.

SHAW, Aaron, a Representative from Illinois; born near Goshen, Orange County, N. Y., December 19, 1811; attended Montgomery Academy, New York; studied law in Goshen, N. Y.; was admitted to the bar in 1833 and commenced practice in Lawrenceville, Ill.; delegate to the first Internal Improvement Convention of Illinois; elected State's attorney by the Legislature of Illinois in 1842; member of the State house of representatives in 1850; elected as a Democrat to the Thirty-fifth Congress (March 4, 1857–March 3, 1859); was not a candidate for renomination in 1858; again a member of the State house of representatives in 1860; circuit judge of the fourth judicial district of Illinois 1863–1869; elected to the Forty-eighth Congress (March 4, 1883–March 3, 1885); was not a candidate for renomination in 1884; resumed the practice of law; died in Olney, Richland County, Ill., January 7, 1887; interment in Haven Hill Cemetery.

SHAW, Albert Duane, a Representative from New York; born in Lyme, Jefferson County, N. Y., December 21, 1841; attended Belleville and Union Academies and St. Lawrence University, Canton, N. Y.; enlisted as a private in Company A, Thirty-fifth Regiment, New York Volunteers, in June 1861 and served out the term of enlistment; appointed a special agent of the War Department in 1863, stationed at provost marshal's headquarters in Watertown, N. Y., and served until the close of the war; member of the State assembly in 1866; appointed colonel of the Thirty-sixth Regiment, New York National Guard, in 1867, and resigned to accept the position of United States consul at Toronto, Canada, in 1868; promoted to United States consul at Manchester, England, in 1878; elected department commander of the Grand Army of the Republic of New York in 1896; unanimously elected commander in chief at the national encampment in 1899; elected as a Republican to the Fifty-sixth Congress to fill the vacancy caused by the death of Charles A. Chickering; reelected to the Fifty-seventh Congress and served from November 6, 1900, until his death in Washington, D. C., on February 10, 1901, before the close of the Fifty-sixth Congress; interment in Brookside Cemetery, Watertown, Jefferson County, N. Y.

SHAW, Frank Thomas, a Representative from Maryland; born in Woodsboro, Frederick County, Md., October 7, 1841; attended the common schools and was graduated from the medical department of the University of Maryland at Baltimore in 1864; engaged in the practice of medicine in Uniontown, Carroll County, Md., until November 1873; elected clerk of the circuit court for Carroll County in 1873; reelected in

1879 and served until 1885, when he resigned; elected as a Democrat to the Forty-ninth and Fiftieth Congresses (March 4, 1885–March 3, 1889); unsuccessful candidate for renomination in 1888; member of the State house of delegates in 1890; State tax commissioner 1890–1894; appointed by President Cleveland as collector of customs for the port of Baltimore and served from May 5, 1894, to May 24, 1898; presidential elector on the Democratic ticket of Wilson and Marshall in 1912; adviser to the clerk of the circuit court 1915–1921; retired and resided in Westminster, Carroll County, Md., until his death, February 24, 1923; interment in Westminster Cemetery.

SHAW, George Bullen, a Representative from Wisconsin; born in Alma, Allegany County, N. Y., on March 12, 1854; moved to Eau Claire, Wis., in 1856 with his father; attended the public schools and was graduated from the International Business College, Chicago, Ill., in 1871; engaged in the lumber manufacturing business; member of the Common Council of Eau Claire 1876–1887; mayor of Eau Claire in 1888 and 1889; delegate to the Republican National Convention at Chicago in 1884; supreme chancellor of the Knights of Pythias of the World from July 1890 to August 1892; elected as a Republican to the Fifty-third Congress and served from March 4, 1893, until his death in Eau Claire, Wis., August 27, 1894; interment in Lake View Cemetery.

SHAW, Guy Loren, a Representative from Illinois; born on a farm near Summer Hill, Pike County, Ill., May 16, 1881; attended the public schools and the College of Agriculture of the University of Illinois at Urbana; engaged in agricultural pursuits and the development of overflow lands along the Illinois River; delegate to the State constitutional convention in 1920; elected as a Republican to the Sixty-seventh Congress (March 4, 1921–March 3, 1923); unsuccessful candidate for reelection in 1922 to the Sixty-eighth Congress; engaged in the real-estate business in Beardstown, Cass County, Ill., and Urbana, Champaign County, Ill.; moved to Normal, McLean County, Ill., and continued agricultural pursuits, farm management, and the real-estate business; died in Normal, Ill., May 19, 1950; interment in Bloomington Cemetery, Bloomington, Ill.

SHAW, Henry (son of Samuel Shaw), a Representative from Massachusetts; born near Putney, Windham County, Vt., in 1788; completed preparatory studies; studied law; was admitted to the bar and commenced practice in Albany, N. Y., in 1810; moved to Lanesboro, Mass., in 1813; elected as a Federalist to the Fifteenth and Sixteenth Congresses (March 4, 1817–March 3, 1821); unsuccessful candidate for renomination in 1820; member of the State house of representatives 1824–1830 and 1833; served in the State senate in 1835; presidential elector on the National-Republican ticket of Clay and Sergeant in 1832; unsuccessful candidate for Governor of Massachusetts in 1845; moved to New York City in 1848; member of the Board of Education of New York City in 1849; member of the New York City Common Council 1850–1851; member of the New York State Assembly in 1853; moved to Newburgh, N. Y., in 1854; died in Peekskill, Westchester County, N. Y., October 17, 1857; interment in the Lower Cemetery, Lanesboro, Mass.

SHAW, Henry Marchmore, a Representative from North Carolina; born in Newport, R. I., November 20, 1819; completed preparatory studies; was graduated from the medical department of the University of Pennsylvania at Philadelphia in 1838 and began practice in Indiantown, Camden County, N. C.; elected as a Democrat to the Thirty-third Congress (March 4, 1853–March 3, 1855); unsuccessful candidate for reelection to the Thirty-fourth Congress; elected to the Thirty-fifth Congress (March 4, 1857–March 3, 1859); unsuccessful candidate for reelection to the Thirty-sixth Congress; served as a colonel in the Confederate Army during the Civil War and was killed near New Bern, N. C., November 1, 1864; interment in the cemetery at Shawboro, Currituck County, N. C.

SHAW, John Gilbert, a Representative from North Carolina; born near Fayetteville, Cumberland County, N. C., January 16, 1859; attended the common schools; engaged in the naval-stores business; studied law; was admitted to the bar in 1888 and commenced practice in Fayetteville; member of the State house of representatives in 1888; prosecuting attorney for Cumberland County 1890–1894; presidential elector on the Democratic ticket of Cleveland and Stevenson in 1892; elected as a Democrat to the Fifty-fourth Congress (March 4, 1895–March 3, 1897); unsuccessful candidate for reelection in 1896 to the Fifty-fifth Congress; resumed the practice of law in Fayetteville, N. C., until his death in that city on July 21, 1932; interment in Cross Creek Cemetery.

SHAW, Samuel (father of Henry Shaw), a Representative from Vermont; born in Dighton, Mass., in December 1768; received a limited schooling; moved to Putney, Vt.; studied medicine and commenced practice in Castleton, Vt., in 1789; imprisoned for a bitter denunciation of President Adams, but liberated by the people; member of the State house of representatives 1800–1807; elected as a Democrat to the Tenth Congress to fill the vacancy caused by the resignation of James Witherell; reelected to the Eleventh and Twelfth Congresses and served from September 6, 1808, to March 3, 1813; served in the United States Army as hospital surgeon from April 6, 1813, to June 15, 1815, when he was honorably discharged; reinstated on September 13, 1815; appointed post surgeon April 18, 1818, and resigned on December 31, 1818; died in Clarendon Springs, Rutland County, Vt., October 23, 1827; interment in Castleton Cemetery, Castleton, Vt.

SHAW, Tristram, a Representative from New Hampshire; born in Hampton, Rockingham County, N. H., May 23, 1786; completed preparatory studies; held several local offices in Exeter, N. H.; elected to the Twenty-sixth and Twenty-seventh Congresses (March 4, 1839–March 3, 1843); died in Exeter, Rockingham County, N. H., March 14, 1843; interment in Bride Hill Cemetery, Hampton, N. H.

SHEAFE, James, a Representative and a Senator from New Hampshire; born in Portsmouth, N. H., November 16, 1755; completed preparatory studies and was graduated from Harvard College in 1774; engaged in mercantile pursuits; member of the State house of representatives 1788–1790; member of the State senate in 1791, 1793, and 1799; member of the executive council in 1799; elected as a Federalist to the Sixth Congress (March 4, 1799–March 3, 1801); elected to the United States Senate and served from March 4, 1801, until his resignation on June 14, 1802; unsuccessful candidate for Governor of New Hampshire in 1816; died in Portsmouth, Rockingham County, N. H., December 5, 1829; interment in St. John's Church Cemetery.

SHEAKLEY, James, a Representative from Pennsylvania; born in Sheakleyville, Mercer County, Pa., April 24, 1829; attended the common schools and Meadville (Pa.) Academy; learned the trade of cabinetmaker; moved to California in 1851 and engaged in the mining of gold; returned to Pennsylvania and settled in Greenville in 1855; engaged in mercantile pursuits and in 1864 in the production and shipment of petroleum; school director of Greenville, Pa., 1864–1868; elected as a Democrat to the Forty-fourth Congress (March 4, 1875–March 3, 1877); un-

successful candidate for reelection in 1876 to the Forty-fifth Congress; appointed United States commissioner of schools of Alaska by President Cleveland in July 1887 and served five years; studied law and was admitted to the bar in the United States District Court of Alaska in 1888; delegate to the Democratic National Convention at Chicago in 1892 which nominated Cleveland and Stevenson; Governor of Alaska 1893–1897; again returned to Greenville, Pa., in 1898; mayor of Greenville 1909–1913; elected justice of the peace in 1914 and served until his death in Greenville, Pa., on December 10, 1917; interment in Shenango Valley Cemetery.

SHEATS, Charles Christopher, a Representative from Alabama; born in Walker County, Ala., April 10, 1839; attended the common schools; elected a member of the secession convention in 1860 but refused to sign the ordinance of secession; member of the State house of representatives in 1861 and expelled for his adherence to the Union in 1862; was imprisoned on a charge of treason by the Confederate authorities, but could not obtain a trial, and was not released until after the close of the Civil War; unsuccessful candidate for election in 1864 to the Thirty-ninth Congress; member of the constitutional convention in 1865; studied law; was admitted to the bar in 1867 and commenced practice in Decatur; presidential elector on the Republican ticket of Grant and Colfax in 1868 and of Grant and Wilson in 1872; appointed by President Grant consul at Elsinore, Denmark, May 31, 1869, and served until elected to Congress; elected as a Republican to the Forty-third Congress (March 4, 1873–March 3, 1875); unsuccessful candidate for reelection in 1874 to the Forty-fourth Congress; died in Decatur, Morgan County, Ala., May 27, 1904; interment in McKendree Cemetery, near Decatur.

SHEEHAN, Timothy Patrick, a Representative from Illinois; born in Chicago, Ill., February 21, 1909; attended St. Pius Grammar School and Joseph Medill High School; was graduated from Northwestern University in 1931, majoring in accounting; with Silver Brook Beverage Co. and Swedish Produce Co., food importers and wholesalers, since 1932 and president and treasurer since 1945; elected as a Republican to the Eighty-second and to the three succeeding Congresses (January 3, 1951–January 3, 1959); unsuccessful candidate for reelection in 1958 to the Eighty-sixth Congress; unsuccessful Republican candidate for mayor of Chicago in 1959 and for election in 1960 to the Eighty-seventh Congress; resumed his importing and wholesale business; is a resident of Chicago, Ill.

SHEFFER, Daniel, a Representative from Pennsylvania; born in York, Pa., May 24, 1783; attended the common schools and Harvard University; studied medicine in Philadelphia and commenced practice at York Springs, Adams County, Pa.; associate judge of Adams County, Pa., 1813–1837; Democratic presidential elector on the Jackson ticket in 1824; elected as a Democrat to the Twenty-fifth Congress (March 4, 1837–March 3, 1839); unsuccessful candidate for reelection in 1838 to the Twenty-sixth Congress; resumed the practice of his profession; was a delegate to the Democratic National Convention at Baltimore in 1848 which nominated Cass and Butler; died at York Springs, Pa., February 16, 1880; interment in the Old Lutheran Cemetery.

SHEFFEY, Daniel, a Representative from Virginia; born in Frederick, Frederick County, Md., in 1770; pursued classical studies; apprenticed as a shoemaker in his father's shop; moved to Wytheville, Va., in 1791; worked at his trade and at the same time studied law; was admitted to the bar July 1, 1802, and commenced the practice of his profession in Wytheville; moved to Abbeville and later to Staunton, where he continued the practice of law; member of the State house of delegates 1800–1804; served in the State senate 1804–1808; elected as a Federalist to the Eleventh and to the three succeeding Congresses (March 4, 1809–March 3, 1817); again a member of the State house of delegates in 1822 and 1823; died in Staunton, Augusta County, Va., December 3, 1830.

SHEFFIELD, William Paine, a Representative and a Senator from Rhode Island; born in New Shoreham, Block Island, Newport County, R. I., August 30, 1820; completed preparatory studies; attended Kingston Academy, Rhode Island, and was graduated from the law department of Harvard University in 1843; was admitted to the bar in 1844 and commenced practice in Newport, R. I.; delegate to the State constitutional conventions in 1841 and 1842; member of the State house of representatives 1842–1845; moved to Tiverton, R. I.; again elected to the State house of representatives, and served from 1849 to 1853; returned to Newport, R. I.; again a member of the State house of representatives 1857–1861; elected as a Republican candidate to the Thirty-seventh Congress (March 4, 1861–March 3, 1863); resumed the practice of law; appointed in 1871 one of the commissioners to revise the State laws; again served in the State house of representatives 1875–1884; appointed as a Republican to the United States Senate to fill the vacancy caused by the death of Henry B. Anthony and served from November 19, 1884, to January 20, 1885; resumed the practice of his profession; died in Newport, R. I., June 2, 1907; interment in the Island Cemetery.

SHEFFIELD, William Paine (son of the preceding), a Representative from Rhode Island; born in Newport, R. I., June 1, 1857; attended Phillips Academy, Andover, Mass., 1869–1873 and was graduated from Brown University, Providence, R. I., in 1877; studied law at the University of Paris and the law department of Harvard University; was admitted to the bar in 1880 and commenced practice in Newport, R. I.; commissioner on abolishing the Narragansett Tribe of Indians in 1880; appointed colonel on the staff of Gov. George Peabody Wetmore; member of the State house of representatives 1885–1887, 1889, 1890, 1894–1896, and 1899–1901; member of the commission to revise the State constitution in 1897; elected as a Republican to the Sixty-first Congress (March 4, 1909–March 3, 1911); unsuccessful candidate for reelection in 1910 to the Sixty-second Congress and in 1912 for election to the Sixty-third Congress; member of the Republican National Committee in 1913; member of the committee to revise the State constitution in 1918; died in Exeter, Washington County, R. I., October 19, 1919; interment in the Island Cemetery, Newport, R. I.

SHELDEN, Carlos Douglas, a Representative from Michigan; born in Walworth, Walworth County, Wis., June 10, 1840; moved with his parents to Houghton County, Mich., in 1847; attended the Union School, Ypsilanti, Mich., and returned to his home in the fall of 1861; served throughout the Civil War as captain in the Twenty-third Regiment, Michigan Volunteer Infantry; at the end of his service returned to Houghton and engaged in mining and the real-estate business; member of the State house of representatives in 1892; served in the State senate in 1894; elected as a Republican to the Fifty-fifth, Fifty-sixth, and Fifty-seventh Congresses (March 4, 1897–March 3, 1903); unsuccessful candidate for renomination in 1902; died in Houghton, Mich., June 24, 1904; interment in Forest Hill Cemetery.

SHELDON, Lionel Allen, a Representative from Louisiana; born in Worcester, Otsego County, N. Y., August 30, 1828; moved with his parents to Lagrange, Ohio; attended the district school and Oberlin College, Ohio, 1848–1850 and was graduated from the Fowler Law School, Poughkeepsie, N. Y., in 1853; was admitted to the bar the same year and commenced practice in Elyria, Lorain County, Ohio; probate judge of Lorain County, Ohio, in 1856 and 1857; delegate to the Republican National Convention at Philadelphia in 1856; commissioned brigadier general of the militia by Governor Chase; served in the Union Army during the Civil War; appointed lieutenant colonel of the Forty-second Regiment, Ohio Volunteer Infantry, November 27, 1861, and promoted to the rank of colonel March 14, 1862; brevetted brigadier general of Volunteers March 13, 1865, "for faithful and meritorious services"; honorably mustered out December 2, 1864; settled in New Orleans, La., and practiced law 1864–1879; elected as a Republican to the Forty-first, Forty-second, and Forty-third Congresses (March 4, 1869–March 3, 1875); unsuccessful candidate for reelection in 1874 to the Forty-fourth Congress; presidential elector on the Republican ticket of Hayes and Wheeler in 1876; returned to Ohio in 1879; delegate to the Republican National Convention at Chicago in 1880; Governor of the Territory of New Mexico 1881–1885; one of the receivers of the Texas and Pacific Railway 1885–1887; moved to Los Angeles, Calif., in 1888 and engaged in the practice of law; delegate to the Republican National Convention at St. Louis in 1896; moved to Pasadena, Calif., and died in that city January 17, 1917; remains were cremated at Mount View Cemetery and the ashes placed in the vault of C. F. Lamb & Salisbury Co.

SHELDON, Porter, a Representative from New York; born in Victor, Ontario County, N. Y., on September 29, 1831; completed preparatory studies; studied law; was admitted to the bar in 1854 at Batavia, N. Y., and commenced practice in Randolph, Cattaraugus County, N. Y.; moved to Rockford, Ill., in 1857 and continued the practice of law; member of the Illinois constitutional convention in 1861; returned to Jamestown, N. Y., in 1865 and continued the practice of law; elected as a Republican to the Forty-first Congress (March 4, 1869–March 3, 1871); unsuccessful candidate for renomination in 1870; resumed the practice of his profession; presidential elector on the Democratic ticket of Tilden and Hendricks in 1876; died in Jamestown, Chautauqua County, N. Y., on August 15, 1908; interment in Lakeview Cemetery.

SHELL, George Washington, a Representative from South Carolina; born near Laurens, Laurens County, S. C., November 13, 1831; attended the common schools and Laurens Academy; engaged in agricultural pursuits; entered the Confederate Army as a private in April 1861 and served throughout the Civil War, attaining the rank of captain; resumed agricultural pursuits; member of the State Democratic executive committee in 1886 and 1887; chosen president of the State Farmers' Association in 1888; clerk of court of Laurens County 1888–1896; elected as a Democrat to the Fifty-second and Fifty-third Congresses (March 4, 1891–March 3, 1895); was not a candidate for renomination in 1894; retired to his plantation near Laurens, Laurens County, S. C., and died there December 15, 1899; interment in Chestnut Ridge Cemetery.

SHELLABARGER, Samuel, a Representative from Ohio; born near Enon, Clark County, Ohio, on December 10, 1817; attended the county schools and was graduated from Miami University, Oxford, Ohio, in 1841; studied law; was admitted to the bar and commenced practice in Springfield, Ohio, in 1846; member of the State house of representatives in 1852 and 1853; elected as a Republican to the Thirty-seventh Congress (March 4, 1861–March 3, 1863); unsuccessful candidate for reelection in 1862 to the Thirty-eighth Congress; elected to the Thirty-ninth and Fortieth Congresses (March 4, 1865–March 3, 1869); declined to be a candidate for renomination in 1868; Minister to Portugal from April 21 to December 31, 1869; again elected to the Forty-second Congress (March 4, 1871–March 3, 1873); was not a candidate for renomination in 1872; member of the United States Civil Service Commission in 1874 and 1875; continued the practice of law until his death in Washington, D. C., August 7, 1896; interment in Ferncliff Cemetery, Springfield, Ohio.

SHELLEY, Charles Miller, a Representative from Alabama; born in Sullivan County, Tenn., December 28, 1833; moved with his father to Selma, Ala., in 1836; received a limited schooling; became an architect and builder; during the Civil War entered the Confederate Army in February 1861 as lieutenant and was stationed first at Fort Morgan and afterward attached to the Fifth Alabama Regiment; was commissioned brigadier general and served under Gen. Joseph E. Johnston and General Hood; elected as a Democrat to the Forty-fifth and Forty-sixth Congresses (March 4, 1877–March 3, 1881); presented credentials as a Member-elect to the Forty-seventh Congress, but the election was contested by James Q. Smith and the seat declared vacant July 20, 1882; subsequently elected to fill the vacancy thus caused and served from November 7, 1882, to March 3, 1883; presented credentials as a Member-elect to the Forty-eighth Congress and served from March 4, 1883, to January 9, 1885, when he was succeeded by George H. Craig, who contested the election; returned to Birmingham, Jefferson County, Ala., and engaged in promoting the industrial interests of that region until his death in that city January 20, 1907; interment in Oak Hill Cemetery, Talladega, Ala.

SHELLEY, John Francis, a Representative from California; born in San Francisco, Calif., September 3, 1905; attended the parochial and public schools; graduated from the law school of the University of San Francisco in 1932; was admitted to the bar and commenced the practice of law in California; elected to the State senate in 1938, and reelected in 1942, serving as Democratic floor leader 1938–1946; unsuccessful Democratic candidate for Lieutenant Governor in 1946; president of San Francisco Labor Council from January 1937 to May 1949 and then became secretary; elected president of the California American Federation of Labor in 1947, reelected in 1948 and 1949; delegate to the Democratic National Conventions in 1940, 1944, 1948, 1952, 1956, and 1960; served in temporary service, United States Coast Guard, during World War II on detached duty; elected as a Democrat to the Eighty-first Congress to fill the vacancy caused by the death of Richard J. Welch; reelected to the Eighty-second and to the four succeeding Congresses and served from November 8, 1949, to January 3, 1961. *Reelected to the Eighty-seventh Congress.*

SHELTON, Samuel Azariah, a Representative from Missouri; born near Waterloo, Lauderdale County, Ala., September 3, 1858; moved with his widowed mother to Webster County, Mo., in 1869; attended the common schools, Mountain Dale Academy, and the Seymour and Marshfield High Schools; taught school; engaged in agricultural pursuits 1881–1930; clerk of the circuit court of Webster County 1895–1899; studied law; was admitted to the bar in 1901 and commenced practice in Marshfield, Webster County, Mo.; postmaster of Marshfield 1906–1910; prosecuting attorney of Webster County 1914–1916; chairman of the Republican county committee for four terms; elected as a Republican to the Sixty-seventh Congress (March 4, 1921–March 3, 1923); declined to be a candidate for reelection; resumed the practice of law in Marshfield, Mo., where he died September 13, 1948; interment in Marshfield Cemetery.

SHEPARD, Charles Biddle, a Representative from North Carolina; born in New Bern, Craven County, N. C., December 5, 1807; attended private schools of his native city and was graduated from the University of North Carolina at Chapel Hill in 1827; studied law; was admitted to the bar in 1828 and commenced practice in New Bern, N. C.; elected to the State house of representatives to fill out the unexpired term of Charles Spaight and served in 1831 and 1832; elected as a Democrat to the Twenty-fifth and Twenty-sixth Congresses (March 4, 1837–March 3, 1841); resumed the practice of his profession; died in New Bern, N. C., October 31, 1843; interment in Cedar Grove Cemetery.

SHEPARD, William, a Representative from Massachusetts; born in Westfield, Mass., December 1, 1737; attended the common schools; engaged in agricultural pursuits; served in the French and Indian wars for six years; member of the committee of correspondence for Westfield in 1774; lieutenant colonel of Minutemen in April 1775; entered the Continental Army in May 1775 as lieutenant colonel; commissioned colonel of the Fourth Massachusetts Regiment October 6, 1776, and served throughout the Revolutionary War; member of the State house of representatives in 1785 and 1786; selectman for Westfield, Mass., 1784–1787; chosen major general of the Fourth Division, Massachusetts Militia, in 1786 and was complimented by the General Court of Massachusetts for his gallantry while holding that position for the successful defense of the Springfield Arsenal during Shays' Rebellion in 1786; presidential elector for the first and second elections under the Constitution in 1788 and 1792 and voted for Washington and Adams; member of the Governor's council of Massachusetts 1792–1796; appointed in 1796 to treat with the Penobscot Indians and in 1797 with the Six Nations; was elected to the Fifth, Sixth, and Seventh Congresses (March 4, 1797–March 3, 1803); resumed his agricultural pursuits; died in Westfield, Mass., November 16, 1817; interment in the Mechanic Street Cemetery.

SHEPARD, William Biddle, a Representative from North Carolina; born in New Bern, N. C., May 14, 1799; completed preparatory studies; attended the University of North Carolina at Chapel Hill in 1813; was graduated from the University of Pennsylvania at Philadelphia; studied law; was admitted to the bar and commenced practice in Camden County, later removing to Elizabeth City, Pasquotank County, N. C.; also engaged in banking; elected as a National-Republican to the Twenty-first and to the three succeeding Congresses (March 4, 1829–March 3, 1837); was not a candidate for renomination in 1836; member of the State senate 1838–1840 and 1848–1850; member of the board of trustees of the University of North Carolina 1838–1852; died in Elizabeth City, N. C., June 20, 1852; interment in St. Paul's Churchyard, Edenton, N. C.

SHEPLER, Matthias, a Representative from Ohio; born in Westmoreland County, Pa., November 11, 1790; received a limited schooling; served in the War of 1812; moved to Ohio in April 1818 and settled in Bethlehem Township, Stark County; engaged in agricultural pursuits; justice of the peace for thirty years; county commissioner for two terms; member of the State house of representatives in 1829; served in the State senate in 1832; elected as a Democrat to the Twenty-fifth Congress (March 4, 1837–March 3, 1839); declined to be a candidate for renomination in 1838; moved to Navarre, Stark County, Ohio, in 1860, where he died April 7, 1863; interment in Shepler Church Cemetery, near Navarre, Ohio.

SHEPLEY, Ether, a Senator from Maine; born in Groton, Mass., November 2, 1789; attended Groton Academy and was graduated from Dartmouth College, Hanover, N. H., in 1811; studied law; was admitted to the bar in 1814 and began practice in Saco, Maine (until 1820 a district of Massachusetts); member of the Massachusetts House of Representatives in 1819; delegate to the Maine constitutional convention in 1820; United States attorney for the district of Maine 1821–1833; member of the Maine Senate 1833–1836; moved to Portland, Maine; elected as a Democrat to the United States Senate and served from March 4, 1833, to March 3, 1836, when he resigned; justice of the supreme court of Maine 1836–1848 and chief justice 1848–1855; was not a candidate for renomination in 1854; appointed sole commissioner to revise the public laws of Maine on April 1, 1856; resumed the practice of his profession; died in Portland, Cumberland County, Maine, January 15, 1877; interment in Evergreen Cemetery.

SHEPPARD, Harry Richard, a Representative from California; born in Mobile, Ala., January 10, 1885; attended the public schools; studied law; employed in transportation department of the Santa Fe Railroad; active committee member of the Brotherhood of Railroad Trainmen; engaged in the copper business in Alaska; traveled on three continents in behalf of business interests; president and general manager of King's Beverage and King's Laboratories Corps. of California until 1934; elected as a Democrat to the Seventy-fifth and to the eleven succeeding Congresses (January 3, 1937–January 3, 1961). *Reelected to the Eighty-seventh Congress.*

SHEPPARD, John Levi (father of Morris Sheppard), a Representative from Texas; born in Bluffton, Chambers County, Ala., April 13, 1852; moved with his mother to Morris County, Tex.; attended the common schools; studied law; was admitted to the bar and commenced practice in Daingerfield, Morris County, Tex., in 1879; district attorney of the fifth judicial district of Texas 1882–1888; district judge of the same district 1888–1896; temporary chairman of the Democratic State convention in 1892; appointed delegate to the Bimetallic Convention in Chicago in 1893; delegate to the Democratic National Convention at Chicago in 1896; served as the Texas member of the presidential notification committee which met in New York City in August 1896; elected as a Democrat to the Fifty-sixth and Fifty-seventh Congresses and served from March 4, 1899, until his death in Texarkana, Bowie County, Tex., October 11, 1902; interment in Rose Hill Cemetery.

SHEPPARD, Morris (son of John Levi Sheppard), a Representative and a Senator from Texas; born in Wheatville, Morris County, Tex., May 28, 1875; attended the common schools of Daingerfield, Pittsburg, Cumby, Austin, and Linden; was graduated from the academic department of the University of Texas at Austin in 1895, from the law department of the same university in 1897, and from the law department of Yale University in 1898; sovereign banker, or national treasurer, of the Woodmen of the World for many years; elected first president of the Texas Fraternal Congress in Dallas in 1901; was admitted to the bar and commenced practice in Pittsburg, Camp County, Tex., in 1898; moved to Texarkana in 1899 and continued the practice of his profession; elected as a Democrat to the Fifty-seventh Congress to fill the vacancy caused by the death of his father, John L. Sheppard; reelected to the Fifty-eighth and to the four succeeding Congresses and served from November 15, 1902, to February 3, 1913, when he resigned; elected to the United States Senate on January 29, 1913, to fill the vacancy in the term ending March 3, 1913, caused by the resignation of Joseph W. Bailey, and on the same day was also elected for the term commencing March 4, 1913; reelected in 1918, 1924, 1930, and again in 1936; did not qualify until February 3, 1913, the date of his resignation from the House, and served until his death in Washington, D. C., April 9, 1941; interment in Hillcrest Cemetery, Texarkana, Tex.

SHEPPERD, Augustine Henry, a Representative from North Carolina; born in Rockford, Surry County, N. C., February 24, 1792; completed preparatory studies; studied law; was admitted to the bar and commenced practice in Surry County, N. C.; member of the State house of representatives 1822–1826; presidential elector on the Democratic ticket of Jackson and Calhoun in 1824; elected to the Twentieth and to the five succeeding Congresses (March 4, 1827–March 3, 1839); unsuccessful candidate for reelection in 1838 to the Twenty-sixth Congress; elected as a Whig to the Twenty-seventh Congress (March 4, 1841–March 3, 1843); presidential elector on the Whig ticket of Clay and Frelinghuysen in 1844; elected to the Thirtieth and Thirty-first Congresses (March 4, 1847–March 3, 1851); declined to be a candidate for reelection in 1850; resumed the practice of his profession; died at "Good Spring," Salem (now Winston-Salem), Forsyth County, N. C., July 11, 1864; interment in Salem Cemetery.

SHERBURNE, John Samuel, a Representative from New Hampshire; born in Portsmouth, N. H., in 1757; was graduated from Dartmouth College, Hanover, N. H., in 1776 and from the law department of Harvard University; was admitted to the bar and commenced practice in Portsmouth, N. H., in 1776; served in the Revolutionary Army and lost a leg at the Battle of Butts Hill, Rhode Island, August 29, 1778; attained the rank of brigade major of staff; elected to the Third and Fourth Congresses (March 4, 1793–March 3, 1797); United States district attorney for New Hampshire 1801–1804; appointed judge of the United States District Court for the District of New Hampshire and served from May 1804 until his death in Portsmouth, N. H., August 2, 1830.

SHEREDINE, Upton, a Representative from Maryland; born near Baltimore, Baltimore County, Md., in 1740; moved to a farm near Liberty, Frederick County, Md., in 1754; pursued academic studies; delegate to the State constitutional convention in 1776; member of the State house of delegates in 1777; served in the State senate 1776–1781; judge of the county court of appeals in 1777; member of the special court which tried, convicted, and sentenced Tories July 25, 1781; judge of the orphans court of Frederick County in 1777 and served many years; associate judge of the fifth judicial district in 1791; elected as a Democrat to the Second Congress (March 4, 1791–March 3, 1793); appointed in 1798 commissioner of the fourth division of Maryland for the valuation of land and houses and the enumeration of slaves; died on his estate, "Midhill," near Liberty, Frederick County, Md., January 14, 1800; interment in a private cemetery on his estate.

SHERIDAN, George Augustus, a Representative from Louisiana; born in Millbury, Mass., February 22, 1840; moved with his parents to Chicago, Ill., in 1858; completed preparatory studies; engaged in the publishing business; during the Civil War enlisted in the Union Army and served as captain of Company D, Eighty-eighth Regiment, Illinois Volunteer Infantry, until October 28, 1864, when he resigned; moved to New Orleans, La., in 1866; served as brigadier general of militia on Governor Warmouth's staff; sheriff of Carroll Parish, La., in 1867; elected as a Liberal to the Forty-third Congress (March 4, 1873–March 3, 1875); appointed recorder of deeds for the District of Columbia May 17, 1878; and served until May 17, 1881, when he resigned; died in the National Soldiers' Home, Virginia, October 7, 1896; interment in the Arlington National Cemetery, Fort Myer, Va.

SHERIDAN, John Edward, a Representative from Pennsylvania; born in Waterbury, New Haven County, Conn., September 15, 1902; attended the public schools; was graduated from the University of Pennsylvania at Philadelphia in 1925 and from the law department of Temple University, Philadelphia, Pa., in 1931; was admitted to the bar in 1931 and commenced practice in Philadelphia, Pa.; counsel to the coroner of Philadelphia in 1933 and 1934; served as deputy attorney general of Pennsylvania 1934–1937; member of the Board of Revision of Taxes of Philadelphia County in 1937; Pennsylvania counsel for Delaware River Bridge Commission in 1938 and 1939; delegate to the Democratic National Conventions in 1932, 1936, 1940, and 1944; elected as a Democrat to the Seventy-sixth Congress to fill the vacancy caused by the death of J. Burrwood Daly; reelected to the Seventy-seventh, Seventy-eighth, and Seventy-ninth Congresses and served from November 7, 1939, to January 3, 1947; was an unsuccessful candidate for reelection in 1946 to the Eightieth Congress; engaged in the practice of law; member of County Board of Law Examiners 1954–; is a resident of Philadelphia, Pa.

SHERLEY, Joseph Swagar, a Representative from Kentucky; born in Louisville, Jefferson County, Ky., November 28, 1871; attended the public schools; was graduated from the Louisville High School in 1889 and from the law department of the University of Virginia at Charlottesville in 1891; was admitted to the bar the same year and commenced practice in Louisville, Ky.; elected as a Democrat to the Fifty-eighth and to the seven succeeding Congresses (March 4, 1903–March 3, 1919); unsuccessful candidate for reelection in 1918 to the Sixty-sixth Congress; director of the division of finance of the United States Railroad Administration from April 1919 to September 1920, when he resigned; resumed the practice of law in Washington, D. C.; died while on a visit in Louisville, Ky., February 13, 1941; interment in Cave Hill Cemetery.

SHERMAN, James Schoolcraft, a Representative from New York and a Vice President of the United States; born in Utica, N. Y., October 24, 1855; attended the public schools; pursued academic and collegiate courses and was graduated from Hamilton College, Clinton, N. Y., in 1878; studied law; was admitted to the bar in 1880 and commenced practice in Utica, N. Y.; president of the Utica Trust & Deposit Co. and of the New Hartford Canning Co.; mayor of Utica in 1884; delegate to the Republican National Convention at Minneapolis in 1892; chairman of the New York State Republican conventions in 1895 and 1900; elected as a Republican to the Fiftieth and Fifty-first Congresses (March 4, 1887–March 3, 1891); unsuccessful candidate for reelection in 1890 to the Fifty-second Congress; elected to the Fifty-third and to the seven succeeding Congresses (March 4, 1893–March 3, 1909); was not a candidate for reelection, having been nominated as the Republican candidate for Vice President; elected Vice President of the United States in 1908 and served from March 4, 1909, until his death; renominated for Vice President in June 1912; died in Utica, Oneida County, N. Y., October 30, 1912; interment in Forest Hill Cemetery.

SHERMAN, John, a Representative and a Senator from Ohio; born in Lancaster, Fairfield County, Ohio, on May 10, 1823; attended the common schools and Homer Academy, Lancaster, Ohio, 1835–1837; junior rodman of an engineer corps in 1839; studied law; was admitted to the bar in 1844 and began practice in Mansfield, Ohio; delegate to the Whig National Convention at Philadelphia in 1848 and at Baltimore in 1852, serving as secretary of the former convention; moved to Cleveland, Ohio, in 1853; president of the first Ohio Republican State convention in 1855; elected as a Republican to the Thirty-fourth and to the three succeeding Congresses and served from

March 4, 1855, to March 21, 1861, when he resigned; elected in 1861 as a Republican to the United States Senate to fill the vacancy caused by the resignation of Salmon P. Chase; reelected in 1866 and 1872 and served from March 21, 1861, until his resignation on March 8, 1877; appointed Secretary of the Treasury in the Cabinet of President Hayes on March 8, 1877, and served until March 3, 1881; elected to the the United States Senate in the place of James A. Garfield, who had been elected President of the United States; reelected in 1886 and 1892 and served from March 4, 1881, until his resignation on March 4, 1897; appointed Secretary of State in the Cabinet of President McKinley and served from March 5, 1897, until his resignation on April 25, 1898; retired to private life; died in Washington, D. C., October 22, 1900; interment in Mansfield Cemetery, Mansfield, Richland County, Ohio.

SHERMAN, Judson W., a Representative from New York; born in that State in 1808; completed preparatory studies; held several local offices in Angelica, N. Y., where he resided; clerk of Allegany County, N. Y., 1831–1837; deputy treasurer of the State of New York about 1850; elected as a Republican to the Thirty-fifth Congress (March 4, 1857–March 3, 1859); appointed captain and commissary of subsistence of Volunteers on September 7, 1861, was assigned to duty with Brigadier General Wood's brigade, and resigned his commission November 9, 1861; retired from political activity and lived in retirement until his death; died at Anglica, Allegany County, N. Y., on November 12, 1881; interment in Until the Day Dawn Cemetery.

SHERMAN, Lawrence Yates, a Senator from Illinois; born near Piqua, Miami County, Ohio, November 8, 1858; moved with his parents to Illinois in 1859; attended the common schools, Lee's Academy in Coles County, and McKendree College, Lebanon, Ill.; studied law; was admitted to the bar in 1882 and commenced practice in Macomb, Ill.; city attorney 1885–1887; judge in McDonough County 1886–1890; member of the State house of representatives 1897–1905 and served as speaker 1899–1903; Lieutenant Governor and ex officio president of the State senate 1905–1909; president of the State board of administration of public charities 1909–1913; continued the practice of law in Springfield, Ill.; delegate to the Republican National Conventions in 1912, 1920, 1924, and 1928; elected as a Republican to the United States Senate to fill the vacancy caused by the unseating of William Lorimer; reelected in 1914 and served from March 26, 1913, to March 3, 1921; voluntarily retired from political activity and resumed the practice of law in Springfield, Ill.; moved to Daytona Beach, Fla., in 1924 and continued the practice of law; also engaged in the investment business; retired from active business pursuits in 1933; died in Daytona Beach, Fla., September 15, 1939; interment in Montrose Cemetery, Effingham County, Ill.

SHERMAN, Roger, a Delegate, a Representative, and a Senator from Connecticut; born in Newton, Mass., April 19, 1721; moved with his parents to Stoughton (now Canton), Mass., in 1723; attended the public schools; learned the shoemaker's trade; moved to New Milford, Conn., in 1743; surveyor of New Haven County in 1745; studied law; was admitted to the bar in February 1754 and practiced; member of the Connecticut Assembly 1755, 1756, 1758–1761, and 1764–1766; justice of the peace for Litchfield County 1755–1761, and of the quorum 1759–1761; moved to New Haven, Conn., in June 1761; justice of the peace and quorum for New Haven County in 1765 and 1766; served in the State senate 1766–1785; judge of the superior court 1766, 1767, and 1773–1788; member of the council of safety 1777–1779; Member of the Continental Congress 1774–1781, 1783, and 1784; a signer of the

Declaration of Independence and a member of the committee which drafted it; member of the committee to prepare the Articles of Confederation; the only Member of the Continental Congress who signed all four of the great State papers—the Declaration of 1774, the Declaration of Independence, the Articles of Confederation, and the Federal Constitution; mayor of New Haven from 1784 until his death; delegate to the Federal Constitutional Convention at Philadelphia in 1787; elected to the First Congress (March 4, 1789–March 3, 1791); elected to the United States Senate to fill the vacancy caused by the resignation of William S. Johnson and served from June 13, 1791, until his death in New Haven, Conn., July 23, 1793; interment in the Grove Street Cemetery.

SHERMAN, Socrates Norton, a Representative from New York; born in Barre, Washington County, Vt., July 22, 1801; attended the grade schools and high school; studied medicine and was graduated from Mount Castleton Medical College in 1824; moved to Ogdensburg, St. Lawrence County, N. Y., in 1825 and engaged in the practice of medicine; elected as a Republican to the Thirty-seventh Congress (March 4, 1861–March 3, 1863); declined to be a candidate for renomination in 1862; during the Civil War was mustered into the service as major and surgeon of the Thirty-fourth Regiment, New York Volunteer Infantry, and was mustered out October 7, 1865, as brevet lieutenant colonel, United States Volunteers; resumed the practice of medicine at Ogdensburg, N. Y., where he died February 1, 1873; interment in Ogdensburg Cemetery.

SHERRILL, Eliakim, a Representative from New York; born in Greenville, Ulster County, N. Y., February 16, 1813; attended the public schools; tanner and farmer; held several local offices; major in the State militia; elected as a Whig to the Thirtieth Congress (March 4, 1847–March 3, 1849); member of the State senate in 1854; during the Civil War organized the One Hundred and Twenty-sixth New York Volunteer Regiment and became its colonel; was wounded at Harpers Ferry, W. Va., on September 15, 1862, but remained in the service; commanded the Third Brigade, Third Division, Second Army Corps, after Colonel Willard's death on July 2, 1863, at the Battle of Gettysburg, until he was mortally wounded on July 3, 1863, and died the next day; interment in the Washington Street Cemetery, Geneva, Ontario County, N. Y.

SHERROD, William Crawford, a Representative from Alabama; born in Courtland, Lawrence County, Ala., August 17, 1835; attended the common schools, a preparatory school at Edgefield, N. C., and the University of North Carolina at Chapel Hill in 1851 and 1852; returned to Courtland and engaged in planting; member of the State house of representatives in 1859 and 1860; delegate to the Democratic National Convention at Charleston, S. C., in 1860; during the Civil War served as a colonel under Gen. N. B. Forrest in the Confederate Army; elected as a Democrat to the Forty-first Congress (March 4, 1869–March 3, 1871); was not a candidate for renomination in 1870 to the Forty-second Congress; again engaged in planting; member of the State senate in 1875; moved to Wichita Falls, Wichita County, Tex., in 1893, engaged in farming and ranching, and died there on March 24, 1919; interment in Riverside Cemetery.

SHERWIN, John Crocker, a Representative from Illinois; born in Gouverneur, St. Lawrence County, N. Y., February 8, 1838; was educated in the common schools, Gouverneur Wesleyan Seminary in New York, and Lombard College, Galesburg, Ill.; studied law; was admitted to the bar and practiced; county clerk of Kane County, Ill.; served as city attorney of Aurora, Ill.; enlisted in the Union Army during the Civil War in the Eighty-ninth Regiment, Illinois Volunteer Infantry, and served until the close of the war; elected as a Republican to the Forty-sixth and Forty-seventh Congresses (March 4, 1879–March 3, 1883); was not a candidate for renomination in 1882; resumed the practice of law; died at Benton Harbor, Mich., January 1, 1904; interment in Spring Lake Cemetery, Aurora, Ill.

SHERWOOD, Henry, a Representative from Pennsylvania; born in Bridgeport, Conn., October 9, 1813; moved with his parents to Catharine, Chemung County, N. Y., in 1817; attended the common schools; during the Texas war for independence served in the Texas Army under Sam Houston in 1836 and 1837; moved to Tioga County and settled in Wellsboro, Pa., in 1840; studied law; was admitted to the bar in 1847 and practiced his profession in Wellsboro; elected burgess of Wellsboro; elected as a Democrat to the Forty-second Congress (March 4, 1871–March 3, 1873); unsuccessful candidate for reelection in 1872 to the Forty-third Congress; president of the Wellsboro & Lawrenceville Railroad and of the Pennsylvania division of the Pine Creek road; died in Wellsboro, Tioga County, Pa., on November 10, 1896; interment in the Wellsboro Cemetery.

SHERWOOD, Isaac R., a Representative from Ohio; born in Stanford, Dutchess County, N. Y., August 13, 1835; attended the common schools, the Hudson River Institute, Claverack, N. Y., Antioch College, Yellow Springs, Ohio, and the Ohio Law College, Poland, Ohio; editor of the Williams County Gazette, Bryan, Ohio, in 1857; elected probate judge of Williams County in October 1860; resigned at the beginning of the Civil War and enlisted April 22, 1861, as a private in the Fourteenth Regiment, Ohio Volunteer Infantry; commissioned first lieutenant and adjutant of the One Hundred and Eleventh Ohio Volunteer Infantry, September 6, 1862; major, February 13, 1863; lieutenant colonel, February 12, 1864; brevetted brigadier general of Volunteers, February 27, 1865; honorably mustered out June 27, 1865; settled in Toledo, Ohio, and was editor of the Toledo Daily Commercial; political editorial writer on the Cleveland Leader; secretary of state of Ohio in 1868 and 1870; organized and established the Bureau of Statistics of the State of Ohio in 1869; elected as a Republican to the Forty-third Congress (March 4, 1873–March 3, 1875); was not a candidate for renomination in 1874; proprietor and editor of the Toledo Journal 1875–1884; elected probate judge of Lucas County in 1878 and 1881; editor of the Canton News-Democrat 1885–1895; author of several books: elected as a Democrat to the Sixtieth and to the six succeeding Congresses (March 4, 1907–March 3, 1921); unsuccessful candidate for reelection in 1920 to the Sixty-seventh Congress; again elected to the Sixty-eighth Congress (March 4, 1923–March 3, 1925); unsuccessful candidate for reelection in 1924 to the Sixty-ninth Congress; retired from public life and returned to Toledo, Ohio, where he died October 15, 1925; interment in Woodlawn Cemetery.

SHERWOOD, Samuel, a Representative from New York; born in Kingsbury, Washington County, N. Y., April 24, 1779; completed preparatory studies; began the study of law at the age of fifteen in Kingston, Ulster County, and in 1798 moved to Delhi, Delaware County, N. Y., where he continued his legal studies; was admitted to the bar in 1800 and practiced in Delhi, N. Y.; elected as a Federalist to the Thirteenth Congress (March 4, 1813–March 3, 1815); was not a candidate for renomination to the Fourteenth Congress; resumed the practice of his profession in Delhi and in New York City, N. Y., where he moved in 1830; retired from active practice in 1858; died in New York City on October 31, 1862; interment in Woodlawn Cemetery, Delhi, N. Y.

SHERWOOD, Samuel Burr, a Representative from Connecticut; born in Northfield Society (later Weston), Conn., November 26, 1767; graduated from Yale College in 1786; studied law; was admitted to the bar and began practice in that part of Fairfield which is now Westport, Conn.; member of the State house of representatives 1809–1815; served in the State senate in 1816; elected as a Federalist to the Fifteenth Congress (March 4, 1817–March 3, 1819); resumed the practice of his profession until 1831, when he retired from professional life; died in Westport, Fairfield County, Conn., on April 27, 1833; interment in Evergreen Cemetery.

SHIEL, George Knox, a Representative from Oregon; born in Ireland in 1825; immigrated to the United States and settled in New Orleans, La.; moved to Ohio; studied law; was admitted to the bar and practiced; moved to Oregon in 1854 and practiced law in Salem; successfully contested as a Democrat the election of Andrew J. Thayer to the Thirty-seventh Congress and served from July 30, 1861, to March 3, 1863; was not a candidate for renomination in 1862; was barred from practicing law, as he would not take the oath of allegiance, and lived in retirement until he was accidentally killed in Salem, Marion County, Oreg., December 12, 1893; interment in the Odd Fellows Cemetery.

SHIELDS, Benjamin Glover, a Representative from Alabama; born in Abbeville, S. C., in 1808; moved with his father to Clarke County, Ala.; resided in Demopolis, Marengo County, Ala.; completed preparatory studies; member of the State house of representatives in 1834; elected as a Whig to the Twenty-seventh Congress (March 4, 1841–March 3, 1843); commissioned in 1845 by President Polk United States Chargé d'Affaires to Venezuela, where he remained until January 7, 1850; moved to Texas and engaged in planting until his death.

SHIELDS, Ebenezer J., a Representative from Tennessee; born in Georgia, December 22, 1778; moved to Tennessee in 1809 and settled on Robertson Fork Creek near Lynnville, Giles County; completed preparatory studies; was graduated from the University of Nashville, Tennessee, in 1827; studied law; was admitted to the bar and commenced practice in Pulaski, Tenn.; member of the State house of representatives 1833–1835; elected as a Whig to the Twenty-fourth and Twenty-fifth Congresses (March 4, 1835–March 3, 1839); unsuccessful candidate for reelection in 1838 to the Twenty-sixth Congress; resumed the practice of law in Pulaski, Tenn.; moved to Memphis, Tenn., in 1844 and continued the practice of his profession; died near La Grange, Fayette County, Tex., April 21, 1846.

SHIELDS, James, a Representative from Ohio; born in Banbridge, County Down, Ireland, April 13, 1762; received a good common-school education; entered the University of Glasgow, Scotland, in 1782 and was graduated in 1786; attended medical college for two years; immigrated to the United States in July 1791 and settled in Frederick County, Va., where he taught school; moved to Butler County, Ohio, in 1801; returned to Virginia and became a citizen of the United States in 1804; returned to Ohio in 1807; member of the State house of representatives 1806–1827; presidential elector on the Democratic ticket of Jackson and Calhoun in 1828; elected as a Jackson Democrat to the Twenty-first Congress (March 4, 1829–March 3, 1831); was killed through the accidental overturning of a stagecoach near Venice, Butler County, Ohio, August 13, 1831; interment in Venice Cemetery, Venice, Ohio.

SHIELDS, James (nephew of the preceding), a Senator from Illinois, Minnesota, and Missouri; born in Altmore, County Tyrone. Ireland, May 10, 1810; attended a hedge school, private schools, and pursued classical studies; immigrated to the United States in 1823; studied law; was admitted to the bar in 1832 and commenced practice in Kaskaskia, Randolph County, Ill.; member of the State house of representatives in 1836; auditor of the State in 1839; judge of the supreme court of Illinois in 1843; Commissioner of the General Land Office 1845–1847; during the Mexican War was commissioned brigadier general of Volunteers July 1, 1846; brevetted major general April 18, 1847, "for gallant and meritorious conduct at the Battle of Cerro Gordo, Mexico"; honorably discharged July 24, 1848; appointed Governor of Oregon Territory by President Polk; resigned in 1849; elected as a Democrat to the United States Senate from Illinois for the term commencing March 4, 1849; upon his appearance to take his seat on March 5, 1849, a resolution was presented raising the question of his eligibility; took his seat on March 6, 1849, but on March 15, 1849, the Senate declared his election void on the ground that he had not been a citizen of the United States the number of years required by the Constitution; again elected for the same term and served from October 27, 1849, to March 3, 1855; unsuccessful candidate for reelection; moved to Minnesota in 1855; upon the admission of Minnesota as a State into the Union was elected to the United States Senate and served from May 11, 1858, to March 3, 1859; unsuccessful candidate for reelection; moved to California; during the Civil War served in the Union Army as brigadier general of Volunteers from August 19, 1861, to March 28, 1863, when he resigned and returned to California; moved to Carrollton, Mo., and resumed the practice of law; member of the State house of representatives in 1874 and 1879; appointed adjutant general of Missouri in 1877; served as railroad commissioner; elected to the United States Senate from Missouri on January 22, 1879, to fill the vacancy caused by the death of Lewis V. Bogy and served from January 27, 1879, to March 3, 1879; declined to be a candidate for renomination; died in Ottumwa, Wapello County, Iowa, June 1, 1879; interment in St. Mary's Cemetery, Carrollton, Carroll County, Mo.

SHIELDS, John Knight, a Senator from Tennessee; born at "Clinchdale," near Bean's Station, Grainger County, Tenn., August 15, 1858; was educated by private tutors; studied law; was admitted to the bar in 1879 and practiced in Grainger and adjoining counties until 1893; chancellor of the twelfth chancery division in 1893 and 1894; resumed the practice of law in Morristown, Hamblen County, Tenn., 1894–1902; delegate to the Democratic National Convention at Chicago in 1896 which nominated Bryan and Sewall and at St. Louis in 1904 which nominated Parker and Davis; elected associate justice of the supreme court of Tennessee and served from 1902 to 1910; reelected in 1910 and appointed chief justice, which office he held until 1913, when he resigned, having been nominated as a candidate for Senator; elected as a Democrat to the United States Senate in 1913; reelected in 1918 and served from March 4, 1913, to March 3, 1925; unsuccessful candidate for renomination in 1924; resumed the practice of law in Knoxville, Tenn.; died at his country estate, "Clinchdale," near Knoxville, September 30, 1934; interment in Memorial Cemetery, Knoxville, Tenn.

SHINN, William Norton, a Representative from New Jersey; born in Burlington County, N. J., October 24, 1782; attended the public schools; engaged in agricultural pursuits; sheriff of Burlington County 1825–1828; member of the State general assembly in 1828; served in the State council 1829–1831; chairman of the Democratic State central committee in 1832; elected as a Jackson Democrat to the Twenty-third and Twenty-fourth Congresses (March 4, 1833–March 3, 1837); resumed agricultural pursuits; president of the Burlington Agricultural Association in

1853 and 1854; elected a director of the Camden & Amboy Railroad Co.; died in Mount Holly, Burlington County, N. J., on August 18, 1871; interment in Mount Holly Cemetery.

SHIPHERD, Zebulon Rudd, a Representative from New York; born in Granville, Washington County, N. Y., November 15, 1768; completed preparatory studies; studied law; was admitted to the bar and commenced the practice of his profession in Granville, N. Y., was elected as a Federalist to the Thirteenth Congress (March 4, 1813–March 3, 1815); resumed the practice of his profession in Granville; trustee of Middlebury College, Middlebury, Vt., 1819–1841; moved to Moriah, Essex County, about 1830, where he died November 1, 1841; interment in the Moriah Corners Cemetery.

SHIPLEY, George Edward, a Representative from Illinois; born in Richland County, near Olney, Ill., April 21, 1927; attended the East Richland High School, Olney, Ill., and graduated from Olney (Ill.) High School in 1950; during World War II served as a private in the United States Marine Corps from December 1944 until discharged in May 1947, with service in the South Pacific; chief deputy sheriff of Richland County, Ill., 1950–1954 and sheriff 1954–1958; owner of a restaurant in Olney, Ill.; elected as a Democrat to the Eighty-sixth Congress (January 3, 1959–January 3, 1961). *Reelected to the Eighty-seventh Congress.*

SHIPPEN, William, a Delegate from Pennsylvania; born in Philadelphia, Pa., October 1, 1712; pursued preparatory studies; studied medicine and practiced his profession in Philadelphia; was one of the founders of the Public Academy and a trustee in 1749; was one of the twenty-four founders of the College of Philadelphia, which afterward became the University of Pennsylvania, and a trusteee 1749–1779; one of the founders of the College of New Jersey (now Princeton University) and a trustee from 1765 to 1796; was a member of the American Philosophical Society, of which he was vice president in 1768 and for many years thereafter; Member of the Continental Congress 1778–1780; resumed the practice of medicine in Philadelphia; died in Germantown, Pa., November 4, 1801; interment in the First Presbyterian Church Cemetery, Philadelphia, Pa.

SHIPSTEAD, Henrik, a Senator from Minnesota; born in Burbank, Kandiyohi County, Minn., January 8, 1881; attended the public schools at New London, Minn., and the State normal school at St. Cloud, Minn.; was graduated from the dental department of Northwestern University, Chicago, Ill., in 1903 and practiced dentistry in Glenwood, Minn., 1904–1920; served as a member of the charter commission of Glenwood in 1911 and 1912; mayor of Glenwood 1911–1913; member of the State house of representatives in 1917; moved to Minneapolis in 1920 and resumed the practice of dentistry; elected on the Farmer-Labor ticket in 1922 to the United States Senate; reelected in 1928, 1934, and as a Republican in 1940 and served from March 4, 1923, to January 3, 1947; unsuccessful candidate for renomination in 1946; member of the Minnesota Academy of Science; retired; died in Alexandria, Minn., June 26, 1960; interment in Kinkead Cemetery.

SHIRAS, George, 3d, a Representative from Pennsylvania; born in Allegheny, Pa., January 1, 1859; attended the public schools and Phillips Academy, Andover, Mass.; was graduated from Cornell University, Ithaca, N. Y., in 1881 and from the law department of Yale College in 1883; was admitted to the Connecticut and Pennsylvania bars in 1883 and commenced the practice of his profession in Pittsburgh, Pa.; member of the State house of representatives in 1889 and 1890; unsuccessful candidate

for the Republican nomination for Congress in 1890; elected as an Independent Republican with Democratic endorsement to the Fifty-eighth Congress (March 4, 1903–March 3, 1905); did not seek renomination in 1904 to the Fifty-ninth Congress; after retirement from Congress resided in Washington, D. C., Ormond Beach, Fla., and Marquette, Mich.; naturalist; engaged in biological research and wildlife photography; died in Marquette, Mich., March 24, 1942; interment in Park Cemetery.

SHIVELY, Benjamin Franklin, a Representative and a Senator from Indiana; born near Osceola, St. Joseph County, Ind., March 20, 1857; attended the common schools and the Northern Indiana Normal School at Valparaiso, Ind.; taught school 1874–1880; engaged in journalism 1880–1884; secretary of the National Anti-Monopoly Association in 1883; president of the board of Indiana University in 1884; elected as a National Anti-Monopolist to the Forty-eighth Congress to fill the vacancy caused by the resignation of William H. Calkins and served from December 1, 1884, to March 3, 1885; was graduated from the law department of the University of Michigan at Ann Arbor in 1886; was admitted to the bar and commenced practice in South Bend, Ind.; elected as a Democrat to the Fiftieth, Fifty-first, and Fifty-second Congresses (March 4, 1887–March 3, 1893); was not a candidate for renomination in 1892; resumed the practice of law in South Bend, Ind.; unsuccessful Democratic candidate for Governor of Indiana in 1896; unsuccessful candidate for election in 1906 to the Sixtieth Congress; elected to the United States Senate in 1909; reelected in 1914 and served from March 4, 1909, until his death in Washington, D. C., March 14, 1916; interment in the Brookville Cemetery, Brookville, Pa.

SHOBER, Francis Edwin (father of Francis Emanuel Shober), a Representative from North Carolina; born in Salem (now Winston-Salem), N. C., March 12, 1831; attended the common schools and the Moravian School, Bethlehem, Pa.; was graduated from the University of North Carolina at Chapel Hill in 1851; studied law; was admitted to the bar in 1853 and commenced practice in Salisbury, N. C., in 1854; member of the State house of commons in 1862 and 1864; served in the State senate in 1865; elected as a Democrat to the Forty-first and Forty-second Congresses (March 4, 1869–March 3, 1873); was not a candidate for renomination in 1872; delegate to the State constitutional convention in 1875; county judge of Rowan County in 1877 and 1878; appointed Chief Clerk of the United States Senate in the Forty-fifth Congress; upon the death of Secretary John C. Burch in the Forty-seventh Congress was appointed Acting Secretary of the Senate and served from October 24, 1881, to March 3, 1883; delegate to the Democratic National Conventions in 1880 and 1884; again a member of the State senate in 1887; resumed the practice of his profession; died in Salisbury, Rowan County, N. C., May 29, 1896; interment in Oakdale Cemetery.

SHOBER, Francis Emanuel (son of Francis Edwin Shober), a Representative from New York; born in Salisbury, N. C., October 24, 1860; studied under private tutors; was graduated from St. Stephen's College, Annandale, N. Y., in 1880; engaged in ministerial and educational work in Dutchess County, N. Y.; reporter on the News-Press of Poughkeepsie; pastor of St. John's Episcopal Church at Barrytown, N. Y., 1880–1891; editor of the Rockaway Journal at Far Rockaway, N. Y.; member of the editorial staff of the New York World; elected as a Democrat to the Fifty-eighth Congress (March 4, 1903–March 3, 1905); unsuccessful candidate for renomination in 1904; deputy tax appraiser of the State of New York in 1907 and 1908; resumed newspaper work; editor of the New York American until his death in New York City October 7, 1919; interment in Worcester Cemetery, Danbury, Fairfield County, Conn.

SHOEMAKER, Francis Henry, a Representative from Minnesota; born on a farm in Flora Township, Renville County, Minn., April 25, 1889; self-educated with mother's assistance; engaged in agricultural pursuits and as editor, writer, traveler, lecturer, and organizer and investigator for many farm and labor organizations; charter member and organizer of the Minnesota Farmer-Labor Party; assisted in organizing the Federated Farmer-Labor Party at Chicago in 1924; was nominated for Vice President of the United States, but declined; editor and publisher of the People's Voice, Green Bay, Wis., 1921–1927, and of the Organized Farmer, Red Wing, Minn., in 1928; elected as a Farmer-Laborite to the Seventy-third Congress (March 4, 1933–January 3, 1935); was not a candidate for renomination in 1934 to the Seventy-fourth Congress but was an unsuccessful candidate for nomination for United States Senator; then became an unsuccessful Independent candidate for reelection to the Seventy-fourth Congress; unsuccessful for election in 1942 to the Seventy-eighth Congress; resumed agricultural pursuits near North Redwood, Minn.; died in Minneapolis, Minn., July 24, 1958; interment in Zion Cemetery, Flora Township, Renville County, Minn

SHOEMAKER, Lazarus Denison, a Representative from Pennsylvania; born in Kingston, Luzerne County, Pa., November 5, 1819; attended Nazareth Hall, Nazareth, Pa., and Kenyon College, Gambier, Ohio; was graduated from Yale College in 1840; studied law; was admitted to the bar in 1842 and commenced practice in Wilkes-Barre, Pa.; member of the State senate 1866–1870; elected as a Republican to the Forty-second and Forty-third Congresses (March 4, 1871–March 3, 1875); was not a candidate for renomination in 1874; resumed the practice of his profession; also engaged in banking; died in Wilkes-Barre, Pa., September 9, 1893; interment in Forty Fort Cemetery, Forty Fort, Luzerne County, Pa.

SHONK, George Washington, a Representative from Pennsylvania; born in Plymouth, Luzerne County, Pa., April 26, 1850; attended the public schools and Wyoming Seminary, Kingston, Pa.; was graduated from Wesleyan University, Middletown, Conn., in 1873; studied law; was admitted to the bar of Luzerne County, Pa., September 29, 1876, and commenced the practice of law in Wilkes-Barre; elected as a Republican to the Fifty-second Congress (March 4, 1891–March 3, 1893); declined to be a candidate for renomination in 1892; again resumed the practice of his profession in Wilkes-Barre; was also interested in coal mining in Pennsylvania; died in Washington, D. C., while en route to Richmond, Va., on a business trip, August 14, 1900; interment in Shawnee Cemetery, Plymouth, Pa.

SHORT, Dewey, a Representative from Missouri; born in Galena, Stone County, Mo., April 7, 1898; attended the public school, Galena High School, and Marionville (Mo.) College; during the First World War served in the Infantry; was graduated from Baker University, Baldwin City, Kans., in 1919 and from Boston (Mass.) University in 1922; attended Harvard University, Cambridge, Mass.; Heidelberg University and the University of Berlin, Germany; Oxford University, Oxford, England; professor of ethics, psychology, and political philosophy at Southwestern College, Winfield, Kans., in 1923, 1924, and 1926–1928; pastor of the Grace Methodist Episcopal Church, Springfield, Mo., in 1927; elected as a Republican to the Seventy-first Congress (March 4, 1929–March 3, 1931); unsuccessful candidate for reelection in 1930 to the Seventy-second Congress; resumed his former professional pursuits; delegate to the Republican National Convention in 1932; again elected to the Seventy-fourth and to the ten succeeding Congresses (January 3, 1935–January 3, 1957); unsuccessful candidate for reelection in 1956 to the Eighty-fifth Congress; received one hundred and

eight votes for Vice Presidential nomination at the Republican National Convention in 1940; delegate to the Inter-parliamentary Union at Oslo, Norway, in 1939 and at Cairo, Egypt, in 1947; congressional delegate to inspect atrocity camps in Germany in 1945; alternate delegate to signing of United States-Japanese Security Pact in 1951; Assistant Secretary of the Army from March 15, 1957, to January 20, 1961; is a resident of Washington, D. C., and Galena, Mo.

SHORT, Don Levingston, a Representative from North Dakota; born in La Mars, Plymouth County, Iowa, June 22, 1903; moved with parents to a ranch in Billings County, near Medora, N. Dak., in February 1904; attended Medora grade and high schools and St. James School, Faribault, Minn.; agricultural short course at Montana State College at Bozeman in 1918 and 1919; graduated from Pillsbury Military Academy, Owatonna, Minn., in 1921; student at the University of Minnesota 1922–1926; farmer and rancher; county supervisor, Farm Security Administration, in 1937 and 1938; president of Medora Grazing Association in 1938 and 1939; president of North Dakota Stockmen's Association 1943–1945; director, Mandan (N. Dak.) Production Credit Association 1945–1958; member, North Dakota Livestock Sanitary Board, 1946–1956; vice president, American National Cattlemen's Association, in 1954 and 1955; president, National Beef Council, in 1956 and 1957; chairman, North Dakota Beef Council, 1956–1958; State representative from the thirty-ninth district in 1957 session of North Dakota State Legislature assembly; member of the Theodore Roosevelt State Centennial Commission in 1958; elected as a Republican to the Eighty-sixth Congress (January 3, 1959–January 3, 1961). *Reelected to the Eighty-seventh Congress.*

SHORTER, Eli Sims, a Representative from Alabama; born in Monticello, Jasper County, Ga., March 15, 1823; attended the common schools and was graduated in law from Yale College in 1844; was admitted to the bar and commenced practice in Eufaula, Ala., in 1844; also engaged in agricultural pursuits; elected as a Democrat to the Thirty-fourth and Thirty-fifth Congresses (March 4, 1855–March 3, 1859); resumed the practice of law in Eufaula, Ala.; during the Civil War served in the Confederate Army as colonel of the Eighteenth Regiment, Alabama Volunteer Infantry; died in Eufaula, Ala., April 29, 1879; interment in Fairview Cemetery.

SHORTRIDGE, Samuel Morgan, a Senator from California; born in Mount Pleasant, Henry County, Iowa, August 3, 1861; moved to California with his parents, who settled in San Jose in 1875; attended the public schools and the Hastings College of Law at San Francisco, Calif.; was admitted to the bar in 1884 and commenced the practice of his profession in San Francisco, Calif.; presidential elector on the Republican ticket in 1888, 1900, and again in 1908; elected as a Republican to the United States Senate in 1920; reelected in 1926 and served from March 4, 1921, to March 3, 1933; unsuccessful candidate for renomination in 1932; resumed the practice of law; special attorney, Justice Department, Washington, D. C., from October 13, 1939, to October 30, 1943; died in Atherton, Calif., January 15, 1952; interment in Oak Hill Cemetery, San Jose, Calif.

SHOTT, Hugh Ike, a Representative and a Senator from West Virginia; born in Staunton, Augusta County, Va., September 3, 1866; attended the Staunton public schools; apprenticed as a printer; later became a reporter and editorial writer; moved to Bluefield, W. Va., in 1893; served as a clerk in the railway mail service in 1895; became publisher and editor of the Bluefield Daily Telegraph in 1896; served as postmaster of Bluefield from January 1903 to July 1912; member of the West Virginia Semicentennial Commission in 1912 and 1913; elected as a Republican to the Seventy-first and Seventy-second Congresses (March 4, 1929–March 3, 1933); was an unsuccessful candidate for reelection in 1932 to the Seventy-third Congress; was an unsuccessful candidate for election to the United States Senate in 1936; elected to the United States Senate to fill the vacancy caused by the resignation of Matthew M. Neely and served from November 18, 1942, to January 3, 1943; was not a candidate for the full term; continued as editor and publisher of the Bluefield Daily Telegraph until his death in Bluefield, W. Va., October 12, 1953; interment in Monte Vista Cemetery.

SHOUP, George Laird, a Senator from Idaho; born in Kittanning, Armstrong County, Pa., June 15, 1836; attended the public schools of Freeport and Slate Lick; moved with his father to Illinois in June 1852; engaged in agricultural pursuits and stock raising near Galesburg, Ill., until 1858; moved to Colorado in 1859; engaged in mining and mercantile pursuits until 1861; during the Civil War enlisted in Captain Backus' independent company of scouts in September 1861 and soon thereafter was commissioned a second lieutenant; was ordered to Fort Union, N. Mex., in 1862; continued scouting duty on the Canadian, Pecos, and Red Rivers until 1863; during this time was promoted to first lieutenant; ordered to the Arkansas River; had been assigned in 1862 to the Second Regiment, Colorado Volunteer Infantry, but retained on duty in the Cavalry service; assigned to the First Regiment, Colorado Volunteer Cavalry, in May 1863; member of the convention to prepare a constitution for the proposed State of Colorado in 1864; returned to active duty in the Army; commissioned colonel of the Third Regiment, Colorado Volunteer Cavalry, in September 1864 and mustered out in Denver; engaged in mercantile pursuits in Virginia City, Mont., in 1866 and later in Salmon City, Idaho; county treasurer in 1868; county commissioner in 1868 and 1869; superintendent of schools of Lemhi County in 1871; member of the Territorial house of representative in 1874; a member of the Territorial council in 1878; delegate to the Republican National Convention at Chicago in 1880; member of the Republican National Committee 1880–1884 and 1888–1892; United States commissioner for Idaho at the World's Cotton Centennial Exposition in New Orleans, La., in 1884 and 1885; Governor of Idaho Territory in 1889 and 1890; upon the admission of Idaho as a State into the Union was elected its first Governor, October 1, 1890, but resigned in December of that year, having been elected Senator; elected as a Republican to the United States Senate in 1890; reelected in 1895 and served from December 18, 1890, to March 3, 1901; was the caucus nominee of his party, who were in the minority, for reelection; died in Boise, Idaho, December 21, 1904; interment in the Masonic Cemetery.

SHOUSE, Jouett, a Representative from Kansas; born in Midway, Woodford County, Ky., December 10, 1879; moved with his parents to Mexico, Mo., in 1892; attended the public schools and the University of Missouri at Columbia; moved to Lexington, Ky., in 1898 and engaged in newspaper work until 1911; moved to Kinsley, Kans., in 1911 and engaged in agricultural pursuits and livestock raising; vice president and treasurer of the Mexican lines of the Kansas, Mexico & Orient Railroad; director of the Kinsley Bank; member of the State senate 1913–1915; elected as a Democrat to the Sixty-fourth and Sixty-fifth Congresses (March 4, 1915–March 3, 1919); unsuccessful candidate for reelection; Assistant Secretary of the Treasury from March 5, 1919, to November 15, 1920; delegate to the Democratic National Conventions in 1920, 1924, and 1932; engaged in the practice of law in Kansas City, Mo., and Washington, D. ·C.; resides in Washington, D. C.

SHOWALTER, Joseph Baltzell, a Representative from Pennsylvania; born near Smithfield, Fayette County, Pa., February 11, 1851; attended the public schools and Georges Creek Academy at Smithfield; taught school in West Virginia, Indiana, and Illinois 1867–1873; moved to Chicora, Pa., in 1873 and engaged in the production of petroleum and natural gas; studied medicine at Long Island College Hospital, Brooklyn, N. Y., in 1883; was graduated from the College of Physicians and Surgeons, Baltimore, Md., in 1884; practiced medicine in Chicora, Pa., from 1884 to 1890, when he again engaged in the production of petroleum and natural gas; member of the State house of representatives in 1887 and 1888; served in the State senate 1889–1892; elected as a Republican to the Fifty-fifth Congress to fill the vacancy caused by the death of James J. Davidson; reelected to the Fifty-sixth and Fifty-seventh Congresses and served from April 20, 1897, to March 3, 1903; was not a candidate for reelection; resumed his former business pursuits and resided in Butler, Pa.; moved to Pittsburgh, Pa., and then to Washington, D. C.; also engaged in the development of land in southern Florida; died in Washington, D. C., December 3, 1932; interment in North Cemetery, Butler, Pa.

SHOWER, Jacob, a Representative from Maryland; born in Manchester, Baltimore County, Md., February 22, 1803; was a drummer boy in the War of 1812; attended private schools at Emmitsburg, Md., and was graduated from the medical department of the University of Maryland at Baltimore in 1825; commenced the practice of his profession in Carroll County, Md.; charter member of the first Andrew Jackson Club in the State in 1824; Democratic member of the State house of delegates 1834–1840; clerk of the circuit court of Carroll County 1842–1850; delegate to the State constitutional convention in 1851; elected as an Independent to the Thirty-third Congress (March 4, 1853–March 3, 1855); resumed medical practice; died in Manchester, Md., May 25, 1879.

SHREVE, Milton William, a Representative from Pennsylvania; born in Chapmanville, Venango County, Pa., May 3, 1858; attended the Edinboro State Normal School and Allegheny College, Meadville, Pa.; was graduated from Bucknell University, Lewisburg, Pa., in 1884; studied law; was admitted to the bar in Erie County and commenced practice in Erie, Pa.; district attorney of Erie County 1899–1902; member of the State house of representatives 1907–1912 and in the session of 1911 succeeded to the speakership; appointed a member of Perry's Victory Centennial Commission; elected as a Republican to the Sixty-third Congress (March 4, 1913–March 3, 1915); unsuccessful candidate for reelection in 1914 to the Sixty-fourth Congress; resumed the practice of law in Erie; also engaged in banking and interested in several manufacturing plants; member of the appeals draft board during the First World War; again elected to the Sixty-sixth and to the six succeeding Congresses (March 4, 1919–March 3, 1933); unsuccessful candidate for reelection in 1932 to the Seventy-third Congress; resumed the practice of law in Erie, Pa., until his death there on December 23, 1939; interment in Erie Cemetery.

SHUFORD, Alonzo Craig, a Representative from North Carolina; born on a farm near Newton, Catawba County, N. C., March 1, 1858; attended the common schools and Newton College; engaged in agricultural pursuits; joined the Farmers Alliance in 1889; made county lecturer and later district lecturer; delegate to the labor conference at St. Louis, Mo., in February 1892; also a delegate to the Populist convention at Omaha, Nebr., in July 1892; elected vice president of the State Alliance in 1894; elected as a Populist to the Fifty-fourth and Fifty-fifth Congresses (March 4, 1895–March 3, 1899); unsuccessful candidate for renomination in 1898; resumed agricultural pursuits near Newton, N. C.; presidential elector on the Progressive ticket of La Follette and Wheeler in 1924; retired from active business pursuits in 1928 and moved to Chapel Hill, N. C., where he died on February 8, 1933; interment in Chapel Hill Cemetery.

SHUFORD, George Adams, a Representative from North Carolina; born in Asheville, Buncombe County, N. C., September 5, 1895; attended the public schools and the University of North Carolina 1913–1915; graduated from the University of Georgia at Athens in 1917; was admitted to the Georgia bar in 1917; during the First World War entered the first officers training camp at Fort McPherson, Ga., in May 1917; was commissioned a second lieutenant in August 1917 and assigned to the One Hundred and Nineteenth Infantry Regiment of the Thirtieth Combat Division; commissioned a first lieutenant in January 1918 and served in the United States and France; was discharged at Camp Jackson, S. C., April 28, 1919; was admitted to the North Carolina bar in August 1920 and commenced practice in Asheville, N. C.; chairman of Buncombe County board of elections 1940–1942; served in the State house of representatives 1945–1947; State superior court judge 1947–1949; elected as a Democrat to the Eighty-third, Eighty-fourth, and Eighty-fifth Congresses (January 3, 1953–January 3, 1959); had been renominated for the Eighty-sixth Congress but later withdrew because of ill health; resumed the practice of law; resides in Asheville, N. C.

SHULL, Joseph Horace, a Representative from Pennsylvania; born at Martins Creek, Northampton County, Pa., August 17, 1848; attended the public schools and Blair Hall, Blairstown, N. J.; took a special course at Lafayette College, Easton, Pa.; was graduated from the University of New York and in 1873 from the Bellevue Hospital Medical College, both in New York City; taught in the public schools of Pennsylvania for four years; studied law; was admitted to the bar in 1879 and commenced practice in Stroudsburg, Monroe County, Pa.; editor of the Monroe Democrat 1881–1886; member of the State Senate 1886–1891; elected as a Democrat to the Fifty-eighth Congress (March 4, 1903–March 3, 1905); unsuccessful candidate for renomination in 1904; resumed the practice of law and medicine; was a contract surgeon during the First World War; died in Stroudsburg, Pa., August 9, 1944; interment in Stroudsburg Cemetery.

SHULTZ, Emanuel, a Representative from Ohio; born in Stouchsburg, Berks County, Pa., July 25, 1819; attended the public schools; apprenticed to the trade of shoemaker; moved to Miamisburg, Montgomery County, Ohio, in 1838; engaged in mercantile pursuits, banking, and the manufacture of paper; member of the State constitutional convention in 1873; member of the State house of representatives 1875–1877; elected as a Republican to the Forty-seventh Congress (March 4, 1881–March 3, 1883); unsuccessful candidate for renomination in 1882; again engaged in paper making; appointed postmaster of Miamisburg and served from August 2, 1889, to January 17, 1894; died in Miamisburg, Ohio, November 5, 1912; interment in Hill Grove Cemetery.

SIBLEY, Henry Hastings (son of Solomon Sibley), a Delegate from the Territories of Wisconsin and Minnesota; born in Detroit, Mich., February 20, 1811; attended the Detroit Academy and also studied under private tutors; studied law; moved to Sault Ste. Marie in 1828 and engaged in mercantile pursuits until 1829, when he moved to Mackinac and entered the service of the American Fur Co.; justice of the peace in 1831; moved to the mouth of the Minnesota River in 1834 and engaged in fur trading; in 1835 built the first stone house at Mendota (now in the State of Minnesota), which house is at present in the custody of the Daughters of the American Revolution; elected as a Delegate from the Territory of Wisconsin to the Thirtieth Congress to fill the vacancy caused by the disqualification of John H. Tweedy and served from October 30, 1848, to March 3, 1849; upon the formation of the Territory of Minnesota was elected as a Delegate to the Thirty-first and Thirty-second Congresses and served from July 7, 1849, to March 3, 1853; declined to be a candidate for renomination; member of the Territorial Legislature of Minnesota in 1855; member of the constitutional convention of Minnesota in 1857, and served as president; Governor of Minnesota 1858–1860; regent of the State university 1860–1869 and president of the board of regents 1876–1891; during the Civil War served in the Union Army as brigadier general of Volunteers from September 29, 1862, to March 4, 1863, and from March 20, 1863, to November 29, 1865, when he was brevetted major general of Volunteers "for efficient and meritorious services"; honorably mustered out April 30, 1866; moved to St. Paul, Minn.; interested in banking, railroads, and other public corporations; president of the St. Paul Gas Co. in 1866; president of the Minnesota Historical Society 1879–1891; unsuccessful candidate for election to the Forty-seventh Congress; appointed by President Arthur in 1883 as president of the commission to settle damage claims of the Ojibway Indians resulting from the construction of national reservoirs; died in St. Paul, Minn., February 18, 1891; interment in Oakland Cemetery.

SIBLEY, Jonas, a Representative from Massachusetts; born in Sutton, Mass., on March 7, 1762; completed preparatory studies; selectman 1801–1803 and again in 1819; town moderator 1802–1827; town treasurer 1806–1816; member of the State house of representatives 1806–1822 and 1827–1829; member of the State senate in 1826; presidential elector on the Democratic ticket of Monroe and Tompkins in 1820; delegate to the State constitutional convention in 1820; elected as a Democrat to the Eighteenth Congress (March 4, 1823–March 3, 1825); unsuccessful candidate for reelection; engaged in agricultural pursuits; died in Sutton, Worcester County, Mass., February 5, 1834; interment in Center Cemetery.

SIBLEY, Joseph Crocker, a Representative from Pennsylvania; born in Friendship, Allegany County, N. Y., February 18, 1850; in 1859 moved with his parents to Boston, N. Y.; attended the county schools and the local academies at Springville and Friendship; taught school and studied medicine; engaged in the oil-refining business in Franklin, Pa., and also in manufacturing and agricultural pursuits; mayor of Franklin, Pa., in 1879; nominated by the Democrats, People's Party, and Prohibitionists of the Twenty-sixth District (though he was a resident of the Twenty-seventh) as their candidate for the Fifty-third Congress; was elected to the Fifty-third Congress (March 4, 1893–March 3, 1895); unsuccessful candidate of the Democratic and Populist Parties for reelection in 1894 to the Fifty-fourth Congress and for election in 1896 to the Fifty-fifth Congress; elected as a Democrat to the Fifty-sixth Congress (March 4, 1899–March 3, 1901); elected as a Republican to the Fifty-seventh, Fifty-eighth, and Fifty-ninth Congresses (March 4, 1901–March 3, 1907); declined renomination in 1906; was nominated for Congress in 1910, but declined to make the campaign because of ill health; chairman of the Republican State convention in 1902; resumed his former manufacturing and agricultural pursuits; died at his home, "River Ridge Farm," near Franklin, Pa., May 19, 1926; interment in Franklin Cemetery.

SIBLEY, Mark Hopkins, a Representative from New York; born in Great Barrington, Mass., in 1796; completed preparatory studies; studied law; was admitted to the bar and commenced practice in Canandaigua, N. Y., in 1814; member of the State assembly in 1834 and 1835; elected as a Whig to the Twenty-fifth Congress (March 4, 1837–March 3, 1839); member of the State senate in 1841; judge of Ontario County 1847–1851; resumed the practice of his profession; died in Canandaigua, Ontario County, N. Y., September 8, 1852; interment in West Avenue Cemetery.

SIBLEY, Solomon (father of Henry Hastings Sibley), a Delegate from the Territory of Michigan; born in Sutton, Mass., October 7, 1769; completed preparatory studies, and in 1794 was graduated from the College of Rhode Island at Providence; studied law; was admitted to the bar in 1795 and commenced practice in Marietta, Ohio; moved to Detroit, Mich., in 1797 and continued the practice of law; was a member of the Territorial legislature of Northwest Territory in 1799; mayor of Detroit, Mich., in 1806; president of the board of trustees of Detroit in 1815; auditor of Michigan Territory 1814–1817; United States attorney, Michigan Territory, by appointment of President Madison 1815–1823; elected to the Sixteenth Congress to fill the vacancy caused by the resignation of William W. Woodbridge; reelected to the Seventeenth Congress and served from November 20, 1820, to March 3, 1823; was not a candidate for reelection in 1822; judge of the supreme court of Michigan Territory 1824–1837; resumed the practice of law; died in Detroit, Mich., April 4, 1846; interment in Elmwood Cemetery.

SICKLES, Daniel Edgar, a Representative from New York; born in New York City October 20, 1825; attended New York University; apprenticed as a printer; studied law; was admitted to the bar in 1846 and commenced practice in New York City; member of the State assembly in 1847; major of the Twelfth Regiment, New York National Guard, in 1852; corporation attorney in 1853; secretary of the legation at London by appointment of President Franklin Pierce 1853–1855; member of the State senate in 1856 and 1857; elected as a Democrat to the Thirty-fifth and Thirty-sixth Congresses (March 4, 1857–March 3, 1861); was not a candidate for renomination in 1860; served in the Civil War; colonel of the Seventeenth Regiment, New York Volunteer Infantry, June 20, 1861; brigadier general of Volunteers September 3, 1861; major general of Volunteers November 29, 1862; colonel of the Forty-second United States Infantry July 28, 1866; honorably mustered out January 1, 1868; retired with rank of major general April 14, 1869; brevetted brigadier general March 2, 1867, "for gallant and meritorious services in the Battle of Fredericksburg, Va.," and major general March 2, 1867, "for gallant and meritorious services in the Battle of Gettysburg, Pa."; awarded the Medal of Honor October 30, 1897, "for most distinguished gallantry in action at Gettysburg, Pa., July 2, 1863, both before and after the loss of a leg, while serving as major general of Volunteers commanding the Third Army Corps"; intrusted with a special mission to the South American Republics in 1865; declined the positions of Minister to Holland and to Mexico; Envoy Extraordinary and Minister Plenipotentiary to Spain by appointment of President Grant 1869–1875; chairman of the New York State Civil Service Commission in 1888 and 1889; sheriff of New York City in 1890; elected as a Democrat to the Fifty-third Congress (March 4, 1893–March 3, 1895); unsuccessful for reelection in 1894 to the Fifty-fourth Congress; retired from public life and resided in New York City until his death there May 3, 1914; interment in Arlington National Cemetery, Fort Myer, Va.

SICKLES, Nicholas, a Representative from New York; born in Kinderhook, Ulster County, N. Y., September 11, 1801; attended private schools and Kinderhook Academy; studied law; was admitted to the bar in 1823 and commenced practice in Kingston, N. Y.; elected as a Democrat to the Twenty-fourth Congress (December 7, 1835–March 3, 1837); prosecuting attorney of Ulster County, N. Y., in 1836 and 1837; served as surrogate of Ulster County from January 1, 1844, until his death in Kingston, Ulster County, N. Y., May 13, 1845; interment in Houghtaling Burying Ground.

SIEGEL, Isaac, a Representative from New York; born in New York City April 12, 1880; attended the public schools and pursued a supplementary course of study in New York City; was graduated from New York University Law School in 1901; was admitted to the bar May 26, 1902, and commenced practice in New York City; was appointed special deputy attorney general for the prosecution of election frauds in 1909 and 1910; elected as a Republican to the Sixty-fourth and to the three succeeding Congresses (March 4, 1915–March 3, 1923); was not a candidate for renomination in 1922; during the First World War was a member of the overseas commission which visited France and Italy during July and August 1918; delegate to the Republican National Conventions in 1916, 1920, 1924, and 1936; resumed the practice of law; appointed as a magistrate of New York City on July 4, 1939, and served until September 14, 1940, when he was appointed to the bench; justice of the domestic relations court of New York City until his death in that city on June 29, 1947; interment in Field Cemetery, Brooklyn, N. Y.

SIEMINSKI, Alfred Dennis, a Representative from New Jersey; born in Jersey City, Hudson County, N. J., August 23, 1911; attended the public schools, New York Military Academy, Cornwall-on-the-Hudson, N. Y., and Hun School, Princeton, N. J.; was graduated from Princeton University in 1934; student Harvard Law School in 1935 and 1936; comptroller and vice president of Brunswick Laundry, Jersey City, N. J., since 1937; enlisted as a private in the United States Army in 1942; served in Italian campaign with the Ninety-second Buffalo Division in 1944 and 1945; captain, Military Government Division in Austria, in 1945 and 1946; served with Tenth Corps in Korea in 1950; discharged to Infantry Reserve as a major in 1950 and promoted to lieutenant colonel in 1960; awarded the Legion of Merit; elected as a Democrat to the Eighty-second and to the three succeeding Congresses (January 3, 1951–January 3, 1959); unsuccessful candidate for renomination in 1958; alternate delegate to the Democratic National Convention in 1952; administrative vice president of the Hun School; engaged in education and project development; is a resident of Jersey City, N. J.

SIKES, Robert Louis Fulton, a Representative from Florida; born in Isabella, near Sylvester, Worth County, Ga., June 3, 1906; attended the public schools; was graduated from the University of Georgia at Athens in 1927 and from the University of Florida at Gainesville in 1929; engaged in the publishing business at Crestview, Fla., since 1933; served in the State house of representatives 1936–1939; elected as a Democrat to the Seventy-seventh and Seventy-eighth Congresses and served from January 3, 1941, until his resignation on October 19, 1944, to enter the United States Army during World War II; elected to the Seventy-ninth and to the seven succeeding Congresses (January 3, 1945–January 3, 1961). *Reelected to the Eighty-seventh Congress.*

SILER, Eugene, a Representative from Kentucky; born in Williamsburg, Whitley County, Ky., June 26, 1900; attended the public schools; graduated from Cumberland College, Williamsburg, Ky., in 1920 and from the University of Kentucky at Lexington in 1922; law student at Columbia University in 1922 and University of Kentucky until 1924; was admitted to the bar in 1923 and commenced the practice of law in Williamsburg, Ky.; during the First World War served as an enlisted man in the United States Navy, and in World War II served as a captain in the United States Army 1942–1945; elected judge of the Court of Appeals of Kentucky in 1945 and served until January 1, 1949; unsuccessful Republican candidate for Governor of Kentucky in 1951; trustee of Cumberland College; director of the Bank of Williamsburg and Kingsport Grocery Co.; elected as a Republican to the Eighty-fourth, Eighty-fifth, and Eighty-sixth Congresses (January 3, 1955–January 3, 1961). *Reelected to the Eighty-seventh Congress.*

SILL, Thomas Hale, a Representative from Pennsylvania; born in Windsor, Conn., October 11, 1783; completed preparatory studies, and was graduated from Brown University, Providence, R. I., in 1804; studied law; was admitted to the bar in 1809 and commenced practice in Lebanon, Ohio; moved to Erie, Pa., in 1813 and resumed the practice of law; member of the staff of General Wallace and also a member of the Minutemen of the State militia; deputy United States marshal 1816–1818; deputy attorney general in 1819; member of the State house of representatives in 1823; elected as a National-Republican to the Nineteenth Congress to fill the vacancy caused by the death of Patrick Farrelly and served from March 14, 1826, to March 3, 1827; elected to the Twenty-first Congress (March 4, 1829–March 3, 1831); declined to be a candidate for renomination in 1830; president of the United States branch bank at Erie, Pa., in 1837; member of the State constitutional convention in 1837 and 1838; presidential elector on the Whig ticket of Taylor and Fillmore in 1848; postmaster of Erie, Pa., 1847–1853; served as a director of the Erie Academy for more than thirty years; engaged in the practice of his profession until his death in Erie, Pa., on February 7, 1856; interment in Erie Cemetery.

SILSBEE, Nathaniel, a Representative and a Senator from Massachusetts; born in Salem, Mass., on January 14, 1773; attended private schools; was a shipmaster; engaged in mercantile pursuits in 1812; held several local offices; elected as a Democrat to the Fifteenth and Sixteenth Congresses (March 4, 1817–March 3, 1821); was not a candidate for renomination; elected to the State house of representatives in 1821; member of the State senate 1823–1825, serving as president; presidential elector in 1824, voting for John Quincy Adams; elected as a Democrat to the United States Senate to fill the vacancy caused by the resignation of James Lloyd; reelected in 1829 and served from May 31, 1826, to March 3, 1835; declined to be a candidate for reelection; delegate to the Whig State convention in 1832, serving as president; presidential elector in 1836, voting for Daniel Webster; resumed mercantile pursuits in Salem, Mass., where he died on July 14, 1850; interment in Harmony Grove Cemetery.

SILVESTER, Peter (grandfather of Peter Henry Silvester), a Representative from New York; born at Shelter Island, Long Island, N. Y., in 1734; completed preparatory studies; studied law; was admitted to the bar in 1763 and practiced in Albany, N. Y.; member of the Albany Common Council in 1772; member of the committee of safety in 1774; served in the First and Second Provincial Congresses in 1775 and 1776; moved to Kinderhook, N. Y., and practiced law; appointed judge of the court of common pleas of Columbia County in 1786; regent of the University of the State of New York 1787–1808; elected to the First and Second Congresses (March 4, 1789–March 3, 1793); served in the State assembly in 1788; member of the State senate 1796–1800; again served in the State assembly 1803–1806; retired from public life; died in Kinderhook, Columbia County, N. Y., October 15, 1808; interment in Old Van Schaack Cemetery, over which the Reformed Dutch Church was built in 1814.

SILVESTER, Peter Henry (grandson of Peter Silvester), a Representative from New York; born in Kinderhook, Columbia County, N. Y., February 17, 1807; attended Kinderhook Academy, and was graduated from Union College, Schenectady, N. Y., in 1827; studied law; was admitted to the bar in 1830 and practiced his profession in Coxsackie, N. Y.; elected as a Whig to the Thirtieth and Thirty-first Congresses (March 4, 1847–March 3, 1851); retired from public affairs and spent the remaining years of his life on one of his farms in the village of Coxsackie, Greene County, N. Y., until his death on November 29, 1882; interment in Kinderhook Cemetery, Kinderhook, Columbia County, N. Y.

SIMKINS, Eldred, a Representative from South Carolina; born in Edgefield, S. C., August 30, 1779; attended a private academy at Willington, Abbeville District, S. C., and was graduated from South Carolina College (now the University of South Carolina) at Columbia; attended Litchfield (Conn.) Law School for three years; was admitted to the bar in 1805 and commenced practice in Edgefield, S. C., in 1806; member of the State house of representatives; served in the State senate 1810–1812; Lieutenant Governor of the State 1812–1814; elected as a Democrat to the Fifteenth Congress to fill the vacancy caused by the resignation of John C. Calhoun; reelected to the Sixteenth Congress and served from January 24, 1818, to March 3, 1821; declined to be a candidate for renomination; again a member of the State house of representatives in 1824; resumed the practice of his profession and also engaged in planting; died in Edgefield, Edgefield County, S. C., November 17, 1831; interment in Cedar Fields, the family burial ground, near Edgefield, S. C.

SIMMONS, Furnifold McLendel, a Representative and a Senator from North Carolina; born on his father's plantation near Pollocksville, Jones County, N. C., January 20, 1854; attended a private school and Wake Forest (N. C.) College; was graduated from Trinity College (now Duke University), Durham, N. C., in 1873; studied law; was admitted to the bar January 3, 1875; moved to New Bern, Craven County, N. C., in 1876 and commenced the practice of law; elected as a Democrat to the Fiftieth Congress (March 4, 1887–March 3, 1889); unsuccessful candidate for reelection in 1888 to the Fifty-first Congress; resumed the practice of his profession in New Bern; in the campaigns of 1892, 1898, 1900, 1902, 1904, and 1906 was chairman of the Democratic State executive committee of North Carolina; appointed by President Cleveland as collector of internal revenue for the fourth district of North Carolina in 1893 and served until 1897; member of the Democratic National Committee 1924–1928; elected as a Democrat to the United States Senate in 1900, 1906, 1912, 1918, and again in 1924, and served from March 4, 1901, to March 3, 1931; unsuccessful candidate for renomination in 1930; retired in 1931 and resided in New Bern, N. C., until his death there on April 30, 1940; interment in Cedar Grove Cemetery.

SIMMONS, George Abel, a Representative from New York; born in Lyme, N. H., September 8, 1791; attended the district school; was graduated from Dartmouth College, Hanover, N. H., in 1816; moved to Lansingburg, Rensselaer County, N. Y., and was principal of the local academy; studied law; was admitted to the bar in 1825 and commenced practice in Keeseville, Essex County, N. Y.; member of the State assembly 1840–1842; member of the State constitutional convention in 1846; elected as a Whig to the Thirty-third and Thirty-fourth Congresses (March 4, 1853–March 3, 1857); was not a candidate for reelection in 1856; resumed the practice of his profession in Keeseville, N. Y., where he died October 27, 1857; interment in Evergreen Cemetery.

SIMMONS, James Fowler, a Senator from Rhode Island; born on a farm near Little Compton, Newport County, R. I., September 10, 1795; attended Mr. Fowler's private school in Newport, R. I.; moved to Providence, R. I., in 1812; employed in various manufacturing concerns in Rhode Island and Massachusetts; engaged in the manufacture of yarn at Simmonsville, N. H., in 1822; moved to Johnston, R. I., in 1827 and resumed the manufacture of yarns and engaged in agricultural pursuits; member of the State house of representatives 1828–1841; elected as a Whig to the United States Senate and served from March 4, 1841, to March 3, 1847; unsuccessful candidate for reelection in 1846 and for election in 1850 to the United States Senate; returned to Johnston, R. I., and resumed his former pursuits; again elected to the United States Senate and served from March 4, 1857, to August 15, 1862, when he resigned; resumed his former manufacturing pursuits; died in Johnston, R. I., July 10, 1864; interment in North End Cemetery, Providence, R. I.

SIMMONS, James Samuel (nephew of Milton George Urner), a Representative from New York; born near Liberty, Frederick County, Md., November 25, 1861; attended the public schools and the local academy at Liberty; was graduated from Frederick College; moved to Roanoke, Va., in 1880 and engaged in the real-estate business; moved to Niagara Falls, N. Y., in 1894 and continued in the real-estate business; chairman of the Republican city committee in 1907 and 1908; elected as a Republican to the Sixty-first and Sixty-second Congresses (March 4, 1909–March 3, 1913); unsuccessful candidate for reelection in 1912 to the Sixty-third Congress; delegate to the Republican National Convention at Chicago in 1912; resumed the real-estate business in Niagara Falls, N. Y., and also, in 1927, in St. Petersburg, Fla., where he maintained his winter home; died in St. Petersburg, Fla., November 28, 1935; interment in Riverdale Cemetery, Lewiston, N. Y.

SIMMONS, Robert Glenmore, a Representative from Nebraska; born in Scotts Bluff County, near Scottsbluff, Nebr., December 25, 1891; attended the public schools and Hastings (Nebr.) College 1909–1911; was graduated from the law college of the University of Nebraska at Lincoln in 1915; was admitted to the bar the same year and commenced practice in Gering, Nebr.; elected prosecuting attorney of Scotts Bluff County in 1916; during the First World War enlisted in the Army on October 15, 1917, qualified as a balloon observer and licensed spherical balloon pilot, and was commissioned as a second lieutenant in the Air Service March 12, 1918, being discharged January 14, 1919; State commander of the American Legion in 1921; president of the University of Nebraska Alumni Association in 1922; elected as a Republican to the Sixty-eighth and to the four succeeding Congresses (March 4, 1923–March 3, 1933); unsuccessful candidate for reelection in 1932 to the Seventy-third Congress and for election to the United States Senate in 1934 and again in 1936; resumed the practice of law in Lincoln, Nebr.; elected chief justice of Nebraska in 1938, in which capacity he is now serving; deputy judge, administrative tribunal of the International Labour Organization, Geneva, Switzerland, in 1955; is a resident of Lincoln, Nebr.

SIMMS, Albert Gallatin (husband of Ruth Hanna McCormick), a Representative from New Mexico; born in Washington, Hempstead County, Ark., October 8, 1882; attended private schools and the University of Arkansas at Fayetteville; moved to Monterrey, Mexico, in 1906 and was employed as an accountant; moved to Silver City, N. Mex., in 1912; studied law; was admitted to the bar in 1915 and practiced law at Albuquerque, N. Mex., until 1919; during the First World War served as field director for the American Red Cross at Camp Cody, N. Mex.;

engaged in banking, serving as president of a national bank in Albuquerque 1920–1924 and as president of a mortgage company since 1924; member of the city council 1920–1922; member and chairman of the board of county commissioners of Bernalillo County 1920–1922; member of the New Mexico House of Representatives 1925–1927; elected as a Republican to the Seventy-first Congress (March 4, 1929–March 3, 1931); unsuccessful candidate for reelection in 1930 to the Seventy-second Congress; member of the Republican National Committee 1932–1934; banker, farmer, and rancher; is a resident of Albuquerque, N. Mex.

SIMMS, William Emmett, a Representative from Kentucky; born near Cynthiana, Harrison County, Ky., January 2, 1822; attended the public schools, and was graduated from the law department of Transylvania University, Lexington, Ky., in 1846; was admitted to the bar in 1846 and commenced practice in Paris, Bourbon County, Ky.; served as captain throughout the Mexican War; member of the State house of representatives 1849–1851; was elected as a Democrat to the Thirty-sixth Congress (March 4, 1859–March 3, 1861); unsuccessful candidate for reelection in 1860 to the Thirty-seventh Congress; on October 21, 1861, during the Civil War, was appointed to the temporary rank of colonel in the Confederate Army; appointed lieutenant colonel in the Provisional Army of the Confederate States, December 24, 1861, and was assigned to the First Battalion, Kentucky Cavalry; resigned February 17, 1862, having been chosen Senator from Kentucky to the Confederate States Congress; member of the Senate of the First and Second Confederate Congresses and also served in President Davis' Cabinet; engaged in agricultural pursuits; died on his estate, "Mount Airy," near Paris, Bourbon County, Ky., June 25, 1898; interment in Paris Cemetery.

SIMON, Joseph, a Senator from Oregon; born in Bechtheim, Germany, February 7, 1851; immigrated to the United States with his parents, who settled in Portland, Oreg., in 1857; attended the public schools; studied law; was admitted to the bar in 1872 and commenced practice in Portland, Oreg.; member of the city council 1877–1880; secretary of the Republican State central committee in 1878, serving as chairman in 1880, 1884, and in 1886; member of the State senate 1880–1898, serving as president in 1889, 1891, 1895, and 1897, and at the special session of 1898; delegate to the Republican National Conventions in 1892 and 1900; member of the National Republican Committee 1892–1896; elected as a Republican to the United States Senate October 8, 1898, to fill the vacancy in the term commencing March 4, 1897, and served until March 3, 1903; was not a candidate for reelection; mayor of Portland, Oreg., 1909–1911; resumed the practice of law; died in Portland, Oreg., February 14, 1935; interment in Beth Israel Cemetery.

SIMONDS, William Edgar, a Representative from Connecticut; born in Collinsville, town of Canton, Hartford County, Conn., November 24, 1842; attended the public school and Collinsville High School, and was graduated from Connecticut State Normal School at New Britain in 1860; taught school; during the Civil War enlisted as a private in Company A, Twenty-fifth Regiment, Connecticut Volunteer Infantry, August 18, 1862; promoted to sergeant major before being mustered into the United States service; promoted to second lieutenant of Company I of his regiment at the Battle of Irish Bend, Louisiana, April 24, 1863; discharged from service by reason of expiration of term August 26, 1863; was graduated from Yale Law School in 1865; was admitted to the bar and commenced practice in Hartford, Conn.; member of the State house of representatives in 1883 and 1885, and served as speaker in the latter year; elected as a Republican to the Fifty-first Congress

(March 4, 1889–March 3, 1891); unsuccessful candidate for reelection in 1890 to the Fifty-second Congress; United States Commissioner of Patents 1891–1893; received the decoration of chevalier of the Legion of Honor from the Republic of France in 1893; resumed the practice of his profession; died in Hartford, Conn., March 14, 1903; interment in Canton Center Cemetery, Canton, Conn.

SIMONS, Samuel, a Representative from Connecticut; born in Bridgeport, Conn., in 1792; pursued an academic course; held several local offices; taught school; studied medicine and commenced practice in Bridgeport, Fairfield County, Conn.; member of the State house of representatives in 1830; director of the Housatonic Railroad; trustee of the Bridgeport Savings Bank; elected as a Democrat to the Twenty-eighth Congress (March 4, 1843–March 3, 1845); resumed the practice of medicine in Bridgeport, Conn., where he died January 13, 1847; interment in Mountain Grove Cemetery.

SIMONTON, Charles Bryson, a Representative from Tennessee; born in Tipton County, Tenn., September 8, 1838; was graduated from Erskine College, Due West, S. C., in August 1859; during the Civil War enlisted as a private in Company C, Ninth Tennessee Infantry, Confederate Army, in 1861; subsequently became second lieutenant and then captain; was severely wounded in the Battle of Perryville October 8, 1862, and disabled from any further active duty during the war; elected clerk of the circuit court of Tipton County in March 1870; studied law; was admitted to the bar in 1873 and commenced practice in Covington, Tenn.; member of the State house of representatives in 1877 and 1878; editor of the Tipton Record in Covington, Tipton County, Tenn.; elected as a Democrat to the Forty-sixth and Forty-seventh Congresses (March 4, 1879–March 3, 1883); chairman of the Democratic State convention in 1886; presidential elector on the Democratic ticket of Cleveland and Stevenson in 1892; president of the Covington city school board 1892–1903; United States district attorney for the district of Tennessee 1895–1898; died in Covington, Tenn., June 10, 1911; interment in Munford Cemetery.

SIMONTON, William, a Representative from Pennsylvania, born in West Hanover Township, near Harrisburg, Pa., February 12, 1788; received his early education from his mother and later attended a private school; was graduated from the medical department of the University of Pennsylvania at Philadelphia in 1810 and practiced his profession while residing on his farm near Hummelstown, Dauphin County, Pa.; elected auditor of Dauphin County in 1823 and served three years; one of the original supporters of the free-school system established by the act of 1834; elected as a Whig to the Twenty-sixth and Twenty-seventh Congresses (March 4, 1839–March 3, 1843); died in South Hanover, Pa., May 17, 1846; interment in the Old Hanover Cemetery, north of Shellsville, Pa.

SIMPKINS, John, a Representative from Massachusetts; born in New Bedford, Bristol County, Mass., June 27, 1862; attended the public schools of Yarmouth and St. Mark's School, Southboro, Mass.; was graduated from Harvard University, Cambridge, Mass., in 1885; served in the State senate in 1890 and 1891; presidential elector on the Republican ticket of Harrison and Reid in 1892; president of the Republican Club of Massachusetts in 1892 and 1893; member of the Republican State committee 1892–1894; elected as a Republican to the Fifty-fourth and Fifty-fifth Congresses and served from March 4, 1895, until his death in Washington, D. C., on March 27, 1898; interment in Woodside Cemetery, Yarmouth, Barnstable County, Mass.

SIMPSON, Edna Oakes (widow of Sidney E. Simpson), a Representative from Illinois; born in Carrollton, Greene County, Ill., October 26, 1891; elected as a Republican to the Eighty-sixth Congress (January 3, 1959–January 3, 1961); did not seek renomination in 1960; is a resident of Carrollton, Ill.

SIMPSON, James, Jr., a Representative from Illinois; born in Chicago, Ill., January 7, 1905; attended St. Paul's School in Concord, N. H., 1919–1922, Westminster School, Salisbury, Conn., 1922–1925, and later a student at Harvard University; director of Marshall Field & Co., 1931–1960; trustee of Provident Hospital 1928–1936; elected as a Republican to the Seventy-third Congress (March 4, 1933–January 3, 1935); unsuccessful candidate for renomination in 1934; was admitted to the Illinois bar in 1939; owner and operator of farms near Wadsworth, Lake County, Ill., and Rapidan, Culpeper County, Va.; during World War II entered the United States Marine Corps in 1943 and served thirty-six months, with twenty-four months in the Pacific area, and was discharged as a captain; civilian aide to Secretary of the Army Robert Stevens in 1953 and 1954; died at his farm near Wadsworth, Ill., February 29, 1960; interment in Graceland Cemetery, Chicago, Ill.

SIMPSON, Jeremiah (Jerry), a Representative from Kansas; born on Prince Edward Island, Canada, March 31, 1842; moved with his parents to Oneida County, N. Y., in 1848; attended the public schools; at the age of fourteen became a sailor and followed nautical pursuits from 1856 to 1879; served in the Civil War in Company A, Twelfth Regiment, Illinois Volunteer Infantry; moved to Barber County, Kans., in 1878 and settled near Medicine Lodge; engaged in farming and stock raising; on two occasions was an unsuccessful candidate for election on the Independent ticket to the Kansas House of Representatives from Barber County; elected as a Populist to the Fifty-second and Fifty-third Congresses (March 4, 1891–March 3, 1895); unsuccessful candidate for reelection in 1894 to the Fifty-fourth Congress; elected to the Fifty-fifth Congress (March 4, 1897–March 3, 1899); unsuccessful candidate for reelection in 1898 to the Fifty-sixth Congress; resumed his former pursuits; died in Wichita, Kans., October 23, 1905; interment in Maple Grove Cemetery.

SIMPSON, Kenneth Farrand, a Representative from New York; born in New York City, N. Y., May 4, 1895; attended private schools in New York City and Hill School, Pottstown, Pa.; was graduated from Yale University, New Haven, Conn., in 1917 and from the law department of Harvard University, Cambridge, Mass., in 1922; during the First World War served as captain, Three Hundred and Second Field Artillery, with one year of overseas service; commandant, American School Detachment University of Aix-Marseilles, in 1919; decorated with the Palmes Academiques by the French Minister of Public Instruction and Fine Arts; was admitted to the bar in 1922 and commenced practice in New York City, N. Y.; assistant United States attorney, southern district of New York, 1925–1927; chairman of Republican county committee 1935–1940; member of Republican National Conventions in 1936 and 1940; elected as a Republican to the Seventy-seventh Congress and served from January 3, 1941, until his death in New York City, N. Y., January 25, 1941; interment in Hudson City Cemetery, Hudson, N. Y.

SIMPSON, Richard Franklin, a Representative from South Carolina; born in Laurens, S. C., March 24, 1798; was graduated from South Carolina College (now the University of South Carolina) at Columbia in 1816; studied law; was admitted to the bar in 1819 and began practice in Pendleton,

S. C.; held several local offices; served as major during the Seminole War in 1835; member of the State senate 1835–1841; elected as a Democrat to the Twenty-eighth, Twenty-ninth, and Thirtieth Congresses (March 4, 1843–March 3, 1849); declined to be a candidate for renomination in 1848; engaged in agricultural pursuits; member of the secession convention in 1860 and signed the ordinance of secession; died in Pendleton, Anderson County, S. C., October 28, 1882; interment in the family cemetery near that city.

SIMPSON, Richard Murray, a Representative from Pennsylvania; born in Huntingdon, Pa., August 30, 1900; attended the public schools; was graduated from the University of Pittsburgh, Pittsburgh, Pa., in 1923 and from Georgetown Law School, Washington, D. C., in 1942; during the First World War served as a private in the Three Hundred and First Company, Tank Corps; engaged in the insurance business 1923–1937; served in the State house of representatives 1935–1937; elected as a Republican to the Seventy-fifth Congress to fill the vacancy caused by the death of Benjamin K. Focht; reelected to the Seventy-sixth and to the ten succeeding Congresses and served from May 11, 1937, until his death in the naval hospital, Bethesda, Md., January 7, 1960; interment in Riverview Cemetery, Huntingdon, Pa.

SIMPSON, Sidney Elmer (Sid) (husband of Edna Oakes Simpson), a Representative from Illinois; born in Carrollton, Greene County, Ill., September 20, 1894; attended the public schools and was graduated from Carrollton High School; during the First World War served in the United States Army, with overseas service; owner of Simpson Motor Co. and Simpson Bus Co.; served as chairman of the Greene County Republican Committee; member of the executive committee of the County Chairman's Association of Illinois; city treasurer of Carrollton, Ill., for one term; member of Carrollton Board of Education; elected as a Republican to the Seventy-eighth and to the seven succeeding Congresses and served from January 3, 1943, until his death; had been renominated to the Eighty-sixth Congress; died in Pittsfield, Ill., October 26, 1958; interment in Carrollton City Cemetery, Carrollton, Ill.

SIMS, Alexander Dromgoole (nephew of George Coke Dromgoole), a Representative from South Carolina; born near Randals Ordinary, Brunswick County, Va., June 12, 1803; attended the rural schools of his native county and at the age of sixteen entered the University of North Carolina at Chapel Hill; was graduated from Union College, Schenectady, N. Y., in 1823; read law with General Dromgoole in Brunswick County, Va., and later was admitted to practice; moved to South Carolina in 1826 and settled in Darlington; assumed charge of Darlington (S. C.) Academy in 1827; was admitted to the bar of South Carolina in 1829 and practiced in Darlington; also engaged in literary pursuits; member of the State house of representatives 1840–1844; elected as a Democrat to the Twenty-ninth and Thirtieth Congresses and served from March 4, 1845, until his death; had been reelected in 1848 to the Thirty-first Congress; died in Kingstree, Williamsburg County, S. C., November 22, 1848; interment in First Baptist Cemetery, Darlington, Darlington County, S. C.

SIMS, Hugo Sheridan, Jr., a Representative from South Carolina; born in Orangeburg, S. C., October 14, 1921; attended the public schools; graduated from Wofford College, Spartanburg, S. C., in 1941; editor of the Times and Democrat, daily newspaper, Orangeburg, S. C., in 1941 and 1942; during World War II enlisted in the United States Army as a private in April 1942; commissioned a captain in November 1944 and commanded Company A, Five Hundred and First Parachute Infantry, One Hundred and First Airborne Division; discharged in October 1945 after serving overseas from January 1944 to September 1945; awarded the Distinguished Service Cross, Silver Star, and decorations from France, Belgium, and Netherlands; graduated from the law school of the University of South Carolina at Columbia in 1947; was admitted to the bar August 28, 1947, and commenced the practice of law in Orangeburg, S. C.; member of the State house of representatives in 1947 and 1948; elected as a Democrat to the Eighty-first Congress (January 3, 1949–January 3, 1951); unsuccessful candidate for renomination in 1950; reentered the Army on January 3, 1951, and assigned as a captain with the Eighty-second Airborne Division at Fort Bragg, N. C., and served until December 1951; resumed the practice of law; resides in Orangeburg, S. C.

SIMS, Leonard Henly, a Representative from Missouri; born in Burke County, N. C., February 6, 1807; received a limited schooling; moved to Rutherford County, Tenn., in 1830 and engaged in agricultural pursuits; member of the Tennessee House of Representatives for two terms; settled near Springfield, Green County, Mo., in 1839 and continued agricultural pursuits; member of the Missouri State House of Representatives 1842–1846; elected as a Democrat to the Twenty-ninth Congress (March 4, 1845–March 3, 1847); returned to Rutherford County, Tenn., in 1847 and continued farming; moved to Independence County, Ark., in 1859, settled on a farm near Batesville, and engaged in cotton raising and farming; served in the Arkansas State Senate 1866–1870 and 1874–1878; died on his plantation near Batesville, Independence County, Ark., February 28, 1886; interment in the family plot on his farm.

SIMS, Thetus Willrette, a Representative from Tennessee; born near Waynesboro, Wayne County, Tenn., April 25, 1852; attended a private school at Martins Mills; moved with his parents to Savannah, Hardin County, Tenn., in 1862; attended Savannah (Tenn.) College and was graduated from the law department of Cumberland University, Lebanon, Tenn., in June 1876; was admitted to the bar the same year and commenced practice in Linden, Perry County, Tenn.; superintendent of public instruction for Perry County, Tenn., 1882–1884; presidential elector on the Democratic ticket of Cleveland and Stevenson in 1892; elected as a Democrat to the Fifty-fifth and to the eleven succeeding Congresses (March 4, 1897–March 3, 1921); unsuccessful candidate for renomination in 1920 to the Sixty-seventh Congress; resumed the practice of law in Lexington, Henderson County, Tenn.; retired from active business pursuits in 1930 and moved to Washington, D. C., where he died December 17, 1939; interment in Rock Creek Cemetery.

SINCLAIR, James Herbert, a Representative from North Dakota; born near St. Marys, Ontario, Canada, October 9, 1871; moved with his parents to Cooperstown, Griggs County, N. Dak., in 1883; attended the public schools and was graduated from Mayville (N. Dak.) State Normal School; superintendent of schools of Cooperstown, N. Dak., 1896–1898; register of deeds of Griggs County 1899–1905; organized the First National Bank of Binford and served as cashier 1905–1908; moved to Kenmare, Ward County, in March 1908; engaged in agricultural pursuits and in the real-estate business; member of the State house of representatives 1915–1919; elected as a Republican to the Sixty-sixth and to the seven succeeding Congresses (March 4, 1919–January 3, 1935); unsuccessful candidate for renomination in 1934; Republican member of the Special Mexican Claims Commission 1936–1939; retired from active business and political life in 1939; died in Miami, Fla., September 5, 1943; the remains were cremated and the ashes deposited under a red flowering hibiscus on the grounds of his home.

SINGISER, Theodore Frelinghuysen, a Delegate from the Territory of Idaho; born in Churchtown, Cumberland County, Pa., March 15, 1845; attended the common schools; learned the art of printing; during the Civil War enlisted in the Union Army as a private in Company E, Sixth Regiment, Pennsylvania Reserves, June 6, 1861; participated in the campaigns and battles of the Army of the Potomac up to and including Antietam; honorably discharged in February 1863; reentered the Army in June 1863 as captain of Company A, Twentieth Regiment, Pennsylvania Volunteer Cavalry, and was in active service with his command until the spring of 1865, when honorably discharged; assistant assessor of internal revenue in 1866 and 1867; engaged in mercantile and editorial pursuits; studied law; was admitted to the bar in Washington, D. C., in 1878; employed in the United States Treasury from June 1, 1875, to May 31, 1879; appointed receiver of public moneys at Oxford, Idaho, in February 1879; engaged in mining in Idaho and Utah; secretary of the Territory of Idaho in 1880; Acting Governor of Idaho during the winter of 1881–1882; elected as a Republican to the Forty-eighth Congress (March 4, 1883–March 3, 1885); unsuccessful candidate for reelection in 1884 to the Forty-ninth Congress; receiver of public moneys at Mitchell, Dak. (now South Dakota), 1885–1889; again engaged in mining, and resided at Salt Lake City, Utah, until his death; died at Mercy Hospital in Chicago, Ill., on January 23, 1907; interment in Chestnut Hill Cemetery, Mechanicsburg, Cumberland County, Pa.

SINGLETON, James Washington, a Representative from Illinois; born in Paxton, Frederick County, Va., November 23, 1811; attended Winchester (Va.) Academy; moved to Mount Sterling, Brown County, Ill., in 1834; studied medicine and practiced; studied law; was admitted to the bar in 1838 and commenced practice in Mount Sterling; engaged in agricultural pursuits; elected brigadier general of the Illinois Militia in 1844 and took a conspicuous part in the so-called Mormon War; delegate to the State constitutional conventions in 1847 and 1861; member of the State house of representatives 1850–1854; moved to Quincy, Adams County, Ill., in 1854; was again a member of the State house of representatives in 1861; was appointed in 1862 by Governor Yates as a member of the commission to confer with the British and Canadian authorities on the establishment of continuous water communication between the United States and Canada; unsuccessful candidate for election in 1868 to the Forty-first Congress; constructed the Quincy & Toledo and the Quincy, Alton & St. Louis Railroads and served as president of both companies; elected as a Democrat to the Forty-sixth and Forty-seventh Congresses (March 4, 1879–March 3, 1883); returned to his farm "Boscobel," near Quincy, Ill., and engaged in farming and the raising of fine stock; moved to Baltimore, Md., about 1891, and died there on April 4, 1892; interment in Mount Hebron Cemetery, Winchester, Frederick County, Va.

SINGLETON, Otho Robards, a Representative from Mississippi; born near Nicholasville, Jessamine County, Ky., October 14, 1814; attended the common schools; was graduated from St. Joseph's College, Bardstown, Ky., and from the law department of the University of Lexington; was admitted to the bar in 1838 and commenced practice in Canton, Madison County, Miss.; member of the State house of representatives in 1846 and 1847; served in the State senate 1848–1854; presidential elector on the Democratic ticket of Pierce and King in 1852; elected as a Democrat to the Thirty-third Congress (March 4, 1853–March 3, 1855); unsuccessful candidate for reelection; elected to the Thirty-fifth and Thirty-sixth Congresses and served from March 4, 1857, until January 12, 1861, when he

withdrew; Representative from Mississippi in the Confederate Congress 1861–1865; elected as a Democrat to the Forty-fourth and to the five succeeding Congresses (March 4, 1875–March 3, 1887); was not a candidate for renomination in 1886; died in Washington, D. C., January 11, 1889; interment in Canton Cemetery, Canton, Madison County, Miss.

SINGLETON, Thomas Day, a Representative from South Carolina; born near Kingstree, S. C.; attended the common schools; held several local offices; elected as a Nullifier to the Twenty-third Congress and served without having qualified, from March 3, 1833, until his death in Raleigh, N. C., November 25, 1833, while en route to Washington, D. C.; interment in Congressional Cemetery, Washington, D. C.

SINNICKSON, Clement Hall (grandnephew of Thomas Sinnickson), a Representative from New Jersey; born in Salem, Salem County, N. J., September 16, 1834; attended private schools, and the Polytechnic Institute at Troy, N. Y.; was graduated from Union College, New York, in 1855; studied law; was admitted to the bar in 1858 and commenced the practice of law in Salem, N. J.; during the Civil War served as captain in the Union Army; elected as a Republican to the Forty-fourth and Forty-fifth Congresses (March 4, 1875–March 3, 1879); resumed the practice of law in Salem; delegate to the Republican National Convention at Chicago in 1880; appointed judge of the court of common pleas in 1896 and reappointed in 1901 and 1906; died in Salem, N. J., on July 24, 1919; interment in St. John's Episcopal Cemetery.

SINNICKSON, Thomas (granduncle of Clement Hall Sinnickson), a Representative from New Jersey; born near Salem, Salem County, N. J., December 21, 1744; completed preparatory studies; engaged in mercantile pursuits; served as captain in the Revolutionary Army; held several local offices; member of the State general assembly in 1777, 1782, 1784, 1785, 1787, and 1788; elected to the First Congress (March 4, 1789–March 3, 1791); elected to the Fifth Congress (March 4, 1797–March 3, 1799); presidential elector on the Federalist ticket and voted for Adams and Pinckney; died in Salem, N. J., May 15, 1817; interment in St. John's Episcopal Cemetery.

SINNICKSON, Thomas (nephew of the preceding), a Representative from New Jersey; born in Salem, Salem County, N. J., December 13, 1786; completed preparatory studies; engaged in mercantile pursuits; judge of the court of errors and appeals of New Jersey; member of the State general assembly; judge of the court of common pleas for twenty years; elected to the Twentieth Congress to fill the vacancy caused by the death of Hedge Thompson and served from December 1, 1828, to March 3, 1829; died in Salem, Salem County, N. J., February 17, 1873; interment in St. John's Episcopal Cemetery.

SINNOTT, Nicholas John, a Representative from Oregon; born in The Dalles, Wasco County, Oreg., December 6, 1870; attended the public schools and Wasco Independent Academy at The Dalles; was graduated from the University of Notre Dame, Indiana, in 1892; studied law; was admitted to the bar in 1895 and commenced practice at The Dalles, Oreg.; elected to the State senate in 1909 and 1911; elected as a Republican to the Sixty-third and to the seven succeeding Congresses and served from March 4, 1913, until his resignation effective May 31, 1928; appointed by President Coolidge on April 18, 1928, as a judge of the United States Court of Claims, at Washington, D. C., in which capacity he served until his death in Washington, D. C., July 20, 1929; interment in St. Peters Cemetery, The Dalles, Oreg.

SIPE, William Allen, a Representative from Pennsylvania; born near Harrisonville, Fulton County, Pa., July 1, 1844; attended the public schools, and Cassville Academy, Cassville, Huntingdon County, Pa.; during the Civil War enlisted in the Union Army in 1862 and served in Company K, One Hundred and Forty-ninth Regiment, Pennsylvania Volunteer Infantry; was discharged for disability the same year; studied law; was admitted to the bar in August 1865 and practiced in Huntingdon, Pa.; moved to Indianapolis, Ind., in January 1867, to Pittsburgh, Pa., in December 1868, and continued the practice of law; elected as a Democrat to the Fifty-second Congress to fill the vacancy caused by the death of Alexander K. Craig; reelected to the Fifty-third Congress and served from December 5, 1892, to March 3, 1895; unsuccessful candidate for reelection in 1894 to the Fifty-fourth Congress; resumed the practice of law in Pittsburgh, Pa., until he retired in 1921; moved to San Diego, Calif., where he died on September 10, 1935; interment in Highwood Cemetery, Pittsburgh, Pa.

SIROVICH, William Irving, a Representative from New York; born in York, York County, Pa., March 18, 1882; moved to New York City, N. Y., with his parents in 1888; attended the public schools; was graduated from the College of the City of New York in 1902 and from the College of Physicians and Surgeons of Columbia University, New York City, in 1906; commenced the practice of medicine in New York City in 1906; also engaged as a lecturer, editor, and playwright, several of his plays being produced on Broadway; member of the fifth district school board 1906–1926; appointed as a member of the commission to inquire into the subject of widows' pensions and of the State pension commission in 1913; appointed a member of the State charities convention in 1914; served as superintendent of Peoples Hospital, New York City, 1910–1927; appointed commissioner of child welfare in 1919 and served until 1931; elected as a fellow of the American College of Surgeons in 1924; unsuccessful candidate for election in 1924 to the Sixty-ninth Congress; elected as a Democrat to the Seventieth and to the six succeeding Congresses and served from March 4, 1927, until his death; president of the Industrial National Bank, New York City, 1929–1932; delegate to the Interparliamentary Union Congress held at Bucharest, Rumania, in 1931; died in New York City, N. Y., December 17, 1939; interment in Mount Hebron Cemetery, Flushing, Long Island, N. Y.

SISK, Bernice Frederic, a Representative from California; born in Montague, Tex., December 14, 1910; at the age of six years moved with his parents to Donley County, Tex.; attended the Whitefish School and high school at Abernathy and Meadow, Tex.; attended Abilene Christian College 1929–1931; assisted his father in the operation of a cotton farm; moved to the San Joaquin Valley of California in 1937 and was employed in a food processing plant until 1941; during World War II served as a civilian flight dispatcher at the Sequoia Air Force training field, Visalia, Calif., from 1941 to 1945; employed with LeMoss-Smith Tire Co. in Fresno, Calif., 1945–1954; elected as a Democrat to the Eighty-fourth, Eighty-fifth, and Eighty-sixth Congresses (January 3, 1955–January 3, 1961). *Reelected to the Eighty-seventh Congress.*

SISSON, Frederick James, a Representative from New York; born in Wells Bridge, Otsego County, N. Y., March 31, 1879; attended the public schools and the high school at Unadilla, N. Y.; was graduated from Hamilton College, Clinton, N. Y., in 1904; principal of Vernon (N. Y.) High School 1904–1910; studied law; was admitted to the bar in 1911 and commenced practice in Utica, N. Y.; sheriff's attorney in 1913 and corporation counsel for the city of Utica in 1914; unsuccessful candidate for election in 1922 to the Sixty-eighth Congress and in 1928 to the Seventy-first Congress; member of the Whitesboro (N. Y.) Board of Education 1925–1933, serving as president 1926–1930; elected as a Democrat to the Seventy-third and Seventy-fourth Congresses (March 4, 1933–January 3, 1937); unsuccessful candidate for reelection in 1936 to the Seventy-fifth Congress; continued the practice of law in Utica, N. Y., and Washington, D. C., until his retirement in 1945; died in Washington, D. C., October 20, 1949; interment in Mount Olivet Cemetery, Whitesboro, N. Y.

SISSON, Thomas Upton, a Representative from Mississippi; born near McCool, Attala County, Miss., September 22, 1869; moved with his father to Choctaw County, Miss.; attended the common schools and the French Camp Academy, Mississippi; was graduated from Southwestern Presbyterian University, Clarkesville, Tenn., in 1889; principal of Carthage High School in 1889 and 1890 and of the graded schools of Kosciusko, Attala County, Miss., 1890–1892; studied law at the University of Mississippi at Oxford and was graduated from the law department of Cumberland University, Lebanon, Tenn.; was admitted to the bar at Memphis, Tenn., in 1894 and commenced practice in Winona, Montgomery County, Miss.; member of the State senate in 1898; presidential elector on the Democratic ticket of Bryan and Stevenson in 1900; district attorney of the fifth judicial district 1903–1907; elected as a Democrat to the Sixty-first and to the six succeeding Congresses (March 4, 1909–March 3, 1923); unsuccessful candidate for reelection in 1922 to the Sixty-eighth Congress; died in Washington, D. C., September 26, 1923; interment in Oak Hill Cemetery, Winona, Miss.

SITES, Frank Crawford, a Representative from Pennsylvania; born in Shippensburg, Cumberland County, Pa., December 24, 1864; moved with his parents to Harrisburg, Pa., in 1875; attended the public schools; learned the trade of watchmaker and jeweler; and afterward engaged in that business at Harrisburg; director on the Harrisburg school board 1903–1912; appointed postmaster of Harrisburg June 3, 1913, and served until his successor was appointed June 20, 1922; secretary-treasurer of the National Association of Postmasters 1913–1922; elected as a Democrat to the Sixty-eighth Congress (March 4, 1923–March 3, 1925); unsuccessful candidate for reelection in 1924 to the Sixty-ninth Congress; returned to Harrisburg and engaged in the bond businesss; died in Harrisburg, Pa., May 23, 1935; interment in East Harrisburg Cemetery.

SITGREAVES, Charles, a Representative from New Jersey; born in Easton, Pa., April 22, 1803; moved with his parents to New Jersey in 1806; pursued classical studies; studied law; was admitted to the bar in Easton in 1824 and commenced practice in Phillipsburg, Warren County, N. J.; member of the State general assembly 1831–1833; major commandant in the State militia 1828–1838; member of the town council in 1834 and 1835; served in the State senate 1851–1854; president of the Belvidere & Delaware Railroad Co.; mayor of Phillipsburg, N. J., in 1861 and 1862; president of the National Bank of Phillipsburg 1856–1878; elected as a Democrat to the Thirty-ninth and Fortieth Congresses (March 4, 1865–March 3, 1869); was not a candidate for renomination in 1868; engaged in banking and railroading; died in Phillipsburg, N. J., March 17, 1878; interment in Seventh Street Cemetery, Easton, Pa.

SITGREAVES, John, a Delegate from North Carolina; born in England in 1757; attended Eton College; immigrated to the United States and settled in New Bern, N. C.; studied law; was admitted to the bar and commenced practice in New Bern, N. C.; during the Revolutionary War attained the rank of lieutenant, later serving as military aide to General Caswell; commissioner in charge of confiscated property; clerk of the State senate in 1778 and 1779; Member of the Continental Congress in 1784 and 1785; member of the State house of commons in 1784 and 1786–1789, serving as speaker in 1787 and 1788; United States district judge for North Carolina from 1789 until his death in Halifax, N. C., March 4, 1802; interment in the City Cemetery, Raleigh, N. C.

SITGREAVES, Samuel, a Representative from Pennsylvania; born in Philadelphia, Pa., March 16, 1764; pursued classical studies; studied law; was admitted to the bar in Philadelphia, Pa., September 3, 1783, and began practice in Easton, Pa., in 1786; delegate to the State constitutional convention in 1790; elected as a Federalist to the Fourth and Fifth Congresses and served from March 4, 1795, until his resignation in 1798; one of the managers appointed by the House of Representatives in 1798 to conduct the impeachment proceedings against William Blount, a Senator from Tennessee; appointed United States commissioner to Great Britain under the Jay treaty, regarding British claims, August 11, 1798; burgess of Easton 1804–1807; treasurer of Northampton County 1816–1819; resumed the practice of law; president of the Easton Bank 1815–1827; died in Easton, Pa., April 4, 1827; interment in Easton Cemetery.

SITTLER, Edward Lewis, Jr., a Representative from Pennsylvania; born in Greensburg, Westmoreland County, Pa., April 21, 1908; moved with his parents to Uniontown, Fayette County, Pa., in August 1908; attended the public schools; was graduated from Uniontown High School in 1926 and from Brown University, Providence, R. I., in 1930; salesman for an ice cream company 1931–1937; elected to the Uniontown School Board in 1934 and served as president of the board in 1936 and 1937; field underwriter for Mutual Life Insurance Co. of New York 1937–; chartered life underwriters designation, American College of Life Underwriters, in 1940; during World War II enlisted as a private in the United States Army in February 1943 and served in the Ordnance Department in the European Theater until released to the Inactive Reserve as a captain in August 1946; mayor of Uniontown 1948–1951; elected as a Republican to the Eighty-second Congress (January 3, 1951–January 3, 1953); unsuccessful candidate for reelection in 1952 to the Eighty-third Congress; resumed insurance business; elected Republican State committeeman for Fayette County in April 1960; resides in Uniontown, Pa.

SKELTON, Charles, a Representative from New Jersey; born in Buckingham Township, Bucks County, Pa., April 19, 1806; moved to Trenton, N. J., about 1829; attended the country schools and Trenton Academy; engaged in mercantile pursuits; moved to Philadelphia, Pa., in 1835; was graduated from Jefferson Medical College at Philadelphia in 1838 and commenced the practice of his profession in that city; returned to Trenton, N. J., in 1841; superintendent of the public schools of Trenton in 1848; elected as a Democrat to the Thirty-second and Thirty-third Congresses (March 4, 1851–March 3, 1855); member of the common council 1873–1875; died in Trenton, N. J., May 20, 1879; interment in City Cemetery, Hamilton Square, Mercer County, N. J.

SKILES, William Woodburn, a Representative from Ohio; born in Stoughstown, Cumberland County, Pa., December 11, 1849, moved with his parents to Richland County, Ohio, in 1854; attended the district schools; taught school for several years; was graduated from Baldwin University, Berea, Ohio, in 1876; studied law; was admitted to the bar July 24, 1878, and commenced the practice of his profession in Shelby, Ohio; interested as a stockholder and director in various manufac-

turing enterprises; president of the Citizens Bank from 1893 until his death; president and member of the city school board 1885–1904; member of the Republican State central committee 1900–1904; elected as a Republican to the Fifty-seventh and Fifty-eighth Congresses and served from March 4, 1901, until his death in Shelby, Richland County, Ohio, January 9, 1904; interment in Oakland Cemetery.

SKINNER, Charles Rufus, a Representative from New York; born in Union Square, Oswego County, N. Y., August 4, 1844; attended the common schools and Clinton Liberal Institute; was graduated from Mexico Academy, New York, in 1866; taught in the common schools and also in the two secondary schools he had attended; editor of the Watertown Daily Times 1870–1874; member of the board of education of Watertown, N. Y., 1875–1884; member of the State assembly 1877–1881; elected as a Republican to the Forty-seventh Congress to fill the vacancy caused by the resignation of Warner Miller; reelected to the Forty-eighth Congress and served from November 8, 1881, to March 3, 1885; was not a candidate for renomination in 1884; member of the Board of Visitors to the United States Military Academy at West Point in 1884; editor of the Watertown Daily Republican from July 1, 1885, to January 1, 1886; city editor of the Watertown Daily Times from January to July 1886; deputy State superintendent of public instruction 1886–1892; supervisor of teachers' training classes and teachers' institutes in the State department of public instruction 1892–1895; State superintendent of public instruction 1895–1904, putting into execution the State law requiring that during school hours the United States flag shall fly over every public school of the State; elected president of the National Education Association in 1897; assistant appraiser of merchandise for the port of New York 1906–1911; librarian of the State assembly in 1913 and 1914 and served as legislative librarian 1915–1925 with residence in Albany, N. Y.; retired from public activities in 1926; died while on a visit to his son in Pelham Manor, N. Y., June 30, 1928; remains were cremated and the ashes interred in Brookside Cemetery, Watertown, N. Y.

SKINNER, Harry (brother of Thomas Gregory Skinner), a Representative from North Carolina; born near Hertford, Perquimans County, N. C., May 25, 1855; attended Hertford Academy and was graduated from the law department of the University of Kentucky at Lexington; was admitted to the bar in 1876 and commenced practice in Greenville, Pitt County, N. C.; member of the town council in 1878; member of Governor Jarvis' staff and served as aide-de-camp 1879–1886; chairman of the Democratic executive committee of the First Congressional District 1880–1890; chairman of the Democratic executive committee of Pitt County 1880–1892; member of the State house of representatives in 1891 and 1892; chairman of the Populist executive committee of Pitt County 1892–1896; member of the State central committee 1892–1896; trustee of the University of North Carolina at Chapel Hill 1890–1896; elected as a Populist to the Fifty-fourth and Fifty-fifth Congresses (March 4, 1895–March 3, 1899); unsuccessful candidate for reelection in 1898 to the Fifty-sixth Congress; United States district attorney for the eastern district of North Carolina 1902–1910; resumed the practice of his profession in Greenville, N. C.; president of the North Carolina Bar Association in 1915 and 1916; vice president and member of the general council of the American Bar Association; died in Greenville, N. C., May 19, 1929; interment in Cherry Hill Cemetery.

SKINNER, Richard, a Representative from Vermont; born in Litchfield, Conn., May 30, 1778; completed preparatory studies and was graduated from Litchfield Law School; was admitted to the bar in 1800 and commenced practice in Manchester, Vt.; State's attorney for Bennington County 1801–1813 and 1819; judge of probate for the Manchester district 1806–1813; elected as a Democrat to the Thirteenth Congress (March 4, 1813–March 3, 1815); unsuccessful candidate for reelection in 1814 to the Fourteenth Congress; resumed the practice of law; assistant judge of the State supreme court in 1815 and 1816; declined the office of chief justice in 1817; member of the State house of representatives in 1815 and 1818, serving as speaker in the latter year; Governor of Vermont 1820–1823; chief justice of the supreme court of Vermont from 1823 until 1828, when he retired; interested in public education and served as president of the northeastern branch of the American Educational Society; trustee of Middlebury College; died in Manchester, Bennington County, Vt., May 23, 1833; interment in Dellwood Cemetery.

SKINNER, Thomas Gregory (brother of Harry Skinner), a Representative from North Carolina; born near Hertford, Perquimans County, N. C., January 22, 1842; attended private schools, Friends Academy, Belvidere, N. C., Horners Military School, Oxford, N. C., and the University of North Carolina at Chapel Hill; entered the Confederate Army in May 1861 and served with the First Regiment, North Carolina Volunteers, until the close of the Civil War, attaining the rank of lieutenant; studied law; was admitted to the bar in 1868 and commenced practice in Hertford, N. C.; delegate to several Democratic State conventions between 1870 and 1902; elected as a Democrat to the Forty-eighth Congress on November 20, 1883, to fill the vacancy caused by the death of Walter F. Pool; reelected to the Forty-ninth Congress and served from November 20, 1883, to March 3, 1887; again elected to the Fifty-first Congress (March 4, 1889–March 3, 1891); declined to be a candidate for renomination in 1890 to the Fifty-second Congress; resumed the practice of his profession in Hertford, N. C.; delegate to the Democratic National Convention at Chicago in 1892 which nominated Cleveland and Stevenson and at St. Louis in 1904 which nominated Parker and Davis; member of the State senate in 1899 and 1900; died in Baltimore, Md., on December 22, 1907; interment in Holy Trinity Churchyard, Hertford, N. C.

SKINNER, Thomson Joseph, a Representative from Massachusetts; born in Colchester, Conn., May 24, 1752; completed preparatory studies; moved to Massachusetts; member of the Massachusetts House of Representatives in 1781, 1785, 1789, 1800, and 1801; served in the State senate 1786–1788, 1790–1797, 1802, and 1803; delegate to the State convention which ratified the Constitution of the United States February 6, 1788; judge of the court of common pleas 1788–1807; presidential elector in 1792 and voted for Washington and Adams; State treasurer in 1806 and 1807; elected as a Democrat to the Fourth Congress to fill the vacancy caused by the resignation of Theodore Sedgwick; reelected to the Fifth Congress and served from January 27, 1797, to March 3, 1799; elected to the Eighth Congress and served from March 4, 1803, to August 10, 1804, when he resigned; died in Boston, Mass., on January 20, 1809.

SLACK, John Mark, Jr., a Representative from West Virginia; born in Charleston, Kanawha County, W. Va., March 18, 1915; attended the public schools in Charleston, W. Va., and Virginia Military Institute at Lexington; engaged in real-estate, construction, and investment business in Charleston, W. Va.; member of Kanawha County Court 1948–1952; Kanawha County assessor 1952–1958; elected as a Democrat to the Eighty-sixth Congress (January 3, 1959–January 3, 1961). *Reelected to the Eighty-seventh Congress.*

SLADE, Charles, a Representative from Illinois; born in England; immigrated to the United States with his parents, who settled in Alexandria, Va.; attended the public schools; moved to Carlyle, St. Clair County, Ill.; engaged in mercantile pursuits; held several local offices; member of the State house of representatives in 1820 and 1826; elected as a Democrat to the Twenty-third Congress and served from March 4, 1833, until his death near Vincennes, Ind., July 26, 1834.

SLADE, William, a Representative from Vermont; born in Cornwall, Vt., May 9, 1786; attended the public schools, and was graduated from Middlebury (Vt.) College in 1807; studied law; was admitted to the bar in 1810 and commenced practice in Middlebury; engaged in editorial work; presidential elector on the Democratic ticket of Madison and Gerry in 1812; established and was the editor of the Columbian Patriot 1814–1816; secretary of state of Vermont 1815–1822; judge of the Addison County Court; clerk in the Department of State, Washington, D. C., 1823–1829; elected as a Whig to the Twenty-second Congress to fill the vacancy caused by the death of Rollin C. Mallary; reelected to the Twenty-third and to the four succeeding Congresses and served from November 1, 1831, to March 3, 1843; reporter of decisions of the State supreme court in 1843 and 1844; Governor of Vermont 1844–1846; corresponding secretary of the Board of National Popular Education 1846–1859; died in Middlebury, Addison County, Vt., on January 18, 1859; interment in West Cemetery.

SLATER, James Harvey, a Representative and a Senator from Oregon; born near Springfield, Sangamon County, Ill., December 28, 1826; attended the common schools; moved to California in 1849; settled in Corvallis, Oreg., in 1850; studied law; was admitted to the bar in 1854; clerk of the district court of the Territory of Oregon for Benton County 1853–1856; member of the Territorial assembly in 1857 and 1858; member of the State house of representatives in 1859; published the Oregon Weekly Union at Corvallis 1859–1861; district attorney for the fifth judicial district of Oregon in 1868; presidential elector on the Democratic ticket of Seymour and Blair in 1868; elected as a Democrat to the Forty-second Congress (March 4, 1871–March 3, 1873); elected to the United States Senate and served from March 4, 1879, to March 3, 1885; resumed the practice of law in La Grande, Oreg.; member of the State railroad commission 1889–1891; died in La Grande, Oreg., January 28, 1899; interment in Masonic Cemetery.

SLATTERY, James Michael, a Senator from Illinois; born in Chicago, Ill., July 29, 1878; attended the parochial schools and St. Ignatius College, Chicago, Ill.; employed as a secretary with the building departments of the city of Chicago in 1905; was graduated from Illinois College of Law at Chicago in 1908; was admitted to the bar the same year and commenced practice in Chicago, Ill.; member of the faculty, Illinois College of Law, 1909–1912; superintendent of public service, Cook County, Ill., 1910–1912; secretary of Webster College of Law, Chicago, Ill., 1912–1914; counsel for the Lincoln Park Commission in 1933 and 1934 and for the Chicago Park District 1934–1936; chairman of the Illinois Commerce Commission 1936–1939; delegate to the Democratic State conventions 1930–1940 and to the Democratic National Conventions in 1936 and 1940; appointed as a Democrat to the United States Senate to fill the vacancy caused by the death of James Hamilton Lewis and served from April 14, 1939, to November 21, 1940, when a duly elected successor qualified; was an unsuccessful candidate for election to fill the vacancy; resumed the practice of law in Chicago, Ill.; died at his summer home at Lake Geneva, Wis., August 28, 1948; interment in Calvary Cemetery, Evanston, Ill.

SLAUGHTER, Roger Caldwell, a Representative from Missouri; born near Odessa, Lafayette County, Mo., July 17, 1905; attended the public schools at Independence, Mo., and was graduated from Princeton University, Princeton, N. J., in 1928; read law in the office of Hon. Henry L. Jost, Kansas City, Mo., and attended the Kansas City School of Law; was admitted to the bar in 1932 and commenced practice in Kansas City; served as assistant prosecutor of Jackson County, Mo., 1932–1936; member of the board of directors of the school district of Kansas City, Mo., 1940–1942; elected as a Democrat to the Seventy-eighth and Seventy-ninth Congresses (January 3, 1943–January 3, 1947); unsuccessful candidate for renomination in 1946; engaged in the practice of law in Kansas City, Mo., where he now resides.

SLAYDEN, James Luther (uncle of Maury Maverick), a Representative from Texas; born in Mayfield, Graves County, Ky., June 1, 1853; upon the death of his father in 1869 moved with his mother to New Orleans, La.; attended the common schools, and Washington and Lee University, Lexington, Va.; moved to San Antonio, Tex., in 1876; became a cotton merchant and ranchman; member of the State house of representatives in 1892; declined to be a candidate for renomination; engaged in agricultural pursuits and mining; appointed as one of the eight envoys to the centennial celebration of the Mexican Republic in September 1910; appointed by Andrew Carnegie as one of the original trustees of the Carnegie Endowment for International Peace in October 1910; president of the American Peace Society for several years; elected as a Democrat to the Fifty-fifth and to the ten succeeding Congresses (March 4, 1897–March 3, 1919); declined renomination in 1918; managed an orchard in Virginia, a ranch in Texas, and mines in Mexico; died in San Antonio, Tex., February 24, 1924; interment in Mission Park Cemetery.

SLAYMAKER, Amos, a Representative from Pennsylvania; born in London Lands, Lancaster County, Pa., on March 11, 1755; received a limited schooling; engaged in agricultural pursuits; built and operated a hotel on the Lancaster and Philadelphia pike and was one of the promoters and proprietors of the stage line operated over that road; during the Revolutionary War served as an ensign in the company of Capt. John Slaymaker; member of an association formed for the suppression of Tory activities in Lancaster County; justice of the peace of Salisbury Township; county commissioner 1806–1810; served in the State senate in 1810 and 1811; elected to the Thirteenth Congress to fill the vacancy caused by the resignation of James Whitehill and served from October 11, 1814, to March 3, 1815; died in Salisbury, Lancaster County, Pa., June 12, 1837.

SLEMONS, William Ferguson, a Representative from Arkansas; born near Dresden, Weakley County, Tenn., March 15, 1830; attended Bethel College; moved to Arkansas in 1852; studied law; was admitted to the bar in 1855 and practiced in Monticello, Drew County; member of the Arkansas State convention in 1861; entered the Confederate Army in July 1861 and served as colonel in Price's Cavalry throughout the Civil War; resumed the practice of law; district attorney 1866–1868; elected as a Democrat to the Forty-fourth, Forty-fifth, and Forty-sixth Congresses (March 4, 1875–March 3, 1881); was not a candidate for renomination in 1880; resumed the practice of his profession in Monticello, Ark.; county and probate judge of Drew County 1903–1907; justice of the peace 1908–1918; died in Monticello, Ark., December 10, 1918; interment in Union Ridge Cemetery, near Monticello, Ark.

SLEMP, Campbell (father of Campbell Bascom Slemp), a Representative from Virginia; born near Turkey Cove, Lee County, Va., December 2, 1839; attended a private school and Emory and Henry College, Emory, Va.; interested in agricultural pursuits and also engaged in the real-estate business; during the Civil War served in the Confederate Army as captain and lieutenant colonel of the Twenty-first Virginia Battalion and colonel of the Sixty-fourth Regiment, composed of Infantry and Cavalry; member of the house of delegates 1879–1882; unsuccessful Republican candidate for Lieutenant Governor in 1889; presidential elector on the Republican ticket of Harrison and Morton in 1888 and of Harrison and Reid in 1892; elected as a Republican to the Fifty-eighth, Fifty-ninth, and Sixtieth Congresses and served from March 4, 1903, until his death in Big Stone Gap, Wise County, Va., October 13, 1907; interment in the family cemetery in Lee County, Va.

SLEMP, Campbell Bascom (son of Campbell Slemp), a Representative from Virginia; born at Turkey Cove, Lee County, Va., September 4, 1870; attended the public schools; served as a page in the Virginia House of Representatives in 1881 and 1882; was graduated from Virginia Military Institute at Lexington in 1891; studied law in the University of Virginia at Charlottesville; was admitted to the bar in 1901 and commenced practice at Big Stone Gap, Wise County, Va.; commandant of cadets at Marion Military Institute for one year; professor of mathematics at Virginia Military Institute for several years, resigning in 1901 to enter professional and business life at Big Stone Gap, Va.; was chairman of the Republican State committee from 1905 to 1918, when he was elected a member of the Republican National Committee; was elected as a Republican to the Sixtieth Congress to fill the vacancy caused by the death of his father, Campbell Slemp; was reelected to the Sixty-first and to the six succeeding Congresses and served from December 17, 1907, to March 3, 1923; declined to be a candidate for reelection in 1922; was appointed secretary to President Calvin Coolidge on September 4, 1923, and served until March 4, 1925, when he resigned; continued the practice of his profession in Big Stone Gap, Va., and in Washington, D. C., until 1932, when he retired and resided at Big Stone Gap, Va.; died, August 7, 1943, in a hospital at Knoxville, Tenn., where he had gone for treatment; interment in the family cemetery at Turkey Cove, Va.

SLIDELL, John, a Representative and a Senator from Louisiana; born in New York City in 1793; was graduated from Columbia College (later Columbia University), New York City, in 1810; studied law; was admitted to the bar in New York City and practiced in New Orleans 1819–1835; member of the State house of representatives; unsuccessful candidate for election in 1828 to the Twenty-first Congress; United States district attorney 1829–1833; elected as a State Rights Democrat to the Twenty-eighth and Twenty-ninth Congresses and served from March 4, 1843, until his resignation November 10, 1845; appointed Minister to Mexico in 1845, but that Government refused to accept him; offered the mission to Central America, but declined; elected to the United States Senate to fill the vacancy caused by the resignation of Pierre Soule; was reelected, and served from December 5, 1853, to February 4, 1861, when he resigned; on November 8, 1861, while on a mission from the Confederate States to England and France, was taken from the British mail steamer *Trent*, sailing from Habana to England, and confined in Fort Warren, Boston Harbor; was later released and sailed for England January 1, 1862; died in Cowes, Isle of Wight, England, July 26, 1871; interment in the private cemetery of the Saint-Roman family at Villejuif, near Paris, France, in the Département de la Seine.

SLINGERLAND, John I., a Representative from New York; born in Jerusalem, Albany County, N. Y., March 1, 1804; attended the public schools; engaged in agricultural pursuits;

member of the State assembly in 1843 and 1844; elected as a Republican to the Thirtieth Congress (March 4, 1847–March 3, 1849); was not a candidate for renomination in 1848; resumed agricultural pursuits; again a member of the State assembly, in 1860 and 1861; died in Slingerland, N. Y., October 26, 1861; interment in the Slingerland family mausoleum.

SLOAN, Andrew, a Representative from Georgia; born in McDonough, Henry County, Ga., June 10, 1845; attended the common schools, Marshall College, Griffin, Ga., and Bethany (W. Va.) College; studied law; was admitted to the bar in 1866 and practiced; solicitor of Henry County in 1866; moved to Savannah, Ga.; deputy collector of customs in 1867; resigned, and resumed the practice of law; assistant United States district attorney in 1869; later appointed district attorney and served until 1872, when he resigned, acting at the same time as local counsel for the United States in regard to the cotton claims and also with the mixed commission on British and American claims; successfully contested as a Republican the election of Morgan Rawls to the Forty-third Congress and served from March 24, 1874, to March 3, 1875; moved to New Mexico in 1881 and settled in Silver City, where he died September 22, 1883; interment in the City Cemetery.

SLOAN, Andrew Scott (brother of Ithamar Conkey Sloan), a Representative from Wisconsin; born in Morrisville, Madison County, N. Y., June 12, 1820; attended the public schools and Morrisville Academy; studied law; was admitted to the bar in 1842 and commenced practice in Morrisville, N. Y.; clerk of the Madison County Court 1847–1849; moved to Wisconsin in 1854 and settled at Beaver Dam, Dodge County, where he continued the practice of law; member of the State assembly in 1857; mayor of Beaver Dam in 1857, 1858, and again in 1879; appointed in 1858 as judge of the circuit court for the third district; elected as a Republican to the Thirty-seventh Congress (March 4, 1861–March 3, 1863); was not a candidate for renomination in 1862; resumed the practice of law; unsuccessful candidate of the Union Party for election in 1864 to the Thirty-ninth Congress; clerk of the United States District Court for Wisconsin 1864–1866; judge of the Dodge County Court 1868–1874; attorney general of Wisconsin 1874–1878; judge of the circuit court for the thirteenth judicial district from January 1882 until his death; died at Beaver Dam, Wis., on April 8, 1895; interment in Oakwood Cemetery.

SLOAN, Charles Henry, a Representative from Nebraska; born in Monticello, Jones County, Iowa, May 2, 1863; attended the public schools, and was graduated from the Iowa State Agricultural College at Ames in 1884; moved to Fairmont, Nebr., the same year; superintendent of the city schools 1884–1887; studied law; was admitted to the bar in 1887 and commenced practice in Fairmont; moved to Geneva, Fillmore County, in 1891 and continued the practice of law; director of the Geneva State Bank; prosecuting attorney of Fillmore County 1890–1894; member of the State senate 1894–1896; chairman of the Republican State convention in 1903; elected as a Republican to the Sixty-second and to the three succeeding Congresses (March 4, 1911–March 3, 1919); did not seek renomination in 1918; elected to the Seventy-first Congress (March 4, 1929–March 3, 1931); unsuccessful for reelection in 1930 to the Seventy-second Congress; resumed the practice of law in Geneva, Nebr., and also engaged in banking; died in Geneva, Nebr., on June 2, 1946; interment in Geneva Cemetery.

SLOAN, Ithamar Conkey (brother of Andrew Scott Sloan), a Representative from Wisconsin; born in Morrisville, Madison County, N. Y., May 9, 1822; attended the common schools; studied law; was admitted to the bar in Oneida County, N. Y., in 1848 and commenced practice; moved to Janesville, Wis., in 1854 and resumed the practice of his profession; district attorney of Rock County, Wis., 1858–1862; elected as a Republican to the Thirty-eighth and Thirty-ninth Congresses (March 4, 1863–March 3, 1867); moved to Madison, Wis., in 1875; dean of the law department of the University of Wisconsin; special counsel for the State of Wisconsin 1874–1879 in the Granger law cases; died in Janesville, Rock County, Wis., December 24, 1898; interment in Oak Hill Cemetery.

SLOAN, James, a Representative from New Jersey; born in that State; engaged in agricultural pursuits; assessor of Newton township for several years; held several other local offices; elected to the Eighth, Ninth, and Tenth Congresses (March 4, 1803–March 3, 1809); was not a candidate for renomination; died in Gloucester County, N. J., in November 1811.

SLOANE, John, a Representative from Ohio; born in York, Pa., in 1779; moved to Ohio in early youth; completed preparatory studies; member of the State house of representatives 1803–1805 and in 1807; colonel of militia in the War of 1812; United States receiver of public moneys at Canton, Ohio, 1808–1816 and at Wooster 1816–1819; elected as a Whig to the Sixteenth and to the four succeeding Congresses (March 4, 1819–March 3, 1829); appointed clerk of the court of common pleas of Wayne County in 1831 and served several years; secretary of state of Ohio 1841–1844; Treasurer of the United States from November 27, 1850, to April 6, 1853; retired from political life and active business pursuits; died in Wooster, Ohio, May 15, 1856; interment in Oak Hill Cemetery.

SLOANE, Jonathan, a Representative from Ohio; born in Pelham, Mass, in November 1785; completed preparatory studies, and was graduated from Williams College, Williamstown, Mass., in 1812; studied law; was admitted to the bar in 1816 and commenced practice in Ravenna, Ohio; was also general agent of the Tappan family for the sale of lands; prosecuting attorney of Portage County in 1819; member of the State house of representatives 1820–1822; served in the State senate in 1826 and 1827; elected as a Whig to the Twenty-third and Twenty-fourth Congresses (March 4, 1833–March 3, 1837); declined to be a candidate for renomination in 1836; retired from business activities on account of ill health; died in Ravenna, Portage County, Ohio, April 25, 1854; interment in Evergreen Cemetery.

SLOCUM, Henry Warner, a Representative from New York; born in Delphi, Onondaga County, N. Y., September 24, 1827; was graduated from the United States Military Academy at West Point and commissioned as a second lieutenant, First Artillery, July 1, 1852; served in the Seminole War and was promoted to first lieutenant March 3, 1855; resigned his commission October 31, 1856; settled in Syracuse, N. Y.; studied law while in the Army; was admitted to the bar in 1858 and practiced in Syracuse, N. Y.; member of the State assembly in 1859; during the Civil War entered the Union Army as colonel of the Twenty-eighth New York Volunteers in May 1861; wounded at the first Battle of Bull Run; promoted to brigadier general of Volunteers August 9, 1861; major general of Volunteers July 4, 1862; resigned his commission September 28, 1865, and settled in Brooklyn, N. Y., where he continued the practice of law; unsuccessful Democratic candidate for secretary of state of New York; presidential elector on the Democratic ticket of Seymour and Blair in 1868; elected as a Democrat to the Forty-first and Forty-second Congresses (March 4, 1869–March 3, 1873); was not a candidate for renomination in 1872; resumed the practice of law; was appointed president of the department of city works in 1876; elected as a Representative at Large from New York to the Forty-eighth Congress (March 4, 1883–March 3, 1885); died in Brooklyn, N. Y., April 14, 1894; interment in Greenwood Cemetery.

SLOCUMB, Jesse, a Representative from North Carolina; born in Spring Bank, Dobbs (later Wayne) County, N. C., in 1780; completed preparatory studies; engaged in agricultural pursuits; held several local offices; member of the court of pleas and quarter sessions of the county; register of deeds 1802–1808; elected as a Federalist to the Fifteenth and Sixteenth Congresses and served from March 4, 1817, until his death in Washington, D. C., December 20, 1820; interment in Congressional Cemetery.

SLOSS, Joseph Humphrey, a Representative from Alabama; born in Somerville, Ala., October 12, 1826; completed preparatory studies; studied law; was admitted to the bar and commenced practice in St. Louis, Mo.; moved to Edwardsville, Ill., in 1849; member of the Illinois State House of Representatives in 1858 and 1859; returned to Alabama; during the Civil War served in the Confederate Army; mayor of Tuscumbia, Ala.; elected as a Conservative Democrat to the Forty-second and Forty-third Congresses (March 4, 1871–March 3, 1875); unsuccessful candidate for reelection in 1874 to the Forty-fourth Congress; appointed United States marshal for the northern district of Alabama February 10, 1877, and served until September 6, 1882; clerk of the Federal court at Huntsville, Ala.; engaged in agricultural pursuits near Huntsville; moved to Memphis, Tenn., where he died January 27, 1911; interment in Maple Hill Cemetery, Huntsville, Ala.

SMALL, Frank, Jr., a Representative from Maryland; born on a farm in Temple Hills, Prince Georges County, Md., July 15, 1896; attended the public schools and received technical education at the National Automobile College in 1914 and 1915; worked on father's farm and also operated several farms of his own; engaged in banking and the automobile business 1923–1957; served in the State house of delegates in 1927 and 1928; member of the board of county commissioners 1930–1934; member of the Republican State Central Committee 1934–1942, serving as chairman for four years; member of the Maryland Racing Commission 1937–1952, serving as chairman in 1951 and 1952; president of Clinton Bank, Clinton, Md., 1938– ; president of the National Association of State Racing Commissioners in 1951 and 1952; elected as a Republican to the Eighty-third Congress (January 3, 1953–January 3, 1955); was unsuccessful for reelection in 1954 to the Eighty-fourth Congress; president of Clinton Realty Co., 1954– ; Maryland Commissioner of Motor Vehicles from April 29, 1955, to April 15, 1957; director of National Capital Bank, American Savings & Loan Association, and Washington Petroleum Products Corp.; is a resident of Clinton, Md.

SMALL, John Humphrey, a Representative from North Carolina; born in Washington, Beaufort County, N. C., August 29, 1858; attended private schools and Trinity College (later Duke University), Durham, N. C.; taught school 1876–1880; studied law; was admitted to the bar in 1881 and commenced practice in Washington, N. C.; elected reading clerk of the State senate in 1881; superintendent of public instruction of Beaufort County, N. C., in 1881; solicitor of the inferior court of Beaufort County 1882–1885; editor of the Washington Gazette 1883–1886; attorney of the Board of Commissioners of Beaufort County 1888–1896; member of the city council 1887–1890; mayor of Washington, N. C., in 1889 and 1890; delegate to all Democratic State conventions from 1889 to 1920; presidential elector on the Democratic ticket of Bryan and Sewall in 1896; elected as a Democrat to the Fifty-sixth and to the ten succeeding Congresses (March 4, 1899–March 3, 1921); declined to be a candidate for renomination in 1920; resumed the practice of his profession in Washington, D. C., until 1931 when he retired from active pursuits; returned to Washington, N. C., where he died on July 13, 1946; interment in Oakdale Cemetery.

SMALL, William Bradbury, a Representative from New Hampshire; born in Limington, Maine, May 17, 1817; moved with his parents to Ossipee, N. H.; attended the public schools and Phillips Exeter Academy, Exeter, N. H.; studied law; was admitted to the bar in 1846 and commenced practice in Newmarket, N. H.; solicitor of Rockingham County, N. H.; member of the State house of representatives in 1865; served in the State senate in 1870; elected as a Republican to the Forty-third Congress (March 4, 1873–March 3, 1875); was not a candidate for renomination in 1874; resumed the practice of law and also engaged in banking; died in Newmarket, N. H., April 7, 1878; interment in Riverside Cemetery.

SMALLS, Robert, a Representative from South Carolina; born in Beaufort, S. C., April 5, 1839; was of the Negro race; moved to Charleston, S. C., in 1851; appointed pilot in the United States Navy and served in that capacity on the monitor *Keokuk* in the attack on Fort Sumter; also served as pilot in the quartermaster's department; promoted to the rank of captain for gallant and meritorious conduct December 1, 1863; placed in command of the *Planter* and served until that vessel was placed out of commission in 1866; member of the State constitutional convention in 1868; served in the State house of representatives in 1868; member of the State senate 1870–1872; delegate to the Republican National Convention at Philadelphia in 1872 and at Cincinnati in 1876; elected as a Republican to the Forty-fourth and Forty-fifth Congresses (March 4, 1875–March 3, 1879); unsuccessful candidate for reelection in 1878 to the Forty-sixth Congress; successfully contested the election of George D. Tillman to the Forty-seventh Congress and served from July 19, 1882, to March 3, 1883; unsuccessful candidate for reelection in 1882; elected to the Forty-eighth Congress to fill the vacancy caused by the death of Edmund W. M. Mackey; reelected to the Forty-ninth Congress and served from March 18, 1884, to March 3, 1887; unsuccessful for reelection in 1886 to the Fiftieth Congress; collector of the port of Beaufort, S. C., 1897–1913; died in Beaufort, S. C., February 22, 1915; interment in the Tabernacle Baptist Church Cemetery.

SMART, Ephraim Knight, a Representative from Maine; born in Prospect (now Searsport), Maine, September 3, 1813; attended the common schools; completed preparatory studies under private tutors and attended Maine Wesleyan Seminary at Readfield; studied law; was admitted to the bar in 1838 and commenced practice in Camden, Knox County, Maine; appointed postmaster of Camden in 1838; member of the State senate in 1841 and 1842; appointed aide-de-camp with the rank of lieutenant colonel on the staff of Governor Fairfield in 1842; moved to Missouri in 1843 and continued the practice of his profession; returned to Camden, Maine, the following year and resumed the practice of law; again appointed postmaster of Camden in 1845; elected as a Democrat to the Thirtieth Congress (March 4, 1847–March 3, 1849); elected to the Thirty-second Congress (March 4, 1851–March 3, 1853); collector of customs at Belfast 1853–1858; established the Maine Free Press in 1854, and served as editor for three years; member of the State house of representatives in 1858; unsuccessful candidate for Governor of Maine in 1860; again served in the State senate in 1862; moved to Biddeford, York County, Maine, in 1869 and established the Maine Democrat; died in Camden, Maine, September 29, 1872; interment in the Mountain Street Cemetery.

SMART, James Stevenson, a Representative from New York; born in Baltimore, Md., June 14, 1842; moved with his parents to Coila, Washington County, N. Y., in 1849; attended Cambridge (N. Y.) Academy and Union College, Schenectady, N. Y., and was graduated from Jefferson College, Canonsburg, Pa., in 1863; during the Civil War entered the Union Army in January 1864 as first lieutenant in the Sixteenth Regiment of New York Heavy Artillery; served in the Army of the James until the second expedition to Fort Fisher; promoted to a captaincy, and was honorably discharged in August 1865; engaged in newspaper work at Cambridge, N. Y., in 1865 and published the Washington County Post; elected as a Republican to the Forty-third Congress (March 4, 1873–March 3, 1875); was not a candidate for renomination in 1874; appointed collector of internal revenue for the northern district of New York and served from March 31, 1883, until November 9, 1885; member of the Republican State central committee for many years; died in Cambridge, Washington County, N. Y., September 17, 1903; interment in Woodland Cemetery.

SMATHERS, George Armistead (nephew of William H. Smathers), a Representative and a Senator from Florida; born in Atlantic City, N. J., November 14, 1913; moved to Miami, Fla., in 1919; attended the public schools of Dade County, Fla.; was graduated from the University of Florida at Gainesville in 1936 and from its law school in 1938; was admitted to the bar in 1938 and commenced practice in Miami, Fla.; assistant United States district attorney 1940–1942; during World War II served in the United States Marine Corps from May 1942 until discharged as a major in October 1945; special assistant to the attorney general from October 1945 until his resignation in January 1946 to begin his campaign for Representative in Congress; elected as a Democrat to the Eightieth and Eighty-first Congresses (January 3, 1947–January 3, 1951); was not a candidate for renomination in 1950; elected to the United States Senate in 1950 for the term commencing January 3, 1951; reelected in 1956 for the term ending January 3, 1963.

SMATHERS, William Howell (uncle of George A. Smathers), a Senator from New Jersey; born on a plantation near Waynesville, Haywood County, N. C., January 7, 1891; attended the public schools and Washington and Lee University, Lexington, Va.; was graduated from the law department of the University of North Carolina at Chapel Hill in 1911; was admitted to the bar in 1912 and commenced practice in Atlantic City, N. J.; judge of the common pleas court of Atlantic City, N. J., 1922–1932; member of the State supreme court commission since 1923; special master in chancery in 1924; first assistant attorney general of New Jersey 1934–1936; elected a member of the State senate in 1935; delegate at large to the Democratic National Conventions in 1936, 1940, and 1948; elected as a Democrat to the United States Senate for the term beginning January 3, 1937, but was not sworn in until April 15, 1937, being a member of the State senate until that time, and served until January 3, 1943; unsuccessful candidate for reelection in 1942; engaged in the practice of law in Atlantic City, N. J., until his retirement; returned to Waynesville, N. C., where he resided until his death in Asheville, N. C., September 24, 1955; interment in Green Hill Cemetery, Waynesville, N. C.

SMELT, Dennis, a Representative from Georgia; born near Savannah, Ga., about 1750; received a limited schooling; participated in the Revolutionary War; elected to the Ninth Congress to fill the vacancy caused by the resignation of Joseph Bryan; reelected to the Tenth and Eleventh Congresses and served from September 1, 1806, to March 3, 1811; was not a candidate for reelection to the Twelfth Congress.

SMILIE, John, a Representative from Pennsylvania; born in Ireland in 1741; immigrated to the United States and settled in Pennsylvania in 1760; attended the public schools; served in the Revolutionary War; moved to Fayette, Pa., in 1780; was a member of the State house of representatives 1784–1786; member of the State constitutional convention in 1790; served in the State senate from 1790 to 1793, when he resigned; elected as a Democrat to the Third Congress (March 4, 1793–March 3, 1795); Democratic presidential elector in 1796; elected to the Sixth and to the six succeeding Congresses and served from March 4, 1799, until his death; had been reelected to the Thirteenth Congress, but died in Washington, D. C., December 30, 1812, before the close of the Twelfth Congress; interment in the Congressional Cemetery.

SMITH, Abraham Herr, a Representative from Pennsylvania; born near Millersville, Manor Township, in Lancaster County, Pa., March 7, 1815; attended Professor Beck's Academy at Lititz, Lancaster County, Pa.; was graduated from Dickinson College, Carlisle, Pa., in 1840; studied law; was admitted to the bar in 1842 and commenced practice in Lancaster, Lancaster County, Pa.; member of the State house of representatives in 1843 and 1844; served in the State senate in 1845; elected as a Republican to the Forty-third and to the five succeeding Congresses (March 4, 1873–March 3, 1885); unsuccessful for renomination in 1884; resumed the practice of law; died in Lancaster, Pa., February 16, 1894; interment in Woodward Hill Cemetery.

SMITH, Addison Taylor, a Representative from Idaho; born near Cambridge, Guernsey County, Ohio, September 5, 1862; attended the public schools of Cambridge, Ohio; was graduated from the Cambridge High School in 1882, from the Iron City Commercial College, Pittsburgh, Pa., in 1883, from the law department of George Washington University, Washington, D. C., in 1895, and from the National Law School, Washington, D. C., in 1896; was admitted to the District of Columbia bar in 1899 and to the Idaho bar in 1905; secretary to Senator George Laird Shoup 1891–1901 and to Senator Weldon B. Heyburn 1903–1912; secretary to the Republican State central committee of Idaho 1904–1911; register of the United States land office at Boise, Idaho, in 1907 and 1908; member of the Republican National congressional committee 1917–1927; elected as a Republican to the Sixty-third and to the nine succeeding Congresses (March 4, 1913–March 3, 1933); unsuccessful candidate for reelection in 1932 to the Seventy-third Congress; associate member of the Board of Veterans' Appeals of the Veterans' Administration from 1934 until his retirement in 1942; director of the Columbia Institution for the Deaf (now Gallaudet College), Washington, D. C., from 1937 until his death; died in Washington, D. C., July 5, 1956; interment in Rock Creek Cemetery.

SMITH, Albert, a Representative from Maine; born in Hanover, Mass., January 3, 1793; attended the common schools, and was graduated from Brown University, Providence, R. I., in 1813; studied law; was admitted to the bar and commenced practice in Portland, Maine, in 1817; member of the State house of representatives in 1820; was United States marshal for the district of Maine 1830–1838; was elected as a Democrat to the Twenty-sixth Congress (March 4, 1839–March 3, 1841); unsuccessful candidate for reelection in 1840 to the Twenty-seventh Congress; retired; died in Boston, Mass., on May 29, 1867; interment in Mount Auburn Cemetery, Cambridge, Mass.

SMITH, Albert, a Representative from New York, born in Cooperstown, Otsego County, N. Y., June 22, 1805; completed preparatory studies; moved to Batavia, Genesee County, N. Y.; studied law; was admitted to the bar and practiced; held several local offices; member of the State assembly in 1840; elected as a Republican to the Twenty-eighth and Twenty-ninth Congresses (March 4, 1843–March 3, 1847); moved to Milwaukee, Wis., in 1849 and resumed the practice of law; justice of the peace 1851–1859; judge of the Milwaukee County Court 1859–1870; died in Milwaukee, Wis., August 27, 1870; interment in Forest Home Cemetery.

SMITH, Arthur, a Representative from Virginia; born at "Windsor Castle," near Smithfield, Isle of Wight County, Va., November 15, 1785; attended an academy at Smithfield, Va., and was graduated from William and Mary College, Williamsburg, Va.; studied law; was admitted to the bar in 1808 and commenced practice in Smithfield, Va.; also engaged in agricultural pursuits; served as colonel in the War of 1812; member of the State house of delegates 1818–1820; elected to the Seventeenth and Eighteenth Congresses (March 4, 1821–March 3, 1825); was not a candidate for renomination in 1824; resumed the practice of law; member of the house of delegates 1836–1841; died in Smithfield, Va., March 30, 1853; interment in the family burying ground on Windsor Castle estate, near Smithfield, Va.

SMITH, Ballard, a Representative from Virginia; born in Hanover County, Va.; served as lieutenant in the Army during the Revolutionary War; member of the State house of delegates 1810–1813; elected to the Fourteenth, Fifteenth, and Sixteenth Congresses (March 4, 1815–March 3, 1821); again a member of the State house of delegates 1824–1826, 1836, and 1837.

SMITH, Bernard, a Representative from New Jersey; born in Morristown, N. J., July 5, 1776; completed preparatory studies collector of customs in 1809 and 1810; postmaster of New Brunswick 1810–1819; elected to the Sixteenth Congress (March 4, 1819–March 3, 1821); did not seek renomination in 1820; appointed register of the land office at Little Rock, Ark., in 1821, and settled in that State; secretary to the Governor of Arkansas 1825–1828; appointed by Governor Izard as subagent of the Quapaw Indians in 1825, and served until his death in Little Rock, Ark., July 16, 1835; interment in Mount Holly Cemetery.

SMITH, Caleb Blood, a Representative from Indiana; born in Boston, Mass., April 16, 1808; moved with his parents to Ohio in 1814; attended Miami University, Oxford, Ohio, 1825–1826; studied law; was admitted to the bar in 1828 and commenced practice in Connersville, Fayette County, Ind.; founded and edited the Indiana Sentinel in 1832; member of the State house of representatives 1833–1837, 1840, and 1841, and served as speaker in 1836; presidential elector on the Whig ticket of Harrison and Tyler in 1840; elected as a Whig to the Twenty-eighth, Twenty-ninth, and Thirtieth Congresses (March 4, 1843–March 3, 1849); appointed by President Zachary Taylor, at the close of his term, a member of the board to investigate claims of American citizens against Mexico; moved to Cincinnati, Ohio, and practiced his profession; presidential elector on the Republican ticket of Frémont and Dayton in 1856; member of the peace convention of 1861 held in Washington, D. C., in an effort to devise means to prevent the impending war; appointed Secretary of the Interior in the Cabinet of President Lincoln and served from March 5, 1861, to January 1, 1863, when he resigned to become judge of the United States District Court for the District of Indiana, in which capacity he served until his death in Indianapolis, Marion County, Ind., January 7, 1864; interment in the City Cemetery, Connersville, Ind.

SMITH, Charles Bennett, a Representative from New York; born in Sardinia, Erie County, N. Y., September 14, 1870; attended the district schools, and was graduated from Arcade

Academy in 1886; engaged in agricultural pursuits, subsequently became a railroad telegraph operator, and later pursued newspaper work in Buffalo; reporter on the Buffalo Courier 1890–1893; became managing editor of the Buffalo Times in 1894, which position he resigned to take editorial charge of the Buffalo Evening Enquirer and the Buffalo Morning Courier; subsequently relinquished the editorship of the Enquirer, but continued as chief editor of the Courier from 1897 to 1910; in the meantime was appointed a member of the Buffalo Board of School Examiners and served two years as its chairman; elected as a Democrat to the Sixty-second and to the three succeeding Congresses (March 4, 1911–March 3, 1919); unsuccessful candidate for reelection in 1918 to the Sixty-sixth Congress; engaged in commercial and industrial pursuits in Buffalo, N. Y.; superintendent of Standards and Purchases, Albany, N. Y., from 1935 until his death; died in Wilmington Notch, Essex County, N. Y., May 21, 1939; interment in Mount Olivet Cemetery, Tonawanda, Erie County, N. Y.

SMITH, Charles Brooks, a Representative from West Virginia; born in Elizabeth, Wirt County, Va. (now West Virginia), February 24, 1844; attended a private school at Parkersburg; during the Civil War enlisted on March 1, 1864, in Company I of the First West Virginia Cavalry of the Union Army; promoted to second lieutenant of the company March 5, 1864, and was honorably discharged on July 8, 1865; engaged in the mercantile business; recorder of Wood County in 1875; member of the city council of Parkersburg, W. Va., in 1876; mayor of Parkersburg 1878–1880; sheriff and treasurer of Wood County 1880–1884; delegate at large to the Republican National Convention at Chicago in 1888 which nominated Harrison and Morton; successfully contested as a Republican the election of James Monroe Jackson to the Fifty-first Congress and served from February 3, 1890, to March 3, 1891; unsuccessful candidate for reelection to the Fifty-second Congress in 1890; became engaged in the fire insurance business; died in Parkersburg, Wood County, W. Va., December 7, 1899; interment in Mount Olivet Cemetery.

SMITH, Clyde Harold (husband of Margaret Chase Smith), a Representative from Maine; born on a farm near Harmony, Somerset County, Maine, June 9, 1876; moved with his parents to Hartland, Maine, in 1891; attended the rural schools and Hartland (Maine) Academy; taught school; served in the State house of representatives 1899–1903 and 1919–1923; engaged in the retail clothing and hardware business in 1901; superintendent of schools of Hartland 1903–1906; member of the board of selectmen of Hartland 1904–1907; moved to Skowhegan, Maine, having been elected sheriff of Somerset County and served from 1905 to 1909; engaged in the retail sales of automobiles, the hardware and plumbing business, and the newspaper publishing business in Skowhegan; later engaged in banking and the real-estate business; member of the board of selectmen of Skowhegan 1914–1932; chairman of the board of directors for locating and building the State reformatory for women in 1917; served in the State senate 1923–1929; chairman of the State highway commission 1928–1932; member of the Governor's council 1933–1937; elected as a Republican to the Seventy-fifth and Seventy-sixth Congresses and served from January 3, 1937, until his death in Washington, D. C., April 8, 1940; interment in Pine Grove Cemetery, Hartland, Maine.

SMITH, Daniel, a Senator from Tennessee; born in Stafford County, Va., October 28, 1748; attended William and Mary College, Williamsburg, Va.; became a surveyor; moved to Augusta County, Va.; deputy surveyor of Augusta County in 1773; justice of the peace in 1776; major of the Washington Militia; high sheriff of Augusta County in 1780; commissioned colonel in the Second Battalion and fought in several battles of the Revolution; moved to Sumner County, Tenn., at the close of the war; appointed by President Washington secretary of the Territory South of the River Ohio January 7, 1790; member of the State constitutional convention of 1796; made the first map of Tennessee; general of State milita; appointed to the United States Senate to fill the vacancy caused by the resignation of Andrew Jackson and served from October 6, 1798, to March 3, 1799; Democratic presidential elector in 1800, and voted for Jefferson and Burr; elected to the United States Senate and served from March 4, 1805, to March 31, 1809, when he resigned; engaged in agricultural pursuits; died at his home, "Rock Castle," near Hendersonville, Sumner County, Tenn., June 6, 1818; interment in the family burial ground near his home.

SMITH, David Highbaugh, a Representative from Kentucky; born near Hammonville, Hart County, Ky., December 19, 1854; attended the public schools and the colleges at Horse Cave, Leitchfield, and Hartford, Ky.; studied law; was admitted to the bar in 1876 and commenced practice in Hodgenville, Larue County, Ky.; superintendent of common schools for Larue County in 1878; county attorney for Larue County 1878–1881; member of the State house of representatives 1881–1883; served in the State senate 1885–1893, and as president pro tempore 1891–1893; elected as a Democrat to the Fifty-fifth and to the four succeeding Congresses (March 4, 1897–March 3, 1907); was not a candidate for renomination in 1906; one of the managers appointed by the House of Representatives in 1905 to conduct the impeachment proceedings against Charles Swayne, judge of the United States District Court for the Northern District of Florida; resumed the practice of law; president of the Farmers' National Bank of Hodgenville, Ky.; died in Hodgenville, Ky., December 17, 1928; interment in Red Hill Cemetery.

SMITH, Delazon, a Senator from Oregon; born in New Berlin, Chenango County, N. Y., October 5, 1816; was graduated from Oberlin College, Ohio, in 1837; studied law and was admitted to the bar; in 1838 established the New York Watchman in Rochester, N. Y., of which he was editor for two years; published and edited the True Jeffersonian and the Western Herald in Rochester in 1840, and in 1841 founded the Western Empire in Dayton, Ohio; special United States commissioner to Quito, Ecuador, 1842–1845; moved to the Territory of Iowa in 1846 and entered the ministry; moved to the Territory of Oregon in 1852; edited the Oregon Democrat; member of the Territorial house of representatives 1854–1856; delegate to the State constitutional convention in 1857; upon the admission of Oregon as a State into the Union was elected as a Democrat to the United States Senate and served from February 14 to March 3, 1859; unsuccessful candidate for reelection; was an unsuccessful candidate for Democratic presidential elector in 1860; died in Portland, Oreg., on November 19, 1860; interment in the City Cemetery, Albany, Linn County, Oreg.

SMITH, Dietrich Conrad, a Representative from Illinois; born in Ost Friesland, Hanover, Germany, April 4, 1840; immigrated to the United States with his parents, who settled in Pekin, Tazewell County, Ill., about 1850; attended the public schools of Pekin, Ill., and Quincy College, Quincy, Ill.; during the Civil War served in the Union Army as lieutenant in Company I, Eighth Regiment, Illinois Volunteer Infantry; left the service as captain of Company C, One Hundred and Thirty-ninth Regiment, Illinois Volunteer Infantry; lay delegate to the Methodist General Conference in 1872; organizer of the German College at Mount Pleasant in 1874; member of board of trustees of that institution for many years; member of the State house of representatives 1876–1878; engaged in banking and manu-

facturing and also in the construction and management of railroads in Illinois; sent as a delegate to the Ecumenical Conference of the Methodist Church held in London, England, about 1880; elected as a Republican to the Forty-seventh Congress (March 4, 1881–March 3, 1883); unsuccessful candidate for reelection in 1882 to the Forty-eighth Congress; again engaged in banking; retired from public life; died in Pekin, Ill., April 18, 1914; interment in Lakeside Cemetery.

SMITH, Edward Henry, a Representative from New York; born in Smithtown, Long Island, Suffolk County, N. Y., May 5, 1809; attended private schools; engaged in agricultural pursuits; served as justice of the peace in the township of Smithtown 1833–1843, assessor 1840–1843, and supervisor 1856–1860; elected as a Democrat to the Thirty-seventh Congress (March 4, 1861–March 3, 1863); was not a candidate for renomination in 1862; resumed farming in Suffolk County, N. Y.; died in Smithtown, N. Y., August 7, 1885; interment in St. James' Protestant Episcopal Cemetery, St. James, Long Island, N. Y.

SMITH, Ellison DuRant, a Senator from South Carolina; born in Lynchburg, Sumter (now Lee) County, S. C., August 1, 1866; attended the private and public schools of Lynchburg, Stewart's School at Charleston, S. C., and the University of South Carolina at Columbia; was graduated from Wofford College at Spartanburg, S. C., in 1889; member of the State house of representatives 1896–1900; engaged in mercantile and agricultural pursuits; one of the principal figures in the organization of the Southern Cotton Association at New Orleans in January 1905; field agent and general organizer in the cotton protective movement 1905–1908, his territory covering the entire South; elected as a Democrat to the United States Senate in 1908; reelected in 1914, 1920, 1926, 1932, and again in 1938, and served from March 4, 1909, until his death; unsuccessful candidate for renomination in 1944; died in Lynchburg, S. C., on November 17, 1944; interment in St. Luke's Cemetery.

SMITH, Francis Ormand Jonathan, a Representative from Maine; born in Brentwood, N. H., November 23, 1806; attended Phillips Exeter Academy, Exeter, N. H.; studied law; was admitted to the bar and commenced practice in Portland, Maine, in 1826; division advocate of the fifth division of the circuit court-martial in Maine 1829–1834; served in the State house of representatives in 1831; member of the State senate in 1833 and served as its president; elected as a Democrat to the Twenty-third, Twenty-fourth, and Twenty-fifth Congresses (March 4, 1833–March 3, 1839); unsuccessful candidate for reelection in 1838 to the Twenty-sixth Congress; assisted Professor Morse in perfecting and introducing the electric telegraph; again a member of the State house of representatives in 1863 and 1864; died in Deering (later Woodfords), Maine, October 14, 1876; interment on his estate, "Forest Home"; reinterment in Evergreen Cemetery, Portland, Maine.

SMITH, Francis Raphael, a Representative from Pennsylvania; born in Philadelphia, Pa., September 25, 1911; attended the parochial school and was graduated from Roman Catholic High School, Philadelphia, Pa., in 1929, from St. Joseph's College, Philadelphia, Pa., in 1933, and from the law department of Temple University, Philadelphia, Pa., in 1938; bank examiner with Pennsylvania State Banking Department in 1938 and 1939; unsuccessful candidate for election in 1938 to the State house of representatives; elected as a Democrat to the Seventy-seventh Congress (January 3, 1941–January 3, 1943); unsuccessful candidate for reelection in 1942 to the Seventy-eighth Congress; United States marshal for the eastern district of Pennsylvania from January 29, 1943, until his resignation on April 30, 1945;

was appointed collector of internal revenue at Philadelphia on May 1, 1945, and served in that capacity until 1952; insurance commissioner, Commonwealth of Pennsylvania, 1955–; is a resident of Philadelphia, Pa.

SMITH, Frank Ellis, a Representative from Mississippi; born in Sidon, Leflore County, Miss., February 21, 1918; attended the public schools of Sidon and Greenwood, Miss.; was graduated from Sunflower Junior College, Moorhead, Miss., in 1936 and from the University of Mississippi in 1941; entered the United States Army as a private on February 9, 1942; graduate of Field Artillery officers candidate school; served in Europe as a captain with the Two Hundred and Forty-third Field Artillery Battalion, Third Army; was discharged to Reserves as a major of Field Artillery on February 13, 1946; awarded Bronze Star; editor of Greenwood Morning Star in 1946 and 1947; newspaperman and writer; student at American University, Washington, D. C., in 1946; legislative assistant to United States Senator John Stennis 1947–1949; member of State senate 1948–1950; member of Mississippi Historical Commission; elected as a Democrat to the Eighty-second and to the four succeeding Congresses (January 3, 1951–January 3, 1961). *Reelected to the Eighty-seventh Congress.*

SMITH, Frank Leslie, a Representative and a Senator from Illinois; born in Dwight, Livingston County, Ill., November 24, 1867; attended the public schools and graduated from the high school of his native city; taught school for several years; engaged in banking, real estate, insurance, and agricultural pursuits in 1893; member of the Republican State central committee 1902–1925, and served as chairman in 1918, 1920, and 1924; internal-revenue collector 1905–1909; delegate to the Republican National Conventions in 1904, 1908, 1912, 1920, 1924, 1932, 1936, 1940, 1944, and 1948; elected as a Republican to the Sixty-sixth Congress (March 4, 1919–March 3, 1921); was not a candidate for renomination in 1920, but was an unsuccessful candidate for the Republican nomination for United States Senator; resumed his former business pursuits in Dwight, Ill.; appointed chairman of the State Public Utilities Commission (now State Commerce Commission) in 1921; reappointed in 1925, and served until his resignation in 1926; presented credentials as a Senator-designate to the United States Senate under appointment of December 16, 1926, to fill the vacancy caused by the death of William B. McKinley in the term ending March 3, 1927, but was not permitted to qualify; presented credentials as a Senator-elect to the United States Senate for the term beginning March 4, 1927, but was not permitted to qualify and subsequently tendered his resignation on February 9, 1928; elected a member of the Republican National Committee in 1932; unsuccessful candidate for election in 1930 to the Seventy-second Congress; continued in real-estate and insurance business and agricultural pursuits; was chairman of the board of directors of the First National Bank of Dwight, Ill., until his death there August 30, 1950; interment in Oak Lawn Cemetery.

SMITH, Frank Owens, a Representative from Maryland; born in Smithville, Calvert County, Md., August 27, 1859; attended the private and public schools of the county, North Mount Institute, West Virginia, and Bethel Military Academy, Virginia; served in the United States Revenue Service at Baltimore, Md., during the first Cleveland administration; resigned in 1889; organized the Calumet Canning Co. in 1889 and engaged in a general merchandise business in 1890; engaged in manufacturing flour and feed 1898–1910; appointed State tobacco inspector by Governor Warfield in 1904 and reappointed in 1906; unsuccessful candidate for election to the State senate in 1911; chief engrossing clerk of the State senate in 1911; elected as a Democrat to the Sixty-third Congress (March 4,

1913–March 3, 1915); unsuccessful candidate for renomination in 1914; engaged in fruit growing in Dunkirk, Calvert County, Md., until his death on January 29, 1924; interment in Mount Zion Cemetery, Lothian, Ann Arundel County, Md.

SMITH, Frederick Cleveland, a Representative from Ohio; born in Shanesville, Tuscarawas County, Ohio, July 29, 1884; attended the public schools; graduated in osteopathy at Kirksville, Ohio, and practiced there for several years; went abroad and continued his study of medicine in Frankfurt, Germany, and in Vienna, Austria; in 1917 was licensed to practice medicine and surgery in the State of Ohio and commenced practice at Marion, Ohio; founded the Frederick C. Smith Clinic in 1920; mayor of Marion, Ohio, from January 1936 until January 1, 1939, when he resigned, having been elected to Congress; elected as a Republican to the Seventy-sixth and to the five succeeding Congresses (January 3, 1939–January 3, 1951); was not a candidate for renomination in 1950; resumed his medical profession; died in Marion, Ohio, July 16, 1956; interment in Marion Cemetery.

SMITH, George, a Representative from Pennsylvania; was elected to the Eleventh and Twelfth Congresses (March 4, 1809–March 3, 1813).

SMITH, George Joseph, a Representative from New York; born in Kingston, Ulster County, N. Y., November 7, 1859; attended the public schools; engaged in banking and the manufacturing business in New York City and Kingston; chairman of the Republican county committee in 1898; treasurer of the Republican State committee in 1899; delegate to numerous Republican State conventions and also to the Republican National Convention at Philadelphia in 1909; elected as a Republican to the Fifty-eighth Congress (March 4, 1903–March 3, 1905); declined to be a candidate for reelection; engaged in the real estate and wholesale grocery business in New York City; died in Atlantic City, N. J., December 24, 1913; interment in Wiltwyck Cemetery, Kingston, N. Y.

SMITH, George Luke, a Representative from Louisiana; born in New Boston, Hillsboro County, N. H., December 11, 1837; completed preparatory studies and attended Union College, Schenectady, N. Y.; during the Civil War served in the Union Army; at the close of the war moved to Shreveport, La., and engaged in mercantile pursuits; held several local offices; member of the State house of representatives 1870–1872; proprietor of the Shreveport Southwestern Telegram; president of the Shreveport Savings Bank & Trust Co.; elected as a Republican to the Forty-third Congress to fill the vacancy caused by the death of Representative-elect Samuel Peters and served from November 24, 1873, to March 3, 1875; unsuccessful candidate for reelection in 1874 to the Forty-fourth Congress; appointed collector of customs at the port of New Orleans by President Hayes and served from May 4, 1878, to February 20, 1879; moved to Hot Springs, Ark., and engaged in the real-estate business until his death in that city on July 9, 1884; interment in the West Street Cemetery, Milford, N. H.

SMITH, George Ross, a Representative from Minnesota; born in St. Cloud, Stearns County, Minn., May 28, 1864; attended the public schools and Sauk Centre (Minn.) Academy; was graduated from the law school of the University of Minnesota at Minneapolis in 1893; was admitted to the bar in 1893 and commenced practice in Minneapolis; member of the State house of representatives in 1903; judge of the probate court of Hennepin County, Minn., 1907–1913; elected as a Republican to the Sixty-third and Sixty-fourth Congresses (March 4, 1913–

March 3, 1917); unsuccessful candidate for reelection in 1916 to the Sixty-fifth Congress; resumed the practice of law and taught law classes at Minneapolis-Minnesota Law School; died in Minneapolis, Minn., November 7, 1952; interment in St. Mary's Cemetery.

SMITH, George Washington, a Representative from Illinois; born in Putnam County, Ohio, August 18, 1846; moved with his father to Wayne County, Ill., in 1850; learned the blacksmith trade; attended the common schools, and was graduated from the literary department of McKendree College, Lebanon, Ill., in 1868; studied law in Fairfield, Ill.; was graduated from the law department of the Indiana University at Bloomington in 1870; was admitted to the bar the same year and commenced practice in Murphysboro, Jackson County, Ill.; presidential elector on the Republican ticket of Garfield and Arthur in 1880; master in chancery 1880–1888; elected as a Republican to the Fifty-first and to the nine succeeding Congresses and served from March 4, 1889, until his death in Murphysboro, Ill., November 30, 1907, before the convening of the Sixtieth Congress; interment in the City Cemetery.

SMITH, Gerrit, a Representative from New York; born in Utica, N. Y., March 6, 1797; moved to Peterboro in 1806; attended an academy in Clinton, N Y.; was graduated from Hamilton College, Clinton, N. Y., in 1818; studied law; engaged in the management of a large estate which he inherited; delegate to the State conventions in 1824 and 1828; was admitted to the bar in 1853 and commenced practice in Peterboro, N. Y.; elected as an Ultra-Abolitionist to the Thirty-third Congress and served from March 4, 1853, until August 7, 1854, when he resigned; resumed the practice of his profession, and was a publicist and philanthropist; he revived the Anti-Dramshop Party, but was a delegate to the Republican National Convention at Philadelphia in 1872 and supported Grant; died in New York City December 28, 1874; interment in Peterboro Cemetery, Peterboro, Madison County, N. Y.

SMITH, Gomer Griffith, a Representative from Oklahoma; born on a farm near Kansas City, Jackson County, Mo., July 11, 1896; attended the common and high schools of Missouri; was graduated from Rockingham Academy, Kansas City, Mo., in 1915; taught in a country school near Excelsior Springs, Clay County, Mo., 1916–1918; studied law; was admitted to the Missouri bar in 1920, to the Oklahoma bar in 1922, and commenced practice in Oklahoma City, Okla.; elected as a Democrat to the Seventy-fifth Congress to fill the vacancy caused by the death of Robert P. Hill and served from December 10, 1937, to January 3, 1939; was not a candidate for renomination in 1938, but was an unsuccessful candidate for the Democratic nomination for United States Senator; resumed the practice of law in Oklahoma City, where he died May 26, 1953; interment in Rose Hill Mausoleum.

SMITH, Green Clay (son of John Speed Smith), a Representative from Kentucky; born in Richmond, Madison County, Ky., July 4, 1826; pursued academic studies; served in the Mexican War; commissioned second lieutenant in the First Regiment, Kentucky Volunteer Infantry, June 9, 1846; honorably mustered out June 8, 1847; was graduated from Transylvania University, Lexington, Ky., in 1849; studied law; was admitted to the bar in 1852 and commenced practice in Covington, Ky.; was school commissioner 1853–1857; member of the State house of representatives 1861–1863; during the Civil War was commissioned colonel of the Fourth Regiment, Kentucky Volunteer Cavalry, April 4, 1862; brigadier general of Volunteers July 2, 1862; resigned December 1, 1863; brevetted

major general of Volunteers March 13, 1865, "for meritorious services during the Civil War"; elected as a Union candidate to the Thirty-eighth and Thirty-ninth Congresses and served from March 4, 1863, until his resignation in 1866, having been appointed Governor of Montana Territory; appointed by President Johnson as Governor of Montana Territory and served from July 13, 1866, until April 9, 1869, when he resigned; moved to Washington, D. C., where he was ordained to the Baptist ministry; became an evangelist; was the candidate of the National Prohibition Party in 1876 for President of the United States; pastor of the Metropolitan Baptist Church in Washington, D. C., from 1890 until his death, June 29, 1895; interment in Arlington National Cemetery, Fort Myer, Va.

SMITH, H. Allen, a Representative from California; born in Dixon, Lee County, Ill., October 8, 1909; attended the public schools; moved to Los Angeles, Calif., in 1924 and attended Hollywood High School and the University of California at Los Angeles; graduated from the University of Southern California in 1930 and the law school of the same university in 1933; was admitted to the bar in 1934 and practiced law in Los Angeles, Calif., until December 1935; special agent for the Federal Bureau of Investigation from December 1935 until August 1942; manager of plant protection, Lockheed Aircraft Corp., from August 1942 to August 1944; resumed the practice of law in Los Angeles, Calif., in 1944; member of the State assembly 1948–1956; delegate to Republican National Convention in 1960; elected as a Republican to the Eighty-fifth and Eighty-sixth Congresses (January 3, 1957–January 3, 1961). *Reelected to the Eighty-seventh Congress.*

SMITH, Henry, a Representative from Wisconsin; born in Baltimore, Md., July 22, 1838; moved with his parents to Massillon, Stark County, Ohio, and later, in 1844, to Milwaukee, Wis.; attended the public schools; became a millwright; member of the common council of Milwaukee 1868–1872; served in the State assembly in 1878; again a member of the common council 1880–1882 and 1884–1887; city comptroller 1882–1884; elected as the People's Party candidate to the Fiftieth Congress (March 4, 1887–March 3, 1889); unsuccessful candidate for relection in 1888 to the Fifty-first Congress; was an architect and builder; elected a member of the board of aldermen of Milwaukee, Wis., in 1898 and served until his death; died in Milwaukee, Wis., September 16, 1916; remains were cremated and the ashes interred in Union Cemetery.

SMITH, Henry Cassorte, a Representative from Michigan; born in Canandaigua, Ontario County, N. Y., June 2, 1856; moved with his father to a farm near Palmyra, Lenawee County, Mich., in 1857; attended the common schools; was graduated from Adrian College, Michigan, in 1878; taught school; studied law; was admitted to the bar September 25, 1880, and commenced practice in Adrian, Lenawee County, Mich.; city attorney of Adrian; delegate to the Republican National Convention at St. Louis in 1896; elected as a Republican to the Fifty-sixth and Fifty-seventh Congresses (March 4, 1899–March 3, 1903); was an unsuccessful candidate for renomination in 1902; resumed the practice of law in Adrian, Mich., and died there on December 7, 1911; interment in Oakwood Cemetery.

SMITH, Hezekiah Bradley, a Representative from New Jersey; born in Bridgewater, Windsor County, Vt., July 24, 1816; attended the common schools; learned the trade of cabinetmaker; settled in Lowell, Mass., about 1840 and engaged in the manufacture of woodworking machinery; invented a machine for which he was awarded a gold medal by the Massachusetts Mechanical Association; subsequently took out more than forty patents for original inventions; moved to Smithville, Burlington County, N. J., in 1865 and continued the manufacture of wood-working machinery; also manufactured the Star bicycle; made the first steam-driven vehicle operated in New Jersey; elected as a Democrat and Greenbacker to the Forty-sixth Congress (March 4, 1879–March 3, 1881); unsuccessful candidate for reelection in 1880 to the Forty-seventh Congress; resumed his former business activities; member of the State senate 1883–1885; died in Smithville, N. J., November 3, 1887; interment in the Pine Street Cemetery, Mount Holly, Burlington County, N. J.

SMITH, Hiram Ypsilanti, a Representative from Iowa; born in Piqua, Miami County, Ohio, March 22, 1843; moved with his parents to Rock Island, Ill., in 1850, and to Des Moines, Iowa, in 1854; attended the public schools; in 1861 enlisted in the State militia for service against the Indians; appointed a clerk in the Post Office Department, Washington, D. C., and served from January 1862 to February 1864; transferred to the Treasury Department, from which he resigned in August 1865; was graduated from the Albany (N. Y.) Law School in 1866; was admitted to the bar the same year and commenced practice in Des Moines, Iowa; district attorney of the fifth judicial district of Iowa 1875–1879; member of the State senate 1882–1884; elected as a Republican to the Forty-eighth Congress to fill the vacancy caused by the resignation of John A. Kasson and served from December 2, 1884, to March 3, 1885; was not a candidate for reelection to the Forty-ninth Congress; resumed the practice of law; died in Des Moines, Iowa, November 4, 1894; interment in Woodland Cemetery.

SMITH, Hoke, a Senator from Georgia; born in Newton, Catawba County, N. C., September 2, 1855; educated principally by his father, Dr. H. H. Smith, who was a professor in the University of North Carolina at Chapel Hill; studied law in Atlanta, Ga.; was admitted to the bar in 1873 and commenced practice in Atlanta, Ga.; became owner of the Atlanta Evening Journal in 1887 and served as editor and president until 1900; delegate to the Democratic National Convention in 1892; appointed Secretary of the Interior in the Cabinet of President Cleveland and served from March 4, 1893, to September 1, 1896; resumed the practice of law in Atlanta, Ga.; served as president of the Atlanta Board of Education 1896–1907; Governor of Georgia from July 1907 to July 1909; unsuccessful candidate for renomination in 1908; again served as Governor from July 1, 1911, until his resignation on November 15, 1911, having previously been elected Senator; elected as a Democrat to the United States Senate on July 12, 1911, to fill the vacancy caused by the death of Alexander S. Clay, but did not assume these duties until later, preferring to continue as Governor; reelected to the Senate in 1914 and served from November 16, 1911, to March 3, 1921; unsuccessful candidate for renomination in 1920; resumed the practice of his profession in Washington, D. C., and Atlanta, Ga.; died in Atlanta, Ga., November 27, 1931; interment in Oakland Cemetery.

SMITH, Horace Boardman, a Representative from New York; born in Whitingham, Windham County, Vt., August 18, 1826; pursued classical studies, and was graduated from Williams College, Williamstown, Mass., in 1847; studied law; was admitted to the bar in 1850 and began practice in Elmira, N. Y.; held several local offices; judge of Chemung County in 1859 and 1860; elected as a Republican to the Forty-second and Forty-third Congresses (March 4, 1871–March 3, 1875); was not a candidate for renomination in 1874; resumed the practice of law in Elmira, Chemung County, N. Y., until 1883; justice of the

supreme court of New York State 1883–1888; retired to his home at Elmira, where he died on December 26, 1888; interment in Woodlawn Cemetery.

SMITH, Howard Alexander, a Senator from New Jersey; born in New York, N. Y., January 30, 1880; attended the Cutler School in New York City; was graduated from Princeton University, Princeton, N. J., in 1901 and from the law department of Columbia University, New York, N. Y., in 1904; was admitted to the bar the same year and commenced the practice of law in New York City, N. Y.; moved to Colorado Springs, Colo., in 1905 and continued the practice of law until 1917; during the First World War served in the United States Food Administration in Colorado and Washington, D. C.; member of postwar relief organizations in 1918; moved to Princeton, N. J., in 1919 and served as executive secretary of Princeton University until 1927; lecturer in the department of politics at Princeton University 1927–1930; resumed the practice of law in New York City 1932–1941; member of the New Jersey Republican State Committee 1934–1945, serving as treasurer 1934–1941 and as chairman 1941–1943; member of the Republican National Committee in 1942 and 1943; member of the Republican Postwar Advisory Council, which met at Mackinac Island, Mich., in September 1943; elected as a Republican to the United States Senate to fill the vacancy in the term ending January 3, 1947, caused by the death of W. Warren Barbour; reelected in 1946 and again in 1952, and served from December 7, 1944, to January 3, 1959; was not a candidate for renomination in 1958; special consultant on foreign affairs to the Secretary of State from October 3, 1959, to March 1, 1960; is a resident of Princeton, N. J.

SMITH, Howard Worth, a Representative from Virginia; born in Broad Run, Fauquier County, Va., February 2, 1883; attended the public schools; was graduated from Bethel Military Academy, Warrenton, Va., in 1901 and from the law department of the University of Virginia at Charlottesville in 1903; was admitted to the bar in 1904 and commenced practice in Alexandria, Va.; assistant general counsel, Alien Property Custodian, in 1917 and 1918; served as Commonwealth attorney of Alexandria, Va., 1918–1922; judge of the corporation court of Alexandria 1922–1928; judge of the sixteenth judicial circuit of Virginia 1928–1930; also engaged in banking, farming, and dairying; elected as a Democrat to the Seventy-second and to the fourteen succeeding Congresses (March 4, 1931–January 3, 1961). *Reelected to the Eighty-seventh Congress.*

SMITH, Isaac, a Representative from New Jersey; born in Trenton, N. J., in 1740; was graduated from Princeton College in 1755; teacher in that institution 1755–1758; studied medicine and commenced practice in Trenton, N. J.; colonel in the Hunterdon County Militia in 1776 and 1777; elected as a Federalist to the Fourth Congress (March 4, 1795–March 3, 1797); appointed by President Washington a commissioner to treat with the Seneca Indians in 1797; associate justice of the supreme court of New Jersey 1777–1804; was a presidential elector on the Democratic ticket of Jefferson and Burr in 1800; first president of the Trenton Banking Co. 1805–1807; died in Trenton, Mercer County, N. J., on August 29, 1807; interment in the First Presbyterian Churchyard.

SMITH, Isaac, a Representative from Pennsylvania; born in Chester County, Pa., January 4, 1761; attended the common schools; engaged in agricultural pursuits near Level Corners, Lycoming County, Pa.; member of the State house of representatives 1806–1808; elected as a Democrat to the Thirteenth Congress (March 4, 1813–March 3, 1815); resumed agricultural pursuits and also engaged in the occupation of millwright; died on his farm at Level Corners, near Jersey Shore, Lycoming County, Pa., April 4, 1834; interment in the Pine Creek Presbyterian Churchyard; reinterment in Jersey Shore Cemetery, Jersey Shore, Lycoming County, Pa.

SMITH, Israel, a Representative and a Senator from Vermont; born in Suffield, Conn., April 4, 1759; was graduated from Yale College in 1781; studied law; was admitted to the bar and commenced practice in Rupert, Vt.; member of the State house of representatives from Rupert in 1785 and 1788–1791; moved to Rutland, Vt.; delegate to the State constitutional convention in 1791; upon the admission of Vermont as a State into the Union was elected as a Democrat to the Second Congress; reelected to the Third and Fourth Congresses and served from October 17, 1791, to March 3, 1797; unsuccessful candidate for reelection; member of the State house of representatives in 1797; appointed chief justice of the State supreme court in 1797; elected to the Seventh Congress (March 4, 1801–March 3, 1803); did not seek renomination, having become a candidate for Senator; elected to the United States Senate and served from March 4, 1803, until his resignation on October 1, 1807; Governor of Vermont in 1807 and 1808; Democratic presidential elector in 1808; died in Rutland, Vt., December 2, 1810; interment in the West Street Cemetery.

SMITH, James, a Delegate from Pennsylvania; born in Ireland in 1713; immigrated to the United States with his father in 1727 and settled in Pennsylvania; pursued classical studies; attended the Philadelphia Academy (now the University of Pennsylvania); worked as a surveyor in Cumberland County; studied law; was admitted to the bar in 1745 and began practice in Shippensburg, Pa.; moved to York, Pa., and engaged in the manufacture of iron; delegate to the provisional conference in Philadelphia; delegate to the State convention in January 1775; organized the Pennsylvania Militia and the two regiments of the Flying Camp in Perth Amboy, N. J., in 1776; Member of the Continental Congress 1776–1778; a signer of the Declaration of Independence; member of the State house of representatives in 1780; brigadier general of State militia; State councilor; resumed the practice of his profession in York, York County, Pa., and died there on July 11, 1806; interment in the First Presbyterian Churchyard.

SMITH, James, Jr., a Senator from New Jersey; born in Newark, N. J., June 12, 1851; attended private schools and St. Mary's College, Wilmington, Del.; engaged in the dry-goods and importing business, later becoming a manufacturer of leather in Newark, N. J.; member of the board of aldermen of Newark 1883–1887; declined the nomination for mayor of Newark in 1884; president of the first board of works of Newark; chairman of the New Jersey delegations to the Democratic National Conventions at Chicago in 1884, 1892, and 1896; elected as a Democrat to the United States Senate and served from March 4, 1893, to March 3, 1899; resumed the manufacture of leather, and also engaged in banking and newspaper publishing; unsuccessful candidate for election to the United States Senate in 1911; died in Newark, N. J., April 1, 1927; interment in Holy Sepulcher Cemetery.

SMITH, James Strudwick, a Representative from North Carolina; born near Hillsboro, Orange County, N. C., October 15, 1790; attended a private school near Hillsboro and Hillsboro Academy; was graduated from Jefferson Medical College, Philadelphia, Pa., in 1818, and practiced medicine near Hillsboro and later near Chapel Hill, Orange County; elected as a Democrat to the Fifteenth and Sixteenth Congresses (March 4, 1817–March 3, 1821); unsuccessful candidate for renomination;

resumed the practice of medicine; member of the State house of commons in 1821 and 1822; delegate to the State constitutional convention in 1835; died near Chapel Hill, N. C., in August 1859; interment in a private cemetery on his farm.

SMITH, Jedediah Kilburn, a Representative from New Hampshire; born in Amherst, N. H., November 7, 1770; completed preparatory studies; studied law; was admitted to the bar and commenced practice at Amherst in 1800; member of the State house of representatives in 1803; member of the State senate 1804–1806 and 1809; elected to the Tenth Congress (March 4, 1807–March 3, 1809); unsuccessful candidate for the United States Senate in 1810; councilor 1810–1815; postmaster at Amherst from May 19, 1819, until his successor was appointed on March 15, 1826; associate justice of the court of common pleas 1816–1821, and of the court of sessions 1821–1823; chief justice of the court of sessions 1823–1825; died in Amherst, Hillsborough County, N. H., December 17, 1828.

SMITH, Jeremiah (brother of Samuel Smith, of New Hampshire, and uncle of Robert Smith), a Representative from New Hampshire; born in Peterboro, N. H., November 29, 1759; received instruction from a private tutor; attended Harvard College in 1777; during the Revolutionary War served under General Stark in the Battle of Bennington; returned to Harvard College and completed the sophomore year; entered Queen's (now Rutgers) College, New Jersey, from which he was graduated in 1780; studied law; was admitted to the bar in 1786 and commenced practice in Peterboro, N. H.; member of the State house of representatives 1788–1791; member of the constitutional convention in 1791 and 1792; elected as a Federalist to the Second and to the three succeeding Congresses and served from March 4, 1791, until his resignation July 26, 1797; moved to Exeter, N. H.; United States district attorney for New Hampshire from 1797 to 1800; judge of probate of Rockingham County 1800–1802; appointed, under authority of the act of February 13, 1801, by President Adams judge of the United States circuit court February 20, 1801, and served until March 8, 1802, when the court was abolished by the act of that date; chief justice of the Superior Court of Judicature of New Hampshire 1802–1809; presidential elector on the Federalist ticket of Pinckney and King in 1808; Governor of New Hampshire in 1809 and 1810; chief Justice of the Supreme Judicial Court of New Hampshire 1813–1816; resumed the practice of law, from which he retired in 1820; president of a bank and treasurer of Phillips Exeter Academy; moved to Dover, and died there September 21, 1842; interment in Winter Street (also called Old) Cemetery, Exeter, N. H.

SMITH, John, a Senator from Ohio; born in Hamilton County, Ohio, in 1735; prepared for the ministry, and was pastor of the First Baptist Church in Columbia, Lorain County, Ohio, in 1790; member of the Territorial legislature 1799–1803; upon the admission of Ohio as a State into the Union was elected as a Democrat to the United States Senate and served from April 1, 1803, to April 25, 1808, when he resigned at the request of the Ohio Legislature on account of charges, which resulted in the attempt to expel him from the Senate, of having been connected with the conspiracy of Burr and Blennerhasset, when sent by President Jefferson on a special mission to Louisiana and Florida in 1804 to judge the attitude of Spanish officers there toward the United States; the motion to expel him from the Senate failed by one vote; died in Cincinnati, Ohio, June 10, 1816.

SMITH, John, a Representative from Virginia; born at "Shooter's Hill," near Locust Hill, Middlesex County, Va., May 7, 1750; resided for a time with his aunt at "Fleets Bay" in Northumberland County, Va.; moved to Frederick County,

Va., in 1773 and engaged in planting at "Hackwood," near Winchester, where he acquired a large acreage of land; commissioned by the Governor as one of the King's justices in 1773; appointed a colonel by the Council of Safety of Virginia on January 8, 1776; promoted to a lieutenant of county militia by Gov. Patrick Henry on March 6, 1777; commissioned lieutenant-colonel commandant by Gov. Henry Lee on March 6, 1793, brigadier general by Gov. James Monroe on December 21, 1801, and major general of the Third Division of Virginia State Troops on January 26, 1811, in which capacity he served until his death; served in Dunmore's War with the Indians in 1774, the Revolutionary War, and the War of 1812; member of the State house of delegates 1779–1783; unsuccessful candidate for election as a delegate from Frederick County in 1788 to consider the ratification of the First Federal Constitution at Richmond; served in the State senate 1792–1795; reelected in 1796; elected as a Democrat to the Seventh and to the six succeeding Congresses (March 4, 1801–March 3, 1815); resumed agricultural pursuits; died at the home of his granddaughter at "Rockville," near Middletown, Frederick County, Va., on March 5, 1836; interment in the family burying ground at "Hackwood," near Winchester, Va.; reinterred in Mount Hebron Cemetery, Winchester, Va., in 1890.

SMITH, John, a Representative and a Senator from New York; born in Mastic, Long Island, N. Y., February 12, 1752; completed preparatory studies; member of the State assembly 1784–1799; delegate to the convention which adopted the Federal Constitution in 1788; elected as a Democrat to the Sixth Congress to fill the vacancy caused by the death of Jonathan N. Havens; reelected to the Seventh and Eighth Congresses and served from February 6, 1800, until his resignation, effective February 23, 1804; elected on February 4, 1804, to the United States Senate to fill the vacancy caused by the resignation of De Witt Clinton; reelected, and served from February 23, 1804, to March 3, 1813; United States marshal for the district of New York from July 29, 1813, to June 19, 1815; major general of the New York Militia at the time of his death in Mastic, Long Island, N. Y., August 12, 1816; interment in the family cemetery on Smiths Point, N. Y.

SMITH, John (father of Worthington Curtis Smith), a Representative from Vermont; born in Barre, Mass., August 12, 1789; attended the common schools; moved to St. Albans, Vt.; studied law; was admitted to the bar in 1810 and commenced practice in St. Albans, Vt.; State's attorney for Franklin County 1826–1832; member of the State house of representatives 1827–1837, and served as speaker from 1831 to 1833; elected as a Democrat to the Twenty-sixth Congress (March 4, 1839–March 3, 1841); unsuccessful candidate for reelection in 1840 to the Twenty-seventh Congress; engaged in the construction of railroads; died in St. Albans, Vt., November 26, 1858; interment in Greenwood Cemetery.

SMITH, John Ambler, a Representative from Virginia; born at Village View, near Dinwiddie Court House, Dinwiddie County, Va., September 23, 1847; attended the rural school and was educated at David Turner's high school at Richmond; was graduated from the law department of the Richmond (Va.) College (later the University of Virginia); was admitted to the bar in 1867 and commenced the practice of law in Richmond, Va.; appointed commissioner in chancery of the courts of Richmond in 1868; served as Commonwealth attorney of Charles City and New Kent Counties; member of the State senate in 1869; elected as a Republican to the Forty-third Congress (March 4, 1873–March 3, 1875); unsuccessful candidate for renomination in 1874; resumed the practice of law in Washing-

ton, D. C.; member of the immigration commission to London; died in Washington, D. C., on January 6, 1892; interment in Glenwood Cemetery.

SMITH, John Armstrong, a Representative from Ohio; born in Hillsboro, Ohio, September 23, 1814; pursued classical studies, and was graduated from Miami University, Oxford, Ohio, in 1834; studied law; was admitted to the bar in 1835 and commenced practice in Hillsboro, Ohio; served in the State house of representatives in 1841; member of the State constitutional convention of Ohio in 1850; elected as a Republican to the Forty-first and Forty-second Congresses (March 4, 1869–March 3, 1873); resumed the practice of law; member of the State constitutional convention of 1873; died in Hillsboro, Ohio, March 7, 1892; interment in Hillsboro Cemetery.

SMITH, John Cotton, a Representative from Connecticut; born in Sharon, Conn., on February 12, 1765; completed preparatory studies; was graduated from Yale College in 1783; studied law; was admitted to the bar and began practice in Sharon, Conn., in 1787; member of the State house of representatives in 1793, 1796, and 1800, and served as speaker in 1800; elected as a Federalist to the Sixth Congress to fill the vacancy caused by the resignation of Jonathan Brace; reelected to the Seventh, Eighth, and Ninth Congresses and served from November 17, 1800, until his resignation in August 1806; judge of the supreme court of Connecticut in 1809; Lieutenant Governor in 1810; Governor 1813–1818; unsuccessful candidate for Governor on the Federalist ticket in 1817; president of the American Board of Commissioners for Foreign Missions; president of the Connecticut Bible Society; retired to his estate near Sharon, Litchfield County, Conn., where he died December 7, 1845; interment in Hillside Cemetery.

SMITH, John Hyatt, a Representative from New York; born in Saratoga, N. Y., April 10, 1824; taught by his father; employed for a time as a clerk in Detroit, Mich., and later as a bank clerk in Albany, N. Y., and while in the latter position studied theology; after ordination his first pastorate was in Poughkeepsie, N. Y., in 1848; officiated in Cleveland, Ohio, for three years, in Buffalo, N. Y., 1855–1860, and in Philadelphia, Pa., 1860–1866; during the Civil War served in Virginia with the United States Christian Commission in 1862; chaplain of the Forty-seventh Regiment, National Guard of New York, in 1869; continued his ministerial duties in Brooklyn, N. Y., 1866–1880; elected as an Independent Republican and Democratic candidate to the Forty-seventh Congress (March 4, 1881–March 3, 1883); appointed by President Arthur a commissioner to inspect the Pacific Railroad, after which he resumed a pastorate in Brooklyn, N. Y., where he died December 7, 1886; interment in Greenwood Cemetery.

SMITH, John Joseph, a Representative from Connecticut; born in Waterbury, New Haven County, Conn., January 25, 1904; attended the public schools; was graduated from Yale University, New Haven, Conn., in 1925 and from the law department of the same university in 1927; was admitted to the bar in 1927 and commenced practice in Waterbury, Conn.; served in the Field Artillery Reserves 1925–1935; elected as a Democrat to the Seventy-fourth and to the three succeeding Congresses and served from January 3, 1935, until his resignation on November 4, 1941, having been appointed a United States district judge for the district of Connecticut, in which capacity he is now serving; is a resident of West Hartford, Conn.

SMITH, John M. C., a Representative from Michigan; born in Belfast, Ireland, February 6, 1853; immigrated to the United

States in 1855 with his parents, who settled near Plymouth, Ohio; attended the public schools; moved to Charlotte, Mich., in 1867; engaged in agricultural pursuits and also worked as a mason; was graduated from the academic department of the University of Michigan at Ann Arbor in 1879 and from the law department in 1880; was admitted to the bar in 1882 and commenced practice in Detroit; prosecuting attorney of Eaton County 1885–1888; president of the First National Bank of Charlotte in 1898; also engaged in manufacturing and agricultural pursuits; member of the board of aldermen in 1903; member of the State constitutional convention in 1908; elected as a Republican to the Sixty-second and to the four succeeding Congresses (March 4, 1911–March 3, 1921); voluntarily retired and was not a candidate for renomination; elected to the Sixty-seventh Congress to fill the vacancy caused by the death of William H. Frankhouser; reelected to the Sixty-eighth Congress and served from June 28, 1921, until his death in Charlotte, Mich., March 30, 1923; interment in Maple Hill Cemetery.

SMITH, John Quincy, a Representative from Ohio; born near Waynesville, Warren County, Ohio, November 5, 1824; attended the common schools and Miami University, Oxford, Ohio; engaged in agricultural pursuits; member of the State senate in 1860 and 1861; served in the State house of representatives in 1862 and 1863; again a member of the State house of representatives in 1872 and 1873; elected as a Republican to the Forty-third Congress (March 4, 1873–March 3, 1875); unsuccessful candidate for reelection in 1874 to the Forty-fourth Congress; United States Commissioner of Indian Affairs 1875–1877; appointed United States consul general to Montreal, Canada, and served from 1878 until he resigned in 1882; died in Oakland, Clinton County, Ohio, December 30, 1901; interment in Miami Cemetery, Waynesville, Ohio.

SMITH, John Speed (father of Green Clay Smith), a Representative from Kentucky; born near Nicholasville, Jessamine County, Ky., July 1, 1792; attended a private school in Mercer County; served in the Indian campaign of 1811 as a private; studied law; was admitted to the bar in 1812 and commenced practice in Richmond, Ky.; during the War of 1812 enlisted as a private, and subsequently promoted to major; aide-de-camp to General Harrison with the rank of colonel; member of the State house of representatives in 1819; elected as a Democrat to the Seventeenth Congress to fill the vacancy caused by the resignation of George Robertson and served from August 6, 1821, to March 3, 1823; was not a candidate for renomination in 1822; again a member of the State house of representatives in 1827, 1830, 1839, 1841, and 1845, and served as speaker in 1827; United States district attorney for Kentucky 1828–1832; member of the State senate 1846–1850; died in Richmond, Ky., June 6, 1854; interment in Richmond Cemetery.

SMITH, John T., a Representative from Pennsylvania; born in Philadelphia, Pa.; attended the common schools of his native city; elected as a Democrat to the Twenty-eighth Congress (March 4, 1843–March 3, 1845).

SMITH, John Walter, a Representative and a Senator from Maryland; born at Snow Hill, Md., February 5, 1845; attended private schools and Union Academy; engaged in the lumber business in Maryland, Virginia, and North Carolina· president of the First National Bank of Snow Hill and director in many business and financial institutions; elected a member of the State senate in 1889, 1893, and 1897, and served as president of the senate during the session of 1894; elected as a Democrat to the Fifty-sixth Congress and served from March 4, 1899, until his resignation on January 12, 1900; Governor of Maryland 1900–1904; delegate at large to the Democratic National Conventions in 1900 and 1904; elected as a Democrat to the United States Senate to fill the vacancy caused by the death of William Pinkney Whyte; reelected in 1909 and 1914 and served from March 25, 1908, to March 3, 1921; unsuccessful for reelection in 1920; retired to private life and died in Baltimore, Md., April 19, 1925; interment in the Presbyterian Cemetery, Snow Hill, Md.

SMITH, Jonathan Bayard, a Delegate from Pennsylvania; born in Philadelphia, Pa., February 21, 1742; received a thorough English education, and was graduated from Princeton College in 1760; secretary of the Philadelphia Committee of Safety 1775–1777; Member of the Continental Congress in 1777 and 1778; prothonotary of the court of common pleas in 1777 and 1778; appointed justice of the court of common pleas in 1778; one of the founders in 1779 of the University of the State of Pennsylvania and a member of its board of trustees until its consolidation in 1791 with the College of Philadelphia into the University of Pennsylvania, serving as a trustee of the latter institution until his death; also a trustee of Princeton College from 1779 until 1808; served on the board of aldermen of Philadelphia 1792–1794; auditor general of Pennsylvania in 1794; died in Philadelphia, Pa., June 16, 1812; interment in the graveyard of the Second Presbyterian Church.

SMITH, Joseph Luther, a Representative from West Virginia; born in Marshes (now Glen Daniel), Raleigh County, W. Va., May 22, 1880; attended public and private schools; employed as a "printer's devil" by the Raleigh Register, Beckley, W. Va., and acquired that publication which he edited and managed until 1911; also engaged in the real-estate and banking business; mayor of Beckley 1904–1929; member of the State senate 1909–1913; elected as a Democrat to the Seventy-first and to the seven succeeding Congresses (March 4, 1929–January 3, 1945); was not a candidate for renomination in 1944; engaged in banking administrative business, and is a resident of Beckley, W. Va.

SMITH, Joseph Showalter, a Representative from Oregon; born in Connellsville, Fayette County, Pa., June 20, 1824; attended the common schools; crossed the Plains, arriving in Oregon City in the spring of 1844; engaged in splitting rails and other manual labor; moved to Salem, Oreg., and taught school; studied law and was admitted to the bar; moved to Olympia, Wash., in 1853; was elected to the Territorial house of representatives in 1856, and served as speaker; was appointed United States attorney for Washington Territory by President Buchanan March 12, 1857; returned to Salem, Oreg., in 1858 and practiced law for twelve years; elected as a Democrat to the Forty-first Congress (March 4, 1869–March 3, 1871); moved to Portland, Oreg., in 1870 and resumed the practice of his profession; unsuccessful Democratic candidate for Governor of Oregon in 1882; died in Portland, Oreg., July 13, 1884; interment in Riverview Cemetery.

SMITH, Josiah, a Representative from Massachusetts; born in Pembroke, Mass., February 26, 1738; was graduated from Harvard College in 1774; studied law; was admitted to the bar and practiced; member of the State house of representatives in 1789 and 1790; served in the State senate 1792–1794 and in 1797; State treasurer in 1797; elected to the Seventh Congress (March 4, 1801–March 3, 1803); was not a candidate for renomination in 1802; died in Pembroke, Plymouth County, Mass., April 4, 1803; interment in Pembroke Cemetery.

SMITH, Lawrence Henry, a Representative from Wisconsin; born in Racine, Boone County, Wis., September 15, 1892; attended the public schools and the State Teachers College,

Milwaukee, Wis.; graduated from the Marquette University Law School, Milwaukee, Wis., in 1923; was admitted to the bar the same year and commenced the practice of law in Racine, Wis.; during the First World War served as a first lieutenant of Infantry, Thirty-second Division, 1917–1919; elected as a Republican to the Seventy-seventh Congress to fill the vacancy caused by the death of Stephen Bolles; reelected to the Seventy-eighth and to the seven succeeding Congresses and served from August 29, 1941, until his death in the United States Capitol, Washington, D. C., January 22, 1958; interment in West Lawn Memorial Park, Racine, Wis.

SMITH, Madison Roswell, a Representative from Missouri; born on a farm near Glenallen, Bollinger County, Mo., July 9, 1850; attended the public schools and Central College in Fayette, Mo.; studied law and was admitted to the bar in 1874; taught school; began the practice of law at Marble Hill, Bollinger County, Mo., in 1877; prosecuting attorney of Bollinger County 1878–1882; served in the State senate 1884–1888; declined to be a candidate for reelection; served as editor of reports for the St. Louis court of appeals for four years and resigned; delegate to the Democratic National Conventions in 1896 and 1912; elected as a Democrat to the Sixtieth Congress (March 4, 1907–March 3, 1909); unsuccessful candidate for reelection in 1908 to the Sixty-first Congress; organizer and secretary of the Federal Trust Co., of St. Louis, 1909–1912; Minister to Haiti from 1912 until his resignation in 1914; continued the practice of his profession in Farmington, Mo., where he died June 18, 1919; interment in the Masonic Cemetery.

SMITH, Marcus Aurelius, a Delegate and a Senator from Arizona; born near Cynthiana, Harrison County, Ky., January 24, 1851; attended the common schools; taught school in Bourbon County, Ky.; was graduated from Transylvania University, Lexington, Ky., in 1872 and from the law department of the University of Kentucky at Lexington; was admitted to the bar and practiced; prosecuting attorney for the city of Lexington; moved to San Francisco, and practiced law 1879–1881; moved to Tombstone, Ariz., in 1881 and continued the practice of law; prosecuting attorney for the Tombstone district in 1882; elected as a Democrat to the Fiftieth and to the three succeeding Congresses (March 4, 1887–March 3, 1895); elected to the Fifty-fifth Congress (March 4, 1897–March 3, 1899); elected to the Fifty-seventh Congress (March 4, 1901–March 3, 1903); elected to the Fifty-ninth and Sixtieth Congresses (March 4, 1905–March 3, 1909); was not a candidate for election to the Fifty-fourth, Fifty-sixth, and Fifty-eighth Congresses; upon the admission of Arizona as a State into the Union was elected to the United States Senate for the term ending March 3, 1915; reelected in 1914 and served from March 27, 1912, to March 3, 1921; unsuccessful candidate for reelection in 1920; appointed March 3, 1921, by President Wilson as a member of the International Joint Commission, created to prevent disputes regarding the use of the boundary waters between the United States and Canada, and served until his death in Washington, D. C., April 7, 1924; interment in Battle Grove Cemetery, Cynthiana, Ky.

SMITH, Margaret Chase (widow of Clyde Harold Smith), a Representative and a Senator from Maine; born in Skowhegan, Somerset County, Maine, December 14, 1897; attended the public schools and was graduated from the high school at Skowhegan, Maine, in 1916; taught school in Skowhegan, Maine, in 1916 and 1917; business executive for country newspaper and a woolen company 1919–1930; member of the Republican State committee 1930–1936; secretary to husband while he was in Congress 1937–1940; permanent chairman of the Republican

State convention in 1944; elected as a Republican to the Seventy-sixth Congress to fill the vacancy caused by the death of her husband, Clyde H. Smith; reelected to the Seventy-seventh and to the three succeeding Congresses and served from June 3, 1940, to January 3, 1949; did not seek renomination in 1948; elected as a Republican to the United States Senate in 1948, and again in 1954, and served from January 3, 1949, to January 3, 1961. *Reelected in 1960 for the term ending January 3, 1967.*

SMITH, Martin Fernard, a Representative from Washington; born in Chicago, Cook County, Ill., May 28, 1891; attended the public schools, Lewis Institute, Chicago, Ill., and Northwestern University, Evanston, Ill.; moved to Hoquiam, Wash., in 1911 and completed law studies commenced in Chicago; was admitted to the bar in 1912 and commenced practice in Hoquiam, Wash.; served as municipal judge of Hoquiam 1914–1917; during the First World War served as a private in the Coast Artillery Corps from October 9, 1918, to December 15, 1918; member of the city council 1926–1928; mayor of Hoquiam 1928–1930; elected as a Democrat to the Seventy-third and to the four succeeding Congresses (March 4, 1933–January 3, 1943); unsuccessful candidate for reelection in 1942 to the Seventy-eighth Congress; delegate to the Democratic National Convention at Philadelphia in 1936; appointed a member of the Board of Immigration Appeals, Justice Department, on April 1, 1943, and served until his resignation on April 29, 1944; unsuccessful candidate in 1944 for the Democratic nomination for United States Senator; appointed special assistant to the Attorney General of the United States on September 26, 1944, and served until his death in Bethesda, Md., October 25, 1954; interment in Arlington National Cemetery, Fort Myer, Va.

SMITH, Melancthon, a Delegate from New York; born in Jamaica, Long Island, N. Y., May 7, 1744; was educated by his parents; as a youth clerked in a store at Poughkeepsie, N. Y.; engaged in business in Poughkeepsie, N. Y.; delegate to the First Provincial Congress in New York, May 22, 1775; served in the Continental Line Regiment which was organized June 30, 1775; organized and became captain of the Dutchess County Minutemen; secret service commissioner and sheriff of Dutchess County, N. Y., in 1777 and 1778; moved to New York City in 1785 and engaged in mercantile pursuits; Member of the Continental Congress 1785–1788; member of the State convention that met at Poughkeepsie and ratified the Federal Constitution July 26, 1788; served in the State assembly in 1791; died in New York City July 29, 1798; interment in Jamaica Cemetery, Jamaica, Queens County, N. Y.

SMITH, Meriwether, a Delegate from Virginia; born at "Bathurst," on Piscataway Creek, near Dunnsville, Essex County, Va., in 1730; completed preparatory studies; was a signer of the articles of the Westmoreland association in 1766, which was pledged to use no articles of British importation; member of Essex Committee on Safety in 1774; member of the house of burgesses in 1774 and 1775; delegate to the Revolutionary conventions of 1775 and 1776; member of the State house of delegates 1776–1778; member of the Continental Congress 1778–1782; again a member of the State house of delegates in 1781, 1782, 1785, and 1788; delegate to the State convention which adopted the Federal Constitution June 26, 1788; died at "Marigold," near Ozeana, Essex County, Va., January 25, 1790; interment on his estate at "Bathurst," near Dunnsville, Essex County, Va.

SMITH, Nathan (brother of Nathaniel Smith and uncle of Truman Smith), a Senator from Connecticut; born in Woodbury, Conn., January 8, 1770; received a thorough English education; attended Litchfield Law School; was admitted to the bar in 1792 and commenced the practice of his profession in New Haven, Conn.; prosecuting attorney for New Haven County 1817–1835; delegate to the State constitutional convention in 1818; unsuccessful candidate for Governor of Connecticut in 1825; appointed United States attorney for the district of Connecticut February 8, 1829; member of the State house of representatives 1833–1835; elected as a Whig to the United States Senate and served from March 4, 1833, until his death in Washington, D. C., December 6, 1835; interment in the Grove Street Cemetery, New Haven, Conn.

SMITH, Nathaniel (brother of Nathan Smith and uncle of Truman Smith), a Representative from Connecticut; born in Woodbury, Conn., January 6, 1762; attended the common schools; engaged in agricultural pursuits and was also a cattle dealer; studied law; was admitted to the bar in 1787 and commenced the practice of his profession in Woodbury, Conn.; member of the State house of representatives 1789–1795; elected as a Federalist to the Fourth and Fifth Congresses (March 4, 1795–March 3, 1799); declined to be a candidate for renomination in 1798; served in the State senate 1800–1805; judge of the supreme court of Connecticut 1806–1819; delegate to the Hartford Convention of 1814; died in Woodbury, Litchfield County, Conn., March 9, 1822; interment in the Episcopal Church Cemetery.

SMITH, Neal Edward, a Representative from Iowa; born in Hedrick, Keokuk County, Iowa, March 23, 1920; attended the elementary and high schools of Packwood, Iowa, Missouri University College of Liberal Arts in 1945 and 1946, Syracuse University Schools of Public and Business Administration 1946–1948; graduated from Drake University Law School in 1950; was admitted to the bar in 1950 and commenced the practice of law in Des Moines, Iowa; also lives on and operates a farm in Polk County, near Altoona, Iowa; during World War II served in the Army Air Force 1942–1945; awarded nine battle stars, Air Medal, four Oak Leaf Clusters, and Order of the Purple Heart; assistant county attorney for Polk County, Iowa, in 1951 and 1952; national president, Young Democratic Clubs of America, 1953–1955; elected as a Democrat to the Eighty-sixth Congress (January 3, 1959–January 3, 1961). *Reelected to the Eighty-seventh Congress.*

SMITH, O'Brien, a Representative from South Carolina; born in Ireland about 1756; came to South Carolina just after the close of the Revolutionary War, taking the oath of allegiance to the Government of the United States July 31, 1784; member of the State assembly in 1796; served in the State senate in 1803; elected to the Ninth Congress (March 4, 1805–March 3, 1807); died April 27, 1811; interment in the burial ground of the colonial Chapel of Ease of St. Bartholomew's Parish, Colleton County, S. C., later in ruins and then called "the Burnt Church," near Jacksonboro, S. C.

SMITH, Oliver Hampton, a Representative and a Senator from Indiana; born on Smiths Island, near Trenton, N. J., October 23, 1794; attended the common schools; moved to Indiana in 1817 and settled in Rising Sun; moved to Lawrenceburg, Ind., in 1818; studied law; was admitted to the bar in 1820 and commenced practice in Connersville, Ind.; member of the State house of representatives 1822–1824; prosecuting attorney for the third judicial district in 1824 and 1825; elected as a Jackson Democrat to the Twentieth Congress (March 4, 1827–March 3, 1829); unsuccessful candidate for reelection in 1828 to the Twenty-first Congress; elected as a Whig to the United States Senate and served from March 4, 1837, to March 3,

1843; unsuccessful candidate for reelection; moved to Indianapolis, Ind., and resumed the practice of law; declined to be a candidate for Governor of Indiana in 1845; engaged in the railroad business in Indianapolis; died in Indianapolis, Ind., March 19, 1859; interment in Crown Hill Cemetery.

SMITH, Perry, a Senator from Connecticut; born in Woodbury, Conn., May 12, 1783; completed preparatory studies; studied law at the Litchfield Law School; was admitted to the bar and commenced the practice of law in New Milford, Conn., in 1807; member of the State house of representatives in 1822, 1823, 1835, and 1836; judge of probate court 1833–1835; appointed postmaster of New Milford May 9, 1829; and served until March 24, 1837, when he resigned, having been elected Senator; elected as a Democrat to the United States Senate and served from March 4, 1837, to March 3, 1843; died in New Milford, Litchfield County, Conn., on June 8, 1852; interment in Center Cemetery.

SMITH, Richard, a Delegate from New Jersey; born in Burlington, N. J., March 22, 1735; educated under private teachers and in Friends' schools; studied law; was admitted to the bar in 1762 and practiced in Philadelphia, Pa., and later in Burlington, N. J.; commissioned county clerk of Burlington on December 7, 1762; Member of the Continental Congress from July 23, 1774, to June 12, 1776, when he resigned; was one of the signers of the petition to the King, being the last effort of the Colonies to avert an armed conflict; member of the State council in 1776; elected treasurer of New Jersey and served from 1776 to February 15, 1777, when he resigned; moved to Laurens, N. Y., in 1790 and thence to Philadelphia in 1799; died near Natchez, Miss.; September 17, 1803; interment in Natchez Cemetery.

SMITH, Robert (nephew of Jeremiah Smith and Samuel Smith of New Hampshire), a Representative from Illinois; born in Peterborough, Hillsboro County, N. H., June 12, 1802; attended the public schools and New Ipswich Academy; taught school; engaged in mercantile pursuits in 1822 and in the manufacturing of textile goods in Northfield, N. H., in 1823; studied law; was admitted to the bar and practiced; moved to Illinois and settled in Alton in 1832 and again engaged in mercantile pursuits; elected captain in the State militia in 1832; extensive land owner and engaged in the real-estate business; member of the State house of representatives 1836–1840; elected enrolling and engrossing clerk of the State house of representatives in 1840 and 1842; elected as a Democrat to the Twenty-eighth, Twenty-ninth, and Thirtieth Congresses (March 4, 1843–March 3, 1849); elected to the Thirty-fifth Congress (March 4, 1857–March 3, 1859); served as paymaster during the Civil War; interested in water-power development and railroad enterprises; died in Alton, Ill., December 21, 1867; interment in Alton City Cemetery.

SMITH, Robert Barnwell, a Representative and a Senator from South Carolina. (See RHETT, Robert Barnwell.)

SMITH, Samuel, a Representative and a Senator from Maryland; born in Carlisle, Pa., July 27, 1752; moved with his father to Baltimore, Md., in 1759; attended the public schools and was graduated from Princeton College; engaged in mercantile pursuits; served in the Revolutionary War as captain, major, and lieutenant colonel, and for his masterly defense of Fort Mifflin Congress gave him a vote of thanks and a sword; engaged in the shipping business; member of the State house of delegates 1790–1792; at the time of the threatened war with France in 1794 was appointed brigadier general of militia, and commanded Maryland's quota during the Whisky Rebellion; during the War of 1812 served as major general of militia in the defense of Baltimore; elected as a Democrat to the Third and to the four succeeding Congresses (March 4, 1793–March 3, 1803); did not seek renomination in 1802, having become a candidate for Senator; elected to the United States Senate in 1802; appointed and subsequently elected for the ensuing term and served from March 4, 1803, to March 3, 1815; elected President pro tempore of the Senate December 2, 1805, March 18, 1806, March 2, 1807, and April 16, 1808; elected to the Fourteenth Congress to fill the vacancy caused by the resignation of Nicholas R. Moore; reelected to the Fifteenth, Sixteenth, and Seventeenth Congresses and served from January 31, 1816, to December 17, 1822, when he resigned, having been elected Senator; elected to the United States Senate to fill the vacancy caused by the death of William Pinkney; reelected in 1826 and served from December 17, 1822, to March 3, 1833; mayor of Baltimore, Md., in 1837; retired from public life; died in Baltimore April 22, 1839; interment in the Old Westminster Burying Ground.

SMITH, Samuel, a Representative from Pennsylvania; associate judge of Erie County, Pa., from 1803 to 1805, when he resigned; elected to the Ninth Congress to fill the vacancy caused by the resignation of John B. C. Lucas; reelected to the Tenth and Eleventh Congresses and served from November 7, 1805, to March 3, 1811; unsuccessful candidate for reelection in 1810 to the Twelfth Congress.

SMITH, Samuel (brother of Jeremiah Smith and uncle of Robert Smith), a Representative from New Hampshire; born in Peterboro, N. H., November 11, 1765; attended Phillips Exeter Academy, Exeter, N. H., and Phillips Academy, Andover, Mass.; engaged in mercantile pursuits; served as moderator in town meetings 1794–1811; elected as a Federalist to the Thirteenth Congress (March 4, 1813–March 3, 1815); was not a candidate for renomination in 1814; resumed his former business pursuits, and in 1828 engaged in the manufacture of paper and cotton goods; died in Peterboro, N. H., April 25, 1842; interment in the Village Cemetery.

SMITH, Samuel A., a Representative from Pennsylvania; born in Harrow, Nockamixon Township, Bucks County, Pa., in 1795; attended the common schools; commissioned justice of the peace for the Rockhill-Milford district before he was twenty-one years of age; register of wills for Bucks County 1824–1829; was brigade inspector of militia for the Bucks and Montgomery County district; resigned in 1832; elected as an Independent Democrat to the Twenty-first Congress to fill in part the vacancies caused by the resignations of George Wolf and Samuel D. Ingham; reelected to the Twenty-second Congress and served from October 13, 1829, to March 3, 1833; member of the State senate 1841–1843; was appointed associate judge of the courts of Bucks County by Governor Porter in 1844 and served until 1849; engaged in mercantile pursuits in Doylestown, Pa., and later in Point Pleasant, Pa.; member and presiding officer of many Democratic county conventions; died in Point Pleasant, Bucks County, Pa., May 15, 1861; interment in the Presbyterian Churchyard, Doylestown, Pa.

SMITH, Samuel Axley, a Representative from Tennessee; born in Monroe County, Tenn., June 26, 1822; received a limited education; taught school; studied law; was admitted to the bar in 1845 and commenced practice in Cleveland, Tenn.; district attorney general 1845–1850; delegate to the Democratic National Convention at Baltimore in 1848; elected as a Democrat to the Thirty-third, Thirty-fourth, and Thirty-fifth Congresses (March 4, 1853–March 3, 1859); unsuccessful candidate for reelection in 1858 to the Thirty-sixth Congress; appointed by President Buchanan to be Commissioner of the General Land Office and served from January 18 to February 12, 1860, when he resigned; during the Civil War was appointed by the Governor of the State of Tennessee on November 16, 1861, an agent to collect arms for the Confederate Army; died at Ladd Springs, Polk County, Tenn., November 25, 1863; interment in Amos Ladd's Burial Ground.

SMITH, Samuel William, a Representative from Michigan; born in Independence Township, Oakland County, Mich., August 23, 1852; attended the common schools in Clarkston and Detroit; began teaching school in 1869; served as superintendent of schools in Waterford Township, Mich., in 1875 and at the same time served as principal of the school at Waterford, Mich.; studied law; was admitted to the bar in 1877 and was graduated from the law department of the University of Michigan at Ann Arbor in 1878; commenced the practice of law in Pontiac, Mich.; prosecuting attorney of Oakland County 1880–1884; served in the State senate 1885–1887; elected as a Republican to the Fifty-fifth and to the eight succeeding Congresses (March 4, 1897–March 3, 1915); was not a candidate for reelection to the Sixty-fourth Congress; moved to Detroit, Mich., in 1913 and continued the practice of law; died in Detroit, Mich., June 19, 1931; interment in Oak Hill Cemetery, Adrian, Mich.

SMITH, Sylvester Clark, a Representative from California; born near Mount Pleasant, Henry County, Iowa, August 26, 1858; attended the district schools and Howe's Academy at Mount Pleasant; taught school in Winfield, Iowa; moved to California in 1879 and engaged in agricultural pursuits; taught school in Colusa and Kern Counties in 1883; studied law; was admitted to the bar in 1885 and commenced practice in Bakersfield, Calif.; employed to edit the Kern County Echo; resumed the practice of law; member of the State senate 1894–1902; unsuccessful candidate for election in 1902 to the Fifty-eighth Congress; elected as a Republican to the Fifty-ninth and to the three succeeding Congresses and served from March 4, 1905, until his death in Los Angeles, Calif., January 26, 1913; interment in Union Cemetery.

SMITH, Thomas, a Delegate from Pennsylvania; born near Cruden, Aberdeenshire, Scotland, in 1745; pursued preparatory studies; attended the University of Edinburgh, Scotland; immigrated to the United States and settled in Bedford, Pa., February 9, 1769; deputy surveyor in 1769; studied law; was admitted to the bar and commenced the practice of his profession in 1772; deputy register of wills and prothonotary in 1773; justice of the peace in 1774; member of the committee of correspondence in 1775; served in the Revolutionary Army as a deputy colonel of militia; delegate to the State constitutional convention in 1776; member of the State house of representatives 1776–1780; Member of the Continental Congress 1780–1782; judge of the court of common pleas in 1791; judge of the Pennsylvania Supreme Court 1794–1809; died in Philadelphia, Pa., on March 31, 1809; interment in Christ Churchyard.

SMITH, Thomas, a Representative from Pennsylvania; born in Pennsylvania; resided in Tinicum Township, Delaware County, Pa.; member of the State house of representatives in 1806 and 1807; elected as a Federalist to the Fourteenth Congress (March 4, 1815–March 3, 1817); moved to Darby Township (later Darby Borough) in 1815; justice of the peace at the time of his death in Darby, Delaware County, Pa., on January 29, 1846; interment in St. James's (Old Swedes) Cemetery, Paschall (now a part of Philadelphia), Pa.

SMITH, Thomas, a Representative from Indiana; born in Fayette County, Pa., May 1, 1799; moved to Rising Sun, Ind., in 1818; learned the trade of tanner; moved to Versailles, Ind., in 1821 and established a tanyard; became a colonel in the militia; member of the State house of representatives in 1829, 1830, and 1833–1836; served in the State senate 1836–1839; elected as a Democrat to the Twenty-sixth Congress (March 4, 1839–March 3, 1841); unsuccessful candidate for election in 1840 to the Twenty-seventh Congress; elected to the Twenty-eighth and Twenty-ninth Congresses (March 4, 1843–March 3, 1847); was not a candidate for renomination in 1846; retired to private life; delegate to the State constitutional convention in 1850; died in Versailles, Ripley County, Ind., April 12, 1876; interment in Cliff Hill Cemetery.

SMITH, Thomas Alexander, a Representative from Maryland; born near Greenwood, Sussex County, Del., September 3, 1850; moved with his parents to Ridgely, Md., in 1856; attended the public schools and Denton (Md.) Academy; taught school in Delaware, Maryland, and Michigan; returned to Ridgely, Md., where he was postmaster from August 4, 1885, to November 25, 1889; engaged in the mercantile business; appointed station agent of the Philadelphia, Wilmington & Baltimore Railroad; member of the board of school commissioners for Caroline County 1889–1893; member of the State senate in 1894 and 1896; unsuccessful candidate for comptroller of the State treasury in 1897; was chief of the Maryland Bureau of Statistics and Information 1900–1904; first vice president of the National Association of Labor Statisticians in 1903 and 1904; member of the board of State aid and charities in 1904 and 1905; one of the founders of the Bank of Ridgely and served as its first president; elected as a Democrat to the Fifty-ninth Congress (March 4, 1905–March 3, 1907); unsuccessful candidate for reelection in 1906 to the Sixtieth Congress; was a delegate to the Farmers' National Congress of the United States held at Madison, Wis., in 1908 and at Lincoln, Nebr., in 1910; land commissioner of Maryland 1908–1912; appointed internal-revenue agent for the district of Maryland in 1915 and served until January 1, 1920; retired from public life and active pursuits in 1922, and resided in Ridgely, Caroline County, Md.; died, while on a visit, in Newark, Del., May 1, 1932; interment in Denton Cemetery, Ridgely, Md.

SMITH, Thomas Francis, a Representative from New York; born in New York City, July 24, 1865; attended the common schools, St. Francis Xavier College, Manhattan College, and the New York Law School from 1899 to 1901; official stenographer in the building department in 1892 and in the eighth district municipal court in 1894; reporter on the New York World and the New York Tribune; clerk of the city court 1898-1917; was admitted to the bar in 1911 and commenced practice in New York City; delegate to the State constitutional convention in 1915 and to the Democratic National Convention at St. Louis in 1916 which nominated Woodrow Wilson for a second term; elected as a Democrat to the Sixty-fifth Congress to fill the vacancy caused by the death of Michael F. Conry; reelected to the Sixty-sixth Congress and served from April 12, 1917, to March 3, 1921; was not a candidate for renomination in 1920; public administrator of New York from April 1, 1921, until his death in a taxicab accident in New York City April 11, 1923; interment in Calvary Cemetery, Long Island City, N. Y.

SMITH, Thomas Vernor, a Representative from Illinois; born in Blanket, Brown County, Tex., April 26, 1890; attended the public schools; was graduated from the University of Texas at Austin in 1915 and from the University of Chicago, Chicago, Ill., in 1922; during the First World War entered the military service September 3, 1918, and served as a private in the United States Army at Camp Bowie, Tex., until discharged on January 28, 1919; member of the faculty of Texas Christian University 1916–1918, the University of Texas 1919–1921, and the University of Chicago 1923–1948; author of numerous books; editor of the International Journal of Ethics 1931–1948; member of the State senate 1935–1938; chairman of the Illinois Legislative Council in 1937 and 1938; elected as a Democrat to the Seventy-sixth Congress (January 3, 1939–January 3, 1941); unsuccessful candidate for reelection in 1940 to the Seventy-seventh Congress; resumed his pursuits as a writer and author; during World War II served in the Army of the United States, as a lieutenant colonel and later as a colonel, from June 1, 1943, to February 28, 1946; served as director of education of the Allied Control Commission in Italy from November 24, 1943, to November 11, 1944; resumed his profession as a writer and teacher at University of Syracuse; is a resident of Syracuse, N. Y.

SMITH, Truman (nephew of Nathan Smith and Nathaniel Smith), a Representative and a Senator from Connecticut; born in Roxbury, Conn., November 27, 1791; completed preparatory studies; was graduated from Yale College in 1815; studied law; was admitted to the bar in 1818 and commenced practice in Litchfield, Conn.; member of the State house of representatives in 1831, 1832, and 1834; elected as a Whig to the Twenty-sixth and Twenty-seventh Congresses (March 4, 1839–March 3, 1843); declined renomination in 1842; presidential elector on the Whig ticket of Clay and Frelinghuysen in 1844; elected to the Twenty-ninth and Thirtieth Congresses (March 4, 1845–March 3, 1849); delegate to the Whig National Convention at Philadelphia in 1848 which nominated General Taylor for President and was chairman of the Whig National Committee during the campaign; declined the appointment of Secretary of the Interior in the Cabinet of President Taylor; elected to the United States Senate and served from March 4, 1849, until his resignation May 24, 1854; resumed the practice of his profession in New York City in 1854, with residence in Stamford, Conn.; appointed by President Lincoln as judge of the court of arbitration in New York, under the treaty of 1862 with Great Britain for the suppression of the slave trade, and served from 1862 to 1870; retired from active business life in 1872; died in Stamford, Fairfield County, Conn., May 3, 1884; interment in Woodland Cemetery.

SMITH, Walter Inglewood, a Representative from Iowa; born in Council Bluffs, Pottawattamie County, Iowa, July 10, 1862; attended the common schools; studied law; was admitted to the bar in 1882 and commenced practice in Council Bluffs, Iowa; judge of the fifteenth judicial district of Iowa 1890–1900; elected as a Republican to the Fifty-sixth Congress to fill the vacancy caused by the resignation of Smith McPherson and on the same day was elected to the Fifty-seventh Congress; reelected to the Fifty-eighth and to the four succeeding Congresses and served from December 3, 1900, to March 15, 1911, when he resigned to accept an appointment on the bench; appointed by President Taft to be United States circuit judge for the eighth judicial circuit and served from March 16, 1911, until his death in Council Bluffs, Iowa, on January 27, 1922; interment in Fairview Cemetery.

SMITH, William, a Delegate and a Representative from Maryland; born in Donegal Township, Lancaster County, Pa., April 12, 1728; moved to Baltimore, Md., May 1, 1761; appointed a member of the committee of correspondence in 1774; member of the committee of observation in 1775; one of a committee appointed by Congress to constitute a naval board in 1777; Member of the Continental Congress in 1777 and 1778; one of a committee to organize the defense of Baltimore and to address and receive Gen. George Washington in 1781; engaged in mercantile pursuits; elected as a Federalist to the First Congress (March 4, 1789–March 3, 1791); First Auditor of the United States Treasury July 16 to November 27, 1791; presidential elector in 1796; member of the State senate in 1801; died in Baltimore, Md., on March 27, 1814; interment in the Old Westminster Graveyard.

SMITH, William, a Senator from South Carolina; born in South Carolina in 1762; attended Alexander's Academy, Bullocks Creek, York District, S. C.; was graduated from Mount Sion Collegiate Institute, Winnsboro, S. C., in 1780; studied law and was admitted to the bar in 1784; settled in Pinckneyville, S. C., and later in Yorkville (now York), S. C., and practiced law; also was engaged as a planter; member of the State senate from 1803 to 1808, and served as president of that body 1806–1808; judge of the South Carolina Circuit Court 1808–1816; elected December 4, 1816, as a Democrat to the United States Senate to fill the vacancy caused by the resignation of John Taylor; on the same day was elected for the term commencing March 4, 1817, and served from December 4, 1816, to March 3, 1823; unsuccessful candidate for reelection; member of the State house of representatives in 1824 and 1825 and resigned; again elected to the United States Senate to fill the vacancy caused by the death of John Gaillard and served from November 29, 1826, to March 3, 1831; unsuccessful candidate for reelection in 1830; received the seven electoral votes of Georgia for Vice President of the United States in 1829; member of State senate 1831 and 1832; moved to Louisiana in 1832, and to a farm near Huntsville, Madison County, Ala., in 1833; member of the Alabama House of Representatives 1836–1840; declined the appointment of Associate Justice of the Supreme Court of the United States tendered by President Jackson in 1829 and 1836; presidential elector on the Democratic ticket of Van Buren and Johnson in 1836; trustee of Alexandria College of Pinckney District in 1797, of Bethel Academy in 1818, and of South Carolina College 1805–1816; died at his estate "Calhoun Place," on the Maysville Pike, near Huntsville, Ala., June 26, 1840; interment in the family burial ground on the estate; reinterment in Maple Hill Cemetery, Huntsville, Ala.

SMITH, William, a Representative from South Carolina; born in Bucks County, Pa., September 20, 1751; educated at best schools of his time; removed to South Carolina with his father in 1765; planter, of Spartan District; during the Revolutionary War took part in "Snow Campaign" against Cherokee Indians in 1775; lieutenant in expedition against Cherokees in 1776; captain in militia in 1777 and stationed in Wood's Fort on Tyger River; ordered to Georgia in December 1778, under General Lincoln; in Battle of Stono in June 1779; fought near Wofford's Iron Works, Hanging Rock, and Musgrove's Mill, August 1780; in Battle of Blackstocks, siege of Fort Granby, at Guilford Courthouse, Quinby Bridge, and affair at the Juniper, and in the capture of some British vessels at Watboo Landing under Colonel Wade Hampton; promoted to major in 1780; fought after the fall of Charles Town until end of war; county court judge, 1785–1797; South Carolina Senate from Spartan District 1790–1796; elected to Fifth Congress (March 4, 1797–March 3, 1799); again a member of the South Carolina Senate from Spartan District 1810–1818; died in Spartan District June 22, 1837; probably buried in Glenn Springs section of Spartanburg.

SMITH, William, a Representative from Virginia; born in Chesterfield, Va.; completed preparatory studies; member of the State house of delegates in 1782; elected to the Seventeenth, Eighteenth, and Nineteenth Congresses (March 4, 1821–March 3, 1827).

SMITH, William, a Representative from Virginia; born in Marengo, King George County, Va., September 6, 1797; attended private schools in Virginia and Plainfield Academy in Connecticut; studied law; was admitted to the bar and commenced practice in Culpeper, Culpeper County, Va., in 1818; established a line of United States mail and passenger post coaches through Virginia, the Carolinas, and Georgia in 1831; member of the State senate from 1836 to 1841, when he resigned; successfully contested as a Democrat the election of Linn Banks to the Twenty-seventh Congress and served from March 4, 1841, to March 3, 1843; unsuccessful candidate for reelection in 1842 to the Twenty-eighth Congress; moved to Fauquier County; presidential elector on the Democratic ticket of Polk and Dallas in 1844; Governor of Virginia 1846–1849, and unsuccessful candidate for election to the United States Senate during that period; moved to California in April 1849; president of the first Democratic State convention in 1850; returned to Virginia in December 1852; elected to the Thirty-third and to the three succeeding Congresses (March 4, 1853–March 3, 1861); during the Civil War served in the Confederate Army as colonel of the Forty-ninth Regiment of Virginia Infantry, and subsequently was promoted to brigadier general and major general; served in the Confederate Congress in 1862; again Governor of Virginia in 1864; returned to his estate, "Monterosa," near Warrenton, Va., in June 1865; engaged in agricultural pursuits; member of the State house of delegates 1877–1879; died in Warrenton, Fauquier County, Va., May 18, 1887; interment in Hollywood Cemetery, Richmond, Va.

SMITH, William Alden, a Representative and a Senator from Michigan; born in Dowagiac, Cass County, Mich., May 12, 1859; attended the common schools; moved with his parents to Grand Rapids in 1872; appointed a page in the Michigan House of Representatives in 1875; studied law; was admitted to the bar and commenced practice in Grand Rapids in 1883; general counsel of the Chicago & West Michigan Railway and the Detroit Lansing & Northern Railroad; assistant secretary of the Michigan State Senate in 1883; served as State game warden 1887–1891; elected as a Republican to the Fifty-fourth and to the six succeeding Congresses and served from March 4, 1895, until his resignation, effective February 9, 1907, having been elected Senator; was elected to the United States Senate January 15, 1907, for the term beginning March 4, 1907; subsequently elected on February 6, 1907, to fill the vacancy in the term ending March 3, 1907, caused by the death of Russell A. Alger; reelected in 1913, and served from February 9, 1907, to March 3, 1919; was not a candidate for renomination in 1918; constructed a railroad in Michigan in 1898 and became owner of the Lowell & Hastings Railroad in 1900; became owner and publisher of the Grand Rapids Herald in 1906; chairman of the board of directors of a transit company operating a line of steamboats from Chicago to various Lake Michigan ports; died in Grand Rapids, Mich., on October 11, 1932; interment in Woodlawn Cemetery.

SMITH, William Alexander, a Representative from North Carolina; born in Warren County, N. C., January 9, 1828; attended the common schools; engaged in agricultural pursuits; member of the State constitutional convention in 1865; member of the State senate in 1870; president of the North Carolina Railroad in 1868 and of the Yadkin River Railroad; elected as a Republican to the Forty-third Congress (March 4, 1873–March 3, 1875); died in Richmond, Va., May 16, 1888; interment in Hollywood Cemetery.

SMITH, William Ephraim, a Representative from Georgia; born in Augusta, Richmond County, Ga., March 14, 1829; pursued an academic course; studied law; was admitted to the bar in 1846, under a special act of the legislature, and practiced in Albany, Ga.; also a planter; ordinary of Dougherty County, Ga., in 1853; solicitor general of the southwest circuit 1858–1860; during the Civil War enlisted in the Confederate Army as a first lieutenant in the Fourth Georgia Volunteer Infantry; elected captain in April 1862; elected to the house of representatives of the Second Confederate Congress in 1863; declined the office of circuit judge of Georgia in 1874; elected as a Democrat to the Forty-fourth, Forty-fifth, and Forty-sixth Congresses (March 4, 1875–March 3, 1881); was not a candidate for renomination in 1880; resumed the practice of law; president of the Democratic State convention in 1886; served in the State senate 1886–1888; died in Albany, Dougherty County, Ga., March 11, 1890; interment in Oakview Cemetery.

SMITH, **William Jay**, a Representative from Tennessee; born in Birmingham, England, September 24, 1823; immigrated to the United States and settled in Orange County, N. Y.; attended the common schools; learned the printing trade; moved to Tennessee in 1846; during the Mexican War, in 1847, served in a regiment from that State; moved to Hardeman County, Tenn., and engaged in horticulture; during the Civil War served in the Union Army 1861–1865, and was brevetted brigadier general; delegate to the State constitutional convention in 1865; member of the State house of representatives in 1866 and 1867; served in the State senate in 1884 and 1885; surveyor of the port of Memphis, Tenn., 1871–1883; elected as a Republican to the Forty-first Congress (March 4, 1869–March 3, 1871); unsuccessful candidate for reelection; engaged in the real-estate business and in banking; delegate to the Republican National Convention at Cincinnati in 1876; died in Memphis, Tenn., November 29, 1913; interment in Elmwood Cemetery.

SMITH, **William Loughton**, a Representative from South Carolina; born in Charleston, S. C., in 1758; attended preparatory schools in England 1770–1774; studied law in the Middle Temple at London, England, in 1774; pursued higher studies in Geneva 1774–1778; returned to Charleston, S. C., in 1783; was admitted to the bar in 1784 and commenced practice in Charleston; engaged in agricultural pursuits on his estate near Charleston; member of the privy council in 1784; member of the State house of representatives 1784–1788; warden of the city of Charleston in 1786; elected as a Federalist to the First and to the four succeeding Congresses and served from March 4, 1789, until July 10, 1797, when he resigned; appointed United States Minister to Portugal and Spain on July 10, 1797, and served until September 9, 1801, when he took leave of absence; commissioned Minister to the Ottoman Porte on February 11, 1799, but did not reach that court; returned to Charleston; unsuccessful Federalist candidate for election in 1804, 1806, and 1808 to the Ninth, Tenth, and Eleventh Congresses; lieutenant in the State militia in 1808; again a member of the State house of representatives in 1808; president of the Santee Canal Co.; vice president of the Charleston Library Society and of the St. Cecilia Society; engaged in literary pursuits; died in Charleston, S. C., December 19, 1812; interment in St. Philip's Churchyard.

SMITH, **William Nathan Harrell**, a Representative from North Carolina; born in Murfreesboro, N. C., September 24, 1812; attended the common schools in Murfreesboro, N. C., Kingston, R. I., and Colchester and East Lyme, Conn.; was graduated from Yale College in 1834 and from Yale Law School in 1836; was admitted to the bar and commenced practice in Murfreesboro, N. C., in 1839; held several local offices; was a member of the State house of commons in 1840, 1858, 1865, and 1866; served in the State senate in 1848; solicitor of the first

judicial district of North Carolina for eight years; elected as a Democrat to the Thirty-sixth Congress (March 4, 1859–March 3, 1861); unsuccessful candidate for Speaker, lacking one vote of election; served in the Confederate Congress 1862–1865; delegate to the Democratic National Convention at New York City in 1868; chief justice of the North Carolina Supreme Court 1878–1889; died in Raleigh, N. C., November 14, 1889; interment in Oakwood Cemetery.

SMITH, **William Orlando**, a Representative from Pennsylvania; born in Reynoldsville, Jefferson County, Pa., June 13, 1859; attended the public schools; learned the printing trade; publisher of the Reynoldsville Herald 1876–1879; worked in the Government Printing Office, Washington, D. C., 1879–1884; one of a company of ten printers to establish the Washington Craftsman, for awhile the organ of the International Typographical Union, and was its first associate editor; returned to Punxsutawney, Pa., in 1884 and successively edited the Punxsutawney Tribune and the Punxsutawney Spirit; member of the State house of representatives 1889–1898; editor of the Bradford (Pa.) Daily Era in 1891; purchased a half interest in the Punxsutawney Spirit in January 1892; elected as a Republican to the Fifty-eighth and Fifty-ninth Congresses (March 4, 1903–March 3, 1907); was not a candidate for renomination in 1906; presidential elector on the Republican ticket of Taft and Sherman in 1908 and of Taft and Butler in 1912; was chairman of the local exemption board for Jefferson County during the First World War; resumed newspaper interests in Punxsutawney, Jefferson County, Pa.; died while a patient in a Cleveland, Ohio, hospital on May 12, 1932; interment in Circle Hill Cemetery, Punxsutawney, Pa.

SMITH, **William Robert**, a Representative from Texas; born near Tyler, Smith County, Tex., August 18, 1863; attended the country schools, and was graduated from Sam Houston Normal Institute, Huntsville, Tex., in 1883; studied law; was admitted to the bar in 1885 and practiced in Tyler until February 1888; moved to Colorado, Mitchell County, Tex., and continued the practice of law; judge of the thirty-second judicial district of Texas 1897–1903; was elected as a Democrat to the Fifty-eighth and to the six succeeding Congresses (March 4, 1903–March 3, 1917); unsuccessful candidate for renomination in 1916; moved to El Paso, Tex., in October 1916 and practiced his profession; appointed United States district judge for the western district of Texas and served from April 12, 1917, until his death in El Paso, Tex., August 16, 1924; interment in Evergreen Cemetery.

SMITH, **William Russell**, a Representative from Alabama; born in Russellville, Ky., March 27, 1815; moved at an early age to Huntsville, Ala.; pursued classical studies and attended the University of Alabama at Tuscaloosa; studied law; was admitted to the bar and commenced practice in Greensboro, Ala., in 1835; served as captain of Alabama State troops in the campaign against the Creek Indians in 1836; moved to Tuscaloosa, Ala., where he continued the practice of law and also engaged in newspaper work; founded and edited the Mirror; mayor of Tuscaloosa in 1839; author of several books and plays; member of the State house of representatives 1841–1843; elected brigadier general of militia in 1845; judge of the seventh judicial circuit in 1850 and 1851; elected as a Union Whig to the Thirty-second and Thirty-third Congresses and as the candidate of the American Party to the Thirty-fourth Congress (March 4, 1851–March 3, 1857); unsuccessful candidate for reelection in 1856 to the Thirty-fifth Congress; member of the State constitutional convention in 1861 and opposed and voted against secession; during the Civil War served in the Confederate Army as colonel of the Twenty-sixth Alabama Regiment; Representative in the First and Second Confederate Congresses; president of the University of Alabama 1869–1871; resumed the practice of his profession and engaged in historical and literary pursuits; died in Washington, D. C., on February 26, 1896; interment in Tuscaloosa, Ala.; reinterment in Mount Olivet Cemetery, Washington, D. C.

SMITH, William Stephens, a Representative from New York; born on Long Island, N. Y., November 8, 1755; was graduated from the College of New Jersey (now Princeton University) in 1774; studied law for a short time; served in the Revolutionary Army as aide-de-camp to General Sullivan in 1776; was on the staff of General Lafayette in 1780 and 1781, and then transferred to the staff of General Washington; fought in twenty-two engagements in the Revolution; secretary of the Legation at London in 1784; returned to America in 1788; appointed by President Washington to be United States marshal for the district of New York in 1789, and later supervisor of revenue; one of the originators of the Society of the Cincinnati, and served as its president 1795–1797; appointed by President John Adams surveyor of the port of New York in 1800; moved to Lebanon, N. Y., in 1807; elected as a Federalist to the Thirteenth Congress (March 4, 1813–March 3, 1815); credentials of his election to the Fourteenth Congress were presented, but he did not qualify, and on December 13, 1815, Westel Willoughby, Jr., successfully contested his election; died in Smith Valley, town of Lebanon, Madison County, N. Y., on June 10, 1816; interment in the Lines Hill Cemetery, between Smyrna and Sherburne, N. Y.

SMITH, Willis, a Senator from North Carolina; born in Norfolk, Va., December 19, 1887; at death of father, when two years of age, moved with his mother to North Carolina and attended the public schools in Elizabeth City; was graduated from Atlantic Collegiate Institute, Elizabeth City, N. C., in 1905, Trinity College (now Duke University), Durham, N. C., in 1910, and from the law school of Duke University in 1912; was admitted to the bar in 1912 and commenced the practice of law in Raleigh, N. C.; during the First World War served in the United States Army at Fort Monroe, Va.; inheritance tax attorney of North Carolina 1915–1920; member of the State house of representatives 1928–1932, serving as speaker in 1931; member of commission preparing rules for Federal courts in North Carolina in 1933; delegate to the Democratic National Convention in 1944; member of board of trustees of Patrick Henry Memorial Foundation; trustee of Duke University and chairman of the board from 1946 to 1953; observer at Nuremburg Trials in 1946; United States delegate to the Interparliamentary Union in Istanbul, Turkey, in 1951, and served as chairman of the American delegation to the Interparliamentary Union in Bern, Switzerland, in 1952; elected as a Democrat to the United States Senate on November 7, 1950, to fill the vacancy caused by the death of J. Melville Broughton and served from November 27, 1950, until his death in the naval hospital at Bethesda, Md., June 26, 1953; interment in Oakwood Cemetery, Raleigh, N. C.

SMITH, Wint, a Representative from Kansas; born in Mankato, Jewell County, Kans., October 7, 1893; attended the public schools and was graduated from the Mankato High School; during the First World War served in the United States Army as a combat Infantry officer from May 11, 1917, to September 4, 1919, with twenty-four months' service overseas; was graduated from the University of Kansas at Lawrence in 1920 and from Yale University Law School, New Haven, Conn., in 1922; was admitted to the bar in 1923 and commenced practice in Kansas City, Kans.; was admitted to practice in all Federal courts,

including the United States Supreme Court in 1934; assistant attorney general 1931–1940; attorney for Kansas Highway Commission 1931–1940; during World War II served as lieutenant colonel and commanding officer of the Six Hundred and Thirty-fifth Tank Destroyer Battalion from May 1941 to December 1945, with twenty-two months' service overseas; resumed the practice of law; elected as a Republican to the Eightieth and to the six succeeding Congresses (January 3, 1947–January 3, 1961); was not a candidate for renomination in 1960; is a resident of Mankato, Kans.

SMITH, Worthington Curtis (son of John Smith, of Vermont), a Representative from Vermont; born in St. Albans, Franklin County, Vt., April 23, 1823; pursued classical studies, and was graduated from the University of Vermont at Burlington in 1843; studied law, but did not practice; engaged in the iron trade; during the Civil War assisted in raising the First Regiment, Vermont Volunteer Infantry; member of the State house of representatives in 1863; served in the State senate in 1864 and 1865, and was elected president pro tempore of that body in 1865; elected as a Republican to the Fortieth, Forty-first, and Forty-second Congresses (March 4, 1867–March 3, 1873); president of St. Albans Foundry Co.; died in St. Albans, Vt., January 2, 1894; interment in Greenwood Cemetery.

SMITHERS, Nathaniel Barratt, a Representative from Delaware; born in Dover, Del., October 8, 1818; was graduated from Lafayette College, Pennsylvania, in 1836; studied law; was admitted to the bar and commenced practice in Dover, Del., in 1840; secretary of state of Delaware January 20 to November 23, 1863; elected as a Republican to the Thirty-eighth Congress to fill the vacancy caused by the death of William Temple and served from December 7, 1863, to March 3, 1865; unsuccessful candidate for reelection in 1864 to the Thirty-ninth Congress; resumed the practice of law in Dover; delegate to the Republican National Convention at Baltimore in 1864; died in Dover, Kent County, Del., January 16, 1896; interment in the Old Methodist Cemetery.

SMITHWICK, John Harris, a Representative from Florida; born near Orange, Cherokee County, Ga., July 17, 1872; attended the public schools; was graduated from Reinhardt Normal College, Waleska, Ga., in 1895 and from the law department of Cumberland University, Lebanon, Tenn., in 1897; was admitted to the bar in 1898 and commenced the practice of his profession in Moultrie, Ga.; moved to Pensacola, Fla., in 1906 and continued the practice of his profession; elected as a Democrat to the Sixty-sixth and to the three succeeding Congresses (March 4, 1919–March 3, 1927); unsuccessful candidate for renomination in 1926; engaged in the real-estate business in Fort Myers, Lee County, Fla., and in Washington, D. C.; retired in 1932, due to ill health, and resided in Moultrie, Ga., until his death on December 2, 1948; interment in Westview Cemetery.

SMOOT, Reed, a Senator from Utah; born in Salt Lake City, Utah, January 10, 1862; moved with his parents to Provo, Utah County, Utah, in 1874; attended the common schools and the University of Utah at Salt Lake City; was graduated from the Brigham Young Academy (now Brigham Young University) at Provo in 1880; engaged in banking, mining, livestock raising, and in the manufacture of woolen goods; delegate to the Republican National Conventions in 1908, 1912, 1916, 1920, and 1924; appointed by President Harding a member of the World War Foreign Debt Commission in 1922; elected as a Republican to the United States Senate in 1902; reelected in 1908, 1914, 1920, and again in 1926, and served from March 4, 1903, to March 3, 1933; unsuccessful candidate for reelection in 1932; moved to

Salt Lake City, Utah, in 1933 and retired from active business pursuits; served as one of the twelve apostles of the Church of Jesus Christ of Latter Day Saints (Mormon Church) and at the time of his death was next in line to succeed the president of the quorum and third to succeed the president; died in St. Petersburg, Fla., while on a visit, February 9, 1941; interment in Provo Burial Park, Provo, Utah.

SMYSER, Martin Luther, a Representative from Ohio; born on a farm in Plaine Township, Wayne County, Ohio, April 3, 1851; attended the common schools, and was graduated from Wittenberg College, Springfield, Ohio, in 1870; studied law; was admitted to the bar in 1872 and practiced in Wooster; elected prosecuting attorney of Wayne County in 1872 and served one term; delegate to the Republican National Conventions at Chicago in 1884 and 1888; elected to the Fifty-first Congress (March 4, 1889–March 3, 1891); unsuccessful candidate for reelection in 1890 to the Fifty-second Congress; resumed the practice of law in Wooster; elected to the Fifty-ninth Congress (March 4, 1905–March 3, 1907); unsuccessful candidate for reelection in 1906 to the Sixtieth Congress; continued the practice of law in Wooster, Ohio, until his death in that city May 6, 1908; interment in Wooster Cemetery.

SMYTH, Alexander, a Representative from Virginia; born on the Island of Rathlin, Ireland, in 1765; immigrated to the United States and settled in Botetourt County, Va., in 1775; completed preparatory studies; studied law; was admitted to the bar and commenced practice in Abingdon, Va.; moved to Wythe County, Va.; member of the State house of delegates in 1792, 1796, 1801, 1802, and 1804–1808; served in the State senate in 1808 and 1809; served in the United States Army as colonel of a regiment of riflemen from July 8, 1808, to July 6, 1812, and as an inspector general with the rank of brigadier general from July 6, 1812, to March 3, 1813; resumed the practice of his profession; again a member of the State house of delegates in 1816, 1817, 1826, and 1827; was elected to the Fifteenth and to the three succeeding Congresses (March 4, 1817–March 3, 1825); elected to the Twentieth and Twenty-first Congresses and served from March 4, 1827, until his death in Washington, D. C., April 17, 1830; interment in the Congressional Cemetery.

SMYTH, George Washington, a Representative from Texas; born in North Carolina, May 16, 1803; moved with his parents to Alabama, and later to Murfreesboro, Tenn.; attended the common schools and the college at Murfreesboro; moved to Texas, then a part of the Republic of Mexico, in 1828, and settled in the municipality of Bevell, Zavalas Colony (now Jasper County); appointed by the Mexican Government as surveyor, and later made commissioner of titles; delegate to the General Consultation of Texas at San Felipe de Austin in 1835; member of the Texas State convention and a signer of the declaration of independence of Texas in 1836; also a signer of the constitution of the Republic of Texas; appointed by President Lamar, of Texas, commissioner in charge of the boundary line between the Republic of Texas and the United States; engaged in agricultural pursuits; deputy in the Congress of the Republic of Texas in 1845, and assisted in framing the constitution of the State of Texas; elected commissioner of the general land office of the State in 1848; elected as a Democrat to the Thirty-third Congress (March 4, 1853–March 3, 1855); declined a renomination to the Thirty-fourth Congress; served in the Confederate Army during the Civil War; member of the State constitutional convention in 1866; died in Austin, Tex., February 21, 1866, while attending a session of the convention; interment in the State Cemetery.

SMYTH, William, a Representative from Iowa; born in Eden, County Tyrone, Ireland, January 3, 1824; attended the rural schools; completed preparatory studies; immigrated to the United States in 1838 with his parents, who settled in Pennsylvania; moved to Iowa in 1844; attended the University of Iowa at Iowa City; studied law; was admitted to the bar in 1847 and commenced practice in Marion, Iowa; prosecuting attorney of Linn County 1848–1853; was appointed judge of the district court for the fourth judicial district of Iowa in 1853 and served until his resignation in 1857; resumed the practice of law; in 1858 served as chairman of the commission to codify and revise the State laws; during the Civil War served in the Union Army for two years as colonel of the Thirty-first Regiment, Iowa Volunteer Infantry; elected as a Republican to the Forty-first Congress and served from March 4, 1869, until his death; renominated in 1870 and was a candidate for reelection at the time of his death; died in Marion, Iowa, September 30, 1870; interment in Oak Shade Cemetery.

SNAPP, Henry (father of Howard Malcolm Snapp), a Representative from Illinois; born in Livonia, Livingston County, N. Y., June 30, 1822; moved with his parents to Rochester, N. Y., in 1825; attended the common schools of that city; moved to Homer, Will County, Ill., in 1833, where he completed his common-school education; studied law; was admitted to the bar in 1843 and commenced practice in Joliet, Will County, Ill.; member of the State senate from 1869 to 1871; elected as a Republican to the Forty-second Congress to fill the vacancy caused by the resignation of Burton C. Cook and served from December 4, 1871, to March 3, 1873; declined to be a candidate for renomination in 1872; resumed the practice of his profession in Joliet, Ill., where he died on November 26, 1895; interment in Oakwood Cemetery.

SNAPP, Howard Malcolm (son of Henry Snapp), a Representative from Illinois; born in Joliet, Will County, Ill., September 27, 1855; attended the Eastern Avenue school and Forest University in Chicago, Ill., 1872–1875; studied law; was admitted to the bar in 1878 and commenced practice in Globe, Ariz.; returned to Joliet, Ill., and continued the practice of law; master in chancery for Will County, Ill., from 1884 to 1903; elected chairman of the Will County Republican central committee in 1893; delegate to the Republican National Conventions in 1896 and 1908; was elected as a Republican to the Fifty-eighth and to the three succeeding Congresses (March 4, 1903–March 3, 1911); was not a candidate for renomination in 1910; resumed the practice of law in Joliet, Ill.; presidential elector on the Republican ticket of Coolidge and Dawes in 1924; died in Joliet, Ill., August 14, 1938; interment in Elmhurst Cemetery.

SNEED, William Henry, a Representative from Tennessee; born in Davidson County, Tenn., August 27, 1812; completed preparatory studies; moved with his father's family to Rutherford County, Tenn.; studied law; was admitted to the bar in 1834 and commenced practice in Murfreesboro, Tenn.; member of the State senate 1843–1845; moved to Knoxville, Tenn., in 1845 and resumed the practice of law; elected as the candidate of the American Party to the Thirty-fourth Congress (March 4, 1855–March 3, 1857); declined to be a candidate for renomination in 1856 and also for nomination as circuit judge; resumed the practice of law; died in Knoxville, Tenn., September 18, 1869; interment in the Old Gray Cemetery.

SNELL, Bertrand Hollis, a Representative from New York; born in Colton, St. Lawrence County, N. Y., December 9, 1870; attended the public schools; was graduated from the State normal school at Potsdam, N. Y., in 1889 and from Amherst (Mass.)

College in 1894; began his business career as a bookkeeper and afterward became secretary and manager of the Raquette River Paper Co. in Potsdam; in 1904 organized the Canton Lumber Co. in Potsdam; president and manager of the Phenix Cheese Co. of New York City; owner of the Snell Power Plant, of Higley Falls, N. Y.; director of the Northern New York Trust Co., the Agricultural Insurance Co. of Watertown, N. Y., and Gould Pumps, Inc., Seneca Falls, N. Y.; vice president of the Northern New York Development League 1908–1910; member of the Republican State Committee 1914–1944; delegate to all Republican National Conventions 1916–1940, serving as chairman in 1932 and 1936; president, board of trustees of Clarkson College, Potsdam, N. Y., 1920–1945; member, board of trustees of Potsdam State Teachers College 1910–1948, Potsdam Public Library, and A. B. Hepburn Memorial Hospital, Ogdensburg, N. Y.; elected as a Republican to the Sixty-fourth Congress to fill the vacancy caused by the death of Edwin A. Merritt, Jr.; reelected to the Sixty-fifth and to the ten succeeding Congresses and served from November 2, 1915, to January 3, 1939; was not a candidate for renomination in 1938; minority leader from the Seventy-second Congress to the Seventy-fifth Congress, inclusive; publisher of the Potsdam Courier-Freeman newspaper 1934–1949; in 1941 became owner and manager of New York State Oil Co., of Kansas; died in Potsdam, N. Y., February 2, 1958; interment in Bayside Cemetery.

SNIDER, Samuel Prather, a Representative from Minnesota; born in Mount Gilead, Morrow County, Ohio, October 9, 1845; attended the public schools, the local high school at Mount Gilead, Ohio, and Oberlin College, Ohio; during the Civil War enlisted as a private soldier in the Sixty-fifth Regiment, Ohio Volunteer Infantry; served in Kentucky, Tennessee, Georgia, Alabama, and Mississippi, and as a captain in west Tennessee in the Thirteenth United States Colored Infantry; after the war engaged in commercial pursuits in New York; moved to Minnesota in 1876 and settled in Minneapolis; organized and built the Midland Railway in southern Minnesota; engaged in agricultural pursuits and the mining of iron ore; member of the State house of representatives 1884–1888; elected as a Republican to the Fifty-first Congress (March 4, 1889–March 3, 1891); unsuccessful candidate for reelection in 1890 to the Fifty-second Congress; delegate to the Republican National Convention at Minneapolis in 1892; retired from active business pursuits and resided in Minneapolis, Minn., until his death at the Minnesota Soldiers' Home in Minneapolis, Minn., September 24, 1928; interment in Lakewood Cemetery.

SNODGRASS, Charles Edward (nephew of Henry Clay Snodgrass), a Representative from Tennessee; born near Sparta, White County, Tenn., December 28, 1866; attended the common schools; studied law; was admitted to the bar and commenced practice in Crossville, Tenn., in 1888; never held or sought any elective office until his election to Congress; elected as a Democrat to the Fifty-sixth and Fifty-seventh Congresses (March 4, 1899–March 3, 1903); unsuccessful candidate for renomination in 1902; judge of the fifth judicial circuit of Tennessee; appointed and subsequently elected judge of the court of appeals upon the reorganization of that court and served from 1925 to 1934; retired to private life in Crossville, Tenn., where he died August 3, 1936; interment in the Crossville City Cemetery.

SNODGRASS, Henry Clay (uncle of Charles Edward Snodgrass), a Representative from Tennessee; born near Sparta, White County, Tenn., March 29, 1848; attended Sparta Academy; studied law at Cumberland University, Lebanon, Tenn.; was admitted to the bar in 1870 and commenced practice in Sparta,

Tenn.; also engaged in agricultural pursuits; during the Civil War served as a private in the Confederate Army; attorney general of the fifth judicial circuit 1878–1884; elected as a Democrat to the Fifty-second and Fifty-third Congresses (March 4, 1891–March 3, 1895); unsuccessful candidate for reelection in 1894 to the Fifty-fourth Congress; delegate to the Democratic National Convention at Chicago in 1896, which nominated Bryan and Sewall; resumed the practice of his profession in Sparta, White County, Tenn.; moved to Gould, Okla., and engaged in agricultural pursuits; died in Altus, Okla., April 22, 1931; interment in Altus Cemetery.

SNODGRASS, John Fryall, a Representative from Virginia; born in Berkeley County, Va. (now West Virginia), March 2, 1804; completed preparatory studies; studied law; was admitted to the bar in 1843 and commenced practice in Parkersburg, Va.; delegate to the State constitutional convention in 1850 and 1851; elected as a Democrat to the Thirty-third Congress and served from March 4, 1853, until his death in Parkersburg, Va. (now West Virginia), June 5, 1854.

SNOOK, John Stout, a Representative from Ohio; born near Antwerp, Paulding County, Ohio, on December 18, 1862; was graduated from the Antwerp grade schools in 1881; attended the Ohio Wesleyan University, Delaware, Ohio; was graduated from the law school of Cincinnati College in May 1887; was admitted to the bar the same year and began practice in Antwerp, Ohio; moved to Paulding, Ohio, in 1890 and continued the practice of his profession; elected as a Democrat to the Fifty-seventh and Fifty-eighth Congresses (March 4, 1901–March 3, 1905); was not a candidate for renomination in 1904; resumed the practice of law in Paulding; delegate to the Democratic National Conventions in 1912 and 1932; judge of the court of common pleas 1913–1915; elected to the Sixty-fifth Congress (March 4, 1917–March 3, 1919); was an unsuccessful candidate for reelection in 1918 to the Sixty-sixth Congress; again engaged in the practice of his profession; judge of the court of common pleas from 1930 to 1938, when he retired; died in Paulding, Ohio, September 19, 1952; interment in Live Oak Cemetery.

SNOVER, Horace Greeley, a Representative from Michigan; born in Romeo, Macomb County, Mich., September 21, 1847; attended the public schools and Dickenson Institute at Romeo; was graduated from the academic department of the University of Michigan at Ann Arbor in 1869 and from the law department in 1871; was admitted to the bar and practiced in Wichita, Kans., in 1871 and 1872; moved to Romeo, Mich., in 1873 and to Port Austin, Huron County, Mich., in 1874 and continued the practice of law; also engaged in banking; principal of the public schools of Port Austin for two years; probate judge of Huron County from January 1, 1881, to January 1, 1885; elected as a Republican to the Fifty-fourth and Fifty-fifth Congresses (March 4, 1895–March 3, 1899); was not a candidate for renomination in 1898; after leaving Congress retired from active business pursuits and moved to Port Huron, Mich.; died in Port Huron July 21, 1924; interment in Lakeside Cemetery.

SNOW, Donald Francis, a Representative from Maine; born in Bangor, Penobscot County, Maine, September 6, 1877; attended the grade and high schools of his native city; was graduated from Bowdoin College, Brunswick, Maine, in 1901 and from the law school of the University of Maine at Orono in 1904; was admitted to the bar in 1904 and commenced practice in Bangor, Maine; city solicitor of Bangor 1906–1910 and prosecuting attorney of Penobscot County 1911–1913; elected as a Republican to the Seventy-first and Seventy-second Congresses (March 4, 1929–March 3, 1933); unsuccessful candidate for renomination in 1932; engaged in literary work in Washington, D. C., 1933–1935; moved to Gorham, Cumberland County, Maine, in 1936 and engaged in poultry farming until 1945; secretary for the E. C. Jones Insurance Corp., Portland, Maine, and later had his own insurance business; died in Gorham, Maine, February 12, 1958; interment in Evergreen Cemetery, Portland, Maine.

SNOW, Herman Wilber, a Representative from Illinois; born in Michigan City, La Porte County, Ind., July 3, 1836; moved with his parents to Madisonville, Ky.; attended the public schools; moved to Sheldon, Iroquois County, Ill.; taught school several years; studied law; was admitted to the bar and practiced; during the Civil War enlisted as a private in the One Hundred and Thirty-ninth Regiment, Illinois Volunteer Infantry; served in Illinois, Missouri, and Kentucky and rose to the rank of captain; after expiration of his first enlistment reenlisted in the One Hundred and Fifty-first Regiment, Illinois Volunteer Infantry, and was promoted to the rank of lieutenant colonel; provost marshal general of Georgia on Major General Steedman's staff; was with his regiment when Brigadier General Wofford surrendered 10,400 Confederate troops to Steedman at Kingston, Ga.; at the expiration of his service taught in the Chicago High School for three years; returned to Sheldon and engaged in banking; member of the State house of representatives 1872–1874; elected as a Democrat to the Fifty-second Congress (March 4, 1891–March 3, 1893); unsuccessful candidate for reelection in 1892 to the Fifty-third Congress; Sergeant at Arms of the National House of Representatives during the Fifty-third Congress; moved to Kankakee, Kankakee County, Ill., and resumed banking; died in Kankakee, Ill., August 25, 1914; interment in Mound Grove Cemetery.

SNOW, William W., a Representative from New York; born in Heath, Franklin County, Mass., April 27, 1812; attended the public schools; learned the trade of wool-carder and cloth dresser; moved to Oneonta, Otsego County, N. Y., in 1831; engaged in the wool-carding business in 1841 and the following year entered the tin and hardware business; also engaged in agricultural pursuits; member of the State assembly in 1844; elected as a Democrat to the Thirty-second Congress (March 4, 1851–March 3, 1853); again a member of the State assembly in 1870; served as supervisor of the town of Oneonta in 1873 and 1874; served as State excise commissioner in 1877; member of the village board of trustees; engaged in banking; died in Oneonta, N. Y., September 3, 1886; interment in Riverside Cemetery.

SNYDER, Adam Wilson, a Representative from Illinois; born in Connellsville, Fayette County, Pa., October 6, 1799; attended the common schools; moved to Cahokia, Ill., in 1817; studied law; was admitted to the bar in 1820 and commenced practice in Cahokia; appointed prosecuting attorney for the first judicial district in 1822; resigned in 1823; engaged in agricultural pursuits 1824–1832; member of the State senate in 1830; reelected in 1832; served as a captain throughout the Black Hawk War; moved to Belleville, Ill., in 1833; unsuccessful candidate for election in 1834 to the Twenty-fourth Congress; elected as a Van Buren Democrat to the Twenty-fifth Congress (March 4, 1837–March 3, 1839); was not a candidate for renomination in 1838; elected to the State senate in 1840, and resigned in 1841; presidential elector on the Democratic ticket of Van Buren and Johnson in 1840; nominated as a candidate for Governor of Illinois, but died before the election; died in Belleville, St. Clair County, Ill., May 14, 1842; interment in Green Mount Cemetery, near Belleville, Ill.

SNYDER, Charles Philip, a Representative from West Virginia; born in Charleston, Kanawha County, Va. (now West Virginia), June 9, 1847; pursued an academic course; studied law; was admitted to the bar and practiced; prosecuting attorney of Kanawha County, W. Va., 1876–1884; was elected as a Democrat to the Forty-eighth Congress to fill the vacancy caused by the resignation of John E. Kenna; reelected to the Forty-ninth and Fiftieth Congresses and served from May 15, 1883, to March 3, 1889; judge of the criminal court of Kanawha County 1890–1896; United States consul to Ciudad Porfirio Diaz, Mexico, 1897–1901; retired from all activities; died in Vineland, Cumberland County, N. J., August 21, 1915; interment in Spring Hill Cemetery, Charleston, W. Va.

SNYDER, Homer Peter, a Representative from New York; born in Amsterdam, Amsterdam County, N. Y., December 6, 1863; attended the common schools; was employed in various capacities in knitting mills until 1887; moved to Little Falls, N. Y., in 1887 and continued employment in knitting mills; engaged in the manufacture of knitting machinery in 1890 and, later, of bicycles and other wheeled vehicles; director and vice president of the Little Falls National Bank; served one term as school commissioner in 1895 and two terms as fire and police commissioner of Little Falls in 1910 and 1911; unsuccessful candidate for election in 1912 to the Sixty-third Congress; elected as a Republican to the Sixty-fourth and to the four succeeding Congresses (March 4, 1915–March 3, 1925); was not a candidate for reelection in 1924; delegate to the Republican National Conventions at Chicago in 1916 and 1920; resumed his former manufacturing pursuits; died in Little Falls, N. Y., December 30, 1937; interment in the Church Street Cemetery.

SNYDER, John, a Representative from Pennsylvania; born in Selinsgrove, Snyder County, Pa., January 29, 1793; attended the rural schools; served in the War of 1812 as captain of Selinsgrove Rifle Volunteers, Pennsylvania Militia; connected with the Snyder Spring Oil Co. and paper mills; elected to the Twenty-seventh Congress (March 4, 1841–March 3, 1843); unsuccessful candidate for reelection to the Twenty-eighth Congress; resumed former business pursuits; died in Selinsgrove, Snyder County, Pa., August 15, 1850; interment in the New Lutheran Cemetery.

SNYDER, John Buell, a Representative from Pennsylvania; born on a farm in Upper Turkeyfoot Township, Somerset County, Pa., July 30, 1877; attended the public schools, and the summer sessions of Harvard University, Cambridge, Mass., and Columbia University, New York, N. Y.; was graduated from Lock Haven (Pa.) Teachers College; principal of schools at Stoyestown, Rockwood, and Berlin, Somerset County, 1901–1906, and of Perry Township Union High School 1906–1912; western Pennsylvania manager of the Macmillan Company, educational publishers, 1912–1932; member of the board of education of Perry Township, Pa., 1922–1932; legislative representative for Pennsylvania school directors during sessions of the State legislature 1921–1923; member of the National Commission of One Hundred for Study and Survey of Rural Schools in the United States 1922–1924; elected as a Democrat to the Seventy-third and to the six succeeding Congresses and served from March 4, 1933, until his death in Pittsburgh, Pa., on February 24, 1946, while on his way to Uniontown, Pa., to attend a business meeting; interment in Mount Washington Cemetery, Perryopolis, Pa.

SNYDER, Melvin Claude, a Representative from West Virginia; born in Albright, Preston County, W. Va., October 29, 1898; attended the public schools; during the First World War enlisted in the United States Army and served as a private in

1918; was graduated in 1923 from the West Virginia University Law School at Morgantown; was admitted to the bar the same year and commenced practice in Kingwood, W. Va.; mayor of Kingwood in 1926; prosecuting attorney for Preston County, W. Va., 1929–1944; during World War II served in the United States Army from January 6, 1941, until his discharge as a colonel on January 30, 1946; awarded Legion of Merit; director of Surplus Property for Division of Territories and Island Possessions, Department of Interior, in 1946; was elected as a Republican to the Eightieth Congress (January 3, 1947–January 3, 1949); unsuccessful candidate for reelection in 1948 to the Eighty-first Congress and for election in 1950 to the Eighty-second Congress; circuit court judge, eighteenth judicial circuit, West Virginia, since January 1, 1953; is a resident of Kingwood, W. Va.

SNYDER, Oliver P., a Representative from Arkansas; born in Missouri November 13, 1833; completed preparatory studies; moved to Arkansas in 1853; engaged in scientific and literary pursuits and at the same time studied law; was admitted to the bar and practiced in Pine Bluff; member of the State house of representatives in 1864 and 1865; delegate to the State constitutional convention in 1867; presidential elector on the Republican ticket of Grant and Colfax in 1868; served in the State senate 1868–1871; member of the committee to revise and rearrange the statutes of Arkansas in 1868; elected as a Republican to the Forty-second and Forty-third Congresses (March 4, 1871–March 3, 1875); unsuccessful candidate for renomination in 1874; resumed the practice of his profession; elected treasurer of Jefferson County in 1882 and served until his death in Pine Bluff, Jefferson County, Ark., November 22, 1882; interment in Bellewood Cemetery.

SOLLERS, Augustus Rhodes, a Representative from Maryland; born near Prince Frederick, Calvert County, Md., May 1, 1814; studied law; was admitted to the bar in 1836 and commenced practice in Prince Frederick; elected as a Whig to the Twenty-seventh Congress (March 4, 1841–March 3, 1843); resumed the practice of law; delegate to the State constitutional convention in 1851; elected to the Thirty-third Congress (March 4, 1853–March 3, 1855); presidential elector on the Democratic ticket of Buchanan and Breckinridge in 1856; resumed the practice of law at Prince Frederick, and died near there November 26, 1862; interment in St. Paul's Churchyard, near Prince Frederick, Md.

SOMERS, Andrew Lawrence, a Representative from New York; born in Brooklyn, N. Y., March 21, 1895; attended St. Teresa's Academy in Brooklyn, Brooklyn College Preparatory School, Manhattan College, and New York University in New York City; engaged in dry color and chemical business; during the First World War enlisted on July 18, 1917, as a hospital apprentice, second class, United States Naval Reserve Force; subsequently served as ensign in the Naval Reserve Flying Corps and was then appointed a naval aviator on September 17, 1918; proceeded to foreign service on September 30, 1918, and served until honorably discharged March 4, 1919; delegate to the Democratic National Convention at Houston, Tex., in 1928; elected as a Democrat to the Sixty-ninth and to the twelve succeeding Congresses and served from March 4, 1925, until his death in St. Albans, Long Island, N. Y., April 6, 1949; interment in Holy Cross Cemetery, Brooklyn, N. Y.

SOMERS, Peter J., a Representative from Wisconsin; born at Menominee Falls, Waukesha County, Wis., April 12, 1850; attended the common schools, the Whitewater Normal School, and the Waukesha Academy; studied law; was admitted to the bar in 1874 and commenced practice in Milwaukee, Wis.; attorney of the city of Milwaukee 1882–1884; elected to the common council in 1890, and upon its organization became its president; a member of the board of trustees of the public library; mayor of Milwaukee 1890–1893; elected as a Democrat to the Fifty-third Congress to fill the vacancy caused by the resignation of John L. Mitchell and served from August 27, 1893, to March 3, 1895; was not a candidate for renomination in 1894; resumed the practice of law in Milwaukee; moved to Reno, Nev., in 1905 and continued the practice of law; chairman of the State Democratic central committee from 1907 to 1909; appointed district judge of Esmeralda County in 1908, and elected in 1910 for the term ending January 1, 1914; again engaged in the practice of law; died in Los Angeles, Calif., February 15, 1924; interment in Calvary Cemetery.

SOMES, Daniel Eton, a Representative from Maine; born in Meredith (now Laconia), N. H., May 20, 1815; received an academic education; moved to Biddeford, Maine, in 1846; established the Eastern Journal, later known as the Union and Journal; engaged in the manufacture of loom harnesses, reed twine, and varnishes; mayor of Biddeford 1855–1857; president of the City Bank of Biddeford 1856–1858; elected as a Republican to the Thirty-sixth Congress (March 4, 1859–March 3, 1861); member of the peace convention of 1861 held in Washington, D. C., in an effort to devise means to prevent the impending war; engaged in the practice of patent law in Washington, D. C., until his death in that city on February 13, 1888; interment in Rock Creek Cemetery.

SORG, Paul John, a Representative from Ohio; born in Wheeling, Va. (now West Virginia), September 23, 1840; attended the common schools; moved with his parents to Cincinnati, Ohio, in 1852; apprenticed to the molder's trade; attended night school in Cincinnati; engaged in the tobacco manufacturing industry in 1864; served in the Union Army during the Civil War; elected as a Democrat to the Fifty-third Congress to fill the vacancy caused by the death of George W. Houk; reelected to the Fifty-fourth Congress and served from May 21, 1894, to March 3, 1897; was not a candidate for renomination in 1896; toured Europe in 1897, and spent some time at Carlsbad, Germany; returned to Ohio, settled in Middletown, and resumed his former business activities; died in Middletown, Butler County, Ohio, on May 28, 1902; interment in Woodside Cemetery.

SOSNOWSKI, John Bartholomew, a Representative from Michigan; born in Detroit, Mich., December 8, 1883; attended the parochial and Army schools; during the Spanish-American War enlisted as a private in the Seventh Regiment, United States Cavalry, and served in Cuba and the Philippine Islands; after the close of the war continued in the service and was on detached duty at the United States Military Academy, West Point, N. Y.; was honorably discharged on December 26, 1906; returned to Detroit, Mich., and engaged in the real estate and brokerage business; captain and adjutant in the Thirty-first Regiment, Infantry, National Guard of Michigan, from 1909 to 1916, with service on the Mexican border in 1916; member and chairman of the board of water commissioners of the city of Detroit 1918–1924; Federal appeal agent at Detroit for the United States Selective Service during the First World War; elected as a Republican to the Sixty-ninth Congress (March 4, 1925–March 3, 1927); unsuccessful candidate for renomination in 1926; resumed the real estate and brokerage business in Detroit, Mich.; delegate to the Republican National Conventions in 1932, 1936, 1940, and 1944; unsuccessful candidate for election in 1942 to the Seventy-eighth Congress, in 1944 to the

Seventy-ninth Congress, and in 1946 to the Eightieth Congress; hearing examiner, Michigan Liquor Control Commission, 1947–1951; retired; is a resident of Detroit, Mich.

SOULE, Nathan, a Representative from New York; born in that State; resided at Fort Plain; completed preparatory studies; elected to the Twenty-second Congress (March 4, 1831–March 3, 1833); member of the State assembly in 1837.

SOULÉ, Pierre, a Senator from Louisiana; born in Castillon, near Bordeaux, France, August 28, 1801; attended the Jesuit College at Toulouse and later an academy in Bordeaux until fifteen years of age; worked as a shepherd boy in the Pyrennes for a year; taught school; went to Paris, France, and engaged in journalism; imprisoned for publishing revolutionary articles in 1825, but escaped to England; went to Haiti in 1826, and thence to the United States, settling in Baltimore, Md.; later went to New Orleans, then to Tennessee, and finally settled in Kentucky, where he worked as a gardener and learned English; studied law; was admitted to the bar and commenced practice in New Orleans, La.; member of the State senate in 1845; elected as a State Rights Democrat to the United States Senate to fill the vacancy caused by the death of Alexander Barrow and served from January 21 to March 3, 1847; again elected to the United States Senate and served from March 3, 1849, to April 11, 1853, when he resigned; Minister to Spain from 1853 until his resignation in 1855; author of the Ostend Manifesto in 1854, outlining the attitude the United States should take in regard to Cuba; resumed the practice of law in New Orleans, La.; was opposed to secession, but abided by the action of his State; when New Orleans was captured he was arrested and imprisoned in Fort Lafayette for several months; later served on the staff of General Beauregard during the defense of Charleston, and was made brigadier general for special service; moved to Habana, Cuba, but subsequently returned to New Orleans, La., and died there March 26, 1870; interment in St. Louis Cemetery No. 2.

SOUTH, Charles Lacy, a Representative from Texas; born on a farm near Damascus, Washington County, Va., July 22, 1892; moved with his parents to Callahan County, Tex., in 1898 and to Coleman County, Tex., in 1914; attended the public schools and Simmons University at Abilene, Tex., in 1915 and 1916; taught in the Coleman County, Tex., public schools 1914–1920; served as superintendent of schools of Coleman County 1921–1925; studied law and was admitted to the bar in 1925; served as county judge 1925–1931 and as district attorney for the thirty-fifth judicial district 1930–1934; elected as a Democrat to the Seventy-fourth and to the three succeeding Congresses (January 3, 1935–January 3, 1943); unsuccessful candidate for renomination in the first primary in 1942 and later withdrew; engaged in the practice of law in Coleman, Tex.; member of the State house of representatives in 1947 and 1948; is a resident of Austin, Tex.

SOUTHALL, Robert Goode, a Representative from Virginia; born at Amelia Court House, Amelia County, Va., December 26, 1852; attended the Washington Academy and High School of Amelia County; deputy clerk of Nottaway County in 1873 and 1874; was graduated from the law department of the University of Virginia at Charlottesville in 1876; was admitted to the bar in 1877 and commenced practice at Amelia Court House; prosecuting attorney for Amelia County, Va., 1884–1902; delegate to the Democratic National Conventions in 1888 and 1896; member of the State house of delegates 1899–1904; elected as a Democrat to the Fifty-eighth and Fifty-ninth Congresses (March 4, 1903–March 3, 1907); resumed the practice of his profession

in Amelia County, Va.; served as a judge of the fourth judicial circuit court of Virginia from January 1912, until his death in Baltimore, Md., May 25, 1924; interment in Amelia Cemetery, Amelia Court House, Va.

SOUTHARD, Henry (father of Isaac Southard and Samuel Lewis Southard), a Representative from New Jersey; born in Hempstead, Long Island, N. Y., October 7, 1747; moved with his parents to Basking Ridge, N. J., in 1755; attended the common schools and worked on a farm; served as a private and later as wagon master during the Revolutionary War; engaged in agricultural pursuits; justice of the peace 1787–1792; member of the State general assembly 1797–1799 and in 1811; elected as a Democrat to the Seventh and to the four succeeding Congresses (March 4, 1801–March 3, 1811); elected to the Fourteenth, Fifteenth, and Sixteenth Congresses (March 4, 1815–March 3, 1821); resumed farming; died in Basking Ridge, Somerset County, N. J., May 22, 1842; interment in Basking Ridge Cemetery.

SOUTHARD, Isaac (son of Henry Southard and brother of Samuel Lewis Southard), a Representative from New Jersey; born in Basking Ridge, Somerset County, N. J., August 30, 1783; educated at the classical school of his native city; engaged in the general merchandise business until 1814; appointed deputy collector of internal revenue for Somerset County; appointed a major of the Second Battalion, Second Regiment, Somerset Brigade, on February 17, 1815; promoted to lieutenant colonel February 10, 1816, and colonel in November 1817; served as aide to Maj. Gen. Peter I. Stryker of the Uniformed Militia, Third Division, as late as 1829; was a director in the State bank at Morristown, N. J.; appointed one of the lay judges of the court of common pleas of Somerset on November 13, 1820; commissioned a justice of the peace on November 16, 1820; moved to Somerville, N. J.; county clerk of Somerset County 1820–1830; elected as a Clay Democrat to the Twenty-second Congress (March 4, 1831–March 3, 1833); unsuccessful candidate for reelection in 1832 to the Twenty-third Congress; appointed a master and examiner in chancery by Gov. Elias P. Seeley in 1833; colonel in the New Jersey State Militia; State treasurer of New Jersey 1837–1843; resided in Trenton, N. J., for several years; lived in retirement until his death in Somerville, N. J., September 18, 1850; interment in the Old Cemetery.

SOUTHARD, James Harding, a Representative from Ohio; born near Toledo, Washington Township, Lucas County, Ohio, January 20, 1851; attended the public schools and was graduated from Cornell University, Ithaca, N. Y., in 1874; studied law; was admitted to the bar in 1877 and commenced practice in Toledo, Ohio; appointed assistant prosecuting attorney of Lucas County in 1882; twice elected prosecuting attorney of the county, and served in that office six years; elected as a Republican to the Fifty-fourth and to the five succeeding Congresses (March 4, 1895–March 3, 1907); unsuccessful candidate for reelection in 1906 to the Sixtieth Congress; resumed the practice of law in Toledo, Ohio, until his death there February 20, 1919; interment in Woodlawn Cemetery.

SOUTHARD, Milton Isaiah, a Representative from Ohio; born in Hanover, Licking County, Ohio, October 20, 1836; completed preparatory studies; was graduated from the Denison University, Granville, Ohio; studied law; was admitted to the bar in 1863 and commenced practice in Toledo, Ohio; prosecuting attorney for Muskingum County, Ohio, 1867–1871; elected as a Democrat to the Forty-third, Forty-fourth, and Forty-fifth Congresses (March 4, 1873–March 3, 1879); moved to New York City and practiced law; died in Zanesville, Muskingum County, Ohio, May 4, 1905; interment in Woodlawn Cemetery.

SOUTHARD, Samuel Lewis (son of Henry Southard and brother of Isaac Southard), a Senator from New Jersey; born in Basking Ridge, Somerset County, N. J., June 9, 1787; attended the village school; was graduated from the College of New Jersey (now Princeton College) in 1804; engaged as tutor in a private family near Fredericksburg, Va., in 1805; studied law, and was admitted to the bar in Virginia in 1809; returned to New Jersey and commenced practice in Flemington in 1811; appointed law reporter of the supreme court by the State legislature in 1814; member of the State general assembly from October 14 to October 31, 1815, when he resigned, having been appointed to the State supreme court bench; associate justice of the New Jersey Supreme Court 1815–1820; moved to Trenton, N. J.; recorder of Trenton in 1818; presidential elector on the Democratic ticket of Monroe and Tompkins in 1820; appointed and subsequently elected to the United States Senate to fill the vacancy caused by the resignation of James J. Wilson and served from January 26, 1821, to March 3, 1823, when he resigned, having been tendered a Cabinet portfolio by President Monroe; it is a remarkable circumstance that Senator Southard and his father, Representative Henry Southard, should both be Members of the Sixteenth Congress, and more especially for both to be members of the joint committee of the two Houses which reported the famous Missouri compromise measure; Secretary of the Navy from September 6, 1823, to March 3, 1829; Secretary of War ad interim in 1824; Secretary of the Treasury ad interim from March 7 to July 1, 1825; attorney general of New Jersey 1829–1833; elected Governor of New Jersey October 26, 1832, and served until February 23, 1833, when he resigned to become Senator; elected as a Whig to the United States Senate in 1833; reelected in 1839, and served from March 4, 1833, until his death; was President pro tempore of the Senate from March 4, 1841, to May 31, 1842, when he resigned from this office; died in Fredericksburg, Va., June 26, 1842; interment in the Congressional Cemetery, Washington, D. C.

SOUTHGATE, William Wright, a Representative from Kentucky; born in Newport, Campbell County, Ky., November 27, 1800; educated in private schools and by private tutors; was graduated from Transylvania College, Lexington, Ky.; moved to Covington, Kenton County, Ky.; studied law; was admitted to the bar in 1821 and commenced practice in Lexington, Ky.; prosecuting attorney 1825–1827; member of the State house of representatives in 1827, 1832, and 1836; elected as a Whig to the Twenty-fifth Congress (March 4, 1837–March 3, 1839); resumed the practice of law; presidential elector on the Whig ticket of Harrison and Tyler in 1840 and of Clay and Frelinghuysen in 1844; died in Covington, Ky., December 26, 1849; interment in Linden Grove Cemetery.

SOUTHWICK, George Newell, a Representative from New York; born in Albany, N. Y., March 7, 1863; attended private and public schools; was graduated from the Albany High School in 1879 and from Williams College, Williamstown, Mass., in 1884; attended the Albany Law School; early in 1885 entered the service of the Albany Morning Express in both an editorial and a reportorial capacity; official reporter of the legislature for the Associated Press 1886–1888; in the last-mentioned year became managing editor of the Morning Express and early in 1889 of the Albany Evening Journal; chairman of the Republican State convention in 1896; elected as a Republican to the Fifty-fourth and Fifty-fifth Congresses (March 4, 1895–March 3, 1899); unsuccessful candidate for reelection in 1898 to the Fifty-sixth Congress; elected to the Fifty-seventh and to the four succeeding Congresses (March 4, 1901–March 3, 1911); was not a candidate for renomination in 1910; died in Albany, N. Y., October 17, 1912; interment in Albany Rural Cemetery.

SOWDEN, William Henry, a Representative from Pennsylvania; born in Liskeard, England, June 6, 1840; immigrated to the United States in 1846 with his father, who settled in Philadelphia; later went to live with friends in Allentown, Pa.; attended the public schools and Allentown Academy; served in the Civil War as a corporal in Company D, One Hundred and Twenty-eighth Pennsylvania Volunteer Infantry, and served from August 13, 1862, to May 19, 1863; was wounded in the Battle of Antietam; studied law; was admitted to the bar in 1864, and after graduation from Harvard Law School in 1865 commenced practice in Allentown, Pa.; served as solicitor of Lehigh County in 1868; district attorney in 1872–1874; unsuccessful candidate for Lieutenant Governor in 1874; unsuccessful candidate for election in 1876 to the Forty-fifth Congress; delegate to the Democratic National Convention in 1884; city solicitor of Allentown in 1886; elected as a Democrat to the Forty-ninth and Fiftieth Congresses (March 4, 1885–March 3, 1889); was not a candidate for reelection in 1888; resumed the practice of law; city solicitor of Allentown 1900–1902; delegate to the Democratic National Convention in 1900; unsuccessful Republican candidate to the Fifty-ninth Congress in 1904; elected solicitor of Lehigh County in 1906; died in Allentown, Pa., March 3, 1907; interment in Union Cemetery.

SPAIGHT, Richard Dobbs (grandfather of Richard Spaight Donnell), a Delegate and a Representative from North Carolina; born in New Bern, N. C., March 25, 1758; received his early schooling in Ireland and attended the University of Glasgow in Scotland; returned home in 1778 and joined the Continental Army as aide-de-camp to General Caswell; member of the North Carolina House of Commons 1781–1783; Member of the Continental Congress 1782–1785; delegate to the Federal Constitutional Convention at Philadelphia in 1787 and to the State constitutional convention in 1788; Governor of North Carolina 1792–1795; elected as a Democrat to the Fifth Congress to fill the vacancy caused by the death of Nathan Bryan; reelected to the Sixth Congress and served from December 10, 1798, to March 3, 1801; member of the State senate in 1801 and 1802; was wounded in a duel with John Stanly, his successor in Congress, from the effects of which he died on September 6, 1802, in New Bern, N. C.; interment in the family sepulcher at "Clermont," near New Bern, N. C.

SPAIGHT, Richard Dobbs, Jr. (son of the preceding), a Representative from North Carolina; born in New Bern, N. C., in 1796; attended the New Bern Academy, and was graduated from the University of North Carolina at Chapel Hill in 1815; studied law; was admitted to the bar in 1818 and commenced practice in New Bern; member of the State house of commons 1819–1822; elected as a Democrat to the Eighteenth Congress (March 4, 1823–March 3, 1825); unsuccessful candidate for reelection in 1824 to the Nineteenth Congress; member of the State senate in 1825 and 1826; Governor of North Carolina 1835–1837; delegate to the Democratic State convention in 1835; engaged in agricultural pursuits; died in New Bern, N. C., May 2, 1850; interment in the family sepulcher at "Clermont," near New Bern, N. C.

SPALDING, Burleigh Folsom, a Representative from North Dakota; born on a farm near Craftsbury, Orleans County, Vt., December 3, 1853; attended the Lyndon Literary Institute, Lyndon, Vt., and was graduated from Norwich University, Northfield, Vt., in 1877; studied law in Montpelier, Vt.; was admitted to the bar in 1880 and commenced practice in Fargo, Dak. (now North Dakota); superintendent of public instruction of Cass County, Dak., 1882–1884; member of the commission to relocate the capital of the Territory of Dakota and build the capitol in 1883; member of the North Dakota constitutional convention in 1889; member of the joint commission provided by the enabling act to divide the property and archives of the Territory of Dakota between the States of North Dakota and South Dakota; chairman of the Republican State central committee of North Dakota 1892–1894 and of the Cass County Republican committee 1896–1898; elected as a Republican to the Fifty-sixth Congress (March 4, 1899–March 3, 1901); did not seek renomination in 1900; elected to the Fifty-eighth Congress (March 4, 1903–March 3, 1905); unsuccessful candidate for renomination in 1904; appointed in 1907 and elected in 1908 an associate justice of the North Dakota Supreme Court; became chief justice in 1911 and served until 1915; resumed the practice of law in Fargo, N. Dak., in 1915; delegate to most Republican Territorial and State conventions 1888–1933; delegate to the Republican National Convention in 1924; died in Fargo, N. Dak., March 17, 1934; interment in Riverside Cemetery.

SPALDING, George, a Representative from Michigan; born in Blairgowrie, Perthshire, Scotland, on November 12, 1836; immigrated to the United States in 1843 with his parents, who settled in Buffalo, N. Y.; attended the public schools; accompanied his parents to Monroe, Mich.; taught school in 1860 and 1861; during the Civil War entered the United States Army June 20, 1861, as a private in Company A, Fourth Regiment, Michigan Volunteer Infantry, and was subsequently promoted to sergeant; first lieutenant August 5, 1861; captain January 13, 1862; lieutenant colonel of the Eighteenth Michigan Infantry July 18, 1862; colonel Twelfth Tennessee Cavalry February 24, 1864; brevetted brigadier general of Volunteers March 21, 1865, "for valuable services during the campaign in Tennessee"; mustered out of the service October 24, 1865; appointed postmaster of Monroe, Mich., July 27, 1866, and served until December 15, 1870; special agent of the Treasury Department 1871–1875; mayor of Monroe in 1876; president of the board of education; studied law, and was admitted to the bar in 1878; member of the board of control of the State Industrial Home for Girls 1885–1897; was elected as a Republican to the Fifty-fourth and Fifty-fifth Congresses (March 4, 1895–March 3, 1899); unsuccessful candidate for renomination in 1898; again appointed postmaster of Monroe, Mich., on February 20, 1899, and served until February 13, 1907; resumed the practice of law and also engaged in agricultural pursuits; president of the First National Bank of Monroe, Mich., until his death there September 13, 1915; interment in Woodlawn Cemetery.

SPALDING, Rufus Paine, a Representative from Ohio; born in West Tisbury, Mass., May 3, 1798; was graduated from Yale College in 1817; studied law and was admitted to the bar; moved to Little Rock, Ark., in 1820 and commenced practice; moved to Warren, Ohio, in 1821 and practiced his profession until 1835, when he moved to Ravenna, Ohio, and continued the practice of law; member of the State house of representatives 1839–1842, and served one term as speaker; associate judge of the Ohio Supreme Court 1849–1852; resumed the practice of law in Cleveland, Ohio; elected as a War Democrat to the Thirty-eighth, Thirty-ninth, and Fortieth Congresses (March 4, 1863–March 3, 1869); was not a candidate for renomination in 1868; resumed the practice of law; died in Cleveland, Ohio, August 29, 1886; interment in Lake View Cemetery.

SPALDING, Thomas, a Representative from Georgia; born in Frederica, St. Simons Island, Glynn County, Ga., March 26, 1774; attended the common schools of Georgia and Florida and a private school in Massachusetts; studied law; was admitted to the bar about 1790, but did not practice; engaged extensively in agricultural pursuits; member of the State house of representa-

tives in 1794; member of the State constitutional convention in 1798; moved to McIntosh County, Ga., in 1803; served in the State senate; successfully contested the election of Cowles Mead to the Ninth Congress and served from December 24, 1805, until his resignation in 1806; trustee of the McIntosh County Academy in 1807; one of the founders of the Bank of Darien and of the branch in Milledgeville, Ga., and president for many years; engaged in the planting of sea-island cotton, residing on Sapelo Island, Ga.; introduced into Georgia the culture of cane and the process of making sugar; experimented in silk culture and vineyards with imported vines; commissioner on the part of the State of Georgia to determine the boundary line between Georgia and the Territory of Florida in 1826; commissioner from the Federal Government to Bermuda to negotiate relative to property taken or destroyed in the South by the British in the War of 1812; president of the convention at Milledgeville, Ga., in 1850 which resolved that the State of Georgia would resist any act of Congress abolishing slavery and died, while en route home, at the residence of his son, near Darien, Ga., January 5, 1851; interment in St. Andrew's Cemetery.

SPANGLER, David, a Representative from Ohio; born in Sharpsburg, Washington County, Md., on December 2, 1796; moved with his parents to Zanesville, Ohio, in 1802; attended the public schools; worked at the blacksmith's trade; engaged in mercantile pursuits; studied law; was admitted to the bar in 1824 and commenced practice in Zanesville; unsuccessful candidate for election to the State house of representatives in 1830; moved to Coshocton, Ohio, in 1832 and continued the practice of law; elected as a Whig to the Twenty-third and Twenty-fourth Congresses (March 4, 1833–March 3, 1837); declined to be a candidate for renomination in 1836 and for the nomination for Governor of Ohio in 1844; died in Coshocton, Ohio, on October 18, 1856; interment in South Lawn Cemetery.

SPANGLER, Jacob, a Representative from Pennsylvania; born in York, Pa., November 28, 1767; attended the York County Academy; engaged in surveying; served as a trumpeter in Captain McClellan's light horse company of York in 1799; county commissioner in 1800; postmaster of York 1795–1812; deputy surveyor of York County 1796–1815; again county commissioner in 1814; elected as a Federalist to the Fifteenth Congress and served from March 4, 1817, until his resignation on April 20, 1818; surveyor general of Pennsylvania 1818–1821; commander of the State militia, with title of general; chief escort of General Lafayette from York to Harrisburg on his visit to the United States in 1825; clerk of York County Court until 1830; again surveyor general of Pennsylvania from 1830 to 1836; died in York, Pa., June 17, 1843; interment in Prospect Hill Cemetery.

SPARKMAN, John Jackson, a Representative and a Senator from Alabama; born on a farm near Hartselle, Morgan County, Ala., December 20, 1899; attended the rural schools and the Morgan County High School, Hartselle, Ala.; during the First World War was a member of the Students Army Training Corps; was graduated from the University of Alabama at Tuscaloosa in 1921 and from its law school in 1923; was admitted to the bar in 1925 and commenced practice in Huntsville, Madison County, Ala.; instructor at Huntsville (Ala.) College 1925–1928; served as a United States commissioner, Huntsville, Ala., in 1930 and 1931; member of the Organized Reserves since 1921, with present rank of lieutenant colonel; served as trustee of Athens (Ala.) College since 1936; elected as a Democrat to the Seventy-fifth and to the five succeeding Congresses and served from January 3, 1937, to November 5, 1946, when he resigned; served as majority whip in 1946; was reelected to the Eightieth

Congress on November 5, 1946, and at the same time was elected to the United States Senate to fill the vacancy caused by the death of John H. Bankhead 2d for the term ending January 3, 1949; following the election resigned from the House of Representatives and began duties in the Senate November 6, 1946; reelected in 1948 and again in 1954 for term ending January 3, 1961; representative of the United States to the fifth general assembly of the United Nations in 1950; unsuccessful Democratic candidate for Vice President of the United States in 1952. *Reelected in 1960 for the term ending January 3, 1967.*

SPARKMAN, Stephen Milancthon, a Representative from Florida; born on a farm in Hernando County, Fla., July 29, 1849; attended the common schools; taught school 1867–1870; studied law; was admitted to the bar in 1872 and commenced practice in Tampa, Fla.; State's attorney for the sixth judicial circuit 1878–1887; declined the position of circuit judge for the sixth judicial circuit in 1888 and also the appointment of associate justice of the supreme court of the State in 1891; member of the county Democratic executive committee 1890–1894 and served as chairman in 1890 and 1891; member of the State Democratic executive committee 1892–1896, serving as chairman; delegate to the Democratic National Convention in 1892; elected as a Democrat to the Fifty-fourth and to the ten succeeding Congresses (March 4, 1895–March 3, 1917); did not seek renomination in 1916; resumed the practice of law in Tampa, Fla.; president of the board of port commissioners until 1920; died while on a visit in Washington, D. C., September 26, 1929; interment in Woodlawn Cemetery, Tampa, Fla.

SPARKS, Charles Isaac, a Representative from Kansas; born on a farm near Ontario, in Jackson Township, Boone County, Iowa, December 20, 1872; educated in the rural schools and Simpson College, Indianola, Iowa; was graduated from the law department of the State University of Iowa at Iowa City in 1896; was admitted to the bar the same year and commenced practice in Boone, Iowa; served as prosecuting attorney of Boone County 1899–1902; chairman of the Republican county committee in 1898; moved to Goodland, Sherman County, Kans., in 1907 and continued the practice of law; served as city attorney and was a member of the Goodland School Board; judge of the thirty-fourth judicial district of Kansas 1915–1929; elected as a Republican to the Seventy-first and Seventy-second Congresses (March 4, 1929–March 3, 1933); unsuccessful candidate for reelection in 1932 to the Seventy-third Congress; resumed the practice of his profession in Goodland, Kans., until his death there on April 30, 1937; interment in the Goodland Cemetery.

SPARKS, William Andrew Jackson, a Representative from Illinois; born near New Albany, Ind., November 19, 1828; moved with his parents to Illinois in 1836; attended the public schools; taught school, and was graduated from McKendree College, Lebanon, Ill., in 1850; studied law; was admitted to the bar in 1851 and commenced practice in Carlyle, Ill.; United States land receiver for the Edwardsville (Ill.) land office 1853–1856; presidential elector on the Democratic ticket of Buchanan and Breckinridge in 1856; member of the State house of representatives in 1856 and 1857; served in the State senate in 1863 and 1864; delegate to the Democratic National Convention in 1868; elected as a Democrat to the Forty-fourth and to the three succeeding Congresses (March 4, 1875–March 3, 1883); did not seek renomination in 1882; resumed the practice of law; appointed by President Cleveland as Commissioner of the United States General Land Office and served from March 26, 1885, to March 26, 1888; resumed the practice of law at Carlyle and Springfield, Ill.; died in St. Louis, Mo., May 7, 1904; interment in St. Mary's Catholic Cemetery, Carlyle, Ill.

SPAULDING, Elbridge Gerry, a Representative from New York; born in Summer Hill, Cayuga County, N. Y., on February 24, 1809; completed preparatory studies; studied law; was admitted to the bar in 1836 and commenced practice in Batavia, Genesee County, N. Y.; moved to Buffalo, N. Y., in 1834; mayor of Buffalo in 1847; member of the State assembly in 1848; elected as a Whig to the Thirty-first Congress (March 4, 1849–March 3, 1851); was not a candidate for renomination in 1850; treasurer of the State of New York in 1854 and 1855; elected as a Union candidate to the Thirty-sixth and Thirty-seventh Congresses (March 4, 1859–March 3, 1863); was not a candidate for renomination in 1862 to the Thirty-eighth Congress; organized the Farmers & Mechanics' National Bank in Buffalo in 1864; died in Buffalo, N. Y., May 5, 1897; interment in Forest Lawn Cemetery.

SPAULDING, Oliver Lyman, a Representative from Michigan; born in Jaffrey, Cheshire County, N. H., August 2, 1833; completed preparatory studies, and was graduated from Oberlin (Ohio) College in 1855; moved to Michigan and taught school; studied law; was admitted to the bar in 1858 and commenced practice in St. Johns, Mich.; regent of the University of Michigan at Ann Arbor 1858–1864; during the Civil War served in the Union Army; commissioned a captain in the Twenty-third Regiment Michigan Volunteers August 1, 1862; major February 13, 1863; lieutenant colonel April 6, 1863; colonel April 16, 1864; brevetted brigadier general of Volunteers June 25, 1865, "for faithful and meritorious services during the war"; honorably mustered out June 28, 1865; resumed the practice of law in St. Johns, Mich.; secretary of state of Michigan 1866–1870; member of the Republican State committee 1871–1878; declined the position of United States district judge of the Territory of Utah in 1871; special agent of the United States Treasury Department 1875–1881; elected as a Republican to the Forty-seventh Congress (March 4, 1881–March 3, 1883); unsuccessful candidate for reelection in 1882 to the Forty-eighth Congress; chairman of the commission sent to the Sandwich Islands to investigate alleged violations of the Hawaiian reciprocity treaty in 1883; again a special agent of the United States Treasury in 1885, 1889, and 1890; Assistant Secretary of the Treasury 1890–1893 and 1897–1903; president of the first International American Customs Congress, held in New York City in January 1903; again a special agent of the United States Treasury 1903–1909; customs agent 1909–1916; died in Washington, D. C., July 30, 1922; interment in Arlington National Cemetery, Fort Myer, Va.

SPEAKS, John Charles, a Representative from Ohio; born in Canal Winchester, Franklin County, Ohio, February 11, 1859; attended the public schools; engaged in milling and the lumber business; fish, game, and conservation officer of Ohio 1907–1918; member of the Ohio National Guard for more than forty years, advancing from private to brigadier general; during the Spanish-American War served as major of the Fourth Regiment, Ohio Volunteer Infantry, participating in the Puerto Rican campaign; commanded the Second Brigade of the Ohio National Guard on the Mexican Border in 1916; during the First World War commanded the Seventy-third Brigade, Thirty-seventh Division, from the call of troops until March 1, 1918; unsuccessful candidate for election in 1918 to the Sixty-sixth Congress; elected as a Republican to the Sixty-seventh and to the four succeeding Congresses (March 4, 1921–March 3, 1931); unsuccessful candidate for reelection in 1930 to the Seventy-second Congress, and for election in 1932 to the Seventy-third Congress, and in 1934 to the Seventy-fourth Congress; retired from active business pursuits; died in Columbus, Ohio, November 6, 1945; interment in Union Grove Cemetery, Canal Winchester, Ohio.

SPEARING, James Zacharie, a Representative from Louisiana; born in Alto, Cherokee County, Tex., April 23, 1864; moved with his parents to New Orleans, La., in 1866; attended the public schools; left school and went to work in 1877; was graduated from the law department of Tulane University, New Orleans, La., in 1886; was admitted to the bar in 1886 and commenced practice in New Orleans; member of the Orleans Parish school board 1908–1912; member of the State board of education 1912–1916; again a member of the Orleans Parish school board 1916–1920, serving as president in 1919 and 1920; alternate delegate to the Democratic National Convention at Baltimore in 1912; elected as a Democrat to the Sixty-eighth Congress to fill the vacancy caused by the death of H. Garland Dupré; reelected to the Sixty-ninth, Seventieth, and Seventy-first Congresses and served from April 22, 1924, to March 3, 1931; unsuccessful candidate for renomination in 1930; resumed the practice of law in New Orleans, La.; died in New Orleans, La., November 2, 1942; interment in Metairie Cemetery.

SPEED, Thomas, a Representative from Kentucky; born in Charlotte County, Va., October 25, 1768; taught by his father; moved with his parents to Kentucky in 1782; employed in the office of the clerk of the general court; engaged in mercantile pursuits at Danville and Bardstown in 1790; also engaged in agricultural pursuits; clerk of the Bullitt and Nelson circuit courts; served as major of Volunteers in the War of 1812; elected to the Fifteenth Congress (March 4, 1817–March 3, 1819); unsuccessful candidate for reelection; resumed agricultural pursuits; contributed articles to the National Intelligencer, Washington, D. C.; member of the State house of representatives in 1821, 1822, and again in 1840; was a member of the Whig Party when it was organized; died on his farm, near Bardstown, Nelson County, Ky., February 20, 1842; interment on his farm, "Cottage Grove," near Bardstown, Ky.

SPEER, Emory, a Representative from Georgia; born in Culloden, Monroe County, Ga., September 3, 1848; pursued classical studies, and was graduated from the University of Georgia at Athens in 1869; entered the Confederate Army at the age of sixteen as a volunteer in the Fifth Kentucky Regiment, Lewis brigade, and remained with that command throughout the Civil War; studied law; was admitted to the bar in 1869 and commenced practice in Athens, Ga.; solicitor general of Georgia 1873–1876; unsuccessful candidate for election to the Forty-fifth Congress to fill the unexpired term of Benjamin H. Hill; elected as an Independent Democrat to the Forty-sixth and as an Independent to the Forty-seventh Congresses (March 4, 1879–March 3, 1883); unsuccessful candidate for reelection in 1882; United States attorney for the northern district of Georgia 1883–1885; district judge of the southern Federal judicial district of Georgia 1885–1918; dean of Mercer University Law School 1893–1918; died in Macon, Ga., December 13, 1918; interment in Riverside Cemetery.

SPEER, Peter Moore, a Representative from Pennsylvania; born near Oil City, Venango County, Pa., December 29, 1862; attended the country schools, Allegheny College, Meadville, Pa., and the Westminster College, New Wilmington, Pa.; was graduated from Washington and Jefferson College, Washington, Pa., in 1887; studied law; was admitted to the bar in 1889 and commenced practice in Oil City, Venango County, Pa.; district attorney of Venango County 1891–1893; city solicitor of Oil City 1895–1906; member of the State house of representatives in 1897 and 1898; elected as a Republican to the Sixty-second Congress (March 4, 1911–March 3, 1913); unsuccessful candidate for reelection in 1910 to the Sixty-third Congress; resumed the practice of law in Oil City, Pa.; moved to New York City, N. Y.,

in 1918 and continued the practice of law; assistant general counsel for the Standard Oil Co. 1918–1922, general counsel and member of the board of directors 1922–1928, and vice president 1928–1932; retired from active business pursuits in 1932; died in New York City, August 3, 1933; interment in Kensico Cemetery, near White Plains, N. Y.

SPEER, Robert Milton, a Representative from Pennsylvania; born in Cassville, Huntingdon County, Pa., September 8, 1838; attended Cassville Academy; taught school; studied law; was admitted to the bar in 1859 and commenced practice in Huntingdon, Pa.; elected assistant clerk of the State house of representatives in 1863; elected as a Democrat to the Forty-second and Forty-third Congresses (March 4, 1871–March 3, 1875); was not a candidate for renomination in 1874; delegate to the Democratic National Conventions in 1872 and 1880; resumed the practice of law and in 1876 became one of the proprietors of the Huntingdon Monitor; unsuccessful candidate for election in 1880 to the Forty-seventh Congress; presidential elector on the Democratic ticket of Cleveland and Thurman in 1888; died in New York City January 17, 1890; interment in Riverview Cemetery, Huntingdon, Pa.

SPEER, Thomas Jefferson, a Representative from Georgia; born in Monroe County, Ga., August 31, 1837; attended the common schools; engaged in mercantile pursuits and as a planter; elected justice of the peace in 1861 and reelected in 1865; appointed collector of Confederate taxes for Pike County in June 1863, serving until the cessation of hostilities; elected justice of the inferior court for Pike County in 1865, serving until July 1868; delegate to the State constitutional convention 1867–1868; member of the State senate 1868–1870; elected as a Republican to the Forty-second Congress and served from March 4, 1871, until his death in Barnesville, Lamar County, Ga., August 18, 1872; interment in Zebulon Street Cemetery.

SPEIGHT, Jesse, a Representative from North Carolina and a Senator from Mississippi; born in Greene County, N. C., September 22, 1795; attended the country schools; member of the State house of commons in 1820 and served as speaker; member of the State senate 1823–1827; elected from North Carolina to the Twenty-first and to the three succeeding Congresses (March 4, 1829–March 3, 1837); was not a candidate for renomination; moved to Plymouth, Miss.; member of the State senate 1841–1844 and served as president; elected as a Democrat to the United States Senate from Mississippi and served from March 4, 1845, until his death in Columbus, Miss., May 1, 1847; interment in Friendship Cemetery.

SPENCE, Brent, a Representative from Kentucky; born in Newport, Campbell County, Ky., December 24, 1874; attended public and private schools; was graduated from the law department of the University of Cincinnati, Cincinnati, Ohio, in 1895; was admitted to the bar the same year and commenced practice in Newport, Ky.; member of the State senate 1904–1908; city solicitor of Newport, Ky., 1916–1924; elected as a Democrat to the Seventy-second and to the fourteen succeeding Congresses (March 4, 1931–January 3, 1961). *Reelected to the Eighty-seventh Congress.*

SPENCE, John Selby (uncle of Thomas Ara Spence), a Representative and a Senator from Maryland; born near Snow Hill, Worcester County, Md., February 29, 1788; attended the common schools; was graduated from the medical department of the University of Pennsylvania at Philadelphia in 1809 and practiced in Worcester County, Md.; was a member of the State house of delegates; served in the State senate; elected as a Democrat to the Eighteenth Congress (March 4, 1823–March 3, 1825); elected to the Twenty-second Congress (March 4, 1831–March 3, 1833); elected to the United States Senate to fill the vacancy caused by the death of Robert H. Goldsborough; reelected in 1837, and served from December 31, 1836, until his death near Berlin, Worcester County, Md., October 24, 1840; interment in the Episcopal Churchyard.

SPENCE, Thomas Ara (nephew of John Selby Spence), a Representative from Maryland; born near Accomac Court House, Accomac County, Va., February 20, 1810; pursued academic studies and attended a local academy; was graduated from Yale College in 1829; studied law; was admitted to the bar and commenced practice at Snow Hill, Md.; elected as a Whig to the Twenty-eighth Congress (March 4, 1843–March 3, 1845); was not a candidate for renomination; later affiliated with the Republican Party; owned large iron-ore properties in Worcester County; judge for Worcester County and the twelfth judicial circuit 1857–1867; practiced his profession in Salisbury, Wicomico County, Md.; assistant attorney general for the Post Office Department 1872–1877; died in Washington, D. C., on November 10, 1877; interment in Makamie Memorial Church Cemetery, Snow Hill, Worcester County, Md.

SPENCER, Ambrose (father of John Canfield Spencer), a Representative from New York; born in Salisbury, Litchfield County, Conn., December 13, 1765; attended Yale College, and was graduated from Harvard University in 1783; studied law; was admitted to the bar and commenced practice in Hudson, Columbia County, N. Y.; city clerk 1786–1793; member of the State assembly 1793–1795; served in the State senate 1795–1804; assistant attorney general in 1796; attorney general of New York 1802–1804; presidential elector in 1808; justice of the State supreme court 1804–1819 and chief justice 1819–1823; resumed the practice of law in Albany, N. Y.; elected as a Democrat to the Twenty-first Congress (March 4, 1829–March 3, 1831); unsuccessful candidate for reelection; one of the managers appointed by the House of Representatives in 1830 to conduct the impeachment proceedings against James H. Peck, United States judge for the district of Missouri; mayor of Albany 1824–1826; moved to Lyons, N. Y., in 1839 and engaged in agricultural pursuits; president of the Whig National Convention at Baltimore in 1844; died in Lyons, N. Y., March 13, 1848; interment in Lyons Rural Cemetery.

SPENCER, Elijah, a Representative from New York; born in Columbia County, N. Y., in 1775; received a limited education; moved to Jerusalem (later Benton), N. Y., in 1791 and engaged in agricultural pursuits; supervisor of the town of Benton 1810–1819; member of the State assembly in 1819; elected as a Democrat to the Seventeenth Congress (March 4, 1821–March 3, 1823); again supervisor of Benton 1826–1828; member of the State constitutional convention in 1846; resumed agricultural pursuits; died in Benton, N. Y., December 15, 1852; interment in Lake View Cemetery, Penn Yan, N. Y.

SPENCER, George Eliphaz, a Senator from Alabama; born in Champion, Jefferson County, N. Y., November 1, 1836; pursued classical studies; attended Montreal College, Canada; moved to Iowa; secretary of the State senate in 1856; studied law; was admitted to the bar in 1857 and practiced; during the Civil War entered the Union Army as a captain, and when he resigned from the service, July 4, 1865, was brevetted brigadier general for gallantry on the field; resumed the practice of law in Decatur, Ala.; appointed register in bankruptcy for the fourth district of Alabama in May 1867; upon the readmission of Alabama to representation was elected as a Republican to the United States Senate; reelected in 1872, and served from July 13, 1868, to March 3, 1879; retired to his ranch in Nevada; died in Washington, D. C., February 19, 1893; interment in Arlington National Cemetery, Fort Myer, Va.

SPENCER, George Lloyd, a Senator from Arkansas; born in Sarcoxie, Jasper County, Mo., March 27, 1893; moved to Okolona, Ark., in 1902; attended the public schools, Peddie School at Hightstown, N. J., and Henderson College at Arkadelphia, Ark.; during the First World War served in the United States Navy as a seaman, second class, in 1918; lieutenant commander in the United States Naval Reserve 1931–1943; moved to Hope, Ark., in 1921 and engaged in banking and farming; delegate to the Democratic State convention at Little Rock, Ark., in 1942; appointed as a Democrat to the United States Senate to fill the vacancy caused by the resignation of John E. Miller and served from April 1, 1941, to January 3, 1943; was not a candidate for nomination to the full term; during World War II served in the United States Navy in 1943; chairman, mayor's advisory committee, Hope, Ark., 1949–1954; member, Hope Municipal Water & Light Commission, 1955–; director, Arkansas-Louisiana Gas Co., Shreveport, La., 1956–; commissioner, Southwest Arkansas Water District, 1958–; Arkansas executive vice president of Red River Valley Association 1960–; is a resident of Hope, Ark.

SPENCER, James Bradley, a Representative from New York; born in Salisbury, Conn., April 26, 1781; received a limited education; moved to Franklin County, N. Y., and settled in Fort Covington; raised a company for the War of 1812, and served as Captain in the Twenty-ninth United States Infantry; appointed a local magistrate in 1814; surrogate of Franklin County 1828–1837; appointed loan commissioner in 1829; member of the State assembly in 1831 and 1832; presidential elector on the Democratic ticket of Jackson and Van Buren in 1832; elected as a Democrat to the Twenty-fifth Congress (March 4, 1837–March 3, 1839); died in Fort Covington, N. Y., March 26, 1848; interment probably in the Old Cemetery near Fort Covington.

SPENCER, James Grafton, a Representative from Mississippi; born near Port Gibson, Claiborne County, Miss., September 13, 1844; attended private schools and Oakland College in 1861; during the Civil War enlisted in the Confederate Army as a private in Cowan's battery of Light Artillery; served until the close of the Civil War in the Army of Mississippi and Tennessee; returned to his home and engaged in agricultural pursuits; member of the State house of representatives 1892–1894; elected as a Democrat to the Fifty-fourth Congress (March 4, 1895–March 3, 1897); engaged in the real estate and insurance business; died in Port Gibson, Miss., February 22, 1926; interment in Wintergreen Cemetery.

SPENCER, John Canfield (son of Ambrose Spencer), a Representative from New York; born in Hudson, N. Y., January 8, 1788; was graduated from Union College, Schenectady, N. Y., in 1806; studied law; was admitted to the bar in 1809 and commenced practice in Canandaigua, N. Y.; served in the War of 1812; Judge Advocate General in 1813; postmaster of Canandaigua, N. Y.; assistant attorney general for western New York in 1815; elected as a Democrat to the Fifteenth Congress (March 4, 1817–March 3, 1819); was not a candidate for renomination in 1818; member of the State assembly in 1820 and 1821, and served one year as speaker; served in the State senate 1824–1828; special attorney general to prosecute the abductors of Morgan; again a member of the State assembly in 1831 and 1832; secretary of state of New York in 1839; appointed Secretary of War by

President Tyler October 12, 1841, and served until March 3, 1843; Secretary of the Treasury March 3, 1843, to May 2, 1844, when he resigned; died in Albany, N. Y., May 18, 1855; interment in Albany Rural Cemetery.

SPENCER, Joseph, a Delegate from Connecticut; born in East Haddam, Conn., October 3, 1714; completed preparatory studies; studied law; was admitted to the bar and practiced; held several local offices; judge of probate in 1753; served in the French war in 1758; member of the Connecticut Council in 1776; brigadier general in the Continental Army; commissioned major general August 9, 1776, and resigned June 14, 1778, because Congress had ordered an investigation of his military conduct in 1777; Member of the Continental Congress in 1778 and 1779; again a member of the Connecticut Council in 1780 and was annually reelected until his death in East Haddam, Conn., on January 13, 1789; interment in Millington Green Cemetery; reinterment in Nathan Hale Park in 1904.

SPENCER, Richard, a Representative from Maryland; born at "Spencer Hall," Talbot County, Md., October 29, 1796; attended the common schools; studied law in Baltimore and was admitted to the Talbot County bar in 1819; moved to his farm, "Solitude," near St. Michaels, Md., in 1822 and engaged in agricultural pursuits; member of the State house of delegates 1823–1825; engaged in literary pursuits and in 1828 he contributed to the establishment of the Eastern Shore Whig and controlled that paper until 1834; elected as a Democrat to the Twenty-first Congress (March 4, 1829–March 3, 1831); unsuccessful candidate for reelection in 1830 to the Twenty-second Congress; again a member of the State house of delegates in 1833 and 1834; was an unsuccessful candidate for reelection in 1835; moved to Georgia in 1837 and engaged in cotton planting; moved to Alabama in 1852 and settled at "Cottage Hill," near Mobile, where he died September 3, 1868; interment probably on his estate, "Cottage Hill."

SPENCER, Selden Palmer, a Senator from Missouri; born in Erie, Pa., September 16, 1862; attended the public schools of his native city and the Hopkins Grammar School, New Haven, Conn.; was graduated from Yale College in 1884 and from the Washington University Law School, St. Louis, Mo., in 1886; was admitted to the bar in 1886 and commenced practice in St. Louis; professor of medical jurisprudence in the Missouri Medical College at St. Louis in 1886; member of the State house of representatives in 1895 and 1896; judge of the circuit court of St. Louis 1897–1903; captain in the Missouri Home Guard and chairman of the draft board in 1917 and 1918; elected as a Republican to the United States Senate to fill the vacancy caused by the death of William J. Stone; reelected in 1920, and served from November 6, 1918, until his death; delegate to the Republican National Conventions in 1920 and 1924; died at Walter Reed Hospital, Washington, D. C., on May 16, 1925; interment in Bellefontaine Cemetery, St. Louis, Mo.

SPENCER, William Brainerd, a Representative from Louisiana; born on "Home Plantation," in Catahoula Parish, La., February 5, 1835; received his early schooling under private tutors; was graduated from Centenary College, Jackson, La., in 1855 and from the law department of the University of Louisiana at New Orleans in 1857; was admitted to the bar in 1857 and commenced practice in Harrisonburg, La.; served in the Confederate Army, with the rank of captain, until 1863, when he was captured; remained a prisoner of war at Johnsons Island, Ohio, until the close of the Civil War; resumed the practice of law in Vidalia, La., in 1866; successfully contested as a Democrat the election of Frank Morey to the Forty-fourth Congress and served from June 8, 1876, to January 8, 1877, when he resigned to accept a judicial appointment; appointed associate justice of the Louisiana Supreme Court January 9, 1877, which position he held until his resignation April 3, 1880; again resumed the practice of law in New Orleans, La.; died in Jalapa, Mexico, February 12, 1882; interment in Magnolia Cemetery, Baton Rouge, La.

SPERRY, Lewis, a Representative from Connecticut; born at East Windsor Hill, town of South Windsor, Conn., January 23, 1848; attended the district school and Monson Academy, Monson, Mass.; was graduated from Amherst College, Amherst, Mass., in 1873; studied law; was admitted to the bar in March 1875 and commenced practice in Hartford, Conn.; member of the State house of representatives in 1876; elected as a Democrat to the Fifty-second and Fifty-third Congresses (March 4, 1891–March 3, 1895); unsuccessful candidate for reelection in 1894 to the Fifty-fourth Congress; again resumed the practice of his profession in Hartford, Conn.; died at East Windsor Hill, town of South Windsor, Hartford County, Conn., June 22, 1922; interment in South Windsor Cemetery.

SPERRY, Nehemiah Day, a Representative from Connecticut; born in Woodbridge, New Haven County, Conn., July 10, 1827; attended the common schools and a private school in New Haven; engaged in agricultural pursuits and worked in a mill; taught school for several years; became a member of a building and contracting firm; member of the common council in 1853; alderman of the city in 1854; secretary of state of Connecticut in 1855 and 1856; delegate to the Republican National Conventions in 1856, 1864, and 1888; member and secretary of the national and executive committees; chairman of the Republican State committee for a number of years; chairman of the recruiting committee of New Haven during the Civil War; appointed July 16, 1861, by President Lincoln as postmaster of New Haven; reappointed and served until removed by President Cleveland January 20, 1886; again postmaster at New Haven and served from January 9, 1890, until March 15, 1894; elected as a Republican to the Fifty-fourth and to the seven succeeding Congresses (March 4, 1895–March 3, 1911); was not a candidate for renomination in 1910; retired from active pursuits; died in New Haven, Conn., on November 13, 1911; interment in Evergreen Cemetery.

SPIGHT, Thomas, a Representative from Mississippi; born near Ripley, Tippah County, Miss., October 25, 1841; attended the common schools, Ripley Academy, Purdy (Tenn.) College, and the La Grange (Tenn.) Synodical College; during the Civil War enlisted in the Confederate Army as a private in 1861; promoted to the rank of lieutenant the same year; in 1862 became captain of Company B, Thirty-fourth Regiment, Mississippi Volunteer Infantry, and served until the close of the war; taught school and also engaged in agricultural pursuits; studied law; was admitted to the bar in 1875 and commenced practice in Ripley, Miss.; member of the State house of representatives 1874–1880; established the Southern Sentinel in 1879, retiring from the newspaper business five years later; presidential elector on the Democratic ticket of Hancock and English in 1880; prosecuting attorney of the third judicial district 1884–1892; elected as a Democrat to the Fifty-fifth Congress to fill the vacancy caused by the resignation of William V. Sullivan; reelected to the Fifty-sixth and to the five succeeding Congresses and served from July 5, 1898, to March 3, 1911; unsuccessful candidate for renomination in 1910; again resumed the practice of his profession and also engaged in religious work until his death in Ripley, Miss., January 5, 1924; interment in Ripley Cemetery.

SPINK, Cyrus, a Representative from Ohio; born in Berkshire County, Mass., March 24, 1793; moved to Stark County, Ohio, in 1815; taught school for several years in Kendall, Stark County, Ohio; appointed deputy surveyor of Wayne County in October 1815 and served until December 1816; county surveyor from 1816 to 1821, serving also for a time as district surveyor; county auditor in 1820 and 1821; member of the State house of representatives in 1821 and 1822; employed in the register's office at Wooster 1822–1824; appointed register by President Monroe in 1824; reappointed by President Adams in 1828 and served until 1832; engaged in mercantile pursuits in Wooster; presidential elector on the Whig ticket of Clay and Frelinghuysen in 1844; member of the State board of equalization in 1846; delegate to the Whig National Convention at Baltimore in 1852; appointed by Governor Chase one of the directors of the Ohio Penitentiary in 1856; elected as a Republican to the Thirty-sixth Congress and served from March 4, 1859, until his death in Wooster, Wayne County, Ohio, on May 31, 1859; interment in Wooster Cemetery.

SPINK, Solomon Lewis, a Delegate from the Territory of Dakota; born in Whitehall, Washington County, N. Y., March 20, 1831; completed preparatory studies and was graduated from Castleton (Vt.) Seminary; taught school several years; studied law; was admitted to the bar in 1856 and commenced practice in Burlington, Iowa; moved to Paris, Ill., in 1860 and became the editor and publisher of the Prairie Beacon; member of the State house of representatives in 1864; moved to Yankton, Dak., in 1865, having been appointed by President Lincoln, the day before his assassination, as secretary of the Territory of North Dakota, in which position he served until 1869; was elected as a Republican to the Forty-first Congress (March 4, 1869–March 3, 1871); unsuccessful candidate for reelection in 1870 to the Forty-second Congress; resumed the practice of his profession in Yankton, S. Dak.; unsuccessful candidate for election in 1876 to the Forty-fifth Congress; died in Yankton, S. Dak., September 22, 1881; interment in the City Cemetery.

SPINNER, Francis Elias, a Representative from New York; born in Mohawk, German Flats, Herkimer County, N. Y., January 21, 1802; was educated by his father; served an apprenticeship at both harness making and candy making; engaged in mercantile pursuits in 1824; entered the State militia and was subsequently promoted to the rank of major general; appointed deputy sheriff in 1829; sheriff of Herkimer County 1834–1837; appointed one of the commissioners for the construction of the State lunatic asylum at Utica in 1838; engaged in banking as cashier and later president of the Mohawk Bank; State inspector of turnpikes; commissioner and supervisor of schools; appointed auditor and deputy naval officer in charge of the port of New York in 1845 and served four years; elected as a Democrat to the Thirty-fourth Congress and as a Republican to the Thirty-fifth and Thirty-sixth Congresses (March 4, 1855–March 3, 1861); was not a candidate for renomination in 1860 to the Thirty-seventh Congress; appointed by President Lincoln as Treasurer of the United States and served from March 16, 1861, until his resignation on July 1, 1875; successfully urged the employment of women in the Treasury Department; withdrew from public life and spent the winters in Florida; died in Jacksonville, Fla., December 31, 1890; interment in Mohawk Cemetery, Mohawk, N. Y.

SPINOLA, Francis Barretto, a Representative from New York; born at Stony Brook, Long Island, N. Y., March 19, 1821; attended Quaker Hill Academy in Dutchess County; studied law; was admitted to the bar in 1844 and commenced practice in Brooklyn, N. Y.; elected alderman of the second ward in Brooklyn in 1846 and 1847; reelected in 1849 and served for four years; member of the State assembly in 1855; served in the State senate 1858–1861; delegate to the Democratic National Convention at Charleston in 1860; harbor commissioner; during the Civil War was appointed brigadier general of Volunteers October 2, 1862, "for meritorious conduct in recruiting and organizing a brigade of four regiments and accompanying them to the field"; honorably discharged from the service in August 1865, after having been twice wounded; alternate to the Democratic National Convention at Chicago in 1884; engaged in the insurance business and banking; elected as a Democrat to the Fiftieth, Fifty-first, and Fifty-second Congresses and served from March 4, 1887, until his death in Washington, D. C., April 14, 1891; interment in Greenwood Cemetery, Brooklyn, N. Y.

SPOONER, Henry Joshua, a Representative from Rhode Island; born in Providence, R. I., August 6, 1839; attended the common schools, and was graduated from Brown University, Providence, R. I., in 1860; studied law; during the Civil War entered the Union Army in 1862 as second lieutenant in the Fourth Regiment, Rhode Island Volunteer Infantry; served in the Armies of the Potomac and the James, mostly in the Ninth Army Corps; shortly after the Battle of Antietam was promoted to first lieutenant and adjutant of the same regiment; mustered out of service in 1865; was admitted to the bar in 1865 and commenced practice in Providence, R. I.; commander of the department of Rhode Island, Grand Army of the Republic, in 1877; member of the State house of representatives 1875–1881, serving as speaker 1879–1881; elected as a Republican to the Forty-seventh Congress to fill the vacancy caused by the resignation of Nelson W. Aldrich; reelected to the Forty-eighth and to the three succeeding Congresses and served from December 5, 1881, to March 3, 1891; unsuccessful candidate for reelection in 1890 to the Fifty-second Congress; again a member of the State house of representatives in 1902; resumed the practice of law in Providence, R. I., and died in that city February 9, 1918; interment in Swan Point Cemetery.

SPOONER, John Coit, a Senator from Wisconsin; born in Lawrenceburg, Dearborn County, Ind., January 6, 1843; moved to Wisconsin with his parents, who settled in Madison, June 1, 1859; attended the common schools and was graduated from the University of Wisconsin at Madison, in 1864; during the Civil War enlisted as a private in Company D, Fortieth Regiment, and subsequently was captain of Company A, Fiftieth Regiment, Wisconsin Volunteer Infantry; brevetted major at the close of the war; private and military secretary of Gov. Lucius Fairchild, of Wisconsin; studied law; was admitted to the bar in 1867 and served as assistant attorney general of the State until 1870; moved to Hudson, Wis., and practiced law from 1870 to 1884; member of the State assembly in 1872; member of the board of regents of Wisconsin University; elected as a Republican to the United States Senate and served from March 4, 1885, to March 3, 1891; was the caucus nominee of his party, who were in the minority, for reelection; chairman of the Wisconsin delegation to the Republican National Conventions in 1888 and 1896; unsuccessful Republican candidate for Governor of Wisconsin in 1892; moved from Hudson to Madison in 1893; again elected to the United States Senate in 1897; reelected in 1903, and served from March 4, 1897, until his resignation, effective April 30, 1907; engaged in the practice of law in New York City; declined the position of Secretary of the Interior in the Cabinet of President McKinley in 1898; declined the appointment as a member of the United States and British Joint High Commission tendered by President

McKinley in 1898; declined the portfolio of Attorney General of the United States in the Cabinet of President McKinley in 1901; delegate to the Republican National Convention in 1904; declined the position of Secretary of State in the Cabinet of President Taft; died in New York City, June 11, 1919; interment in Forest Hill Cemetery, Madison, Wis.

SPRAGUE, Charles Franklin (grandson of Peleg Sprague), a Representative from Massachusetts; born in Boston, Mass., June 10, 1857; attended the public schools, and was graduated from Harvard University in 1879; studied law at the Harvard Law School and the Boston University and was admitted to the bar in Boston; member of the Boston Common Council in 1889 and 1890; member of the State house of representatives in 1891 and 1892; served as chairman of the board of park commissioners of the city of Boston in 1893 and 1894; served in the State senate in 1895 and 1896; elected as a Republican to the Fifty-fifth and Fifty-sixth Congresses (March 4, 1897–March 3, 1901); declined to be a candidate for renomination in 1900 to the Fifty-seventh Congress; died in Providence, R. I., on January 30, 1902; interment in Mount Auburn Cemetery, Watertown, Mass.

SPRAGUE, Peleg, a Representative from New Hampshire; born in Rochester, Mass., December 10, 1756; clerked in a store in Littleton, Mass.; attended Harvard College, and was graduated from Dartmouth College, Hanover, N. H., in 1783; studied law; was admitted to the bar in 1785 and commenced practice in Winchendon, Mass.; moved to Keene, N. H., in 1787; selectman 1789–1791; county solicitor for Cheshire County in 1794; member of the State house of representatives in 1797; elected to the Fifth Congress to fill the vacancy caused by the resignation of Jeremiah Smith and served from December 15, 1797, to March 3, 1799: declined to be a candidate for renomination in 1798; died in Keene, N. H., April 20, 1800; interment in the Washington Street Cemetery.

SPRAGUE, Peleg (grandfather of Charles Franklin Sprague), a Representative and a Senator from Maine; born in Duxbury, Mass., April 27, 1793; was graduated from Harvard University, Cambridge, Mass., in 1812; studied law at the Litchfield Law School; was admitted to the bar in 1815 and commenced practice in Augusta, Maine; moved to Hallowell, Kennebec County, Maine, in 1817 and continued the practice of law; member of the Maine House of Representatives in 1821 and 1822; was one of the corporate members of the Maine Historical Society, founded in 1822; elected to the Nineteenth, Twentieth, and Twenty-first Congresses and served from March 4, 1825, until his resignation, effective March 3, 1829, at the close of the Twentieth Congress, having been elected Senator; elected as a National-Republican to the United States Senate and served from March 4, 1829, to January 1, 1835, when he resigned; again resumed the practice of law in Boston, Mass., in 1840; presidential elector on the Whig ticket of Harrison and Tyler in 1840; United States district judge of Massachusetts 1841–1865; died in Boston, Mass., October 13, 1880; interment in Mount Auburn Cemetery, Cambridge, Mass.

SPRAGUE, William, a Representative from Michigan; born in Providence, R. I., February 23, 1809; attended the public schools; moved to Michigan and settled in Kalamazoo; studied theology and was ordained as a minister; presiding elder of the Methodist Episcopal Church, Kalamazoo district, 1844–1848; elected as a Whig to the Thirty-first Congress (March 4, 1849–March 3, 1851); retired to his farm near Oshtemo, Kalamazoo County, Mich.; died in Kalamazoo, Mich., September 19, 1868; interment in Mountain Home Cemetery.

SPRAGUE, William, a Representative and a Senator from Rhode Island; born in Cranston, R. I., November 3, 1799; pursued classical studies; engaged in mercantile pursuits; member of the State house of representatives, serving as speaker 1832–1835; elected as a Whig to the Twenty-fourth Congress (March 4, 1835–March 3, 1837); declined to be a candidate for renomination in 1836; Governor of Rhode Island in 1838 and 1839; elected to the United States Senate to fill the vacancy caused by the death of Nathan F. Dixon and served from February 18, 1842, to January 17, 1844, when he resigned; presidential elector on the Whig ticket of Taylor and Fillmore in 1848; engaged in the manufacture of cotton and paint; died in Providence, R. I., on October 19, 1856; interment in Swan Point Cemetery.

SPRAGUE, William (nephew of the preceding), a Senator from Rhode Island; born in Cranston, R. I., September 12, 1830; attended the common schools and Irving Institute, Tarrytown, N. Y.; engaged in the calico-printing business and the manufacture of locomotives; elected Governor of Rhode Island on the Unionist ticket and served from 1860 to 1863; was colonel Marine Artillery Rhode Island Militia in 1860; tendered a commission as brigadier general in 1861, but declined to accept; elected as a Republican to the United States Senate; reelected, and served from March 4, 1863, to March 3, 1875; was not a candidate for renomination; trustee of Brown University in 1866; was an unsuccessful candidate for Governor of Rhode Island in 1883; engaged in agricultural pursuits at the county seat, near Narragansett Pier, R. I.; died in Paris, France, September 11, 1915; interment in Swan Point Cemetery, Providence, R. I.

SPRAGUE, William Peter, a Representative from Ohio; born near Malta, Morgan County, Ohio, May 21, 1827; attended the country schools; engaged in mercantile pursuits when quite young and continued in active business until 1864; member of the State senate 1860–1863; moved to McConnelsville, Ohio, in 1866, and engaged in banking; elected as a Republican to the Forty-second and Forty-third Congresses (March 4, 1871–March 3, 1875); was not a candidate for renomination in 1874; resumed the banking business at Malta, Ohio; died in McConnelsville, Morgan County, Ohio, March 3, 1899; interment in Riverview Cemetery.

SPRIGG, James Cresap (brother of Michael Cresap Sprigg), a Representative from Kentucky; born in Frostburg, Md., in 1802; completed preparatory studies; moved to Shelbyville, Shelby County, Ky.; studied law; was admitted to the bar and practiced; held several local offices; member of the State house of representatives 1830–1834 and 1837–1840; elected to the Twenty-seventh Congress (March 4, 1841–March 3, 1843); unsuccessful candidate as an Independent for reelection in 1842 to the Twenty-eighth Congress; resumed the practice of law; again a member of the State house of representatives in 1852, and served until his death in Shelbyville, Ky., October 3, 1852; interment in Grove Hill Cemetery.

SPRIGG, Michael Cresap (brother of James Cresap Sprigg), a Representative from Maryland; born in Frostburg, Md., July 1, 1791; completed preparatory studies; held a number of local offices; member of the State house of delegates in 1821, 1823, 1837, 1840, and 1844; president of the Chesapeake & Ohio Canal Co. in 1841 and 1842; presidential elector on the Monroe ticket in 1820; elected as a Democrat to the Twentieth and Twenty-first Congresses (March 4, 1827–March 3, 1831); died in Cumberland, Allegany County, Md., December 18, 1845; interment in Rose Hill Cemetery.

SPRIGG, Richard, Jr. (nephew of Thomas Sprigg), a Representative from Maryland; born in Prince Georges County, Md.; member of the State house of delegates in 1792 and 1793; elected to the Fourth Congress to fill the vacancy caused by the resignation of Gabriel Duval; reelected to the Fifth Congress and served from May 5, 1796, to March 3, 1799; elected to the Seventh Congress and served from March 4, 1801, until his resignation February 11, 1802; appointed associate judge of the Maryland Court of Appeals on January 27, 1806.

SPRIGG, Thomas (uncle of Richard Sprigg, Jr.), a Representative from Maryland; born in Prince Georges County, Md., in 1747; served during the Revolutionary War as ensign in the Maryland Battalion of the Flying Camp from September to December 1776; appointed the first register of wills of Washington County, Md., in 1777, and served until September 29, 1780, when he resigned; appointed lieutenant of Washington County by the Governor and Council of Maryland December 21, 1779; elected to the Third and Fourth Congresses (March 4, 1793–March 3, 1797); died in Washington County, Md., December 13, 1809.

SPRIGGS, John Thomas, a Representative from New York; born in Peterborough, Northamptonshire, England, April 5, 1825; immigrated to the United States with his parents, who settled in Whitesboro, Oneida County, N. Y., in 1836; attended Hamilton College, Clinton, N. Y., and was graduated from Union College, Schenectady, N. Y., in 1848; studied law; was admitted to the bar in 1848 and commenced practice in Whitesboro, N. Y.; prosecuting attorney of Oneida County in 1853; county treasurer in 1854; delegate to the Democratic National Convention at Baltimore in 1860; mayor of Utica 1868–1880; delegate to the Democratic National Convention at Baltimore in 1872 which nominated Greeley and Brown and at Cincinnati in 1880 which nominated Hancock and English; elected as a Democrat to the Forty-eighth and Forty-ninth Congresses (March 4, 1883–March 3, 1887); unsuccessful candidate for reelection in 1886 to the Fiftieth Congress; resumed the practice of law; died in Utica, N. Y., December 23, 1888; interment in Whitesboro Cemetery, Whitesboro, N. Y.

SPRINGER, Raymond Smiley, a Representative from Indiana; born on a farm in Rush County, near Dunreith, Ind., April 26, 1882; attended the public schools, Earlham College, Richmond, Ind., and Butler University, Indianapolis, Ind.; was graduated from the Indiana Law School at Indianapolis in 1904; was admitted to the bar in 1904 and commenced practice in Connersville, Fayette County, Ind.; county attorney of Fayette County, Ind., 1908–1914; judge of the thirty-seventh judicial circuit of Indiana 1916–1922; during the First World War served as a captain of Infantry, Eighty-fourth Division, in 1918; lieutenant colonel of the Officers' Reserve Corps 1918–1946; unsuccessful candidate for Governor of Indiana in 1932 and 1936; elected as a Republican to the Seventy-sixth and to the four succeeding Congresses and served from January 3, 1939, until his death in Connersville, Ind., August 28, 1947; interment in Dale Cemetery.

SPRINGER, William Lee, a Representative from Illinois; born in Sullivan, Ind., April 12, 1909; attended the public schools of Sullivan and Culver Military Academy at Culver, Ind.; was graduated from DePauw University, Greencastle, Ind., in 1931, and from the law school of the University of Illinois in 1935; was admitted to the bar in 1935 and commenced the practice of law in 1936 in Champaign, Ill.; State's attorney of Champaign County, Ill., 1940–1942; served in the United States Navy from March 1942 as an officer, with nineteen months foreign duty,

until discharged as a lieutenant in the Naval Reserve on September 22, 1945; county judge of Champaign County 1946–1950; elected as a Republican to the Eighty-second and to the four succeeding Congresses (January 3, 1951–January 3, 1961). *Reelected to the Eighty-seventh Congress.*

SPRINGER, William McKendree, a Representative from Illinois; born near New Lebanon, Sullivan County, Ind., May 30, 1836; moved to Jacksonville, Ill., with his parents in 1848; attended the public schools in New Lebanon and Jacksonville and the Illinois College at Jacksonville; was graduated from the University of Indiana at Bloomington in 1858; studied law; was admitted to the bar in 1859 and practiced in Lincoln and Springfield, Ill.; secretary of the State constitutional convention in 1862; traveled in Europe 1868–1871; member of the State house of representatives in 1871 and 1872; elected as a Democrat to the Forty-fourth and to the nine succeeding Congresses (March 4, 1875–March 3, 1895); was an unsuccessful candidate for reelection in 1894 to the Fifty-fourth Congress; again resumed the practice of law in Washington, D. C., in 1895; United States judge for the northern district of Indian Territory and chief justice of the United States Court of Appeals of Indian Territory by appointment of President Cleveland 1895–1900; again engaged in the practice of his profession in Washington, D. C., where he died on December 4, 1903; interment in Oak Ridge Cemetery, Springfield, Ill.

SPROUL, Elliott Wilford, a Representative from Illinois; born in Apohaqui, Kings County, New Brunswick, Canada, December 28, 1856; attended the public schools; moved to Boston, Mass., in 1879 and to Chicago, Ill., in 1880, and engaged in the building and contracting business; was naturalized in 1886; member of the Chicago City Council 1896–1899; delegate to the Republican National Convention at Chicago in 1920; member of the board of directors of the Chicago Public Library 1919–1921; elected as a Republican to the Sixty-seventh and to the four succeeding Congresses (March 4, 1921–March 3, 1931); unsuccessful candidate for reelection in 1930 to the Seventy-second Congress; retired from political and business activities in 1931, and resided in Chicago, Ill., until his death there on June 22, 1935; interment in Mount Hope Cemetery.

SPROUL, William Henry, a Representative from Kansas; born on a farm near Livingston, Overton County, Tenn., October 14, 1867; attended the public schools and Alpine Academy in Overton County, Tenn.; in 1883 moved to Kansas with his parents, who settled in Cherokee County; worked on a farm and in the mines; attended high school at Columbus, Kans., and the Kansas Normal College at Fort Scott; taught school at Columbus 1888–1892; was graduated from the Kansas State University Law School in 1894; was admitted to the bar in 1894 and commenced practice in Sedan, Kans.; prosecuting attorney of Chautauqua County 1897–1901; mayor of Sedan 1921–1923; engaged in agricultural pursuits and stock raising; was also interested in the oil and gas business; elected as a Republican to the Sixty-eighth and to the three succeeding Congresses (March 4, 1923–March 3, 1931); was not a candidate for renomination, but was an unsuccessful candidate for nomination for United States Senator in 1930; resumed his former business pursuits; died in a hospital in Kansas City, Mo., December 27, 1932; interment in Greenwood Cemetery, Sedan, Kans.

SPRUANCE, Presley, a Senator from Delaware; born in Kent County, Del., September 11, 1785; pursued preparatory studies; engaged in manufacturing and mercantile pursuits in Smyrna, Del.; delegate to the State constitutional convention in 1831; member of the State senate in 1828, 1840, and 1846, and served as its president; elected as a Whig to the United States Senate and served from March 4, 1847, to March 3, 1853; was not a candidate for renomination in 1852; resumed his business pursuits; died in Smyrna, Del., February 13, 1863; interment in the Presbyterian Cemetery.

SQUIRE, Watson Carvosso, a Senator from Washington; born in Cape Vincent, Jefferson County, N. Y., May 18, 1838; attended the public schools at Hannibal, Oswego County, N. Y., Falley Seminary, Fulton, N. Y., and Fairfield Seminary, Herkimer County, N. Y.; was graduated from the Wesleyan University, Middletown, Conn., in 1859; principal of the Moravia (N. Y.) Institute; during the Civil War enlisted in Company F, Nineteenth Regiment, New York Volunteer Infantry, in 1861 for three months' service; promoted to the rank of first lieutenant; after five months' service was mustered out; was graduated from the Cleveland Law School in 1862; was admitted to the bar the same year and commenced practice in Cleveland, Ohio; raised a company of sharpshooters, of which he was commissioned captain; participated in the Battles of Chickamauga, Chattanooga, Nashville, and Resaca, and other engagements; made judge advocate of the district of Tennessee, with headquarters in Nashville; discharged with the rank of captain of the Seventh Independent Company, Ohio Sharpshooters, July 28, 1865; brevetted as major, lieutenant colonel, and colonel, each rank to date from July 28, 1866, in recognition of services rendered during the war; subsequently employed with the Remington Arms Co.; purchased large holdings in the Territory of Washington in 1876 and moved to Seattle in 1879; Governor of the Territory of Washington 1884–1887; upon the admission of Washington as a State into the Union in 1889 was elected as a Republican to the United States Senate; reelected in 1891, and served from November 20, 1889, to March 3, 1897; unsuccessful candidate for reelection in 1897; retired from the practice of law and devoted his time to management of his properties in Seattle; organizer and president of the Union Trust Co. (later Squire Investment Co.); died in Seattle, Wash., June 7, 1926; interment in Washelli Cemetery.

STACK, Edmund John, a Representative from Illinois; born in Chicago, Ill., January 31, 1874; attended the grammar and high schools of Chicago; was graduated from the law department of Lake Forest (Ill.) University in 1895; was admitted to the bar the same year and commenced the practice of his profession in Chicago, Ill.; appointed assistant corporation counsel of Chicago and, later, chief trial attorney; unsuccessful candidate for election in 1906 to the Sixtieth Congress; elected as a Democrat to the Sixty-second Congress (March 4, 1911–March 3, 1913); unsuccessful candidate for renomination in 1912; resumed the practice of law; died in Chicago, Ill., April 12, 1957; interment in Calvary Cemetery, Evanston, Ill.

STACK, Michael Joseph, a Representative from Pennsylvania; born in Listowel, County Kerry, Ireland, September 29, 1888; attended the national school of his native city; immigrated to the United States in 1903 and settled in Philadelphia, Pa.; attended St. Joseph's College, Philadelphia, Pa., and was graduated from St. Mary's University, Baltimore, Md., in 1910; employed by a railroad company at Detroit, Mich., 1910–1917; during the First World War enlisted on July 17, 1917, as a private in the Medical Detachment, Three Hundred and Sixtieth Infantry; participated in the St. Mihiel offensive and the Villers-en-Haye and Puvenelle defensive sectors, and was discharged February 17, 1919; was wounded and decorated with the Order of the Purple Heart; after the war became engaged in the real-estate business in Philadelphia, Pa.; elected as a Democrat to the Seventy-fourth and Seventy-fifth Congresses (January 3, 1935–

January 3, 1939); unsuccessful Democratic candidate for renomination in 1938 and was an unsuccessful Royal Oak candidate for reelection in 1938 to the Seventy-sixth Congress; resumed the real-estate business; died in Philadelphia, Pa., December 14, 1960; interment in St. Denis Cemetery, Havertown, Pa.

STACKHOUSE, Eli Thomas, a Representative from South Carolina; born in Little Rock, Marion County, S. C., March 27, 1824; attended the common schools; worked on his father's farm; taught school for several years; later engaged in agricultural pursuits; enlisted in the Confederate Army January 9, 1861, and served throughout the Civil War, attaining the rank of colonel of the Eighth Regiment, South Carolina Volunteers; wounded in the Battles of Antietam, Gettysburg, and Chickamauga; member of the State house of representatives 1862–1868; member of the first board of trustees of Clemson Agricultural and Mechanical College of South Carolina in 1887; first president of the South Carolina State Farmers' Alliance in 1888; elected as a Democrat to the Fifty-second Congress and served from March 4, 1891, until his death in Washington, D. C., June 14, 1892; interment in Little Rock Cemetery, Little Rock, S. C.

STAFFORD, William Henry, a Representative from Wisconsin; born in Milwaukee, Wis., October 12, 1869; attended the public schools, and was graduated from Harvard University Law School in 1893; was admitted to the bar in 1894 and commenced practice in Milwaukee, Wis.; elected as a Republican to the Fifty-eighth and to the three succeeding Congresses (March 4, 1903–March 3, 1911); unsuccessful candidate for renomination in 1910; resumed the practice of his profession in Milwaukee, Wis.; elected to the Sixty-third, Sixty-fourth, and Sixty-fifth Congresses (March 4, 1913–March 3, 1919); unsuccessful candidate for reelection in 1918 to the Sixty-sixth Congress; elected to the Sixty-seventh Congress (March 4, 1921–March 3, 1923); unsuccessful candidate for reelection in 1922 to the Sixty-eighth Congress and for election in 1926 to the Seventieth Congress; elected to the Seventy-first and Seventy-second Congresses (March 4, 1929–March 3, 1933); unsuccessful candidate for renomination in 1932 and for the Republican nomination for United States Senator in 1938; resumed the practice of law; died in Milwaukee, Wis., April 22, 1957; interment in Forest Home Cemetery.

STAGGERS, Harley Orrin, a Representative from West Virginia; born in Keyser, Mineral County, W. Va., August 3, 1907; attended the public schools of Mineral County, W. Va.; was graduated from Emory and Henry College, Emory, Va., in 1931; graduate work at Northwestern University in 1933 and Duke University in 1935; coach and teacher of science at Norton (Va.) High School 1931–1933; head coach of Potomac State College, Keyser, W. Va., 1933–1935; sheriff of Mineral County, W. Va., 1937–1941; right-of-way agent, State Road Commission of West Virginia, in 1941 and 1942; West Virginia State Director, Office of Government Reports (later Office of War Information) in 1942; during World War II was a lieutenant commander in the United States Naval Air Corps with service as a navigator in the Atlantic and Pacific Theaters of War 1942–1946; elected as a Democrat to the Eighty-first and to the five succeeding Congresses (January 3, 1949–January 3, 1961). *Reelected to the Eighty-seventh Congress.*

STAHLE, James Alonzo, a Representative from Pennsylvania; born in West Manchester Township, York County, Pa., January 11, 1829; attended the common schools and York Academy; learned the printing trade; later became a merchant tailor; organized the Ellsworth Zouaves in 1861 and in August of that year, together with his company of forty recruits, enlisted as Company A in the Eighty-seventh Regiment, Pennsylvania Volunteers, for service in the Civil War; promoted to major January 1, 1863, and to lieutenant colonel May 9, 1863; honorably discharged at the expiration of his term of service October 13, 1864; deputy collector of internal revenue at York, Pa., from May 3, 1869, to July 3, 1885; engaged in agricultural pursuits; elected as a Republican to the Fifty-fourth Congress (March 4, 1895–March 3, 1897); was not a candidate for renomination in 1896; resumed agricultural pursuits; died on his estate near York, Pa., December 21, 1912; interment in Prospect Hill Cemetery, York, Pa.

STAHLNECKER, William Griggs, a Representative from New York; born in Auburn, Cayuga County, N. Y., June 20, 1849; moved with his parents to Brooklyn and later to New York City; pursued an academic course, and attended the University of New York in New York City; studied law; was admitted to practice; engaged in mercantile pursuits; member of the New York Produce Exchange; moved to Yonkers in 1880; mayor of Yonkers, N. Y., 1884–1886; delegate to the Democratic State convention at Saratoga in June 1884; delegate to the Democratic National Convention at Chicago in 1884, which nominated Grover Cleveland, of New York, for President and Thomas A. Hendricks, of Indiana, for Vice President; elected as a Democrat to the Forty-ninth and to the three succeeding Congresses (March 4, 1885–March 3, 1893); retired from political activity because of illness; engaged in the practice of law; died in Yonkers, N. Y., March 26, 1902; interment in Sleepy Hollow Cemetery, Tarrytown, N. Y.

STALKER, Gale Hamilton, a Representative from New York; born in Long Eddy, Sullivan County, N. Y., November 7, 1889; attended the grade and high schools, Scranton (Pa.) Business College, and the night schools of New York City; moved to Elmira, Chemung County, N. Y., and engaged in the lumber business and also in banking; elected as a Republican to the Sixty-eighth and to the five succeeding Congresses (March 4, 1923–January 3, 1935); was not a candidate for renomination in 1934; retired from political activities and is a resident of Arlington, Va.

STALLINGS, Jesse Francis, a Representative from Alabama; born near Manningham, Butler County, Ala., April 4, 1856; completed preparatory studies, and was graduated from the University of Alabama at Tuscaloosa in 1877; studied law at that university; was admitted to the bar in April 1880 and commenced practice in Greenville, Ala.; elected by the legislature of Alabama as solicitor for the second judicial circuit in November 1886 and served until his resignation in September 1892; delegate to the Democratic National Convention at St. Louis in 1888, which nominated Grover Cleveland, of New York, for President; elected as a Democrat to the Fifty-third and to the three succeeding Congresses (March 4, 1893–March 3, 1901); was not a candidate for renomination in 1900; resumed the practice of his profession in Birmingham, Ala.; president of the Lincoln Reserve Life Insurance Co. 1912–1928; died in Birmingham, Ala., on March 18, 1928; interment in Elmwood Cemetery.

STALLWORTH, James Adams, a Representative from Alabama; born in Evergreen, Conecuh County, Ala., April 7, 1822; attended Old Field Piney Woods Schools; engaged as a planter; studied law; was admitted to the bar in 1848 and commenced practice in Evergreen, Ala.; member of the State house of representatives 1845–1848; solicitor for the second judicial circuit of Alabama in 1850 and 1855; unsuccessful candidate for election in 1854 to the Thirty-fourth Congress;

elected as a Democrat to the Thirty-fifth and Thirty-sixth Congresses and served from March 4, 1857, to January 21, 1861, when he withdrew; died near Evergreen, Conecuh County, Ala., August 31, 1861; interment in Evergreen Cemetery.

STANARD, Edwin Obed, a Representative from Missouri; born in Newport, Sullivan County, N. H., January 5, 1832; moved with his parents to the Territory of Iowa in 1836; completed preparatory studies; moved to St. Louis, Mo., in 1853; taught school in Illinois in 1854 and 1855; was graduated from St. Louis (Mo.) Commercial College in 1855; engaged in the commission business in 1856 and later in the milling business at St. Louis; Lieutenant Governor of Missouri 1869–1871; elected as a Republican to the Forty-third Congress (March 4, 1873–March 3, 1875); unsuccessful candidate for reelection in 1874 to the Forty-fourth Congress; engaged in the manufacture of flour; died in St. Louis, Mo., March 12, 1914; interment in Bellefontaine Cemetery.

STANBERY, William, a Representative from Ohio; born in Essex County, N. J., August 10, 1788; received an academic education; studied law in New York City and was admitted to the bar; moved to Ohio in 1809; settled in Newark, Licking County, and practiced law; member of the State senate in 1824 and 1825; elected as a Jacksonian Democrat to the Twentieth Congress to fill the vacancy caused by the death of William Wilson; reelected to the Twenty-first and Twenty-second Congresses and served from October 9, 1827, to March 3, 1833; unsuccessful candidate for renomination in 1832; resumed the practice of law; died in Newark, Ohio, January 23, 1873; interment in Cedar Hill Cemetery.

STANDIFER, James, a Representative from Tennessee; born in Sequatchie Valley, near Dunlap, Tenn.; attended the common schools and was graduated from the University of Tennessee at Knoxville; elected as a Whig to the Eighteenth Congress (March 4, 1823–March 3, 1825); elected to the Twenty-first and to the four succeeding Congresses and served from March 4, 1829, until his death near Kingston, Tenn., August 20, 1837, while on his way to Washington, D. C.; interment in the Baptist Cemetery, Kingston, Tenn.

STANDIFORD, Elisha David, a Representative from Kentucky; born near Louisville, Jefferson County, Ky., December 28, 1831; attended the common schools and St. Mary's College, near Lebanon, Ky.; was graduated from the Kentucky School of Medicine and commenced practice in Louisville; abandoned the practice of medicine and engaged in agricultural pursuits and other enterprises; member of the State senate in 1868 and 1871; elected as a Democrat to the Forty-third Congress (March 4, 1873–March 3, 1875); declined a renomination in 1874 to the Forty-fourth Congress; president of the Louisville & Nashville Railroad Co. 1875–1879; engaged in banking and agricultural pursuits; died in Louisville, Ky., July 26, 1887; interment in Cave Hill Cemetery.

STANFIELD, Robert Nelson, a Senator from Oregon; born in Umatilla, Umatilla County, Oreg., July 9, 1877; attended the public schools and the State normal school at Weston, Oreg.; engaged in the livestock industry and also interested in banking in Echo and Baker, Oreg.; member of the State house of representatives 1913–1917, serving as speaker in 1917; elected as a Republican to the United States Senate in 1920 and served from March 4, 1921, to March 3, 1927; unsuccessful candidate for reelection on the Independent ticket in 1926; resumed his former business pursuits; died in Weiser, Idaho, April 13, 1945; interment in Hillcrest Cemetery.

STANFILL, William Abner, a Senator from Kentucky; born in Barbourville, Knox County, Ky., January 16, 1892; attended the public schools and Union College; was graduated from the law department of the University of Kentucky at Lexington in 1912; was admitted to the bar the same year and commenced practice in Barbourville, Ky.; moved to Hazard, Ky., in 1916 and continued the practice of law; member of the board of regents of Morehead State Teachers College 1927–1931; member of the board of governors of the Kentucky Children's Home at Lyndon, Ky., 1933–1936; chairman of the Republican State central committee 1944–1948; appointed as a Republican to the United States Senate to fill the vacancy caused by the resignation of Albert B. Chandler and served from November 19, 1945, to November 5, 1946, when a successor was elected; was not a candidate for nomination to the vacancy in 1946; resumed the practice of law and is a resident of Lexington, Ky.

STANFORD, Leland, a Senator from California; born in Watervliet, N. Y., March 9, 1824; pursued an academic course; studied law; was admitted to practice in 1848; moved to Port Washington, Wis., the same year and engaged in the practice of law; moved to California in 1852 and opened a general store at Michigan Bluff; in 1855 moved to Sacramento and engaged in mercantile pursuits on a large scale; one of the "big four" who built the Central Pacific Railroad, serving as its president in 1863; founder of Leland Stanford Junior University; delegate to the Republican National Convention in 1860; Governor of California 1861–1863; elected as a Republican to the United States Senate in 1885; reelected in 1891 and served from March 4, 1885, until his death in Palo Alto, Calif., June 21, 1893; interment in a mausoleum on the grounds of Stanford University.

STANFORD, Richard (grandfather of William Robert Webb), a Representative from North Carolina; born near Vienna, Md., March 2, 1767; completed preparatory studies; moved to Hawfields, N. C., about 1793 and established an academy; elected as a Democrat to the Fifth and to the nine succeeding Congresses and served from March 4, 1797, until his death in Georgetown, D. C., April 9, 1816; interment in Congressional Cemetery, Washington, D. C.

STANLEY, Augustus Owsley, a Representative and a Senator from Kentucky; born in Shelbyville, Ky., May 21, 1867; attended the State college at Lexington, Ky., and was graduated from Centre College, Danville, Ky., in 1889; professor of belles-lettres at Christian College and principal of Mackville Academy 1891–1893; studied law; was admitted to the bar in 1894 and commenced practice in Flemingsburg, Ky.; presidential elector on the Democratic ticket of Bryan and Stevenson in 1900; elected as a Democrat to the Fifty-eighth and to the five succeeding Congresses (March 4, 1903–March 3, 1915); unsuccessful candidate for reelection to the Sixty-fourth Congress; Governor of Kentucky from December 7, 1915, to May 18, 1919, when he resigned, having been elected Senator; elected to the United States Senate in 1918 for the term commencing March 4, 1919, but, preferring to continue as Governor, did not qualify until May 19, 1919, and served until March 3, 1925; unsuccessful candidate for reelection in 1924; resumed the practice of law in Washington, D. C.; appointed to the International Joint Commission on May 9, 1930, and on March 7, 1933, was elected chairman, in which capacity he served until his resignation February 1, 1954; died in Washington, D. C., August 13, 1958; interment in Frankfort Cemetery, Frankfort, Ky.

STANLEY, Thomas Bahnson, a Representative from Virginia; born on a farm near Spencer, Henry County, Va., July 16, 1890; attended the local public schools and Eastman Business College, Poughkeepsie, N. Y.; engaged in furniture manufacturing since 1924; dairy farmer and livestock breeder; member of State house of delegates 1930–1946, serving as speaker 1942–1946; elected as a Democrat to the Seventy-ninth Congress to fill the vacancy caused by the resignation of Thomas G. Burch and at the same time was elected to the Eightieth Congress; reelected to the Eighty-first, Eighty-second, and Eighty-third Congresses, and served from November 5, 1946, until his resignation February 3, 1953, having entered the campaign for Governor; elected Governor of Virginia for the term commencing January 1954 and ending January 1958; trustee of Randolph-Macon College; vice president and director of First National Bank, Bassett, Va.; is a resident of Stanleytown, Va.

STANLEY, Winifred Claire, a Representative from New York; born in New York City, N. Y., August 14, 1909; attended the public schools in New York City and Buffalo, N. Y.; was graduated from the Arts College of the University of Buffalo in 1930 and from its law school in 1933; was admitted to the bar in 1934 and commenced practice in Buffalo, N. Y.; first woman to serve as assistant district attorney of Erie County, N. Y., 1938–1943; elected as a Republican to the Seventy-eighth Congress (January 3, 1943–January 3, 1945); was not a candidate for renomination in 1944; appointed counsel to the New York State Employees' Retirement System January 1, 1945, and served until March 31, 1955; assistant attorney general, New York State Law Department, Albany, N. Y.; is a resident of Buffalo, N. Y.

STANLY, Edward (son of John Stanly), a Representative from North Carolina; born in New Bern, N. C., July 13, 1810; attended New Bern Academy, and was graduated from the American Literary, Scientific, and Military Academy, Norwich University, in 1829; studied law; was admitted to the bar in 1832 and commenced practice in Washington, Beaufort County, N. C.; elected as a Whig to the Twenty-fifth, Twenty-sixth, and Twenty-seventh Congresses (March 4, 1837–March 3, 1843); unsuccessful candidate for reelection in 1842 to the Twenty-eighth Congress; member of the State house of representatives 1844–1846, 1848, and 1849, serving as speaker in 1846; attorney general of North Carolina in 1847; elected to the Thirty-first and Thirty-second Congresses (March 4, 1849–March 3, 1853); unsuccessful candidate for reelection in 1852 to the Thirty-third Congress; moved to California in 1853 and practiced law in San Francisco; unsuccessful Republican candidate for Governor of California in 1857; during the Civil War was appointed Military Governor of eastern North Carolina May 26, 1862, with rank of brigadier general, and served until March 2, 1863, when he resigned; returned to California and resumed the practice of law; died in San Francisco, Calif., July 12, 1872; interment in Mountain View Cemetery, Oakland, Calif.

STANLY, John (father of Edward Stanly), a Representative from North Carolina; born in New Bern, N. C., April 9, 1774; received his early education from private tutors; attended Princeton University; studied law; was admitted to the bar in 1799 and practiced; clerk and master in equity; member of the State house of commons in 1798 and 1799; elected to the Seventh Congress (March 4, 1801–March 3, 1803); elected to the Eleventh Congress (March 4, 1809–March 3, 1811); resumed the practice of his profession; again a member of the State house of commons 1812–1815, 1818, 1819, 1823–1825, and 1826; died in New Bern, N. C., August 2, 1834; interment in Episcopal Cemetery.

STANTON, Benjamin, a Representative from Ohio; born in Mount Pleasant, Jefferson County, Ohio, June 4, 1809; pursued academic studies; learned the tailor's trade; studied law; was admitted to the bar in 1834 and commenced practice in Bellefontaine, Ohio; member of the State senate in 1841 and 1843; delegate to the State constitutional convention in 1850; elected as a Whig to the Thirty-second Congress (March 4, 1851–March 3, 1853); elected to the Thirty-fourth, Thirty-fifth, and Thirty-sixth Congresses (March 4, 1855–March 3, 1861); Lieutenant Governor of Ohio in 1862; moved to Martinsburg, W. Va., in 1865, and practiced law; moved to Wheeling, W. Va., in 1867 and continued the practice of law; died in Wheeling, W. Va., June 2, 1872; interment in Greenwood Cemetery.

STANTON, Frederick Perry, a Representative from Tennessee; born in Alexandria, Va., December 22, 1814; pursued classical studies, and was graduated from Columbian College (now George Washington University), Washington, D. C., in 1833; taught school; studied law; was admitted to the bar and commenced practice in Memphis, Tenn.; elected as a Democrat to the Twenty-ninth and to the four succeeding Congresses (March 4, 1845–March 3, 1855); Governor of Kansas Territory 1858–1861; moved to Virginia and subsequently settled in Florida; died in Stanton, Fla., June 4, 1894; interment in South Lake Weir Cemetery, South Lake Weir, Fla.

STANTON, Joseph, Jr., a Senator and a Representative from Rhode Island; born in Charlestown, R. I., July 19, 1739; served in the expedition against Canada in 1759; member of the State house of representatives 1768–1774; served as colonel in the Revolutionary Army; delegate to the State constitutional convention in 1790; elected as a Democrat to the United States Senate and served from June 7, 1790, to March 3, 1793; again a member of the State house of representatives 1794–1800; elected as a Democrat to the Seventh, Eighth, and Ninth Congresses (March 4, 1801–March 3, 1807); died in Charlestown, R. I., in 1807; interment in the family cemetery.

STANTON, Richard Henry, a Representative from Kentucky; born in Alexandria, Va., September 9, 1812; completed preparatory studies; attended Alexandria Academy; studied law; was admitted to the bar and began practice in Maysville, Ky., in 1835; editor of the Maysville Monitor 1835–1842; postmaster of Maysville; elected as a Democrat to the Thirty-first, Thirty-second, and Thirty-third Congresses (March 4, 1849–March 3, 1855); unsuccessful candidate for reelection in 1854 to the Thirty-fourth Congress; presidential elector on the Democratic ticket of Buchanan and Breckinridge in 1856; State's attorney 1858–1861; delegate to the Democratic National Convention at New York City in 1868; district judge 1868–1874; resumed the practice of law until his retirement in 1885; died in Maysville, Ky., March 20, 1891; interment in Maysville Cemetery.

STANTON, William Henry, a Representative from Pennsylvania; born in New York City July 28, 1843; moved with his parents to Carbondale, Pa., and subsequently to Archbald, Pa.; attended the public schools in Archbald and St. John's College, near Montrose, Pa.; studied law; was admitted to the bar in Scranton, Pa., in 1868 and commenced practice in that city; prosecuting attorney of the mayor's court of Scranton 1872–1874; served in the State senate in 1875 and 1876; elected as a Democrat to the Forty-fourth Congress to fill the vacancy caused by the resignation of Winthrop W. Ketchum and served from November 7, 1876, to March 3, 1877; was not a candidate for election to the Forty-fifth Congress; elected judge of the Luzerne County Court of Common Pleas in 1877; served with Judges Harding and Handley at the organization of the courts of the newly created county of Lackawanna October 24, 1878; resigned in 1879; resumed the practice of law in Scranton, Pa., and died there March 28, 1900; interment in West Side Catholic Cemetery.

STARIN, John Henry (grandson of Thomas Sammons), a Representative from New York; born in Sammonsville, Fulton County (then a part of Montgomery County), N. Y., August 27, 1825; pursued an academic course in Esperance, N. Y.; began the study of medicine in 1842; established and conducted a drug and medicine business in Fultonville 1845–1858; postmaster of Fultonville, N. Y., 1848–1852; founder and president of the Starin City River & Harbor Transportation Co.; director of the North River Bank, New York City, and the Mohawk River National Bank; also interested in agriculture and stock raising; elected as a Republican to the Forty-fifth and Forty-sixth Congresses (March 4, 1877–March 3, 1881); president of Fultonville National Bank 1883–1909; engaged in railroading; member of the New York City Rapid Transit Commission; died in New York City March 21, 1909; interment in Starin mausoleum, Fultonville Cemetery, Fultonville, N. Y.

STARK, Benjamin, a Senator from Oregon; born in New Orleans, La., June 26, 1820; pursued classical studies, and was graduated from Union School, New London, Conn., and Hebron Academy; engaged in mercantile pursuits in New York City 1835–1848, and also studied law; moved to San Francisco, Calif., and engaged in mercantile pursuits in 1849 and 1850, moving to Portland, Oreg., the latter year; was admitted to the bar in 1850 and commenced practice in Portland, Oreg.; member of the Territorial house of representatives in 1852; served in the Oregon Indian hostilities in 1853 with the rank of colonel; member of the State house of representatives in 1860; appointed as a Democrat to the United States Senate to fill the vacancy caused by the death of Edward D. Baker and served from October 29, 1861, to September 12, 1862, when a successor was elected; was not a candidate for election; resumed the practice of law; delegate to the Democratic National Convention at Chicago in 1864; moved to New London, Conn.; delegate from Connecticut to the Democratic National Convention at New York City in 1868; member of the board of aldermen of New London, Conn., in 1873 and 1874; member of the State house of representatives in 1874; member of the Connecticut State Prison Commission; died in New London, Conn., October 10, 1898; interment in Cedar Grove Cemetery.

STARK, William Ledyard, a Representative from Nebraska; born in Mystic, New London County, Conn., July 29, 1853; was graduated from Mystic Valley Institute, Mystic, Conn., in 1872; moved to Wyoming, Stark County, Ill.; taught school and clerked in a store; attended the Union College of Law, Chicago, Ill.; was admitted to the bar by the supreme court of Illinois in January 1878; moved to Aurora, Nebr., in February 1878; served as superintendent of city schools; deputy district attorney; judge of the Hamilton County Court; served as a major and judge advocate general of the Nebraska National Guard; unsuccessful Populist candidate for election in 1895 to the Fifty-fourth Congress; elected as a Democrat to the Fifty-fifth, Fifty-sixth, and Fifty-seventh Congresses (March 4, 1897–March 3, 1903); unsuccessful Fusionist candidate for reelection in 1902 to the Fifty-eighth Congress; retired, and resided in Aurora, Nebr.; died at Tarpon Springs, Fla., November 11, 1922; interment in the City Cemetery, Aurora, Nebr.

STARKEY, Frank Thomas, a Representative from Minnesota; born in St. Paul, Ramsey County, Minn., February 18, 1892; attended the public schools; business representative of the Milk Drivers Union 1917–1933 and 1942–1944; member of the State house of representatives 1923–1933, serving as chief clerk in 1933; member of the State Industrial Commission 1933–1939; vice president of the Minnesota State Federation of Labor for twelve years, serving as director of its research division 1939–1942;

member of the Ramsey County Civil Service Commission 1942–1944; elected as a Democrat to the Seventy-ninth Congress (January 3, 1945–January 3, 1947); unsuccessful for reelection in 1946 to the Eightieth Congress; writer for trade magazines; commissioner, Department of Employment Security, St. Paul, Minn., since April 1, 1955; is a resident of St. Paul, Minn.

STARKWEATHER, David Austin, a Representative from Ohio; born in Preston, Conn., January 21, 1802; received an academic education; studied law; was admitted to the bar in 1825 and commenced practice in Mansfield, Ohio; moved to Canton, Ohio, in 1827 and continued the practice of law; judge of one of the higher courts in Stark County, Ohio; member of the State house of representatives 1833–1835; served in the State senate 1836–1838; elected as a Democrat to the Twenty-sixth Congress (March 4, 1839–March 3, 1841); resumed the practice of law in Cleveland, Ohio; elected to the Twenty-ninth Congress (March 4, 1845–March 3, 1847); unsuccessful candidate for reelection in 1846 to the Thirtieth Congress; presidential elector on the Cass and Butler ticket in 1848; chairman of the Democratic National Convention at Baltimore in 1852; Minister to Chile 1854–1857; discontinued active pursuits and lived in retirement until his death in Cleveland, Ohio, on July 12, 1876; interment in Lake View Cemetery.

STARKWEATHER, George Anson, a Representative from New York; born in Preston, Conn., May 19, 1794; attended the common schools, and was graduated from Union College, Schenectady, N. Y., in 1819; studied law; was admitted to the bar and practiced in Cooperstown, N. Y.; elected as a Democrat to the Thirtieth Congress (March 4, 1847–March 3, 1849); again resumed the practice of his profession in Milwaukee, Wis., 1853–1868; died in Cooperstown, N. Y., October 15, 1879; interment in Lakewood Cemetery.

STARKWEATHER, Henry Howard, a Representative from Connecticut; born in Preston, Conn., April 29, 1826; attended the common schools; studied law; was admitted to the bar and commenced practice in Norwich, Conn.; member of the State house of representatives in 1856; delegate to the Republican National Conventions at Chicago in 1860 and 1868; postmaster of Norwich, Conn., 1861–1865; elected as a Republican to the Fortieth and to the four succeeding Congresses and served from March 4, 1867, until his death in Washington, D. C., on January 28, 1876; interment in Yantic Cemetery, Norwich, Conn.

STARNES, Joe, a Representative from Alabama; born in Guntersville, Marshall County, Ala., March 31, 1895; attended the public schools; taught school in Marshall County, Ala., 1912–1917; during the First World War served overseas as a second lieutenant in the Fifty-third Infantry, Sixth Division, in 1918 and 1919; decorated with the Silver Star; was graduated from the law department of the University of Alabama at Tuscaloosa in 1921; was admitted to the bar the same year and commenced practice at Guntersville, Ala.; member of the One Hundred and Sixty-Seventh Infantry, Alabama National Guard, since 1923, advancing through the ranks to colonel; member of the State board of education 1933– and became vice chairman in January 1948; elected as a Democrat to the Seventy-fourth and to the four succeeding Congresses (January 3, 1935–January 3, 1945); unsuccessful candidate for renomination in 1944; during World War II served as a colonel of Infantry in the European Theater of Operations and in the Army of Occupation from January 4, 1945, until discharged on February 22, 1946; resumed the practice of law and is a resident of Guntersville, Ala.

STARR, John Farson, a Representative from New Jersey; born in Philadelphia, Pa., March 25, 1818; completed preparatory studies; moved to Camden, N. J., in 1844; one of the founders of the Camden Iron Works; engaged in mercantile pursuits; president of the First National Bank of Camden for over thirty years, up to the time of his death; elected as a Republican to the Thirty-eighth and Thirty-ninth Congresses (March 4, 1863–March 3, 1867); was not a candidate for renomination in 1866; died in Atlantic City, N. J., August 9, 1904; interment in Harleigh Cemetery, Camden, N. J.

STAUFFER, S. Walter, a Representative from Pennsylvania; born in Walkersville, Frederick County, Md., August 13, 1888; attended the public schools; worked in father's store as a boy, as a farmhand at harvest time, and as a canning factory employee; took preparatory college work at Conway Hall, Carlisle, Pa., in 1906 and 1907; graduated from Dickinson College, Carlisle, Pa., in 1912; moved to York, Pa., in 1915; engaged in the manufacture of lime, crushed stone, and refractory dolomite 1916–1936; formed a business partnership in 1929 with his brother, Southern Farms, Walkersville, Md., in aging and curing hams; trustee of Dickinson College since 1930; president of National Lime Association, Washington, D. C., 1936–1946; chairman of York City Housing Authority 1949–1952; vice president and chairman of executive committee, York County Gas Co., 1950–1960; director of First National Bank, York, Pa., Columbia Water Co., J. E. Baker Co., Farmers Fire Insurance Co., and York Water Co.; owner of a large tract of woodland and engaged in timbering operations 1947–1960; elected as a Republican to the Eighty-third Congress (January 3, 1953–January 3, 1955); was an unsuccessful candidate for reelection in 1954 to the Eighty-fourth Congress; elected to the Eighty-fifth Congress (January 3, 1957–January 3, 1959); unsuccessful candidate for reelection in 1958 to the Eighty-sixth Congress; is a resident of York, Pa.

STEAGALL, Henry Bascom, a Representative from Alabama; born in Clopton, Dale County, Ala., May 19, 1873; attended the common schools and the Southeast Alabama Agricultural School at Abbeville; was graduated from the law department of the University of Alabama at Tuscaloosa in 1893; was admitted to the bar the same year and commenced practice in Ozark, Ala.; county solicitor of Dale County 1902–1908; member of the State house of representatives in 1906 and 1907; member of the State Democratic executive committee 1906–1910; prosecuting attorney of the third judicial circuit 1907–1914; delegate to the Democratic National Convention at Baltimore in 1912; elected as a Democrat to the Sixty-fourth and to the fourteen succeeding Congresses and served from March 4, 1915, until his death in Washington, D. C., November 22, 1943; interment in the City Cemetery, Ozark, Ala.

STEARNS, Asahel, a Representative from Massachusetts; born in Lunenburg, Mass., June 17, 1774; was graduated from Harvard University in 1797; studied law; was admitted to the bar and commenced the practice of law in Chelmsford, Mass.; member of the State senate in 1813; moved to Charlestown, Mass., in 1815; elected as a Federalist to the Fourteenth Congress (March 4, 1815–March 3, 1817); served in the State house of representatives in 1817; professor of law at Harvard University from 1817 to 1829; again served as a member of the State senate in 1830 and 1831; died in Cambridge, Mass., February 5, 1839; interment in Mount Auburn Cemetery.

STEARNS, Foster Waterman, a Representative from New Hampshire; born in Hull, Plymouth County, Mass., July 29, 1881; attended the public schools; was graduated from Amherst

(Mass.) College in 1903, Harvard University, Cambridge, Mass., in 1906, and Boston (Mass.) College in 1915; librarian of the Museum of Fine Arts, Boston, Mass., 1913–1917; State librarian of Massachusetts in 1917; during the First World War served as a first lieutenant with the Sixteenth Infantry, First Division, and at the General Headquarters of the American Expeditionary Forces in France from November 27, 1917, until discharged August 5, 1919; wounded in action; decorated with the Order of the Silver Star and the Order of the Purple Heart (United States); Privy Chamberlain of Sword and Cape to Pope Pius XI and Knight of the Sovereign Military Order of Malta; assistant military attaché to Belgium in 1919; served in the Department of State, Washington, D. C., in 1920 and 1921; third secretary of the American Embassy, attached to the United States High Commission, in Constantinople 1921–1923; second secretary of the American Embassy at Paris in 1923 and 1924; librarian of Holy Cross College, Worcester, Mass., 1925–1930; moved to Hancock, N. H., in 1927; member of the State house of representatives in 1937 and 1938; delegate to the Republican National Conventions at Philadelphia in 1940 and 1948; Regent of the Smithsonian Institution 1941–1945; elected as a Republican to the Seventy-sixth, Seventy-seventh, and Seventy-eighth Congresses (January 3, 1939–January 3, 1945); was not a candidate for renomination in 1944, but was an unsuccessful candidate for the Republican nomination for United States Senator; engaged in foreign educational work; in 1942 became a director of the Rumford Printing Co. of Concord, N. H.; moved to Exeter, N. H., in 1948, where he died June 4, 1956; interment in Exeter Cemetery.

STEARNS, Ozora Pierson, a Senator from Minnesota; born in De Kalb, St. Lawrence County, N. Y., January 15, 1831; moved to Ohio in 1833 with his parents, who settled in Lake County; attended Oberlin (Ohio) College, and was graduated from the University of Michigan in 1858 and from the law department of that university in 1860; was admitted to the bar in 1860 and commenced practice in Rochester, Minn.; elected prosecuting attorney of Olmstead County in 1861; mayor of Rochester 1866–1868; served in the Union Army during the Civil War as a lieutenant in the Ninth Regiment, Minnesota Volunteer Infantry, and as colonel of the Thirty-ninth Regiment, United States Colored Troops; was mustered out in December 1865; elected as a Republican to the United States Senate on January 18, 1871, to fill the vacancy caused by the death of Daniel S. Norton and served from January 23 to March 3, 1871; was not a candidate for reelection; moved to Duluth, Minn., in 1872 and practiced law; judge of the eleventh judicial district of Minnesota 1874–1895; regent of the University of Minnesota at Minneapolis 1890–1895; died in Pacific Beach, Calif., June 2, 1896; remains were cremated in Los Angeles and the ashes interred in Forest Hill Cemetery, Duluth, St. Louis County, Minn.

STEBBINS, Henry George, a Representative from New York; born in Ridgefield, Conn., September 15, 1811; attended private schools; moved to New York; engaged in banking; colonel of the Twelfth Regiment; president of the Dramatic Fund Association; president of the Academy of Music; elected as a War Democrat to the Thirty-eighth Congress and served from March 4, 1863, until his resignation on October 24, 1864; engaged as a stock broker; president of the New York Stock Exchange; appointed president of the Central Park Commission; chairman of the committee of seventy; died in New York City December 9, 1881; interment in Greenwood Cemetery, Brooklyn, N. Y.

STECK, Daniel Frederic, a Senator from Iowa; born in Ottumwa, Wapello County, Iowa, December 16, 1881; attended the common schools; was graduated from the law department of the University of Iowa at Iowa City in 1906; was admitted to the bar the same year and commenced practice in Ottumwa; during the First World War reported for service on July 15, 1917, as captain of Company C, One Hundred and Ninth Field Signal Battalion, Thirty-fourth Division, and served in France with his company from October 12, 1918, to April 27, 1919; was honorably discharged at Camp Dodge, Iowa, May 31, 1919; resumed the practice of law in Ottumwa; delegate to the Democratic National Conventions in 1924 and 1928; successfully contested as a Democrat the election of Smith W. Brookhart to the United States Senate and served from April 12, 1926, to March 3, 1931; was an unsuccessful candidate for reelection in 1930; again resumed the practice of his profession; special assistant to the United States Attorney General 1933–1947; retired; died in Ottumwa, Iowa, December 31, 1950; interment in Ottumwa Cemetery.

STEDMAN, Charles Manly, a Representative from North Carolina; born in Pittsboro, Chatham County, N. C., January 29, 1841; moved with his parents to Fayetteville, N. C., in 1853; attended Pittsboro Academy and Donaldson Academy at Fayetteville; was graduated from the University of North Carolina at Chapel Hill in 1861; during the Civil War served as a private in the Fayetteville Independent Light Infantry Company, First North Carolina Regiment, and later as major in the Forty-fourth North Carolina Regiment; served with Lee's army during the entire war and was wounded three times; returned to Chatham County and taught school at Pittsboro one year; studied law; was admitted to the bar in 1865 and commenced practice in Wilmington, N. C., in 1867; delegate to the Democratic National Convention at Cincinnati in 1880, which nominated Winfield S. Hancock, of Pennsylvania, for President and William H. English, of Indiana, for Vice President; Lieutenant Governor of North Carolina 1884–1888; unsuccessful candidate for nomination as Governor in 1888 and again in 1903; moved to Asheville, N. C., in 1891, to Greensboro, N. C., in 1898, and continued the practice of law; president of the North Carolina Bar Association in 1900 and 1901; director of the North Carolina Railroad in 1909 and 1910, during which time he served as president; trustee of the University of North Carolina 1899–1915; director of the Guilford Battle Ground Company 1898–1917; elected as a Democrat to the Sixty-second and to the nine succeeding Congresses and served from March 4, 1911, until his death in Washington, D. C., September 23, 1930; interment in Cross Creek Cemetery, Fayetteville, N. C.

STEDMAN, William, a Representative from Massachusetts; born in Cambridge, Mass., January 21, 1765; was graduated from Harvard University in 1784; studied law; was admitted to the bar in 1787 and practiced in Lancaster, Charlestown, and Worcester; appointed justice of the peace in 1790; town clerk of Lancaster 1795–1800; member of the State house of representatives in 1802; executive chancellor of Lancaster, 1803–1807; elected as a Federalist to the Eighth and to the three succeeding Congresses and served from March 4, 1803, until his resignation July 16, 1810; clerk of Worcester County Courts 1810–1816; late in life moved to Newburyport, Essex County, Mass., where he died August 31, 1831; interment in Old Hill Burying Ground.

STEED, Thomas Jefferson, a Representative from Oklahoma; born on a farm near Rising Star, Eastland County, Tex., March 2, 1904; attended the public schools of Konawa, Okla.; connected with Oklahoma daily newspapers for twenty years, including four years as managing editor of Shawnee News and Star; enlisted during World War II on October 29, 1942, as a private in Antiaircraft Artillery and released from active duty in May 1944 with rank of second lieutenant; joined Office of War Information July 1, 1944, and served with information division in India-Burma Theater until December 1945; elected as a Democrat to the Eighty-first and to the five succeeding Congresses (January 3, 1949–January 3, 1961). *Reelected to the Eighty-seventh Congress.*

STEELE, George Washington, a Representative from Indiana; born near Connersville, Fayette County, Ind., December 13, 1839; attended the common schools and Ohio Wesleyan University at Delaware; studied law; was admitted to the bar and commenced practice in Hartford City, Ind.; during the Civil War enlisted in the Eighth Regiment, Indiana Volunteer Infantry, but due to a full quota, was mustered instead into the Twelfth Indiana Regiment on May 2, 1861, and served with this regiment and with the One Hundred and First Indiana Regiment until the close of the war, serving his first year in the Army of the Potomac and the other three years in the Army of the Cumberland and with Sherman in his march to the sea; mustered out as lieutenant colonel in July 1865; commissioned and served in the Fourteenth Regiment, United States Infantry, from February 23, 1866, to February 1, 1876; resigned and engaged in agricultural pursuits and pork packing until 1882; declined an appointment as director of the Union Pacific Railroad; first Governor of Oklahoma Territory in 1890 and 1891; elected as a Republican to the Forty-seventh and to the three succeeding Congresses (March 4, 1881–March 3, 1889); member of the Board of Managers of the National Military Home from April 21, 1890, to December 10, 1904; elected to the Fifty-fourth and to the three succeeding Congresses (March 4, 1895–March 3, 1903); governor of the National Military Home in Marion, Ind., from December 11, 1904, to May 31, 1915, when he resigned; died in Marion, Grant County, Ind., July 12, 1922; interment in Odd Fellows Cemetery.

STEELE, Henry Joseph, a Representative from Pennsylvania; born in Easton, Northampton County, Pa., May 10, 1860; attended the public schools, and was graduated from Stevens College of Business in 1875; studied law; was admitted to the bar on May 16, 1881, and commenced practice in Easton, Pa.; member of the board of education 1889–1893; city solicitor 1889–1895; delegate to the State constitutional convention in 1891; president of the Pennsylvania Bar Association in 1914; elected as a Democrat to the Sixty-fourth, Sixty-fifth, and Sixty-sixth Congresses (March 4, 1915–March 3, 1921); declined to be a candidate for renomination in 1920; resumed the practice of law in Easton, Pa.; served as a director of the Lehigh Valley Transit Co. and of the Pennsylvania Motor Co.; member of the board of trustees of Easton Hospital at the time of his death; died in Easton, Pa., March 19, 1933; interment in Easton Cemetery.

STEELE, John, a Representative from North Carolina; born in Salisbury, N. C., November 1, 1764; attended Clio's Nursery, near Statesville, N. C., and the English School, Salisbury, N. C.; farmer; assessor in 1784; town commissioner in 1787; member of the State house of commons in 1787, 1788, 1794, 1795, 1806, and 1811–1813; delegate to the Hillsborough convention in 1788; special commissioner from North Carolina to treat with the Cherokee and Chickasaw Indians from 1788 to 1790: elected as a Federalist to the First and Second Congresses (March 4, 1789–March 3, 1793); appointed Comptroller of the Treasury July 1, 1796; reappointed by both President John Adams and President Jefferson and served until December 15, 1802, when he resigned; member of the board of commissioners to determine the boundary line between North Carolina and Georgia 1805–1814; died August 14, 1815, in Salisbury, N. C., having been on the same day again elected to the State house of commons; interment in Chestnut Hill Cemetery.

STEELE, John Benedict, a Representative from New York; born in Delhi, N. Y., March 28, 1814; attended Delaware Academy at Delhi and was graduated in law from Williams College, Williamstown, Mass.; was admitted to the bar of Otsego County in 1839 and commenced practice in Cooperstown, N. Y.; district attorney of Otsego County 1841–1847; moved to Kingston in 1847; elected special judge of Ulster County in 1850; elected as a Democrat to the Thirty-seventh and Thirty-eighth Congresses (March 4, 1861–March 3, 1865); was an unsuccessful candidate for renomination in 1864 to the Thirty-ninth Congress; was again a candidate for the nomination in 1866, but died on the eve of the primary; was accidentally killed in Rondout, near Kingston, N. Y., September 24, 1866; interment in Wiltwyck Cemetery, Kingston, N. Y.

STEELE, John Nevett, a Representative from Maryland; born in Weston, Dorchester County, Md., February 22, 1796; resided on an estate called "Indian Town," near Vienna, Md.; completed preparatory studies; studied law; was admitted to the bar in 1819 and commenced practice in Dorchester County, Md.; member of the State house of delegates 1822–1824, 1829, and 1830; elected as a Whig to the Twenty-third Congress to fill the vacancy caused by the death of Littleton P. Dennis; reelected to the Twenty-fourth Congress and served from May 29, 1834, to March 3, 1837; unsuccessful Whig candidate for Governor of Maryland in 1838; engaged in agricultural pursuits; died in Cambridge, Md., August 13, 1853; interment in Christ Protestant Episcopal Church Cemetery.

STEELE, Leslie Jasper, a Representative from Georgia; born near Decatur, De Kalb County, Ga., November 21, 1868; attended the public and private schools of Decatur and was graduated from Emory College, Oxford, Ga., in 1893; taught school 1893–1898; was graduated from the law department of Georgia University, Athens, Ga., in 1899; was admitted to the bar the same year and commenced practice in Decatur, Ga.; member of the De Kalb County Board of Education 1902–1921; mayor of Decatur 1915–1920; served in the State house of representatives 1915–1919; city and county attorney 1921–1925; elected as a Democrat to the Seventieth and Seventy-first Congresses and served from March 4, 1927, until his death in Washington, D. C., on July 24, 1929; interment in Decatur Cemetery, Decatur, Ga.

STEELE, Thomas Jefferson, a Representative from Iowa; born near Rushville, Rush County, Ind., March 19, 1853; attended the public schools and Axline Seminary, Fairfax, Iowa; taught school in central and western Iowa; studied law at Sheldon, Iowa; engaged in the hardware business and in banking at Wayne, Nebr.; county clerk of Wayne County, Nebr., 1884–1886; moved to Sioux City, Iowa, in 1897 and became a livestock commission merchant; elected as a Democrat to the Sixty-fourth Congress (March 4, 1915–March 3, 1917); unsuccessfully contested the election of George C. Scott to the Sixty-fifth Congress; resumed business as commission merchant; unsuccessful candidate for election in 1918 to the Sixty-sixth Congress; died in Sioux City, Iowa, March 20, 1920; interment in Graceland Park Cemetery.

STEELE, Walter Leak, a Representative from North Carolina; born at Steeles Mills (later Littles Mills), near Rockingham, Richmond County, N. C., April 18, 1823; attended the common schools, Randolph-Macon College, Lynchburg, Va., and Wake Forest (N. C.) College; was graduated from the University of North Carolina at Chapel Hill in 1844; member of the State house of commons in 1846, 1848, 1850, and 1854; trustee of the University of North Carolina from 1852 until his death; served in the State senate in 1852 and 1858; delegate to the Democratic National Conventions at Charleston and Baltimore in 1860; secretary of the State convention in 1861 which passed the ordinance of secession; studied law; was admitted to the bar in 1865 and commenced practice in Rockingham, N. C.; presidential elector on the Democratic ticket of Tilden and Hendricks in 1876; elected as a Democrat to the Forty-fifth and Forty-sixth Congresses (March 4, 1877–March 3, 1881); declined to be a candidate for renomination in 1880 to the Forty-seventh Congress; engaged in cotton manufacturing and banking; died in Baltimore, Md., where he had undergone a surgical operation, on October 16, 1891; interment in Leak Cemetery, near Rockingham, Richmond County, N. C.

STEELE, William Gaston, a Representative from New Jersey; born in Somerville, Somerset County, N. J., December 17, 1820; attended the public schools and Somerville Academy; engaged in banking; elected as a Democrat to the Thirty-seventh and Thirty-eighth Congresses (March 4, 1861–March 3, 1865); engaged in the brokerage business; died in Somerville, Somerset County, N. J., April 22, 1892; interment in Somerville City Cemetery.

STEELE, William Randolph, a Delegate from the Territory of Wyoming; born in New York City, July 24, 1842; received an academic education; studied law; was admitted to the bar and practiced; during the Civil War served in the Second Army Corps from 1861 to 1865; discharged with the rank of captain and brevet lieutenant colonel; moved to the Territory of Wyoming in 1869 and engaged in the practice of law in Cheyenne; elected as a member of the Territorial legislative council in 1871 and served until March 4, 1873, when he resigned, having been elected to Congress; elected as a Democrat to the Forty-third and Forty-fourth Congresses (March 4, 1873–March 3, 1877); unsuccessful candidate for reelection in 1876 to the Forty-fifth Congress; moved to Deadwood, S. Dak., and resumed the practice of law; mayor of Deadwood 1894–1896; died in Deadwood November 30, 1901; interment in Mount Moriah Cemetery.

STEENERSON, Halvor, a Representative from Minnesota; born at Pleasant Springs, near Madison, Dane County, Wis., June 30, 1852; moved with his parents to Sheldon, Houston County, Minn., in 1853; attended the county schools and the high school in Rushford, Minn.; studied law at the Union College of Law in Chicago; was admitted to the bar in 1878 and commenced practice in Lanesboro, Minn.; moved to Crookston, Polk County, Minn., in 1880; prosecuting attorney of Polk County 1881–1883; city attorney of Crookston; member of the State senate 1883–1887; delegate to the Republican National Conventions at Chicago in 1884 and 1888; elected as a Republican to the Fifty-eighth and to the nine succeeding Congresses (March 4, 1903–March 3, 1923); unsuccessful candidate for reelection in 1922 to the Sixty-eighth Congress; vice president of the American group of the Interparliamentary Union; resumed the practice of law in Crookston, Minn., and died there November 22, 1926; interment in Oakdale Cemetery.

STEENROD, Lewis, a Representative from Virginia; born near Wheeling, Ohio County, Va. (now West Virginia), May 27, 1810; attended the common schools; studied law; was admitted to the bar in 1835 and commenced practice in Wheeling; elected as a Democrat to the Twenty-sixth, Twenty-seventh, and Twenty-eighth Congresses (March 4, 1839–March 3, 1845); served in the State senate from 1853 to 1856; resumed the practice of his profession; died near Wheeling, Ohio County, W. Va., October 3, 1862; interment in Stone Church Cemetery, Elm Grove, W. Va.

STEFAN, Karl, a Representative from Nebraska; born on a farm near Zebrakov, Bohemia, March 1, 1884; immigrated to the United States in 1885 with his parents, who settled in Omaha, Douglas County, Nebr.; attended the public schools in Omaha, Nebr., and later the Y.M.C.A. night school; private in the Illinois National Guard; lieutenant in the Nebraska National Guard; served as inspector of telegraph in Philippine Constabulary 1904–1906; moved to Norfolk, Nebr., in 1909; instructor, Morse and Continental codes, during the First World War; served as telegrapher and later as city editor of the Norfolk Daily News until 1924; radio commentator and contributor to newspapers and magazines until 1934; president of the Stefan Co., publishers' agent for magazines and newspapers; member of congressional committee aiding inauguration of Philippine Commonwealth Government, Manila, P. I., 1935; delegate to the Interparliamentary Union, Oslo, Norway, in 1939; official adviser, United Nations Conference, San Francisco, Calif., in 1945; elected as a Republican to the Seventy-fourth and to the eight succeeding Congresses and served from January 3, 1935, until his death in Washington, D. C., October 2, 1951; interment in Prospect Hill Cemetery, Norfolk, Nebr.

STEIWER, Frederick, a Senator from Oregon; born on a farm near Jefferson, Marion County, Oreg., October 13, 1883; attended the public schools; was graduated from Oregon State Agricultural College at Corvallis in 1902 and from the University of Oregon at Eugene in 1906; studied law; was admitted to the bar in 1908 and commenced practice in Pendleton, Umatilla County, in 1909; also interested in agricultural pursuits; deputy district attorney in 1909 and 1910 and district attorney 1912–1916; member of the State senate in 1916 and 1917; enlisted in the United States Army during the First World War and served from August 1917 to March 1919 in the Sixty-fifth Field Artillery, with rank of first lieutenant; elected as a Republican to the United States Senate in 1926; reelected in 1932 and served from March 4, 1927, until January 31, 1938, when he resigned; delegate to the Republican National Convention in Cleveland in 1936; continued the practice of law in Washington, D. C., until his death there February 3, 1939; interment in Arlington National Cemetery, Fort Myer, Va.

STENGER, William Shearer, a Representative from Pennsylvania; born in Fort London, Franklin County, Pa., February 13, 1840; attended the public schools; was graduated from Franklin and Marshall College, Lancaster, Pa., in 1858; studied law; was admitted to the bar in 1860 and commenced practice in Chambersburg, Pa.; executive director of the Philadelphia Record; district attorney of Franklin County 1862–1871; elected as a Democrat to the Forty-fourth and Forty-fifth Congresses (March 4, 1875–March 3, 1879); unsuccessful candidate for reelection in 1878 to the Forty-sixth Congress; resumed the practice of his profession; secretary of the Commonwealth of Pennsylvania 1883–1887; died in Philadelphia, Pa., March 29, 1918; interment in Falling Spring Presbyterian Church Cemetery.

STENGLE, Charles Irwin, a Representative from New York; born in Savageville, Accomack County, Va., December 5, 1869; attended the public schools; was graduated from Goldey College, Wilmington, Del., in 1890; chaplain of the Delaware House of Representatives in 1898; engaged in newspaper work in Norfolk and Fredericksburg, Va., and in New York City 1910–1917; secretary of the municipal civil service commission of New York City from January 1, 1918, to January 1, 1923, when he resigned; lecturer in favor of pensions for disabled Federal civil employees; elected as a Democrat to the Sixty-eighth Congress (March 4, 1923–March 3, 1925); was not a candidate for renomination in 1924 to the Sixty-ninth Congress; appointed by President

Coolidge in 1925 as a lieutenant colonel, Specialist Reserves, attached to The Adjutant General's Office; editor of the National Farm News; legislative representative of the American Federation of Government Employees from 1934 until his retirement in August 1953; died at Shaftos Corner, New Shrewsbury, N. J., November 23, 1953; interment in Monmouth Memorial Park.

STENNIS, John Cornelius, a Senator from Mississippi; born near De Kalb, Kemper County, Miss., August 3, 1901; attended the county schools; was graduated from Kemper County Agricultural High School, Scooba, Miss., in 1919, from Mississippi State College in 1923, and from the law department of the University of Virginia at Charlottesville in 1928; was admitted to the bar in 1928 and commenced practice in De Kalb, Miss.; member of the State house of representatives 1928–1932; district prosecuting attorney 1932–1937; circuit judge 1937–1947; delegate to the Democratic National Convention at Philadelphia in 1948; elected as a Democrat to the United States Senate on November 4, 1947, to fill the vacancy caused by the death of Theodore G. Bilbo and served from November 5, 1947, to January 3, 1953; reelected in 1952 and again in 1958 for the term ending January 3, 1965.

STEPHENS, Abraham P., a Representative from New York; born near New City, Rockland County, N. Y., February 18, 1796; justice of the peace; elected as a Democrat to the Thirty-second Congress (March 4, 1851–March 3, 1853); died in Nyack, Rockland County, N. Y., November 25, 1859; interment in Oak Hill Cemetery.

STEPHENS, Alexander Hamilton, a Representative from Georgia; born near Crawfordville, Taliaferro County, Ga., on February 11, 1812; attended private and public schools; was graduated from the University of Georgia at Athens in 1832; taught school eighteen months; studied law; was admitted to the bar in Crawfordville in 1834; member of the State house of representatives 1836–1841; served in the State senate in 1842; elected to the Twenty-eighth Congress to fill the vacancy caused by the resignation of Mark A. Cooper; reelected to the Twenty-ninth and to the six succeeding Congresses and served from October 2, 1843, to March 3, 1859; was not a candidate for renomination in 1858; presidential elector on the Democratic ticket of Douglas and Johnson in 1860; successively supported Harrison, Clay, Taylor, Pierce, and Buchanan for the Presidency; member of the secession convention of Georgia in 1861, which elected him to the Confederate Congress, and was chosen by that Congress as Vice President of the provisional government; elected Vice President of the Confederacy; one of the commissioners representing the Confederacy at the Hampton Roads conference in February 1865; after the Civil War was imprisoned in Fort Warren, Boston Harbor, for five months, until October 1865; elected to the United States Senate in 1866 by the first legislature convened under the new State constitution, but did not present his credentials, as the State had not been readmitted to representation; elected as a Democrat to the Forty-third Congress to fill the vacancy caused by the death of Ambrose R. Wright; reelected to the Forty-fourth and to the three succeeding Congresses and served from December 1, 1873, until his resignation November 4, 1882; elected Governor of Georgia in 1882 and served until his death in Atlanta, Ga., March 4, 1883; interment in a vault in Oakland Cemetery; reinterment on his estate, "Liberty Hall," near Crawfordville, Ga.

STEPHENS, Ambrose Everett Burnside, a Representative from Ohio; born in Crosby Township, Hamilton County, Ohio, June 3, 1862; attended the public schools, and Chickering's Institute of Cincinnati; studied law; was admitted to the bar

in 1902 and commenced practice in Cincinnati; captain in the Ohio National Guard 1901–1903 and colonel in 1910 and 1911; clerk of the Hamilton County Courts 1911–1917; commander in chief of the Sons of Veterans in 1915 and 1916; elected as a Republican to the Sixty-sixth and to the three succeeding Congresses and served from March 4, 1919, until his death; had been reelected to the Seventieth Congress; died in North Bend, Ohio, February 12, 1927; interment in Maple Grove Cemetery, Cleves, Hamilton County, Ohio.

STEPHENS, Dan Voorhees, a Representative from Nebraska; born in Bloomington, Monroe County, Ind., on November 4, 1868; attended the common schools and Valparaiso College, Indiana; settled in Fremont, Dodge County, Nebr., in 1887; studied law; taught school; county superintendent of schools in Dodge County 1890–1894; author of books on education; engaged in agricultural pursuits, manufacturing, publishing, and banking; delegate to the Democratic National Conventions in 1904, 1908, 1920, 1924, and 1932; elected as a Democrat to the Sixty-second Congress to fill the vacancy caused by the death of James P. Latta; elected to the Sixty-third, Sixty-fourth, and Sixty-fifth Congresses and served from November 7, 1911, to March 3, 1919; unsuccessful candidate for reelection in 1918 to the Sixty-sixth Congress; resumed his former business pursuits; member of the State board of education of Nebraska 1923–1926; died in Fremont, Nebr., January 13, 1939, and the remains were cremated.

STEPHENS, Hubert Durrett, a Representative and a Senator from Mississippi; born in New Albany, Union County, Miss., July 2, 1875; attended the public schools, and was graduated from the law department of the University of Mississippi at Oxford in 1896; was admitted to the bar the same year and commenced practice in New Albany; district attorney for the second district of Mississippi 1907–1910; elected as a Democrat to the Sixty-second and to the four succeeding Congresses (March 4, 1911–March 3, 1921); was not a candidate for reelection in 1920 to the Sixty-seventh Congress; resumed the practice of law in New Albany; elected to the United States Senate in 1922; reelected in 1928 and served from March 4, 1923, to January 3, 1935; unsuccessful candidate for renomination in 1934; served as a director of the Reconstruction Finance Corporation in 1935 and 1936; continued the practice of law in Washington, D. C., until 1941, when he retired to his farm in Union County, Miss., and engaged in agricultural pursuits; died March 14, 1946, at his country home near New Albany, Miss.; interment in Pythian Cemetery.

STEPHENS, John Hall, a Representative from Texas; was born in Shelby County, Tex., on November 22, 1847; attended the common schools in Mansfield, Tarrant County, Tex.; was graduated from Mansfield College, and from the law department of Cumberland University, Lebanon, Tenn., in 1872; was admitted to the bar in 1873 and practiced in Montague, Montague County, and Vernon, Wilbarger County, Tex.; member of the State senate 1886–1888; resumed the practice of law in Vernon, Tex.; elected as a Democrat to the Fifty-fifth and to the nine succeeding Congresses (March 4, 1897–March 3, 1917); unsuccessful candidate for renomination in 1916; moved to Monrovia, Los Angeles County, Calif., in 1917, and died there November 18, 1924; interment in East View Cemetery, Vernon, Tex.

STEPHENS, Philander, a Representative from Pennsylvania; born near Montrose, Susquehanna County, Pa., in 1788; received a limited education; engaged in agricultural and mercantile pursuits; coroner in 1815; county commissioner in 1818; sheriff in 1821; member of the State house of representatives in 1824 and

1825; elected as a Jacksonian Democrat to the Twenty-first and Twenty-second Congresses (March 4, 1829–March 3, 1833); was not a candidate for renomination in 1832; resumed agricultural and mercantile pursuits; died probably in Springville, Susquehanna County, Pa., July 8, 1842; interment in Stephens Burying Ground, Dimock Township, Susquehanna County, Pa.

STEPHENS, William Dennison, a Representative from California; born in Eaton, Preble County, Ohio, December 26, 1859; attended the public schools and was graduated from Eaton High School; taught country school; studied law; engaged in the construction and operation of railroads in Ohio, Indiana, Iowa, and Louisiana 1880–1887; moved to Los Angeles, Calif., in 1887; engaged in the wholesale and retail grocery business 1888–1909; was a member of the board of education in 1906; major and commissary of the First Brigade, California National Guard, 1904–1914; president of the Los Angeles Chamber of Commerce in 1907; mayor of Los Angeles in 1909; elected as a Republican to the Sixty-second, Sixty-third, and Sixty-fourth Congresses and served from March 4, 1911, to July 22, 1916, when he resigned, having been appointed Lieutenant Governor of California; served as Lieutenant Governor from January 2 to March 15, 1917, when he became Governor; Governor of California 1917–1923; was admitted to the bar in 1920; resided in Los Angeles, Calif., until his death on April 25, 1944; interment in Rosedale Cemetery.

STEPHENSON, Benjamin, a Delegate from Illinois Territory; born in Kentucky; moved to Illinois Territory in 1809 and settled in Randolph County; appointed as the first sheriff of Randolph County by Governor Edwards June 28, 1809; moved to Edwardsville, Madison County, and engaged in the general mercantile business; appointed adjutant general of the Territory in 1813; served as a colonel in two campaigns during the War of 1812; elected on September 3, 1814, as a Democrat to Congress for a term of two years (Thirteenth and Fourteenth Congresses); was not a candidate for renomination in 1816; served as receiver of public moneys in the land office at Edwardsville from April 29, 1816, until his death; delegate to the convention in 1818 which framed the first State constitution; president of the Bank of Edwardsville in 1819; died in Edwardsville, Ill., October 10, 1822.

STEPHENSON, Isaac (brother of Samuel Merritt Stephenson), a Representative and a Senator from Wisconsin; born in Yorkton near Fredericton, in York County, New Brunswick, Canada, June 18, 1829; attended the common schools for a time and helped his father, who was a farmer and lumberman; when fourteen years of age, moved to Bangor, Maine, and thence to Milwaukee, Wis., in 1845; engaged in lumber pursuits in Escanaba, Mich.; moved to Marinette in 1858 and enlarged his business activities to include every phase of lumbering; held various local offices; member of the Wisconsin State Assembly in 1866 and 1868; founder and president of the Stephenson Banking Co. in 1873; delegate to the Republican National Conventions in 1880 and 1892; elected as a Republican to the Forty-eighth, Forty-ninth, and Fiftieth Congresses (March 4, 1883–March 3, 1889); was not a candidate for renomination in 1888; resumed the lumber business in Marinette, Wis.; elected in 1907 as a Republican to the United States Senate to fill the vacancy caused by the resignation of John C. Spooner; reelected in 1909 and served from May 17, 1907, to March 3, 1915; died in Marinette, Wis., on March 15, 1918; interment in Forest Home Cemetery.

STEPHENSON, James, a Representative from Virginia; born in Gettysburg, Pa., March 20, 1764; moved to Martinsburg, Va. (now West Virginia); volunteer rifleman under General St. Clair in his Indian expedition in 1791; brigade inspector; member of the State house of delegates 1800–1803; elected as a Federalist to the Eighth Congress (March 4, 1803–March 3, 1805); again a member of the State house of delegates in 1806 and 1807; elected to the Eleventh Congress (March 4, 1809–March 3, 1811); elected to the Seventeenth Congress to fill the vacancy caused by the death of Thomas Van Swearingen; reelected to the Eighteenth Congress and served from October 28, 1822, to March 3, 1825; died in Martinsburg, Va. (now West Virginia), August 7, 1833.

STEPHENSON, Samuel Merritt (brother of Isaac Stephenson), a Representative from Michigan; born in Hartland, in Carleton County, New Brunswick, Canada, December 23, 1831; moved with his parents to Maine, and later, in 1846, to Delta County, Mich., and engaged in lumbering; moved to Menominee, Mich., in 1858; interested in real estate, lumbering, general merchandising, and agricultural pursuits; was chairman of the board of supervisors of Menominee County for several years; member of the State house of representatives in 1877 and 1878; served in the State senate in 1879, 1880, 1885, and 1886; presidential elector on the Republican ticket of Garfield and Arthur in 1880; delegate to the Republican National Conventions at Chicago in 1884 and 1888; elected as a Republican to the Fifty-first and to the three succeeding Congresses (March 4, 1889–March 3, 1897); resumed the lumber business; died in Menominee, Mich., July 31, 1907; interment in Riverside Cemetery.

STERETT, Samuel, a Representative from Maryland; born in Carlisle, Pa., in 1758; moved with his parents to Baltimore, Md., in 1761; completed preparatory studies; was graduated from the University of Pennsylvania at Philadelphia; held several local offices; member of the independent company (military) of Baltimore merchants in 1777; appointed private secretary to the President of Congress in November 1782; member of the State senate in 1789; elected as an Anti-Federalist to the Second Congress (March 4, 1791–March 3, 1793); secretary of the Maryland Society for Promoting the Abolition of Slavery in 1791; member of the Baltimore committee of safety in 1812; served as captain of an independent company at the Battle of North Point September 12, 1814; wounded at the Battle of Bladensburg; grand marshal at Baltimore at the laying of the foundation stone of the Baltimore & Ohio Railroad, July 4, 1828; died in Baltimore, Md., July 12, 1833; interment in the burying ground of Westminster Church.

STERIGERE, John Benton, a Representative from Pennsylvania; born in Upper Dublin Township, near Ambler, Montgomery County, Pa., July 31, 1793; worked on a farm and attended school; taught at Puffs Church School; appointed justice of the peace in 1818; member of the State house of representatives 1821–1824; studied law; was admitted to the bar November 17, 1829, and commenced practice in Norristown, Pa.; elected as a Democrat to the Twentieth and Twenty-first Congresses (March 4, 1827–March 3, 1831); delegate to the State convention to revise the constitution in 1838; member of the State senate 1839 and 1843–1846; delegate to the Democratic National Convention at Baltimore in 1852; retired from public life and edited the Register; appointed by the State assembly as chairman of a commission to improve the town of Norristown; died in Norristown, Montgomery County, Pa., October 13, 1852; interment in Upper Dublin Lutheran Church Cemetery, Ambler, Pa.

STERLING, Ansel (brother of Micah Sterling), a Representative from Connecticut; born in Lyme, New London County, Conn., February 3, 1782; attended the common schools; studied law; was admitted to the bar in 1805 and commenced practice in Salisbury, Conn.; moved to Sharon, Litchfield County, in 1808 and continued the practice of his profession; member of the

State house of representatives in 1815, 1818–1821, 1825, 1826, 1829, and 1835–1837, and served as clerk of the house in the sessions of 1815 and 1818–1820; elected to the Seventeenth and Eighteenth Congresses (March 4, 1821–March 3, 1825); resumed legal practice; chief justice of the court of common pleas of Litchfield County 1838–1840; died in Sharon, Conn., November 6, 1853; interment in Sharon Burying Ground.

STERLING, Bruce Foster, a Representative from Pennsylvania; born in Masontown, Fayette County, Pa., September 28, 1870; attended the public schools of Masontown and the California State Normal School, California, Pa.; was graduated from the University of West Virginia at Morgantown in 1895; studied law; was admitted to the bar in 1896 and commenced practice in Uniontown, Pa.; member of the State house of representatives in 1906; delegate to the Democratic National Conventions in 1912, 1920, and 1924; elected as a Democrat to the Sixty-fifth Congress (March 4, 1917–March 3, 1919); unsuccessful candidate for reelection in 1918 to the Sixty-sixth Congress; resumed the practice of law; elected register of wills and clerk of the orphans court of Fayette County, Pa., in 1935, 1939, and 1943; died at Uniontown, Pa., on April 26, 1945; interment in Oak Grove Cemetery.

STERLING, John Allen (brother of Thomas Sterling), a Representative from Illinois; born near Le Roy, McLean County, Ill., February 1, 1857; attended the public schools, and was graduated from the Illinois Wesleyan University at Bloomington in 1881; superintendent of the public schools of Lexington, Ill., 1881–1883; studied law; was admitted to the bar in December 1884 and commenced practice in Bloomington, Ill.; State's attorney of McLean County 1892–1896; member of the Republican State central committee 1896–1898; elected as a Republican to the Fifty-eighth and to the four succeeding Congresses (March 4, 1903–March 3, 1913); one of the managers appointed by the House of Representatives in 1912 to conduct the impeachment proceedings against Robert W. Archbald, judge of the United States Commerce Court; unsuccessful candidate for reelection to the Sixty-third Congress; elected to the Sixty-fourth and Sixty-fifth Congresses and served from March 4, 1915, until his death near Pontiac, Ill., as the result of an automobile accident, October 17, 1918; interment in Park Hill Cemetery, Bloomington, Ill.

STERLING, Micah (brother of Ansel Sterling), a Representative from New York; born in Lyme, Conn., November 5, 1784; was graduated from Yale College in 1804; studied law at the Litchfield (Conn.) Law School; was admitted to the bar in 1809 and commenced the practice of law in Adams, Jefferson County, N. Y.; moved to Watertown, N. Y., in 1809 and continued the practice of his profession; held several local offices; treasurer of the village of Watertown in 1816; served as a director of the Jefferson County Bank; elected as a Federalist to the Seventeenth Congress (March 4, 1821–March 3, 1823); resumed the practice of law; member of the State senate 1836–1839; died in Watertown, N. Y., April 11, 1844; interment in Brookside Cemetery.

STERLING, Thomas (brother of John Allen Sterling), a Senator from South Dakota; born near Amanda, Fairfield County, Ohio, February 21, 1851; moved with his parents to McLean County, Ill., in 1854; attended the public schools, and was graduated from Illinois Wesleyan University at Bloomington in 1875; superintendent of schools of Bement, Ill., 1875–1877; studied law; was admitted to the bar in 1878 and commenced practice in Springfield, Ill.; city prosecuting attorney in 1880 and 1881; moved to the Territory of Dakota and located in Northville, Spink County, in 1882; moved to Redfield in 1886 and continued the practice of law; district attorney of Spink County, Dak., 1886–1888; member of the State constitutional convention in 1889; member of the State senate in 1890; dean of the college of law of the University of South Dakota at Vermillion 1901–1911; elected in 1913 as a Republican to the United States Senate; reelected in 1918, and served from March 4, 1913, to March 3, 1925; unsuccessful candidate for renomination in 1924; engaged in the practice of law in Washington, D. C., and also served on the faculty of National University Law School; appointed by President Coolidge in 1925 as field secretary of the Commission for the Celebration of the Two Hundredth Anniversary of the Birth of George Washington; died in Washington, D. C., August 26, 1930; interment in Cedar Hill Cemetery.

STETSON, Charles, a Representative from Maine; born in New Ipswich, Hillsborough County, N. H., November 2, 1801; moved with his parents to Hampden, Penobscot County, Maine, in 1802; attended Hampden Academy, and was graduated from Yale College in 1823; studied law; was admitted to the bar and commenced practice in Hampden in 1826; admitted to the bar of the United States Supreme Court in 1828; held various local offices; moved to Bangor, Maine, in 1833; judge of the Bangor Municipal Court 1834–1839; member of the common council of Bangor in 1843 and 1844; member of the State executive council 1845–1848; elected as a Democrat to the Thirty-first Congress (March 4, 1849–March 3, 1851); unsuccessful candidate for renomination in 1850 to the Thirty-second Congress; resumed the practice of his profession; affiliated with the Republican Party in 1860; died in Bangor, Maine, March 27, 1863; interment in Mount Hope Cemetery.

STETSON, Lemuel, a Representative from New York; born in Champlain, Clinton County, N. Y., March 13, 1804; attended the public schools and Plattsburg Academy; studied law; was admitted to the bar in 1824 and commenced practice in Keeseville, Essex County, N. Y.; member of the State assembly in 1835, 1836, and 1842; district attorney of Clinton County 1838–1843; elected as a Democrat to the Twenty-eighth Congress (March 4, 1843–March 3, 1845); member of the State constitutional convention in 1846; again a member of the State assembly in 1846; moved to Plattsburg, N. Y., in 1847; judge of Clinton County 1847–1851; delegate to the Democratic National Convention at Baltimore in 1860; resumed the practice of law; died in Plattsburg, N. Y., May 17, 1868; interment in Riverside Cemetery.

STEVENS, Aaron Fletcher, a Representative from New Hampshire; born in Londonderry, Rockingham County, N. H., August 9, 1819; attended Pinkerton Academy, Derry, N. H., and Crosby's Nashua Literary Institute, Nashua, N. H.; at the age of sixteen was apprenticed to the trade of machinist and worked as a journeyman for several years; studied law; was admitted to the bar and commenced practice in Nashua, Hillsborough County, N. H.; member of the State house of representatives in 1845; held several local offices; during the Civil War served in the Union Army as major of the First Regiment, New Hampshire Volunteer Infantry, as colonel of the Thirteenth New Hampshire Volunteer Infantry, and was brevetted brigadier general; delegate to the Whig National Convention at Baltimore in 1852; president of the common council of Nashua in 1853 and 1854; solicitor of Hillsborough County 1856–1861; city solicitor of Nashua in 1859, 1860, 1865, 1872, and 1875–1877; elected as a Republican to the Fortieth and Forty-first Congresses (March 4, 1867–March 3, 1871); unsuccessful candidate for reelection in 1870 to the

Forty-second Congress; again a member of the State house of representatives 1876–1884; resumed the practice of law; died in Nashua, N. H., May 10, 1887; interment in Nashua Cemetery.

STEVENS, Bradford Newcomb, a Representative from Illinois; born in Boscawen, Merrimack County, N. H., January 3, 1813; attended schools in New Hampshire and at Montreal, Canada, and was graduated from Dartmouth College, Hanover, N. H., in 1835; taught school six years in Hopkinsville, Ky., and New York City; moved to Bureau County, Ill., in 1846; engaged in mercantile and agricultural pursuits; county surveyor; mayor of Tiskilwa, Ill.; elected as an Independent Democrat to the Forty-second Congress (March 4, 1871–March 3, 1873); resumed mercantile and agricultural pursuits; died in Tiskilwa, Bureau County, Ill., November 10, 1885; interment in Mount Bloom Cemetery.

STEVENS, Charles Abbot (brother of Moses Tyler Stevens and cousin of Isaac Ingalls Stevens), a Representative from Massachusetts; born in North Andover (then a part of Andover), Essex County, Mass., August 9, 1816; attended Franklin Academy at North Andover; manufacturer of flannels and broadcloths at Ware, Hampshire County, Mass., in 1841; member of the State house of representatives in 1853; delegate to the Republican National Conventions at Chicago in 1860 and 1868; served as a member of the Governor's council 1867–1870; unsuccessful for election in 1874 to the Forty-fourth Congress; was subsequently elected as a Republican to the Forty-third Congress to fill the vacancy caused by the death of Alvah Crocker and served from January 27 to March 3, 1875; resumed the manufacturing business; died in New York City, N. Y., April 7, 1892; interment in Aspen Grove Cemetery, Ware, Mass.

STEVENS, Frederick Clement, a Representative from Minnesota; born in Boston, Mass., January 1, 1861; moved with his parents to Searsport, Maine; attended the common schools of Rockland; was graduated from Bowdoin College, Brunswick, Maine, in 1881 and from the law department of the University of Iowa at Iowa City in 1884; was admitted to the bar in 1884 and commenced practice in St. Paul, Minn.; member of the State house of representatives 1888–1891; elected as a Republican to the Fifty-fifth and to the eight succeeding Congresses (March 4, 1897–March 3, 1915); unsuccessful candidate for reelection in 1914 to the Sixty-fourth Congress; engaged in the practice of law until his death in St. Paul, Minn., July 1, 1923; interment in Oakland Cemetery.

STEVENS, Hestor Lockhart, a Representative from Michigan; born in Lima, Livingston County, N. Y., October 1, 1803; attended the common schools; studied law; was admitted to the bar and commenced practice in Rochester, N. Y.; major general of militia of western New York; moved to Pontiac, Mich.; elected as a Democrat to the Thirty-third Congress (March 4, 1853–March 3, 1855); resumed the practice of law in Washington, D. C.; died in Georgetown, D. C., May 7, 1864; interment in Oak Hill Cemetery.

STEVENS, Hiram Sanford, a Delegate from the Territory of Arizona; born in Weston, Windsor County, Vt., March 20, 1832; received a limited education; farmer; in 1851 enlisted in Company I, First United States Dragoons for service in New Mexico; participated in engagements against the Apaches in 1852 and 1854; honorably discharged at Fort Thorn, N. Mex., in 1856, moving to Tucson, Ariz., where he engaged in general merchandising and the supplying of forage for the Army; elected to the Arizona Territorial House of Representatives in 1868; served in the Territorial council 1871–1873; assessor and supervisor of Pima County; served as treasurer of Tucson in 1871; elected as a Democrat to the Forty-fourth and Forty-fifth Congresses (March 4, 1875–March 3, 1879); unsuccessful candidate for renomination in 1878; engaged in mercantile pursuits and cattle growing; died in Tucson, Ariz., March 22, 1893; interment in Old Tucson Cemetery; reinterment in Evergreen Cemetery.

STEVENS, Isaac Ingalls (cousin of Charles Abbot Stevens and Moses Tyler Stevens), a Delegate from the Territory of Washington; born in North Andover (then a part of Andover), Essex County, Mass., March 25, 1818; attended Phillips Academy, Andover, Mass., and was graduated from the United States Military Academy at West Point at the head of the class in 1839; entered the Corps of Engineers and served on the staff of General Scott in Mexico; assistant in charge of the Coast Survey Office in Washington, D. C.; organized and commanded the northern Pacific exploration party which explored and surveyed the route for a railway from St. Paul to Puget Sound in 1853; resigned his commission as major in the Corps of Engineers to become Governor; Governor of the Territory of Washington from 1853 to 1857; was a candidate for the Democratic nomination to Congress in 1855, but withdrew; elected as a Democrat to the Thirty-fifth and Thirty-sixth Congresses (March 4, 1857–March 3, 1861); was not a candidate for renomination in 1860; delegate to the Democratic National Conventions at Charleston in April 1860 and at Baltimore in June 1860; during the Civil War entered the Union Army as a colonel of the Seventy-ninth New York Highlanders; appointed brigadier general and later major general in command of a division; killed at the Battle of Chantilly, Virginia, September 1, 1862; interment in Island Cemetery, Newport, R. I.

STEVENS, James, a Representative from Connecticut; born in that part of Stamford (Ponus Street) which is now the town of New Canaan, Fairfield County, Conn., July 4, 1768; studied law; was admitted to the bar and commenced practice in Stamford, Conn.; member of the State house of representatives 1804, 1805, 1808–1810, 1814, 1815, 1817, and 1818; judge of probate, Stamford district, in 1819; elected as a Democrat to the Sixteenth Congress (March 4, 1819–March 3, 1821); justice of the peace at Stamford 1819–1826; postmaster of Stamford, Conn., from May 17, 1822 to October 5, 1829; judge of Fairfield County Court in 1823; resumed the practice of law in Stamford, Conn., and died there April 4, 1835; interment in St. John's and St. Andrew's Episcopal Cemetery.

STEVENS, John, a Delegate from New Jersey; born in Perth Amboy, N. J., in 1715; merchant and shipowner; engaged in trading with the West Indies and Madeira; large landowner and mine owner in Hunterdon, Union, and Somerset Counties; member of the general colonial assembly in 1751; during the French and Indian War was active in raising troops and money for Crown Point in 1755; helped build blockhouses at Drake's Fort, Normenach, and Philipsburg; was a member of the defense committee to protect New York and New Jersey against Indian depredations; commissioner to the Indians in 1758; paymaster of Colonel Schuyler's regiment, the "Old Blues," 1756–1760; as a resident of New York City in 1765 was one of the committee of four who prevented the issue of stamps under the infamous stamp act; in 1774 was appointed a commissioner to define the boundary line between New York and New Jersey; vice president of the council of New Jersey 1770–1782; served as president of the council of East Jersey proprietors in 1783; Member of the Continental Congress in 1783 and 1784; presided over the State constitutional convention December 18, 1787; died in Hoboken, Hudson County, N. J., May 10, 1792; interment in the Frame Meeting House Cemetery, Hunterdon County, N. J.

STEVENS, Moses Tyler (brother of Charles Abbot Stevens and cousin of Isaac Ingalls Stevens), a Representative from Massachusetts; born in North Andover (then a part of Andover), Essex County, Mass., October 10, 1825; attended Franklin Academy at North Andover; was graduated from Phillips Academy, Andover, in 1842; attended Dartmouth College, Hanover, N. H., in 1842 and 1843; engaged in the manufacture of woolen goods in North Andover; served as president of the Andover National Bank; member of the Massachusetts State House of Representatives in 1861; served in the Massachusetts State Senate in 1868; elected as a Democrat to the Fifty-second and Fifty-third Congresses (March 4, 1891–March 3, 1895); was not a candidate for renomination in 1894 to the Fifty-fourth Congress; resumed his interests in the manufacturing business; died in North Andover, Mass., March 25, 1907; interment in Ridgewood Cemetery.

STEVENS, Raymond Bartlett, a Representative from New Hampshire; born in Binghamton, Broome County, N. Y., June 18, 1874; moved with his parents to Lisbon, Grafton County, N. H., in 1876; attended the public schools, Boston Latin School, Harvard University, and Harvard Law School; was admitted to the bar in 1899 and commenced practice in Lisbon, N. H.; member of the State house of representatives in 1909, 1911, 1913, and 1923; member of the State constitutional convention in 1912; elected as a Democrat to the Sixty-third Congress (March 4, 1913–March 3, 1915); was not a candidate for renomination in 1914, having become a candidate for Senator; unsuccessful candidate for election to the United States Senate in 1914; special counsel of the Federal Trade Commission 1915–1917; United States representative to the Allied Maritime Transport Council in 1917 and 1918; vice chairman of the United States Shipping Board 1917–1920; delegate to the Democratic National Conventions in 1920 and 1924; appointed adviser in foreign affairs to the King of Siam in January 1926, in which capacity he served until 1935, except for a six-month period during 1933 when he was a member of the Federal Trade Commission; member of the Federal Tariff Commission 1935–1942, serving as chairman 1937–1942; died at Indianapolis, Ind., May 18, 1942; interment on the grounds of the family residence at Landaff, N. H.

STEVENS, Robert Smith, a Representative from New York; born in Attica, Wyoming County, N. Y., March 27, 1824; prepared for college under a tutor; pursued an academic course; studied law; was admitted to the bar in 1846; moved to Kansas, and engaged in the practice of law; subsequently became extensively interested in real estate, in the development of coal lands, and in the management and building of railroads; member of the State house of representatives; retired from active business pursuits in 1880 and returned to New York; engaged in agricultural pursuits; elected as a Democrat to the Forty-eighth Congress (March 4, 1883–March 3, 1885); unsuccessful candidate for reelection in 1884 to the Forty-ninth Congress; after the expiration of his term in Congress retired from public life because of ill health; resumed agricultural pursuits; died in Attica, Wyoming County, N. Y., on February 23, 1893; interment in Forest Hill Cemetery.

STEVENS, Thaddeus, a Representative from Pennsylvania; born in Danville, Caledonia County, Vt. April 4, 1792; attended Peacham Academy and the University of Vermont at Burlington; was graduated from Dartmouth College, Hanover, N. H., in 1814; moved to Pennsylvania in 1814; studied law; was admitted to the bar in 1816 and commenced practice in Gettysburg; member of the State house of representatives 1833–1835, 1837, and 1841; delegate to the State constitutional convention in 1838; appointed as a canal commissioner in 1838; moved to Lancaster, Pa., in 1842; elected as a Whig to the Thirty-first and Thirty-second Congresses (March 4, 1849–March 3, 1853); elected as a Republican to the Thirty-sixth and to the four succeeding Congresses and served from March 4, 1859, until his death; chairman of the managers appointed by the House of Representatives in 1868 to conduct the impeachment proceedings against Andrew Johnson, President of the United States; died in Washington, D. C., on August 11, 1868; interment in Shreiner's Cemetery, Lancaster, Pa.

STEVENSON, Adlai Ewing, a Representative from Illinois and a Vice President of the United States; born in Christian County, Ky., October 23, 1835; moved with his parents to Bloomington, Ill., in 1852; attended Illinois Wesleyan University at Bloomington and Centre College, Danville, Ky.; studied law; was admitted to the bar in 1858 and commenced practice in Metamora, Woodford County, Ill.; master in chancery 1860–1864; presidential elector on the Democratic ticket of McClellan and Pendleton in 1864; district attorney 1865–1868; elected as a Democrat to the Forty-fourth Congress (March 4, 1875–March 3, 1877); unsuccessful candidate for reelection in 1876 to the Forty-fifth Congress; elected to the Forty-sixth Congress (March 4, 1879–March 3, 1881); unsuccessful candidate for reelection in 1880 to the Forty-seventh Congress; delegate to the Democratic National Conventions at Chicago in 1884 and 1892; First Assistant Postmaster General 1885–1889; elected Vice President of the United States on the Democratic ticket headed by Grover Cleveland; was inaugurated March 4, 1893, and served until March 3, 1897; member of the commission to Europe in 1897 to try to secure international bimetallism; was an unsuccessful Democratic candidate for Vice President of the United States in 1900 and for Governor of Illinois in 1908; retired from public and political activities and resided in Bloomington, Ill.; died in Chicago, Ill., June 14, 1914; interment in Bloomington Cemetery, Bloomington, Ill.

STEVENSON, Andrew (father of John White Stevenson), a Representative from Virginia; born in Culpeper County, Va., January 21, 1784; pursued classical studies; attended William and Mary College, Williamsburg, Va.; studied law; was admitted to the bar and commenced practice in Richmond, Va.; member of the State house of delegates 1809–1816 and 1818–1821 and served as speaker 1812–1815; unsuccessful candidate in 1814 and 1816 for election to Congress; elected as a Democrat to the Seventeenth and to the six succeeding Congresses and served from March 4, 1821, until his resignation, because of ill health, June 2, 1834; served as Speaker of the United States House of Representatives 1827–1834; Minister to Great Britain 1836–1841; engaged in agricultural pursuits at "Blenheim," Albemarle County, Va.; in 1845 was elected a member of the board of visitors of the University of Virginia at Charlottesville, and in 1856 was elected rector; died at his home, "Blenheim," January 25, 1857; interment in Enniscothy Cemetery, Albemarle County, Va.

STEVENSON, James S., a Representative from Pennsylvania; born in York County, Pa., in 1780; completed preparatory studies; studied law; was admitted to the bar and practiced; member of the State house of representatives in 1822 and 1823; president of the board of canal commissioners of the State, which position he held until the time of his death; elected to the Nineteenth and Twentieth Congresses (March 4, 1825–March 3, 1829); unsuccessful candidate for reelection in 1828 to the Twenty-first Congress; engaged in manufacturing in Pittsburgh, Pa., until his death in that city October 16, 1831; interment in First Presbyterian Cemetery.

STEVENSON, Job Evans, a Representative from Ohio; born in Yellow Bud, Ross County, Ohio, February 10, 1832; completed preparatory studies; studied law; was admitted to the bar and commenced the practice of his profession in Chillicothe, Ohio; also engaged in agricultural pursuits; member of the State senate 1863–1865; solicitor of Chillicothe 1859–1862; unsuccessful candidate for election in 1864 to the Thirty-ninth Congress; moved to Cincinnati, Ohio, in 1865; was elected as a Republican to the Forty-first and Forty-second Congresses (March 4, 1869–March 3, 1873); resumed the practice of law in Cincinnati, Ohio; large landowner; retired from active practice of his profession and resided in Lexington and Corinth, Ky.; died in Corinth, Ky., July 24, 1922; interment in Yellow Bud Cemetery, Yellow Bud, Ohio.

STEVENSON, John White (son of Andrew Stevenson), a Representative and a Senator from Kentucky; born in Richmond, Va., May 4, 1812; attended Hampden-Sidney Academy, Virginia, and was graduated from the University of Virginia at Charlottesville in 1832; studied law; was admitted to the bar and commenced practice in Vicksburg, Miss; moved to Covington, Kenton County, Ky., in 1841; county attorney; member of the State house of representatives 1845–1849; delegate to the State constitutional convention in 1849; one of three commissioners appointed to revise the civic and criminal code of the State in 1850 and 1851; delegate to the Democratic National Conventions in 1848, 1852 and 1856; presidential elector on the Democratic tickets of Pierce and King in 1852 and Buchanan and Breckinridge in 1856; elected as a Democrat to the Thirty-fifth and Thirty-sixth Congresses (March 4, 1857–March 3, 1861); unsuccessful candidate for reelection in 1860 to the Thirty-seventh Congress; Lieutenant Governor of Kentucky in 1867; became Governor September 13, 1867, upon the death of Gov. John L. Helm; subsequently elected Governor in 1868 and served until 1871, when he resigned, having been elected a Senator; elected as a Democrat to the United States Senate and served from March 4, 1871, to March 3, 1877; was not a candidate for reelection; became a professor in the Cincinnati Law School; chairman of the Democratic National Convention at Cincinnati in 1880; president of the American Bar Association in 1884 and 1885; died in Covington, Ky., August 10, 1886; interment in Spring Grove Cemetery, Cincinnati, Ohio.

STEVENSON, William Francis, a Representative from South Carolina; born in what is now Loray, near Statesville, Iredell County, N. C., November 23, 1861; attended the public schools and was tutored by his father; worked on the farm every crop season until he entered college; teacher in the public schools in 1879 and 1880; was graduated from Davidson College, Davidson, N. C., in 1885; again engaged in teaching in Cheraw, S. C., 1885–1887, studying law at the same time; was admitted to the bar in 1887 and commenced practice in Chesterfield, S. C., the same year; moved to Cheraw in 1892 and continued the practice of law; member of the Democratic executive committee of Chesterfield County 1888–1914, serving as chairman 1896–1902; mayor of Cheraw in 1895 and 1896; member of the State house of representatives 1896–1902, serving as speaker 1900–1902; declined to be a candidate for reelection; interested in various business enterprises in Chesterfield County; district counsel for the Seaboard Air Line Railway 1900–1917; member of the Democratic State executive committee 1901–1942; general counsel for the State dispensary commission 1907–1911; and directed through the Supreme Court of the United States the litigation which resulted in the termination of the State dispensary; again a member of the State house of representatives 1910–1914; elected as a Democrat to the Sixty-fifth Congress to fill the vacancy caused by the death of Representative-elect David E.

Finley; reelected to the Sixty-sixth and to the six succeeding Congresses and served from March 4, 1917, to March 3, 1933; was an unsuccessful candidate for renomination in 1932 to the Seventy-third Congress; member of the Federal Home Loan Bank Board, Washington, D. C., 1933–1939, serving as chairman in 1933; retired to private life; died in Washington, D. C., on February 12, 1942; interment in St. David's Episcopal Church Cemetery, Cheraw, S. C.

STEVENSON, William Henry, a Representative from Wisconsin; born in Kenosha, Wis., September 23, 1891; moved to La Crosse, Wis., with his parents in 1894; attended the grade and high schools; was graduated from Teachers College, La Crosse, Wis., in 1912; taught in the high schools of Holmen, Neillsville, and Madison, Wis., 1912–1916; was graduated from the University of Wisconsin at Madison in 1919 and from its law department in 1920; was admitted to the bar in 1920 and commenced practice in Richland Center, Wis.; appointed circuit court commissioner and divorce counsel of Richland County in 1922 and served until 1924; district attorney of Richland County 1924–1926; moved to La Crosse, Wis., in 1930 and continued the practice of his profession; served as district attorney of La Crosse County, Wis., 1935–1941; elected as a Republican to the Seventy-seventh and to the three succeeding Congresses (January 3, 1941–January 3, 1949); was an unsuccessful candidate for renomination in 1948 to the Eighty-first Congress; admitted to practice before United States Supreme Court in 1946; resumed the practice of law until his retirement on May 1, 1957; resides in Onalaska, Wis.

STEWARD, Lewis, a Representative from Illinois; born near Hollisterville, Wayne County, Pa., November 21, 1824; attended the common schools; in 1838 moved with his parents to Kendall County, Ill.; studied law; was admitted to the bar about 1860 but never practiced; engaged in agricultural pursuits and became an extensive landowner; also engaged in the manufacture of harvesters, mowers, and binders at Plano and later at West Pullman; unsuccessful Democratic candidate for Governor of Illinois in 1876; elected as a Democrat to the Fifty-second Congress (March 4, 1891–March 3, 1893); unsuccessful candidate for reelection in 1892 to the Fifty-third Congress and for election in 1894 to the Fifty-fourth Congress; resumed his former manufacturing activities; also interested in agricultural pursuits; died in Plano, Kendall County, Ill., August 27, 1896; interment in Plano Cemetery.

STEWART, Alexander, a Representative from Wisconsin; born in Fredericton, York County, New Brunswick, Canada, September 12, 1829; attended the common schools of his native city; moved to Marathon County, Wis., in 1849, and settled where the city of Wausau is now located; engaged in the lumber business; delegate to the Republican National Convention at Chicago in 1884, which nominated Blaine and Logan; elected as a Republican to the Fifty-fourth, Fifty-fifth, and Fifty-sixth Congresses (March 4, 1895–March 3, 1901); was not a candidate for renomination in 1900 to the Fifty-seventh Congress; retired from active business pursuits and resided in Washington, D. C., until his death on May 24, 1912; interment in Pine Grove Cemetery, Wausau, Wis.

STEWART, Andrew, a Representative from Pennsylvania; born near Uniontown, Fayette County Pa., on June 11, 1791; received a good education; taught school; was graduated from Washington College (now Washington and Jefferson College), Washington, Pa.; studied law; was admitted to the bar in 1815 and commenced practice in Uniontown; member of the State house of representatives 1815–1818; was appointed by

President Monroe as United States attorney for the western district of Pennsylvania and served from 1818 to 1820, when he resigned; elected as a Democrat to the Seventeenth and to the three succeeding Congresses (March 4, 1821–March 3, 1829); one of the originators of the project to build the Chesapeake & Ohio Canal; elected to the Twenty-second and Twenty-third Congresses (March 4, 1831–March 3, 1835); unsuccessful candidate for reelection in 1834 to the Twenty-fourth Congress; was elected as a Whig to the Twenty-eighth, Twenty-ninth, and Thirtieth Congresses (March 4, 1843–March 3, 1849); declined to be a candidate for renomination; unsuccessful candidate for the nomination for Vice President in 1848; declined the appointment as Secretary of the Treasury in the Cabinet of President Taylor; affiliated with the Republican Party; unsuccessful candidate for election in 1870 to the Forty-second Congress; largely interested in building and real estate until his death in Uniontown, Fayette County, Pa., July 16, 1872; interment in Union Cemetery.

STEWART, Andrew (son of the preceding), a Representative from Pennsylvania; born in Uniontown, Fayette County, Pa., April 6, 1836; attended Sewickley Academy, Sewickley, Pa., and Madison College, Uniontown, Pa.; studied medicine and attended Jefferson Medical College, Philadelphia, Pa.; during the Civil War enlisted as a private in the Eighty-fifth Regiment, Pennsylvania Volunteer Infantry, and was promoted to first lieutenant; regimental adjutant October 1, 1861; captain and assistant adjutant general, Second Brigade, Casey's division, September 1, 1862; brevetted major of Volunteers for gallant service at Plymouth, N. C., May 20, 1864, and lieutenant colonel of Volunteers October 25, 1865, for meritorious service during the war; honorably mustered out February 2, 1866; was captured at Plymouth, N. C., and confined in Libby, Macon, Charleston, Columbia, and other southern prisons for over a year; unsuccessful candidate for election in 1874 to the Forty-fourth Congress; delegate to the Republican National Convention at Cincinnati in 1876, which nominated Rutherford B. Hayes, of Ohio, for President and William A. Wheeler, of New York, for Vice President; presented credentials as a Republican Member-elect to the Fifty-second Congress and served from March 4, 1891, to February 26, 1892, when he was succeeded by Alexander K. Craig, who contested his election; unsuccessful candidate for election to the Fifty-second Congress to fill the vacancy caused by the death of Alexander K. Craig; engaged in the manufacture of paper pulp and lumber; died in Stewarton, Fayette County, Pa., November 9, 1903; interment in Union Cemetery, Uniontown, Pa.

STEWART, Arthur Thomas (Tom), a Senator from Tennessee; born in Dunlap, Sequatchie County, Tenn., January 11, 1892; attended the public schools, Pryor Institute, Jasper, Tenn., Emory (Ga.) College; and Cumberland University, Lebanon, Tenn.; studied law; was admitted to the bar in 1913 and commenced practice in Birmingham, Ala.; returned to Jasper, Tenn., in 1915; moved to Winchester, Tenn., in 1919 and continued the practice of law; elected district attorney general of the eighteenth circuit of Tennessee and served from September 29, 1923, until his resignation on January 16, 1939, having previously been elected Senator; delegate to the Democratic National Conventions in 1940, 1944, 1948, and 1956; elected as a Democrat to the United States Senate on November 8, 1938, for the term ending January 3, 1943, to fill the vacancy caused by the death of Nathan L. Bachman, but, preferring to continue as district attorney general, did not assume his senatorial duties until January 16, 1939; reelected in 1942 for the term ending January 3, 1949; unsuccessful candidate for renomination in 1948; resumed the practice of law; is a resident of Nashville, Tenn.

STEWART, Charles, a Delegate from New Jersey; born in Gortlea, County Donegal, Ireland, in 1729; immigrated to the United States in 1750; engaged in agricultural pursuits; was commissioned lieutenant colonel of militia in Hunterdon County, N. J., April 10, 1771; active in pre-Revolutionary movements; commissioned colonel of a battalion of Minutemen on February 15, 1776; appointed commissary general of issues by the Continental Congress on June 18, 1777; Member of the Continental Congress from November 1, 1784, to November 7, 1785; died in Flemington, N. J., on June 24, 1800; interment in Old Stone Church, Bethlehem Township, Hunterdon County, N. J.

STEWART, Charles, a Representative from Texas; born in Memphis, Tenn., May 30, 1836; moved to Texas in 1845 with his parents, who settled in Galveston; attended the common schools; studied law; was admitted to the bar in 1854 and commenced the practice of law in Marlin, Falls County, Tex.; prosecuting attorney for the thirteenth judicial district from 1856 to 1860; delegate to the secession convention in 1861; enlisted in the Confederate Army and served throughout the Civil War, first in the Tenth Regiment of Texas Infantry and later in Baylor's Cavalry; moved to Houston in 1866 and resumed the practice of law; was city attorney of Houston 1874–1876; member of the State senate 1878–1882; elected as a Democrat to the Forty-eighth and to the four succeeding Congresses (March 4, 1883–March 3, 1893); was not a candidate for renomination in 1892; resumed the practice of his profession in Houston, Tex.; died in the Santa Rosa Hospital, San Antonio, Tex., September 21, 1895; interment in Glenwood Cemetery, Houston, Tex.

STEWART, David, a Senator from Maryland; born in Baltimore, Md., September 13, 1800; completed preparatory studies; attended Princeton University, and was graduated from Union College, Schenectady, N. Y., in 1819; studied law; was admitted to the bar about 1821 and commenced practice in Baltimore, Md.; appointed as a Whig to the United States Senate to fill the vacancy caused by the resignation of Reverdy Johnson and served from December 6, 1849, to January 12, 1850, when a successor was elected; was not a candidate for election to fill the vacancy; resumed the practice of his profession in Baltimore, Md., where he died January 5, 1858; interment in the Stewart vault in "Old Westminster" Burying Ground.

STEWART, David Wallace, a Senator from Iowa; born in New Concord, Muskingum County, Ohio, January 22, 1887; attended the common schools; was graduated from Geneva College, Beaver Falls, Pa., in 1911; high-school teacher and athletic coach 1911–1914; was graduated from the law department of the University of Chicago in 1917; was admitted to the bar the same year and commenced practice in Sioux City, Iowa; during the First World War served overseas as first sergeant in Company K, Thirteenth Regiment, United States Marine Corps, from July 12, 1918, to September 13, 1919, when he was honorably discharged; resumed the practice of law in Sioux City, Iowa; delegate to the Republican State conventions in 1922 and 1924; president of the Sioux City Chamber of Commerce in 1925; appointed and subsequently elected as a Republican to the United States Senate to fill the vacancy caused by the death of Albert B. Cummins and served from August 7, 1926, to March 3, 1927; was not a candidate for renomination in 1926; resumed the practice of his profession; president of the board of trustees of Morningside College; is a resident of Sioux City, Iowa.

STEWART, Jacob Henry, a Representative from Minnesota; born in Clermont, Columbia County, N. Y., January 15, 1829; moved with his parents to Peekskill, N. Y.; attended the common schools and was graduated from Phillips Academy, Peekskill; attended Yale College; studied medicine, and was graduated from the University Medical College of New York City in 1851; commenced the practice of medicine in Peekskill, N. Y.; moved to St. Paul, Minn., in 1855; medical officer of Ramsey County in 1856; member of the State senate in 1858 and 1859; during the Civil War served as a surgeon in the Union Army in 1861; captured at the first Battle of Bull Run; was paroled and allowed to care for the wounded at Sudley Church Hospital; surgeon general of the State of Minnesota 1857–1863; mayor of St. Paul in 1864, 1868, and 1872–1874; postmaster of St. Paul 1865–1870; elected as a Republican to the Forty-fifth Congress (March 4, 1877–March 3, 1879); was not a candidate for renomination in 1878; surveyor general of Minnesota 1879–1882; resumed the practice of medicine in St. Paul, Minn., and died there August 25, 1884; interment in Oakland Cemetery.

STEWART, James, a Representative from North Carolina; born in Scotland November 11, 1775; received a liberal education; immigrated to the United States and settled near Stewartsville, Richmond County, N. C.; engaged in mercantile and agricultural pursuits; member of the State house of commons in 1798 and 1799; served in the State senate 1802–1804 and 1813–1815; elected to the Fifteenth Congress to fill the vacancy caused by the death of Alexander McMillan and served from January 5, 1818, to March 3, 1819; resumed mercantile and agricultural pursuits; died near Laurinburg, Richmond County, N. C., on December 29, 1821; interment in the Old Stewartsville Cemetery, near Laurinburg.

STEWART, James Augustus, a Representative from Maryland; born at "Tobacco Stick" (now Madison), Dorchester County, Md., November 24, 1808; attended the local schools; studied law in Baltimore, Md.; was admitted to the bar in 1829 and commenced practice in Cambridge, Dorchester County, Md.; also engaged in the building of ships and houses; unsuccessful candidate for election in 1838 to the Twenty-sixth Congress; member of the State house of delegates 1843–1845; elected as a Democrat to the Thirty-fourth, Thirty-fifth, and Thirty-sixth Congresses (March 4, 1855–March 3, 1861); was not a candidate for renomination in 1860; resumed the practice of his profession in Cambridge; member of the Court of Appeals of Maryland and chief justice of the circuit court from 1867 until his death in Cambridge, Md., April 3, 1879; interment in Christ Protestant Episcopal Church Cemetery.

STEWART, James Fleming, a Representative from New Jersey; born in Paterson, N. J., June 15, 1851; attended the public and private schools of Paterson; was graduated from the law department of the University of New York at New York City in 1870; was admitted to the bar the same year and commenced the practice of law in New York City; returned to Paterson, N. J., and continued the practice of law in 1875; recorder (criminal magistrate) of the city of Paterson 1890–1895; elected as a Republican to the Fifty-fourth and to the three succeeding Congresses (March 4, 1895–March 3, 1903); was an unsuccessful candidate for reelection in 1902 to the Fifty-eighth Congress; resumed the practice of law in Paterson, N. J., where he died on January 21, 1904; interment in Cedar Lawn Cemetery.

STEWART, John, a Representative from Pennsylvania; completed preparatory studies; member of the State house of representatives 1789–1796; elected as a Democrat to the Sixth Congress to fill the vacancy caused by the death of Thomas Hartley; reelected to the Seventh and Eighth Congresses and served from January 15, 1801, to March 3, 1805; died in Elmwood, near York, Spring Garden Township, Pa., in 1820; interment on his estate near Elmwood.

STEWART, John, a Representative from Connecticut; born in Chatham, Conn., February 10, 1795; completed preparatory studies; became engaged in shipbuilding and in the mercantile business in Middle Haddam; member of the State house of representatives in 1830; served in the State senate 1832–1837; judge of the county court of Middletown; elected as a Democrat to the Twenty-eighth Congress (March 4, 1843–March 3, 1845); unsuccessful candidate for reelection in 1844 to the Twenty-ninth Congress; resumed shipbuilding pursuits; again a member of the State senate in 1846; again served in the house of representatives in 1854; died in Chatham, Middlesex County, Conn., September 16, 1860; interment in Union Hill Cemetery at Middle Haddam, Chatham, Conn.

STEWART, John David, a Representative from Georgia; born near Fayetteville, Fayette County, Ga., August 2, 1833; attended the common schools and Marshall College, Griffin, Ga.; taught school two years in Griffin, Spalding County, Ga.; studied law; was admitted to the bar in 1856 and commenced practice in Griffin, Ga.; probate judge of Spalding County 1858–1860; lieutenant and captain in the Thirteenth Georgia Regiment during the Civil War; member of the State house of representatives 1865–1867; studied theology; was ordained as a minister of the Baptist Church in 1871; mayor of Griffin in 1875 and 1876; judge of the superior court from November 7, 1879, to January 1, 1886, when he resigned to become a candidate for Congress; elected as a Democrat to the Fiftieth and Fifty-first Congresses (March 4, 1887–March 3, 1891); unsuccessful candidate for renomination in 1890; engaged in the practice of his profession until his death in Griffin, Ga., January 28, 1894; interment in Oak Hill Cemetery.

STEWART, John George, a Representative from Delaware; born in Wilmington, New Castle County, Del., June 2, 1890; attended the grade and high schools of Wilmington and the University of Delaware at Newark; engaged in the landscape construction business 1919–1942; member of the Delaware Athletic Commission 1931–1934; commissioner on the Delaware Emergency Relief Commission in 1934; elected as a Republican to the Seventy-fourth Congress (January 3, 1935–January 3, 1937); unsuccessful candidate for reelection in 1936 to the Seventy-fifth Congress; member of the staff of the United States Senate Committee on the District of Columbia 1947–1951; special engineer to the lands division of the Department of Justice and Corps of Engineers in 1952 and 1953; civil engineer in Hollywood, Fla., in 1954; appointed Architect of the Capitol August 16, 1954, and assumed duties October 1, 1954; is a resident of Wilmington, Del.

STEWART, John Knox, a Representative from New York; born in Perth, Fulton County, N. Y., October 20, 1853; moved with his parents to Amsterdam in 1860; attended the public schools and Amsterdam Academy; engaged in the manufacture of paper until 1885, when he engaged in the manufacture of textiles; sewer commissioner of the city 1885–1890; a director of the Farmers' National Bank of Amsterdam and of the Chuctanunda Gas Light Co.; vice president of the Amsterdam Board of Trade; member of the State assembly in 1889; elected as a Republican to the Fifty-sixth and Fifty-seventh Congresses (March 4, 1899–March 3, 1903); unsuccessful candidate for renomination in 1902; resumed the manufacture of textiles and continued in that business until his death in Amsterdam, N. Y., June 27, 1919; interment in Greenhill Cemetery.

STEWART, John Wolcott, a Representative and a Senator from Vermont; born in Middlebury, Addison County, Vt., November 24, 1825; was graduated from the Middlebury Academy in 1846; studied law; was admitted to the bar in 1850 and commenced practice in Middlebury, Vt.; prosecuting attorney of Addison County 1852–1854; member of the State house of representatives in 1856, 1865–1867, and 1876, serving as speaker 1865–1867 and 1876; delegate to the Republican National Convention at Chicago in 1860; served in the State senate in 1861 and 1862; Governor of Vermont 1870–1872; elected as a Republican to the Forty-eighth and to the three succeeding Congresses (March 4, 1883–March 3, 1891); declined to be a candidate for renomination in 1890; engaged in the banking business at Middlebury; appointed to the United States Senate March 24, 1908, to fill the vacancy caused by the death of Redfield Proctor and served from March 24, 1908, to October 21, 1908, when a successor was elected; retired from political life and active business pursuits and resided in Middlebury, Vt., until his death on October 29, 1915; interment in West Cemetery.

STEWART, Paul, a Representative from Oklahoma; born in Clarksville, Johnson County, Ark., February 27, 1892; moved with his parents to Poteau, Indian Territory, in 1894 and to Red River County, Choctaw Nation, Indian Territory (now a part of McCurtain County, Okla.) in 1897; self-educated; entered the mercantile business at the age of thirteen at Spencerville, Indian Territory; in 1910 moved his mercantile business to Haworth, Okla., where he continued its operation until 1919; was admitted to the bar in 1915 and commenced the practice of law; postmaster at Haworth 1914–1922; served in the Oklahoma State House of Representatives 1922–1926; moved to Antlers Okla., in 1929; editor, owner, and publisher of the Antlers (Okla.) American, a weekly newspaper, 1929–1950; member of the State senate 1926–1942, serving as Democratic floor leader in 1929 and 1930 and as president pro tempore in 1933 and 1934; Acting Governor in 1933; engaged in cattle raising, farming, and hotel business; elected as a Democrat to the Seventy-eighth and Seventy-ninth Congresses (January 3, 1943–January 3, 1947); was not a candidate for renomination in 1946 to the Eightieth Congress; resumed newspaper publishing business until his death in Antlers, Okla., on November 13, 1950; interment in City Cemetery.

STEWART, Percy Hamilton, a Representative from New Jersey; born in Newark, Essex County, N. J., January 10, 1867; attended the public schools; was graduated from Yale College, New Haven, Conn., in 1890 and from Columbia Law School, New York City, N. Y., in 1893; was admitted to the bar the same year and commenced practice in New York City; treasurer and member of the executive committee of the Military Training Camps Association during the First World War and active in recruiting and selecting officers for the various branches of the service; was appointed by the Secretary of War as a civilian aide to the Adjutant General of the United States Army, representing the State of New Jersey; mayor of Plainfield, N. J., in 1912 and 1913; chairman of the Union County Democratic committee in 1914 and of the Washington Rock Park Commission of New Jersey 1915–1921; member of the New Jersey State Board of Education 1919–1921 and of the New Jersey State Highway Commission 1923–1929; delegate to the Democratic National Conventions in 1920 and 1928; elected as a Democrat to the Seventy-second Congress to fill the vacancy caused by the death of Ernest R. Ackerman and served from December 1, 1931, to March 3, 1933; was not a candidate for renomination in 1932, but was an unsuccessful candidate for election to the United States Senate; resumed the practice of law until his retirement in 1941; died in Plainfield, N. J., June 30, 1951; interment in Hillside Cemetery.

STEWART, Thomas Elliott, a Representative from New York; born in New York City September 22, 1824; completed preparatory studies; studied law; was admitted to the bar in 1847 and commenced practice in New York City; member of the board of education in 1854; served in the State assembly in 1865 and 1866; member of the Republican State committee 1866–1868; elected as a Conservative Republican to the Fortieth Congress (March 4, 1867–March 3, 1869); was not a candidate for renomination in 1868 to the Forty-first Congress; resumed the practice of his profession in New York City; chairman of the Liberal Republican general committee of New York City in 1872; park commissioner of New York City 1874–1876; died in New York City on January 9, 1904; interment in Center Cemetery, New Milford, Litchfield County, Conn.

STEWART, William, a Representative from Pennsylvania; born in Mercer, Mercer County, Pa., September 10, 1810; attended the public schools; was graduated from Jefferson College, Canonsburg, Pa.; studied law; was admitted to the bar and commenced practice in Mercer, Pa.; member of the State senate; elected as a Republican to the Thirty-fifth and Thirty-sixth Congresses (March 4, 1857–March 3, 1861); resumed the practice of law; died in Mercer, Pa., on October 17, 1876; interment in Mercer Cemetery.

STEWART, William Morris, a Senator from Nevada; born in Galen, near Lyons, Wayne County, N. Y., August 9, 1827; moved with his parents to Mesopotamia Township, Trumbull County, Ohio; attended Lyons Union School and West Farmington Academy; teacher of mathematics at Lyons Union School; attended Yale College in 1849 and 1850; moved to San Francisco, Calif., in May 1850 and engaged in mining in Nevada County; studied law; was admitted to the bar in 1852 and commenced practice in Nevada City, Calif.; district attorney in 1852; attorney general of California in 1854; moved to Virginia City, Nev., in 1860; involved in early mining litigation and in the development of the Comstock lode; member of the Territorial council in 1861; member of the State constitutional convention in 1863; upon the admission of Nevada as a State into the Union was elected as a Republican to the United States Senate; reelected in 1869 and served from December 15, 1864, to March 3, 1875; resumed the practice of law in Nevada, California, and the Pacific coast generally; again elected as a Republican to the United States Senate in 1887; reelected in 1893 and 1899 and served from March 4, 1887, to March 3, 1905; declined to be a candidate for reelection in 1905; lived in retirement until his death in Washington, D. C., April 23, 1909; remains were cremated and the ashes deposited in Laurel Hill Cemetery, San Francisco, Calif.

STIGLER, William Grady, a Representative from Oklahoma; born in Stigler, Haskell County, Indian Territory (now Oklahoma), July 7, 1891; attended the public schools; was graduated from Northeastern State College, Tahlequah, Okla., in 1912; attended the law school of the University of Oklahoma at Norman; during the First World War served as a second lieutenant in the Three Hundred and Fifty-seventh Infantry of the Ninetieth Division in 1918 and 1919, with overseas service in the St. Mihiel and Meuse-Argonne engagements and with the Army of Occupation; attended the University of Grenoble, France, in 1919; was admitted to the Oklahoma bar in 1920 and commenced practice in Stigler, Okla.; city attorney of Stigler, Okla., 1920–1924; served in the State senate 1924–1932, serving as president pro tempore in 1931; lieutenant colonel in the Forty-fifth Division of the Oklahoma National Guard 1925–1938; elected as a Democrat to the Seventy-eighth Congress to fill the vacancy caused by the resignation of Jack

Nichols; reelected to the Seventy-ninth and to the three succeeding Congresses and served from March 28, 1944, until his death in Stigler, Okla., August 21, 1952; interment in Stigler Cemetery.

STILES, John Dodson, a Representative from Pennsylvania; born in Town Hill, Luzerne County, Pa., January 15, 1822; completed preparatory studies; studied law; was admitted to the bar in 1844 and practiced in Allentown, Lehigh County; elected district attorney of Lehigh County in 1853 and served three years; delegate to the Democratic National Convention at Cincinnati in 1856 which nominated Buchanan and Breckinridge, at Chicago in 1864 which nominated McClellan and Pendleton, and at New York City in 1868 which nominated Seymour and Blair; was also a delegate to the Union National Convention at Philadelphia in 1866; elected as a Democrat to the Thirty-seventh Congress to fill the vacancy caused by the death of Thomas B. Cooper; reelected to the Thirty-eighth Congress and served from June 3, 1862, to March 3, 1865; again elected to the Forty-first Congress (March 4, 1869–March 3, 1871); was not a candidate for renomination in 1870; resumed the practice of law; died in Allentown, Pa., October 29, 1896; interment in Fairview Cemetery.

STILES, William Henry (grandson of Joseph Clay), a Representative from Georgia; born in Savannah, Ga., January 1, 1808; completed preparatory studies; studied law at Yale College; was admitted to the bar in 1831 and commenced practice in Savannah, Ga.; solicitor general for the eastern district of Georgia 1833–1836; elected as a Democrat to the Twenty-eighth Congress (March 4, 1843–March 3, 1845); appointed on April 19, 1845, by President Polk as Chargé d'Affaires to Austria and served until October 1849; resumed the practice of law in Savannah; member of the State house of representatives and served as speaker in 1858; delegate from the State at large to the commercial congress held at Montgomery, Ala., in 1858; delegate to the Democratic National Convention at Baltimore in 1860; served as colonel in the Confederate Army during the Civil War; engaged in literary pursuits; died in Savannah, Ga., December 20, 1865; interment in Laurel Grove Cemetery.

STILLWELL, Thomas Neel, a Representative from Indiana; born in Stillwell, Ohio, August 29, 1830; received a thorough English education; attended Oxford and College Hill Colleges; studied law; was admitted to the bar in 1852 and began practice in Anderson, Ind.; member of the State house of representatives in 1856; served in the Union Army during the Civil War; elected as a Republican to the Thirty-ninth Congress (March 4, 1865–March 3, 1867); was not a candidate for renomination in 1866; Minister Resident to Venezuela in 1867 and 1868; served as president of the First National Bank of Anderson, Ind., until his death; died in Anderson as the result of a gunshot wound January 14, 1874; interment in Maplewood Cemetery.

STINESS, Walter Russell, a Representative from Rhode Island; born in Smithfield, Providence County, R. I., March 13, 1854; attended the public schools, and was a student at Brown University, Providence, R. I., in 1873 and 1874; served in the city council in 1875; was graduated from Boston University Law School in 1877; was admitted to the bar the same year and commenced practice in Providence, R. I.; member of the State house of representatives 1878–1881; clerk of the justice court of Providence 1879–1885; aide-de-camp on the staff of Gov. A. O. Bourn 1883–1885; State railroad commissioner 1888–1891; assistant judge advocate general of Rhode Island 1888–1898; judge advocate general 1898–1913; member of the State senate 1904–1909; chairman of the commission to revise the statutes of Rhode Island in 1909; United States attorney for the district of Rhode Island 1911–1914; elected as a Republican to the Sixty-fourth and to the three succeeding Congresses (March 4, 1915–March 3, 1923); was not a candidate for renomination in 1922; lived in retirement in Warwick, R. I., until his death there March 17, 1924; interment in Swan Point Cemetery, Providence, R. I.

STIRK, Samuel, a Delegate from Georgia; born in Savannah, Ga.; clerk of executive council in 1777; lieutenant colonel in Georgia militia 1778–1779; elected as a Delegate to the Continental Congress on August 16, 1781; attorney general of Georgia in 1781 and reelected in 1783; justice of Chatham County 1786–1789.

STIVERS, Moses Dunning, a Representative from New York; born near Beemerville, Sussex County, N. J., December 30, 1828; attended common and private schools and Mount Retirement Seminary in Wantage, Sussex County, N. J.; moved with his father to Ridgebury, N. Y., in 1845 and completed his education; taught school; engaged in mercantile pursuits in Ridgebury and later in Middletown, N. Y., 1855–1864; clerk of Orange County 1864–1867 and resided in Goshen, N. Y.; returned to Middletown and became proprietor of the Orange County Press in 1868 and was also one of the proprietors and editors of the Middletown Daily Press; appointed by President Grant as United States collector of internal revenue for the eleventh district of New York in 1869 and served until 1883; delegate to the Republican National Convention at Chicago in 1880; president of the New York State Press Association in 1887; trustee of Middletown State Hospital for the Insane; engaged in banking; unsuccessful Republican candidate for election in 1884 to the Forty-ninth Congress to fill the vacancy caused by the death of Lewis Beach and for election in 1886 to the Fiftieth Congress; elected as a Republican to the Fifty-first Congress (March 4, 1889–March 3, 1891); was not a candidate for renomination in 1890; engaged in banking; died in Middletown, N. Y., February 2, 1895; interment in Hillside Cemetery.

STOBBS, George Russell, a Representative from Massachusetts; born in Webster, Worcester County, Mass., February 7, 1877; attended the public schools of Webster, and Phillips Exeter Academy, Exeter, N. H.; was graduated from Harvard University, Cambridge, Mass., in 1899 and from its law department in 1902; was admitted to the bar in 1902 and commenced practice in Worcester, Mass.; special justice for the central district court of Worcester 1909–1916; captain in the State Guard of Massachusetts 1917–1920; assistant district attorney for the middle district of Massachusetts 1917–1921; trustee of Worcester Public Library 1922–1928; elected as a Republican to the Sixty-ninth, Seventieth, and Seventy-first Congresses (March 4, 1925–March 3, 1931); was not a candidate for renomination in 1930; one of the managers appointed by the House of Representatives in 1926 to conduct the impeachment proceedings against George W. English, judge of the United States District Court for the Eastern District of Illinois; major and subsequently lieutenant colonel in the Judge Advocate General's Department, Officers' Reserve Corps, 1927–1942; delegate to the Interparliamentary Congress, London, England, in 1930; delegate to the Republican National Convention in 1932, and to the Republican State conventions in 1940 and 1942; resumed the practice of law in Worcester, Mass., where he now resides.

STOCKBRIDGE, Francis Brown, a Senator from Michigan; born in Bath, Maine, April 9, 1826; attended the common schools; clerk in a wholesale house in Boston 1843–1847; moved to Chicago, Ill., and opened a lumber yard; moved to Saugatuck, Allegan County, Mich., in 1851 and engaged in the operation of sawmills; also interested in mercantile pursuits; moved to Kalamazoo, Mich., in 1863 and engaged in the lumber business; member of the State house of representatives in 1869; served as a member of the State senate in 1871; elected as a Republican to the United States Senate in 1887; reelected in 1893 and served from March 4, 1887, until his death in Chicago, Ill., on April 30, 1894; interment in Mountain Home Cemetery, Kalamazoo, Mich.

STOCKBRIDGE, Henry, Jr., a Representative from Maryland; born in Baltimore, Md., September 18, 1856; attended public and private schools and Williston Academy, Easthampton, Mass.; was graduated from Amherst (Mass.) College in 1877 and from the law school of the University of Maryland at Baltimore in 1878; was admitted to the bar in the latter year and commenced practice in Baltimore; employed on the editorial staff of the Baltimore Herald and later with the Baltimore American; appointed as an examiner in equity by the supreme bench of Baltimore in December 1882; elected as a Republican to the Fifty-first Congress (March 4, 1889–March 3, 1891); declined to be a candidate for renomination in 1890; served as United States commissioner of immigration for the port of Baltimore 1891–1893; elected judge of the supreme bench of Baltimore in November 1896 and served until 1911; regent of the University of Maryland 1907–1920; appointed judge of the Maryland Court of Appeals on April 13, 1911, and was elected in November 1911 for a term of fifteen years; died in Baltimore, Md., March 22, 1924; interment in Loudon Park Cemetery.

STOCKDALE, Thomas Ringland, a Representative from Mississippi; born near West Union Church, Greene County, Pa., March 28, 1828; was graduated from Jefferson College, Canonsburg, Pa., in 1856; moved to Pike County, Miss., in 1857 and taught school; was graduated from the University of Mississippi at Oxford in 1859; studied law; was admitted to the bar in 1859 and practiced in Woodville, Miss., 1859–1861; during the Civil War enlisted in the Confederate Army as a private in the Sixteenth Mississippi Infantry in 1861, being promoted successively to lieutenant, adjutant, and major of that regiment; elected major of Stockdale's battalion of Cavalry in 1863 and commanded the outposts of the Army at Fort Hudson until it was invested; commissioned lieutenant colonel of the Fourth Mississippi Cavalry in 1864; at the close of the war resumed the practice of law in Summit, Miss.; delegate to the Democratic National Convention at New York in 1868; was presidential elector on the Democratic tickets of Greeley and Brown in 1872 and Cleveland and Hendricks in 1884; elected as a Democrat to the Fiftieth and to the three succeeding Congresses (March 4, 1887–March 3, 1895); was an unsuccessful candidate for renomination; appointed judge of the State supreme court December 1, 1896; died in Summit, Pike County, Miss., January 8, 1899; interment in Woodlawn Cemetery.

STOCKMAN, Lowell, a Representative from Oregon; born on a farm near Helix, Umatilla County, Oreg., April 12, 1901; attended the public schools at Pendleton, Oreg.; was graduated from Oregon State University at Corvallis in 1922; engaged in agricultural pursuits in 1922; elected as a Republican to the Seventy-eighth and to the four succeeding Congresses (January 3, 1943–January 3, 1953); was not a candidate for renomination in 1952; retired, and resides in Bellevue, Wash.

STOCKSLAGER, Strother Madison, a Representative from Indiana; born in Mauckport, Harrison County, Ind., May 7, 1842; attended the common schools, Corydon High School, and Indiana University at Bloomington; taught school; served in the Union Army during the Civil War as second lieutenant and captain in the Thirteenth Indiana Volunteer Cavalry, which he had assisted to organize; was mustered out as captain and returned to Mauckport; deputy county auditor of Harrison County 1866–1868; deputy county clerk of Harrison County 1868–1870; appointed by President Andrew Johnson as assessor of internal revenue in 1867, but was not confirmed by the United States Senate; studied law; was admitted to the bar in Corydon, Ind., in 1871 and practiced in Indiana and Kentucky; member of the State senate 1874–1878; editor of the Corydon Democrat 1879–1882; elected as a Democrat to the Forty-seventh and Forty-eighth Congresses (March 4, 1881–March 3, 1885); was an unsuccessful candidate for renomination in 1884 to the Forty-ninth Congress; resumed the practice of law in Corydon; appointed assistant commissioner of the General Land Office on October 1, 1885, and commissioner on March 27, 1888; resigned March 4, 1889, but remained in charge until June 20, 1889; continued the practice of law in Washington, D. C.; was an unsuccessful Democratic candidate for election in 1894 to the Fifty-fourth Congress; delegate to the Democratic National Convention at Chicago in 1896, which nominated William J. Bryan for President; served as legal expert in the Department of Labor in 1918; resumed the practice of law in Washington, D. C., until his death there on June 1, 1930; interment in Arlington National Cemetery, Fort Myer, Va.

STOCKTON, John Potter (son of Robert Field Stockton), a Senator from New Jersey; born in Princeton, N. J., August 2, 1826; attended private schools, and was graduated from Princeton College in 1843; studied law; was admitted to the bar in 1846 and practiced in Princeton and Trenton, N. J.; State reporter to the court of chancery 1852–1858; served as United States Minister to Italy from 1857 until 1861; presented credentials as a Democratic Senator-elect to the United States Senate and served from March 15, 1865, to March 27, 1866, when the Senate declared the seat vacant; elected as a Democrat to the United States Senate and served from March 4, 1869, to March 3, 1875; resumed the practice of his profession; attorney general of New Jersey 1877–1892; delegate to all Democratic National Conventions from 1864 until his death; died in New York City January 22, 1900; interment in Princeton Cemetery, Princeton, N. J.

STOCKTON, Richard (grandfather of Richard Stockton Field), a Delegate from New Jersey; born at "Morven," near Princeton, Somerset County, N. J., October 1, 1730; attended Nottingham Academy in Cecil County, Md., and was graduated in the first class from Princeton College, in 1748; studied law; was admitted to the bar in 1754 and commenced practice in Princeton, N. J.; member of the executive council of New Jersey from November 2, 1768, to June 17, 1776; associate justice of the State supreme court from February 28, 1774, to June 17, 1776; elected as a Member of the Continental Congress on June 22, 1776; reelected on November 30, 1776, but declined the latter election on December 2, 1776; a signer of the Declaration of Independence; unsuccessful candidate for Governor of New Jersey on August 31, 1776; elected chief justice of the State supreme court on August 31, 1776, but declined the office; while in Congress served as chairman of a committee to inspect the northern army at Ticonderoga; was taken prisoner by the Tories near Freehold, N. J., on November 30, 1776, and confined in the provost jail in New York City until December 29, 1776, when he was released; resumed the practice of law; died at "Morven," near Princeton, N. J., February 28, 1781; interment in Quaker Cemetery, Princeton, N. J.

STOCKTON, Richard (son of the preceding and father of Robert Field Stockton), a Senator and a Representative from New Jersey; born in Princeton, N. J., April 17, 1764; tutored privately; was graduated from Princeton College in 1779; studied law; was admitted to the bar in 1784 and commenced practice in Princeton, N. J.; presidential elector on the Washington and Adams ticket in 1792; elected as a Federalist to the United States Senate to fill the vacancy caused by the resignation of Frederick Frelinghuysen and served from November 12, 1796, to March 3, 1799; declined to be a candidate for reelection; again presidential elector on the Federalist ticket in 1800 and voted for John Adams and Charles C. Pinckney; unsuccessful candidate for Governor of New Jersey in 1801; member of the State general assembly 1813–1815; elected to the Thirteenth Congress (March 4, 1813–March 3, 1815); declined to be a candidate for renomination to the Fourteenth Congress; resumed the practice of his profession; died at "Morven," near Princeton, Mercer County, N. J., March 7, 1828; interment in Princeton Cemetery, Princeton, N. J.

STOCKTON, Robert Field (son of the preceding and father of John Potter Stockton), a Senator from New Jersey; born in Princeton, N. J., August 20, 1795; was privately tutored; attended Princeton College; entered the United States Navy in 1811 and attained the rank of commodore; was sent to the Pacific coast in October 1845 and, in cooperation with the land forces, captured the Mexican capital of California and organized a civil government; returned home and resigned his commission May 28, 1850; elected as a Democrat to the United States Senate and served from March 4, 1851, until his resignation on January 10, 1853; president of the Delaware & Raritan Canal 1853–1866; member of the peace convention of 1861 held in Washington, D. C., in an effort to devise means to prevent the impending war; retired from public life; died in Princeton, N. J., October 7, 1866; interment in Princeton Cemetery.

STODDARD, Ebenezer, a Representative from Connecticut; born in Union, Tolland County, Conn., May 6, 1785; attended Woodstock Academy in 1802 and in 1803, and was graduated from Brown University, Providence, R. I., in 1807; studied law; was admitted to the bar in 1810 and commenced practice in West Woodstock, Conn.; elected to the Seventeenth and Eighteenth Congresses (March 4, 1821–March 3, 1825); served in the State senate 1825–1827; Lieutenant Governor of Connecticut in 1833 and 1835–1837; practiced law; died in West Woodstock, Conn., on August 19, 1847; interment in Bungay Cemetery.

STODDERT, John Truman, a Representative from Maryland; born in Smith Point, Nanjemoy, Charles County, Md., October 1, 1790; studied under private teachers and was graduated from Princeton College in 1810; studied law; was admitted to the bar and practiced; served in the War of 1812; member of the State house of delegates in 1820; elected as a Jackson Democrat to the Twenty-third Congress (March 4, 1833–March 3, 1835); engaged in agricultural pursuits; died at the "Wicomico House," West Hatton estate, in Charles County, Md., July 19, 1870; interment in the family burying ground on his estate.

STOKELY, Samuel, a Representative from Ohio; born in Washington, Pa., January 25, 1796; attended private schools; was graduated from Washington College (now Washington and Jefferson College), Washington, Pa., in 1813; studied law; was admitted to the bar and commenced practice in Steubenville, Ohio, in 1817; United States land receiver in 1827 and 1828; member of the State senate in 1837 and 1838; elected as a Whig to the Twenty-seventh Congress (March 4, 1841–March 3, 1843); resumed the practice of law in Steubenville, Jefferson County, Ohio, where he died May 23, 1861; interment in Union Cemetery.

STOKES, Edward Lowber, a Representative from Pennsylvania; born in Philadelphia, Pa., September 29, 1880; attended the public schools, and was graduated from St. Paul's School, Concord, N. H.; employed as a clerk for a trust company and later became engaged as an investment dealer; unsuccessful candidate for election to the State house of representatives in 1930; elected as a Republican to the Seventy-second Congress to fill the vacancy caused by the death of George S. Graham; reelected to the Seventy-third Congress and served from November 3, 1931, to January 3, 1935; was not a candidate for renomination in 1934; retired, and resides in Newtown Square, Pa.

STOKES, James William, a Representative from South Carolina; born near Orangeburg, S. C., December 12, 1853; attended the common schools, and was graduated from Washington and Lee University, Lexington, Va., in 1876; taught school for twelve years; was graduated in medicine from Vanderbilt University, Nashville, Tenn.; engaged in agricultural pursuits in 1889; president of the State Farmers' Alliance; member of the State senate in 1890; delegate to the Democratic National Convention at Chicago in 1892; presidential elector on the Democratic ticket of Cleveland and Stevenson in 1892; unsuccessful candidate for election in 1892 to the Fifty-third Congress; presented credentials as a Democratic Member-elect to the Fifty-fourth Congress and served from March 4, 1895, to June 1, 1896, when the seat was declared vacant; elected to fill the vacancy thus caused; reelected to the Fifty-fifth, Fifty-sixth, and Fifty-seventh Congresses and served from November 3, 1896, until his death in Orangeburg, Orangeburg County, S. C., July 6, 1901; interment in Sunnyside Cemetery.

STOKES, Montfort, a Senator from North Carolina; born in Lunenburg County, Va., March 12, 1762; completed preparatory studies; at the age of fourteen entered the merchant service, and the same year enlisted in the Continental Navy under Commodore Stephen Decatur; was captured by the British the same year and confined for seven months on the British prison ship *Jersey* in New York Harbor; after the Revolutionary War settled in North Carolina and engaged in planting; assistant clerk of the State senate 1786–1790; clerk of the superior court of Rowan County, N. C., in 1790; elected as United States Senator in 1804, but declined; trustee of the University of North Carolina at Chapel Hill 1805–1838; moved from Salisbury, N. C., about 1812 and settled in Wilkesboro, N. C.; elected as a Democrat to the United States Senate to fill the vacancy caused by the resignation of James Turner; elected at same time for the full term and served from December 4, 1816, to March 3, 1823; member of the State senate 1826–1829; served in the State house of commons in 1829 and 1830; president in 1830 of the Board of Visitors to the United States Military Academy at West Point; Governor of North Carolina from 1830 to 1832, when he resigned; Democratic presidential elector in 1804, 1812, 1824, and 1828; appointed by President Jackson in 1832 as a member of the Board of Indian Commissioners and resided at Fort Gibson in what is now Oklahoma; was later appointed as a commissioner to negotiate treaties with various tribes of Indians in the West and Southwest; appointed agent for the Cherokee Indians in 1837, serving in this capacity until September 8, 1842, when he was made subagent for the Senecas, Shawnees, and Quapaws; died at Fort Gibson November 4, 1842; interment in Fort Gibson Cemetery.

STOKES, William Brickly, a Representative from Tennessee; born in Chatham County, N. C., September 9, 1814; attended the common schools; moved to Tennessee; engaged in agricultural pursuits; member of the State house of representatives 1849–1852; served in the State senate in 1855 and 1856; elected as a Whig to the Thirty-sixth Congress (March 4, 1859–March 3, 1861); entered the Union Army May 15, 1862, during the Civil War, as major of Tennessee Volunteers; promoted to colonel and subsequently brevetted major general; honorably discharged March 10, 1865; studied law; was admitted to the bar in 1867 and commenced practice in Alexandria, De Kalb County, Tenn.; upon the readmission of the State of Tennessee to representation was elected as a Republican to the Thirty-ninth, Fortieth, and Forty-first Congresses and served from July 24, 1866, to March 3, 1871; unsuccessful candidate for reelection in 1870 to the Forty-second Congress; supervisor of internal revenue for Tennessee; resumed the practice of law; died in Alexandria, Tenn., March 14, 1897; interment in East View Cemetery.

STOLL, Philip Henry, a Representative from South Carolina; born in Little Rock, Marion (now Dillon) County, S. C., November 5, 1874; attended the public schools; was graduated from Wofford College, Spartanburg, S. C., in 1897; teacher in the public schools 1897–1901; studied law; was admitted to the bar in 1901 and commenced practice in Kingstree, Williamsburg County, S. C.; member of the State house of representatives 1904–1906; solicitor of the third judicial circuit from 1908 to 1917, when he resigned; chairman of the Democratic county committee and member of the Democratic State committee 1908–1918; commissioned as a major in the Judge Advocate General's Department of the United States Army in 1917; promoted to the rank of lieutenant colonel in 1918 and served throughout the First World War; elected as a Democrat to the Sixty-sixth Congress to fill the vacancy caused by the death of J. Willard Ragsdale; reelected to the Sixty-seventh Congress and served from October 7, 1919, to March 3, 1923; unsuccessful candidate for renomination in 1922; resumed the practice of law; elected as a judge of the third judicial circuit of South Carolina in 1931 and served until December 6, 1946, when he retired; died in Columbia, S. C., October 29, 1958; interment in Williamsburg Presbyterian Cemetery, Kingstree, S. C.

STONE, Alfred Parish, a Representative from Ohio; born in Worthington, Mass., June 28, 1813; attended the common schools; moved to Columbus, Ohio, in 1832 and engaged in mercantile pursuits; elected as a Democrat to the Twenty-eighth Congress to fill the vacancy caused by the death of Heman A. Moore and served from October 8, 1844, to March 3, 1845; was not a candidate for renomination; appointed State treasurer by Governor Chase in 1857 to fill the vacancy caused by the resignation of W. H. Gibson; was elected and reelected to the same office and served until 1862; appointed as collector of internal revenue for the Columbus district of Ohio in 1862 and served until his death in Columbus, Ohio, August 2, 1865; interment in Green Lawn Cemetery.

STONE, Charles Warren, a Representative from Pennsylvania; born in Groton, Middlesex County, Mass., June 29, 1843; attended Lawrence Academy at Groton, and was graduated from Williams College, Williamstown, Mass., in 1863; moved to Pennsylvania in 1863 and settled in Warren; superintendent of schools of Warren County in 1865; studied law; was admitted to the bar in 1867 and commenced practice in Warren; trustee of Pennsylvania State College; member of the State house of representatives in 1870 and 1871; served in the State senate in 1877 and 1878; Lieutenant Governor of Pennsylvania 1879–1883; appointed secretary of the Commonwealth on January 18, 1887, and served until his resignation to accept nomination for Congress; elected as a Republican to the Fifty-first Congress to fill the vacancy caused by the death of Lewis F. Watson; reelected to the Fifty-second and to the three succeeding Congresses and

served from November 4, 1890, to March 3, 1899; unsuccessful candidate for reelection in 1898 to the Fifty-sixth Congress; unsuccessful candidate for Governor of Pennsylvania in 1898; resumed the practice of law; died at his home near Warren, Pa., August 15, 1912; interment in Oakland Cemetery, Pleasant Township, Warren County, Pa.

STONE, Claudius Ulysses, a Representative from Illinois; born on a farm in Menard County, near Greenview, Ill., May 11, 1879; attended the rural school and Western Normal College, Bushnell, Ill.; at the age of seventeen taught in the Bee Grove rural school in Menard County for one year; principal of Brimfield (Ill.) Public Schools for two years; during the Spanish-American War served as a corporal in Company K, Fourth Illinois Volunteer Infantry, from May 1898 to May 1899 with service in Cuba; studied law at the University of Michigan at Ann Arbor and at George Washington University, Washington, D. C.; elected superintendent of schools for Peoria County, Ill., in 1902, reelected in 1906 and served until 1910; president of the Association of County Superintendents of Schools of Illinois in 1909; was admitted to the bar in 1909 and commenced practice in Peoria, Ill.; elected as a Democrat to the Sixty-second, Sixty-third, and Sixty-fourth Congresses (March 4, 1911–March 3, 1917); unsuccessful candidate for reelection in 1916 to the Sixty-fifth Congress; postmaster of Peoria from 1917 until he resigned in October 1920 to practice law; master in chancery of the circuit court of Peoria County from June 5, 1928, to January 20, 1945; editor and publisher of the Peoria Star from December 1938 until his retirement in 1949 due to illness; died in Peoria, Ill., November 13, 1957; interment in Parkview Memorial Cemetery.

STONE, David, a Representative and a Senator from North Carolina; born at Hope, near Windsor, Bertie County, N. C., February 17, 1770; attended Windsor Academy, and was graduated from Princeton College in 1788; studied law; was admitted to the bar in 1790 and commenced practice in Halifax, N. C.; member of the State house of commons 1791–1794; judge of the supreme court of North Carolina 1794–1798; elected as a Democrat to the Sixth Congress (March 4, 1799–March 3, 1801); elected to the United States Senate and served from March 4, 1801, until his resignation about February 17, 1807; Governor of North Carolina 1808–1810; again elected to the United States Senate and served from March 4, 1813, until his resignation on December 24, 1814; resumed the practice of law; died on his plantation near Raleigh, Wake County, N. C., October 7, 1818; interment in the family burial ground on the banks of the Neuse River, near Raleigh, N. C.

STONE, Eben Francis, a Representative from Massachusetts; born in Newburyport, Essex County, Mass., August 3, 1822; attended North Andover Academy, and was graduated from Harvard University in 1843 and from Harvard Law School in 1846; was admitted to the bar in 1847 and commenced practice in Newburyport, Mass.; president of the common council in 1851; served in the State senate in 1857, 1858, and 1861; enlisted in the Union Army during the Civil War and commanded the Forty-eighth Regiment, Massachusetts Volunteer Militia, during its term of service; mayor of Newburyport in 1867; member of the State house of representatives in 1867, 1877, 1878, and 1880; elected as a Republican to the Forty-seventh, Forty-eighth, and Forty-ninth Congresses (March 4, 1881–March 3, 1887); was not a candidate for renomination in 1886; after his retirement from Congress resumed the practice of law in Newburyport, Mass., where he died January 22, 1895; interment in Oakhill Cemetery.

STONE, Frederick (grandson of Michael Jenifer Stone), a Representative from Maryland; born in Charles County, Md.,

February 7, 1820; was graduated from St. John's College, Annapolis, Md., in 1839; studied law; was admitted to the bar in 1841 and began practice in Port Tobacco, Md.; appointed by the legislature in 1852 as one of the commissioners to revise the rules of pleading and practice in the State courts; member of the State house of delegates in 1864 and 1865; elected as a Democrat to the Fortieth and Forty-first Congresses (March 4, 1867–March 3, 1871); unsuccessful candidate for reelection in 1870 to the Forty-second Congress; associate judge of the court of appeals 1881–1890; died near La Plata, Md., October 17, 1899; interment in Mount Rest Cemetery, La Plata, Md.

STONE, James W., a Representative from Kentucky; born in Taylorsville, Spencer County, Ky., in 1813; attended the common schools; studied law; was admitted to the bar and practiced; held several local offices; member of the State house of representatives in 1837 and 1839; elected as a Democrat to the Twenty-eighth Congress (March 4, 1843–March 3, 1845); unsuccessful candidate for reelection in 1844 to the Twenty-ninth Congress; elected to the Thirty-second Congress (March 4, 1851–March 3, 1853); unsuccessful candidate for reelection in 1852 to the Thirty-third Congress; died in Taylorsville, Ky., October 13, 1854.

STONE, John Wesley, a Representative from Michigan; born in Wadsworth, Medina County, Ohio, July 18, 1838; attended the public schools and Spencer (Ohio) Academy; moved to Allegan County, Mich., in 1856; elected county clerk of Allegan County in 1860; studied law; was admitted to the bar in January 1862 and practiced; reelected county clerk in 1862; prosecuting attorney 1864–1870; president of Allegan Village in 1872; circuit judge of the twentieth judicial circuit of Michigan from April 1873 until his resignation on November 1, 1874; moved to Grand Rapids, Mich., and practiced law; elected as a Republican to the Forty-fifth and Forty-sixth Congresses (March 4, 1877–March 3, 1881); was not a candidate for renomination in 1880; appointed by President Chester A. Arthur as United States attorney for the western Michigan district in 1882; moved to Houghton, Mich., in 1887 and resumed the practice of law; elected circuit judge of the twenty-fifth Michigan circuit in April 1890 and served until December 31, 1909; elected justice of the State supreme court in April 1909 for the term ending December 31, 1917; reelected in 1916 and served until his death in Lansing, Mich., March 24, 1922; interment in Park Cemetery, Marquette, Mich.

STONE, Joseph Champlin, a Representative from Iowa; born in Westport, Essex County, N. Y., July 30, 1829; moved to Iowa Territory in 1844; attended the public schools; was graduated from the medical department of St. Louis University, Missouri, in 1854 and practiced; during the Civil War enlisted as a private in the Union Army and was made adjutant of the First Iowa Cavalry; promoted to captain and assistant adjutant general of Volunteers in 1862 and served until the end of the war; resumed the practice of medicine in Burlington, Iowa; elected as a Republican to the Forty-fifth Congress (March 4, 1877–March 3, 1879); again engaged in the practice of his profession; died in Burlington, Iowa, December 3, 1902; interment in Aspen Grove Cemetery.

STONE, Michael Jenifer (brother of Thomas Stone and grandfather of Frederick Stone), a Representative from Maryland; born at "Equality," near Port Tobacco, Charles County, Md., in 1747; completed preparatory studies; member of the State house of delegates 1781–1783; member of the State convention that ratified the Federal Constitution in 1788; elected to the First Congress (March 4, 1789–March 3, 1791); ap-

pointed judge of the first judicial district of Maryland in 1791; died in Charles County, Md., in 1812; interment on his estate, "Equality," near Port Tobacco, Charles County, Md.

STONE, Thomas (brother of Michael Jenifer Stone), a Delegate from Maryland; born at Poynton Manor, Charles County, Md., in 1743; completed preparatory studies; studied law; was admitted to the bar in 1764 and commenced practice in Frederick, Md.; moved to Charles County, Md., in 1771; member of the State senate 1779–1783; a signer of the Declaration of Independence; Member of the Continental Congress 1775–1779, 1784, and 1785; died in Alexandria, Va., October 5, 1787; interment in the garden of his estate, Habre de Venture, Port Tobacco, Charles County, Md.

STONE, Ulysses Stevens, a Representative from Oklahoma; born on a farm near Weldon, De Witt Township, De Witt County, Ill., December 17, 1878; moved with his parents to Jones, Okla., in 1894; attended the country schools and the University of Oklahoma at Norman; engaged in the banking business at Jones, Okla., 1894–1905 and as an oil operator at Norman and Oklahoma City in 1905; was an unsuccessful candidate for Governor of Oklahoma in 1918 and for election to the United States Senate in 1926; elected as a Republican to the Seventy-first Congress (March 4, 1929–March 3, 1931); was an unsuccessful candidate for reelection in 1930 to the Seventy-second Congress and for election in 1934 to the Seventy-fourth Congress; resumed activities as an oil operator and also interested in investments and real estate; is a resident of Oklahoma City, Okla.

STONE, William, a Representative from Tennessee; born in Sevier County, Tenn. (then North Carolina), January 26, 1791; completed preparatory studies; held several local offices; was a captain in the Creek War and subsequently commissioned brigadier general for gallantry in the Battle of the Horseshoe; served with General Jackson in the Battle of New Orleans; was presented a cane by Congress for bravery in the Battle of Tippecanoe; unsuccessful Whig candidate for election in 1836 to the Twenty-fifth Congress; subsequently elected to the Twenty-fifth Congress to fill the vacancy caused by the death of James Standifer and served from September 14, 1837, to March 3, 1839; unsuccessful candidate for reelection to the Twenty-sixth Congress; died in Delphi (later Davis), Sequatchie County, Tenn., February 18, 1853; interment in the family burying ground at Delphi.

STONE, William Alexis, a Representative from Pennsylvania; born near Wellsboro, Delmar Township, Tioga County, Pa., April 18, 1846; attended the public schools and the State normal school at Mansfield, Tioga County, Pa.; served in the Civil War as second lieutenant of Company A, One Hundred and Eighty-seventh Regiment, Pennsylvania Volunteer Infantry; after the war became a lieutenant colonel in the State National Guard; studied law in Wellsboro, Pa.; was admitted to the bar in 1870 and practiced in Wellsboro and Pittsburgh, Pa.; district attorney of Tioga County from 1874 to 1876, when he resigned and moved to Pittsburgh, Pa.; served as United States attorney for the western district of Pennsylvania 1880–1886; elected as a Republican to the Fifty-second and to the three succeeding Congresses and served from March 4, 1891, until his resignation on November 9, 1898; Governor of Pennsylvania from 1899 to 1903; resumed the practice of his profession in Pittsburgh, Pa.; prothonotary of the eastern district of Pennsylvania and served from January 1, 1916, until his death in Philadelphia, Pa., on March 1, 1920; interment in Wellsboro Cemetery, Wellsboro, Pa.

STONE, William Henry, a Representative from Missouri; born in Shawangunk, N. Y., November 7, 1828; attended the common schools; moved to St. Louis, Mo., in 1848 and engaged in the manufacture of iron; became president of the St. Louis Hot Pressed Nut & Bolt Company upon its organization in 1867; served in the Missouri State House of Representatives; member of the St. Louis Board of Water Commissioners from July 5, 1871, to November 15, 1873, when he resigned, having been elected to Congress; elected as a Democrat to the Forty-third and Forty-fourth Congresses (March 4, 1873–March 3, 1877); was not a candidate for renomination in 1876 to the Forty-fifth Congress; resumed business interests; died in Asbury Park, N. J., July 9, 1901; interment in Bellefontaine Cemetery, St. Louis, Mo.

STONE, William Joel, a Representative and a Senator from Missouri; born near Richmond, Madison County, Ky., May 7, 1848; attended the public schools of Richmond, Ky.; was graduated from the University of Missouri at Columbia in 1867; studied law; was admitted to the bar in 1869 and commenced practice in Bedford, Ind.; moved to Columbia, Mo., where he was city attorney for a few months in 1870, and later in the same year moved to Nevada, Mo., and continued the practice of law; prosecuting attorney of Vernon County, Mo., in 1873 and 1874; presidential elector on the Democratic ticket of Tilden and Hendricks in 1876; elected as a Democrat to the Forty-ninth, Fiftieth, and Fifty-first Congresses (March 4, 1885–March 3, 1891); was not a candidate for renomination in 1890; Governor of Missouri 1893–1897; moved to Jefferson City, Mo., in 1893; member of the Democratic National Committee 1896–1904, serving as vice chairman 1900–1904; moved to St. Louis in 1897 and continued the practice of law; returned to Jefferson City in 1903; elected to the United States Senate and took his seat March 4, 1903; reelected in 1909 and again in 1914 and served until his death; was chairman of the Senate Committee on Foreign Relations during the First World War; died in Washington, D. C., April 14, 1918; interment in Deepwood Cemetery, Nevada, Vernon County, Mo.

STONE, William Johnson, a Representative from Kentucky; born in Kuttawa, Caldwell (now Lyon) County, Ky., June 26, 1841; attended the common schools and Q. M. Tyler's Collegiate Institute in Cadiz, Trigg County; studied law; during the Civil War served as captain in the Confederate Army; engaged in agricultural pursuits; member of the State house of representatives in 1867, 1875, and 1883, serving as speaker in 1875; elected as a Democrat to the Forty-ninth and to the four succeeding Congresses (March 4, 1885–March 3, 1895); engaged in mercantile pursuits in Kuttawa, Lyon County; Confederate pension commissioner of Kentucky in 1912 and served until his death in Frankfort, Ky., March 12, 1923; interment in New Bethel Cemetery, Lyon County, Ky.

STORER, Bellamy, a Representative from Ohio; was born in Portland, Maine, March 26, 1796; attended private schools in his native city; entered Bowdoin College, Brunswick, Maine, in 1809; studied law in Boston; was admitted to the bar in Portland in 1817 and commenced practice in Cincinnati, Ohio, the same year; elected as a Whig to the Twenty-fourth Congress (March 4, 1835–March 3, 1837); declined to be a candidate for renomination in 1836 to the Twenty-fifth Congress; presidential elector on the Whig ticket of Clay and Frelinghuysen in 1844; professor in Cincinnati Law School 1855–1874; judge of the superior court of Cincinnati from its organization in 1854 until 1872, when he resigned; resumed the practice of law, and died in Cincinnati, Ohio, on June 1, 1875; interment in Spring Grove Cemetery.

STORER, Bellamy (son of the preceding and uncle of Nicholas Longworth), a Representative from Ohio; born in Cincinnati, Ohio, August 28, 1847; attended the common schools of that city and Dixwell's private Latin school, Boston, Mass.; was graduated from Harvard University in 1867 and from the law school of Cincinnati College in 1869; was admitted to the bar in 1869 and commenced practice in Cincinnati; assistant United States attorney for the southern district of Ohio in 1869 and 1870; elected as a Republican to the Fifty-second and Fifty-third Congresses (March 4, 1891–March 3, 1895); was not a candidate for renomination in 1894; resumed the practice of law; Assistant Secretary of State in 1897; Envoy Extraordinary and Minister Plenipotentiary to Belgium from May 4, 1897, to April 11, 1899, to Spain from April 12, 1899, to September 26, 1902, and to Austria-Hungary from September 26, 1902, to March 1906; resumed the practice of law; died in Paris, France, November 12, 1922; interment in Le Cimetière Neuf, Marvejols, France.

STORER, Clement, a Representative and a Senator from New Hampshire; born in Kennebunk, Maine, September 20, 1760; completed preparatory studies; studied medicine in Portsmouth, N. H., and in Europe; engaged in the practice of medicine in Portsmouth; captain of militia, and held successive ranks to that of major general; member of the State house of representatives 1810–1812, serving one year as speaker; elected to the Tenth Congress (March 4, 1807–March 3, 1809); elected to the United States Senate to fill the vacancy caused by the resignation of Jeremiah Mason and served from June 27, 1817, to March 3, 1819; high sheriff of Rockingham County 1818–1824; died in Portsmouth, N. H., November 21, 1830; interment in North Cemetery.

STORKE, Thomas More, a Senator from California; born in Santa Barbara, Calif., November 23, 1876; attended the public schools and was graduated from Leland Stanford Junior University, Palo Alto, Calif., in 1898; editor and publisher of Santa Barbara News-Press and its predecessors since 1901; rancher and citrus fruit grower; delegate to the Democratic National Conventions in 1924, 1932, and 1936; appointed as a Democrat to the United States Senate to fill the vacancy caused by the resignation of William Gibbs McAdoo and served from November 9, 1938, to January 3, 1939; was not a candidate for election for the full term; member of the board of regents of University of California 1955–1960; is a resident of Santa Barbara, Calif.

STORM, Frederic, a Representative from New York; born in Alsace, France, July 2, 1844; immigrated to the United States in 1846 with his parents, who settled in New York City; attended the public schools of New York City; engaged in the cigar manufacturing business; member of the State constitutional convention in 1894; elected to the State assembly in 1895; member of the Queens County Republican committee 1894–1900 and was three times its chairman; founder of Flushing Hospital; elected as a Republican to the Fifty-seventh Congress (March 4, 1901–March 3, 1903); unsuccessful candidate for reelection in 1902 to the Fifty-eighth Congress; after leaving Congress engaged in banking in Bayside; founded the Bayside National Bank in 1905 and was its president until his resignation in 1920; resided in Bayside, Flushing, N. Y., until his death in that city on June 9, 1935; interment in Flushing Cemetery, Flushing, N. Y.

STORM, John Brutzman, a Representative from Pennsylvania; born in Hamilton Township, Monroe County, Pa., September 19, 1838; attended the common schools, and was graduated from Dickinson College, Carlisle, Pa., in 1861; studied law; was admitted to the bar in 1863 and commenced practice in Stroudsburg, Monroe County; county superintendent of public schools for seven years; elected as a Democrat to the Forty-second and Forty-third Congresses (March 4, 1871–March 3, 1875); was not a candidate for renomination in 1874; elected to the Forty-eighth and Forty-ninth Congresses (March 4, 1883–March 3, 1887); was not a candidate for renomination in 1886; resumed the practice of law; president judge of the forty-third judicial district of Pennsylvania; died in Stroudsburg, Monroe County, Pa., on August 13, 1901; interment in Stroudsburg Cemetery.

STORRS, Henry Randolph (brother of William Lucius Storrs), a Representative from New York; born in Middletown, Conn., September 3, 1787; was graduated from Yale College in 1804; studied law; was admitted to the bar in 1807 and commenced practice in Champion, Jefferson County, N. Y.; later practiced in Whitesboro and Utica, N. Y.; elected as a Federalist to the Fifteenth and Sixteenth Congresses (March 4, 1817–March 3, 1821); unsuccessful candidate for renomination in 1820; elected to the Eighteenth and to the three succeeding Congresses (March 4, 1823–March 3, 1831); one of the managers appointed by the House of Representatives in 1830 to conduct the impeachment proceedings against James H. Peck, United States judge for the district of Missouri; presiding judge of the court of common pleas of Oneida County 1825–1829; moved to New York City and practiced law; died in New Haven, Conn., July 29, 1837; interment in Grove Street Cemetery.

STORRS, William Lucius (brother of Henry Randolph Storrs), a Representative from Connecticut; born in Middletown, Conn., March 25, 1795; was graduated from Yale College in 1814; studied law; and was admitted to the bar in Whitestown, N. Y., in 1817; returned to Connecticut the same year and commenced practice in Middletown; member of the State house of representatives 1827–1829 and again in 1834; served as speaker in 1834; elected to the Twenty-first and Twenty-second Congresses (March 4, 1829–March 3, 1833); was not a candidate for renomination in 1832; elected as a Whig to the Twenty-sixth Congress and served from March 1839 until his resignation in June 1840; appointed associate judge of the Connecticut Supreme Court in 1840 and promoted to chief justice in 1856, in which capacity he served until his death; professor of law in the Wesleyan University at Middletown 1841–1846; professor of law at Yale College in 1846 and 1847; died in Hartford, Conn., June 25, 1861; interment in Old North Cemetery.

STORY, Joseph, a Representative from Massachusetts; born in Marblehead, Mass., September 18, 1779; attended Marblehead Academy; was graduated from Harvard University in 1798; studied law; was admitted to the bar in 1801 and commenced practice in Salem; member of the State house of representatives 1805–1807; elected as a Democrat to the Tenth Congress to fill the vacancy caused by the death of Jacob Crowninshield and served from May 23, 1808, to March 3, 1809; was not a candidate for renomination in 1808; again a member of the State house of representatives in 1811, and served as speaker; published commentaries on the Constitution, and also other works; appointed by President Madison as an Associate Justice of the Supreme Court of the United States and served from 1811 until his death; elected as an overseer of Harvard University in 1818 and as professor of law in the same institution in 1829, a position which he held until his death; delegate to the State constitutional convention in 1820; declined the position of chief justice of the Massachusetts Supreme Court in 1831; died in Cambridge, Mass., September 10, 1845; interment in Mount Auburn Cemetery.

STOUGHTON, William Lewis, a Representative from Michigan; born in Bangor, N. Y., March 20, 1827; attended Kirkland, Painesville, and Madison Academies in Ohio; studied law in Ohio, Indiana, and Michigan 1849–1851; was admitted to the bar and commenced practice in Sturgis, Mich., in 1851; prosecuting attorney 1855–1859; delegate to the Republican National Convention at Chicago in 1860, which nominated Lincoln and Hamlin; appointed by President Lincoln as United States district attorney for the Michigan district in March 1861, but resigned a few months later to enter the Union Army; served as colonel and brigadier general and was promoted to the rank of major general by brevet; resigned in August 1864 because of ill health and resumed the practice of his profession in Sturgis, St. Joseph County, Mich., in 1865; member of the Michigan State Constitutional Convention in 1867; attorney general of Michigan in 1867 and 1868; elected as a Republican to the Forty-first and Forty-second Congresses (March 4, 1869–March 3, 1873); again engaged in the practice of his profession in May 1874; died in Sturgis, Mich., on June 6, 1888; interment in Oak Lawn Cemetery.

STOUT, Byron Gray, a Representative from Michigan; born in Richmond, Ontario County, N. Y., January 12, 1829; moved with his parents to Michigan in 1831; attended the common schools; was graduated from the University of Michigan at Ann Arbor in 1851; studied law; superintendent and principal of Pontiac High School in 1853 and 1854; member of the State house of representatives in 1855 and 1857, serving as speaker in the latter year; member of the State senate in 1860 and served as president pro tempore; member of the Union Convention of Conservatives at Philadelphia in 1866; delegate to the Democratic National Conventions in 1868, 1880, and 1888; engaged in private banking prior to 1869; elected as a Democrat to the Fifty-second Congress (March 4, 1891–March 3, 1893); was not a candidate for reelection in 1892 to the Fifty-third Congress; president of the Oakland County Bank 1893–1896; died in Pontiac, Oakland County, Mich., June 19, 1896; interment in Oak Hill Cemetery.

STOUT, Lansing, a Representative from Oregon; born in Watertown, Jefferson County, N. Y., March 27, 1828; attended the public schools; studied law; was admitted to the bar; moved to Placer County, Calif., in 1852 and commenced the practice of law; member of the California Assembly in 1855; moved to Portland, Oreg., in 1857 and continued the practice of his profession; judge of the Multnomah County Court in 1858; was elected as a Democrat to the Thirty-sixth Congress (March 4, 1859–March 3, 1861); was not a candidate for renomination in 1860; resumed the practice of his profession in Portland; instrumental in securing the daily overland mail between Portland and Sacramento and the payment of the Oregon and Washington Territory Indian war debt; elected to the Oregon Senate in June 1868 and served until his death in Portland, Multnomah County, Oreg., March 4, 1871; interment in Riverview Cemetery.

STOUT, Tom, a Representative from Montana; born in New London, Ralls County, Mo., May 20, 1879; attended the common schools, Warrenburg (Mo.) State Normal School, and the University of Missouri at Columbia; taught school; studied law; was admitted to the Missouri bar in 1901 but did not practice; moved to Lewistown, Mont., in 1902; engaged in the newspaper business and was editor and publisher of the Fergus County Democrat 1902–1916 and the Lewistown Democrat News 1916–1946; delegate to the Democratic National Convention at Denver in 1908 and to all State conventions from 1904 to 1946; member of the State senate of Montana 1911–1913; elected as a

Democrat to the Sixty-third and Sixty-fourth Congresses (March 4, 1913–March 3, 1917); was not a candidate for renomination in 1916; member of the Montana Public Service Commission 1930–1932; elected to the State house of representatives in 1942, 1944, and 1946; editoral writer for the Billings (Mont.) Gazette from April 1, 1947, to February 29, 1960; resides in Billings, Mont.

STOVER, John Hubler, a Representative from Missouri; born in Aaronsburg, Center County, Pa., April 24, 1833; completed preparatory studies at Bellefonte Academy; studied law; was admitted to the bar in 1857 and commenced practice in Bellefonte, Pa.; held several local offices; district attorney of Center County 1860–1862; during the Civil War enlisted in the Union Army in 1861 as a private, and was successively a captain and a major; commissioned as a colonel of the One Hundred and Eighty-fourth Regiment, Pennsylvania Volunteer Infantry; after the war moved to Versailles, Morgan County, Mo., and resumed the practice of law; district attorney of Morgan County from 1866 to 1868; elected as a Republican to the Fortieth Congress to fill the vacancy caused by the resignation of Joseph W. McClurg and served from December 7, 1868, to March 3, 1869; was not a candidate for renomination in 1868; resumed the practice of his profession; engaged in the real-estate business and was also interested in mining pursuits at Versailles, Mo.; delegate to the Centennial Exposition at Philadelphia in 1876; unsuccessful candidate for election in 1876 to the Forty-fifth Congress; died at Aurora Springs, Mo., October 27, 1889; interment in the City Cemetery, Versailles, Morgan County, Mo.

STOW, Silas, a Representative from New York; born in Middlefield, Middlesex County, Conn., December 21, 1773; attended the common schools; studied law, but never practiced; moved to Lowville, Lewis County, N. Y., and engaged in agricultural pursuits; became land agent for Nicholas Low and moved to Oneida County in 1797; appointed judge of Oneida County, January 28, 1801; returned to Lewis County; elected as a Federalist to the Twelfth Congress (March 4, 1811–March 3, 1813); sheriff of Lewis County in 1814 and 1815; judge of the same county 1815–1823; died in Lowville, N. Y., January 19, 1827; interment in East State Street Burying Ground.

STOWELL, William Henry Harrison, a Representative from Virginia; born in Windsor, Vt., July 26, 1840; attended the public schools in Boston, Mass., and was graduated from Boston Latin School in 1860; engaged in mercantile pursuits; moved to Virginia in 1865; collector of internal revenue for the fourth district in 1869; elected as a Republican to the Forty-second, Forty-third, and Forty-fourth Congresses (March 4, 1871–March 3, 1877); was not a candidate for renomination in 1876; delegate to the Republican National Convention at Cincinnati in 1876; moved to Appleton, Wis., in 1880 and engaged in paper manufacturing; moved to Duluth, Minn., in 1886 and engaged in paper and steel manufacturing; president of the Manufacturers Bank of West Duluth 1889–1895; resided for awhile in St. Paul, Minn., and then in Washington, D. C.; correspondent in Paris, France, for various newspapers; author of several books on historical subjects; moved to Amherst, Mass., in 1914, where he died on April 27, 1922; interment in Woodlawn Cemetery, New York City, N. Y.

STOWER, John G., a Representative from New York; born in Madison, Madison County, N. Y.; completed preparatory studies; elected as a Jacksonian Democrat to the Twentieth Congress (March 4, 1827–March 3, 1829); member of the State senate in 1833 and 1834.

STRADER, Peter Wilson, a Representative from Ohio; born in Shawnee, Warren County, N. J., November 6, 1818; moved with his parents to Lebanon, Ohio, in 1819; attended the common schools; worked in a printing office for three years; moved to Cincinnati, Hamilton County, Ohio, in 1835; connected with the steamboat interests on the Ohio and Mississippi Rivers as a clerk and an engineer 1835–1848; general ticket agent of the Little Miami Railroad 1848–1867; elected as a Democrat to the Forty-first Congress (March 4, 1869–March 3, 1871); was not a candidate for renomination in 1870; resumed his former business interests; moved to Ashtabula, Ohio, in 1876, where he died February 25, 1881; interment in Spring Grove Cemetery, Cincinnati, Ohio.

STRAIT, Horace Burton, a Representative from Minnesota; born in Potter County, Pa., January 26, 1835; attended the common schools; moved with his parents to Indiana in 1846; settled near Jordan, Minn., in 1855 and engaged in agricultural pursuits; moved to Shakopee, Minn., in 1860 and conducted a general store; during the Civil War entered the Union Army in 1862 as captain in the Ninth Regiment, Minnesota Volunteer Infantry, being promoted to major in 1864; served at the close of the war as inspector general on the staff of General McArthur; honorably discharged in 1865; trustee of Minnesota Hospital for the Insane in 1866; mayor of Shakopee in 1870, 1871, and 1872; engaged in mercantile pursuits, manufacturing, and banking; elected as a Republican to the Forty-third, Forty-fourth, and Forty-fifth Congresses (March 4, 1873–March 3, 1879); unsuccessful candidate for reelection in 1878 to the Forty-sixth Congress; elected to the Forty-seventh, Forty-eighth, and Forty-ninth Congresses (March 4, 1881–March 3, 1887); withdrew from political life; resumed banking at Shakopee and also engaged in agricultural pursuits; died February 25, 1894, on a train at Juarez, Mexico, en route to the United States; interment in Valley Cemetery, Shakopee, Minn.

STRAIT, Thomas Jefferson, a Representative from South Carolina; born in Chester District, S. C., December 25, 1846; attended the common schools of Mayesville, S. C., and Cooper Institute, Mississippi; during the Civil War entered the Confederate Army in 1862 and served throughout the war, first in Company A, Sixth Regiment of Infantry, and later as sergeant in Company H, Twenty-fourth Regiment, Gist's brigade; engaged in agricultural pursuits; taught school in Ebenezer, York County, S. C., in 1880; was graduated from South Carolina Medical College at Charleston in 1885 and practiced medicine; member of the State senate 1890–1893; elected as an Alliance Democrat to the Fifty-third, Fifty-fourth, and Fifty-fifth Congresses (March 4, 1893–March 3, 1899); unsuccessful candidate for renomination in 1898 to the Fifty-sixth Congress; resumed the practice of his profession in Lancaster, S. C., and died there on April 18, 1924; interment in Westside Cemetery.

STRANAHAN, James Samuel Thomas, a Representative from New York; born in Peterboro, Madison County, N. Y., April 25, 1808; attended the common schools and Cazenovia Seminary; founded the town of Florence, Oneida County, N. Y., in 1832; engaged in the lumber business; postmaster of Florence; member of the State assembly in 1838; moved to Newark, N. J., in 1840; engaged in building railroads; moved to Brooklyn, N. Y., in 1845; elected alderman of that city in 1848; elected as a Whig to the Thirty-fourth Congress (March 4, 1855–March 3, 1857); unsuccessful candidate for reelection in 1856 to the Thirty-fifth Congress; appointed as a member of the metropolitan police commission on January 1, 1857; presidential elector on the Republican tickets of Lincoln and Hamlin in 1860 and Harrison and Morton in 1888; president of the board of trustees of Prospect

Park, Brooklyn, N. Y.; director of the first Brooklyn Bridge and presided at its dedication May 28, 1884; died at his summer home at Saratoga Springs, N. Y., September 3, 1898; interment in Greenwood Cemetery, Brooklyn, N. Y.

STRANGE, Robert, a Senator from North Carolina; born in Manchester, Va., September 20, 1796; attended private schools in Virginia, New Oxford Academy, and Washington College (now Washington and Lee University), Lexington, Va.; was graduated from Hampden-Sidney College, Virginia; moved to Fayetteville, N. C., in 1815; studied law; was admitted to the bar and practiced in Fayetteville; member of the State house of commons 1821–1823 and in 1826; judge of the superior court of North Carolina 1827–1836; elected as a Democrat to the United States Senate to fill the vacancy caused by the resignation of Willie P. Mangum and served from December 5, 1836, to November 16, 1840, when he resigned; resumed the practice of law in Fayetteville, Cumberland County, N. C.; solicitor for the fifth judicial district of North Carolina; engaged in literary pursuits; died in Fayetteville, N. C., February 19, 1854; interment in the family burial ground at "Myrtle Hill," near Fayetteville, N. C.

STRATTON, Charles Creighton (uncle of Benjamin Franklin Howey), a Representative from New Jersey; born in Swedesboro, Gloucester County, N. J., March 6, 1796; attended the common schools; was graduated from Rutgers College, New Brunswick, N. J., in 1814; engaged in agricultural pursuits; member of the State general assembly in 1821, 1823, and again in 1829; elected as a Whig to the Twenty-fifth Congress (March 4, 1837–March 3, 1839); presented credentials as a Member-elect to the Twenty-sixth Congress, but the House declined to seat him; reelected to the Twenty-seventh Congress (March 4, 1841–March 3, 1843); was not a candidate for renomination in 1842; member of the State constitutional convention in 1844; Governor of New Jersey from January 21, 1845, to January 17, 1848; resumed agricultural pursuits; owing to ill health resided in Europe in 1857 and 1858; died in Swedesboro, N. J., March 30, 1859; interment in the Episcopal Cemetery.

STRATTON, John, a Representative from Virginia; born at "Old Castle," near Eastville, Northampton County, Va., August 19, 1769; attended the common schools; studied law; was admitted to the bar and practiced; member of the State house of delegates 1779–1792; elected to the Seventh Congress (March 4, 1801–March 3, 1803); died, while visiting his sister, in Norfolk, Va., May 10, 1804; interment in St. Paul's Church Cemetery.

STRATTON, John Leake Newbold, a Representative from New Jersey; born in Mount Holly, Burlington County, N. J., November 27, 1817; attended private schools at Mount Holly; prepared for college at Mendham; was graduated from Princeton College in 1836; studied law; was admitted to the bar in 1839 and commenced practice in Mount Holly; elected as a Republican to the Thirty-sixth and Thirty-seventh Congresses (March 4, 1859–March 3, 1863); was not a candidate for renomination in 1862; resumed the practice of law; delegate to the Union National Convention of Conservatives at Philadelphia in 1866; president of the Farmers' National Bank of Mount Holly in 1875; died in Mount Holly, N. J., on May 17, 1899; interment in St. Andrews Cemetery.

STRATTON, Nathan Taylor, a Representative from New Jersey; born in Pilesgrove Township, Salem County, N. J., near Swedesboro, March 17, 1813; attended the common schools; moved to Mullica Hill, N. J., in 1829 and clerked in a store, becoming a partner of his employer in 1835; conducted his own business 1840–1886; member of the State general assembly 1843–1844; justice of the peace 1844–1847; also engaged in the real-estate business and in agricultural pursuits; held several local offices; elected as a Democrat to the Thirty-second and Thirty-third Congresses (March 4, 1851–March 3, 1855); was not a candidate for renomination in 1854; again engaged in mercantile pursuits; elected as a member of the Harrison Township committee in 1865; served as State tax commissioner; trustee of the State reform school for boys at Jamesburg, N. J., 1865–1887; delegate to the Union National Convention of Conservatives at Philadelphia in 1866; unsuccessful candidate for election in 1880 to the Forty-seventh Congress; died in Mullica Hill, N. J., March 9, 1887; interment in the Baptist Cemetery.

STRATTON, Samuel Studdiford, a Representative from New York; born in Yonkers, Westchester County, N. Y., September 27, 1916; at age of three months moved with parents to Schenectady, N. Y.; attended the public schools of Schenectady and Rochester, N. Y., and Blair Academy, Blairstown, N. J.; graduated from University of Rochester in 1937, Haverford (Pa.) College in 1938, and Harvard University in 1940; executive secretary to Representative Thomas H. Eliot of Massachusetts 1940–1942; during World War II was commissioned an ensign in the United States Naval Reserve on June 26, 1942; attended the Naval Japanese Language School, Boulder, Colo.; served in the Southwest Pacific Theater as naval combat intelligence officer on the staff of Gen. Douglas MacArthur from Brisbane, Australia, to Tokyo, Japan; participated with the Army in combat landings at Hollandia and Biak in New Guinea and Lingayan Gulf in the Philippines; separated from the service as a lieutenant in 1946; twice awarded the Bronze Star Medal with combat V; at the close of the war interrogated Japanese supreme commander in the Philippines, Gen. Tomoyuki Yamashita, who was later hanged as a war criminal; deputy secretary-general of the Far Eastern Commission, Washington, D. C., 1946–1948; elected city councilman of Schenectady, N. Y., in 1949, reelected in 1953 and served until 1956; recalled to active naval duty as a lieutenant commander during the Korean emergency and served as instructor at the Naval Intelligence School, Washington, D. C., 1951–1953; member of Schenectady Municipal Housing Authority 1950–1955, serving as chairman in 1951; mayor of Schenectady 1956–1959; member of board of trustees University of Rochester; registered representative with First Albany Corporation since 1957; elected as a Democrat to the Eighty-sixth Congress (January 3, 1959–January 3, 1961). *Reelected to the Eighty-seventh Congress.*

STRATTON, William Grant, a Representative from Illinois; born in Ingleside, Lake County, Ill., February 26, 1914; attended the public schools, and was graduated from the University of Arizona at Tucson in 1934; elected as a Republican to the Seventy-seventh Congress (January 3, 1941–January 3, 1943); was not a candidate for renomination in 1942; State treasurer of Illinois in 1943 and 1944, and 1950–1952; during World War II served as a lieutenant in the United States Navy in 1945 and 1946; again elected in 1946 to the Eightieth Congress (January 3, 1947–January 3, 1949); was not a candidate for renomination in 1948; delegate to the Republican National Conventions in 1952, 1956 and 1960; Governor of Illinois 1953–1961; unsuccessful for reelection as Governor in 1960; engaged in livestock farming at Cantrall, Ill.; is a resident of Morris, Ill.

STRAUB, Christian Markle, a Representative from Pennsylvania; born in Milton, Pa., in 1804; studied law; was admitted to the bar; prothonotary of Schuylkill County in 1845; sheriff of Schuylkill County in 1849; elected as a Democrat to the Thirty-third Congress (March 4, 1853–March 3, 1855); member of the State senate 1856–1858; died in Washington, D. C.; interment in Pottsville, Pa

STRAUS, Isidor, a Representative from New York; born in Otterberg, Rhenish Bavaria, Germany, February 6, 1845; immigrated to the United States in 1854 with his mother and settled in Talbotton, Ga., where his father had previously provided a home; attended Collinsworth Institute and prepared for West Point Military Academy, but did not enter due to the Civil War; moved to New York City in 1865 and engaged in mercantile pursuits; elected as a Democrat to the Fifty-third Congress to fill the vacancy caused by the resignation of Ashbel P. Fitch and served from January 30, 1894, to March 3, 1895; was not a candidate for reelection in 1894 to the Fifty-fourth Congress; resumed the mercantile business in New York City; member of the New York and New Jersey Bridge Commission; perished in the wreck of the steamship *Titanic* on April 15, 1912; the body was subsequently recovered and interred in the family vault in Beth-El Cemetery, Fresh Pond Road, Brooklyn, N. Y.

STRAWBRIDGE, James Dale, a Representative from Pennsylvania; born in Liberty Township, Montour County, Pa., April 7, 1824; attended the common schools; was graduated from Princeton College in 1844 and from the medical department of the University of Pennsylvania at Philadelphia in 1847; engaged in the practice of medicine at Danville, Pa.; during the Civil War entered the Army as a brigade surgeon of Volunteers and served throughout the war; confined in Libby Prison for three months; resumed the practice of medicine at Danville; elected as a Republican to the Forty-third Congress (March 4, 1873–March 3, 1875); again engaged in the practice of his profession; died in Danville, Pa., July 19, 1890; interment in Fairview Cemetery.

STREET, Randall S., a Representative from New York; born in Catskill, N. Y., in 1780; pursued classical studies; studied law; was admitted to the bar and began practice in Poughkeepsie; district attorney for the second judicial district from February 1810 to February 1811 and from March 1813 to February 1815; lieutenant colonel of militia in the War of 1812; elected as a Democrat to the Sixteenth Congress (March 4, 1819–March 3, 1821); moved to Monticello, N. Y., about 1825; continued the practice of law until his death in Monticello, N. Y., November 21, 1841; interment in Poughkeepsie, N. Y.

STRICKLAND, Randolph, a Representative from Michigan; born in Dansville, N. Y., February 4, 1823; attended the common schools; moved to Michigan in 1844 and taught school in Ingham County; studied law; was admitted to the bar in 1849 and commenced practice in De Witt, Clinton County, Mich.; moved to St. Johns, Clinton County, and continued the practice of law; elected prosecuting attorney for Clinton County in 1852, 1854, 1856, 1858, and 1862; member of the State senate in 1861 and 1862; provost marshal of the Sixth Congressional District 1863–1865; delegate to the Republican National Conventions in 1856 and 1868; elected as a Republican to the Forty-first Congress (March 4, 1869–March 3, 1871); was an unsuccessful candidate for renomination in 1870; resumed the practice of law; died in Battle Creek, Mich., May 5, 1880; interment in De Witt Cemetery, De Witt, Mich.

STRINGER, Lawrence Beaumont, a Representative from Illinois; born near Atlantic City, N. J., February 24, 1866; moved with his parents to Lincoln, Ill., in 1876; attended the public schools; was graduated from Lincoln University (later Lincoln College) in 1887; reporter on a local paper; member of the State house of representatives 1890–1892; entered the

Chicago College of Law (law department of Lake Forest University), and was graduated therefrom in 1896, taking a postgraduate course the following year; returned to Lincoln, Ill., in 1898 and commenced the practice of his profession; delegate to the Democratic State convention in 1900 and served as chairman; member of the State senate 1900–1904; unsuccessful Democratic candidate for Governor of Illinois in 1904; appointed chief justice of the Illinois State Court of Claims in 1905 and served until 1913; unsuccessful candidate for the Democratic nomination for United States Senator in 1908; elected as a Democrat to the Sixty-third Congress (March 4, 1913–March 3, 1915); did not seek renomination in 1914, having again become a candidate for Senator, but was unsuccessful; resumed the practice of law; unsuccessful candidate for justice of the supreme court of Illinois in 1924; elected judge of Logan County in 1918 and served until his death; died in Lincoln, Ill., December 5, 1942; interment in Union Cemetery.

STRINGFELLOW, Douglas R., a Representative from Utah; born in Draper, Utah, September 24, 1922; attended the public schools; moved to Odgen, Utah, in 1935 and graduated from high school in 1941; attended Weber College in 1941 and 1942, Ohio State University in 1943, and the University of Cincinnati in 1943 and 1944; took special schooling in radio announcing and production at Broadcasters Network Studios in Hollywood in 1947; during World War II entered the military service on November 4, 1942; separated as a private, first class, on November 8, 1945; awarded the Purple Heart Medal for injuries received in France on November 19, 1944; also the Good Conduct Medal, American Campaign Medal, World War II Victory Medal, European-African-Middle Eastern Campaign Medal with one Bronze Service Star for participation in the Rhineland Campaign, and the Combat Infantryman Badge; State chairman of the Young Republican League in 1946; served a Latter Day Saint's Mission in Northern California in 1947 and 1948; announcer and executive for radio station 1949–1952; recipient of Freedom Foundation Award and State Junior Chamber of Commerce Distinguished Service Award in 1950, Eagles Lodge Civil Service Award in 1951, and took second place in American Legion Operation Comeback National Contest in 1951; elected as a Republican to the Eighty-third Congress (January 3, 1953–January 3, 1955); renominated in 1954 but withdrew and was not a candidate for reelection to the Eighty-fourth Congress; engaged as a newscaster, Mutual Broadcasting System, Intermountain Network, Station KALL; is a resident of Bountiful, Utah.

STRODE, Jesse Burr, a Representative from Nebraska; born in Farmers Township, Fulton County, Ill., February 18, 1845; attended the public and high schools and was graduated from Abingdon (Ill.) College; during the Civil War enlisted in Company G, Fiftieth Regiment, Illinois Volunteer Infantry, September 10, 1861, and served as sergeant until January 1864; reenlisted and was promoted to rank of second lieutenant, serving with his regiment during the Atlanta campaign, the march to the sea through the Carolinas and Virginia, and the grand review in Washington, D. C.; mustered out in July 1865; principal of the graded schools of Abingdon 1865–1873; was twice elected mayor and six times councilman of Abingdon; studied law; moved to Plattsmouth, Nebr., May 1, 1879; was admitted to the bar in November 1879 and commenced practice in Plattsmouth; district attorney 1882–1888; moved to Lincoln in 1887 and practiced law; judge of the district court in 1892; elected as a Republican to the Fifty-fourth and Fifty-fifth Congresses (March 4, 1895–March 3, 1899); was not a candidate for renomination in 1898; resumed the practice of law; prosecuting attorney for the third district of Nebraska; department commander of the Grand Army of the Republic in 1919 and 1920; died in Lincoln, Nebr., on November 10, 1924; interment in Wyuka Cemetery.

STROHM, John, a Representative from Pennsylvania; born in Little Britain (later Fulton) Township, near Centerville, Lancaster County, Pa., October 16, 1793; attended the public schools; taught school for several years; moved to Providence, Pa.; member of the State house of representatives 1831–1833; served in the State senate 1834–1842, being speaker in 1842; elected as a Whig to the Twenty-ninth and Thirtieth Congresses (March 4, 1845–March 3, 1849); surveyor and justice of the peace in Providence Township for several years; delegate to the Whig National Convention at Baltimore in 1852; delegate to the State convention in 1869; died in Lancaster, Pa., September 12, 1884; interment in the Mennonite Cemetery.

STRONG, Caleb, a Senator from Massachusetts; born in Northampton, Mass., January 9, 1745; studied under private tutors; was graduated from Harvard College in 1764; studied law; was admitted to the bar and commenced practice in 1772; member of the committee of correspondence and safety in 1774 and 1775; member of the State house of representatives 1776–1778; served in the State senate 1780–1788; county attorney 1776–1800; member of the national convention in Philadelphia which framed the Constitution of the United States, but illness in his family compelled his absence before the convention was ended; member of the Massachusetts constitutional convention which ratified the Constitution of the United States; elected as a Federalist to the United States Senate; reelected in 1793, and served from March 4, 1789, to June 1, 1796, when he resigned; presidential elector on the Federalist ticket of Pinckney and King in 1809; Governor of Massachusetts 1800–1807 and 1812–1816; died in Northampton, Mass., November 7, 1819; interment in Bridge Street Cemetery.

STRONG, James, a Representative from New York; born in Windham, Conn., in 1783; was graduated from the University of Vermont at Burlington in 1806; moved to Hudson, Columbia County, N. Y.; elected as a Federalist to the Sixteenth Congress (March 4, 1819–March 3, 1821); elected to the Eighteenth and to the three succeeding Congresses (March 4, 1823–March 3, 1831); died in Chester, Morris County, N. J., on August 8, 1847.

STRONG, James George, a Representative from Kansas; born in Dwight, Livingston County, Ill., April 23, 1870; attended the public schools of Dwight, Ill., 1876–1879, the Episcopal Mission of Greenwood Agency, S. Dak., 1879–1880, the public school at St. Marys, Kans., 1882–1887, and Baker University, Baldwin, Kans., 1887–1889; moved to Blue Rapids, Kans., in 1891; engaged in the real estate, loan, and insurance businesses; also studied law; was admitted to the bar in 1895 and commenced practice in Blue Rapids; also interested in mercantile and agricultural pursuits; city attorney 1896–1911; organized the Blue Rapids Telephone Co. in 1905; assistant attorney general of Marshall County in 1911 and 1912; delegate to the Republican National Conventions in 1912 and 1928; organized and developed the Marshall County Power & Light Co. in 1912; member of the school board 1913–1916; prosecuting attorney of Marshall County in 1916 and 1917; elected as a Republican to the Sixty-sixth and to the six succeeding Congresses (March 4, 1919–March 3, 1933); unsuccessful for renomination in 1932; appointed first assistant treasurer of the Home Owners' Loan Corporation in 1933 and served until his death in Washington, D. C., on January 11, 1938; interment in Fairmount Cemetery, Blue Rapids, Kans.

STRONG, Jedediah, a Delegate from Connecticut; born in Litchfield, Conn., November 7, 1738; was graduated from Yale College in 1761; studied law; was admitted to the bar in 1764 and commenced the practice of his profession in Litchfield; member of the State house of representatives 1771–1801; town clerk 1773–1789; member of the committee on inspection in 1774 and 1775, and was made commissary of supplies for the Army in 1775; elected as a Delegate to the Continental Congress in 1779 but declined; clerk of the State house of representatives 1779–1788; associate judge of the Litchfield County Court 1780–1791; Member of the Continental Congress 1782–1784; delegate to the Connecticut convention to ratify the Constitution of the United States in 1788; served as a member of the Governor's council, or upper house, in 1789 and 1790; died in Litchfield, Conn., August 21, 1802; interment in the West Burying Ground.

STRONG, Julius Levi, a Representative from Connecticut; born in Bolton, Tolland County, Conn., November 8, 1828; attended Wesleyan University, Middletown, Conn., and Union College, Schenectady, N. Y.; member of the State house of representatives in 1852; served in the State senate in 1853; studied law at National Law School, Balston Spa, N. Y.; was admitted to the bar in 1853 and commenced practice in Hartford, Conn.; again a member of the State house of representatives, in 1855; prosecuting attorney in 1864 and 1865; president of the common council; elected as a Republican to the Forty-first and Forty-second Congresses and served from March 4, 1869, until his death in Hartford, Conn., September 7, 1872; interment in Cedar Hill Cemetery.

STRONG, Luther Martin, a Representative from Ohio; born near Tiffin, Seneca County, Ohio, June 23, 1838; attended the common schools and Aaron Schuyler's Academy, Republic, Ohio; taught school; during the Civil War enlisted as a private in the Forty-ninth Regiment, Ohio Volunteer Infantry, early in 1861; elected captain of Company G and afterward promoted to major and lieutenant colonel; senior officer of the regiment and in command thereof from about the time of the fall of Atlanta until after the Battle of Nashville, but could not be commissioned colonel because the regiment had become greatly reduced in numbers; resigned March 13, 1865, because of a wound; studied law; was admitted to the bar by the supreme court of Ohio January 30, 1867; moved to Kenton and practiced his profession; member of the board of education; was elected to the State senate in 1879 and 1881; appointed judge of the court of common pleas by Governor Foster in 1883 to fill an unexpired term; elected as a Republican to the Fifty-third and Fifty-fourth Congresses (March 4, 1893–March 3, 1897); unsuccessful candidate for renomination in 1896 to the Fifty-fifth Congress; engaged in agricultural pursuits; died in Kenton, Ohio, April 26, 1903; interment in Grove Cemetery.

STRONG, Nathan Leroy, a Representative from Pennsylvania; born in Troy (now Summerville), Jefferson County, Pa., November 12, 1859; attended the public schools; was a telegraph operator and railroad agent 1877–1894; studied law; was admitted to the bar in 1891 and commenced practice in Brookville, Jefferson County, Pa., in 1893; district attorney of Jefferson County 1895–1900; engaged in the development of mineral lands in Jefferson and Armstrong Counties 1901–1916; promoted the building of the Pittsburgh & Shawmut Railroad; president of the Mohawk Mining Co.; engaged in banking; president of the Brookville Park Association; president of the Jefferson County Agricultural Association; president of the Lake Erie-Allegheny River Canal Association; elected as a Republican to the Sixty-fifth and to the eight succeeding Congresses (March 4, 1917–

January 3, 1935); unsuccessful candidate for reelection in 1934 to the Seventy-fourth Congress; resumed his former business activities; died in Brookville, Pa., December 14, 1939; interment in Brookville Cemetery.

STRONG, Selah Brewster, a Representative from New York; born in Brookhaven, Suffolk County, N. Y., May 1, 1792; received a preliminary education and was graduated from Yale College in 1811; studied law; was admitted to the bar in 1814 and began practice in New York City; during the War of 1812 was commissioned as an ensign and quartermaster in the Tenth Regiment, Third Brigade, New York City and County Troops, and in 1815 was promoted successively to lieutenant and captain; master in chancery in 1817; moved to Brookhaven in 1820; district attorney for Suffolk County from 1821 to 1847, except for nine months in 1830; appointed judge advocate of the First Division of the New York State Infantry in 1825; elected as a Democrat to the Twenty-eighth Congress (March 4, 1843–March 3, 1845); was not a candidate for renomination in 1844; resumed the practice of law; appointed March 27, 1846, as circuit judge by Governor Wright and was confirmed, but did not accept; judge of the supreme court for the second judicial district from June 7, 1847, to January 1, 1860; member of the State constitutional convention in 1867; died at his home, "St. George's Manor," Setauket, Long Island, N. Y., November 29, 1872; interment in a private lot on his estate.

STRONG, Solomon, a Representative from Massachusetts; born in Amherst, Mass., March 2, 1780; was graduated from Williams College, Williamstown, Mass., in 1798; studied law; was admitted to the bar in Northampton, Mass., in 1800 and commenced the practice of law; member of the State senate in 1812 and 1813; judge of the circuit court of common pleas in 1818 and judge of the court of common pleas from 1821 until his resignation in 1842; elected as a Federalist to the Fourteenth and Fifteenth Congresses (March 4, 1815–March 3, 1819); was not a candidate for renomination in 1818; again a member of the State senate in 1843 and 1844; died in Leominster, Mass., on September 16, 1850; interment in Evergreen Cemetery.

STRONG, Stephen, a Representative from New York; born in Lebanon, Conn., October 11, 1791; moved to New York; attended Hamilton College, Clinton, N. Y.; studied law; was admitted to the bar in 1822 and practiced; district attorney of Tioga County 1836–1838 and 1844–1847; judge of Tioga County 1838–1843; elected as a Democrat to the Twenty-ninth Congress (March 4, 1845–March 3, 1847); resumed the practice of law in Owego, N. Y.; again judge of Tioga County 1855–1859; moved to Watertown, Jefferson County, N. Y., in 1861 and practiced law; died in Watertown, N. Y., April 15, 1866.

STRONG, Sterling Price, a Representative from Texas; born on a farm near Jefferson City, Cole County, Mo., August 17, 1862; moved to Texas in 1871 with his parents, who settled in Montague County; attended the rural schools of Montague County, Tex., and was graduated from Eastman's National Business College, Poughkeepsie, N. Y., in 1884; county clerk of Montague County 1884–1888 and 1898–1904; engrossing clerk of the State senate in 1889; county and district clerk of Hale County 1889–1892; traveling salesman 1892–1898 and 1911–1932; cashier in the National Bank of Bowie, Tex., 1908–1911; member of Texas State Democratic executive committee 1900–1902; unsuccessful candidate for Lieutenant Governor of Texas in 1930; elected as a Democrat to the Seventy-third Congress (March 4, 1933–January 3, 1935); unsuccessful candidate for renomination in 1934; died in Dallas, Tex., March 28, 1936; interment in Old Oak Cliff Cemetery.

STRONG, Theron Rudd (cousin of William Strong of Pennsylvania), a Representative from New York; born in Salisbury, Conn., November 7, 1802; attended the common schools; studied law at Litchfield Law School; was admitted to the bar in 1821 and commenced practice in Palmyra, Wayne County, N. Y.; master and examiner in chancery for several years; held several local offices; district attorney of Wayne County from 1835 to 1839; elected as a Democrat to the Twenty-sixth Congress (March 4, 1839–March 3, 1841); member of the State assembly in 1842; associate justice of the supreme court of New York 1851–1859 and judge of the court of appeals in 1859; moved to Rochester, N. Y., in 1860 and resumed the practice of his profession; returned to New York City in 1867 and continued the practice of law until his death May 14, 1873; interment in Mount Hope Cemetery, Rochester, N. Y.

STRONG, William, a Representative from Vermont; born in Lebanon, Conn., in 1763; moved with his parents to Hartford, Vt., in 1764; self-educated; engaged extensively in land surveying; member of the State house of representatives in 1798, 1799, 1801, and 1802; sheriff of Windsor County from 1802 to 1810; elected as a Democrat to the Twelfth and Thirteenth Congresses (March 4, 1811–March 3, 1815); again a member of the State house of representatives 1815–1818; judge of the supreme court of Windsor County 1819–1821; elected to the Sixteenth Congress (March 4, 1819–March 3, 1821); member of the council of censors in 1834; died in Hartford, Windsor County, Vt., January 28, 1840; interment in Quechee Cemetery.

STRONG, William (cousin of Theron Rudd Strong), a Representative from Pennsylvania; born in Somers, Conn., May 6, 1808; attended Munson Academy, Massachusetts, and was graduated from Yale College in 1828; taught school in New Haven, Conn.; studied law; was admitted to the bar in 1832 and commenced practice in Reading, Pa.; elected as a Democrat to the Thirtieth and Thirty-first Congresses (March 4, 1847–March 3, 1851); did not seek renomination in 1850; associate justice of the supreme court of Pennsylvania 1857–1868; practiced law in Philadelphia, Pa.; appointed as an Associate Justice of the Supreme Court of the United States in 1870 and served until December 1880, when he retired; resumed the practice of law; died at Lake Minnewassa, N. Y., August 19, 1895; interment in Charles Evans Cemetery, Reading, Pa.

STROTHER, George French (father of James French Strother), a Representative from Virginia; born in Stevensburg, Culpeper County, Va., in 1783; attended William and Mary College, Williamsburg, Va.; studied law; was admitted to the bar and commenced practice in Culpeper; member of the State house of delegates 1806–1809; elected as a Democrat to the Fifteenth and Sixteenth Congresses and served from March 4, 1817, until his resignation February 10, 1820; receiver of public moneys at St. Louis, Mo.; died in St. Louis November 28, 1840; interment in Christ Church Cemetery; reinterment in Bellefontaine Cemetery in 1860.

STROTHER, James French (son of George French Strother), a Representative from Virginia; born in Culpeper, Va., September 4, 1811; completed preparatory studies and attended St. Louis University, Missouri; studied law; was admitted to the bar and commenced practice in Washington, Rappahannock County, Va.; member of the State house of delegates 1840–1851, serving as speaker in 1851; delegate to the State constitutional convention in 1850; elected as a Whig to the Thirty-second Congress (March 4, 1851–March 3, 1853); resumed the practice of law in Culpeper, Va.; died near Culpeper, Va., September 20, 1860; interment in the Masonic Cemetery.

STROTHER, James French (grandson of the preceding), a Representative from West Virginia; born near Pearisburg, Giles County, Va., June 29, 1868; attended the public schools, Pearisburg Academy, and Virginia Agricultural and Mechanical College at Blacksburg; deputy collector of internal revenue at Lynchburg, Va., 1890–1893; studied law at the University of Virginia at Charlottesville; was admitted to the bar in 1894 and commenced practice in Pearisburg; settled in Welch, McDowell County, W. Va., in 1895 and continued the practice of law; United States commissioner 1897–1901; appointed judge of the criminal court of McDowell County by Gov. Albert B. White on January 1, 1905; was thrice elected and served until September 30, 1924, when he resigned, having been nominated for Congress; elected as a Republican to the Sixty-ninth and Seventieth Congresses (March 4, 1925- March 3, 1929); was not a candidate for renomination in 1928; because of failing health, retired from public activities; died in Welch, W. Va., April 10, 1930; interment in Monte Vista Cemetery, Bluefield, W. Va.

STROUSE, Myer, a Representative from Pennsylvania; born in Oberstrau, Bavaria, Germany, December 16, 1825; immigrated to the United States in 1832 with his father, who settled in Pottsville, Schuylkill County, Pa.; attended private schools; edited the North American Farmer in Philadelphia 1848–1852; studied law; was admitted to the bar in 1855 and commenced practice in Pottsville; elected as a Democrat to the Thirty-eighth and Thirty-ninth Congresses (March 4, 1863–March 3, 1867); was not a candidate for renomination in 1866; resumed the practice of law; was attorney and solicitor for the "Molly Maguires," a secret organization in the mining regions of Pennsylvania, in 1876 and 1877; died in Pottsville, Pa., February 11, 1878; interment in Odd Fellows Cemetery.

STROWD, William Franklin, a Representative from North Carolina; born near Chapel Hill, Orange County, N. C., December 7, 1832; attended the country schools, Bingham private school at Melvane, the local academy at High Hill, and Graham Institute; moved to Chatham County in 1861 and engaged in agricultural pursuits; during the Civil War served as a private in the Confederate Army; member of the State constitutional convention in 1875; unsuccessful Populist candidate for election in 1892 to the Fifty-third Congress; elected as a Populist to the Fifty-fourth and Fifty-fifth Congresses (March 4, 1895–March 3, 1899); was not a candidate for renomination in 1898; resumed agricultural pursuits in Chatham County; discontinued activities in 1908 and lived in retirement until his death December 12, 1911, at the residence of his son in Chapel Hill, N. C.; interment in Chapel Hill Cemetery.

STRUBLE, Isaac S., a Representative from Iowa; born near Fredericksburg, Va., November 3, 1843; moved to Iowa with his parents, who settled in Johnson County; attended the common schools; during the Civil War enlisted at the age of seventeen and served three years as a private in Company F, Twenty-second Iowa Regiment, Volunteer Infantry; attended the University of Iowa in Iowa City; studied law; was admitted to the bar in 1870 and commenced practice in Ogle County, Ill.; settled in Le Mars, Plymouth County, Iowa, in 1872; elected as a Republican to the Forty-eighth and to the three succeeding Congresses (March 4, 1883–March 3, 1891); unsuccessful candidate for renomination in 1890; resumed the practice of law; died in Le Mars, Iowa, on February 17, 1913; interment in Le Mars Cemetery.

STRUDWICK, William Francis, a Representative from North Carolina; born at "Stag Park," near Wilmington, New Hanover County, N. C.; received a limited education; engaged in agricultural pursuits; delegate to the State convention in 1789; served in the State senate 1792–1797; held several local offices; elected as a Federalist to the Fourth Congress to fill the vacancy caused by the resignation of Absalom Tatom and served from November 28, 1796, to March 3, 1797; member of the State house of representatives 1801–1803; resumed agricultural interests; died in North Carolina in 1812; interment in a private cemetery on his estate at "Hawfields," Orange County, N. C.

STUART, Alexander Hugh Holmes (cousin of Archibald Stuart), a Representative from Virginia; born in Staunton, Va., April 2, 1807; attended Staunton Academy, and William and Mary College, Williamsburg, Va.; was graduated from the University of Virginia at Charlottesville in 1828; studied law; was admitted to the bar in 1828 and commenced practice in Staunton; member of the State house of delegates 1836–1839; elected as a Whig to the Twenty-seventh Congress (March 4, 1841–March 3, 1843); unsuccessful candidate for reelection in 1842 to the Twenty-eighth Congress; presidential elector on the Whig ticket of Clay and Frelinghuysen in 1844 and of Taylor and Fillmore in 1848; served as Secretary of the Interior in the Cabinet of President Fillmore from September 16, 1850, to March 6, 1853; member of the State senate 1857–1861; member of the State secession convention in 1861; delegate to the National Convention of Conservatives at Philadelphia in 1866; presented credentials as a Member-elect to the Thirty-ninth Congress in 1865 but was not admitted; chairman of the committee of nine, which was instrumental in restoring Virginia to the Union in 1870; member of the State house of delegates from 1874 to 1877; rector of the University of Virginia from 1874 to 1882; president of the Virginia Historical Society; resumed the practice of law; died in Staunton, Va., February 13, 1891; interment in Thornrose Cemetery.

STUART, Andrew, a Representative from Ohio; born near Pittsburgh, Pa., August 3, 1823; moved to Pittsburgh with his mother in 1834; attended school three months; was self-instructed through reading newspapers; worked in a newspaper office; moved to Steubenville, Ohio, in 1850; was editor of the American Union 1850–1857; elected as a Democrat to the Thirty-third Congress (March 4, 1853–March 3, 1855); unsuccessful candidate for reelection; engaged in the shipping business on the Gulf of Mexico and in the transportation of mails and supplies from Leavenworth, Kans., to Santa Fe, N. Mex.; resided in Washington, D. C., from 1869 until his death, April 30, 1872; interment in Union Cemetery, Steubenville, Ohio.

STUART, Archibald (cousin of Alexander Hugh Holmes Stuart), a Representative from Virginia; born in Lynchburg, Va., December 2, 1795; attended private schools and completed preparatory studies; served as an officer in the War of 1812; studied law; was admitted to the bar and practiced in Lynchburg, Campbell County, Va.; member of the State house of delegates in 1830 and 1831; delegate to the State conventions of 1829, 1830, 1850, and 1851; elected as a Whig to the Twenty-fifth Congress (March 4, 1837–March 3, 1839); unsuccessful candidate for reelection in 1838 to the Twenty-sixth Congress; resumed the practice of law; served in the State senate 1852–1854; died at his home, "Laurel Hill," Patrick County, Va., September 20, 1855; interment in the Stuart family cemetery at Laurel Hill, Patrick County, Va.

STUART, Charles Edward, a Representative and a Senator from Michigan; born near Waterloo, Columbia County, N. Y., November 25, 1810; studied law; was admitted to the bar in 1832 and commenced practice in Waterloo; moved to Michigan in 1835 and settled in Kalamazoo; member of the State house of representatives in 1842; elected as a Democrat to the Thirtieth Congress to fill the vacancy caused by the death of Edward Bradley, who never qualified, and served from December 6, 1847, to March 3, 1849; unsuccessful candidate for reelection in 1848 to the Thirty-first Congress; elected to the Thirty-second Congress (March 4, 1851–March 3, 1853); elected to the United States Senate and served from March 4, 1853, to March 3, 1859; was not a candidate for renomination; resumed the practice of law; delegate to the Democratic National Conventions at Charleston, S. C., and at Baltimore, Md., in 1860 and to the National Convention of Conservatives at Philadelphia in 1866; during the Civil War raised and equipped the Thirteenth Regiment, Michigan Volunteer Infantry, of which he was commissioned colonel, but resigned because of ill health; died in Kalamazoo, Mich., May 19, 1887; interment in Mountain Home Cemetery.

STUART, David, a Representative from Michigan; born in Brooklyn, N. Y., March 12, 1816; studied law; was admitted to the bar and commenced practice in Detroit, Mich.; elected as a Democrat to the Thirty-third Congress (March 4, 1853–March 3, 1855); unsuccessful candidate for reelection in 1854 to the Thirty-fourth Congress; moved to Chicago, Ill.; enlisted in the Union Army during the Civil War and was commissioned lieutenant colonel of the Forty-second Regiment, Illinois Volunteer Infantry, July 22, 1861; colonel of the Fifty-fifth Regiment, Illinois Volunteer Infantry, October 31, 1861; appointed brigadier general of Volunteers November 29, 1862, but the Senate declined to confirm the nomination March 11, 1863; resigned April 3, 1863; resumed the practice of law in Detroit, Mich., and died there September 12, 1868; interment in Elmwood Cemetery.

STUART, John Todd, a Representative from Illinois; born near Lexington, Ky., November 10, 1807; was graduated from Centre College, Danville, Ky., in 1826; studied law; was admitted to the bar in 1828 and commenced practice in Springfield, Sangamon County, Ill.; subsequently became a law partner of Abraham Lincoln; major in the Black Hawk War in 1832; member of the State house of representatives 1832–1836; unsuccessful candidate for election in 1836 to the Twenty-fifth Congress; elected as a Whig to the Twenty-sixth and Twenty-seventh Congresses (March 4, 1839–March 3, 1843); was not a candidate for renomination in 1842; member of the State senate 1848–1852; was the unsuccessful Constitutional-Union candidate for Governor of Illinois in 1860; elected as a Democrat to the Thirty-eighth Congress (March 4, 1863–March 3, 1865); resumed the practice of law; died in Springfield, Sangamon County, Ill., November 23, 1885; interment in Oak Ridge Cemetery.

STUART, Philip, a Representative from Maryland; born near Fredericksburg, Va., in 1760; completed his preparatory education; moved to Maryland; served in the Revolutionary Army as a lieutenant in the Third Continental Dragoons; wounded at Eutaw Springs September 8, 1781; transferred to Baylor's dragoons November 9, 1782; lieutenant, Second Artillerists and Engineers, June 5, 1798; resigned November 15, 1800; served in the War of 1812; elected as a Federalist to the Twelfth and to the three succeeding Congresses (March 4, 1811–March 3, 1819); died in Washington, D. C., August 14, 1830; interment in the Congressional Cemetery.

STUBBLEFIELD, Frank Albert, a Representative from Kentucky; born in Murray, Calloway County, Ky., April 5, 1907; attended the public schools and Murray High School; student at University of Arizona in 1927; graduated from the University of Kentucky College of Commerce in 1932; engaged

in the retail drug business in Murray, Ky., since 1933; member of city council, Murray, Ky., 1939–1943; during World War II served as a lieutenant in the United States Navy; member of the Kentucky Railroad Commission since 1951; elected as a Democrat to the Eighty-sixth Congress (January 3, 1959–January 3, 1961). *Reelected to the Eighty-seventh Congress.*

STUBBS, Henry Elbert, a Representative from California; born in Nampa, Coleman County, Tex., March 4, 1881; attended the public schools in Groesbeck, Tex., and Phillips University, Enid, Okla.; was ordained a minister of the Christian Church in 1911 and served as pastor of the Christian Church in Frederick, Okla., 1911–1914 and 1918–1921, and in Kingfisher, Okla., 1914–1917; moved to California in 1921 and served as pastor of the Christian Church in Tulare, Calif., 1921–1923 and of the Santa Maria (Calif.) Christian Church from 1923 until elected to Congress; elected as a Democrat to the Seventy-third, Seventy-fourth, and Seventy-fifth Congresses and served from March 4, 1933, until his death in Washington, D. C., February 28, 1937; interment in Santa Maria Cemetery, Santa Maria, Calif.

STUDLEY, Elmer Ebenezer, a Representative from New York; born on a farm near East Ashford, Cattaraugus County, N. Y., September 24, 1869; attended the district schools; was graduated from Springville (N. Y.) High School in 1888 and from Cornell University, Ithaca, N. Y., in 1894; reporter on Buffalo newspapers in 1894 and 1895; served in the New York National Guard 1894–1898 and during the Spanish-American War was commissioned as a first lieutenant in the Two Hundred and Second Regiment, New York Volunteer Infantry, serving in Cuba in 1898 and 1899; studied law; was admitted to the bar in 1895 and practiced in Buffalo, N. Y., 1895–1898; moved to Raton, Colfax County, N. Mex., in 1899 and practiced law until 1917; served as a Republican in the Territorial house of representatives in 1907; member of the New Mexico Statutory Revision Commission in 1907; district attorney of Colfax and Union Counties, N. Mex., in 1909 and 1910; candidate for presidential elector on the Progressive ticket of Roosevelt and Johnson in 1912; member of the New Mexico Board of Water Commissioners 1913–1915; delegate to the Progressive National Convention at Chicago in 1916; moved to New York City, N. Y., in 1917 and continued the practice of law; deputy attorney general of New York in 1924; United States commissioner for the eastern district of New York in 1925 and 1926; New York State departmental commander of the Veterans of Foreign Wars in 1930; elected as a Democrat to the Seventy-third Congress (March 4, 1933–January 3, 1935); was not a candidate for renomination in 1934; resumed the practice of law; appointed by President Franklin D. Roosevelt in February 1935 as a member of the Board of Veterans' Appeals and served until his death in Flushing, Long Island, N. Y., on September 6, 1942; interment in Flushing Cemetery.

STULL, Howard William, a Representative from Pennsylvania; born on a farm near Johnstown, Cambria County, Pa., April 11, 1876; attended the public schools, Johnstown High School, and State Normal School (later State Teachers' College), Indiana, Pa.; employed as a store clerk 1887–1894 and as a railroad clerk in 1894 and 1895; taught school at Ferndale and Dale, Pa., 1895–1897; served as post office clerk at Johnstown in 1897 and 1898 and as assistant postmaster 1899–1904; moved to Washington, D. C., in 1905 and served as an assistant division chief in the United States Treasury Department 1905–1908; was graduated from the law department of George Washington University, Washington, D. C., in 1908; was admitted to the bar the same year and commenced practice in Colville, Stevens County, Wash., in 1909; prosecuting attorney of Stevens County,

Wash., in 1911, 1912, 1915, and 1916; alternate delegate to the Republican National Convention in 1916; delegate to the Republican State convention in 1916; returned to Johnstown, Pa., in 1917 and continued the practice of law; elected as a Republican to the Seventy-second Congress to fill the vacancy caused by the resignation of J. Russell Leech and served from April 26, 1932, to March 3, 1933; was not a candidate for renomination in 1932; resumed the practice of law; died in Johnstown, Pa., April 22, 1949; interment in Grandview Cemetery.

STUMP, Herman, a Representative from Maryland; born on Oakington farm, in Harford County, Md., August 8, 1837; pursued classical studies; studied law; was admitted to the bar in 1856 and commenced practice in Bel Air, Md.; also interested in agricultural pursuits; elected to the State senate in 1878, serving as president in 1880; chairman of the Democratic State convention in 1879; elected as a Democrat to the Fifty-first and Fifty-second Congresses (March 4, 1889–March 3, 1893); was not a candidate for renomination; appointed Superintendent of Immigration by President Cleveland April 8, 1893, and served until July 16, 1897; resumed the practice of law in Bel Air, Md.; died at his home, "Waverly," near Bel Air, Md., January 9, 1917; interment in St. Mary's Cemetery, Emmorton, Md.

STURGEON, Daniel, a Senator from Pennsylvania; born in Mount Pleasant, York (later Adams) County, Pa., October 27, 1789; attended the common schools; moved to western Pennsylvania in 1804 with his parents, who settled near Pittsburgh; was graduated from Jefferson College, Canonsburg, Pa. (later Washington and Jefferson College, Washington, Pa.), and Jefferson Medical College, Philadelphia, Pa.; commenced the practice of medicine in Uniontown, Pa., in 1813; appointed county coroner; member of the State house of representatives 1818–1824; member of the State senate 1825–1830, serving as president from 1828 to 1830; auditor general of Pennsylvania 1830–1836; State treasurer in 1838 and 1839; elected as a Democrat to the United States Senate to fill the vacancy in the term commencing March 4, 1839, caused by the failure of the legislature to elect; reelected and served from January 14, 1840, to March 3, 1851; was not a candidate for reelection; appointed by President Franklin Pierce as treasurer of the United States Mint in Philadelphia, Pa., and served from May 3, 1853, to June 13, 1858; engaged in banking; died in Uniontown, Fayette County, Pa., July 3, 1878; interment in Oak Grove Cemetery.

STURGES, Jonathan (father of Lewis Burr Sturges), a Delegate and a Representative from Connecticut; born in Fairfield, Conn., August 23, 1740; was graduated from Yale College in 1759; was admitted to the bar in May 1772 and commenced practice in Fairfield, Conn.; member of the State house of representatives in 1772 and 1773–1784; justice of the peace in 1773; Member of the Continental Congress from 1774 to 1787; judge of the probate court for the district of Fairfield in 1775; again a member of the State house of representatives in 1786; elected to the First and Second Congresses (March 4, 1789–March 3, 1793); associate justice of the State supreme court 1793–1805; Federalist presidential elector in 1796 and voted for John Adams for President; presidential elector on the Federalist ticket of Pinckney and King in 1804; died in Fairfield, Fairfield County, Conn., October 4, 1819; interment in the Old Burying Ground.

STURGES, Lewis Burr (son of Jonathan Sturges), a Representative from Connecticut; born in Fairfield, Conn., March 15, 1763; was graduated from Yale College in 1782; engaged in mercantile pursuits in New Haven; returned to Fairfield, Conn., in 1786; clerk of the probate court for the district of Fairfield 1787–1791; member of the State house of representa-

tives 1794–1803; elected as a Federalist to the Ninth Congress to fill in part the vacancies caused by the resignations of Calvin Goddard and Roger Griswold; reelected to the Tenth and to the four succeeding Congresses and served from September 16, 1805, to March 3, 1817; moved to Norwalk, Huron County, Ohio, where he died March 30, 1844; interment in St. Paul's Episcopal Churchyard.

STURGISS, George Cookman, a Representative from West Virginia; born in Poland, Mahoning County, Ohio, August 16, 1842; attended country schools; moved to Morgantown, Va. (now West Virginia), in 1859; attended Monongalia Academy, Morgantown, W. Va., and taught in that school for a short time; studied law; was admitted to the bar in 1863 and commenced practice at Morgantown; during the Civil War served as a clerk under Maj. James V. Boughner, paymaster of United States Volunteers; county superintendent of free schools 1865–1869; member of the West Virginia House of Delegates 1870–1872; prosecuting attorney of the county 1872–1880; Republican nominee for Governor of the State in 1880; appointed by President Harrison as United States attorney for the district of West Virginia in 1889 and served four years; first president of the State board of trade and of the State association for the promotion of good roads; elected as a Republican to the Sixtieth and Sixty-first Congresses (March 4, 1907–March 3, 1911); unsuccessful candidate for reelection in 1910 to the Sixty-second Congress; trustee of American University, Washington, D. C.; was instrumental in the construction of the Morgantown & Kingwood Railroad; judge of the circuit court 1912–1920; engaged in the practice of law at Morgantown, Monongalia County, W. Va., until his death on February 26, 1925; interment in Oak Grove Cemetery.

STURTEVANT, John Cirby, a Representative from Pennsylvania; born in Spring Township, Crawford County, Pa., February 20, 1835; attended the common schools; engaged in teaching and farming; officer in the State house of representatives at Harrisburg in 1861, 1862, and 1864; delegate to seven Republican State conventions from 1865 to 1890; member of the State house of representatives in 1865 and in 1866; moved to Conneautville, Pa., in 1867; engaged in the hardware business until 1873, and in manufacturing and milling until 1888; also engaged in banking, serving as cashier and president of the First National Bank of Conneautville; presidential elector on the Republican ticket of Benjamin Harrison and Levi P. Morton in 1888; elected as a Republican to the Fifty-fifth Congress (March 4, 1897–March 3, 1899); was not a candidate for renomination in 1898; resumed banking interests in Conneautville, Crawford County, Pa., and died there December 20, 1912; interment in Conneautville Cemetery.

SULLIVAN, Christopher Daniel, a Representative from New York; born in New York City, July 14, 1870; attended the public schools, St. James Parochial School, and St. Mary's Academy, in New York City; engaged in the real-estate business in 1904; elected as a member of the State senate in 1906; reelected in 1908, 1910, 1912, and 1914, and served until 1916, when he was elected to Congress; was elected as a Democrat to the Sixty-fifth and to the eleven succeeding Congresses (March 4, 1917–January 3, 1941); was not a candidate for renomination in 1940; resided in New York City, until his death there August 3, 1942; interment in Calvary Cemetery, Woodside, Long Island, N. Y.

SULLIVAN, George (son of John Sullivan), a Representative from New Hampshire; born in Durham, N. H., August 29, 1771; was graduated from Harvard University in 1790; studied law; was admitted to the bar and commenced practice in Exeter,

Rockingham County, N. H., in 1793; member of the State house of representatives in 1805; attorney general of New Hampshire in 1805 and 1806; elected to the Twelfth Congress (March 4, 1811–March 3, 1813); again a member of the State house of representatives in 1813; served in the State senate in 1814 and 1815; again attorney general of the State 1816–1835; died in Exeter, N. H., April 14, 1838; interment in the Old Cemetery (Winter Street).

SULLIVAN, James (brother of John Sullivan), a Delegate from Massachusetts; born in Berwick, Maine (then a part of Massachusetts), April 22, 1744; completed preparatory studies; studied law; was admitted to the bar about 1782 and commenced practice in Biddeford; King's attorney for York County; active in pre-Revolutionary movements; member of the Provincial Congress of Massachusetts in 1774 and 1775; member of the general court in 1775 and 1776; justice of the superior court 1776–1782; Member of the Continental Congress in 1782; member of the executive council in 1787; judge of probate for Suffolk County in 1788; State attorney general 1790–1807; Governor of Massachusetts in 1807 and 1808; died in Boston, Mass., December 10, 1808; interment in Central Boston Common Cemetery.

SULLIVAN, John (brother of James Sullivan and father of George Sullivan), a Delegate from New Hampshire; born in Somersworth, N. H., February 17, 1740; received a limited education; studied law; was admitted to the bar and commenced practice in Durham in 1760; took an active part in pre-Revolutionary movements; Member of the Continental Congress in 1774 and 1775; during the Revolution was appointed as a brigadier general; later promoted to major general, and from June 1775 until early in 1780 was an active participant in many major engagements and received the thanks of Washington and the approbation of Congress; resigned on account of ill health; again a Member of the Continental Congress in 1780 and 1781; attorney general of New Hampshire 1782–1786; President of New Hampshire in 1786 and 1787; member of the convention that ratified the Federal Constitution; speaker of the State house of representatives; presidential elector in 1789; again chosen President of New Hampshire; appointed by President Washington judge of the United States District Court of New Hampshire in September 1789 and held that office until his death in Durham, N. H., January 23, 1795; interment in the Sullivan family cemetery.

SULLIVAN, John Andrew, a Representative from Massachusetts; born in Boston, Mass., May 10, 1868; attended the common and high schools; was graduated from the Boston University Law School in 1896; was admitted to the bar the same year and commenced practice in Boston, Mass.; member of the State senate 1900–1902; elected as a Democrat to the Fifty-eighth and Fifty-ninth Congresses (March 4, 1903–March 3, 1907); declined to be a candidate for renomination; resumed the practice of law in Boston, Mass.; appointed a member of the Boston Finance Commission in July 1907 and served until the commission expired; in June 1909 became chairman of the permanent finance commission; resigned in 1914 to become corporation counsel of Boston; lecturer on municipal government in Harvard University in 1912 and 1913; lecturer at Boston University Law School 1920–1925; resumed the practice of his profession in Boston; died in Scituate, Mass., May 31, 1927; interment in Holy Cross Cemetery, Malden, Mass.

SULLIVAN, John Berchmans (husband of Leonor Kretzer Sullivan), a Representative from Missouri; born in Sedalia, Pettis County, Mo., October 10, 1897; attended St. Patrick's parochial school in Sedalia, Mo.; moved to St. Louis, Mo., in 1910; was graduated from Gonzaga Hall (St. Louis University

High School) in 1914 and from St. Louis University in 1918; during the First World War enlisted in the United States Army and served as a private in the Infantry; was graduated from the law department of the St. Louis University in 1922; was admitted to the bar in 1921 and commenced practice in St. Louis, Mo.; delegate to the Democratic State conventions in 1928, 1932, and 1940; associate city counselor of St. Louis 1936–1938; secretary to the mayor of St. Louis 1938–1940; secretary and lawyer member of the smoke elimination committee of the city of St. Louis and author of the smoke elimination ordinance; elected as a Democrat to the Seventy-seventh Congress (January 3, 1941–January 3, 1943); unsuccessful candidate for reelection in 1942 to the Seventy-eighth Congress; elected to the Seventy-ninth Congress (January 3, 1945–January 3, 1947); unsuccessful candidate for reelection in 1946 to the Eightieth Congress; special assistant to the United States Attorney General in 1947 and 1948; elected to the Eighty-first and Eighty-second Congresses and served from January 3, 1949, until his death in the naval hospital at Bethesda, Md., January 29, 1951; interment in Calvary Cemetery, St. Louis, Mo.

SULLIVAN, Leonor Kretzer (widow of John Berchmans Sullivan), a Representative from Missouri; born in St. Louis, Mo.; attended public and private schools; also attended Washington University, St. Louis, Mo., night classes for training in selected and special subjects; taught business arithmetic and accounting and also served as placement director of the St. Louis Comptometer School; member of the St. Louis League of Women Voters since 1941; served as administrative aide to her husband, John B. Sullivan, 1942–1951, and as secretary to Representative Irving of Missouri until May 1952, when she resigned to campaign for congressional nomination; first woman elected to the House of Representatives from Missouri; elected as a Democrat to the Eighty-third and to the three succeeding Congresses (January 3, 1953–January 3, 1961). *Reelected to the Eighty-seventh Congress.*

SULLIVAN, Maurice Joseph, a Representative from Nevada; born in San Rafael, Marin County, Calif., December 7, 1884; attended the parochial school and Sacred Heart College, San Francisco, Calif.; Lieutenant Governor of Nevada 1915–1926 and 1939–1942; during the First World War was adjutant general of Nevada, disbursing officer of the United States Government, and draft executive of Nevada; colonel in the United States Army 1922–1932; was admitted to the bar in 1923 and commenced practice in Carson City, Nev.; also a mining operator; principal owner of the Wood-Sullivan Hardware Co.; elected as a Democrat to the Seventy-eighth Congress (January 3, 1943–January 3, 1945); unsuccessful candidate for renomination in 1944; resumed the practice of law in Reno, Nev., until his death there August 9, 1953; interment in Mater Dolorosa Cemetery.

SULLIVAN, Patrick Joseph, a Senator from Wyoming; born on a farm west of Bantry, County Cork, Ireland, March 17, 1865; attended a nearby national school; immigrated to America in April 1888, landing in New York, and the following June went to the Territory of Wyoming; engaged in sheep raising in Rawlins, Carbon County; moved to Casper, Natrona County, in 1892; interested in banking, the production of oil, and various other enterprises; served as a member of the house of representatives of the Wyoming State Legislature 1894–1896 and 1898–1900; mayor of Casper in 1897 and 1898; chairman of the Republican State central committee for twenty years and represented the State and party in several national conventions; appointed as a Republican to the United States Senate to fill the vacancy caused by the death of Francis E. Warren and served from December 5, 1929, to November 20, 1930, when a successor was elected and qualified; was not a candidate for election to fill the vacancy;

continued his former business pursuits until his death in Santa Barbara, Calif., April 8, 1935; interment in Highland Cemetery, Casper, Wyo.

SULLIVAN, Patrick Joseph, a Representative from Pennsylvania; born in Pittsburgh, Allegheny County, Pa., October 12, 1877; attended public and parochial schools; employed in the Homestead Axle Works, Homestead, Pa., 1890–1900, and in the steel mills at Pittsburgh, Pa., 1900–1909; member of the city council 1906–1909; served as alderman 1910–1929; police magistrate 1916–1923; member of the board of assessment and tax revision, Allegheny County, Pa., 1923–1929; elected as a Republican to the Seventy-first and Seventy-second Congresses (March 4, 1929–March 3, 1933); unsuccessful candidate for renomination in 1932; city police magistrate in Pittsburgh, Pa., from 1936 until his death there December 31, 1946; interment in Calvary Cemetery.

SULLIVAN, Timothy Daniel, a Representative from New York; born in New York City July 23, 1862; attended the public schools; engaged in the real estate and theatrical business; elected to the State assembly in 1886 and served until 1894; member of the State senate 1894–1903; elected as a Democrat to the Fifty-eighth and Fifty-ninth Congresses and served from March 4, 1903, to July 27, 1906, when he resigned; served in the State senate in 1908 and 1910; elected to the Sixty-third Congress and served from March 4, 1913, until accidentally killed by a locomotive near Pelham Parkway, New York City, August 31, 1913; interment in Calvary Cemetery, Long Island City, N. Y.

SULLIVAN, William Van Amberg, a Representative and a Senator from Mississippi; born near Winona, Montgomery County, Miss., December 18, 1857; attended the common schools near Sardis, in Panola County, and the University of Mississippi at Oxford; was graduated from Vanderbilt University, Nashville, Tenn., in 1875; was admitted to the bar in 1875 and commenced practice in Austin, Tunica County; moved to Oxford, Lafayette County, Miss., in 1877; member of the board of city aldermen; delegate to the Democratic National Conventions at Chicago in 1892 and 1896; elected as a Democrat to the Fifty-fifth Congress and served from March 4, 1897, to May 31, 1898, when he resigned, having been appointed Senator; appointed and subsequently elected to the United States Senate to fill the vacancy caused by the death of Edward C. Walthall and served from May 31, 1898, to March 3, 1901; retired from active business and resided in Washington, D. C.; died in Oxford, Miss., March 21, 1918; interment in St. Peter's Cemetery.

SULLOWAY, Cyrus Adams, a Representative from New Hampshire; born in Grafton, Grafton County, N. H., June 8, 1839; attended the common schools, Colby Academy, and Kimball Academy; studied law in Franklin, N. H.; was admitted to the bar in 1863 and commenced practice in Manchester, N. H.; member of the State house of representatives in 1872, 1873, and 1887–1893; elected as a Republican to the Fifty-fourth and to the eight succeeding Congresses (March 4, 1895–March 3, 1913); unsuccessful candidate for reelection in 1912 to the Sixty-third Congress; elected to the Sixty-fourth and Sixty-fifth Congresses and served from March 4, 1915, until his death in Washington, D. C., March 11, 1917; interment in the City Cemetery, Franklin, N. H.

SULZER, Charles August (brother of William Sulzer), a Delegate from the Territory of Alaska; born in Roselle, Union County, N. J., February 24, 1879; attended the public schools, Pingry School, Elizabeth, N. J., Berkeley Academy, New York City, and the United States Military Academy, West Point, N. Y.; during the Spanish-American War served with the Fourth Regiment, New Jersey Volunteer Infantry; moved to Alaska in 1902 and engaged in mining; member of the Alaska Territorial Senate in 1914; presented credentials as a Democratic Delegate-elect to the Sixty-fifth Congress and served from March 4, 1917, to January 7, 1919, when he was succeeded by James Wickersham, who contested his election; presented credentials as a Delegate-elect to the Sixty-sixth Congress and served from March 4, 1919, until his death in Sulzer, Alaska, April 28, 1919, before the convening of Congress; interment in Evergreen Cemetery, Elizabeth, N. J.

SULZER, William (brother of Charles August Sulzer), a Representative from New York; born in Elizabeth, N. J., March 18, 1863; attended the public schools and Columbia College, New York City; studied law; was admitted to the bar in 1884 and commenced practice in New York City; member of the State assembly 1889–1894; speaker in 1893; delegate to the Democratic National Conventions in 1892, 1896, 1900, 1904, 1908, and 1912; elected as a Democrat to the Fifty-fourth and to the eight succeeding Congresses and served from March 4, 1895, to December 31, 1912, when he resigned, having been elected Governor of New York for the term commencing January 1, 1913, and served until October 18, 1913, when he was removed from office; elected as an independent to the State assembly November 4, 1913; independent candidate for Governor in 1914; declined the nomination for President in 1916 by the American Party; engaged in the practice of law in New York City until his death there November 6, 1941; interment in Evergreen Cemetery, Hillside, N. J.

SUMMERS, George William, a Representative from Virginia; born near Alexandria, Va., March 4, 1804; attended school at Charleston, Va. (now West Virginia) and Washington College (now Washington and Lee University), Lexington, Va.; was graduated from the Ohio University at Athens in 1826; studied law; was admitted to the bar in 1827 and commenced practice in Charleston, Va.; member of the State house of delegates 1830–1832 and 1834–1836; elected as a Whig to the Twenty-seventh and Twenty-eighth Congresses (March 4, 1841–March 3, 1845); unsuccessful candidate for reelection in 1844 to the Twenty-ninth Congress; elected as a delegate to the State constitutional convention in 1850; unsuccessful Whig candidate for Governor in 1851; judge of the eighteenth judicial circuit of Virginia 1852–1858; member of the peace conference held at Washington, D. C., in 1861 in an effort to devise means to prevent the impending war; delegate to the secession convention in 1861 at Richmond, Va.; resumed the practice of his profession; died in Charleston, W. Va., September 19, 1868; interment in Walnut Grove Cemetery, Putnam County, W. Va.

SUMMERS, John William, a Representative from Washington; born near Valeene, Orange County, Ind., April 29, 1870; attended the public schools; worked on a farm, clerked in a village store, and taught school in Indiana and Texas; was graduated from the Southern Indiana Normal College at Mitchell, Ind., in 1889 and from the Kentucky School of Medicine at Louisville in 1892; pursued postgraduate studies in the Louisville Medical College and in New York, London, Berlin, and the University of Vienna, Austria; commenced the practice of medicine in Mattoon, Ill.; moved to Walla Walla, Wash., in 1908 and continued the practice of medicine; also engaged in agricultural pursuits and fruit raising; member of the State house of representatives in 1917; member of the Washington National Guard in 1917 and 1918; later served as a lieutenant colonel in the medical section of the Reserve Corps; elected as a Republican to the Sixty-sixth and to the six succeeding Congresses (March 4, 1919–March 3, 1933); unsuccessful candidate for reelection in 1932 to the Seventy-third Congress, and for election in 1934 to the Seventy-fourth Congress and in 1936 to the Seventy-fifth Congress; resumed former pursuits; died in Walla Walla, Wash., on September 25, 1937; interment in Mountain View Cemetery.

SUMNER, Charles, a Senator from Massachusetts; born in Boston, Mass., January 6, 1811; attended the Boston Latin School; was graduated from Harvard University in 1830 and from the Harvard Law School in 1833; was admitted to the bar the following year and commenced the practice of law in Boston, Mass.; appointed reporter of the United States circuit court; lectured at the Harvard Law School 1835–1837; traveled extensively in Europe from December 1837 until May 1840; declined the Whig nomination in 1846 for election to the Thirtieth Congress; one of the founders of the Free-Soil Party in 1848; unsuccessful candidate for election in 1848 on the Free-Soil ticket to the Thirty-first Congress; elected to the United States Senate in 1851, after a prolonged contest, by a coalition of Democratic and Free-Soil Parties; reelected as a Republican in 1857, 1863, and 1869, and served from April 24, 1851, until his death; was assaulted by Representative Preston Brooks, of South Carolina, May 22, 1856, while in his seat in the Senate, and was absent on account of injuries received until December 5, 1859; died in Washington, D. C., March 11, 1874; interment in Mount Auburn Cemetery, Cambridge, Mass.

SUMNER, Charles Allen, a Representative from California; born in Great Barrington, Mass., on August 2, 1835; attended Trinity College, Hartford, Conn.; studied law; was admitted to the bar and engaged in patent practice; moved to California in 1856 and settled in San Francisco; editor of the Herald and Mirror in 1861; during the Civil War was appointed November 26, 1862, to be captain and assistant quartermaster of United States Volunteers, and served until his resignation on March 30, 1864; moved to Virginia City, Nev.; member of the State senate 1865–1868 and served as president pro tempore for one session; returned to San Francisco in 1868 and became editor of the Herald; was elected as a Democrat to the Forty-eighth Congress (March 4, 1883–March 3, 1885); unsuccessful candidate for reelection in 1884 to the Forty-ninth Congress; resumed the practice of law; died in San Francisco, Calif., January 31, 1903; interment in the George H. Thomas Post plot at the Presidio.

SUMNER, Daniel Hadley, a Representative from Wisconsin; born in Malone, Franklin County, N. Y., September 15, 1837; moved to Michigan in 1843 with his parents, who settled in Richland; attended the common schools and Prairie Seminary, Richland, Mich.; studied law; was admitted to the bar in 1868 and commenced practice in Kalamazoo, Mich.; moved to Oconomowoc, Wis., in 1868 and practiced law; also published the La Belle Mirror; moved to Waukesha, Wis., in 1870 and continued the practice of his profession; town superintendent of schools; member of the county board of supervisors; district attorney of Waukesha County in 1876 and 1877; elected as a Democrat to the Forty-eighth Congress (March 4, 1883–March 3, 1885); was not a candidate for renomination in 1884; resumed the practice of law; died in Waukesha, Wis., May 29, 1903; interment in Prairie Home Cemetery.

SUMNER, Jessie, a Representative from Illinois; born in Milford, Iroquois County, Ill., July 17, 1898; attended the public schools; was graduated from Girton School, Winnetka, Ill., in 1916 and Smith College, Northampton, Mass., in 1920; studied law at the University of Chicago, Chicago, Ill.; Columbia University, New York, N. Y., and Oxford University, England;

also studied briefly at Wisconsin University in Madison and New York University School of Commerce in New York City; was admitted to the bar in 1923 and practiced in Chicago, Ill.; employed at the Chase National Bank in New York City in 1928; returned to Milford, Ill., in 1932 and resumed the practice of law; served as county judge of Iroquois County, Ill., in 1937; director of Sumner National Bank, Sheldon, Ill.; elected as a Republican to the Seventy-sixth and to the three succeeding Congresses (January 3, 1939–January 3, 1947); was not a candidate for renomination in 1946; resumed activity in the family business of farming and banking; is a resident of Milford, Ill.

SUMNERS, Hatton William, a Representative from Texas; born near Fayetteville, Lincoln County, Tenn., May 30, 1875; moved to Garland, Dallas County, Tex., in 1893; studied law; was admitted to the bar in 1897 and commenced practice in Dallas, Tex.; elected prosecuting attorney of Dallas County in 1900 and served two terms; president of the district and county attorney's association of Texas in 1906 and 1907; elected as a Democrat to the Sixty-third and to the sixteen succeeding Congresses (March 4, 1913–January 3, 1947); was not a candidate for renomination in 1946; retired from public activities, and is a resident of Dallas, Tex.

SUMTER, Thomas (grandfather of Thomas De Lage Sumter), a Representative and a Senator from South Carolina; born in Hanover County, Va., August 14, 1734; attended the common schools and received a college education; engaged in surveying; moved to South Carolina about 1760 and settled on a plantation near Stateburg; lieutenant colonel of the Sixth Continental Regiment in the Revolutionary Army; attained the rank of brigadier general of militia in 1780; voted the thanks of Congress in January 1781; member of the State senate in 1781 and 1782; elected to the privy council in 1782; elected a Delegate to the Continental Congress in 1783, but declined to accept; delegate to the State convention which ratified the Constitution and which he opposed; elected as a Democrat to the First and Second Congresses (March 4, 1789–March 3, 1793); was not a candidate for renomination in 1792; elected to the Fifth, Sixth, and Seventh Congresses and served from March 4, 1797, to December 15, 1801, when he resigned; elected as a Democrat to the United States Senate on December 3, 1801, to fill the vacancy caused by the resignation of Charles Pinckney; reelected in 1805 and served from December 15, 1801, until his resignation on December 16, 1810; retired from public life and lived on his plantation near Stateburg, S. C.; elected a delegate to the State Rights and Free Trade Convention at Charleston, S. C., in 1832, but on account of his advanced age did not serve; died on his plantation "South Mount," near Stateburg, S. C., June 1, 1832; interment in the private burial ground on the family estate.

SUMTER, Thomas De Lage (grandson of Thomas Sumter), a Representative from South Carolina; born in Germantown, Pa., November 14, 1809; attended the common schools at Edgehill, near Stateburg, S. C.; was graduated from the United States Military Academy at West Point, N. Y., in 1835; entered the United States Army as first lieutenant the same year and served until 1841, attaining the rank of colonel; engaged in the war against the Seminole Indians; moved to Stateburg, S. C.; elected as a Democrat to the Twenty-sixth and Twenty-seventh Congresses (March 4, 1839–March 3, 1843); was not a candidate for renomination; engaged in teaching, surveying, and agricultural pursuits; connected as agent with the South Carolina Railroad Co.; died on his plantation, "South Mount," near Stateburg, S. C., July 2, 1874; interment in the private burial ground on his estate.

SUNDSTROM, Frank Leander, a Representative from New Jersey; born in Massena, St. Lawrence County, N. Y., January 5, 1901; attended the public schools; newspaper reporter and editor 1918–1920; was graduated from Cornell University, Ithaca, N. Y., in 1924; football coach at Indiana University at Bloomington in 1924; engaged in the banking business in New York City in 1925; chairman of the East Orange Republican Committee 1940–1946; elected as a Republican to the Seventy-eighth, Seventy-ninth, and Eightieth Congresses (January 3, 1943–January 3, 1949); unsuccessful candidate for reelection in 1948 to the Eighty-first Congress; vice president and director, Schenley Distillers, 1954–; vice president and director of public relations, Schenley Industries, Inc., 1955–; stockbroker in New York City; is a resident of East Orange, N. J.

SUTHERLAND, Daniel Alexander, a Delegate from the Territory of Alaska; born in Pleasant Bay on Cape Breton Island, Canada, April 17, 1869; moved with his parents to Essex, Mass., in 1876; attended the public schools; was employed as a grocer's clerk, and subsequently engaged in the fish business; moved to Circle City, Alaska, in 1898, to Nome in 1900, and thence to Juneau in 1909; engaged in mining and fishing; member of the Territorial senate 1912–1920, serving as president in 1915; during the First World War enrolled in the United States Naval Reserve and served until honorably discharged on July 30, 1921; elected as a Republican to the Sixty-seventh and to the four succeeding Congresses (March 4, 1921–March 3, 1931); was not a candidate for renomination in 1930; purchasing agent for the Ogontz (Pa.) School 1931–1950; died in Abington, Pa., March 24, 1955; remains were cremated and deposited in St. Paul's Church Cemetery, Elkins Park, Pa.

SUTHERLAND, George, a Representative and a Senator from Utah; born in Buckinghamshire, England, March 25, 1862; immigrated to the United States in 1864 with his parents, who settled in Springville, Utah County, Utah; received a common-school and academic education; studied law at the University of Michigan at Ann Arbor; was admitted to the bar in 1883 and commenced practice in Provo, Utah; unsuccessful candidate for mayor of Provo, Utah, in 1890; unsuccessful candidate for Territorial representative in Congress in 1892; member of the State senate 1896–1900; delegate to the Republican National Conventions in 1900, 1904, 1908, and 1912; elected as a Republican to the Fifty-seventh Congress (March 4, 1901–March 3, 1903); declined to be a candidate for reelection in 1902 to the Fifty-eighth Congress; elected to the United States Senate in 1904; reelected in 1910, and served from March 4, 1905, to March 3, 1917; unsuccessful candidate for reelection; president of the American Bar Association in 1916 and 1917; counsel for the United States in the Norway-United States arbitration at The Hague in 1922; appointed by President Harding on September 5, 1922, an Associate Justice of the Supreme Court of the United States; entered upon the duties of that office on October 2, 1922, and served until his retirement on January 18, 1938; died in Stockbridge, Mass., July 18, 1942; interment in the Abbey Mausoleum, Arlington, Va.

SUTHERLAND, Howard, a Representative and a Senator from West Virginia; born near Kirkwood, St. Louis County, Mo., September 8, 1865; attended the public schools of the county and the city of St. Louis; was graduated from the literary department of Westminster College, Fulton, Mo., in 1889; edited a daily and weekly newspaper at Fulton; moved to Washington, D. C., in 1890; employed in the Census Office in 1890; studied law at Columbian (now George Washington) University, Washington, D. C.; moved to Elkins, Randolph County, W. Va., in 1893; engaged in the coal and railroad business and later in the coal and timberland business; member of the State senate 1908–1912; elected as a Republican to the Sixty-third and Sixty-fourth Congresses (March 4, 1913–March 3, 1917); did not seek renomination in 1916, having become a candidate for Senator; elected to the United States Senate in 1916 and served from March 4, 1917, to March 3, 1923; unsuccessful candidate for reelection in 1922; resumed his former business activities in Elkins, W. Va.; delegate at large to the Republican National Convention at Cleveland in 1924; vice president of the West Virginia Board of Trade; chairman of the West Virginia Good Roads Commission; member of the board of trustees of Davis and Elkins Presbyterian College; appointed Alien Property Custodian by President Coolidge on December 24, 1925, and served until April 24, 1933, when he resigned and retired from public life; was a resident of Washington, D. C., until his death March 12, 1950; interment in Maplewood Cemetery, Elkins, W. Va.

SUTHERLAND, Jabez Gridley, a Representative from Michigan; born in Van Buren, Onondaga County, N. Y., October 6, 1825; completed preparatory studies; studied law; was admitted to the bar in 1848 and commenced practice in Saginaw, Mich.; prosecuting attorney of Saginaw County, Mich., in 1848 and 1849; delegate to the State constitutional conventions in 1850 and 1867; member of the State house of representatives in 1853; judge of the tenth circuit court of Michigan from 1863 to 1871, when he resigned to enter Congress; elected as a Democrat to the Forty-second Congress (March 4, 1871–March 3, 1873); was not a candidate for renomination in 1872; moved to Salt Lake City in 1873; resumed the practice of law; in 1881 elected first president of the Salt Lake Bar Association; a member of the faculty of what is now the University of Utah in 1889; president of the Territorial Bar Association in 1894 and 1895; moved to California in 1897; died in Berkeley, Calif., November 20, 1902; interment in Mount Olivet Cemetery, Salt Lake City, Utah.

SUTHERLAND, Joel Barlow, a Representative from Pennsylvania; born in Gloucester County, N. J., February 26, 1792; attended the common schools, and was graduated from the University of Pennsylvania at Philadelphia in 1812; served in the War of 1812 as assistant surgeon to the "Junior Artillerists of Philadelphia," transferred to the line, and was appointed in 1814 lieutenant colonel of rifles in the State militia; member of the State house of representatives 1813–1816; physician to Lafayette; founder of Jefferson Medical College at Philadelphia; served in the State senate in 1816 and 1817; abandoned medicine for the practice of law; elected as a Jackson Democrat to the Twentieth and to the four succeeding Congresses (March 4, 1827–March 3, 1837); unsuccessful Whig candidate for reelection in 1836 to the Twenty-fifth Congress and for election in 1838 to the Twenty-sixth Congress; associate judge of the court of common pleas of Philadelphia, Pa., in 1833 and 1834; retired to private life; died in Philadelphia, Pa., November 15, 1861; interment in the Old Pine Street Presbyterian Church Cemetery.

SUTHERLAND, Josiah, a Representative from New York; born in the township of Stanford, near the village of Stissing, Dutchess County, N. Y., June 12, 1804; attended the district school, and was graduated from Union College, Schenectady, N. Y., in 1824; studied law in Waterford and Hudson; was admitted to the bar in 1828 and commenced practice in the village of Johnstown, Livingston Township, N. Y.; district attorney for Columbia County 1832–1843; moved to Hudson, N. Y., in 1838 and continued the practice of law; elected as a Democrat to the Thirty-second Congress (March 4, 1851–March 3, 1853); was not a candidate for renomination; moved to New York City in 1857 and continued the practice of law; associate justice of the supreme court of New York 1857–1871; member and presiding judge of the court of general sessions 1872–1878; resumed the practice of law in New York City, and died there May 25, 1887; interment in Woodlawn Cemetery.

SUTHERLAND, Roderick Dhu, a Representative from Nebraska; born in Scotch Grove, Jones County, Iowa, April 27, 1862; attended the common schools and Amity College, College Springs, Iowa; taught school; studied law; was admitted to the bar in 1888 and commenced practice in Nelson, Nuckolls County, Nebr.; prosecuting attorney of Nuckolls County 1890–1896; served as chairman of the Populist State convention in 1899; appointed by Governor Poynter a delegate to the trust conference held in Chicago in September 1899; elected as a Populist to the Fifty-fifth and Fifty-sixth Congresses (March 4, 1897–March 3, 1901); unsuccessful candidate for reelection in 1900 to the Fifty-seventh Congress; delegate to the Populist National Convention held in Sioux Falls, S. Dak., in May 1900; also a delegate to the Democratic National Convention at Kansas City, Mo., in 1900 which nominated Bryan and Stevenson, and at Denver, Colo., in 1908 which nominated Bryan and Kern; resumed the practice of his profession in Nelson, Nebr.; died in Kansas City, Kans., October 18, 1915; interment in Evergreen Cemetery, Nelson, Nebr.

SUTPHIN, William Halstead, a Representative from New Jersey; born in Browntown, Middlesex County, N. J., August 30, 1887; attended the public schools of Matawan, N. J., and the Woods Business College, Brooklyn, N. Y.; attended the officers training camp at Plattsburg, N. Y., in 1915; mayor of Matawan, Monmouth County, N. J., 1915–1916 and 1921–1926; served on the Mexican border in 1916 with B Troop, First Squadron, New Jersey Cavalry; during the First World War served in France from December 1917 to May 1919; discharged as captain in the Air Service; factory representative for asphalt roofing 1920–1931; elected as a Democrat to the Seventy-second and to the five succeeding Congresses (March 4, 1931–January 3, 1943); unsuccessful candidate for reelection in 1942 to the Seventy-eighth Congress; vice president of the M. J. Merkin Paint Co. in New York City, N. Y.; retired in 1951 and moved to Rumbley, Somerset County, Md.

SUTTON, James Patrick (Pat), a Representative from Tennessee; born on a farm near Wartrace, Bedford County, Tenn., October 31, 1915; attended the public schools of Wartrace, Tenn., and Cumberland University Law School, Lebanon, Tenn.; graduated from Middle Tennessee State College at Murfreesboro in 1939; during World War II served in the United States Navy 1942–1946; awarded the Distinguished Service Cross, Silver Star, Purple Heart with Oak Leaf Cluster, Presidential Unit Citation with Oak Leaf Cluster, Navy Unit Citation with Cluster, and Army Distinguished Unit Citation; elected as a Democrat to the Eighty-first, Eighty-second, and Eighty-third Congresses (January 3, 1949–January 3, 1955); unsuccessful candidate for the Democratic nomination for United States Senator in 1954; investment securities broker; is a resident of Phoenix, Ariz.

SWAN, John, a Delegate from North Carolina; born in Pasquotank County, N. C., in 1760; tutored under Rev. Charles Earl, an English minister missionary of the Society for the Propagation of the Gospel, at Edenton, N. C.; attended William and Mary College, Williamsburg, Va., about 1780; appointed a Delegate to the Continental Congress to fill the vacancy caused by the resignation of John Baptista Ashe and served from March 22 to November 1, 1788; engaged in agricultural pursuits; urged the adoption by North Carolina of the proposed Constitution of the United States; died in 1793; interment on the grounds of his plantation, "The Elms," in Pasquotank County, N. C.

SWAN, Samuel, a Representative from New Jersey; born near Scotch Plains, Somerset County, N. J., in 1771; studied medicine, and practiced in Boundbrook, N. J., 1800–1806 and in Somerville, N. J., 1806–1809; commissioned as sheriff of Somerset County October 13, 1804, for two years; county clerk 1809–1820; elected to the Seventeenth and to the four succeeding Congresses (March 4, 1821–March 3, 1831); did not seek renomination in 1830 to the Twenty-second Congress; affiliated with the Whig Party; resumed the practice of medicine; died at Boundbrook, N. J., August 24, 1844; interment in the De Groot vault in the Presbyterian Cemetery.

SWANK, Fletcher B., a Representative from Oklahoma; born near Bloomfield, Davis County, Iowa, April 24, 1875; moved with his parents to Beef Creek, Indian Territory, in 1888; worked on farms and ranches until 1897; attended an academy in Noble, Okla., and University of Oklahoma at Norman; superintendent of schools of Cleveland County, Okla., 1903–1907; private secretary to Congressman Scott Ferris in 1907 and 1908; attended the law department of Georgetown University, Washington, D. C., in 1907 and 1908, and was graduated from Cumberland University, Lebanon, Tenn., in 1909; was admitted to the bar in 1909 and commenced practice in Norman, Cleveland County, Okla.; judge of the county court of Cleveland County, Okla., 1911–1915; judge of the fourteenth judicial district of Oklahoma from 1915 to September 1920, when he resigned; elected as a Democrat to the Sixty-seventh and to the three succeeding Congresses (March 4, 1921–March 3, 1929); unsuccessful candidate for reelection in 1928 to the Seventy-first Congress; elected to the Seventy-second and Seventy-third Congresses (March 4, 1931–January 3, 1935); unsuccessful candidate for renomination in 1934; retired from public and political activities; died in Norman, Okla., March 16, 1950; interment in Odd Fellows Cemetery.

SWANN, Edward, a Representative from New York, born near Madison, Madison County, Fla., March 10, 1862; attended the common schools and was graduated from the law department of Columbia College (now University), New York City, in 1886; was admitted to the bar the same year and commenced practice in New York City; elected as a Democrat to the Fifty-seventh Congress to fill the vacancy caused by the death of Amos J. Cummings and served from November 4, 1902, to March 3, 1903; was not a candidate for renomination in 1902; resumed the practice of law in New York City; elected judge of the court of general sessions, New York City, and served from January 1, 1908, until his resignation in 1916; district attorney for New York County 1916–1922; retired from public and political activities; died in Sewalls Point, Jensen Beach, Fla., September 19, 1945; interment in St. Peters Episcopal Cemetery, Fernandina, Fla.

SWANN, Thomas, a Representative from Maryland; born in Alexandria, Va., February 3, 1809; attended Columbian College (now George Washington University), Washington, D. C., and the University of Virginia at Charlottesville; studied law; was appointed by President Jackson as secretary of the United States Neapolitan Commission; moved to Baltimore, Md., in 1834; director and president of the Baltimore & Ohio Railroad 1847–1853; president of the Northwestern Virginia Railroad; mayor of Baltimore 1856–1860; elected by the Union Party as Governor of Maryland and served from 1865 to 1869; elected as a Democrat to the United States Senate in 1866, but did not serve, preferring to continue as Governor; elected as a Democrat to the Forty-first and to the four succeeding Congresses (March 4, 1869–March 3, 1879); died on his estate, "Morven Park," near Leesburg, Va., July 24, 1883; interment in Greenmount Cemetery, Baltimore, Md.

SWANSON, Charles Edward, a Representative from Iowa; born on a farm near Galesburg, Knox County, Ill., January 3, 1879; in 1890 moved to Iowa with his parents, who settled on a farm in Ringgold County; attended the public schools of Galesburg, Ill., and Clearfield, Iowa; was graduated from Knox College, Galesburg, Ill., in 1902, and from the law department of Northwestern University, Evanston, Ill., in 1907; principal of schools, Altona, Ill., 1902–1904; was admitted to the bar in 1907 and commenced practice in Council Bluffs, Iowa; prosecuting attorney of Pottawattamie County, Iowa, 1915–1922; delegate to several Republican State conventions; elected as a Republican to the Seventy-first and Seventy-second Congresses (March 4, 1929–March 3, 1933); unsuccessful candidate for reelection in 1932 to the Seventy-third Congress and for election in 1934 to the Seventy-fourth Congress; resumed the practice of law; chairman, City Board of Tax Review, 1949–; is a resident of Council Bluffs, Iowa.

SWANSON, Claude Augustus, a Representative and a Senator from Virginia; born in Swansonville, Pittsylvania County, Va., March 31, 1862; attended the public schools; taught school; attended the Virginia Agricultural and Mechanical College (now the Virginia Polytechnic Institute) at Blacksburg; was graduated from Randolph-Macon College, Ashland, Va., in 1885 and from the law department of the University of Virginia at Charlottesville in 1886; was admitted to the bar in 1886 and commenced practice in Chatham, Pittsylvania County, Va.; elected as a Democrat to the Fifty-third and to the six succeeding Congresses and served from March 4, 1893, until his resignation, effective January 30, 1906; unsuccessful candidate for nomination as Governor in 1901; Governor of Virginia 1906–1910; appointed as a Democrat to the United States Senate on August 1, 1910, to fill the vacancy in the term ending March 3, 1911, caused by the death of John W. Daniel; again appointed, on February 28, 1911, and subsequently elected to fill the vacancy caused by the death of John W. Daniel, who had been reelected for the term commencing March 4, 1911; reelected in 1916, 1922, and in 1928, and served from August 1, 1910, until March 3, 1933, when he resigned to accept a Cabinet portfolio; served as the American delegate to the Disarmament Conference at Geneva, Switzerland, in 1932; appointed Secretary of the Navy in the Cabinet of President Franklin D. Roosevelt and served from March 4, 1933, until his death while on a visit at Rapidan Camp in the Blue Ridge Mountains, near Criglersville, Madison County, Va., July 7, 1939; funeral services were held in the Chamber of the United States Senate; interment in Hollywood Cemetery, Richmond, Va.

SWANWICK, John, a Representative from Pennsylvania; born in 1740; engaged in mercantile pursuits in Philadelphia, Pa., and was also interested in literature, having published a volume of poetry; elected as a Democrat to the Fourth and Fifth Congresses and served from March 4, 1795, until his death in Philadelphia, Pa., August 1, 1798; interment in St. Peter's Churchyard.

SWART, Peter, a Representative from New York; born in Schoharie, N. Y., July 5, 1752; attended the common schools; studied law; was admitted to the New York bar and commenced the practice of law in Schoharie; judge of the court of common pleas of Schoharie County in 1795; member of the New York State Assembly in 1798 and 1799; elected to the Tenth Congress (March 4, 1807–March 3, 1809); sheriff of Schoharie County in 1810 and 1813; served in the New York State Senate 1817–1820; resumed the practice of his profession in Schoharie, N. Y., and died there on November 3, 1829; interment in the Old Stone Fort Cemetery.

SWARTZ, Joshua William, a Representative from Pennsylvania; born in Lower Swatara Township, Dauphin County, Pa., June 9, 1867; raised on his father's farm; attended the rural schools, Lebanon Valley College, and Williamsport Commercial School; was graduated from the law department of Dickinson College, Carlisle, Pa., in 1892; was admitted to the bar the same year and commenced practice in Harrisburg, Pa.; member of the State house of representatives 1915–1917; elected as a Republican to the Sixty-ninth Congress (March 4, 1925–March 3, 1927); declined to become a candidate for reelection in 1926; resumed the practice of law until his death in Harrisburg, Pa., May 27, 1959; interment in Paxtang Cemetery, Paxtang, Pa.

SWASEY, John Philip, a Representative from Maine; born in Canton, Oxford County, Maine, September 4, 1839; attended the Canton public schools, Dearborn Academy, Hebron Academy, Maine State Seminary, and Tufts College, Medford, Mass.; during the Civil War enlisted in the Union Army and was appointed first lieutenant of Company K, Seventeenth Regiment, Maine Volunteer Infantry; studied law; was admitted to the bar in 1863 and commenced practice in Canton; town clerk and treasurer of Canton in 1866 and 1867; county attorney of Oxford County, Maine, 1868–1870; assessor of internal revenue in 1869 and 1870; member of the State house of representatives in 1874; served in the State senate in 1875 and 1876; member of Governor Robie's council in 1883 and 1884; elected on November 3, 1908, as a Republican to the Sixtieth Congress to fill the vacancy caused by the resignation of Charles E. Littlefield and at the same time was elected to the Sixty-first Congress and served from November 3, 1908, to March 3, 1911; unsuccessful candidate for reelection in 1910 to the Sixty-second Congress; resumed the practice of his profession at Canton, Maine, where he died May 27, 1928; interment in Pine Grove Cemetery.

SWEARINGEN, Henry, a Representative from Ohio; born in the Panhandle of Virginia about 1792; moved to Ohio and settled near Steubenville; sheriff of Jefferson County, Ohio, 1824–1828 and 1830–1832; elected as a Democrat to the Twenty-fifth Congress to fill the vacancy caused by the resignation of Daniel Kilgore; reelected to the Twenty-sixth Congress and served from December 3, 1838, to March 3, 1841; died on board ship while en route to his home from the State of California and was buried at sea.

SWEAT, Lorenzo De Medici, a Representative from Maine; born in Parsonsfield, Maine, May 26, 1818; was graduated from Bowdoin College, Brunswick, Maine, in 1837 and from the law department of Harvard University in 1840; was admitted to the bar and commenced practice in New Orleans, La., in 1841; returned to Maine and settled in Portland; held several local offices, including city solicitor, 1856–1860; member of the State senate in 1862; elected as a Democrat to the Thirty-eighth Congress (March 4, 1863–March 3, 1865); unsuccessful candidate for reelection in 1864 to the Thirty-ninth Congress and for election in 1866 to the Fortieth Congress; delegate to the Union National Convention at Philadelphia in 1868; while attending the Democratic National Convention at Philadelphia in 1872 was chosen a member of the National committee and served four years; honorary commissioner to the World's Expositions at Paris in 1867 and at Vienna in 1873; died in Portland, Maine, July 26, 1898; interment in Evergreen Cemetery.

SWEENEY, Martin Leonard, a Representative from Ohio; born in Cleveland, Cuyahoga County, Ohio, April 15, 1885; attended the parochial and public schools; was graduated from the Cleveland Law School of Baldwin-Wallace College, Cleveland, Ohio, in 1914; employed as a laborer 1901–1903; as a hoisting engineer 1904–1908, and as a salesman 1910–1913; member of the State house of representatives in 1913 and 1914; was admitted to the bar in 1914 and commenced practice in Cleveland, Ohio; judge of the municipal court of Cleveland 1924–1932; delegate to the Democratic National Convention at Chicago in 1932; elected as a Democrat to the Seventy-second Congress to fill the vacancy caused by the death of Charles A. Mooney; reelected to the Seventy-third and to the four succeeding Congresses and served from November 3, 1931, to January 3, 1943; unsuccessful candidate for renomination in 1942; unsuccessful for Democratic nomination for mayor of Cleveland, Ohio, in 1933 and in 1941; and for the gubernatorial nomination in 1944; practiced law in Cleveland, Ohio, until his death there May 1, 1960; interment in Calvary Cemetery.

SWEENEY, William Northcut, a Representative from Kentucky; born in Liberty, Casey County, Ky., May 5, 1832; attended the common schools and Bethany (W. Va.) College; studied law; was admitted to the bar in 1853 and commenced practice in Liberty, Ky.; moved to Owensboro, Daviess County, in 1853; prosecuting attorney of Daviess County 1854–1858; presidential elector on the Democratic ticket of Douglas and Johnson in 1860; elected as a Democrat to the Forty-first Congress (March 4, 1869–March 3, 1871); was renominated in 1870, but declined to accept the nomination; resumed the practice of law in Owensboro, Ky., and died there April 21, 1895; interment in Elmwood Cemetery.

SWEENY, George, a Representative from Ohio; born near Gettysburg, Pa., February 22, 1796; pursued academic studies and was graduated from Dickinson College, Carlisle, Pa.; studied law; was admitted to the bar and commenced practice in Gettysburg in 1820; moved to Bucyrus, Crawford County, Ohio, in 1830; was prosecuting attorney of Crawford County in 1838; elected to the Twenty-sixth and Twenty-seventh Congresses (March 4, 1839–March 3, 1843); was not a candidate for renomination in 1842; resumed the practice of his profession; moved to Geneseo, Henry County, Ill., in 1853, and continued the practice of law; returned to Bucyrus, Ohio, in 1856; was again elected prosecuting attorney of Crawford County; retired from the practice of his profession and engaged in literary and scientific pursuits; died in Bucyrus, Ohio, October 10, 1877; interment in Oakwood Cemetery.

SWEET, Burton Erwin, a Representative from Iowa; born on a farm near Waverly, Bremer County, Iowa, December 10, 1867; attended the common schools and the Iowa State Normal School at Cedar Falls; was graduated from Cornell College, Mount Vernon, Iowa, in 1893 and from the law department of the University of Iowa at Iowa City in 1895; was admitted to the bar in 1895 and commenced practice in Waverly, Iowa; city solicitor of Waverly 1896–1899; member of the State house of representatives 1900–1904; delegate to the Republican National Convention at Chicago in 1904; member of the Republican State central committee 1902–1906; elected as a Republican to the Sixty-fourth and to the three succeeding Congresses (March 4, 1915–March 3, 1923); did not seek renomination in 1922, having become a candidate for Senator; unsuccessful candidate for United States Senator in the Republican primary election of 1922 and again in 1924; resumed the practice of law; died in Waverly, Iowa, January 3, 1957; interment in Harlington Cemetery.

SWEET, Edwin Forrest, a Representative from Michigan; born in Dansville, Livingston County, N. Y., November 21, 1847; attended the common schools; was graduated from the literary department of Yale College in 1871 and from the law department of Michigan University at Ann Arbor in 1874; was admitted to the bar 1874 and commenced practice in Grand Rapids, Mich., in 1876; member of the board of education 1899–1906; mayor of Grand Rapids 1904–1906; elected as a Democrat to the Sixty-second Congress (March 4, 1911–March 3, 1913); unsuccessful candidate for reelection in 1912 to the Sixty-third Congress; Assistant Secretary of Commerce 1913–1921; unsuccessful candidate for Governor of Michigan in 1916; member of the board of education of Grand Rapids 1923–1926; member of the city commission 1926–1928; operated a grain and stock ranch in North Dakota; resided in Grand Rapids, Mich., until 1928 when he retired and moved to Ojai, Calif., where he died April 2, 1935; interment in Oakhill Cemetery, Grand Rapids, Mich.

SWEET, John Hyde, a Representative from Nebraska; born in Milford, Otsego County, N. Y., September 1, 1880; moved to Palmyra, Nebr., with his parents in 1885; attended the Palmyra grade and high schools, the University of Nebraska at Lincoln, and the Lincoln (Nebr.) Business College; employed as a court reporter in western Nebraska in 1899 and 1900; wholesale grocer in Nebraska City 1902–1909; engaged in the newspaper publishing business at Nebraska City, Nebr., in 1909; delegate to the Progressive National Convention at Chicago in 1912 which nominated Theodore Roosevelt and Hiram W. Johnson on the Progressive (Bull Moose) ticket; elected as a Republican to the Seventy-sixth Congress to fill the vacancy caused by the death of George H. Heinke and served from April 9, 1940, to January 3, 1941; was not a candidate for renomination in 1940; resumed the newspaper publishing business in Nebraska City, Nebr.

SWEET, Thaddeus C., a Representative from New York; born in Phoenix, Oswego County, N. Y., November 16, 1872; attended the public schools; was graduated from Phoenix Academy and High School; entered business and for two years served as a traveling salesman; in 1895 began the manufacture of paper and was president of the Sweet Paper Manufacturing Co.; also engaged in banking; town clerk of Phoenix 1896–1899; delegate to most all Republican National Conventions 1908–1927; member New York State Assembly 1910–1920, serving as speaker 1914–1920; elected as a Republican to the Sixty-eighth Congress to fill the vacancy caused by the death of Luther W. Mott; reelected to the Sixty-ninth and Seventieth Congresses and served from November 6, 1923, until his death as the result of an airplane accident at Whitney Point, Broome County, N. Y., May 1, 1928; interment in the Rural Cemetery, Phoenix, N. Y.

SWEET, Willis, a Representative from Idaho; born at Alburg Springs, Vt., January 1, 1856; attended the common schools and the University of Nebraska at Lincoln; learned the printer's trade in Lincoln, Nebr.; moved to Moscow, Latah County, Idaho, in September 1881; studied law; was admitted to the bar in 1889 and commenced practice in Moscow; appointed United States attorney for Idaho in May 1888; judge of the first judicial district of Idaho from November 19, 1889, to January 1, 1890; appointed associate justice of Idaho Supreme Court November 25, 1889; first president of the board of regents of the University of Idaho 1889–1893; upon the admission of Idaho as a State into the Union was elected as a Republican to the Fifty-first Congress; reelected to the Fifty-second and Fifty-third Congresses and served from October 1, 1890, to March 3, 1895; was not a candidate for renomination in 1894; unsuccessful candidate for election to the United States Senate in 1896; resumed the practice of his profession in Coeur d'Alene, Kootenai County, Idaho; attorney general for Puerto Rico 1903–1905; editor of a newspaper in San Juan, P. R., from 1913 until his death there July 9, 1925; interment in Santurce Cemetery

SWEETSER, Charles, a Representative from Ohio; born in Dummerston, Vt., January 22, 1808; moved with his parents to Delaware, Ohio, in 1817; attended the public schools; engaged in mercantile pursuits; studied law; was admitted to the bar in 1832 and commenced practice in Delaware, Delaware County, Ohio; elected as a Democrat to the Thirty-first and Thirty-second Congresses (March 4, 1849–March 3, 1853); resumed the practice of law; died in Delaware, Ohio, April 14, 1864; interment in Oak Grove Cemetery.

SWENEY, Joseph Henry, a Representative from Iowa; born in Warren County, Pa., October 2, 1845; attended the public schools of Pennsylvania and Iowa; was graduated from the law department of the University of Iowa at Iowa City in 1880; was admitted to the bar the same year and commenced practice in Osage, Mitchell County, Iowa; also engaged in banking and agricultural pursuits; during the Civil War enlisted in the Union Army and served as sergeant in Company K, Twenty-seventh Regiment, Iowa Volunteer Infantry; colonel of the Sixth Regiment National Guard of Iowa for four years and brigadier and inspector general of the State; member of the State senate 1883–1891, serving as president pro tempore in 1886; elected as a Republican to the Fifty-first Congress (March 4, 1889–March 3, 1891); unsuccessful candidate for reelection in 1890 to the Fifty-second Congress; resumed the practice of law in Osage, Iowa; died while on a visit in Norfolk, Va., November 11, 1918; interment in Osage Cemetery, Osage, Iowa.

SWICK, Jesse Howard, a Representative from Pennsylvania; born near New Brighton, Beaver County, Pa., August 6, 1879; attended the public schools and Geneva College, Beaver Falls, Pa.; taught school in Beaver County, Pa., 1895–1900; graduated from Hahnemann Medical College of Philadelphia in 1906; served as an interne in the Children's Homeopathic Hospital of Philadelphia in 1905 and 1906, and Homeopathic Hospital of Pittsburgh, Pa., in 1906; moved to Beaver Falls, Pa., in 1906 and commenced the practice of medicine; president of the Beaver Falls Bureau of Health 1907–1914; during the First World War served as a first lieutenant and later as a captain in the Medical Corps of the United States Army, with overseas service, from August 31, 1917, to May 9, 1919; after the war resumed the practice of medicine in Beaver Falls, Pa.; also interested in banking and the manufacturing of steel products; member of the Beaver Falls City Council 1925–1927; elected as a Republican to the Seventieth and to the three succeeding Congresses (March 4, 1927–January 3, 1935); was an unsuccessful candidate for reelection in 1934 to the Seventy-fourth Congress; resumed the practice of medicine until August 1945, when he retired; died in Beaver Falls, Pa., November 17, 1952; interment in Concord Cemetery, North Sewickley Township, Beaver County, Pa.

SWIFT, Benjamin, a Representative and a Senator from Vermont; born in Amenia, N. Y., April 3, 1781; moved with his father to Bennington, Vt., in 1786; completed preparatory studies; studied law; was admitted to the bar in 1806 and commenced practice in Bennington; moved to Manchester and then to St. Albans in 1809; practiced law and also engaged in banking and agricultural pursuits; member of the State house of representatives in 1813, 1825, and 1826; elected as a Federalist to the Twentieth and Twenty-first Congresses (March 4, 1827–March 3, 1831); was not a candidate for renomination in 1830; elected to the United States Senate and served from March 4, 1833, to March 3, 1839; was not a candidate for renomination in 1839; resumed the practice of law and agricultural pursuits; died in St. Albans, Vt., on November 11, 1847; interment in the Old Cemetery, South Main Street.

SWIFT, George Robinson, a Senator from Alabama; born at Swift Post Office, Baldwin County, Ala., December 19, 1887; attended the public schools of Baldwin County, Ala., the University Military School, Mobile, Ala., and the University of Alabama at Tuscaloosa; engaged in the lumber industry at Bon Secour, Ala., 1907–1912; Knoxo, Miss., 1912–1922; and Atmore, Ala., in 1922; served in the Alabama House of Representatives 1931–1935; member of the State senate 1935–1939; served as State highway director from January 1943 to June 1946; appointed as a Democrat to the United States Senate to fill the vacancy caused by the death of John H. Bankhead 2d and served from June 15, 1946, to November 5, 1946, when a successor was elected; was not a candidate for election to the vacancy in 1946; member of Alabama State Senate 1947–1951; president of Southern Pine Association from April 1954 to April 1955; president, Swift-Hunter Lumber Co., of Atmore, Ala., where he resides.

SWIFT, Oscar William, a Representative from New York; born in Paines Hollow, Herkimer County, N. Y., April 11, 1869; moved to Michigan with his parents, who settled in Adrian in 1877; attended the public schools and the University of Michigan at Ann Arbor; was graduated from the New York Law School, New York City, in 1896; was admitted to the bar in 1897 and commenced practice in New York City; elected as a Republican to the Sixty-fourth and Sixty-fifth Congresses (March 4, 1915–March 3, 1919); unsuccessful candidate for reelection in 1918 to the Sixty-sixth Congress; resumed law practice in New York City; died in Brooklyn, N. Y., June 30, 1940; interment in Kensico Cemetery, Valhalla, N. Y.

SWIFT, Zephaniah, a Representative from Connecticut; born in Wareham, Plymouth County, Mass., February 27, 1759; moved with his parents to Lebanon, New London County, Conn.; completed preparatory studies; was graduated from Yale College in 1778; studied law; was admitted to the bar and commenced practice in Windham, Conn.; member of the State house of representatives 1787–1793, serving as speaker in 1792; clerk of the house for four sessions; elected as a Federalist to the Third and Fourth Congresses (March 4, 1793–March 3, 1797); resumed the practice of law at Windham; also engaged in literary pursuits; secretary of the French mission in 1800; judge of the supreme court in 1801 and chief justice 1806–1819; member of the New England Federalists Convention at Hartford in 1814; again a member of the State house of representatives 1820–1822; died in Warren, Trumbull County, Ohio, while on a visit to a son, September 27, 1823; interment in Oakwood Cemetery.

SWINBURNE, John, a Representative from New York; born at Deer River, Lewis County, N. Y., May 30, 1820; attended the public schools and academies in Denmark and Lowville, Lewis County, and an academy in Fairfield, Herkimer County; was graduated from the Albany Medical College in 1847 and commenced practice as a physician and surgeon; during the Civil War was appointed in 1861 chief medical officer on the staff of Gen. John F. Rathbone and placed in charge of the depot for recruits in Albany; appointed by Governor Morgan in May 1862 auxiliary Volunteer surgeon at the front with the rank of medical superintendent of New York wounded troops and reappointed June 13 by Governor Seymour; appointed by the Surgeon General of the United States Army and assigned to duty at Savage Station by General McClellan; taken prisoner of war June 29, 1862; appointed by Governor Seymour in 1864 health officer of the port of New York and reappointed by Governor Fenton in 1866, holding the position six years; in charge of the American Ambulance Corps during the siege of Paris by the

Prussians in 1870 and 1871; elected mayor of Albany in 1882 and counted out, but after fourteen months' litigation was awarded the office by the courts; elected as a Republican to the Forty-ninth Congress (March 4, 1885–March 3, 1887); resumed the practice of his profession; died in Albany, N. Y., March 28, 1889; interment in Albany Rural Cemetery.

SWINDALL, Charles, a Representative from Oklahoma; born at College Mound, near Terrell, Kaufman County, Tex., February 13, 1876; attended the public schools and Vanderbilt University, Nashville, Tenn.; was graduated from the law department of Cumberland University, Lebanon, Tenn., in 1897; was admitted to the bar the same year and commenced practice in Woodward, Okla.; prosecuting attorney of Day (later Ellis) County 1898–1900; returned to Woodward in 1900 and continued the practice of law; delegate to the Republican National Convention at Chicago in 1916; during the First World War took an active part in American Red Cross work; elected as a Republican to the Sixty-sixth Congress to fill the vacancy caused by the death of Dick T. Morgan, and served from November 2, 1920, to March 3, 1921; unsuccessful candidate for renomination in 1920 to the Sixty-seventh Congress; resumed the practice of law in Woodward, Okla.; appointed April 26, 1924, judge of the twentieth judicial district of Oklahoma, in which capacity he served until 1929; justice of the State supreme court 1929–1934; resumed the practice of law in Oklahoma City, Okla., until his death there June 19, 1939; interment in Memorial Park Cemetery.

SWING, Philip David, a Representative from California; born in San Bernardino, San Bernardino County, Calif., November 30, 1884; attended the public schools, and was graduated from Leland Stanford (Calif.) Junior University in 1905; first lieutenant in the California National Guard 1906–1908; studied law; was admitted to the bar in 1907 and commenced practice in San Bernardino; city attorney of Brawley, Calif., in 1908 and 1909; deputy district attorney of Imperial County 1908–1911 and district attorney 1911–1915; chief counsel of the Imperial Irrigation District 1916–1919; judge of the superior court of Imperial County 1919–1921; delegate to the Republican State conventions at Sacramento, Calif., 1920–1932, serving as chairman in 1926; during the First World War served as a private in the Officers Training Camp at Camp Taylor, Ky., in 1918; elected as a Republican to the Sixty-seventh and to the five succeeding Congresses (March 4, 1921–March 3, 1933); was not a candidate for renomination in 1932; resumed law practice; appointed a member of the California State Water Resources Board (now California Water Commission) in 1945; reappointed in 1950 and served until 1958; is a resident of San Diego, Calif.

SWITZER, Robert Mauck, a Representative from Ohio; born near Gallipolis, Gallia County, Ohio, March 6, 1863; attended the district schools, Gallia Academy, and Rio Grande College; taught school 1883–1887; deputy sheriff of Gallia County 1888–1892; attended the law departments of the University of Virginia at Charlottesville and the Ohio State University of Columbus; was admitted to the bar in 1892 and commenced practice in Gallipolis, Ohio; prosecuting attorney of Gallia County 1893–1900; delegate to the Republican National Conventions in 1900 and 1920; presidential elector on the Republican ticket of William Howard Taft and John S. Sherman in 1908; elected as a Republican to the Sixty-second and to the three succeeding Congresses (March 4, 1911–March 3, 1919); was an unsuccessful candidate for renomination in 1918 to the Sixty-sixth Congress; resumed the practice of law; city solicitor of Gallipolis, Ohio; died in Gallipolis, Ohio, on October 28, 1952; interment in Mound Hill Cemetery.

SWOOPE, Jacob, a Representative from Virginia; born in Philadelphia, Pa.; attended the common schools; moved to Staunton, Va., in 1789 and engaged in the mercantile business; held several local offices; elected the first mayor of Staunton under the new charter of 1801; reelected in 1804; elected as a Federalist to the Eleventh Congress (March 4, 1809–March 3, 1811); declined to be a candidate for renomination in 1810; member of the State constitutional convention in 1812; presidential elector on the Federalist ticket of King and Davis in 1812; died in Staunton, Va., in 1832; interment in Trinity Episcopal Churchyard.

SWOOPE, William Irvin (nephew of John Patton), a Representative from Pennsylvania; born in Clearfield, Clearfield County, Pa., October 3, 1862; attended the public schools, Hill School, Pottstown, Pa., and Phillips Academy, Andover, Mass.; was graduated from the law department of Harvard University in 1886; was admitted to the bar December 6, 1886, and practiced law in Minnesota, Nebraska, and also at Bellefonte, Pa., where he was elected burgess; returned to Clearfield, Pa., in 1892 and continued the practice of law; county chairman and district attorney for Clearfield County 1901–1907; delegate to the Republican National Convention at Chicago in 1916; deputy attorney general for Pennsylvania 1919–1923; elected as a Republican to the Sixty-eighth and Sixty-ninth Congresses (March 4, 1923–March 3, 1927); declined to be a candidate for renomination in 1926; resumed the practice of law in Clearfield, Pa., until his death there October 9, 1930; interment in Hillcrest Cemetery.

SWOPE, Guy Jacob, a Representative from Pennsylvania; born in Meckville, Berks County, Pa., December 26, 1892; attended the public schools, Keystone State Teachers College, Kutztown, Pa., and Columbia University School of International Affairs; taught school in Lebanon County, Pa., 1909–1913; served as United States internal revenue agent 1913–1918; engaged as a public accountant 1919–1934; budget secretary of Pennsylvania 1935–1937; elected as a Democrat to the Seventy-fifth Congress (January 3, 1937–January 3, 1939); unsuccessful candidate for reelection in 1938 to the Seventy-sixth Congress; engaged as an accountant in 1939; auditor of Puerto Rico from January 15, 1940, to February 2, 1941; Governor of Puerto Rico from February 3, 1941, to August 6, 1941; director of the Division of Territories and Island Possessions, Interior Department, from August 7, 1941, to October 15, 1942; district director, Office of Price Administration, Harrisburg, Pa., from October 16, 1942, to July 27, 1943; during World War II served as a lieutenant commander and later as a commander in the United States Naval Reserve, Military Government Branch, from July 28, 1943, to November 14, 1946, retiring as captain in 1958; awarded the Legion of Merit by General MacArthur; engaged as a civilian chief, National Government Division, General Headquarters, Tokyo, Japan, from February 12, 1947, to March 9, 1948; special assistant to Pennsylvania State treasurer from August 1, 1948, to May 3, 1949; served as special assistant to the American High Commissioner in Germany from July 1949 to March 1954; was an unsuccessful candidate for election in 1956 to the Eighty-fifth Congress; certified public accountant; director and comptroller of Lake Asphalt & Petroleum Co. of Pennsylvania 1956–1961; deputy State treasurer, Commonwealth of Pennsylvania, since May 1, 1961; is a resident of Harrisburg, Pa.

SWOPE, John Augustus, a Representative from Pennsylvania; born in Gettysburg, Adams County, Pa., December 25, 1827; attended the common schools at Gettysburg, Pa., and Mount St. Mary's Academy, Emmitsburg, Md.; was graduated from Princeton College in 1847 and from the medical department of the University of Pennsylvania at Philadelphia, but discontinued the practice of medicine after a few years and engaged in mercantile pursuits in Baltimore; returned to Gettysburg and became president of the Gettysburg National Bank in 1879; also engaged in manufacturing and agricultural pursuits; elected in 1884 as a Democrat to the Forty-eighth Congress to fill the vacancy caused by the death of William A. Duncan and served from December 23, 1884, to March 3, 1885; subsequently elected in 1885 to the Forty-ninth Congress to fill the vacancy caused by the death of Mr. Duncan, who had been reelected, and served from November 3, 1885, to March 3, 1887; was not a candidate for renomination in 1886; moved to Washington, D. C., and engaged in banking until his death there on December 6, 1910; interment in Evergreen Cemetery, Gettysburg, Pa.

SWOPE, King, a Representative from Kentucky; born in Danville, Boyle County, Ky., August 10, 1893; attended the common schools; was graduated from Centre College, Danville, Ky., in 1914 and from the law department of the University of Kentucky at Lexington in 1916; was admitted to the bar in 1915 and commenced practice in Lexington, Ky.; presidential elector on the Republican ticket of Hughes and Fairbanks in 1916; enlisted and served during the First World War as captain of Infantry; elected as a Republican to the Sixty-sixth Congress to fill the vacancy caused by the death of Harvey Helm and served from August 2, 1919, to March 3, 1921; unsuccessful candidate for reelection in 1920 to the Sixty-seventh Congress; appointed aide-de-camp with the rank of colonel on the staff of Gov. Edwin P. Morrow in 1919; resumed the practice of law; chairman of the Republican executive committee of Fayette County, Ky., 1928–1931; appointed and subsequently elected a judge of the circuit court of the twenty-second judicial district of Kentucky and served from 1931 to 1940; unsuccessful Republican candidate for Governor in 1935 and 1939; delegate to the Republican National Conventions in 1936, 1940, and 1944; chairman of the Republican State convention in 1936; member of the judicial council of Kentucky 1931–1940; died in Lexington, Ky., April 23, 1961; interment in Lexington Cemetery.

SWOPE, Samuel Franklin, a Representative from Kentucky; born in Bourbon County, Ky., March 1, 1809; attended the rural schools of Bourbon and Scott Counties and the Georgetown (Ky.) College; studied law; was admitted to the bar March 1, 1830, and commenced practice in Georgetown, Ky.; moved to Falmouth, Pendleton County, Ky., in 1832 and continued the practice of law; member of the State house of representatives 1837–1839 and in 1841; served in the State senate 1844–1848; elected by the American Party to the Thirty-fourth Congress (March 4, 1855–March 3, 1857); was not a candidate for renomination in 1856; affiliated with the Republican Party in 1856; engaged in the practice of law at Falmouth, Ky., until his death April 19, 1865; interment in Riverside Cemetery.

SYKES, George, a Representative from New Jersey; born near Sykesville, Burlington County, N. J., September 20, 1802; educated by private teachers; became a surveyor and conveyancer; elected as a Democrat to the Twenty-eighth Congress (March 4, 1843–March 3, 1845); elected to the Twenty-ninth Congress to fill the vacancy caused by the death of Samuel G. Wright, and served from November 4, 1845, to March 3, 1847; resumed his former pursuits; member of the council of properties of West Jersey; member of the State assembly 1877–1879; died near Columbia, Mansfield Township, Burlington County, N. J., February 25, 1880; interment in Upper Springfield Cemetery, near Wrightstown, N. J.

SYKES, James, a Delegate from Delaware; born in 1725; studied law; was admitted to the bar and commenced practice; lieutenant in Capt. Caesar Rodney's company of Dover Militia in 1756; member of the council of safety in 1776; delegate to the State constitutional convention held at New Castle, Del., in 1776; member of the Continental Congress in 1777 and 1778; clerk of the peace 1777–1792; prothonotary of Kent County 1777–1793; served in the State council in 1780; member of the State legislature which ratified the Federal Constitution on December 7, 1787; again a delegate to the State constitutional convention in 1790; presidential elector in 1792 and voted for Washington and Adams; judge of the High Court of Errors and Appeals of Delaware; died in Dover, Del., April 4, 1792; interment in the burial ground of Christ Church.

SYMES, George Gifford, a Representative from Colorado; born in Ashtabula County, Ohio, April 28, 1840; attended the common schools; studied law; was admitted to the bar and practiced; during the Civil War enlisted as a private in Company B, Second Regiment, Wisconsin Volunteers, April 12, 1861; wounded in the first Battle of Bull Run; adjutant of the Twenty-fifth Regiment, Wisconsin Infantry; served in the Sioux Indian campaign of 1862 and in the Vicksburg campaign of 1863; was in the Atlanta campaign of 1864 and wounded in the Battle of Atlanta July 22, 1864; commissioned colonel of the Forty-fourth Regiment, Wisconsin Volunteers, in August 1864; commanded the post at Paducah, Ky., during the summer of 1865; mustered out August 28, 1865; practiced law in Paducah, Ky.; associate justice of the supreme court of Montana Territory 1869–1871; resumed the practice of law in Helena, Mont.; moved to Denver, Colo., in 1874; elected as a Republican to the Forty-ninth and Fiftieth Congresses (March 4, 1885–March 3, 1889); engaged in the management of his estate and in the practice of law; died in Denver, Colo., November 3, 1893; interment in Fairmount Cemetery.

SYMINGTON, William Stuart, a Senator from Missouri; born in Amherst, Hampshire County, Mass., June 26, 1901; soon after his birth the family moved to Baltimore, Md.; attended the public schools; worked during summer vacations as an office boy at age of twelve years and as a machinist apprentice at age of fourteen years; after graduation from high school, enlisted as a private in the United States Army at seventeen years of age and was discharged as a second lieutenant; after military service went to Yale University, graduating in 1923, and worked summers as a reporter on a Baltimore newspaper; went to Rochester, N. Y., and worked as an iron moulder and lathe operator 1923–1926, studying mechanical and electrical engineering at night and by correspondence; executive with several radio and steel companies 1926–1937; moved to St. Louis, Mo., and became president of the Emerson Electric Manufacturing Co., 1938–1945; chairman of Surplus Property Board July 1945 to September 1945; Surplus Property Administrator September 1945 to January 1946; Assistant Secretary of War for Air from February 1946 to September 1947; first Secretary of the Air Force from September 1947 to April 1950; chairman of National Security Resources Board April 1950 to May 1951; Reconstruction Finance Corporation Administrator May 1951 to January 1952, from which office he resigned to run for nomination as United States Senator; awarded Medal of Merit in 1947 and Distinguished Service Medal in 1952; elected as a Democrat to the United States Senate in 1952 for the term commencing January 3, 1953; reelected in 1958 for the term ending January 3, 1965.

SYMMES, John Cleves, a Delegate from New Jersey; born in Riverhead, Long Island, N. Y., July 21, 1742; completed preparatory studies; moved to New Jersey; chairman of the committee of safety of Sussex County in 1774; member of the State council in 1778; served in the Revolutionary Army; chief justice of the State supreme court 1777–1787; Member of the Continental Congress in 1785 and 1786; moved to the Northwest Territory and settled in North Bend, below Cincinnati; appointed one of the three judges of the Northwest Territory in 1788 and held the position until Ohio was admitted into the Union; died in Cincinnati, Ohio, February 26, 1814; interment in Congress Green Cemetery, North Bend, Ohio.

SYPHER, Jacob Hale, a Representative from Louisiana; born near Millerstown, Perry County, Pa., June 22, 1837; received a liberal education, and was graduated from Alfred (N. Y.) University in 1859; taught school in Cleveland, Ohio; during the Civil War entered the Union Army as a private in Company A, First Ohio Light Artillery; promoted to first lieutenant of Company B, October 8, 1861; resigned February 3, 1864; later, on August 11, 1864, served as colonel of the Eleventh United States Colored Heavy Artillery; brevetted brigadier general of Volunteers March 13, 1865, "for faithful and meritorious services during the war"; honorably mustered out October 2, 1865; after the war bought a plantation in northern Louisiana, but about two years later commenced the study of law; was admitted to the bar and practiced in New Orleans, La.; delegate to the Republican National Convention at Chicago in 1868; upon readmission of the State of Louisiana to representation was elected as a Republican to the Fortieth Congress and served from July 18, 1868, to March 3, 1869; contested the election of Louis St. Martin to the Forty-first Congress, but the House decided that neither was entitled to the seat; subsequently elected to the Forty-first Congress to fill the vacancy thus created; reelected to the Forty-second Congress and served from November 7, 1870, to March 3, 1873; presented credentials as a Member-elect to the Forty-third Congress and served from March 4, 1873, to March 3, 1875, when he was succeeded by Effingham Lawrence, who contested the election; unsuccessful candidate for election in 1874 to the Forty-fourth Congress; resumed the practice of law in Washington, D. C.; died in Baltimore, Md., May 9, 1905; interment in the Arlington National Cemetery, Fort Myer, Va.

T

TABER, John, a Representative from New York; born in Auburn, Cayuga County, N. Y., May 5, 1880; attended the public schools; was graduated from Yale University in 1902 and from New York Law School in 1904; was admitted to the bar November 15, 1904, and commenced practice in Auburn, N. Y.; supervisor of Cayuga County in 1905 and 1906; special judge of the county court 1910–1918; delegate to the Republican National Conventions in 1920, 1924, and 1936; chairman of the Cayuga County Republican committee 1920–1925; president of the Auburn Chamber of Commerce in 1922; elected as a Republican to the Sixty-eighth and to the eighteen succeeding Congresses (March 4, 1923–January 3, 1961). *Reelected to the Eighty-seventh Congress.*

TABER, Stephen (son of Thomas Taber 2d), a Representative from New York; born in Dover, Dutchess County, N. Y., March 7, 1821; completed preparatory studies; moved to Queens County and engaged in agricultural pursuits; member of the State assembly in 1860 and 1861; elected as a Democrat to the Thirty-ninth and Fortieth Congresses (March 4, 1865–March 3, 1869); assisted in organizing the Long Island North Shore Transportation Co. in 1861 and served as its president for several years; director of the Long Island Railroad Co.; became the first president of the Roslyn Savings Bank in 1876 and

served in this capacity for a number of years; died in New York City April 23, 1886; interment in Roslyn Cemetery, Roslyn, Long Island, N. Y.

TABER, Thomas, 2d (father of Stephen Taber), a Representative from New York; born in Dover, Dutchess County, N. Y., May 19, 1785; attended the common schools; engaged in agricultural pursuits; member of the State assembly in 1826; elected as a Democrat to the Twentieth Congress to fill the vacancy caused by the resignation of Thomas J. Oakley and served from November 5, 1828, to March 3, 1829; died in Roslyn, Long Island, N. Y., March 21, 1862; interment in the Friends Cemetery, Westbury, Long Island, N. Y.

TABOR, Horace Austin Warner, a Senator from Colorado; born in Holland, Orleans County, Vt., November 26, 1830; attended the common schools and received instruction from a private tutor; moved to Quincy, Mass., and then to Augusta, Maine, where he worked at the stonecutter's trade; moved to Kansas in 1855 and settled in Riley County; engaged in agricultural pursuits; member of the Topeka Legislature when it was dispersed by order of President Pierce; moved to Denver, Colo., in 1859 and in the following year to California Gulch (now Leadville); engaged in mining and mercantile pursuits; postmaster of Leadville from February 19 to December 18, 1878; city mayor in 1878 and 1879; treasurer of Lake County; Lieutenant Governor of Colorado in 1878–1884; elected as a Republican to the United States Senate to fill the vacancy caused by the resignation of Henry M. Teller and served from January 27 to March 3, 1883; was not a candidate for reelection; postmaster of Denver, Colo., from January 14, 1898, until his death April 10, 1899; interment in Mount Calvary Cemetery.

TACKETT, Boyd, a Representative from Arkansas; born near Black Springs, Montgomery County, Ark., May 9, 1911; moved with his parents to Glenwood, Pike County, Ark., and attended the public schools; student at Arkansas Polytechnic College at Russellville 1930–1932, Ouachita College, Arkadelphia, Ark., in 1932 and 1933, and graduated from the University of Arkansas Law School at Fayetteville in 1935; was admitted to the bar in 1935 and practiced law in Glenwood, Murfreesboro, and Nashville, Ark.; member of the State legislature 1937–1941; elected prosecuting attorney of the ninth judicial circuit of Arkansas and served from January 1, 1941, until his enlistment in the Armed Services; during World War II served as a corporal in the United States Army Signal Corps from October 4, 1943, until discharged on November 5, 1944; resumed law practice in Nashville, Ark.; State police commissioner, Little Rock, Ark., 1945–1948; elected as a Democrat to the Eighty-first and Eighty-second Congresses (January 3, 1949–January 3, 1953); was not a candidate for renomination in 1952 but was unsuccessful for the Democratic gubernatorial nomination; resumed the practice of law; is a resident of Texarkana, Ark.

TAFFE, John, a Representative from Nebraska; born in Indianapolis, Ind., January 30, 1827; completed preparatory studies; studied law; was admitted to the bar in Indianapolis, Ind.; moved to Nebraska in 1856; member of the Territorial house of representatives in 1858 and 1859; member of the Territorial council in 1860 and 1861 and served as president; during the Civil War enlisted in the Union Army and served as major in the Second Regiment, Nebraska Volunteer Cavalry; returned to Omaha, Nebr.; elected as a Republican to the Fortieth, Forty-first, and Forty-second Congresses (March 4, 1867–March 3, 1873); resumed the practice of law; receiver of the public land office in North Platte, Nebr., where he died March 14, 1884; interment in Prospect Hill Cemetery, Omaha, Nebr.

TAFT, Charles Phelps (uncle of Robert Alphonso Taft), a Representative from Ohio; born in Cincinnati, Ohio, December 21, 1843; attended the common schools, and was graduated from Phillips Academy, Andover, Mass., in 1860, from Yale College in 1864, and from Columbia College Law School of New York City in 1866; was admitted to the bar in 1866; went to Germany and was graduated from the University of Heidelberg in 1867; commenced the practice of law in Cincinnati, Ohio, in 1869; member of the State house of representatives 1871–1873; became owner and editor of the Cincinnati Times-Star in 1879; member of the board of sinking-fund trustees of the city of Cincinnati for sixteen years and served as president 1898–1908; elected as a Republican to the Fifty-fourth Congress (March 4, 1895– March 3, 1897); was not a candidate for renomination in 1896 to the Fifty-fifth Congress; resumed the newspaper business in Cincinnati, Ohio; presidential elector at large on the Republican ticket of Theodore Roosevelt and Charles W. Fairbanks in 1904; president of the Ohio Electoral College in 1905; delegate to the Republican National Conventions at Chicago in 1908 and in 1912 which nominated the presidential ticket of William H. Taft and James S. Sherman; director in various corporations, particularly public utilities; also engaged in the collection of fine arts and in 1927 made a gift of his collection valued at several million dollars to the Cincinnati Institute of Fine Arts; died in Cincinnati, Ohio, December 31, 1929; interment in Spring Grove Cemetery.

TAFT, Kingsley Arter, a Senator from Ohio; born in Cleveland, Cuyahoga County, Ohio, July 19, 1903; attended the public schools of Cleveland and Cleveland Heights High School; was graduated from Amherst College, Amherst, Mass., in 1925 and from the law school of Harvard University, Cambridge, Mass., in 1928; editor of the Harvard Law Review in 1927 and 1928; was admitted to the bar in 1928; practiced law in Cleveland, Ohio, through 1948; member of the Ohio House of Representatives in 1933 and 1934; member of the Shaker Heights Board of Education 1940–1942, serving as president in 1942; during World War II was commissioned as a captain in the United States Army in 1942; promoted to major in 1945 and awarded the Army Commendation Ribbon with Oak Leaf Cluster in 1946; separated from the service June 13, 1946; trustee of Baldwin-Wallace College and formerly of the Welfare Federation of Cleveland; elected as a Republican to the United States Senate on November 5, 1946, to fill the vacancy in the term ending January 3, 1947, caused by the resignation of Harold H. Burton; was not a candidate for election to the full term; elected in 1948 as judge of the Ohio Supreme Court; reelected in 1954 and again in 1960 for the term ending January 2, 1967; is a resident of Columbus, Ohio.

TAFT, Robert Alphonso (son of President William Howard Taft and nephew of Charles Phelps Taft), a Senator from Ohio; born in Cincinnati, Ohio, September 8, 1889; attended the public schools of Cincinnati, Ohio, and of Manila, Philippine Islands, and Taft School, Watertown, Conn.; was graduated from Yale University, New Haven, Conn., in 1910 and from Harvard Law School, Cambridge, Mass., in 1913; was admitted to the Ohio bar in 1913 and commenced practice in Cincinnati, Ohio; director in a number of business enterprises in Cincinnati; assistant counsel, United States Food Administration, in 1917 and 1918; counsel, American Relief Administration, in 1919; member of the Ohio House of Representatives 1921–1926, serving as speaker in 1926; served in the Ohio Senate in 1931 and 1932; delegate to the Republican National Conventions in 1932, 1940, and 1944; elected as a Republican to the United States Senate in 1938; reelected in 1944 and again in 1950 and served from January 3, 1939, until his death; unsuccessful in 1952 for the Republican nomination for President of the United States; died in New York City, N. Y., July 31, 1953; memorial services were held in the rotunda of the Capitol; interment in Indian Hill Episcopal Church Cemetery (Indian Hill), Cincinnati, Ohio.

TAGGART, Joseph, a Representative from Kansas; born near Waukon, Allamakee County, Iowa, June 15, 1867; attended the district school; moved to Salina, Kans., in 1885; was graduated from the Salina Normal University in 1890; taught school in Bavaria, Kans., in 1892 and 1893; studied law; was admitted to the bar in 1893 and commenced the practice of his profession in Salina, Kans., moving shortly thereafter to Kansas City, Kans.; prosecuting attorney of Wyandotte County 1907–1911; elected as a Democrat to the Sixty-second Congress to fill the vacancy caused by the death of Alexander C. Mitchell; reelected to the Sixty-third and Sixty-fourth Congresses and served from November 7, 1911, to March 3, 1917; unsuccessful candidate for reelection in 1916 to the Sixty-fifth Congress; served as captain in the Quartermaster Corps of the United States Army during the First World War; resumed the practice of law in Kansas City, Kans.; appointed judge of the Kansas Court of Industrial Relations in 1924; died in the veterans' hospital at Wadsworth, Kans., on December 3, 1938; interment in Mount Vernon Cemetery, Atchison, Kans.

TAGGART, Samuel, a Representative from Massachusetts; born in Londonderry, N. H., March 24, 1754; completed preparatory studies; was graduated from Dartmouth College, Hanover, N. H., in 1774; studied theology and was licensed to preach in 1776; was ordained to the Presbyterian ministry on February 19, 1777, and installed as pastor of a church in Colrain, Mass.; journeyed as a missionary through western New York; elected as a Federalist to the Eighth and to the six succeeding Congresses (March 4, 1803–March 3, 1817); was not a candidate for renomination in 1816; continued his service as pastor of the Colrain Presbyterian Church until October 28, 1818, when he resigned; died on his farm in Colrain, Franklin County, Mass., April 25, 1825; interment in Chandler Hill Cemetery.

TAGGART, Thomas, a Senator from Indiana; born in County Monaghan, Ireland, November 17, 1856; immigrated to the United States in 1861 with his parents, who settled in Xenia, Greene County, Ohio; attended the common schools; moved to Garrett, Ind., in 1874 and to Indianapolis, Ind., in 1877 and was employed in a restaurant and later engaged in the restaurant and hotel business; auditor of Marion County 1886–1894; chairman of the Democratic State committee 1892–1894, and district chairman for twelve years; mayor of Indianapolis 1895– 1901; member of the Democratic National Committee 1900–1912, and served as chairman 1900–1908; delegate to all the Democratic National Conventions from 1900 to 1924; president of the French Lick Hotel Co.; appointed as a Democrat to the United States Senate to fill the vacancy caused by the death of Benjamin F. Shively and served from March 20 to November 7, 1916; was unsuccessful candidate for election in 1916 to fill the vacancy; resumed his former business pursuits in Indianapolis and French Lick, Ind.; elected chairman of the board of directors of the Fletcher National Bank, Indianapolis, Ind., in 1924; member of the George Rogers Clark Commission 1927–1929; died in Indianapolis, Ind., on March 6, 1929; interment in Crown Hill Cemetery.

TAGUE, Peter Francis, a Representative from Massachusetts; born in Boston, Mass., June 4, 1871; attended the public schools and graduated from Frothingham and English High Schools; engaged in the blacksmith and contractor supply business and later in the manufacture of chemicals; member of the Boston Common Council 1894–1896; member of the State house of representatives in 1897 and 1898 and in 1913 and 1914; served in the State senate in 1899 and 1900; elected as a Democrat to the Sixty-fourth and Sixty-fifth Congresses (March 4, 1915–March 3, 1919); successfully contested the election of John F. Fitzgerald to the Sixty-sixth Congress; unsuccessful candidate for mayor in 1917; reelected to the Sixty-seventh and Sixty-eighth Congresses and served from October 23, 1919, to March 3, 1925; was an unsuccessful candidate for reelection in 1924 to the Sixty-ninth Congress; resumed the manufacture of chemicals in Boston, Mass.; appointed assessor of Boston in 1930; chairman of the election commission of Boston in 1930; appointed postmaster in 1936, serving as acting postmaster until April 2, 1937, when he took the oath as postmaster, and served until his death in Boston, Mass., September 17, 1941; interment in Holy Cross Cemetery, Malden, Mass.

TAIT, Charles, a Senator from Georgia; born near the present town of Hanover, Hanover County, Va., February 1, 1768; moved to Wilkes County, Ga., in 1783 with his parents, who settled near Petersburg; completed preparatory studies; attended Wilkes Academy, Washington, Ga., in 1786 and 1787, and Cokesburg College, Abingdon, Md., in 1788; professor of French in Cokesburg College 1789–1794; studied law while teaching, and was admitted to the bar in Elbert County in 1795; rector and professor in Richmond Academy in Augusta 1795–1798; commenced the practice of law in Elbert County in 1798; presiding judge of the western circuit court of Georgia 1803–1809; elected as a Democrat to the United States Senate to fill the vacancy caused by the resignation of John Milledge; was reelected in 1813 and served from November 27, 1809, to March 3, 1819; moved to Wilcox County, Ala., in 1819; appointed by President Monroe as United States district judge for Alabama on May 10, 1820, and served until 1826, when he resigned; engaged as a planter near Claiborne, Ala.; declined a mission to Great Britain in 1828; died near Claiborne, Ala., October 7, 1835; interment in Dry Forks Cemetery on his country estate, Wilcox County, Ala.

TALBERT, William Jasper, a Representative from South Carolina; born near Edgefield, Edgefield County, S. C., October 6, 1846; attended the common schools in Greenwood and Due West Academy at Abbeville, and was graduated from Erskine College, Due West, S. C.; during the Civil War served in the Confederate Army as a private, Company F, Fifth South Carolina Reserves, as a substitute for his father B. M. Talbert, who was discharged December 17, 1862; enlisted at Richmond, Va., September 15, 1864, as a private, Company B, Infantry Regiment, Hampton Legion, South Carolina; engaged in agricultural pursuits near Parksville, McCormick County, S. C.; member of the State house of representatives 1880–1884; served in the State senate 1884–1888; superintendent of the State penitentiary 1891–1893; delegate to the Democratic National Convention at Chicago in 1892; mayor of Parksville 1895–1900; president of the Democratic State convention in 1899; held various positions in the Farmers' Alliance; elected as a Democrat to the Fifty-third and to the four succeeding Congresses (March 4, 1893–March 3, 1903); was not a candidate for renomination in 1902, having become an aspirant for the gubernatorial nomination; unsuccessful candidate in the second primary for the Democratic nomination for Governor in 1902; voluntarily retired from public life and resumed agricultural pursuits near Parksville, McCormick County, S. C.; moved to McCormick, S. C., in 1927 and lived in retirement until his death in Greenwood Hospital, Greenwood, S. C., February 5, 1931; interment in Parksville Cemetery, Parksville, S. C.

TALBOT, Isham, a Senator from Kentucky; born near Talbot, Bedford County, Va., in 1773; moved with his father to Harrodsburg, Ky.; completed preparatory studies; studied law; was admitted to the bar and commenced practice in Versailles, Ky.; moved to Frankfort, Ky., and continued the practice of law; member of the State senate 1812–1815; elected to the United States Senate to fill the vacancy caused by the resignation of Jesse Bledsoe and served from January 3, 1815, to March 3, 1819; again elected to the United States Senate to fill the vacancy caused by the resignation of William Logan and served from October 19, 1820, to March 3, 1825; resumed the practice of law; died near Frankfort, Ky., September 25, 1837; interment in the State Cemetery, Frankfort, Ky.

TALBOT, Joseph Edward, a Representative from Connecticut; born in Naugatuck, New Haven County, Conn., March 18, 1901; attended the public schools; was graduated from Dartmouth College, Hanover, N. H., in 1922 and from Yale Law School, New Haven, Conn., in 1925; was admitted to the bar in 1925 and commenced practice in Naugatuck and Waterbury, Conn.; prosecuting attorney, Naugatuck, Conn., 1928–1933 and judge 1935–1937; State treasurer 1939–1941; workmen's compensation commissioner for the fifth district of Connecticut in 1941 and 1942; elected as a Republican to the Seventy-seventh Congress in a special election to fill the vacancy caused by the resignation of J. Joseph Smith; reelected to the Seventy-eighth and Seventy-ninth Congresses and served from January 20, 1942, to January 3, 1947; was not a candidate for renomination in 1946; unsuccessful candidate for the gubernatorial nomination in 1946; unsuccessful candidate for election to the United States Senate in 1950; appointed a member of the United States Tariff Commission in April 1953; reappointed in May 1959 for a six-year term ending June 16, 1965, serving as vice chairman 1953–1959 and as chairman 1959– ; chairman, Committee on Reciprocity Information, 1959– ; is a resident of Naugatuck, Conn.

TALBOT, Silas, a Representative from New York; born in Dighton, Bristol County, Mass., January 11, 1751; completed preparatory studies; went to sea on a coasting vessel; engaged in mercantile pursuits in Providence, R. I.; lieutenant and captain in the Revolutionary Army; promoted to the rank of major October 10, 1777, and to lieutenant colonel October 29, 1778; commissioned captain in the Continental Navy September 17, 1779; captured by the British in November 1780 and imprisoned in England until 1781, when he was exchanged and sent to Cherbourg, France; returned to America and resided in Philadelphia, Pa.; moved to Albany, N. Y., and engaged in agricultural pursuits; member of the State assembly in 1792 and 1793; elected as a Federalist to the Third Congress (March 4, 1793–March 3, 1795); again commissioned by President Washington May 11, 1798, a captain in the United States Navy; resigned September 21, 1801; died in New York City on June 30, 1813; interment in Trinity Churchyard.

TALBOTT, Albert Gallatin (uncle of William Clayton Anderson), a Representative from Kentucky; born near Paris, Bourbon County, Ky., April 4, 1808; moved with his parents to Clark County in 1813 and to Jessamine County in 1818; attended Forrest Hill Academy, Jessamine County, Ky.; studied law, but did not practice; engaged in agricultural pursuits and general trading in 1831; moved to Mercer County in 1838 and engaged in the real-estate business; moved to Danville, Boyle County, Ky., in 1846; delegate to the State constitutional convention in 1849; member of the State house of representatives in 1850; elected as a Democrat to the Thirty-fourth and Thirty-fifth Congresses (March 4, 1855–March 3, 1859); resumed real-estate pursuits; served in the State senate 1869–1873; again a member of the State house of representatives in 1883; moved to Pennsylvania and settled near Chestnut Hill, and engaged in agricultural pursuits and stock raising; died in Philadelphia, Pa., on September 9, 1887; interment in Bellevue Cemetery, Danville, Ky.

TALBOTT, Joshua Frederick Cockey, a Representative from Maryland; born near Lutherville, Baltimore County, Md., July 29, 1843; attended the public schools; began the study of law in 1862; joined the Confederate Army in 1864 and served as a private in the Second Maryland Cavalry throughout the remainder of the Civil War; was admitted to the bar in 1866 and began the practice of law in Towson, Baltimore County, Md.; prosecuting attorney for Baltimore County 1871–1875; unsuccessful candidate for reelection; delegate to the Democratic National Convention at St. Louis in 1876; elected as a Democrat to the Forty-sixth, Forty-seventh, and Forty-eighth Congresses (March 4, 1879–March 3, 1885); was not a candidate for reelection in 1884; appointed insurance commissioner of Maryland in October 1889 and resigned in January 1893, having been elected to Congress; elected to the Fifty-third Congress (March 4, 1893–March 3, 1895); unsuccessful candidate for reelection in 1894 to the Fifty-fourth Congress; resumed the practice of law in Towson; unsuccessful candidate for election in 1900 to the Fifty-seventh Congress; delegate to the Democratic National Convention at St. Louis in 1904 and at Denver in 1908; elected to the Fifty-eighth and to the seven succeeding Congresses and served from March 4, 1903, until his death in Lutherville, Md., on October 5, 1918; interment in Sherwood Cemetery, Cockeysville, Baltimore County, Md.

TALCOTT, Charles Andrew, a Representative from New York; born in Oswego, Oswego County, N. Y., June 10, 1857; attended the public schools and Utica Free Academy; was graduated from Princeton University in 1879; studied law; was admitted to the bar in 1881 and commenced practice in Utica, N. Y.; clerk of the city court 1881–1883; city counsel of Utica in 1886; member of the board of police and fire commissioners 1888–1892; trustee of the Utica Public Library 1893–1901; mayor of the city of Utica 1902–1906; elected as a Democrat to the Sixty-second and Sixty-third Congresses (March 4, 1911–March 3, 1915); unsuccessful candidate for reelection in 1914 to the Sixty-fourth Congress; engaged in the practice of law until his death in Utica, N. Y., February 27, 1920; interment in Forest Hill Cemetery.

TALIAFERRO, Benjamin, a Representative from Georgia; born in Virginia in 1750; completed preparatory studies; served in the Revolutionary War as a lieutenant in the rifle corps commanded by General Morgan; was promoted to captain; captured by the British at Charleston in 1780; after independence had been established he settled in Georgia in 1785; member of the State senate and its president; delegate to the State constitutional convention in 1798; elected to the Sixth and Seventh Congresses and served from March 4, 1799, until his resignation in 1802; judge of the superior court; trustee of Georgia University; died in Wilkes County, Ga., September 3, 1821.

TALIAFERRO, James Piper, a Senator from Florida; born in Orange, Orange County, Va., September 30, 1847; attended the common schools and the William Dinwiddie School in Greenwood, Va.; during the Civil War enlisted in the Confederate Army in 1864 and served until the close of the war; resumed his studies in college; moved to Jacksonville, Fla., in 1866; engaged in the lumber business and other commercial enterprises; also engaged in the building of railroads; president of the First

National Bank of Tampa; elected as a Democrat to the United States Senate to fill the vacancy in the term beginning March 4, 1899; appointed and subsequently reelected in 1905 and served from April 20, 1899, to March 3, 1911; was an unsuccessful candidate for reelection in 1910, again resumed his former business and commercial pursuits in Jacksonville, Duval County, Fla., until 1920 when he retired from active business pursuits; died in Jacksonville, Fla., October 6, 1934; interment in Evergreen Cemetery.

TALIAFERRO, John, a Representative from Virginia; born on the estate, "Hays," near Fredericksburg, King George County, Va., in 1768; attended the common schools; studied law; was admitted to the bar and commenced practice in Fredericksburg, Va.; elected as a Democrat to the Seventh Congress (March 4, 1801–March 3, 1803); presidential elector on the Democratic ticket of Jefferson and Clinton in 1804; successfully contested the election of John P. Hungerford to the Twelfth Congress and served from November 29, 1811, to March 3, 1813; unsuccessfully contested the election of John P. Hungerford to the Thirteenth Congress; presidential elector on the Democratic ticket of Monroe and Tompkins in 1820; elected to the Eighteenth Congress to fill the vacancy caused by the death of William L. Ball; reelected to the Nineteenth, Twentieth, and Twenty-first Congresses and served from March 24, 1824, to March 3, 1831; elected as a Whig to the Twenty-fourth and to the three succeeding Congresses (March 4, 1835–March 3, 1843); librarian of the United States Treasury Department from 1850 until his death at his residence, "Hagley," near Fredericksburg, King George County, Va., August 12, 1852; interment on his farm, "Hagley."

TALLE, Henry Oscar, a Representative from Iowa; born on a farm near Albert Lea, Freeborn County, Minn., January 12, 1892; educated in rural schools and Luther Academy, Albert Lea, Minn.; was graduated from Luther College, Decorah, Iowa, in 1917; pursued graduate work at University of Minnesota, Boston University, Emerson College, and University of Chicago; during the First World War served in the United States Navy as an enlisted man and as an officer 1917–1919; teacher and superintendent of schools, Rugby and Rolette, N. Dak., in 1919 and 1920; teacher in Luther Academy, Albert Lea, Minn., in 1920 and 1921; professor of economics, Luther College, Decorah, Iowa, 1921–1938; treasurer of Luther College 1932–1938; elected as a Republican to the Seventy-sixth and to the nine succeeding Congresses (January 3, 1939–January 3, 1959); unsuccessful candidate for reelection in 1958 to the Eighty-sixth Congress; assistant administrator for program policy of the Housing and Home Finance Agency, Washington, D. C., from February 2, 1959, to February 19, 1961; is a resident of Decorah, Iowa.

TALLMADGE, Benjamin (father of Frederick Augustus Tallmadge), a Representative from Connecticut; born in Brookhaven, Long Island, N. Y., February 25, 1754; moved to Litchfield, Conn., in 1783; was graduated from Yale College in 1773; superintendent of Wethersfield High School 1773–1776; served throughout the whole period of the Revolutionary War; commissioned lieutenant in the Continental Line June 20, 1776; promoted to captain of dragoons December 15, 1776; major April 7, 1777, and colonel September 5, 1779; led the expedition which captured Fort George and destroyed the magazines of the British Army at Oyster Bay, Long Island, for which he received the public tribute of the Continental Congress; in charge of Maj. John André until his execution; was appointed postmaster at Litchfield, Conn., in 1792; first president of the Phoenix Branch Bank; treasurer and later president of the Society of the Cincinnati; elected as a Federalist to the Seventh and to the seven succeeding Congresses (March 4, 1801–March 3, 1817); declined to be a candidate for renomination; engaged in mercantile pursuits and was an importer; also interested in banking; died in Litchfield, Conn., March 7, 1835; interment in the East Cemetery.

TALLMADGE, Frederick Augustus (son of Benjamin Tallmadge), a Representative from New York; born in Litchfield, Conn., August 29, 1792; completed preparatory studies, and was graduated from Yale College in 1811; studied law in the Litchfield Law School; was admitted to the bar in 1811 and commenced practice in New York City in 1813; served as captain in the War of 1812; member of the board of aldermen of New York City in 1834; served as common councilman in 1836; member of the State senate 1837–1840, and during the last session served as president pro tempore; recorder of the city of New York 1841–1846; elected as a Whig to the Thirtieth Congress (March 4, 1847–March 3, 1849); was not a candidate for renomination in 1848; again recorder of the city of New York 1848–1851; superintendent of the Metropolitan police 1857–1862; clerk of the New York Court of Appeals 1862–1865; resumed the practice of law in New York City; returned to Litchfield, Conn., in 1869, and died there on September 17, 1869; interment in the East Cemetery.

TALLMADGE, James, Jr., a Representative from New York; born in Stanfordville, Dutchess County, N. Y., January 20, 1778; was graduated from Brown University, Providence, R. I., in 1798; secretary to Governor Clinton 1798–1800; studied law; was admitted to the bar in 1802 and practiced in Poughkeepsie, N. Y., and in New York City; served in the War of 1812 and commanded a company of home guards in defense of New York; elected as a Democrat to the Fifteenth Congress to fill the vacancy caused by the death of Henry B. Lee and served from June 6, 1817, to March 3, 1819; declined to be a candidate for renomination in 1818 to the Sixteenth Congress; delegate to the State constitutional conventions in 1821 and 1846; member of the State assembly in 1824; Lieutenant Governor of New York 1824–1826; president of New York University 1830–1846; died in New York City September 29, 1853; interment in Marble Cemetery.

TALLMADGE, Nathaniel Pitcher, a Senator from New York; born in Chatham, Columbia County, N. Y., February 8, 1795; was graduated from Union College, Schenectady, N. Y., in 1815; studied law; was admitted to the bar in 1818 and commenced practice in Poughkeepsie, N. Y.; member of the State assembly in 1828; served in the State senate 1830–1833; elected as a Democrat to the United States Senate in 1833; reelected in 1839, and served from March 4, 1833, to June 17, 1844, when he resigned, having been appointed by President Tyler to be Governor of Wisconsin Territory, with residence in Fond du Lac; served as Governor of Wisconsin Territory until his removal from office on May 13, 1845; devoted himself to writing religious tracts; died in Battle Creek, Mich., November 2, 1864; interment in Rienzi Cemetery, Fond du Lac, Wis.

TALLMAN, Peleg, a Representative from Massachusetts; born in Tiverton, R. I., July 24, 1764; attended the public schools; served in the Revolutionary War on the privateer *Trumbull,* and lost an arm in an engagement in 1780; was captured and imprisoned in England and Ireland 1781–1783; engaged in mercantile pursuits in Bath, Maine (until 1820 a district of Massachusetts); elected as a Democrat to the Twelfth Congress (March 4, 1811–March 3, 1813); declined to be a candidate for renomination; overseer of Bowdoin College, Brunswick, Maine, 1802–1840; member of the Maine Senate in

1821 and 1822; died in Bath, Maine, March 12, 1840; interment in Maple Grove Cemetery; reinterment in Forest Hills Cemetery, Roxbury, Mass.

TALMADGE, Herman Eugene, a Senator from Georgia; born on a farm near McRae, Telfair County, Ga., August 9, 1913; attended the public schools in McRae; moved to Atlanta, Ga., in 1930 and attended Druid Hills High School; graduated from the University of Georgia at Athens in 1936; was admitted to the bar in 1936 and commenced the practice of law in Atlanta, Ga.; volunteered for service in the United States Navy in 1941; served as an ensign with the Sixth Naval District at Charleston, S. C., and with the Third Naval District in New York after graduating from midshipman's school at Northwestern University in 1942; participated in the invasion of Guadalcanal aboard the U. S. S. *Tryon;* served as flag secretary to the commandant of naval forces in New Zealand from June 1943 to April 1944 and then as executive officer of the U. S. S. *Dauphin* and participated in the battle of Okinawa; was present in Tokyo Bay at Japanese surrender; attained rank of lieutenant commander and was discharged in November 1945; upon the death of his father, Governor-elect Eugene Talmadge, was elected to the governorship by the State legislature in 1947; served sixty-seven days, then vacated the office due to a decision of the State supreme court; elected in September 1948 to fill the unexpired term; reelected in 1950 and served until January 10, 1955; owns and operates two farms; delegate to the Democratic National Convention in 1952; elected as a Democrat to the United States Senate for the term commencing January 3, 1957, and ending January 3, 1963.

TANNEHILL, Adamson, a Representative from Pennsylvania; born in Frederick County, Md., May 23, 1750; attended the public schools; served in the Revolutionary War as captain of riflemen; moved to Pennsylvania and engaged in agricultural pursuits near Pittsburgh; held several local offices; brigadier general of Pennsylvania Volunteers in the United States service from September 25 to December 31, 1812; elected as a Democrat to the Thirteenth Congress (March 4, 1813–March 3, 1815); unsuccessful candidate for reelection in 1814 to the Fourteenth Congress; resumed farming; died near Pittsburgh, Allegheny County, Pa., December 23, 1820; interment in the churchyard of the First Presbyterian Church; reinterment in Allegheny Cemetery, Pittsburgh, Pa., in 1849.

TANNER, Adolphus Hitchcock, a Representative from New York; born in Granville, Washington County, N. Y., May 23, 1833; completed preparatory studies; studied law; was admitted to the bar in 1854 and commenced practice in Whitehall, N. Y.; during the Civil War entered the Union Army in 1862 as a captain; was subsequently commissioned lieutenant colonel of the One Hundred and Twenty-third Regiment, New York Volunteer Infantry, and served until the close of the war; elected as a Republican to the Forty-first Congress (March 4, 1869–March 3, 1871); resumed the practice of law in Whitehall, Washington County, N. Y., and died there January 14, 1882; interment in Evergreen Cemetery, Salem, N. Y.

TAPPAN, Benjamin, a Senator from Ohio; born in Northampton, Mass., May 25, 1773; attended the public schools; became a printer and engraver; studied law; was admitted to the bar in Hartford, Conn., and commenced practice in Ravenna, Ohio, in 1799; member of the State senate in 1803; moved to Steubenville, Ohio, in 1809 and continued the practice of law; served in the War of 1812 as an aide to Gen. William Wadsworth; held several local offices; county judge and, in 1816, judge of the Fifth Ohio Circuit Court of Common Pleas; was presidential elector on the Democratic ticket of Jackson and

Van Buren in 1832; United States district judge of Ohio in 1833; elected as a Democrat to the United States Senate and served from March 4, 1839, to March 3, 1845; died in Steubenville, Jefferson County, Ohio, April 12, 1857; interment in Union Cemetery.

TAPPAN, Mason Weare, a Representative from New Hampshire; born in Newport, Sullivan County, N. H., October 20, 1817; moved to Bradford, N. H., with his parents; attended private schools and the Hopkinton and Meriden Academies; studied law; was admitted to the bar in 1841 and commenced practice in Bradford, N. H.; served in the State house of representatives 1853–1855; elected as a Republican to the Thirty-fourth, Thirty-fifth, and Thirty-sixth Congresses (March 4, 1855–March 3, 1861); was not a candidate for renomination in 1860; during the Civil War served in the Union Army as colonel of the First Regiment, New Hampshire Volunteer Infantry; again a member of the State house of representatives in 1860 and 1861; resumed the practice of law; appointed attorney general of the State in 1876, which position he held until his death in Bradford, Merrimack County, N. H., October 25, 1886; interment in Pleasant Hill Cemetery.

TARBOX, John Kemble, a Representative from Massachusetts; born in Methuen, near Lawrence, Mass., May 6, 1838; pursued classical studies; engaged in newspaper work; studied law; was admitted to the bar in 1860 and practiced; during the Civil War served in the Union Army as first lieutenant in the Eighth Regiment, Massachusetts Volunteer Infantry; member of the State house of representatives in 1868, 1870, and 1871; served in the State senate in 1872; mayor of Lawrence in 1873 and 1874; elected as a Democrat to the Forty-fourth Congress (March 4, 1875–March 3, 1877); unsuccessful candidate for reelection in 1876 to the Forty-fifth Congress; city solicitor of Lawrence, Mass., in 1882 and 1883; State insurance commissioner 1884–1887; died in Boston, Mass., May 28, 1887; interment in Bellevue Cemetery, Lawrence, Mass.

TARR, Christian, a Representative from Pennsylvania; born in Baltimore, Md., May 25, 1765; received a limited schooling; moved to Westmoreland County, Pa., in 1794 and engaged in agricultural pursuits; engaged in the manufacture of pottery in Fayette County, Pa.; elected to the Fifteenth and Sixteenth Congresses (March 4, 1817–March 3, 1821); member of the State house of representatives in 1821 and 1822; appointed on October 31, 1827, superintendent of the road which had been built by the United States Government from Cumberland, Md., to Wheeling, Va. (now West Virginia), and served until March 20, 1829; died in Washington Township, Fayette County, Pa., February 24, 1833; interment in the Methodist Graveyard, Brownsville, Pa.

TARSNEY, John Charles, a Representative from Missouri; born in Medina, Lenawee County, Mich., November 7, 1845; attended the common schools; during the Civil War enlisted in the Fourth Regiment, Michigan Volunteer Infantry, in August 1862; mustered out of the service in June 1865; attended high school in Hudson, Mich.; was graduated from the law department of the University of Michigan at Ann Arbor in 1869; was admitted to the bar the same year and commenced practice in Hudson, Mich.; moved to Kansas City, Mo., in 1872; city attorney of Kansas City in 1874 and 1875; elected as a Democrat to the Fifty-first, Fifty-second, and Fifty-third Congresses (March 4, 1889–March 3, 1895); presented credentials as a Member-elect to the Fifty-fourth Congress and served from March 4, 1895, to February 27, 1896, when he was succeeded by Robert T. Van Horn, who contested his election; appointed by President Cleveland associate justice of the supreme court

of Oklahoma Territory in 1896 and served until 1899; returned to Kansas City, Mo., in 1899 and resumed the practice of law; died in Kansas City, Mo., September 4, 1920; interment in Mount St. Mary's Cemetery.

TARSNEY, Timothy Edward, a Representative from Michigan; born in Ransom, Hillsdale County, Mich., February 4, 1849; attended the common and high schools; worked on the Government roads in Tennessee until the close of the Civil War, when he returned to Michigan and settled in Saginaw; was employed as an engineer in a sawmill; became a marine engineer in 1867; continued his studies at night and in the wintertime; was graduated from the law department of the University of Michigan at Ann Arbor in 1872; was admitted to the bar the same year and commenced practice in East Saginaw, Mich.; elected justice of the peace in 1873, but resigned after one year's service; city attorney from 1875 to 1878, when he resigned; unsuccessful candidate for election in 1880 to the Forty-seventh Congress; delegate at large to the Democratic National Convention at Chicago in 1884; elected as a Democrat to the Forty-ninth and Fiftieth Congresses (March 4, 1885–March 3, 1889); unsuccessful candidate for reelection in 1888 to the Fifty-first Congress; moved to Detroit, Mich., in 1893 and resumed the practice of law; corporation counsel of Detroit 1900–1908; died in Detroit, Mich., June 8, 1909; interment in Calvary Cemetery, Saginaw, Mich.

TARVER, Malcolm Connor, a Representative from Georgia; born in Rural Vale, Whitfield County, Ga., September 25, 1885; attended the public schools; was graduated from the law department of Mercer University, Macon, Ga., in 1904; was admitted to the bar the same year and commenced practice in Dalton, Ga.; member of the State house of representatives 1909–1912; served in the State senate in 1913 and 1914; judge of the superior courts, Cherokee Circuit, Ga., 1917–1927; elected as a Democrat to the Seventieth and to the nine succeeding Congresses (March 4, 1927–January 3, 1947); unsuccessful candidate for renomination in 1946; resumed the practice of law; died in Dalton, Ga., March 5, 1960; interment in West Hill Cemetery.

TATE, Farish Carter, a Representative from Georgia; born in Japser, Pickens County, Ga., November 20, 1856; attended the common schools and North Georgia Agricultural College in Dahlonega, Ga.; studied law; was admitted to the bar in 1880 and commenced practice at Jasper, Ga.; member of the general assembly of Georgia 1882–1887; member of the Democratic State executive committee 1884–1887 and 1890–1892; delegate to the Democratic State convention in 1888; elected as a Democrat to the Fifty-third and to the five succeeding Congresses (March 4, 1893–March 3, 1905); unsuccessful candidate for renomination in 1904 to the Fifty-ninth Congress; appointed United States district attorney for the northern district of Georgia by President Theodore Roosevelt; reappointed by President Taft, and served from 1905 to 1913; resumed the practice of law in Jasper, Ga., and died there February 7, 1922; interment in the Tate family cemetery.

TATE, Magnus, a Representative from Virginia; born in Berkeley County, Va. (now West Virginia), in 1760; studied law; was admitted to the bar and practiced; engaged in agricultural pursuits; appointed justice of the Berkeley County Court May 19, 1798; sheriff of Berkeley County in 1819 and 1820; member of the house of delegates of Virginia in 1797, 1803, 1809, and 1810; elected as a Federalist to the Fourteenth Congress (March 4, 1815–March 3, 1817); died near Martinsburg, Va. (now West Virginia), March 30, 1823.

TATGENHORST, Charles, Jr., a Representative from Ohio; born in Cincinnati, Hamilton County, Ohio, August 19, 1883; educated in the public schools of Cincinnati; was graduated from Cincinnati Law School in 1910; was admitted to the bar the same year and commenced practice in Cincinnati; assistant city solicitor for Cincinnati 1914–1919; moved to Cleves, Ohio, in 1919 and continued the practice of law; elected as a Republican to the Seventieth Congress to fill the vacancy caused by the death of Ambrose E. B. Stephens and served from November 8, 1927, to March 3, 1929; was not a candidate for renomination in 1928; again resumed the practice of his profession in Cincinnati, Ohio; elected judge of the court of appeals of the first appellate district of Ohio on November 3, 1936, and served until February 8, 1937; Ohio State bar examiner 1938–1942; in January 1941 became a member of the Ohio State Banking Board; director of Cincinnati Street Railway Co. and Sullivan Electric Co.; died in Cincinnati, Ohio, January 13, 1961; interment in Spring Grove Cemetery.

TATOM, Absalom, a Representative from North Carolina; born in that State in 1742; sergeant in the Greenville (N. C.) Militia in 1763; during the Revolutionary War was commissioned first lieutenant in the First North Carolina Continental Regiment September 1, 1775; promoted to the rank of captain June 29, 1776; resigned from the Continental Army on September 19, 1776; enlisted as assistant quartermaster and keeper of the arsenal in the State service at Hillsborough, N. C., August 15, 1778; was contractor for Hillsborough in 1778; major of detachment of the North Carolina Light Horse February 12, 1779; was clerk of Randolph County Court in 1779; elected to the State house of commons, but was unseated because he already held the office of county clerk; was district auditor for Hillsborough in 1781; one of three commissioners appointed by Congress to survey lands granted to Continental soldiers in the western territory (later Tennessee) in 1782; private secretary to Gov. Thomas Burke in 1782; State tobacco agent in 1782; elected surveyor of North Carolina by the Continental Congress in May 1785; commissioner to sign State paper money in December 1785; served as a delegate to the constitutional convention in 1788; elected as a Republican to the Fourth Congress and served from March 4, 1795, to June 1, 1796, when he resigned; again served in the State house of commons 1797–1802; died in Raleigh, N. C., on December 20, 1802; interment in the Old City Cemetery.

TATTNALL, Edward Fenwick, a Representative from Georgia; born in Savannah, Ga., in 1788; educated in England; held several local offices; solicitor general from November 1816 to September 1817, when he resigned; member of the State house of representatives in 1818 and 1819; elected to the Seventeenth and to the three succeeding Congresses and served from March 4, 1821, until his resignation in 1827 before the convening of the Twentieth Congress; first captain of the Savannah Volunteer Guards; died in Savannah, Chatham County, Ga., November 21, 1832; interment in Bonaventure Cemetery.

TATTNALL, Josiah, a Senator from Georgia; born at Bonaventure, near Savannah, Ga., in 1764; completed preparatory studies; went with his father to England at the outbreak of the Revolutionary War and attended Eaton College; ran away from England and enlisted under Gen. Anthony Wayne in 1782; colonel of a regiment of State troops in 1793 for protection against the Indians, and was promoted to brigadier general in 1801; member of the State house of representatives in 1795 and 1796; elected to the United States Senate to fill the vacancy caused by the resignation of James Jackson and served from February 20, 1796, to March 3, 1799; Governor of Georgia in 1801 and 1802; re-

signed in November 1802; died in Nassau, New Providence, British West Indies, June 6, 1803; interment in Bonaventure Cemetery, Savannah, Ga.

TAUL, Micah (grandfather of Taul Bradford), a Representative from Kentucky; born in Bladensburg, Md., May 14, 1785; moved to Kentucky with his parents in 1787; attended private school; studied law; was admitted to the bar in 1801 and commenced practice in Monticello, Ky.; clerk of Wayne County Courts in 1801; served as a colonel of Wayne County Volunteers in the War of 1812; elected as a Democrat to the Fourteenth Congress (March 4, 1815–March 3, 1817); declined to be a candidate for renomination in 1816; resumed the practice of law; moved to Winchester, Tenn., in 1826 and continued the practice of law; moved to Mardisville, Talladega County, Ala., in 1846 and engaged in agricultural pursuits until his death there on May 27, 1850; interment on his plantation at Mardisville.

TAULBEE, William Preston, a Representative from Kentucky; born near Mount Sterling, in Morgan County, Ky., October 22, 1851; attended the common schools and was tutored by his father; was ordained for the ministry and admitted to the Kentucky conference of the Methodist Episcopal Church South; elected clerk of the Magoffin County Court in 1878 and reelected in 1882; studied law and was admitted to the bar in 1881; elected as a Democrat to the Forty-ninth and Fiftieth Congresses (March 4, 1885–March 3, 1889); was not a candidate for renomination; was shot by Charles E. Kincaid in the Capitol Building, Washington, D. C., February 28, 1890, and died from the effects of the wounds at Providence Hospital, in that city, March 11, 1890; interment in the family burying ground near Mount Sterling, Ky.

TAURIELLO, Anthony Francis, a Representative from New York; born in Buffalo, Erie County, N. Y., August 14, 1899; attended the public schools; was graduated from the law school of Cumberland University, Lebanon, Tenn., in 1929; was admitted to the Tennessee bar in 1929 and commenced the practice of law in Nashville, Tenn.; member of the Erie County (N. Y.) Board of Supervisors from October 1933 to December 1937, and Buffalo Common Council 1938–1941; deputy city treasurer 1942–1945; examiner for Reconstruction Finance Corporation, Buffalo, N. Y., from April 1946 to November 1946 and with War Assets Administration from November 1946 to May 1947; again a member of the Buffalo Common Council in 1948; delegate to the Democratic National Convention in 1936 and alternate delegate in 1960; elected as a Democrat to the Eighty-first Congress (January 3, 1949–January 3, 1951); was an unsuccessful candidate for reelection in 1950 to the Eighty-second Congress, and for election in 1952 to the Eighty-third Congress; retail liquor dealer; again elected a member of Buffalo Common Council and served from 1954 to 1957; resides in Buffalo, N. Y.

TAVENNER, Clyde Howard, a Representative from Illinois; born in Cordova, Rock Island County, Ill., February 4, 1882; attended the common schools; learned the printer's trade; engaged as editorial writer; went abroad in 1909, and wrote on the tariff systems of the several European countries visited; director of publicity for the Democratic National Congressional Committee in 1910 and 1912; elected as a Democrat to the Sixty-third and Sixty-fourth Congresses (March 4, 1913–March 3, 1917); unsuccessful candidate for reelection in 1916 to the Sixty-fifth Congress; visited Russia, Japan, and the Philippine Islands in 1919, and on his return wrote a series of articles on the question of Philippine independence; founded a monthly magazine, the Philippine Republic, in Washington, D. C., in 1923, and also engaged in the publishing business; visited Europe, the Near East, and the Far East in 1931 and 1932 as a member of a mission from the Philippine Islands; legislative analyst to the House Committee on Rules in 1939; died in Washington, D. C., February 6, 1942; interment in the Congressional Cemetery.

TAWNEY, James Albertus, a Representative from Minnesota; born in Mount Pleasant Township, near Gettysburg, Adams County, Pa., January 3, 1855; apprenticed with his father as a blacksmith; subsequently learned the trade of machinist; moved to Winona, Minn., August 1, 1877, where he was employed as a blacksmith and machinist until January 1, 1881; attended the law department of the University of Wisconsin at Madison; was admitted to the bar in 1882 and commenced practice in Winona, Winona County, Minn.; member of the State senate of Minnesota in 1890; elected as a Republican to the Fifty-third and to the eight succeeding Congresses (March 4, 1893–March 3, 1911); unsuccessful candidate for renomination in 1910; member of the International Joint Commission, created to prevent disputes regarding the use of boundary waters between the United States and Canada, from March 11, 1911, until his death, serving as chairman of the United States section from September 17, 1911, to December 1, 1914; died at Excelsior Springs, Clay County, Mo., June 12, 1919; interment in Woodlawn Cemetery, Winona, Minn.

TAYLER, Robert Walker, a Representative from Ohio; born in Youngstown, Mahoning County, Ohio, November 26, 1852; attended the public schools, and was graduated from Western Reserve College, Cleveland, Ohio, in 1872; taught in the high school in New Lisbon (now Lisbon), Ohio; superintendent of schools 1873–1875; editor of the Buckeye State, a newspaper, in New Lisbon, Ohio, from January 1875 to November 1876, studying law at the same time; was admitted to the bar in April 1877 and commenced practice in East Liverpool, Columbiana County, Ohio; prosecuting attorney of Columbiana County 1880–1885; resumed the practice of law in Lisbon, Ohio; moved to New York in 1890; returned to Lisbon in 1892; elected as a Republican to the Fifty-fourth and to the three succeeding Congresses (March 4, 1895–March 3, 1903); declined to be a candidate in 1902 for renomination; resumed the practice of law in Youngstown, Ohio; appointed by President Theodore Roosevelt to be United States district judge for the northern district of Ohio February 2, 1905; moved to Cleveland, Ohio, and died there November 25, 1910; interment in Lisbon Cemetery, Lisbon, Ohio.

TAYLOR, Abner, a Representative from Illinois; born in Bangor, Penobscot County, Maine, in 1829; moved with his parents to Champaign County, Ohio, in 1832, thence to Fort Dodge, Iowa, and subsequently to Chicago, Ill., in 1860; engaged in extensive contracting, building, and mercantile pursuits, and participated in the construction of the Texas State capitol; member of the Illinois House of Representatives from 1884 to 1886; delegate to the Republican National Convention at Chicago in 1884 which nominated Blaine and Logan; elected as a Republican to the Fifty-first and Fifty-second Congresses (March 4, 1889–March 3, 1893); was not a candidate for renomination in 1892; resumed the building and contracting business; died in Washington, D. C., April 13, 1903; interment in Rock Creek Cemetery.

TAYLOR, Alexander Wilson, a Representative from Pennsylvania; born in Indiana, Indiana County, Pa., March 22, 1815; pursued classical studies; attended the Indiana Academy and Jefferson College, Canonsburg, Pa., and was graduated from the law school at Carlisle, Pa.; was admitted to the bar in 1841 and commenced practice in Indiana, Pa.; clerk of the court of Indiana County 1845–1848; member of the State

house of representatives in 1859 and 1860; elected as a Republican to the Forty-third Congress (March 4, 1873–March 3, 1875); again resumed the practice of law; died in Indiana, Pa., May 7, 1893; interment in Greenwood Cemetery.

TAYLOR, Alfred Alexander (son of Nathaniel Green Taylor and brother of Robert Love Taylor), a Representative from Tennessee; born in Happy Valley, Carter County, Tenn., August 6, 1848; attended Duffield Academy, Elizabethton, Tenn., Buffalo Institute (later Milligan College), Tennessee, and the schools of Edge Hill and Pennington Seminary, New Jersey; studied law; was admitted to the bar in 1874 and commenced practice in Jonesboro, Washington County, Tenn.; member of the State house of representatives in 1875 and 1876; candidate for presidential elector on the Republican ticket of Hayes and Wheeler in 1876 and on the Garfield and Arthur ticket in 1880; unsuccessful Republican candidate for Governor in 1886, being defeated by his brother, Robert; delegate to the Republican National Convention at Chicago in 1888; elected as a Republican to the Fifty-first, Fifty-second, and Fifty-third Congresses (March 4, 1889–March 3, 1895); declined to be a candidate in 1894 for renomination; engaged in the practice of law in Johnson City, Tenn.; engaged as a lecturer and also interested in agricultural pursuits; candidate for presidential elector on the Republican ticket of Hughes and Fairbanks in 1916; Governor of Tennessee 1921–1923; again engaged in lecturing and in agricultural pursuits and resided at Milligan College, Carter County, Tenn.; died while on a visit in Johnson City, Tenn., November 25, 1931; interment in Monta Vista Cemetery.

TAYLOR, Arthur Herbert, a Representative from Indiana; born at Caledonia Springs, Canada, February 29, 1852; moved with his parents to Yates County, N. Y., in 1856; attended the local school; taught school for several years; moved to Indianapolis, Ind., in 1869; studied law; was admitted to the bar in 1873 and commenced practice in Indianapolis, Ind.; moved to Petersburg, Ind., in 1874 and continued the practice of law; prosecuting attorney for the eleventh judicial circuit of Indiana 1880–1884; elected as a Democrat to the Fifty-third Congress (March 4, 1893–March 3, 1895); unsuccessful candidate for reelection in 1894 to the Fifty-fourth Congress; resumed the practice of law in Petersburg, Ind., until his death February 20, 1922; interment in Walnut Hills Cemetery.

TAYLOR, Benjamin Irving, a Representative from New York; born in New York City December 21, 1877; attended the public schools; was graduated from the high school in New Rochelle, N. Y., and from Columbia Law School in New York City in 1899; was admitted to the bar the same year and commenced practice in Port Chester, Westchester County, N. Y.; supervisor of Harrison, Westchester County, 1905–1913; elected as a Democrat to the Sixty-third Congress (March 4, 1913–March 3, 1915); unsuccessful candidate for reelection in 1914 to the Sixty-fourth Congress; resumed the practice of law in Port Chester, N. Y.; again elected supervisor of Harrison, N. Y., in 1921, and served in that capacity, with the exception of two years, until December 1945, when he retired because of illness; died in Harrison, N. Y., September 5, 1946; interment in Kensico Cemetery, Valhalla, N. Y.

TAYLOR, Caleb Newbold, a Representative from Pennsylvania; born near Newportville, Bristol Township, Bucks County, Pa., July 27, 1813; completed preparatory studies; engaged in agricultural pursuits; delegate to the Whig State convention at Harrisburg in 1832; unsuccessful candidate for election to Congress in 1848, 1850, and again in 1852; presidential elector; delegate to numerous State conventions; delegate to the Republican National Convention at Chicago in 1860 which nominated Lincoln and Hamlin; elected as a Republican to the Fortieth Congress (March 4, 1867–March 3, 1869); successfully contested the election of John R. Reading to the Forty-first Congress and served from April 13, 1870, to March 3, 1871; engaged in banking; president of the Farmers' National Bank of Bucks County, Bristol, Pa., from 1875 until his death at his home, "Sunbury Farm," near Newportville, Bristol Township, Pa., November 15, 1887; interment in the Friends Burying Ground, Bristol, Pa.

TAYLOR, Chester William (son of Samuel Mitchell Taylor), a Representative from Arkansas; born in Verona, Lee County, Miss., July 16, 1883; moved to Pine Bluff, Ark., with his parents; attended the public schools in Pine Bluff, Ark.; studied law at Georgetown University Law School, Washington, D. C.; deputy State auditor 1908–1910; deputy secretary of state in 1911; deputy State treasurer in 1911 and 1912; secretary to his father 1913–1921; elected as a Democrat to the Sixty-seventh Congress to fill the vacancy caused by the death of his father, Samuel M. Taylor, and served from October 31, 1921, to March 3, 1923; was not a candidate for renomination in 1922; engaged in the general insurance business at Pine Bluff, Ark., and later as an official in the State department of conservation at Little Rock, until his death in Pine Bluff, Ark., July 17, 1931; interment in Bellewood Cemetery.

TAYLOR, Dean Park, a Representative from New York; born in Troy, Rensselaer County, N. Y., January 1, 1902; attended the public schools and Colgate University, Hamilton, N. Y.; was graduated from Union University Department of Law, Schenectady, N. Y., in 1926; was admitted to the bar the same year and commenced practice in Troy, N. Y.; served as assistant United States attorney, northern district of New York, 1927–1930; chairman of the Rensselaer County Republican Committee in 1938; delegate to the Republican National Convention at Philadelphia in 1940; trustee of Russell Sage College; director of the Union National Bank and of the Niagara Mohawk Power Co.; elected as a Republican to the Seventy-eighth and to the eight succeeding Congresses (January 3; 1943–January 3, 1961); was not a candidate for renomination in 1960; resumed the practice of law; is a resident of Troy, N. Y.

TAYLOR, Edward Livingston, Jr., a Representative from Ohio; born in Columbus, Ohio, August 10, 1869; attended the public schools and was graduated from the Columbus High School; studied law; was admitted to the bar in 1891 and commenced practice in Columbus; prosecuting attorney of Franklin County 1899–1904; elected as a Republican to the Fifty-ninth and to the three succeeding Congresses (March 4, 1905–March 3, 1913); unsuccessful candidate for reelection in 1912 to the Sixty-third Congress; continued the practice of law in Columbus, Ohio, until his death there March 10, 1938; interment in Greenlawn Cemetery.

TAYLOR, Edward Thomas, a Representative from Colorado; born on a farm near Metamora, Woodford County, Ill., June 19, 1858; attended the common schools of Illinois and Kansas, and was graduated from the high school at Leavenworth, Kans., in 1881; moved to Leadville, Lake County, Colo.; principal of Leadville High School in 1881 and 1882; was graduated from the law department of the University of Michigan at Ann Arbor in 1884; was admitted to the bar the same year and commenced the practice of law in Leadville, Colo.; superintendent of schools of Lake County in 1884; deputy district attorney in 1885; moved to Glenwood Springs, Colo., in 1887; resumed the

practice of his profession; district attorney of the ninth judicial district 1887–1889; member of the State senate 1896–1908, and served as president pro tempore for one term; city attorney 1896–1900; county attorney in 1901 and 1902; elected as a Democrat to the Sixty-first and to the sixteen succeeding Congresses and served from March 4, 1909, until his death in Denver, Colo., September 3, 1941; interment in a mausoleum in Rosebud Cemetery, Glenwood Springs, Colo.

TAYLOR, Ezra Booth, a Representative from Ohio; born in Nelson, Portage County, Ohio, July 9, 1823; attended the common and select schools and academies; studied law; was admitted to the bar and commenced practice in Portage County in 1845; elected prosecuting attorney in 1854; moved to Warren, Trumbull County, Ohio, in 1861; during the Civil War enrolled as a private in Company A, One Hundred and Seventy-first Ohio Infantry, on April 27, 1864; was mustered into service on May 5, 1864, and was honorably discharged on August 20, 1864; elected judge of the court of common pleas for the ninth judicial district of Ohio and served from March 1877 to September 1880, when he resigned; elected as a Republican to the Forty-sixth Congress to fill the vacancy caused by the resignation of James A. Garfield; reelected to the Forty-seventh and to the five succeeding Congresses and served from December 13, 1880, to March 3, 1893; declined to be a candidate for renomination in 1892; resumed the practice of his profession; died in Warren, Trumbull County, Ohio, January 29, 1912; interment in the Warren mausoleum at Oakwood Cemetery.

TAYLOR, George, a Delegate from Pennsylvania; born in Ireland in 1716; pursued academic studies; immigrated to the United States in 1736 and settled at Warwick Furnace and later at Coventry Forge, Chester County, Pa.; engaged in the manufacture of iron; moved to Durham, Pa., in 1755; justice of the peace in 1757, 1761, and 1763; moved to Easton, Pa., in 1763; member of the provincial assembly 1764–1769; justice of the peace for Northampton County 1764–1772; appointed judge of the county court in 1770; again a member of the provincial assembly in 1775; colonel of Pennsylvania Militia in 1775; returned to Durham in 1775; Member of the Continental Congress in 1776 and 1777; member of the First Supreme Executive Council in 1777; signer of the Declaration of Independence; returned to Easton, Pa., in 1780, where he died February 23, 1781; interment in St. John's Lutheran Church Cemetery; reinterment in the Easton Cemetery.

TAYLOR, George, a Representative from New York; born in Wheeling, Va. (now West Virginia), October 19, 1820; completed preparatory studies; studied medicine and law; was admitted to the bar and practiced in Indiana; moved to Alabama in 1844, and to Brooklyn, N. Y., in 1848, where he continued the practice of law; held several local offices; elected as a Democrat to the Thirty-fifth Congress (March 4, 1857–March 3, 1859); unsuccessful candidate for reelection in 1858 to the Thirty-sixth Congress; resumed the practice of law in Washington, D. C., until his death there January 18, 1894; interment in Rock Creek Cemetery.

TAYLOR, George Washington, a Representative from Alabama; born on "Roselawn" plantation near Montgomery, Montgomery County, Ala., January 16, 1849; attended private schools; during the Civil War, while a schoolboy in Columbia, S. C., enlisted in the Confederate Army in November 1864; served a few weeks with the South Carolina State Troops on the coast near Savannah, Ga., and then enlisted as a private in Company D, First Regiment, South Carolina Cavalry; served as a courier in that regiment until the end of the war; was graduated from the University of South Carolina at Columbia in 1867; taught school in Mobile, Ala., and studied law; was admitted to the bar in Mobile, Ala., in November 1871 and commenced practice in Butler, Choctaw County, Ala., in 1872; member of the State house of representatives in 1878 and 1879; State solicitor for the first judicial circuit of Alabama 1880–1892; declined a third term; moved to Demopolis, Marengo County, Ala., in 1883; elected as a Democrat to the Fifty-fifth and to the eight succeeding Congresses (March 4, 1897–March 3, 1915); was not a candidate for renomination in 1914; resumed the practice of law in Demopolis, Ala.; chairman of the State Democratic convention which called the constitutional convention in 1901; was a delegate to the Democratic National Convention at San Francisco in 1920 which nominated the Presidential ticket of James M. Cox and Franklin D. Roosevelt; died in Rome, Ga., while on a visit in that city, on December 21, 1932; interment in Oakwood Cemetery, Montgomery, Ala.

TAYLOR, Glen Hearst, a Senator from Idaho; born in Portland, Multnomah County, Oreg., April 12, 1904; moved to a homestead near Kooskia, Idaho, in 1906; attended the public schools of Idaho; joined a dramatic stock company in 1919; owner and manager of various entertainment enterprises since 1926; unsuccessful Democratic candidate for election to the United States Senate in 1940 and 1942; elected as a Democrat to the United States Senate in 1944 for the term commencing January 3, 1945, and ending January 3, 1951; unsuccessful candidate for renomination in 1950; in 1948 was defeated as a Progressive for election as Vice President of the United States; unsuccessful Democratic candidate for election to the United States Senate in 1954 and for the nomination in 1956; president of Coryell Construction Co. 1950–1952; and of Taylor Topper, Inc., of Millbrae, Calif., since 1957; is a resident of Pocatello, Idaho.

TAYLOR, Herbert Worthington, a Representative from New Jersey; born in Belleville, Essex County, N. J., February 19, 1869; attended the public schools, and was graduated from the law school of the University of New York, New York City, in 1891; was admitted to the New York bar the same year and to the New Jersey bar in 1897, and practiced in New York City and Newark, N. J.; member of the common council of Newark 1899–1903; member of the State assembly in 1904 and 1905; chairman of the Essex County Republican committee 1913–1917; delegate to the Republican National Convention at Chicago in 1916; county counsel of Essex County 1916–1921; elected as a Republican to the Sixty-seventh Congress (March 4, 1921–March 3, 1923); unsuccessful candidate for renomination in 1922; resumed the practice of law in Newark, N. J.; elected to the Sixty-ninth Congress (March 4, 1925–March 3, 1927); unsuccessful candidate for reelection in 1926 to the Seventieth Congress; resumed the practice of law in Newark, N. J., where he died on October 15, 1931; interment in East Ridgelawn Cemetery, Delawanna, N. J.

TAYLOR, Isaac Hamilton, a Representative from Ohio; born near New Harrisburg (later Hibbetts), Carroll County, Ohio, April 18, 1840; attended the common schools and completed an academic course; studied law; was admitted to the bar in 1867 and commenced practice in Carrollton, Ohio; clerk of court in Carroll County, Ohio, 1870–1877; elected as a Republican to the Forty-ninth Congress (March 4, 1885–March 3, 1887); was not a candidate for renomination in 1886; moved to Canton, Ohio, and resumed the practice of law; delegate to the Republican National Convention at Minneapolis in 1892 which nominated Benjamin Harrison, of Indiana, for a second term; judge of the court of common pleas from 1889 to 1901, when he re-

signed; engaged in the practice of his profession in Canton, Ohio, until 1922, when he discontinued active pursuits and lived in retirement; died at Congress Lake, near Hartville, Stark County, Ohio, December 18, 1936; interment in Westlawn Cemetery, Canton, Ohio.

TAYLOR, James Alfred, a Representative from West Virginia; born near Ironton, Lawrence County, Ohio, September 25, 1878; attended the public schools; employed in a printing office in Ironton, Ohio; moved to Alderson, W. Va., and engaged in the newspaper business; moved from Greenbrier County to Fayette County in 1905; served as a noncommissioned officer in the West Virginia National Guard 1908–1911; member of the State house of representatives 1916–1918, 1920–1922, 1930–1932, and 1936–1938, serving as speaker 1930–1932; elected as a Democrat to the Sixty-eighth and Sixty-ninth Congresses (March 4, 1923–March 3, 1927); was an unsuccessful candidate for reelection in 1926 to the Seventieth Congress; resumed the newspaper publishing business; unsuccessful Democratic candidate for the gubernatorial nomination in 1928; presidential elector in 1933; served as secretary of the West Virginia Liquor Commission 1941–1945; elected a member of the Fayette County Board of Education in 1946 for a six-year term; died in Montgomery, W. Va., on June 9, 1956; interment in Huse Memorial Park, Fayetteville, W. Va.

TAYLOR, James Willis, a Representative from Tennessee; born near Lead Mine Bend, Union County, Tenn., August 28, 1880; attended the public schools, Holbrook Normal College, Fountain City, Tenn., and the American Temperance University, Harriman, Tenn.; taught school for several years; was graduated from the law department of Cumberland University, Lebanon, Tenn., in 1902; was admitted to the bar the same year; moved to La Follette, Campbell County, Tenn., and commenced practice; postmaster at La Follette 1904–1909; served as mayor 1910–1913 and in 1918 and 1919; insurance commissioner for the State of Tennessee in 1913 and 1914; chairman of the Republican State executive committee in 1917 and 1918; elected as a Republican to the Sixty-sixth and to the ten succeeding Congresses and served from March 4, 1919, until his death; member of the Republican National Executive Committee 1929–1939; died in La Follette, Tenn., November 14, 1939; interment in Woodlawn Cemetery.

TAYLOR, John, a Senator from Virginia; born at Mill Farm, near Bowling Green, Caroline County, Va., May 17, 1754; educated by private tutors, and was graduated from William and Mary College, Williamsburg, Va., in 1770; studied law; was admitted to the bar and commenced practice in Caroline County in 1774; served in the Revolutionary War as major and colonel; member of the State house of delegates 1779–1785 and 1796–1800; lieutenant colonel in Gen. Alexander Spotswood's Legionary Corps, serving under General Lafayette; retired from the practice of law and engaged in agricultural pursuits; elected as a Democrat to the United States Senate to fill the vacancy caused by the resignation of Richard Henry Lee; reelected in 1793, and served from October 18, 1792, until his resignation on May 11, 1794; presidential elector in 1797 and voted for Adams and Jefferson; appointed to the United States Senate to fill the vacancy caused by the death of Stevens T. Mason and served from June 4 to December 7, 1803, when a successor was elected; was not a candidate for election to fill the vacancy; elected to the United States Senate to fill the vacancy caused by the resignation of James Pleasants; reelected in 1823, and served from December 18, 1822, until his death in Caroline County, Va., August 20, 1824; interment on "Hazelwood" farm, near Port Royal, Caroline County, Va.

TAYLOR, John, a Representative and a Senator from South Carolina; born near Granby, S. C., May 4, 1770; attended Mount Sion Institute, and was graduated from Princeton College in 1790; studied law; was admitted to the bar in 1793 and commenced practice in Columbia, S. C.; also engaged in planting; member of the State house of representatives 1796–1802, 1804, 1805; circuit court solicitor in 1805 and 1806; served as first intendent of Columbia in 1806 and 1807; elected as a Democrat to the Tenth and Eleventh Congresses and served from March 4, 1807, until his resignation on December 30, 1810; elected to the United States Senate on December 19, 1810, to fill the vacancy caused by the resignation of Thomas Sumter, and was also elected on December 20, 1810, for the full term beginning March 4, 1811, and served from December 31, 1810, until his resignation in November 1816; served in the State senate 1818–1826; unsuccessful candidate for reelection in 1826; Governor of South Carolina 1826–1828; trustee of South Carolina College (now the University of South Carolina) at Columbia and director of the Columbia Theological Seminary (Presbyterian); died at Camden, Kershaw County, S. C., April 16, 1832; interment in the family burial ground at Columbia, Richland District, S. C.

TAYLOR, John, a Representative from South Carolina; presidential elector on the Jefferson and Clinton ticket in 1805; elected to the Fourteenth Congress (March 4, 1815–March 3, 1817); unsuccessful candidate for reelection in 1816 to the Fifteenth Congress and for election in 1820 to the Seventeenth Congress.

TAYLOR, John Clarence, a Representative from South Carolina; born in Honea Path, Anderson County, S. C., March 2, 1890; attended the public schools and Fruitland Institute, Hendersonville, N. C.; was graduated from the law department of the University of South Carolina at Columbia in 1919; during the First World War attended the Officers' Training School at Camp Johnston, Fla., in 1918 and was discharged into the Reserves at the end of the war; was admitted to the bar in 1919; engaged in agricultural pursuits; clerk of court and register of deeds for Anderson County, S. C., from 1920 until elected to Congress; elected as a Democrat to the Seventy-third, Seventy-fourth, and Seventy-fifth Congresses (March 4, 1933–January 3, 1939); was an unsuccessful candidate for renomination in 1938 to the Seventy-sixth Congress; resumed his former business pursuits, giving major attention to farming interests; is a resident of Anderson, S. C.

TAYLOR, John James, a Representative from New York; born in Leominster, Worcester County, Mass., April 27, 1808; attended the common schools, New Ipswich Academy, and Groton Academy; was graduated from Harvard University in 1829; engaged in teaching for a short time; moved to Troy, N. Y., in 1830; studied law; was admitted to the bar in 1834 and commenced practice in Greene, Chenango County, N. Y.; moved to Owego, N. Y., in 1834 and continued the practice of law; appointed district attorney of Tioga County in 1838, and served until 1843, when he resigned; member of the village board of trustees in 1839, 1843, and 1848; first chief engineer of the fire department in 1844; member of the State constitutional convention in 1846; unsuccessful candidate for election in 1850 to the Thirty-second Congress; elected as a Democrat to the Thirty-third Congress (March 4, 1853–March 3, 1855); resumed the practice of his profession; tendered the appointment of commissioner to settle the northwestern boundary of the United States by President Franklin Pierce, but declined the position; unsuccessful Democratic candidate for Lieutenant Governor of New York in 1858; president of the village of Owego in 1859; engaged in banking; elected vice president and later president of the Southern Central Railway Co., later the Auburn division of the Lehigh Valley Railroad Co.; died in Owego, Tioga County, N. Y., July 1, 1892; interment in Evergreen Cemetery.

TAYLOR, John Lampkin, a Representative from Ohio; born in Stafford County, near Fredericksburg, Va., March 7, 1805; completed preparatory studies; studied law in Washington, D. C.; was admitted to the bar in 1828 and commenced practice in Chillicothe, Ross County, Ohio, in 1829; major general in the State militia for several years; elected as a Whig to the Thirtieth and to the three succeeding Congresses (March 4, 1847–March 3, 1855); served as a clerk in the Interior Department from May 1, 1870, until his sudden death at his desk in Washington, D. C., September 6, 1870; interment in the family burying ground on the Taylor ancestral estate, "Mansfield," near Louisa, Louisa County, Va.

TAYLOR, John May, a Representative from Tennessee; born in Lexington, Henderson County, Tenn., May 18, 1838; attended the Male Academy in Lexington and the Union University, Murfreesboro, Tenn.; was graduated from the law department of Cumberland University, Lebanon, Tenn., in 1861; was admitted to the bar the same year and commenced practice in Lexington; during the Civil War enlisted in the Confederate Army; was elected first lieutenant in June 1861 and promoted to captain; elected major in the Twenty-seventh Tennessee Regiment in 1862; mayor of Lexington in 1869 and 1870; delegate to the State constitutional convention of Tennessee in 1870; attorney general of the eleventh judicial circuit of Tennessee 1870–1878; delegate to the Democratic National Convention at Cincinnati in 1880; member of the State house of representatives in 1881 and 1882; elected as a Democrat to the Forty-eighth and Forty-ninth Congresses (March 4, 1883–March 3, 1887); presidential elector on the Democratic ticket of Cleveland and Stevenson in 1892; member of the State senate in 1892; resumed the practice of law; was appointed judge of the criminal court for the eleventh judicial circuit in 1895 and subsequently elected for a six-year term, serving until the court was abolished; elected in August 1902 as a judge of the court of chancery appeals (name changed to court of civil appeals by the legislature); reelected in 1910 for a period of eight years and served until his death; died in Lexington, Tenn., February 17, 1911; interment in Lexington Cemetery.

TAYLOR, John W., a Representative from New York; born in Charlton, N. Y., March 26, 1784; received his early education at home; was graduated from Union College, Schenectady, N. Y., in 1803; studied law; was admitted to the bar in 1807 and commenced practice in Ballston Spa, N. Y.; organized the Ballston Center Academy; justice of the peace in 1808; member of the State assembly in 1812 and 1813; elected as a Democrat to the Thirteenth and to the nine succeeding Congresses (March 4, 1813–March 3, 1833); unsuccessful candidate for reelection in 1832 to the Twenty-third Congress; served as Speaker during the second session of the Sixteenth Congress and during the Nineteenth Congress; resumed the practice of law in Ballston Spa, N. Y.; member of the State senate in 1840 and 1841, but resigned in consequence of a paralytic stroke; moved to Cleveland, Ohio, in 1843, and died there September 8, 1854; interment in the City Cemetery, Ballston Spa, Saratoga County, N. Y.

TAYLOR, Jonathan, a Representative from Ohio; born near Mansfield, Conn., in 1796; moved to Newark, Ohio; completed an academic course; studied law; was admitted to the bar and commenced practice in Newark; appointed by the Governor a commissioner to settle the boundary dispute between Ohio and Michigan; brigadier general in the State militia; member of the State house of representatives 1831–1833; served in the State senate 1833-1836; elected as a Democrat to the Twenty-sixth Congress (March 4, 1839-March 3, 1841); died in Newark, Licking County, Ohio, in April 1848; interment in the Old Cemetery; reinterment in Cedar Hill Cemetery.

TAYLOR, Joseph Danner, a Representative from Ohio; born in Goshen Township, Belmont County, Ohio, November 7, 1830; attended the common schools and Madison College at Antrim; taught school 1854-1856, and was principal of the Fairview High School in 1857; studied law in Cincinnati, Ohio, and was admitted to the bar in 1859; was graduated from the Cincinnati Law College in 1860 and commenced practice in Cambridge, Guernsey County, Ohio, the same year; owner of the Guernsey Times 1861-1871; during the Civil War entered the Union Army as a captain in the Eighty-eighth Regiment, Ohio Volunteer Infantry; was judge advocate of the Department of Indiana in 1863 and 1864; citizen judge advocate in Indianapolis, Ind., in 1865; prosecuting attorney of Guernsey County, Ohio, 1863-1866; delegate to the Philadelphia Loyalist Convention in 1866; member of the Cambridge School Board 1870-1877; delegate to the Republican National Conventions in 1876 and 1880; elected as a Republican to the Forty-seventh Congress to fill the vacancy caused by the death of Jonathan T. Updegraff; reelected to the Forty-eighth Congress and served from January 2, 1883, to March 3, 1885; unsuccessful candidate for reelection in 1884 to the Forty-ninth Congress; elected to the Fiftieth, Fifty-first, and Fifty-second Congresses (March 4, 1887-March 3, 1893); died in Cambridge, Ohio, September 19, 1899; interment in the South Cemetery.

TAYLOR, Miles, a Representative from Louisiana; born in Saratoga Springs, N. Y., July 16, 1805; received a liberal education; moved to Bayou Lafourche, La.; studied medicine, but never practiced; studied law; was admitted to the bar and commenced practice in Donaldsonville, Ascension Parish, La.; moved to New Orleans, La., about 1847; held several local offices; appointed by the Governor in 1849 as a member of a committee to revise the Civil Code, the Code of Procedure, and the Statutes of Louisiana; elected as a Democrat to the Thirty-fourth, Thirty-fifth, and Thirty-sixth Congresses and served from March 4, 1855, to February 5, 1861, when he withdrew; chairman of the Douglas National Executive Committee in 1869; resumed the practice of law in New Orleans, La., and was a leader of the sugar growers in Louisiana for many years; died in Saratoga Springs, N. Y., September 23, 1873; interment on the family plantation, "Front Scattery," near Belle Alliance, Assumption Parish, La.

TAYLOR, Nathaniel Green (father of Alfred Alexander Taylor and Robert Love Taylor), a Representative from Tennessee; born in Happy Valley, Carter County, Tenn., December 29, 1819; was educated in private schools and Washington College, near Jonesboro, Tenn.; was graduated from Princeton College in 1840; studied law; was admitted to the bar in 1841 and commenced practice in Elizabethton, Carter County, Tenn.; presidential elector on the Whig ticket of Scott and Graham in 1852; elected as a Whig to the Thirty-third Congress to fill the vacancy caused by the death of Brookins Campbell, who never qualified, and served from March 30, 1854, to March 3, 1855; unsuccessful candidate for reelection in 1854 to the Thirty-fourth Congress; presidential elector on the Constitutional Union ticket of Bell and Everett in 1860; member of the relief association formed for the aid of war sufferers in east Tennessee and lectured in their behalf throughout the East; upon the readmission of Tennessee to representation was elected to the Thirty-ninth Congress and served from July 24, 1866, to March 3, 1867; was not a candidate for renomination in 1866,

Commissioner of Indian Affairs from March 26, 1867, to April 21, 1869, when he retired, and devoted himself to farming and preaching the Gospel; died in Happy Valley, Carter County, Tenn., April 1, 1887; interment in the old Taylor private cemetery.

TAYLOR, Nelson, a Representative from New York; born in South Norwalk, Conn., June 8, 1821; attended the common schools; enlisted for the Mexican War as a captain in the First Regiment, New York Volunteer Infantry, August 1, 1846, and was sent to California in 1846 just before the outbreak of the war; was honorably mustered out September 18, 1848; upon the annexation of California he remained there and engaged in business at Stockton; member of the State senate 1850-1856; president of the board of trustees of the State insane asylum 1850-1856; elected sheriff of San Joaquin County in 1855; moved to New York City; was graduated from the law department of Harvard University in 1860; was admitted to the bar and practiced; unsuccessful Democratic candidate for election in 1860 to the Thirty-seventh Congress; served in the Union Army during the Civil War; was commissioned colonel of the Seventy-second Regiment, New York Volunteer Infantry, July 23, 1861; was in command of troops at Harlem during the draft riots in New York City; brigadier general of Volunteers September 7, 1862; resigned from the service January 19, 1863; resumed the practice of law in New York City; elected as a Democrat to the Thirty-ninth Congress (March 4, 1865-March 3, 1867); unsuccessful candidate for reelection in 1866 to the Fortieth Congress; moved to South Norwalk, Conn., in 1869 and continued the practice of law; served several times as city attorney; died in South Norwalk, Fairfield County, Conn., January 16, 1894; interment in Riverside Cemetery.

TAYLOR, Robert, a Representative from Virginia; born at Orange Court House, Va., April 29, 1763; completed preparatory studies; studied law; was admitted to the bar in 1783 and commenced practice at Orange Court House, Va.; held several local offices; member of the State senate 1804-1815, and served as president pro tempore; elected to the Nineteenth Congress (March 4, 1825-March 3, 1827); was not a candidate for renomination in 1826; devoted his attention to the management of his plantation; died on his estate, "Meadow Farm," in Orange County, Va., July 3, 1845; interment in the family burying ground at "Meadow Farm."

TAYLOR, Robert Love (son of Nathaniel Green Taylor and brother of Alfred Alexander Taylor), a Representative and a Senator from Tennessee; born in Happy Valley, Carter County, Tenn., July 31, 1850; attended Pennington Seminary and Buffalo Institute (later Milligan College), Tennessee; engaged in making bar iron and in tobacco raising; studied law in Jonesboro, Tenn.; was admitted to the bar in 1878 and practiced in Elizabethton and Jonesboro; elected as a Democrat to the Forty-sixth Congress (March 4, 1879-March 3, 1881); unsuccessful candidate for reelection in 1880 to the Forty-seventh Congress and for election in 1882 to the Forty-eighth Congress; practiced law and also engaged in the newspaper business in Johnson City, Tenn., in 1880; presidential elector on the Democratic ticket of Cleveland and Hendricks in 1884; pension agent at Knoxville, Tenn., 1885-1887; was Governor of Tennessee 1887-1891; presidential elector on the Democratic ticket of Cleveland and Stevenson in 1892; resumed the practice of law in Chattanooga, Tenn.; again served as Governor of Tennessee from 1897 to 1899; elected as a Democrat to the United States Senate in January 1907 for the term beginning March 4, 1907, and served until his death in Washington, D. C., March 31, 1912; interment in the Old Gray Cemetery, Knoxville, Tenn.; reinterred in Monta Vista Cemetery, Johnson City, Tenn., in 1938.

TAYLOR, Roy Arthur, a Representative from North Carolina; born in Vader, Lewis County, Wash., January 31, 1910; moved to Candler, N. C., in 1910 and attended the public schools of Buncombe County, N. C.; graduated from Asheville-Biltmore College in 1929, Maryville College in 1931, and from Asheville University Law School in 1936; was admitted to the bar in 1936 and commenced the practice of law in Asheville, N. C.; during World War II served in the United States Navy from 1943 until discharged as a lieutenant in 1946; member of the North Carolina General Assembly 1947–1953; Buncombe County attorney 1949–1960; member of board of trustees of Asheville-Biltmore College since 1949; elected as a Democrat to the Eighty-sixth Congress to fill the vacancy caused by the death of David M. Hall and served from June 25, 1960, to January 3, 1961. *Reelected to the Eighty-seventh Congress.*

TAYLOR, Samuel Mitchell (father of Chester William Taylor), a Representative from Arkansas; born near Fulton, Itawamba County, Miss., May 25, 1852; attended the public schools; studied law; was admitted to the bar in Tupelo, Miss., and commenced practice in 1876; member of the State house of representatives in 1879 and 1880; moved to Pine Bluff, Jefferson County, Ark., in 1887, where he continued the practice of law; prosecuting attorney of the eleventh judical district of Arkansas 1888–1892; delegate to the Democratic National Convention at Chicago in 1896; temporary chairman of the Democratic State convention in 1910; elected as a Democrat to the Sixty-third Congress; subsequently elected to the Sixty-second Congress to fill the vacancy caused by the resignation of Joseph T. Robinson; reelected to the Sixty-fourth and to the three succeeding Congresses and served from January 15, 1913, until his death in Washington, D. C., September 13, 1921; interment in Bellewood Cemetery, Pine Bluff, Ark.

TAYLOR, Vincent Albert, a Representative from Ohio; born in Bedford, Cuyahoga County, Ohio, December 6, 1845; attended the common schools; enlisted in Company H, One Hundred and Fiftieth Regiment, Ohio Volunteer Infantry, in May 1864 and in August of the same year in Company H, One Hundred and Seventy-seventh Regiment, Ohio Volunteer Infantry, and served until the close of the Civil War; engaged in manufacturing pursuits; member of the Ohio Senate 1888–1890; elected as a Republican to the Fifty-second Congress (March 4, 1891–March 3, 1893); was not a candidate for renomination in 1892; president of the Taylor Chair Co., and a resident of Bedford, Ohio, until his death there December 2, 1922; interment in Bedford Cemetery.

TAYLOR, Waller, a Senator from Indiana; born in Lunenburg County, Va., before 1786; attended the common schools; studied law; was admitted to the bar and practiced in Virginia; member of the State house of delegates 1800–1802; moved to Vincennes, Ind., in 1804 and continued the practice of law; appointed chancellor of Indiana Territory in 1807; appointed major in the Territorial militia in 1807; served as aide-de-camp to Gen. William H. Harrison in the War of 1812, and was promoted to adjutant general in 1814; upon the admission of Indiana as a State into the Union in 1816 was elected as a Democrat to the United States Senate; reelected, and served from December 11, 1816, to March 3, 1825; died while on a visit to his old home in Lunenburg County, Va., August 26, 1826; interment in the family burial ground near Lunenburg, Va.

TAYLOR, William, a Representative from New York; born in Suffield, Hartford County, Conn., October 12, 1791; moved with his parents to Onondaga County, N. Y.; attended the public schools; studied medicine and was admitted to practice; elected as a Democrat to the Twenty-third, Twenty-fourth, and Twenty-fifth Congresses (March 4, 1833–March 3, 1839); resumed the practice of his chosen profession; member of the State assembly in 1841 and 1842; delegate to the State constitutional convention in 1846; died in Manlius, N. Y., September 16, 1865; interment in Christ Church Cemetery.

TAYLOR, William, a Representative from Virginia; born in Alexandria, Va. (then included in the District of Columbia), April 5, 1788; completed preparatory studies; studied law; was admitted to the bar and commenced practice in Staunton, Va.; moved to Lexington, Va., in 1813; became a member of the bar; Commonwealth attorney for the county court of Rockbridge 1817–1843; Commonwealth attorney for the circuit court of Pocahontas County 1817–1843; member of the house of delegates in 1821; elected as a Democrat to the Twenty-eighth and Twenty-ninth Congresses and served from March 4, 1843, until his death in Washington, D. C., January 17, 1846; interment in the Congressional Cemetery.

TAYLOR, William Penn, a Representative from Virginia; born in Fredericksburg, Spotsylvania County, Va.; received a limited schooling; held several local offices; elected as a Whig to the Twenty-third Congress (March 4, 1833–March 3, 1835); was an unsuccessful candidate for reelection in 1834 to the Twenty-fourth Congress; died at "Hayfield," Caroline County, Va., near Fredericksburg, Va.; interment in the family graveyard at "Hayfield."

TAYLOR, Zachary, a Representative from Tennessee; born near Brownsville, Haywood County, Tenn., May 9, 1849; attended J. I. Hall's School near Covington, Tenn., and was graduated from the Virginia Military Institute at Lexington as senior captain July 4, 1872, and from the law department of Cumberland University, Lebanon, Tenn., in January 1874; was admitted to the bar and commenced practice in Covington, Tenn., in 1878; served in the State senate in 1880; postmaster of Covington, Tenn., from July 1, 1883, to January 1, 1885, when he resigned; elected as a Republican to the Forty-ninth Congress (March 4 1885–March 3, 1887); unsuccessful candidate for reelection in 1886 to the Fiftieth Congress; moved to Memphis, Tenn., and engaged in the general life insurance business; elected as a delegate to the Republican National Convention at St. Louis in 1896; moved to San Antonio, Tex.; died in Ellendale, Shelby County, Tenn., February 19, 1921; interment in Mount Pisgah Cemetery.

TAZEWELL, Henry (father of Littleton Waller Tazewell), a Senator from Virginia; born in Brunswick County, Va., November 15, 1753; attended the rural schools; was graduated from William and Mary College at Williamsburg in 1772; studied law; was admitted to the bar and commenced practice in 1773; member of the provincial house of burgesses in 1775; delegate to the State constitutional convention of 1775 and 1776; judge of the State supreme court 1785–1793 and chief justice from 1789 to 1793; judge of the high court of appeals in 1793; elected to the United States Senate to fill the vacancy caused by the resignation of John Taylor and served from December 29, 1794, until his death; elected President pro tempore of the Senate December 7, 1795; died in Philadelphia, Pa., January 24, 1799; interment in Christ Church Cemetery.

TAZEWELL, Littleton Waller (son of Henry Tazewell), a Representative and a Senator from Virginia; born in Williamsburg, James City County, Va., December 17, 1774; was graduated from William and Mary College at Williamsburg in 1792; studied law; was admitted to the bar in 1796 and commenced practice in James

City County; member of the State house of delegates 1796–1800; elected as a Democrat to the Sixth Congress to fill the vacancy caused by the resignation of John Marshall and served from November 26, 1800, to March 3, 1801; moved to Norfolk, Va., in 1802; member of the Virginia House of Delegates in 1816; one of the commissioners of claims under the treaty with Spain ceding Florida in 1820; declined appointment as Minister to Great Britain; elected to the United States Senate to fill the vacancy caused by the death of John Taylor; reelected, and served from December 7, 1824, to July 16, 1832, when he resigned; delegate to State convention in 1829; elected President pro tempore of the Senate July 9, 1832; Governor of Virginia from 1834 until his resignation in 1836; retired from public life; died in Norfolk, Va., May 6, 1860; interment on his estate on the Eastern Shore of Virginia; reinterment in 1866 in Elmwood Cemetery, Norfolk, Va.

TEAGUE, Charles McKevett, a Representative from California; born in Santa Paula, Ventura County, Calif., September 18, 1909; attended the public schools; was graduated from Stanford University in 1931 and from Stanford Law School in 1934; was admitted to the bar in 1934 and commenced the practice of law in Los Angeles and Ventura, Calif.; during World War II served in the United States Air Force 1942–1946; awarded Air Force commendation ribbon; director of McKevett Corp. and Teague-McKevett Co.; elected as a Republican to the Eighty-fourth, Eighty-fifth, and Eighty-sixth Congresses (January 3, 1955–January 3, 1961). *Reelected to the Eighty-seventh Congress.*

TEAGUE, Olin Earl, a Representative from Texas; born in Woodward, Okla., April 6, 1910; attended Texas Agricultural and Mechanical College at College Station 1928–1932; employed in the post office at College Station, Tex., 1932–1940; resigned his position as superintendent of South Station on October 5, 1940, to enlist in the United States Army, being commissioned a first lieutenant; commanded the First Battalion, Three Hundred and Fourteenth Infantry, Seventy-ninth Division; was in combat six months, wounded several times, and awarded the Silver Star with two clusters, Bronze Star, Purple Heart with two clusters, Combat Infantryman's Badge, Army Commendation Ribbon, and the Croix de Guerre with Palm; was discharged as a colonel at Walter Reed General Hospital September 6, 1946; elected as a Democrat to the Seventy-ninth Congress to fill the vacancy caused by the resignation of Luther A. Johnson; reelected to the Eightieth and to the six succeeding Congresses and served from August 24, 1946, to January 3, 1961. *Reelected to the Eighty-seventh Congress.*

TEESE, Frederick Halstead, a Representative from New Jersey; born in Newark, N. J., October 21, 1823; was graduated from Princeton College in 1843; studied law; was admitted to the bar in 1846 and commenced practice in Newark, N. J.; member of the State house of assembly in 1860 and 1861, serving as speaker in 1861; presiding judge of the court of common pleas of Essex County from 1864 until his resignation in 1872; elected as a Democrat to the Forty-fourth Congress (March 4, 1875–March 3, 1877); declined the nomination for reelection in 1876 to the Forty-fifth Congress; resumed the practice of law; died in New York City January 7, 1894; interment in Mount Pleasant Cemetery, Newark, N. J.

TEIGAN, Henry George, a Representative from Minnesota; born in Forest City, Winnebago County, Iowa, August 7, 1881; attended the public schools, Luther Academy, Albert Lea, Minn., and Central College, Pella, Iowa; was graduated from Valparaiso (Ind.) University in 1908; taught in the Iowa rural schools 1900–1904, at Des Lacs, N. Dak., in 1909 and 1910, and

at Logan, N. Dak , 1912–1913; secretary of North Dakota State Socialist Party 1913–1916; moved to Minneapolis, Minn., in 1917; secretary of National Nonpartisan League 1916–1923; secretary to Senator Magnus Johnson 1923–1925; editor and newspaper writer 1923–1933; served in the State senate 1933–1935; elected as a Farmer-Laborite to the Seventy-fifth Congress (January 3, 1937–January 3, 1939); unsuccessful candidate for reelection in 1938 to the Seventy-sixth Congress and in 1940 for election to the Seventy-seventh Congress; resumed newspaper and editorial work in Minneapolis, Minn., until his death on March 12, 1941; interment in Hillside Cemetery.

TELFAIR, Edward (father of Thomas Telfair), a Delegate from Georgia; born in "Town Head," Scotland, in 1735; was graduated from the Kirdcudbright Grammar School and subsequently acquired a thorough commercial training; immigrated to the United States in 1758 as agent of a commercial house and settled in Virginia; moved to Halifax, N. C.; established a commission house in Savannah, Ga., in 1766; also engaged in the sawmill business and agricultural pursuits; active in pre-Revolutionary movements of 1774; member of the council of safety in 1775 and 1776; delegate to the Provincial Congress at Savannah in 1776; member of the committee of intelligence and other important committees in 1776; Member of the Continental Congress 1778–1782, 1784–1785, 1788–1789; one of the signers of the Articles of Confederation and a delegate to the convention to ratify the Constitution of the United States; commissioner to treat with the Cherokee Indians in 1783; designated agent on the part of Georgia to settle the northern boundary of the Commonwealth in February 1783; Governor of Georgia in 1786 and 1790–1793; entertained President Washington at his home in Augusta in May 1791; died in Savannah, Ga., September 17, 1807; interment in Bonaventure Cemetery.

TELFAIR, Thomas (son of Edward Telfair), a Representative from Georgia; born in Savannah, Ga., March 2, 1780; was graduated from Princeton College in 1805; studied law; was admitted to the bar and commenced practice in Savannah, Ga.; elected as a Democrat to the Thirteenth and Fourteenth Congresses (March 4, 1813–March 3, 1817); died in Savannah, Ga., February 18, 1818; interment in Bonaventure Cemetery.

TELLER, Henry Moore, a Senator from Colorado; born in Granger, Allegany County, N. Y., May 23, 1830; attended Rushford Academy and Alfred (N. Y.) University; taught school; studied law and was admitted to the bar in Binghamton, N. Y., in 1858; moved to Illinois in 1858 and to Colorado in 1861; major general of Colorado Militia 1862–1864; upon the admission of Colorado as a State into the Union was elected as a Republican to the United States Senate; reelected, and served from November 15, 1876, until his resignation on April 17, 1882, to accept a Cabinet position; appointed Secretary of the Interior in the Cabinet of President Arthur and served from April 17, 1882, to March 4, 1885; elected as a Republican to the United States Senate in 1885 and 1891, as an Independent Silver Republican in 1897, and as a Democrat in 1903, and served from March 4, 1885, to March 3, 1909; declined to be a candidate for renomination; member of the United States Monetary Commission in 1908; engaged in the practice of law until his death in Denver, Colo., February 23, 1914; interment in Fairmount Cemetery.

TELLER, Isaac (nephew of Abraham Henry Schenck), a Representative from New York; born in Matteawan, Dutchess County, N. Y., February 7, 1799; completed preparatory studies; held several local offices; elected as a Democrat to the Thirty-third Congress to fill the vacancy caused by the resignation of

Gilbert Dean and served from November 7, 1854, to March 3, 1855; engaged in agricultural pursuits; died in Matteawan (now Beacon), N. Y., April 30, 1868; interment in the Rural Cemetery, Fishkill, Dutchess County, N. Y.

TELLER, Ludwig, a Representative from New York; born in New York City (Borough of Manhattan), N. Y., June 22, 1911; educated in the public schools; graduated from New York University in 1936 and from the law school of the same university in 1935; was admitted to the bar in 1936 and commenced the practice of law in New York City; expert consultant to Labor Relations Board, War Department, in 1942; trial examiner, New York State Labor Relations Board, 1942–1946; during World War II served as a senior lieutenant in the United States Navy as communications officer in Atlantic convoy, and as labor relations officer, Ninth Naval District, Chicago, Ill., 1943–1945; lieutenant commander, United States Naval Reserve, since 1959; served on the faculty of New York University Law School 1947–1950 and professor of law at New York Law School since 1950; author of several law treatises and articles in legal periodicals; member of the State assembly 1950–1956; elected as a Democrat to the Eighty-fifth and Eighty-sixth Congresses (January 3, 1957–January 3, 1961); was unsuccessful for the Democratic nomination in 1960 and also for election as a Liberal candidate to the Eighty-seventh Congress; is a resident of New York City, N. Y.

TEMPLE, Henry Willson, a Representative from Pennsylvania; born in Belle Center, Logan County, Ohio, March 31, 1864; attended the common schools; was graduated from Geneva College, Beaver Falls, Pa., in 1883 and from the Covenanter Theological Seminary, Allegheny, Pa., in 1887, pastor of churches at Baxter, Leechburg, and Washington, Pa.; adjunct professor of political science 1898–1905 and professor of history and political science in Washington and Jefferson College, Washington, Pa., 1905–1913; elected as a Progressive Republican to the Sixty-third Congress (March 4, 1913–March 3, 1915); unsuccessful Progressive Republican candidate for reelection to succeed himself in 1914 to the Sixty-fourth Congress; elected as a Republican to the Sixty-fourth Congress to fill the vacancy caused by the death of William M. Brown; reelected to the Sixty-fifth and to the seven succeeding Congresses and served from November 2, 1915, to March 3, 1933; unsuccessful candidate for reelection in 1932 to the Seventy-third Congress; professor of international relations in Washington and Jefferson College from 1933 until his retirement in 1947; died in Washington, Pa., January 11, 1955; interment in Washington Cemetery.

TEMPLE, William, a Representative from Delaware; born in Queen Anne County, Md., February 28, 1814; completed preparatory studies; moved to Smyrna, Del., and engaged in mercantile pursuits; member of the State house of representatives in 1844 and served as speaker; served in the State senate 1845–1854; Acting Governor of Delaware from May 1846 to January 1847; elected as a Democrat to the Thirty-eighth Congress and served from March 4, 1863, until his death before the convening of the Congress; died in Smyrna, Del., May 28, 1863; interment in the Episcopal Cemetery.

TEMPLETON, Thomas Weir, a Representative from Pennsylvania; born in Plymouth, Luzerne County, Pa., November 8, 1867; attended the public schools and was graduated from Wyoming Seminary, Kingston, Pa.; studied law; was admitted to the bar in 1899 but did not practice; prothonotary of Luzerne County 1904–1907; engaged in business as a florist at Kingston; elected as a Republican to the Sixty-fifth Congress (March 4, 1917–March 3, 1919); was not a candidate for renomi-

nation in 1918; superintendent of grounds and buildings at the State capitol 1920–1923; resumed the florist business in Kingston, Pa.; died in Plymouth, Pa., September 5, 1935; interment in Edgehill Cemetery, West Nanticoke, Pa.

TENER, John Kinley, a Representative from Pennsylvania; born in County Tyrone, Ireland, July 25, 1863; immigrated to the United States with his parents, who settled in Pittsburgh, Pa., in 1872; attended the public and high schools; was employed by manufacturing firms and corporations in and about Pittsburgh; engaged as a professional baseball player 1885–1890; entered the banking business in Charleroi, Pa., in 1901, serving as cashier and later as president of the First National Bank; elected as a Republican to the Sixty-first Congress and served from March 4, 1909, to January 16, 1911, when he resigned, having been elected Governor; Governor of Pennsylvania 1911–1915; president of the National League of Professional Baseball Clubs 1914–1918; elected a director of the Philadelphia National League Baseball Club in 1931; engaged in the insurance business until his death; died in Pittsburgh, Pa., May 19, 1946; interment in Homewood Cemetery.

TENEROWICZ, Rudolph Gabriel, a Representative from Michigan; born in Budapest, Austria, June 14, 1890; immigrated to the United States in 1892 with his parents, who settled in Adrian, Pa.; attended the parochial schools in that city, St. Cyril and Methodius Seminary, Orchard Lake, Mich., St. Bonaventure's College, Allegany, N. Y., and St. Ignatius College, Chicago, Ill.; was graduated in medicine from Loyola University, Chicago, Ill., in 1912; practiced medicine and surgery in Chicago, Ill., 1912–1923; during the First World War served from September 10, 1917, as a first lieutenant in the Medical Corps of the United States Army until his discharge on December 26, 1918; captain in the Medical Reserve Corps 1919–1934; postgraduate course in surgery at Illinois Post Graduate School at Chicago, Ill.; moved to Hamtramck, Wayne County, Mich., in 1923 and continued the practice of medicine and surgery; mayor of Hamtramck 1928–1932 and 1936–1938; member of the Wayne County Board of Supervisors for seven years; elected as a Democrat to the Seventy-sixth and Seventy-seventh Congresses (January 3, 1939–January 3, 1943); unsuccessful candidate for renomination in 1942 and for election as a Republican in 1948, 1950, 1952, and 1954; resumed the practice of medicine and surgery in Hamtramck, Mich.

TEN EYCK, Egbert, a Representative from New York; born in Schodack, Rensselaer County, N. Y., April 18, 1779; was graduated from Williams College, Williamstown, Mass., in 1799; studied law; was admitted to the bar in 1807 and commenced practice in Watertown, N. Y.; member of the State assembly in 1812 and 1813 and served as speaker; supervisor of Jefferson County in 1816; trustee of the village of Watertown in 1816; one of the incorporators of the Jefferson County National Bank; first secretary of the Jefferson County Agricultural Society in 1817; president of the village of Watertown in 1820; delegate to the State constitutional convention in 1822; elected to the Eighteenth Congress (March 4, 1823–March 3, 1825); presented credentials as a Member-elect to the Nineteenth Congress and served from March 4 to December 15, 1825, when he was succeeded by Daniel Hugunin, Jr., who contested his election; was judge of the Jefferson County Courts for nine years; died in Watertown, Jefferson County, N. Y., April 11, 1844; interment in Brookside Cemetery.

TEN EYCK, John Conover, a Senator from New Jersey; born in Freehold, Monmouth County, N. J., March 12, 1814; completed preparatory studies under private tutors; studied law;

was admitted to the bar in 1835 and commenced practice in Burlington, N. J.; prosecuting attorney for Burlington County 1839–1849; delegate to the State constitutional convention in 1844; elected as a Republican to the United States Senate and served from March 4, 1859, to March 3, 1865; unsuccessful candidate for reelection; delegate to the Republican National Convention in 1860; appointed a member of a commission to revise the New Jersey constitution April 24, 1875, and for a time was president of the commission; died in Mount Holly, N. J., August 24, 1879; interment in St. Andrew's Cemetery.

TEN EYCK, Peter Gansevoort, a Representative from New York; born in Bethlehem, Albany County, N. Y., November 7, 1873; was educated in the common schools in Normansville, the Albany Academy, and the Rensselaer Polytechnic Institute, Troy, N. Y.; engaged in civil and signal engineering for fifteen years; signal engineer of the New York Central Lines; chief engineer of the Federal Railway Signal Co. in 1903 and later its vice president and general manager; served seven years in the Third Signal Corps, Third Brigade, National Guard of New York; connected with several business enterprises; elected as a Democrat to the Sixty-third Congress (March 4, 1913–March 3, 1915); unsuccessful candidate for reelection in 1914 to the Sixty-fourth Congress; delegate to the Democratic National Convention at San Francisco in 1920; elected to the Sixty-seventh Congress (March 4, 1921–March 3, 1923); declined to be a candidate for renomination in 1922; engaged in agricultural pursuits near Albany, N. Y.; died at his summer residence, "Indian Ladder Farms," Altamont, N. Y., September 2, 1944; interment in the Rural Cemetery, Albany, N. Y.

TENNEY, Samuel, a Representative from New Hampshire; born in Byfield, Mass., November 27, 1748; attended Dummer Academy, Byfield, Mass.; was graduated from Harvard College in 1772; taught school in Andover, Mass.; studied medicine and began practice in Exeter, N. H.; surgeon in the Revolutionary War; returned to Exeter at the close of the war and continued the practice of his profession; delegate to the State constitutional convention in 1788; judge of probate for Rockingham County 1793–1800; elected to the Sixth Congress to fill the vacancy caused by the resignation of William Gordon; reelected to the Seventh, Eighth, and Ninth Congresses and served from December 8, 1800, to March 3, 1807; pursued literary, historical, and scientific studies; died in Exeter, N. H., February 6, 1816; interment in the Old Cemetery.

TERRELL, George Butler, a Representative from Texas; born in Alto, Cherokee County, Tex., December 5, 1862; attended the public schools, Sam Houston Teachers' College, Huntsville, Tex., and Baylor University, Waco, Tex.; taught school in Cherokee County, Tex., 1886–1903; member of the State teachers' examining board in 1897 and 1902, and of the State textbook commission in 1903; engaged in agricultural pursuits and in stock raising near Alto, Tex., in 1903; presidential elector on the Democratic ticket of Parker and Davis in 1904; member of the State house of representatives 1898–1902, 1906–1912, 1916–1920, 1930–1932; elected commissioner of agriculture of Texas in 1920, serving by reelection until 1931; elected as a Democrat to the Seventy-third Congress (March 4, 1933–January 3, 1935); was not a candidate for renomination in 1934; resumed agricultural pursuits and resided at Alto, Tex., until his death there on April 18, 1947; interment in the Old Palestine Cemetery, near Alto, Tex.

TERRELL, James C., a Representative from Georgia; born in Franklin County, Ga., November 7, 1806; studied law; was admitted to the bar by an act of the legislature and practiced in Carnesville, Ga.; member of the State house of representatives 1830–1834; elected as a Union Democrat to the Twenty-fourth Congress and served from March 4 to July 8, 1835, when he resigned, before Congress convened, on account of ill health; died at Carnesville, Franklin County, Ga., December 1, 1835.

TERRELL, Joseph Meriwether, a Senator from Georgia; born in Greenville, Meriwether County, Ga., June 6, 1861; attended the common schools; studied law; was admitted to the bar in 1882 and commenced practice in Greenville, Ga.; served in the State house of representatives 1884–1887; member of the State senate in 1890; attorney general of Georgia 1892–1902; Governor of Georgia from October 1902 to July 1907; resumed the practice of law in Atlanta, Ga.; appointed as a Democrat to the United States Senate to fill the vacancy caused by the death of Alexander S. Clay and served from November 17, 1910, to July 14, 1911, when he resigned; again resumed the practice of his profession in Atlanta, Ga., and died there November 17, 1912; interment in the City Cemetery, Greenville, Ga.

TERRELL, William, a Representative from Georgia; born in Fairfax County, Va., in 1778; moved with his parents to Georgia; pursued classical studies; was graduated from the medical department of the University of Pennsylvania at Philadelphia and commenced practice in Sparta, Hancock County, Ga.; member of the State house of representatives 1810–1813; held various local offices; elected as a Democrat to the Fifteenth and Sixteenth Congresses (March 4, 1817–March 3, 1821); declined to be a candidate for renomination in 1820; resumed the practice of medicine; died in Sparta, Ga., July 4, 1855; interment in Sparta Cemetery.

TERRY, David Dickson (son of William Leake Terry), a Representative from Arkansas; born in Little Rock, Pulaski County, Ark., January 31, 1881; attended the public schools, the Bethel Military Academy in Fauquier County, Va., and the University of Virginia at Charlottesville; was graduated from the law department of the University of Arkansas at Fayetteville in 1903; later attended the University of Chicago, Chicago, Ill.; was admitted to the bar in 1903 and commenced practice in Little Rock, Ark.; during the First World War enlisted on June 5, 1918, later commissioned a second lieutenant of Infantry in the Infantry School of Fire, Camp Perry, Ohio, and Fourteenth Replacement Battalion, Camp Pike, Ark., and was discharged on December 20, 1918; member of the Little Rock School Board 1929–1933; member of the State house of representatives in 1933; elected as a Democrat to the Seventy-third Congress to fill the vacancy caused by the resignation of Heartsill Ragon; reelected to the Seventy-fourth and to the three succeeding Congresses and served from December 19, 1933, to January 3, 1943; was not a candidate for renomination in 1942, but was an unsuccessful candidate for nomination for United States Senator; engaged in the practice of law; director of the Division of Flood Control Water and Soil Conservation of the Arkansas Resources and Development Commission 1945–1953; is a resident of Little Rock, Ark.

TERRY, Nathaniel, a Representative from Connecticut; born in Enfield, Conn., January 30, 1768; attended the common schools, Dartmouth College, and was graduated from Yale College in 1786; studied law; was admitted to the bar in 1790 and commenced practice in Enfield; moved to Hartford in 1796; commander of the Governor's Foot Guard of Hartford 1802–1813; judge of the Hartford County Court from 1807 to 1809, when he resigned; member of the State house of representatives 1804–1815; elected to the Fifteenth Congress (March

4, 1817–March 3, 1819); memder of the State constitutional convention in 1818; president of the Hartford Fire Insurance Co. 1810–1835; president of the Hartford Bank 1819–1828; mayor of Hartford 1824–1831; served as a general in the State militia; died in New Haven, Conn., June 14, 1844; interment in Old North (Spring Grove) Cemetery, Hartford, Conn.

TERRY, William, a Representative from Virginia; born in Amherst County, Va., August 14, 1824; attended an "old field school" in Amherst County; was graduated from the University of Virginia at Charlottesville in 1848; taught school; studied law; was admitted to the bar in 1851 and commenced practice in Wytheville, Va.; engaged in newspaper work; served in the Confederate Army as a lieutenant in the Fourth Regiment, Virginia Infantry; promoted to major in 1862, colonel in February 1864, and commissioned brigadier general May 20, 1864; was the last commander of the famous "Stonewall Jackson" Brigade of the Confederate Army; resumed the practice of law in Wytheville; elected as a Conservative to the Forty-second Congress (March 4, 1871–March 3, 1873); unsuccessful candidate for renomination in 1872; elected to the Forty-fourth Congress (March 4, 1875–March 3, 1877); unsuccessful candidate for renomination in 1876; delegate to the Democratic National Convention in 1880 which nominated Gen. Winfield S. Hancock for President; resumed the practice of law; drowned while trying to ford Reed Creek, near Wytheville, Va., September 5, 1888; interment in East End Cemetery, Wytheville, Va.

TERRY, William Leake (father of David Dickson Terry), a Representative from Arkansas; born near Wadesboro, Anson County, N. C., September 27, 1850; moved with his parents to Tippah County, Miss., in 1857 and to Pulaski County, Ark., in 1861; attended Bingham's Military Academy, North Carolina, and was graduated from Trinity College, North Carolina, in June 1872; studied law; was admitted to the bar in November 1873 and practiced; member of the city council 1877–1879; member of the State senate in 1878 and 1879, serving as president of the senate in the session of 1879; city attorney of Little Rock, Ark., 1879–1885; unsuccessful candidate for election in 1886 to the Fiftieth Congress; elected as a Democrat to the Fifty-second and to the four succeeding Congresses (March 4, 1891–March 3, 1901); unsuccessful candidate for renomination in 1900; resumed the practice of law in Little Rock, Ark., and died there November 4, 1917; interment in Calvary Cemetery.

TEST, John, a Representative from Indiana; born in Salem, N. J., November 12, 1771; moved with his parents to Philadelphia, Pa., and attended the common schools; moved to Fayette County, Pa., and operated Fayette Chance Furnace for several years; moved to Cincinnati, Ohio, and then to Brookville, Franklin County, Ind., and operated a grist mill; studied law; was admitted to the bar and began practice in Brookville, Ind.; held several local offices; judge of the third district circuit 1816–1819; elected as a Clay Democrat to the Eighteenth and Nineteenth Congresses (March 4, 1823–March 3, 1827); unsuccessful candidate for reelection in 1826 to the Twentieth Congress; elected as a Whig to the Twenty-first Congress (March 4, 1829–March 3, 1831); presiding judge of the Indiana circuit court; moved to Mobile, Ala., and resumed the practice of law; died near Cambridge City, Wayne County, Ind., October 9, 1849; interment in Cambridge City, Ind.

TEWES, Donald Edgar, a Representative from Wisconsin; born in Merrill, Lincoln County, Wis., August 4, 1916; was graduated from Trinity Lutheran School, Merrill High School, Valparaiso (Ind.) University in 1938, and from University of Wisconsin Law School in 1940; was admitted to the bar and commenced the practice of law in Merrill, Wis.; during World War II entered the service as a private in 1942; became combat intelligence officer with the Fourteenth United States Air Force's Flying Tigers with twenty-five combat missions in the China-Burma-India Theater and was discharged as a major in 1946; awarded the Air Medal; president of Tewes Plastics Corp., Waukesha, Wis., 1947–; elected as a Republican to the Eighty-fifth Congress (January 3, 1957–January 3, 1959); unsuccessful candidate for reelection in 1958 to the Eighty-sixth Congress; is a resident of Waukesha, Wis.

THACHER, George, a Delegate and a Representative from Massachusetts; born in Yarmouth, in the county of Barnstable, Mass., April 12, 1754; prepared for college by a private instructor; was graduated from Harvard College in 1776; studied law; was admitted to the bar in 1778 and commenced practice in York, Maine; moved to Biddeford, Maine, in 1782; Member of the Continental Congress in 1787; elected as a Federalist to the First and to the five succeeding Congresses (March 4, 1789–March 3, 1801); did not seek renomination in 1800, having accepted a judicial appointment; district judge in Maine 1792–1800; associate judge of the supreme court of Massachusetts 1800–1820; delegate in 1819 to the constitutional convention of Maine, which until 1820 was a district of Massachusetts; again a judge of the supreme court of Maine 1820–1824; died in Biddeford, Maine, April 6, 1824; interment in Woodlawn Cemetery.

THACHER, Thomas Chandler, a Representative from Massachusetts; born in Yarmouth Port, Mass., July 20, 1858; attended the public schools; was graduated from Adams Academy, Quincy, Mass., in 1878 and from Harvard University in 1882; became engaged in the wool business at Boston in 1882; president of the Barnstable County Agricultural Society; president of the Cape Cod Pilgrim Memorial Association; chairman of the Yarmouth Port Planning Board; served as chairman of the Provincetown Tercentenary Commission in 1920; elected as a Democrat to the Sixty-third Congress (March 4, 1913–March 3, 1915); unsuccessful candidate for reelection in 1914; writer on business topics and also engaged in his former business pursuits; died in Boston, Mass., April 11, 1945; interment in Woodside Cemetery, Yarmouth Port, Mass.

THATCHER, Maurice Hudson, a Representative from Kentucky; born in Chicago, Cook County, Ill., August 15, 1870; moved to Butler County, Ky., and settled near Morgantown in 1874; attended public and private schools; engaged in agricultural pursuits; was employed in a newspaper office and in various county offices; elected clerk of the circuit court of Butler County in 1892 and served from January 1, 1893, until his resignation in 1896; studied law in Frankfort, Ky.; was admitted to the bar in 1898 and commenced practice in Frankfort; assistant attorney general of Kentucky 1898–1900; moved to Louisville, Ky., in 1900; assistant United States attorney for the western district of Kentucky 1901–1906; State examiner and inspector for Kentucky 1908–1910; member of the Isthmian Canal Commission and civil governor of the Canal Zone 1910–1913; resumed the practice of law in Louisville, Ky.; member of the board of public safety 1917–1919 and department counsel 1919–1923 for the city of Louisville; elected as a Republican to the Sixty-eighth and to the four succeeding Congresses (March 4, 1923–March 3, 1933); in 1932 was nominated for the House of Representatives, but subsequently relinquished that nomination to become his party's candidate for the United States Senate but was unsuccessful; resumed the practice of law in Washington, D. C.; vice president and general counsel of the Gorgas Memorial Institute of Tropical and Preventative Medicine, Inc., Washington, D. C.; is a resident of Louisville, Ky.

THATCHER, Samuel, a Representative from Massachusetts; born in Cambridge, Mass., July 1, 1776; was graduated from Harvard University in 1793; studied law; was admitted to the bar in 1797 and commenced practice in New Gloucester, Maine (then a district of Massachusetts); moved to Warren in 1800; member of the Massachusetts House of Representatives 1801–1811; was elected as a Democrat to the Seventh Congress to fill the vacancy caused by the resignation of Silas Lee; reelected to the Eighth Congress and served from December 6, 1802, to March 3, 1805; was an unsuccessful candidate for reelection in 1804 to the Ninth Congress; sheriff of Lincoln County, Maine, 1814–1821; member of the Maine House of Representatives in 1824; moved to Bangor, Maine, in 1860, and died there July 18, 1872; interment in Mount Hope Cemetery.

THAYER, Andrew Jackson, a Representative from Oregon; born in Lima, Livingston County, N. Y., November 27, 1818; attended the common schools; studied law; was admitted to the bar in 1849 and commenced practice in Lima; crossed the continent in 1853 and settled on a farm near Corvallis, Benton County, Oreg.; resumed the practice of law and also engaged in agricultural pursuits; appointed by President Buchanan United States attorney for the district of Oregon on March 2, 1859, and resigned after six months' service, having become a candidate for Congress; presented credentials as a Democratic Member-elect to the Thirty-seventh Congress and served from March 4 to July 30, 1861, when he was succeeded by George K. Shiel, who contested his election; district attorney for the second district of Oregon 1862–1864; served as circuit judge of the second judicial district of Oregon from 1870 until his death in Corvallis, Oreg., April 28, 1873; interment in Crystal Lake Cemetery.

THAYER, Eli (father of John Alden Thayer), a Representative from Massachusetts; born in Mendon, Worcester County, Mass., June 11, 1819; attended the common schools, the academies in Bellingham and Amherst, Mass., and the Worcester Manual Labor School; taught school in Douglas, Mass., in 1835 and 1836 and in Hopkington, R. I., in 1842; had charge of the boys' high school in Providence, R. I., in 1844; was graduated from Brown University at Providence in 1845 and was an instructor in Worcester Academy 1845–1848; studied law and was admitted to the bar, but did not practice; founded the Oread Collegiate Institute, a school for young women, in 1848; member of the Worcester School Board in 1852; alderman of Worcester in 1852 and 1853; member of the State house of representatives in 1853 and 1854; while in the legislature secured a charter, and originated and organized the New England Emigrant Aid Co., which had for its purpose the sending out of an advance colony of antislavery settlers to Kansas, which resulted in that Territory becoming an antislave State; elected as a Republican to the Thirty-fifth and Thirty-sixth Congresses (March 4, 1857–March 3, 1861); unsuccessful candidate for reelection in 1860 to the Thirty-seventh Congress; delegate accredited from Oregon to the Republican National Convention at Chicago in 1860; engaged in railroad and other business pursuits; unsuccessful candidate for election in 1872 to the Forty-third Congress; died in Worcester, Mass., April 15, 1899; interment in Hope Cemetery.

THAYER, Harry Irving, a Representative from Massachusetts; born in Pembroke, Plymouth County, Mass., September 10, 1869; attended the public schools of Hanover, Mass.; engaged in the leather business; organizer and president of the Thayer-Ross Co.; president of the New England Shoe and Leather Association 1916–1921; was president of the Tanners' Council of the United States in 1920 and 1921; during the First World War was chairman of the Wakefield Chapter of the American Red Cross and served until 1924, when he resigned; also served as chairman of the Liberty bond sales committee and war chest; was a delegate to the Republican National Convention at Cleveland in 1924; elected as a Republican to the Sixty-ninth Congress and served from March 4, 1925, until his death in Wakefield, Middlesex County, Mass., March 10, 1926; interment in Lakeside Cemetery.

THAYER, John Alden (son of Eli Thayer), a Representative from Massachusetts; born in Worcester, Mass., December 22, 1857; attended the grade and high schools of Worcester; was graduated from Harvard University in 1879; taught school; studied law at Columbia College of Law at New York City; was admitted to the bar in 1889 and commenced practice in Worcester; clerk of the central district court of Worcester 1892–1897; elected as a Democrat to the Sixty-second Congress (March 4, 1911–March 3, 1913); unsuccessful candidate for reelection in 1912 to the Sixty-third Congress; delegate to the Democratic National Convention at Baltimore in 1912; appointed postmaster of Worcester, Mass., by President Wilson in February 1915, which position he held until his death, which occurred in Worcester, Mass., July 31, 1917; interment in Hope Cemetery.

THAYER, John Milton (uncle of Arthur Laban Bates), a Senator from Nebraska; born in Bellingham, Mass., January 24, 1820; was graduated from Brown University, Providence, R. I., in 1847; moved to Nebraska in 1854 and engaged in agricultural pursuits; studied law; was admitted to the bar in 1855 and commenced practice in Omaha, Nebr.; brigadier general and major general of the Territorial forces operating against the Pawnee Indians 1855–1861; captured the Pawnees and placed them on reservations in 1859; member of the Territorial State senate in 1860; delegate to the State constitutional convention in 1860; during the Civil War served in the Union Army; commissioned colonel of the First Regiment, Nebraska Volunteer Infantry, July 21, 1861; promoted to brigadier general of Volunteers October 4, 1862; appointment expired March 4, 1863; brigadier general of Volunteers March 13, 1863; brevetted major general of Volunteers March 13, 1865, for "gallant and meritorious services during the war"; resigned July 19, 1865; returned to Omaha, Nebr.; member of the State constitutional convention in 1866; upon the admission of Nebraska as a State into the Union was elected as a Republican to the United States Senate and served from March 1, 1867, to March 3, 1871; unsuccessful candidate for reelection in 1871; appointed by President Grant as Governor of the Territory of Wyoming and served from 1875 to 1879; department commander of the Grand Army of the Republic of Nebraska in 1886; Governor of Nebraska 1887–1891; resumed the practice of law in Lincoln, Nebr., and died there March 19, 1906; interment in Wyuka Cemetery.

THAYER, John Randolph, a Representative from Massachusetts; born in Douglas, Worcester County, Mass., March 9, 1845; attended the common schools and Nichols Academy in Dudley, Worcester County, and was graduated from Yale College in 1869; studied law; was admitted to the bar in 1871 and commenced practice in Worcester, Mass.; served in the city council 1874–1876 and as alderman 1878–1880; was one of the trustees of Nichols Academy for fifteen years; was an unsuccessful candidate for district attorney in 1876; member of the State house of representatives in 1880 and 1881; unsuccessful candidate for mayor of Worcester in 1886; served in the State senate in 1890 and 1891; unsuccessful candidate for election in 1892 to the Fifty-third Congress; elected as a Democrat to the Fifty-sixth, Fifty-seventh, and Fifty-eighth Congresses (March

4, 1899–March 3, 1905); was not a candidate for renomination in 1904; resumed the practice of law in Worcester, Mass., where he died December 19, 1916; interment in the Rural Cemetery.

THAYER, Martin Russell, a Representative from Pennsylvania; born in Dinwiddie County, near the city limits of Petersburg, Va., January 27, 1819; attended the Mount Pleasant Classical Institute in Amherst, Mass., and Amherst College; moved with his father to Philadelphia, Pa., in 1837; was graduated from the University of Pennsylvania at Philadelphia in 1840; studied law; was admitted to the bar in 1842 and commenced practice in Philadelphia; commissioner to revise the revenue laws of Pennsylvania in 1862; elected as a Republican to the Thirty-eighth and Thirty-ninth Congresses (March 4, 1863–March 3, 1867); declined to be a candidate for renomination in 1866; resumed the practice of law; judge of the district court of Philadelphia 1867–1874; president judge of the court of common pleas of Philadelphia from 1874 until his resignation in 1896; elected by the judges of the common pleas court prothonotary of Philadelphia in 1896; also engaged in literary pursuits; died in Philadelphia, Pa., October 14, 1906; interment in St. James the Less Church Cemetery.

THEAKER, Thomas Clarke, a Representative from Ohio; born in York County, Pa., February 1, 1812; attended the common schools; moved to Bridgeport, Belmont County, Ohio, in 1830; became a machinist and wheelwright; was elected as a Republican to the Thirty-sixth Congress (March 4, 1859–March 3, 1861); was an unsuccessful candidate for reelection in 1860 to the Thirty-seventh Congress; member of the board of commissioners to investigate the Patent Office in 1864, and later was appointed a member of the board of examiners in chief; served as Commissioner of Patents from August 17, 1865, to January 20, 1868; engaged in the practice of patent law in Washington, D. C., until his death in Oakland, Md., July 16, 1883; interment in Weeks Cemetery, near Bridgeport, Ohio.

THIBODEAUX, Bannon Goforth, a Representative from Louisiana; born on St. Bridget plantation, near Thibodeaux, Terrebonne Parish, La., December 22, 1812; attended the country schools; studied law in Hagerstown, Md.; was admitted to the bar and commenced practice in Lafourche and Terrebonne Parishes, La.; member of the State constitutional conventions in 1845 and 1852; held several local offices; elected to the Twenty-ninth and Thirtieth Congresses (March 4, 1845–March 3, 1849); resumed the practice of law in Terrebonne and Lafourche Parishes, La.; sugar planter and manufacturer; died in Terrebonne Parish, La., March 5, 1866; interment in the Halfway Cemetery, near Houma, La.

THILL, Lewis Dominic, a Representative from Wisconsin; born in Milwaukee, Wis., October 18, 1903; attended the public and parochial schools and was graduated from Marquette University, Milwaukee, Wis., in 1926; attended Harvard Graduate School, Cambridge, Mass., and Northwestern University, Evanston, Ill.; was graduated from the law department of the University of Wisconsin at Madison in 1931; was admitted to the bar in 1932 and commenced practice in Milwaukee, Wis.; elected as a Republican to the Seventy-sixth and Seventy-seventh Congresses (January 3, 1939–January 3, 1943); unsuccessful candidate for reelection in 1942 to the Seventy-eighth Congress and in 1944 to the Seventy-ninth Congress; lawyer; also real-estate and investment broker; is a resident of Elm Grove, Wis.

THISTLEWOOD, Napoleon Bonaparte, a Representative from Illinois; born near Harrington, Kent County, Del., March 30, 1837; attended the public schools; moved to Mason, Ill., in 1858 and engaged in mercantile pursuits; during the Civil War enlisted in the Union Army in 1862; commissioned by Gov. Richard Yates September 24, 1864, as captain of Company C, Ninety-eighth Regiment, Illinois Volunteer Infantry; served in the Army of the Cumberland, in Wilder's brigade, and with Wilson's Cavalry Corps, and was wounded at Selma, Ala., April 2, 1865; returned to Mason and resumed business pursuits; moved to Cairo, Ill., and engaged in the commission business; mayor of Cairo, Ill., 1879–1883 and again 1897–1901; department commander of the Grand Army of the Republic for Illinois in 1901; elected as a Republican to the Sixtieth Congress to fill the vacancy caused by the death of George W. Smith; reelected to the Sixty-first and Sixty-second Congresses and served from February 15, 1908, to March 3, 1913; unsuccessful candidate for reelection in 1912 to the Sixty-third Congress; retired from public and business life, and was a resident of Cairo, Ill., until his death in that city September 15, 1915; interment in Beech Grove Cemetery, Mounds, Ill.

THOM, William Richard, a Representative from Ohio; born in Canton, Stark County, Ohio, July 7, 1885; attended the public and high schools; engaged as a newspaper reporter 1905–1909; attended Western Reserve University, Cleveland, Ohio, 1909–1911; served as private secretary to Congressman John J. Whitacre 1911–1913; member of the United States House of Representatives Press Galleries in 1915 and 1916; was graduated from the law department of Georgetown University, Washington, D. C., in 1916; was admitted to the bar in 1917 and commenced practice in Canton, Ohio; member of the park commission of Canton 1920–1932; unsuccessful candidate for the Democratic nomination to Congress in 1920; elected as a Democrat to the Seventy-third, Seventy-fourth, and Seventy-fifth Congresses (March 4, 1933–January 3, 1939); unsuccessful candidate for reelection in 1938 to the Seventy-sixth Congress; resumed the practice of law; elected to the Seventy-seventh Congress (January 3, 1941–January 3, 1943); unsuccessful candidate for reelection in 1942 to the Seventy-eighth Congress; elected to the Seventy-ninth Congress (January 3, 1945–January 3, 1947); unsuccessful candidate for reelection in 1946 to the Eightieth Congress; resumed the practice of law; delegate to the Democratic National Convention in 1956; died in Canton, Ohio, August 28, 1960; interment in West Lawn Cemetery.

THOMAS, Albert, a Representative from Texas; born in Nacogdoches, Tex., April 12, 1898; attended the public schools; during the First World War served as a second lieutenant in the United States Army; was graduated from Rice Institute, Houston, Tex., in 1920 and from the law department of the University of Texas at Austin in 1926; was admitted to the bar in 1927 and began practice in Nacogdoches, Tex.; county attorney of Nacogdoches County, Tex., 1927–1930; assistant United States district attorney for the southern district of Texas 1930–1936; elected as a Democrat to the Seventy-fifth and to the eleven succeeding Congresses (January 3, 1937–January 3, 1961). *Reelected to the Eighty-seventh Congress.*

THOMAS, Benjamin Franklin, a Representative from Massachusetts; born in Boston, Mass., February 12, 1813; moved with his parents to Worcester in 1819; attended Lancaster Academy, and was graduated from Brown University, Providence, R. I., in 1830; studied law in Cambridge, Mass.; was admitted to the bar in 1833 and commenced practice in Worcester, Mass.; held several local offices; member of the State house of representatives in 1842; commissioner of bankruptcy in 1842; judge of probate 1844–1848; presidential elector on the Whig ticket of Taylor and Fillmore in 1848; judge of the Massachusetts Supreme Court from 1853 to 1859, when he resigned; continued the practice of law in

Boston, Mass.; elected as a Conservative Unionist to the Thirty-seventh Congress to fill the vacancy caused by the resignation of Charles F. Adams and served from June 11, 1861, to March 3, 1863; declined a renomination; again engaged in the practice of law; nominated by Governor Bullock for chief justice of the supreme court of Massachusetts in 1868, but the nomination was not confirmed by the council; died at his home in Beverly Farms, Mass., September 27, 1878; interment in Forrest Hill Cemetery, Boston, Mass.

THOMAS, Charles Randolph, a Representative from North Carolina; born in Beaufort, Carteret County, N. C., February 7, 1827; attended a private school in Hillsboro, N. C., and was graduated from the University of North Carolina at Chapel Hill in 1849; studied law; was admitted to the bar in 1850 and commenced practice in Beaufort, N. C.; moved to New Bern, N. C., and continued the practice of law; member of the State constitutional convention in 1861; secretary of state of North Carolina in 1864; appointed by the Governor president of the Atlantic & North Carolina Railroad in 1867; judge of the superior court 1868–1870; elected as a Republican to the Forty-second and Forty-third Congresses (March 4, 1871–March 3, 1875); unsuccessful candidate for renomination in 1874; resumed the practice of law in New Bern, N. C., and died there February 18, 1891; interment in Cedar Grove Cemetery.

THOMAS, Charles Randolph (son of the preceding), a Representative from North Carolina; born in Beaufort, Carteret County, N. C., August 21, 1861; attended New Bern (N. C.) Academy and Emerson Institute, Washington, D. C.; was graduated from the University of North Carolina at Chapel Hill in 1881; studied law with his father and at the law school of Judges R. P. Dick and John H. Dillard at Greensboro, N. C.; was admitted to the bar in 1882 and commenced practice in New Bern, N. C.; member of the State house of representatives in 1887; attorney for Craven County 1890–1896; elected by the State legislature a trustee of the University of North Carolina in 1893; member of the Democratic State executive committee; presidential elector on the Democratic ticket of Bryan and Sewall in 1896; elected as a Democrat to the Fifty-sixth and to the five succeeding Congresses (March 4, 1899–March 3, 1911); declined to be a candidate for renomination in 1910; resumed the practice of law in New Bern, N. C.; delegate to the Democratic National Convention at New York City in 1924; moved on account of his wife's health to Waynesville, Haywood County, N. C., in 1925 and engaged in the active practice of his profession; appointed in September 1926 as emergency judge of the superior court by the Governor of North Carolina; resumed the practice of law in Waynesville, N. C.; died while a patient in a Norfolk, Va., hospital March 8, 1931; interment in Cedar Grove Cemetery, New Bern, N. C.

THOMAS, Charles Spalding, a Senator from Colorado; born in Darien, McIntosh County, Ga., December 6, 1849; attended private schools in Georgia and Connecticut, and was graduated from the law department of the University of Michigan at Ann Arbor in 1871; was admitted to the bar in April 1871 and commenced practice in Denver, Colo.; city attorney in 1875 and 1876; delegate to the Democratic National Conventions in 1880, 1896, 1900, 1904, and 1908; member of the Democratic National Committee 1884–1896; unsuccessful candidate for election to the United States Senate in 1888; Governor of Colorado 1899–1901; temporary chairman of the Democratic National Convention at Kansas City, Mo., in 1900; elected as a Democrat to the United States Senate in 1913 to fill the vacancy caused by the death of Charles J. Hughes, Jr.; reelected in 1914, and served from January 15, 1913, to March 3, 1921; unsuccessful independ-

ent candidate on the Nationalist ticket for reelection in 1920; special assistant to the Attorney General of the United States in 1922; resumed the practice of law; died in Denver, Colo., June 24, 1934; the remains were cremated and the ashes interred in Fairmount Cemetery.

THOMAS, Christopher Yancy, a Representative from Virginia; born in Pittsylvania County, Va., March 24, 1818; attended the common schools, and was graduated from a private academy in 1838; studied law; was admitted to the bar in 1844 and commenced practice in Martinsville, Henry County, Va.; served in the State senate 1860–1864; member of the commission to settle the boundary line between Virginia and North Carolina; treasurer of Henry County; prosecuting attorney for Henry County; member of the State constitutional convention in 1868; elected to the State house of delegates in 1869; successfully contested as a Republican the election of Alexander M. Davis to the Forty-third Congress and served from March 5, 1874, to March 3, 1875; unsuccessful candidate for reelection in 1874 to the Forty-fourth Congress; resumed the practice of law; died in Martinsville, Va., February 11, 1879; interment in the family cemetery at Leatherwood, Henry County, Va.

THOMAS, David, a Representative from New York; born in Pelham, Mass., June 11, 1762; completed preparatory studies; served as a volunteer in 1777; joined the Fifth Massachusetts Regiment as a corporal in 1781, and later became sergeant in the Third Massachusetts Regiment; moved to Salem, Washington County, N. Y., in 1784, where he conducted a tavern for several years; commissioned captain in the State militia in 1786; rose to the rank of major general of the northern division of the Militia of New York in 1805; engaged in mercantile pursuits; member of the State assembly 1794 and 1798–1800; supervisor of the town of Salem 1797–1800; justice of the peace 1798–1801, 1804, and 1811; elected as a Democrat to the Seventh and to the three succeeding Congresses and served from March 4, 1801, to May 1, 1808, when he resigned; served as treasurer of the State of New York from February 5, 1808, to February 8, 1810, and again from February 18, 1812, to February 10, 1813; moved to Providence, R. I., where he died November 11, 1831; interment in Evergreen Cemetery, Salem, N. Y.

THOMAS, Elbert Duncan, a Senator from Utah; born in Salt Lake City, Utah, June 17, 1883; attended the public schools; was graduated from the University of Utah at Salt Lake City in 1906; served as a missionary of Latter Day Saints Church in Japan 1907–1912; student traveler in Asia and Europe in 1912 and 1913; instructor of Latin and Greek at the University of Utah 1914–1916 and secretary of board of regents 1917–1922; served as major, inspector general's department, Utah National Guard, and United States Reserves, 1917–1926; professor of political science at the University of Utah 1924–1933; member of Carnegie International Conference of American Professors in 1926; delegate to the Interparliamentary Union at Budapest in 1936 and at Paris in 1937; delegate to the International Labor Organization Conference at Philadelphia in 1944, at Paris in 1945, at Montreal in 1946, at Geneva in 1947, and at San Francisco in 1948; member of the Thomas Jefferson Memorial Commission since 1933, serving as chairman since 1944; member of the Board of Columbia Institution for the Deaf 1939–1947; delegate to the Democratic National Convention at Philadelphia in 1948; author; elected as a Democrat to the United States Senate in 1932; reelected in 1938 and again in 1944 and served from March 4, 1933, to January 3, 1951; unsuccessful candidate for reelection in 1950; appointed high commissioner of United

States trust territories of the Pacific and served from January 8, 1951, until his death in Honolulu, Hawaii, February 11, 1953; interment in City Cemetery, Salt Lake City, Utah.

THOMAS, Francis, a Representative from Maryland; born in that part of Frederick County, Md., close to South Mountain, known as Merryland tract, February 3, 1799; attended St. John's College, Annapolis, Md.; studied law; was admitted to the bar in 1820 and commenced practice in Frankville, Md.; member of the State house of delegates in 1822, 1827, and 1829, and served the last year as speaker; elected as a Democrat to the Twenty-second and to the four succeeding Congresses (March 4, 1831–March 3, 1841); president of the Chesapeake & Ohio Canal Co. in 1839 and 1840; Governor of Maryland 1841–1844; was an unsuccessful candidate for reelection as Governor in 1844; member of the Maryland State Constitutional Convention in 1850; elected as a Union Republican to the Thirty-seventh and to the three succeeding Congresses (March 4, 1861–March 3, 1869); served as a delegate to the Loyalist Convention at Philadelphia in 1866; collector of internal revenue 1870–1872; United States Minister to Peru from March 25, 1872, to July 9, 1875; retired from public and professional life and devoted his time to agricultural pursuits; was killed by a locomotive while walking on the railroad tracks near Frankville, Md., January 22, 1876; interment in a vault in Rose Hill Cemetery, Cumberland, Md.

THOMAS, George Morgan, a Representative from Kentucky; born near Poplar Flat, Lewis County, Ky., November 23, 1828; educated in the common schools; taught school two years; was school commissioner from 1850 to 1859; studied law; was admitted to the bar in 1851 and practiced; elected prosecuting attorney of Lewis County in 1854 and served for four years; a member of the State house of representatives 1859–1863; Commonwealth attorney for the tenth judicial district 1862–1868; Republican presidential elector in 1864, 1868, and 1872; county judge in 1868; unsuccessful Republican candidate for Lieutenant Governor of Kentucky in 1871; again a member of the State house of representatives in 1872 and 1873; circuit judge of the fourteenth judicial district 1874–1880; United States district attorney 1881–1885; elected as a Republican to the Fiftieth Congress (March 4, 1887–March 3, 1889); appointed Solicitor of Internal Revenue by President McKinley on May 20, 1897, and served until May 31, 1901; retired from public life; died in Vanceburg, Lewis County, Ky., January 7, 1914; interment in Greenlawn Cemetery.

THOMAS, Henry Franklin, a Representative from Michigan; born in Tompkins, Jackson County, Mich., December 17, 1843; attended the common schools and Albion (Mich.) College in 1859; enlisted in 1862 during the Civil War as a private in the Seventh Regiment, Michigan Volunteer Cavalry; was promoted to first sergeant of Company D, and in July 1864 to second lieutenant; renewed his studies in the Ypsilanti Normal School; was graduated from the medical department of Michigan University at Ann Arbor in 1868 and commenced practice in Constantine, St. Joseph County, Mich.; moved to Allegan, Mich., in 1870; member of the State house of representatives in 1873 and 1874; served in the State senate in 1875 and 1876; delegate to the Republican National Convention at Chicago in 1884; elected as a Republican to the Fifty-third and Fifty-fourth Congresses (March 4, 1893–March 3, 1897); was an unsuccessful candidate for renomination in 1896; surgeon in the Michigan Soldiers' Home in 1907 and 1908; member of the Michigan pardon board in 1909 and 1910; retired from the practice of medicine; died in Allegan, Mich., April 16, 1912; interment in Oak Hill Cemetery, Ann Arbor, Mich.

THOMAS, Isaac, a Representative from Tennessee; born in Sevierville, Tenn., November 4, 1784; after the death of his parents he moved to Winchester, Tenn., in 1800; self-educated; studied law; was admitted to the bar in 1808 and practiced in Winchester; elected as a Democrat to the Fourteenth Congress (March 4, 1815–March 3, 1817); moved to Alexandria, Rapides Parish, La., in 1819; resumed the practice of law; purchased vast tracts of land adjoining Alexandria and became one of the largest landowners and slaveholders in Louisiana; was the first man to introduce the cultivation of sugar cane in central Louisiana; also engaged in mercantile pursuits and in the operation of sawmills and steamboats; served as brigadier general of the Louisiana Militia; served in the State senate 1823–1827; moved to California in 1849; returned to Alexandria, La., where he died on February 2, 1859; interment in the Flint lot, in Rapides Cemetery, Pineville, La.

THOMAS, James Houston, a Representative from Tennessee; born in Iredell County, N. C., September 22, 1808; attended the rural schools; was graduated from Jackson College, Columbia, Tenn., in 1830; studied law; was admitted to the bar in 1831 and commenced practice in Columbia, Tenn.; attorney general of Tennessee 1836–1842; elected as a Democrat to the Thirtieth and Thirty-first Congresses (March 4, 1847–March 3, 1851); unsuccessful candidate for reelection in 1850 to the Thirty-second Congress; elected to the Thirty-sixth Congress (March 4, 1859–March 3, 1861); resumed the practice of law in Columbia, Tenn.; died near Fayetteville, Lincoln County, Tenn., on August 4, 1876; interment in St. John's Cemetery, Ashwood, Maury County, Tenn.

THOMAS, Jesse Burgess, a Delegate from Indiana Territory and a Senator from Illinois; born in Elizabethtown (now Hagerstown), Md., in 1777; moved with his parents to Bracken County, Ky., in 1779; attended the common schools; clerk of Bracken County Court 1799–1803; studied law in Mason County, Ky.; was admitted to the bar in 1803 and commenced practice in Lawrenceburg, Ind.; appointed deputy attorney general of Indiana Territory August 23, 1805; member of the Territorial house of representatives 1805–1808, and served as speaker of the house from September 26, 1805, to October 24, 1808; elected as a Delegate from Indiana Territory to the Tenth Congress to fill the vacancy caused by the resignation of Benjamin Parke and served from October 22, 1808, to March 3, 1809; moved to Kaskaskia in 1809, then to Cahokia, and later to Edwardsville, Ill.; upon the organization of Illinois Territory was appointed judge of the United States court for the northwestern judicial district and served from 1809 to 1818; delegate to the State constitutional convention in 1818, and served as president of that body; upon the admission of Illinois as a State into the Union was elected as a Whig to the United States Senate; reelected in 1823, and served from December 3, 1818, to March 3, 1829; declined to be a candidate for reelection in 1829; moved to Mount Vernon, Ohio, in 1829; delegate to the Whig National Convention at Harrisburg, Pa., in 1839; died in Mount Vernon, Ohio, May 4, 1853; interment in Mound View Cemetery.

THOMAS, John, a Senator from Idaho; born on a farm in Phillips County, Kans., January 4, 1874; attended the rural schools, the high school in Phillipsburg, Kans., and the Central Normal College at Great Bend, Kans.; taught school, serving as superintendent of schools of Phillips County, Kans., 1898–1903; served as register of land office at Colby, Kans., 1906–1909; moved to Gooding, Idaho, in 1909; engaged in banking and livestock business; mayor of Gooding, 1917–1919; chairman of the Republican State central committee of Idaho 1922–1924; member of the Republican National Committee 1925–1933;

appointed and subsequently elected as a Republican to the United States Senate to fill the vacancy caused by the death of Frank R. Gooding and served from June 30, 1928, to March 3, 1933; unsuccessful candidate for reelection in 1932; resumed former business pursuits; again appointed and subsequently elected to the United States Senate to fill the vacancy caused by the death of William E. Borah; reelected in 1942, and served from January 27, 1940, until his death in Washington, D. C., November 10, 1945; interment in Elmwood Cemetery, Gooding, Idaho.

THOMAS, John Chew, a Representative from Maryland; born in Perryville, Cecil County, Md., October 15, 1764; attended private schools; was graduated from the University of Pennsylvania at Philadelphia in 1783; moved to "Fairland," in Anne Arundel County, Md., about 1789; studied law; and was admitted to the bar in Philadelphia, Pa., December 15, 1787, but did not engage in extensive practice; elected as a Federalist to the Sixth Congress (March 4, 1799–March 3, 1801); declined to be a candidate for reelection; moved to Pennsylvania; died near Leiperville, Pa., May 10, 1836; interment in the Friends Cemetery, near Chester, Pa.

THOMAS, John Lewis, Jr., a Representative from Maryland; born in Baltimore, Md., May 20, 1835; completed preparatory studies; studied law; was admitted to the bar in 1856 and commenced practice in Cumberland, Md.; city counselor of Cumberland in 1856 and 1857; moved to Baltimore, Md., in 1857 and continued the practice of law; city solicitor of Baltimore 1860–1862; delegate to the State constitutional convention in 1863; State's attorney 1863–1865; elected as a Republican to the Thirty-ninth Congress to fill the vacancy caused by the resignation of Edwin H. Webster and served from December 4, 1865, to March 3, 1867; was an unsuccessful Republican candidate for reelection in 1866 to the Fortieth Congress; collector of the port of Baltimore, Md., from 1869 to 1873, and from 1877 to 1882; died in Baltimore, Md., on October 15, 1893; interment in Greenmount Cemetery.

THOMAS, John Parnell, a Representative from New Jersey; born in Jersey City, Hudson County, N. J., January 16, 1895; attended the public schools of Allendale, N. J., the high school at Ridgewood, N. J., and the University of Pennsylvania at Philadelphia; during the First World War served overseas as a second lieutenant in Company B, Three Hundred and Sixth Infantry, and first lieutenant and captain in Headquarters, Regimental Staff of the Fiftieth Infantry, 1917–1919; engaged in investment securities pursuits 1920–1938 and in the insurance business in New York, N. Y., since 1938; member of the borough council of Allendale, N. J., in 1925; mayor of Allendale 1926–1930; member of State house of assembly 1935–1937; elected as a Republican to the Seventy-fifth and to the six succeeding Congresses and served from January 3, 1937, until his resignation January 2, 1950; editor and publisher of three weekly newspapers in Bergen County, N. J., 1951–1955; real-estate solicitor in 1955 and 1956; defeated for the Republican nomination for Congress in 1954; engaged in investment securities; resides in St. Petersburg, Fla.

THOMAS, John Robert, a Representative from Illinois; born in Mount Vernon, Jefferson County, Ill., October 11, 1846; attended the common schools and Hunter Collegiate Institute, Princeton, Ind.; served in the Union Army during the Civil War, and rose from the rank of private to that of captain of Company D, One Hundred and Twentieth Regiment, Indiana Volunteer Infantry; studied law; was admitted to the bar in 1869 and practiced; city attorney of Metropolis, Ill., 1869 and 1870; served as State's attorney 1871–1874; elected as a Republican to the Forty-sixth and to the four succeeding Congresses (March 4, 1879–March 3, 1889); was not a candidate for renomination in 1888; resumed the practice of law in Muskogee, Okla.; United States judge in the Indian Territory from June 30, 1897, to June 30, 1901; nominated for judge of the supreme court by the first Republican State convention of Oklahoma, but declined the nomination; member of the Oklahoma State Code Commission 1908–1910; resumed the practice of law in Muskogee, Okla.; died in McAlester, Okla., January 19, 1914; interment in Green Hill Cemetery, Muskogee, Okla.; reinterment in Arlington National Cemetery, Fort Myer, Va.

THOMAS, John William Elmer, a Representative and a Senator from Oklahoma; born on a farm near Greencastle, Putnam County, Ind., September 8, 1876; attended the common schools; was graduated from the Central Normal College (now Canterbury), Danville, Ind., in 1897 and from De Pauw University, Greencastle, Ind., in 1900; studied law; was admitted to the Indiana bar in 1897 and to the Oklahoma bar in 1900, and commenced practice in Oklahoma City, Okla.; moved to Lawton, Okla., in 1901 and continued the practice of law; member of the first State senate in 1907 and served until 1920, when he resigned; served as president pro tempore 1910–1913; delegate to all Democratic State conventions 1907–1950; delegate to all Democratic National Conventions since 1924; chairman of the Democratic State convention in 1910; unsuccessful candidate for election in 1920 to the Sixty-seventh Congress; elected as a Democrat to the Sixty-eighth and Sixty-ninth Congresses (March 4, 1923–March 3, 1927); was not a candidate for renomination in 1926, having become a candidate for United States Senator; elected as a Democrat to the United States Senate in 1926; reelected in 1932, 1938, and again in 1944, and served from March 4, 1927, to January 3, 1951; unsuccessful candidate for renomination in 1950; engaged in the practice of law in Washington, D. C., until August 1957; returned to Lawton, Okla., where he now resides.

THOMAS, Lot, a Representative from Iowa; born near Markleysburg, Fayette County, Pa., October 17, 1843; attended the public schools and Vermillion Institute, Hayesville, Ohio; moved to Iowa in 1868; taught school in New Virginia, Warren County; attended the law department of the University of Iowa at Iowa City, and was admitted to the bar in 1870; moved to Buena Vista County and settled at Storm Lake in 1870; practiced law; judge of the fourteenth judicial district of Iowa from 1885 until his resignation August 26, 1898, having become a candidate for Congress; elected as a Republican to the Fifty-sixth, Fifty-seventh, and Fifty-eighth Congresses (March 4, 1899–March 3, 1905); unsuccessful candidate for renomination in 1904; on account of illness did not engage in active business pursuits; died on a train near Yuma, Ariz., March 17, 1905, while en route to Los Angeles, Calif.; interment in Storm Lake Cemetery, Storm Lake, Iowa.

THOMAS, Ormsby Brunson, a Representative from Wisconsin; born in Sandgate, Bennington County, Vt., August 21, 1832; moved with his parents to Wisconsin in 1836; attended the common schools and Burr Seminary, Manchester, Vt.; was graduated from the National Law School, Poughkeepsie, N. Y., in 1856; was admitted to the bar in Albany, N. Y., in 1856 and commenced practice in Prairie du Chien, Wis.; district attorney of Crawford County, Wis.; served in the Union Army during the Civil War as captain of Company D, Thirty-first Regiment, Wisconsin Volunteer Infantry; member of the State assembly in 1862, 1865, and 1867; served in the State senate in 1880 and 1881; presidential elector on the Republican ticket of Grant and Wilson in 1872; elected as a Republican to the Forty-ninth,

Fiftieth, and Fifty-first Congresses (March 4, 1885–March 3, 1891); was an unsuccessful candidate for reelection in 1890 to the Fifty-second Congress; resumed the practice of law in Prairie du Chien, Wis., and died there October 24, 1904; interment in Evergreen Cemetery.

THOMAS, Philemon, a Representative from Louisiana; born in Orange County, Va., February 9, 1763; attended the common schools; served in the Revolutionary War; moved to Kentucky and settled in Mason County; delegate to the convention which framed the constitution of the State of Kentucky; member of the Kentucky House of Representatives 1796–1799; served in the State senate 1800–1803; moved to Louisiana in 1806 and settled on the banks of the lower Mississippi River; member of the Louisiana House of Representatives; leader of an uprising against the Spanish authorities, who exercised authority over what is now Mississippi and Louisiana, and commanded the forces which captured the Spanish fort at Baton Rouge in 1810; major general of Louisiana Militia in 1814 and 1815 and served in that capacity in the War of 1812; moved to Baton Rouge, La.; elected as a Democrat to the Twenty-second and Twenty-third Congresses (March 4, 1831–March 3, 1835); died in Baton Rouge, La., November 18, 1847; interment in the Old American Graveyard; reinterment in the National Cemetery at Baton Rouge, La.

THOMAS, Phillip Francis, a Representative from Maryland; born in Easton, Talbot County, Md., September 12, 1810; attended the academy in Easton, and was graduated from Dickinson College, Carlisle, Pa., in 1830; studied law; was admitted to the bar in 1831 and commenced practice in Easton, Md.; delegate to the State constitutional convention in 1836; member of the State house of delegates in 1838, 1843, and 1845; elected as a Democrat to the Twenty-sixth Congress (March 4, 1839–March 3, 1841); declined to be a candidate for renomination in 1840; resumed the practice of law; Governor of Maryland 1848–1851; judge of the land office court of eastern Maryland; Comptroller of the United States Treasury 1851–1853; collector of the port of Baltimore, Md., 1853–1860; declined the position of Treasurer of the United States tendered him by President Buchanan; United States Commissioner of Patents from February 16 to December 10, 1860; appointed Secretary of the Treasury in the Cabinet of President Buchanan and served from December 10, 1860, to January 11, 1861; again a member of the State house of delegates in 1863; presented credentials as a Senator-elect to the United States Senate for the term beginning March 4, 1867, but was not seated; elected as a Democrat to the Forty-fourth Congress (March 4, 1875–March 3, 1877); declined to be a candidate for renomination in 1876; unsuccessful candidate for election to the United States Senate in 1878; again elected a member of the State house of delegates in 1878 and 1883; delegate to the Democratic State convention in 1883; resumed the practice of law in Easton, Md.; died in Baltimore, Md., October 2, 1890; interment in Spring Hill Cemetery, Easton, Md.

THOMAS, Richard, a Representative from Pennsylvania; born in West Whiteland, Pa., December 30, 1744; educated at home by private teachers; served in the Revolutionary Army as colonel of the First Regiment, Chester County Volunteers; elected as a Federalist to the Fourth, Fifth, and Sixth Congresses (March 4, 1795–March 3, 1801); engaged in agricultural pursuits; died in Philadelphia, Pa., January 19, 1832; interment in the Friends Western Burial Ground.

THOMAS, Robert Young, Jr., a Representative from Kentucky; born near Russellville, Logan County, Ky., July 13, 1855; attended the common schools, and was graduated from Bethel College, Russellville, Ky., in 1878; studied law; was ad-

mitted to the bar in 1881 and commenced practice in Central City, Ky.; also engaged in journalism; member of the State house of representatives in 1886 and 1887; elected Commonwealth attorney for the seventh judicial district of Kentucky in 1903 for a term of six years; elected as a Democrat to the Sixty-first and to the eight succeeding Congresses and served from March 4, 1909, until his death at Red Boiling Springs, Macon County, Tenn., September 3, 1925; interment in Evergreen Cemetery, Greenville, Ky.

THOMAS, William Aubrey, a Representative from Ohio; born in Y Bynea, near Llanelly, Wales, June 7, 1866; immigrated to the United States in 1868 with his parents, who settled in Niles, Ohio; attended the public schools of Niles, Mount Union College, Alliance, Ohio, and later Rensselaer Polytechnic Institute, Troy, N. Y.; analytical chemist at Niles 1886–1888; engaged in the iron and steel business; president of the Mahoning Steel Co.; secretary and director of the Niles Fire Brick Co.; elected as a Republican to the Fifty-eighth Congress to fill the vacancy caused by the resignation of Charles W. F. Dick; reelected to the Fifty-ninth, Sixtieth, and Sixty-first Congresses and served from November 8, 1904, to March 3, 1911; unsuccessful candidate for reelection in 1910 to the Sixty-second Congress; moved to Jenifer, Ala., in 1918, and continued his interest in the manufacture of iron, steel, and firebrick; president of the Jenifer Iron Co.; died in Talladega, Ala., September 8, 1951; interment in Oakhill Cemetery, Youngstown, Ohio.

THOMAS, William David, a Representative from New York; born in Middle Granville, Washington County, N. Y., March 22, 1880; attended the grade and high schools; was graduated from the Albany College of Pharmacy, Albany, N. Y., in 1904; moved to Hoosick Falls, Rensselaer County, N. Y., in 1905 and was employed as a pharmacist, later engaging in the retail drug business; also interested in banking; served as town clerk 1917–1925; member of the State assembly in 1925 and 1926; served as treasurer of Rensselaer County 1927–1933; chairman of the Republican county committee 1927–1934; elected as a Republican to the Seventy-third Congress to fill the vacancy caused by the death of James S. Parker; reelected to the Seventy-fourth Congress and served from January 30, 1934, until his death in Washington, D. C., May 17, 1936; interment in Maple Grove Cemetery, Hoosick Falls, N. Y.

THOMASON, Robert Ewing, a Representative from Texas; born in Shelbyville, Bedford County, Tenn., May 30, 1879; moved to Gainesville, Cooke County, Tex., with his parents in 1880; attended the public schools; was graduated from Southwestern University, Georgetown, Tex., in 1898 and from the law department of the University of Texas at Austin in 1900; was admitted to the bar in 1900 and commenced practice in Gainesville, Tex.; prosecuting attorney of Cooke County, Tex., 1902–1906; moved to El Paso, Tex., in 1911 and continued the practice of law; member of the State house of representatives 1917–1921, and served as speaker in 1920 and 1921; mayor of El Paso 1927–1931; elected as a Democrat to the Seventy-second and to the eight succeeding Congresses and served from March 4, 1931, until his resignation on July 31, 1947, having been appointed United States district judge for the western district of Texas, in which capacity he is now serving; is a resident of El Paso, Tex.

THOMASSON, William Poindexter, a Representative from Kentucky; born in New Castle, Henry County, Ky., October 8, 1797; completed preparatory studies; served in Captain Duncan's company in the War of 1812; studied law; was admitted to the bar and commenced practice in Corydon, Ind., before he was twenty-one years of age; member of the State house of representatives 1818–1820; prosecuting attorney of Corydon in 1818; moved to Louisville, Ky., in 1841; elected as a Whig to the Twenty-eighth and Twenty-ninth Congresses (March 4, 1843–March 3, 1847); declined to be a candidate for renomination; moved to Chicago, Ill., and resumed the practice of law; during the Civil War served in the Union Army in the Seventy-first Regiment, New York Volunteer Infantry; died near La Grange, Oldham County, Ky., December 29, 1882; interment in Cave Hill Cemetery, Louisville, Ky.

THOMPSON, **Albert Clifton,** a Representative from Ohio; born in Brookville, Jefferson County, Pa., January 23, 1842; attended the common schools and Jefferson College, Canonsburg, Pa.; studied law; served in the Union Army during the Civil War as second lieutenant of Company B, One Hundred and Fifth Regiment, Pennsylvania Volunteer Infantry; promoted to captain of Company K in the same regiment November 28, 1861, and served until March 23, 1863, when he was discharged on account of wounds received in the second Battle of Bull Run; resumed the study of law; was admitted to the bar December 13, 1864, and commenced practice in Portsmouth, Ohio, in 1865; elected probate judge of Scioto County, Ohio, in October 1869; elected common pleas judge of the seventh judicial district of Ohio in October 1881; elected as a Republican to the Forty-ninth, Fiftieth, and Fifty-first Congresses (March 4, 1885–March 3, 1891); unsuccessful candidate for renomination in 1890; resumed the practice of law; appointed by President McKinley chairman of the commission to revise and codify the criminal and penal laws of the United States June 21, 1897; appointed United States judge for the southern district of Ohio September 13, 1898, and served until his death in Cincinnati, Ohio, on January 26, 1910; interment in Greenlawn Cemetery, Portsmouth, Ohio.

THOMPSON, **Benjamin,** a Representative from Massachusetts; born in Charlestown, Mass., August 5, 1798; attended the public schools; engaged in mercantile pursuits; member of the State house of representatives 1830–1831 and 1833–1836; served in the State senate in 1841; elected as a Whig to the Twenty-ninth Congress (March 4, 1845–March 3, 1847); declined to be a candidate for renomination in 1846; elected to the Thirty-second Congress and served from March 4, 1851, until his death in Charlestown, Mass., September 24, 1852; interment in the Congressional Cemetery, Washington, D. C.

THOMPSON, **Charles James,** a Representative from Ohio; born in Wapakoneta, Auglaize County, Ohio, January 24, 1862; attended the public schools and the Ohio Wesleyan University, Delaware, Ohio; learned the art of printing 1876–1879; worked as a journeyman printer in various cities in Ohio, Indiana, and Illinois 1879–1884; returned to Wapakoneta in 1885 and was employed as a bookkeeper until 1889; moved to Defiance, Ohio, in 1889 and was owner and publisher of the Defiance Express until 1902; member of the Republican State central committee in 1893 and 1894; postmaster of Defiance 1898–1915; unsuccessful candidate for mayor in 1915; elected as a Republican to the Sixty-sixth and to the five succeeding Congresses (March 4, 1919–March 3, 1931); unsuccessful candidate for reelection in 1930 to the Seventy-second Congress; retired from business pursuits; died in Albuquerque, N. Mex., while on a visit, March 27, 1932; interment in Riverside Cemetery, Defiance, Ohio.

THOMPSON, **Charles Perkins,** a Representative from Massachusetts; born in Braintree, Norfolk County, Mass., July 30, 1827; attended the public schools, the Hollis Institute of Braintree, and Amherst (Mass.) College; studied law; was admitted to the bar in 1854 and commenced practice in Gloucester, Mass., in 1857; United States assistant district attorney from 1855 to 1857; member of the State house of representatives in 1871 and 1872; delegate to the Democratic National Convention at Baltimore in 1872; elected as a Democrat to the Forty-fourth Congress (March 4, 1875–March 3, 1877); unsuccessful candidate for reelection in 1876 to the Forty-fifth Congress; resumed the practice of law; city solicitor of Gloucester, Mass., in 1874, 1875, 1877, and 1879; unsuccessful Democratic candidate for Governor of Massachusetts in 1880 and again in 1881; served as judge of the superior court of Massachusetts from 1885 until his death in Gloucester, Mass., January 19, 1894; interment in Oak Grove Cemetery.

THOMPSON, **Charles Winston,** a Representative from Alabama; born near Tuskegee, Macon County, Ala., December 30, 1860; attended the common schools and Park High School in Tuskegee, Ala.; was graduated from Bryant and Stratton's Business College, Louisville, Ky., in 1878; engaged in mercantile pursuits; president of the Bank of Tuskegee, Ala.; county superintendent of education for Macon County 1886–1888; appointed in 1896 lieutenant colonel on the staff of Gov. Joseph F. Johnston and served in that capacity until the end of the Governor's term; member of the State senate in 1898; elected as a Democrat to the Fifty-seventh and Fifty-eighth Congresses and served from March 4, 1901, until his death in Washington, D. C., March 20, 1904; interment in the City Cemetery, Tuskegee, Ala.

THOMPSON, **Chester Charles,** a Representative from Illinois; born in Rock Island, Ill., September 19, 1893; attended the grade and high schools; engaged in the plastering contracting business 1910–1932; during the First World War served as a corporal in Headquarters Company of the Twenty-fifth Coast Artillery in 1918 and 1919; treasurer of Rock Island County, Ill., 1922–1926; mayor of Rock Island 1927–1933; member of the Democratic State central committee 1930–1932; elected as a Democrat to the Seventy-third, Seventy-fourth, and Seventy-fifth Congresses (March 4, 1933–January 3, 1939); unsuccessful candidate for reelection in 1938 to the Seventy-sixth Congress; appointed on November 15, 1939, as president and chairman of the board of the Inland Waterways Corporation, which was then owned by the United States Government and under the supervision of the Secretary of Commerce, and served until his resignation August 15, 1944; president of the American Waterways Operators, Inc., from August 1944 until his retirement in 1957; is a resident of Rock Island, Ill.

THOMPSON, **Clark Wallace,** a Representative from Texas; born in La Crosse, Wis., August 6, 1896; moved to Oregon in 1901 with his parents, who settled in Cascade Locks; attended the common schools and the University of Oregon at Eugene; during the First World War enlisted as a private on May 25, 1917, in the United States Marine Corps; promoted to corporal on December 20, 1917, and served until honorably discharged on December 15, 1918; commissioned a second lieutenant in the Marine Corps Reserve on December 16, 1918; moved to Galveston, Tex., in 1919; engaged in the insurance business until 1920 and the retail dry goods business 1920–1931, when he engaged as a public relations counsel; elected as a Democrat to the Seventy-third Congress to fill the vacancy caused by the death of Clay Stone Briggs, serving from June 24, 1933, to January 3, 1935; was not a candidate for renomination in 1934; resumed activities as a public relations counsel; delegate to the State Democratic convention at Austin in 1936; organized the Fifteenth Battalion, Marine Corps Reserve, in Galveston County, Tex., in 1936 and was called to active duty on November 1,

1940; served as a lieutenant colonel with the Second Marine Division in the Pacific and later returned to Marine Headquarters to head Division of Reserve; promoted to colonel on October 18, 1942, and placed on the retired list on June 1, 1946; resumed his activities as a public relations counsel; elected to the Eightieth Congress to fill the vacancy caused by the death of Joseph J. Mansfield; reelected to the Eighty-first and to the five succeeding Congresses and served from August 23, 1947, to January 3, 1961. *Reelected to the Eighty-seventh Congress.*

THOMPSON, Fountain Land, a Senator from North Dakota; born near Scottsville, Macoupin County, Ill., November 18, 1854; moved to Girard, Macoupin County, Ill., in 1865; attended the grammar and high schools in Girard; studied law and was admitted to the bar, but did not engage in extensive practice; member of the board of supervisors of Macoupin County; engaged in mercantile pursuits in 1872; moved to Dakota Territory and settled on a farm near Cando, Towner County, in 1888; delegate to the first Democratic county convention that assembled after statehood and was chosen chairman; judge of Towner County Court 1890–1894; engaged in the real-estate business and banking in Cando and also in agricultural pursuits; school director; member of the Cando Board of Aldermen; mayor of Cando; appointed as a Democrat to the United States Senate to fill the vacancy caused by the death of Martin N. Johnson and served from November 10, 1909, to January 31, 1910, when he resigned; resumed his former business activities in Cando, N. Dak., until his retirement in 1921; moved to Los Angeles, Calif., where he resided until his death on February 4, 1942; interment in Hollywood Cemetery.

THOMPSON, Frank, Jr., a Representative from New Jersey; born in Trenton, Mercer County, N. J., July 26, 1918; attended parochial and public schools; was graduated from Wake Forest (N. C.) College in 1941 and from Wake Forest Law School in 1948; during World War II served in the United States Navy 1941–1948; commanded the U. S. S. LCI (L) 428 and LCI (Rocket) Squadrons 63 and 48; received three combat decorations for action at Iwo Jima and Okinawa; commanded the United States Naval Reserve Battalion 4–22 and completed a seventeen-month tour of active duty, from August 1950 to January 1952, on the staff of the commander, Eastern Sea Frontier, and released from active duty January 1, 1952; was admitted to the bar in 1948 and commenced the practice of law in Trenton, N. J.; member of the State house of assembly 1950–1954, serving as assistant minority leader in 1950 and minority leader in 1954; elected as a Democrat to the Eighty-fourth, Eighty-fifth, and Eighty-sixth Congresses (January 3, 1955–January 3, 1961). *Reelected to the Eighty-seventh Congress.*

THOMPSON, George Western, a Representative from Virginia; born in St. Clairsville, Ohio, May 14, 1806; was graduated from Jefferson (now Washington and Jefferson) College, Pennsylvania, in 1824; studied law in Richmond, Va.; was admitted to the bar in 1826 and commenced practice in St. Clairsville, Ohio, in 1828; moved to western Virginia in 1837; appointed deputy postmaster at Wheeling in 1838; appointed on a commission to settle jurisdiction of the Ohio River between Virginia and Ohio; United States attorney for the western district of Virginia by appointment of President James K. Polk 1848–1850; elected as a Democrat to the Thirty-second Congress and served from March 4, 1851, until his resignation on July 30, 1852; was elected judge of the circuit court of Virginia in 1852 and reelected in 1860; was removed from office in 1861 on refusal to take the oath of office to support what he believed unconstitutional action to set up the present State of West Virginia; retired from the practice of his profession and

resided on his estate near Wheeling, Ohio County, W. Va., until his death February 24, 1888; interment in Elm Grove Cemetery, Wheeling, W. Va.

THOMPSON, Hedge, a Representative from New Jersey; born in Salem, N. J., January 28, 1780; pursued an academic course; was graduated from the medical department of the University of Pennsylvania at Philadelphia in 1802 and practiced his profession in Salem; member of the General Assembly of New Jersey in 1805; served in the State council in 1819; appointed associate judge of Salem County, N. J., in 1815 and again in 1824; served as collector for Salem County from 1826 to 1828; elected to the Twentieth Congress and served from March 4, 1827, until his death in Salem, N. J., on July 23, 1828; interment in St. John's Protestant Episcopal Churchyard.

THOMPSON, Jacob, a Representative from Mississippi; born in Leasburg, Caswell County, N. C., May 15, 1810; attended the public schools and Bingham Academy in Orange County; was graduated from the University of North Carolina at Chapel Hill in 1831; member of the faculty of the University of North Carolina in 1831 and 1832; studied law; was admitted to the bar in 1834 and commenced practice in Pontotoc, Miss., in 1835; elected as a Democrat to the Twenty-sixth and to the five succeeding Congresses (March 4, 1839–March 3, 1851); unsuccessful candidate for reelection in 1850 to the Thirty-second Congress; declined an appointment to the United States Senate tendered by Governor Brown in 1845; appointed Secretary of the Interior in the Cabinet of President Buchanan and served from March 6, 1857, to January 8, 1861, when he resigned; served as inspector general in the Confederate Army during the Civil War; confidential agent of the Confederacy to Canada in 1864 and 1865; traveled throughout Europe in 1866 and 1867; settled in Memphis, Tenn., in 1868 and managed the affairs of his extensive holdings; died in Memphis, Tenn., March 24, 1885; interment in Elmwood Cemetery.

THOMPSON, James, a Representative from Pennsylvania; born in Middlesex, Butler County, Pa., October 1, 1806; completed preparatory studies; learned the printer's trade; studied law; was admitted to the bar in 1829 and commenced practice in Erie, Pa.; member of the State house of representatives 1832–1834 and in 1855 and served as speaker in 1834; presidential elector on the Democratic ticket of Van Buren and Johnson in 1836; delegate to the State constitutional convention in 1838; presiding judge of sixth judicial district court 1838–1844; elected as a Democrat to the Twenty-ninth, Thirtieth, and Thirty-first Congresses (March 4, 1845–March 3, 1851); was not a candidate for renomination in 1850; resumed the practice of his profession; associate justice of the supreme court of Pennsylvania from 1857 to 1866, and served as chief justice of that court from 1866 to 1872; again engaged in the practice of law; died in Philadelphia, Pa., January 28, 1874; interment in Woodlands Cemetery.

THOMPSON, Joel, a Representative from New York; born in Stanford, Dutchess County, N. Y., October 3, 1760; attended the common schools in Smyrna, N. Y.; studied law; was admitted to the bar and practiced in Duanesburg, and Sherburne, N. Y.; during the Revolutionary War enlisted in April 1779, serving four months in Capt. Smith Sutherland's New York company, stationed at Fort Independence; reenlisted in the fall of 1779, serving two months in Capt. Roger Sutherland's company and Colonel Brinton Paine's New York regiment, stationed at Fishkill; again enlisted in May 1780, serving two months under Lieut. Stephen Haight, guarding public stores and the jail at Poughkeepsie; member of the State assembly in 1798, 1803, and

1804, serving one term as member from Albany County and two terms as member from Chenango County; assistant justice of the court of common pleas of Chenango County from July 1799 to June 1807, when he became judge of Chenango County, serving until March 16, 1814; elected as a Federalist to the Thirteenth Congress (March 4, 1813–March 3, 1815); resumed the practice of law in Sherburne, N. Y.; died in Brooklyn, N. Y., February 8, 1843; interment in Greenwood Cemetery.

THOMPSON, John, a Representative from New York; born in Litchfield, Conn., March 20, 1749; attended the common schools; at the age of fourteen moved with his parents to Stillwater, N. Y.; appointed justice of Stillwater Township in 1788; member of the State assembly in 1788 and 1789; elected as a Democrat to the Sixth Congress (March 4, 1799–March 3, 1801); delegate to the New York State Constitutional Convention in 1801; was appointed by Governor Clinton in 1791 as first judge of Saratoga County and held this office until 1809; elected to the Tenth and Eleventh Congresses (March 4, 1807–March 3, 1811); retired to private life; died in Stillwater, Saratoga County, N. Y., in 1823; interment in a cemetery at Stillwater, N. Y.

THOMPSON, John, a Representative from New York; born in Rhinebeck, Dutchess County, N. Y., July 4, 1809; was graduated from Union College, Schenectady, N. Y., and later from Yale College; studied law; was admitted to the bar and commenced practice in Poughkeepsie, N. Y.; elected as a Republican to the Thirty-fifth Congress (March 4, 1857–March 3, 1859); resumed the practice of law; died in New Hamburg, Dutchess County, N. Y., June 1, 1890; interment in Poughkeepsie Rural Cemetery, Poughkeepsie, N. Y.

THOMPSON, John Burton, a Representative and a Senator from Kentucky; born near Harrodsburg, Ky., December 14, 1810; completed preparatory studies; studied law; was admitted to the bar and practiced in Harrodsburg, Ky.; Commonwealth attorney; served in the State senate from 1829 to 1833; member of the State house of representatives in 1835 and 1837; elected as a Whig to the Twenty-sixth Congress to fill the vacancy caused by the death of Simeon H. Anderson; reelected to the Twenty-seventh Congress and served from December 7, 1840, to March 3, 1843; elected to the Thirtieth and Thirty-first Congresses (March 4, 1847–March 3, 1851); Lieutenant Governor of Kentucky in 1852; elected to the United States Senate and served from March 4, 1853, to March 3, 1859; died in Harrodsburg, Mercer County, Ky., January 7, 1874; interment in Spring Hill Cemetery.

THOMPSON, John McCandless (brother of William George Thompson), a Representative from Pennsylvania; born near Butler, Butler County, Pa., January 4, 1829; attended the common schools and Witherspoon Institute; studied law; was admitted to the bar in 1854 and began practice in Butler, Pa.; member of the State house of representatives in 1859 and 1860, and served one year as speaker; entered the Union Army during the Civil War and served as major and subsequently as lieutenant colonel of the One Hundred and Thirty-fourth Regiment, Pennsylvania Volunteer Infantry; delegate to the Republican National Convention at Chicago in 1868; elected as a Republican to the Forty-third Congress to fill the vacancy caused by the resignation of Ebenezer McJunkin and served from December 22, 1874, to March 3, 1875; elected to the Forty-fifth Congress (March 4, 1877–March 3, 1879); was not a candidate for renomination in 1878; resumed the practice of his profession; died in Butler, Pa., September 3, 1903; interment in Butler Cemetery.

THOMPSON, Joseph Bryan, a Representative from Oklahoma; born near Sherman, Grayson County, Tex., April 29, 1871; attended the public schools, and was graduated from Savoy College in Fannin County, Tex., in 1890; studied law; was admitted to the bar in 1892 and commenced practice in Purcell, Indian Territory; moved to Ardmore, Indian Territory; appointed commissioner for the United States court in 1893 and returned to Purcell, Indian Territory; resigned in 1897; moved to Pauls Valley and resumed the practice of law; delegate to the Democratic National Conventions in 1900, 1904, and 1908; member of the Democratic Territorial committee 1896–1904; chairman of the Democratic State committee in 1906 and 1908; served in the State senate 1910–1914; elected as a Democrat to the Sixty-third and to the three succeeding Congresses and served from March 4, 1913, until his death on a train near Martinsburg, W. Va., while en route to his home at Pauls Valley, Okla., September 18, 1919; interment in Mount Olivet Cemetery, Pauls Valley, Okla.

THOMPSON, Philip, a Representative from Kentucky; born on Shawnee Run, near Harrodsburg, Mercer County, Ky., August 20, 1789; received a limited education; served as a lieutenant in the War of 1812; held several local offices; studied law; was admitted to the bar and commenced practice in Hartford, Ohio County, Ky.; moved to Owensboro, Daviess County, Ky.; member of the State house of representatives; elected to the Eighteenth Congress (March 4, 1823–March 3, 1825); resumed the practice of law in Owensburg, Ky., where he died November 25, 1836; interment in the Moseley burying ground on Firth Street; reinterment in Rural Hill (later Elmwood) Cemetery in 1856.

THOMPSON, Philip Burton, Jr., a Representative from Kentucky; born in Harrodsburg, Mercer County, Ky., October 15, 1845; attended the common schools and the University of Kentucky at Lexington; during the Civil War entered the Confederate Army at the age of sixteen and served throughout the war; studied law; was admitted to the bar in 1866 and commenced practice in Harrodsburg; was city attorney of Harrodsburg 1867–1869; was appointed in 1869 and subsequently elected Commonwealth attorney for the thirteenth judicial district of Kentucky, serving until 1874; reelected in 1874 and served until 1878, when he resigned, having been elected to Congress; elected as a Democrat to the Forty-sixth, Forty-seventh, and Forty-eighth Congresses (March 4, 1879–March 3, 1885); delegate to the Democratic National Convention at Chicago in 1884; moved to New York City and resumed the practice of law; died in Washington, D. C., December 15, 1909; interment in Spring Hill Cemetery, Harrodsburg, Ky.

THOMPSON, Philip Rootes, a Representative from Virginia; born near Fredericksburg, Va., March 26, 1766; was educated by private tutors; was graduated from William and Mary College, Williamsburg, Va.; studied law; was admitted to the bar and commenced practice in Fairfax, Va.; member of the State house of delegates 1793–1797; elected as a Democrat to the Seventh, Eighth, and Ninth Congresses (March 4, 1801–March 3, 1807); resumed the practice of law; died in Kanawha County, Va. (now West Virginia), July 27, 1837; interment at Coals Mouth (now St. Albans), W. Va.

THOMPSON, Richard Wigginton, a Representative from Indiana; born near Culpeper Court House, Culpeper County, Va., June 9, 1809; pursued classical studies; moved to Louisville, Ky., in 1831; clerked in a store; moved to Lawrence County, Ind., in 1831; taught school; studied law; was admitted to the bar in 1834 and began practice in Bedford, Lawrence County,

Ind.; member of the State house of representatives 1834–1836; served in the State senate 1836–1838 and for a short time as president pro tempore; presidential elector on the Whig ticket of Harrison and Tyler in 1840; elected as a Whig to the Twenty-seventh Congress (March 4, 1841–March 3, 1843); was not a candidate for renomination in 1842; moved to Terre Haute, Ind., in 1843; city attorney in 1846 and 1847; elected as a Whig to the Thirtieth Congress (March 4, 1847–March 3, 1849); declined a renomination; declined the appointment of Minister to Austria which was tendered him by President Taylor, the office of recorder of the General Land Office tendered by President Fillmore, and a seat on the bench of the Court of Claims tendered by President Lincoln; commander of Camp Thompson, Ind., and provost marshal 1861–1865; appointed by President Lincoln collector of internal revenue for the seventh district of Indiana and served one term; presidential elector on the Republican ticket of Lincoln and Johnson in 1864; delegate to the Republican National Convention at Chicago in 1868 and at Cincinnati in 1876; judge of the fifth Indiana circuit court 1867–1869; appointed Secretary of the Navy in the Cabinet of President Hayes and served from March 12, 1877, until his resignation December 21, 1880; chairman of the American Committee of the Panama Canal Co. in 1881; director of the Panama Railroad Co. 1881–1888; died in Terre Haute, Ind., February 9, 1900; interment in High Lawn Cemetery.

THOMPSON, Robert Augustine (father of Thomas Larkin Thompson), a Representative from Virginia; born near Culpeper Court House, Culpeper County, Va., February 14, 1805; attended a private school at Gallipolis, Ohio, and the University of Virginia at Charlottesville, Va.; studied law; was admitted to the bar in 1826 and commenced practice in Charleston, Kanawha County, Va. (now West Virginia); member of the State senate 1839–1846; presidential elector on the Democratic ticket of Polk and Dallas in 1844; elected as a Democrat to the Thirtieth Congress (March 4, 1847–March 3, 1849); declined to be a candidate for reelection; delegate to the Democratic National Convention at Baltimore in 1852; member of the board of visitors to the University of Virginia in 1852; moved to San Francisco, Calif., in 1853; appointed in 1853 a member of a commission to settle private land claims in California; appointed by the Governor a reporter of the California Supreme Court in 1870; member of the justices' court of San Francisco from 1870 until his death in San Francisco, Calif., August 31, 1876; interment in Laurel Hill Cemetery.

THOMPSON, Ruth, a Representative from Michigan; born in Whitehall, Muskegon County, Mich., September 15, 1887; attended the public schools; graduated from Muskegon Business College in 1905; studied law while employed in a law office 1918–1924; was admitted to the bar; registrar of probate court of Muskegon County for eighteen years; judge of probate, Muskegon County, 1925–1937; member of the State house of representatives 1939–1941; with Social Security Board, Washington, D. C., in 1941 and 1942, Labor Department in 1942, Adjutant General's Office 1942–1945; Headquarters Command, Frankfurt, Germany, and Copenhagen, Denmark, in 1945 and 1946; member and chairman State Prison Commission for Women for four years; private practice of law in Michigan; elected as a Republican to the Eighty-second, Eighty-third, and Eighty-fourth Congresses (January 3, 1951–January 3, 1957); unsuccessful candidate for renomination in 1956 to the Eighty-fifth Congress; is a resident of Whitehall, Mich.

THOMPSON, Theo Ashton, a Representative from Louisiana; born in Ville Platte, Evangeline Parish, La., March 31, 1916; attended the public schools and the Louisiana State University

1932–1934, completing course in higher accounting; engaged in State government service as traveling auditor for State highway commission 1934–1940; transferred to State department of finance in 1940 and assisted in State reorganization plan; Louisiana representative at the national assembly of the States in the development of the civil defense program in Chicago, Ill., in 1942; during World War II served in the United States Army Air Force 1942–1946; served as State budget officer and financial adviser to the Louisiana Legislature, designing and installing a complete accounting system for all State agencies, 1948–1952; chairman of the board of trustees of the State employees retirement system 1947–1953; represented the United States Department of State in Louisiana in training foreign representatives in principles of democracy in 1950 and 1951; elected as a Democrat to the Eighty-third and to the three succeeding Congresses (January 3, 1953–January 3, 1961). *Reelected to the Eighty-seventh Congress.*

THOMPSON, Thomas Larkin (son of Robert Augustine Thompson), a Representative from California; born in Charleston, Va. (now West Virginia), May 31, 1838; attended the common schools and Buffalo Academy, Virginia (now West Virginia); moved to California in 1855 and settled in Sonoma County; established the Petaluma Journal the same year; purchased the Sonoma Democrat in 1860, and was the editor of that paper; delegate to the Democratic National Convention at Cincinnati in 1880 and at Chicago in 1892; secretary of state of California 1882–1886; declined to be a candidate for renomination; elected as a Democrat to the Fiftieth Congress (March 4, 1887–March 3, 1889); unsuccessful candidate for reelection in 1888 to the Fifty-first Congress; appointed on April 4, 1891, commissioner from California to the World's Fair at Chicago; Minister to Brazil from April 24, 1893, to May 27, 1897; died in Santa Rosa, Sonoma County, Calif., February 1, 1898; interment in the Rural Cemetery.

THOMPSON, Thomas Weston, a Representative and a Senator from New Hampshire; born in Boston, Mass., March 15, 1766; attended Dummer Academy, Byfield, Mass.; was graduated from Harvard University in 1786; studied law; was admitted to the bar in 1791 and practiced in Salisbury, N. H., 1791–1810; postmaster of Salisbury, N. H., 1798–1803; trustee of Dartmouth College, Hanover, N. H., 1801–1821; moved to Concord, N. H., in 1810 and continued the practice of law; member of the State house of representatives in 1807, 1808, 1813, and 1814, and served as speaker in 1813 and 1814; elected to the Ninth Congress (March 4, 1805–March 3, 1807); State treasurer of New Hampshire 1809–1811; elected to the United States Senate to fill the vacancy caused by the death of Nicholas Gilman and served from June 24, 1814, to March 3, 1817; died in Concord, N. H., on October 1, 1821; interment in the Old North Cemetery.

THOMPSON, Waddy, Jr., a Representative from South Carolina; born in Pickensville (now Pickens), Ninety-sixth District, S. C., January 8, 1798; moved to Greenville with his parents in his infancy; received his early education in neighboring schools, and was graduated from South Carolina College (now the University of South Carolina), at Columbia in 1814; studied law; was admitted to the bar in 1819 and began practice in Edgefield, S. C.; moved to Greenville, S. C., and continued the practice of law; member of the State house of representatives from 1826 to 1830; elected solicitor of the western circuit in 1830; presidential elector in 1832 and cast the vote for John Floyd for President and Henry Lee for Vice President; brigadier general of militia in 1832; elected as a Whig to the Twenty-fourth Congress to fill the vacancy caused by the death of Warren R. Davis; reelected to the Twenty-fifth and Twenty-sixth Congresses and served from September 10, 1835, to March 3, 1841; was not a candidate for renomination in 1840; appointed Envoy Extraordinary and Minister Plenipotentiary to Mexico and served from February 10, 1842, to March 9, 1844; moved to Madison, Fla., and engaged in cotton planting; appointed solicitor general of a circuit in 1868; died while on a visit to Tallahassee, Fla., November 23, 1868; interment in the Episcopal Cemetery.

THOMPSON, Wiley, a Representative from Georgia; born in Amelia County, Va., September 23, 1781; moved to Elberton, Elbert County, Ga.; served as a commissioner of the Elbert County Academy in 1808; served in the State senate 1817–1819; was appointed major general of the Fourth Division of the Georgia Militia in November 1817 and served until November 1824, when he resigned; elected as a Democrat to the Seventeenth and to the five succeeding Congresses (March 4, 1821–March 3, 1833); was a delegate to the State constitutional convention in 1833; murdered by the Seminole Indians at Fort King, Fla., on December 28, 1835; interment in the private burial ground on his estate at Elberton, Ga.

THOMPSON, William, a Representative from Iowa; born in Fayette County, Pa., November 10, 1813; attended the common schools; moved to Iowa and settled in Mount Pleasant; member of the Territorial house of representatives in 1843; secretary of the State constitutional convention in 1846; elected as a Democrat to the Thirtieth Congress (March 4, 1847–March 3, 1849); presented credentials as a Member-elect to the Thirty-first Congress and served from March 4, 1849, to June 29, 1850, when the seat was declared vacant; served in the Union Army during the Civil War; commissioned captain in the First Iowa Volunteer Cavalry on July 31, 1861; promoted to major on May 18, 1863, and colonel on June 20, 1864; brevetted brigadier general of Volunteers on March 13, 1865, "for gallant and meritorious services," and was honorably mustered out on March 15, 1866; recommissioned captain in the Seventh Cavalry, Regular Army, on July 28, 1866; brevetted major on March 2, 1867, "for gallant and meritorious service in action at Prairie Grove, Ark."; lieutenant colonel on March 2, 1867, "for gallant and meritorious service in action at Bayou Metoe, Ark."; retired from the Army on December 15, 1875, and became editor of the Iowa State Gazette; died in Tacoma, Pierce County, Wash., on October 6, 1897; interment in Tacoma Cemetery.

THOMPSON, William George (brother of John McCandless Thompson), a Representative from Iowa; born near Butler, Butler County, Pa., January 17, 1830; attended the common schools and the Witherspoon Institute in Butler, Pa.; studied law and was admitted to the bar in 1853; moved to Iowa the same year and settled in Marion, Linn County, where he commenced the practice of law; prosecuting attorney of Linn County 1854–1856; member of the State senate 1856–1860; served during the Civil War as major of the Twentieth Regiment, Iowa Volunteer Infantry, in 1862; presidential elector on the Republican ticket of Lincoln and Johnson in 1864; district attorney for the eighth judicial district for six years; appointed chief justice of the Territory of Idaho and served from January 13, 1879, until his resignation in April of that year; elected as a Republican to the Forty-sixth Congress to fill the vacancy caused by the death of Rush Clark; reelected to the Forty-seventh Congress and served from October 14, 1879, to March 3, 1883; declined to be a candidate for renomination in 1882; served on the city council of Marion; member of the State house of representatives 1885–1887; judge of the eighteenth judicial district of Iowa 1894–1906; moved to Kenwood Park, Linn County, Iowa, in 1896; retired from public life and died in Kenwood Park, Iowa, April 2, 1911; interment in Oak Shade Cemetery, Marion, Iowa.

THOMPSON, William Henry, a Senator from Nebraska; born in Perrysville, Ashland County, Ohio, December 14, 1853; attended the common schools and received private instruction; attended Upper Iowa University at Fayette 1872–1875, and was graduated from the law department of the State University of Iowa at Iowa City in 1877; was admitted to the bar the same year and commenced practice at Brush Creek (now Arlington), Iowa; moved to Grand Island, Hall County, Nebr., in 1881 and continued the practice of law; also interested in banking; served as city attorney of Grand Island in 1887 and 1888; unsuccessful candidate for election in 1890 to the Fifty-second Congress; delegate to the Democratic National Conventions in 1892, 1896, 1900, 1904, and 1908; member of the board of trustees of Grand Island College in 1893; served as mayor 1895–1898; member of the Democratic National Committee 1896–1900 and 1920–1924; unsuccessful candidate for Governor of Nebraska in 1902; member of the State commission for erection of a new capitol; served as judge of the supreme court of Nebraska 1924–1931; appointed as a Democrat to the United States Senate to fill the vacancy caused by the death of Robert B. Howell and served from May 24, 1933, to November 6, 1934, when a successor was elected; was not a candidate for election to this vacancy; retired to private life; died in Grand Island, Nebr., on June 6, 1937; interment in Grand Island Cemetery.

THOMPSON, William Howard, a Senator from Kansas; born in Crawfordsville, Montgomery County, Ind., October 14, 1871; moved with his parents to Nemaha County, Kans., in 1880; attended the public schools; was graduated from the Seneca Normal School in 1886 and from the Lawrence Business College in 1891; official court reporter of the twenty-second judicial district of Kansas 1891–1894; studied law; was admitted to the bar in 1894 and commenced practice in Seneca; clerk of the Kansas Court of Appeals in Topeka and practiced law from 1897 to 1901; moved to Iola, Kans., in 1901 and continued the practice of law; was county attorney of Allen County; moved to Garden City in 1905; judge of the thirty-second judicial district of Kansas from 1906 to 1913, when he resigned, having been elected Senator; elected as a Democrat to the United States Senate in 1912 and served from March 4, 1913, to March 3, 1919; unsuccessful candidate for reelection to the United States Senate in 1918; delegate to the Democratic National Convention at St. Louis in 1916; resumed the practice of law at Kansas City, Kans., in 1919; moved to Tulsa, Okla., in 1923 and practiced law in Kansas City and Tulsa; moved to Washington, D. C., in 1927, where he continued the practice of law, and died there on February 9, 1928; interment in Glenwood Cemetery.

THOMSON, Alexander, a Representative from Pennsylvania; born in Franklin County, Pa., January 12, 1788; apprenticed as a sickle maker; moved to Bedford, Pa.; received a limited schooling; studied law; was admitted to the bar in 1816 and commenced practice in Chambersburg, Franklin County, Pa.; held several local offices; member of the State house of representatives; elected to the Eighteenth Congress to fill the vacancy caused by the resignation of John Tod; reelected to the Nineteenth Congress and served from December 6, 1824, to May 1, 1826, when he resigned; mayor of Lancaster, Pa.; president judge of the sixteenth judicial district of Pennsylvania 1827–1841; professor in the law school of Marshall College, Lancaster, Pa.; died in Chambersburg, Pa., August 2, 1848; interment in Falling Spring Presbyterian Cemetery.

THOMSON, Charles Marsh, a Representative from Illinois; born in Chicago, Ill., February 13, 1877; attended the public schools and the Chicago Manual Training School; was graduated from Washington and Jefferson College, Washington, Pa., in 1899 and from the Northwestern University Law School, Evanston, Ill., in 1902; was admitted to the bar in the latter year and commenced practice in Chicago, Ill.; elected a member of the city council in 1908, 1910, and again in 1912; elected as a Progressive Republican to the Sixty-third Congress (March 4, 1913–March 3, 1915); unsuccessful candidate for reelection in 1914 to the Sixty-fourth Congress; elected judge of the circuit court of Cook County in 1915; reelected in 1921; appointed justice of the Appellate Court of Illinois in 1917; reappointed in 1921 and served until June 1927; resumed the practice of his profession in Chicago; trustee of the Chicago & Eastern Illinois Railroad Co. from 1933 to 1939, when he was appointed trustee of the Chicago & North Western Railroad, in which capacity he served until his death; died in Chicago, Ill., December 30, 1943; interment in Rosehill Cemetery.

THOMSON, Edwin Keith, a Representative from Wyoming; born in New Castle, Weston County, Wyo., February 8, 1919; attended the public schools in Beulah, Wyo., and Spearfish, S. Dak.; was graduated from the University of Wyoming Law School in 1941; during World War II was called to active duty on March 24, 1941; commanded Second Battalion, Three Hundred and Sixty-second Infantry Regiment, Ninety-first Division; released from active duty as a lieutenant colonel on January 24, 1946; awarded Combat Infantryman's Badge, Purple Heart, Legion of Merit, Bronze Star Medal, and the Italian Cross of Valor; was admitted to the bar in 1941 and commenced the practice of law in Cheyenne, Wyo., in February 1946; delegate to the Republican National Convention in 1952; member of the State house of representatives 1952–1954; elected as a Republican to the Eighty-fourth, Eighty-fifth, and Eighty-sixth Congresses and served from January 3, 1955, until his death; did not seek renomination to the Eighty-seventh Congress but was elected to the United States Senate on November 8, 1960, for the term commencing January 3, 1961; died in Cody, Wyo., December 9, 1960; interment in Arlington National Cemetery, Fort Myer, Va.

THOMSON, John, a Representative from Ohio; born in Ireland November 20, 1780; immigrated with his parents to the United States in 1787; completed preparatory studies; studied medicine, and in 1806 moved to New Lisbon, Ohio, and practiced; served in the State senate in 1814, 1815, and 1817–1820; member of the State house of representatives in 1816; elected as a Democrat to the Nineteenth Congress (March 4, 1825–March 3, 1827); unsuccessful candidate for reelection in 1826 to the Twentieth Congress; elected to the Twenty-first and to the three succeeding Congresses (March 4, 1829–March 3, 1837); was not a candidate for renomination in 1836; resumed the practice of medicine; died in New Lisbon (now Lisbon), Columbiana County, Ohio, December 2, 1852; interment in New Lisbon Cemetery.

THOMSON, John Renshaw, a Senator from New Jersey; born in Philadelphia, Pa., September 25, 1800; attended the common schools in Princeton, N. J., and the College of New Jersey (now Princeton University), but left in the junior year to engage in mercantile pursuits; went to China in 1817 and became a merchant in Canton; United States consul at that port 1823–1825; returned to the United States and settled in Princeton, N. J.; director and secretary of the Delaware & Raritan Canal Co.; connected with the Philadelphia & Trenton Railroad Co. as president and later as treasurer; member of the State constitutional convention in 1844; unsuccessful Democratic candi-

date for Governor of New Jersey in 1844; elected as a Democrat to the United States Senate to fill the vacancy caused by the resignation of Robert F. Stockton; reelected in 1857, and served from March 4, 1853, until his death in Princeton, N. J., September 12, 1862; interment in the Princeton Cemetery.

THOMSON, Mark, a Representative from New Jersey; born in Norriton Township, near Norristown, Montgomery County, Pa., in 1739; engaged in milling; was justice of the peace of Sussex County in 1773; member of the provincial convention in 1774 and of the Provincial Congress in 1775; was commissioned lieutenant colonel of the First Regiment, Sussex County (N. J.) Militia, July 22, 1775; lieutenant colonel in Col. Charles Stewart's Battalion of Minutemen February 15, 1776; colonel of the First Regiment, Sussex County Militia, July 10, 1776; colonel of the Battalion of Detached New Jersey Militia July 18, 1776; member of the State general assembly in 1779; served in the State council 1786–1788; appointed lieutenant colonel and aide-de-camp on the staff of Gov. Richard Howell, of New Jersey, June 10, 1793; elected as a Federalist to the Fourth and Fifth Congresses (March 4, 1795–March 3, 1799); died in Marksboro, Sussex (later Warren) County, N. J., December 14, 1803; interment in the Presbyterian Church Cemetery.

THORINGTON, James, a Representative from Iowa; born in Wilmington, N. C., May 7, 1816; moved with his parents to Montgomery, Ala., in 1827; attended the common schools, the military school in Fayetteville, N. C., 1830–1832, and the University of Alabama at Tuscaloosa 1832–1835; studied law in Montgomery, Ala.; engaged in trading and trapping on the upper Missouri and Columbia Rivers 1837–1839; moved to Davenport, Iowa, in 1839; was admitted to the bar in 1844 and commenced practice in Davenport; mayor of Davenport 1843–1847; probate judge of Scott County 1843–1851; clerk of the district court of Scott County 1846–1854; elected as a Whig to the Thirty-fourth Congress (March 4, 1855–March 3, 1857); was not a candidate for renomination in 1856; affiliated with the Republican Party; sheriff of Scott County 1859–1863; recorder 1864–1868; was appointed consul at Aspinwall, Colombia, January 21, 1873; appointed commercial agent at the same city May 27, 1873, and served in both positions until October 21, 1882; died while on a visit to his daughter at Santa Fe, N. Mex., June 13, 1887; interment in Oakdale Cemetery, Davenport, Iowa.

THORKELSON, Jacob, a Representative from Montana; born in Egersund, Norway, September 24, 1876; attended elementary schools; immigrated to the United States in 1892 and studied navigation; engaged as a navigator in 1896 and served as master of ocean-going ships 1900–1907; served with the Virginia Naval Reserve 1897–1899; was graduated from the College of Physicians and Surgeons, University of Maryland, at Baltimore in 1911, and served as a member of the faculty 1911–1913; moved to Dillon, Beaverhead County, Mont., in 1913, to Warmsprings, Deer Lodge County, Mont., in 1915, and to Butte, Silver Bow County, Mont., in 1920, and practiced medicine and surgery; served in the United States Naval Reserve 1936–1939 with rank of lieutenant commander; elected as a Republican to the Seventy-sixth Congress (January 3, 1939–January 3, 1941); unsuccessful candidate for renomination in 1940; resumed the practice of medicine and surgery; unsuccessful candidate for the Republican nomination for United States Senator in 1942 and for Governor in 1944; died in Butte, Mont., November 20, 1945; interment in Holy Cross Cemetery.

THORNBERRY, William Homer, a Representative from Texas; born in Austin, Travis County, Tex., January 9, 1909; attended the public schools; was graduated from the University of Texas in 1932 and from the law school of the same university in 1936; was admitted to the bar in 1936 and commenced the practice of law in Austin, Tex.; member of the State house of representatives 1936–1941; district attorney of the fifty-third judicial district of Texas from 1941 until his resignation in 1942 to enlist in the United States Navy; during World War II served in the United States Navy from July 1942 until discharged as a lieutenant commander in February 1946; member of the Austin City Council 1946–1948, serving as mayor pro tempore in 1947 and 1948; delegate at large to the Democratic National Convention in 1956; elected as a Democrat to the Eighty-first and to the five succeeding Congresses (January 3, 1949–January 3, 1961). *Reelected to the Eighty-seventh Congress.*

THORNBURGH, Jacob Montgomery, a Representative from Tennessee; born in New Market, Jefferson County, Tenn., July 3, 1837; completed preparatory studies; studied law; was admitted to the bar in 1861 and commenced practice in Jefferson County; during the Civil War entered the Union Army as a private and was promoted to lieutenant colonel of the Fourth Regiment, Tennessee Volunteer Cavalry, July 11, 1863; returned to Jefferson County, Tenn., and practiced law; moved to Knoxville, Tenn., in 1867; appointed attorney general of the third judicial circuit of Tennessee in 1866, and elected in 1868 and 1870; United States commissioner at the International Exposition held at Vienna, Austria, in 1872; elected as a Republican to the Forty-third, Forty-fourth, and Forty-fifth Congresses (March 4, 1873–March 3, 1879); was not a candidate for renomination in 1878; delegate to the Republican National Conventions in 1872, 1876, and 1880; retired from public life and resumed the practice of law in Knoxville, Tenn., where he died September 19, 1890; interment in the Old Gray Cemetery.

THORNTON, Anthony, a Representative from Illinois; born near Paris, Bourbon County, Ky., November 9, 1814; attended the common schools and Centre College, Danville, Ky.; was graduated from Miami University, Ohio, in 1834; studied law; was admitted to the bar and commenced practice in Shelbyville, Ill., in 1836; major of militia during the war with Mexico; delegate to the State constitutional conventions in 1847 and 1862; member of the State house of representatives in 1850; elected as a Democrat to the Thirty-ninth Congress (March 4, 1865–March 3, 1867); was not a candidate for renomination in 1866; resumed the practice of law; justice of the supreme court of Illinois from 1870 to 1873, when he resigned; president of the State bar association for four terms; chairman of the State board of arbitration 1895–1897; died in Shelbyville, Shelby County, Ill., on September 10, 1904; interment in Glenwood Cemetery.

THORNTON, John Randolph, a Senator from Louisiana; born on Notoway plantation, near Bayou Goula, Iberville Parish, La., August 25, 1846; moved with his parents to Rapides Parish, La., in 1853; attended Parker Seminary, Pineville, La., the McGruder Institute, Baton Rouge, La., and the Louisiana Seminary (afterwards the State university) at Pineville until 1863; enlisted in the Confederate Army and served until the close of the Civil War in Company B, Second Louisiana Cavalry; engaged in agricultural pursuits until 1877; studied law; was admitted to the bar in 1877 and commenced practice in Rapides Parish; judge of Rapides Parish 1878–1880; delegate to the State constitutional convention in 1898; member of the board of supervisors of the State university 1904–1910; one of the three Louisiana commissioners attending the conference on uniform laws for the United States, and served as vice president of that body 1909–1916; appointed as a Democrat to the United States Senate on August 27, 1910, and subsequently elected to fill the

vacancy caused by the death of Samuel D. McEnery and served from December 7, 1910, to March 3, 1915; was not a candidate for reelection to the Senate; appointed by President Wilson a member of the Board of Ordnance and Fortification and served from 1915 to 1917; resumed the practice of law in Alexandria, Rapides Parish, La., and died there December 28, 1917; interment in Rapides Cemetery, Pineville, La.

THORNTON, Matthew, a Delegate from New Hampshire; born in Ireland in 1714; immigrated to the United States in 1716 with his father, who settled in Wiscasset, Maine; moved to Worcester, Mass.; completed preparatory studies; studied medicine and commenced practice in Londonderry, N. H., in 1740; surgeon of New Hampshire troops in the expedition against Cape Breton; member of the New Hampshire Assembly when it was organized in 1758 and again in 1760 and 1761; justice of the peace; delegate to the first Provincial Congress in 1775 and served as its president; chairman of the committee of safety in 1775; speaker of the general assembly from January 5, to September 12, 1776; colonel of the State militia during the Revolutionary War; Member of the Continental Congress in 1776 and 1778; a signer of the Declaration of Independence; chief justice of the court of common pleas; judge of the superior court of New Hampshire 1776–1782; moved to Exeter, N. H., in 1779; member of the general assembly in 1783; served in the State senate in 1784; State councilor in 1785; moved to Merrimack, N. H., in 1789, where he purchased a farm and spent his remaining years in literary pursuits; died in Newburyport, Mass., June 24, 1803; interment in Thornton's Ferry Cemetery, Merrimack, N. H.

THORP, Robert Taylor, a Representative from Virginia; born near Oxford, Granville County, N. C., March 12, 1850; attended Horner Academy, Oxford, N. C., and was graduated from the law department of the University of Virginia at Charlottesville in 1870; was admitted to the bar in 1870 and commenced practice in Boydton, Mecklenburg County, Va., in 1871; Commonwealth attorney for that county 1877–1895; successfully contested as a Republican the election of William R. McKenney to the Fifty-fourth Congress and served from May 2, 1896, to March 3, 1897; successfully contested the election of Sydney P. Epes to the Fifty-fifth Congress and served from March 23, 1898, to March 4, 1899; unsuccessful candidate for reelection in 1898 to the Fifty-sixth Congress; moved to Norfolk, Va., and continued the practice of law; moved to Virginia Beach, Va., in 1934 and died November 26, 1938; interment in Forest Lawn Cemetery, Norfolk, Va.

THORPE, Roy Henry, a Representative from Nebraska; born near Greensburg, Decatur County, Ind., December 13, 1874; attended the country schools and Greensburg (Ind.) High School; studied pharmacy, medicine, and law; engaged in evangelistic work and was known as "The boy tramp orator of 1896"; was employed as a salesman in Du Quoin, Ill., 1897–1904, and in Shenandoah, Iowa, 1905–1919; engaged in secret-service work in the State of Iowa in 1917 and 1918; moved to Nebraska in 1919 and settled in Lincoln, where he resumed the occupation of salesman; elected as a Republican to the Sixty-seventh Congress to fill the vacancy caused by the resignation of C. Frank Reavis and served from November 7, 1922, to March 3, 1923; was not a candidate for renomination to the Sixty-eighth Congress; unsuccessful candidate for election in 1924 to the Sixty-ninth Congress; traveled as a sales organizer and later engaged in the insurance business; died in Lincoln, Nebr., September 19, 1951; interment in Wyuka Cemetery.

THROCKMORTON, James Webb, a Representative from Texas; born in Sparta, White County, Tenn., on February 1,

1825; attended the common schools; moved with his father to Collin County, Tex., in 1841; studied medicine in Princeton, Ky., and practiced in Collin County; served as surgeon during the Mexican War; studied law; was admitted to the bar and commenced practice in McKinney, Collin County, Tex.; member of the State house of representatives 1851–1856; candidate for presidential elector on the Whig ticket of Scott and Graham in 1852; served in the State senate 1856–1861; member of the secession convention of Texas in 1861; during the Civil War served as captain and major in the Confederate Army from the spring of 1861 until November 1863; brigadier general of State troops in 1864 and commander on the northwest border of the State; again a member of the State senate in 1865; delegate to the reconstruction convention under President Johnson's proclamation and chosen the presiding officer of that body in 1866; elected Governor of Texas and was inaugurated August 8, 1866; removed by order of General Sheridan August 9, 1867; resumed the practice of law in Collin County, Tex.; elected as a Democrat to the Forty-fourth and Forty-fifth Congresses (March 4, 1875–March 3, 1879); was not a candidate for renomination in 1878; resumed the practice of his profession; elected to the Forty-eighth and Forty-ninth Congresses (March 4, 1883–March 3, 1887); declined to be a candidate for renomination in 1886; presidential elector on the Democratic ticket of Hancock and English in 1880; unsuccessful candidate for election as United States Senator in 1881; resumed the practice of law; delegate to the Democratic National Convention at Chicago in 1892; died in McKinney, Collin County, Tex., April 21, 1894; interment in Pecan Grove Cemetery.

THROOP, Enos Thompson, a Representative from New York; born in Johnstown, Montgomery County, N. Y., August 21, 1784; attended the common schools; studied law; was admitted to the bar in 1806 and commenced practice in Auburn, N. Y.; clerk of Cayuga County 1811–1815; elected as a Democrat to the Fourteenth Congress and served from March 4, 1815, to June 4, 1816, when he resigned; unsuccessful candidate for reelection in 1816 to the Fifteenth Congress; circuit judge of New York 1823–1827; elected Lieutenant Governor of New York in 1828, and became Governor when Martin Van Buren was appointed Secretary of State of the United States March 12, 1829; elected Governor of New York and served from 1830 to 1833; naval officer of the port of New York 1833–1838; appointed Chargé d'Affaires to the Two Sicilies on February 6, 1838, and served until January 12, 1842; engaged in the management of his large estate and resided in Kalamazoo, Mich., 1847–1867; returned to his estate "Willowbrook," near Auburn, Cayuga County, N. Y., and died there November 1, 1874; interment in St. Peter's Churchyard, Auburn, N. Y.

THROPP, Joseph Earlston, a Representative from Pennsylvania; born in Valley Forge, Chester County, Pa., October 4, 1847; attended the public schools and Friends Central High School, Philadelphia, Pa., and was graduated as a civil engineer from the Polytechnic College of Pennsylvania in 1868; went to the Middle Northwest and engaged in his profession, constructing docks at Duluth and Fond du Lac, Wis., attaining the position of railroad division engineer; moved to Conshohocken, Pa., in 1870 and engaged in the manufacture of pig iron; subsequently became owner of the Earlston Furnaces, Everett, Pa., in 1888; elected as a Republican to the Fifty-sixth Congress (March 4, 1899–March 3, 1901); was an unsuccessful candidate for reelection in 1900 to the Fifty-seventh Congress; retired from active business pursuits and resided in Washington, D. C., and Miami, Fla.; died while on a visit in Quebec, Canada, July 27, 1927; interment in West Laurel Hill Cemetery, Philadelphia, Pa.

THRUSTON, Buckner, a Senator from Kentucky; born in Petsoe Parish, Gloucester County, Va., February 9, 1764; pursued preparatory studies; was graduated from William and Mary College at Williamsburg, Va., in 1783; studied law; moved to Lexington, Fayette County, Va. (now Kentucky), in 1788; was admitted to the bar and commenced the practice of law; member of the Virginia Assembly in 1789; after Kentucky was organized as a State was elected clerk of the first State senate in 1792; appointed one of Kentucky's three commissioners to settle the boundary dispute between the States of Kentucky and Virginia; district judge of Kentucky in 1791; judge of the circuit court in 1802 and 1803; appointed United States judge of the court of the Territory of Orleans in 1804, but declined; elected as a Democrat to the United States Senate and served from March 4, 1805, to December 18, 1809, when he resigned, having been appointed to a judicial position; appointed judge of the United States Circuit Court for the District of Columbia and served from December 18, 1809, until his death in Washington, D. C., on August 30, 1845; interment in the Congressional Cemetery.

THURMAN, Allen Granberry, a Representative and a Senator from Ohio; born in Lynchburg, Va., November 13, 1813; moved with his father to Chillicothe, Ohio, in 1819; attended the Chillicothe Academy; private secretary to Gov. Robert Lucas in 1834; studied law; was admitted to the bar in 1835 and practiced in Ross County, Ohio; elected as a Democrat to the Twenty-ninth Congress (March 4, 1845–March 3, 1847); declined to be a candidate for renomination in 1846; resumed the practice of law; associate justice of the supreme court of Ohio 1851–1854 and chief justice 1854–1856; unsuccessful Democratic candidate for Governor of Ohio in 1867; elected as a Democrat to the United States Senate; reelected in 1874, and served from March 4, 1869, to March 3, 1881; appointed a member of the Electoral Commission created by act of Congress approved January 29, 1877, to decide the contests in various States in the presidential election of 1876; unsuccessful candidate for reelection to the United States Senate in 1881; resumed the practice of law in Columbus, Ohio; delegate to the Democratic National Conventions in 1876, 1880, and 1884; declined to be a candidate for the nomination of Governor in 1887; unsuccessful candidate for Vice President of the United States on the Democratic ticket of Cleveland and Thurman in 1888; died in Columbus, Franklin County, Ohio, December 12, 1895; interment in Green Lawn Cemetery.

THURMAN, John Richardson, a Representative from New York; born in New York City October 6, 1814; was graduated from Columbia College in 1835; moved to Warren County, near Chestertown, N. Y., and engaged in agricultural pursuits; held several local offices; elected as a Whig to the Thirty-first Congress (March 4, 1849–March 3, 1851); declined to be a candidate for renomination in 1850; devoted his attention to the management of his estate; died at Friends Lake, Chester Township, Warren County, N. Y., July 24, 1854; interment in the family cemetery; reinterment in Oakwood Cemetery, Troy, Rensselaer County, N. Y.

THURMOND, James Strom, a Senator from South Carolina; born in Edgefield, S. C., December 5, 1902; attended the public schools; was graduated from Clemson (S. C.) College in 1923; taught in South Carolina high schools 1923–1929; Edgefield County Superintendent of Education 1929–1933; completed South Carolina law course and was admitted to the bar in 1930; city and county attorney 1930–1938; member of the State senate 1933–1938; trustee of Winthrop College, Rock Hill, S. C., 1936–1938; served as circuit judge from 1938 until World War II, when he took leave of absence on April 17, 1942, to enter upon active duty in the United States Army; served with the First Army, attached to the Eighty-second Airborne Division for the invasion of Europe and later transferred to the Pacific Theater; was discharged as a lieutenant colonel on January 20, 1946; awarded the Legion of Merit, Bronze Star Medal, Bronze Arrowhead, Army Commendation Ribbon, Purple Heart, Presidential Distinguished Unit Citation with five battle stars, Order of the Crown by the Belgian Government, and the French Croix de Guerre; returned to his position as circuit judge, but resigned in May 1946; Governor of South Carolina 1947–1951; unsuccessful as a States Rights candidate for President of the United States in 1948; unsuccessful for the Democratic nomination for United States Senator in 1950; practiced law in Aiken, S. C., 1951–1955; delegate to the Democratic National Conventions in 1932, 1936, 1948, 1952, 1956, and 1960; president of Aiken Federal Savings and Loan Association 1951–1955; chairman of Southern Governors Conference in 1950; appointed as a Democrat to the United States Senate to fill the vacancy caused by the death of Burnet R. Maybank and served from December 24, 1954, to January 3, 1955; had been previously elected as a write-in candidate in November 1954 for the term commencing January 3, 1955, and ending January 3, 1961, but due to a promise made to the voters in the 1954 election, resigned as of April 4, 1956; again elected as a Democrat in November 1956 to fill the vacancy caused by his own resignation and served from November 7, 1956, to January 3, 1961. *Reelected in 1960 for the term ending January 3, 1967.*

THURSTON, Benjamin Babock, a Representative from Rhode Island; born in Hopkinton, R. I., June 29, 1804; attended the common schools; engaged in mercantile pursuits; member of the State house of representatives 1831–1837; presidential elector on the Democratic ticket of Van Buren and Johnson in 1836; Lieutenant Governor of Rhode Island in 1838; elected as a Democrat to the Thirtieth Congress (March 4, 1847–March 3, 1849); unsuccessful candidate for reelection in 1848 to the Thirty-first Congress; elected to the Thirty-second, Thirty-third, and Thirty-fourth Congresses (March 4, 1851–March 3, 1857); was not a candidate for renomination in 1856; after leaving Congress moved to New London, Conn.; member of the board of aldermen in 1862 and 1863; member of the State house of representatives in 1869 and 1870; resumed mercantile pursuits; died in New London, Conn., May 17, 1886; interment in Cedar Grove Cemetery.

THURSTON, John Mellen, a Senator from Nebraska; born in Montpelier, Vt., August 21, 1847; moved with his parents to Madison, Wis., in 1854 and two years later to Beaver Dam, Wis.; attended the public schools and was graduated from Wayland University, Beaver Dam, Wis.; studied law; was admitted to the bar May 21, 1869, and commenced practice in Omaha, Nebr.; member of the city council 1872–1874; city attorney of Omaha 1874–1877; member of the State house of representatives 1875–1877; appointed assistant attorney of the Union Pacific Railroad in 1877 and general solicitor in 1888; presidential elector on the Republican ticket of Garfield and Authur in 1880; delegate to the Republican National Conventions at Chicago in 1884 which nominated Blaine and Logan and in 1888 which nominated Harrison and Morton, and at Philadelphia in 1900 which nominated McKinley and Roosevelt; temporary chairman of the Republican National Convention at Chicago in 1888; unsuccessful Republican candidate for United States Senator in 1893; elected as a Republican to the United States Senate and served from March 4, 1895, to March 3, 1901; was not a candidate for reelection; chairman of the Republican National Convention at St. Louis in 1896; appointed United

States commissioner to the St. Louis Exposition March 6, 1901; moved to Washington, D. C., and resumed the practice of law; returned to Omaha, Nebr., and practiced law until his death August 9, 1916; remains were cremated at Forest Lawn Cemetery, Omaha, Nebr., and the ashes interred in the Congressional Cemetery, Washington, D. C.

THURSTON, Lloyd, a Representative from Iowa; born in Osceola, Clarke County, Iowa, March 27, 1880; attended the public schools; during the Spanish-American War enlisted on June 13, 1898, as a private in Company I, Fifty-first Regiment, Iowa Volunteer Infantry, and served with this company during the Philippine Insurrection, and was honorably discharged on November 2, 1899; was graduated from the law department of the University of Iowa at Iowa City in 1902; was admitted to the bar the same year and commenced practice in Osceola, Clarke County, Iowa; captain in the National Guard of Iowa 1902–1906; prosecuting attorney of Clarke County 1906–1910; during the First World War served with the rank of captain in Company C, Twenty-sixth Battalion, United States Guards, at Fort Crook, Nebr.; member of the State senate 1920–1924; elected as a Republican to the Sixty-ninth and to the six succeeding Congresses (March 4, 1925–January 3, 1939); was not a candidate for renomination in 1938, but was an unsuccessful candidate for the Republican nomination for United States Senator; lawyer; is a resident of Osceola, Iowa.

THURSTON, Samuel Royal, a Delegate from the Territory of Oregon; born in Monmouth, Kennebec County, Maine, April 15, 1816; attended Wesleyan Seminary, Readfield, Maine, and Dartmouth College, Hanover, N. H.; was graduated from Bowdoin College, Brunswick, Maine, in 1843; studied law; was admitted to the bar in 1844 and commenced practice in Brunswick, Cumberland County, Maine; moved to Burlington, Iowa, in 1845 and continued the practice of law; editor of the Iowa Gazette; moved to Oregon City, Oreg., in 1849 and engaged in the practice of his profession; when the Territory of Oregon was formed was elected as a Democrat to the Thirty-first Congress (March 4, 1849–March 3, 1851); died while at sea April 9, 1851, en route to his home from Washington, D. C., and was buried in Acapulco, Mexico; reinterment in the Odd Fellows Cemetery, Salem, Marion County, Oreg.

THYE, Edward John, a Senator from Minnesota; born on a farm near Frederick, Brown County, S. Dak., April 26, 1896; moved in early childhood to Minnesota with his parents who settled on a farm near Northfield, Rice County; attended the public schools, Tractor and Internal Combustion School in 1913, and American Business College in 1915 and 1916; during the First World War enlisted as a private in the United States Army Air Corps in 1917 and promoted through the ranks to second lieutenant with overseas service; tractor expert, Minneapolis, Minn., in 1919; salesman 1920–1922; in 1922 engaged in agricultural pursuits; appraiser for Federal land bank in 1933 and 1934; deputy commissioner of agriculture for State of Minnesota 1939–1942; elected Lieutenant Governor of Minnesota in 1942 and succeeded to governorship on April 27, 1943; elected Governor in 1944 and served until January 1947; elected as a Republican to the United States Senate in 1946 and again in 1952 and served from January 3, 1947, to January 3, 1959; unsuccessful candidate for reelection in 1958; resumed his agricultural interests; is a resident of Northfield, Minn.

TIBBATTS, John Wooleston, a Representative from Kentucky; born in Lexington, Ky., June 12, 1802; pursued classical studies; studied law; was admitted to the bar in 1826 and commenced practice in Newport, Campbell County, Ky.; held several local offices; elected as a Democrat to the Twenty-eighth and Twenty-ninth Congresses (March 4, 1843–March 3, 1847); served as colonel in the Mexican War; resumed the practice of law in Newport, Ky., and died there July 5, 1852; interment in Evergreen Cemetery.

TIBBITS, George, a Representative from New York; born in Warwick, R. I., January 14, 1763; pursued classical studies; engaged in business in Lansingburg, N. Y., in 1784; moved to Troy, N. Y., in 1797 and became engaged in extensive mercantile pursuits; member of the State assembly in 1800; elected as a Federalist to the Eighth Congress (March 4, 1803–March 3, 1805); was not a candidate for renomination in 1804; member of the State senate 1815–1818; unsuccessful Federalist candidate for Lieutenant Governor of New York in 1816; was a member of the commission on State prisons which rendered a favorable report on the Auburn Prison system in 1824; member of the commission which had charge of the construction of Sing Sing Prison; mayor of Troy, N. Y., from 1830 to 1836; died in Troy, Rensselaer County, N. Y., July 19, 1849; interment in Oakwood Cemetery.

TIBBOTT, Harve, a Representative from Pennsylvania; born near Ebensburg, Cambria County, Pa., May 27, 1885; attended the public schools; was graduated from the school of pharmacy of the University of Pittsburgh in 1906; engaged in the retail drug business and as a pharmacist in Ebensburg, Pa., in 1906; treasurer of the William Penn Highway Association 1913–1915; treasurer of Cambria County, Pa., 1932–1935; member of the Republican State committee in 1936 and 1937; president of the First National Bank of Ebensburg since 1938; elected as a Republican to the Seventy-sixth and to the four succeeding Congresses (January 3, 1939–January 3, 1949); unsuccessful candidate for reelection in 1948 to the Eighty-first Congress; is a resident of Ebensburg, Pa.

TICHENOR, Isaac, a Senator from Vermont; born in Newark, N. J., February 8, 1754; completed preparatory studies; was graduated from Princeton College in 1775; studied law in Schenectady, N. Y.; appointed assistant commissary general in 1777 and was stationed in Bennington, Vt.; was admitted to the bar and commenced practice in Bennington, Vt., at the close of the Revolutionary War; member of the State house of representatives 1781–1784, serving as speaker in 1783; agent from the State to Congress to present Vermont's claim for admission into the Union in 1782; State councilor 1787–1792; one of the commissioners to settle the boundary question with New York in 1789; associate justice of the State supreme court 1790–1794, and chief justice in 1795 and 1796; member of the State board of censors 1792–1813; elected as a Federalist to the United States Senate to fill the vacancy caused by the resignation of Moses Robinson; reelected for the term commencing March 4, 1797, and served from October 18, 1796, to October 17, 1797, when he resigned, having been elected Governor; Governor of Vermont 1797–1806 and again in 1808; unsuccessful candidate for reelection in 1809; again elected to the United States Senate and served from March 4, 1815, to March 3, 1821; resumed the practice of his profession; died in Bennington, Vt., December 11, 1838; interment in the Village Cemetery, Old Bennington, Vt.

TIERNEY, William Laurence, a Representative from Connecticut; born in Norwalk, Fairfield County, Conn., August 6, 1876; attended the public schools; was graduated from Fordham University, New York City, N. Y., in 1898 and from New York Law School in 1900; was admitted to the bar in 1900 and commenced practice in New York City, N. Y.; moved to Denver, Colo., in 1905 and to Greenwich, Conn., in 1912, continuing the practice of law; judge of Greenwich court 1912–1914; elected as a Democrat to the Seventy-second Congress (March 4, 1931–March 3, 1933); unsuccessful candidate for reelection in 1932 to the Seventy-third Congress; resumed the practice of law in Greenwich, Conn., and New York City, N. Y.; State counsel for the Home Owners' Loan Corporation in 1934 and 1935; engaged in banking and the practice of law in Greenwich, Conn., until his death there April 13, 1958; interment in St. Mary's Cemetery.

TIFFIN, Edward, a Senator from Ohio; born in Carlisle, England, June 19, 1766; attended the common schools; studied medicine; immigrated to the United States in 1784 and settled in Charles Town, Va. (now West Virginia); attended lectures in the medical department of the University of Pennsylvania at Philadelphia in 1789; entered the ministry of the Methodist Episcopal Church in 1790; moved to Chillicothe, Ohio, in 1796 and engaged in preaching and the practice of medicine; member of the Territorial house of representatives in 1799, serving as speaker; president of the convention that formed the constitution of Ohio in 1802; elected as the first Governor of the State in 1803 and reelected in 1805; elected as a Democrat to the United States Senate and served from March 4, 1807, to March 3, 1809, when he resigned; elected to the State house of representatives in 1809, serving as speaker; resumed the practice of medicine in Chillicothe, Ohio; appointed by President Madison as the first Commissioner of the General Land Office and served from 1812 to 1814; with the consent of the President and the Senate he exchanged offices with Josiah Meigs and became surveyor general of the Northwest Territory, which position he held until removed by President Jackson July 1, 1829; died in Chillicothe, Ross County, Ohio, August 9, 1829; interment in Grand View Cemetery.

TIFT, Nelson, a Representative from Georgia; born in Groton, Conn., July 23, 1810; attended the village school; moved to Key West, Fla., with his father in 1826, to Charleston, Charleston County, S. C., in 1830, and engaged in the mercantile business; moved to Georgia and engaged in mercantile pursuits at Augusta, Richmond County, in 1835, at Hawkinsville, Pulaski County, in March 1836, and at Albany, Baker (now Dougherty) County, in October 1836; founder of the Augusta (Ga.) Guards in 1835; founder of the city of Albany, Ga., in 1836; served as justice of the peace; delegate from Baker County to the State convention held in Milledgeville, Ga., in 1839, to reduce the membership of the State legislature; elected to the Baker County Inferior Court on July 5, 1840; reelected in January 1841 and again in 1849; elected colonel of Baker County (Ga.) Militia in 1840; member of the State house of representatives in 1841, 1847, and 1851–1852; founder in 1845 of the Albany Patriot and served as editor and publisher until 1858; during the Civil War was connected with the Confederate States Navy Supply Department with the rank of captain; upon the readmission of Georgia to representation was elected as a Democrat to the Fortieth Congress and served from July 25, 1868, to March 3, 1869; presented credentials as a Member-elect to the Forty-first Congress, but was not permitted to qualify; contested the subsequent election of Richard H. Whiteley to the Forty-first Congress, but no action was taken thereon; conducted an extensive plantation and operated lumber, flour, and corn-meal mills; also instrumental in promoting the building of several railroads, serving as president; delegate to the State constitutional convention in 1877; died in Albany, Dougherty County, Ga., on November 21, 1891; interment in Oakview Cemetery.

TILDEN, Daniel Rose, a Representative from Ohio; born in Lebanon, Conn., November 5, 1804; attended the public schools; resided several years in Virginia and South Carolina; moved to

Garrettsville, Ohio, about 1828, and thence to Warren, Ohio; studied law; was admitted to the bar in 1836 and commenced practice in Ravenna, Portage County, Ohio; prosecuting attorney of Portage County 1838–1841; elected as a Whig to the Twenty-eighth and Twenty-ninth Congresses (March 4, 1843–March 3, 1847); delegate to the Whig National Convention at Philadelphia in 1848 and at Baltimore in 1852; moved to Cleveland, Ohio, in 1852; elected probate judge of Cuyahoga County and served from 1855 to 1888; died in Cleveland, Ohio, March 4, 1890; remains were cremated at Buffalo, N. Y., and the ashes deposited in the Buffalo Crematory.

TILGHMAN, Matthew, a Delegate from Maryland; born at the "Hermitage," near Centerville, Queen Annes County, Md., February 17, 1718; was tutored privately; justice of the peace for Talbot County; member of the Maryland House of Delegates 1751–1777, serving as speaker 1773–1775; president of the Revolutionary convention that directed the affairs of the colony 1774–1777; member of the committee appointed to draw up the protest against the Stamp Act; chairman of the committee of correspondence in 1774; Member of the Continental Congress 1774–1777; was summoned from his seat in Congress to attend the convention at Annapolis, Md., convening June 21, 1776, and served as president of that body, it being during his service in Annapolis that the Declaration of Independence, which he supported, was adopted and signed at Philadelphia; chairman of the committee of safety in 1775; chairman of the committee which prepared the first declaration and charter of rights and plan of government (constitution) for the State of Maryland; resigned his seat in Congress and was elected as a member of the State senate in 1777; reelected, but resigned before the expiration of his term; was an extensive land owner and engaged in planting; died at his home "Rich Neck," near Claiborne, Talbot County, Md., May 4, 1790; interment in the family cemetery at "Rich Neck."

TILLINGHAST, Joseph Leonard (great-grandson of Thomas Tillinghast), a Representative from Rhode Island; was born in Taunton, Mass., in 1791; moved to Rhode Island and pursued classical studies; published the Providence Gazette in 1809; studied law; was admitted to the bar in 1811 and began practice in Providence, R. I.; member of the State house of representatives 1826–1833, serving as speaker 1829–1832; elected as a Whig to the Twenty-fifth, Twenty-sixth, and Twenty-seventh Congresses (March 4, 1837–March 3, 1843); was not a candidate for renomination; trustee of Brown University at Providence 1833–1844; died in Providence, R. I., December 30, 1844; interment in North Burial Ground.

TILLINGHAST, Thomas (great-grandfather of Joseph Leonard Tillinghast), a Representative from Rhode Island; born in East Greenwich, R. I., August 21, 1742; completed preparatory studies; member of the State house of representatives in 1772 and 1773; held several offices under Revolutionary authorities; again a member of the State house of representatives 1778–1780; judge of the court of common pleas in 1779; member of the council of war; associate justice of the State supreme court 1780–1797; elected to the Fifth Congress to fill the vacancy caused by the resignation of Elisha R. Potter and served from November 13, 1797, to March 3, 1799; elected to the Seventh Congress (March 4, 1801–March 3, 1803); died in East Greenwich, R. I., August 26, 1821.

TILLMAN, Benjamin Ryan (brother of George Dionysius Tillman), a Senator from South Carolina; born near Trenton, Edgefield County, S. C., August 11, 1847; pursued an academic course; left school in July 1864, during the Civil War, to join the Confederate Army, but was stricken with a severe illness; engaged in agricultural pursuits; delegate to all Democratic State and National Conventions from 1890 to 1918; Governor of South Carolina 1890–1894; founded Clemson Agricultural and Mechanical College, Fort Hill, S. C., in 1893; established Winthrop Normal and Industrial College, Rock Hill, S. C., in 1895; member of the State constitutional convention in 1895; elected as a Democrat to the United States Senate in 1894 and took his seat March 4, 1895; reelected in 1901, 1907, and 1913 and served from March 4, 1895, until his death; was chairman of the Senate Committee on Naval Affairs during the First World War; died in Washington, D. C., July 3, 1918; interment in Ebenezer Cemetery, Trenton, S. C.

TILLMAN, George Dionysius (brother of Benjamin Ryan Tillman), a Representative from South Carolina; born near Curryton, Edgefield County, S. C., August 21, 1826; pursued an academic course in Penfield, Ga., and in Greenwood, S. C.; attended Harvard University, but did not graduate; studied law; was admitted to the bar in 1848 and commenced practice in Edgefield, S. C.; member of the State house of representatives 1854–1860; enlisted during the Civil War and served in the Third Regiment of South Carolina State troops in 1862; shortly after its disbandment entered the Second Regiment of South Carolina Artillery, in which he served until the close of the war; again a member of the State house of representatives in 1864; member of the State constitutional convention in 1865, held under the reconstruction proclamation of President Johnson; served in the State senate in 1865; unsuccessful candidate for election in 1876 to the Forty-fifth Congress; elected as a Democrat to the Forty-sixth Congress (March 4, 1879–March 3, 1881); presented credentials as a Member-elect to the Forty-seventh Congress and served from March 4, 1881, to June 19, 1882, when he was succeeded by Robert Smalls, who contested the election; elected to the Forty-eighth and to the four succeeding Congresses (March 4, 1883–March 3, 1893); unsuccessful candidate for renomination in 1892; engaged in agricultural pursuits and also as a publicist; member of the State constitutional convention in 1895; unsuccessful candidate for election as Governor of South Carolina in 1898; died in Clarks Hill, McCormick County, S. C., February 2, 1902; interment in the Bethlehem Baptist Church Community Cemetery.

TILLMAN, John Newton, a Representative from Arkansas; born near Springfield, Greene County, Mo., December 13, 1859; attended the common schools; was graduated from the University of Arkansas at Fayetteville in 1880; taught school; studied law; was admitted to the bar in 1883 and commenced practice in Fayetteville, Washington County, Ark.; clerk of the circuit court of Washington County 1884–1889; served in the State senate 1888–1892; prosecuting attorney of the fourth judicial circuit 1892–1898; judge of the same circuit court 1900–1905; president of the University of Arkansas 1905–1912; elected as a Democrat to the Sixty-fourth and to the six succeeding Congresses (March 4, 1915–March 3, 1929); one of the managers appointed by the House of Representatives in 1926 to conduct the impeachment proceedings against George W. English, judge of the United States District Court for the Eastern District of Illinois; did not seek renomination in 1928; died in Fayetteville, Ark., March 9, 1929; interment in Evergreen Cemetery.

TILLMAN, Lewis (nephew of Barclay Martin), a Representative from Tennessee; born near Shelbyville, Bedford County, Tenn., August 18, 1816; attended the common schools and pursued an academic course; served in the Seminole War as a private; engaged in agricultural pursuits; clerk of the circuit court of Bedford County 1852–1860; colonel of State militia before the Civil War; editor of a newspaper in Shelbyville, Tenn.; clerk and master of the chancery court 1865–1869; elected as a Republican to the Forty-first Congress (March 4, 1869–March 3, 1871); was not a candidate for renomination in 1870; engaged in agricultural pursuits; died in Shelbyville, Bedford County, Tenn., May 3, 1886; interment in Willow Mount Cemetery.

TILLOTSON, Thomas, a Representative from New York; born in Maryland in 1750; received a thorough education; studied medicine and practiced; during the Revolutionary War was commissioned first lieutenant in the Maryland Militia in 1776; appointed by Congress as physician and surgeon general of the Northern Department of the Army in 1780 and served until the close of the war; settled in New York and engaged in the practice of medicine; member of the State assembly from Red Hook, Dutchess County, from 1788 to 1790; served in the State senate 1791–1799; member of the council of appointment in 1791; elected to the Seventh Congress, but did not qualify or take his seat and resigned August 10, 1801; secretary of state of New York from August 10, 1801, to March 15, 1806, and from February 16, 1807, to June 31, 1808; retired from public life; died in Rhinebeck, Dutchess County, N. Y., May 5, 1832; interment in the vault in the rear of Rhinebeck Reformed Dutch Church.

TILSON, John Quillin, a Representative from Connecticut; born in Clearbranch, Unicoi County, Tenn., April 5, 1866; attended public and private schools at Flag Pond, in his native county, and also at Mars Hill, Madison County, N. C.; was graduated from Carson-Newman College, Jefferson City, Tenn., in 1888, from Yale University, New Haven, Conn., in 1891, and from the law department of the same university in 1893; was admitted to the bar in 1897 and commenced practice in New Haven, Conn.; enlisted as a volunteer during the war with Spain and served as second lieutenant in the Sixth Regiment, United States Volunteer Infantry; member of the State house of representatives 1904–1908, serving as speaker the last two years; elected as a Republican to the Sixty-first and Sixty-second Congresses (March 4, 1909–March 3, 1913); unsuccessful candidate for reelection in 1912 to the Sixty-third Congress; served on the Mexican border as lieutenant colonel of the Second Infantry, Connecticut National Guard, in 1916; elected to the Sixty-fourth and to the eight succeeding Congresses and served from March 4, 1915, until his resignation on December 3, 1932; Republican majority leader in the Sixty-ninth, Seventieth, and Seventy-first Congresses; was not a candidate for renomination in 1932; delegate to the Republican National Convention at Chicago in 1932; resumed practice of law in Washington, D. C., and New Haven, Conn.; special lecturer at Yale University on parliamentary law and procedure and author of a book on that subject in 1935; awarded British Medal of King George and Italian Grand Officer of the Crown for charitable work among children after World War II; died in New London, N. H., August 14, 1958; interment in private burial grounds on the family farm, Clearbranch, Tenn.

TILTON, James, a Delegate from Delaware; born in Kent County, Del., June 1, 1745; attended Nottingham Academy, Maryland; was graduated from the medical department of the University of Pennsylvania in 1771 and commenced practice in Dover, Del.; entered the Revolutionary Army as surgeon, and in 1777 was in charge of the military hospital at Princeton, N. J.; after peace was declared resumed the practice of his profession in Dover, Del.; Member of the Continental Congress 1783–1785; moved to Wilmington, Del.; Government commissioner of loans 1785–1801; served several years as a member of the State house of representatives; Surgeon General of the United States Army 1813–1815; died near Wilmington, Del., May 14, 1822; interment in Wilmington and Brandywine Cemetery.

TIMBERLAKE, Charles Bateman, a Representative from Colorado; born in Wilmington, Clinton County, Ohio, September 25, 1854; attended the common schools and Earlham College, Richmond, Ind., 1871–1874; taught school; moved to Colorado in 1885, and settled near Holyoke, Phillips County; engaged in agricultural pursuits and stock raising; member of the Republican State committee 1892–1910; superintendent of schools of Phillips County 1889–1895; county clerk 1895–1897; appointed receiver of the United States land office at Sterling, Colo., on July 1, 1897, and served until April 30, 1914; elected as a Republican to the Sixty-fourth and to the eight succeeding Congresses (March 4, 1915–March 3, 1933); unsuccessful candidate for renomination in 1932; engaged in banking in Sterling, Colo., until his death there on May 31, 1941; interment in Grand View Cemetery, Fort Collins, Colo.

TINCHER, Jasper Napoleon, a Representative from Kansas; born near Browning, Sullivan County, Mo., November 2, 1878; moved with his parents to Medicine Lodge, Barber County, Kans., in 1892; attended the common and high schools; taught school in Hardtner, Kans., from 1896 until February 1899; worked and studied in a law office and was admitted to the bar in May 1899; commenced the practice of law in Medicine Lodge, Kans.; also interested in farming and stock raising; elected as a Republican to the Sixty-sixth and to the three succeeding Congresses (March 4, 1919–March 3, 1927); was not a candidate for renomination in 1926; moved to Hutchinson, Kans., in 1926 and practiced law until his death there on November 6, 1951; interment in Memorial Park Cemetery.

TINKHAM, George Holden, a Representative from Massachusetts; born in Boston, Suffolk County, Mass., October 29, 1870; attended the public and private schools; was graduated from Harvard University, Cambridge, Mass., in 1894; member of the Boston Common Council in 1897 and 1898; studied law at Harvard Law School; was admitted to the bar in 1899 and commenced practice in Boston; member of the board of aldermen 1900–1902; served in the State senate 1910–1912; was the first American to fire a shot against the Austrians at Capo d'Argine, on the Piave River, December 11, 1917; the title of "Chevalier della Corona d'Italia" was proffered him by the King of Italy, but was not accepted because of the provision in the Constitution forbidding such acceptance without the consent of Congress; the letters patent and insignia of the title are in the possession of the Department of State; life member of the Massachusetts Society of Mayflower Descendants and of the Society of Massachusetts Bay in New England; elected as a Republican to the Sixty-fourth and to the thirteen succeeding Congresses (March 4, 1915–January 3, 1943); was not a candidate for renomination in 1942; continued the practice of law in Boston, Mass., until his retirement; died in Cramerton, N. C., August 28, 1956; interment in Forest Hills Cemetery, Boston, Mass.

TIPTON, John, a Senator from Indiana; born near Sevierville, Sevier County, Tenn., August 14, 1786; received a limited schooling; moved to Harrison County, Ind., in 1807 and engaged in agricultural pursuits; served with the "Yellow Jackets" in the Tippecanoe campaign and subsequently attained the rank of brigadier general of militia; served as sheriff of Harrison County, Ind., 1815–1819; member of the State house of representatives 1819–1823; one of the commissioners to select a site for a new capital for Indiana in 1820; commissioner to determine the boundary line between Indiana and Illinois; appointed United States Indian agent for the Pottawatamie and Miami tribes in March 1823; laid out the city of Logansport, Ind., April 10, 1828; elected as a Democrat to the United States Senate on December 9, 1831, to fill the vacancy caused by the death of James Noble; reelected in 1832 and served from January 3, 1832, to March 3, 1839; due to poor health declined to be a candidate for reelection in 1838, died in Logansport, Cass County, Ind., on April 5, 1839; interment in Mount Hope Cemetery.

TIPTON, Thomas Foster, a Representative from Illinois; born near Harrisburg, Franklin County, Ohio, August 29, 1833; attended the public schools; moved with his parents to McLean County, Ill., in 1843; studied law; was admitted to the bar in 1854 and commenced the practice of law; State attorney for the eighth judicial district of Illinois in 1867 and 1868; elected circuit judge of the eighth judicial circuit in 1870, and upon the reorganization of the circuit court under the new constitution was reelected circuit judge of the fourteenth judicial circuit; elected as a Republican to the Forty-fifth Congress (March 4, 1877–March 3, 1879); unsuccessful candidate for reelection in 1878 to the Forty-sixth Congress; again elected circuit judge and served from 1891 to 1897; resumed the practice of law; died in Bloomington, McLean County, Ill., February 7, 1904; interment in Evergreen Cemetery.

TIPTON, Thomas Weston, a Senator from Nebraska; born in Cadiz, Ohio, August 5, 1817; attended Allegheny College, Meadville, Pa.; pursued classical studies, and was graduated from Madison College, Pennsylvania, in 1840; studied law; was admitted to the bar in 1844 and commenced the practice of law; member of the Ohio State House of Representatives in 1845; appointed to a position in the United States Land Office in 1849 and served until 1852; resumed the practice of law in McConnelsville, Ohio, in 1853; was ordained a minister of the Methodist Episcopal Church in 1856; moved to Brownsville, Nebr., about 1859 and joined the Congregational Church; member of the Nebraska constitutional convention in 1859; member of the Territorial council in 1860; during the Civil War was appointed chaplain of the First Regiment, Nebraska Volunteer Infantry, 1861–1865; assessor of internal revenue for Nebraska in 1865; member of the State constitutional convention in 1867; upon the admission of Nebraska as a State into the Union was elected as a Republican to the United States Senate; reelected in 1869 and served from March 1, 1867, to March 3, 1875; resumed the practice of law; unsuccessful candidate for Governor of Nebraska in 1880; died in Washington, D. C., November 26, 1899; interment in Rock Creek Cemetery.

TIRRELL, Charles Quincy, a Representative from Massachusetts; born in Sharon, Norfolk County, Mass., December 10, 1844; attended the common schools, and was graduated from Dartmouth College, Hanover, N. H., in 1866; served as principal of Peacham (Vt.) Academy for one year and of the high school at St. Johnsbury, Vt., for two years; studied law; was admitted to the bar in 1870 and commenced practice in Boston, Mass.; member of the State house of representatives in 1872; moved to Natick, Mass., in 1873; served in the State senate in 1881 and 1882; presidential elector on the Republican ticket of Harrison and Morton in 1888; elected as a Republican to the Fifty-seventh and to the four succeeding Congresses and served from March 4, 1901, until his death in Natick, Mass., July 31, 1910; interment in Dell Park Cemetery.

TITUS, Obadiah, a Representative from New York; born in what is now Millbrook, Dutchess County, N. Y., January 20, 1789; studied law; was admitted to the bar and commenced practice in the town of Washington, Dutchess County; served as captain of Infantry in the War of 1812; elected county judge; elected sheriff of Dutchess County in 1828; elected as a Democrat to the Twenty-fifth Congress (March 4, 1837–March 3,

1839); unsuccessful candidate for reelection in 1838 to the Twenty-sixth Congress; resumed the practice of law; died in the town of Washington, Dutchess County, N. Y., September 2, 1854; interment in Nine Partners (Friends) Burial Ground at Millbrook, N. Y.

TOBEY, Charles William, a Representative and a Senator from New Hampshire; born in Roxbury, Mass., July 22, 1880; attended the public schools and Roxbury (Mass.) Latin School; moved to Temple, N. H., in 1903, and engaged in the raising of poultry; also engaged in insurance, agriculture, banking, and manufacturing; member of the State house of representatives in 1915, 1916, 1919, 1920, 1923, and 1924, serving as speaker in 1919 and 1920; served in the State senate as president in 1925 and 1926; Governor of New Hampshire in 1929 and 1930; trustee of Colby Junior College, New London, N. H.; elected as a Republican to the Seventy-third, Seventy-fourth, and Seventy-fifth Congresses (March 4, 1933–January 3, 1939); was not a candidate for renomination in 1938; elected to the United States Senate in 1938; reelected in 1944 and again in 1950 and served from January 3, 1939, until his death; United States adviser, UNESCO Conference in Paris, November 7, 1952, to December 10, 1952; member of the United States delegation to the International Monetary Conference held in Bretton Woods, N. H., in 1944; died in the naval hospital at Bethesda, Md., July 24, 1953; interment in Miller Cemetery, Temple, N. H.

TOD, John, a Representative from Pennsylvania; born in Hartford, Conn., in 1779; attended the common schools and Yale College; moved to Bedford, Pa., in 1800; taught school while studying law; was admitted to the bar in 1803 and commenced practice in Bedford, Pa.; clerk to the county commissioners of Bedford County in 1806 and 1807; member of the State house of representatives 1810–1813, serving twice as speaker; served in the State senate and acted as president 1814–1816; elected as a Democrat to the Seventeenth and Eighteenth Congresses and served from March 4, 1821, until his resignation in 1824; president judge of the court of common pleas for the sixteenth judicial district 1824–1827; appointed associate judge of the State supreme court in 1827; died in Bedford, Bedford County, Pa., in March 1830; interment in Bedford Cemetery.

TODD, Albert May, a Representative from Michigan; born near Nottawa, St. Joseph County, Mich., June 3, 1850; attended the district school and was graduated from Sturgis (Mich.) High School; studied for some time at Northwestern University, Evanston, Ill.; traveled abroad in 1875, studying foreign institutions and governments; moved to Kalamazoo, Mich.; engaged in business as a manufacturing chemist; unsuccessful Prohibition candidate for Governor in 1894; elected as a fusion candidate to the Fifty-fifth Congress (March 4, 1897–March 3, 1899); unsuccessful Democratic candidate for reelection in 1898 to the Fifty-sixth Congress; resumed his former manufacturing pursuits in Kalamazoo; member of the Society of Chemical Industry, Public Ownership League of America, and other civil and scientific organizations; founded a museum of art and a library of ten thousand rare books and illuminated manuscripts; engaged in literary pursuits and also in cultivating aromatic and medicinal plants; president of the A. M. Todd Co., manufacturing chemists; died in Kalamazoo, Mich., October 6, 1931; interment in Mountain Home Cemetery.

TODD, John Blair Smith, a Delegate from the Territory of Dakota; born in Lexington, Ky., April 4, 1814; moved with his parents to Illinois in 1827; attended private schools; was graduated from the United States Military Academy, West Point,

N. Y., in 1837; commissioned second lieutenant in the Sixth Infantry July 1, 1837, first lieutenant December 10, 1837, and captain November 8, 1843; served in the Florida War 1837–1842 and in the war with Mexico; resigned from the Army September 16, 1856; became an Indian trader and settled in Fort Randall, Dak.; studied law; was admitted to the bar in 1861 and commenced the practice of law in Yankton, Dak.; during the Civil War was appointed brigadier general of Volunteers in the Union Army September 19, 1861, which appointment expired July 17, 1862; when the Territory of Dakota was formed was elected as a Democrat to the Thirty-seventh Congress and served from December 9, 1861, to March 3, 1863; successfully contested the election of William Jayne to the Thirty-eighth Congress and served from June 17, 1864, to March 3, 1865; unsuccessful candidate for reelection in 1864 to the Thirty-ninth Congress; engaged in mercantile pursuits and the practice of his profession; served as speaker of the Territorial house of representatives in 1866 and 1867; unsuccessful candidate for election in 1868 to the Forty-first Congress; retired from public life; died in Yankton County, Dak. (now South Dakota), January 5, 1872; interment in Yankton Cemetery.

TODD, Lemuel, a Representative from Pennsylvania; born in Carlisle, Pa., July 29, 1817; pursued classical studies, and was graduated from Dickinson College, Carlisle, Pa., in 1839; studied law; was admitted to the bar in 1841 and commenced practice in Carlisle; elected to the Thirty-fourth Congress (March 4, 1855–March 3, 1857); unsuccessful Union candidate for reelection in 1856 to the Thirty-fifth Congress; during the Civil War served in the Union Army as major of the First Regiment, Pennsylvania Volunteer Reserve Corps; inspector general of Pennsylvania on the Governor's staff; elected as a Republican to the Forty-third Congress (March 4, 1873–March 3, 1875); was not a candidate for renomination in 1874; resumed the practice of law; died in Carlisle, Cumberland County, Pa., May 12, 1891; interment in Ashland Cemetery.

TOLAN, John Harvey, a Representative from California; born in St. Peter, Nicollet County, Minn., January 15, 1877; attended the public schools; moved to Anaconda, Mont., in 1897; was graduated from the law department of the University of Kansas at Lawrence in 1902; was admitted to the bar the same year and commenced the practice of law in Anaconda, Mont.; attorney of Deer Lodge County, Mont., 1904–1906; moved to Oakland, Calif., in 1914 and continued the practice of law; elected as a Democrat to the Seventy-fourth and to the five succeeding Congresses (January 3, 1935–January 3, 1947); was not a candidate for renomination in 1946 to the Eightieth Congress; retired from political activities; died in a hospital at Westwood, Calif., on June 30, 1947; interment in Holy Sepulchre Cemetery, Hayward, Calif.

TOLAND, George Washington, a Representative from Pennsylvania; born in Philadelphia, Pa., February 8, 1796; attended the common schools; was graduated from Princeton College in 1816; held several local offices; elected as a Whig to the Twenty-fifth, Twenty-sixth, and Twenty-seventh Congresses (March 4, 1837–March 3, 1843); died in Philadelphia, Pa., January 30, 1869; interment in Laurel Hill Cemetery.

TOLL, Herman, a Representative from Pennsylvania; graduated from Temple University School of Law, Philadelphia, Pa.; was admitted to the bar and commenced the practice of law in Philadelphia, Pa., in 1930; member of the Pennsylvania Prison Society, Philadelphia Housing Association, and the board of directors of the Crusader Savings & Loan Association; in 1950 was elected to the State legislature from the sixteenth legislative

district in Philadelphia and reelected in 1952, 1954, and 1956; elected as a Democrat to the Eighty-sixth Congress (January 3, 1959–January 3, 1961). *Reelected to the Eighty-seventh Congress.*

TOLLEFSON, Thor Carl, a Representative from Washington; born in Perley, Norman County, Minn., May 2, 1901; moved to Tacoma, Wash., in 1912; attended the public schools; was graduated from Lincoln High School in 1924 and from the University of Washington Law School at Seattle in 1930; was admitted to the bar in 1930 and commenced practice in Tacoma, Wash.; prosecutor of Pierce County 1938–1946; delegate to the Republican State conventions in 1936, 1938, 1940, 1942, and 1944; was elected as a Republican to the Eightieth and to the six succeeding Congresses (January 3, 1947–January 3, 1961). *Reelected to the Eighty-seventh Congress.*

TOLLEY, Harold Sumner, a Representative from New York; born in Honesdale, Wayne County, Pa., January 16, 1894; moved with his parents to Binghamton, N. Y., in 1903; attended the public schools; was graduated from Syracuse University, New York, in 1916; studied for the ministry and took a postgraduate course at Drew Theological Seminary, Madison, N. J.; director of religious education at the Metropolitan (Methodist Episcopal) Temple, New York City, in 1916 and 1917; abandoned the ministry to enlist in the military forces of the United States during the First World War and served from May 13, 1917, to July 25, 1919, attaining the rank of captain of Infantry; participated in the Meuse-Argonne offensive with the First Army, American Expeditionary Forces; was commissioned a captain in the United States Officers' Reserve Corps; engaged in the retail shoe business; elected as a Republican to the Sixty-ninth Congress (March 4, 1925–March 3, 1927); unsuccessful candidate for renomination in 1926; delegate to the Republican State convention in 1926; resumed his former business pursuits; commissioner of public welfare, city of Binghamton, from January 1932 to April 1937; in 1937 was appointed area director for New York State Department of Social Welfare, assigned to the western New York area, and served until his death; died in Kenmore, N. Y., May 20, 1956; interment in Forest Lawn Cemetery, Buffalo, N. Y.

TOMLINSON, Gideon, a Representative and a Senator from Connecticut; born in Stratford, Conn., December 31, 1780; completed preparatory studies, and was graduated from Yale College in 1802; studied law; was admitted to the bar and commenced practice in Fairfield, Conn., in 1807; clerk of the State house of representatives in 1817; member of the State house of representatives in 1818, serving as speaker; elected as a Democrat to the Sixteenth and to the three succeeding Congresses (March 4, 1819–March 3, 1827); Governor of Connecticut from 1827 to 1831, when he resigned; elected to the United States Senate and served from March 4, 1831, to March 3, 1837; trustee of Trinity College 1832–1836; retired to private life; died in Fairfield, Conn., October 8, 1854; interment in the Old Congregational Cemetery.

TOMLINSON, Thomas Ash, a Representative from New York; born in New York City in March 1802; attended the schools of Champlain and Plattsburgh, N. Y.; studied law; was admitted to the bar and commenced practice in Keeseville, N. Y., in 1823; mill owner and dealer in lands; served as colonel in the State militia; member of the State assembly in 1835 and 1836; elected as a Whig to the Twenty-seventh Congress (March 4, 1841–March 3, 1843); resumed the practice of law and also engaged in the real-estate business; unsuccessful for election to the United States Senate in 1859; died in Keeseville, N. Y., June 18, 1872; interment in Evergreen Cemetery.

TOMPKINS, Arthur Sidney, a Representative from New York; born in Middleburg, Schoharie County, N. Y., August 26, 1865; moved with his parents to West Nyack, N. Y., in 1866; attended the public schools of Clarkstown and Nyack until 1878; studied law; was admitted to the bar in 1886 and commenced practice in Nyack, Rockland County, N. Y.; police justice of Nyack, N. Y., 1887–1889; elected chairman of the Rockland County Republican committee in 1888; member of the State assembly in 1890; delegate to all Republican State conventions from 1888 to 1906; delegate or alternate to all Republican National Conventions from 1888 to 1900; county judge and surrogate of Rockland County 1893–1898; connected in an official way with various local organizations; member of the Union League Club of New York; elected as a Republican to the Fifty-sixth and Fifty-seventh Congresses (March 4, 1899–March 3, 1903); was not a candidate for renomination in 1902; resumed the practice of law in Nyack, N. Y.; elected justice of the supreme court of New York in 1906; reelected in 1920 and 1934; raised to the appellate division of the supreme court of New York in January 1930 and served until his retirement in 1936; presidential elector on the Republican ticket of Landon and Knox in 1936; died in Nyack N. Y., January 20, 1938; interment in Oak Hill Cemetery.

TOMPKINS, Caleb (brother of Daniel D. Tompkins), a Representative from New York; born near Scarsdale, Westchester County, N. Y., December 22, 1759; member of the State assembly 1804–1806; judge of the court of common pleas and county court of Westchester County 1807–1811 and 1820–1824; elected to the Fifteenth and Sixteenth Congresses (March 4, 1817–March 3, 1821); died in Scarsdale, Westchester County, N. Y., January 1, 1846; interment in the First Presbyterian Church Cemetery, White Plains, N. Y.

TOMPKINS, Christopher, a Representative from Kentucky; born in Green County, Ky., March 24, 1780; completed preparatory studies; studied law; was admitted to the bar and commenced practice in Glasgow; member of the State house of representatives in 1805; elected to the Twenty-second and Twenty-third Congresses (March 4, 1831–March 3, 1835); again a member of the State house of representatives in 1835 and 1836; presidential elector on the Whig ticket of Harrison and Granger in 1837; resumed the practice of law; died in Glasgow, Barren County, Ky., August 9, 1858; interment in the family burying ground at Glasgow.

TOMPKINS, Cydnor Bailey (father of Emmett Tompkins), a Representative from Ohio; born near St. Clairsville, Belmont County, Ohio, November 8, 1810; moved with his parents to Morgan County in 1831 and settled near McConnelsville; completed preparatory studies, and was graduated from the Ohio University at Athens in 1835; studied law; was admitted to the bar in 1837 and commenced practice in McConnelsville, Morgan County, Ohio; served as recorder of McConnelsville in 1840; prosecuting attorney of Morgan County 1848–1851; street commissioner of McConnelsville in 1850; member of the Republican State convention in 1855; elected as a Republican to the Thirty-fifth and Thirty-sixth Congresses (March 4, 1857–March 3, 1861); unsuccessful candidate for renomination in 1860; resumed the practice of law; died in McConnelsville, Ohio, July 23, 1862; interment in McConnelsville Cemetery.

TOMPKINS, Daniel D. (brother of Caleb Tompkins), a Vice President of the United States; born in Fox Meadows (later Scarsdale), Westchester County, N. Y., June 21, 1774; completed preparatory studies; was graduated from Columbia College, New York City, in 1795; studied law; was admitted to the bar in 1797 and began practice in New York City; delegate to the State constitutional convention in 1801; member of the State assembly in 1803; elected as a Democrat to the Ninth Congress, but resigned before the beginning of the congressional term to accept an appointment as associate justice of the State supreme court, in which capacity he served from 1804 to 1807; Governor of New York 1807–1817; one of the founders of the New York Historical Society; declined an appointment as Secretary of State of the United States tendered by President Madison; elected Vice President of the United States on the Democratic ticket of Monroe and Tompkins in 1816; reelected on the same ticket in 1820 and served from March 4, 1817, to March 3, 1825; delegate to the State constitutional convention in 1821, serving as its president; died in Tompkinsville, Staten Island, N. Y., June 11, 1825; interment in the Minthorne vault in St. Mark's Churchyard, New York City.

TOMPKINS, Emmett (son of Cydnor Bailey Tompkins), a Representative from Ohio; born in McConnelsville, Morgan County, Ohio, September 1, 1853; moved to Athens County, Ohio, in 1865; attended the public schools and Ohio University at Athens; studied law; was admitted to the bar in 1875 and commenced practice in Athens, Ohio; city solicitor in 1876 and 1877; mayor of Athens 1877–1879; prosecuting attorney of Athens County in 1879; delegate to the Republican State conventions in 1879, 1881, and 1883; member of the State house of representatives 1886–1890; moved to Columbus, Ohio, in 1889- member of the board of trustees of Ohio University; elected as a Republican to the Fifty-seventh Congress (March 4, 1901–March 3, 1903); resumed the practice of law in Columbus, Ohio; appointed trustee of Ohio University in 1908; died in Columbus, Ohio, December 18, 1917; remains were cremated in Cincinnati, Ohio, and the ashes returned to his home in Columbus, Ohio.

TOMPKINS, Patrick Watson, a Representative from Mississippi; born in Kentucky in 1804; received a limited education; studied law; was admitted to the bar and commenced practice in Vicksburg, Warren County, Miss.; judge of the circuit court; elected as a Whig to the Thirtieth Congress (March 4, 1847–March 3, 1849); moved to California during the gold rush of 1849; died in San Francisco, Calif., May 8, 1853; interment in Yerba Buena Cemetery.

TONGUE, Thomas H., a Representative from Oregon; born in Lincolnshire, England, June 23, 1844; attended the public schools in England; immigrated to the United States with his parents, who settled in Washington County, Oreg., November 23, 1859; attended Tualatin (Wash.) Academy, and was graduated from the Pacific University, Forest Grove, Washington County, Oreg., in 1868; moved to Hillsboro, Washington County, Oreg., in 1868; studied law; was admitted to the bar in 1870 and commenced practice in Hillsboro; chairman of the Republican State convention in 1890; served in the State senate 1888–1892; delegate to the Republican National Convention at Minneapolis in 1892, which nominated Benjamin Harrison, of Indiana, for President for a second term; again chairman of the Republican State convention, in 1894; elected as a Republican to the Fifty-fifth, Fifty-sixth and Fifty-seventh Congresses and served from March 4, 1897, until his death; had been reelected to the Fifty-eighth Congress; died in Washington, D. C., January 11, 1903; interment in the private family cemetery adjoining the Masonic Cemetery at Hillsboro, Oreg.

TONRY, Richard Joseph, a Representative from New York; born in Brooklyn, N. Y., September 30, 1893; educated in the public and high schools, Randolph Military Academy, Montclair, N. J., and Pratt Institute, Brooklyn, N. Y.; during the First

World War served as a sergeant in the United States Marine Corps 1917–1921; engaged in the real-estate and the insurance brokerage business in 1921; served in the State assembly 1922–1929; member of the New York City Board of Aldermen 1930–1934; elected as a Democrat to the Seventy-fourth Congress (January 3, 1935–January 3, 1937); unsuccessful candidate for renomination in 1936; delegate to the Democratic State conventions in 1938, 1940, 1942, and 1946; journal clerk of the National House of Representatives 1943–1946; in 1947 was appointed a commissioner of appraisal for the corporation counsel in the city of New York; real-estate and insurance broker; is a resident of Brooklyn, N. Y.

TOOLE, Joseph Kemp, a Delegate from the Territory of Montana; born in Savannah, Andrew County, Mo., May 12, 1851; attended the public schools in St. Joseph, Mo., and the Western Military Academy, Newcastle, Ky.; moved to Helena, Mont., in 1870; studied law; was admitted to the bar in 1871 and commenced practice in Helena, Mont.; district attorney of the third judicial district of Montana 1872–1876; member of the Territorial house of representatives 1879–1881; member and president of the Territorial council 1881–1883; delegate to the State constitutional conventions at Helena, Mont., in 1884 and 1889; elected as a Democrat to the Forty-ninth and Fiftieth Congresses (March 4, 1885–March 3, 1889); did not seek renomination in 1888, having become a gubernatorial candidate; elected as the first Governor of Montana and served from November 8, 1889, until January 1, 1893; resumed the practice of law in Helena; delegate to the Democratic National Conventions in 1892 and 1904; again elected Governor in November 1900; reelected in 1904 and served from January 7, 1901, until April 1, 1908, when he resigned on account of ill health; lived in retirement, dividing his time between his home in Helena, Mont., and San Francisco, Calif.; died in Helena, Mont., March 11, 1929; interment in Resurrection Cemetery.

TOOMBS, Robert, a Representative and a Senator from Georgia; born in Wilkes County, Ga., July 2, 1810; attended the University of Georgia at Athens, and was graduated from Union College, Schenectady, N. Y., in 1828; studied law at the University of Virginia at Charlottesville; was admitted to the bar and commenced practice in Washington, Wilkes County, Ga., in 1828; commanded a company in the Creek War in 1836; member of the State house of representatives 1837–1840 and 1841–1844; Whig candidate for speaker of the house in 1842; delegate to the Democratic National Convention at Baltimore in 1844; elected as a State Rights Democrat to the Twenty-ninth and to the three succeeding Congresses (March 4, 1845–March 3, 1853); elected to the United States Senate in 1852; reelected in 1858 and served from March 4, 1853, to February 4, 1861, when he withdrew; member of the State sovereignty convention at Milledgeville, Ga., January 16, 1861; during the Civil War served in the Confederate Provisional Congress; Secretary of State of the Confederate States; brigadier general in the Confederate Army; went to Europe after the war; returned to his home in Washington, Ga., in 1867; delegate to the State constitutional convention in 1877; died in Washington, Ga., December 15, 1885; interment in Rest Haven Cemetery.

TORRENS, James H., a Representative from New York; born in New York City, N. Y., September 12, 1874; elected as a Democrat to the Seventy-eighth Congress to fill the vacancy caused by the resignation of Joseph A. Gavagan; reelected to the Seventy-ninth Congress and served from February 29, 1944, to January 3, 1947; was not a candidate for renomination in 1946; retired; died in New York City, N. Y., April 5, 1952; interment in Gate of Heaven Cemetery, Mount Pleasant, N. Y.

TOUCEY, Isaac, a Representative and a Senator from Connecticut; born in Newtown, Fairfield County, Conn., November 5, 1796; pursued classical studies; studied law; was admitted to the bar in 1818 and began practice in Hartford, Conn.; prosecuting attorney of Hartford County 1822–1835; elected as a Democrat to the Twenty-fourth and Twenty-fifth Congresses (March 4, 1835–March 3, 1839); unsuccessful candidate for reelection in 1838 to the Twenty-sixth Congress; again prosecuting attorney of Hartford County 1842–1844; unsuccessful Democratic candidate for Governor of Connecticut in 1845; there being no choice by the people at the election held for Governor in 1846, he was elected to that office by the legislature; again defeated for Governor in 1847; appointed Attorney General of the United States in the Cabinet of President Polk and served from June 21, 1848, to March 3, 1849; served in the State senate in 1850; member of the State house of representatives in 1852; elected as a Democrat to the United States Senate for the term commencing March 4, 1851, and served from May 12, 1852, to March 3, 1857; declined to be a candidate for reelection; appointed Secretary of the Navy in the Cabinet of President James Buchanan and served from March 6, 1857, to March 3, 1861; resumed the practice of his profession; died in Hartford, Hartford County, Conn., July 30, 1869; interment in Cedar Hill Cemetery.

TOU VELLE, William Ellsworth, a Representative from Ohio; born in Celina, Mercer County, Ohio, November 23, 1862, attended the public schools and was graduated from Celina High School in 1879; appointed postmaster of Celina, Ohio, on May 27, 1885, and served until June 14, 1888, when a successor was appointed; was graduated from Cincinnati Law School in 1889; was admitted to the bar the same year and commenced practice in Celina; elected as a Democrat to the Sixtieth and Sixty-first Congresses (March 4, 1907–March 3, 1911); did not seek renomination in 1910; resumed the practice of law; president of the First National Bank of Celina; died in Celina, Ohio, August 14, 1951; interment in North Grove Cemetery.

TOWE, Harry Lancaster, a Representative from New Jersey; born in Jersey City, N. J., November 3, 1898; attended the public schools of Passaic, N. J., and the United States Naval Academy 1918–1920; was graduated from New Jersey Law School at Newark in 1925; was admitted to the bar the same year and commenced practice in Rutherford, N. J.; United States commissioner 1929–1931; special assistant attorney general of New Jersey 1931–1934; member of the State house of assembly in 1941 and 1942; elected as a Republican to the Seventy-eighth and to the four succeeding Congresses and served from January 3, 1943, until his resignation September 7, 1951, to become an assistant attorney general of New Jersey, in which capacity he served until October 31, 1953; engaged in the practice of law in Hackensack, N. J.; secretary and general counsel of publishing firm of Medical Economics, Inc.; is a resident of Tenafly, N. J.

TOWEY, Frank William, Jr., a Representative from New Jersey; born in Jersey City, Hudson County, N. J., November 5, 1895; attended Manresa Hall Grammar School and St. Peters High School, Jersey City, N. J.; was graduated from Holy Cross College, Worcester, Mass., in 1916 and from the law department of Fordham University, New York City, N. Y., in 1919; commissioned as a second lieutenant of Infantry, United States Army, in September 1918, and served until honorably discharged in January 1919; was admitted to the bar in 1920 and commenced practice in Newark, N. J.; elected as a Democrat to the Seventy-fifth Congress (January 3, 1937–January 2, 1939); unsuccessful candidate for reelection in 1938 to the Seventy-sixth Congress; resumed the practice of law; member of State of New Jersey

Selective Appeal Board from October 1940 to April 1947; assistant to the Attorney General of the United States, Department of Justice, at New York City since 1943; is a resident of Caldwell, Essex County, N. J.

TOWNE, Charles Arnette, a Representative and a Senator from Minnesota and a Representative from New York; born near Pontiac, Oakland County, Mich., on November 21, 1858; attended the common schools; was graduated from Owosso (Mich.) High School, and from the University of Michigan at Ann Arbor in 1881; studied law; was admitted to the bar in 1886 and commenced practice in Lansing, Mich.; moved to Duluth, Minn., in 1890 and continued the practice of law; judge advocate general of Minnesota 1893–1895; elected as a Republican to the Fifty-fourth Congress (March 4, 1895–March 3, 1897); unsuccessful Democratic candidate for reelection in 1896 to the Fifty-fifth Congress and for election in 1898 to the Fifty-sixth Congress; declined the nomination for Vice President of the United States by the national conventions of the Populist and Silver Republican Parties in 1900; unsuccessful Democratic candidate for election to the United States Senate in 1900; appointed as a Democrat to the United States Senate to fill the vacancy caused by the death of Cushman K. Davis and served from December 5, 1900, to January 28, 1901, when a successor was elected and qualified; moved to New York City in June 1901 and resumed the practice of law; delegate to the Democratic National Convention at St. Louis in 1904; elected as a Democrat from New York to the Fifty-ninth Congress (March 4, 1905–March 3, 1907); died in Tucson, Ariz., October 22, 1928, while on a speaking tour on behalf of the Democratic ticket of Smith and Robinson; interment in Evergreen Cemetery, Tucson, Ariz.

TOWNER, Horace Mann, a Representative from Iowa; born in Belvidere, Boone County, Ill., October 23, 1855; attended the public and high schools of Belvidere, the University of Chicago, and Union College of Law; was admitted to the bar in 1877 and commenced practice in Prescott, Adams County, Iowa; moved to Corning, Adams County, Iowa, in 1880, having been elected county superintendent of schools, in which capacity he served until 1884, when he resumed the practice of law; elected judge of the third judicial district of Iowa in 1890 and served until January 1, 1911; lectured on constitutional law in the University of Iowa 1902–1911; elected as a Republican to the Sixty-second and to the six succeeding Congresses and served from March 4, 1911, to April 1, 1923, when he resigned to become Governor of Puerto Rico, in which capacity he served until his resignation on September 29, 1929; resumed the practice of law in Corning, Iowa, until his death on November 23, 1937; interment in Walnut Grove Cemetery.

TOWNS, George Washington Bonaparte, a Representative from Georgia; born in Wilkes County, Ga., May 4, 1801; received a limited education; studied law; was admitted to the bar in 1824 and began practice in Montgomery, Ala.; returned to Georgia in 1826 and continued the practice of law at Talbotton; member of the State house of representatives in 1829 and 1830; served in the State senate 1832–1834; elected as a Union Democrat to the Twenty-fourth Congress and served from March 4, 1835, to September 1, 1836, when he resigned; reelected to the Twenty-fifth Congress (March 4, 1837–March 3, 1839); was not a candidate for reelection in 1838 to the Twenty-sixth Congress; again elected as a Democrat to the Twenty-ninth Congress to fill the vacancy caused by the resignation of Washington Poe and served from January 5, 1846, to March 3, 1847; unsuccessful candidate for reelection in 1846 to the Thirtieth Congress; Governor of Georgia 1847–1851; resumed the practice of law; died in Macon, Ga., July 15, 1854; interment in Rose Hill Cemetery.

TOWNSEND, Amos, a Representative from Ohio; born in Brownsville, Fayette County, Pa., in 1821; attended the common schools of Pittsburgh, Pa.; clerked in a store in Pittsburgh; moved to Mansfield, Ohio, in 1839 and engaged in mercantile pursuits; served as United States marshal during the Kansas troubles; moved to Cleveland, Ohio, in 1858 and engaged in the wholesale grocery business; member of the city council 1866–1876, serving as president for seven years; member of the State constitutional convention in 1873; elected as a Republican to the Forty-fifth, Forty-sixth, and Forty-seventh Congresses (March 4, 1877–March 3, 1883); declined renomination; member of a wholesale food-packing firm; died while on a visit to St. Augustine, Fla., March 17, 1895; interment in Lake View Cemetery, Cleveland, Ohio.

TOWNSEND, Charles Champlain, a Representative from Pennsylvania; born in Allegheny (now a part of Pittsburgh), Pa., November 24, 1841; attended the common schools and Western University, Pittsburgh, Pa.; manufacturer of wire rivets and nails; served two years in the Union Army during the Civil War as a private in Company A, Ninth Regiment, Pennsylvania Volunteer Reserve Corps, and later as adjutant of the First Pennsylvania Volunteer Cavalry; elected as a Republican to the Fifty-first Congress (March 4, 1889–March 3, 1891); was not a candidate for renomination in 1890 to the Fifty-second Congress; again engaged in manufacturing; died in New Brighton, Beaver County, Pa., on July 10, 1910; interment in Grove Cemetery.

TOWNSEND, Charles Elroy, a Representative and a Senator from Michigan; born near Concord, Jackson County, Mich., August 15, 1856; attended the common schools in Concord and Jackson and the literary department of the University of Michigan at Ann Arbor in 1877; taught school at Concord 1881–1886; register of deeds 1886–1897; studied law; was admitted to the bar in 1895 and commenced the practice of his profession in Jackson, Mich.; elected as a Republican to the Fifty-eighth and to the three succeeding Congresses (March 4, 1903–March 3, 1911); elected to the United States Senate in 1910; reelected in 1916 and served from March 4, 1911, to March 3, 1923; unsuccessful candidate for reelection in 1922; appointed on April 16, 1923, as a member of the International Joint Commission created to regulate the use of the boundary waters between the United States and Canada, in which capacity he served until his death in Jackson, Mich., August 3, 1924; interment in Maple Grove Cemetery, Concord, Mich.

TOWNSEND, Dwight, a Representative from New York; born in New York City September 26, 1826; was educated at the grammar school of Columbia College, New York City; engaged in the sugar business in the early sixties; member of the original board of the Equitable Life Assurance Society from 1859 to 1865; elected as a Democrat to the Thirty-eighth Congress to fill the vacancy caused by the resignation of Henry G. Stebbins and served from December 5, 1864, to March 3, 1865; elected to the Forty-second Congress (March 4, 1871–March 3, 1873); resumed his former business pursuits in 1875; died in New York City October 29, 1899; interment in Greenwood Cemetery, Brooklyn, N. Y.

TOWNSEND, Edward Waterman, a Representative from New Jersey; born in Cleveland, Ohio, February 10, 1855; attended private and public schools in that city; went to San Francisco, Calif., in 1875 and engaged in newspaper and literary work; moved to New York City, N. Y., in 1893 and continued his reportorial and literary pursuits; in 1900 became a resident of Montclair, Essex County, N. J.; author of novels, plays, short stories, as well as a textbook on the Constitution of the United States; elected as a Democrat to the Sixty-second and Sixty-third Congresses (March 4, 1911–March 3, 1915); unsuccessful candidate for reelection in 1914 to the Sixty-fourth Congress; served as postmaster of Montclair, N. J., 1915–1923; moved to New York City in 1924 and resumed newspaper and literary pursuits; member of the National Institute of Arts and Letters; died in New York City, N. Y., March 15, 1942; interment in Forest Hills Cemetery, Utica, N. Y.

TOWNSEND, George, a Representative from New York; born in Lattingtown, township of Oyster Bay, Queens County, N. Y., in 1769; engaged in agricultural pursuits; elected as a Democrat to the Fourteenth and Fifteenth Congresses (March 4, 1815–March 3, 1819); died in Lattingtown, township of Oyster Bay, Queens County, N. Y., August 17, 1844.

TOWNSEND, Hosea, a Representative from Colorado; born in Greenwich, Huron County, Ohio, June 16, 1840; attended the common schools and Western Reserve College, Cleveland, Ohio, in 1860; left school to enter the Union Army during the Civil War and enlisted in the Second Regiment, Ohio Volunteer Cavalry, in 1861; promoted to lieutenant, but resigned in 1863 on account of disability; studied law; was admitted to the bar in Cleveland, Ohio, in 1864 and commenced practice in Memphis, Tenn., in 1865; member of the State house of representatives in 1869; moved to Colorado in 1879 and settled in Silver Cliff in 1881; elected as a Republican to the Fifty-first and Fifty-second Congresses (March 4, 1899–March 3, 1893); unsuccessful for renomination in 1892; delegate to the Republican National Convention at Minneapolis in 1892, which nominated the presidential ticket of Harrison and Reid; United States judge for the southern district of the Indian Territory 1897–1907; died in Ardmore, Okla., March 4, 1909; interment in Woodlawn Cemetery, Norwalk, Huron County, Ohio.

TOWNSEND, John Gillis, Jr., a Senator from Delaware; born on a farm in Worcester County, Md., near Selbyville, Del., May 31, 1871; attended the rural schools; moved to Selbyville, Sussex County, Del., in 1895 and engaged in banking; also interested in manufacturing and agricultural pursuits; member of the State house of representatives 1901–1903; delegate to the Republican National Conventions in 1908, 1924, and 1928; colonel on the respective staffs of Governors Lea, Pennevill, and Miller; Governor of Delaware 1917–1921; elected as a Republican to the United States Senate in 1928; reelected in 1934 and served from March 4, 1929, to January 3, 1941; unsuccessful candidate for reelection in 1940; member of the Mount Rushmore National Memorial Commission in 1939 and 1940; member of the board of trustees of Washington College in Chestertown, Md., American University in Washington, D. C., and Goucher College in Baltimore, Md.; resumed banking, agricultural pursuits, and the raising of poultry; is a resident of Selbyville, Del.

TOWNSEND, Martin Ingham, a Representative from New York; born in Hancock, Mass., February 6, 1810; moved with his parents to Williamstown, Mass, in 1816; attended the common schools, and was graduated from Williams College, Williamstown, Mass., in 1833; studied law; was admitted to the bar in 1836 and commenced practice in Troy, N. Y.; district attorney of Rensselaer County 1842–1845; delegate to the State constitutional convention in 1867 and 1868; regent of New York University 1873–1903; elected as a Republican to the Forty-fourth and Forty-fifth Congresses (March 4, 1875–March 3, 1879); declined to be a candidate for renomination in 1878; United States district attorney for the northern district of New York 1879–1887; member of the State constitutional convention in 1890; retired from legal practice in 1901; died in Troy, N. Y., March 8, 1903; interment in Oakwood Cemetery.

TOWNSEND, Washington, a Representative from Pennsylvania; born in West Chester, Chester County, Pa., January 20, 1813; attended a private school and West Chester Academy; engaged as a bank teller 1828–1844; studied law; was admitted to the bar in 1844 and commenced practice in West Chester, Pa.; prosecuting attorney of Chester County in 1848; deputy attorney under Attorneys General Darragh and Cooper; cashier of the Bank of Chester County 1849–1857; delegate to the Whig National Convention at Baltimore in 1852; delegate to the Republican National Convention at Chicago in 1860; elected as a Republican to the Forty-first and to the three succeeding Congresses (March 4, 1869–March 3, 1877); was not a candidate for renomination in 1876; again resumed the practice of his profession in West Chester, Chester County, Pa.; president of the Bank of Chester County 1879–1894; died in West Chester, Pa., March 18, 1894; interment in Oakland Cemetery, near West Chester.

TOWNSHEND, Norton Strange, a Representative from Ohio; born in Clay-Coaton, Northamptonshire, England, December 25, 1815; in 1830 immigrated to the United States with his parents, who settled in Avon, Ohio; educated himself by the use of his father's library; taught a district school for a short time; studied medicine, and was graduated from the University of Physicians and Surgeons in New York in 1840; delegate to the World's Antislavery Convention in London, England, in 1840; studied medicine in the hospitals of London, Paris, Edinburgh, and Dublin; returned to Ohio and engaged in the practice of medicine in Avon, Ohio, in 1841; moved to Elyria, Ohio; member of the State house of representatives in 1848 and 1849; delegate to the State constitutional convention in 1850; elected as a Democrat to the Thirty-second Congress (March 4, 1851–March 3, 1853); member of the State senate in 1854 and 1855; medical inspector of the United States Army with the rank of lieutenant colonel 1863–1865; engaged in agricultural pursuits near Avon, Ohio; director of the State board of agriculture 1858–1869 and 1886–1889; professor of agriculture in Iowa Agricultural College in 1869; appointed in 1870 as one of the first trustees of Ohio Agricultural and Mechanical College; resigned in 1873 to become professor of agriculture in the new State college and served until his resignation in 1892, when he became professor emeritus; died in Columbus, Ohio, July 13, 1895; interment in Protestant Cemetery, Avon Center, Ohio.

TOWNSHEND, Richard Wellington, a Representative from Illinois; born near Upper Marlboro, Prince Georges County, Md., April 30, 1840; moved to Washington, D. C., in 1846; attended public and private schools; page in the National House of Representatives; moved to Cairo, Alexander County, Ill., in 1858; taught school in Fayette County; studied law; was admitted to the bar in 1862 and commenced practice in McLeansboro, Ill.; clerk of the circuit court of Hamilton County 1863–1868; prosecuting attorney for the twelfth judicial circuit of Illinois 1868–1872; member of the Democratic State central committee in 1864, 1865, 1874, and 1875; delegate to the Democratic National Convention at Baltimore in 1872; moved to Shawneetown, Gallatin County, Ill., in 1873 and resumed the practice of law; elected as a Democrat to the Forty-fifth and to the six succeeding Congresses and served from March 4, 1877, until his death in Washington, D. C., March 9, 1889; interment in Rock Creek Cemetery.

TRACEWELL, Robert John, a Representative from Indiana; born near Front Royal, Warren County, Va., May 7, 1852; moved with his parents to Corydon, Harrison County, Ind., in 1854; attended the public schools of Corydon, and was graduated from Hanover (Ind.) College in 1874; studied law; was admitted to the bar in 1875 and commenced practice in Corydon, Ind.; elected as a Republican to the Fifty-fourth Congress (March 4, 1895–March 3, 1897); unsuccessful candidate for reelection in 1896 to the Fifty-fifth Congress; appointed by President McKinley as Comptroller of the Treasury and served from March 4, 1897, to June 15, 1914, when he resigned; moved to Evansville, Ind., in 1914 and resumed the practice of law; elected judge of the superior court of Vanderburg County, Ind., in 1918; renominated in 1922, but died in Evansville, Ind , on July 28, 1922, before the election; interment in Cedar Hill Cemetery, Corydon, Harrison County, Ind.

TRACEY, Charles, a Representative from New York; born in Albany, N. Y., May 27, 1847; was graduated from the Albany Academy in 1866; served in the Papal Zouaves at Rome, Italy, portions of the years 1867–1870; appointed aide-de-camp to Governor Tilden, of New York, January 1, 1877; appointed manager of the House of Refuge in Hudson, N. Y., by Governor Cleveland and reappointed by Governor Hill in 1886; engaged in the distilling business; elected as a Democrat to the Fiftieth Congress to fill the vacancy caused by the death of Nicholas T. Kane; reelected to the Fifty-first, Fifty-second, and Fifty-third Congresses and served from November 8, 1887, to March 3, 1895; was an unsuccessful candidate for reelection in 1894 to the Fifty-fourth Congress; resumed business activities in Albany and Rochester, N. Y.; died at Watkins Glen, Schuyler County, N. Y., on March 24, 1905; interment in St. Agnes Cemetery, Albany, N. Y.

TRACEY, John Plank, a Representative from Missouri; born in Wayne County, Ohio, September 18, 1836; attended the public schools of Ohio and Indiana; studied law; taught school; moved to Missouri in 1858; during the Civil War enlisted as a private in the Union Army March 1, 1862, and served until March 10, 1865, when he was mustered out with the rank of first lieutenant; commissioned lieutenant colonel of Missouri Enrolled Militia in April 1865; was admitted to the bar in May 1865 and commenced practice in Stockton, Cedar County, Mo.; presidential elector on the Republican ticket of Grant and Colfax in 1868; moved to Springfield, Greene County, Mo., in 1874 and engaged in journalism; unsuccessful candidate for railroad commissioner in 1878; commissioned United States marshal for the western district of Missouri February 4, 1890, and served until March 4, 1894; elected as a Republican to the Fifty-fourth Congress (March 4, 1895–March 3, 1897); unsuccessful candidate for reelection in 1896 to the Fifty-fifth Congress; member of the State house of representatives in 1903 and 1904; superintendent of the Soldiers' Home at St. James, Mo., in 1909 and 1910; engaged in newspaper work in Springfield, Mo., where he died July 24, 1910; interment in Hazelwood Cemetery.

TRACY, Albert Haller (brother of Phineas Lyman Tracy), a Representative from New York; born in Norwich, Conn., June 17, 1793; pursued classical studies; studied medicine; moved to New York State in 1811; abandoned medicine and studied law; was admitted to the bar and commenced practice in Buffalo, N. Y., in 1815; elected as a Democrat to the Sixteenth, Seventeenth, and Eighteenth Congresses (March 4, 1819–March 3, 1825); declined a judgeship tendered by Gov. De Witt Clinton and a Cabinet position offered by President John Q. Adams; member of the State senate 1830–1837; unsuccessful Whig candidate for election to the United States Senate in 1839; tendered a portfolio in the Cabinet of President Tyler, but declined; died in Buffalo, N. Y., September 19, 1859.

TRACY, Andrew, a Representative from Vermont; born in Hartford, Vt., December 15, 1797; attended Royalton and Randolph Academies, and also Dartmouth College, Hanover, N. H., for two years; taught school; studied law; was admitted to the bar in 1826 and commenced practice in Quechee, Windsor County, Vt.; moved to Woodstock, Vt., in 1838 and continued the practice of law; member of the State house of representatives 1833–1837; served in the State senate in 1839; was an unsuccessful candidate for election in 1840 to the Twenty-seventh Congress; again a member of the State house of representatives 1843–1845 and served as speaker; elected as a Whig to the Thirty-third Congress (March 4, 1853–March 3, 1855); declined to be a candidate for renomination in 1854 to the Thirty-fourth Congress; resumed the practice of his profession; died in Woodstock, Vt., on October 28, 1868; interment in Old Cemetery on River Street.

TRACY, Henry Wells, a Representative from Pennsylvania; born in Ulster Township, Bradford County, Pa., September 24, 1807; completed preparatory studies; attended Angelica Seminary in Allegany County, N. Y.; studied law; engaged in mercantile pursuits and as a road contractor in Standing Stone, Pa., Havre de Grace, Md., and Towanda, Pa.; delegate to the Republican National Convention at Chicago in 1860, which nominated Abraham Lincoln for President; member of the State house of representatives in 1861 and 1862; elected as an Independent Republican to the Thirty-eighth Congress (March 4, 1863–March 3, 1865); collector of the port of Philadelphia in 1866; resumed mercantile pursuits; died at Standing Stone, Bradford County, Pa., April 11, 1886; interment in the Brick Church Cemetery, Wysox, Pa.

TRACY, Phineas Lyman (brother of Albert Haller Tracy), a Representative from New York; born in Norwich, Conn., on December 25, 1786; was graduated from Yale College in 1806; engaged in teaching for two years; studied law; was admitted to the bar in 1811 and commenced practice in the village of Madison, Madison County, N. Y.; moved to Batavia, Genesee County, about 1815 and continued the practice of law; elected as a Whig to the Twentieth Congress to fill the vacancy caused by the resignation of David E. Evans; reelected to the Twenty-first and Twenty-second Congresses and served from November 5, 1827, to March 3, 1833; declined to be a candidate for renomination; presidential elector on the Whig ticket of Harrison and Tyler in 1840; appointed presiding judge of Genesee County Court in 1841, and continued in that office until 1846, when he retired from public life; died in Batavia, N. Y., December 22, 1876; interment in Batavia Cemetery.

TRACY, Uri, a Representative from New York; born in Norwich, West Farms (later Franklin), Conn., February 8, 1764; was graduated from Yale College in 1789; became a Presbyterian clergyman and missionary to the Indians; moved to Oxford, N. Y., in 1791; first principal of Oxford Academy in 1794; first sheriff of Chenango County and served from 1798 until his resignation in August 1801; elected county clerk and served from 1801 to 1815; member of the State assembly in 1803; first postmaster of Oxford 1802–1805; elected as a Democrat to the Ninth Congress (March 4, 1805–March 3, 1807); elected to the Eleventh and Twelfth Congresses (March 4, 1809–March 3, 1813); appointed first judge of Chenango County July 8, 1819, and served until February 1823; died in Oxford, N. Y., July 21, 1838; interment in Riverview Cemetery.

TRACY, Uriah, a Representative and a Senator from Connecticut; born in Franklin, Conn., February 2, 1755; was graduated from Yale College in 1778; studied law; was admitted to the bar in 1781 and commenced practice in Litchfield, Conn.; major general of militia; member of the State house of representatives 1788–1793, serving as speaker in 1793; State's attorney for Litchfield County 1794–1799; elected as a Federalist to the Third and Fourth Congresses and served from March 4, 1793, until his resignation, effective October 13, 1796; elected to the United States Senate to fill the vacancy caused by the resignation of Jonathan Trumbull; reelected in 1801 and 1807, and served from October 13, 1796, until his death; President pro tempore of the Senate May 14, 1800; died in Washington, D. C., July 19, 1807; interment in Congressional Cemetery.

TRAEGER, William Isham, a Representative from California; born in Porterville, Tulare County, Calif., February 26, 1880; attended the grammar and high schools of Porterville; during the Spanish-American War served as a private in Company E, First Battalion, California Infantry, later known as Sixth Regiment, California Volunteer Infantry, and served from May 11 to December 15, 1898; was graduated from Leland Stanford Junior University in 1901; moved to Los Angeles in 1902 and engaged as athletic coach at Pomona College and later at the University of California; attended the law department of the University of Southern California at Los Angeles; deputy United States marshal 1903–1906; deputy sheriff of Los Angeles County 1907–1911; was admitted to the bar in 1909 and commenced the practice of law; deputy clerk of the California Supreme Court 1911–1921; sheriff of Los Angeles County 1921–1932; elected as a Republican to the Seventy-third Congress (March 4, 1933–January 3, 1935); unsuccessful candidate for reelection in 1934 to the Seventy-fourth Congress; died in Los Angeles, Calif., January 20, 1935; interment in Rosedale Cemetery.

TRAFTON, Mark, a Representative from Massachusetts; born in Bangor, Maine (then a district of Massachusetts), August 1, 1810; completed preparatory studies; studied theology and was ordained pastor of a church in Westfield, Mass.; elected as the candidate of the American Party to the Thirty-fourth Congress (March 4, 1855–March 3, 1857); unsuccessful candidate for reelection in 1856 to the Thirty-fifth Congress; resumed his ministerial duties and was pastor of a church in Mount Wollaston, Norfolk County, Mass.; died in West Somerville, Middlesex County, Mass., March 8, 1901; interment in Peabody Cemetery, Springfield, Mass.

TRAIN, Charles Russell, a Representative from Massachusetts; born in Framingham, Mass., October 18, 1817; attended the common schools, Framingham Academy, and was graduated from Brown University, Providence, R. I., in 1837; studied law at Harvard University; was admitted to the bar and commenced practice in Framingham, Mass., in 1841; member of the State house of representatives in 1847 and 1848; district attorney 1848–1854; declined the appointment of Associate Justice of the Supreme Court of the United States in 1852; delegate to the State constitutional convention in 1853; delegate to the Republican National Convention at Philadelphia in 1856; member of the Governor's council in 1857 and 1858; elected as Republican to the Thirty-sixth and Thirty-seventh Congresses (March 4, 1859–March 3, 1863); was not a candidate for renomination in 1862; one of the managers appointed by the House of Representatives in 1862 to conduct the impeachment proceedings against West H. Humphreys, United States judge for the several districts of Tennessee; during the Civil War served in the Union Army as a volunteer aide-de-camp to General McClellan; delegate to the Republican National Convention at Baltimore in 1864; moved to Boston, Mass.; again served in the State house of representatives 1868–1871; attorney general of Massachusetts 1871–1878; resumed the practice of law; died while on a visit in Conway, Carroll County, N. H., July 28, 1885; interment in Edgell Grove Cemetery, Framingham, Mass.

TRAMMELL, Park, a Senator from Florida; born in Macon County, Ala., April 9, 1876; moved to Florida, in his infancy, with his parents who settled on a farm near Lakeland, Polk County; attended the common schools in Florida; studied law at the Vanderbilt University, Nashville, Tenn., and was graduated from Cumberland University, Lebanon, Tenn., in 1899; was admitted to the bar in 1899 and commenced practice in Lakeland, Fla.; engaged as a fruit grower and for a while owned and edited a newspaper; mayor of Lakeland 1899–1903; served in the State house of representatives in 1902; member of the State senate 1904–1908, serving as president in 1905; attorney general of Florida 1909–1913; Governor of Florida 1913–1917; elected in 1916 as a Democrat to the United States Senate; reelected in 1922, 1928, and again in 1934, and served from March 4, 1917, until his death in Washington, D. C., May 8, 1936; interment in Roselawn Cemetery, Lakeland, Fla.

TRANSUE, Andrew Jackson, a Representative from Michigan; born in Clarksville, Ionia County, Mich., January 12, 1903; attended the local schools and was graduated from the Detroit (Mich.) College of Law in 1926; was admitted to the bar in 1926 and commenced the practice of law in Flint, Mich., in 1927; prosecuting attorney of Genesee County 1933–1937; elected as a Democrat to the Seventy-fifth Congress (January 3, 1937–January 3, 1939); unsuccessful candidate for reelection in 1938 to the Seventy-sixth Congress; resumed the practice of law in Flint, Mich., where he now resides.

TRAPIER, Paul, a Delegate from South Carolina; born in Prince George's Parish, Winyah, near Georgetown, S. C., in 1749; educated in England, where he attended Eton College 1763–1765; admitted pensioner, St. John's College, Cambridge, March 20, 1766; admitted to the Middle Temple, London, February 17, 1767; member of the Provincial Congress and the committee of safety for Georgetown, S. C.; member of the South Carolina General Assembly in 1776; justice of the peace in 1776; served in the Revolutionary War as captain of the Georgetown Artillery; Member of the Continental Congress in 1777 and 1778; died at his home near Georgetown, S. C., on July 8, 1778; interment in the churchyard of Prince George, Winyah, Georgetown, S. C.

TRAYNOR, Philip Andrew, a Representative from Delaware; born in Wilmington, New Castle County, Del., May 31, 1874; attended the public schools, Goldey Business College, Wilmington, Del., and the University of Delaware at Newark; was graduated in 1895 from the dental department of the University of Pennsylvania at Philadelphia and commenced the practice of dentistry in Wilmington, Del.; during the First World War served as a dental examiner; a fellow of the American College of Dentistry; member of the State board of dentistry 1918–1943, serving as chairman of the board since 1922; delegate to the State Democratic convention in 1936; vice president and member of the board of trustees of Ferris Industrial School for Boys 1938–1942; elected as a Democrat to the Seventy-seventh Congress (January 3, 1941–January 3, 1943); unsuccessful candidate for reelection in 1942 to the Seventy-eighth Congress; resumed the practice of his chosen profession; elected as a Democrat to the Seventy-ninth Congress (January 3, 1945–January 3, 1947); unsuccessful candidate for reelection in 1946 to the Eightieth Congress; resumed the practice of dentistry at Wilmington, Del., where he now resides.

TREADWAY, Allen Towner, a Representative from Massachusetts; was born in Stockbridge, Berkshire County, Mass., on September 16, 1867; attended the public schools, and was graduated from Amherst (Mass.) College in 1886; engaged in the hotel business; member of the State house of representatives in 1904; member of the State senate 1908–1911, and served as president 1909–1911; elected as a Republican to the Sixty-third and to the fifteen succeeding Congresses (March 4, 1913–January 3, 1945); was not a candidate for renomination in 1944; retired from public and political activities and resided in Stockbridge, Mass., and Washington, D. C.; died in Washington, D. C., February 16, 1947; interment in Stockbridge Cemetery, Stockbridge, Mass.

TREADWELL, John, a Delegate from Connecticut; born in Farmington, Hartford County, Conn., November 23, 1745; completed preparatory studies; was graduated from Yale College in 1767; studied law; was admitted to the bar and commenced practice in Farmington, Conn.; member of the State house of representatives 1776–1785; clerk of the court of probate 1777–1784; member of the Governor's council in 1785; Member of the Continental Congress in 1785 and 1786; member of the State council 1786–1797; judge of the court of common pleas; delegate to the State convention in 1788 which ratified the Federal Constitution; judge of probate and the supreme court of errors 1789–1809; Lieutenant Governor of Connecticut 1798–1809; Governor of Connecticut 1809–1811; delegate to the State constitutional convention in 1818; died in Farmington, Conn., August 18, 1823; interment in the Old Cemetery.

TREDWAY, William Marshall, a Representative from Virginia; born near Farmville, Prince Edward County, Va., August 24, 1807; completed preparatory studies; was graduated from Hampden-Sidney College, Prince Edward County, Va., in 1827; studied law; was admitted to the bar in 1830 and commenced practice in Danville, Va.; elected as a Democrat to the Twenty-ninth Congress (March 4, 1845–March 3, 1847); unsuccessful candidate for reelection in 1846 to the Thirtieth Congress; delegate to the Democratic State convention in 1850; member of the secession convention of Virginia in 1861; judge of the circuit court of Virginia 1870–1879; resumed the practice of law in Chatham, Va., and died there May 1, 1891; interment in Chatham Cemetery.

TREDWELL, Thomas (grandfather of Thomas Treadwell Davis), a Representative from New York; born in Smithtown, Long Island, N. Y., February 6, 1743; was graduated from Princeton College in 1764; studied law; was admitted to the bar and began practice in Plattsburg, N. Y.; delegate to the Provincial Congress of New York in 1774 and 1775; delegate to the State constitutional convention in 1776 and 1777; member of the State assembly 1777–1783; judge of the court of probate 1778–1787; served in the State senate 1786–1789; surrogate of Suffolk County 1787–1791; delegate to the State convention which ratified the Constitution of the United States in 1788; elected to the Second Congress to fill the vacancy caused by the death of James Townsend; reelected to the Third Congress and served from May 1791 to March 3, 1795; delegate to the State constitutional convention in 1801; again a member of the State senate 1803–1807; surrogate of Clinton County 1807–1831; died in Plattsburg, Clinton County, N. Y., December 30, 1831; interment in a private burial ground in the town of Beekmantown (north of Plattsburg), overlooking Tredwell's Bay, on the State road.

TRELOAR, William Mitchellson, a Representative from Missouri; born near Linden, Iowa County, Wis., September 21, 1850; attended the common schools; moved to Mount Pleasant, Iowa, in 1864 and attended the high school and the Iowa Wesleyan University at Mount Pleasant; moved to Missouri in 1872; taught English and music in Mount Pleasant College, Huntsville, Mo., 1872–1875; moved to Mexico, Audrain County, Mo., in

1875 and taught in the Synodical Female College in Fulton, Hardin College in Mexico, Mo., and the public schools of Mexico, Mo.; delegate to the Republican State convention in 1894; elected as a Republican to the Fifty-fourth Congress (March 4, 1895–March 3, 1897); unsuccessful candidate for reelection in 1896 to the Fifty-fifth Congress; appointed by President William McKinley on March 22, 1898, postmaster of Mexico, Mo., and served until March 16, 1904; engaged in the music publishing business at Kansas City, Mo., in 1905; moved to St. Louis, Mo., in 1915 and continued the music publishing business; also engaged in teaching and composing music; served as election judge 1920–1924; died in St. Louis, Mo., July 3, 1935; interment in Bellefontaine Cemetery.

TREMAIN, Lyman, a Representative from New York; born in Durham, Greene County, N. Y., June 14, 1819; attended the common schools and Kinderhook Academy; studied law; was admitted to the bar in 1840 and commenced practice in Durham, N. Y.; elected supervisor of Durham in 1842; appointed district attorney in 1844; elected surrogate and county judge of Greene County in 1846; unsuccessful candidate for reelection in 1851; moved to Albany, N. Y., in 1853 and practiced law; elected, as a Democrat, attorney general of New York in 1858; unsuccessful candidate for reelection in 1860; unsuccessful Republican candidate for Lieutenant Governor of New York in 1862; member of the State assembly 1866–1868, serving as speaker in 1867; elected as a Republican to the Forty-third Congress (March 4, 1873–March 3, 1875); was not a candidate for renomination in 1874; resumed the practice of law in Albany; died in New York City, while on a visit, November 30, 1878; interment in the Rural Cemetery, Albany, N. Y.

TREZVANT, James, a Representative from Virginia; born in Sussex County, Va.; completed preparatory studies; studied law; was admitted to the bar and commenced practice in Jerusalem, Va.; attorney general of Virginia; delegate to the State constitutional convention in 1820; served in the State house of delegates; elected to the Nineteenth, Twentieth, and Twenty-first Congresses (March 4, 1825–March 3, 1831); died in Southampton County, Va., September 2, 1841.

TRIBBLE, Samuel Joelah, a Representative from Georgia; born on a farm near Carnesville, Franklin County, Ga., November 15, 1869; attended the common schools and the University of George at Athens; studied law; was admitted to the bar in 1891 and commenced practice in Athens, Ga.; solicitor of the city court 1899–1904; solicitor general of the western circuit of Georgia 1904–1908; continued the practice of law in Athens until elected to Congress; elected as a Democrat to the Sixty-second, Sixty-third, and Sixty-fourth Congresses and served from March 4, 1911, until his death; had been reelected in 1916 to the Sixty-fifth Congress; died in Washington, D. C., December 8, 1916; interment in Oconee Cemetery, Athens, Ga.

TRIGG, Abram (brother of John Johns Trigg), a Representative from Virginia; born on his father's estate, near Old Liberty (now Bedford), Va., in 1750; completed academic studies; studied law; was admitted to the bar and commenced practice in Montgomery County, Va.; lived on his estate, "Buchanan's Bottom," on New River; held local offices, such as clerk and judge, and various other offices in Montgomery County; served in the Revolutionary War as lieutenant colonel of militia in 1782 and later as general of militia in Virginia; delegate to the Virginia convention of 1788 that ratified the Constitution of the United States; elected to the Fifth and to the five succeeding Congresses (March 4, 1797–March 3, 1809); died and was buried on the family estate.

TRIGG, Connally Findlay, a Representative from Virginia; born in Abingdon, Washington County, Va., September 18, 1847; attended the common schools; studied law; was admitted to the bar in 1870 and commenced practice in Abingdon, Va.; during the Civil War was a private in the First Virginia Cavalry and also served in the Confederate States Navy; elected Commonwealth attorney for Washington County in 1872, which position he held until he resigned in 1884 to become a candidate for Congress; elected as a Democrat to the Forty-ninth Congress (March 4, 1885–March 3, 1887); resumed the practice of law; died in Abingdon, Va., April 23, 1907; interment in Sinking Spring Cemetery.

TRIGG, John Johns (brother of Abram Trigg), a Representative from Virginia; born on his father's estate near Old Liberty (now Bedford), Va., in 1748; received a liberal schooling; engaged in agricultural pursuits; raised a company of militia in Bedford County, Va., in 1775; was commissioned captain March 23, 1778; promoted to the rank of major in 1781, and served throughout the Revolution; served under Washington at the siege of Yorktown; member of the State convention which ratified the Federal Constitution in 1788; lieutenant colonel of militia in 1791; major of the Second Battalion, Tenth Regiment of Militia, in 1793; justice of the peace of Bedford County; served as a member of the Virginia House of Delegates 1784–1792; elected to the Fifth and to the three succeeding Congresses and served from March 4, 1797, until his death on his estate, near Old Liberty, Bedford County, Va., on May 17, 1804; interment in burial grounds on his estate.

TRIMBLE, Carey Allen, a Representative from Ohio; born in Hillsboro, Highland County, Ohio, September 13, 1813; attended Pestalostian School in Philadelphia, Pa., and Stubb's Classical School in Newport, Ky.; was graduated from Ohio University at Athens in 1833 and from Cincinnati Medical College in 1836; taught for four years; practiced medicine in Chillicothe, Ohio; elected as a Republican to the Thirty-sixth and Thirty-seventh Congresses (March 4, 1859–March 3, 1863); unsuccessful candidate for reelection; resumed medical practice; moved to Columbus, Ohio, where he died May 4, 1887; interment in Grand View Cemetery, Chillicothe, Ohio.

TRIMBLE, David, a Representative from Kentucky; born in Frederick County, Va., in June 1782; was graduated from William and Mary College, Williamsburg, Va., in 1899; studied law; was admitted to the bar and commenced legal practice in Mount Sterling, Ky.; served in the War of 1812 as brigade quartermaster of the First Brigade, Kentucky Mounted Militia, and later as a private in the Battalion of Kentucky Mounted Infantry Volunteers commanded by Major Dudley; elected as a Democrat to the Fifteenth and to the four succeeding Congresses (March 4, 1817–March 3, 1827); was an unsuccessful candidate for reelection to the Nineteenth Congress; died at Trimble's Furnace, Greenup County, Ky., October 20, 1842.

TRIMBLE, James William, a Representative from Arkansas; born in Osage, Carroll County, Ark., February 3, 1894; attended the public schools; was graduated from the University of Arkansas at Fayetteville in 1917; was admitted to the bar in 1925 and commenced practice in Berryville, Carroll County, Ark.; during the First World War served in the United States Army as a private and was assigned to the Adjutant General's Office, Little Rock, Ark.; county official of Carroll County, Ark., 1920–1928; prosecuting attorney of the fourth judicial circuit of Arkansas 1930–1938; judge of the fourth judicial circuit of Arkansas 1938–1944; elected as a Democrat to the Seventy-ninth and to the seven succeeding Congresses (January 3, 1945–January 3, 1961). *Reelected to the Eighty-seventh Congress.*

TRIMBLE, John, a Representative from Tennessee; born in Roane County, Tenn., February 7, 1812; pursued classical studies under a private tutor and at the University of Nashville; studied law; was admitted to the bar and commenced practice in Nashville, Tenn.; attorney general of Tennessee 1836–1842; member of the State house of representatives in 1843 and 1844; served in the State senate in 1845 and 1846, and in 1859 and 1861, when he resigned because of the secession of the State; United States attorney from April 1862 until August 1864, when he resigned; served in the State senate from 1865 to 1867; elected as a Republican to the Fortieth Congress (March 4, 1867–March 3, 1869); died in Nashville, Tenn., February 23, 1884.

TRIMBLE, Lawrence Strother, a Representative from Kentucky; born near Flemingsburg, Fleming County, Ky., August 26, 1825; completed preparatory studies; studied law; was admitted to the bar in 1847 and commenced practice in Paducah, Ky.; member of the State house of representatives in 1851 and 1852; judge of the equity and criminal court of the first judicial circuit of Kentucky 1856–1860; president of the New Orleans & Ohio Railroad Co. 1860–1865; unsuccessful candidate for election in 1868 to the Thirty-eighth Congress; elected as a Democrat to the Thirty-ninth, Fortieth, and Forty-first Congresses (March 4, 1865–March 3, 1871); unsuccessful candidate for renomination in 1870; resumed the practice of law; moved to Albuquerque, N. Mex., in 1879 and continued the practice of law until 1889, when he retired; died in Albuquerque, N. Mex., August 9, 1904; interment in Fairview Cemetery.

TRIMBLE, South, a Representative from Kentucky; born near Hazel Green, Wolfe County, Ky., April 13, 1864; attended the public schools of Frankfort and Excelsior Institute; engaged in agricultural pursuits near Frankfort, Ky.; member of the State house of representatives 1898–1900, serving as speaker in 1900, holding this office during the memorable Goebel election contest; elected as a Democrat to the Fifty-seventh, Fifty-eighth, and Fifty-ninth Congresses (March 4, 1901–March 3, 1907); did not seek renomination in 1906, but was an unsuccessful Democratic candidate for Lieutenant Governor of Kentucky; Clerk of the National House of Representatives from April 4, 1911, to May 18, 1919; retired from public life and operated a plantation near Selma, Ala.; again served as Clerk of the National House of Representatives from December 7, 1931, until his death in Washington, D. C., November 23, 1946; interment in Frankfort Cemetery, Frankfort, Ky.

TRIMBLE, William Allen, a Senator from Ohio; born in Woodford, Ky., April 4, 1786; was graduated from Transylvania College, Lexington, Ky.; studied law; was admitted to the bar in 1811 and commenced practice in Highland County, Ohio; adjutant in the campaign against the Pottawatomie Indians in 1812; major of Ohio Volunteers May 7, 1812; taken prisoner at the capture of Detroit; major of the Twenty-sixth United States Infantry March 18, 1813; brevetted lieutenant colonel September 17, 1814, for gallantry at Fort Erie, where he was severely wounded; lieutenant colonel of the First United States Infantry November 30, 1814; transferred to the Eighth United States Infantry May 17, 1815; resigned March 1, 1819; elected to the United States Senate and served from March 4, 1819, until his death in Washington, D. C., December 13, 1821; interment in the Congressional Cemetery.

TRIPLETT, Philip, a Representative from Kentucky; born in Madison County, Ky., December 24, 1799; attended the common schools of central Kentucky near Franklin, and in Scott County; studied law in Owensboro, Daviess County, Ky.; was admitted to the bar and commenced practice in Owensboro in 1824;

member of the State house of representatives in 1824; presidential elector on the Whig ticket of Harrison and Granger in 1836; elected as a Whig to the Twenty-sixth and Twenty-seventh Congresses (March 3, 1839–March 3, 1843); was not a candidate for reelection in 1842; presidential elector on the Whig ticket of Clay and Frelinghuysen in 1844; delegate to the State constitutional convention in 1849; died in Owensboro, Ky., March 30, 1852; interment in Elwood Cemetery.

TRIPPE, Robert Pleasant, a Representative from Georgia; born near Monticello, Jasper County, Ga., December 21, 1819; moved with his father to Monroe County and settled near Culloden; attended Randolph-Macon College, Ashland, Va., and was graduated from the Old Franklin College (later the University of Georgia) at Athens in 1839; studied law; was admitted to the bar in 1840 and commenced practice in Forsyth, Ga.; member of the State house of representatives 1849–1852; unsuccessful candidate for election in 1852 to the Thirty-third Congress; elected as a Whig to the Thirty-fourth and Thirty-fifth Congresses (March 4, 1855–March 3, 1859); was not a candidate for renomination in 1858 having become a candidate for State senator; served in the State senate in 1859 and 1860; Member of the First Confederate Congress; served in the Confederate Army during the Civil War 1862–1865; resumed the practice of law in Forsyth, Ga.; associate judge of the State supreme court from 1873 until 1875, when he resigned; again resumed the practice of law in Atlanta, Ga., and died there July 22, 1900; interment in Forsyth Cemetery, Forsyth, Ga.

TROTTER, James Fisher, a Senator from Mississippi; born in Brunswick County, Va., November 5, 1802; moved with his father to eastern Tennessee; attended private schools; studied law; was admitted to the bar in 1820 and commenced practice in Hamilton, Monroe County, Miss., in 1823; member of the State house of representatives 1827–1829; served in the State senate 1829–1833; judge of the circuit court of Mississippi in 1833; appointed as a Democrat to the United States Senate to fill the vacancy caused by the resignation of John Black and served from January 22 to July 10, 1838, when he resigned; judge of the supreme court of Mississippi from 1839 until his resignation in 1842; moved to Holly Springs, Marshall County, Miss., and resumed the practice of law in 1840; vice chancellor of the northern district of Mississippi 1855–1857; professor of law at the University of Mississippi 1860–1862; appointed circuit judge in 1866 and served until his death in Holly Springs, Miss., March 9, 1866; interment in Hill Crest Cemetery.

TROTTI, Samuel Wilds, a Representative from South Carolina; born in Barnwell, S. C., July 18, 1810; attended the common schools; was graduated from South Carolina College (now University of South Carolina) at Columbia in 1832; studied law; was admitted to the bar and practiced; served in the Seminole War; member of the State house of representatives; elected to the Twenty-seventh Congress to fill the vacancy caused by the resignation of Sampson H. Butler and served from December 17, 1842, to March 3, 1843; resumed the practice of law; died in Buckhead, Fairfield District (now county), S. C., June 24, 1856.

TROUP, George Michael, a Representative and a Senator from Georgia; born at McIntosh Bluff, on Tombigbee River, Ala. (then a part of Georgia), September 8, 1780; received preliminary education at home and in the schools of Savannah, Ga.; attended Erasmus Hall, Flatbush, N. Y., and was graduated from Princeton College in 1797; studied law; was admitted to the bar and commenced practice in Savannah, Ga., in 1799; member of the State house of representatives 1803–1805; unsuccessful candidate for election to the Ninth Congress to fill the vacancy caused by the resignation of Joseph Bryan; elected as a Democrat to the Tenth and to the three succeeding Congresses (March 4, 1807–March 3, 1815); was not a candidate for renomination in 1814; retired to his plantation in Laurens County; elected as a State Rights Democrat to the United States Senate for the term beginning March 4, 1817; subsequently elected to fill the vacancy in the term ending March 3, 1817, caused by the resignation of William W. Bibb, and served from November 13, 1816, until September 23, 1818, when he resigned; unsuccessful candidate for Governor in 1820; Governor of Georgia 1823–1827; again elected to the United States Senate and served from March 4, 1829, to November 8, 1833, when he resigned; in 1852 declined the nomination of the Southern Rights Party of Alabama for the Presidency; died while on a visit to one of his plantations in Montgomery County, Ga., April 26, 1856; interment on the Rosemont plantation, Montgomery County, Ga.

TROUT, Michael Carver, a Representative from Pennsylvania; born in Hickory Township, Mercer County, Pa., September 30, 1810; received a very limited education; employed as a hatter for three years and then became a carpenter and contractor; served as president of the Hickory Township School Board for twenty years; elected burgess of Sharon in 1841; recorder of Mercer County, Pa., 1842–1845; prothonotary 1846–1851; elected as a Democrat to the Thirty-third Congress (March 4, 1853–March 3, 1855); unsuccessful candidate for reelection; engaged in iron manufacturing, banking, and coal mining; died in Hickory Township, Pa., June 25, 1873; interment in Morefield Cemetery, Hickory Township, near Sharon, Pa.

TROUTMAN, William Irvin, a Representative from Pennsylvania; born in Shamokin, Northumberland County, Pa., January 13, 1905; attended the public schools; was graduated from Franklin and Marshall College, Lancaster, Pa., in 1927, and from the University of Pennsylvania Law School at Philadelphia in 1930; was admitted to the bar in 1930 and commenced practice in Shamokin; special attorney for Pennsylvania 1939-1943; elected as a Republican to the Seventy-eighth Congress and served from January 3, 1943, until his resignation on January 2, 1945; did not seek renomination in 1944; member of the Pennsylvania State senate in 1945; elected judge of the Court of Common Pleas of Northumberland County, Pa., for a ten-year term and assumed his duties on January 7, 1946; reelected in November 1955 for term ending January 1966; is a resident of Shamokin, Pa.

TROWBRIDGE, Rowland Ebenezer, a Representative from Michigan; born in Horseheads, Chemung County, N. Y., June 18, 1821; moved with his parents in 1821 to Oakland County, Mich.; was graduated from Kenyon College, Gambier, Ohio, in 1841; engaged in agricultural pursuits; member of the State senate 1856–1860; elected as a Republican to the Thirty-seventh Congress (March 4, 1861–March 3, 1863); unsuccessful candidate for reelection; elected to the Thirty-ninth and Fortieth Congresses (March 4, 1865–March 3, 1869); unsuccessful candidate for renomination; resumed agricultural pursuits; Commissioner of Indian Affairs in 1880 and 1881; died in Birmingham, Mich., April 20, 1881; interment in Greenwood Cemetery.

TRUAX, Charles Vilas, a Representative from Ohio; born on a farm near Sycamore, Wyandot County, Ohio, February 1, 1887; attended the public schools and was graduated from Sycamore High School; engaged in the implement business and afterward in agricultural pursuits, specializing in raising and breeding registered swine; editor of the Swine World 1916–1921; appointed director of agriculture of Ohio by Gov. A. V. Donahey in 1913 and served until 1929; unsuccessful candidate for election to the

United States Senate in 1928; engaged in the life insurance business in Columbus, Ohio, in 1928; was elected as a Democrat to the Seventy-third and Seventy-fourth Congresses and served from March 4, 1933, until his death in Washington, D. C., August 9, 1935; interment in Pleasant View Cemetery, Sycamore, Ohio.

TRUMAN, Harry S., a Senator from Missouri, a Vice President, and a President of the United States; born in Lamar, Barton County, Mo., May 8, 1884; moved with his parents to a farm in Jackson County, Mo., in 1888; attended the public schools in Independence, Mo.; engaged in agricultural pursuits; during the First World War was commissioned a first lieutenant on June 22, 1917, and later a captain, and served with Battery D, One Hundred and Twenty-ninth Field Artillery, United States Army, with service overseas, until his discharge as a major on May 6, 1919; colonel of Field Artillery, United States Army Reserve Corps, 1927–1945; engaged in the haberdashery business 1919–1921; studied law at Kansas City (Mo.) Law School; judge of the Jackson County Court 1922–1924 and presiding judge 1926–1934; elected as a Democrat to the United States Senate in 1934; reelected in 1940 and served from January 3, 1935, until his resignation on January 17, 1945; elected Vice President of the United States on the Democratic ticket with Franklin Delano Roosevelt in 1944; inaugurated January 20, 1945, and upon the death of President Roosevelt, April 12, 1945, became President of the United States; elected in 1948 for the term ending January 20, 1953; is a resident of Independence, Mo.

TRUMBO, Andrew, a Representative from Kentucky; born in Montgomery (now Bath) County, Ky., September 15, 1797; attended the common schools; employed in the county clerk's office; studied law; was admitted to the bar and commenced practice in Owingsville, Ky., in 1824; clerk of Bath County in 1830; Commonwealth attorney for Bath County in 1830; elected as a Whig to the Twenty-ninth Congress (March 4, 1845–March 3, 1847); presidential elector on the Democratic ticket of Cass and Butler in 1848; resumed the practice of law; moved to Franklin County, Ky.; died in Frankfort, Ky., August 21, 1871; interment in the City Cemetery, Owingsville, Ky.

TRUMBULL, Jonathan (brother of Joseph Trumbull), a Representative and a Senator from Connecticut; born in Lebanon, Conn., March 26, 1740; was graduated from Harvard College in 1759; member of the Colonial Legislature of Connecticut, and served as speaker of the house; served in the Continental Army as a paymaster 1776–1780; appointed secretary and first aide-de-camp to General Washington in 1780; elected as a Federalist to the First, Second, and Third Congresses (March 4, 1789–March 3, 1795), serving as Speaker in the Second Congress; did not seek reelection, having become a candidate for Senator; elected to the United States Senate and served from March 4, 1795, to June 10, 1796, when he resigned; Lieutenant Governor of Connecticut from 1796 until the death of Governor Wolcott on December 1, 1797, when be became Acting Governor; was reelected for eleven consecutive terms, and served as chief executive of the State from 1797 until his death in Lebanon, Conn, August 7, 1809; interment in the Old Cemetery.

TRUMBULL, Joseph (brother of Jonathan Trumbull), a Delegate from Connecticut; born in Lebanon, Conn., March 11, 1737; was graduated from Harvard College in 1756; Member of the Continental Congress in 1774 and 1775; served in the Continental Army as commissary general with the rank of colonel from July 19, 1775, to August 2, 1777; was commissioner of the board of war from 1777 until his resignation in April 1778 on account of ill health; died in Lebanon, Conn., July 23, 1778; interment in the Old Cemetery.

TRUMBULL, Joseph, a Representative from Connecticut; born in Lebanon, Conn., December 7, 1782; completed preparatory studies; was graduated from Yale College in 1801; studied law; was admitted to the bar in 1803 at Windham, Conn., and commenced practice in Hartford, Conn.; in 1828 became president of the Hartford Bank and later of the Providence, Hartford & Fishkill Railroad Co.; member of the State house of representatives in 1832; elected as a Whig to the Twenty-third Congress to fill the vacancy caused by the resignation of William W. Ellsworth and served from December 1, 1834, to March 3, 1835; resigned the presidency of the bank in November 1839; elected to the Twenty-sixth and Twenty-seventh Congresses (March 4, 1839–March 3, 1843); again a member of the State house of representatives in 1848; Governor of Connecticut in 1849 and 1850; again elected to the State house of representatives in 1851; died in Hartford, Conn., August 4, 1861; interment in the Old North Cemetery.

TRUMBULL, Lyman, a Senator from Illinois; born in Colchester, Conn., October 12, 1813; attended Bacon Academy; taught school in Connecticut 1829–1833; studied law; was admitted to the bar and commenced practice in Greenville, Ga.; moved to Belleville, Ill.; member of the State house of representatives in 1840; secretary of state of Illinois in 1841 and 1842; justice of the supreme court of Illinois 1848–1853; elected as a Republican to the Thirty-fourth Congress in 1854, but before the beginning of the Congress was elected to the United States Senate; reelected in 1861 and again in 1867, and served from March 4, 1855, to March 3, 1873; resumed the practice of law in Chicago, Ill.; unsuccessful Democratic candidate for Governor of Illinois in 1880; died in Chicago, Ill., June 25, 1896; interment in Oakwoods Cemetery.

TUCK, Amos, a Representative from New Hampshire; born in Parsonsfield, Maine, August 2, 1810; attended Effingham and Hampton Academies; was graduated from Dartmouth College, Hanover, N. H., in 1835; studied law; was admitted to the bar in 1838 and commenced practice in Exeter, N. H.; trustee of Dartmouth College; principal of Hampton Academy 1836–1838; member of the State house of representatives in 1842; elected as an independent to the Thirtieth, Thirty-first, and Thirty-second Congresses (March 4, 1847–March 3, 1853); unsuccessful candidate for reelection; delegate to the Republican National Conventions in 1856 and 1860; delegate to the peace convention held in Washington, D. C., in 1861 in an effort to devise means to prevent the impending war; naval officer of the port of Boston 1861–1865; resumed the practice of law and also engaged in railroad building; died in Exeter, N. H., December 11, 1879; interment in Exeter Cemetery.

TUCK, William Munford, a Representative from Virginia; born near High Hill, Halifax County, Va., September 28, 1896; attended the public schools; during the First World War served in the United States Marines from June 1918 to July 1919; attended the College of William and Mary and was graduated from Washington and Lee University, Lexington, Va., in 1921; was admitted to the bar the same year and commenced practice in South Boston, Va.; chairman of the Virginia State Democratic Central Committee in 1952; delegate to all State Democratic Conventions beginning in 1920; Democratic elector at large in 1936; delegate at large to the Democratic National Conventions in 1948 and 1952; member of the State house of delegates 1924–1932; served in the State Senate 1932–1942; Lieutenant Governor of Virginia 1942–1946; elected Governor of Virginia in November 1945 and served the term beginning January 1946 and ending January 1950; resumed the practice of law; elected as a Democrat to the Eighty-third Congress to fill the vacancy caused by the resignation of Thomas B. Stanley; reelected to the Eighty-fourth, Eighty-fifth, and Eighty-sixth Congresses and served from April 14, 1953, to January 3, 1961. *Reelected to the Eighty-seventh Congress.*

TUCKER, Ebenezer, a Representative from New Jersey; born at Tuckers Beach, Burlington County, N. J., November 15, 1758; attended the common schools; served in the Revolution under General Washington at the Battle of Long Island and other engagements; judge of the court of common pleas, justice of the court of quarter sessions, and judge of the orphans' court of Burlington County from 1820 to 1825; moved to what is now Tuckerton, N. J., which was named after him, where he engaged in mercantile pursuits and shipbuilding; postmaster of Tuckerton from 1806 to 1825, when he resigned to take up his duties in Congress; elected to the Nineteenth and Twentieth Congresses (March 4, 1825–March 3, 1929); was not a candidate for renomination; first collector of revenue of the port of Tuckerton; again postmaster of Tuckerton from 1831 until his death in Tuckerton, N. J., September 5, 1845; interment in the Old Methodist Cemetery.

TUCKER, George (cousin of Henry St. George Tucker), a Representative from Virginia; born in the town of St. Georges, Bermuda, on August 20, 1775; immigrated to Virginia about 1790; was graduated from William and Mary College, Williamsburg, Va., in 1797; studied law with Judge St. George Tucker at William and Mary College; was admitted to the bar and commenced practice in Richmond, Va.; moved to Pittsylvania County, Va., and was elected Commonwealth attorney of the county; member of the State house of delegates in 1815; moved to Lynchburg, Va., in 1818 and continued the practice of law; elected as a Democrat to the Sixteenth, Seventeenth, and Eighteenth Congresses (March 4, 1819–March 3, 1825); was appointed by Thomas Jefferson as the first professor of moral philosophy at the University of Virginia, which chair then embraced finance and economics; resigned as professor in 1845 and moved to Philadelphia; author and prolific writer on finance, economics, banking, and historical subjects; died in Sherwood, Albemarle County, Va., April 10, 1861; interment in the University of Virginia Cemetery, Albemarle County, Va.

TUCKER, Henry St. George (father of John Randolph Tucker, cousin of George Tucker, and nephew of Thomas Tudor Tucker), a Representative from Virginia; born in Williamsburg, Va., December 29, 1780; pursued classical studies; was graduated from William and Mary College, Williamsburg, Va., in 1798; later studied law under his father, Prof. St. George Tucker, and was graduated in 1801; was admitted to the bar and commenced practice in Winchester, Va.; captain of Cavalry in the War of 1812; elected to the Fourteenth and Fifteenth Congresses (March 4, 1815–March 3, 1819); was not a candidate for renomination in 1818; in 1816 spoke and voted against the bill to increase the salaries of Members of Congress and declined to accept the increase; chancellor of the fourth judicial district of Virginia 1824–1831; during this period he maintained a private law school, from which many of the most distinguished lawyers of the State came; president of the court of appeals of Virginia 1831–1841, and was the youngest member of the court when appointed; professor of law at the University of Virginia at Charlottesville from 1841 to 1845, when he resigned; was the author in 1842 of the honor system for students adopted at the university; declined the portfolio of Attorney General of the United States tendered by President Jackson; author of Tucker's Commentaries, universally used in Virginia and in many of the Southern States, and also of a treatise on natural law and on the formation of the Constitu-

tion of the United States, which were textbooks at the University of Virginia; died in Winchester, Va., August 28, 1848; interment in Mount Hebron Cemetery.

TUCKER, Henry St. George (son of John Randolph Tucker and grandson of the preceding), a Representative from Virginia; born in Winchester, Frederick County, Va., April 5, 1853; attended a private school in Richmond, Va., during the Civil War and a private preparatory school at Middleburg, Va., 1865–1871; was graduated from the law department of Washington and Lee University, Lexington, Va., in 1876; was admitted to the bar the same year and commenced practice in Staunton, Va.; elected as a Democrat to the Fifty-first and to the three succeeding Congresses (March 4, 1889–March 3, 1897); was not a candidate for renomination in 1896; elected professor of constitutional law and equity in Washington and Lee University in 1897; dean of the law school of the same university in 1900, and dean of the school of law and diplomacy in George Washington University, Washington, D. C., in 1905; president of the Jamestown Exposition Co., succeeding Gen. Fitzhugh Lee, 1905–1907; president of the American Bar Association in 1905; unsuccessful Democratic candidate for the nomination of Governor in 1909 and again in 1921; edited Tucker on the Constitution; author of Woman Suffrage by Constitutional Amendment and Limitations on the Treaty Making Power; elected as a Democrat to the Sixty-seventh Congress to fill the vacancy caused by the death of Henry D. Flood; reelected to the Sixty-eighth and to the four succeeding Congresses and served from March 21, 1922, until his death in Lexington, Va., July 23, 1932; interment in the Presbyterian Cemetery.

TUCKER, John Randolph (son of Henry St. George Tucker), a Representative from Virginia: born in Winchester, Frederick County, Va., on December 24, 1823; attended a private school and Richmond Academy, and was graduated from the University of Virginia at Charlottesville in 1844; was admitted to the bar in 1845 and commenced practice in Winchester, Va.; presidential elector on the Democratic ticket of Pierce and King in 1852 and of Buchanan and Breckinridge in 1856; attorney general of Virginia 1857–1865; professor of equity and public law at Washington and Lee University, Lexington, Va., in 1870; elected as a Democrat to the Forty-fourth and to the five succeeding Congresses (March 4, 1875–March 3, 1887); declined to be a candidate for renomination in 1886; elected professor of constitutional law at Washington and Lee University in 1888, and served until his death; author of Tucker on the Constitution; president of the American Bar Association in 1894; died in Lexington, Va., February 13, 1897; interment in Mount Hebron Cemetery, Winchester, Va.

TUCKER, Starling, a Representative from South Carolina; born in Halifax County, N. C., in 1770; moved to Mountain Shoals (now Enoree), S. C.; received a limited education; held several local offices; member of the State house of representatives; elected to the Fifteenth and to the six succeeding Congresses (March 4, 1817–March 3, 1831); died in Mountain Shoals (now Enoree), S. C., January 3, 1834; interment in the private burial ground on the family estate west of Enoree, S. C.

TUCKER, Thomas Tudor (uncle of Henry St. George Tucker), a Delegate and a Representative from South Carolina; born in Port Royal, Bermuda, June 25, 1745; attended the common schools; studied medicine at the University of Edinburgh, Scotland; moved to South Carolina and practiced medicine; served as a surgeon in the Revolutionary War; Member of the Continental Congress in 1787 and 1788; elected as a Federalist to the First and Second Congresses (March 4, 1789–March 3,

1793); appointed United States Treasurer by President Jefferson and served from December 1, 1801, until his death in Washington, D. C., May 2, 1828; interment in Congressional Cemetery.

TUCKER, Tilghman Mayfield, a Representative from Mississippi; born near Lime Stone Springs, N. C., February 5, 1802; completed preparatory studies; engaged in agricultural pursuits; moved to Hamilton, Miss.; studied law; was admitted to the bar and commenced practice in Columbus, Miss.; member of the State house of representatives 1831–1835; served in the State senate 1838–1841; Governor of Mississippi 1841–1843; elected as a Democrat to the Twenty-eighth Congress (March 4, 1843–March 3, 1845); retired to his plantation home, "Cottonwood," in Louisiana; died at the home of his father near Bexar, Marion County, Ala., April 3, 1859.

TUFTS, John Quincy, a Representative from Iowa; born near Aurora, Dearborn County, Ind., July 12, 1840; moved to Iowa in 1852 with his parents, who settled in Muscatine County; attended the common schools and Cornell College, Mount Vernon, Iowa; moved to Cedar County, Iowa, in 1858; engaged in agricultural pursuits; member of the State house of representatives in 1870, 1872, and 1874; elected as a Republican to the Forty-fourth Congress (March 4, 1875–March 3, 1877); United States Indian agent of Indian Territory 1879–1887; moved to Los Angeles, Calif.; engaged in the real-estate business; president of the Los Angeles Board of Aldermen 1892–1896; died in Los Angeles, Calif., August 10, 1908; interment in Rosedale Cemetery.

TULLY, Pleasant Britton, a Representative from California; born in Henderson County, Tenn., on March 21, 1829; moved to Arkansas with his father, who settled in Phillips County in 1838; attended public and private schools; moved to California in 1853 and engaged in mining; resided in Gilroy, Calif., after 1857; studied law; was admitted to the bar and practiced; delegate at large to the State constitutional convention in 1879; elected as a Democrat to the Forty-eighth Congress (March 4, 1883–March 3, 1885); resumed the practice of law; died in Gilroy, Santa Clara County, Calif., March 24, 1897; interment in the Masonic Cemetery.

TUMULTY, Thomas James, a Representative from New Jersey; born in Jersey City, Hudson County, N. J., March 2, 1913; graduated from Xavier High School and attended Holy Cross University; graduated from Fordham University, New York City, N. Y., in 1935, from Seton Hall, South Orange, N. J., in 1938 and from John Marshall Law School, Jersey City, N. J., in 1938; admitted to the bar in 1940 and commenced the practice of law in Jersey City, N. J.; professor of public speaking at Seton Hall in 1940 and 1941; director of student activities at John Marshall Law School 1939–1941; teacher of public speaking at St. Aloysius High School in Jersey City in 1949 and 1950; during World War II served in the United States Army as an enlisted man in 1943 and 1944; served in the State house of assembly 1944–1952, serving as minority leader in 1951; assistant corporation counsel for Jersey City 1943–1954; delegate to the Democratic National Convention in 1952; secretary to the mayor of Jersey City in 1952 and 1953; elected as a Democrat to the Eighty-fourth Congress (January 3, 1955–January 3, 1957); unsuccessful for reelection to the Eighty-fifth Congress; special counsel Urban Renewal for Jersey City in 1957; deputy mayor of Jersey City 1958–1960; lawyer; resides in Jersey City, N. J.

TUNNELL, James Miller, a Senator from Delaware; born in Clarksville, Sussex County, Del., August 2, 1879; attended the public schools; was graduated from Franklin College (now com-

bined with Muskingum College at New Concord, Ohio) in 1900; taught in the public schools, advancing to principal of schools at Frankford, Selbyville, and Ocean View, Del., 1903–1907; studied law; was admitted to the bar in 1907 and commenced practice in Georgetown, Del.; delegate to the Democratic National Conventions in 1916, 1940, 1944, and 1952; president of the board of education of Georgetown, Del., 1919–1932; unsuccessful Democratic candidate for election to the United States Senate in 1924; elected as a Democrat to the United States Senate in 1940 and served from January 3, 1941, to January 3, 1947; unsuccessful candidate for reelection in 1946; president of Georgetown Trust Co.; a director of the First National Bank of Frankford and the Georgetown Citizen's Loan & Mortgage Co.; trustee of Muskingum College, New Concord, Ohio; owned and operated a number of farms in Sussex County, Del.; died in Philadelphia, Pa., November 14, 1957; interment in Blackwater Church Cemetery, near Clarksville, Del.

TURLEY, Thomas Battle, a Senator from Tennessee; born in Memphis, Tenn., April 5, 1845; attended the public schools; served throughout the Civil War as a private in the Confederate Army; was graduated from the law department of the University of Virginia at Charlottesville in 1867; was admitted to the bar in 1870 and commenced practice in Memphis, Tenn.; appointed as a Democrat and subsequently elected to the United States Senate to fill the vacancy caused by the death of Isham G. Harris and served from July 20, 1897, to March 3, 1901; declined to be a candidate for renomination and resumed the practice of law in Memphis, Tenn.; died in Memphis, Tenn., July 1, 1910; interment in Elmwood Cemetery.

TURNBULL, Robert, a Representative from Virginia; born in Lawrenceville, Brunswick County, Va., January 11, 1850; attended Rock Spring Academy, and was graduated from the law department of the University of Virginia at Charlottesville in 1871; was admitted to the bar in 1871 and commenced practice in Lawrenceville, Va.; clerk of Brunswick County 1891–1910; member of the State senate 1894–1898; delegate to the State constitutional convention in 1901; delegate to the Democratic National Conventions in 1896 and 1904; elected as a Democrat to the Sixty-first Congress to fill the vacancy caused by the death of Francis R. Lassiter; reelected to the Sixty-second Congress and served from March 8, 1910, to March 3, 1913; unsuccessful candidate for renomination in 1912; resumed the practice of law in Lawrenceville; clerk of the circuit court of Brunswick County from 1916 until his death, January 22, 1920; interment in Lawrenceville Cemetery, Lawrenceville, Va.

TURNER, Benjamin Sterling, a Representative from Alabama; born near Weldon, Halifax County, N. C., March 17, 1825; was of the Negro race and raised as a slave; received no early education; moved to Alabama in 1830 and by clandestine study obtained a fair education; engaged in mercantile pursuits; elected tax collector of Dallas County in 1867; councilman of the city of Selma in 1869; elected as a Republican to the Forty-second Congress (March 4, 1871–March 3, 1873); unsuccessful candidate for reelection in 1872 to the Forty-third Congress; delegate to the Republican National Convention at Chicago in 1880; engaged in agricultural pursuits in Alabama; died in Selma, Dallas County, Ala., March 21, 1894; interment in Live Oak Cemetery.

TURNER, Charles, Jr., a Representative from Massachusetts; born in Duxbury, Mass., June 20, 1760; received a common-school education at Duxbury and Scituate, Mass.; was commissioned an adjutant in the Massachusetts State Militia in 1787; promoted to major in 1790, and held the rank of lieutenant colonel commandant 1798–1812; appointed first postmaster of Scituate, Mass., in 1800; justice of the peace; member of the State house of representatives in 1803 and 1805–1808; successfully· contested as a War Democrat the election of William Baylies to the Eleventh Congress; reelected to the Twelfth Congress and served from June 28, 1809, to March 3, 1813; unsuccessful candidate for reelection to the Thirteenth Congress; served in the State senate in 1816; again a member of the State house of representatives in 1817, 1819, and 1823; appointed steward of the Marine Hospital at Chelsea, Mass.; delegate to the State constitutional convention in 1820; engaged in agricultural pursuits; died in Scituate, Plymouth County, Mass., May 16, 1839; interment in the burial ground of the First Parish of Norwell (formerly Scituate).

TURNER, Charles Henry, a Representative from New York; born in Wentworth, Grafton County, N. H., May 26, 1861; attended the common schools; moved to New York City in November 1879; attended Columbia College, New York City, 1886–1888; engaged in the ice business; unsuccessful candidate for State senator in 1888; elected as a Democrat to the Fifty-first Congress to fill the vacancy caused by the resignation of Frank T. Fitzgerald and served from December 9, 1889, to March 3, 1891; was not a candidate for renomination in 1890; Doorkeeper in the National House of Representatives 1891–1893; studied law; was admitted to the bar in 1897 and commenced practice in Washington, D. C.; appointed assistant district attorney for the District of Columbia July 16, 1903, and served until his resignation September 1, 1911; appointed special assistant to the United States attorney for the District of Columbia November 27, 1911, and served until his death in Wentworth, N. H., August 31, 1913; interment in Wentworth Cemetery.

TURNER, Clarence Wyly, a Representative from Tennessee; born on a farm near Clydeton, Humphreys County, Tenn., October 22, 1866; attended the public schools, a preparatory school in Edgewood, Dickson County, Tenn., and National Normal Institute, Lebanon, Ohio; was graduated from the law department of Northern Indiana Normal College at Valparaiso in 1904; was admitted to the bar the same year and commenced practice at Waverly, Humphreys County, Tenn.; editor of the Waverly Sentinel; chairman of the Democratic committee of Humphreys County for fifteen years; member of the State senate 1900, 1901, and 1909–1912; delegate to the Democratic National Convention in 1920; elected mayor of Waverly, Tenn., in 1920; city attorney; elected as a Democrat to the Sixty-seventh Congress to fill the vacancy caused by the death of Lemuel P. Padgett and served from November 7, 1922, to March 3, 1923; was not a candidate for reelection in 1922 to the Sixty-eighth Congress; returned to Waverly, Tenn., and engaged in banking and agricultural pursuits; served as county judge of Humphreys County 1924–1933; elected to the Seventy-third and to the three succeeding Congresses and served from March 4, 1933, until his death in Washington, D. C., March 23, 1939; interment in Marable Cemetery, Waverly, Tenn.

TURNER, Daniel (son of James Turner), a Representative from North Carolina; born near Warrenton, Warren County, N. C., September 21, 1796; completed preparatory studies; was graduated from the United States Military Academy at West Point in 1814, and commissioned second lieutenant of Artillery the same year; served in the War of 1812 as acting assistant engineer; resigned his commission May 17, 1815; student for two years at William and Mary College, Williamsburg, Va.; moved to North Carolina; member of the North Carolina House of Commons 1819–1823; elected as a Democrat to the Twentieth Congress (March 4, 1827–March 3, 1829); was not a candidate

for renomination; principal of the Warrenton (N. C.) Female Seminary; superintending engineer of the construction of public works at the Mare Island (Calif.) Navy Yard from September 16, 1854, until his death there July 21, 1860; interment in Mare Island Naval Cemetery.

TURNER, Erastus Johnson, a Representative from Kansas; born in Lockport, Erie County, Pa., December 26, 1846; attended college in Henry, Ill., in 1859 and 1860; moved to Bloomfield, Iowa, in 1860; enlisted in Company E, Thirteenth Regiment, Iowa Volunteer Infantry, in 1864 and served until the close of the Civil War; attended Adrian (Mich.) College 1866–1868; was admitted to the bar in 1871 and commenced practice at Bloomfield, Iowa; moved to Hoxie, Sheridan County, Kans., in 1879 and resumed the practice of law; member of the State house of representatives 1881–1885; secretary of the Kansas Board of Railroad Commissioners from April 1, 1883, to August 1, 1886; elected as a Republican to the Fiftieth and Fifty-first Congresses (March 4, 1887–March 3, 1891); was not a candidate for renomination in 1890; practiced law several years in Washington, D. C.; moved to Seattle, Wash., in 1905 and continued the practice of law; retired from active pursuits in 1916 and moved to Los Angeles, Calif., where he died February 10, 1933; interment in Forest Lawn Mausoleum, Glendale, Calif.

TURNER, George, a Senator from Washington; born in Edina, Knox County, Mo., February 25, 1850; attended the common schools; served as United States military telegraph operator with the Union forces during the Civil War 1861–1865; studied law; was admitted to the bar in 1869 and commenced practice in Mobile, Ala.; United States marshal for the southern and middle districts of Alabama 1876–1880; delegate to the Republican National Conventions in 1876, 1880, and 1884; appointed associate justice of the supreme court for the Territory of Washington and served from July 4, 1884, to February 15, 1888; resumed the practice of law in Spokane, Wash., in 1888; also interested in mining; member of the Territorial convention in 1889 that framed the constitution of the new State of Washington; unsuccessful candidate for election as a Republican to the United States Senate in 1889 and 1893; elected as a Fusionist to the United States Senate and served from March 4, 1897, to March 3, 1903; was not a candidate for reelection to the Senate; resumed the practice of law in Spokane, Wash.; member of the Alaska Boundary Tribunal in 1903; unsuccessful Democratic candidate for Governor in 1904; counsel for the United States at The Hague in the northeastern fisheries arbitration with Great Britain in 1910; appointed by President Taft as a member of the International Joint Commission, created to prevent disputes regarding the use of boundary waters between the United States and Canada, and served from December 18, 1911, to February 28, 1914; counsel for the United States before the International Joint Commission 1918–1924; died in Spokane, Wash., January 26, 1932; interment in Greenwood Cemetery.

TURNER, Henry Gray, a Representative from Georgia; born near Henderson, Franklin County, N. C., March 20, 1839; attended the common schools and the University of Virginia at Charlottesville in 1857; moved to Brooks County, Ga., in 1859 and taught school; enlisted in the Confederate Army as a private in 1861, and served throughout the Civil War, attaining the rank of captain; severely wounded at the Battle of Gettysburg; studied law; was admitted to the bar in 1865 and commenced practice in Quitman, Ga.; presidential elector on the Democratic ticket of Greeley and Brown in 1872; member of the State house of representatives 1874–1876; delegate to the Democratic National Convention at St. Louis in 1876; again served in the State house of representatives in 1878 and 1879;

elected as a Democrat to the Forty-seventh and to the seven succeeding Congresses (March 4, 1881–March 3, 1897); declined to be a candidate for renomination in 1896; resumed the practice of law in Quitman, Ga.; appointed associate justice of the supreme court of Georgia in 1903; died in Raleigh, N. C., June 9, 1904; interment in West End Cemetery, Quitman, Ga.

TURNER, James (father of Daniel Turner), a Senator from North Carolina; born in Southampton County, Va., December 20, 1766; moved with his father to Warren County, N. C., in 1770; attended the common schools; engaged in planting; served as a private in a company of North Carolina Volunteers during the Revolutionary War; member of the State house of commons 1797–1800; served in the State senate in 1801 and 1802; Governor of North Carolina 1802–1805; elected as a Democrat to the United States Senate in 1805; reelected in 1811 and served from March 4, 1805, to November 21, 1816, when he resigned on account of ill health; died on his plantation, "Bloomsbury," near Warrenton, Warren County, N. C., January 15, 1824; interment in Bloomsbury Cemetery.

TURNER, James, a Representative from Maryland; born near Bel Air, Harford County, Md., November 7, 1783; completed preparatory studies at the Classic Academy of Madonna, Maryland; captain of militia in the War of 1812; moved to Parkton, Baltimore County, in 1811 and established the first large dairy farm at Parkton; collector of State and county taxes in 1817; served as a justice of the peace in 1824; member of the State house of delegates 1824–1833; elected as a Democrat to the Twenty-third and Twenty-fourth Congresses (March 4, 1833–March 3, 1837); unsuccessful candidate for reelection; again served in the State house of delegates in 1837 and 1838; member of the State senate 1855–1859; engaged in farming at Parkton, Md., until his death March 28, 1861; interment in Bethel Cemetery, near Madonna, Harford County, Md.

TURNER, Oscar, a Representative from Kentucky; born in New Orleans, La., February 3, 1825; moved with his parents to Fayette County, Ky., in 1826; completed preparatory studies; moved to Ballard County, Ky., in 1843; was graduated from the law department of Transylvania University, Lexington, Ky., in 1847; Commonwealth attorney 1851–1855; was admitted to the bar and practiced until 1861; served in the State senate 1867–1871; elected as an Independent Democrat to the Forty-sixth, Forty-seventh, and Forty-eighth Congresses (March 4, 1879–March 3, 1885); resumed the practice of law; died in Louisville, Ky., on January 22, 1896; interment in Cave Hill Cemetery.

TURNER, Oscar (son of the preceding), a Representative from Kentucky; born in Woodlands, Ballard County, Ky., October 19, 1867; attended the public schools of Washington, D. C., and Louisville (Ky.) Rugby School; studied law at the University of Louisville, and graduated from the University of Virginia in 1886; traveled extensively; was admitted to the bar and commenced practice in Louisville, Ky., in 1891; elected as a Democrat to the Fifty-sixth Congress (March 4, 1899–March 3, 1901); declined to be a candidate for renomination in 1900; resumed the practice of law; died in Louisville, Ky., July 17, 1902; interment in Cave Hill Cemetery.

TURNER, Smith Spangler, a Representative from Virginia; born in Warren County, Va., November 21, 1842; cadet at the Virginia Military Institute, Lexington, Va., when the Civil War commenced, and was subsequently given an honorary diploma; enlisted in the Confederate Army in 1861; served with Gen. T. J. Jackson as drill officer; an officer of Pickett's

division during the remainder of the war; near the close of the war was badly injured and disfigured by an explosion of gunpowder; taught mathematics in a female seminary in Winchester, Va., 1865–1867; studied law; was admitted to the bar in 1869 and commenced practice in Front Royal, Va.; member of the State house of delegates 1869–1872; prosecuting attorney for Warren County, Va., 1874–1879; member of the State board of visitors of the Virginia Military Institute for eight years; elected as a Democrat to the Fifty-third Congress to fill the vacancy caused by the resignation of Charles T. O'Ferrall; reelected to the Fifty-fourth Congress and served from January 30, 1894, to March 3, 1897; was not a candidate for renomination in 1896; died in Front Royal, Va., April 8, 1898; interment in Prospect Hill Cemetery.

TURNER, Thomas, a Representative from Kentucky; born in Richmond, Madison County, Ky., September 10, 1821; attended the Richmond Academy, and was graduated from Centre College, Danville, Ky., in September 1840; studied law at the Transylvania Law School, Lexington, Ky.; was admitted to the bar in 1842 and commenced practice in Richmond, Ky.; Commonwealth attorney in 1845, and resigned in 1846; served in the Mexican War as a private in Captain Stone's company of Col. Roger Hanson's regiment; moved to Mount Sterling, Montgomery County, Ky., in November 1854 and continued the practice of law; member of the State house of representatives 1861–1863; elected as a Democrat to the Forty-fifth and Forty-sixth Congresses (March 4, 1877–March 3, 1881); unsuccessful candidate for reelection in 1880 to the Forty-seventh Congress; resumed the practice of law; died in Mount Sterling, Ky., on September 11, 1900; interment in Macpelah Cemetery.

TURNER, Thomas Johnston, a Representative from Illinois; born in Trumbull County, Ohio, April 5, 1815; completed preparatory studies; moved with his parents to Butler County, Pa., in 1825; moved to Lake County, Ind., in 1837 and to Freeport, Ill., in 1838; studied law; was admitted to the bar in 1840 and commenced practice in Freeport; judge of the probate court of Stephenson County in 1842; postmaster of Freeport in 1844; State district attorney in 1845; established the first weekly newspaper (Prairie Democrat) in Stephenson County; elected as a Democrat to the Thirtieth Congress (March 4, 1847–March 3, 1849); member of the State house of representatives in 1854, serving as speaker; elected first mayor of Freeport, Ill., in 1855; delegate to the peace convention held in Washington, D. C., in 1861 in an effort to devise means to prevent the impending war; during the Civil War enlisted in the Union Army May 24, 1861, and served as colonel of the Fifteenth Regiment, Illinois Volunteer Infantry; resigned on account of ill health in 1862; member of the constitutional convention in 1863; unsuccessful Democratic candidate for United States Senator in 1871; moved to Chicago in 1871 and resumed the practice of law; died at Hot Springs, Ark., April 4, 1874; interment in the City Cemetery, Freeport, Ill.

TURNEY, Hopkins Lacy, a Representative and a Senator from Tennessee; born at Dixon Springs, Smith County, Tenn., October 3, 1797; apprenticed to the tailor's trade; served in the Seminole War in 1818; studied law; was admitted to the bar and commenced practice in Jasper, Tenn.; moved to Winchester, Tenn., and continued the practice of law; member of the State house of representatives 1828–1838; elected as a Democrat to the Twenty-fifth, Twenty-sixth, and Twenty-seventh Congresses (March 4, 1837–March 3, 1843); elected to the United States Senate and served from March 4, 1845, to March 3, 1851; resumed the practice of law; died in Winchester, Tenn., August 1, 1857; interment in Winchester Cemetery.

TURNEY, Jacob, a Representative from Pennsylvania; born in Greensburg, Westmoreland County, Pa., February 18, 1825; completed preparatory studies and attended Greensburg Academy; apprenticed as a printer; studied law; was admitted to the bar in 1849 and commenced practice in Greensburg, Pa.; district attorney for Westmoreland County 1850–1855; presidential elector on the Democratic ticket of Buchanan and Breckinridge in 1856; member of the State senate 1858–1860 and was elected president in 1859; unsuccessful candidate for State senator in 1871; elected as a Democrat to the Forty-fourth and Forty-fifth Congresses (March 4, 1875–March 3, 1879); again resumed the practice of law; died in Greensburg, Pa., on October 4, 1891; interment in St. Clair Cemetery.

TURPIE, David, a Senator from Indiana; born in Hamilton County, Ohio, July 8, 1828; was graduated from Kenyon College, Gambier, Ohio, in 1848; studied law; was admitted to the bar in 1849 and commenced practice in Logansport, Cass County, Ind.; member of the State house of representatives in 1852 and 1858; appointed by Governor Wright as judge of the court of common pleas and served from 1854 to 1856; judge of the circuit court in 1856; elected as a Democrat to the United States Senate to fill the vacancy caused by the expulsion of Jesse D. Bright and served from January 14 to March 3, 1863; moved to Monticello, Ind., in 1865; returned to Logansport in 1868; moved to Indianapolis, Ind., in 1872 and continued the practice of law; member of the State house of representatives, serving as speaker in 1874 and 1875; one of the three commissioners to revise the laws of Indiana in 1878 and 1881; appointed United States district attorney for Indiana in August 1886 and served until March 3, 1887; again elected as a Democrat to the United States Senate in 1887; reelected in 1893 and served from March 4, 1887, to March 3, 1899; unsuccessful candidate for reelection; delegate to the Democratic National Convention in 1888; retired from public life; died in Indianapolis, Ind., April 21, 1909; interment in Crown Hill Cemetery.

TURPIN, Charles Murray, a Representative from Pennsylvania; born in Kingston, Luzerne County, Pa., March 4, 1878; attended the public and high schools and Wyoming Seminary, Kingston, Pa.; served as a corporal in the United States Army during the Spanish-American War in Company F, Ninth Pennsylvania Volunteer Infantry; member of the Pennsylvania National Guard 1896–1901, serving as second lieutenant, first lieutenant, and captain; employed as a carpenter, grocery clerk, and a steamboat captain before graduating from the dental department of the University of Pennsylvania at Philadelphia in 1904; commenced the practice of dentistry in Kingston, Pa., in 1905; member of the board of education 1916–1922; burgess of Kingston 1922–1926, and prothonotary of Luzerne County 1926–1929; elected as a Republican to the Seventy-first Congress to fill the vacancy caused by the death of John J. Casey; reelected to the Seventy-second, Seventy-third, and Seventy-fourth Congresses and served from June 4, 1929, to January 3, 1937; unsuccessful candidate for reelection in 1936 to the Seventy-fifth Congress; appointed assistant chief clerk, Luzerne County assessor's office, Wilkes-Barre, Pa.; died in Kingston, Pa., June 4, 1946; interment in Forty Fort Cemetery, Forty Fort, Pa.

TURPIN, Louis Washington, a Representative from Alabama; born in Charlottesville, Albemarle County, Va., February 22, 1849; his parents having died he moved to Alabama with his sister and settled in Perry County in 1858; self-educated; engaged in agricultural pursuits; tax assessor of Hale County 1873–1880; chairman of the Democratic committee of Hale County for six years; unsuccessful candidate for nomination to the Forty-eighth Congress; presented credentials as a Democratic Member-elect to the Fifty-first Congress and served from March 4, 1889, to June 4, 1890, when he was succeeded by John V. McDuffie, who contested his election; elected to the Fifty-second and Fifty-third Congresses (March 4, 1891–March 3, 1895); unsuccessful candidate for renomination; retired from politics and engaged in planting; died in Greensboro, Ala., February 3, 1903; interment in the City Cemetery.

TURRILL, Joel, a Representative from New York; born in Shoreham, Vt., February 22, 1794; attended the common school; was graduated from Middlebury College in 1816; studied law in Newburgh, N. Y.; moved to Oswego, Oswego County, N. Y.; was admitted to the bar in 1819 and commenced practice in Oswego; justice of the peace; county judge 1828–1833; member of the State assembly in 1831; elected as a Jackson Democrat to the Twenty-third and Twenty-fourth Congresses (March 4, 1833–March 3, 1837); was not a candidate for reelection in 1836; district attorney for Oswego County 1838–1840; surrogate of Oswego County in 1843; United States consul to the Sandwich Islands 1845–1850; died in Oswego, N. Y., December 28, 1859; interment in Riverside Cemetery.

TUTHILL, Joseph Hasbrouck (nephew of Selah Tuthill), a Representative from New York; born in Blooming Grove, Orange County, N. Y., February 25, 1811; attended common and private schools; moved with his parents to Shawangunk, Ulster County, N. Y., in 1824; engaged in mercantile and agricultural pursuits; moved to New York City in 1828, and continued his mercantile pursuits; moved to Ulsterville, N. Y., in 1832, where he engaged in business; moved to Ellenville, N. Y., in 1834; member of the Ulster County Board of Supervisors in 1842, 1843, 1861, 1862, 1865–1870; clerk of Ulster County 1843–1847; served as president of the Ellenville Glass Works; unsuccessful candidate for election in 1866 to Congress; elected as a Democrat to the Forty-second Congress (March 4, 1871–March 3, 1873); retired from public life; died in Ellenville, N. Y., July 27, 1877; interment in Fantinekill Cemetery, near Ellenville, N. Y.

TUTHILL, Selah (uncle of Joseph Hasbrouck Tuthill), a Representative from New York; born in Blooming Grove, Orange County, N. Y., October 26, 1771; attended public and private schools; member of the State assembly from Ulster County in 1805 and from Orange County in 1820; elected to the Seventeenth Congress and served from March 4, 1821, until his death in Goshen, N. Y., September 7, 1821; interment in Riverside Cemetery, Marlboro, Ulster County, N. Y.

TUTTLE, William Edgar, Jr., a Representative from New Jersey; born in Horseheads, Chemung County, N. Y., December 10, 1870; was graduated from Horseheads High School and Elmira Free Academy in 1887 and attended Cornell University, Ithaca, N. Y., for two years; was engaged in the lumber business in Westfield, N. J.; delegate to the Democratic National Convention in 1908 which nominated Bryan and Kern and in 1916 which nominated Wilson and Marshall; elected as a Democrat to the Sixty-second and Sixty-third Congresses (March 4, 1911–March 3, 1915); unsuccessful candidate for reelection in 1914 to the Sixty-fourth Congress; resumed the lumber business; United States commissioner to the Panama Exposition in 1916; president of the State board of conservation and development in 1919; State commissioner of banking and insurance in 1921; died in Westfield, Union County, N. J., February 11, 1923; interment in Maple Grove Cemetery, Horseheads, N. Y.

TWEED, William Marcy, a Representative from New York; born in New York City April 3, 1823; completed preparatory studies; learned the trade of chair maker; alderman in New York

City in 1852 and 1853; elected as a Democrat to the Thirty-third Congress (March 4, 1853–March 3, 1855); unsuccessful candidate for reelection in 1854 to the Thirty-fourth Congress; school commissioner in 1856 and 1857; member of the board of supervisors for New York County in 1858; defeated as the peace candidate for sheriff in 1861; deputy street commissioner 1861–1870; elected to the State senate in 1867 and 1869, serving four years; again elected in 1871, but was not permitted to take his seat; commissioner of the department of public works in 1870; tried in 1874 on charges of official embezzlement, found guilty, and sentenced to twelve years' imprisonment; escaped in December 1875 and was captured in Spain; brought back to the United States on a man-of-war; again confined in prison in New York City from November 23, 1876, until his death, April 12, 1878; interment in Greenwood Cemetery, Brooklyn, N. Y.

TWEEDY, John Hubbard, a Delegate from the Territory of Wisconsin; born in Danbury, Fairfield County, Conn., November 9, 1814; was graduated from Yale College in 1834 and from the Yale Law School in 1836; was admitted to the bar in July 1836; moved to Milwaukee, Wis., in October 1836 and commenced practice; commissioner and receiver of canal lands 1839–1841; member of the Territorial council in 1842; delegate to the State constitutional convention in 1846; elected as a Whig to the Thirtieth Congress and served from March 4, 1847, until that portion of the Territory of Wisconsin in which he resided was admitted as a State into the Union on May 29, 1848; was not a candidate for renomination in 1848; unsuccessful Whig candidate for Governor in 1848; member of the State assembly in 1853; engaged in railroad development and served as director of the Milwaukee & Mississippi Railroad and the Milwaukee & Watertown Railroad; died in Milwaukee, Wis., November 12, 1891; interment in Wooster Cemetery, Danbury, Conn.

TWEEDY, Samuel, a Representative from Connecticut; born at Nine Partners, Dutchess County, N. Y., March 8, 1776; moved to Danbury, Fairfield County, Conn.; member of the State house of representatives in 1818, 1820, and 1824; served in the State senate 1826–1828; held many local offices; elected as a Whig to the Twenty-third Congress (March 4, 1833–March 3, 1835); died in Danbury, Conn., on July 1, 1868; interment in Wooster Cemetery.

TWICHELL, Ginery, a Representative from Massachusetts; born in Athol, Mass., August 26, 1811; attended the common schools; at the age of nineteen he became interested in stage coaches; was the proprietor of several lines and in that connection received many important contracts for carrying the mails; in 1848 engaged in railroading; president of the Boston & Worcester Railway in 1857; delegate to the Republican National Convention in 1864 which nominated Abraham Lincoln for a second term; elected as a Republican to the Fortieth, Forty-first, and Forty-second Congresses (March 4, 1867–March 3, 1873); was not a candidate for renomination in 1872; president of the Atchison, Topeka & Santa Fe Railway Co. 1870–1874; president of the Boston, Barre & Gardner Railroad Co. 1873–1878; died in Brookline, Norfolk County, Mass., July 23, 1883; interment in the Rural Cemetery, Worcester, Mass.

TWYMAN, Robert Joseph, a Representative from Illinois; born in Indianapolis, Marion County, Ind., June 18, 1897; attended Georgetown University, Washington, D. C.; employed in foreign service by the Department of State; during the First World War served as an ensign in the United States Navy; employed by a public utility company in Guatemala, Central America, in 1919; during World War II accepted a commission in the United States Navy in February 1941 and served until September 1945; engaged in manufacturing and distributing construction machinery; elected as a Republican to the Eightieth Congress (January 3, 1947–January 3, 1949); unsuccessful candidate for reelection in 1948 to the Eighty-first Congress; resumed business interests until retirement; resides in Stuart, Fla.; is a legal resident of Chicago, Ill.

TYDINGS, Millard Evelyn, a Representative and a Senator from Maryland; born in Havre de Grace, Harford County, Md., April 6, 1890; attended the public schools of Harford County; was graduated from Maryland Agricultural College (now the University of Maryland) in 1910; engaged in civil engineering with the Baltimore & Ohio Railroad in West Virginia in 1911; studied law at the University of Maryland Law School, Baltimore, Md.; was admitted to the bar and commenced practice in Havre de Grace in 1913; member of the State house of delegates 1915–1921; speaker of the house 1919–1921; served as a private on the Mexican border at Eagle Pass, Tex., from June to November 1916; enlisted as a private in the First World War on April 6, 1917; became second lieutenant April 7, 1917, first lieutenant August 6, 1917, and captain January 12, 1918; sailed for France in June 1918; participated in the defense of the center sector, Haute-Alsace, from July to September 1918, and in the Meuse-Argonne from September 1918 until the signing of the Armistice on November 11, 1918; promoted to major, One Hundred and Eleventh Machine Gun Battalion, September 4, 1918, and to lieutenant colonel and division machine-gun officer on November 7, 1918; awarded the Distinguished Service Medal, the Distinguished Service Cross, the Distinguished Service Star of the Commonwealth of the Philippines, and received citations for meritorious and conspicuous service from Generals Pershing, Morton, and Upton; served in Germany with the Army of Occupation; honor graduate, School of Musketry, Fort Sill, Okla., and the Second Corps Machine Gun School, Chatillon-sur-Seine; also graduated from the Army Center of Artillery Studies, Trier, Germany; discharged from the service May 31, 1919; author of "Machine Gunners of the Blue and Gray," "Before and After Prohibition," and "Counter-Attack"; member of the State senate 1921–1923; elected as a Democrat to the Sixty-eighth and Sixty-ninth Congresses (March 4, 1923–March 3, 1927); was not a candidate for renomination in 1926, having become a candidate for United States Senator; elected as a Democrat to the United States Senate in 1926, 1932, 1938, and again in 1944 and served from March 4, 1927, to January 3, 1951; was an unsuccessful candidate for reelection in 1950; nominated in 1956 as Democratic candidate for the United States Senate but withdrew before election due to ill health; engaged in the practice of law in Washington, D. C., and Baltimore, Md.; died at his farm, "Oakington," near Havre de Grace, Md., February 9, 1961; interment in Angel Hill Cemetery.

TYLER, Asher, a Representative from New York; born in Bridgewater, Oneida County, N. Y., May 10, 1798; was graduated from Hamilton College, Clinton, N. Y., in 1817; studied law; was admitted to the bar and commenced practice in Ellicottville, Cattaraugus County, N. Y., in 1836; agent of the Devereaux Land Co., with headquarters at Ellicottville, and subsequently served in a like capacity for the Erie Co.; held several local offices; elected as a Whig to the Twenty-eighth Congress (March 4, 1843–March 3, 1845); moved to Elmira in 1846 and engaged in railroad operations; one of the incorporators of the Elmira Rolling Mill Co.; died in Elmira, N. Y., August 1, 1875; interment in Woodlawn Cemetery.

TYLER, David Gardiner (son of John Tyler), a Representative from Virginia; born in East Hampton, Long Island, N. Y., July 12, 1846; completed preparatory studies in a private school in Charles City County, Va., and entered Washington College (now Washington and Lee University), Lexington, Va., in 1862, leaving there in 1863 to join the Confederate Army; served as a private in the Rockbridge Artillery, First Virginia Battalion, Army of Northern Virginia, surrendering at Appomattox; went to Europe in October 1865 and for two years attended the Polytechnic School at Karlsruhe, Grand Duchy of Baden; returned to the United States in 1867 and was graduated from the law department of Washington College in 1869; was admitted to the bar in 1870 and commenced practice in Richmond, Va.; director of the State lunatic asylum in Williamsburg, Va., 1884–1887; presidential elector on the Democratic ticket of Cleveland and Thurman in 1888; served in the State senate in 1891 and 1892; member of the board of visitors of William and Mary College, Williamsburg, Va.; elected as a Democrat to the Fifty-third and Fifty-fourth Congresses (March 4, 1893–March 3, 1897); unsuccessful candidate for renomination in 1896; resumed the practice of his profession; again served in the State senate 1900–1904; elected judge of the fourteenth judicial circuit of Virginia in 1904; reelected in 1908 and 1912, and served until his death; died at "Sherwood Forest," Charles City County, Va., September 5, 1927; interment in Hollywood Cemetery, Richmond, Va.

TYLER, James Manning, a Representative from Vermont; born in Wilmington, Windham County, Vt., April 27, 1835; attended the Brattleboro Academy and was graduated from the Law University of Albany, N. Y.; was admitted to the bar in September 1860 and commenced practice in Wilmington, Vt.; member of the State house of representatives in 1863 and 1864; State's attorney in 1866 and 1867; trustee of the Vermont Asylum for the Insane 1875–1926; elected as a Republican to the Forty-sixth and Forty-seventh Congresses (March 4, 1879–March 3, 1883); declined to be a candidate for renomination in 1882; resumed the practice of his profession in Brattleboro, Vt.; appointed a judge of the supreme court of the State in September 1887 and served until his resignation December 1, 1908; president of the Vermont National Bank 1917–1923; president of the Vermont-Peoples' National Bank in 1923 and 1924; retired from active business pursuits; died in Brattleboro, Windham County, Vt., October 13, 1926; interment in Prospect Hill Cemetery.

TYLER, John (father of David Gardiner Tyler), a Representative and a Senator from Virginia, a Vice President and a President of the United States; was born in Charles City County, Va., March 29, 1790; attended private schools, and was graduated from William and Mary College, Williamsburg, Va., in 1807; studied law; was admitted to the bar in 1809 and commenced practice in Charles City County; captain of a military company in 1813; member of the State house of delegates 1811–1816; member of the council of state in 1816; elected as Democratic-Republican to the Fourteenth Congress to fill the vacancy caused by the death of John Clopton; reelected to the Fifteenth and Sixteenth Congresses and served from December 16, 1817, to March 3, 1821; declined to be a candidate for renomination in 1820 because of impaired health; again a member of the State house of delegates 1823–1825; Governor of Virginia 1825–1827; elected to the United States Senate in 1827; reelected in 1833 and served from March 4, 1827, to February 29, 1836, when he resigned; elected President pro tempore of the Senate March 3, 1835; member of the State constitutional convention in 1829 and 1830; was nominated for Vice President of the United States in 1835; president of the Virginia African Colonization Society in 1838; again a member of the State house of delegates in 1839; elected Vice President of the United States on the Whig ticket of Harrison and Tyler in 1840; was inaugurated

March 4, 1841, and served until the death of President Harrison April 4, 1841; took the oath of office as President of the United States April 6, 1841, and served until March 3, 1845; chancellor of William and Mary College in 1859; delegate to and president of the peace convention held in Washington, D. C., in 1861 in an effort to devise means to prevent the impending war; delegate to the Confederate Provisional Congress in 1861; elected to the House of Representatives of the Confederate Congress, but died in Richmond, Va., January 18, 1862, before the assembling of the Congress; interment in Hollywood Cemetery, where a monument has been erected over his remains by the Congress of the United States.

TYNDALL, William Thomas, a Representative from Missouri; born in Sparta, Christian County, Mo., January 16, 1862; attended the public schools, Henderson Academy at Sparta, and Sparta Academy; engaged in teaching at Sparta 1884–1895; studied law; was admitted to the bar in 1893 and commenced practice in Sparta; appointed postmaster of Sparta, Mo., by President Harrison and served from March 23, 1891, to November 14, 1893; again appointed postmaster by President McKinley, and served from December 8, 1897, to January 7, 1905; elected as a Republican to the Fifty-ninth Congress (March 4, 1905–March 3, 1907); unsuccessful candidate for reelection in 1906 to the Sixtieth Congress; resumed the practice of law in Sparta, Mo.; moved to Bartlesville, Okla., in 1912 and continued the practice of law until his death there November 26, 1928; interment in a mausoleum in White Rose Cemetery.

TYNER, James Noble, a Representative from Indiana; born in Brookville, Franklin County, Ind., January 17, 1826; pursued an academic course, and was graduated from Brookville Academy in 1844; spent ten years in business; studied law; was admitted to the bar in 1857 and commenced practice in Peru, Ind.; secretary of the State senate 1857–1861; presidential elector on the Republican ticket of Lincoln and Hamlin in 1860; special agent of the Post Office Department 1861–1866; elected as a Republican to the Forty-first Congress to fill the vacancy caused by the resignation of Representative-elect Daniel D. Pratt; reelected to the Forty-second and Forty-third Congresses and served from March 4, 1869, to March 3, 1875; appointed by President Grant as Governor of Colorado, but declined; appointed Second Assistant Postmaster General, serving from February 26, 1875, to July 12, 1876, and as Postmaster General from July 12, 1876, to March 3, 1877; appointed First Assistant Postmaster General, and served from March 16, 1877, until his resignation on October 29, 1881; delegate to the International Postal Congress at Paris in 1878 and at Washington in 1897; Assistant Attorney General for the Post Office Department from March 21, 1889, to May 27, 1893, and again from May 6, 1897, to April 27, 1903; died in Washington, D. C., December 5, 1904; interment in Oak Hill Cemetery.

TYSON, Jacob, a Representative from New York; born in Staten Island, N. Y., October 8, 1773; attended the common schools; moved to Richmond, N. Y.; studied law; was admitted to the bar and practiced; supervisor of the town of Castletown, Richmond County, 1811–1821; served as judge of Richmond County 1822–1840; elected to the Eighteenth Congress (March 4, 1823–March 3, 1825); member of the State senate in 1828; died in Staten Island, N. Y., July 16, 1848; interment in the Reformed Protestant Dutch Church Cemetery, Port Richmond, Staten Island, N. Y.

TYSON, Job Roberts, a Representative from Pennsylvania; born in Philadelphia, Pa., February 8, 1803; completed preparatory studies; taught school in Hamburg, Pa.; studied law;

was admitted to the bar in 1827 and commenced practice in Philadelphia, Pa.; also engaged in literary pursuits; held several local offices; served in the State house of representatives; elected as a Whig to the Thirty-fourth Congress (March 4, 1855–March 3, 1857); retired from active life; died on his estate, "Woodlawn," Montgomery County, Pa., June 27, 1858; interment in South Laurel Hill Cemetery, Philadelphia, Pa.

TYSON, John Russell, a Representative from Alabama; born in Lowndes County, Ala., November 28, 1856; attended the public schools; was graduated from Howard College, Marion, Ala., in 1877 and from Washington and Lee University, Lexington, Va., in 1879; studied law; was admitted to the Alabama bar in 1879 and commenced the practice of law in Hayneville, Ala.; member of the Alabama State House of Representatives in 1880; moved to Montgomery, Ala., in 1884 and resumed the practice of law; elected a member of the city council in May 1889 and its president in May 1891, resigning in October 1892, having been appointed to the circuit court; served as judge of the circuit court 1892–1898; associate justice of the supreme court of Alabama 1898–1906, and served as chief justice from November 1906 to February 28, 1909, when he resigned; resumed the practice of law in Montgomery, Ala.; elected a Democrat to the Sixty-seventh and Sixty-eighth Congresses, and served from March 4, 1921, until his death in a hospital at Rochester, Minn., on March 27, 1923; interment in Oakwood Cemetery, Montgomery, Ala.

TYSON, Lawrence Davis, a Senator from Tennessee; born on a farm near Greenville, Pitt County, N. C., July 4, 1861; attended the county schools and Greenville Academy, and was graduated from the United States Military Academy at West Point in 1883; professor of military science and tactics in the University of Tennessee at Knoxville 1891–1895, and was graduated in law from that university in 1894; was admitted to the bar in 1894 and commenced practice in Knoxville; served with the Ninth Regiment, United States Infantry, until 1895, when he resigned his commission; volunteered in 1898 for service during the Spanish-American War, and was appointed by President McKinley as colonel of the Sixth Regiment, United States Volunteer Infantry, which he recruited, trained, and took to Puerto Rico; was mustered out March 15, 1899; engaged in the practice of law at Knoxville and later in manufacturing, retiring from the practice of law; brigadier general and inspector general of the National Guard of Tennessee 1902–1908; member of the Tennessee State House of Representatives and served as speaker 1903–1905; delegate at large to the Democratic National Convention in 1908; was an unsuccessful candidate for election to the United States Senate in 1913; volunteered for service at the outbreak of the First World War and was commissioned brigadier general in command of all National Guard troops of Tennessee; later commissioned by President Woodrow Wilson as a brigadier general and assigned to the Fifty-ninth Brigade, Thirtieth Division; trained troops at Camp Sevier, Greenville, S. C.; embarked for France May 10, 1918, in command of the Thirtieth Division, landing at Calais; participated in engagements at the Canal sector, Belgium, July 1 to August 30, 1918; Ypres-Lys offensive, Belgium, August 30 to September 2, 1918; Somme offensive, France, September 5 to October 20, 1918; was honorably discharged on April 16, 1919; awarded the Distinguished Service Medal for exceptionally meritorious and distinguished service; resumed newspaper pursuits; was an unsuccessful candidate for the Democratic nomination for Vice President in 1920; elected as a Democrat to the United States Senate and served from March 4, 1925, until his death in a sanitarium at Strafford, Pa., on August 24, 1929; interment in Old Gray Cemetery, Knoxville, Tenn.

U

UDALL, Stewart Lee (brother of Morris K. Udall), a Representative from Arizona; born in St. John, Apache County, Ariz., January 31, 1920; attended the public schools and the Eastern Arizona Junior College for one year; during World War II enlisted and engaged in combat operations over Europe as a gunner with the Fifteenth Air Force until 1944; graduated from the law school of the University of Arizona at Tucson in 1948; was admitted to the bar in 1948 and commenced the practice of law in Tucson, Ariz.; trustee of School District 16 in 1954; elected as a Democrat to the Eighty-fourth and to the three succeeding Congresses and served from January 3, 1955, until his resignation January 18, 1961; appointed Secretary of the Department of the Interior by President John F. Kennedy and took the oath of office January 21, 1961; is a resident of Tucson, Ariz.

UDREE, Daniel, a Representative from Pennsylvania; born in Philadelphia, Pa., August 5, 1751; attended the common schools; moved to Berks County and engaged in mercantile pursuits; member of the State house of representatives 1799–1805; elected as a Democrat to the Thirteenth Congress to fill the vacancy caused by the resignation of John M. Hyneman and served from October 12, 1813, to March 3, 1815; unsuccessful candidate for reelection in 1814 to the Fourteenth Congress; elected to the Sixteenth Congress to fill the vacancy caused by the resignation of Joseph Hiester and served from December 26, 1820, to March 3, 1821; elected to the Eighteenth Congress; subsequently elected to the Seventeenth Congress to fill the vacancy caused by the death of Ludwig Worman and served from December 10, 1822, to March 3, 1825; was not a candidate for renomination in 1824; resumed mercantile pursuits; died in Reading, Pa., July 15, 1828; interment in Oley Cemetery, Oley, Pa.

ULLMAN, Albert Conrad, a Representative from Oregon; born in Great Falls, Cascade County, Mont., March 9, 1914; attended the public schools in Snohomish, Wash.; graduated from Whitman College, Walla Walla, Wash., in 1935; taught in Port Angeles (Wash.) High School 1935–1937; graduated from Columbia University, New York City, N. Y., in 1939; commissioned an ensign in the United States Navy in 1942, and served as communications officer in the South and Southwest Pacific until December 1945; now commander, United States Naval Reserve; engaged in the real-estate and building business since 1946 in Baker, Oreg.; elected as a Democrat to the Eighty-fifth and Eighty-sixth Congresses (January 3, 1957–January 3, 1961). *Reelected to the Eighty-seventh Congress.*

UMSTEAD, William Bradley, a Representative and a Senator from North Carolina; born on a farm near Mangum's store in Mangum Township, Durham County, N. C., May 13, 1895; attended the county public schools and was graduated from the University of North Carolina at Chapel Hill in 1916; taught school in Kinston, N. C., in 1916 and 1917; during the First World War served as a lieutenant in the Three Hundred and Seventeenth Machine Gun Battalion, Eighty-first Division, United States Army, from August 15, 1917, to April 9, 1919, with service overseas; studied law at Trinity College (now Duke University) 1919–1921; was admitted to the bar in 1920 and commenced practice in Durham, N. C., in 1921; prosecuting attorney of the Durham County Recorders Court 1922–1926; solicitor of the tenth judicial district 1927–1933; member of the board of trustees of the University of North Carolina; chairman of the State Democratic executive committee 1944–1947; delegate to the Democratic National Convention in 1948; elected as a Democrat to the Seventy-third, Seventy-fourth, and Seventy-fifth Congresses (March 4, 1933–January 3, 1939); was not a candidate for renomination in 1938; resumed the practice of law in Durham, N. C.; appointed to the United States Senate to fill the vacancy caused by the death of Josiah W. Bailey and served from December 18, 1946, to December 30, 1948; was an unsuccessful candidate for the nomination to fill the vacancy and also for the full term; resumed the practice of law; Governor of North Carolina from January 1953 until his death in Durham, N. C., November 7, 1954; interment in Mount Tabor Church Cemetery in Mangum Township, Durham County, N. C.

UNDERHILL, Charles Lee, a Representative from Massachusetts; born in Richmond, Henrico County, Va., July 20, 1867; moved to Massachusetts in 1872 with his parents, who settled in Somerville; attended the common schools; was office boy, coal teamster, and blacksmith; subsequently engaged in the manufacture and sale of hardware in Somerville, Middlesex County, Mass.; served in the State house of representatives in 1902, 1903, 1908–1913, 1917, and 1918; member of the State constitutional convention in 1917 and 1918; elected as a Republican to the Sixty-seventh and to the five succeeding Congresses (March 4, 1921–March 3, 1933); was not a candidate for renomination in 1932 to the Seventy-third Congress; engaged in real-estate development in Washington, D. C., from 1933 until he retired from active business in 1941; died in a hospital in New York City, N. Y., January 28, 1946; interment in Mount Auburn Cemetery, Cambridge, Mass.

UNDERHILL, Edwin Stewart, a Representative from New York; born in Bath, Steuben County, N. Y., October 7, 1861; attended the common schools of his native city and Haverling High School at Bath; was graduated from Yale College, New Haven, Conn., in 1881; engaged in journalism and became editor of the Steuben Farmers' Advocate at Bath; presidential elector on the Democratic ticket of Cleveland and Thurman in 1888; became editor and publisher of the Corning (N. Y.) Daily Democrat (later the Corning Evening Leader) in 1899; elected as a Democrat to the Sixty-second and Sixty-third Congresses (March 4, 1911–March 3, 1915); was not a candidate for renomination in 1914; resumed the newspaper publishing business in Corning, N. Y.; during the First World War served as food administrator for Steuben County; engaged in banking, serving as vice president of the Farmers & Mechanics' Trust Co., Bath, N. Y.; delegate to the Democratic National Convention at Houston, Tex., in 1928; died as the result of an automobile accident in Coopers, Steuben County, N. Y., February 7, 1929; interment in Grove Cemetery, Bath, N. Y.

UNDERHILL, John Quincy, a Representative from New York; born in New Rochelle, Westchester County, N. Y., February 19, 1848; attended private and public schools and the College of the City of New York; engaged in the insurance business; village trustee of New Rochelle in 1877; elected village president in 1878 and reelected in 1880; served as town auditor; member of the board of education for several years; connected with the Westchester Fire Insurance Co. for nineteen years, serving as president and treasurer; elected as a Democrat to the Fifty-sixth Congress (March 4, 1899–March 3, 1901); was not a candidate for renomination in 1900; discontinued active business pursuits and lived in retirement; died in New Rochelle, N. Y., May 21, 1907; interment in Beechwoods Cemetery.

UNDERHILL, Walter, a Representative from New York; born in New York City September 12, 1795; completed preparatory studies; trustee of the house of refuge; treasurer of New York City for several years; served on the board of managers of the Society for the Reformation of Juvenile Delinquents in the city of New York 1845–1866, serving as treasurer 1857–1866, when he retired; elected as a Whig to the Thirty-first Congress (March 4, 1849–March 3, 1851); was not a candidate for renomination in 1850; president of the Mechanics & Traders' Insurance Co., New York City, from 1853 until his death in Whitestone, Long Island, N. Y., August 17, 1866; interment in Woodlawn Cemetery, New York City.

UNDERWOOD, John William Henderson, a Representative from Georgia; born in Ellenton, Ga., November 20, 1816; completed preparatory studies; studied law; was admitted to the bar in 1835 and commenced practice in Clarkesville, Ga.; solicitor general of the western judicial circuit of Georgia 1843–1847; delegate to the State constitutional convention in 1850; delegate to the Democratic State convention in 1857; member of the State house of representatives 1857–1859 and served as speaker; elected as a Democrat to the Thirty-sixth Congress and served from March 4, 1859, to January 23, 1861, when he withdrew and joined the Confederacy; served as brigade inspector during the Civil War; resumed the practice of law in Rome, Ga.; judge of the superior court of Georgia 1867–1869 and 1873–1882; delegate to the Democratic National Convention at New York City in 1868; appointed by President Arthur in 1884 a member of the first United States Tariff Commission; died in Rome, Floyd County, Ga., on July 18, 1888; interment in Myrtle Hill Cemetery.

UNDERWOOD, Joseph Rogers (brother of Warner Lewis Underwood and grandfather of Oscar Wilder Underwood), a Representative and a Senator from Kentucky; born in Goochland County, Va., October 24, 1791; moved to Barren County, Ky., in 1803 and lived with his uncle; attended the common schools and was graduated from Transylvania College, Lexington, Ky., in 1811; studied law in Lexington; served in the War of 1812 as a lieutenant in the Thirteenth Regiment, Kentucky Infantry; was admitted to the bar in 1813 and commenced the practice of law in Glasgow, Ky.; served as town trustee and county auditor until 1823; member of the State house of representatives 1816–1819; moved to Bowling Green, Ky., in 1823; presidential elector on the Clay ticket in 1824; member of the State house of representatives in 1825 and 1826; unsuccessful Whig candidate for Lieutenant Governor of Kentucky in 1828; judge of the court of appeals 1828–1835; elected as a Whig to the Twenty-fourth and to the three succeeding Congresses (March 4, 1835–March 3, 1843); declined to be a candidate for renomination; resumed the practice of law; presidential elector on the Whig ticket of Clay and Frelinghuysen in 1844; member of the State house of representatives in 1846 and served as speaker; elected as a Whig to the United States Senate and served from March 4, 1847, to March 3, 1853; was not a candidate for reelection; served in the State house of representatives in 1861; delegate to the Democratic National Convention at Chicago in 1864; resumed the practice of law and also engaged in agricultural pursuits; died near Bowling Green, Ky., August 23, 1876; interment in Fairview Cemetery, Bowling Green, Ky.

UNDERWOOD, Mell Gilbert, a Representative from Ohio; born at Rose Farm, Morgan County, Ohio, January 30, 1892; attended the public schools and was graduated from the New Lexington High School in 1911; taught in the public schools of New Lexington for several years; studied law at the Ohio State University at Columbus; was admitted to the bar in 1915 and commenced practice in New Lexington, Perry County, Ohio; prosecuting attorney of Perry County 1917–1921; unsuccessful Democratic candidate for election in 1920 to the Sixty-seventh Congress; elected as a Democrat to the Sixty-eighth and to the

six succeeding Congresses and served from March 4, 1923, to
April 10, 1936, when he resigned, having been appointed a judge
of the United States District Court for the Southern District of
Ohio, in which capacity he is still serving; is a resident of New
Lexington, Ohio.

UNDERWOOD, Oscar Wilder (grandson of Joseph Rogers
Underwood), a Representative and a Senator from Alabama;
born in Louisville, Jefferson County, Ky., May 6, 1862; attended
the common schools, the Rugby School, Louisville, Ky., and the
University of Virginia at Charlottesville; studied law; was admitted to the bar in 1884 and commenced practice in Birmingham, Ala.; chairman of the Democratic executive committee for
the ninth district in 1892; presented credentials as a Democratic
Member-elect to the Fifty-fourth Congress and served from
March 4, 1895, to June 9, 1896, when he was succeeded by Truman H. Aldrich, who contested his election; elected as a Democrat
to the Fifty-fifth and to the eight succeeding Congresses (March
4, 1897–March 3, 1915); did not seek renomination in 1914,
having become a candidate for Senator; Democratic floor leader
of the House of Representatives 1911–1915; candidate for the
Democratic presidential nomination in 1912 and 1924; elected to
the United States Senate in 1914; reelected in 1920, and served
from March 4, 1915, to March 3, 1927; declined to be a candidate
for reelection in 1926; floor leader of his party in the Senate 1921–
1923, and then declined reelection; represented the United States
as a member of the Conference on Limitation of Armament in
1921 and 1922; represented the United States as a delegate to the
Sixth International Conference of American States at Habana,
Cuba, in 1928; retired to his estate, "Woodlawn Mansion," near
Accotink, Fairfax County, Va., and engaged in literary pursuits
until his death there on January 25, 1929; interment in Woodlawn
Cemetery, Birmingham, Ala.

UNDERWOOD, Thomas Rust, a Representative and a Senator from Kentucky; born in Hopkinsville, Christian County,
Ky., March 3, 1898; attended the public schools; was graduated
from the University of Kentucky at Lexington in 1917; started
newspaper career in 1917; during the First World War served in
the Students Army Training Corps at the University of Kentucky
in 1918; general manager of Lexington (Ky.) Herald 1931–1935
and editor 1935–1956; member of the State planning board
1931–1935; secretary of the State racing commission 1931–1943
and in 1947 and 1948; secretary of the National Association of
State Racing Commissioners 1934–1948; became assistant to the
Director, Office of Economic Stabilization, in 1943; elected as a
Democrat to the Eighty-first Congress; reelected to the Eighty-
second Congress and served from January 3, 1949, until his
resignation March 17, 1951; appointed to the United States
Senate to fill the vacancy in the term ending January 3, 1955,
caused by the death of Virgil M. Chapman, and served from
March 19, 1951, to November 4, 1952; unsuccessful candidate
for election in 1952 to fill the vacancy; resumed editorial duties
with the Lexington Herald; died in Lexington, Ky., June 29,
1956; interment in Lexington Cemetery.

UNDERWOOD, Warner Lewis (brother of Joseph Rogers
Underwood), a Representative from Kentucky; born in Goochland County, Va., on August 7, 1808; completed preparatory
studies; moved to Kentucky in 1825; was graduated from the
University of Virginia at Charlottesville in 1829; studied law;
was admitted to the bar and commenced practice in Bowling
Green, Ky., in 1830; moved to Texas in 1834; attorney general
for the eastern district of Texas; declined a position in General
Houston's Cabinet; returned to Bowling Green, Ky., in 1840;
member of the State house of representatives in 1848; served in
the State senate 1849–1853; elected as the candidate of the

American Party to the Thirty-fourth and Thirty-fifth Con-
gresses (March 4, 1855–March 3, 1859); was not a candidate for
renomination; United States consul to Glasgow, Scotland, from
July 17, 1862, until September 30, 1864; returned to the United
States and practiced law in San Francisco, Calif.; returned to
Kentucky in 1866 and resumed the practice of law; died near
Bowling Green, Ky., March 12, 1872; interment in Fairview
Cemetery, Bowling Green, Ky.

UPDEGRAFF, Jonathan Taylor, a Representative from Ohio;
born near Mount Pleasant, Jefferson County, Ohio, May 13, 1822;
attended private schools and Franklin College; studied medicine;
was graduated from the University of Pennsylvania at Philadelphia
in 1845 and later from medical schools in Edinburgh and
Paris; practiced his profession, but devoted a large share of his
time to agricultural pursuits; served as a surgeon in the Union
Army during the Civil War; presidential elector on the Republican ticket of Grant and Wilson in 1872; served in the State senate
in 1872 and 1873; delegate to the Republican State convention
in 1873 and to the Republican National Convention at Cincinnati
in 1876; elected as a Republican to the Forty-sixth and Forty-
seventh Congresses and served from March 4, 1879, until his
death in Mount Pleasant, Ohio, November 30, 1882; had been
reelected to the Forty-eighth Congress; interment in Updegraff
Cemetery, near Mount Pleasant, Ohio; reinterment in Short Creek
Cemetery, west of Mount Pleasant, in 1926.

UPDEGRAFF, Thomas, a Representative from Iowa; born
in Tioga County, Pa., April 3, 1834; attended private schools,
the University of Notre Dame, Indiana, and an academy in
Binghamton, N. Y.; clerk of the district court of Clayton County,
Iowa, 1856–1860; studied law; was admitted to the bar in
1860 and commenced practice in McGregor, Iowa; member
of the State house of representatives in 1878; elected as a Republican to the Forty-sixth and Forty-seventh Congresses (March
4, 1879–March 3, 1883); unsuccessful candidate for reelection
in 1882 to the Forty-eighth Congress; member of the board of
education and city solicitor of McGregor, Iowa; delegate to the
Republican National Convention at Chicago in 1888; elected to
the Fifty-third, Fifty-fourth, and Fifty-fifth Congresses (March
4, 1893–March 3, 1899); unsuccessful candidate for renomination
in 1898; engaged in the practice of his profession until his death
in McGregor, Iowa, on October 4, 1910; interment in Pleasant
Grove Cemetery.

UPDIKE, Ralph Eugene, a Representative from Indiana; born
in Brookville, Franklin County, Ind., May 27, 1894; attended
the public schools of Whitcomb and Brookville, Dodds Army and
Navy Academy, Washington, D. C., Columbia University, New
York, N. Y., and Purdue University, Lafayette, Ind.; during the
First World War served overseas as a sergeant with the Seventy-
fourth Company, Sixth Regiment, Second Division, United States
Marines, 1916–1919; was five times wounded in action; studied
law; was admitted to the bar in 1920; was graduated from the
law department of Indiana University in 1923 and commenced
practice in Indianapolis, Ind.; member of the State house of
representatives 1923–1925; special judge of the city of Indianapolis in 1923 and 1924; special judge of the superior court of
Marion County in 1925 and 1926; elected as a Republican to
the Sixty-ninth and Seventieth Congresses (March 4, 1925–
March 3, 1929); unsuccessful candidate for reelection in 1928
to the Seventy-first Congress; special attorney in the Bureau of
Internal Revenue 1929–1933; delegate to the Republican National Convention at Cleveland in 1926; resumed the practice of
law in Indianapolis, Ind., and Washington, D. C., until March
2, 1942, when he was commissioned a captain in the United States
Marine Corps Reserve; served overseas in the South Pacific

with the First Marine Division, Fleet Marine Force, and was inactivated June 15, 1945; resumed the practice of law in Indianapolis, Ind., and Washington, D. C., until his retirement; died in Arlington, Va., September 16, 1953; interment in Arlington National Cemetery, Fort Myer, Va.

UPHAM, Charles Wentworth (cousin of George Baxter Upham and Jabez Upham), a Representative from Massachusetts; born in St. John, New Brunswick, Canada, May 4, 1802; served as an apothecary's apprentice; worked on a farm in Nova Scotia, immigrated to the United States in 1816 and settled in Boston, Mass.; was graduated from the theological department of Harvard University in 1821; was ordained to the ministry and officiated in Salem, Mass., 1824–1844; member of the State house of representatives 1840–1849; unsuccessful Whig candidate for election to the Thirty-second Congress; mayor of Salem, Mass., in 1852; delegate to the State constitutional convention in 1853; elected as a Whig to the Thirty-third Congress (March 4, 1853–March 3, 1855); unsuccessful candidate for reelection in 1854 to the Thirty-fourth Congress; member of the State senate in 1857 and 1858, serving as president; again a member of the State house of representatives in 1859 and 1860; died in Salem, Mass., on June 15, 1875; interment in Harmony Grove Cemetery.

UPHAM, George Baxter (brother of Jabez Upham and cousin of Charles Wentworth Upham), a Representative from New Hampshire; born in Brookfield, Mass., December 27, 1768; attended the common schools and Phillips Exeter Academy, Exeter, N. H.; was graduated from Harvard University in 1789; studied law; was admitted to the bar in 1792 and commenced practice in Claremont, N. H.; solicitor for Cheshire County 1796–1804; elected to the Seventh Congress (March 4, 1801–March 3, 1803); declined to be a candidate for reelection to the Eighth Congress; member of the State house of representatives 1804–1813 and again in 1815, serving as speaker of the house in 1809 and 1815; served in the State senate in 1814; resumed the practice of law and also interested in banking; died in Claremont, N. H., on February 10, 1848; interment in Pleasant Street Cemetery.

UPHAM, Jabez (brother of George Baxter Upham and cousin of Charles Wentworth Upham), a Representative from Massachusetts; born in Brookfield, Mass., August 23, 1764; was graduated from Harvard University in 1785; studied law; was admitted to the bar and commenced practice in Sturbridge, Mass.; moved to Claremont, N. H., and thence to Brookfield, Mass., where he continued the practice of law; member of the State house of representatives 1804–1806 and in 1811; elected to the Tenth and Eleventh Congresses, and served from March 4, 1807, until his resignation in 1810; died in Brookfield, Mass., November 8, 1811; interment in New Cemetery, West Brookfield, Mass.

UPHAM, Nathaniel, a Representative from New Hampshire; born in Deerfield, N. H., June 9, 1774; pursued classical studies and attended the Phillips Exeter Academy, Exeter, N. H., in 1793; engaged in mercantile pursuits at Gilmanton in 1794, at Deerfield in 1796, at Portsmouth in 1801, and at Rochester in 1802 and afterward; member of the State house of representatives 1807–1809; governor's counselor in 1811 and 1812; elected as a Democrat to the Fifteenth, Sixteenth, and Seventeenth Congresses (March 4, 1817–March 3, 1823); declined to be a candidate for renomination in 1822 because of failing health; returned to Rochester, N. H., and became interested in educational work; died in Rochester, N. H., July 10, 1829; interment in Old Rochester Cemetery.

UPHAM, William, a Senator from Vermont; born in Leicester, Mass., August 5, 1792; moved with his father to Montpelier, Vt., in 1802; attended the district schools, the Montpelier Academy, and was privately tutored; studied law; was admitted to the bar in 1811 and commenced practice in Montpelier, Vt., in 1812; served in the State house of representatives in 1827 and 1828; State's attorney for Washington County in 1829; again a member of the State house of representatives in 1830; elected as a Whig to the United States Senate in 1843; reelected in 1849 and served from March 4, 1843, until his death in Washington, D. C., January 14, 1853; interment in the Congressional Cemetery.

UPSHAW, William David, a Representative from Georgia; born near Newnan, Coweta County, Ga., October 15, 1866; attended the country schools, the public schools of Atlanta, Ga., and Mercer University, Macon, Ga.; engaged in agricultural and mercantile pursuits until physically incapacitated by an accident; since then a writer and lecturer; founded "The Golden Age," a magazine of militant christian citizenship, at Atlanta, Ga., February 22, 1906; elected as a Democrat to the Sixty-sixth and to the three succeeding Congresses (March 4, 1919–March 3, 1927); unsuccessful candidate for renomination in 1926; vice chairman of the Scandinavian Commercial Commission; nominated for President by the Prohibition Party in 1932; unsuccessful candidate for the Democratic nomination for United States Senator in 1942; resumed his former pursuits as a lecturer, evangelist, and writer; vice president of the Linda Vista Baptist Bible College and Seminary and member of the faculty, San Diego, Calif.; at the age of seventy-two was ordained a minister of the Baptist Church; died in Glendale, Calif., November 21, 1952; interment in Forest Lawn Cemetery.

UPSON, Charles, a Representative from Michigan; born in Southington, Conn., March 19, 1821; attended the district and select schools of Southington; taught school in Farmington, Conn., 1840–1842; studied law at the Yale Law School in 1844; removed to Constantine, St. Joseph County, Mich., in 1845; taught school in 1846 and 1847; deputy county clerk of St. Joseph County in 1847; admitted to the bar in 1847 and commenced practice in Kalamazoo, Mich.; county clerk in 1848 and 1849; prosecuting attorney 1852–1854; member of the State senate in 1855 and 1856; moved to Coldwater, Mich., in 1856 and continued the practice of law; member of the State board of railroad commissioners in 1857; attorney general of Michigan in 1861 and 1862; elected as a Republican to the Thirty-eighth, Thirty-ninth, and Fortieth Congresses (March 4, 1863–March 3, 1869); was not a candidate for renomination in 1868; judge of the fifteenth circuit court from 1869 until his resignation December 31, 1872; member of the commission to revise the State constitution in 1873; declined appointment as Commissioner of Indian Affairs in 1876; mayor of the city of Coldwater in 1877; again a member of the State senate in 1880; retired from public life and resumed the practice of his profession; died in Coldwater, Mich., September 5, 1885; interment in Oak Grove Cemetery.

UPSON, Christopher Columbus, a Representative from Texas; born near Syracuse, Onondaga County, N. Y., October 17, 1829; attended the common schools and Williams College, Williamstown, Mass.; studied law; was admitted to the bar in 1851 and commenced practice in Syracuse, N. Y., in 1851; moved to San Antonio, Tex., in 1854 and engaged in the practice of law; during the Civil War served in the Confederate Army as a volunteer aide, with the rank of colonel, on the staff of Gen. W. H. C. Whiting; appointed by the Confederacy associate justice of Arizona in 1862; presidential elector on the

Democratic ticket of Tilden and Hendricks in 1876; elected as a Democrat to the Forty-sixth Congress to fill the vacancy caused by the death of Gustave Schleicher; reelected to the Forty-seventh Congress and served from April 15, 1879, to March 3, 1883; unsuccessful candidate for renomination in 1882; resumed the practice of law in San Antonio, Tex., and died there February 8, 1902; interment in Confederate Cemetery.

UPSON, William Hanford, a Representative from Ohio; born in Worthington, Franklin County, Ohio, on January 11, 1823; attended Tallmadge Academy, pursued classical studies, and was graduated from Western Reserve College, Hudson, Ohio, in 1842; studied law one year in the law department of Yale College and in Painesville, Ohio; was admitted to the bar in 1845 and commenced practice in Akron, Ohio, in 1846; prosecuting attorney of Summit County 1848–1850; member of the State senate 1853–1855; delegate to the Republican National Conventions in 1864 and 1876; elected as a Republican to the Forty-first and Forty-second Congresses (March 4, 1869–March 3, 1873); was not a candidate for renomination in 1872; appointed associate justice of the supreme court of Ohio in 1883; elected judge of the circuit court of Ohio in 1884 and served until 1894; resumed the practice of law; died in Akron, Ohio, April 13, 1910; interment in Glendale Cemetery.

UPTON, Charles Horace, a Representative from Virginia; born in Salem, Mass., August 23, 1812; attended the public schools; was graduated from Bowdoin College, Brunswick, Maine, in 1834; moved to Falls Church, Va., in 1836 and engaged in agricultural and literary pursuits; held several local offices; presented credentials as a Republican Member-elect to the Thirty-seventh Congress under an election held on May 23, 1861, and served until February 27, 1862, when the House declared he was not entitled to the seat; appointed by President Lincoln in 1863 United States consul to Switzerland and served from July 9, 1863, until his death in Geneva, Switzerland, June 17, 1877; interment in the Congressional Cemetery, Washington, D. C.

UPTON, Robert William, a Senator from New Hampshire; born in Boston, Mass., February 3, 1884; attended the public schools; was graduated from Boston University Law School in 1907; admitted to the Massachusetts and New Hampshire bars in 1907 and commenced practice in Concord, N. H.; member of the State house of representatives in 1911; delegate to the New Hampshire State Constitutional Conventions in 1918, 1930, 1938, and 1948, serving as president in 1948; chairman of the New Hampshire Republican State Committee in 1936 and vice chairman from 1937 to 1952; delegate to the Republican National Conventions in 1940, 1944, 1948, 1956, and chairman of delegation in 1960; appointed as a Republican to the United States Senate to fill the vacancy caused by the death of Charles W. Toby and served from August 14, 1953, to November 7, 1954; unsuccessful candidate for nomination to fill the vacancy; resumed law practice; member, Mixed Board, Clemency and Parole, Bonn, Germany, from March 15 to June 30, 1956; special ambassador to Liberia in 1956 for inauguration of President Tubman; is a resident of Concord, N. H.

URNER, Milton George (uncle of James Samuel Simmons), a Representative from Maryland; born in the Liberty district, Frederick County, Md., July 29, 1839; attended the common schools, Freeland Seminary, Montgomery County, Pa., and Dickinson Seminary, Williamsport, Pa.; engaged in teaching in his native county 1859–1862; studied law; was admitted to the bar in 1863 and commenced practice in Frederick, Md.; State's attorney for Frederick County 1871–1875; presidential

elector on the Republican ticket of Hayes and Wheeler in 1876; elected as a Republican to the Forty-sixth and Forty-seventh Congresses (March 4, 1879–March 3, 1883); was not a candidate for renomination in 1882; resumed the practice of his profession in Frederick, Md.; became local attorney for the Pennsylvania Railroad Co. in 1887; member of the State senate 1888–1890; appointed naval officer at the port of Baltimore by President Harrison in 1890; engaged in banking and other business enterprises; trustee of several educational institutions; died in Frederick, Md., February 9, 1926; interment in Mount Olivet Cemetery.

UTT, James Boyd, a Representative from California; born in Tustin, Orange County, Calif., March 11, 1899; attended the public schools of Orange County, student at Santa Ana Junior College in 1942 and 1943; engaged in agricultural and citrus processing; served in the State assembly 1932–1936; inheritance tax appraiser in the State controller's office 1936–1952; graduated from the University of Southern California Law School in 1946; was admitted to the bar in 1947 and commenced the practice of law in Santa Ana, Calif.; elected as a Republican to the Eighty-third and to the three succeeding Congresses (January 3, 1953–January 3, 1961). _Reelected to the Eighty-seventh Congress._

UTTER, George Herbert, a Representative from Rhode Island; born in Plainfield, Union County, N. J., July 24, 1854; moved with his parents to Westerly, R. I., in 1861; attended the public schools of Westerly and Alfred (N. Y.) Academy; was graduated from Amherst College, Massachusetts, in 1877; engaged as a printer and newspaper publisher in Westerly, R. I.; personal aide on the staff of Gov. A. O. Bourn 1883–1885; member of the State house of representatives 1885–1889, serving as speaker the last year; served in the State senate 1889–1891; secretary of state of Rhode Island 1891–1894; Lieutenant Governor in 1904; Governor of Rhode Island in 1905 and 1906; elected as a Republican to the Sixty-second Congress and served from March 4, 1911, until his death in Westerly, R. I., November 3, 1912; interment in Riverbend Cemetery.

UTTERBACK, Hubert (cousin of John Gregg Utterback), a Representative from Iowa; born on a farm near Hayesville, Keokuk County, Iowa, June 28, 1880; attended the rural schools and Hedrick (Iowa) Normal and Commercial College; was graduated from Drake University, Des Moines, Iowa, in 1908; studied law; was admitted to the bar in 1906 and commenced practice in Des Moines, Iowa; instructor in the law department of Drake University 1908–1935; lecturer on law, Still College, Des Moines, Iowa, 1911–1933; judge of police court of Des Moines 1912–1914; judge of the ninth Iowa judicial district 1915–1927; served as chairman of the Des Moines and Polk County Chapter of the American National Red Cross 1916–1928 and of the Iowa State Red Cross Chapters 1919–1934; member of the Iowa State Conference of Social Work and served as chairman of the legislative committee 1923–1925; served as vice president of the Iowa Humane Society; served as an associate justice of the State supreme court from December 5, 1932, to April 16, 1933; elected as a Democrat to the Seventy-fourth Congress (January 3, 1935–January 3, 1937); was not a candidate for renomination but was an unsuccessful candidate for nomination as United States Senator in 1936; chairman of the State parole board 1937–1940; State Democratic National committeeman 1937–1940; died in Des Moines, Iowa, on May 12, 1942; interment in Glendale Cemetery.

UTTERBACK, John Gregg (cousin of Hubert Utterback), a Representative from Maine; born in Franklin, Johnson County, Ind., July 12, 1872; attended the public schools of his native city; employed in a carriage factory 1889–1892; engaged as a traveling salesman 1892–1905, during which time he resided in Jackson, Mich., Rochester, N. Y., and Winchester, Mass.; settled in Bangor, Maine, in 1905 and engaged in the retail sale of carriages and later in the retail sale of automobiles; served as councilman in 1912 and 1913, as alderman in 1913 and 1914, and as mayor of Bangor in 1914 and 1915; chairman of the Maine Motor Vehicle Conference Committee in 1930; delegate to the Democratic National Convention at Chicago in 1932; elected as a Democrat to the Seventy-third Congress (March 4, 1933–January 3, 1935); was an unsuccessful candidate for reelection in 1934 to the Seventy-fourth Congress; was appointed a United States marshal for the district of Maine in 1935 and served until his resignation in 1944; resumed the automobile business and was president of the Utterback Corp.; died in Bangor, Maine, July 11, 1955; interment in Mount Hope Cemetery.

V

VAIL, George, a Representative from New Jersey; born in Morristown, Morris County, N. J., July 21, 1809; completed preparatory studies; attended Morris Academy at Morristown; engaged in the manufacture of telegraph instruments; member of the State general assembly in 1843 and 1844; appointed by the Governor of New Jersey to represent the State at the World's Fair in London, England, in 1851; unsuccessful candidate for election in 1850 to the Thirty-second Congress; elected as a Democrat to the Thirty-third and Thirty-fourth Congresses (March 4, 1853–March 3, 1857); appointed February 3, 1858, by President James Buchanan, as consul to Glasgow, Scotland, and served until August 10, 1861; returned to the United States and settled in Morristown, N. J., where he engaged in literary pursuits; member of the court of pardons; judge of the New Jersey Court of Errors and Appeals 1865–1871; retired from public life; died in Morristown, N. J., May 23, 1875; interment in First Presbyterian Church Cemetery.

VAIL, Henry, a Representative from New York; born near Milbrook, Dutchess County, N. Y., in 1782; received a limited schooling; engaged in the retail mercantile business 1806–1815 and in wholesale mercantile pursuits 1815–1832; elected as a Democrat to the Twenty-fifth Congress (March 4, 1837–March 3, 1839); unsuccessful candidate for reelection in 1838 to the Twenty-sixth Congress; resumed his former business pursuits in Troy, Rensselaer County, N. Y., and died there June 25, 1853; interment in Oakwood Cemetery.

VAIL, Richard Bernard, a Representative from Illinois; born in Chicago, Cook County, Ill., August 31, 1895; attended the public schools, the School of Commerce, the Chicago Technical College, and the John Marshall Law School; during the First World War served in the United States Army as a lieutenant of Infantry; engaged in the manufacture of steel products; elected as a Republican to the Eightieth Congress (January 3, 1947–January 3, 1949); unsuccessful candidate for reelection in 1948 to the Eighty-first Congress; elected to the Eighty-second Congress (January 3, 1951–January 3, 1953); unsuccessful candidate for reelection in 1952 to the Eighty-third Congress and for election in 1954 to the Eighty-fourth Congress; chairman of the board of directors of the Vail Manufacturing Co., Chicago, Ill.; died in Chicago, Ill., July 29, 1955; interment in Holy Sepulchre Cemetery, Worth, Ill.

VAILE, William Newell, a Representative from Colorado; born in Kokomo, Howard County, Ind., June 22, 1876; moved with his parents to Denver, Colo., in 1881; attended the public schools, and was graduated from Yale University in 1898; during the Spanish-American War served as a private in the First Regiment of the Connecticut Volunteer Field Artillery from May 19, 1898, to October 25, 1898; studied law at the University of Colorado and Harvard Law School; was admitted to the bar in 1901 and commenced the practice of law in Denver, Colo.; served on the Mexican border from June 28 to December 1, 1916, as a second lieutenant in the First Separate Battalion, National Guard of Colorado; elected as a Republican to the Sixty-sixth and to the four succeeding Congresses and served from March 4, 1919, until his death in Rocky Mountain National Park, Colo., on July 2, 1927; interment in Fairmount Cemetery, Denver, Colo.

VALENTINE, Edward Kimble, a Representative from Nebraska; born in Keosauqua, Van Buren County, Iowa, June 1, 1843; attended the common schools; learned the trade of a printer; during the Civil War enlisted in the Union Army and served in the Sixty-seventh Regiment, Illinois Volunteer Infantry; promoted to second lieutenant and honorably discharged; in the spring of 1863 reenlisted as a private in the Seventh Iowa Volunteer Cavalry; promoted to adjutant of the regiment and served until June 1866, having been twice brevetted for "efficient and meritorious services"; settled in Omaha, Nebr., in 1866; appointed register of the United States land office at West Point, Nebr., and served from May 17, 1869, to September 30, 1871; studied law; was admitted to the bar in 1869 and commenced practice at West Point, Nebr.; elected judge of the sixth judicial district in 1875; elected as a Republican to the Forty-sixth, Forty-seventh, and Forty-eighth Congresses (March 4, 1879–March 3, 1885); declined to be a candidate for renomination in 1884; Sergeant-at-Arms of the United States Senate from June 30, 1890, to August 6, 1893; resumed the practice of law in West Point, Nebr.; moved to Chicago, Ill., in 1908 and lived in retirement until his death April 11, 1916; interment in Union Ridge Cemetery, Norwood Park, Ill.

VALK, William Weightman, a Representative from New York; born in Charleston, S. C., October 12, 1806; attended the local school and was graduated from the University of South Carolina at Columbia in 1830; studied medicine and commenced practice in Bridgeport, Conn.; served as assistant surgeon on the U. S. frigate *Constellation*; went to California about 1849 during the gold rush; finally settled in Flushing, Long Island, N. Y., and continued the practice of medicine until elected to Congress; elected as a candidate of the American Party to the Thirty-fourth Congress (March 4, 1855–March 3, 1857); unsuccessful candidate for reelection in 1856 to the Thirty-fifth Congress; during the Civil War was surgeon in the Second Regiment, Maryland Volunteer Infantry; appointed a clerk in the United States Pension Office at Washington, D. C., in 1867 and served until his death in that city September 20, 1879; interment in Flushing Cemetery, Flushing, Queens County, N. Y.

VALLANDIGHAM, Clement Laird (uncle of John A. McMahon), a Representative from Ohio; born in New Lisbon, Columbiana County, Ohio, July 29, 1820; attended a classical school conducted by his father and Jefferson College, Canonsburg, Pa.; moved to Maryland and for two years was a preceptor in Union Academy at Snow Hill; moved to New Lisbon, Ohio, in 1840; studied law; was admitted to the bar in 1842 and commenced practice in Dayton, Ohio; member of the State house of representatives in 1845 and 1846; edited the Western Empire 1847–1849; was an unsuccessful candidate for election in 1854 to the Thirty-fourth Congress; delegate to the Democratic National Convention at Cincinnati in 1856; successfully contested as a Democrat the election of Lewis D. Campbell to the Thirty-fifth Congress; reelected to the Thirty-sixth and Thirty-seventh Congresses and served from May 25, 1858, to March 3, 1863; unsuccessful candidate for reelection in 1862 to the Thirty-eighth Congress; arrested by the Union military authorities in 1863 for treasonable utterance and banished to the Confederate States; went from Wilmington, N. C., to Bermuda and thence to Canada, where he remained until June 1864; during his exile was an unsuccessful Democratic candidate for Governor of Ohio in 1863; delegate to the Democratic National Convention at Chicago in 1864 which nominated McClellan and Pendleton and at New York City in 1868 which nominated Seymour and Blair; unsuccessful candidate for election to the United States Senate in 1869; died in Lebanon, Ohio, June 17, 1871; interment in Woodland Cemetery, Dayton, Ohio.

VAN AERNAM, Henry, a Representative from New York; born in Marcellus, Onondaga County, N. Y., March 11, 1819; pursued an academic course; studied medicine at the Geneva and Willoughby Medical Colleges and practiced his profession; member of the State assembly in 1858; during the Civil War served in the Union Army as a surgeon in the One Hundred and Fifty-fourth Regiment, New York Volunteer Infantry, from September 26, 1862, to November 5, 1864; elected as a Republican to the Thirty-ninth and Fortieth Congresses (March 4, 1865–March 3, 1869); appointed as Commissioner of Pensions May 1, 1869, and served until May 31, 1871, when he resigned; elected to the Forty-sixth and Forty-seventh Congresses (March 4, 1879–March 3, 1883); resumed the practice of medicine in Franklinville, Cattaraugus County, N. Y., and died there June 1, 1894; interment in Mount Prospect Cemetery.

VAN ALEN, James Isaac (half brother of Martin Van Buren), a Representative from New York; born in Kinderhook, Columbia County, N. Y., in 1776; attended the common schools; city clerk of Kinderhook 1797–1801; member of the State constitutional conventions in 1801 and 1803; justice of the peace 1801–1804; member of the State assembly in 1804; surrogate of Columbia County 1804–1808 and 1815–1822; elected as a Federalist to the Tenth Congress (March 4, 1807–March 3, 1809); died in Newburgh, N. Y., on December 23, 1870; interment in Kinderhook Cemetery, Kinderhook, N. Y.

VAN ALEN, John Evert, a Representative from New York; born in Kinderhook, Columbia County, N. Y., in 1749; completed preparatory studies; moved to De Freestville in 1778 and engaged in extensive farming operations; surveyed the town of Greenbush in 1790 and conducted a general store there; engaged in civil engineering and surveying; assistant court justice in Rensselaer County in 1791; elected to the Third, Fourth, and Fifth Congresses and served from March 4, 1793, to March 3, 1799; member of the State assembly in 1800 and 1801; died in March 1807.

VAN ALSTYNE, Thomas Jefferson, a Representative from New York; born in Richmondville, Schoharie County, N. Y., July 25, 1827; attended the common schools, Moravia (N. Y.) Academy, and Hartwick (N. Y.) Seminary, and was graduated from Hamilton College, Clinton, N. Y., in 1848; studied law in Albany, N. Y.; was admitted to the bar in 1849 and commenced practice in that city; served as judge advocate with the rank of major during the Civil War; judge of Albany County 1871–1882; elected as a Democrat to the Forty-eighth Congress (March 4, 1883–March 3, 1885); unsuccessful candidate for reelection in 1884 to the Forty-ninth Congress; resumed the practice of law; mayor of Albany, N. Y., 1898–1900; died in Albany, N. Y., October 26, 1903; interment in the Rural Cemetery.

VAN AUKEN, Daniel Myers, a Representative from Pennsylvania; born in Montague, Sussex County, N. J., January 15, 1826; attended the common schools and Deckertown Academy; was graduated from Union College, Schenectady, N. Y., in 1852; studied law; was admitted to the Pennsylvania bar in 1855 and commenced the practice of law in Milford, Pa.; served as prosecuting attorney of Pike County 1855–1859; elected as a Democrat to the Fortieth and Forty-first Congresses (March 4, 1867–March 3, 1871); was not a candidate for reelection in 1870 to the Forty-second Congress; resumed the practice of law in Milford, Pa.; served as district attorney of Pike County, Pa., 1893–1896 and 1899–1903; continued the practice of law until his death in Milford, Pa., on November 7, 1908; interment in Milford Cemetery.

VAN BUREN, John, a Representative from New York; born in Kingston, Ulster County, N. Y., May 13, 1799; was graduated from Union College, Schenectady, N. Y., in 1818; studied law; was admitted to the bar and commenced practice in Kingston, N. Y.; member of the State assembly in 1831; judge of Ulster County 1836–1841; elected as a Democrat to the Twenty-seventh Congress (March 4, 1841–March 3, 1843); resumed the practice of law; district attorney of Ulster County 1846–1850; died in Kingston, N. Y., January 16, 1855; interment in Old Houghtaling Cemetery.

VAN BUREN, Martin (half brother of James Isaac Van Alen), a Senator from New York and a Vice President and a President of the United States; born in Kinderhook, Columbia County, N. Y., December 5, 1782; attended the district schools and Kinderhook Academy; studied law; was admitted to the bar in New York City and commenced practice in Kinderhook, N. Y., in 1803; moved to Hudson, N. Y., in 1809; surrogate of Columbia County 1808–1813; member of the State senate 1813–1820; attorney general of New York 1815–1819; delegate to the State constitutional convention in 1821; elected as a Democrat to the United States Senate; reelected in 1827, and served from March 4, 1821, until December 20, 1828, when he resigned, having been elected Governor; served as Governor of New York from January 1 to March 12, 1829, when he resigned to enter the Cabinet; appointed Secretary of State in the Cabinet of President Andrew Jackson and served from March 28, 1829, until his resignation, effective May 23, 1831, when he was commissioned Minister to Great Britain; the Senate rejected his nomination January 25, 1832, and he returned to the United States; elected, as a Democrat, Vice President of the United States on the ticket with Andrew Jackson and served from March 4, 1833, to March 3, 1837; elected, as a Democrat, President of the United States and served from March 4, 1837, to March 3, 1841; unsuccessful candidate for reelection as President on the Democratic ticket in 1840 and on the Free-Soil ticket in 1848; withdrew from political life and retired to his country home, "Lindenwald," in Kinderhook, N. Y., where he died July 24, 1862; interment in Kinderhook Cemetery.

VANCE, John Luther, a Representative from Ohio; born in Gallipolis, Gallia County, Ohio, July 19, 1839; attended the public schools and Gallia Academy, Ohio; was graduated from the Cincinnati Law School in April 1861, and was admitted to the bar the same year; during the Civil War enlisted in April 1861 in the Union Army and served successively as captain, major, and lieutenant colonel in the Fourth Regiment, West Virginia Volunteer Infantry; mustered out in December 1864; established and published the Gallipolis Bulletin in 1867; commenced the practice of law in Gallipolis, Ohio, in 1870; delegate to the Democratic National Convention at Baltimore in 1872; elected as a Democrat to the Forty-fourth Congress (March

4, 1875–March 3, 1877); unsuccessful candidate for reelection in 1876 to the Forty-fifth Congress; resumed his former newspaper pursuits; president of the Ohio River Improvement Association from shortly after 1877 until his death; died in Gallipolis, Ohio, on June 10, 1921; interment in Pine Street Cemetery.

VANCE, Joseph, a Representative from Ohio; born in Catfish (now Washington), Washington County, Pa., March 21, 1786; moved with his father to Vanceburg, Ky., in 1788 and to Urbana, Ohio, in 1805; engaged in agricultural pursuits; captain of a rifle company in 1811 and 1812; during the War of 1812 served successively as major, colonel, brigadier general, and major general of Ohio Militia; member of the State house of representatives in 1812, 1813, 1815, 1816, 1818, and 1819; delegate to the State constitutional convention in 1820; engaged in mercantile pursuits at Urbana and Perrysburg, Ohio; laid out the city of Findlay in Hancock County; elected as a Democrat to the Seventeenth and to the six succeeding Congresses (March 4, 1821–March 3, 1835); unsuccessful candidate for reelection in 1834 to the Twenty-fourth Congress; Governor of Ohio 1836–1838; member of the State senate 1840–1841; elected as a Whig to the Twenty-eighth and Twenty-ninth Congresses (March 4, 1843–March 3, 1847); was not a candidate for renomination in 1846; delegate to the Whig National Convention at Philadelphia in 1848; delegate to the State constitutional convention in 1851; retired from public life and active business pursuits; died near Urbana, Champaign County, Ohio, August 24, 1852; interment in Oak Dale Cemetery.

VANCE, Robert Brank (uncle of Zebulon Baird Vance), a Representative from North Carolina; born on Reems Creek, near Asheville, Buncombe County, N. C., in 1793; attended the common schools and Newton Academy, Asheville, N. C.; studied medicine at the medical school of Dr. Charles Harris in Cabarrus County, N. C.; commenced the practice of medicine in Asheville, N. C., in 1818; held several local offices; elected as a Democrat to the Eighteenth Congress (March 4, 1823–March 3, 1825); unsuccessful candidate for reelection in 1824 to the Nineteenth Congress and for election in 1826 to the Twentieth Congress; was mortally wounded by Hon. Samuel P. Carson, the successful candidate, who challenged him to a duel, fought at Saluda Gap, N. C., because of a derogatory remark made during the campaign of 1826, to the effect that the latter's father had turned Tory during the Revolutionary War; died the following day near Saluda Gap, N. C., 1827; interment in the family burial ground on Reems Creek, near Asheville, N. C.

VANCE, Robert Brank (nephew of the preceding and brother of Zebulon Baird Vance), a Representative from North Carolina; born on Reems Creek, near Asheville, Buncombe County, N. C., April 24, 1828; attended the common schools; engaged in mercantile and agricultural pursuits; clerk of the court of pleas and quarter sessions 1848–1856; during the Civil War was elected captain of a company in the Confederate Army; twice elected colonel of the Twenty-ninth North Carolina Regiment; appointed brigadier general in 1863; elected as a Democrat to the Forty-third and to the five succeeding Congresses (March 4, 1873–March 3, 1885); unsuccessful candidate for renomination in 1884 to the Forty-ninth Congress; United States Assistant Commissioner of Patents from April 11, 1885, to April 4, 1889, when he resigned; returned to North Carolina and settled in Alexander; member of the State house of representatives 1894–1896; died in Alexander, near Asheville, N. C., November 28, 1899; interment in Riverside Cemetery, Asheville, N. C.

VANCE, Robert Johnstone, a Representative from Connecticut; born in New York City, N. Y., March 15, 1854; attended the common schools; moved to New Britain, Conn., in 1870; attended the high school; city clerk of New Britain from 1878 until his resignation in 1887, having been elected a Representative; became editor and publisher of the New Britain Herald in 1881; member of the State house of representatives in 1886; elected as a Democrat to the Fiftieth Congress (March 4, 1887–March 3, 1889); unsuccessful candidate for reelection in 1888 to the Fifty-first Congress; resumed his former business pursuits; labor commissioner of Connecticut 1893–1895; mayor of New Britain, Conn., in 1896 and 1897; delegate to the State constitutional convention in 1902; died in Montreat, N. C., where he had gone in search of better health, June 15, 1902; interment in Fairview Cemetery, New Britain, Conn.

VANCE, Zebulon Baird (brother of Robert Brank Vance), a Representative and a Senator from North Carolina; born on Reems Creek, near Asheville, Buncombe County, N. C., May 13, 1830; attended the common schools of Buncombe County, Washington (Tenn.) College, and the University of North Carolina at Chapel Hill; studied law; was admitted to the bar in 1852 and commenced practice in Asheville, N. C.; elected prosecuting attorney of Buncombe County in 1852; member of the State house of commons in 1854; elected as a Democrat to the Thirty-fifth Congress to fill the vacancy caused by the resignation of Thomas L. Clingman; reelected to the Thirty-sixth Congress and served from December 7, 1858, to March 3, 1861; during the Civil War entered the Confederate Army as a captain in May 1861, and was promoted to the rank of colonel in August 1861; Governor of North Carolina 1862–1866; delegate to the Democratic National Convention at New York City in 1868 which nominated Seymour and Blair; elected to the United States Senate in November 1870, but did not present his credentials; unsuccessful Democratic candidate for election to the United States Senate in 1872; again Governor of North Carolina 1876–1878; elected as a Democrat to the United States Senate; reelected in 1884 and 1890, and served from March 4, 1879, until his death in Washington, D. C., April 14, 1894; funeral services were held in the Chamber of the United States Senate; interment in Riverside Cemetery, Asheville, N. C.

VAN CORTLANDT, Philip (brother of Pierre Van Cortlandt, Jr.), a Representative from New York; born in New York City August 21, 1749; pursued classical studies; attended Coldenham Academy and was graduated from King's College (later Columbia University) in 1768; engaged as a civil engineer; member of the Provincial Congress in 1775; during the War of the Revolution served as lieutenant colonel and was mustered out of the service with the rank of brigadier general for gallant conduct at the siege of Yorktown under General Lafayette; delegate to the State convention which adopted the Federal Constitution in 1788; served as supervisor of the town of Cortland, and as school commissioner and road master; member of the State assembly 1788–1790; served in the State senate 1791–1793; elected as a Democrat to the Third and to the seven succeeding Congresses (March 4, 1793–March 3, 1809); engaged in agricultural pursuits; accompanied General Lafayette on his tour through the United States in 1831; was a charter member of the Society of the Cincinnati; died at Van Cortlandt Manor, Croton on Hudson, Westchester County, N. Y., on November 1, 1831; interment in Hillside Cemetery, Peekskill, N. Y.

VAN CORTLANDT, Pierre, Jr. (brother of Philip Van Cortlandt), a Representative from New York; born at Van Cortlandt Manor, Croton, Westchester County, N. Y., August

29, 1762; pursued classical studies; was graduated from Queen's College (later Rutgers College), New Brunswick, N. J., in 1783; studied law in the office of Alexander Hamilton; was admitted to the bar and commenced practice; retired from his law practice and devoted his time managing his estate in Westchester County; presidential elector on the Jefferson ticket in 1800; member of the State assembly in 1811 and 1812; elected as a Democrat to the Twelfth Congress (March 4, 1811–March 3, 1813); presidential elector on the Harrison ticket in 1840; founded and was president of the Westchester County Bank at Peeks-kill, N. Y., from 1833 until his death there July 13, 1848; inter-ment in Hillside Cemetery.

VANDENBERG, Arthur Hendrick, a Senator from Michigan; born in Grand Rapids, Mich., March 22, 1884; attended the public schools and studied law at the University of Michigan at Ann Arbor; editor and publisher of the Grand Rapids Herald 1906–1928; author; member of Grand Rapids Charter Commis-sion in 1912; chairman of Michigan commission to place the statue of Zachariah Chandler in the United States Capitol in 1913; chairman of the Michigan Republican State conventions in 1916 and 1928; member of the Republican State central committee 1912–1918; appointed as a Republican to the United States Senate on March 31, 1928, to fill the vacancy caused by the death of Woodbridge N. Ferris, and on November 6, 1928, was elected to fill this vacancy and also for the term ending January 3, 1935; reelected in 1934, 1940, and again in 1946, and served from March 31, 1928, until his death; delegate to the United Nations Conference at San Francisco in 1945; delegate to the United Nations General Assembly at London and New York in 1946; United States adviser to the Council of Foreign Ministers at London, Paris, and New York in 1946; delegate to Pan American Conference at Rio de Janeiro, Brazil, in 1947; President pro tempore of the Senate from January 4, 1947, to January 3, 1949; given Collier Award for Distinguished Congressional Service in 1946 and 1949; died in Grand Rapids, Mich., April 18, 1951; interment in Oak Hill Cemetery.

VANDERPOEL, Aaron, a Representative from New York; born in Kinderhook, Columbia County, N. Y., February 5, 1799; pursued classical studies; studied law; was admitted to the bar in 1820 and commenced practice in Kinderhook, N. Y.; member of the State assembly 1826–1830; elected as a Demo-crat to the Twenty-third and Twenty-fourth Congresses (March 4, 1833–March 3, 1837); unsuccessful candidate for reelection in 1836 to the Twenty-fifth Congress; elected to the Twenty-sixth Congress (March 4, 1839–March 3, 1841); retired from Congress and settled in New York City; judge of the superior court 1842–1850; died in New York City July 18, 1870; interment in Woodlawn Cemetery.

VANDERVEER, Abraham, a Representative from New York; born in Kings County, N. Y., in 1781; attended the common schools; county clerk of Kings County 1816–1821 and 1822–1837; upon its organization was elected treasurer of the Brooklyn Savings Bank; elected as a Democrat to the Twenty-fifth Congress (March 4, 1837–March 3, 1839); was not a can-didate for renomination in 1838; died in Brooklyn, N. Y., July 21, 1839; interment in Reformed Dutch Cemetery.

VANDEVER, William, a Representative from Iowa and from California; born in Baltimore, Md., March 31, 1817; at-tended the common schools and pursued an academic course; moved to Illinois in 1839 and to Iowa in 1851; studied law; was admitted to the bar in 1852 and commenced practice in Dubuque, Iowa; elected as a Republican to the Thirty-sixth and Thirty-seventh Congresses and served from March 4, 1859,

to September 24, 1861, when he was mustered into the Union Army as colonel of the Ninth Regiment, Iowa Volunteer Infan-try, never having resigned his seat in Congress; promoted to brigadier general of Volunteers in 1862 and brevetted a major general in 1865; member of the peace convention of 1861 held in Washington, D. C., in an effort to devise means to prevent the impending war; resumed the practice of law in Dubuque, Iowa; appointed United States Indian inspector by President Grant in 1873, and served until 1877; moved to San Buena-ventura, Calif., in 1884; elected as a Republican from Cali-fornia to the Fiftieth and Fifty-first Congresses (March 4, 1887–March 3, 1891); was not a candidate for renomination in 1890; retired from public life; died in Ventura, Calif., July 23, 1893; interment in Ventura Cemetery.

VANDIVER, Willard Duncan, a Representative from Missouri; born near Moorefield, Hardy County, Va. (now West Virginia), March 30, 1854; moved to Missouri with his parents, who settled on a farm in Boone County in 1857, and to Fayette in 1872; attended the common schools, and was graduated from Central College, Fayette, Mo., in 1877; studied law; professor of natural science in Bellevue Institute, Caledonia, Mo., 1877–1880, and served as its president 1880–1889; accepted the chair of science in the State normal school at Cape Girardeau, Mo., in 1889, and became its president in 1893 and served until 1897; dele-gate to the Democratic State conventions in 1896, 1898, 1918, and 1920 and served as chairman in 1918; elected as a Democrat to the Fifty-fifth and to the three succeeding Congresses (March 4, 1897–March 3 1905); was not a candidate for renomination in 1904; chairman of the State executive committee in 1904; delegate to the Democratic National Convention at St. Louis in 1904 which nominated Alton B. Parker for President and Henry G. Davis for Vice President; State insurance commissioner of Missouri 1905–1909; vice president of the Central States Life Insurance Co. 1910–1912; Assistant Treasurer of the United States 1913–1921; president of the Missouri Society Sons of the American Revolution 1919–1921; traveled abroad in 1922; settled on a farm near Columbia, Mo., and engaged in agricul-tural pursuits and lecturing; was author of many biographical sketches published and is credited with the authorship of the famous expression "I'm from Missouri, you've got to show me"; died in Columbia, Mo., May 30, 1932; interment in the Columbia Cemetery.

VAN DUZER, Clarence Dunn, a Representative from Nevada; born near Mountain City, Nev., May 4, 1866; attended public and private schools in Nevada and California, and the University of California at Berkeley; was graduated from the State Uni-versity of Nevada at Reno in 1889, and from the law department of Georgetown University, Washington, D. C., in 1893; was admitted to practice before the supreme court of the District of Columbia in 1893; appointed by the Governor of Nevada in 1892 State land agent with residence in Washington, D. C., and served until 1897; served as private secretary to Senator Francis G. Newlands for five years; returned to Nevada and became interested in mining; elected district attorney of Humboldt County in 1898; member of the State house of representatives 1900–1902 and served as speaker; elected as a Democrat to the Fifty-eighth and Fifty-ninth Congresses (March 4, 1903–March 3, 1907); was not a candidate for renomination in 1906; resumed his mining interests until 1922 when he moved to Passaic, N. J., and engaged in newspaper work; died in Passaic, N. J., Septem-ber 28, 1947; remains were cremated and the ashes scattered on the Humboldt River near Winnemucca, Nev.

VAN DYKE, Carl Chester, a Representative from Minne-sota; born in Alexandria, Douglas County, Minn., February 18,

1881; attended the common and high schools of Alexandria; taught school in Douglas County 1899–1901; during the Spanish-American War served as a private in Company B, Fifteenth Regiment, Minnesota Volunteer Infantry; was graduated from the St. Paul Law School; was admitted to the bar at St. Paul in 1916, but did not engage in extensive practice; elected commander in chief of the United Spanish War Veterans September 6, 1918; elected as a Democrat to the Sixty-fourth, Sixty-fifth, and Sixty-sixth Congresses and served from March 4, 1915, until his death in Washington, D. C., May 20, 1919; interment in a mausoleum in Forest Cemetery, St. Paul, Minn.

VAN DYKE, John, a Representative from New Jersey; born in Lamington, Somerset County, N. J., April 3, 1807; completed preparatory studies; studied law; was admitted to the bar in 1836 and commenced practice in New Brunswick, N. J.; prosecuting attorney of Middlesex County in 1841; mayor of New Brunswick in 1846 and 1847; president of the Bank of New Jersey at New Brunswick; elected as a Whig to the Thirtieth and Thirty-first Congresses (March 4, 1847–March 3, 1851); declined to be a candidate for renomination in 1850; resumed the practice of law; delegate to the Republican National Convention at Philadelphia in 1856 which nominated Frémont and Dayton; judge of the New Jersey Supreme Court 1859–1866; moved to Minnesota in 1868 and settled in Wabasha, Wabasha County; member of the State senate in 1872 and 1873; judge of the third judicial district of Minnesota 1873–1878; died in Wabasha, Minn., December 24, 1878; interment in Riverview Cemetery.

VAN DYKE, Nicholas, a Delegate from Delaware; born in New Castle County, Del., September 25, 1738; studied law in Philadelphia, Pa.; was admitted to the bar in 1765 and commenced practice in New Castle County; delegate to the State constitutional convention in July 1776; elected a member of the Council of Delaware in 1777, serving as speaker in 1779; appointed judge of admiralty February 21, 1777; Member of the Continental Congress 1777–1782; a signer of the Articles of Confederation; served as President of Delaware from February 1, 1783, to October 27, 1786; died in New Castle County, Del., February 19, 1789; interment in Immanuel Churchyard, New Castle, Del.

VAN DYKE, Nicholas (son of the preceding), a Representative and a Senator from Delaware; born in New Castle, Del., December 20, 1769; was graduated from Princeton College in 1788; studied law; was admitted to the bar in New Castle, Del., in 1792 and commenced the practice of law; member of the State house of representatives in 1799; elected as a Federalist to the Tenth Congress to fill the vacancy caused by the resignation of James M. Broom; reelected to the Eleventh Congress, and served from October 6, 1807, to March 3, 1811; served in the State senate 1815–1817; elected to the United States Senate in 1817; reelected in 1823, and served from March 4, 1817, until his death in New Castle, Del., on May 21, 1826; interment in Immanuel Churchyard.

VAN EATON, Henry Smith, a Representative from Mississippi; born in Anderson Township, Hamilton County, Ohio, September 14, 1826; was graduated from Illinois College, Jacksonville, Ill., in 1848; moved to Woodville, Miss., in 1848; taught school; studied law; was admitted to the bar in 1855 and commenced practice in Woodville, Wilkinson County; elected district attorney in 1857; member of the State house of representatives in 1859; enlisted in the Confederate Army and served throughout the Civil War; resumed the practice of law in Woodville, Miss., in 1865; appointed chancellor of the tenth Mississippi

district in 1880; elected as a Democrat to the Forty-eighth and Forty-ninth Congresses (March 4, 1883–March 3, 1887); appointed by President Cleveland a member of the Board of Visitors to the United States Naval Academy at Annapolis in 1887; member of a commission to examine and report upon the last completed portion of the Northern Pacific Railroad in 1888; died in Woodville, Miss., May 30, 1898; interment in Evergreen Cemetery.

VAN GAASBECK, Peter, a Representative from New York; born in Ulster County, N. Y., September 27, 1754; attended the grammar schools and became a man of prominence in the county and State; engaged in mercantile pursuits in Kingston, N. Y.; was a captain and major in the Ulster County Militia during the Revolutionary War; elected as an Anti-Federalist to the Third Congress (March 4, 1793–March 3, 1795); died in Kingston, N. Y., in 1797; interment in First Reformed Dutch Churchyard.

VAN HORN, Burt, a Representative from New York; born in Newfane, Niagara County, N. Y., October 28, 1823; was raised on a farm; attended the common schools, Yates Academy in Orleans County, Hamilton College (now Colgate University), Hamilton, N. Y.; engaged in agricultural pursuits in Niagara County, and later in the manufacture of cloth; member of the State assembly 1858–1860; elected as a Republican to the Thirty-seventh Congress (March 4, 1861–March 3, 1863); elected to the Thirty-ninth and Fortieth Congresses (March 4, 1865–March 3, 1869); was not a candidate for renomination in 1868; moved to Lockport, N. Y., in 1867; resumed farming and also engaged in the loaning of money; collector of internal revenue at Rochester, N. Y., 1877–1882; died in Lockport, N. Y., April 1, 1896; interment in Glenwood Cemetery.

VAN HORN, George, a Representative from New York; born in Otsego, Otsego County, N. Y., February 5, 1850; attended the common schools, the Cooperstown Seminary, and the New Berlin Academy; studied law; was admitted to the bar in February 1871 and practiced in Cooperstown, N. Y.; elected clerk of Otsego County in 1881 and reelected in 1884; elected supervisor of Otsego, and twice reelected; member of the Democratic county committee; elected as a Democrat to the Fifty-second Congress (March 4, 1891–March 3, 1893); unsuccessful candidate for reelection in 1892 to the Fifty-third Congress; engaged in banking, and was vice president of the Second National Bank of Cooperstown, N. Y., until his death there on May 3, 1904; interment in Lakewood Cemetery.

VAN HORN, Robert Thompson, a Representative from Missouri; born in East Mahoning, Indiana County, Pa., May 19, 1824; attended the common schools; apprenticed to a printer; moved to Ohio in 1844 and settled in Pomeroy; studied law; was admitted to the bar about 1850 and commenced practice in Pomeroy, Ohio; moved to Kansas City, Mo., in 1855; member of the board of aldermen in 1857; postmaster of Kansas City 1857–1861; established and edited the Kansas City Journal; elected mayor of Kansas City in 1861 and again in 1864; enlisted in the Union Army during the Civil War and served as lieutenant colonel of the Twenty-fifth Regiment, Missouri Volunteer Infantry; member of the State senate 1862–1864; elected as a Republican to the Thirty-ninth, Fortieth, and Forty-first Congresses (March 4, 1865–March 3, 1871); was not a candidate for renomination in 1870; chairman of the Republican State central committee 1874–1876; collector of internal revenue for the sixth district of Missouri 1875–1881; delegate to the Republican National Conventions in 1864, 1868, 1872, 1876, 1880, and 1884; member of the Republican National

Committee in 1872 and 1884; elected as a Republican to the Forty-seventh Congress (March 4, 1881–March 3, 1883); successfully contested the election of John C. Tarsney to the Fifty-fourth Congress and served from February 27, 1896, to March 3, 1897; unsuccessful candidate for renomination in 1896; retired from editorship of the Kansas City Journal in 1897; died on his estate, "Honeywood," at Evanston Station, near Kansas City, Mo., January 3, 1916; interment in Mount Washington Cemetery, Kansas City, Mo.

VAN HORNE, Archibald, a Representative from Maryland; appointed adjutant of the Fourteenth Regiment of the Maryland Militia, April 18, 1798; commissioned captain May 26, 1802; member of the State house of delegates 1801–1803 and 1805, and served as speaker in the latter year; resigned November 11, 1805; elected to the Tenth and Eleventh Congresses (March 4, 1807–March 3, 1811); again a member of the State house of delegates 1814–1816; elected to the State senate in 1816 and served until his death in Prince Georges County, Md., in 1817.

VAN HORNE, Espy, a Representative from Pennsylvania; born in Lycoming County, Pa., in 1795; elected as a Democrat to the Nineteenth and Twentieth Congresses (March 4, 1825–March 3, 1829); died in Williamsport, Pa., August 25, 1829.

VAN HORNE, Isaac, a Representative from Pennsylvania; born in Tollbury Township, Bucks County, Pa., January 13, 1754; apprenticed as a carpenter and cabinetmaker; elected ensign of a company of militia in 1775; appointed ensign in the Continental Army by the committee of safety and in January 1776 was assigned to Capt. John Beatty's Company in Col. Samuel McGaw's Regiment; held as a prisoner of war from November 1776 to May 1778 when he was exchanged; served as first lieutenant, captain lieutenant, and captain until the close of the Revolutionary War; justice of the peace for Tollbury Township for several years; coroner of Bucks County four years; member of the State house of representatives in 1796 and 1797; declined to be a candidate for reelection; elected as a Democrat to the Seventh and Eighth Congresses (March 4, 1801–March 3, 1805); moved to Zanesville, Muskingum County, Ohio, in 1805; receiver of the land office at Zanesville from 1805 to December 1826 when he resigned; died in Zanesville, Ohio, February 2, 1834; interment in Woodlawn Cemetery.

VAN HOUTEN, Isaac B., a Representative from New York; born in Clarkstown (now New City), Rockland County, N. Y., June 4, 1776; attended the common schools; engaged in milling and agricultural pursuits; member of the State assembly 1833–1835; elected as a Democrat to the Twenty-third Congress (March 4, 1833–March 3, 1835); resumed his former business pursuits; died in Clarkstown (now New City), N. Y., August 16, 1850; interment in the family burying ground on his estate near Clarkstown.

VANIK, Charles Albert, a Representative from Ohio; born in Cleveland, Cuyahoga County, Ohio, April 7, 1913; attended the public schools; was graduated from Adelbert College of Western Reserve University, Cleveland, Ohio, in 1933, and from Western Reserve University Law School in 1936; was admitted to the bar in 1936 and commenced the practice of law in Cleveland, Ohio; member of Cleveland City Council in 1938 and 1939; served in the State senate 1940–1942; member of the Cleveland Board of Education in 1941 and 1942; during World War II enlisted in the United States Naval Reserve as an ensign in 1942 and served with amphibious forces of the Atlantic and Pacific Fleets; participated in the invasion of North Africa, Sicily, and

Okinawa; released from active duty as a lieutenant in December 1945; appointed a member of the Cleveland Library Board in January 1946; elected judge of Cleveland Municipal Court in 1947 and reelected in 1949 for a six-year term, but resigned in March 1954 to campaign for Congress; served as referee with Ohio Industrial Commission; legal adviser to the Ohio highway director; elected as a Democrat to the Eighty-fourth, Eighty-fifth, and Eighty-sixth Congresses (January 3, 1955–January 3, 1961). *Reelected to the Eighty-seventh Congress.*

VANMETER, John Inskeep, a Representative from Ohio; born near Moorefield, Hardy County, Va. (now West Virginia), in February 1798; attended William and Mary College, Williamsburg, Va., and was graduated from Princeton (N. J.) College in 1821; studied law at the school of Judge Gould in Litchfield, Conn.; was admitted to the bar of Virginia in 1822 and commenced practice in Moorefield, Va.; member of the Virginia House of Delegates in 1824; retired from practice; moved to Pike County, Ohio, in 1826 and engaged in agricultural pursuits; member of the State house of representatives in 1836; served in the State senate in 1838; elected as a Whig to the Twenty-eighth Congress (March 4, 1843–March 3, 1845); unsuccessful candidate for reelection in 1844 to the Twenty-ninth Congress; affiliated with the Democratic Party in 1856; moved to Chillicothe, Ross County, Ohio, in 1855, where he resided until his death August 3, 1875; interment in Grand View Cemetery.

VAN NESS, John Peter, a Representative from New York; born in Ghent (formerly Claverly), Columbia County, N. Y., in 1770; completed preparatory studies and attended Columbia College in New York City; studied law and was admitted to the bar, but never practiced; Democratic presidential elector in 1800 and cast his vote for Jefferson and Burr; elected as a Democrat to the Seventh Congress to fill the vacancy caused by the resignation of John Bird and served from October 6, 1801, to January 17, 1803, when his seat was declared forfeited, as he had accepted and exercised the office of major of militia in the District of Columbia bestowed on him by President Jefferson; he then made Washington his home; president of the second council in 1803; promoted to the rank of lieutenant colonel commandant of the first legion of militia in 1805, brigadier general in 1811, and major general in 1813; alderman of the city of Washington in 1829; mayor 1830–1834; second vice president of the Washington National Monument Society in 1833; president of the commissioners of the Washington Canal in 1834; president of the branch bank of the United States at Washington, D. C.; first president of the National Metropolitan Bank from 1814 until his death in Washington, D. C., March 7, 1846; interment in a mausoleum at Oak Hill Cemetery.

VAN NUYS, Frederick, a Senator from Indiana; born in Falmouth, Rush County, Ind., April 16, 1874; attended the public schools; was graduated from Earlham College, Richmond, Ind., in 1898 and from the Indiana Law School at Indianapolis, Ind., in 1900; was admitted to the bar in 1900 and commenced practice in Shelbyville, Ind., moving shortly afterward to Anderson, Ind.; served as prosecuting attorney of Madison County, Ind., 1906–1910; member of the State senate 1913–1916, serving as president pro tempore in 1915; moved to Indianapolis, Ind., in 1916 and continued the practice of law; chairman of the Democratic State committee in 1917 and 1918; served as United States attorney, district of Indiana, 1920–1922; elected as a Democrat to the United States Senate in 1932, reelected in 1938, and served from March 4, 1933, until his death on a farm near Vienna, Fairfax County, Va., on January 25, 1944; interment in East Maplewood Cemetery, Anderson, Ind.

VAN PELT, William K., a Representative from Wisconsin; born in Glenbeulah, Sheboygan County, Wis., March 10. 1905; moved with his parents to Fond du Lac, Wis., and attended the public schools, graduating from high school in 1924; owner and operator of City Fuel Co., Fond du Lac, Wis., in 1939; chairman of Fond du Lac County Republican Committee 1944–1950; delegate to the Republican National Convention in 1944 and an alternate delegate in 1948; elected as a Republican to the Eighty-second and to the four succeeding Congresses (January 3, 1951–January 3, 1961). *Reelected to the Eighty-seventh Congress.*

VAN RENSSELAER, Henry Bell (son of Stephen Van Rensselaer), a Representative from New York; born at the Manor House in Albany, N. Y., May 14, 1810; was graduated from the United States Military Academy at West Point in 1831; commissioned brevet second lieutenant of the Fifth Regiment, United States Infantry, July 1, 1831, and resigned January 27, 1832; engaged in agricultural pursuits near Ogdensburg, N. Y.; elected as a Whig to the Twenty-seventh Congress (March 4, 1841–March 3, 1843); was associated with mining enterprises; upon the outbreak of the Civil War reentered the military service with the rank of brigadier general in the Union Army and was appointed chief of staff under Gen. Winfield Scott; served as inspector general with the rank of colonel from 1862 until his death; died in Cincinnati, Ohio, March 23, 1864; interment in Grace Episcopal Churchyard, Jamaica, Long Island, N. Y.

VAN RENSSELAER, Jeremiah (father of Solomon Van Vechten Van Rensselaer and cousin of Killian Killian Van Rensselaer), a Representative from New York; born in that State August 27, 1738; completed preparatory studies at the manor house, "Rensselaerswyck," and in private schools in Albany; was graduated from Princeton College in 1758; took an active interest in the Revolutionary War and was a member of the Albany Committee of Safety; elected to the First Congress (March 4, 1789–March 3, 1791); unsuccessful candidate for reelection in 1790 to the Second Congress; member of the New York State Assembly in 1789; member of the first board of directors of the Bank of Albany in 1792 and president of that bank 1798–1806; Democratic presidential elector in 1800 and cast his vote for Jefferson and Burr; Lieutenant Governor of New York 1801–1804; curator of the Evangelical Lutheran Seminary at Albany in 1804; died in Albany, N. Y., February 19, 1810; interment in the Dutch Reformed Cemetery.

VAN RENSSELAER, Killian Killian (cousin of Jeremiah Van Rensselaer and uncle of Solomon Van Vechten Van Rensselaer), a Representative from New York; born in Greenbush, Rensselaer County, N. Y., June 9, 1763; completed preparatory studies and attended Yale College; studied law; was admitted to the bar in 1784 and commenced practice in Claverack, N. Y.; private secretary to Gen. Philip Schuyler; elected as a Democrat to the Seventh and to the four succeeding Congresses (March 4, 1801–March 3, 1811); resumed the practice of law; died in Albany, N. Y., on June 18, 1845; interment in a private cemetery at Greenbush, N. Y.

VAN RENSSELAER, Solomon Van Vechten (son of Jeremiah Van Rensselaer and nephew of Killian Killian Van Rensselaer), a Representative from New York; born in Greenbush, Rensselaer County, N. Y., August 6, 1774; completed preparatory studies; entered the United States Army; was promoted to captain of a volunteer company, and later, on January 8, 1799, to major; was mustered out in June 1800; adjutant general of State militia in 1801, 1810, and 1813; served in the War of 1812 as lieutenant colonel of New York Volunteers; elected as a Federalist to the Sixteenth and Seventeenth Congresses and served from March 4, 1819, to January 14, 1822, when he resigned; postmaster of Albany, N. Y., 1822–1839 and 1841–1843; delegate from New York at the opening of the Erie Canal November 4, 1825; died near Albany, N. Y., April 23, 1852; interment in North Dutch Church Cemetery, Albany, N. Y.; reinterment in Albany Rural Cemetery.

VAN RENSSELAER, Stephen (father of Henry Bell Van Rensselaer), a Representative from New York; born in New York City November 1, 1764; completed preparatory studies and attended Princeton College; was graduated from Harvard University in 1782; major of militia in 1786, colonel in 1788, and major general in 1801; member of the State assembly 1789–1791, 1798, and 1818; served in the State senate 1791–1796; elected Lieutenant Governor of New York in 1795; served as major general of Volunteers in the War of 1812; member of the canal commission 1816–1839, and served fourteen years as its president; member of the State constitutional convention in 1821; founded the Rensselaer Polytechnic Institute at Troy in 1824; was a supporter of John Quincy Adams and was elected to the Seventeenth Congress to fill the vacancy caused by the resignation of Solomon Van Vechten Van Rensselaer; reelected to the Eighteenth, Nineteenth, and Twentieth Congresses and served from February 27, 1822, to March 3, 1829; was not a candidate for reelection; devoted his time to landed interests and to educational and public welfare matters; regent of the University of New York 1819–1839; died in Albany, N. Y., January 26, 1839; interment in the family burying ground; reinterment in Albany Rural Cemetery.

VAN SANT, Joshua, a Representative from Maryland; born in Millington, Kent County, Md., December 31, 1803; moved with his parents to Wilmington, Del., in 1807 and to Philadelphia, Pa., in 1812; attended the common schools; moved to Baltimore, Md.; engaged in hat making in 1817, became journeyman, and continued at that trade until 1835; unsuccessful candidate as a Jackson Democrat to the State house of delegates in 1833 and 1834; delegate to the State constitutional convention in 1836; postmaster of Baltimore 1839–1841; member of the State house of delegates in 1845; commissioner of Baltimore finances March 1, 1846, to March 1, 1855; trustee of the city and county almshouse 1847–1853 and in 1861; commissioner of public schools 1852–1854, and served as president in 1854; elected as a Democrat to the Thirty-third Congress (March 4, 1853–March 3, 1855); unsuccessful candidate for reelection to the Thirty-fourth Congress in 1854; presidential elector on the Democratic ticket of Breckinridge and Lane in 1860; delegate to the State constitutional convention in 1867; director of the Maryland State Penitentiary 1867–1869, serving two years as president; member of the board of trustees of the McDonough Educational Fund and Institute 1867–1871, serving as president in 1871; member and president of the board for Bay View Asylum 1868–1870; mayor of Baltimore 1871–1875; declined to be a candidate for renomination; appointed city comptroller of Baltimore in July 1876 and served until January 1881; was afterward elected to that office and served until his death in Baltimore, Md., April 8, 1884; interment in Greenmount Cemetery.

VAN SCHAICK, Isaac Whitbeck (uncle of Aaron Van Schaick Cochrane), a Representative from Wisconsin; born in Coxsackie, Greene County, N. Y., December 7, 1817; attended the common schools; engaged extensively in the manufacture of glue; moved to Chicago in 1857, and to Wisconsin in 1861 and engaged in the flour-milling business in Milwaukee; elected to the Milwaukee Common Council in 1871; member of the State assembly 1873–1875; served in the State senate 1877–1882; elected as a Republican to the Forty-ninth Congress (March 4, 1885–March 3, 1887); declined to be a candidate for renomination in 1886; elected to the Fifty-first Congress (March 4, 1889–March 3,

1891); was not a candidate for renomination in 1890; unsuccessful candidate for State senator in 1890; moved to Catonsville, Baltimore County, Md., in 1894, where he lived in retirement until his death there August 22, 1901; interment in Athens Cemetery, Athens, N. Y.

VAN SWEARINGEN, Thomas, a Representative from Virginia; born near Shepherdstown, Jefferson County, Va. (now West Virginia), May 5, 1784; attended the common schools; member of the State house of delegates 1814–1816; elected to the Sixteenth and Seventeenth Congresses and served from March 4, 1819, until his death in Shepherdstown, Va., August 19, 1822; interment in Elmwood Cemetery.

VAN TRUMP, Philadelph, a Representative from Ohio; born in Lancaster, Fairfield County, Ohio, November 15, 1810; attended the public schools; learned the art of printing and subsequently became editor of the Gazette and Enquirer at Lancaster; studied law; was admitted to the bar and commenced practice in Lancaster on May 14, 1838; delegate to the Whig National Convention at Baltimore in 1852; unsuccessful candidate of the American Party for Governor in 1856; delegate to the Bell and Everett State convention in 1860 and served as president; judge of the court of common pleas 1862–1867; unsuccessful candidate for supreme judge of Ohio in 1863, 1864, and 1865; elected as a Democrat to the Fortieth, Forty-first, and Forty-second Congresses (March 4, 1867–March 3, 1873); was not a candidate for renomination in 1872; served as president of the Democratic State convention in 1869; resumed the practice of law in Lancaster, Ohio, and died there on July 31, 1874; interment in Elmwood Cemetery.

VAN VALKENBURGH, Robert Bruce, a Representative from New York; born in Prattsburg, Steuben County, N. Y., September 4, 1821; attended Franklin Academy, Prattsburg, N. Y.; studied law; was admitted to the bar and commenced practice in Bath, N. Y.; member of the State assembly in 1852 and again in 1857 and 1858; was in command of the recruiting depot in Elmira, N. Y., and organized seventeen regiments for the Civil War; elected as a Republican to the Thirty-seventh and Thirty-eighth Congresses (March 4, 1861–March 3, 1865); served as colonel of the One Hundred and Seventh Regiment, New York Volunteer Infantry, and was its commander at the Battle of Antietam; Acting Commissioner of Indian Affairs in 1865; appointed Minister Resident to Japan January 18, 1866, and served until November 11, 1869; settled in Florida; appointed associate justice of the State supreme court on May 20, 1874, and served until his death in Suwanee Springs, near Live Oak, Suwanee County, Fla., August 1, 1888; interment in Old St. Nicholas Cemetery, on the south side of the St. Johns River, south of Jacksonville, Fla.

VAN VOORHIS, Henry Clay, a Representative from Ohio; born in Nashport, Muskingum County, Ohio, May 11, 1852; attended the public schools and Denison University, Granville, Ohio; studied law and was admitted to the bar in 1874; was graduated from the Cincinnati Law School in 1875 and commenced practice in Zanesville, Ohio, the same year; delegate to the Republican National Conventions in 1884 and 1916; president of the Citizens' National Bank of Zanesville 1885–1893; elected as a Republican to the Fifty-third and to the five succeeding Congresses (March 4, 1893–March 3, 1905); declined to be a candidate for renomination in 1904; again became president of the Citizens' National Bank of Zanesville, Ohio, in 1905; member of the board of trustees of Marietta (Ohio) College; died in Zanesville, Ohio, December 12, 1927; interment in Greenwood Cemetery.

VAN VOORHIS, John, a Representative from New York; born in Decatur, Otsego County, N. Y., on October 22, 1826; pursued an academic course; studied law; was admitted to the bar in 1851 and commenced practice in Elmira, Chemung County, N. Y.; member of the board of education in 1857; city attorney in 1859; appointed collector of internal revenue for the twenty-eighth district of New York and served from September 1, 1862, to March 31, 1863; delegate to the Republican National Convention at Baltimore in 1864; elected as a Republican to the Forty-sixth and Forty-seventh Congresses (March 4, 1879–March 3, 1883); unsuccessful candidate for reelection in 1882 to the Forty-eighth Congress; resumed the practice of law in Rochester, N. Y.; elected to the Fifty-third Congress (March 4, 1893–March 3, 1895); unsuccessful candidate for renomination in 1894 to the Fifty-fourth Congress; resumed the practice of law in Rochester, N. Y., and died there on October 20, 1905; interment in Mount Hope Cemetery.

VAN VORHES, Nelson Holmes, a Representative from Ohio; born in Washington County, Pa., January 23, 1822; moved to Athens County, Ohio, in 1832 and engaged in agricultural pursuits; apprenticed to a printer for six years; editor and proprietor of the Athens Messenger 1844–1861; member of the State house of representatives 1850–1872 and served four years as speaker; elected probate judge in 1854, but resigned; unsuccessful candidate for election in 1858 to the Thirty-sixth Congress; delegate to the Republican National Convention at Chicago in 1860; entered the Union Army as a private in 1861 and was mustered out as colonel; elected as a Republican to the Forty-fourth and Forty-fifth Congresses (March 4, 1875–March 3, 1879); unsuccessful candidate for reelection in 1878 to the Forty-sixth Congress; died in Athens, Athens County, Ohio, December 4, 1882; interment in West Union Street Cemetery.

VAN WINKLE, Marshall (grandnephew of Peter G. Van Winkle), a Representative from New Jersey; born in Jersey City, N. J., September 28, 1869; attended the public schools; studied law; was admitted to the bar in 1890 and commenced practice in Hoboken, N. J.; appointed counsel to the county tax board in 1895, holding this position until his resignation to accept an appointment as the assistant prosecutor of the pleas of Hudson County, N. J.; unsuccessful candidate for election in 1900 to the Fifty-seventh Congress; assistant prosecutor of pleas from 1902 to 1905, when he resigned to become a candidate for Congress; elected as a Republican to the Fifty-ninth Congress (March 4, 1905–March 3, 1907); was not a candidate for renomination in 1906; resumed the practice of law in Jersey City, N. J.; advisory master in chancery, matrimonial division, 1933–1939; wrote and published law reference books; died in Oceanport, N. J., May 10, 1957; interment in Fairview Mausoleum, Fairview, N. J.

VAN WINKLE, Peter Godwin (granduncle of Marshall Van Winkle), a Senator from West Virginia; born in New York City, N. Y., September 7, 1808; completed preparatory studies; studied law; was admitted to the bar and commenced practice in Parkersburg, Wood County, Va. (now West Virginia), in 1835; president of the town board of trustees 1844–1850; member of the Virginia State constitutional convention in 1850; was treasurer and later president of the Northwestern Virginia Railroad Co. in 1852; member of the Wheeling reorganization convention in 1861; delegate to the State convention which framed the constitution of West Virginia; served in the West Virginia House of Delegates in 1863; upon the admission of West Virginia as a State into the Union was elected as a Unionist to the United States Senate and served from August 4, 1863, to March 3, 1869; delegate to the Southern Loyalist Convention at Philadelphia, Pa., in 1866; upon the expiration of his term as Senator he resided in Parkersburg, W. Va., where he died April 15, 1872; interment in River View Cemetery.

VAN WYCK, Charles Henry, a Representative from New York and a Senator from Nebraska; born in Poughkeepsie, Dutchess County, N. Y., May 10, 1824; completed preparatory studies and graduated from Rutgers College, New Brunswick, N. J., in 1843; studied law; was admitted to the bar in 1847 and commenced the practice of law; moved to Bloomingburg, Sullivan County, N. Y.; district attorney 1850–1856; elected as a Republican from New York to the Thirty-sixth and Thirty-seventh Congresses (March 4, 1859–March 3, 1863); entered the Union Army as colonel of the Tenth Legion, or Fifty-sixth Regiment, New York Volunteers, and commanded it during the Civil War; brevetted brigadier general for services during the war; elected to the Fortieth Congress (March 4, 1867–March 3, 1869); successfully contested the election of George W. Greene to the Forty-first Congress and served from February 17, 1870, to March 3, 1871; moved to Nebraska in 1874, settled on a farm in Otoe County, and engaged in agricultural pursuits; delegate to the State constitutional convention in 1876; member of the State senate 1876–1880; elected as a Republican to the United States Senate from Nebraska and served from March 4, 1881, to March 3, 1887; unsuccessful candidate for reelection; unsuccessful Populist candidate for Governor of Nebraska in 1892; retired from political life and active business pursuits; died in Washington, D. C., October 24, 1895; interment in Milford Cemetery, Milford, Pa.

VAN WYCK, William William, a Representative from New York; born near Fishkill, Dutchess County, N. Y., August 9, 1777; attended the public schools and Fishkill Academy; engaged in agricultural pursuits; elected as a Democrat to the Seventeenth and Eighteenth Congresses (March 4, 1821–March 3, 1825); moved to Sudley, Fairfax County, Va., and engaged in planting; returned to Dutchess County, N. Y., and died in Fishkill, N. Y., August 27, 1840; interment in the Dutch Reformed Churchyard.

VAN ZANDT, James Edward, a Representative from Pennsylvania; born in Altoona, Blair County, Pa., December 18, 1898; attended the public schools and the Pennsylvania Railroad Apprentice School, Altoona, Pa.; apprenticed as a molder in the Pennsylvania Railroad shops at Altoona in 1916; served in various departments until 1938, when he became district passenger agent; during the First World War enlisted as an apprentice seaman in the United States Navy on April 30, 1917, and served two years overseas; honorably discharged on August 22, 1919, with rank of chief quartermaster; member of the United States Naval Reserve 1919–1943 with rank of lieutenant; national commander of the Veterans of Foreign Wars 1934–1936; elected as a Republican to the Seventy-sixth, Seventy-seventh, and Seventy-eighth Congresses and served from January 3, 1939, until his resignation September 24, 1943; while a Member of Congress was called to active duty in September 1941 and served until January 1942 with the Pacific Fleet in the Hawaiian area and in escort convoy duty in the North Atlantic; reentered the service in September 1943 as a lieutenant commander and was assigned to the Pacific area until discharged as a captain on January 25, 1946; elected in 1946 to the Eightieth and to the six succeeding Congresses (January 3, 1947–January 3, 1961). *Reelected to the Eighty-seventh Congress.*

VARDAMAN, James Kimble, a Senator from Mississippi; born near Edna, Jackson County, Tex., July 26, 1861; moved to Mississippi in 1868 with his parents, who settled in Yalabusha County; attended the public schools; studied law in Carrollton,

Miss.; was admitted to the bar in 1881 and commenced practice in Winona, Miss.; became editor of the Winona Advance; moved to Greenwood, Miss., where he continued the practice of law and also engaged in the newspaper business; member of the State house of representatives 1890–1896 and served as speaker in 1894; unsuccessful candidate for Governor of Mississippi in 1895 and again in 1899; presidential elector on the Democratic ticket of Cleveland and Stevenson in 1892 and of Bryan and Sewall in 1896; publisher of the Greenwood Commonwealth 1896–1903 and the Issue 1908–1912; during the Spanish-American War served as captain and major in the Fifth United States Volunteer Infantry; Governor of Mississippi 1904–1908; unsuccessful candidate for election to the United States Senate in 1907 and 1910; elected as a Democrat to the United States Senate in 1912 and served from March 4, 1913, to March 3, 1919; unsuccessful candidate for reelection in 1918 and for election in 1922; retired from active business pursuits in 1922 and moved to Birmingham, Ala., where he died June 25, 1930; interment in Lakewood Memorial Park, Jackson, Miss.

VARE, William Scott, a Representative and a Senator from Pennsylvania; born in Philadelphia, Pa., December 24, 1867; attended the public schools; at the age of fifteen years entered the mercantile business, and became a general contractor in 1893; member of the select council of Philadelphia 1898–1901; recorder of deeds for Philadelphia 1902–1912; delegate to the Republican National Conventions in 1908, 1912, 1916, 1920, and 1924; elected as a member of the State senate on April 24, 1912, and at the same time was elected as a Republican to the Sixty-second Congress to fill the vacancy caused by the death of Henry H. Bingham; reelected to the Sixty-third and to the four succeeding Congresses and served from April 24, 1912, until January 2, 1923, when he resigned; reelected to the Sixty-eighth and Sixty-ninth Congresses (March 4, 1923–March 3, 1927); was not a candidate for reelection in 1926, having become a candidate for United States Senator; presented credentials as a Senator-elect to the United States Senate for the term beginning March 4, 1927, but was not permitted to qualify, eventually being unseated on December 6, 1929; resumed his former business and political activities; died in Atlantic City, N. J., August 7, 1934; interment in West Laurel Hill Cemetery, Philadelphia, Pa.

VARNUM, James Mitchell (brother of Joseph Bradley Varnum), a Delegate from Rhode Island; born in Dracut, Middlesex County, Mass., December 17, 1748; was graduated from the College of Rhode Island, Warren, R. I. (later Brown University, Providence, R. I.), in 1769; studied law; was admitted to the bar in 1771 and commenced practice in East Greenwich, R. I.; served in the Revolutionary Army, and was colonel of the "Kentish Guards" in 1774 and of Varnum's Rhode Island Regiment in 1775; commissioned colonel of the Ninth Continental Infantry in 1776; brigadier general of State troops December 12, 1776; brigadier general in the Continental Army February 21, 1777, and was honorably discharged March 5, 1779; appointed major general of State militia in May 1779; resumed the practice of law in East Greenwich, R. I.; Member of the Continental Congress 1780–1782, 1786, and 1787; appointed a judge of the United States Court in the Northwest Territory in 1787; moved to Marietta, Ohio, in 1788, and died there January 10, 1789; interment in Mound Cemetery.

VARNUM, John, a Representative from Massachusetts; born in Dracut, Middlesex County, Mass., June 25, 1778; was graduated from Harvard University in 1798; studied law; was admitted to the bar and commenced practice in Haverhill, Mass., in 1802; was elected as a Federalist to the State senate in 1811; moved to Lowell, Mass.; elected to the Nineteenth, Twentieth, and Twenty-first Congresses (March 4, 1825–March 3, 1831); returned to Lowell, Mass., and later moved to Niles, Berrien County, Mich., where he died July 23, 1836; interment in Silverbrook Cemetery.

VARNUM, Joseph Bradley (brother of James Mitchell Varnum), a Representative and a Senator from Massachusetts; born in Dracut, Middlesex County, Mass., January 29, 1750; completed preparatory studies; served in the Revolutionary Army; member of the State house of representatives 1780–1784; served in the State senate 1786–1788 and in 1795; commissioned colonel of the Seventh Regiment of Massachusetts Militia April 4, 1787, brigadier general November 22, 1802, and major general June 12, 1805; delegate to the State convention that ratified the Federal Constitution in 1788; justice of the court of common pleas; chief justice of the court of general sessions 1811–1815; elected to the Fourth and to the eight succeeding Congresses and served from March 4, 1795, to June 29, 1811, when he resigned, having been elected Senator; Speaker of the House during the Tenth and Eleventh Congresses; elected to the United States Senate in 1811 to fill the vacancy in the term commencing March 4, 1811, and served from June 8, 1811, to March 3, 1817; elected President pro tempore of the Senate December 6, 1813; delegate to the State constitutional convention in 1820; again a member of the State senate 1817–1821; died in Dracut, Mass., September 21, 1821; interment in Varnum Cemetery.

VAUGHAN, Horace Worth, a Representative from Texas; born near Jefferson, Marion County, Tex., December 2, 1867; attended the common schools of Linden, Cass County, Tex.; studied law; was admitted to the bar in 1885 and commenced practice in Texarkana, Tex., in 1886; city attorney of Texarkana 1890–1898; prosecuting attorney of Bowie County 1898–1906; district attorney for the fifth judicial district of Texas 1906–1910; member of the State senate in 1910; elected as a Democrat to the Sixty-third Congress (March 4, 1913–March 3, 1915); unsuccessful candidate for reelection in 1914 to the Sixty-fourth Congress; appointed by President Woodrow Wilson as United States district attorney at Honolulu, Hawaii, and served from December 22, 1915, to March 22, 1916; United States district judge in Hawaii from May 15, 1916, to April 4, 1922; died in Honolulu, Hawaii, November 10, 1922; interment in Nuuanu Cemetery.

VAUGHAN, William Wirt, a Representative from Tennessee; born in LaGuardo (now Martha), Wilson County, Tenn., July 2, 1831; attended the common schools and was graduated from Cumberland University, Lebanon, Tenn.; studied law; was admitted to the bar in 1860 and commenced practice in Brownsville, Tenn.; elected as a Democrat to the Forty-second Congress (March 4, 1871–March 3, 1873); unsuccessful candidate for reelection in 1872 to the Forty-third Congress; resumed the practice of law in Brownsville; one of the prime movers in the building of the Chesapeake & Ohio Railroad branch from Brownsville to Newbern, and was president of the system at the time of his death; became a candidate for election in 1878 to the Forty-sixth Congress, but died in Crockett Mills, near Alamo, Crockett County, Tenn., August 19, 1878, while canvassing the district; interment in Oakwood Cemetery, Brownsville, Tenn.

VAUGHN, Albert Clinton, Sr., a Representative from Pennsylvania; born in West Catasauqua, Lehigh County, Pa., October 9, 1894; attended the public schools in Whitehall Township; was graduated from Whitehall High School in 1910 and from Allentown (Pa.) Business College in 1911; also completed an extension course in business administration; during the First World War served as a yeoman in the United States Navy; for twenty-five years engaged in private industry, including engineering, administrative, and sales positions; elected a school director in Whitehall Township in 1929 for a six-year term; executive assistant to the late Representative Charles L. Gerlach in 1945 and to former Representative Franklin H. Lichtenwalter in 1947 and served until taking his seat in Congress; elected as a Republican to the Eighty-second Congress and served from January 3, 1951, until his death in Fullerton, Lehigh County, Pa., September 1, 1951; interment in Fairview Cemetery, West Catasauqua, Pa.

VAUX, Richard, a Representative from Pennsylvania; born in Philadelphia, Pa., December 19, 1816; educated by private tutors at the Friends Select School in Philadelphia and Bolmar's French School, Westchester, Pa.; studied law and was admitted to the bar in Philadelphia in 1837; secretary of legation under Andrew Stevenson, United States Minister to Great Britain, for one year; declined appointment as secretary of legation at St. Petersburg; made a tour of the Continent; returned to Philadelphia in 1839; member of the State house of representatives in 1839; delegate to the Democratic State convention at Harrisburg in 1840; commenced the practice of law in Philadelphia in 1840; recorder of deeds of Philadelphia 1842–1849; appointed by the State supreme court as inspector of the State penitentiary for the eastern district of Pennsylvania in 1842, and served as secretary and later as president of the board of inspectors until his death; unsuccessful candidate for mayor of Philadelphia in 1842, 1845, and 1854; elected mayor of Philadelphia in 1856; member of the board of city trusts 1859–1866, serving as president 1863–1865; elected as a Democrat to the Fifty-first Congress to fill the vacancy caused by the death of Samuel J. Randall and served from May 20, 1890, to March 3, 1891; unsuccessful candidate for reelection in 1890 to the Fifty-second Congress; retired from public life; died in Philadelphia, Pa., March 22, 1895; interment in Laurel Hill Cemetery.

VEEDER, William Davis, a Representative from New York; born in Guilderland, Albany County, N. Y., May 19, 1835; completed preparatory studies; studied law; was admitted to the bar and commenced the practice of law in Brooklyn, N. Y., in 1858; served in the State assembly in 1865 and 1866; delegate to the Democratic State conventions in 1875 and 1877; member of the State constitutional convention in 1867 and 1868; surrogate of Kings County, N. Y., 1867–1877; elected as a Democrat to the Forty-fifth Congress (March 4, 1877–March 3, 1879); was not a candidate for renomination in 1878; resumed the practice of law in Brooklyn; member of the State constitutional convention in 1887 and 1888; died in Brooklyn, N. Y., December 2, 1910; interment in Voorheesville Cemetery, Voorheesville, N. Y.

VEHSLAGE, John Herman George, a Representative from New York; born in New York City December 20, 1842; attended the public schools; left school to become a clerk in the retail grocery business; engaged in the coal and wood business; joined the Third Cavalry, New York National Guard, in 1863 and was commissioned a captain by Gov. Horatio Seymour on February 15, 1864; appointed inspector of rifle practice with the rank of captain and continued in service until 1880, when the regiment was mustered out by order of Governor Cornell; remained as supernumerary until November 12, 1883, when he received an honorable discharge from Gov. Grover Cleveland; member of the State assembly 1894–1896; appointed presidential elector on the Democratic ticket of Bryan and Sewall in 1896, but resigned, having received the Democratic nomination for Congress; elected as a Democrat to the Fifty-fifth Congress (March 4, 1897–March 3, 1899); unsuccessful candidate for renomination in 1898 to the Fifty-sixth Congress; retired from active business pursuits; died in New York City on July 21, 1904; interment in the Lutheran Cemetery, Brooklyn, N. Y.

VELDE, Harold Himmel, a Representative from Illinois; born on a farm near Parkland, Tazewell County, Ill., April 1, 1910; attended rural grade and high schools; student at Bradley University, Peoria, Ill., 1927–1929; was graduated from Northwestern University, Evanston, Ill., in 1931 and from the University of Illinois Law School at Champaign in 1937; athletic coach and teacher of Hillsdale (Ill.) Community High School 1931–1935; was admitted to the bar in 1937 and commenced the practice of law in Pekin, Ill.; during World War II served as a private in the Signal Corps of the United States Army in 1942 and 1943; special agent of the Federal Bureau of Investigation in sabotage and counter-espionage division 1943–1946; elected county judge of Tazewell County in 1946 and served until 1949; member of the board of trustees of Pekin Public Hospital since 1938; elected as a Republican to the Eighty-first and to the three succeeding Congresses (January 3, 1949–January 3, 1957); was not a candidate for renomination in 1956; engaged in the practice of law in Urbana, Ill., and Washington, D. C.; resides in Urbana, Ill.

VENABLE, Abraham Bedford (uncle of Abraham Watkins Venable), a Representative and a Senator from Virginia; born on "State Hill" farm, near Prince Edward Court House (now Worsham), Prince Edward County, Va., November 20, 1758; attended Hampden-Sidney (Va.) College, and was graduated from Princeton College in 1780; engaged as a planter in his native county; studied law; was admitted to the bar in 1784 and commenced practice at Prince Edward Court House; elected to the Second and to the three succeeding Congresses (March 4, 1791–March 3, 1799); was not a candidate for renomination in 1798; elected to the United States Senate to fill the vacancy caused by the death of Stevens T. Mason and served from December 7, 1803, to June 7, 1804, when he resigned to become president of the first national bank organized in Virginia; perished at the burning of the theater in Richmond, Va., December 26, 1811; interment of ashes, with those of other fire victims, under a stone in front of the altar in Monumental Church, Richmond, Va.

VENABLE, Abraham Watkins (nephew of Abraham Bedford Venable), a Representative from North Carolina; born in Springfield, Prince Edward County, Va., October 17, 1799; was graduated from Hampden-Sidney (Va.) College in 1816; studied medicine for two years; was graduated from Princeton College in 1819; studied law; was admitted to the bar in 1821 and commenced practice in Prince Edward and Mecklenburg Counties, Va.; moved to North Carolina in 1829; presidential elector on the Democratic ticket of Jackson and Van Buren in 1832 and of Van Buren and Johnson in 1836; elected as a Democrat to the Thirtieth, Thirty-first, and Thirty-second Congresses (March 4, 1847–March 3, 1853); unsuccessful candidate for renomination in 1852 to the Thirty-third Congress; presidential elector on the Democratic ticket of Breckinridge and Lane in 1860; delegate from the State of North Carolina to the Provisional Confederate Congress in 1861; member of the house of representatives of the Confederate Congress 1862–1864; retired from public life and active business pursuits; died in Oxford, N. C., on February 24, 1876; interment in the Shiloh Presbyterian Churchyard, Granville County, N. C.

VENABLE, Edward Carrington, a Representative from Virginia; born near Farmville, Prince Edward County, Va., January 31, 1853; attended the local school, McCabe's University High School, Petersburg, Va., and the University of Virginia at Charlottesville; taught school for three years; moved to Peters-

burg, Va., in 1876 and engaged in mercantile pursuits; delegate to the Democratic State convention in 1886; presented credentials as a Democratic Member-elect to the Fifty-first Congress and served from March 4, 1889, to September 23, 1890, when he was succeeded by John M. Langston, who successfully contested his election; resumed his former business pursuits; died in Baltimore Md., December 8, 1908; interment in Blandford Cemetery, Petersburg, Va.

VENABLE, William Webb, a Representative from Mississippi; born in Clinton, Hinds County, Miss., September 25, 1880; moved with his parents to Memphis, Tenn., returned to Clinton, Miss., in 1891; attended public and private schools; was graduated from Mississippi College at Clinton in 1898, from the University of Mississippi at Oxford in 1899, and from the law department of Cumberland University, Lebanon, Tenn., in 1905; was admitted to the bar in 1905 and commenced practice in Meridian, Miss.; prosecuting attorney of Lauderdale County from April to October 1910, when he was appointed district attorney; served in the latter capacity until January 1, 1915, when he resigned; judge of the tenth judicial district of Mississippi from 1915 until his resignation in December 1916; elected as a Democrat to the Sixty-fourth Congress to fill the vacancy caused by the death of Samuel A. Witherspoon; reelected to the Sixty-fifth and Sixty-sixth Congresses and served from January 4, 1916, to March 3, 1921; unsuccessful for renomination; practiced law Clarksdale, Miss.; died in a hospital in New Orleans, La., August 2, 1948; interment in Magnolia Cemetery, Meridian, Miss.

VERPLANCK, Daniel Crommelin (father of Gulian Crommelin Verplanck), a Representative from New York; born in New York City March 19, 1762; was educated under private tutors; was graduated from Columbia College (now Columbia University), New York City, in 1788; studied law; was admitted to the bar and commenced practice in New York City in 1789; also engaged in banking; elected as a Federalist to the Eighth Congress to fill the vacancy caused by the death of Isaac Bloom; reelected to the Ninth and Tenth Congresses and served from October 17, 1803, to March 3, 1809; was not a candidate for renomination in 1808; resumed the practice of law; judge of the court of common pleas of Dutchess County 1828–1830; died at his home, "Mount Gulian," near Fishkill, Dutchess County, N. Y., March 29, 1834; interment in Trinity Church Cemetery, Fishkill, N. Y.

VERPLANCK, Gulian Crommelin (son of Daniel Crommelin Verplanck), a Representative from New York; born in New York City August 6, 1786; pursued classical studies, and was graduated from Columbia College (now Columbia University), New York City, in 1801; studied law and was admitted to the bar in 1807; member of the State assembly 1820–1823; professor of the evidences of Christianity at the Protestant Episcopal General Theological Seminary, New York City, 1821–1824; elected as a Democrat to the Nineteenth and to the three succeeding Congresses (March 4, 1825–March 3, 1833); was not a candidate for renomination in 1832; unsuccessful Whig candidate for mayor of New York City in 1834; member of the State senate 1838–1841; governor of the city hospital 1823–1865; regent of the State university 1826–1870 and vice chancellor 1858–1870; president of the board of commissioners of immigration 1846–1870; member of the State constitutional convention in 1867 and 1868; member of the New York Historical Society; died in New York City on March 18, 1870; interment in Trinity Churchyard, Fishkill, Dutchess County, N. Y.

VERREE, John Paul, a Representative from Pennsylvania; born at "Verree Mills," on Pennypack Creek, near what is now Fox Chase Station, Philadelphia, Pa., March 9, 1817;

completed preparatory studies; engaged in the manufacture of iron and subsequently was a dealer in edged tools and also in iron and steel; member of the select council of Philadelphia 1851–1857, serving as president 1853–1857; elected as a Republican to the Thirty-sixth and Thirty-seventh Congresses (March 4, 1859–March 3, 1863); declined to be a candidate for renomination in 1862; resumed his former manufacturing pursuits; also interested in life insurance and served as president of a company; president of the Philadelphia Union League in 1875 and 1876; retired from active business pursuits; died at "Verree Mills," Philadelphia, Pa., June 27, 1889; interment in Cedar Hill Cemetery, Frankford (now a part of Philadelphia), Pa.

VEST, George Graham, a Senator from Missouri; born in Frankfort, Franklin County, Ky., December 6, 1830; was graduated from Centre College, Danville, Ky., in 1848 and from the law department of Transylvania University, Lexington, Ky., in 1853; was admitted to the bar in 1853 and commenced practice in Georgetown, Mo.; moved to Boonville, Mo., in 1856; Democratic presidential elector on the Douglas and Johnson ticket in 1860; member of the State house of representatives in 1860 and 1861; judge advocate in General Price's Confederate forces in Missouri in 1862; served in the house of representatives of the Confederate Congress from February 1862 to January 12, 1865, when he resigned, having been appointed to fill a vacancy in the Confederate Senate; resumed the practice of law in Sedalia, Mo., in 1865; moved to Kansas City in 1877; elected as a Democrat to the United States Senate; reelected in 1885, 1891, and 1897, and served from March 4, 1879, to March 3, 1903; on account of failing health retired from public life and resided at Sweet Springs, Saline County, Mo., until his death August 9, 1904; interment in Bellefontaine Cemetery, St. Louis, Mo.

VESTAL, Albert Henry, a Representative from Indiana; born on a farm near Frankton, Madison County, Ind., January 18, 1875; attended the common schools; worked in steel mills and factories; attended the Indiana State Normal School at Terre Haute; taught school for several years; was graduated from the law department of the Valparaiso (Ind.) University in 1896; was admitted to the bar the same year and commenced practice in Anderson, Ind.; prosecuting attorney of the fiftieth judicial circuit 1900–1906; unsuccessful candidate for the Republican nomination for Congress in 1908; unsuccessful candidate for election in 1914 to the Sixty-fourth Congress; elected as a Republican to the Sixty-fifth and to the seven succeeding Congresses and served from March 4, 1917, until his death; in 1920 was sent to England by the United States Government to investigate the metric system of measurements abroad; served as Republican whip of the National House of Representatives 1925–1931; died in Washington, D. C., April 1, 1932; interment in East Maplewood Cemetery, Anderson, Ind.

VIBBARD, Chauncey, a Representative from New York; born in Galway, Saratoga County, N. Y., November 11, 1811; attended the common schools and was graduated from Mott's Academy for Boys, Albany, N. Y.; clerk in a wholesale grocery store in Albany, N. Y.; moved to New York City, and in 1834 went to Montgomery, Ala.; returned to New York and settled in Schenectady; was appointed chief clerk of the Utica & Schenectady Railroad Co. in 1836; became a railroad freight and ticket agent in 1848; consolidated the many little railroads of western New York into one system under the name of the New York Central Railroad Co., serving as its first general superintendent 1853–1865; elected as a Democrat to the Thirty-seventh Congress (March 4, 1861–March 3, 1863); declined to be a candidate for renomination in 1862; during the Civil War served as director and superintendent of military railroads in

1862; presidential elector on the Democratic ticket of McClellan and Pendleton in 1864; first president of the Family Fund Insurance Co. 1864–1867; moved to New York City in 1865; became one of the owners of a line of steamers running between New York City and Albany; also a director and stockholder in the original elevated railroad in Greenwich Street, New York City; interested in the development of southern railroads and South and Central American enterprises at the time of his retirement in 1889; died in Macon, Ga., June 5, 1891; interment in Riverside Cemetery.

VICKERS, George, a Senator from Maryland; born in Chestertown, Kent County, Md., November 19, 1801; pursued an academic course; employed in the county clerk's office for several years; studied law; was admitted to the bar in 1832 and commenced practice in Chestertown, Md.; delegate to the Whig National Convention at Baltimore in 1852; major general of the State militia in 1861; presidential elector on the Democratic ticket of McClellan and Pendleton in 1864; vice president of the Union National Convention of Conservatives in Philadelphia in 1866; member of the State senate in 1866 and 1867; elected as a Democrat to the United States Senate to fill the vacancy caused by the action of the Senate in declining to permit Philip F. Thomas to qualify, and served from March 7, 1868, to March 3, 1873; resumed the practice of law in Chestertown, Md., and died there October 8, 1879; interment in Chester Cemetery.

VIDAL, Michel, a Representative from Louisiana; born in the city of Carcassonne, Languedoc, France, October 1, 1824; attended college; immigrated to the Republic of Texas at the time of the administration of President Anson Jones; moved to Louisiana when Texas was annexed to the United States; engaged in literary and scientific pursuits; engaged as associate editor with several American and French papers of this country and Canada; moved to Opelousas, La., in 1867; founded and became editor of the St. Landry Progress; editor of the New York Courrier des États-Unis and the New Orleans Picayune; at the close of the Civil War was appointed by General Sheridan a registrar for the city of New Orleans; delegate to the State constitutional convention in 1867 and 1868; upon the readmission of the State of Louisiana to representation was elected as a Republican to the Fortieth Congress and served from July 18, 1868, to March 3, 1869; appointed a United States commissioner under the convention concluded with Peru in 1868 for the adjustment of claims of citizens of either country; appointed by President Grant as United States consul at Tripoli and served from April 5, 1870, to October 12, 1876.

VIELE, Egbert Ludovicus, a Representative from New York; born in Waterford, Saratoga County, N. Y., June 17, 1825; attended Albany (N. Y.) Academy; was graduated from the United States Military Academy, West Point, N. Y., July 1, 1847; commissioned brevet second lieutenant in the Second United States Infantry; served in the Mexican War in 1847 and 1848; promoted to second lieutenant, First United States Infantry, September 8, 1847; promoted to first lieutenant in 1850; resigned in 1853; became a civil and military engineer; appointed State engineer of New Jersey in 1855; appointed engineer in chief of Central Park, New York City, in 1856; appointed engineer of Prospect Park, Brooklyn, in 1860; appointed captain of the Engineer Corps of the Seventh New York Regiment in 1860; appointed brigadier general of United States Volunteers in 1861; military governor of Norfolk, Va., in 1862; resigned October 20, 1863; engaged in civil engineering; appointed president of the department of public parks in New York City in 1884; elected as a Democrat to the Forty-ninth Congress (March 4, 1885–March 3, 1887); unsuccessful candidate for reelection in 1886 to the Fiftieth Congress; resumed his former business pursuits and also engaged in literary work; died in New York City April 22, 1902; interment in Post Cemetery, West Point, Orange County, N. Y.

VILAS, William Freeman, a Senator from Wisconsin; born in Chelsea, Orange County, Vt., July 9, 1840; moved with his parents to Madison, Dane County, Wis., in 1851; attended the common schools; was graduated from the University of Wisconsin at Madison in 1858 and from the law department of the University of Albany, New York, in 1860; was admitted to the bar and commenced practice in Madison, Wis., July 9, 1860; enlisted in the Union Army during the Civil War; captain of Company A, Twenty-third Regiment, Wisconsin Volunteer Infantry, and afterward major and lieutenant colonel of the regiment; professor of law at the University of Wisconsin; regent of the university 1880–1885; one of three revisers appointed by the Wisconsin Supreme Court in 1875 to prepare a revised body of the statute law, and which was adopted in 1878; member of the State assembly in 1885; delegate to the Democratic National Conventions in 1876, 1880, 1884, 1892, and 1896, and served as permanent chairman of the convention in 1884; Postmaster General of the United States in the Cabinet of President Cleveland from March 7, 1885, to January 16, 1888, when he became Secretary of the Interior of the United States, and served until March 6, 1889; elected as a Democrat to the United States Senate January 28, 1891, and served from March 4, 1891, to March 3, 1897; was not a candidate for renomination in 1896; regent of the University of Wisconsin 1898–1905; resumed the practice of law; member of the commission to provide for the construction of the State capitol in 1907; died in Madison, Wis., August 28, 1908; interment in Forest Hill Cemetery.

VINCENT, Beverly Mills, a Representative from Kentucky; born in Brownsville, Edmonson County, Ky., March 28, 1890; attended the public schools, Western Kentucky State Teachers College at Bowling Green, and the law department of the University of Kentucky at Lexington; was admitted to the bar in 1915 and commenced practice in Brownsville, Ky.; county judge of Edmonson County, Ky., 1916–1918; during the First World War served as a private in Battery A, Seventy-second Field Artillery, from August 27, 1918, to January 9, 1919; assistant attorney general of Kentucky in 1919 and 1920; member of the State senate 1929–1933; presidential elector on the Democratic ticket of Roosevelt and Garner in 1932; attorney general of Kentucky from 1936 until his resignation in March 1937; elected as a Democrat to the Seventy-fifth Congress to fill the vacancy caused by the death of Glover H. Cary; reelected to the Seventy-sixth, Seventy-seventh, and Seventy-eighth Congresses and served from March 3, 1937, to January 3, 1945; was not a candidate for renomination in 1944; resumed the practice of law and also interested in agricultural pursuits; is a resident of Brownsville, Ky.

VINCENT, Bird J., a Representative from Michigan; born near Clarkston, Oakland County, Mich., March 6, 1880; attended the public schools of Oakland and Midland Counties and Ferris Institute; was graduated from the law department of the University of Michigan at Ann Arbor in 1905; was admitted to the bar the same year and commenced practice in Saginaw; assistant prosecuting attorney of Saginaw County 1909–1914 and prosecuting attorney from 1915 to 1917, when he resigned to enter the Army; during the First World War served ten months in France as first lieutenant of the Sixth Train Headquarters and in the Three Hundred and Second Train Headquarters; city attorney of Saginaw 1919–1923; elected as a Republican to the Sixty-eighth and to the four succeeding Congresses and

served from March 4, 1923, until his death July 18, 1931, on board the transport *Henderson*, while en route to the United States from Honolulu, Hawaii; interment in Forest Lawn Cemetery, Saginaw, Mich.

VINCENT, Earl W., a Representative from Iowa; born in Washington County, near Keota, Iowa, March 27, 1886; attended the rural schools; was graduated from Keota High School in 1904, from Monmouth (Ill.) College in 1909, and from the law department of the University of Iowa at Iowa City in 1912; was admitted to the bar in 1912 and commenced practice in Guthrie Center, Iowa; prosecuting attorney of Guthrie County 1919–1922; member of the Iowa House of Representatives 1923–1927; elected as a Republican to the Seventieth Congress to fill the vacancy caused by the resignation of William R. Green and served from June 4, 1928, to March 3, 1929; unsuccessful candidate for renomination in 1928; resumed the practice of law in Guthrie Center, Iowa; delegate to the Republican State convention in 1930; appointed judge of the fifth judicial district of Iowa in February 1945, and served until his death in Guthrie Center, Iowa, May 22, 1953; interment in Union Cemetery.

VINCENT, William Davis, a Representative from Kansas; born near Dresden, Weakley County, Tenn., October 11, 1852; moved with his parents to Riley County, Kans., in 1858 and to Manhattan, Kans., in 1864; attended the public schools and the State agricultural college in Manhattan, Kans.; engaged in business in Manhattan 1872–1876; moved to Clay Center, Kans., in 1878 and engaged in mercantile pursuits; elected as a member of the city council in 1880; one of the nominees of the Greenback Party for presidential elector in 1884; member of the State board of railroad commissioners in 1893 and 1894; elected as a Populist to the Fifty-fifth Congress (March 4, 1897–March 3, 1899); engaged in the hardware business in Clay Center, Clay County, Kans., until his death in St. Louis, Mo., February 28, 1922; interment in Greenwood Cemetery, Clay Center, Kans.

VINING, John, a Delegate, a Representative, and a Senator from Delaware; born in Dover, Kent County, Del., December 23, 1758; studied law; was admitted to the bar in 1782 and commenced practice in New Castle County; Member of the Continental Congress 1784–1786; member of the State house of representatives in 1787 and 1788; elected to the First and Second Congresses (March 4, 1789–March 3, 1793); was not a candidate for renomination in 1792; member of the State senate in 1793; elected to the United States Senate and served from March 4, 1793, to January 19, 1798, when he resigned; died in Dover, Del., in February 1802; interment in Episcopal Cemetery.

VINSON, Carl, a Representative from Georgia; born in Milledgeville, Baldwin County, Ga., November 18, 1883; attended the Georgia Military College at Milledgeville, and was graduated from Mercer University Law School, Macon, Ga., in 1902; was admitted to the bar in 1902 and commenced practice in Milledgeville; prosecuting attorney of Baldwin County, Ga., 1906–1909; member of the State house of representatives 1909–1912, serving as speaker pro tempore in 1911 and 1912; appointed judge of the county court of Baldwin County and served from October 3, 1912, to November 2, 1914, when he resigned, having been elected to Congress; elected as a Democrat to the Sixty-third Congress to fill the vacancy caused by the resignation of Thomas W. Hardwick; reelected to the Sixty-fourth and to the twenty-two succeeding Congresses and served from November 3, 1914, to January 3, 1961. *Reelected to the Eighty-seventh Congress.*

VINSON, Frederick Moore (Fred), a Representative from Kentucky; born in Louisa, Lawrence County, Ky., January 22, 1890; attended the public schools; was graduated from the law department of Centre College, Danville, Ky., in 1911; was admitted to the bar the same year and commenced practice in Louisa; city attorney of Louisa in 1914 and 1915; served in the United States Army during the First World War; Commonwealth attorney for the thirty-second judicial district of Kentucky 1921–1924; elected as a Democrat to the Sixty-eighth Congress to fill the vacancy caused by the resignation of William J. Fields; reelected to the Sixty-ninth and Seventieth Congresses and served from January 12, 1924, to March 3, 1929; unsuccessful candidate for reelection in 1928 to the Seventy-first Congress; resumed the practice of law in Kentucky; again elected to the Seventy-second and to the three succeeding Congresses and served from March 4, 1931, to May 12, 1938, when he resigned, having been appointed by President Franklin D. Roosevelt an associate justice of the United States Court of Appeals for the District of Columbia and subsequently designated by Chief Justice Stone on March 2, 1942, as chief judge of the United States Emergency Court of Appeals; served in each capacity until his resignation May 27, 1943, to become Director of the Office of Economic Stabilization, in which capacity he served until March 5, 1945; Federal Loan Administrator from March 6 to April 3, 1945; director of War Mobilization and Reconversion from April 4 to July 22, 1945; appointed Secretary of the Treasury by President Harry S. Truman and served from July 23, 1945, to June 23, 1946; appointed and took the oath of office as Chief Justice of the United States on June 24, 1946, and served until his death in Washington, D. C., September 8, 1953; interment in Pinehill Cemetery, Louisa, Ky.

VINTON, Samuel Finley, a Representative from Ohio; born in South Hadley, Mass., September 25, 1792; was graduated from Williams College, Williamstown, Mass., in 1814; studied law; was admitted to the bar in 1816 and commenced practice in Gallipolis, Ohio; held several local offices; elected as a Whig to the Eighteenth and to the six succeeding Congresses (March 4, 1823–March 3, 1837); declined to be a candidate for renomination in 1836; presidential elector on the Whig ticket of Harrison and Tyler in 1840; elected to the Twenty-eighth and to the three succeeding Congresses (March 4, 1843–March 3, 1851); was not a candidate for renomination in 1850; unsuccessful candidate for election as Governor of Ohio in 1851; appointed by President Lincoln in 1862 to appraise the slaves emancipated in the District of Columbia; died in Washington, D. C., May 11, 1862; interment in Pine Street Cemetery, Gallipolis, Gallia County, Ohio.

VOIGT, Edward, a Representative from Wisconsin; born in Bremen, Germany, December 1, 1873; in 1883 immigrated to the United States with his parents, who settled in Milwaukee, Wis.; attended the public schools; employed in law and insurance office for several years; was graduated from law department of the University of Wisconsin at Madison in 1899; was admitted to the bar the same year and commenced practice in Sheboygan, Wis.; district attorney of Sheboygan County 1905–1911; city attorney for Sheboygan 1913–1917; elected as a Republican to the Sixty-fifth and to the four succeeding Congresses (March 4, 1917–March 3, 1927); was not a candidate for reelection in 1926 to the Seventieth Congress; delegate to the Republican National Convention in 1924; resumed the practice of law in Sheboygan, Wis.; elected in 1928 as a judge of the fourth judicial circuit of Wisconsin; reelected in 1934, and served from January 1929 until his death at his summer home at Crystal Lake, near Sheboygan, Wis., August 26, 1934; interment in Forest Home Cemetery, Milwaukee, Wis.

VOLK, Lester David, a Representative from New York; born in Brooklyn, N. Y., September 17, 1884; attended the public and high schools; was graduated from Long Island Medical School in 1906 and from St. Lawrence University Law School in 1911; engaged in the practice of medicine since 1906; editor of the Medical Economist; was admitted to the bar in 1913 and engaged in the practice of law; elected as a Progressive to the New York Assembly in 1912; declined to be a candidate for renomination; coroner's physician in 1914; during the First World War served as first lieutenant in the Medical Corps with the American Expeditionary Forces in 1918 and 1919; was largely instrumental in securing the soldiers' bonus granted by the State of New York; judge advocate of the Veterans of Foreign Wars for the State of New York in 1922; delegate to the Republican State conventions in 1920, 1924, 1942, and 1946; elected as a Republican to the Sixty-sixth Congress to fill the vacancy caused by the resignation of Reuben L. Haskell; reelected to the Sixty-seventh Congress and served from November 2, 1920, to March 3, 1923; unsuccessful candidate for reelection in 1922 to the Sixty-eighth Congress; member from New York City on the American Waterways Commission in 1924; assistant attorney general of New York State from March 1, 1943, to January 15, 1958; is a resident of Brooklyn, N. Y.

VOLLMER, Henry, a Representative from Iowa; born in Davenport, Iowa, July 28, 1867; attended the public and high schools of Davenport; distributing clerk of the Fiftieth Congress in 1887 and 1888; studied law at the University of Iowa at Iowa City and Georgetown University, Washington, D. C.; was admitted to the bar in 1889 and commenced practice in Davenport, Iowa; member of the board of aldermen of Davenport in 1889; served as mayor of Davenport from 1893 to 1897; member of the board of education 1898–1901; corporation counsel in 1913 and 1914; elected as a Democrat to the Sixty-third Congress to fill the vacancy caused by the death of Irvin S. Pepper and served from February 10, 1914, to March 3, 1915; unsuccessful candidate for reelection in 1914 to the Sixty-fourth Congress; resumed the practice of his profession; died in Piedmont, Calif., August 25, 1930; the remains were cremated and the ashes placed in a crypt in the California Crematorium.

VOLSTEAD, Andrew John, a Representative from Minnesota; born near Kenyon, Goodhue County, Minn., October 31, 1860; attended the public schools of the district and St. Olaf's College, Northfield, Minn.; was graduated from Decorah Institute, Decorah, Iowa, in 1881; studied law; was admitted to the bar in 1883 and commenced practice in Lac qui Parle County, Minn.; moved to Grantsburg, Wis., in 1885, and in the following year to Granite Falls, Yellow Medicine County, Minn.; member of the board of education and served as president; city attorney of Granite Falls; prosecuting attorney of Yellow Medicine County 1886–1902; mayor of Granite Falls 1900–1902; elected as a Republican to the Fifty-eighth and to the nine succeeding Congresses (March 4, 1903–March 3, 1923); unsuccessful candidate for reelection in 1922 to the Sixty-eighth Congress; resumed the practice of law, and resided in Granite Falls, Minn., until his death there January 20, 1947; interment in City Cemetery.

VOORHEES, Charles Stewart (son of Daniel Wolsey Voorhees), a Delegate from the Territory of Washington; born in Covington, Fountain County, Ind., June 4, 1853; attended Wabash College, Crawfordsville, Ind., and was graduated from Georgetown College, Washington, D. C., June 26, 1873; studied law; was admitted to the bar in 1875 and commenced practice in Terre Haute, Ind.; moved to the Territory of Washington in 1882 and settled in Colfax; prosecuting attorney for Whitman County 1882–1885; elected as a Democrat to the Forty-ninth and Fiftieth Congresses (March 4, 1885–March 3, 1889); unsuccessful candidate for reelection in 1888; resumed the practice of law in Colfax, Wash.; moved to Spokane, Wash., and continued the practice of law until his death there December 26, 1909; interment in Greenwood Cemetery.

VOORHEES, Daniel Wolsey (father of Charles Stewart Voorhees), a Representative and a Senator from Indiana; born in Liberty Township, Butler County, Ohio, September 26, 1827; moved with his parents to Indiana in early childhood; attended the common schools of Veedersburg, Ind.; was graduated from the Indiana Asbury (now De Pauw) University at Greencastle in 1849; studied law; was admitted to the bar in 1851 and commenced practice in Covington, Ind.; moved to Terre Haute and continued the practice of law; unsuccessful candidate for election in 1856 to the Thirty-fifth Congress; United States district attorney for Indiana 1858–1861; elected as a Democrat to the Thirty-seventh and Thirty-eighth Congresses (March 4, 1861–March 3, 1865); presented credentials as a Member-elect to the Thirty-ninth Congress and served from March 4, 1865, to February 23, 1866, when he was succeeded by Henry D. Washburn, who contested the election; elected to the Forty-first and Forty-second Congresses (March 4, 1869–March 3, 1873); unsuccessful candidate for reelection in 1872 to the Forty-third Congress; appointed and subsequently elected to the United States Senate to fill the vacancy caused by the death of Oliver H. P. T. Morton; reelected in 1885 and again in 1891, and served from November 6, 1877, to March 3, 1897; unsuccessful candidate for reelection; died in Washington, D. C., April 9, 1897; interment in Highland Lawn Cemetery, Terre Haute, Ind.

VOORHIS, Charles Henry, a Representative from New Jersey; born in Spring Valley, Bergen County, N. J., March 13, 1833; attended the district schools; was graduated from Rutgers College, New Brunswick, N. J., in 1853; moved to Jersey City; studied law; was admitted to the bar in 1856 and commenced practice in Jersey City, N. J.; delegate to the Republican National Convention at Baltimore in 1864; presiding judge of Bergen County, N. J., in 1868 and 1869; one of the organizers of the Hackensack Improvement Commission in 1869 and also of the Hackensack Academy; organized and served as first president of the Hackensack Water Co. in 1873; became interested in banking; elected as a Republican to the Forty-sixth Congress (March 4, 1879–March 3, 1881); was not a candidate for reelection in 1880 to the Forty-seventh Congress; resumed his former business pursuits; died in Jersey City, N. J., April 15, 1896; interment in New York Cemetery, Hackensack, Bergen County, N. J.

VOORHIS, Horace Jerry, a Representative from California; born in Ottawa, Franklin County, Kans., April 6, 1901; attended the public schools in Ottawa, Kans., Oklahoma City, Okla., Peoria, Ill., and Pontiac, Mich.; was graduated from Yale University, New Haven, Conn., in 1923 and from Claremont (Calif.) College in 1928; worked in a factory, handled freight on the railroads, and worked as a cowboy in Wyoming; traveling representative for Young Men's Christian Association in Germany in 1923 and 1924; worked in an automobile assembling plant in Charlotte, N. C., in 1924 and 1925; teacher in Allendale Farm School, Lake Villa, Ill., in 1925 and 1926 and Dray Cottage Home for Boys, Laramie, Wyo., in 1926 and 1927; headmaster and trustee of Voorhis School for Boys, San Dimas, Calif., 1928–1938; lecturer at Pomona College, Claremont, Calif., 1930–1935; unsuccessful candidate for the State assembly in 1934; elected as a Democrat to the Seventy-fifth and to the four succeeding Congresses (January 3, 1937–January 3, 1947); unsuccessful

candidate for reelection in 1946 to the Eightieth Congress; author; executive director of the Cooperative League of the United States of America and executive secretary of Cooperative Health Federation of America, Chicago, Ill., since April 1, 1947; resides in Chicago, Ill.

VORYS, John Martin, a Representative from Ohio; born in Lancaster, Fairfield County, Ohio, June 16, 1896; attended the public schools in Lancaster and Columbus, Ohio; during the First World War served overseas as a pilot in the United States Naval Air Service, retiring to inactive service in 1919 with rank of lieutenant; was graduated from Yale University, New Haven, Conn., in 1919 and from Ohio State University Law School at Columbus in 1923; teacher in the College of Yale, Changsha, China, in 1919 and 1920; assistant secretary, American delegation, Conference on Limitation of Armament, Washington, D. C., in 1921 and 1922; was admitted to the bar in 1923 and commenced practice in Columbus, Ohio; member of the State house of representatives in 1923 and 1924; served in the State senate in 1925 and 1926; director of aeronautics of Ohio in 1929 and 1930; elected as a Republican to the Seventy-sixth and to the nine succeeding Congresses (January 3, 1939–January 3, 1959); did not seek renomination in 1958; delegate to the United Nations Assembly in 1951; regent of Smithsonian Institution 1949–1959; resumed the practice of law; is a resident of Columbus, Ohio.

VOSE, Roger, a Representative from New Hampshire; born in Milton, Norfolk County, Mass., February 24, 1763; moved to New Hampshire in 1766 with his parents, who settled near Walpole, Cheshire County; was graduated from Harvard University in 1790; studied law; was admitted to the bar in 1793 and commenced practice in Walpole, N. H.; member of the State senate in 1809, 1810, and 1812; elected as a Federalist to the Thirteenth and Fourteenth Congresses (March 4, 1813–March 3, 1817); member of the State house of representatives in 1818; chief justice of the court of common pleas 1818–1820; chief justice of the court of sessions 1820–1825; resumed the practice of law; died in Walpole, N. H., October 26, 1841; interment in the Village Cemetery.

VREELAND, Albert Lincoln, a Representative from New Jersey; born in East Orange, Essex County, N. J., July 2, 1901; attended the public schools; served as ambulance driver for the American Red Cross in 1918 and 1919; was graduated from the New York Electrical School in New York City in 1919, the Peddie School, Hightstown, N. J., in 1922, and the New Jersey Law School at Newark in 1925; was admitted to the bar in 1927 and commenced practice in East Orange, N. J.; assistant city counsel and city prosecutor of East Orange 1929–1934; judge of the recorder's court of East Orange 1934–1938; elected as a Republican to the Seventy-sixth and Seventy-seventh Congresses (January 3, 1939–January 3, 1943); was a captain in the United States Army Reserve and on December 9, 1941, was granted leave of absence from the House of Representatives to go on active duty and assigned to the Military Intelligence Section of the War Department; transferred to the Seventy-sixth Infantry Division in April 1942; commissioned a major in Infantry on July 17, 1942, and on July 18, 1942, by Presidential directive, was ordered back to the House of Representatives; was not a candidate for renomination in 1942; reentered the Army on January 4, 1943, and served two years in Australia and New Guinea; commissioned a lieutenant colonel on August 27, 1944, and ordered to inactive duty August 27, 1945; colonel, A. I., USAR (retired); police commissioner of East Orange, N. J., 1945–1951; public relations officer for the Celanese Corporation of America 1945–1956; resumed the practice of law and is a resident of East Orange, N. J.

VREELAND, Edward Butterfield, a Representative from New York; born in Cuba, Allegany County, N. Y., December 7, 1856; was graduated from Friendship Academy in 1877; moved to Salamanca, Cattaraugus County, N. Y., in 1869; superintendent of the public schools at Salamanca, N. Y., 1877–1882; studied law; was admitted to the bar in 1881, but did not engage in active practice; engaged in banking and in the oil and insurance business; became president of the Salamanca Trust Co. in 1891; served as postmaster of Salamanca 1889–1893; was elected as a Republican to the Fifty-sixth Congress to fill the vacancy caused by the resignation of Warren B. Hooker; reelected to the Fifty-seventh and to the five succeeding Congresses and served from November 7, 1899, to March 3, 1913; declined to be a candidate for renomination in 1912; appointed a member of the National Monetary Commission, serving as vice chairman 1909–1912; resumed former business pursuits in Salamanca, N. Y., until January 1, 1936, when he retired from active business; died in Salamanca, N. Y., May 8, 1936; interment in Wildwood Cemetery.

VROOM, Peter Dumont, a Representative from New Jersey; born in Hillsboro, Somerset County, N. J., December 12, 1791; attended the common schools and the Somerville (N. J.) Academy; was graduated from Columbia College, New York City, in 1808; studied law; was admitted to the bar in 1813 and commenced practice in Hillsboro; moved to Somerville in 1821; member of the State general assembly in 1826, 1827, and 1829; became a sergeant at law in 1828; elected Governor of New Jersey as a Jackson Democrat in 1829, 1830, and 1831; unsuccessful candidate for reelection in 1832, but again elected in 1833, 1834, 1835, and 1836; on account of ill health declined to become a candidate for renomination; was appointed a commissioner to adjust the claims of the Choctaw Indians in 1837; elected as a Democrat to the Twenty-sixth Congress (March 4, 1839–March 3, 1841); unsuccessful candidate for reelection in 1840 to the Twenty-seventh Congress; moved to Trenton, N. J., and resumed the practice of law; delegate to the State constitutional convention in 1844; presidential elector on the Democratic ticket of Pierce and King in 1852; appointed chief justice of the supreme court of New Jersey in 1853, but declined; appointed Minister to Prussia on May 24, 1853, and served until August 10, 1857; again resumed the practice of law; delegate to the peace convention held in Washington, D. C., in 1861 in an effort to devise means to prevent the impending war; reporter of the supreme court of New Jersey 1862–1872; commissioner of the sinking fund of New Jersey from 1864 until his death; presidential elector on the Democratic ticket of Seymour and Blair in 1868; died in Trenton, N. J., November 18, 1873; interment in the cemetery of the First Reformed Dutch Church, Somerville, N. J.

VURSELL, Charles Wesley, a Representative from Illinois; born in Salem, Marion County, Ill., February 8, 1881; attended the public schools of Marion County, Ill.; hardware merchant in 1904; sheriff of Marion County 1910–1914; member of the State house of representatives 1914–1916; owner and publisher of the Salem Republican 1916–1948; elected as a Republican to the Seventy-eighth and to the seven succeeding Congresses (January 3, 1943–January 3, 1959); unsuccessful candidate for reelection in 1958 to the Eighty-sixth Congress; is a resident of Salem, Ill.

W

WACHTER, Frank Charles, a Representative from Maryland; born in Baltimore, Md., September 16, 1861; attended private schools and St. Paul's Evangelical School at Baltimore, Md.; learned the trade of clothing cutter and in 1892 engaged in the cloth-shrinking business; member of the jail board of Baltimore 1896–1898; unsuccessful candidate for police commissioner of Baltimore in 1898; elected as a Republican to the Fifty-sixth and to the three succeeding Congresses (March 4, 1899–March 3, 1907); was not a candidate for renomination in 1906; resumed his former business pursuits in Baltimore; member of the board of managers of Maryland Penitentiary from 1909 until his death in Baltimore, Md., on July 1, 1910; interment in Loudon Park Cemetery.

WADDELL, Alfred Moore, a Representative from North Carolina; born in Hillsboro, Orange County, N. C., September 16, 1834; attended Bingham's School and Caldwell Institute in Hillsboro; was graduated from the University of North Carolina at Chapel Hill in 1853; studied law; was admitted to the bar in 1855 and began practice in Wilmington, New Hanover County, N. C.; clerk of a court of equity 1858–1861; delegate to the Constitutional Union National Convention at Baltimore in 1860, which nominated Bell and Everett; engaged in newspaper work; edited the Wilmington Daily Herald in 1860 and 1861; served as lieutenant colonel of the Third Cavalry, Forty-first North Carolina Regiment, during the Civil War; elected as a Democrat to the Forty-second and to the three succeeding Congresses (March 4, 1871–March 3, 1879); unsuccessful candidate for reelection in 1878 to the Forty-sixth Congress; resumed the practice of law and also engaged in literary pursuits; editor of the Charlotte Journal-Observer in 1881 and 1882; delegate to the Democratic National Conventions in 1880 and 1896; presidential elector on the Democratic ticket of Cleveland and Thurman in 1888; mayor of Wilmington 1898–1904; died in Wilmington, N. C., March 17, 1912; interment in Oakdale Cemetery.

WADDILL, Edmund, Jr., a Representative from Virginia; born in Charles City County, Va., May 22, 1855; educated by private tutors and attended Norwood Academy; deputy clerk of the courts of Charles City, New Kent, Hanover, and Henrico Counties and of the circuit court of the city of Richmond; studied law privately and in the University of Virginia at Charlottesville; was admitted to the bar in 1877 and commenced the practice of law in Richmond in 1878; judge of the Henrico County Court in 1880; resigned in 1883 to accept the position of United States attorney for the eastern district of Virginia, which position he held until 1885; member of the State house of delegates from 1886 to March 4, 1889, when he resigned; unsuccessful Republican candidate for election in 1886 to the Fiftieth Congress; successfully contested as a Republican the election of George D. Wise to the Fifty-first Congress and served from April 12, 1890, to March 3, 1891; was not a candidate for renomination in 1890; resumed the practice of law in Richmond, Va.; delegate to the Republican National Conventions in 1892 and 1896; appointed judge of the District Court of the United States for the Eastern District of Virginia March 22, 1908, and served until June 2, 1921, when he was appointed as judge of the United States Circuit Court of Appeals for the fourth circuit and was presiding judge at the time of his death in Richmond, Va., April 9, 1931; interment in Hollywood Cemetery.

WADDILL, James Richard, a Representative from Missouri; born in Springfield, Greene County, Mo., November 22, 1842; attended private schools and Springfield College; during the Civil War enlisted as a private in the Union Army and served from 1861 to 1863, when he resigned, having attained the rank of first lieutenant; studied law; was admitted to the bar in 1864 and commenced practice in Springfield, Mo.; prosecuting attorney of Greene County 1874–1876; elected as a Democrat to the Forty-sixth Congress (March 4, 1879–March 3, 1881); resumed the practice of law and also engaged in mining operations near Joplin, Mo.; died in Deming, Luna County, N. Mex., June 14, 1917; interment in Mountain View Cemetery.

WADE, Benjamin Franklin (brother of Edward Wade), a Senator from Ohio; born in Feeding Hills, near Springfield, Hampden County, Mass., October 27, 1800; received his early education from his mother; moved with his parents to Andover, Ohio, in 1821; taught school; studied medicine in Albany, N. Y., 1823–1825; returned to Ohio; studied law; was admitted to the bar in 1828 and commenced the practice of law in Jefferson, Ashtabula County, Ohio; prosecuting attorney of Ashtabula County 1835–1837; member of the State senate in 1837 and 1838; president judge of the third judicial court of Ohio 1847–1851; elected as a Whig to the United States Senate to fill the vacancy in the term commencing March 4, 1851, caused by the failure of the legislature to elect; reelected as a Republican in 1856 and again in 1863 and served from March 15, 1851, to March 3, 1869; unsuccessful candidate for renomination in 1868; elected President pro tempore of the Senate March 2, 1867, and served until March 3, 1869; delegate to the Southern Loyalist Convention at Philadelphia in 1866; candidate for Vice President in the Republican National Convention at Chicago in 1868; resumed the practice of law in Jefferson, Ohio, in 1869; appointed a Government director of the Pacific Railroad; member of the Santo Domingo Commission in 1871; chairman of the Ohio delegation in the Republican National Convention at Cincinnati in 1876; died in Jefferson, Ashtabula County, Ohio, on March 2, 1878; interment in Oakdale Cemetery.

WADE, Edward (brother of Benjamin Franklin Wade), a Representative from Ohio; born in West Springfield, Hampden County, Mass., November 22, 1802; received a limited schooling; moved to Andover, Ashtabula County, Ohio, in 1821; studied law; was admitted to the bar in 1827 and commenced practice in Jefferson, Ashtabula County, Ohio; justice of the peace of Ashtabula County in 1831; moved to Unionville in 1832; prosecuting attorney of Ashtabula County 1833; moved to Cleveland in 1837; elected as a Free-Soil candidate to the Thirty-third Congress (March 4, 1853–March 3, 1855); reelected as a Republican to the Thirty-fourth, Thirty-fifth, and Thirty-sixth Congresses (March 4, 1855–March 3, 1861); was not a candidate for renomination in 1860; died in East Cleveland, Cuyahoga County, Ohio, August 13, 1866; interment in Woodland Cemetery, Cleveland, Ohio.

WADE, Martin Joseph, a Representative from Iowa; born in Burlington, Chittenden County, Vt., October 20, 1861; moved to Iowa with his parents at an early age; attended the common schools and St. Joseph's College (later Columbia University), Dubuque, Iowa; was graduated from the law department of the University of Iowa at Iowa City in 1886; was admitted to the bar the same year and practiced in Iowa City, Johnson County, Iowa, 1886–1893; judge of the eighth judicial district of Iowa 1893–1903; lecturer in the law department of the University of Iowa 1891–1903 and professor of medical jurisprudence 1895–1905; president of the Iowa State Bar Association in 1897 and 1898; elected as a Democrat to the Fifty-eighth Congress (March 4, 1903–March 3, 1905); unsuccessful candidate for reelection in 1904 to the Fifty-ninth Congress; resumed the practice of his profession in Iowa City, Iowa; delegate to the Democratic National Conventions in 1904 and 1912; appointed judge of the United States District Court for the Southern District of Iowa in 1915 and served until his death April 16, 1931, in Los Angeles, Calif., while on a visit in that State; interment in St. Joseph's Cemetery, Iowa City, Iowa.

WADE, William Henry, a Representative from Missouri; born near Springfield, Clark County, Ohio, November 3, 1835; attended the common schools, Grove Academy, and Antioch College, Yellow Springs, Ohio; engaged in agricultural pursuits; during the Civil War enlisted in the Union Army April 17, 1861, and was mustered out April 26, 1866; moved to Missouri in May 1866 and resumed agricultural pursuits; member of the State house of representatives 1881–1884; elected as a Republican to the Forty-ninth, Fiftieth, and Fifty-first Congresses (March 4, 1885–March 3, 1891); unsuccessful candidate for reelection to the Fifty-second Congress; again engaged in agricultural pursuits; died in Springfield, Greene County, Mo., January 13, 1911; interment in Maple Park Cemetery.

WADLEIGH, Bainbridge, a Senator from New Hampshire; born in Bradford, Merrimack County, N. H., January 4, 1831; attended the common schools and Kimball Union Academy, Plainfield, N. H.; studied law; was admitted to the bar in 1850 and commenced practice in Milford, Hillsborough County, N. H.; served six terms as town moderator; member of the State house of representatives in 1855, 1856, 1859, 1860, and 1869–1872; elected as a Republican to the United States Senate and served from March 4, 1873, to March 3, 1879; unsuccessful candidate for reelection in 1878; resumed the practice of law in Boston, Mass., where he died January 24, 1891; interment in West Street Cemetery, Milford, N. H.

WADSWORTH, James, a Delegate from Connecticut; born in Durham, Middlesex County, Conn., July 8, 1730; received a thorough English training, and was graduated from Yale College in 1748; studied law and was admitted to the bar; town clerk 1756–1786; justice of the peace in 1762; appointed judge of the New Haven County Court in 1773 and promoted to presiding judge five years later; member of the committee of safety; served in the Revolutionary Army as a colonel and brigadier general of Connecticut Militia, and as a second major general 1777–1779; Member of the Continental Congress 1783–1786; member of the State executive council 1785–1789; State comptroller in 1786 and 1787; member of the State convention in 1788 to ratify the Federal Constitution which he opposed, and refused to take the oath of allegiance; died in Durham, Conn., September 22, 1817; interment in the Old Cemetery.

WADSWORTH, James Wolcott, a Representative from New York; born in Philadelphia, Pa., October 12, 1846; attended Hopkins Grammar School, New Haven, Conn.; served in the Civil War as captain on the staff of Gen. G. K. Warren and was made brevet major for gallant service at Five Forks; after the war settled in Geneseo, N. Y., and engaged in agricultural pursuits; supervisor of Geneseo 1873–1876; member of the State assembly in 1878 and 1879; State comptroller in 1880 and 1881; elected as a Republican to the Forty-seventh Congress to fill the vacancy caused by the resignation of Eldridge G. Lapham; reelected to the Forty-eighth Congress and served from November 8, 1881, to March 3, 1885; elected to the Fifty-second and to the seven succeeding Congresses (March 4, 1891–March 3, 1907); unsuccessful candidate for reelection in 1906 to the Sixtieth Congress; elected president of the board of managers for the National Home for Disabled Volunteer Soldiers; actively interested in better education; engaged in agricultural pursuits and interested in livestock; member of the New York State Constitutional Convention in 1914; was for many years president of the Genesee Valley National Bank, but resigned about 1924 due to advanced age; died in Washington, D. C., on December 24, 1926; interment in the family plot in Temple Hill Cemetery, Geneseo, N. Y.

WADSWORTH, James Wolcott, Jr. (son of the preceding), a Senator and a Representative from New York; born in Geneseo, N. Y., August 12, 1877; received preparatory education at St. Mark's School, Southboro, Mass.; was graduated from Yale University, New Haven, Conn., in 1898; during the Spanish-American War served with Battery A, Pennsylvania Field Artillery, in the Puerto Rican campaign in 1898; engaged in livestock and agricultural pursuits near Geneseo, N. Y., since 1899 and as manager of a ranch in Texas 1911–1915; member of the State assembly 1905–1910, serving as speaker 1906–1910; delegate to the Republican National Conventions in 1908, 1912, 1916, 1920, 1924, 1928, and 1940; elected as a Republican to the United States Senate in 1914; reelected in 1920 and served from March 4, 1915, to March 3, 1927; unsuccessful candidate for reelection in 1926; resumed agricultural pursuits; elected to the Seventy-third and to the eight succeeding Congresses (March 4, 1933–January 3, 1951); was not a candidate for renomination in 1950; appointed by President Truman chairman of the National Security Training Commission in June 1951 and served until his death in Washington, D. C., June 21, 1952; interment in Temple Hill Cemetery, Geneseo, N. Y.

WADSWORTH, Jeremiah, a Delegate and a Representative from Connecticut; born in Hartford, Conn., July 12, 1743; attended the common schools; went to sea in 1761; became first mate of a vessel and subsequently master; prominently identified with pre-Revolutionary movements and served as deputy and commissary general 1775–1778 during the Revolution; Member of the Continental Congress in 1787 and 1788; member of the Connecticut convention that ratified the Federal Constitution in 1788; elected as a Federalist to the First, Second, and Third Congresses (March 4, 1789–March 3, 1795); was not a candidate for reelection; member of the State house of representatives in 1795 and of the State executive council 1795–1801; engaged in agricultural pursuits; died in Hartford, Conn., April 30, 1804; interment in Ancient Burying Ground.

WADSWORTH, Peleg, a Representative from Massachusetts; born in Duxbury, Mass., May 6, 1748; attended public and private schools, and was graduated from Harvard College in 1769; engaged in mercantile pursuits in Kingston, Mass.; served in the Revolutionary Army as an aide to Gen. Artemas Ward in 1776; engineer under General Thomas in 1776 and 1777; brigadier general of militia in 1777; adjutant general of Massachusetts in 1778; moved to Portland, Maine (then a district of Massachusetts), in 1784 and became a land agent; served in the Massachusetts Senate in 1792; elected to the Third and to the six succeeding Congresses (March 4, 1793–March 3, 1807); moved to Oxford County, Maine, in 1807 to survey and improve a large tract of land granted to him by the Government; died in Hiram, Oxford County, Maine, November 12, 1829; interment in the family cemetery at Wadsworth Hall.

WADSWORTH, William Henry, a Representative from Kentucky; born in Maysville, Mason County, Ky., July 4, 1821; attended town and county private schools; was graduated from Augusta College, Bracken County, Ky., in 1841; studied law; was admitted to the bar in 1844 and commenced practice in Maysville, Ky.; member of the State senate 1853–1856; presidential elector on the Constitutional Union ticket of Bell and Everett and president of the electoral college of Kentucky in 1860; elected as a Unionist to the Thirty-seventh and Thirty-eighth Congresses (March 4, 1861–March 3, 1865); was not a candidate for renomination in 1864; during the Civil War served as aide to General Nelson, with the rank of colonel, at the Battle of Ivy Mountain; was tendered the appointment of Minister to Austria by President Grant, but declined; appointed United States commissioner to Mexico, under the treaty of Washington for the adjustment of claims, by President Grant in 1869; elected as a Republican to the Forty-ninth Congress (March 4, 1885–March 3, 1887); was not a candidate for renomination in 1886; resumed the practice of law; died in Maysville, Mason County, Ky., April 2, 1893; interment in Maysville Cemetery.

WAGENER, David Douglas, a Representative from Pennsylvania; born in Easton, Pa., October 11, 1792; attended the common schools; captain of the Easton Union Guards 1816–1829; engaged in mercantile pursuits; elected as a Democrat to the Twenty-third and to the three succeeding Congresses (March 4, 1833–March 3, 1841); established the Easton Bank in 1852 and was its president until his death in Easton, Northampton County, Pa., October 1, 1860; interment in Easton Cemetery.

WAGGAMAN, George Augustus, a Senator from Louisiana; born at "Fairview," near Cambridge, Dorchester County, Md., in 1790; completed preparatory studies under private tutors; studied law; was admitted to the bar in Caroline County, Md., in 1811; served in the War of 1812 under General Jackson at New Orleans; settled in Baton Rouge, La., and commenced the practice of law in 1813; attorney general of the third district of Louisiana in 1813; judge of the third judicial circuit court in 1818; assistant judge of the criminal court in New Orleans in 1819; interested in sugar-cane growing; secretary of state of Louisiana 1830–1832; elected as a National-Republican to the United States Senate to fill the vacancy caused by the resignation of Edward Livingston and served from November 15, 1831, to March 3, 1835; resumed the practice of law in New Orleans and also again engaged in sugar-cane planting; participated as a principal in a duel and received injuries from which he died in New Orleans, La., March 22, 1843; interment in Girod Cemetery.

WAGNER, Earl Thomas, a Representative from Ohio; born in Cincinnati, Hamilton County, Ohio, April 27, 1908; attended parochial and public schools; was graduated from the Salmon P. Chase College of Law, Cincinnati, Ohio, in 1930; was admitted to the bar in September 1930 and commenced the practice of law in Cincinnati, Ohio; district counsel of Home Owners Loan Corporation in 1933 and 1934; special counsel to the attorney general of Ohio in 1937 and 1938; city solicitor of Sharonville, Ohio, in 1938 and 1939; member of the board of education of the Cincinnati school district 1944–1947; elected as a Democrat to the Eighty-first Congress (January 3, 1949–January 3, 1951); unsuccessful candidate for reelection in 1950 to the Eighty-second Congress, for election in 1952 to the Eighty-third Congress, and for election in 1954 to the Eighty-fourth Congress; resumed the practice of law; city solicitor of Addyston, Ohio, in 1952 and 1953; secretary of Pasquale Foods, Inc., of Indiana and general counsel for Pasquale Foods, Inc., of Ohio, Indiana, Kentucky, Alabama, and Florida; resides in Westwood, Cincinnati, Ohio.

WAGNER, Peter Joseph, a Representative from New York; born at Wagners Hollow in the town of Palatine, Montgomery County, N. Y., August 14, 1795; moved to Fort Plain, N. Y., with his parents in 1805; completed preparatory studies; attended Fairfield Academy in 1810 and 1811; was graduated from Union College, Schenectady, N. Y., in 1816; studied law; was admitted to the bar in September 1819 and commenced practice at Fort Plain, N. Y.; also engaged in agricultural pursuits and banking; unsuccessful candidate for election in 1834 to the Twenty-fourth Congress; elected as a Whig to the Twenty-sixth Congress (March 4, 1839–March 3, 1841); continued the practice of law at Fort Plain until May 1873, when he retired; died at Fort Plain, Montgomery County, N. Y., September 13, 1884; interment in Fort Plain Cemetery.

WAGNER, Robert Ferdinand, a Senator from New York; born in Nastatten, Province Hessen-Nassau, Germany, June 8, 1877; immigrated with his parents to the United States in 1885, and settled in New York City; attended the public schools; was graduated from the College of the City of New York in 1898 and from New York (N. Y.) Law School in 1900; was admitted to the bar in 1900 and commenced practice in New York City; member of the State assembly 1905–1908; served in the State senate 1909–1918, the last eight years as Democratic floor leader; chairman of the State Factory Investigating Committee 1911–1915; Acting Lieutenant Governor in 1914; delegate to the New York constitutional conventions in 1915 and 1938; justice of the supreme court of New York 1919–1926; delegate to the United Nations Monetary and Financial Conference at Bretton Woods in 1944; elected as a Democrat to the United States Senate in 1926; reelected in 1932, 1938, and again in 1944, and served from March 4, 1927, until his resignation on June 28, 1949, due to ill health; died in New York City, N. Y., May 4, 1953; interment in Calvary Cemetery, Queens, New York, N. Y.

WAGONER, George Chester Robinson, a Representative from Missouri; born in Cincinnati, Ohio, September 3, 1863; attended the public schools and Beaumont Hospital Medical College, St. Louis, Mo.; president of the Wagoner Undertaking Co. and secretary and treasurer of the H. H. Wagoner Realty Co., St. Louis, Mo.; successfully contested as a Republican the election of James J. Butler to the Fifty-seventh Congress and served from February 26 to March 3, 1903; declined to be a candidate for renomination in 1904; resumed business activities; died in St. Louis, Mo., April 27, 1946; interment in Bellefontaine Cemetery.

WAINWRIGHT, Jonathan Mayhew, a Representative from New York; born in New York City, N. Y., December 10, 1864; was graduated from Columbia College and Columbia School of Political Science, New York City, in 1884, and from Columbia Law School in 1886; was admitted to the bar the same year and practiced in New York City and in Westchester County, N. Y.; served in the Twelfth Infantry of the New York National Guard successively as second lieutenant, first lieutenant, captain, major, and lieutenant colonel 1889–1903; also served in the war with Spain as captain of the Twelfth Regiment, New York Volunteers; president of the Westchester County Bar Association 1904–1906; member of the State assembly 1902–1908; served in the State senate 1909–1913; appointed as a member of the first New York State Workmen's Compensation Commission in 1914 and served until 1915; served as lieutenant colonel, inspector general's department, New York National Guard, on the Mexican border in 1916; during the First World War served as a lieutenant colonel in the Twenty-seventh Division throughout its entire service in this country, France, and Belgium, 1917–1919, participating in all of its engagements; awarded the Distinguished Service Medal, the Croix de Guerre with Palm (Belgium), the decoration of officer of the Legion of Honor (French), and the New York State Conspicuous Service Cross; Assistant Secretary of War from March 14, 1921, to March 4, 1923, when he resigned; elected as a Republican to the Sixty-eighth and to the three succeeding Congresses (March 4, 1923–March 3, 1931); was not a candidate for renomination in 1930; resumed the practice of law; member of the Westchester County Park Commission 1930–1937; died in Rye, N. Y., June 3, 1945; interment in Greenwood Union Cemetery.

WAINWRIGHT, Stuyvesant, a Representative from New York; born in New York City, N. Y., March 16, 1921; moved to East Hampton, N. Y., in 1927; graduated from Westminster School, Simsbury, Conn.; interrupted legal studies at Yale University when twenty years of age to enlist as a private in the United States Army on January 30, 1942; attended officers candidate school; went overseas December 30, 1943, rose through the ranks, and was commanding officer of O. S. S. units of the First Army as it moved through Europe; returned to the States June 10, 1945, and spent the last three months of his service as adviser on intelligence coordination in the War Department in Washington, D. C.; was discharged as a captain December 13, 1945; awarded five battle stars and the Croix de Guerre; lieutenant colonel in the Active Army Reserve; resumed legal studies and graduated from Yale University Law School in 1947; was admitted to the bar in 1948 and commenced practice in New York City, N. Y.; elected as a Republican to the Eighty-third and to the three succeeding Congresses (January 3, 1953–January 3, 1961); unsuccessful candidate for reelection in 1960 to the Eighty-seventh Congress; is a resident of Wainscott, N. Y.

WAIT, John Turner, a Representative from Connecticut; born in New London, Conn., August 27, 1811; moved with his mother to Norwich, Conn.; attended the common schools and Trinity College, Hartford, Conn., for two years; engaged in mercantile pursuits; studied law; was admitted to the bar in 1836 and began practice in Norwich; State's attorney for the county of New London 1842–1844 and 1846–1854; unsuccessful candidate for election as Lieutenant Governor in 1854, 1855, 1856, and 1857; presidential elector on the Republican ticket of Lincoln and Johnson in 1864; served in the State senate in 1865 and 1866, the latter year as president pro tempore; member of the State house of representatives in 1867, 1871, and 1873, serving as speaker in 1867; elected as a Republican to the Forty-fourth Congress to fill the vacancy caused by the death of Henry H. Starkweather; reelected as a Republican to the Forty-fifth and to the four succeeding Congresses and served from April 12, 1876, to March 3, 1887; was not a candidate for renomination in 1886; resumed the practice of his profession; died in Norwich, Conn., April 21, 1899; interment in Yantic Cemetery.

WAKEFIELD, James Beach, a Representative from Minnesota; born in Winsted, Conn., March 21, 1825; attended the public schools at Westfield, Mass., and Jonesville, N. Y.; was graduated from Trinity College, Hartford, Conn., in 1846; studied law in Painesville, Lake County, Ohio; was admitted to the bar and commenced practice in Delphi, Ind., in 1852; moved to Shakopee, Minn., in 1854; first judge of the probate court of Faribault County, Minn.; elected as a member of the State house of representatives in 1858, 1863, and 1866, serving as speaker in the session of 1866; member of the State senate 1867–1869; appointed receiver of the United States Land Office at Winnebago City, Minn., June 1, 1869, and served until January 15, 1875, when he resigned; Lieutenant Governor of Minnesota 1875–1877; elected as a Republican to the Forty-eighth and Forty-ninth Congresses (March 4, 1883–March 3, 1887); retired from public life; died at Blue Earth, Faribault County, Minn., August 25, 1910; interment in Evergreen Cemetery, Painesville, Ohio.

WAKEMAN, Abram, a Representative from New York; born in Greenfield Hill, Fairfield County, Conn., May 31, 1824; completed preparatory studies and was graduated from Herkimer Academy, New York; studied law at Little Falls, N. Y.; was admitted to the bar and commenced practice in New York City in 1847; member of the State assembly in 1850 and 1851; elected as a Whig, supported by the American Party, to the Thirty-fourth Congress (March 4, 1855–March 3, 1857); unsuccessful Republican candidate for reelection in 1856 to the Thirty-fifth Congress; delegate to the Republican National

Convention at Philadelphia in 1856; at the outbreak of the Civil War raised the Eighty-first Pennsylvania Volunteers; postmaster of New York City from March 21, 1862, to September 18, 1864; surveyor of the port of New York City; resumed the practice of law; died in New York City June 29, 1889; interment in Greenwood Cemetery, Brooklyn, N. Y.

WAKEMAN, Seth, a Representative from New York; born in Franklin, Vt., January 15, 1811; attended the common schools; moved to Batavia, N. Y., where he studied law; was admitted to the bar and commenced the practice of law; district attorney for Genesee County 1850–1856; member of the State assembly in 1856 and 1857; member of the State constitutional convention in 1867 and 1868; elected as a Republican to the Forty-second Congress (March 4, 1871–March 3, 1873); was not a candidate for renomination in 1872; resumed the practice of law; died in Batavia, Genesee County, N. Y., January 4, 1880; interment in Elmwood Cemetery.

WALBRIDGE, David Safford, a Representative from Michigan; born in Bennington, Vt., July 30, 1802; attended the common schools; moved to New York in 1820 and engaged in mercantile and agricultural pursuits at Geneseo from 1820 to 1826 and at Jamestown from 1826 to 1842; moved to Kalamazoo, Mich., in 1842; again engaged in mercantile pursuits; became a large landowner and stock raiser; member of the State house of representatives in 1848; served two terms in the State senate; served as permanent chairman of the first Republican State convention held "under the oaks" July 6, 1854, at Jackson, Mich.; elected as a Republican to the Thirty-fourth and Thirty-fifth Congresses (March 4, 1855–March 3, 1859); resumed his former pursuits; appointed postmaster of Kalamazoo by President Johnson; died in Kalamazoo, Mich., June 15, 1868; interment in Mountain Home Cemetery.

WALBRIDGE, Henry Sanford (cousin of Hiram Walbridge), a Representative from New York; born in Norwich, Conn., April 8, 1801; attended school in Bennington, Vt.; moved to Ithaca, Tompkins County, N. Y., in 1820; studied law; was admitted to the bar and commenced practice in Ithaca; clerk of the board of supervisors of Tompkins County in 1824; member of the State assembly in 1829; president of the village council of Ithaca, Tompkins County, in 1829 and again in 1842; again a member of the State assembly in 1846; elected as a Whig to the Thirty-second Congress (March 4, 1851–March 3, 1853); declined to be a candidate for renomination in 1852; trustee of Ithaca Academy 1858–1868; judge and surrogate of Tompkins County 1859–1868; moved to Leonia, N. J., in 1868 and practiced law in New York City; killed in a railroad accident at Bergen Tunnel near Hoboken, N. J., January 27, 1869; interment in Ithaca City Cemetery, Ithaca, N. Y.

WALBRIDGE, Hiram (cousin of Henry Sanford Walbridge), a Representative from New York; born in Ithaca, Tompkins County, N. Y., February 2, 1821; moved to Ohio with his parents, who settled in Toledo in 1836; attended the public schools and the University of Ohio at Athens; studied law; was admitted to the bar in 1842 and commenced practice in Toledo; appointed brigadier general of militia in 1843; moved to New York and engaged in mercantile pursuits at Buffalo; member of the board of aldermen; moved to New York City in 1847 and continued mercantile pursuits; elected as a Democrat to the Thirty-third Congress (March 4, 1853–March 3, 1855); declined to be a candidate for renomination in 1854; resumed his former pursuits in New York City; unsuccessful Union candidate for election in 1862 to the Thirty-eighth Congress; president of the International Commercial Convention held in Detroit, Mich., July 11,

1865; elected as a delegate to the Southern Loyalist Convention at Philadelphia in 1866; died in New York City December 6, 1870; interment in Glenwood Cemetery, Washington, D. C.

WALCOTT, Frederic Collin, a Senator from Connecticut; born in New York Mills, Oneida County, N. Y., February 19, 1869; attended the public schools of Utica, N. Y.; was graduated from Lawrenceville (N. J.) School in 1886, from Phillips Academy, Andover, Mass., in 1887, and from Yale University, New Haven, Conn., in 1891; moved to New York City, N. Y., in 1907 and engaged in the manufacture of cotton cloth and in banking; moved to Norfolk, Litchfield County, Conn., in 1910, but continued his business connections in New York City until 1921, when he retired from active business pursuits; during the First World War served with the United States Food Administration as assistant to Herbert Hoover; was decorated by the Government of France with the Legion of Honor and by Poland with the Officer's Cross; president of the Connecticut Board of Fisheries and Game 1923–1928 and chairman of the Connecticut Water Commission 1925–1928; delegate to the Republican National Conventions in 1924, 1928, and 1932; member of the State senate 1925–1929, serving as president pro tempore 1927–1929; elected as a Republican to the United States Senate and served from March 4, 1929, to January 3, 1935; unsuccessful candidate for reelection in 1934; appointed commissioner of welfare of Connecticut in July 1935 and served until July 1939; trustee of the American Geological Society 1924–1948 and of Bethume Cookman College, Daytona, Fla., 1922–1948; member of the advisory committee of the Human Welfare Group of Yale University 1920–1948; Regent of the Smithsonian Institution 1941–1948; died in Stamford, Conn., on April 27, 1949; interment in Center Cemetery, Norfolk, Conn.

WALDEN, Hiram, a Representative from New York; born in Pawlet, Vt., August 21, 1800; attended the district schools; moved to Berne, Albany County, N. Y., in 1818 and to Waldenville, Schoharie County, N. Y., in 1821; engaged in the manufacture of axes; major general of militia; member of the State assembly in 1836; was one of the supervisors of the town of Wright in 1842; elected as a Democrat to the Thirty-first Congress (March 4, 1849–March 3, 1851); was not a candidate for renomination in 1850 to the Thirty-second Congress; resumed his former manufacturing pursuits; was also employed in the customhouse in New York City; discontinued his active business pursuits and lived in retirement until his death in Waldenville, N. Y., July 21, 1880; interment in Pine Grove Cemetery, Berne, Albany County, N. Y.

WALDEN, Madison Miner, a Representative from Iowa; born near Scioto, Brush Creek, Adams County, Ohio, October 6, 1836; moved to Iowa in 1852; attended Denmark Academy, Lee County, Iowa, and Wesleyan College, Mount Pleasant, Iowa, and was graduated from Wesleyan University, Delaware, Ohio, in 1859; during the Civil War served in the Union Army as captain in the Sixth Regiment, Iowa Volunteer Infantry, and the Eighth Regiment, Iowa Volunteer Cavalry, from May 1861 to May 1865; taught school; published the Centerville (Iowa) Citizen 1865–1874; member of the State house of representatives in 1866 and 1867; served in the State senate in 1868 and 1869; Lieutenant Governor of Iowa in 1870; elected as a Republican to the Forty-second Congress (March 4, 1871–March 3, 1873); unsuccessful candidate for renomination in 1872; engaged in agricultural pursuits and coal mining in Centerville, Appanoose County, Iowa; was appointed chief clerk in the office of the Solicitor of the Treasury in 1889 and served until his death in Washington, D. C., July 24, 1891; interment in Oakland Cemetery, Centerville, Iowa.

WALDO, George Ernest, a Representative from New York; born in Brooklyn, N. Y., January 11, 1851; attended the public schools of Scotland, Conn., and Brooklyn, N. Y., Doctor Fitch's Academy, South Windham, Conn., Natchaug High School, Willimantic, Conn., and studied two years in Cornell University, Ithaca, N. Y., class of 1872; studied law in New York City; was admitted to the bar in Poughkeepsie, N. Y., in 1876 and practiced in New York City 1876–1883 and in Ulysses, Nebr., 1883–1889; village attorney of Ulysses, Nebr., for several years; for four years a member of the board of trustees and school director of Ulysses High School; returned to New York City in 1889; member of the New York Assembly in 1896; commissioner of records of Kings County, N. Y., 1899–1904; delegate to the Republican National Convention at Philadelphia in 1900; elected as a Republican to the Fifty-ninth and Sixtieth Congresses (March 4, 1905–March 3, 1909); was not a candidate for renomination in 1908; resumed the practice of law in New York City; moved to Los Angeles, Calif., in 1913, to Pasadena, Calif., in 1918, and continued the practice of his profession; died in Pasadena, Calif., June 16, 1942; remains were cremated and the ashes deposited in the New Cemetery, Scotland, Conn.

WALDO, Loren Pinckney, a Representative from Connecticut; born in Canterbury, Conn., February 2, 1802; attended the common schools; taught school; engaged in agricultural pursuits; moved to Tolland, Conn., in 1823; studied law; was admitted to the bar in 1825 and commenced practice in Somers; superintendent of schools; postmaster of Somers in 1829 and 1830; returned to Tolland in 1830; member of the State house of representatives 1832–1834 and in 1839; clerk of the State house of representatives in 1833; State's attorney 1837–1849; judge of probate for Tolland district in 1842 and 1843; member in 1847 of the committee to revise the statutes; a member of the State house of representatives in 1847 and 1848; elected as a Democrat to the Thirty-first Congress (March 4, 1849–March 3, 1851); unsuccessful candidate for reelection in 1850 to the Thirty-second Congress; commissioner of the school fund of Connecticut; Commissioner of Pensions under President Pierce from March 17, 1853, until January 10, 1856, when he resigned to become judge of the superior court of Connecticut 1856–1863; moved to Hartford, Conn., and resumed the practice of his profession; again a member of a committee to revise the statutes, in 1864; died in Hartford, Conn., September 8, 1881; interment in Cedar Hill Cemetery.

WALDO, William Frederick, a Representative from New York; born in Buffalo, N. Y., August 26, 1882; attended the common schools; apprenticed as a plumber and later engaged as a plumbing contractor; elected a member of the board of aldermen of Buffalo in 1912 and 1913; member of the New York Republican State committee in 1916; elected as a Republican to the Sixty-fifth Congress (March 4, 1917–March 3, 1919); unsuccessful for reelection in 1918 to the Sixty-sixth Congress; resumed former business pursuits; delegate to the Republican National Convention at Chicago in 1920; sheriff of Erie County, N. Y., 1921–1923; died in Snyder (a suburb of Buffalo), N. Y., April 16, 1930; interment in Forest Lawn Cemetery.

WALDRON, Alfred Marpole, a Representative from Pennsylvania; born in Philadelphia, Pa., September 21, 1865; educated in the public schools of Philadelphia; engaged in the insurance business; member of the Philadelphia Select Council 1911–1924; member of the Republican city committee 1916–1936; delegate to the Republican National Conventions in 1924, 1928, and 1932; elected as a Republican to the Seventy-third Congress (March 4, 1933–January 3, 1935); did not seek renomination in 1934; resumed the insurance business; died in Philadelphia, Pa., June 28, 1952; interment in North Cedar Hill Cemetery.

WALDRON, Henry, a Representative from Michigan; born in Albany, N. Y., October 11, 1819; attended Albany Academy, and was graduated from Rutgers College, New Brunswick, N. J., in 1836; moved to Michigan in 1837 and was employed as a civil engineer in railroad work; settled in Hillsdale, Mich., in 1839; member of the State legislature in 1843; built the first warehouse on the line of the Michigan Southern Railroad in 1843; a director of the Michigan Southern Railroad 1846–1848; active in promoting the construction of the Detroit, Hillsdale & Southwestern Railroad and served as its first president; president of the Second National Bank of Hillsdale from the date of its organization until 1876; presidential elector on the Whig ticket of Taylor and Fillmore in 1848; elected as a Republican to the Thirty-fourth, Thirty-fifth, and Thirty-sixth Congresses (March 4, 1855–March 3, 1861); was not a candidate for renomination in 1860; elected to the Forty-second, Forty-third, and Forty-fourth Congresses (March 4, 1871–March 3, 1877); declined to be a candidate for renomination in 1876; elected president of the First National Bank of Hillsdale in 1876 and served until his death in Hillsdale, Hillsdale County, Mich., September 13, 1880; interment in Oak Grove Cemetery.

WALES, George Edward, a Representative from Vermont; born in Westminster, Windham County, Vt., May 13, 1792; attended the common schools; studied law in Westminster and Woodstock, Vt.; was admitted to the bar in 1812 and commenced practice at Hartford, Vt.; treasurer of the White River Bridge Co. in 1818; member of the State house of representatives 1822–1824 and served as speaker; elected to the Nineteenth and Twentieth Congresses (March 4, 1825–March 3, 1829); unsuccessful candidate for reelection in 1828 to the Twenty-first Congress; resumed the practice of his profession; town clerk of Hartford, Windsor County, Vt., 1840–1860; judge of probate for the Hartford district 1847–1850; died in Hartford, Vt., January 8, 1860; interment in Hartford Cemetery.

WALES, John, a Senator from Delaware; born in New Haven, Conn., July 31, 1783; pursued preparatory studies, and was graduated from Yale College in 1801; studied law; was admitted to the bar in 1801 and commenced the practice of law at New Haven, Conn.; moved to Philadelphia, Pa., and continued his practice; removed to Baltimore, Md., in 1813, where he remained until 1815; moved to Wilmington, Del., in 1815 and was president of the National Bank of Wilmington and Brandywine; secretary of state of Delaware 1845–1849; elected to the United States Senate to fill the vacancy caused by the resignation of John M. Clayton and served from February 3, 1849, to March 3, 1851; unsuccessful candidate for reelection in 1851; one of the founders of Delaware College, Newark, Del.; died in Wilmington, Del., on December 3, 1863; interment in Wilmington and Brandywine Cemetery.

WALKER, Amasa, a Representative from Massachusetts; born in East Woodstock, Conn., May 4, 1799; moved with his parents to North Brookfield, Mass.; attended the district school; in 1814 entered commercial life in North Brookfield; in 1825 moved to Boston, where he engaged in mercantile pursuits until 1840; delegate to the Democratic National Convention at Buffalo, N. Y., in 1836; delegate to the first international peace conference at London in 1843 and at Paris in 1849; lecturer on political economy at Oberlin College, Ohio, 1842–1848; member of the Massachusetts House of Representatives in 1849; served in the State senate in 1850; secretary of state of Massachusetts in 1851 and 1852; member of the State constitutional convention in 1853; lecturer on political economy at Harvard University 1853–1860; again a member of the State house of representatives in 1860; elected as a Republican to the Thirty-seventh Congress to fill the vacancy caused by the death of Goldsmith F. Bailey and served from December 1, 1862, to March 3, 1863; was not a candidate for election to the Thirty-eighth Congress; presidential elector on the Republican ticket of Lincoln and Hamlin in 1860; lecturer on political economy at Amherst College, Amherst, Mass., 1859–1869; author of several books on political economy; died in North Brookfield, Mass., October 29, 1875; interment in Maple Street Cemetery.

WALKER, Benjamin, a Representative from New York; born in London, England, in 1753; attended the Blue-Coat School; immigrated to the United States and settled in New York City; served in the Revolutionary War as aide-de-camp to General von Steuben and subsequently as a member of the staff of General Washington; naval officer of customs at the port of New York from March 21, 1791, to February 20, 1798; moved to Fort Schuyler (now Utica), N. Y., in 1797; agent of the great landed estate of the Earl of Bath; elected as a Democrat to the Seventh Congress (March 4, 1801–March 3, 1803); declined to be a candidate for renomination in 1802; died in Utica, N. Y., January 13, 1818; interment in the Old Village Burying Ground on Water Street; reinterment, June 17, 1875, in Forest Hill Cemetery.

WALKER, Charles Christopher Brainerd, a Representative from New York; was born in Drewsville, near Keene, N. H., June 27, 1824; completed preparatory studies; moved to Corning, Steuben County, N. Y., in 1848; postmaster of Corning 1856–1860; was a contractor and also engaged in the hardware and lumber business; during the Civil War served as brigade quartermaster with the rank of captain in the New York State Militia; delegate to the Democratic National Conventions at Charleston in 1860 and at Baltimore in 1872; elected as a Democrat to the Forty-fourth Congress (March 4, 1875–March 3, 1877); resumed former business activities; member of the board of control of the New York Agricultural Experiment Station from June 10, 1885, until his death in Corning, N. Y., January 26, 1888; interment in Palmyra Cemetery, Palmyra, Wayne County, N. Y.

WALKER, David (brother of George Walker and grandfather of James David Walker), a Representative from Kentucky; born in Brunswick County, Va.; attended public and private schools; served in the Revolutionary War as a private under General Lafayette; was at the surrender of Cornwallis at Yorktown; moved to Logan County, Ky.; clerk of county and circuit courts; member of the State house of representatives 1793–1796; served as major on the staff of Governor Shelby of Kentucky in the Battle of the Thames during the War of 1812; elected to the Fifteenth and Sixteenth Congresses and served from March 4, 1817, until his death in Washington, D. C., March 1, 1820; interment in the Congressional Cemetery.

WALKER, Felix, a Representative from North Carolina; born on the south branch of the Potomac River, in Hampshire County, Va. (now West Virginia), July 19, 1753; attended country school on the Congaree River, near Columbia, S. C., and in Burke County, N. C.; moved with his father to what became Lincoln County, N. C., and in 1768, to what became Rutherford County, N. C.; was employed as a merchant's clerk at Charleston, S. C., in 1769; also engaged in agricultural pursuits; in company with Daniel Boone and others formed the settlement of Boonsboro, Ky., in 1775; clerk of the court of Washington district (most of which is now in Tennessee) in 1775 and 1776 and of the county court of Washington County (now chiefly in Tennessee) in 1777 and 1778; fought in the Revolutionary and Indian wars; about 1776 was lieutenant in Captain Richardson's company in the rifle regiment

from Mecklenburg County commanded by James Stuger, and also was captain of a company of light dragoons on the Nolachucky River; clerk of court of Rutherford County, N. C., 1779–1787; member of the State house of commons in 1792, 1799–1802, and 1806; resumed agricultural pursuits and was also a trader and land speculator in Haywood County, N. C.; elected as a Democrat to the Fifteenth, Sixteenth, and Seventeenth Congresses (March 4, 1817–March 3, 1823); unsuccessful candidate for reelection in 1822 to the Eighteenth Congress; moved to Mississippi about 1824 and engaged in agricultural pursuits and trading; died in Clinton, Hinds County, Miss., in 1828; interment probably in a private cemetery.

WALKER, Francis (brother of John Walker), a Representative from Virginia; born at "Castle Hill," near Cobham, Albemarle County, Va., June 22, 1764; magistrate of Albemarle County; colonel of the Eighty-eighth Regiment, Virginia Militia; member of the State house of delegates 1788–1791 and 1797–1801; elected to the Third Congress (March 4, 1793–March 3, 1795); died at "Castle Hill," near Cobham, Va., in March 1806; interment in the family cemetery at "Castle Hill."

WALKER, Freeman, a Senator from Georgia; born in Charles City, Va., October 25, 1780; attended the common schools moved to Augusta, Ga., in 1797; studied law; was admitted to the bar in 1802 and commenced practice in Augusta; member of the State house of representatives 1807–1811; mayor of Augusta in 1818 and 1819; elected as a Democrat to the United States Senate to fill the vacancy caused by the resignation of John Forsyth and served from November 6, 1819, to August 6, 1821, when he resigned; again mayor of Augusta in 1823; died in Augusta, Richmond County, Ga., September 23, 1827; interment in Spring Hill Cemetery.

WALKER, George (brother of David Walker), a Senator from Kentucky; born in Culpeper County, Va., in 1763; attended the common schools; during the Revolutionary War served under Generals Green and Morgan in 1780 and 1781; moved to Jessamine County, Ky., in 1794; studied law; was admitted to the bar and commenced practice in Nicholasville, Ky., in 1799; a commissioner of the Kentucky River Co. in 1801; member of the State senate 1810–1814; appointed to the United States Senate to fill the vacancy caused by the resignation of George M. Bibb and served from August 30 to December 16, 1814, when a successor was elected; died in Nicholasville, Ky., in 1819; interment on his estate near Nicholasville.

WALKER, Gilbert Carlton, a Representative from Virginia; born in South Gibson, Susquehanna County, Pa., August 1, 1833; received a thorough English training, and was graduated from Hamilton College, Clinton, N. Y., in 1854; studied law; was admitted to the bar in 1855 and practiced in Owego, Broome County, N. Y., 1855–1859 and in Chicago, Ill., 1859–1864; moved to Norfolk, Va., in 1864 and continued the practice of law; also engaged in banking; Governor of Virginia 1869–1874; elected as a Conservative to the Forty-fourth Congress and as a Democrat to the Forty-fifth Congress (March 4, 1875–March 3, 1879); was not a candidate for renomination in 1878; settled in Binghamton, N. Y., in 1879 and practiced law; moved to New York City in 1881 and continued the practice of law; served as president of the New York Underground Railroad Co.; died in New York City, N. Y., May 11, 1885; interment in Spring Forest Cemetery, Binghamton, N. Y.

WALKER, Isaac Pigeon, a Senator from Wisconsin; born near Wheeling, Va. (now West Virginia), November 2, 1815; moved to Danville, Ill., in early youth; attended the common schools; was employed as a clerk in a store; studied law; was admitted to the bar in 1834 and commenced practice in Springfield; served one term in the State house of representatives; presidential elector on the Democratic ticket of Van Buren and Johnson in 1840; moved to Wisconsin Territory in 1841, settled in Milwaukee, and continued the practice of law; member of the special session of the fifth legislative assembly October 18 to 27, 1847; member of the Territorial legislature in 1847 and 1848; upon the admission of Wisconsin as a State into the Union was elected as a Democrat to the United States Senate; reelected in 1849 and served from June 8, 1848, to March 3, 1855; engaged in agricultural pursuits in Waukesha County; returned to Milwaukee and resumed the practice of law; died there March 29, 1872; interment in Forest Home Cemetery.

WALKER, James Alexander, a Representative from Virginia; born near Mount Meridian, Augusta County, Va., August 27, 1832; attended private schools, and was graduated from Virginia Military Institute, Lexington, Va., in 1852; studied law in the University of Virginia at Charlottesville in 1854 and 1855; was admitted to the bar in 1856 and commenced practice in Newbern, Pulaski County, Va., in 1856; attorney for the Commonwealth in 1860; during the Civil War entered the Confederate Army in April 1861 as captain of the Pulaski Guards, afterwards Company C, Fourth Virginia Infantry, Stonewall Brigade; promoted to lieutenant colonel and assigned to the Thirteenth Virginia Infantry in July 1861, becoming colonel in March 1862; was promoted to brigadier general and assigned as commander of the Stonewall Brigade in May 1863; commanded Early's old division at the surrender of Appomattox; severely wounded at Spotsylvania Court House May 12, 1864; member of the house of delegates of Virginia in 1871 and 1872; elected Lieutenant Governor of Virginia in 1877; until 1893 was a member of the Democratic Party; elected as a Republican to the Fifty-fourth and Fifty-fifth Congresses (March 4, 1895–March 3, 1899); unsuccessful candidate for reelection in 1898 to the Fifty-sixth Congress; resumed the practice of his profession; died in Wytheville, Wythe County, Va., October 21, 1901; interment in East End Cemetery.

WALKER, James David (grandson of David Walker, nephew of John McLean, of Illinois, and cousin of Wilkinson Call), a Senator from Arkansas; born near Russellville, Logan County, Ky., December 13, 1830; attended private schools in Kentucky and Ozark Institute and Arkansas College, Fayetteville, Ark.; moved to Arkansas in 1847; studied law; was admitted to the bar in 1850 and commenced practice in Fayetteville, Washington County, Ark.; judge of the circuit court, fourth judicial district; during the Civil War served as colonel of the First Regiment, Arkansas Infantry, Confederate Army; captured at Oak Hills, Mo., in 1861 and imprisoned for two years; resumed the practice of law in Fayetteville, Ark., in 1865; solicitor general of the State of Arkansas; presidential elector on the Democratic ticket of Tilden and Hendricks in 1876; elected as a Democrat to the United States Senate and served from March 4, 1879, to March 3, 1885; declined to be a candidate for reelection in 1884; resumed the practice of law in Fayetteville, Ark., and died there on October 17, 1906; interment in the Walker family cemetery.

WALKER, James Peter, a Representative from Missouri; born near Memphis, Lauderdale County, Tenn., March 14, 1851; attended the public schools and the boys' college at Durhamville, Tenn.; employed in early youth as a clerk in a country store; moved to Missouri in 1867 and settled near Kennett, Dunkin County; engaged in agricultural pursuits; moved to Point Pleasant, New Madrid County, in 1871 and engaged in transportation on the Mississippi River; engaged in the dry-goods business at Dexter, Mo., in 1876, and later, in 1882, in the buying and selling of grain; delegate to the Democratic National Convention at Cincinnati in 1880, which nominated Hancock and English; unsuccessful candidate for the Democratic nomination for Congress in 1884· elected as a Democrat to the Fiftieth and Fifty-first Congresses and served from March 4, 1887, until his death; had been unanimously nominated as the Democratic candidate for reelection to the Fifty-second Congress on the day of his death; died July 19, 1890, in Dexter, Stoddard County, Mo.; interment in Dexter Cemetery.

WALKER, John (brother of Francis Walker), a Delegate and a Senator from Virginia; born at "Castle Hill," near Cobham, Albemarle County, Va., February 13, 1744; received private schooling and was graduated from William and Mary College, Williamsburg, Va., in 1764; moved to "Belvoir," Albemarle County, and engaged in planting; commissioned with his father to make special terms with the Indians at Fort Pitt, Pa., so as to retain their friendship during the Revolutionary War; with the rank of colonel served as extra aide to Gen. George Washington in 1777; was commended by George Washington to Patrick Henry for confidential service; studied law; was admitted to the bar and commenced the practice of law; Member of the Continental Congress in 1780; appointed to the United States Senate to fill the vacancy caused by the death of William Grayson and served from March 31 to November 9, 1790, when a successor was elected; was not a candidate for reelection; resumed his agricultural pursuits; died near Madison Mills, Orange County, Va., December 2, 1809; interment in the family cemetery on the Belvoir estate near Cismont, Va.

WALKER, John Randall, a Representative from Georgia; born near Blackshear, Pierce County, Ga., February 23, 1874; attended the public schools; was graduated from Jasper (Fla.) Normal College in 1895 and from the law department of the University of Georgia at Athens in 1898; was admitted to the bar and commenced practice in Valdosta, Lowndes County, Ga., in 1900; member of the State house of representatives in 1907 and 1908; elected as a Democrat to the Sixty-third, Sixty-fourth, and Sixty-fifth Congresses (March 4, 1913–March 3, 1919); unsuccessful candidate for renomination in 1918; moved to Eldorado, Ark., and resumed the practice of law; returned to Blackshear, Ga., where he died; interment in the Walker family burying grounds in Pierce County, Ga.

WALKER, John Williams (father of Percy Walker), a Senator from Alabama; born in Amelia County, Va., August 12, 1783; attended a private school; was graduated from Princeton College in 1806; studied law; was admitted to the bar in 1810 and commenced practice in Huntsville, Ala.; member of the Territorial house of representatives in 1817 and served as speaker; president of the State constitutional convention in 1819; upon the admission of Alabama as a State into the Union was elected as a Democrat to the United States Senate and served from December 14, 1819, to December 12, 1822, when he resigned; died in Huntsville, Madison County, Ala., April 23, 1823; interment in Maple Hill Cemetery.

WALKER, Joseph Henry, a Representative from Massachusetts; born in Boston, Mass., December 21, 1829; moved with his parents to Hopkinton in 1830 and to Worcester, Mass., in 1843; attended the public schools; engaged in the manufacture of boots and shoes; established the business of manufacturing leather in Chicago, Ill., in 1868; member of the common council of Worcester 1852–1854; served in the State house of representatives in 1879, 1880, and 1887; elected as a Republican to the Fifty-first and to the four succeeding Congresses (March 4,

1889–March 3, 1899); unsuccessful candidate for reelection in 1898 to the Fifty-sixth Congress; resumed his former business pursuits; died in Worcester, Mass., April 3, 1907; interment in the Rural Cemetery.

WALKER, Lewis Leavell, a Representative from Kentucky; born in Lancaster, Garrard County, Ky., February 15, 1873; attended Lancaster (Ky.) Academy, Garrard College, Lancaster, Ky., and Central University, Richmond, Ky.; studied law; was admitted to the bar in 1894 and commenced practice in Lancaster, Ky.; also engaged in banking; prosecuting attorney of Garrard County in 1901; city attorney of Lancaster 1907–1910; served as trustee of the University of Kentucky, at Lexington, Ky., 1908–1915; judge of the thirteenth judicial district of Kentucky in 1910 and 1911; elected as a Republican to the Seventy-first Congress (March 4, 1929–March 3, 1931); was not a candidate for renomination in 1930; continued the practice of law in Lancaster, Ky., until his death there on June 30, 1944; interment in Lancaster Cemetery.

WALKER, Percy (son of John Williams Walker), a Representative from Alabama; born in Huntsville, Madison County, Ala., in December 1812; completed preparatory studies; was graduated from the medical department of the University of Pennsylvania at Philadelphia in 1835; commenced the practice of medicine in Mobile, Ala.; served in the campaign against the Creek Indians; studied law; was admitted to the bar and practiced in Mobile; State's attorney for the sixth judicial district; member of the State house of representatives in 1839, 1847, and 1853; elected by the American Party to the Thirty-fourth Congress (March 4, 1855–March 3, 1857); declined to be a candidate for renomination in 1856; died in Mobile, Ala., December 31, 1880; interment in Magnolia Cemetery.

WALKER, Robert James, a Senator from Mississippi; born in Northumberland, Pa., July 23, 1801; was graduated from the University of Pennsylvania at Philadelphia in 1819; studied law; was admitted to the bar in 1821 and commenced practice in Pittsburgh, Pa., the following year; chairman of the Pennsylvania State Democratic committee in 1823; moved to Natchez, Miss., in 1826 and continued the practice of law; elected judge of the State supreme court about 1828, but declined; elected as a Democrat to the United States Senate; reelected, and served from March 4, 1835, to March 5, 1845, when he resigned; Secretary of the Treasury in the Cabinet of President James K. Polk and served from March 6, 1845, until his resignation on March 6, 1849; declined the mission to China tendered by President Pierce in 1853; resumed the practice of law; was appointed Governor of Kansas April 10, 1857, but resigned in December 1857; United States financial agent to Europe in 1863 and 1864; again engaged in the practice of law at Washington, D. C., and died there November 11, 1869; interment in Oak Hill Cemetery.

WALKER, Robert Jarvis Cochran, a Representative from Pennsylvania; born near West Chester, Chester County, Pa., October 20, 1838; attended school at East Hampton and old Cambridge, Mass.; was graduated from the law department of Harvard University in 1858; was admitted to the bar in 1859 and commenced practice in Philadelphia; director of the first school district of Pennsylvania; twice elected to the council of Philadelphia; purchased the Saturday Evening Post in 1874 and was its editor for a short time; engaged in the production of oil; moved to Williamsport, Lycoming County, Pa., in 1875 and engaged in land, lumber, and coal developments; elected as a Republican to the Forty-seventh Congress (March 4, 1881–March 3, 1883); declined to be a candidate for renomi-

nation in 1882 but his name was presented by his friends; returned to Philadelphia in 1890 and became a manufacturing chemist; died in Philadelphia, Pa., December 19, 1903; interment in Laurel Hill Cemetery.

WALKER, Walter, a Senator from Colorado; born in Marion, Crittenden County, Ky., April 3, 1883; attended the public and high schools; moved to Grand Junction, Colo., in 1903 and engaged in the daily newspaper business, later becoming editor, manager, and chief owner of the Grand Junction Daily Sentinel; delegate to the Democratic National Conventions in 1924, 1928, 1932, and 1936; chairman of the Democratic State committee 1930–1932; appointed as a Democrat to the United States Senate to fill the vacancy caused by the death of Charles W. Waterman and served from September 26, 1932, until December 6, 1932, when a duly elected successor qualified; unsuccessful candidate for election in 1932 to fill this vacancy; resumed former activities as publisher of the Daily Sentinel in Grand Junction, Colo., until his death; presidential elector on the Democratic ticket of Roosevelt and Garner in 1936; died in Grand Junction, Colo., October 8, 1956; interment in Orchard Mesa Cemetery.

WALKER, William Adams, a Representative from New York; born in New Hampshire June 5, 1805; attended the common schools and Northampton Law School; was admitted to the bar but never engaged in the practice of law; moved to New York City in 1832; appointed principal of a public school in New York City; county superintendent of common schools 1843–1847; member of the board of aldermen in 1846; defeated for reelection in 1847; served as commissioner of jurors until elected to Congress; elected as a Democrat to the Thirty-third Congress (March 4, 1853–March 3, 1855); declined to be a candidate for renomination in 1854 to the Thirty-fourth Congress; defeated for election to the board of aldermen in 1857; died in Irvington, West Chester County, N. Y., December 18, 1861; interment in Sleepy Hollow Cemetery, Tarrytown, N. Y.

WALL, Garret Dorset (father of James Walter Wall), a Senator from New Jersey; born in Middletown, N. J., March 10, 1783; completed preparatory studies; studied law; was licensed as an attorney in 1804 and as a counselor in 1807 and commenced practice in Burlington, N. J.; served in the War of 1812 and commanded a volunteer regiment from Trenton; clerk of the State supreme court 1812–1817; quartermaster general of the State 1815–1837; member of the State general assembly in 1827; United States district attorney for New Jersey in 1829; elected Governor of New Jersey in 1829, but declined to serve; elected as a Democrat to the United States Senate and served from March 4, 1835, to March 3, 1841; unsuccessful candidate for reelection; judge of the Court of Errors and Appeals of New Jersey from 1848 until his death in Burlington, N. J., November 22, 1850; interment in the churchyard of St. Mary's Church.

WALL, James Walter (son of Garret Dorset Wall), a Senator from New Jersey; born in Trenton, N. J., May 26, 1820; was tutored privately in Flushing, N. Y., and was graduated from Princeton College in 1838; studied law; was admitted to the bar in 1841 and commenced practice in Trenton; served as commissioner in bankruptcy; moved to Burlington, N. J., in 1847; mayor of the city in 1850; was tendered the Democratic nomination for Congress in 1850, but declined; unsuccessful candidate for election in 1854 to the Thirty-fourth Congress; elected as a Democrat to the United States Senate to fill the vacancy caused by the death of John R. Thompson and served from January 14 to March 3, 1863; unsuccessful candidate for reelection; resumed the practice of law in Burlington; also engaged in literary pursuits; in 1869 moved to Elizabeth, N. J., where he died June 9, 1872; interment in the churchyard of St. Mary's Protestant Episcopal Church, Burlington, N. J.

WALL, William, a Representative from New York; born in Philadelphia, Pa., March 20, 1800; received a limited schooling; learned the trade of ropemaking and worked as a journeyman; became a manufacturer of rope; moved to Kings County, Long Island, N. Y., in 1822; trustee, commissioner of highways, supervisor, member of the board of finance, and commissioner of waterworks of Williamsburg (now a part of New York City); mayor of Williamsburg in 1853; was one of the incorporators and for a number of years president of the Williamsburg Savings Bank; also one of the founders of the Williamsburg City Bank (later the First National Bank) and of the Williamsburg Dispensary; elected as a Republican to the Thirty-seventh Congress (March 4, 1861–March 3, 1863); declined to be a candidate for renomination in 1862; delegate to the Loyalist Convention at Philadelphia in 1866; retired to private life; died in Brooklyn, N. Y., April 20, 1872; interment in Greenwood Cemetery.

WALLACE, Alexander Stuart, a Representative from South Carolina; born near York, S. C., December 30, 1810; received a limited schooling; engaged in planting in his native county; member of the State house of representatives 1854–1858; successfully contested as a Republican the election of William D. Simpson to the Forty-first Congress; reelected to the Forty-second, Forty-third, and Forty-fourth Congresses and served from May 27, 1870, to March 3, 1877; unsuccessful candidate for reelection in 1876 to the Forty-fifth Congress; engaged in agricultural pursuits until his death near York, S. C., June 27, 1893; interment in Rose Hill Cemetery, York, S. C.

WALLACE, Daniel, a Representative from South Carolina; born near Laurens, S. C., May 9, 1801; received a limited schooling; moved to Union County in 1833; major general of State militia; studied law; was admitted to the bar and practiced in Union and Jonesville, Union County, S. C.; also engaged in agricultural pursuits; member of the State house of representatives 1844–1848; elected as a Whig to the Thirtieth Congress to fill the vacancy caused by the death of James A. Black; reelected to the Thirty-first and Thirty-second Congresses and served from June 12, 1848, to March 3, 1853; resumed agricultural pursuits; died in Jonesville, S. C., May 13, 1859; interment in Old Presbyterian Cemetery, Union, S. C.

WALLACE, David, a Representative from Indiana; born near Lewistown, Mifflin County, Pa., April 4, 1799; moved with his parents to Brookville, Ind., in 1817; was graduated from the United States Military Academy at West Point, N. Y., in 1821, and was appointed assistant professor of mathematics in that institution, resigning in 1822; returned to Brookville, Ind.; studied law; was admitted to the bar in 1824 and practiced; member of the State house of representatives 1828–1830; moved to Covington, Ind., in 1830 and continued the practice of law; Lieutenant Governor of Indiana 1831–1837; Governor 1837–1840; settled in Indianapolis and continued the practice of law; elected as a Whig to the Twenty-seventh Congress (March 4, 1841–March 3, 1843); unsuccessful candidate for reelection to the Twenty-eighth Congress; resumed the practice of law in Indianapolis; delegate to the State constitutional convention in 1850; judge of the court of common pleas of Marion County from 1856 until his death in Indianapolis, Ind., September 4, 1859; interment in Crown Hill Cemetery.

WALLACE, Henry Agard, a Vice President of the United States; born on a farm near Orient, Adair County, Iowa, October

7, 1888; attended the public schools and West Des Moines (Iowa) High School; was graduated from Iowa State College at Ames in 1910; served on the editorial staff of Wallace's Farmer, Des Moines, Iowa, 1910–1924 and was editor 1924–1929; editor of Wallaces' Farmer and Iowa Homestead 1929–1933; experimented with breeding high-yielding strains of corn 1913–1933; in 1915 devised the first corn-hog ratio charts indicating probable course of markets; author of many publications on agriculture; chairman of the Agricultural Round Table, Williamstown, Mass., in 1927; delegate to the International Conference of Agricultural Economics held at South Devon, England, in 1929; delegate to the Democratic National Conventions at Chicago in 1940 and 1944; appointed Secretary of Agriculture in the Cabinet of President Franklin D. Roosevelt on March 4, 1933, and served until September 2, 1940, when he resigned, having been nominated for Vice President; elected on November 5, 1940, as Vice President of the United States on the Democratic ticket with President Franklin D. Roosevelt, and was inaugurated January 20, 1941, for the term ending January 20, 1945; was not a candidate for reelection as Vice President in 1944; appointed Secretary of Commerce and served from March 2, 1945, to September 20, 1946; unsuccessful Progressive candidate for election as President of the United States in 1948; resumed his farming interests; is a resident of South Salem, N. Y.

WALLACE, James M., a Representative from Pennsylvania; born in Hanover Township, Lancaster (now Dauphin) County, Pa., in 1750; pursued preparatory studies in Philadelphia; participated in the Revolution as a member of Capt. James Roger's, Col. Timothy Green's, and Capt. William Brown's companies, and at the close of the war was major of a battalion of Associators; commanded a company of rangers in defense of the frontier in 1779; became major of the Dauphin County Militia in 1796; one of the commissioners of the county 1799–1801; member of the State house of representatives 1806–1810; elected to the Fourteenth Congress to fill the vacancy caused by the declination of Amos Ellmaker to serve; reelected to the Fifteenth and Sixteenth Congresses and served from October 10, 1815, to March 3, 1821; declined to be a candidate for renomination and retired to his farm; died near Hummelstown, West Hanover Township, Dauphin County, Pa., December 17, 1823; interment in the Old Derry Church Graveyard, Derry (now Hershey), Pa.

WALLACE, John Winfield, a Representative from Pennsylvania; born near Beaver Falls, Beaver County, Pa., December 20, 1818; attended Darlington (Pa.) Academy, where he afterward taught; was graduated from Jefferson Medical College at Philadelphia in 1846 and commenced the practice of medicine in Darlington; moved to New Castle, Pa., in 1850; held several local offices; elected as a Republican to the Thirty-seventh Congress (March 4, 1861–March 3, 1863); unsuccessful candidate for reelection in 1862 to the Thirty-eighth Congress; during the Civil War served as paymaster in the Union Army; several times a delegate to State and National conventions; presidential elector on the Republican ticket of Grant and Wilson in 1872 and of Harrison and Morton in 1888; elected as a Republican to the Forty-fourth Congress (March 4, 1875–March 3, 1877); was not a candidate for renomination in 1876; resumed the practice of medicine in New Castle, Lawrence County, Pa., where he died June 24, 1889; interment in Grandview Cemetery, near Beaver Falls, Beaver County, Pa.

WALLACE, Jonathan Hasson, a Representative from Ohio; born in St. Clair Township, Columbiana County, Ohio, October 31, 1824; attended the common schools, and was graduated from Washington College (now Washington and Jefferson University), Washington, Pa., in 1844; studied law; was admitted to the bar and commenced the practice of law in New Lisbon, Ohio; prosecuting attorney of Columbiana County in 1851 and 1853; successfully contested as a Democrat the election of William McKinley, Jr., to the Forty-eighth Congress and served from May 27, 1884, to March 3, 1885; unsuccessful candidate for reelection in 1884 to the Forty-ninth Congress; appointed judge of the court of common pleas by Governor Hoadley on March 5, 1885, to fill a vacancy and served one year; continued the practice of law until his death in Lisbon, Ohio, October 28, 1892; interment in Lisbon Cemetery.

WALLACE, Nathaniel Dick, a Representative from Louisiana; born in Columbia, Maury County, Tenn., October 27, 1845; attended the common schools, and was graduated from Trinity College, Dublin, Ireland, in 1865; returned to the United States in 1867, and engaged in the commission business at New Orleans, La., in 1878; twice elected president of the New Orleans Produce Exchange; active in manufacturing enterprises; elected as a Democrat to the Forty-ninth Congress to fill the vacancy caused by the death of Michael Hahn and served from December 9, 1886, to March 3, 1887; was not a candidate for renomination in 1886 to the Fiftieth Congress; president of Consumers Ice Co., New Orleans, from 1886 until his death July 16, 1894, in Kenilworth, near Asheville, N. C., where he had gone for the summer; interment in Metairie Cemetery, New Orleans, La.

WALLACE, Robert Minor, a Representative from Arkansas; born in New London, Union County, Ark., August 6, 1856; attended the common schools, and was graduated from Arizona Seminary, Arizona, La., in 1876; studied law; was admitted to the bar at Little Rock, Ark., in 1879 and commenced the practice of law in El Dorado, Ark.; member of the State house of representatives in 1881 and 1882; United States post-office inspector 1887–1891; prosecuting attorney for the thirteenth judicial circuit of Arkansas in 1891 and 1892; assistant United States attorney in 1894; elected as a Democrat to the Fifty-eighth and to the three succeeding Congresses (March 4, 1903–March 3, 1911); unsuccessful candidate for renomination in 1910 to the Sixty-second Congress; resumed the practice of his profession at Hot Springs and Little Rock and also engaged in lecturing for the Chautauqua and for the Anti-Saloon League; moved to Magnolia, Ark., where he died on November 9, 1942; interment in Magnolia Cemetery.

WALLACE, Rodney, a Representative from Massachusetts; born in New Ipswich, Hillsborough County, N. H., December 21, 1823; attended the common schools; engaged in the manufacture of paper; was a member of the select council of Fitchburg, Mass., in 1864, 1865, and 1867; served in the State house of representatives in 1873; member of the Governor's council 1880–1882; elected as a Republican to the Fifty-first Congress (March 4, 1889–March 3, 1891); was not a candidate for renomination in 1890 to the Fifty-second Congress; again engaged in the manufacture of paper; died in Fitchburg, Worcester County, Mass., on February 27, 1903; interment in Laurel Hill Cemetery.

WALLACE, William Andrew, a Senator from Pennsylvania; born in Huntingdon, Pa., November 28, 1827; moved with his parents to Clearfield, Pa., in 1836; attended the local schools; studied law; was admitted to the bar before he was twenty years of age and commenced practice in Clearfield; also taught school in Clearfield; delegate to the Democratic State convention in 1861; member of the State senate 1863–1875 and served as speaker in 1871; delegate to the Democratic National Conven-

tions in 1864, 1872, 1876, 1880, 1884, and 1892, and was chairman of the Pennsylvania delegation in 1872 and 1876; chairman of the Democratic State central committee 1865–1868; member of the commission to suggest amendments to the constitution of Pennsylvania in 1874; elected as a Democrat to the United States Senate and served from March 4, 1875, to March 3, 1881; unsuccessful candidate for reelection in 1880; resumed the practice of law in Clearfield; again a member of the State senate 1882–1887; became interested in the development of the bituminous coal fields of the Clearfield region, with offices in New York City, N. Y.; also served as president of the Beech Creek Railroad; died in New York City, May 22, 1896; interment in Hillcrest Cemetery, Clearfield, Pa.

WALLACE, William Copeland, a Representative from New York; born in Brooklyn, N. Y., May 21, 1856; was graduated from Adelphi Academy, Brooklyn, N. Y., in 1873, from Wesleyan University, Middletown, Conn., in 1876, and from the law department of Columbia College (now Columbia University), New York City, in 1878; commenced the practice of law in New York City; assistant United States attorney for the southern district of New York 1880–1883; appointed judge advocate general on the staff of Governor Morton in 1894; elected as a Republican to the Fifty-first Congress (March 4, 1889–March 3, 1891); unsuccessful candidate for reelection in 1890 to the Fifty-second Congress; delegate to several Republican National Conventions; resumed the practice of his profession in Brooklyn, N. Y.; also engaged extensively in banking; died at his summer home in Warwick, Orange County, N. Y., September 4, 1901; interment in Greenwood Cemetery, Brooklyn, N. Y.

WALLACE, William Henson, a Delegate from the Territories of Washington and Idaho; born in Troy, Miami County, Ohio, July 19, 1811; attended the common schools of Indiana; studied law; was admitted to the bar and practiced; moved to Iowa in 1837; appointed colonel of State troops; appointed receiver of public money at Fairfield, Iowa; moved to the Territory of Washington in 1853; member of the Territorial council in 1855 and 1856 and served as president of the council; appointed Governor of the Territory of Washington in 1861, but did not qualify, having been elected as a Republican a Delegate from the Territory of Washington to the Thirty-seventh Congress (March 4, 1861–March 3, 1863); was appointed as the first Governor of the Territory of Idaho in 1863; elected as a Republican a Delegate from the Territory of Idaho to the Thirty-eighth Congress and served from February 1, 1864, to March 3, 1865; died in Steilacoom, Pierce County, Wash., on February 7, 1879; interment in Fort Steilacoom Cemetery.

WALLEY, Samuel Hurd, a Representative from Massachusetts; born in Boston, Mass., August 31, 1805; attended the common schools and Phillips Academy, Andover, Mass.; attended Yale College in 1822 and was graduated from Harvard University in 1826; studied law; was admitted to the Suffolk bar in 1831 and practiced in Boston and Roxbury; engaged in banking; treasurer of the Vermont Central Railroad; promoter and first treasurer of the Wisconsin Central Railroad; member of the State house of representatives in 1836 and 1840–1846, serving as speaker 1844–1846; corporate member of the American Board of Commissioners of Foreign Missions 1848–1867; elected as a Whig to the Thirty-third Congress (March 4, 1853–March 3, 1855); unsuccessful candidate for reelection in 1854 to the Thirty-fourth Congress; unsuccessful Whig candidate for Governor of Massachusetts in 1855; president of the Revere National Bank; died at Nantasket Beach, Plymouth County, Mass., on August 27, 1877; interment in Mount Auburn Cemetery, Cambridge, Mass.

WALLGREN, Monrad Charles, a Representative and a Senator from Washington; born in Des Moines, Iowa, April 17, 1891; moved with his parents to Galveston, Tex., in 1894 and to Everett, Wash., in 1901; attended the public schools and business college of Everett, Wash.; graduated from Washington State School of Optometry at Spokane in 1914; engaged in the retail jewelry and optical business 1915–1932; during the First World War enlisted as a private in the Coast Artillery Corps of the Washington National Guard on February 5, 1917; commissioned as a second lieutenant at the Coast Artillery School at Fort Monroe, Va., and served in the Sixty-third Regiment, Coast Artillery Corps, and later as instructor in heavy field artillery at the coast guard defenses of Puget Sound, Wash., until discharged March 12, 1919; adjutant of the Third Battalion of the Washington National Guard in 1921 and 1922; elected as a Democrat to the Seventy-third and to the three succeeding Congresses and served from March 4, 1933, until his resignation, effective December 19, 1940; elected November 5, 1940, to the United States Senate for the term commencing January 3, 1941; subsequently appointed to the United States Senate to fill the vacancy caused by the resignation of Lewis B. Schwellenbach in the term ending January 3, 1941, and served from December 19, 1940, to January 9, 1945, when he resigned; Governor of the State of Washington from January 1945 to January 1949; appointed as a member of the Federal Power Commission in 1949 for the term ending in June 1954, but resigned October 1, 1951; engaged in citrus growing in the Coachella Valley, Calif., and the development of uranium claims at Twenty-nine Palms, Calif.; died in Olympia Wash., September 18, 1961, due to injuries suffered in an automobile accident; interment in Evergreen Cemetery, Everett, Wash.

WALLHAUSER, George Marvin, a Representative from New Jersey; born in Newark, Essex County, N. J., February 10, 1900; attended the grade schools and graduated from Barringer High School, Newark, N. J., in 1918; during the First World War served as a hospital corpsman in the United States Naval Reserve 1918–1922; graduated from the University of Pennsylvania in 1922; associated with United States Realty & Investment Co., Newark, N. J., in 1928, serving on board of directors and as treasurer and vice president in 1940; enrolled in Columbia University in 1941 and completed courses in real-estate appraising in 1942; chairman, Maplewood (N. J.) Planning Board, 1946–1954; trustee, Maplewood Community Service; member, Maplewood Township Committee, 1954–1957; member, National Board of Directors, Family Service Association of America; member, Essex County Highway Right-of-Way Commission, 1957–1959; director, Maplewood Savings & Loan Association and Maplewood Bank & Trust Co.; member, board of trustees, Maplewood Library, 1957–1959; elected as a Republican to the Eighty-sixth Congress (January 3, 1959–January 3, 1961). *Reelected to the Eighty-seventh Congress.*

WALLIN, Samuel, a Representative from New York; born in Easton, Northampton County, Pa., July 31, 1856; moved with his parents to Amsterdam, Montgomery County, N. Y., in 1864; attended the public schools and Amsterdam Academy; engaged in the manufacture of carpets and rugs; served as alderman 1889–1892; mayor of Amsterdam in 1901 and 1902; elected as a Republican to the Sixty-third Congress (March 4, 1913–March 3, 1915); was not a candidate for renomination in 1914; resumed his business activities in Amsterdam, N. Y., where he died December 1, 1917; interment in Green Hill Cemetery.

WALLING, Ansel Tracy, a Representative from Ohio; born in Otsego County, N. Y., January 10, 1824; moved to Erie County, Pa., where he attended a local academy; studied medicine and practiced a short time; learned the art of printing; moved to Ohio in 1843 and engaged in newspaper work; clerk of the State legislature in 1851 and 1852; studied law; was admitted to the bar in 1852 and practiced; moved to Keokuk, Iowa, and was editor of the Daily Times 1855–1858; delegate to the Democratic National Convention at Cincinnati in 1856; returned to Ohio in 1861 and settled in Circleville, Pickaway County, where he resumed the practice of law; member of the State senate in 1865; served in the State house of representatives in 1867 and was elected speaker pro tempore; elected as a Democrat to the Forty-fourth Congress (March 4, 1875–March 3, 1877); unsuccessful candidate for renomination; again engaged in the practice of law; died in Circleville, Ohio, June 22, 1896; interment in Forest Cemetery.

WALLS, Josiah Thomas, a Representative from Florida; born in Winchester, Frederick County, Va., December 30, 1842; was of the Negro race; received a limited schooling; engaged in truck farming; moved to Florida; delegate to the State constitutional convention in 1868; served in the State senate 1869–1872; presented credentials as a Member-elect to the Forty-second Congress and served from March 4, 1871, to January 29, 1873, when he was succeeded by Silas L. Niblack, who contested his election; elected as a Republican to the Forty-third Congress (March 4, 1873–March 3, 1875); presented credentials as a Member-elect to the Forty-fourth Congress and served from March 4, 1875, to April 19, 1876, when he was succeeded by Jesse J. Finley, who contested his election; resumed his occupation as truck farmer; died in Tallahassee, Fla., May 5, 1905; interment in the Negro Cemetery.

WALN, Robert, a Representative from Pennsylvania; born in Philadelphia, Pa., February 22, 1765; received a limited schooling; engaged in mercantile pursuits and in East India and China trade; member of the State legislature for several years; member of the city council of Philadelphia and served as president of the select council; elected as a Federalist to the Fifth Congress to fill the vacancy caused by the death of John Swanwick; reelected to the Sixth Congress and served from December 3, 1798, to March 3, 1801; became interested in the operation of ironworks and during the War of 1812 erected a cotton factory in Trenton; served as president of the Philadelphia Insurance Co. and as a trustee of the University of Pennsylvania; died in Philadelphia, Pa., January 24, 1836; interment in Friends' Arch Street Burial Ground.

WALSH, Allan Bartholomew, a Representative from New Jersey; born in Trenton, N. J., August 29, 1874; attended Immaculate Conception Parochial School and the public schools of Trenton; employed with an electrical concern in Trenton 1900–1911; member of the State house of assembly in 1910 and 1911; secretary of the Mercer County Board of Taxation in 1912 and 1913; elected as a Democrat to the Sixty-third Congress (March 4, 1913–March 3, 1915); unsuccessful candidate for reelection in 1914 to the Sixty-fourth Congress; engaged in the real-estate brokerage business; served as an internal-revenue agent in New Jersey and Wisconsin from 1915 to 1920, when he resigned to engage in private practice as a consultant and adviser in the field of federal laws; again appointed as an internal-revenue agent and served from 1933 until 1940, when he retired due to physical disability and resided in Palm Beach, Fla.; died in New York City, N. Y., August 5, 1953; interment in Our Lady of Lourdes Cemetery, Trenton, N. J.

WALSH, Arthur, a Senator from New Jersey; born in Newark, Essex County, N. J., February 26, 1896; educated in the public schools, by private tutor, and at the New York University

School of Commerce at New York City; began his career as a recording violinist for Thomas A. Edison in 1915 and later held executive positions with the Edison enterprises; during the First World War served as a sergeant in the United States Marine Corps 1917–1919; lieutenant in the United States Naval Reserve 1929–1932; colonel in the New Jersey National Guard 1941–1943; member of the New Jersey Workmen's Compensation Investigating Commission in 1932 and 1933; served as New Jersey director of the Federal Housing Administration in 1934 and 1935 and as deputy and later as assistant administrator at Washington, D. C., 1935–1938; delegate to the Democratic National Convention at Philadelphia in 1936; presidential elector in 1940 on the Democratic ticket of Roosevelt and Wallace; member of the New Jersey State Board of Regents in 1941 and 1942; member of the board of directors of the American-Russian Chamber of Commerce in 1943; commissioner of the Port of New York Authority in 1943; appointed as a Democrat to the United States Senate to fill the vacancy caused by the death of W. Warren Barbour and served from November 26, 1943, to December 7, 1944, when a duly elected successor qualified; was not a candidate for election to the vacancy in 1944; resumed his former business pursuits; died in a hospital in New York City, N. Y., December 13, 1947; interment in Gate of Heaven Cemetery, East Hanover, N. J.

WALSH, David Ignatius, a Senator from Massachusetts; born in Leominster, Worcester County, Mass., November 11, 1872; attended the public schools; was graduated from Holy Cross College, Worcester, Mass., in 1893 and from Boston University Law School in 1897; was admitted to the bar and commenced practice at Fitchburg, Mass., in 1897, later practicing in Boston; member of the State house of representatives in 1900 and 1901; Lieutenant Governor of Massachusetts in 1913 and Governor in 1914 and 1915; delegate at large to all Democratic National Conventions from 1912 to 1944; delegate at large to the Massachusetts constitutional convention in 1917 and 1918; elected as a Democrat to the United States Senate and served from March 4, 1919, to March 3, 1925; unsuccessful candidate for reelection in 1924; resumed the practice of law in Boston; elected to the United States Senate in 1926 to fill the vacancy caused by the death of Henry Cabot Lodge and took his seat December 6, 1926; reelected in 1928, 1934, and again in 1940 for the term ending January 3, 1947; unsuccessful candidate for reelection in 1946; retired from political activities and resided in Clinton, Mass., until his death; died at Brighton, Mass., June 11, 1947; interment in St. John's Cemetery, Lancaster, Mass.

WALSH, James Joseph, a Representative from New York; born in New York City May 22, 1858; attended the public schools and St. James' Parochial School; was graduated from Manhattan College in 1877 and from the law department of Columbia University, both in New York City, in 1879; was admitted to the bar in 1880 and commenced practice in New York City; inspector of common schools 1889–1894; presented credentials as a Democratic Member-elect to the Fifty-fourth Congress and served from March 4, 1895, to June 2, 1896, when he was succeeded by John M. Mitchell, who had contested his election; resumed the practice of law in New York City; appointed city magistrate in 1905, which office he held until his death in New York City on May 8, 1909; interment in Calvary Cemetery, Long Island City, N. Y.

WALSH, John Richard, a Representative from Indiana; born in Martinsville, Morgan County, Ind., May 22, 1913; attended the public schools; was graduated from Indiana University Law School in 1934; was admitted to the bar July 27, 1934, and engaged in the practice of law in Martinsville, Ind., until 1941;

Morgan County attorney in 1935 and 1936; deputy attorney general of Indiana in 1941; during World War II served in the United States Army with the Thirty-fifth Infantry Division from May 18, 1942, until discharged as a technical sergeant June 15, 1943; in 1943 continued the practice of law in Anderson, Ind.; chief deputy prosecuting attorney of Madison County, Ind., in 1945 and 1946; probate commissioner for Madison County Circuit Court in 1948; elected as a Democrat to the Eighty-first Congress (January 3, 1949–January 3, 1951); unsuccessful candidate for reelection in 1950 to the Eighty-second Congress and for election in 1954 to the Eighty-fourth Congress; member of board of directors and secretary-treasurer, State Security Life Insurance Co., Anderson, Ind., 1953–1958; secretary of state of Indiana from December 1, 1958, to November 30, 1960; is a resident of Anderson, Ind.

WALSH, Joseph, a Representative from Massachusetts; born in Boston (Brighton), Mass., December 16, 1875; attended public schools in Falmouth, Mass., and Boston University Law School; was admitted to the bar in 1906 and practiced in New Bedford; served as a fish culturist and clerk in the United States Bureau of Fisheries at Woods Hole, Mass., 1900–1905; also engaged in newspaper reporting in Boston and New Bedford, Mass.; member of the State house of representatives in 1905; presidential elector on the Republican ticket of Taft and Butler in 1912; elected as a Republican to the Sixty-fourth and to the three succeeding Congresses and served from March 4, 1915, to August 2, 1922, when he resigned to accept a judicial position; appointed August 2, 1922, as a justice of the superior court of Massachusetts, in which capacity he served until his death in New Bedford, Mass., January 13, 1946; interment in St. Mary's Cemetery.

WALSH, Michael, a Representative from New York; born in Youghal, near Cork, Ireland, March 8, 1810; completed preparatory studies; was graduated from Trinity College, Dublin, Ireland; immigrated to the United States and settled in Baltimore, Md.; learned the trade of lithographic printer; moved to New York City; member of the State assembly in 1839; in 1843 established the Subterranean, which he stopped after two years when convicted for the publication of a libel; elected as a member of the State assembly in 1846 and again in 1848; elected as a Democrat to the Thirty-third Congress (March 4, 1853–March 3, 1855); unsuccessful candidate for reelection in 1854 to the Thirty-fourth Congress; after his term in Congress was employed as a newspaper reporter; died in New York City March 18, 1859; interment in Greenwood Cemetery, Brooklyn, N. Y.

WALSH, Patrick, a Senator from Georgia; born in Ballingarry, County Limerick, Ireland, January 1, 1840; immigrated to the United States in 1852 with his parents, who settled in Charleston, S. C.; became a journeyman printer in 1857; attended night schools, Charleston High School, and Georgetown University, Washington, D. C., 1859–1861; returned to Charleston and entered the State military service; moved to Augusta, Ga., in 1862 and for thirty-two years was connected with the press of that city, most of the time as manager and editor of the Augusta Chronicle; treasurer and general manager of the Southern Associated Press: member of the city council of Augusta in 1870; member of the State house of representatives in 1872, 1874, and 1876; delegate at large to the Democratic National Convention at Chicago in 1884, which nominated Grover Cleveland, of New York, for President and Thomas A. Hendricks, of Indiana, for Vice President; member of the Democratic National Executive Committee for four years; member of the World's Columbian Exposition Commission at Chicago in 1893; appointed as a Democrat to the United States Senate to fill the vacancy caused by the death of Alfred H. Colquitt; subsequently elected and served from April 2, 1894, to March 3, 1895; unsuccessful candidate for renomination in 1894; resumed his newspaper interests; mayor of Augusta 1897–1899; died in Augusta, Ga., March 19, 1899; interment in the City Cemetery.

WALSH, Thomas James, a Senator from Montana; born at Two Rivers, Manitowoc County, Wis., June 12, 1859; attended the public schools, and was graduated from the law department of the University of Wisconsin at Madison in 1884; taught school; was admitted to the bar in 1884 and commenced practice at Redfield, Spink County, S. Dak.; moved to Helena, Mont., in 1890 and continued the practice of law; unsuccessful candidate for election in 1906 to the Sixtieth Congress; delegate to the Democratic National Conventions in 1908, 1912, 1916, 1920, and 1924; permanent chairman of the Democratic National Conventions at New York City in 1924 and at Chicago in 1932; elected as a Democrat to the United States Senate in 1912; reelected in 1918, 1924, and 1930 and served from March 4, 1913, until his death on March 2, 1933, on a train near Wilson, N. C., while en route to Washington, D. C., to accept the appointment as Attorney General in President Franklin D. Roosevelt's Cabinet; funeral services were held in the Chamber of the United States Senate; interment in Resurrection Cemetery, Helena, Mont.

WALSH, Thomas Yates, a Representative from Maryland; born in Baltimore, Md., in 1809; completed preparatory studies and attended St. Mary's College at Baltimore 1821–1824; studied law; was admitted to the bar on July 30, 1832, and commenced practice in Baltimore; member of the city council in 1847 and 1848; elected as a Whig to the Thirty-second Congress (March 4, 1851–March 3, 1853); unsuccessful candidate for reelection in 1852 to the Thirty-third Congress; resumed the practice of law; died in Baltimore, Md., January 20, 1865; interment in St. Paul's Protestant Episcopal Cemetery.

WALSH, William, a Representative from Maryland; born near Tullamore, County Kings, Ireland, May 11, 1828; attended a local school; immigrated to the United States in 1842 and settled in Virginia; was graduated from Mount St. Mary's College, Emmitsburg, Md.; studied law; was admitted to the bar in Virginia in 1850 and commenced practice in Cumberland, Md., in 1852; presidential elector on the Democratic ticket of Breckinridge and Lane in 1860 and of Greeley and Brown in 1872; member of the State constitutional convention in 1867; elected as a Democrat to the Forty-fourth and Forty-fifth Congresses (March 4, 1875–March 3, 1879); declined to be a candidate for renomination in 1878; resumed the practice of law; died in Cumberland, Md., May 17, 1892; interment in St. Patrick's Cemetery.

WALTER, Francis Eugene, a Representative from Pennsylvania; born in Easton, Northampton County, Pa., May 26, 1894; attended the public schools, preparatory school at Princeton, N. J., Lehigh University, Bethlehem, Pa., and George Washington University and Georgetown University, Washington, D. C.; during both World Wars served in the air service of the United States Navy; was admitted to the bar in 1919 and commenced practice in Easton, Pa.; director of the Broad Street Trust Co., Philadelphia, Pa., and of the Easton National Bank, Easton, Pa.; solicitor of Northampton County, Pa., 1928–1933; trustee of the Easton (Pa.) Hospital; delegate to the Democratic National Convention at Houston in 1928; elected as a Democrat to the Seventy-third and to the thirteen succeeding Congresses (March 4, 1933–January 3, 1961). *Reelected to the Eighty-seventh Congress.*

WALTERS, Anderson Howell, a Representative from Pennsylvania; born in Johnstown, Cambria County, Pa., May 18, 1862; attended the public schools, and was graduated from Johnstown

High School in 1878; employed as a telegrapher and clerk with the Pennsylvania Railroad Co. 1878–1880; entered the service of the Johnstown Water Co. and the Johnstown Gas Co. in 1881 and was assistant superintendent of these companies in 1889 and general manager and secretary 1895–1902; delegate to the Republican State conventions in 1890, 1892, 1898, and 1904; delegate to the Republican National Convention at St. Louis in 1896, which nominated William McKinley, of Ohio, for President, and Garret A. Hobart, of New Jersey, for Vice President; chairman of the Republican city committee 1896–1899; member of the Republican State committee 1898–1902; member of the Johnstown City Council 1900–1904; editor and proprietor of the Johnstown Tribune from 1902 until his death; elected as a member of the board of trustees of the Johnstown Savings Bank in 1907; elected as a Republican to the Sixty-third Congress (March 4, 1913–March 3, 1915); was not a candidate for renomination; elected to the Sixty-sixth and Sixty-seventh Congresses (March 4, 1919–March 3, 1923); was not a candidate for renomination; elected to the Sixty-ninth Congress (March 4, 1925–March 3, 1927); was not a candidate for renomination; died in Johnstown, Pa., December 7, 1927; interment in Grandview Cemetery.

WALTHALL, Edward Cary, a Senator from Mississippi; born in Richmond, Va., April 4, 1831; pursued an academic course and attended St. Thomas Hall, Holly Springs, Miss.; studied law; was admitted to the bar in 1852 and commenced practice in Coffeeville, Miss.; elected district attorney for the tenth judicial district of Mississippi in 1856 and reelected in 1859; during the Civil War entered the Confederate Army as a lieutenant in the Fifteenth Mississippi Regiment and was subsequently elected lieutenant colonel; elected colonel of the Twenty-ninth Mississippi Regiment in the spring of 1862 and was promoted to brigadier general in December 1862 and to major general in June 1864; resumed the practice of law in Coffeeville; moved to Grenada, Miss., in 1871 and continued the practice of law until March 1885; appointed as a Democrat to the United States Senate to fill the vacancy caused by the resignation of Lucius Q. C. Lamar; was subsequently elected to fill the vacancy; reelected in 1889 and served from March 9, 1885, to January 24, 1894, when he resigned; was again elected for the term beginning March 4, 1895, and served from that date until his death in Washington, D. C., April 21, 1898; funeral services were held in the Chamber of the United States Senate; interment in Holly Springs Cemetery, Holly Springs, Miss.

WALTON, Charles Wesley, a Representative from Maine; born in Mexico, Oxford County, Maine, December 9, 1819; attended the common schools and was instructed at home and by private tutors; studied law; was admitted to the bar in Oxford, Maine, in 1841 and commenced practice in Mexico, Maine, in 1843; also practiced law in Dixfield, Maine; attorney for Oxford County 1847–1851; moved to Auburn, Maine, in 1855 and continued the practice of law; attorney for Androscoggin County 1857–1860; elected as a Republican to the Thirty-seventh Congress and served from March 4, 1861, to May 26, 1862, when he resigned to accept a judicial appointment; associate justice of the State supreme court 1862–1897; was not a candidate for reappointment; retired from public life and resided in Portland, Cumberland County, Maine, until his death on January 24, 1900; interment in Evergreen Cemetery.

WALTON, Eliakim Persons, a Representative from Vermont; born in Montpelier, Vt., February 17, 1812; attended the common schools; apprenticed to a printer; studied law, but did not practice; engaged in journalism and compiling; editor of "Walton's Vermont Register"; organizer and first president of the Editors and Publishers' Association, holding the office of president for more than twenty years; after the retirement of his father in 1853 was sole proprietor of the Watchman until 1868; served in the State house of representatives in 1853; elected as a Republican to the Thirty-fifth, Thirty-sixth, and Thirty-seventh Congresses (March 4, 1857–March 3, 1863); declined to be a candidate for reelection and returned to his editorial and literary labors; delegate to the Republican National Convention at Baltimore in 1864; member of the State constitutional convention in 1870; served in the State senate in 1875 and 1877; trustee of the University of Vermont and of the State agricultural college 1875–1887; president of the Vermont Historical Society 1876–1890; died in Montpelier, Washington County, Vt., December 19, 1890; interment in Green Mount Cemetery.

WALTON, George (brother of John Walton and cousin of Matthew Walton), a Delegate and a Senator from Georgia; born near Farmville, Cumberland County, Va., in 1750; attended the common schools; moved to Savannah, Ga., in 1769; studied law; was admitted to the bar 1774 and commenced practice in Savannah, Ga.; secretary of the Provincial Congress in 1775 and a member of the committee of intelligence; member of the council of safety in 1775 and later president of that body; member of the State house of representatives; Member of the Continental Congress 1776–1778, 1780–1781, 1787–1788; a signer of the Declaration of Independence; served in the Revolutionary War and was captured at Savannah; colonel in the First Georgia Battalion; Governor of Georgia in 1779; commissioner to treat with the Indians at Easton, Pa., and to negotiate a treaty with the Cherokees in Tennessee in 1783; chief justice of Georgia 1783–1786; member of the Augusta Board of Commissioners in 1784 and 1785; represented Georgia in the settlement of the boundary line between South Carolina and Georgia in 1786; elected as a delegate to the convention to frame the Federal Constitution in 1787, but declined; again Governor of Georgia in 1789; was appointed first judge of the superior courts of the eastern judicial circuit in 1790; chairman of the reception committee and delivered the address of welcome upon the occasion of President Washington's visit to Augusta in 1791; again chief justice of Georgia in 1793; appointed to the United States Senate to fill the vacancy caused by the resignation of James Jackson and served from November 16, 1795, to February 20, 1796, when a successor was elected; trustee of Richmond Academy and of the University of Georgia; moved to Augusta; appointed judge of the middle circuit of Georgia and served from 1799 until his death at his home, "Meadow Garden," near Augusta, Richmond County, Ga., February 2, 1804; interment in Rosney Cemetery; reinterment in 1848 beneath the monument in front of the courthouse on Greene Street, Augusta, Ga.

WALTON, John (brother of George Walton and cousin of Matthew Walton), a Delegate from Georgia; born in Virginia in 1738; became a planter near Augusta, Ga.; delegate from St. Paul Parish to the Provincial Congress at Savannah, Ga., in 1775; elected to the Continental Congress February 26, 1778; signed the Articles of Confederation on behalf of Georgia on July 24, 1778; held office of surveyor of Richmond County for several years; died at New Savannah, Ga., in 1783.

WALTON, Matthew (cousin of George Walton and John Walton), a Representative from Kentucky; received a limited schooling; member of the conventions held in Danville in 1785 and 1787; member of the first State constitutional convention in 1792; member of the State house of representatives in 1792, 1795, and 1808; presidential elector on the Democratic ticket of Madison and Clinton in 1809; elected to the Eighth and Ninth Congresses (March 4, 1803–March 3, 1807); died in Springfield, Ky., January 18, 1819; interment in Springfield Cemetery.

WALTON, William Bell, a Representative from New Mexico; born in Altoona, Blair County, Pa., January 23, 1871; attended the public schools, and South Jersey Institute, Bridgeton, N. J.; moved to New Mexico in 1891; studied law; was admitted to the bar in 1893 and commenced practice at Deming, N. Mex.; member of the State house of representatives in 1901 and 1902; clerk of Grant County 1903–1906; delegate to the Democratic National Convention at Denver in 1908; chairman of the State Democratic central committee in 1910; member of the State constitutional convention in 1911; served in the State senate 1912–1916; elected as a Democrat to the Sixty-fifth Congress (March 4, 1917–March 3, 1919); did not seek renomination, having become a candidate for Senator; unsuccessful candidate for election to the United States Senate in 1918; resumed the practice of law in Silver City, N. Mex.; elected district attorney of the sixth judicial district November 2, 1926; reelected in 1928 and served until 1932; continued the practice of law until 1934, when he retired from active pursuits; died in Silver City, N. Mex., April 14, 1939; interment in the Masonic Cemetery.

WALWORTH, Reuben Hyde, a Representative from New York; born in Bozrah, Conn., October 26, 1788; moved to New York with his parents, who settled on a farm near Hoosick in 1796; attended the common schools; taught school; studied law; was admitted to the bar in 1809 and commenced practice in Plattsburgh in 1810; master in chancery and circuit judge in 1811; served in the War of 1812; aide-de-camp to Gen. Benjamin Mooers and division judge advocate with rank of colonel; elected as a Democrat to the Seventeenth Congress (March 4, 1821–March 3, 1823); was not a candidate for renomination in 1822; judge of the fourth judicial district of New York 1823–1828; moved to Saratoga Springs, Saratoga County, N. Y., in October 1828; chancellor of the State of New York from 1828 to 1848, when the office of chancellor was abolished; unsuccessful candidate for election as Governor in 1848; appointed as an Associate Justice of the United States Supreme Court by President Tyler in 1844, but was not confirmed by the Senate; died in Saratoga Springs, N. Y., November 27, 1867; interment in Greenridge Cemetery.

WAMPLER, Fred, a Representative from Indiana; born in Carriers Mills, Saline County, Ill., October 15, 1909; moved with parents to Terre Haute, Ind., in 1911 and attended the public schools; graduated from Indiana State Teachers College in 1931 and in 1940; athletic director at Bluffton (Ohio) High School 1931–1933; terminal manager for Norwalk Truck Line, South Bend, Ind., in 1935 and 1936; athletic director, Washington Court House, Ohio, in 1936 and 1937; head football coach at Gerstmeyer Tech, Terre Haute, Ind., in 1937 and 1938; during World War II served from January 1944 as a gunnery officer in the United States Navy, with service in the Pacific Theater until discharged as a lieutenant in 1946; served as commanding officer, Naval Reserve, activating training center at Terre Haute, Ind., 1946–1949; sports director for station WTHI, Terre Haute, Ind., 1947–1949; during the Korean conflict was recalled to active duty as executive officer aboard troop transport and served from January 1950 to March 1954; promoted to commander, United States Naval Reserve, May 11, 1960; elected as a Democrat to the Eighty-sixth Congress (January 3, 1959–January 3, 1961); unsuccessful candidate for reelection in 1960 to the Eighty-seventh Congress; appointed to the Indiana-Illinois Wabash Valley Interstate Commission on March 13, 1961; is a resident of Terre Haute, Ind.

WAMPLER, William Creed, a Representative from Virginia; born in Pennington Gap, Lee County, Va., April 21, 1926; attended the public schools in Bristol, Va.; during World War II enlisted on May 21, 1943, in the United States Navy as a seaman and served for twenty-seven months until discharged September 29, 1945; member of the Naval Reserve, V–6; resumed his education and was graduated from Virginia Polytechnic Institute, Blacksburg, Va., in 1948 and studied law at the University of Virginia 1948–1950; reporter, Bristol, Va.–Tennessean in 1950 and 1951; reporter, editorial writer, Big Stone Gap (Va.) Post 1951; reporter, copy editor, Bristol Herald Courier in 1951 and 1952; member of board of visitors of Emory and Henry College, Emory, Va.; Republican assistant campaign manager for Ninth Congressional District elections in 1948; president of the Young Republican Federation of Virginia in 1950 and served as keynote speaker and permanent chairman of the Ninth District Republican Convention the same year; elected as a Republican to the Eighty-third Congress (January 3, 1953–January 3, 1955); was an unsuccessful candidate for reelection in 1954 to the Eighty-fourth Congress; with Atomic Energy Commission from January 1955 to March 1956; unsuccessful candidate for election in 1956 to the Eighty-fifth Congress; vice president and general manager of Wampler Brothers Furniture Co., Bristol, Va., where he resides.

WANGER, Irving Price, a Representative from Pennsylvania; born in North Coventry, Chester County, Pa., March 5, 1852; attended the public schools of North Coventry and Pottstown, and Hill School in Pottstown; deputy prothonotary of Chester County in 1871; commenced the study of law at Norristown in 1872; deputy prothonotary of Montgomery County 1873–1875; was admitted to the bar December 18, 1875, and commenced the practice of law in Norristown, Pa.; elected burgess of Norristown in 1878; delegate to the Republican National Convention at Chicago in 1880, which nominated the presidential ticket of Garfield and Arthur; elected district attorney of Montgomery County in 1880 and again in 1886; served as chairman of the Montgomery County Republican committee in 1889; unsuccessful candidate for election in 1890 to the Fifty-second Congress; elected as a Republican to the Fifty-third and to the eight succeeding Congresses (March 4, 1893–March 3, 1911); unsuccessful candidate for reelection in 1910 to the Sixty-second Congress; lived for a short time in Wilmington, Del.; resumed the practice of his profession in Media and Norristown, Pa., in 1920; died in Norristown, Pa., January 14, 1940; interment in Mount Zion Cemetery, Pottstown, Pa.

WARBURTON, Herbert Birchby, a Representative from Delaware; born in Wilmington, New Castle County, Del., September 21, 1916; attended the public schools of Wilmington, Del., and Reading, Pa.; graduated from Wilmington High School in February 1934, from University of Delaware, Newark, Del., in June 1938, and from Dickinson School of Law, Carlisle, Pa., in June 1941; took reserve officers training course at University of Delaware and commissioned a second lieutenant; began active Army duty as first lieutenant of the One Hundred and Twenty-second Antiaircraft Battalion in September 1941 and assigned to several posts throughout the United States; graduated from Command and General Staff School, Fort Leavenworth, Kans., in September 1945 and served on temporary duty with Military Intelligence at the Pentagon, Washington, D. C.; assigned to Central Intelligence Command Center, Fort George G. Meade, Md., as a student and became battalion commander in October 1945; was relieved from active duty as a major in December 1945; was admitted to the Delaware bar in absentia in April 1942 and began the practice of law in Wilmington, Del., in January 1946; city solicitor 1949–1952; elected as a Republican to the Eighty-third Congress (January 3, 1953–January 3, 1955); was not a candidate for renomination in 1954 but was an unsuccessful candidate for election to the United States Senate; appointed

special assistant to Secretary of Labor James P. Mitchell March 2, 1955, and served until November 7, 1957; general counsel, Post Office Department, from November 7, 1957, to January 20, 1961; investment broker; resides in Bethesda, Md.

WARBURTON, Stanton, a Representative from Washington; was born in Sullivan County, Pa., April 13, 1865; moved to Iowa with his parents, who settled in Cherokee in 1868; attended the public schools; was graduated from Cherokee (Iowa) High School in 1884 and from Coe College, Cedar Rapids, Iowa, in 1888; moved to Tacoma, Wash., in 1888; studied law; was admitted to the bar in 1889 and commenced practice in Tacoma; member of the State senate 1896–1904; elected as a Republican to the Sixty-second Congress (March 4, 1911–March 3, 1913); unsuccessful candidate for reelection in 1912 to the Sixty-third Congress; resumed the practice of law in Tacoma, Wash.; died in Boston, Mass., December 24, 1926, while undergoing medical treatment; interment in Mountain View Burial Park, Tacoma, Wash.

WARD, Aaron (uncle of Elijah Ward), a Representative from New York; was born in Sing Sing (now Ossining), N. Y., on July 5, 1790; completed preparatory studies in Mount Pleasant Academy; served in the War of 1812 as lieutenant and captain in the Twenty-ninth Infantry; studied law; was admitted to the bar and commenced practice at Sing Sing; district attorney for Westchester County; served in the State militia as colonel, brigadier general, and major general; elected as a Democrat to the Nineteenth and Twentieth Congresses (March 4, 1825–March 3, 1829); was not a candidate for reelection; elected to the Twenty-second, Twenty-third, and Twenty-fourth Congresses (March 4, 1831–March 3, 1837); was not a candidate for reelection to the Twenty-fifth Congress; elected to the Twenty-seventh Congress (March 4, 1841–March 3, 1843); unsuccessful candidate for reelection to the Twenty-eighth Congress; delegate to the State constitutional convention in 1846; unsuccessful Democratic candidate for secretary of state in 1855; trustee of Mount Pleasant Academy; died at the home of his son-in-law in Georgetown, D. C., March 2, 1867; interment in Dale Cemetery, Ossining, N. Y.

WARD, Andrew Harrison, a Representative from Kentucky; was born near Cynthiana, Harrison County, Ky., on January 3, 1815; attended the county schools and Transylvania University, Lexington, Ky.; clerk on a steamboat on the Tombigbee River for several years; studied law; was admitted to the bar in 1844 and commenced practice in Cynthiana, Ky.; city attorney of Cynthiana in 1860; unsuccessful candidate for election to the State house of representatives in 1861; member of the State house of representatives 1863–1865; unsuccessful candidate for election in 1864 to the Thirty-ninth Congress; elected as a Democrat to the Thirty-ninth Congress to fill the vacancy caused by the resignation of Green Clay Smith and served from December 3, 1866, to March 3, 1867; was not a candidate for renomination in 1866; resumed the practice of law and subsequently became president of the National Bank of Cynthiana; died in Cynthiana, Ky., April 16, 1904; interment in Battle Grove Cemetery.

WARD, Artemas, a Delegate and a Representative from Massachusetts; born in Shrewsbury, Mass., November 26, 1727; attended the common schools and was prepared for college by a private tutor; was graduated from Harvard College in 1748; justice of the peace in 1752; a representative in the general assembly many terms and served in the executive council; lieutenant colonel in the provincial army during the French and Indian War; appointed brigadier general by the provincial congress of Massachusetts on October 27, 1774, and was made commander in chief of the Massachusetts forces on May 19, 1775; appointed by the Continental Congress as major general on June 17, 1775, and was, until the arrival of General Washington, in command of the forces besieging Boston; chief justice of the court of common pleas of Worcester County in 1776 and 1777; president of the Massachusetts Executive Council 1777–1779; member of the State house of representatives 1779–1785, serving as speaker in 1785; Member of the Continental Congress from January 1780 to May 1782, when he resigned; elected as a Federalist to the Second and Third Congresses (March 4, 1791–March 3, 1795); his home in Shrewsbury, Mass., is owned by Harvard University and maintained as a permanent memorial to him; died in Shrewsbury, Mass., October 28, 1800; interment in Mountain View Cemetery.

WARD, Artemas, Jr. (son of the preceding), a Representative from Massachusetts; born in Shrewsbury, Mass., January 9, 1762; was graduated from Harvard University in 1783; studied law; was admitted to the bar in 1783 and commenced the practice of law in Weston; member of the State house of representatives 1796–1800 and again in 1811; moved to Charlestown in 1800; member of the board of overseers of Harvard University 1810–1844; elected as a Federalist to the Thirteenth and Fourteenth Congresses (March 4, 1813–March 3, 1817); served in the State senate in 1818 and 1819; member of the State constitutional convention in 1820; chief justice of the court of common pleas from 1820 to 1839; died in Boston, Mass., October 7, 1847.

WARD, Charles Bonnell, a Representative from New York; born in Newark, N. J., April 27, 1879; attended the public schools and was graduated from Pennsylvania Military College at Chester in 1899; moved to New York and settled in Debruce, Sullivan County, in 1903; engaged in agricultural pursuits; editor and owner of the Liberty Register at Liberty, N. Y., 1910–1928; elected as a Republican to the Sixty-fourth and to the four succeeding Congresses (March 4, 1915–March 3, 1925); declined to be a candidate for reelection in 1924 to the Sixty-ninth Congress; resumed agricultural pursuits; owner and operator of the Debruce Inn Club until his death; died at Liberty, N. Y., May 27, 1946; interment in Mount Pleasant Cemetery, Newark, N. J.

WARD, David Jenkins, a Representative from Maryland; born in Salisbury, Wicomico County, Md., September 17, 1871; attended the public schools; engaged in agricultural pursuits, lumbering, and the mercantile business at Salisbury, Md.; member of the State house of delegates 1915–1917; chairman of the Democratic State central committee of Wicomico County 1918–1926; member of the State senate 1926–1934 and from 1938 until his resignation in 1939; elected as a Democrat to the Seventy-sixth Congress to fill the vacancy caused by the resignation of T. Alan Goldsborough; reelected to the Seventy-seventh and Seventy-eighth Congresses and served from June 6, 1939, to January 3, 1945; was an unsuccessful candidate for renomination in 1944; resumed the mercantile, lumber, and real-estate businesses; died in Salisbury, Md., February 18, 1961; interment in Parsons Cemetery.

WARD, Elijah (nephew of Aaron Ward), a Representative from New York; born in Sing Sing (now Ossining), N. Y., September 16, 1816; pursued classical studies; engaged in commercial pursuits in New York City and at the same time attended the law department of New York University; was admitted to the bar in 1843 and commenced practice in New York City; judge advocate general of the State 1853–1855; delegate to the Democratic National Convention at Cincinnati in 1856, which nominated James Buchanan, of Pennsylvania, for President, and John C. Breckinridge, of Kentucky, for Vice President; elected as a Democrat to the Thirty-fifth Congress (March 4, 1857–March 3, 1859); unsuccessful candidate for reelection in 1858 to the Thirty-sixth Congress; elected to the Thirty-seventh and Thirty-eighth Congresses (March 4, 1861–March 3, 1865); unsuccessful candidate for reelection in 1864 to the Thirty-ninth Congress; traveled in Europe for two years, after which he resumed the practice of law in New York City; elected to the Forty-fourth Congress (March 4, 1875–March 3, 1877); unsuccessful candidate for reelection in 1876 to the Forty-fifth Congress; died in Roslyn, Nassau County, N. Y., February 7, 1882; interment in Woodlawn Cemetery, New York City, N. Y.

WARD, Hallett Sydney, a Representative from North Carolina; born near Gatesville, Gates County, N. C., August 31, 1870; attended the public schools; was graduated from the law department of the University of North Carolina at Chapel Hill in 1893; was admitted to the bar the same year and commenced practice in Winton, N. C.; member of the State senate in 1899 and 1901; mayor of Plymouth, N. C., in 1902 and 1903; solicitor of the first judicial district of North Carolina 1904–1910; moved to Washington, N. C., in November 1904 and engaged in the practice of law; elected as a Democrat to the Sixty-seventh and Sixty-eighth Congresses (March 4, 1921–March 3, 1925); declined to be a candidate for renomination in 1924; resumed the practice of law; served in the State senate in 1931; died in Washington, N. C., March 31, 1956; interment in Oakdale Cemetery.

WARD, Hamilton, a Representative from New York; born in Salisbury, Herkimer County, N. Y., July 3, 1829; attended the common schools and was privately tutored; studied law; was admitted to the bar and commenced practice in Phillipsville (now Belmont), N. Y., in 1851; district attorney of Allegany County 1856–1859 and 1862–1865; appointed in 1862 by the Governor as commissioner to raise and equip troops for the Civil War; elected as a Republican to the Thirty-ninth, Fortieth, and Forty-first Congresses (March 4, 1865–March 3, 1871); was not a candidate for renomination in 1870; delegate to nearly all State conventions from 1858 to 1890; attorney general of New York in 1880 and 1881; member of the State constitutional commission in 1890; appointed and subsequently elected justice of the State supreme court and served from 1891 until his death in Belmont, Allegany County, N. Y., December 28, 1898; interment in Forest Hill Cemetery.

WARD, James Hugh, a Representative from Illinois; born in Chicago, Ill., November 30, 1853; attended the public schools of Chicago, and was graduated from the University of Notre Dame, Indiana, in 1873; attended the Union College of Law in Chicago, and was graduated in 1876; was admitted to the bar in July 1876, and practiced; was elected supervisor of the town of West Chicago in 1879; was presidential elector on the Democratic ticket of Cleveland and Hendricks in 1884; elected as a Democrat to the Forty-ninth Congress (March 4, 1885–March 3, 1887); did not seek renomination in 1886; resumed the practice of his profession in Chicago, Cook County, Ill. where he died on August 15, 1916; interment in Calvary Cemetery.

WARD, Jasper Delos, a Representative from Illinois; born in Java, Wyoming County, N. Y., February 1, 1829; attended Allegheny College, Meadville, Pa., in 1849 and 1850; studied law; was admitted to the bar in 1852 and commenced practice in Chicago, Ill.; member of the board of aldermen of Chicago in 1855, 1856, 1859, and 1860; during the Civil War enlisted in the Western Engineers Regiment in 1861 and served for about eight months; member of the State senate 1862–1870; elected as a Republican to the Forty-third Congress (March 4, 1873–March 3, 1875); unsuccessful candidate for reelection in 1874 to the Forty-fourth Congress; United States attorney for the northern district of Illinois 1875–1877; moved to Colorado in 1877 and settled in Leadville; appointed by Governor Pitkin as judge of the fifth judicial district of Colorado and served from March 5, 1881, to January 3, 1882, declining to be a candidate for election to the same office; moved to Denver, Colo., and resumed the practice of law; died in Denver, Colo., August 6, 1902; interment in Fairmount Cemetery.

WARD, Jonathan, a Representative from New York; born in the town of Eastchester, N. Y., September 21, 1768; received a limited schooling; assessor of Eastchester in 1791; sheriff of Westchester County 1802–1806; served in the State senate in 1807; member of the council of appointment in 1809; elected as a Democrat to the Fourteenth Congress (March 4, 1815–March 3, 1817); member of the State constitutional convention in 1821; surrogate of Westchester County 1828–1840; died in the town of Eastchester, N. Y., September 28, 1842.

WARD, Marcus Lawrence, a Representative from New Jersey; born in Newark, N. J., November 9, 1812; received a limited schooling; engaged in candle manufacturing; delegate to the Republican National Convention at Chicago in 1860 and at Baltimore in 1864; unsuccessful candidate for Governor of New Jersey in 1862; presidential elector on the Republican ticket of Lincoln and Johnson in 1864; elected Governor in 1865 and served from January 16, 1866, to January 18, 1869; was chairman of the Republican National Committee in 1866; elected as a Republican to the Forty-third Congress (March 4, 1873–March 3, 1875); unsuccessful candidate for reelection in 1874 to the Forty-fourth Congress; died in Newark, N. J., April 25, 1884; interment in Mount Pleasant Cemetery.

WARD, Matthias, a Senator from Texas; born in Elbert County, Ga., October 13, 1805; was raised in Madison County, Ala.; received a college education in Huntsville, Ala.; taught school two years; studied law; moved to the Republic of Texas in 1836 and settled in Bowie, Montague County, and subsequently in Clarksville, Red River County, in 1845; engaged in trading; served a number of years in the Congress of the Republic of Texas; moved to Jefferson, Marion County, Tex.; served in the State senate; delegate to the Democratic National Conventions in 1852 and 1856; delegate to the Democratic State convention at Austin in 1856 and served as president; appointed as a Democrat to the United States Senate to fill the vacancy caused by the death of J. Pinckney Henderson and served from September 27, 1858, to December 5, 1859, when a successor was elected; died at Warm Springs, near Raleigh, N. C., October 5, 1861; interment in the Old City Cemetery, Nashville, Tenn.

WARD, Samuel, a Delegate from Rhode Island; born in Newport, R. I., May 27, 1725; educated privately; settled in Westerly, R. I., in 1745; engaged in agricultural pursuits; member of the general assembly 1756–1759; one of the founders of Rhode Island College (now Brown University), Providence, R. I., in 1756; chief justice of Rhode Island in 1761 and 1762; Governor under the royal charter in 1762, 1763, and 1765–1767; trustee of Brown University 1764–1776; was an active patriot and a friend and correspondent of Washington and Franklin; Member of the Continental Congress 1774–1776; died in Philadelphia, Pa., March 26, 1776; interment in the churchyard of the First Baptist Church, Philadelphia, Pa.; reinterment in the Old Cemetery, Newport, R. I., in 1860.

WARD, Thomas, a Representative from New Jersey; born in Newark, N. J., about 1759; completed preparatory studies; studied law; was admitted to the bar and commenced practice in Newark, N. J.; served as captain and major during the Whisky Insurrection in 1794; sheriff of Essex County, N. J., in 1797; elected one of the judges of the Essex County Court in 1804 and reelected in 1809; member of the legislative council in 1808 and 1809; elected as a Democrat to the Thirteenth and Fourteenth Congresses (March 4, 1813–March 3, 1817); was senior officer of the New Jersey Cavalry at the time of his death in Newark, N. J., March 4, 1842; interment in the churchyard of the First Presbyterian Church.

WARD, Thomas Bayless, a Representative from Indiana; born in Marysville, Union County, Ohio, April 27, 1835; moved with his parents to La Fayette, Ind., in May 1836; attended Wabash College, Crawfordsville, Ind., and was graduated from Miami University, Oxford, Ohio, in June 1855; clerk of the city of La Fayette in 1855 and 1856; studied law; was admitted to the bar in 1857 and commenced the practice of his profession in La Fayette, Ind.; city attorney in 1859 and 1860; mayor of La Fayette 1861–1865; judge of the superior court of Tippecanoe County, Ind., 1875–1880; elected as a Democrat to the Forty-eighth and Forty-ninth Congresses (March 4, 1883–March 3, 1887); was not a candidate for renomination in 1886 to the Fiftieth Congress; resumed the practice of his profession in La Fayette, Tippecanoe County, Ind., where he died January 1, 1892; interment in Springvale Cemetery.

WARD, William, a Representative from Pennsylvania; born in Philadelphia, Pa., January 1, 1837; attended Girard College, Philadelphia, Pa.; learned the art of printing in the office of the Delaware County Republican, Chester, Pa.; studied law; was admitted to the bar in August 1859 and commenced practice in Chester; also engaged in the land business and banking; member of the city council of Chester and city solicitor; elected as a Republican to the Forty-fifth, Forty-sixth, and Forty-seventh Congresses (March 4, 1877–March 3, 1883); was not a candidate for renomination in 1882; resumed the practice of his profession and his former business pursuits in Chester, Pa., where he died February 27, 1895; interment in the Rural Cemetery.

WARD, William Lukens, a Representative from New York; born in Pemberwick, town of Greenwich, Fairfield County, Conn., September 2, 1856; moved to Port Chester, N. Y., with his parents in 1863; attended Friends Seminary, New York City, and the school of mines of Columbia College, New York City (class of 1878); engaged in the manufacture of bolts, nuts, and rivets in Port Chester, N. Y.; presidential elector on the Republican ticket of McKinley and Hobart in 1896; delegate to many Republican State and National Conventions 1896–1933; chairman of the Republican State committee for several years; elected as Republican to the Fifty-fifth Congress (March 4, 1897–March 3, 1899); resumed his former manufacturing pursuits in Port Chester, Westchester County, N. Y.; member of the Republican National Committee 1904–1912; died in a hospital in New York City, N. Y., July 16, 1933; interment in the family mausoleum in Kensico Cemetery, Valhalla, N. Y.

WARD, William Thomas, a Representative from Kentucky; born in Amelia County, Va., August 9, 1808; attended the common schools and St. Mary's College, near Lebanon, Ky.; studied law; was admitted to the bar and commenced practice in Greensburg, Ky.; served in the Mexican War as major of the Fourth Kentucky Volunteers in 1847 and 1848; member of the State house of representatives in 1850; elected as a Whig to the Thirty-second Congress (March 4, 1851–March 3, 1853); was not a candidate for renomination in 1852; commissioned brigadier general in 1861 and served throughout the Civil War; brevetted major general in 1865; resumed the practice of law in Louisville, Ky., where he died October 12, 1878; interment in Cave Hill Cemetery.

WARDWELL, Daniel, a Representative from New York; born in Bristol, R. I., May 28, 1791; was graduated from Brown University, Providence, R. I., in 1811; studied law; was admitted to the bar and commenced practice in Rome, N. Y.; moved to Mannsville, N. Y., in 1814; judge of the court of common pleas for Jefferson County, N. Y.; elected to the State assembly 1825–1828; was elected as a Republican to the Twenty-second, Twenty-third, and Twenty-fourth Congresses (March 4, 1831–March 3, 1837); was not a candidate for renomination in 1836; returned to Rome, N. Y., and resumed the practice of law; died in Rome, Oneida County, N. Y., March 27, 1878; interment in Maplewood Cemetery, Mannsville, Jefferson County, N. Y.

WARE, Nicholas, a Senator from Georgia; born in Caroline County, Va., in 1769; moved with his parents to Edgefield, S. C., and a few years later to Augusta, Ga.; received a thorough English education; studied medicine for a time; then studied law in Augusta and at Litchfield (Conn.) Law School; was admitted to the bar and commenced practice in Augusta; member of the State house of representatives 1808–1811, 1814, and 1815; mayor of Augusta 1819–1821; elected to the United States Senate to fill the vacancy caused by the resignation of Freeman Walker and served from November 10, 1821, until his death in New York City September 7, 1824; interment under the annex of Grace Church.

WARE, Orie S., a Representative from Kentucky; born in Peach Grove, Pendleton County, Ky., May 11, 1882; attended the public schools of Covington, Ky.; was graduated from the private academy of Prof. George W. Dunlap, at Independence, Ky., in 1899, and from the law department of the University of Cincinnati at Cincinnati, Ohio, in 1903; was admitted to the bar in 1903 and commenced practice in Covington, Ky.; also engaged in banking, serving as a director of the First National Bank and Trust Co.; delegate to all Democratic State conventions 1910–1939; served as postmaster of Covington from September 1, 1914, to July 1, 1921; Commonwealth attorney of the sixteenth judicial circuit, serving from January 1, 1922, to February 1, 1927, when he resigned; elected as a Democrat to the Seventieth Congress (March 4, 1927–March 3, 1929); was not a candidate for renomination in 1928 to the Seventy-first Congress; resumed the practice of law in Covington and resides in Kenton County, near Independence, Ky.

WARFIELD, Henry Ridgely, a Representative from Maryland; born in Anne Arundel County, Md., September 14, 1774; completed preparatory studies; held several local offices; settled in Frederick, Md.; elected as a Federalist to the Sixteenth, Seventeenth, and Eighteenth Congresses (March 4, 1819–March 3, 1825); died in Frederick, Md., March 18, 1839.

WARNER, Adoniram Judson, a Representative from Ohio; born in Wales, near Buffalo, N. Y., January 13, 1834; moved with his parents to Wisconsin at the age of eleven; attended school in Beloit, Wis., and New York Central College, McGrawville, N. Y.; principal of Lewistown (Pa.) Academy, superintendent of the public schools of Mifflin County, and principal of Mercer Union School, Pennsylvania, 1856–1861; during the Civil War was commissioned captain in the Tenth Pennsylvania Reserves July 21, 1861, lieutenant colonel May 14, 1862, colonel April 25, 1863, and colonel of the Veteran Reserve Corps November 15, 1863; brevetted brigadier general March 13, 1865,

"for gallant and meritorious services during the war," and was mustered out November 17, 1865; studied law; was admitted to the bar in Indianapolis, Ind., in 1865 but never practiced; at the conclusion of the war returned to Pennsylvania, and in 1866 moved to Marietta, Ohio; engaged in the oil, coal, and railroad businesses; elected as a Democrat to the Forty-sixth Congress (March 4, 1879–March 3, 1881); unsuccessful candidate for reelection in 1880 to the Forty-seventh Congress; elected to the Forty-eighth and Forty-ninth Congresses (March 4, 1883–March 3, 1887); was not a candidate for reelection in 1886; delegate to the Democratic National Convention at Chicago in 1896; engaged in street railway construction in the District of Columbia and in railroad construction in Ohio; from about 1898 until six months before his death engaged in transportation and power development in Georgia; died in Marietta, Washington County, Ohio, August 12, 1910; interment in Oak Grove Cemetery.

WARNER, Hiram, a Representative from Georgia; born in Williamsburg, Hampshire County, Mass., on October 29, 1802; received a good common-school training and acquired some knowledge of the classics; in 1819 moved to Georgia and taught school for three years; studied law; was admitted to the bar and commenced practice in Knoxville, Crawford County, Ga., in 1825; served in the general assembly 1828–1831; declined reelection; moved to Talbotton in 1830 and continued the practice of his profession; moved to Greenville; elected judge of the State superior court and served from 1833 to 1840; judge of the State supreme court from 1846 to 1853, when he resigned; elected as a Democrat to the Thirty-fourth Congress (March 4, 1855–March 3, 1857); declined to be a candidate for reelection in 1856; appointed by Governor Jenkins as judge of the Coweta Circuit Court and served from 1865 to 1867, when he was appointed chief justice of the State supreme court; was subsequently elected and served until 1880, when he resigned; died in Atlanta, Ga., June 30, 1881; interment in Town Cemetery, Greenville, Meriwether County, Ga.

WARNER, John De Witt, a Representative from New York; born on a farm in the town of Reading, Schuyler County, N. Y., October 30, 1851; moved with his parents to Big Stream (later Glenora), N. Y., and in 1860 settled in Rock Stream, Yates County, N. Y.; completed preparatory studies; attended the district schools and Starkey Seminary, Eddytown, N. Y.; was graduated from Cornell University in 1872; edited the Ithaca Daily Leader for a few months; professor in the Ithaca and Albany Academies for four years; was graduated from Albany Law School in 1876; was admitted to the bar the same year and commenced practice in New York City in 1877; elected as a Democrat to the Fifty-second and Fifty-third Congresses (March 4, 1891–March 3, 1895); declined to be a candidate for renomination in 1894; resumed the practice of law in New York City; president of the Art Commission of New York City 1902–1905; was president of the American Free Trade League 1905–1909; special counsel for the dock department to advise on terminal work in 1911 and 1912; served on the commission to revise the New York banking laws in 1913; also engaged in literary pursuits; engaged in the practice of law until his death in New York City May 27, 1925; interment in Rock Stream Cemetery, Rock Stream, Yates County, N. Y.

WARNER, Levi (brother of Samuel Larkin Warner), a Representative from Connecticut; born in Wethersfield, Hartford County, Conn., October 10, 1831; completed preparatory studies; attended the law department of Yale College, New Haven, Conn., and Dane Law School, Cambridge, Mass.; was admitted to the bar in 1859 and commenced practice in

Fairfield County, Conn.; moved to Norwalk, Conn., in 1858 and continued the practice of law; elected as a Democrat to the Forty-fourth Congress to fill the vacancy caused by the resignation of William H. Barnum; reelected to the Forty-fifth Congress and served from December 4, 1876, to March 3, 1879; was not a candidate for renomination in 1878; resumed the practice of law; died in Norwalk, Conn., April 12, 1911; interment in Riverside Cemetery.

WARNER, Richard, a Representative from Tennessee; born near Chapel Hill, Marshall County, Tenn., September 19, 1835; attended the public schools and was graduated from the law department of Cumberland University, Lebanon, Tenn., in 1858; was admitted to the bar the same year and commenced practice in Lewisburg, Tenn.; during the Civil War served in the Confederate Army 1861–1865; returned to Lewisburg, Tenn., and resumed the practice of law; member of the State house of representatives in 1878; delegate to the convention that framed the new constitution of Tennessee in 1870; elected as a Democrat to the Forty-seventh and Forty-eighth Congresses (March 4, 1881–March 3, 1885); unsuccessful candidate for renomination in 1884; resumed the practice of law in Lewisburg, Tenn.; died in Nashville, Tenn., March 4, 1915; interment in Warner Cemetery, near Chapel Hill, Tenn.

WARNER, Samuel Larkin (brother of Levi Warner), a Representative from Connecticut; born in Wethersfield, Hartford County, Conn., June 14, 1828; attended Wilbraham Academy, Wilbraham, Mass., and the law department of Yale College; was graduated from the law department of Harvard University in 1854; was admitted to the bar in Boston, Mass., in 1854; commenced the practice of law in Portland, Middlesex County, Conn., in 1855; member of the State house of representatives in 1858; moved to Middletown in 1860; mayor 1862–1866; delegate to the Republican National Convention at Baltimore in 1864, serving as one of the secretaries of the convention; elected as a Republican to the Thirty-ninth Congress (March 4, 1865–March 3, 1867); was not a candidate for renomination; resumed the practice of law; delegate at large to the Republican National Conventions in 1888 and 1892; died in Middletown, Conn., on February 6, 1893; interment in Indian Hill Cemetery.

WARNER, Vespasian, a Representative from Illinois; born in Mount Pleasant (now Farmer City), De Witt County, Ill., April 23, 1842; moved with his parents to Clinton, Ill., in 1843; attended the common and select schools in Clinton and Lombard University, Galesburg, Ill.; studied law in Clinton; during the Civil War enlisted as a private in Company E, Twentieth Regiment, Illinois Volunteer Infantry, June 13, 1861; promoted to sergeant June 23, 1861, second lieutenant February 4, 1862, captain and commissary of subsistence February 10, 1865; brevetted major March 13, 1865, "for meritorious services," and was mustered out July 13, 1866; was graduated from the law department of Harvard University in 1868; was admitted to the bar the same year and commenced the practice of law in Clinton, Ill.; presidential elector on the Republican ticket of Harrison and Morton in 1888; elected as a Republican to the Fifty-fourth and to the four succeeding Congresses (March 4, 1895–March 3, 1905); served as Commissioner of Pensions from March 4, 1905, to November 25, 1909; engaged in business in Clinton, Ill., as a banker and realty owner and agent; died in Clinton, De Witt County, Ill., on March 31, 1925; interment in Woodlawn Cemetery.

WARNER, Willard, a Senator from Alabama; born in Granville, Licking County, Ohio, on September 4, 1826; attended country school near Roseville, Muskingum County, Ohio; was graduated from Marietta College, Ohio, in 1845; engaged in mercantile pursuits at Cincinnati in 1852 and later became manager of the Newark (Ohio) Machine Works; delegate to the Republican National Conventions at Chicago in 1860 and 1868; served in the Union Army during the Civil War; commissioned major in the Seventy-sixth Regiment, Ohio Volunteer Infantry, December 3, 1861, lieutenant colonel December 15, 1863, colonel of the One Hundred and Eightieth Regiment, Ohio Volunteer Infantry, October 27, 1864; brevetted brigadier general of Volunteers March 13, 1865, "for gallant and meritorious services in the Georgia, Tennessee, and North Carolina campaigns" and major general March 13, 1865, "for gallant and meritorious conduct during the war"; was mustered out July 12, 1865; served two years in the Ohio Senate; moved to Prattville, Autauga County, Ala., in 1867 and engaged in cotton planting; member of the State house of representatives in 1868; held several local offices; upon the readmission of the State of Alabama to representation was elected as a Republican to the United States Senate and served from July 13, 1868, to March 3, 1871; unsuccessful candidate for reelection; collector of customs of the port of Mobile, Ala., in 1871 and 1872; declined the appointment as Governor of New Mexico in 1872 and also that of Minister to Argentina; moved to Tecumseh, Ala., in 1873 and organized the Tecumseh Iron Co., of which he served as general manager; again a delegate to the Republican National Conventions in 1876, 1880, and 1888; in 1890 moved to Chattanooga, Tenn., where he engaged in banking and was a director in several corporations; member of the Tennessee House of Representatives in 1897 and 1898; died in Chattanooga, Tenn., November 23, 1906; interment in Cedar Hill Cemetery, Newark, Ohio.

WARNER, William, a Representative and a Senator from Missouri; born in Shullsburg, Lafayette County, Wis., June 11, 1840; attended the common schools and the University of Michigan at Ann Arbor; studied law; was admitted to the bar in 1861 and commenced practice in Kansas City, Mo.; enlisted in 1862 in the Thirty-third Regiment, Wisconsin Volunteer Infantry; was mustered out at the close of the Civil War with the rank of major in the Forty-fourth Regiment, Wisconsin Volunteer Infantry; returned to Kansas City, Mo., in 1865 and resumed the practice of law; city attorney in 1867; circuit attorney in 1868; mayor of Kansas City, Mo., in 1872; elected as a Republican to the Forty-ninth and Fiftieth Congresses (March 4, 1885–March 3, 1889); was not a candidate for renomination in 1888; elected commander in chief of the Grand Army of the Republic in 1888; unsuccessful Republican candidate for Governor in 1892; United States district attorney for the western district of Missouri in 1870, 1882, 1898, and 1902; chairman of the Republican State committee in 1884 and 1885; delegate to the Republican National Conventions in 1872, 1884, 1888, 1892, and 1896; unsuccessful candidate for Governor of Missouri in 1892; elected as a Republican to the United States Senate and served from March 18, 1905, to March 3, 1911; was not a candidate for reelection; resumed the practice of law; appointed as civilian member of the Board of Ordnance and Fortifications; member of the Board of Managers of the National Home for Disabled Volunteer Soldiers; died in Kansas City, Mo., October 4, 1916; interment in Elmwood Cemetery.

WARNOCK, William Robert, a Representative from Ohio; born in Urbana, Ohio, August 29, 1838; attended the public schools; taught school in Urbana 1856–1868; was graduated from Ohio Wesleyan University, Delaware, Ohio, in 1861; commenced the study of law in 1861; during the Civil War entered the Union Army July 21, 1862, as captain of Company G, Ninety-fifth Regiment, Ohio Volunteer Infantry; promoted to major July 28, 1863, "for gallantry at Vicksburg," and brevetted lieutenant colonel March 15, 1865, "for gallantry at the Battle of Nashville"; chief of staff for the eastern district of Mississippi from April to August 1865; mustered out August 14, 1865; resumed the study of law; was admitted to the bar in 1866 and commenced practice in Urbana; prosecuting attorney 1868–1872; member of the board of school examiners of Champaign County 1870–1876; served as trustee of Ohio Wesleyan University for twenty-five years; member of the State senate in 1876 and 1877; judge of the court of common pleas in the second district of Ohio 1879–1889; president of the National Bank of Urbana; elected as a Republican to the Fifty-seventh and Fifty-eighth Congresses (March 4, 1901–March 3, 1905); was not a candidate for renomination; resumed the practice of law; United States pension agent at Columbus, Ohio, 1906–1910; commander of the department of Ohio, Grand Army of the Republic, in 1913 and 1914; died in Urbana, Ohio, July 30, 1918; interment in Oakdale Cemetery.

WARREN, Cornelius, a Representative from New York; born in Phillipstown, Putnam County, N. Y., March 15, 1790; completed preparatory studies; studied law; was admitted to the bar and commenced the practice of law; appointed judge of the court of common pleas in 1841; elected as a Whig to the Thirtieth Congress (March 4, 1847–March 3, 1849); died at Cold Spring, Putnam County, N. Y., July 28, 1849; interment in the Old Cemetery.

WARREN, Edward Allen, a Representative from Arkansas; born near Eutaw, Green County, Ala., May 2, 1818; completed preparatory studies; studied law; was admitted to the bar in 1843 and commenced the practice of law in Clinton, Miss.; member of the State house of representatives in 1845 and 1846; moved to Arkansas in 1847 and settled in Camden, where he continued the practice of his profession; member of the State house of representatives in 1848 and 1849, serving as speaker in 1849; judge of the circuit court of the sixth district of Arkansas; elected as a Democrat to the Thirty-third Congress (March 4, 1853–March 3, 1855); elected to the Thirty-fifth Congress (March 4, 1857–March 3, 1859); resumed the practice of law; died in Prescott, Nevada County, Ark., July 2, 1875; interment in Moscow Cemetery, near Prescott, Ark.

WARREN, Francis Emroy, a Senator from Wyoming; born in Hinsdale, Berkshire County, Mass., June 20, 1844; attended the common schools and Hinsdale Academy; during the Civil War enlisted in the Forty-ninth Regiment, Massachusetts Volunteer Infantry, and served as a private and noncommissioned officer until he was mustered out of the service; received the Congressional Medal of Honor for gallantry on the battlefield at the siege of Port Hudson; later served as captain in the Massachusetts Militia; engaged in farming and stock raising in Massachusetts; moved to Wyoming (then a part of the Territory of Dakota) in 1868; became interested in the real estate, mercantile, livestock, and lighting businesses in Cheyenne; member of the Territorial senate in 1873 and 1874 and served as president of that body; member of the city council in 1873 and 1874; treasurer of Wyoming in 1876, 1879, 1882, and 1884: again a member of the Territorial senate in 1884 and 1885; mayor of Cheyenne in 1885; delegate to the Republican National Convention at Chicago in 1888; chairman of the Wyoming delegation to the Republican National Conventions in 1900, 1904, 1908, and 1912; chairman of the Republican Territorial central committee; appointed Governor of the Territory of Wyoming by President Arthur in February 1885 but was removed by President Cleveland in November 1886; again appointed Governor by President Harrison in March 1889,

and served until elected; elected as the first Governor of the State on September 11, 1890; resigned as Governor on November 24, 1890, having been elected Senator; elected as a Republican to the United States Senate November 18, 1890, and served until March 4, 1893; resumed agricultural pursuits and stock raising; again elected to the United States Senate in 1895; reelected in 1901, 1907, 1913, 1918, and again in 1924, and served from March 4, 1895, until his death in Washington, D. C., November 24, 1929; funeral services were held in the Chamber of the United States Senate; interment in Lakeview Cemetery, Cheyenne, Wyo.

WARREN, Joseph Mabbett, a Representative from New York; born in Troy, N. Y., January 28, 1813; attended the local schools, and in 1827 entered Rensselaer Polytechnic Institute at Troy; was graduated from the Washington (now Trinity) College, Hartford, Conn., in 1834; worked as a clerk in New York for a year and returned to Troy, N. Y., where he engaged in the wholesale grocery business for several years; entered the wholesale hardware business in 1840; one of the directors of the Bank of Troy and of the United National Bank of Troy, and president of the Bank of Troy 1853–1865; trustee of Rensselaer Polytechnic Institute; mayor of Troy in 1852; appointed as a commissioner of the Troy Water Works Company in 1855 and served until 1867, when he resigned; elected as a Democrat to the Forty-second Congress (March 4, 1871–March 3, 1873); was not a candidate for renomination in 1872; resumed his former business activities in Troy, N. Y., where he died September 9, 1896; interment in the Warren Chapel, Oakwood Cemetery.

WARREN, Lindsay Carter, a Representative from North Carolina; born in Washington, Beaufort County, N. C., December 16, 1889; pursued preparatory studies at Bingham School, Asheville, N. C., 1903–1906; attended the University of North Carolina at Chapel Hill 1906–1908; studied law at the same university in 1911 and 1912; was admitted to the bar in 1912 and commenced practice in Washington, N. C.; attorney of Beaufort County 1912–1925; chairman of the Democratic executive committee of Beaufort County 1912–1925; member of the State senate in 1917, 1919, 1959, and 1961, serving as president pro tempore in 1919; member of the State code commission for compiling the consolidated statutes in 1919; chairman of the legal advisory board and Government appeal agent for Beaufort County during the First World War; chairman of the special legislative committee in 1920 on workmen's compensation acts; member of the State house of representatives in 1923; member of the board of trustees of the University of North Carolina 1921–1925; elected as a Democrat to the Sixty-ninth and to the seven succeeding Congresses and served from March 4, 1925, until his resignation on October 31, 1940, having been appointed Comptroller General of the United States for a fifteen-year term, serving from November 1, 1940, until his retirement for physical disability on May 1, 1954; had been renominated to the Seventy-seventh Congress, but later withdrew; delegate to Democratic National Conventions in 1932 and 1940; chairman of the Democratic State conventions in 1930, 1934, and temporary chairman and keynoter in 1938; resides in Washington, N. C.

WARREN, Lott, a Representative from Georgia; born in Burke County, near Augusta, Richmond County, Ga., October 30, 1797; attended the common schools; moved to Dublin, Laurens County, Ga., in 1816; served as a second lieutenant of Volunteers in the expedition against the Seminoles in 1818; studied law; was admitted to the bar in 1821 and commenced practice in Dublin, Laurens County, Ga.; was also a regularly ordained Baptist minister, but never filled a definite charge; moved to Marion in 1825; elected major of the State militia in

1823; member of the State house of representatives in 1824 and 1831; served in the State senate in 1830; solicitor general and judge of the southern circuit of Georgia 1831–1834; moved to Americus, Sumter County, in 1836; elected as a Whig to the Twenty-sixth and Twenty-seventh Congresses (March 4, 1839–March 3, 1843); was not a candidate for renomination in 1842; moved to Albany in 1842; was judge of the superior court of Georgia 1843–1852; resumed the practice of his profession; died in Albany, Dougherty County, Ga., June 17, 1861; interment in Riverside Cemetery.

WARREN, William Wirt, a Representative from Massachusetts; born in Brighton (now a part of Boston), Mass., February 27, 1834; pursued classical studies, and was graduated from Harvard University in 1856; studied law; was admitted to the bar and commenced practice in 1857; assessor of internal revenue in the seventh Massachusetts district in 1865; delegate to the Democratic National Convention in New York City in 1868, which nominated Seymour and Blair; member of the State senate in 1870; elected as a Democrat to the Forty-fourth Congress (March 4, 1875–March 3, 1877); unsuccessful candidate for reelection in 1876 to the Forty-fifth Congress; engaged in the practice of law until his death in Boston, Mass., May 2, 1880; interment in Evergreen Cemetery.

WARWICK, John George, a Representative from Ohio; born in County Tyrone, Province of Ulster, Ireland, December 23, 1830; attended the common schools of his native land; immigrated with his brother to the United States about 1850 and resided in Philadelphia, Pa., for a short time; moved to Navarre, Stark County, Ohio, and became a bookkeeper in a dry-goods establishment; moved to Massillon, Ohio, and clerked in a dry-goods store, subsequently becoming interested in flour milling, coal mining, and agricultural pursuits; also was a promoter of railroad construction; elected as Lieutenant Governor of Ohio and served from 1884 to 1886; unsuccessful candidate for reelection in 1886; elected as a Democrat to the Fifty-second Congress and served from March 4, 1891, until his death in Washington, D. C., August 14, 1892; interment in Protestant Cemetery, Massillon, Stark County, Ohio.

WASHBURN, Cadwallader Colden (brother of Israel Washburn, Jr., Elihu Benjamin Washburne, and William Drew Washburn), a Representative from Wisconsin; born in Livermore, Androscoggin County, Maine, April 22, 1818; completed preparatory studies and taught school in Wiscasset, Maine, in 1838 and 1839; moved to Davenport, Iowa, in 1839 and was employed in the geological survey of that State; moved to Rock Island, Ill., and studied law; elected surveyor of Rock Island County, Ill., in 1840; moved to Wisconsin and settled in Mineral Point, Iowa County, in 1842; was admitted to the bar the same year and commenced practice at Mineral Point; founder of the Mineral Point Bank in 1852; elected as a Republican to the Thirty-fourth, Thirty-fifth, and Thirty-sixth Congresses (March 4, 1855–March 3, 1861); declined to be a candidate for renomination in 1860; moved to La Crosse, Wis., in 1861; delegate to the peace convention held in Washington, D. C., in 1861 in an effort to devise means to prevent the impending war; served in the Union Army during the Civil War; colonel of the Second Regiment, Wisconsin Volunteer Cavalry, February 6, 1862; brigadier general of Volunteers July 16, 1862; major general November 29, 1862; resigned May 25, 1865, and returned to La Crosse, Wis.; elected to the Fortieth and Forty-first Congresses (March 4, 1867–March 3, 1871); was not a candidate for renomination in 1870; Governor of Wisconsin 1872–1874; unsuccessful candidate for reelection in 1873; engaged in the manufacture of lumber; owned and operated large flour mills

in Minneapolis, Minn.; served as president of the Wisconsin Historical Society; founded the Washburn Observatory at the University of Wisconsin and the public library in La Crosse; died May 15, 1882, at Eureka Springs, Carroll County, Ark., while on a visit at the springs for his health; interment in Oak Grove Cemetery, La Crosse, Wis.

WASHBURN, Charles Grenfill, a Representative from Massachusetts; born in Worcester, Mass., January 28, 1857; was graduated from Worcester Polytechnic Institute in 1875 and from Harvard University in 1880; studied law; was admitted to the Suffolk bar in 1887; connected with various manufacturing enterprises in Worcester; member of the State house of representatives in 1897 and 1898; served in the State senate in 1899 and 1900; member of the committee to revise the corporation laws of Massachusetts in 1902; was a delegate to the Republican National Conventions at Chicago in 1904 and 1916; was elected as a Republican to the Fifty-ninth Congress to fill the vacancy caused by the death of Rockwood Hoar; reelected to the Sixtieth and Sixty-first Congresses and served from December 18, 1906, to March 3, 1911; unsuccessful candidate for reelection in 1910 to the Sixty-second Congress; director of the Federal Reserve Bank of Boston; president of the Washburn Co. of Worcester, Mass., until his death at Lenox, Berkshire County, Mass., May 25, 1928; interment in Rural Cemetery, Worcester, Mass.

WASHBURN, Henry Dana, a Representative from Indiana; born in Windsor, Vt., March 28, 1832; attended the common schools; became a tanner and a currier; taught school for several years; moved to Vermillion County, Ind., in 1850; was graduated from the New York State and National Law Schools; was admitted to the bar in 1853 and commenced the practice of law in Newport, Vermillion County, Ind.; county auditor 1854–1861; during the Civil War enlisted on August 16, 1861, and served in the Union Army as lieutenant colonel of the Eighteenth Regiment, Indiana Volunteer Infantry; promoted to colonel July 15, 1862; brevetted brigadier general of Volunteers December 15, 1864, and major general July 26, 1865, "for gallant and meritorious services during the war"; mustered out August 26, 1865; successfully contested as a Republican the election of Daniel W. Voorhees to the Thirty-ninth Congress; reelected to the Fortieth Congress and served from February 23, 1866, to March 3, 1869; was not a candidate for renomination in 1868 to the Forty-first Congress; appointed surveyor general of Montana in 1869 and served until his death; in 1870 headed an expedition to find the headwaters of the Yellowstone River and discovered what is now known as Yellowstone Park; Mount Washburn, Mont., is named for him; returned to Clinton, Vermillion County, Ind., where he died on January 26, 1871; interment in Riverside Cemetery.

WASHBURN, Israel, Jr. (brother of Elihu Benjamin Washburne, Cadwallader Colden Washburn, and William Drew Washburn), a Representative from Maine; born in Livermore, Androscoggin County, Maine, June 6, 1813; attended the common schools and was educated by private tutors; studied law; was admitted to the bar in 1834 and commenced practice in Orono, Penobscot County, Maine; member of the State house of representatives in 1842 and 1843; elected as a Whig to the Thirty-second and Thirty-third Congresses, as a Republican to the Thirty-fourth, Thirty-fifth, and Thirty-sixth Congresses and served from March 4, 1851, to January 1, 1861, when he resigned, having been elected Governor; Governor of Maine in 1861 and 1862; declined to be a candidate for renomination; appointed by President Lincoln as collector of customs at Portland, Maine, and served from October 31, 1863, until March 16, 1877, when he resigned; served as president of the board of trustees of Tufts

College, Medford, Mass.; engaged in literary pursuits; died in Philadelphia, Pa., on May 12, 1883; interment in Mount Hope Cemetery, Bangor, Maine.

WASHBURN, William Barrett, a Representative and a Senator from Massachusetts; born in Winchendon, Worcester County, Mass., January 31, 1820; attended Westminster and Hancock Academies, and was graduated from Yale College in 1844; employed as a clerk in Orange 1844–1847; engaged in manufacturing pursuits in Erving, Franklin County, Mass., 1847–1857; served in the State senate in 1850; member of the State house of representatives 1853–1855; moved to Greenfield in 1858 and engaged in banking; elected as a Republican to the Thirty-eighth and to the four succeeding Congresses and served from March 4, 1863, to December 5, 1871, when he resigned, having been elected Governor; Governor of Massachusetts from January 1872 to May 1, 1874, when he resigned, having been elected a Senator; elected to the United States Senate to fill the vacancy caused by the death of Charles Sumner and served from April 17, 1874, to March 3, 1875; was not a candidate for reelection; president of the Greenfield National Bank; member of the board of trustees of Smith College at Northampton; director of the Connecticut River Railroad; alumnus trustee of Yale College 1872–1881; member of the board of overseers of Amherst (Mass.) College; died in Springfield, Hampden County, Mass., October 5, 1887; interment in Green River Cemetery, Greenfield, Franklin County, Mass.

WASHBURN, William Drew (brother of Israel Washburn, Jr., Elihu Benjamin Washburne, and Cadwallader Colden Washburn), a Representative and a Senator from Minnesota; born in Livermore, Androscoggin County, Maine, on January 14, 1831; attended the common schools, and was graduated from Bowdoin College, Brunswick, Maine, in 1854; studied law in Bangor, Maine; was admitted to the bar in 1857 and commenced the practice of his profession in Minneapolis, Minn., where he had settled early in 1857; appointed as United States surveyor general of Minnesota by President Lincoln in 1861 and served until 1865, residing in St. Paul while holding that office; returned to Minneapolis and engaged in different manufacturing industries; director, principal owner, and for many years managing agent, of the Minneapolis Water Power Co.; projector and president of the Minneapolis & St. Louis Railway Co.; member of the State house of representatives 1861–1865, 1871, 1874, 1880, and 1882; elected as a Republican to the Forty-sixth, Forty-seventh, and Forty-eighth Congresses (March 4, 1879–March 3, 1885); elected to the United States Senate and served from March 4, 1889, to March 3, 1895; unsuccessful candidate for reelection; resumed manufacturing pursuits and also engaged in railroad building; died in Minneapolis, Minn., July 29, 1912; interment in Lakewood Cemetery.

WASHBURNE, Elihu Benjamin (brother of Israel Washburn, Jr., Cadwallader Colden Washburn, and William Drew Washburn), a Representative from Illinois; born in Livermore, Androscoggin County, Maine, September 23, 1816; attended the common schools; printer's apprentice; assistant editor of the Kennebec Journal, Augusta; studied law at Kents' Hill Seminary in 1836 and at Harvard Law School in 1839; was admitted to the bar in 1840; moved to Galena, Jo Daviess County, Ill., in 1840 and commenced the practice of law; delegate to the Whig National Conventions at Baltimore in 1844 and 1852; unsuccessful candidate for election in 1848 to the Thirty-first Congress; elected as a Whig to the Thirty-third and to the eight succeeding Congresses and served from March 4, 1853, to March 6, 1869, when he resigned; appointed as Secretary of State in the Cabinet of President Grant, but resigned a few

days afterward to accept a diplomatic mission to France; upon the declaration of the Franco-Prussian War he protected with the American flag the Paris legations of the various German states; remained in Paris during the siege and was the only foreign minister who continued at his post during the days of the Commune; protected not only Germans but all the foreigners left by their ministers; served as Minister until 1877, when he returned and settled in Chicago, Ill.; engaged in literary pursuits; served as president of the Chicago Historical Society 1884–1887; died in Chicago, Ill., October 22, 1887; interment in Greenwood Cemetery, Galena, Ill.

WASHINGTON, George, a Delegate from Virginia and the first President of the United States; born at "Wakefield," near Popes Creek, Westmoreland County, Va., February 22, 1732; in early childhood moved with his parents to an estate in Stafford County, Va., on the east side of the Rappahannock River, opposite Fredericksburg; attended an "old field" school, with Hobby, the sexton of the parish, as his first instructor; after the death of his father in 1743 he returned to Popes Creek to reside with his elder half brother, Augustine Washington, and attended a private school kept by a Mr. Williams; went to the Mount Vernon estate in his seventeenth year to reside with his brother Lawrence and engaged in the surveying of lands; appointed adjutant general of a military district in Virginia with the rank of major in 1751; in November 1753 was sent by Lieutenant Governor Dinwiddie, of Virginia, to conduct important business with the French Army in the Ohio Valley; in 1754 was promoted to the rank of lieutenant colonel and served in the French and Indian war, becoming aide-de-camp to General Braddock in 1755; appointed by the legislature as commander in chief of colonial forces, and from 1755 to 1758 engaged in recruiting and organizing troops for colonial defense; commanded a successful expedition to Fort Duquesne in 1758; engaged in agriculture at Mount Vernon, and served as a magistrate and as a member of the colonial house of burgesses 1758–1774; delegate to the Williamsburg convention of August 1773; Member of the First and Second Continental Congresses in 1774 and 1775; unanimously chosen June 15, 1775, as commander in chief of all the forces raised or to be raised; commanded the armies throughout the war for independence and received the special thanks and recognition of Congress upon eight separate occasions; resigned his commission December 23, 1783, and returned to private life at Mount Vernon; was delegate to, and president of, the national convention that framed the Federal Constitution in Philadelphia in 1787; unanimously elected as the first President of the United States, being inaugurated April 30, 1789, in New York City; unanimously reelected; retired March 3, 1797, after declining a renomination; issued his farewell address to the people of the United States in September 1796; again appointed as lieutenant general and commander of the United States Army July 3, 1798, and served until his death December 14, 1799, in Mount Vernon, Va., after a short illness; interment in the vault at Mount Vernon on December 18, 1799.

WASHINGTON, George Corbin (grandnephew of George Washington), a Representative from Maryland; born on "Haywood Farms," near Oak Grove, Westmoreland County, Va., August 20, 1789; attended Harvard University; studied law, but devoted himself to agricultural pursuits on his plantation in Maryland; resided for the most part at Dumbarton Heights, in Georgetown, D. C.; elected to the Twentieth, Twenty-first, and Twenty-second Congresses (March 4, 1827–March 3, 1833); was not a candidate for renomination in 1832; was elected to the Twenty-fourth Congress (March 4, 1835–March 3, 1837); was not a candidate for renomination on the Whig ticket in

1836; president of the Chesapeake & Ohio Canal Co.; was appointed by President Tyler in 1844 as a commissioner to adjust and settle the claims arising under the treaty of 1835 with the Cherokee Indians; died in Georgetown, D. C., July 17, 1854; interment in Oak Hill Cemetery.

WASHINGTON, Joseph Edwin, a Representative from Tennessee; was born on the family homestead, "Wessyngton," near Cedar Hill, Robertson County, Tenn., November 10, 1851; received his early instruction at home; was graduated from Georgetown College, Washington, D. C., June 26, 1873; studied law with the first law class organized at Vanderbilt University, Nashville, Tenn., in 1874, and was admitted to the bar, but never practiced; engaged in agricultural pursuits; member of the State house of representatives in 1876–1878; presidential elector on the Democratic ticket of Hancock and English in 1880; elected as a Democrat to the Fiftieth and to the four succeeding Congresses (March 4, 1887–March 3, 1897); was not a candidate for renomination in 1896; appointed road commissioner and had charge of the road construction work of Robertson County; member of the board of trustees of Vanderbilt University; director of the Nashville, Chattanooga & St. Louis and Nashville & Decatur Railroads; resumed agricultural pursuits upon the family homestead, "Wessyngton," in Robertson County, Tenn., where he died August 28, 1915; interment in the family burying ground on his estate.

WASHINGTON, William Henry, a Representative from North Carolina; born near Goldsboro, Wayne County, N. C., February 7, 1813; studied law; was admitted to the bar in 1835 and commenced practice in New Bern, Craven County, N. C.; was elected as a Whig to the Twenty-seventh Congress (March 4, 1841–March 3, 1843); declined to be a candidate for renomination in 1842; served in the State house of commons in 1843 and 1846; member of the State senate in 1848, 1850, and 1852; resumed the practice of law; died in New Bern, N. C., August 12, 1860; interment in Cedar Grove Cemetery.

WASIELEWSKI, Thaddeus Francis Boleslaw, a Representative from Wisconsin; born in Milwaukee, Wis., December 2, 1904; attended the parochial schools and South Division High School of his native city; was graduated from the University of Michigan at Ann Arbor in 1927, and from the law department of Marquette University, Milwaukee, Wis., in 1931; was admitted to the bar in 1931 and commenced practice in Milwaukee, Wis.; served as census supervisor in 1940; elected as a Democrat to the Seventy-seventh, Seventy-eighth, and Seventy-ninth Congresses (January 3, 1941–January 3, 1947); unsuccessful Democratic candidate for renomination in 1946 and an unsuccessful Independent candidate for election in 1946 to the Eightieth Congress; engaged in the practice of law in Milwaukee, Wis., where he now resides.

WASKEY, Frank Hinman, a Delegate from the Territory of Alaska; born in Lake City, Wabasha County, Minn., April 20, 1875; attended the public schools of Minneapolis; moved to Alaska in February 1898, located in Nome, and engaged in mining; president of a mining company; director of a bank and also of a publishing company, both in Nome; elected as a Democrat to the Fifty-ninth Congress as the first Delegate from Alaska and served from August 14, 1906, to March 3, 1907; was not a candidate for renomination in 1906; prospected for minerals in Alaska until 1955; United States commissioner at Fortuna Ledge, Alaska, 1915–1918; during the First World War served as registration officer, food commissioner, and chairman of the council of national defense at Fortuna Ledge, Alaska; fur buyer and curio dealer 1911–1956; resides in Olney, Md.

WASON, Edward Hills, a Representative from New Hampshire; born in New Boston, Hillsborough County, N. H., September 2, 1865; attended public and private schools and Francestown (N. H.) Academy; was graduated from New Hampshire College of Agriculture and Mechanic Arts at Hanover in 1886 and from Boston (Mass.) University Law School in 1890; was admitted to the bar in 1890 and commenced practice in Nashua, N. H.; sergeant at arms, assistant clerk, and later clerk of the State senate; member of the Nashua Board of Education 1891–1895, serving as its president in 1895; city solicitor of Nashua in 1894 and 1895; president of the common council in 1897 and 1898; served in the State house of representatives in 1899, 1909, and 1913; member of the State constitutional conventions in 1902 and 1912; solicitor of Hillsborough County 1903–1907; president of the Citizens' Guaranty Savings Bank of Nashua 1904–1941; also engaged in agricultural pursuits in Merrimack, N. H., 1906–1941; alderman of Nashua 1906–1908; elected as a Republican to the Sixty-fourth and to the eight succeeding Congresses (March 4, 1915–March 3, 1933); was not a candidate for renomination in 1932; retired from public life in 1933 and resided on his estate near New Boston, N. H., where he died February 6, 1941; interment in New Boston Cemetery.

WATERMAN, Charles Winfield, a Senator from Colorado; born in Waitsfield, Washington County, Vt., November 2, 1861; attended the rural schools, and St. Johnsbury Academy; was graduated from the University of Vermont at Burlington in 1885; taught school in Connecticut and also at Fort Dodge, Iowa, 1885–1888; was graduated from the law school of the University of Michigan at Ann Arbor in 1889; was admitted to the bar the same year and commenced practice in Denver, Colo.; delegate to the Republican National Conventions in 1920 and 1924; elected as a Republican to the United States Senate in 1926 and served from March 4, 1927, until his death in Washington, D. C., August 27, 1932; remains were cremated and the ashes deposited in Cedar Hill Cemetery.

WATERS, Russell Judson, a Representative from California; born in Halifax, Windham County, Vt., June 6, 1843; moved with his parents to Franklin County, Mass., in 1846; attended the district schools; learned the machinist's trade in Shelburne Falls, Mass.; taught school at Charlemont Center, Mass.; was graduated from Franklin Institute (later Arms Academy), Shelburne Falls, Mass., where he later was professor of Latin and mathematics; moved to Chicago, Ill., in 1867; studied law; was admitted to the bar in 1868 and practiced in Chicago until 1886; moved to California and settled in Redlands in 1886; city attorney of Redlands in 1888; moved to Los Angeles in 1894; president of the Pasadena Consolidated Gas Co.; treasurer of the Los Angeles Chamber of Commerce, vice president of the Citizens' Bank, and connected with many public institutions; elected as a Republican to the Fifty-sixth Congress (March 4, 1899–March 3, 1901); was not a candidate for renomination in 1900; resumed banking as president of the Citizens' National Bank, Los Angeles; president of the California Cattle Co., San Jacinto, Calif., 1903–1911; president of the San Jacinto Water Co. in 1910 and 1911; died in Los Angeles, Calif., September 25, 1911; interment in Hollywood Cemetery.

WATKINS, Albert Galiton, a Representative from Tennessee; born near Jefferson City, Jefferson County, Tenn., May 5, 1818; was graduated from Holston College, Tennessee; studied law; was admitted to the bar and began practice at Panther Springs, Tenn., in 1839; member of the State house of representatives in 1845; presidential elector on the Whig ticket of Taylor and Fillmore in 1848; elected as a Whig to the Thirty-first and Thirty-second Congresses (March 4, 1849–March 3, 1853); unsuccessful candidate for reelection in 1852 to the Thirty-third Congress; elected as a Democrat to the Thirty-fourth and Thirty-fifth Congresses (March 4, 1855–March 3, 1859); was not a candidate for renomination in 1858; engaged in the ministry; died in Mooresburg, Hawkins County, Tenn., November 9, 1895; interment in Westview Cemetery, Jefferson City, Tenn.

WATKINS, Arthur Vivian, a Senator from Utah; born in Midway, Wasatch County, Utah, December 18, 1886; attended the public schools, Brigham Young University, Provo, Utah, 1903–1906, and New York University, New York, N. Y., in 1909 and 1910; was graduated from Columbia University Law School, New York, N. Y., in 1912; was admitted to the bar the same year and commenced practice in Vernal, Utah; engaged in newspaper work in 1914; assistant county attorney of Salt Lake County in 1914 and 1915; engaged in agricultural pursuits 1919–1925; district judge of the fourth judicial district of Utah 1928–1933; unsuccessful candidate for the Republican nomination to Congress in 1936; elected as a Republican to the United States Senate in 1946 and reelected in 1952 and served from January 3, 1947, to January 3, 1959; was an unsuccessful candidate for reelection in 1958; member of the Indian Claims Commission, Washington, D. C., since August 15, 1959; resides in Arlington, Va.

WATKINS, Elton, a Representative from Oregon; born in Newton, Newton County, Miss., July 6, 1881; attended the common schools of Mississippi, and Webb School of Bell Buckle, Tenn.; was graduated from Washington and Lee University, Lexington, Va., Georgetown University Law School, and George Washington Law School, Washington, D. C.; after leaving college was employed by the Federal Bureau of Investigation, Department of Justice, Washington, D. C., until 1912, when he moved to Oregon; was admitted to the Oregon bar the same year and commenced the practice of law in Portland; prosecutor, Oregon Bar Association, 1914–1918; assistant United States district attorney in 1919; during the First World War was again employed by the Federal Bureau of Investigation; presidential elector on the Democratic ticket in 1920, 1940, and 1944; elected as a Democrat to the Sixty-eighth Congress (March 4, 1923–March 3, 1925); unsuccessful candidate for reelection in 1924 to the Sixty-ninth Congress; unsuccessful Democratic candidate for election to the United States Senate in 1930 and for nomination in 1932; unsuccessful candidate for mayor of Portland in 1932 and in 1940; resumed the practice of law in Portland, Oreg., until his death there June 24, 1956; interment in Greenwood Hills Cemetery.

WATKINS, John Thomas, a Representative from Louisiana; born in Minden, Webster Parish, La., January 15, 1854; attended the common schools and spent three years in Cumberland University, Lebanon, Tenn.; studied law; was admitted to the bar in 1878 and commenced the practice of law in Minden; judge of the district court 1892–1904; resumed the practice of law; elected as a Democrat to the Fifty-ninth and to the seven succeeding Congresses (March 4, 1905–March 3, 1921); unsuccessful candidate for renomination in 1920; engaged in the practice of law in Washington, D. C., until his death on April 25, 1925; interment in Murrell Cemetery, Minden, La.

WATMOUGH, John Goddard, a Representative from Pennsylvania; born in Wilmington, Del., December 6, 1793; pursued classical studies and was graduated from Princeton College; also did postgraduate work in the University of Pennsylvania at Philadelphia; served in the War of 1812 as corporal in the Fourth Company, Fourth Detachment, Pennsylvania Militia, from May 13 to July 31, 1813; appointed second lieutenant in the Regular Army September 2, 1813; brevetted first lieutenant August 15, 1814, for gallant conduct in the defense of Fort Erie, Canada, and resigned on October 1, 1816; elected to the Twenty-second and Twenty-third Congresses (March 4, 1831–March 3, 1835); unsuccessful Whig candidate for reelection in 1834 to the Twenty-fourth Congress; high sheriff of Philadelphia in 1835 and 1836; surveyor of the port of Philadelphia 1841–1845; discontinued active pursuits in 1854 and lived in retirement until his death in Philadelphia, Pa., November 27, 1861; interment in Christ Church Cemetery.

WATRES, Laurence Hawley, a Representative from Pennsylvania; born in Scranton, Lackawanna County, Pa., July 18, 1882; attended the public schools, and Hill School, Pottstown, Pa.; was graduated from Princeton (N. J.) University in 1904 and from the law school of Harvard University, Cambridge, Mass., in 1907; was admitted to the bar in 1907 and commenced practice in Scranton, Pa.; during the First World War served from September 26, 1916, as captain in the One Hundred and Eighth Machine Gun Battalion of the Twenty-eighth Division; wounded in action near the Vesle River; promoted to major and discharged May 28, 1919; awarded the Distinguished Service Cross and the Purple Heart Medal; after the war assisted in reorganizing the One Hundred and Ninth Infantry Regiment of the Pennsylvania National Guard and served as lieutenant colonel; elected as a Republican to the Sixty-eighth and to the three succeeding Congresses (March 4, 1923–March 3, 1931); was not a candidate for renomination in 1930; resumed the practice of law in Scranton, Pa., until 1951; moved to East Orange, N. J., where he now resides.

WATSON, Clarence Wayland, a Senator from West Virginia; born in Fairmont, Marion County, W. Va., May 8, 1864; attended the public schools of Marion County; employed in the coal-mining industry, and later organized a number of coal companies, serving as president of the Consolidation Coal Co., from 1903 to 1911; delegate to the Democratic National Convention at Denver in 1908; elected as a Democrat to the United States Senate to fill the vacancy caused by the death of Stephen B. Elkins and served from February 1, 1911, to March 3, 1913; was the caucus nominee of his party, which was in the minority, for reelection; commissioned lieutenant colonel in the Ordnance Department of the Army in March 1918 and served with the American Expeditionary Forces in France until January 1919; in 1918, while overseas, was nominated for United States Senator, but was unsuccessful in the election; again served as president of the Consolidation Coal Co., until 1928; also owned a stock farm and training stables; served as chairman of the board of directors of the Elk Horn Coal Corporation, later moving to Cincinnati, Ohio, to serve as president of the corporation; died in Cincinnati, Ohio, May 24, 1940; interment in Woodlawn Cemetery, Fairmont, W. Va.

WATSON, Cooper Kinderdine, a Representative from Ohio; born in Jefferson County, Ky., June 18, 1810; pursued preparatory studies; studied law; was admitted to the bar and commenced practice in Delaware, Ohio; moved to Marion, Ohio; unsuccessful candidate for prosecuting attorney of Marion County in 1839; moved to Tiffin, Ohio, and practiced law for twenty years or more; elected as a Free-Soiler to the Thirty-fourth Congress (March 4, 1855–March 3, 1857); unsuccessful candidate for reelection in 1856 to the Thirty-fifth Congress; resumed the practice of law; moved to Sandusky, Ohio; member of the State constitutional convention in 1871; appointed judge of the court of common pleas in 1876 and served until his death in Sandusky, Erie County, Ohio, May 20, 1880; interment in Greenlawn Cemetery, Tiffin, Seneca County, Ohio.

WATSON, David Kemper, a Representative from Ohio; born near London, Madison County, Ohio, on June 18, 1849; was graduated from Dickinson College, Carlisle, Pa., in 1871 and from the law department of Boston University in 1873; was admitted to the bar and commenced practice; assistant United States district attorney for the southern district of Ohio during the administration of President Arthur; elected attorney general of Ohio in 1887 and reelected in 1889; special counsel for the United States in the suits brought by the Government against the Pacific railroads in 1892; elected as a Republican to the Fifty-fourth Congress (March 4, 1895–March 3, 1897); unsuccessful candidate for reelection in 1896 to the Fifty-fifth Congress; appointed by President McKinley as a member of the commission to revise and codify the laws of the United States; resumed the practice of law; died in Columbus, Ohio, September 28, 1918; interment in Greenlawn Cemetery.

WATSON, Henry Winfield, a Representative from Pennsylvania; born in Bucks County, Pa., June 24, 1856; educated in private schools; studied law; was admitted to the bar in 1881 and commenced the practice of his profession in Philadelphia; member of the Historical Society of Pennsylvania and the Historical Society of Bucks County; president of the Washington, Potomac & Chesapeake Railway Co.; director of several banks and of the Langhorne Water Co.; elected as a Republican to the Sixty-fourth and to the nine succeeding Congresses and served from March 4, 1915, until his death in Langhorne, Pa., on August 27, 1933; interment in the Brandywine Cemetery, Wilmington, Del.

WATSON, James, a Senator from New York; born in Woodbury, Conn., April 6, 1750; completed preparatory studies; was graduated from Yale College in 1776; commissioned lieutenant in a Connecticut regiment in 1776, captain January 1, 1777, and resigned July 15, 1777; studied law; was admitted to the bar and practiced; appointed in 1780 by the assembly as a purchasing commissary for the Connecticut Line; moved to New York City in 1786; engaged in mercantile pursuits; member of the State assembly in 1791 and 1794–1796, serving as speaker in 1794; regent of New York University 1795–1806; served in the State senate 1796–1798; elected as a Democrat to the United States Senate to fill the vacancy caused by the resignation of John Sloss Hobart and served from August 17, 1798, to March 19, 1800, when he resigned to accept an appointment by President Adams as United States naval officer at New York City, N. Y.; unsuccessful Federalist candidate for Lieutenant Governor in 1801; member of the Society of the Cincinnati; organizer and first president of the New England Society in New York City, N. Y., from 1805 until his death there May 15, 1806.

WATSON, James Eli, a Representative and a Senator from Indiana; born in Winchester, Randolph County, Ind., November 2, 1863; was graduated from Winchester High School in 1881; entered De Pauw University, Greencastle, Ind., the same year and remained until 1885; studied law; was admitted to the bar in 1886 and commenced practice in Winchester; unsuccessful candidate for presidential elector on the Republican ticket of Harrison and Reid in 1892; moved to Rushville, Ind., in 1893 and resumed the practice of law; elected as a Republican to the Fifty-fourth Congress (March 4, 1895–March 3, 1897); unsuccessful candidate for renomination in 1896; elected to the Fifty-sixth and to the four succeeding Congresses (March 4, 1899–March 3, 1909); was not a candidate for renomination in 1908; Republican candidate for Governor of Indiana in 1908; resumed the practice of his profession in Rushville, Ind.; presided over the Republican State conventions in 1904, 1906, 1912, 1918, 1920, 1924, and 1926; delegate at large to nine Republican

National Conventions and served as chairman of the committee on resolutions in the convention of 1920; elected to the United States Senate to fill the vacancy caused by the death of Benjamin F. Shively; reelected in 1920 and 1926, and served from November 8, 1916, to March 3, 1933; unsuccessful candidate for reelection in 1932; continued the practice of law in Washington, D. C., until his death there on July 29, 1948; interment in Cedar Hill Cemetery.

WATSON, Lewis Findlay, a Representative from Pennsylvania; born in Crawford County, Pa., April 14, 1819; attended the common schools; engaged in mercantile pursuits at Titusville in 1832; moved to Warren, Pa., in 1835 and continued his former pursuits until 1837; clerk in the office of the recorder in 1838; studied law at Warren Academy 1839–1840; resumed his former mercantile pursuits until 1860; engaged as an opertaor in lumber and in the production of petroleum 1860–1875; organized and was the first president of the Conewango Valley Railroad Co. in 1861; elected president of the Warren Savings Bank at its organization in 1870; elected as a Republican to the Forty-fifth Congress (March 4, 1877–March 3, 1879); elected to the Forty-seventh Congress (March 4, 1881–March 3, 1883); elected to the Fifty-first Congress and served from March 4, 1889, until his death in Washington, D. C., August 25, 1890; interment in Oakland Cemetery, Warren, Pa.

WATSON, Thomas Edward, a Representative and a Senator from Georgia; born in Columbia County, near Thomson, Ga., September 5, 1856; attended the common schools and Mercer University, Macon, Ga.; engaged in teaching for two years; studied law; was admitted to the bar in 1875 and commenced practice in Thomson, McDuffie County, Ga., in 1876; also engaged in agricultural pursuits; member of the State house of representatives in 1882 and 1883; presidential elector for the State at large on the Democratic ticket of Cleveland and Thurman in 1888; engaged in agricultural pursuits; elected as a Populist to the Fifty-second Congress (March 4, 1891–March 3, 1893); unsuccessful candidate for reelection in 1892 to the Fifty-third Congress and in 1894 for election to the Fifty-fourth Congress; resumed the practice of law in Thomson, Ga.; nominated for Vice President at the Populist National Convention at St. Louis in 1896 and for President by the People's Party in 1904; conducted a magazine for many years and later engaged in the newspaper business; author of several books and numerous sketches; elected as a Democrat to the United States Senate and served from March 4, 1921, until his death in Washington, D. C., September 26, 1922; interment in Thomson Cemetery, Thomson, Ga.

WATSON, Walter Allen, a Representative from Virginia; born in Nottoway County, Va., November 25, 1867; attended "old field" school, and was graduated from Hampden-Sidney College, Virginia, in 1887; studied law in the University of Virginia at Charlottesville in 1888 and 1889; was admitted to the bar in 1893 and commenced practice in Nottoway and adjoining counties of Virginia; member of the State senate 1891–1895; Commonwealth attorney 1895–1904; member of the Democratic State committee in 1901 and 1902; circuit judge of the fourth judicial circuit of Virginia 1904–1912; elected as a Democrat to the Sixty-third and to the three succeeding Congresses and served from March 4, 1913, until his death in Washington, D. C., December 24, 1919; interment in the family cemetery on his estate, "Woodland," Nottoway County, Va.

WATTERSON, Harvey Magee (father of Henry Watterson), a Representative from Tennessee; born at "Beechgrove," the family homestead, in Bedford County, Tenn., November 23,

1811; pursued classical studies; studied law; was admitted to the bar and commenced practice in Shelbyville, Bedford County, Tenn.; established and edited a paper in Shelbyville, Tenn., in 1831; member of the State house of representatives in 1835; elected as a Democrat to the Twenty-sixth and Twenty-seventh Congresses (March 4, 1839–March 3, 1843); declined to be a candidate for reelection in 1842 to the Twenty-eighth Congress; sent by President Tyler on a diplomatic mission to Buenos Aires, where he remained for a year; member of the State senate 1845–1847, and served as speaker; editor and proprietor of the Nashville Union 1847–1851 and editor of the Washington Union in 1851; delegate to the Democratic National Convention at Baltimore in 1860, and was a presidential elector on the Douglas and Johnson ticket the same year; appointed by President Johnson as one of a commission to investigate conditions in the States "lately in rebellion"; practiced law in Washington, D. C., for fourteen years; moved to Louisville, Ky.; member of the editorial staff of the Louisville Courier-Journal; died in Louisville, Ky., October 1, 1891; interment in Cave Hill Cemetery.

WATTERSON, Henry (son of Harvey Magee Watterson and nephew of Stanley Matthews), a Representative from Kentucky; born in Washington, D. C., February 16, 1840; completed preparatory studies under private tutors; attended the Academy of the Diocese of Pennsylvania in Philadelphia, Pa.; engaged in newspaper work as correspondent and editorial writer; his first newspaper employment was on the Washington States, a Democratic paper, 1858–1861; became editor of the Republican Banner in Nashville, Tenn., in 1861; during the Civil War entered the Confederate service; aide to Gen. N. B. Forrest; was on the staff of Gen. Leonidas Polk; chief of scouts in Gen. Joseph E. Johnston's army; edited the Chattanooga Rebel in 1862 and 1863; resumed newspaper pursuits in Nashville after the war; moved to Louisville, Ky., in 1867 and purchased the Louisville Journal, consolidated it with the Courier, and served as editor of the Louisville Courier-Journal for fifty years; temporary chairman of the Democratic National Convention at St. Louis in 1876; elected as a Democrat to the Forty-fourth Congress to fill the vacancy caused by the death of Edward Y. Parsons and served from August 12, 1876, to March 3, 1877; declined to be a candidate for renomination in 1876; delegate to the Democratic National Conventions in 1880, 1884, 1888, and 1892; died in Jacksonville, Fla., December 22, 1921; interment in Cave Hill Cemetery, Louisville, Ky.

WATTS, John, a Representative from New York; born in New York City, August 27, 1749; completed preparatory studies; studied law; last recorder of New York under the Crown; member of the State assembly 1791–1793, serving as speaker of that body in 1792 and 1793; member of the commission to build Newgate Prison, New York City, 1796–1799; elected to the Third Congress (March 4, 1793–March 3, 1795); judge of Westchester County from 1802 to 1807; founded and endowed the Leake and Watts Orphan House; died in New York City September 3, 1836; interment in a vault in Trinity Churchyard.

WATTS, John Clarence, a Representative from Kentucky; born in Nicholasville, Jessamine County, Ky., July 9, 1902; attended the public schools; was graduated from the University of Kentucky in 1925 and from its law school in 1927; was admitted to the bar in 1927 and commenced the practice of law in Nicholasville, Ky.; also operates a farm; police judge of Nicholasville, Ky., 1929–1933; county attorney of Jessamine County, Ky., 1933–1945; member of the State house of representatives in 1947 and 1948, serving as floor leader; commissioner of motor transportation for State of Kentucky 1948–1951; elected as a Democrat to the Eighty-second Congress to fill the

vacancy caused by the resignation of Thomas R. Underwood; reelected to the Eighty-third and to the three succeeding Congresses and served from April 14, 1951, to January 3, 1961. *Reelected to the Eighty-seventh Congress.*

WATTS, John Sebrie, a Delegate from the Territory of New Mexico; born in Boone County, Ky., January 19, 1816; moved to Indiana, where he completed preparatory studies; was graduated from Indiana University at Bloomington; studied law; was admitted to the bar and practiced; member of the State house of representatives in 1846 and 1847; associate justice of the United States court in the Territory of New Mexico from 1851 to 1854, when he resigned; resumed the practice of law; elected as a Republican to the Thirty-seventh Congress (March 4, 1861–March 3, 1863); delegate to the Republican National Convention at Baltimore in 1864; took an active part in equipping troops for the Union Army during the Civil War; appointed chief justice of the supreme court of New Mexico July 11, 1868, by President Johnson, and served in that capacity one year; resumed the practice of law in Santa Fe; returned to Bloomington, Monroe County, Ind., where he died June 11, 1876; interment in Rose Hill Cemetery.

WAUGH, Daniel Webster, a Representative from Indiana; born near Bluffton, Wells County, Ind., March 7, 1842; attended the country schools and the high school in Bluffton; during the Civil War enlisted in the Union Army in 1861 in Company A, Thirty-fourth Regiment, Indiana Volunteer Infantry, and served until honorably discharged in September 1864; taught school; engaged in agricultural pursuits; studied law; was admitted to the bar in 1866; settled in Tipton, Ind., in 1867 and practiced; judge of the thirty-sixth judicial circuit 1884–1890; elected as a Republican to the Fifty-second and Fifty-third Congresses (March 4, 1891–March 3, 1895); declined to be a candidate for renomination in 1894; resumed the practice of law; died in Tipton, Ind., March 14, 1921; interment in the mausoleum adjoining Green Lawn Cemetery.

WAYNE, Anthony (father of Isaac Wayne), a Representative from Georgia; born in East Town, Chester County, Pa., January 1, 1745; attended Philadelphia Academy; became a land surveyor and was employed for a time in Nova Scotia; returned to Chester County, Pa.; member of the colonial house of representatives in 1774 and 1775; served in the Revolutionary Army as colonel of the Fourth Regiment of Pennsylvania troops; commissioned as brigadier general February 21, 1777; received a gold medal and the thanks of Congress and a similar testimonial from the Pennsylvania Assembly for the capture of Stony Point; brevetted major general October 10, 1783; elected to the Pennsylvania Assembly in 1784; moved to Georgia and settled upon a tract of land granted him by that State for his military service; delegate to the State convention which ratified the Constitution of the United States in 1788; presented credentials as a Member-elect to the Second Congress and served from March 4, 1791, to March 21, 1792, when the seat was declared vacant; declined to be a candidate for reelection in 1792; again entered the service of the United States Army, as major general and General in Chief of the Army; concluded a treaty August 3, 1795, with the hostile Indians northwest of the Ohio River; died in Presque Isle (now Erie), Pa., December 15, 1796; remains were moved in 1809 and interred in St. David's Episcopal Church Cemetery, Radnor, Pa.

WAYNE, Isaac (son of Anthony Wayne), a Representative from Pennsylvania; born near Paoli, Chester County, Pa., in 1772; attended the common schools and was graduated from Dickinson College, Carlisle, Pa.; studied law; was admitted to the Chester County bar in 1795; member of the State house of representatives 1799–1801 and in 1806; served in the State senate in 1810; during the War of 1812 was captain of a troop of Pennsylvania Horse, raised and equipped by himself, and was subsequently colonel of the Second Regiment, Pennsylvania Volunteer Infantry; unsuccessful Federalist candidate for Governor in 1814; elected to the Eighteenth Congress (March 4, 1823–March 3, 1825); engaged in agricultural pursuits; died in Chester County, Pa., October 25, 1852; interment in St. David's Episcopal Church Cemetery, Radnor, Pa.

WAYNE, James Moore, a Representative from Georgia; born in Savannah, Ga., in 1790; completed preparatory studies and was graduated from Princeton College in 1808; studied law in New Haven, Conn.; was admitted to the bar in 1810 and commenced practice in Savannah, Ga.; entered the military service during the War of 1812, and served as an officer in the Georgia Hussars; member of the State house of representatives in 1815 and 1816; mayor of Savannah 1817–1819; judge of the court of common pleas and oyer and terminer of Savannah 1820–1822; judge of the superior court of Savannah from 1822 to 1828; elected as a Jackson Democrat to the Twenty-first, Twenty-second, and Twenty-third Congresses and served from March 4, 1829, to January 13, 1835, when he resigned to accept a judicial position; had been reelected to the Twenty-fourth Congress; appointed as an Associate Justice of the Supreme Court of the United States and served from January 14, 1835, until his death in Washington, D. C., on July 5, 1867; interment in Laurel Grove Cemetery, Savannah, Chatham County, Ga.

WEADOCK, Thomas Addis Emmet, a Representative from Michigan; born in Ballygarrett, County Wexford, Ireland, on January 1, 1850; immigrated to the United States in infancy with his parents, who settled on a farm near St. Marys, Auglaize County, Ohio; educated in the common schools and the Union School at St. Marys; taught school in the counties of Auglaize, Shelby, and Miami for five years; was graduated from the law department of the University of Michigan at Ann Arbor in March 1873; was admitted to the bar the same year and commenced practice in Bay City, Mich.; assisted in making an abstract of title to the real estate in Bay County; served in the State militia 1874–1877; prosecuting attorney of Bay County in 1877 and 1878; chairman of the Democratic State conventions in 1883 and 1894; mayor of Bay City 1883–1885; member of the board of education of Bay City in 1884; elected as a Democrat to the Fifty-second and Fifty-third Congresses (March 4, 1891–March 3, 1895); declined to be a candidate for reelection in 1894; delegate at large to the Democratic National Convention at Chicago in 1896 which nominated Bryan and Sewall; resumed the practice of law in Bay City, and later moved to Detroit, and continued to practice; unsuccessful Democratic candidate for judge of the supreme court of Michigan in 1904; appointed a professor of law in the University of Detroit in 1912; appointed an associate justice of the State supreme court in 1933; died in Detroit, Mich., November 18, 1938; interment in St. Patrick's Cemetery, Bay City, Mich.

WEAKLEY, Robert, a Representative from Tennessee; born in Halifax County, Va., July 20, 1764; attended Princeton (N. J.) schools; joined the Revolutionary Army at the age of sixteen and served until the close of the Revolutionary War; moved in 1785 to that part of North Carolina which later became Tennessee and engaged in agricultural pursuits; member of the North Carolina convention that ratified the Constitution of the United States in 1789; member of the first State house of representatives in 1796; elected to the Eleventh Congress (March 4, 1809–March 3, 1811); appointed United States commissioner to treat with the Chickasaw Indians in 1819; member of the State senate in 1823 and 1824, serving as president in 1823; member of the State constitutional convention in 1834; died near Nashville, Tenn., February 4, 1845; interment in the family vault at "Lockland," on his estate in the suburbs of Nashville.

WEARIN, Otha Donner, a Representative from Iowa; born on a farm near Hastings, Mills County, Iowa, January 10, 1903; attended the country schools; was graduated from Tabor (Iowa) Academy in 1920 and from Grinnell (Iowa) College in 1924; served as treasurer of Wearin, Iowa, rural school district 1926–1928; engaged in agricultural pursuits and also as an author and editor; attended the International Institute of Agriculture at Rome, Italy, in 1927; delegate to all Democratic State conventions 1924–1960; member of the State house of representatives 1928–1932; delegate to the Iowa State Democratic judicial convention in 1930 and served as chairman; delegate to the International Midwest Aeronautics Convention at Minneapolis in 1930; alternate delegate to the Democratic National Convention in 1932 and delegate in 1936 and 1940; elected as a Democrat to the Seventy-third, Seventy-fourth, and Seventy-fifth Congresses (March 4, 1933–January 3, 1939); was not a candidate for renomination in 1938 but was an unsuccessful candidate for the Democratic nomination for United States Senator; resumed agricultural pursuits; member of the Alien Enemy Hearing Board for the southern district of Iowa 1941–1944; member of the Democratic State Central Committee 1948–1952; member of Mills County Board of Education; unsuccessful for Democratic nomination for United States Senator in 1950 and for Governor of Iowa in 1952; resides at Hastings, Iowa.

WEATHERFORD, Zadoc Lorenzo, a Representative from Alabama; born on a farm in Marion County, Ala., near Vina, Franklin County, February 4, 1888; attended the public schools; was graduated from the medical department of the University of Tennessee at Memphis in 1914; served as an interne in St. Joseph Hospital, Memphis, Tenn., 1914–1916; moved to Red Bay, Ala., in 1916 and commenced general medical practice; during the First World War served from August 26, 1917, as battalion surgeon in the Three Hundred and Twenty-sixth Infantry and was discharged on October 6, 1920; severely wounded in Argonne Forest, France, and was awarded the Purple Heart Medal; was subdistrict medical officer, United States Veterans' Bureau, Montgomery, Ala., 1922–1924; resumed medical practice in Red Bay, Ala.; also interested in banking and agricultural pursuits, with farming interests in both Alabama and Mississippi; served in the State senate from 1939 until elected to Congress; elected as a Democrat to the Seventy-sixth Congress to fill the vacancy caused by the death of William B. Bankhead and served from November 5, 1940, to January 3, 1941; was not a candidate for the full term; resumed his medical profession, retiring from active practice January 1, 1958; mayor of Red Bay, Ala., 1945–1948; vice chairman Franklin County Democratic Committee 1933–; president of the Bank of Red Bay 1938–; is a resident of Red Bay, Ala.

WEAVER, Archibald Jerard (grandfather of Phillip H. Weaver), a Representative from Nebraska; born in Dundaff, Susquehanna County, Pa., April 15, 1844; attended the common schools; was graduated from Wyoming Seminary, Kingston, Pa., and a member of the faculty 1864–1867; was graduated from the law department of Harvard University in 1869; was admitted to the bar in Boston, Mass., in 1869; moved to Falls City, Nebr., in 1869 and commenced the practice of law; member of the State constitutional conventions in 1871 and 1875; district attorney for the first district of Nebraska in 1872; elected judge of the first judicial district of Nebraska in

1875; reelected in 1879 and resigned in 1883; was elected as a Republican to the Forty-eighth and Forty-ninth Congresses (March 4, 1883–March 3, 1887); did not seek renomination in 1886, having become a candidate for Senator; unsuccessful candidate for election to the United States Senate in 1887; resumed the practice of law; died in Falls City, Richardson County, Nebr., April 18, 1887; interment in Steele Cemetery.

WEAVER, Claude, a Representative from Oklahoma; born in Gainesville, Cooke County, Tex., March 19, 1867; attended the public schools; was graduated from the law department of the University of Texas at Austin in 1887; was admitted to the bar the same year and practiced in Gainesville, Tex., 1887–1895; assistant prosecuting attorney of Cooke County, Tex., in 1892; moved to Pauls Valley, Indian Territory, in 1895 and engaged in the practice of law; moved to Oklahoma City, Okla., in 1902; member of Oklahoma City Board of Freeholders in 1910; elected as a Democrat to the Sixty-third Congress (March 4, 1913–March 3, 1915); unsuccessful candidate for renomination in 1914 and for election to fill a vacancy in the Sixty-sixth Congress in 1919; postmaster of Oklahoma City, Okla., by appointment of President Woodrow Wilson 1915–1923; acting county attorney of Oklahoma County in 1926; legal adviser and secretary to the Governor, William H. Murray, 1931–1934; district judge of thirteenth Oklahoma district in 1934 and 1935; returned to the practice of law; died in Oklahoma City, Okla., May 19, 1954; interment in Fairlawn Cemetery.

WEAVER, James Baird, a Representative from Iowa; born in Dayton, Ohio, June 12, 1833; moved with his parents to Michigan in 1835 and subsequently moved to Iowa and settled on a farm near Bloomfield; attended the common schools; moved to Bloomfield, Iowa; studied law at Bloomfield 1853–1856; was graduated from the Cincinnati Law School in April 1856; was admitted to the bar in 1856 and commenced practice in Bloomfield; during the Civil War enlisted as a private in the Second Regiment, Iowa Volunteer Infantry, in April 1861; commissioned first lieutenant of Company G May 27, 1861; major July 25, 1862; colonel November 10, 1862; brevetted brigadier general of Volunteers March 13, 1864, "for gallant and meritorious services"; mustered out May 27, 1864; elected district attorney for the second judicial district of Iowa in 1866 and served four years; appointed assessor of internal revenue for the first district of Iowa by President Johnson March 25, 1867, and served until May 20, 1873; elected as a Greenbacker to the Forty-sixth Congress (March 4, 1879–March 3, 1881); was not a candidate for renomination in 1880, having become a candidate for President of the United States; was nominated at Chicago in 1880 by the National Greenback Party as their candidate for President of the United States and received about 350,000 votes; was elected to the Forty-ninth Congress and reelected as the Democratic and Greenback-Laborite candidate to the Fiftieth Congress (March 4, 1885–March 3, 1889); unsuccessful candidate for reelection in 1888 to the Fifty-first Congress; People's Party candidate for President in 1892, receiving twenty-two electoral votes; mayor of Colfax, Iowa, 1901–1903; died in Des Moines, Iowa, February 6, 1912; interment in Woodland Cemetery.

WEAVER, Phillip Hart (grandson of Archibald Jerard Weaver), a Representative from Nebraska; born in Falls City, Richardson County, Nebr., April 9, 1919; attended the public schools of Falls City and Lincoln, Nebr.; student at St. Benedicts College, Atchison, Kans., in 1938 and 1939; graduated from the University of Nebraska at Lincoln in 1942; staff announcer for radio stations KGNF, KFAB, KFOR, and KVAK 1938–1940; during World War II entered the Armed Services June 1, 1942, and assigned to command, staff, and liaison duties with the Seventeenth Airborne Division, First Allied Airborne Army, and Headquarters, Berlin District; participated in campaigns in Ardennes, Rhineland, and Central Europe; was discharged as a captain in March 1946; awarded Combat Infantryman's Badge and Bronze Star; engaged in the insurance and finance business, Falls City, Nebr., 1946–1949; director, Falls City Wholesale & Supply, Inc., since 1946; civilian administrative assistant to the G–1, Fifth Army, Chicago, Ill., in 1949 and 1950; owner of Weaver Motor Sales, Falls City, Nebr., since 1950; elected as a Republican to the Eighty-fourth, Eighty-fifth, and Eighty-sixth Congresses (January 3, 1955–January 3, 1961). *Reelected to the Eighty-seventh Congress.*

WEAVER, Walter Lowrie, a Representative from Ohio; born in Montgomery County, Ohio, April 1, 1851; attended the public schools and Monroe Academy, and was graduated from Wittenberg College, Springfield, Ohio, in 1870; studied law; was admitted to the bar in 1872 and commenced practice in Springfield, Ohio; elected prosecuting attorney of Clark County in 1874, 1880, 1882, and 1885; elected as a Republican to the Fifty-fifth and Fifty-sixth Congresses (March 4, 1897–March 3, 1901); unsuccessful candidate for renomination in 1900; appointed associate justice Choctaw-Chickasaw citizens' court at McAlester, Okla., in 1902; returned to Springfield, Ohio, in 1904 and resumed the practice of law; died in Springfield, Clark County, Ohio, May 26, 1909; interment in Ferncliff Cemetery.

WEAVER, Zebulon, a Representative from North Carolina; born in Weaverville, Buncombe County, N. C., May 12, 1872; attended the public schools, and was graduated from Weaver College at Weaverville in 1889; studied law at the University of North Carolina at Chapel Hill; was admitted to the bar in 1894 and commenced practice in Asheville, N. C.; member of the State house of representatives 1907–1909; served in the State senate 1913–1915; presented credentials as a Democratic Member-elect to the Sixty-fifth Congress and served from March 4, 1917, to March 1, 1919, when he was succeeded by James J. Britt, who contested his election; elected to the Sixty-sixth and to the four succeeding Congresses (March 4, 1919–March 3, 1929); unsuccessful candidate for reelection in 1928 to the Seventy-first Congress; elected to the Seventy-second and to the seven succeeding Congresses (March 4, 1931–January 3, 1947); unsuccessful candidate for renomination in 1946; resumed the practice of law in Asheville, N. C., until his death there October 29, 1948; interment in Riverside Cemetery.

WEBB, Edwin Yates, a Representative from North Carolina; born in Shelby, Cleveland County, N. C., May 23, 1872; attended the Shelby Military Institute, and was graduated from Wake Forest (N. C.) College in June 1893; studied law at the University of North Carolina at Chapel Hill in 1893 and 1894; was admitted to the bar in 1894 and commenced practice in Shelby; entered the University of Virginia Law School at Charlottesville in 1896 and completed a postgraduate course; member of the State senate in 1901; appointed a trustee of Wake Forest College in 1898; appointed trustee of the Agricultural and Mechanical College of Raleigh by the legislature in 1899 and served two years; chairman of the Democratic senatorial district in 1896; chairman of the Democratic county executive committee 1898–1902; temporary chairman of the Democratic State convention in 1900; elected as a Democrat to the Fifty-eighth and to the eight succeeding Congresses and served from March 4, 1903, to November 10, 1919, when he resigned to accept a judicial position; one of the managers appointed by the House of Representatives in 1912 to conduct impeachment proceedings against Robert W. Archbald, judge of the United States Commerce Court; appointed United States district judge for the western district of North Carolina November 5, 1919, and served until his retirement March 1, 1948; died while visiting in Wilmington, N. C., February 7, 1955; interment in Sunset Cemetery, Shelby, N. C.

WEBB, William Robert (grandson of Richard Slanford), a Senator from Tennessee; born near Mount Tirzah, Person County, N. C., November 11, 1842; attended private schools, and was a student in Bingham's School, Oaks, N. C., 1856–1860; served with the Confederate Army in Company H, Fifteenth Regiment, North Carolina Infantry, during the Civil War and was wounded at the Battle of Malvern Hill, Virginia, July 1, 1862; returned to North Carolina in July 1865; was graduated from the University of North Carolina at Chapel Hill in 1868; taught at Horner's School, Oxford, N. C., 1868–1870; founded the first training school west of the Allegheny Mountains at Culleoka, Tenn., in 1870; moved the school to Bell Buckle, Tenn., in 1886; was a State Credit and Gold Democrat in 1896 and a delegate to the convention in Indianapolis in 1896 which nominated Palmer and Buckner for President and Vice President of the United States; elected as a Democrat to the United States Senate to fill the vacancy caused by the death of Robert L. Taylor and served from January 24, 1913, to March 3, 1913; was not a candidate for reelection in 1913; continued the occupation of teaching until his death in Bell Buckle, Tenn., December 19, 1926; interment in Hazelwood Cemetery.

WEBBER, Amos Richard, a Representative from Ohio; born in Hinckley, Medina County, Ohio, January 21, 1852; attended the public schools of Hinckley, and was graduated from Baldwin University, Berea, Ohio, in 1876; studied law; was admitted to the bar in 1876 and commenced practice in Elyria, Ohio; prosecuting attorney of Lorain County 1884–1890; judge of the court of common pleas of Lorain County 1900–1903; elected as a Republican to the Fifty-eighth Congress to fill the vacancy caused by the death of William W. Skiles; reelected to the Fifty-ninth Congress and served from November 8, 1904, to March 3, 1907; unsuccessful candidate for renomination in 1906; resumed the practice of law in Elyria, Ohio; engaged in literary pursuits; again elected in 1922 judge of the court of common pleas, serving until his retirement in 1935; died in Elyria, Ohio, February 25, 1948; interment in Ridgelawn Cemetery.

WEBBER, George Washington, a Representative from Michigan; born in Newbury, Orange County, Vt., November 25, 1825; attended the common schools and the academy at Alfred, Allegany County, N. Y.; moved to Michigan in 1852 and settled in Manistee County, where he engaged in farming, lumbering, manufacturing, and mercantile pursuits; moved to Ionia, Ionia County, in 1858 and continued the lumber and mercantile business; engaged in the banking business at Ionia in 1870; elected president of the Second National Bank of Ionia in 1872, a position which he held until the time of his death; mayor of Ionia in 1874 and 1875; elected as a Republican to the Forty-seventh Congress (March 4, 1881–March 3, 1883); was not a candidate for renomination in 1882; resumed his former business activities; died in Ionia, Mich., January 15, 1900; interment in Highland Park Cemetery.

WEBER, John Baptiste, a Representative from New York; born in Buffalo, N. Y., September 21, 1842; attended public and private schools and the Central School of Buffalo; enlisted in the Civil War as a private in the Forty-fourth Regiment, New York Volunteer Infantry, August 7, 1861, and was rapidly promoted, attaining the rank of colonel of the Eighty-ninth United States Colored Infantry; engaged in the wholesale grocery business; assistant postmaster of Buffalo 1871–1873;

sheriff of Erie County 1874–1876; elected as a Republican to the Forty-ninth and Fiftieth Congresses (March 4, 1885–March 3, 1889); unsuccessful candidate for reelection in 1888 to the Fifty-first Congress; delegate to the Republican National Convention at Chicago in 1888; grade-crossing commissioner of the city of Buffalo 1888–1908; commissioner of immigration at the port of New York 1890–1893; commissioner general of the Pan American Exposition at Buffalo in 1901; retired from active business pursuits; died in Lackawanna, N. Y., on December 18, 1926; interment in Forest Lawn Cemetery, Buffalo, N. Y.

WEBSTER, Daniel, a Representative from New Hampshire and a Representative and a Senator from Massachusetts; born in Salisbury (now Franklin), N. H., January 18, 1782; attended district schools and Phillips Exeter Academy, Exeter, N. H., and was graduated from Dartmouth College, Hanover, N. H., in 1801; principal of an academy at Fryeburg, Maine, in 1802; studied law; was admitted to the bar in March 1805 and commenced practice in Boscawen, near Salisbury, N. H.; moved to Portsmouth, N. H., in 1807 and continued the practice of law; elected as a Federalist from New Hampshire to the Thirteenth and Fourteenth Congresses (March 4, 1813–March 3, 1817); unsuccessful candidate for reelection in 1816 to the Fifteenth Congress; moved to Boston, Mass., in 1816; presidential elector on the Monroe and Tompkins ticket in 1820; delegate to the State constitutional convention in 1820; elected from Massachusetts to the Eighteenth, Nineteenth, and Twentieth Congresses and served from March 4, 1823, to May 30, 1827, when he was elected to the United States Senate for the term beginning March 4, 1827; reelected in 1833 and 1839 and served until his resignation, effective February 22, 1841; nominated by the Massachusetts Legislature for President in 1836 and received the electoral vote of the State; appointed Secretary of State by President Harrison and again by President Tyler and served from March 5, 1841, to May 9, 1843; again elected as a Whig to the United States Senate and served from March 4, 1845, to July 22, 1850, when he resigned; appointed Secretary of State by President Fillmore and served from July 22, 1850, until his death in Marshfield, Mass., October 24, 1852; interment in the Winslow Cemetery.

WEBSTER, Edwin Hanson, a Representative from Maryland; born near Churchville, Harford County, Md., March 31, 1829; received a classical training; attended the Churchville (Md.) Academy and the New London Academy, Chester County, Pa., and was graduated from Dickinson College, Carlisle, Pa., in 1847; taught school; studied law; was admitted to the bar in 1851 and commenced practice in Bel Air, Harford County, Md.; member of the State senate 1855–1859; presidential elector on the American Party ticket of Fillmore and Donelson in 1856; during the Civil War was colonel of the Seventh Regiment, Maryland Volunteer Infantry, and served in 1862 and 1863; was elected as a Republican to the Thirty-sixth and to the three succeeding Congresses and served from March 4, 1859, until his resignation in July 1865 when he was appointed collector of customs at the port of Baltimore, and served from July 27, 1865, to April 15, 1869; resumed the practice of his profession in Bel Air; was again appointed by President Arthur, on February 17, 1882, and served until February 23, 1886; in 1882 he engaged in banking, which he followed until his death; died in Bel Air, Md., April 24, 1893; interment in Calvary Cemetery, near Churchville, Md.

WEBSTER, John Stanley, a Representative from Washington; born in Cynthiana, Harrison County, Ky., February 22, 1877; attended the public schools and Smith's Classical School for Boys; studied law at the University of Michigan at Ann Arbor 1897–1899; was admitted to the bar in 1899 and commenced practice in Cynthiana, Ky.; prosecuting attorney of Harrison County, Ky., 1902–1906; moved to Spokane, Wash., in May 1906; chief assistant prosecuting attorney for Spokane County 1907–1909; judge of the superior court of Spokane County 1909–1916; lecturer on criminal and elementary law in Gonzaga University, Spokane, Wash.; associate justice of the State supreme court 1916–1918; elected as a Republican to the Sixty-sixth, Sixty-seventh, and Sixty-eighth Congresses and served from March 4, 1919, to May 8, 1923, when he resigned to become United States district judge for the eastern district of Washington, in which capacity he served until August 31, 1939, when he retired due to ill health; is a resident of Spokane, Wash.

WEBSTER, Taylor, a Representative from Ohio; born in Pennsylvania October 1, 1800; moved with his parents to Ohio in 1806, where he received a limited schooling; attended Miami University, Oxford, Ohio, for a short time; editor and publisher of the Western Telegraph, Hamilton, Ohio, 1828–1836; clerk of the State house of representatives in 1829; member of the State house of representatives in 1830 and served as speaker; elected as a Jackson Democrat to the Twenty-third, Twenty-fourth, and Twenty-fifth Congresses (March 4, 1833–March 3, 1839); clerk of court of Butler County, Ohio, 1842–1846; resumed his former business pursuits; moved to New Orleans, La., in 1863 and was employed in a clerical position; died in New Orleans, La., April 27, 1876; interment in Lafayette Cemetery No. 1.

WEDEMEYER, William Walter, a Representative from Michigan; born near Lima Township, Washtenaw County, Mich., March 22, 1873; attended the district schools and Ann Arbor High School; was graduated from the law department of the University of Michigan at Ann Arbor in 1895; member of the board of school examiners in 1894 and 1895; was admitted to the bar in 1895; county commissioner of schools 1895–1897; deputy commissioner of railroads for Michigan 1897–1899; commenced the practice of law at Ann Arbor in 1899; chairman of the Republican State convention in 1903; American consul at Georgetown, British Guiana, during the summer of 1905; member of the Republican State central committee 1906–1910; elected as a Republican to the Sixty-second Congress and served from March 4, 1911, until his death; was an unsuccessful candidate for reelection in 1912 to the Sixty-third Congress; while on an official visit to Colon, Panama, was accidentally drowned in the harbor of that port on January 2, 1913; remains were never recovered.

WEEKS, Edgar (cousin of John Wingate Weeks), a Representative from Michigan; born at Mount Clemens, Macomb County, Mich., August 3, 1839; attended the public schools; learned the trade of printer; studied law, and was admitted to the bar in January 1861; during the Civil War served in Company B, Fifth Regiment, Michigan Volunteer Infantry, and was first sergeant of the company; first lieutenant and adjutant of the Twenty-second Michigan Infantry in 1862; captain in 1863; appointed assistant inspector general of the Third Brigade, Second Division, Reserve Corps, Army of the Cumberland, in 1863; was mustered out in December 1863; proprietor and editor of a Republican newspaper in Mount Clemens, Mich.; commenced the practice of law in Mount Clemens in 1866; prosecuting attorney 1867–1870; appointed judge of probate of Macomb County 1870–1876; unsuccessful candidate for election in 1884 to the Forty-ninth Congress; elected as a Republican to the Fifty-sixth and Fifty-seventh Congresses (March 4, 1899–March 3, 1903); unsuccessful candidate for renomination in 1902; resumed the practice of law; died in Mount Clemens, Mich., December 17, 1904; interment in Clinton Grove Cemetery.

WEEKS, John Eliakim, a Representative from Vermont; born in Salisbury, Addison County, Vt., June 14, 1853; attended the country schools and Middlebury High School; after leaving school assisted on the home farm for several years; engaged in the banking business since 1882; assistant judge of Addison County 1884–1886; served in the State house of representatives in 1888; moved to Middlebury, Vt., in 1896; member of the State senate in 1896; elected trustee of the State industrial school (later the Weeks School) in 1898; associate judge 1902–1904; again served in the State house of representatives in 1912 and 1915, serving as speaker in 1915; director of State institutions 1917–1923; commissioner of public welfare 1923–1926; Governor of Vermont 1927–1931; elected as a Republican to the Seventy-second Congress (March 4, 1931–March 3, 1933); was not a candidate for renomination in 1932; resumed his banking interests; died in Middlebury, Vt., September 10, 1949; interment in Salisbury Cemetery, Salisbury, Vt.

WEEKS, John Wingate (great uncle of John Wingate Weeks), a Representative from New Hampshire; born in Greenland, Rockingham County, N. H., March 31, 1781; attended the common schools; learned the carpenter's trade; during the War of 1812 recruited a company for the Eleventh Regiment of United States Infantry and served as its captain; promoted to the rank of major; after the war resided in Coos County, N. H., where he held several local offices; elected to the Twenty-first and Twenty-second Congresses (March 4, 1829–March 3, 1833); died in Lancaster, Coos County, N. H., April 3, 1853; interment in the Old Cemetery.

WEEKS, John Wingate (father of Sinclair Weeks and cousin of Edgar Weeks), a Representative and a Senator from Massachusetts; born near Lancaster, N. H., April 11, 1860; attended the common schools; taught school; was graduated from the United States Naval Academy, Annapolis, Md., in 1881; served in the United States Navy as a midshipman 1881–1883; resigned from the Navy June 26, 1883, and took up the profession of civil engineering; became engaged in the banking and brokerage business in Boston, Mass., 1888–1914; served in the Massachusetts Naval Brigade 1890–1900, acting as commander the last six years; moved to Newton, Mass., in 1893; chairman of the Republican State convention in 1895; member of the Board of Visitors to the United States Naval Academy in 1896; served in the Spanish-American War as a lieutenant in the Volunteer Navy from April 23 to October 28, 1898, later accepting a reserve commission as rear admiral; placed on the Massachusetts Volunteer Militia retired list with rank of rear admiral on April 10, 1900; member of the board of aldermen of Newton, Mass., 1899–1902; city mayor in 1902 and 1903; elected as a Republican to the Fifty-ninth and to the four succeeding Congresses and served from March 4, 1905, until his resignation effective March 4, 1913, when he resigned to become United States Senator; elected to the United States Senate and served from March 4, 1913, to March 3, 1919; unsuccessful candidate for reelection in 1918; received 105 votes for the presidential nomination in the Republican National Convention at Chicago in 1916; delegate to the Republican National Convention at Chicago in 1920; appointed Secretary of War by President Harding March 4, 1921, and again by President Coolidge, and served until October 13, 1925, when he resigned on account of ill health; died in Lancaster, N. H., July 12, 1926; remains were cremated and the ashes interred in Arlington National Cemetery, Fort Myer, Va.

WEEKS, Joseph (grandfather of Joseph Weeks Babcock), a Representative from New Hampshire; born in Warwick, Mass., February 13, 1773; attended the common schools; moved to Richmond, N. H.; engaged in agricultural pursuits; town clerk of Richmond, N. H., 1802–1822; member of the State house of representatives 1807–1809, 1812, 1813, 1821–1826, 1830, and 1832–1834; associate judge of the court of common pleas 1823 and 1827; elected as a Democrat to the Twenty-fourth and Twenty-fifth Congresses (March 4, 1835–March 3, 1839); died in Winchester, Cheshire County, N. H., August 4, 1845.

WEEKS, Sinclair (son of John Wingate Weeks), a Senator from Massachusetts; born in West Newton, Middlesex County, Mass., June 15, 1893; attended the public schools and graduated from Newton (Mass.) High School in 1910; was graduated from Harvard University, Cambridge, Mass., in 1914; engaged in the banking business at Boston, Mass., 1914–1923; served on the Mexican border with the Massachusetts National Guard in 1916; during the First World War served from July 25, 1917, as a lieutenant and later as a captain of the One Hundred and First Field Artillery in the Twenty-sixth Division, participating in all its engagements, and was discharged April 30, 1919; engaged in the manufacture of metal products 1923–1953; alderman of Newton 1923–1930, mayor 1930–1935; chairman of the Republican State Committee 1936–1938; member of the Republican National Committee 1941–1953, serving as treasurer 1940–1944; delegate to the Republican National Conventions in 1932, 1940, 1944, 1948, 1952, and 1956; appointed as a Republican to the United States Senate to fill the vacancy caused by the resignation of Henry Cabot Lodge, Jr., and served from February 8, 1944, to December 19, 1944, a successor having been elected; was not a candidate for election to the vacancy; overseer, Harvard University 1948–1954; Secretary of Commerce in the Cabinet of President Eisenhower from January 21, 1953, until his resignation November 10, 1958; financier and industrialist; is a resident of Lancaster, N. H.

WEEMS, Capell Lane, a Representative from Ohio; born in Whigville, Noble County, Ohio, July 7, 1860; attended the common schools and normal academy, Caldwell, Ohio; studied law; was admitted to the bar in 1883 and commenced practice in Caldwell; elected prosecuting attorney of Noble County in 1884; member of the State house of representatives in 1888 and 1889; moved to St. Clairsville in 1890; prosecuting attorney of Belmont County 1890–1896; elected as a Republican to the Fifty-eighth Congress to fill the vacancy caused by the resignation of Joseph J. Gill; reelected to the Fifty-ninth and Sixtieth Congresses and served from November 3, 1903, to March 3, 1909; resumed the practice of law and was solicitor for the Pennsylvania Railroad; died in Steubenville, Ohio, January 5, 1913; interment in Union Cemetery, St. Clairsville, Ohio.

WEEMS, John Crompton, a Representative from Maryland; born in Waterloo, Calvert County, Md., in 1778; attended St. John's College, Annapolis, Md.; engaged in planting; elected as a Democrat to the Nineteenth Congress to fill the vacancy caused by the resignation of Joseph Kent; reelected to the Twentieth Congress and served from February 1, 1826, to March 3, 1829; resumed agricultural pursuits; died on his plantation, "Loch Eden," in Anne Arundel County, Md., January 20, 1862; interment in a private cemetery on his estate.

WEFALD, Knud, a Representative from Minnesota; born in Kragero, Norway, November 3, 1869; attended the local schools and high school of his native land; immigrated to the United States in 1887 and in 1896 settled in Hawley, Clay County, Minn., engaged in agricultural pursuits; also manager and part owner of a lumber business; member of the village council of Hawley, serving as president in 1907–1912, 1917, and 1918; member of the State house of representatives 1913–1915; elected on the Farmer-Labor ticket to the Sixty-eighth and Sixty-ninth

Congresses (March 4, 1923–March 3, 1927); unsuccessful candidate for reelection in 1926 to the Seventieth Congress; resumed his former business pursuits; editor of a Norwegian newspaper at Fargo, N. Dak., 1929–1931; executive secretary of the commission of administration and finance of Minnesota in 1931 and 1932; served as railroad and warehouse commissioner of Minnesota from January 1933 until his death; died in St. Paul, Minn., October 25, 1936; interment in Hawley Cemetery, Hawley, Minn.

WEICHEL, Alvin F., a Representative from Ohio; born in Sandusky, Ohio, September 11, 1891; attended the public schools of Sandusky, Ohio; during the First World War enlisted on December 14, 1917, and assigned to Company P, Ordnance Training Camp, and later to Headquarters Supply Company at Camp Hancock, Ga., and was discharged a sergeant January 31, 1919; appointed second lieutenant, Ordnance Section, Officers' Reserve Corps, December 10, 1918, and commission terminated December 8, 1928; was graduated from Ferris Institute, Big Rapids, Mich., from the University of Michigan at Ann Arbor, and from the Michigan College of Law in 1924; was admitted to the bar in 1924; served as commissioner of insolvents for the State of Ohio; prosecuting attorney of Erie County, Ohio, 1931–1937; served as special counsel for the attorney general of Ohio; lecturer, School Police Administration, Ohio State University, Columbus, Ohio; elected as a Republican to the Seventy-eighth and to the five succeeding Congresses (January 3, 1943–January 3, 1955); was not a candidate for renomination in 1954; resumed the practice of law; died in Sandusky, Ohio, November 27, 1956; interment in Calvary Cemetery.

WEIDEMAN, Carl May, a Representative from Michigan; born in Detroit, Mich., March 5, 1898; attended the public schools and the University of Michigan at Ann Arbor from 1914 until the outbreak of the First World War; attended the Naval Officers Training School at Ann Arbor, Mich.; enlisted in the United States Navy as an apprentice seaman; member of the United States Naval Reserve 1918–1922; graduated from the Detroit (Mich.) College of Law in 1921 but was previously admitted to the bar in 1920; commenced practice in Detroit, Mich.; delegate to the Democratic State conventions 1932–1942 and to the Democratic National Convention at Philadelphia in 1936; elected as a Democrat to the Seventy-third Congress (March 4, 1933–January 3, 1935); unsuccessful candidate for renomination in 1934; resumed the practice of law in Detroit, Mich.; elected circuit court commissioner of Wayne County, Mich., in 1936, 1942, and 1948, and served from January 1, 1937, to April 30, 1950; circuit judge for the third judicial circuit of the State of Michigan May 1, 1950– ; resides in Grosse Pointe Park, Mich.

WEIGHTMAN, Richard Hanson, a Delegate from the Territory of New Mexico; born in Washington, D. C., December 28, 1816; attended private schools in Washington, D. C., and Alexandria, Va.; was graduated from the University of Virginia at Charlottesville in 1834; attended the United States Military Academy at West Point 1835–1837; studied law; was admitted to the bar in 1841 in the District of Columbia, but did not practice; moved to St. Louis, Mo., and on May 28, 1846, was elected captain of Clark's Battalion, Missouri Volunteer Light Artillery, in the Mexican War; served with distinction at the Battle of Sacramento, near Chihuahua, Mexico, February 28, 1847, and was mustered out as a captain in June 1847, at New Orleans, where he served as Additional Paymaster, Volunteers, in the Army in 1848 and 1849; moved to New Mexico in 1851 and edited a newspaper in Santa Fe; appointed agent for Indians in New Mexico in July 1851; elected as a Democrat and the Territory's first Delegate to the Thirty-second Congress (March 4, 1851–March 3, 1853);

was not a candidate for reelection in 1852; resumed newspaper work; moved to Kickapo and Atcheson, Kans., in 1858, and went to Independence, Mo., in 1861; elected colonel, First Regiment Cavalry, Eighth Division, Missouri State Guard, Confederate States Army, June 11, 1861; promoted to command of First Brigade, Eighth Division, June 20, 1861; distinguished himself at the Battle of Carthage, Mo., July 5, 1861; killed while commanding the First Brigade at Wilson Creek, Mo., August 10, 1861; interment on the battlefield near Springfield, Mo.

WEIS, Jessica McCullough, a Representative from New York; born in Chicago, Ill., July 8, 1901; moved to Rochester, N. Y., in 1921; attended the Franklin School, Buffalo, N. Y.; graduate of Miss Wright's School, Bryn Mawr, Pa., and Madam Rieffel's School, New York City, N. Y.; appointed to Inter-American Commission of Women; vice chairman, Monroe County Republican Committee, 1937–1952; president, National Federation of Republican Women, in 1940 and 1941; member of the Republican National Committee since 1944; delegate at large to the Republican National Conventions in 1940, 1944, 1948, 1952, and 1956; appointed by President Eisenhower in 1953 as a member of the National Civil Defense Advisory Council, reappointed in 1956, and served until 1959; member of the board of Rochester Convalescent Hospital for Children since 1926 and the Women's Board of the Genesee Hospital since 1927; elected as a Republican to the Eighty-sixth Congress (January 3, 1959–January 3, 1961). *Reelected to the Eighty-seventh Congress.*

WEISS, Samuel Arthur, a Representative from Pennsylvania; born in Krotowocz, Poland, April 15, 1902; immigrated to the United States in 1903 with his parents, who settled in Glassport, Pa.; attended the public schools; graduated from Duquesne University, Pittsburgh, Pa., in 1925 and from the law department of the same university in 1927; was admitted to the bar in 1927 and commenced practice in Pittsburgh, Pa.; referee for high school and college football games since 1923; director of the Roselia Maternity Hospital, Pittsburgh, Pa.; member of the athletic council of Duquesne University; served in the State house of representatives 1935–1939; elected as a Democrat to the Seventy-seventh, Seventy-eighth, and Seventy-ninth Congresses and served from January 3, 1941, until his resignation on January 7, 1946; elected in November 1945 a judge of Common Pleas Court of Allegheny County, Pa., for the term commencing in January 1946; reelected in 1955 for the term ending January 1966; resides in Pittsburgh, Pa.

WEISSE, Charles Herman, a Representative from Wisconsin; born near Sheboygan Falls, Sheboygan County, Wis., October 24, 1866; attended the public schools and St. Paul Lutheran School; in 1880 started to work in a tannery and became a partner in 1888; president of the city council of Sheboygan Falls, Wis., 1893–1896; treasurer of the school board 1897–1900; delegate to the Democratic National Conventions in 1904 and 1908; unsuccessful Democratic candidate for election in 1900 to the Fifty-seventh Congress; elected as a Democrat to the Fifty-eighth and to the three succeeding Congresses (March 4, 1903–March 3, 1911); was not a candidate for renomination in 1910 to the Sixty-second Congress; engaged in the manufacture of leather and in various other business enterprises in his native city; accidentally killed in Sheboygan Falls, Wis., October 8, 1919; interment in Falls Cemetery.

WELBORN, John, a Representative from Missouri; born near Aullville, Lafayette County, Mo., on November 20, 1857; attended the public schools; studied law at Warrensburg (Mo.) State Normal School; was admitted to the bar in 1880 and practiced in Lexington, Lafayette County, Mo.; city recorder

in 1890 and 1891; mayor of Lexington 1896–1920; delegate to the Republican National Convention in 1900; elected as a Republican to the Fifty-ninth Congress (March 4, 1905–March 3, 1907); unsuccessful candidate for reelection in 1906 to the Sixtieth Congress; resumed the practice of law; died in Lexington, Mo., October 27, 1907; interment in Machpelah Cemetery.

WELCH, Adonijah Strong, a Senator from Florida; born in East Hampton, Conn., April 12, 1821; attended the public schools; moved to Michigan in 1839 and settled in Jonesville; was graduated from the University of Michigan at Ann Arbor in 1846; studied law, and was admitted to the bar in 1847; principal of the Jonesville (Mich.) High School 1847–1849; principal of the Michigan State Normal School, Ypsilanti, Mich., 1851–1865; trustee of the Michigan Agricultural College at East Lansing; during the Civil War served as a field officer in the Second Regiment, Michigan Volunteer Cavalry; moved to Pensacola, Fla., in 1865, and later to Jacksonville, where he established a lumber mill and also engaged in orange growing; chairman of the Republican State committee in 1868; upon the readmission of the State of Florida to representation was elected as a Republican to the United States Senate and served from June 25, 1868, to March 3, 1869; declined a renomination to accept the presidency of the Iowa State Agricultural College at Ames, Iowa, and served from 1869 to 1884, when he resigned; commissioner to inspect foreign colleges of agriculture in 1882 and 1883; professor of psychology and history in the Iowa State Agricultural College 1885–1889; was an author and engaged in educational work; died in Pasadena, Los Angeles County, Calif., March 14, 1889; interment in the Iowa State College Cemetery, Ames, Iowa.

WELCH, Frank, a Representative from Nebraska; born at Bunker Hill, Charlestown, Mass., February 10, 1835, moved with his parents to Boston in early childhood; was graduated from the Boston High School; adopted the profession of civil engineering; moved to the Territory of Nebraska in 1857 and engaged in mercantile pursuits at Decatur, Burt County; served as postmaster of Decatur; served in the Territorial council in 1864; member of the Territorial house of representatives in 1865 and 1866, serving as presiding officer in 1865; register of the land office at West Point, Nebr., 1871–1876; elected as a Republican to the Forty-fifth Congress and served from March 4, 1877, until his death in Neligh, Nebr., September 4, 1878; interment in Forest Hills Cemetery, Jamaica Plain, Mass.

WELCH, John, a Representative from Ohio; born near New Athens, Harrison County, Ohio, October 28, 1805; received a liberal schooling and was graduated from Franklin College; moved to Athens County in 1828 and settled in Rome Township; engaged in the milling business; studied law; was admitted to the bar and commenced practice in Athens, Ohio, in 1833; prosecuting attorney of Athens County 1841–1843; member of the State senate 1845–1847; elected as a Whig to the Thirty-second Congress (March 4, 1851–March 3, 1853); declined to be a candidate for renomination in 1852; delegate to the Whig National Convention at Baltimore in 1852; resumed the practice of law; member of the electoral college and cast his vote for John C. Frémont in 1856; judge of the court of common pleas 1862–1865; associate justice of the supreme court of Ohio 1865–1878 and was chief justice in 1877 and 1878; died in Athens, Ohio, August 5, 1891; interment in West Union Street Cemetery.

WELCH, Philip James, a Representative from Missouri; born in St. Joseph, Buchanan County, Mo., April 4, 1895; educated in the public schools; engaged in the furniture business 1916–1931;

treasurer of city of St. Joseph 1932–1936 and mayor 1936–1946; delegate to Democratic National Convention in 1940; assistant director of Reconstruction Finance Corporation, Kansas City, Mo., in 1946 and 1947; elected as a Democrat to the Eighty-first and Eighty-second Congresses (January 3, 1949–January 3, 1953); was not a candidate for renomination in 1952 to the Eighty-third Congress but was unsuccessful for the Democratic gubernatorial nomination; is a resident of St. Joseph, Mo.

WELCH, Richard Joseph, a Representative from California; born in Monroe County, N. Y., February 13, 1869; educated in the public schools; moved to California in early boyhood and settled in San Francisco; served in the State senate 1901–1913; harbor master for the port of San Francisco 1903–1907; supervisor of the city and county of San Francisco from 1916 until September 30, 1926, when he resigned, having been elected to Congress; elected as a Republican to the Sixty-ninth Congress to fill the vacancy caused by the death of Lawrence J. Flaherty; reelected to the Seventieth and to the eleven succeeding Congresses and served from August 31, 1926, until his death in a hospital in Needles, Calif., September 10, 1949; interment in Holy Cross Cemetery, San Francisco, Calif.

WELCH, William Wickham, a Representative from Connecticut; born in Norfolk, Litchfield County, Conn., December 10, 1818; studied medicine; was graduated from the medical department of Yale College in 1839 and commenced practice in Norfolk; member of the State house of representatives 1848–1850; served in the State senate in 1851 and 1852; elected by the American Party to the Thirty-fourth Congress (March 4, 1855–March 3, 1857); resumed the practice of his profession; again a member of the State house of representatives in 1869 and 1881; died in Norfolk, Conn., July 30, 1892; interment in Center Cemetery.

WELKER, Herman, a Senator from Idaho; born in Cambridge, Washington County, Idaho, December 11, 1906; was graduated from Weiser High School and from the law school of the University of Idaho at Moscow in 1929; was admitted to the bar in 1929; while still in college was appointed prosecuting attorney of Washington County, Idaho, was reelected twice, and held that position until 1935; moved to Los Angeles, Calif., in 1936 and practiced law until 1943; during World War II served as an enlisted man in the United States Air Corps in 1943 and 1944; returned to Payette, Idaho, and practiced law 1944–1950; also interested in farming and livestock raising in Idaho; member of the State senate from Payette County, Idaho, 1948–1950; elected as a Republican to the United States Senate in 1950 and served from January 3, 1951, to January 3, 1957; unsuccessful candidate for reelection in 1956; engaged in the practice of law and farming; died in the National Institutes of Health, Bethesda, Md., October 30, 1957; interment in Arlington National Cemetery, Fort Myer, Va.

WELKER, Martin, a Representative from Ohio; born in Knox County, Ohio, April 25, 1819; attended the common schools; studied law; was admitted to the bar in 1840 and commenced practice at Millersburg, Ohio; clerk of the court of common pleas for Holmes County 1846–1851; unsuccessful candidate for election in 1852 to the Thirty-third Congress; judge of the sixth judicial district of Ohio 1852–1857; moved to Wooster, Ohio, in 1857; Lieutenant Governor of Ohio in 1857 and 1858 on the ticket with Salmon P. Chase; declined to be a candidate for renomination in 1858; was appointed aide-de-camp, with rank of colonel, to the Governor of Ohio August 10, 1861; judge advocate general of the State of Ohio in 1861; superintendent of drafting with rank of colonel under Governor

Tod August 15, 1862; assistant adjutant general in 1862; during the Civil War enlisted in the Union Army as a private in Company I, One Hundred and Eighty-eighth Regiment, Ohio Volunteer Infantry, February 16, 1865; mustered out September 21, 1865; unsuccessful candidate for election in 1892 to the Thirty-eighth Congress; elected as a Republican to the Thirty-ninth, Fortieth, and Forty-first Congresses (March 4, 1865–March 3, 1871); was not a candidate for renomination in 1870 to the Forty-second Congress; appointed United States judge for the northern district of Ohio by President Ulysses S. Grant in 1873 and served until 1889, when he retired; professor of political science and international law at Wooster University 1873–1890; died in Wooster, Ohio, on March 15, 1902; interment in Wooster Cemetery.

WELLBORN, Marshall Johnson, a Representative from Georgia; born near Eatonton, Putnam County, Ga., May 29, 1808; attended the University of Georgia at Athens; studied law; was admitted to the bar in 1826 and practiced in Columbus, Ga.; held several local offices; member of the State house of representatives in 1833 and 1834; judge of the superior court of Georgia 1838–1842; elected as a Democrat to the Thirty-first Congress (March 4, 1849–March 3, 1851); studied theology and was ordained as a Baptist minister in 1864 and continued in the ministry until his death in Columbus, Ga., October 16, 1874; interment in Oakland Cemetery, Atlanta, Ga.

WELLBORN, Olin, a Representative from Texas; born in Cumming, Forsyth County, Ga., June 18, 1843; attended the common schools, Emory College, Oxford, Ga., and the University of North Carolina at Chapel Hill; enlisted in the Confederate Army in 1861 and served throughout the Civil War, attaining the rank of captain in Company B, Fourth Georgia Cavalry; at the close of the war settled in Atlanta, Ga.; studied law; was admitted to the bar in 1866 and commenced the practice of law in Atlanta; moved to Dallas, Tex., in 1871 and continued the practice of his profession; elected as a Democrat to the Forty-sixth and to the three succeeding Congresses (March 4, 1879–March 3, 1887); unsuccessful candidate for renomination in 1886 to the Fiftieth Congress; moved to San Diego, Calif., in 1887 and continued the practice of his profession for six years; moved to Los Angeles, Calif., in 1893; appointed by President Cleveland as United States judge of the southern district of California in 1895, which office he held until January 20, 1915, when he retired; died in Los Angeles, Calif., December 6, 1921; interment in Rosedale Cemetery.

WELLER, John B., a Representative from Ohio and a Senator from California; born in Hamilton, Butler County, Ohio, February 22, 1812; attended the public schools and Miami University, Hamilton, Ohio; studied law; was admitted to the bar and practiced in Hamilton, Butler County, Ohio; prosecuting attorney of Butler County 1833–1836; elected as a Democrat from Ohio to the Twenty-sixth, Twenty-seventh, and Twenty-eighth Congresses (March 4, 1839–March 3, 1845); was not a candidate for renomination in 1844; served in the Mexican War as a lieutenant colonel and colonel in 1846 and 1847; unsuccessful candidate for Governor of Ohio in 1848; member of the commission to establish the boundary line between California and Mexico in 1849 and 1850; resigned from the commission in the latter year, moved to California, and engaged in the practice of law; elected as a Union Democrat from California to the United States Senate for the term commencing March 4, 1851, and served from January 30, 1852, to March 3, 1857; Governor of California 1858–1860; appointed Minister to Mexico on November 7, 1860, and served until May 14, 1861; delegate to the Democratic National Convention at Chicago in 1864;

moved to New Orleans, La., in 1867 and continued the practice of law; died in New Orleans, La., August 17, 1875; interment in Lone Mountain Cemetery, San Francisco, Calif.

WELLER, Luman Hamlin, a Representative from Iowa; born in Bridgewater, Litchfield County, Conn., on August 24, 1833; received a common-school and an academic training; attended the State normal school at New Britain, and the Suffield (Conn.) Literary Institute; moved to Chickasaw County, Iowa, in 1859 and engaged in agricultural pursuits; justice of the peace in 1865; unsuccessful independent candidate for the State house of representatives in 1867; studied law; was admitted to the bar in 1869 and commenced practice in Bradford, Iowa; elected as the candidate of the National Greenback and the Democratic Parties to the Forty-eighth Congress (March 4, 1883–March 3, 1885); unsuccessful candidate for reelection in 1884 to the Forty-ninth Congress; resumed the practice of law and also engaged in agricultural pursuits near Nashua, Iowa; for twenty years was proprietor and editor of the Farmers' Advocate, a weekly paper, published at Independence, Iowa; upon the organization of the People's Party in 1890 was appointed as a member of its national committee, and served until his death; served as president of the Chosen Farmers of America; twice unsuccessful candidate for judge of the supreme court of Iowa; was an unsuccessful candidate of the People's Party for Governor of Iowa in 1901; died in a sanitarium at Minneapolis, Minn., March 2, 1914; interment in Greenwood Cemetery, near Nashua, Chickasaw County, Iowa.

WELLER, Ovington Eugene, a Senator from Maryland; born in Reisterstown, Baltimore County, Md., on January 23, 1862; attended the public schools and was graduated from the Reisterstown High School in 1877; entered the United States Naval Academy, Annapolis, Md., September 22, 1877, and was graduated in 1881; after two years of service in the Navy he was honorably discharged June 30, 1883; employed as a clerk in the Post Office Department, Washington, D. C., 1883–1887; was graduated from the National Law School, Washington, D. C., in 1887; was admitted to the bar in 1888 and practiced law for three years; then engaged in banking and in manufacturing; member of the stock brokerage firm of Hornblower & Weeks, of Boston and New York; retired in 1901 and traveled extensively; chairman of the State Roads Commission of Maryland 1912–1916; unsuccessful candidate for Governor of Maryland in 1915; delegate at large and chairman of the Maryland delegation to the Republican National Convention at Chicago in 1916; treasurer of the Republican National Senatorial Committee 1918–1920; elected as a Republican to the United States Senate in 1920 and served from March 4, 1921, to March 3, 1927; unsuccessful candidate for reelection in 1926; delegate at large and chairman of the Maryland delegation to the Republican National Convention in 1924; resumed the practice of law in Baltimore, Md., until his death there January 5, 1947; interment in Arlington National Cemetery, Fort Myer, Va.

WELLER, Royal Hurlburt, a Representative from New York; born in New York City, July 2, 1881; attended the public schools and the College of the City of New York; was graduated from the New York Law School in 1901; was admitted to the bar in 1902 and commenced practice in New York City; assistant district attorney of New York County from 1911 to 1917, when he resigned to reenter the practice of law; counsel for the Alien Property Custodian in 1918 and 1919; member of the American and the New York Bar Associations, the Academy of Political Science, and the Seventh Regiment Veterans' Association; elected as a Democrat to the Sixty-eighth, Sixty-ninth, and Seventieth Congresses and served from March 4, 1923, until

his death; had been reelected to the Seventy-first Congress; died in New York City, N. Y., March 1, 1929; interment in Woodlawn Cemetery.

WELLING, Milton Holmes, a Representative from Utah; born in Farmington, Davis County, Utah, January 25, 1876; attended the common schools, the Latter-day Saints' University, and the University of Utah at Salt Lake City; engaged in agricultural and mercantile pursuits and also in banking; was elected a member of the board of trustees of Brigham Young College, Logan, Utah, in 1906; served in the State house of representatives 1911–1915; elected as a Democrat to the Sixty-fifth and Sixty-sixth Congresses (March 4, 1917–March 3, 1921); did not seek renomination, having become a candidate for Senator; unsuccessful Democratic candidate for the United States Senate in 1920; director of registration for the State of Utah 1925–1928; elected secretary of state of Utah in 1928; reelected in 1932 and served until January 1, 1937; trustee of Utah State Agricultural College 1926–1936; regent of University of Utah 1928–1936; appointed by Secretary of Interior Harold L. Ickes to make a survey of public grazing lands in 1937 and 1938; resumed agricultural and mining operations; in January 1943 accepted war service appointment as auditor with Army Air Forces and also served with the War Assets Administration at Salt Lake City, Utah, until his death May 28, 1947; interment in Fielding Cemetery, Fielding, Utah.

WELLINGTON, George Louis, a Representative and a Senator from Maryland; born in Cumberland, Allegany County, Md., January 28, 1852; attended a German school and received private instruction; served as a clerk in the Second National Bank of Cumberland in 1870, and later was teller; appointed treasurer of Allegany County in 1882 and served until 1888; again appointed treasurer in 1890; delegate to the Republican National Conventions at Chicago in 1884 and 1888; unsuccessful candidate of the Republican Party for election as comptroller of Maryland in 1889; assistant treasurer of the United States at Baltimore 1890–1893; unsuccessful candidate for election to the Fifty-third Congress; elected as a Republican to the Fifty-fourth Congress (March 4, 1895–March 3, 1897); elected to the United States Senate and served from March 4, 1897, to March 3, 1903; was not a candidate for reelection; supported William Jennings Bryan, Democrat, for President in 1900 on the anti-imperialism issue; unsuccessful candidate on the Progressive ticket for election to the United States Senate in 1913; engaged in civic activities; was president of two banks and interested in the electric railways and electric lighting companies of Cumberland, Md.; died in that city March 20, 1927; interment in Rose Hill Cemetery.

WELLS, Alfred, a Representative from New York; born in Dagsboro, Sussex County, Del., May 27, 1814; pursued classical studies; studied law; was admitted to the bar in 1837 and commenced practice in Ithaca, Tompkins County, N. Y.; one of the owners of the Ithaca Journal and Advertiser 1839–1853; district attorney of Tompkins County, N. Y., 1845–1847; judge of Tompkins County Court from 1847 to 1851; attended the Anti-Nebraska Conventions at Saratoga and Auburn in 1854; elected as a Republican to the Thirty-sixth Congress (March 4, 1859–March 3, 1861); unsuccessful candidate for renomination in 1860; appointed United States assessor of internal revenue at Ithaca in 1862 and served until his death in Ithaca, N. Y., July 18, 1867; interment in the City Cemetery.

WELLS, Daniel, Jr., a Representative from Wisconsin; born in West Waterville, Maine, July 16, 1808; attended the public schools; taught school; engaged in the mercantile business at

Palmyra, Maine; moved to Milwaukee, Wis., in 1838 and engaged in banking and lumbering pursuits; appointed probate judge of Milwaukee in 1838; member of the Territorial council 1838–1840; elected as a Democrat to the Thirty-third and Thirty-fourth Congresses (March 4, 1853–March 3, 1857); was not a candidate for renomination in 1856; engaged in the development of railroads; a director of the Chicago, Milwaukee & St. Paul Railroad in 1865 and 1866; president of the La Crosse & Milwaukee Railroad, the Southern Minnesota Railroad, and the St. Paul & Minnesota Valley Railroad; died in Milwaukee, Wis., March 18, 1902; interment in Forest Home Cemetery.

WELLS, Erastus, a Representative from Missouri; born in Sackets Harbor, Jefferson County, N. Y., December 2, 1823: attended the public schools; moved to St. Louis, Mo., in 1842; established the first omnibus line in that city, and subsequently inaugurated the first street railroad company; member of the board of aldermen of St. Louis 1853–1867; president of the Missouri Railroad Co. 1859–1883; elected as a Democrat to the Forty-first and to the three succeeding Congresses (March 4, 1869–March 3, 1877): unsuccessful candidate for reelection in 1876 to the Forty-fifth Congress; elected to the Forty-sixth Congress (March 4, 1879–March 3, 1881); was not a candidate for renomination in 1880; president of the Laclede Gas Light Co. 1880–1883; retired from active business; died in St. Louis, Mo., October 2, 1893; interment in Bellefontaine Cemetery.

WELLS, Guilford Wiley, a Representative from Mississippi; born in Conesus Center, Livingston County, N. Y., February 14, 1840; attended the Genesee Wesleyan Seminary and College, Lima, N. Y.; during the Civil War enlisted in the Union Army as a private in the Twenty-seventh New York Infantry May 21, 1861; promoted to second lieutenant in the One Hundred and Thirtieth New York Infantry in 1862 and subsequently to first lieutenant and captain in the Nineteenth New York Cavalry; wounded in the Battle of Trevillian Station, Virginia, June 12, 1864; mustered out February 10, 1865, as a lieutenant colonel; was graduated from the law department of Columbian College (later George Washington University); Washington, D. C., in 1867; was admitted to the bar in 1867 and commenced practice in Holly Springs, Miss.; United States attorney for the northern district of Mississippi 1870–1875; elected as an administration Republican to the Forty-fourth Congress (March 4, 1875–March 3, 1877); declined to be a candidate for renomination in 1876; consul general at Shanghai, China, from June 23, 1877, to May 26, 1879; settled in Los Angeles, Calif., in 1879 and resumed the practice of law; died in Santa Monica, Calif., March 21, 1909; interment in Evergreen Cemetery, Los Angeles, Calif.

WELLS, John, a Representative from New York; born in Johnstown, Fulton County, N. Y., July 1, 1817; attended Johnstown Academy, and was graduated from Union College, Schenectady, N. Y., in 1835; studied law; was admitted to the bar in 1839 and commenced practice in Palmyra, N. Y.; returned to Johnstown, N. Y., and continued the practice of law; elected judge of Fulton County and served from June 1847 until his resignation in December 1851, having been elected to Congress; elected as a Whig to the Thirty-second Congress (March 4, 1851–March 3, 1853); declined to be a candidate for reelection in 1852 to the Thirty-third Congress; resumed the practice of law and also engaged in literary pursuits; died in Johnstown, N. Y., May 30, 1877; interment in Johnstown Cemetery.

WELLS, John Sullivan, a Senator from New Hampshire; born in Durham, Strafford County, N. H., October 18, 1803; attended Pembroke (N. H.) Academy; studied law; was admitted to the bar in 1828 and practiced in Guildhall, Vt., 1828–1835; moved to Lancaster, N. H., in 1836 and continued the practice of law until 1846; solicitor of Coos County 1838–1847; moved to Exeter, Rockingham County, N. H., and resumed the practice of law; member of the State house of representatives 1839–1841, serving as speaker in 1841; attorney general of New Hampshire in 1847; member and president of the State senate in 1851 and 1852; appointed to the United States Senate to fill the vacancy caused by the death of Moses Norris and served from January 16 to March 3, 1855; died in Exeter, N. H., August 1, 1860.

WELLS, Owen Augustine, a Representative from Wisconsin; born in Catskill, Greene County, N. Y., February 4, 1844; moved with his parents to a farm near Empire, Fond du Lac County, Wis., in 1850; attended public and private schools; studied law; was admitted to the bar in 1870 and commenced practice in Fond du Lac; also engaged in agricultural pursuits and stock raising; appointed by President Cleveland as collector of internal revenue for the third Wisconsin district in 1885, serving until 1887, when that district was consolidated with the Milwaukee district; delegate to the Democratic National Convention at St. Louis in 1888 and to the Gold Democratic National Convention at Indianapolis in 1896, also to numerous State conventions of his party in Wisconsin; elected as a Democrat to the Fifty-third Congress (March 4, 1893–March 3, 1895); unsuccessful candidate for reelection in 1894 to the Fifty-fourth Congress; declined to accept any public office and resumed the practice of law in Fond du Lac; retired from active practice and business in 1901 and resided in Fond du Lac, Wis., until his death there on January 29, 1935; interment in Rienzi Cemetery.

WELLS, William Hill, a Senator from Delaware; born in Burlington, N. J., January 7, 1769; received a liberal schooling; engaged in mercantile pursuits at Dagsboro and Millsboro, Del.; studied law; was admitted to the bar and practiced at Georgetown, Del.; moved to Dover, Del.; member of the General Assembly of Delaware 1794–1798; elected to the United States Senate to fill the vacancy caused by the death of Joshua Clayton and served from January 17, 1799, to November 6, 1804, when he resigned; again elected to the United States Senate to fill the vacancy caused by the resignation of James A. Bayard and served from May 28, 1813, to March 3, 1817; was not a candidate for reelection in 1816; resumed the practice of law and was interested in the oil business in Pennsylvania, where the town of Wellsboro was named in his honor; died near Dagsboro, Sussex County, Del., on March 11, 1829; interment in Prince Georges Churchyard, near Dagsboro.

WELSH, George Austin, a Representative from Pennsylvania; born near Bay View, Cecil County, Md., August 9, 1878; attended the country schools and the public schools of Philadelphia, Pa.; took business and academic courses at Temple University, Philadelphia, Pa.; engaged as a legislative stenographer and reporter from 1895 to 1901; graduated from the law department of Temple University in 1905; was admitted to the bar the same year and commenced practice in Philadelphia; secretary to the mayor of Philadelphia in 1905 and 1906; assistant solicitor for Philadelphia in 1906 and 1907; assistant district attorney for Philadelphia County 1907–1922; secretary of Temple University 1914–1938, serving as first vice president since 1938; president of the Republican district executive committee 1914–1932; attended officers' training camp at Fort Niagara, N. Y., from May 9 to August 10, 1917; member of the Board of Education of Philadelphia County 1921–1932; elected as a Republican to the Sixty-eighth and to the four succeeding Congresses and served from March 4, 1923, until his resignation, effective May 31, 1932, having been appointed judge of the United States district court for the eastern district of Pennsylvania, in which capacity he served until 1957, when he retired as judge to become senior judge; is a resident of Philadelphia, Pa.

WELTY, Benjamin Franklin, a Representative from Ohio; born near Bluffton, Allen County, Ohio, August 9, 1870; attended the common schools and the Tri-State Normal College of Indiana; was graduated from the Ohio Northern University at Ada in 1894 and from the University of Michigan at Ann Arbor in 1896; studied law; was admitted to the bar in 1896 and commenced practice in Lima, Allen County, Ohio; city solicitor of Bluffton 1897–1909; served as a private during the Spanish-American War; prosecuting attorney of Allen County 1905–1910; lieutenant colonel in the Ohio National Guard 1908–1913; special counsel to the State attorney general 1911–1913; special assistant in the United States Department of Justice 1913–1915; elected as a Democrat to the Sixty-fifth and Sixty-sixth Congresses (March 4, 1917–March 3, 1921); unsuccessful candidate for reelection in 1920 to the Sixty-seventh Congress; employed with Inland Waterways Association 1921–1924; resumed the practice of law until 1951, when he retired; is a resident of Lima, Ohio.

WEMPLE, Edward, a Representative from New York; born in Fultonville, Montgomery County, N. Y., October 23, 1843; attended the common schools in Fultonville and Ashland Academy in Green County, and was graduated from Union College, Schenectady, N. Y., in 1866; studied law for a time and then engaged in the foundry business; served as president of the village of Fultonville in 1873; supervisor of the town of Glen 1874–1876; member of the State assembly in 1877 and 1878; elected as a Democrat to the Forty-eighth Congress (March 4, 1883–March 3, 1885); unsuccessful candidate for reelection in 1884; continued his former business pursuits; was presidential elector on the Democratic ticket of Cleveland and Hendricks in 1884 and of Cleveland and Stevenson in 1892; served in the State senate in 1885; elected comptroller of the State of New York in 1887, and served two terms; unsuccessful candidate for reelection; died in Fultonville, N. Y., December 18, 1920; interment in Maple Avenue Cemetery.

WENDOVER, Peter Hercules, a Representative from New York; born in New York City August 1, 1768; received a liberal schooling; held several local offices; member of the volunteer fire department of New York City in 1796; delegate to the State constitutional conventions in 1801 and 1821; member of the State assembly in 1804; elected as a Democrat to the Fourteenth, Fifteenth, and Sixteenth Congresses (March 4, 1815–March 3, 1821); sheriff of New York County 1822–1825; died in New York City September 24, 1834; interment in the Dutch Reformed Church Cemetery.

WENE, Elmer H., a Representative from New Jersey; born on a farm near Pittstown, Hunterdon County, N. J., May 1, 1892; attended the public schools and Rutgers University, New Brunswick, N. J.; in 1918 engaged in agricultural pursuits and the hatching and raising of poultry near Vineland, N. J.; also lectured on the poultry industry in the leading agricultural colleges; served on the New Jersey State board of agriculture 1925–1934; member of the board of directors of the Newcomb Hospital, Vineland, N. J., in 1935 and 1936; elected as a Democrat to the Seventy-fifth Congress (January 3, 1937–January 3, 1939); unsuccessful candidate for reelection in 1938 to the Seventy-sixth Congress; member of the Board of Chosen Freeholders of Cumberland County, N. J., 1939–1941; again elected to the Seventy-seventh and Seventy-eighth Congresses (January 3, 1941–January 3, 1945); was not a candidate for renomination in 1944, but was an unsuccessful candidate for election to the United States Senate; resumed agricultural pursuits and poultry raising; also president and owner of two radio stations in New Jersey; in 1945 was adviser to the Secretary of Agriculture; elected to the State senate in 1946; delegate to the New Jersey State constitutional convention in 1947; on June 26, 1948, was given a recess appointment by President Truman as Under Secretary of Agriculture; unsuccessful Democratic candidate for Governor of New Jersey in 1949; unsuccessful candidate for election in 1950 to the Eighty-second Congress; was unsuccessful for the gubernatorial nomination in 1953; died in Philadelphia, Pa., on January 25, 1957; interment in Locust Grove Cemetery, Quakertown, Pa.

WENTWORTH, John (grandson of John Wentworth, Jr.), a Representative from Illinois; born in Sandwich, Carroll County, N. H., March 5, 1815; educated in the common schools and academies at Gilmanton, Wolfeboro, and New Hampton, N. H., and South Berwick, Maine; taught school for several years, and contributed political articles to newspapers; was graduated from Dartmouth College, Hanover, N. H., in 1836; moved to Chicago, Ill., in 1836, where he engaged as a clerk in a law office, and also studied law; editor and manager of the Chicago Democrat; appointed aide-de-camp to Governor Carlin in 1838; attended the law department of Harvard University in 1841; was admitted to the bar in 1841 and commenced practice in Chicago, Ill.; elected as a Democrat to the Twenty-eighth and to the three succeeding Congresses (March 4, 1843–March 3, 1851); elected to the Thirty-third Congress (March 4, 1853–March 3, 1855); Republican mayor of Chicago 1857–1863; delegate to the State constitutional convention in 1861; elected as a Republican to the Thirty-ninth Congress (March 4, 1865–March 3, 1867); resumed the practice of law; died in Chicago, Ill., October 16, 1888; interment in Rosehill Cemetery.

WENTWORTH, John, Jr. (grandfather of John Wentworth), a Delegate from New Hampshire; born at Salmon Falls, Strafford County, N. H., July 17, 1745; prepared for college by private tutors; was graduated from Harvard College in 1768; studied law; was admitted to the bar and commenced practice in Dover, N. H., in 1771; register of probate of Strafford County 1773–1787; appointed on January 10, 1774, a member of the committee of correspondence; member of the State house of representatives 1776–1780; appointed in June 1777 a member of the State committee of safety; served as moderator 1777–1786; Member of the Continental Congress in 1778 and 1779; one of the signers of the Articles of Confederation; member of the State council 1780–1784; served in the State senate 1784–1786; died in Dover, N. H., on January 10, 1787; interment in Pine Hill Cemetery.

WENTWORTH, Tappan, a Representative from Massachusetts; born in Dover, N. H., February 24, 1802; received a liberal schooling; studied law; was admitted to the bar in 1826 and commenced practice in York County, Maine; moved to Lowell, Mass., in 1833 and continued the practice of law; member of the common council 1836–1841; served in the State house of representatives in 1851, 1859, 1860, 1863, and 1864; member of the State senate in 1848, 1849, 1865, and 1866; elected as a Whig to the Thirty-third Congress (March 4, 1853–March 3, 1855); unsuccessful candidate for reelection in 1854 to the Thirty-fourth Congress; engaged in the practice of his profession until his death in Lowell, Mass., June 12, 1875; interment in Lowell Cemetery.

WERDEL, Thomas Harold, a Representative from California; born in Emery, Hanson County, S. Dak., September 13, 1905; moved with his parents to Kern County, Calif., in 1915; attended the public schools and Kern County Union High School; was graduated from the University of California at Berkeley in 1930 and from the University of California Law School in 1936; was admitted to the bar in 1936 and commenced the practice of law in Bakersfield, Calif.; member of the California State Assembly from the thirty-ninth district in the legislative sessions of 1943 and 1945; elected as a Republican to the Eighty-first and Eighty-second Congresses (January 3, 1949–January 3, 1953); was an unsuccessful candidate for reelection in 1952 to the Eighty-third Congress; resumed the practice of law; third party candidate for Vice President of the United States in 1956; resides in Bakersfield, Calif.

WERNER, Theodore B., a Representative from South Dakota; born in Ossian, Winneshiek County, Iowa, June 2, 1892; attended the public and parochial schools; moved to Rapid City, S. Dak., in 1909; engaged in the newspaper publishing and commercial printing business; editor and publisher of the Gate City Guide since 1912; served as postmaster of Rapid City 1915–1923; commissioner of Rapid City 1927–1930; served as mayor in 1929 and 1930; unsuccessful Democratic candidate for election in 1930 to the Seventy-second Congress; elected as a Democrat to the Seventy-third and Seventy-fourth Congresses (March 4, 1933–January 3, 1937); unsuccessful candidate for reelection in 1936 to the Seventy-fifth Congress; resumed the newspaper publishing business; is a resident of Rapid City, S. Dak.

WERTZ, George M., a Representative from Pennsylvania; born near Johnstown, Cambria County, Pa., July 19, 1856; attended the public schools, Ebensburg (Pa.) Academy, and the National Normal School, Lebanon, Ohio; taught school 1876–1884; school director 1886–1894; county commissioner 1893–1896; sheriff of Cambria County 1897–1901; member of the State senate 1908–1912, serving as president pro tempore in 1911 and 1912; organized and directed the Johnstown (Pa.) Daily Leader 1911–1917; comptroller of Cambria County 1914–1916; elected as a Republican to the Sixty-eighth Congress (March 4, 1923–March 3, 1925); unsuccessful candidate for renomination in 1924; engaged in the real-estate business until his death in Johnstown, Pa., November 19, 1928; interment in Grand View Cemetery.

WEST, Charles Franklin, a Representative from Ohio; born in Mount Vernon, Knox County, Ohio, January 12, 1895; attended the public schools; was graduated from Ohio Wesleyan University, Delaware, Ohio, in 1918; attended Harvard University, Cambridge, Mass., in 1920 and 1922–1924; served as American vice consul at Naples, Italy, in 1918 and 1919; instructor of government at the College of Wooster, Wooster, Ohio, 1920–1922 and at Harvard University, Cambridge, Mass., 1922–1924; professor of political science at Denison University, Granville, Ohio, 1924–1930; elected as a Democrat to the Seventy-second and Seventy-third Congresses (March 4, 1931–January 3, 1935); was not a candidate for renomination in 1934 but was an unsuccessful candidate for the Democratic nomination for United States Senator; served as special assistant to the governor of the Farm Credit Administration from February 25, 1935, to August 4, 1935; appointed Under Secretary of the Interior on August 5, 1935, and served until May 10, 1938; delegate to the Democratic National Convention at Philadelphia in 1936; member of United States Processing Tax Board of Review until October 1940; engaged in private business 1940–1947; became professor of political science at Akron (Ohio) University in 1947; received the Democratic nomination in 1954 to the Eighty-fourth Congress but withdrew before the November election; died in Bradenton, Fla., December 27, 1955; interment in Mound View Cemetery, Mount Vernon, Ohio.

WEST, George, a Representative from New York; born in Bradninch, Devonshire County, England, February 17, 1823; attended the common schools; immigrated to the United States in February 1849 and settled at Ballston Spa., Saratoga County, N. Y.; engaged in paper manufacturing; member of the State assembly 1872–1876; delegate to the Republican National Convention at Chicago in 1880; president of the First National Bank of Ballston Spa; elected as a Republican to the Forty-seventh Congress (March 4, 1881–March 3, 1883); unsuccessful candidate for reelection in 1882 to the Forty-eighth Congress; elected to the Forty-ninth and Fiftieth Congresses (March 4, 1885–March 3, 1889); was not a candidate for renomination in 1888; resumed his former business activities; died in Ballston Spa, N. Y., September 20, 1901; interment in Ballston Spa Cemetery.

WEST, Joseph Rodman, a Senator from Louisiana; born in New Orleans, La., September 19, 1822; moved with his parents to Philadelphia in 1824; educated in private schools; attended the University of Pennsylvania in 1836 and 1837; moved to New Orleans in 1841; captain attached to Maryland and District of Columbia Volunteers in the Mexican War from July 17, 1847, to August 10, 1848; moved to California in 1849 and engaged in newspaper work in San Francisco; proprietor of the San Francisco Price Current; during the Civil War entered the Union Army as lieutenant of the First Regiment, California Volunteer Infantry, August 13, 1861; promoted to the rank of colonel May 1, 1862; brigadier general of Volunteers October 25, 1862; brevetted major general January 4, 1866, "for faithful and meritorious services"; served in Arizona, New Mexico, and Arkansas, and led expedition which resulted in the death of the Apache chieftain, Mangus Coloradas, January 16, 1863; honorably mustered out at San Antonio, Tex., January 4, 1866; returned to New Orleans, La.; deputy United States marshal; auditor for customs 1867–1871; elected as a Republican to the United States Senate and served from March 4, 1871, to March 3, 1877; was not a candidate for reelection; member of the Board of Commissioners of the District of Columbia 1882–1885; retired from public life in 1885; died in Washington, D. C., October 31, 1898; interment in Arlington National Cemetery, Fort Myer, Va.

WEST, Milton Horace, a Representative from Texas; born on a farm near Gonzales, Gonzales County, Tex., June 30, 1888; attended the public schools and the West Texas Military Academy at San Antonio; served with Company C, Texas Rangers, in 1911 and 1912; studied law; was admitted to the bar in 1915 and began practice in Floresville, Tex.; moved to Brownsville, Tex., in 1917 and continued the practice of law; district attorney for the twenty-eighth judicial district of Texas 1922–1925 and assistant district attorney 1927–1930; member of the State house of representatives 1930–1933; elected as a Democrat to the Seventy-third Congress to fill the vacancy caused by the resignation of John N. Garner; reelected to the Seventy-fourth and to the six succeeding Congresses and served from April 22, 1933, until his death; was not a candidate for renomination in 1948; died in Walter Reed Hospital, Washington, D. C., October 28, 1948; interment in Buena Vista Cemetery, Brownsville, Tex.

WEST, William Stanley, a Senator from Georgia; was born near Buena Vista, Marion County, Ga., on August 23, 1849; moved with his parents to Lowndes (now Brooks) County, Ga., where he was reared; attended the country schools and preparatory schools at Lookout Mountain, Tenn., and Penfield, Ga.; taught school about four years; was graduated from the law department of Mercer University, Macon, Ga., in 1876 and from the literary department in 1880; was admitted to the bar in 1876 and commenced practice in Statenville, Ga.; moved to

Valdosta, Lowndes County, Ga.; engaged as a planter and mill-man; also interested in other enterprises; member of the State house of representatives 1892–1901; served in the State senate 1901–1906, serving as president in 1905 and 1906; chairman of the board of trustees of South Georgia State Normal College at Valdosta and ex officio member of the board of trustees of the University of Georgia at Athens; delegate to many Democratic State conventions; delegate at large to the Democratic National Convention at Denver in 1908 which nominated the presidential ticket of William J. Bryan, of Nebraska, for President and John W. Kern, of Indiana, for Vice President; appointed to the United States Senate to fill the vacancy caused by the death of Augustus O. Bacon and served from March 2 to November 3, 1914, when a successor was elected and qualified; resumed his occupation as planter and lumberman; died in Valdosta, Ga., on December 22, 1914; interment in Sunset Hill Cemetery.

WESTBROOK, John, a Representative from Pennsylvania; born in Sussex County, N. J., January 9, 1789; moved with his parents to Pike County, Pa., in 1792 and settled near Dingmans Ferry; attended private schools; engaged in lumbering and agricultural pursuits; colonel in the State militia in 1812; sheriff of Pike County in 1817; member of the State house of representatives in 1833; elected as a Democrat to the Twenty-seventh Congress (March 4, 1841–March 3, 1843); declined to be a candidate for reelection in 1842 to the Twenty-eighth Congress; resumed agricultural pursuits; died near Dingmans Ferry, Pike County, Pa., October 8, 1852; interment in Laurel Hill Cemetery, Milford, Pa.

WESTBROOK, Theodoric Romeyn, a Representative from New York; born in Fishkill, Dutchess County, N. Y., November 20, 1821; attended the common schools, and was graduated from Rutgers College, New Brunswick, N. J., in 1838; studied law; was admitted to the bar in 1843 and commenced practice in Kingston, Ulster County, N. Y.; elected as a Democrat to the Thirty-third Congress (March 4, 1853–March 3, 1855); declined to be a candidate for renomination in 1854; resumed the practice of his profession at Kingston, N. Y.; elected a justice of the supreme court in 1873; died while holding court in Troy, Rensselaer County, N. Y., on October 6, 1885; interment in Wiltwyck Cemetery, Kingston, N. Y.

WESTCOTT, James Diament, Jr., a Senator from Florida; born in Alexandria, Va., May 10, 1802; moved to New Jersey, where he received a liberal schooling; studied law; was admitted to the bar in 1824 and commenced practice; clerk in the Consular Bureau, Washington, D. C.; secretary of Florida Territory 1830–1834; United States attorney for the middle district of Florida 1834–1836; served in the Territorial house of representatives in 1832; delegate to the constitutional convention in 1838 and 1839 which framed the first constitution of the State; upon the admission of Florida as a State into the Union was elected as a Democrat to the United States Senate and served from July 1, 1845, to March 3, 1849; was not a candidate for reelection in 1848; settled in New York City in 1850 and practiced law; moved to Canada in 1862; died in Montreal, Canada, January 19, 1880; interment in City Cemetery, Tallahassee, Fla.

WESTERLO, Rensselaer, a Representative from New York; born in Albany, N. Y., April 29, 1776; was graduated from Columbia College, New York City, in 1795; studied law; was admitted to the bar and practiced; elected as a Federalist to the Fifteenth Congress (March 4, 1817–March 3, 1819); was not a candidate for reelection; resumed the practice of law; died in Albany, N. Y., April 18, 1851; interment in the Albany Rural Cemetery.

WESTLAND, Alfred John, a Representative from Washington; born in Everett, Snohomish County, Wash., December 14, 1904; attended the local schools and was graduated from the University of Washington Law School, Seattle, Wash., in 1926; engaged in the cotton goods business in New York City, N. Y., and Chicago, Ill., 1926–1930; in the investment brokerage business in Chicago, Ill., 1930–1936, and in Seattle, Wash., 1936–1941; enlisted in the United States Navy in the summer of 1940 and was commissioned a lieutenant (jg) in November 1940; was called to active duty May 1, 1941, serving the last two years aboard the U. S. Carrier *Independence* in the Pacific until separated from the service as a commander in February 1946; returned to Everett, Wash., and operated own insurance agency until 1954; elected as a Republican to the Eighty-third and to the three succeeding Congresses (January 3, 1953–January 3, 1961). *Reelected to the Eighty-seventh Congress.*

WETHERED, John, a Representative from Maryland; born near Wetheredville, Baltimore County, Md., on May 8, 1809; completed preparatory studies; held several local offices; engaged in the manufacture of woolen goods at Wetheredville, Md.; elected as a Democrat to the Twenty-eighth Congress (March 4, 1843–March 3, 1845); resumed the manufacture of woolen goods; delegate from Baltimore County to the State convention which framed the constitution of Maryland in 1867; retired from active pursuits in 1868 and lived on his estate, "Ashland," near Catonsville, Md., where he died February 15, 1888; interment in Greenmount Cemetery, Baltimore, Md.

WETMORE, George Peabody, a Senator from Rhode Island; born during a visit of his parents abroad, in London, England, August 2, 1846; received his early education at a private school; was graduated from Yale College in 1867 and from the law department of Columbia College, New York City, in 1869; was admitted to the bar of Rhode Island and of New York in 1869, but never practiced; trustee of the Peabody Museum of Natural History in Yale University; trustee of the Peabody Education Fund, president of the Newport Hospital, and a director of other associations; presidential elector on the Republican ticket of Garfield and Arthur in 1880 and of Blaine and Logan in 1884; member of the commission that built the new Rhode Island statehouse; Governor of Rhode Island in 1885 and 1886; unsuccessful candidate for a third term; unsuccessful candidate for election to the United States Senate in 1889; elected as a Republican to the United States Senate in 1894; reelected in 1900 and served from March 4, 1895, to March 3, 1907; elected January 22, 1908, to fill the vacancy caused by the failure of the legislature to elect in the term commencing March 4, 1907, and served until March 3, 1913; declined to be a candidate for reelection in 1912; died in Boston, Mass., on September 11, 1921; interment in Island Cemetery, Newport, R. I.

WEVER, John Madison, a Representative from New York; born in Ganges, Allegan County, Mich., February 24, 1847; attended the common schools and Albion (Mich.) College; during the Civil War entered the Union Army at the age of sixteen and served in the Army of the Cumberland and the Army of the Ohio; at the close of the war settled in Plattsburg, Clinton County, N. Y., and engaged in banking; elected county treasurer of Clinton County in 1884 and reelected in 1887; elected as a Republican to the Fifty-second and Fifty-third Congresses (March 4, 1891–March 3, 1895); was not a candidate for renomination in 1894 to the Fifty-fourth Congress; cashier and later president of the Merchants' National Bank of Plattsburg, N. Y.; died in Plattsburg, N. Y., September 27, 1914; interment in Riverside Cemetery.

WEYMOUTH, George Warren, a Representative from Massachusetts; born in West Amesbury (now Merrimac), Mass., August 25, 1850; attended the public schools and the Merrimac High School; moved to Fitchburg, Mass., in 1882 and engaged in the carriage business; later became manager of the Simonds Rolling Machine Co.; trustee of the Fitchburg Savings Bank 1891–1901 and director of the Fitchburg National Bank 1892–1901; director in other corporations; member of the common council of Fitchburg in 1886; served in the State house of representatives in 1896; delegate to the Republican National Convention at St. Louis in 1896 which nominated McKinley and Hobart; elected as a Republican to the Fifty-fifth and Fifty-sixth Congresses (March 4, 1897–March 3, 1901); was not a candidate for renomination in 1900; moved to Fairhaven; president of the Atlas Tack Corp. of Fairhaven, Mass., 1897–1910; killed in an automobile accident near Bingham, Maine, September 7, 1910; interment in Riverside Cemetery, Fairhaven, Bristol County, Mass.

WHALEY, Kellian Van Rensalear, a Representative from Virginia and from West Virginia; born in Onondaga County, near Utica, N. Y., May 6, 1821; moved to Ohio and attended the public schools; moved to Virginia in 1842, settled in Ceredo, and engaged in the lumbering business; elected as a Republican from Virginia to the Thirty-seventh Congress (March 4, 1861–March 3, 1863); during the Civil War recruited several regiments for the Union Army; upon the admission of West Virginia as a State into the Union was elected to the Thirty-eighth and Thirty-ninth Congresses and served from December 7, 1863, to March 3, 1867; was not a candidate for renomination in 1866; delegate to the Republican National Convention at Baltimore in 1864; collector of customs at Brazos de Santiago, Tex., in 1868; returned to West Virginia and settled in Point Pleasant, Mason County, where he died May 20, 1876; interment in Lone Oak Cemetery.

WHALEY, Richard Smith, a Representative from South Carolina; born in Charleston, S. C., July 15, 1874; attended the Episcopal High School, Alexandria, Va., and was graduated from the law department of the University of Virginia at Charlottesville in 1897; was admitted to the bar in 1897 and commenced practice in Charleston, S. C.; member of the State house of representatives 1900–1913; served as speaker 1907–1910 and as speaker pro tempore in 1913; presiding officer of the Democratic State convention in 1910 and of the Democratic city convention in 1911; delegate to the Democratic National Conventions in 1912 and 1920; elected as a Democrat to the Sixty-third Congress to fill the vacancy caused by the death of George S. Legare; reelected to the Sixty-fourth, Sixty-fifth, and Sixty-sixth Congresses and served from April 29, 1913, to March 3, 1921; was not a candidate for renomination in 1920; resumed the practice of law; appointed commissioner of the United States Court of Claims in 1925; appointed judge of the Court of Claims by President Hoover in 1930, and was designated chief justice in 1939; retired as chief justice in 1947; died in Charleston, S. C., November 8, 1951; interment in Magnolia Cemetery.

WHALLEY, John Irving, a Representative from Pennsylvania; born in Barnesboro, Cambria County, Pa., September 14, 1902; attended the public schools and Cambria Rowe Business College; engaged in the automobile, banking, and coal businesses; member of advisory board of Johnstown College, University of Pittsburgh; chairman of Somerset County Redevelopment Authority and Windber Planning Commission; member of Windber School Board 1935–1947; member of the State house of representatives 1951–1955 and served in the State senate 1955–1960; elected as a Republican to the Eighty-sixth Congress to fill the vacancy caused by the death of Douglas H. Elliott and served from November 8, 1960, to January 3, 1961. *Reelected to the Eighty-seventh Congress.*

WHALLON, Reuben, a Representative from New York; born in Bedminster, Somerset County, N. J., December 7, 1776; attended the common schools; moved to Argyle, Washington County, N. Y.; appointed justice of the peace for the township of Argyle March 13, 1806, and served until 1811; moved to Essex, Essex County, N. Y., in 1814; was a large landowner, farmer, merchant, mill owner, and ironmaster; served as captain and major in the New York State Militia 1803–1814; member of the State assembly in 1808, 1809, and 1811; supervisor of the town of Essex in 1818, 1819, 1827, and 1828; first judge of Essex County Court of Common Pleas 1831–1838; elected as a Jackson Democrat to the Twenty-third Congress (March 4, 1833–March 3, 1835); again engaged in his former business pursuits; died on his estate at Whallons Bay, town of Essex, N. Y., on April 15, 1843; interment in Whallons Bay Cemetery.

WHARTON, Charles Stuart, a Representative from Illinois; born in Aledo, Mercer County, Ill., April 22, 1875; moved to Chicago with his parents in 1878; attended the public schools; was graduated from the law department of the University of Michigan at Ann Arbor in 1896; was admitted to the bar in 1896 and commenced practice in Chicago, Ill.; prosecuting attorney for the town of Lake in 1899; appointed assistant city attorney of Chicago in 1903; elected as a Republican to the Fifty-ninth Congress (March 4, 1905–March 3, 1907); unsuccessful candidate for reelection in 1906 to the Sixtieth Congress; resumed the practice of law in Chicago, Ill.; member of the board of exemption and Government appeal agent at Chicago during the First World War; served as an assistant corporation counsel in 1919; appointed assistant State's attorney in 1920 and served in this capacity until December 1923, when he resigned; resumed the practice of law in Chicago, Ill., until 1929; operated a restaurant; author of several books; died in Chicago, Ill., September 4, 1939; interment in Mount Hope Cemetery.

WHARTON, James Ernest, a Representative from New York; born in Binghamton, Broome County, N. Y., October 4, 1899; attended the public schools of Richmondville, N. Y.; was graduated from Union University and from Albany Law School; during the First World War served with the United States Army; was admitted to the bar in 1923; employed with the Travelers Insurance Co., 1920–1929; commenced the private practice of law in 1929 at Richmondville, N. Y.; owns and operates a farm; district attorney of Schoharie County, N. Y., 1932–1935; elected surrogate, county judge, and judge of children's court of Schoharie County 1941–1947; elected as a Republican to the Eighty-second and to the four succeeding Congresses (January 3, 1951–January 3, 1961). *Reelected to the Eighty-seventh Congress.*

WHARTON, Jesse (grandfather of Wharton Jackson Green), a Representative and a Senator from Tennessee; born in Covesville, Albemarle County, Va., July 29, 1782; completed preparatory studies; studied law; was admitted to the bar and commenced practice in Albemarle County; moved to Tennessee; elected to the Tenth Congress (March 4, 1807–March 3, 1809); appointed to the United States Senate to fill the vacancy caused by the resignation of George W. Campbell and served from March 17, 1814, to October 10, 1815, when a successor was elected; resumed the practice of his profession; member of the Board of Visitors to the United States Military Academy, West Point, N. Y., in 1832; died in Nashville, Tenn., July 22, 1833; interment in Mount Olivet Cemetery.

WHARTON, Samuel, a Delegate from Delaware; born in Philadelphia, Pa., May 3, 1732; received a liberal schooling; engaged in mercantile pursuits; goods of the firm with which he was associated were destroyed by the Indians and for indemnification a large tract of land bordering on the Ohio River and comprising about one-fourth of the present State of West Virginia was made over to him; signed the nonimportation resolutions of 1765; while in England to secure a confirmation of the grant some of his correspondence with Benjamin Franklin was discovered and, with Franklin, he was forced to flee to France; returned to Philadelphia in 1780; Member of the Continental Congress from Delaware in 1782 and 1783; justice of the peace for the district of Southwark 1784–1786; judge of the court of common pleas 1790–1791 and resigned in the latter year; died at his country home near Philadelphia, Pa., in March 1800.

WHEAT, William Howard, a Representative from Illinois; born in Kahoka, Clark County, Mo., February 19, 1879; attended the public schools of Brookfield and Chillicothe, Mo., and Chaddock College and Gem City Business College, Quincy, Ill.; clerk in clothing stores in Quincy and Bloomington, Ill.; moved to Thomasboro, Ill., in 1900, becoming engaged as bookkeeper and later cashier of a bank; in 1909 moved to Rantoul, Ill., and served as vice president and president of banking institutions; also interested in agriculture; school treasurer of Rantoul, Ill., for a number of years; unsuccessful candidate for election to the Seventy-fifth Congress; elected as a Republican to the Seventy-sixth, Seventy-seventh, and Seventy-eighth Congresses and served from January 3, 1939, until his death in Washington, D. C., January 16, 1944; interment in Maplewood Cemetery, Rantoul, Ill.

WHEATON, Horace, a Representative from New York; born in New Milford, Litchfield County, Conn., February 24, 1803; moved with his parents to Pompey, Onondaga County, N. Y., in 1810; received a limited schooling; was graduated from Pompey (N. Y.) Academy; engaged in mercantile pursuits; member of the State assembly in 1834; one of the commissioners to build a railroad between Syracuse and Utica; postmaster of Pompey, N. Y., 1840–1842; supervisor of Pompey; city treasurer; elected as a Democrat to the Twenty-eighth and Twenty-ninth Congresses (March 4, 1843–March 3, 1847); was not a candidate for renomination in 1846; moved to Syracuse, N. Y., in 1846; mayor of Syracuse 1851–1853; city treasurer of Syracuse in 1857 and 1858; engaged in hardware, saddlery, and mercantile pursuits; died in Syracuse, N. Y., June 23, 1882; interment in Oakwood Cemetery.

WHEATON, Laban, a Representative from Massachusetts; born in Mansfield, Bristol County, Mass., on March 13, 1754; attended Wrentham (Mass.) Academy; was graduated from Harvard College in 1774; studied theology under private instructor at Woodstock, Conn.; also studied law; was admitted to the bar in 1788 and commenced practice in Milton, Mass.; judge of the Bristol County Court; member of the State house of representatives 1803–1808 and again in 1825; elected as a Federalist to the Eleventh and to the three succeeding Congresses (March 4, 1809–March 3, 1817); appointed chief justice of the court of common pleas of Bristol County May 18, 1810, which position he held until appointed chief justice of the court of sessions on May 25, 1819, for life; died in Norton, Bristol County, Mass., March 23, 1846; interment in Norton Cemetery.

WHEELER, Burton Kendall, a Senator from Montana; born in Hudson, Middlesex County, Mass., February 27, 1882; attended the common schools, and was graduated from Hudson High School in 1900; worked as a stenographer in Boston, Mass.; was graduated from the law department of the University of Michigan at Ann Arbor in 1905; was admitted to the bar the same year and commenced practice in Butte, Silver Bow County, Mont.; member of the State house of representatives 1910–1912; United States district attorney for Montana 1913–1918; resumed the practice of law in Butte; unsuccessful Democratic candidate for Governor of Montana in 1920; elected as a Democrat to the United States Senate in 1922 for the term ending March 3, 1929; unsuccessful candidate for Vice President of the United States in 1924 on the ticket nominated by the Conference for Progressive Political Action with Robert M. La Follette as the nominee for President; reelected to the United States Senate in 1928, 1934, and 1940 and served from March 4, 1923, to January 3, 1947; unsuccessful candidate for renomination in 1946; engaged in the practice of law in Washington, D. C., where he now resides

WHEELER, Charles Kennedy, a Representative from Kentucky; born near Hopkinsville, Christian County, Ky., April 18, 1863; received his early education from a private tutor; was graduated from Southwestern University, Clarksville, Tenn., in 1879 and from the Lebanon Law School, Lebanon, Tenn., in 1880; was admitted to the bar the same year through the enactment of a special grant by the State legislature, and commenced practice in Paducah, McCracken County, Ky.; presidential elector on the Democratic ticket of Cleveland and Stevenson in 1892; city solicitor of Paducah 1894–1896; elected as a Democrat to the Fifty-fifth, Fifty-sixth, and Fifty-seventh Congresses (March 4, 1897–March 3, 1903); did not seek renomination in 1902; practiced law in Paducah, Ky., until his death in that city June 15, 1933; interment in Oak Grove Cemetery.

WHEELER, Ezra, a Representative from Wisconsin; born in Chenango County, N. Y., December 23, 1820; received a liberal preparatory schooling and was graduated from Union College, Schenectady, N. Y., in 1842; moved to Berlin, Green Lake County, Wis., in 1849; studied law; was admitted to the bar and commenced practice in Berlin, Wis.; member of the State assembly in 1853; judge of Green Lake County 1854–1862; elected as a Democrat to the Thirty-eighth Congress (March 4, 1863–March 3, 1865); resumed the practice of law in Berlin, Wis.; on account of ill health, moved to Pueblo, Colo., in 1870; appointed register of the land office at Pueblo on June 27, 1871, and served until his death in that city on September 19, 1871; interment in Oakwood Cemetery, Berlin, Wis.

WHEELER, Frank Willis, a Representative from Michigan; born in Chaumont, Jefferson County, N. Y., March 2, 1853; attended the common schools; moved to Michigan in 1864 with his parents, who settled in East Saginaw; attended the Saginaw High School and the Ypsilanti State Normal School; engaged in boatbuilding; moved to West Bay City, Mich., in 1876; became master of the Saginaw River Tug Association; engaged in shipbuilding at the Bay Cities for many years; elected as a Republican to the Fifty-first Congress (March 4, 1889–March 3, 1891); was not a candidate for renomination in 1890; engaged in his former pursuits until 1899, when he moved to Detroit; returned to Saginaw in 1917 and organized the Saginaw Shipbuilding Co., and was engaged in building boats for the United States Government; died in Saginaw, Mich., August 9, 1921; interment in Elm Lawn Cemetery, Bay City, Mich.

WHEELER, Grattan Henry, a Representative from New York; born near Providence, R. I., August 25, 1783; attended public and preparatory schools; moved to New York with his parents, who settled in Steuben County about 1800; agriculturist and lumberman near Wheeler, N. Y.; member of the

State assembly in 1822, 1824, and 1826; served in the State senate 1826–1830; elected to the Twenty-second Congress (March 4, 1831–March 3, 1833); unsuccessful candidate for reelection to the Twenty-third Congress; resumed former pursuits; presidential elector on the Whig ticket of Harrison and Tyler in 1840; died in Wheeler, Steuben County, N. Y., March 11, 1852; interment in a private cemetery on the Wheeler homestead.

WHEELER, Hamilton Kinkaid, a Representative from Illinois; born in Ballston Township, Saratoga County, N. Y., August 5, 1848; moved to Illinois in 1852 with his parents, who settled near Grant Park, Kankakee County; attended public and private schools in Kankakee County; studied law; was admitted to the bar in 1871 and commenced practice in the city of Kankakee; member of the State senate in 1884; elected as a Republican to the Fifty-third Congress (March 4, 1893–March 3, 1895); was not a candidate for renomination in 1894 to the Fifty-fourth Congress; resumed the practice of law in Kankakee, Ill.; delegate to the Republican National Conventions in 1896 and 1900; died in Kankakee, Ill., July 19, 1918; interment in Mound Grove Cemetery.

WHEELER, Harrison H., a Representative from Michigan; born at Farmers Creek, Lapeer County, Mich., March 22, 1839; attended the common schools; taught school until 1861; during the Civil War enlisted in the Union Army November 1, 1861, as a private in Company C, Tenth Regiment, Michigan Volunteer Infantry; promoted to second lieutenant in June 1862; first lieutenant of Company E, same regiment, in April 1863; captain of Company F, same regiment, in April 1865; wounded at Buzzards Roost Gap, Kenesaw Mountain, and at Jonesboro, Ga., during the Atlanta campaign; settled in Bay City, Mich., at the close of the war; elected clerk of Bay County in 1866; studied law; was admitted to the bar in 1868 and commenced practice in Bay City; member of the State senate in 1870 and 1872; moved to Ludington, Mason County, Mich., in 1873; appointed circuit judge in 1874 and later elected to the office; resigned in June 1878; appointed postmaster April 16, 1878, and served until his successor was appointed, April 26, 1882; resumed the practice of law in Ludington; elected as a Democrat to the Fifty-second Congress (March 4, 1891–March 3, 1893); unsuccessful candidate for reelection in 1892 to the Fifty-third Congress; appointed United States pension agent at Detroit February 8, 1894, and served until his death; died at Farmers Creek, near Lapeer, Mich., while on a visit, July 28, 1896; interment in Lakeview Cemetery, Ludington, Mich.

WHEELER, John, a Representative from New York; born in Humphreysville (now Seymour), New Haven County, Conn., February 11, 1823; attended the common schools at Cheshire, Conn.; moved to New York City in 1843 and was engaged in the hotel business with his father; became a dry-goods clerk; elected as a Democrat to the Thirty-third and Thirty-fourth Congresses (March 4, 1853–March 3, 1857); declined to be a candidate for renomination in 1856 to the Thirty-fifth Congress; commissioner and president of the Department of Taxes and Assessments of New York City 1872–1880; member of the Board of Estimates and Apportionments and commissioner of accounts of New York City; was a lawyer, but did not practice; died in New York City April 1, 1906; interment in Woodlawn Cemetery.

WHEELER, Joseph, a Representative from Alabama; born in Augusta, Ga., September 10, 1836; attended local schools and the Episcopal Academy, Cheshire, Conn.; was graduated from the United States Military Academy at West Point, N. Y.,

July 1, 1859; brevetted second lieutenant of First Dragoons; attended the Cavalry School at Carlisle, Pa., from October 1, 1859, to July 18, 1860; transferred to the Mounted Rifles June 26, 1860; second lieutenant September 1, 1860, and served in New Mexico; resigned from the United States Army February 27, 1861, the resignation being accepted April 22, 1861; during the Civil War was appointed lieutenant of Artillery in the Confederate Army on April 3, 1861; successively promoted to the grade of colonel, brigadier general, and major general, and was commissioned lieutenant general in February 1865; in 1862 was assigned to the command of the Army Corps of Cavalry of the Western Army, continuing in that position until the war closed; took part in over 400 engagements; was wounded three times, and had sixteen horses shot under him; by joint resolution of the Confederate Congress received the thanks of that body for successful military operations; for the defense of the city of Aiken received the thanks of the State of South Carolina; senior Cavalry general of the Confederate Armies May 11, 1864; studied law; was admitted to the bar and engaged in practice at Wheeler, Ala., and also became a planter; presented credentials as a Democratic Member-elect to the Forty-seventh Congress and served from March 4, 1881, to June 3, 1882, when he was succeeded by William M. Lowe, who contested his election; subsequently elected to the same Congress to fill the vacancy caused by the death of William M. Lowe and served from January 15 to March 3, 1883; elected as a Democrat to the Forty-ninth and to the seven succeeding Congresses and served from March 4, 1885, to April 20, 1900, when he resigned; served in the Spanish-American War; commissioned major general of Volunteers May 4, 1898, and assigned to command of a Cavalry division, United States Army; commanded at the Battle of Las Guasimas (first victory of United States Army overseas) June 24, 1898; engaged in all the conflicts in front of Santiago which terminated in the surrender of the Spanish Army; senior member of the commission which negotiated the surrender of Santiago and the Spanish Army in Cuba; during the Philippine Insurrection commanded the First Brigade, Second Division, Eighth Army Corps, in the Tarlac campaign and in several other operations in central Luzon from July 8, 1899, to January 24, 1900; commissioned brigadier general in the United States Regular Army June 16, 1900; retired September 10, 1900; author of many books on military and civil matters; retired from active pursuits and traveled in Europe and Mexico; died while visiting his sister in Brooklyn, N. Y., January 25, 1906; interment in Arlington National Cemetery, Fort Myer, Va.

WHEELER, Loren Edgar, a Representative from Illinois; born in Havana, Mason County, Ill., October 7, 1862; attended the public schools and Graylock Institute, South Williamstown, Mass.; moved to Springfield, Ill., in 1880 and engaged in the ice and coal business until 1910 when he became identified with the advertising business; member of the board of aldermen 1895–1897; mayor of Springfield 1897–1901; delegate to the Republican National Convention at Philadelphia in 1900; postmaster of Springfield 1901–1913; elected as a Republican to the Sixty-fourth and to the three succeeding Congresses (March 4, 1915–March 3, 1923); unsuccessful candidate for reelection in 1922 to the Sixty-eighth Congress; again elected to the Sixty-ninth Congress (March 4, 1925–March 3, 1927); unsuccessful candidate for reelection in 1926 to the Seventieth Congress; continued his former business activities in Springfield, Ill., until his death there on January 8, 1932; interment in Oak Ridge Cemetery.

WHEELER, Nelson Platt, a Representative from Pennsylvania; born in Portville, Cattaraugus County, N. Y., November 4, 1841; attended the public schools and academies in Olean and Deposit, N. Y.; became a surveyor and civil engineer; moved to Endeavor, Forest County, Pa.; engaged in the lumber business and also interested in agricultural pursuits and banking; elected county commissioner in 1866; held various township offices; member of the State house of representatives in 1878 and 1879; declined to be a candidate for renomination; elected as a Republican to the Sixtieth and Sixty-first Congresses (March 4, 1907–March 3, 1911); unsuccessful candidate for renomination in 1910, but the primary election being contested, his opponent subsequently withdrew and he was tendered the congressional nomination, but declined; resumed his former business pursuits in Endeavor, Pa.; owing to ill health, moved to Pasadena, Los Angeles County, Calif., in 1915, and died there on March 3, 1920; interment in Mountain View Cemetery.

WHEELER, William Almon, a Representative from New York and a Vice President of the United States; born in Malone, Franklin County, N. Y., June 19, 1819; completed preparatory studies; attended the Franklin Academy at Malone and the University of Vermont at Burlington; studied law; was admitted to the bar in 1845 and practiced in Malone, N. Y.; for several years district attorney for Franklin County, N. Y.; member of the State assembly in 1850 and 1851; served in the State senate in 1858 and 1859; elected as a Republican to the Thirty-seventh Congress (March 4, 1861–March 3, 1863); delegate to the State constitutional conventions in 1867 and 1868; elected to the Forty-first and to the three succeeding Congresses (March 4, 1869–March 3, 1877); was not a candidate for reelection, having been nominated in 1876 as the Republican candidate for Vice President; elected Vice President of the United States on the Republican ticket of Hayes and Wheeler in 1876; retired from public life and active business pursuits because of ill health; died in Malone, N. Y., June 4, 1887; interment in Morningside Cemetery.

WHEELER, William McDonald, a Representative from Georgia; born near Alma, Bacon County, Ga., July 11, 1915; attended the public schools and South Georgia College at Douglas, Middle Georgia College at Cochran, and Georgia Teachers College at Statesboro; engaged in agricultural pursuits; taught school and also served as principal of the junior high schools in Bacon and Appling Counties 1936–1941; during World War II enlisted as a private in the Army Air Forces on May 30, 1942; was promoted through the ranks to captain and discharged on June 4, 1946; elected as a Democrat to the Eightieth and to the three succeeding Congresses (January 3, 1947–January 3, 1955); unsuccessful candidate for renomination in 1954; employed with the Georgia Motor Vehicle Division in the Internal Revenue Department, Atlanta, Ga., in 1955 and 1956; engaged in sales and public relations; is a resident of Alma, Ga.

WHELCHEL, Benjamin Frank, a Representative from Georgia; born in Lumpkin County, near Gainesville, Ga., December 16, 1895; attended the public schools; studied law privately in Gainesville, Ga.; was admitted to the bar in 1925 and commenced the practice of law in Gainesville, Ga.; judge of the city court of Hall County 1932–1934; elected as a Democrat to the Seventy-fourth and to the four succeeding Congresses (January 3, 1935–January 3, 1945); was not a candidate for renomination in 1944; resumed the practice of law; died in Gainesville, Ga., May 11, 1954; interment in West View Abbey, Atlanta, Ga.

WHERRY, Kenneth Spicer, a Senator from Nebraska; born in Liberty, Gage County, Nebr., February 28, 1892; attended the public schools, and was graduated from Pawnee City (Nebr.) High School, and from the University of Nebraska at Lincoln in 1914; attended Harvard University, Cambridge, Mass., in 1915 and 1916; during the First World War served in the United States Navy Flying Corps in 1917 and 1918; engaged in the sale of automobiles, implements, furniture, and in livestock farming; studied law; was admitted to the bar and commenced practice in Pawnee City, Nebr.; member of the Pawnee City, Nebr., Council in 1927 and 1929; mayor of Pawnee City 1929–1931 and 1938–1943; served in the State senate 1929–1932; unsuccessful candidate for Governor in 1933; unsuccessful candidate for nomination for United States Senator in 1935; Republican State chairman 1939–1942; western director for the Republican National Committee in twenty-two States west of the Mississippi River in 1941 and 1942; elected as a Republican to the United States Senate in 1942; reelected in 1948 and served from January 3, 1943, until his death; Republican Senate whip 1944–1948 and Republican leader of the Senate 1949–1951; died in Washington, D. C., November 29, 1951; interment in Pawnee City Cemetery, Pawnee City, Nebr.

WHIPPLE, Thomas, Jr., a Representative from New Hampshire; born in Lebanon, Grafton County, N. H., in 1787; completed preparatory studies; moved to Warren, N. H., in 1811; studied medicine in Haverhill and Hanover, N. H., and was graduated from Dartmouth College, Hanover, N. H., in 1814; commenced practice in Wentworth, N. H.; member of the State house of representatives 1818–1820; elected to the Seventeenth and to the three succeeding Congresses (March 4, 1821–March 3, 1829); resumed the practice of medicine; died in Wentworth, Grafton County, N. H., January 23, 1835.

WHIPPLE, William, a Delegate from New Hampshire; born in Kittery, York County, Maine, January 14, 1730; became a sailor and engaged in the slave trade; abandoned sailor life; liberated his slaves and engaged in mercantile pursuits in Portsmouth, N. H.; delegate to the Provincial Congress at Exeter in 1775; Member of the Continental Congress in 1775, 1776, and 1778; declined to be a candidate for renomination; one of the signers of the Declaration of Independence; commissioned a brigadier general in 1777; member of the State assembly 1780–1784; participated in several battles in the Revolutionary War; appointed judge of the State supreme court in 1782; financial receiver for New Hampshire 1782–1784; died in Portsmouth, N. H., November 28, 1785; interment in the North Cemetery.

WHITACRE, John Jefferson, a Representative from Ohio; born in Decatur, Burt County, Nebr., December 28, 1860; attended the public schools, Hiram (Ohio) College, and the University of Michigan at Ann Arbor; engaged as a manufacturer of hollow building tile; delegate to the Democratic National Convention at Baltimore in 1912; unsuccessful candidate in 1908 to the Sixty-first Congress; elected as a Democrat to the Sixty-second and Sixty-third Congresses (March 4, 1911–March 3, 1915); resumed his former manufacturing pursuits; president of the Whitacre Engineering Co. and the Whitacre-Greer Fireproofing Co.; died in Miami, Fla., December 2, 1938; interment in Magnolia Cemetery, Magnolia, Ohio.

WHITAKER, John Albert (grandson of Addison Davis James), a Representative from Kentucky; born in Russellville, Logan County, Ky., October 31, 1901; attended the public schools, Bethel College, and the University of Kentucky; studied law; was admitted to the bar in 1926 and commenced practice in Russellville, Ky.; county attorney of Logan County, Ky., 1928–1948; delegate to all State conventions 1924–1950; elected as a Democrat to the Eightieth Congress to fill the vacancy caused by the resignation of Earle C. Clements; reelected to the Eighty-first and Eighty-second Congresses and served from April 17, 1948, until his death in Russellville, Ky., December 15, 1951; interment in Maple Grove Cemetery.

WHITCOMB, James, a Senator from Indiana; born near Windsor, Windsor County, Vt., December 1, 1795; was graduated from Transylvania University, Lexington, Ky., in 1819; studied law; was admitted to the bar and commenced practice in Bloomington, Ind., in 1824; prosecuting attorney for Monroe County in 1826; member of the State senate 1830–1836; appointed by President Jackson as Commissioner of the General Land Office October 21, 1836, and served until July 6, 1841; resumed the practice of law in Terre Haute, Ind.; Governor of Indiana 1843–1849; elected as a Democrat to the United States Senate and served from March 4, 1849, until his death in New York City October 4, 1852; interment in Crown Hill Cemetery, Indianapolis, Ind.

WHITE, Addison (cousin of John White), a Representative from Kentucky; born in Abingdon, Washington County, Va., May 1, 1824; received an academic education; was graduated from Princeton College in 1844; engaged in agricultural pursuits and cotton raising; elected as a Whig to the Thirty-second Congress (March 4, 1851–March 3, 1853); during the Civil War served in the Confederate Army; moved to Huntsville, Ala., and resumed agricultural pursuits; died in Huntsville, Ala., February 4, 1909; interment in Maple Hill Cemetery.

WHITE, Albert Smith, a Representative and a Senator from Indiana; born at "The Clove," near Washingtonville, Orange County, N. Y., October 24, 1803; was graduated from Union College, Schenectady, N. Y., in 1822; studied law; was admitted to the bar in 1825 and practiced; moved to LaFayette, Ind., in 1829; assistant clerk of the State house of representatives in 1830 and 1831 and clerk from 1832 to 1835; unsuccessful candidate for election in 1832 to the Twenty-third Congress; presidential elector on the Whig ticket of Harrison and Granger in 1836; elected as a Whig to the Twenty-fifth Congress (March 4, 1837–March 3, 1839); was not a candidate for renomination in 1838; president of several railroads; elected to the United States Senate and served from March 4, 1839, to March 3, 1845; declined to be a candidate for reelection; moved to Stockwell, Ind., and resumed the practice of law; elected as a Republican to the Thirty-seventh Congress (March 4, 1861–March 3, 1863); was not a candidate for renomination in 1862; appointed by President Lincoln one of three commissioners to adjust the claims of citizens of Minnesota and Dakota against the Government for Indian depredations; appointed judge of the United States Court for the District of Indiana on January 18, 1864, and served until his death in Stockwell, Ind., September 24, 1864; interment in Greenbush Cemetery, Lafayette, Ind.

WHITE, Alexander, a Representative from Virginia; born in Frederick County, Va., in 1738; studied law at the Inner Temple, London, in 1762 and attended Gray's Inn in 1763; member of the State house of delegates 1782–1786 and in 1788; delegate to the State convention in 1788; elected as a Federalist to the First and Second Congresses (March 4, 1789–March 3, 1793); again a member of the State house of delegates 1799–1801; appointed by President Washington May 18, 1795, one of the three commissioners to lay out the city of Washington, D. C., and erect the public buildings, and served until May 1, 1802, when the board was abolished; died on his estate, "Woodville," in Frederick County, Va., September 19, 1804.

WHITE, Alexander, a Representative from Alabama; born in Franklin, Williamson County, Tenn., October 16, 1816; moved with his parents to Courtland, Ala., in 1821; pursued an academic course and attended the University of Tennessee at Knoxville; served in the Seminole War in 1836; moved to Talladega, Ala., in 1837; studied law; was admitted to the bar in 1838 and commenced practice in Talladega; elected as a Union Whig to the Thirty-second Congress (March 4, 1851–March 3, 1853); moved to Selma, Ala., in 1856 and continued the practice of law; delegate to the State constitutional convention in 1865; member of the State house of representatives in 1872; elected as a Republican to the Forty-third Congress (March 4, 1873–March 3, 1875); unsuccessful candidate for reelection in 1874 to the Forty-fourth Congress; appointed an associate justice of the United States Court for the Territory of Utah in 1875, serving only a few months; moved to Dallas, Tex., in 1876 and resumed the practice of law; died in Dallas December 13, 1893; interment in Greenwood Cemetery.

WHITE, Alexander Colwell, a Representative from Pennsylvania; was born near Kittanning, Armstrong County, Pa., December 12, 1833; attended the public schools; taught school; attended the Jacksonville Institute and the Dayton Union Academy; moved to Jefferson County, Pa., in 1860 where he studied law; was admitted to the bar in 1862, and commenced practice in Punxsutawney, Pa.; during the Civil War enlisted in the Union Army as a private in Company I, Eighth Regiment, Pennsylvania Volunteer Infantry; moved to Brookville, Jefferson County, Pa., and continued the practice of his profession; elected district attorney in 1867 and 1870; elected as a Republican to the Forty-ninth Congress (March 4, 1885–March 3, 1887); was not a candidate for reelection in 1886 to the Fiftieth Congress; resumed the practice of his profession; justice of the peace for Rose Township; died near Brookville, Pa., June 11, 1906; interment in Brookville Cemetery.

WHITE, Allison, a Representative from Pennsylvania; born in Pine Township, near Jersey Shore, Pa., December 21, 1816; attended the public schools, and was graduated from Allegheny College, Meadville, Crawford County, Pa.; studied law; was admitted to the bar and commenced practice in Lock Haven, Pa.; was elected as a Democrat to the Thirty-fifth Congress (March 4, 1857–March 3, 1859); unsuccessful candidate for reelection in 1858 to the Thirty-sixth Congress; engaged in the lumber and coal business at Philadelphia; died in Philadelphia, Pa., on April 5, 1886; interment in Highland Cemetery, Lock Haven, Clinton County, Pa.

WHITE, Bartow, a Representative from New York; born in Yorktown, Westchester County, N. Y., November 7, 1776; attended the common schools and completed preparatory studies; studied medicine with his father, Dr. Ebenezer White, and commenced practice in Fishkill, N. Y., in 1800; elected to the Nineteenth Congress (March 4, 1825–March 3, 1827); resumed the practice of medicine; presidential elector on the Whig ticket of Harrison and Tyler in 1840; died in Fishkill, Dutchess County, N. Y., December 12, 1862; interment in the Dutch Reformed Church Cemetery.

WHITE, Benjamin, a Representative from Maine; born in Goshen (now Vienna), Maine, May 13, 1790; attended the common schools; moved to Winthrop, Maine, in 1802 and was employed on a farm until 1808 when he entered Farmington Academy; taught school for several years; during the War of 1812 was in Augusta, Maine, and assisted in raising troops, later serving as a noncommissioned officer with troops stationed at Castine and Eastport, Maine; again engaged in teaching in Montville, Maine, until 1821, when he also engaged in the sawmill business and agricultural pursuits; served as town selectman; member of the State house of representatives in 1829, 1841, and 1842; elected as a Democrat to the Twenty-eighth Congress (March 4, 1843–March 3, 1845); resumed his former pursuits; died in Montville, Maine, on June 7, 1860; interment in Halldale Cemetery, North Montville, Maine.

WHITE, Campbell Patrick, a Representative from New York; born in Ireland November 30, 1787; received a limited education; immigrated to the United States in 1816 and engaged in mercantile pursuits in New York City; elected as a Jackson Democrat to the Twenty-first and to the three succeeding Congresses and served from March 4, 1829, until his resignation in 1835, which occurred before the convening of the Twenty-fourth Congress; resumed mercantile pursuits; appointed quartermaster general of the State militia on January 24, 1831; delegate to the New York State constitutional convention in 1845; retired from active business pursuits and resided in New York City, where he died February 12, 1859; interment in St. Paul's Cemetery.

WHITE, Cecil Fielding, a Representative from California; born in Temple, Bell County, Tex., December 12, 1900; attended the public schools of Fort Smith, Ark.; spent most of early youth and boyhood in Fort Smith, Ark.; at sixteen years of age joined the United States Army and served on the Mexican Border and at the outbreak of the First World War went to France as a sergeant in the One Hundred and Forty-second Field Artillery, Thirty-ninth Division, 1916–1919; with George H. McFadden Bros., cotton brokers, as telegrapher and later appointed assistant manager of the Los Angeles, Calif., office; in 1926 associated with the California Cotton Mills of Oakland, Calif., and sent to Fresno, Calif., as manager of their cotton merchandising department; founded and operated the Cecil F. White & Co., 1930–1932; manager of Cockrell & Co., Little Rock, Ark., and Memphis, Tenn., 1933–1935; manager of Frierson & Co., Memphis, Tenn., in 1935 and 1936; vice president and manager of the R. G. Hamilton & Co., Fresno, Calif., 1936–1941; in 1937 founded the Pinedale Compress & Warehouse Co. at Fresno, Calif.; owner and operator of the Cecil F. White Ranches, Inc., Devils Den, Calif.; in 1944 delegate to Democratic State Convention in 1948; elected as a Democrat to the Eighty-first Congress (January 3, 1949–January 3, 1951); unsuccessful candidate for reelection in 1950 to the Eighty-second Congress; engaged in cotton compressing business; resides in Orinda, Calif.

WHITE, Chilton Allen, a Representative from Ohio; born in Georgetown, Brown County, Ohio, February 6, 1826; attended the public schools; taught school; served in the Mexican War with Company G, First Regiment, Ohio Volunteers; studied law; was admitted to the bar in 1848 and commenced the practice of law in Georgetown, Ohio; prosecuting attorney of Brown County from 1852 to 1854; member of the State senate in 1859 and 1860; elected as a Democrat to the Thirty-seventh and Thirty-eighth Congresses (March 4, 1861–March 3, 1865); unsuccessful for reelection in 1864 to the Thirty-ninth Congress; resumed the practice of law in Georgetown; delegate to the State constitutional convention in 1873; unsuccessful candidate for secretary of state in 1896; died in Georgetown, Ohio, December 7, 1900; interment in Confidence Cemetery.

WHITE, Compton Ignatius, a Representative from Idaho; born in Baton Rouge, La., July 31, 1877; at an early age moved with his parents to Rankin County, Miss., and to Clark Fork, Bonner County, Idaho, in 1890; attended the public schools, Metropolitan Business College, Chicago, Ill., and Gonzaga University, Spokane, Wash.; railway telegraph operator 1897–1903, trainman 1903–1906, and conductor 1906–1910; engaged in agricultural, lumbering, and mining work in Clark Fork; also engaged in stock raising; member of the board of trustees of Clark Fork; delegate to the Democratic National Conventions in 1928, 1932, and 1936; unsuccessful candidate for election in 1930 to the Seventy-second Congress; elected as a Democrat to the Seventy-third and to the six succeeding Congresses

(March 4, 1933–January 3, 1947); unsuccessful candidate for reelection in 1946 to the Eightieth Congress; elected to the Eighty-first Congress (January 3, 1949–January 3, 1951); was not a candidate for renomination in 1950 but was unsuccessful for the Democratic nomination for United States Senator; defeated for the Democratic nomination for Congress in 1952; resumed stock raising and mining interests at Clark Fork, Idaho; died in Spokane, Wash., March 31, 1956; interment in the family cemetery, east of Clark Fork, Idaho.

WHITE, David, a Representative from Kentucky; born in 1785; completed preparatory studies; studied law; was admitted to the bar and commenced practice in New Castle, Ky.; member of the State house of representatives in 1826; elected to the Eighteenth Congress (March 4, 1823–March 3, 1825); died in Franklin County, Ky., October 19, 1834.

WHITE, Dudley Allen, a Representative from Ohio; born in New London, Huron County, Ohio, January 3, 1901; attended the public schools and was graduated from the New London High School in 1918; during the First World War served as an enlisted man in the United States Navy; employed with a rubber company in Akron, Ohio, in 1919 and 1920, and also engaged in the insurance business; moved to Uhrichsville, Ohio, and engaged in the dry-goods business in 1920 and 1921; returned to New London, Ohio, and became associated with a company manufacturing regalia and uniforms 1921–1925; entered the newspaper business at Norwalk, Ohio, in 1925, later becoming editor and general manager; delegate to the Republican National Conventions in 1928, 1948, and an alternate in 1932 and 1956; State commander of the American Legion in Ohio in 1929 and 1930; trustee of Bowling Green State University for five years; elected as a Republican to the Seventy-fifth and Seventy-sixth Congresses (January 3, 1937–January 3, 1941); did not seek renomination in 1940, but was unsuccessful for the Republican nomination for United States Senator; during World War II was called to active duty in the United States Navy in 1942 as a lieutenant commander; promoted to captain and served as director of recruiting and induction until 1946; awarded the Legion of Merit; director of the Citizens National Bank and president of Sandusky Broadcasting Co., of Norwalk, Ohio; served as executive director of President Eisenhower's Commission on Intergovernmental Relations in 1954 and 1955; president and publisher of the Norwalk Reflector-Herald and the Sandusky Register at time of death: died in Delaware, Ohio, October 14, 1957; interment in Woodlawn Cemetery, Norwalk, Ohio.

WHITE, Edward Douglass (son of James White), a Representative from Louisiana; born in Nashville, Tenn., in March 1795; moved with his father to what is now St. Martin Parish, La., in 1799; attended the common schools, and was graduated from the University of Nashville, Tennessee, in 1815; studied law; was admitted to the bar and commenced practice in Donaldsonville, La.; was appointed judge of the city court of New Orleans and moved there in 1825; elected to the Twenty-first, Twenty-second, and Twenty-third Congresses and served from March 4, 1829, to November 15, 1834, when he resigned; Governor of Louisiana from 1834 to 1838; moved to Thibodaux; elected as a Whig to the Twenty-sixth and Twenty-seventh Congresses (March 4, 1839–March 3, 1843); resumed the practice of his profession; also engaged as a planter; died in New Orleans, La., April 18, 1847; interment in St. Joseph's Catholic Cemetery, Thibodaux, La.

WHITE, Edward Douglass (son of the preceding), a Senator from Louisiana; born near Thibodaux, Lafourche Parish, La., November 3, 1845; attended Mount St. Mary's College, near Emmitsburg, Md., the Jesuit College in New Orleans, La., and Georgetown College, Washington, D. C.; served in the Confederate Army during the Civil War; studied law; was admitted to the bar and commenced practice in New Orleans, La., in 1868; member of the State senate 1874–1878; upon the death of Justice Egan, was appointed January 10, 1879, as associate justice of the supreme court of Louisiana and served until April 5, 1880; resumed the practice of law; elected as a Democrat to the United States Senate and served from March 4, 1891, until his resignation, effective March 12, 1894; appointed Associate Justice of the Supreme Court of the United States by President Cleveland on February 19, 1894, and qualified on March 12, 1894; appointed Chief Justice of the United States December 12, 1910, took the oath of office December 19, 1910, and served until his death in Washington, D. C., May 19, 1921; interment in Oak Hill Cemetery.

WHITE, Francis, a Representative from Virginia; born near Winchester, Frederick County, Va.; attended the common schools at Winchester; engaged in agricultural pursuits; elected a member of the State house of delegates in 1794, 1809–1813, and 1818; elected to the Thirteenth Congress (March 4, 1813–March 3, 1815); served in the State senate in 1823 and 1824; appointed sheriff of Hampshire County, Va. (now West Virginia), on December 9, 1823, by the Governor; died in Hampshire County, on the Capon River, in November 1826.

WHITE, Francis Shelley (Frank), a Senator from Alabama; born in Prairie, Noxubee County, Miss., March 13, 1847; attended the common schools and was tutored at home; during the Civil War served in the Confederate Army as a private in Company F, First Mississippi Cavalry, and also with Gen. Nathan B. Forrest; was captured near the close of the war at Selma, Ala.; after the close of the war engaged in agricultural pursuits until 1868; studied law; was admitted to the bar in 1869 and commenced practice in West Point, Miss.; was a member of the State house of representatives in 1875, 1882, and 1883; moved to Birmingham, Jefferson County, Ala., in 1886 and continued the practice of law; president of the Democratic State convention in 1900; delegate to the Democratic National Convention at Kansas City in 1900 and to the State constitutional convention in 1901; chairman of the Democratic State executive committee 1908–1910; elected as a Democrat to the United States Senate to fill the vacancy caused by the death of Joseph F. Johnston and served from May 11, 1914, to March 3, 1915; was not a candidate for renomination; resumed the practice of his profession until his death in Birmingham, Ala., August 1, 1922; interment in Elmwood Cemetery.

WHITE, Frederick Edward, a Representative from Iowa; born in Prussia, Germany, January 19, 1844; immigrated to the United States in 1857 with his mother, who settled on a farm in Keokuk County, Iowa; during the Civil War joined the Eighth Regiment, Iowa Volunteer Infantry, in 1861 but was rejected on account of age; enlisted in February 1862 in the Thirteenth Regiment, Iowa Volunteer Infantry, and was mustered out in August 1865; returned to Keokuk County and engaged in agricultural pursuits and stock raising; elected as a Democrat to the Fifty-second Congress (March 4, 1891–March 3, 1893); unsuccessful candidate for reelection in 1892 to the Fifty-third Congress; retired from public life and resumed agricultural pursuits; died in Sigourney, Keokuk County, Iowa, January 14, 1920; interment in Sigourney Cemetery.

WHITE, George, a Representative from Ohio; born in Elmira, Chemung County, N. Y., August 21, 1872; moved with his parents to Titusville, Crawford County, Pa., in 1874; attended the common schools; was graduated from the local high school in 1891 and from Princeton College in 1895; taught school for several years; mined in the Klondike 1898–1901; moved to Washington County, Ohio, in 1902 and settled in Marietta; engaged in the production of oil; member of the State house of representatives 1905–1908; unsuccessful candidate for election in 1908 to the Sixty-first Congress; elected as a Democrat to the Sixty-second and Sixty-third Congresses (March 4, 1911–March 3, 1915); unsuccessful candidate for reelection in 1914 to the Sixty-fourth Congress; elected to the Sixty-fifth Congress (March 4, 1917–March 3, 1919); was an unsuccessful candidate for reelection in 1918 to the Sixty-sixth Congress; served as chairman of the Democratic National Committee from July 1920 to November 1921; resumed his former activities in the oil business; Governor of Ohio 1931–1935; chairman of the Northwest Territory (Federal) Commission in 1938; vice chairman of the Marietta College Board of Trustees; vice president and a director of People's Banking & Trust Co. of Marietta, Ohio; died in West Palm Beach, Fla., December 15, 1953; interment in Oak Grove Cemetery, Marietta, Ohio.

WHITE, George Elon, a Representative from Illinois; born in Millbury, Worcester County, Mass., March 7, 1848; attended the public schools; during the Civil War enlisted as a private in the Fifty-seventh Regiment, Massachusetts Veteran Volunteers, in which he served under General Grant in the Army of the Potomac, from the Battle of the Wilderness until the surrender of General Lee at Appomattox Court House; after the close of the war entered a commercial college in Worcester, Mass.; moved to Chicago, Ill., in 1867 and engaged in the lumber business and also became interested in banking; member of the board of aldermen of Chicago; member of the State senate 1878–1886; elected as a Republican to the Fifty-fourth and Fifty-fifth Congresses (March 4, 1895–March 3, 1899); unsuccessful candidate for reelection in 1898 to the Fifty-sixth Congress; resumed his former business pursuits in Chicago, Ill., and served as president of the White Lumber Co.; died in Chicago, Ill., on May 17, 1935; interment in the mausoleum in Rosehill Cemetery.

WHITE, George Henry, a Representative from North Carolina; born in Rosindale, Bladen County, N. C., December 18, 1852; was of the Negro race; attended the public schools, and was graduated from Howard University, Washington, D. C., in 1877; studied law; was admitted to the bar in 1879 and commenced practice in New Bern, N. C.; principal of the State Normal School of North Carolina; member of the State house of representatives in 1880; served in the State senate in 1884; solicitor and prosecuting attorney for the second judicial district of North Carolina 1886–1894; delegate to the Republican National Conventions in 1896 and 1900; elected as a Republican to the Fifty-fifth and Fifty-sixth Congresses (March 4, 1897–March 3, 1901); was not a candidate for renomination in 1900 to the Fifty-seventh Congress; resumed the practice of law and also engaged in banking; died in Philadelphia, Pa., December 28, 1918; interment in Eden Cemetery.

WHITE, Harry, a Representative from Pennsylvania; born in Indiana, Indiana County, Pa., January 12, 1834; attended Indiana (Pa.) Academy, and was graduated from Princeton College in 1854; studied law; was admitted to the bar in June 1855 and commenced practice in Indiana, Pa.; during the Civil War entered the Union Army as major of the Sixty-seventh Regiment, Pennsylvania Volunteer Infantry, on December 13, 1861; mustered out February 22, 1865; brevetted a brigadier general of Volunteers March 2, 1865; member of the State senate during his military service and attended its sessions in the winter of 1862–1863; reelected to the State senate and served from 1865 to 1874, being speaker at the close of the last term; delegate to the State constitutional convention in 1872; unsuccessful candidate for Governor of Pennsylvania in 1872; elected as a Republican to the Forty-fifth and Forty-sixth Congresses (March 4, 1877–March 3, 1881); was not a candidate for renomination in 1880; elected a judge of Indiana County, Pa., in 1884; reelected in 1894 and served until 1904; resumed the practice of law and engaged in banking; died in Indiana, Pa., June 23, 1920; interment in Oakland Cemetery.

WHITE, Hays Baxter, a Representative from Kansas; born near Fairfield, Jefferson County, Iowa, on September 21, 1855; attended the rural schools of his native county; engaged in agricultural pursuits; moved to Jewell County, Kans., in 1875 and engaged in agricultural pursuits near Mankato; taught school at Mankato in 1876; member of the State house of representatives 1888–1890; member of the State senate 1900–1904; mayor of Mankato in 1914 and 1915; member of the State tax commission in 1915–1918; elected as a Republican to the Sixty-sixth and to the four succeeding Congresses (March 4, 1919–March 3, 1929); election unsuccessfully contested by W. H. Clark; was not a candidate for renomination in 1928; retired from active pursuits in 1929; died in Mankato, Kans., September 29, 1930; interment in Mount Hope Cemetery.

WHITE, Hugh, a Representative from New York; born in Whitestown, Oneida County, N. Y., on December 25, 1798; attended the common schools; was graduated from Hamilton College, Clinton, N. Y., in 1823; studied law but did not practice; entered business at Chittenango in 1825 and afterwards at Rondout; active in the building of the Michigan Southern & Northern Indiana Railroad; moved to Cohoes, N. Y., in 1830; was greatly interested in the development of water power from the Mohawk River; organized the Rosendale Cement Works; elected as a Republican to the Twenty-ninth, Thirtieth, and Thirty-first Congresses (March 4, 1845–March 3, 1851); resumed his business activities; died in Waterford, N. Y., October 6, 1870; interment in Albany Rural Cemetery.

WHITE, Hugh Lawson, a Senator from Tennessee; born in Iredell County, N. C., October 30, 1773; moved with his parents in 1785 to that part of North Carolina which now is Knox County, Tenn.; participated in the expedition against the Cherokees under General Sevier; pursued classical studies in Philadelphia, Pa., and studied law in Lancaster, Pa.; was admitted to the bar in 1796 and commenced practice in Knoxville, Tenn.; private secretary to Governor Blount; judge of the State supreme court 1801–1807; served in the State senate 1807–1809; appointed United States district attorney in 1808; judge of the supreme court 1809–1815; chosen president of the State bank in 1815; again a member of the State senate 1817–1825; elected to the United States Senate to fill the vacancy caused by the resignation of Andrew Jackson; reelected in 1829 and 1835 and served from October 28, 1825, to January 13, 1840, when he resigned because he could not conscientiously obey the instructions of his constituents; chosen President pro tempore of the Senate December 3, 1832; received the electoral votes of Tennessee and Georgia in 1836 for President of the United States; died in Knoxville, Tenn., April 10, 1840; interment in First Presbyterian Church Cemetery.

WHITE, James (father of Edward Douglass White), a Delegate from North Carolina and from the Territory South of the River Ohio (now the State of Tennessee); born in Philadelphia, Pa., June 16, 1749; attended a Jesuit College in St. Omer, France; returned to the United States and studied medicine in the

University of Pennsylvania at Philadelphia; also studied law; moved to North Carolina and settled in Davidson County; member of the North Carolina General Assembly in 1785; Member of the Continental Congress from North Carolina 1786–1788; superintendent of Indian affairs for the southern district in 1786; after the creation of the Territory South of the River Ohio (later the State of Tennessee) in 1790, served in the house of representatives of the first Territorial legislature from Davidson County in 1794; elected as a Delegate to the Third and Fourth Congresses from the Territory South of the River Ohio and served from September 3, 1794, to June 1, 1796, when the Territory was admitted into the Union as the State of Tennessee; moved to Louisiana in 1799; appointed judge of Attakapas district in 1804 and later of St. Martin Parish; died in Attakapas, La., in October 1809.

WHITE, James Bain, a Representative from Indiana; born in Stirlingshire, Scotland, June 26, 1835; attended the common schools; immigrated to the United States in 1854 and settled in Fort Wayne, Ind.; a calico printer and a tailor until the outbreak of the Civil War; enlisted as a private in Company I, Thirteenth Regiment, Indiana Volunteers; elected captain of the company and served until December 1862, when he resigned; was wounded in the Battle of Shiloh April 7, 1862; elected a member of the common council of Fort Wayne, Ind., in 1874; operated a department store; engaged in the manufacture of wheels and was also interested in banking; elected as a Republican to the Fiftieth Congress (March 4, 1887–March 3, 1889); unsuccessful candidate for reelection in 1888 to the Fifty-first Congress; delegate to the Republican National Convention at Minneapolis in 1892, which nominated Harrison and Reid; commissioner to the World's Columbian Exposition at Chicago in 1893; died in Fort Wayne, Ind., October 9, 1897; interment in Linwood Cemetery.

WHITE, James Bamford, a Representative from Kentucky; born near Winchester, Clark County, Ky., on June 6, 1842; attended the common schools and the Mount Zion Academy, Macon County, Ill.; entered the Confederate Army in the fall of 1863 and served in the commands of Generals Breckinridge and Morgan until the close of the Civil War, when he was honorably discharged; engaged in teaching at Irvine, Estill County, Ky.; studied law while teaching; was admitted to the bar in 1867 and commenced the practice of law in Irvine; prosecuting attorney of Estill County 1872–1880; elected as a Democrat to the Fifty-seventh Congress (March 4, 1901–March 3, 1903); continued the practice of his profession in Irvine, Ky., until his retirement in 1919; died in Irvine, Ky., March 25, 1931; interment in Oakdale Cemetery.

WHITE, John (cousin of Addison White and uncle of John Daugherty White), a Representative from Kentucky; born near Cumberland Gap (now Middlesboro), Ky., February 14, 1802; received a limited schooling; studied law; was admitted to the bar and commenced practice in Richmond, Madison County, Ky.; member of the State house of representatives in 1832; elected as a Whig to the Twenty-fourth and to the four succeeding Congresses (March 4, 1835–March 3, 1845); served as Speaker of the House of Representatives in the Twenty-seventh Congress; appointed judge of the nineteenth judicial district of Kentucky and served from February 8, 1845, until his death in Richmond, Ky., September 22, 1845; interment in the State Cemetery, Frankfort, Franklin County, Ky.

WHITE, John Daugherty (nephew of John White), a Representative from Kentucky; born near Manchester, Clay County. Ky., January 16, 1849; attended a private school until 1865 and Eminence (Ky.) College and the University of Kentucky at

Lexington until 1870; was graduated from the law department of the University of Michigan at Ann Arbor in 1872; also attended the medical department of the same institution; declined a nomination for clerk of the court of appeals of Kentucky in 1874; was admitted to the bar by the Kentucky Court of Appeals in 1875 and practiced; elected as a Republican to the Forty-fourth Congress (March 4, 1875–March 3, 1877); declined to be a candidate for renomination; chairman of the Kentucky Republican State convention at Louisville in 1879; member of the State house of representatives in 1879 and 1880; resigned in 1880; endorsed and reelected without opposition during the sitting of the legislature; chairman of the Kentucky delegation to the Republican National Convention at Chicago in 1880, which nominated James A. Garfield, of Ohio, for President and Chester A. Arthur, of New York, for Vice President; unsuccessful Republican candidate for the United States Senate in 1881; elected as a Republican to the Forty-seventh and Forty-eighth Congresses (March 4, 1881–March 3, 1885); declined to be a candidate for renomination in 1884 and resumed the practice of law in Louisville, Ky.; unsuccessful candidate of the State Prohibition Party for Governor of Kentucky in 1903; unsuccessful candidate of the Progressive Party for judge of the Kentucky Court of Appeals in 1912; died near Manchester, Ky., January 5, 1920; interment in the family burying ground near Manchester, Clay County, Ky.

WHITE, Joseph Livingston, a Representative from Indiana; born in Cherry Valley, Otsego County, N. Y.; completed preparatory studies; studied law in Utica, N. Y.; was admitted to the bar, and commenced practice in Madison, Ind.; elected as a Whig to the Twenty-seventh Congress (March 4, 1841–March 3, 1843); moved to New York City and resumed the practice of law; presidential elector on the Whig ticket of Clay and Frelinghuysen in 1844; while on a business trip to Nicaragua, Central America, he was shot by a Mr. Gavett as he was leaving the ship at Corinto (Punta Ycacos), Nicaragua, January 5, 1861, dying at Corinto on January 12; interment in the cemetery at Corinto, Nicaragua.

WHITE, Joseph M., a Delegate from Florida Territory; born in Franklin County, Ky., May 10, 1781; completed preparatory studies; studied law; was admitted to the bar and practiced; moved to Pensacola, Fla., in 1821; one of the commissioners under the act of Congress of May 8, 1822, "for ascertaining claims and titles to lands within the Territory of Florida"; elected as a Democrat to the Nineteenth and to the five succeeding Congresses (March 4, 1825–March 3, 1837); unsuccessful candidate for reelection to the Twenty-fifth Congress; author of a "New Collection of Laws, Charters, etc., of Great Britain, France, and Spain Relating to Cessions of Lands, with the Laws of Mexico," in two volumes published in 1839; died in St. Louis, Mo., October 19, 1839.

WHITE, Joseph Worthington, a Representative from Ohio; born in Cambridge, Guernsey County, Ohio, October 2, 1822; attended the common schools and Cambridge Academy; engaged in mercantile pursuits; studied law; was admitted to the bar in 1844, and commenced practice in Cambridge; prosecuting attorney of Guernsey County 1845–1847; mayor of Cambridge; delegate to the Democratic National Convention in 1860; elected as a Democrat to the Thirty-eighth Congress (March 4, 1863–March 3, 1865); unsuccessful for reelection in 1864 to the Thirty-ninth Congress; resumed the practice of law; died in Cambridge, Ohio, August 6, 1892; interment in the South Cemetery.

WHITE, Leonard, a Representative from Massachusetts; born in Haverhill, Essex County, Mass., May 3, 1767; was graduated from Harvard University in 1787; member of the

State house of representatives in 1809; held many local offices; elected as a Democrat to the Twelfth Congress (March 4, 1811–March 3, 1813); town clerk of Haverhill; cashier of the Merrimack Bank of Haverhill 1814–1836; died in Haverhill, Mass., October 10, 1849; interment in Pentucket Cemetery.

WHITE, Michael Doherty, a Representative from Indiana; born in Clark County, Ohio, September 8, 1827; moved with his parents to Tippecanoe County, Ind., in 1829; pursued classical studies; moved to Crawfordsville, Crawfordsville County, Ind., in 1848; attended the county seminary and Wabash College, Crawfordsville; clerked in a store for one year; studied law; was admitted to the bar in 1854 and commenced the practice of his profession in Crawfordsville; law partner of Gen. Lew Wallace; prosecuting attorney of Montgomery and Boone Counties 1854–1856; member of the State senate 1860–1864; elected as a Republican to the Forty-fifth Congress (March 4, 1877–March 3, 1879); was not a candidate for renomination in 1878; continued the practice of law in Crawfordsville, Ind., until 1911, and died there on February 6, 1917; interment in the Masonic Cemetery.

WHITE, Milo, a Representative from Minnesota; born in Fletcher, Franklin County, Vt., August 17, 1830; attended the common schools and Bakersfield Academy; moved to Chatfield, Fillmore County, Minn., in 1855 and engaged in mercantile pursuits; chairman of the board of supervisors of Chatfield upon its organization in 1858; served in the State senate 1872–1876, 1881, and 1882; elected as a Republican to the Forty-eighth and Forty-ninth Congresses (March 4, 1883–March 3, 1887); unsuccessful candidate for election in 1898 to the Fifty-sixth Congress; resumed mercantile pursuits; mayor of Chatfield for several terms; member of the school board until his death in Chatfield, Minn., May 18, 1913; interment in Chatfield Cemetery.

WHITE, Phillips, a Delegate from New Hampshire; born in Haverhill, Mass., on October 28, 1729; completed preparatory studies and attended Harvard College; during the French and Indian War was an officer in the colonial army at Lake George in 1755; moved to New Hampshire; member of the State house of representatives 1775–1782, and served as speaker in 1775 and 1782; probate judge of Rockingham County, N. H., 1776–1790; Member of the Continental Congress in 1782 and 1783; councilor 1792–1794; retired to his farm near South Hampton, N. H.; died in South Hampton on June 24, 1811; interment in the Old Cemetery.

WHITE, Phineas, a Representative from Vermont; born in South Hadley, Hampshire County, Mass., October 30, 1770; was graduated from Dartmouth College, Hanover, N. H., in 1797; studied law; was admitted to the bar in 1800 and commenced practice in Pomfret, Vt.; register of probate for Windsor County 1800–1809; county attorney in 1813; judge of Windham County in 1814, 1815, 1817, and 1820; also judge of probate of the district of Westminster in 1814 and 1815; member of the constitutional convention in 1814; served in the State house of representatives 1815–1820; elected as a Democrat to the Seventeenth Congress (March 4, 1821–March 3, 1823); member of the State constitutional convention in 1836; served in the State senate in 1836 and 1837; trustee of Middlebury College; died in Putney, Windham County, Vt., on July 6, 1847; interment in Maple Grove Cemetery.

WHITE, Samuel, a Senator from Delaware; born near Dover, Mispillion Hundred, Kent County, Del., in 1770; attended Cokesbury College, Maryland; studied law; was admitted to the bar in 1793 and commenced practice in Dover, Del.; served two years as a captain in the United States Army; adjutant general of Delaware in 1803; appointed and subsequently elected as a Federalist to the United States Senate to fill the vacancy caused by the resignation of Henry Latimer; reelected in 1803 and 1809 and served from February 28, 1801, until his death in Wilmington, Del., November 4, 1809; interment in the Old Swede Churchyard.

WHITE, Sebastian Harrison, a Representative from Colorado; born on a farm near Maries County, Mo., December 24, 1864; was reared and attended the rural schools in Dallas County and the Marionville (Mo.) Collegiate Institute (later the Ozark Wesleyan College at Carthage, Mo.); taught school for several years; elected president of the Hickory County Teachers Institute in 1886; elected superintendent of schools of Hickory County in 1887; while a teacher studied law; was admitted to the bar in 1889 and commenced practice in Pueblo, Colo.; delegate to the Democratic State convention in 1892; chairman of the Pueblo County Democratic central committee in 1892; served as city attorney of Pueblo 1897–1899; public trustee of Pueblo County 1900–1903 and 1905–1909; district attorney of the tenth judicial district 1904–1908; elected justice of the State supreme court in 1908 for a term of ten years 1909–1919, and served as chief justice from 1917 until 1918, when he retired; engaged in the practice of law in Denver, Colo., in 1919; elected as a Democrat to the Seventieth Congress to fill the vacancy caused by the death of William N. Vaile and served from November 15, 1927, to March 3, 1929; unsuccessful candidate for reelection in 1928 to the Seventy-first Congress; resumed the practice of law in Denver, Colo.; died in a hospital in Colorado Springs, Colo., December 21, 1945; remains were cremated in Fairmount Cemetery, Denver, Colo., and the ashes scattered over the cemetery.

WHITE, Stephen Mallory, a Senator from California; born in San Francisco, Calif., January 19, 1853; moved with his parents to Santa Cruz County, Calif.; attended private and common schools and St. Ignatius College in San Francisco; was graduated from Santa Clara College, Santa Clara, Calif., in 1871; studied law; was admitted to the bar April 14, 1874, and commenced practice in Los Angeles, Calif.; district attorney of Los Angeles County in 1882; member of the State senate 1886–1890, serving as president pro tempore both sessions, and in 1888 became, by virtue of his office, Lieutenant Governor; member of the board of regents of the University of California; delegate to the Democratic National Conventions in 1888 and 1892; was an unsuccessful candidate for election to the United States Senate in 1890; elected as a Democrat to the United States Senate and served from March 4, 1893, to March 3, 1899; delegate to the Democratic National Convention at Kansas City in 1900, which nominated Bryan and Stevenson; died in Los Angeles, Calif., February 21, 1901; interment in Calvary Cemetery.

WHITE, Stephen Van Culen, a Representative from New York; born in Chatham County, N. C., August 1, 1831; moved to Illinois with his parents, who settled near Otterville, Jersey County, Ill.; attended the free school founded by Dr. Silas Hamilton in Otterville, Ill., and was graduated from Knox College, Galesburg, Ill., in 1854; entered a mercantile house in St. Louis, Mo.; studied law and was admitted to the bar November 4, 1856; moved to Des Moines, Iowa, in 1856, and practiced law until January 1, 1865; acting United States district attorney for Iowa in 1864; moved to New York City in 1865 and engaged in banking; member of the New York Stock Exchange; was an astronomer and upon the organization of

the American Astronomical Society in 1883 was elected its first president; elected as a Republican to the Fiftieth Congress (March 4, 1887–March 3, 1889); was not a candidate for renomination in 1888 to the Fifty-first Congress; resumed the practice of law; died in Brooklyn, N. Y., January 18, 1913; interment in Greenwood Cemetery.

WHITE, Wallace Humphrey, Jr. (grandson of William Pierce Frye), a Representative and a Senator from Maine; born in Lewiston, Androscoggin County, Maine, August 6, 1877; attended the public schools of Lewiston; was graduated from Bowdoin College, Brunswick, Maine, in 1899; assistant clerk to the Committee on Commerce, United States Senate, and secretary to the President pro tempore of the Senate, Senator Frye, of Maine, 1899–1903; studied law; was admitted to the bar of the District of Columbia in 1902 and of Maine in 1903, and commenced practice in Lewiston, Maine; elected as a Republican to the Sixty-fifth and to the six succeeding Congresses (March 4, 1917–March 3, 1931); was not a candidate for renomination in 1930, having become a candidate for Senator; appointed by President Coolidge as a delegate to the Pan American Electrical Communications Conference at Mexico City in 1924; elected as a member of the American group of the Interparliamentary Union in 1925; selected by the Secretary of State as a delegate to the International Telegraph Conference at Paris, France, in 1925; designated by the Secretary of State as unofficial observer to attend meetings of the International Committee on Wireless Telegraphy, held at Geneva in 1927, and elected a member of this committee the same year; appointed by President Coolidge as a delegate of the United States to the International Radio Telegraphic Conference in Washington in 1927; appointed as chairman of the United States delegation to the International Conference on Safety of Life at Sea, held at London, England, in 1929; selected by the Secretary of State to head the delegation to the meeting of the International Technical Consulting Committee on Radio Communication, held at Copenhagen, Denmark, in 1931; appointed by President Franklin D. Roosevelt as chairman of the delegation to the International Radio Conference, held in Cairo, Egypt, in 1938; member of the board of overseers of Bowdoin College; elected to the United States Senate in 1930; reelected in 1936 and again in 1942 and served from March 4, 1931, to January 3, 1949; was not a candidate for renomination in 1948; served as minority leader of the Senate in the Seventy-ninth Congress and as majority leader in the Eightieth Congress; retired from all political and business activities; died in Auburn, Maine, March 31, 1952; interment in Mount Auburn Cemetery.

WHITE, Wilbur McKee, a Representative from Ohio; born near Hillsboro, Highland County, Ohio, February 22, 1890; educated in the rural schools and the Hillsboro High School; was graduated from the Marietta (Ohio) College in 1914; engaged in teaching at Marietta, Ohio, in 1914 and 1915; correspondent for a Dayton, Ohio, newspaper in 1916; served in the United States Army on the Mexican border as a private and first sergeant in Company H, Third Ohio Infantry, in 1916; during the First World War served from August 15, 1917, as a first lieutenant and later as a captain in the Three Hundred and Thirty-second Regiment, United States Infantry, in Italy and France, and was discharged May 21, 1919; was decorated with the Italian Cross of Merit; associated with the Toledo Times in 1919 in various capacities until 1925; managing editor of the Toledo Times 1925–1930 and associate editor in 1930 and 1931; elected as a Republican to the Seventy-second Congress (March 4, 1931–March 3, 1933); unsuccessful candidate for reelection in 1932 to the Seventy-third Congress and for election in 1940 to the Seventy-seventh Congress; employed in a glass manufacturing concern in 1933; served as secretary and as executive director of the Safety Glass Association 1934–1958; engaged in independent highway safety work 1958–1961; retired; is a resident of Hillsboro, Ohio.

WHITE, William John, a Representative from Ohio; born at Rice Lake, Ontario, Canada, October 7, 1850; moved to the United States in 1857 with his parents, who settled in Cleveland, Ohio; attended the district schools; entered business as a candy maker in 1869, and later began the manufacture of chewing gum; mayor of West Cleveland in 1889; elected as a Republican to the Fifty-third Congress (March 4, 1893–March 3, 1895); declined to be a candidate for renomination in 1894; was first president of the American Chicle Co. and later president of the W. J. White Chicle Co.; died in Cleveland, Ohio, on February 16, 1923; interment in Lake View Cemetery.

WHITEAKER, John, a Representative from Oregon; born in Dearborn County, near Fort Wayne, Ind., May 4, 1820; was self-educated, and early engaged in agricultural pursuits and stock raising; moved to the Pacific coast in 1849, and settled in Lane County, Oreg., in 1852; elected judge of probate for Lane County in 1855; member of the Territorial legislature in 1857; Governor of the State of Oregon 1858–1862; member of the State house of representatives in 1866 and 1868, and served as speaker; again elected to the State house of representatives in 1870; member of the State board of equalization in 1872, and served as chairman; member of the commission to examine, report upon, and receive the locks and canal at the falls of the Willamette River; member of the State senate 1876–1880, and served as president of the sessions of 1876 and 1878; elected as a Democrat to the Forty-sixth Congress (March 4, 1879–March 3, 1881); was an unsuccessful candidate for reelection in 1880 to the Forty-seventh Congress; appointed internal-revenue collector for the district of Oregon (with residence in Portland), and served from June 20, 1885, to February 27, 1890; moved to Eugene, Lane County, Oreg., in 1889 and died there October 2, 1902; interment in the Masonic Cemetery.

WHITEHEAD, Joseph, a Representative from Virginia; born near Mount Airy, Pittsylvania County, Va., October 31, 1867; attended the public schools of his native city; was graduated from the academic department of Richmond College (now the University of Richmond), Richmond, Va., in 1889, and from the law department of the University of Virginia at Charlottesville in 1892; was admitted to the bar the same year and commenced the practice of law in Chatham, Pittsylvania County, Va.; served in the State senate 1899–1904; elected as a Democrat to the Sixty-ninth, Seventieth, and Seventy-first Congresses (March 4, 1925–March 3, 1931); unsuccessful candidate for renomination in 1930; resumed the practice of his chosen profession until his death at Chatham, Va., on July 8, 1938; interment in Chatham Cemetery.

WHITEHEAD, Thomas, a Representative from Virginia; born in Lovingston, Nelson County, Va., December 27, 1825; received a limited schooling; engaged in mercantile pursuits; studied law; was admitted to the bar in 1849 and commenced practice in Amherst, Va.; during the Civil War served in the Confederate Army as captain of Company E, Second Virginia Cavalry, 1861–1865; elected to the State senate in 1865, but did not qualify; elected prosecuting attorney for Amherst County in 1866 and again in 1869, resigning in November 1873, having been elected to Congress; elected as a Conservative to the Forty-third Congress (March 4, 1873–March 3, 1875); was not a candidate for renomination in 1874; editor of

the Lynchburg News in 1876 and the Lynchburg Advance in 1880; resumed the practice of law; elected commissioner of agriculture for the State of Virginia in 1888 and served in this capacity until his death; died near Lynchburg, Campbell County, Va., July 1, 1901; interment in Spring Hill Cemetery, Lynchburg, Va.

WHITEHILL, James (son of John Whitehill and nephew of Robert Whitehill), a Representative from Pennsylvania; born in Strasburg, Lancaster County, Pa., on January 31, 1762; studied law; was admitted to the bar and commenced practice in Strasburg; associate judge of the Lancaster County Court from January 3, 1811, to February 1, 1813, when he resigned, having been elected to Congress; served in the War of 1812 as major general of Pennsylvania Militia; elected to the Thirteenth Congress and served from March 4, 1813, to September 1, 1814, when he resigned; engaged in mercantile pursuits in Strasburg; burgess of Strasburg in 1816; again associate judge of the county court from October 17, 1820, until his death in Strasburg, Pa., on February 26, 1822; interment in the Presbyterian Church Cemetery, Leacock, Lancaster County, Pa.

WHITEHILL, John (father of James Whitehill and brother of Robert Whitehill), a Representative from Pennsylvania; born in Salisbury Township, Lancaster County, Pa., December 11, 1729; completed preparatory studies; studied law; was admitted to the bar and commenced practice in Lancaster County; was appointed justice of the peace and justice of the orphans' court of Lancaster County March 31, 1777; member of the State house of representatives 1780–1782 and 1793; member of the council of censors in 1783; was delegate to the supreme executive council in 1784; member of the State convention for the adoption of the Federal Constitution in 1787; associate judge of Lancaster County in 1791; elected to the Eighth and Ninth Congresses (March 4, 1803–March 3, 1807); died in Salisbury Township, Lancaster County, Pa., September 16, 1815; interment in Pequea Presbyterian Church Cemetery.

WHITEHILL, Robert (brother of John Whitehill and uncle of James Whitehill), a Representative from Pennsylvania; born in Pequea, Lancaster County, Pa., July 21, 1738; attended the common schools; purchased a large tract of land in Cumberland County, settled upon it, and erected the first stone house in the county; member of the State constitutional convention in July 1776 that approved the Declaration of Independence; member of the council of safety in 1777; delegate to the State constitutional convention in 1790; member of the State house of representatives 1797–1800; served in the State senate 1801–1804, and was speaker of the senate in 1804 during the impeachment trials of the supreme court judges of Pennsylvania; elected to the Ninth Congress to fill the vacancy caused by the death of John A. Hanna; reelected to the Tenth and to the three succeeding Congresses and served from November 7, 1805, until his death at Lauther Manor, Cumberland County, Pa., April 8, 1813; interment in the Silver Spring Presbyterian Church Cemetery, Hampden Township, near Camp Hill, Pa.

WHITEHOUSE, John Osborne, a Representative from New York; born in Rochester, Strafford County, N. H., July 19, 1817; received a common-school education; moved to New York City, N. Y., in 1835 and was engaged as a clerk until 1839, when he moved to Brooklyn, N. Y., and engaged as a merchant and manufacturer of shoes; moved to Poughkeepsie, Dutchess County, N. Y., in 1860 and continued the shoe manufacturing business; elected as a Liberal Democrat to the Forty-third and Forty-fourth Congresses (March 4, 1873–March 3, 1877); was not a candidate for reelection in 1876 to the Forty-fifth Congress;

resumed the shoe manufacturing business; also interested in banking and railroading; owner of the Daily News 1872–1880; died in Poughkeepsie, N. Y., August 24, 1881; interment in Greenwood Cemetery, Brooklyn, N. Y.

WHITELAW, Robert Henry, a Representative from Missouri; born on a farm near Lloyds, Essex County, Va., January 30, 1854; moved with his father to Cape Girardeau County, Mo., in 1856; returned to Essex County, Va., in 1866; attended private schools in Tappahannock and Staunton, Va., and the law department of the University of Michigan at Ann Arbor; was admitted to the bar in 1873 and commenced practice in Cape Girardeau, Mo.; city attorney in 1873; prosecuting attorney of Cape Girardeau County 1874–1878; member of the State house of representatives in 1883 and 1887; elected as a Democrat to the Fifty-first Congress to fill the vacancy caused by the death of James Peter Walker and served from November 4, 1890, to March 3, 1891; was not a candidate for election in 1890 to the Fifty-second Congress; resumed the practice of law in Cape Girardeau, Mo.; retired from active law practice in 1927 and moved to Blodgett, Mo., and in 1934 to Blytheville, Ark., where he died on July 27, 1937; interment in Lorimier Cemetery, Cape Girardeau, Mo.

WHITELEY, Richard Henry, a Representative from Georgia; born in County Kildare, Ireland, December 22, 1830; immigrated to the United States in 1836 with his parents, who settled in Georgia; received private instruction in elementary education; engaged in manufacturing; studied law; was admitted to the bar in 1860 and commenced practice in Bainbridge, Ga.; opposed secession, but after the adoption of the ordinance entered the Confederate Army and served throughout the Civil War, attaining the rank of major; member of the State constitutional convention in 1867; unsuccessful candidate for election in 1866 to the Fortieth Congress; presented credentials as a Senator-elect to the United States Senate on July 15, 1870, to fill the vacancy in the term beginning March 4, 1865, but as the election took place prior to the readmission of Georgia into the Union was not admitted to a seat; elected as a Republican to the Forty-first Congress to fill the vacancy caused by the House declaring Nelson Tift not entitled to the seat; reelected to the Forty-second and Forty-third Congresses and served from December 22, 1870, to March 3, 1875; unsuccessful candidate for reelection to the Forty-fourth Congress and for election to the Forty-fifth Congress; moved to Boulder, Colo., in 1877 and resumed the practice of his profession; died in Boulder, Colo., September 26, 1890; interment in the Masonic Cemetery.

WHITELEY, William Gustavus, a Representative from Delaware; born near Newark, Del., August 7, 1819; attended Bullock's School at Wilmington, Del., and was graduated from Princeton College in 1838; studied law; was admitted to the bar in 1841 and began practice in Wilmington, Del.; prothonotary of New Castle County 1852–1856; elected as a Democrat to the Thirty-fifth and Thirty-sixth Congresses (March 4, 1857–March 3, 1861); was not a candidate for renomination in 1860; again prothonotary of New Castle County 1862–1867; mayor of Wilmington, Del., 1875–1878; member of commission to settle fishery disputes between New Jersey and Delaware in 1877; census enumerator for Delaware in 1880; associate judge of the superior court of Delaware from March 31, 1884, until his death in Wilmington, Del., April 23, 1886; interment in Bridgeton Cemetery, Bridgeton, N. J.

WHITENER, Basil Lee, a Representative from North Carolina; born in York County, S. C., May 14, 1915; educated in public schools of Gaston County; graduated from Lowell High School in 1931 and from Rutherford College in 1933; attended University of South Carolina 1933–1935; graduated from Duke University in 1937; admitted to the North Carolina bar the same year and commenced the practice of law in Gastonia, N. C.; member of the State house of representatives in 1941 and renominated in 1942 but resigned to enter the United States Navy; served as gunnery officer during World War II and was separated from the service in November 1945 with rank of lieutenant; appointed solicitor, fourteenth solicitorial district, in January 1946 and elected in November 1946, reelected in 1950 and 1954, and served until December 31, 1956; delegate to the Democratic National Convention 1948; elected as a Democrat to the Eighty-fifth and Eighty-sixth Congresses (January 3, 1957–January 3, 1961). *Reelected to the Eighty-seventh Congress.*

WHITESIDE, Jenkin, a Senator from Tennessee; born in Lancaster, Pa., in 1772; pursued preparatory studies; studied law and was admitted to the bar; moved to Tennessee and commenced practice in Knoxville; one of the commissioners of Knoxville in 1801 and 1802; elected to the United States Senate in 1809 to fill the vacancy caused by the resignation of Daniel Smith; reelected the same year and served from April 11, 1809, to October 8, 1811, when he resigned; resumed the practice of law; died in Nashville, Tenn., September 25, 1822; interment was probably in the Old Cemetery west of the Nashville sulphur spring.

WHITESIDE, John, a Representative from Pennsylvania; born near Lancaster, Pa., in 1773; attended the common schools and Chestnut Level Academy; employed on his father's farm; later engaged in the hotel business and operated a distillery; justice of the peace; member of the State house of representatives in 1810 and 1811; elected as a Democrat to the Fourteenth and Fifteenth Congresses (March 4, 1815–March 3, 1819); resumed the hotel business in Lancaster, Pa.; register of wills; again a member of the State house of representatives in 1825; died in Lancaster, Pa., July 28, 1830; interment in Lancaster Cemetery.

WHITFIELD, John Wilkins, a Delegate from the Territory of Kansas; born in Franklin, Williamson County, Tenn., March 11, 1818; attended the local schools; served in the Mexican War in 1846; moved to Independence, Mo., in 1853 to serve as Indian agent to the Pottawatomies at Westport, Mo., and to the Arkansas Indians in 1855 and 1856; upon the admission of the Territory of Kansas to representation was elected as a Democrat to the Thirty-third Congress and served from December 20, 1854, to March 3, 1855; presented credentials as a Delegate-elect to the Thirty-fourth Congress and served from March 4, 1855, to August 1, 1856, when the seat was declared vacant; again elected to the Thirty-fourth Congress to fill the vacancy caused by the action of the House of Representatives in declaring the seat vacant and served from December 9, 1856, to March 3, 1857; register of the land office at Doniphan, Kans., 1857–1861; began his military career as captain of the Twenty-seventh Texas Cavalry in 1861; promoted to the rank of major in 1862; engaged in the Battles of Pea Ridge and Iuka in 1862; cited by General Price for "dashing boldness and steady courage"; promoted to the rank of colonel; engaged in the cavalry battle near Spring Hill in 1863; again cited for "skill and valor"; commissioned brigadier general May 9, 1863; at the close of the war in 1865 went to Texas and settled in Lavaca County and engaged in agricultural pursuits and stock raising; member of the State house of representatives; died near Hallettsville, Lavaca County, Tex., October 27, 1879; interment in Hallettsville Cemetery.

WHITING, Justin Rice, a Representative from Michigan; born in Bath, Steuben County, N. Y., February 18, 1847; moved to Michigan in 1849 with his parents, who settled in St. Clair; attended the public schools and the University of Michigan at Ann Arbor 1863–1865; engaged as a merchant and manufacturer; mayor of St. Clair in 1879; member of the State senate in 1882; elected by the combined votes of Democrats and Greenbackers to the Fiftieth Congress and reelected to the Fifty-first, Fifty-second, and Fifty-third Congresses (March 4, 1887–March 3, 1895); resumed his former business pursuits in St. Clair; unsuccessful Democratic candidate for Governor in 1898 and also for election in 1900 to the Fifty-seventh Congress; chairman of the Democratic State central committee; died in St. Clair, Mich., January 31, 1903; interment in Hillside Cemetery.

WHITING, Richard Henry (uncle of Ira Clifton Copley), a Representative from Illinois; born in West Hartford, Conn., January 17, 1826; attended the common schools; moved to Altona, Ill., in 1850, thence to Galesburg, Ill., in 1860, where he built a gas works; during the Civil War served in the Union Army as paymaster of Volunteers 1862–1866; appointed assessor of internal revenue for the fifth district of Illinois in February 1870, serving until May 20, 1873, when the office was abolished; appointed collector of internal revenue for the same district May 20, 1873, with office at Peoria, Ill., and served until his resignation on March 4, 1875, having been elected to Congress; elected as a Republican to the Forty-fourth Congress (March 4, 1875–March 3, 1877); was not a candidate for renomination in 1876; delegate to the Republican National Convention at Chicago in 1884, which nominated the presidential ticket of James G. Blaine and John A. Logan; died in New York City May 24, 1888; interment in Springdale Cemetery, Peoria, Ill.

WHITING, William, a Representative from Massachusetts; born in Concord, Mass., on March 3, 1813; attended Concord Academy, and was graduated from Harvard University in 1833; taught school in Plymouth and Concord, Mass.; was graduated from the law department of Harvard University in 1838; was admitted to the bar the same year and commenced practice in Boston; solicitor of the War Department 1862–1865; presidential elector on the Republican ticket of Grant and Colfax in 1868; elected as a Republican to the Forty-third Congress and served from March 4, 1873, until death in Boston, Mass., June 29, 1873; interment in Sleepy Hollow Cemetery, Concord, Mass.

WHITING, William, a Representative from Massachusetts; born in Dudley, Worcester County, Mass., May 24, 1841; attended the public schools; was graduated from Amherst College, Amherst, Mass.; engaged in the manufacture of paper in Holyoke, Mass., in 1865; member of the State senate in 1873; city treasurer of Holyoke in 1876 and 1877; mayor of Holyoke in 1878 and 1879; delegate to the Republican National Convention at Cincinnati in 1876 and at St. Louis in 1896; elected as a Republican to the Forty-eighth, Forty-ninth, and Fiftieth Congresses (March 4, 1883–March 3, 1889); was not a candidate for renomination in 1888; commissioner to the World's Exposition in Paris, France, in 1900; resumed his former manufacturing pursuits; died in Holyoke, Hampden County, Mass., January 9, 1911; interment in Forestdale Cemetery.

WHITLEY, James Lucius, a Representative from New York; born in Rochester, N. Y., May 24, 1872; attended the public schools; was graduated from the Rochester Free Academy and from the law department of Union University, Albany, N. Y., in 1898; during the Spanish-American War served as a sergeant in the Seventh Battery, United States Volunteers; was admitted to the bar in 1899 and commenced practice in Rochester,

N. Y.; author; served as assistant corporation counsel, city of Rochester, in 1900 and 1901; chief examiner of the Civil Service Commission 1902–1904; member of the State assembly 1905–1910; served in the State senate 1918–1928; delegate to the Republican State conventions for twenty years; elected as a Republican to the Seventy-first, Seventy-second, and Seventy-third Congresses (March 4, 1929–January 3, 1935); unsuccessful candidate for reelection in 1934 to the Seventy-fourth Congress; returned to the practice of law; died in Rochester, N. Y., May 17, 1959; interment in Mount Hope Cemetery.

WHITMAN, Ezekiel, a Representative from Massachusetts and from Maine; born in East Bridgewater, Mass., March 9, 1776; was graduated from Brown University, Providence, R. I., in 1795; studied law; was admitted to the bar and practiced in New Gloucester, Maine (until 1820 a district of Massachusetts), 1799–1807 and in Portland, Maine, 1807–1852; unsuccessful candidate for election in 1806 to the Tenth Congress; elected as a Federalist from Massachusetts to the Eleventh Congress (March 4, 1809–March 3, 1811); member of the executive council in 1815 and 1816; elected to the Fifteenth and Sixteenth Congresses (March 4, 1817–March 3, 1821); delegate to the convention in 1819 that framed the first State constitution of Maine; elected to the Seventeenth Congress from Maine and served from March 4, 1821, to June 1, 1822, when he resigned; judge of the court of common pleas of Maine 1822–1841; unsuccessful candidate for election in 1838 to the Twenty-sixth Congress; served as chief justice of the Massachusetts State Supreme Court 1841–1848; retired in 1852 and returned to East Bridgewater, Mass., where he died on August 1, 1866.

WHITMAN, Lemuel, a Representative from Connecticut; born in Farmington, Conn., June 8, 1780; completed preparatory studies; was graduated from Yale College in 1800; taught in a seminary in Bermuda in 1801; studied law and was graduated from the Litchfield Law School; was admitted to the bar and commenced practice in Farmington; appointed judge of the superior court in 1818; associate judge of the Hartford County Court 1819–1821, and chief judge 1821–1823; one of a committee of three to prepare a revision of the statutes of the State in 1821; member of the State senate in 1822; elected as a Democrat to the Eighteenth Congress (March 4, 1823–March 3, 1825); resumed the practice of law; again a member of the State house of representatives in 1831 and 1832; died in Farmington, Conn., on November 13, 1841.

WHITMORE, Elias, a Representative from New York; born in Pembroke, N. H., March 2, 1772; completed preparatory studies; moved to New York and settled in Windsor; engaged in mercantile pursuits; elected as a Democrat to the Nineteenth Congress (March 4, 1825–March 3, 1827); resumed his former business pursuits in Windsor, N. Y., until his death in that city December 26, 1853; interment in the Village Cemetery.

WHITMORE, George Washington, a Representative from Texas; born in McMinn County, Tenn., on August 26, 1824; attended the public schools; moved to Texas in 1848; studied law; was admitted to the bar and practiced in Tyler, Smith County, Tex.; member of the State house of representatives in 1852, 1853, and 1858; district attorney for the ninth judicial district in 1866; appointed register in bankruptcy in 1867; upon the readmission of Texas to representation was elected as a Republican to the Forty-first Congress and served from March 30, 1870, to March 3, 1871; unsuccessful candidate for reelection in 1870 to the Forty-second Congress; resumed the practice of law; died in Tyler, Tex., October 14, 1876; interment in Oakwood Cemetery.

WHITNEY, Thomas Richard, a Representative from New York; born in New York City May 2, 1807; pursued classical studies and engaged in newspaper work; member of the State assembly in 1854 and 1855; elected as the candidate of the American Party to the Thirty-fourth Congress (March 4, 1855–March 3, 1857); died in New York City April 12, 1858; interment in Greenwood Cemetery, Brooklyn, N. Y.

WHITTEMORE, Benjamin Franklin, a Representative from South Carolina; born in Malden, Middlesex County, Mass., May 18, 1824; attended the public schools of Worcester, and received an academic education at Amherst; engaged in mercantile pursuits until 1859; studied theology and became a minister in the Methodist Episcopal Church of the New England Conference in 1859; during the Civil War served as chaplain of the Fifty-third Regiment, Massachusetts Volunteers, and later with the Thirtieth Regiment, Veteran Volunteers; after the war settled in Darlington, S. C.; delegate to the State constitutional convention in 1867; elected president of the Republican State executive board in 1867; founded the New Era in Darlington; member of the State senate in 1868; delegate to the Republican National Convention at Chicago in 1868; upon the readmission of South Carolina to representation was elected as a Republican to the Fortieth and Forty-first Congresses and served from July 18, 1868, to February 24, 1870, when he resigned, pending the investigation of his conduct in connection with certain appointments to the United States Military and Naval Academies; presented credentials of a second election to the same Congress on June 18, 1870, but the House declined to allow him to take his seat; again a member of the State senate in 1877; resigned from the State senate and returned to Massachusetts, settling in Woburn; became a publisher; died in Montvale, a suburb of Woburn, Mass., on January 25, 1894; interment in the Salem Street Cemetery, Woburn, Mass.

WHITTEN, Jamie Lloyd, a Representative from Mississippi; born in Cascilla, Tallahatchie County, Miss., April 18, 1910; attended the public schools and the literary and law departments of the University of Mississippi at Oxford; was admitted to the bar in 1932 and commenced practice at Charleston, Miss.; principal of the Cascilla School in Tallahatchie County, Miss., in 1930 and 1931; member of the State house of representatives in 1931 and 1932; district attorney of the seventeenth district of Mississippi 1933–1937 and 1939–1941; elected as a Democrat to the Seventy-seventh Congress to fill the vacancy caused by the resignation of Wall Doxey; reelected to the Seventy-eighth and to the eight succeeding Congresses and served from November 4, 1941, to January 3, 1961. *Reelected to the Eighty-seventh Congress.*

WHITTHORNE, Washington Curran, a Representative and a Senator from Tennessee; born near Farmington, Marshall County, Tenn., April 19, 1825; attended the common schools, an academy in Arrington, Williamson County, and Campbell Academy, Lebanon, Tenn.; was graduated from the University of Tennessee at Knoxville in 1843; studied law and was admitted to the bar in 1845 at Columbia, Maury County, Tenn.; served as auditor's clerk and in other positions in the Government service until 1848, when he commenced the practice of law in Columbia, Tenn.; member of the State senate 1855–1858; member of the State house of representatives and speaker in 1859; presidential elector on the Breckinridge and Lane ticket in 1860; during the Civil War served as assistant adjutant general in the provisional army of Tennessee in 1861 and in the Confederate service as adjutant general of the State 1861–1865; his political disabilities were removed by act of Congress approved July 15, 1870; elected as a Democrat to the Forty-second and to the five

succeeding Congresses (March 4, 1871–March 3, 1883); appointed and subsequently elected as a Democrat to the United States Senate to fill the vacancy caused by the resignation of Howell E. Jackson and served from April 16, 1886, to March 3, 1887; elected to the Fiftieth and Fifty-first Congresses (March 4, 1887–March 3, 1891); died in Columbia, Tenn., September 21, 1891; interment in Rose Hill Cemetery.

WHITTINGTON, William Madison, a Representative from Mississippi; born in Little Springs, Franklin County, Miss., May 4, 1878; attended the public schools of Franklin County; was graduated from Mississippi College at Clinton in 1898 and from the law department of the University of Mississippi at Oxford in 1899; was admitted to the bar in 1899 and commenced practice in Roxie, Franklin County, Miss., January 1, 1901; in January 1904 moved to Greenwood, Miss., where he continued the practice of law and also engaged in agricultural pursuits; member of the city council, Greenwood, Miss., from January 1, 1907, to January 1, 1911; chairman of the local board for selective service of Leflore County during the First World War; member of the State senate from January 1, 1916, to January 1, 1920; reelected in 1923 for a four-year term and served from January 1 to August 16, 1924, when he resigned to accept the Democratic nomination for Representative in Congress; delegate to the Democratic National Conventions in 1920, 1928, 1936, 1940, and 1948; elected as a Democrat to the Sixty-ninth and to the twelve succeeding Congresses (March 4, 1925–January 3, 1951); was not a candidate for renomination in 1950; resumed the practice of law; is a resident of Greenwood, Miss.

WHITTLESEY, Elisha (uncle of William Augustus Whittlesey and cousin of Frederick Whittlesey and Thomas Tucker Whittlesey), a Representative from Ohio; born in Washington, Conn., October 19, 1783; in early youth moved with his parents to Salisbury, Conn.; attended the common schools at Danbury; studied law in Danbury; was admitted to the bar of Fairfield County and practiced in Danbury and Fairfield County; also practiced in New Milford, Conn., in 1805; moved to Canfield, Mahoning County, Ohio, in 1806; practiced law and taught school; prosecuting attorney of Mahoning County; served as military and private secretary to Gen. William Henry Harrison and as brigade major in the Army of the Northwest in the War of 1812; member of the State house of representatives in 1820 and 1821; elected to the Eighteenth and to the seven succeeding Congresses and served from March 4, 1823, to July 9, 1838, when he resigned; Sixth Auditor of the Treasury from March 18, 1841, until December 18, 1843, when he resigned and resumed the practice of law in Canfield; was one of the founders of the Whig Party; appointed general agent of the Washington Monument Association in 1847; appointed by President Taylor as First Comptroller of the Treasury and served from May 31, 1849, to March 26, 1857, when he was removed by President Buchanan; was reappointed by President Lincoln April 10, 1861, and served until his death in Washington, D. C., January 7, 1863; interment in the Canfield Village Cemetery, Canfield, Mahoning County, Ohio.

WHITTLESEY, Frederick (cousin of Elisha Whittlesey and Thomas Tucker Whittlesey), a Representative from New York; born in New Preston, Conn., June 12, 1799; pursued academic studies; was graduated from Yale College in 1818; studied law; was admitted to the bar in Utica, N. Y., in 1821 and commenced practice in Cooperstown, N. Y., early in 1822; later in the year moved to Rochester, N. Y.; treasurer of Monroe County in 1829 and 1830; elected as a Whig to the Twenty-second and Twenty-third Congresses (March 4, 1831–March 3, 1835);

resumed the practice of law; city attorney of Rochester in 1838; vice chancellor of the eighth judicial district of New York 1839–1847; justice of the State supreme court in 1847 and 1848; professor of law at Genesee College in 1850 and 1851; died in Rochester, N. Y., September 19, 1851; interment in Mount Hope Cemetery.

WHITTLESEY, Thomas Tucker (cousin of Elisha Whittlesey and Frederick Whittlesey), a Representative from Connecticut; born in Danbury, Conn., December 8, 1798; attended the public schools, and was graduated from Yale College in 1817; attended Litchfield Law School; was admitted to the bar in 1818 and commenced practice in Danbury, Conn.; served as probate judge; elected as a Van Buren Democrat to the Twenty-fourth Congress to fill the vacancy caused by the death of Zalmon Wildman; reelected to the Twenty-fifth Congress and served from April 29, 1836, to March 3, 1839; unsuccessful candidate for reelection in 1838 to the Twenty-sixth Congress; moved to Pheasant Branch, near Madison, Wis., in 1846; resumed the practice of law and also engaged in agricultural pursuits; member of the State senate in 1853 and 1854; died at Pheasant Branch, Dane County, Wis., August 20, 1868; interment in Forest Hill Cemetery, Madison, Wis.

WHITTLESEY, William Augustus (nephew of Elisha Whittlesey), a Representative from Ohio; born in Danbury, Conn., July 14, 1796; attended the common schools, and was graduated from Yale College in 1816; taught school; moved to Canfield, Ohio, in 1818; studied law; was admitted to the bar in 1821 and commenced practice in Canfield; moved to Marietta, Ohio, in 1821; auditor of Washington County 1825–1837; member of the State house of representatives in 1839 and 1840; elected as a Democrat to the Thirty-first Congress (March 4, 1849–March 3, 1851); did not seek renomination in 1850; resumed the practice of law; mayor of Marietta in 1856, 1860, and 1862; died in Brooklyn, N. Y., where he had gone for medical treatment, on November 6, 1866; interment in Mound Cemetery, Marietta, Ohio.

WHYTE, William Pinkney, a Senator from Maryland; born in Baltimore, Md., August 9, 1824; was instructed by a private teacher and attended Baltimore College; engaged in banking in Baltimore 1842–1844; studied law in Baltimore, and attended the law school of Harvard University in 1844 and 1845; was admitted to the bar in 1846 and practiced in Baltimore; served in the State house of delegates in 1847 and 1848; judge advocate of a court-martial at the Naval Academy in 1848; unsuccessful candidate for election in 1850 to the Thirty-second Congress; comptroller of the treasury of Maryland 1853–1855; declined a reelection; delegate to the Democratic National Convention at New York in 1868; appointed to the United States Senate to fill the vacancy caused by the resignation of Reverdy Johnson and served from July 13, 1868, to March 3, 1869; was not a candidate for renomination in 1868; elected Governor of Maryland in 1871 and served from January 10, 1872, to March 4, 1874, when he resigned having been elected Senator; counsel for Maryland before the arbitration board in the boundary dispute between Virginia and Maryland in 1874; elected as a Democrat to the United States Senate and served from March 4, 1875, to March 3, 1881; unsuccessful candidate for reelection in 1880; mayor of Baltimore in 1881 and 1882; attorney general of Maryland 1887–1891; declined appointment as a delegate to the Congress of South American Republics; chairman of a commission to frame a new charter for the city of Baltimore in 1897 and 1898; city solicitor 1900–1903; appointed and subsequently elected to the United States Senate to fill the vacancy caused by the death of Arthur Pue Gorman and served from June 8, 1906, until his death in Baltimore, Md., March 17, 1908; interment in Greenmount Cemetery.

WICK, William Watson, a Representative from Indiana; born in Canonsburg, Washington County, Pa., February 23, 1796; moved with his parents to Western Reserve in 1800; completed preparatory studies; moved to Cincinnati, Ohio, in 1816; taught school; studied medicine until 1818 and then law; was admitted to the bar in Franklin, Johnson County, Ind., in 1819 and commenced practice in Connersville, Fayette County, Ind., in 1820; clerk of the State house of representatives 1820; assistant clerk of the State senate 1821; president judge of the fifth judicial State circuit 1822–1825; secretary of state 1825–1829; prosecuting attorney of the fifth judicial circuit 1829–1831; again president judge 1834–1837; elected as a Democrat to the Twenty-sixth Congress (March 4, 1839–March 3, 1841); unsuccessful candidate for reelection in 1840 to the Twenty-seventh Congress; resumed the practice of law in Indianapolis; elected to the Twenty-ninth and Thirtieth Congresses (March 4, 1845–March 3, 1849); was not a candidate for renomination; president judge for a third time, serving from 1850 to 1853; postmaster of Indianapolis, Ind., from April 9, 1853, to April 6, 1857; adjutant general in the State militia; moved to Franklin, Ind., in 1857, where he continued the practice of law, and died there May 19, 1868; interment in Greenlawn Cemetery.

WICKERSAHM, James, a Delegate from the Territory of Alaska; born in Patoka, Marion County, Ill., August 24, 1857; attended the common schools; studied law; was admitted to the bar in 1880 and commenced practice in Springfield, Sangamon County, Ill.; served in the Governor's guards, Springfield Militia; moved to Washington Territory in 1883; probate judge of Pierce County, Wash., 1884–1888; city attorney of Tacoma, Wash., in 1894; member of the State house of representatives in 1898; moved to Eagle, Alaska, when appointed United States district judge for the Territory of Alaska in 1900; moved to Nome in 1901, to Valdez in 1902, and to Fairbanks in 1903; served as district judge until January 1908, when he resigned to run for Congress; elected as a Republican to the Sixty-first and to the three succeeding Congresses (March 4, 1909–March 3, 1917); successfully contested the election of Charles A. Sulzer to the Sixty-fifth Congress and served from January 7 to March 3, 1919; successfully contested the election of Charles A. Sulzer to the Sixty-sixth Congress and served from March 1 to March 3, 1921, succeeding George B. Grigsby, who had qualified on credentials of a special election held to fill the vacancy caused by the death of Mr. Sulzer, which occurred while the contest was pending; was not a candidate for renomination in 1920; moved to Juneau, Alaska, in 1921 and resumed the practice of law; elected to the Seventy-second Congress (March 4, 1931–March 3, 1933); unsuccessful candidate for reelection in 1932 to the Seventy-third Congress; continued the practice of law in Juneau, Alaska; writer on ethnological and historical subjects; editor of Alaska Territory Law Reports, and of Old Yukon and Alaskan literature; died in Juneau, Alaska, October 24, 1939; remains were cremated and the ashes deposited in Old Tacoma Cemetery, Tacoma, Wash.

WICKERSHAM, Victor Eugene, a Representative from Oklahoma; born on a farm near Lone Rock, Baxter County, Ark., February 9, 1906; moved to Mangum, Greer County, Okla., with his parents in 1915; educated in the public schools of Oklahoma; employed in the office of the county clerk of Greer County, Okla., 1924–1926; court clerk of Greer County 1926–1935; served as chief clerk of the board of affairs of the State of Oklahoma in 1935 and 1936; engaged as a building contractor in Oklahoma City in 1937 and 1938 and in the life-insurance business 1938–1941; elected as a Democrat to the Seventy-seventh Congress to fill the vacancy caused by the death of Sam C. Massingale; reelected to the Seventy-eighth and Seventy-ninth Congresses and served from April 1, 1941, to January 3, 1947; unsuccessful candidate for renomination in 1946; elected to the Eighty-first and to the three succeeding Congresses (January 3, 1949–January 3, 1957); unsuccessful candidate for renomination in 1956 and for the Democratic nomination in 1958; real-estate and investment broker. *Elected to the Eighty-seventh Congress.*

WICKES, Eliphalet, a Representative from New York; born in Huntington, Long Island, N. Y., April 1, 1769; during the Revolution was employed as an express rider, and at the storming of Stony Point, July 15, 1779, when only ten years of age, bore the news to General Gates at Providence, R. I.; studied law; was admitted to the bar and commenced practice in Jamaica, Long Island, N. Y.; elected to the Ninth Congress (March 4, 1805–March 3, 1807); appointed July 1, 1797, the first postmaster of Jamaica, Long Island, N. Y., and served until April 1, 1806; reappointed January 1, 1807, and served until April 27, 1835; district attorney of Queens County 1818–1821; master in chancery; died in Troy, N. Y., on June 7, 1850; interment in Oakwood Cemetery.

WICKHAM, Charles Preston, a Representative from Ohio; born in Norwalk, Huron County, Ohio, September 15, 1836; attended the public schools and the Norwalk Academy; learned the printer's trade; was graduated from the Cincinnati Law School; admitted to the bar in 1858 and practiced in Norwalk, Ohio; during the Civil War enlisted as a private in Company D, Fifty-fifth Regiment, Ohio Volunteers, in September 1861 and was mustered out of the service July 11, 1865; attained the ranks of first lieutenant, captain, major, and lieutenant colonel; was commissioned lieutenant colonel by brevet "for gallant and meritorious services in the Carolinas"; resumed the practice of law in Norwalk in 1865; prosecuting attorney 1866–1870; elected judge of the court of common pleas of the fourth judicial district in 1880 and 1885; resigned in 1886; elected as a Republican to the Fiftieth and Fifty-first Congresses (March 4, 1887–March 3, 1891); unsuccessful candidate for renomination; resumed the practice of law; died in Norwalk, Ohio, March 18, 1925; interment in Woodlawn Cemetery.

WICKLIFFE, Charles Anderson (grandfather of Robert Charles Wickliffe and John Crepps Wickliffe Beckham), a Representative from Kentucky; born near Springfield, Washington County, Ky., June 8, 1788; completed preparatory studies; studied law; was admitted to the bar in 1809 and commenced practice in Bardstown; served in the War of 1812; was aide to General Winlock; member of the State house of representatives in 1812 and 1813; again entered the Army as aide to General Caldwell; again a member of the State house of representatives in 1822, 1823, and 1833–1835, and served as speaker in 1834; elected as a Democrat to the Eighteenth and to the four succeeding Congresses (March 4, 1823–March 3, 1833); was not a candidate for renomination; one of the managers appointed by the House of Representatives in 1830 to conduct the impeachment proceedings against James H. Peck, United States judge for the district of Missouri; Lieutenant Governor in 1836; became Governor upon the death of Governor Clark and served from October 5, 1839, to September 1840; Postmaster General from October 13, 1841, to March 6, 1845; sent on a secret mission by President Polk to the Republic of Texas in 1845; member of the State constitutional convention in 1849; member of the peace conference held at Washington, D. C., in 1861 in an effort to devise means to prevent the impending war; elected as a Union Whig to the Thirty-seventh Congress (March 4, 1861–March 3, 1863); did not seek renomination; unsuccessful candidate for Governor in 1863; delegate to the Democratic National Convention at Chicago in 1864; died near Ilchester, Md., October 31, 1869; interment in Bardstown Cemetery, Bardstown, Ky.

WICKLIFFE, Robert Charles (grandson of Charles Anderson Wickliffe and cousin of John Crepps Wickliffe Beckham), a Representative from Louisiana; born in Bardstown, Ky., May 1, 1874, while his parents were on a visit to relatives in that State; attended the public schools of St. Francisville, La.; was graduated from Centre College, Danville, Ky., in 1895 and from the law department of Tulane University, New Orleans, La., in 1897; was admitted to the bar in 1898 and commenced practice in St. Francisville, La.; member of the State constitutional convention in 1898; enlisted as a private in Company E, First Regiment, Louisiana Volunteer Infantry, during the Spanish-American War; was mustered out of the service in October 1898; returned to West Feliciana Parish; district attorney of the twenty-fourth judicial district of Louisiana 1902–1906; elected as a Democrat to the Sixty-first and Sixty-second Congresses and served from March 4, 1909, until his death; chosen as a delegate to the Democratic National Convention at Baltimore in 1912, but was killed on June 11, 1912, a short time before the convention met, while crossing a railroad bridge in Washington, D. C.; interment in Cave Hill Cemetery, Louisville, Ky.

WIDGERY, William, a Representative from Massachusetts; probably born in Devonshire, England, about 1753; immigrated to America with his parents, who settled in Philadelphia; attended the common schools; engaged in shipbuilding; served in the Revolutionary War as a lieutenant on a privateer; studied law; was admitted to the bar and commenced practice in Portland, Maine (until 1820 a district of Massachusetts), about 1790; member of the Massachusetts House of Representatives 1787–1793 and 1795–1797; delegate to the State constitutional convention in 1788; served in the State senate in 1794; member of the executive council in 1806 and 1807; elected as a Democrat to the Twelfth Congress (March 4, 1811–March 3, 1813); unsuccessful for reelection in 1812 to the Thirteenth Congress; judge of the court of common pleas 1813–1821; died in Portland, Maine, July 31, 1822; interment in the Eastern Cemetery.

WIDNALL, William Beck, a Representative from New Jersey; born in Hackensack, Bergen County, N. J., March 17, 1906; attended the public schools; graduated from Brown University, Providence, R. I., in 1926 and from the New Jersey Law School (now part of Rutgers University) in 1931; was admitted to the bar in 1932 and commenced the practice of law in Hackensack, N. J.; member of the State house of assembly 1946–1950; elected as a Republican to the Eighty-first Congress to fill the vacancy caused by the resignation of J. Parnell Thomas; reelected to the Eighty-second and to the four succeeding Congresses and served from February 6, 1950, to January 3, 1961. *Reelected to the Eighty-seventh Congress.*

WIER, Roy William, a Representative from Minnesota; born in Redfield, Spink County, S. Dak., February 25, 1888; moved with his parents in 1896 to Minneapolis, Hennepin County, Minn.; attended the public schools and North High School; learned the telephone and electrical trade, later going into theatrical stage-lighting work; during the First World War served in the United States Army for eighteen months, with overseas service; since 1920 has been active in the trade-union movement in Minneapolis and has been officially a representative of the Trades and Labor Assembly of Minneapolis; member of the State house of representatives 1933–1939; member of the Minneapolis Board of Education 1939–1948 and the board of directors of Hennepin County Red Cross; elected as a Democrat to the Eighty-first and to the five succeeding Congresses (January 3, 1949–January 3, 1961); unsuccessful candidate for reelection in 1960 to the Eighty-seventh Congress; is a resident of Minneapolis, Minn.

WIGFALL, Louis Tresvant, a Senator from Texas; was born near Edgefield, Edgefield District, S. C., April 21, 1816; pursued classical studies; attended South Carolina College (now the University of South Carolina) at Columbia; served as a lieutenant of Volunteers in the Seminole War in Florida in 1835; attended the law department of the University of Virginia at Charlottesville; was admitted to the bar in 1839 and commenced practice in Edgefield, S. C.; moved to Marshall, Tex., in 1848; member of the State house of representatives in 1849 and 1850; delegate to the State convention in 1857; served in the State senate 1857–1860; elected as a Democrat to the United States Senate to fill the vacancy caused by the death of J. Pinckney Henderson and served from December 5, 1859, until March 23, 1861, when he withdrew; served in the Confederate Army during the Civil War; represented the State of Texas in the Confederate Congress; after the war moved to London, England; returned to the United States in 1873 and settled in Baltimore, Md.; died in Galveston, Tex., while on a lecture tour, February 18, 1874; interment in the Episcopal Cemetery.

WIGGINTON, Peter Dinwiddie, a Representative from California; born in Springfield, Sangamon County, Ill., September 6, 1839; moved to Wisconsin with his parents in 1843; completed preparatory studies and attended the University of Wisconsin at Madison; studied law; was admitted to the bar in 1859 and practiced; editor of the Dodgeville (Wis.) Advocate; moved to Snelling, Merced County, Calif., in 1862, and continued the practice of law; district attorney of Merced County 1864–1868; elected as a Democrat to the Forty-fourth Congress (March 4, 1875–March 3, 1877); successfully contested the election of Romualdo Pocheco to the Forty-ninth Congress and served from February 7, 1878, to March 3, 1879; settled in San Francisco in 1880 and resumed the practice of law; nominated by the American Party as candidate for Vice President in 1888 in place of James R. Geer; died in Oakland, Calif., July 7, 1890; interment in Mountain View Cemetery.

WIGGLESWORTH, Richard Bowditch, a Representative from Massachusetts; born in Boston, Mass., April 25, 1891; was graduated from Milton Academy, Milton, Mass., in 1908, from Harvard University, Cambridge, Mass., in 1912, and from the law department of the same university in 1916; assistant private secretary to the Governor General of the Philippine Islands in 1913; admitted to the bar in 1916 and commenced practice in Boston, Mass.; during the First World War served overseas as captain, Battery E, and as commanding officer, First Battalion, Three Hundred and Third Field Artillery, Seventy-sixth Division, 1917–1919; legal adviser to the Assistant Secretary of the Treasury in charge of foreign loans and railway payments, and secretary of the World War Debt Commission 1922–1924; assistant to the agent general for reparation payments, Berlin, Germany, 1924–1927; general counsel and Paris representative for organizations created under the Dawes plan in 1927 and 1928; elected as a Republican to the Seventieth Congress to fill the vacancy caused by the death of Louis A. Frothingham; reelected to the Seventy-first and to the fourteen succeeding Congresses and served from November 6, 1928, until his resignation November 13, 1958; was not a candidate for renomination in 1958; United States Ambassador to Canada from January 28, 1959, until his death in Boston, Mass., October 22, 1960; interment in Arlington National Cemetery, Fort Myer, Va.

WIKE, Scott, a Representative from Illinois; born in Meadville, Pa., April 6, 1834; moved with his parents to Quincy, Ill., in 1838 and to Pike County in 1844; was graduated from Lombard University, in Galesburg, in 1857; studied law; admitted to the bar in 1858; was graduated from Harvard Law School, Cambridge, Mass., in 1859 and commenced practice the same year in Pittsfield, Pike County, Ill.; member of the State house of representatives 1863–1867; elected as a Democrat to the Forty-fourth Congress (March 4, 1875–March 3, 1877); unsuccessful candidate for renomination in 1876 to the Forty-fifth Congress; elected to the Fifty-first and Fifty-second Congresses (March 4, 1889–March 3, 1893); unsuccessful candidate for renomination in 1892; appointed an Assistant Secretary of the Treasury during the second administration of President Cleveland and served from July 1, 1893, to May 4, 1897; resumed the practice of law in Pittsfield, Ill.; died near Barry, Pike County, Ill., January 15, 1901.

WILBER, David (father of David Forrest Wilber), a Representative from New York; born near Quaker Street, Schenectady County, N. Y., October 5, 1820; moved with his parents to Milford, Otsego County, N. Y.; attended the common schools; engaged in the lumbering trade, hop business, and agricultural pursuits; member of the board of supervisors of Otsego County in 1858, 1859, 1862, 1865, and 1866; director of the Albany & Susquehanna Railroad; director of the Second National Bank of Cooperstown, N. Y.; president of the Wilber National Bank of Oneonta 1874–1890; elected as a Republican to the Forty-third Congress (March 4, 1873–March 3, 1875); was not a candidate for renomination in 1874; elected to the Forty-sixth Congress (March 4, 1879–March 3, 1881); was not a candidate for renomination in 1880; delegate to the Republican National Conventions at Chicago in 1880 and 1888; moved to Oneonta, N. Y., in 1886; again elected as a Republican to the Fiftieth Congress; reelected to the Fifty-first Congress, but owing to ill health took the oath of office at his home and never attended a session; served from March 4, 1887, until his death in Oneonta, Otsego County, N. Y., April 1, 1890; interment in Glenwood Cemetery.

WILBER, David Forrest (son of David Wilber), a Representative from New York; born in Milford, Otsego County, N. Y., December 7, 1859; attended the public schools; was graduated from Cazenovia (N. Y.) Seminary in 1879; engaged in the hop business at Milford in 1879 and at Oneonta, N. Y., in 1880; also interested in the real-estate business, agricultural pursuits, and stock breeding; twice represented Oneonta on the board of supervisors; member of the State tuberculosis commission in 1894; vice president and director of the Wilber National Bank of Oneonta 1883–1896; president of the Holstein-Friesian Association of America in 1894 and of the American Cheviot Sheep Association of the United States and Canada; trustee of the Cazenovia Seminary; elected as a Republican to the Fifty-fourth and Fifty-fifth Congresses (March 4, 1895–March 3, 1899); was not a candidate for renomination in 1898; served as United States consul to Barbados 1903–1905; served as consul general to Singapore 1905–1907, Halifax 1907–1909, Kobe 1909–1910, Vancouver 1910–1913, Zurich 1913–1915, Genoa 1915–1921, and Auckland and Wellington 1922–1923; retired in June 1923 and returned to Oneonta, N. Y., to care for his business interests; presidential elector on the Republican ticket of Coolidge and Dawes in 1924; member of the Republican State committee 1924–1927; died at his summer camp at Upper Dam, Oxford County, Maine, August 14, 1928; interment in Glenwood Cemetery, Oneonta, N. Y.

WILBOUR, Isaac, a Representative from Rhode Island; born in Little Compton, R. I., April 25, 1763; completed preparatory studies; studied law; was admitted to the bar in 1793 and practiced; also engaged in agricultural pursuits; held various local offices from 1793 to 1800; member of the State house of representatives in 1805 and 1806 and served as speaker the last year; Lieutenant Governor in 1806 and 1807 and Acting Governor in

1806; elected as a Federalist to the Tenth Congress (March 4, 1807–March 3, 1809); unsuccessful candidate for reelection in 1808 to the Eleventh Congress and for election in 1812 to the Thirteenth Congress; in 1807 received a commission from Governor Fenner, appointing him as his successor to the United States Senate for the remainder of the term ending March 3, 1811, which he declined; again Lieutenant Governor in 1810 and 1811; associate justice of the supreme court of Rhode Island in 1818 and chief justice from 1819 to 1827, when he resigned; died in Little Compton, R. I., on October 4, 1837; interment in the Seaconnet Cemetery.

WILCOX, James Mark, a Representative from Florida; born in Willacoochee, Atkinson County, Ga., May 21, 1890; attended the public schools and Emory College, Atlanta, Ga.; was graduated from the law department of Mercer University, Macon, Ga., in 1910; was admitted to the bar the same year and commenced practice in Hazelhurst, Ga.; solicitor of Jeff Davis County, Ga., 1911–1918; moved to Brunswick, Ga., in 1919 and to West Palm Beach, Fla., in 1925, continuing the practice of law; city attorney of West Palm Beach 1928–1933; a member of the taxation committee of President Hoover's Conference on Home Ownership in 1931; elected as a Democrat to the Seventy-third, Seventy-fourth, and Seventy-fifth Congresses (March 4, 1933–January 3, 1939); was not a candidate for renomination in 1938, but was an unsuccessful candidate for the Democratic nomination for United States Senator; resumed the practice of law in Miami, Fla.; attorney general for the Dade County Port Authority from 1945 until his death; died at his farm near White Springs, Fla., February 3, 1956; interment in Woodlawn Park Cemetery, Miami, Fla.

WILCOX, Jeduthun (father of Leonard Wilcox), a Representative from New Hampshire; born in Middletown, Conn., November 18, 1768; studied law; was admitted to the bar in 1802 and commenced practice in Orford, N. H.; member of the State house of representatives 1809–1811; elected as a Federalist to the Thirteenth and Fourteenth Congresses (March 4, 1813–March 3, 1817); died in Orford, Grafton County, N. H., July 18, 1838; interment in Orford Cemetery.

WILCOX, John A., a Representative from Mississippi; born in Greene County, N. C., April 18, 1819; moved to Tennessee; attended the common schools; moved to Mississippi and settled in Aberdeen; secretary of the State senate; served in the Mexican War as lieutenant, adjutant, and lieutenant colonel; elected as a Union Whig to the Thirty-second Congress (March 4, 1851–March 3, 1853); unsuccessful candidate for reelection in 1852 to the Thirty-third Congress; moved to Texas in 1853; member of the Confederate Congress; died in Richmond, Va., February 7, 1864; interment in Hollywood Cemetery.

WILCOX, Leonard (son of Jeduthun Wilcox), a Senator from New Hampshire; born in Hanover, N. H., January 29, 1799; was graduated from Dartmouth College, Hanover, N. H., in 1817; studied law; was admitted to the bar in 1820 and commenced practice in Orford, Grafton County, N. H.; member of the State house of representatives 1828–1834; judge of the superior court 1838–1840; bank commissioner 1838–1842; appointed as a Democrat to the United States Senate to fill the vacancy caused by the resignation of Franklin Pierce; subsequently elected and served from March 1, 1842, to March 3, 1843; resumed the practice of law; judge of the court of common pleas of New Hampshire in 1847 and 1848; again appointed judge of the superior court June 26, 1848, and served until his death in Orford, N. H., June 18, 1850; interment in the West Congregational Churchyard.

WILCOX, Robert William, a Delegate from the Territory of Hawaii; born in Kahalu, Honuaula, island of Maui, Hawaiian Islands, February 15, 1855; attended the Haleakala Boarding School, Makawao, island of Maui; taught school at Honuaula for several years; elected to the legislature as a representative from Wailukua, island of Maui, in 1880; later pursued an academic course in the Royal Military Academy, Turin, Italy, 1881–1885 and became a sublieutenant of artillery; entered the Royal Application School for Engineer and Artillery Officers in Turin in 1885; recalled by the Hawaiian Government in 1887; moved to San Francisco, Calif., in 1887 and engaged in the surveying business; returned to Hawaii in 1889 and became leader of the revolution of 1889; tried for treason but acquitted by a Hawaiian jury; elected to the legislature as a representative from Honolulu in 1890 and from Koolauloa, island of Oahu, in 1892; again a revolutionary leader in 1895 in an effort to restore Liliuokalani to the throne; was court-martialed and sentenced to death, but the sentence was commuted to thirty-five years; pardoned by President Dole in 1898; elected the first Delegate from Hawaii to the Fifty-sixth Congress; reelected to the Fifty-seventh Congress and served from November 6, 1900, to March 3, 1903; unsuccessful candidate for reelection in 1902 to the Fifty-eighth Congress; died in Honolulu, Hawaii, October 23, 1903; interment in the Catholic Cemetery.

WILDE, Richard Henry, a Representative from Georgia; born in Dublin, Ireland, September 24, 1789; immigrated to the United States in 1797 with his parents, who settled in Baltimore, Md.; received a limited schooling; moved to Augusta, Ga., in 1802; engaged in mercantile pursuits; studied law; was admitted to the bar in 1809 and commenced practice in Augusta; solicitor general of the superior court of Richmond County and by virtue of this office attorney general of Georgia 1811–1813; elected as a Democrat to the Fourteenth Congress (March 4, 1815–March 3, 1817); unsuccessful candidate for reelection in 1816 to the Fifteenth Congress; elected to the Eighteenth Congress to fill the vacancy caused by the resignation of Thomas W. Cobb and served from February 7 to March 3, 1825; unsuccessful candidate for reelection in 1824 to the Nineteenth Congress and for election in 1826 to the Twentieth Congress; subsequently elected to the Twentieth Congress to fill the vacancy caused by the resignation of John Forsyth; reelected to the Twenty-first, Twenty-second, and Twenty-third Congresses and served from November 17, 1827, to March 3, 1835; unsuccessful candidate for reelection in 1834 to the Twenty-fourth Congress; engaged in literary pursuits while traveling in Europe 1835–1840; moved to New Orleans in 1843 and continued the practice of law; professor of constitutional law in the University of Louisiana at New Orleans; died in New Orleans, La., September 10, 1847; interment in a vault in a cemetery in New Orleans; reinterred at Sand Hill family burying ground near Augusta, Ga., in 1854 and again in 1886 in the City Cemetery, Augusta, Ga.

WILDER, Abel Carter, a Representative from Kansas; born in Mendon, Worcester County, Mass., March 18, 1828; completed preparatory studies; engaged in mercantile pursuits; moved to Rochester, N. Y., and continued mercantile pursuits; moved to Leavenworth, Kans., in 1857 and again engaged in mercantile pursuits; delegate to the Osawatomie convention in 1859; delegate to the Republican National Convention at Chicago in 1860 and elected its chairman; served as a captain in the Kansas brigade for one year in the Civil War; elected as a Republican to the Thirty-eighth Congress (March 4, 1863–March 3, 1865); delegate to the Republican National Conventions in 1864, 1868, and 1872; returned to Rochester, N. Y., in 1865 and published the Morning and Evening Express until 1868, when he retired from active business pursuits; elected mayor of Rochester in 1872, but resigned in 1873; died in San Francisco, Calif., December 22, 1875, while there for his health; interment in Mount Hope Cemetery, Rochester, N. Y.

WILDER, William Henry, a Representative from Massachusetts; born in Belfast, Waldo County, Maine, May 14, 1855; moved with his parents to Massachusetts in 1866; attended the common schools; engaged in the mercantile and manufacturing business at Gardner, Mass.; president of the Wilder Industries (Inc.); studied law; admitted to the bar in 1900; was admitted to practice before the United States Supreme Court in 1909; studied the monetary systems in Europe in 1909 and wrote many articles and pamphlets on monetary questions; elected as a Republican to the Sixty-second and Sixty-third Congresses and served from March 4, 1911, until his death in Washington, D. C., September 11, 1913; interment in Crystal Lake Cemetery, Gardner, Worcester County, Mass.

WILDMAN, Zalmon, a Representative from Connecticut; born in Danbury, Fairfield County, Conn., February 16, 1775; completed preparatory studies; manufacturer of hats; established the first hat stores in Charleston, S. C., and Savannah, Ga., in 1802; first president of Danbury National Bank 1824–1826; member of the State house of representatives in 1818 and 1819; appointed postmaster of Danbury, Conn., and served from April 9, 1805, to May 26, 1835; elected as a Democrat to the Twenty-fourth Congress and served from March 4, 1835, until his death in Washington, D. C., December 10, 1835; interment in Wooster Cemetery, Danbury, Conn.

WILDRICK, Isaac, a Representative from New Jersey; born in Marksboro, Warren County, N. J., March 3, 1803; attended the common schools; engaged in agricultural pursuits near Blairstown, Warren County, N. J.; constable from 1827 to 1832; coroner 1829–1831; justice of the peace 1834–1839; judge in 1839; sheriff 1839–1841; director of the county poorhouse 1842–1848; member freeholder 1845–1848; elected as a Democrat to the Thirty-first and Thirty-second Congresses (March 4, 1849–March 3, 1853); was not a candidate for renomination in 1852; resumed agricultural pursuits; again a freeholder 1856–1859; member of the State assembly 1882–1885; died in Blairstown, N. J., March 22, 1892; interment in the Presbyterian Cemetery, Marksboro, N. J.

WILEY, Alexander, a Senator from Wisconsin; born in Chippewa Falls, Chippewa County, Wis., May 26, 1884; attended the public schools, Augsburg College, Minneapolis, Minn., and the University of Michigan at Ann Arbor; was graduated from the law department of the University of Wisconsin at Madison in 1907; was admitted to the bar the same year and commenced practice in Chippewa Falls, Wis.; district attorney of Chippewa County 1909–1915; also engaged in agricultural pursuits and banking; delegate to the Interparliamentary Union Conference in Oslo, Norway, in 1939, and to the Empire Parliamentary Conference in Bermuda, Bahamas Islands, in 1946; elected as a Republican to the United States Senate in 1938 for the term commencing January 3, 1939; reelected in 1944, 1950, and again in 1956 for the term ending January 3, 1963.

WILEY, Ariosto Appling (brother of Oliver Cicero Wiley), a Representative from Alabama; born in Clayton, Barbour County, Ala., November 6, 1848; moved with his parents to Troy, Pike County, Ala.; attended the common schools and was graduated from Emory and Henry College, Emory, Va., in 1870; studied law; was admitted to the bar in 1871 and commenced practice in Clayton, Ala.; moved to Montgomery, Ala., the same year and continued the practice of law; was cap-tain of a Cavalry troop of the Alabama National Guard and later a lieutenant colonel commanding the Second Regiment of Infantry of the Alabama National Guard; member of the State house of representatives in 1884, 1885, 1888, 1889, 1896, and 1897; served in the State senate 1890–1893, 1898, and 1899; appointed by President McKinley on June 9, 1898, lieutenant colonel of the Fifth Regiment, United States Volunteer Infantry, and served during the Spanish-American War; legal adviser and chief of staff to Gen. Henry W. Lawton in Santiago, Cuba, and assisted Gen. Leonard Wood in the establishment of civil government in the eastern Province; delegate to the Democratic National Convention at St. Louis in 1888; presidential elector on the Democratic ticket of Cleveland and Thurman in 1888; elected as a Democrat to the Fifty-seventh and to the three succeeding Congresses and served from March 4, 1901, until his death at Hot Springs, Bath County, Va., June 17, 1908; interment in Oakwood Cemetery, Montgomery, Ala.

WILEY, James Sullivan, a Representative from Maine; born in Mercer, Somerset County, Maine, January 22, 1808; moved to Bethel, Oxford County, Maine, in 1826; attended Gould's Academy and was graduated from Colby College, Waterville, Maine, in 1836; moved to Dover, Maine, and was an instructor in Foxcroft Academy; studied law; was admitted to the Piscataquis County bar in 1839 and commenced practice in Dover; elected as a Democrat to the Thirtieth Congress (March 4, 1847–March 3, 1849); resumed the practice of law in Dover; moved to Fryeburg, Maine, in 1889 and continued the practice of law until his death in that city on December 21, 1891; interment in Smart Hill Cemetery.

WILEY, John McClure, a Representative from New York; born in Londonderry, Ireland, August 11, 1846; immigrated to the United States in 1850 with his parents, who settled in Erie County, N. Y.; attended the common schools; engaged in mercantile pursuits and the real-estate business in Colden, N. Y.; member of the State assembly in 1871 and 1872; delegate to the Democratic National Conventions in 1884, 1888, and 1892; elected as a Democrat to the Fifty-first Congress (March 4, 1889–March 3, 1891); declined to be a candidate for renomination in 1890; appointed on April 24, 1893, by President Cleveland, consul at Bordeaux, France, and served until July 31, 1897; retired from public life; resided in Jacksonville, Fla., during the winter and in Colden, N. Y., during the summer months; died in St. Catharines, Ontario, Canada, August 13, 1912; interment in Crown Hill Cemetery, Indianapolis, Ind.

WILEY, Oliver Cicero (brother of Ariosto Appling Wiley), a Representative from Alabama; born in Troy, Pike County, Ala., January 30, 1851; attended the common schools; member of the town council for five years; chairman of the Democratic executive committee of Pike County 1884–1886; member of the Democratic State executive committee in 1888; alternate delegate to the Democratic National Conventions in 1888 and 1892; was president of the Alabama Midland Railway during its construction, from 1887 to 1892; president of the board of directors of the State normal college at Troy, Ala.; director of the Farmers & Merchants' National Bank at Troy; vice president and general manager of the Standard Chemical & Oil Co. at Troy; elected as a Democrat to the Sixtieth Congress to fill the vacancy caused by the death of his brother, Ariosto Appling Wiley, and served from November 3, 1908, to March 3, 1909; died in Troy, Ala., October 18, 1917; interment in Oakwood Cemetery.

WILEY, William Halsted, a Representative from New Jersey; born in New York City July 10, 1842; attended private schools; was graduated from the College of the City of New

York in 1861; during the Civil War entered the Union Army in 1860 as a member of the Seventh New York Volunteers; was promoted to first lieutenant of Volunteers in 1862 and mustered out with the rank of brevet major in 1864 by the consolidation of his regiment; was graduated from the Rensselaer Polytechnic Institute, Troy, N. Y., in 1866; attended the Columbia College School of Mines in 1868; engaged in civil engineering and also as a superintendent of a mine for several years; member of the township committee of East Orange, N. J., 1886–1888, and president one year; in 1897 was president of one of the juries at the International Exposition in Brussels and a member of the superior jury; received the decoration of the Order of Leopold from the King of Belgium in 1897; appointed by the Governor of New Jersey a member of the commission for the Louisiana Purchase Exposition at St. Louis, Mo., in 1904; elected as a Republican to the Fifty-eighth and Fifty-ninth Congresses (March 4, 1903–March 3, 1907); was an unsuccessful candidate for renomination in 1906; elected to the Sixty-first Congress (March 4, 1909–March 3, 1911); unsuccessful candidate for reelection in 1910 to the Sixty-second Congress; a publisher in New York City, with residence in East Orange, N. J.; during the First World War served as the representative of the American Society of Mechanical Engineers on the National Preparedness Committee and became its chairman; died in East Orange, Essex County, N. J., May 2, 1925; interment in Rosedale Cemetery.

WILFLEY, Xenophon Pierce, a Senator from Missouri; born near Mexico, Audrain County, Mo., March 18, 1871; attended the country schools; was graduated from Clarksburg College in 1891 and from Central College, at Fayette in 1894; taught in Central College one year and in Sedalia High School for three years; was graduated from the Washington University Law School at St. Louis, Mo., in 1899 and commenced practice in that city; chairman of the board of election commissioners of St. Louis in 1917 and 1918; appointed as a Democrat to the United States Senate to fill the vacancy caused by the death of William J. Stone and served from April 30 to November 5, 1918, when a successor was elected; unsuccessful candidate for the nomination to fill the vacancy in 1918; resumed the practice of his profession; president of the Missouri Bar Association in 1925; died in St. Louis, Mo., May 4, 1931; interment in Oak Grove Cemetery.

WILKIN, James Whitney (father of Samuel Jones Wilkin), a Representative from New York; born in Wallkill, Orange (now Ulster) County, N. Y., in 1762; served in the Revolutionary War; was graduated from Princeton College in 1785; studied law; was admitted to the bar in 1788 and began practice in Goshen, N. Y.; member of the State assembly in 1800; entered the State militia and rose through successive grades to the rank of major general; served in the State senate 1801–1804 and 1811–1814; member of the State assembly in 1808 and 1809, and served as speaker in the latter year; member of the council of appointment in 1802, 1811, and 1813; elected as a Democrat to the Fourteenth Congress to fill the vacancy caused by the resignation of Jonathan Fisk; reelected to the Fifteenth Congress and served from June 7, 1815, to March 3, 1819; unsuccessful candidate for United States Senator in 1815; county clerk of Orange County 1819–1821; county treasurer for several years; died in Goshen, N. Y., February 23, 1845; interment in Slate Hill Cemetery.

WILKIN, Samuel Jones (son of James Whitney Wilkin), a Representative from New York; born in Goshen, Orange County, N. Y., December 17, 1793; was graduated from Princeton College in 1812; studied law; was admitted to the bar in 1815 and began practice in Goshen; member of the State

assembly in 1824 and 1825; elected as a Democrat to the Twenty-second Congress (March 4, 1831–March 3, 1833); unsuccessful Whig candidate for election in 1844 as Lieutenant Governor of New York; member of the State senate in 1848 and 1849; canal appraiser in 1850; died in Goshen, N. Y., March 11, 1866; interment in Slate Hill Cemetery.

WILKINS, Beriah, a Representative from Ohio; born near Richwood, Union County, Ohio, July 10, 1846; attended the common schools of Marysville, Ohio; during the Civil War enlisted as a private in Company H, One Hundred and Thirty-sixth Regiment, Ohio Volunteer Infantry, May 2, 1864, and served until honorably discharged August 31, 1864; engaged in banking in Uhrichsville, Tuscarawas County, Ohio; member of the State senate 1880 and 1881; member of the Democratic State central committee in 1882; elected as a Democrat to the Forty-eighth, Forty-ninth, and Fiftieth Congresses (March 4, 1883–March 3, 1889); settled in Washington, D. C.; became majority owner and publisher of the Washington Post in 1889, and later, in 1894, acquired the entire stock ownership of the paper, serving as editor until his death; died in Washington, D. C., June 7, 1905; interment in Rock Creek Cemetery.

WILKINS, William, a Senator and a Representative from Pennsylvania; born in Carlisle, Pa., December 20, 1779; attended Dickinson College, Carlisle, Pa.; studied law; was admitted to the bar December 28, 1801, and commenced practice in Pittsburgh, Pa.; assisted in organizing the Pittsburgh Manufacturing Co. in 1810; was the first president of the Bank of Pittsburgh; president of the common council 1816–1819; member of the State house of representatives in 1820, resigning December 18, 1820; president judge of the fifth judicial district of Pennsylvania 1821–1824; judge of the United States District Court for Western Pennsylvania 1824–1831; unsuccessful candidate for election in 1826 to the Twentieth Congress; elected to the Twenty-first Congress, but resigned before qualifying; elected as a Democrat and Anti-Mason to the United States Senate and served from March 4, 1831, to June 30, 1834, when he resigned; appointed United States Minister to Russia and served from June 1834 to December 1835; received the electoral vote of Pennsylvania for Vice President in 1833; elected as a Democrat to the Twenty-eighth Congress and served from March 4, 1843, to February 14, 1844, when he resigned; appointed Secretary of War by President Tyler February 15, 1844; entered upon his duties February 20, 1844, and served until March 6, 1845; member of the State senate 1855–1857; major general of the Pennsylvania Home Guards in 1862; died in "Homewood," near Pittsburgh, Allegheny County, Pa., June 23, 1865; interment in Homewood Cemetery, Wilkinsburg, Pa.

WILKINSON, Morton Smith, a Representative and a Senator from Minnesota; born in Skaneateles, Onondaga County, N. Y., January 22, 1819; attended the common schools; moved to Illinois in 1837 and was employed in railroad work two years; returned to Skaneateles in 1840; studied law; was admitted to the bar in 1842 and commenced practice in Eaton Rapids, Eaton County, Mich., in 1843; moved to Stillwater, Washington County, Minn., in 1847; elected to the first legislature of Minnesota Territory in 1849; register of deeds of Ramsey County 1851–1853; moved to Mankato in 1858; member of the board of commissioners to prepare a code of laws for the Territory of Minnesota in 1858; elected as a Republican to the United States Senate and served from March 4, 1859, to March 3, 1865; unsuccessful candidate for reelection; delegate to the Republican National Convention at Baltimore in 1864; elected as a Republican to the Forty-first Congress (March 4, 1869–March 3, 1871); unsuccessful candidate for renomination in 1870; moved to Wells, Faribault County; member of the State senate 1874–1877; was prosecuting attorney of Faribault County 1880–1884; resumed the practice of his profession; died in Wells, Minn., February 4, 1894; interment in Glenwood Cemetery, Mankato, Blue Earth County, Minn.

WILKINSON, Theodore Stark, a Representative from Louisiana; born on Point Celeste plantation in Plaquemines Parish, near New Orleans, La., December 18, 1847; educated by private tutors and attended the common schools; was graduated from Washington and Lee University, Lexington, Va., in 1870; engaged in sugar planting in 1870; member of the school board of Plaquemines Parish; member and president of the board of levee commissioners for the third levee district; elected as a Democrat to the Fiftieth and Fifty-first Congresses (March 4, 1887–March 3, 1891); declined to be a candidate for renomination in 1890; chairman of the Louisiana antilottery convention in 1892; collector of the port of New Orleans 1893–1898; unsuccessful candidate for Governor in 1898; again engaged in sugar planting; delegate to the Democratic National Convention in Baltimore in 1912; died in New Orleans, La., on February 1, 1921; interment in Metairie Cemetery.

WILLARD, Charles Wesley, a Representative from Vermont; born in Lyndon, Caledonia County, Vt., June 18, 1827; was graduated from Dartmouth College, Hanover, N. H., in 1851; studied law; was admitted to the bar and commenced practice in Montpelier in 1853; secretary of state of Vermont 1855 and 1856; declined a reelection; member of the State senate 1860 and 1861; became editor and publisher of the Montpelier Freeman in 1861; elected as a Republican to the Forty-first, Forty-second, and Forty-third Congresses (March 4, 1869–March 3, 1875); unsuccessful candidate for reelection in 1874 to the Forty-third Congress; resumed the practice of law in Montpelier; member of the commission to revise the laws of Vermont in 1879 and 1880; died in Montpelier, Vt., on June 8, 1880; interment in Green Mount Cemetery.

WILLARD, George, a Representative from Michigan; born in Bolton, Vt., March 20, 1824; attended school and received instruction from his father; moved with his parents to Battle Creek, Mich., in 1836; was graduated from Kalamazoo (Mich.) College in 1844; taught school and also studied theology, and was ordained a minister of the Episcopal Church in 1848; rector of churches in Coldwater, Battle Creek, and Kalamazoo, Mich., until 1863; professor of Latin in Kalamazoo (Mich.) College in 1863 and 1864; engaged in newspaper work in Battle Creek, Calhoun County, Mich.; member of the Michigan State Board of Education 1857–1863; regent of the University of Michigan at Ann Arbor 1863–1872; member of the State house of representatives in 1866 and 1867; member of the State constitutional convention in 1867; delegate to the Republican National Convention at Philadelphia in 1872; elected as a Republican to the Forty-third and Forty-fourth Congresses (March 4, 1873–March 3, 1877); was not a candidate for renomination in 1876; resumed newspaper work in Battle Creek, Mich.; editor and owner of the Battle Creek Journal until his death in Battle Creek, Mich., March 26, 1901; interment in Oak Hill Cemetery.

WILLCOX, Washington Frederick, a Representative from Connecticut; born in Killingworth, Middlesex County, Conn., August 22, 1834; prepared for college at a private school, Madison Academy, and Hopkins Grammar School, New Haven; was graduated from Yale Law School in 1862; was admitted to the bar the same year and commenced practice in Deep River, Middlesex County, Conn.; member of the State house of representatives in 1862 and 1863; served in the State senate in 1875

and 1876; State's attorney 1875–1883; elected as a Democrat to the Fifty-first and Fifty-second Congresses (March 4, 1889–March 3, 1893); was not a candidate for renomination in 1892; resumed the practice of law in Deep River, Conn., and also engaged in banking; State railroad commissioner 1897–1905; died at his home in Chester, Conn., March 8, 1909; interment in Fountain Hill Cemetery, Deep River, Conn.

WILLETT, William Forte, Jr., a Representative from New York; born in Brooklyn, N. Y., November 27, 1869; attended the public schools of his native city, and was graduated from the law department of New York University, New York City, in 1895; was admitted to the bar the following year and commenced the practice of his profession in New York City; elected as a Democrat to the Sixtieth and Sixty-first Congresses (March 4, 1907–March 3, 1911); was not a candidate for renomination in 1910; engaged in the real-estate business; died in New York City, N. Y., February 12, 1938; interment in Evergreen Cemetery, Brooklyn, N. Y.

WILLEY, Calvin, a Senator from Connecticut; born in East Haddam, Conn., September 15, 1776; attended the common schools; studied law; was admitted to the bar in 1798 and commenced practice in Chatham, Conn.; moved to Stafford, Conn., in 1800; member of the State house of representatives in 1805 and 1806; postmaster of Stafford Springs, Conn., 1806–1808; moved to Tolland, Tolland County, Conn., in 1808; again a member of the State house of representatives in 1810, 1812, 1820, and 1821; postmaster of Tolland 1812–1816; probate judge of Stafford district 1818–1825; served in the State senate in 1823 and 1824; presidential elector in 1824 and voted for John Quincy Adams; elected as a Democrat to the United States Senate for the term commencing March 4, 1825, and served from May 4, 1825, to March 3, 1831; resumed the practice of law in Tolland, Conn.; died in Stafford, Conn., August 23, 1858; interment in Skungamaug Cemetery, Tolland, Conn.

WILLEY, Earle Dukes, a Representative from Delaware; born in Greenwood, Sussex County, Del., July 21, 1889; attended the public schools and George Washington University Law School, Washington, D. C.; was graduated from Dickinson College, Carlisle, Pa., in 1911; principal of Greenwood High School 1911–1915; secretary to Hon. Thomas W. Miller, Washington, D. C., 1915–1917; was admitted to the bar in 1920 and commenced practice in Dover, Del.; State librarian 1917–1921; deputy attorney general and prosecuting attorney for Kent County, Del., 1921–1931; judge of the court of common pleas of Kent County 1931–1939 and of the juvenile court of Kent and Sussex Counties 1933–1939; unsuccessful candidate for Lieutenant Governor in 1940; secretary of state 1941–1943; trustee of the University of Delaware, of the Elizabeth W. Murphey School for Orphan Children, and of the State College for Colored Students; elected as a Republican to the Seventy-eighth Congress (January 3, 1943–January 3, 1945); unsuccessful candidate for reelection in 1944 to the Seventy-ninth Congress; resumed the practice of law in Dover, Del., until his death March 17, 1950; interment in St. Johnstown Cemetery, near Greenwood, Del.

WILLEY, Waitman Thomas, a Senator from Virginia and from West Virginia; born in Monongalia County, Va., in what is now a part of Marion County, W. Va., October 18, 1811; was graduated from Madison (Pa.) College in 1831; studied law; was admitted to the bar in 1833 and commenced practice in Morgantown, Va. (now West Virginia); appointed clerk of the county court of Monongalia County in October 1841 and later clerk of the circuit superior court, and held both positions until 1852; delegate to the Virginia constitutional convention in 1850 and

1851; delegate to the Constitutional Union National Convention at Baltimore in 1860, which nominated Bell and Everett; elected to the United States Senate from Virginia to fill the vacancy caused by the retirement of James M. Mason and served from July 9, 1861, to March 3, 1863; delegate to the State constitutional convention of West Virginia; upon the admission of West Virginia as a State into the Union was elected to the United States Senate; reelected in 1865 and served from August 4, 1863, to March 3, 1871; delegate to the Republican National Convention at Cincinnati in 1876, which nominated Hayes and Wheeler; again served as clerk of the county court of Monongalia County 1882–1896; retired from public life; died in Morgantown, W. Va., May 2, 1900; interment in Oak Grove Cemetery.

WILLFORD, Albert Clinton, a Representative from Iowa; born in Vinton, Benton County, Iowa, September 21, 1877; attended the country and town schools and Tilford's Academy, Vinton, Iowa; employed as chief engineer of the electric light, power, and water company at Vinton 1900–1907; moved to Waterloo, Black Hawk County, Iowa, in 1907 and engaged in the manufacture of ice until 1910, when he engaged in the seed, feed, and coal business; trustee of the Waterloo Public Library 1918–1930; served on the Black Hawk County Jury Commission 1922–1924; president of the Iowa Stationary Engineers Association for one year; president of the Izaak Walton League of America for Iowa 1927–1929 and served as a National and State director; president of the Waterloo Baseball Club 1923–1927; elected as a Democrat to the Seventy-third Congress (March 4, 1933–January 3, 1935); unsuccessful candidate for reelection in 1934 to the Seventy-fourth Congress and for election in 1936 to the Seventy-fifth Congress; resumed his former pursuits in Waterloo, Iowa, until his death there on March 10, 1937; interment in Memorial Park Cemetery.

WILLIAMS, Abram Pease, a Senator from California; was born in New Portland, Somerset County, Maine, February 3, 1832; attended the common schools and completed an academic course at North Anson (Maine) Academy 1846–1848; attended normal school at Farmington, Maine, 1848–1853; taught school at North Anson; moved to Fairfield, Somerset County, Maine, in 1853 and engaged in mercantile pursuits; moved to California in 1858 and engaged in mining in Tuolumne County; resumed mercantile pursuits in 1859; moved to San Francisco in 1861 and became an importer, stock raiser, and farmer; one of the founders of the San Francisco Board of Trade, serving as its first president; member of the San Francisco Chamber of Commerce; chairman of the finance committee and treasurer of the Republican State committee in 1880; chairman of the latter committee in 1884; elected as a Republican to the United States Senate to fill the vacancy caused by the death of John F. Miller and served from August 4, 1886, to March 3, 1887; was not a candidate for renomination in 1887; resumed the wholesale mercantile business in San Francisco, Calif., where he died October 17, 1911; interment in Maplewood Cemetery, Fairfield, Maine.

WILLIAMS, Alpheus Starkey, a Representative from Michigan; born in Saybrook, Middlesex County, Conn., September 20, 1810; was graduated from Yale College in 1831; studied law; was admitted to the bar in 1837 and commenced practice in Detroit, Mich.; judge of probate 1840–1844; editor of the Detroit Daily Advertiser 1843–1847; served in the war with Mexico; commissioned lieutenant colonel of the First Michigan Infantry December 8, 1847; mustered out July 29, 1848; postmaster of Detroit 1849–1853; during the Civil War was commissioned brigadier general of Michigan Volunteers April 24, 1861, and of United States Volunteers May 17, 1861; brevetted

major general of Volunteers January 12, 1865, "for marked ability and energy"; mustered out January 15, 1866; Minister Resident to San Salvador 1866–1869; elected as a Democrat to the Forty-fourth and Forty-fifth Congresses and served from March 4, 1875, until his death in Washington, D. C., December 20, 1878; interment in Elmwood Cemetery, Detroit, Mich.

WILLIAMS, Andrew, a Representative from New York; born in Ormstown, Province of Quebec, Canada, August 27, 1828; received a limited schooling; engaged in mercantile pursuits; immigrated to the United States in 1852 and settled in Plattsburg, N. Y.; engaged in the manufacture of nails 1863–1865, and subsequently in the mining of iron ore, in the lumber trade, and in the manufacture of horseshoe nails and wagons; one of the organizers of the Iron National Bank at Plattsburg in 1881 and served as its president until 1888; elected as a Republican to the Forty-fourth and Forty-fifth Congresses (March 4, 1875–March 3, 1879); was not a candidate for renomination in 1878; member of the board of supervisors of Dannemora for two years and for a number of years represented Plattsburg in a like capacity; superintendent of the Plattsburg waterworks 1889–1902; elected county treasurer in 1890; reelected in 1893, 1896, 1899, 1902, and 1905; member of the board of education; died in Plattsburg, N. Y., October 6, 1907; interment in Riverside Cemetery.

WILLIAMS, Archibald Hunter Arrington (nephew of Archibald Hunter Arrington), a Representative from North Carolina; born near Louisburg, Franklin County, N. C., October 22, 1842; attended the common schools and Emory and Henry College, Emory, Va.; enlisted as a private in the Confederate Army during the Civil War; served four years in the Army of Northern Virginia, and at the surrender at Appomattox was captain of his company; severely wounded in the Battle of Gettysburg; after the war engaged in agricultural pursuits and in retail trade in Oxford, Granville County, N. C.; was instrumental in completing and making successful the Oxford & Henderson Railroad, and was for several years its president; member of the State house of representatives 1883–1885; elected as a Democrat to the Fifty-second Congress (March 4, 1891–March 3, 1893); unsuccessful candidate for reelection in 1892 to the Fifty-third Congress; died in Chase City, Mecklenburg County, Va., September 5, 1895; interment in Elmwood Cemetery, Oxford, N. C.

WILLIAMS, Arthur Bruce, a Representative from Michigan; born in Ashland, Ashland County, Ohio, January 27, 1872; attended the common schools of Eaton County, and was graduated from Olivet College, in that county, in 1892; was admitted to the bar in 1894 and commenced practice at Battle Creek, Mich.; interested in agricultural pursuits at his summer home, Gull Lake, Mich.; director of the Old National Bank, Battle Creek; vice president and general counsel of the Postum Cereal Co.; president of the Michigan Manufacturers' Association; elected as a Republican to the Sixty-eighth Congress to fill the vacancy caused by the death of John M. C. Smith; reelected to the Sixty-ninth Congress and served from June 19, 1923, until his death in Baltimore, Md., May 1, 1925; interment in Maple Hill Cemetery, Charlotte, Eaton County, Mich.

WILLIAMS, Benjamin, a Representative from North Carolina; born near Smithfield, Johnston County, N. C., January 1, 1751; attended the country schools; engaged in agricultural pursuits; member of the provincial congress in 1774 and 1775; served in the Revolutionary Army as second lieutenant; promoted to captain in the Second Regiment July 19, 1776; promoted to colonel for gallantry at Guilford, N. C., July 12, 1781;

member of the State house of commons in 1779, 1785, and 1789; member of the State senate in 1781, 1784, 1786, and 1788; elected to the Third Congress (March 4, 1793–March 3, 1795); was not a candidate for renomination; Governor of North Carolina 1799–1802, 1807, and 1808, again a member of the State senate in 1809; died in Moore County, N. C., July 20, 1814; interment in the family cemetery in Moore County, near Carbonton, N. C.

WILLIAMS, Charles Grandison, a Representative from Wisconsin; born in Royalton, Niagara County, N. Y., October 18, 1829; pursued an academic course and studied law in Rochester, N. Y.; moved to Wisconsin in 1856 and settled in Janesville; was admitted to the bar and commenced practice in Janesville; presidential elector on the Republican ticket of Grant and Colfax in 1868; served in the State senate 1869–1872; twice chosen president pro tempore of that body; elected as a Republican to the Forty-third and to the four succeeding Congresses (March 4, 1873–March 3, 1883); unsuccessful candidate for reelection in 1882 to the Forty-eighth Congress; resumed the practice of law; died in Watertown, Codington County, S. Dak., March 30, 1892; interment in Oak Hill Cemetery, Janesville, Rock County, Wis.

WILLIAMS, Christopher Harris (grandfather of John Sharp Williams), a Representative from Tennessee; born near Hillsboro, Orange County, N. C., December 18, 1798; pursued an academic course and attended the University of North Carolina at Chapel Hill; studied law; was admitted to the bar about 1820 and practiced; elected as a Whig to the Twenty-fifth, Twenty-sixth, and Twenty-seventh Congresses (March 4, 1837–March 3, 1843); unsuccessful candidate for reelection in 1842 to the Twenty-eighth Congress; delegate to several State and National conventions; was elected to the Thirty-first and Thirty-second Congresses (March 4, 1849–March 3, 1853); was not a candidate for renomination in 1852; resumed the practice of law in Lexington, Henderson County, Tenn., and died there November 27, 1857; interment in Lexington Cemetery.

WILLIAMS, Clyde, a Representative from Missouri; born on a farm near Grubville, Jefferson County, Mo., October 13, 1873; attended the county schools, De Soto High School, and the State normal school at Cape Girardeau; was graduated from the law department of the University of Missouri at Columbia in 1901; was admitted to the bar the same year and commenced practice in De Soto, Mo.; prosecuting attorney of Jefferson County 1902–1908; delegate to a number of Democratic State conventions and permanent chairman in 1938; elected as a Democrat to the Seventieth Congress (March 4, 1927–March 3, 1929); unsuccessful candidate for reelection in 1928 to the Seventy-first Congress; resumed the practice of law; elected to the Seventy-second and to the five succeeding Congresses (March 4, 1931–January 3, 1943); unsuccessful candidate for reelection in 1942 to the Seventy-eighth Congress; engaged in legal work for the Reconstruction Finance Corporation in Washington, D. C., 1943–1945; served as president of the Jefferson Trust Co. in Hillsboro and president of the Bank of Hillsboro; died in St. Louis, Mo., November 12, 1954; interment in Hillsboro Cemetery, Hillsboro, Mo.

WILLIAMS, David Rogerson, a Representative from South Carolina; born in Robbins Neck, S. C., March 8, 1776; attended school at Wrentham, Mass., and Rhode Island College (now Brown University), Providence, R. I.; studied law; was admitted to the bar in 1797 and practiced for three years in Providence, R. I.; editor and proprietor of the City Gazette and Weekly Carolina Gazette of Charleston, S. C., 1801–1803; engaged in cotton planting and manufacturing in Darlington

County, S. C., from 1803 until his death; built the first cottonseed-oil mill in South Carolina; elected as a Democrat to the Ninth and Tenth Congresses (March 4, 1805–March 3, 1809); elected to the Twelfth Congress (March 4, 1811–March 3, 1813); brigadier general in the United States Army July 9, 1813, to April 6, 1814, when he resigned; Governor of South Carolina 1814–1816; member of the State senate from 1824 until he was accidentally killed November 17, 1830, while superintending the construction of a bridge over Lynchs Creek, Witherspoons Ferry, on the road to Georgetown, Georgetown County, S. C.; interment on his plantation near Society Hill, Darlington County, S. C.

WILLIAMS, Elihu Stephen, a Representative from Ohio; born in New Carlisle, Clark County, Ohio, January 24, 1835; educated in the common schools and attended Antioch College, Yellow Springs, Ohio, two years; studied law in Dayton, Ohio, and was admitted to the bar in 1861; during the Civil War enlisted as a private in the Seventy-first Regiment, Ohio Volunteer Infantry, in October 1861; commissioned first lieutenant February 14, 1862; promoted to captain February 10, 1863; detailed to the command of the military post at Carthage, Smith County, Tenn., in September 1863 and remained there until the close of the war; attorney general of the sixth judicial district of Tennessee from April 1865 to 1867; member of the Tennessee House of Representatives 1867–1869; moved to Troy, Miami County, Ohio, in January 1875; elected as a Republican to the Fiftieth and Fifty-first Congresses (March 4, 1887–March 3, 1891); editor of the Buckeye; died in Troy, Ohio, December 1, 1903; interment in Riverside Cemetery.

WILLIAMS, George Fred, a Representative from Massachusetts; born in Dedham, Norfolk County, Mass., July 10, 1852; attended private schools, and was graduated from the Dedham High School in 1868 and from Dartmouth College, Hanover, N. H. in 1872; studied at the Universities of Heidelberg and Berlin; taught school in West Brewster, Mass., in 1872 and 1873; became a reporter on the Boston Globe; member of the Dedham school committee; studied law at Boston University, Boston, Mass.; was admitted to the bar in 1875 and practiced in Boston; edited Williams' Citations of Massachusetts Cases in 1878 and volumes 10 to 17 of the Annual Digest of the United States 1880–1887; member of the State house of representatives in 1890; elected as a Democrat to the Fifty-second Congress (March 4, 1891–March 3, 1893); unsuccessful candidate for reelection in 1892 to the Fifty-third Congress; was an unsuccessful Democratic nominee for Governor in 1895, 1896, and 1897; resumed the practice of law in Boston, Mass.; delegate to several State conventions; delegate to the Democratic National Conventions in 1896, 1900, 1904 and 1908; Minister to Greece and Montenegro in 1913 and 1914; resumed the practice of law until his retirement in 1930; died in Brookline, near Boston, Mass., July 11, 1932; interment in the Old Village Cemetery, Dedham, Mass.

WILLIAMS, George Henry, a Senator from Oregon; born in New Lebanon, Columbia County, N. Y., March 23, 1823; completed preparatory studies; studied law; was admitted to the bar in 1844 and commenced practice at Fort Madison, Lee County, Iowa; judge of the first judicial district of Iowa 1847–1852; presidential elector on the Democratic ticket of Pierce and King in 1852; was chief justice of the Territory of Oregon 1853–1857; reappointed by President Buchanan but declined; member of the State constitutional convention of Oregon in 1858; elected as a Union Republican to the United States Senate and served from March 4, 1865, to March 3, 1871; unsuccessful candidate for reelection; Attorney General of the United States in the Cabinet of President Grant from January

10, 1872, to May 15, 1875; was nominated by President Grant as Chief Justice of the Supreme Court of the United States, but subsequently his name was withdrawn; mayor of Portland, Oreg., 1902–1905; died in Portland, Oreg., April 4, 1910; interment in Riverview Cemetery.

WILLIAMS, George Howard, a Senator from Missouri; born in California, Moniteau County, Mo., on December 1, 1871; attended the public schools; was graduated from the California (Mo.) High School in 1889, from the preparatory department of Drury College, Springfield, Mo., in 1890, from Princeton (N. J.) University in 1894, and from the Washington University Law School, St. Louis, Mo., in 1897; was admitted to the bar in 1897 and commenced practice in St. Louis; judge of the circuit court of the city of St. Louis 1906–1912; delegate at large to the Missouri constitutional convention in 1922 and 1923; appointed as a Republican to the United States Senate to fill the vacancy caused by the death of Selden P. Spencer and served from May 25, 1925, to December 5, 1926, when a duly elected successor qualified; was an unsuccessful candidate for election to fill the vacancy in 1926; resumed the practice of law in St. Louis until January 1, 1943, when he retired and moved to Sarasota, Fla.

WILLIAMS, George Short, a Representative from Delaware; born in Ocean View, Sussex County, Del., October 21, 1877; attended the public schools and Wilmington Conference Academy, Dover, Del.; was graduated from Dickinson College, Carlisle, Pa., in 1900; instructor in Ironwood (Mich.) High School 1902–1904; engaged in the lumber business in Delaware and North Carolina 1905–1923; also interested in banking; mayor of Millsboro, Del., 1921–1927; treasurer of the State of Delaware 1929–1933; president of the State board of education 1927–1934; deputy motor vehicle commissioner 1935–1937; delegate to the Republican National Convention at Philadelphia in 1940; elected as a Republican to the Seventy-sixth Congress (January 3, 1939–January 3, 1941); unsuccessful candidate for reelection to the Seventy-seventh Congress; motor vehicle commissioner 1941–1946; administrative assistant to Senator John J. Williams from January 1947 to January 1959; is a resident of Millsboro, Del.

WILLIAMS, Guinn, a Representative from Texas; born near Beuela, Calhoun County, Miss., April 22, 1871; moved with his parents to Texas and settled in Decatur, Wise County, in 1876; attended the public schools; was graduated from the commercial branch of Transylvania College, Lexington, Ky., in 1890; engaged in the livestock business, agricultural pursuits, and banking; county clerk of Wise County, Tex., 1898–1902; member of the State senate from 1920 to May 1922, when he resigned, having been elected to Congress; elected as a Democrat to the Sixty-seventh Congress to fill the vacancy caused by the death of Lucian W. Parrish; reelected to the Sixty-eighth and to the four succeeding Congresses and served from May 13, 1922, to March 3, 1933; was not a candidate for renomination in 1932 to the Seventy-third Congress; manager of the Regional Agricultural Credit Corporation in San Angelo, Tex., in 1933; also engaged in the livestock business and ranching; died in San Angelo, Tex., on January 9, 1948; interment in Decatur Cemetery, Decatur, Tex.

WILLIAMS, Harrison Arlington, Jr., a Representative and a Senator from New Jersey; born in Plainfield, Union County, N. J., December 10, 1919; attended the public schools; graduated from Oberlin College in 1941; engaged in newspaper work in Washington, D. C., and studied at Georgetown University Foreign Service School until called to active duty as a seaman in the United States Naval Reserve December 17, 1941, serving on a minesweeper, as a pilot, and as a naval aviation instructor; after his discharge from the service as a lieutenant (jg) in December 1945, was employed in the steel industry for a short time, then entered Columbia University Law School, graduating in 1948; was admitted to the bar and commenced practice in New Hampshire in 1948; returned to Plainfield, N. J., in 1949 and continued to practice law; was an unsuccessful candidate for the State house of assembly in 1951 and for city councilman in 1952; elected as a Democrat to the Eighty-third Congress to fill the vacancy caused by the resignation of Clifford Case; reelected to the Eighty-fourth Congress and served from November 3, 1953, to January 3, 1957; unsuccessful candidate for reelection in 1956 to the Eighty-fifth Congress; elected to the United States Senate in 1958 for the term commencing January 3, 1959, and ending January 3, 1965.

WILLIAMS, Henry, a Representative from Massachusetts; born in Taunton, Bristol County, Mass., November 30, 1805; completed preparatory studies; studied law; was admitted to the bar in 1829 and commenced practice in Taunton, Mass.; member of the State house of representatives in 1834; served in the State senate in 1836 and 1837; elected as a Democrat to the Twenty-sixth Congress (March 4, 1839–March 3, 1841); unsuccessful candidate for reelection in 1840 to the Twenty-seventh Congress; was elected to the Twenty-eighth Congress (March 4, 1843–March 3, 1845); resumed the practice of law; died in Taunton, Mass., on May 8, 1887; interment in Mount Pleasant Cemetery.

WILLIAMS, Hezekiah, a Representative from Maine; born near Woodstock, Vt., July 28, 1798; was graduated from Dartmouth College, Hanover, N. H., in 1820; studied law; was admitted to the bar and commenced practice in Castine, Hancock County, Maine, in 1825; register of probate for Hancock County 1824–1838; selectman of Castine 1833–1835; trustee of the school fund in 1834; member of school committee in 1840; served in the State senate 1839–1841; again a selectman of Castine in 1843 and 1844; elected as a Democrat to the Twenty-ninth and Thirtieth Congresses (March 4, 1845–March 3, 1849); resumed the practice of law; died in Castine, Maine, October 23, 1856; interment in Castine Cemetery.

WILLIAMS, Isaac, Jr., a Representative from New York; born in Goshen, Conn., April 5, 1777; received a limited schooling; moved with his father to Otsego County, N. Y., in 1793; was appointed undersheriff of Otsego County in 1810; afterward appointed sheriff by the council of appointment in 1811 and served until 1813; successfully contested as a Democrat the election of John M. Bowers to the Thirteenth Congress to fill the vacancy caused by the death of William Dowse and served from December 20, 1813, to March 3, 1815; elected to the Fifteenth Congress (March 4, 1817–March 3, 1819); again elected to the Eighteenth Congress (March 4, 1823–March 3, 1825); unsuccessful Adam's candidate for sheriff in 1828; died in Cooperstown, Otsego County, N. Y., November 9, 1860; interment in Warren Cemetery, Otsego, N. Y.

WILLIAMS, James, a Representative from Delaware; born in Philadelphia, Pa., August 4, 1825; completed preparatory studies; moved to Kenton, Kent County, Del., in 1844 and engaged in agricultural pursuits; member of the State house of representatives in 1856 and 1862; served in the State senate in 1866 and 1871; delegate to the Democratic National Convention at Baltimore in 1872; elected as a Democrat to the Forty-fourth and Forty-fifth Congresses (March 4, 1875–March 3, 1879); was not a candidate for renomination in 1878; resumed agricultural pursuits; moved to Smyrna, Del., in 1891 and continued farming until his death on April 12, 1899; interment in St. Peter's Cemetery.

WILLIAMS, James Douglas, a Representative from Indiana; born in Pickaway County, Ohio, January 16, 1808; moved with his parents to Indiana and settled in Knox County in 1818; received a limited education; engaged in agricultural pursuits; justice of the peace of Vincennes, Ind., 1839–1843; from 1855 was identified with the State board of agriculture for sixteen years, serving four years as its president; member of the State house of representatives in 1843, 1847, 1851, 1856, and 1868; served in the State senate in 1858, 1862, and 1870; delegate to the Democratic National Convention at Baltimore in 1872; was the caucus nominee of his party, which was in the minority, for United States Senator in 1872; was elected as a Democrat to the Forty-fourth Congress and served from March 4, 1875, to December 1, 1876, when he resigned, having been elected Governor; Governor of Indiana from 1877 until his death in Indianapolis, Ind., November 20, 1880; interment in Walnut Grove Cemetery, near Monroe City, Knox County, Ind.

WILLIAMS, James Robert, a Representative from Illinois; born in Carmi, White County, Ill., December 27, 1850; attended the common schools; was graduated from Indiana State University at Bloomington in 1875 and from Union College of Law, Chicago, Ill., in 1876; was admitted to the bar in 1876 and commenced practice in Carmi, Ill.; master in chancery 1880–1882; county judge of White County 1882–1886; was a nominee for presidential elector on the Democratic ticket of Cleveland and Thurman in 1888; elected as a Democrat to the Fifty-first Congress to fill the vacancy caused by the death of Richard W. Townsend; reelected to the Fifty-second and Fifty-third Congresses and served from December 2, 1889, to March 3, 1895; elected to the Fifty-sixth, Fifty-seventh, and Fifty-eighth Congresses (March 4, 1899–March 3, 1905); resumed the practice of his profession; died in Loma Linda, San Bernardino County, Calif., November 8, 1923; interment in Maple Ridge Cemetery, Carmi, Ill.

WILLIAMS, James Wray, a Representative from Maryland; born in that State October 8, 1792; completed preparatory studies; member of the State house of delegates; was speaker in 1830; elected as a Democrat to the Twenty-seventh Congress and served from March 4, 1841, until his death on Priestford farm, Deer Creek, Harford County, Md., December 2, 1842; interment in the family cemetery on Priestford farm.

WILLIAMS, Jared, a Representative from Virginia; born in Montgomery County, Md., March 4, 1766; pursued classical studies; engaged in agricultural pursuits; member of the State house of delegates from 1812 to 1817; elected as a Jackson Democrat to the Sixteenth, Seventeenth, and Eighteenth Congresses (March 4, 1819–March 3, 1825); presidential elector on the Democratic ticket of Jackson and Calhoun in 1828; died near Newton, Va., January 2, 1831.

WILLIAMS, Jared Warner, a Representative and a Senator from New Hampshire; born in West Woodstock, Conn., December 22, 1796; was graduated from Brown University, Providence, R. I., in 1818; studied law in the Litchfield (Conn.) Law School; was admitted to the bar in 1822 and commenced practice in Lancaster, Coos County, N. H.; member of the State house of representatives in 1830 and 1831; served in the State senate 1832–1834; again a member of the State house of representatives in 1835 and 1836; elected as a Democrat to the Twenty-fifth and Twenty-sixth Congresses (March 4, 1837–

March 3, 1841); was Governor of New Hampshire 1847–1849; appointed to the United States Senate to fill the vacancy caused by the death of Charles G. Atherton and served from November 29, 1853, to July 15, 1854, when representation under the appointment expired; died in Lancaster, N. H., September 29, 1864; interment in Summer Street Cemetery.

WILLIAMS, Jeremiah Norman, a Representative from Alabama; born near Louisville, Barbour County, Ala., May 29, 1829; attended the preparatory schools of Barbour County and was graduated from the University of South Carolina at Columbia in 1852; studied law in Montgomery and Tuskegee; was admitted to the bar in 1855 and commenced practice in Clayton, Barbour County, Ala.; volunteered for service in the Confederate Army during the Civil War and was made captain of the Clayton Guards, later becoming major of the First Regiment, Alabama Infantry; elected a member of the State house of representatives in 1872, but was not allowed to take his seat; elected as a Democrat to the Forty-fourth and Forty-fifth Congresses (March 4, 1875–March 3, 1879); chancellor of the third division 1893–1899; resumed the practice of law in Clayton, Ala.; member of the State constitutional convention in 1901; died in Clayton, Ala., May 8, 1915; interment in the City Cemetery.

WILLIAMS, John, a Delegate from North Carolina; born in Hanover County, Va., March 14, 1731; moved to North Carolina in 1745 with his parents, who settled in Granville County; donated the land and laid out the town of Williamsboro, N. C.; studied law; was admitted to the bar and commenced practice in Williamsboro; one of the founders of the University of North Carolina at Chapel Hill; deputy attorney general in 1768; delegate to the Provincial Congress of 1775; member of the State house of commons in 1777 and 1778 and served as speaker; Member of the Continental Congress in 1778 and 1779; judge of the supreme court of North Carolina from 1779 until his death in Montpelier, near Williamsboro, N. C., October 10, 1799; interment in the family cemetery, Montpelier, N. C.

WILLIAMS, John, a Representative from New York; born in Barnstable, England, in September 1752; received a liberal education; studied medicine and surgery in St. Thomas Hospital, London; served for one year as surgeon's mate on an English man-of-war; immigrated to America in 1773 and settled in New Perth, Charlotte County (now Salem, Washington County), N. Y.; engaged in an extensive medical practice; member of the State Provincial Congress in 1775, to which body he was reelected and served until its dissolution in 1777; appointed surgeon of the State forces in 1775; colonel of the Charlotte County Regiment in 1776 and retained command throughout the Revolutionary War; served in the State senate in 1777 and 1778; member of the State assembly in 1781 and 1782; again a member of the State senate 1782–1785; appointed a member of the first board of regents of New York University in 1784; brigadier general of militia in 1786; delegate to the State convention for the ratification of the Federal Constitution in 1788; member of the council of appointment in 1789; elected to the Fourth and Fifth Congresses (March 4, 1795–March 3, 1799); was a large landholder; a promoter and director of a company organized to build the Erie Canal as a private enterprise, the project later being taken over and completed by the State; judge of the county court; died in Salem, N. Y., July 22, 1806; interment in Salem Cemetery.

WILLIAMS, John (brother of Lewis Williams and Robert Williams, father of Joseph Lanier Williams, and cousin of Marmaduke Williams), a Senator from Tennessee; born in Surry County, N. C., January 29, 1778; completed preparatory studies; captain in the Sixth Regiment, United States Infantry, from April 1799 to June 1800; studied law in Salisbury, N. C.; was admitted to the bar of Knox County, Tenn., in 1803 and commenced practice in Knoxville, Tenn.; captain of regular troops in the War of 1812, and was colonel of a regiment of East Tennessee Mounted Volunteers in the expedition against the Seminoles in Florida in 1812 and 1813; colonel of the Thirty-ninth Regiment, United States Infantry, June 18, 1813, and subsequently served under General Jackson in the expedition against the Creek Indians in Alabama; participated in the decisive Battle of Horse-Shoe Bend March 27, 1813; elected to the United States Senate to fill the vacancy caused by the resignation of George W. Campbell; was subsequently appointed to fill the vacancy in the regular term caused by a recess of the legislature; was then elected and served from October 10, 1815, to March 3, 1823; unsuccessful candidate for reelection; appointed by President John Quincy Adams as Chargé d'Affaires to the Central American Federation and served from December 29, 1825, to December 1, 1826; member of the State senate in 1827 and 1828; declined appointment as justice of the State supreme court; died near Knoxville, Tenn., August 10, 1837; interment in the First Presbyterian Church Cemetery.

WILLIAMS, John, a Representative from New York; born in Utica, N. Y., January 7, 1807; spent his youth and completed preparatory studies in Sackets Harbor, N. Y.; moved to Rochester, N. Y., in 1824 and engaged in mercantile pursuits and the manufacture of flour; member of the board of aldermen in 1844; mayor of Rochester in 1853; elected as a Democrat to the Thirty-fourth Congress (March 4, 1855–March 3, 1857); again engaged in the milling business 1858–1870; was major general of the Seventh Division of the National Guard at the time of his death; excise commissioner and manager of the house of refuge in 1870; city treasurer from 1871 until his death; died in Rochester, N. Y., March 26, 1875; interment in Mount Hope Cemetery.

WILLIAMS, John Bell, a Representative from Mississippi; born in Raymond, Hinds County, Miss., December 4, 1918; attended the public schools; was graduated from Hinds Junior College, Raymond, Miss., in 1936, from the University of Mississippi at Oxford in 1938, and from Jackson (Miss.) School of Law in 1940; was admitted to the bar in 1940 and commenced practice in Raymond, Miss.; during World War II enlisted as an aviation cadet in the United States Army, November 5, 1941; was commissioned as a pilot July 3, 1942; only surviving member of a five-man crew involved in an airplane accident in South America in March 1943; retired from active duty at Lawson General Hospital, Atlanta, Ga., on April 29, 1944; prosecuting attorney of Hinds County, Miss., from May 20, 1944, to October 1, 1946; elected as a Democrat to the Eightieth and to the six succeeding Congresses (January 3, 1947–January 3, 1961). *Reelected to the Eighty-seventh Congress.*

WILLIAMS, John James, a Senator from Delaware; born on a farm near Frankford, Sussex County, Del., May 17, 1904; attended the public schools and was graduated from Frankford High School; moved to Millsboro, Del., in 1922 and engaged in the grain business; elected as a Republican to the United States Senate in 1946 for the term commencing January 3, 1947; reelected in 1952 and again in 1958 for the term ending January 3, 1965.

WILLIAMS, John McKeown Snow, a Representative from Massachusetts; born in Richmond, Henrico County, Va., August 13, 1818; moved to Boston, Mass.; attended the public schools;

engaged in mercantile pursuits and was also a shipowner; member of the State house of representatives in 1856; served in the State senate in 1858; presidential elector on the Republican ticket of Grant and Colfax in 1868; elected as a Republican to the Forty-third Congress (March 4, 1873–March 3, 1875); unsuccessful candidate for reelection in 1874 to the Forty-fourth Congress; resumed his former business pursuits; died in Cambridge, Middlesex County, Mass., March 19, 1886; interment in Mount Auburn Cemetery.

WILLIAMS, John Sharp (grandson of Christopher Harris Williams), a Representative and a Senator from Mississippi; born in Memphis, Tenn., July 30, 1854; after the death of his parents moved to the family homestead of his mother in Yazoo County, Miss.; attended private schools, the Kentucky Military Institute near Frankfort, the University of the South, Sewanee, Tenn., the University of Virginia at Charlottesville, and the University of Heidelberg, at Baden, Germany; subsequently studied law at the University of Virginia and in Memphis, Tenn.; was admitted to the bar in Shelby County, Tenn., in 1877; moved to Yazoo City, Miss., in December 1878; engaged in the practice of law and also interested in cotton planting; delegate to the Democratic National Convention at Chicago in 1892; elected as a Democrat to the Fifty-third and to the seven succeeding Congresses (March 4, 1893–March 3, 1909); was not a candidate for renomination in 1908; Democratic minority leader in the Fifty-eighth, Fifty-ninth, and Sixtieth Congresses; temporary chairman of the Democratic National Convention at St. Louis in 1904 which nominated Parker and Davis; elected to the United States Senate in 1910; reelected in 1916 and served from March 4, 1911, to March 3, 1923; declined to be a candidate for renomination in 1922; was a delegate to the Democratic National Convention at Baltimore in 1912, which nominated Wilson and Marshall; retired from public life and lived on his plantation, "Cedar Grove," near Yazoo City, Miss., until his death there September 27, 1932; interment in the family cemetery on his plantation.

WILLIAMS, John Stuart, a Senator from Kentucky; born near Mount Sterling, Montgomery County, Ky., July 10, 1818; attended the common schools; was graduated from Miami University, Oxford, Ohio, in 1839; studied law; was admitted to the bar in 1840 and commenced practice in Paris, Bourbon County, Ky.; served in the Mexican War, first as a captain of an independent company attached to the Sixth Regiment, United States Infantry, and afterward as a colonel of the Fourth Regiment, Kentucky Volunteers; member of the State house of representatives in 1851 and 1853; during the Civil War served in the Confederate Army as a colonel in 1861; promoted to brigadier general in April 1862 and surrendered with the army of Gen. Joseph E. Johnston April 26, 1865; engaged in agricultural pursuits, with residence in Winchester, Ky.; again a member of the State house of representatives in 1873 and 1875; was an unsuccessful candidate for election as Governor in 1875; presidential elector on the Democratic ticket of Samuel J. Tilden and Thomas A. Hendricks in 1876; elected as a Democrat to the United States Senate and served from March 4, 1879, to March 3, 1885; was an unsuccessful candidate for reelection; engaged in agricultural pursuits; died in Mount Sterling, Ky., on July 17, 1898; interment in Winchester Cemetery, Winchester, Ky.

WILLIAMS, Jonathan, a Representative from Pennsylvania; born in Boston, Mass., May 20, 1750; completed preparatory studies and worked in a bank in Boston; went to France as secretary to Benjamin Franklin in 1770 and served until 1775, part of this time as commercial agent for the United

States; studied military science; returned to the United States in 1785 and settled in Philadelphia; was judge of the court of common pleas; entered the United States Army as major of the Second Regiment of Artillerists and Engineers February 16, 1801; inspector of fortifications from December 14, 1801, to June 1, 1802; commanded the post at West Point, N. Y., and was the first Superintendent of the United States Military Academy in 1802; was retained as major of Engineers April 1, 1802; lieutenant colonel and Chief of Engineers July 3, 1802; resigned June 20, 1803, on a question of rank; resumed the rank of lieutenant colonel and Chief of Engineers at President Jefferson's request April 19, 1805; promoted to the rank of colonel February 23, 1808; planned and built the inner forts for the defense of New York Harbor; resigned July 31, 1812; returned to Philadelphia, Pa., and engaged in literary and scientific pursuits; was the author of several military and philosophical papers; elected to the Fourteenth Congress and served from March 4, 1815, until his death, before the assembling of the Congress, in Philadelphia, Pa., May 16, 1815.

WILLIAMS, Joseph Lanier (son of John Williams, of Tennessee), a Representative from Tennessee; born near Knoxville, Knox County, Tenn., October 23, 1810; completed preparatory studies; attended the University of East Tennessee and the United States Military Academy at West Point; studied law; was admitted to the bar and commenced practice in Knoxville, Tenn.; elected as a Whig to the Twenty-fifth, Twenty-sixth, and Twenty-seventh Congresses (March 4, 1837–March 3, 1843); unsuccessful candidate for renomination in 1842; engaged in the practice of law in Washington, D. C.; appointed judge of the United States District Court of Dakota Territory by President Lincoln; died in Knoxville, Tenn., December 14, 1865; interment in Old Gray Cemetery.

WILLIAMS, Lemuel, a Representative from Massachusetts; born in Taunton, Mass., June 18, 1747; was graduated from Harvard College in 1765; studied law; was admitted to the bar and practiced in Bristol and Worcester Counties, Mass.; town clerk of New Bedford, Mass., 1792–1800; elected to the Sixth, Seventh, and Eighth Congresses (March 4, 1799–March 3, 1805); member of the State house of representatives in 1806; resumed the practice of law; died in Acushnet, Mass., November 8, 1828; interment in Acushnet Cemetery.

WILLIAMS, Lewis (brother of John Williams, of Tennessee, and Robert Williams and cousin of Marmaduke Williams), a Representative from North Carolina; born in Surry County, N. C., February 1, 1782; was graduated from the University of North Carolina at Chapel Hill in 1808; member of the State house of commons in 1813 and 1814; elected to the Fourteenth and to the thirteen succeeding Congresses and served from March 4, 1815, until his death; was known as the "Father of the House"; died in Washington, D. C., February 23, 1842; interment in Panther Creek Cemetery, Surry County, N. C.

WILLIAMS, Marmaduke (cousin of John Williams, of Tennessee, Lewis Williams, and Robert Williams), a Representative from North Carolina; born in Caswell County, N. C., April 6, 1774; completed preparatory studies; studied law; was admitted to the bar and practiced; member of the State senate in 1802; elected as a Democrat to the Eighth, Ninth, and Tenth Congresses (March 4, 1803–March 3, 1809); was not a candidate for renomination; moved to Mississippi Territory in 1810 and later to Huntsville, Madison County, Ala.; in 1818 settled in Tuscaloosa, Ala.; delegate to the State constitutional convention in 1819 and the same year was an unsuccessful candidate for Governor of Alabama; member of the State house of representa-

tives 1821–1839; judge of the Tuscaloosa County Court 1832–1842; died in Tuscaloosa, Ala., October 29, 1850; interment in Greenwood Cemetery.

WILLIAMS, Morgan B., a Representative from Pennsylvania; born in Rhandir-Mwyn, parish of Llanfair-ar-y-Bryn, Carmarthenshire, Wales, September 17, 1831; attended the public schools; went to Australia in 1856; returned to Wales in August 1861; immigrated to the United States in March 1862 and settled in Scranton, Pa., where he worked in the coal mines; moved to Wilkes-Barre, Pa., in September 1865; appointed superintendent for the Lehigh & Wilkes-Barre Coal Co., which position he held for fourteen years; member of the school board and of the city council for twelve years; alternate delegate to the Republican National Convention at Chicago in 1884; served in the State senate in 1884; member of the Chicago World's Fair Commission; elected as a Republican to the Fifty-fifth Congress (March 4, 1897–March 3, 1899); unsuccessful candidate for reelection in 1898 to the Fifty-sixth Congress; engaged in coal mining, and was vice president and general manager of the Red Ash Coal Co.; died in Wilkes-Barre, Pa., October 13, 1903; interment in Hollenback Cemetery.

WILLIAMS, Nathan, a Representative from New York; was born in Williamstown, Mass., December 19, 1773; attended the common schools in Bennington, Vt.; moved with his parents to Troy, N. Y., in 1786; studied law; was admitted to the bar in 1795 and commenced practice in Utica, N. Y.; assisted in the establishment of Utica Public Library, of which he was librarian for a number of years; president of the village corporation; president of the Manhattan Bank; district attorney for the sixth district 1801–1813; elected as a Democrat to the Ninth Congress (March 4, 1805–March 3, 1807); served in the War of 1812 under his brother-in-law, Gen. Jacob Brown; member of the State assembly 1816–1818 and in 1819; regent of the University of the State of New York from January 28, 1817, to February 13, 1824; district attorney of Oneida County 1818–1821; delegate to the State constitutional convention in 1821; judge of the circuit court 1823–1833; appointed clerk of the State supreme court in 1834 and moved to Geneva, Ontario County, N. Y., where he died September 25, 1835; interment in the "Burying Ground," Utica, Oneida County, N. Y.; reinterment in Forest Hill Cemetery.

WILLIAMS, Reuel, a Senator from Maine; born in Hallowell, Maine, June 2, 1783; attended Hallowell Academy; studied law; was admitted to the bar in 1802 and commenced practice in Augusta, Maine; member of the State house of representatives 1822–1826 and 1829–1832; served in the State senate in 1827 and 1828; commissioner of public buildings in 1831; presidential elector on the Democratic ticket of Van Buren and Johnson in 1836; elected February 22, 1837, as a Democrat to the United States Senate to fill the vacancy caused by the resignation of Ether Shepley and served from March 4, 1837, to February 15, 1843, when he resigned; manager of a railroad for twelve years; died in Augusta, Maine, on July 25, 1862; interment in the family cemetery on the banks of the Kennebec River, Augusta, Maine.

WILLIAMS, Richard, a Representative from Oregon; born in Findlay, Hancock County, Ohio, November 15, 1836; attended the common schools; moved to Monroe County, Oreg., in 1851; was educated at the Willamette University, Salem, Oreg.; studied law; was admitted to the bar in 1857 and commenced practice in Kirbyville, Josephine County, Oreg.; moved to Portland, Oreg., in 1865 and practiced law; unsuccessful Republican candidate for election in 1874 to the Forty-fourth Congress; elected as a Republican to the Forty-fifth Congress (March 4, 1877–March 3, 1879); was not a candidate for renomination in 1878; resumed the practice of law in Portland, Oreg.; elected a member of the Portland School Board in 1890 and served for twenty years; died in Portland, Oreg., June 19, 1914; interment in Riverview Cemetery.

WILLIAMS, Robert (brother of John Williams, of Tennessee, and Lewis Williams and cousin of Marmaduke Williams), a Representative from North Carolina; born in Prince Edward County, Va., July 12, 1773; moved with his parents to Surry County, N. C.; received a liberal education; studied law; was admitted to the bar and commenced practice in what is now Rockingham County; member of the State senate 1792–1795; elected to the Fifth, Sixth, and Seventh Congresses (March 4, 1797–March 3, 1803); appointed by President Jefferson in 1803 a member of a commission to ascertain the rights of persons claiming lands west of the Pearl River in Mississippi Territory and served in this capacity until 1807; Governor of Mississippi Territory from May 10, 1805, to March 3, 1809, when he resigned; subsequently resided in Mississippi and North Carolina, where he practiced law and engaged in planting; adjutant general of North Carolina; moved to Ouachita, Union Parish, La., where he died January 25, 1836; interment on his plantation near Monroe, Ouachita Parish, La.

WILLIAMS, Seward Henry, a Representative from Ohio; born in Amsterdam, Montgomery County, N. Y., November 7, 1870; attended the common schools, the Amsterdam Academy, Williams College, Williamstown, Mass., and Princeton College; was graduated in law from Washington and Lee University, Lexington, Va., in 1895; was admitted to the bar in 1895 and commenced practice the same year; city solicitor of Lorain, Ohio, 1901–1904; member of the State house of representatives 1910–1913; elected as a Republican to the Sixty-fourth Congress (March 4, 1915–March 3, 1917); unsuccessful candidate for reelection in 1916 to the Sixty-fifth Congress; resumed the practice of law; died in Lorain, Ohio, September 2, 1922; interment in Elmwood Cemetery.

WILLIAMS, Sherrod, a Representative from Kentucky; born in Pulaski County, Ky., in 1804; moved with his parents to Wayne County; received a limited education; learned the trade of brickmaker in Monticello when about fifteen years of age; studied law; was admitted to the bar and practiced; member of the State house of representatives 1829–1834 and in 1846; elected as a Whig to the Twenty-fourth, Twenty-fifth, and Twenty-sixth Congresses (March 4, 1835–March 3, 1841); was not a candidate for reelection; moved to one of the Southern States, where he died.

WILLIAMS, Thomas, a Representative from Pennsylvania; born in Greensburg, Westmoreland County, Pa., August 28, 1806; attended the common schools, and was graduated from Dickinson College, Carlisle, Pa., in 1825; studied law; was admitted to the bar in 1828 and commenced practice in Greensburg, Pa.; moved to Pittsburgh, Pa., in 1832 and continued the practice of law; served in the State senate 1838–1841; elected as a Republican to the Thirty-eighth, Thirty-ninth, and Fortieth Congresses (March 4, 1863–March 3, 1869); one of the managers appointed by the House of Representatives in 1868 to conduct the impeachment proceedings against Andrew Johnson, President of the United States; was not a candidate for renomination in 1868 to the Forty-first Congress, and lived in retirement until his death in Allegheny City, Pa., on June 16, 1872; interment in Allegheny Cemetery, Pittsburgh, Pa.

WILLIAMS, Thomas, a Representative from Alabama; born near Richmond, Greensville County, Va., on August 11, 1825; attended preparatory schools and was graduated from the University of East Tennessee, Knoxville, Tenn.; studied law; was admitted to the bar in 1852 and commenced practice in Wetumpka, Elmore County, Ala.; justice of the peace; register in chancery; appointed prison inspector in 1872; member of the State house of representatives in 1878; elected as a Democrat to the Forty-sixth, Forty-seventh, and Forty-eighth Congresses (March 4, 1879–March 3, 1885); engaged in agricultural pursuits and resided in Wetumpka, Ala., until his death April 13, 1903; interment in the City Cemetery.

WILLIAMS, Thomas Hickman, a Senator from Mississippi; born in Williamson County, Tenn., January 20, 1801; attended the common schools; moved to Mississippi and settled in Pontotoc County; engaged in planting; appointed and subsequently elected as a Democrat to the United States Senate to fill the vacancy caused by the resignation of James F. Trotter and served from November 12, 1838, to March 3, 1839; secretary and treasurer of the University of Mississippi at Oxford 1845–1851; known as "Father of the State University," being the first to propose it and also aiding to secure it; died on his plantation south of Pontotoc, Pontotoc County, Miss., May 3, 1851; interment in the private cemetery on the family estate.

WILLIAMS, Thomas Hill, a Senator from Mississippi; born in North Carolina in 1780; completed preparatory studies; studied law; was admitted to the bar and practiced; register of the land office for the Territory of Mississippi in 1805; appointed secretary of the Territory June 1, 1805; Acting Governor from April 22 to June 3, 1806, when he resigned as secretary; reappointed secretary June 1, 1807; again Acting Governor from March to June 1809; collector of customs at New Orleans in 1810; delegate to the State constitutional convention; upon the admission of Mississippi as a State into the Union was elected as a Democrat to the United States Senate; reelected in 1823 and served from December 10, 1817, to March 3, 1829; moved to Tennessee, where he died, in Robertson County, in 1840.

WILLIAMS, Thomas Scott, a Representative from Connecticut; born in Wethersfield, Conn., June 26, 1777; completed preparatory studies; was graduated from Yale College in 1794; studied law; was admitted to the bar in 1799 and commenced practice in Mansfield, Conn.; moved to Hartford, Conn., in 1803; appointed attorney of the board of managers of the school fund of Hartford 1809–1810; served in the State house of representatives in 1813, 1815, and 1816; clerk of the house in 1815 and 1816; elected to the Fifteenth Congress (March 4, 1817–March 3, 1819); again a member of the State house of representatives in 1819, 1825, and 1827–1829; appointed in 1829 an associate judge of the supreme court of errors and of the superior court, and in May 1834 appointed chief justice, holding the position until his resignation in May 1847; mayor of Hartford 1831–1835; resigned from public office; president of the American Tract Society of New York from May 1848 until his death; died in Hartford, Conn., December 22, 1861; interment in Old North Cemetery.

WILLIAMS, Thomas Sutler, a Representative from Illinois; born in Louisville, Clay County, Ill., February 14, 1872; attended Willis district school, Louisville High School, and Austin College, Effingham, Ill.; studied law; was admitted to the bar in 1897 and commenced practice in Louisville; city attorney 1897–1899; member of the State house of representatives 1899–1901; mayor of Louisville 1907–1909; prosecuting attorney of Clay County 1908–1915; became the owner and publisher of the Clay

County Republican at Louisville in 1920; moved to Harrisburg, Salina County, Ill., in 1926; elected as a Republican to the Sixty-fourth and to the seven succeeding Congresses and served from March 4, 1915, until his resignation November 11, 1929, having been appointed a judge for the Court of Claims of the United States and served until his death in Washington, D. C., April 5, 1940; interment in Cedar Hill Cemetery.

WILLIAMS, Thomas Wheeler, a Representative from Connecticut; born in Stonington, Conn., September 28, 1789; attended the public schools; at the age of fifteen was employed as a clerk in New York City, and before he was twenty-one was employed on a business mission to Norway, Sweden, and Russia; for about eight years was engaged in the shipping business; moved to New London, Conn., in 1818; engaged in the whaling business, in which he became a dominant figure; elected as a Whig to the Twenty-sixth and Twenty-seventh Congresses (March 4, 1839–March 3, 1843); member of the State house of representatives in 1846 and 1847; presidential elector on the Whig ticket of Taylor and Fillmore in 1848; president of the New London, Willimantic and Palmer Railroad (later the New London Northern Railroad) in 1847 and for many years thereafter; died in New London, Conn., December 31, 1874; interment in Cedar Grove Cemetery.

WILLIAMS, William, a Delegate from Connecticut; born in Lebanon, Conn., April 28, 1731; completed preparatory studies; was graduated from Harvard College in 1751; studied theology for a year; engaged in mercantile pursuits; town clerk of Lebanon 1753–1796; member of a military expedition to Lake George in 1755; member of the State house of representatives 1757–1761, 1763–1776, and 1780–1784, serving as speaker in 1775 and 1781–1783; Member of the Continental Congress 1776–1778, 1783, and in 1784; a signer of the Declaration of Independence; member of the council of safety during the Revolution; judge of the county court of Windham 1776–1804; judge of probate for the Windham district 1776–1808; became an assistant councilor in 1780 and served as assistant and as councilor for twenty-four years; member of the Connecticut convention in 1787 that ratified the Constitution of the United States; died in Lebanon, Conn., August 2, 1811; interment in the Old Cemetery.

WILLIAMS, William, a Representative from New York; born in Bolton, Conn., September 6, 1815; received a common-school education; clerk in a bank in Windham, Conn.; moved to Sandusky, Ohio, in 1838, and to Buffalo, N. Y., in 1839, where he engaged in banking; also served as a railroad manager and president; member of the State assembly in 1866 and 1867; elected as a Democrat to the Forty-second Congress (March 4, 1871–March 3, 1873); unsuccessful candidate for reelection in 1872 to the Forty-third Congress; withdrew from public life and active business pursuits, and lived in retirement until his death in Buffalo, N. Y., September 10, 1876; interment in Forest Lawn Cemetery.

WILLIAMS, William, a Representative from Indiana; born near Carlisle, Cumberland County, Pa., May 11, 1821; attended the common schools and received a very limited education; studied law; was admitted to the bar in 1845 and commenced practice in Warsaw, Kosciusko County, Ind.; treasurer of Kosciusko County in 1852; resigned the office of treasurer in order to become a candidate for Lieutenant Governor; unsuccessful candidate for Lieutenant Governor in 1853; managed the Bank of Warsaw for several years; director of the Fort Wayne and Chicago Railway 1854–1856; director of the Michigan City prison 1859–1862; during the Civil War served in the Union Army as commandant of Camp Allen, Fort Wayne, Ind., in 1862

and as paymaster of Volunteers, with headquarters at Louisville, Ky., until the close of the war; elected as a Republican to the Fortieth and to the three succeeding Congresses (March 4, 1867–March 3, 1875); was not a candidate for renomination in 1874; resumed the practice of law in Warsaw, Ind.; appointed by President Arthur as Chargé d'Affaires to Paraguay and Uruguay April 12, 1882, and served until February 14, 1885, when he resigned; returned to Warsaw, Ind., in 1885 and retired from active business pursuits; died in Warsaw April 22, 1896; interment in Oakwood Cemetery.

WILLIAMS, William Brewster, a Representative from Michigan; born in Pittsford, Monroe County, N. Y., July 28, 1826; attended the common schools and received an academic education; was graduated from the State and National Law School, Ballston Spa, N. Y., in 1851; was admitted to the bar the same year and commenced practice in Rochester, N. Y.; moved to Allegan, Mich., in 1855; judge of probate 1857–1865; member of the State senate 1866–1870, serving as president pro tempore in 1869; member of the State constitutional convention in 1867; appointed by the Governor in 1871 a member of the State board for the supervisory control of the charitable, penal, and beneficiary institutions, which position he resigned upon his election to Congress; elected as a Republican to the Forty-third Congress to fill the vacancy caused by the death of Wilder D. Foster; reelected to the Forty-fourth Congress and served from December 1, 1873, to March 3, 1877; was not a candidate for renomination in 1876; railroad commissioner of Michigan 1877–1883; resumed the practice of law; died in Allegan, Mich., March 4, 1905; interment in Oakwood Cemetery.

WILLIAMS, William Elza, a Representative from Illinois; born near Detroit, Pike County, Ill., May 5, 1857; attended the public schools and Illinois College, Jacksonville, Ill.; studied law; was admitted to the bar in 1880 and practiced in Detroit and Pittsfield, Ill.; State's attorney of Pike County 1886–1892; member of the board of aldermen of Pittsfield; member of the board of education; became trial lawyer for the City Railway Co. of Chicago in 1903; elected as a Democrat to the Fifty-sixth Congress (March 4, 1899–March 3, 1901); resumed the practice of law in Pittsfield, Ill.; elected to the Sixty-third and Sixty-fourth Congresses (March 4, 1913–March 3, 1917); unsuccessful candidate for reelection in 1916 to the Sixty-fifth Congress and for election in 1918 to the Sixty-sixth Congress; continued the practice of law until his death in Pittsfield, Ill., September 13, 1921; interment in Pittsfield West Cemetery.

WILLIAMS, William Robert, a Representative from New York; born in Brookfield, Madison County, N. Y., August 11, 1884; moved to Cassville, Oneida County, N. Y., with his parents in 1891; attended the public schools of Bridgewater, N. Y.; started working at an early age on a farm, in a general store, and in a post office; salesman with Standard Oil Co., of New York, 1907–1910; engaged in farming at Cassville, N. Y.; member of the State assembly 1935–1943; sheriff of Oneida County 1943–1951; elected as a Republican to the Eighty-second and to the three succeeding Congresses (January 3, 1951–January 3, 1959); was not a candidate for renomination in 1958; retired and resides in Cassville, N. Y.

WILLIAMSON, Ben Mitchell, a Senator from Kentucky; born in White Post, Pike County, Ky., October 16, 1864; attended the rural schools of Kentucky and Bethany (W. Va.) College; engaged in the wholesale hardware business at Catlettsburg, Ky., 1886–1924 and at Ashland, Ky., in 1924; also engaged in banking and in the mining of coal; one of the founders of the Kentucky Crippled Children's Commission, serving as president

1924–1941; member of the board of charities and correction for the State of Kentucky in 1929 and 1930; served as a director of the International Society for Crippled Children; elected as a Democrat to the United States Senate on November 4, 1930, to fill the vacancy caused by the resignation of Frederic M. Sackett and served from December 1, 1930, to March 3, 1931; was not a candidate for election to the full term; resumed the wholesale hardware business at Ashland, Ky., with residence in Catlettsburg, Ky.; also interested financially in various other business enterprises; died while a patient in a Cincinnati, Ohio, hospital June 23, 1941; interment in Ashland Cemetery Mausoleum, Ashland, Ky.

WILLIAMSON, Hugh, a Delegate and a Representative from North Carolina; born on Oterara Creek, in West Nottingham Township, Pa., December 5, 1735; attended the common schools; prepared for college at Newark, Del., and was graduated from the University of Pennsylvania at Philadelphia in 1757; studied theology, and was licensed to preach in 1758; resigned, owing to ill health, in 1760; professor of mathematics in the College of Philadelphia; studied medicine in Edinburgh, Scotland, and Utrecht, Holland; returned to Philadelphia and practiced there until 1773; became a member of the American Philosophical Society, and was sent abroad as a member of the commission to observe the transits of Venus and Mercury in 1773; at the time of the "Boston Tea Party" he was examined in England by the privy council regarding it; returned to America in 1776 and settled in Edenton, N. C.; engaged in mercantile pursuits; during the Revolutionary War was surgeon general of the North Carolina troops 1779–1782; member of the State house of commons in 1782; Member of the Continental Congress 1782–1785, 1787, and 1788; delegate to the convention which framed the Federal Constitution in 1787 and a member of the State convention which adopted it in 1789; elected as a Federalist to the First and Second Congresses (March 4, 1789–March 3, 1793); moved to New York City in 1793; engaged extensively in literary pursuits until his death in New York City, May 22, 1819; interment in the Apthrop tomb in Trinity Churchyard.

WILLIAMSON, John Newton, a Representative from Oregon; born near Junction City, Lane County, Oreg., November 8, 1855; attended the country schools; became a student at Williamette University, Salem, Oreg., and pursued a classical course until within three months of graduation, when he was stricken with rheumatism and never returned to graduate; moved to Prineville, Oreg., and engaged in livestock raising; sheriff of Cook County 1886–1888; member of the State house of representatives 1888–1898; served in the State senate 1900–1902; elected as a Republican to the Fifty-eighth and Fifty-ninth Congresses (March 4, 1903–March 3, 1907); declined to be a candidate for renomination in 1906; engaged in stock raising and agricultural pursuits; appointed by President Harding as postmaster at Prineville, Cook County, Oreg., March 21, 1922; reappointed on May 18, 1926, and served until June 30, 1934, when he retired to his farm in Central Oregon; died in Prineville, Oreg., August 29, 1943; interment in the Masonic Cemetery.

WILLIAMSON, William, a Representative from South Dakota; born near New Sharon, Mahaska County, Iowa, October 7, 1875; moved with his parents to Plankinton, Aurora County, S. Dak., in 1882; attended the public schools and the Wayne (Nebr.) Normal School; engaged in agricultural pursuits and also taught school for several years; was graduated from the University of South Dakota at Vermilion in 1903 and from the law department of that university in 1905; while at college was editor of the Coyote, the college annual, and of the Volante, the college weekly newspaper; was admitted to the bar in 1905

and commenced practice in Oacoma, Lyman County, S. Dak.; founder, with his brother, of the Murdo Coyote and the Prairie Sun; prosecuting attorney of Lyman County 1905–1911; circuit judge of the eleventh judicial district 1911–1921; delegate to the Republican National Convention at Chicago in 1912; elected as a Republican to the Sixty-seventh and to the five succeeding Congresses (March 4, 1921–March 3, 1933); unsuccessful candidate for reelection in 1932 to the Seventy-third Congress; resumed the practice of law in Rapid City, S. Dak.; special assistant attorney general of South Dakota and assigned as general counsel for the Public Utilities Commission 1939–1951; vice president, member of the board of directors, and general counsel of the Rushmore Mutual Life Insurance Co. 1950–; member of the Mount Rushmore National Memorial Commission 1928–; is a resident of Rapid City, S. Dak.

WILLIAMSON, William Durkee, a Representative from Maine; born in Canterbury, Conn., July 31, 1779; moved in boyhood with his father to Amherst, Mass; attended the common schools and Williams College, Williamstown, Mass.; was graduated from Brown University, Providence, R. I., in 1804; studied law; was admitted to the bar and commenced practice in Bangor, Maine (then a district of Massachusetts), in 1807; State's attorney for Hancock County 1808–1815; postmaster of Bangor, Maine, 1810–1821; member of the Massachusetts State Senate from 1816 until the separation of Maine from Massachusetts in 1820; served in the Maine State Senate in 1820 and 1821 and was elected its president both years; as president of the senate he became Governor upon the resignation of Governor King in 1821; elected as a Democrat to the Seventeenth Congress (March 4, 1821–March 3, 1823); was not a candidate for renomination in 1822; judge of probate for Penobscot County 1824–1840; bank commissioner 1838–1841; an original member of the Maine Historical Society; died in Bangor, Maine, May 27, 1846; interment in Mount Hope Cemetery.

WILLIE, Asa Hoxie, a Representative from Texas; born in Washington, Wilkes County, Ga., October 11, 1829; attended private schools and pursued an academic course; moved to Washington County, Tex., in 1846 and settled in Brenham; studied law; was admitted to the bar in 1848 and commenced practice in Brenham; district attorney of the third judicial district of Texas 1852–1854; during the Civil War served in the Confederate Army under General Gregg with the rank of major; moved to Galveston, Tex., in 1866; elected associate justice of the Texas Supreme Court the same year but was removed in 1867 by the military commander: elected as a Democrat to the Forty-third Congress (March 4, 1873–March 3, 1875); declined to be a candidate for renomination in 1874; resumed the practice of law in Galveston; elected chief justice of the Texas Supreme Court in November 1882 and served until his resignation March 3, 1888; resumed the practice of law; died in Galveston, Tex., March 16, 1899; interment in Episcopal Cemetery.

WILLING, Thomas, a Delegate from Pennsylvania; born in Philadelphia, Pa., December 19, 1731; completed preparatory studies in Bath, England; studied law in London at the Inner Temple; returned to Philadelphia and engaged in mercantile pursuits until 1793; member of the common council in 1755; alderman in 1759; associate justice of the city court October 2, 1759; justice of the court of common pleas February 28, 1761; mayor of Philadelphia in 1763; associate justice of the supreme court of Pennsylvania 1767–1777; member of the committee of correspondence in 1774 and of the committee of safety in 1775; served in the colonial house of representatives; Member of the Continental Congress in 1775 and 1776; president of the Bank of North America; first president of the Bank of the United States 1791–1811; resumed mercantile pursuits; died in Philadelphia, Pa., January 19, 1821; interment in Christ Churchyard.

WILLIS, Albert Shelby, a Representative from Kentucky; born in Shelbyville, Shelby County, Ky., January 22, 1843; attended the common schools, and was graduated from the Louisville (Ky.) Male High School in 1860; taught school four years; was graduated from the Louisville Law School in 1866; was admitted to the bar and commenced the practice of law in Louisville; presidential elector on the Democratic ticket of Greeley and Brown in 1872; prosecuting attorney for Jefferson County 1874–1877; elected as a Democrat to the Forty-fifth and to the four succeeding Congresses (March 4, 1877–March 3, 1887); unsuccessful candidate for renomination in 1886; resumed the practice of law; appointed Minister to Hawaii by President Cleveland in 1893 and served until his death in Honolulu, Hawaii, January 6, 1897; interment in Cave Hill Cemetery, Louisville, Ky.

WILLIS, Benjamin Albertson, a Representative from New York; born in Roslyn, Queens County, N. Y., March 24, 1840; was graduated from Union College in 1861; studied law; was admitted to the bar in 1862 and commenced practice in New York City; during the Civil War enlisted in the Union Army in 1862; captain in the One Hundred and Nineteenth New York Volunteers, and subsequently colonel of the Twelfth Regiment, New York State Volunteers; honorably discharged in 1864; resumed the practice of law; member of the State assembly 1872–1878; elected as a Democrat to the Forty-fourth and Forty-fifth Congresses (March 4, 1875–March 3, 1879); unsuccessful candidate for reelection in 1878 to the Forty-sixth Congress; engaged in the practice of law and also in the real-estate business; died in New York City on October 14, 1886; interment in Friends Cemetery, Westbury, Long Island; reinterment in Woodlawn Cemetery.

WILLIS, Edwin Edward, a Representative from Louisiana; born in Arnaudville, St. Martin Parish, La., October 2, 1904; graduated from St. Martin Parish public schools and from the law school of Loyola University, New Orleans, La., in 1926; was admitted to the bar in 1926 and commenced the practice of law in New Orleans, La., and in St. Martinville, La., since 1936; law lecturer in evening classes 1926–1936; owner and operator of a plantation in St. Martin Parish; elected to the State senate in January 1948 and served until elected to Congress; delegate to Democratic National Convention in 1956; elected as a Democrat to the Eighty-first and to the five succeeding Congresses (January 3, 1949–January 3, 1961). *Reelected to the Eighty-seventh Congress.*

WILLIS, Francis, a Representative from Georgia; born in Frederick County, Va., January 5, 1745; received a liberal education; served as captain and colonel in the Revolutionary War in 1777 and 1778; moved to Wilkes County, Ga., in 1784; elected to the Second Congress (March 4, 1791–March 3, 1793); moved to Maury County, Tenn.; died January 25, 1829.

WILLIS, Frank Bartlett, a Representative and a Senator from Ohio; born in Lewis Center, Delaware County, Ohio, December 28, 1871; attended the common schools and the Galena (Ohio) High School; was graduated from the Ohio Northern University at Ada in 1894; studied law; was admitted to the bar in 1906; professor of history and economics at Ohio Northern University 1894–1906; professor of economics and law 1906–1910; member of the State house of

representatives 1900–1904; was elected as a Republican to the Sixty-second and Sixty-third Congresses and served from March 4, 1911, to January 9, 1915, when he resigned, having been elected Governor; Governor of Ohio 1915–1917; delegate to the Republican National Convention at Chicago in 1916 and nominated Theodore E. Burton as a candidate for President; delegate to the Republican National Convention at Chicago in 1920 and nominated Warren G. Harding as a candidate for President; elected as a Republican to the United States Senate in 1920 for the term commencing March 4, 1921, and subsequently appointed in January 1921 to fill the vacancy in the term ending March 3, 1921, caused by the resignation of Warren G. Harding; reelected in 1926 and served from January 14, 1921, until his death; delegate to the Republican National Convention at Cleveland in 1924; died in Delaware, Ohio, March 30, 1928; interment in Oak Grove Cemetery.

WILLIS, Jonathan Spencer, a Representative from Delaware; born in Oxford, Talbot County, Md., April 5, 1830; attended the district schools and studied under private tutors; taught school seven years and then entered the ministry of the Methodist Episcopal Church; served charges in Maryland, Delaware, Philadelphia, Pa., New York City, N. Y., and Stamford, Conn.; retired from the ministry in 1884; settled on a farm near Milford, Del., and engaged in fruit growing; unsuccessful Republican candidate for election in 1892 to the Fifty-third Congress; elected as a Republican to the Fifty-fourth Congress (March 4, 1895–March 3, 1897); unsuccessful candidate for reelection in 1896 to the Fifty-fifth Congress; engaged in agricultural pursuits; died in Milford, Sussex County, Del., November 24, 1903; interment in Barrett's Chapel Cemetery, near Frederica, Kent County, Del.

WILLIS, Raymond Eugene, a Senator from Indiana; born in Waterloo, De Kalb County, Ind., August 11, 1875; attended the public schools and was graduated from Wabash College, Crawfordsville, Ind., in 1896; learned the printer's trade in Waterloo, Ind.; moved to Angola, Ind., and engaged in the newspaper publishing business in 1898; postmaster of Angola in 1910–1914; during the First World War served as chairman of Steuben County Council of Defense in 1917 and 1918; member of the State house of representatives 1919–1921; unsuccessful candidate for election to the United States Senate in 1938; elected as a Republican to the United States Senate in 1940 for the term ending January 3, 1947; was not a candidate for renomination in 1946; resumed the publishing business as president of the Steuben Printing Co.; trustee of Tri-State College at Angola; died in Angola, Ind., March 21, 1956; interment in Circle Hill Cemetery.

WILLITS, Edwin, a Representative from Michigan; born at Otto, Cattaraugus County, N. Y., April 24, 1830; moved to Michigan with his parents in September 1836; was graduated from the University of Michigan at Ann Arbor in June 1855; settled in Monroe, Monroe County, Mich., in April 1856; editor of the Monroe Commercial 1856–1861; studied law; was admitted to the bar in December 1857 and commenced practice in Monroe; prosecuting attorney of Monroe County 1860–1862; member of the State board of education 1860–1872; appointed postmaster of Monroe January 1, 1863, by President Lincoln, and removed by President Johnson October 15, 1866; member of the commission to revise the constitution of the State in 1873; elected as a Republican to the Forty-fifth, Forty-sixth, and Forty-seventh Congresses (March 4, 1877–March 3, 1883); was not a candidate for renomination in 1882; principal of the State normal school at Ypsilanti 1883–1885; president of the Michigan Agricultural College 1885–1889; First Assistant Secretary of

Agriculture under Secretaries Rusk and Morton and served from March 23, 1889, to December 31, 1893; continued the practice of law in Washington, D. C., until his death there October 22, 1896; interment in Woodlawn Cemetery, Monroe, Mich.

WILLOUGHBY, Westel, Jr., a Representative from New York; born in Goshen, Conn., November 20, 1769; moved to Newport, N. Y.; studied medicine and engaged in practice; appointed judge of the court of common pleas of Herkimer County in 1805 and served until 1821; president of the Herkimer County Medical Society 1806–1816 and 1818–1836; served in the State assembly in 1808 and 1809; president of the College of Physicians and Surgeons for the Western District of New York 1812–1844; member of the medical staff of the militia and served in the War of 1812; successfully contested as a Democrat the election of William S. Smith to the Fourteenth Congress and served from December 13, 1815, to March 3, 1817; founded the town of Willoughby, Ohio, and also Willoughby College (now a part of Syracuse University); died in Newport, Herkimer County, N. Y., October 3, 1844; interment in the First Baptist Church Cemetery.

WILMOT, David, a Representative and a Senator from Pennsylvania; born in Bethany, Pa., January 20, 1814; completed preparatory studies in the academy at Aurora, N. Y.; studied law; was admitted to the bar of Bradford County, Pa., in 1834 and commenced practice in Towanda, Bradford County, Pa.; delegate to the State Democratic convention at Harrisburg in 1844; elected as a Democrat to the Twenty-ninth, Thirtieth, and Thirty-first Congresses (March 4, 1845–March 3, 1851); was not a candidate for renomination in 1850; delegate to the Free-Soil Democratic convention at Herkimer in 1847, State Democratic convention at Harrisburg in 1848, and National Free-Soil Convention at Utica, N. Y., in 1848; was the author of the "Wilmot proviso" relative to slavery in newly annexed territory; supported the Free-Soil ticket in 1848 and took a leading part in the founding of the Republican Party in 1854, being the Pennsylvania member of the National executive committee; presiding judge of the thirteenth judicial district 1853–1861; delegate to the Republican National (preliminary) Convention at Pittsburgh in 1856, Pennsylvania State Republican convention at Philadelphia in 1856, and the Republican National Convention at Philadelphia in 1856; drafted the first Republican platform in 1856; unsuccessful Republican candidate for Governor of Pennsylvania in 1857; delegate to and temporary chairman of the Republican National Convention at Chicago in 1860; elected as a Republican to the United States Senate to fill the vacancy caused by the resignation of Simon Cameron and served from March 14, 1861, to March 3, 1863; was not a candidate for reelection in 1862; member of the peace convention of 1861, held in Washington, D. C., in an effort to devise means to prevent the impending war; appointed by President Lincoln a judge of the United States Court of Claims in 1863 and served until his death in Towanda, Pa., March 16, 1868; interment in Riverside Cemetery.

WILSHIRE, William Wallace, a Representative from Arkansas; born in Shawneetown, Gallatin County, Ill., on September 8, 1830; educated in the country schools; spent three years in California in gold mining, from 1852 to 1855, when he returned to his home in Port Byron and engaged in the coal mining and mercantile business; studied law, and was admitted to the bar in 1859; during the Civil War entered the Union Army as major in the One Hundred and Twenty-sixth Regiment, Illinois Volunteer Infantry, and served from July 16, 1862, to July 16, 1864, when he resigned his commission on account of ill health; after the war located in Little Rock, Ark., and com-

menced the practice of law; appointed solicitor general of the State in 1867; chief justice of the State supreme court from 1868 to 1871, when he resigned and resumed the practice of law; presented credentials as a Republican Member-elect to the Forty-third Congress and served from March 4, 1873, to June 16, 1874, when he was succeeded by Thomas M. Gunter, who contested his election; elected as a Conservative to the Forty-fourth Congress (March 4, 1875–March 3, 1877); was not a candidate for renomination in 1876; engaged in the practice of law in Washington, D. C., where he died August 19, 1888; interment in Mount Holly Cemetery, Little Rock, Ark.

WILSON, Alexander, a Representative from Virginia; born in that State; completed preparatory studies; member of the State house of delegates in 1803 and in 1804; elected to the Eighth Congress to fill the vacancy caused by the resignation of Andrew Moore; reelected to the Ninth and Tenth Congresses and served from December 4, 1804, to March 3, 1809.

WILSON, Benjamin, a Representative from West Virginia; born in Wilsonburg, Harrison County, Va. (now West Virginia), April 30, 1825; attended the Northwestern Virginia Academy at Clarksburg and the law school in Staunton, Va.; was admitted to the bar in 1848 and commenced practice in Clarksburg, Harrison County, Va. (now West Virginia); Commonwealth attorney for Harrison County 1852–1860; member of the State constitutional convention in 1861; presidential elector on the Democratic ticket of Seymour and Blair in 1868; member of the State constitutional convention of West Virginia in 1871; delegate to the Democratic National Convention at Baltimore in 1872; unsuccessful candidate for election in 1872 to the Forty-third Congress; elected as a Democrat to the Forty-fourth and to the three succeeding Congresses (March 4, 1875–March 3, 1883); Assistant Attorney General of the United States 1885–1893; died in Clarksburg, W. Va., April 26, 1901; interment in the Odd Fellows Cemetery.

WILSON, Earl, a Representative from Indiana; born on a farm near Huron, Lawrence County, Ind., on April 18, 1906; attended the public schools and Purdue University, Lafayette, Ind.; was graduated from the Coyne Electrical School, Chicago, Ill., in 1928 and from Indiana University at Bloomington in 1931; taught high school in Dubois, White, and Decatur Counties, Ind., 1931–1938; high-school principal in Jackson County, Ind., in 1939 and 1940; elected as a Republican to the Seventy-seventh and to the eight succeeding Congresses (January 3, 1941–January 3, 1959); unsuccessful candidate for reelection in 1958 to the Eighty-sixth Congress. *Elected to the Eighty-seventh Congress.*

WILSON, Edgar, a Representative from Idaho; born in Armstrong County, Pa., near the city of Pittsburgh, February 25, 1861; attended the public schools; was graduated from the law department of the University of Michigan at Ann Arbor in 1884 and admitted to the bar; moved to Idaho in 1884, settled in Boise City and commenced the practice of law; elected city attorney of Boise City in 1887 and district attorney in 1888; member of the constitutional convention that framed the State constitution in 1890; elected as a Republican to the Fifty-fourth Congress (March 4, 1895–March 3, 1897); was not a candidate for reelection, having been nominated as a candidate for the bench; unsuccessful candidate for justice of the State supreme court in 1896; elected as a Silver Republican, with the indorsement of the Democratic Party, to the Fifty-sixth Congress (March 4, 1899–March 3, 1901); resumed the practice of law in Boise, Idaho, where he died January 3, 1915; interment in Morris Hill Cemetery.

WILSON, Edgar Campbell (son of Thomas Wilson of Virginia and father of Eugene McLanahan Wilson), a Representative from Virginia; born in Morgantown, Monongalia County, Va. (now West Virginia), October 18, 1800; completed preparatory studies; studied law; was admitted to the bar June 24, 1832, and commenced practice in Morgantown; elected as a Whig to the Twenty-third Congress (March 4, 1833–March 3, 1835); was an unsuccessful candidate for reelection in 1834 to the Twenty-fourth Congress; resumed the practice of law in Morgantown; appointed prosecuting attorney in the circuit court of Marion County in 1842; died in Morgantown, Va. (now West Virginia), April 24, 1860; interment in Oak Grove Cemetery.

WILSON, Emmett (grandson of Augustus Emmett Maxwell), a Representative from Florida; born during the temporary residence of his parents at Belize, British Honduras, Central America, September 17, 1882; moved with his parents to Chipley, Fla.; attended the public schools and Florida State College at Tallahassee; employed as a railroad telegrapher and later as a stenographer; was graduated from the law department of the John B. Stetson University at De Land in 1904; was admitted to the bar the same year and commenced practice in Marianna, Fla.; moved to Pensacola in 1906 and continued the practice of law; appointed assistant United States attorney for the northern district of Florida February 1, 1907, and United States attorney for the same district October 7, 1907, holding the position until March 1909; State's attorney for the first judicial circuit of Florida 1911–1913; elected as a Democrat to the Sixty-third and Sixty-fourth Congresses (March 4, 1913–March 3, 1917); unsuccessful candidate for renomination in 1916; resumed the practice of law in Pensacola, Fla., and died there May 29, 1918; interment in St. John's Cemetery.

WILSON, Ephraim King, a Representative from Maryland; born near Snow Hill, Somerset (now Worcester) County, Md., September 15, 1771; received instruction in private schools and was graduated from Princeton College in 1790; studied law; was admitted to the bar in 1792 and commenced practice in Snow Hill, Md.; presidential elector on the Democratic ticket of Jefferson and Clinton in 1804; elected as a Democrat to the Twentieth and Twenty-first Congresses (March 4, 1827–March 3, 1831); was not a candidate for renomination in 1830 to the Twenty-second Congress; resumed the practice of law until his death in Snow Hill, Md., on January 2, 1834; interment in the Makemie Presbyterian Churchyard.

WILSON, Ephraim King (son of the preceding), a Representative and a Senator from Maryland; born in Snow Hill, Worcester County, Md., December 22, 1821; attended Union Academy at Snow Hill and Washington Academy, Princess Anne, Md.; was graduated from Jefferson College, Canonsburg, Pa., in 1840; taught school for six years; studied law; was admitted to the bar in 1848 and commenced practice in Snow Hill, Md.; member of the State house of delegates in 1847; presidential elector on the Democratic ticket of Pierce and King in 1852; on account of impaired health abandoned the practice of law in 1867 and retired to his farm; examiner and treasurer of the school board of Worcester County in 1868; elected as a Democrat to the Forty-third Congress (March 4, 1873–March 3, 1875); declined to be a candidate for renomination in 1874; judge of the first judicial circuit of Maryland 1878–1884; elected as a Democrat in 1884 to the United States Senate and served from March 4, 1885, until his death; had been reelected in 1890 for the term beginning March 4, 1891; died in Washington, D. C., February 24, 1891; interment in Makemie Presbyterian Churchyard, Snow Hill, Md.

WILSON, Eugene McLanahan (son of Edgar Campbell Wilson, grandson of Thomas Wilson of Virginia, and great-grandson of Isaac Griffin), a Representative from Minnesota; born in Morgantown, Monongalia County, Va. (now West Virginia), December 25, 1833; attended the common schools and Morgantown Academy; was graduated from Jefferson College, Canonsburg, Pa., in 1852; studied law; was admitted to the bar in 1855 and commenced practice in Winona, Minn.; United States attorney for the district of Minnesota with residence in Minneapolis 1857–1861; continued the practice of law in Minneapolis; served in the Union Army during the Civil War as captain of Company A, First Minnesota Mounted Rangers; elected as a Democrat to the Forty-first Congress (March 4, 1869–March 3, 1871); was not a candidate for renomination in 1870; resumed the practice of law; elected mayor of Minneapolis in 1872 and 1874; unsuccessful candidate for election in 1874 to the Forty-fourth Congress; delegate to the Democratic National Convention at St. Louis in 1876; member of the State senate in 1878 and 1879; unsuccessful candidate for Governor in 1888; died while on a visit to regain his health in Nassau, New Providence Island, British West Indies, April 10, 1890; interment in Lakewood Cemetery, Minneapolis, Minn.

WILSON, Francis Henry, a Representative from New York; born in Clinton, Oneida County, N. Y., February 11, 1844; lived in Utica, N. Y., until ten years of age, when he moved with his parents to the Westmoreland farm; attended the district school, Dwight's Preparatory School, Clinton, N. Y., and was graduated from Yale College in 1867; taught in a preparatory school four years; was graduated from the Columbia College Law School, New York City, in 1875; was admitted to the bar in 1882 and commenced practice in New York City; one of the founders of the Union League Club and its president in 1888 and 1889; elected as a Republican to the Fifty-fourth and Fifty-fifth Congresses and served from March 4, 1895, to September 30, 1897, when he resigned to become postmaster; appointed postmaster of Brooklyn, N. Y., and served from October 1897 until December 1901; resumed the practice of law; died in Brooklyn, N. Y., September 25, 1910; interment in Greenwood Cemetery.

WILSON, Frank Eugene, a Representative from New York; born in Roxbury, Delaware County, N. Y., December 22, 1857; attended the public schools and the Poughkeepsie Military Academy; was graduated from the Jefferson Medical College, Philadelphia, Pa., in 1882; practiced medicine in Pleasant Valley, Dutchess County, N. Y., until April 1888; moved to Brooklyn, N. Y., in 1888 and continued the practice of medicine; senior physician, a director, and member of the board of governors of the Bushwick Hospital and visiting physician to the Swedish Hospital, both of Brooklyn, N. Y.; elected as a Democrat to the Fifty-sixth, Fifty-seventh, and Fifty-eighth Congresses (March 4, 1899–March 3, 1905); unsuccessful candidate for reelection in 1904 to the Fifty-ninth Congress; delegate to the Democratic National Convention at Kansas City in 1900; elected to the Sixty-second and Sixty-third Congresses (March 4, 1911–March 3, 1915); was not a candidate for renomination in 1914; resumed the practice of medicine in Brooklyn, N. Y., until his death there July 12, 1935; remains were cremated and the ashes deposited in Roxbury Cemetery, Roxbury, N. Y.

WILSON, George Allison, a Senator from Iowa; born on a farm near Menlo, Adair County, Iowa, April 1, 1884; attended the rural schools and was graduated from Menlo High School; later attended Grinnell (Iowa) College and was graduated from the law school of the State University of Iowa at Iowa City in 1907; was admitted to the bar the same year and commenced practice in Des Moines, Iowa; assistant county attorney of

Polk County, Iowa, 1912–1914 and county attorney in 1915 and 1916; district judge 1917–1921; member of the State senate 1925–1935; Governor of Iowa 1939–1943; elected as a Republican to the United States Senate for the term beginning January 3, 1943, but was not sworn in until January 14, 1943, continuing as Governor during the interim, and served from January 14, 1943, to January 3, 1949; unsuccessful candidate for reelection in 1948; resumed the practice of law; died in Des Moines, Iowa, September 8, 1953; interment in Glendale Cemetery.

WILSON, George Howard, a Representative from Oklahoma; born in Mattoon, Coles County, Ill., August 21, 1905; moved with his parents to Oklahoma and attended the public schools of Enid; graduated from Phillips University, Enid, Okla., in 1926; student at the University of Michigan Law School in 1926 and 1927, and graduated from the law school of the University of Oklahoma in 1929; was admitted to the bar in 1928 and commenced the practice of law in 1929 in Enid, Okla.; deputy district court clerk of Garfield County, Okla., in 1928; special agent, Federal Bureau of Investigation, 1934–1938; city attorney of Enid, Okla., 1939–1942; during World War II served as a colonel in Judge Advocate General's Department, United States Army, with overseas duty in the South Atlantic Theater of Operations 1942–1946; elected as a Democrat to the Eighty-first Congress (January 3, 1949–January 3, 1951); unsuccessful for reelection in 1950 to the Eighty-second Congress; director of Oklahoma State Crime Bureau in 1951; State judge, Superior Court, Garfield County, Okla., 1952–; is a resident of Enid, Okla.

WILSON, George Washington, a Representative from Ohio; born in Brighton, Clark County, Ohio, February 22, 1840; attended the common schools and Antioch College, Yellow Springs, Ohio; during the Civil War enlisted in the Ninety-fourth Regiment, Ohio Volunteer Infantry, August 8, 1862; commissioned second lieutenant and later first lieutenant; first lieutenant in the First Regiment, United States Veteran Volunteer Engineers, July 2, 1864, and afterward captain; mustered out October 1, 1865; studied law; was admitted to the bar August 7, 1866, and practiced in London, Ohio; prosecuting attorney of Madison County 1866–1870; member of the State house of representatives 1871–1874; served in the State senate 1877–1881; elected as a Republican to the Fifty-third and Fifty-fourth Congresses (March 4, 1893–March 3, 1897); resumed the practice of law in London, Ohio; delegate to the Republican National Convention at St. Louis in 1896; mayor of New London; prosecuting attorney of Madison County; died in London, Ohio, November 27, 1909; interment in Kirkwood Cemetery.

WILSON, Henry, a Representative from Pennsylvania; born in Dauphin, Dauphin County, Pa., in 1778; completed preparatory studies; studied law in Harrisburg, Pa.; was admitted to the bar December 21, 1812, and commenced practice in Allentown, Pa.; prothonotary and clerk of Lehigh County Courts 1815–1821; elected as a Democrat to the Eighteenth and Nineteenth Congresses and served from March 4, 1823, until his death in Allentown, Pa., August 14, 1826; interment in Union Cemetery.

WILSON, Henry, a Senator from Massachusetts and a Vice President of the United States; born in Farmington, N. H., February 16, 1812; worked on a farm; attended the common schools; his parents' name was Colbaith, and his name was Jeremiah Jones Colbaith until he was twenty-one years of age, when he had it changed by the legislature to Henry Wilson; moved to Natick, Mass., in 1833 and learned the shoemaker's trade; traveled in the South in 1836; returned to New Hampshire and attended the Strafford, Wolfsboro, and Concord Acad-

emies for short periods; taught school in Natick, Mass., where he later engaged in the manufacture of shoes; member of the State house of representatives in 1841 and 1842; served in the State senate 1844–1846 and 1850–1852, serving as president in 1851 and 1852; delegate to the Whig National Convention at Philadelphia in 1848, but withdrew from the party on its rejection of the antislavery resolutions; owner and editor of the Boston Republican 1848–1851; delegate to the Free-Soil National Convention at Pittsburgh in 1852 and served as president; unsuccessful candidate on the Free-Soil ticket for election in 1852 to the Thirty-third Congress; delegate to the State constitutional convention in 1853; unsuccessful Free-Soil candidate for Governor of Massachusetts in 1853; elected to the United States Senate by a coalition of Free-Soilers, Americans, and Democrats to fill the vacancy caused by the resignation of Edward Everett; reelected in 1859, 1865, and 1871, and served from January 31, 1855, to March 3, 1873, when he resigned to become Vice President; in 1861 he raised and commanded for a time the Twenty-second Regiment, Massachusetts Volunteer Infantry; elected Vice President of the United States on the Republican ticket with President Grant and served from March 4, 1873, until his death in the Capitol Building at Washington, D. C., November 22, 1875; interment in Old Dell Park Cemetery, Natick, Mass.

WILSON, Isaac, a Representative from New York; born in Middlebury, Vt., June 25, 1780; served in the War of 1812 as captain of Cavalry; moved to Genesee County, N. Y.; member of the State assembly in 1816 and 1817; served in the State senate 1818–1821; judge of the Genesee County Court from May 9, 1821, to February 10, 1823; presented credentials as a Member-elect to the Eighteenth Congress and served from March 4, 1823, to January 7, 1824, when he was succeeded by Parmenio Adams, who contested his election; again judge of the Genesee County Court from February 2, 1830, to January 23, 1836; moved to Batavia, Kane County, Ill.; appointed postmaster of Batavia on February 6, 1841, and served until July 21, 1846, when his successor was appointed; died in Batavia, Ill., on October 25, 1848; interment in East Batavia Cemetery.

WILSON, James, a Delegate from Pennsylvania; born in Carskerdo, near St. Andrews, Scotland, September 14, 1742; attended the Universities of St. Andrews, Glasgow, and Edinburgh; immigrated to the United States in 1765; resided in New York City until 1766, when he moved to Philadelphia, Pa.; tutor in the College of Philadelphia (now the University of Pennsylvania); studied law; was admitted to the bar in 1767; practiced in Reading and Carlisle, Pa., and for a short time, during Howe's occupation of Philadelphia, in Annapolis, Md.; also engaged in literary pursuits; Member of the Continental Congress in 1775, 1776, 1782, 1783, and 1785–1787; active in pre-Revolutionary movements; chosen colonel of the Fourth Battalion of Associators in 1775; advocate general for France in America and guided that country's legal relations to the Confederation; member of the board of war; brigadier general of the State militia; a signer of the Declaration of Independence; a delegate from Pennsylvania to the convention which framed the Federal Constitution and a delegate to the State convention which adopted it; settled in Philadelphia in 1778 and resumed the practice of law; suggested and outlined the first financial system in 1780; Associate Justice of the United States Supreme Court 1789–1798; first professor of law in the College of Philadelphia in 1790 and in the University of Pennsylvania when they were united in 1791; died in Edenton, N. C., August 28, 1798; interment in the Johnston burial ground on the Hayes plantation near Edenton, N. C.; reinterment in Christ Churchyard, Philadelphia, Pa., in 1906.

WILSON, James, a Representative from New Hampshire; born in Peterboro, N. H., August 16, 1766; attended Phillips Academy, Andover, Mass., and was graduated from Harvard University in 1789; studied law; was admitted to the bar in 1792 and commenced practice in Peterboro, N. H.; member of the State house of representatives 1803–1808 and 1812–1814; elected as a Federalist to the Eleventh Congress (March 4, 1809–March 3, 1811); was not a candidate for renomination in 1810; resumed the practice of law; moved to Keene, Cheshire County, N. H., in 1815 and continued the practice of law; died in Keene, N. H., January 4, 1839; interment in Woodland Cemetery.

WILSON, James (son of the preceding), a Representative from New Hampshire; born in Peterboro, N. H., March 18, 1797; attended the academies at New Ipswich, Atkinson, and Exeter; moved with his parents to Keene, N. H., in 1815; was graduated from Middlebury College in 1820; member of the State militia 1820–1840 and successively promoted from captain to major general; studied law; was admitted to the bar in 1823 and commenced practice in Keene, Cheshire County, N. H.; member of the State house of representatives 1825–1837, 1840, and 1846, and served as speaker in 1828; unsuccessful candidate for Governor in 1835 and 1838; delegate to the Whig National Convention at Harrisburg, Pa., in 1840; surveyor general of public lands in the Territories of Wisconsin and Iowa 1841–1845; elected as a Whig to the Thirtieth and Thirty-first Congresses and served from March 4, 1847, to September 9, 1850, when he resigned; appointed one of the commissioners to settle private land claims in California in 1851 and served in this capacity until 1853; settled in San Francisco and remained there until 1867, when he returned to Keene, N. H.; was offered a brigadier general's commission in the Army by President Lincoln during the Civil War, but declined to accept on account of his age; again a member of the State house of representatives in 1871 and 1872; died in Keene, N. H., May 29, 1881; interment in Woodland Cemetery.

WILSON, James, a Representative from Pennsylvania; born in Millerstown (now Fairfield), Pa., April 28, 1779; attended the common schools; learned the trade of cabinetmaker; engaged in mercantile pursuits and also interested in the real-estate business; justice of the peace 1811–1822; elected as a Democrat to the Eighteenth, Nineteenth, and Twentieth Congresses (March 4, 1823–March 3, 1829); again a justice of the peace 1830–1859; engaged in the real-estate business; died in Gettysburg, Adams County, Pa., July 19, 1868; interment in Evergreen Cemetery.

WILSON, James (father of John Lockwood Wilson), a Representative from Indiana; born in Crawfordsville, Montgomery County, Ind., April 9, 1825; was graduated from Wabash College, Crawfordsville, Ind., in 1842; studied law; was admitted to the bar in 1848 and commenced practice in Crawfordsville, Ind.; served in the Mexican War from June 17, 1846, to June 16, 1847; during the Civil War was appointed captain of Volunteers November 26, 1862, and honorably discharged December 6, 1865, as brevet lieutenant colonel; elected as a Republican to the Thirty-fifth and Thirty-sixth Congresses (March 4, 1857–March 3, 1861); Minister to Venezuela from 1866 until his death in Caracas, Venezuela, August 8, 1867; interment in Oak Hill Cemetery, Crawfordsville, Ind.

WILSON, James, a Representative from Iowa; born on a farm in Ayrshire, Scotland, August 16, 1835; immigrated to the United States in 1852 with his parents, who settled in Norwich, Conn.; moved to Iowa in 1855 and located in Traer, Tama County; attended the public schools and Grinnell (Iowa) College; engaged in agricultural pursuits; taught school; member of the State house of representatives 1867–1871, serving as speaker in 1870 and 1871; regent of the State university 1870–1874; elected as a Republican to the Forty-third and Forty-fourth Congresses (March 4, 1873–March 3, 1877); member of the Iowa Railway Commission 1878–1883; presented credentials as a Member-elect to the Forty-eighth Congress and served from March 4, 1883, until the closing day, March 3, 1885, when he was succeeded by Benjamin T. Frederick, who contested his election; director of the agricultural experiment station and professor of agriculture in the Iowa Agricultural College at Ames 1891–1897; was Secretary of Agriculture in the Cabinets of Presidents McKinley, Roosevelt, and Taft, and served from March 5, 1897, to March 3, 1913; editor of the Agricultural Digest; died in Traer, Iowa, August 26, 1920; interment in Buckingham Cemetery.

WILSON, James Clifton, a Representative from Texas; born in Palo Pinto, Palo Pinto County, Tex., June 21, 1874; attended the public schools and Weatherford (Tex.) College; was graduated from the law department of the University of Texas at Austin in 1896; was admitted to the bar the same year and commenced practice in Weatherford, Tex.; assistant prosecuting attorney of Parker County 1898–1900 and prosecuting attorney 1902–1908; chairman of the Democratic county executive committee 1908–1912; moved to Fort Worth in November 1912 and served as assistant district attorney of Tarrant County until July 1913; United States attorney for the northern district of Texas from July 1913 to March 1917; elected as a Democrat to the Sixty-fifth and Sixty-sixth Congresses and served from March 4, 1917, to March 3, 1919, when he resigned; appointed by President Woodrow Wilson as United States district judge for the northern district of Texas, serving from March 13, 1919, until his retirement in 1947; died in Fort Worth, Tex., August 3, 1951; interment in Rose Hill Cemetery.

WILSON, James Falconer, a Representative and a Senator from Iowa; born in Newark, Licking County, Ohio, October 19, 1828; pursued an academic course; apprenticed to the harness-maker's trade 1841–1850; studied law; was admitted to the bar in 1851 and practiced in Newark, Ohio, 1851–1853; moved to Fairfield, Jefferson County, Iowa, in 1853 and resumed the practice of law; member of the constitutional convention of Iowa in 1857; member of the State house of representatives in 1857 and 1859; served in the State senate 1859–1861 and was its president in 1861; delegate to the Republican National Convention at Chicago in 1860; elected as a Republican to the Thirty-seventh Congress to fill the vacancy caused by the resignation of Samuel R. Curtis; reelected to the Thirty-eighth, Thirty-ninth, and Fortieth Congresses and served from October 8, 1861, to March 3, 1869; was not a candidate for renomination in 1868; one of the managers appointed by the House of Representatives in 1868 to conduct the impeachment proceedings against Andrew Johnson, President of the United States; was tendered the position of Secretary of State in the Cabinet of President Grant, which he declined, and was subsequently appointed by President Grant as Government director of the Union Pacific Railroad and served eight years; unsuccessful candidate for the Republican nomination for United States Senator in 1872; elected as a Republican to the United States Senate in 1882; reelected in 1888 and served from March 4, 1883, to March 3, 1895; was not a candidate for reelection in 1894; died in Fairfield, Iowa, April 22, 1895; interment in Fairfield-Evergreen Cemetery.

WILSON, James Jefferson, a Senator from New Jersey; born in Essex County, N. J., in 1775; attended the common schools; editor and publisher of the True American of Trenton 1801–1824; clerk in the State general assembly in 1804; judge advocate and captain, Hunterdon Brigade, New Jersey Militia, in 1806; surrogate of Hunterdon County in 1808; member of the State general assembly 1809–1811; brigadier general and adjutant general of New Jersey in 1810; resigned November 4, 1812; reappointed brigadier general and adjutant general of New Jersey February 12, 1814; captain in the Third Regiment, Hunterdon Brigade, April 15 to May 6, 1814; captain in Maj. Isaac Andruss' detachment, New Jersey Militia, from August 15, 1814, until September 18, 1814; resigned as adjutant general November 22, 1814; brigadier general and quartermaster general of New Jersey 1821–1824; elected as a Democrat to the United States Senate and served from March 4, 1815, to January 8, 1821, when he resigned; was an unsuccessful candidate for reelection November 8, 1820; appointed postmaster of Trenton, N. J., in 1821, and served until his death in that city July 28, 1824; interment in the First Baptist Church Cemetery.

WILSON, Jeremiah Morrow, a Representative from Indiana; born near Lebanon, Warren County, Ohio, November 25, 1828; completed preparatory studies; studied law; was admitted to the bar and practiced; moved to Indiana and settled in Connersville and continued the practice of law; judge of the court of common pleas 1860–1865; elected judge of the circuit court in October 1865 and served until his election to Congress; elected as a Republican to the Forty-second and Forty-third Congresses (March 4, 1871–March 3, 1875); was not a candidate for reelection in 1874; resumed the practice of his profession in Washington, D. C., where he died September 24, 1901; interment in Rock Creek Cemetery.

WILSON, John, a Representative from South Carolina; born at Wilson's Ferry (now Pelzer), Anderson County, S. C., August 11, 1773; attended the common schools; engaged in agricultural pursuits in Anderson County, near Golden Grove, S. C.; also operated a public ferry across the Saluda River at what is now known as Pelzer; elected to the Seventeenth, Eighteenth, and Nineteenth Congresses (March 4, 1821–March 3, 1827); unsuccessful candidate for reelection in 1826 to the Twentieth Congress; died at his home near Golden Grove, in Anderson County, S. C., August 13, 1828; interment in the family cemetery on his plantation, which is now a part of the industrial city of Pelzer, S. C.

WILSON, John, a Representative from Massachusetts; born in Peterboro, N. H., January 10, 1777; was graduated from Harvard University in 1799; studied law; was admitted to the bar in 1802 at Peterboro, N. H., and commenced practice in Belfast, Maine (then a district of Massachusetts); served as a captain in the State militia; elected as a Federalist to the Thirteenth Congress (March 4, 1813–March 3, 1815); unsuccessful candidate for reelection in 1814 to the Fourteenth Congress; resumed the practice of his profession in Belfast; was elected to the Fifteenth Congress (March 4, 1817–March 3, 1819); unsuccessful candidate for renomination in 1818; engaged in the practice of law until his death in Belfast, Maine, August 9, 1848; interment in Grove Cemetery.

WILSON, John Frank, a Delegate from the Territory of Arizona; born near Pulaski, Giles County, Tenn., May 7, 1846; moved with his parents to Alabama; attended the common schools and Rhuhama (Ala.) College; served in the Confederate Army as a member of Company B, First Battalion, Volunteer Infantry, and later on staff duty under General Hindman until 1863, after which he served as lieutenant colonel of a regiment;

studied law; was admitted to the bar in 1866 and commenced practice in Fayetteville, Ark.; member of the State house of representatives in 1877 and 1878; prosecuting attorney for the fourth judicial district in 1885 and 1886; moved to the Territory of Arizona; settled in Prescott in 1887 and continued the practice of law; member of the constitutional convention in 1891; probate judge of Yavapai County 1893–1895; delegate to the Democratic National Convention at Chicago in 1896; appointed attorney general of the Territory of Arizona by Governor Franklin and served during 1896 and 1897; elected as a Democrat to the Fifty-sixth Congress (March 4, 1899–March 3, 1901); elected to the Fifty-eighth Congress (March 4, 1903–March 3, 1905); was not a candidate for renomination in 1900 and 1904; resumed the practice of his profession; died in Prescott, Ariz., April 7, 1911; interment in Mountain View Cemetery.

WILSON, John Haden, a Representative from Pennsylvania; born in Nashville, Tenn., August 20, 1867; moved with his parents to Harmony, Butler County, Pa., the same year; attended the public schools; was graduated from Harmony (Pa.) Collegiate Institute, Zelienople (Pa.) Academy, and from Grove City (Pa.) College; studied law and was admitted to the bar in Butler, Pa., in 1893; taught school; commenced the practice of law in Butler in 1896; member of the Pennsylvania National Guard for three years and served during the Homestead riots; was solicitor for the city of Butler 1906–1934, except while a Member of Congress; delegate to the Democratic National Conventions in 1916, 1932, 1936, and 1940; elected as a Democrat to the Sixty-sixth Congress to fill the vacancy caused by the death of Representative-elect Edward E. Robbins and served from March 4, 1919, to March 3, 1921; unsuccessful candidate for reelection in 1920 to the Sixty-seventh Congress; resumed the practice of law; served as judge of the several courts of Butler County, Pa., 1933–1943; died in Butler, Pa., on January 28, 1946; interment in North Cemetery.

WILSON, John Henry, a Representative from Kentucky; born in Crab Orchard, Lincoln County, Ky., January 30, 1846; pursued preparatory studies; was graduated from Tusculum College, Greeneville, Tenn., in June 1870; studied law; was admitted to the bar in September 1871 and commenced practice in Barbourville, Knox County, Ky.; was also greatly interested in agricultural pursuits and the construction of the Dixie Highway; member of the State senate 1883–1887; elected as a Republican to the Fifty-first and Fifty-second Congresses (March 4, 1889–March 3, 1893); unsuccessful candidate for reelection in 1892 to the Fifty-third Congress; resumed the practice of his profession in Barbourville, Ky.; died at the home of his daughter in Louisville, Ky., January 14, 1923; interment in Barbourville Cemetery.

WILSON, John Lockwood (son of James Wilson of Indiana), a Representative and a Senator from Washington; born in Crawfordsville, Montgomery County, Ind., August 7, 1850; attended the common schools; messenger on the staff of Col. James Wilson during the Civil War; was graduated from Wabash College, Crawfordsville, Ind., in 1874; studied law; was admitted to the bar in 1878 and commenced practice in Crawfordsville; member of the Indiana House of Representatives in 1880; appointed by President Arthur as receiver of public moneys at Spokane Falls and Colfax in 1882 and served until 1887; delegate to the Republican National Convention at Chicago in 1888; upon the admission of Washington as a State into the Union was elected as a Republican to the Fifty-first Congress; reelected to the Fifty-second and Fifty-third Congresses and served from November 20, 1889, to February 18, 1895, when he resigned to become Senator; elected to the United States Senate on February

1, 1895, to fill the vacancy in the term commencing March 4, 1893, but did not assume his senatorial duties until February 19, 1895; served until March 3, 1899; was an unsuccessful candidate for reelection in 1898; engaged in the publication of the Seattle Post-Intelligencer, Seattle, Wash.; died in Washington, D. C., on November 6, 1912; interment in Oak Hill Cemetery, Crawfordsville, Ind.

WILSON, John Thomas, a Representative from Ohio; born in Bell, Highland County, Ohio, April 16, 1811; received a limited schooling; engaged in mercantile and agricultural pursuits; during the Civil War was appointed first lieutenant of Company E, Seventieth Regiment, Ohio Volunteer Infantry, November 2, 1861, and was discharged as captain November 27, 1862, on account of age and ill health; member of the State senate 1863–1866; elected as a Republican to the Fortieth, Forty-first, and Forty-second Congresses (March 4, 1867–March 3, 1873); unsuccessful candidate for reelection in 1872 to the Forty-third Congress; engaged in the handling of loans and mortgages; died in Tranquillity (near what is now known as Seaman), Adams County, Ohio, on October 6, 1891; interment in Tranquillity Cemetery.

WILSON, Joseph Franklin, a Representative from Texas; born in Corsicana, Navarro County, Tex., March 18, 1901; attended the elementary school at Corsicana; at the age of twelve moved to Memphis, Tex. (in the Panhandle), and attended the public schools until 1916; during the First World War enrolled at Peacock Military College, San Antonio, Tex., from September 1917 to June 1918 and at Tennessee Military Institute at Sweetwater from September 1918 to June 1919, advancing through the grades to first sergeant; graduated from Baylor University Law School, Waco, Tex., in 1923; was admitted to the bar the same year and commenced practice in Dallas, Tex.; delegate to the Democratic National Convention in 1936; chairman of the Dallas County Democratic Executive Committee 1942–1945; district judge of the criminal district court of Texas in 1943 and 1944; elected as a Democrat to the Eightieth and to the three succeeding Congresses (January 3, 1947–January 3, 1955); was not a candidate for renomination in 1954; appointed judge of Criminal District Court No. 1, Dallas, Tex., in 1955, in which capacity he is still serving; resides in Dallas, Tex.

WILSON, Joseph Gardner (cousin of James Willis Nesmith), a Representative from Oregon; born in Acworth, Sullivan County, N. H., December 13, 1826; moved with his parents to Cincinnati, Ohio, in 1828 and later to a farm near Reading, Hamilton County; attended the district schools until 1840 and Cary's Academy from 1840 to 1842; was graduated from Marietta (Ohio) College in 1846; professor in Farmer's College, near Cincinnati, in 1849; traveled through New England during 1850; was graduated from the Cincinnati Law School in 1852 and was admitted to the bar; moved to Oregon Territory in 1852 and commenced the practice of law in Salem, Oreg.; clerk of the Territorial legislature in 1853; first secretary of the Willamette Woolen Co. when it was established in 1854; prosecuting attorney of Marion County 1860–1862; associate judge of the State supreme court 1864–1866 and 1868–1870; unsuccessful candidate for election in 1870 to the Forty-second Congress; resumed the practice of his profession; elected as a Republican to the Forty-third Congress and served from March 4, 1873, until his death in Marietta, Ohio, July 2, 1873; interment in Pioneer Cemetery, The Dalles, Oreg.

WILSON, Nathan, a Representative from New York; born in Bolton, Worcester County, Mass., December 23, 1758; moved with his family to Greenwich, Hampshire County, Mass., where he attended school; served two enlistments in Massachusetts regiments during the Revolutionary War in 1777 and 1780; fought in the second battle of Stillwater and was present at Burgoyne's surrender at Saratoga; moved to New Perth (now Salem), Washington County, N. Y.; enlisted as a private in the Sixteenth Regiment, Albany County Militia; appointed by Governor George Clinton in 1791 adjutant in Washington County Militia Regiment; town collector in 1801 and 1802; sheriff of Washington County 1802–1806; elected as a Democrat to the Tenth Congress to fill the vacancy caused by the resignation of David Thomas and served from June 3, 1808, to March 3, 1809; justice of the peace 1808–1816; engaged in agricultural pursuits; died near Salem, Washington County, N. Y., July 25, 1834; interment in Evergreen Cemetery, Salem, N. Y.

WILSON, Riley Joseph, a Representative from Louisiana; born near Goldonna, Winn Parish, La., November 12, 1871; attended the public schools and Beeson College, Arcadia, La.; was graduated from Iuka (Miss.) Normal Institute in 1894; principal of Harrisonburg High School 1895–1897; studied law; was admitted to the bar in 1898 and commenced practice in Harrisonburg, La.; member of the State constitutional convention in 1898; edited the Catahoula News 1898–1904; member of the State house of representatives 1900–1904; district attorney of the eighth judicial district from December 1, 1904, until his resignation on May 1, 1910, to accept a judicial appointment; judge of the eighth judicial district from May 1, 1910, until his resignation on December 1, 1914, having been elected to Congress; delegate to the Democratic National Convention at San Francisco in 1920; elected as a Democrat to the Sixty-fourth and to the ten succeeding Congresses (March 4, 1915–January 3, 1937); unsuccessful candidate for renomination in 1936; unsuccessful candidate for Governor in 1928; retired from public and political activities; died in Ruston, La., February 23, 1946; interment in Greenwood Cemetery.

WILSON, Robert, a Senator from Missouri; born near Staunton, Va., in November 1803; moved to Howard County, Mo., in 1820; taught school; probate judge of Howard County in 1825; clerk of the circuit and county courts 1829–1840; appointed brigadier general of the State forces in 1837 and served during the so-called Mormon war; studied law; was admitted to the bar and commenced practice in 1840; moved to Huntsville, Mo.; member of the State house of representatives in 1844; moved to Andrew County, Mo., in 1852; served in the State senate in 1854; chosen as a Union delegate to the State convention called to determine the attitude on secession in 1861 and elected vice president of the convention, later acting as president; appointed as a Unionist to the United States Senate to fill the vacancy caused by the expulsion of Waldo P. Johnson and served from January 17, 1862, to November 13, 1863, when a successor was elected; engaged in agricultural pursuits; died in Marshall, Saline County, Mo., on May 10, 1870; interment in Mount Mora Cemetery, St. Joseph, Mo.

WILSON, Robert Carleton, a Representative from California; born in Calexico, Imperial County, Calif., April 5, 1916; attended the public schools; moved to San Diego, Calif., in 1928 and worked as a newsboy, grocery clerk, and theater usher while attending San Diego State College; also attended Otis Art Institute; worked as a milk route salesman and merchandising manager for a dairy; during World War II operated Conship Commissary; served in the Coast Guard Reserve (Port Security Service) and as a private in the United States Army; partner and vice president of an advertising agency in San Diego; elected as a Republican to the Eighty-third and to the three succeeding Congresses (January 3, 1953–January 3, 1961). *Reelected to the Eighty-seventh Congress.*

WILSON, Robert Patterson Clark, a Representative from Missouri; born in Boonville, Cooper County, Mo., August 8, 1834; moved with his parents to Platte County; attended William Jewell College, Liberty, Mo., and was graduated from Centre College, Danville, Ky., in 1853; studied law; was admitted to the bar in 1854 and commenced practice in Seguin, Tex., in 1855; returned to Missouri in 1858; moved to Leavenworth, Kans., in 1860; was a member of the first State house of representatives of Kansas from March to June 4, 1861; returned to Missouri in 1861; member of the State house of representatives of Missouri in 1871 and 1872 and served as speaker both years; presidential elector on the Democratic ticket of Greeley and Brown in 1872; member of the State senate in 1879 and 1880; delegate to the Democratic National Convention at St. Louis in 1888; president of the school board of Platte City, Mo.; elected as a Democrat to the Fifty-first Congress to fill the vacancy caused by the death of James N. Burnes; reelected to the Fifty-second Congress and served from December 2, 1889, to March 3, 1893; resumed the practice of his profession in Platte City, Platte County, Mo.; died in Kansas City, Mo., December 21, 1916; interment in Marshall Cemetery, Platte City, Mo.

WILSON, Stanyarne, a Representative from South Carolina; born in Yorkville (now York), S. C., January 10, 1860; attended Kings Mountain Military School and Washington and Lee University, Lexington, Va.; studied law; was admitted to the bar by an act of the legislature in 1880, then being a minor; settled in Spartanburg, Spartanburg County, S. C., in 1881; practiced law and was also interested in cotton manufactures, gold mining, iron works, and agriculture; member of the State house of representatives 1884–1886 and 1890–1892; served in the State senate 1892–1895; member of the State constitutional convention in 1895; elected as a Democrat to the Fifty-fourth, Fifty-fifth, and Fifty-sixth Congresses (March 4, 1895–March 3, 1901); continued the practice of law in Spartanburg, S. C., and later in Richmond, Va., where he moved in 1913; returned to Spartanburg, S. C., in January 1928, and died there February 14, 1928; interment in Church of the Advent Cemetery.

WILSON, Stephen Fowler, a Representative from Pennsylvania; born in Columbia, Pa., September 4, 1821; received an academic education; studied law; was admitted to the bar and practiced; held several local offices; member of the State senate 1863–1865 and served in one session after he had been elected a Representative to Congress; delegate to the Republican National Convention at Baltimore in 1864; elected as a Republican to the Thirty-ninth and Fortieth Congresses (March 4, 1865–March 3, 1869); appointed additional judge of the fourth judicial district of Pennsylvania in 1871 to fill a vacancy; elected additional judge and served ten years; appointed associate justice of the supreme court of the Territory of New Mexico by President Arthur on October 16, 1884; president judge of the fourth judicial district of Pennsylvania from 1887 to 1889; resumed the practice of his profession in Wellsboro, Tioga County, Pa., where he died March 30, 1897; interment in Wellsboro Cemetery.

WILSON, Thomas (father of Edgar Campbell Wilson and grandfather of Eugene McLanahan Wilson), a Representative from Virginia; born in Staunton, Va., September 11, 1765; studied law in Staunton, Va.; was admitted to the bar September 21, 1789, and commenced practice in Morgantown, Va. (now West Virginia); member of the State senate 1792–1795; served in the State house of delegates in 1799 and 1800; again a member of the State senate 1800–1804; elected as a Federalist to the Twelfth Congress (March 4, 1811–March 3, 1813); again a member of the State house of delegates in 1816 and 1817; resumed the practice of law; died in Morgantown, Va., January 24, 1826; interment in Oak Grove Cemetery.

WILSON, Thomas, a Representative from Pennsylvania; born near Sunbury, Northumberland County, Pa., in 1772; attended the common schools; had the contract for supplying the western forts of the United States from Niagara to New Orleans; engaged in shipbuilding in Erie, Pa., in 1805; built vessels for commerce on the Great Lakes; burgess of Erie in 1807; town clerk in 1808; treasurer of Erie County 1809–1812; county commissioner in 1811; justice of the peace; elected as a Democrat to the Thirteenth Congress to fill the vacancy caused by the resignation of Abner Lacock; reelected to the Fourteenth Congress and served from May 4, 1813, to March 3, 1817; member of the State house of representatives 1817–1820; prothonotary and clerk of court of Erie County 1819–1824; died in Erie, Pa., October 4, 1824.

WILSON, Thomas, a Representative from Minnesota; born in Dungannon, County Tyrone, Ireland, May 16, 1827; attended the common schools; immigrated to the United States in 1839 with his parents, who settled in Venango County, Pa.; was graduated from Allegheny College, Meadville, Pa., in 1852; studied law; was admitted to the bar in February 1855 and commenced practice in Winona, Minn.; member of the Minnesota constitutional convention in 1857; judge of the third judicial district court 1857–1864; associate justice of the supreme court of Minnesota in 1864; chief justice from 1864 to July 1869, when he resigned; resumed the practice of law; member of the State house of representatives 1880–1882; served in the State senate 1882–1885; elected as a Democrat to the Fiftieth Congress (March 4, 1887–March 3, 1889); unsuccessful candidate for reelection; unsuccessful candidate for Governor in 1890; delegate to the Democratic National Convention at Chicago in 1892; general counsel for the Chicago, St. Paul, Minneapolis & Omaha Railroad until his death in St. Paul, Minn., April 3, 1910; interment in Woodlawn Cemetery, Winona, Minn.

WILSON, Thomas Webber, a Representative from Mississippi; born in Coldwater, Tate County, Miss., January 24, 1893; attended the public schools of his native city; was graduated from the law department of the University of Mississippi at Oxford in 1913; was admitted to the bar the same year and commenced the practice of law in Laurel, Miss.; prosecuting attorney of Jones County 1915–1919; district attorney for the twelfth judicial district of Mississippi 1919–1923; elected as a Democrat to the Sixty-eighth, Sixty-ninth, and Seventieth Congresses (March 4, 1923–March 3, 1929); was not a candidate for renomination in 1928 but was an unsuccessful candidate for the nomination for United States Senator; engaged in the private practice of law 1928–1933; appointed a Federal judge for the Virgin Islands and served from 1933 until 1935; member of the Parole Board in the Justice Department, Washington, D. C., 1935–1947; died in Coldwater, Miss., January 31, 1948; interment in Magnolia Cemetery.

WILSON, William, a Representative from Pennsylvania; was elected to the Fourteenth and Fifteenth Congresses (March 4, 1815–March 3, 1819).

WILSON, William, a Representative from Ohio; born in New Boston, Hillsboro County, N. H., March 19, 1773; attended the public schools and was graduated from Dartmouth College, Hanover, N. H., in 1797; studied law in Johnstown, N. Y., and was admitted to the bar; moved to Ohio and settled in Chillicothe about 1805; engaged in the practice of law; moved to

Newark, Ohio, in 1808, having been appointed chief judge of the court of common pleas, and served until 1823; elected to the Eighteenth, Nineteenth, and Twentieth Congresses and served from March 4, 1823, until his death in Newark, Licking County, Ohio, June 6, 1827; interment in the Old Cemetery; reinterment on March 23, 1853, in Cedar Hill Cemetery.

WILSON, William Bauchop, a Representative from Pennsylvania; born in Blantyre, Scotland, April 2, 1862; immigrated to this country with his parents, who settled in Arnot, Tioga County, Pa., in 1870; attended the common schools; engaged in coal mining 1871–1898; international secretary-treasurer of the United Mine Workers of America 1900–1908; elected as a Democrat to the Sixtieth, Sixty-first, and Sixty-second Congresses (March 4, 1907–March 3, 1913); unsuccessful candidate for reelection in 1912 to the Sixty-third Congress and for election in 1914 to the Sixty-fourth Congress; appointed Secretary of Labor in the Cabinet of President Wilson and served from March 5, 1913, to March 5, 1921; during the First World War was a member of the Council of National Defense; member of the Federal Board for Vocational Education 1914–1921 and also chairman of the board in 1920 and 1921; appointed on March 4, 1921, a member of the International Joint Commission, created to prevent disputes regarding the use of the boundary waters between the United States and Canada, and served until March 21, 1921, when he resigned; unsuccessful candidate for election to the United States Senate in 1926; engaged in mining and agricultural pursuits near Blossburg, Tioga County, Pa.; died on a train near Savannah, Ga., May 25, 1934; interment in Arbon Cemetery, Blossburg, Pa.

WILSON, William Edward, a Representative from Indiana; born in Mount Vernon, Posey County, Ind., March 9, 1870; attended the public schools and the Evansville Commercial College, with which he was associated as teacher, principal, and owner from 1888 to 1904; retired from school work and engaged in the insurance business at Evansville, Ind.; deputy auditor of Vanderburg County, Ind., 1910–1912; clerk of the circuit court of Vanderburg County 1912–1920; unsuccessful candidate for election in 1920 to the Sixty-seventh Congress; elected as a Democrat to the Sixty-eighth Congress (March 4, 1923–March 3, 1925); unsuccessful candidate for reelection in 1924 to the Sixty-ninth Congress; engaged in banking and was later employed by the Chrysler Corp.; died in Evansville, Ind., September 29, 1948; interment in Oak Hill Cemetery.

WILSON, William Henry, a Representative from Pennsylvania; born in Philadelphia, Pa., December 6, 1877; attended the public and high schools and was graduated from the law department of the University of Pennsylvania at Philadelphia in 1898; was admitted to the bar in 1899 and commenced the practice of law in Philadelphia, Pa.; served as assistant city solicitor 1900–1909; member of the State house of representatives 1913–1915; served as director of public safety, Philadelphia, 1916–1920; elected as a Republican to the Seventy-fourth Congress (January 3, 1935–January 3, 1937); unsuccessful candidate for reelection in 1936 to the Seventy-fifth Congress; retired from active business pursuits and traveled extensively; died in Santa Barbara, Calif., August 11, 1937; remains were cremated and placed in Forest Lawn Memorial Park, Glendale, Calif.

WILSON, William Lyne, a Representative from West Virginia; born near Charles Town, Jefferson County, Va. (now West Virginia), May 3, 1843; attended Charles Town Academy; was graduated from Columbian College (now George Washington University), Washington, D. C., in 1860 and subsequently studied in the University of Virginia at Charlottesville; during the Civil War served in the Confederate Army as a private in the Twelfth Virginia Cavalry; taught for several years in Columbian College, during which time he was graduated from its law school; was admitted to the bar in 1869 and commenced practice in Charles Town, W. Va.; delegate to the Democratic National Convention at Cincinnati in 1880; presidential elector on the Democratic ticket of Hancock and English in 1880; chosen president of the West Virginia University at Morgantown and entered upon the office September 4, 1882; elected as a Democrat to the Forty-eighth and to the five succeeding Congresses (March 4, 1883–March 3, 1895); Postmaster General in the Cabinet of President Cleveland and served from April 4, 1895, to March 5, 1897; president of the Washington and Lee University, Lexington, Va.; died in Lexington, Rockbridge, County, Va., October 17, 1900; interment in Edgehill Cemetery, Charles Town, W. Va.

WILSON, William Warfield, a Representative from Illinois; born in Ohio, Bureau County, Ill., March 2, 1868; attended the public schools of Ohio, Ill., and the University of Michigan at Ann Arbor; was graduated from the Chicago-Kent College of Law in 1893; was admitted to the bar the same year and commenced practice in Chicago, Ill.; elected as a Republican to the Fifty-eighth and to the four succeeding Congresses (March 4, 1903–March 3, 1913); unsuccessful candidate for election in 1912 to the Sixty-third Congress; elected to the Sixty-fourth, Sixty-fifth, and Sixty-sixth Congresses (March 4, 1915–March 3, 1921); was not a candidate for renomination in 1920; appointed general counsel of the Alien Property Custodian of the United States in 1922, serving until 1927; resumed the practice of law; died in Chicago, Ill., July 22, 1942; interment in Union Cemetery, Ohio, Ill.

WINANS, Edwin Baruch, a Representative from Michigan; born in Avon, Livingston County, N. Y., May 16, 1826; moved with his parents to Michigan in 1834; attended Albion College, Michigan; went to California and engaged in mining on the North Yuba River, near Placerville, in 1850; worked in different parts of the State until 1857; returned to Michigan in 1858 and settled in Hamburg, Livingston County, where he engaged in agricultural pursuits; member of the State house of representatives 1861–1865; delegate to the State constitutional convention of May 15, 1867; probate judge of Livingston County 1877–1881; elected as a Democrat to the Forty-eighth and Forty-ninth Congresses (March 4, 1883–March 3, 1887); resumed agricultural pursuits in Livingston County, Mich.; Governor of Michigan 1891–1893; died in Hamburg, Mich., July 4, 1894; interment in Hamburg Cemetery.

WINANS, James January, a Representative from Ohio; born in Maysville, Ky., June 7, 1818; moved with his parents to Greene County, Ohio; attended the common schools and the University of Lexington, Kentucky; studied law; was admitted to the bar in Lexington, Ky., in 1841 and commenced practice in Indiana; moved to Xenia, Greene County, Ohio, in 1843 and continued the practice of law; clerk of the Greene County Courts 1845–1851; served in the State senate in 1857; member of the State house of representatives in 1863; judge of the court of common pleas 1864–1871; elected as a Republican to the Forty-first Congress (March 4, 1869–March 3, 1871); unsuccessful candidate for reelection in 1870 to the Forty-second Congress; resumed the practice of law; died in Xenia, Ohio, April 28, 1879; interment in Woodlawn Cemetery.

WINANS, John, a Representative from Wisconsin; born in Vernon, Sussex County, N. J., September 27, 1831; studied law and was admitted to the bar in 1855; moved to Janesville,

Rock County, Wis., in 1857 and practiced his profession; member of the board of aldermen of Janesville in 1861; city attorney 1865–1875; member of the State assembly in 1874, 1882, 1887, and 1891; delegate to the Democratic National Convention at Chicago in 1864; served as colonel on the staff of Governor Taylor in 1874 and 1875; mayor of Janesville 1885–1887; elected as an Independent Democrat to the Forty-eighth Congress (March 4, 1883–March 3, 1885); was not a candidate for renomination in 1884; engaged in the practice of law in Janesville, Wis., until his death January 17, 1907; interment in Oak Hill Cemetery.

WINCHESTER, Boyd, a Representative from Kentucky; born in Ascension Parish, La., September 23, 1836; pursued preparatory studies; attended Centre College, Danville, Ky., and the University of Virginia at Charlottesville; was graduated from the law department of the University of Louisville, Kentucky, in 1857 and commenced practice in Louisville; member of the State senate in 1867 and 1868; when he resigned; presidential elector on the Democratic ticket of Seymour and Blair in 1868 and of Cleveland and Hendricks in 1884; elected as a Democrat to the Forty-first and Forty-second Congresses (March 4, 1869–March 3, 1873); was not a candidate for renomination in 1872; resumed the practice of law in Louisville, Ky.; president of an insurance company 1875–1877; president of the Democratic State convention in 1884; appointed Minister Resident and consul general to Switzerland and served from 1885 to 1889; writer and lecturer; died in Louisville, Ky., May 18, 1923; interment in Cave Hill Cemetery.

WINDOM, William, a Representative and a Senator from Minnesota; born in Belmont County, Ohio, on May 10, 1827; pursued an academic course at Martinsburg, Ohio; studied law; was admitted to the bar in 1850 and commenced practice in Mount Vernon, Ohio; prosecuting attorney of Knox County in 1852; moved to Winona, Winona County, Minn., in 1855; elected as a Republican to the Thirty-sixth and to the four succeeding Congresses (March 4, 1859–March 3, 1869); appointed to the United States Senate to fill the vacancy in the term ending March 3, 1871, caused by the death of Daniel S. Norton, until the legislature could elect a successor, and served from July 15, 1870, to January 22, 1871, when a successor was elected to complete the term; elected to the United States Senate in 1871; reelected in 1877 and served from March 4, 1871, to March 7, 1881, when he resigned to accept a Cabinet portfolio; appointed Secretary of the Treasury by President Garfield on March 5, 1881, and served from March 8, 1881, until his resignation, effective November 14, 1881, having been elected Senator; reelected to the United States Senate on October 26, 1881, to fill the vacancy caused by his own resignation, and served from November 15, 1881, to March 3, 1883; unsuccessful candidate for reelection in 1883; moved to New York City in 1883 and practiced law; appointed Secretary of the Treasury in the Cabinet of President Benjamin Harrison on March 5, 1889, and served from March 7, 1889, until his death in New York City on January 29, 1891; interment in Rock Creek Cemetery, Washington, D. C.

WINFIELD, Charles Henry, a Representative from New York; born in Crawford, N. Y., April 22, 1822; completed preparatory studies; studied law; was admitted to the bar in 1846 and commenced practice in Goshen, N. Y.; district attorney for Orange County 1850–1856; elected as a Democrat to the Thirty-eighth and Thirty-ninth Congresses (March 4, 1863–March 3, 1867); was not a candidate for renomination in 1866; resumed the practice of his profession; died in Walden, N. Y., June 10, 1888; interment in Wallkill Valley Cemetery.

WING, Austin Eli, a Delegate from Michigan; born in Conway, Hampshire County, Mass., February 3, 1792; in early youth moved with his parents to Marietta, Ohio; attended the common schools, the academy at Chillicothe, Ohio, and Athens College, Ohio; was graduated from Williams College, Williamstown, Mass., in 1814; moved to Detroit, Mich.; elected as a Whig to the Nineteenth and Twentieth Congresses (March 4, 1825–March 3, 1829); moved to Monroe, Mich.; elected to the Twenty-second Congress (March 4, 1831–March 3, 1833); affiliated with the Whig Party after its formation; member of the State house of representatives in 1842; served as a member of the board of regents of the University of Michigan from 1845 until 1850; appointed United States marshal for the district of Michigan on February 24, 1846, and served until 1849; died in Cleveland, Ohio, on August 27, 1849; interment in Woodlawn Cemetery, Monroe, Mich.

WINGATE, Joseph Ferdinand, a Representative from Maine; born in Haverhill, Essex County, Maine (until 1820 a district of Massachusetts), June 29, 1786; received a limited schooling; engaged in the mercantile business in Bath, Maine; member of the Massachusetts House of Representatives in 1818 and 1819; collector of customs at the port of Bath 1820–1824; elected as a Democrat to the Twentieth and Twenty-first Congresses (March 4, 1827–March 3, 1831); moved to Windsor, Maine; died in South Windsor, Kennebec County, Maine; interment in Rest Haven Cemetery.

WINGATE, Paine, a Delegate, a Senator, and a Representative from New Hampshire; born in Amesbury, Mass., May 14, 1739; was graduated from Harvard College in 1759; studied theology, and was ordained a minister of the Congregational Church at Hampton Falls, Rockingham County, N. H., December 14, 1763, holding a pastorate in that town until 1776; moved to Stratham, Rockingham County, N. H., in 1776 and engaged in agricultural pursuits; member of the State constitutional convention in 1781; served in the State house of representatives in 1783; Member of the Continental Congress in 1787 and 1788; elected as a Federalist to the United States Senate and served from March 4, 1789, to March 3, 1793; elected to the Third Congress (March 4, 1793–March 3, 1795); again a member of the State house of representatives in 1795; served as judge of the superior court of New Hampshire 1798–1809; withdrew from political life and resumed agricultural pursuits; died in Stratham, N. H., on March 7, 1838; interment in Stratham Cemetery.

WINGO, Effiegene (Locke) (widow of Otis Theodore Wingo and great-great-great-granddaughter of Matthew Locke), a Representative from Arkansas; born in Lockesburg, Sevier County, Ark., April 13, 1883; attended public and private schools and Union Female College, Oxford, Miss.; was graduated from Maddox Seminary, Little Rock, Ark., in 1901; moved to Texarkana, Ark., in 1895 and to De Queen, Ark., in 1897; elected as a Democrat on November 4, 1930, to the Seventy-first Congress to fill the vacancy caused by the death of her husband, Otis Theodore Wingo, and on the same day was elected to the Seventy-second Congress and served from November 4, 1930, to March 3, 1933; was not a candidate for renomination in 1932; co-founder in 1934 of National Institute of Public Affairs, Washington, D. C.; engaged in educational and research work; is a resident of De Queen, Sevier County, Ark.

WINGO, Otis Theodore (husband of Effiegene Wingo), a Representative from Arkansas; born in Weakley County, Tenn., June 18, 1877; attended the public schools, Bethel College at McKenzie, Tenn., McFerrin College at Martin, Tenn., and

Valparaiso (Ind.) University; taught school; studied law; was admitted to the bar in 1900 and commenced practice in De Queen, Sevier County, Ark.; member of the State senate 1907–1909; resumed the practice of his profession in De Queen, Ark.; elected as a Democrat to the Sixty-third and to the eight succeeding Congresses and served from March 4, 1913, until his death in a hospital at Baltimore, Md., October 21, 1930; interment in Rock Creek Cemetery, Washington, D. C.

WINN, Richard, a Representative from South Carolina; born in Fauquier County, Va., in 1750; attended the common schools; moved to Georgia and then to Fairfield County in South Carolina in 1768; served as a clerk in a countinghouse; engaged in cotton buying and other mercantile pursuits, and was a land surveyor; entered the Revolutionary Army as a lieutenant and attained the rank of colonel of State militia; after the war was promoted to the rank of major general of militia; appointed superintendent of Indian affairs for the Creek Nation in 1788; elected as a Democrat to the Third and Fourth Congresses (March 4, 1793–March 3, 1797); elected to the Seventh Congress to fill the vacancy caused by the resignation of Thomas Sumter; reelected to the Eighth and to the four succeeding Congresses and served from January 24, 1803, to March 3, 1813; moved to Tennessee in 1813; became a planter, and continued in the mercantile business until his death on his plantation at Duck River, Maury County, Tenn., December 19, 1818; interment at Winnsboro, Fairfield County, S. C.

WINN, Thomas Elisha, a Representative from Georgia; born near Athens, Clarke County, Ga., May 21, 1839; attended Carrollton (Ga.) Masonic Institute, and was graduated from Emory and Henry College, Emory, Va., in 1860; studied law; was admitted to the bar in 1861 and commenced practice in Alpharetta, Milton County, Ga.; solicitor of the county court of Milton County; during the Civil War entered the Confederate Army as a first lieutenant in 1861; was soon promoted to captain, afterward, a major, and finally a lieutenant colonel, Twenty-fourth Regiment, Georgia Infantry, and served with Lee's army until the close of the Civil War; engaged in agricultural pursuits in 1868; county school commissioner of Gwinnett County from 1876 to 1890, when he resigned; elected as an Alliance Democrat to the Fifty-second Congress (March 4, 1891–March 3, 1893); did not seek renomination in 1892 to the Fifty-third Congress; resumed agricultural pursuits in Greene County, Ga.; died in Atlanta, Ga., on June 5, 1925; interment in Ridge Grove Cemetery, near Greensboro, Greene County, Ga.

WINSLOW, Samuel Ellsworth, a Representative from Massachusetts; born in Worcester, Mass., April 11, 1862; attended the public schools; was graduated from Worcester Classical High School in 1880, from Williston Seminary, Easthampton, Mass., in 1881, and from Harvard University in 1885; engaged in the manufacture of skates; appointed as a colonel on the staff of Governor Brackett in 1890; chairman of the Republican city committee of Worcester 1890–1892; chairman of the Republican State committee in 1893 and 1894; delegate to the Republican National Convention at Chicago in 1908 which nominated William H. Taft, of Ohio, for President and James S. Sherman, of New York, for Vice President; elected as a Republican to the Sixty-third and to the five succeeding Congresses (March 4, 1913–March 3, 1925); was not a candidate for renomination in 1924; appointed by President Coolidge in 1926 as a member of the United States Board of Mediation, for the disposition of disputes between carriers and their employees, and was subsequently chosen chairman, serving until 1934; moved in 1935 to Worcester, Mass., where he died July 11, 1940; remains were cremated and the ashes interred in Hope Cemetery.

WINSLOW, Warren, a Representative from North Carolina; born in Fayetteville, Cumberland County, N. C., January 1, 1810; was graduated from the University of North Carolina at Chapel Hill in 1827; studied law; was admitted to the bar and commenced practice in Fayetteville; member of the State senate, and served as speaker; Acting Governor of North Carolina in December 1854; elected as a Democrat to the Thirty-fourth, Thirty-fifth, and Thirty-sixth Congresses (March 4, 1855–March 3, 1861); died in Fayetteville, N. C., August 16, 1862; interment in Cross Creek Cemetery.

WINSTEAD, William Arthur, a Representative from Mississippi; born near Philadelphia, Neshoba County, Miss., January 6, 1904; attended the public schools, Clarke Memorial College, Newton, Miss., and the University of Alabama at Tuscaloosa; was graduated from Mississippi Southern College at Hattiesburg in 1931; engaged in agricultural pursuits; superintendent of education of Neshoba County, Miss., 1935–1942; elected as a Democrat to the Seventy-eighth and to the eight succeeding Congresses (January 3, 1943–January 3, 1961). *Reelected to the Eighty-seventh Congress.*

WINSTON, Joseph, a Representative from North Carolina; born in Louisa County, Va., June 17, 1746; moved in 1766 to that part of Rowan County which later became Stokes County, N. C.; participated in expeditions against the hostile frontier Indians; member of the Hillsboro convention in 1775; member of the commission that concluded a treaty with the Cherokees in 1777; appointed entry taker for Surry County in 1778; chief ranger of Surry County; served as major in the Revolutionary Army; commanded the right wing at the Battle of Kings Mountain in October 1780, and was presented with a sword by the legislature of North Carolina for his gallantry there; member of the State senate in 1790, 1791, 1802, 1807, and 1812; elected to the Third Congress (March 4, 1793–March 3, 1795); presidential elector on the Democratic ticket of Jefferson and Burr in 1800; elected to the Eighth and Ninth Congresses (March 4, 1803–March 3, 1807); died near Germanton, Stokes County, N. C., April 21, 1815; interment in the family burial ground near Germanton; reinterment on Guilford Battle Grounds, N. C.

WINTER, Charles Edwin, a Representative from Wyoming; born in Muscatine, Iowa, September 13, 1870; attended the public schools and Iowa Wesleyan University at Mount Pleasant; was graduated from the Nebraska Wesleyan University at Lincoln in 1892; studied law; was admitted to the bar in 1895 and commenced practice in Omaha, Nebr.; moved to Encampment, Carbon County, Wyo., in 1902 and to Casper, Natrona County, Wyo., in 1903; delegate to the Republican National Convention at Chicago in 1908; delegate to the Republican State convention at Lander, Wyo., in 1908; judge of the sixth judicial district of Wyoming 1913–1919; chairman of the Liberty Loan Committee and Council of National Defense of Natrona County during the First World War; resigned from the bench and resumed the practice of law at Casper, Wyo.; elected as a Republican to the Sixty-eighth, Sixty-ninth, and Seventieth Congresses (March 4, 1923–March 3, 1929); was not a candidate for renomination in 1928, but was an unsuccessful candidate for election to the United States Senate; attorney general of Puerto Rico in 1932 and 1933, and served as Acting Governor; resumed the practice of law; died in Casper, Wyo., April 22, 1948; interment in Highland Cemetery.

WINTER, Elisha I., a Representative from New York; born in New York City, July 15, 1781; moved about 1806 to that portion of the township of Peru, Clinton County, which was later included in the township of Ausable, and engaged in mining ore; was elected as a Federalist to the Thirteenth Congress (March 4, 1813–March 3, 1815); unsuccessful candidate for reelection in 1814 to the Fourteenth Congress; moved to a farm near Lexington, Ky., and engaged as a planter; was also instrumental in building the first railroad in that locality, and subsequently became president of the Lexington & Ohio Railroad; died in Lexington, Fayette County, Ky., June 30, 1849; interment in Lexington Cemetery.

WINTER, Thomas Daniel, a Representative from Kansas; born in Columbus, Cherokee County, Kans., July 7, 1896; attended the public and high schools; during the First World War served as a private in the United States Air Corps in 1918 and 1919; court reporter of the district court of Crawford County, Kans., 1921–1927; studied law; was admitted to the bar in 1926 and commenced practice in Girard, Kans.; assistant county attorney of Crawford County, Kans., in 1927 and 1928 and county attorney in 1929 and 1930; commissioner of public utilities of Girard 1933–1935; commissioner of finance of Girard 1936–1938; elected as a Republican to the Seventy-sixth and to the three succeeding Congresses (January 3, 1939–January 3, 1947); unsuccessful candidate for renomination in 1946; returned to Girard, Kans., and continued to practice law; died in Pittsburg, Kans., November 7, 1951; interment in Park Cemetery, Columbus, Kans.

WINTHROP, Robert Charles, a Representative and a Senator from Massachusetts; born in Boston, Mass., May 12, 1809; attended Roxbury High School, and was graduated from Harvard University in 1828; studied law with Daniel Webster; was admitted to the bar in 1831 and practiced in Boston; member of the State house of representatives 1835–1840, and served as speaker 1838–1840; elected as a Whig to the Twenty-sixth Congress to fill the vacancy caused by the resignation of Abbott Lawrence; reelected to the Twenty-seventh Congress and served from November 9, 1840, to May 25, 1842, when he resigned; subsequently elected to the Twenty-seventh Congress to fill the vacancy caused by the resignation of his successor, Nathan Appleton; reelected to the Twenty-eighth and to the three succeeding Congresses and served from November 29, 1842, to July 30, 1850, when he again resigned to become Senator; was Speaker of the House of Representatives during the Thirtieth Congress and a portion of the Thirty-first Congress; appointed to the United States Senate on July 27, 1850, to fill the vacancy caused by the resignation of Daniel Webster and served from July 30, 1850, to February 1, 1851, when a successor was elected; unsuccessful candidate for election to the vacancy in 1851; was an unsuccessful candidate for Governor of Massachusetts the same year; was presidential elector on the Whig ticket of Scott and Graham in 1852; engaged in literary, historical, and philanthropic pursuits; died in Boston, Mass., November 16, 1894; interment in Mount Auburn Cemetery, Cambridge, Middlesex County, Mass.

WISE, George Douglas (cousin of John Sergeant Wise and Richard Alsop Wise and nephew of Henry Alexander Wise), a Representative from Virginia; born at "Deep Creek," the Wise estate in Accomack County, near Onancock, Va., June 4, 1831; was graduated from Indiana University at Bloomington; studied law in William and Mary College, Williamsburg, Va.; was admitted to the bar and commenced practice in Richmond, Henrico County, Va.; captain in the Confederate Army during the Civil War; Commonwealth attorney of the city of Richmond from 1870 to 1889, when he resigned; elected as a Democrat to the Forty-seventh and to the three succeeding Congresses (March 4, 1881–March 3, 1889); presented credentials as a Member-elect to the Fifty-first Congress and served from March 4, 1889, to April 10, 1890, when he was succeeded by Edmund Waddill, Jr., who contested his election; elected to the Fifty-second and Fifty-third Congresses (March 4, 1891–March 3, 1895); died in Richmond, Va., February 4, 1898; interment in Hollywood Cemetery.

WISE, Henry Alexander (father of John Sergeant Wise and Richard Alsop Wise and uncle of George Douglas Wise), a Representative from Virginia; born in Drummondtown, Accomack County, Va., December 3, 1806; was privately tutored until his twelfth year and then entered Margaret Academy, near Pungoteague, Accomack County; was graduated from Washington College, Pennsylvania, in 1825; studied law in Winchester, Va.; was admitted to the bar in 1828 and commenced practice in Nashville, Davidson County, Tenn.; returned to Virginia in 1830; held several local offices; elected as a Jackson Democrat to the Twenty-third and Twenty-fourth Congresses, as a Whig to the Twenty-fifth, Twenty-sixth, and Twenty-seventh Congresses, and as a Tyler Democrat to the Twenty-eighth Congress and served from March 4, 1833, until his resignation on February 12, 1844; declined the portfolio of the Navy in the Cabinet of President Tyler in 1841; was appointed Minister to France in 1843, but was not confirmed; Minister to Brazil 1844–1847; presidential elector on the Democratic ticket of Cass and Butler in 1848; delegate to the State constitutional convention in 1850; was presidential elector on the Democratic ticket of Pierce and King in 1852; Governor of Virginia 1856–1860; served in the Confederate Army during the Civil War; resumed the practice of law in Richmond, Henrico County, Va.; served on the commission to fix the boundary line between Virginia and Maryland; died in Richmond, Va., September 12, 1876; interment in Hollywood Cemetery.

WISE, James Walter, a Representative from Georgia; born near McDonough, Henry County, Ga., March 3, 1868; attended the common schools; studied law at Emory College, Oxford, Ga.; was admitted to the bar in 1892 and commenced practice in Fayetteville, Fayette County, Ga., in January 1893; member of the State house of representatives 1902–1908; was mayor of Fayetteville 1904–1906; solicitor general of the Flint judicial circuit 1908–1912; elected as a Democrat to the Sixty-fourth and to the four succeeding Congresses (March 4, 1915–March 3, 1925); declined to be a candidate for renomination in 1924; owing to prolonged illness was unable to qualify for or attend the Sixty-eighth Congress; died in Atlanta, Fulton County, Ga., on September 8, 1925; interment in McDonough Cemetery, McDonough, Ga.

WISE, John Sergeant (son of Henry Alexander Wise, grandson of John Sergeant, brother of Richard Alsop Wise, and cousin of George Douglas Wise), a Representative from Virginia; born in Rio de Janeiro, Brazil, December 27, 1846, while his father was United States Minister to that country; attended preparatory schools in Goochland and Princess Anne Counties, Va., and the Virginia Military Institute at Lexington in 1862; participated with the institute cadets in the Battle of New Market during the Civil War and was slightly wounded; subsequently became a lieutenant in the Confederate Army; was graduated from the law department of the University of Virginia at Charlottesville in 1867; was admitted to the bar the same year and commenced practice in Richmond, Henrico County, Va.; United States attorney for the eastern district of Virginia from May 1882 to March 1883, when he resigned, having been elected to Congress; elected as a Readjuster to the Forty-eighth Congress (March 4, 1883–March 3, 1885); was not a candidate for renomination in 1884; unsuccessful Republican candidate for Governor of Virginia in 1885; moved to New York City and engaged in the practice of his profession; died at the summer home of his son, near Princess Anne, Somerset County, Md., May 12, 1913; interment in Hollywood Cemetery, Richmond, Va.

WISE, Morgan Ringland, a Representative from Pennsylvania; born in West Bethlehem, Washington County, Pa., June 7, 1825; attended the public schools; taught school; crossed the Plains and engaged in gold mining in California in 1850; while there volunteered, under Major Stammins, to defend the miners against the depredations of the Indians; returned to Pennsylvania, and was graduated from Waynesburg College, Pennsylvania, in 1856; engaged in agricultural pursuits; member of the State house of representatives from 1874 to 1878; elected as a Democrat to the Forty-sixth and Forty-seventh Congresses (March 4, 1879–March 3, 1883); was not a candidate for renomination in 1882; moved to Arizona and engaged in cattle raising; consular agent at Nogales, Mexico, from February 20, 1888, to May 31, 1900; died in Coraopolis, Pa., on April 13, 1903; interment in Greenmount Cemetery, Waynesburg, Pa.

WISE, Richard Alsop (son of Henry Alexander Wise, grandson of John Sergeant, brother of John Sergeant Wise, and cousin of George Douglas Wise), a Representative from Virginia; born in Philadelphia, Pa., September 2, 1843; attended private schools in Richmond, Va., Harrison's Academy, Albemarle County, Va., and William and Mary College, Williamsburg, Va., for two years; during the Civil War served in the Confederate Army as a private in Stuart's cavalry and as assistant inspector general of Wise's brigade, Army of Northern Virginia; was graduated in medicine from the Medical College of Virginia in 1867 and practiced; professor in William and Mary College 1869–1881; delegate to all Republican State conventions from 1879 to 1900; superintendent of the Eastern Lunatic Asylum of Virginia 1882–1885; member of the State house of delegates 1885–1887; clerk of the circuit and county courts of the city of Williamsburg and county of James City 1888–1894; delegate to the Republican National Conventions in 1892, 1896, and 1900; successfully contested as a Republican the election of William A. Young to the Fifty-fifth Congress and served from April 26, 1898, to March 3, 1899; was again successful in contesting the election of William A. Young to the Fifty-sixth Congress and served from March 12, 1900, until his death in Williamsburg, Va., December 21, 1900; interment in Hollywood Cemetery, Richmond, Va.

WISNER, Henry, a Delegate from New York; born near Florida, Orange County, N. Y., in 1720; completed academic studies; invested in real estate and built a gristmill near Goshen, N. Y.; assistant justice of the court of common pleas; member of the colonial assembly 1759–1769; delegate to the New York provincial convention in 1775; Member of the Continental Congress 1774–1776; voted for the Declaration of Independence, but was absent at the time it was signed, attending the Provincial Congress in New York, to which he had just been elected; member of the Provincial Congress in 1776 and 1777; erected three powder mills in the vicinity of Goshen, Orange County, N. Y., and supplied powder to the Continental Army during the Revolution; one of the committee that framed the first constitution of New York in 1777; member of the commission to provide for fortifying the Hudson River, which constructed forts at West Point and placed the chain across the river in 1777 and 1778; served in the State senate 1777–1782; established an academy at Goshen in 1784; member of the first board of regents of the University of the State of New York 1784–1787; served as a member of the State convention that ratified the Federal Constitution in 1788; died in Goshen, N. Y., on March 4, 1790; interment in the Old Wallkill Cemetery, Phillipsburg, N. Y.

WITCHER, John Seashoal, a Representative from West Virginia; born in Cabell County, Va. (now West Virginia), July 15, 1839; attended the public schools; elected clerk of the circuit court of Cabell County in 1861; during the Civil War enrolled in the Union Army as a first lieutenant, Third Regiment, West Virginia Volunteer Cavalry, December 13, 1862; promoted to captain September 8, 1863, major May 23, 1864, lieutenant colonel May 6, 1865; brevetted colonel of Volunteers March 13, 1865, for "gallant and meritorious services during the Shenandoah campaign of 1864 and the final campaign around Richmond and Petersburg, Va., in the spring of 1865, and especially at the Battle of Fords Station, Virginia"; brigadier general of Volunteers March 3, 1865, "for like services"; honorably mustered out June 30, 1865; member of the State house of delegates in 1865; secretary of state of West Virginia 1866–1869; elected as a Republican to the Forty-first Congress (March 4, 1869–March 3, 1871); unsuccessful candidate for reelection in 1870 to the Forty-second Congress; appointed by President Grant as collector of internal revenue for the third district of West Virginia and served from April 1, 1871, to October 1, 1876; served as United States pension agent at Washington, D. C., from July 7, 1878, to October 3, 1880; major and paymaster, United States Army, from October 5, 1880, until he retired September 8, 1899; moved to Salt Lake City, Utah, in 1891, and died there July 8, 1906; interment in Mount Olivet Cemetery.

WITHERELL, James, a Representative from Vermont; born in Mansfield, Mass., June 16, 1759; completed preparatory studies; served in the Revolutionary Army as a member of the Eleventh Massachusetts Regiment 1775–1783; studied medicine and was licensed to practice in 1788; moved to Hampton, Vt., in 1788 and to Fair Haven, Vt., in 1789 and continued the practice of his profession; member of the State house of representatives 1798–1802; associate county judge 1801–1803; judge of Rutland County 1803–1806; executive councilor 1802–1806; elected as a Democrat to the Tenth Congress and served from March 4, 1807, to May 1, 1808, when he resigned; appointed United States judge for the Territory of Michigan in 1808 and served until 1828, when he resigned to become secretary of the Territory; during the War of 1812 was in command of the troops at Detroit in the absence of General Hull, and was taken prisoner when the latter surrendered; lived in Fair Haven, Vt., while on parole; was exchanged and returned to his duties in Detroit; secretary of Michigan Territory by appointment of President John Quincy Adams 1828–1830; died in Detroit, Mich., January 9, 1838; interment in the Russell Street Cemetery; reinterment in Elmwood Cemetery.

WITHERS, Garrett Lee, a Senator and a Representative from Kentucky; born on a farm in Webster County, near Clay, Ky., June 21, 1884; student of Providence M. and F. Academy and Southern Normal School, Bowling Green, Ky.; was admitted to the bar in 1908; practicing attorney in Webster County, Ky., 1911–1953; served as clerk of Webster County Circuit Court 1910–1912 and as master commissioner 1913–1917; member of Kentucky Highway Commission 1932–1936; referee in bankruptcy 1941–1945; appointed commissioner, Kentucky Department of Highways, December 10, 1947, serving until January 17, 1949; appointed as a Democrat to the United States Senate to fill the vacancy caused by the resignation of Alben W. Barkley, and served from January 20, 1949, to November 26, 1950, a successor having been elected; was not a candidate for election to the vacancy; member of the Kentucky House of Representatives in 1951; elected as a Democrat to the Eighty-second Congress to fill the vacancy caused by the death of John A. Whitaker; reelected to the Eighty-third Congress and served from

August 2, 1952, until his death in the naval hospital at Bethesda, Md., April 30, 1953; interment in the I. O. O. F. Cemetery, Clay, Ky.

WITHERS, Robert Enoch (cousin of Thomas Withers Chinn), a Senator from Virginia; born near Lynchburg, Campbell County, Va., September 18, 1821; attended private schools; was graduated from the medical department of the University of Virginia at Charlottesville in 1841 and commenced practice in Campbell County; moved to Danville, Pittsylvania County, Va., in 1858; during the Civil War entered the Confederate Army as major of Infantry in April 1861 and was promoted to colonel of the Eighteenth Virginia Infantry, which he commanded until retired in consequence of numerous disabling wounds; appointed to command the post at Danville, Va., which position he held until the close of the war; moved to Lynchburg, Va., in January 1866 and established the Lynchburg News, a daily paper devoted to the interests of the Conservative Party; nominated for Governor by that party, but withdrew in favor of the nominee of the Liberal Republicans; presidential elector on the Democratic ticket of Greeley and Brown in 1872; elected Lieutenant Governor in 1873; elected as a Conservative to the United States Senate and served from March 4, 1875, to March 3, 1881; unsuccessful candidate for reelection in 1881; appointed by President Cleveland as United States consul at Hong Kong, China, on April 28, 1885, and served until March 31, 1889, when he resigned; returned to Wytheville, Wythe County, Va.; died at "Ingleside," Wytheville, Va., September 21, 1907; interment in the East End Cemetery.

WITHERSPOON, John, a Delegate from New Jersey; born in Gifford, Haddingtonshire, Scotland, February 5, 1723; completed preparatory studies; was graduated from Edinburgh University in 1739; studied theology at Edinburgh; was licensed in 1743 and ordained minister of the parish of Beith in 1745; was the author of various pamphlets dealing with controversial religious subjects; installed pastor at Paisley June 16, 1757; moderator of the synod of Glasgow and Ayr in 1758; declined calls to Rotterdam in 1759, Dundee in 1762, and Dublin in 1766; also declined the presidency of the College of New Jersey (now Princeton University) in 1766, but accepted the second invitation of that institution, and was inaugurated as president August 17, 1768; became a leader of Presbyterians in America; member of the committee on correspondence from Somerset County July 28, 1775; member of the Provincial Congress of New Jersey from June 10 to June 22, 1776; Member of the Continental Congress from June 22, 1776, to December 1, 1779, from December 1, 1780, to December 1, 1781, and from May 20 to November 5, 1782; a signer of the Declaration of Independence; member of the secret committee of the Congress on the conduct of the war and member of the board of war in 1778; member of the State council in 1780; drafted the instructions of June 1781 to the American peace commissioners; served in the State general assembly in 1783 and 1789; member of the State convention to ratify the Federal Constitution in 1787; after the war returned to Princeton, where he continued his duties as president, although retiring later to his farm, "Tusculum," near Princeton, N. J.; continued his interest in public affairs; throughout his life was a prolific writer, and after his death his works were collected and published; became blind in 1792; died on his farm near Princeton, N. J., November 15, 1794; interment in the presidents' lot in the Witherspoon Street Graveyard, Princeton, N. J.

WITHERSPOON, Robert (great-great-grandfather of Robert Witherspoon Hemphill), a Representative from South Carolina; born near Kingstree, Williamsburg County, S. C., January 29, 1767; attended the best schools of the community; elected State treasurer in 1800 and served one term; was a member of the State house of representatives 1806–1808; elected as a Democrat to the Eleventh Congress (March 4, 1809–March 3, 1811); declined to be a candidate for reelection; had large planting interests in Sumter County, S. C.; opposed the nullification act in 1832; died near Mayesville, Sumter County, S. C., October 11, 1837; interment in the Salem Brick Church Cemetery.

WITHERSPOON, Samuel Andrew, a Representative from Mississippi; born near Columbus, Lowndes County, Miss., May 4, 1855; attended the public schools; in 1872 moved with his mother to Oxford, Miss.; was graduated from the University of Mississippi at Oxford in 1876; professor in the University of Mississippi 1876–1879; studied law; was admitted to the bar in 1879 and commenced practice in Meridian, Lauderdale County, Miss., the same year; elected as a Democrat to the Sixty-second, Sixty-third, and Sixty-fourth Congresses and served from March 4, 1911, until his death in Meridian, Miss., November 24, 1915; interment in Rose Hill Cemetery.

WITHROW, Gardner Robert, a Representative from Wisconsin; born in La Crosse, Wis., October 5, 1892; attended the grade and high schools; after two years of legal training engaged in railroading as a fireman and conductor 1912–1931; member of the Wisconsin Assembly in 1926 and 1927; served as State representative for the railroad brotherhoods 1928–1931; elected as a Republican to the Seventy-second and Seventy-third Congresses and as a Progressive to the Seventy-fourth and Seventy-fifth Congresses (March 4, 1931–January 3, 1939); unsuccessful candidate for reelection in 1938 to the Seventy-sixth Congress, and for election in 1940 to the Seventy-seventh Congress and in 1942 to the Seventy-eighth Congress; resumed activities as State representative for the Brotherhood of Railroad Trainmen; elected as a Republican to the Eighty-first and to the five succeeding Congresses (January 3, 1949–January 3, 1961); did not seek renomination in 1960; is a resident of La Crosse, Wis.

WITTE, William Henry, a Representative from Pennsylvania; born in Columbia, Morris County, N. J., October 4, 1817; moved to Springtown, Bucks County, Pa., and attended the common schools; moved to Philadelphia in 1840; engaged in mercantile pursuits and the real-estate business; elected as a Democrat to the Thirty-third Congress (March 4, 1853–March 3, 1855); engaged in newspaper work and resumed real-estate interests; died in Philadelphia, Pa., November 24, 1876; interment in Durham Cemetery, Durham, Bucks County, Pa.

WOFFORD, Thomas Albert, a Senator from South Carolina; born in Madden Station, Laurens County, S. C., September 27, 1908; attended New Prospect Elementary School and Laurens High School; graduated from the University of South Carolina at Columbia in 1928 and from Harvard Law School in 1931; was admitted to the bar in 1931 and commenced the practice of law in Greenville, S. C.; assistant solicitor of thirteenth judicial circuit in 1935 and 1936; assistant United States district attorney 1937–1944; member, board of trustees, Winthrop College 1944–1956; appointed as a Democrat to the United States Senate to fill the vacancy caused by the resignation of Strom Thurmond and served from April 5, 1956, to November 6, 1956; was not a candidate to fill the vacancy; engaged in general practice of law; is a resident of Greenville, S. C.

WOLCOTT, Edward Oliver, a Senator from Colorado; born in Long Meadow, Hampden County, Mass., March 26, 1848; attended the common schools, Yale College, and Norwich

(Conn.) Academy; served in the One Hundred and Fiftieth Regiment, Ohio Volunteer Infantry, during the Civil War; was graduated from the law department of Harvard University in 1871; moved to Blackhawk, Gilpin County, Colo., in September 1871 and taught school; moved to Georgetown, Clear Creek County, Colo., in December 1871 and was admitted to the practice of law; elected district attorney in 1876; moved to Denver in 1879; member of the State senate 1879–1882; elected in 1889 as a Republican to the United States Senate; reelected in 1895 and served from March 4, 1889, to March 3, 1901; resumed the practice of his profession in Denver, Colo.; delegate to the Republican National Conventions in 1892 and 1900; died in Monte Carlo, Principality of Monaco, March 1, 1905; remains were cremated in Paris, France, and the ashes interred in Woodlawn Cemetery, New York City.

WOLCOTT, Jesse Paine, a Representative from Michigan; born in Gardner, Worcester County, Mass., March 3, 1893; attended the common and high schools at Gardner, Mass., and the Detroit (Mich.) Technical Institute; was graduated from the Detroit College of Law, Detroit, Mich., in 1915; was admitted to the bar the same year and commenced practice in Detroit, Mich.; during the First World War served overseas as a second lieutenant in a machine-gun company of the Twenty-sixth Infantry, First Division, 1917–1919; after the war settled in Port Huron, Mich., and resumed the practice of law; assistant police judge of Port Huron in 1921; assistant prosecuting attorney of St. Clair County, Mich., 1922–1926; prosecuting attorney 1927–1930; elected as a Republican to the Seventy-second and to the twelve succeeding Congresses (March 4, 1931–January 3, 1957); was not a candidate for renomination in 1956; member, Federal Deposit Insurance Corporation since 1958; resides in Chevy Chase, Md.

WOLCOTT, Josiah Oliver, a Senator from Delaware; born in Dover, Del., October 31, 1877; attended the public schools and Wilmington Conference Academy, Dover, Del., and was graduated from Wesleyan University, Middletown, Conn., in 1901; studied law; was admitted to the bar in 1904 and commenced practice in Wilmington, Del.; member of the American Bar Association; deputy attorney general of Delaware 1909–1913; attorney general of Delaware 1913–1917; elected as a Democrat to the United States Senate and served from March 4, 1917, to July 2, 1921, when he resigned to accept a judicial position; appointed chancellor of Delaware in 1921 and served until his death in Dover, Del., November 11, 1938; interment in Lake Side Methodist Episcopal Cemetery.

WOLCOTT, Oliver, a Delegate from Connecticut; born in Windsor, Conn., December 1, 1726; was graduated from Yale College in 1747; commissioned a captain by the Governor of New York in 1747; raised a company of Volunteers and served on the northwestern frontier until the peace of Aix-la-Chapelle; returned to Connecticut and settled in Litchfield; studied medicine, but did not practice; elected sheriff of the newly organized county of Litchfield, Conn., in 1751; member of the State council 1774–1786 and at the same time judge of the county court of common pleas; judge of probate for the Litchfield district many years; major general of militia; appointed by the Continental Congress in 1775 as one of the commissioners of Indian affairs for the northern department, intrusted with the task of inducing the Iroquois Indians to remain neutral; Member of the Continental Congress 1775–1778 and 1780–1784; a signer of the Declaration of Independence; commander of the fourteen Connecticut regiments sent for the defense of New York in 1776, and divided his time between Army service and service in Congress; commanded a brigade of militia which took part

in the defeat of General Burgoyne in 1777; Lieutenant Governor of Connecticut 1786–1796; elected Governor in 1796 and served until his death in Litchfield, Conn., December 1, 1797; interment in the East Cemetery.

WOLF, George, a Representative from Pennsylvania; born in Allen Township, Northampton County, Pa., August 12, 1777; pursued preparatory studies; studied law; was admitted to the bar in 1799 and commenced practice in Easton, Pa.; postmaster of Easton in 1802 and 1803; clerk of the orphans' court of Northampton County 1803–1809; member of the State house of representatives in 1814; elected as a Democrat to the Eighteenth Congress to fill the vacancy caused by the resignation of Thomas J. Rogers; reelected to the Nineteenth, Twentieth, and Twenty-first Congresses and served from December 9, 1824, until his resignation in 1829 before the convening of the Twenty-first Congress; Governor of Pennsylvania 1829–1835; was an unsuccessful candidate for reelection in 1834; first Comptroller of the Treasury of the United States from June 18, 1836, to February 23, 1838; appointed collector of customs of the port of Philadelphia in 1838 and served until his death in Philadelphia, Pa., on March 11, 1840; interment in Harrisburg Cemetery, Harrisburg, Pa.

WOLF, Harry Benjamin, a Representative from Maryland; born in Baltimore, Md., June 16, 1880; attended the public schools of Baltimore, and was graduated from the law department of the University of Maryland at Baltimore in 1901; was admitted to the bar the same year and commenced the practice of law in Baltimore; also engaged in the real-estate business and hotel-property investments; member of the State house of delegates 1906–1908; elected as a Democrat to the Sixtieth Congress (March 4, 1907–March 3, 1909); unsuccessful candidate for reelection in 1908 to the Sixty-first Congress; resumed the practice of his profession and other business interests in Baltimore, Md.; died in Baltimore, Md., February 17, 1944; interment in Hebrew Friendship Cemetery.

WOLF, Leonard George, a Representative from Iowa; born on a farm in Dane County, near Mazomanie, Wis., October 29, 1925; attended the public schools of Mazomanie, Wis.; during World War II served in the United States Navy 1944–1946, with service in the Pacific Theater; graduated from the University of Wisconsin in agricultural economics in 1949 and moved to Elkader, Iowa, the same year; retail feed dealer in Elkader, Iowa, 1952–1958; also public speaker and lecturer; unsuccessful candidate for election in 1956 to the Eighty-fifth Congress; elected as a Democrat to the Eighty-sixth Congress (January 3, 1959–January 3, 1961); unsuccessful candidate for reelection in 1960 to the Eighty-seventh Congress; in 1961 was appointed special assistant to the director, International Cooperation Administration Mission in Brazil; is a resident of Elkader, Iowa.

WOLF, William Penn, a Representative from Iowa; born in Harrisburg, Stark County, Ohio, December 1, 1833; attended the public schools and Holbrook Seminary; moved to Cedar County, Iowa, in 1856; studied law; was admitted to the bar in 1859 and commenced practice in Tipton, Cedar County, Iowa; superintendent of public schools; member of the State house of representatives in 1863 and 1864; during the Civil War served in the Union Army as captain of Company I, Forty-sixth Regiment, Iowa Volunteer Infantry; wounded in action July 24, 1864; appointed assistant assessor of internal revenue in 1865; member of the State senate 1867–1869; elected as a Republican to the Forty-first Congress to fill the vacancy caused by the death of William Smyth and served from December 6, 1870, to March 3, 1871; resumed the practice of law in Tipton, Iowa; again a member of the State house of representatives 1881–1885, and was chosen speaker in 1884; elected judge of the eighteenth judicial district in the fall of 1894 and continued in this capacity until his death in Tipton, Iowa, on September 19, 1896; interment in the Masonic Cemetery.

WOLFE, Simeon Kalfius, a Representative from Indiana; born near Georgetown, Floyd County, Ind., February 14, 1824; attended Floyd County schools, and was graduated from the law department of the University of Indiana at Bloomington in 1850; was admitted to the bar in 1851 and commenced practice in Corydon, Harrison County, Ind.; presidential elector on the Democratic ticket of Buchanan and Breckinridge in 1856; edited and published the Corydon Democrat from 1857 to 1865; member of the State senate 1860–1864; delegate to the Democratic National Conventions at Charleston and Baltimore in 1860; moved to New Albany in 1870 and continued the practice of law; elected as a Democrat to the Forty-third Congress (March 4, 1873–March 3, 1875); was not a candidate for renomination in 1874; resumed the practice of law; judge of the Floyd and Clark circuit court 1880–1884; died in New Albany, Floyd County, Ind., November 18, 1888; interment in Fairview Cemetery.

WOLFENDEN, James, a Representative from Pennsylvania; born in Cardington, Delaware County, Pa., on July 25, 1889; attended the public schools, the Friends' Central School, and Penn Charter Academy, Philadelphia, Pa.; engaged in the manufacture of cotton and woolen goods, Cardington, Pa.; elected as a Republican to the Seventieth Congress to fill the vacancy caused by the death of Thomas S. Butler; reelected to the Seventy-first and to the eight succeeding Congresses and served from November 6, 1928, to January 3, 1947; was not a candidate for renomination in 1946; retired from political activities; died in Philadelphia, Pa., April 8, 1949; interment in Friends Cemetery, Upper Darby, Pa.

WOLFF, Joseph Scott, a Representative from Missouri; born on a farm in Westmoreland County near Greensburg, Pa., June 14, 1878; attended the public schools; served with the Fourth United States Cavalry in the Philippine Islands during the Spanish-American War 1899–1901; moved to St. Louis, Mo., in 1901; was graduated from the dental department of Washington University, St. Louis, Mo., in 1905 and practiced his profession in St. Louis and Festus, Mo.; mayor of Festus, Jefferson County, Mo., 1907–1911 and 1915–1917; member of the State house of representatives 1913–1915; was graduated from the St. Louis College of Law and Finance in 1923; was admitted to the bar the same year and commenced practice in Festus, Mo.; elected as a Democrat to the Sixty-eighth Congress (March 4, 1923–March 3, 1925); unsuccessful candidate for reelection in 1924 to the Sixty-ninth Congress; moved to Kansas City in 1924 and continued the practice of dentistry and law until retirement in 1957; died in Kansas City, Mo., February 27, 1958; interment in Gambel Cemetery, Festus, Mo.

WOLFORD, Frank Lane, a Representative from Kentucky; born near Columbia, Adair County, Ky., September 2, 1817; attended the common schools; studied law; was admitted to the bar and commenced practice in Liberty, Casey County, Ky.; member of the State house of representatives in 1847, 1848, 1865, and 1866; presidential elector on the Democratic ticket of McClellan and Pendleton in 1864 and of Seymour and Blair in 1868; during the Civil War served as colonel of the First Kentucky Volunteer Cavalry 1861–1864; adjutant general of the State of Kentucky in 1867 and 1868; elected as a Democrat to the Forty-eighth and Forty-ninth Congresses (March 4, 1883–March 3, 1887); unsuccessful candidate for reelection in 1886 to the Fiftieth Congress; continued the practice of law in Columbia, Ky., until his death there August 2, 1895; interment in Columbia Cemetery.

WOLVERTON, Charles Anderson, a Representative from New Jersey; born in Camden, N. J., October 24, 1880; attended the public schools, and was graduated from the law department of the University of Pennsylvania at Philadelphia in 1900; was admitted to the bar in 1901 and began practice in Camden, N. J.; assistant prosecutor of Camden County, N. J., 1906–1913; special assistant attorney general of New Jersey in 1913 and 1914; member of the State house of assembly 1915–1918, serving as speaker in 1918; Federal food administrator for Camden County 1917–1919; prosecutor of pleas of Camden County 1918–1923; alternate delegate to the Republican National Convention at Chicago in 1920; elected as a Republican to the Seventieth and to the fifteen succeeding Congresses (March 4, 1927–January 3, 1959); was not a candidate for renomination in 1958; resumed the practice of law in Camden, N. J.; is a resident of Merchantville, N. J.

WOLVERTON, John Marshall, a Representative from West Virginia; born in Big Bend, Calhoun County, W. Va., January 31, 1872; attended country schools and Glenville and Fairmont State Normal Schools; was graduated from the law department of the West Virginia University at Morgantown in 1901; was admitted to the bar the same year and commenced practice in Grantsville, Calhoun County, W. Va.; moved to Richwood in 1904; mayor of Richwood in 1918 and 1919; prosecuting attorney of Nicholas County 1913–1917 and 1921–1925; elected as a Republican to the Sixty-ninth Congress (March 4, 1925–March 3, 1927); unsuccessful candidate for reelection in 1926 to the Seventieth Congress; elected to the Seventy-first Congress (March 4, 1929–March 3, 1931); unsuccessful candidate for reelection in 1930 to the Seventy-second Congress, and for election in 1932 to the Seventy-third Congress and in 1936 to the Seventy-fifth Congress; resumed the practice of law in Richwood, W. Va., where he died August 19, 1944; interment in the Odd Fellows Cemetery.

WOLVERTON, Simon Peter, a Representative from Pennsylvania; born in Rush Township, Northumberland County, Pa., January 28, 1837; attended the common schools and Danville (Pa.) Academy, and was graduated from Lewisburg University (now Bucknell University), Lewisburg, Pa., in 1860; principal of Sunbury (Pa.) Academy 1860–1862; studied law; was admitted to the bar in 1862 and commenced practice in Sunbury; during the Civil War raised a company of emergency men, of which he was made captain in 1862, and served in the Eighteenth Regiment, Pennsylvania Volunteers; chosen captain of Company F, Thirty-sixth Regiment, Pennsylvania Volunteers, in June 1863; member of the State senate in 1878, 1880, and 1884; Democratic nominee for the United States Senate in the joint convention of 1884; elected as a Democrat to the Fifty-second and Fifty-third Congresses (March 4, 1891–March 3, 1895); was not a candidate for renomination in 1894; continued the practice of law; died in Sunbury, Northumberland County, Pa., October 25, 1910; interment in Pomfret-Manor Cemetery.

WOOD, Abiel, a Representative from Massachusetts; born in Wiscasset, Maine (then a district of Massachusetts), July 22, 1772; attended the common schools; engaged in mercantile pursuits; member of the Massachusetts House of Representatives 1807–1811, and again in 1816; presidential elector on the

Federalist ticket of Clinton and Ingersoll in 1812; elected as a Federalist to the Thirteenth Congress (March 4, 1813–March 3, 1815); unsuccessful candidate for reelection in 1814 to the Fourteenth Congress; delegate to the constitutional convention of Maine in 1819; State councilor of Maine in 1820 and 1821; resumed mercantile pursuits and also engaged in shipping; bank commissioner for Maine until his death in Belfast, Waldo County, Maine, October 26, 1834, while on an official visit; interment in Woodlawn Cemetery, Wiscasset, Lincoln County, Maine.

WOOD, Alan, Jr. (nephew of John Wood), a Representative from Pennsylvania; born in Philadelphia, Pa., July 6, 1834; attended private schools; employed in his father's mill at Delaware Iron Works, near Wilmington, Del.; moved to Conshohocken, Montgomery County, Pa., in 1857; engaged in iron manufacturing and banking; elected as a Republican to the Forty-fourth Congress (March 4, 1875–March 3, 1877); was not a candidate for renomination in 1876; resumed his former business activities and also engaged in agricultural pursuits; president of the Alan Wood Iron & Steel Co.; died in Philadelphia, Pa., October 31, 1902; interment in Woodland Cemetery.

WOOD, Amos Eastman, a Representative from Ohio; born in Ellisburg, N. Y., January 2, 1810; attended the common schools; moved to Sandusky County, Ohio, in 1833 and engaged in agricultural pursuits; member of the State house of representatives 1840–1842; served in the State senate in 1845; elected as a Democrat to the Thirty-first Congress to fill the vacancy caused by the death of Rudolphus Dickinson and served from December 3, 1849, until his death in Fort Wayne, Ind., November 19, 1850; interment in Woodville Cemetery, Woodville, Sandusky County, Ohio.

WOOD, Benjamin (brother of Fernando Wood), a Representative from New York; born in Shelbyville, Shelby County, Ky., October 13, 1820; moved to New York City with his parents; attended the public schools; entered the shipping business; purchased the Daily News in 1860 and was its editor and publisher until his death; chairman of Democratic Editors in 1860; elected as a Democrat to the Thirty-seventh and Thirty-eighth Congresses (March 4, 1861–March 3, 1865); member of the State senate in 1866 and 1867; elected to the Forty-seventh Congress (March 4, 1881–March 3, 1883); died in New York City February 21, 1900; interment in Calvary Cemetery, Long Island City, N. Y.

WOOD, Benson, a Representative from Illinois; born near Bridgewater, Susquehanna County, Pa., on March 31, 1839; attended the common schools, Montrose (Pa.) Academy, and Wyoming (Pa.) Seminary; moved to Illinois in 1859 and for two years was principal of a village school in Lee County; during the Civil War enlisted as first lieutenant of Company C, Thirty-fourth Regiment, Illinois Volunteer Infantry, September 7, 1861; promoted to captain May 1, 1862; honorably discharged January 29, 1863; was graduated from the law department of the University of Chicago in 1864; was admitted to the bar in 1864 and engaged in the practice of law in Effingham, Effingham County, Ill.; member of the State house of representatives in 1872; delegate to the Republican National Convention at Cincinnati in 1876 and at Chicago in 1888; mayor of Effingham 1881–1883; elected as a Republican to the Fifty-fourth Congress (March 4, 1895–March 3, 1897); was an unsuccessful candidate for reelection in 1896 to the Fifty-fifth Congress; resumed the practice of law in Effingham, Ill.; president of the Illinois Bar Association in 1899 and 1900; president of the Effingham State Bank 1903–1912, and chairman of the board of directors 1912–1915; died in Effingham, Ill., on August 27, 1915; interment in Oakridge Cemetery.

WOOD, Bradford Ripley, a Representative from New York; born in Westport, Conn., September 3, 1800; attended the common schools, and was graduated from Union College at Schenectady, N. Y., in 1824; was engaged in teaching and lecturing; studied law at the Litchfield (Conn.) Law School; was admitted to the bar in 1827 and commenced practice in Albany, N. Y.; on May 29, 1827, was made solicitor in the court of chancery of New York State, and on June 6, 1830, rose to the position of chancellor of the same court; became counselor in the New York Supreme Court in 1835 and in the United States Supreme Court in 1845; member of the Albany County board of supervisors in 1844; was elected as a Democrat to the Twenty-ninth Congress (March 4, 1845–March 3, 1847); unsuccessful candidate for reelection in 1846 to the Thirtieth Congress; was a member of the board of trustees of Union College 1848–1872; president of the Young Men's Temperance Society in 1851; trustee of Williams College, Williamstown, Mass., and the Albany Law School; vice president of the Albany Medical College; one of the founders of the Republican Party in New York State in 1856; vice president of the American Home Missionary Society; founder of the First Congregational Church in Albany; United States Minister to Denmark from 1861 to 1865; died in Albany, N. Y., September 26, 1889; interment in Albany Rural Cemetery, Albany County, N. Y.

WOOD, Ernest Edward, a Representative from Missouri; born in Chico, Butte County, Calif., August 24, 1875; attended the public schools and was graduated from the Stockton (Calif.) High School in 1892; appointed as a cadet to the United States Military Academy at West Point in 1893 and remained two years; studied law; was admitted to the bar in 1898 and commenced practice in St. Louis, Mo.; presented credentials as a Democratic Member-elect to the Fifty-ninth Congress and served from March 4, 1905, to June 23, 1906, when he was succeeded by Harry M. Coudrey, who contested his election; moved to Los Angeles, Calif., in 1907 and resumed the practice of law; died in Los Angeles, Calif., January 10, 1952; interment in Hollywood Cemetery, Hollywood, Calif.

WOOD, Fernando (brother of Benjamin Wood), a Representative from New York; born in Philadelphia, Pa., June 14, 1812; attended the public schools; moved with his father to New York City in 1820; was engaged in business as a shipping merchant in 1831; was elected as a Tammany Democrat to the Twenty-seventh Congress (March 4, 1841–March 3, 1843); unsuccessful candidate for reelection in 1842 to the Twenty-eighth Congress; appointed by Secretary of State John C. Calhoun dispatch agent for the State Department at the port of New York; reappointed to the position by Secretary of State James Buchanan and served from 1844 to 1847; unsuccessful candidate for mayor of New York in 1850 and in 1867; retired as a shipping merchant in 1850; mayor of New York City in 1855–1858, 1861, and 1862; elected as a Democrat to the Thirty-eighth Congress (March 4, 1863–March 3, 1865); unsuccessful candidate for reelection in 1864 to the Thirty-ninth Congress; elected to the Fortieth and to the seven succeeding Congresses and served from March 4, 1867, until his death at Hot Springs, Ark., February 13, 1881, before the beginning of the Forty-seventh Congress, to which he had been reelected; interment in Trinity Cemetery, New York City.

WOOD, Ira Wells, a Representative from New Jersey; born in Wilkes-Barre, Pa., on June 19, 1856; was graduated from Princeton College in 1877; studied law; was admitted to the bar in 1880 and commenced practice in Trenton, N. J.; was a member of the city board of education 1894–1896; served in the city council 1896–1900; president of the Board of Trade of Trenton

1896–1900; member of the State assembly in 1899 and 1900; commissioner for New Jersey to the Louisiana Purchase Exposition held in St. Louis, Mo., in 1904; delegate to the Interparliamentary Peace Union at Brussels, Belgium, in 1905; president of the Republican Club at Trenton; elected as a Republican to the Fifty-eighth Congress to fill the vacancy caused by the resignation of William M. Lanning; reelected to the Fifty-ninth and to the three succeeding Congresses and served from November 8, 1904, to March 3, 1913; declined to be a candidate for reelection to the Sixty-third Congress; retired from active pursuits and resided in Trenton, N. J., until his death there on October 5, 1931; interment in Mercer Cemetery.

WOOD, John (uncle of Alan Wood, Jr.), a Representative from Pennsylvania; born in Philadelphia, Pa., September 6, 1816; attended the Friends Society schools of Philadelphia; employed by his father in the manufacture of tools and agricultural machinery 1832–1840; engaged in the manufacture of iron and steel near Wilmington, Del., 1841–1844; moved to Conshohocken, Montgomery County, Pa., in 1844 and engaged in the milling of iron and steel; first burgess of Conshohocken, Pa.; elected as a Republican to the Thirty-sixth Congress (March 4, 1859–March 3, 1861); was not a candidate for renomination in 1860; resumed his former manufacturing pursuits; died in Conshohocken, Pa., May 28, 1898; interment in Montgomery Cemetery, Norristown, Montgomery County, Pa.

WOOD, John Jacob, a Representative from New York; born in Clarkstown (now New City), Rockland County, N. Y., February 16, 1784; town clerk of Clarkstown 1809–1812; inspector of schools in 1815, 1823, 1829–1831, 1835–1836; elected as a Jackson Democrat to the Twentieth Congress (March 4, 1827–March 3, 1829); again inspector of schools 1829–1831, 1835–1837; surrogate of Rockland County in 1837; delegate to the State constitutional convention in 1846; died at New City, Rockland County, N. Y., May 20, 1874; interment in Old Wood Burying Ground.

WOOD, John M., a Representative from Maine; born in Minisink, Orange County, N. Y., November 17, 1813; attended the common schools; engaged in railroad construction in New Jersey; moved to Portland, Maine, in 1846; was one of the contractors in the construction of the Atlantic & St. Lawrence Railroad; also engaged in banking; member of the State house of representatives in 1852 and 1853; owner and publisher of the Portland Daily Advertiser 1853–1857; elected as a Republican to the Thirty-fourth and Thirty-fifth Congresses (March 4, 1855–March 3, 1859); contractor for building the Air Line Railroad between Woonsocket and New Haven, Conn.; died while on a visit in Boston, Mass., December 24, 1864; interment in Greenwood Cemetery, Brooklyn, N. Y.

WOOD, John Stephens, a Representative from Georgia; born on a farm near Ball Ground, Cherokee County, Ga., February 8, 1885; attended the public schools and the North Georgia Agricultural College at Dahlonega; was graduated from the law department of Mercer University, Macon, Ga., in 1910; was admitted to the bar the same year and commenced practice in Jasper, Ga.; member of the State house of representatives in 1917; served as solicitor general of the Blue Ridge judicial circuit of Georgia 1921–1925, and as judge of superior courts of the Blue Ridge judicial circuit 1925–1931; elected as a Democrat to the Seventy-second and Seventy-third Congresses (March 4, 1931–January 3, 1935); unsuccessful candidate for renomination in 1934; resumed the practice of law; elected to the Seventy-ninth and to the three succeeding Congresses (January 3, 1945–January 3, 1953); was not a candidate for renomination in 1952; resumed law practice in Canton, Ga., where he now resides.

WOOD, John Travers, a Representative from Idaho; born in Wakefield, England, November 25, 1878; immigrated to the United States with his parents in 1889 and settled in Woodridge, N. Dak.; naturalized in 1901; attended the public schools; taught school for six years after self-study and passage of teacher's examination; graduated from Detroit College of Medicine in 1904 and practiced medicine in Hannah, N. Dak., for one year; moved to Coeur d'Alene, Idaho, in 1905 and licensed to practice medicine in 1906; surgeon for Chicago, Milwaukee & St. Paul Railroad 1910–1950; mayor of Coeur d'Alene in 1911 and 1912; founder and first president of Coeur d'Alene Hospital in 1908; during the First World War served as a lieutenant in the Medical Corps; physician, writer, lecturer, and a student of history and philosophy; elected as a Republican to the Eighty-second Congress (January 3, 1951–January 3, 1953); was an unsuccessful candidate for reelection in 1952 to the Eighty-third Congress; resumed the practice of medicine; died in Coeur d'Alene, Idaho, November 2, 1954; interment in Forest Cemetery.

WOOD, Joseph, a Delegate from Georgia; born in Pennsylvania in 1712; moved to Sunbury, St. John's Parish (afterward Liberty County), Ga., about 1774; served in the Revolutionary War as major, lieutenant colonel, and colonel of the Second Pennsylvania Battalion, which later became the Third Pennsylvania Regiment, and was on duty in Canada in 1776; returned to Georgia and engaged in planting; member of the State council of safety; Member of the Continental Congress 1777–1778; died on his plantation near Sunbury, Ga., in September 1791.

WOOD, Reuben Terrell, a Representative from Missouri; born on a farm near Springfield, Greene County, Mo., August 7, 1884; attended the public schools and received private instructions; apprenticed as a cigar maker in Springfield, Mo., in 1898; employed as a labor organization officer 1902–1912; served as president of the Missouri State Federation of Labor 1912–1932; during the First World War served on the State advisory board of the United States Fuel Administration and on the Missouri division of the United States Food Administration; elected as a Democrat to the Seventy-third and to the three succeeding Congresses and served from March 4, 1933, to January 3, 1941; was an unsuccessful candidate for election in 1940 to the Seventy-seventh Congress; resumed office as president of the Missouri State Federation of Labor until his retirement in May 1953; member of the Missouri Constitutional Convention in 1944; died in Springfield, Mo., July 16, 1955; interment in Greenlawn Cemetery.

WOOD, Silas, a Representative from New York; born in West Hills, near Huntington, Suffolk County, N. Y., September 14, 1769; pursued classical studies; was graduated from Princeton College in 1789 and during the five succeeding years was a teacher at that institution; studied law; was admitted to the bar and commenced practice in Huntington, N. Y.; was appointed district attorney of Suffolk County in 1818 and 1821; was elected as a Democrat to the Sixteenth and to the four succeeding Congresses (March 4, 1819–March 3, 1829); unsuccessful candidate for reelection in 1828 to the Twenty-first Congress; retired from all business and political activities; died in Huntington, N. Y., March 2, 1847; interment in the Old Public Cemetery on Main Street.

WOOD, Thomas Jefferson, a Representative from Indiana; born in Athens County, Ohio, September 30, 1844; moved with his parents to Vigo County, Ind., in 1853; attended the common schools; taught school two years; studied law in Terre Haute, Ind., and was graduated from the law department of the University of Michigan at Ann Arbor in 1867; moved to Crown

Point, Lake County, Ind., in November 1867 and practiced law; corporation treasurer 1870–1872; prosecuting attorney of Lake County 1872–1876; member of the State senate 1878–1882; elected as a Democrat to the Forty-eighth Congress (March 4, 1883–March 3, 1885); unsuccessful candidate for reelection; resumed the practice of law; died in Crown Point, Ind., October 13, 1908; interment in Maplewood Cemetery.

WOOD, Walter Abbott, a Representative from New York; born in Mason, N. H., October 23, 1815; moved to New York in 1816 with his parents, who settled in Rensselaerville; attended the common schools; moved to Hoosick Falls in 1835; became an inventor and manufacturer of reapers, mowers, and binders; elected as a Republican to the Forty-sixth and Forty-seventh Congresses (March 4, 1879–March 3, 1883); was not a candidate for renomination; returned to Hoosick Falls, N. Y., and resumed his former pursuits; died in Hoosick Falls, N. Y., January 15, 1892; interment in Maple Grove Cemetery.

WOOD, William Robert, a Representative from Indiana; born in Oxford, Benton County, Ind., on January 5, 1861; attended the public schools of Oxford, and was graduated from the law department of the University of Michigan at Ann Arbor in 1882; was admitted to the bar the same year and commenced practice in LaFayette, Tippecanoe County; prosecuting attorney of Tippecanoe County 1890–1894; member of the State senate 1896–1914, and served as president pro tempore 1899–1907; Republican floor leader of the State senate for four sessions; delegate to the Republican National Conventions in 1912, 1916, 1920, and 1924; chairman of the Republican National congressional committee 1920–1933; elected as a Republican to the Sixty-fourth and to the eight succeeding Congresses (March 4, 1915–March 3, 1933); unsuccessful candidate for reelection in 1932 to the Seventy-third Congress; died while on a visit in New York City, N. Y., March 7, 1933; interment in Spring Vale Cemetery, LaFayette, Ind.

WOODARD, Frederick Augustus, a Representative from North Carolina; born near Wilson, Wilson County, N. C., February 12, 1854; attended private schools in Wilson County; studied law at the law school of Chief Justice Richmond Mumford Pearson; was admitted to the bar in 1873 and commenced practice in Wilson, N. C.; vice president of the First National Bank of Wilson; elected as a Democrat to the Fifty-third and Fifty-fourth Congresses (March 4, 1893–March 3, 1897); unsuccessful candidate for reelection to the Fifty-fifth Congress; resumed the practice of law in Wilson, N. C., and died there May 8, 1915; interment in Maplewood Cemetery.

WOODBRIDGE, Frederick Enoch, a Representative from Vermont; born in Vergennes, Addison County, Vt., August 29, 1818; was graduated from the University of Vermont at Burlington in 1840; studied law; was admitted to the bar in 1843 and commenced practice in Vergennes; member of the State house of representatives in 1849, 1857, and 1858; mayor of Vergennes for five years; State auditor 1850–1852; prosecuting attorney 1854–1858; engaged in the construction of railroads; member of the State senate in 1860 and 1861 and served as president pro tempore in the latter year; elected as a Republican to the Thirty-eighth, Thirty-ninth, and Fortieth Congresses (March 4, 1863–March 3, 1869); resumed the practice of his profession; died in Vergennes, Vt., April 25, 1888; interment in Prospect Cemetery.

WOODBRIDGE, William, a Delegate and a Senator from Michigan; born in Norwich, Conn., August 20, 1780; moved with his father to Marietta, Ohio, in 1791 but in a few years returned to Litchfield, Conn., and studied law; returned to Ohio in 1799; was admitted to the Ohio bar in 1806 and commenced the practice of law in Marietta; member of the State house of representatives in 1807; prosecuting attorney for New London (now Washington) County, Ohio, 1808–1814; served in the State senate 1808–1814; moved to Detroit, Mich.; collector of customs at Detroit, Mich., from January 24, 1814, to June 12, 1829; appointed secretary of Michigan Territory on October 5, 1814, and served until appointed judge of the Territory on January 15, 1828; elected as a Delegate to the Sixteenth Congress and served from March 4, 1819, to August 9, 1820, when he resigned; was judge of the supreme court of Michigan Territory from 1828 to 1832; delegate to the State constitutional convention in 1835; member of the State senate in 1837; Governor of Michigan in 1840 and 1841; elected by a combination of Whigs and Democrats to the United States Senate and served from March 4, 1841, to March 3, 1847; retired from public life and devoted his time to horticulture; died in Detroit, Mich., October 20, 1861; interment in Elmwood Cemetery.

WOODBURN, William, a Representative from Nevada; born in County Wicklow, Ireland, April 14, 1838; immigrated with his parents to the United States in 1849; attended St. Charles College, Maryland; studied law; was admitted to the bar in 1866 and commenced the practice of law in Virginia City, Nev.; district attorney of Storey County, Nev., in 1871 and 1872; elected as a Republican to the Forty-fourth Congress (March 4, 1875–March 3, 1877); elected to the Forty-ninth and Fiftieth Congresses (March 4, 1885–March 3, 1889); resumed the practice of his profession in Virginia City, Storey County, Nev.; unsuccessful candidate for election in 1892 to the Fifty-third Congress; died in Carson City, Nev., January 15, 1915; interment in St. Theresa Cemetery.

WOODBURY, Levi, a Senator from New Hampshire; born in Francestown, N. H., December 22, 1789; was graduated from Dartmouth College, Hanover, N. H., in 1809; studied law in Litchfield, Conn., Boston, Mass., and Exeter, N. H.; was admitted to the bar in 1812 and practiced in Francestown, N. H., 1813–1816; appointed judge of the superior court of New Hampshire in 1816; moved to Portsmouth, N. H., in 1819; Governor of New Hampshire in 1823 and 1824; member of the State house of representatives in 1825 and served as speaker; elected as a Democrat to the United States Senate for the term beginning March 4, 1825, and served from March 16, 1825, to March 3, 1831; was nominated for the State senate in 1831 but declined; was Secretary of the Navy in the Cabinet of President Jackson from May 23, 1831, to June 30, 1834, when he was appointed Secretary of the Treasury, serving until March 3, 1841; appointed chief justice of the superior court of New Hampshire but declined to serve; again elected to the United States Senate and served from March 4, 1841, to November 20, 1845, when he resigned; declined the British mission; appointed Associate Justice of the Supreme Court of the United States to fill the vacancy caused by the death of Joseph Story and served from November 20, 1845, until his death in Portsmouth, N. H., September 4, 1851; interment in Harmony Grove Cemetery.

WOODCOCK, David, a Representative from New York; was born in Williamstown, Berkshire County, Mass., in 1785; attended the public schools; studied law; was admitted to the bar and practiced; moved to Ithaca, Seneca (now Tompkins) County, N. Y.; commissioned postmaster of Ithaca November 19, 1808; appointed master of the court of chancery in 1808; member of the State assembly in 1814 and 1815; appointed district attorney of Tompkins County in April 1817; surrogate and assistant attorney general of the State in 1817; president of the Cayuga Steamboat Co. in 1819; elected as a Democrat to the Seventeenth Congress (March 4, 1821–March 3, 1823); president and trustee of the village of Ithaca in 1823, 1824, and 1826; resumed the practice of law; again a member of the State assembly in 1826; took a prominent part in the Anti-Masonic Crusade and State Convention at Utica, N. Y., in 1827; elected to the Twentieth Congress (March 4, 1827–March 3, 1829); unsuccessful candidate for reelection in 1828 to the Twenty-first Congress; resumed the practice of his profession; died in Ithaca, N. Y., September 18, 1835; interment in the City Cemetery.

WOODFORD, Stewart Lyndon, a Representative from New York; born in New York City September 3, 1835; was graduated from Columbia College (now Columbia University), New York City, in 1854; studied law; was admitted to the bar in 1857 and commenced practice in New York City; delegate to the Republican National Convention held at Chicago in 1860; assistant attorney for the United States in New York City in 1861 and in 1862; during the Civil War served in the Union Army; lieutenant colonel of the One Hundred and Twenty-seventh New York Volunteers September 8, 1862; colonel of the One Hundred and Third United States Colored Infantry March 3, 1865; brevetted brigadier general of Volunteers May 12, 1865, "for zealous, efficient, and generally meritorious conduct in the discharge of duties"; resigned August 23, 1865; was first Union military commander of Charleston, S. C., and of Savannah, Ga.; Lieutenant Governor of New York 1867–1869; unsuccessful candidate for Governor in 1870; delegate to the Republican National Convention held at Philadelphia in 1872; presidential elector on the Republican ticket of Grant and Wilson in 1872 and president of the Electoral College; elected as a Republican to the Forty-third Congress and served from March 4, 1873, to July 1, 1874, when he resigned; United States attorney for the southern district of New York from 1877 to 1883; appointed United States Envoy Extraordinary and Minister Plenipotentiary to Spain on June 19, 1897, and served until September 20, 1898, when he resigned; resumed the practice of law in New York City and died there February 14, 1913; interment in Woodland Cemetery, Stamford, Conn.

WOODHOUSE, Chase Going, a Representative from Connecticut; born in Victoria, British Columbia, Canada; attended the public schools in San Francisco, Calif., Aberdeen, S. Dak., and Science Hill School, Shelbyville, Ky.; graduated from McGill University at Montreal, Canada, in 1912; took graduate work at the University of Berlin and the University of Chicago, Chicago, Ill.; professor of economics at Connecticut College in New London, Conn., 1934–1946; managing director, Institute of Women's Professional Relations at Connecticut College, 1929–1946; taught economics at Smith College in Northampton, Mass., 1918–1925, and at summer sessions at Teachers College of Columbia University in New York City, N. Y., University of Texas at Austin, and the University of Iowa at Iowa City; personnel director, Woman's College, University of North Carolina at Greensboro, 1929–1934; senior economist, Bureau of Home Economics, United States Department of Agriculture, 1926–1928; consultant, National Roster of Scientific and Specialized Personnel, War Manpower Commission, 1942–1944; chairman of New London Democratic Town Committee in 1942 and 1943; secretary of state of Connecticut in 1941 and 1942; president of the Connecticut Federation of Democratic Women's Clubs 1943–1948, and honorary president since; author of several books and articles on women's work and education; elected as a Democrat to the Seventy-ninth Congress (January 3, 1945–January 3, 1947); unsuccessful candidate for reelection in 1946 to the Eightieth Congress; executive director, women's

division, Democratic National Committee, Washington, D. C., from February 1947 to April 1948; visiting expert on the staff of Gen. Lucius Clay, Allied Military Governor of Germany, in 1948; again elected to the Eighty-first Congress (January 3, 1949–January 3, 1951); unsuccessful candidate for reelection in 1950 to the Eighty-second Congress; special assistant to the Director of Price Stabilization 1951–1953; director of service bureau, Beatrice Fox Auerbach Foundation, 1954–; is a resident of Baltic, Conn.

WOODMAN, Charles Walhart, a Representative from Illinois; born in Aalborg, Denmark, March 11, 1844; was educated in the schools of his native country; followed the sea 1860–1863; arrived in Philadelphia, Pa., in 1863 and immediately enlisted in the Gulf Squadron of the United States Navy; moved to Chicago, Ill., in 1865; graduated from the law department of Chicago University in 1871; was admitted to the Illinois bar the same year and commenced practice in Chicago; appointed prosecuting attorney of the lower courts in 1877; appointed justice of the peace by the judges of Cook County in 1881; elected as a Republican to the Fifty-fourth Congress (March 4, 1895–March 3, 1897); unsuccessful candidate for reelection in 1896 to the Fifty-fifth Congress; engaged in the practice of his profession until his death; died in Elgin, Ill., March 18, 1898; interment in Rose Hill Cemetery, Chicago, Ill.

WOODRUFF, George Catlin, a Representative from Connecticut; born in Litchfield, Conn., on December 1, 1805; was graduated from Yale College in 1825; studied law; was admitted to the bar in 1827 and began practice in Litchfield; postmaster of Litchfield from January 4, 1832, to January 27, 1842, and from September 2, 1842, to September 28, 1846; member of the State house of representatives in 1851, 1866, and 1874; elected as a Democrat to the Thirty-seventh Congress (March 4, 1861–March 3, 1863); unsuccessful candidate for reelection in 1862 to the Thirty-eighth Congress; continued the practice of law until his death in Litchfield, Conn., November 21, 1885; interment in East Cemetery.

WOODRUFF, John, a Representative from Connecticut; born in West Hartford, Hartford County, Conn., February 12, 1826; received a limited schooling; moved to Catskill, Greene County, N. Y., in 1835; returned to Connecticut in 1841 and settled in Bristol, where he worked in a clock factory until 1845; moved to New Haven in 1845, where he began his public career; elected a member of the common council in 1848 and served several terms; member of the general assembly in 1852; elected by the American Party to the Thirty-fourth Congress (March 4, 1855–March 3, 1857); unsuccessful candidate for reelection in 1856 to the Thirty-fifth Congress; elected to the Thirty-sixth Congress (March 4, 1859–March 3, 1861); upon establishment of the office in 1862 was appointed collector of internal revenue for the second district of Connecticut and served until his death in New Haven, Conn., May 20, 1868; interment in Evergreen Cemetery.

WOODRUFF, Roy Orchard, a Representative from Michigan; born at Eaton Rapids, Eaton County, Mich., March 14, 1876; attended the common schools and the high school of Eaton Rapids; apprenticed to the printing business 1891–1899; enlisted as a corporal in Company G, Thirty-third Regiment, Michigan Volunteer Infantry, during the Spanish-American War; saw active service and was mustered out; was graduated from the dental department of the College of Medicine, Detroit, Mich., in 1902 and practiced dentistry in Bay City, Mich., 1902–1911; mayor of Bay City 1911–1913; elected as a Progressive Republican to the Sixty-third Congress (March 4, 1913–March

3, 1915); was not a candidate for renomination in 1914; served for two years in the First World War as an Infantry officer, acquiring the rank of major during his service in France; elected as a Republican to the Sixty-seventh and to the fifteen succeeding Congresses (March 4, 1921–January 3, 1953); was not a candidate for renomination in 1952 to the Eighty-third Congress; died in Washington, D. C., February 12, 1953; interment in Elm Lawn Cemetery, Bay City, Mich.

WOODRUFF, Thomas M., a Representative from New York; born in New Jersey, May 3, 1804; elected as a Democrat to the Twenty-ninth Congress (March 4, 1845–March 3, 1847); employed as a cabinetmaker and later engaged in the furniture business in New York City; died in New York City, March 28, 1855; interment in the First Presbyterian Church Cemetery, Newark, N. J.

WOODRUM, Clifton Alexander, a Representative from Virginia; born in Roanoke, Roanoke County, Va., April 27, 1887; attended the public schools of his native city and the University College of Medicine (now combined with the Medical College of Virginia), Richmond, Va.; became a registered pharmacist and engaged in his profession in Roanoke; studied law at Washington and Lee University, Lexington, Va.; was admitted to the bar in 1908 and commenced practice in Roanoke, Va.; Commonwealth attorney of Roanoke 1917–1919; judge of the Hustings Court of Roanoke 1919–1922; elected as a Democrat to the Sixty-eighth and to the eleven succeeding Congresses and served from March 4, 1923, until his resignation on December 31, 1945, to become president of the American Plant Food Council, Inc.; died in Washington, D. C., October 6, 1950; interment in Fairview Cemetery, Roanoke, Va.

WOODS, Frank Plowman, a Representative from Iowa; born near Sharon, Walworth County, Wis., December 11, 1868; attended the public schools and the Northern Indiana Normal School, Valparaiso, Ind.; moved to Estherville, Emmett County, Iowa, in 1887 and worked in a newspaper office for two years; engaged in the mortgage-loan business and private banking; chairman of the Republican State central committee in 1906 and 1907; elected as a Republican to the Sixty-first and to the four succeeding Congresses (March 4, 1909–March 3, 1919); unsuccessful candidate for renomination in 1918; chairman of the Republican National Congressional Committee 1913–1918; engaged in literary pursuits; resided in Altadena, Calif., until his death there April 25, 1944; interment in Mountain View Cemetery.

WOODS, Henry (brother of John Woods), a Representative from Pennsylvania; born in Bedford, Bedford County, Pa., in 1764; received a limited schooling; attended the subscription schools of Bedford County, Pa.; took an active part in pre-Revolutionary affairs; studied law; was admitted to the bar in 1792 and commenced practice in Bedford, Pa.; elected to the Sixth and Seventh Congresses (March 4, 1799–March 3, 1803); engaged as a land speculator; died in Bedford, Pa., in 1826.

WOODS, James Pleasant, a Representative from Virginia; born near Roanoke, Roanoke County, Va., February 4, 1868; attended the common schools; was graduated from Roanoke College in 1892; studied law at the University of Virginia at Charlottesville in 1892 and 1893; was admitted to the bar in the latter year and commenced practice in Roanoke, Va.; mayor of Roanoke 1898–1900; elected as a Democrat to the Sixty-fifth and Sixty-sixth Congresses to fill the vacancies caused by the resignation of Carter Glass; was reelected to the Sixty-seventh Congress and served from February 25, 1919, to

March 3, 1923; unsuccessful candidate for renomination in 1922; delegate to the Democratic National Convention at San Francisco in 1920; president of the board of trustees of Roanoke College; member of the board of trustees of the Randolph-Macon system of colleges; rector of the board of visitors of the Virginia Polytechnic Institute; resumed the practice of law; died in Roanoke, Va., July 7, 1948; interment in Evergreen Burial Park.

WOODS, John (brother of Henry Woods), a Representative from Pennsylvania; born in Bedford, Bedford County, Pa., in 1761; studied law; was admitted to the bar in Washington County, Pa., in December 1783, in Westmoreland County and Fayette County in 1784, in Allegheny County on December 16, 1788, and in Bedford County in 1791; practiced extensively in those counties; assisted in laying out the city of Pittsburgh in 1784; presidential elector in 1796; member of the State senate in 1797; elected as a Federalist to the Fourteenth Congress (March 4, 1815–March 3, 1817); owing to illness never attended or qualified; died in Brunswick County, Va., December 16, 1816, while on a journey to the South to regain his health.

WOODS, John, a Representative from Ohio; born in Johnstown, Dauphin County, Pa., October 18, 1794; moved with his parents to Ohio, where he attended the common schools; served in the War of 1812; after the war operated a school near Springborough for two years; studied law; was admitted to the bar in 1819 and commenced the practice of his profession in Hamilton, Butler County, Ohio; prosecuting attorney of Butler County 1820–1825; elected as a Whig to the Nineteenth and Twentieth Congresses (March 4, 1825–March 3, 1829); unsuccessful candidate for reelection in 1828 to the Twenty-first Congress; became editor and publisher of the Hamilton Intelligencer in 1829; State auditor of Ohio from 1845 to 1851; president of the Cincinnati, Hamilton & Indianapolis Railroad; died in Hamilton, Ohio, July 30, 1855; interment in Greenwood Cemetery.

WOODS, Samuel Davis, a Representative from California; born in Mount Pleasant, Maury County, Tenn., September 19, 1845; moved with his parents to Stockton, Calif., in February 1850; attended the public schools; studied law; was admitted to the California bar in April 1875 and engaged in practice in Stockton and in the city and county of San Francisco; elected as a Republican to the Fifty-sixth Congress to fill the vacancy caused by the resignation of Marion De Vries; reelected to the Fifty-seventh Congress and served from December 3, 1900, to March 3, 1903; was not a candidate for reelection in 1902 to the Fifty-eighth Congress; resumed the practice of law in San Francisco, Calif., and died there December 24, 1915; interment in Mount Olivet Cemetery, San Mateo County, Calif.

WOODS, William, a Representative from New York; born in Washington County, N. Y., in 1790; received a limited schooling; moved to Bath, Steuben County, N. Y., in 1813; studied law; was admitted to the bar and practiced in Bath, N. Y.; member of the State assembly 1823–1825; elected as a Democrat to the Eighteenth Congress to fill the vacancy caused by the resignation of William B. Rochester and served from November 3, 1823, to March 3, 1825; resumed the practice of his profession; surrogate of Steuben County 1827–1835; died in Bath, N. Y., August 7, 1837; interment in Grove Cemetery.

WOODSON, Samuel Hughes, a Representative from Kentucky; born near Charlottesville, Albemarle County, Va., September 15, 1777; completed preparatory studies; studied law; was admitted to the bar in 1802 and commenced practice in Nicholasville, Jessamine County, Ky.; first clerk of Jessamine

County Circuit Court 1803–1819, after the admission of Kentucky as a State into the Union; elected to the Seventeenth Congress (March 4, 1821–March 3, 1823); unsuccessful candidate for reelection in 1822 to the Eighteenth Congress; resumed the practice of his profession in Nicholasville; member of the State house of representatives in 1825 and 1826; died at "Chaumiere," Jessamine County, Ky., July 28, 1827; interment in the Crocket Burying Ground.

WOODSON, Samuel Hughes (son of the preceding), a Representative from Missouri; born near Nicholasville, Jessamine County, Ky., October 24, 1815; attended the public schools; was graduated from Centre College, Danville, Ky., and the law department of Transylvania University, Lexington, Ky.; was admitted to the bar in 1838 and commenced the practice of law in Independence, Jackson County, Mo., in 1840; member of the State house of representatives in 1853 and 1854; delegate to the State constitutional convention in 1855; elected on the American Party ticket to the Thirty-fifth and Thirty-sixth Congresses (March 4, 1857–March 3, 1861); was not a candidate for renomination in 1860; resumed the practice of his profession in Independence; became affiliated with the Democratic Party; was judge of the twenty-fourth judicial circuit of Missouri from March 1875 until his death in Independence, Mo., June 23, 1881; interment in Woodlawn Cemetery.

WOODWARD, George Washington, a Representative from Pennsylvania; born in Bethany, Wayne County, Pa., March 26, 1809; attended Geneva Seminary (now Hobart College), Geneva, N. Y., and Wilkes-Barre (Pa.) Academy; studied law; was admitted to the bar in 1830 and commenced practice in Wilkes-Barre, Pa.; delegate to the State constitutional convention in 1837; president judge of the fourth judicial district 1841–1851; unsuccessful candidate for United States Senator in 1845; nominated in 1845 by President Polk a Justice of the Supreme Court of the United States but was not confirmed by the Senate; associate judge of the supreme court of Pennsylvania 1852–1863 and chief justice 1863–1867; unsuccessful Democratic candidate for Governor in 1863; elected as a Democrat to the Fortieth Congress to fill the vacancy caused by the death of Charles Denison; reelected to the Forty-first Congress and served from November 21, 1867, to March 3, 1871; was not a candidate for renomination in 1870; delegate to the Democratic National Convention at New York City in 1868; unsuccessful candidate for president judge of the eleventh judicial district in 1870; moved to Philadelphia in 1871 and continued the practice of his profession; was a delegate to the State constitutional convention in 1873; traveled abroad in 1874 and died in Rome, Italy, on May 10, 1875; interment in Hollenback Cemetery, Wilkes-Barre, Pa.

WOODWARD, Gilbert Motier, a Representative from Wisconsin; born in Washington, D. C., December 25, 1835; educated in the common schools; studied law; was admitted to the bar in 1861 and commenced practice in La Crosse, Wis., in February 1860; served more than three years in the Union Army during the Civil War as a private, first sergeant, second lieutenant, first lieutenant, and adjutant in the Second Regiment, Wisconsin Volunteer Infantry; district attorney of La Crosse County 1866–1873; mayor of the city of La Crosse in 1874 and 1875; city attorney 1876–1882; elected as a Democrat to the Forty-eighth Congress (March 4, 1883–March 3, 1885); unsuccessful for reelection in 1884 to the Forty-ninth Congress; resumed the practice of law in La Crosse, Wis.; unsuccessful Democratic candidate for Governor of Wisconsin in 1886; delegate to the Democratic National Convention at St. Louis in 1888; died in La Crosse, Wis., March 13, 1913; interment in Oak Grove Cemetery.

WOODWARD, Joseph Addison, a Representative from South Carolina; born in Winnsboro, Fairfield County, S. C., on April 11, 1806; received an academic training and was graduated from the University of South Carolina at Columbia; studied law; was admitted to the bar and practiced; member of the State house of representatives 1837–1843; elected as a Democrat to the Twenty-eighth and to the four succeeding Congresses (March 4, 1843–March 3, 1853); declined to be a candidate for reelection in 1852 to the Thirty-third Congress; moved to Alabama and resumed the practice of his profession; died in Talladega, Talladega County, Ala., on August 3, 1885; interment in Oak Hill Cemetery.

WOODWARD, William, a Representative from South Carolina; elected to the Fourteenth Congress (March 4, 1815–March 3, 1817).

WOODWORTH, James Hutchinson, a Representative from Illinois; born in Greenwich, N. Y., December 4, 1804; received a limited schooling; moved to Fabius, Onondaga County, N. Y., and taught school; engaged in mercantile pursuits in 1823; inspector of the common schools in 1826; moved to Erie, Pa., in 1827; justice of the peace 1829–1832; moved to Chicago, Ill., in 1833 and engaged in the dry-goods business; served in the State senate 1839–1842; member of the State house of representatives 1842–1847; owner and manager of the Chicago Hydraulic Flouring Mills for ten years; member of the Chicago City Council 1845–1848; mayor of Chicago 1848–1850; elected as a Republican to the Thirty-fourth Congress (March 4, 1855–March 3, 1857); retired to private life until appointed by Governor Yates to serve on the board of auditors on war claims; served as president of the Merchants & Mechanics' Bank of Chicago and was president of the Treasury Bank of Chicago at the time of his death; one of the founders of Chicago University; died in Highland Park, Ill., March 26, 1869; interment in Oakland Cemetery, Chicago, Ill.

WOODWORTH, Laurin Dewey, a Representative from Ohio; born in Windham, Portage County, Ohio, September 10, 1837; attended the common schools, Windham (Ohio) Academy, Hiram (Ohio) College, and the Ohio State University at Columbus; studied law at Union Law College, Cleveland, Ohio; was admitted to the bar in 1859 and commenced practice in Ravenna, Ohio; member of the Portage County Board of School Examiners; during the Civil War served in the Union Army as major of the One Hundred and Fourth Ohio Volunteer Infantry from July 1862 to December 1862; moved to Youngstown, Mahoning County, Ohio, in 1864 and resumed the practice of law; elected to the State senate in 1867; reelected in 1869 and served as president pro tempore; elected as a Republican to the Forty-third and Forty-fourth Congresses (March 4, 1873–March 3, 1877); was an unsuccessful candidate for renomination in 1876 to the Forty-fifth Congress; continued the practice of law in Youngstown, Ohio, until his death there on March 13, 1897; interment in Windham Cemetery, Windham, Portage County, Ohio.

WOODWORTH, William W., a Representative from New York; born in New London, Conn., March 16, 1807; moved to Hyde Park, Dutchess County, N. Y., in 1834; received a limited schooling; supervisor of Hyde Park in 1838, 1841, and 1843; appointed judge of Dutchess County in 1838 and reappointed in 1843; unsuccessful candidate for election in 1842 to the Twenty-eighth Congress; elected as a Democrat to the Twenty-ninth Congress (March 4, 1845–March 3, 1847); unsuccessful candidate for renomination in 1846; held interests in Cuba and formed a stock company of the Hudson River State Co. at

Clinton, N. Y.; contractor for building a section of the Hudson River Railroad; moved to Yonkers, N. Y., December 1, 1849, and engaged in the real-estate business and banking; elected president of Yonkers in 1857 and 1858; elected receiver of taxes in 1870; died in Yonkers, N. Y., February 13, 1873; interment in Oakland Cemetery.

WOODYARD, Harry Chapman, a Representative from West Virginia; born in Spencer, Roane County, W. Va., November 13, 1867; attended the common schools; engaged in the wholesale grocery and lumber business; member of the State senate in 1898; elected as a Republican to the Fifty-eighth and to the three succeeding Congresses (March 4, 1903–March 3, 1911); unsuccessful candidate for reelection in 1910 to the Sixty-second Congress; elected to the Sixty-fourth Congress to fill the vacancy caused by the death of Hunter H. Moss, Jr.; re-elected to the Sixty-fifth, Sixty-sixth, and Sixty-seventh Congresses and served from November 7, 1916, to March 3, 1923; unsuccessful candidate for reelection in 1922 to the Sixty-eighth Congress; elected to the Sixty-ninth Congress (March 4, 1925–March 3, 1927); was not a candidate for reelection to the Seventieth Congress; resumed his former business pursuits; died in Spencer, W. Va., on June 21, 1929; interment in Spencer Mausoleum.

WOOMER, Ephraim Milton, a Representative from Pennsylvania; born in Jonestown, Lebanon County, Pa., January 14, 1844; attended the common schools; during the Civil War enlisted in Company A, Ninety-third Regiment, Pennsylvania Volunteer Infantry, in September 1861; promoted to sergeant; wounded twice at Salem Heights and lost a leg in the Battle of the Wilderness May 5, 1864; discharged from the hospital September 9, 1865; taught school until 1869; engaged in mercantile pursuits; clerk of the orphans' court of Lebanon County 1869–1872; cashier of the People's Bank of Lebanon; member of the council of the borough of Lebanon 1884–1886; president of the select council of the city of Lebanon 1886–1890; delegate to the Republican National Convention at Chicago in 1888; elected as a Republican to the Fifty-third and Fifty-fourth Congresses (March 4, 1893–March 3, 1897); unsuccessful candidate for renomination in 1896; again engaged in banking; died in Lebanon, Pa., November 29, 1897; interment in Mount Lebanon Cemetery.

WOOTEN, Dudley Goodall, a Representative from Texas; born near Springfield, Greene County, Mo., June 19, 1860; moved in infancy with his parents to Texas during the Civil War; attended private schools in Paris, Tex., and was graduated from Princeton College in 1875; attended Johns Hopkins University, Baltimore, Md., and was graduated from the law department of the University of Virginia at Charlottesville; was admitted to the bar in 1880 and practiced in Austin, Tex.; prosecuting attorney of Austin 1884–1886; moved to Dallas, Tex., in 1888; judge of the Dallas County district court 1890–1892; presidential elector on the Democratic ticket of Cleveland and Stevenson in 1892; member of the State house of representatives in 1898 and 1899; delegate to the National Antitrust Conference at Chicago in 1899; member of the executive council of the National Civic Federation in 1900; delegate to the National Tax Conference at Buffalo in 1901; elected as a Democrat to the Fifty-seventh Congress to fill the vacancy caused by the death of Robert E. Burke and served from July 13, 1901, to March 3, 1903; unsuccessful candidate for renomination in 1902; continued the practice of law in Seattle, Wash.; served as special judge of the superior court at various times; delegate to the National Rivers and Harbors Congress in 1912; delegate to the National Conservation Congress in 1913; ap-

pointed a member of the State board of higher curricula by the Governor in 1919; author of several historical works and numerous articles in literary and law periodicals; tendered the position of professor of law at the University of Notre Dame, Notre Dame, Ind., in 1924, and served until his health forced him to take leave of absence in November 1928; died, while on a visit, in Austin, Tex., on February 7, 1929; interment in Calvary Cemetery, Seattle, Wash.

WORCESTER, Samuel Thomas, a Representative from Ohio; born in Hollis, Hillsborough County, N. H., August 30, 1804; attended the common schools, and was graduated from Harvard University in 1830; studied law; was admitted to the bar in 1835 and began practice in Norwalk, Huron County, Ohio; member of the State senate in 1849 and 1850; served as judge of the court of common pleas in 1859 and 1860; elected as a Republican to the Thirty-seventh Congress to fill the vacancy caused by the resignation of John Sherman and served from July 4, 1861, to March 3, 1863; resumed the practice of law and engaged in literary pursuits; died in Nashua, Hillsboro County, N. H., on December 6, 1882; interment in the South Cemetery, Hollis, N. H.

WORD, Thomas Jefferson, a Representative from Mississippi; born in Surry County, N. C.; member of the State house of commons in 1832; moved to Mississippi and settled in Pontotoc, Pontotoc County; contested the election of Samuel J. Gholson to the Twenty-fifth Congress, and the election was set aside by the House; subsequently elected as a Whig to fill the vacancy caused by this action, and served from May 30, 1838, to March 3, 1839.

WORKS, John Downey, a Senator from California; born near Rising Sun, Ohio County, Ind., March 29, 1847; attended private schools; during the Civil War served in the Tenth Regiment, Indiana Volunteer Cavalry, of the Union Army; studied law; was admitted to the bar in 1868 and commenced practice in Vevay, Ind.; member of the State house of representatives 1878–1880; moved to San Diego, Calif., in 1883 and continued the practice of law; judge of the superior court of San Diego County in 1886 and 1887; associate justice of the supreme court of California 1888–1891; moved to Los Angeles in 1896; president of the city council of Los Angeles in 1910; elected as a Republican to the United States Senate and served from March 4, 1911, to March 3, 1917; was not a candidate for renomination; resumed the practice of law for a short time; died in Los Angeles, Calif., June 6, 1928; remains were cremated and the ashes deposited in Inglewood Cemetery.

WORLEY, Francis Eugene, a Representative from Texas; born in Lone Wolf, Kiowa County, Okla., October 10, 1908; moved to Shamrock, Tex., in 1922; attended the public schools, the Texas Agricultural and Mechanical College at College Station in 1927 and 1928, and the law school of the University of Texas at Austin 1930–1935; was admitted to the bar in 1935 and commenced practice in Shamrock, Tex.; member of the State house of representatives from 1935 to 1940, when he resigned, having been elected to Congress; served as a lieutenant commander in the United States Navy from December 1941 to August 1942, while a Member of Congress; elected as a Democrat to the Seventy-seventh and to the four succeeding Congresses and served from January 3, 1941, until his resignation, effective April 3, 1950; appointed an associate judge of the United States Court of Customs and Patent Appeals, Washington, D. C., and served from April 4, 1950, to May 3, 1959; appointed chief judge for a ten-year term commencing May 4, 1959; resides in Arlington, Va.

WORMAN, Ludwig, a Representative from Pennsylvania; born in Tinicum Township, Bucks County, Pa., in 1761; received a limited schooling; learned the tanning business; moved to Earl Township, Berks County, Pa., in 1784 and established a tannery; elected as a Federalist to the Seventeenth Congress and served from March 4, 1821, until his death; unsuccessful candidate for reelection in 1822 to the Eighteenth Congress; died in Earl Township, Berks County, Pa., October 17, 1822; interment in Earl Township Cemetery.

WORTENDYKE, Jacob Reynier, a Representative from New Jersey; born in Chestnut Ridge, near Hackensack, Bergen County, N. J., November 27, 1818; completed preparatory studies under a private tutor; was graduated from Rutgers College, New Brunswick, N. J., 1839; taught school for ten years; studied law; was admitted to the bar in 1853 and commenced practice in Jersey City, N. J.; elected as a Democrat to the Thirty-fifth Congress (March 4, 1857–March 3, 1859); unsuccessful candidate for reelection in 1858 to the Thirty-sixth Congress; resumed the practice of law; trustee of Rutgers College 1862–1868; president of the water board, Jersey City, 1860–1868; president of the Riparian Commission of New Jersey 1865–1868; delegate to the Democratic National Convention at New York City in 1868; died in Jersey City, N. J., November 7, 1868; interment in the Dutch Reformed Church Cemetery, Park Ridge, Bergen County, N. J.

WORTHINGTON, Henry Gaither, a Representative from Nevada; born in Cumberland, Md., February 9, 1828; completed preparatory studies; studied law; was admitted to the bar and commenced practice in Tuolumne County, Calif.; traveled in Central America and Mexico and upon his return settled in San Francisco, Calif.; member of the State house of representatives in 1861; moved to Nevada in 1862 and settled in Austin; upon the admission of Nevada as a State into the Union was elected as a Republican to the Thirty-eighth Congress and served from October 31, 1864, to March 3, 1865; collector of the port of Charleston, S. C.; served as United States Minister to Uruguay and the Argentine Republic in 1868 and 1869 by appointment of President Andrew Johnson; United States district judge; major general of militia; defeated by two votes for election to the United States Senate; served as a pallbearer at the funeral of President Abraham Lincoln; died in Washington, D. C., July 29, 1909; interment in Congressional Cemetery.

WORTHINGTON, John Tolley Hood, a Representative from Maryland; born at "Shewan," near Baltimore, Baltimore County, Md., November 1, 1788; received a limited schooling; engaged in agricultural pursuits; elected as a Democrat to the Twenty-second Congress (March 4, 1831–March 3, 1833); unsuccessful candidate for reelection in 1832 to the Twenty-third Congress and for election in 1834 to the Twenty-fourth Congress; elected to the Twenty-fifth and Twenty-sixth Congresses (March 4, 1837–March 3, 1841); resumed agricultural pursuits; died at "Shewan," Baltimore County, Md., April 27, 1849; interment in a private cemetery on his farm; reinterment in St. John's Episcopal Churchyard, Worthington Valley, Baltimore County, Md.

WORTHINGTON, Nicholas Ellsworth, a Representative from Illinois; born in Brooke County, Va. (now West Virginia), March 30, 1836; was graduated from Allegheny College, Meadville, Pa.; studied law; was admitted to the bar in 1860 and commenced practice in Peoria, Ill.; superintendent of schools of Peoria County 1865–1872; member of the State board of education 1869–1872; elected as a Democrat to the Forty-eighth and Forty-ninth Congresses (March 4, 1883–March 3, 1887); unsuccessful candidate for reelection in 1886 to the Fiftieth Congress and for election in 1888 to the Fifty-first Congress; resumed the practice of law; elected circuit judge of the tenth judicial district of Illinois in 1891; reelected in 1897, and served until his retirement June 15, 1915; appointed by President Cleveland a member of the commission to investigate labor strikes in 1894; died in Peoria, Ill., March 4, 1916; interment in Springdale Cemetery.

WORTHINGTON, Thomas, a Senator from Ohio; born in Jefferson County, Va. (now West Virginia), on July 16, 1773; completed preparatory studies; moved to Ross County, Ohio, in 1798; member of the first and second Territorial legislatures 1799–1801; delegate to the State constitutional convention in 1803; elected as a Democrat to the United States Senate and served from April 1, 1803, to March 3, 1807; member of the State house of representatives in 1807; again elected to the United States Senate to fill the vacancy caused by the resignation of Return J. Meigs, Jr., and served from December 15, 1810, until December 1, 1814, when he resigned, having been elected Governor; Governor of Ohio 1814–1818; canal commissioner from 1818 until his death; again a member of the State house of representatives in 1821 and 1822; died in New York City June 20, 1827; interment in Grandview Cemetery, Chillicothe, Ross County, Ohio.

WORTHINGTON, Thomas Contee (nephew of Benjamin Contee), a Representative from Maryland; born near Annapolis, Anne Arundel County, Md., November 25, 1782; received a limited schooling; served as a captain in the War of 1812; brigadier general of the Ninth Brigade, Maryland Militia, 1818–1847; studied law; was admitted to the bar in 1817 and commenced practice in Annapolis, Md.; member of the executive council in 1830 under the first State constitution; moved to Frederick, Frederick County, Md., in 1818 and continued the practice of law; member of the State house of representatives in 1818; elected as a Democrat to the Nineteenth Congress (March 4, 1825–March 3, 1827); resumed the practice of law in Frederick, Md., and died there on April 12, 1847; interment in Mount Olivet Cemetery.

WREN, Thomas, a Representative from Nevada; born in McArthurstown, Ohio, January 2, 1826; received a common-school education; moved with his parents to Illinois; crossed the Plains to California in 1850; engaged in mining for three years; deputy clerk of Eldorado County, Calif., 1855–1857; studied law; was admitted to the bar and commenced practice in Downeyville, Calif.; moved to Nevada in 1863, where he resided successively in Austin, Hamilton, Pioche, Eureka, and Reno, being engaged in the practice of law at each place; city attorney of Austin 1874–1876; president and attorney for the Richmond Mining Co. in Eureka; member of the State house of representatives in 1875; elected as a Republican to the Forty-fifth Congress (March 4, 1877–March 3, 1879); resumed the practice of law; died in Reno, Nev., February 5, 1904; interment in the Masonic Cemetery.

WRIGHT, Ashley Bascom, a Representative from Massachusetts; born in Hinsdale, Berkshire County, Mass., May 25, 1841; attended the public schools and Lincoln Academy at Hinsdale; moved to North Adams, Mass., in 1861; appointed chief deputy collector of internal revenue for the tenth district of Massachusetts in 1861; resigned in 1865 and engaged in mercantile pursuits; elected selectman; commissioner for the county of Berkshire 1884–1887 and chairman for one year; member of the State executive council in 1890 and 1891; elected as a Republican to the Fifty-third, Fifty-fourth, and Fifty-fifth Congresses and served from March 4, 1893, until his death in North Adams, Berkshire County, Mass., August 14, 1897; interment in Hinsdale Cemetery.

WRIGHT, Augustus Romaldus, a Representative from Georgia; born in Wrightsboro, Ga., June 16, 1813; attended the public schools at Appling, Ga., the grammar school, Franklin College, and the University of Georgia at Athens; studied law at Litchfield (Conn.) Law School; was admitted to the bar in 1835 and commenced practice in Crawfordville, Ga., moving the following year to Cassville; served as judge of the superior courts of the Cherokee circuit from 1842 until he resigned in 1849 to resume the practice of law; moved to Rome, Ga., in 1855 and continued the practice of law; elected as a Democrat to the Thirty-fifth Congress (March 4, 1857–March 3, 1859); delegate to Georgia Secession Convention (opposing secession) and to the Confederate Secession Convention; offered provisional governorship of Georgia by President Lincoln, but declined; served as a member of the Confederate Congress; during the Civil War organized Wright's Legion, which was mustered in with the Thirty-eighth Georgia Infantry; after the Civil War resumed the practice of law at Rome, Ga.; member of the Georgia Constitutional Convention of 1877; died March 31, 1891, at his home "Glenwood," later a part of the Berry School, near Rome, Ga.; interment in Myrtle Hill Cemetery.

WRIGHT, Charles Frederick (brother of Myron Benjamin Wright), a Representative from Pennsylvania; born in Forest Lake Township, Susquehanna County, Pa., on May 3, 1856; attended the public schools, and was graduated from the Montrose (Pa.) Academy in 1874; teller of the First National Bank of Montrose, Pa., 1875–1881; was assistant cashier, cashier, and president of the First National Bank of Susquehanna Depot 1882–1899; delegate to the Republican National Convention at St. Louis in 1896; elected as a Republican to the Fifty-sixth, Fifty-seventh, and Fifty-eighth Congresses (March 4, 1899–March 3, 1905); was not a candidate for renomination in 1904; delegate to the Republican National Conventions at Chicago which nominated Roosevelt and Fairbanks in 1904 and Taft and Sherman in 1908; State treasurer 1911–1913; commissioner of public service in 1915 and 1916; resumed banking pursuits; died in Susquehanna, Pa., November 10, 1925; interment in Evergreen Cemetery.

WRIGHT, Daniel Boone, a Representative from Mississippi; born near Mount Pleasant, Giles County, Tenn., February 17, 1812; attended the common schools and was graduated from Cumberland University, Lebanon, Tenn., in 1837; studied law; was admitted to the bar in 1840 and commenced practice in Ashland, Benton County, Miss.; moved to Salem (later Hudsonville), Benton County, Miss., in 1850 and continued the practice of law and also engaged in agricultural pursuits; elected as a Democrat to the Thirty-third and Thirty-fourth Congresses (March 4, 1853–March 3, 1857); was not a candidate for renomination in 1856; resumed the practice of law at Ashland, Miss.; during the Civil War was appointed, on April 16, 1862, lieutenant colonel of the Thirty-fourth Regiment of Mississippi Infantry in the Confederate Army; was wounded at Perryville on October 8, 1862, and captured the next day and sent to Camp Chase, Ohio; was exchanged at City Point, Va., on April 2, 1863; resigned August 5, 1863, because of disability resulting from wounds received at Perryville, Ky.; appointed colonel of Cavalry to take effect June 6, 1864, and served as a judge of military courts in Gen. N. B. Forrest's Cavalry Division; was captured on May 18, 1865, and surrendered at La Grange, Tenn., but was subsequently paroled; resumed the practice of his profession in Ashland, Miss., and was also interested in agricultural pur-

suits in Benton County; died in Ashland, Miss., December 27, 1887; interment in the McDonald (private) Cemetery, near Ashland, Miss.

WRIGHT, Edwin Ruthvin Vincent, a Representative from New Jersey; born in Hoboken, N. J., January 2, 1812; completed preparatory studies; engaged in newspaper work in 1835; editor of the Jersey Blue in 1836, a newspaper published in Hoboken, N. J.; studied law; was admitted to the bar in 1839 and commenced practice in Jersey City; subsequently settled in Hudson City and continued the practice of law; member of the State council in 1843; district attorney for Hudson County 1851–1855; mayor of Hudson, N. J., in 1855; elected as a Democrat to the Thirty-ninth Congress (March 4, 1865–March 3, 1867); owing to ill health, was not a candidate for renomination in 1866 to the Fortieth Congress; elected Governor of New Jersey in 1869; retired from public and business life; died in Jersey City, N. J., January 21, 1871; interment in Hoboken Cemetery, New Durham, Hudson County, N. J.

WRIGHT, George Grover (brother of Joseph Albert Wright), a Senator from Iowa; born in Bloomington, Monroe County, Ind., March 24, 1820; attended private schools and was graduated from Indiana University at Bloomington in 1839; studied law in Rockville, Ind.; was admitted to the bar in 1840 and commenced practice in Keosauqua, Van Buren County, Iowa; prosecuting attorney of Van Buren County in 1847 and 1848; member of the State senate 1849–1851; justice of the State supreme court 1854–1870; served as president of the Iowa Agricultural Society from 1860 to 1865; moved to Des Moines, Iowa, in 1865; one of the founders of the College of Law, University of Iowa; professor in the law department of the State university 1865–1871; elected as a Republican to the United States Senate and served from March 4, 1871, to March 3, 1877; was not a candidate for reelection; resumed the practice of his profession in Des Moines and also engaged in banking; president of the American Bar Association in 1887 and 1888; died in Des Moines, Iowa, on January 11, 1896; interment in Woodland Cemetery.

WRIGHT, George Washington, a Representative from California; was born in Concord, Mass., on June 4, 1816; attended the public schools; employed in the business department of the Boston Courier in 1835 and later engaged in mercantile pursuits in Boston; moved to California and settled in San Francisco in 1849; again engaged in mercantile pursuits and also became interested in banking and mining; one of the founders of the banking house of Palmer, Cook & Co. in San Francisco; upon the admission of California as a State into the Union was elected as an Independent to the Thirty-first Congress and served from September 11, 1850, to March 3, 1851; declined to be a candidate for renomination; affiliated with the Republican Party and was an ardent supporter of John C. Frémont for President of the United States in 1856; moved to Washington, D. C.; toward the close of the Civil War he built, at Buffalo, N. Y., the *Commodore Perry*, a steam revenue vessel with side screw propellers; returned to Washington, D. C., and served as attorney of the Choctaw Indians; declined the portfolio of Secretary of the Interior in the Cabinet of President Johnson; retired from political life and engaged in private scientific work; was also interested in the prosecution of certain claims pending before Congress; moved to Dorchester, Mass., in 1880 and retired from active pursuits; died in Dorchester, Mass., April 7, 1885; interment in Sleepy Hollow Cemetery, Concord, Middlesex County, Mass.

WRIGHT, Hendrick Bradley, a Representative from Pennsylvania; born in Plymouth, Luzerne County, Pa., April 24,

1808; attended the Wilkes-Barre Grammar School, and was graduated from Dickinson College, Carlisle, Pa., in 1829; studied law; was admitted to the bar November 8, 1831, and commenced practice in Wilkes-Barre, Luzerne County; appointed district attorney for Luzerne County in 1834; member of the State house of representatives 1841–1843 and served the last year as speaker; delegate to the Democratic National Convention at Baltimore in 1844 which nominated Polk and Dallas, and served as temporary and permanent chairman; delegate to the subsequent Democratic National Conventions which nominated Cass and Butler at Baltimore in 1848, Pierce and King at Baltimore in 1852, Buchanan and Breckinridge at Cincinnati in 1856, Douglas and Johnson at Baltimore in 1860, Seymour and Blair at New York City in 1868, and Tilden and Hendricks at St. Louis in 1876; elected as a Democrat to the Thirty-third Congress (March 4, 1853–March 3, 1855); unsuccessful candidate for reelection in 1854 to the Thirty-fourth Congress; elected to the Thirty-seventh Congress to fill the vacancy caused by the death of George W. Scranton and served from July 4, 1861, to March 3, 1863; resumed the practice of his profession; elected to the Forty-fifth and Forty-sixth Congresses (March 4, 1877–March 3, 1881); although declining to be a candidate for reelection in 1880 to the Forty-seventh Congress, he received over four thousand votes; died in Wilkes-Barre, Pa., September 2, 1881; interment in Hollenback Cemetery.

WRIGHT, James Assion, a Representative from Pennsylvania; born in Carnegie, Allegheny County, Pa., on August 11, 1902; attended the public schools; was graduated from Holy Cross College, Worcester, Mass., in 1923 and from the law department of the University of Pittsburgh, Pittsburgh, Pa., in 1927; was admitted to the bar in 1927 and commenced practice in Carnegie, Pa.; served as assistant county solicitor of Allegheny County, Pa., 1935–1941; elected as a Democrat to the Seventy-seventh and Seventy-eighth Congresses (January 3, 1941–January 3, 1945); unsuccessful candidate for reelection in 1944 to the Seventy-ninth Congress; resumed the practice of law and is a resident of Pittsburgh, Pa.

WRIGHT, James Claud, Jr., a Representative from Texas; born in Fort Worth, Tarrant County, Tex., December 22, 1922; attended the public schools of Fort Worth and Dallas, Tex.; student at Weatherford (Tex.) College and the University of Texas; during World War II enlisted in the United States Air Force in December 1941; commissioned in 1942 and flew combat missions in the South Pacific; was awarded the Distinguished Flying Cross; partner in a national trade extension and advertising firm; mayor of Weatherford, Tex.; member of the State house of representatives; served as president of the League of Texas Municipalities in 1953; elected as a Democrat to the Eighty-fourth, Eighty-fifth, and Eighty-sixth Congresses (January 3, 1955–January 3, 1961). *Reelected to the Eighty-seventh Congress.*

WRIGHT, John Crafts, a Representative from Ohio; born in Wethersfield, Conn., August 17, 1783; completed preparatory studies; learned the trade of printer; moved to Troy, N. Y., and edited the Troy Gazette for several years; studied law in Litchfield, Conn.; was admitted to the bar and commenced practice in Steubenville, Ohio, in 1809; United States district attorney in 1817; was elected as an Adams Democrat to the Seventeenth Congress, but resigned on March 3, 1821, before the beginning of the congressional term; reelected to the Eighteenth, Nineteenth, and Twentieth Congresses (March 4, 1823–March 3, 1829); unsuccessful candidate for reelection in 1828 to the Twenty-first Congress; elected to the Ohio Supreme Court in 1831 and served until February 2, 1835, when he resigned;

moved to Cincinnati in 1835 and engaged in newspaper work, and for thirteen years published the Cincinnati Gazette; director of the Cincinnati, Hamilton & Dayton Railway Co.; delegate to and honorary president of the peace congress held in Washington, D. C., in 1861 in an effort to devise means to prevent the impending war, and died while serving in that capacity at Washington, D. C., February 13, 1861; interment in Spring Grove Cemetery, Cincinnati, Ohio.

WRIGHT, John Vines, a Representative from Tennessee; born in Purdy, McNairy County, Tenn., June 28, 1828; completed preparatory studies; attended the University of Tennessee at Knoxville, where he pursued courses in medicine and law, graduating from the law department; was admitted to the bar and commenced practice in Purdy, Tenn.; elected as a Democrat to the Thirty-fourth, Thirty-fifth, and Thirty-sixth Congresses (March 4, 1855–March 3, 1861); during the Civil War served in the Confederate Army as colonel of the Thirteenth Regiment, Tennessee Infantry, in 1861; elected to the First and Second Confederate Congresses; judge of the circuit court of Tennessee; chancellor and judge of the State supreme court; practiced law in Nashville, Tenn., 1865–1886; unsuccessful candidate as an Anti-Repudiation Democrat for Governor of Tennessee in 1880; was chairman of the Northwest Indian Commission in 1886 and member of the commission to treat with the Great Sioux Nation in Dakota; appointed to the law division of the General Land Office in 1887 and served until his death in Washington, D. C., June 11, 1908; interment in Rock Creek Cemetery.

WRIGHT, Joseph Albert (brother of George Grover Wright), a Representative and a Senator from Indiana; born in Washington, Pa., April 17, 1810; moved to Indiana about 1820 with his parents, who settled in Bloomington, Monroe County; attended the common schools; was graduated from Indiana University at Bloomington in 1825; studied law; was admitted to the bar in 1829 and commenced practice in Rockville, Parke County, Ind.; member of the State house of representatives in 1833; served in the State senate in 1840; elected as a Democrat to the Twenty-eighth Congress (March 4, 1843–March 3, 1845); unsuccessful candidate for reelection in 1844 to the Twenty-ninth Congress; Governor of Indiana 1849–1857; appointed by President Buchanan as Envoy Extraordinary and Minister Plenipotentiary to Prussia on June 1, 1857, and served until July 1, 1861; appointed to the United States Senate to fill the vacancy caused by the expulsion of Jesse D. Bright and served from February 24, 1862, to January 14, 1863; was not a candidate for the succeeding term; appointed United States commissioner to the Hamburg Exhibition in 1863; again appointed Envoy Extraordinary and Minister Plenipotentiary to Prussia on June 30, 1865, and served until his death in Berlin, Germany, May 11, 1867; interment in New York City.

WRIGHT, Myron Benjamin (brother of Charles Frederick Wright), a Representative from Pennsylvania; born at Forest Lake, Susquehanna County, Pa., June 12, 1847; attended the common schools and pursued an academic course; taught school; clerk in the First National Bank of Susquehanna in 1865 and 1866; elected assistant cashier of the bank in 1867 and cashier in 1869; interested in several financial, business, and manufacturing enterprises; elected as a Republican to the Fifty-first, Fifty-second, and Fifty-third Congresses and served from March 4, 1889, until his death before the close of the Fifty-third Congress; had been reelected to the Fifty-fourth Congress; died while on a trip for the benefit of his health in Trenton, Canada, November 13, 1894; interment in the Grand Street Cemetery, Susquehanna, Pa.

WRIGHT, Robert (cousin of Turbutt Wright), a Senator and a Representative from Maryland; born at "Narborough," near Chestertown, Queen Annes County, Md., November 20, 1752; attended the common schools and Washington College, Chestertown, Md.; studied law; was admitted to the bar in 1773 and commenced practice in Chestertown; served in the Revolutionary War as private, lieutenant, and later as captain; member of the State house of delegates in 1776 and 1784; served in the State senate in 1787; elected as a Democrat to the United States Senate on November 19, 1801, for the term commencing March 4, 1801, and served until his resignation on November 12, 1806, having been elected Governor; delegate to the Farmers' National Convention in 1803; Governor of Maryland 1806–1809; clerk of Queen Annes County in 1810; elected to the Eleventh and Twelfth Congresses to fill the vacancies caused by the resignation of John Brown; reelected to the Thirteenth and Fourteenth Congresses and served from November 29, 1810, to March 3, 1817; unsuccessful candidate for reelection in 1816 to the Fifteenth Congress; elected to the Seventeenth Congress (March 4, 1821–March 3, 1823); was not a candidate for renomination in 1822; district judge of the lower Eastern Shore district of Maryland from 1823 until his death at "Blakeford," Queen Annes County, Md., September 7, 1826; interment in the private burying ground of the DeCourcy family at "Cheston-on-Wye," Queen Annes County, Md.

WRIGHT, Samuel Gardiner, a Representative from New Jersey; born in Wrightstown, N. J., November 18, 1781; was mainly self-educated; engaged in mercantile pursuits in Philadelphia, Pa., with a country place near Imlaystown, N. J.; owned several iron furnaces in New Jersey and Delaware; was elected as a Whig to the Twenty-ninth Congress and served from March 4, 1845, until his death near Imlaystown, Monmouth County, N. J., July 30, 1845, before the assembling of Congress; interment in the East Branch Cemetery, near Imlaystown, N. J.

WRIGHT, Silas, Jr., a Representative and a Senator from New York; born in Amherst, Mass., May 24, 1795; moved with his father to Wyebridge, Vt., in 1796; was graduated from Middlebury (Vt.) College in 1815; moved to Sandy Hill, Washington County, N. Y., in 1816; studied law; was admitted to the bar in January 1819 and commenced practice in Canton, St. Lawrence County, N. Y.; surrogate of St. Lawrence County 1821–1824; member of the State senate 1824–1827; appointed brigadier general of State militia in 1827; elected as a Democrat to the Twentieth Congress and served from March 4, 1827, to February 16, 1829, when he resigned; successfully contested the election of George Fisher to the Twenty-first Congress, but declined to qualify; appointed comptroller of the State of New York in 1829 and served until 1833; delegate to the Democratic National Convention at Baltimore in 1832 which nominated Andrew Jackson for President and Martin Van Buren for Vice President; elected to the United States Senate to fill the vacancy caused by the resignation of William L. Marcy; reelected in 1837 and served from January 4, 1833, to November 26, 1844, when he resigned, having been elected Governor; was nominated as the Democratic candidate for Vice President of the United States at the Baltimore Convention in 1844, but declined the nomination; Governor of New York 1844–1846; unsuccessful candidate for reelection; died in Canton, N. Y., August 27, 1847; interment in Old Canton Cemetery.

WRIGHT, Turbutt (cousin of Robert Wright), a Delegate from Maryland; born at "White Marsh," near Chester ·Mills (now Centerville), Queen Annes County, Md., on February 5, 1741; engaged in agricultural pursuits; member of the General Assembly of Maryland in 1773 and 1774; one of the signers of the Association of Freemen of Maryland July 26, 1775; member of the Maryland constitutional convention in 1776; appointed February 3, 1777, by the council of Maryland as a member of the council of safety to fill the place of James Lloyd Chamberlaine, resigned, and served until the dissolution of the council on March 21, 1777; commissioned a justice of Queen Annes County in 1779; register of wills of Queen Annes County in 1779 and 1780; Member of the Continental Congress in 1781 and 1782; again served in the State general assembly in 1781 and 1782; subscribed (with others, including George Washington) in 1783 to a fund for the purpose of establishing Washington College at Chestertown, Kent County, Md.; died on his estate, "White Marsh," near Centerville, Md., in 1783; interment in the family burial plot on the homestead.

WRIGHT, William, a Representative and a Senator from New Jersey; born in Clarksville, Rockland County, N. Y., November 13, 1790; attended the public schools; was a volunteer for the defense of Stonington, Conn., in the War of 1812; learned the saddler's trade and engaged in business in Bridgeport, Conn., in 1815; moved to Newark, N. J., in 1821; mayor of Newark 1840–1843; elected as a Clay Whig to the Twenty-eighth and Twenty-ninth Congresses (March 4, 1843–March 3, 1847); unsuccessful candidate for Governor of New Jersey in 1847; delegate to the Whig National Convention at Philadelphia in 1848; affiliated with the Democratic Party in 1850; elected as a Democrat to the United States Senate and served from March 4, 1853, to March 3, 1859; unsuccessful candidate for reelection in 1858; again elected to the United States Senate and served from March 4, 1863, until his death in Newark, N. J., November 1, 1866; interment in Mount Pleasant Cemetery.

WRIGHT, William Carter, a Representative from Georgia; born on a farm in Carroll County, Ga., January 6, 1866; moved with his parents to Newnan, Coweta County, Ga., in 1869; attended the common and high schools of Newnan; studied law; was admitted to the bar in 1886 and commenced practice in Newnan, Ga.; also interested in banking and agricultural pursuits; city attorney for Newnan 1892–1895; solicitor of the city court of Newnan 1894–1903; member of the board of education 1910–1918; chairman of the Democratic State executive committee in 1910 and 1911; elected as a Democrat to the Sixty-fifth Congress to fill the vacancy caused by the resignation of William C. Adamson; reelected to the Sixty-sixth and to the six succeeding Congresses and served from January 24, 1918, to March 3, 1933; did not seek renomination in 1932; died in Newnan, Ga., June 11, 1933; interment in Oak Hill Cemetery.

WURTS, John, a Representative from Pennsylvania; born in Flanders, Morris County, N. J., August 13, 1792; after his father's death in 1793 the family resided in Montville, Morris County, and subsequently moved to Philadelphia, Pa.; was graduated from Princeton College in 1813; studied law; was admitted to the bar in 1816 and commenced practice in Philadelphia, Pa.; member of the State house of representatives in 1817; served in the State senate in 1820; elected as a National-Republican to the Nineteenth Congress (March 4, 1825–March 3, 1827); was not a candidate for renomination; United States district attorney 1827–1831; member of the city council of Philadelphia; president of the Delaware & Hudson Canal Co. 1831–1858; went abroad for his health in 1859; died in Rome, Italy, on April 23, 1861; interment in the family cemetery at Pleasant Mills, near Batsto, Atlantic County, N. J.

WURZBACH, Harry McLeary, a Representative from Texas; born in San Antonio, Tex., May 19, 1874; attended the public schools, and was graduated from the law department of Washington and Lee University, Lexington, Va., in 1896; was admitted to the bar the same year and commenced practice in San Antonio, Tex.; during the Spanish-American War volunteered as a private in Company F, First Regiment, Texas Volunteer Infantry; after the war moved to Seguin, Tex., in 1900 and continued the practice of law; prosecuting attorney of Guadalupe County 1900–1902; judge of Guadalupe County 1904–1910; elected as a Republican to the Sixty-seventh and to the three succeeding Congresses (March 4, 1921–March 3, 1929); successfully contested the election of Augustus McCloskey to the Seventy-first Congress; reelected to the Seventy-second Congress and served from February 10, 1930, until his death; delegate at large from Texas to the Republican National Convention at Cleveland in 1924; died in San Antonio, Tex., November 6, 1931; interment in Military Cemetery.

WYANT, Adam Martin, a Representative from Pennsylvania; born near Kittanning, Armstrong County, Pa., September 15, 1869; attended the public schools, Mount Pleasant Institute, and Bucknell University, Lewisburg, Pa.; was graduated from the University of Chicago in 1895; moved to Greensburg, Westmoreland County, Pa., in 1896; studied law; was admitted to the Westmoreland County Bar in 1902 and commenced the practice of law in Greensburg; interested in coal mining and other business enterprises; elected as a Republican to the Sixty-seventh and to the five succeeding Congresses (March 4, 1921–March 3, 1933); was an unsuccessful candidate for reelection in 1932 to the Seventy-third Congress; resumed his former business pursuits; died in Greensburg, Pa., on January 5, 1935; interment in St. Clair Cemetery.

WYNKOOP, Henry, a Delegate and a Representative from Pennsylvania; born in Northampton Township, Bucks County, Pa., March 2, 1737; completed English and classical studies; member of the Pennsylvania Assembly in 1760 and 1761; associate justice of Bucks County Courts 1764–1777 and president judge 1777–1789; member of the committee of observation in 1774; delegate to the provincial conferences of July 15, 1774, and June 18, 1775; major of Bucks County Associated Battalions; member of the general committee of safety in 1776 and 1777; Member of the Continental Congress from 1779 to 1783; justice of the high court of errors and appeals from 1783 to 1789; elected to the First Congress (March 4, 1789–March 3, 1791); appointed associate justice of Bucks County, Pa., and served until his death in that county on March 25, 1816; interment in the graveyard of the Low Dutch Reformed Church, Richboro, Pa.

WYNN, William Joseph, a Representative from California; born in San Francisco, Calif., June 12, 1860; attended the public schools of San Francisco; apprenticed to the machinist's trade and subsequently worked in the principal manufacturing establishments of San Francisco; member of the board of supervisors of the city and county of San Francisco from January 8, 1902, to March 4, 1903; elected by a fusion of the Union Labor and Democratic Parties to the Fifty-eighth Congress (March 4, 1903–March 3, 1905); unsuccessful candidate for reelection in 1904 to the Fifty-ninth Congress; engaged in the insurance business in San Francisco, Calif., until his death in that city January 4, 1935; interment in Holy Cross Cemetery, Colma, Calif.

WYNNS, Thomas, a Representative from North Carolina; born near Barfields, Hertford County, N. C., in 1764; received his education in England; captured at sea on a vessel called the *Fair American* in 1780, and with several other colonists was carried to London; returned to North Carolina and settled as a planter in Hertford County; one of the first trustees of the

University of North Carolina at Chapel Hill; member of the North Carolina House of Commons in 1787; delegate to the State convention for the ratification of the Federal Constitution in 1788 and 1789; served in the North Carolina State Senate 1790–1802 and 1807–1817; presidential elector on the Federalist ticket of Adams and Pinckney in 1800 and of Pinckney and King in 1808; elected as a Federalist to the Seventh Congress to fill the vacancy caused by the death of Charles Johnston; reelected to the Eighth and Ninth Congresses and served from December 7, 1802, to March 3, 1807; resumed planting in Hertford County; member of the North Carolina Executive Council 1818–1824; brigadier general of militia; died near Winton, Hertford County, N. C., on June 3, 1825; interment in Maneys Cemetery, near Maneys Ferry, N. C.

WYTHE, George, a Delegate from Virginia; born near Back River, Elizabeth City County, Va., in 1726; privately instructed by his mother and attended William and Mary College, Williamsburg, Va.; studied law; was admitted to the bar in 1746 and commenced practice in Elizabeth City County in 1755; moved to Williamsburg about 1755; member of the house of burgesses 1758–1768; appointed a member of the committee of correspondence in 1759; moved to his estate in Elizabeth City County in 1763; clerk of the house of burgesses 1768–1775; returned to Williamsburg in 1768; Member of the Continental Congress 1775–1777; a signer of the Declaration of Independence; speaker of the house of delegates in 1777; judge of the Virginia Chancery Court in 1777; appointed sole chancellor of Virginia in 1778; professor of law in William and Mary College from 1779 to 1791, when he resigned and moved to Richmond, Va.; conducted a private school in Richmond and continued teaching until his death; served as a member of the Federal Constitutional Convention at Philadelphia, Pa., in 1787 which adopted the Constitution and was also a member of the State constitutional convention in 1788 which ratified it; was a presidential elector on the Democratic ticket of Jefferson and Burr in 1800 and of Jefferson and Clinton in 1804; emancipated his slaves, furnishing them with means of support until they were able to care for themselves; died in Richmond, Va., June 8, 1806; interment in St. John's Churchyard.

Y

YANCEY, Bartlett (cousin of John Kerr), a Representative from North Carolina; born near Yanceyville, Caswell County, N. C., February 19, 1785; attended a private school and Hyco Academy in Caswell County; student at the University of North Carolina at Chapel Hill 1804–1806; studied law; was admitted to the bar in 1807 and practiced; elected to the Thirteenth and Fourteenth Congresses (March 4, 1813–March 3, 1817); declined to be a candidate for renomination in 1816; member of the State senate and served as its presiding officer 1817–1827; declined the appointment as Minister to Peru tendered by President John Quincy Adams in 1826, and also declined an appointment to the supreme court of North Carolina; died near Yanceyville, N. C., August 30, 1828; interment in the family cemetery upon the homestead.

YANCEY, Joel, a Representative from Kentucky; born in Albemarle County, Va., October 21, 1773; member of the State house of representatives 1809–1811; served in the State senate 1816–1820 and 1824–1827, elected as a Democrat to the Twentieth and Twenty-first Congresses (March 4, 1827–March 3, 1831); unsuccessful candidate for reelection in 1830 to the Twenty-second Congress; died in Barren County, Ky., in April 1838; interment in that county.

YANCEY, William Lowndes (uncle of Joseph Haynsworth Earle), a Representative from Alabama; born at the Falls of the Ogeechee, Warren County, Ga., August 10, 1814; attended preparatory school and Williams College, Williamstown, Mass.; studied law in Sparta, Ga., was admitted to the bar in 1834 and commenced practice in Greenville, S. C.; moved to Cahawba, Ala., in 1836; temporarily abandoned the practice of law and became a cotton planter; editor of the Cahawba Democrat and the Cahawba Gazette; moved to Wetumpka, Ala., in 1839 and resumed the practice of law; member of the State house of representatives in 1841; served in the State senate in 1843; elected as a Democrat to the Twenty-eighth Congress to fill the vacancy caused by the resignation of Dixon H. Lewis; reelected to the Twenty-ninth Congress and served from December 2, 1844, to September 1, 1846, when he resigned; moved to Montgomery, Ala., in 1846; delegate to the Democratic National Convention in 1848, 1856, and 1860; presidential elector on the Democratic ticket of Buchanan and Breckinridge in 1856; member of the State constitutional convention which convened in Montgomery January 7, 1861; appointed chairman of the commission sent to Europe in 1861 to present the Confederate cause to the Governments of England and France; elected to the first Confederate States Senate February 21, 1862; died at his plantation home, near Montgomery, Ala., July 28, 1863; interment in Oakwood Cemetery.

YANGCO, Teodoro Rafael, a Resident Commissioner from the Philippine Islands; born in San Antonio, Province of Zambales, Philippine Islands, on November 9, 1861; attended the Ateneo de Manila (Jesuit College), and was graduated from the University of St. Thomas in 1881; pursued a commercial course in London, England, 1882–1886; engaged in the construction and repair of vessels, in the operation of a line of ferries, and also in mercantile pursuits; director of a life insurance company and interested in various commercial and charitable organizations in Manila; elected as a Nationalist a Resident Commissioner to the United States, and served from March 4, 1917, to March 3, 1920; was not a candidate for renomination in 1920; resumed his former business activities in Manila, Philippine Islands, until his death on April 20, 1939; interment in the Cementerio del Norte.

YAPLE, George Lewis, a Representative from Michigan; born in Leonidas, St. Joseph County, Mich., on February 20, 1851; moved with his parents to Mendon, Mich., in 1857; attended the common schools and Albion (Mich.) College; was graduated from the Northwestern University, Evanston, Ill., in 1871 and completed a postgraduate course in 1874; studied law; was admitted to the bar in 1872, but was engaged in agricultural pursuits until 1877, when he commenced the practice of law at Mendon, Mich.; unsuccessful Greenback candidate for election in 1880 to the Forty-seventh Congress; elected on the Union ticket to the Forty-eighth Congress (March 4, 1883–March 3, 1885); unsuccessful candidate for reelection in 1884 to the Forty-ninth Congress; unsuccessful candidate for election as Governor in 1886; delegate to the Democratic National Convention at St. Louis in 1888, which nominated Grover Cleveland of New York for President and Allen G. Thurman of Ohio for Vice President; resumed the practice of law in Mendon, Mich.; circuit judge of the fifteenth circuit of Michigan 1894–1911; became a member of the Republican Party in 1916; retired from active pursuits and resided in Mendon, Mich., until his death December 16, 1939; interment in Mendon Cemetery.

YARBOROUGH, Ralph Webster, a Senator from Texas; born in Chandler, Henderson County, Tex., June 8, 1903; attended the public schools of Chandler and graduated from Tyler (Tex.) High School; attended the United States Military Academy, West Point, N. Y., in 1919 and 1920 and the Sam Houston State Teachers College, Huntsville, Tex., in 1921; taught school for three years in Delta and Martin Springs, Henderson County, Tex.; spent one year working and studying foreign trade and international relations in Europe, mostly in Germany as assistant secretary for the American Chamber of Commerce in Berlin; served in the Thirty-sixth Division, Texas National Guard, from private to staff sergeant, 1923–1926; worked as a harvest hand in the wheat fields of Oklahoma and as a tank builder in the boom oil town of Borger, Tex., in 1926; graduated from the University of Texas Law School in 1927; was admitted to the bar and commenced the practice of law in El Paso, Tex.; served as assistant attorney general of Texas 1931–1934; wrote Texas' first underground water conservation law in 1931; member of the original board of directors of the Lower Colorado River Authority in 1935; unsuccessful candidate for State attorney general in 1938; lectured on land law at University of Texas Law School in 1935; served as district judge of the Fifty-third Judicial district, Austin, Tex., 1936–1941, and for three years was presiding judge for the third administrative judicial district; during World War II served in Army ground forces with the Ninety-seventh Infantry Division with combat duty in Europe and with occupation forces in Japan from February 1, 1943, until discharged as a lieutenant colonel in June 1946; member of Texas Board of Law Examiners 1947–1951; unsuccessful for the gubernatorial nomination in 1952, 1954, and 1956; elected as a Democrat to the United States Senate in a special election April 2, 1957, to fill the vacancy caused by the resignation of Price Daniel and served from April 29, 1957, to January 3, 1959; reelected in 1958 for the term ending January 3, 1965.

YARDLEY, Robert Morris, a Representative from Pennsylvania; born in Yardley, Bucks County, Pa., October 9, 1850; attended public and private schools in Yardley and Doylestown; studied law; was admitted to the bar in 1872 and commenced practice in Doylestown, Pa.; district attorney of Bucks County 1880–1884; delegate to the Republican National Convention at Chicago in 1884; elected as a Republican to the Fiftieth and Fifty-first Congresses (March 4, 1887–March 3, 1891); declined to be a candidate for renomination in 1890; resumed the practice of law in Bucks County; member of the Doylestown School Board; director of several financial and public service corporations; died in Doylestown, Pa., December 8, 1902; interment in Doylestown Cemetery.

YATES, Abraham (uncle of Peter Waldron Yates), a Delegate from New York; born in Albany, N. Y., August 23, 1724; completed preparatory studies; sheriff of Albany County 1755–1759; deputy to the Provincial Convention in 1775; delegate to the Provincial Congress 1775–1777, and served as president pro tempore of that body November 2, 1775, August 10, 1776, and as president August 28, 1776; member of the council of appointment in 1777; member of the first and second councils of safety May 3, 1777, to January 7, 1778; served in the State senate 1778–1790; receiver of Albany in 1778 and 1779; first postmaster of Albany in 1783; Member of the Continental Congress in 1787 and 1788; mayor of Albany 1790–1796; presidential elector on the Washington and Adams ticket in 1792; died in Albany, N. Y., June 30, 1796; interment in Albany Rural Cemetery.

YATES, John Barentse, a Representative from New York; born in Schenectady, N. Y., February 1, 1784; completed preparatory studies and was graduated from Union College at Schenectady in 1802; studied law; was admitted to the bar in 1805 and commenced practice in Schenectady; served in the War of 1812 under Gen. Wade Hampton on the northern frontier and was subsequently appointed aide-de-camp to Gov. Daniel D. Tompkins; elected as a Democrat to the Fourteenth Congress (March 4, 1815–March 3, 1817); did not seek renomination in 1816; aided in the construction of the Welland Canal; founded the Yates Polytechnic Institute in 1825; moved to Chittenango in 1816; judge of Madison County in 1835 and 1836; elected a member of the State assembly in 1836 and served until his death in Chittenango, N. Y., July 10, 1836; interment in Walnut Grove Cemetery, near Chittenango, N. Y.

YATES, Peter Waldron (nephew of Abraham Yates), a Delegate from New York; born in Albany, N. Y., August 23, 1747; studied law; was admitted to the bar and commenced practice in Albany; member of the committee on correspondence in 1775; resigned and was reelected, but declined to serve; regent of the University of the State of New York in 1784; served in the State assembly in 1784 and 1785; Member of the Continental Congress 1785–1787; resumed the practice of law; died in Caughnawaga, N. Y., March 9, 1826.

YATES, Richard, a Representative and a Senator from Illinois; born in Warsaw, Gallatin County, Ky., January 18, 1818; attended the common schools; moved with his father to Springfield, Ill., in 1831, and subsequently settled in Berlin (now New Berlin), Sangamon County; was graduated from Illinois College, Jacksonville, Ill., in 1835; studied law at Transylvania University, Lexington, Ky.; was admitted to the bar in 1837 and commenced practice in Jacksonville, Ill.; member of the State house of representatives 1842–1845, 1848, and 1849; elected as a Whig to the Thirty-second and Thirty-third Congresses (March 4, 1851–March 3, 1855); unsuccessful candidate for reelection in 1854 to the Thirty-fourth Congress; delegate to the Republican State convention in 1854 and to the Republican National Conventions at Chicago in 1860 which nominated Lincoln and in 1868 which nominated Grant; Governor of Illinois 1861–1865; was the caucus nominee of his party, which was in the minority, for Senator in 1863; elected as a Union Republican to the United States Senate, and served from March 4, 1865, to March 3, 1871; was not a candidate for reelection; died suddenly in St. Louis, Mo., November 27, 1873, while returning from Arkansas, where he had gone as a United States commissioner, appointed by President Grant, to inspect a land subsidy railroad; interment in Diamond Grove Cemetery, Jacksonville, Ill.

YATES, Richard (son of the preceding), a Representative from Illinois; born in Jacksonville, Morgan County, Ill., December 12, 1860; attended public schools and Illinois Woman's College, Jacksonville, Ill., 1870–1874; city editor of the Daily Courier in 1878 and 1879, and of the Daily Journal 1881–1883; was graduated from the Illinois College, Jacksonville, Ill., in 1880 and from the law department of the University of Michigan at Ann Arbor in 1884; commenced practice in Jacksonville, Ill.; city attorney of Jacksonville 1885–1890; private in Company I, Fifth Infantry, Illinois National Guard 1885–1890; county judge of Morgan County 1894–1897; United States collector of internal revenue for the eighth internal revenue district 1897–1900; Governor of Illinois 1901–1904; member of the State public utilities commission 1914–1917; assistant attorney general of the State of Illinois in 1917 and 1918; elected as a Republican to the Sixty-sixth and to the six succeeding Congresses (March 4, 1919–March 3, 1933); unsuccessful for renomination in 1928 to the Seventy-first Congress but was later appointed nominee and elected in place of Henry R. Rathbone, deceased; unsuccessful for reelection in 1932 to the Seventy-third Congress; resided in Harbor Springs, Mich., and Springfield, Ill., while engaged in writing his memoirs; died in Springfield, Ill., April 11, 1936; interment in Diamond Grove Cemetery, Jacksonville, Ill.

YATES, Sidney Richard, a Representative from Illinois; born in Chicago, Ill., August 27, 1909; attended the elementary and high schools in Chicago; graduated from the University of Chicago in 1931 and from its law school in 1933; was admitted to the bar in 1933 and commenced the practice of law in Chicago, Ill.; assistant attorney for Illinois State bank receiver 1935–1937; assistant attorney general attached to Illinois Commerce Commission as traction attorney 1937–1940; served as a lieutenant in the United States Navy 1944–1946; editor of "Bulletin of Decalogue Society of Lawyers," in 1947; elected as a Democrat to the Eighty-first and to the five succeeding Congresses (January 3, 1949–January 3, 1961). *Reelected to the Eighty-seventh Congress.*

YEAMAN, George Helm, a Representative from Kentucky; born in Hardin County, Ky., November 1, 1829; completed preparatory studies; studied law; was admitted to the bar in 1852 and commenced practice in Owensboro, Ky.; judge of Davis County in 1854; member of the State house of representatives in 1861; elected as a Unionist to the Thirty-seventh Congress to fill the vacancy caused by the death of James S. Jackson; reelected to the Thirty-eighth Congress and served from December 1, 1862, to March 3, 1865; unsuccessful candidate for reelection in 1864 to the Thirty-ninth Congress; United States Minister to Denmark 1865–1870; resigned in 1870 and settled in New York City; lecturer on constitutional law at Columbia College; president of the Medico-Legal Society of New York; author of several books, articles, and pamphlets on various subjects; died in Jersey City, N. J., February 23, 1908; interment in Webb Memorial Chapel, Madison, N. J.

YEATES, Jesse Johnson, a Representative from North Carolina; born near Murfreesboro, Hertford County, N. C., May 29, 1829; attended private schools and Emory and Henry College, Emory, Va.; studied law; was admitted to the bar in 1855 and commenced practice in Murfreesboro; prosecuting attorney of Hertford County 1855–1860; member of the State house of commons 1860–1862; solicitor of the first judicial district 1860–1866; served in the Confederate Army as captain and major of the Thirty-first North Carolina Infantry during the Civil War; member of the Governor's council during Governor Worth's administration; declined appointment by Governor Holden as judge of the first judicial district in 1868; delegate to the Democratic State convention in 1871; member of the State constitutional convention in 1871; elected as a Democrat to the Forty-fourth and Forty-fifth Congresses (March 4, 1875–March 3, 1879); successfully contested the election of Joseph J. Martin to the Forty-sixth Congress and served from January 29 to March 3, 1881; declined to be a candidate for renomination in 1880; resumed the practice of his profession in Washington, D. C., and died there on September 5, 1892; interment in Glenwood Cemetery.

YELL, Archibald, a Representative from Arkansas; born in North Carolina in 1797; moved to Tennessee in his youth and settled in Bedford County; took part in the Creek campaign; participated in the War of 1812 and served under General Jackson at the Battle of New Orleans; studied law; was admitted to the bar of Tennessee and commenced practice in Fayetteville, Lincoln County, Tenn., and continued until 1832; declined the governorship of the Territory of Florida; appointed judge of the Territory of Arkansas by President Jackson in 1832, with residence at Fayetteville, Ark., and served until 1835; upon the admission of Arkansas as a State into the Union was elected as a Van Buren Democrat to the Twenty-fourth Congress; reelected to the Twenty-fifth Congress and served from August 1, 1836, to March 3, 1839; Governor of Arkansas 1840–1844; resigned in

1844; elected to the Twenty-ninth Congress and served from March 4, 1845, to July 1, 1846, when he resigned to take part in the Mexican War; served as colonel of the First Regiment, Arkansas Volunteer Cavalry, and was killed in the Battle of Buena Vista February 22, 1847; interment in Fayetteville Cemetery, Fayetteville, Ark.

YOAKUM, Charles Henderson, a Representative from Texas; born near Tehuacana, Lincoln (now Limestone) County, Tex., July 10, 1849; attended Larissa College in Cherokee County and Cumberland College; studied law; was admitted to the bar in 1874 and commenced practice in Emory, Rains County, Tex.; served as prosecuting attorney for Rains County in 1876; moved to Hunt County in 1883 and continued the practice of law in Greenville; district attorney for the eighth judicial district 1886–1890; member of the State senate 1892–1896; elected as a Democrat to the Fifty-fourth Congress (March 4, 1895–March 3, 1897); continued the practice of law in Greenville, Tex., until 1900, when he moved to Los Angeles, Calif.; returned to Texas in 1904; died in Fort Worth, Tex., January 1, 1909; interment in Myrtle Cemetery, Ennis, Tex.

YOCUM, Seth Hartman, a Representative from Pennsylvania; born in Catawissa, Columbia County, Pa., August 2, 1834; attended the rural schools; went to Philadelphia in 1850 and learned the printer's trade; taught school for several years; was graduated from Dickinson College, Carlisle, Pa., in 1860; during the Civil War entered the Union Army as a private and was promoted to first lieutenant of the Fifth Pennsylvania Cavalry; studied law; was admitted to the Schuylkill County bar in 1865 and commenced practice in Ashland, Pa.; moved to Bellefonte, Center County, in 1873 and continued the practice of law; district attorney of Center County 1875–1879; elected as Republican to the Forty-sixth Congress (March 4, 1879–March 3, 1881); was not a candidate for renomination in 1880; moved to Johnson City, Tenn., and engaged in the tanning business; mayor of Johnson City, Tenn., in 1885; moved to Pasadena, Calif., and became engaged in the orange-growing business; died in Santa Monica, Calif., April 19, 1895; interment in Mountain View Cemetery, Pasadena, Calif.

YODER, Samuel S., a Representative from Ohio; born in Berlin, Holmes County, Ohio, August 16, 1841; attended the common schools and Wooster (Ohio) University, and was graduated from the University of Michigan at Ann Arbor; during the Civil War enlisted in the Union Army in the One Hundred and Twenty-eighth Regiment, Ohio Volunteer Infantry, April 19, 1862; rose to the rank of lieutenant and served until the end of the war; studied medicine and practiced in Bluffton, Ohio; mayor of Bluffton 1868–1878; moved to Lima, Ohio, in 1878; studied law; was admitted to the bar in 1880 and commenced practice in Lima; member of the Democratic State executive committee 1883–1885; judge of the probate court of Allen County from February 1882 to October 1886, when he resigned, having been elected to Congress; elected as a Democrat to the Fiftieth and Fifty-first Congresses (March 4, 1887–March 3, 1891); was not a candidate for renomination in 1890; Sergeant at Arms of the National House of Representatives from December 8, 1891, to August 7, 1893; continued the practice of law and also engaged in the real-estate business in Washington, D. C., until his death, May 11, 1921; interment in Arlington National Cemetery, Fort Myer, Va.

YON, Thomas Alva, a Representative from Florida; born near Blountstown, Calhoun County, Fla., March 14, 1882; at the age of five years moved with his parents to a farm in Jackson County, Fla.; attended rural schools, and was graduated from Lanier Southern Business College, Macon, Ga., in 1903; returned to Bloumtstown, Fla., the same year and engaged in mercantile pursuits until 1906; engaged as a traveling salesman at Tallahassee, Fla., 1906–1927; delegate to the Democratic National Convention at San Francisco in 1920; elected as a Democrat to the Seventieth, Seventy-first, and Seventy-second Congresses (March 4, 1927–March 3, 1933); unsuccessful candidate for renomination in 1932; special and commercial agent in the Bureau of Foreign and Domestic Commerce, United States Department of Commerce, Washington, D. C., 1933–1940; assistant investigator, Division of Investigation, General Accounting Office, from 1941 until his retirement in January 1946; engaged in development and sale of his Florida real estate holdings 1946–; is a resident of Tallahassee, Fla.

YORK, Tyre, a Representative from North Carolina; born in Rockford, Surry County, N. C., May 4, 1836; attended the common schools; studied medicine at the Charleston (S. C.) Medical College and commenced practice in Traphill, Wilkes County, N. C., in 1859; also engaged in agricultural pursuits; served during the latter part of the Civil War as surgeon of the Wilkes County Home Guards; was a member of the State house of representatives in 1865, 1866, 1879, and 1887; served in the State senate in 1876 and 1881; elected as a Liberal Democrat to the Forty-eighth Congress (March 4, 1883–March 3, 1885); did not seek renomination in 1884 to the Forty-ninth Congress, having become a gubernatorial candidate; unsuccessful candidate for Governor of North Carolina in 1884; resumed agricultural pursuits; died in Traphill, N. C., January 28, 1916; interment in Traphill Cemetery.

YORKE, Thomas Jones, a Representative from New Jersey; born at Hancocks Bridge, Salem County, N. J., March 25, 1801; attended the common schools and the Salem Academy; during the War of 1812 served as a scout for the United States forces; studied law, but did not practice; engaged in mercantile pursuits at Salem; county collector of Salem County in 1830; judge of the Salem County court of common pleas in 1833, 1834, and 1845–1854 and for a portion of the latter term was presiding judge; member of the State general assembly in 1835; elected as a Whig to the Twenty-fifth Congress (March 4, 1837–March 3, 1839); presented credentials as a Member-elect to the Twenty-sixth Congress, but the House declined to seat him; elected to the Twenty-seventh Congress (March 4, 1841–March 3, 1843); director of the West Jersey Railroad Co., serving as secretary and treasurer in 1853 and as president 1866–1875; also president of the Cape May & Millville Railroad Co.; served as director at various times of the Swedesborough Railroad Co., Salem Railroad Co., Camden & Philadelphia Ferry Co., and West Jersey Marl & Transportation Co.; died in Salem, N. J., April 4, 1882; interment in St. John's Episcopal Cemetery.

YORTY, Samuel William, a Representative from California; born in Lincoln, Lancaster County, Nebr., October 1, 1909; attended the public schools of Lincoln, Nebr.; moved to Los Angeles, Calif., in 1927; completed prelegal work and studied law at Southwestern University and La Salle University; also studied at University of Southern California 1946–1950, and extension courses at University of California in 1948; was admitted to the bar in 1939 and commenced the practice of law in Los Angeles, Calif.; member of the State assembly 1936–1940; during World War II served as a captain, Combat Intelligence, United States Air Corps, with service in New Guinea and the Philippine Islands 1942–1945; again a member of the State assembly in 1949 and 1950; elected as a Democrat to the Eighty-second and Eighty-third Congresses (January 3, 1951–January 3, 1955); was not a candidate for renomination in 1954 but was unsuccessful for election to the United States Senate; unsuccessful for Democratic nomination as United States Senator in 1956; resumed the practice of law; elected mayor of Los Angeles in May 1961 for a four-year term; resides in Studio City, Calif.

YOST, Jacob, a Representative from Virginia; born in Staunton, Augusta County, Va., April 1, 1853; attended the public schools and Mossy Creek Academy; learned the printing trade and was associated in publishing the Valley Virginian; engaged in civil engineering; presidential elector on the Republican ticket of Garfield and Arthur in 1880; unsuccessful Republican candidate for election in 1884 to the Forty-ninth Congress; elected mayor of Staunton in May 1886 and served until January 1887, when he resigned, having been elected to Congress; elected as a Republican to the Fiftieth Congress (March 4, 1887–March 3, 1889); unsuccessful candidate for reelection in 1888 to the Fifty-first Congress; elected to the Fifty-fifth Congress (March 4, 1897–March 3, 1899); declined to be a candidate for renomination in 1898; engaged in the management and development of iron ore and coal lands; discontinued active business pursuits in 1924; moved to Palo Alto, Calif., in 1925 and lived there in retirement until his death on January 25, 1933; interment in Thornrose Cemetery, Staunton, Va.

YOST, Jacob Senewell, a Representative from Pennsylvania; born in Pottsgrove Township, near Pottstown, Montgomery County, Pa., July 29, 1801; attended the common schools and Fourth Street Academy, Philadelphia, Pa.; engaged in agricultural pursuits; publisher and editor of the La Fayette (Pa.) Aurora; member of the State house of representatives 1836–1839; elected as a Democrat to the Twenty-eighth and Twenty-ninth Congresses (March 4, 1843–March 3, 1847); resumed agricultural pursuits near Pottstown, Pa.; United States marshal for the eastern district of Pennsylvania at Philadelphia, Pa., by appointment of President James Buchanan and served from 1857 until his resignation in 1860; resumed agricultural pursuits; died in Pottstown, Pa., on March 7, 1872; interment in Edgewood Cemetery.

YOUMANS, Henry Melville, a Representative from Michigan; born in Otego, Otsego County, N. Y., May 15, 1832; attended the common schools; was in the employ of the York & Erie Railroad Co., on the Susquehanna division, for ten years; moved to East Saginaw, Mich., in 1862; engaged in the manufacture of lumber and salt 1863–1878; moved to St. Clair County, Mich., in 1878 and engaged in farming and lumbering until 1884 when he returned to East Saginaw; mayor of East Saginaw in 1886 and 1887; served four terms as alderman; held all the positions of honor under the municipal government of East Saginaw; elected as a Democrat to the Fifty-second Congress (March 4, 1891–March 3, 1893); unsuccessful candidate for reelection in 1892 to the Fifty-third Congress; member of the State senate in 1896 and 1897; engaged in agricultural pursuits at Bridgeport, Mich., until his death in Saginaw, Mich., July 8, 1920; interment in Brady Hill Cemetery.

YOUNG, Augustus, a Representative from Vermont; born in Arlington, Bennington County, Vt., March 20, 1784; completed preparatory studies; studied law; was admitted to the bar in 1810 and commenced practice in Stowe, Vt.; moved to Craftsbury, Vt., in 1812; member of the State house of representatives 1821–1824, 1826, 1828–1830, and 1832; State's attorney for Orleans County 1824–1828; judge of probate in 1830 and 1831; served in the State senate 1836–1838; elected as a Whig to the Twenty-seventh Congress (March 4, 1841–March 3, 1843); declined to be a candidate for renomination in 1842; resumed the practice of law and engaged in literary pursuits;

moved to St. Albans in 1847; assistant judge of the Franklin County Court 1851–1854; died in St. Albans, Vt., June 17, 1857; interment in Greenwood Cemetery.

YOUNG, Bryan Rust (brother of William Singleton Young and uncle of John Young Brown), a Representative from Kentucky; born near Bardstown, Nelson County, Ky., January 14, 1800; attended the common schools and was graduated from the University of Louisville, Louisville, Ky.; studied medicine and practiced his profession in Nelson County, Ky.; member of State house of representatives in 1858–1859, 1861–1862, and 1863–1864; elected as a Democrat to the Twenty-ninth Congress (March 4, 1845–March 3, 1847); resumed the practice of medicine; presidential elector on the Democratic ticket of Cass and Butler in 1848; died in Elizabethtown, Ky., May 14, 1882; interment in Elizabethtown Cemetery.

YOUNG, Clarence Clifton, a Representative from Nevada; born in Lovelock, Pershing County, Nev., November 7, 1922; attended the public schools of his native city; graduated from the University of Nevada in Reno in 1943; during World War II served in the United States Army ground forces from May 1943 to October 1946, with twenty months' overseas duty in the European Theater with the One Hundred and Third Infantry Division, and was discharged as a major; after military service, graduated from Harvard Law School in 1949; was admitted to the Nevada bar in 1949 and commenced practice in Reno, Nev.; public administrator of Washoe County 1950–1952; State president of the Young Republicans of Nevada in 1952; elected as a Republican to the Eighty-third and Eighty-fourth Congresses (January 3, 1953–January 3, 1957); was not a candidate for renomination in 1956 but was an unsuccessful candidate for election to the United States Senate; engaged in the practice of law in Reno, Nev.

YOUNG, Ebenezer, a Representative from Connecticut; born in Killingly, Windham County, Conn., on December 25, 1783; was graduated from Yale College in 1806; studied law; was admitted to the bar and commenced practice in Westfield (now Danielson), Conn.; engaged in the manufacture of cloth at East Killingly, Conn.; elected as a Federalist a member of the State house of representatives in 1810, 1811, 1816, and 1817; served in the State senate 1823–1825; again a member of the State house of representatives 1826–1828, serving as speaker in 1827 and 1828; elected to the Twenty-first, Twenty-second, and Twenty-third Congresses (March 4, 1829–March 3, 1835); died in West Killingly, Conn., August 18, 1851; interment in Westfield Cemetery, Danielson, Conn.

YOUNG, George Morley, a Representative from North Dakota; born in Lakelet, Huron County, Ontario, Canada, December 11, 1870; when a boy moved to the United States and settled in St. Charles, Mich.; attended the public schools; was graduated from the law department of the University of Minnesota at Minneapolis in 1894; was admitted to the bar the same year and commenced practice in Valley City, N. Dak.; member of the board of aldermen in 1898 and 1899; member of the State house of representatives 1900–1902; served in the State senate 1904–1908 and was president pro tempore during the entire term; elected as a Republican to the Sixty-third and to the five succeeding Congresses and served from March 4, 1913, to September 2, 1924, when he resigned to accept a judicial position; appointed as a member of the United States Customs Court at New York City in 1924; served as associate judge until 1932 and as presiding judge until his death in New York City, N. Y., May 27, 1932; interment in Woodbine Cemetery, Valley City, N. Dak.

YOUNG, **Hiram Casey,** a Representative from Tennessee; born in Tuscaloosa, Tuscaloosa County, Ala., December 14, 1828; moved with his parents to a farm near Byhalia, Marshall County, Miss., in 1838; attended the local schools and was tutored by his father and also attended Marshall Institute in Marshall County, Miss.; studied law; was admitted to the bar in 1859 and commenced practice in Memphis, Tenn.; served in the Civil War 1861–1865 as lieutenant colonel of Cavalry and on the brigade staff; Assistant Inspector General, First Division of Cavalry, in 1864; elected as a Democrat to the Forty-fourth, Forty-fifth, and Forty-sixth Congresses (March 4, 1875–March 3, 1881); unsuccessful candidate for reelection in 1880; elected to the Forty-eighth Congress (March 4, 1883–March 3, 1885); was not a candidate for renomination; resumed the practice of law; died in Memphis, Tenn., August 17, 1899; interment in Elmwood Cemetery.

YOUNG, **Horace Olin,** a Representative from Michigan; born in New Albion, Cattaraugus County, N. Y., August 4, 1850; attended the common schools and high school of Albion, N. Y., and Randolph (N. Y.) Institute; moved to Ishpeming, Mich.; engaged in accounting; studied law; was admitted to the bar in 1879 and commenced practice in Ishpeming, Mich.; member of the State house of representatives in 1879; prosecuting attorney of Marquette County 1886–1896; elected as a Republican to the Fifty-eighth and to the four succeeding Congresses (March 4, 1903–March 3, 1913); presented credentials as a Member-elect to the Sixty-third Congress and served from March 4, 1913, until his resignation, effective May 16, 1913, while a contest for the seat was pending; president of the Miners' National Bank in Ishpeming; died in Ishpeming, Mich., August 5, 1917; interment in the City Cemetery.

YOUNG, **Isaac Daniel,** a Representative from Kansas; born near Pleasantville, Marion County, Iowa, on March 29, 1849; attended high school and Oskaloosa College in Iowa; began teaching at the age of fifteen and continued in that profession for ten years; moved to Mitchell County, Kans., in 1874 and settled on a homestead in Turkey Creek Township; engaged in agricultural pursuits for eleven years; superintendent of public instruction of Mitchell County, Kans., 1876–1880; member of the State senate 1884–1888; moved to Beloit, Kans., in 1885; studied law; was admitted to the bar in 1889 and commenced practice in Beloit, Kans.; again a member of the State senate 1904–1908; elected as a Republican to the Sixty-second Congress (March 4, 1911–March 3, 1913); unsuccessful for reelection in 1912; delegate to nearly all Republican conventions; resumed the practice of law in Beloit, Kans., until his death December 10, 1927; interment in Elmwood Cemetery.

YOUNG, **James,** a Representative from Texas; born in Henderson, Rusk County, Tex., July 18, 1866; attended the public schools; was graduated from the law department of the University of Texas at Austin in July 1891; was admitted to the bar the same year and commenced practice in Kaufman, Tex.; elected as a Democrat to the Sixty-second and to the four succeeding Congresses (March 4, 1911–March 3, 1921); declined to be a candidate for renomination in 1920; again engaged in the practice of law in Kaufman, Tex.; unsuccessful candidate for the Democratic gubernatorial nomination in 1930; moved to Henderson, Tex., in 1931, and continued the practice of law until 1937, when he moved to Dallas, Tex., where he died April 29, 1942; interment in the Kaufman Cemetery, Kaufman, Tex.

YOUNG, **James Rankin,** a Representative from Pennsylvania; born in Philadelphia, Pa., March 10, 1847; attended the common schools and Philadelphia High School; during the Civil War enlisted in the Union Army in June 1863 in the Thirty-second Regiment, Pennsylvania Volunteer Infantry, and served during the Gettysburg campaign; one of the founders of the Philadelphia Evening Star in 1866; attended all Republican National Conventions 1864–1908; served as chief of the Washington bureau of the New York Tribune from June 1866 to December 1870; chief executive clerk of the United States Senate from December 1873 to March 1879; chief clerk of the Department of Justice from September 1882 to December 1883; again chief executive clerk of the United States Senate from December 1883 to April 1892; elected as a Republican to the Fifty-fifth, Fifty-sixth, and Fifty-seventh Congresses (March 4, 1897–March 3, 1903); superintendent of the Dead Letter Office of the Post Office Department 1905–1913; superintendent of the postal savings depository in Philadelphia until 1915; retired and was a resident of Washington, D. C., until his death December 18, 1924; interment in Glenwood Cemetery.

YOUNG, **John,** a Representative from New York; born in Chelsea, Orange County, Vt., June 12, 1802; moved to New York State in 1806 with his parents, who settled in Conesus, Livingston County, where he attended the public schools; studied law; was admitted to the bar in 1829 and commenced practice in Geneseo, N. Y.; member of the State assembly in 1833, 1844, and 1845; elected as a Whig to the Twenty-fourth Congress to fill the vacancy caused by the resignation of Philo C. Fuller and served from November 9, 1836, to March 3, 1837; declined to be a candidate for reelection in 1836; elected to the Twenty-seventh Congress (March 4, 1841–March 3, 1843); was not a candidate for reelection in 1842; Governor of New York 1847–1849; delegate to the Whig National Convention at Philadelphia in 1848; appointed assistant treasurer of the United States at New York June 28, 1849, and served until his death in New York City April 23, 1852; interment in Temple Hill Cemetery, Geneseo, N. Y.

YOUNG, **John Andrew,** a Representative from Texas; born in Corpus Christi, Nueces County, Tex., November 10, 1916; attended the Incarnate Word Academy and Corpus Christi College-Academy; graduated from St. Edwards University, Austin, Tex., in 1937 and from the University of Texas School of Law in 1940; was admitted to the bar in 1940 and commenced the practice of law; volunteered for service in the United States Navy in 1941, before Pearl Harbor, served in all theaters of war, and was separated from the service in 1945 as a lieutenant commander; awarded the Presidential Unit Citation for service beyond the call of duty; assistant county attorney of Nueces County in 1946; assistant district attorney of Nueces County 1947–1950; county attorney in 1951 and 1952; county judge of Nueces County 1953–1956; elected as a Democrat to the Eighty-fifth and Eighty-sixth Congresses (January 3, 1957–January 3, 1961). *Reelected to the Eighty-seventh Congress.*

YOUNG, **John Duncan,** a Representative from Kentucky; born in Owingsville, Bath County, Ky., September 22, 1823; attended the common schools; studied law; was admitted to the bar in 1854 and practiced in Owingsville, Ky., and later engaged in agricultural pursuits; acting marshal of Kentucky during the administration of President Pierce; elected judge of the quarterly court of Bath County in 1858 and served four years; again elected in 1866 and served until 1867 when he resigned, having been elected to Congress; presented credentials as a Member-elect to the Fortieth Congress in 1867, but was not permitted to qualify; elected as a Democrat to the Forty-third Congress (March 4, 1873–March 3, 1875); was not a candidate for renomination in 1874; resumed agricultural pursuits; State railroad commissioner of Kentucky 1884–1889;

again served as judge of the quarterly court of Bath County 1890–1895; died in Mount Sterling, Ky., December 26, 1910; interment in Machpelah Cemetery.

YOUNG, John Smith, a Representative from Louisiana; born near Raleigh, Wake County, N. C., November 4, 1834; moved with his father to Fayette County, Tenn., in 1836, and to Columbia County, Ark., in 1848; was graduated from Centenary College, Jackson, La., in 1855; moved to Homer, Claiborne Parish, La., in September 1855; studied law; was admitted to the bar in 1860 and practiced in Homer; during the Civil War enlisted in the Confederate Army as a private May 3, 1861, and was successively promoted until he attained the rank of lieutenant colonel; returned to Homer at the close of the war and resumed the practice of law; judge of Claiborne Parish Court 1870–1872; member of the State house of representatives 1872–1876; judge of the eleventh judicial district of Louisiana 1876–1878; elected as a Democrat to the Forty-fifth Congress to fill the vacancy caused by the death of John E. Leonard and served from November 5, 1878, to March 3, 1879; was not a candidate for renomination in 1878; resumed the practice of law in Homer, La.; moved to Monroe, La., and later to Shreveport in 1880, where he continued the practice of his profession; sheriff of Caddo Parish 1892–1900; died in Shreveport, La., October 11, 1916; interment in Oakland Cemetery.

YOUNG, Lafayette, a Senator from Iowa; born near Eddyville, Monroe County, Iowa, May 10, 1848; attended country schools and night school in St. Louis, in which city he learned the printing trade; founded and published the Atlantic (Iowa) Telegraph 1871–1890; member of the State senate 1874–1886; established the Des Moines Capital March 30, 1890, and was editor at the time of his death; was with General Shafter's expedition in Cuba as a war correspondent in 1898; delegate to the Republican National Conventions in 1900 and 1908; at the former convention nominated Theodore Roosevelt for Vice President of the United States; presidential elector on the Republican ticket of Taft and Sherman in 1908; appointed to the United States Senate to fill the vacancy caused by the death of Jonathan P. Dolliver and served from November 12, 1910, to April 11, 1911, when a successor was elected; unsuccessful candidate for election to fill this vacancy; war correspondent for four months in Europe in 1915; Chautauqua lecturer in 1915; established the Sunday Capital April 6, 1919; chairman of the State council for defense for Iowa during the First World War; was made a knight of the Order of Leopold II of Belgium in recognition of his work in raising funds in Iowa for the children of Belgium; died in Des Moines, Iowa, November 15, 1926; interment in Woodlawn Cemetery.

YOUNG, Milton Ruben, a Senator from North Dakota; born in Berlin, La Moure County, N. Dak., on December 6, 1897; attended the public and high schools of La Moure County, the North Dakota State Agricultural College at Fargo, and Graceland College, Lamoni, Iowa; engaged in agricultural pursuits near Berlin, N. Dak.; member of the State house of representatives in 1932; served in the State senate from 1934 until his resignation in March 1945; elected president pro tempore in 1941 and majority leader in 1943; appointed and subsequently elected as a Republican to the United States Senate to fill the vacancy caused by the death of John Moses and served from March 12, 1945, to January 3, 1951; reelected in 1950 and again in 1956 for the term ending January 3, 1963.

YOUNG, Pierce Manning Butler, a Representative from Georgia; born in Spartanburg, Spartanburg County, S. C., on November 15, 1836; moved with his parents to Georgia in

1839; studied under private tutors, and was graduated from Georgia Military Institute at Marietta in 1856; studied law; entered the United States Military Academy, West Point, N. Y., in 1857 and resigned two months before graduation to enter the Confederate Army as a second lieutenant; served throughout the Civil War, attaining the rank of major general; settled in Cartersville, Ga., after the war and engaged in agricultural pursuits; upon the readmission of the State of Georgia to representation was elected as a Democrat to the Fortieth Congress and served from July 25, 1868, to March 3, 1869; presented credentials as a Member-elect to the Forty-first Congress, but the House decided he was not entitled to the seat; subsequently elected to fill the vacancy thus caused; reelected to the Forty-second and Forty-third Congresses and served from December 22, 1870, to March 3, 1875; unsuccessful candidate for renomination in 1874; delegate to the Democratic National Conventions in 1872, 1876, and 1880; resumed agricultural pursuits; appointed United States commissioner to the Paris Exposition in 1878; consul general at St. Petersburg (later Leningrad), Russia, 1885–1887; envoy Extraordinary and Minister Plenipotentiary to Guatemala and Honduras by appointment of President Grover Cleveland 1893–1896; died in the Presbyterian Hospital, New York City, July 6, 1896; interment in Oak Hill Cemetery, Cartersville, Ga.

YOUNG, Richard, a Representative from New York; born in Londonderry, Ireland, August 6, 1846; immigrated to the United States in 1851 with his parents, who settled in Philadelphia, Pa.; attended the public schools and was graduated from Crittenden's Commercial College in Philadelphia; moved to Flatbush, N. Y., in 1866 and engaged in an extensive leather trade in New York City; member of the board of school commissioners of Brooklyn 1895–1902; park commissioner for the Boroughs of Brooklyn and Queens in 1902 and 1903; engaged in banking and also interested in numerous corporations and business enterprises; elected as a Republican to the Sixty-first Congress (March 4, 1909–March 3, 1911); declined to be a candidate for reelection in 1910; resumed his interest in the leather industry, serving as chairman of the board of directors of the Richard Young Co., in New York City; also engaged in banking and various business enterprises in Brooklyn and resided in Flatbush, Brooklyn, N. Y., until his death there June 9, 1935; interment in Greenwood Cemetery.

YOUNG, Richard Montgomery, a Senator from Illinois; born in Fayette County, Ky., February 20, 1798; attended the country schools and Forest Hill Academy, Jessamine County, Ky.; studied law, and was admitted to the bar in Kentucky in 1816; member of the Kentucky Militia; moved to Illinois in 1817 and commenced the practice of law in Jonesboro; appointed captain in the Illinois Militia; member of the State house of representatives 1820–1822; served as circuit judge of the fifth circuit from 1825 to January 2, 1837, when he resigned, having been elected to the United States Senate; elected as a Democrat to the United States Senate and served from March 4, 1837, to March 3, 1843; member of the mission to England to negotiate a loan for the State of Illinois in 1839; associate justice of the State supreme court from 1843 to 1847, when he resigned; appointed by President Polk as Commissioner of the General Land Office and served from 1847 to 1849; Clerk of the National House of Representatives from April 17, 1850, to March 4, 1851; resumed the practice of law in Washington, D. C., where he died November 28, 1861; interment in the Congressional Cemetery.

YOUNG, Stephen Marvin, a Representative and a Senator from Ohio; born on a farm near Norwalk, Huron County, Ohio, May 4, 1889; attended the public schools, and Kenyon and Adelbert Colleges; was graduated from the law department of Western

Reserve University, Cleveland, Ohio, in 1911; was admitted to the bar the same year and commenced practice in Norwalk, Ohio; member of the State house of representatives 1913–1917; assistant prosecuting attorney of Cuyahoga County in 1917 and 1918; served as a private in Company F, Third Ohio Infantry, on the Mexican border in 1916, and during the First World War served in the Field Artillery; awarded the Victory Medal; chief assistant prosecuting attorney of Cuyahoga County in 1919 and 1920; unsuccessful candidate for attorney general in 1922; unsuccessful Democratic candidate for the gubernatorial nomination in 1930; member of the Ohio Commission on Unemployment Insurance in 1931 and 1932; elected as a Democrat to the Seventy-third and Seventy-fourth Congresses (March 4, 1933–January 3, 1937); was not a candidate for renomination in 1936, but was an unsuccessful candidate for the gubernatorial nomination; special counsel to the attorney general of Ohio 1937–1939; elected to the Seventy-seventh Congress (January 3, 1941–January 3, 1943); unsuccessful candidate for reelection in 1942 to the Seventy-eighth Congress; during World War II was commissioned a major in the United States Army January 13, 1943; served in North Africa and Italy, and later as allied military governor of Reggio Emilia, Italy; discharged as a lieutenant colonel February 18, 1946; awarded the Bronze Star, European-African-Middle Eastern Theater Campaign Medal with four battle stars, Commendation of Gen. Mark W. Clark, Victory Medal, and Order of the Crown of Italy; resumed the practice of law in Cleveland, Ohio, and Washington, D. C.; elected to the Eighty-first Congress (January 3, 1949–January 3, 1951); unsuccessful candidate for reelection in 1950 to the Eighty-second Congress; in 1956 was defeated for attorney general of Ohio; elected as a Democrat to the United States Senate for the term commencing January 3, 1959, and ending January 3, 1965.

YOUNG, Thomas Lowry, a Representative from Ohio; born in Killyleagh, County Down, Ireland, December 14, 1832; immigrated to the United States with his parents in 1847; enlisted in the United States Army as a musician and advanced through the ranks to first sergeant of Company A, Third Artillery, and served from March 25, 1848, to January 28, 1858; settled in Cincinnati and was instructor in the State reform school; during the Civil War was captain of Benton Cadets, Missouri Volunteers, September 6, 1861; resigned December 10, 1861; commissioned major of the One Hundred and Eighteenth Regiment, Ohio Volunteer Infantry, September 17, 1862; lieutenant colonel April 17, 1863; colonel April 11, 1864; brevetted brigadier general of Volunteers March 13, 1865, "for gallant and meritorious services in the Battle of Resaca, Ga."; resigned September 14, 1864; was graduated from the Cincinnati Law School; was admitted to the bar in 1865 and commenced practice in Cincinnati, Ohio; assistant city auditor of Cincinnati in 1865; member of the State house of representatives 1866–1868; elected recorder of Hamilton County in 1867; appointed supervisor of internal revenue in 1868; delegate to the Republican National Convention at Chicago in 1868; member of the State senate 1871–1873; Lieutenant Governor in 1875; Acting Governor of Ohio in 1877; elected as a Republican to the Forty-sixth and Forty-seventh Congresses (March 4, 1879–March 3, 1883); unsuccessful candidate for renomination in 1882; resumed the practice of law; member of the board of public affairs of Cincinnati 1886–1888; died in Cincinnati, Ohio, July 20, 1888; interment in Spring Grove Cemetery.

YOUNG, Timothy Roberts, a Representative from Illinois; born in Dover, N. H., November 19, 1811; completed preparatory studies; attended Phillips Exeter (N. H.) Academy and was graduated from Bowdoin College, Brunswick, Maine, in 1835; studied law in Dover, N. H., and was admitted to the bar; moved to Marshall, Ill., in the spring of 1838 and practiced law for ten years; elected as a Democrat to the Thirty-first Congress (March 4, 1849–March 3, 1851); moved to Mattoon, Ill., and became interested in the manufacture of plug tobacco, in which he continued for ten years; engaged in agricultural pursuits near Casey, Clark County, Ill.; died at Oilfield, near Casey, Ill., May 12, 1898; interment in Marshall Cemetery, Marshall, Ill.

YOUNG, William Albin, a Representative from Virginia; born in Norfolk, Va., May 17, 1860; attended the public schools and St. Mary's Academy at Norfolk; studied law, but abandoned it before obtaining a license and devoted himself to mercantile pursuits; clerk of the circuit and corporation courts of the city of Norfolk for six years; delegate to the Democratic National Convention at Chicago in 1892; presented credentials as a Member-elect to the Fifty-fifth Congress and served from March 4, 1897, to April 26, 1898, when he was succeeded by Richard A. Wise, who contested his election; presented credentials as a Member-elect to the Fifty-sixth Congress and served from March 4, 1899, to March 12, 1900, when he was again succeeded by Richard A. Wise, who contested his election; engaged in the real-estate business at Norfolk, Va., where he died March 12, 1928; interment in St. Mary's Cemetery.

YOUNG, William Singleton (brother of Bryan Rust Young and uncle of John Young Brown), a Representative from Kentucky; born near Bardstown, Nelson County, Ky., April 10, 1790; studied medicine with Dr. Bemiss, of Bloomfield, and was graduated from the University of Louisville, Louisville, Ky.; commenced practice in Bloomfield, Nelson County, Ky.; moved to Elizabethtown, Hardin County, Ky., in 1814 and continued the practice of law; elected as a Democrat to the Nineteenth Congress; reelected to the Twentieth Congress and served from March 4, 1825, until his death in Elizabethtown, September 20, 1827, before the assembling of the Twentieth Congress; interment in Elizabethtown Cemetery.

YOUNGBLOOD, Harold Francis, a Representative from Michigan; born in Detroit, Wayne County, Mich., August 7, 1907; attended the public schools; was graduated from St. Joseph's Commercial College in 1927; employed in Detroit office of the secretary of state of Michigan in 1927 and 1928; member of staff of Wayne County Board of Auditors 1928–1935; engaged as a plumbing and heating contractor in 1940; elected as a Republican to the Eightieth Congress (January 3, 1947–January 3, 1949); unsuccessful candidate for reelection in 1948 to the Eighty-first Congress; special assistant to the Director of Foreign Operations Administration in Berlin area in 1954 and 1955; engaged in construction contracting; is a resident of Tucson, Ariz.

YOUNGDAHL, Oscar Ferdinand, a Representative from Minnesota; born in Minneapolis, Minn., October 13, 1893; attended the public schools and Hamline University, St. Paul, Minn.; was graduated from Gustavus Adolphus College, St. Peter, Minn., in 1916; principal of Ortonville (Minn.) High School and instructor of dramatics and public speaking 1916–1918; during the First World War served as a seaman second class in the United States Navy in 1918 and 1919; engaged in the sale of bonds and securities 1919–1925; was graduated from the Minnesota College of Law at Minneapolis in 1925; was admitted to the bar the same year and commenced practice in Minneapolis, Minn.; unsuccessful candidate for attorney general in 1936; elected as a Republican to the Seventy-sixth and Seventy-seventh Congresses (January 3, 1939–January 3, 1943); unsuccessful candidate for renomination in 1942; resumed the practice of law until his death in Minneapolis, Minn., February 3, 1946; interment in Lakewood Cemetery.

YOUNGER, Jesse Arthur, a Representative from California; born in Albany, Linn County, Oreg., April 11, 1893; moved to Kirkland, Wash., in 1904; attended the public schools; graduated from the University of Washington at Seattle in 1915 and served as graduate manager of athletics until 1917; during the First World War was called into Federal service in August 1917 with the Washington National Guard; served overseas for ten months with the Forty-eighth Coast Artillery Corps, and discharged as a captain in June 1919; served as vice president, director, and manager of the mortgage loan department of the Seattle Title Trust Co., 1920–1930; president of the Seattle Mortgage Loan Co., 1930–1934; regional appraiser for the Home Owners Loan Corporation, assistant appraiser-adviser for the Home Loan Bank Board, and Chief of the Savings and Loan Division of the Federal Home Loan Bank Board 1934–1937; moved to San Mateo, Calif., in 1937; executive vice president of Citizens Federal Savings & Loan Association in San Francisco 1937–1952; elected as a Republican to the Eighty-third and to the three succeeding Congresses (January 3, 1953–January 3, 1961). *Reelected to the Eighty-seventh Congress.*

YULEE, David Levy (formerly David Levy), a Delegate and a Senator from Florida; born in St. Thomas, West Indies, June 12, 1810; immigrated to the United States with his father, who settled in Norfolk, Va.; attended a private school in Norfolk, Va.; studied law in St. Augustine, Fla., where he went as a lad to his father's plantation in 1824; was admitted to the bar in 1836 and practiced in St. Augustine, Fla.; clerk to the Territorial legislature in 1841; elected as a Republican a Delegate to the Twenty-seventh and Twenty-eighth Congresses (March 4, 1841–March 3, 1845); did not seek renomination, having become a candidate for the Senate; delegate to the first State constitutional convention in 1845; upon the admission of Florida as a State into the Union was elected to the United States Senate and served from July 1, 1845, to March 3, 1851; by an act of the Florida Legislature and at his request his name was changed to David Levy Yulee, and the United States Senate on January 12, 1846, ordered his name changed upon its rolls and journals in conformity with the act; again elected in January 1855 and served from March 4, 1855, until his withdrawal January 21, 1861; president of the Atlantic & Gulf Railroad; served in the Confederate Congress throughout the Civil War; was a prisoner of state at Fort Pulaski in 1865; moved to Washington, D. C., in 1880; died at the Clarendon Hotel, New York City, October 10, 1886, while en route to his home in Washington, D. C., after a visit to Bermuda; interment in Oak Hill Cemetery, Washington, D. C.

Z

ZABLOCKI, Clement John, a Representative from Wisconsin; born in Milwaukee, Wis., November 18, 1912; attended parochial school and Marquette University High School; graduated from Marquette University in 1936; taught high school in Milwaukee in 1938 and 1939; organist and choir director 1932–1948; member of the State senate 1942–1948; chairman of the Democratic State Convention in 1948; alternate delegate to the Democratic National Conventions in 1952 and 1956 and delegate in 1960; was an unsuccessful candidate for the office of city controller of Milwaukee in 1948; United States delegate to the fourteenth session of the United Nations General Assembly in 1959; major in the United States Air Force Reserve; in 1957 was unsuccessful for the senatorial nomination to fill a vacancy in the United States Senate; elected as a Democrat to the Eighty-first and to the five succeeding Congresses (January 3, 1949–January 3, 1961). *Reelected to the Eighty-seventh Congress.*

ZELENKO, Herbert, a Representative from New York; born in New York City, N. Y., March 16, 1906; attended Public School No. 40 in the Bronx and Stuyvesant High School; graduated from Columbia University in 1926 and from Columbia Law School in 1928; was admitted to the bar in 1929 and commenced the practice of law in New York City, N. Y.; lecturer, Practicing Law Institute and Law Science Institute; former assistant United States attorney for the southern district of New York; elected as a Democrat to the Eighty-fourth, Eighty-fifth, and Eighty-sixth Congresses (January 3, 1955–January 3, 1961). *Reelected to the Eighty-seventh Congress.*

ZENOR, William Taylor, a Representative from Indiana; born near Corydon, Harrison County, Ind., April 30, 1846; attended the common schools and the seminary of James G. May; studied law in New Albany, Ind.; was admitted to the bar in 1870 and commenced practice in Corydon; moved to Leavenworth, Crawford County, Ind., in 1871 and continued the practice of law; prosecuting attorney of Crawford and Harrison Counties 1879–1885; judge of the third judicial circuit 1885–1897; elected as a Democrat to the Fifty-fifth and to the four succeeding Congresses (March 4, 1897–March 3, 1907); resumed the practice of law in Corydon, Ind.; moved to New Albany, Ind., in 1910 and continued the practice of law until his death there June 2, 1916; interment in Cedar Hill Cemetery, Corydon, Ind.

ZIEGLER, Edward Danner, a Representative from Pennsylvania; born in Bedford, Bedford County, Pa., March 3, 1844; attended the common schools, and was graduated from Pennsylvania College at Gettysburg in 1865; engaged in teaching in the York County Academy; studied law; was admitted to the bar on November 4, 1868, and commenced practice in York, Pa.; commissioner's clerk in 1871 and 1872; counsel to the board of commissioners; district attorney of York County 1881–1883; delegate to the Democratic National Convention at Chicago in 1884; elected as a Democrat to the Fifty-sixth Congress (March 4, 1899–March 3, 1901); unsuccessful candidate for renomination in 1900; resumed the practice of law; appointed by the judge of the court of common pleas of York County auditor of the offices of prothonotary, register of wills, clerk of the court, treasurer, and recorder of York County and served from 1923 to 1925; resumed the practice of law in York, Pa., until his death there on December 21, 1931; interment in Prospect Hill Cemetery.

ZIHLMAN, Frederick Nicholas, a Representative from Maryland; born in Carnegie, Allegheny County, Pa., October 2, 1879; moved to Maryland with his parents, who settled in Cumberland in 1882; attended the public schools; entered a glass factory in 1890 and apprenticed as a glass blower; president of the local flint-glass workers' union 1904–1909 and was a member of the national executive board in 1905 and 1906; president of the Allegany Trades Council 1904–1909; president of the Maryland State Federation of Labor in 1906 and 1907; member of the Maryland State Senate 1909–1917, serving as Republican floor leader in 1914 and 1916; engaged in the real estate and insurance business in Cumberland, Md., in 1912; was an unsuccessful candidate for election in 1914 to the Sixty-fourth Congress; elected as a Republican to the Sixty-fifth and to the six succeeding Congresses (March 4, 1917–March 3, 1931); was an unsuccessful candidate for reelection in 1930 to the Seventy-second Congress, and for election in 1934 to the Seventy-fourth Congress; resumed his former business pursuits in Cumberland, Md., where he died on April 22, 1935; interment in St. John's Cemetery, Forest Glen, Md.

ZIMMERMAN, Orville, a Representative from Missouri; born on a farm near Glenallen, Bollinger County, Mo., December 31, 1880; attended the public schools and Mayfield-Smith Academy, Marble Hill, Mo.; was graduated from the Southeast Missouri State College at Cape Girardeau in 1904 and from the law department of the University of Missouri at Columbia in 1911; principal of Dexter (Mo.) High School 1904–1908; was admitted to the bar in 1911 and commenced practice in Kennett, Mo.; during the First World War served as a private in the United States Army in 1918; member of the board of education of Kennett, Mo., 1928–1936; member of the board of regents of Southeast Missouri State College 1933–1948; elected as a Democrat to the Seventy-fourth and to the six succeeding Congresses and served from January 3, 1935, until his death in Washington, D. C., April 7, 1948; interment in Oak Ridge Cemetery, Kennett, Mo.

ZIONCHECK, Marion Anthony, a Representative from Washington; born in Kety, Galicia, Poland, December 5, 1901; immigrated to the United States in 1905 with his parents who settled in Seattle, Wash.; attended the public schools and was graduated from Olympia High School in 1918; attended the University of Washington at Seattle from 1919 until graduated from the law department in 1929, working between times to pay his expenses; was admitted to the bar the same year and commenced practice in Seattle, Wash.; delegate to the Democratic State conventions in 1932 and 1934; elected as a Democrat to the Seventy-third and Seventy-fourth Congresses and served from March 4, 1933, until his death in Seattle, Wash., August 7, 1936; interment in Evergreen Cemetery.

ZOLLICOFFER, Felix Kirk, a Representative from Tennessee; born in Bigbyville, Maury County, Tenn., May 19, 1812; attended the "old field" schools and Jackson College, Columbia, Tenn.; became a printer; engaged in newspaper work in Paris, Tenn., 1828–1830, Knoxville, Tenn., in 1831 and 1832, and Huntsville, Ala., 1835–1843; elected State printer of Tennessee in 1835; served as a lieutenant in the war against the Seminoles in Florida in 1836; owner and editor of the Columbia Observer and the Southern Agriculturist in 1837; editor of the Republican Banner, the State organ of the Whig Party, in 1843; comptroller of the State treasury 1845–1849; served in the State senate 1849–1852; delegate to the Whig National Convention at Baltimore in 1852; elected as a State Rights Whig to the Thirty-third, Thirty-fourth, and Thirty-fifth Congresses (March 4, 1853–March 3, 1859); declined to be a candidate for renominaton in 1858; member of the peace convention of 1861 held in Washington, D. C., in an effort to devise means to prevent the impending war; during the Civil War served in the Confederate Army as brigadier general; commanded ten thousand troops in east Tennessee; one of the Tennessee generals whose figure is carved on Stone Mountain, Atlanta, Ga.; died from wounds received near Mill Springs, Ky., January 19, 1862; interment in the Old City Cemetery, Nashville, Tenn.

ZUBLY, John Joachim, a Delegate from Georgia; born in St. Gall, Switzerland, August 27, 1724; immigrated to America and settled in South Carolina; was engaged as a clerk in Wando Neck; ordained to the ministry in 1744; was the first pastor of the Presbyterian Church in Savannah (later the Independent Presbyterian Church) in 1760; prominent in early Revolutionary movements; served in the Provincial Congress of Georgia in 1775; Member of the Continental Congress from July 4, 1775, to November 1775, when he resigned; was accused of having furnished information to Sir James Wright, the royal governor, and narrowly escaped severe punishment; was banished from the State and one-half of his property was confiscated; resided in South Carolina 1777–1779; returned to Georgia ·and resumed pastoral duties in Savannah, where he died July 23, 1781; interment in what was later known as Colonial Park.